Broadcasting & Cable Yearbook 1994

A Broadcasting® & R.R. Bowker® Publication

Volume 1

FORMERLY
Broadcasting & Cable Market Place
and
Broadcasting Yearbook

R.R. Bowker
A Reed Reference Publishing Company
New Providence, New Jersey

Broadcasting & Cable Yearbook
is compiled by
R.R. Bowker
A Reed Reference Publishing Company

Leigh C. Yuster-Freeman, Publisher
Dean Hollister, Vice President, Production-Directories

Andrew Grabois, Editorial Director
Elizabeth A. Onaran, Managing Editor
Kimberly A. Willard, Senior Editor

Joseph A. Esser, Aimee Koval-Jurista, M. Michelle Mahlstadt,
Carole J. Rafferty, Stacy A. Stanford, Associate Editors
Kimberley B. Jenkins, Michael Kondrak. Erica Milowitz, Assistant Editors

Judy Redel, Research Director
Tanya Hurst, Senior Research Editor
Jason Doerr, Associate Research Editor
Jeffrey Schumow, Assistant Research Editor

Robin Fagan, Administrative Assistant

Peter Simon, Senior Vice President, Database Publishing

Broadcasting & Cable magazine
Cahners Publishing Company
A Division of Reed Publishing (USA) Inc.

Peggy Conlon, Publisher
Donald V. West, Senior Vice President and Editor
Harry Jessell, Executive Editor
Mark K. Miller, Managing Editor

Jennifer Allen, Production Manager

ADVERTISING
Classified Advertising/NJ
Randy Mysel, Vice President, Planning
Susan Towne, Director, Advertising Sales

Display Advertising/NY
Lawrence W. Oliver, Associate Publisher

Display Advertising/DC
Doris Kelly, Sales Service Manager

Display Advertising/CA
Gary Rubin, National Marketing Director & Director of Syndication Advertising

---

Published by R.R. Bowker, A Reed Reference Publishing Company

Copyright © 1994 by Reed Elsevier Inc. All rights reserved.

No part of this publication may be reproduced or transmitted
in any form or by any means, nor stored in any information storage
and retrieval system, without prior written permission of R.R. Bowker,
121 Chanlon Road, New Providence, New Jersey 07974.

International Standard Book Number 0-8352-3438-X (Set)
International Standard Book Number 0-8352-3439-8 (Vol. 1)
International Standard Book Number 0-8352-3440-1 (Vol. 2)
International Standard Serial Number 0000-1511
Library of Congress Serial Card Number 71-649524

Printed and bound in the United States of America.

ISBN 0-8352-3438-X

No payment is either solicited or accepted for the inclusion of entries in this publication. R.R. Bowker has used its best efforts in collecting and preparing material for inclusion in this publication, but does not warrant that the information herein is complete or accurate, and does not assume, and hereby disclaims, any liability to any person for any loss or damage caused by errors or omissions in this publication, whether such errors or omissions result from negligence, accident or any other cause.

Table of Contents

HE
8664
.B76
1994
v.1

VOLUME I

Preface	v
User's Guide	vii
Glossary of Terms	xi
List of Abbreviations	xii
Brief History of Broadcasting and Cable	xiii
Year in Review 1993	xxi

Section A
Law and Regulation, Government Agencies and Ownership

Table of Contents	A-1
Law and Regulation	A-2
Government Agencies	A-50
Ownership	A-54

Section B
Radio

Table of Contents	B-1
Key to Listings	B-2
Directory of Radio Stations in the United States and Canada	B-3
U.S. AM Stations by Call Letters	B-451
U.S. FM Stations by Call Letters	B-460
Canadian AM Stations by Call Letters	B-473
Canadian FM Stations by Call Letters	B-474
Table of FM Allotments	B-475
College, University and School-Owned Radio	B-484
U.S. AM Stations by Frequency	B-486
U.S. FM Stations by Frequency	B-502
Canadian AM Stations by Frequency	B-525
Canadian FM Stations by Frequency	B-527
Radio Formats	B-529
U.S. and Canadian Radio Programming Formats	B-542
Programming on Radio Stations in the United States and Canada	B-543
Special Programming on Radio Stations in the United States and Canada	B-573
Radio Market Statistics	B-591

Section C
Television

Table of Contents	C-1
Key to Listings	C-2
Directory of Television Stations in the United States and Canada	C-3
Television Stations by Call Letters	C-90
Low Power Television Stations	C-94
Spanish-Language Television Stations	C-110
Experimental Television Stations	C-111
U.S. Independent Television Stations	C-112
College, University and School-Owned Television Stations	C-113
U.S. Television Stations Broadcasting in Stereo	C-114
Television Stations by Channel	C-115
Television Assignments by State	C-120
Television Market Statistics	C-123

Section D
Cable

Table of Contents	D-1
Key to Listings	D-2
Directory of Multiple System Operators (MSOs), Independent Owners & Cable Systems in the U.S. and Canada	D-3
Geographical Index to Large Cable Systems & MSOs in the U.S. and Canada	D-55
Broadcasters in Cable Television	D-66
Cable Market Statistics	D-68

Section E
Satellites and Other Carriers

Table of Contents	E-1
Satellite Owners and Operators	E-2
Satellite Guide to the Sky	E-3
Satellite Resale and Common Carriers	E-4
Direct Broadcast Satellites	E-9
Teleports	E-10
Microwave	E-12
Wireless Cable Operators	E-13
Multipoint Distribution Services	E-14
Multichannel Multipoint Distribution Services	E-17

Section F
Advertising and Marketing Services

Table of Contents	F-1
Advertising and Marketing Services (Advertising Agencies; Media Buying/Planning Services; Barter Services; Radio, TV & Cable Representatives; Public Relations & Publicity)	F-2

Section G
Programming Services

Table of Contents	G-1
Producers, Distributors, Production and Other Services	G-2
Radio Programming Services	G-36
Television Programming Services	G-62
Cable Programming Services	G-78
Other Programming Services	G-89

Section H
Services and Suppliers

Table of Contents	H-1
Equipment Manufacturers, Distributors and Technical Services	H-2
Professional Services (Brokers; Consultants; Finance Services; Research Services; Engineering & Technical Consultants; Law Firms; Talent Agents; Executive Search Services)	H-59
Professional Cards	H-105

Section I
Associations, Events, Education and Awards

Table of Contents	I-1
Associations	I-2
Events	I-20
Education	I-25
Awards	I-32

Section J
Books, Periodicals, Videos

Table of Contents	J-1
Books on Broadcasting, Cable and Mass Media	J-2
Periodicals on Broadcasting, Cable and Mass Media	J-16
Videos on Broadcasting and Cable	J-31

Section K
Indexes

Index to Sections	K-1
Index to Radio & Television by State/Possession/Province	K-8
Index to Advertisers	K-9

VOLUME II

Preface	v
User's Guide	vii
Year in Review	xi
Radio, Television & Cable Yellow Pages	1

Broadcasting & Cable Yearbook 1994

Preface

The 1994 edition of **Broadcasting & Cable Yearbook** continues the traditions set by the original **Yearbook,** combined with innovations introduced in the 1992 and 1993 editions.

The need for complete and reliable information has become increasingly more important as the broadcasting and cable industries continue to grow and expand. **Broadcasting & Cable Yearbook 1994** continues to meet that need with a well-organized tabbed format containing current and timely information in all areas related to broadcasting and cable.

The **1994 Yearbook** continues to be organized in 11 sections to enable easy and almost effortless access to the wealth of information supplied in this directory.

The order of sections in this edition is the same as the prior (1993) edition: The section on **Law and Regulation (FCC), Government Agencies and Ownership** is **Section A** in the front of Volume I. **Section B - Radio** and **Section C - Television** each contain a **Call Letter Index** and the marketplace statistics and maps appropriate to each.

The focus on cable—from the impending involvement of the telephone companies, to the freeze on cable rates imposed by the FCC, to the re-establishment of the Cable Bureau—demands accurate and complete information on the cable industry. Coverage in the **Cable Section - Section D** includes most MSOs and independent owners and their systems with 1,000 or more subscribers. Feedback on the organization of the cable information continues to be very positive. Therefore, we continue to list the entire organization, that is the MSO or independent owner and its cable systems. Access to companies serving particular areas is provided by the geographic index. Cable marketplace statistics are also included in this section.

Satellites and Other Services - Section E continues to include expanding broadcasting and cable services—313 MMDS/Multichannel Multipoint Distribution Services and 11 Wireless Cable Operators, with 12 Barter Service companies included in **Section F - Advertising and Marketing Services,** and seven Regional Cable TV News Program Networks in **Programming Services - Section G.**

Participation in conferences and trade shows is important in any industry, especially with industry and worldwide changes happening so rapidly. Forty-eight trade shows for the radio, television, and cable industries, are provided in an alphabetical listing, in addition to the subject listing. The information on trade shows is drawn from the annual directory **Trade Show Week Data Book,** also published by R.R. Bowker.

A listing of 461 industry-related books published in the past five years is also included from the **Books in Print** database, in addition to the selection of 204 titles provided by Professor Christopher H. Sterling, Director, National Center for Communication Studies, George Washington University.

One of the best means of keeping up with news and industry developments is with periodical literature. Two listings of industry-related periodicals are included—the first is a selection of 75 domestic and foreign periodicals compiled by Professor Christopher H. Sterling, and the second is a listing of 461 U.S. periodicals drawn from the **Ulrich's International Periodicals Directory** database.

Videos have become an integral part of classroom, office and home, as they provide an excellent means of study and entertainment. The 122 industry-related videos included in this edition are largely for adult audiences, and have been taken from **Bowker's Complete Video Directory** database.

Broadcasting & Cable Yearbook 1994 continues to be provided in two volumes. The **Industry Yellow Pages** are contained in Volume II, making the main volume easier to use, and enabling separate shelf storage and use of the yellow pages.

Each edition of **Broadcasting & Cable Yearbook** is compiled by mailing questionnaires to all current and to possible new entrants indentified throughout the year. Entrant questionnaires are mailed from approximately August through October each year—we urge all entrants to provide updated information throughout the year and to return the questionnaires by mail or fax even if there are no corrections. The editorial address is **Broadcasting & Cable Yearbook,** 121 Chanlon Road, New Providence, NJ 07974, FAX: (908) 771-7704.

In addition to the questionnaires, data collection and updating are provided by the **Broadcasting & Cable** magazine staff and other outside sources. The contributions of the outside sources are an invaluable part of **Broadcasting & Cable Yearbook,** and I extend my appreciation to Sherm Brodey and Paula Odom, Arbitron; Louisa Nielsen, Broadcast Education Association; T. Glyn Finley, Electronic Industries Association; Paula Friedman, Federal Communications Bar Association; Maureen Peratino and Sandy Bailey, FCC; Christopher Sterling, George Washington University; Louise O'Gara, ISCI; John Kompass, K-B, Ltd.; Elise Adde, National Cable Television Association; Maria Zimmann and Diane Buono, The Nielsen Co.; Robert Emeritz, Pike & Fischer, Inc.; and the Radio Advertising Bureau.

This 1994 edition of **Broadcasting & Cable Yearbook** contains information on 12,939 radio stations, of which 5,266 are AM and 7,673 are FM, 1,919 television stations, and 500 MSOs and independent owners, which collectively own 656 larger cable systems. Arrangements for classified advertising (professional cards, tie-ins, station headers, boldface listings, annotations) in **Broadcasting & Cable Yearbook** is coordinated by Susan Towne, (908) 771-6744. Display advertising, including tabs, for **Broadcasting & Cable Yearbook** is coordinated by Larry Oliver, (212) 340-9860.

Mailing lists of the radio stations, television stations, and cable MSOs listed in **Broadcasting & Cable Yearbook** are available through Cahners Direct Marketing Services in Illinois. Contact Susan Knuth at (800) 323-4958.

A book of this magnitude requires the efforts of many dedicated people working together—and that was duly accomplished with tremendous spirit and talent. My heartfelt appreciation to Dean Hollister, Vice President, Production-Directories, Andrew Grabois, Editorial Director, and Elizabeth Onaran, Managing Editor, for their untiring efforts and dedication in producing this edition with the many changes and enhancements, and to Kim Willard, Senior Editor, and Joe Esser, Associate Editor, and the fine staff of editorial associates and assistants for tackling all of the work entailed with this book with fervor and dedication. My thanks also to Judy Redel, Research Director, Tanya Hurst, Senior Re-

Preface

search Editor, Jason Doerr, Associate Research Editor, and Jeffrey Schumow, Assistant Research Editor, for their tireless efforts. My appreciation also to everyone at **Broadcasting and Cable** magazine—specifically Don West, Senior Vice President and Editor, Mark Miller, Managing Editor, Harry Jessell, Executive Editor, and Doris Kelley, Sales Service Manager—for continuing to be an active partner in the compilation of this publication. Sincere appreciation also to Peter Simon, Senior Vice President, Database Publishing, and to all members of the Systems, Operations, Advertising, Manufacturing and Marketing departments for their roles in the completion of this 1994 edition.

Finally, I would like to thank each and every person that provided comments on the 1993 directory. The **Yearbook** is your information tool, and your feedback is essential. We strongly encourage you to contact us with suggestions and comments for future editions, as well as comments on this 1994 edition.

We trust that you will find this source of information on the broadcasting and cable industries valuable, accurate, well-organized and easy to use.

Leigh C. Yuster-Freeman
Publisher

User's Guide

Broadcasting & Cable Yearbook has been reorganized into two volumes for easier access to the great amount of the data compiled into this directory. **Volume I** contains eleven sections (A through K) and **Volume** II contains the *Radio, Television & Cable Yellow Pages.*

Data may be found through various access points, as well as by browsing through a particular section:

Table of Contents **on page iii.** Provides a general overview of the entire publication by section.

Table of Contents **for each section.** The first page of each section has a detailed table of contents for that section only.

Indexes in Section K:

Index to Sections

Index to Radio and Television by State/Possession/Province

Index to Advertisers

Note on Abbreviations: Abbreviations are used throughout this directory to conserve space. Abbreviations are explained in the *List of Abbreviations,* which can be found in this section.

Note on Filing Rules: Acronyms and initials appear first in the alphabetical order of most listings in this book (except the radio & television directories).

This *User's Guide* provides general guidelines by section and includes specific instructions only *when needed.*

VOLUME I

Section A

Law and Regulation, Government Agencies and Ownership

The *Table of Contents* on the first page provides an overview of the entire section.

This section is divided into three parts: 1) *Law & Regulation,* 2) *Government Agencies,* and 3) *Ownership.*

Law and Regulation

FCC Executives and Staff includes a listing of executives and staff by department; information provided includes department phone numbers and titles. Also included is a flowchart of FCC operations.

FCC Rules and Regulations outlines the rules and regulations as set by the Federal Communications Commission. The first page contains a brief table of contents as a guide to FCC rules paragraph headings. This listing is updated and maintained with the cooperation of Pike & Fischer Inc., publisher of *Pike & Fischer Radio Regulation* and *Pike & Fischer's Broadcast Rules Service.*

Cable Regulations is an outline of federal cable television rules, including current regulations and developments.

The *Industry Standard Coding Identification System (ISCI)* is described in this section. The *NAB Television and Radio Codes* have been suspended; the description is included here for historical purposes only.

Government Agencies

Government Agencies of Interest to Broadcasting and Cable are listed, those in the U.S. first and then agencies in Canada. Information provided includes address (headquarters and other locations), phone, personnel and/or committee members.

U.S. State Cable Regulatory Agencies lists the agencies alphabetically by state, regardless of the agency name.

Ownership

Television Ownership Transfers is a comprehensive history of television station transfers from the inception of authorized commercial service through December 1993. Transfers are listed by state, city, then call letters.

Note: Information contained here has been obtained from **Broadcasting & Cable** magazine's regular columns "For the Record" and "Changing Hands."

1993 Station Sales provides information on station sales of one million dollars and higher. The sales transactions are provided in price sequence with the highest price first. Information provided is price, the properties, the seller, and the buyer. This information is provided by the **Broadcasting & Cable** magazine staff.

A chart of *40 Years of Station Transactions* lists the dollar volume of transactions approved by the FCC from 1954 to 1993. The figures for 1993 are in bold type. Information included in this chart is tracked weekly by the **Broadcasting & Cable** magazine staff.

Group Ownership includes individuals and companies with multiple station holdings—those controlling three or more radio stations and/or two or more television stations. The listing is in alphabetical sequence by company and includes call letters, city and state of stations owned, and the name, address, phone and fax of the group.

Note: Notations in the television directory regarding group ownership and cross-ownership are cross-referenced to information listed here.

Newspaper/Magazine Cross-Ownership with Broadcasting Stations includes companies that have interests in both broadcasting and newspaper or magazine publishing. Minority interests are indicated where information is available. In many instances stations and publications are owned by the same interests, but operations are entirely separate. The listing is in alphabetical sequence by company and includes the company name, address, phone and fax, the name of each newspaper and/or magazine with the city and state in which they are published and the call letters of each station with the city and state in which they operate.

Note: Notations in the television directory regarding group ownership and cross-ownership are cross-referenced to information listed here.

Broadcasting Stations Associated with Newspaper/Magazine Ownership is a state-by-state (or province) cross-reference listing of broadcasting stations and the publishing companies or newspapers with which the companies outlined in the prior listing are associated. The U.S. is listed first, followed by Canada. The listing is by state or province, then by city, then by call letters.

Section B

Radio

The *Table of Contents* on the first page provides an overview of the entire section.

A sample radio station listing with a key to all of the elements contained in an entry is provided on the second page of this section.

The *Directory of Radio Stations in the U.S. and Canada* is organized by state or province, then city, then call letters (except when two or more stations are co-owned; the lead station is listed first, with the trail station immediately following). Stations in the United States are listed first; the stations in Canada follow.

Immediately following the above directory are *Miscellaneous Radio Services:* Armed Forces Radio, Radio Free Europe, U.S. International Radio, and Voice of America. Each of these listings contain contact information, personnel (when available), and a description of the service.

U.S. AM & FM Stations By Call Letters and *Canadian AM & FM Stations By Call Letters* list radio stations alphabetically by call letters, followed by city (or province) and state or possession.

Note: Access to radio stations by call letters is also available through the *Radio, Television & Cable Yellow Pages* located in Volume II. Radio stations are listed alphabetically within the *Yellow Pages.*

The following listings have pulled together specific data from the radio station listings and FCC sources to aid the user in compiling research, etc. Once a radio station has been identified, refer to the *Directory of Radio Stations in the United States and Canada* for complete information.

Table of FM Allotments contains the channels (other than noncommercial, educational channels 201-220) designated for use in communities in the United States, its territories and possessions as of November 1993. The listing is by state, then by city, with the channel listed next to the city.

College, University and School-Owned Radio Stations is a listing by state, then by city, then by call letters of college, university and school-owned radio stations in the United States.

U.S. AM Stations by Frequency are listed by state, then by city, under the frequency heading, which is listed in ascending, numeric sequence. Clear stations appear in boldface type. Refer to the frequency heading to determine if the station is on a clear regional or local frequency. For an explanation of AM station classes, see the *Brief History of Broadcasting and Cable* within this section.

U.S. FM Stations by Frequency are listed by state, then by city under the frequency and channel number. Frequencies are listed in ascending numeric order.

Canadian AM Stations by Frequency are listed by province, then by city, under the frequency heading, which is listed in ascending numeric sequence.

Canadian FM Stations by Frequency are listed by province, then by city under the frequency heading, which is listed in ascending numeric sequence.

Radio Formats Defined describes programming and the specific radio formats currently included in the *Directory of Radio Stations in the U.S. and Canada.* The formats are listed alphabetically.

Radio Formats by State and Possession and *Radio Formats by Province* include the number of AM and FM stations in each state or province, with a breakdown of the number of commercial and noncommercial stations, followed by a

User's Guide

ranked tally of formats. Note: This tally includes only those stations that have provided format information.

U.S. and Canada Radio Programming Formats is a chart that provides totals for format usage in the United States and Canada, broken down by AM/FM and commercial/noncommercial.

Programming on Radio Stations in the United States and Canada provides a quick reference to regular programming formats by radio format, by state or province, then city, then by call letters.

Special Programming on Radio Stations in the United States and Canada provides a quick reference to foreign-language and other specialized programming, such as Agriculture and Farm, Polish language, etc., by radio format, by state or province, then city, then by call letters.

Radio Market Statistics

U.S. Radio Markets contains the Arbitron population ranking in alphabetical sequence by radio market (city). The two charts that follow, *U.S. Radio Markets: Arbitron Metro Survey Area Ranking*, and *U.S. Radio Markets: Population Ranking* provide additional information to assist in the use of *U.S. Radio Markets.*

The next four charts and tables, *Growth of Radio Broadcasting Pre-Television 1922-1945*, *U.S. Radio Set Sales 1958-1992*, *Record of Radio Station Growth Since Television Began* and *U.S. Radio Audiences*, include explanatory notes regarding the data included in the chart, or the organization of the data.

Section C

Television

The *Table of Contents* on the first page provides an overview of the entire section.

A sample television station listing with a key to all of the elements contained in an entry is provided on the second page of this section.

The *Directory of Television Stations in the United States and Canada* is organized by state or province, then city, then call letters (except when two or more noncommercial stations are co-owned; the lead station is listed first in the proper alpha position, with the trail station following). Stations in the United States are listed first; the stations in Canada follow.

U.S. Television Stations By Call Letters and *Canadian Television By Call Letters* lists television stations alphabetically by call letters, followed by city (or province) and state or possession.

Note: Access to television stations by call letters is also available through the *Radio, Television & Cable Yellow Pages*, located in Volume II. Television stations are listed alphabetically within the *Yellow Pages.*

The following listings pull together specific data from the television station listings and FCC sources to aid the user in compiling research, etc. Once a television station has been identified, refer to the *Directory of Television Stations in the United States and Canada* for complete information.

Low Power Television Stations are listed by state, then by city, then by call letters. Information provided includes date station first went on air (when available), licensee, contact and address.

Spanish-Language Television Stations that operate within the United States or near the U.S. border are listed by state, then by market, then by call letters and city. Channel numbers are also provided.

Experimental Television Stations is an alphabetical list of stations authorized by the FCC as of January 1994.

U.S. Independent Television Stations are listed by state, then city, then call letters.

College, University and School-Owned Television Stations are listed by state, then city, then call letters.

U.S. Television Stations Broadcasting in Stereo are listed by state, then city, then call letters.

Television Stations by Channel in the United States and Canada are listed by channel, then by state, then city, then call letters. The frequency is included with each U.S. channel.

Television Assignments by State contains the channels designated for the listed communities in the United States, its territories and possessions by state, then city. Channels designated with an asterisk (*) are assigned for use by noncommercial educational broadcast stations only. A station on a channel identified by a plus (+) or minus (-) mark is required to operate with its carrier frequencies offset 10 khz above or below, respectively, the nominal carrier frequencies.

Television Market Statistics

The *Arbitron ADI Market Atlas* lists Arbitron's 209 ADI (Area of Dominant Influence) markets for 1993-1994 alphabetically by city.

The two charts that follow the atlas, *Multi-City ADI Cross-Reference* and *Non-ADI Markets* provide additional information to assist in use of the atlas.

The two charts, *Television Markets Ranked by Size* and *Television Markets by Nielsen Marketing Research Territory* provide market information from two distinct compilation and reporting methods.

The *Top 100 Companies* provides company and revenue data according to the Electronic Communications Index (ECI).

The next four charts and tables, *How Network Delivery Varies by Market*, *U.S. Sales of Television Receivers 1983-1992*, *Record of Television Station Growth Since Television Began* and *U.S. Television Audiences*, include explanatory notes regarding the data included in the charts, or the organization of the data.

Section D

Cable

The *Table of Contents* on the first page provides an overview of the entire section.

A sample MSO/Cable System listing with a key to all of the elements contained in an entry is provided on the second page of this section.

The *Directory of Multiple Systems Operators (MSOs), Independent Owners & Cable Systems in the United States and Canada* contains information on U.S. or Canadian MSOs and independent owners followed by information on their individual large cable systems with 20,000 subscribers or more. Information on their smaller cable systems, those with less than 20,000 subscribers, is included when available. The listings are in alphabetical sequence by MSO.

The *Geographical Index to Large Cable Systems & MSOs in the U.S. and Canada* provides state and city access to the large cable systems, listed with the individual MSOs.

Broadcasters in Cable Television lists companies and individuals in alphabetical sequence that have at least partial ownership in radio or TV stations and in MSOs (multiple system operators) or individual cable systems but are not necessarily MSOs.

Cable Market Statistics

Cable Penetration by Market is a listing that contains the number of cable homes and the percentage of cable penetration as compiled by A.C. Nielsen Company. The information is listed by Nielsen's Designated Market Areas (DMAs). The next three charts provide an overview of the top 50 DMAs ranked by percentage of cable penetration, cable television households and television households, respectively. The fourth chart provides an overview of the *Bottom 50 DMA Ranked by Percentage of Cable Penetration.*

The last chart in this section, *Top 50 MSOs*, provides the number of subscribers for the top 50 MSOs covered in the *Directory of Multiple Systems Operators (MSOs), Independent Owners & Cable Systems in the United States and Canada.*

Section E

Satellites and Other Carriers

The *Table of Contents* on the first page provides an overview of the entire section.

Satellite Owners and Operators are listed alphabetically by company name. Information provided includes address, phone, personnel and a brief description.

Satellite Guide to the Sky, a chart, provides a broad satellite perspective of each carrier and its satellites currently in space.

Satellite Resale and Common Carriers are listed alphabetically by company name. Information provided includes address, phone, personnel and a brief description of services.

Direct Broadcast Satellites are listed alphabetically by company name. Information provided includes address, phone, personnel and a brief description of services.

Teleports are listed by state (although the state is not shown), then city, then company name. Information provided includes address, phone, personnel, ownership and a brief description of services.

Microwave services are listed alphabetically by company name. Information provided includes address, phone, personnel, regional offices and a brief description of services.

Wireless Cable companies are listed alphabetically. Information provided includes address, phone, personnel and a brief description of services.

Multipoint Distribution Services or MDS systems are listed by state, then city, then company name with address.

Multichannel Multipoint Distribution Services or MMDS systems are listed by state, then city, then company name with address.

Section F

Advertising and Marketing Services

The *Table of Contents* on the first page is an overview of the entire section.

Advertising Agencies Handling Major Radio and Television Accounts is an alphabetical listing by company. Information provided is name, address, phone number and executives. Fax number, address of regional or satellite offices, and additional contacts are supplied as appropriate.

Independent Media Buying/Planning Services is an alphabetical listing by company. Information provided is name, address, phone number. Fax number, address of regional or satellite offices, additional contacts, and a brief description of services are supplied when provided.

Barter Service Companies lists companies alphabetically by name. Information includes address, phone, personnel and a brief description of services.

Radio, Television Station and Cable Representatives is an alphabetical listing by company. Information provided is name, address, phone number. Fax number, address of regional or satellite offices, and additional contacts are supplied as appropriate. Representatives in the United States are listed first, with Canadian representatives following.

Public Relations, Publicity and Promotion Services is an alphabetical listing by company. Information provided is name, address, phone number. Fax number, address of regional or satellite offices, additional contacts, and a brief description of services may also be supplied.

Section G

Programming Services

This section is divided into five parts: 1) *Producers, Distributors, Production and Other Services*, an alphabetical compilation of various services with subject access, 2) *Radio Programming Services,* 3) *Television Programming Services,* 4) *Cable Programming Services,* and 5) *Other Programming Services.*

The first page provides a *Table of Contents,* an overview of the entire section.

Producers, Distributors, Production and Other Services is provided in two parts: the *Subject Index* lists the company name under one or more appropriate subjects, and the *Alphabetical Index* lists the complete name, address, phone, fax, personnel and a brief description of the company.

When a company name is not known, search under an appropriate subject in the *Subject Index.* When a company has been identified, turn to the *Alphabetical Index* for complete information on that company.

Radio Programming Services

Major National Radio Networks is an alphabetical listing of the major radio networks, i.e., CBS. Full contact information, address, phone, fax, personnel, and all divisions are supplied. If a network is also involved in TV, that information is also listed here, as well as under *Major National Television Networks.*

Public Broadcasting - Radio is an alphabetical listing of public radio organizations and networks. Information provided includes address, phone, executives and directors.

Radio Program Networks is an alphabetical listing of the national radio program networks, more specialized (as far as programming is concerned) than the major national radio networks. Information provided includes address, phone, executives and a brief description.

Regional Radio Networks is an alphabetical listing of radio networks serving certain states or regions. Information provided includes address, phone, executives, and the area served.

Unwired Radio Networks is an alphabetical listing of non-interconnected networks of radio or TV stations which can be purchased as a group by advertisers. Information provided includes address, phone and executives.

Canadian Radio Networks is an alphabetical listing of radio networks in Canada. Information provided includes address, phone and executives.

Radio News Services is an alphabetical listing of audio news services. Information provided includes address, phone, personnel and a brief description.

Radio Format Providers is an alphabetical listing of firms that provide specific music or talk formats to radio stations. Information provided includes address, phone, executives, and types of programming offered.

Television Programming Services

Major National Television Networks is an alphabetical listing of the major TV networks, i.e., ABC. Full contact information, address, phone, fax, personnel, and divisions are supplied. If a network is also involved in radio, that information is also listed here, as well as under *Major National Radio Networks.*

Public Broadcasting - Television is an alphabetical listing of the public TV organizations and networks. Information provided includes address, phone, executives, and directors.

Television Program Networks is an alphabetical listing of the national TV program networks, more specifically targeted than the major national TV networks. Information provided includes address, phone, executives and types of programming offered.

Regional Television Networks is an alphabetical listing of TV networks serving certain states or regions. Information provided includes address, phone, executives, and the area served.

Unwired Television Networks is an alphabetical listing of non-interconnected networks of TV or radio stations which can be purchased as a group by advertisers. Information provided includes address, phone, and executives.

Canadian Television Networks is an alphabetical listing of TV networks in Canada. Information provided includes address, phone and executives.

Television News Services is an alphabetical listing of video news services. Information provided includes address, phone, personnel and a brief description.

Closed Circuit Television is an alphabetical listing of closed circuit TV services. Information provided includes address, phone, executives and a description of the services offered.

Cable Programming Services

Pay Cable Services is an alphabetical listing of premium and pay-per-view cable services. Information provided includes address, phone, executives and a brief description of the type of services provided.

Basic Cable Services is an alphabetical listing of cable video networks and superstations. Information provided includes address, phone, executives and a brief description of the services offered.

Automated Cable Channel Programmers is an alphabetical listing of video alpha-numeric text services, often with enhanced graphics, that provide news, weather, sports, business information and program guide information. Information provided includes address, phone, contacts, and type of text available.

Audio Cable Programming Services is an alphabetical listing of audio programming and cable radio services available for cable channels not occupied by TV stations or cable networks. Music formats, religious and international programs, and background music for alpha-numeric channels are available. Information provided includes address, phone and type of audio programs offered.

Regional Cable Television News Services is an alphabetical listing of regional cable news services. Information includes address, phone, personnel and a brief description of services.

Cable Sports Services is an alphabetical listing of national and regional cable sports networks. Information provided includes address, phone, executives and a description of the type of sports programming offered.

Canadian Cable Programming Services is an alphabetical listing of Canadian cable networks, pay TV services and specialty services. Information provided includes address, phone and type of service available.

Other Programming Services

Music Licensing Groups is an alphabetical listing of organizations that provide licenses for the public performance of musical compositions. Information provided includes address, phone, executives and a brief description.

Videotext Operations is an alphabetical listing of organizations that provide news or other text via a two-way interactive service that uses either two-way cable or telephone lines. Information provided includes address, phone, executives and a brief description.

Teletext Operations is an alphabetical listing of firms or TV stations that transmit news or other text via an unused portion of a standard television signal. Information provided includes address, phone, personnel and a brief description.

Subcarrier/VBI Services is an alphabetical listing of firms that provide audio programs or video text or data using portions of FM or TV signals. Information provided includes address, phone, executives and services offered.

Section H

Services and Suppliers

This section is divided into two parts: 1) *Technological Services* and 2) *Professional Services.*

The *Table of Contents* on the first page is an overview of the entire section.

Technological Services

Equipment Manufacturers and Distributors and Technical Services is provided in two parts: the *Subject Index* lists the company name under one or more appropriate subjects, and the *Alphabetical Index* lists the complete name, address, phone, fax, personnel and a brief description of the company.

When a company name is not known, search under an appropriate subject in the *Subject Index.* When a company has been identified, turn to the *Alphabetical Index* for complete information on that company.

Professional Services

Station and Cable Television Brokers lists in alphabetical sequence by company name brokers or brokerage firms that service the media field specifically. Information provided includes address, phone, fax, personnel and a brief description of services.

Consultants lists individuals or companies that provide a variety of services to the media field, i.e., strategic planning, management, facilities design, etc. Listings are in alphabetical sequence by company name and include address, phone, fax, personnel and a brief description of services.

Station Financing Services lists individuals or companies that provide a variety of financial services to the communications industries. Listings are in alphabetical sequence by company name and include address, phone, fax, personnel and a brief description of services.

Research Services is an alphabetical listing of various tracking, monitoring and research services that serve the broadcasting and cable industries. Information provided includes address, phone, fax, personnel, regional or satellite offices, and a brief description of the services.

Engineering and Technical Consultants is an alphabetical listing by company or individual; individuals are listed by the last name. Information provided includes address, phone, fax, personnel and a brief description of the services (when supplied). An asterisk (*) indicates membership in the Association of Federal Communications Consulting Engineers.

Law Firms Active in Communications Law is an alphabetical listing of firms or individuals that

User's Guide

practice before the FCC as reported by radio and television stations, brokers, consultants and the attorneys themselves. Information was also gleaned from the Martindale-Hubbell database, Martindale-Hubbell, New Providence, N.J., and the Federal Communications Bar Association. Many, but not all, are members of the Federal Communications Bar Association. Information provided includes address, phone, fax, attorneys. A brief description may also be provided.

Talent Agents and Managers is an alphabetical listing by company name. Information provided includes address, phone, fax, personnel, regional or satellite offices, and a brief description.

Employment and Executive Search Services is an alphabetical listing by company name. Information provided includes address, phone, fax, personnel, regional or satellite offices, and a brief description.

Section I
Associations, Events, Education, Awards

The *Table of Contents* on the first page provides an overview of the entire section.

Associations

Major National Associations includes those organizations with large memberships and a large roster of departments and personnel. These associations tend to have strong voices in the broadcasting and cable industries. The associations are listed alphabetically by their full names; acronyms are provided in parentheses. Information provided includes the headquarters address and phone, and various personnel—officers, boards, representatives, committees.

National Associations includes all national associations and professional societies. Cross-references for the *Major National Associations* are included. Listings are alphabetical by full name. Information provided includes headquarters address, phone and executive personnel.

State Broadcast Associations and *State Cable Associations* are listed by state (regardless of the association name). Information provided includes headquarters address, phone and executive personnel.

Union/Labor Groups are listed alphabetically by the union or labor group's full name. Information provided includes headquarters address, phone, executive personnel and regional offices.

Events

Trade Shows Alphabetical Index lists trade shows alphabetically by name with a "see reference" to subject area in *Trade Shows By Category* where the full listing appears.

Trade Shows By Category lists alphabetically by subject category national and state conferences and trade shows for the communications industries. Trade shows and conferences are listed alphabetically by the name of the show within subject category. Information provided includes show management contacts and may include show sponsor, show management statement, show facts—location & dates of scheduled shows, estimated number of attendees, profile of exhibitors and profile of attendees.

Education

Schools Specializing in Radio-TV-Cable includes only those educational institutions that specialize in professional or technical courses in broadcasting. The listing is alphabetical by the name of the school. Information provided includes address, phone, personnel, other branch locations, and a brief description of the type of training provided or a listing of the courses offered.

Universities and Colleges lists institutions alphabetically by state in three parts: 1) *Universities and Colleges Offering Degrees in Broadcasting*, 2) *Universities and Colleges Offering Broadcasting Courses*, and 3) *Two-Year Colleges Offering Programs in Broadcasting*. The name and address is provided. Degrees offered may also be listed.

Additional information on educational opportunities in broadcasting, cable and communications may be obtained from the *Broadcast Education Association*, Washington, D.C.

Awards

Major Broadcasting & Cable Awards is an alphabetical listing by the name of the award, which may or may not include the sponsoring body. Note: Abbreviations and acronyms appear first in the alphabetical sequence. If a sponsor presents more than one award, each award is listed separately. The awards included are presented in the areas of broadcasting, cable, and the media. Entries include a description of the award, entrant deadline dates, and contact information.

Section J
Books, Periodicals, Videos

The *Table of Contents* on the first page provides an overview of the entire section.

Books is divided into two parts:

Books on Broadcasting, Cable and Mass Media, An Annotated Bibliography was compiled by Christopher H. Sterling. The bibliography annotates a selection of the most useful recent books listed by author, or title when no author is available. Information provided includes title, author, number of pages, price, name of publisher and a brief description.

Books on Broadcasting and Cable is an alphabetical listing by title of books on broadcasting, cable, satellites, and mass media published largely between 1989 and 1993 from the *Books in Print* data base, published by R.R. Bowker, New Providence, N.J. Information provided includes title, author, number of pages, publication date, price, binding, ISBN, and publisher name with city and state.

Periodicals is divided into two parts:

Periodicals on Broadcasting, Cable and Mass Media, An Annotated Bibliography, was compiled by Christopher H. Sterling. The bibliography annotates a selection of important periodicals issued domestically and abroad, listed by title. Information provided includes, title, frequency, publisher name and address, and a brief description.

Periodicals on Broadcasting and Cable is an alphabetical listing by title of periodicals on broadcasting, cable, satellites, and mass media published in the U.S. and Canada, from the *Ulrich's International Periodicals Directory* data base, published by R.R. Bowker, New Providence, N.J. Information provided includes title, frequency (codes are explained in the List of Abbreviations), price, year founded, ISSN, publisher name, address and phone, format, and a brief description.

Videos on Broadcasting and Cable is an alphabetical listing by title of videos on broadcasting, cable, satellites, and mass media produced in the U.S. from *Bowker's Complete Home Video Directory* data base (available on CD-ROM as *Variety's Video Directory Plus*), published by R.R. Bowker, New Providence, N.J. Information provided includes title, year produced, length, narrator(s), host(s) and/or featured person(s), a brief description, and producer name and address. Audience is largely adult.

Section K
Indexes

The *Index to Sections* provides keyword access to the listings, indexes and information included in this directory.

The *Index to Radio and Television by State/Possession/Province* is a one-page quick reference to the first page of each state, possession or province for both the radio and television directories.

The *Index to Advertisers* is an alphabetical listing of each display and classified advertiser and includes the page number where the ad can be found.

VOLUME II
Radio, Television & Cable Yellow Pages

The *Radio, Television & Cable Yellow Pages* lists each radio and TV station, cable MSO, large cable system, and all the personnel included in each of these directories. There are two types of *Yellow Page* listings: a station or company listing, and a personal listing. The station or company listings include the station call letters or company name, city and state, phone number, and section letter reference to Volume I (where the full entry is listed). The personal listings include the person's name (last name first), the station or company name, city and state, phone number, and section letter reference to Volume I (where the full entry is listed).

Note: If a person is connected with two or more stations or systems, that person will have two or more (multiple) listings. Multiple listings and same names (i.e., John Smith) will appear in order by state, then city.

Glossary of Terms Used in *Broadcasting & Cable Yearbook*

AM—Amplitude modulation. Also referring to audio service broadcast over 535 khz-1705 khz.

Analog—A continuous electrical signal that carries information in the form of variable physical values, such as amplitude or frequency modulation.

Basic cable service—Package of programming on cable systems eligible for regulation by local franchising authorities under 1992 Cable Act, including all local broadcast signals and PEG (public, educational and government) access channels.

Cable television—System that transmits original programming, and programming of broadcast television stations, to consumers over wired network (see page xvii).

CC—Closed captioning. Method of transmitting textual information over television channel's vertical blanking interval; transmissions are deciphered with decoders; decoded transmissions appear as text superimposed over television image.

CED—Capacitance electronic disk (RCA videodisk).

Clear channel—AM radio station allowed to dominate its frequency with up to 50 kw of power; their signals are generally protected for distance of up to 750 miles at night.

Closed circuit—The method of transmission of programs or other material that limits its target audience to a specific group rather than the general public.

Coaxial cable—Cable with several common axis lines under protective sheath used for television signal transmissions.

Common carrier—Telecommunication company that provides communications transmission services to the public.

DAB—Digital audio broadcasting. Modulations for sending digital rather than analog audio signals by either terrestrial or satellite transmitter with audio response up to compact disc quality (20 khz).

DBS—Direct broadcast satellite. High powered satellite authorized to broadcast direct to homes (see page xviii).

Digital—A discontinuous electrical signal that carries information in binary fashion. Data is represented by a specific sequence of off-on electrical pulses.

Directional antenna—An antenna that directs most of its signal strength in a specific direction rather than at equal strength in all directions. Used chiefly in AM radio operation.

Downlink—Earth station used to receive signals from satellites.

Earth station—Equipment used for transmitting or receiving satellite communications.

EDTV—Enhanced-definition television. Proposed intermediate systems for evolution to full HDTV, usually including slightly improved resolution and sound, with a wider (16:9) aspect ratio.

Effective competition—Market status under which cable TV systems are exempt from regulation of basic tier rates by local franchising authorities, as defined in 1992 Cable Act. To claim effective competition, a cable system must compete with at least one other multichannel provider that is available to at least 50% of an area's households and is subscribed to by more than 15% of the households.

EFT—Electronic funds transfer.

EM—Electronic mail (commonly referred to as E-mail).

Encryption—System for scrambling signals to prevent unauthorized reception.

ENG—Electronic news gathering.

ETV—Educational television.

Fiber optic cable—Wires made of glass fiber used to transmit video, audio, voice or data providing vastly wider bandwidth than standard coaxial cable.

Field—Half of the video information in the frame of a video picture. The NTSC system displays 59.94 fields per second.

FM—Frequency modulation. Also referring to audio service broadcast over 88 mhz-108 mhz.

Footprint—Area on earth within which a satellite's signal can be received.

Frame—A full video picture. The NTSC system displays 29.97 525-line frames per second.

Frequency—The number of cycles a signal is transmitted per second, measured in hertz.

Geostationary orbit—Orbit 22,300 miles above earth's equator where satellites circle earth at same rate earth rotates.

ghz—Gigahertz. One billion hertz (cycles) per second.

HDTV—High-definition television (see page xviii).

Headend—Facility in cable system from which all signals originate. (Local and distant television stations, and satellite programming, are picked up and amplified for retransmission through system.)

Hertz—A measurement of frequency. One cycle per second equals one hertz (hz).

HUT—Households using television.

Independent television—Television stations that are not affiliated with networks and that do not use the networks as a primary source of their programming.

Information services—Broad term used to describe full range of audio, video and data transmission services that can be transmitted over the air or by cable.

Interlaced scanning—Television transmission technique in which each frame is divided into two fields. NTSC system interleaves odd-numbered lines with even-numbered lines at a transmission rate of 59.94 fields per second.

ITFS—Instructional Television Fixed Service (see page xviii).

khz—Kilohertz. One thousand hertz (cycles) per second.

LED—Light emitting diode. Type of semiconductor that lights up when activated by voltage.

LO—Local origination channel.

LPTV—Low-power television (see page xvii).

LV—LaserVision (optical videodisk).

MDS—Multipoint distribution service (see page xviii).

mhz—Megahertz. One million hertz (cycles) per second.

Microwave—Frequencies above 1,000 mhz.

MSO—Multiple cable systems operator.

Must carry—Legal requirement that cable operators carry local broadcast signals. Cable systems with 12 or fewer channels must carry at least three broadcast signals; systems with 12 or more channels must carry up to one-third of their capacity; systems with 300 or fewer subscribers are exempt. The 1992 Cable Act requires broadcast station to waive must-carry rights if it chooses to negotiate retransmission compensation (see "Retransmission consent").

NTSC—National Television System Committee. Committee that recommended current American standard color television.

PCM—Pulse code modulation. Conversion of voice signals into digital code.

PCS—Personal Communications Service. New digital wireless telephone technology, with smaller and less expensive outdoor cells and consumer telephone sets than current cellular service. Cable television operators are among the entreprenuers for PCS. Also called PCN (Personal Communications Network).

PPV—Pay-per-view.

Program access—Prohibition on exclusive programming contracts between cable operators and program services controlled by cable operators, designed to give alternative multichannel distributors (such as wireless cable and DBS) the opportunity to bid for established cable services (such as CNN or Nickelodeon). The rule expires in 2002.

Progressive scanning—TV system where video frames are transmitted sequentially, unlike interlaced scanning in which frames are divided into two fields.

PSA—Public service announcment.

PTV—Public television.

Public radio—Radio stations and networks that are operated on a noncommercial basis.

Public television—Television stations and networks that operate as noncommercial ventures.

RCC—Radio common carrier. Common carriers whose major businesses include radio paging and mobile telephone services.

Retransmission consent—Local TV broadcasters' right to negotiate a carriage fee with local cable operators, as provided in 1992 Cable Act.

SCA—Subsidiary communications authorizations. Authorizations granted to FM broadcasters for using subcarriers on their channels for other communications services.

Shortwave—Transmissions on frequencies of 6-25 mhz.

SHF—Super high frequency.

Signal-to-noise ratio—The ratio between the strength of an electronically produced signal to interfering noises in the same bandwidth.

SMATV—Satellite master antenna television (see page xviii).

STV—Subscription television (see page xviii).

Superstation—Local television station whose signal is retransmitted via satellite to cable systems beyond reach of over-the-air signal.

Tariff—Common carrier's statement describing services it offers and rates it charges.

Teletext—A one-way electronic publishing service that can be transmitted over the vertical blanking interval of a standard television signal or the full channel of a television station or cable television system. The major use today is for closed-captioning.

Translator—Broadcast station that rebroadcasts signals of other stations without originating its own programming.

Transponder—Satellite transmitter/receiver that picks up signals transmitted from earth, translates them into new frequencies and amplifies them before retransmitting them back to ground.

UHF—Ultra high frequency band (300 mhz-3,000 mhz), which includes TV channels 14-83.

Uplink—Earth station used for transmitting to satellite.

VCR—Videocassette recorder.

VHF—Very high frequencies (30 mhz-300 mhz), which include TV channels 2-13 and FM radio.

Videotext—Two-way interactive service that uses either two-way cable or telephone lines to connect a central computer to a television screen.

VTR—Videotape recorder.

List of Abbreviations Used in *Broadcasting & Cable Yearbook*

*	noncommercial
a	annual
A&E	Arts & Entertainment
actg	acting
ADI	Area of Dominant Influence
admin	administrative
adv	advertising
affil	affiliate
affrs	affairs
AFRTS	Armed Forces Radio and TV Service
alt	alternate
APR	American Public Radio
ant	antenna
AOR	album-oriented rock
AP	Associated Press
assn	association
assoc	associate
asst	assistant
atty	attorney
aur	aural
aux	auxiliary
bcst	broadcast
bcstg	broadcasting
bcstr	broadcaster
bd	board
BET	Black Entertainment Television
bi-m	every two months
bk rev	book reviews
bldg	building
bor	borough
btfl	beautiful
bus	business
C-SPAN	Cable Satellite Public Affairs Network
CATV	community antenna television
CBC	Canadian Broadcasting Corp.
CBN	Christian Broadcasting Network
CEO	chief executive officer
ch	channel
CH	critical hours
chg	charge
CHR	contemporary hit radio
chmn	chairman
circ	circulation
coml	commercial
contemp	contemporary
COO	chief operating officer
coord	coordinator
CP	construction permit
CRTC	Canadian Radio-television and Telecommunications Commission
C&W	country & western
D	day
d	daily
DA	directional antenna
dance rev	dance reviews
DBS	direct broadcast satellite
dev	development
dir	director
div	diverse
dups	duplicates
edit	editor
Eds	editors
Ed Bd	Editorial Board
educ	educational
engr	engineer
engrg	engineering
EPG	Electronic Program Guide
ERP	effective radiated power
ESPN	Entertainment & Sports Programming Network
ETV	educational television
exec	executive
FCC	Federal Communications Commission
film rev	film reviews
fortn	fortnightly
Fr	French
g	ground
gen	general
Ger	German
govt	government
HAAT	height above average terrain
HBO	Home Box Office
horiz	horizontal polarization
hqtrs	headquarters
ind	independent
info	information
instal	installation
ISBN	International Standard Book Number
ISSN	International Standard Serial Number
illus	illustrations
irreg	irregular
It	Italian
khz	kilohertz
kw	kilowatts
loc	local
LPTV	low power television
LS	local sunset
lstng	listening
lw	long wave
m	meters
MBS	Mutual Broadcasting System
MDS	Multipoint Distribution Service
mdse	merchandising
mfg	manufacturing
mgng	managing
mgr	manager
mgmt	management
mhz	megahertz
mi	miles
mktg	marketing
MMDS	Multichannel Multipoint Distribution Service
mo	month
mod	modification
MOR	middle of the road
MSO	multiple system operator
mthy	monthly
MTV	Music Television
mus	music
music rev	music reviews
mw	medium wave
N	night
na	not available
NAB	National Association of Broadcasters
natl	national
net	network
nwspr	newspaper
off	officer
opns	operations
own	owner
per	personnel
play rev	play reviews (theatre reviews)
Pol	Polish
pop	population
PR	public relations
pres	president
prod	production, producer
prog	program
progmg	programming
progsv	progressive
prom	promotion
PSA	presunrise authority, public service announcement
ptnr	partner
pub affrs	public affairs
publ	publicity
q	quarterly
quad	quadraphonic
record rev	record reviews
rel	relations
relg	religion
rep	representative
RFE	Radio Free Europe
rgn	region
rgnl	regional
RL	Radio Liberty
rsch	research
s-a	twice annually
s-m	twice monthly
s-w	twice weekly
sec	secretary
sep	separate
sh	shares
SH	specified hours
SIN	Spanish International Network
sls	sales
SMATV	satellite master antenna television
Sp	Spanish
spec	special
sr	senior
ST	shares time
stn	station
sub	subscriber
supt	superintendent
supvr	supervisor
svcs	services
sw	short wave
t	terrain
tech	technical
tele rev	television reviews
3/m	three times a month
3/y	three times a year
TNN	The Nashville Network
traf	traffic
trans	translators
treas	treasurer
twp	township
TWX	Teletypewriter Exchange
U	unlimited
UHF	ultra high frequency
UPI	United Press International
var	variety
vert	vertical polarization
VHF	very high frequency
video rev	video reviews
vis	visual
VOA	Voice of America
vp	vice president
w	watts
wkly	weekly

Brief History of Broadcasting and Cable

An overview of the evolution and development of radio, TV, cable and other mass communication media. Compiled by the **Broadcasting & Cable** magazine news staff.

One of the most dramatic developments of 20th-century technology has been the use of radio waves—electromagnetic radiations traveling at the speed of light—for communication. Radio communication designed for reception by the public at large is known as "broadcasting." Radio waves of different frequencies (number of cycles per second) can be "tuned." Hence, signals from many sources can be received on a radio set without interfering with each other.

In everyday language, the term "radio" refers to aural (sound) broadcasting, which is received from amplitude-modulated (AM) or frequency-modulated (FM) stations. "Television," another form of radio, is received from stations making both visual and aural transmissions. AM radio, sometimes called standard broadcasting, was the earliest broadcast service and operates on relatively low "medium" frequencies. FM and TV are newer and occupy considerably higher frequency bands.

Radio communication was born of many minds and developments. In the 1860s, a Scottish physicist, James Clerk Maxwell, predicted the existence of radio waves. Heinrich Rudolph Hertz, a German physicist, later demonstrated that rapid variations of electric current can be projected into space in the form of waves similar to those of light and heat. (His contributions have been honored internationally by the adoption of Hertz as a synonym for cycles per second.) In 1895, an Italian engineer, Guglielmo Marconi, transmitted radio signals for a short distance, and at the turn of the century, conducted successful transatlantic tests.

The first practical application of radio was for ship-to-ship and ship-to-shore telegraphic communication. Marine disasters early demonstrated the speed and effectiveness of radiotelegraphy for saving life and property at sea.

This new communication medium was first known as "wireless." American use of the term "radio" is traced to about 1912 when the Navy, feeling that "wireless" was too inclusive, adopted the word "radiotelegraph." The use of the word "broadcast" (originally a way to sow seed) stems from early U.S. naval references to "broadcast" of orders to the fleet. Now it is used to describe radio service to the public.

The origin of the first voice broadcast is a subject for debate. Claims to that distinction range from "Hello, Rainey," said to have been transmitted by Nathan B. Stubblefield to a neighbor, Rainey T. Wells, in a demonstration near Murray, Ky., in 1892, to an impromptu program from Brant Rock, Mass., by Reginald A. Fessenden in 1906, which was picked up by nearby ships.

There were other early experimental audio transmissions. Lee De Forest put singer Enrico Caruso on the air in 1910, and there were transatlantic voice tests by the Bell Telephone Co. in Arlington, Va., in 1915. But it was not until after World War I that regular broadcasting began.

The identity of the "first" broadcasting station also is a matter of conflicting claims. This is due largely to the fact that some pioneer AM broadcast stations developed from experimental operations. Although KDKA Pittsburgh did not receive a regular broadcasting license until Nov. 7, 1921, it furnished programs under a different authorization before that date. Records of the Department of Commerce, which then supervised radio, indicate that the first station to receive a regular broadcasting license was WBZ, Springfield, Mass., on Sept. 15, 1921. (WBZ is now assigned to Boston.)

There was experimental network operation over telephone lines as early as 1922. In that year, WJZ (now WABC) New York and WGY Schenectady, N.Y., broadcast the World Series. Early in 1923, WEAF (now WNBC) New York and WNAC Boston picked up a football game from Chicago. Later that same year, WEAF and WGY were connected with KDKA Pittsburgh and KYW Chicago (now Philadelphia) to carry talks made at a dinner in New York. President Coolidge's message to Congress was broadcast by six stations in 1923.

In 1926, the National Broadcasting Co., a subsidiary of the Radio Corporation of America, started the first regular network with 24 stations. For its first coast-to-coast hookup, in 1927, it broadcast a football game. In that same year, the Columbia Broadcasting System, first called the Columbia Phonograph Broadcasting System, was organized.

For some years NBC operated two networks, the Red and the Blue, but when the FCC adopted chain-broadcasting rules in the early 1940s, one organization was prohibited from operating two networks serving the same area at the same time. RCA sold the Blue Network to Edward J. Noble in 1943. It ultimately became the American Broadcasting Co. (In 1968, ABC itself was given a limited exception to the dual-network rule in order to operate four radio networks, each providing a specific service.)

FM and TV broadcasting emerged from their experimental stage just before U.S. entry into World War II. Wartime restrictions retarded expansion of radio facilities, although the emergency produced new techniques and apparati that are in use today. In the decades following the war, broadcasting expanded domestically, and the development of communication satellites has opened new possibilities for international relay.

Regulation of Broadcasting

The Wireless Ship Act of 1910 applied to use of radio by ships, but the Radio Act of 1912 was the first domestic law for general control of radio. It made the Secretary of Commerce and Labor (then a single department) responsible for licensing radio stations and operators.

Early broadcasting was experimental and, therefore, noncommercial. In 1919, radiotelephone experiments were enabled to operate as "limited commercial stations." In 1922, the wavelength of 360 meters (approximately 830 khz) was assigned for the transmission of "important news items, entertainment, lectures, sermons and similar matter."

Recommendations of the first National Radio Conference in 1922 resulted in further regulations by the Secretary of Commerce. A new type of AM broadcast station came into being, with minimum power of 500 watts and maximum of 1,000 watts (1 kilowatt). Two frequencies (750 and 833 khz) were assigned for program transmission.

So rapid was the development of AM broadcasting that, upon recommendation of subsequent National Radio Conferences in 1923 and 1924, the Department of Commerce allocated 550 to 1,500 khz for standard broadcast and authorized operating power up to 5,000 watts (5 kilowatts).

Increasing numbers of AM stations caused so much interference that, in 1925, a fourth National Radio Conference asked for a limitation on broadcast time and power. The Secretary of Commerce was unable to deal with the situation because court decisions held that the Radio Act of 1912 did not give him this authority. As a result, many broadcasters changed their frequencies and increased their power and operating time at will, regardless of the effect on other stations, producing bedlam on the air.

In 1926, President Coolidge urged Congress to remedy matters. The result was the Dill-White Radio Act of 1927.

Federal Radio Commission—The Radio Act of 1927 created a five-member Federal Radio Commission to issue station licenses, allocate frequency bands to various services, assign specific frequencies to individual stations and control station power. The same act delegated to the Secretary of Commerce authority to inspect radio stations, to examine and license radio operators and to assign radio call signs.

Much of the early effort of the Federal Radio Commission was required to straighten out the confusion in the broadcast band. It was impossible to accommodate the 732 broadcast stations then operating. New regulations caused about 150 of them to surrender their licenses.

Communications Act of 1934—At the request of President Roosevelt, the Secretary of Commerce in 1933 appointed an interdepartmental committee to study electronic communications. The committee recommended that Congress establish a single agency to regulate all interstate and foreign communication by wire and radio, including telegraph, telephone and broadcast.

The Communications Act of 1934 created the Federal Communications Commission for this unified regulation. This is the statute under which the FCC operates and which it enforces. Several of its provisions were taken from the earlier Radio Act.

Federal Communications Commission—The FCC began operating on July 11, 1934, as an independent federal agency headed by seven commissioners, who are appointed by the President with the advice and consent of the Senate. Under legislation passed in 1982, the FCC was cut back to five commissioners in June 1983.

FCC Broadcast Regulation—One of the FCC's major activities is the regulation of broadcasting. This has three phases.

The first is the allocation of space in the radio frequency spectrum to the broadcast services and to many nonbroadcast services which also must be accommodated. In view of the tremendously increased use of radio technology in recent decades, the competing demands for frequencies are among the commission's most pressing problems. Fortunately, as technology has advanced, frequencies higher and higher in the spectrum have become usable. Apart from the frequencies used for broadcasting, frequencies in other portions of the spectrum are allocated for "broadcast auxiliary" use by remote pickup and other transmitters auxiliary to main broadcast stations (see Auxiliary Broadcast Services).

The second phase of regulation is the assignment of stations in each service within the allocated frequency bands, with specific location, frequency and power. The chief consideration, although by no means the only one, is to avoid interference with other stations on the same channel (frequency) or channels adjacent in the spectrum. If an application is granted, the applicant for a new station or for changed facilities receives a construction permit. Later, when the station is built and it is capable of operating as proposed, a license to operate is issued.

The third phase is regulation of existing stations: inspection to see that stations are operating in accordance with FCC rules and technical provisions of their authorizations, modifying the authorizations when necessary, assigning station call letters, licensing transmitter operators, processing requests to assign the station license to another party or transfer control of the licensee corporation and processing applications for renewal of license. At renewal time, the commission reviews the station's record to see if it is operating in the public interest.

Although educational and other noncommercial stations share the airwaves, the American broadcasting system for the most part is a commercial system. In this respect it is supported by revenues from those who advertise goods or services to the audience. Advertising messages are presented as commercial "spot announcements" before, during and after programs, or as a part of "sponsored" programs.

Broadcast stations are licensed to serve the public interest, convenience and necessity. By law, each license must contain a statement that the licensee does not have any right to operate the station or use the frequency beyond the term of license. The maximum term of license for a radio station is seven years; the maximum term of license for a television station is five years.

Under requirements of the Communications Act, applicants must be legally, technically and financially qualified, and they must show that their proposed operation would be in the public interest. They must be citizens of the United States. Corporations with alien officers or directors or with more than one-fifth of the capital stock controlled by foreign interests may not be licensed.

Penalties for violation of FCC rules by broadcast stations, depending upon the degree of seriousness, range from reprimands, fines and short-term probationary licenses to denial of license renewal, or even license revocation. Cease-and-desist orders may also be issued.

In 1965, the commission provided for public inspection of certain records of broadcast stations in the communities they serve. These are mainly duplicate copies of records in the public files of the commission in Washington, and include licenses, records of ownership, applications to the FCC and related material, network affiliation contracts and employment reports.

The commission is forbidden by law from censoring programs. The Communications Act, Section 326, states: "Nothing in this Act shall be understood or construed to give the commission the power of censorship over the radio communications of signals transmitted by any radio station, and no regulation or condition shall be promulgated or fixed by the commission which shall interfere with the right of free speech by means of radio communication." Despite the prohibition, the federal government has promulgated limited rules and laws regulating content of broadcast stations.

Fairness Doctrine—In a highly controversial move, the FCC voted in August 1987 to eliminate the fairness doctrine, which required broadcast stations to air issues of public importance and to present all sides of the issues. While most broadcasters cheered the action as one that elevated their First Amendment standing, many members of Congress called for resurrection of doctrine in federal law.

Only the general fairness doctrine was repealed. The fairness corollaries—the personal attack rule and the political editorializing rule—are still on the books. Broadcast organizations have petitioned for their deletion, but thus far the FCC has failed to act.

The doctrine stems from a policy on editorializing announced in 1949, and supported by a 1959 amendment to the Communications Act. It obligates broadcasters "to afford reasonable opportunity for the discussion of conflicting views of public importance." In 1967, the commission adopted specific rules requiring stations to notify persons when personal attacks were made on them in discussion of controversial public issues (with certain exceptions such as newscasts). The same requirement was also applied to station editorials endorsing or opposing a political candidate. These rules were upheld by the Supreme Court in 1969.

Section 315—Section 315 of the Communications Act provides: (a) "If any licensee shall permit any person who is a legally qualified candidate for any public office to use a broadcasting station, he shall afford equal opportunities to all other such candidates for that office in the use of such broadcasting station; provided that such licensee shall have no power of censorship over the material broadcast under the provisions of this section. No obligation is hereby imposed upon any licensee to allow the use of its station by any such candidate ... (b) The charges made for the use of any broadcast station for any of the purposes set forth in this section shall not exceed the charges made for comparable use of such station for other purposes ..." In 1959, the act was amended to exempt from the equal-time requirement appearances by candidates on newscasts, news interviews and other news coverage.

A problem in connection with this statute is that it requires a station presenting one candidate to afford equal opportunities to "all" other legally qualified candidates for the same office, including, often, some who have no chance of prevailing in the election. In 1960, Congress suspended this requirement for the presidential election, thus making possible the broadcast debates between the Democratic and Republican candidates without stations having to give equal time to the numerous other presidential candidates representing small parties. A similar provision on a permanent basis is contained in legislation passed by Congress in September 1970.

Advertising—Congress passed a law late in 1990 that limits the amount of advertising in children's TV programming (12.5 minutes per hour on weekends and 10.5 minutes per hour on weekdays). The FCC had eliminated advertising time limits for all types of programming in 1984 as part of a general deregulation of TV broadcasting.

Stations and producers of advertising are expected to cooperate in controlling the sound volume (loudness) of commercials.

"Payola" and "Rigged Quiz Shows"—Revelations about programs in the late 1950s led to amendments to the Communications Act in 1960. These made more explicit a station's obligation to make an announcement when money or other consideration is received for the presentation of broadcast material (e.g., money received by a disk jockey for playing a record). They made illegal the presentation of programs purporting to be contests of knowledge or skill where the result is in any way prearranged.

Lotteries and Fraud—Congress, in January 1975, modified the law to permit the broadcasting of information or advertisements on a lawful state-operated lottery by stations in that state or adjacent states. A month later, the FCC amended its rules to conform to the changes. The U.S. Criminal Code prohibits broadcasting of lotteries other than state-operated. To be regarded as a "lottery," a giveaway arrangement must involve a prize, chance and "consideration." A number of commission and court decisions have dealt with these concepts in particular situations, especially as to what is "consideration." (It has been held, for instance, that having to go in a particular store or listen to a particular program is not "consideration.")

Indecency—Broadcasting of obscene or indecent programming is against the law. Enforcement of the obscenity prohibition is up to the Justice Department, but it is left to the FCC to take care of indecency.

In 1978, the Supreme Court affirmed the FCC's authority to act against stations that broadcast indecency during times when the likelihood of children being in the audience was high. It was not until April 1987 that the FCC began enforcing the law in earnest, however. Since then, it has generated a small, but steady, stream of fines against stations.

Congress adopted a 24-hour indecency ban in 1988 that was reversed in the courts. First Amendment advocates argued the ban violated the 1978 Supreme Court decision. Congress tried again in 1992, passing an indecency band covering all except the "safe harbor" hours of midnight-6 a.m. But again the courts rejected the rules, saying the "safe harbor" was arbitrary. At year's end, the FCC was planning a proceeding to craft and justify a new "safe harbor."

Networks—The commission does not license networks as such, only individual stations. Station licensees are subject to the chain broadcasting regulations adopted by the commission in 1941 to further competition in broadcasting. These rules have been supplemented by further regulations adopted from time to time.

The principal regulations affecting broadcast networks are the financial interest and syndication rules, which limit networks' ability to own and syndicate the programming they air.

After one of the longest and most bitter fights the FCC has ever experienced, the agency voted in April 1991 to relax the rules. That was little solace to the networks, who believed that the rules were unwarranted and should have been repealed in their entirety.

After a federal court said the rules were still unjustified, the FCC further relaxed them in early 1993. All that remained were restrictions on the networks' actually selling programs in syndication, and they were set to expire in 1995.

Also in 1993, a federal judge in Los Angeles lifted consent decrees that restricted the networks much as the original FCC rules did. Without the judge's action, the FCC liberalization of its rules would have meant little.

Monopoly—Commission rules prohibit the same person or group from owning more than four radio stations or one TV station in the same locality. (Ownership is limited to just three radio stations in small markets with fewer than 15 total stations.) Nationally, the FCC permits ownership of up to 18 AM and 18 FM stations and 12 TV stations. The TV stations may not operate in markets collectively containing more than 25% of the nation's TV homes.

Licensees are now also prohibited from owning an AM and a TV station in the same locality, although the FCC in 1988 implemented a liberal waiver policy that has resulted in a number of new radio-TV combinations. The FCC also has regulations pending to allow broadcast networks to acquire up to 10% of the nation's cable homes passed and 50% of homes passed in a locality. Still prohibited: common ownership of TV stations and newspapers or TV stations and cable systems in the same market.

The commission is considering relaxing the TV ownership rules to allow an owner to own either two UHF stations or one VHF and one UHF station per locality.

Receivers—The advent of "wireless" prompted amateurs and others interested in listening in on Morse code radiotelegraph transmissions to acquire receiving sets. Homemade sets with crystal detectors gradually gave way to commercially manufactured receivers. Then the rise of broadcasting aroused public interest in owning sets, battery-operated at first, to receive regular programs. Receivers operated by house current came on the market about 1928. Development of the transistor in 1948 led to their use in place of tubes in sets. Successive stages in TV receiver development have taken sets from black-and-white to color, and VHF-only to all-channel (VHF and UHF) capability (see chapter on TV Broadcast).

The commission does not license receivers. However, it does require manufacturers to limit radiation that may interfere with radio or TV reception.

Call Letters—International agreement provides for national identification of a radio station by the first letter or first two letters of its assigned call signal, and for this purpose the alphabet is apportioned among nations. Broadcast stations in the United States use call letters beginning with K or W. Generally, those beginning with K are assigned to stations west of the Mississippi River while W is assigned east of the Mississippi.

During radio's infancy, most of the broadcast stations were in the East. As inland stations developed, the Mississippi River was made the dividing line between K and W calls. However, KDKA Pittsburgh and some other eastern stations authorized before this system went into effect have retained their K calls, and similarly some pioneer stations west of the Mississippi have kept their W calls. Most of the early broadcast call signs contained only three letters. These combinations were soon exhausted and stations were assigned four-letter calls. Since many AM licensees also operate FM and TV stations, a common practice is to use the AM call letters followed by "-FM" or "-TV."

National Defense—In cooperation with military and civil defense agencies, the commission has established the Emergency Broadcast System, based on voluntary participation by the broadcast industry. EBS facilities are for the primary purpose of giving emergency warning and advice to the public in event of attack, but they are put to peacetime use in alerting audiences to serious weather and other emergencies threatening life and property.

Broadcast Operation

Frequencies and Station Assignments—Radio frequencies differ in characteristics, and each service is assigned to a frequency band to suit its needs.

The AM aural service, sometimes called standard broadcast, occupies the band from 535 khz to 1705 khz. Radio waves travel with the same speed as light, and are of different "frequencies" (cycles per second) and "wavelengths" (distance between points in successive cycles). "Frequency" and "wavelength" vary inversely with each other. The latter term was formerly used generally to describe a particular radio wave, and still is in some other countries; but in the United States the use of "frequency" is much more common. The usable frequency spectrum has constantly expanded upward with developing technology, so that what were once "high" frequencies are near the low end of the total spectrum used. AM stations are assigned at 10 khz intervals beginning at 540 khz.

FM broadcasting occupies the frequencies from 88 to 108 mhz, with 100 channels of 200 khz width each, the lowest 20 of them reserved for educational use. Both the center frequency (e.g., "93.1 mhz") and the designated channel number from 201 to 300 are used (e.g., "channel 201" is "88.1 mhz"), although channel numbers are not in popular usage since they are not on FM receivers.

In television, where wider channels are required to carry both picture and sound, each channel is 6 mhz wide. The very high frequency (VHF) portion of the television service occupies the frequencies 54 to 72 mhz (channels 2, 3 and 4), 76 to 88 mhz (channels 5 and 6) and 174 to 216 mhz (channels 7 through 13). The ultra high frequency (UHF) portion of the television service occupies the frequencies from 470 to 890 mhz (channels 14 through 83). Designated channel numbers identify the frequency assignments (e.g., 54-60 mhz is "Channel 2"). There is no "channel 1" in television.

Although "AM" and "FM" are often used to refer to the standard broadcast and FM broadcast services, these terms more properly apply to the methods, "amplitude modulation" and "frequency modulation," used to impress aural or visual intelligence on the carrier wave. The "AM" principle is used not only in the standard broadcast service but also in the picture portion of television and in the international "shortwave" service. The "FM" principle is used both in the FM broadcast service and in the sound portion of television.

In all the broadcast services, the same aural or visual channel can be used in different places if the stations are far enough apart not to interfere with one another or with stations on adjacent or technically related channels. A TV station may be required to "offset" 10 khz above or below its normal carrier frequency. The channel assigned to such a station is then designated "plus" or "minus" as the case may be. This makes more TV assignments possible and reduces the possibility of interference.

AM and FM Systems—Without being too technical, this is how an aural station works:

A person talks into a microphone as if it were a telephone. His voice sets up vibrations of varying intensity and frequency. The lower the pitch the slower the vibration. A cycle, or wavelength, is one complete performance of a vibration.

In the microphone, these vibrations are converted into electrical impulses which are then greatly amplified at the transmitter before being put on the "carrier" wave. The intensity and frequency of the carrier wave are constant. This wave, by itself, does not transmit music or speech, so it is varied to correspond with fluctuations of the speech or music received at the microphone. This is called "modulation."

In AM broadcast, the audio waves are impressed on the carrier wave in a manner to cause its amplitude (or power) to vary with the audio waves. The frequency of the carrier remains constant. This is known as amplitude modulation. In frequency modulation (FM), the amplitude remains unchanged but the frequency is varied in a manner corresponding to the voice or music to be transmitted.

These modulated waves radiate from the antenna tower at approximately 186,000 miles per second (the speed of light). Some of them follow the contour of the ground and are called "groundwaves." Others dart upward and are called "skywaves." At night, the skywave portions of transmissions in the standard broadcast (AM) frequencies are reflected back to earth by electrical particles in the "ionosphere" portion of the atmosphere. This gives the listener a choice of more distant AM stations at night, but also increases interference. Daytime reception is largely dependent upon groundwaves.

Radio waves may pass through buildings and other objects but are subject to absorption or interference. As in the case of ripples on water, radio vibrations weaken with distance. Seasonal disturbances and sunspot periods can throw them off course and cause "freak" reception.

AM broadcast stations use "medium waves." That is to say, they transmit 540,000 to 1,600,000 waves a second, or 540 to 1600 khz. At 540,000 waves a second, the distance between waves is approximately 1,800 feet.

The so-called "shortwave" (international long-distance) broadcast stations transmit in the frequency range 6 mhz to 25 mhz. These waves are sent out one after another so rapidly that the distance between their crests (wave length) is only about 37 to 150 feet.

FM and TV stations, broadcasting in the very high and ultra high frequencies, send out even shorter, or very short, waves. (The word "shortwave" came into use before there was technology to use these other parts of the spectrum.)

The modulated radio wave from the radio station is picked up by the home receiving antenna. In other words, the wave sets up in the receiving antenna a current having the same frequency characteristics as the one transmitted. In the receiver, the audio and carrier waves are separated by a device called a detector or demodulator. The carrier wave, no longer needed, is dissipated while the audio wave is relayed to the loudspeaker where it is transformed back into the sound that is heard by the listener. (Television operation is discussed in TV Broadcast.)

Stereophonic Service—Stereophony is not really a 20th century innovation but dates back to experiments performed over wire lines by telephone engineers in the 1880's. Even at that time, contemporary accounts spoke of being able to "localize" a singer's position on an opera stage by virtue of the signal strength in either the right or left telephone. Over the next few decades, there were other experiments in transmitting binaural sound, but the general impetus to development came only with post-World War II technology in which multiplexing techniques were applied to FM broadcasting. In 1959, the National Stereophonic Radio Committee was created to examine the many proposed systems of FM stereo and submit a final recommendation to the commission. In the summer of 1960, six systems were field tested over KDKA-FM (now WPNT) Pittsburgh, with receivers set up at Uniontown, Pa. The system of stereo transmission proposed by the General Electric Co. and the Zenith Corp. was adopted, with broadcasting authorized to start on June 1, 1961. The FCC authorized AM stereo in 1982, but refused to select a standard from among five incompatible systems. In July 1982, KDKA(AM) Pittsburgh and KTSA(AM) San Antonio, Tex., began AM stereo programming with a Kahn system, the first to win FCC acceptance. The Motorola system ultimately emerged as the most popular system. Under a congressional mandate, the FCC in 1993 finally picked a stereo standard. And to no one's surprise, it was Motorola's.

Nonetheless, AM stereo has not caught on, principally because many AM stations have given up on music formats and no longer care. Stereo did nothing to overcome AM's other weaknesses as a music medium: susceptibility to interference and low fidelity.

Television stereo was approved by the FCC in spring 1984. Although the FCC did not adopt a single standard, it did provide interference protection for an industry committee-selected Zenith/dbx transmission system. The authorization allowed not only for stereocasts, but also a second audio program channel for bilingual or narrative broadcasts and a third channel for professional uses. Noncommercial WTTW(TV) Chicago became the first stereo TV broadcaster in August 1984. Within one year, 100 stations were providing multichannel sound. TV stereo is now commonplace.

Transmitting Antenna—In the AM service, antenna height above ground is not usually a matter of much importance. The entire antenna structure acts as the antenna and usually varies in height with the frequency of the transmission. Few AM antennas exceed 1,000 feet in height and most are considerably less. By contrast, in FM and TV, where transmission follows "line of sight," service depends on the location of the receiver in relation to the transmitting antenna. Here, antenna height is extremely important. While FM and TV antennas themselves are short, they are often situated, for greater overall height, atop natural or man-made structures, such as tall buildings, mountain tops, or tall towers specifically built for this purpose.

In the interest of safe air navigation, authorizations for broadcast transmitting antennas must usually be coordinated with the Federal Aviation Administration. Those over a certain height (usually 200 feet) must be painted and lighted. To further minimize the hazard to air traffic, shared use of tall towers, or location of all tall antennas of a given area on an "antenna farm" is encouraged.

Radio and TV broadcasters must also limit public and occupational exposure to radio frequency radiation emissions from antenna towers. Following enactment of new regulations by the FCC in January 1986, exposure levels will be routinely considered for construction permits of new or modified facilities and for renewal applications. The rules also apply to TV translators, low power TV, satellite earth station transmitters and experimental stations.

"Directional antennas" consist of more than one radiating element (the tower in AM), with phasing of the radiation from a series of towers so arranged that radiations cancel each other in some directions and reinforce each other in other directions. Sometimes they are used to increase radiation and service in a particular direction. More commonly, the purpose is to restrict radiation in one or more directions, usually to avoid interference to other stations.

As AM stations began to multiply on shared channels, it became necessary to employ directional antennas to prevent interference. Since 1937, directional antennas have helped new stations squeeze into the congested AM broadcast band. Most full-time (day and night) AM stations operate directionally at night. Directional antenna arrays can produce "figure eight" and more complicated service patterns. A complete array may include 12 towers. Directional antennas also are used in international communication and microwave relay to beam transmissions to particular points. Some FM and TV stations now use directional antennas.

AM Broadcast

AM is the oldest system of broadcasting. The pioneer AM service started operation on the 535-1605 khz band. In a sweeping reform of the service in 1991, the AM extended the upper end of the band to 1705 khz.

Classes of AM Stations—As part of its reforms, the FCC adopted a new classification system.

Classes of AM Broadcast Channels and Stations—Clear channel. A clear channel is one on which stations are assigned to serve wide areas. These stations are protected from objectionable interference within their primary service areas and, depending on the class of the station, their secondary service areas. Stations operating on these channels are classified as follows:

(1) Class A station. A Class A station is an unlimited time station that operates on a clear channel and is designed to render primary and secondary service over an extended area and at relatively long distances from its transmitter. Its primary service area is protected from objectionable interference from other stations on the same and adjacent channels, and its secondary service area is protected from interference from other stations on the same channel. The operating power shall not be less than 10 kw nor more than 50 kw.

(2) Class B station. A Class B station is an unlimited time station which is designed to render service only over a primary service area. Class B stations are authorized to operate with a minimum power of 250 watts and a maximum power of 50 kw or 10 kw for stations that are authorized to operate in the 1605-1705 khz band.

(3) Class D station. A Class D station operates either daytime, limited time or unlimited time with nighttime power less than 250 watts. Class D stations shall operate with daytime powers not less than 250 watts nor more than 50 kw. Nighttime operations of Class D stations are not afforded protection and must protect all Class A and Class B operations during nighttime hours. New Class D stations that had not been previously licensed as Class B will not be authorized.

Regional Channel. A regional channel is one on which Class B and Class D stations may operate and serve primarily a principal center of population and the rural area contiguous thereto.

Local Channel. A local channel is one on which stations operate unlimited time and serve primarily a community and the suburban and rural areas immediately contiguous thereto.

(4) Class C station. A Class C station is a station operating on a local channel and is designed to render service only over a primary service area that may be reduced if found to cause interference with other stations. The power shall not be less than 250 watts, nor more than 1 kw. Class C stations that are licensed to operate with 100 watts may continue to do so.

Day and Night Service—Of the two types of signals—groundwave and skywave—groundwave service is steadier, more reliable and is called "primary" service. Skywave or "secondary" service is available at night because skywave signals, lost in the daylight, are reflected from the ionosphere. Since skywaves cover tremendous distances, Class A stations can render skywave service across 700 miles or more. This service is subject to "fading," varying with changes in such factors as time of day, weather, latitude, atmospheric noise and sunspot activity, hence the name "secondary." Because of the high power and extent of protection required for skywave signals to afford useful service, only Class A stations are authorized for skywave service.

Because skywave transmission is a factor in the AM frequencies at night, the number of AM stations operating at night must be limited. Therefore, slightly more than half of U.S. AM stations are licensed for daytime-only operation, sunrise to sunset, although on many frequencies most of them are also permitted to operate, usually with reduced power, starting at 6 a.m. when that is before sunrise (so-called "presunrise" operation). More than 2,000 such stations may operate up to two hours after local sunset.

In the early 1960s, the AM band was experiencing congestion and interference. At the same time, some service needs, such as night-time primary service to large portions of the country, were not being met. Therefore, in 1964, the assignment rules for new AM stations, or for more powerful facilities, were tightened to prevent interference and preserve the AM potential for more efficient use.

Facilities authorized from 1964 to 1968 involved minimal interference and provided the first local radio outlets for a number of communities. Still, there were unfulfilled service needs, particularly at night, and so in July 1968, the commission stopped accepting AM applications while it studied how to utilize the limited potential for new stations in the AM band. At that time, there were 4,215 AM stations on the air in this country; another 100 that had been previously authorized were expected to come on the air in succeeding months. There were more than twice as many AM as FM stations on the air.

The next year, new rules were proposed under which the commission would, to a greater extent, regard AM and FM as a single aural service. New AM stations would be authorized only where they would bring a primary service to a substantial area not receiving such service from existing AM or FM stations, and would not be granted if an FM channel were available which would bring the same service benefits. FM development would be encouraged because of technical qualities of this service, including ample nighttime coverage and relative lack of interference when new stations were added.

FM Broadcast

Frequency modulation broadcast has several advantages over the older amplitude modulation. FM has higher fidelity characteristics and is freer of static, fading and background overlapping of other stations.

FM's greater tonal range is due primarily to the fact that it uses a wider channel than that employed for AM broadcast. Then, too, it occupies a higher portion of the radio spectrum where there is less static and other noise than at lower frequencies. FM receivers have the particular ability to suppress weaker stations and other interference.

Since the frequencies on which FM operates do not ordinarly reflect back to earth from ionospheric layers (in skywaves), it is possible for many scattered FM stations to use the same frequency without interference, night or day, unlike the AM band.

History—The principle of frequency modulation has long been known, but its advantages for broadcasting were not realized until shortly before World War II. Largely as a result of interest evoked by extensive developmental work by Edwin H. Armstrong in the 1930s, the commission authorized increased FM experimentation, and in 1940, after extensive public hearings, provided for FM operation to start Jan. 1, 1941. It set apart 35 channels for commercial and five channels for noncommercial educational FM.

On Oct. 31, 1940, the commission granted construction permits for the first 15 FM stations. By the end of that year, there were 10 more. Though all radio construction was frozen during World War II, more than 40 prewar FM stations continued to serve some 400,000 receivers.

FM stations were initially assigned call letters with numerals added, but in 1943 the present letter system was adopted. There is optional use of the suffix "FM" to distinguish these stations from jointly operated AM stations.

Because of skywave interference experienced on the original FM band of 42-50 mhz per second, the commission in 1945 moved FM to its present higher and less vulnerable position of 88-108 mhz. At the same time, it increased the number of channels to 100, providing 80 for commercial and 20 for noncommercial educational use.

FM Zones and Classes—In 1962, the commission revised its commercial FM rules to divide the country into three zones (instead of the previous two). Zone I includes part or all of 18 northeastern states, plus the District of Columbia; Zone I-A is limited to Southern California, and Zone II includes the rest of the country.

Three classes of commercial FM stations (instead of the previous two) were created. Class A stations are assigned to all zones; Class B stations are assigned to Zones I and I-A, and Class C stations are assigned to Zone II.

Class A stations are low-powered with a maximum of 6 kw effective radiated power. The maximum power for Class B stations is 50 kw and for Class C, 100 kw.

An important factor in FM operation is the height of the antenna above surrounding terrain (see earlier section on Transmitting Antennas, line-of-sight transmission). Therefore, stations have maximum antenna heights in relation to power; 300 feet above average terrain for Class A, 500 feet for Class B and 2,000 feet for Class C. If the antenna height above average terrain is greater, power must be reduced commensurately. Minimum power requirements are also prescribed.

FM reception varies with location of the receiver in relation to the transmitting antenna. With maximum power and antenna height, good service extends about 15 miles for Class A stations, 33 miles for Class B, and 64 miles for Class C. The rules also include minimum mileage separations between stations on the same or adjacent channels. This is to protect the service from interference.

Subsidiary FM Service—To aid FM broadcasters, the commission in 1955 enabled them to apply for subsidiary communications authorizations for supplemental service such as background music. Sometimes called "functional music," this specialized service is offered to stores, factories and other business subscribers.

Originally, subsidiary communications were permitted on a simplex basis, the station devoting part of the time on its channel to regular broadcasting and part to this specialized service. Later, rules were adopted requiring subsidiary communications to be on a multiplex basis, that is, using one or more subchannels with the main channel used for regular broadcasting. The FCC permits FM broadcasters to use their subcarriers for a broad variety of new services.

TV Broadcast

Television broadcasting is synchronous transmission of visual and aural programs. The picture phase is accomplished by sending a rapid succession of electrical impulses which the receiver transforms into scenes and images. Here is a brief explanation of a complex process.

Monochrome—The scene to be televised is focused on a special tube in the television camera which has a small "screen" covered with about 367,000 microscopic dots of a special photo-sensitive substance. This can be likened to a tiny motion picture screen and is called a "mosaic." The varying light from each part of the scene being televised falls upon these dots and gives them an electrical charge, the strength depending upon the amount of light falling upon the individual dots. Thus each dot becomes a tiny storage battery and the scene is formed in a pattern of electrical charges on the mosaic.

The mosaic is "scanned" by a tiny beam of electrons, no larger than the head of a pin, moving from left to right and progressing downward (just as the printed page is read by the human eye). This complete process is repeated 60 times per second, and the horizontal lines of alternate scanning are interlaced so that 30 complete pictures or "frames" composed of 525 horizontal lines are produced each second.

As the electron beam strikes each dot on the mosaic, the dot is discharged through the electron beam and the electrical impulses produced are used to modulate the signals of the TV transmitter. Each time the dots are discharged by the electron beam they are recharged by the light produced by the succeeding scene falling upon them. The succession of individual "still" scenes creates the illusion of motion just as in the case of motion pictures made on film.

The reproduction by the TV receiver of the pictures transmitted is just the reverse of the transmission. The incoming succession of electrical impulses is separated from the "carrier" and, after amplification, is impressed on the picture tube grid and progresses downward on the face of the picture tube.

The face of the tube is coated with a material which fluoresces or gives off light at the point where it is struck by the electron beam. In the absence of a television signal, the whole face of the picture tube is illuminated equally by a series of closely spaced horizontal lines. When a TV signal is placed on the grid of the picture tube, it controls the strength of the electron beam and hence the amount of light on the face of the tube. If the scanning of the electron beam in the picture tube is kept in perfect step with the scanning of the electron beam in the TV camera, the picture tube will reproduce the lights and shadows of the subject scene, and the succession of such scenes produces the illusion of motion.

In brief, the picture seen by the viewer is actually produced by a flickering spot of light moving rapidly across and down the face of the picture tube. The viewer sees the "whole" picture because the screen continues to glow for a tiny fraction of a second after the electron beam has passed. Coupled with the retentive ability of the eye, this creates the illusion that the picture is there all the time. The high rate of repetition of the picture produced by the beam minimizes flicker and lends smoothness to motion.

The TV transmitter is, in effect, two separate units. One sends out the picture and the other the sound. Visual transmission is by amplitude modulation. Sound transmission is by frequency modulation.

Color—In color TV, a brightness component is transmitted in much the same manner as the black-and-white picture signal is sent. In addition, a color component is transmitted at the same time on a subcarrier frequency located between the visual and aural carrier frequencies.

Color standards are based on a simultaneous system of color transmission. Signals representing red, blue and green are transmitted simultaneously. These are the "primary colors," and when they are combined in various amounts, they produce all other colors. A magnifying-glass examination of the scene on a receiver will reveal that it is made up only of red, blue and green dots, no matter what color is being shown. Even scenes not transmitted in color and seen as varying shades of gray to white are made up of red, blue and green dots.

Only color receivers have the special picture tubes and the necessary circuitry to illuminate the colored dots. Under the "compatible color" system, color programs can be received in black-and-white on monochrome sets, and black-and-white programs can be received as they are on color sets.

TV History—Men of many lands contributed to the development of television. Like aural radio, TV was made possible by electronic discoveries in the late 19th and early 20th centuries. In 1884, Paul Nipkow, a German, patented a scanning disk for transmitting pictures by wireless. In this country, Charles F. Jenkins began his study of the subject about 1890. The English physicist, E.E. Fournier d'Albe, conducted experiments in the early 1900s. In 1915, Marconi predicted "visible telephone."

In 1923, physicist Vladimir Zworykin, a Russian-born American, applied for a patent on the iconoscope camera tube. In the years following, there were experiments by E.F.W. Alexanderson and Philo T. Farnsworth in this country and John L. Baird in England. An experimental TV program, in which Secretary of Commerce Herbert Hoover participated, was sent by wire between New York and Washington by the Bell Telephone Laboratories in 1927. The next year Bell experimentally televised outdoor programs.

The Federal Radio Commission (predecessor of the Federal Communications Commission) reported that a few broadcast stations were experimenting with television in 1928. In that year, WGY Schenectady, N.Y., broadcast the first TV drama. Large-screen TV was demonstrated by Radio Corp. of America (now RCA Corp.) at a New York theater in 1930. RCA tested outdoor TV pickup at Camden, N.J., in 1936.

By 1937, there were 17 experimental TV stations operating. The first incumbent U.S. President seen on TV was Franklin D. Roosevelt, when he opened the New York World's Fair in 1939. That year saw the first telecast of a major league baseball game, a college football game and a professional boxing match. In 1940, the Republican and Democratic conventions were first televised. Pioneer use of coaxial cable for long-distance relay was made for the Republican convention.

The first President's message to Congress over network TV was that of Harry S Truman in 1950. The first TV debate between presidential candidates was in 1960 between John F. Kennedy and Richard M. Nixon. The first presidential message to Congress televised in color was that of President Lyndon B. Johnson in 1966.

Early Commercial Operation—The Journal Co. of Milwaukee, now licensee of WTMJ-TV, filed the first application to broadcast TV on a commercial basis. At a 1940 hearing the FCC found industry divided on technology and standards, but a committee appointed to work on the questions reached agreement on the present standards of 525 lines and 30 frames per second, and on Apr. 30, 1941, the commission authorized commercial TV operations to start the following July 1 on 10 commercial stations which were on the air by May 1942, six continuing during the war.

In 1945 the commission allocated 13 VHF channels between 44 and 216 mhz for commercial television, but it noted that there was not enough spectrum space below 300 mhz for an adequate nationwide system. Twelve of the VHF channels had to be shared with nonbroadcast two-way radio services. To prepare for TV expansion, the UHF frequencies between 480 and 920 mhz were made available for experimental TV and those between 1,245 and 1,325 mhz for TV relay.

In 1948, because of interference with commercial TV, the VHF sharing was ended. TV channel 1 (44-50 mhz) was deleted and assigned to land mobile or two-way radio service.

TV Proceedings 1948-1951—As the commission had foreseen, it was increasingly evident that the available channels were too few for nationwide service. On Sept. 30, 1948, the commission stopped granting new TV applications in order to study the situation. This was the so-called TV "freeze" order. On July 11, 1949, comprehensive changes were proposed to improve and extend TV service. These included engineering standards, opening UHF channels for TV, consideration of color systems, reservation of channels for noncommercial educational use and a national assignment plan for all channels.

Color was considered first. Three competitive systems were offered for commission consideration. They were the "field sequential" system of Columbia Broadcasting System, the RCA "dot sequential" system and the Color Television Inc. "line sequential" system. The commission found that the field sequential system was the only one that met its criteria for color operation, even though this system could not be received in monochrome on existing receivers (the others claimed theirs could). This method of operation was adopted in 1950, but the door was left open for development of a better system.

CBS began limited color broadcasts on June 25, 1951, but ran into problems. Because of a materials shortage, Defense Mobilization Chief Charles E. Wilson, in October 1951, requested the suspension of manufacture of color TV sets for the public and interest in the field sequential system lagged.

Thereafter, new standards for "compatible color," receivable both in color and monochrome, were developed by RCA and advocated by the industry through its National Television System Committee. These standards were adopted by the commission on Dec. 17, 1953.

Freeze Lifted 1952—On Apr. 14, 1952, the commission reopened TV to expansion. It added 70 UHF channels (between 470 and 890 mhz) to the 12 VHF channels (54-216 mhz). It adopted a table making more than 2,000 channel assignments to nearly 1,300 communities. These included 242 assignments for noncommercial educational use.

The minimum effective radiated visual power of TV stations was set at 100 watts. The maximum varies with antenna height. (No minimum height above average terrain is specified.) On VHF channels 2-6, maximum power is 100 kw; on channels 7-13 it is 316 kw; and on UHF channels 14-83 it is 5,000 kw. With very high antennas, the amount of power is reduced.

Separation of stations on the same channels is determined by three geographic zones. In Zone I, minimum co-channel separation is 170 miles for VHF channels and 155 for UHF. This zone covers Massachusetts, Rhode Island, Connecticut, New Jersey, Maryland, Pennsylvania, Delaware, District of Columbia, Ohio, Indiana, Illinois and parts of Maine, New Hampshire, Vermont, New York, Virginia, West Virginia, Michigan and Wisconsin.

In Zone II, minimum co-channel separation is 190 miles for VHF and 175 miles for UHF channels. This zone includes Kentucky, Tennessee, North and South Carolina, Missouri, Iowa, Minnesota, Arkansas, Kansas, Nebraska, Oklahoma, North and South Dakota, Utah, Idaho, Arizona, New Mexico, Montana, Wyoming, Nevada, Colorado, Oregon, Washington, California, Alaska, Hawaii and parts of Maine, New Hampshire, Vermont, New York, Virginia, West Virginia, Georgia, Alabama, Mississippi, Louisiana, Michigan, Wisconsin and Texas.

In Zone III, the separation is 220 miles for VHF and 205 miles for UHF channels. This zone includes Florida and parts of Georgia, Alabama, Louisiana, Mississippi and Texas.

The first commercial TV grants after the freeze were made July 11, 1952, to three Denver stations. The first commercial UHF station to go on the air was KPTV Portland, Ore., on Sept. 20, 1952.

TV Service—Commercial TV stations are required to broadcast at least 28 hours a week, at least two hours every day, although they are allowed a shorter schedule when they begin operation.

TV service may be expanded to new areas through use of "satellite" stations—regular stations largely rebroadcasting the programs of parent stations—and "translators," lower power automatic installations which pick up and rebroadcast programs of parent stations on a different frequency. The rules also provide that UHF stations may use "boosters," low-power stations rebroadcasting on the same frequency, to fill in "shadow" areas within their normal service areas. These have not proved satisfactory and none are now in operation. Rebroadcasting requires the consent of the originating stations.

Unlike AM networking over ordinary telephone wires, TV networking requires special relay adjuncts. Network TV was made possible in large measure by the development of coaxial cable and microwave relay facilities. As early as 1937, motion pictures were televised and sent over the coaxial cable link between New York and Philadelphia. Network operation was begun by WNBT (now WNBC-TV) New York City, WRGB Schenectady, and WPTZ (now KYW-TV) Philadelphia in 1944.

Regular coaxial-cable relay service was inaugurated between Washington and New York in 1946. The following year microwave relay service was extended as far as Boston. A Midwestern relay system, opened in 1948, was joined with the Eastern system in 1949. The first link in the transcontinental relay system was opened between New York and Chicago in 1950. It reached San Francisco the following year and on Sept. 4, 1951, it carried telecasts of the Japanese peace treaty conference there.

Today, all three broadcast networks are using satellites to distribute programming to many of their affiliates. Of the three, NBC has the most extensive satellite network. It serves directly via satellite more than 170 of its affiliates.

UHF Development—Economic and technical problems have impeded full utilization of the UHF channels. Because of the large number of VHF-only receivers originally in use, advertisers preferred VHF stations which limited UHF revenues.

In 1956, the commission outlined plans to promote comparable TV facilities as a means of extending service throughout the nation. In the years following, it considered and rejected the idea of moving all or most of TV to the UHF band. It sought the cooperation of industry to find ways to increase the range of UHF stations. It made certain areas all-UHF and took other steps to put UHF and VHF on a more competitive basis. In 1966, it revised the table of channel assignments to make additional UHF assignments.

Public Broadcasting

AM—Educational institutions were among the pioneers in experimental broadcasting, and held many early AM licenses.

By 1925, educational groups had 171 AM licenses. For various reasons, notably the increased competition from commercial broadcasting, most of these stations were off the air by 1934 when the FCC was created. However, there are still two dozen educational stations operating in the AM broadcast band, although there are no longer any educational allocations there (see section on FM below).

As directed by Section 307(c) of the Communications Act, the commission in 1934 studied a proposal that Congress allocate fixed percentages of radio facilities for nonprofit programs. On Jan. 22, 1935, the FCC recommended against such a statutory allocation but recognized the need for extending broadcasting to education. It expressed its intention "actively to assist the determination of the rightful place of broadcasting in education and to see that it is used in that place."

FM Educational Stations—When regular FM broadcasting was authorized in 1941, five channels were authorized for noncommercial educational use as a substitution for AM allocations previously made to education.

In 1945, as part of an extensive revision of frequency allocations, the commission reserved 20 FM channels between 88 and 92 mhz for noncommercial educational FM stations. This part of the FM band is contiguous to the commercial portion, and FM receivers can tune both noncommercial and commercial stations. Since then, the number of noncommercial educational FM stations has grown slowly but steadily.

In 1948, the commission authorized 10 watt operation on educational FM channels. With such low-power equipment, easily installed and operated, schools may broadcast to a limited area of two to five miles for an outlay of a few thousand dollars. High-power equipment may be added when desired. In 1951, as a further aid, the commission authorized remote control operation of low-power educational stations. Approximately half of all educational FM stations use power of 10 watts.

Educational FM stations traditionally have been assigned on an individual-application "demand" basis, as AM stations are assigned. To permit planned development of the 20 reserved channels, it is proposed to adopt a table of assignments like that adopted in 1963 for commercial FM channels to allocate specific frequencies to communities.

Stations in the educational FM service are licensed principally to school systems, colleges and universities for student-teacher programs as well as for public education and information.

TV Educational Stations—The commission allocated TV facilities for noncommercial educational use after a lengthy study in the general television proceedings (see Broadcast). It determined that "the need for noncommercial educational stations has been amply demonstrated," that it would take longer for the educational service to be developed than for the commercial service, and that special channels should be reserved. Consequently, in 1952, channel assignments were made to 242 communities exclusively for noncommercial educational stations. Forty-six of these were made to primary educational centers. Of the total 242 channels, 80 were VHF and 162 UHF. There have been more assignments since. In 1966, a revised table of channel assignments was adopted for UHF, containing many more educational assignments than before. The new table contains altogether over 615 educational TV assignments in the mainland states, more than a third of all channel assignments.

The first educational TV station to go on the air was KUHT Houston on May 25, 1953. The first state educational TV network was established in Alabama on April 28, 1955.

A 1962 law enabled the Department of Health, Education and Welfare to make matching federal grants of money to build educational TV stations, and a 1967 law extended these benefits to educational radio.

Public broadcasting in its present form emerged with the passage of the Public Broadcasting Act of 1967. That act authorized the establishment of the Corporation for Public Broadcasting, whose primary function is to funnel federal funds to qualified noncommercial licensees. National Public Radio was established in 1971 to provide interconnection and programming service for public radio stations. The Public Broadcasting Service started operating in 1970. PBS provides interconnection and distributes programming to public television stations.

Cable Television

Cable TV got its start as CATV (community antenna television) in the late 1940s when entrepreneurs seized upon it as a method for boosting television receiver sales in areas that were underserved or unserved by standard broadcast stations. According to legend, one backwoods Pennsylvania appliance dealer rigged a large antenna on a mountaintop, then connected it to homes in the area with a network of wires. The gentleman's system reportedly did stimulate receiver sales, and his idea caught on.

After it was discovered that CATV could present consumers with better reception and could, via microwave relay stations, be used to import television signals from distant television stations, CATV systems began sprouting up in areas that already were served by local broadcast stations.

During the 1960s, equipment was developed that increased the capacity of CATV systems to 20 channels. Further advancements in the early 1970's permitted the transmission of more than 100 channels over dual-cable systems.

Attempts to wire the major urban areas in the early 1970's largely fell flat, with major companies discovering that laying coaxial cable in cities was far more expensive than they thought and that there wasn't an overwhelming demand for CATV in those areas, which were already well served by standard broadcast stations.

Demand for cable increased dramatically, however, in the mid-1970's when Time Inc.'s Home Box Office began distributing its pay TV service via satellite. Other entrepreneurs followed HBO's lead, distributing programming of their own, via satellite, and cable started looking far more attractive to consumers in suburban and urban areas. By the early 1980's, most cities were either wired or franchising battles were being fought for the right to wire them.

The FCC started regulating cable TV in April 1965, adopting rules for CATV systems served by microwave. The commission required CATV operators to carry the signals of local stations and to refrain from duplicating the programs of local stations (by carrying other stations broadcasting the same programs) within 15 days of the local broadcast.

In 1966, the commission required all cable TV systems to carry local and nearby stations (the must-carry rules), and to protect their programs from duplications. Nonetheless, the 15-day protection requirement was repealed, and cable operators were required to provide that protection only on the day of the broadcast. In 1969, the broadcast requirements of fairness and sponsor identification were extended to cable.

In 1972, the FCC began deregulating cable, dropping most of its cable regulations over the next 10 years. In 1980, the FCC eliminated its distant-signal and syndicated exclusivity rules, and the Court of Appeals in New York upheld that decision the following year. In July 1985, The Court of Appeals in Washington repealed the must-carry rules. In August 1986, the FCC issued new rules which are much less burdensome on cable operators, but they too failed to pass judicial muster.

In 1984, Congress essentially deregulated cable with passage of the Cable Communications Policy Act of 1984. The law removed local franchising authorities' rights to regulate cable rates. It also banned crossownership of cable television systems and cable programming networks with telephone companies in their local telephone service areas.

Before long, pressure mounted for a new law to reregulate the cable industry. In 1992 Congress enacted the Cable Television Consumer Protection and Competition Act over the only veto by President Bush ever to be overturned. Several cable system operators and program networks have pending suits to overturn major provisions of the Act.

The Act reinstates local regulation of basic-tier rates for systems not subject "effective competition," requires cable programmers controlled by cable operators to make their services available to cable's competitors, and grants broadcasters must carry and retransmission consent rights.

In implementing the Act in April 1993, the FCC adopted rate regulations and ordered roll backs to bring rates in line with benchmarks—the lower rates cable systems would charge if they were subject to head to head competition. At the time, the FCC claimed the rollbacks would save consumers $1.5 billion.

However, as the regulations went into effect, many subscribers saw their actual monthly bills go up. The reason: systems were allowed to increase or decrease rates for particular services as long as the average monthly rate did not increase.

The must carry/retransmission consent provision gave broadcasters the option of requiring carriage on local cable systems or negotiating for a carriage fee. Most broadcast stations who opted for the latter failed to win compensation, although some managed to negotiate for cable channels with which they planned to launch new programming services.

The cable industry's challenge of the retransmission consent/must carry was pending before the Supreme Court at year's end.

The 1992 Act did not repeal the 1984 Act's ban against telephone companies' owning cable systems or providing other kinds of video services in their telephone service areas.

But in 1993, the U.S. District Court in Alexandria, Va., agreed with Bell Atlantic that the crossownership ban was unconstitutional. The ruling applied only to Bell Atlantic. But several other telephone companies have mounted similar challenges to the ban.

Related Technologies

Satellites—In presenting programmers and common carriers with a relatively inexpensive alternative for transmitting their services nationally, satellites have probably done more to speed the communications revolution than any other technology.

A satellite, in essence, is a radio relay station in the sky, one that receives transmissions from the earth, then retransmits them back to receiving stations on the ground. The satellite's actual transmitter/receivers are called transponders; they are generally able to relay a single color TV channel (or 1,000 telephone conversations) at any one time, but methods for increasing that capacity are being developed. Most communications satellites have either 16 or 24 transponders.

Communications satellites are launched into positions 22,300 miles above the equator, where they orbit the earth at the same rate the earth is rotating, which makes them appear to be stationary and permits the use of fixed earth stations.

The first live transatlantic telecast was relayed by Telstar I on July 10, 1962. That same year's Communications Satellite Act provided for the U.S. portion of a global satellite system that would be operated by the Communications Satellite Corp., a private corporation subject to federal regulation.

Intelsat I on Apr. 2, 1965, became the first commercial satellite to be put into orbit with its foreign partners in the International Telecommunications Satellite Consortium. During the following year, some 80 hours of television were transmitted between the U.S. and Europe.

The real rush for satellite video transmission didn't begin until after 1975, when Time Inc.'s Home Box Office began transmitting its pay-TV programming over RCA's Satcom I to cable systems scattered across the country. Over the past 10 years, scores of companies have followed HBO's lead. By late last year, most of the transponders on three satellites were dedicated to the distribution of cable programming.

Cable programmers aren't alone in realizing the benefits of satellite distribution. The Public Broadcasting Service started transmitting programming via satellite to its noncommercial affiliates in 1978, and in the mid-1980s the major commercial networks have switched to satellites for the distribution of their programming as well.

Although the FCC has traditionally regulated domestic satellites as common carriers, it has been loosening its grasp. In 1982, the commission permitted some operators to sell transponders on their satellites (they previously have had to lease those on a first-come, first-served basis, at rates approved by the FCC). The commision decided to reduce orbital spacing between satellites to two degrees. This move will be phased in over several years and will permit more satellites to be launched.

Subscription Television (STV)—The major difference between STV and conventional TV is that you have to pay for the former.

STV stations are standard VHF or UHF television stations that scramble their signals. The STV operater then charges customers a fee for a decoder to decipher the scrambled signals.

Authorized in December 1968, STV did not really get off the ground until the late 1970's. It grew rapidly for a few years, and counted about 1.4 million subscribers in the summer of 1982. But it's been in a steep decline ever since, the victim of piracy and stiff competition from cable systems offering more channels for less money.

Low-Power Television (LPTV)—LPTV stations are essentially television translator stations (stations that have traditionally been limited to rebroadcasting the signals of full-service stations) that are permitted to originate programming.

In authorizing the service in 1982, the FCC estimated that as many as 4,000 new stations would be spawned by the rules, adding to the more than 4,000 existing translators that can rise to LPTV status simply by notifying the FCC. However, the new medium has gotten off to a slow start, raising doubts about whether it will ever meet the FCC's original expectations.

Under the rules, LPTV stations were given "secondary status," which essentially means they cannot interfere with full-power stations. They were also limited to 10 watts VHF and 1,000 watts UHF.

LPTV stations have few regulatory obligations and there are no crossownership or multiple-ownership restrictions. The stations must observe statutory prhobitions against broadcast of obscenities and lotteries; however, they only have limited equal time and fairness doctrine obligations.

Wireless Cable—More than an oxymoron, wireless cable is a pay television service that delivers multiple cable programming services to subscribers via omnidirectional microwave (2 ghz) broadcasts. To receive the broadcast, subscribers are equipped with special antennas and tuners.

Wireless cable operators use a combination of 2 ghz channels licensed to three different services: the multipoint distribution service (MDS), the Instructional Television Fixed Service (ITFS), and the Operational Fixed Service (OFS). There are 31 such channels available in each market.

MDS is a common carrier service. Wireless cable operators may own and program certain MDS channels, or lease the capacity from others. ITFS is a broadcasting service, intended primarily for nonprofit groups interested in broadcasting instructional programming. The FCC permits ITFS licensees to lease a portion of each of their channels to wireless cable operators as long as a "substantial portion" is retained for its intended educational purpose. OFS is regulated by the FCC's Private Radio Bureau.

Direct Broadcast Satellites (DBS)—The FCC authorized the direct broadcast satellite service in 1982, but the first DBS satellite was not launched until December 1993 and actual service is not to begin until April 1994.

In between, several companies stumbled in the DBS business. The most notable failure was Comsat's Satellite Television Corp. The first DBS applicant, it dropped its plans in November 1984 after five and half years of planning and $140 million.

DBS satellites work the same way as other communications satellites, beaming signals to stationary satellite antennas scattered over vast areas—countries or even continents. But since the DBS birds are more powerful, their signals can be received with relatively small antennas—in most cases, just 18-inches across.

In 1990, Hughes, NBC, Cablevision and Rupert Murdoch's News Corp. announced plans to combine forces to pursue the business, but never did.

As a manufacturer of satellites, Hughes had the greatest incentive to get DBS off the ground. Not giving up, it struck a deal with United States Satellite Broadcasting, a subsidiary of Hubbard Broadcasting, which was among the first DBS applicant in 1982.

Under terms of the agreement, Hughes built a 16-transponder satellite, sold five to USSB and kept 11 for its own DBS venture, DirecTV. Hughes successfully launched the satellite in December 1993.

With the help of digital video compression, DirecTV and USSB expect to begin offering in April 1994 around 150 channels of service to subscribers with 18-inch dish antennas. RCA plans to retail the dishes for around $700.

Between them, DirecTV and USSB will offer most of the major basic and pay cable services. DirecTV also hopes to offer a wide selection of movies on a pay-per-view basis.

Although the DirecTV and USSB services are the only "true" DBS services on the horizion, they are braced for keen competition from PrimeStar, a consortium of cable operators who are planning a DBS-like service using a conventional medium power communications satellite. The service will comprise 80 channels, but subscribers will need a slightly larger dish to receive them—perhaps one-meter. Is their a significant marketplace difference between an 18-inch dish and a one-meter dish? It will be up to the public to decide.

Satellite Master Antenna Systems (SMATV)—SMATV systems, cloned from cable systems, look like cable systems, and, in most cases, are operated like them. The essential difference is that SMATV systems operate on private property—apartment buildings, condominium complexes or private housing developments and mobile home parks. Instead of getting a franchise (the right to string or bury wire along city streets and rights of way) from local governments, SMATV operators sign contracts with property owners, allowing them to bring cable television into the homes on the property.

In most cases, that's done by hooking up an earth station that's aimed at a cable satellite to a multi-unit building's master antenna system. In other cases, it also sometimes involves wiring buildings with nonexistent or inadequate master antenna systems and interconnecting two or more buildings of a single complex with overhead or underground cable. One advantage SMATV operators have over their cable counterparts is that they are free from regulation. Because they don't need a municipal franchise, they aren't burdened with the local regulations that go along with those. Since SMATV operators are generally excluded from the FCC's definition of a cable system, they are also exempt from federal regulation.

High-Definition Television (HDTV)—The term "HDTV" is used to describe the series of video production, transmission and display technologies providing television with wider screens than the current National Television Systems Committee system (16:9 compared to the current 4:3), at least twice the NSTC's resolution, vastly improved color fidelity and compact disk-quality digital audio.

The most widely known HDTV video production system was developed by the Japanese Broadcast Corp. (NHK). First demonstrated in the U.S. in 1982, the NHK system records video with 1,125 scanning lines of information at a field rate of 60 hertz. NHK was also the first to demonstrate HDTV in terrestrial and satellite transmission with its MUSE (multiple sub-Nyquist encoding) system.

Transmission of HDTV is currently an issue before the FCC. In 1987, the commission established an industry advisory committee on advanced television service to recommend a transmission system for standardization.

The advisory committee oversaw the testing of several systems vying to become the national HDTV broadcast standard. The system proponents included General Instrument, NHK; a joint effort by AT&T and Zenith Electronics, and the Advanced Television Research Consortium (Sarnoff Research, Philips Research, Thomson Consumer Electronics and NBC).

With testing nearing completion in May 1993, the leading proponents reached an agreement to work together and merge their systems and produce a single standard. Among other things, the so-called "grand alliance" agreed to use a process called "progressive scanning" to build the picture on the screen.

Most of the technical characteristics of the system were finalized last fall. However, a modulation or transmission system was not expected to be selected until early 1994. Full prototype testing of the "grand alliance" system is likely in the fall of 1994.

Auxiliary Broadcast Services—Broadcasters take portable or mobile transmitters to the scene of events to relay aural programs back to the station for on-the-spot coverage of sporting events, parades, conventions, fairs, disasters and other newsworthy events. These remote-broadcast pickup stations use frequencies in the 26, 153 and 450 mhz portions of the spectrum.

TV stations also use small portable transmitters operating in the 2, 7 and 13 ghz-per-second (microwave) portions of the spectrum for visual coverage of out-of-studio events.

Other Broadcast Activity

International Broadcast—Under international agreement, certain high-frequency bands are allocated for broadcast between nations.

Authorizations for non-government international broadcast stations in the United States are issued by the FCC. Only a handful of these international stations are now authorized. A single station uses a number of frequencies between 5950 and 26100 khz, and it may need more than one transmitter because of seasonal considerations and other factors in broadcasting different programs simultaneously to different parts of the world. The minimum power for these stations, sometimes known as short-wave stations, is 50 kw.

During World War II, international broadcast stations in the United States were taken over temporarily by the Office of War Information and the Office of Inter-American Affairs of the Department of State, which programmed them in the interest of the war effort.

Under the peacetime program of the Department of State, the United States Information Agency broadcasts daily in many languages to other parts of the world through the Voice of America. VOA stations are not licensed or regulated by the FCC. There are about 30 VOA transmitters in the United States and about 70 located in foreign countries.

VOA is not the U.S.'s only foreign broadcast service. Radio Liberty and Radio Free Europe, funded by Congress and supervised by the Board of International Broadcasting, serve as surrogate stations for the countries to which they broadcast—the former Soviet Union, in the case of RL, and other countries of the Eastern bloc in the case of RFE.

Year in Review:
Broadcasting and Cable 1993

Broadcasting

There were 11,543 radio stations operating in the United States at the end of 1993. Of these, 4,948 were commercial AM stations, 4,945 were commercial FMs and 1,650 were noncommercial FMs. There were 1,516 operating television stations: 558 commercial VHFs, 595 commercial UHFs, 123 noncommercial VHFs and 240 noncommercial UHFs. Most commercial TVs are network affiliated; approximately 443 operate as independents.

No single entity may own more than 18 AM, 18 FM and 12 TV stations. In TV, the entity is permitted to own 12 TV stations as long as they don't reach more than 25% of the nation's television homes. UHFs are assessed for only half of a market's television homes. Group broadcasters who buy interests in stations more than half owned by minorities are able to own up to 21 AM, 21 FM and 14 TV stations, and are able to reach 30% of the nation's television households through their TVs, as long as two of the stations in each service are controlled by minorities.

Newspaper owners may no longer purchase broadcast properties in the same market, nor may radio station owners acquire TV stations there, nor TV owners acquire radio outlets. TV stations may no longer acquire cable TV franchises in the same city, and networks may not own cable systems at all.

In 1992, according to estimates by the Television Bureau of Advertising and the Radio Advertising Bureau, commercial broadcasting had total advertising revenues of approximately $35.9 billion. Television advertising accounted for $27.1 billion (75.4%) of revenues; radio advertising, for approximately $8.8 billion (24.6%). Public broadcasting had a 1992 income of $1.8 billion—20.9% from the federal government.

In 1992, television billings for stations and networks amounted to $9.5 billion (national network), $7.6 billion (national non-network), $8.0 billion (local), and $2.0 billion (national syndication), according to estimates by the Television Bureau of Advertising. The Radio Advertising Bureau estimated radio billings for stations and networks were $388,000,000 (national network), $1,479,000,000 (national non-network), and $6,899,000,000 (local).

There are more than 93 million U.S. homes (99% of all homes) with television sets, about 70% of which have more than one set. About 92 million homes have color. It is estimated that about 80.6% of TV homes are equipped with a VCR, and that about 64% are linked with cable systems, according to Arbitron Television. There are an estimated 576 million radio sets in the U.S., 367 million (64%) of them in homes and 209 million (36%) out of homes.

The average American home watches TV seven hours and 5 minutes a day, according to Nielsen Media Research statistics for the 1992-1993 season. And the latest study by The Roper Organization (commissioned by the National Association of Broadcasters and the Network Television Association) shows that 69% of the U.S. public turns to TV as the source of most of its news, and that 56% ranks it as the most believable news source.

The average 30-second prime-time network television announcement now costs $100,000 (spots on a top-rated series cost $325,000; low-rated spots average about $50,000). An estimated 135 million people watched the 1994 Super Bowl telecast. Thirty-second announcements during that event cost $900,000. Thirty-second announcements on individual TV stations range from $20,000 in top-rated specials in major markets to as low as $10 in the second-hundred markets. Radio spots cost from $1,500 or more in major markets to less than a dollar in small towns.

Cable

There are 11,600 operating cable systems in the U.S., serving some 33,000 communities. Another 100 franchises are approved but not built. Texas has the most systems (890) and California the most subscribers (6 million). Operating systems currently reach about 56 million subscribers, perhaps over 147 million people—62.4% of the nation's TV households. The largest (Time Warner Cable in New York) has over 900,000 subscribers. Some have fewer than 100. Tele-Communications Inc. is the largest multiple system operator (MSO), with more than 10 million subscribers. Industry revenues last year totaled approximately $22 billion. Most systems offer 30 or more channels. Systems constructed after March 1972 must have a minimum 20-channel capacity. The average monthly fee (basic service) is $21. Costs of laying cable range from $10,000 per mile in rural areas to $100,000 in urban areas and up to $300,000 where underground cable is required. An estimated 5,600 systems originate programing in their own studios; the average is 23 hours weekly. Equipment costs are as low as $30,000 for a small black-and-white operation and $200,000 for a color studio.

Over 2,550 systems (22% of all systems) accept advertising on their local origination channels (excluding automated channels), with rates from $2 to $600 per 30-second spot. Most cable systems derive less than 5% of their gross revenues from advertising. Pay cable is on approximately 9,100 systems and reaches 41 million subscribers in 50 states. Most pay cable operators are reporting close to 74% penetration of their subscriber count. Home Box Office Inc. initiated the first national satellite interconnected pay network Sept. 30, 1975, using transponder time leased on the Satcom satellite. Aside from contracting for packaged pay programs, like HBO, cable operators can lease a channel to a pay program operator or secure their own programing directly from a supplier. Many systems have multiple cross-ownership ties.

Although wireless cable systems offer programming similar to cable systems, the subscriber receives the programming in a different way. A wireless cable system uses a microwave transmitter to send video programming to the rooftop antennas of subscribers. According to the Wireless Cable Association, there are more than 160 wireless cable systems.

Another potential alternative to cable is provided by DBS (direct broadcast satellites). Although none are yet operating, nine permittees have construction grants for DBS systems. Two permittees—United States Satellite Broadcasting Co. and DirecTv Inc.—expect to be operating by April 1994. The nine permittees are authorized to transmit via high-power satellites to small antennas on the ground. Midpower DBS systems also transmit via satellite but require bigger antennas on the ground.

Section A

Law and Regulation, Government Agencies and Ownership

Table of Contents

Table of Contents... A-1
Law and Regulation
   Federal Communications Commission Executives and Staff........... A-2
   Federal Communications Commission Rules and Regulations......... A-5
   Cable Regulations A-32
   Industry Standard Coding Identification System (ISCI) A-48
   National Association of Broadcasters Television and Radio Codes..... A-49
Government Agencies
   Government Agencies of Interest to Broadcasting and Cable
      United States A-50
      Canada A-52
   U.S. State Cable Regulatory Agencies........................... A-53
Ownership
   Television Ownership Transfers............................... A-54
   1993 Station Sales A-90
   40 Years of Station Transactions A-95
   Group Ownership A-96
   Newspaper/Magazine Cross-Ownership with Broadcasting Stations... A-118
   Broadcasting Stations Associated with
      Newspaper/Magazine Ownership........................... A-124

# Federal Communications Commission Executives and Staff

Headquarters: 1919 M St. N.W., Washington 20554. (202) 632-7260.

Commissioners and Assistants

James H. Quello, Mich. (632-7557), Room 802. Democrat, assumed office April 30, 1974; term expires June 30, 1996. Brian F. Fontes, sr advisor; Robert Corn-Revere, legal advisor; Ginger Clark, confidential asst.

Andrew C. Barrett, Ill. (632-7116), Room 826. Republican, assumed office Sep. 8, 1989; term expires June 30, 1995. Lisa Smith, legal advisor; James Coltharp, special advisor; Byron F. Marchant, sr legal advisor; Betty Freeman, confidential asst.

Ervin S. Duggan, Ga. (632-6996), Room 832. Democrat, assumed office Feb. 28, 1990; term expires June 30, 1994. John C. Hollar, sr legal advisor; Linda Oliver, legal advisor; Randall S. Coleman, legal advisor; Linda A. Botbyl, confidential asst.

Administrative Departments

Office of Managing Director
Room 852

Andrew S. Fishel, mng dir (632-6390); Alan R. McKie, deputy mng dir; Eileen B. Savell, asst mgt; Walker Feaster, assoc mng dir prog analysis; Marilyn McDermett, assoc mng dir opns; Michael Gilbride, acting assoc mng dir info mgmt; Alan R. McKie, acting assoc mng dir public info & ref svcs; Michelle A. Oppenheimer, assoc mng dir human resources mgmt. Network Products Division: Eric Kanner, chief. Customer Solutions Division: Edward McCarthy, chief. Computer Applications Division: John Giuli, chief. Financial Management Division: (vacant), chief. Operations Management and Services Division: Jeffrey R. Ryan, chief; John Winston, acting chief office of small business activities.

PIRS Management Team
Room 242

Public Information & Reference Services Managers: Alan McKie, acting assoc mng dir (632-6390); Kathy Fagan, acting deputy dir opns/acting chief reference opns div; Patti Grace Smith, deputy dir policy; Public Services Division: Martha Contee, chief (632-0260 & 632-7260). Records Management Division: Bill Cline, chief (632-7513); Sheryl Segal, sr info tech mgr (632-0260). Public Policy Planning Branch: Stan Felder, chief (Room 244, 632-0244). Mass Media Adjudication Branch: Sharon Jenkins, chief (Room 242F, 632-0272). Library Branch: Gloria Thomas, chief (Room 639, 632-7100). Consumer Assistance Branch: Mickey Williams, chief (Room 254, 632-7260).

Office of the Secretary
Room 222

William F. Caton, acting sec (632-6410). Agenda Branch: LaVera Marshall, chief. Publications Branch: Shirley Suggs, chief. Audio Visual Management Office: Daniel Oliver.

Inspector General
Room 752

James Warwick, inspector gen (632-0471); Paul Brachfeld, dir audits (632-0471); Robert Andary, counsel & dir investigations (632-0441).

Office of Legislative Affairs
Room 808

Stephen Klitzman, assoc dir (632-6405).

Office of Public Affairs
Room 202

(vacant), dir (632-5050); Maureen P. Peratino, deputy dir. News Media Division (Room 202): Stephen Svab, chief (632-5050).

Office of Plans and Policy
Room 822

Robert Pepper, chief (653-5940); (vacant), deputy chief.

Office of International Communications
Room 658

(vacant), dir (632-0932); James Ball, acting dir.

Review Board
Room 211, 2000 L Street

Joseph A. Marino, chmn (632-7180); Norman B. Blumenthal, bd member; Marjorie R. Greene, bd member; Leland J. Blair, deputy chief for law; Allan Sacks, chief for law; Audrey L. Allison, sr atty.

Office of Administrative Law Judges
Room 224, 2000 L Street

Joseph Stirmer, chief admin law judge (632-7680). Admin law judges: Joseph Chachkin, John M. Frysiak, Joseph Gonzalez, Edward Luton, Walter C. Miller, Richard L. Sippel, Arthur Steinburg.

Office of General Counsel
Room 614

Renee Licht, acting gen counsel (632-7020); Lauren J. Belvin, deputy gen counsel; Sara Seidman, special asst.

Litigation Division: Daniel M. Armstrong, chief (632-7112); John E. Ingle, deputy assoc gen counsel (litigation); Jane Mago, asst gen counsel (trial & enforcement).

Administrative Law Division: Sheldon M. Guttmann, chief (632-6990); Susan Steiman, deputy assoc gen counsel; David Solomon, asst gen counsel; Lawrence Schaffner, asst gen counsel; Magalie Salas, asst gen counsel.

Adjudication Division: John I. Riffer, chief (632-7220).

Office of Engineering and Technology
Room 7002, 2025 M St. N.W., Washington

Thomas P. Stanley, chief engr (632-7060); Bruce A. Franca, deputy chief engr (632-7060); Steven S. Kaminer, legal counsel (653-8100); R. Allan Stillwell, econ advisor (653-8103).

Program Management Staff: Lawrence P. Petak, chief (653-8103).

Authorization Evaluation Division: Julius P. Knapp, chief (301-725-1585); Robert M. Bromery, deputy chief, hqtrs (202-653-7315). Engineering Evaluation Branch: David L. Means, chief (301-725-1585). Equipment Authorization Branch: Charles M. Cobbs, chief (301-725-1585). Sampling and Measurements Branch: L. Art Wall, chief (301-725-1585). Technical Standards Branch: Richard B. Engelman, chief (202-653-6288).

Spectrum Engineering Division: (vacant), chief; William R. Torak, deputy chief (632-7025). Frequency Allocations Branch: David R. Siddall, chief (653-8108). Frequency Liaison Branch: H. Franklin Wright, chief (653-8141). Propagation Analysis Branch: William A. Daniel, chief (632-7025). Telecommunications Analysis Branch: H. John Morgan, chief (632-7025). Treaty Branch: Francis K. Williams, chief (653-8126).

Bureaus

Mass Media Bureau
Room 314

Roy J. Stewart, chief (632-6460); Karl Kensinger, special asst; Roderick K. Porter, William Johnson, deputy chiefs; William Hassinger, asst chief engr; Robert Ratcliffe, asst chief law; Janet S. Amaya, asst chief mgmt & personnel (632-7191).

Audio Services Division (Room 302): Larry D. Eads, chief (632-6485); Linda Blair, Stuart Bedell, asst chiefs. Data Management Staff: Gary Kalagian, supervisory electronics engr. AM Branch: James Burtle, chief (254-9570); Peter Rubenstein, asst branch chief law. FM Branch: Dennis Williams, chief (632-6908); Edwin Jorgensen, asst branch chief law; Robert Greenberg, asst branch chief engr. **Auxiliary Services Branch (Room 408, 1919 M St. N.W.):** Alan Schneider, chief (634-6307).

Cable Services Division (Room 914): Alexandra M. Wilson, chief (416-0856). Technical Services Branch: Ronald Parver, chief (Room 201, 2033 M St., 416-0903); John Wong, deputy chief (Room 201, 2033 M St., 416-0903); Broadcast Signal Carriage Branch: (vacant), chief. Basic Rates & Certification Branch: (vacant), chief. Cable Programming Service Rates & Appeals Branch: (vacant), chief. Cable Ownership & Industry Analysis Branch: (vacant), chief. Program Access Branch: (vacant), chief. Consumer Complaints & Inquiries Branch: (vacant), chief. Cable Information Line: (202-632-0004).

Enforcement Division: (Room 8202, 2025 M St. N.W.) Charles W. Kelley, chief (632-6968); Edythe Wise, asst chief. Complaints and Investigations Branch: Norman Goldstein, chief (632-7048). Equal Employment Opportunity Branch: Glenn A. Wolfe, chief (632-7069). Fairness/Political Programming Branch: Milton O. Gross, chief (632-7586). Hearing Branch: Charles Dziedzic, chief (632-6402).

Policy and Rules Division: (Room 8010, 2025 M St. N.W.) Douglas Webbink, chief (632-5414); Bruce Romano, deputy chief; Beverly McKittrick, asst chief; Larry Olson, international chief. International Staff—Notifications Group: James Ballis (254-3394). Negotiations Group: Henry Straube (632-6955). Legal Branch: David Horowitz, chief (632-7792). Engineering Policy Branch: (vacant), chief (632-9660). Policy Analysis Branch: Judith Herman, chief (632-6302). Allocations Branch: Michael Ruger, chief (634-6530); Victoria McCauley, asst chief.

Video Services Division: (Room 702) Barbara Kriesman, chief (632-6993); James J. Brown, Larry A. Miller, asst chiefs. Television Branch: Clay Pendarvis, chief (632-6357). Low Power TV Branch: Keith Larson, chief (632-3894). Distribution Services Branch: (vacant), chief (632-9356).

Private Radio Bureau
Room 5002, 2025 M St. N.W., Washington

Ralph A. Haller, chief (632-6940); Beverly G. Baker, deputy chief; Kent Nakamura, legal counsel to bureau chief; Ron Netro, engrg advisor to bureau chief; Jennifer Bush, asst chief for mgmt; Special Services Division: Robert McNamara, chief (632-7197). Land Mobile and Microwave Division: Richard J. Shiben, chief (632-7597). Licensing Division: Gary L. Stanford, chief (717-337-1311).

Common Carrier Bureau
Room 500

Elle J. Mulcare, asst chief, mgmt (632-6934); Gerald P. Vaughan, deputy bureau chief for opns (632-6910); Kathleen Levitz, deputy bureau chief for policy (632-6910); Jill Ross-Meltzer, assoc bureau chief (632-6910); David Kresche, legal asst to the chief (632-6910); Kelly Cameron, legal asst to the chief (632-6910); Roxanne McElvane, asst to the chief (632-6910). Enforcement Division: Gregory Weiss, acting chief (632-4890). Domestic Facilites Division: James Keegan, chief (634-1860). Mobile Services Division: John Cimko Jr., chief (632-6400). Tariff Division: Gregory J. Vogt, chief (632-6387). Accounting and Audits Division: Kenneth Moran, chief (634-1861). Industry Analysis Division: Peyton

Federal Communications Commission Executives and Staff

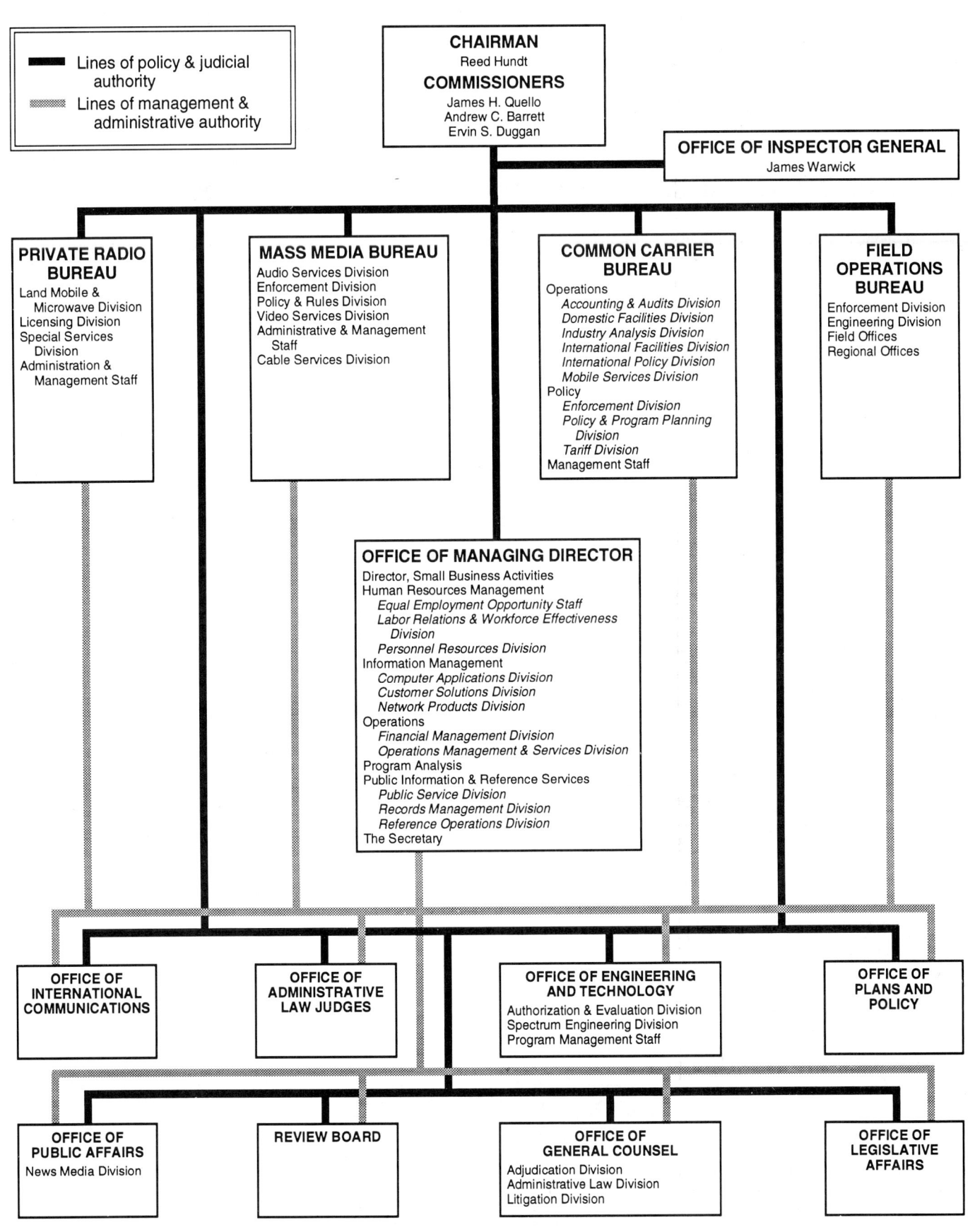

Broadcasting & Cable Yearbook 1994

… Wynns, chief (632-0745). Policy and Program Planning Division: James Schlichting, chief (632-9342). International Facilities Division: George Li, chief (632-7834); Wendell Harris, asst bureau chief international (632-3214). Economics: Thomas Spavins, asst chief (632-6910).

Field Operations Bureau
Room 734

Richard M. Smith, chief (632-6980); Arlan K. van Doorn, deputy chief; Michael J. Marcus, asst bureau chief for tech; Lawrence Clance, asst chief law; Robert Crisman, asst for mgmt; William A. Luther, asst for international. Enforcement Division: Mary Beth Richards, chief. Engineering Division: Kenneth R. Nichols, chief. Emergency Broadcast System: M. Helena Mitchell, chief. Program Development & Evaluation Staff: James A. Davis, chief.

Regional Directors

Duluth, Ga. 30136-4958: 3575 Koger Blvd. (404) 279-4621. Carl E. Pyron, rgnl dir.
Quincy, Mass. 02169-7495: One Batterymarch Park. (617) 770-4023. Joseph P. Casey, rgnl dir.
Park Ridge, Ill. 60068-1460: 1550 Northwest Hwy. (312) 353-0393. Russell D. Monie, rgnl dir.
Kansas City, Mo. 64133-4895: 8800 E. 63rd St. (816) 353-9035. Dennis P. Carlton, rgnl dir.
Hayward, Calif. 94545-2756: 3777 Depot Rd. (510) 732-9046. S. Marti-Volkoff, acting rgnl dir.
Kirkland, Wash. 98034-6927: 11410 N.E. 122nd Way. (206) 821-9037. William E. Johnson, rgnl dir.

Field Offices

Allegan, Mich. 49010-9437. Box 89. (616) 673-2063. Melvyn H. Hyman, engr in charge.
Anchorage 99502. 6721 Raspberry Rd. (907) 243-2153. Marlene Windel, engr in charge.
Duluth, Ga. 30136-4958. 3575 Koger Blvd. (404) 279-4621. Fred L. Broce, engr in charge.
Baltimore 21201-2802. 31 Hopkins Plaza. (410) 962-2729. Robert M. Mroz, engr in charge.
Belfast, Me. 04915-0470. Box 470. (207) 338-4088. Barry A. Bohac, engr in charge.
Quincy, Mass. 02169-7495. One Batterymarch Park. (617) 770-4023. Vincent F. Kajunski, engr in charge.
Buffalo, N.Y. 14202-2398. 111 W. Huron St. (716) 846-4511. David A. Viglione, engr in charge.
Park Ridge, Ill. 60068-1460. 1550 Northwest Hwy. (312) 353-0195. Will Gray, acting engr in charge.
Dallas 75243-3429. 9330 LBJ Freeway. (214) 235-3369. James D. Wells, engr in charge.
Lakewood, Colo. 80228-2213. 165 S. Union Blvd. (303) 969-6497. Robert D. Weller, engr in charge.
Farmington Hills, Mich. 48335-1552. 24897 Hathaway St. (313) 226-6078. Irby C. Tallant, engr in charge.
Douglas, Ariz. 85608-0006. Box 6. (602) 364-8414. Stephen Y. Tsuya, engr in charge.
Custer, Wash. 98240-9303. 1330 Loomis Trail Rd. (206) 354-4892. Jack W. Bazhaw, engr in charge.
Grand Island, Neb. 68802-1588. Box 1588. (308) 381-4721. James H. Berrie Jr., engr in charge.
Waipahu, Hawaii 96797-1030. Box 1030. (808) 677-3318. Jack Shedletsky, engr in charge.
Houston 77008-1775. 1225 North Loop West. (713) 861-6200. Loyd P. Perry, engr in charge.
Kansas City, Mo. 64133-4895. 8800 E. 63rd St. (816) 353-3773. James A. Dailey, engr in charge.
Kingsville, Tex. 78363-0632. Box 632. (512) 592-2531. Oliver K. Long, engr in charge.
Columbia, Md. 21045-9998. Box 250. (301) 725-3474. Robert J. Douchis, engr in charge.
Livermore, Calif. 94551-0311. Box 311. (510) 447-3614. Thomas N. Van Stavern, engr in charge.
Cerritos, Calif. 90701-3684. 18000 Studebaker Rd. (310) 809-2096. James R. Zoulek, engr in charge.
Miami, Fla. 33166-4668. 8390 N.W. 53rd St. (305) 526-7420. John L. Theimer, engr in charge.
New Orleans 70123-3333. 800 W. Commerce Rd. (504) 589-2095. James C. Hawkins, engr in charge.
New York 10014-4870. 201 Varick St. (212) 620-3437. Alexander J. Zimny, engr in charge.
Virginia Beach, Va. 23455-3725. 1200 Communications Circle. J. Jerry Freeman, engr in charge. (804) 441-6472.
Langhorne, Pa. 19047-1859. 2300 E. Lincoln Hwy. (215) 752-1324. John Rahtes, engr in charge.
Portland, Ore. 97204-2898. 1220 S.W. 3rd Ave. (503) 326-4114. Charles W. Craig, engr in charge.
Powder Springs, Ga. 30073-0085. Box 85. (404) 943-5420. Donald E. Taylor, engr in charge.
St. Paul, Minn. 55101-1467. 316 N. Robert St. (612) 290-3819. Albert S. Jarratt Jr., engr in charge.
San Diego 92111-2216. 4542 Ruffner St. (619) 467-0549. William H. Grigsby, engr in charge.
Hayward, Calif. 94545-2756. 3777 Depot Rd. (510) 732-9046. Phillip Kane, acting engr in charge.
Hato Rey, P.R. 00918-1731. 747 Federal Bldg. (809) 766-5567. William C. Berry, engr in charge.
Kirkland, Wash. 98034-6972. 11410 N.E. 122nd Way. (206) 821-9037. Gary P. Soulshy, engr in charge.
Tampa 33607-2356. 2203 N. Lois Ave. (813) 228-2872. Ralph M. Barlow, engr in charge.
Vero Beach, Fla. 32961-1730. Box 1730. Robert C. McKinney, engr in charge. (407) 778-3755.

Past Membership

Members of Former Federal Radio Commission
Feb. 23, 1927 - July 10, 1934

Colonel John F. Dillon, Calif., March 15, 1927-Oct. 8, 1927 (Deceased).
Henry A. Bellows, Minn., March 15, 1927-Oct. 31, 1927 (Deceased).
Admiral W.H.C. Bullard, Pa., March 15, 1927-Nov. 24, 1927 (Deceased).
Sam Pickard, Kan., Nov. 1, 1927-Jan. 31, 1929.
Orestes H. Caldwell, N.Y., March 15, 1927-Feb. 23, 1929.
Eugene O. Sykes, Miss., March 15, 1927-July 10, 1934 (Deceased).
Harold A. Lafount, Utah, Nov. 14, 1927-July 10, 1934 (Deceased).
Ira E. Robinson, W. Va., March 29, 1928-Jan. 15, 1932 (Deceased).
General C. McK. Saltzman, Iowa, May 2, 1929-July 19, 1932 (Deceased).
Thad H. Brown, Ohio, Jan. 21, 1932-July 10, 1934 (Deceased).
James H. Hanley, Neb., April 1, 1933-July 10, 1934 (Deceased).

Past Members of the Federal Communications Commission

Hampson Gary, Tex., July 11, 1934-Jan. 1, 1935 (Deceased).
Irvin Stewart, Tex., July 11, 1934-June 30, 1937 (Deceased).
Eugene O. Sykes, Miss., July 11, 1934-April 5, 1939 (Deceased).
Thad H. Brown, Ohio, July 11, 1934-June 30, 1940 (Deceased).
George H. Payne, N.Y., July 11, 1934-June 30, 1943 (Deceased).
Norman S. Case, R.I., July 11, 1934-June 30, 1945 (Deceased).
Paul Atlee Walker, Okla., July 11, 1934-June 30, 1953 (Deceased).
Anning S. Prall, N.Y., Jan. 17, 1935-July 23, 1937 (Deceased).
T.A.M. Craven, D.C., Aug. 25, 1937-June 30, 1944; July 2, 1956-March 25, 1963 (Deceased).
Frank R. McNinch, N.C., Oct. 1, 1937-Aug. 31, 1939 (Deceased).
Frederick I. Thompson, Ala., April 13, 1939-June 30, 1941 (Deceased).
James Lawrence Fly, Tex., Sept. 1, 1939-Nov. 13, 1944 (Deceased).
Ray C. Wakefield, Calif., March 22, 1941-June 30, 1947 (Deceased).
Clifford J. Durr, Ala., Nov. 1, 1941-June 30, 1948 (Deceased).
Ewell K. Jett, Md., Feb. 15, 1944-Dec. 31, 1947 (Deceased).
Paul A. Porter, Ky., Dec. 21, 1944-Feb. 25, 1946 (Deceased).
Rosel H. Hyde, Idaho, April 17, 1946-Oct. 31, 1969 (Deceased).
Charles R. Denny Jr., D.C., March 30, 1945-Oct. 31, 1947.
William H. Willis, Vt., July 23, 1945-March 6, 1946 (Deceased).
Edward Mount Webster, D.C., April 10, 1947-June 30, 1956 (Deceased).
Robert Franklin Jones, Ohio, Sept. 5, 1947-Sept. 19, 1952 (Deceased).
Wayne Coy, Ind., Dec. 29, 1947-Feb. 21, 1952 (Deceased).
George Edward Sterling, Me., Jan. 2, 1948-Sept. 30, 1954.
Frieda Barkin Hennock, N.Y., July 6, 1948-June 30, 1955 (Deceased).
Robert T. Bartley, Tex., March 6, 1952-June 30, 1972 (Deceased).
Eugene H. Merrill, Utah, Oct. 6, 1952-April 15, 1953 (Recess Appointee) (Deceased).
John C. Doerfer, Wis., April 15, 1953-March 21, 1960.
Robert E. Lee, Ill., Oct. 6, 1953-June 30, 1981 (Deceased).
George C. McConnaughey, Ohio, Oct. 4, 1954-June 30, 1957 (Deceased).
Richard A. Mack, Fla., July 7, 1955-March 3, 1958 (Deceased).
Frederick W. Ford, W.Va., Aug. 29, 1957-Dec. 31, 1964 (Deceased).
John S. Cross, Ark., May 23, 1958-Sept. 30, 1962 (Deceased).
Charles H. King, Mich., July 19, 1960-March 2, 1961 (Recess Appointee).
Newton N. Minow, Ill., March 2, 1961-June 1, 1963.
E. William Henry, Tenn., Oct. 2, 1962-April 30, 1966.
Kenneth A. Cox, Wash., March 26, 1963-Sept. 1, 1970.
Lee Loevinger, Minn., June 11, 1963-June 30, 1968.
James J. Wadsworth, N.Y., May 5, 1965-Oct. 31, 1969 (Deceased).
Thomas J. Houser, Ill., Jan. 6, 1971-Oct. 5, 1971.
Robert Wells, Kan., Nov. 6, 1969-Nov. 1, 1971.
Nicholas Johnson, Iowa, July 1, 1966-Dec. 5, 1973.
H. Rex Lee, D.C., Oct. 28, 1968-Dec. 31, 1973.
Dean Burch, Ariz., Oct. 31, 1969-March 8, 1974.
Charlotte T. Reed, Ill., Oct. 8, 1971-June 30, 1976.
Richard E. Wiley, Ill., Jan. 5, 1972-Oct. 13, 1977.
Benjamin L. Hooks, Tenn., July 5, 1972-July 25, 1977.
Glenn O. Robinson, Minn., July 10, 1974-Aug. 30, 1976.
Abbott M. Washburn, Minn., July 10, 1974-Oct. 1, 1982.
Margita E. White, Va., Sept. 23, 1976-Feb. 28, 1979.
Charles D. Ferris, Mass., Oct. 17, 1977-April 10, 1981.
Tyrone Brown, Va., Nov. 15, 1977-Jan. 31, 1981.
Joseph R. Fogarty, R.I., Sept. 17, 1976-June 30, 1983.
Anne Jones, Mass., April 7, 1979-May 31, 1983.
Stephen A. Sharp, Ohio, Oct. 4, 1982-June 30, 1983.
Henry M. Rivera, N.M., Aug. 10, 1981-Sept. 15, 1985.
Mark S. Fowler, Canada, May 18, 1981-April 17, 1987.
Mimi Weyforth Dawson, Mo., July 6, 1981-Dec. 3, 1987.
Dennis R. Patrick, Calif., Dec. 2, 1983-Aug. 7, 1989.
Patricia Diaz Dennis, N.M., June 25, 1986-Sept. 29, 1989.

Federal Communications Commission Rules and Regulations

Definitions	A-5
Allocations	A-6
Multiple Ownership	A-12
Studio Location, Program Originations	A-14
Operating Schedules	A-14
Operator Requirements	A-17
Personal Attacks, Political Broadcasts	A-17
Equal Employment Opportunities	A-19
Network Affiliation	A-19
Network Interests & Syndication	A-21
Common Antenna Site	A-21
Reports to be Filed	A-21
License Renewals	A-24
Modifications of Unbuilt Facilities	A-25
Station Identification	A-25
Sponsored Programs	A-26
Public Notice	A-26
Rebroadcasts	A-26
Recordings, Tapes & Films	A-27
Time	A-27
Children's Programs	A-27
Political Broadcasts	A-27
Candor, Truthful Responses to FCC	A-28
Revocations, Modifications, Suspensions	A-28
Suspension of Operator Licenses	A-29
Logs & Records	A-29
Lotteries	A-29
Hoaxes	A-29
Tender Offers & Proxy Statements	A-29
Censorship	A-29
Forfeitures	A-29
Station Application Procedure	A-30

Compiled with the cooperation of Pike & Fischer Inc., publisher of Pike & Fischer Radio Regulation, Pike & Fischer Broadcast Rules Service, Pike & Fischer's Broadcast Rules on Disk and Pike & Fischer's Broadcast Forms on Disk. Correct to December 31, 1993.

§73.14 AM broadcast definitions.

AM broadcast band—The band of frequencies extending from 535 to 1705 kHz.

AM broadcast channel—The band of frequencies occupied by the carrier and the upper and lower sidebands of an AM broadcast signal with the carrier frequency at the center. Channels are designated by their assigned carrier frequencies. The 117 carrier frequencies assigned to AM broadcast stations begin at 540 kHz and are in successive steps of 10 kHz to 1700 kHz. See §73.21 for the classification of AM broadcast channels.

AM broadcast station—A broadcast station licensed for the dissemination of radio communications intended to be received by the public and operated on a channel in the AM broadcast band.

Amplitude modulated stage—The radio-frequency stage to which the modulator is coupled and in which the carrier wave is modulated in accordance with the system of amplitude modulation and the characteristics of the modulating wave.

Amplitude modulator stage—The last amplifier stage of the modulating wave which amplitude modulates a radio-frequency stage.

Antenna current—The radio-frequency current in the antenna with no modulation.

Antenna input power—The product of the square of the antenna current and the antenna resistance at the point where the current is measured.

Antenna resistance—The total resistance of the transmitting antenna system at the operating frequency and at the point at which the antenna current is measured.

Blanketing—The interference which is caused by the presence of an AM broadcast signal of one volt per meter (v/m or greater intensity in the area adjacent to the antenna of the transmitting station. The 1 v/m contour is referred to as the blanket contour and the area within this contour is referred to as the blanket area.

Carrier-amplitude regulation—The change in amplitude of the carrier wave in an amplitude-modulated transmitter when modulation is applied under conditions of symmetrical modulation.

Combined audio harmonics—The arithmetical sum of the amplitudes of all the separate harmonic components. Root sum square harmonic readings may be accepted under conditions prescribed by the FCC.

Critical directional antenna—An AM broadcast directional antenna that is required, by the terms of a station authorization, to be operated with the relative currents and phases within the antenna elements at closer tolerances of deviation than those permitted under §73.62 and observed with a high precision monitor capable of measuring these parameters.

Critical hours—The two hour period immediately following local sunrise and the two hour period immediately preceding local sunset.

Daytime—The period of time between local sunrise and local sunset.

Dominant station—A Class I station, as defined in §73.21.

Effective field; Effective field strength—The root-mean-square (RMS) value of the inverse distance fields at a distance of 1 kilometer from the antenna in all directions in the horizontal plane. The term field strength is synonymous with the term field intensity as contained elsewhere in this Part.

Equipment performance measurements—The measurements performed to determine the overall performance characteristics of a broadcast transmission system from point of program origination at main studio to sampling of signal as radiated.

Experimental period—The time between 12 midnight local time and local sunrise, used by AM stations for tests, maintenance and experimentation.

Frequency departure—The amount of variation of a carrier frequency or center frequency from its assigned value.

Incidental phase modulation—The peak phase deviation (in radians) resulting from the process of amplitude modulation.

Input power—Means the product of the direct voltage applied to the last radio stage and the total direct current flowing to the last radio stage, measured without modulation.

Intermittant service area—Means the area receiving service from the groundwave of a broadcast station but beyond the primary service area and subject to some interference and fading.

Last radio stage—The radio-frequency power amplifier stage which supplies power to the antenna.

Left (or right) signal—The electrical output of a microphone or combination of microphones placed so as to convey the intensity, time, and location of sounds originated predominantly to the listener's left (or right) of the center of the performing area.

Left (or right) stereophonic channel—The left (or right) signal as electrically reproduced in reception of AM stereophonic broadcasts.

Main channel—The band of audio frequencies from 50 to 10,000 hz which amplitude modulates the carrier.

Maximum percentage of modulation—The greatest percentage of modulation that may be obtained by a transmitter without producing in its output harmonics of the modulating frequency in excess of those permitted by these regulations. (See §73.1570)

Maximum rated carrier power—The maximum power at which the transmitter can be operated satisfactorily and is determined by the design of the transmitter and the type and number of vacuum tubes or other amplifier devices used in the last radio stage.

Model I facility—A station operating in the 1605-1705 kHz band featuring fulltime operation with stereo, competitive technical quality, 10 kw daytime power, 1 kw nighttime power, non-directional antenna (or a simple directional antenna system), and separated by 400-800 km from other co-channel stations.

Model II facility—A station operating in the 535-1605 kHz band featuring fulltime operation, competitive technical quality, wide area daytime coverage with nighttime coverage at least 15% of the daytime coverage.

Modulated stage—The radio frequency stage to which the modulator is coupled and in which the continuous wave (carrier wave) is modulated in accordance with the system of modulation and the characteristics of the modulating wave.

Modulator stage—The last amplifier stage of the modulating wave which modulates in a radio-frequency stage.

Nighttime—The period of time between local sunset and local sunrise.

Nominal power—The antenna input power less any power loss through a dissipative network and, for directional antennas, without consideration of adjustments specified in subparagraphs (b)(1) and (b)(2) of 73.51 of the rules. However, for AM broadcast applications granted or filed before June 3, 1985, nominal power is specified in a system of classifications which include the following values: 50 kw, 25 kw, 10 kw, 5 kw, 2.5 kw, 1 kw, 0.5 kw and 0.25 kw. The specified nominal power for any station in this group of stations will be retained until action is taken on or after June 3, 1985, which involves a change in the technical facilities of the station.

Plate modulation—The modulation produced by introduction of the modulating wave into the plate circuit of any tube in which the carrier frequency wave is present.

Primary service area—Means the service area of a broadcast station in which the groundwave is not subject to objectionable interference or objectionable fading.

Proof of performance measurements or antenna proof of performance measurements—The measurements of field strengths made to determine the radiation pattern or characteristics of an AM directional antenna system.

Secondary service area—Means the service area of a broadcast station served by the skywave and not subject to objectionable interference and in which the signal is subject to intermittent variations in strength.

Secondary AM station—Any AM station, except a Class I station, operating on a Class I frequency.

Stereophonic channel—The band of audio frequencies from 50 to 10,000 Hz containing the stereophonic information which modulates the radio frequency carrier.

Stereophonic crosstalk—An undesired signal occurring in the main channel from modulation of the stereophonic channel or that occuring in the stereophonic channel from modulation of the main channel.

Stereophonic pilot tone—An audio tone of fixed or variable frequency modulating the carrier during the transmission of stereophonic programs.

Stereophonic separation—The ratio of the electrical signal caused in the right (or left) stereophonic channel to the electrical signal caused in the left (or right) stereophonic channel by the transmission of only a right (or left) signal.

Sunrise and sunset—For each particular location and during any particular month, the time of sunrise and sunset as specified in the instrument of authorization (see §73.1209).

White area—The area or population which does not receive interference-free primary service from an authorized AM station or does not receive a signal strength of at least 1 mV/m from an authorized FM station.

In AM, FM, TV rules ...

§73.1530 Portable test stations—A portable test station is one that is moved from place to place for making field strength and ground conductivity measurements, for selecting station transmitter sites, and conducting other specialized propagation tests. Portable test stations are not normally used while in motion, and may not be used for the transmission of programs intended to be received by the public.

§73.1700 Broadcast day. The term broadcast day means that period of time between the station's sign-on and its sign-off.

§73.1720 Daytime. Operation is permitted during the hours between average monthly local sunrise and average monthly local sunset.

(a) The controlling times for each month of the year are stated in the station's instrument of authorization. Uniform sunrise and sunset times are specified for all of the days of each month, based upon the actual times of sunrise and sunset for the fifteenth day of the month adjusted to the nearest quarter hour. Sunrise and sunset times are derived by using the standardized procedure and the tables in the 1946 American Nautical Almanac issued by the United States Naval Observatory.

Allocations

In AM rules ...

§73.21 Classes of AM broadcast channels and stations.

(a) Clear channel. A clear channel is one on which stations are assigned to serve wide areas. These stations are protected from objectionable interference within their primary service areas and, depending on the class of station, their secondary service areas. Stations operating on these channels are classified as follows:

(1) Class A station. A Class A station is an unlimited time station that operates on a clear channel and is designed to render primary and secondary service over an extended area and at relatively long distances from its transmitter. Its primary service area is protected from objectionable interference from other stations on the same and adjacent channels, and its secondary service area is protected from interference from other stations on the same channel. (See §73.182). The operating power shall not be less than 10 kw nor more than 50 kw. (Also see §73.25(a)).

(2) Class B station. A Class B station is an unlimited time station which is designed to render service only over a primary service area. Class B stations are authorized to operate with a minimum power of 0.25 kw (or, if less than 0.25 kw, an equivalent RMS antenna field of at least 141 mV/m at 1 km) and a maximum power of 50 kw, or 10 kw for stations that are authorized to operate in the 1605-1705 kHz band.

(3) Class D station. A Class D station operates either daytime, limited time or unlimited time with nighttime power less than 0.25 kw and an equivalent RMS antenna field of less than 141 mV/m at one km. Class D stations shall operate with daytime powers not less than 0.25 kw nor more than 50 kw. Nighttime operations of Class D stations are not afforded protection and must protect all Class A and Class B operations during nighttime hours. New Class D stations that had not been previously licensed as Class B will not be authorized.

(b) Regional Channel. A regional channel is one on which Class B and Class D stations may operate and serve primarily a principal center of population and the rural area contiguous thereto.

Note: Until the North American Regional Broadcasting Agreement (NARBA) is terminated with respect to the Bahama Islands and the Dominican Republic, radiation toward those countries from a Class B station may not exceed the level that would be produced by an omnidirectional antenna with a transmitted power of 5 kw, or such lower level as will comply with NARBA requirements for protection of stations in the Bahama Islands and the Dominican Republic against objectionable interference.

(c) Local channel. A local channel is one on which stations operate unlimited time and serve primarily a community and the suburban and rural areas immediately contiguous thereto.

(1) Class C station. A Class C station is a station operating on a local channel and is designed to render service only over a primary service area that may be reduced as a consequence of interference in accordance with §73.182. The power shall not be less than 0.25 kw, nor more than 1 kw. Class C stations that are licensed to operate with 0.1 kw may continue to do so.

§73.24 Broadcast facilities; showing required. An authorization for a new standard broadcast station or increase in facilities of an existing station will be issued only after a satisfactory showing has been made in regard to the following, among others:

(a) That the proposed assignment will tend to effect a fair, efficient and equitable distribution of radio service among the several states and communities.

(b) That a proposed new station (or a proposed change in the facilities of an authorized station) complies with the pertinent requirements of §73.37.

(c) That the applicant is financially qualified to construct and operate the proposed station.

(d) That the applicant is legally qualified. That the applicant (or the person or persons in control of an applicant corporation or other organization) is of good character and possesses other qualifications sufficient to provide a satisfactory public service.

(e) That the technical equipment proposed, the location of the transmitter, and other technical phases of operation comply with the regulations governing the same, and the requirements of good engineering practice.

(f) That the facilities sought are subject to assignment as requested under existing international agreements and the rules and regulations of the Commission.

(g) That the population within the 1 m/v contour does not exceed 1.0 percent of the population within the 25 mv/m contour: Provided, however, that where the number of persons within the 1 m/v contour is 300 or less the provisions of this subparagraph are not applicable.

(h) That, in the case of an application for a Class B or Class D station on a clear channel, the proposed station would radiate, during two hours following local sunrise and two hours preceding local sunset, in any direction toward the 0.1 mv/m groundwave contour of a co-channel United States Class A station, no more than the maximum radiation values permitted under the provisions of §73.187.

(i) That, for all stations, the daytime 5 mv/m contour encompasses the entire principal community to be served. That, for stations in the 535-1605 kHz band, 80% of the principal community is encompassed by the nighttime 5 mV/m contour or the nighttime interference-free contour, whichever value is higher. That, for stations in the 1605-1705 kHz band, 50% of the principal community is encompassed by the 5 mV/m contour or the nighttime interference-free contour, whichever value is higher. That, Class D stations with nighttime authorizations need not demonstrate such coverage during nighttime operation.

(j) That the public interest, convenience and necessity will be served through the operation under the proposed assignment.

§73.25 Clear channels: Class A, Class B and Class D stations. The frequencies in the following tabulations are designated as clear channels and assigned for use by the classes of stations given:

(a) On each of the following channels, one Class A station may be assigned, operating with power of 50 kw: 640, 650, 660, 670, 700, 720, 750, 760, 770, 780, 820, 830, 840, 870, 880, 890, 1020, 1030, 1040, 1100, 1120, 1160, 1180, 1200 and 1210 kHz. In Alaska, these frequencies can be used by Class A stations subject to the conditions set forth in §73.182(a)(1)(ii). On the channels listed in this paragraph, Class B and Class D stations may be assigned.

(b) To each of the following channels there may be assigned Class A, Class B and Class D stations: 680, 710, 810, 850, 940, 1000, 1060, 1070, 1080, 1090, 1110, 1130, 1140, 1170, 1190, 1500, 1510, 1520, 1530, 1540, 1550 and 1560 kHz.

NOTE: Until superseded by a new agreement, protection of the Bahama Islands shall be in accordance with NARBA. Accordingly, a Class A, Class B or Class D station on 1540 kHz shall restrict its signal to a value no greater than 4 uV/m groundwave or 25 uV/m-10% skywave at any point of land in the Bahama Islands, and such stations operating nighttime (i.e., sunset to sunrise at the location of the U.S. station) shall be located not less than 650 miles from the nearest point of land in the Bahama Islands.

(c) Class A, Class B and Class D stations may be assigned on 540, 690, 730, 740, 800, 860, 900, 990, 1010, 1050, 1220, 1540, 1570, and 1580 kHz.

§73.26 Regional channels: Class B and Class D stations.

(a) The following frequencies are designated as regional channels and are assigned for use by Class B and Class D stations: 550, 560, 570, 580, 590, 600, 610, 620, 630, 790, 910, 920, 930, 950, 960, 970, 980, 1150, 1250, 1260, 1270, 1280, 1290, 1300, 1310, 1320, 1330, 1350, 1360, 1370, 1380, 1390, 1410, 1420, 1430, 1440, 1460, 1470, 1480, 1590, 1600, 1610, 1620, 1630, 1640, 1650, 1660, 1670, 1680, 1690, and 1700 kHz.

(b) Additionally, in Alaska, Hawaii, Puerto Rico and the U.S. Virgin Islands the frequencies 1230, 1240, 1340, 1400, 1450 and 1490 kHz are designated as Regional channels, and are assigned for use by Class B stations. Stations formerly licensed to these channels in those locations as Class C stations are redesignated as Class B stations.

§73.27 Local Channels; Class C stations. Within the coterminous 48 states, the following frequencies are designated as local channels, and are assigned for use by Class C stations: 1230, 1240, 1340, 1400, 1450, and 1490 kHz.

§73.28 Assignments of stations to channels. (a) The Commission will not make an AM station assignment that does not conform with international requirements and restrictions on spectrum use that the United States has accepted as a signatory to treaties, conventions, and other international agreements. See §73.1650 for a list of pertinent treaties, conventions and agreements, and §73.23 for procedural provisions relating to compliance with them.

(c) Engineering standards now in force domestically differ in some respects from those specified for international purposes. The engineering standards specified for international purposes (see §73.1650, International Agreements) will be used to determine: (1) The extent to which interference might be caused by a proposed station in the United States to a station in another country; and (2) whether the United States should register an objection to any new or changed assignment notified by another country. The domestic standards in effect in the United States will be used to determine the extent to which interference exists or would exist from a foreign station where the value of such interference enters into a calculation of: (1) the service to be rendered by a proposed operation in the United States; or (2) the permissible interfering signal from one station in the United States to another United States station.

§73.29 Class C stations on regional channels. No license will be granted for the operation of a Class C station on a regional channel.

§73.30 Petition for authorization of an allotment in the 1605-1705 kHz band.

(a) Any party interested in operating an AM broadcast station on one of the ten channels in the 1605-1705 kHz band must file a petition for the establishment of an allotment to its community of license. Each petition must include the following information:

(1) name of community for which allotment is sought; (2) frequency and call letters of the petitioner's existing AM operation; and (3) statement as to whether or not AM stereo operation is proposed for the operation in the 1605-1705 kHz band.

(b) Petitions are to be filed during a filing period to be determined by the Commission. For each filing period, eligible stations will be allotted channels based on the following steps:

(1) Stations are ranked in descending order according to the calculated improvement factor.

(2) The station with the highest improvement factor is initially allotted the lowest available channel.

(3) Successively, each station with the next lowest improvement factor is allotted an available channel taking into account the possible frequency and location combinations and relationship to previously selected allotments. If a channel is not available for the subject station, previous allotments are examined with respect to an alternate channel, the use of which would make a channel available for the subject station.

(4) When it has been determined that, in accordance with the above steps, no channel is available for the subject station, that station is no longer considered and the process continues to the station with the next lowest improvement factor.

(c) If awarded an allotment, a petitioner will have sixty (60) days from the date of public notice of selection to file an application for construction permit on FCC Form 301. (See §§73.24 and 73.37(e) for filing requirements.) Unless instructed by the Commission to do otherwise, the application shall specify Model I facilities. (See §73.14.) Upon grant of the application and subsequent construction of the authorized facility, the applicant must file a license application on FCC Form 302.

NOTE 1: Until further notice by the Commission, the filing of these petitions is limited to licensees of existing AM stations (excluding Class C stations) operating in the 535-1605 kHz band. First priority will be assigned to Class D stations located within the primary service contours of U.S. Class A stations that are licensed to serve communities of 100,000 or more for which there exists no local full-time aural service.

NOTE 2: Selection among competing petitions will be based on interference reduction. Notwithstanding the exception contained in NOTE 5, within each operational category, the station demonstrating the highest value of improvement factor will be afforded the highest priority for an allotment, with the next priority assigned to the station with next lowest value, and so on, until available allotments are filled.

NOTE 3: The Commission will periodically evaluate the progress of the movement of stations from the 535-1605 kHz band to the 1605-1705 kHz band to determine whether the 1605-1705 kHz band should continue to be administered on an allotment basis or modified to an assignment method. If appropriate, the Commission will later develop further procedures for use of the 1605-1705 kHz band by existing station licensees and others.

NOTE 4: Other than the exception specified in NOTE 1, existing fulltime stations are considered first for selection as described in NOTE 2. In the event that an allotment availability exists for which no fulltime station has filed a relevant petition, such allotment may be awarded to a licensed Class D station. If more than one Class D station applies for this migration opportunity, the following priorities will be used in the selection process: First priority - A Class D station located within the 0.5 mV/m-50% contour of a U.S. Class A station and licensed to serve a community of 100,000 or more, for which there exists no local fulltime aural service; Second priority - Class D stations ranked in order of improvement factor, from highest to lowest, considering only those stations with improvement factors greater than zero.

NOTE 5: The preference for AM stereo in the expanded band will be administered as follows: when an allotment under consideration (candidate allotment) conflicts with one or more previously selected allotments (established allotments) and cannot be accommodated in the expanded band, the candidate allotment will be substituted for the previously established allotment provided that: the petitioner for the candidate allotment has made a written commitment to the use of AM stereo and the petitioner for the established allotment has not; the difference between the ranking factors associated with the candidate and established allotments does not exceed 10% of the ranking factor of the candidate allotment; the substitution will not require the displacement of more than one established allotment; and both the candidate allotment and the established allotment are within the same priority group.

In FM rules ...

§73.35 Calculation of improvement factors.
(a) A petition for an allotment (see §73.30) in the 1605-1705 kHz band filed by an existing fulltime AM station licensed in the 535-1605 kHz band will be ranked according to the station's calculated improvement factor. (See §73.30.) Improvement factors relate to both nighttime and daytime interference conditions and are based on two distinct considerations: (1) service area lost by other stations due to interference caused by the subject station, and (2) service area of the subject station. These considerations are represented by a ratio. The ratio consists, where applicable, of two separate additive components, one for nighttime and one for daytime. For the nighttime component, to determine the numerator of the ratio (first consideration), calculate the RSS and associated service area of the stations (co- and adjacent channel) to which the subject station causes nighttime interference. Next, repeat the RSS and service area calculations excluding the subject station. The cumulative gain in the above service areas is the numerator of the ratio. The denominator (second consideration) is the subject station's interference-free service area. For the daytime component, the composite amount of service lost by co-channel an adjacent channel stations, each taken individually, that are affected by the subject station, excluding the effects of other assignments during each study, will be used as the numerator of the daytime improvement factor. The denominator will consist of the actual daytime service area (0.5 mV/m contour) less any area lost to interference from other assignments. The value of this combined ratio will constitute the petitioner's improvement factor. Notwithstanding the requirements of §73.153, for uniform comparisons and simplicity, measurement data will not be used for determining improvement factors and FCC Figure M-3 ground conductivity values are to be used exclusively in accordance with the pertinent provisions of §73.183(c)(1).

§73.201. Numerical designation of FM broadcast channels. The FM broadcast band consists of that portion of the radio frequency spectrum between 88 megacycles per second (mHz) and 108 mHz. It is divided into 100 channels of 200 kHz each. For convenience, the frequencies available for FM broadcasting (including those assigned to noncommercial educational broadcasting) are given numerical designations which are shown in the table below:

Freq.	Ch. No.	Freq.	Ch. No.
88.1 mhz	201	98.1 mhz	251
88.3 mhz	202	98.3 mhz	252
88.5 mhz	203	98.5 mhz	253
88.7 mhz	204	98.7 mhz	254
88.9 mhz	205	98.9 mhz	255
89.1 mhz	206	99.1 mhz	256
89.3 mhz	207	99.3 mhz	257
89.5 mhz	208	99.5 mhz	258
89.7 mhz	209	99.7 mhz	259
89.9 mhz	210	99.9 mhz	260
90.1 mhz	211	100.1 mhz	261
90.3 mhz	212	100.3 mhz	262
90.5 mhz	213	100.5 mhz	263
90.7 mhz	214	100.7 mhz	264
90.9 mhz	215	100.9 mhz	265
91.1 mhz	216	101.1 mhz	266
91.3 mhz	217	101.3 mhz	267
91.5 mhz	218	101.5 mhz	268
91.7 mhz	219	101.7 mhz	269
91.9 mhz	220	101.9 mhz	270
92.1 mhz	221	102.1 mhz	271
92.3 mhz	222	102.3 mhz	272
92.5 mhz	223	102.5 mhz	273
92.7 mhz	224	102.7 mhz	274
92.9 mhz	225	102.9 mhz	275
93.1 mhz	226	103.1 mhz	276
93.3 mhz	227	103.3 mhz	277
93.5 mhz	228	103.5 mhz	278
93.7 mhz	229	103.7 mhz	279
93.9 mhz	230	103.9 mhz	280
94.1 mhz	231	104.1 mhz	281
94.3 mhz	232	104.3 mhz	282
94.5 mhz	233	104.5 mhz	283
94.7 mhz	234	104.7 mhz	284
94.9 mhz	235	104.9 mhz	285
95.1 mhz	236	105.1 mhz	286
95.3 mhz	237	105.3 mhz	287
95.5 mhz	238	105.5 mhz	288
95.7 mhz	239	105.7 mhz	289
95.9 mhz	240	105.9 mhz	290
96.1 mhz	241	106.1 mhz	291
96.3 mhz	242	106.3 mhz	292
96.5 mhz	243	106.5 mhz	293
96.7 mhz	244	106.7 mhz	294
96.9 mhz	245	106.9 mhz	295
97.1 mhz	246	107.1 mhz	296
97.3 mhz	247	107.3 mhz	297
97.5 mhz	248	107.5 mhz	298
97.7 mhz	249	107.7 mhz	299
97.9 mhz	250	107.9 mhz	300

§73.202. Table of Allotments.
(a) General. The following Table of Allotments contains the channels (other than noncommercial educational Channels 201-220) designated for use in communities in the United States, its territories, and possessions. All listed channels are for Class B stations in Zones I and I-A and for Class C stations in Zone II unless otherwise specifically designated.

(1) Channels designated with an asterisk may only be used by noncommercial educational broadcast stations. Noncommercial educational FM allotments (Channels 201-220) available for use in various communities in Arizona, California, New Mexico, and Texas are listed in §73.504. The rules governing the use of noncommercial educational channels in other communities are contained in §73.501.

(2) Each channel listed in the Table of Allotments reflects the class of station that is authorized, or has an application filed, to use it based on the minimum and maximum facility requirements for each class contained in §73.211.

NOTE: The provisions of this subparagraph [(a)(2)] become effective March 1, 1987.

(b) Table of FM Allotments. [EDITOR'S NOTE: Channel assignments by cities are reprinted in the AM-FM directory and are not repeated here.]

§73.203. Availability of channels.
(a) Except as provided for in paragraph (b) of this section, applications may be filed to construct FM broadcast stations only at the communities and on the channels and classes contained in the FM Table of Allotments (§73.202(b)). Applications that fail to comply with this requirement, whether or not accompanied by a petition to amend the Table, will not be accepted for tender.

(b) Applications filed on a first-come, first served basis may propose a lower or higher class adjacent, intermediate frequency or co-channel. Applications for the modification of an existing FM broadcast station may propose a lower or higher class adjacent, intermediate frequency or co-channel, or a same class adjacent channel. In these cases, the applicant need not file a petition for rule making to amend the Table of Allotments (§73.202(b)) to specify the modified channel class.

Note: Changes in channel and/or class by application are limited to modifications on first, second and third adjacent channels, intermediate frequency (IF) channels, and co-channels which require no other changes to the FM Table of Allotments. Applications requesting such modifications must meet either the minimum spacing requirements of §73.207 at the site specified in the application, without resort to the provisions of the Commission's Rules permitting short spaced stations as set forth in §§73.213-73.215 or demonstrate by a separate exhibit attached to the application the existence of a suitable allotment site that fully complies with §§73.207 and 73.315, without resort to §§73.213-73.215.

§73.205. Zones.
For the purpose of allotments and assignments, the United States is divided into three zones as follows:

(a) Zone I consists of that portion of the United States located within the confines of the following lines drawn on the United States Albers Equal Area Projection Map (based on standard parallels 29½ and 45½; North American datum); Beginning at the most easterly point on the State boundary line between North Carolina and Virginia; thence in a straight line to a point on the Virginia, West Virginia boundary line located at North Latitude 37 49' and West Longitude 80 12' 30"; thence westerly along the southern boundary lines of the States of West Virginia, Ohio, Indiana, and Illinois to a point at the junction of the Illinois, Kentucky, and Missouri state boundary lines; thence northerly along the western boundary line of the State of Illinois to a point at the junction of the Illinois, Iowa, and Wisconsin state boundary lines; thence, easterly along the northern state boundary line of Illinois to the 90th meridian; thence north along this meridian to the 43.5- parallel; thence east along the parallel to the United States-Canada border; thence southerly and following that border until it again intersects the 43.5- parallel; thence east along this parallel to the 71st meridian; thence in a straight line to the intersection of the 69th meridian and the 45th parallel; thence east along the 45th parallel to the Atlantic Ocean. When any of the above lines pass through a city, the city shall be considered to be located in Zone I. (See Figure I of §73.699 [in complete copy of Rules]).

(b) Zone IA consists of Puerto Rico, the Virgin Islands, and that portion of the State of California which is located south of the 40th parallel.

(c) Zone II consists of Alaska, Hawaii and the rest of the United States which is not located in either Zone I or Zone IA.

73.207 Minimum distance separations between stations.
(a) Except for assignments made pursuant to §§73.213 or 73.215, FM allotments and assignments must be separated from other allotments and assignments on the same channel (co-channel) and five pairs of adjacent channels by not less than the minimum distances specified in paragraphs (b) and (c) of this section. The Commission will not accept petitions to amend the Table of Allotments unless the reference points meet all of the minimum distance separation requirements of this section. The Commission will not accept applications for new stations, or applications to change the channel or location of existing assignments, unless transmitter sites meet the minimum distance separation requirements of this section, or such applications conform to the requirements of §§73.213 or 73.215. However, applications to modify the facilities of stations with short-spaced antenna locations authorized pursuant to prior waivers of the distance separation requirements may be accepted, provided that such applications propose to maintain or improve that particular spacing deficiency. Class D (secondary) assignments are subject only to the distance separation requirements contained in paragraph (b)(3) of this section. (See §73.512 for rules governing the channel and location of Class D (secondary) assignments.)

(b) The distances listed in Tables A, B and C apply to allotments and assignments on the same channel and each of five pairs of adjacent channels. The five pairs of adjacent channels are the first (200 kHz above and 200 kHz below the channel under consideration), the second (400 kHz above and below), the third (600 kHz above and below), the fifty-third (10.6 mHz above and below), and the fifty-fourth (10.8 mHz above and below). The distances in the Tables apply regardless of whether the proposed station class appears first or second in the "Relation" column of the table.

(1) Domestic allotments and assignments must be separated from each other by not less than the distances in Table A which follows:

(2) Under the Canada-United States FM Broadcasting Agreement, domestic U.S. allotments and assignments within 320 kilometers (199 miles) of the common border must be separated from Canadian allotments and as-

signments by not less than the distances given in Table B, which follows. When applying Table B, U.S Class C2 allotments and assignments are considered to be Class B; also, U.S. Class C3 allotments and assignments and U.S. Class A assignments operating with more than 3 kw ERP and 100 meters antenna HAAT (or equivalent lower ERP and higher antenna HAAT based on a class contour distance of 24 km) are considered to be Class B1.

(3) Under the Mexico-United States FM Broadcasting Agreement, domestic U.S. allotments and assignments within 320 kilometers (199 miles) of the common border must be separated from Mexican allotments and assignments by not less than the distances given in Table C, which follows. When applying Table C, U.S. Class C2, C3 and B1 allotments and assignments are considered to be Class B; U.S. Class C1 allotments and assignments are considered to be Class C; also, U.S. Class A assignments operating with more than 3 kw ERP and 91 meters antenna height above average terrain (or equivalent lower ERP and higher antenna HAAT based on Annex IV of the Agreement) are considered to be Class B.

(c) The distances listed below apply only to allotments and assignments on Channel 253 (98.5 mHz). The Commission will not accept petitions to amend the Table of Allotments, applications for new stations, or applications to change the channel or location of existing assignments where the following minimum distances (between transmitter sites, in kilometers) from any TV Channel 6 allotment or assignment are not met:

Minimum Distance Separation from TV Channel 6 (82-88 mhz)

FM Class	TV Zone I	TV Zones II & III
A	17	22
B1	19	23
B	22	26
C3	19	23
C2	22	26
C1	29	33
C	36	41

§73.210 Station classes.

(a) The rules applicable to a particular station, including minimum and maximum facilities requirements, are determined by its class. Possible class designations depend upon the zone in which the station's transmitter is located. The zones are defined in §73.205. Allotted station classes are indicated in the Table of Allotments, §73.202. Class A, B1 and B stations may be authorized in Zones I and I-A. Class A, C3, C2, C1 and C stations may be authorized in Zone II.

(b) The power and antenna height requirements for each class are set forth in §73.211. If a station has an ERP and an antenna HAAT such that it cannot be classified using the maximum limits and minimum requirements in §73.211, its class shall be determined using the following procedure:

(1) Determine the reference distance of the station using the procedure in paragraph (b)(1)(i) of §73.211. If this distance is less than or equal to 28 km, the station is Class A; otherwise,

(2) For a station in Zone I or Zone I-A, except for Puerto Rico and the Virgin Islands:

(i) If this distance is greater than 28 km and less than or equal to 39 km, the station is Class B1.

(ii) If this distance is greater than 39 km and less than or equal to 52 km, the station is Class B.

(3) For a station in Zone II:

(i) If this distance is greater than 28 km and less than or equal to 39 km, the station is Class C3.

(ii) If this distance is greater than 39 km and less than or equal to 52 km, the station is Class C2.

(iii) If this distance is greater than 52 km and less than or equal to 72 km, the station is Class C1.

(iv) If this distance is greater than 72 km and less than or equal to 92 km, the station is Class C.

(4) For a station in Puerto Rico or the Virgin Islands:

(i) If this distance is less than or equal to 42 km, the station is Class A.

(ii) If this distance is greater than 42 km and less than or equal to 46 km, the station is Class B1.

(iii) If this distance is greater than 46 km and less than or equal to 78 km, the station is Class B.

§73.211 Power and antenna height requirements.

(a) Minimum requirements.

(1) Except as provided in paragraphs (a)(3) and (b)(2) of this section, FM stations must operate with a minimum effective radiated power (ERP) as follows:

(i) The minimum ERP for Class A stations is 0.1 kw.

(ii) The ERP for Class B1 stations must exceed 6 kw.

(iii) The ERP for Class B stations must exceed 25 kw.

(iv) The ERP for Class C3 stations must exceed 6 kw.

(v) The ERP for Class C2 stations must exceed 25 kw.

(vi) The ERP for Class C1 stations must exceed 50 kw.

(vii) The minimum ERP for Class C stations is 100 kw.

(2) Class C stations must have an antenna height above average terrain (HAAT) of at least 300 meters (984 feet). No minimum HAAT is specified for Classes A, B1, B, C3, C2, or C1 stations.

(3) Stations of any class except Class A may have an ERP less than that specified in paragraph (a)(1) of this section, provided that the reference distance, determined in accordance with paragraph (b)(1)(i) of this section, exceeds the distance to the class contour for the next lower class. Class A stations may have an ERP less than 100 watts provided that the reference distance, determined in accordance with paragraph (b)(1)(i) of this section, equals or exceeds 6 kilometers.

(b) Maximum limits.

(1) Except for stations located in Puerto Rico or the Virgin Islands, the maximum ERP in any direction, reference HAAT and distance to the class contour for each FM station class are listed below:

Station Class	*Maximum ERP*	*Reference HAAT in meters (ft.)*	*Class contour distance in kilometers*
A	6 kw (7.8 dBk)	100 (328)	28
B1	25 kw (14.0 dBk)	100 (328)	39
B	50 kw (17.0 dBk)	150 (492)	52
C3	25 kw (14.0 dBk)	100 (328)	39
C2	50 kw (17.0 dBk)	150 (492)	52
C1	100 kw (20.0 dBk)	299 (981)	72
C	100 kw (20.0 dBk)	600 (1968)	92

(i) The reference distance of a station is obtained by finding the predicted distance to the 1 mV/m contour using Figure 1 of §73.333 and then rounding to the nearest kilometer. Antenna HAAT is determined using the procedure in §73.313. If the HAAT so determined is less than 30 meters (100 feet), a HAAT of 30 meters must be used when finding the predicted distance to the 1 mV/m contour.

(ii) If a station's ERP is equal to the maximum for its class, its antenna HAAT must not exceed the reference HAAT, regardless of the reference distance. For example, a Class A station operating with 6 kw ERP may have an antenna HAAT of 100 meters, but not 101 meters, even though the reference distance is 28 km in both cases.

(iii) Except as provided in paragraph (b)(3) of this section, no station will be authorized in Zone I or I-A with an ERP equal to 50 kw and a HAAT exceeding 150 meters. No station will be authorized in Zone II with an ERP equal to 100 kw and a HAAT exceeding 600 meters.

(2) If a station has an antenna HAAT greater than the reference HAAT for its class, its ERP must be lower than the class maximum such that the reference distance does not exceed the class contour distance. If the antenna HAAT is so great that the station's ERP must be lower than the minimum ERP for its class (specified in paragraphs (a)(1) and (a)(3) of this section), that lower ERP will become the minimum for that station.

(3) For stations located in Puerto Rico or the Virgin Islands, the maximum ERP in any direction, reference HAAT, and distance to the class contour for each FM station class are listed below:

Station Class	*Maximum ERP*	*Reference HAAT in meters (ft.)*	*Class contour distance in kilometers*
A	6 kw (7.8 dBk)	240 (787)	42
B1	25 kw (14.0 dBk)	150 (492)	46
B	50 kw (17.0 dBk)	472 (1549)	78

(c) Existing stations. Stations authorized prior to March 1, 1984 that do not conform to the requirements of this section, may continue to operate as authorized. Stations operating with facilities in excess of those specified in paragraph (b) of this section may not increase their effective radiated powers or extend their 1 mV/m field strength contour beyond the location permitted by their present authorizations. The provisions of this section will not apply to applications to increase facilities for those stations operating with less than the minimum power specified in paragraph (a) of this section.

§73.213 Grandfathered short-spaced stations.

(a) Stations at locations authorized prior to November 16, 1964 that did not meet the separation distances required by §73.207 and have remained short-spaced since that time may be modified or relocated provided that the predicted distance to the 1 mV/m field strength contour is not extended toward the 1 mV/m field strength contour of any short-spaced station. Mutual increase in the facilities of such stations up to the limits set forth in §73.211 may be permitted pursuant to an agreement between the affected stations and a showing of public interest. See §73.4235.

(b) Stations at locations authorized prior to May 17, 1989 that did not meet the IF separation distances required by §73.207 and have remained short-spaced since that time may be modified or relocated provided that the overlap area of the two stations' 36 mV/m field strength contours is not increased.

(c) Short spacings involving at least one Class A allotment or authorization. Stations that became short-spaced on or after November 16, 1964 (including stations that do not meet the minimum distance separation requirements of paragraph (c)(1) of this section and that propose to maintain or increase their existing distance separations) may be modified or relocated in accordance with paragraph (c)(1) or (c)(2) of this section, except that this provision does not apply to stations that became short spaced by grant of applications filed after October 1, 1989, or filed pursuant to §73.215. If the reference coordinates of an allotment are short spaced to an authorized facility or another allotment (as a result of the revision of §73.207 in the Second Report and Order in MM Docket No. 88-375), an application for the allotment may be authorized, and subsequently modified after grant, in accordance with paragraph (c)(1) or (c)(2) of this section only with respect to such short spacing. No other stations will be authorized pursuant to these paragraphs.

(1) Applications for authorization under requirements equivalent to those of prior rules. Each application for authority to operate a Class A station with no more than 3000 watts ERP and 100 meters antenna HAAT (or equivalent lower ERP and higher antenna HAAT based on a class contour distance of 24 km) must specify a transmitter site that meets the minimum distance separation requirements in this paragraph. Each application for authority to operate a Class A station with more than 3000 watts ERP (up to a maximum of 5800 watts) but with an antenna HAAT lower than 100 meters such that the distance to the predicted 0.05 mV/m (34 dB uV/m) F(50,10) field strength contour does not exceed 98 km must specify a transmitter site that meets the minimum distance separation requirements in this paragraph. Each application for authority to operate an FM station of any class other than Class A must specify a transmitter site that meets the minimum distance separation requirements in this paragraph with respect to Class A stations operating pursuant to this paragraph or paragraph (c)(2) of this section, and that meets the minimum distance separation requirements of §73.207 with respect to all other stations.

(2) Applications for authorization of Class A facilities greater than 3000 watts ERP and 100 meters HAAT. Each application to operate a Class A station with an ERP and HAAT such that the reference distance would exceed 24 kilometers must contain an exhibit demonstrating the consent of the licensee of each co-channel, first, second, or third adjacent channel station (for which the requirements of §73.207 are not met) to a grant of that application. Each such application must specify a transmitter site that meets the applicable IF-related channel distance separation requirements of §73.207. Applications that specify a new transmitter site which is short-spaced to an FM station other than another Class A station which is seeking a mutual increase in facilities may be granted only if no alternative fully-spaced site or less short-spaced site is available. Licensees of Class A stations seeking mutual increases in facilities need not show that a fully-spaced site or less short-spaced site is available. Applications submitted pursuant to the provisions of this paragraph may be granted only if such action is consistent with the public interest.

§73.215 Contour protection for short-spaced assignments.

The Commission will accept applications that specify short-spaced antenna locations (locations that do not meet the domestic co-channel and adjacent channel minimum distance separation requirements of §73.207); provided that, such applications propose contour protection, as defined in paragraph (a) of this section, with all short-spaced assignments, applications and allotments, and meet the other applicable requirements of this section. Each application to be processed pursuant to this section must specifically request such processing on its face, and must include the necessary exhibit to demonstrate that the requisite contour protection will be provided. Such applications may be granted when the Commission determines that such action would serve the public interest, convenience, and necessity.

(a) Contour protection. Contour protection, for the purpose of this section, means that on the same channel and on the first, second and third adjacent channels, the

Federal Communications Commission Rules and Regulations

predicted interfering contours of the proposed station do not overlap the predicted protected contours of other short-spaced assignments, applications and allotments, and the predicted interfering contours of other short-spaced assignments, applications and allotments do not overlap the predicted protected contour of the proposed station.

(1) The protected contours, for the purpose of this section, are defined as follows: For all Class B and B1 stations on Channels 221 through 300 inclusive, the F(50,50) field strengths along the protected contours are 0.5 mV/m (54 dBu) and 0.7 mV/m (57 dBu), respectively. For all other stations, the F(50,50) field strength along the protected contour is 1.0 mV/m (60 dBu).

(2) The interfering contours, for the purpose of this section, are defined as follows. For co-channel stations, the F(50,10) field strength along the interfering contour is 20 dB lower than the F(50,50) field strength along the protected contour for which overlap is prohibited. For first adjacent channel stations (+/-200 kHz), the F(50,10) field strength along the interfering contour is 6 dB lower than the F(50,50) field strength along the protected contour for which overlap is prohibited. For both second and third adjacent channel stations (+/-400 kHz and +/-600 kHz), the F(50,10) field strength along the interfering contour is 40 dB higher than the F(50,50) field strength along the protected contour for which overlap is prohibited.

(3) The locations of the protected and interfering contours of the proposed station and the other short-spaced assignments, applications and allotments must be determined in accordance with the procedures of paragraphs (c), (d)(2) and (d)(3) of §73.313, using data for as many radials as necessary to accurately locate the contours.

(4) Stations in Puerto Rico and the Virgin Islands may submit application for short spaced locations provided the predicted distance to their 1 mV/m field strength contour is not extended toward the 1 mV/m contour of any short-spaced station.

(b) Applicants requesting short-spaced assignments pursuant to this section must take into account the following factors in demonstrating that contour protection is achieved:

(1) The ERP and antenna HAAT of the proposed station in the direction of the contours of other short-spaced assignments, applications and allotments. If a directional antenna is proposed, the pattern of that antenna must be used to calculate the ERP in particular directions. See §73.316 for additional requirements for directional antennas.

(2) The ERP and antenna HAAT of other short-spaced assignments, applications and allotments in the direction of the contours of the proposed station. The ERP and antenna HAATs in the directions of concern must be determined as follows:

(i) For vacant allotments, contours are based on the presumed use, at the allotment's reference point, of the maximum ERP that could be authorized for the station class of the allotment, and antenna HAATs in the directions of concern that would result from a nondirectional antenna mounted at a standard eight-radial antenna HAAT equal to the reference HAAT for the station class of the allotment.

(ii) For existing stations that were not authorized pursuant to this section, including stations with authorized ERP that exceeds the maximum ERP permitted by §73.211 for the standard eight-radial antenna HAAT employed, and for applications not requesting authorization pursuant to this section, contours are based on the presumed use of the maximum ERP for the applicable station class (as specified in §73.211), and the antenna HAATs in the directions of concern that would result from a nondirectional antenna mounted at a standard eight-radial antenna HAAT equal to the reference HAAT for the applicable station class, without regard to any other restrictions that may apply (e.g., zoning laws, FAA constraints, application of §73.213).

(iii) For stations authorized pursuant to this section, except stations with authorized ERP that exceeds the maximum ERP permitted by §73.211 for the standard eight-radial antenna HAAT employed, contours are based on the use of the authorized ERP in the directions of concern, and HAATs in the directions of concern derived from the authorized standard eight-radial antenna HAAT. For stations with authorized ERP that exceeds the maximum ERP permitted by §73.211 for the standard eight-radial antenna HAAT employed, authorized under this section, contours are based on the presumed use of the maximum ERP for the applicable station class (as specified in §73.211), and antenna HAATs in the directions of concern that would result from a nondirectional antenna mounted at a standard eight-radial antenna HAAT equal to the reference HAAT for the applicable station class, without regard to any other restrictions that may apply.

(iv) For applications containing a request for authorization pursuant to this section, except for applications to continue operation with authorized ERP that exceeds the maximum ERP permitted by §73.211 for the standard eight-radial antenna HAAT employed, contours are based on the use of the proposed ERP in the directions of concern, and antenna HAATs in the directions of concern derived from the proposed standard eight-radial antenna HAAT. For applications to continue operation with an ERP that exceeds the maximum ERP permitted by §73.211 for the standard eight-radial HAAT employed, if processing is requested under this section, contours are based on the presumed use of the maximum ERP for the applicable station class (as specified in §73.211), and antenna HAATs in the directions of concern that would result from a nondirectional antenna mounted at a standard eight-radial antenna HAAT equal to the reference HAAT for the applicable station class, without regard to any other restrictions that may apply.

NOTE: Applicants are cautioned that the antenna HAAT in any particular direction of concern will not usually be the same as the standard eight-radial antenna HAAT or the reference HAAT for the station class.

(c) Applications submitted for processing pursuant to this section are not required to propose contour protection of any assignment, application or allotment for which the minimum distance separation requirements of §73.207 are met, and may, in the directions of those assignments, applications and allotments, employ the maximum ERP permitted by §73.211 for the standard eight-radial antenna HAAT employed.

(d) Stations authorized pursuant to this section may be subsequently authorized on the basis of compliance

MINIMUM DISTANCE SEPARATION REQUIREMENTS—U.S. STATIONS
in Kilometers (miles)

Relation	Co-channel	200 khz	400/600 khz	10.6/10.8 mhz
A to A	115 (71)	72 (45)	31 (19)	10 (6)
A to B1	143 (89)	96 (60)	48 (30)	12 (7)
A to B	178 (111)	113 (70)	69 (43)	15 (9)
A to C3	142 (88)	89 (55)	42 (26)	12 (7)
A to C2	166 (103)	106 (66)	55 (34)	15 (9)
A to C1	200 (124)	133 (83)	75 (47)	22 (14)
A to C	226 (140)	165 (103)	95 (59)	29 (18)
B1 to B1	175 (109)	114 (71)	50 (31)	14 (9)
B1 to B	211 (131)	145 (90)	71 (44)	17 (11)
B1 to C3	175 (109)	114 (71)	50 (31)	14 (9)
B1 to C2	200 (124)	134 (83)	56 (35)	17 (11)
B1 to C1	233 (145)	161 (100)	77 (48)	24 (15)
B1 to C	259 (161)	193 (120)	105 (65)	31 (19)
B to B	241 (150)	169 (105)	74 (46)	20 (12)
B to C3	211 (131)	145 (90)	74 (44)	17 (11)
B to C2	241 (150)	169 (105)	74 (46)	20 (12)
B to C1	270 (168)	195 (121)	79 (49)	27 (17)
B to C	274 (170)	217 (135)	105 (65)	35 (22)
C3 to C3	153 (95)	99 (62)	43 (27)	14 (9)
C3 to C2	177 (110)	117 (73)	56 (35)	17 (11)
C3 to C1	211 (131)	144 (90)	76 (47)	24 (15)
C3 to C	237 (147)	176 (109)	96 (60)	31 (19)
C2 to C2	190 (118)	130 (81)	58 (36)	20 (12)
C2 to C1	224 (139)	158 (98)	79 (49)	127 (17)
C2 to C	249 (155)	188 (117)	105 (65)	35 (22)
C1 to C1	290 (152)	177 (110)	82 (51)	34 (21)
C1 to C	270 (168)	209 (130)	105 (65)	41 (25)
C to C	290 (180)	241 (150)	105 (65)	48 (30)

MINIMUM DISTANCE SEPARATION REQUIREMENTS—U.S. TO CANADIAN STATIONS
in Kilometers

Relation	Co-channel 0 khz	Adjacent Channels 200 khz	400 khz	I.F. 600 khz	10.6/10.8 mhz
A to A	132	85	45	37	8
A to B1	180	113	62	54	16
A to B	206	132	76	69	16
A to C1	239	164	98	90	32
A to C	242	177	108	100	32
B1 to B1	197	131	70	57	24
B1 to B	223	149	84	71	24
B1 to C1	256	181	106	92	40
B1 to C	259	195	116	103	40
B to B	237	164	94	74	24
B to C1	271	195	115	95	40
B to C	274	209	125	106	40
C1 to C1	292	217	134	101	48
C1 to C	302	230	144	111	48
C to C	306	241	153	113	48

MINIMUM DISTANCE SEPARATION REQUIREMENTS—U.S. TO MEXICAN STATIONS
in Kilometers (miles)

Relation	Co-channel	200 khz	400/600 khz	10.6/10.8 mhz
A to A	105 (65)	65 (40)	25 (15)	8 (5)
A to B	175 (110)	105 (65)	65 (40)	16 (10)
A to C	210 (130)	170 (105)	105 (65)	8 (5)
A to D	95 (60)	50 (30)	25 (15)	8 (5)
B to B	240 (150)	170 (105)	65 (40)	25 (15)
B to C	270 (170)	215 (215)	105 (65)	40 (25)
B to D	170 (105)	95 (60)	65 (40)	16 (10)
C to C	290 (180)	240 (150)	105 (65)	48 (30)
C to D	200 (125)	155 (95)	105 (65)	25 (15)
D to D	18 (11)	10 (6)	5 (3)	3 (2)

Broadcasting & Cable Yearbook 1994

Federal Communications Commission Rules and Regulations

with the domestic minimum separation distance requirements of §73.207, upon filing of an FCC Form 301 or FCC Form 340 (as appropriate) requesting a modification of authorization.

(e) The Commission will not accept applications that specify a short-spaced antenna location for which the following minimum distance separation requirements, in kilometers (miles), are not met:

Relation	Co-channel	200 kHz	400/600 kHz
A to A	92 (57)	49 (30)	29 (18)
A to B1	119 (74)	72 (45)	46 (29)
A to B	143 (89)	96 (60)	67 (42)
A to C3	119 (74)	72 (45)	40 (25)
A to C2	143 (89)	89 (55)	53 (33)
A to C1	178 (111)	111 (69)	73 (45)
A to C	203 (126)	142 (88)	93 (58)
B1 to B1	143 (89)	96 (60)	48 (30)
B1 to B	178 (111)	114 (71)	69 (43)
B1 to C3	143 (89)	96 (60)	48 (30)
B1 to C2	175 (109)	114 (71)	55 (34)
B1 to C1	200 (124)	134 (83)	75 (47)
B1 to C	233 (145)	165 (103)	95 (59)
B to B	211 (131)	145 (90)	71 (44)
B to C3	178 (111)	114 (70)	69 (43)
B to C2	211 (131)	145 (90)	71 (44)
B to C1	241 (150)	169 (105)	77 (48)
B to C	270 (168)	195 (121)	105 (65)
C3 to C3	142 (88)	89 (55)	42 (26)
C3 to C2	166 (103)	106 (66)	55 (34)
C3 to C1	200 (124)	133 (83)	75 (47)
C3 to C	226 (140)	165 (103)	95 (59)
C2 to C2	177 (110)	117 (73)	56 (35)
C2 to C1	211 (131)	144 (90)	76 (47)
C2 to C	237 (147)	176 (109)	96 (60)
C1 to C1	224 (139)	158 (98)	79 (49)
C1 to C	249 (155)	188 (117)	105 (65)
C to C	270 (168)	209 (130)	105 (65)

§73.220 Restrictions on use of channels.

a) The Frequency 89.1 mHz (Channel 206) is reserved in the New York City metropolitan area for the use of the United Nations with the equivalent of an antenna height of 150 meters (492 feet) above average terrain and effective radiated power of 20 kilowatts, and the FCC will make no assignments which would cause objectionable interference with such use.

(b) In Alaska, FM broadcast stations operating on Channels 221-300 (92.1-107.9 mHz) shall not cause harmful interference to and must accept interference from non-Government fixed operations authorized prior to January 1, 1982.

§73.23 AM broadcast station applications affected by international agreements.

(a) Except as provided in paragraph (b) of this section, no application for an AM station will be accepted for filing if authorization of the facilities requested would be inconsistent with international commitments of the United States under treaties and other international agreements, arrangements and understandings. (See list of such international instruments in §73.1650(b).) Any such application that is inadvertently accepted for filing will be dismissed.

(b) AM applications that involve conflicts only with the North American Regional Broadcasting Agreement (NARBA), but that are in conformity with the remaining treaties and other international agreements listed in §73.1650(b) and with the other requirements of Part 73, will be granted subject to such modifications as the FCC may subsequently find appropriate, taking international considerations into account.

(c) In the case of any application designated for hearing on issues other than those related to consistency with international relationships and as to which no final decision has been rendered, whenever action under this section becomes appropriate because of inconsistency with international relationships, the applicant involved shall, notwithstanding the provisions of §§73.3522 and 73.3571, be permitted to amend its application to achieve consistency with such relationships. In such cases the provisions of §73.3605(c) will apply.

(d) In some circumstances, special international considerations may require that the FCC, in acting on applications, follow procedures different from those established for general use. In such cases, affected applicants will be informed of the procedures to be followed.

In Noncommercial FM rules ...

§73.506 Classes of noncommercial educational FM stations and channels.

(a) Noncommercial educational stations operating on the channels specified in §73.501 are divided into the following classes:

(1) A Class D educational station is one operating with no more than 10 watts transmitter power output.

(2) A Class D educational (secondary) station is one operating with no more than 10 watts transmitter power output in accordance with the terms of §73.512 or which has elected to follow these requirements before they become applicable under the terms of §73.512.

(3) Noncommercial educational FM (NCE-FM) stations with more than 10 watts transmitter power output are classified as Class A, B1, B, C3, C2, C1, or C depending on the station's effective radiated power and antenna height above average terrain, and on the zone in which the station's transmitter is located, on the same basis as set forth in §§73.210 and 73.211 for commercial stations.

(b) Any noncommercial educational station except Class D may be assigned to any of the channels listed in §73.501. Class D noncommercial educational FM stations applied for or authorized prior to June 1, 1980, may continue to operate on their authorized channels subject to the provisions of §73.512.

§73.507 Minimum distance separations between stations.

(a) Minimum distance separations. No application for a new station, or change in channel or transmitter site or increase in facilities of an existing station, will be granted unless the proposed facilities will be located so as to meet the adjacent channel distance separations specified in §73.207(a) for the class of station involved with respect to assignment on Channels 221, 222, and 223 listed in §73.201 (except where in the case of an existing station the proposed facilities fall within the provisions of §73.207(b)), or where a Class D station is changing frequency to comply with the requirements of §73.512.

(b) Stations authorized as of September 10, 1962, which do not meet the requirements of paragraph (a) of this section and §73.511, may continue to operate as authorized; but any application to change facilities will be subject to the provision of this section.

(c)(1) Stations separated in frequency by 10.6 or 10.8 mHz (53 or 54 channels) from allotments or assignments on non-reserved channels will not be authorized unless they conform to the separations in Table A given in §73.207.

(2) Under the United States-Mexican FM Broadcasting Agreement, for stations and assignments differing in frequency by 10.6 to 10.8 mHz (53 or 54 channels), U.S. noncommercial educational FM allotments and assignments must meet the separations given in Table C of §73.207 to Mexican allotments or assignments in the border area.

In TV rules ...

§73.603. Numerical designation of television channels. (a)

Chan. No.	Freq. Band (Megacycles)	Chan. No.	Freq. Band (Megacycles)
2	54-60	43	644-650
3	60-66	44	650-656
4	66-72	45	656-662
5	76-82	46	662-668
6	82-88	47	668-674
7	174-180	48	674-680
8	180-186	49	680-686
9	186-192	50	686-692
10	192-198	51	692-698
11	198-204	52	698-704
12	204-210	53	704-710
13	210-216	54	710-716
14	470-476	55	716-722
15	476-482	56	722-728
16	482-488	57	728-734
17	488-494	58	734-740
18	494-500	59	740-746
19	500-506	60	746-752
20	506-512	61	752-758
21	512-518	62	758-764
22	518-524	63	764-770
23	524-530	64	770-776
24	530-536	65	776-782
25	536-542	66	782-788
26	542-548	67	788-794
27	548-554	68	794-800
28	554-560	69	800-806
29	560-566	70	806-812
30	566-572	71	812-818
31	572-578	72	818-824
32	578-584	73	824-830
33	584-590	74	830-836
34	590-596	75	836-842
35	596-602	76	842-848
36	602-608	77	848-854
37	608-614	78	854-860
38	614-620	79	860-866
39	620-626	80	866-872
40	626-632	81	872-878
41	632-638	82	878-884
42	638-644	83	884-890

(b) In Alaska, television broadcast stations operating on Channel 5 (76-82 mHz) and on Channel 6 (82-88 mHz) shall not cause harmful interference to and must accept interference from non-Government fixed operations authorized prior to January 1, 1982.

(c) Channel 37, 608-614 mHz, is reserved exclusively for the radio astronomy service.

(d) In Hawaii, the frequency band 488-494 mHz is allocated for non-broadcast use. This frequency band (Channel 17) will not be assigned in Hawaii for use by television broadcast stations.

§73.606. Table of Assignments.

(a) The following Table of Assignments contains the channels assigned to the listed communities in the United States, its territories, and possessions. Channels designated with an asterisk are assigned for use by noncommercial educational broadcast stations only. A station on a channel identified by a plus or a minus mark is required to operate with its carrier frequencies offset 10 kHz above or below, respectively, the normal carrier frequencies.

(b) Table of Allotments. [EDITOR'S NOTE: Channel assignments by cities are reprinted in the TV directory and are not repeated here.]

§73.607. Availability of channels.

(a) Applications may be filed to construct television broadcast stations only on the channels assigned in the Table of Allotments [§73.606(b)] and only in the communities listed therein. Applications which fail to comply with this requirement, whether or not accompanied by a petition to amend the Table, will not be accepted for filing. However, applications specifying channels which accord with publicly announced FCC orders changing the Table of Allotments will be accepted for filing even though such applications are tendered before the effective dates of such channel changes.

(b) [Deleted; see note on next page]. A channel assigned to a community listed in the Table of Assignments is available upon application in any unlisted community which is located within 15 miles of the listed community. In addition, a channel assigned to a community listed in the Table of Assignments and not designated for use by noncommercial educational stations only, is available upon application in any other community within 15 miles thereof which, although listed in the table, is assigned only a channel designated for use only by noncommer-

Minimum Distance Separation Requirements in kilometers (miles)

Relation	Co-channel	200 khz	400/600 khz	10.6/10.8 mhz
A to A	105 (65)	64 (40)	27 (17)	8 (5)
A to B1	138 (86)	88 (55)	48 (30)	11 (6)
A to B	163 (101)	105 (65)	69 (43)	14 (9)
A to C3	138 (86)	84 (52)	42 (26)	11 (6)
A to C2	163 (101)	105 (65)	55 (34)	14 (9)
A to C1	960 (122)	129 (80)	74 (46)	21 (13)
A to C	222 (138)	161 (100)	94 (58)	28 (17)

Federal Communications Commission Rules and Regulations

cial educational stations. Where channels are assigned to two or more communities listed in combination in the Table of Assignments the provisions of this paragraph shall apply separately to each community so listed. The distance between communities shall be determined by the distance between the respective coordinates thereof as set forth in the publication of the United States Department of Commerce entitled Air Line Distances Between Cities in the United States. (This publication may be purchased from the Government Printing Office, Washington, D.C.) If said publication does not contain the coordinates of either or both communities the coordinates of the main post office in either or both of such communities shall be used. The method to be followed in making the measurements is set forth in §73.611(d).

[EDITOR'S NOTE: Subsection (b) was deleted by order adopted 2-17-83 (Docket No. 82-320). Applications on file on the date of adoption will be processed under the former rule; all applications filed after that date will be accepted only if tendered as valid competing applications to applications already found acceptable by the staff under the rule.]

§73.609. Zones.
a) For the purpose of allotment and assignment, the United States is divided into three zones as follows:
(1) Zone I consists of that portion of the United States located within the confines of the following lines drawn on the United States Albers Equal Area Projection Map (based on standard parallels 29 1/2 and 45 1/2; North American datum); Beginning at the most easterly point on the state boundary line between North Carolina and Virginia; thence a straight line to a point on the Virginia-West Virginia boundary line located at North Latitude 37 49' and West Longitude 80 12'30"; thence westerly along the southern boundary lines of the states of West Virginia, Ohio, Indiana and Illinois to a point at the junction of the Illinois, Kentucky, and Missouri state boundary lines; thence northerly along the western boundary line of the state of Illinois to a point at the junction of the Illinois, Iowa, and Wisconsin state boundary lines; thence easterly along the northern state boundary line of Illinois to the 90th meridian; thence north along this meridian to the 43.5 parallel; thence east along this parallel to the United States-Canada border; thence southerly and following that border until it again intersects the 43.5 parallel; thence east along this parallel to the 71st meridian; thence in a straight line to the intersection of the 69th meridian and the 45th parallel; thence east along the 45th parallel; to the Atlantic Ocean. When any of the above lines pass through a city, the city shall be considered to be located in Zone I. (See Figure 1 of §73.699).

(2) Zone II consists of that portion of the United States which is not located in either Zone I or Zone III, and Puerto Rico, Alaska, Hawaiian Islands and the Virgin Islands.

(3) Zone III consists of that portion of the United States located south of a line, drawn on the United States Albers Equal Area Projection Map (based on standard parallels 29 1/2 and 45 1/2; North American datum), beginning at a point on the east coast of Georgia and the 31st parallel and ending at the United States-Mexican border, consisting of arcs drawn with a 241.4 kilometer (150 mile) radius to the north from the following specified points:

	North Latitude	West Longitude
a)	29° 40' 00"	83° 24' 00"
b)	30° 07' 00"	84° 12' 00"
c)	30° 31' 00"	86° 30' 00"
d)	30° 48' 00"	87° 58' 30"
e)	30° 00' 00"	90° 38' 30"
f)	30° 04' 30"	93° 19' 00"
g)	29° 46' 00"	95° 05' 00"
h)	28° 43' 00"	96° 30' 30"
i)	27° 52' 30"	97° 32' 00"

When any of the above arcs pass through a city, the city shall be considered to be located in Zone II. (See Figure 2 of §73.699.)

§73.610. Minimum distance separations between stations.
(a) The provisions of this section relate to allotment separations and station separations. Petitions to amend the Table of Allotments [§73.606(b)] other than those also expressly requesting amendment of this section or §73.609 will be dismissed and all applications for new television broadcast stations or for changes in the transmitter sites of existing stations will not be accepted for filing if they fail to comply with the requirements specified in paragraphs (b), (c) and (d) of this section.

NOTE: Licensees and permittees of television broadcast stations which were operating on April 14, 1952 pursuant to one or more separations below those set forth in §3.610 may continue to so operate, but in no event may they further reduce the separations below the minimum. As the existing separations of such stations are increased, the new separations will become the required minimum separations until separations are reached which comply with the requirements of §73.610. Thereafter the provisions of said section shall be applicable.

(b) Minimum co-channel allotment and station separations:

(1) Zone	Channels 2-13	Channels 14-28
	Kilometers (Miles)	
I	272.7 (169.5 mi.)	248.6 (154.5 mi.)
II	304.9 (189.5 mi.)	280.8 (174.5 mi.)
III	353.2 (219.5 mi.)	329.0 (204.5 mi.)

(2) The minimum co-channel distance separation between a station in one zone and a station in another zone shall be that of the zone requiring the lower separation.

(c) Minimum allotment and station adjacent channel separations applicable to all zones:

(1) Channels 2-13	95.7 km (59.5 mi.)
Channels 14-69	87.7 km (54.5 mi.)

(2) Due to the frequency spacing which exists between channels 4 and 5, between channels 6 and 7, and between channels 13 and 14, the minimum adjacent channel separations specified above shall not be applicable to these pairs of channels [see §73.603(a)].

(d) In addition to the requirements of paragraphs (a), (b) and (c) of this section, the minimum assignment and

Table IV of Sec. 73.698—UHF Mileage Separations

(1)	(2) 20 miles (I.F. beat)	(3) 20 miles (Intermodulation)	(4) 55 miles (Adjacent channel)	(5) 60 miles (Oscillator)	(6) 60 miles (Sound image)	(7) 75 miles (Picture image)
14	22		16-19	15	21	29	30
15	23		17-20	14, 16	22	29	30
16	24		14, 18-21	15, 17	23	30	31
17	25		14-15, 19-22	16, 18	24	31	32
18	26		14-16, 20-23	17, 19	25	32	33
19	27		14-17, 21-24	18, 20	26	33	34
20	28		15-18, 22-25	19, 21	27	34	35
21	29		16-19, 23-26	20, 22	28, 14	35	36
22	30, 14	17-20, 24-27	21, 23	29, 15	36	37
23	31, 15	18-21, 25-28	22, 24	30, 16	37	38
24	32, 16	19-22, 26-29	23, 25	31, 17	38	39
25	33, 17	20-23, 27-30	24, 26	32, 18	39	40
26	34, 18	21-24, 28-31	25, 27	33, 19	40	41
27	35, 19	22-25, 29-32	26, 28	34, 20	41	42
28	36, 20	23-26, 30-33	27, 29	35, 21	42, 14	43
29	37, 21	24-27, 31-34	28, 30	36, 22	43, 15	44, 14
30	38, 22	25-28, 32-35	29, 31	37, 23	44, 16	45, 15
31	39, 23	26-29, 33-36	30, 32	38, 24	45, 17	46, 16
32	40, 24	27-30, 34-37	31, 33	39, 25	46, 18	47, 17
33	41, 25	28-31, 35-38	32, 34	40, 26	47, 19	48, 18
34	42, 26	29-32, 36-39	33, 35	41, 27	48, 20	49, 19
35	43, 27	30-33, 37-40	34, 36	42, 28	49, 21	50, 20
36	44, 28	31-34, 38-41	35, 37	43, 29	50, 22	51, 21
37	45, 29	32-35, 39-42	36, 38	44, 30	51, 23	52, 22
38	46, 30	33-36, 40-43	37, 39	45, 31	52, 24	53, 23
39	47, 31	34-37, 41-44	38, 40	46, 32	53, 25	54, 24
40	48, 32	35-38, 42-45	39, 41	47, 33	54, 26	55, 25
41	49, 33	36-39, 43-46	40, 42	48, 34	55, 27	56, 26
42	50, 34	37-40, 44-47	41, 43	49, 35	56, 28	57, 27
43	51, 35	38-41, 45-48	42, 44	50, 36	57, 29	58, 28
44	52, 36	39-42, 46-49	43, 45	51, 37	58, 30	59, 29
45	53, 37	40-43, 47-50	44, 46	52, 38	59, 31	60, 30
46	54, 38	41-44, 48-51	45, 47	53, 39	60, 32	61, 31
47	55, 39	42-45, 49-52	46, 48	54, 40	61, 33	62, 32
48	56, 40	43-46, 50-53	47, 49	55, 41	62, 34	63, 33
49	57, 41	44-47, 51-54	48, 50	56, 42	63, 35	64, 34
50	58, 42	45-48, 52-55	49, 51	57, 43	64, 36	65, 35
51	59, 43	46-49, 53-56	50, 52	58, 44	65, 37	66, 36
52	60, 44	47-50, 54-57	51, 53	59, 45	66, 38	67, 37
53	61, 45	48-51, 55-58	52, 54	60, 46	67, 39	68, 38
54	62, 46	49-52, 56-59	53, 55	61, 47	68, 40	69, 39
55	63, 47	50-53, 57-60	54, 56	62, 48	69, 41	70, 40
56	64, 48	51-54, 58-61	55, 57	63, 49	70, 42	71, 41
57	65, 49	52-55, 59-62	56, 58	64, 50	71, 43	72, 42
58	66, 50	53-56, 60-63	57, 59	65, 51	72, 44	73, 43
59	67, 51	54-57, 61-64	58, 60	66, 52	73, 45	74, 44
60	68, 52	55-58, 62-65	59, 61	67, 53	74, 46	75, 45
61	69, 53	56-59, 63-66	60, 62	68, 54	75, 47	76, 46
62	70, 54	57-60, 64-67	61, 63	69, 55	76, 48	77, 47
63	71, 55	58-61, 65-68	62, 64	70, 56	77, 49	78, 48
64	72, 56	59-62, 66-69	63, 65	71, 57	78, 50	79, 49
65	73, 57	60-63, 67-70	64, 66	72, 58	79, 51	80, 50
66	74, 58	61-64, 68-71	65, 67	73, 59	80, 52	81, 51
67	75, 59	62-65, 69-72	66, 68	74, 60	81, 53	82, 52
68	76, 60	63-66, 70-73	67, 69	75, 61	82, 54	83, 53
69	77, 61	64-67, 71-74	68, 70	76, 62	83, 55	54
70	78, 62	65-68, 72-75	69, 71	77, 63	56	55
71	79, 63	66-69, 73-76	70, 72	78, 64	57	56
72	80, 64	67-70, 74-77	71, 73	79, 65	58	57
73	81, 65	68-71, 75-78	72, 74	80, 66	59	58
74	82, 66	69-72, 76-79	73, 75	81, 67	60	59
75	83, 67	70-73, 77-80	74, 76	82, 68	61	60
76	68	71-74, 78-81	75, 77	83, 69	62	61
77	69	72-75, 79-82	76, 78		63	62
78	70	73-76, 80-83	77, 79		64	63
79	71	74-77, 81-83	78, 80		65	64
80	72	75-78, 82-83	79, 81		66	65
81	73	76-79, 83	80, 82		67	66
82	74	77-80	81, 83		68	67
83	75	78-81	82		69	68

station separations between stations on channels 14-69, inclusive, as set forth in Table II of §—73.698 must be met in either rule making proceedings looking towards the amendment of the Table of Assignments (§—73.606 (b)) or in licensing proceedings. No channel listed in column (1) of Table II of §—73.698 [see box] will be assigned to any city, and no application for an authorization to operate on such a channel will be granted unless the mileage separations indicated at the top of columns (2)-(7), inclusive, are met with respect to each of the channels listed in those columns and parallel with the channel in column (1).

(e) The zone in which the transmitter of a television station is located or proposed to be located determines the applicable rules with respect to co-channel mileage separations where the transmitter is located in a different zone from that in which the channel to be employed is located.

(f) The distances listed below apply only to allotments and assignments on Channel 6 (82-88 mHz). The Commission will not accept petitions to amend the Table of Allotments, applications for new stations, or applications to change the channel or location of existing assignments where the following minimum distances (between transmitter sites, in kilometers) from any FM Channel 253 allotment or assignment are not met:

FM Class	TV Zone I	TV Zones II & III
A	17	22
B1	19	23
B	22	26
C3	19	23
C2	22	26
C1	29	33
C	36	41

§73.614. Power and antenna height requirements.

(a) Minimum requirements. Applications will not be accepted for filing if less than 10 dbk (100 watts) horizontally polarized visual effective radiated power in any horizontal direction. No minimum antenna height above average terrain is specified.

(b) Maximum power. Applications will not be accepted for filing if they specify a power which exceeds the maximum permitted boundaries specified in the following formulas:

Channel Nos.	Maximum visual effective radiated power in db above one kilowatt (dBk)
2-6	20 dBk (100 kw)
7-13	25 dBk (316 kw)
14-83	37 dBk (5000 kw)

(6) The effective radiated power in any horizontal or vertical direction may not exceed the maximum values permitted by this section and Figure 3 and 4 of §73.1700.

(7) The effective radiated power at any angle above the horizontal shall be as low as the state of the art permits, and in the same vertical plane may not exceed the effective radiated power in either the horizontal direction or below the horizontal, whichever is greater.

(c) The zone in which the transmitter of a television station is located or proposed to be located determines the applicable rules with respect to maximum antenna heights and powers for VHF stations when the transmitter is located in Zone I and the channel to be employed is located in Zone II, or the transmitter is located in Zone II and the channel to be employed is located in Zone I.

In AM, FM, TV rules ...

§73.1635 Special temporary authorizations (STA). A special temporary authorization (STA) is the authority granted to a permittee or licensee to permit the operation of a broadcast facility for a limited period at a specified variance with the terms of the station authorization or requirements of the FCC rules applicable to the particular class of station.

(1) A request for an STA should be filed with FCC in Washington, D.C. at least 10 days prior to the date of the proposed operation.

(2) The request is to be made by letter and shall fully describe the proposed operation and the necessity for the requested STA. Such letter requests shall be signed by the licensee or the licensee's representative.

(3) A request for an STA necessitated by unforeseen equipment damage or failure may be made without regard to the procedural requirements of this section (e.g., via telegram or telephone). Any request made pursuant to this paragraph shall be followed by a written confirmation request confirming to the requirements of paragraph (a)(2) above. Confirmation requests shall be submitted within 24 hours. (See also §73.1680 Emergency Antennas).

(4) An STA may be granted for an initial period not to exceed 180 days. A limited number of extensions of such authorizations may be granted for additional periods not exceeding 180 days per extension. An STA necessitated by technical or equipment problems, however, may, in practice, be granted for an initial period not to exceed 90 days with a limited number of extensions not to exceed 90 days per extension. The permittee or licensee must demonstrate that any further extensions requested are necessary and that all steps to resume normal operation are being undertaken in an expeditious and timely fashion.

(5) Certain rules permit temporary operation at variance without prior authorization from the FCC when notification is filed as prescribed in the particular rules. See §73.62, Directional Antenna System Tolerances; §73.157, Antenna Testing During Daytime; §73.1250, Broadcasting Emergency Information; §73.1615, Operation During Modification of Facilities; and §73.1680, Emergency Antennas.

(b) An STA may be modified or cancelled by the FCC without prior notice or right to hearing.

(c) No request by an AM station for temporary authority to extend its hours of operation beyond those authorized by its regular authorization wili be accepted or granted by the FCC except in emergency situations confirming with the requirements of §73.3542. Application for Emergency Authorization. See also §73.1250, Broadcasting Emergency Information.

§73.1650 International agreements.

(a) The Rules in this Part 73, and authorizations for which they provide, are subject to compliance with the international obligations and undertakings of the United States. Accordingly, all provisions in this Part 73 are subject to compliance with applicable requirements, restrictions and procedures accepted by the United States that have been established by or pursuant to treaties or other international agreements, arrangements or understandings to which the United States is a signatory, including applicable annexes, protocols, resolutions, recommendations and other supplementing documents associated with such international instruments.

(b) The United States is a signatory to the following treaties and other international agreements that relate, in whole or in part, to AM, FM or TV broadcasting:

(1) The following instruments of the International Telecommunication Union:

(i) Constitution;

(ii) Convention;

(iii) Radio Regulations.

(2) Regional Agreements for the Broadcasting Service in Region 2

(i) MF Broadcasting 535-1605 kHz, Rio de Janeiro, 1981.

(ii) MF Broadcasting 1605-1705 kHz, Rio de Janeiro, 1988.

(3) Bi-lateral Agreements between the United States and Canada relating to: (i) AM Broadcasting; (ii) FM Broadcasting; (iii) TV Broadcasting.

(4) Bi-lateral Agreements between the United States and Mexico relating to: (i) AM Broadcasting; (ii) FM Broadcasting; (iii) TV Broadcasting.

(5) Bi-lateral Agreement between the United States and the Bahama Islands relating to presunrise operations by AM stations.

(6) North American Regional Broadcasting Agreement (NARBA), which, for the United States, remains in effect with respect to the Dominican Republic and the Bahama Islands.

The documents listed in this paragraph are available for inspection in the Office of the Chief, Policy and Rules Division, Mass Media Bureau, FCC, Washington, D.C. Copies may be purchased from the FCC Copy Contractor, whose name may be obtained from the FCC Consumer Assistance Office.

In FCC Policies ...

§73.4107 FM broadcast assignments, increasing availability of.

(a) See First Report and Order, MM Docket 84-231, FCC 86-640, adopted December 19, 1984, 50 FR 3514, January 25, 1985.

(b) See Second Report and Order, MM Docket No. 84-231, FCC 85-124, adopted March 14, 1985. 50 FR 15558, April 19, 1985.

(c) See Memorandum Opinion and Order, MM Docket No. 84-231, FCC 86-76, adopted February 10, 1986. 51 FR 9210, March 18, 1986.

(d) See Public Notice, 51 FR 26009, July 18, 1986.

Multiple Ownership

§73.3555 Multiple Ownership.

(a)(1) Radio Contour Overlap Rule. No license for an AM or FM broadcasting station shall be granted to any party (including all parties under common control) if the grant of such license will result in overlap of the principal community contour of that station and the principal community contour of any other broadcasting station directly or indirectly owned, operated, or controlled by the same party, except that such license may be granted in connection with a transfer or assignment from an existing party with such interests, or in the following circumstances:

(i) In radio markets with 14 or fewer commercial radio stations, a party may own up to 3 commercial radio stations, no more than 2 of which are in the same service (AM or FM), provided that the owned stations, if other than a single AM and FM station combination, represent less than 50 percent of the stations in the market.

(ii) In radio markets with 15 or more commercial radio stations, a party may own up to 2 AM and 2 FM commercial stations, provided, however, that evidence that grant of any application will result in a combined audience share exceeding 25 percent will be considered prima facie inconsistent with the public interest.

NOTE: When evaluating audience share evidence submitted under 73.3555(a)(1)(ii), the Commission will consider data that eliminates statistical anomalies, provides a better focused survey area or includes revenue data or other relevant information. Where applicants certify that they do not have readily available audience share data, they may substitute other information that can serve as a proxy for such data. See Memorandum Opinion and Order in MM Docket No. 91-140, FCC 92-361 (released September 4, 1992).

(iii) Overlap between two stations in different services is permissible if neither of those two stations overlaps a third station in the same service.

(2)(i) Where the principal community contours of two radio stations overlap and a party (including all parties under common control) with an attributable ownership interest in one such station brokers more than 15 percent of the broadcast time per week of the other such station, that party shall be treated as if it has an interest in the brokered station subject to the limitations set forth in paragraphs (a) and (e) of this section. This limitation shall apply regardless of the source of the brokered programming supplied by the party to the brokered station.

(ii) Every time brokerage agreement of the type described in paragraph (a)(2)(i) of this section shall be undertaken only pursuant to a signed written agreement that shall contain a certification by the licensee or permittee of the brokered station verifying that it maintains ultimate control over the station's facilities, including specifically control over station finances, personnel and programming, and by the brokering station that the arrangement complies with the provisions of paragraphs (a)(1) and (e)(1) of this section.

(iii) Any party operating in conflict with the requirements of paragraph (a)(2)(ii) of this section on the effective date of this rule shall come into compliance within one year thereafter.

(3) For purposes of this paragraph:

(i) The "principal community contour" for AM stations is the predicted or measured 5 mV/m groundwave contour computed in accordance with 73.183 or 73.186 and for FM stations is the predicted 3.16 mV/m contour computed in accordance with 73.313.

(ii) The number of stations in a radio market, is the number of commercial stations whose principal community contours overlap, in whole or in part, with the principal community contours of the stations in question (i.e., the station for which an authorization is sought and any station in the same service that would be commonly owned whose principal community contour overlaps the principal community contour of that station). In addition, if the area of overlap between the stations in question is overlapped by the principal community contour of a commonly owned station or stations in a different service (AM or FM), the number of stations in the market includes stations whose principal community contours overlap the principal community contours of such commonly owned station or stations in a different service.

(iii) A station's "audience share" is the average number of persons age 12 or older on an average quarter hour basis, Monday-Sunday, 6 a.m.-midnight, who listen to the station, expressed as a percentage of the average number of persons listening to AM and FM stations in that radio metro market or a recognized equivalent, in which a majority of the overlap between the stations in question takes place. The "combined audience share" is the total audience share of all AM or FM stations that would be under common ownership or control following a proposed acquisition. In situations where no metro market or recognized equivalent exists, the relevant audience share data is the data for all counties that are within the principal community contours of the stations in question, in whole or in part.

(iv) "Time brokerage" is the sale by a licensee of discrete blocks of time to a "broker" that supplies the programming to fill that time and sells the commercial spot announcements in it.

(b) Television Contour Overlap (Duopoly) Rule. No license for a TV broadcast station shall be granted to any party (including all parties under common control) if the grant of such license will result in overlap of the Grade B contour of that station (computed in accordance with 73.684) and the Grade B contour of any other TV broadcast station directly or indirectly owned, operated, or controlled by the same party.

(c) One-to-a-Market Ownership Rule. No license for an AM, FM or TV broadcast station shall be granted to any party (including all parties under common control) if such party directly or indirectly owns, operates or controls one or more such broadcast stations and the grant of such license will result in:

(1) The predicted or measured 2 mV/m groundwave contour of an existing or proposed AM station, computed in accordance with 73.183 or 73.186, encompassing the entire community of license of an existing or proposed TV broadcast station(s) or the Grade A contour(s) of the TV broadcast station(s), computed in accordance with 73.684, encompassing the entire community of license of the AM station; or

(2) The predicted 1 mV/m contour of an existing or proposed FM station, computed in accordance with 73.313, encompassing the entire community of license of an existing or proposed TV broadcast station(s) or the Grade A contour(s) of the TV broadcast station(s), computed in accordance with 73.684, encompassing the entire community of license of the FM station.

(d) Daily Newspaper Cross-Ownership Rule. No license for an AM, FM or TV broadcast station shall be granted to any party (including all parties under common control) if such party directly or indirectly owns, operates or controls a daily newspaper and the grant of such license will result in:

(1) The predicted or measured 2 mV/m contour for an AM station, computed in accordance with 73.183 or 73.186, encompassing the entire community in which such newspaper is published; or

(2) The predicted 1 mV/m contour for an FM station, computed in accordance with 73.313, encompassing the entire community in which such newspaper is published; or

(3) The Grade A contour for a TV station, computed in accordance with 73.684, encompassing the entire community in which such newspaper is published.

(e)(1) National Multiple Ownership Rule. No license for a commercial AM, FM or TV broadcast station shall be granted, transferred or assigned to any party (including all parties under common control) if the grant, transfer or assignment of such license would result in such party or any of its stockholders, partners, members, officers or directors, directly or indirectly, owning, operating or controlling, or having a cognizable interest in:

(i) More than 18 AM or more than 18 FM stations, or more than 20 AM or more than 20 FM stations two years after the effective date of this rule, provided, however, that an entity may have an attributable but noncontrolling interest in an additional 3 AM and 3 FM stations that are small business controlled or minority controlled.

(ii) More than 14 television stations, or

(iii) More than 12 television stations that are not minority controlled.

(2) No license for a commercial TV broadcast station shall be granted, transferred or assigned to any party (including all parties under common control) if the grant, transfer or assignment of such license would result in such party or any of its stockholders, partners, members, officers or directors, directly or indirectly, owning, operating or controlling, or having a cognizable interest in, either:

(i) TV stations which have an aggregate national audience reach exceeding thirty (30) percent, or

(ii) TV stations which have an aggregate national audience reach exceeding twenty-five (25) percent and which are not minority controlled.

(3) For purposes of this paragraph:

(i) "National audience reach" means the total number of television households in the Arbitron Area of Dominant Influence (ADI) markets in which the relevant stations are located divided by the total national television households as measured by ADI data at the time of a grant, transfer or assignment of a license. For purposes of making this calculation, UHF television stations shall be attributed with 50 percent of the television households in their television market. Where the relevant application forms require a showing with respect to audience reach and the application relates to an area where Arbitron ADI market data are unavailable, then the applicant shall make a showing as to the number of television households in its market. Upon such a showing, the Commission shall make a determination as to the appropriate audience reach to be attributed to the applicant.

(ii) "TV broadcast station" or "TV station" exclude stations which are primarily satellite operations.

(iii) "Minority-controlled" means more than 50 percent owned by one or more members of a minority group.

(iv) "Minority" means Black, Hispanic, American Indian, Alaska Native, Asian and Pacific Islander.

(v) "Small business" means an individual or business entity which, at the time of application to the Commission had, including all affiliated entities under common control, annual revenues of less than $500,000 and assets of less than $1,000,000.

(f) This section is not applicable to noncommercial educational FM and noncommercial educational TV stations.

NOTE 1: The word control as used herein is not limited to majority stock ownership, but includes actual working control in whatever manner exercised.

NOTE 2: In applying the provisions of this section, ownership and other interests in broadcast licensees, cable television systems and daily newspapers will be attributed to their holders and deemed cognizable pursuant to the following criteria:

(a) Except as otherwise provided herein, partnership and direct ownership interests and any voting stock interest amounting to 5% or more of the outstanding voting stock of a corporate broadcast licensee, cable television system or daily newspaper will be cognizable;

(b) No minority voting stock interest will be cognizable if there is a single holder of more than 50% of the outstanding voting stock of the corporate broadcast licensee, cable television system or daily newspaper in which the minority interest is held;

(c) Investment companies, as defined in 15 USC §80a-3, insurance companies and banks holding stock through their trust departments in trust accounts will be considered to have a cognizable interest only if they hold 10% or more of the outstanding voting stock of a corporate broadcast license, cable television system or daily newspaper, or if any of the officers or directors of the broadcast licensee, cable television system or daily newspaper are representatives of the investment company, insurance company or bank concerned. Holdings by a bank or insurance company will be aggregated if the bank or insurance company has any right to determine how the stock will be voted. Holdings by investment companies will be aggregated if under common management.

(d) Attribution of ownership interests in a broadcast licensee, cable television system or daily newspaper that are held indirectly by any party through one or more intervening corporations will be determined by successive multiplication of the ownership percentages for each link in the vertical ownership chain and application of the relevant attribution benchmark to the resulting product, except that whereever the ownership percentage for any link in the chain exceeds 50%, it shall not be included for purposes of this multiplication. [For example, if A owns 10% of company X, which owns 60% of company Y, which owns 25% of Licensee, then X's interest in Licensee would be 25% (the same as Y's interest since X's interest in Y exceeds 50%), and A's interest in Licensee would be 2.5% (0.1 x 0.25). Under the 5% attribution benchmark, X's interest in Licensee would be cognizable, while A's interest would not be cognizable.]

(e) Voting stock interests held in trust shall be attributed to any person who holds or shares the power to vote such stock, to any person who has the sole power to sell such stock, and to any person who has the right to revoke the trust at will or to replace the trustee at will. If the trustee has a familial, personal or extratrust business relationship to the grantor or beneficiary, as appropriate, will be attributed with the stock interests held in trust. An otherwise qualified trust will be ineffective to insulate the grantor or beneficiary from attribution with the trust's assets unless all voting stock interests held by the grantor or beneficiary in the relevant broadcast licensee, cable television system or daily newspaper are subject to said trust.

(f) Holders of non-voting stock shall not be attributed an interest in the issuing entity. Holders of debt and instruments such as warrants, convertible debentures, options or other non-voting interests with rights of conversion to voting interests shall not be attributed unless and until conversion is effected.

(g)(1) A limited partnership interest shall be attributed to a limited partner unless that partner is not materially involved, directly or indirectly, in the management or operation of the media-related activities of the partnership and the licensee or system so certifies.

(2) In order for a licensee or system to make the certification set forth in paragraph (a)(1) of this section, it must verify that the partnership agreement or certificate of limited partnership, with respect to the particular limited partner exempt from attribution, establishes that the exempt limited partner has no material involvement, directly or indirectly, in the management or operation of the media activities of the partnership. The criteria which would assure adequate insulation for purposes of this certification are described in the Memorandum Opinion and Order in MM Docket No. 83-46, FCC 85-252 (released June 24, 1985) as modified on reconsideration in Memorandum Opinion and Order in MM Docket No. 83-46, FCC 86-410 (released November 28, 1986). Irrespective of the terms of the certificate of limited partnership or partnership agreement, however, no such certificate shall be made if the individualor entity making the certification has actual knowledge of any material involvement of the limited partners in the management or operation of the media-related business of the partnership.

(h) Officers and directors of a broadcast licensee, cable television system or daily newspaper are considered to have a cognizable interest in the entity with which they are so associated. If any such entity engages in businesses in addition to its primary business of broadcasting, cable television service or newspaper publication, it may request the Commission to waive attribution for any officer or director whose duties and responsibilities are wholly unrelated to its primary business. The officers and directors of a parent company of a broadcast licensee, cable television system or daily newspaper, with an attributable interest in any such subsidiary entity, shall be deemed to have a cognizable interest in the subsidiary unless the duties and responsibilities of the officer or director involved are wholly unrelated to the broadcast licensee, cable television system or daily newspaper subsidiary, and a statement properly documenting this fact is submitted to the Commission. [This statement may be included on the appropriate Ownership Report]. The officers and directors of a sister corporation of a broadcast licensee, cable television system or daily newspaper shall not be attributed with ownership of these entities by virtue of such status.

(i) Discrete ownership interests will be aggregated in determining whether or not an interest is cognizable under this section. An individual or entity will be deemed to have a cognizable investment if:

(1) the sum of the interests held by or through passive investors is equal to or exceeds 10 percent; or

(2) the sum of the interests other than those held by or through passive investors is equal to or exceeds 5 percent; or

(3) the sum of the interests computed under (1) plus the sum of the interests computed under (2) is equal to or exceeds 10 percent.

NOTE 3: In cases where record and beneficial ownership of voting stock is not identical (e.g., bank nominees holding stock as record owners for the benefit of mutual funds, brokerage houses holding stock in street names for the benefit of customers, investment advisors holding stock in their own names for the benefit of clients, and insurance companies holding stock), the party having the right to determine how the stock will be voted will be considered to own it for purposes of these rules.

NOTE 4: Paragraphs (a) through (e) of this section will not be applied so as to require divestiture, by any licensee, of existing facilities, and will not apply to applications for increased power for Class C stations, to applications for assignment of license or transfer of control filed in accordance with §73.3540(f) or §73.3541(b) of this part, or to applications for assignment of license or transfer of control to heirs or legatees by will or intestacy if no new or increased overlap would be created between commonly owned, operated or controlled broadcast stations in the same service and if no new encompassment of communities proscribed in paragraphs (c) and (d) of this section as to commonly owned, operated, or controlled broadcast stations or daily newspapers would result. Said paragraphs will apply to all applications for new stations, to all other applications for assignment or transfer, and to all applications for major changes in existing stations except major changes that will result in overlap of contours of broadcast stations in the same service with each other no greater than already existing. (The resulting areas of overlap of contours of such broadcast stations with each other in such major change cases may consist partly or entirely of new terrain. However, if the population in the resulting areas substantially exceeds that in the previously existing overlap areas, the Commission will not grant the application if it finds that to do so would be against the public interest, convenience, or necessity.) Commonly owned, operated, or controlled broadcast stations with overlapping contours or with community-encompassing contours prohibited by this section may not be assigned or transferred to a single person, group, or entity, except as provided above in this note and by §73.3555(a). If a commonly owned, operated, or controlled broadcast station and daily newspaper fall within the encompassing proscription of this section, the station may not be assigned to a single person, group or entity if the newspaper is being simultaneously sold to such single person, group or entity.

NOTE 5: Paragraphs (a)-(e) of this section will not be applied to cases involving television stations which are "satellite" operations. Such cases will be considered in accordance with the analysis set forth in the Report and Order in MM Docket No. 87-8, FCC 91-182 (released July 8, 1991) in order to determine whether common ownership, operation, or control of the stations in question would be in the public interest. An authorized and operating "satellite" television station the Grade B contour of which overlaps that of a commonly owned, operated, or controlled "non-satellite" parent television broadcast station, or the Grade A contour of which completely encompasses the community of publication of a commonly owned, operated, or controlled daily newspaper, or the community of license of a commonly owned, operated, or controlled AM or FM broadcast station, or the community of license of which is completely encompassed by the 2 mV/m contour of such AM broadcast station or the 1 mV/m contour of such FM broadcast station may subsequently become a "non-satellite" station under the circumstances described in the aforementioned Report and Order in MM Docket No. 87-8. However, such commonly owned, operated, or controlled "non-satellite" television stations with Grade B overlap or such commonly owned, operated, or controlled "non-satellite" television stations and AM or FM stations with the aforementioned community encompassment, may not be transferred or assigned to a single person, group, or entity except as provided in NOTE 4. Nor shall any application for assignment or transfer concerning such "non-satellite" stations be granted if the assignment or transfer would be to the same person, group or entity to which the commonly owned, operated, or controlled newspaper is proposed to be transferred, except as provided in NOTE 4.

NOTE 6. For the purposes of this section a daily newspaper is one which is published four or more days per week, which is in the English language and which is circulated generally in the community of publication. A college newspaper is not considered as being circulated generally.

NOTE 7: The Commission will entertain requests to waive the restrictions of paragraph (c) of this section on a case-by-case basis. The Commission will look favorably upon waiver applications that meet either of the following two standards: (1) those involving radio and television station combinations in the top 25 television markets where there will be at least 30 separately owned, operated and controlled broadcast licensees after the proposed combination, as determined by counting television licensees in the relevant ADI television market and radio licensees in the relevant television metropolitan market; or (2) those involving "failed" broadcast stations that have not been operated for a substantial period of time, e.g., four months, or that are involved in bankruptcy proceedings. For the purposes of determining the top 25 ADI television markets, the relevant ADI television market and the relevant television metropolitan market for each prospective combination, we will use the most recent Arbitron Ratings Television ADI Market Guide. We will determine the number of radio stations in the relevant television metropolitan market and the number of television licensees within the relevant ADI television market based on the most recent Commission ownership records. Other waiver requests will be evaluated on a more rigorous case-by-case basis, as set forth in the Second Report and Order in MM Docket No. 87-7, FCC 88-407, released February 23, 1989, and Memorandum Opinion and Order in MM Docket No. 87-7, FCC 89-256, released August 4, 1989.

NOTE 8: Paragraph (a)(1) of this section will not apply to an application for an AM station license in the 535-1605 kHz band where grant of such application will result in the overlap of 5 mV/m groundwave contours of the proposed station and that of another AM station in the 535-1605 kHz band that is commonly owned, operated or controlled if the applicant shows that a significant reduction in interference to adjacent or co-channel stations would accompany such common ownership. Such AM overlap cases will be considered on a case-by-case basis to determine whether common ownership, operation or control of the stations in question would be in the public interest. Applicants in such cases must submit a contingent application for the major or minor facilities change needed to achieve the interference reduction along with the application which seeks to create the 5 mV/m overlap situation.

NOTE 9: Paragraph (a)(1) of this section will not apply to an application for an AM station license in the 1605-1705 kHz band where grant of such application will result in the overlap of the 5 mV/m groundwave contours of the proposed station and that of another AM station in the 535-1605 kHz band that is commonly owned, operated or controlled. Paragraphs (d)(1)(i) and (d)(1)(ii) of this section will not apply to an application for an AM station license in the 1605-1705 kHz band by an entity that owns, operates, controls or has a cognizable interest in AM radio stations in the 535-1605 kHz band.

NOTE 10: Authority for joint ownership granted pursuant to NOTE 9 will expire at 3:00 a.m. local time on the fifth anniversary of the date of issuance of a construction permit for an AM radio station in the 1605-1705 kHz band.

§73.3556 Duplication of programming on commonly owned or time brokered stations.

(a) No commercial AM or FM radio station shall operate so as to devote more than 25 percent of the total hours in its average broadcast week to programs that duplicate those of any station in the same service (AM or FM) which is commonly owned or with which it has a time brokerage agreement if the principal community contours (predicted or measured 5 mV/m groundwave for AM stations and predicted 3.16 mV/m for FM stations) of the stations overlap and the overlap constitutes more than 50 percent of the total principal community contour service area of either station.

(b) For purposes of this section, duplication means the broadcasting of identical programs within any 24 hour period.

(c) Any party engaged in a time brokerage arrangement which conflicts with the requirements of paragraph (a) of this section on the effective date of this rule shall bring that arrangement into compliance within one year thereafter.

Studio Location, Program Originations

In AM, FM and TV rules...

§73.1120 Station location. Each AM, FM and TV broadcast station will be licensed to the principal community or other political subdivision which it primarily serves. This principal community (city, town or other political subdivision) will be considered to be the geographical station location.

§73.1125 Station main studio location.

(a) Each AM, FM and TV broadcast station shall maintain a main studio within the station's principal community contour as defined in §§73.24(i) (%mV/m daytime contour), 73.315(a) and 73.685(a), respectively, of this chapter, except:

(1) AM stations licensed as synchronous amplifier transmitters (AM boosters) or,

(2) AM stations whose main studio is located at the collocated main studio-transmitter site of a commonly-owned AM station licensed to the same principal community or,

(3) Any AM, FM or TV broadcast station whose main studio is located in the community which the station is licensed to serve at a point situated outside the principal community contour or,

(4) AM, FM or TV stations, when good cause exists for locating the main studio outside the station's principal community contour and that to do so would be consistent with the operation of the station in the public interest.

(b) Relocation of the main studio may be made:

(1) From one point to another within the principal community contour or from a point outside the principal community contour to one within it, without specific FCC authority, but notification to the FCC in Washington shall be made promptly; however,

(2) From a point within the principal community contour to one outside it or from one such point outside the community contour to another, only by first securing modification of construction permit or license (FCC Forms 301 for commercial stations and 340 for noncommercial educational stations).

(3) Exceptions to paragraph (b)(2) of this section are:

(i) Relocation of the main studio of an FM station to the collocated main studio-transmitter site of a commonly owned AM station licensed to the same principal community;

(ii) Relocation of the main studio from one point to another within the principal community of license or from a point outside the principal community to one within it; and

(iii) Notification to the FCC in Washington shall be made promptly of such relocations described in (b)(3)(i) and (b)(3)(ii) of this section.

(c) Each AM, FM and TV broadcast station shall maintain a local telephone number in its community of license or a toll-free number.

(d) Where the principal community to be served does not have specifically defined political boundaries, applications will be considered on a case-by-case basis by the FCC to determine if the main studio is located within the principal community to be served.

NOTE: AM stations that simulcast on a frequency in the 535-1605 kHz band and on a frequency in the 1605-1705 kHz band need only have the studio be located within the 5 mV/m contour of the lower band operation during the term of the simultaneous operating authority. Upon termination of the 535-1605 kHz band portion of the dual frequency operation, the above rule shall then become applicable to the remaining operation in the 1605-1705 kHz band.

Operating Schedules

For AM stations ...

§73.72 Operation during the experimental period.

(a) An AM station may operate during the experimental period (the time between midnight and sunrise, local time) on its assigned frequency and with its authorized power for the routine testing and maintenance of its transmitting system, and for conducting experimentation under an experimental authorization; provided no interference is caused to other stations maintaining a regular operating schedule within such period.

(b) No station licensed for daytime or specified hours of operation may broadcast any regular or scheduled program during this period.

(c) The licensee of an AM station shall operate or refrain from operating its station during the experimental period as directed by the FCC to facilitate frequency measurements or for the determination of interference.

Pre-sunrise service authorization (PSRA) and post-sunset service authorization (PSSA).

(a) To provide maximum uniformity in early morning operation compatible with interference considerations, and to provide for additional service during early evening hours for Class D stations, provisions are made for pre-sunrise service and postsunset service. The permissible power for presunrise or postsunset service authorizations shall not exceed 500 watts, or the authorized daytime or critical hours power (whichever is less). Calculation of the permissible power shall consider only co-channel stations for interference protection purposes.

(b) Pre-sunrise service authorizations (PSRA) permit:

(1) Class D stations operating on Mexican, Bahamian, and Canadian priority Class A clear channels to commence PSRA operation at 6:00 a.m. local time and to continue such operation until the sunrise times specified in their basic instruments of authorization.

(2) Class D stations situated outside 0.5 mv/m 50% skywave contours of co-channel U.S. Class A stations to commence PSRA operation at 6:00 a.m. local time and to continue such operation until sunrise times specified in their basic instruments of authorization.

(3) Class D stations located within co-channel 0.5 mv/m 50% skywave contours of U.S. Class A stations, to commence PSRA operation either at 6:00 a.m. local time, or at sunrise at the nearest Class A station located east of the Class D station (whichever is later), and to continue such operation until the sunrise times specified in their basic instruments of authorization.

(4) Class B and Class D stations on regional channels to commence PSRA operation at 6:00 a.m. local time and to continue such operation until local sunrise times specified in their basic instruments of authorization.

(c) Extended Daylight Saving Time Pre-Sunrise Authorizations: (1) Between the first Sunday in April and the end of the month of April, Class D stations will be permitted to conduct pre-sunrise operation beginning at 6:00 a.m. local time with a maximum power of 500 watts (not to exceed the station's regular daytime or critical hours power), reduced as necessary to comply with the following requirements:

(i) Full protection is to be provided as specified in applicable international agreements.

(ii) Protection is to be provided to the 0.5 mV/m groundwave signals of co-channel U.S. Class A stations; protection to the 0.5 mV/m 50% skywave signals of these stations is not required.

(iii) In determining the protection to be provided, the effect of each interfering signal will be evaluated separately. The presence of interference from other stations will not reduce or eliminate the required protection.

(iv) Notwithstanding the requirements of paragraph (c)(1)(ii) and (iii) of this section, the stations will be permitted to operate with a minimum power of 10 watts unless a lower power is required by international agreement.

(2) The Commission will issue appropriate authorizations to Class D stations not previously eligible to operate during this period. Class D stations authorized to operate during this pre-sunrise period may continue to operate under their current authorization.

(d) Postsunset service authorizations (PSSA) permit:

(1) Class D stations located on Mexican, Bahamian, and Canadian priority Class A clear channels to commence PSSA operation at sunset times specified in their basic instruments of authorization and to continue for two hours after such specified times.

(2) Class D stations situated outside 0.5 mv/m 50% skywave contours of co-channel U.S. Class A stations to commence PSSA operations at sunset times specified in their basic instruments of authorization and to continue for two hours after such specified times.

(3) Class D stations located within co-channel 0.5 mv/m 50% skywave contours of U.S. Class A stations to commence PSSA operation at sunset times specified in their basic instruments of authorization and to continue such operation until two hours past such specified times, or until sunset at the nearest Class A station located west of the Class D station, whichever is earlier. Class D stations located west of the Class A station do not qualify for PSSA operation.

(4) Class III daytime only stations to commence PSSA operation at sunset times specified on their basic instruments of authorization and to continue such operation until two hours past such specified times.

(e) Procedural Matters. (1) Applications for PSRA and PSSA operation are not required. Instead, the FCC will calculate the periods of such operation and the power to be used puusuant to the provisions of this Section and the protection requirements contained in applicable international agreements. Licensees will be duly notified of permissible power and times of operation. Presunrise and Postsunset service authority permits operation on a secondary basis and does not confer license rights. No request for such authority need be filed. However, stations intending to operate PSRA or PSSA shall submit by letter, signed as specified in §73.3513, the following information;

(i) Licensee name, station call letters and station location,

(ii) Indication as to whether PSRA operation, PSSA operation, or both, is intended by the station,

(iii) A description of the method whereby any necessary power reduction will be achieved.

(2) Upon submission of the required information, such operation may begin without further authority.

(f) Technical criteria. Calculations to determine whether there is objectionable interference will be determined in accordance with the AM Broadcast Technical Standards, §§73.182 through 73.190, and applicable international agreements. Calculations will be performed using daytime antenna systems, or critical hours antenna systems when specified on the license. In performing calculations to determine assigned power and times for commencement of PSRA and PSSA operation, the following standards and criteria will be used:

(1) Class D stations operating in accordance with paragraphs (b)(1), (b)(2), (d)(1) and (d)(2) of this section are required to protect the nighttime 0.5 mV/m 50% skywave contours of co-channel Class A stations. Where a 0.5 mV/m 50% skywave signal from the Class A station is not produced, the 0.5 mV/m groundwave contour shall be protected.

(2) Class D stations are required to fully protect foreign Class B and Class C stations when operating PSRA and PSSA; Class D stations operating PSSA are required to fully protect U.S. Class B stations. For purposes of determining protection, the nighttime RSS limit will be used in the determination of maximum permissible power.

(3) Class D stations operating in accordance with paragraphs (d)(2) and (d)(3) of this section are required to restrict maximum 10% skywave radiation at any point on the daytime 0.1 mV/m groundwave contour of a co-channel Class A station to 25 uV/m. The location of the 0.1 mV/m contour will be determined by use of Figure M3, Estimated Ground Conductivity in the United States. When the 0.1 mV/m contour extends beyond the national boundary, the international boundary shall be considered the 0.1 mV/m contour.

(4) Class B and Class D stations oon regional channels perating PSRA and PSSA (Class D only) are required to provide full protection to co-channel foreign Class B and Class C stations.

(5) Class D stations on regional channels operating PSSA beyond 6:00 p.m. local time are required to fully protect U.S. Class B stations.

(6) The protection that Class D stations on regional channels are required to provide when operating PSSA until 6:00 p.m. local time is as follows:

(i) For the first half-hour of PSSA operation, protection will be calculated at sunset plus 30 minutes at the site of the Class D station;

(ii) For the second half-hour of PSSA operation, protection will be calculated at sunset plus one hour at the site of the Class D station;

(iii) For the second hour of PSSA operation, protection will be calculated at sunset plus two hours at the site of the Class D station;

(iv) Minimum powers during the period until 6:00 p.m. local time shall be permitted as follows:

Calculated Power	Adjusted Minimum Power
From 1 to 45 watt	50 watts
Above 45 watts to 70 watts	75 watts
Above 70 watts to 10C watts	100 watts

(7) For protection purposes, the nighttime RSS limit will be used in the determination of maximum permissible power.

(g) Calculations made under paragraph (d) of this section may not take outstanding PSRA or PSSA operations into account, nor will the grant of a PSRA or PSSA confer any degree of interference protection on the holder thereof.

(h) Operation under a PSRA or PSSA is not mandatory, and will not be included in determing compliance with the requirements of §73.1740. To the extent actually undertaken, however, pre-sunrise operation will be considered by the FCC in determing overall compliance with the past programming representations and station policy concerning commercial matter.

(i) The PSRA or PSSA is secondary to the basic instrument of authorization with which it is to be associated. The PSRA or PSSA may be suspended, modified, or withdrawn by the FCC without prior notice or right to hearing, if necessary to resolve interference conflicts, to implement agreements with foreign governments, or in other circumstances warranting such action. Moreover, the PSRA or PSSA does not extend beyond the term of the basic authorization.

(j) The Commission will periodically recalculate maximum permissible power and times for commencing PSRA and PSSA for each Class D station operating in accordance with paragraph (c) of this section. The Commission will calculate the maximum power at which each individual station may conduct presunrise operations during extended daylight saving time and shall issue conforming authorizations. These original notifications and subsequent notifications should be associated with the station's authorization. Upon notification of new power and time of commencing operation, affected stations shall make necessary adjustments within 30 days.

(k) A PSRA and PSSA does not require compliance with §73.45, 73.182, and 73.1560 where the operation might otherwise be considered as technically substandard. Further, the requirements of paragraphs (a)(5), (b)(2), (c)(2), and (d)(2) of §73.1215 concerning the scale ranges of transmission system indicating instruments are waived for PSRA and PSSA operation except for the radio frequency ammeters used in determining antenna input power.

(l) A station having an antenna monitor incapable of functioning at the authorized PSRA and PSSA power when using a directional antenna shall take the monitor reading using unmodulated carrier at the authorized daytime power immediately prior to commencing PSRA or PSSA operations. Special conditions as the FCC may deem appropriate may be included for PSRA or PSSA to insure operation of the transmitter and associated equipment in accordance with all phases of good engineering practice.

For TV stations...

§73.653 Operation of TV aural and visual transmitters. The aural and visual transmitters may be operated independently of each other or, if operated simultaneously, may be used with different and unrelated program material.

For AM, FM and TV stations ...

§73.1250 Broadcasting emergency information.

(a) Emergency situations in which the broadcasting of information is considered as furthering the safety of life and property include, but are not limited to the following: Tornadoes, hurricanes, floods, tidal waves, earthquakes, icing conditions, heavy snows, widespread fires, discharge of toxic gasses, widespread power failures, industrial explosions, civil disorders and school closings and changes in school bus schedules resulting from such conditions. See also §73.3542, Application for Emergency Authorization, for requirements involving emergency situations not covered by this section for which prior operating authority must be requested.

(b) If requested by responsible public officials, a station may, at its discretion, and without further FCC authority, transmit emergency point-to-point messages for the purpose of requesting or dispatching aid and assisting in rescue operations.

(c) If the Emergency Broadcast System (EBS) is activated for a national level emergency while a local or state level emergency operation is in progress, the national level EBS operation shall take precedence. If, during the broadcasting of local or state emergency information, the attention signal described in §73.906 is used, the broadcasts are considered as being carried out under a state level or local level EBS operational plan.

(d) Any emergency operation undertaken in accordance with this section may be terminated by the FCC if required in the public interest.

(e) Immediately upon cessation of an emergency during which broadcast facilities were used for the transmission of point-to-point messages under paragraph (b) of this section, or when daytime facilities were used during nighttime hours by an AM station in accordance with paragraph (f) of this section, a report in letter form shall be forwarded to the FCC in Washington, D.C., setting forth the nature of the emergency, the dates and hours of the broadcasting of emergency information, and a brief description of the material carried during the emergency. A certification of compliance with the noncommercialization provision of paragraph (f) of this section must accompany the report where daytime facilities are used during nighttime hours by an AM station, together with a detailed showing, under the provisions of that paragraph, that no other broadcast service existed or was adequate.

(f) AM stations may, without further FCC authority, use their full daytime facilities during nighttime hours to broadcast emergency information (examples listed in paragraph (a) of this section), when necessary to the safety of life and property, in dangerous conditions of a general nature and when adequate advance warning cannot be given with the facilities authorized, because of skywave interference impact on other stations assigned to the same channel, such operation may be undertaken only if regular, unlimited-time service, is non-existent, inadequate from the standpoint of coverage, or not serving the public need. All operation under this paragraph must be conducted on a noncommercial basis. Recorded music may be used to the extent necessary to provide program continuity.

(g) Broadcasting of emergency information shall be confined to the hours, frequencies, powers and modes of operation specified in the station license, except as otherwise provided for AM stations in paragraph (f) of this section.

(h) Any emergency information transmitted by a TV station in accordance with this section shall be transmitted both aurally and visually or only visually. TV stations may use any method of visual presentation which results in a legible message conveying the essential emergency information. Methods which may be used include, but are not necessarily limited to, slides, electronic captioning, manual methods (e.g., hand printing) or mechanical printing processes. However, when emergency operation is being conducted under a national, state or local level Emergency Broadcast System (EBS) plan, emergency information shall be transmitted both aurally and visually.

§73.1500 Automatic transmission systems (ATS). An automatic transmission system consists of monitoring devices, control, and alarm circuitry, arranged so that they interact automatically to operate a broadcast station's transmitter and maintain technical parameters within licensed values.

(a) Licensees of AM, FM or TV broadcast stations may utilize an automatic transmission system (ATS) in lieu of either direct or remote control of the station transmitting system.

(b) No authorization from the FCC is required to operate the transmitter using an automatic transmission system. Prior to commencing use of the ATS, the station chief operator, technical director, or consulting engineer shall certify in writing to the station licensee that the system has been installed, tested, and fully complies with all prescribed technical standards of the rules applicable to the particular class of station.

(c) Broadcast stations operating automatic transmission systems must be provided with one or more ATS duty operator points. Each such point shall have a means to turn the transmitting apparatus off at all times.

(d) Whenever an automatic transmission system duty operator point is established at a location other than the main studio or transmitter, notification of that location must be sent to the FCC is Washington, D.C. within 3 days of initial use of the point. This notification is not required if responsible station personnel may be contacted at the transmitter or studio site during hours of operation when the ATS duty operator is elsewhere.

(e) The ATS must incorporate circuits that will terminate station transmission within 3 minutes if the adjustment controls do not correct an operating condition which is capable of causing interference.

(f) The transmitting apparatus must be manually activated at the beginning of each broadcast period.

(g) For AM station operation, the ATS may incorporate a means to transmit emergency information under the provisions of §73.1250(f).

§73.1510 Experimental authorizations.

(a) Licensees of broadcast stations may obtain experimental authorizations to conduct technical experimentation directed toward improvement of the technical phases of operation and service, and for such purposes may use a signal other than the normal broadcast program signal.

(b) Experimental authorizations may be requested by filing an informal application with the FCC in Washington, D.C., describing the nature and purpose of the experimentation to be conducted, the nature of the experimental signal to be transmitted, and the proposed schedule of hours and duration of the experimentation. Experimental authorizations shall be posted with the station license.

(c) Experimental operations are subject to the following conditions:

(1) The authorized power of the station may not be exceeded, except as specifically authorized for the experimental operations.

(2) Emissions outside the authorized bandwidth must be attenuated to the degree required for the particular type of station.

(3) The experimental operations may be conducted at any time the station is authorized to operate, but the minimum required schedule of programing for the class and type of station must be met. AM stations also may conduct experimental operations during the experimental period (12 midnight local time to local sunrise) and at additional hours if permitted by the experimental authorization provided no interference is caused to other stations maintaining a regular operating schedule within such period(s).

(4) If an experimental authorization permits the use of additional facilities or hours of operation for experimental purposes, no sponsored programs or commercial announcements may be transmitted during such experimentation.

(5) The licensee may transmit regularly scheduled programing concurrently with the experimental transmissions if there is no significant impairment of service.

(6) No charges may be made, either directly or indirectly, for the experimentation; however, normal charges may be made for regularly scheduled programing transmitted concurrently with the experimental transmissions.

(d) The FCC may request a report of the research, experimentation and results at the conclusion of the experimental operations.

§73.1515 Special field test authorizations.

(a) A special field test authorization may be issued to conduct field strength surveys to aid in the selection of suitable sites for broadcast transmission facilities, determine coverage areas, or to study other factors influencing broadcast signal propagation. The applicant for the authorization must be qualified to hold a license under Section 303(l)(1) of the Communications Act.

(b) Requests for authorizations to operate a transmitter under a special field test authorization must be in writing using an informal application in letter form, signed by the applicant and including the following information:

(1) Purpose, duration and need for the survey.

(2) Frequency, transmitter output powers and time of operation.

(3) A brief description of the test antenna system, its estimated effective radiated field and height above ground or average terrain, and the geographic coordinates of its proposed location(s).

(c) Operation under a special field test authorization is subject to the following conditions:

(1) No objectionable interference will result to the operation of other authorized radio services; in this connection, the power requested shall not exceed that necessary for the purposes of the test.

(2) The carriers will be unmodulated except for the transmission of a test pattern on a visual TV transmitter, and for hourly voice station identification on aural AM, FM and TV transmitters.

(3) The transmitter output power or antenna input power may not exceed those specified in the test authorization and the operating power must be maintained at a constant value for each phase of the tests.

(4) The input power to the final amplifier stage, and the AM antenna current or the FM or TV transmitter output power must be observed and recorded at half hour intervals and at any time that the power is adjusted or changed. Copies of these records must be submitted to the FCC with the required report.

(5) The test equipment may not be permanently installed, unless such installation has been separately authorized. Mobile units are not deemed permanent installations.

(6) Test transmitters must be operated by or under the immediate direction of an operator holding a commercial radio operator license (any class, unless otherwise endorsed).

(7) A report, containing the measurements, their analysis and other results of the survey shall be filed with the FCC in Washington, D.C. within sixty (60) days following the termination of the test authorization.

(8) The test transmission equipment, installation and operation thereof need not comply with the requirements of FCC Rules and Standards except as specified in this section if the equipment, installation and operation are consistent with good engineering principles and practices.

(d) A special field test authorization may be modified or terminated by notification from the FCC if in its judgment such action will promote the public interest, convenience and necessity.

§73.1520 Operation for tests and maintenance.

(a) Broadcast stations may be operated for tests and maintenance of their transmitting systems on their assigned frequencies using their licensed operating power and antennas during their authorized hours of operation without specific authorization from the FCC.

(b) Licensees of AM stations may operate for tests and maintenance during the hours from 12 midnight local time to local sunrise, if no interference is caused to other stations maintaining a regular operating schedule within such period. No AM station licensed for daytime or "specified hours" of operation may broadcast any regular or scheduled programs during this period of test and maintenance operation.

(c) Licensees of AM stations may obtain special antenna test authorizations, and operate under the provisions described in §73.157, to operate with nighttime facilities during daytime hours in conducting directional antenna field strength and antenna proof of performance measurements.

73.1705 Time of operation.

(a) Commercial and noncommercial educational TV and commercial FM stations will be licensed for unlimited time operation. Application may be made for voluntary share-time operation.

(b) Noncommercial educational FM stations will be licensed for unlimited and share time operation according to the provisions of §73.561.

(c) AM stations in the 535-1705 kHz band will be licensed for unlimited time. In the 535-1605 kHz band, stations that apply for share time and specified hours operation may also be licensed. AM stations licensed to operate daytime-only and limited-time may continue to do so; however, no new such stations will be authorized, except for fulltime stations that reduce operating hours to daytime-only for interference reduction purposes.

§73.1715 Share time. Operation is permitted by two or more broadcast stations using the same channel in accordance with a division of hours mutually agreed upon and considered part of their licenses.

(a) If the licenses of stations authorized to share time do not specify hours of operation, the licensees shall endeavor to reach an agreement for a definite schedule of periods of time to be used by each. Such agreement shall be in writing and each licensee shall file it in triplicate original with each application to the FCC in Washington, D.C. for renewal of license. If and when such written agreements are properly filed in conformity with this section, the file mark of the FCC will be affixed thereto, one copy will be retained by the FCC, and one copy returned to the licensee to be posted with the station license and considered as a part thereof.If the license specifies a proportionate time division, the agreement shall maintain this proportion. If no proportionate time division is specified in the license, the licensees shall agree upon a division of time. Such division of time shall not include simultaneous operation of the stations unless specifically authorized by the terms of the license.

(b) If the licensees of stations authorized to share time are unable to agree on a division of time, the FCC in Washington, D.C. shall be so notified by a statement filed with the applications for renewal of licenses. Upon receipt of such statement, the FCC will designate the applications for a hearing and, pending such hearing, the operating schedule previously adhered to shall remain in full force and effect.

(c) A departure from the regular schedule in a time-sharing agreement will be permitted only in cases where an agreement to that effect is put in writing, is signed by the licensees of the stations affected thereby and filed in triplicate by each licensee with the FCC in Washington, D.C. prior to the time of the proposed change. If time is of the essence, the actual departure in operating schedule may precede the actual filing of written agreement; provided appropriate notice is sent to the FCC.

(d) If the license of an AM station authorized to share time does not specify the hours of operation, the station may be operated for the transmission of regular programs during the experimental period provided an agreement thereto is reached with the other stations with which the broadcast day is shared: and further provided, such operation is not in conflict with §73.72 (Operating during the experimental period). Time-sharing agreements for operation during the experimental period need not be submitted to the FCC.

(e) Noncommercial educational FM stations are authorized for share-time operation according to the provisions of §73.561.

§73.1720 Daytime. Operation is permitted during the hours between average monthly local sunrise and average monthly local sunset.

(a) The controlling times for each month of the year are stated in the station's instrument of authorization. Uniform sunrise and sunset times are specified for all of the days of each month, based upon the actual times of sunrise and sunset for the fifteenth day of the month adjusted to the nearest quarter hour. Sunrise and sunset times are derived by using the standardized procedure and the table in the 1946 American Nautical Almanac issued by the United States Naval Observatory.

Limited time.

(a) Operation is applicable only to Class B (secondary) AM stations on a clear channel with facilities authorized before November 30, 1959. Operation of the secondary station is permitted during daytime and until local sunset if located west of the Class A station on the channel, or until local sunset at the Class A station if located east of that station. Operation is also permitted during nighttime hours not used by the Class A station or stations on the channel.

(b) No authorization will be granted for: (1) A new limited time station; (2) A limited time station operating on a changed frequency; (3) A limited time station with a new transmitter site materially closer to the 0.1 mv/m contour of a co-channel U.S. Class A station during the hours after local sunset in which the limited station is permitted to operate by reason of location east of the Class A station; or (4) Modification of the operating facilities of a limited time station resulting in increased radiation toward any point on the 0.1 mv/m contour of a co-channel U.S. Class A station during the hours after local sunset in which the limited time station is permitted to operate by reason of location east of the Class A station.

(c) The licensee of a secondary station which is authorized to operate limited time and which may resume operation at the time the Class A station (or stations) on the same channel ceases operation shall, with each application for renewal of license, file in triplicate a copy of its regular operating schedule. It shall bear a signed notation by the licensee of the Class A station of its objection or lack of objection thereto. Upon approval of such operating schedule, the FCC will affix its file mark and return one copy to the licensee authorized to operate limited time. This shall be posted with the station license and considered as a part thereof. Departure from said operating schedule will be permitted only pursuant to §73.1715 (Share time).

§73.1730 Specified hours.

(a) Specified hours stations must operate in accordance with the exact hours specified in their license. However, such stations, operating on local channels, unless sharing time with other stations, may operate at hours beyond those specified in their licenses to carry special events programming. When such programs are carried during nighttime hours, the station's authorized nighttime facilities must be used.

(b) Other exceptions to the adherence to the schedule of specified hours of operation are provided in §73.72 (Operating during the experimental period), §73.1250 (Broadcasting emergency information) and §73.1740 (Minimum operating schedule).

§73.1735 AM station operating pre-sunrise and post-sunset. Certain classes of AM stations are eligible to operate pre-sunrise and/or post-sunset for specified periods with facilities other than those specified on their basic instruments of authorization. Such pre-sunrise and post-sunset operation is authorized pursuant to the provisions of §73.99 of the rules.

73.1740 Minimum operating schedule.

(a) All commercial broadcast stations are required to operate not less than the following minimum hours:

(1) AM and FM stations. Two-thirds of the total hours they are authorized to operate between 6 a.m. and 6 p.m. local time and two-thirds of the total hours they are authorized to operate between 6 p.m. and midnight, local time, each day of the week except Sunday.

(i) Class D stations which have been authorized nighttime operations need comply only with the minimum requirements for operation between 6 a.m. and 6 p.m., local time.

(2) TV stations. (i) During the first 36 months of operation, not less than 2 hours daily in any 5 broadcast days per calendar week and not less than a total of: (A) 12 hours per week during the first 18 months. (B) 16 hours per week during the 19th through 24th months. (C) 20 hours per week during the 25th through 30th months. (D) 24 hours per week during the 31st through 36th months.

(ii) After 36 months of operation, not less than 2 hours in each day of the week and not less than a total of 28 hours per calendar week.

(iii) Visual transmissions of test patterns, slides, or still pictures accompanied by unrelated aural transmissions may not be counted in computing program service (see §73.653).

(3) Operation includes the period during which the station is operated pursuant to temporary authorization or program tests, as well as during the license period.

(4) In the event that causes beyond the control of a licensee make it impossible to adhere to the operating schedule of this section or to continue operating, the station may limit or discontinue operation for a period of not more than 30 days without further authority from the FCC. Notification must be sent to the FCC in Washington, D.C. not later than the 10th day of limited or discontinued operation. During such period, the licensee shall continue to adhere to the requirements in the station license pertaining to the lighting of antenna structures. In the event normal operation is restored prior to the expiration of the 30-day period, the licensee will so notify the FCC of this date. If the causes beyond the control of the licensee make it impossible to comply within the allowed period, informal written request shall be made to the FCC no later than the 30th day for such additional time as may be deemed necessary.

(b) Noncommercial educational AM and TV stations are not required to operate on a regular schedule and no minimum hours of operation are specified; but the hours of actual operation during a license period shall be taken into consideration in the renewal of noncommercial educational AM and TV broadcast licenses. Noncommercial educational FM stations are subject to the operating schedule requirements according to the provisions of §73.561.

Operator Requirements

In AM rules ...

§73.61 AM directional antenna field strength measurements.

(a) Each AM station using a directional antenna system must make field strength measurements at the monitoring point locations specified in the instrument of authorization, as often as necessary to ensure that the field at those points does not exceed the values specified in the station authorization. Additionally, stations not having an approved sampling system must make the measurements once each calendar quarter at intervals not exceeding 120 days. The provision of this paragraph supersedes any schedule specified on a station license issued prior to January 1, 1986. The results of the measurements are to be entered into the station log pursuant to the provisions of §73.1820.

(b) Partial proof of performance measurements using the procedures described in §73.154 must be made whenever the licensee has reason to believe that the radiated field may be exceeding the limits for which the station was most recently authorized to operate.

(c) A station may be directed to make a partial proof of performance by the FCC whenever there is an indication that the antenna is not operating as authorized.

In AM, FM and TV rules ...

§73.1580 Transmission system inspections.

(a) Each AM, FM and TV station licensee or permittee must conduct a complete inspection of the transmitting system and all required monitors as often as necessary to ensure proper station operation.

(b) The results of the inspections required by subsection (a) of this section are to be entered in the station maintenance log as specified in §73.1830(a)(1)(ix).

§73.1860 Transmitter duty operators.

(a) Each AM, FM or TV broadcast station must have at least one person holding a commercial radio operator license or permit (any class, unless otherwise endorsed) on duty in charge of the transmitter during all periods of broadcast operation. The operator must be on duty at the transmitter location, a remote control point, an ATS monitor and alarm point, or a position where extension meters are installed under the provisions of §73.1550.

(b) The transmitter operator must be able to observe the required transmitter and monitor metering to determine deviations from normal indications. The operator must also be able to make the necessary adjustments from the normal operator duty position, except as provided for in §73.1550.

(c) It is the responsibility of the station licensee to ensure that each transmitter operator is fully instructed and capable to perform all necessary observations and adjustments of the transmitting system and other associated operating duties to ensure compliance with the rules and station authorization.

(d) The transmitter duty operator may, at the discretion of the license and chief operator, be employed for other duties or operation of other transmitting stations if such other duties will not interfere with the proper operation of the broadcast transmission system.

§73.1870 Chief operators.

(a) The licensee of each AM, FM or TV broadcast station must designate a person holding a commercial radio operator license or permit (any class, unless otherwise endorsed) to serve as the station's chief operator. At times when the chief operator is unavailable or unable to act (e.g., vacations, sickness), the licensee shall designate another licensed operator as the acting chief operator on a temporary basis.

(b) Chief operators shall be employed or serve on the following basis:

(1) The chief operator for an AM station using a directional antenna or operating with greater than 10 kw authorized power, or of a TV station is to be an employee of the station on duty for whatever number of hours each week the station licensee determines is necessary to keep the station's technical operation in compliance with FCC rules and the terms of the station authorization.

(2) Chief operators for non-directional AM stations operating with authorized powers not exceeding 10 kw and FM stations may be either an employee of the station or engaged to serve on a contract basis for whatever number of hours each week the licensee determines is necessary to keep the station's technical operation in compliance with the FCC rules and terms of the station authorization.

(3) The designation of the chief operator must be in writing with a copy of the designation posted with the operator license. Agreements with chief operators serving on a contract basis must be in writing with a copy kept in station files.

(c) The chief operator is responsible for completion of the following duties specified in this paragraph below. When these duties are delegated to other persons, the chief operator shall maintain supervisory oversight sufficient to know that each requirement has been fulfilled in a timely and correct manner.

(1) Weekly (or monthly for stations using automatic transmission systems) inspections and calibrations of the transmission system, required monitors, metering, and control systems; and any necessary repairs or adjustments where indicated.

(2) Periodic AM field monitoring point measurements, equipment performance measurements, or other tests as specified in the rules or terms of the station license.

(3) Review of the station operating system inspections to determine if the entries are being made correctly or if the station authorization. Upon completion of the review, the chief operator or his designee is to make a notation of any discrepancies observed and date and sign the log; initiate necessary corrective action, and advise the station licensee of any condition which is a repetitive problem.

Personal Attacks and Political Broadcasts

In AM, FM, TV rules ...

§73.1910 Fairness Doctrine. The Fairness Doctrine is contained in Section 315(a) of the Communications Act of 1934, as amended, which provides that broadcasters have certain obligations to afford reasonable opportunity for the discussion of conflicting views on issues of public importance. See FCC public notice Fairness Doctrine and the Public Interest Standards, 39 FR 26372. Copies may be obtained from the FCC upon request.

§73.1920 Personal attacks.

(a) When, during the presentation of views on a controversial issue of public importance, an attack is made upon the honesty, character, integrity or like personal qualities of an identified person or group, the licensee shall, within a reasonable time and in no event later than one week after the attack, transmit to the persons or group attacked: (1) Notification of the date, time and identification of the broadcast; (2) A script or tape (or an accurate summary if a script or tape is not available) of the attack; and (3) An offer of a reasonable opportunity to respond over the licensee's facilities.

(b) The provisions of paragraph (a) of this Section shall not apply to broadcast material which falls within one or more of the following categories: (1) Personal attacks on foreign groups or foreign public figures; (2) Personal attacks occurring during uses by legally qualified candidates. (3) Personal attacks made during broadcasts not included in (b)(2) and made by legally qualified candidates, their authorized spokespersons, or those associated with them in the campaign, on other such candidates, their authorized spokespersons or persons associated with the candidates in the campaign; and (4) Bona fide newscasts, bona fide news interviews, and on-the-spot coverage of bona fide news events, including commentary or analysis contained in the foregoing programs.

(c) The provisions of paragraph (a) of this section shall be applicable to editorials of the licensee, except in the case of noncommercial educational stations since they are precluded from editorializing (Section 399(a), Communications Act).

§73.1930 Political editorials.

(a) Where a licensee, in an editorial, (1) endorses or (2) opposes a legally qualified candidate or candidates, the licensee shall, within 24 hours after the editorial, transmit to, respectively, (i) the other qualified candidate or candidates for the same office or (ii) the candidate opposed in the editorial, (A) notification of the date and the time of the editorial, (B) a script or tape of the editorial and (C) an offer of a reasonable opportunity for the candidate or a spokesman of the candidate to respond over the licensee's facilities. Where such editorials are broadcast on the day of the election or within 72 hours prior to the day of the election, the licensee shall comply with the provisions of this paragraph sufficiently far in advance of the broadcast to enable the candidate or candidates to have a reasonable opportunity to prepare a response and to present it in a timely fashion.

(b) Inasmuch as noncommercial educational stations may not engage in editorializing nor may support nor oppose any candidate for political office (Section 399, Communications Act), the provisions of paragraph (a) of this section do not apply to such stations.

§73.1940 Legally qualified candidates for public office.

(a) A legally qualified candidate for public office is any person who:

(1) Has publicly announced his or her intention to run for nomination or office;

(2) Is qualified under the applicable local, State or Federal law to hold the office for which he or she is a candidate; and

(3) Has met the qualifications set forth in either paragraphs (b), (c), (d) or (e) of this section.

(b) A person seeking election to any public office including that of President or Vice President of the United States, or nomination for any public office except that of President or Vice President, by means of a primary, general or special election, shall be considered a legally qualified candidate if, in addition to meeting the criteria set forth in paragraph (a) of this section, that person:

(1) Has qualified for a place on the ballot, or

(2) Has publicly committed himself or herself to seeking election by the write-in method and is eligible under applicable law to be voted for by sticker, by writing in his or her name on the ballot or by other method, and makes a substantial showing that he or she is a bona fide candidate for nomination or office.

(c) A person seeking election to the office of President or Vice President of the United States shall, for the purposes of the Communications Act and the rules thereunder, be considered legally qualified candidates only in those States or territories (or the District of Columbia) in which they have met the requirements set forth in paragraphs (a) and (b) of this section: except, that any such person who has met the requirements set forth in paragraphs (a) and (b) of this section in at least 10 States (or 9 and the District of Columbia) shall be considered a legally qualified candidate for election in all States, territories and the District of Columbia for purposes of this Act.

(d) A person seeking nomination to any public office, except that of President or Vice President of the United States, by means of a convention, caucus or similar procedure, shall be considered a legally qualified candidate if, in addition to meeting the requirements set forth in paragraph (a) of this section, that person makes a substantial showing that he or she is a bona fide candidate for such nomination: except, that no person shall be considered a legally qualified candidate for nomination by the means set forth in this paragraph prior to 90 days before the beginning of the convention, caucus or similar procedure in which he or she seeks nomination.

(e) A person seeking nomination for the office of President or Vice President of the United States shall, for the purposes of the Communications Act and the rules thereunder, be considered a legally qualified candidate only in those States or territories (or the District of Columbia) in which, in addition to meeting the requirements set forth in paragraph (a) of this section:

(1) He or she, or proposed delegates on his or her behalf, have qualified for the primary or Presidential preference ballot in that State, territory or the District of Columbia, or

(2) He or she has made a substantial showing of a bona fide candidacy for such nomination in that State, territory or the District of Columbia: except, that any such person meeting the requirements set forth in paragraphs (a)(1) and (2) of this section in at least 10 States (or nine and the District of Columbia) shall be considered a legally qualified candidate for nomination in all States, territories and the District of Columbia for purposes of this act.

(f) The term "substantial showing" of a bona fide candidacy as used in paragraphs (b), (d) and (e) of this section means evidence that the person claiming to be a candidate has engaged to a substantial degree in activities commonly associated with political campaigning. Such activities normally would include making campaign speeches, distributing campaign literature, issuing press releases, maintaining a campaign committee, and establishing campaign headquarters (even though the headquarters in some instances might be the residence of the candidate or his or her campaign manager). Not all of the listed activities are necessarily required in each case to demonstrate a substantial showing, and there may be activities not listed herein which would contribute to such a showing.

§73.1941 Equal opportunities.

(a) General requirements. Except as otherwise indicated in §73.1944, no station licensee is required to permit the use of its facilities by any legally qualified candidate for public office, but if any licensee shall permit any such candidate to use its facilities, it shall afford equal opportunities to all other candidates for that office to use such facilities. Such licensee shall have no power of censorship over the material broadcast by any such candidate. Appearance by a legally qualified candidate on any: (1) bona fide newscast; (2) bona fide news interview; (3) bona fide news documentary (if the appearance of the candidate is incidental to the presentation of the subject or subjects covered by the news documentary); or (4) on-the-spot coverage of bona fide news events (including, but not limited to political conventions and activities incidental thereto) shall not be deemed to be of use to a broadcasting station. (Section 315(a) of the Communications Act.)

(b) Uses. As used in this section and 73.1942, the term "use" means candidate appearance (including by voice or picture) that is not exempt under 73.1941(a)(1)-(4) and that is controlled, approved or sponsored by the candidate or the candidate's authorized Committee after the candidate becomes legally qualified.

(c) Timing of request. A request for equal opportunities must be submitted to the licensee within 1 week of the day on which the first prior use giving rise to the right of equal opportunities occurred; provided, however, that where the person was not a candidate at the time of such first prior use, he or she shall submit his or her request within 1 week of the first subsequent use after he or she has become a legally qualified candidate for the office in question.

(d) Burden of proof. A candidate requesting equal opportunities of the licensee or complaining of noncompliance to the Commission shall have the burden of proving that he or she and his or her opponent are legally qualified candidates for the same public office.

(e) Discrimination between candidates. In making time available to candidates for public office, no licensee shall make any discrimination between candidates in practices, regulations, facilities, or services for or in connection with the service rendered pursuant to this part, or make or give any preference to any candidate for public office or subject any such candidate to any prejudice or disadvantage; nor shall any licensee make any contract or other agreement which shall have the effect of permitting any legally qualified candidate for any public office to broadcast to the exclusion of other legally qualified candidates for the same public office.

§73.1942 Candidate rates.

(a) Charges for use of stations. The charges, if any, made for the use of any broadcasting station by any person who is a legally qualified candidate for any public office in connection with his or her campaign for nomination for election, or election, to such office shall not exceed:

(1) During the 45 days preceding the date of a primary or primary runoff election and during the 60 days preceding the date of a general or special election in which such person is a candidate, the lowest unit charge of the station for the same class and amount of time for the same period.

(i) A candidate shall be charged no more per unit than the station charges its most favored commercial advertisers for the same classes and amounts of time for the same periods. Any station practices offered to commercial advertisers that enhance the value of advertising spots must be disclosed and made available to candidates on equal terms. Such practices include but are not limited to any discount privileges that affect the value of advertising, such as bonus spots, time-sensitive make goods, preemption priorities, or any other factors that enhance the value of the announcement.

(ii) The Commission recognizes non-preemptible, preemptible with notice, immediately preemptible and run-of-schedule as distinct classes of time.

(iii) Stations may establish and define their own reasonable classes of immediately preemptible time so long as the differences between such classes are based on one or more demonstrable benefits associated with each class and are not based solely upon price or identity of the advertiser. Such demonstrable benefits include, but are not limited to, varying levels of preemption protection, scheduling flexibility, or associated privileges, such as guaranteed time-sensitive make goods. Stations may not use class distinctions to defeat the purpose of the lowest unit charge requirement. All classes must be fully disclosed and made available to candidates.

(iv) Stations may establish reasonable classes of preemptible with notice time so long as they clearly define all such classes, fully disclose them and make them available to candidates.

(v) Stations may treat non-preemptible and fixed position as distinct classes of time provided that stations articulate clearly the differences between such classes, fully disclose them, and make them available to candidates.

(vi) Stations shall not establish a separate, premium-priced class of time sold only to candidates. Stations may sell higher-priced non-preemptible or fixed time to candidates if such a class of time is made available on a bona fide basis to both candidates and commercial advertisers, and provided such class is not functionally equivalent to any lower-priced class of time sold to commercial advertisers.

(vii) [Reserved]

(viii) Lowest unit charge may be calculated on a weekly basis with respect to time that is sold on a weekly basis, such as rotations through particular programs or dayparts. Stations electing to calculate the lowest unit charge by such a method must include in that calculation all rates for all announcements scheduled in the rotation, including announcements aired under long-term advertising contracts. Stations may implement rate increases during election periods only to the extent that such increases constitute "ordinary business practices," such as seasonal program changes or changes in audience ratings.

(ix) Stations shall review their advertising records periodically throughout the election period to determine whether compliance with this section requires that candidates receive rebates or credits. Where necessary, stations shall issue rebates or credits promptly.

(x) Unit rates charged as part of any package, whether individually negotiated or generally available to all advertisers, must be included in the lowest unit charge calculation for the same class and length of time in the same time period. A candidate cannot be required to purchase advertising in every program or daypart in a package as a condition for obtaining package unit rates.

(xi) Stations are not required to include non-cash promotional merchandising incentives in lowest unit charge calculations; provided, however, that all such incentives must be offered to candidates as part of any purchases permitted by the licensee. Bonus spots, however, must be included in the calculation of the lowest unit charge calculation.

(xii) Make goods, defined as the rescheduling of preempted advertising, shall be provided to candidates prior to election day if a station has provided a time-sensitive make good during the year preceding the pre-election periods, respectively set forth in paragraph (a)(1) of this section to any commercial advertiser who purchased time in the same class.

(xiii) Stations must disclose and make available to candidates any make good policies provided to commercial advertisers. If a station places a make good for any commercial advertiser or other candidate in a more valuable program or daypart, the value of such make good must be included in the calculation of the lowest unit charge for that program or daypart.

(2) At any time other than the respective periods set forth in paragraph (a)(1) of this section, stations may charge legally qualified candidates for public office no more than the charges made for comparable use of the station by commercial advertisers. The rates, if any, charged all such candidates for the same office shall be uniform and shall not be rebated by any means, direct or indirect. A candidate shall be charged no more than the rate the station would charge for comparable commercial advertising. All discount privileges otherwise offered by a station to commercial advertisers must be disclosed and made available upon equal terms to all candidates for public office.

(b) If a station permits a candidate to use its facilities, the station shall make all discount privileges offered to commercial advertisers, including the lowest unit charges for each class and length of time in the same time period and all corresponding discount privileges, available upon equal terms to all candidates. This duty includes an affirmative duty to disclose to candidates information about rates, terms, conditions and all value-enhancing discount privileges offered to commercial advertisers. Stations may use reasonable discretion in making the disclosure; provided, however, that the disclosure includes, at a minimum, the following information:

(1) a description and definition of each class of time available to commercial advertisers sufficiently complete to allow candidates to identify and understand what specific attributes differentiate each class;

(2) a description of the lowest unit charge and related privileges (such as priorities against preemption and make goods prior to specific deadlines) for each class of time offered to commercial advertisers;

(3) a description of the station's method of selling preemptible time based upon advertiser demand, commonly known as the "current selling level," with the stipulation that candidates will be able to purchase at these demand-generated rates in the same manner as commercial advertisers;

(4) an approximation of the likelihood of preemption for each kind of preemptible time; and

(5) an explanation of the station's sales practices, if any, that are based on audience delivery, with the stipulation that candidates will be able to purchase this kind of time, if available to commercial advertisers.

(c) Once disclosure is made, stations shall negotiate in good faith to actually sell time to candidates in accordance with the disclosure.

(d) This rule (73.1942) shall not apply to any station licensed for noncommercial operation.

§73.1943 Political file.

(a) Every licensee shall keep and permit public inspection of a complete and orderly record (political file) of all requests for broadcast time made by or on behalf of a candidate for public office, together with an appropriate notation showing the disposition made by the licensee of such requests, and the charges made, if any, if the request is granted. The "disposition" includes the schedule of time purchased, when spots actually aired, the rates charged, and the classes of time purchased.

(b) When free time is provided for use by or on behalf of candidates, a record of the free time provided shall be placed in the political file.

(c) All records required by this paragraph shall be placed in the political file as soon as possible and shall be retained for a period of two years. As soon as possible means immediately absent unusual circumstances.

§73.1944 Reasonable access.

(a) Section 312(a)(7) of the Communications Act provides that the Commission may revoke any station license or construction permit for willful or repeated failure to allow reasonable access to, or to permit purchase of, reasonable amounts of time for the use of a broadcasting station by a legally qualified candidate for Federal elective office on behalf of his candidacy.

(b) Weekend access. For purposes of providing reasonable access, a licensee shall make its facilities available for use by federal candidates on the weekend before the election if the licensee has provided similar access to commercial advertisers during the year preceding the relevant election period. Licensees shall not discriminate between candidates with regard to weekend access.

Equal Employment Opportunities

In AM, FM, TV rules ...

§73.2080 Equal employment opportunities.

(a) General EEO policy. Equal opportunity in employment shall be afforded by all licensees or permittees of commercially or noncommercially operated AM, FM, TV or international broadcast stations (as defined in this part) to all qualified persons, and no person shall be discriminated against in employment because of race, color, religion, national origin or sex.

(b) EEO program. Each broadcast station shall establish, maintain, and carry out, a positive continuing program of specific practices designed to assure equal opportunity in every aspect of station employment policy and practice. Under the terms of its programs, a station shall:

(1) Define the responsibility of each level of management to ensure a positive application and vigorous enforcement of the policy of equal opportunity, and establish a procedure to review and control managerial and supervisory performance.

(2) Inform its employees and recognized employee organizations of the positive equal employment opportunity policy and program and enlist their cooperation.

(3) Communicate its equal employment opportunity policy and program and its employment needs to sources of qualified applicants without regard to race, color, religion, national origin or sex, and solicit their recruitment assistance on a continuing basis.

(4) Conduct a continuing program to exclude all unlawful forms of prejudice or discrimination based upon race, color, religion, national origin or sex, from its personnel policies and practices and working conditions; and

(5) Conduct a continuing review of job structure and employment practices and adopt positive recruitment, job design, and other measures needed in order to ensure genuine equality of opportunity to participate fully in all organizational units, occupations and levels of responsibility.

(c) EEO program requirements. A broadcast station's equal employment opportunity program should reasonably address itself to the specific areas set forth below, to the extent possible, and to the extent that they are appropriate in terms of the station's size, location, etc.:

(1) Disseminate its equal opportunity program to job applicants and employees. For example, this requirement may be met by:

(i) Posting notices in the station's office and other places of employment, informing employees, and applicants for employment, of their equal employment opportunity rights. Where it is appropriate, such equal employment opportunity notices should be posted in languages other than English;

(ii) Placing a notice in bold type on the employment application informing prospective employees that discrimination because of race, color, religion, national origin or sex is prohibited;

(iii) Seeking the cooperation of labor unions, if represented at the station, in the implementation of its EEO program and the inclusion of nondiscrimination provisions in union contracts;

(iv) Utilizing media for recruitment purposes in a manner that will contain no indication, either explicit or implicit, of a preference for one sex over another and that can be reasonably expected to reach minorities and women.

(2) Use minority organizations, organizations for women, media, educational institutions and other potential sources of minority and female applicants, to supply referrals whenever job vacancies are available in its operation. For example, this requirement may be met by:

(i) Placing employment advertisements in media that have significant circulation among minorities residing and/or working in the recruiting area;

(ii) Recruiting through schools and colleges, including those located in the station's local area, with significant minority-group enrollments;

(iii) Contacting, both orally and in writing, minority and human relations organizations, leaders and spokesmen to encourage referral of qualified minority or female applicants;

(iv) Encouraging current employees to refer minority or female applicants;

(v) Making known to recruitment sources in the employer's immediate area that qualified minority members and females are being sought for consideration whenever you hire and that all candidates will be considered on a nondiscriminatory basis.

(3) Evaluate its employment profile and job turnover against the availability of minorities and women in its recruitment area. For example, this requirement may be met by:

(i) Comparing the composition of the relevant labor area with composition of the station's workforce;

(ii) Where there is underrepresentation of either minorities and/or women, examining the company's personnel policies and practices to assure that they do not inadvertently screen out any group and take appropriate action where necessary. Data on representation of minorities and women in the available labor force are generally available on a metropolitan statistical area (MSA) or county basis.

(4) Undertake to offer promotions of qualified minorities and women in a nondiscriminatory fashion to positions of greater responsibility. For example, this requirement may be met by:

(i) Instructing those who make decisions on placement and promotion that qualified minority employees and females are to be considered without discrimination, and that job areas in which there is little or no minority or female representation should be reviewed;

(ii) Giving qualified minority and female employees equal opportunity for positions which lead to higher positions. Inquiring as to the interest and skills of all lower paid employees with respect to any of the higher paid positions.

(5) Analyze its efforts to recruit, hire and promote minorities and women and address any difficulties encountered in implementing its equal employment opportunity program. For example, this requirement may be met by:

(i) Avoiding use of selection techniques or tests that have the effect of discriminating against qualified minority groups or females;

(ii) Reviewing seniority practices to ensure that such practices are nondiscriminatory;

(iii) Examining rates of pay and fringe benefits for employees having the same duties, and eliminating any inequities based upon race or sex discrimination.

(d) Mid-term review for television broadcast stations. The Commission will conduct a mid-term review of the employment practices of each broadcast television station at two and one-half years following the station's most recent license expiration date as specified in §73.1020 of these rules. The Commission will use the employment profile information provided on the first two Form 395-B reports submitted following such license expiration date to determine whether the television station's employment profiles as compared to the applicable labor force data are in compliance with the Commission's processing criteria. Television broadcast stations whose employment profiles fall below the processing criteria will receive a letter noting any necessary improvements identified as a result of the review.

Network Affiliation

In AM rules ...

§73.132. Territorial exclusivity. No licensee of an AM broadcast station shall have any arrangement with a network organization which prevents or hinders another station serving substantially the same area from broadcasting the network's programs not taken by the former station, or which prevents or hinders another station serving a substantially different area from broadcasting any program of the network organization: provided, however, that this section does not prohibit arrangements under which the station is granted first call within its primary service area upon the network's programs. The term network organization means any organization originating program material, with or without commercial messages, and furnishing the same to stations interconnected so as to permit simultaneous broadcast by all or some of them. However, arrangements involving only stations under common ownership, or only the rebroadcast by one station of programing from another with no compensation other than a lump-sum payment by the station rebroadcasting, are not considered arrangements with a network organization. The term arrangement means any contract arrangement or understanding, express or implied.

In FM rules ...

§73.232.

EDITOR'S NOTE: Same as §73.132.

In TV rules ...

§73.658. Affiliation agreements.

(a) Exclusive affiliation of station. No license shall be granted to a television broadcast station having any contract, arrangement, or understanding, express or implied, with a network organization under which the station is prevented or hindered from, or penalized for, broadcasting the programs of any other network organization. (The term network organization as used herein includes national and regional network organizations. See chapter VII, J. of Report on Chain Broadcasting.)

(b) Territorial exclusivity. No license shall be granted to a television broadcast station having any contract, arrangement, or understanding, express or implied, with a network organization which prevents or hinders another broadcast station in the same community from broadcasting the network's programs not taken by the former stations, or which prevents or hinders another broadcast station located in a different community from broadcasting any program of the network organization. This regulation shall not be construed to prohibit any contract, arrangement, or understanding between a station and a network organization pursuant to which the station is granted the first call in its community upon the program of the network organization. As employed in this paragraph the term community is defined as the community specified in the instrument of authorization as the location of the station.

(c) [Reserved]

(d) Station commitment of broadcast time. No license shall be granted to a television broadcast station having any contract, arrangement, or understanding, express or implied, with any network organization, which provides for optioning of the station's time to the network organization, or which has the same restraining effect as time optioning. As used in this section, time optioning is any contract, arrangement, or understanding, express or implied, between a station and a network organization which prevents or hinders the station from scheduling programs before the network agrees to utilize the time during which such programs are scheduled, or which requires the station to clear time already scheduled when the network organization seeks to utilize the time.

(e) Right to reject programs. No license shall be granted to a television broadcast station having any contract, arrangement, or understanding, express or implied, with a network organization which, with respect to programs offered or already contracted for pursuant to an affiliation contract, prevents or hinders the station from (1) rejecting or refusing network programs which the station reasonably believes to be unsatisfactory or unsuitable or contrary to the public interest, or (2) substituting a program which in the station's opinion, is of greater local or national importance.

(f) Network ownership of stations. No license shall be granted to a network organization, or to any person directly or indirectly controlled by or under common control of a network organization, for a television broadcast station in any locality where the existing television broadcast stations are so few or of such unequal desirability (in terms of coverage, power, frequency, or other related matters) that competition would be substantially restrained by such licensing. (The word control as used in this section is not limited to full control but includes such a measure of control as would substantially affect the availability of the station to other networks.)

(g) Dual network operation. No license shall be issued to a television broadcast station affiliated with a network organization which maintains more than one network of television broadcast stations: Provided that this section shall not be applicable, if such networks are not operated simultaneously, or if there is no substantial overlap in the territory served by the group of stations comprising each such network.

(h) Control by networks of station rates. No license shall be granted to a television broadcast station having any contract, arrangement, or understanding, express or implied, with a network organization under which the station is prevented or hindered from, or penalized for, fixing or altering its rates for the sale of broadcast time for other than the network's programs.

(i) No license shall be granted to a television broadcast station which is represented for the sale of non-network time by a network organization or by an organization directly or indirectly controlled by or under common control with a network organization, if the station has any contract, arrangement, or understanding, express or implied, which provides for the affiliation of the station with such network organization; provided, however, that this rule shall not be applicable to stations licensed to a network organization or to a subsidiary of a network organization.

(j) [Deleted]

(k) Prime time access rule. Effective September 8, 1975, commercial television stations owned by or affiliated with a national television network in the 50 largest television markets (see Note 1 to this paragraph) shall devote, during the four hours of prime time (7-11 p.m. E.T. and P.T., 6-10 p.m. C.T. and M.T.), no more than three hours to the presentation of programs from a national network, programs formerly on a national network (off-network programs) other than feature films, or, on Saturdays, feature films; provided, however, that the following categories of programs need not be counted toward the three-hour limitation:

(1) On nights other than Saturdays, network or off-network programs designed for children, public affairs programs or documentary programs (see Note 2 to this paragraph for definitions).

(2) Special news programs dealing with fast-breaking news events, on-the-spot coverage of news events or other material related to such coverage, and political broadcasts by or on behalf of legally qualified candidates for public office.

(3) Regular network news broadcasts up to half hour, when immediately adjacent to a full hour of continuous locally produced news or locally produced public affairs programing.

(4) Runovers of live network broadcast of sporting events, where the event has been reasonably scheduled to conclude before prime time or occupy only a certain amount of prime time, but the event has gone beyond its expected duration due to circumstances not reasonably foreseeable by the networks or under their control. This exemption does not apply to post-game material.

(5) In the case of stations in the Mountain and Pacific time zones, on evenings when network prime time programing consists of a sports event or other program broadcast live and simultaneously throughout the contiguous 48 states, such stations may assume that the network's schedule that evening occupies no more of prime time in these time zones than it does in the Eastern and Central time zones.

(6) Network broadcasts of an international sports event (such as the Olympic Games), New Year's Day college football games, or any other network programing of a special nature other than motion pictures or other sports events, when the network devotes all of its time on the same evening to the same programing, except brief incidental fill material.

NOTE 1: The top 50 markets to which this paragraph applies are the 50 largest markets in terms of average prime time audience for all stations in the market. For broadcast years before fall 1980, the 50 markets are the largest 50 as listed in the Arbitron publication Television Markets and Rankings Guide, generally published in November, which will apply for the broadcast year starting the following fall, except that, for 1978-79, Syracuse-Elmira will not be included and the Salt Lake City market will be included. For broadcast years starting in the fall of 1980 and thereafter, the 50 largest markets to which this paragraph applies will be determined at three-year intervals, on the basis of the average of two Arbitron February/March audience surveys occurring roughly 2-1/2 years and roughly 3-1/2 years before the start of the three-year period. The 50 markets to which this paragraph will apply for three years from fall 1980 to fall 1983 will be determined by an average of the prime time audience figures (all market stations combined) contained in the reports of Arbitron February/March 1977 and February/March 1978 audience surveys. Shortly after the results of the 1978 survey are available the Commission will issue a list of the 50 largest markets to which this paragraph will apply from fall 1980 to fall 1983. The same procedure will take place, on the basis of February/March 1980 and 1981 surveys, for the three-year period from fall 1983 to fall 1986.

NOTE 2: As used in this paragraph, the term programs designed for children means programs primarily designed for children aged 2 through 12. The term documentary programs means programs which are nonfictional and educational or informational, but not including programs where the information is used as part of a contest among participants in the program, and not including programs relating to the visual entertainment arts (stage, motion pictures or television) where more than 50% of the program is devoted to the presentation of entertainment material itself. The term public affairs programs means talks, commentaries, discussions, speeches, editorials, political programs, documentaries, forums, panels, roundtables, and similar programs primarily concerning local, national, and international public affairs.

NOTE 3: The provisions of this paragraph apply only to U.S. commercial television broadcast stations in the 50 states, and not to stations in Puerto Rico or the Virgin Islands, foreign stations or noncommercial educational television or "public" television stations (either by way of restrictions on their exclusivity or on exclusivity against them).

NOTE 4: New stations authorized in any community of a hyphenated market listed in §76.51 of this chapter or in any community of a hyphenated market listed in the ARB Television Market Analysis (for markets below the top-100 markets) are subject to the same rules as previously existing stations therein. New stations authorized in other communities are considered stations in separate markets unless and until §76.51 is amended by Commission action, or the ARB listing is changed.

(l) Broadcast of the programs of more than one network. The provisions of this paragraph govern and limit the extent to which, after October 1, 1971, commercial television stations in the 50 States of the United States, which are regular affiliates of one of the three national television networks, may broadcast programs of another network, in markets where there are two such affiliated stations and one or more operational VHF or UHF stations having reasonably comparable facilities which are not regular affiliates of any network. Whether or not the stations in a particular market come within the provisions of this paragraph is determined by whether, as of July 1 of each year with respect to programs beginning October 1, or as of January 1 of each year with respect to programs beginning April 1, there are in the market the stations specified in the last sentence.

(1) Definitions. As used in this paragraph, the following terms have the meaning given:

(i) Station means a commercial television station in the 50 States of the United States.

(ii) Operational station means a station authorized and operating as of June 10 (with respect to programs beginning October 1) or as of December 10 (with respect to programs beginning April 1), or as a station authorized and which gives notice to the Commission by such June 10 or December 10 date that it sill be on the air by such October 1 or April 1 date (including request for program test authority if none has previously been given), and commit itself to remain on the air for six months after such October 1 or April 1 date. Such notice shall be received at the Commission by the June 10 or December 10 date mentioned, and shall show that copies thereof have been sent to the three national networks and to the licensees of all operating television stations in the market.

(iii) Affiliated station means a station having a regular affiliation with one of the three national television networks, under which it serves as that network's primary outlet for the presentation of its programs in a market. It includes any arrangement under which the network looks primarily to this station rather than other stations for the presentation of its programs and the station chiefly presents the programs of this network rather than another network.

(iv) Unaffiliated station means a station not having an affiliation arrangement as defined in this subparagraph with a national television network, even though it may have other types of agreements or pre-program arrangements with it.

(v) Network means a national organization distributing programs for a substantial part interconnection facilities.

(vi) Unaffiliated network means a network not having an affiliated station (as defined in this paragraph) in a particular market, even though it may have other types of agreements or pre-program arrangements.

(vii) Market means the television markets of the United States, and the stations in them, as identified in the latest publication of American Research Bureau (ARB), together with any stations which have since become operational in the same communities.

(viii) Evening programing means programming (regular programs or specials) starting and concluding on a network between the hours of 7:30 p.m. and 11 p.m. local time (except 6:30 p.m. and 10 p.m. in the Central time zone), plus all programs other than regular newscasts starting on the network between 7 and 7:30 p.m. local time (6 and 6:30 p.m. local time in the Central time zone). It does not include portions broadcast after 7 p.m. of programs starting earlier, or portions broadcast after 11 p.m. of programs starting earlier.

(ix) Specials means programs not carried on the network at least as often as once a week. It includes both programs scheduled very well in advance and those scheduled very shortly before broadcast on the network.

(x) Reasonably comparable facilities means station transmitting facilities (effective radiated power and effective antenna height above average terrain) such that the station's Grade B coverage area is at least two-thirds as large (in square kilometers) as the smallest of the market affilated stations' Grade B coverage areas. Where one or both of the affiliates is licensed to a city different from that of the unaffiliated station, the term reasonably comparable facilities also includes the requirement that the unaffiliated station must put a predicted Grade A or better signal over all of the city of license of the other regular (non-satellite) station(s), except that where one of the affiliated stations is licensed to the same city as the unaffiliated station, and puts a Grade B but not a Grade A signal over the other city of license, the unaffiliated station will be considered as having reasonably comparable facilities if it too puts a predicted Grade B signal over all of the other city of license.

(2) Taking programs from unaffiliated networks. No affiliated station, in a market covered by this paragraph, shall take and broadcast, from an unaffiliated network, any programming of the times and types specified in this subparagraph, unless the conditions specified have first been met:

(i) Any evening programming (as defined in this paragraph), unless and until the entire schedule of such programs has been offered by the unaffiliated network to the unaffiliated station as provided in subparagraph (4) of this paragraph, and the unaffiliated station has either accepted 15 hours per week of such programs, plus additional special hours when part of the "special" is included in the 15 hours, or has accepted a lesser amount and indicated that it does not wish to carry any more. Such acceptance shall be governed by the provisions of subparagraph (4) of this paragraph.

(ii) Any programming beginning on the network between 12 noon and 7 p.m. on Saturdays, Sundays and holidays, and consisting of sports events (without limitation, college football and basketball, professional football, baseball, ice hockey, golf, tennis, horse racing and auto racing), unless and until the program has first been offered to the unaffiliated station and that station has indicated that it does not wish to accept it.

(iii) Any programming broadcast after 11 p.m. local time (except 10 p.m. local time in the Central time zone) which is a continuation of programs starting earlier and carried by the unaffiliated station; or any material broadcast after 7 p.m. (6 p.m. in the Central time zone) which is a continuation of sports programs beginning earlier and carried by the unaffiliated station.

(iv) Any program presented in the same week by the unaffiliated station.

(3) Carriage of programs of a network which has an affiliate. No affiliated station in a market covered by this paragraph shall broadcast, from another network which has an affiliated station in the market, any evening programming or Saturday, Sunday or holiday sports programming, unless such programming has been offered to the unaffiliated station in the market and the latter has indicated that it does not wish to carry it.

(4) Offer and acceptance (i) the offer by a network referred to in this paragraph means an offer to the unaffiliated station of the programs for broadcast. Programs so offered cannot be withdrawn by the network until the following April 1 or October 1, unless the station does not in fact broadcast the program as accepted, in which case the provisions of paragraph (1) (4) (ii) shall apply, or unless the program is cancelled on the network, in which case the replacement or substitute program shall be offered to the station as a new program under paragraph (l) (2) or (l) (3). If a program accepted by the unaffiliated station is shifted in time, the station may exercise its right of first call either with respect to the program at its new time, or the previous time segment, at its option.

(ii) The acceptance referred to in paragraphs (1) (2) and (3) means that the unaffiliated station agrees to broadcast the program accepted, at its live network time or a delayed time acceptable to the network, unless in its judgment the program is not in the public interest or it wishes to substitute a local, or other live, program for it. The provisions of §73.658(a), prohibiting agreements which hinder the presentation of the programs of other networks, shall not apply to material covered by this paragraph. If a program is not presented in a particular week or at a delayed time acceptable to the network, the network may place this particular broadcast of the program on another station; and if this occurs more than 4 times in any 13-week period the network may withdraw the program from the station without obligation to offer it any additional programming. The unaffiliated station is free to seek and obtain other terms of acceptance from the network; but the offer of programming by the network on the foregoing terms satisfies its obligations under this paragraph.

(iii) The offer by the network shall, to the extent possible, be on or before July 15 with respect to programs beginning in the fall season, and by January 15 with respect to programs presented after April 1, or otherwise as soon as possible. The unaffiliated station's acceptance or indication of non-acceptance shall be within two weeks after the date of the offer; where any negotiations between the network and the station concerning particular programs are involved, programs not accepted within 30 days of the date of the offer shall be deemed not accepted.

NOTE 1: If there are in a particular market two affiliated stations and two (or more) operational unaffiliated stations with reasonably comparable facilities, the provisions of paragraph (l) shall require an offer of programming to each: but the 15-hour-per-week first call provision applies to the total programming taken by all such stations.

NOTE 2: The provisions of paragraph (l) do not apply to a market in which there are two VHF affiliated U.S. stations, and a foreign VHF station to which a national U.S. television network transmits programs pursuant to authority granted under Section 325 of the Communications Act of 1934, as amended, and which serves as that network's primary affiliate in the market.

(m)(1) Territorial exclusivity in non-network arrangements. No television station shall enter into any contract, arrangement or understanding, expressed or implied, with a non-network program producer, distributor, or supplier, or other person which prevents or hinders another television station located in a community over 56.3 kilometers (35 miles) away, as determined by the reference points contained in §76.53 of this chapter, (if reference points for a community are not listed in §76.53, the location of the main post office will be used) from broadcasting any program purchased by the former station from such non-network program-producer, distributor, supplier or any other person except that a TV station may secure exclusivity against a television station licensed to another designated community in a hyphenated market specified in the market listing as contained in §76.51 of this chapter for those 100 markets listed, and for markets not listed in §76.51 of this chapter, the listing as contained in the ARB Television Market Analysis for the most recent year at the time that the exclusivity contract, arrangement, or understanding is complete under practices of the industry. As used in this subsection, the term community as defined as the community specified in the instrument of authorization as the location of the station.

(2) Notwithstanding paragraph (m)(1), a television station may enter into a contract, arrangement, or understanding with a producer, supplier, or distributor of a non-network program if that contract, arrangement, or understanding provides that the broadcast station has exclusive national rights such that no other television station in the United States may broadcast the program.

NOTE 1: Contracts, arrangements, or understandings that are complete under the practices of the industry prior to August 7, 1973, will not be disturbed. Extensions or renewals of such agreements are not permitted because they would in effect be new agreements without competitive bidding. However, such agreements that were based on the broadcaster's advancing "seed money" for the production of a specific program or series that specify two time periods — a tryout period and period thereafter for general exhibition — may be extended or renewed as contemplated in the basic agreement.

NOTE 2: It is intended that the top 100 major television markets listed in §76.51 of this chapter shall be used for the purposes of this rule and that the listing of the top 100 television markets appearing in the ARB Television Market Analysis shall not be used. The reference in this rule to the listing of markets in the ARB Television Market Analysis refers to hyphenated markets below the top-100 markets contained in the ARB Television Market Analysis. If a community is listed in a hyphenated market in §76.51 and is also listed in one of the Markets in the ARB listing, the listing in §76.51 shall govern.

NOTE 3: The provisions of this paragraph apply only to U.S. commercial television broadcast stations in the 50 states, and not to stations in Puerto Rico or the Virgin Islands, foreign stations or noncommercial educational television or "public" television stations (either by way of restrictions on their exclusivity or on exclusivity against them).

NOTE 4: New stations authorized in any community of a hyphenated market listed in §76.51 of this chapter or in any community of a hyphenated market listed in the ARB Television Market Analysis (for markets below the top-100 markets) are subject to the same rules as previously existing stations therein. New stations authorized in other communities are considered stations in separate markets unless and until §76.51 is amended by Commission action, or the ARB listing is changed.

Network Financial Interests and Syndication

In TV rules ...

§73.659 Television network financial interests and syndication rights in first-run programs.

(a) No television network, other than an "emerging network" defined in §73.662(g), may hold or acquire continuing financial interests or syndication rights in any first-run non-network program or series distributed in the United States unless the network has solely produced the program or series.

§73.660 Television network participation in program syndication.

(a) No television network, other than an "emerging network" as defined in §73.662(g), may actively syndicate any prime time entertainment or first-run non-network program to television stations within the United States. Any such programs for which a television network holds syndication rights shall be syndicated domestically through an independent syndicator.

(b) Where a television network, other than an "emerging network" as defined in §73.662(g), has syndication rights in prime time entertainment programming, such programming shall be made available for non-network broadcast exhibition within the United States no later than the earlier of: (1) the end of the fourth year after network exhibition of such a series has commenced, or the subsequent anniversary of that date as to all programs in that series aired after the fourth year, or (2) one hundred eighty (180) days after network exhibition of such a series or program is completed.

§73.661 Network television program ownership and syndication reports. (a) A television network shall maintain reports identifying all network prime time entertainment programs, whether aired on its own or another network, and all first-run non-network programs, in which the network holds or acquires financial interests or syndication rights. The network shall identify the name of the program, the type of program (network or first-run), the nature of the interest or right held in the program, the dates the program (if a network program) began and ended its network run, and the date the program (if a first-run program) first appeared in syndication. Where a network has, before June 5, 1993, but not on or before August 1, 1972, acquired an interest or right in a program presented to the public, the network shall identify the party that initiated negotiations that led to network acquisition of such interest or right. Any contract or agreement creating or conveying a financial interest or syndication right shall be made available to the Commission upon request.

(b) For any television network that actively syndicates any prime time entertainment program or any first-run non-network program, the network shall maintain reports that list the sales to broadcast stations of any such programming it actively syndicates; provided, however, that with respect to sales of programs to broadcast stations outside the United States, the network may either redact the identity of such stations (if contracts are provided as part of the reports) or report the market (city and country) to which a specific program is syndicated rather than the identity of the station. Any contract or agreement creating or conveying the right to engage actively in syndication sales shall be made available to the Commission upon request.

(c) For the programs described under paragraph (a) of this section, a television network shall maintain reports that identify the independent syndicator who holds the active syndication rights, the date on which the independent syndicator obtained such rights, and the network's owned and operated and affiliated stations that have obtained the program for exhibition from the independent syndicator. Any contract or agreement entered into between a network and an independent syndicator creating or conveying the right to engage in syndication shall be made available to the Commission upon request.

(d) Each television network shall certify in writing that it is in compliance with §§73.659-73.661 of this part.

(e) An "emerging network" as defined in §73.662(g) of this part, is exempt from compliance with the requirements of paragraphs (a)-(d) of this section until it provides to interconnected affiliates, on a regular basis, 16 hours of prime time programming per week (exclusive of live coverage of bona fide news events of national importance).

(f) The records maintained pursuant to paragraphs (a)-(d) of this section shall be filed with the Commission and placed in the public file of each station owned and operated by the network semi-annually before the first regular business day of September and March of each year. Such records shall be maintained in the public file until the remaining syndication rules expire.

§73.662 Definitions for television network financial interest, syndication, and prime time access rules. For purposes of 73.658(k), 73.659, 73.660, and 73.661:

(a) A "continuing financial interest" is a right to receive revenue from the non-network broadcast or syndicated use of a television program by a network.

(b) "Entertainment programs" include series, made-for-television movies, mini-series, and entertainment specials, and do not include sports, public affairs, or news programs.

(c) An "independent syndicator" is one not owned or controlled, in full or in part, by a television network.

(d) A "prime time" program is one that has network exhibition during the hours of 7-11 p.m. eastern and pacific time or 6-10 p.m. central and mountain time.

(e) A program "solely produced by a network" is a program in which the network, directly or through a production entity it owns or controls, is the sole copyright owner, has full financial responsibility and full business and production control.

(f) A "television network" is any person, entity, or corporation providing on a regular basis fifteen (15) hours of prime time programming per week (exclusive of live coverage of bona fide news events of national importance) to interconnected affiliates that reach, in aggregate, at least seventy-five (75) percent of television households nationwide; and/or any person, entity, or corporation controlling, controlled by, or under common control with such person, entity, or corporation. Not included within this definition is any television network formed for the purpose of producing, distributing, or syndicating program material for educational, noncommercial, or public broadcasting exhibition, or for non-English language exhibition, or that predominantly distributes programming involving the direct sale of products or services.

NOTE: "National audience reach" for purposes of this definition is the total number of United States television households in the Arbitron Area of Dominant Influence (ADI) markets in which the stations or regular television station affiliates of the network are located, divided by the total national television households as measured by the most current ADI data publicly available at the start of each television season. "Regular basis" means providing, on average for the prior six months, more than the specified number of hours of programming per week.

(g) an "emerging network" is an entity not meeting the definition of a "television network," as set forth in paragraph (f) of this section, on June 5, 1993, but which subsequently meets this definition.

Common Antenna Site

§73.635. Use of common antenna site. No television license or renewal of a television license will be granted to any person who owns, leases, or controls a particular site which is peculiarly suitable for television broadcasting in a particular area and (a) which is not available for use by other television licensees; and (b) no other comparable site is available in the area; and (c) where the exclusive use of such site by the applicant or licensee would unduly limit the number of television stations that can be authorized in a particular area or would unduly restrict competition among television stations.

Reports to be Filed

All broadcast stations ...

§73.3526 Local public inspection file of commercial stations.

(a) Records to be maintained. Every applicant for a construction permit for a new station in the commercial broadcast services shall maintain for public inspection a file containing the material described in paragraph (a)(1) of this section. Every permittee or licensee of an AM, FM or TV station in the commercial broadcast services shall maintain for public inspection a file containing the material described in paragraphs (a)(1), (2), (3), (4), (5), (6), (7) and (10) of this section. In addition, every permittee or licensee of a TV station shall maintain for public inspection a file containing the material described in paragraphs (a)(8) of this section; every permittee or licensee of an AM or FM station shall maintain for public inspection a file containing material described in paragraph (a)(9) of this section. The material to be contained in the file is as follows:

(1) A copy of every application tendered for filing, with respect to which local public notice is required to be given under the provisions of §73.3580 or §73.3594; and all exhibits, letters and other documents tendered for filing as part thereof; all amendments thereto, copies of all documents incorporated therein by reference, all correspondence between the FCC and the applicant pertaining to the application after it has been tendered for filing, and copies of Initial Decisions and Final Decisions in hearing cases pertaining thereto, which according to the provisions of §0.451 through §0.461 of the rules are open for public inspection at the offices of the FCC. Information incorporated by reference which is already in the local file need not be duplicated if the entry making the reference sufficiently identifies the information so that it may be found in the file, and if there has been no change in the document since the date of filing and the applicant, after making the reference, so states. If petitions to deny are filed against the application, and have been duly served on the applicant, a statement that such a petition has been filed shall appear in the local file together with the name and address of the party filing the petition. The file shall also contain a copy of every written citizen agreement. For purposes of this section, a citizen agreement is a written agreement between a broadcast applicant, permittee, or licensee, and one or more citizens or citizen groups, entered for primarily noncommercial pur-

poses. This definition includes those agreements that deal with goals or proposed practices directly or indirectly affecting station operation in the public interest, in areas such as but not limited to community ascertainment, programing, and employment. It excludes common commercial agreements such as advertising contracts; union, employment, and personal services contracts; network affiliation, syndication, program supply contracts and so on. However, the mere inclusion of commercial terms in a primarily noncommercial agreement such as provision for payment of fees for future services of the citizen-parties [see Report and Order, Docket 19518, 57 FCC 2d 494 [35 RR 2d 1542] (1976). would not cause the agreement to be considered commercial for purposes of this section.

NOTE: Applications tendered for filing on or before May 13, 1965, which are subsequently designated for hearing after May 13, 1965, with local notice being given pursuant to the provisions of §73.3594, and material related to such applications, need not be placed in the file required to be kept by this section. Applications tendered for filing after May 13, 1965, which contain major amendments to applications tendered for filing on or before May 13, 1965, with local notice of the amending application being given pursuant to the provisions of §73.3580, need not be placed in the file required to be kept by this section.

(2) A copy of every application tendered for filing by the licensee or permittee for such station which is not included in paragraph (a)(1) of this section and which involves changes in program service, which requests an extension of time in which to complete construction of a new station, or which requests consent to involuntary assignment or transfer, or to voluntary assignment or transfer not resulting in a substantial change in ownership or control and which may be applied for on FCC Form 316; and copies of all exhibits, letters, and other documents filed as part thereof, all amendments thereto, all correspondence between the FCC and the applicant pertaining to the application after it has been tendered for filing, and copies of all documents incorporated therein by reference, which according to the provisions of §0.451 through §0.461 of these rules are open for public inspection at the offices of the FCC. Information incorporated by reference which is already in the local file need not be duplicated if the entry making the reference sufficiently identifies the information so that it may be found in the file, and there has been no change in the document since the date of filing and the licensee, after making the reference, so states. If petitions to deny are filed against the application, and have been duly served on the applicant, a statement that such a petition has been filed shall appear in the local file together with the name and address of the party filing the petition.

NOTE: The engineering section of the applications mentioned in paragraphs (a)(1) and (2) of this section, and material related to the engineering section, need not be kept in the file required to be maintained by this paragraph. If such engineering section contains service contour maps submitted with that section, copies of such maps and information (State, county, city, street address, or the identifying information) showing main studio and transmitter locations shall be kept in the file.

(3) A copy of every ownership report or supplemental ownership report filed by the licensee or permittee for such station after May 13, 1965, pursuant to the provisions of this part; and copies of all exhibits, letters, and other documents filed as part thereof, all amendments thereto, all correspondence between the permittee or licensee and the FCC pertaining to the reports after they have been filed, and all documents incorporated therein by reference, including contracts listed in such reports in accordance with the provisions of §73.3615(a)(4)(i) and which according to the provisions of §0.451 through §0.461 of the rules are open for public inspection at the offices of the FCC. Information incorporated by reference which is already in the local file need not be duplicated if the entry making the reference sufficiently identifies the information so that it may be found in the file, and if there has been no change in the document since the date of filing and the licensee or permittee, after making the reference, so states.

(4) Such records as are required to be kept by §73.1940 concerning broadcasts by candidates for public office.

(5) A copy of every annual employment report filed by the licensee or permittee for such station pursuant to the provisions of this part; and copies of all exhibits, letters and other documents filed as part thereof, all amendments thereto, and all correspondence between the permittee or licensee and the FCC pertaining to the reports after they have been filed and all documents incorporated therein by reference and which according to the provisions of §0.451 through §0.461 of the rules are open for public inspection at the offices of the FCC.

(6) The Public and Broadcasting—A Procedure Manual [see FCC 74-942, 39 32288, September 5, 1974.]

(7) Letters received from members of the public as are required to be retained by §73.1202.

(8)(i) For commercial TV broadcast stations, every three months a list of programs that have provided the station's most significant treatment of community issues during the preceding 3 month period. The list for each calendar quarter is to be filed by the tenth day of the succeeding calendar quarter (e.g., January 10 for the quarter October - December, April 10 for the quarter January - March, etc.). The list shall include a brief narrative describing what issues were given significant treatment and the programming that provided this treatment. The description of the programs should include, but is not limited to, the time, date, duration and title of each program in which the issue was treated.

(ii) For commercial TV broadcast stations, records sufficient to permit substantiation of the station's certification, in its license renewal application, of compliance with the commercial limits on children's programming established in 47 USC §303a and 47 CFR §73.670.

(iii) For commercial TV broadcast stations, on either an anuual or quarterly basis, records demonstrating the extent to which the licensee responded to the educational and informational needs of children in their overall programming, including programming specifically designed to serve such needs. These records may also reflect any special nonbroadcast efforts by the licensee which enhance the educational and informational value of such programming to children and any special efforts by the licensee to produce or support programming broadcast by another television station in the licensee's marketplace, which is specifically designed to serve the educational and informational needs of children. These records shall include a summary of the licensee's programming response, nonbroadcast efforts and support for other stations' programming directed to the educational and informational needs of children, and shall reflect the most significant programming related to such needs which the licensee has aired. Licensees may make their children's programming records part of their issues/programs list or keep them as a separate list. Such records should indicate, at a minimum, the time, date, duration and a brief description of the program or nonbroadcast effort the licensee has made to serve the educational and informational needs of children.

(9) For commercial AM and FM broadcast stations, every three months a list of programs that have provided the station's most significant treatment of community issues during the preceding 3 month period. The list for each calendar quarter is to be filed by the tenth day of the succeeding calendar quarter (e.g., January 10 for the quarter October - December, April 10 for the quarter January - March, etc.). The list shall include a brief narrative describing what issues were given significant treatment and the programming that provided this treatment. The description of the programs should include, but is not limited to, the time, date, duration and title of each program in which the issue was treated.

(10) Each applicant for renewal of license shall, within seven days of the last day of the broadcast of the local public notice of filing announcements required pursuant to §73.3580(h), place in the station's local public inspection file a statement certifying compliance with this requirement. The dates and times that the pre-filing and post-filing notices were broadcast and the text thereof shall be made part of the certifying statement.

(11) Every television broadcast station owned or controlled by a television network shall maintain the records required by §73.661. These records shall be maintained in the file until the remaining syndication rules expire.

(12) For commercial radio stations, a copy of every agreement or contract involving time brokerage of the licensee's station or of another station by the licensee, with confidential or proprietary information redacted where appropriate.

(b) Responsibility in case of assignment or transfer.

(1) In some cases involving applications for consent to assignment of broadcast station construction permits or licenses, with respect to which public notice is required to be given under the provisions of §73.3580 or §73.3594, the file mentioned in paragraph (a) of this section shall be maintained by the assignor. If the assignment is consented to by the FCC and consummated, the assignee shall maintain the file commencing with the date on which notice of the consummation of the assignment is filed with the FCC. The file maintained by the assignee shall cover the period both before and after the time when the notice of consumation of assignment was filed. The assignee is responsible for obtaining copies of the necessary documents from the assignor or from the FCC files.

(2) In cases involving applications for consent to transfer of control of a permittee or licensee of a broadcast station, the file mentioned in paragraph (a) of this section shall be maintained by the permittee or licensee.

(c) Station to which records pertain. The file need contain only applications, ownership reports, and related material that concern the station for which the file is kept. Applications, permittees, and licensees need not keep in the file copies of such applications, reports, and material which pertain to other stations with regard to which they may be applicants, permittees or licensees, except to the extent that such information is reflected in the materials required to be kept under the provisions of this section.

(d) Location of records. The file shall be maintained at the main studio of the station, where such studio is located in the community to which the station is licensed or where such studio is located outside the community of license pursuant to authorization granted under §73.1125(a) of the Rules prior to July 16, 1987, or at any accessible place (such as a public registry for documents or an attorney's office) in the community to which the station is or is proposed to be licensed. The file shall be available for public inspection at any time during regular business hours.

(e) Period of retention. The records specified in paragraph (a)(4) of this section shall be retained for periods specified in §73.1940 (2 years). The manual specified in paragraph (a)(6) of this section shall be retained indefinitely. The letters specified in paragraph (a)(7) of this section shall be retained for the period specified in §73.1202 (3 years). The "significant treatment of community issues" list and the records demonstrating the station's response to the educational and informational needs of children specified in paragraph (a)(8) of this section shall be retained by commercial broadcast television licensees for the term of license (5 years). Commercial AM and FM radio licensees shall retain the "significant treatment of community issues" list specified in paragraph (a)(9) of this section for the term of license (7 years). The certification specified in paragraph (a)(10) of this section shall be retained for the period specified in §73.3580 (for as long as the application to which it refers). The records specified in paragraph (a)(12) of this section shall be retained as long as the contract or agreement is in force. The records specified in paragraphs (a)(1), (2), (3) and (5) of this section shall be retained as follows:

(1) The applicant for a construction permit for a new station shall maintain such a file so long as the application is pending before the FCC or any proceeding involving that application is pending before the courts. (If the application is granted, subparagraph (2) below shall apply.)

(2) The permittee or licensee shall maintain such a file so long as an authorization to operate the station is outstanding, and shall permit public inspection of the material as long as it is retained by the licensee even though the request for inspection is made after the conclusion of a required retention period specified in this paragraph. However, material which is voluntarily retained after the required retention time may be kept in a form and place convenient to the licensee, and shall be made available to the inquiring party, in good faith after written request, at a time and place convenient to both the party and the licensee. Applications and related material placed in the file shall be retained for a period beginning with the date that they are tendered for filing and ending with the expiration of one license term (five (5) years for television and seven (7) years for radio licensees) or until the grant of the first renewal application of the television or radio broadcast station in question, whichever is later, with two exceptions:

(i) Engineering material pertaining to a former mode of operation need not be retained longer than 3 years after a station commences operation under a new or modified mode; and

(ii) Material having a substantial bearing on a matter which is the subject of a claim against the licensee, or relating to an FCC investigation or a complaint to the FCC of which the licensee has been advised, shall be retained until the licensee is notified in writing that the material may be discarded, or, if the matter is a private one, the claim has been satisfied or is barred by statute of limitations. Where an application or related material incorporates by reference material in earlier applications and material concerning programming and related matters (Section IV and related material), the material so referred to shall be retained as long as the application referring to it. If a written agreement is not incorporated in an application tendered for filing with the FCC, the starting date of the retention period for that agreement is the date the agreement is executed.

(f) Copies of any material required to be in the public file of any applicant for a construction permit, or permittee or licensee of any commercial TV or radio station shall be available for machine reproduction upon request made in person, provided the requesting party shall pay the reasonable cost of reproduction. Requests for machine copies shall be fulfilled at a location specified by the applicant, permittee or licensee, within a reasonable period of time which, in no event, shall be longer than seven days unless reproduction facilities are unavailable in the applicant's, permittee's or licensee's community. The applicant, permittee or licensee is not required to honor requests made by mail, but may do so if it chooses.

§73.3612 Annual employment report. Each licensee or permittee of a commercially or non-commercially operated AM, FM, television, or international broadcast station with five or more fulltime employees shall file with the Commission on or before May 31 of each year, on FCC Form 395, an annual employment report.

§73.3613 Filing of contracts. Each licensee or permittee of a commercial or noncommercial AM, FM, TV or International broadcast station shall file with the FCC copies of the following contracts, instruments, and documents together with amendments, supplements, and cancellations (with the substance of oral contracts reported in writing), within 30 days of execution thereof:

(a) Network service: Network affiliation contracts between stations and networks will be reduced to writing and filed as follows:

(1) All network affiliation contracts, agreements or understandings between a TV broadcast or low power TV station and a national network. For the purposes of this paragraph the term network means any person, entity or corporation which offers an interconnected program serivice on a regular basis for 15 or more hours per week to at least 25 affiliated television licensees in 10 or more states; and/or any person, entity or corporation controlling, controlled by, or under common control with such person, entity or corporation.

(2) Each such filing on or after May 1, 1969, initially shall consist of a written instrument containing all of the terms and conditions of such contract, agreement or understanding without reference to any other paper or document by incorporation or otherwise. Subsequent filings may simply set forth renewal, amendment or change, as the case may be, of a particular contract previously filed in accordance herewith.

(3) The FCC shall also be notified of the cancellation or termination of network affiliations, contracts for which are required to be filed by this section.

(b) Ownership or control: Contracts, instruments or documents relating to the present or future ownership or control of the licensee or permittee or of the licensee's or permittee's stock, rights or interests therein, or relating to changes in such ownership or control shall include but are not limited to the following:

(1) Articles of partnership, association, and incorporation, and changes in such instruments;

(2) Bylaws, and any instruments effecting changes in such bylaws:

(3) Any agreement, document or instrument providing for the assignment of a license or permit, or affecting, directly or indirectly, the ownership or voting rights of the licensee's or permittee's stock (common or preferred, voting or nonvoting), such as:

(i) Agreements for transfer of stock;

(ii) Instruments for the issuance of new stock; or

(iii) Agreements for the acquisition of licensee's or permittee's stock by the issuing licensee or permittee corporation. Pledges, trust agreements, options to purchase stock and other executory agreements are required to be filed. However, trust agreements or abstracts thereof are not required to be filed, unless requested specifically by the FCC. Should the FCC request an abstract of the trust agreement in lieu of the trust agreement, the licensee or permittee will submit the following information concerning the trust:

(A) Name of trust;

(B) Duration of trust;

(C) Number of shares of stock owned;

(D) Name of beneficial owner of stock;

(F) Name of the party or parties who have the power to vote or control the vote or control the vote of the shares; and

(G) Any conditions on the powers of voting the stock or any unusual characteristics of the trust.

(4) Proxies with respect to the licensee's or permittee's stock running for a period in excess of 1 year, and all proxies, whether or not running for a period of 1 year, given without full and detailed instructions binding the nominee to act in a specified manner. With respect to proxies given without full and detailed instructions, a statement showing the number of such proxies, by whom given and received, and the percentage of outstanding stock represented by each proxy shall be submitted by the licensee or permittee within 30 days after the stockholders' meeting in which the stock covered by such proxies has been voted. However, when the licensee or permittee is a corporation having more than 50 stockholders, such complete information need be filed only with respect to proxies given by stockholders who are officers or directors, or who have 1% or more of the corporation's voting stock. When the licensee or permittee is a corporation having more than 50 stockholders and the stockholders giving the proxies are not officers or directors or do not hold 1% or more of the corporation's stock, the only information required to be filed is the name of any person voting 1% or more of the stock by proxy, the number of shares voted by proxy by such person, and the total number of shares voted at the particular stockholders' meeting in which the shares were voted by proxy.

(5) Mortgage or loan agreements containing provisions restricting the licensee's or permittee's freedom of operation, such as those affecting voting rights, specifying or limiting the amount of dividends payable, the purchase of new equipment, or the maintenance of current assets.

(6) Any agreement reflecting a change in the officers, directors or stockholders of a corporation, other than the licensee or permittee, having an interest, direct or indirect, in the licensee or permittee as specified by §73.3615.

(c) Personnel:

(1) Management consultant agreements with independent contractors; contracts relating to the utilization in a management capacity of any person other than an officer, director, or regular employee of the licensee or permittee; station management contracts with any persons, whether or not officers, directors, or regular employees, which provide for both a percentage of profits and a sharing in losses; or any similar agreements.

(2) The following contracts, agreements, or understandings need not be filed: Agreements with persons regularly employed as general or station managers or salesmen; contracts with program managers or program personnel; contracts with attorneys, accountants or consulting radio engineers; contracts with performers; contracts with station representatives; contracts with labor unions; or any similar agreements.

(d) Time brokerage agreements: Time brokerage agreements involving radio stations, where the licensee (including all parties under common control) is the brokering entity, there is a principal community contour (predicted or measured 5 mV/m groundwave for AM stations and predicted 3.16 mV/m for FM stations) overlap with the brokered station, and more than 15 percent of the time of the brokered station, on a weekly basis, is brokered by that licensee. Confidential or proprietary information may be redacted where appropriate but such information shall be made available for inspection upon request by the FCC.

(e) The following contracts, agreements, or understandings need not be filed but shall be kept at the station and made available for inspection by any authorized representative of the FCC: contracts relating to the sale of television broadcast time to "time brokers" for resale; subchannel leasing agreements for Subsidiary Communications Authorization operation; franchise/leasing agreements for operation of telecommunications services on the TV vertical blanking interval; time sales contracts with the same sponsor for 4 or more hours per day, except where the length of the events (such as athletic contests, musical programs, and special events) broadcast pursuant to the contract is not under control of the station; and contracts with chief operators.

§73.3615 Ownership reports.

(a) With the exception of sole proprietorships and partnerships composed entirely of natural persons, each licensee of a commercial AM, FM, or TV broadcast station shall file an Ownership Report on FCC Form 323 once a year, on the anniversary of the date that its renewal application is required to be filed. Licensees owning multiple stations with different anniversary dates need file only one Report per year on the anniversary of their choice, provided that their Reports are not more than one year apart. A licensee with a current and unamended Report on file at the Commission may certify that it has reviewed its current Report and that it is accurate, in lieu of filing a new report. Ownership Reports shall provide the following information as of a date not more than 60 days prior to the filing of the Report:

(1) In the case of an individual, the name of such individual;

(2) In the case of a partnership, the name of each partner and the interest of each partner. Except as specifically noted below, the names of limited partners shall be reported. A limited partner need not be reported, regardless of the extent of its ownership, if the limited partner is not materially involved, directly or indirectly, in the management or operation of the licensee and the licensee so certifies.

(i) Any change in partners or in their rights will require prior consent of the FCC upon an application for consent to assignment of license or permit. If such change involves less than a controlling interest, the application for FCC consent to such changes may be made upon FCC Form 316.

(3) In the case of a corporation, association, trust, estate, or receivership, the data applicable to each:

(i)(A) The name, residence, citizenship, and stockholding of every officer, director, trustee, executor, administrator, receiver, partner, member of an association, and any stockholder which holds stock accounting for 5% or more of the votes of the corporation, except that an investment company, insurance company, or bank trust department need be reported only if it holds stock amounting to 10% or more of the votes, provided that the licensee certifies that such entity has made no attempt to influence, directly or indirectly, the management or operations of the licensee, and that there is no representation on the licensee's board or among its officers by any person professionally or otherwise associated with the entity.

(B) A licensee shall report any separate interests known to the licensee to be held ultimately by the same individual or entity, whether those interests are held in custodial accounts, by individual holding corporations or otherwise, if, when aggregated:

(1) the sum of all interests except those held by or through "passive investors" is equal to or exceeds 5 percent; or

(2) the sum of all interests held by or through passive investors is equal to or exceeds 10 percent; or

(3) the sum of the interests computed under (1) plus the sum of the interests computed under (2) is equal to or exceeds 10 percent.

(c) If the majority of the voting stock of a corporate licensee is held by a single individual or entity, no other stockholding need be reported for that licensee;

(ii) Full information as to family relationship or business association between two or more officials and/or stockholders, trustees, executors, administrators, receivers, and members of any association;

(iii) Capitalization with a description of the classes and voting power of stock authorized by the corporate charter or other appropriate legal instrument and the number of shares of each class issued and outstanding; and

(iv) Full information with respect to the interest and identity of any person having any direct, indirect, fiduciary, or beneficial interest in the licensee or in its stock accounting for 5% or more of its votes. For example:

(A) Where A is the trustee of stock held for beneficiary B, A shall be reported if A votes the stock or has the sole or shared power to dispose of the stock; B or any other party shall be reported if B or such party votes the stock or has sole power to dispose of the stock or has the power to revoke the trust or replace the trustee at will;

(B) Where X is not a natural person and has attributable ownership interests in the licensee under §73.3555 of the rules, regardless of its position in the vertical ownership chain, an Ownership Report shall be filed for X which, except as specifically noted below, must contain the same information as required of a licensee. If X has a voting stockholder interest in the licensee, only those voting interests of X that are cognizable after application of the multiplier described in NOTE 2(d) of §73.3555 of the rules, if applicable, shall be reported. If X is a corporation, whether or not its interest in the licensee is by virtue of its ownership of voting stock, the officers and directors shall be reported. With respect to those officers and directors shall be reported. With respect to those officers and directors whose duties and responsibilities are wholly unrelated to the licensee, and who wish to be relieved of attribution in the licensee, the name, title and duties of these officers and directors, with statements properly documenting that their duties do not involve the licensee, shall be reported.

(4) In the case of all licensees:

(i) A list of contracts will in effect be required to be filed with the FCC §73.3613 showing the date of execution and expiration of each contract; and

(ii) Any interest which the licensee may have in any other broadcast station.

(b) Except as specifically noted below, each permittee of a commercial AM, FM or TV broadcast station shall file an Ownership Report on FCC Form 323 (1) within 30 days of the date of grant by the FCC of an application for construction permit and (2) on the date that it applies for a station license. The Ownership Report of the permittee shall give the information required by the applicable portions of paragraph (a) of this section. A permittee with a current and unamended Report on file at the Commission may certify that it has reviewed its current Report and it is accurate, in lieu of filing a new Report.

(c) Before any change is made in the organization, capitalization, officers, directors, or stockholders of a corporation other than licensee or permittee, which results in a change in the control of the licensee or permittee, prior FCC consent must be received under §73.3540. A transfer of control takes place when an individual or group in privity, gains or loses affirmative or negative (50%) control. See instructions on FCC Form 323 (Ownership Report).

(d) Each licensee of a noncommercial educational AM, FM or TV broadcast station shall file an Ownership Report on FCC Form 323-E at the time the application for renewal of station license is required to be filed. Licensees owning more than one noncommercial educational AM, FM or TV broadcast station need file only one Ownership report at 5 year intervals for TV stations and 7 year intervals for AM and FM stations. Ownership Reports shall give the following information as of a date not more than 30 days prior to the filing of the Ownership Report:

(1) The following information as to all officers, members of governing board, and holders of 1% or more ownership interest (if any): Name, residence, office held, citizenship, principal profession or occupation, and by whom appointed or elected.

(2) Full information with respect to the interest and identity of any individual, organization, corporation, association, or any other entity which has direct or indirect control over the licensee or permittee.

(3) A list of all contracts still in effect required by §73.3613 to be filed with the FCC, showing the date of execution and expiration of each contract. (4) Any interest which the licensee or permittee or any of its officers, members of the governing board, and holders of 1% or more ownership interest (if any) held in any other broadcast station.

(e) Each permittee of a noncommercial educational AM, FM or TV broadcast station shall file an Ownership Report on FCC Form 323-E within 30 days of the date of grant by the FCC of an application for original construction permit. The Ownership Report of the permittee shall give the information required by the applicable form.

(f) A supplemental Ownership Report on FCC Form 323-E shall be filed by each licensee or permittee within 30 days after any change occurs in the information required by the Ownership Report from that previously reported. Such report should include, without limitation: (1) An change in organization; or

(2) Any change in officers or directors;

(3) Any transaction affecting the ownership (direct or indirect) or voting rights with respect to the licensee or permittee (or with respect to any stock interest therein).

(g) A copy of all Ownership and supplemental Ownership Reports and related material filed pursuant to this section shall be maintained and made available for public inspection locally as required by §73.3526 and §73.3527.

License Renewals

General ...

§73.3523 Dismissal of applications in renewal proceedings.

(a) Any applicant for a construction permit, that has filed an application that is mutually exclusive with an application for the renewal of a license of an AM, FM or television station (hereinafter "competing applicant"), and seeks to dismiss or withdraw its application and thereby remove a conflict between applications pending before the Commission, must obtain the approval of the Commission.

(b) If a competing applicant seeks to dismiss or withdraw its application prior to the Initial Decision stage of the hearing on its application, it must submit to the Commission a request for approval of the dismissal or withdrawal of its application, a copy of any written agreement related to the dismissal or withdrawal of its application, and an affidavit setting forth:

(1) A certification that neither the applicant nor its principals has received or will receive any money or other consideration in exchange for dismissing or withdrawing its application;

(2) A statement that its application was not filed for the purpose of reaching or carrying out an agreement with any other applicant regarding the dismissal or withdrawal of its application; and

(3) The terms of any oral agreement relating to the dismissal or withdrawal of its application.

In addition, within 5 days of the applicant's request for approval, each remaining competing applicant and the renewal applicant must submit an affidavit setting forth:

(4) A certification that neither the applicant nor its principals has paid or will pay any money or other consideration in exchange for the dismissal or withdrawal of the application; and

(5) The terms of any oral agreement relating to the dismissal or withdrawal of the application.

(c) If a competing applicant seeks to dismiss or withdraw its application after the Initial Decision stage of the hearing on its application, it must submit to the Commission a request for approval of the dismissal or withdrawal of its application, a copy of any written agreement related to the dismissal or withdrawal, and an affidavit setting forth:

(1) A certification that neither the applicant nor its principals has received or will receive any money or other consideration in excess of the legitimate and prudent expenses of the applicant;

(2) The exact nature and amount of any consideration paid or promised;

(3) An itemized accounting of the expenses for which it seeks reimbursement;

(4) A statement that its application was not filed for the purpose of reaching or carrying out an agreement with any other applicant regarding the dismissal or withdrawal of its application; and

(5) The terms of any oral agreement relating to the dismissal or withdrawal of its application.

In addition, within 5 days of the applicant's request for approval, each remaining party to any written or oral agreement must submit an affidavit setting forth:

(6) A certification that neither the applicant nor its principals has paid or will pay money or other consideration in excess of the legitimate and prudent expenses of the withdrawing applicant in exchange for the dismissal or withdrawal of the application; and

(7) The terms of any oral agreement relating to the dismissal or withdrawal of its application.

(d) For the purposes of this section:

(1) Affidavits filed pursuant to this section shall be executed by the applicant, permittee, or licensee, if an individual; a partner having personal knowledge of the facts, if a partnership; or an officer having personal knowledge of the facts, if a corporation or association.

(2) An application shall be deemed to be pending before the Commission from the time an application is filed with the Commission until an order of the Commission granting or denying the application is no longer subject to reconsideration by the Commission or to review by any court.

(3) "Legitimate and prudent expenses" are those expenses reasonably incurred by an applicant in preparing, filing, and prosecuting its application.

(4) "Other consideration" consists of financial concessions, including but not limited to the transfer of assets or the provision of tangible pecuniary benefit, as well as non-financial concessions that confer any type of benefit on the recipient.

§73.3539 Application for renewal of license.

(a) Unless otherwise directed by the Federal Communications Commission, an application for renewal of license shall be filed not later than the first day of the fourth full calendar month prior to the expiration date of the license sought to be renewed, except that applications for renewal of license of an experimental broadcast station shall be filed not later than the first day of the second full calendar month prior to the expiration date of the license sought to be renewed. If any deadline prescribed in this paragraph falls on a non-business day, the cut-off shall be the close of business of the first full business day thereafter.

(b) No application for renewal of license of any broadcast station will be considered unless there is on file with the Commission, the information, if any, currently required by §73.3611-73.3615, inclusive, for the particular class of station. The renewal application shall include a reference by date and file number to such information on file.

(c) Whenever the Commission regards an application for a renewal of license as essential to the proper conduct of a hearing or investigation, and specifically directs that it be filed by a certain date, such application shall be filed within the time thus specified. If the licensee fails to file such application within the prescribed time, the hearing or investigation shall proceed as if such renewal application has been received.

(d) Renewal application forms, titles and numbers are listed in §73.35000, Applications and Report Forms.

§73.3584 Procedures for filing petitions to deny.

(a) Except in the case of applications for new low power TV, TV translator or TV booster stations, for major changes in the existing facilities of such stations, or for applications for a change in output channel tendered by displaced low power TV and TV translator stations pursuant to §73.3572(a)(1), any party in interest may file with the Commission a Petition to Deny any application (whether as originally filed or if amended so as to require a new file number pursuant to §§73.3571(j), 73.3572(b), 73.3573(b), 73.3574(b) or 73.3578) for which local notice pursuant to §73.3580 is required, provided such petitions are filed prior to the day such applications are granted or designated for hearing; but where the FCC issues a public notice pursuant to the provisions of §§73.3571(c), 73.3572(c) or 73.3573(d), establishing a "cutoff" date, such petitions must be filed by the date specified. In the case of applications for transfers and assignments of construction permits or station licenses, Petitions to Deny must be filed not later than 30 days after issuance of a public notice of the acceptance for filing of the applications. In the case of applications for renewal of license, Petitions to Deny may be filed at any time up to the last day for filing mutually exclusive applications under §73.3516(e). Requests for extension of time to file Petitions to Deny applications for new broadcast stations or major changes in the facilities of existing stations or applications for renewal of license will not be granted unless all parties concerned, including the applicant, consent to such requests, or unless a compelling showing can be made that unusual circumstances make the filing of a timely petition impossible and the granting of an extension warranted.

(b) Except in the case of applications for new low power TV or TV translator stations, for major changes in the existing facilities of such stations, the applicant may file an opposition to any Petition to Deny, and the petitioner a reply to such opposition in which allegations of fact or denials thereof shall be supported by affidavit of a person or persons with personal knowledge thereof. The times for filing such oppositions and replies shall be those provided in §1.45 except that as to a Petition to Deny an application for renewal of license, an opposition thereto may be filed within 30 days after the Petition to Deny is filed, and the party that filed the Petition to Deny may reply to the opposition within 20 days after the opposition is due or within 20 days after opposition is filed, whichever is longer. The failure to file an opposition or reply will not necessarily be construed as an admission of fact or argument contained in a pleading.

(c) In the case of applications for new low power TV, TV translator or TV booster stations, for major changes in the existing facilities of such stations, or for applications for a change in output channel tendered by displaced low power TV and TV translator stations pursuant to §73.3572(a)(1), any party in interest may file with the FCC a Petition to Deny any application (whether as originally filed or if amended so as to require a new file number pursuant to §73.3572(b)) for which local notice pursuant to §73.3580 is required, provided such petitions are filed within 30 days of the FCC Public Notice proposing the application for grant (applicants may file oppositions within 15 days after the Petition to Deny is filed); but where the FCC selects a tentative permittee pursuant to §1.1601 et seq., Petitions to Deny shall be accepted only if directed against the tentative selectee and filed after issuance of and within 15 days of FCC Public Notice announcing the tentative selectee. The applicant may file an opposition within 15 days after the Petition to Deny is filed. In cases in which the minimum diversity preference provided for in §1.1623(f)(1) has been applied, an "objection to diversity claim," and opposition thereto may be filed against any applicant receiving a diversity preference, within the same time period provided herein for Petitions and Oppositions. In all pleadings, allegations of fact or denials thereof shall be supported by appropriate certification. However, the FCC may announce, by the Public Notice announcing the acceptance of the last-filed mutually exclusive application, that a notice of Petition to Deny will be required to be filed no later than 30 days after issuance of the Public Notice.

(1) If so announced, a Petition to Deny filed against an applicant will not be accepted if filed by a party which failed to timely file a notice of petition, and make service of the notice of petition pursuant to §1.47, unless good cause is shown for the failure to file the notice. Good cause includes allegations based on facts that could not previously be discovered with diligence, and fraud or suppression of evidence by the tentative selectee.

(2) The notice of Petition to Deny shall be limited to two pages. The notice shall include specific allegations that concisely state the reasons why the applicant lacks the qualifications to be a licensee or why a grant of the application would be inconsistent with the public interest. The notice shall be supported by certification made by a person or persons having personal knowledge thereof.

(d) Untimely Petitions to Deny, as well as other pleadings in the nature of a Petition to Deny, and any other pleadings or supplements which do not lie as a matter of law or are otherwise procedurally defective, are subject to return by the FCC's staff without consideration.

§73.3588 Dismissal of petitions to deny or withdrawal of informal objections in renewal proceedings.

(a) Whenever a petition to deny or an informal objection has been filed against any application, and the filing party seeks to dismiss or withdraw the petition to deny or the informal objection, either unilaterally or in exchange for financial consideration, that party must file with the Commission a request for approval of the dismissal or withdrawal, a copy of any written agreement related to the dismissal or withdrawal, and an affidavit setting forth:

(1) A certification that neither the petitioner nor its principals has received or will receive any money or other consideration in excess of legitimate and prudent expenses in exchange for the dismissal or withdrawal of the petition to deny;

(2) The exact nature and amount of any consideration received or promised;

(3) An itemized accounting of the expenses for which it seeks reimbursement; and

(4) The terms of any oral agreement related to the dismissal or withdrawal of the petition to deny.

In addition, within 5 days of petitioner's request for approval, each remaining party to any written or oral agreement must submit an affidavit setting forth:

(5) A certification that neither the applicant nor its principals has paid or will pay money or other consideration in excess of the legitimate and prudent expenses of the petitioner in exchange for dismissing or withdrawing the petition to deny; and

(6) The terms of any oral agreement relating to the dismissal or withdrawal of the petition to deny.

(b) Citizens' agreements. For purposes of this section, citizens agreements include agreements arising whenever a petition to deny or informal objection has been filed against any application and the filing party seeks to dismiss or withdraw the petition or objection in exchange for non-financial consideration (e.g., programming, ascertainment or employment initiatives). The parties to such an agreement must file with the Commission a joint request for approval of the agreement, a copy of any written agreement, and an affidavit executed by each party setting forth:

(1) Certification that neither the petitioner, nor any person or organization related to the petitioner, has received or will receive any money or other consideration in connection with the citizens' agreement other than legitimate and prudent expenses incurred in prosecuting the petition to deny;

(2) Certification that neither the petitioner, nor any person or organization related to the petitioner is or will be involved in carrying out, for a fee, any programming, ascertainment, employment or other non-financial initiative referred to in the citizens' agreement; and

(3) The terms of any oral agreement.

(c) For the purposes of this section:

(1) Affidavits filed pursuant to this section shall be executed by the applicant, permittee, or licensee, if an individual; a partner having personal knowledge of the facts, if a partnership; or an officer having personal knowledge of the facts, if a corporation or association.

(2) A petition shall be deemed to be pending before the Commission from the time a petition is filed with the Commission until an order of the Commission granting or denying the petition is no longer subject to reconsideration by the Commission or to review by any court.

(3) "Legitimate and prudent expenses" are those expenses reasonably incurred by a petitioner in preparing, filing, and prosecuting its petition for which reimbursement is being sought.

(4) "Other consideration" consists of financial concessions, including but not limited to the transfer of assets or the provision of tangible pecuniary benefit, as well as non-financial concessions that confer any type of benefit on the recipient.

§73.3589 Threats to file petitions to deny or informal objections.

(a) No person shall make or receive any payments in exchange for withdrawing a threat to file or refraining from filing a petition to deny or an informal objection. For purposes of this section, reimbursement by an applicant of the legitimate and prudent expenses of a potential petitioner or objector incurred reasonably and directly in preparing to file a petition to deny will not be considered to be payment for refraining from filing a petition to deny or informal objection. Payments made directly to a potential petitioner or objector, or a person related to a potential petitioner or objector, to implement non-financial promises are prohibited unless specifically approved by the Commission.

(b) Whenever any payment is made in exchange for withdrawing a threat to file or refraining from filing a petition to deny or informal objection, the licensee must file with the Commission a copy of any written agreement related to the dismissal or withdrawal, and an affidavit setting forth:

(1) Certification that neither the would-be petitioner, nor any person or organization related to the would-be petitioner, has received or will receive any money or other consideration in connection with the citizens' agreement other than legitimate and prudent expenses reasonably incurred in preparing to file the petition to deny;

(2) Certification that unless such arrangement has been specifically approved by the Commission, neither the would-be petitioner, nor any person or organization related to the would-be petitioner, is or will be involved in carrying out, for a fee, any programming ascertainment, employment or other non-financial initiative referred to in the citizens' agreement; and

(3) The terms of any oral agreement.

(c) For purposes of this section:

(1) Affidavits filed pursuant to this section shall be executed by the licensee, if an individual; a partner having personal knowledge of the facts, if a partnership; or an officer having personal knowledge of the facts, if a corporation or association.

(2) "Legitimate and prudent expenses" are those expenses reasonably incurred by a would-be petitioner in preparing to file its petition for which reimbursement is being sought.

(3) "Other consideration" consists of financial concessions, including but not limited to the transfer of assets or the provision of tangible pecuniary benefit, as well as non-financial concessions that confer any type of benefit on the recipient.

§73.3601 Simultaneous modification and renewal of license. When an application is granted by the FCC necessitating the issuance of a modified license less than 60 days prior to the expiration date of the license sought to be modified, and an application for renewal of the license is granted subsequent or prior thereto (but within 30 days of expiration of the present license), the modified license as well as the renewal license shall be issued to conform to the combined action of the FCC.

§73.1020 Station license period.

(a) Initial licenses for broadcast stations will ordinarily be issued for a period running until the date specified in this section for the state or territory in which the station is located. If issued after such date, it will run to the next renewal date determined in accordance with this section. Radio broadcasting stations will ordinarily be renewed for 7 years and TV broadcast stations will be renewed for 5 years. However, if the FCC finds that the public interest, convenience, and necessity will be served thereby, it may issue either an initial license or a renewal thereof for a lesser term. The time of expiration of normally issued initial and renewal licenses will be 3 a.m., local time, on the following dates and therafter at 7-year intervals for radio broadcast stations and at 5-year intervals for television broadcast stations located in:

(1) Maryland, District of Columbia, Virginia and West Virginia: (i) Radio stations, October 1, 1988; (ii) Television stations, October 1, 1991.

(2) North Carolina and South Carolina: (i) Radio stations, December 1, 1988; (ii) Television stations, December 1, 1991.

(3) Florida, Puerto Rico and Virgin Islands: (i) Radio stations, February 1, 1989; (ii) Television stations, February 1, 1992.

(4) Alabama and Georgia: (i) Radio stations, April 1, 1989; (ii) Television stations, April 1, 1992.

(5) Arkansas, Louisiana and Mississippi: (i) Radio stations, June 1, 1989; (ii) Television stations, June 1, 1992.

(6) Tennessee, Kentucky and Indiana: (i) Radio stations, August 1, 1989; (ii) Television stations, August 1, 1987.

(7) Ohio and Michigan: (i) Radio stations, October 1, 1989; (ii) Television stations, October 1, 1987.

(8) Illinois and Wisconsin: (i) Radio stations, December 1, 1989; (ii) Television stations, December 1, 1987.

(9) Iowa and Missouri: (i) Radio stations, February 1, 1990; (ii) Television stations, February 1, 1988.

(10) Minnesota, North Dakota, South Dakota, Montana and Colorado: (i) Radio stations, April 1, 1990; (ii) Television stations, April 1, 1988.

(11) Kansas, Oklahoma and Nebraska: (i) Radio stations, June 1, 1990; (ii) Television stations, June 1, 1988.

(12) Texas: (i) Radio stations, August 1, 1990; (ii) Television stations, August 1, 1988.

(13) Wyoming, Nevada, Arizona, Utah, New Mexico and Idaho: (i) Radio stations, October 1, 1990; (ii) Television stations, October 1, 1988.

(14) California: (i) Radio stations, December 1, 1990; (ii) Television stations, December 1, 1988.

(15) Alaska, American Samoa, Guam, Hawaii, Mariana Islands, Oregon and Washington: (i) Radio stations, February 1, 1991; (ii) Television stations, February 1, 1989.

(16) Connecticut, Maine, Massachusetts, New Hampshire, Rhode Island and Vermont: (i) Radio stations, April 1, 1991; (ii) Television stations, April 1, 1989.

(17) New Jersey and New York: (i) Radio stations, June 1, 1991; (ii) Television stations, June 1, 1989.

(18) Delaware and Pennsylvania: (i) Radio stations, August 1, 1991: (ii) Television stations, August 1, 1989.

(b) For the cutoff date for the filing of applications mutually exclusive with, and petitions to deny, renewal applications, see §73.3516(e).

Modification of Unbuilt Facilities

§73.3535 Application to modify authorized but unbuilt facilities, or to assign transfer control of an unbuilt facility.

(a) If a permittee finds it necessary to file either an application to modify its authorized, but unbuilt facilities, or an assignment/transfer application, such application shall be filed within the first nine months of the issuance of the original construction permit for radio and other broadcast and auxiliary stations, or within twelve months of the issuance of the original construction permit for television facilities. Before such application can be granted, the permittee or assignee must certify that it will immediately begin building after the modification is granted or the assignment is consummated.

(b) Modification and assignment applications filed after the time periods stated in paragraph (a) will not be granted absent a showing that one of the following three criteria applies: (1) construction is complete and testing is underway looking toward prompt filing of a license application; (2) substantial progress has been made i.e., demonstration that equipment is on order or on hand, site aquired, site cleared and construction proceeding toward completion; or (3) no progress has been made for reasons clearly beyond the control of the permittee (such as delays caused by governmental budgetary processes and zoning problems) but the permittee has taken all possible steps to expeditiously resolve the problem and proceed with construction. A certification by the permittee or the assignee that it immediately will begin building after the modification is granted or the assignment is consumated is also necessary. A seller must make the "one of three criteria" showing in an assignment application.

(c) If the modification is granted, the time period allowed for construction will be six months from the issuance of the authorization to modify or the remainder of the construction period, whichever is longer. Also, in the case of an assignment the time period allowed for construction will be twelve months from the consummation of the assignment or the remainder of the construction period, whichever is longer. The extension will be given subject to the condition that the modification is completed or the assignment consummated. Failure to modify or consummate within the time allowed will result in cancellation of the construction permit.

(d) We will not entertain an application for modification of an authorized but unbuilt facility or an application for assignment or transfer of control of an unbuilt facility if filed after the expiration of the initial construction period.

All broadcast stations ...

§73.1201 Station identification.

(a) When regularly required. Broadcast station identification announcements shall be made: (1) at the beginning and ending of each hour of operation, and (2) hourly, as close to the hour as feasible, at a natural break in program offerings. Television broadcast stations may make these announcements visually or aurally.

(b) Content. (1) Official station identification shall consist of the station's call letters immediately followed by the community or communities specified in its license as the station's location: provided, that the name of the licensee or the station's frequency or channel number, or both, as stated on the station's license may be inserted between the call letters and station location. No other insertion is permissible.

(2) A station may include in its official station identification the name of any additional community or communities, but the community to which the station is licensed must be named first.

(c) Channel. (1) Generally. Except as provided in this paragraph, in making the identification announcement the call letters shall be given only on the channel of the station identified thereby.

(2) Simultaneous AM (535-1605 kHz) and AM (1605-1705 kHz) broadcasts. If the same licensee operates an AM broadcast station in the 535-1605 kHz band and an AM broadcast station in the 1605-1705 kHz band with both stations licensed to the same community and simultaneously broadcasts the same programs over the facilities of both such stations, station identification announcements may be made jointly for both stations for periods of such simultaneous operation..

(3) Satellite operation. When programming of a broadcast station is rebroadcast simultaneously over the facilities of a satellite station, the originating station may make identification announcements for the satellite station for periods of such simultaneous operation.

(i) In the case of a television broadcast station, such announcements, in addition to the information required by paragraph (b) (1) of this section, shall include the number of the channel on which each station is operating.

(ii) In the case of aural broadcast stations, such announcements, in addition to the information required by paragraph (b) (1) of this section, shall include the frequency on which each station is operating.

(d) Subscription television stations (STV). The requirements for official station identification applicable to TV stations will apply to Subscription TV stations except, during STV-encoded programing such station identification is not required. However, a station identification announcement will be made immediately prior to and following the encoded-Subscription TV program period.

Announcement of Sponsored Programs

§73.1212 Sponsorship identification; list retention; related requirements.

(a) When a broadcast station transmits any matter for which money, service, or other valuable consideration is either directly or indirectly paid or promised to, or charged or accepted by such station, the station, at the time of the broadcast, shall announce:

(1) that such matter is sponsored, paid for, or furnished, either in whole or in part, and

(2) by whom or on whose behalf such consideration was supplied: provided, however, that "service or other valuable consideration" shall not include any service or property furnished either without or at a nominal charge for use on, or in connection with, a broadcast unless it is so furnished in consideration for an identification of any person, product, service, trademark, or brand name beyond an identification reasonably related to the use of such service or property on the broadcast.

(i) For the purposes of this section, the term "sponsored" shall be deemed to have the same meaning as "paid for."

(ii) In the case of any television political advertisement concerning candidates for public office, the sponsor shall be identified with letters equal to or greater than four (4) percent of the vertical picture height that air for not less than four (4) seconds.

(b) The licensee of each standard broadcast station shall exercise reasonable diligence to obtain from its employes, and from other persons with whom it deals directly in connection with any program matter for broadcast, information to enable such licensee to make the announcement required by this section.

(c) In any case where a report has been made to a broadcast station, as required by Section 507 of the Communications Act of 1934, as amended, of circumstances which would have required an announcement under this section had the consideration been received by such broadcast station, an appropriate announcement shall be made by such station.

(d) In the case of any political broadcast matter or any broadcast matter involving the discussion of a controversial issue of public importance for which any film, record, transcription, talent, script, or other material or service of any kind is furnished, either directly or indirectly, to a station as an inducement for broadcasting such matter, an announcement shall be made both at the beginning and conclusion of such broadcast on which such material or service is used that such film, record, transcription, talent, script, or other material or service has been furnished to such station in connection with the transmission of such broadcast matter: provided, however, that in the case of any broadcast of 5 minutes duration or less, only one such announcement need be made either at the beginning or conclusion of the broadcast.

(e) The announcement required by this section shall, in addition to stating the fact that the broadcast matter was sponsored, paid for or furnished, fully and fairly disclose the true identity of the person or persons or corporation, committee, association or other unincorporated group, or other entity by whom or on whose behalf such payment is made or promised, or from whom or on whose behalf such services or other valuable consideration is received, or by whom the material or services referred to in paragraph (d) of this section are furnished. Where an agent or other person or entity contracts or otherwise makes arrangements with a station on behalf of another, and such fact is known or by the exercise of reasonable diligence, as specified in paragraph (b) of this section, could be known to the station, the announcement shall disclose the identity of the person or persons or entity on whose behalf such agent is acting instead of the name of such agent. Where the material broadcast is political matter or matter involving the discussion of a controversial issue of public importance and a corporation, committee, association or other unincorporated group, or other entity is paying for or furnishing the broadcast matter, the station shall, in addition to making the announcement required by this section, require that a list of the chief executive officers or members of the executive committee as of the board of directors of the corporation, committee, association or other unincorporated group, or other entity, shall be made available for public inspection at the location specified by the licensee under §73.3526 of this chapter. If the broadcast is originated by a network, the list may, instead, be retained at the headquarters office of the network or at the location where the originating station maintains its public inspection file under §73.3526 of this chapter. Such lists shall be kept and made available for a period of two years.

(f) In the case of broadcast matter advertising commercial products or services, an announcement stating the sponsor's corporate or trade name, or the name of the sponsor's product, when it is clear that the mention of the name of the product constitutes a sponsorship identification, shall be deemed sufficient for the purposes of this section and only one such announcement need be made at any time during the course of the broadcast.

(g) The announcement otherwise required by Section 317(a) of the Communications Act of 1934, as amended, is waived with respect to the broadcast of "want ad" or classified advertisements sponsored by an individual. The waiver granted in this paragraph shall not extend to a classified advertisement or want ad sponsored by any form of business enterprise, corporate or otherwise. Whenever sponsorship announcements are omitted pursuant to this paragraph the licensee shall observe the following conditions:

(1) Maintain a list showing the name, address and (where available) the telephone number of each advertiser;

(2)[Reserved]

(3) Make this list available to members of the public who have a legitimate interest in obtaining the information contained in the list. Such list must be maintained for a period of two years after broadcast.

(h) Any announcement required by Section 317(b) of the Communciations Act of 1934, as amended, is waived with respect to feature motion picture film produced initially and primarily for theatre exhibition.

NOTE: The waiver heretofore granted by the commission in its report and order adopted November 16, 1960 (FCC 60-1369; 40 FCC 95), continues to apply to programs filmed or recorded on or before June 20, 1963, when §73.654, the predecessor television rule, went into effect.

(i) Commission interpretations in connection with the provisions of the sponsorship identification rules are contained in the commission's public notice, entitled "Applicability of Sponsorship Identification Rules," dated May 6, 1963 (40 FCC 141), as modified by public notice, dated April 21, 1975 (FCC 75-418). Further interpretations are printed in full in various volumes of the Federal Communciations Commission reports.

[EDITOR'S NOTE: In a statement issued in 1950, the FCC warned that the sponsor or his product must be identified by a distinctive name and not by one merely descriptive of the type of business or product. The following are acceptable, the Commission said: "Henry Smith offers you ...," or "Smith Stove Co. offers you ...," or "Ajax Pens brings you ..." The following are not acceptable: "Write to the Comb Man ...," or "Send your money to Nylons, Box ..." or "This program is sponsored by your Sink man ..."]

Public Notice

In AM, FM and TV ...

§73.1202. Retention of letters received from the public.

(a) All written comments and suggestions received from the public by licensees of commercial AM, FM and TV broadcast stations regarding operation of their station shall be maintained in the local public inspection file, unless the letter writer has requested that the letter not be made public or when the licensee feels that it should be excluded from public inspection because of the nature of its content, such as a defamatory or obscene letter.

(1) Letters shall be retained in the local public inspection file for three years from the date on which they are received by the licensee.

(2) Letters received by TV licensees only shall be placed in one of the following separated subject categories: programming or nonprogramming. If comments in a letter relate to both categories, the licensee shall file it under the category to which the writer has given the greater attention.

Rebroadcasts

§73.1207 Rebroadcasts. (a) The term "rebroadcast" means reception by radio of the programs or other transmissions of a broadcast or any other type of radio station, and the simultaneous or subsequent retransmission of such programs or transmissions by a broadcast station.

(1) As used in this section, "program" includes any complete program or part thereof.

(2) The transmission of a program from its point of origin to a broadcast station entirely by common carrier facilities, whether by wire line or radio, is not considered a rebroadcast.

(3) The broadcasting of a program relayed by a remote pickup broadcast station is not considered a rebroadcast.

(b) No broadcast station may retransmit the program, or any part thereof, of another U.S. broadcast station without the express authority of the originating station. A copy of the written consent of the licensee originating the program must be kept by the licensee of the station retransmitting such program and made available to the FCC upon request.

(1) Stations originating emergency communications under a Detailed State EBS Operation Plan are deemed to have conferred rebroadcast authority to other participating stations.

(2) Permission must be obtained from the originating station to rebroadcast any subsidiary communications transmitted by means of a multiplex subcarrier or the vertical blanking interval of a television signal.

(3) Programs originated by the Voice of America (VOA) and the Armed Forces Radio and Television Services (AFRTS) cannot, in general, be cleared for domestic rebroadcast, and may therefore be retransmitted only by special arrangements among the parties concerned.

(4) Except as otherwise provided by international agreement, programs originated by foreign broadcast stations may be retransmitted without the consent of the originating station.

(c) The transmission of messages of nonbroadcast stations may be rebroadcast under the following conditions:

(1) Messages originated by privately-owned nonbroadcast stations other than those in the Amateur and Citizens Band (CB) Radio Services may be broadcast only upon receipt of prior permission from the non-broadcast licensee. Additionally, messages transmitted by common carrier stations may be rebroadcast only upon prior permission of the originator of the message as well as the station licensee.

(2) Except as provided in paragraph (d) of this section, messages originated entirely by non-broadcast stations owned and operated by the Federal Government may be rebroadcast only upon receipt of prior permission from the government agency originating the messages.

(3) Messages orginated by stations in the Amateur and Citizens Band (CB) radio services may be rebroadcast at the discretion of broadcast station licensees.

(d) The rebroadcasting of time signals originated by the Naval Observatory and the National Bureau of Standards and messages from the National Weather Service stations is permitted without specific authorization under the following procedures:

(1) Naval Observatory Time Signals. (i) The time signals rebroadcast must be obtained by direct radio reception from a naval radio station, or by land line circuits. (ii) Announcement of the time signal must be made without reference to any commercial activity. (iii) Identification of the Naval Observatory as the source of the time signal must be made by an announcement, substantially as follows: "With the signal, the time will be ... courtesy of the U.S. Naval Observatory." (iv) Schedules of time signal broadcasts may be obtained upon request from the Superintendent, U.S. Naval Observatory, Washington, D.C. 20390.

(2) National Bureau of Standards Time Signals. (i) Time signals for rebroadcast must be obtained by direct radio reception from a National Bureau of Standards (NBS) station. (ii) Use of receiving and rebroadcasting equipment must not delay the signals by more than 0.05 second. (iii) Signals must be rebroadcast live, not from tape or other recording. (iv) Voice or code announcements of the call signs of NBS stations are not to be rebroadcast. (v) Identification of the origin of the service and the source of the signals must be made by an announcement substantially as follows: "At the tone, 11 hours 25 minutes Coordinated Universal Time. This is a rebroadcast of a continuous service furnished by the National Bureau of Standards, Ft. Collins, Colo." No commercial sponsorship of this announcement is permitted and none may be implied. (vi) Schedules of time signal broadcasts may be obtained from, and notice of use of NBS time signals for rebroadcast must be forwarded semiannually to: National Bureau of Standards,

WWV/WWVB, 2000 East County Road 58, Ft. Collins, Colo 80524. (vii) In the rebroadcasting of NBS time signals, announcements will not state that they are standard frequency transmissions. Voice announcements of Coordinated Universal Time are given in voice every minute. Each minute, except the first of the hour, begins with an 0.8 second long tone of 1000 hertz at WWV and 1200 hertz tone at WWVH. The first minute of every hour begins with an 0.8 second long tone of 1500 hertz at both stations. This tone is followed by a 3-second pause, then the announcement, "National Bureau of Standards Time." This is followed by another 3-second pause before station identification. This arrangement allows broadcast stations sufficient time to retransmit the hour time tone and the words "National Bureau of Standards Time" either by manual or automatic switching. (viii) Time signals or scales made up from integration of standard frequency signals broadcast from NBS stations may not be designated as national standard scales of time or attributed to the NBS as originator. For example, if a broadcasting station transmits time signals obtained from a studio clock which is periodically calibrated against the NBS time signals from WWV or WWVH, such signals may not be announced as NBS standard time or as having been originated by the NBS.

(3) National Weather Service Messages. (i) Messages of the National Weather Service must be rebroadcast within 1 hour of receipt. (ii) If advertisements are given in connection with weather rebroadcast, these advertisements must not directly or indirectly convey an endorsement by the U.S. Government of the products or services so advertised. (iii) Credit must be given to indicate that the rebroadcast message originates with the National Weather Service.

Recordings, Tapes and Films

§73.1206 Broadcast of telephone conversations. Before recording a telephone conversation for broadcast, or broadcasting such a conversation simultaneously with its occurrence, a licensee shall inform any party to the call of the licensee's intention to broadcast the conversation, except where such party is aware, or may be presumed to be aware from the circumstances of the conversation, that it is being or likely will be broadcast. Such awareness is presumed to exist only when the other party to the call is associated with the station (such as an employe or part-time reporter), or where the other party originates the call and it is obvious that it is in connection with a program in which the station customarily broadcasts telephone conversations.

73.1208 Broadcast of taped, filmed, or recorded material.

(a) Any taped, filmed or recorded program material in which time is of special significance, or by which an affirmative attempt is made to create the impression that it is occuring simultaneously with the broadcast, shall be announced at the beginning as taped, filmed or recorded. The language of the announcement shall be clear and in terms commonly understood by the public. For television stations, the announcement may be made visually or aurally.

(b) Taped, filmed or recorded announcements which are of a commercial, promotional or public service nature need not be identified as taped, filmed, or recorded.

Time

For AM, FM and TV ...

§73.1209 References to time. Unless specifically designated as "standard (non-advanced)" or "advanced," all references to time contained in this part, and in license documents and other authorizations issued thereunder, shall be understood to mean *local* time; i.e., the time legally observed in the community.

Children's Programs

In TV Rules ...

§73.670 Commercial limits in children's programs. No commercial television broadcast station licensee shall air more than 10.5 minutes of commercial matter per hour during children's programming on weekends, or more than 12 minutes of commercial matter per hour on weekdays.

NOTE 1: Commercial matter means air time sold for purposes of selling a product or service.

NOTE 2: For purposes of this section, children's programming refers to programs originally produced and broadcast primarily for an audience of children 12 years old and younger.

§73.671 Educational and informational programming for children.

(a) Each commercial television broadcast station licensee has an obligation to serve, over the term of its license, the educational and informational needs of children through the licensee's overall programming, including programming specifically designed to serve such needs.

(b) Any special nonbroadcast efforts which enhance the value of children's educational and informational television programming, and any special effort to produce or support educational and informational television programming by another station in the licensee's marketplace, may also contribute to meeting the licensee's obligation to serve, over the term of its license, the educational and informational needs of children.

NOTE: For purposes of this section, educational and informational television programming is any television programming which furthers the positive development of children 16 years of age and under in any respect, including the child's intellectual/cognitive or social/emotional needs.

§73.672 Educational and informational programming for children on noncommercial television.

(a) Each noncommercial television broadcast station licensee has an obligation to serve, over the term of its license, the educational and informational needs of children through the licensee's overall programming, including programming specifically designed to serve such needs.

(b) Any special nonbroadcast efforts which enhance the value of children's educational and informational television programming, and any special effort to produce or support educational and informational television programming by another station in the licensee's marketplace, may also contribute to meeting the licensee's obligation to serve, over the term of its license, the educational and informational needs of children.

NOTE: For purposes of this section, educational and informational television programming is any television programming which furthers the positive development of children 16 years of age and under in any respect, including the child's intellectual/cognitive or social/emotional needs.

Political Broadcasts

For AM, FM and TV ...

§73.1940 Broadcasts by candidates for public office.

(a) Definitions. (1) A legally qualified candidate for public office is any person who: (a) has publicly announced his or her intention to run for nomination or office; (b) is qualified under the applicable local, state or federal law to hold the office for which he or she is a candidate; and, (c) has met the qualifications set forth in either subparagraphs (2), (3), or (4), below.

(2) A person seeking election to any public office including that of President or Vice President of the United States, or nomination for any public office except that of President or Vice President, by means of a primary, general or special election, shall be considered a legally qualified candidate if, in addition to meeting the criteria set forth in subparagraph (1) above, that person: (a) has qualified for a place on the ballot, or (b) has publicly committed himself or herself to seeking election by the write-in method and is eligible under applicable law to be voted for by sticker, by writing in his or her name on the ballot or by other methods, and makes a substantial showing that he or she is a bona fide candidate for nomination or office.

Persons seeking election to the office of President or Vice President of the United States shall, for the purposes of the Communications Act and the rules thereunder, be considered legally qualified candidates only in those states or territories (or the District of Columbia) in which they have met the requirements set forth in paragraph (a)(1) and (2) of this rule: Except, that any such person who has met the requirements set forth in paragraph (a)(1) and (2) in at least 10 states (or nine and the District of Columbia) shall be considered a legally qualified candidate for election in all states, territories and the District of Columbia for purposes of this Act.

(3) A person seeking nomination to any public office, except that of President or Vice President of the United States, by means of a convention, caucus or similar procedure, shall be considered a legally qualified candidate if, in addition to meeting the requirements set forth in paragraph (a)(1) above, that person makes a substantial showing that he or she is a bona fide candidate for such nomination: Except, that no person shall be considered a legally qualified candidate for nomination by the means set forth in this paragraph prior to 90 days before the beginning of the convention, caucus or similar procedure in which he or she seeks nomination.

(4) A person seeking nomination for the office of President or Vice President of the United States shall, for the purposes of the Communications Act and the rules thereunder, be considered a legally qualified candidate only in those states or territories or the District of Columbia in which, in addition to meeting the requirements set forth in paragraph (a)(1) above, (a) he or she, or proposed delegates on his or her behalf, have qualified for the primary or Presidential preference ballot in that state, territory or the District of Columbia, or (b) he or she has made a substantial showing of bona fide candidacy for such nomination in that state, territory or the District of Columbia; Except, that any such person meeting the requirements set forth in paragraph (a)(1) and (4) in at least ten states (or nine and the District of Columbia) shall be considered a legally qualified candidate for nomination in all states, territories and the District of Columbia for purposes of this Act.

(5) The term "substantial showing" of bona fide candidacy as used in paragraphs (a)(2), (3) and (4) above means evidence that the person claiming to be a candidate has engaged to a substantial degree in activities commonly associated with political campaigning. Such activities normally would include making campaign speeches, distributing campaign literature, issuing press releases, maintaining a campaign committee, and establishing campaign headquarters (even though the headquarters in some instances might be the residence of the candidate or his campaign manager). Not all of the listed activities are necessarily required in each case to demonstrate a substantial showing, and there may be activities not listed herein which would contribute to such a showing.

(b) Charges for use of stations. The charges, if any, made for the use of any broadcasting station by any person who is a legally qualified candidate for any public office in connection with his campaign for nomination for election, or reelection, to such office shall not exceed (1) during the 45 days preceding the date of a primary or primary runoff election and during the 60 days preceding the date of a general or special election in which such person is a candidate, the lowest unit charge of the station for the same class and amount of time for the same period, and (2) at any other time, the charges made for comparable use of such station by other users thereof. The rates, if any, charged all such candidates for the same office shall be uniform and shall not be rebated by any means direct or indirect. A candidate shall be charged no more than the rate the station would charge if the candidate were a commercial advertiser whose advertising was directed to promoting its business within the same area as that encompassed by the particular office for which such person is a candidate. All discount privileges otherwise offered by a station to commercial advertisers shall be available upon equal terms to all candidates for public office. (3) This paragraph shall not apply to any station which is not licensed for commercial operation.

(c) Discrimination between candidates. In making time available to candidates for public office, no licensee shall make any discrimination between candidates in practices, regulations, facilities, or services for or in connection with the service rendered pursuant to this part, or make or give any preference to any candidate for public office or subject any such candidate to any prejudice or disadvantage; nor shall any licensee make any contract or other agreement which shall have the effect of permitting any legally qualified candidate for any public office to broadcast to the exclusion of other legally qualified candidates for the same public office.

(d) See §73.3526 and §73.3527.

(e) Time of request. A request for equal opportunities must be submitted to the licensee within one week of the day on which the first prior use, giving rise to the right of equal opportunities, occurred: provided, however, that where the person was not a candidate at the time of such first prior use, he shall submit his request within one week of the first subsequent use after he has become a legally qualified candidate for the office in question.

(f) Burden of proof. A candidate requesting equal opportunities of the licensee, or complaining of noncompliance to the Commission shall have the burden of proving that he and his opponent are legally qualified candidates for the same public office.

(g) General requirements. (1) Except as otherwise indicated in paragraph (g)(2) of this section, no station licensee is required to permit the use of its facilities by any legally qualified candidate for public office, but if any licensee shall permit any such candidate to use its facilities, it shall afford equal opportunities to all other candidates for that office to use such facilities. Such licensee shall have no power of censorship over the material broadcast by any such candidate. Appearance by a legally qualified candidate on any (i) bona fide newscast, (ii) bona fide news interview, (iii) bona fide news documentary (if the appearance of the candidate is incidental to the presentation of the subject covered by the news documentary), or (iv) on-the-spot coverage of bona fide news events (including, but not limited to political conventions and activities incidental thereto) shall not be deemed to be use of a broadcasting station. (Section 315(a) of the Communications Act.)

(2) Section 312(a)(7) of the Communications Act provides that the Commission may revoke any station license or construction permit for willful or repeated failure to allow reasonable access to, or to permit purchase of, reasonable amounts of time for the use of a broadcasting station by a legally qualified candidate for federal elective office on behalf of his candidacy.

(h) Political broadcasting primer. A detailed study of these rules regarding broadcasts by candidates for federal and non-federal public office is available in the FCC public notice of July 20, 1978, "The Law of Political Broadcasting and Cablecasting". Copies may be obtained from the FCC upon request.

Candor; Truthful Responses to FCC

§73.1015 Truthful written statements and responses to Commission inquiries and correspondence. The Commission or its representatives may, in writing, require from any applicant, permittee or licensee written statements of fact relevant to a determination whether an application should be granted or denied, or to a determination whether a license should be revoked, or to some other matter within the jurisdiction of the Commission, or, in the case of a proceeding to amend the FM or Television Table of Allotments, require from any person filing an expression of interest, written statements of fact relevant to that allotment proceeding. No applicant, permittee or licensee, or person who files an expression of interest shall in any response to Commission correspondence or inquiry or in any application, pleading, report or any other written statement submitted to the Commission, make any misrepresentation or willful material omission bearing on any matter within the jurisdiction of the Commission.

NOTE: Section 73.1015 is limited in application to written matter. It implies no change in the Commission's existing policies respecting the obligation of applicants, permittees and licensees in all instances to respond truthfully to requests for information deemed necessary to the proper execution of the Commission's functions.

Revocations, Modifications, Suspensions

All Classes of Station Licenses ...

§1.87 Modification of license or construction permit on motion of the Commission.

(a) Whenever it appears that a station license or construction permit should be modified, the Commission will notify the licensee or permittee in writing of the proposed action and reasons therefore and afford the licensee or permittee at least thirty days to protest such order of modification, except that, where safety of life or property is involved, the Commission may by order provide a shorter period of time.

(b) The notification required in paragraph (a) of this section may be effectuated by a notice of proposed rulemaking in regard to a modification or addition of an FM or television channel to the Table of Allotments (§§73.202 and 73.504) or Table of Assignments (§73.606). The Commission shall send a copy of any such notice of proposed rulemaking to the affected licensee or permittee by certified mail, return receipt requested.

(c) Any other licensee or permittee who believes that its license or permit would be modified by the proposed action may also protest the proposed action before its effective date.

(d) Any protest filed pursuant to this section shall be subject to the requirements of Section 309 of the Communications Act of 1934, as amended, for petitions to deny.

(e) In any case where a hearing is conducted pursuant to the provisions of this section, both the burden of proceeding with the introduction of evidence and the burden of proof shall be upon the Commission except that, with respect to any issue that pertains to the question of whether the proposed action would modify the license or permit of a person filing a protest pursuant to paragraph (c) of this section, such burdens shall be as prescribed by the Commission.

(f) In order to utilize the right to a hearing and the opportunity to appear and give evidence upon the issues specified in any hearing order, the licensee or permittee, in person or by his attorney, shall, within the period of time as may be specified in the hearing order, file with the Commission a written statement stating that he or she will appear at the hearing and present evidence on the matters specified in the hearing order.

(g) The right to file a protest or have a hearing shall, unless good cause is shown in a petition to be filed not later than five days before the lapse of time specified in paragraphs (a) or (f) of this section, be deemed waived:

(1) In case of failure to timely file the protest as required by paragraph (a) of this section or a written statement as required by paragraph (f) of this section.

(2) In case of filing a written statement provided for in paragraph (f) of this section but failing to appear at the hearing, either in person or by counsel.

(h) Where the right to file a protest or have a hearing is waived, the licensee or permittee will be deemed to have consented to the modification as proposed and a final decision may be issued by the Commission accordingly. Irrespective of any waiver as provided for in paragraph (g) of this section or failure by the licensee or permittee to raise a substantial and material question of fact concerning the proposed modification in his protest, the Commission may, on its own motion, designate the proposed modification for hearing in accordance with this section.

(i) Any order of modification issued pursuant to this section shall include a statement of the findings and grounds and reasons therefore, shall specify the effective date of the modification, and shall be served on the licensee or permittee.

§1.89 Notice of violations.

(a) Except in cases of willfulness or those in which public health, interest, or safety requires otherwise, any person who holds a license, permit or other authorization appearing to have violated any provision of the Communications Act or any provision of this chapter will, before revocation, suspension, or cease and desist proceedings are instituted, be served with a written notice calling these facts to his or her attention and requesting a statement concerning the matter. FCC Form 793 may be used for this purpose. The Notice of Violation may be combined with a Notice of Apparent Liability to Monetary Forfeiture. In such event, notwithstanding the Notice of Violation, the provisions of §1.80 apply and not those of §1.89.

(b) Within 10 days from receipt of notice or such other period as may be specified, the recipient shall send a written answer, in duplicate, directly to the Commission office originating the official notice. If an answer cannot be sent or an acknowledgment cannot be made within such 10-day period by reason of illness or other unavoidable circumstance, acknowledgment and answer shall be made at the earliest practicable date with a satisfactory explanation of the delay.

(c) The answer to each notice shall be complete in itself and shall not be abbreviated by reference to other communications or answers to other notices. In every instance the answer shall contain a statement of action taken to correct the condition or omission complained of and to preclude its recurrence. In addition:

(1) If the notice related to violations that may be due to the physical or electrical characteristics of transmitting apparatus and any new apparatus is to be installed, the answer shall state the date such apparatus was ordered, the name of the manufacturer, and the promised date of delivery. If the installation of such apparatus requires a construction permit, the file number of the application shall be given, or if a file number has not been assigned by the Commission, such identification shall be given as will permit ready identification of the application.

(2) If the notice of violation relates to lack of attention to or improper operation of the transmitter, the name and license number of the operator in charge (where applicable) shall be given.

§1.91 Revocation and/or cease and desist proceedings: hearings.

(a) If it appears that a station license or construction permit should be revoked and/or that a cease and desist order should be issued, the Commission will issue an order directing the person to show cause why an order of revocation and/or a cease and desist order, as the facts may warrant, should not be issued.

(b) An order to show cause why an order of revocation and/or a cease and desist order should not be issued will contain a statement of the matters with respect to which the Commission is inquiring and will call upon the person to whom it is directed (the respondent) to appear before the Commission at a hearing, at a time and place stated in the order, but not less than thirty days after the receipt of such order, and give evidence upon the matters specified in the order to show cause. However, if safety of life or property is involved, the order to show cause may specify a hearing date less than thirty days from the receipt of such order.

(c) To avail himself of such opportunity for hearing, the respondent, personally or by his attorney, shall file with the Commission, within thirty days of the service of the order or such shorter period as may be specified therein, a written appearance stating that he will appear at the hearing and present evidence on the matters specified in the order. The Commission in its discretion may accept a late appearance. However, an appearance tendered after the specific time has expired will not be accepted unless accompanied by a petition stating with particularity the facts and reasons relied on to justify such late filing. Such petition for acceptance of late appearance will be granted only if the Commission determines that the facts and reasons stated therein constitute good cause for failure to file on time.

(d) Hearings on the matters specified in such orders to show cause shall accord with the practice and procedure prescribed in this subpart and Subpart B of this part, with the following exception: (1) In all such revocation and/or cease and desist hearings, the burden of proceeding with the introduction of evidence and the burden of proof shall be upon the Commission; and (2) the Commission may specify in a show cause order, when the circumstances of the proceeding require expedition, a time less than that prescribed in §1.276 and §1.277 within which the initial decision in the proceeding shall become effective, exceptions to such initial decision must be filed, parties must file request for oral argument, and parties must file notice of intention to participate in oral argument.

(e) Correction or promise to correct the conditions or matters complained of in a show cause order shall not preclude the issuance of a cease and desist order. Corrections or promises to correct the conditions or matters complained of, and the past record of the licensee, may, however, be considered in determining whether a revocation and/or cease and desist order should be issued.

(f) Any order of revocation and/or cease and desist order issued after hearing pursuant to this section shall include a statement of findings and the grounds therefore, shall specify the effective date of the order, and shall be served on the person to whom such order is directed.

§1.92 Revocation and/or cease and desist proceedings: after waiver of hearing.

(a) After the issuance of an order to show cause, pursuant to §1.91, calling upon a person to appear at a hearing before the Commission, the occurrence of any one of the following events or circumstances will constitute a waiver of such hearing and the proceeding thereafter will be conducted in accordance with the provisions of this section.

(1) The respondent fails to file a timely written appearance as prescribed in §1.91(c) indicating that he will appear at a hearing and present evidence on the matters specified in the order.

(2) The respondent, having filed a timely written appearance as prescribed in §191(c), fails in fact to appear in person or by his attorney at the time and place of the duly scheduled hearing.

(3) The respondent files with the Commission, within the time specified for a written appearance in §191(c), a written statement expressly waiving his rights to a hearing.

(b) When a hearing is waived under the provisions of paragraph (a)(1) or (3) of this section, a written statement signed by the respondent denying or seeking to mitigate or justify the circumstances or conduct complained of in the order to show cause may be submitted within the time specified in §1.91(c). The Commission in its discretion may accept a late statement. However, a statement tendered after the specified time has expired will not be accepted unless accompanied by a petition stating with particularity the facts and reasons relied on to justify such late filing. Such petitions for acceptance of a late statement will be granted only if the Commission determines that the facts and reasons stated therein constitute good cause for failure to file on time.

(c) Whenever a hearing is waived by the occurrence of any of the events or circumstances listed in paragraph (a) of this section, the Chief Hearing Examiner (or the presiding officer if one has been designated) shall, at the earliest practicable date, issue an order reciting the events or circumstances constituting a waiver of hearing, terminating the hearing proceeding, and certifying the case to the Commission. Such order shall be served upon the respondent.

(d) After a hearing has been terminated pursuant to paragraph (c) of this section, the Commission will act upon the matters specified in the order to show cause in the regular course of business. The Commission will determine on the basis of all the information available to it from any source, including such further proceedings as may be warranted, if a revocation order and/or a cease and desist order should issue, and if so, will issue such order. Otherwise, the Commission will issue an order dismissing the proceeding. All orders specified in this paragraph will include a statement of the findings of the Commission and the grounds and reasons therefore, will specify the effective date thereof, and will be served upon the respondent.

(e) Corrections or promise to correct the conditions or matters complained of in a show cause order shall not preclude the issuance of a cease and desist order. Corrections or promises to correct the conditions or matters complained of, and the past record of the licensee, may, however, be considered in determining whether a revocation and/or cease and desist order should be issued.

Suspension of Operator Licenses

§1.85 Suspension of operator licenses. Whenever grounds exist for suspension of an operator license, as provided in Section 303(m) of the Communications Act, the Chief of the Safety and Special Radio Services Bureau, with respect to amateur operator licenses, or the Chief of the Field Engineering and Monitoring Bureau, with respect to commercial operator licenses, may issue an order suspending the operator license. No order of suspension in any operators' license shall take effect until 15 days' notice in writing of the cause for the proposed suspension has been given to the operator licensee, who may make written application to the Commission at any time within said 15 days for a hearing upon such order. The notice to the operator licensee shall not be effective until actually received by him, and from that time he shall have 15 days in which to mail the said application. In the event that physical conditions prevent mailing of the application before the expiration of the 15-day period, the application shall then be mailed as soon as possible thereafter, accompanied by a satisfactory explanation of the delay. Upon receipt by the Commission of such application for hearing, said order of suspension shall be designated for hearing by the Chief, Safety and Special Radio Services Radio Bureau or the Chief, Field Engineering Bureau, as the case may be, and said order of suspension shall be held in abeyance until the conclusion of the hearing. Upon the conclusion of said hearing, the Commission may affirm, modify or revoke said order of suspension. If the license is ordered suspended, the operator shall send his operator license to the office of the Commission in Washington, D.C., on or before the effective date of the order, or, if the effective date has passed at the time notice is received, the license shall be sent to the Commission forthwith.

Logs and Records

§1.6 Availability of station logs and records for Commission inspection.

(a) Station records and logs shall be made available for inspection or duplication at the request of the Commission or its representative. Such logs or records may be removed from the licensee's possession by a Commission representative or, upon request, shall be mailed by the licensee to the Commission by either registered mail, return receipt requested, or certified mail, return receipt requested. The return receipt shall be retained by the licensee as part of the station records until such records or logs are returned to the licensee. A receipt shall be furnished when the logs or records are removed from the licensee's possession by a Commission representative and this receipt shall be retained by the licensee as part of the station records until such records or logs are returned to the licensee. When the Commission has no further need for such records or logs, they shall be returned to the licensee. The provisions of this rule shall apply solely to those station logs and records which are required to be maintained by the provisions of this chapter.

(b) Where records or logs are maintained as the official records of a recognized law enforcement agency and the removal of the records from the possession of that law enforcement agency will hinder its law enforcement activities, such records will not be removed pursuant to this section if the Chief of the law enforcement agency shall promptly certify in writing to the Federal Communications Commission that the removal of the logs or records will hinder law enforcement activities of the agency, and stating insofar as feasible the basis for his decision and the date when it can reasonably be expected that such records may be released to the Federal Communications Commission.

Lotteries

§73.1211 Broadcast of lottery information.

(a) No licensee of an AM, FM or television broadcast station, except as in paragraph (c) of this section, shall broadcast any advertisement of or information concerning any lottery, gift enterprise, or similar scheme, offering prizes dependent in whole or in part upon lot or chance, or any list of the prizes drawn or awarded by means of any such lottery, gift enterprise or scheme, whether said list contains any part or all of such prizes. (18 USC §1304, 62 Stat 763).

(b) The determination whether a particular program comes within the provisions of paragraph (a) of this section depends on the facts of each case. However, the Commission will in any event consider that a program comes within the provisions of paragraph (a) of this section to any person whose selection is dependent in whole or in part upon lot or chance, if as a condition of winning or competing for such prize, such winner or winners, are required to furnish any money, or thing of value or are required to have in their possession any product sold, manufactured, furnished or distributed by a sponsor of a program broadcast on the station in question.

(c) The provisions of paragraphs (a) and (b) of this section shall not apply to an advertisement, list of prizes or other information concerning:

(1) A lottery conducted by a State acting under authority of State law which is broadcast by a radio or television station licensed to a location in that State or any other State which conducts such a lottery. (18 USC §1307; 88 Stat 1916).

(2) Fishing contests exempted under 18 USC §1305 (not conducted for profit, i.e., all receipts fully consumed in defraying the actual costs of operation).

(3) Any gaming conducted by an Indian Tribe pursuant to the Indian Gaming Regulatory Act (25 USC §2701 et seq.).

(4) A lottery, gift enterprise or similar scheme, other than one described in paragraph (c)(1) of this section, that is authorized or not otherwise prohibited by the State in which it is conducted and which is:

(i) conducted by a not-for-profit organization or a governmental organization (18 USC §1307; 102 Stat 3205); or

(ii) conducted as a promotional activity by a commercial organization and is clearly occasional and is ancillary to the primary business of that organization. (18 USC §1307(a); 102 Stat 3205.)

(d) For the purposes of paragraph (c) of this section, "Lottery" means the pooling of proceeds derived from the sale of tickets or chances and allotting those proceeds or parts thereof by chance to one or more chance takers or ticket purchasers. It does not include the placing or accepting of bets or wagers on sporting events or contests.

(2) For purposes of paragraph (c)(4)(i) of this section, the term "not-for-profit organization" means any organization that would qualify as tax exempt under Section 502 of the Internal Revenue Code of 1986.

§1304 (Of U.S. Criminal Code) Broadcasting Lottery Information.—Whoever broadcasts by means of any radio station for which a license is required by any law of the U.S. or whoever, operating any such station, knowingly permits the broadcasting of any advertisement or information concerning any lottery, gift enterprise, or similar scheme, offering prizes dependent in whole or in part upon lot or chance, or any list of the prizes drawn or awarded by means of any such lottery, gift enterprise, or scheme, whether said list contains any part or all of such prizes, shall be fined not more than $1,000 or imprisoned not more than one year, or both.

Each day's broadcasting shall constitute a separate offense.

Hoaxes

§73.1217 Broadcast hoaxes. No licensee or permittee of any broadcast station shall broadcast false information concerning a crime or catastrophe if (a) the licensee knows this information is false, (b) it is foreseeable that broadcast of the information will cause substantial public harm, and (c) broadcast of the information does in fact directly cause substantial public harm. Any programming accompanied by a disclaimer will be presumed not to pose foreseeable harm if the disclaimer clearly characterizes the program as a fiction and is presented in a way that is reasonable under the circumstances.

NOTE 1: For purposes of this rule, "public harm" must begin immediately, and cause direct and actual damage to property or to the health or safety of the general public, or diversion of law enforcement or other public health and safety authorities from their duties. The public harm will be deemed foreseeable if the licensee could expect with a significant degree of certainty that public harm would occur. A "crime" is any act or omission that makes the offender subject to criminal punishment by law. A "catastrophe" is a disaster or imminent disaster involving violent or sudden events affecting the public.

Tender Offers and Proxy Statements

§73.4266 Tender offers and proxy statements. See Policy Statement, MM Docket No. 85-218, FCC 86-67 [59 RR 2d 1536], adopted January 30, 1986. 51 FR 9794, March 21, 1986.

Censorship

§326 (of Communications Act) Nothing in this Act shall be understood to give the Commission the power of censorship over the radio communications or signals transmitted Commission which shall interfere with the right of free speech by means of radio communications.

§73.3999 Enforcement of 18 USC §1464 (Restrictions on the transmission of obscene and indecent language).

(a) No licensee of a radio or television broadcast station shall broadcast any material which is obscene.

(b) No licensee of a public broadcast station, as defined in 47 USC §397(6), that goes off the air at or before 12 midnight shall broadcast on any day between 6 a.m. and 10 p.m. any material which is indecent.

(c) No licensee of a radio or television broadcast station not described in paragraph (b) of this section shall broadcast on any day between 6 a.m. and 12 midnight any material which is indecent.

Forfeitures

§503 (of Communications Act) (a) Any person who shall deliver messages for interstate or foreign transmission to any carrier, or for whom as sender or receiver, any such carrier shall transmit any interstate or foreign wire or radio communication, who shall knowingly by employee, agent, officer, or otherwise, directly or indirectly, by or through any means or device whatsoever, receive or accept from such common carrier any sum of money or any other valuable consideration as a rebate or offset against the regular charges for transmission of such messages as fixed by the schedules of charges provided for in this Act, shall in addition to any other penalty provided by this Act forfeit to the Unites States a sum of money three times the amount of money so received or accepted and three times the value of any other consideration so receieved or accepted, to be ascertained by the trial court; and in the trial of said action all such rebates or other considerations so received or accepted for a period of six years prior to the commencement of the action, may be included therein, and the amount recovered shall be three times the total amount of money, or three times the total value of such consideration, so received or accepted, or both, as the case may be.

(b) (1) Any person who is determined by the Commission, in accordance with paragraph (3) or (4) of this subsection, to have

(A) willfully or repeatedly failed to comply substantially with the terms and conditions of any license, permit, certificate, or other instrument or authorization issued by the Commission;

(B) willfully or repeatedly failed to comply with any of the provisions of this Act or of any rule, regulation, or order issued by the Commission under this Act or under any treaty convention, or other agreement to which the United States is a party and which is binding upon the United States;

(C) violated any provision of Section 317(c) or 509(a) of this Act; or

(D) violated any provision of Sections 1304, 1343, or 1464 of Title 18, United States Code;

(1) shall be liable to the United States for a forfeiture penalty. A forfeiture penalty under this subsection shall be in addition to any other penalty provided for by this Act; except that this subsection shall not apply to any conduct which is subject to forfeiture under Title II, Part II or III of Title III, or Section 507 of this Act.

(2) The amount of any forfeiture penalty determined under this subsection shall not exceed $2,000 for each violation. Each day of a continuing violation shall constitute a separate offense, but the total forfeiture penalty which may be imposed under this subsection, for acts or ommissions described in paragraph (1) of this subsection and set forth in the notice or the notice of apparent liability issued under this subsection, shall not exceed

(A)$20,000, if the violator is (i) a common carrier subject to the provisions of this Act, (ii) a broadcast station licensee or permittee, or (iii) a cable television operator; or

(B)$5,000, in any case not covered by subparagraph. (A) The amount of such forfeiture penalty shall be assessed by the Commission, or its designee, by written notice. In determining the amount of such a forfeiture penalty, the Commission or its designee shall take into account the nature, circumstances, extent, and gravity of the prohibited acts committed and, with respect to the violator, the degree of culpability, any history of prior offenses, ability to pay, and such other matters as justice may require.

(3)(A) At the discretion of the Commission, a forfeiture penalty may be determined against a person under this subsection after notice and an opportunity for a hearing before the Commission or an administrative law judge thereof in accordance with Section 554 of Title 5, United States Code. Any person against whom a forfeiture penalty is determined under this paragraph may obtain review thereof pursuant to Section 402(a).

(B) If any person fails to pay an assessment of a forfeiture penalty determined under subparagraph (A) of this paragraph, after it has become, a final and unappealable order or after the appropriate court has entered final judgment in favor of the Commission, the Commission shall refer the matter to the Attorney General of the United States, who shall recover the amount assessed in any appropriate district court of the United States. In such action, the validity and appropriateness of the final order imposing the forfeiture penalty shall not be subject to review.

(4) Except as provided in paragraph (3) of this subsection, no forfeiture penalty shall be imposed under this subsection against any person unless and until—

(A) the Commission issues a notice of apparent liability, in writing, with respect to such person;

(B) such notice has been received by such person, or until the Commission has sent such notice to the last known address of such person, by registered or certified mail; and

(C) such person is granted an opportunity to show, in writing, within such reasonable period of time as the Commission prescribes by rule or regulation, why no such forfeiture penalty should be imposed. Such a notice shall (1) identify each specific provision, term, and condition of any Act, rule, regulation, order, treaty, convention, or other agreement, license, permit, certificate, instrument, or authorization which such person apparently violated or with which such person apparently failed to comply; (ii) set forth the nature of the act or omission charged against such person and the facts upon which such charge is based; and (iii) state the date on which such conduct occurred. Any forfeiture penalty determined under this paragraph shall be recoverable pursuant to Section 504(a) of this Act.

(5) No forfeiture liability shall be determined under this subsection against any person, if such person does not hold a license, permit, certificate, or other authorization issued by the Commission, unless, prior to the notice required by paragraph (3) of this subsection or the notice of apparent liability required by paragraph (4) of this subsection, such person (A) is sent a citation of the violation charged; (B) is given a reasonable opportunity for a personal interview with an official of the Commission, at the field office of the Commission which is nearest to such person's place of residence; and (C) subsequently engages in conduct of the type described in such citation. The provisions of this paragraph shall not apply, however, if the person involved is engaging in activities for which a license, permit, certificate, or other authorization is required, or is a cable television system operator, or if the person involved is transmitting on frequencies assigned for use in a service in which individual station operation is authorized by rule pursuant to Section 307(e). Whenever the requirements of this paragraph are satisfied with respect to a particular person, such person shall not be entitled to receive any additional citation of the violation charged, with respect to any conduct of the type described in the citation sent under this paragraph.

(6) No forfeiture penalty shall be determined or imposed against any person under this subsection if—

(A) such person holds a broadcast station license issued under Title III of this Act and if the violation charged occured more than one year prior to the date of issuance of the required notice or notice of apparent liability, or prior to the date of commencement of the current term of such license, whichever is earlier so long as such violation occurred within three years prior to the date of issuance of such required notice; or

(B) such person does not hold a broadcast station license issued under Title III of this Act and if the violation charged occured more than one year prior to the date of issuance of the required notice or notice of apparent liability.

[EDITOR's NOTE: Section 504 provides for recovery of forfeitures by the government in federal district courts, and for remission or mitigation of forfeitures.]

Station Application Procedure

Any qualified citizen, company, or group may apply to the Federal Communications Commission for authority to construct a standard (AM), frequency modulation (FM), or television (TV) broadcast station.

Licensing of these facilities is prescribed by the Communications Act of 1934, as amended, which sets up certain basic requirements. In general, applicants must satisfy the Commission that they are legally, technically and financially qualified, and that operation of the proposed station would be in the public interest.

Full details of the licensing procedure and station operation are in Part 1 of the Commission's rules, "Practice and Procedure" and Part 73 "Radio Broadcast Services." This includes technical standards for AM, FM and TV stations, and TV and FM channel (frequency) assignments by states and communities. Copies of the complete rules may be purchased from the Superintendent of Documents, Government Printing Office, Washington 20402. (202) 783-3238.

Most applicants retain engineering and legal services in preparing their applications. The Commission does not perform technical or other special studies for prospective applicants nor does it recommend individual lawyers or engineers. Names of firms and individuals practicing before the Commission are listed in various trade publications.

The following is a summary of the consecutive steps to be followed in applying for authorization to build and operate a broadcast station. The application procedure is substantially the same whether the facility sought is AM, FM or TV.

Selecting a Facility

An applicant must make his own search for a frequency on which he can operate without causing or receiving interference from existing stations and stations proposed in pending applications. AM broadcast stations operate on "local," "regional," or "clear" channels. Stations of 250 watts power nighttime and up to 1 kilowatt daytime serve small communities; stations of 500 watts to 5 kilowatts cover population centers and surrounding areas; stations of 10 to 50 kilowatts are for large area coverage, particularly at night.

An FM station applicant must request an FM channel assigned to the community in which he proposes to operate. Power, antenna height and station separation are governed by the zone in which the station is located.

The Commission authorizes three classes of commercial FM stations and three zones. Class A stations use power from 100 watts to 3 kilowatts to cover a radius of about 15 miles; Class B stations, 5 kilowatts to 50 kilowatts for 40-mile service and Class C, 25 kilowatts to 100 kilowatts for 65-mile range.

Noncommercial educational FM stations are in a separate category and may operate with power as low as 100 watts. FM stations as well as AM stations may engage in stereophonic broadcasting, for which no special application is required.

An applicant for a TV station must request a VHF (Very High Frequency) or a UHF (Ultra High Frequency) channel assignment to the community in which he proposes to operate, or a place having no channel assignment within 15 miles of that community. Power depends upon the kind of channel used (VHF or UHF) and station separation is determined by three zones. TV "translator" stations serve remote communities by picking up and rebroadcasting the programs of outside stations, with the latter's permission. "Low power" TV stations may originate programing and/or operate subscription service. They operate on any VHF channel or on any unassigned UHF channel, provided they do not cause objectionable interference to full service stations. Low power channels are to be allocated on a demand basis. There is a "Community Antenna Relay Service" for non-common carrier microwave facilities to relay TV signals to cable TV systems.

Applying for a Construction Permit

FCC Form 301, "Application for Authority to Construct a New Broadcast Station or Make Changes in an Existing Station" is utilized when applying for a construction permit. This form covers AM, FM, or TV broadcast, with the exception educational applicants (who use FCC Form 340), FM and TV translators (Form 346) and FM booster stations (Form 349P). These forms require information about the citizenship and character of the applicant, as well as financial, technical and other qualifications, plus details about the transmitting apparatus to be used, antenna and studio locations, and the service proposed. Triplicate copies are required. Nonprofit educational institutions apply for new or changed instructional TV fixed stations on Form 330-P.

Applicants Must Give Local Notice

Applicants for new broadcast stations, license renewals, station sales or major changes in existing stations must give local public notice of their plans and also of any subsequent designation of their applications for hearing. This is done over the applicant's local station (if any) and by advertising in the local newspaper. It affords an opportunity for public comment on these applications to the Commission. Applicants and stations also must maintain public reference files in their respective localities.

Applicants for new broadcast stations and major changes in existing facilities must be placed on a cut-off list. The cut-off procedure entails issuance of a public notice announcing that an application has been accepted for filing and establishing a date by which competing applications and petitions to deny may be filed. The cut-off is usually about 30 days from the release date of the notice. Prior to the cut-off date, an application cannot be processed.

Applications generally are processed in the order in which accepted. They are reviewed for engineering, legal and financial data by the Mass Media Bureau which, under delegated authority, acts on routine applications and reports to the Commission those involving policy or other particular considerations. If an application has no engineering or other conflicts and no valid protests have been received, the applicant is found qualified. Assuming all other requirements are met, the application may be granted without hearing and a construction permit issued. All such grants are announced by the Commission. Petitions for reconsideration of grants made without hearing can be filed within 30 days but must show good cause why the objections were not raised before the grant.

Hearing Procedure

In instances where it appears that an application does not conform to the Commission's rules and regulations or that serious interference would be caused, if there is protest of merit, or if there are other serious questions of a technical, legal or financial character, a hearing is usually required. The FCC must accord a hearing to competing applications filed within specified time limits.

In designating an application for hearing, the Commission gives public notice of the issues for the information of the applicant and others concerned. The hearing notice generally allows the applicant 60 days or more in which to prepare. Even after the hearing has been set, an applicant may amend his application to resolve engineering or other problems, if he or she so requests. (Commission approval is required for all mergers or situations in which a competing applicant withdraws on payment of expenses.) Hearings customarily are conducted by an Administrative Law Judge (ALJ).

Within 20 days after the close of a record by the ALJ, each party and the Chief of the FCC Broadcast Bureau can file proposed findings of fact and conclusions to support their contentions. After review of the evidence and statements, the ALJ issues an initial decision.

An applicant or any other party in interest wishing to contest the initial decision has 30 days from the date on which the initial decision was issued to file exceptions. In all cases heard by an ALJ, the Commission or its Review Board may hear oral argument and may adopt, modify or reverse the ALJ's initial decision. In cases where the Review Board has acted on the exceptions, an appeal from its decision may be taken to the FCC within 30 days. However the Commission may deny an appeal for review without stating its reasons. Court appeals may be filed within 30 days following release of the final decision, in which case the Commission's action is stayed pending court decision.

Construction Permit

When an application is granted a construction permit is issued. The new permittee may then request call letters that, if they are available and conform to the rules, are issued. A period of 60 days from date of the construction permit is provided in which construction shall begin, and a maximum of ten months (AM, FM, FM and TV translators and ITFS) thereafter for completion (or twelve months in all) and a maximum of 16 months (commercial and educational television [UHF-VHF]) thereafter for completion (or 18 months in all). If the permittee is unable to build his station within the time specified, he must apply for extension of time on Form 701 ("Application for Additional Time to Construct a Radio Station"), giving

Federal Communications Commission Rules and Regulations

reasons. Upon completion of construction, the permittee conducts equipment tests and in the case of a nondirectional station, the permittee may begin program tests prior to filing a license application. However, a license application must be filed within 10 days of commencement of program tests.

Licenses

The final step is to apply for the actual license on Form 302 ("Application for New Broadcast Station License"), or one of the following: Form 330-L (Instructional TV Fixed stations), Form 341 (Noncommercial Educational FM stations), Form 347 (TV and FM translators), or Form 349L (FM boosters). Applicants must show compliance with all terms, conditions and obligations in the original applications and the construction permit.

Not until he applies for a license can the holder of a construction permit for a directional station request authority to conduct program tests. The license application form provides a space for program tests requests, or it can be made separately. A station license and program test authority are issued if no new cause or circumstance has come to the attention of the Commission that would make operation of the station contrary to public interest.

Renewals

An applicant for renewal of a station license must show that he has operated according to the terms of his authorization and the promises made in obtaining it. Most renewal applications are made on Form 303 ("Application for Renewal of Broadcast Station License"). However, Instructional TV Fixed stations use Form 330-R; noncommercial educational licensees use Form 341; TV and FM translators Form 348 and FM boosters Form 349R.

Pending the disposition of any Commission hearing or other proceeding involving license renewal or revocation considerations, the station continues to operate even though its license term may have expired.

Sales and Transfers

If the holder of a construction permit or license desires to assign it to someone else, he makes application on Form 314 ("Application for Consent to Assignment of Radio Broadcast Station Construction Permit or License"). Should the permittee or licensee wish to transfer corporate control, he applies on Form 315 ("Application for Consent to Transfer Control of Corporation Holding Radio Broadcast Station Construction Permit or License"). Form 316 ("Application for Assignment or Transfer Short Form") may be used when the transfer or assignment involves no substantial change in interest. Sales of stations held less than three years are subject to hearing except in case of death, hardship or other mitigating circumstances beyond the licensee's control.

Construction Changes

Applicants for authority to make construction changes in existing stations apply on the same form used for a construction permit for the type of station involved.

Printed Rules

FCC rules may be obtained only through the Government Printing Office, Washington, D.C. 20402. The rules on FCC practice and procedure are contained in Volume I. The broadcast rules are contained in Volume III. Orders should be sent to the Government Printing Office direct (not through the FCC).

Applications Forms

Application forms may be obtained from the FCC's Operations Support Division, Service and Supply Branch, Room B-10, 1919 M St. N.W., Washington, D.C. 20554. (202) 632-7272.

Cable Regulations

Cable television is regulated primarily by the FCC and by state and local governments. The federal Cable Communications Policy Act of 1984 imposed additional regulations on cable systems, but more important, it set limits on state and local regulation. Significant modifications to the Cable Act were made by the Cable Television Consumer Protection and Competition Act of 1992, P.L. 102-385, approved October 5, 1992.

The following contains selected and edited rules of the FCC and provisions of the Cable Communications Act, current through December 31, 1993.

Definitions (§76.5).

Basic cable service. For the purposes of regulating rates of cable systems found not to be subject to effective competition, basic cable service is the tier of service regularly provided to all subscribers that includes the retransmission of all must-carry broadcast television signals as defined in TK to TK of the rules (or, in the absence of at least three must-carry signals, any unaltered broadcast television signals) and the public, educational and governmental channels, if required by a franchising authority under Title VI of the Communuications Act.

Cable service. The one-way transmission to subscribers of video programming, or other programming service; and, subscriber interaction, if any, which is required for the selection of such video programming or other programming service. For the purposes of this definition, "video programming" is programming provided by, or generally considered comparable to programming provided by, a television broadcast station; and, "other programming service" is information that a cable operator makes available to all subscribers generally.

Cable system or cable television system. A facility consisting of a set of closed transmission paths and associated signal generation, reception, and control equipment that is designed to provide cable service which includes video programming and which is provided to multiple subscribers within a community, but such term does not include (1) a facility that serves only to retransmit the television signals of one or more television broadcast stations; (2) a facility that serves only subscribers in one or more multiple unit dwellings under common ownership, control or management unless such facility or facilities uses any public right-of-way; (3) a facility of a common carrier which is subject, in whole or in part, to the provisions of Title II of the Communications Act of 1934, as amended, except that such facility shall be considered a cable system to the extent such facility is used in the transmission of video programming directly to subscribers; or (4) any facilities of any electric utility used solely for operating its electric utility systems.

Cable system operator. Any person or group of persons (1) who provides cable service over a cable system and directly or through one or more affiliates owns a significant interest in such a cable system; or (2) who otherwise controls or is responsible for, through any arrangement, the management and operation of such a cable system.

Cablecasting. Programming (exclusive of broadcast signals) carried on a cable television system. See paragraphs (y), (z), and (aa) (Classes II, III and IV cable television channels) of this section.

Rural area. A community unit with a density of less than thirty households per route mile of coaxial and/or fiber optic cable trunk and feeder line.

Television station; television broadcast station. Any television broadcast station operating on a channel regularly assigned to its community by §73.606 of this chapter, and any television broadcast station licensed by a foreign government: provided, however, that a television broadcast station licensed by a foreign government shall not be entitled to assert a claim to carriage, program exclusivity, or retransmission consent authorization pursuant to Subpart D or F of this part, but may otherwise be carried if consistent with the rules on any service tier.

§76.7 Special relief and must-carry complaint procedures.

(a)(1) Petitions for special relief. On petition by a cable television system operator, a franchising authority, an applicant, permittee, or licensee of a television broadcast or translator station, or by any other interested person, the Commission may waive any provision of the rules relating to cable television systems, impose additional or different requirements, or issue a ruling on a complaint or disputed question.

(2) Complaints filed pursuant to §76.61. In response to a complaint filed by a television broadcast station under §76.61 (must-carry complaint), the Commission may order a cable television system operator to commence or resume carriage of the complaining station, or position or reposition the complaining station's channel on the cable television system, pursuant to Subpart D of this Part.

(b) The petition for special relief or must-carry complaint may be submitted informally, by letter, but shall be accompanied by a certificate of service on any cable television system operator, franchising authority, station licensee, permittee, or applicant, or other interested person who may be directly affected if the relief requested is granted.

(c)(1) The petition for special relief or must-carry complaint shall state the relief requested. It shall state fully and precisely all pertinent facts and considerations relied on to demonstrate the need for the relief requested and to support a determination that a grant of such relief would serve the public interest. Factual allegations shall be supported by affidavit of a person or persons with actual knowledge of the facts, and exhibits shall be verified by the person who prepares them.

(2) A petition for special relief or must-carry complaint shall set forth all steps taken by the parties to resolve the problem, except where the only relief sought is a clarification or interpretation of the rules.

(3) An original and two (2) copies of the petition for special relief or must-carry complaint, and all subsequent pleadings shall be filed in accordance with §0.401(a) of this chapter, except that petitions for special relief requiring fees as set forth at Part 1, Subpart G of this chapter must be filed in accordance with §0.401(b) of this chapter. Must-carry complaints filed pursuant to §76.61 are not covered by Part 1, Subpart G of this chapter and do not require fees.

(4)(i) Must-carry complaints filed pursuant to §76.61(a) (Complaints regarding carriage of local commercial television stations) shall be accompanied by the notice from the complainant to the cable television system operator (§76.61(a)(1)), and the cable television system operator's response (§76.61(a)(2)), if any. If no timely response was received, the complaint should so state.

(ii) Must-carry complaints filed pursuant to §76.61 (b) (Complaints regarding carriage of qualified local NCE television stations) should be accompanied by any relevant correspondence between the complainant and the cable television system operator.

(iii) No must-carry complaint filed pursuant to §76.61 will be accepted by the Commission if filed more than sixty (60) days after the date of the specific event described in this paragraph. Must-carry complaints filed pursuant to §76.61(a) or §76.61(b) should affirmatively state the specific event upon which the complaint is based, and shall establish that the complaint is being filed within sixty (60) days of such specific event. With respect to must-carry complaints filed pursuant to §76.61(a), the specific event shall be

(A) The denial by a cable television system operator of a request for carriage or channel position contained in the notice required by §76.61(a)(1), or

(B) The failure to respond to such notice within the time period allowed by §76.61(a)(2). With respect to must-carry complaints filed pursuant to §76.61(b), the specific event shall be when the complainant first believes that the cable television system operator has failed to comply with the applicable provisions of Subpart D of this Part.

(d) Interested persons may submit comments or oppositions to a petition for special relief or a must-carry complaint within twenty (20) days after the date of public notice of the filing of such petition or complaint. For good cause shown in the petition for special relief or must-carry complaint, the Commission may, by letter or telegram to known interested persons, specify an altered time for such submissions. Comments or oppositions shall be served on the petitioner or complainant and on all persons listed in petitioner's or complainant's certificate of service, and shall contain a detailed full showing, supported by affidavit, of any facts or considerations relied on.

(e) The petitioner or complainant may file a reply to the comments or oppositions within ten (10) days after their submission, which shall be served on all persons who have filed pleadings and shall also contain a detailed full showing, supported by affidavit, of any additional facts or considerations relied on. For good cause shown, the Commission may specify a shorter time for the filing of reply comments.

(f) The Commission, after consideration of a petition for special relief and the responsive pleadings, may determine whether the public interest would be served by the grant, in whole or in part, or denial of the request, or may issue a ruling on the complaint or dispute. The Commission will resolve must-carry complaints pursuant to paragraphs (a)(4) and (b)(2) of §76.61. The Commission may specify other procedures, such as oral argument, evidentiary hearing, or further written submissions directed to particular aspects, as it deems appropriate. In the event that an evidentiary hearing is required, the Commission will determine, on the basis of the pleadings and such other procedures as it may specify, whether temporary relief should be afforded any party pending the hearing and the nature of any such temporary relief.

(g) On a finding that the public interest so requires, the Commission may determine that a system community unit operating or proposing to operate in a community located outside of the 48 contiguous states shall comply with provisions of Subparts D, F, and G of this part in addition to the provisions thereof otherwise applicable.

Note: Each party filing a petition, comments, opposition or other pleading pursuant to §76.7 is responsible for the continuing accuracy and completeness of all information in such document. The provisions of §1.65 of this chapter are wholly applicable to pleadings involving §76.7, except that where specific provisions of the latter conflict with the former, the specific provisions of §76.7 are controlling, e.g., where requirements for service on specified parties of certain information may vary.

Network nonduplication; extent of protection (§76.92).

(a) Upon receiving notification pursuant to §76.94, a cable community unit located in whole or in part within the geographic zone for a network program, the network nonduplication rights to which are held by a commercial television station licensed by the Commission, shall not carry that program as broadcast by any other television signal, except as otherwise provided below.

(b) For purposes of this section, the order of nonduplication priority of television signals carried by a community unit is as follows:

(1) First, all television broadcast stations within whose specified zone the community of the community unit is located, in whole or in part;

(2) Second, all smaller market television broadcast stations within whose secondary zone the community of the community unit is located, in whole or in part.

(c) For purposes of this section, all noncommercial educational television broadcast stations licensed to a community located in whole or in part within a major television market as specified in §76.51 shall be treated in the same manner as a major market commercial television broadcast station, and all noncommercial educational television broadcast stations not licensed to a community located in whole or in part within a major television market shall be treated in the same manner as a smaller market television broadcast station.

(d) Any community unit operating in a community to which a 100-watt or higher power translator is located within the predicted Grade B signal contour of the television broadcast station that the translator station retransmits, and which translator is carried by the community unit shall, upon request of such translator station licensee or permittee, delete the duplicating network programming of any television broadcast station whose reference point (see §76.53) is more than 88.5 km (55 miles) from the community of the community unit. [§76.53, "Reference points," omitted. - Ed.]

(e) Any community unit which operates in a community located in whole or in part within the secondary zone of a smaller market television broadcast station is not required to delete the duplicating network programming of any major market television broadcast station whose reference point (see §76.53) is also within 88.5 km (55 miles) of the community of the community unit. [§76.53, "Reference points," omitted. - Ed.]

(f) A community unit is not required to delete the duplicating network programming of any television broadcast station which is significantly viewed in the cable television community pursuant to §76.54.

NOTE: With respect to network programming, the geographic zone within which the television station is entitled to enforce network nonduplication protection and priority of shall be that geographic area agreed upon between the network and the television station. In no event shall such rights exceed the area within which the television station may acquire broadcast territorial exclusivity rights as defined in §73.658(m), except that small market television stations shall be entitled to a secondary protection zone of 32.2 additional kilometers (20 additional miles).

(g) A community unit is not required to delete the duplicating network programming of any qualified NCE television broadcast station that is carried in fulfillment of the cable television system's mandatory signal carriage obligations, pursuant to §76.56.

Parties entitled to network nonduplication protection (76.93).

Television broadcast station licensees shall be entitled to exercise nonduplication rights pursuant to §76.92 in accordance with the contractual provisions of the network-affiliate agreement.

Notification (§76.94).

(a) In order to exercise nonduplication rights pursuant to §76.92, television stations shall notify each cable television system operator of the nonduplication sought in accordance with the requirements of this section. Except as otherwise provided in paragraph (b) of this section, nonduplication protection notices shall include the following information:

(1) The name and address of the party requesting nonduplication protection and the television broadcast station holding the nonduplication right;

(2) The name of the program or series (including specific episodes where necessary) for which protection is sought; and

(3) The dates on which protection is to begin and end.

(b) Broadcasters entering into contracts providing for network nonduplication protection shall notify affected cable systems within 60 calendar days of the signing of such a contract; provided, however, that for such contracts signed before May 5, 1989, a broadcaster may provide notice on or before June 19, 1989. In the event the broadcaster is unable based on the information contained in the contract, to furnish all the information required by paragraph (a) of this section at that time, the broadcaster must provide modified notices that contain the following information:

(1) The name of the network (or networks) which has (or have) extended nonduplication protection to the broadcaster;

(2) The time periods by time of day (local time) and by network (if more than one) for each day of the week that the broadcaster will be broadcasting programs from that network (or networks) and for which nonduplication protection is requested; and

(3) The duration and extent (e.g., simultaneous, same-day, seven-day, etc.) of the nonduplication protection which has been agreed upon by the network (or networks) and the broadcaster.

(c) Except as otherwise provided in paragraph (d) of this section, a broadcaster shall be entitled to nonduplication protection beginning on the later of:

(1) The date specified in its notice (as described in paragraphs (a) or (b) of this section, whichever is applicable) to the cable television system; or

(2) The first day of the calendar week (Sunday-Saturday) that begins 60 days after the cable television system receives notice from the broadcaster.

(d) A broadcaster shall provide the following information to the cable television system under the following circumstances:

(1) In the event the protection specified in the notices described in paragraphs (a) or (b) of this section has been limited or ended prior to the time specified in the notice, or in the event a time period, as identified to the cable system in a notice pursuant to paragraph (b) of this section, for which a broadcaster has obtained protection is shifted to another time of day or another day (but not expanded), the broadcaster shall, as soon as possible, inform each cable television system operator that has previously received the notice of all changes from the original notice. Notice to be furnished "as soon as possible" under this subsection shall be furnished by telephone, telegraph, facsimile, overnight mail or other similar expedient means.

(2) In the event the protection specified in the modified notices described in paragraph (b) of this section has been expanded, the broadcaster shall, at least 60 calendar days prior to broadcast of a protected program entitled to such expanded protection, notify each cable system operator that has previously received notice of all changes from the original notice.

(e) In determining which programs must be deleted from a television signal, a cable television system operator may rely on information from any of the following sources published or otherwise made available.

(1) Newspapers or magazines of general circulation.

(2) A television station whose programs may be subject to deletion. If a cable television system asks a television station for information about its program schedule, the television station shall answer the request:

(i) Within ten business days following the television station's receipt of the request; or

(ii) Sixty days before the program or programs mentioned in the request for information will be broadcast; whichever comes later.

(3) The broadcaster requesting exclusivity.

(f) A broadcaster exercising exclusivity pursuant to §76.92 shall provide to the cable system, upon request, an exact copy of those portions of the contracts, such portions to be signed by both the network and the broadcaster, setting forth in full the provisions pertinent to the duration, nature, and extent of the nonduplication terms concerning broadcast signal exhibition to which the parties have agreed.

Exceptions (§76.95).

(a) The provisions of sections §76.92-§76.94 shall not apply to a cable system serving fewer than 1,000 subscribers. Within 60 days following the provision of service to 1,000 subscribers, the operator of each such system shall file a notice to that effect with the Commission, and serve a copy of that notice on every television station that would be entitled to exercise network nonduplication protection against it.

(b) Network nonduplication protection need not be extended to a higher priority station for one hour following the scheduled time of completion of the broadcast of a live sports event by that station or by a lower priority station against which a cable community unit would otherwise be required to provide nonduplication protection following the scheduled time of completion.

Effective dates (§76.97).

The network nonduplication protection and exceptions thereto outlined in sections §76.92-§76.95 shall become enforceable on January 1, 1990. The rules in effect on May 18, 1988 will remain operative until January 1, 1990.

Syndicated program exclusivity: extent of protection (§76.151).

Upon receiving notification pursuant to §76.155, a cable community unit located in whole or in part within the geographic zone for a syndicated program, the syndicated exclusivity rights to which are held by a commercial television station licensed by the Commission, shall not carry that program as broadcast by any other television signal, except as otherwise provided below.

NOTE: With respect to each syndicated program, the geographic zone within which the television station is entitled to enforce syndicated exclusivity rights shall be that geographic area agreed upon between the non-network program supplier, producer or distributor and the television station. In no event shall such zone exceed the area within which the television station has acquired broadcast territorial exclusivity rights as defined in §73.658(m). To the extent rights are obtained for any hyphenated market named in §76.51, such rights shall not exceed those permitted under §73.658(m) for each named community in that market.

Parties entitled to syndicated exclusivity (§76.153).

(a) Television broadcast station licensees shall be entitled to exercise exclusive rights pursuant to §76.151 in accordance with the contractual provisions of their syndicated program license agreements, consistent with §76.159.

(b) Distributors of syndicated programming shall be entitled to exercise exclusive rights pursuant to §76.151 for a period of one year from the initial broadcast syndication licensing of such programming anywhere in the United States; provided, however, that distributors shall not be entitled to exercise such rights in areas in which the programming has already been licensed.

Notification (§76.155).

(a) In order to exercise exclusivity rights pursuant to §76.151, distributors or television stations shall notify each cable television system operator of the exclusivity sought in accordance with the requirements of this section. Syndicated program exclusivity notices shall include the following information:

(1) The name and address of the party requesting exclusivity and the television broadcast station or other party holding the exclusive right;

(2) The name of the program or series (including specific episodes where necessary) for which exclusivity is sought;

(3) The dates on which exclusivity is to begin and end.

(b) Broadcasters entering into contracts on or after August 18, 1988, which contain syndicated exclusivity protection shall notify affected cable systems within sixty calendar days of the signing of such a contract. Broadcasters who have entered into contracts prior to August 18, 1988, and who comply with the requirements specified in §76.159 shall notify affected cable systems on or before June 19, 1989; provided, however, that with respect to such pre-August 18, 1988, contracts that require amendment in order to invoke the provisions of these rules, notification may be given within sixty calendar days of the signing of such amendment. A broadcaster shall be entitled to exclusivity protection beginning on the later of:

(1) The date specified in its notice to the cable television system; or

(2) The first day of the calendar week (Sunday-Saturday) that begins 60 days after the cable television system receives notice from the broadcaster.

(c) In determining which programs must be deleted from a television broadcast signal, a cable television system operator may rely on information from any of the following sources published or otherwise made available.

(1) Newspapers or magazines of general circulation;

(2) A television station whose programs may be subject to deletion. If a cable television system asks a television station for information about its program schedule, the television station shall answer the request:

(i) Within 10 business days following the television station's receipt of the request; or

(ii) Sixty days before the program or programs mentioned in the request for information will be broadcast; whichever comes later.

(3) The distributor or television station requesting exclusivity.

(d) In the event the exclusivity specified in paragraph (a) of this section has been limited or has ended prior to the time specified in the notice, the distributor or broadcaster who has supplied the original notice shall, as soon as possible, inform each cable television system operator that has previously received the notice of all changes from the original notice. In the event the original notice specified contingent dates on which exclusivity is to begin and/or end, the distributor or broadcaster shall, as soon as possible, notify the cable television system operator of the occurrence of the relevant contingency. Notice to be furnished "as soon as possible" under this subsection shall be furnished by telephone, telegraph, facsimile, overnight mail or other similar expedient means.

Exceptions (§76.156).

(a) Notwithstanding the requirements of sections §76.151-§76.155, a broadcast signal is not required to be deleted from a cable community when that cable community unit falls, in whole or in part, within that signal's Grade B contour, or when the signal is significantly viewed pursuant to §76.54 in the cable community.

(b) The provisions of sections §76.151-§76.155 shall not apply to a cable system serving fewer than 1,000 subscribers. Within 60 days following the provision of service to 1,000 subscribers, the operator of each such system shall file a notice to that effect with the Commission, and serve a copy of that notice on every television station that would be entitled to exercise syndicated exclusivity protection against it.

Exclusivity contracts (§76.157).

A distributor or television station exercising exclusivity pursuant to §76.151 shall provide to the cable system, upon request, an exact copy of those portions of the exclusivity contracts, such portions to be signed by both the distributor and the television station, setting forth in full the provisions pertinent to the duration, nature, and extent of the exclusivity terms concerning broadcast signal exhibition to which the parties have agreed.

Indemnification contracts (§76.158).

No licensee shall enter into any contract to indemnify a cable system for liability resulting from failure to delete programming in accordance with the provisions of this subpart unless the licensee has a reasonable basis for concluding that such program deletion is not required by this subpart.

Requirements for invocation of protection (§76.159).

For a station licensee to be eligible to invoke the provisions of this subpart, it must have a contract or other written indicia that it holds syndicated exclusivity rights for the exhibition of the program in question. Contracts entered on or after August 18, 1988, must contain the following words: "the licensee [or substitute name] shall, by the terms of this contract, be entitled to invoke the protection against duplication of programming imported under the Compulsory Copyright License, as provided in §76.151 of the FCC Rules [or 'as provided in the FCC's syndicated exclusivity rules']." Contracts entered into prior to August 18, 1988, must contain either the foregoing language or a clear and specific reference to the licensee's authority to exercise exclusivity rights as to the specific programming against cable television broadcast signal carriage by the cable system in question upon the contingency that the government reimposed syndicated exclusivity protection. In the absence of such a specific reference in contracts entered into prior to August 18, 1988, the provisions of these rules may be invoked only if (a) the contract is amended to include the specific language referenced above or (b) a specific written acknowledgement is obtained, from the party from whom the broadcast exhibition rights were obtained that the existing contract was intended, or should now be construed by agreement of the parties, to include such rights. A general acknowledgement by a supplier of exhibition rights that specific contract language was intended to convey rights under these rules will be accepted with respect to all contracts containing that specific language. Nothing in this section shall be construed as a grant of exclusive rights to a broadcaster where such rights are not agreed to by the parties.

Substitutions (§76.161).

Whenever, pursuant to the requirements of the syndicated exclusivity rules, a community unit is required to delete a television program on a broadcast signal that is permitted to be carried under the Commission's Rules, such community unit may, consistent with these rules and the sports blackout rules at 47 CFR §76.67, substitute a program from any other television broadcast station. Programs substituted pursuant to this section may be carried to their completion.

Effective dates (§76.163).

No cable system shall be required to delete programming pursuant to the provisions of sections §76.151-§76.159 prior to January 1, 1990.

Carriage of Other Television Signals (§76.60).

A cable system may carry the signals of any television station including low power television stations, television translator stations, foreign television stations, subscription television broadcasts, satellite distributed program services, direct broadcast satellite stations and programming from any other source. A cable system may also carry any ancillary service transmission on the vertical blanking interval or the aural baseband of any television broadcast signal including, but not limited to, multichannel television sound and teletext.

Manner of Carriage (§76.62).

Where a television broadcast signal is carried by a cable system, the signal shall be carried without material degradation and programs broadcast shall be carried in full, without deletion or alteration of any portion thereof.

Notification (§76.63).

Where the signal of a local television broadcast station, as described in §76.5(gg)(1)-(gg)(3) of this part, is carried by a cable television system that is subject to the provisions of §76.501(b)(1) of this part, the operator of such cable system shall provide written notice to the licensee of a local television station at least 30 days prior to either discontinuing carriage of the station's broadcast signal or carrying that signal on a different cable channel.

Input selector switches and consumer education (§76.66).

(a) A cable system operator shall offer to supply to each new subscriber and each existing subscriber an input selector switch for each separate television receiver for which cable service is provided by the cable operator. The operator shall comply with the following in offering the switch and installing cable service:

(1) Offer to supply and install a switch for all new and existing subscribers within six months of June 10, 1987, and thereafter on an annual basis until June 10, 1992, unless the subscriber already has an input selector switching device or his/her television receiver has such a device built in;

(2) A cable operator may charge for purchase or lease of switches and associated hardware and may separately charge for installation of switches for existing subscribers. A cable operator may not charge new subscribers a separate fee for switch installation.

(i) A cable operator may offer to inspect and/or install antenna grounding systems for outdoor antennas and shall separately charge for such services.

(3) A cable system operator is not required to provide a switch to any subscriber who declines the required offer, but is not thereby relieved from making the offer to any such subscriber thereafter on an annual basis;

(4) The switch offer shall be made using text chosen by the cable operator that includes the following points:

(i) An offer to supply an input selector switch for each separate television receiver to which cable service is provided;

(ii) The switch connects both to the cable service and an antenna, and enables selection between cable service and off-the-air broadcast television signals;

(iii) If the subscriber already has switching capability, either in a separate device or as a built-in feature of his/her television receiver, an additional switch may not be needed;

(iv) If the subscriber desires switching capability, he/she may have the cable system install a switch or may obtain a switch from it with written self-installation instructions;

(v) Switching capability may be obtained from other suppliers; and,

(vi) For the subscriber's convenience, attach an offer response form to be returned to the cable system's business office.

(5) Comply with the following requirements with respect to antennas:

(i) If an antenna is present, the operator shall not recommend that the antenna be removed;

(ii) If an antenna is not present, the operator shall inform the subscriber that the switch will be operational only if it is connected to an antenna;

(iii) Where the operator installs a switch and an antenna is present, it shall connect the switch to that existing antenna.

(iv) Cable operators must provide to subscribers information on the potential for interference related to the input selector switch and the associated connections and suggest measures to take to avoid such problems. Such suggestions must include the recommendations that shielded coaxial cable be used between the receiver and the switch terminals and that at least four feet of shielded coaxial cable be used for connecting switch terminals to any unshielded antenna leads.

(b) Individual cable subscribers are not required to purchase or lease input selector switches from their cable system. Subscribers may obtain such switches from suppliers other than their cable systems. Although cable subscribers are encouraged to establish and maintain independent access to off-the-air broadcast signals, they are not required to do so.

(c) The cable system operator shall provide the following information to each subscriber at the time of installation of cable service and to existing subscribers, in writing, by November 1, 1989, and annually thereafter to all subscribers. Operators may use whatever language they deem appropriate to convey the following:

(1) The cable system is not required to carry any off-the-air broadcast signal; but, of course, may choose to do so; thus,

(2) [Reserved]

(3) It may be necessary to use an antenna, in conjunction with an input selector switch, to access broadcast signals available off-the-air and not carried by the cable system;

(4) A description of the function of an input selector switch and state that its purpose is to aid the viewer in preserving independent access to off-the-air television service;

(5) That input selector switches may be obtained from suppliers other than the cable system and that there may be a range of switch options available, such as simple manual cable/broadcast switches, multiple input source switches, electronic switches, remote control switches, and receivers with built-in switches;

(6) Identify for their subscribers, by call sign and channel number, any full service broadcast signals not carried on the cable system whose predicted Grade B contour covers any portion of the cable community or that are "significantly viewed" in the cable community, as defined in §76.5(i) of the rules (the list of stations must be current to within one month of the distribution of the information required pursuant to this paragraph);

(7) Indicate that questions related to input selector switches should be directed to a specified individual at the cable system and provide a telephone number at which that person can be reached.

Sports broadcasts (§76.67).

(a) No community unit located in whole or in part within the specified zone of a television broadcast station licensed to a community in which a sports event is taking place, shall, on request of the holder of the broadcast rights to that event, or its agent, carry the live television broadcast of that event if the event is not available live on a television broadcast signal carried by the community unit meeting the criteria specified in sections §76.5(gg)(1)-(gg)(3) of this part. For purposes of this section, if there is no television station licensed to the community in which the sports event is taking place, the applicable specified zone shall be that of the television station licensed to the community with which the sports event or local team is identified, or, if the event or local team is not identified with any particular community, the nearest community to which a television station is licensed.

(b) Notification of the programming to be deleted pursuant to this section shall include the following information:

(1) As to programming to be deleted from television broadcast signals regularly carried by the community unit:

(i) The name and address of the party requesting the program deletion;

i) The date, time and expected duration of the sports event the television broadcast of which is to be deleted;

(iii) The call letters of the television broadcast station(s) from which the deletion is to be made.

(2) As to programming to be deleted from television broadcast signals not regularly carried by the community unit:

(i) The name and address of the party requesting the program deletion;

(ii) The date, time and expected duration of the sports event the television broadcast of which is to be deleted.

(c) Notifications given pursuant to this section must be received, as to regularly scheduled events, not later than the Monday preceding the calendar week (Sunday-Saturday) during which the program deletion is to be made. Notifications as to events not regularly scheduled and revisions of notices previously submitted, must be received within twenty-four (24) hours after the time of the telecast to be deleted is known, but in any event no later than twenty-four (24) hours from the time the subject telecast is to take place.

(d) Whenever, pursuant to this section, a community unit is required to delete a television program on a signal regularly carried by the community unit, such community unit may, consistent with the rules contained in Subpart F of this part, substitute a program from any other television broadcast station. A program substituted may be carried to its completion, and the community unit need not return to its regularly carried signal until it can do so without interrupting a program already in progress.

(e) The provisions of this section shall not be deemed to require the deletion of any portion of a television signal which a community unit was lawfully carrying prior to March 31, 1972.

(f) The provisions of this section shall not apply to any cable television system having fewer than 1000 subscribers.

Exemption from input selector switch rules (§76.70).

(a) In any case of cable systems serving communities where no portion of the community is covered by the predicted Grade B contour of at least one full service broadcast television station or noncommercial educational television translator station operating with 5 or more watts output power and where the signals of no such broadcast stations are "significantly viewed" in the county where such a cable system is located, the cable system shall be exempt from the provisions of §76.66 of this chapter. Cable systems may be eligible for this exemption where they demonstrate with engineering studies prepared in accordance with §73.686 of this chapter or other showings that broadcast signals meeting the above criteria are not actually viewable within the community.

(b) Where a new full service broadcast television station, or new noncommercial educational television translator station with 5 or more watts, or an existing such station of either type with newly upgraded facilities provides predicted Grade B service to a community served by a cable system previously exempt under paragraph (a) of this section, or the signal of any such broadcast station is newly determined to be "significantly viewed" in the county where such a cable system is located, the cable system at that time is required to comply fully with the provisions of §76.66 of this chapter. Cable systems may retain their exemption under paragraph (a) of this section where they demonstrate with engineering studies prepared in accordance with §73.686 of this chapter or other showings that broadcast signals meeting the above criteria are not actually viewable within the community.

Origination cablecasts by legally qualified candidates for public office; equal opportunities (§76.205).

(a) General requirements. No cable television system is required to permit the use of its facilities by any legally qualified candidate for public office, but if any system shall permit any such candidate to use its facilities, it shall afford equal opportunities to all other candidates for that office to use such facilities. Such system shall have no power of censorship over the material broadcast by any such candidate. Appearance by a legally qualified candidate on any: (1) bona fide newscast; (2) bona fide news interview; (3) bona fide news documentary (if the appearance of the candidate is incidental to the presentation of the subject or subjects covered by the news documentary); or (4) on-the-spot coverage of bona fide news events (including but not limited to political conventions and activities incidental thereto), shall not be deemed to be use of a system. (Section 315(a) of the Communications Act.)

(b) Uses. As used in this section and §76.206, the term "use" means candidate appearance (including by voice or picture) that is not exempt under §76.205(a)(1)-(4) and that is controlled, approved or sponsored by the candidate or the candidate's authorized Committee after the candidate becomes legally qualified.

(c) Timing of request. A request for equal opportunities must be submitted to the system within one week of the day on which the first prior use giving rise to the right of equal opportunities occurred; provided, however, that where the person was not a candidate at the time of such first prior use, he or she shall submit his or her request within one week of the first subsequent use after he or she has become a legally qualified candidate for the office in question.

(d) Burden of proof. A candidate requesting equal opportunities of the system or complaining of noncompliance to the Commission shall have the burden of proving that he or she and his or her opponent are legally qualified candidates for the same public office.

(e) Discrimination between candidates. In making time available to candidates for public office, no system shall make any discrimination between candidates in practices, regulations, facilities, or services for or in connection with the service rendered pursuant to this part, or make or give any preference to any candidate for public office or subject any such candidate to any prejudice or disadvantage; nor shall any system make any contract or other agreement which shall have the effect of permitting any legally qualified candidate for any public office to cablecast to the exclusion of other legally qualified candidates for the same public office.

Candidate rates (§76.206).

(a) Charges for use of cable television systems. The charges, if any, made for the use of any system by any person who is a legally qualified candidate for any public office in connection with his or her campaign for nomination for election, or election, to such office shall not exceed:

(1) During the 45 days preceding the date of a primary or primary runoff election and during the 60 days preceding the date of a general or special election in which such person is a candidate, the lowest unit charge of the system for the same class and amount of time for the same period.

(i) A candidate shall be charged no more per unit than the system charges its most favored commercial advertisers for the same classes and amounts of time for the same periods. Any system practices offered to commercial advertisers that enhance the value of advertising spots must be disclosed and made available to candidates upon equal terms. Such practices include but are not limited to any discount privileges that affect the value of advertising, such as bonus spots, time-sensitive make goods, preemption priorities, or any other factors that enhance the value of the announcement.

(ii) The Commission recognizes non-preemptible, preemptible with notice, immediately preemptible and run-of-schedule as distinct classes of time.

(iii) Systems may establish and define their own reasonable classes of immediately preemptible time so long as the differences between such classes are based on one or more demonstrable benefits associated with each class and are not based solely upon price or identity of the advertiser. Such demonstrable benefits include, but are not limited to, varying levels of preemption protection, scheduling flexibility, or associated privileges, such as guaranteed time-sensitive make goods. Systems may not use class distinctions to defeat the purpose of the lowest unit charge requirement. All classes must be fully disclosed and made available to candidates.

(iv) Systems may establish reasonable classes of preemptible with notice time so long as they clearly define all such classes, fully disclose them and make them available to candidates.

(v) Systems may treat non-preemptible and fixed position as distinct classes of time provided that systems articulate clearly the differences between such classes, fully disclose them, and make them available to candidates.

(vi) Systems shall not establish a separate, premium-priced class of time sold only to candidates. Systems may sell higher-priced non-preemptible or fixed time to candidates if such a class of time is made available on a bona fide basis to both candidates and commercial advertisers, and provided such class is not functionally equivalent to any lower-priced class of time sold to commercial advertisers.

(vii) [Reserved]

(viii) Lowest unit charge may be calculated on a weekly basis with respect to time that is sold on a weekly basis, such as rotations through particular programs or dayparts. Systems electing to calculate the lowest unit charge by such a method must include in that calculation all rates for all announcements scheduled in the rotation, including announcements aired under long-term advertising contracts. Systems may implement rate increases during election periods only to the extent that such increases constitute "ordinary business practices," such as seasonal program changes or changes in audience ratings.

(ix) Systems shall review their advertising records periodically throughout the election period to determine whether compliance with this section requires that candidates receive rebates or credits. Where necessary, systems shall issue such rebates or credits promptly.

(x) Unit rates charged as part of any package, whether individually negotiated or generally available to all advertisers, must be included in the lowest unit charge calculation for the same class and length of time in the same time period. A candidate cannot be required to purchase advertising in every program or daypart in a package as a condition for obtaining package unit rates.

(xi) Systems are not required to include non-cash promotional merchandising incentives in lowest unit charge calculations; provided, however, that all such incentives must be offered to candidates as part of any purchases permitted by the system. Bonus spots, however, must be included in the calculation of the lowest unit charge calculation.

(xii) Make goods, defined as the rescheduling of preempted advertising, shall be provided to candidates prior to election day if a system has provided a time-sensitive make good during the year preceding the pre-election periods, respectively set forth in paragraph (a)(1) of this section to any commercial advertiser who purchases time in the same class.

(xiii) Systems must disclose and make available to candidates any make good policies provided to commercial advertisers. If a system places a make good for any commercial advertiser or other candidate in a more valuable program or daypart, the value of such make good must be included in the calculation of the lowest unit charge for that program or daypart.

(2) At any time other than the respective periods set forth in paragraph (a)(1) of this section, systems may charge legally qualified candidates for public office no more than the charges made for comparable use of the system by commercial advertisers. The rates, if any, charged all such candidates for the same office shall be uniform and shall not be rebated by any means, direct or indirect. A candidate shall be charged no more than the rate the system would charge for comparable commercial advertising. All discount privileges otherwise offered by a system to commercial advertisers must be disclosed and made available upon equal terms to all candidates for public office.

(b) If a system permits a candidate to use its cablecast facilities, the system shall make all discount privileges offered to commercial advertisers, including the lowest unit charges for each class and length of time in the same time period and all corresponding discount privileges, available on equal terms to all candidates. This duty includes an affirmative duty to disclose to candidates information about rates, terms, conditions and all value-enhancing discount privileges offered to commercial advertisers. Systems may use reasonable discretion in making the disclosure; provided, however, that the disclosure includes, at a minimum, the following information:

(1) a description and definition of each class of time available to commercial advertisers sufficiently complete enough to allow candidates to identify and understand what specific attributes differentiate each class;

(2) a description of the lowest unit charge and related privileges (such as priorities against preemption and make goods prior to specific deadlines) for each class of time offered to commercial advertisers;

(3) a description of the system's method of selling preemptible time based upon advertiser demand, commonly known as the "current selling level," with the stipulation that candidates will be able to purchase at these demand-generated rates in the same manner as commercial advertisers;

(4) an approximation of the likelihood of preemption for each kind of preemptible time; and

(5) an explanation of the system's sales practices, if any, that are based on audience delivery, with the stipulation that candidates will be able to purchase this kind of time, if available to commercial advertisers.

(c) Once disclosure is made, systems shall negotiate in good faith to actually sell time to candidates in accordance with the disclosure.

Political file (§76.207).

(a) Every cable television system shall keep and permit public inspection of a complete and orderly record (political file) of all requests for cablecast time made by or on behalf of a candidate for public office, together with an appropriate notation showing the disposition made by the system of such requests, and the charges made, if any, if the request is granted. The "disposition" includes the schedule of time purchased, when spots actually aired, the rates charged, and the classes of time purchased.

(b) When free time is provided for use by or on behalf of candidates, a record of the free time provided shall be placed in the political file.

(c) All records required by this paragraph shall be placed in the political file as soon as possible and shall be retained for a period of two years. As soon as possible means immediately absent unusual circumstances.

Fairness Doctrine; Personal Attacks; Political Editorials (§76.209).

(a) A cable television system operator engaging in origination cablecasting shall afford reasonable opportunity for the discussion of conflicting views on issues of public importance.

(b) When, during such origination cablecasting, an attack is made upon the honesty, character, integrity, or like personal qualities of an identified person or group, the cable television system operator shall, within a reasonable time and in no event later than one (1) week after the attack, transmit to the person or group attacked: (1) notification of the date, time, and identification of the cablecast; (2) a script or tape (or an accurate summary if a script or tape is not available) of the attack; and (3) an offer of a reasonable opportunity to respond over the system's facilities.

(c) the provisions of paragraph (b) of this section shall not apply to cablecast material which falls within one or more of the following categories:

(1) Personal attacks on foreign groups or foreign public figures;

(2) Personal attacks occurring during uses by legally qualified candidates;

(3) Personal attacks made during cablecasts not included in paragraph (b)(2) of this section and made by legally qualified candidates, their authorized spokespersons or persons associated with the candidates in the campaign; and

(4) Bona fide newscasts, bona fide news interviews, and on-the-spot coverage of bona fide news events (including commentary or analysis contained in the foregoing programs, but, the provisions of paragraph (b) of this section shall be applicable to editorials of the cable television system operator).

(d) Where a cable television system operator, in an editorial, (1) endorses or (2) opposes a legally qualified candidate or candidates, the system operator shall, within 24 hours of the editorial, transmit to respectively (i) the other qualified candidate or candidates for the same office, or (ii) the candidate opposed in the editorial, (a) notification of the date, time, and channel of the editorial; (b) a script or tape of the editorial; and (c) an offer of a reasonable oppourtunity for a candidate or a spokesman of the candidate to respond over the system's facilities: provided, however, that where such editorials are cablecast within 72 hours prior to the day of the election, the system operator shall comply with the provisions of this paragraph sufficiently far in advance of the broadcast to enable the candidate or candidates to have a reasonable opportunity to prepare a response and to present it in a timely fashion.

Lotteries (§76.213).

(a) No cable television system operator, except as in paragraph (c), when engaged in origination cablecasting shall transmit or permit to be transmitted on the origination cablecasting channel or channels any advertisement of or information concerning any lottery, gift, enterprise, or similar scheme, offering prizes dependent in whole or in part upon lot or chance, or any list of prizes drawn or awarded by means of any such lottery, gift enterprise, or scheme, whether said list contains any part or all of such prizes.

(b) The determination whether a particular program comes within the provisions of paragraph (a) of this section depends on the facts of each case. However, the Commission will in any event consider that a program comes within the provisions of paragraph (a) of this section if in connection with such program a prize consisting of money or thing of value is awarded to any person whose selection is dependent in whole or in part upon lot or chance, if as a condition of winning or competing for such prize, such winner or winners are required to furnish any money or thing of value or are required to have in their possession any product sold, manufactured, furnished, or distributed by a sponsor of a program cablecast on the system in question.

(c) The provisions of paragraphs (a) and (b) of this section shall not apply to advertisements or lists of prizes or information concerning:

(1) A lottery conducted by a State acting under authority of State law which is transmitted:

(i) by a cable system located in that State,

(ii) by a cable system located in another State which conducts such a lottery, or

(iii) by a cable system located in another State which is integrated with a cable system described in paragraphs (c)(1)(i) or (ii) of this section, if termination of the receipt of such transmission by the cable systems in such other State would be technically infeasible.

(2) Any gaming conducted by an Indian Tribe pursuant to the Indian Gaming Regulatory Act (25 USC section 2701 et seq.).

(d) For the purposes of paragraph (c) lottery means the pooling of proceeds derived from the sale of tickets or chances and allotting those proceeds or parts thereof by chance to one or more chance takers or ticket purchasers. It does not include the placing or accepting of bets or wagers on sporting events or contests.

(e) For purposes of paragraph (c)(3)(i) of this section, the term "not for profit organization" means any organization that would qualify as tax exempt under Section 501 of the Internal Revenue Code of 1986.

Sponsorship Identification; List Retention; Related Requirements (§76.221).

(a) When a cable television system operator engaged in origination cablecasting presents any matter for which money, service, or other valuable consideration is either directly or indirectly paid or promised to, or charged or accepted by such cable television system operator, the cable television system operator, at the time of the cablecast, shall announce (i) that such matter is sponsored, paid for, or furnished, either in whole and or in part, and (ii) by whom or on whose behalf such consideration was supplied: provided, however, that "service or other valuable consideration" shall not include any service or property furnished either without or at a nominal charge for use on, or in connection with, a cablecast unless it is so furnished in consideration for an identification of any person, product, service, trademark, or brand name beyond an identification reasonably related to the use of such service or property on the cablecast. In the case of any political advertisement cablecast under this subsection that concerns candidates for public office, the sponsor shall be identified with letters equal to or greater than four percent of the vertical picture height that air for not less than four seconds.

(b) Each cable television system operator engaged in origination cablecasting shall exercise reasonable diligence to obtain from its employes, and from other persons with whom it deals directly in connection with any matter for cablecasting, information to enable such system operator to make the announcement required by this section.

(c) In the case of any political origination cablecast or any origination cablecast matter involving the discussion of public controversial issues for which any film, record, transcription, talent, script or other material or service of any kind is furnished, either directly or indirectly, to a cable television system operator as an inducement for cablecasting such matter, an announcement shall be made both at the beginning and conclusion of such cablecast on which such material or service is used that such film record, transcription, talent, script or other material or service has been furnished to such cable television system operator in connection with the transmission of such cablecast matter: provided, however, that in the case of any cablecast of five minutes' duration or less, only one such announcement need be made either at the beginning or conclusion of the cablecast.

(d) The announcement required by this section shall, in addition to stating the fact that the origination cablecasting matter was sponsored, paid for or furnished, fully and fairly disclose the true identity of the person or persons, or corporation, committee, association or other unincorporated group, or other entity by whom or on whose behalf such payment is made or promised or from whom or on whose behalf such services or other valuable consideration is received, or by whom the material or services referred to in paragraph (c) of this section are furnished. Where an agent or other person or entity contracts or otherwise makes arrangements with a cable television system operator on behalf of another, and such fact is known or by the exercise of reasonable diligence, as specified in paragraph (b) if this section, could be known to the system operator, the announcement shall disclose the identity of the person or persons or entity on whose behalf such agent is acting instead of the name of such agent. Where the origination cablecasting material is political matter or matter involving the discussion of controversial issue of public importance and a corporation, committee, association or other unincorporated group, or other entity that is paying for or furnishing the matter, the system operator shall, in addition to making the announcement required by this section, require that a list of the chief executive officers or members of the executive committee or of the board of directors of the corporation, committee, association or other unincorporated group, or other entity shall be made available for public inspection at the local office of the system. Such lists shall be kept and made available for a period of two years.

(e) In the case of origination cablecast matter advertising commercial products or services, an announcement stating the sponsor's corporate or trade name, or the name of the sponsor's product, when it is clear that the mention of the name of the product constitutes a sponsorship identification, shall be deemed sufficient for the purposes of this section and only one such announcement need be made at any time during trhe course of the cablecast.

(f) The announcement otherwise required by this section is waived with respect to the origination cablecast of "want ad" or classified advertisements sponsored by an individual. The waiver granted in this paragraph shall not extend to a classified advertisement or want ad sponsorship by any form of business enterprise, corporate or otherwise. Whenever sponsorship announcements are omitted pursuant to this paragraph, the cable television system operator shall observe the following conditions:

(1) Maintain a list showing name, address and (where available) the telephone number of each advertiser;

(2) Make this list available to the members of the public who have a legitimate interest in obtaining the information contained in the list.

(g) The announcements required by this section are waived with respect to feature motion picture films produced initially and primarily for theater exhibition.

Commercial Limits in Children's Programs (§76.225).

(a) No cable operator shall air more than 10.5 minutes of commercial matter per hour during children's programming on weekends, or more than 12 minutes of commercial matter per hour on weekdays.

(b) This rule shall not apply to programs aired on a broadcast television channel which the cable operator passively carries, or to access channels over which the cable operator may not exercise editorial control, pursuant to 47 USC 531(e) and 532(c)(2).

(c) Cable operators must maintain records sufficient to verify compliance with this rule and make such records available to the public. Such records must be retained for a period sufficient to cover the limitations period specified in 47 USC 503(b)(6)(B).

NOTE 1: Commercial matter means air time sold for purposes of selling a product or service.

NOTE 2: For purposes of this section, children's programming refers to programs originally produced and broadcast primarily for an audience of children 12 years old and younger.

Cross-Ownership (§76.501).

(a) No cable television system (including all parties under common control) shall carry the signal of any television broadcast station if such system directly or indirectly owns, operates, controls, or has an interest in a TV broadcast station whose predicted Grade B contour, computed in accordance with §73.684 of Part 73 of this chapter, overlaps in whole or in part the service area of such system (i.e., the area within which the system is serving subscribers).

(b)(1) A cable television system (including all parties under common control) may directly or indirectly own, operate, control, or have an interest in a national television network (such as ABC, CBS, or NBC) only if such a system does not pass more than:

(i) 10 percent of homes passed on a nationwide basis when aggregated with all other cable systems in which the network holds such a cognizable interest, and

(ii) 50 percent of homes passed within any one ADI, except that a cable television system facing a competing system will not be counted toward this 50-percent limit.

(2) The requirements of paragraph (b)(1) of this section are applied at the acquisition date, except that a party with no prior attributable interests in a broadcast network or cable systems may exceed these limits in connection with a purchase of these operations from a party with such existing network-cable interests. Paragraph (b) of this section will not be applied so as to require divestiture of existing facilities.

(3) For purposes of paragraph (b) of this section:

(i) "Homes passed" is defined as the number of homes to which cable service is currently available whether or not a given household subscribes to the service.

(ii) "ADI" is defined as the Arbitron Area of Dominant Influence.

(iii) A "competing system" is faced by a network-owned cable system where the cable system provides service in the same area as another independently owned, multichannel video delivery system, as specified in §76.33(a)(2)(ii) of the rules. In order to be counted, such multichannel competitor must be capable of providing a package of local broadcast signals integrated within the service.

NOTE 1: The word "control" as used herein is not limited to majority stock ownership, but includes actual working control in whatever manner exercised.

NOTE 2: In applying the provisions of this section, ownership and other interests will be attributed to their holders and deemed cognizable pursuant to the following criteria:

(a) Except as otherwise provided herein, partnership and direct ownership interest and any voting stock interest amounting to 5% or more of the outstanding voting stock of a corporate broadcast licensee or cable television system will be cognizable;

(b) No minority voting stock interest will be cognizable if there is a single holder of more than 50% of the outstanding voting stock of the corporate broadcast licensee or cable television system in which the minority interest is held;

(c) Investment companies, as defined in 15 USC 80a-3, insurance companies and banks holding stock through their trust departments in trust accounts will be considered to have a cognizable interest only if they hold 10% or more of the outstanding voting stock of a corporate broadcast licensee or cable television system, or if any of the officers or directors of the broadcast licensee or cable television system are representatives of the investment company, insurance company or bank concerned. Holdings by a bank or insurance company will be aggregated if the bank or insurance company has any right to determine how the stock will be voted. Holdings by investment companies will be aggregated if under common management;

(d) Attribution of ownership interests in a broadcast licensee or cable television system that are held indirectly by any party through one or more intervening corporations will be determined by successive multiplication of the ownership percentages for each link in the vertical ownership chain and application of the relevant attribution benchmark to the resulting product, except that wherever the ownership percentage for any link in the chain exceeds 50%, it shall not be included for purposes of this multiplication. [For example, if A owns 10% of company X, which owns 60% of company Y, which owns 25% of "Licensee," then X's interest in "Licensee" would be 25% (the same as Y's interest since X's interest in Y exceeds 50%), and A's interest in "Licensee" would be 2.5% (0.1 x 0.25). Under the 5% attribution benchmark, X's interest in "Licensee" would be cognizable, while A's interest would not be cognizable.]

(e) Voting stock interests held in trust shall be attributed to any person who holds or shares the power to vote such stock, to any person who has the power to sell such stock, and to any person who has the right to revoke the trust at will or to replace the trustee at will. If the trustee has a familial, personal or extra-trust business relationship to the grantor or the beneficiary, the grantor or beneficiary, as appropriate, will be attributed with the stock interests held in trust. An otherwise qualified trust will be ineffective to insulate the grantor or beneficiary from attribution with the trust's assets unless all voting stock interests held by the grantor or beneficiary in the relevant broadcast licensee or cable television system are subject to said trust.

(f) Holders of non-voting stock shall not be attributed an interest in the issuing entity. Holders of debt and instruments such as warrants, convertible debentures, options or other non-voting interests with rights of conversion to voting interests shall not be attributed unless and until conversion is effected.

(g)(1) A limited partnership interest shall be attributed to a limited partner unless that partner is not materially involved, directly or indirectly, in the management or operation of the media-related activities of the partnership and the licensee or system so certifies.

(2) In order for a licensee or system to make the certification set forth in paragraph (g)(1) of this NOTE, it must verify that the partnership agreement or certificate of limited partnership, with respect to the particular limited partner exempt from attribution, establishes that the exempt limited partner has no material involvement, directly or indirectly, in the management or operation of the media activities of the partnership. The criteria which would assure adequate insulation for purposes of this certification are described in the Memorandum Opinion and Order in MM Docket No. 83-46, FCC 85-252 (released June 24, 1985) as modified on reconsideration in MM Docket No. 83-46, FCC 86-410 (released November 28, 1986). Irrespective of the terms of the certificate of limited partnership or partnership agreement, however, no such certification shall be made if the individual or entity making the certification has actual knowledge of any material involvement of the limited partners in the management or operation of the media-related businesses of the partnership.

(h) Officers and directors of a broadcast licensee or cable television system are considered to have a cognizable interest in the entity with which they are so associated. If any such entity engages in businesses in addition to its primary business of broadcasting or cable television service, it may request the Commission to waive attribution for any officer or director whose duties and responsibilities are wholly unrelated to its primary business. The officers and directors of a parent company of a broadcast licensee or a cable television system, with an attributable interest in any such subsidiary entity, shall be deemed to have a cognizable interest in the subsidiary unless the duties and responsibilities of the officer or director involved are wholly unrelated to the broadcast licensee or cable television system subsidiary, and a statement properly documenting this fact is submitted to the Commission. (This statement may be included on appropriate Ownership Report.) The officers and directors of a sister corporation of a broadcast licensee or cable television system shall not be attributed with ownership of these entities by virtue of such status.

(i) Discrete ownership interests will be aggregated in determining whether or not an interest is cognizable under this section. An individual or entity will be deemed to have a cognizable investment if:

(1) The sum of the interests held by or through "passive investors" is equal to or exceeds 10 percent; or

(2) The sum of the interests other than those held by or through "passive investors" is equal to or exceeds 5 percent; or

(3) The sum of the interests computed under paragraph (i)(1) of this NOTE plus the sum of the interests computed under paragraph (i)(2) of this NOTE is equal to or exceeds 10 percent.

NOTE 3: In cases where record and beneficial ownership of voting stock is not identical (e.g., bank nominees holding stock as record owners for the benefit of mutual funds, brokerage houses holding stock in street names for benefit of customers, investment advisors holding stock in their own names for the benefit of clients, and insurance companies holding stock), the party having the right to determine how the stock will be voted will be considered to own it for purposes of this subpart.

NOTE 4: Paragraph (a) of this section will not be applied so as to require the divestiture of ownership interests proscribed herein solely because of the transfer of such interests to heirs or legatees by will or intestacy, provided that the degree or extent of the proscribed cross-ownership is not increased by such transfer.

(c) Effective date. The provisions of paragraph (a) of this section are not effective until November 8, 1987, as to ownership interests proscribed herein if such interests were in existence on or before July 1, 1970 (e.g., if a franchise were in existence on or before July 1, 1970), and will be applied to cause divestiture as to ownership interests proscribed herein only where the cable system is, directly or indirectly, owned, operated, controlled by, or has an interest in a non-satellite television broadcast station which places a principal community contour encompassing the entire community and there is no other commercial non-satellite television broadcast station placing a principal community contour encompassing the entire community.

Cable Television System Reports (§76.403)

The operator of every operational cable television system shall correct and/or furnish information in response to forms, encompassing each community unit, mailed to said operator by the Commission. These include:

Community unit data; "Annual Report of Cable Television System," Form 325, Schedule 1.

Physical system data; "Annual Report of Cable Television System," Form 325, Schedule 2.

Operator ownership data; "Annual Report of Cable Television System," Form 325, Schedules 3 and 4.

These forms shall be completed and returned to the Commission within 60 days after the date of mailing by the Commission.

NOTE: The operator of a cable television system having fewer than 1000 subscribers shall only be required to file Schedules 1 and 2 of Form 325 for each community unit.

Lockbox Enforcement (§76.11)

Any party aggrieved by the failure or refusal of a cable operator to provide a lockbox as provided for in title VI of the Communications Act may petition the Commission for relief in accordance with the provisions and procedures set forth in §76.7 for petitions for special relief.

Registration Statement Required (§76.12).

A separate unit shall be authorized to commence operation only after filing with the Commission the following information:

(a) The legal name of the operator, Entity Identification or Social Security number, and whether the operator is an individual, private association, partnership, or corporation. If the operator is a partnership, the legal name of the partner responsible for communications with the Commission shall be supplied;

(b) The assumed name (if any) used for doing business in the community;

(c) The mail address, including zip code, and the telephone number to which all communications are to be directed;

(d) The date the system provided service to 50 subscribers;

(e) The name of the community area served and the county in which it is located;

(f) The television broadcast signals to be carried which previously have not been certified or registered.

Scope of Application (§76.300).

(a) The provisions of §§76.302, 76.306, and 76.307 are applicable to all cable television systems.

(b) The provisions of §76.301 and §76.305 are not applicable to any cable television system serving fewer than 1,000 subscribers.

Copies of Rules (§76.301).

The operator of a cable television system shall have a current copy of Part 76, and is expected to be familiar with the rules governing cable television systems.

Required record keeping for must-carry purposes (§76.302).

(a) Effective June 17, 1993, the operator of every cable television system shall maintain for public inspection a file containing a list of all broadcast television stations carried by its system in fulfillment of the must-carry requirements pursuant to §76.56 of the rules. Such list shall include the call sign, community of license, broadcast channel number, cable channel number, and in the case of a noncommercial educational broadcast station, whether that station was carried by the cable system on March 29, 1990.

(b) The operator of every cable television system shall maintain for public inspection the designation and location of its principal headend.

(c) Such records must be maintained in accordance with the provisions of §76.305(b).

(d) Upon written request from any person, a cable operator is required to provide the list of signals specified in paragraph (a) of this section in writing within 30 days of receipt of such request.

Records to be Maintained Locally by Cable Television System Operators for Public Inspection (§76.305).

(a) Records to be maintained. The operator of every cable television system having 1,000 or more subscribers shall maintain for public inspection a file containing a copy of all records which are required to be kept by §76.205(d) (origination cablecasts by candidates for public office); §76.221(f) (sponsorship identification); §76.79 (EEO records available for public inspection); §76.601(c) (proof of performance test data; §76.601(e) (signal leakage logs and repair records); and §76.701(h) (records for leased access).

(b) Location of records. The public inspection file shall be maintained at the office which the system operator maintains for ordinary collection of subscriber charges, resolution of subscriber complaints, and other business or at any accessible place in the community served by the system unit(s) (such as a public registry for documents or an attorney's office). The public inspection file shall be available for public inspection at any time during regular business hours.

(c) Period of retention. The records specified in paragraph (a) of this section shall be retained for the period specified in §§76.205(d), 76.221(f), 76.79, 76.601(c), and 76.601(e), respectively.

(d) Reproduction of records. Copies of any material in the public inspection file shall be available for machine reproduction upon request made in person, provided the requesting party shall pay the reasonable cost for reproduction. Request for machine copies shall be fulfilled at a location specified by the system operator, within a reasonable period of time, which in no event shall be longer than seven days. The system Operator is not required to honor requests made by mail but may do so if it so chooses.

System Inspection (§76.307).

The operator of a cable television system shall make the system, its public inspection file (if required by §76.305), and its records of subscribers available for inspection upon request by an authorized representative of the Commission at any reasonable hour.

Customer Service Obligations (§76.309).

(a) A cable franchise authority may enforce the customer service standards set forth in paragraph (c) of this section against cable operators. The franchise authority must provide affected cable operators ninety (90) days written notice of its intent to enforce standards.

(b) Nothing in this section should be construed to prevent or prohibit:

(1) A franchising authority and a cable operator from agreeing to customer service requirements that exceed the standards set forth in paragraph (c) of this section;

(2) A franchising authority from enforcing, through the end of the franchise term, pre-existing customer service requirements that exceed the standards set forth in paragraph (c) of this section and are contained in current franchise agreements;

(3) Any State or any franchising authority from enacting or enforcing any consumer protection law, to the extent not specifically preempted herein; or

(4) The establishment or enforcement of any State or municipal law or regulation concerning customer service that imposes customer service requirements that exceed, or address matters not addressed by, the standards set forth in paragraph (c) of this section.

(c) Effective July 1, 1993, a cable operator shall be subject to the following customer service standards:

(1) Cable system office hours and telephone availability:

(i) The cable operator will maintain a local, toll-free or collect call telephone access line which will be available to its subscribers 24 hours a day, seven days a week.

(A) Trained company representatives will be available to respond to customer telephone inquiries during normal business hours.

(B) After normal business hours, the access line may be answered by a service or an automated response system, including an answering machine. Inquiries received after normal business hours must be responded to by a trained company representative on the next business day.

(ii) Under normal operating conditions, telephone answer time by a customer representative, including wait time, shall not exceed thirty (30) seconds when the connection is made. If the call needs to be transferred, transfer time shall not exceed thirty (30) seconds. These standards shall be met no less than ninety (90) percent of the time under normal operating conditions, measured on a quarterly basis.

(iii) The operator will not be required to acquire equipment or perform surveys to measure compliance with the telephone answering standards above unless an historical record of complaints indicates a clear failure to comply.

(iv) Under normal operating conditions, the customer will receive a busy signal less than three (3) percent of the time.

(v) Customer service center and bill payment locations will be open at least during normal business hours and will be conveniently located.

(2) Installations, outages and service calls. Under normal operating conditions, each of the following four standards will be met no less than ninety five (95) percent of the time measured on a quarterly basis:

(i) Standard installations will be performed within seven (7) business days after an order has been placed. "Standard" installations are those that are located up to 125 feet from the existing distribution system.

(ii) Excluding conditions beyond the control of the operator, the cable operator will begin working on "service interruptions" promptly and in no event later than 24 hours after the interruption becomes known. The cable operator must begin actions to correct other service problems the next business day after notification of the service problem.

(iii) The "appointment window" alternatives for installations, service calls, and other installation activities will be either a specific time or, at maximum, a four-hour time block during normal business hours. (The operator may schedule service calls and other installation activities outside of normal business hours for the express convenience of the customer.)

(iv) An operator may not cancel an appointment with a customer after the close of business on the business day prior to the scheduled appointment.

(v) If a cable operator representative is running late for an appointment with a customer and will not be able to keep the appointment as scheduled, the customer will be contacted. The appointment will be rescheduled, as necessary, at a time which is convenient for the customer.

(3) Communications between cable operators and cable subscribers:

(i) Notifications to subscribers:

(A) The cable operator shall provide written information on each of the following areas at the time of installation of service, at least annually to all subscribers, and at any time upon request:

(1) Products and services offered;

(2) Prices and options for programming services and conditions of subscription to programming and other services;

(3) Installation and service maintenance policies;

(4) Instructions on how to use the cable service;

(5) Channel positions of programming carried on the system; and

(6) Billing and complaint procedures, including the address and telephone number of the local franchise authority's cable office.

(B) Customers will be notified of any changes in rates, programming services or channel positions as soon as possible through announcements on the cable system and in writing. Notice must be given to subscribers a minimum of thirty (30) days in advance of such changes if the change is within the control of the cable operator. In addition, the cable operator shall notify subscribers thirty (30) days in advance of any significant changes in the other information required by the preceding paragraph.

(ii) Billing:

(A) Bills will be clear, concise and understandable. Bills must be fully itemized, with itemizations including, but not limited to, basic and premium service charges and equipment charges. Bills will also clearly delineate all activity during the billing period, including optional charges, rebates and credits.

(B) In case of a billing dispute, the cable operator must respond to a written complaint from a subscriber within thirty (30) days.

(iii) Refunds: Refund checks will be issued promptly, but no later than either:

(A) The customer's next billing cycle following resolution of the request or thirty (30) days, whichever is earlier, or

(B) The return of the equipment supplied by the cable operator if service is terminated.

(iv) Credits: Credits for service will be issued no later than the customer's next billing cycle following the determination that a credit is warranted.

(4) Definitions:

(i) Normal Business Hours: The term "normal business hours" means those hours during which most similar businesses in the community are open to serve customers. In all cases, "normal business hours" must include some evening hours at least one night per week and/or some weekend hours.

(ii) Normal Operating Conditions: The term "normal operating conditions" means those service conditions which are within the control of the cable operator. Those conditions which are not within the control of the cable operator include, but are not limited to, natural disasters, civil disturbances, power outages, telephone network outages, and severe or unusual weather conditions. Those conditions which are ordinarily within the control of the cable operator include, but are not limited to, special promotions, pay-per-view events, rate increases, regular peak or seasonal demand periods, and maintenance or upgrade of the cable system.

(iii) Service Interruption: The term "service interruption" means the loss of picture or sound on one or more cable channels.

Equal Employment Opportunity Requirements

Scope of Application (§76.71).

(a) The provisions of the subpart shall apply to any corporation, partnership, association, joint-stock company, or trust engaged primarily in the management or operation of any cable system. Cable entities subject to these provisions include those systems defined in §76.5(a) of the rules and all satellite master antenna systems serving 50 or more subscribers.

(b) Employment units. The provisions of this subpart shall apply to cable entities as employment units. Each cable entity may be considered a separate employment unit; however, where two or more cable entities are under common ownership or control and are interrelated in their local management, operation and utilization of employes, they shall constitute a single employment unit.

(c) Headquarters office. A multiple cable operator shall treat as a separate unit each headquarters office to the extent the work of that office is primarily related to the operation of more than one employment unit as described in paragraph (b) of this section.

General EEO Policy (§76.73).

(a) Equal opportunity in employment shall be afforded by each cable entity to all qualified persons, and no person shall be discriminated against in employment by such entity because of race, color, religion, national origin, age or sex.

(b) Each employment unit shall establish, maintain and carry out a positive program of specific practices designed to assure equal opportunity to every aspect of cable system employment policy and practice. Under the terms of its program, an employment unit shall:

(1) Define the responsibility of each level of management to ensure a positive application and vigorous enforcement of its policy of equal opportunity, and establish a procedure to review and control managerial and supervisory performance;

(2) Inform its employes and recognized employe organizations of the positive equal employment opportunity policy and program and enlist their cooperation;

(3) Communicate its equal employment opportunity policy and program and its employment needs to sources of qualified applicants without regard to race, color, religion, national origin, age or sex, and solicit their recruitment assistance on a continuing basis;

(4) Conduct a continuing program to exclude every form of prejudice or discrimination based upon race, color, religion, national origin, age or sex, and solicit their recruitment assistance on a continuing basis;

(5) Conduct a continuing review of job structure and employment practices and adopt positive recruitment, training, job design and other measures needed to ensure genuine equality of opportunity to participate fully in all organizational units, occupations and levels of responsibilty.

EEO Program Requirements (§76.75).

An employment unit's equal employment opportunity program should reasonably address itself to the specific areas set forth below, to the extent possible and to the extent that they are appropriate in terms of employment unit size, location, etc.:

(a) Disseminate its equal employment opportunity program to job applicants, employes and those with whom it regularly does business. For example, this requirement may be met by:

(1) Posting notices in the employment unit's office and places of employment informing employes and applicants for employment of their equal employment opportunity rights, and their right to notify the Equal Employment Opportunity Commission, the Federal Communications Commission or other appropriate agency, if they believe they have been discriminated against. Where a significant percentage of employes, employment applicants or residents of the community of a cable television system or the relevant labor area are Hispanic, such notices should be posted in Spanish and English. Similar use should be made of other languages in such posted equal opportunity notices, where appropriate;

(2) Placing a notice in bold type on the employment application informing prospective employes that discrimination because of race, color, religion, national origin, age or sex is prohibited and that they may notify the Equal Employment Commission, the Federal Communications Commission or other appropriate agency if they believe they have been discriminated against.

(b) Use minority organizations, organizations for women, media, educational institutions and other potential sources of minority and female applicants, to supply referrals whenever job vacancies are available in its operation. For example, this requirement may be met by:

(1) Placing employment advertisements in media that have significant circulation among minority-group people in the recruiting area;

(2) Recruiting through schools and colleges with significant minority-group enrollments;

(3) Maintaining systematic contacts with minority and human relations organizations, leaders and spokesmen to encourage referral of qualified minority or female applicants;

(4) Encouraging current employes to refer minority or female applicants;

(5) Making known to the appropriate recruitment sources in the employer's immediate area that qualified minority members and females are being sought for consideration whenever the employment unit hires.

(c) Evaluate its employment profile and job turnover against the availability of minorities and women in its franchise area. For example, this requirement may be met by:

(1) Comparing composition of relevant labor area with the composition of the entity's employes;

(2) Comparing its employes, within each job category, with the people available for such positions;

(3) Where there is underrepresentation of either minorities and/or women, examining the company's personnel policies and practices to assure that they do not inadvertently screen out any protected group and take appropriate action where necessary.

NOTE: These data are generally available on a metropolitan statistical area (MSA), primary metropolitan statistical area (PMSA) or county basis.

(d) Undertake to offer promotions of minorities and women in a non-discriminatory fashion to positions of greater responsibility. For example, this requirement may be met by:

(1) Instructing those who make decisions on placement and promotion that minority employes and females are to be considered without discrimination, and that the job areas in which there is little or no minority or female representation should be reviewed to determine whether this results from discrimination;

(2) Giving minority groups and female employes equal opportunity for positions which lead to higher positions. Inquiring as to the interest and skills of all lower paid employes with respect to any of the higher paid position, followed by assistance, counseling and effective measures to enable employes with interest and potential to qualify themselves for such positions;

(3) Providing opportunity to perform overtime work on a basis that does not discriminate against qualified minority group or female employes.

(e) Encourage minority and female entrepreneurs to conduct business with all parts of its operation. For example, this requirement may be met by:

(1) Recruiting as wide as possible a pool of qualified entrepreneurs from sources such as employe referals, community groups, contractors, associations and other sources likely to be representative of minority and female interests.

(f) Analyze the results of its efforts to recruit, hire, promote and use the services of minorities and women and explain any difficulties encountered in implementing its equal employment opportunity program. For example, this requirement may be met by:

(1) Where union agreements exist, cooperating with the union or unions in the development of programs to assure qualified minority persons or females of equal opportunity for employment, and including an effective nondiscrimination clause in new or renegotiated union agreements;

(2) Avoiding use of selection techniques or tests that have the effect of discriminating against qualified minority groups or females;

(3) Reviewing seniority practices to ensure that such practices are nondiscriminatory;

(4) Examining rates of pay and fringe benefits for employes having the same duties, and eliminating any inequities based upon race or sex discrimination.

Reporting Requirements (§76.77).

(a) Annual employment report. Each employment unit with six or more full-time employes shall file an annual employment report (FCC Form 395A) with the Commission on or before May 1 of each year. Employment data on the annual employment report shall reflect the figures from any one payroll period in January, February or March of the year during which the report is filed. Unless instructed otherwise by the FCC, the same payroll period shall be used for each successive annual employment report.

(b) Certification of Compliance. The Commission will use the information submitted on Form 395A to determine whether cable systems are in compliance with the provisions of this subpart. Cable systems found to be in compliance with these rules will receive a Certificate of Compliance.

(c) Investigations. The Commission will investigate each cable system at least once every five years. Cable systems are required to submit supplemental investigation information with their regular Form 395A reports in the years they are investigated.

Records Available for Public Inspection (§76.79).

(a) A copy of every annual employment report, and any other employment report filed with the Commission, and complaint report that has been filed with the Commission, and copies of all exhibits, letters and other documents filed as part thereof, all amendments thereto, all correspondence between the cable entity and the Commission pertaining to the reports after they have been filed in all documents incorporated therein by reference, unless specifically exempted from the requirement, are open for public inspection at the offices of the Commission in Washington, D.C.

(b) Every employment unit shall maintain for public inspection a file containing copies of all annual reports. Each document shall be retained for a period of five years. The file shall be maintained at the central office and at every location with more than five full-time employes. A headquarters employment unit file and a file containing a consolidated set of all documents pertaining to the other employment units of a multiple cable operator shall be maintained at the central office of the headquarters employment unit. The cable entity shall provide reasonable accomodations at these locations for undisturbed inspection of his equal employment opportunity records by members of the public during regular business hours.

Closed captioning (§76.606).

(a) The requirements for closed captioning are as follows:

(1) As of June 30, 1992, the operator of each cable television system shall not take any action to remove or alter closed captioning data contained on line 21 of the vertical blanking interval; and

(2) As of July 1, 1993, the operator of each cable television system shall deliver intact closed captioning data contained on line 21 of the vertical blanking interval, as it arrives at the headend or from another origination source, to subscriber terminals and (when so delivered to the cable system) in a format that can be recovered and displayed by decoders meeting §15.119 of the Rules.

Resolution of complaints (§76.607).

Cable system operators shall establish a process for resolving complaints from subscribers about the quality of the television signal delivered. These records shall be maintained for at least a one-year period. Aggregate data based upon these complaints shall be made available for inspection by the Commission and franchising authorities, upon request. Subscribers shall be advised, at least once each calendar year, of the procedures for resolution of complaints by the cable system operator, including the address of the responsible officer of the local franchising authority.

NOTE: Prior to being referred to the Commission, complaints from subscribers about the quality of the television signal delivered must be referred to the local franchising authority and the cable system operator.

Cable Act of 1984, as amended 1992

Cable Channels for Public, Educational, or Governmental Use (Sec. 611).

(a) A franchising authority may establish requirements in a franchise with respect to the designation or use of channel capacity for public, educational, or governmental use only to the extent provided in this section.

(b) A franchising authority may in its request for proposals require as part of a franchise, and may require as part of a cable operator's proposal for a franchise renewal, subject to section 626, that channel capacity be designated for public, educational, or governmental use, and channel capacity on institutional networks be designated for educational or governmental use, and may require rules and procedures for the use of the channel capacity pursuant to this section.

(c) A franchising authority may enforce any requirement in any franchise regarding the providing or use of such channel capacity. Such enforcement authority includes the authority to enforce any provisions of the franchise for services, facilities, or equipment proposed by the cable operator which relate to public, educational, or governmental use of channel capacity, whether or not required by the franchising authority pursuant to subsection (b).

(d) In the case of any franchise under which the channel capacity is designated under subsection (b), the franchising authority shall prescribe:

(1) rules and procedures under which the cable operator is permitted to use such channel capacity for the provision of other services if such channel capacity is not being used for the purposes designated, and

(2) rules and procedures under which such permitted use shall cease.

(e) Subject to section 624(d), a cable operator shall not exercise any editorial control over any public, educational, or governmental use of channel capacity provided pursuant to this subsection.

(f) For the purposes of this section, the term "institutional network" means a communication network which is constructed or operated by the cable operator and which is generally available only to subscribers who are not residential subscribers.

Cable Channels for Commercial Use. (Sec. 612)

(a) The purpose of this section is to promote competition in the delivery of diverse sources of video programming and to assure that the widest possible diversity of information sources are made available to the public from cable systems in a manner consistent with growth and development of cable systems.

(b)(1) A cable operator shall designate channel capacity for commercial use by persons unaffiliated with the operator in accordance with the following requirements:

(A) An operator of any cable system with 36 or more (but not more than 54) activated channels shall designate 10 percent of such channels which are not otherwise required for use (or the use of which is not prohibited) by Federal law or regulation.

(B) An operator of any cable system with 55 or more (but no more than 100) activated channels shall designate 15 percent of such channels which are not otherwise required for use (or the use of which is not prohibited) by Federal law or regulation.

(C) An operator of any cable system with more than 100 activated channels shall designate 15 percent of all such channels.

(D) An operator of any cable system with fewer than 36 activated channels shall not be required to designate channel capacity for commercial use by persons unaffiliated with the operator, unless the cable system is required to provide such channel capacity under the terms of the franchise in effect on the date of the enactment of this title.

(E) An operator of any cable system in operation on the date of the enactment of this title shall not be required to remove any service actually being provided on July 1, 1984, in order to comply with this section, but shall make channel capacity available for commercial use as such capacity becomes available until such time as the cable operator is in full compliance with this section.

(2) Any Federal agency, State, or franchising authority may not require any cable system to designate channel capacity for commercial use by unaffiliated persons in excess of the capacity specified in paragraph (1), except as otherwise provided in this section.

(3) A cable operator may not be required, as part of a request for proposals or as part of a proposal for renewal, subject to section 626, to designate channel capacity for any use (other than commercial use by unaffiliated persons under this section) except as provided in sections 611 and 637, but a cable operator may offer in a franchise, or proposal for renewal thereof, to provide, consistent with applicable law, such capacity for other than commercial use by such persons.

(4) A cable operator may use any unused channel capacity designated pursuant to this section until the use of such channel capacity is obtained, pursuant to a written agreement, by a person unaffiliated with the operator.

(5) For the purposes of this section, the term "commercial use" means the provision of video programming, whether or not for profit.

(6) Any channel capacity which has been designated for public, educational, or governmental use may not be considered as designated under this section for commercial use for purpose of this section.

(c)(1) If a person unaffiliated with the cable operator seeks to use channel capacity designated pursuant to subsection (b) for commercial use, the cable operator shall establish, consistent with the purpose of this section, and with rules prescribed by the Commission under paragraph (4), the price, terms, and conditions of such use which are at least sufficient to assure that such use will not adversely affect the operation, financial condition, or market development of the cable system.

(2) A cable operator shall not exercise any editorial control over any video programming provided pursuant to this section, or in any other way consider the content of such programming, except that an operator may consider such content to the minimum extent necessary to establish a reasonable price for the commercial use of designated channel capacity by an unaffiliated person.

(3) Any cable system channel designated in accordance with this section shall not be used to provide a cable service that is being provided over such system on the date of the enactment of this title, if the provision of such programming is intended to avoid the purpose of this section.

(4)(A) The Commission shall have the authority to:

(i) determine the maximum reasonable rates that a cable operator may establish pursuant to paragraph (1) for commercial use of designated channel capacity, including the rate charged for the billing of rates to subscribers and for the collection of revenue from subscribers by the cable operator for such use;

(ii) establish reasonable terms and conditions for such use, including those for billing and collection; and

(iii) establish procedures for the expedited resolution of disputes concerning rates or carriage under this section.

(B) Within 180 days after the date of enactment of this paragraph, the Commission shall establish rules for determining maximum reasonable rates under subparagraph (A)(i), for establishing terms and conditions under subparagraph (A)(ii), and for providing procedures under subparagraph (A)(iii).

(d) Any person aggrieved by the failure or refusal of a cable operator to make channel capacity available for use pursuant to this section may bring an action in the district court of the United States for the judicial district in which the cable system is located to compel that such capacity be made available. If the court finds that the channel capacity sought by such person has not been made available in accordance with this section, or finds that the price, terms, or conditions, established by the cable operator are unreasonable, the court may order such system to make available to such person the channel capacity sought, and further determine the appropriate price, terms, or conditions, for such use consistent with subsection (c), and may award actual damages if it deems such relief appropriate. In any such action, the court shall not consider any price, term, or condition established between an operator and an affiliate for comparable services.

(e)(1) Any person aggrieved by the failure or refusal of a cable operator to make channel capacity available pursuant to this section may petition the Commission for relief under this subsection upon a showing of prior adjudicated violations of this section. Records of previous adjudications resulting in a court determination that the operator has violated this section shall be considered as sufficient for the showing necessary under this subsection. If the Commission finds that the channel capacity sought by such person has not been made available in accordance with this section, or that the price, terms, or conditions established by such system are unreasonable under subsection (c), the Commission shall, by rule or order, require such operator to make available such channel capacity under price, terms, and conditions consistent with subsection (c).

(2) In any case in which the Commission finds that the prior adjudicated violations of this section constitute a pattern or practice of violations by an operator, the Commission may also establish any further rule or order necessary to assure that the operator provides the diversity of information sources required by this section.

(3) In any case in which the Commission finds that the prior adjudicated violations of this section constitute a pattern or practice of violations by any person who is an operator of more than one cable system, the Commission may also establish any further rule or order necessary to assure that such person provides the diversity of information sources required by this section.

(f) In any action brought under this section in any Federal district court or before the Commission, there shall be a presumption that the price, terms, and conditions for use of channel capacity designated pursuant to subsection (b) are reasonable and in good faith unless shown by clear and convincing evidence to the contrary.

(g) Notwithstanding Sections 621(c) and 623(a), at such time as cable systems with 36 or more activated channels are available to 70 percent of households within the United States and are subscribed to by 70 percent of the households to which such systems are available, the Commission may promulgate any additional rules necessary to provide diversity of information sources. Any rules promulgated by the Commission pursuant to this subsection shall not preempt authority expressly granted to franchising authorities under this title.

(h) Any cable service offered pursuant to this section shall not be provided, or shall be provided subject to conditions, if such cable service in the judgment of the franchising authority or the cable operator is obscene, or is in conflict with community standards in that it is lewd, lascivious, filthy, or indecent or is otherwise unprotected by the Constitution of the United States. This subsection shall permit a cable operator to enforce prospectively a written and published policy of prohibiting programming that the cable operator reasonably believes describes or depicts sexual or excretory activities or organs in a patently offensive manner as measured by contemporary community standards.

(i)(1) Notwithstanding the provisions of subsections (b) and (c), a cable operator required by this section to designate channel capacity for commercial use may use any such channel capacity for the provision of programming from a qualified minority programming source or from any qualified educational programming source, whether or not such source is affiliated with the cable operator. The channel capacity used to provide programming from a qualified minority programming source or from any qualified educational programming source pursuant to this subsection may not exceed 33 percent of the channel capacity designated pursuant to this section. No programming provided over a cable system on July 1, 1990, may qualify as minority programming or educational programming on that cable system under this subsection.

(2) For purposes of this subsection, the term "qualified minority programming source" means a programming source which devotes substantially all of its programming to coverage of minority viewpoints, or to programming directed at members of minority groups, and which is over 50 percent minority-owned, as the term "minority" is defined in Section 309(i)(3)(C)(ii).

(3) For purposes of this subsection, the term "qualified educational programming source" means a programming source which devotes substantially all of its programming to educational or instructional programming that promotes public understanding of mathematics, the sciences, the humanities, and the arts and has a documented annual expenditure on programming exceeding

$15,000,000. The annual expenditure on programming means all annual costs incurred by the programming source to produce or acquire programs which are scheduled to be televised, and specifically excludes marketing, promotion, satellite transmission and operational costs, and general administrative costs.

(4) Nothing in this subsection shall substitute for the requirements to carry qualified noncommercial educational television stations as specified under Section 615.

(j)(1) Within 120 days following the date of the enactment of this subsection, the Commission shall promulgate regulations designed to limit the access of children to indecent programming, as defined by Commission regulations, and which cable operators have not voluntarily prohibited under subsection (h) by:

(A) requiring cable operators to place on a single channel all indecent programs, as identified by program providers, intended for carriage on channels designated for commercial use under this section;

(B) requiring cable operators to block such single channel unless the subscriber requests access to such channel in writing; and

(C) requiring programmers to inform cable operators if the program would be indecent as defined by Commission regulations.

(2) Cable operators shall comply with the regulations promulgated pursuant to paragraph (1).

Ownership Restrictions (Sec. 613).

(a)(1) It shall be unlawful for any person to be a cable operator if such person, directly or through one or more affiliates, owns or controls, the licensee of a television broadcast station and the predicted grade B contour of such station covers any portion of the community served by such operator's cable system.

(2) It shall be unlawful for a cable operator to hold a license for multichannel multipoint distribution service, or to offer satellite master antenna television service separate and apart from any franchised cable service, in any portion of the franchise area served by that cable operator's cable system. The Commission:

(A) shall waive the requirements of this paragraph for all existing multichannel multipoint distribution services and satellite master antenna television services which are owned by a cable operator on the date of enactment of this paragraph; and

(B) may waive the requirements of this paragraph to the extent the Commission determines is necessary to ensure that all significant portions of a franchise area are able to obtain video programming.

(b)(1) It shall be unlawful for any common carrier, subject in whole or in part to Title II of this Act, to provide video programming directly in subscribers in its telephone service area, either directly or indirectly through an affiliate owned by, operated by, controlled by, or under common control with the common carrier.

(2) It shall be unlawful for any common carrier, subject in whole or in part to Title II of this Act, to provide channels of communications or pole line conduit space, or other rental arrangements, to any entity which is directly or indirectly owned by, operated by, controlled by, or under common control with such common carrier, if such facilities or arrangements are to be used for, or in connection with, the provision of video programming directly to subscribers in the telephone service area of the common carrier.

(3) This subsection shall not apply to any common carrier to the extent such carrier provides telephone exchange service in any rural area (as defined by the Commission).

(4) In those areas where the provision of video programming directly to subscribers through a cable system demonstrably could not exist except through a cable system owned by, operated by, controlled by, or affiliated with the common carrier involved, or upon other showing of good cause, the Commission may, on petition for waiver, waive the applicability of paragraphs (1) and (2) of this subsection. Any such waiver shall be made in accordance with §63.56 of Title 47, Code of Federal Regulations (as in effect Sept. 20, 1984) and shall be granted by the Commission upon a finding that the issuance of such waiver is justified by the particular circumstances demonstrated by the petitioner, taking into account the policy of this subsection.

(c) The Commission may prescribe rules with respect to the ownership or control of cable systems by persons who own or control other media of mass communications which serve the same community served by a cable system.

(d) Any State or franchising authority may not prohibit the ownership or control of a cable system by any person because of such person's ownership or control of any other media of mass communications or other media interests. Nothing in this section shall be construed to prevent any State or franchising authority from prohibiting the ownership or control of a cable system in a jurisdiction by any person (1) because of such person's ownership or control of any other cable system in such jurisdiction; or (2) in circumstances in which the State or franchising authority determines that the acquisition of such a cable system may eliminate or reduce competition in the delivery of cable service in such jurisdiction.

(e)(1) Subject to paragraph (2), a State or franchising authority may hold any ownership interest in any cable system.

(2) Any State or franchising authority shall not exercise any editorial control regarding the content of any cable service on a cable system in which such governmental entity holds ownership interest (other than programming on any channel designated for educational or governmental use), unless such control is exercised through an entity separate from the franchising authority.

(f)(1) In order to enhance effective competition, the Commission shall, within one year after the date of enactment of the Cable Television Consumer Protection and Competition Act of 1992, conduct a proceeding:

(A) to prescribe rules and regulations establishing reasonable limits on the number of cable subscribers a person is authorized to reach through cable systems owned by such person, or in which such person has an attributable interest;

(B) to prescribe rules and regulations establishing reasonable limits on the number of channels on a cable system that can be occupied by a video programmer in which a cable operator has an attributable interest; and

(C) to consider the necessary and appropriateness of imposing limitations on the degree to which multichannel video programming distributors may engage in the creation or production of video programming.

(2) In prescribing rules and regulations under paragraph (1), the Commission shall, among other public interest objectives:

(A) ensure that no cable operator or group of cable operators can unfairly impede, either because of the size of any individual operator or because of joint actions by a group of operators of sufficient size, the flow of video programming from the video programmer to the consumer;

(B) ensure that cable operators affiliated with video programmers do not favor such programmers in determining carriage on their cable systems or do not unreasonably restrict the flow of the video programming of such programmers to other video distributors;

(C) take particular account of the market structure, ownership patterns, and other relationships of the cable television industry, including the nature and market power of the local franchise, the joint ownership of cable systems and video programmers, and the various types of non-equity controlling interests;

(D) account for any efficiencies and other benefits that might be gained through increased ownership or control;

(E) make such rules and regulations reflect the dynamic nature of the communications marketplace;

(F) not impose limitations which would bar cable operators from serving previously unserved rural areas; and

(G) not impose limitations which would impair the development of diverse and high quality video programming.

(g) This section shall not apply to prohibit any combination of any interests held by any person on July 1, 1984, to the extent of the interests so held as of such date, if the holding of such interests was not inconsistent with any applicable Federal or State law or regulations in effect on that date.

(h) For purposes of this section, the term "media of mass communications" shall have the meaning given such term under Section 309(i)(3)(C)(i) of this Act.

Carriage of Local Commercial Television Signals (Sec. 614).

(a) Carriage Obligations. Each cable operator shall carry, on the cable system of that operator, the signals of local commercial television stations and qualified low power stations as provided by this section. Carriage of additional broadcast television signals on such system shall be at the discretion of such operator, subject to Section 325(b).

(b) Signals Required:

(1) In general. (A) A cable operator of a cable system with 12 or fewer usable activated channels shall carry the signals of at least three local commercial television stations, except that if such a system has 300 or fewer subscribers, it shall not be subject to any requirements under this section so long as such system does not delete from carriage by that system any signal of a broadcast television station.

(B) A cable operator of a cable system with more than 12 usable activated channels shall carry the signals of local commercial television stations, up to one-third of the aggregate number of usable activated channels of such system.

(2) Selection of signals. Whenever the number of local commercial television stations exceeds the maximum number of signals a cable system is required to carry under paragraph (1), the cable operator shall have discretion in selecting which such stations shall be carried on its cable system, except that:

(A) under no circumstances shall a cable operator carry a qualified low power station in lieu of a local commercial television station; and

(B) if the cable operator elects to carry an affiliate of a broadcast network (as such term is defined by the Commission by regulation), such cable operator shall carry the affiliate of such broadcast network whose city of license reference point, as defined in §76.53 of Title 47, Code of Federal Regulations (in effect on January 1, 1991), or any successor regulation thereto, is closest to the principal headend of the cable system.

(3) Content to be carried. (A) A cable operator shall carry in its entirety, on the cable system of that operator, the primary video, accompanying audio, and line 21 closed caption transmission of each of the local commercial television stations carried on the cable system and, to the extent technically feasible, program-related material carried in the vertical blanking interval or on subcarriers. Retransmission of other material in the vertical blanking internal or other nonprogram-related material (including teletext and other subscription and advertiser-supported information services) shall be at the discretion of the cable operator. Where appropriate and feasible, operators may delete signal enhancements, such as ghost-canceling, from the broadcast signal and employ such enhancements at the system headend or headends.

(B) The cable operator shall carry the entirety of the program schedule of any television station carried on the cable system unless carriage of specific programming is prohibited, and other programming authorized to be substituted, under §76.67 or Subpart F of Part 76 of Title 47, Code of Federal Regulations (as in effect on January 1, 1991), or any successor regulations thereto.

(4) Signal quality:

(A) Nondegradation; technical specifications. The signals of local commercial television stations that a cable operator carries shall be carried without material degradation. The Commission shall adopt carriage standards to ensure that, to the extent technically feasible, the quality of signal processing and carriage provided by a cable system for the carriage of local commercial television stations will be no less than that provided by the system for carriage of any other type of signal.

(B) Advanced television. At such time as the Commission prescribes modifications of the standards for television broadcast signals, the Commission shall initiate a proceeding to establish any changes in the signal carriage requirements of cable television systems necessary to ensure cable carriage of such broadcast signals of local commercial television stations which have been changed to conform with such modified standards.

(5) Duplication not required. Notwithstanding paragraph (1), a cable operator shall not be required to carry the signal of any local commercial television station that substantially duplicates the signal of another local commercial television station which is carried on its cable system, or to carry the signals of more than one local commercial television station affiliated with a particular broadcast network (as such term is defined by regulation). If a cable operator elects to carry on its cable system a signal which substantially duplicates the signal of another local commercial television station carried on the cable system, or to carry on its system the signals of more than one local commercial television station affiliated with a particular broadcast network, all such signals shall be counted toward the number of signals the operator is required to carry under paragraph (1).

(6) Channel positioning. Each signal carried in fulfillment of the carriage obligations of a cable operator under this section shall be carried on the cable system channel number on which the local commercial television station is broadcast over the air, or on the channel on which it was carried on July 19, 1985, or on the channel on which it was carried on January 1, 1992, at the election of the station, or on such other channel number as is mutually agreed upon by the station and the cable operator. Any dispute regarding the positioning of a local commercial television station shall be resolved by the Commission.

(7) Signal availability. Signals carried in fulfillment of the requirements of this section shall be provided to every subscriber of a cable system. Such signals shall be viewable via cable on all television receivers of a subscriber which are connected to a cable system by a cable operator or for which a cable operator provides a connection. If a cable operator authorizes subscribers to install additional receiver connections, but does not provide the subscriber with such connections, or with the

equipment and materials for such connections, the operator shall notify such subscribers of all broadcast stations carried on the cable system which cannot be viewed via cable without a converter box and shall offer to sell or lease such a converter box to such subscribers at rates in accordance with Section 623(b)(3).

(8) Identification of signals carried. A cable operator shall identify, upon request by any person, the signals carried on its system in fulfillment of the requirements of this section.

(9) Notification. A cable operator shall provide written notice to a local commercial television station at least 30 days prior to either deleting from carriage or repositioning that station. No deletion or repositioning of a local commercial television station shall occur during a period in which major television ratings services measure the size of audiences of local television stations. The notification provisions of this paragraph shall not be used to undermine or evade the channel positioning or carriage requirements imposed upon cable operators under this section.

(10) Compensation for carriage. A cable operator shall not accept or request monetary payment or other valuable consideration in exchange either for carriage of local commercial television stations in fulfillment of the requirements of this section or for the channel positioning rights provided to such stations under this section, except that:

(A) any such station may be required to bear the costs associated with delivering a good quality signal or a baseband video signal to the principal headend of the cable system;

(B) a cable operator may accept payments from stations which would be considered distant signals under Section 111 of Title 17, United States Code, as indemnification for any increased copyright liability resulting from carriage of such signal; and

(C) a cable operator may continue to accept monetary payment or other valuable consideration in exchange for carriage or channel positioning of the signal of any local commercial television station carried in fulfillment of the requirements of this section, through, but not beyond, the date of expiration of an agreement thereon between a cable operator and a local commercial television station entered into prior to June 26, 1990.

(c) Low Power Station Carriage Obligation:

(1) Requirement. If there are not sufficient signals of full power local commercial television stations to fill the channels set aside under subsection (b):

(A) a cable operator of a cable system with a capacity of 35 or fewer usable activated channels shall be required to carry one qualified low power station; and

(B) a cable operator of a cable system with a capacity of more than 35 usable activated channels shall be required to carry two qualified low power stations.

(2) Use of public, educational, or governmental channels. A cable operator required to carry more than one signal of a qualified low power station under this subsection may do so, subject to approval by the franchising authority pursuant to Section 611, by placing such additional station on public, educational, or governmental channels not in use for their designated purposes.

(d) Remedies:

(1) Complaints by broadcast stations. Whenever a local commercial television station believes that a cable operator has failed to meet its obligations under this section, such station shall notify the operator, in writing, of the alleged failure and identify its reasons for believing that the cable operator is obligated to carry the signal of such station or has otherwise failed to comply with the channel positioning or repositioning or other requirements of this section. The cable operator shall, within 30 days of such written notification, respond in writing to such notification and either commence to carry the signal of such station in accordance with the terms requested or state its reasons for believing that it is not obligated to carry such signal or is in compliance with the channel positioning and repositioning and other requirements of this section. A local commercial television station that is denied carriage or channel positioning or repositioning in accordance with this section by a cable operator may obtain review of such denial by filing a complaint with the Commission. Such complaint shall allege the manner in which such cable operator has failed to meet its obligations and the basis for such allegations.

(2) Opportunity to respond. The Commission shall afford such cable operator an opportunity to present data and arguments to establish that there has been no failure to meet its obligations under this section.

(3) Remedial actions; dismissal. Within 120 days after the date a complaint is filed, the Commission shall determine whether the cable operator has met its obligations under this section. If the Commission determines that the cable operator has failed to meet such obligations, the Commission shall order the cable operator to reposition the complaining station or, in the case of an obligation to carry a station, to commence carriage of the station and to continue such carriage for at least 12 months. If the Commission determines that the cable operator has fully met the requirements of this section, it shall dismiss the complaint.

(e) Input Selector Switch Rules Abolished. No cable operator shall be required:

(1) to provide or make available any input selector switch as defined in 76.5(mm) of Title 47, Code of Federal Regulations, or any comparable device; or

(2) to provide information to subscribers about input selector switches or comparable devices.

(f) Regulations by Commission. Within 180 days after the date of enactment of this section, the Commission shall, following a rulemaking proceeding, issue regulations implementing the requirements imposed by this section. Such implementing regulations shall include necessary revisions to update §76.51 of Title 47 of the Code of Federal Regulations.

(g) Sales Presentations and Program Length Commercials:

(1) Carriage pending proceeding. Pending the outcome of the proceeding under paragraph (2), nothing in this Act shall require a cable operator to carry on any tier, or prohibit a cable operator from carrying on any tier, the signal of any commercial television station or video programming service that is predominantly utilized for the transmission of sales presentations or program length commercials.

(2) Proceeding concerning certain stations. Within 270 days after the date of enactment of this section, the Commission, notwithstanding prior proceedings to determine whether broadcast television stations that are predominantly utilized for the transmission of sales presentations or program length commercials are serving the public interest, convenience, and necessity, shall complete a proceeding in accordance with this paragraph to determine whether broadcast television stations that are predominantly utilized for the transmission of sales presentations or program length commercials are serving the public interest, convenience, and necessity. In conducting such proceeding, the Commission shall provide appropriate notice and opportunity for public comment. The Commission shall consider the viewing of such stations, the level of competing demands for the spectrum allocated to such stations, and the role of such stations in providing competition to nonbroadcast services offering similar programming. In the event that the Commission concludes that one or more of such stations are serving the public interest, convenience, and necessity, the Commission shall qualify such stations as local commercial television stations for purposes of subsection (a). In the event that the Commission concludes that one or more of such stations are not serving the public interest, convenience, and necessity, the Commission shall allow the licensees of such stations a reasonable period within which to provide different programming, and shall not deny such stations a renewal expectancy solely because their programming consisted predominantly of sales presentations or program length commercials.

(h) Definitions:

(1) Local commercial television station:

(A) In general. For purposes of this section, the term "local commercial television station" means any full power television broadcast station, other than a qualified noncommercial educational television station within the meaning of Section 615(l)(1), licensed and operating on a channel regularly assigned to its community by the Commission that, with respect to a particular cable system, is within the same television market as the cable system.

(B) Exclusions. The term "local commercial television station" shall not include:

(i) low power television stations, television translator stations, and passive repeaters which operate pursuant to Part 74 of Title 47, Code of Federal Regulations, or any successor regulations thereto;

(ii) a television broadcast station that would be considered a distant signal under Section 111 of Title 17, United States Code, if such station does not agree to indemnify the cable operator for any increased copyright liability resulting from carriage on the cable system; or

(iii) a television broadcast station that does not deliver to the principal headend of a cable system either a signal level of -45 dBm for UHF signals or -49 dBm for VHF signals at the input terminals of the signal processing equipment, if such station does not agree to be responsible for the costs of delivering to the cable system a signal of good quality or a baseband video signal.

(C) Market determinations. (i) For purposes of this section, a broadcasting station's market shall be determined in the manner provided in §73.3555(d)(3)(i) of Title 47, Code of Federal Regulations, as in effect on May 1, 1991, except that, following a written request, the Commission may, with respect to a particular television broadcast station, include additional communities within its television market or exclude communities from such station's television market to better effectuate the purposes of this section. In considering such requests, the Commission may determine that particular communities are part of more than one television market.

(ii) In considering requests filed pursuant to clause (i), the Commission shall afford particular attention to the value of localism by taking into account such factors as:

(I) whether the station, or other stations located in the same area, have been historically carried on the cable system or systems within such community;

(II) whether the television station provides coverage or other local service to such community;

(III) whether any other television station that is eligible to be carried by a cable system in such community in fulfillment of the requirements of this section provides news coverage of issues of concern to such community or provides carriage or coverage of sporting and other events of interest to the community; and

(IV) evidence of viewing patterns in cable and noncable households within the areas served by the cable system or systems in such community.

(iii) A cable operator shall not delete from carriage the signal of a commercial television station during the pendency of any proceeding pursuant to this subparagraph.

(iv) In the rulemaking proceeding required by subsection (f), the Commission shall provide for expedited consideration of requests filed under this subparagraph.

(2) Qualified low power station. The term "qualified low power station" means any television broadcast station conforming to the rules established for Low Power Television Stations contained in Part 74 of Title 47, Code of Federal Regulations, only if:

(A) such station broadcasts for at least the minimum number of hours of operation required by the Commission for television broadcast stations under Part 73 of Title 47, Code of Federal Regulations;

(B) such station meets all obligations and requirements applicable to television broadcast stations under Part 73 of Title 47, Code of Federal Regulations, with respect to the broadcast of nonentertainment programming; programming and rates involving political candidates, election issues, controversial issues of public importance, editorials, and personal attacks; programming for children; and equal employment opportunity; and the Commission determines that the provision of such programming by such station would address local news and informational needs which are not being adequately served by full power television broadcast stations because of the geographic distance of such full power stations from the low power station's community of license;

(C) such station complies with interference regulations consistent with its secondary status pursuant to Part 74 of Title 47, Code of Federal Regulations;

(D) such station is located no more than 35 miles from the cable system's headend, and delivers to the principal headend of the cable system an over-the-air signal of good quality, as determined by the Commission;

(E) the community of license of such station and the franchise area of the cable system are both located outside of the largest 160 Metropolitan Statistical Areas, ranked by population, as determined by the Office of Management and Budget on June 30, 1990, and the population of such community of license on such date did not exceed 35,000; and

(F) there is no full power television broadcast station licensed to any community within the county or other political subdivision (of a State) served by the cable system.

Nothing in this paragraph shall be construed to change the secondary status of any low power station as provided in Part 74 of Title 47, Code of Federal Regulations, as in effect on the date of enactment of this section.

Carriage of Noncommercial Educational Television (Sec. 615).

(a) Carriage obligations. In addition to the carriage requirements set forth in Section 614, each cable operator of a cable system shall carry the signals of qualified noncommercial educational television stations in accordance with the provisions of this section.

(b) Requirements to carry qualified stations:

(1) General requirement to carry each qualified station. Subject to paragraphs (2) and (3) and subsection (e), each cable operator shall carry, on the cable system of that cable operator, any qualified local noncommercial educational television station requesting carriage.

(2)(A) Systems with 12 or fewer channels. Notwithstanding paragraph (1), a cable operator of a cable system with 12 or fewer usable activated channels shall be required to carry the signal of one qualified local noncommercial educational television station; except that a cable operator of such a system shall comply with subsection (c) and may, in its discretion, carry the signals of other qualified noncommercial educational television stations.

(B) In the case of a cable system described in subparagraph (A) which operates beyond the presence of any qualified local noncommercial educational television station:

(i) the cable operator shall import and carry on that system the signal of one qualified noncommercial educational television station;

(ii) the selection for carriage of such a signal shall be at the election of the cable operator; and

(iii) in order to satisfy the requirements for carriage specified in this subsection, the cable operator of the system shall not be required to remove any other programming service actually provided to subscribers on March 29, 1990; except that such cable operator shall use the first channel available to satisfy the requirements of this subparagraph.

(3) Systems with 13 to 36 channels. (A) Subject to subsection (c), a cable operator of a cable system with 13 to 36 usable activated channels:

(i) shall carry the signal of at least one qualified local noncommercial educational television station but shall not be required to carry the signals of more than three such stations, and

(ii) may, in its discretion, carry additional such stations.

(B) In the case of a cable system described in this paragraph which operates beyond the presence of any qualified local noncommercial educational television station, the cable operator shall import and carry on that system the signal of at least one qualified noncommercial educational television station to comply with subparagraph (A)(i).

(C) The cable operator of a cable system described in this paragraph which carries the signal of a qualified local noncommercial educational station affiliated with a State public television network shall not be required to carry the signal of any additional qualified local noncommercial educational television stations affiliated with the same network if the programming of such additional stations is substantially duplicated by the programming of the qualified local noncommercial educational television station receiving carriage.

(D) A cable operator of a system described in this paragraph which increases the usable activated channel capacity of the system to more than 36 channels on or after March 29, 1990, shall, in accordance with the other provisions of this section, carry the signal of each qualified local noncommercial educational television station requesting carriage, subject to subsection (e).

(c) Continued carriage of existing stations. Notwithstanding any other provision of this section, all cable operators shall continue to provide carriage to all qualified local noncommercial educational television stations whose signals were carried on their systems as of March 29, 1990. The requirements of this subsection may be waived with respect to a particular cable operator and a particular such station, upon the written consent of the cable operator and the station.

(d) Placement of additional signals. A cable operator required to add the signals of qualified local noncommercial educational television stations to a cable system under this section may do so, subject to approval by the franchising authority pursuant to Section 611, by placing such additional stations on public, educational, or governmental channels not in use for their designated purposes.

(e) Systems with more than 36 channels. A cable operator of a cable system with a capacity of more than 36 usable activated channels which is required to carry the signals of three qualified local noncommercial educational television stations shall not be required to carry the signals of additional such stations the programming of which substantially duplicates the programming broadcast by another qualified local noncommercial educational television station requesting carriage. Substantial duplication shall be defined by the Commission in a manner that promotes access to distinctive noncommercial educational television services.

(f) Waiver of nonduplication rights. A qualified local noncommercial educational television station whose signal is carried by a cable operator shall not assert any network nonduplication rights it may have pursuant to §76.92 of Title 47, Code of Federal Regulations, to require the deletion of programs aired on other qualified local noncommercial educational television stations whose signals are carried by that cable operator.

(g) Conditions of carriage:

(1) Content to be carried. A cable operator shall retransmit in its entirety the primary video, accompanying audio, and line 21 closed caption transmission of each qualified local noncommercial educational television station whose signal is carried on the cable system, and, to the extent technically feasible, program-related material carried in the vertical blanking interval, or on subcarriers, that may be necessary for receipt of programming by handicapped persons or for educational or language purposes. Retransmission of other material in the vertical blanking interval or on subcarriers shall be within the discretion of the cable operator.

(2) Bandwidth and technical quality. A cable operator shall provide each qualified local noncommercial educational television station whose signal is carried in accordance with this section with bandwidth and technical capacity equivalent to that provided to commercial television broadcast stations carried on the cable system and shall carry the signal of each qualified local noncommercial educational television station without material degradation.

(3) Changes in carriage. The signal of a qualified local noncommercial educational television station shall not be repositioned by a cable operator unless the cable operator, at least 30 days in advance of such repositioning, has provided written notice to the station and all subscribers of the cable system. For purposes of this paragraph, repositioning includes (A) assignment of a qualified local noncommercial educational television station to a cable system channel number different from the cable system channel number to which the station was assigned as of March 29, 1990, and (B) deletion of the station from the cable system. The notification provisions of this paragraph shall not be used to undermine or evade the channel positioning or carriage requirements imposed upon cable operators under this section.

(4) Good quality signal required. Notwithstanding the other provisions of this section, a cable operator shall not be required to carry the signal of any qualified local noncommercial educational television station which does not deliver to the cable system's principal headend a signal of good quality or a baseband video signal, as may be defined by the Commission.

(5) Channel positioning. Each signal carried in fulfillment of the carriage obligations of a cable operator under this section shall be carried on the cable system channel number on which the qualified local noncommercial educational television station is broadcast over the air, or on the channel on which it was carried on July 19, 1985, at the election of the station, or on such other channel number as is mutually agreed upon by the station and the cable operator. Any dispute regarding the positioning of a qualified local noncommercial educational television station shall be resolved by the Commission.

(h) Availability of signals. Signals carried in fulfillment of the carriage obligations of a cable operator under this section shall be available to every subscriber as part of the cable system's lowest priced service tier that includes the retransmission of local commercial television broadcast signals.

(i) Payment for carriage prohibited:

(1) In general. A cable operator shall not accept monetary payment or other valuable consideration in exchange for carriage of the signal of any qualified local noncommercial educational television station carried in fulfillment of the requirements of this section, except that such a station may be required to bear the cost associated with delivering a good quality signal or a baseband video signal to the principal headend of the cable system.

(2) Distant signal exception. Notwithstanding the provisions of this section, a cable operator shall not be required to add the signal of a qualified local noncommercial educational television station not already carried under the provision of subsection (c), where such signal would be considered a distant signal for copyright purposes unless such station indemnifies the cable operator for any increased copyright costs resulting from carriage of such signal.

(j) Remedies:

(1) Complaint. Whenever a qualified local noncommercial educational television station believes that a cable operator of a cable system has failed to comply with the signal carriage requirements of this section, the station may file a complaint with the Commission. Such complaint shall allege the manner in which such cable operator has failed to comply with such requirements and state the basis for such allegations.

(2) Opportunity to respond. The Commission shall afford such cable operator an opportunity to present data, views, and arguments to establish that the cable operator has complied with the signal carriage requirements of this section.

(3) Remedial actions; dismissal. Within 120 days after the date a complaint is filed under this subsection, the Commission shall determine whether the cable operator has complied with the requirements of this section. If the Commission determines that the cable operator has failed to comply with such requirements, the Commission shall state with particularity the basis for such findings and order the cable operator to take such remedial action as is necessary to meet such requirements. If the Commission determines that the cable operator has fully complied with such requirements, the Commission shall dismiss the complaint.

(k) Identification of signals. A cable operator shall identify, upon request by any person, those signals carried in fulfillment of the requirements of this section.

(l) Definitions. For purposes of this section:

(1) Qualified noncommercial educational television station. The term "qualified noncommercial educational television station" means any television broadcast station which:

(A)(i) under the rules and regulations of the Commission in effect on March 29, 1990, is licensed by the Commission as a noncommercial educational television broadcast station and which is owned and operated by a public agency, nonprofit foundation, corporation, or association; and

(ii) has as its licensee an entity which is eligible to receive a community service grant, or any successor grant thereto, from the Corporation for Public Broadcasting, or any successor organization thereto, on the basis of the formula set forth in Section 396(k)(6)(B); or

(B) is owned and operated by a municipality and transmits predominantly noncommercial programs for educational purposes.

Such term includes (I) the translator of any noncommercial educational television station with five watts or higher power serving the franchise area, (II) a full-service station or translator if such station or translator is licensed to a channel reserved for noncommercial educational use pursuant to §73.606 of Title 47, Code of Federal Regulations, or any successor regulations thereto, and (III) such stations and translators operating on channels not so reserved as the Commission determines are qualified as noncommercial educational stations.

(2) Qualified local noncommercial educational television station. The term "qualified local noncommercial educational television station" means a qualified noncommercial educational television station:

(A) which is licensed to a principal community whose reference point, as defined in §76.53 of Title 47, Code of Federal Regulations (as in effect on March 29, 1990), or any successor regulations thereto, is within 50 miles of the principal headend of the cable system; or

(B) whose Grade B service contour, as defined in §73.683(a) of such title (as in effect on March 29, 1990), or any successor regulations thereto, encompasses the principal headend of the cable system.

Regulation of Carriage Agreements (Sec. 616).

(a) Regulations. Within one year after the date of enactment of this section, the Commission shall establish regulations governing program carriage agreements and related practices between cable operators or other multichannel video programming distributors and video programming vendors. Such regulations shall:

(1) include provisions designed to prevent a cable operator or other multichannel video programming distributor from requiring a financial interest in a program service as a condition for carriage on one or more of such operator's systems;

(2) include provisions designed to prohibit a cable operator or other multichannel video programming distributor from coercing a video programming vendor to provide, and from retaliating against such a vendor for failing to provide, exclusive rights against other multichannel video programming distributors as a condition of carriage on a system;

(3) contain provisions designed to prevent a multichannel video programming distributor from engaging in conduct the effect of which is to unreasonably restrain the ability of an unaffiliated video programming vendor to compete fairly by discriminating in video programming distribution on the basis of affiliation or nonaffiliation of vendors in the selection, terms, or conditions for carriage of video programming provided by such vendors;

(4) provide for expedited review of any complaints made by a video programming vendor pursuant to this section;

(5) provide for appropriate penalties and remedies for violations of this subsection, including carriage; and

(6) provide penalties to be assessed against any person filing a frivolous complaint pursuant to this section.

(b) Definition. As used in this section, the term "video programming vendor" means a person engaged in the production, creation, or wholesale distribution of video programming for sale.

Sales of Cable Systems (Sec. 617).

(a) 3-year holding period required. Except as provided in this section, no cable operator may sell or otherwise transfer ownership in a cable system within a 36-month period following either the acquisition or initial construction of such system by such operator.

(b) Treatment of multiple transfers. In the case of a sale of multiple systems, if the terms of the sale require the buyer to subsequently transfer ownership of one or more such systems to one or more third parties, such transfers shall be considered a part of the initial transaction.

(c) Exceptions. Subsection (a) shall not apply to:

(1) any transfer of ownership interest in any cable system which is not subject to Federal income tax liability;

(2) any sale required by operation of any law or any act of any Federal agency, any State or political subdivision thereof, or any franchising authority; or

(3) any sale, assignment, or transfer, to one or more purchasers, assignees, or transferees controlled by, controlling, or under common control with, the seller, assignor, or transferor.

(d) Waiver authority. The Commission may, consistent with the public interest, waive the requirement of subsection (a), except that, if the franchise requires franchise authority approval of a transfer, the Commission shall not waive such requirements unless the franchise authority has approved the transfer. The Commission shall use its authority under this subsection to permit appropriate transfers in the cases of default, foreclosure, or other financial distress.

(e) Limitation on duration of franchising authority power to disapprove transfers. In the case of any sale or transfer of ownership of any cable system after the 36-month period following acquisition of such system, a franchising authority shall, if the franchise requires franchising authority approval of a sale or transfer, have 120 days to act upon any request for approval of such sale or transfer that contains or is accompanied by such information as is required in accordance with Commission regulations and by the franchising authority. If the franchising authority fails to render a final decision on the request within 120 days, such request shall be deemed granted unless the requesting party and the franchising authority agree to an extension of time.

General Franchise Requirements (Sec. 621).

(a)(1) A franchising authority may award, in accordance with the provisions of this title, one or more franchises within its jurisdiction; except that a franchising authority may not grant an exclusive franchise and may not unreasonably refuse to award an additional competitive franchise. Any applicant whose application for a second franchise has been denied by a final decision of the franchising authority may appeal such final decision pursuant to the provisions of Section 635 for failure to comply with this subsection.

(2) Any franchise shall be construed to authorize the construction of a cable system over public rights-of-way, and through easements, which is within the area to be served by the cable system and which have been dedicated for compatible uses, except that in using such easements the cable operator shall ensure:

(A) that the safety, functioning, and appearance of the property and the convenience and safety of other persons not be adversely affected by the installation or construction of facilities necessary for a cable system;

(B) that the cost of the installation, construction, operation, or removal of such facilities be borne by the cable operator or subscriber, or a combination of both; and

(C) that the owner of the property be justly compensated by the cable operator for any damages caused by the installation, construction, operation, or removal of such facilities by the cable operator.

(3) In awarding a franchise or franchises, a franchising authority shall assure that access to cable service is not denied to any group of potential residential cable subscribers because of the income of the residents of the local cable area in which the group resides.

(4) In awarding a franchise, the franchising authority:

(A) shall allow the applicant's cable system a reasonable period of time to become capable of providing cable service to all households in the franchise area;

(B) may require adequate assurance that the cable operator will provide adequate public, educational, and governmental access channel capability, facilities, or financial support; and

(C) may require adequate assurance that the cable operator has the financial, technical, or legal qualifications to provide cable service.

(b)(1) Except to the extent provided in paragraph (2) and subsection (f), a cable operator may not provide cable service without a franchise.

(2) Paragraph (1) shall not require any person lawfully providing cable service without a franchise on July 1, 1984, to obtain a franchise unless the franchising authority so requires.

(c) Any cable system shall not be subject to regulation as a common carrier or utility by reason of providing any cable service.

(d)(1) A State or the Commission may require the filing of informational tariffs for any intrastate communications service provided by a cable system, other than cable service, that would be common carrier subject, in whole or in part, to title II of this Act. Such informational tariffs shall specify the rates, terms and conditions for the provision of such service, including whether it is made available to all subscribers generally, and shall take effect on the date specified therein.

(2) Nothing in this title shall be construed to affect the authority of any State to regulate any cable operator to the extent that such operator provides any communication service other than cable service, whether offered on a common carrier or private contract basis.

(3) For the purposes of this subsection, the term "State" has the meaning given it in section (3)(v).

(e) Nothing in this title shall be construed to affect the authority of any State to license or otherwise regulate any facility or combination of facilities which serves only subscribers in one or more multiple unit dwellings under common ownership, control, or management and which does not use any public right-of-way.

(f) No provision of this Act shall be construed to:

(1) prohibit a local or municipal authority that is also, or is affiliated with, a franchising authority from operating as a multichannel video programming distributor in the franchise area, notwithstanding the granting of one or more franchises by such franchising authority; or

(2) require such local or municipal authority to secure a franchise to operate as a multichannel video programming distributor.

Franchise Fees (Sec. 622).

(a) Subject to the limitation of subsection (b), any cable operator may be required under terms of any franchise to pay a franchise fee.

(b) For any 12-month period, the franchise fee paid by a cable operator with respect to any cable system shall not exceed 5 percent of such cable operator's gross revenues derived in such period from the operation of the cable system. For the purposes of this section, the 12-month period shall be the 12-month period applicable under the franchise for accounting purposes. Nothing in this subsection shall prohibit a franchising authority and a cable operator from agreeing that franchise fees which lawfully could be collected for any such 12-month period shall be paid on a prepaid or deferred basis; except that the sum of the fees paid during the term of the franchise may not exceed the amount, including the time value of money, which would have lawfully been collected if such fees had been paid per annum.

(c) Each cable operator may identify, consistent with the regulations prescribed by the Commission pursuant to Section 623, as a separate line item on each regular bill of each subscriber, each of the following:

(1) The amount of the total bill assessed as a franchise fee and the identity of the franchising authority to which the fee is paid.

(2) The amount of the total bill assessed to satisfy any requirements imposed on the cable operator by the franchise agreement to support public, educational, or governmental channels or the use of such channels.

(3) The amount of any other fee, tax, assessment, or charge of any kind imposed by any governmental authority on the transaction between the operator and the subscriber.

(d) In any court action under subsection (c), the franchising authority shall demonstrate that the rate structure reflects all costs of the franchise fees.

(e) Any cable operator shall pass through to subscribers the amount of any decrease in the franchise fee.

(f) A cable operator may designate that portion of a subscriber's bill attributable to the franchise fee as a separate item on the bill.

(g) For the purposes of this section:

(1) the term "franchise fee" includes any tax, fee, or assessment of any kind imposed by a franchising authority or other governmental entity on a cable operator or cable subscriber, or both, solely because of their status as such.

(2) the term "franchise fee" does not include:

(A) any tax, fee, or assessment of general applicability (including any such tax, fee, or assessment imposed on both utilities and cable operators or their services but not including a tax, fee, or assessment which is unduly discriminatory against cable operators or cable subscribers);

(B) in the case of any franchise in effect on the date of the enactment of this title, payments which are required by the franchise to be made by the cable operator during the term of such franchise for, or in support of the use of, public, educational, or governmental access facilities;

(C) in the case of any franchise granted after such date if enactment, capital costs which are required by the franchise to be incurred by the cable operator for public, educational, or governmental access facilities;

(D) requirements or charges incidental to the awarding or enforcing of the franchise, including payments for bonds, security funds, letters of credit, insurance, indemnification, penalties, or liquidated damages; or

(E) any fee imposed under title 17, United States Code.

(h)(1) Nothing in this Act shall be construed to limit any authority of a franchising authority to impose a tax, fee, or other assessment of any kind on any person (other than a cable operator) with respect to cable service or other communications service provided by such person over a cable system for which charges are assessed to subscribers but not received by the cable operator.

(2) For any 12-month period, the fees paid by such person with respect to any such cable service or other communications service shall not exceed 5 percent of such person's gross revenue derived in such period from the provision of such service over the cable system.

(i) Any Federal agency may not regulate the amount of the franchise fees paid by a cable operator, or regulate the use of funds derived from such fees, except as provided in this section.

Regulation of Rates (Sec. 623).

(a) Competition preference; local and Federal regulation:

(1) In general. No Federal agency or State may regulate the rates for the provision of cable service except to the extent provided under this section and Section 612. Any franchising authority may regulate the rates for the provision of cable service, or any other communications service provided over a cable system to cable subscribers, but only to the extent provided under this section. No Federal agency, State, or franchising authority may regulate the rates for cable service of a cable system that is owned or operated by a local government or franchising authority within whose jurisdiction that cable system is located and that is the only cable system located within such jurisdiction.

(2) Preference for competition. If the Commission finds that a cable system is subject to effective competition, the rates for the provision of cable service by such system shall not be subject to regulation by the Commission or by a State or franchising authority under this section. If the Commission finds that a cable system is not subject to effective competition:

(A) the rates for the provision of basic cable service shall be subject to regulation by a franchising authority, or by the Commission if the Commission exercises jurisdiction pursuant to paragraph (6), in accordance with the regulations prescribed by the Commission under subsection (b); and

(B) the rates for cable programming services shall be subject to regulation by the Commission under subsection (c).

(3) Qualification of franchising authority. A franchising authority that seeks to exercise the regulatory jurisdiction permitted under paragraph (2)(A) shall file with the Commission a written certification that:

(A) the franchising authority will adopt and administer regulations with respect to the rates subject to regulation under this section that are consistent with the regulations prescribed by the Commission under subjection (b);

(B) the franchising authority has the legal authority to adopt, and the personnel to administer, such regulations; and

(C) procedural laws and regulations applicable to rate regulation proceedings by such authority provide a reasonable opportunity for consideration of the views of interested parties.

(4) Approval by Commission. A certification filed by a franchising authority under paragraph (3) shall be effective 30 days after the date on which it is filed unless the Commission finds, after notice to the authority and a reasonable opportunity for the authority to comment, that:

(A) the franchising authority has adopted or is administering regulations with respect to the rates subject to regulation under this section that are not consistent with the regulations prescribed by the Commission under subsection (b);

(B) the franchising authority does not have the legal authority to adopt, or the personnel to administer, such regulations; or

(C) procedural laws and regulations applicable to rate regulation proceedings by such authority do not provide a reasonable opportunity for consideration of the views of interested parties.

If the Commission disapproves a franchising authority's certification, the Commission shall notify the franchising authority of any revisions or modifications necessary to obtain approval.

(5) Revocation of jurisdiction. Upon petition by a cable operator or other interested party, the Commission shall

review the regulation of cable system rates by a franchising authority under this subsection. A copy of the petition shall be provided to the franchising authority by the person filing the petition. If the Commission finds that the franchising authority has acted inconsistently with the requirements of this subsection, the Commission shall grant appropriate relief. If the Commission, after the franchising authority has had a reasonable opportunity to comment, determines that the State and local laws and regulations are not in conformance with the regulations prescribed by the Commission under subsection (b), the Commission shall revoke the jurisdiction of such authority.

(6) Exercise of jurisdiction by Commission. If the Commission disapproves a franchising authority's certification under paragraph (4), or revokes such authority's jurisdiction under paragraph (5), the Commission shall exercise the franchising authority's regulatory jurisdiction under paragraph (2)(A) until the franchising authority has qualified to exercise that jurisdiction by filing a new certification that meets the requirements of paragraph (3). Such new certification shall be effective upon approval by the Commission. The Commission shall act to approve or disapprove any such new certification within 90 days after the date it is filed.

(b) Establishment of basic service tier rate regulations:

(1) Commission obligation to subscribers. The Commission shall, by regulation, ensure that the rates for the basic service tier are reasonable. Such regulations shall be designed to achieve the goal of protecting subscribers of any cable system that is not subject to effective competition from rates for the basic service tier that exceed the rates that would be charged for the basic service tier if such cable system were subject to effective competition.

(2) Commission regulations. Within 180 days after the date of enactment of the Cable Television Consumer Protection and Competition Act of 1992, the Commission shall prescribe, and periodically thereafter revise, regulations to carry out its obligations under paragraph (1). In prescribing such regulations, the Commission:

(A) shall seek to reduce the administrative burdens on subscribers, cable operators, franchising authorities, and the Commission;

(B) may adopt formulas or other mechanisms and procedures in complying with the requirements of subparagraph (A); and

(C) shall take into account the following factors:

(i) the rates for cable systems, if any, that are subject to effective competition;

(ii) the direct costs (if any) of obtaining, transmitting, and otherwise providing signals carried on the basic service tier, including signals and services carried on the basic service tier pursuant to paragraph (7)(B), and changes in such costs;

(iii) only such portion of the joint and common costs (if any) of obtaining, transmitting, and otherwise providing such signals as is determined, in accordance with regulations prescribed by the Commission, to be reasonably and properly allocable to the basic service tier, and changes in such costs;

(iv) the revenues (if any) received by a cable operator from advertising from programming that is carried as part of the basic service tier or from other consideration obtained in connection with the basic service tier;

(v) the reasonably and properly allocable portion of any amount assessed as a franchise fee, tax, or charge of any kind imposed by any State or local authority on the transactions between cable operators and cable subscribers or any other fee, tax, or assessment of general applicability imposed by a governmental entity applied against cable operators or cable subscribers;

(vi) any amount required, in accordance with paragraph (4), to satisfy franchise requirements to support public, educational, or governmental channels or the use of such channels or any other services required under the franchise; and

(vii) a reasonable profit, as defined by the Commission consistent with the Commission's obligations to subscribers under paragraph (1).

(3) Equipment. The regulations prescribed by the Commission under this subsection shall include standards to establish, on the basis of actual cost, the price or rate for:

(A) installation and lease of the equipment used by subscribers to receive the basic service tier, including a converter box and a remote control unit and, if requested by the subscriber, such addressable converter box or other equipment as is required to access programming described in paragraph (8); and

(B) installation and monthly use of connections for additional television receivers.

(4) Costs of franchise requirements. The regulations prescribed by the Commission under this subsection shall include standards to identify costs attributable to satisfying franchise requirements to support public, educational, and governmental channels or the use of such channels or any other services required under the franchise.

(5) Implementation and enforcement. The regulations prescribed by the Commission under this subsection shall include additional standards, guidelines, and procedures concerning the implementation and enforcement of such regulations, which shall include:

(A) procedures by which cable operators may implement and franchising authorities may enforce the regulations prescribed by the Commission under this subsection;

(B) procedures for the expeditious resolution of disputes between cable operators and franchising authorities concerning the administration of such regulations;

(C) standards and procedures to prevent unreasonable charges for changes in the subscriber's selection of services or equipment subject to regulation under this section, which standards shall require that charges for changing the service tier selected shall be based on the cost of such change and shall not exceed nominal amounts when the system's configuration permits changes in service tier selection to be effected solely by coded entry on a computer terminal or by other similarly simple method; and

(D) standards and procedures to assure that subscribers receive notice of the availability of the basic service tier required under this section.

(6) Notice. The procedures prescribed by the Commission pursuant to paragraph (5)(A) shall require a cable operator to provide 30 days' advance notice to a franchising authority of any increase proposed in the price to be charged for the basic service tier.

(7) Components of basic tier subject to rate regulation:

(A) Minimum contents. Each cable operator of a cable system shall provide its subscribers a separately available basic service tier to which subscription is required for access to any other tier of service. Such basic service tier shall, at a minimum, consist of the following:

(i) All signals carried in fulfillment of the requirements of Sections 614 and 615.

(ii) Any public, educational and governmental access programming required by the franchise of the cable system to be provided to subscribers.

(iii) Any signal of any television broadcast station that is provided by the cable operator to any subscriber, except a signal which is secondarily transmitted by a satellite carrier beyond the local service area of such station.

(B) Permitted additions to basic tier. A cable operator may add additional video programming signals or services to the basic service tier. Any such additional signals or services provided on the basic service tier shall be provided to subscribers at rates determined under the regulations prescribed by the Commission under this subsection.

(8) Buy-through of other tiers prohibited:

(A) Prohibition. A cable operator may not require the subscription to any tier other than the basic service tier required by paragraph (7) as a condition of access to video programming offered on a per channel or per program basis. A cable operator may not discriminate between subscribers to the basic service tier and other subscribers with regard to the rates charged for video programming offered on a per channel or per program basis.

(B) Exception; limitation. The prohibition in subparagraph (A) shall not apply to a cable system that, by reason of the lack of addressable converter boxes or other technological limitations, does not permit the operator to offer programming on a per channel or per program basis in the same manner required by subparagraph (A). This subparagraph shall not be available to any cable operator after:

(i) the technology utilized by the cable system is modified or improved in a way that eliminates such technological limitation; or

(ii) 10 years after the date of enactment of the Cable Television Consumer Protection and Competition Act of 1992, subject to subparagraph (C).

(C) Waiver. If, in any proceeding initiated at the request of any cable operator, the Commission determines that compliance with the requirements of subparagraph (A) would require the cable operator to increase its rates, the Commission may, to the extent consistent with the public interest, grant such cable operator a waiver from such requirements for such specified period as the Commission determines reasonable and appropriate.

(c) Regulation of unreasonable rates:

(1) Commission regulations. Within 180 days after the date of enactment of the Cable Television Consumer Protection and Competition Act of 1992, the Commission shall, by regulation, establish the following:

(A) criteria prescribed in accordance with paragraph (2) for identifying, in individual cases, rates for cable programming services that are unreasonable;

(B) fair and expeditious procedures for the receipt, consideration, and resolution of complaints from any subscriber, franchising authority, or other relevant State or local government entity alleging that a rate for cable programming services charged by a cable operator violates the criteria prescribed under subparagraph (A), which procedures shall include the minimum showing that shall be required for a complaint to obtain Commission consideration and resolution of whether the rate in question is unreasonable; and

(C) the procedures to be used to reduce rates for cable programming services that are determined by the Commission to be unreasonable and to refund such portion of the rates or charges that were paid by subscribers after the filing of such complaint and that are determined to be unreasonable.

(2) Factors to be considered. In establishing the criteria for determining in individual cases whether rates for cable programming services are unreasonable under paragraph (1)(A), the Commission shall consider, among other factors:

(A) the rates for similarly situated cable systems offering comparable cable programming services, taking into account similarities in facilities, regulatory and governmental costs, the number of subscribers and other relevant factors;

(B) the rates for cable systems, if any, that are subject to effective competition;

(C) the history of the rates for cable programming services of the system, including the relationship of such rates to changes in general consumer prices;

(D) the rates, as a whole, for all the cable programming, cable equipment, and cable services provided by the system, other that programming provided on a per channel or per program basis;

(E) capital and operating costs of the cable system, including the quality and costs of the customer service provided by the cable system; and

(F) the revenues (if any) received by a cable operator from advertising from programming that is carried as part of the service for which a rate is being established, and changes in such revenues, or from other consideration, obtained in connection with the cable programming services concerned.

(3) Limitation on complaints concerning existing rates. Except during the 180-day period following the effective date of the regulations prescribed by the Commission under paragraph (1), the procedures established under subparagraph (B) of such paragraph shall be available only with respect to complaints filed within a reasonable period of time following a change in rates that is initiated after that effective date, including a change in rates that results from a change in that system's service tiers.

(d) Uniform rate structure required. A cable operator shall have a rate structure, for the provision of cable service, that is uniform throughout the geographic area in which cable service is provided over its cable system.

(e) Discrimination; services for the hearing impaired. Nothing in this title shall be construed as prohibiting any Federal agency, State, or a franchising authority from:

(1) prohibiting discrimination among subscribers and potential subscribers to cable service, except that no Federal agency, State, or franchising authority may prohibit a cable operator from offering reasonable discounts to senior citizens or other economically disadvantaged group discounts; or

(2) requiring and regulating the installation or rental of equipment which facilitates the reception of cable service by hearing impaired individuals.

(f) Negative option billing prohibited. A cable operator shall not charge a subscriber for any service or equipment that the subscriber has not affirmatively requested by name. For purposes of this subsection, a subscriber's failure to refuse a cable operator's proposal to provide such service or equipment shall not be deemed to be an affirmative request for such service or equipment.

(g) Collection of information. The Commission shall, by regulation, require cable operators to file with the Commission or a franchising authority, as appropriate, within one year after the date of enactment of the Cable Television Consumer Protection and Competition Act of 1992 and annually thereafter, such financial information as may be needed for purposes of administering and enforcing this section.

(h) Prevention of evasions. Within 180 days after the date of enactment of the Cable Television Consumer Protection and Competition Act of 1992, the Commission shall, by regulation, establish standards, guidelines, and procedures to prevent evasions, including evasions that result from retiering, of the requirements of this section and shall, thereafter, periodically review and revise such standards, guidelines, and procedures.

(i) Small system burdens. In developing and prescribing regulations pursuant to this section, the Commission shall design such regulations to reduce the administrative burdens and cost of compliance for cable systems that have 1,000 or fewer subscribers.

(j) Rate regulation agreements. During the term of an agreement made before July 1, 1990, by a franchising authority and a cable operator providing for the regulation of basic cable service rates, where there was not effective competition under Commission rules in effect on that date, nothing in this section (or the regulations thereunder) shall abridge the ability of such franchising authority to regulate rates in accordance with such an agreement.

(k) Reports on average prices. The Commission shall annually publish statistical reports on the average rates for basic cable service and other cable programming, and for converter boxes, remote control units, and other equipment, of:

(1) cable systems that the Commission has found are subject to effective competition under subsection (a)(2), compared with

(2) cable systems that the Commission has found are not subject to such effective competition.

(l) Definitions. As used in this section:

(1) The term "effective competition" means that:

(A) fewer than 30 percent of the households in the franchise area subscribe to the cable service of a cable system;

(B) the franchise area is:

(i) served by at least two unaffiliated multichannel video programming distributors each of which offers comparable video programming to at least 50 percent of the households in the franchise area; and

(ii) the number of households subscribing to programming services offered by multichannel video programming distributors other than the largest multichannel video programming distributor exceeds 15 percent of the households in the franchise area; or

(C) a multichannel video programming distributor operated by the franchising authority for that franchise area offers video programming to at least 50 percent of the households in that franchise area.

(2) The term "cable programming service" means any video programming provided over a cable system, regardless of service tier, including installation or rental of equipment used for the receipt of such video programming, other than (A) video programming carried on the basic service tier, and (B) video programming offered on a per channel or per program basis.

Regulation of Services, Facilities, and Equipment (Sec. 624).

(a) Any franchising authority may not regulate the services, facilities, and equipment provided by a cable operator except to the extent consistent with this title.

(b) In the case of any franchise granted after the effective date of this title, the franchising authority, to the extent related to the establishment or operation of a cable system:

(1) in its request for proposals for a franchise (including requests for renewal proposals, subject to section 626), may establish requirements for facilities and equipment, but may not, except as provided in subsection (h), establish requirements for video programming or other information services; and

(2) subject to section 625, may enforce any requirements contained within the franchise:

(A) for facilities and equipment; and

(B) for broad categories of video programming or other services.

(c) In the case of franchise in effect on the effective date of this title, the franchising authority may, subject to section 625, enforce requirements contained within the franchise for the provision of services, facilities, and equipment, whether or not related to the establishment or operation of a cable system.

(d)(1) Nothing in this title shall be contrued as prohibiting a franchising authority and a cable operator from specifying, in a franchise or renewal thereof, that certain cable services shall not be provided or shall be provided subject to conditions, if such cable services are obscene or are otherwise unprotected by the Constitution of the United States.

(2)(A) In order to restrict the viewing of programming which is obscene or indecent, upon the request of a subscriber, a cable operator shall provide (by sale or lease) a device by which the subscriber can prohibit viewing of a particular cable service during periods selected by that subscriber.

(B) Subparagraph (A) shall take effect 180 days after the effective date of this title.

(3)(A) If a cable operator provides a premium channel without charge to cable subscribers who do not subscribe to such premium channel, the cable operator shall, not later than 30 days before such premium channel is provided without charge:

(i) notify all cable subscribers that the cable operator plans to provide a premium channel without charge;

(ii) notify all cable subscribers when the cable operator plans to offer a premium channel without charge;

(iii) notify all cable subscribers that they have a right to request that the channel carrying the premium channel be blocked; and

(iv) block the channel carrying the premium channel upon the request of a subscriber.

(B) For the purpose of this section, the term "premium channel" shall mean any pay service offered on a per channel or per program basis, which offers movies rated by the Motion Picture Association of America as X, NC-17, or R.

(e) Within one year after the date of enactment of the Cable Television Consumer Protection and Competition Act of 1992, the Commission shall prescribe regulations which establish minimum technical standards relating to cable systems' technical operation and signal quality. The Commission shall update such standards periodically to reflect improvements in technology. A franchising authority may require as part of a franchise (including a modification, renewal, or transfer thereof) provisions for the enforcement of the standards prescribed under this subsection. A franchising authority may apply to the Commission for a waiver to impose standards that are more stringent than the standards prescribed by the Commission under this subsection.

(f)(1) Any Federal agency, State, or franchising authority may not impose requirements regarding the provision or content of cable services, except as expressly provided in this title.

(2) Paragraph (1) shall not apply to:

(A) any rule, regulation, or order issued under any Federal law, as such rule, regulation, or order (i) was in effect on September 21, 1983, or (ii) may be amended after such date if the rule, regulation, or order as amended is not inconsistent with the express provisions of this title; and

(B) any rule, regulation, or order under title 17, United States Code.

(g) Notwithstanding any such rule, regulation, or order, each cable operator shall comply with such standards as the Commission shall prescribe to ensure that viewers of video programming on cable systems are afforded the same emergency information as is afforded by the emergency broadcasting system pursuant to Commission regulations in Subpart G of Part 73, Title 47, Code of Federal Regulations.

(h) A franchising authority may require a cable operator to do any one or more of the following:

(1) Provide 30 days' advance written notice of any change in channel assignment or in the video programming service provided over any such channel.

(2) Inform subscribers, via written notice, that comments on programming and channel position changes are being recorded by a designated office of the franchising authority.

(i) Within 120 days after the date of enactment of this subsection, the Commission shall prescribe rules concerning the disposition, after a subscriber to a cable system terminates service, of any cable installed by the cable operator within the premises of such subscriber.

Consumer Electronics Equipment Compatibility (Sec. 624A).

(a) Findings. The Congress finds that:

(1) new and recent models of television receivers and video cassette recorders often contain premium features and functions that are disabled or inhibited because of cable scrambling, encoding, or encryption technologies and devices, including converter boxes and remote control devices required by cable operators to receive programming;

(2) if these problems are allowed to persist, consumers will be less likely to purchase, and electronics equipment manufacturers will be less likely to develop, manufacture, or offer for sale, television receivers and video cassette recorders with new and innovative features and functions; and

(3) cable operators should use technologies that will prevent signal thefts while permitting consumers to benefit from such features and functions in such receivers and recorders.

(b) Compatible interfaces:

(1) Report; regulations. Within one year after the date of enactment of this section, the Commission, in consultation with representatives of the cable industry and the consumer electronics industry, shall report to Congress on means of assuring compatibility between televisions and video cassette recorders and cable systems, consistent with the need to prevent theft of cable service, so that cable subscribers will be able to enjoy the full benefit of both the programming available on cable systems and the functions available on their televisions and video cassette recorders. Within 180 days after the date of submission of the report required by this subsection, the Commission shall issue such regulations as are necessary to assure such compatibility.

(2) Scrambling and encryption. In issuing the regulations referred to in paragraph (1), the Commission shall determine whether and, if so, under what circumstances to permit cable systems to scramble or encrypt signals or to restrict cable systems in the manner in which they encrypt or scramble signals, except that the Commission shall not limit the use of scrambling or encryption technology where the use of such technology does not interfere with the functions of subscribers' television receivers or video cassette recorders.

(c) Rulemaking requirements:

(1) Factors to be considered. In prescribing the regulations required by this section, the Commission shall consider:

(A) the costs and benefits to consumers of imposing compatibility requirements on cable operators and television manufacturers in a manner that, while providing effective protection against theft or unauthorized reception of cable service, will minimize interference with or nullification of the special functions of subscribers' television receivers or video cassette recorders, including functions that permit the subscriber:

(i) to watch a program on one channel while simultaneously using a video cassette recorder to tape a program on another channel;

(ii) to use a video cassette recorder to tape two consecutive programs that appear on different channels; and

(iii) to use advanced television picture generation and display features; and

(B) the need for cable operators to protect the integrity of the signals transmitted by the cable operator against theft or to protect such signals against unauthorized reception.

(2) Regulations required. The regulations prescribed by the Commission under this section shall include such regulations as are necessary:

(A) to specify the technical requirements with which a television receiver or video cassette recorder must comply in order to be sold as "cable compatible" or "cable ready";

(B) to require cable operators offering channels whose reception requires a converter box

(i) to notify subscribers that they may be unable to benefit from the special functions of their television receivers and video cassette recorders, including functions that permit subscribers:

(I) to watch a program on one channel while simultaneously using a video cassette recorder to tape a program on another channel;

(II) to use a video cassette recorder to tape two consecutive programs that appear on different channels; and

(III) to use advanced television picture generation and display features; and

(ii) to the extent technically and economically feasible, to offer subscribers the option of having all other channels delivered directly to the subscribers' television receivers or video cassette recorders without passing through the converter box;

(C) to promote the commercial availability, from cable operators and retail vendors that are not affiliated with cable systems, of converter boxes and of remote control devices compatible with converter boxes;

(D) to require a cable operator who offers subscribers the option of renting a remote control unit:

(i) to notify subscribers that they may purchase a commercially available remote control device from any source that sells such devices rather than renting it from the cable operator; and

(ii) to specify the types of remote control units that are compatible with the converter box supplied by the cable operator; and

(E) to prohibit a cable operator from taking any action that prevents or in any way disables the converter box supplied by the cable operator from operating compatibly with commercially available remote control units.

(d) Review of regulations. The Commission shall periodically review and, if necessary, modify the regulations issued pursuant to this section in light of any actions taken in response to such regulations and to reflect improvements and changes in cable systems, television receivers, video cassette recorders, and similar technology.

Modification of Franchise Obligations (Sec. 625).

(a)(1) During the period a franchise is in effect, the cable operator may obtain from the franchising authority modifications of the requirements of the franchise:

(A) in the case of any such requirements for facilities or equipment, including public, educational, or governmental access facilities or equipment, if the cable operator demonstrates that (i) it is commercially impracticable for the operator to comply with such requirement, and (ii) the proposal by the cable operator for modification of such requirement is appropriate because of commercial impracticability; or

(B) in the case of any such requirement for services, if the cable operator demonstrates that the mix, quality and level of services required by the franchise at the time it was granted will be maintained after such modification.

(2) Any final decision by a franchising authority under this subsection shall be made in a public proceeding. Such decision shall be made within 120 days after receipt of such request by the franchising authority, unless such 120 day period is extended by mutual agreement of the cable operator and the franchising authority.

(b)(1) Any cable operator whose request for modification under subsection (a) has been denied by a final decision of a franchising authority may obtain modification of such franchise requirements pursuant to the provisions of section 635.

(2) In the case of any proposed modification of a requirement for facilities or equipment, the court shall grant such modification only if the cable operator demonstrates to the court that:

(A) it is commercially impracticable for the operator to comply with such requirement; and

(B) the terms of the modification requested are appropriate because of commercial inpracticability.

(3) In the case of any proposed modification of a requirement for services, the court shall grant such modification only if the cable operator demonstrates to the court that the mix, quality, and level of services required by the franchise at the time it was granted will be maintained after such modification.

(c) Notwithstanding subsections (a) and (b), a cable operator may, upon 30 days' advance notice to the franchising authority, rearrange, replace, or remove a particular cable service required by the franchise if:

(1) such service is no longer available to the operator; or

(2) such service is available to the operator only upon the payment of a royalty required under section 801(b)(2) of title 17, United States Code, which the cable operator can document:

(A) is substantially in excess of the amount of such payment required on the date of the operator's offer to provide such service; and

(B) has not been specifically compensated for through a rate increase or other adjustment.

(d) Notwithstanding subsections (a) and (b), a cable operator may take such actions to rearrange a particular service from one service tier to another, or otherwise offer the service, if the rates for all of the service tiers involved in such actions are not subject to regulation under section 623.

(e) A cable operator may not obtain modification under this section of any requirement for services relating to public, educational, or governmental access.

(f) For the purposes of this section, the term "commercially impracticable" means, with respect to any requirement applicable to a cable operator, that it is commercially impracticable for the operator to comply with such requirement as a result of a change in conditions which is beyond the control of the operator and the nonoccurence of which was a basic assumption on which the requirement was based.

Renewal (Sec. 626).

(a)(1) A franchising authority may, on its own initiative during the six-month period which begins with the 36th month before the franchise expiration, commence a proceeding which affords the public in the franchise area appropriate notice and participation for the purpose of (A) identifying the future cable-related community needs and interests, and (B) reviewing the performance of the cable operator under the franchise during the then current franchise term. If the cable operator submits, during such six-month period, a written renewal notice requesting the commencement of such a proceeding, the franchising authority shall commence such a proceeding not later than 6 months after the date such notice is submitted.

(2) The cable operator may not invoke the renewal procedures set forth in subsections (b) through (g) unless:

(A) such a proceeding is requested by the cable operator by timely submission of such notice; or

(B) such a proceeding is commenced by the franchising authority on its own initiative.

(b)(1) Upon completion of a proceeding under subsection (a), a cable operator seeking renewal of a franchise may, on its own initiative or at the request of a franchising authority, submit a proposal for renewal.

(2) Subject to Section 624, any such proposal shall contain such material as the franchising authority may require, including proposals for an upgrade of the cable system.

(3) The franchising authority may establish a date by which such proposal shall be submitted.

(c)(1) Upon submittal by a cable operator of a proposal to the franchising authority for the renewal of a franchise, pursuant to subsection (b) the franchising authority shall provide prompt public notice of such proposal and, during the four-month period which begins on the date of the submission of the cable operator's proposal pursuant to subsection (b), renew the franchise or, issue a preliminary assessment that the franchise should not be renewed and, at the request of the operator or on its own initiative, commence an administrative proceeding, after providing prompt public notice of such proceeding, in accordance with para. (2) to consider whether

(A) the cable operator has substantially complied with the material terms of the existing franchise with applicable law;

(B) the quality of the operator's service, including signal quality, response to consumer complaints, and billing practices, but without regard to the mix or quality of cable services or other services provided over the system, has been reasonable in light of community needs;

(C) the operator has the financial, legal and technical ability to provide the services, facilities, and equipment as set forth in the operator's proposal; and

(D) the operator's proposal is reasonable to meet the future cable-related community needs and interests, taking into account the cost of meeting such needs and interests.

(2) In any proceeding under paragraph (1), the cable operator shall be afforded adequate notice and the cable operator and the franchise authority, or its designee, shall be afforded fair opportunity for full participation, including the right to introduce evidence (including evidence related to issues raised in the proceeding under subsection (a)), to require the production of evidence, and to question witnesses. A transcript shall be made of any such proceeding.

(3) At the completion of a proceeding under this subsection, the franchising authority shall issue a written decision granting or denying the proposal for renewal based upon the record of such proceeding, and transmit a copy of such decision to the cable operator. Such decision shall state the reasons therefor.

(d) Any denial of a proposal for renewal that has been submitted in compliance with subsection (b) shall be based on one or more adverse findings made with respect to the factors described in subparagraphs (A) through (D) of subsection (c)(1), pursuant to the record of the proceeding under subsection (c). A franchising authority may not base a denial of renewal on a failure to substantially comply with the material terms of the franchise under subsection (c)(1)(A) or on events considered under subsection (c)(1)(B) in any case in which a violation of the franchise or the events considered under subsection (c)(1)(B) occur after the effective date of this title unless the franchising authority has provided the operator with notice and the opportunity to cure, or in any case in which it is documented that the franchising authority has waived its right to object, or the cable operator gives written notice of a failure or inability to cure and the franchising authority fails to object within a reasonable time after receipt of such notice.

(e)(1) Any cable operator whose proposal for renewal has been denied by a final decision of a franchising authority made pursuant to this section, or has been adversely affected by a failure of the franchising authority to act in accordance with the procedural requirements of this section, may appeal such final decision or failure pursuant to the provisions of Section 635.

(2) The court shall grant appropriate relief if the court finds that:

(A) any action of the franchising authority, other than harmless error, is not in compliance with the procedural requirements of this section; or

(B) in the event of a final decision of the franchising authority denying the renewal proposal, the operator has demonstrated that the adverse finding of the franchising authority with respect to each of the factors described in subparagraphs (A) through (D) of subsection (c)(1) on which the denial is based is not supported by a preponderance of the evidence, based on the record of the proceeding conducted under subsection (c).

(f) Any decision of a franchising authority on a proposal for renewal shall not be considered final unless all administrative review by the State has occurred or the opportunity therefor has lapsed.

(g) For purposes of this section, the term "franchise expiration" means the date of the expiration of the term of the franchise, as provided under the franchise, as it was in effect on the date of the enactment of this title.

(h) Notwithstanding the provisions of subsections (a) through (g) of this section, a cable operator may submit a proposal for the renewal of a franchise pursuant to this subsection at any time, and a franchising authority may, after affording the public adequate notice and opportunity for comment, grant or deny such proposal at any time (including after proceedings pursuant to this section have commenced). The provisions of subsections (a) through (g) of this section shall not apply to a decision to grant or deny a proposal under this subsection. The denial of a renewal pursuant to this subsection shall not affect action on a renewal proposal that is submitted in accordance with subsections (a) through (g).

(i) Notwithstanding the provisions of subsections (a) through (h), any lawful action to revoke a cable operator's franchise for cause shall not be negated by the subsequent initiation of renewal proceedings by the cable operator under this section.

Conditions of Sale (Sec. 627).

(a) If a renewal of a franchise held by a cable operator is denied and the franchising authority acquires ownership of the cable system or effects a transfer of ownership of the system to another person, any such acquisition or transfer shall be:

(1) at fair market value, determined on the basis of the cable system valued as a going concern but with no value allocated to the franchise itself, or

(2) in the case of any franchise existing on the effective date of this title, at a price determined in accordance with the franchise if such franchise contains provisions applicable to such an acquisition or transfer.

(b) If a franchise held by a cable operator is revoked for cause and the franchising authority acquires ownership of the cable system or effects a transfer of ownership of the system to another person, any such acquisition or transfer shall be:

(1) at an equitable price, or

(2) in the case of any franchise existing on the effective date of this title, at a price determined in accordance with the franchise if such franchise contains provisions applicable to such an acquisition or transfer.

Development of Competition and Diversity in Video Programming Distribution (Sec. 628).

(a) Purpose. The purpose of this section is to promote the public interest, convenience, and necessity by increasing competition and diversity in the multichannel video programming market, to increase the availability of satellite cable programming and satellite broadcast programming to persons in rural and other areas not currently able to receive such programming, and to spur the development of communications technologies.

(b) Prohibition. It shall be unlawful for a cable operator, a satellite cable programming vendor in which a cable operator has an attributable interest, or a satellite broadcast programming vendor to engage in unfair methods of competition or unfair or deceptive acts or practices, the purpose or effect of which is to hinder significantly or to prevent any multichannel video programming distributor from providing satellite cable programming or satellite broadcast programming to subscribers or consumers.

(c) Regulations required:

(1) Proceeding required. Within 180 days after the date of enactment of this section, the Commission shall, in order to promote the public interest, convenience, and necessity by increasing competition and diversity in the multichannel video programming market and the continuing development of communications technologies, prescribe regulations to specify particular conduct that is prohibited by subsection (b).

(2) Minimum contents of regulations. The regulations to be promulgated under this section shall:

(A) establish effective safeguards to prevent a cable operator which has an attributable interest in a satellite cable programming vendor or a satellite broadcast programming vendor from unduly or improperly influencing the decision of such vendor to sell, or the prices, terms and conditions of sale of, satellite cable programming or satellite broadcast programming to any unaffiliated multichannel video programming distributor;

(B) prohibit discrimination by a satellite cable programming vendor in which a cable operator has an attributable interest or by a satellite broadcast programming vendor in the prices, terms, and conditions of sale or delivery of satellite cable programming or satellite broadcast programming among or between cable systems, cable operators, or other multichannel video programming distributors, or their agents or buying groups; except that such a satellite cable programming vendor in which a cable operator has an attributable interest or such a satellite broadcast programming vendor shall not be prohibited from:

(i) imposing reasonable requirements for creditworthiness, offering of service, and financial stability and standards regarding character and technical quality;

(ii) establishing different prices, terms, and conditions to take into account actual and reasonable differences in the cost of creation, sale, delivery, or transmission of satellite cable programming or satellite broadcast programming;

(iii) establishing different prices, terms, and conditions which take into account economies of scale, cost savings, or other direct and legitimate economic benefits reasonably attributable to the number of subscribers served by the distributor; or

(iv) entering into an exclusive contract that is permitted under subparagraph (D);

(C) prohibit practices, understandings, arrangements, and activities, including exclusive contracts for satellite cable programming or satellite broadcast programming between a cable operator an a satellite cable programming vendor or satellite broadcast programming vendor, that prevent a multichannel video programming distributor from obtaining such programming from any satellite cable programming vendor in which a cable operator has an attributable interest or any satellite broadcast programming vendor in which a cable operator has an attributable interest for distribution to persons in areas not served by a cable operator as of the date of enactment of this section; and

(D) with respect to distribution to persons in areas served by a cable operator, prohibit exclusive contracts for satellite cable programming or satellite broadcast programming between a cable operator and a satellite cable programming vendor in which a cable operator has an attributable interest or a satellite broadcast programming vendor in which a cable operator has an attributable interest, unless the Commission determines (in accordance with paragraph (4)) that such contract is in the public interest.

(3) Limitations:

(A) Geographic limitations. Nothing in this section shall require any person who is engaged in the national or regional distribution of video programming to make such programming available in any geographic area beyond which such programming has been authorized or licensed for distribution.

(B) Applicability to satellite retransmissions. Nothing in this section shall apply (i) to the signal of any broadcast affiliate of a national television network or other television signal that is retransmitted by satellite but that is not satellite broadcast programming, or (ii) to any internal satellite communication of any broadcast network or cable network that is not satellite broadcast programming.

(4) Public interest determinations on exclusive contracts. In determining whether an exclusive contract is in the public interest for purposes of paragraph (2)(D), the Commission shall consider each of the following factors with respect to the effect of such contract on the distribution of video programming in areas that are served by a cable operator:

(A) the effect of such exclusive contract on the development of competition in local and national multichannel video programming distribution markets;

(B) the effect of such exclusive contract on competition from multichannel video programming distribution technologies other than cable;

(C) the effect of such exclusive contract on the attraction of capital investment in the production and distribution of new satellite cable programming;

(D) the effect of such exclusive contract on diversity of programming in the multichannel video programming distribution market; and

(E) the duration of the exclusive contract.

(5) Sunset provision. The prohibition required by paragraph (2)(D) shall cease to be effective 10 years after the date of enactment of this section, unless the Commission finds, in a proceeding conducted during the last year of such ten-year period, that such prohibition continues to be necessary to preserve and protect competition and diversity in the distribution of video programming.

(d) Adjudicatory proceeding. Any multichannel video programming distributor aggrieved by conduct that it alleges constitutes a violation of subsection (b), or the regulations of the Commission under subsection (c), may commence an adjudicatory proceeding at the Commission.

(e) Remedies for violations:

(1) Remedies authorized. Upon completion of such adjudicatory proceeding, the Commission shall have the power to order appropriate remedies, including, if necessary, the power to establish prices, terms, and conditions of sale of programming to the aggrieved multichannel video programming distributor.

(2) Additional remedies. The remedies provided in paragraph (1) are in addition to and not in lieu of the remedies available under Title V or any other provision of this Act.

(f) Procedures. The Commission shall prescribe regulations to implement this section. The Commission's regulations shall:

(1) provide for an expedited review of any complaints made pursuant to this section;

(2) establish procedures for the Commission to collect such data, including the right to obtain copies of all contracts and documents reflecting arrangements and understandings alleged to violate this section, as the Commission requires to carry out this section; and

(3) provide for penalties to be assessed against any person filing a frivolous complaint pursuant to this section.

(g) Reports. The Commission shall, beginning not later than 18 months after promulgation of the regulations required by subsection (c), annually report to Congress on the status of competition in the market for the delivery of video programming.

(h) Exemptions for prior contracts:

(1) In general. Nothing in this section shall affect any contract that grants exclusive distribution rights to any person with respect to satellite cable programming and that was entered into on or before June 1, 1990, except that the provisions of subsection (c)(2)(C) shall apply for distribution to persons in areas not served by a cable operator.

(2) Limitation on renewals. A contract that was entered into on or before June 1, 1990, but that is renewed or extended after the date of enactment of this section shall not be exempt under paragraph (1).

(i) Definitions. As used in this section:

(1) The term "satellite cable programming" has the meaning provided under Section 705 of this Act, except that such term does not include satellite broadcast programming.

(2) The term "satellite cable programming vendor" means a person engaged in the production, creation, or wholesale distribution for sale of satellite cable programming, but does not include a satellite broadcast programming vendor.

(3) The term "satellite broadcast programming" means broadcast video programming when such programming is retransmitted by satellite and the entity retransmitting such programming is not the broadcaster or an entity performing such retransmission on behalf of and with the specific consent of the broadcaster.

(4) The term "satellite broadcast programming vendor" means a fixed service satellite carrier that provides service pursuant to Section 119 of Title 17, United States Code, with respect to satellite broadcast programming.

Industry Standard Coding Indentification System (ISCI)

ISCI is a computer-format system for indentifying television commercials, programs and program-related materials. ISCI stands for "Industry Standard Coding Identification" and is the system of TV commercial identification endorsed and accepted by ABC, CBS, NBC, Fox, the Cable Advertising Bureau and the National Association of Broadcasters. The ISCI System is under the control of two parties: The ISCI Commercial System is owned and operated by the American Association of Advertising Agencies and the Association of National Advertisers, and administered by AAAA. The Program System is owned and operated by ISCI Program Systems.

The system provides identity coding for TV commercials, TV programs and music used in both commercials and programs: 1) the TV commercial coding (approximately 4.5 billion eight-character codes) is offered to cover TV commercials of all advertisers under one standard; 2) a portion of the ISCI system (almost 160 million codes) is offered to cover all television programs worldwide...program material of all types, lengths and media which are intended for syndication or other repeat usage; and 3) the final portion of the ISCI system (approximately 17 million codes) are offered to cover all musical compositions in the ASCAP, BMI, SESAC and other performing rights societies as well as "orignal" compositions created specifically for use in TV commercials and programs (present and future) worldwide.

The eight-character (four letters and four numbers) coding is to identify commericals, programs and music on their schedules, leaders, boxes, cartons, cassettes, etc., with all commercials of a single advertiser or "parent" company (if there are divisions, subsidiaries or affiliates) identified by the advertiser's prefix assigned by the ISCI system. For programs and music, the ISCI system licenses a specific eight-character permanent code to each piece of programming and each composition.

For more information concerning the ISCI Commercial System or to purchase an ISCI Commercial Register, which lists the assigned prefixes of over 3,000 advertisers and 1,000 agencies and their assigned codes contact: Louise O'Gara, ISCI, c/o AAAA, 666 3rd Ave., New York 10017. (212) 682-2500. FAX: (212) 682-8391. For information concerning the ISCI Program System, contact: Timothy J. Daly, General Manager. (212) 921-8184.

National Association of Broadcasters (NAB) Television and Radio Codes

Both codes of broadcast standards promulgated by the National Association of Broadcasters have been suspended.

The NAB and U.S. Justice Department agreed to a consent decree abolishing commercial time standards in the television code, in settlement of an antitrust suit brought by the Justice Department (see *Broadcasting Magazine*, July 19, 1982).

Programming standards in the television and radio codes were suspended in 1976 after a U.S. federal judge in Los Angeles ruled that family-viewing provisions of the television code violated the First Amendment.

For texts of the suspended codes, see *Broadcasting/Cablecasting Yearbook 1982*.

U.S. Government Agencies of Interest to Broadcasting and Cable

The following information is current as of December 1993.

Executive Office of the President

The White House. 1600 Pennsylvania Ave. N.W., Washington 20500. (202) 456-1414. George Stephanopoulos, sr advisor on policy & strategy; David Gergen, counselor to the Pres; Mark Gearan, dir of communications; Dee Dee Myers, deputy asst to Pres/press sec; Arthur Jones, deputy press sec; Lorraine Voles, deputy press sec; Ricki Seidman, deputy asst to Pres/deputy dir; David E. Dreyer, deputy asst to Pres/planning dir; Jeff Elder, deputy asst to Pres/media affrs dir; Marla Romash, communications dir to Vice Pres.

Senate Commerce Committee

Suite 508, Dirksen Bldg., Washington 20510-6125. (202) 224-5115.

Members: Ernest F. Hollings (D-S.C.), chmn; Daniel K. Inouye (D-Hawaii); Wendell H. Ford (D-Ky.); J. James Exon (D-Neb.); Byron Dorgan (D-N.D.); John Rockefeller (D-W.Va.); Harlin Mathews (D-Tenn.); John Kerry (D-Mass.); John B. Breaux (D-La.); Richard Bryan (D-Nev.); Charles Robb (R-Va.); John Danforth (R-Mo.); Bob Packwood (R-Ore.); Larry Pressler (R-S.D.); Ted Stevens (R-Alaska); Kay Hutchison (R-Texas); John McCain (R-Ariz.); Conrad Burns (R-Mont.); Slade Gorton (R-Wash.); Trent Lott (R-Miss.).

Communications Subcommittee: Daniel K. Inouye (D-Hawaii), chmn.

Senate Judiciary Committee

Suite 224, Dirksen Bldg., Washington 20510-6275. (202) 224-5225.

Members: Joseph Biden Jr. (D-Del.), chmn; Edward Kennedy (D-Mass.); Howard Metzenbaum (D-Ohio); Dennis DeConcini (D-Ariz.); Patrick Leahy (D-Vt.); Howell Heflin (D-Ala.); Paul Simon (D-Ill.); Herbert Kohl (D-Wisc.); Dianne Feinstein (D-Calif.); Carol Moseley-Braun (D-Ill.); Strom Thurmond (R-S.C.); Orrin Hatch (R-Utah); Alan Simpson (R-Wyo.); Charles Grassley (R-Iowa); Arlen Specter (R-Pa.); Larry Pressler (R-S.D.); William S. Cohen (R-Me.); Hank Brown (R-Colo.).

Senate Appropriations Committee

Rm. SD-118, Dirksen Senate Office Bldg., Washington 20510. (202) 224-3471.

Members: Robert Byrd (D-W.Va.), chmn; Daniel K. Inouye (D-Hawaii); Ernest Hollings (D-S.C.); J. Bennett Johnston (D-La.); Dianne Feinstein (D-Calif.); Patrick Leahy (D-Vt.); Jim Sasser (D-Tenn.); Dennis DeConcini (D-Ariz.); Frank Lautenberg (D-N.J.); Tom Harkin (D-Iowa); Barbara Mikulski (D-Md.); Harry Reid (D-Nev.); Patty Murray (D-Wash.); Herb Kohl (D-Wis.); J. Robert Kerrey (D-Neb.); Mark O. Hatfield (R-Ore.), ranking; Ted Stevens (R-Alaska); Mitch McConnell (R-Ky.); Thad Cochran (R-Miss.); Connie Mack (R-Fla.); Alfonse D'Amato (R-N.Y.); Conrad Burns (R-Mont.); Arlen Specter (R-Pa.); Pete Domenici (R-N.M.); Don Nickles (R-Okla); Phil Gramm (R-Texas); Christopher S. Bond (R-Mo.); Slade Gorton (R-Wash.).

Subcommittee on Commerce, Justice, State, the Judiciary: Ernest Hollings (D-S.C.), chmn.

Subcommittee on Labor, Health & Human Services, & Education: Tom Harkin (D-Iowa), chmn.

House Energy and Commerce Committee

Rm. 2125, Rayburn House Office Bldg., Washington 20515-6115. (202) 225-2927.

Members: John D. Dingell (D-Mich.), chmn; Henry Waxman (D-Calif.); Philip Sharp (D-Ind.); Edward J. Markey (D-Mass.); Gerry Studds (D-Mass.); Richard H. Lehman (D-Calif.); Al Swift (D-Wash.); Cardiss Collins (D-Ill.); Mike Synar (D-Oka.); W.J. (Billy) Tauzin (D-La.); Ron Wyden (D-Ore.); Ralph M. Hall (D-Tex.); Bill Richardson (D-N.M.); Jim Slattery (D-Kan.); John Bryant (D-Tex.); Rick Boucher (D-Va.); Jim Cooper (D-Tenn.); J. Roy Rowland (D-Ga.); Thomas J. Manton (D-N.Y.); Edolophus Towns (D-N.Y.); Frank Pallone (D-N.J.); Craig Washington (D-Tex.); Lynn Schenk (D-Calif.); Sherrod Brown (D-Ohio); Mike Kriedler (D-Wash.); Marjorie M. Mezvinsky (D-Pa.); Blanche Lambert (D-Ark.); Carlos Moorhead (R-Calif.); Thomas J. Bliley Jr. (R-Va.); Jack Fields (R-Tex.); Michael G. Oxley (R-Ohio); Michael Bilirakis (R-Fla.); Dan Schaefer (R-Colo.); Joe Barton (R-Tex.); Alex McMillan (R-N.C.); J. Dennis Hastert (R-Ill.); Fred Upton (R-Mich.); Cliff Stearns (R-Fla.); Bill Paxon (R-N.Y.); Paul Gillmor (R-Ohio); Scott Klug (R-Wis.); Gary Franks (R-Conn.); James Greenwood (R-Pa.); Mike Crapo (R-Idaho).

Telecommunications & Finance Subcommittee: Edward J. Markey (D-Mass.), chmn.

Oversight & Investigations Subcommittee: John D. Dingell (D-Mich.), chmn.

House Judiciary Committee

Rm. 2138, Rayburn House Office Bldg., Washington 20515-6216. (202) 225-3951. Minority Rm. B351-C, (202) 225-6909. Main Committee Rm. 2141. Subcommittee Hearing Rm. 2237, (202) 225-6966. Subcommittee Hearing Rm. 2226, (202) 225-6965. Subcommittee Hearing Rm. B352, (202) 225-5462.

Members: Jack Brooks (D-Tex.), chmn; Don Edwards (D-Calif.); John Conyers Jr. (D-Mich.); Romano L. Mazzoli (D-Ky.); William J. Hughes (D-N.J.); Mike Synar (D-Okla.); Patricia Schroeder (D-Colo.); Dan Glickman (D-Kan.); Barney Frank (D-Mass.); Charles E. Schumer (D-N.Y.); Howard L. Berman (D-Calif.); Rick Boucher (D-Va.); John Bryant Jr. (D-Tex.); George E. Sangmeister (D-Ill.); Craig A. Washington (R-Tex.); John F. Reed (D-R.I.); Jerrold Nadler (D-N.Y.); Robert C. Scott (D-Va.); David Mann (D-Ohio); Melvin L. Watt (D-N.C.); Xavier Becerra (D-Calif.); Hamilton Fish Jr. (R-N.Y.); Carlos J. Moorhead (R-Calif.); Henry J. Hyde (R-Ill.); F. James Sensenbrenner Jr. (R-Wis.); Bill McCollum (R-Fla.); George Gekas (R-Pa.); Howard Coble (R-N.C.); Lamar Smith (R-Tex.); Craig T. James (R-Fla.); Steven Schiff (R-N.M.); Jim Ramstad (R-Min.); George Allen (R-Va.); Elton Gallegly (R-Calif); Charles T. Canady (R-Fla.); Bob Inglis (R-S.C.); Bob Goodlatte (R-Va.).

Subcommittee on Economic & Commercial Law: Jack Brooks (D-Tex.), chmn.

Subcommittee on Civil & Constitutional Rights: Don Edwards (D-Calif.), chmn.

Subcommittee on International Law, Immigration & Refugees: Romano L. Mazzoli (D-Ky.), chmn.

Subcommittee on Intellectual Property & Judicial Administration: William J. Hughes (D-N.J.), chmn.

Subcommittee on Crime & Criminal Justice: Charles E. Schumer (D-N.Y.), chmn.

Subcommittee on Administrative Law & Governmental Relations: John Bryant (D-Tex.), chmn.

House Appropriations Committee

Rm. H218, Capitol Bldg., Washington 20515. (202) 225-2771.

Subcommittee on Commerce, Justice, State, Judiciary & Related Agencies. (202) 225-3351. Neal Smith (D-Iowa), chmn.

Subcommittee on Labor, Health & Human Services, & Education. (202) 225-3508. William H. Natcher (D-Ky.), chmn.

U.S. Supreme Court

One First St. N.E., Washington 20543. (202) 479-3000. Chief Justice of the United States: William H. Rehnquist. Associate Justices: Byron R. White, Harry A. Blackmun, John Paul Stevens, Sandra Day O'Connor, Antonin Scalia, Anthony M. Kennedy, David H. Souter, Clarence Thomas, Ruth Bader Ginsburg. Retired Chief Justice: Warren E. Burger. Retired Associate Justices: William J. Brennan Jr., Lewis F. Powell Jr., Byron R. White, Toni House, dir pub info.

U.S. Court of Appeals for the District of Columbia Circuit

Headquarters: 3rd St. & Constitution Ave. N.W., Washington 20001. (202) 273-0310. Chief Judge: Abner J. Mikva. Ron Garvin, clerk.

U.S. District Court for the District of Columbia

Headquarters: 3rd St. & Constitution Ave. N.W., Washington 20001. (202) 273-0594. Chief Judge: John Garrett Penn; Nancy Mayer-Whittington, clerk.

Department of Agriculture

Headquarters: 14th & Independence Ave. S.W., Washington 20250. (202) 720-8732. Mike Espy, sec; Susan Fertig-Dyks, dir of publ & vis communications.

Department of Commerce

Headquarters: 14th & Constitution Ave. N.W., Washington 20230. (202) 482-2000. Ronald H. Brown, sec; Thomas J. Murrin, deputy sec. Office of Pub Affrs: (202) 377-3263. Marion Blakey, dir of pub affrs. Bureau of Census: Barbara E. Bryant, dir. International Trade Administration: (202) 377-2867. J. Michael Sarren, under sec international trade; Elizabeth Dugan, dir pub affrs. Economic Development Administration: (202) 377-5081. James L. Perry, actg asst sec for economic dev. National Bureau of Standards: (202) 975-2762. Dr. Lyons, dir designate; Richard S. Franzen, chief pub affrs. National Oceanic and Atmospheric Administration: (202) 377-4190. Reed Boatright, dir of pub affrs. Bureau of Economic Analysis: (202) 523-0693. Allen Young, dir. Patent Office: (703) 557-3071. William O. Craig, dir pub affrs. U.S. Travel and Tourism Administration: (202) 377-3811. Rockwell A. Schnabel, under sec for tourism. Minority Business Development Agency: (202) 377-5741. Kenneth E. Bolton, dir.

National Telecommunications and Information Administration. 14th & Constitution N.W., Washington 20230. (202) 482-1551. FAX: (202) 482-1635. Larry Irving, asst sec for C&I.

Department of Defense

Headquarters: Pentagon, Washington 20301. (703) 545-6700.

Dept. of the Army: Gordin R. Sullivan, actg sec; Major Gen Charles W. McClain, Jr., chief of pub affrs. (703) 695-5135.

Dept. of the Navy: John H. Dalton, sec; Rear Admiral Kendell Pease, chief of info. (703) 697-7391.

Dept. of the Air Force: Dr. Sheila E Widnall actg sec; Colonel Edward A. Pardini, dir info mgmt. (703) 697-4191.

Marine Corps: Carl E. Mundy Jr., commandant; Colonel John M. Shotwell, dir pub affrs. (703) 614-1492.

Department of Education

Headquarters: 400 Maryland Ave. S.W., Washington 20202-4133. (202) 708-5366; (202) 401-3000. Richard Riley, sec. (202) 401-3000. Catherine Kahlor, dir pub affrs. (202) 401-3026. Audio Broadcast Service (800) 424-0214; in D.C. (202) 401-1052. Norma Dunkin, confidential asst.

Department of Health and Human Services

Headquarters: 200 Independence Ave. S.W., Washington 20201. (202) 619-0257. Dr. Donna E. Shalala, sec. (202) 690-7000.

Office of Asst Sec for Pub Affrs: Avis LaBelle. (202) 690-6343.

Health Care Financing Administration: Kevin L. Erbe, dir pub info div. (202) 690-6113.

U.S. Government Agencies

Center for Disease Control (Public Health Service): David Satcher, dir of center; Ann Simms, actg dir office pub affrs. (404) 639-3286.

National Institutes of Health (Public Health Service): Anne Thomas, assoc dir communications. (301) 496-5787.

Food and Drug Administration (Public Health Service): Alexander Grant, assoc commissioner for consumer affrs. (301) 443-5006.

Health Resources and Services Administration (Public Health Service): Sylvia Shaffer, actg assoc admin for communications. (301) 443-3376.

Social Security Administration: Phillip Gambino, press off. (410) 965-8904.

Office for Civil Rights: Dennis Hayashi, dir. (202) 619-0403.

Administration for Children, Youth & Families: Josaph Mottola, deputy actg commissioner. (202) 205-8347.

Office of Assistant Secretary for Health: Dr. Phillip Lee, communications news dir. (202) 690-6867.

Office of Assistant Secretary for Planning & Evaluation: David Elwood, asst sec. (202) 690-7858.

Office of Consumer Affairs: Patricia Faley, actg dir. (202) 634-9610.

Office of Refugee Resettlement: Chris Gersten, dir. (202) 401-9246.

Office of the Inspector General: Brian Mitchell, principle deputy inspector gen. (202) 619-3148.

Substance Abuse & Mental Health Services Administration: James Miller, dir communications & external affrs. (301) 443-8956.

Indian Health Service: Michael E. Lincoln actg dir; Patricia A. DeAsis, dir communications. (301) 443-3593.

Department of Justice

Headquarters: Constitution Ave. & 10th St. N.W., Washington 20530. (202) 514-2000. Janet Reno, atty gen; Philip B. Heymann, deputy atty gen; Webster L. Hubbell, assoc atty gen; Drew S. Days, III, solicitor gen: Walter Dellinger, desinate AAG/office of legal counsel; John C.Keeney, actg AAG/criminal; Frank Hunger, designate AAG/civil division; Anne Bingaman, AAG/antitrust; Gerald Torres, designate AAG/environment & natural resources; Michael L. Paup, actg AAG/tax division; James P. Turner, actg AAG/civil rights, Sheila Anthony, designate AAG/legislative affrs; Shirley Ashton Jr., actg AAG/office of justice programs; Steve Colgate, AAG/administration; Eleanor Acheson, designate office of policy dev; Carl Stern, dir office of public affrs; William Sessions, dir FBI, Chris Sale, actg dir immigration & naturalization svc; Richard J. Hankinson, inspector gen; Mary C. Lawton, dir office of intelligence policy & review; Robert M. Yahn, exec sec.

Department of Labor

Headquarters: 200 Constitution Ave. N.W., Washington 20210. (202) 219-6666. Richard Reich, sec. Office of info & pub affrs: (202) 219-7316. Robert Zachariasiewicz, asst sec pub affrs.

Department of State

Headquarters: 2201 C St. N.W., Washington 20520. (202) 647-4000. Warren M. Christopher, sec of state; J. Brian Atwood, under sec for mgmt; Anthony A. Das, actg dir, office of pub communication (Bureau of Pub Affrs), (202) 647-9554; Bradley Holmes, dir, (Bureau of International Communications & Info Policy), (202) 647-5212; John Clark, deputy asst sec for systems opns (IMSO), (202) 647-1000.

Department of Transportation

Headquarters: 400 7th St. S.W., Washington 20590. (202) 366-4000. FAX: (202) 366-7202. Federico Pena, sec; Richard I. Mintz, dir pub affrs, (202) 366-4570.

Federal Highway Administration: (202) 366-0660. Rodney Slater, admin; Steven Akey, dir pub affrs.

Federal Aviation Administration: (202) 267-3883. David Hinson, admin; Robert Buckhorn, actg asst admin pub affrs.

Federal Transit Administration: (202) 366-4043. Godron J. Linton, admin; Peter G. Halpin, dir communication & external affrs.

United States Coast Guard: (202) 267-1587. Admiral J. William Kime, commandant; Capt. Ernes Blanchard, pub affrs staff.

Saint Lawrence Seaway Development Corp.: (202) 366-0110. Stanford Parris, admin; Dennis E. Deuschl, communications dir.

Federal Railroad Administration: (202) 366-0881. Jolene Molitoris, admin.

National Highway Traffic Safety Administration: (202) 366-9550. Barry McCahill, actg dir public & consumer affrs.

Maritime Administration: (202) 366-5807. Albert Herberger, admin; Walter E. Oates, pub affrs off.

Department of the Treasury

Headquarters: 15th & Pennsylvania Ave. N.W., Washington 20220. (202) 622-2000. Lloyd Bentsen, treasury sec; Roger Altman, deputy sec; Desiree Tucker-Sorini, asst sec pub affrs/pub liaison, (202) 622-2920.

Bureau of Alcohol, Tobacco & Firearms: 650 Massachusetts Ave. N.W., Washington 20226. (202) 927-7777. John Magaw, actg dir; James O. Pasco, asst dir cong/media affrs, (202) 927-8490.

Comptroller of the Currency: 250 E St. S.W., Washington 20219. (202) 874-4900. Vjean A. Ludwig, comptroller; Frank Maguire, sr dep comptroller leg/pub affrs, (202) 874-4710.

U.S. Customs Service: 1301 Constitution Ave. N.W., Washington 20229. (202) 927-1000. George Weise, commissioner; Charles Parkinson, asst commissioner for cong/pub affrs, (202) 927-1760; William Anthony, dir pub affrs, (202) 927-0549.

Bureau of Engraving & Printing: 14th & C Sts. S.W., Washington 20227. (202) 874-2000. Peter Daly, dir; Norma Opgrand, dir pub affrs, (202) 874-2005.

Financial Management Service: 401 14th St. N.W., Washington 20227. (202) 874-7000. Russell Morris, commissioner; Andy Montgomery, dir pub affrs, (202) 874-6750.

Internal Revenue Service: 1111 Constitution Ave. N.W., Washington 20224. (202) 622-4115. Margaret Richardson, commissioner; Ellen Murphy, asst to the commissioner pub affrs, (202) 622-4010.

Bureau of the Mint. 633 3rd St. N.W., Washington 20220. (202) 874-6000. David J. Ryder, dir.

Bureau of Public Debt: 999 E St. N.W., Washington 20239. (202) 219-3300. Richard Gregg, commissioner; Pete Hollenbach, dir pub affrs, (202) 219-3302.

U.S. Savings Bond Division: 800 K St. N.W., Washington 20226. (202) 622-0100.

U.S. Secret Service: 1800 G St. N.W., Washington 20223. (202) 435-5700. Guy Caputo, actg dir; Don Edwards, asst dir govt liaison & pub affrs, (202) 535-5708.

Office of Thrift Supervision: 1700 G St. N.W., Washington 20552. (202) 906-6280. Timothy Ryan, dir; William Folwider, dir pub affrs, (202) 906-6804.

United States Information Agency

Headquarters: 301 4th St. S.W., Washington 20547. (202) 619-4700. Assignment edit bcst svcs: (202) 619-1741. Joseph Duffey, dir; Ann T. Pincus, rsch office; Kimberly Marteau, dir public liaison office.

U.S. Advisory Commission on Public Diplomacy

Headquarters: 301 4th St. S.W., Washington 20547. (202) 619-4457. FAX: (202) 619-5489. Tom C. Korologos, chmn; Bruce Gregory, staff dir.

Department of Energy

Headquarters: 1000 Independence Ave. S.W., Washington 20585. (202) 586-5000. FAX: (202) 586-5049. William Taylor, sec; Debra L. Louison, asst department sec inter-governmental affrs; Michael Gauldin, dir pub affrs. Office of External Affrs: (202) 586-5544. Press office: M.J. Jameson, press sec, (202) 586-5806.

Federal Communications Commission

Headquarters: 1919 M St. N.W., Washington 20554. (202) 632-5050. (For full listing of commissioners & staff, see FCC Executives & Staff).

Federal Trade Commission

Headquarters: 6th & Pennsylvania Ave. N.W., Washington 20580. (202) 326-2180. Janet D. Steiger, chmn. Commissioners: Deborah K. Owen; Mary Azcuenaga; Roscoe B. Starek III; Dennis A. Yao; Christian S. White, actg dir bureau of consumer protection; Donald S. Clark, sec; Mary Lou Steptoe, actg dir bureau of competition; Ronald S. Bond, actg dir bureau of economics; Lewis F. Parker, chief admin law judge; Bonnie L. Jansen, dir of office of pub affrs.

National Aeronautics & Space Administration (NASA)

Headquarters: 300 E St. S.W., Washington 20546. (202) 358-0000. Daniel S. Golden, admin; Jeff Vincent, actg assoc admin for pub affrs; James W. McCulla, dir media svcs div; James M. Funkhouser, dir pub svcs div; Robert J. Shafer, dir TV/dev div; David W. Garrett, chief news & info branch; Joseph L. Headlee, chief bcst & audio visual branch.

Emergency Broadcast System Advisory Committee

Headquarters: Federal Communications Commission, 1919 M St. N.W., Washington 20554. (202) 632-3906. FAX: (202) 632-1148. Helena Mitchell, Ph.D., chief.

National Labor Relations Board

Headquarters: 1099 14th St. N.W., Washington 20570-0001. (202) 273-1000. William Gould, chmn; Dennis M. Devaney, John N. Raudabaugh, bd members; Jerry M. Hunter, gen counsel. Div of info: (202) 273-1991. David B. Parker, dir.

National Science Foundation

Headquarters: 4201 Wilson Blvd., Arlington, VA 22230. (703) 306-1067. Raymond E. Bye, actg dir pub affrs; Michael Fluharty, head Media & Public Information; Susan Bartlett, audio visual officer.

Federal Emergency Management Agency

Headquarters: 500 C St. S.W., Washington 20472. Maurice Goodman, dir. (202) 646-4600. FAX: (202) 646-4086.

Securities & Exchange Commission

Headquarters: 450 5th St. N.W., Washington 20549. (202) 272-7450. Members: Richard C. Breeden, chmn; Mary L. Schapiro, Richard Roberts, Carter Beese, commissioners; William Heyman, dir div of mkt regulation; Peter Robinson, dir of pub affrs. Office of the sec: (202) 272-2600. Jonathan Katz, sec pub affrs.

Canadian Government Agencies of Interest to Broadcasting and Cable

The following information is current as of December 1993.

Department of Communications

Head office: Industry Canada, 235 Queens St., 11th Fl., Ottawa, Ont. Canada K1A 0HS. Info svcs: (613) 995-9001. FAX: (613) 952-1231.

Minister: The Hon. Michele Dupuy.

Canadian Radio-Television and Telecommunications Commission

Head office: Ottawa, Ont. Canada K1A ON2. General info: (819) 997-0313; library: (819) 997-4484. FAX: (819) 994-0218.

Full-time members: Keith Spicer, chmn; Fernand Belisle, vice chmn; Louis R. Sherman, vice chmn; David Colville; Adrian Burns; Beverley J. Oda; Edward A. Ross; Sally Reukauf Warren.

Part-time members: Normand F. Carrier, Edmundston, N.B.; Gail Scott, Toronto, Ont.; Robert Gordon, Ottawa, Ont.; Walter Ruest, Rimouski, Que.; Claude Sylvestre, Montreal, Que.

Senior staff mgmt committee: Diane Rheaume, dir gen radio; Peter Fleming, dir gen TV; Wayne Charman, dir gen cable distribution & bcst technology directorate; Bill Allen, dir gen pub affairs; Allan Darling, sec gen; Avrum Cohen, sr gen counsel.

U.S. State Cable Regulatory Agencies

Alaska Public Utilities Commission. 1016 W. Sixth Ave., Suite 400, Anchorage 99501. (907) 276-6222. FAX: (907) 276-0160. Don Schroer, chmn; Robert A. Lohr, exec dir.

Connecticut Department of Public Utility Control. One Central Park Plaza, New Britain 06051. (203) 827-1553. Reginald I. Smith, chmn; Evan Woollacott, vice-chmn.

Delaware Public Service Commission. 1560 S. DuPont Hwy., Dover 19901. (302) 739-4247. Nancy M. Norling, chmn; Robert J. Kennedy, exec dir.

Hawaii Cable Television Division. Dept. of Commerce & Consumer Affairs, Box 541, Honolulu 96809. (808) 586-2620. Clifford K. Higa, dir; Susan Doyle, dep dir; Jasmine Fujiwara Uehara, administrator.

Commonwealth of Massachusetts Cable Television Commission. 100 Cambridge St., Rm. 2003, Boston 02202. (617) 727-6925. Jill Reddish, exec dir; John M. Urban, commissioner.

New Jersey Office of Cable Television. Two Gateway Center, Newark 07102. (201) 648-2670. FAX: (201) 648-2848. Celeste M. Fasone, dir; Charles Russell, dep dir.

New York State Commission on Cable Television. Empire State Plaza, Tower Bldg., Albany 12223. (518) 474-4992. William B. Finneran, chmn; Edward P. Kearse, exec dir.

Rhode Island Division of Public Utilities and Carriers. 100 Orange St., Providence 02903. (401) 277-3500. James J. Malachowski, admin of the division; John A. Notte III, assoc admin for CATV.

Vermont Public Service Board. 89 Main St., City Center Bldg., Montpelier 05602-2701. (802) 828-2358. Richard H. Cowart, chmn.

Television Ownership Transfers

Note: The following directory presents a comprehensive history of television station transfers from the inception of authorized commercial service through December 1993.

Alabama

WJSU-TV Anniston (ch 40)—Licensed to Osborn Communications. Former owner: Anniston Broadcasting Co. (John Price). Sale price: $25.1 million (including KKRD-FM Wichita, KS & WWVA-AM/WOVK-FM Wheeling, WV). FCC approved: March 18, 1987 [Changing Hands, February 2, 1987]. Previous owner: Jacksonville State University Communications Foundation Inc. (nonprofit organization). Sale price: $5.5 million. FCC approved: December 20, 1985 [For the Record, November 18, 1985]. Previous owner: Anniston Broadcasting Co., headed by H. Brandt Ayers & his sister, Elsie Ayers Sanguinetti (each 40%). Sale price: $2.9 million. FCC approved: May 4, 1983 [For the Record, June 6, 1983]. Note: Stn went on air October 26, 1969.

WBMG(TV) Birmingham (ch 42)—Licensed to Roy H. Park Broadcasting of Birmingham Inc. (owned by Park Broadcasting Inc., see Group Ownership). Original owner: Birmingham Television Corp. (see Southern Broadcasting Co. under Group Ownership). Sale price: $4.75 million. FCC approved: June 13, 1973 [For the Record, June 25, 1973].

WBRC-TV Birmingham (ch 6)—Licensed to Great American Broadcasting (see Group Ownership). Previous owner: Taft Broadcasting. Note: part of the Taft Broadcasting reorganization of October 1987. Former owner: Storer Broadcasting Co. (see Group Ownership). Sale price: $6.35 million (with WBRC-AM-FM). FCC approved: May 8, 1957 [For the Record, May 13, 1957]. Note: Storer purchased WBRC-AM-TV for $2.4 million from Eloise S. Hanna in May 1953 [For the Record, June 1, 1953] & was required to sell stns with FCC approval of purchase of WBFH(TV) Wilmington, DE, & WIBG-AM-FM, Philadelphia.

WSGN-TV Birmingham (ch 42, now deleted)—Licensed to Jemison Broadcasting Co. Original owners: Birmingham News Co. Sale price: $300,000 (including WSGN-AM-FM). FCC approved: June 26, 1953 [For the Record, July 6, 1953]. Note: This was part of condition imposed by FCC in granting Birmingham News Co. purchase of WAP(AM), WAFM(FM) & WAFM-TV (now WAPI-AM-FM-TV).

WTTO Birmingham (ch 21)—Licensed to HR Broadcasting Corp. (Albert Krivin, Hal Gaba, Robin French, Hal Roach Studios). Former owner: Arlington Broadcast Group (see Group Ownership). Sale price: $30.5 million (including WCGV-TV, Milwaukee). FCC approved: July 14, 1986 [For the Record, June 16, 1986]. Previous owner: Chapman Radio & TV Corporation (William & George Chapman, 50.2%). (Arlington Broadcast owned 49.8% of stn & completed transfer of control.) Sale price: $1 million. FCC approved: August 3, 1983. Note: Stn began operation April 21, 1982.

WVTM-TV Birmingham (ch 13)—Licensed to KTVI Argyle Inc. (owned by Argyle Television Holding Inc., see Group Ownership). Former owner: WVTM-TV Inc. (owned by Times Mirror Co.). Sale price: $45 million. FCC approved: May 14, 1993 [For the Record, May 31, 1993]. Note: Part of $80 million 2-stn sale with KTVI(TV) St. Louis. Previous owner: Newhouse Broadcasting Co. Sale price: $82 million (including KYVI(TV) St. Louis, MO; WSYR-TV Syracuse, & satellite WSYE-TV Elmira, both NY; & WTPA(TV) Harrisburg, PA. FCC approved: March 27, 1980. [*Broadcasting*, March 31 & April 7, 1980]. Former call letters: WAPI-TV. Original owners: The Television Co. [Ed Norton (75%), Thad Holt (25%)]. Sale price: $2.4 million (including WAPI-AM & WAFM-FM). FCC approved: June 10, 1953, on condition Birmingham News Co. relinquish WSGN-AM-FM-TV Birmingham [For the Record, June 22, 1953]. Original call letters: WAFM-TV. Note: On January 25, 1956, FCC approved $18.7 million purchase of Birmingham News Co. by S.I. Newhouse, which included this stn, two nwsprs & two radio stns [For the Record, January 30, 1956].

WDHN-TV Dothan (ch 18)—Licensed to The Morris Network. Former owner: Hi-Ho Television Stations. [F. Francis D'Addario (33.3%), Jerome Kurtz (33.3%), James D. Ivey (16.6%) & David Antoniak (16.6%)]. Sale price: $6.6 million (including WNGA(TV) Valdosta, GA). FCC approved: July 18, 1986 [For the Record, June 16, 1986]. Previous owner: Southeast Alabama Broadcasting Inc. (Jay B. Bragg, Betts Slingluff & 31 others). Sale price: $310,563. FCC approved: June 26, 1979 [*Broadcasting*, July 16, 1979].

WTVY(TV) Dothan (ch 4)—Licensed to Dothan Holdings II Inc. Former owner: Woods Communications Group Inc. Sale price: assumption of debt in form of 1986 credit agreement with Chemical Bank in amount of $23.25 million. FCC approved: March 16, 1993 [For the Record, April 5, 1993].

WAAY-TV Huntsville (ch 31)—Licensed to Rocket City Television Inc. Previous owner: P. Gunn, J. Cleary, J. Higdon. Sale price: $509,775. FCC approved: 1963. Former call letters: WAFG-TV.

WAFF(TV) Huntsville (ch 48)—Licensed to American Valley Broadcasting Co. (owned by American Family Corp., holding company of American Life Assurance Co., which owns WYEA-TV Columbus, GA). Former owner: Tennessee Valley Radio & Television Corp., 75.8% owned by International Television Corp. [Gerald V. Bull (47.9%), Donald G. Martin (47.9%), et al]. Sale price: $3.35 million. FCC approved: July 1978 [Changing Hands, July 24, 1978]. Former call letters: WYUR-TV. Original owner: Tennessee Valley Radio & Television Corp., 76.8% owned by Frank Whisenant, Benny Digesu & Ned Frazier. Sale price: $891,111. FCC approved: October 24, 1974 [For the Record, November 11, 1974].

WHNT-TV Huntsville (ch 19)—Licensed to New York Times Co. (see Group Ownership). Former owner: North Alabama Broadcasters Inc [Charles Grisham (90%), Tom Percer (10%)]. Sale price: $12 million. FCC approved: February 27, 1980 [For the Record, March 27, 1980].

WZDX(TV) Huntsville (ch 54)—Licensed to Huntsville Television Acquisition Corp. Former owner: Community Service Broadcasting, debtor-in-possession. Sale price: $6.1 million. FCC approved: January 4, 1989.

WALA-TV Mobile (ch 10)—Licensed to Knight-Ridder Broadcasting Inc. Former owner: Universal Communications Corp. (see Evening News Association Stations in Group Ownership). Sale price: $160 million (including KOLD(TV) Tuscon, AZ, & KTVY(TV) Oklahoma City). FCC approved: January 13, 1986 [For the Record, December 16, 1985]. Previous owner: Roywood Corp. [Royal Street Corp. (41%) & others. Royal Street is controlled by Edgar B. Stern & family & owns WDSU-AM-FM-TV New Orleans]. Sale price: $4.75 million. FCC approved: October 29, 1969 [For the Record, November 10, 1969]. Note: Founded in 1953. Sold by W.O. Pape to Roywood Corp. for $3 million in 1964 with WALA(AM) Mobile. Subsequently, Roywood sold WALA(AM) to Stone Representatives for $250,000.

WKRG-TV Mobile (ch 5)—Licensed to Ansley G. Green, et al. Former owner: WKRG Inc. (Kenneth R. Giddens). Sale price: no financial consideration in stock transfer (including WKRG-AM-FM Mobile, AL). FCC approved: June 21, 1991 [For the Record, July 22, 1991]. Previous owners: Giddens & Mobile *Press-Register* for 50%. Sale price: $2.25 million for 50% (included WKRG-AM-FM). FCC approved: September 28, 1966 [For the Record, October 10, 1966]. Note: Founded in 1955 by Giddens, Shirley Rester Conrad & others. Sold in 1958 to Giddens & Mobile *Press-Register* for $1.17 million (with WKRG-AM-FM).

WMPV(TV) Mobile (ch 21)—Licensed to Sonlight Broadcasting System Inc. Former owner: Rel Com Corp. Sale price: $2 million. FCC approved: July 27, 1989 [For the Record, August 14, 1989]. Previous owner: Rel Way Ltd. Sale price: $3 million. FCC approved: December 9, 1988 [For the Record, Jaunary 16, 1989].

WPMI(TV) Mobile (ch 15)—Licensed to Clear Channel Television Co. Former owner: WPMI Television Co. Sale price: approximately $9 million [For the Record, January 16, 1989]. FCC approved: December 8, 1988. Previous owner: Michigan Energy Resources Co., preceded by Hess Broadcasting Corp. Sale price of Michigan-Hess transaction: $11.95 million. FCC approved: September 26, 1985 [For the Record, August 19, 1985].

WCOV-TV Montgomery (ch 20)—Licensed to Woods Communications Corp. (David D. Woods). Former owner: WCOV Inc. (see Gay-Bell Stations in Group Ownership). Sale price: $4 million. FCC approved: September 26, 1985 [For the Record, June 10, 1985]. Previous owners: Oscar P. Covington (26.23%), Clara R. Covington (20.83%), Hugh M. Smith (15.07%), Ethel Covington (13.87%) & Mary R. Covington (2.78%). Sale price: $1.27 million. FCC approved: October 2, 1964 [For the Record, October 12, 1964].

WHOA-TV Montgomery (ch 32)—Licensed to Montgomery Independent Telecasters (owned by Terrapin Communications). Former call letters: WKAB-TV. Former owner: Bahakel Communications. Sale price: $10.22 million. FCC approved: June 10, 1985 [For the Record, May 6, 1985].

WMCF(TV) Montgomery (ch 45)—Licensed to Sonlight Broadcasting System Inc. Former owner: League of Prayer Inc. Sale price: $1.1 million. FCC approved: August 8, 1990. Previous owner: Word of God Fellowship Inc. Sale $2.39 million [For the Record, September 25, 1989]. FCC approved September 11, 1989.

WSFA-TV Montgomery (ch 12)—Licensed to Cosmos Broadcasting Co. (see Group Ownership). Former owner: WKY Television System Inc. Sale price: $2.25 million. FCC approved: September 2, 1959 [For the Record, September 14, 1959]. Note: Founded by David E. Dunn & associates & sold to WKY Television System Inc. in 1955 for $568,589 (with WSFA-AM) [For the Record, February 28, 1955].

WSWS-TV Opelika (ch 66)—Licensed to Robert R. D'Andrea. Former owner: RCH Broadcasting Inc. Sale price: $2.44 million. FCC approved: July 30, 1984.

WAKA(TV) Selma (ch 8)—Licensed to Alabama Telecasters Inc. (owned by Bahakel Communications, see Group Ownership). Former owner: Charles F. Grisham, et al. Sale price: undisclosed. FCC approved: June 10, 1985. Previous owner: Selma TV Inc. Sale price: $100,000. FCC approved: 1971. Stn was off-the-air at the time & resumed operation in 1973.

WCFT-TV Tuscaloosa (ch 33)—Licensed to Federal Broadcasting Co. Former owner: Beacon Broadcasters Ltd., debtors-in-possession. Sale price: $7.5 million. FCC approved: February 20, 1991 [For the Record, March 11, 1991]. Previous owner: Chapman TV of Tuscaloosa Inc. [S.A. Rosenbaum (43.75%), W.S. Smylie (18.75%), Marvin Reuben (8.33%), Jerry P. Keith (4.17%), Margaret G. Smylie (16.67%) & W.S. Smylie III (8.33%)]. Sale price: $25 million (including KYEL-TV Yuma, AZ, & WDAM-TV Laurel-Hattiesburg, MS). FCC approved: July 27, 1983, for WCFT-TV; June 10, 1983, for WDAM-TV [For the Record, August 15, 1983]. Original owners: Lewis N. Manderson Jr., R.S. Holified, C.H. Armstrong, Edwin L. Minges, C.J. Hartley & James D. Kincaid. Sale price: assumption of $121,294 debt. FCC approved: August 23, 1957 [For the Record, September 4, 1967].

Alaska

KDMD(TV) Anchorage (ch 33)—Licensed to GREENTV Corp. Former owner: Echonet Corp. Sale price: $75,000. FCC approved: January 31, 1992 [For the Record, February 17, 1992].

KIMO(TV) Anchorage (ch 13)—Licensed to The Alaska 13 Corp. [Carl A. Bracale Jr. (21%), Duane L. Triplett (17%), Robert L. Lewis (11%) & Richard M. Zook (15%)]. Former owner: Sourdough Broadcasters Inc. (Patricia E. Harpel, sole owner). Sale price: $343,000, including KHAR-AM-FM. FCC approved: May 28, 1971 [For the Record, June 21, 1971]. Original call letters: KHAR-TV. Note: Original owner was Willis R. Harpel. Sold to Sourdough Broadcasters Inc. [W. Harpel (82%), Patricia Harpel (3%), & Sourdough Broadcasters (15%)] for assumption of $250,359.20 debt plus reimbursement for out-of-pocket expenses in amount of $83,610.06, with KHAR-FM. FCC approved: November 9, 1967, for TV; October 31, 1967, for FM [For the Record, November 13, 1967].

KTBY(TV) Anchorage (ch 4)—Licensed to KTBY Inc. (Ronald Bradley). Former owner: Tak Communications Inc. Sale price: $225,000 (transfer of control). FCC approved: December 31, 1984 [For the Record, January 7, 1985]. Original owner: Totem Broadcasting Corp. Sale price: $1.6 million. FCC approved: 1984.

KTUU-TV Anchorage (ch 2)—Licensed to Channel 2 Broadcasting Co. [owned by Zaser & Longston Inc. (Jessica L. Longston)]. Former owner: Midnight Sun Broadcasters Inc. Sale price: $4.6 million (including KFAR-TV Fairbanks, AK). FCC approved: March 6, 1981 [Changing Hands, March 30, 1981]. Former call letters: KENI-TV. Previous owner: Midnight Sun Broadcasting Co. Sale price: $3.5 million (including KENI(AM) Anchorage;

KFAR-AM-TV Fairbanks; KTKN(AM) Ketchikan; & KINY-AM-TV Juneau; all AK). FCC approved: March 17, 1960 [For the Record, March 28, 1960]. Note: Stn founded by Richard R. Rollins & Keith Kiggins as KFIA(TV). Sold to Midnight Sun Broadcasting Co. (Lathrop Co. & others) for $100,000 interest in Midnight Sun. FCC approved: December 29, 1954 [For the Record, January 10, 1955].

KYES(TV) Anchorage (ch 5)—Licensed to Fireweed Communications Corp., owned by Jeremy Lansman (51%) & Carol Schatz (41.5%). Former owner: Fireweed Television, owned by William Hately. Sale price: $100 & assumption of debt. FCC approved: December 11, 1991 [For the Record, January 6, 1992]. Note: Hately retained 7.5% interest in stn.

KATN(TV) Fairbanks (ch 2)—Licensed to The Alaska 13 Corp. (see KIMO(TV) Anchorage). Former owner: Zaser & Longston. Sale price: $2 million. FCC approved: July 18, 1984.

KJUD-TV Juneau (ch 8)—Licensed to The Alaska 13 Corp. (see KIMO(TV) Anchorage). Former owners: Charles M. Gray, et al. Sale price: $275,000. FCC approved: November 24, 1982. Previous owner: Midnight Sun Broadcasters Inc. Sale price: $500,000. FCC approved: December 12, 1981. Previous owner: William J. Wagner. Sale price: $52,250. FCC approved: March 27, 1959 [For the Record, April 6, 1959]. Former call letters: KINY-TV. Note: Founded by Alaska Broadcasting System Inc. in 1956.

KTNL(TV) Sitka (ch 13)—Licensed to Sitka News Bureau, owned by Marty W. Baggin. Former owners: Dan & Kathie Etulain. Sale price: $250,000. FCC approved: January 7, 1992 [For the Record, January 27, 1992]. Previous owner: Ray Paschal, et al. Sale price: $125,000. FCC approved: May 10, 1983.

Arizona

KNAZ(TV) Flagstaff (ch 2)—Licensed to Grand Canyon Television Co. (owned by William A. Franke 51%, Robert Wood Johnson IV 39%, Herold G. Gawthrop 1% & John P. Michaels, see Group Ownership). Former owner: Grand Canyon Television Co. (owned by Capitol Broadcasting Co., see Group Ownership). Sale price: $98,000 (including KMOH-TV Kingman). FCC approved: May 7, 1992 [For the Record, June 15, 1992]. Previous owner: Wendell Elliot, Jr., et al. Sale price: $1.4 million. FCC approved: January 7, 1981 [Changing Hands, February 9, 1981].

KMOH-TV Kingman (ch 6)—Licensed to Grand Canyon Television Co. (owned by William A. Franke 51%, Robert Wood Johnson IV 39%, Herold G. Gawthrop 1% & John P. Michaels, see Group Ownership). Former owner: Grand Canyon Television Co. (owned by Capitol Broadcasting Co., see Group Ownership). Sale price: $98,000 (including KMOH-TV Kingman). FCC approved: May 7, 1992 [For the Record, June 15, 1992].

KPNX(TV) Mesa (ch 12)—Licensed to KPNX Broadcasting Co. (owned by Combined Communications Corp., a subsidiary of Gannett Co. following merger in June 1979). Sale price: $370 million [including KARK-TV Little Rock, AR; KBTV(TV) (now KUSA-TV) Denver; WXIA-TV Atlanta; WPTA(TV) Ft. Wayne, IN; WKLY-TV Louisville; & KOCO-TV Oklahoma City; six AMs & six FMs). FCC approved: June 7, 1979 [*Broadcasting*, June 11, 1979]. Former call letters: KTAR-TV. Note: CCC purchased KTAR Broadcasting Stations (which included KTAR-AM-FM-TV Phoenix; KYUM(AM) Yuma & KYCA(AM) Prescott; all AZ) from John J. Louis & family for $15 million in CCC stock. Founded in 1953 by Harkins Broadcasting Co. (Dwight Harkin, Lorenzo J. Lisonbee & Harry L. Nace estate). Sold as KTYL-TV in 1954 to KTAR Broadcasting Co. for $251,242 in liabilities. Former call letters: KPNX-TV.

KMSB-TV Nogales/Tuscon (ch 11)—Licensed to Mountain States Broadcasting. Former owner: Roadrunner Television (limited partnership with Eugene D. Adelstein, Edward B. Berger & others). Sale price: $13 million. FCC approved: November 11, 1984. Previous owner: IBC. Sale price: $1.98 million plus liabilitites. FCC approved: November 19, 1976 [For the Record, November 29, 1976].

KNXV-TV Phoenix (ch 15)—Licensed to Scripps-Howard Broadcasting Company. Former owner: Arlington Broadcasting (Byron Lasky). Sale price: $26.6 million (including $500,000 non-compete). FCC approved: January 9, 1985.

KOY-TV Phoenix (ch 10, now deleted)—Licensed to Maricopa Broadcasters (KOOL-AM-TV with which it shared time on ch 10). Original owners: KOY Broadcasting Co. Sale Price: $200,000. FCC approved: May 5, 1954 [For the Record, May 10, 1954]. Merged with KOOL-TV, now KTSP(TV).

KPAZ-TV Phoenix (ch 21)—Licensed to Trinity Broadcasting. Former owner: Glad Tidings Church of America. Sale price: assumption of liabilities. FCC approved: 1977. Previous owner: Julius Altschul, trustee (following involuntary transfer of control from Donald B. Thompson, et al) in 1969. Sale price: $400,000. FCC approved: 1970.

KPHO-TV Phoenix (ch 5)—Licensed to Meredith Corp. (see Group Ownership). Original owners: Phoenix TV Inc. Sale price: $1.5 million (with KPHO(AM)). FCC approved: June 25, 1952 [For the Record, June 30, 1952]. Note: stn, originally KTLX(TV), first owned by W.L. Pickens, R.L. Wheelock & H.H. Coffield, then ownership broadened to include some KPHO(TV) stockholders, finally (in 1949) taken over by John C. Mullins & Associates.

KTSP-TV Phoenix (ch 10)—Licensed to Great American Broadcasting. Former owner: Taft Broadcasting (part of the Taft Broadcasting reorganization of October 1987). Previous owner: Gulf United Broadcasting (subsidiary of Gulf United Corp.). Sale price: $755 million [sale included WTSP-TV Tampa-St. Petersburg; KTXH-TV Houston; WGHP-TV High Point, NC; KTXA-TV Arlington (Ft. Worth), TX]. FCC approved: May 30, 1985 [For the Record, April 15, 1985]. Former owners: Tom Chauncey (51.08%), Homer Lane (.81%), & Gulf United Broadcasting. Sale price: $57 million for 51.9%. FCC approved: August 1982 [Changing Hands, September 13, 1982]. Original call letters: KOOL-TV. Note: Original owners were: KOOL Radio-Television Inc., 19.4% sold by Anne Kerney to licensee, KOOL Radio-Television Inc., for $572,970; 7.66% sold by Gene Autry to Tom Chauncey for $484,200. Autry & Chauncey are both stockholders in the KOOL Stations. After the transaction, which included KOOL-AM-FM as well as KOOL-TV, Chauncey held 47.78% of the stock, & Autry 46.07%. The remaining 6.15% of the stock held by Frank Beer. FCC approved: January 1972 [*Broadcasting*, January 31, 1972]. 48.11% of KOOL-TV stock sold by Autry to Gulf United Corp. for about $30 million [balance of stock remaining with Tom Chauncey (51.08%) & Homer Lane (.81%)]. FCC approved: 1981.

KTVK(TV) Phoenix (ch 3)—Licensed to Arizona Television Co., (Delbert Lewis, et al). Former owner: RCR Investments, Norwell Investment Company & 3W Investments. Sale price: $5.9 million. FCC approved: June 1977.

KTVW Phoenix (ch 33)—Licensed to Hallmark Acquisition Inc. Former owner: The Seven Hills Television Co. Sale price: $23 million. FCC approved: May 17, 1989 [For the Record, June 5, 1989].

KGUN-TV Tucson (ch 9)—Licensed to Lee Enterprises Inc. Former owner: May Broadcasting Co. Sale price: $89 million (including KMTV(TV) & 48.8% of KFAB(AM)/KGOR(FM), both Omaha, NE). FCC approved: November 7, 1986 [For the Record, October 6, 1986]. Previous owner: Gilmore Broadcasting Corp. of Arizona (James S. Gilmore). Sale price: $2.91 million. FCC approved: July 31, 1968 [For the Record, August 12, 1968]. Note: Founded by D.W. & Kathleen Ingram in 1955 as KDWI-TV & sold to H.U. Garrett & Associates for $533,000 in 1956. Garrett group sold stn to Henry S. Hilberg & others for $1.44 million in 1960. Gilmore Broadcasting bought stn in 1964 for $4.2 million with WEHT(TV) Evansville, IN.

KOLD-TV Tucson (ch 13)—Licensed to New Vision Television I Inc. (see New Vision Television Inc. in Group Ownership). Former owner: Knight-Ridder Broadcasting Inc. Sale price: $100 million (including WSAV-TV Savannah, GA; WHLT-TV Hattiesburg, MS; WJTV-TV Jackson, MS; WECT-TV Wilmington, NC; KABY-TV Aberdeen, SD; KPRY-TV Pierre, SD; & KSFY-TV Sioux Falls, SD). FCC approved: September 7, 1993 [For the Record, September 27, 1993]. Previous owner: Universal Communications Corp. (see Evening News Association in Group Ownership). Sale price: $160 million (including KTVY(TV) Oklahoma City & WALA(TV) Mobile, AL). FCC approved: January 13, 1986 [For the Record, December 16, 1985]. Original owner: Old Pueblo Broadcasting Co. (Gene Autry & others, see Golden West Broadcasters in Group Ownership). Sale price: $4.1 million. FCC approved: May 21, 1969 [For the Record, June 9, 1969]. Note: Founded by Old Pueblo Broadcasting in January 1953.

KPOL(TV) Tucson (ch 40)—Licensed to Jay S. Zucker. Former owner: Les Von Eberstein, trustee. Sale price: $45,000. FCC approved: October 16, 1991 [For the Record, November 16, 1991].

KTTU-TV Tucson (ch 18)—Licensed to Clear Channel Communications Inc. Former owner: Roman Catholic Church. Sale price: $8.5 million [For the Record, January 30, 1989]. FCC approved: January 11, 1989. Former call letters: KDTU(TV).

KVOA-TV Tucson (ch 4)—Licensed to KVOA Communications Inc. Former owner: Channel Four Television Co. (owned by H & C Communications Inc., see Group Ownership). Sale price: $13.2 million. FCC approved: October 28, 1993 [For the Record, November 15, 1993]. Previous owner: Channel 4-TV Inc. (principally owned by Donald Diamond, Richard Bloch & Donald Pitt). Sale price: $30 million. FCC approved June 28, 1982. [For the Record, July 12, 1982]. Previous owner: KVOA Television Inc. (Pulitzer Publishing Co.). Sale price: $2.72 million. FCC approved: November 24, 1972. Note: Founded by John J. Louis & family. Bought by Clinton D. McKinnon & associates in 1955 for $288,904 plus assumption of obligations amounting to $225,000 (with KVOA). Sold to WGAL Inc. in 1963 for $3.25 million (with KOAT-TV Albuquerque, NM). Sold by WGAL Television Inc. (Steinman Stations) to KVOA Television Inc. in 1968 for $3 million. FCC approved: July 31, 1968 [For the Record, August 12, 1968].

KIVA(TV) Yuma (ch 11, now deleted)—Licensed to Valley Telecasting Co. (Bruce Merrill). Former owners: Floyd B. Odlum & Harry Butcher. Sale price: $500,000. FCC approved: February 1, 1961 [For the Record, February 13, 1961]. Note: stn went dark January 31, 1970, & returned license to FCC. Odlum group took control in 1959 by assuming indebtedness of $241,000. Butcher bought 25% for $150,000. Butcher originally bought the stn from Donald Ellsworth & associates in 1957 for $241,000.

KYAT(TV) Yuma (ch 8, now deleted)—See KFMB-TV San Diego.

KSWT(TV) Yuma (ch 13)—Licensed to KB Media [owned by John A. Radeck (33.3%), William H. Sanders (33.3%), Janice W. Radeck & Kenneth L. Bazzle (33.3%)]. Former owners: Beacon Broadcasters Ltd. (see Group Ownership). Sale price: $1.4 million. FCC approved: April 24, 1991 [For the Record, May 13, 1991]. Former call letters: KYEL-TV. Previous owner: Service Broadcasters Inc. Sale price: $25.75 million (including WCFT-TV Tuscaloosa, AL; & WDAM-TV Laurel-Hattiesburg, MS). FCC approved: July 27, 1983 [Changing Hands, August 15, 1983]. Previous owner: Thaddeus G. Baker & others. Sale price: $1.1 million. FCC approved: September 18, 1978. Former call letters: KBLU-TV. Note: KBLU-TV founded in 1963 by Robert & Patricia Crites & John & Helen Noga. R. Crites acquired his wife's 25% interest in 1965 for $50,000. In 1966 one-third was sold to Paul Morgan & Herman Newhouse for $140,000 (including KBLU(AM)). The group, Desert Telecasting Inc., sold KBLU-AM-TV to Eller Telecasting in 1967 for $500,000. KBLU(AM) is now KAWC(AM); KYUM(AM) is KBLU(AM). Merged with KTAR Inc. to form Combined Communications Inc., October 22, 1969. Sold to R. Crites, Victor Root, Paul Coleman, Thaddeus Baker & others August 2, 1973 along with KBLU(AM) for $550,000. Sold to Chapman TV of Tuscaloosa, AL in 1978, when call letters were changed to the current ones. Chapman became Service Broadcasters Inc.

KYMA(TV) Yuma (ch 11)—Licensed to Sunbelt Broadcasting Co. Former owner: Clyde E. Pettit & A. Bates Butler. Sale price: Pettit & Butler sold combined 55% interest in stn to Sunbelt for $60,000. FCC approved: June 6, 1989 [For the Record, June 26, 1989]. Former call letters: KCAA(TV). Previous owner: Manning Telecasting Inc. (Yuma Television Assoc.), preceded by Cadmus Inc. (trustee in bankruptcy). Sale price of Manning-Cadmus transaction: $30,000. FCC approved: January 30, 1986 [For the Record, April 15, 1985].

Arkansas

KTVE(TV) El Dorado (ch 10)—Licensed to KTVE Inc. (owned by Gray Communications Systems Inc., see Group Ownership). Former owner: Fuqua Stations (see Group Ownership). Sale price: $3.25 million. FCC approved: December 4, 1967 [For the Record, December 11, 1967]. Note: Founded in 1955 by Joe F. Rushton & associates. Former Representative Oren Harris (D-Ark.) bought 25% interest in 1957 for $5,000 but sold back interest in 1958 for return of his $5,000 note. Purchased by William H. Simon in 1960 for reported $1.1 million, with Simon selling 80% to Veterans Broadcasting Co. later that year for $282,000. Sold in 1963 to Fuqua Industries for $650,000 plus assumption of $1.5 million in obligations.

KTVP(TV) Fayetteville (ch 29)—Licensed to Sigma Broadcasting. Former owner: Hernreich Broadcasting (George T. Hernreich). Sale price: $2.5 million (including KHBS(TV) Fort Smith, AR). FCC approved: February 19, 1985. Previous owner: Noark Investment Co. (100% owned by Paul W. Milam Sr., Paul W. Milam, Jr. & Jane R. Horne). Sale price: $215,000. FCC approved: April 30, 1975 [For the Record, May 19, 1975]. Former call letters: KGTO-TV.

KFSM-TV Fort Smith (ch 5)—Licensed to the New York Times Company (see Group Ownership). Former owner: Buford Television Inc. Sale price: $17.5 million. FCC approved: August 6, 1979. [For the Record, August 13, 1979]. Former call letters: KFSA-TV. Note: Donald W. Reynolds, 100% owner of KFSA-TV Inc., which owned KFSM before Buford, had acquired 49% of stn & then the remaining 51% from Harry Pollock in 1959 for $565,000. FCC approved: January 8, 1959 [For the Record, January 19, 1959]. Pollock (16.6% owner) purchased 50% of American TV Co. from George T. Hernreich & Harry Newton Co. for $175,000. FCC approved: March 5, 1958 [For the Record, March 10, 1958]. Hernreich bought 50% from the estate of Hiram S. Nakdimen in 1957 for obligations in excess of $150,000.

KHBS(TV) Fort Smith (ch 40)—Licensed to Sigma Broadcasting (Robert E. & Cynthia Hernreich). Former owner: George T. Hernreich. Sale price: $2.5 million (including KTVP(TV) Fayetteville, AR). FCC approved: February 19, 1985.

KPOM-TV Fort Smith (ch 24)—Licensed to Westark Broadcasting Ltd. Former owner: J.D.G. Television Inc. Sale price: $4.383 million (with KFAA(TV) Rogers, AR). FCC approved: July 25, 1991 [For the Record, August 12, 1991]. Previous owner: Ozark Television Co. (Raymond G. Schindler & family). Sale price: $6.24 million. FCC approved: October 25, 1985 [For the Record, November 11, 1985]. Previous owner: MCM Broadcasting Co. Sale price: $950,000 plus debt assumption. FCC approved: May 18, 1981 [Changing Hands, June 1, 1981]. Note: Schindlers also own KVGL(AM)-KMUZ(FM) La Grange, Tex.

KRZB-TV Hot Springs (ch 26)—Licensed to Bell Equities Inc. Former owner: PPD&G Inc. Sale price: $941,000. FCC approved: May 1987. Previous owner: Razorback TV Broadcasting. Sale price: $200,000. FCC approved: August 1, 1985 [For the Record, June 24, 1985].

KAIT-TV Jonesboro (ch 8)—Licensed to Cosmos Broadcasting. Former owner: Channel Communications Inc. Sale price: $68 million (including KPLC-TV Lake Charles, LA). FCC approved: November 12, 1986 [In Brief, September 29, 1986].

KARK-TV Little Rock (ch 4)—Licensed to KARK-TV Inc. [owned by United Broadcasting Corp: David J. Jones & Larry C. Wallace (20% each); Jerrol W. Jones, Thomas F. McLarty III, John J. Flake & E. Sheffield Nelson (13.75% each); & Karl Eller (5%)]. Former owner: Combined Communication Corp. [subsidiary of Gannett Co. following merger with Gannett Co. in June 1979 (see KPNX(TV) Mesa)]. Sale price: $25 million. FCC approved: February 17, 1983 [Changing Hands, March 7, 1983]. Note: Madeline M. Barton, C.N. Barton & T.K. Barton sold stn to Mullins Broadcasting Co. with KARK-AM-FM for $3.75 million [For the Record, January 24, 1966]. Later, 89.7% of stn sold by Mullins to Combined Communications for $15.18 million, including KBTV(TV) (now KUSA-TV), Denver. FCC approved: January 28, 1972 [For the Record, February 14, 1972].

KATV(TV) Little Rock (ch 7)—Licensed to KATV Inc. (Allbritton Communications Co., see Group Ownership). Former owner: Leake TV Inc. (James C. Leake, who owns 80% WSTE(TV) Fajardo, PR). Sale price: More than $80 million (including KTUL-TV Tulsa, OK). FCC approved: February 14, 1983 [Changing Hands, March 7, 1983].

KLRT(TV) Little Rock (ch 16)—Licensed to Clear Channel Television of Little Rock (subsidiary of Clear Channel Communications Inc.). Former owner: Little Rock Communications Association (headed by Gary Scolard). Sale price: $6.6 million. FCC approved: June 19, 1991 [For the Record, July 8, 1991].

KRTV(TV) Little Rock (ch 16, now deleted)—Licensed to Little Rock Telecasters Inc. (Rowley-Brown Broadcasting. Co.). Original owners: Rowley-Brown Broadcasting Co. & Donald W. Reynolds. Sale price: $52,500 & assumption of $300,000 in liabilities. FCC approved: August 26, 1953 [For the Record, August 31, 1953]. Note: Stn facilities sold to Central South Sale Co., owners of KATV(TV) Pine Bluff, AR, for $400,000 in March 1954 [For the Record, March 8, 1954].

KASN(TV) Pine Bluff (ch 38)—Licensed to Mercury Broadcasting Corp. Former owner: MMC Television Corp. Sale price: $14.29 million assumption of debt. FCC approved: December 24, 1991 [For the Record, February 3, 1992]. Previous owner: Television Corp. of Arkansas. Former call letters: KJTM-TV. Previous owner: Pine Bluff Broadcasting Inc. Sale price of Television Corp.-Pine Bluff transaction: $200,000. FCC approved: May 15, 1985 [For the Record, June 3, 1985]. Former call letters: KMJD(TV).

KVTN(TV) Pine Bluff (ch 25)—Licensed to Agape Church Inc. Purchased CP from Charles R. Shinn for $41,000. FCC approved: June 1987 [For the Record, May 1, 1987]. Former call letters: KZRQ(TV).

KFAA(TV) Rogers (ch 51)—Licensed to Westark Broadcasting. Ltd. Former owner: J. D. G. Television Inc. (owned by Martha Griffin & family). Sale price: $4.38 million (including KPOM-TV Fort Smith, AR). FCC approved: July 25, 1991 [For the Record, August 12, 1991]. Previous owner: MCC Communications (owned by John McCutcheon). Sale price: $6,297 for CP.

California

KBAK-TV Bakersfield (ch 29)—Licensed to Burnham Broadcasting Corp. Former owner: Harriscope Broadcasting Corp. (see Group Ownership). Sale price: $15 million. FCC approved: October 2, 1986 [For the Record, September 1, 1986]. Previous owner: Reeves Broadcasting Corp. Sale price: $1.63 million. FCC approved: April 24, 1964 [For the Record, May 4, 1964]. Note: Founded by Sheldon Anderson as KAFY-TV; sold 51% to San Francisco *Chronicle* in 1953 for $85,000 (with KAFY(AM)), with remainder of stock purchased by nwspr in 1954. Sold to Reeves Broadcasting Corp. for $1.25 million in 1960.

KERO-TV Bakersfield (ch 23)—Licensed to McGraw-Hill Broadcasting Inc. (see Group Ownership). Former owner: Time-Life Broadcasting Inc. Sale price: $57.18 million (including KGTV(TV) San Diego; KMGH-TV Denver; & WRTV(TV) Indianapolis). FCC approved: March 8, 1972 [*Broadcasting*, March 13, 1972; May 15, 1972]. Note: Time-Life bought stn from Transcontinent TV Inc. in 1964 for $1.5 million. FCC approved: February 19, 1964. (See KFMB-TV San Diego). Original owner: Gene DeYoung, et al. Sale price: $2.1 million. FCC approved: 1957.

KGET(TV) Bakersfield (ch 17)—Licensed to KPWR-TV Inc. (owned by Ackerly Communications Inc. (Barry Ackerly, who owns KKTV(TV) Colorado Springs, CO). Former owner: Gillett Group Inc. (George N. Gillett Jr.). Sale price: $6.3 million. FCC approved: October 14, 1983 [Changing Hands, June 13, 1983]. Previous owner: Kern County Broadcasting Co. Sale price: $2.22 million. FCC approved: 1978. Note: Founded by Lincoln & Sylvia Dellar, Edward E. Urner, Bryan J. Coleman & Maurice St. Clair in November 1959. Mr. & Mrs. Dellar, 41.18% owners, bought 23% from Mr. Urner (who acquired KLYD(AM) for his interest), & 17.64% each from Messrs. Coleman & St. Clair for $117,720 in December 1962. Former call letters: KLYD-TV. Sold to Kern County Broadcasting Corp. (see ASI Communications Inc. in Group Ownership) by Dellar Family (Mr. & Mrs. Dellar) for $1.15 million. FCC approved: September 11, 1959 [For the Record, September 22, 1969]. Former call letters: KJTV(TV).

KCPM(TV) Chico (ch 24)—Licensed to Davis-Goldfarb Co. Former owner: Goltrin Communications Inc. Previous owners: Melvin Querio (40%), Jack Koonce (40%), & Telepictures Corp. (20%). Sale price of Goltrin-Querio, et al transaction: $23 million (including KSPR(TV) Springfield, MO, & KMID-TV Midland, TX).

KCFT-TV Concord (ch 42, now deleted)—Licensed to T.V. Hill Inc. [joint venture of Television Communications Inc. (Lindsey H. Spight) & Watson Communication Systems (Herbert M. Watson)]. Former owner: John M. England, trustee of estate of Jerry Basset Inc. Sale price: $13,500, CP only. FCC approved: September 20, 1968 [For the Record, October 7, 1968].

KVEA-TV Corona (ch 52)—Licensed to Estrella Communications. Former owner: Oak Broadcasting Systems Inc. (Oak Industries, 100%). Sale price: $30 million. FCC approved: July 17, 1985 [For the Record: June 10, 1985]. Former call letters: KBSC-TV. Note: Oak Industries acquired additional 50% from A. Jerrold Perenchio for $10 million in 1983. Original owner: Kaiser Broadcasting Corp. (see Group Ownership). Sale price: $1.2 million. FCC approved: August 24, 1976 [For the Record, September 27, 1976]. Original call letters: KMYW(TV).

KECY-TV El Centro (ch 9)—Licensed to Katherine R. Everett & Robinson O. Everett. Former owner: Pacific Media Corp. (John Smart, et al). Sale price: $1.56 million. FCC approved: February 28, 1989 [For the Record, March 20, 1989]. Previous owner: Esquire Inc. Sale price: $1.50 million plus. FCC approved: July 23, 1984. Original owner: Tele-Broadcasters Inc. (United Broadcasting). Sale price: $1.02 million. FCC approved: 1981.

KIEM-TV Eureka (ch 3)—Licensed to Precht Television Associates. Former owner: Ingham Communications. Sale price: $4 million. FCC approved: August 2, 1985. Previous owner: California-Oregon Radio Co. Sale price: $400,000 plus assumption of liabilities. FCC approved: July 29, 1975. Original owner: Redwood Broadcasting Co. Sale price: $800,000. FCC approved: 1961.

KVIQ(TV) Eureka (ch 6)—Licensed to Miller Broadcasting Co. Former owner: California Northwest Broadcasting Corp. (Carl R. & Leah McConnell). Sale price: $3.9 million. FCC approved: June 17, 1986 [For the Record, May 5, 1986]. Previous owners: Carroll R. Hauser (50%), Shasta Telecasting Corp. (50%). Sale price: $83,472. FCC approved: May 18, 1960 [For the Record, May 23, 1960]. Note: Founded by Carroll R. Hauser as KHUM-TV. Sold 50% to Shasta Telecasting Corp. for out-of-pocket expenses. FCC approved: August 2, 1957 [For the Record, August 5, 1957].

KAIL-TV Fresno (ch 53)—Licensed to Tel-America Corp. (A.J. Williams, 100%). Former owners: B.L. Golden & L.W. Fawns. Sale price: $236,500. FCC approved: December 23, 1966 [For the Record, December 26, 1966].

KFSN-TV Fresno (ch 30)—Licensed to Capital Cities Communications Inc. (see Group Ownership). Former owner: Triangle Publications Inc. (owned by Walter H. Annenberg & family). Sale price: $110 million (including WFIL(AM), WIOQ(FM), & WPVI-TV, all Philadelphia; WNHC(AM), WPLR(FM) & WTNH-TV New Haven, CT; KFRE(AM) & KFRE(FM) Fresno, CA; & television program syndication business). Note: Contingent on sale was Capital Cities spin-off of WFIL(AM) & WIOQ(FM) (formerly WFIL-FM) Philadelphia; WNHC(AM) & WPLR(FM) (formerly WNHC-FM) New Haven; & KFRE(AM) & KFYE(FM) (formerly KFRE-FM) Fresno, CA to separate buyers for an aggregate of $14.45 million. FCC approved: February 24, 1971 [*Broadcasting*, March 1, 1971]. Original call letters: KFRE-TV. Note: Triangle purchased stn, then broadcasting on Channel 12, from original owner, California Inland Broadcasting Co. (Paul R. Bartlett, et al), for $3 million (with KFRE-AM-FM). FCC approved: December 30, 1958 [For the Record, January 5, 1959].

KJEO(TV) Fresno (ch 47)—Licensed to Retlaw Enterprises Inc., (Mrs. Walter E. Disney, Sharon Disney Brown, Diane Disney Miller & others). Former owner: Subscription TV. Sale price: $3.65 million. FCC approved: April 17, 1968 [For the Record, April 29, 1968]. Previous owner: Shasta Telecasting. Sale price: $8.65 million. FCC approved: 1966. Note: Founded by J.E. O'Neill & associates. Bought by Shasta Telecasting in 1961 for $3 million.

KSEE(TV) Fresno (ch 24)—Licensed to San Joaquin Communications Corp. (see Granite Broadcasting Corp. in Group Ownership). Former owner: San Joaquin Communications Corp. (see Meredith Corp. in Group Ownership). Sale price: $32 million (including WTVH(TV) Syracuse, NY). FCC approved: August 9, 1993 [For the Record, August 30, 1993]. Previous owner: James K. Herbert, et al. Sale price: $17.61 million. FCC approved: April 8, 1983 [For the Record, May 2, 1983]. Note: Stn went on air June 1, 1953. Sold to Stockholders by McClatchy Newspapers in 1979. Sale price: $13.5 million [*Broadcasting*, November 12, 1979]. Former call letters: KMJ-TV.

KFTV(TV) Hanford (ch 21)—Licensed to Univision Station Group Inc. Former owner: Spanish International Broadcasting Co. (Reynold V. Anselmo, 50%, Emilio Azcarraga, 20%, & others). Previous owner: KSJV Television Inc. (Cy Newman, 41.1%, & others). Sale price of Spanish-KSJV transaction: $40,000 plus assumption of liabilities of $73,000. FCC approved: March 19, 1969 [For the Record, March 31, 1969]. Former call letters: KSJV-TV. Previous owners: George L. Naron & C.B. Sweeney. Former call letters: KDAS-TV. CP sold in February 1966 to KSJV Television Inc. for $90,750.

KABC-TV Los Angeles (ch 7)—Licensed to Capital Cities/ABC Inc. (see Group Ownership). Sale price: $3.417 billion (including WABC(TV) New York; WLS(TV) Chicago; KGO(TV) San Francisco; WXYZ-TV Detroit; & all other ABC broadcasting & publishing operations. FCC approved: November 14, 1985 [For the Record: July 15, 1985]. Note: This was change of ownership when ABC merged with United Paramount Theaters Inc. Original owner: American Broadcasting Co. Original call letters: KECA-TV. FCC approved: February 2, 1953 [For the Record, February 16, 1953].

KCBS-TV Los Angeles (ch 2)—Licensed to CBS Inc. (see Group Ownership). Original owner: Thomas S. Lee Enterprises Inc. (General Tire & Rubber Co.). Former call letters: KNXT(TV). Original call letters: KTSL(TV). Sale price: $3.6 million. FCC approved: December 27, 1950 [For the Record, January 1, 1951]. Note: Licensee sold to General Tire & Rubber Co. from estate of Thomas S. Lee in 1950, with other Don Lee properties for $12.32 million [For the Record, January 1, 1951].

KCOP(TV) Los Angeles (ch 13)—Licensed to KCOP TV Inc. (see Chris Craft Industries in Group Ownership). Former owners: Kenyon Brown, Harry L. (Bing) Crosby, George L. Coleman, Joseph A. Thomas & Alvin G. Flanagan. Sale price: over $5 million in the aggregate. FCC approved: January 28, 1960 [For the Record, February 8, 1960]. Note: Founded by Mrs. Dorothy Schiff Sonneborn as KLAC-TV. Sold to Copley Press for $1.37 million in December 1953 [For the Record, January 4, 1954]. Messrs. Brown, Crosby, Coleman, Thomas & Flanagan bought stn from Copley Press Inc. for $4 million. FCC approved: December 11, 1957 [For the Record, December 16, 1957].

KMEX-TV Los Angeles (ch 34)—Licensed to Los Angeles Unified School District. Former owner: Spanish International Communications Corp.

KNBC(TV) Los Angeles (ch 4)—Licensed to National Broadcasting Co. Inc. General Electric Co. acquired RCA Corp., NBC's parent company, for $6.28 billion. FCC approved: June 5, 1986.

KTLA(TV) Los Angeles (ch 5)—Licensed to Tribune Broadcasting Co. (owned by Chicago Tribune). Former owner: Golden West Associates (KKR Associates). Sale price: $510 million. FCC approved: October 10, 1985. Previous owner: Golden West Broadcasters Inc. (The Signal Companies, Gene Autry & Estate of Ina Mae Autry). Sale price: $245 million. FCC approved: March 28, 1983 [For the Record, April 4, 1983].

KTTV(TV) Los Angeles (ch 11)—Licensed to Fox Television Stations Inc. For details of sale, see WNYW-TV New York. Former owner: Metromedia Inc. (John W. Kluge, chmn & pres, see Group Ownership). Original owners: Los Angeles *Times-Mirror*. Sale price: $10.39 million. FCC approved: May 28, 1963 [For the Record, June 10, 1963].

KWHY-TV Los Angeles (ch 22)—Licensed to Harriscope of L.A. Inc. [(Owned by Burt Harris & SelecTV of California.) Harris is pres & principal own of Harriscope Broadcasting, (see Group Ownership). SelecTV is Marina del Rey, CA-based STV operator.] Former owner: Coast TV Broadcasting Corp. (owned by brothers Wiley, Robert & Hugh Bunn). Sale price: $5.3 million. FCC approved: November 20, 1981 [For the Record, December 14, 1981]. Former owners: Messrs Bunn & Custer, Hugh Murchison Jr., & others sold to Coast TV. FCC approved: June 17, 1966 [For the Record, June 27, 1966]. Former call letters: KPOL-TV. Note: Founded in 1952 as KBIC-TV by John Poole. Sold in 1963 to H. Calvin Young, Martha White Mills & others as KIIX-TV for $180,000. FCC approved: January 23, 1963 [For the Record, January 28, 1963]. Sold to Messrs. Murchison, Straub & others in 1964 for $150,000 & assumption of $205,377 in obligations.

KTRB-TV Modesto (ch 14, now deleted)—Licensed to O'Neill Broadcasting Co. (J.E. O'Neill). Former owners: William H. Bates Jr. & Margie W. Cleary. Sale price: $5,000 (assignment of CP). FCC approved: September 5, 1957 [For the Record, September 16, 1957].

KMST(TV) Monterey (ch 46)—Licensed to Harron-Smith Television Partnership. Former owner: Retlaw Enterprises Inc. [Lillian Truyens (30%), Sharon Lund (30%) & Diane Miller (24%)]. Sale price: $8.2 million. FCC approved: March 11, 1993 [For the Record, March 29, 1993]. Previous owner: Monterey-Salinas TV Inc. [Lynn J. Brinker (25%), Stoddard Johnston, Jones Morris & William Bertram (20% each); & two others]. Sale price: $8.25 million. FCC approved: August 18, 1979 [For the Record, September 17, 1979].

KTVU(TV) Oakland (ch 2)—Licensed to KTVU Inc. (owned by Cox Communications Corp., see Group Ownership). Original owners: Ward D. Ingrim, William D. Pabst, Edwin W. Pauley (each 25%), & others. Sale price: $12.36 million. FCC approved: October 16, 1963 [For the record, October 21, 1963].

KIHS-TV Ontario (ch 46)—Licensed to Silver King Broadcasting (owned by Home Shopping Network Inc., see Group Ownership). Former owner: HBI Acquisition Corp. (owned by DeRance Foundation & Santa Fe Communications, nonprofit Catholic foundations). Sale price: $35 million. FCC approved: October 30, 1986. [For the Record, September 29, 1986]. Previous owner: Hispanic Broadcasters Inc., owned by United Minority Broadcasters Inc. (52%) & Leon Crosby (48%). Principals of UMB, less its largest stockholder Debra Olivas, kept interest in HBI Acquisition Corp. Sale price: $3.7 million. FCC approved: May 25, 1982 [For the Record, June 14, 1982]. Former call letters: KBSA-TV. Previous owner: Broadcasting Service of America (100% owned by Berean Bible Ministries). FCC approved: March 27, 1980 [Changing Hands, April 7, 1980]. Original owner: Broadcasting Service of America, William A. & Ethel J. Myers (51%) & Berean Bible Ministries (49%). Sale price: $602,578. FCC approved: March 12, 1975 [For the Record, March 24, 1975].

KADY-TV Oxnard (ch 63)—Licensed to PZ Entertainment Ltd. Partnership (sole general partner is Riklis Enterprises Inc.). Original owners: Thorne Donnelley Jr. & Donald Sterling. Sale price: $5.5 million. Former call letters: KTIE(TV).

KESQ-TV Palm Springs (ch 42)—Licensed to Gulf-California Broadcast Comm. (owned by EFG Broadcast Corp.). Former owner: Gulf Broadcast Group. Sale price: $4.4 million. FCC approved: August 23, 1985. Previous owner: Pacific Media Corp. (bankrupt corporation). Sale price: $3.75 million. FCC approved: July 27, 1984. Previously sold by receivers, Irving Sulmeyer & Arnold Kupetz, to publicly traded Esquire Inc. (magazine publisher) for $710,000.

KBCP(TV) Paradise (ch 46)—Licensed to Sainte Broadcasting. Former owner: Butte Creek Communications Co. Sale price: $60,000.

KRCR-TV Redding (ch 7)—Licensed to Sacramento Valley TV Inc. (William B. Smulin & others). Former owner: Shasta TV Corp. Sale price: $1.28 million. FCC approved: February 9, 1968 [For the Record, February 19, 1968]. Note: Founded by George Fleharty, Laurence W. Carr, Carl R. McConnell & others. Original call letters: KVIP-TV.

KRCA(TV) Riverside, CA (ch 62)—Licensed to Founce Amusement Enterprises Inc. Former owner: Sunland Broadcasting Co. Sale price: $3.575 million. FCC approved: March 2, 1990. Former call letters: KSLD(TV).

KCCC-TV Sacramento (ch 40, now deleted)—Licensed to Capital TV Co. [Melvin Lord (16.8%); Melvin Lucas, Clarence A. Halien, Henry P. Deane (11.1%); & others). Original owners: Melvin Lucas & group. Sale price: $70,548. FCC approved: October 7, 1959 [For the Record, October 19, 1959].

KCRA-TV Sacramento (ch 3)—Licensed to Kelly Broadcasting Co. (Gerald & C. Vernon Hansen & family). Original owners: 50% owned by the family of the late Ewing C. Kelly. Sale price: $2.8 million for 50% (including KCRA-AM-FM). FCC approved: April 8, 1962 [For the Record, April 23, 1962].

KRBK-TV Sacramento (ch 31)—Licensed to Koplar Communications Inc. (Edward Koplar & family). Former owner: Northern California Broadcasting, debtor-in-possession. Sale price: $7.7 million. FCC approved: January 28, 1981. [Changing Hands, July 14, 1980]. Previous owner: Channel 31 Inc. (Andrew Bartalini, William Crabtree, Della Grayson, Samuel Klor, George W. Artz). Sale price: no consideration. FCC approved: August 25, 1976 [For the Record, October 4, 1976]. Original owner: Hercules Broadcasting Co. (Manning Slater, et al) sold stn to Grayson Television Inc. [Hugh A. Evans (10%), Morris Lavine (25%), Della G. Grayson (15%), Norman Kauffman (15%), et al] for $26,800. FCC approved: December 9, 1970 [For the Record, December 21, 1970]. Original call letters: KRAQ(TV).

KTXL(TV) Sacramento (ch 40)—Licensed to Channel 40 Licensee Inc. (Warburg, Pincus Capital Co. L.P. & Michael Finkelstein). Former owner: Camellia City Telecasters Inc. [Cypress Communications Corp. (71%), Jack F. Matranga, 24%, & others]. Sale price: $56 million. FCC approved: January 31, 1989 [For the Record, February 20, 1989]. Previous transaction: 60% sold by Electronics Capital Corp. (Richard C. Memhard, W. Randolph Tucker, Leon N. Papernow, Richard Burns & others). Sale price: stock transfer for CP. FCC approved: January 5, 1968.

KXTV(TV) Sacramento (ch 10)—Licensed to Great Western Broadcasting Corp. (owned by Belo Broadcasting, see Group Ownership). Former owner: Corinthian Broadcasting. Sale price: $78.1 million. (Transfer is part of a six stn deal totaling $606 million). FCC approved: November 28, 1983 [For the Record, December 19, 1983]. Former call letters: KBET-TV. Note: Corinthian purchased stn from original owner in 1958. Original owner: Sacramento Telecasters Inc. [William Wright & sons (20.55%); John H. Schachte (15.48%); & others]. Sale price: $4.5 million. FCC approved: December 23, 1958 [For the Record, December 29, 1958]. Note: stn was merged with Corinthian Broadcasting into Dunn & Bradstreet Companies Inc. for stock valued at $137 million (including KOTV(TV) Tulsa, OK; KHOU-TV Houston; WISH-TV Indianapolis; & WANE-TV Fort Wayne, IN). FCC approved: April 14, 1971 [*Broadcasting*, April 19, 1971].

KCBA(TV) Salinas (ch 35)—Licensed to Cypress Broadcasting Inc. (owned by Ackerly Communications). Former owner: Sainte Broadcasting Corp. Sale price: $13.1 million. FCC approved: May 22, 1986 [For the Record, April 14, 1986].

KSBW-TV Salinas (ch 8)—Licensed to KSBW Licensee Inc. Former owner: KSBW Inc. (Gillett Broadcasting). Sale price: no cash consideration (including KSBY-TV San Luis Obispo, CA). Application was filed in connection with restructuring of Gillett Holdings Inc., ultimate corporate parent of licensees of stations. FCC approved: July 27, 1992 [For the Record, August 17, 1992]. Previous owner: John Blair & Co. Sale price: $86 million (including KSBY-TV San Luis Obispo, CA, & KOKH-TV Oklahoma City). FCC approved: December 1986 [For the Record, December 1, 1986]. Previous owner: Central California Communications Corp. (principally owned by Elizabeth A. Cohan). Sale price: $16.84 million (including KSBY-TV). FCC approved: February 1979 [For the Record, February 26, 1979].

KCHU(TV) San Bernardino (ch 18, now deleted)—Licensed to Sun Co. of San Bernardino (James A. Guthrie, pres). Original owner: Norman H. Rogers. Sale price: $180,109. FCC approved: January 30, 1963 [For the Record, February 4, 1963].

KSCI-TV San Bernardino (ch 18)—Licensed to KSCI Holding Corp. (Ray L. Beindorf & Thomas Headley). Former owner: World Plan Executive Council-United States (Thomas M. Headley, et al). Sale price: $40.5 million. FCC approved: December 1986 [For the Record, November 3, 1986].

KCST-TV San Diego (ch 39)—Licensed to Gillett Communications Inc. Former owner: KCST-TV Inc. (owned by KKR Associates). Sale price: $1.3 billion (including WSBK-TV Boston; WAGA-TV Atlanta; WITI-TV Milwaukee; WJW-TV Cleveland; & WJBK-TV Detroit). FCC approved: August 1987. Previous owner: Storer Broadcasting Co. (see Group Ownership). (For details of sale, see WJW-TV Cleveland.) Previous owner: Western Telecasters Inc. (100% owned by Bass Brothers Enterprises Inc.) Sale price: $12 million & adjustments. FCC approved: September 26, 1974 [For the Record, October 14, 1974]. Note: Original call letters: KAAR(TV). San Diego Telecasters Inc. (Paul Corriere (44%); Town & Country Development Inc. & Sample-Brown Enterprises (56% each) sold KAAR(TV) to Bass Brothers Enterprises in 1967 for $1.1 million. FCC approved: August 3, 1967 [For the Record, September 11, 1967].

KFMB-TV San Diego (ch 8)—Licensed to Midwest TV Inc. (see Group Ownership). Former owner: Transcontinent TV Corp. Sale price: $10 million (with KFMB-AM-FM). FCC approved: February 19, 1964. Note: TTC acquired KFMB Stations & KERO-TV Bakersfield, CA. through merger with Marietta Broadcasting Inc. (Jack D. Wrather & Edward Petry Inc.) in 1959. Marietta Broadcasting took over stns from Wrather-Alvarez Broadcasting Inc. for $2.9 million for Mrs. Alvarez's 38.9% in 1958. Petry Co. bought 22.2% of Wrather-Alvarez for $633,333 in 1953. Wrather-Alvarez bought KFMB Stations from John A. Kennedy for $3 million in 1953. Mr. Kennedy bought KFMB Stations from Jack Gross for $925,000 in 1951. Wrather-Alvarez bought KERO-TV from Albert E. DeYoung & associates for $2.15 million in 1957.

KGTV(TV) San Diego (ch 10)—Licensed to McGraw-Hill Broadcasting Co. (see Group Ownership). Former owner: Time-Life Broadcast Inc. Sale price: $57.18 million (including KERO-TV Bakersfield, CA; KMGH-TV Denver; & WRTV(TV) Indianapolis). FCC approved: March 8, 1972 [*Broadcasting*, March 13, 1972; May 15, 1972]. Former call letters: KOGO-TV. Note: Founded as KFSD-TV in 1953 by Thomas E. Sharpe & associates. Sold in 1954 to Fox, Wells & Rogers (42.55%) & *Newsweek* Magazine (Washington Post Co.) (46.22%) for $2.2 million. Sold in 1962 to Time-Life Broadcast Inc. for $6.12 million (including KOGO-AM-FM). FCC approved: March 21, 1962 [For the Record, March 26, 1962].

KNSD(TV) San Diego (ch 39)—Licensed to KNSD License Inc. (see SCI Television Inc. in Group Ownership). Former owner: Gillett Communications Inc. Sale price: unknown. (See WAGA-TV Atlanta for details of sale). FCC approved: February 19, 1993 [For the Record, April 26, 1993].

KUSI-TV San Diego (ch 5)—Licensed to San Diego's Fifty One Inc. (headed by Michael D. McKinnon & James A. Gillece). Former owner: University Television Inc. (headed by William Rust & Michael McKinnon). Sale price: $17 million. FCC approved: April 10, 1990.

KBHK-TV San Francisco (ch 44)—Licensed to UTV of San Francisco Inc. (owned by United Television Inc., see Group Ownership). Former owner: Field Communications Corp. [owned by Field Enterprises Inc., Marshall Field (50%) & half-brother Frederick W. Field (50%)]. Sale price: $23 million. FCC approved: May 31, 1983 [For the Record, June 13, 1983]. Original owner: Kaiser Broadcasting Corp. (100%). Sale price: no financial consideration. Note: FCC approved merger of Kaiser Broadcasting Corp.'s five independent UHF's (including KBHK-TV) & Field Communications Corp.'s one independent UHF in May 1973 [*Broadcasting*, May 14, 1973]. Field purchased 77.5% of group for $42.62 million in 1977 including KBHK-TV [*Broadcasting*, August 8, 1977].

KCNS(TV) San Francisco (ch 38)—Licensed to Lynette Ellertson. Former owner: West Coast United Broadcasting Co. Sale price: $93,750. FCC approved: April 17, 1989 [For the Record, May 1, 1989]. Former call letters: KWBB(TV), KVOF-TV. Previous owner: Faith Center, preceded by John M. England, trustee in bankruptcy. Sale price of Center-England transaction: $102,000. FCC approved: May 29, 1973 [For the Record, June 18, 1973]. Original call letters: KUDO(TV).

KDTV(TV) San Francisco (ch 14)—Licensed to Univision Television Group. Former owner: Bahia de San Francisco Co. [principal owner Reynold Anselmo (42%)].

KGO-TV San Francisco (ch 7)—Licensed to Capital Cities/ABC Inc. Former owner: ABC Inc. (see Group Ownership). Sale price: $3.417 billion (including WABC(TV) New York; KABC(TV) Los Angeles; WLS(TV) Chicago; WXYZ-TV Detroit; & all other ABC broadcasting & publishing operations. FCC approved: November 14, 1985 [For the Record, July 15, 1985]. Note: This was change of ownership when ABC merged with United Paramount Theaters Inc. FCC approved: February 9, 1953 [For the Record, February 16, 1953].

KOFY-TV San Francisco (ch 20)—Licensed to Pacifc FM Inc. (Jim Gabbert). Former owner: Leon Crosby. Sale price: $9.85 million. FCC approved: September 5, 1980 [Changing Hands, September 29, 1980]. Former call letters: KTZO-TV. Previous owner: U.S. Communications of California Inc. Sale price: assumption of liabilities to $278,820 per year plus assumption of promissory notes totalling $11,058. FCC approved: January 19, 1972 [For the Record, February 7, 1972]. Note: CP secured by Lawrence A. Harvey. Sold to Leonard & Lily Averett in 1954 (no consideration). Former call letters: KBAY-TV. Purchased by Sherrill C. Corwin in 1957 for $1,750. CP sold by Mr. Corwin to D.H. Overmyer Communications in 1965 for $6,000. 80% of CP sold by D.H. Overmyer Communications to U.S. Communications Corp. in 1967 (with 80% of CPs for WMBO-TV Atlanta; WSCO-TV Newport, KY; WECO-TV Pittsburgh, PA; & KJDO-TV Rosenberg, TX). Sale price: Aggregate of $1 million. FCC approved: December 8, 1967 [For the Record, December 18, 1967].

KPIX(TV) San Francisco (ch 5)—Licensed to Westinghouse Broadcasting Co. (see Group Ownership). Original owners: Associated Broadcasters Inc. (Wesley I. Dumm & Associates). Sale price: $7.5 million. FCC approved: July 2, 1954 [For the Record, July 12, 1954].

***KQEC(TV) San Francisco (ch 32)**—Licensed to KQED Inc. (owned by Bay Area Educational TV Association). Previous owner: Metromedia Inc. (see Group Ownership). Former call letters: KNEW-TV. Donated by gift to Bay Area. FCC approved: September 9, 1970 [*Broadcasting*, September 14, 1970]. Note: Founded by S.H. Patterson in 1954. Original call letters: KSAN-TV. Went dark in 1958. Returned to air as satellite of KICU-TV Visalia-Fresno, CA, in 1966. Sold to Metromedia in 1968 for $1 million. FCC approved: March 20, 1968 [For the Record, April 1, 1968].

KICU-TV San Jose (ch 36)—Licensed to KICU Inc. Former owner: Ralph C. Wilson Industries (owned by Ralph C. Wilson Jr.). Sale price: $34 million. Previous owner Continental Urban Television Corp. Sale price: $14 million. FCC approved: December 1979 [Changing Hands, December 10, 1979]. Former call letters: KGSC-TV.

KLXV-TV San Jose (ch 65)—Licensed to Friendly Bible Church (nonprofit corporation headed by Ray K. Foreman). Original owner: Donald B. Thomson. Sale price: $1.72 million. FCC approved: February 1987 [For the Record, March 2, 1987].

KNTV(TV) San Jose (ch 11)—Licensed to KNTV Inc. (owned by Landmark Communications, see Cross-Ownership). Former owner: Gill Industries [Allen T. Gilliland, Jr. (73.1%) & others]. Sale price: $24.52 million. FCC approved: 1978. [Changing Hands, August 14, 1978]. Original owners: estate of Allen T. Gilliland, Sr. Sale price: $957,825. FCC approved: August 4, 1966 [For the Record, August 15, 1966].

KSTS-TV San Jose (ch 48)—Licensed to Telemundo Group Inc. (formerly John Blair & Co., see Group Ownership). Former owner: National Group Inc. (principally owned by N. J. & Hazel Douglas). Sale price: $10.9+ million. FCC approved: June 1987 [For the Record, July 6, 1987].

KADE(TV) San Luis Obispo (ch 33)—Licensed to Riklis Broadcasting Corp. Former owner: Community Media Corp. Sale price: $825,000. FCC approved: March 23, 1993 [For the Record, April 12, 1993].

KSBY(TV) San Luis Obispo (ch 6)—Licensed to KSBW Licensee Inc. Former owner: KSBW Inc. (Gillett Broadcasting). For details of sale, see KSBW-TV Salinas, CA. FCC approved: July 27, 1992 [For the Record, August 17, 1992]. Previous owner: John Blair & Co. (For details of sale, see KSBW-TV Salinas, CA). FCC approved: November 1986 [For the Record, December 1, 1986]. Previous owner: Central California Communications Corp. (principally owned by Elizabeth A. Cohan). (For details of sale, see KBSW-TV Salinas, CA.) Previous owner: John C. Cohan & Jerome Kantro. Sale price: $127,450. FCC approved: 1957. Former call letters: KVEC-TV. Original owners: Christina M. Jacobson (2/3) & Leslie H. Hacker (1/3). Sale price: $450,000, including KVEC-AM. FCC approved: 1956.

KTBN-TV Santa Ana (ch 40)—Licensed to Trinity Broadcasting Network. Original owner: International Panorama TV Inc., 100% owned by Angel Lerma Maler. Sale price: $1.26 million. FCC approved: August 2, 1974 [For the Record, August 19, 1974].

KEYT(TV) Santa Barbara (ch 3)—Licensed to Smith Broadcasting (principally owned by Robert N. Smith, William Reyner & TA Associates). Former owner: Shamrock Broadcasting Co. Sale price: $30 million. FCC approved: February 1987 [Changing Hands, February 23, 1987]. Previous owner: Key TV Inc. (William F. & Nancy Lutton). Sale price: $9.2 million. FCC approved: October 16, 1984. Original owner: Santa Barbara Broadcasting & TV Corp. Sale price: $1.4 million. FCC approved: March 27, 1957 [For the Record, April 1, 1957].

KCOY-TV Santa Maria (ch 12)—Licensed to Stauffer Communications Inc. Former owner: Central Coast Broadcasters Inc. (Helen Pedotti). Sale price: $7 million. FCC approved: June 17, 1980 [Changing Hands, June 30, 1980]. Previous owner: Dale G. Moore & others. Sale price: $75,000 for 50%. FCC approved: July 9, 1968 [For the Record, July 15, 1968]. Note: Founded by Central Coast Broadcasters Inc. (formerly Central Coast TV, Helen L. Pedotti & others) in 1964.

KFTY(TV) Santa Rosa (ch 50)—Licensed to William B. Grover, trustee in bankruptcy. Original owner: Redwood Empire Broadcasting Co. [Sonoma Productions, gen ptnr (50%), & others]. Sale price: no consideration. FCC approved: July 22, 1974 [For the Record, August 12, 1974].

KOVR(TV) Stockton (ch 13)—Licensed to Robert Bass. Former owner: Anchor Media Corp., Anchor Media Investors II Inc. & Group Management Inc. Sale price: no financial consideration. FCC approved: July 27, 1989. Previous owner: Narragansett Broadcasting Co. Sale price: $162 million [For the Record, December 26, 1988]. FCC approved: December 8, 1988. Previous owner: Wesray Communications Group. Sale price: $104 million. FCC approved: June 13, 1986 [For the Record, April 21, 1986]. Previous owner: Rockefeller Group Inc. (For details of sale, see WCMH(TV) Columbus, OH.) Previous owner: Outlet Company. Sale price: $332 million (including all Outlet TV & radio properties). FCC approved: November 23, 1983. Previous owner: McClatchy Newspapers (see Group Ownership). Sale price: $65 million (then-record price for bcst stn). FCC approved: March 17, 1980 [Changing Hands, March 24, 1980]. Previous owner: Metromedia Inc. (see Group Ownership). Sale price: $7.8 million. FCC approved: July 30, 1964 [For the Record, August 10, 1964]. Note: Founded by H.L. Hoffman in 1954. Sold to Gannett Co. in 1958 for $1.47 million. Purchased by Metromedia Inc. in 1959 for $1.39 million plus assumption of $2.1 million in debts.

KSCH-TV Stockton (ch 58)—Licensed to Commacq Inc. Former owner: SFN Companies. For details of sale, see WAPA-TV San Juan, PR. FCC approved: October 2, 1986 [Changing Hands, July 14, 1986].

KVVG(TV) Tulare (ch 27, now deleted)—Licensed to James Stacy. Former owner: UHF Telecasting Corp. (M.B. Scott & Joseph Justman). Sale price: $10,000 & assumption of liabilities. FCC approved: January 30, 1957 [For the Record, February 4, 1957]. Note: Messrs. Scott & Justman purchased stn in March 1955 from Sheldon Anderson for $350,000 in obligations [For the Record, March 28, 1955].

KVMD(TV) Twentynine Palms (ch 31)—Licensed to Mike Parker. Former owner: Desert 31 Television Inc. Sale price: assumption of debt. FCC approved: November 23, 1992 [For the Record, December 14, 1992].

KMPH(TV) Visalia (ch 26)—Licensed to Pappas Telecasting Inc. (Harry Pappas & wife). Original owner: Pappas Television Inc. (Harry Pappas & 150 others). Sale price: $3.1 million. FCC approved: June 1978 [Changing Hands, June 19, 1978].

Colorado

KKTV(TV) Colorado Springs (Pueblo)(ch 11)—Licensed to Ackerley Inc. (Barry Ackerley). Former owner: Capitol of Colorado Corp. (group owner: T.B. Lansford Stations). Sale price: $15.5 million. FCC approved: January 19, 1983 [For the Record, February 21, 1983]. Note: Founded in 1952. Sold to Willard Garvey in 1963 by Gifford Phillips, James D. & Betty Z. Russell, & Robert D. Ellis for $885,000 with KFMH(FM) Colorado Springs & KGHF(AM) Pueblo, Colo. Sold to Capitol of Colorado Corp. in 1969 for $2.57 million.

KCNC-TV Denver (ch 4)—Licensed to General Electric Broadcasting Co., now a part of NBC after GE's acquisition of RCA Corp., of which NBC was a subsidiary (see Group Ownership). Former owner: Metropolitan Television Co. (William Grant & others). Sale price: $10 million in GE stock plus adjustments (including KOA-AM-FM Denver & KOAA-TV Pueblo, both CO). FCC approved: June 5, 1968 [For the Record, June 10, 1968]. Note: Founded by Bob Hope, James L. Saphier, William Grant & others in 1953. In 1964, 52.5% sold by Messrs. Hope, Saphier & group to Mr. Grant & Denver group for $6.3 million including KOA-AM-FM & KOAA-TV.

KDVR(TV) Denver (ch 31)—Licensed to Renaissance Communications. Former owner: Chase Communications Inc. (headed by Roger M. Freedman). Sale price: $126.6 million in group purchase (For details of sale, see WATL(TV) Atlanta, GA). FCC approved: January 11, 1993 [For the Record, February 1, 1993]. Previous owner: BMA Corporation. Sale price: $12 million. FCC approved: December 29, 1989 [*Broadcasting*, March 20, 1990].

KHBC(TV) Denver (ch 20, now deleted)—Licensed to Denver Post Inc. (Newhouse Newspapers (18.8%) & others). Former owner: Harcourt Brace & World Inc. (William J. Javanovich & others). Sale price: $6,160 (50% of CP). FCC approved: November 22, 1967. Note: Founded in 1966 by Harcourt, Brace & World.

KMGH-TV Denver (ch 7)—Licensed to McGraw-Hill Broadcasting Co. (see Group Ownership). Former owner: Time-Life Broadcast Inc. Sale price: $57.18 million (including KERO-TV Bakersfield & KGTV(TV) San Diego, both CA; & WRTV(TV) Indianapolis). FCC approved: March 8, 1972 [*Broadcasting*, March 13, 1972; May 15, 1972]. Former call letters: KLZ-TV. Original owner: Aladdin Radio & TV Inc. Sale price: $3.5 million (including KLZ-AM-FM). FCC approved: June 25, 1954 [For the Record, July 5, 1954].

KTVD(TV) Denver (ch 20)—Licensed to Twenver Inc. (N. Richard Miller et al). Former owner: Alden Communications of Colorado. Sale price: $500,000 [Changing Hands, January 18, 1988]. Former call letters: KTZO-TV.

KUBD(TV) Denver (ch 59)—Licensed to UHF Channel 59 Corp. (Chas Ergen 80%, David M. Drucker 20%). Former owner: The Denver Channel 59 Partnership Ltd. Sale price: no cash consideration; assignment was filed to reflect tax & legal changes as result of sale of Colorado Broadcasters limited partnership interests. FCC approved: June 16, 1992 [For the Record, July 6, 1992].

KUSA(TV) Denver (ch 9)—Licensed to Combined Communications Corp. (subsidiary of Gannett Co., following merger in June 1979). (For details of merger, see KPNX(TV) Phoenix.) Former owner: Mullins Broadcasting. Sale price: $15.18 million (including KARK-TV Little

Rock, AR). FCC approved: 1972. Former call letters: KBTV(TV). Note: Mullins Broadcasting purchased the stn from loc businessmen in 1955 for $1 million.

KWGN-TV Denver (ch 2)—Licensed to WGN of Colorado Inc. (see WGN Continental Broadcasting Co. in Group Ownership). Former owner: J. Elroy McCaw. Sale price: $3.5 million. FCC approved: March 3, 1966. Former call letters: KCTO(TV). Original owner: O'Fallon Inc. Original call letters: KFEL-TV, later KTVR(TV). Note: Transferred to Eugene P. O'Fallon Trust, September 1953. Transferred to Gotham Broadcasting. for $400,000 & assumption of $300,000 in obligations. FCC approved: July 27, 1955 [For the Record, August 1, 1955]. Fifty percent transferred to Radio Hawaii for payment of half of purchase price & half of obligations. FCC approved: November 16, 1955. Gotham repurchased 50% from Radio Hawaii. Sale price: $150,000. FCC approved: March 25, 1959 [For the Record, April 6, 1959].

KREZ-TV Durango (ch 6)—Licensed to W. Russell Withers, Jr. For details of acquisition, see KREX-TV Grand Junction, CO. Original owners: Floyd & Lieselotte Jeter. Sale price: $2,000. FCC approved: 1964.

KWXU-TV Fort Collins (ch 22)—Licensed to 31 Licensee Inc. (see Renaissance Communications Corp. in Group Ownership). Former owner: Chase Broadcasting of Denver Inc. FCC approved: August 12, 1993 [For the Record, August 30, 1993].

KCWS(TV) Glenwood Springs (ch 3)—Licensed to Royal Publishing Co. Former owner: Western Slope Comm. Sale price: $3.51 million for CP. FCC approved: June 27, 1985 [For the Record, May 20, 1985].

KREX-TV Grand Junction (ch 5)—Licensed to W. Russell Withers Jr. Former owner: E & W Broadcasting Corp. Sale price: $7.32 million (including KREY-TV Montrose & KREZ-TV Durango, both CO). FCC approved: June 5, 1985. Previous owner: Carl Q. Anderson, et al. Sale price: $3.86 million (including KREZ-TV Durango, KREX-AM-FM Grand Junction, & KREY-TV Montrose, all CO). FCC approved: May 15, 1984. Previous owner: XYZ Television Inc. (Roy G. Howell). Note: Mr. Howell, former owner of stns, transferred control while retaining a minority interest for $2 million plus assumption of $75,000 in liabilities, plus $500,000 for 10-year consultant's fee to Mr. Howell (with KREY-TV Montrose & KREZ-TV Durango, both CO). FCC approved: September 21, 1966 [For the Record, October 3, 1966].

KREY-TV Montrose (ch 10)—Licensed to W. Russell Withers Jr. Former owner: E & W Broadcasting Corp. (For details of sale, see KREX-TV Grand Junction). Previous owner: XYZ Television Inc. Note: Originally owned 51% by Mr. Howell & 49% by Carl Q. Anderson. Mr. Howell paid Mr. Anderson $75,000 for the latter's 49% in 1966. FCC approved: May 19, 1966 [For the Record, May 30, 1966].

KOAA-TV Pueblo (ch 5)—Licensed to Sangre de Cristo Communications Inc. (owned 100% by Evening Post Publishing Co., Charleston, SC). Former owner: Sangre de Cristo Broadcasting Corp. (William Grant, 33%; William M. White, 25.6%; Mahlon T. White, 25.6%; & others). Sale price: $4.5 million. FCC approved: August 6, 1976 [For the Record, August 30, 1976]. Note: Founded by Douglas D. Kahle & Robert L. Clinton in 1953. Original call letters: KSCJ-TV. Sold in 1954 to Star Broadcasting (Bankers Life & Casualty Co.) for assumption of obligations amounting to $823,000 (with KCSJ(AM) Pueblo, CO). KOAA-TV sold in 1961 to Metropolitan Television for $1.25 million. Sold in 1968 to Metropolitan Television Co. (William Grant & others) for $1.5 million. FCC approved: June 18, 1968.

KSBS-TV Steamboat Springs (ch 24)—Licensed to F&I TV Inc. Original owner: Steamboat Broadcasting Systems Inc. Sale price: $250,000. FCC approved: January 15, 1992 [For the Record, February 3, 1992].

KHOL-TV Sterling (ch 3, now deleted)—Licensed to Richard B. Steuer. Original owner: Bi-States Co. Sale price: $2,185 (for CP). FCC approved: February 1, 1961 [For the Record, February 6, 1961].

KTVS(TV) Sterling (ch 3)—Licensed to Stauffer Communications. Former owner: Burke Broadcasting Co. of Cheyenne. (For details of sale, see KYCU-TV Cheyenne.) FCC approved: July 8, 1986 [Changing Hands, March 31, 1986]. Previous owner: Wyneco Communications Inc. (a wholly owned subsidiary of Lamb Communications). Sale price: $9.7 million (including KYCU-TV Cheyenne & KSTF(TV) Scottsbluff, NE). FCC approved: October 14, 1983 [For the Record, November 7, 1983]. Former call letters: KFBC-TV. Note: Founded by Frontier Broadcasting Co. in 1964. Sold to Wyenco in 1972 (including KSTF(TV) Scottsbluff, NE; KYCU-TV Cheyenne; & CP for KVRW(TV) Rawlins, WY) for $3 million.

Connecticut

WICC-TV Bridgeport (ch 43, now deleted)—Licensed to Bridgeport Broadcasting Co. (original owner). Connecticut-New York Broadcasters Inc. purchased 80% from Phillip Merryman & Manning Slater. Sale price: $1.22 million (with WICC-AM) & $275,000 to not compete for 10 years. FCC approved: February 25, 1959 [For the Record, March 2, 1959].

WFSB-TV Hartford (ch 3)—Licensed to Post-Newsweek Stations, Connecticut Inc. (see Post-Newsweek Stations Inc. under Group Ownership). Original owner: Broadcast Plaza Inc. (100% owned by Travelers Corp., Hartford, CT). Sale price: $33.9 million. FCC approved: January 30, 1974 [For the Record, February 11, 1974]. Original call letters: WTIC-TV.

WHCT-TV Hartford (ch 18)—Licensed to Astroline Comm. Co. (see Group Ownership). Previous owner: Faith Center Inc. (see Group Ownership). Sale price: $5 million, including non-compete (distress). FCC approved: December 12, 1984. Note: Given to Faith Center by RKO in 1972. FCC approved: February 16, 1972 [*Broadcasting*, February 21, 1972]. Founded as WGTH-TV, 55% owned by RKO General Inc. & 45% owned by Hartford Times. Sold to CBS in 1956 for $650,000. FCC approved: February 23, 1956. Edward D. Taddei & group bought stn from CBS for $250,000. FCC approved: December 23, 1958 [For the Record, December 29, 1958]. Mr. Taddei & Associates sold stn in 1960 to RKO General Inc. for $150,000 plus $245,000 for 10-year lease (and option to purchase for $570,000 at the end of four years). FCC approved: June 1, 1960 [For the Record, June 6, 1960].

WTIC-TV Hartford (ch 61)—Licensed to Renaissance Communications. Former owner: Arch Communications Corp. (Chase Broadcasting Corp.). Sale price: $126.6 million in group purchase (For details of sale, see WATL(TV) Atlanta, GA). FCC approved: January 11, 1993 [For the Record, February 1, 1993]. Previous owner: Arnold L. Chase. Sale price: $1 million. FCC approved: October 30, 1985 [For the Record, November 11, 1985].

WUHF-TV Hartford (ch 61, now deleted)—Licensed to Evans Broadcasting Corp. (Thomas M. Evans). Former owner: Albert G. Hartigan. Sale price: $48,821 for CP. FCC approved: April 24, 1970 [For the Record, May 11, 1970].

WVIT-TV New Britain (ch 30)—Licensed to Viacom Inc. (see Group Ownership). Note: Viacom International Inc. merged with Arsenal Acquiring Corp. September 1987. Sale price: $16 million. FCC approved: March 13, 1978. Former call letters: WHNB. Previous owner: Connecticut TV Inc. (Transcontinental Properties Inc. & H & E Balaban Corp.) Previous owner: NBC. Previous call letters: WNBC(TV). Sale price: $750,000 (with WKNB(AM), later resold). FCC approved: September 23, 1959 [For the Record, October 5, 1959]. Note: Founded by Julian Gross & associates as WKNB-TV & sold to NBC in 1956 for $600,000 (with WKNB(AM)) [For the Record, December 17, 1956].

WTNH-TV New Haven (ch 8)—Licensed to Cook Inlet Communications LP. Former owner: Capital Cities Communications Inc. (see Group Ownership). Sale price: $170 million. FCC approved: November 14, 1985 [For the Record, September 9, 1985]. Former owner: Triangle Publications Inc. (owned by Walter H. Annenberg & family). Sale price: $110 million (including WFIL(AM), WIOQ(FM) & WPVI-TV Philadelphia; WNHC(AM) & WPLR(FM) New Haven, CT; KFRE(AM), KFYE(FM) & KFSN-TV Fresno, CA; & TV prog syndication bus). Contingent on sale was Capital Cities spin-off of WFIL(AM) & WIOQ(FM) (formerly WFIL-FM) Philadelphia; WNHC(AM) & WPLR(FM) (formerly WNHC-FM) New Haven, CT; & KFRE(AM) & KFYE(FM) (formerly KFRE-FM) Fresno, CA, to separate buyers for an aggregate of $14.45 million. FCC approved: February 24, 1971 [*Broadcasting*, March 1, 1971]. Note: Triangle purchased stn from original owners (Aldo DeDominicis, Patrick J. Goode & associates) for $5.4 million (with WNHC-AM-FM). FCC approved: June 20, 1956 [For the Record, July 2, 1956]. Original call letters: WHNC-TV.

WTVU(TV) New Haven (ch 59)—Licensed to Impart Systems Inc. (Albert F. Campbell, Charles Tackman & Robert Tiberiis, executors). Former owners: Impart Systems Inc. (Victor Muscat, owner). Sale price: no consideration. FCC approved: December 30, 1975 [For the Record, January 26, 1976]. Note: previous owner, Conn. Radio Foundation (Richard W. Davis & others), sold CP to Impart Systems Inc. in 1967 for $27,500 plus payment of debts. FCC approved: August 18, 1967 [For the Record, August 28, 1967].

WTXX(TV) Waterbury (ch 20)—Licensed to Counterpoint Communications Inc. Former owner: Channel 20 Associates (joint venture of Esen Associates & Oppenheimer & Co. Esen is owned by Michael Finkelstein & others in Washington law firm of Nixon, Hargrave, Devans & Doyle. Oppenheimer & Co. is a New York investment firm). Sale price: $3.601 million. FCC approved: January 14, 1993 [For the Record, February 8, 1993]. Previous owner: Thomas Television Inc. (owned by B. Preston Gilmore family, who kept co-located WATR-AM-FM). Sale price: $4.5 million. FCC approved, November 9, 1981 [For the Record, December 7, 1981]. Former call letters: WATR-TV.

Delaware

WYUE(TV) Wilmington (ch 12, now deleted)—Licensed to Storer Broadcasting Co. Former owner: Paul F. Harron & associates. Sale price: $5.6 million (including WIBG-AM-FM Philadelphia). FCC approved: March 28, 1957 (conditioned on Storer disposal of WBRC-AM-FM-TV Birmingham, AL.) [For the Record, April 1, 1957]. Former call letters: WPFH(TV). Note: Mr. Harron & associates purchased stns in March 1955 for $3.7 million from J.F. Steinman interests [For the Record, April 4, 1955]. Former call letters: WDEL-TV. Stn permanently left the air in 1958.

District of Columbia

WDCA-TV Washington (ch 20)—Licensed to TVX Broadcast Group (see Group Ownership). Former owner: Taft Broadcasting Co. (see Group Ownership). For details of sale, see KTXH(TV) Houston. FCC approved: February 20, 1987 [*Broadcasting*, November 24, 1986]. Previous owner: Superior Tube Co. [Clarence A. Warden Jr. (21.5%), Paul E. Kelly (1.4%), Richard H. Gavel (20%), & others]. Sale price: $15 million. FCC approved: August 1979 [*Broadcasting*, September 3, 1979]. Note: Founded by Capitol Broadcasting (Milton Grant, A. Dana Hodgdon, Edward Mernone, Alan I. Kay & others) in April 1966. Purchased by Superior Tube for $4.86 million, including liabilities & covenant not to compete. FCC approved: May 7, 1969 [For the Record, May 19, 1969].

WFTY(TV) Washington (ch 50)—Licensed to JASAS Corp. Former owner: Channel 50 Inc. (owned by Hill Bcstg). Sale price: stock, including WUNI-TV Worcester, MA. FCC approved: October 15, 1993 [For the Record, November 8, 1993]. Previous owner: Theodore Ledbetter Jr. Sale price: $15 million. FCC approved: January 17, 1985. Former call letters: WCQR(TV).

WJLA-TV Washington (ch 7)—Licensed to Joseph Allbritton Communications. Former owner: Washington Star Communications. Sale price: $28.5 million (including WMAL-AM-FM, WLVA-TV-AM Lynchburg, VA; & WCIV(TV) Charleston SC). FCC approved: January 1976. Former call letters: WMAL-TV.

WRC-TV Washington (ch 4)—Licensed to NBC, a subsidiary of General Electric Co. (see Group Ownership). Sold as part of RCA Corp. in $6.28 billion acquisition. FCC approved: June 5, 1986.

WTTG(TV) Washington (ch 5)—Licensed to Fox Television Stations Inc. Former owner: Metromedia Inc. Sale price: $2.2 billion (including WNEW-TV New York; KTTV(TV) Los Angeles; WFLD-TV Chicago; KRLD-TV Dallas; & KRIV(TV) Houston). FCC approved: November 14, 1985.

WUSA-TV Washington (ch 9)—Licensed to Gannett Co. Inc. (see Group Ownership). Former owner: Evening News Association (see Group Ownership & Cross-Ownership). Sale price: $717 million for group (see KVUE-TV Austin, TX). Former call letters: WDVM-TV. Previous owner: Post-Newsweek Stations (see Group Ownership & Cross-Ownership). Stn was traded for *Evening News'* WWJ-TV Detroit to comply with FCC's cross-ownership rules. FCC approved: May 1978 [Changing Hands, May 22, 1978]. Former call letters: WTOP-TV. Original owner: Bamberger Broadcasting. Service Inc. Sale price: $1.4 million. FCC approved: July 26, 1950 [For the Record, July 31, 1950]. CBS, 45% owner of WTOP Inc., sold its interest to Washington Post Co., 55% stockholder, for $3.5 million in October 1954. Original call letters: WOIC.

Florida

WFTX(TV) Cape Coral (ch 36)— Licensed to Hulman & Company. Former owner: Wabash Valley Broadcasting Corp. Sale price: Unavailable (including WOGX(TV) Ocala, FL & WTHI-AM-FM-TV Terre Haute, IN). FCC approved: July 13, 1992 [For the Record: November 2, 1992].

***WBCC(TV) Cocoa (ch 18)**—Licensed to Brevard Community College. Former owner: The Glorious Church of God in Christ Inc. Sale price: $300,000. Former call letters: WRES(TV).

WESH-TV Daytona Beach (ch 2)—Licensed to H & C Communications (see Group Ownership). Former owner: Cowles Broadcasting. In 1984, Cowles merged with H & C Communications at $46 per share. Sale price: $182 million (including KCCI-TV Des Moines, IA). Previous owner: Telrad Inc. (John H. Perry Jr., et al). Sale price: $1 million. FCC approved: April 20, 1966. Note: Founded in 1955 by W. Wright Esch, A.B. Esch & Louis Ossinsky Sr. Sold to Perry interests in 1956 for $5,000 plus $150,000 loan. FCC approved: April 25, 1956 [For the Record, May 7, 1956].

WSCV(TV) Fort Lauderdale (ch 51)—Licensed to John Blair Broadcasting. Former owner: Oak Communications Inc. (publicly traded, 50% owner of KBSC(TV) Los Angeles). Sale price: $17.75 million. FCC approved: October 10, 1984. Previous owner: CB TV Corp. [William F. Johns Jr. (38%), Alvin Koenig (22%), Abel Holtz (19%), & three others]. Sale price: $4.1 million. FCC approved: February 29, 1980. [Changing Hands, March 24, 1980]. Former call letters: WKID(TV). Previous owner: Channel 51 Inc. (debtor-in-possession, with Herbert Freehling, receiver). Sale price: $1 million. FCC approved: July 14, 1976 [For the Record, August 2, 1976]. Note: Founded as WSMS-TV in 1968 by Gold Coast Telecasting Co. Sold to Channel 51 Inc. in 1972 for $473,615. FCC approved: January 12, 1972 [*Broadcasting*, January 24, 1972].

WBBH-TV Fort Myers (ch 20)—Licensed to Waterman Broadcasting Corp. of Texas [William Dakos (16.77%), Howard L. Hoffman (5.63%), & 31 others]. Original owner: Broadcasting-Telecasting Services Inc. [Bernard Waterman (90%), his wife Edith (10%)]. Sale price: $7.88 million. FCC approved: July 1979 [*Broadcasting*, July 30, 1979].

WTCE(TV) Fort Pierce (ch 21)—Licensed to Jacksonville Educators Broadcasting Inc. Former owner: Palmetto Broadcasters Associated. Sale price: $630,089. FCC approved: July 6, 1990. Previous owner: Florida Educational Television of the Treasure Coast Inc. Sale price: $76,500 for CP (including CP for WETV(TV) Key West, FL). FCC approved: December 15, 1986 [For the Record, November 17, 1986].

WTVI(TV) Fort Pierce (ch 19, now deleted)—Licensed to Atlantic Broadcasting Co. (Isadore J. Fine & associates). Previous owner: Gene T. Dyer. Sale price: $175,795 for CP. FCC approved: July 6, 1961 [For the Record, July 17, 1961].

WTVX(TV) Fort Pierce (ch 34)—Licensed to Krypton Broadcasting Corp. Former owner: WTWV Inc. Sale price: $8 million. FCC approved: February 1, 1991 [For the Record, February 18, 1991]. Previous owner: Indian River TV Inc. Sale price: $900,000. FCC approved: April 20, 1979.

WFGX(TV) Fort Walton Beach (ch 35)—Licensed to Bowers Network Inc. Former owner: TV 35 Ltd. Sale price: $210,000. FCC approved: January 27, 1992 [For the Record, February 17, 1992]. Previous owner: Family Group Broadcasting. Previous owner: Beacon/Lloyd Broadcast Corp. Sale price of Family-Beacon transaction: $225,000 for 50% of construction permit (Family Group owned other 50%). FCC approved: July 1987. Previous owner: Lloyd Comm. Group (Marvin Palmquist & Family). Sale price: $50,000 for 1% of stn in transfer of control. FCC approved: January 15, 1986 [For the Record, December 9, 1985]. Former call letters: WQAC(TV). Previous owner: William J. Kitchen. Sale price: $100,000 for 51% (transfer of control). FCC approved: January 22, 1985 [For the Record, February 4, 1985].

WCJB(TV) Gainesville (ch 20)—Licensed to Gainesville TV Inc. (owned by Diversified Communications Inc., see Group Ownership). Original owner: Minshall Broadcasting Co. (owned by William E. Minshall (74%) & six other minority stockholders). Sale price: $1.87 million plus $500,000 covenant not to compete. FCC approved: October 12, 1976 [For the Record, November 1, 1976].

WGBZ(TV) Gainesville (ch 61)—Licensed to G.T.L. (principally owned by Louis Frey & Ronald D. Campbell). Former owner: Gator Broadcasting Ltd. Partnership. Sold for assumption of liabilities. FCC approved: May 7, 1987 [For the Record, April 6, 1987].

WAWS(TV) Jacksonville (ch 30)—Licensed to Clear Channel Television Inc. Former owner: Malrite of New York Inc. Sale price: $8.1 million. FCC approved: August 30, 1989 [For the Record, September 18, 1989].

WDUV-TV Jacksonville (ch 30, now deleted)—Licensed to Canasta Broadcasting Co. [Al, Jerome & Irving Lapin (20% each); Alex & Corine Finkel (25%); et al). Former owners: Scott I. Peek (20%); Alvin Leitman, Henry Kramer, David A. Watts, H. George Carrison (each 13.35%); Norman P. Freeman, Gilbert C. Palmer (each 13.33%). Sale price: $24,646 for CP. FCC approved: June 22, 1966 [For the Record, June 27, 1966].

WJEB(TV) Jacksonville, FL (ch 59)—Licensed to Community Educational Television Inc. Former owner: Jacksonville Educators Broadcasting Inc. Sale price: $250,000. FCC approved: December 4, 1990.

WJKS-TV Jacksonville (ch 17)—Licensed to Tampa Television Inc. (owned by Media General Inc., see Group Ownership). Former owner: Ziff Davis Broadcasting, (subsidiary of Ziff Corp.). Sale price: $18 million. FCC approved: October 21, 1982 [For the Record, November 8, 1982]. Note: Ziff sold stn as part of its divestiture of bcst interests [*Broadcasting*, July 26, 1982]. Previous owner: Rust Craft Greeting Cards Inc. Sale price: $70.57 million (including other stns, see WTOV-TV Steubenville, OH). FCC approved: May 10, 1978.

WJXT(TV) Jacksonville (ch 4)—Licensed to Post-Newsweek Stations, Florida Inc. (see Group Ownership). Original owner: Florida Broadcasting Co. (Edward L. Norton, Frank King & Glenn Marshall Jr.). Sale price: $2.47 million (with WMBR-AM-FM). FCC approved: January 28, 1953 [For the Record, February 2, 1953]. Original call letters: WMBR-TV. Note: Sale of WMBR-AM-FM to WWDC Inc. (WWDC Washington) for $375,000. FCC approved: July 31, 1958 [For the Record, August 11, 1958].

WNFT(TV) Jacksonville (ch 47)—Licensed to Krypton Broadcasting Corp. Former owner: North Florida 47 Inc. Sale price: $3.3 million. FCC approved: June 19, 1989.

WQIK-TV Jacksonville (ch 30, now deleted)—Licensed to Southern Radio & Equipment Co. (Carmen Macri). Original owner: E.D. Rivers Sr., majority stockholder. Sale price: $90,000 (including WOBS(AM)) for additional 60% interest (Mr. Macri already owned 21%). FCC approved: July 27, 1955 [For the Record, August 1, 1955]. Original call letters: WOBS-TV.

WTLV(TV) Jacksonville (ch 12)—Licensed to Television 12 of Jacksonville (owned by Harte-Hanks Newspapers, see Cross-Ownership). Original owner: Television 12 of Jacksonville [Thomas McGehee, Frank S. McGehee, Frank E. Pellegrin, et al (51%)]. Sale price: $11.4 million. FCC approved: March 27, 1975 [For the Record, April 14, 1975].

WETV(TV) Key West (ch 13)—Licensed to Palmetto Broadcasters Associated for Communities Inc. Former owner: Florida Educational Television of the Treasure Coast Inc. (For details of sale, see WFET(TV) Fort Pierce, FL) [For the Record, November 17, 1986].

WACX(TV) Leesburg (ch 55)—Licensed to Sharp Communications Inc. (owned by Associated Christian Television System Inc.). Former owner: Sharp Communications (H. James Sharp). Sale price: $1.55 million for 51%. Note: H.J. Sharp sold his 51% interest in stn to ACTS, who already owned remaining 49%. FCC approved: June 8, 1983 [For the Record, July 4, 1983]. Former call letters: WIYE(TV). Stn founded in 1982.

WBSF(TV) Melbourne (ch 43)—Licensed to Blackstar Communications Inc. (owned by John E. Oxendine, Kenneth O. Harris & Wesley S. Williams). Former owner: Press Broadcasting Co. (subsidiary of Asbury Park Press). Sale price: $5 million. FCC approved: February 18, 1988 [For the Record, February 29, 1988]. Former call letters: WMOD(TV). Note: control of stn transferred to Asbury Park Press Inc. for $6.8 million plus 20% of stock of Asbury Park Press.

WIRB(TV) Melbourne (ch 56)—Licensed to WMVP Inc., owned by Robert J. Rich. Former owner: Beach Television Partners. Sale price: $100,000. FCC approved: April 6, 1992 [For the Record, April 27, 1992]. Former call letters: WAYK(TV).

WCIX-TV Miami (ch 6)—Licensed to CBS Inc. Former owner: TVX Broadcast Group. Sale price: $59 million [*Broadcasting*, August 15, 1988]. Previous owner: Taft Broadcasting Co. (see Group Ownership). (For details of sale, see KTXH(TV) Houston.) Previous owner: Coral Television Corp. (subsidiary of General Cinema Corp.). Sale price: $70 million plus trade of WGRZ-TV Buffalo, NY, for WCIX-TV. FCC approved: February 24, 1983 [For the Record, March 14, 1983]. Stn founded in 1967.

WDZL(TV) Miami (ch 39)—Licensed to Channel 39 Inc. (Renaissance Communications Corp.) Former owner: 39 Broadcasting Ltd. (owned by Odyssey TV Inc., also headed by Michael Finkelstein). Sale price: $29.5 million. FCC approved: December 8, 1989 [For the Record, December 26, 1988]. Previous owner: 39 Broadcasting Ltd. Sale price: $11.96 million. FCC approved: April 4, 1984.

WHFT(TV) Miami (ch 45)—Licensed to Trinity Broadcasting of Florida. Former owner: Lester Sumrall Evangelistic Association Inc. (Indiana-based religious bcstr & licensee of WHME-TV South Bend & WHMB-TV Indianapolis, both IN). Sale price: $10 million. FCC approved: May 14, 1980 [Changing Hands, June 2, 1980]. Original owner: Florida Christian Broadcasting Inc. (T.I. Monroe, pres, et al). Sale price: $900,000. FCC approved: June 22, 1976 [For the Record, July 5, 1976]. Original call letters: WFCB-TV.

WLTV(TV) Miami (ch 23)—Licensed to Univision. Former owner: Spanish International Communications Corp. [Fouce Amusement Enterprises Inc.: Frank K. Fouce (51%), Emilio Ascaraga (20%), Reynold V. Anselmo (15%), et al]. Previous owner: Coastal Broadcasting System Inc. (Al Lapin Jr., 94.4%). (For details of sale, see WXTV(TV) Paterson, NJ.) Sale price: $1.44 million. FCC approved: January 6, 1971 [For the Record, January 18, 1971]. Former call letters: WAJA-TV. Previous owner: Coastal Broadcasting System Inc. Sale price: $250,000. FCC approved: October 25, 1967 [For the Record, October 30, 1967]. Previous call letters: WGBS-TV. Previous owner: Storer Broadcasting Co. (see Group Ownership). Note: Former Storer purchase was a combination purchase of a construction permit for ch 27 WMIE-TV Miami for $35,410 & facilities of ch 23 WFTL-TV Fort Lauderdale, FL, for $300,000. Original owners: WMIE-TV, E.D. Rivers Sr. & associates; WFTL-TV Gore Pub. Co., principal owner. FCC approved: December 16, 1954 [For the Record, December 27, 1954].

WMLB(TV) Miami (ch 35)—Licensed to William C. de la Pena. Former owner: New Miami Latino Broadcasting Corp. Sale price: $1.6 million. FCC approved: December 7, 1992 [For the Record, January 4, 1993].

WPLG(TV) Miami (ch 10)—Licensed to Post-Newsweek Stations, Florida Inc. (see Post-Newsweek Stations, Group Ownership). Former owner: L.B. Wilson Inc. (Charles H. Topmiller, Thomas A., Welstead, Jeannette Heinze, William C. Ittman, Jolar Corp. & Essie Rupp). Sale price: $19.6 million, including WCKY(AM) Cincinnati. FCC approved: September 27, 1969 [For the Record, October 6, 1969]. Note: Founded by L.B. Wilson Inc. in November 1961. Original call letters: WLBW-TV.

WSVN(TV) Miami (ch 7)—Licensed to Sunbeam TV Corp. (Sidney D. & Edmund N. Ansin, & others.). Former owner: Catchings Therrel. (Messrs. Ansin will vote 64% of stock.) Sale price: $185,000. FCC approved: October 4, 1967 [For the Record, October 16, 1967]. Former call letters: WCKT(TV).

WTVJ(TV) Miami (ch 4)—Licensed to NBC Subsidiary (WTVJ-TV) Inc. Former owner: WBC Broadcasting Corp. (Kohlberg, Kravis, Roberts & McDonnell). Sale price: $270 million. FCC approved: September 17, 1987 [*Broadcasting*, January 19, 1987]. Previous owner: Wometco Enterprises Inc. Sale price: more than $1 billion (including all Wometco properties: WZZM-TV Grand Rapids, MI; WWHT(TV) Newark; WLOS(TV) Asheville, NC; KVOS-TV Bellingham, WA; WSNL-TV Smithtown, NY; & Wometco Cable TV].

WEVU(TV) Naples (ch 26)—Licensed to Elcom of South Carolina Inc. (see Ellis Communications in Group Ownership). Former owner: FCVS Communications (see Group Ownership). Sale price: $15 million, including WACH-TV Columbia, SC. FCC approved: October 7, 1993 [For the Record, October 25, 1993]. Previous owner: Caloosa Television Corp. (Home News Publishing Co., see Cross-Ownership). Sale price: $4.65 million. FCC approved: June 29, 1992 [For the Record, July 20, 1992]. Original owner: Gulfshore Television Corp. (Richard S. Simpson Jr., R.S. Dean Sr. & Sam Johnson Jr.). Sale price: $2.64 million plus $780,000 in consulting & noncompetition agreements. FCC approved: August 1978 [Changing Hands, September 4, 1978].

WNPL(TV) Naples (ch 46)—Licensed to Southwest Florida Telecommunications (William T. Darling). Former owner: Gerard A. McHale Jr., receiver. Sale price: $650,250. FCC approved: September 1, 1989 [For the Record, September 25, 1989].

WOGX(TV) Ocala (ch 51)—Licensed to Hulman & Company. Former owner: Wabash Valley Broadcasting (Mary R. Hulman, et al). Sale price: Unavailable (including WTHI-AM-FM-TV Terre Haute, IN & WFTX(TV) Cape Coral, FL). FCC approved: July 13, 1992 [For the Record, November 2, 1992]. Notes: Transferors are Jack R. Snyder and Merchants National Bank & Trust Co. of Indianapolis, co-trustees of Anton Hulman Jr. Real Estate & Grace Hulman Descendants Trust, which own 87.04% of licensees of WKOX(AM)-WVBF(FM) Framingham, MA & WJNO(AM)-WRMF(FM) Palm Beach, FL. Previous owner: Big Sun Television Inc. Sale price: $7 million. FCC approved: August 12, 1986 [For the Record, July 21, 1986]. Former call letters: WBSP-TV. Previous owner: Gator Broadcasting Corp. (Thomas P. Hicks, 93.44%). Former call letters: WOCA-TV. Previous owner: Marion Communications Corp. [Thomas P. Hicks (46.72%) & R. Joseph Zeigler (46.72%)]. Sale price: $467 for CP. FCC approved: February 26, 1976 [For the Record, March 15, 1976].

WCPX-TV Orlando (ch 6)—Licensed to First Media Corp. (Richard E. Marriott, et al, see Group Ownership). Former owner: Wesray Communications Corp. Sale price: $200 million. FCC approved: May 30, 1986 [Changing Hands, March 24, 1986]. Previous owner: Rockefeller Group Inc. (For details of sale, see WCMH(TV) Columbus, OH.) Previous owner: The Outlet Co. (see Group Ownership). Sale price: $332 million (including WJAR-TV Providence, RI; KOVR-TV Stockton, CA; WCMH-TV Columbus, OH; KSAT-TV San Antonio, TX; one AM stn, & four FM stns. FCC approved: November 23, 1983. Previous owners: Estate of William S. Cherry Jr. Sale price: $6.1 million (including WBDO-AM-FM). FCC approved: July 17, 1963 [For the Record, July 29, 1963]. Note: Founded by Harold P. Danforth Sr. & associates. Bought by William S. Cherry Jr. & associates in 1957 for $3 million (with WBDO-AM-FM).

WEAL-TV Orlando (ch 18, now deleted)—Licensed to Orange County Broadcasters Inc. Original owner: Carmen Macri, 40% stockholder. Sale price: $29,000 (including WABR(AM)). R.H. Gunckel, 40% stockholder, increased holdings to 60% & James H. Sawyer, 20% stockholder, increased holdings to 40%. FCC approved: November 3, 1955 [For the Record, November 14, 1955].

WFTV(TV) Orlando (ch 9)—Licensed to WFTV Inc. (owned by Cox Communications). Former owner: SFN Companies, affiliate of E.M. Warburg, Pincus & Co. Inc. & Hallmark Cards Inc. Sale price: $185 million. FCC approved: December 13, 1985. Earlier, SFN Cos. were acquired by E. M. Warburg, Pincus & Co. Inc. & Hallmark Cards. Sale price: $425 million (sale included: WJBF(TV) Augusta, GA; WTVM(TV) Columbus, GA; WAPA-TV San Juan, PR; & three Montana radio stns). FCC approved: August 29, 1985. Previous owner: Channel 9 of Orlando Inc. (joint venture of Mid-Florida TV Corp., Channel 9 Inc., TV-9 Inc., Comint Corp., Florida Heartland TV Inc.) Sale price: $125 million. FCC approved: August 10, 1984. Note: Founded in 1958 by Mid-Florida Inc. (John W. Kluge, Joseph L. Brechner & others). Mr. Brechner boosted holdings from 17% to 41.67% in 1959 when he bought stock from Mr. Kluge for $350,000. Former call letters: WLOF-TV.

WOFL(TV) Orlando (ch 35)—Licensed to Meredith Corp., see Group ownership. Former owner: Control Group. Sale price: $16 million (Control Group sold its 60% interest in WOFL to Meredith, which already owned remaining 40%). FCC approved: April 18, 1983 [For the Record, May 9, 1983]. Former call letters: WSWB-TV. Note: Founded by Sun World Broadcasters. It went off the air in 1976 & after protracted litigation returned to the air in October 1979. It was sold to Omega in 1979 for $5.6 million.

WPTV(TV) Palm Beach (ch 5)—Licensed to Scripps-Howard Broadcasting Co. (see Group Ownership). Former owner: John H. Phipps. Sale price: $2 million. FCC approved: December 13, 1961 [For the Record, December 25, 1961]. Note: Founded by Theodore Granik & William H. Cook as WJNO-TV. Sold in 1956 to John H. Phipps for $642,500.

WJHG-TV Panama City (ch 7)—Licensed to WJHG-TV Inc. (owned by Gray Communications, see Group Ownership). Former owners: Mel Wheeler & wife. Sale price: $340,000. FCC approved: June 29, 1960 [For the Record, July 4, 1960]. Former call letters: WJDM-TV. Note: Founded by J.D. Manley as WJDM(TV). Sold to Mr. Wheeler in 1957 for $60,000. FCC approved: November 21, 1957 [For the Record, December 2, 1957].

WMBB-TV Panama City (ch 13)—Licensed to The Spartan Radiocasting Co. Former owner: Buford TV Inc. of Panama. Sale price $10.4 million. FCC approved: March 21, 1990. Previous owner: Octagon Broadcasting Co. (Anthony C. Kupris). Sale price: $12 million. FCC approved: December 5, 1986. Previous owner: Panhandle Broadcasting Co. Sale price: $2.1 million. FCC approved: February 28, 1977 [For the Record, March 21, 1977].

WPGX-TV Panama City (ch 28)—Licensed to Ashling Broadcast Group. Former owner: WMJA Inc. Sale price: $500,000. FCC approved: March 6, 1990.

WEAR-TV Pensacola (ch 3)—Licensed to Heritage Media (formerly Rollins Telecasting Inc., which merged with Heritage in March 1987). Former owner: Charles Smith, Mel Wheeler, et al. Sale price: $1.4 million. FCC approved: 1959.

WJTC-TV Pensacola (ch 44)—Licensed to Mercury Broadcasting Co. Former owner: Channel 44 Ltd. Sale price: $2.25 million. FCC approved: March 30, 1992 [For the Record, April 13, 1992].

WSUN-TV St. Petersburg (ch 38, now deleted)—Licensed to WSUN Inc. [controlled by H.Y. Levinson (52.6%) & Celia D. Levinson (23.58%)]. Former owner: City of St. Petersburg. Sale price: $1.31 million (including WSUN-AM). FCC approved: February 23, 1966 [For the Record, March 7, 1966].

WTSP(TV) St. Petersburg (ch 10)—Licensed to Great American Broadcasting (see Group Ownership). (This was part of the Taft Broadcasting reorganization of October 1987.) Former owner: Gulf Broadcast Group, owned by Gulf United Corp. (see Group Ownership). Sale price: $755 million (including KTSP-TV Phoenix; KTXH-TV Houston; WGHP-TV High Point, NC; KTXA-TV Arlington (Ft. Worth), TX). FCC approved: May 30, 1985 [For the Record, April 15, 1985]. Former call letters: WTSP-TV. Previous owner: Rahall Communications. Sale price: Approx. $30 million (including 4 radio stns). FCC approved: 1977.

WWSB(TV) Sarasota (ch 40)—Licensed to Calkins Newspaper Inc. Former owner: Southern Broadcast Associates. Sale price: Buyer, headed by Grover Friend, previously had 48% interest in stn & now has purchased shares to become majority shareholder. Further details not available [For the Record, July 10, 1989]. FCC approved: June 22, 1989. Previous owner: Sarasota Bradenton TV Co. Sale price: $40.5 million. FCC approved: November 13, 1985 [For the Record, September 16, 1985]. Former call letters: WXLT-TV.

WTXL-TV Tallahassee (ch 27)—Licensed to Media Venture Management Inc. (F. Tracy Lavery 50%, Elio Betty 50%). Former owner: E.T. Broadcasting (owned by F. Tracy Lavery & Elio Betty). Sale price: $5 million. FCC approved: May 26, 1993 [For the Record, June 14, 1993]. Previous owner: Tallahassee 27 Ltd. Partnership (owned by U.S. Communications Group). Sale price: $5.35 million. FCC approved: August 23, 1991 [For the Record, September 9, 1991]. Previous owner: E.C. Allen. Sale price: $3.8 million. FCC approved: January 27, 1984. Former call letters: WECA-TV.

WFLA-TV Tampa (ch 8)—Licensed to Tampa Television Inc. (owned by Media General Inc., see Cross-Ownership). Former Owner: Tribune Co. Sale price: $17.5 million. FCC approved: 1965. Former call letters: WXFL(TV).

WFTS(TV) Tampa (ch 28)—Licensed to Tampa Bay Television Inc. (owned by Scripps-Howard Broadcasting Co., see Group Ownership). Former owner: Capital Cities Communications Inc. Sale price: $246 million (including WXYZ-TV Detroit). FCC approved: November 14, 1985. Previous owner: Family Broadcast Group (Ian Wheeler, et al). Sale price: $30.1 million. FCC approved: July 23, 1984.

WTVT(TV) Tampa (ch 13)—Licensed to WTVT Inc. (Gillett Holdings Inc.). Former owner: Gillett Communications (see Group Ownership). FCC approved: July 27, 1992 [For the Record, August 17, 1992]. Previous owner: Gaylord Broadcasting Co. (see Group Ownership). Sale price: $365 million. FCC approved: April 1987 [For the Record, March 23, 1987]. Original owners: W. Walter Tison & associates. Sale price: $3.5 million plus assumption of $500,000 of liabilities. FCC approved: July 19, 1956 [For the Record, July 30, 1956].

WPBF-TV Tequesta (ch 25)—Licensed to Alan Potamkin. Former owner: Brenda Skipper & Silvia Salinas. Sale price: $5,000 for CP (Brenda Skipper & Silvia Salinas own 100 shares of licensee between them. Pursuant to joint stock purchase option agreement, they have granted buyers option to purchase 96 of their shares. By this assignment they are granting buyers an option to purchase their remaining 4 shares for total of $5,000 & forgiveness of all liabilities incurred by them in connection with monies advanced by corporation to fund operating & construction costs). [For the Record, September 5, 1989]. FCC approved: August 5, 1989.

WBSV(TV) Venice (ch 2)—Licensed to Desoto Broadcasting Inc. Former owner: Venice Broadcasting Corp. Financial details not available for this sale of CP. [For the Record, May 29, 1989]. FCC approved: May 10, 1989.

WPEC(TV) West Palm Beach (ch 12)—Licensed to PEC Communications Inc. Former owner: Gardens Broadcasting Co. (Royal American Industries Inc., 66.7% owned by Bankers Life & Casualty Co.). Sale price: $3.53 million. FCC approved: October 26, 1973 [For the Record, November 12, 1973]. Original call letters: WEAT-TV. Note: Founded by James R. & June H. Meacham in 1954. Sold to RKO General in 1955 for $301,000 (with WEAT(AM)). Sold to Rex Rand & associates in 1957 for $600,000. Rex Rand (80%) & Bertram Lebhar (20%) sold stn to Gardens Broadcasting Co. for $2.1 million (with WEAT(AM)) in 1964. FCC approved: February 25, 1964 [For the Record, March 2, 1964].

Georgia

WTAU-TV (CP) Albany (ch 19)—Licensed to RoPa Communications Inc. Former owner: Albany Television Co. Sale price: $30,000. FCC approved: September 14, 1989 [For the Record, October 2, 1989].

WTSG-TV Albany (ch 31)—Licensed to NewSouth Media. Former owner: Gordon Communications. Sale price: $2.25 million. FCC approved: October 1987 [For the Record, April 27, 1987].

WAGA-TV Atlanta (ch 5)—Licensed to WAGA License Inc. (see SCI Television Inc. in Group Ownership). Former owner: Gillett Communications Inc. Sale price: unknown. (Sale included WSBK-TV Boston, WJBK-TV Detroit, KNSD(TV) San Diego, WITI-TV Milwaukee & WJW-TV Cleveland). FCC approved: February 19, 1993 [For the Record, April 26, 1993]. Previous owner: Storer Communications Inc. (See KCST-TV San Diego for details of sale.)

WATC(TV) Atlanta (ch 57)—Licensed to Action for Communities to Community Television Inc. (see Carolina Christian Broadcasting Inc. in Group Ownership). Former owner: Acorn Television in Action for Communities. Sale price: $79,866 for CP. FCC approved: June 3, 1993 [For the Record, June 28, 1993].

WATL(TV) Atlanta (ch 36)—Licensed to FTS Atlanta Inc. (see Fox Television Stations Inc. in Group Ownership). Former owner: Renaissance Communications. Sale price: $60 million. FCC approved: April 21, 1993 [For the Record, May 10, 1993]. Previous owner: Chase Broadcasting of Washington. Sale price: $126.6 million (base price), $25.4 million noncompete agreement & 131,000 shares of Renaissance preferred stock (including KDVR(TV) Denver, CO, WTIC-TV Hartford, CT, & WXIN(TV) Indianapolis, IN). FCC approved: January 11, 1993 [For the Record, February 1, 1993]. Previous owner: WATL-Inc. (owned by Outlet Communications Group, see Group Ownership). Sale price: $120 million (including WXIN-TV Indianapolis & WTOP(AM)-WASH(FM) Washington). FCC approved: January 22, 1990. [See Changing Hands, August 14, 1989, for details of sale]. Former owner: Rockefeller Group. (For details of sale, see WCMH(TV) Columbus, OH). Previous owner: Outlet Communications. Sale price: $332.1 million in group purchase (see WCMH(TV) Columbus, OH for details). Former owner: ATL Acquisition Corp. (Don Kennedy (30.5%), D.R. Jones (30.5%) & others). Sale price: $27 million. FCC approved: September 6, 1984. Previous owner: U.S. Communications of Georgia Inc. (80% owned by U.S. Communications Corp., controlled by A.V.C. Corp.). Sale price: $23,500 for CP. FCC approved: July 17, 1974 [For the Record, July 29, 1974]. Note: Original owner, Robert W. Rounsaville, sold CP (as WATL-TV) to D.H. Overmyer in 1965 for $100,000. D.H. Overmyer Communications Co. sold CP (as WMBO-TV) in 1967 to U.S. Communications of Georgia Inc. for $1 million (with CPs for KEMO-TV San Francisco; WSCO-TV Newport, Ky.; WECO-TV Pittsburgh & KJDO-TV Rosenberg, TX). FCC approved: December 8, 1967 [For the Record, December 18, 1967].

WGNX(TV) Atlanta (ch 46)—Licensed to WGNX Inc. (owned by the Tribune Broadcasting Co., see Group Ownership). Former Owner: Continental Broadcasting Network Co. (see Christian Broadcasting Network, Group Ownership). Sale price: $32 million. FCC approved: December 19, 1983 [For the Record, December 19, 1983]. Former call letters: WANX-TV. Note: Stn went on air, June 6, 1971.

WVEU(TV) Atlanta (ch 69)—Licensed to HSN Silver King Broadcasting Co. (Home Shopping Network Inc.). Former owner: Broadcasting Corp. of Georgia. Sale price: $13 million, which includes $100,000 non-compete agreement [For the Record, May 29, 1989]. FCC approved: May 10, 1989.

WXIA-TV Atlanta (ch 11)—Licensed to Pacific & Southern Co. (owned by the Gannett Co., see Group Ownership). Former owner: Combined Communications Corp., {(acquired by Gannett in 1979. For details, see KPNX-TV Phoenix.) [Fox, Wells & Rogers (24.4%); Paulette B. Godfrey (10.8%); DeSale Harrison Jr. (8%)]. Combined Communications Corp. & previous owner, Pacific & Southern Broadcasting Co. merged in an exchange of stock (valued in January 1973 at about $38.6 million)]}. FCC approved: January 9, 1974 [*Broadcasting*, January 14, 1974]. Note: Founded by Atlanta *Journal* as WSB-TV. When *Journal* merged with Atlanta *Constitution* in 1950, it sold stn to Broadcasting Inc. for $525,000. In 1953, Broadcasting Inc. sold facilities [WLTV(TV)] to Crosley (later Avco) Broadcasting Corp. for $1.5 million. Crosley sold stn (WLWA-TV) in 1962 to Richard M. Fairbanks & Associates for $2.25 million. Richard M. Fairbanks & others sold stn to Pacific & Southern Broadcasting Co. in 1967 for $15 million, including WIBC-AM-FM, Indianapolis. FCC approved: 1966. Later sold for $12.89 million as WAII-TV in 1967 to Jupiter Broadcasting Co., which later changed its name to Pacific & Southern Broadcasting Co.

WAGT(TV) Augusta (ch 26)—Licensed to WAGT Inc. (owned by Schurz Communications, see Group Ownership). Former owner: Augusta Telecasters [J. Thomas Jones (55%) & Francis Robertson (45%)]. Sale price: $5 million. FCC approved: May 14, 1980 [Changing Hands, June 2, 1980]. Former call letters: WATU-TV.

WJBF(TV) Augusta (ch 6)—Licensed to Commacq Inc. Former owner: SFN Companies Inc., (acquired by affiliates of Warburg, Pincas & Company & Hallmark Company in 1985 for $425 million. For details, see WFTV(TV) Orlando, FL). (For details of Commacq sale, see WAPA-TV San Juan, PR.) FCC approved: October 2, 1986. Previous owner: Western Broadcasting Company. Sale price: $116 million (included WFTV(TV) Orlando, FL; WTVM(TV) Columbus, GA; WAPA-TV San Juan, PR). FCC approved: December 13, 1984. Previous owner: J.B. Fuqua (see Fuqua Industries Stations, Group Ownership). Sale price: $25 million. FCC approved: July 10, 1980 [Changing Hands, July 28, 1980].

WRDW-TV Augusta (ch 12)—Licensed to Television Station Partners (see Group Ownership). Former owner: Ziff-Davis Corp. Sale price: $57 million (including WEYI-TV Saginaw, Mich.; WROC-TV Rochester, N.Y. & WTOV-TV Steubenville, OH). FCC approved: January 18, 1983 [For the Record, February 7, 1983]. Note: Founded by Grover C. Maxwell Sr., Harry W. Jernigan Sr., Judge F. Frederick Kennedy, Allen M. Woodall & W.R. Ringson. Sold to Southeastern Newspapers in 1956 for $1 million [with WRDW(AM)] [For the Record, February 27, 1956]. Sold to the Friendly Group in 1959 for $1.5 million. Later sold to Rust Craft Broadcasting Co. in 1960 for $1.57 million [For the Record, April 25, 1960]. Sold to Ziff-Davis Corp., as part of $69 million deal [*Broadcasting*, May 15, 1978].

WTLH(TV) Bainbridge (ch 49)—Licensed to NewSouth Media (aka Lloyd Communications Group). Former owner: Bainbridge Communications Ltd. (owned by Gregory Capogna). Sale price: $85,000 for CP. FCC approved: September 1987 [For the Record, November 3, 1986].

WBSG-TV Brunswick (ch 21)—CP licensed to WBSG-TV Ltd. Former owner: Richard L. Huff. FCC approved: July 17, 1989 [For the Record, August 7, 1989].

WLTZ(TV) Columbus (ch 38)—Licensed to Columbus Television Inc. (owned by J.C. Lewis Jr.). Former owner: Eagle Broadcasting Co., subsidiary of American Family Corp. (see Group Ownership). Sale price: $3.25 million. FCC approved: June 16, 1981. Former call letters: WYEA-TV. Original owners: Gala Broadcasting Co. (Charles Grisham, Aaron Aronov, Tine W. Davis & Bryghte Godbold, David Rothschild, J. Kyle Spencer, John H. Swift & S. Douglas Smith). Sale price: $1.5 million. FCC approved: February, 1978 [*Broadcasting*, March 13, 1978].

WRBL-TV Columbus (ch 3)—Licensed to TCS Television Partners. Former owner: Columbus Broadcasting Co. (owned by Avant Development Corp). Sale price: $56 million [including WTWO(TV) Terre Haute, IN; & KQTV(TV) St. Joseph, MO (see Changing Hands, February 12, 1990)]. FCC approved: April 6, 1990. Previous owner: Columbus Broadcasting Co. (estate of James W. Woodruff). Sale price: $7 million. FCC approved: September 11, 1978 [Changing Hands, September 18, 1978]. Note: Avant Development is owned by Malcolm I. Glazer, who owns WTWO-TV Terre Haute, IN. Original owner: R.W. Page Corp. Sale price: $2.24 million (including WRBL-AM-FM). FCC approved: 1972.

WTVM(TV) Columbus (ch 9)—Licensed to WTVM Television Inc. Former owner: Pegasus Broadcasting of Columbus, Georgia Inc. Sale price: $45 million. FCC approved: February 16, 1989 [For the Record, March 6, 1989]. Previous owner: Commacq Inc., preceded by SFN Companies Inc. (acquired by E.M. Warburg, Pincus & Co. & Hallmark Cards Inc). (For details of latter sale, see WFTV(TV) Orlando, FL, for details of Commacq sale, see WAPA-TV San Juan, PR.) FCC approved: October 2, 1986. Previous owner: Western Broadcasting Co. Sale price: $116 million (see WJBF(TV) Augusta, GA). FCC approved: December 13, 1984. Previous owner: Fuqua Industries (see WJBF(TV) Augusta, GA). Sale price: $19.5 million. FCC approved: July 10, 1980 [Changing Hands, July 21, 1980]. Previous owner: Martin Theaters of Georgia Inc. (E.D. Martin & Roy E. Martin Jr.). Sale price: Exchange of stock valued at about $19 million, including WTVC(TV) Chattanooga. FCC approved: February 7, 1969 [For the Record, February 17, 1969]. Note: Went on air October 6, 1953, on ch 28. Switched to ch 9 November 3, 1960. See WTVC(TV), Chattanooga.

WELF(TV) Dalton (ch 23)—Licensed to Sonlight Broadcasting System Inc. (see Group Ownership). Former owner: Dalton Television Associates Ltd. Sale price: $195,000 for CP. FCC approved: July 27, 1992 [For the Record, September 21, 1992].

WFXQ(TV) Macon (ch 64)—Licensed to Newsouth Macon Inc. Former owner: Macon Urban Ministries Inc. Sale price: $102,500 for CP. FCC approved: July 14, 1989 [For the Record, July 31, 1989]. Former call letters: WGNM(TV).

WMAZ-TV Macon (ch 13)—Licensed to Multimedia Inc. (see Group Ownership). Stn was transferred in 1967. No details available. Previous owner: Southeastern Broadcasting Corp. Original owners: George P. Rankin Jr., Wilton E. Cobb, & Mr. & Mrs. Wallace Miller. Sale price: $2 million (including WMAZ-AM-FM). FCC approved: March 13, 1963 [For the Record, March 18, 1963].

WMGT(TV) Macon (ch 41)—Licensed to Morris Network Inc. (Charles H. Morris & others). Former owner: Bibb Television Inc. (F.E. Busby). Sale price: $2.8 million. FCC approved: November 30, 1978 [*Broadcasting*, December 18, 1978]. Former call letters: WCWB-TV. Note: Founded by WTVY Inc. (Charles E. Woods) on August 26, 1968. Sold to Bibb for $800,000. FCC approved: August 9, 1974 [*Broadcasting*, August 26, 1974].

WOKA(TV) Macon (ch 47, now deleted)—Licensed to Macon TV Co. (J.C. Barnes & E.K. Cargill). Original owners: W.A. Fickling & WNEX(AM) Macon. Sale price: $1 million & assumption of $260,000 in obligations. FCC approved: April 19, 1955 [For the Record, April 25, 1955].

WTLK-TV Rome (ch 14)—Licensed to Sudbrink Broadcasting Co. Former owner: Rome Television Inc. (owned by American Communications & Television Inc.). Sale price: $250,000 (including CP for WSQY-TV Forest City, NC). FCC approved: August 13, 1986 [For the Record, June 30, 1986]. Former call letters: WZGA(TV), preceded by WAWA-TV.

WSAV-TV Savannah (ch 3)—Licensed to New Vision Television I Inc. (see New Vision Television Inc. in Group Ownership). Former owner: News-Press & Gazette Co. (David R. Bradley 31%, Henry H. Bradley 21%, David R. Bradley Jr. 21%). Sale price: $110 million. FCC approved: September 7, 1993 [For the Record, September 27, 1993]. Note: Part of multi-stn purchase (see KOLD-TV Tucson, AZ]. Original owner: WSAV Inc. (Harben Daniel 52.78%, William K. Jenkins estate 19.83%, Arthur Lucas estate 19.83%, & others). Sale price: $4.75 million & $500,000 covenant not to compete. FCC approved: September 21, 1976 [For the Record, October 11, 1976].

WTOC-TV Savannah (ch 11)—Licensed to American Savannah Broadcasting, owned by American Family Corp. (see Group Ownership). Original owner: Savannah Broadcasting Co. (William T. Knight & family). Sale price: $7.72 million (including WTOC-AM-FM). FCC approved: August 8, 1979 [*Broadcasting*, August 20, 1979]. Note: WTOC-AM-FM were subsequently spun off for $1.2 million.

WCTV(TV) Thomasville (ch 6)—Licensed to John H. Phipps Broadcasting Stations Inc. (John H. Phipps). Original owner: E.D. Rivers Sr. Sale price: $88,700 for expenses & equipment plus assumption of $331,464 in obligations. FCC approved: May 11, 1955 [For the Record, May 23, 1955].

WVGA(TV) Valdosta (ch 44)—Licensed to Tallahassee Channel 27 Inc. (see Group Ownership). Former owner: The Morris Network. Sale price: $850,000. FCC approved: September 4, 1992 [For the Record, September 28, 1992]. Previous owner: Hi-Ho Television Stations. Sale price: $6.6 million (including WDHN(TV) Dothan, AL). FCC approved: July 18, 1986 [For the Record, June 16, 1986].

Hawaii

KGMD-TV Hilo (ch 9)—Licensed to Lee Enterprises Inc. Former owner: Heftel Television-Honolulu Inc. (90% owned by Heftel Broadcasting Corp. & 10% by Lani G. & James Donohoe Jr., daughter & son-in-law of Cecil & Joyce Heftel, principals of Heftel Broadcasting Corp.) Sale price: $10,000. FCC approved: September 10, 1985 (see KGMB-TV Honolulu). Previous owner: Heftel Broadcasting Corp. Former call letters: KPUA-TV. Note: Stn operates as a satellite of KGMB-TV Honolulu.

KHAW-TV Hilo (ch 11)—Licensed to Burnham Broadcasting Co. Former owner: Simpson Communications Inc. (nonprofit corporation owned by Simpson College, Indianola, IA). Sale price: unknown. FCC approved: March 10, 1986. Note: Simpson purchased stn from Western Sun Inc. after Western bought McCoy Broadcasting. (See KHON-TV Honolulu.) FCC approved: March 8, 1979.

KHBC-TV Hilo (ch 2)—Licensed to King Holding Corp. (owned 50% each by Providence Journal Co. & Kelso Partners IV). Former owner: King Broadcasting Co. Sale price: $355 million. FCC approved: August 27, 1991 [For the Record, September 9, 1991]. Note: Part of multi-stn purchase. (See KING-TV Seattle.) Previous owners: Clio Enterprises Inc., preceded by Hilo Broadcasting. Sale price of Clio-Hilo transaction: $325,000. FCC approved: April 1987 [For the Record, March 23, 1987].

KHIK(TV) Hilo (ch 14)—Licensed to LeSea Broadcasting Corp. Former owner: King Broadcasting Co. Sale price: $8,277 for CP. FCC approved: December 7, 1989 [For the Record, December 26, 1989].

KHVO-TV Hilo (ch 13)—Licensed to Tak Communications (see Group Ownership). Former owner: Shamrock Broadcasting Inc. (For details see KITV(TV) Honolulu.)

KBFD(TV) Honolulu (ch 32)—Licensed to Kea Sung Chung. Former owner: Leroy Allen. Sale price: $35,000 for CP. FCC approved: January 7, 1986 [For the Record, December 16, 1985].

KGMB-TV Honolulu (ch 9)—Licensed to Lee Enterprises Inc. Former owner: Heftel Broadcasting-Honolulu Inc., owned by Heftel Broadcasting Corp. (see Group Ownership). Sale price: $10.5 million (including KGMB(AM), KGMD-TV Hilo & KMAU-TV Wailuku; all HI). FCC approved: 1976. Previous owner: Pacific Broadcasting Inc. (80% owned by The Standard Corp.). Note: Mr. & Mrs. Heftel gained control of KGMB-AM-FM-TV Honolulu & KPUA-AM-TV Hilo; both HI, by exchanging all of their stock in Standard Corp. (25%) for all of Standard's stock (80%) in Pacific. Transfer of control involved no cash consideration. The Standard Corp. owns 80% of KUTV(TV) Salt Lake City. FCC approved: September 1972 [*Broadcasting*, September 25, 1972]. Note: Founded by Consolidated Amusement Corp. in 1952. Bought by Hialand Development Corp. in 1958 for $8.7 million including real estate. Honolulu *Star-Bulletin* became 24.5% owner in 1959 & later that year became 100% owner by paying $2.35 million for 75.5% interest. Honolulu *Star-Bulletin* sold stn (with KGMB(AM), KHBC-AM-TV Hilo & KMAU-TV Wailuku; all HI) to Pacific Broadcasting in 1965 for $2.5 million. FCC approved: May 5, 1965 [For the Record, May 10, 1965].

KHAI(TV) Honolulu (ch 20)—Licensed to KHAI Inc. Former owner: Honolulu Family Television Ltd. Sale price: $1.5 million (seller is subsidiary of Media Central Inc., Chattanooga, which filed for bankruptcy in 1987; sale was approved by Federal Bankruptcy Court of Eastern District of Tennessee). FCC approved: August 24, 1989 [For the Record, September 11, 1989].

KHNL(TV) Honolulu (ch 13)—Licensed to King Holding Corp. (owned 50% each by Providence Journal Co. & Kelso Partners IV). Former owner: King Broadcasting Co. (see Group Ownership). Sale price: $355 million. FCC approved: August 27, 1991 [For the Record, September 9, 1991]. Note: Part of multi-stn purchase. (See KING-TV Seattle). Previous owner: Mid-Pacific TV Assoc., owned by Hawaii-Nippon Communications Inc. (50%), Ten Tel Assoc. Inc (30%) & Transpacific TV Inc. (20%). FCC approved: May 5, 1986. Former call letters: KIKU-TV. Previous owner: United Broadcasting. Sale price: $2.3 million. FCC approved: November 28, 1979 [For the Record, December 10, 1979]. Original owners:

David Watumull & associates. Sale price: $700,000. FCC approved: 1966. Original call letters: KTRG-TV.

KHON-TV Honolulu (ch 2)—Licensed to Burnham Broadcasting. Former owner: Western Sun Inc., wholly owned by Des Moines Register & Tribune Company (see Cross-Ownership). Sale price: $47.5 million (including KAII-TV Wailuku, HI). FCC approved: August 23, 1985. Note: McCoy Broadcasting sold KHON-TV, KHAW-TV, KAII-TV & four radio stns (see Group Ownership) to Western as part of $27 million deal. FCC approved: March 8, 1979. Previous owner: Pacific & Southern Broadcasting Inc. (see Combined Communications Corp., Group Ownership). Sale price: $2.88 million (including KHAW-TV Hilo & KAII-TV Wailuku, both HI). FCC approved: January 17, 1973 [*Broadcasting*, January 29, 1973]. Note: Founded as KONA(TV) in 1952 by Herbert M. Richards. Bought by Honolulu Advertiser & J. Elroy McCaw subsequently sold out his interest to John D. Keating. Honolulu *Advertiser* & Keating, jointly, sold stn to Pacific & Southern in 1956 for $2.59 million (with KHAW-TV & KAII-TV). FCC approved: April 28, 1956 [For the Record, May 10, 1956].

KITV(TV) Honolulu (ch 4)—Licensed to Tak Communications Inc. (see Group Ownership). Former owner: Shamrock Broadcasting (owned by Roy E. Disney). Sale price: $50 million (including satellites KMAU(TV) Wailuku & KHVO(TV) Hilo, both HI). FCC approved: January 27, 1987 [For the Record, December 1, 1986]. Previous owner: Western Telestations Inc., owned 100% by Starr Broadcasting Group Inc. (see Group Ownership). Sale price: Part of $24 million deal (see WTVQ-TV Lexington, KY). Previous owner: Western Telestations Inc. [Lawrence S. Berger (51%), Mrs. Fred Goodstein (29%) & others]. Sale price: $4 million [including KHVO(TV)]. FCC approved: June 15, 1973 [For the Record, July 2, 1973]. Former call letters: KHVH-TV. Note: Founded in 1954 as KULA-TV by Dolph-Pettey group. Sold to Albert Zugsmith, Arthur Hogan & others in 1956 for $600,825 (with KULA). Sold to Kaiser Broadcasting in 1958 for $685,000 (with KULA) & call letters changed to KHVH-TV. Sold to Western Telestations (Lawrence S. Berger, et al) for $4.25 million [with KHVH-AM-FM & KHVO(TV)] in 1964. FCC approved: December 16, 1964 [For the Record, December 28, 1964].

KOBN(TV) Honolulu (ch 26)—Licensed to Oceania Broadcasting Network Inc. (Christopher Racine). Former owner: Mount Wilson FM Broadcasters Inc. (headed by Saul Levine). Sale price: $4.3 million (including KVHF(TV) Kailua-Kona, HI). Buyer shall assume certain liabilities & obligations of seller. Purchase price of $4.3 million includes covenant not to compete for period of five years, valued at $250,000. FCC approved: September 20, 1989 [For the Record, October 16, 1989]. Former call letters: KMGT(TV).

KWHE(TV) Honolulu (ch 14)—Licensed to LeSea Broadcasting Corp. (Lester Sumrall, et al). Former owner: Pacific Rim Broadcasting Co. Sale price: $825,000 for CP. FCC approved: August 15, 1986 [For the Record, June 16, 1986]. Former call letters: KDSC-TV.

KLEI(TV) Kailua-Kona (ch 6)—Licensed to Oceania Broadcasting Network Inc. Former call letters: KVHF(TV). See KOBN(TV) Honolulu.

KAII-TV Wailuku (ch 7)—See KHON-TV Honolulu.

KGMV(TV) Wailuku (ch 3)—Licensed to Lee Enterprises Inc. Former owner: Heftel Broadcasting-Maui Inc. (see Heftel Broadcasting Corp., Group Ownership). Sale price: $10,000. FCC approved: September 10, 1985. Previous owner: John S. Young Associates Inc. (John S. Young, 100%). Sale price: $95,000 with grant fee of $1,900. FCC approved: March 7, 1974 [For the Record, March 25, 1974]. Original call letters: KMAU-TV. Note: Honolulu *Star-Bulletin* (see KGMB-TV above) sold stn (with KHBC-AM-TV Hilo & KGMB-AM-TV Honolulu, both HI) to Pacific Broadcasting Inc. (A.L. Glasmann group) in 1965 for $2.5 million. FCC approved: May 5, 1965 [For the Record, May 10, 1965]. Pacific Broadcasting sold stn to John S. Young Associates Inc. Sale price: $1,500 per month rent for 10 years, with Pacific Broadcasting paying KMAU-TV for period of two years. FCC approved: May 5, 1965 [For the Record, May 10, 1965].

KMAU(TV) Wailuku (ch 12)—Licensed to Tak Communications Inc. Former owner: Shamrock Broadcasting Inc. (owned by Roy E. Disney). (For details of sale, see KITV(TV) Honolulu.) Previous owner: Western Telestations (Starr Broadcasting Group, see Group Ownership). Sale price: Part of $24 million deal (see WTVQ-TV Lexington, KY). Former call letters KMVI-TV. Original owner: Maui Publishing (J. Walter Cameron). Sale price: $70,000 (stn is satellite of Starr's KITV(TV) Honolulu). FCC approved: March 27, 1978 [For the Record, April 10, 1978].

KOGG(TV) Wailuku (ch 15)—Licensed to King Holding Corp. (owned 50% each by Providence Journal Co. & Kelso Partners IV) Former owner: King Broadcasting Co. Sale price: $355 million. FCC approved: August 27, 1991 [For the Record, September 9, 1991]. Note: Part of multi-stn purchase. (See KING-TV Seattle.)

Idaho

KBCI-TV Boise (ch 2)—Licensed to Eugene Television Inc. (see Group Ownership). Original owner: Boise Valley Broadcasters Inc. [Robert W. Howell (10.9%), H. Westerman Whillock (5.3%), Mrs. Stanley King (9.9%)]. Sale price: $2 million. FCC approved: August 31, 1976 [For the Record, September 27, 1976]. Original call letters: KBOI-TV.

KTVB(TV) Boise (ch 7)—Licensed to King Holding Corp. (owned 50% each by Providence Journal Co. & Kelso Partners IV) Former owner: King Broadcasting Co. Sale price: $355 million. FCC approved: August 27, 1991 [For the Record, September 9, 1991]. Note: Part of multi-stn purchase (see KING-TV Seattle). Previous owner: Georgia M. Davidson & family. Sale price: $14 million. FCC approved: February 22, 1980 [Changing Hands, March 3, 1980].

KHDT-TV Caldwell (ch 9)—Licensed to Schuyler Broadcasting Corp. (owned by William & Kristine M. Schuyler). Former owner: TRC Communications Inc. (owned by Donald E. Smullin). Sale price: $105,000 for CP. FCC approved: May 21, 1991 [For the Record, June 10, 1991]. Former call letters: KTMW(TV).

KIDK(TV) Idaho Falls (ch 3)—Licensed to Retlaw Enterprises. Former owner: Idaho Falls Broadcasting Co., owned by Price Broadcasting Co. (see Group Ownership). Sale price: $6.8 million. Original owner: Lucille J. Ricks, et al. Sale price: $4 million. FCC approved: October 2, 1984. Former call letters: KID-TV.

KLEW-TV Lewiston (ch 3)—Licensed to Retlaw Enterprises Inc. Former owner: NWG Broadcasting Corp. (John & Roger Noel). Sale price: $17 million (including KIMA-TV Yakima, & KEPR-TV Pasco, both WA). FCC approved: November 25, 1986 [For the Record, October 27, 1986].

KIVI(TV) Nampa (ch 6)—Licensed to Sawtooth Communications Inc. (see Evening Post Broadcasting Co., Cross-Ownership). Former owner: Futura Communications Corp. (Robert V. Hansberger). Sale price: approximately $11.5 million. FCC approved: July 1983 [Changing Hands, August 3, 1983]. Note: Founded in 1974 by co-owned Idaho Television Corp. & Eastern Idaho Television Corp. Sold to Futura for $655,580 in June 20, 1977 [For the Record, July 4, 1977].

KTRV(TV) Nampa (ch 12)—Licensed to Idaho Independent TV Inc. Former owner: Peyton Broadcasting Ltd. Sale price: $4.9 million. FCC approved: April 23, 1985 [For the Record, March 25, 1985].

KPVI(TV) Pocatello (ch 6)—Licensed to Ambassador Media Corp. (William R. Armstrong, pres). Former owner: Futura Communications Corp. (Robert Hansberger). Sale price: $3.2 million, including $500,000 non-complete agreement. FCC approved: October 26, 1983 [For the Record, November 14, 1983]. Original owner: Eastern Idaho TV Corp. Sale price: $655,850. FCC approved: 1977. Stn founded in 1974.

KBYN(TV) Twin Falls (ch 13, now deleted)—Licensed to Boise Valley Broadcasters Inc. (H. Westerman Whillock). Former owner: Samuel H. Bennion. Sale price: $3,000. FCC approved: May 17, 1967 [For the Record, May 29, 1967].

KMVT(TV) Twin Falls (ch 11)—Licensed to Susan Spear Root. Former owner: KMVT Broadcasting Inc. (owned by the Root Company). Sale price: no cash consideration in transfer of estate. FCC approved: January 30, 1991 [For the Record, February 18, 1991]. Previous owner: Western Broadcasting Co. Sale price: $11.4 million. FCC approved: January 6, 1984. Previous owner: KLIX Corp. (Glassman Stations). Sale price: $883,000. FCC approved: 1970. Original owners: J. Robb Brady Trust Co., Frank C. Carman & Grant R. Wrathall. Sale price: $95,598 (with KLIX-AM). FCC approved: March 7, 1956 [For the Record, March 12, 1956]. Original call letters: KLIX-TV.

Illinois

WEHS(TV) Aurora (ch 60)—Licensed to Silver King Broadcasting (owned by Home Shopping Network Inc.). Former owner: Metrowest Corp. (owned by Fred Eychaner). Sale price: $25 million. FCC approved: December 4, 1986 [For the Record, November 10, 1986]. Former call letters: WPWR-TV.

WYZZ-TV Bloomington (ch 43)—Licensed to Bloomington Comco Inc. Former owner: Midwest Television Associates [Paul A. Misch, James I. Bliss, Ren Lafferty, Edward Saari, Steward & Jane Ann Bell Coddington (20% each)]. Sale price: $500,000. FCC approved: June 14, 1985 [For the Record, May 13, 1985]. Former call letters: WBLN(TV). Previous owner: Grace Communications. Sale price: $1.9 million. FCC approved: August 16, 1983. Original owner: Cecil W. Roberts. FCC approved: July 13, 1955 [For the Record, July 18, 1955].

WICD(TV) Champaign (ch 15)—Licensed to Plains TV Corp. (see Group Ownership). Original owners: Gannett Pub. Corp. Sale price: $75,000. FCC approved: July 27, 1960 [For the Record, August 8, 1960]. Original call letters: WDAN-TV.

WBBM-TV Chicago (ch 2)—Licensed to CBS Inc. Original owner: Balaban & Katz Inc. (subsidiary of United Paramount Theaters Inc.). Sale price: $6 million. FCC approved: February 9, 1953 [For the Record, February 16, 1953]. Original call letters: WBKB(TV).

WCFC(TV) Chicago (ch 38)—Licensed to Christian Communications of Chicagoland Inc. Former owner: Chicago Federation of Labor & Industrial Union Council. Sale price: $850,000 for CP. FCC approved: January 16, 1976 [For the Record, February 2, 1976]. Original call letters: WCFL-TV.

WCIU-TV Chicago (ch 26)—Licensed to Weigel Broadcasting Co. (Howard Shapiro 65%). Sale price: acquired additional 35% from J.W. O'Connor for $616,949. FCC approved: March 22, 1977 [For the Record, April 18, 1977].

WFLD(TV) Chicago (ch 32)—Licensed to Fox Television Stations Inc. (see Group Ownership). Former owner: Metromedia Inc. (see Group Ownership). (For details, see WNYW(TV) New York.) Previous owner: Field Communications (wholly owned subsidiary of Field Enterprises Inc.). Sale price: $136 million. FCC approved: February 17, 1983 [For the Record, March 7, 1983]. Note: Founded as WOGO-TV by Television Chicago (Winnebago Television Corp., Transcontinental Properties Inc., & Froelich & Friedland). Sold January 18, 1965 to New Television Chicago Group for $2 million with Froelich & Friedland retaining interest, & Field, 50% owner, obtaining option to purchase remaining 50% for $2.5 million. In 1970, Field bought the remaining 50% from Harry & Elmer Balaban, et al for $2.5 million. FCC approved: April 1, 1970 [For the Record, April 13, 1970]. Kaiser Broadcasting & Field entered into a merger of five independent Kaiser UHFs & WFLD-TV in May 1973 [*Broadcasting*, May 14, 1973]. Field completed purchase of Kaiser/Field group by purchasing 77.5% of this stn plus same interest in KBHK-TV San Francisco; WLVI-TV Cambridge, MA; WKBD-TV Detroit; & WKBS-TV Burlington, NJ, for $42.62 million in 1977 [*Broadcasting*, August 8, 1977].

WIND-TV Chicago (ch 20, now deleted)—Licensed to Westinghouse Broadcasting Co. (see Group Ownership). Original owner: WIND Inc. (Chicago Daily News-Ralph L. Atlass & family). Sale price: $5.3 million (including WIND). FCC approved: November 8, 1956 [For the Record, November 12, 1956].

WLS-TV Chicago (ch 7)—Licensed to Capital Cities/ABC Inc. Former owner: ABC Inc. Sale price: $3.417 billion (including WABC(TV) New York; KABC(TV) Los Angeles; KGO(TV) San Francisco; WXYZ-TV Detroit; plus all other ABC broadcasting & publishing properties). FCC approved: December 1985 [For the Record, July 15, 1985]. Note: This was change of ownership when ABC merged with United Paramount Theatres Inc. Original owner: American Broadcasting Co. FCC approved: February 9, 1953 [For the Record, February 16, 1953]. Former call letters: WBKB-TV. Original call letters: WENR-TV.

WMAQ-TV Chicago (ch 5)—Licensed to National Broadcasting Company Inc. Sale price: General Electric Company acquired RCA Corp., including NBC, for $6.28 billion. FCC approved: June 5, 1986.

WSNS(TV) Chicago (ch 44)—Licensed to Video 44 joint venture [Oak Industries (49%); Harriscope of Chicago Inc. (see Group Ownership) & Essaness Theater Corp. (25.5% each)]. Former owner: Harriscope & Essaness. Sale price: $7.35 million for 49% of stn. FCC approved:

July 11, 1980 [Changing Hands, July 28, 1980]. Previous owners: River Grove Theater Corp., Velma Entertainment Corp. & Riverdale Drive-In Inc. (together 50%) & Harriscope of Chicago Inc. (50%). Original owner: Essaness Television Associates terminated its existence & transferred rights to Essaness TV Corp., which merged into River Grove Theater.

***WXXW-TV Chicago (ch 20)**—Licensed to Chicago Metropolitan Higher Education Council. Former owner: Chicago Educational Television Association. Sale price: $65,000. FCC approved: June 10, 1977 [For the Record, June 27, 1977].

WAND(TV) Decatur (ch 17)—Licensed to WAND TV Inc. (owned by LIN Broadcasting Co., see Group Ownership). Former owner: Metromedia Inc. Sale price: $2 million. FCC approved: December 22, 1965 [For the Record, January 3, 1966]. Former call letters: WTVP(TV). Note: Founded by William A. Schellabarger & Associates. Bought by George A. Bolas & Associates in 1958 for $200,000 plus $20,000 yearly lease of premises for five years. Metromedia bought stn in 1960 for $570,000.

WIFR(TV) Freeport (ch 23)—Licensed to Benedek Broadcasting Inc. (see Group Ownership). Former owner: Worrell Broadcasting Inc., subsidiary of Worrell Newspapers Inc. (see Cross-Ownership). Sale price: $40 million (including WHSV-TV Harrisonburg, VA, & WBNB-TV Charlotte Amalie, VI). FCC approved: November 15, 1986 [For the Record, September 29, 1986]. Former call letters: WIFR-TV. Previous owner: WCEE-TV Inc. (subsidiary of General Media Inc.). Sale price: $3.87 million. FCC approved: April 11, 1977 [For the Record, April 25, 1977]. Former call letters: WCEE-TV. Note: WCEE-TV Inc. (Rock River Television Corp.) & WCEE Inc., both subsidiaries of General Media, merged. FCC approved: February 11, 1975.

WHP-TV Harrisburg (ch 21)—Licensed to WHP Televison Ltd. (Ralph E. Becker). Former owner: WHP Inc. Sale price: $9.25 million. FCC approved: 1993 [For the Record, September 6, 1993].

WSIL-TV Harrisburg (ch 3)—Licensed to WSIL-TV Inc. (see Mel Wheeler Inc., Group Ownership). Former owner: John Kirby, et al. Sale price: $6.6 million (including satellite KPOB-TV Poplar Bluff, MO). FCC approved: May 12, 1983 [For the Record, June 6, 1983]. Note: In 1974 FCC granted involuntary transfer of control of Turner-Farrar Association (partnership) from Harry R. Horning to Bernice Horning, executrix of estate of Mr. Horning. FCC approved: August 30, 1974 [For the Record, September 16, 1974]. Control taken by Turners, excluding B. Horning. Sale price: $578,000 eventually paid for 100% of stn. FCC approved: November 7, 1974 [For the Record, November 25, 1974]. Turner-Farrar sold to group headed by M. Nicholes & John Kirby. Sale price: $2.16 million, including KPOB-TV & 70% of WEBQ-AM-FM Harrisburg [*Broadcasting*, May 11, 1981].

WGBO(TV) Joliet (ch 66)—Licensed to Grant Broadcasting of Chicago. Former owner: Focus Broadcasting of Chicago. Sale price: $2 million plus $7 million loan agreement. FCC approved: October 30, 1985 [For the Record, August 5, 1985]. Former call letters: WFBN(TV).

WTCT(TV) Marion (ch 27)—Licensed to Tri-State Christian TV. Former owner: Dennis Doelitzsch. Sale price: $1.2 million. FCC approved: May 29, 1984. Former call letters: WDDD-TV.

WQAD-TV Moline (ch 8)—Licensed to The New York Times Co. (see Cross-Ownership). Former owner: Quad-Cities Communications Corp. (subsidiary of Des Moines (IA) Register Tribune Co.). Sale price: $25.3 million. Previous owner: Moline Television Corp. Sale price: $9.62 million, plus $375,000 covenant not to compete. FCC approved: July 13, 1977 [For the Record, August 1, 1977].

WCEE(TV) Mount Vernon (ch 13)—Licensed to Sudbrink Broadcasting (see Group Ownership). Former owner: Pyramid Broadcasting. Sale price: $3.6 million. FCC approved: October 30, 1985 [For the Record, September 30, 1985].

WEEK-TV Peoria (ch 25)—Licensed to Granite Broadcasting Corp. (principally owned by W. Don Cornwell). Former owner: Eagle Broadcasting Corp. (owned by Price Communications Corp.). Sale price: $33 million (tax certificate involved). FCC approved: May 1988 [Changing Hands, May 30, 1988]. Previous owner: LDX Group. Sale price: $28 million (including KRCG(TV) Jefferson City, MO). FCC approved: November 11, 1984. Previous owner: West Central Broadcasting. Sale price: $2.93 million. FCC approved: 1972.

WHOI(TV) Peoria (ch 19)—Licensed to Adams Television of Peoria, owned by Paul A. Brissette (see Group Ownership). Former owner: Adams Communications Corp. (see Group Ownership). Sale price: Undisclosed (including WWLP(TV) Springfield, MA; WILX-TV Onondaga, MI; KOSA-TV Odessa & KAUZ-TV Wichita Falls, both TX; WMTV(TV) Madison & WSAW-TV Wausau, both WI; & WTRF-TV Wheeling, WV). FCC approved: December 24, 1991 [For the Record, January 27, 1992]. Previous owner: Forward of Illinois Inc. (see Wesray Communications Corp., Group Ownership). Sale price: $126.5 million (including KOSA-TV Odessa, TX; WTRF-TV Wheeling, WV; WMTV(TV) Madison, WI; & WSAW-TV Wausau, WI). FCC approved: March 1, 1988. Previous owner: Forward Communications. (For details of 1984 sale, see WSAW-TV Wausau, WI.) Previous owner: Mid-America Media Inc. (see Group Ownership). Sale price: $2.75 million. FCC approved: March 24, 1971 [*Broadcasting*, March 29, 1971]. Former call letters: WRAU-TV, WIRL-TV. Note: Founded in 1953 by Hugh R. Norman & Edward C. Schoede. Sold to Hilltop Broadcasting (55.66% owned by Peoria *Star-Journal*) in 1954 for $210,000. Bought by Metromedia Inc. (see Group Ownership) in 1959 for $610,000. Former call letters: WTVH(TV). Purchased by Mid-America Media Inc. in 1965 for $2.2 million. FCC approved: July 21, 1965 [For the Record, July 26, 1965].

WMBD-TV Peoria (ch 31)—Licensed to Midwest TV Inc. (see Group Ownership). Original owners: Charles C. Caley (51%) & John E. Fetzer (49%). Sale Price: $1.85 million (including WMBD-AM-FM). FCC approved: June 15, 1960 [For the Record, June 10, 1960].

KHQA-TV Quincy (ch 7)—Licensed to Benedek Broadcasting. Former owner: Lee Enterprises Inc. Sale price: $13 million. FCC approved: October 30, 1986 [For the Record, September 22, 1986].

WHBF-TV Rock Island (ch 4)—Licensed to Citadel Communications Co. (see Group Ownership). Previous owner: Rock Island Broadcasting Co. (Ann Potter Delong, et al). Sale price: $21 million (including WHBF(AM-FM), to be sold by Citadel). FCC approved: November 28, 1986 [For the Record, November 17, 1986].

WQRF-TV Rockford (ch 39)—Licensed to Petracom Inc. Former owner: Communications Investment Corp. [owned by Ian N. (Sandy) Wheeler, et al]. Sale price: $2 million. FCC approved: September 12, 1989 [For the Record, October 2, 1989]. Previous owner: Orion Broadcast Group. Sale price: $3.75 million. FCC approved: March 31, 1986 [For the Record, March 3, 1986]. Previous owner: Lloyd Hearing Aid Corp. Sale price: $4 million. FCC approved: February 29, 1984.

WREX-TV Rockford (ch 13)—Licensed to WREX Associates (owned by M.L. Media Partners). Former owner: Gilmore Broadcasting Corp. Sale price: $18 million. FCC approved: July 1987 [Changing Hands, June 22, 1987]. Previous owner: WREX-TV Inc. (see Gannett Co. Stations in Group Ownership). Sale price: $6.85 million. FCC approved: August 29, 1969 [For the Record, September 8 1969]. Note: Founded in September 1953 by Swan Hillman & Associates. Sold to WREX-TV Inc. in June 1963 for $3.42 million.

WTVO(TV) Rockford (ch 17)—Licensed to Young Broadcasting Inc. (subsidiary of Adam Young Station Reps). Former owner: Winnebago Television Corp. (Elmer Balaban). Sale price: $18 million. FCC approved: July 27, 1998 [For the Record, August 15, 1988].

WICS(TV) Springfield (ch 20)—Licensed to Guy Gannett Broadcasting. Former owner: WICS Inc. (Larry Israel & Steven Kumble, principals). Sale price: $18 million. FCC approved: January 31, 1985. Previous owner: Plains Television Corp. (see Group Ownership). Sale price: $10.7 million. FCC approved: April 7, 1980 [Changing Hands, April 14, 1980].

WRSP-TV Springfield (ch 55)—Licensed to Springfield Independent TV Co. (owned by Bahakel Communications Inc., see Group Ownership). Former owner: Windmill Broadcasting Co. (group of 23 stockholders headed by William Wingarter, pres). Sale price: $734,000. FCC approved: March 15, 1982 [For the Record, March 29, 1982]. Former call letters: WBHW(TV).

WCCU-TV Urbana (ch 27)—Licensed to Springfield Independent Television Co. Inc. (owned by Bahakel Communications Inc.). Former owner: Urbana Channel 27 Inc. (Gerald Fitzgerald). Sale price: $3 million, estimated. Note: The proposed sale to Springfield Independent Television of the construction permit for $50,000 was dismissed at Urbana's request in 1986. [For the Record, May 26, 1986].

Indiana

WKKF(TV) Anderson (ch 67)—Licensed to Anderson Corp. Former owner: Greater Indianapolis Broadcasters. Sale price: $51,381. FCC approved: September 6, 1985 [For the Record, July 1, 1985]. Previous owner: Indiana Telecasters Inc. Sale price: no financial consideration. FCC approved: February 21, 1985 [For the Record, March 18, 1985].

WINM(TV) Angola (ch 63)—Licensed to Tri-State Christian TV (owned by Garth W. & Christina Coonce, & their daughters, Julie A. Nolan & Victoria M. Clark). Former owner: Tri-State Broadcasting Corp. (owned by Paul E. Paino & his sons, Paul C. & Philip C. Paino). Sale price: $400,000. FCC approved: January 24, 1991 [For the Record, February 11, 1991]. Previous owner: Manna for Modern Man Inc., preceded by James A. Chase. Sale price of Manna-Chase transaction: $300,000. FCC approved: October 1, 1985 [For the Record, August 12, 1985]. Former call letters: WBKZ(TV).

WTTV(TV) Bloomington (ch 4)—Licensed to Atlantic Broadcasting Co. [headed by Better Communications Inc. (60% gen ptnr), CEA Investors Partnership (40% gen ptnr), Barry Baker & Larry D. Marcus]. Former owner: WTTV Inc. (headed by Jim Goodmon, who acquired minority interest in assignee). Sale price: $37 million (including WTTK(TV) Kokomo, IN). FCC approved: May 31, 1991 [For the Record, June 17, 1991]. Previous owner: Tel-Am Associates Ltd., preceded by Teleco Indiana Inc. Sale price of Tel-Am/Teleco transaction: $73 million. FCC approved: March 23, 1984. Previous owner: Sarkes Tarzian Inc. Sale price: $26 million. FCC approved: 1977.

WSJV(TV) Elkhart (ch 28)—Licensed to WSJV Television Inc., owned by Quincy Newspapers (see Quincy Broadcasting Co., Cross-Ownership). Original owner: Truth Publishing Co. (see Truth Radio Corp., Cross-Ownership). Sale price: $3.2 million. FCC approved: March 31, 1975 [For the Record, April 14, 1975].

WEHT(TV) Evansville (ch 25)—Licensed to Gilmore Broadcasting Corp. (see Group Ownership). Former owner: Henry S. Hilberg (17.3% personally & 17.3% as trustee), Edwin G. Richter (20.7%), & others. Sale price: $4.2 million (including KGUN-TV Tucson, AZ). FCC approved: July 20, 1964 [For the Record, July 27, 1964]. Note: Founded in 1953 by Malco Theatres Inc. Sold to Hilberg group in 1956 for $820,000.

WEVV(TV) Evansville (ch 44)—Licensed to Ralph C. Wilson Industries. Former owner: Ohio Valley TV Inc. Sale price: $3.1 million, plus assumption of $1.26 million debt. FCC approved: December 27, 1985 [For the Record, November 25, 1985].

WFIE-TV Evansville (ch 14)—Licensed to Cosmos Broadcasting Corp. Former owner: Orion Broadcasting. Sale price: Sale is part of $110 million Cosmos purchase of Orion Broadcasting, which included WAVE-TV Louisville; WMT-TV Cedar Rapids, IA; WFRV-TV Green Bay, WI; & WJMN-TV Escanaba, MI; & 3 radio stns. Orion spun off WAVE(AM) Louisville; WFRV-TV Green Bay; WJMN-TV Escanaba, MI; & WMT-TV Cedar Rapids, IA to comply with FCC multiple ownership rules [Changing Hands, August 31, 1981]. Original owners: Grand Carlton Corp. (Jesse D. Fine & Family). Sale price: $586,937. FCC approved: July 19, 1956 [For the Record, July 30, 1956].

WTVW(TV) Evansville (ch 7)—Licensed to BANAM Broadcasting Inc. Former owner: Indiana Partners Ltd. (Charles Woods, et al). Sale price: assumption of debt (including KDEB(TV) Springfield, MO; KARD(TV) West Monroe, LA; & KLBK-TV Lubbock, TX). FCC approved: March 16, 1993 [For the Record, April 5, 1993]. Previous owner: Fuqua Industries Inc. Sale price: $21.5 million. FCC approved: November 17, 1980 [Changing Hands, December 1, 1980]. Previous owner: Polaris Corp. Sale price: Stock exchange value at about $3.8 million plus assumption of $3 million in obligations (with 80.8% of KTHI-TV Fargo, ND, & KXOA-AM-FM Sacramento, CA). FCC approved: September 23, 1966 [For the Record, October 3, 1966]. Previous owner: Ferris E. Traylor, Rex Schepp & Miklos Sperling. Sale price: $514,800 for 90.4% of stn. FCC approved: 1962.

WANE-TV Fort Wayne (ch 15)—Licensed to Indiana Broadcasting Corp. (owned by LWWI Broadcasting Inc., see LIN Broadcasting in Group Ownership). Former owner: Belo Broadcasting (see Group Ownership). Sale price: $104.9 million (including WISH-TV Indianapolis). FCC approved: November 28, 1983 [For the Record, December 19, 1983]. Note: Belo purchased stn from Corinthian Broadcasting, a subsidiary of Dun & Bradstreet Companies, as part of a $606 million deal (see KHOU-TV Houston). Belo owned stn for a legal instant

& sold the two stns to LWWI). Universal Broadcasting Co. (C. Bruce McConnell & associates) purchased Fort Wayne Stations in June 1956 from R. Morris Pierce, Frederick W. Wolf, John F. Patt & associates for $800,000 [For the Record, June 25, 1956]. Indiana Broadcasting Co. (owned by J.H. Whitney & Co.) purchased WANE-TV from Universal in October 1956 for $10 million (with WANE-AM & WISH-AM-TV Indianapolis). FCC approved: October 10, 1956 [For the Record, October 15. 1956]. Stn was merged with Corinthian Broadcasting into Dun & Bradstreet Companies Inc. for stock valued at $137 million (with KXTV(TV) Sacramento, CA; KOTV(TV) Tulsa, OK; KHOU-TV Houston; & WISH-TV Indianapolis). FCC approved: April 14, 1971 [*Broadcasting*, April 19, 1971]. Original call letters: WINT(TV).

WFFT-TV Fort Wayne (ch 55)—Licensed to Williams Communications Inc. Former owner: Great Trails Broadcasting Corp. Sale price: unknown. (Sale included WHAG-TV Hagerstown, MD; WING(AM) Dayton, WGTZ(FM) Eaton, WIZE(AM) Springfield, WCOL(AM)/WXGT(FM) Columbus, all OH; WBCS(AM/FM) Milwaukee; & WCII(AM)/WDJX(FM) Louisville.) FCC approved: November 24, 1986 [Changing Hands, September 15, 1986]. Original owner: Ontario Corp. (group of 46 stockholders headed by Van P. Smith, pres & 35% own). Sale price: $3.3 million plus assumption of $450,000 in liabilities. FCC approved: June 1, 1982 [For the Record, June 21, 1982].

WKJG-TV Fort Wayne (ch 33)—Licensed to Corporation for General Trade (owned by Joseph A. Cloutier, trustee, The Joseph R. Cloutier Trust). Former owner: Thirty-Three Inc. (The Corporation for General Trust, owned by Joseph R. Cloutier). Sale price: no financial consideration. FCC approved: March 12, 1990. Previous owner: Wabash Valley Broadcasting Corp. (Anton Hulman Jr., et al). Sale price: $425,000 plus 23% of Wabash Valley Broadcasting. FCC approved: November 23, 1983. Previous owner: Federated Media Inc. (Paul E. Van Hook, pres, & John Dille Jr., chmn of bd). Sale price: $4 million. FCC approved: July 29, 1974 [For the Record, August 19, 1974]. Note: WKJG Inc. purchased stn from original owners (Walter L. Thomas & associates) in 1957. Sale price: $1.92 million (with WKJG). FCC approved: March 13, 1957 [For the Record, March 18, 1957]. WKJG Inc. [John F. Dille, 15%; Truth Publishing Co., controlled by Mr. Dille & his family & publisher of the Elkhart (IN) *Truth* (60%), Walter R. Beardsley (25%)] sold stn to Television Communications Corp. in 1971 for $6 million. FCC approved: March 10, 1971 [*Broadcasting*, March 29, 1971]. Spun off to Federated Media when Television Communications Corp. was sold to Warner Communications, Inc. [*Broadcasting*, February 7, 1972].

WPTA(TV) Fort Wayne (ch 21)—Licensed to Granite Broadcasting Corp. Former owner: Pulitzer Broadcasting Co. Sale price: $25.15 million. FCC approved: September 25, 1989 [For the Record, October 9, 1989]. Previous owner: WPTA(TV) Inc. (Gannett Co.). Sale price: $8.62 million. FCC approved: May 12, 1983 [For the Record, May 23, 1983]. Previous owner: Combined Communications Corp. CCC was acquired by Gannett Co. in 1979. For details, see KPNX-TV Phoenix. Original owner: Sarkes Tarzian Inc. Sale price: $3.62 million. FCC approved: 1973. Note: Stn on air September 28, 1957.

WGMI(TV) Gary (ch 56, now deleted)—Licensed to Family Stations Inc. (see Group Ownership). Previous owner: General Media Television Inc. (Earl B. Glickman, et al). Sale price: $20,000 for CP. FCC approved: February 24, 1971 [For the Record, March 8, 1971].

WHMB-TV Indianapolis (ch 40)—Licensed to LeSea Broadcasting Corp. (nonprofit corporation affiliated with evangelist Lester Sumrall). Original owner: White River Radio Corp. Sale price: $354,618. FCC approved: August 15, 1972 [For the Record, September 4, 1972]. Former call letters: WURD(TV).

WISH-TV Indianapolis (ch 8)—Licensed to Indiana Broadcasting Corp. (owned by LWWI Broadcasting Inc., see LIN Broadcasting, Group Ownership). Former owner: Belo Broadcasting (see Group Ownership). Sale price: $104.9 million, including WANE-TV Fort Wayne. FCC approved: November 28, 1983 [For the Record, December 19, 1983]. Note: Belo purchased stn from Corinthian Broadcasting, a subsidiary of Dun & Bradstreet Companies, as part of a $606 million deal. Belo owned stn for a legal instant, then sold the two stns to LWWI. Indiana Broadcasting Corp. purchased WISH-TV from original owner, Universal Broadcasting Co. (C. Bruce McConnell & associates), in October 1956. Sale price: $10 million (with WISH & WANE-AM-TV Fort Wayne). FCC approved: October 10, 1956 [For the Record, October 15, 1956]. Stn was merged with Corinthian Broadcasting into Dun & Bradstreet Companies Inc., for stock valued at $137 million (with KXTV(TV) Sacramento, CA; KOTV(TV) Tulsa, OK; KHOU-TV Houston; & WANE-TV Fort Wayne, IN). FCC approved: April 14, 1971 [*Broadcasting*, April 19, 1971].

WRTV(TV) Indianapolis (ch 6)—Licensed to McGraw-Hill Broadcasting Co. (see Group Ownership). Former owner: Time-Life Broadcasting Inc. Sale price: $57.18 million (including KERO-TV Bakersfield & KGTV(TV) San Diego, both CA; & KMGH-TV Denver). FCC approved: March 8, 1972 [*Broadcasting*, March 13, 1972; May 15, 1972]. Note: original owner Consolidated TV & Radio Broadcastrs Inc. (Harry M. Bitner interests) sold stn to Time-Life in 1957 as part of a package deal including WFBM(AM); WOOD-AM-TV Grand Rapids, MI; & WTCN-AM-TV Minneapolis for $15.75 million. FCC approved: April 17, 1957 [For the Record, April 22, 1957]. Former call letters: WFBM-TV.

WTHR(TV) Indianapolis (ch 13)—Licensed to VideoIndiana, Inc, subsidiary of The Dispatch Printing Co. (see Group Ownership). Original owner: Avco Broadcasting Corp. (see Group Ownership). Sale price: $17.65 million. FCC approved: August 11, 1975 [For the Record, September 1, 1975]. Original call letters: WLWI(TV).

WXIN(TV) Indianapolis (ch 59)—Licensed to Renaissance Communications. Former owner: Chase Broadcasting of Washington. Sale price: $126.6 million in group purchase (For details of sale, see WATL(TV) Atlanta, GA). FCC approved: January 11, 1993 [For the Record, February 1, 1993]. Previous owner: Outlet Communications Group. Sale price: $120 million [including WATL(TV) Atlanta & WTOP(AM)-WASH(FM) Washington (see Changing Hands, August 14, 1990)]. FCC approved: January 22, 1990. Former owner: Rockefeller Group Inc. (For details of sale, see WCMH(TV) Columbus, OH.) Original owner: Anacomp (80%) & Herb & Mel Simon (20%). Sale price: $22 million. FCC approved: December 26, 1984 [For the Record, January 21, 1985]. Original call letters: WPDS(TV).

WTTK(TV) Kokomo (ch 29)—Licensed to Atlantic Broadcasting Co. [headed by Better Communications Inc. (60% gen ptnr), CEA Investors Partnership (40% gen ptnr), Barry Baker & Larry D. Marcus]. Former owner: WTTV Inc. (headed by Jim Goodmon, who acquired minority interest in assignee). Sale price: $37 million (including WTTV(TV) Bloomington, IN). FCC approved: May 31, 1991 [For the Record, June 17, 1991].

WLFI-TV Lafayette (ch 18)—Licensed to WLFI-TV Inc. (owned by Toledo Blade Co., with various media interests). Former owner: Wooster Republican Printing Co. (Richard F. Shively & brother, Harold). Sale price: $3.15 million. FCC approved: September 13, 1979. Previous owner: Sarkes Tarzian Inc. (see Group Ownership). Sale price: $250,000. FCC approved: November 3, 1967 [For the Record, November 13, 1967]. Former call letters: WFAM-TV. Previous owner: Lafayette Broadcasting Inc. (Henry Rosenthal, et al). Sale price: $65,000. FCC approved: May 15, 1959 [For the Record, May 25, 1959]. Note: Stn was bcstg on Channel 59 at that time & was sold with CP for Channel 18. Original owner: Olney E. Richardson. Sale price: $330,000 (with WASK(AM) Lafayette). FCC approved: February 21, 1957 [For the Record, February 25, 1957].

WMCC(TV) Marion (ch 23)—Licensed to Gerald J. Robinson. Former owner: Mississinewa Communications Corp. Sale price: $52,168 for CP. FCC approved: May 30, 1986. Previous owner: Rodney Funk. Sale price: $52,168 for CP. FCC approved: October 7, 1985 [For the Record, March 4, 1985].

WSFD-TV Marion (ch 31, now deleted)—Licensed to R. David Boyer, trustee in bankruptcy. Former owner: Geneco Broadcasting Inc. (Anthony R. Martin-Trigona (81%) & others). Sale price: no financial consideration. FCC approved: May 8, 1969 [For the Record, May 19, 1969]. Note: Founded in 1962 by Eugene C. Thompson. Controlling interest sold to Northern Indiana Broadcasters (William N. Udell & others) in 1963. Northern Indiana sold 76% to Geneco, October 31, 1968, for $157,000. Original call letters: WTAF(TV).

WIPB(TV) Muncie (ch 49)—Licensed to Ball State University. Original owner: Tri-City Radio Corp. [Donald A. Burton (51%), William F. Craig estate (46.5%) & others]. Sale price: $125,000. FCC approved: October 26, 1971 [For the Record, December 6, 1971]. Original call letters: WLBC-TV.

WHME-TV South Bend (ch 46)—Licensed to Lester Sumrall Evangelistic Association. Former owner: Gordon G. McKenzie, trustee of G & E Religious & Educational Broadcasting Corp. Sale price: $496,000. FCC approved: June 10, 1977 [For the Record, June 27, 1977]. Former call letters: WMSH-TV.

WBAK-TV Terre Haute (ch 38)—Licensed to Terre Haute Independent Broadcasters, owned by Bahakel Broadcasting Co. (see Group Ownership). Former owner: Alpha Broadcasting Corp. Sale price: $649,000. FCC approved: February 28, 1977 [For the Record, March 21, 1977]. Former call letters: WIIL-TV.

WTHI-TV Terre Haute (ch 10)—Licensed to Hulman & Company. Former owner: Wabash Valley Broadcasting Corp. Sale price: Unavailable (including WTHI-AM-FM Terre Haute, WFTX(TV) Cape Coral & WOGX(TV) Ocala, both FL. FCC approved: July 13, 1992 [For the Record, November 2, 1992].

WTWO(TV) Terre Haute (ch 2)—Licensed to TCS Television Partners. Former owner: Illiana Telecasting Corp. (subsidiary of Fabri Development Co., 100% owned by Malcolm I. Glazer). Sale price: $56 million (including WRBL(TV) Columbus, GA, & KQTV(TV) St. Joseph, MO). FCC approved: April 6, 1990. Previous owner: Illiana Telecasting Corp. (James E. Sauter, et al, trustees; see Booth American Co., Group Ownership). Sale price: $4.65 million. FCC approved: July 18, 1975 [For the Record, August 4, 1975]. Note: Illiana forced to sell stn because of common ownership rules. James E. Sauter, et al, purchased stn from James Raymond Livesay (25%), et al, in 1971. Sale price: $5 million. FCC approved: January 6, 1971 [For the Record, January 18, 1971].

***WVUT(TV) Vincennes (ch 22)**—Licensed to Board of Trustees for Vincennes University (Fr. Issac K. Beckes, et al). Previous owner: Board of Trustees for Vincennes University (Clarence J. McCormick, Curtis Shake, et al). Sale price: no financial consideration. FCC approved: September 16, 1976 [For the Record, October 11, 1976]. Note: Transfer, which included *WVUB(FM) Vincennes, was for the purpose of a reconstitution of the bd of dirs.

Iowa

KCRG-TV Cedar Rapids (ch 9)—Licensed to Cedar Rapids TV Co. (owned by Cedar Rapids *Gazette*). Original owners: Myron N. Blank, Harrison E. Spangler & associates (70%) & Cedar Rapids *Gazette* (30%). Sale price: $101,500 for Cedar Rapids *Gazette* purchase of remaining 70% interest (with KCRG-AM). FCC approved: August 12, 1954 [For the Record, August 23, 1954]. Original call letters: KCRI-TV.

KGAN(TV) Cedar Rapids (ch 2)—Licensed to WHYN Stations Corp. (owned by Guy Gannett Broadcasting Services Inc., subsidiary of Guy Gannett Publishing Co.; see Group Ownership). Former owner: Orion Broadcasting Inc. Sale price: $13 million. FCC approved: August 14, 1981. Former call letters: WMT-TV. Note: Sale was spin-off from Orion-Cosmos merger [*Broadcasting*, June 16, 1980]. Original owner: American Broadcasting Systems. Sale price: $7.5 million, including WMT-FM. FCC approved: 1968.

KDAV(TV) Davenport (ch 30)—Licensed to Linton Broadcasting Corp. (Linda & Anthony Estavez). Former owner: Peggy & Donald Tucker. Sale price: $30,997 (stn unbuilt). FCC approved: February 6, 1985 [For the Record, February 18, 1985].

KLJB-TV Davenport (ch 18)—Licensed to Quad Cities Television Acquisition (headed by Milton Grant, John H. Markley, William D. Towe, Gregory B. Maffei, & Huntsville Television Holdings Corp.). Former owner: Davenport Comm. Ltd (headed by Gary Brandt & Richard Greenblatt). Sale price: $3.706 million. FCC approved: April 1, 1991 [For the Record April 15, 1991].

KWQC(TV) Davenport (ch 6)—Licensed to Broad Street Television Corp. Former owner: Palmer Communications Inc. Sale price: $45.82 million. FCC approved: July 19, 1989 [For the Record, August 7, 1989].

KBTV-TV Des Moines (ch 63)—Licensed to Home Town Broadcasters Inc. (owned by John Menard). Former owner: Iowa Television Authority Corp. Sale price: $55,000 for CP. FCC approved: June 9, 1987 [For the Record, April 13, 1987].

KCCI-TV Des Moines (ch 8)—Licensed to KCCI-TV Broadcasting Inc. (owned by H & C Communications). Former owner: Cowles Broadcasting. Sale price: $182.5 million (including WESH-TV Daytona Beach-Orlando, FL). FCC approved: October 24, 1984.

KDSM(TV) Des Moines (ch 17)—Licensed to River City Partners Ltd. (headed by Atlantic Broadcasting Inc.) Former owner: Duchossois Communications Co. of Iowa (headed by Rolland Johnson). Sale price: $1.36 million. FCC approved: January 4, 1991 [For the Record, January 28, 1991]. Previous owner: Independence Broadcasting Corp. (owned by William J. Trout, Raymond J. Gazzo & Carl G. Goldsberry). Sale price: $7.55 million, plus $750,000 consultancy & non-compete agreement. FCC approved: April 19, 1985 [For the Record, March 18, 1985]. Former call letters: KCBR(TV).

KEEH(TV) Des Moines (ch 63, now deleted)—Licensed to Linton Broadcasting. Former owner: Des Moines Central Comm. Sale price: $24,966. FCC approved: February 26, 1985 [For the Record, March 18, 1985].

WHO-TV Des Moines (ch 13)—Licensed to Hughes Broadcasting Partners. Former owner: Palmer Broadcasting Co. Sale price: undisclosed (including KFOR-TV Oklahoma City, & co-owned WHO(AM) & KLYF(FM) Des Moines. FCC approved: November 1991 [Changing Hands, November 18, 1991].

KDUB-TV Dubuque (ch 40)—Licensed to Dubuque TV Ltd. Partnership. Former owner: Birney Imes Jr. & family. Sale price: undisclosed. FCC approved: February 8, 1985. Previous owner: Lloyd Hearing Aid Corp. [Marvin E. Palmquist & Elizabeth L. Palmquist (50% jointly); Andrew Palmquist (16.67%); Mary Palmquist (16.66%); et al]. Sale price: $1.5 million. FCC approved: September 13, 1979 [*Broadcasting*, October 1, 1979]. Note: Stn founded by Dubuque Communications Corp. [Gerald J. Green (30.5%) & Timothy M. Green (30.5%)]. Sold to Lloyd Hearing Aid for $35,000. FCC approved: June 29, 1976 [For the Record, July 19, 1976].

KEII(TV) Dubuque (ch 16, now deleted)—Licensed to Metro Program Network. Former owner: Powell Broadcasting Co. Sale price: no financial consideration (contract filed in amendment). FCC approved: May 22, 1985 [For the Record, June 3, 1985].

KICI-TV Iowa City (ch 20, now deleted)—Licensed to Hawkeye Broadcasting Ltd. (Walter R. Brewster, et al). Former owner: Iowa Television Authority (William B. Newbrough, et al). Sale price: $45,000 for CP. FCC approved: May 30, 1986 [For the Record, May 5, 1986].

KIMT(TV) Mason City (ch 3)—Licensed to Iowa Television Inc. (owned by Spartan Radiocasting). Former owner: Daily Telegraph Printing Co. (Hugh I. Shott & family). Sale price: $36.75 million (including WBTW(TV) Florence, SC). FCC approved: June 12, 1984. Previous owner: Lee Enterprises (see Group Ownership). Sale price: $9.5 million. FCC approved: April 22, 1980 [Changing Hands, May 5, 1980].

KZJB-TV Newton (ch 39)—Licensed to FM Iowa Inc. Former owner: MTN Broadcasting Inc. Sale price: $1.3 million (including KGCI(AM) Marshalltown & KGCI(FM) Grundy Center, both IA). FCC approved: July 2, 1990.

KYOU-TV Ottumwa (ch 15)—Licensed to Public Interest Broadcast Group Inc. (owned by Dean C. Engstrom & Les White). Former owner: Ottumwa Television LP. Sale price: $900. FCC approved: August 1987 [For the Record, April 13, 1987]. Former call letters: KOIA-TV. Previous owner: Haynes Communications Co. Sale price: assumption of liabilities. FCC approved: August 29, 1985 [For the Record, July 15, 1985].

KCAU-TV Sioux City (ch 9)—Licensed to Citadel Communications Co. Ltd. (see Group Ownership). Former owner: Forward of Iowa (see Forward Communications Stations, Group Ownership). Sale price: $15 million. FCC approved: October 1, 1985. Previous owner: People's Broadcasting Corp. (Nationwide Mutual Insurance Co.). Sale price: $3.5 million. FCC approved: October 27, 1965. Original owners: Cowles Broadcasting Co. (see Group Ownership). Sold by Cowles in 1957 to People's for $3 million with WNAX(AM) Yankton, SD. Original call letters: KVTV(TV).

KMEG(TV) Sioux City (ch 14)—Licensed to Maine Broadcasting Systems. Former owner: Gillett Group Inc. Sale price: $4 million. FCC approved: September 23, 1986 [For the Record, August 25, 1986]. Former owner: Medallion Broadcasters Inc. (see Fetzer Broadcasting Stations, Group Ownership). Sale price: $80 million (including WKZQ(TV) Kalamazoo, MI; KOLN(TV) Lincoln & KGIN(TV) Grand Island, both NE). FCC approved: October 29, 1985 [For the Record, September 23, 1985]. Previous owner: Robert B. Donovan & others. Sale price: $930,065. FCC approved: August 13, 1969 [For the Record, August 25, 1969]. Note: Founded in September 1967.

KTIV(TV) Sioux City (ch 4)—Licensed to KTIV Television Co. (owned by American Family Corp., see Group Ownership). Former owner: Black Hawk Broadcasting Co. Sale price: $45 million (including KWWL-TV Waterloo, IA). FCC approved: September 23, 1980. Note: in merger American Family also acquired KWWL-TV (ch 7) Waterloo, Iowa. Black Hawk's other TV & radio properties were spun off to comply with FCC cross-ownership & duopoly rules. Note: original owner KTIV Television Co. [Perkins Brothers Co. (Sioux City *Journal* & *Journal-Tribune*-KSCJ) (50%), Dietrich Dirks (36.75%), & others], sold 50% to Perkins Brothers Co. in 1965, giving Perkins Brothers 100% control. Sale price: $2.2 million for 50%. FCC approved: May 26, 1965 [For the Record, May 31, 1965]. Perkins Brothers then sold stn to Black Hawk Broadcasting for $3.3 million.

KWWL(TV) Waterloo (ch 7)—Licensed to American Black Hawk Broadcasting Co. (owned by American Family Corp., see Group Ownership). (See KTIV(TV) Sioux City, IA for details of sale.)

Kansas

KLBY(TV) Colby (ch 4)—Licensed to Chronicle Broadcasting Inc. Former owner: Channel 4 Broadcasting Ltd. (Sam A. Lunsway, et al). Sale price: $1.38 million. FCC approved: October 10, 1986 [For the Record, September 1, 1986].

KBSD-TV Ensign (ch 6)—Licensed to VS&A Communications Partners. Former owner: KBS Inc. (Smith Broadcasting Group Inc.). (For details of sale, see KWCH-TV Hutchinson, KS). FCC approved: October 26, 1992 [For the Record, November 23, 1992]. Previous owner: Southwest Kansas Television Co. Inc. Former call letters: KTVC(TV).

KSNG(TV) Garden City (ch 11)—Licensed to SJL Inc. (See KSNW(TV) Wichita, KS for details of sale.)

KUPK-TV Garden City (ch 13)—See KAKE-TV Wichita, KS.

KBSL-TV Goodland (ch 10)—Licensed to VS&A Communications Partners. Former owner: KAYS Inc. (Ross Beach Jr., Robert E. Schmidt, & others, see Group Ownership under Kansas State Network). (For details of sale, see KWCH-TV Hutchinson, KS). FCC approved: October 26, 1992 [For the Record, November 23, 1992]. Previous owner: Standard Electronics Corp. Sale price: $152,500. FCC approved: July 13, 1962 [For the Record, July 23, 1962]. Former call letters: KLOE-TV. Previous owner: Leslie E. Whittemore & associates. Sale price: $200,000 in liabilities (sold through bankruptcy proceeding). FCC approved: 1960. Former call letters: KWKT-TV. Original owner: James Blair. Sale price: $5,000 plus assumption of liabilities of $400,000. FCC approved: 1959. Original call letters: KBLR-TV.

KSNC(TV) Great Bend (ch 2)—Licensed to SJL Inc. Former owners: Kansas State Net. (See KSNW(TV) Wichita, KS for details of sale.) Original owners: Elmer C. Wedell & group. Sale price: $1 million (including KGLD(TV) Garden City, KS & KOMC(TV) McCook, NE). FCC approved: June 13, 1962 [For the Record, June 18, 1962].

KBSH-TV Hays (ch 7)—Licensed to VS&A Communications Partners. Former owner: KBS Inc. (For details of sale, see KWCH-TV Hutchinson, KS). FCC approved: October 26, 1992 [For the Record, November 23, 1992].

KWCH-TV Hutchinson (ch 12)—Licensed to VS&A Communications Partners. Former owner: Kansas Broadcasting System Inc. Sale price: Conversion by VS&A Communications of its nonvoting stock in general partner of licensee to voting stock (including satellite stations KBSD-TV Ensign, KBSH-TV Hays & KBSL-TV Goodland, all KS). FCC approved: October 26, 1992 [For the Record, November 23, 1992]. Previous owner: Wichita-Hutchinson Co. (93% owned by Minneapolis Star-Tribune Co.). Sale price: $12 million. FCC approved: November 24, 1982. Original owners: Hutchinson TV Inc. (John P. & Sidney F. Harris, R.J. Laubengayer, Howard O. Peterson & others). Sale price: $1 million. FCC approved: October 19, 1955 [For the Record, October 24, 1955].

KOAM-TV Pittsburg (ch 7)—Licensed to Scarecrow Inc. Former owner: KOAM-TV Acquisition (gen ptnrs: David Croll, William P. Collatos, Richard H. Churchill, Stephen F. Gormley). Sale price: no cash consideration (assignee is subsidiary of Chemical Bank, which made loan in principal amount of $13 million to assignor; parties agreed to resolve default on that loan by having bank temporarily acquire assets of station until buyer is found). FCC approved: May 28, 1993 [For the Record, June 28, 1993]. Former owner: Draper Communications. Sale price: $15.3 million. FCC approved: October 29, 1987 [Changing Hands, August, 10, 1987]. Previous owner: Mid-Continent Telecasting Inc. Sale price: $12 million. FCC approved: October 22, 1984.

KSLN-TV Salina (ch 34, now deleted)—Licensed to Mid-America Broadcasting Corp. [James P. Sunderland (50%), Ralph L. Weir Jr. (25%), Robert K. Weary (25%)]. Former owner: Melvin L. Gleason & family. Sale price: $43,000. FCC approved: February 26, 1964 [For the Record, March 2, 1964].

KSNT(TV) Topeka (ch 27)—Licensed to SJL Inc. Former owner: Topeka Television Inc., subsidiary of Kansas State Network. Sale price: $12 million. FCC approved: August 5, 1988 [For the Record, August 29, 1988]. Previous owner: Studio Broadcast System (subsidiary of Ralph C. Wilson Industries). Sale price: $10 million. FCC approved: August 9, 1982 [Changing Hands, August 9, 1982]. Former call letters: KTSB(TV).

KTKA-TV Topeka (ch 49)—Licensed to Joseph L. Brechner. Former owner: Larry D. Hudson. Sale price: $6.5 million. FCC approved: April 28, 1986 [For the Record, April 7, 1986]. Former call letters: KLDH-TV.

WIBW-TV Topeka (ch 13)—Licensed to Stauffer Communications Inc. (owned by Stauffer Publications Inc., see Group Ownership). Original owner: Capper Publications. Sale price: $7 million (including WIBW(AM) Topeka & KCKN(AM) Kansas City, both KS). FCC approved: December 20, 1956 [For the Record, December 24, 1956]. Note: KCKN(AM) in turn was sold to Cy Blumenthal for $110,000.

KAKE-TV Wichita (ch 10)—Licensed to Chronicle Broadcasting (Chronicle Publishing Co., publisher of San Francisco *Chronicle* & licensee of KRON-TV San Francisco; WOW(TV) Omaha, NE, & Western Communications Inc., cable MSO). Former owner: Sherill Corwin. Sale price (including Kansas Information Network, KAKE-AM, & KUPK-TV Garden City, KS): $27 million. FCC approved: January 21, 1980 [Changing Hands, February 4, 1980].

KSNW(TV) Wichita (ch 3)—Licensed to SJL Inc. (N.Y. group owner principally owned by George Lilly). Former owner: Kansas State Network (George C. & Wilda Gene Hatch Stations). Sale price: approximately $40-45 million (including KSNC(TV) Great Bend & KSNG(TV) Garden City, both KS; & KSNK(TV) McCook, NE). [For the Record, August 29, 1988]. Former owner: Standard Communications. Sale price: $39.5 million (including KSNG(TV); KSNC(TV); KSNF(TV) Joplin, MO; & KSNK(TV)). FCC approved: December 30, 1980.

KWCH-TV Wichita (ch 12)—Licensed to Smith Broadcasting of Kansas Inc. (Smith Broadcasting Group Inc.). Former owner: Beach-Schmidt Group. Sale price: $45 million. [Changing Hands, July 25, 1988].

Kentucky

WBKO(TV) Bowling Green (ch 13)—Licensed to Benedek Broadcasting (see Group Ownership). Former owner: Bluegrass Media (closely held group headed by Clyde G. Payne). Sale price: $4 million. FCC approved: February 14, 1983 [For the Record, March 7, 1983]. Note: Founded as WLTV(TV) in 1962 by Argus Broadcasting Co. (George A. Brown Jr. & J.M. Walters). Sold in 1970 to Professional Telecasting Systems Inc. for $1 million. FCC approved: June 11, 1970 [For the Record, June 22, 1970]. Sold by Professional to Bluegrass for $1.75 million. FCC approved: July 14, 1976 [For the Record, August 19, 1976].

WKNT(TV) Bowling Green (ch 40)—Licensed to Southeastern Communications Inc. Former owner: Word Broadcasting Network. Sale price: $1 million. FCC approved: October 24, 1991 [For the Record, November 11, 1991]. Former call letters: WQQB(TV). Previous owner: JMC Inc. (owned by John M. Cunningham). Sale price: assumption of liabilities for CP. FCC approved: October 3, 1986 [For the Record, July 28, 1986].

WDKY(TV) Danville (ch 56)—Licensed to Superior Communications of Kentucky Ltd. Former owner: Superior Communications Group Inc. (Perry A. Sook). Sale price: no cash consideration (application was filed to request approval for internal reorganization). FCC approved: December 30, 1992 [For the Record, January 25, 1993]. Previous owner: WDKY License Co. Inc. Sale price: $10.3 million. FCC approved: August 19, 1992 [For the Record, September 7, 1992]. Former owner: MMC Television Corp. (Paula S. Baird Pruett). Previous owner: Backe Communications Inc. Sale price: $9.5 million. FCC approved: September 25, 1989 [For the Record, October 16, 1989]. Note: stn began operation February 10, 1986. Former owner: Robert L. Bertram. Sale price: $25,000 for CP. FCC approved: June 21, 1985 [For the Record, April 29, 1985].

WYMT-TV Hazard (ch 57)—Licensed to Kentucky Central TV. Former owner: Hazard TV Co. (William D. Gorman, et al). Sale price: $1 million. FCC approved: May 22, 1985 [For the Record, June 10, 1985]. Former call letters: WKYH-TV.

WKYT-TV Lexington (ch 27)—Licensed to Kentucky Central Television Inc. (Central Bank & Trust Co., executor of estate of Garvice D. Kincaid). Former owner: Kentucky Central Television Inc. (owned 100% by Mid-Central Investment Co.). Sale price: no financial consideration. FCC approved: January 21, 1976 [For the Record, February 9, 1976]. Former call letters: WKXP-TV. Gilmore N. Nunn sold stn (with WLAP-AM-FM) to Community Broadcasting Co. (Frederic Gregg Jr., Harry C. Feingold & Charles H. Wright) in 1957 for $346,000. FCC approved: January 17, 1957 [For the Record, January 28, 1957]. Sold in 1958 to Taft Broadcasting Co. (see Group Ownership) for $100,000, of which $35,000 was paid for in covenant not to compete for five years. FCC approved: May 15, 1958 [For the Record, May 26, 1958]. Sold in 1967 to Kentucky Central Television Inc. for $2.5 million. FCC approved: April 26, 1967 [For the Record, May 8, 1967]. Original call letters: WLAP-TV.

WTVQ-TV Lexington (ch 36)—Licensed to Park Communications, (owned by Roy H. Park, see Group Ownership). Former owner: Shamrock Broadcasting, owned by Roy E. Disney (see Group Ownership). Sale price: $11 million. FCC approved: December 18, 1991 [For the Record, January 20, 1992]. Previous owners: Starr WTVQ Inc. (see Starr Broadcasting Group Inc., Group Ownership). Sale price: $21.6 million (including KHVO(TV) Hilo, KITV(TV) Honolulu, & KMAU(TV) Wailuku, all HI; & 8 radio stns). FCC approved: June 1979 [*Broadcasting*, June 11, 1979]. Original owner: WBLG-TV Inc. (50% owned by Roy B. White Jr. & 50% by Reeves Telecom Corp). Sale price: $1.5 million. FCC approved: November 14, 1973 [For the Record, November 26, 1973]. Original call letters: WBLG-TV. Note: formerly bcst on Channel 62.

WAVE-TV Louisville (ch 3)—Licensed to Cosmos Broadcasting Corp. Sale price: part of $110 million Cosmos purchase of Orion Broadcasting, including WFIE-TV Evansville, IN; WMT-TV Cedar Rapids, IA; WFRV-TV Green Bay, WI; WJMN-TV Escanaba, MI; & 3 radio stns [*Broadcasting*, June 9, 16, 1980]. Note: Cosmos sold WAVE(AM) Louisville; WFRV-TV Green Bay, WI; WJMN-TV Escanaba, MI; & WMT-TV Cedar Rapids, IA to comply with FCC multiple ownership rules [Changing Hands, August 31, 1981].

WDRB-TV Louisville (ch 41)—Licensed to Independence Television Co. (owned by The Toledo Blade Co., see Cross-Ownership). Former owner: Cowles Media Co. (see Group Ownership). Sale price: $10 million. FCC approved: December 5, 1983 [For the Record, January 2, 1984]. Original owners: Consolidated Broadcasting Co. (Owsley & Edgerton Welsh, Arlie Howard, J.P. Morgan & others). Sold to Cowles for $6.5 million. FCC approved: October 26, 1977 [Changing Hands, December 19, 1977].

WEZI(TV) Louisville (ch 21, now deleted)—Licensed to South Central Broadcasting Corp. Former owner: Great Trails Broadcasting Corp. (then owned by Charles Sawyer). Sale price: $25,000 for CP. FCC approved: October 11, 1965 [For the Record, October 18, 1965]. Note: Founded in 1954 by James F. Brownlee, Milton S. Trost, Harold Plunkett, Emmanuel Levi & group as WKLO-TV. Sold to Mr. Sawyer in 1955 for $350,000 with WKLO(AM).

WHAS-TV Louisville (ch 11)—Licensed to WHAS Inc. (owned by the Providence Journal Co., see Group Ownership). Former owner: Barry Bingham, et al. Sale price: $85.7 million. FCC approved: July 30, 1986 [For the Record, July 21, 1986].

WLKY-TV Louisville (ch 32)—Licensed to Pulitzer Broadcasting Co. (see Group Ownership). Former owner: Combined Communications Corp. of Kentucky Inc. (see Gannett Co., Group Ownership). Sale price: $15.4 million. FCC approved: May 12, 1983 [For the Record, May 23, 1983]. Note: Founded by Kentuckiana TV Inc. in 1961. Kentuckiana TV Inc. (George E. & Helen Egger, & others) sold stn to Sonderling Broadcasting Corp. in 1967 for $6.86 million. FCC approved: December 13, 1967 [*Broadcasting*, December 18, 1967]. Purchased from Sonderling by Combined Communications for $8.33 million in 1972. FCC approved: August 9, 1972 [*Broadcasting*, August 14, 1972]. Combined Communications was acquired by Gannett Co. in 1979.

WXIX-TV Newport (Cincinnati, OH) (ch 19)—Licensed to Malrite Communications Group (see Group Ownership). Former owner: Metromedia Inc. Sale price: $45 million. FCC approved: November 8, 1983 [For the Record, December 5, 1983]. Former call letters: WSCO-TV, WNOP-TV. Note: original owners James G. Lang & Dean Stuhlmueller sold CP in 1965 to D.H. Overmyer Communications Corp. (a subsidiary of AVC Corp.) in 1967 for $1 million (with 80% of CPs for KEMO-TV San Francisco; WBMO-TV Atlanta; WECO-TV Pittsburgh, PA; & KJDO-TV Rosenberg, TX). Bought by Metromedia Inc. from U.S. Communications of Ohio for $3 million in 1972 [*Broadcasting*, August 14, 1972].

WROZ(TV) Owensboro (ch 61)—Licensed to Seney Communications. Former owner: Powers Communications. Sale price: $40,000. FCC approved: June 21, 1989 [For the Record, July 10, 1989].

WDKA Paducah (ch 49)—Licensed to Robert W. Sudbrink (Robert W. Sudbrink, 51%, & Marion Sudbrink, 49%, husband & wife). Former owner: MacPherson Broadcasting of Kentucky Inc. Sale price: $200. FCC approved: September 4, 1992 [For the Record, October 19, 1992]. Previous owner: TV 49 (Robert W. Sudbrink). Sale price: $131,000. FCC approved: August 15, 1989 [For the Record, September 5, 1989].

WKPD-TV Paducah (ch 29)—Licensed to Kentucky Authority for Educational TV. Former owner: Lady Sarah McKinney-Smith. FCC approved: February 28, 1978. Previous owner: WDXR-TV Inc. [(George T. Baily (50%) & Lady Sarah McKinney-Smith (50%)]. FCC approved: December 19, 1974 [For the Record, January 13, 1975]. Former call letters: WDXR(TV). Note: FCC approved involuntary transfer of control to Mrs. McKinney-Smith, May 22, 1974 [For the Record, June 10, 1974].

Louisiana

KALB-TV Alexandria (ch 5)—Licensed to Park Broadcasting of Louisiana Inc. Former owner: Lanford Telecasting Co. (see Lanford Stations, Group Ownership). Sale price: $21 million, plus non-compete agreement worth up to $5 million. FCC approved: September 17, 1993 [For the Record, October 11, 1993]. Previous owner: T.B. Lanford (99.2%). Sale price: $333,155 for 48% of stn. FCC approved: January 10, 1957 [For the Record, January 14, 1957]. Note: Mr. Lanford originally owned 47.2% of stn, purchased 52% from W.H. Allen for $200,000 (with KALB-AM-FM). FCC approved: August 31, 1955 [For the Record, September 5, 1955].

WAFB(TV) Baton Rouge (ch 9)—Licensed to American Family Corp. Former owner: Guaranty Broadcasting Corp. [Guaranty Bond & Finance Inc. & Guaranty Income Life Insurance Co., principally owned by George A. Foster Trust (27%), George A. Foster Jr. (10%), & others]. Sale price: $60 million estimated. FCC approved: April 1988. Former call letters: WAFB-TV. Previous owner: Royal Street Corp. (WDSU-AM-FM-TV New Orleans). Sale price: $2.97 million. FCC approved: January 14, 1964 [For the Record, January 20, 1964]. Note: Royal Street Corp. acquired control of WAFB Stations in 1956 from Louis S. Prejean & associates by paying $148,600 for 31.1% of the stock. It previously had owned 26.7%.

WBRZ(TV) Baton Rouge (ch 2)—Licensed to Louisiana Television Broadcasting Co. (99% owned by Baton Rouge Broadcasting Co.). Note: Stn went on air in 1955. 47% was acquired from Lewis Gottlieb, et al for $548,000 in 1958.

WGMB(TV) Baton Rouge (ch 44)—Licensed to Galloway Media Inc, owned by Thomas R. Galloway Sr. (see Group Ownership). Former owners: Sheldon H. Galloway & Karen G. Mire. Sale price: assumption of debt & release from guarantees. FCC approved: December 24, 1991 [For the Record, January 13, 1992].

WRBT-TV Baton Rouge (ch 33)—Licensed to Cyril E. Vetter. Former owner: Rush Broadcasting Corp. [Jules B. Leblanc III (70%) & Vetter (30%)]. Sale price: $742,000. FCC approved: January 9, 1979 [*Broadcasting*, January 29, 1979]. Note: Stn founded by Richard O. Rush, Ramon V. Jarrell & Southern Educators Life Insurance Co., & sold to LeBlanc & Vetter. Sale price: $200,000 plus assumption of liabilities of $2.56 million. FCC approved: March 12, 1976 [For the Record, March 29, 1976].

KNHH(TV) Houma (ch 11)—Licensed to MGM Inc. (dba New Dawn Broadcasting). Former owner: GACO Communications. Sale price: $300,000. FCC approved: November 27, 1985 [For the Record, December 16, 1985].

KATC(TV) Lafayette (ch 3)—Licensed to ML Media Partners (Martin Pompadur, Ralph E. Becker, et al). Former owner: Abellor Corp. (owned by Loyola University). Sale price: $28 million. FCC approved: November 25, 1986 [For the Record, October 6, 1986]. Previous owner: Acadian TV Corp. (Frances Kurzweg, et al). Sale price: $18.5 million. FCC approved: April 29, 1982.

KLFY-TV Lafayette (ch 10)—Licensed to Young Broadcasting of Louisiana Inc [Vincent J. Young (33%) & Adam J. Young (66%)]. Former owner: Texoma Broadcasters Inc. (see KWTX Stations, Group Ownership). Sale price: $51 million. FCC approved: May 28, 1988. Former owners: Camellia Broadcasting [Paul H. DeClouet, Thomas A. DeClouet, Harold Delhommer, J.W. Mitchell, (each 18.75%) & others]. Sale price: $2.69 million. FCC approved: January 27, 1965 [For the Record, February 1, 1965].

KPLC-TV Lake Charles (ch 7)—Licensed to Cosmos Broadcasting Corp. Former owner: Nasco Inc. (owned by Channel Communications, see Group Ownership). Sale price: $68 million (including KAIT-TV Jonesboro, AR). FCC approved: November 13, 1986 [In Brief, September 29, 1986]. Previous owner: Calcasieu Television & Radio Inc. (Lake Charles Television Inc., owned by G. Russell Chambers). Sale price: $18 million. FCC approved: March 31, 1986 [For the Record, February 10, 1986]. Previous owner: Calcasieu Television & Radio Inc. (Harry W. Chesley Jr., Ray Eder, et al). Sale price: $2.05 million. FCC approved: February 18, 1971 [For the Record, March 1, 1971]. Note: Stn was sold by T.B. Lanford (66.6%), Lewis M. Sepaugh Sr. & Jr. (33.3% together), to Calcasieu Television Inc. [Henry W. Chesley Jr. (19.8%); Mary Ann Stein (7.2%); Stan Musial & 12 other stockholders (4.7% each)] in 1964. Sale price: $2 million [with KPLC(AM)]. FCC approved: June 27, 1964 [For the Record, July 13, 1964].

KVHP(TV) Lake Charles (ch 29)—Licensed to Calascieu Communications Inc. Former owner: TMG Inc. (Harold E. Protter, et al). Sale price: $2 million. FCC approved: March 1987 [For the Record, January 26, 1987].

WCCL(TV) New Orleans (ch 49)—Licensed to George S. Flinn Jr. Former owner: Wayne Ducote, chapter 7 trustee for Crescent City Communications Company Inc. Sale price: $135,000. FCC approved: April 30, 1993 [For the Record, May 24, 1993].

WDSU-TV New Orleans (ch 6)—Licensed to Pulitzer Broadcasting Co. Former owner: Cosmos Broadcasting of Louisiana Inc. Sale price: $46.8 million [For the Record, October 9, 1989]. Original owner: WDSU-TV Inc. (wholly owned by Royal Street Corp.). Sale price: $16 million. FCC approved: November 29, 1972 [For the Record, December 11, 1972].

WGNO-TV New Orleans (ch 26)—Licensed to WGNO Inc., owned by Tribune Broadcasting Co. (see Group Ownership). Former owner: General Media Corp. (Earl Hickerson & 80 others). Sale price: $21 million. FCC approved: July 21, 1983 [For the Record, August 8, 1983]. Note: Founded in 1967 as WWOM-TV. Original owner was David W. Wagenvoord. Receiver in bankruptcy Dorothy R. Cowen sold stn in 1971 to Communications Corp. of the South Inc. for $300,000 (for CP). FCC approved: December 29, 1971. Comm. Corp. of the South sold by Cascade Development Corp. to Seymour Smith & family in 1976. Sale price: Exchange of stock. FCC approved: April 30, 1976 [For the Record, May 17, 1976]. License transferred to General Media Inc., for $4 million in 1978. FCC approved: June 26. 1978 [Changing Hands, July 10, 1978].

WJMR-TV New Orleans (ch 20, now deleted)—Licensed to Summit Broadcasting Corp. [George A. Mayoral (85%) & Richard L. Voelker (15%)]. Former owner: Supreme Broadcasting Co. (Mr. & Mrs. Roy A. Nelson & others). Sale price: $393,000 for CP (including WNNR-AM-FM New Orleans). FCC approved: November 20, 1968 [For the Record, December 2, 1968].

WNOL-TV New Orleans (ch 38)—Licensed to TVX Corp. (see Group Ownership). Former owner: Channel 38 Associates (Harold Protter, et al). Sale price: $13.7 million. FCC approved: February 28, 1986 [For the Record, December 30, 1985].

WVUE(TV) New Orleans (ch 8)—Licensed to Burnham Broadcasting (see Group Ownership). Former owner: Gaylord Broadcasting Co. (see Group Ownership). Sale price: $60 million. FCC approved: June 1987 [Changing Hands, January 12, 1987]. Previous owner: Screen Gems Stations (subsidiary of Columbia Pictures Industries). Sale price: $12.5 million. FCC approved: June 30, 1977 [For the Record, July 18, 1977]. Note: Founded in 1958 as merger of Supreme Broadcasting Co. (ch 20 WJMR-TV) (40%), & Coastal Television (60%). Rust Craft bought Supreme Broadcasting's 40% in 1962 for $855,100. Screen Gems Broadcasting of Louisiana Inc. purchased stn from Rust Craft Broadcasting Co. & Coastal TV for $8 million. FCC approved: June 2, 1965.

WWL-TV New Orleans (ch 4)—Licensed to Rampart Operating Partnership. Former owner: Loyola University. Sale price: $102.85 million. FCC approved: May 23, 1990.

KMSS(TV) Shreveport (ch 33)—Licensed to Southwest MultiMedia. Former owner: Media South of Shreveport. Sale price: $7 million. FCC approved: July 1987 [For the Record, May 25, 1987].

KSLA-TV Shreveport (ch 12)—Licensed to VSC Communications Inc. (subsidiary of Viacom International Inc., which merged with Arsenal Acquiring Corp. September 1987). Former owner: KSLA-TV Inc. [Dolores LaVigne (36.32%), Journal Publishing Co. (25.14%), Winston B. Linman (18.45%)]. Sale price: One million shares of Viacom stock valued at approximately $32 million. FCC approved: March 30, 1983 [For the Record, April 18, 1983]. Note: Original owner, Shreveport Television Co. (Henry E. Linam & associates), sold stn in 1960 to KSLA-TV Inc. [Journal Publishing Co. (55%), Dolores LaVigne (20%), Winston B. Linam (10%)] for $3.4 million. FCC approved: May 25, 1960 [For the Record, May 30, 1960]. On May 27, 1976, FCC approved transfer of control of KSLA-TV Inc. among principals. (See former owner above for ownership breakdown). Deal involved $2.82 million [For the Record, June 21, 1976].

KTBS-TV Shreveport (ch 3)—Licensed to KTBS Inc. (Helen H. Wray, Florence H. Wray). Former owner: KTBS Inc. Sale price: no cash consideration; application was filed as result of death of Charles H. Wray, 26.3% shareholder of licensee. FCC approved: August 14, 1992 [For the Record, September 7, 1992].

KARD(TV) West Monroe (ch 14)—Licensed to BANAM Broadcasting Inc. Former owner: Woods Communications Group Inc. Sale price: assumption of debt (including KDEB(TV) Springfield, MO; WTVW(TV) Evansville, IN; & KLBK-TV Lubbock, TX). FCC approved: March 16, 1993 [For the Record, April 5, 1993].

Maine

***WCBB(TV) Augusta (ch 10)**—Licensed to Maine Public Broadcasting Corp. Former owner: University of Maine System. Sale price: no cash consideration (assignment included WMEM-FM-TV Presque Isle, WMEH(FM) Bangor, WMEW(FM) Waterville, WMED-FM-TV Calais, WMEA-FM-TV Portland-Biddeford, WMEB(TV) Orono, all ME. FCC approved: June 23, 1992 [For the Record, July 13, 1992]. Previous owner: Colby-Bates-Bowdoin Educational Telecasting Corp. (Colby, Bates & Bowdoin Colleges). Original owner: Richard S. Roble. Sale price: $6,000. FCC approved: July 27, 1960 [For the Record, August 8, 1960].

WABI-TV Bangor (ch 5)—Licensed to Diversified Communications (see Group Ownership). Sale price: $125,000 for Murray Carpenter's 50% interest (including WABI(AM)). FCC approved: October 7, 1953 [For the Record, October 12, 1953].

WLBZ-TV Bangor (ch 2)—Licensed to WLBZ Television Inc. (owned by Maine Broadcasting System, see Group Ownership). Former owners: Murray Carpenter & wife. Sale price: $600,000. FCC approved: May 15, 1958 [For the Record, May 26, 1958]. Former call letters: WTWO(TV).

WVII-TV Bangor (ch 7)—Licensed to Bangor Communications Inc., (owned by Seaway Comm. Inc., see Group Ownership). Former owner: Eastern Maine Broadcasting System Inc. Sale price: $3.8 million. FCC approved: July 23, 1982. Previous owner: Downeast Television Inc., debtor-in-possession. Sale price: $530,000. FCC approved: January 20, 1976 [For the Record, February 2, 1976]. Original call letters: WEMT(TV).

***WMED-TV Calais (ch 13)**—Licensed to Maine Public Broadcasting Corp. Former owner: University of Maine System. Sale price: no cash consideration (assignment included WMED-FM, WMEM-FM-TV Presque Isle, WMEH(FM) Bangor, WMEW(FM) Waterville, WCBB(TV) Augusta, WMEA-FM-TV Portland-Biddeford, WMEB(TV) Orono, all ME. FCC approved: June 23, 1992 [For the Record, July 13, 1992].

***WMEB(TV) Orono (ch 12)**—Licensed to Maine Public Broadcasting Corp. Former owner: University of Maine System. Sale price: no cash consideration (assignment included WMEM-FM-TV Presque Isle, WMEH(FM) Bangor, WMEW(FM) Waterville, WCBB(TV) Augusta, WMED-FM-TV Calais, WMEA-FM-TV Portland-Biddeford, all ME. FCC approved: June 23, 1992 [For the Record, July 13, 1992].

WMTW-TV Poland Spring (Portland) (ch 8)—Licensed to Harron Broadcasting Co. (owned by Mid New York Broadcasting Stations). Former owner: Dolphin Enterprises Inc. (Jack & Miriam Paar). Sale price: $3.62 million (including WMTW-FM Mt. Washington, NH). FCC approved: November 8, 1967 [For the Record, November 20, 1967]. Original owner: John W. Guider, Horace A. Hildreth, Peter Anderson & others. Sale price: $3 million (with WMTW-FM). FCC approved: April 15, 1964 [For the Record, April 27, 1964].

***WMEA-TV Portland-Biddeford (ch 26)**—Licensed to Maine Public Broadcasting Corp. Former owner: University of Maine System. Sale price: no cash consideration (assignment included WMEA-FM, WMEM-FM-TV Presque Isle, WMEH(FM) Bangor, WMEW(FM) Waterville, WCBB(TV) Augusta, WMED-FM-TV Calais, WMEB(TV) Orono, all ME. FCC approved: June 23, 1992 [For the Record, July 13, 1992].

WAGM-TV Presque Isle (ch 8)—Licensed to Peter P. Kozloski. Former owner: WAGM-TV Inc. (owned by NEPSK Inc.). Sale price: undisclosed (including KIKC-AM-FM Forsyth, MT). FCC approved: March 8, 1991 [For the Record, April 1, 1991]. Previous owner: Aroostook Broadcasting Corp. (see Community Broadcasting Service in Group Ownership). Sale price: $1.76 million. FCC approved: February 8, 1984. Previous owner: Harold D. Glidden. Sale price: $525,000 (with WAGM(AM) & WABM(AM) Houlton, ME). FCC approved: September 26, 1957 [For the Record, September 30, 1957]. Original owner: Harry E. Umphrey, et al. Sale price: $30,000 for Umphrey's 47% of stn. FCC approved: 1956.

***WMEM-TV Presque Isle (ch 10)**—Licensed to Maine Public Broadcasting Corp. Former owner: University of Maine System. Sale price: no cash consideration (assignment included WMEM-FM, WMEA-FM-TV Portland-Biddeford, WMEH(FM) Bangor, WMEW(FM) Waterville, WCBB(TV) Augusta, WMED-FM-TV Calais, WMEB(TV) Orono, all ME. FCC approved: June 23, 1992 [For the Record, July 13, 1992].

Maryland

WHSW(TV) Baltimore (ch 24)—Licensed to Silver King Broadcasting (owned by Home Shopping Network). Former owner: Family Media Inc. Sale price: $15 million. FCC approved: November 6, 1986. Former call letters: WKJL(TV). Previous owner: Look & Live Ministries. Sale price: $543,000 for CP. FCC approved: October 1, 1985 [For the Record, August 5, 1985].

WJZ-TV Baltimore (ch 13)—Licensed to Westinghouse Broadcasting Co. (see Group Ownership). Original owners: Ben Cohen, Herman Cohen & Associates. Sale price: $4.4 million. FCC approved: June 28, 1957 [For the Record, July 1, 1957]. Original call letters: WAAM-TV.

WMAR(TV) Baltimore (ch 2)—Licensed to Scripps-Howard Broadcasting Co. Former owner: Gillett Group Inc. Sale price: $125 million. FCC approved: May 1991 [*Broadcasting*, June 3, 1991]. Previous owner: Times Mirror Broadcasting. Sale price: $200 million plus (including WRLH-TV Richmond, VA). FCC approved: October 31, 1986 [For the Record, July 21, 1986].

WIVQ(TV) Cumberland (ch 52)—Licensed to Beacon Broadcasting Inc. Former owner: Contemporary Communications Inc. Sale price: $20,000 for CP. FCC approved: February 14, 1986 [For the Record, November 25, 1985].

WTBO-TV Cumberland (ch 17, now deleted)—Licensed to Tennessee Valley Broadcasting Corp. Original owners: Maryland Radio Corp. (Howard L. Chernoff & associates). Sale price: $110,000 [with WTBO(AM)]. FCC approved: September 1, 1954 [For the Record, September 16, 1954].

WHAG-TV Hagerstown (ch 25)—Licensed to Williams Communications Inc. Former owner: Great Trails Broadcasting Corp. (Charles Sawyer Family). (For details of this transfer of control, see WFFT-TV Fort Wayne, IN.) FCC approved: November 24, 1986. Previous owner: Henson Aviation Inc. [Richard A. Henson (36%), Sheldon Magazine & brother, Samuel (29.8% each), & Hans Omenitsch (4.4%)]. Sale price: $1.6 million. FCC approved: July 30, 1981 [Changing Hands, September 7, 1981]. Original owner: WHAG TV Inc. [Adler Communications Corp. (51.2%)]. Sale price: $101,350. FCC approved: September 18, 1972 [For the Record, October 30, 1972].

WBOC-TV Salisbury (ch 16)—Licensed to WBOC Inc. (owned by Draper Communications, see Group Ownership). Former owner: WBOC Inc. (see A.S. Abell Co. in Group Ownership). Sale price: $8 million. FCC approved: September 1980 [Changing Hands, September 29, 1980]. Previous owner: John W. Downing & associates. Sale price: $1.21 million [including WBOC(AM)]. FCC approved: July 26, 1961 [For the Record, August 7, 1961].

WMDT(TV) Salisbury (ch 47)—Licensed to Marion B. Brechner, representative to the estate. Former owner: Delmarva Broadcast Services Limited Partnership [owned by Mid-Florida Television Corp. (40% general partner), Joseph L. Brechner (12.5% general partner) & 25 limited partners; Mid-Florida Television Corp. was owned by J. Brechner (51.63%) & 12 others]. Sale price: no financial consideration. FCC approved: December 13, 1990 [For the Record, January 7, 1991]. Previous owner: Fulton P. Jeffers, receiver, who took over control after stn went into receivership. It was formerly owned by Paul Audet. Sale price: $4 million. FCC approved: May 5, 1982 [For the Record, May 24, 1982].

Massachusetts

WCDC(TV) Adams (ch 19)—Licensed to Young Broadcasting Inc. Former owner: Knight-Ridder Broadcasting Inc. Sale price: $32 million (including WTEN(TV) Albany, NY). FCC approved: August 24, 1989 [For the Record, September 11, 1989]. Previous owner: Albany Television Inc. (owned by Poole Broadcasting). Sale price: $49.63 million (including WTEN(TV) Albany, NY; WPRI-TV Providence, RI; & WJRT-TV Flint, MI). FCC approved: 1977. Previous owner: Capital Cities Broadcasting Corp. (see Capital Cities Communications Inc., Group Ownership). Sale price: $19 million (including WTEN(TV) Albany, NY). FCC approved: February 24, 1971 [*Broadcasting*, March 1, 1971]. Note: Capital Cities purchased stn from original owner, Greylock Broadcasting Co., in 1957. Sale price: $379,206. FCC approved: February 7, 1957 [For the Record, February 11, 1957]. Original call letters: WMGT-TV.

WCVB-TV Boston (ch 5)—Licensed to The Hearst Corp. (see Group Ownership). Former owner: Metromedia Inc. Sale price: $450 million. FCC approved: November 14, 1985. Previous owner: Boston Broadcasters (group of 225 stockholders; Leo Beranek, chmn, (5.99%) & Robert Bennett, pres, (3.43%). Sale price: $220 million. FCC approved: April 1, 1982 [*Broadcasting*, April 5, 1982].

WFXT-TV Boston (ch 25)—Licensed to Boston Celtics Communications. Former owner: Fox Television Stations Inc. (see Group Ownership). Sale price: $10 million. FCC approved: April 24, 1990. Previous owner: CBN Continental Broadcasting Network. Sale price: $28 million. FCC approved: November 18, 1986 [For the Record, October 6, 1986]. Former call letters: WXNE-TV.

WDHDH-TV Boston (ch 7)—Licensed to WHDH-TV Inc. (owned by Sunbeam Television Corp.). Former owner: WHDH-TV Inc. (owned by New England TV Corp.). FCC approved: June 3, 1993 [For the Record, June 21, 1993].

WQTV(TV) Boston (ch 68)—Licensed to Boston University (Dr. John Silber). Former owner: WQTV Inc. (owned by Christian Science Monitor Syndicate). Sale price: $3.8 million. FCC approved: September 7, 1993 [For the Record, September 27, 1993]. Previous owner: Boston Star Broadcasting Inc. [owned by Satellite Television & Associated Resources Inc. (50%), John Sullivan (25%), Byron Lasky (18.75%) & Don Speigelman Jr. (6.25%). STAR is a publicly traded Santa Monica, CA-based MDS & STV operator]. Original owner: Boston Heritage Broadcasting Inc. (owned by George Fritzinger, Ed Mank & 11 others). Sale price: $600,000. FCC approved: March 22, 1982 [For the Record, April 12, 1982]. Note: BHB sold WQTV facilities to group that earlier bought operator of its STV franchise for $20 million.

WSBK-TV Boston (ch 38)—Licensed to WSBK License Inc. (see SCI Television Inc. in Group Ownership). Former owner: Gillett Communications. Sale price: unknown. (See WAGA-TV Atlanta for details of sale). FCC approved: February 19, 1993 [For the Record, April 26, 1993]. Previous owner: New Boston Television Inc. (owned by KKR Associates, see Group Ownership). (See KCST-TV San Diego for details of sale.) Previous owner: Storer Broadcasting Co. (For details of sale, see WJW-TV Cleveland.) Previous owners: Boston Catholic Television Center (50%) & Austin A. Harrison (10%). Sale price: $2.27 million. FCC approved: July 27, 1966 [For the Record, August 8, 1966]. Former call letters: WIHS-TV.

WLVI-TV Cambridge (ch 56)—Licensed to Gannett Mass. Broadcasting (see Gannett Co., Group Ownership). Former owner: Field Comm. Corp. (see Group Ownership). Sale price: $47 million. FCC approved: May 12, 1983 [For the Record, May 23, 1983]. Previous owner: Kaiser Broadcasting Corp. Sale price: $42.62 million for 77.5% of group including KBHK-TV San Francisco; WFLD-TV Chicago; WKBD-TV Detroit; WKBS-TV Burlington, NJ (Philadelphia). FCC approved: 1977 [*Broadcasting*, August 8, 1977]. Former call letters: WHXR-TV. Note: sold by Harvey Radio Laboratories Inc. to WKBG Inc. [Kaiser Broadcasting Corp. (50%) & Globe Newspaper Co. (50%)] in 1966 for $1.75 million (including WXHR-AM-FM). FCC approved: October 22, 1966 [For the Record, October 31, 1966]. Kaiser bought 40% of Globe's holdings in 1968. Kaiser Broadcasting Co. acquired the remaining 10% from Globe in 1974 [*Broadcasting*, January 28, 1974]. Former call letters: WKBG-TV.

WVJV-TV Marlborough (ch 66)—Licensed to Silver King Broadcasting (owned by Home Shopping Network Inc.). Former owner: Channel 66 Associates Limited Partnership (John Garabedian plus 204 other investors). Sale price: $19-20 million. FCC approved: September 23, 1986 [For the Record, August 25, 1986].

WLNE(TV) New Bedford (Providence, RI) (ch 6)—Licensed to Freedom WLNE-TV Inc. (owned by Freedom Newspapers Inc., see Cross-Ownership). Former owner: Pulitzer Publishing Co. (see Group Ownership & Cross-Ownership). Sale price: $15.5 million. FCC approved: December 14, 1982. Previous owner: WGAL Television Inc. (owned by Steinman Stations). Sale price: $45 million (including WGAL-TV Lancaster, PA). FCC approved: October 1978 [Changing Hands, October 23, 1978]. Former call letters: WTEV(TV). Original owners: E. Anthony & Sons (55%), New England Television Co. (45%). Sale price: $5.77 million. FCC approved: April 6, 1966 [For the Record, April 11, 1966].

WHRC(TV) Norwell (ch 46)—Licensed to Two If By Sea Broadcasting Corp. Former owner: Massachusetts Channel 46 Corp. Sale price: $900,000. FCC approved: September 11, 1991 [For the Record, September 30, 1991].

WGGB-TV Springfield (ch 40)—Licensed to The WHYN Stations Corp. (see Guy Gannett Broadcasting Services, Group Ownership). Former owners: Hampden-Hampshire Corp. (William Dwight & Charles N. DeRose & families, 50%) & Republican TV Inc. (employee & beneficial funds of Springfield *Republican News & Union*, 50%). Sale price: $3.85 million (including WHYN-AM-FM) plus covenant not to compete. FCC approved: June 7, 1967 [For the Record, June 19, 1967]. Note: Dwight DeRose group originally sold stn to Hampden-Hampshire for $250,000 for 50% interest by Republican TV Inc. (with WHYN-AM-FM). FCC approved: July 21, 1954 [For the Record, July 26, 1954].

WWLP(TV) Springfield (ch 22)—Licensed to Adams Television of Springfield, owned by Paul A. Brissette (see Group Ownership). Former owner: Adams Communications Corp. (see Group Ownership). Sale price: Undisclosed (including WHOI(TV) Peoria, IL; WILX-TV Onondaga, MI; KOSA-TV Odessa & KAUZ-TV Wichita Falls, both TX; WMTV(TV) Madison & WSAW-TV Wausau, both WI; & WTRF-TV Wheeling, WV). FCC approved: December 24, 1991 [For the Record, January 27, 1992]. Original owner: Springfield TV Corp. Sale price: $47.5 million (including WKEF(TV) Dayton, OH & KSTU(TV) Salt Lake City). FCC approved: January 9, 1984.

WCVX-TV Vineyard Haven (ch 58)—Licensed to Cape Television Inc. Former owner: Cape Cod Television Inc. (Sentry Serivces Corp). Sale price: $826,000. FCC approved: June 16, 1992 [For the Record, July 6, 1992]. Previous owner: Donald P. Moore. Sale price: $3.8 million. FCC approved: December 18, 1988.

WHLL-TV Worcester (ch 27)—Licensed to JASAS Corp. Former owner: Sibos Inc. (owned by Central Mass. Television Inc.). Sale price: stock, including WFTY(TV) Washington. FCC approved: October 15, 1993 [For the Record, November 8, 1993]. Previous owner: Melvin Simon & others. Sale price: $8 million. FCC approved: October 18, 1983 [For the Record, November 7, 1983]. Former call letters: WSMW-TV. Note: On air January 2, 1970. Sold to Simon group by State Mutual Life Assurance Co. of America for $550,000. FCC approved: April 21, 1977 [For the Record, May 2, 1977].

WJBZ-TV Worcester (ch 14, now deleted)—Licensed to Capital Communications Corp. (see Springfield TV Broadcasting Corp., Group Ownership). Original owner: Salisbury Broadcasting Corp. [Fox, Wells & Rogers (30.4%); Kenneth P. & Milton P. Higgins (9.9%); & others]. Sale price: 20% stock interest in Springfield TV. FCC approved: October 15, 1958 [For the Record, October 20, 1958]. Original call letters: WWOR-TV. Note: Stn went off the air in 1969.

Michigan

WXON(TV) Allen Park (Detroit) (ch 20)—Licensed to WXON-TV Inc. (principally owned by Aben Johnson). Former owner: United Broadcasting Inc. Sale price: $233,952. FCC approved: June 1972 [*Broadcasting*, June 5, 1972]. Original call letters: WJMY(TV). Note: Founded by Robert M. Paar in 1962. CP sold to Triangle Broadcasting Co. [Robert P. Sanos (20%) & others] in 1962 for $45,000. Sold to United Broadcasting in 1964 for $115,000. FCC approved: July 8, 1964 [For the Record, July 13, 1964].

WBSX(TV) Ann Arbor (ch 31)—Licensed to Blackstar Communications Inc. Former call letters: WIHT(TV). Former owner: Fab Communications Inc. Sale price: $4.35 million [For the Record, July 31, 1989]. FCC approved: July 10, 1989.

WJUE(TV) Battle Creek (ch 43)—Licensed to Western Michigan Christian Broadcasting Inc. Former owner: Margaret Miller. Sale price: $55,467 for CP. FCC approved: October 20, 1992 [For the Record, November 23, 1992].

WUHQ-TV Battle Creek (ch 41)—Licensed to Channel 41 Inc. [John W. & William Lawrence, as family group, (53%)]. Original owner: Channel 41 Inc. [John W. & William Lawrence, as family group, (47%), & others]. Note: acquisition of positive control of licensee through purchase of stock from William Betts, Robert Braun, et al. FCC approved: May 30, 1974 [For the Record, June 17, 1974].

WNEM-TV Bay City (ch 5)—Licensed to Meredith Corp. (see Group Ownership). Former owner: Gerity Broadcasting Co. (James Gerity Jr.). Sale price: $11.5 million. FCC approved: April 16, 1969 [For the Record, April 21, 1969]. Note: Founded by Gerity Broadcasting in February 1954.

WWTV(TV) Cadillac (ch 9)—Licensed to Heritage Broadcasting Co. of Michigan. Former owner: Wilson Communications Inc. (Ralph C. Wilson). Sale price: $10.4 million (including WWUP(TV) Sault Ste. Marie, MI). FCC approved: March 3, 1989 [For the Record, March 20, 1989]. Previous owner: Fetzer Brodcasting Co. [John E. Fetzer (49.99%); Carl E. Lee, A. James Ebel, C.E. Ellerman, et al, (15.7%)]. Sale price: $6 million (including WWUP-TV Sault Ste. Marie, MI). FCC approved: December 28, 1978. Note: original owner Sparton Broadcasting Co. (owned by Sparton Corp., formerly Sparks-Withington Co.)., sold stn to Fetzer Television Inc. in 1958 for $1 million. FCC approved: July 24, 1958 [For the Record, August 4, 1958].

WTOM(TV) Cheboygan (ch 4)—See WPBN-TV Traverse City.

WDIV-TV Detroit (ch 4)—Licensed to Post-Newsweek Stations (see Group Ownership & Cross-Ownership). Original owner: Evening News Association (see Group Ownership & Cross-Ownership). Former call letters: WWJ-TV. Note: Stn was traded for Post-Newsweek's WTOP-TV (now WUSA-TV) Washington, plus $2 million to comply with FCC's cross-ownership rules. FCC approved: May 1978 [Changing Hands, May 22, 1978].

WJBK-TV Detroit (ch 2)—Licensed to WJBK License Inc. (see SCI Television Inc. in Group Ownership). Former owner: Gillett Communications Inc. Sale price: unknown. (See WAGA-TV Atlanta for details of sale). FCC approved: February 19, 1993 [For the Record, April 26, 1993].

WKBD-TV Detroit (ch 50)—Licensed to WKBD Inc. (owned by Paramount Stations Group, see Group Ownership). Former owner: WKBD Inc. (owned by Cox Communications, see Group Ownership). Sale price: $105 million. FCC approved: September 1, 1993 [For the Record, September 13,1993]. Previous owner: Field Communications. Sale price: $70 million. FCC approved: January 30, 1984. Previous owner: Kaiser Broadcasting Co. [77.5% owned by Kaiser Broadcasting Corp. (see Group Ownership) & 22.5% by Field Communications Corp. (owned by Field Enterprises Inc., Chicago)]. Sale price: 77.5% for $42.62 million [including KBHK-TV San Francisco; WFLD-TV Chicago; WLVI-TV Cambridge, MA; & WKBS-TV Burlington, NJ (Philadelphia)]. FCC approved: 1977. Original owner: Kaiser Broadcasting Corp. Note: FCC approved merger of Kaiser Broadcasting Corp.'s five independent UHFs (including WKBD-TV) & Field Communications Corp.'s one independent UHF in May 1973 [*Broadcasting*, May 14, 1973].

WXYZ-TV Detroit (ch 7)—Licensed to Scripps-Howard Broadcasting Co. (see Group Ownership). Former owner: Capital Cities/ABC Inc. Sale price: $246 million (including WFTS-TV Tampa). FCC approved: December 19, 1985. Previous owner: American Broadcasting Companies Inc. (acquired as part of ABC's acquisition by Capital Cities Communications). FCC approved: November 14, 1985. Original owner: American Broadcasting Co. Note: This was change of ownership when ABC merged with United Paramount Theaters Inc. FCC approved: February 9, 1953 [For the Record, February 16, 1953].

WJRT-TV Flint (ch 12)—Licensed to SJL-Michigan, owned by Media-Communications Partners Ltd. (see Group Ownership). Former owner: SJL-Michigan, owned by SJL Management Corp. Sale price: transfer of stock. FCC approved: April 28, 1992 [For the Record, May 18, 1992]. Previous owner: Knight-Ridder Broadcasting Co. Sale price: $39 million. FCC approved: June 6, 1989 [For the Record, June 26, 1989]. Previous owner: Poole Broadcasting Co. Sale price: $49.63 million (including WTEN(TV) Albany, NY; WPRI-TV Providence, RI; & WCDC(TV) Adams, MA). FCC approved: 1978 [Changing Hands, January 9, 1978]. Previous owner: Goodwill Stations Inc. (G.A. Richards trusts, John F. Patt, Worth Kramer & others). Sale price: $6 million. FCC approved: July 29, 1964 [For the Record, August 10, 1964].

WMCN(TV) Grand Rapids (ch 23, now deleted)—Licensed to Peninsular Broadcasting Co. [H&B Balaban Corp. (50%), John D. Loeks (33.3%), Howard W. Freck (16.6%)]. Sale price: $7,500. FCC approved: September 12. 1956 [For the Record, September 17, 1956]. Note: H&B Balaban purchased interest from E.A. McCready & present minority stockholders.

WOOD-TV Grand Rapids (ch 8)—Licensed to LIN-Central Broadcasting Corp. (owned by LIN Broadcasting, see Group Ownership). Former owner: Manhattan Cable Television (owned by Time Inc.). Sale price: $32 million. FCC approved: February 16, 1983 [For the Record, February 23, 1983]. Note: Stn founded August 15, 1949, by Leonard A. Versluis (call letters then WLAV-TV). Sold to Consolidated TV & Radio Broadcasters Inc. (Harry M. Bitner interests) as WOOD-TV in September 1951 for $1.38 million [For the Record, September 24, 1954]. Sold to Manhattan Cable as part of package deal including WOOD-AM-TV & WTCN-AM-TV Minneapolis; & WFBM-AM-TV Indianapolis for $15.75 million. FCC approved: April 17, 1957 [For the Record, April 22, 1957].

WZZM-TV Grand Rapids (ch 13)—Licensed to NTG Inc. Former owner: Western Michigan Broadcasting (owned by Price Communications). Sale price: $120 million (including WAPT-TV Jackson, MS; WSEE-TV Erie, PA; & WNAC-TV Providence, RI). FCC approved: September 11, 1989 [For the Record, September 25, 1989]. Previous owner: KKR Associates (see Group Ownership). Sale price: $62 million. FCC approved: December 19, 1985. Previous owner: Wometco Enterprises Inc. (Wometco was purchased as group by Kohlberg, Kravis, Roberts & McDonnell, see WTVJ(TV) Miami.) Previous owner: Synergistic Communications Corp. [West Michigan Telecasters stockholders (55%), Henry M. Hogan Jr., Paul Neal Averill & Elinor Bunin (45% as a group)]. Sale price: $14 million. FCC approved: December 1978 [Changing Hands, December 19, 1978]. Previous owner: West Michigan Telecasters Inc. (William C. Dempsey & others). Sale price: 55% of Synergistic stock. FCC approved: September 17, 1969 [For the Record, September 29, 1969]. Note: Began operation November 1, 1962, on interim basis whereby all four applicants operated on a cooperative basis. West Michigan Telecasters began operating stn January 25, 1965.

WIIM-TV Iron Mountain (ch 8)—Licensed to Danny Hood Evangelistic Association. Former owner: John R. Powley. Sale price: $500,000. FCC approved: May 14, 1992 [For the Record, June 8, 1992].

WIRN(TV) Ironwood (ch 12, now deleted)—Licensed to Lake Superior Broadcasting Co. (*Marquette* [MI] *Mining Journal*). Former owners: William J. Johnson & wife & others. Sale price: $10,000 for CP. FCC approved: January 8, 1958 [For the Record, January 13, 1958]. Former call letters: WJMS-TV.

WLLA(TV) Kalamazoo (ch 64)—Licensed to Christian Faith Broadcasting. Former owner: Channel 64 Inc. Sale price: $35,000 for CP. FCC approved: January 13, 1986 [For the Record, December 9, 1985].

WWMT(TV) Kalamazoo (ch 3)—Licensed to Gillett Communications Corp. (see Group Ownership). Former owner: Fetzer Broadcasting Co. Sale price: $80 million (including KMEG(TV) Sioux City, IA; KOLN(TV) Lincoln, NE; & KGIN(TV) Grand Island, NE). FCC approved: October 29, 1985 [For the Record, September 23, 1985]. Former call letters: WKZO(TV).

WLNS-TV Lansing (ch 6)—Licensed to Young Broadcasting Inc. Former owner: Backe Communications Inc. Sale price: $72 million (including WKBT(TV) LaCrosse, WI). FCC approved: May 14, 1986 [For the Record, April 14, 1986]. Previous owner: Gross Telecasting. Sale price: $48 million (including WKBT(TV) LaCrosse, WI). FCC approved: April 26, 1984. Former call letters: WJIM-TV.

WSYM-TV Lansing (ch 47)—Licensed to WTMJ Inc. (owned by The (Milwaukee) Journal Co., see Group Ownership, Cross-Ownership). Former owner: F&S Comm-News Inc. (Joel Ferguson, Sol Steadman & Douglas Crist). Sale price: $8.25 million. FCC approved: November 9, 1984 [For the Record, December 3, 1984].

WTOM-TV Lansing (ch 54, now deleted)—Licensed to Inland Broadcasting Co. Original owner: Lansing Broadcasting Co. (John C. Pomeroy & associates). Sale price: Lease with option to purchase at $166,254. FCC approved: September 21, 1954 [For the Record, September 27, 1954]. Original call letters: WILS-TV.

WLUC-TV Marquette (ch 6)—Licensed to Federal Enterprises. Former owner: Gillett Group (see Group Ownership). Sale price: $31 million plus (including KTVO(TV) Kirksville, MO). FCC approved: July 1987. Previous owner: Appleton (WI) Post-Crescent Publishing Co. Sale price: $65 per share (including WEAU-TV Eau Claire & WLUK-TV Green Bay, both WI; KTVO(TV) Ottumwa, IA; WOKR(TV) Rochester, NY; & 2 radio stns). FCC approved: June 14, 1984. Previous owner: Morgan Murphy Stations. Sale price: $3.1 million (including WLUK-TV Green Bay, WI). FCC approved: January 6, 1965. [For the Record, January 11, 1965]. Note: Founded in 1954 as WAGE-TV by Jerome Sill & H.R. Herzberg. Sold in 1955 to *Mining Journal*-Frank Russell group for $20,000 & call letters changed to WDMJ-TV. Control sold in 1959 to Morgan Murphy in stock transaction for overall considerations of $250,000 plus assumption by buying corporation of obligations totaling $102,000 & securing of notes totaling $160,000, with call letters changed to WLUC-TV.

WTLJ(TV) Muskegon (ch 54)—Licensed to Tri-State Christian TV Inc. (see Group Ownership). Former owner: Video Mall Communications Inc. [owned by Marvin D. Sparks (70%), Richard L. Woodby (15%), & John W. Elliott (15%)]. Sale price: $1.47 million cash, $30,000 escrow deposit. FCC approved: January 15, 1992 [For the Record, February 10, 1992]. Previous owner: Miami Valley Christian TV Inc. (headed by Sparks, Vernon Wilson, Homer Speece, Murray Ross, & William Koch). Sale price: $2 million (including WTJC(TV) Springfield, OH). FCC approved: January 15, 1991 [For the Record, February 4, 1991].

WILX-TV Onondaga (ch 10)—Licensed to Adams TV of Lansing Inc., owned by Paul A. Brissette (see Group Ownership). Former owner: Adams Communications Corp. (see Group Ownership). Sale price: Undisclosed (including WHOI(TV) Peoria, IL; KOSA-TV Odessa & KAUZ-TV Wichita Falls, both TX; WMTV(TV) Madison & WSAW-TV Wausau, both WI; & WTRF-TV Wheeling, WV). FCC approved: December 24, 1991 [For the Record, January 27, 1992]. Previous owner: Figgie Communications (owned by Figgie International Inc.). Sale price: $22.5 million. FCC approved: April 8, 1983. [For the Record, April 25, 1983]. Original owner: Television Corp. of Michigan (Howard E. Wilson & family principal owners). Sale price: $12 million. FCC approved: October 6, 1978. [Changing Hands, October 23, 1978]. Note: Stn founded March 15, 1959.

WEYI-TV Saginaw (ch 25)—Licensed to WEYI Inc. (owned by Television Station Partners, see Group Ownership). Former owner: Ziff Corp. Sale price: $57 million (including WRDW-TV Augusta, GA; WROC-TV Rochester, NY; & WTOV-TV Steubenville, OH). FCC approved: January 18, 1983 [For the Record, February 7, 1983). Former call letters: WKNX-TV. Note: Founded by Lake Huron Broadcasting Corp. Sold to Rust Craft on February 17, 1972, for $1.6 million [For the Record, March 13, 1972]. Rust Craft sold to Ziff-Davis in 1979 for $70 million with WJKS-TV Jacksonville, FL; WRDW-TV Augusta, GA; WTOV-TV Steubenville, OH; WROC-TV Rochester, NY; & WRCB-TV Chattanooga.

WGTQ(TV) Sault Ste. Marie (ch 8)— See WGTU(TV) Traverse City.

WWUP-TV Sault Ste. Marie (ch 10)—Licensed to Heritage Broadcasting Co. of Michigan. Former owner: Wilson Communications Inc. (Ralph C. Wilson). Sale price: $10.4 million (including WWTV(TV) Cadillac, MI). FCC approved: March 3, 1989 [For the Record, March 20, 1989]. Previous owner: Fetzer Broadcasting Co. [John E. Fetzer (49.99%); Carl E. Lee, A. James Ebel, C.E. Ellerman, et al (15.7%)]. Sale price: $6 million (including WWTV(TV) Cadillac, MI). (See WWTV(TV) Cadillac, MI.)

WGTU(TV) Traverse City (ch 29)—Licensed to Mark C., Scott L. & Kent R. Adams. Former owner: Stephen Adams (father). Sale included WGTQ(TV) Sault Ste. Marie, MI. FCC approved: September 11, 1989 [For the Record, September 25, 1989]. Previous owner: Michigan Center Broadcasting Inc. (subsidiary of Center Group Broadcasting, see Group Ownership), preceded by Michigan Television Network Inc. (closely held group headed by Harry Calcutt, pres & 12% own). Sale price of Center-Television transaction: $1.8 million. FCC approved: May 25, 1982 [For the Record, June 14, 1982].

WPBN-TV Traverse City (ch 7)—Licensed to WPBN-TV & WTOM-TV Inc. (owned by Beacon Broadcasters Ltd., see Group Ownership). Former owner: WPBN-TV & WTOM-TV Inc. (owned by United States Tobacco Co.). Sale price: $5.15 million (including satellite WTOM(TV) Cheboygan, MI). FCC approved: September 18, 1985 [For the Record, July 15, 1985]. Original owner: Lester Biederman & three others. Sale price: $3.5 million. (including WTOM-TV). FCC approved: September 12, 1979 [*Broadcasting*, October 1, 1979].

Minnesota

KCMT(TV) Alexandria (ch 7)—Licensed to Central Minnesota Television Co. (see Group Ownership). Former owner: Central Minnesota Television Co. (Thomas Barnstuble Jr., Bruce Barnstuble, Harris Widmer, Philip Vogel & Rozel Barnstuble, executors). Sale price: no consideration. FCC approved: November 18, 1974 [For the Record, December 2, 1974]. Note: Earlier in 1974, FCC granted involuntary transfer of control of licensee from Thomas K. Barnstuble to Rozel Barnstuble, Thomas K. Barnstuble Jr., Bruce Barnstuble, Philip Vogel & Harris W. Widmer, executors of estate of Mr. Barstuble. FCC approved: August 26, 1974 [For the Record, September 16, 1974].

KWCM-TV Appleton (ch 10)—Licensed to West Central Minnesota Educational TV Inc. (Phil Greseth). Former owner: West Central Minnesota Educational TV Inc. (Dr. Edward J. Kaufman). Sale price: no financial consideration. FCC approved: 1993 [For the Record, September 20, 1993].

KAAL(TV) Austin (ch 6)—Licensed to Wooster Republican Printing Co. Former owner: News Press & Gazette Co. (David R. Bradley & family, St. Joseph, MO). Sale price: $13.25 million. FCC approved: December 13, 1985 [For the Record, November 4, 1985]. Previous owner: Black Hawk Broadcasting Co. (merged with American Family Corp.). (See KITV-TV Sioux City, IA.) Sale price: $11.5 million. FCC approved: September 17, 1980 [Changing Hands, October 6, 1980]. Former call letters: KAUS-TV. Original owner: Minnesota-Iowa Television Co. (Chester A. Weseman, George Wilson, Martin Bustad, Harold Westby & Albert W. Smith). Sale price: $41,000 (with KAUS(AM) Austin). FCC approved: October 29, 1958 [For the Record, November 3, 1958]. Former call letters: KMMT(TV).

KDLH-TV Duluth (ch 3)—Licensed to Benedek Broadcasting. Former owner: Palmer Broadcast Co. (see Group Ownership). Sale price: $9.5 million. FCC approved: May 23, 1985 [For the Record, June 10, 1985]. Previous owner: KDAL Inc., subsidiary of WGN Continental Broadcasting Co. Sale price: $7.25 million. FCC approved: January 10, 1979. Former call letters: KDAL-TV. Original owner: Red River Broadcasting Co. Sale price: $3.3 million, including KDAL(AM). FCC approved: 1960.

WDIO-TV Duluth (ch 10)—Licensed to Hubbard Broadcasting Inc. Former owner: Channel 10 Inc. (owned by Harcourt Brace Jovanovich Inc.). Sale price: $10.75 million (including satellite WIRT(TV) Hibbing, MN). FCC approved: December 1987. Original owner: Channel 10 Inc., principally owned by Frank Befrea & others. Sale price: $5 million (including WIRT-TV Hibbing, MN). FCC approved: March 31, 1978.

WIRT-TV Hibbing (ch 13)—See WDIO-TV Duluth.

KEYC-TV Mankato (ch 12)—Licensed to Mankato Broadcasting Corp. (owned by United Communications Corp., et al, see Group Ownership). Former owner: Lee Enterprises Inc. (see Group Ownership). Sale price: $5 million. FCC approved: 1977. Original owner: Walter K. Mickelson & associates. Sale price: $400,000 in aggregate. FCC approved: February 24, 1960 [For the Record, February 29, 1960].

KARE(TV) Minneapolis (ch 11)—Licensed to Combined Communications Corp. (see Gannett Co. in Group Ownership). Former owner: WTCN Television Inc. (owned by Metromedia Inc., see Group Ownership). Sale price: $75 million. FCC approved: February 17, 1983 [For the Record, March 7, 1983]. Former call letters: WUSA-TV, WTCN-TV. Note: Founded by Robert Butler & associates in 1953. Sold to Harry M. Bitner interests in 1959 for $1.81 million. Bought by Time-Life Broadcast Inc. in package transaction including WTCN, WOOD-AM-FM-TV Grand Rapids, MI; & WFBM-AM-TV Indianapolis in 1957 for $15.75 million. Purchased by Chris-Craft in 1964 for $3.9 million. FCC approved: August 24, 1964 [For the Record, August 31, 1964]. Bought by Metromedia Inc. for $18 million in 1972 [*Broadcasting*, June 26, 1972].

KITN-TV Minneapolis (ch 29)—Licensed to Clear Channel Communications Inc. (see Group Ownership). Former owner: Nationwide Communications Inc. (see Group Ownership). Sale price: $36 million. FCC approved: October 3, 1993 [For the Record, November 15, 1993]. Previous owner: Channel 29 Television Inc. [owned by Beverly Hills Hotel Corp., which is owned by Ivan Boesky & family (53.2%) & Burton Slatkin & family (46.8%)]. Sale price: $22 million. FCC approved: July 30, 1985. Former call letters: KITN(TV). Original owner: Jonathan Byrd & others. Sale price: $12 million plus other considerations. FCC approved: March 20, 1984 [For the Record, April 2, 1984]. Former call letters: WFBT-TV.

KLGT-TV Minneapolis (ch 23)—Licensed to Sonlight Television Inc., owned by Robert Beale (50%) & Linda R. Brook. Former owner: Estate of KTMA Acquisition Corp., debtor (owned by Donald H. O'Connor). Sale price: $3.3 million. FCC approved: January 17, 1992 [For the Record, February 10, 1992]. Former call letters: KTMA-TV. Previous owner: KTMA-TV Inc. [United Cable TV Corp. (80%) & Buford TV Corp. (20%)]. Sale price: $13.8 million, comprising exchange of stock valued at $9-10 million, $2 million cash & 93% of accounts receivable minus unpaid operating expenses. FCC approved: September 30, 1986 [For the Record, August 25, 1986]. Previous owner: Buford TV Corp. Sale price: $7.5 million for 80% of the stn. FCC approved: September 5, 1984. Previous owner: Viking TV Inc. Sale price: $475,000 for CP. FCC approved: June 26, 1981.

KMSP-TV Minneapolis (ch 9)—Licensed to United TV Inc. (20th Century-Fox Film Corp.). Former owner: National Theaters. Sale price: $4.1 million. FCC approved: October 29, 1959 [For the Record, November 9, 1959]. Note: Founded as KETD-TV by Lee L. Whiting & group. Morris T. Baker & associates bought 75% for $300,000 in 1954 [For the Record, September 20, 1954]. Thomas P. Johnson, Seymour Weintraub & associates bought 100% for $1.14 million plus assumption of obligations amounting to $315,452 (including KEYD(AM), later sold) in 1956 [For the Record, June 4, 1956]. Call letters changed to KMGM-TV when Loew's Inc. bought 25% interest. National Telefilm Assoc. bought 75% interest for $650,000 in 1957 [For the Record, December 2, 1957]; remaining 25% from Loew's Inc. for $130,000 in 1958 [For the Record, February 10, 1958]. National Theaters bought KMGM-TV for $11 million [with WNTA-AM-FM Newark, NJ (New York City area)] in 1959 [For the Record, March 9, 1959].

WCCO-TV Minneapolis (ch 4)—Licensed to WCCO Television Inc., owned by Midwest Radio-Television Inc. [MTC Properties Inc. (53%), Minneapolis Star & Tribune Co. (47%)]. Former owner: Midwest Radio-Television Inc. [Mid-Continent Radio-TV Inc. (53%) & Minneapolis Star & Tribune Co. (47%)]. Sale price: $11.76 million (including WCCO-AM-FM). FCC approved: July 12, 1976 [For the Record, July 26, 1976]. Note: Began operating as WTCN-TV in 1949. Original owner Mid-Continent Radio-TV Inc. [Northwest Publications Inc. (50%) & Minnesota Tribune Co. (50%)] sold stn in 1952 to Midwest Radio-Television Inc. [Mid-Continent Radio-TV Inc. (53%) & CBS (47%)] in an exchange of properties. FCC approved: July 31, 1952 [For the Record, August 4, 1952]. Note: CBS sold its 47% interest to Minneapolis Star & Tribune Co. in November 1954 for $3.95 million.

KTTC(TV) Rochester (ch 10)—Licensed to KTTC Television Inc. (wholly owned subsidiary of Quincy Newspapers Inc.). Former owner: Southern Minnesota Broadcasting Co. (G. David Gentling 100%). Sale price: $4.25 million. FCC approved: May 6, 1976 [For the Record, May 24, 1976]. Note: Began operating as KROC-TV in 1953. Original owner: Southern Minnesota Broadcasting Co. (Agnes P. Gentling & others), transferred control of stn to Southern Minnesota Broadcasting Co. (G. David Gentling & others) in 1963 for $438,000 for 62.7% of stn & KROC(AM). FCC approved: April 1, 1963 [For the Record, April 8, 1963].

KXLT(TV) Rochester (ch 47)—See KXLI(TV) St. Cloud, MN.

KXLI(TV) St. Cloud (ch 41)—Licensed to KXLI Acquisition Corp. Former owner: Halcomm Inc. Sale price: assumption of debt (including KXLT-TV Rochester, MN). FCC approved: August 1990. Original owner: L.E.O. Broadcasting Inc. owned by N. Walter Goins. Merged with Halcomm Inc. FCC approved: May 1987.

KBRR(TV) Thief River Falls (ch 10)—See KVRR(TV) Fargo, ND.

KNMT(TV) Walker (ch 12)—Licensed to Central Minnesota Television Co. (see Group Ownership). Former owner: Central Minnesota Television Co. (Thomas Barnstuble Jr., Bruce Barnstuble, Harris Widmer, Philip Vogel & Rozel Barnstuble, executors). Sale price: no financial consideration. FCC approved: November 18, 1974 [For the Record, December 2, 1974]. Note: Earlier in 1974, FCC granted involuntary transfer of control of licensee from Thomas K. Barnstuble to Rozel Barnstuble, Thomas K. Barnstuble Jr., Bruce Barnstuble, Philip Vogel & Harris W. Widmerm, executors of estate of Mr. Barnstuble. FCC approved: August 26, 1974 [For the Record, September 16, 1974].

Mississippi

WLOX-TV Biloxi (ch 13)—Licensed to WLOX Broadcasting Co. (James S. Love III, Jo Love Little & Mary E. Love McMillan as a family group). Original owners: Estate of J.S. Love Jr., Mrs. J.S. Love Jr., & James S Love III (as a family group). Sale price: $0 (transfer of voting control). FCC approved: May 5, 1978.

WXVT(TV) Greenville (ch 15)—Licensed to Greenville Television. (owned 20% each by John F. Hash, Aubrey L. Collum, Larry Harris, Leon D. Long, & Jo Love Little). Former owner: Big River Broadcasting Co. of Greenville. Sale price: $1.43 million. FCC approved: August 28, 1991 [For the Record, September 16, 1991]. Previous owner: Big River Broadcasting Co. Sale price: $4.8 million. FCC approved: March 5, 1984 [For the Record, March 19, 1984].

WXXV-TV Gulfport (ch 25)—Licensed to Prime Cities Broadcasters Corp. of Mississippi [owned by John B. Tupper (40%), Richard F. Shively (40%), Henry B. Smart (10%), Lawrence C. McQuade (5%), William L. Kepper (5%) & Jon J. Masters]. Former owner: AmSouth Realty (subsidiary of AmSouth Bank N.A.). Sale price: $3.2 million. FCC approved: May 1, 1991 [For the Record, May 20, 1991]. Former owner: Four-O Inc. (debtor in possession), dba Gulf Coast Television. Sale price: $2.43 million (stn in bankruptcy proceeding). FCC approved: December 8, 1990.

WHLT(TV) Hattiesburg (ch 22)—Licensed to New Vision Televison I Inc. (see New Vision Television Inc. in Group Ownership). Former owner: Broadcasters of Mississippi. Sale price: $110 million. FCC approved: September 7, 1993 [For the Record, September 27, 1993]. Note: Part of multi-stn purchase (see KOLD-TV Tucson, AZ). Previous owner: Central Television Inc. Sale price: $55,299 for CP. FCC approved: July 15, 1986. [For the Record, January 7, 1985].

WBUY-TV (CP) Holly Springs (ch 40)—Licensed to Sonlight Broadcasting System Inc. (headed by Paul F. Crouch, pres of Trinity Broadcasting). Former owner: Rel Way Ltd., Relcom Corp. & Texas Mineral Inc. Sale price: $2 million (including WMPV-TV Molile, AL, & WPGD-TV Hendersonville, TN). FCC approved: July 27, 1989 [For the Record, August 14, 1989].

WAPT(TV) Jackson (ch 16)—Licensed to NTG Inc. Former owner: Magnolia Broadcasting Corp. (Price Communications Corp.). Sale price: $120 million (including WZZM-TV Grand Rapids, MI; WSEE-TV Erie, PA; & WNAC-TV Providence, RI). FCC approved: September 11, 1989 [For the Record, September 25, 1989]. Previous owner: Clay Communications Inc. (see Group Ownership). Sale price: $60 million (including WWAY(TV) Wilmington, NC; KJAC-TV Port Arthur & KFDX-TV Wichita Falls, both TX). FCC approved: June 1987. Previous owner: Television America Sixteen Inc. (owned by Lewis Hopper, et al). Sale price: $7.9 million. FCC approved: November 19, 1979. Original owner: American Public Life Broadcasting Co. (owned 100% by American Public Life Insurance Co.). Sale price: $500,000 plus assumption of approximately $3 million in liabilities. FCC approved: March 18, 1976 [For the Record, March 29, 1976].

WDBD(TV) Jackson (ch 40)—Licensed to Pegasus Broadcast Television Ltd. Former owner: D&K Broadcast Properties Ltd. Sale price: $21 million (including WDSI-TV Chattanooga, TN). FCC approved: February 18, 1993 [For the Record, March 8, 1993]. Previous owner: C. Kenneth Still, trustee [seller is trustee in bankruptcy case for Media Central Inc., Chattanooga-based group owner (owned by Morton Kent & family) that is bankrupt]. Former owner: Jackson Family Television Inc. Sale price: $9 million. FCC approved: June 22, 1989 [For the Record, July 10, 1989]. Previous owner: H. Bernard Dixon. Sale price: $2 million. FCC approved: November 6, 1985 [For the Record, October 28, 1985]. Original owner: Brenda Harrison. Sale price: $100,000 for 90% (transfer of control). FCC approved: March 11, 1985 [For the Record, March 25, 1985].

WJTV(TV) Jackson (ch 12)—Licensed to New Vision Television I Inc. (see New Vision Television Inc. in Group Ownership). Former owner: Broadcasters of Mississippi Inc. (owned by the News-Press & Gazette Co., see Cross-Ownership). Sale price: $110 million. FCC approved: September 7, 1993 [For the Record, September 27, 1993]. Note: Part of multi-stn purchase (see KOLD-TV Tucson, AZ). Previous owner: Capitol Broadcasting Co. (see Group Ownership). Sale price: $19 million. FCC approved: March 7, 1983 [For the Record, March 28, 1983]. Note: Stn founded as WSLI-TV March 15, 1954. Original owners plus additional interests formed Capitol Broadcasting in 1955 & changed to the present call letters.

WLBT-TV Jackson (ch 3)—Licensed to TV-3 Inc. (owned by Civic Communications Corp., composed of several former owners plus new interests). Former owner: TV-3 Inc. (a group consisting of 24 shareholders). Sale price: $12.76 million (including WLBM-TV Meridian, MS). FCC approved: December 12, 1983 [For the Record, January 2, 1984]. Note: Stn founded December 28, 1953 by Lamar life Insurance Co. License renewal denied by court decision, June 20, 1969. Interim operations begun by Communications Improvement in June 1971 after FCC approved. TV-3 began operations February 1, 1980.

WDAM-TV Laurel-Hattiesburg (ch 7)—Licensed to Beacon Broadcasters Ltd. (see Group Ownership). Former owner: Service Broadcasters Inc. Sale price: $25 million (including WCFT-TV Tuscaloosa, AL, & KYEL-TV Yuma, AZ). FCC approved: July 27, 1983. [Changing Hands, August 15, 1983]. Note: Stn founded June 8, 1956, on ch 9 by Matison, Matison, Fine & Fine group. Interest (51%) sold to WDSU Broadcasting Corp., September 19, 1956 [For the Record, September 24, 1956]. Began operation on ch 7 September 3, 1959. Sold 43.75% interest to S.A. Rosenblum. FCC approved: December 7, 1960. On September 18, 1978 licensee became Service Broadcasters, ownership held by Rosenblum, Smylie, et al.

WZZV(TV) Magee (ch 34)—Licensed to Signal Mississippi Inc. (Lewis Hopper, Robert Nichols & Walter J. Stiles). Former owner: Wyatt-Clark Broadcasting. Sale price: $92,763 for CP. FCC approved: July 28, 1986 [For the Record, March 31, 1986].

WGBC(TV) Meridian (ch 30)—Licensed to Global Communications Inc. (owned by Charles L. Young). Former owner: TV-3 Inc. (see WLBT-TV Jackson, MS). Sale price: $85,000. FCC approved: March 12, 1991 [For the Record, April 1, 1991]. Stn signed on in 1982. Former call letters: WLBM-TV.

WTOK-TV Meridian (ch 11)—Licensed to WTOK-TV Inc. (owned by United Broadcasting Corp.) Former owner: H&C Communications (see Group Ownership). Sale price: $13.1 million. FCC approved: October 24, 1984. Original owner: Southern TV Corp. (Robert F. Wright, et al). Sale price: $11.25 million. FCC approved: July 28, 1981.

WTZH(TV) Meridian (ch 24)—Licensed to Meridian Broadcasting Partnership. Former owner: Central Television Inc. (Civic Communications Corp.). Sale price: $1.5 million. FCC approved: August 15, 1985 [For the Record, July 15, 1985]. Former call letters: WHTV(TV). Previous owner: TV-3 Inc. (a group of 24 shareholders, including some of the new owners). Sale price: Consideration of $12.76 million (including WLBT-TV Jackson, MS). FCC approved: December 12, 1983 [For the Record, January 2, 1984]. Note: Stn founded June 10, 1968 by Central TV (Frank Delta Communications Corp. Sold to Central TV [Frank Spain (80%), et al] for $30,000). FCC approved: March 23, 1972 [For the Record, April 17, 1972].

WNTZ(TV) Natchez (ch 48)—Licensed to Delta Management Corp. (Charles H. Chatelain). Former owner: Ozone General Partnership (Alan N. Perkins). Sale price: $100,000. FCC approved: September 25, 1992 [For the Record, November 9, 1992]. Previous owner: MISS-LOU Communications Inc. Former owner: Associate Broadcasters Inc. Sale price: $600,000. FCC approved: January 19, 1989 [For the Record, February 6, 1989].

WDKM-TV Vicksburg (ch 35)—Licensed to Television Communications Inc. (Jack Rehburg). Former owner: Vicksburg Broadcasting Group. Sale price: $120,000 for CP. FCC approved: May 29, 1986.

WLOV-TV West Point (ch 27)—Licensed to Love Communications Co. (headed by James S. Love III & Robert R. O'Brien Jr.). Former owner: Venture Systems Inc. (headed by John Dyer). Sale price: $1.65 million. FCC approved: June 24, 1991 [For the Record, July 8, 1991]. Former call letters: WVSB-TV.

Missouri

KBSI(TV) Cape Girardeau (ch 23)—Licensed to Engles Communications Inc. Former owner: Cape Girardeau Family TV Inc. Sale price: $3 million. FCC approved: 1989.

KFVS-TV Cape Girardeau (ch 12)—Licensed to American Hirsch Broadcasting Co. (owned by American Family Corp., see Group Ownership). Original owner: Hirsch Broadcasting Co. (Oscar C. Hirsch & family). Sale price: $22.23 million. FCC approved: April 4, 1979 [*Broadcasting*, April 30, 1979].

KMIZ(TV) Columbia (ch 17)—Licensed to Stauffer Communications Inc. Original owner: Richard & Robert Koenig. Sale price: $5 million. FCC approved: December 13, 1984. Former call letters: KCBJ-TV.

KHQA-TV Hannibal (ch 7)—Licensed to Lee Enterprises Inc. (see Group Ownership). Original owners: Courier Post Pub. Co. (acquired 20% interest in Lee Broadcasting Inc.). FCC approved: July 1, 1953 [For the Record, July 13, 1953].

KRCG(TV) Jefferson City (ch 13)—Licensed to Cardinal Broadcasting Corp. (owned by Price Communications Inc., see Group Ownership). Former owner: LDX Group. Sale price: $28 million (including WEEK-TV Peoria, IL). FCC approved: November 11, 1984. Previous owner: William H. Weldon. Sale price: $3.15 million (including KNOS(AM) Jefferson City & KMOS-TV Sedalia, both MO). FCC approved: July 13, 1966 [For the Record, July 18, 1966].

KODE-TV Joplin (ch 12)—Licensed to Gilmore Broadcasting Corp. (see Group Ownership). Former owner: WSTV Inc. (owned by United Printers & Publishers). Sale price: $1.85 million (including KODE(AM)). FCC approved: May 23, 1962 [For the Record, May 28, 1962]. Previous owner: WSTV Inc. (Jack Berman & associates). Sale price: undisclosed stock transaction. Note: Founded by Austin Harrison & associates as KSWM-TV. Sold in 1956 to WSTV Inc. for $591,000 (with KSWM-AM).

KSNF(TV) Joplin (ch 16)—Licensed to Price Communications Inc. Former owner: Kansas State Network (owned by Standard Communications, see Group Ownership). Sale price: $11.8 million. FCC approved: November 12, 1986 [For the Record, October 6, 1986]. Original owner: Mid America Broadcasting (Virginia S. Hickey, William Burton, et al). Sale price: $1.11 million. FCC approved: April 29, 1975 [For the Record, May 12, 1975]. Former call letters: KTVS(TV).

***KCPT(TV) Kansas City (ch 19)**—Licensed to Public Television 19 Inc. Original owner: School District of Kansas City, MO. Sale price: $22,226. FCC approved: December 10, 1971 [For the Record, February 14, 1972]. Former call letters: KCSD-TV.

KCTV(TV) Kansas City (ch 5)—Licensed to Meredith Corp. (see Group Ownership). Original owner: KCMO Broadcasting Co. (T.L. Evans & Lester E. Cox). Sale price: $2 million (including KCMO-AM-FM). FCC approved: November 12, 1953 [For the Record, November 23, 1953]. Former call letters: KCMO-TV.

KCTY(TV) Kansas City (ch 25, now deleted)—Licensed to Allen B. DuMont Labs Inc. Original owner: Empire Coil Co. Sale price: $1 & assumption of certain obligations. FCC approved: December 31, 1953 [For the Record, January 11, 1954].

KMBC-TV Kansas City (ch 9)—Licensed to The Hearst Corp. (see Group Ownership). Former owner: Metromedia Inc. Sale price: $79 million. FCC approved: April 1, 1982 [*Broadcasting*, April 5, 1982]. Previous owner: Cook Paint & Varnish Co. Sale price: $10.4 million (including KMBC(AM) Kansas City, KMOS-TV Sedalia, both MO; & KFRM(AM) Concordia, KS). FCC approved:

July 26, 1961 [For the Record, August 7, 1961]. Note: KMBC Stations were founded by Arthur B. Church & sold to Cook in 1954 for $1.75 million. Cook, who at that time owned WHB-TV Kansas City (sharing time on ch 9 with KMBC-TV), sold WHB(AM) to Mid-Continent Broadcasting Co. for $400,000 & surrendered the license for WHB-TV.

KSHB-TV Kansas City (ch 41)—Licensed to Scripps-Howard Broadcasting Co. (see Group Ownership). Former owner: Benno C. Schmidt & BMA Corp. Sale price: $7.5 million. FCC approved: September 15, 1977 [For the Record, October 3, 1977]. Original owner: William D. Grant. Sale price: $438,500 for 62% of stn. FCC approved: 1971. Original call letters: KBMA-TV.

KSMO-TV Kansas City (ch 62)—Licensed to Kansas City TV 62 Ltd. Sale price: $10.525 million. FCC approved: April 1990 [Changing Hands, May 7, 1990]. Former call letters: KZKC. Former owner: KZKC Television Inc. Steven B. Engles, gen mgr of KZKC(TV) Kansas City, MO, has interest in Engles Communications, which recently bought KBSI(TV) Cape Girardeau, MO from subsidiary of Media Central. FCC approved: July 31, 1989.

WDAF-TV Kansas City (ch 4)—Licensed to Great American Broadcasting (part of the Taft Broadcasting reorganization October 1987, see Group Ownership). Former owner: Transcontinent TV Corp. Sale price: $26.9 million (including WDAF-AM-FM; WGR-AM-FM-TV Buffalo, NY; & WNEP-TV Scranton, PA). FCC approved: February 19, 1964. Note: Founded by Kansas City *Star* & *Times*. Sold to National Theaters for $7.6 million (with WDAF-AM-FM) in 1958 under divestiture order following consent judgment in 1957 in civil antitrust suit brought by the Department of Justice against the Kansas City Star Co. National Theaters sold stns to TTC for $9.75 million in 1960.

KTVO(TV) Kirksville (ch 3)—Licensed to Federal Enterprises. Former owner: Gillett Group (see Group Ownership). (See WLUC-TV Marquette, MI, for details of sale.) Previous owner: Turner Farrar Association (see Group Ownership). (For details of sale, see WEAU-TV Eau Claire, WI.) FCC approved: June 14, 1984. Previous owner: Turner-Farrar Association (partnership of O.L. Turner, trustee of Turner trust; Ethel M. Turner; & Bernice Horning, executrix of estate of Harry B. Horning). Sale price: no financial consideration. FCC approved: November 7, 1974 [For the Record, November 25, 1974]. Note: Earlier in 1974 FCC granted involuntary transfer of control of Turner-Farrar Association (partnership) from Harry R. Horning to Bernice Horning, executrix of estate of Mr. Horning. FCC approved: August 30, 1974 [For the Record, September 16, 1974].

KPOB-TV Poplar Bluff (ch 15)—See WSIL-TV Harrisburg, IL.

KQTV(TV) St. Joseph (ch 2)—Licensed to to TCS Television Partners. Former owner: Elba Development Corp. (Malcolm Glazer). Sale price: $56 million (including WRBL(TV) Columbus, GA, & WTWO(TV) Terre Haute, IN). FCC approved: April 6, 1990. Previous owner: Amaturo Group Inc. (see Group Ownership). Sale price: $9 million. FCC approved: September 10, 1979 [*Broadcasting*, October 1, 1979]. Note: Founded by Barton Pitts in September 1953. Sold to Kenyon Brown-Bing Crosby group in December 1955 for $550,000 & $200,000 in liabilities. Sold to Jesse D. Fine family in 1957 for $841,091 with KFEQ(AM) St. Joseph. Sold in 1963 to Mid-States Broadcasting Corp. (later Panax Corp.) for $1.75 million with KFEQ(AM) & KLIK(AM) Jefferson City, MO. Panax Corp. (formerly Mid-States Broadcasting) sold stn as KFEQ-TV in 1969 for $3.15 million to Intermedia Inc. which sold it to Amaturo Group Inc. (see Group Ownership) in July 1973 for $4.67 million, including KGRV(FM) St. Louis, MO, & KLYX(FM) Clear Lake City, TX. [*Broadcasting*, July 16, 1973].

KDNL-TV St. Louis (ch 30)—Licensed to Atlantic Broadcasting Co. Former owner: KDNL Inc. (owned by Cox Communications). Sale price: $21.5 million. FCC approved: July 14, 1989 [For the Record, July 31, 1989]. Previous owner: Evans Broadcasting Corp. [Thomas M. Evans (30%), E.P. Evans (30%), B. Loomis (30%), Jack Petrick (10%)]. Sale price: $17 million. FCC approved: November 25, 1981 [Changing Hands, May 19, 1980]. Previous owner: Evans Broadcasting Corp. (Thomas M. Evans 100%). Sale price: no financial consideration. FCC approved: July 8, 1976 [For the Record, August 2, 1976]. Note: Sold in 1968 by Greater St. Louis Television Corp. (Boyd W. Fellows & others) to Evans Broadcasting Corp. for $40,500. FCC approved: July 19, 1968 [For the Record, July 29, 1968].

KMOV(TV) St. Louis (ch 4)—Licensed to Viacom Inc. (Viacom International Inc. merged with Arsenal Acquiting Corp., September 1987.) Former owner: CBS Inc. (see Group Ownership). Sale price: $122.5 million. FCC approved: April 17, 1986. [For the Record, January 13, 1986]. Former call letters: KMOX-TV. Previous owners: Robert T. Convey & associates [St. Louis *Globe-Democrat* (Newhouse interests), 800 N. 12th Inc. (Elzey Roberts), KSTP Inc., & others]. Sale price: $4 million. FCC approved: October 23, 1957 [For the Record, October 28, 1957]. Original call letters: KWK-TV. Note: Conditioned on CBS disposal of permit for ch 11 in St. Louis.

KSDK-TV St. Louis (ch 5)—Licensed to Multimedia Inc. (see Cross-Ownership). Former owner: KSDK Inc. (owned by Pulitzer Publishing Co., see Cross-Ownership). Sale price: $9 million (including WXII-TV Winston Salem, NC, & WFBC(TV) Greenville, SC). FCC approved: February 17, 1983 [For the Record, March 14, 1983; *Broadcasting*, January 9, 1984]. Note: Stn founded February 7, 1947.

KTVI(TV) St. Louis (ch 2)—Licensed to KTVI Argyle Inc. (owned by Argyle Television Holding Inc., see Group Ownership). Former owner: KTVI-TV Inc. (owned by Times Mirror Co., see Group Ownership). Sale price: $35 million. FCC approved: May 14, 1993 [For the Record, May 31, 1993]. Note: Part of $80 million 2-stn sale with WVTM-TV Birmingham, AL. Previous owner: Newhouse Broadcasting Co. Sale price: $82 million (including WAPI-TV Birmingham, AL; KTVI(TV) St. Louis, MO; WSYR-TV Syracuse & satellite WSYE-TV Elmira, both NY; & WTPA(TV) Harrisburg, PA). FCC approved: March 27, 1980 [*Broadcasting*, March 31 & April 7, 1980]. Original owner: Paul E. Peltason (34.1%), Harry Tenenbaum (34.1%), & others (5.8%). Sale price: $7.57 million for 74% of stn. FCC approved: June 10, 1964 [For the Record, June 22, 1964].

KMOS-TV Sedalia 9 (ch 6)—Licensed to Board of Regents, Central Missouri State University. Former owner: Mid-America Television Co. Sale price: $1,000. FCC approved: June 6, 1978. Note: Founded by Milton J. Hinlein & others; sold to Cook Paint & Varnish Co. in 1958 for $50,000. Purchased by Metromedia Inc. & then sold to Jefferson TV Co. (later Mid-America) in 1961 for $200,000.

KDEB(TV) Springfield (ch 27)—Licensed to BANAM Broadcasting Inc. Former owner: Charles Woods TV Corp. Sale price: assumption of debt (including KARD(TV) West Monroe, LA; WTVW(TV) Evansville, IN; & KLBK-TV Lubbock, TX). FCC approved: March 16, 1993 [For the Record, April 5, 1993]. Previous owner: Kenneth E. Meyer (33%), Meyer Communications (17%), H.C. Wattner (15%) & others. Sale price: $13 million. FCC approved: March 18, 1985 [For the Record, February 18, 1985]. Previous owner: Steve W. Ball, Inks Franklin & Burks Development Co. Sale price: $1 million. FCC approved: January 31, 1978. Former call letters: KMTC-TV.

KOLR(TV) Springfield (ch 10)—Licensed to Independent Broadcasting Co. [J.H.G. Cooper (25%), John O. Cooper (26%), James H. Cooper (26%)]. Previous owner: Independent Broadcasting Co. (J.H.G. Cooper 77%). FCC granted relinquishment of positive control of licensee through transfer of stock. FCC approved: August 30, 1974 [For the Record, September 16, 1974].

KSPR(TV) Springfield (ch 33)—Licensed to Davis-Goldfarb Co. Former owner: Telepictures Broadcasting KSPR Corp. (owned by Lorimar-Telepictures Corp., see Group Ownership). (See KCPM-TV Chico, CA, for details of sale.) Original owner: Springfield Television Associates Ltd. Sale price: $3.47 million. FCC approved: December 12, 1984.

KYTV(TV) Springfield (ch 3)—Licensed to KY-3 Inc. (owned by Schurz Comm Inc.). Former owner: Harte-Hanks Communications Inc. Sale price: $50.8 million. FCC approved: February 1987 [For the Record, January 19, 1987]. Previous owner: Springfield Television Inc. Sale price: $20 million plus $582,500 for covenant not to compete. FCC approved: October 13, 1978 [Changing Hands, October 30, 1978]. Note: Harte-Hanks acquired Southern Communications in merger [*Broadcasting*, June 26, 1978]. Fifty percent of voting stock of Springfield Television Inc., transferred from Lester L. Cox (749 shares) & his wife, Claudine B. Cox (one share), & Lynn E. Bussey (749 shares) & wife, Virginia Cox Bussey (one share), to same persons dba Grand Prairie Investment Co. of which they are sole owners, in same proportion. Sale price: no consideration. FCC approved: October 29, 1970 [For the Record, November 16, 1979].

Montana

KPQD(TV) Billings (ch 6)—Licensed to Big Horn Communications Inc. (headed by Thomas Hendrickson). Former owner: BHC Associates Ltd. (owned by Tom Curtis & the estate of Dan Coon). Sale price: $200,000 for CP. FCC approved: May 3, 1991 [For the Record, June 3, 1991].

KTVQ(TV) Billings (ch 2)—Licensed to KTVQ Communications Inc. (subsidiary of Cordillera Communications, see Group Owners). Former owner: KTVQ Inc. (SJL of Montana Associates Ltd., owned by George D. Lilly). Sale price: $6.8 million. FCC approved: March 16, 1992 [For the Record, April 6, 1992]. Previous owner: The Montana Network (owned by Joseph S. Sample). Sale price: $18.90 million (including KXLF-TV Butte, KRTV(TV) Great Falls & KPAX-TV Missoula, all MT). FCC approved: December 21, 1983. Original owners: Joseph S. Sample, J. Carter Johnson, C.L. Crist & others. Sale price: $540,075 (with KOOK-AM). FCC approved: December 13, 1956 [For the Record, December 24, 1956]. Original call letters: KOOK-TV.

KULR-TV Billings (ch 8)— Licensed to KULR Corp. (owned by Dix Communications, see Group Ownership). Former owner: Harriscope Broadcasting Corp. (see Group Ownership). Sale price: $12.2 million (including KTWO-TV Casper, WY). FCC approved: December 12, 1986 [For the Record, November 3, 1986]. Previous owners: Rex H. Baker, Arthur Miller & Thor Myhre. Sale price: $350,000. FCC approved: March 8, 1967 [For the Record, March 13, 1967]. Previous owners: Paul Crain, Dan Snyder & associates. Sale price: $33,000 for 51% of the stn. FCC approved: 1965. Former call letters: KGHL-TV. Original owners: P. N. Fortin (50%), Warren J. Hancock (25%) & Kenneth L. Hancock (25%). Sale price: $745,000. FCC approved: 1962.

KCTZ(TV) Bozeman (ch 7)—Licensed to Big Horn Communications Inc. Former owner: Bee Broadcasting Associates. Sale price: $335,000 for CP.

KTVM(TV) Butte (ch 6)—See KECI-TV Missoula, MT.

KXLF-TV Butte (ch 4)—Licensed to Evening Post Publishing Co. Former owner: SJL Inc. (George D. Lilly & David McCurdy). (For details of sale see KPAX-TV Missoula, MT.) FCC approved: October 31, 1986 [For the Record, September 29, 1986]. Previous owner: The Montana Network (owned by Joseph S. Sample). (See KTVQ(TV) Billings for sale details.) Previous owner: Ed Craney & group. Sale price: $1.75 million (including KXLF(AM) & KXLJ-AM-TV Helena, MT). FCC approved: January 18, 1961 [For the Record, January 30, 1961]. Note: Mr. Sample immediately sold the Helena stns to Helena TV Inc. for $400,000 (see KTVH(TV) Helena).

KFBB-TV Great Falls (ch 5)—Licensed to MDM Broadcasting Inc., owned by Dix Stations (see Group Ownership). Former owner: Advance Corp. (principally owned by estate of late Donald P. Nathanson). Sale price: $5.2 million. FCC approved: April 26, 1982 [For the Record, May 17, 1982]. Previous owner: Harriscope Broadcasting Corp. Sale price: unknown. FCC approved: April 21, 1977. Previous owner: David E. Bright, Ernest L. Scanlon, Daniel T. O'Shea. Sale price: $850,000. FCC approved: May 23, 1962 [For the Record, June 4, 1962]. Original owner: Joseph P. Wilkins & associates. Sale price: $616,000. FCC approved: 1960.

KRTV(TV) Great Falls (ch 3)—Licensed to Evening Post Publishing Co. Former owner: SJL Inc. (George D. Lilly & David McCurdy). (For details of sale, see KPAX-TV Missoula, MT.) FCC approved: October 31, 1986 [For the Record, September 29, 1986]. Previous owner: Garryowen-Cascade TV Inc. (See KTVQ(TV) Billings, MT, for sale details.) Previous owner: Snyder & Associates (Dan Snyder, estate of Paul Crain, & others). Sale price: $1 million & liabilities. FCC approved: February 28, 1969 [For the Record, March 3, 1969]. Note: founded in 1958. Construction permit sold that year by Francis N. & Robert R. Laird to Snyder & Associates for $59,680 & cancellation of $19,000 debt owed to Snyder by Lairds. Former call letters: KCTL(TV).

KTVH(TV) Helena (ch 12)—Licensed to KTVH Inc. (Donald Bradley & Lyle Courtnage). Former owner: Capital City Television Inc. (owned by Lynn Koch & his wife, Karen). Sale price: $1.5 million. FCC approved: July 30, 1985. Former call letters: KTVG(TV). Previous owners: Tim Babcock (56.67%) & Bob Magness (43.33%). Sale price: $850,000. FCC approved: November 29, 1979 [For the Record, December 24, 1979]. Former call letters: KBLL-TV. Original call letters: KXLJ-TV. Note: 56.677% sold to Mr Babcock by Paul McAdam & A.W. Scribner. Sale price: $201,421.45 (including 56.677% of KBLL(AM) Helena). FCC approved: December 18, 1968 [For the Record, December 23, 1968].

Broadcasting & Cable Yearbook 1994
A-72

Founded by Ed Craney & associates in 1958. Bought by Joseph S. Sample for $1.7 million in 1961 (with KXLF-AM-TV Butte, & KBLL(AM) Helena, both Montana). Mr. Sample immediately sold the KBLL(AM) stn to W.L. Piehl & associates for $400,000. Mr. Piehl & associates sold KBLL(AM) stn to Capital City Television (Paul McAdam, A.W. Scribner & Bob Magness) for $5,000 plus $255,000 in obligations in 1963.

KCFW-TV Kalispell (ch 9)—See KECI-TV Missoula, MT.

KYUS-TV Miles City (ch 3)—Licensed to Custer Broadcasting Corp. (owned by David G. Rivenes & L. B. Foster). Former owner: KOUS-TV Inc. Sale price: $200,000. FCC approved: March 14, 1986.

KECI-TV Missoula (ch 13)—Licensed to Eagle Communications Inc. [Precht Communications (80%) & Advance Corp. (20%)]. Former owner: Western Broadcasting Co. (Dale Moore Stations). Sale price: $6.5 million plus $300,000 for covenant not to compete for KECI-TV & satellites KCFW-TV Kalispell & KTVM(TV) Butte, both MT. FCC approved: August 24, 1978 [Changing Hands, September 4, 1978]. Former call letters: KGVO-TV. Original owner: A.J. Mosby (78.8%), Aline Mosby (10.1%) & Mary Jane Bader (10.1%). Sale price: $818,841. FCC approved: September 10, 1964 [For the Record, September 21, 1964]. Original call letters: KMSO-TV.

KPAX-TV Missoula (ch 8)—Licensed to Evening Post Publishing Co. Former owner: SJL Inc. (George D. Lilly & David McCurdy). Sale price: $24 million (including KXLF-TV Butte; & KRTV(TV) Great Falls; both MT). FCC approved: October 31, 1986 [For the Record, September 29, 1986].

Nebraska

KCAN(TV) Albion (ch 8)—Licensed to Citadel Communications Co. Former owner: Amaturo Group Inc. Sale price: $3 million ($2.25 million cash & remainder note). FCC approved: January 1987 [For the Record, July 28, 1986]. Former call letters: KBGT-TV. Previous owner: NTV Enterprises Inc. (see Group Ownership). Sale price: $8.5 million (including KHGI-TV Kearney & KSNB-TV Superior, both NE). FCC approved: November 16, 1979. Original owner: Bi-States Co. (F. Wayne Brewster, et al, 100%). Sale price: $1.9 million (including KPHL-TV Hayes Center, KHOL-TV Kearney & KHTL-TV Superior, all NE). FCC approved: April 29, 1974 [For the Record, May 13, 1974]. Original call letters: KCNA-TV.

KGIN-TV Grand Island (ch 11)—See KOLN-TV Lincoln, NE.

KHAS-TV Hastings (ch 5)—Licensed to Nebraska Television Corp. (see Seaton Stations in Group Ownership). Original owner: Nebraska Television Corp. (Seaton Publishing Co., 51.67%). Sale price: no financial consideration. FCC approved: June 19, 1974 [For the Record, July 15, 1974].

KWNB-TV Hayes Center (ch 6)—See KHGI-TV Kearney, NE.

KHGI-TV Kearney (ch 13)—Licensed to Fant Broadcasting Company of Nebraska Inc. Former owner: Gordon Broadcasting Inc. Sale price: $2.05 million (including KSNB-TV Superior & KWNB-TV Hayes Center, both NE). FCC approved: May 14, 1993 [For the Record, May 31, 1993]. Previous owner: Amaturo Group Inc. Sale price: $10 million (including satellites KWNB(TV) Hayes Center & KSNB(TV) Superior, both NE). FCC approved: January 17, 1986 [For the Record, December 16, 1985]. Previous owner: NTV Enterprises Inc. (see Group Ownership). Sale price: $8.5 million (including KBGT-TV Albion, KWNB-TV Hayes Center, & KSNB-TV Superior, all NE). FCC approved: November 16, 1979 [Changing Hands, December 10, 1979]. Original owner: Bi-States Co. (F. Wayne Brewster, et al, 100%). Sale price: $1.9 million (including KBGT-TV Albion, KWNB-TV Hayes Center, & KSNB-TV Superior, all NE). FCC approved: April 29, 1974 [For the Record, May 13, 1974]. Original call letters: KHOL-TV.

KOLN-TV Lincoln (ch 10)—Licensed to Gillett Communications Corp. (see Group Ownership). Former owner: Cornhusker Radio TV Corp. (owned by Fetzer Stations). Sale price: $80 million (including WWMT(TV) Kalamazoo, MI; KMEG(TV) Sioux City, IA; & satellite KGIN-TV Grand Island, NE). FCC approved: October 29, 1985 [For the Record, September 25, 1985]. Original owner: Edward M. O'Shea, Bennett S. Martin & Harold E. Anderson. Sale price: $650,000 (with KOLN-AM). FCC approved: August 19, 1953 [For the Record, August 24, 1953].

***KUON-TV Lincoln (ch 12)**—Licensed to U. of Nebraska. Original owner: Cornhusker Radio & TV Corp. (John E. Fetzer). Sale price: no financial consideration. FCC approved: July 28, 1954 [For the Record, August 2, 1954]. Original call letters: KOLN-TV (now being used on ch 10 Lincoln). Note: Mr. Fetzer bought KOLN-TV Lincoln, ch 12, in 1953 (see KOLN-TV Lincoln, NE). His purchase of KFOR-TV Lincoln on ch 10 for $300,000 from Cornbelt Broadcasting Corp. (Stuart Investment Co.) was approved by FCC March 24, 1954 [For the Record, March 29, 1954]. The ch 12 facility is now KUON-TV; the ch 10 facility is now KOLN-TV.

KSNK(TV) McCook (ch 8)—See KSNC(TV) Great Bend, KS.

KNOP-TV North Platte (ch 2)—Licensed to North Platte Television Inc. (owned 93% by FerRich Broadcasting Co., Richard F. Shively, voting trustee). Former owner: FerRich Broadcasting Co. (Ferris E. Traylor & Richard F. Shively). Sale price: no financial consideration (including KNOP-AM). FCC approved: October 28, 1970 [For the Record, November 16, 1970]. Note: original owners Ray J. Williams, Franklin R. Stewart & Alvin E. Larsen Jr. Sold stn in 1958 to North Platte for $5,000 for CP, plus ownership in permittee by Mr. Williams. North Platte Television Inc. (Rush C. Clark & associates) sold stn (along with KNOP-AM) to FerRich Broadcasting Co. [Ferris E. Traylor (83.33%) & Richard F. Shively (16.67%)] in 1967. Sale price: $216,810 (including KNOP(AM)). FCC approved: June 16, 1967 [For the Record, June 26, 1967]. Original call letters: KWSL-TV.

KETV(TV) Omaha (ch 7)—Licensed to KETV Television Inc. (owned by Pulitzer Publishing, see Group Ownership). Former owner: Channel 7 Corp. (subsidiary of Peter Kiewit Sons' Inc.). Sale price: $9.45 million. FCC approved: February 26, 1976 [For the Record, March 8, 1976]. Original owner: Herald Corp. (owned by Omaha World Publishing Corp.). Sale price: $41.4 million for entire publishing firm with about $5 million allocated to the TV stn. FCC approved: June 5, 1963 [For the Record, June 17, 1963].

KGMC-TV Omaha (ch 15)—Licensed to Pappas Telecasting of the Midlands. Former owner: Mid-America Broadcasting Inc. Sale price: $350,000. FCC approved: June 21, 1990. Former call letters: KPQC(TV).

KMTV(TV) Omaha (ch 3)—Licensed to Lee Enterprises Inc. Original owner: May Broadcasting Co. Sale price: $89 million (including KGUN-TV Tucson, AZ, & 48.8% of KFAB(AM)/KGOR(FM) Omaha, NE). FCC approved: November 16, 1986 [For the Record: September 22, 1986]. Note: May Broadcasting Co. purchased 25% of stn for $550,000 in 1960 from Central Broadcasting Co., thereby raising their holdings to 100%.

WOWT-TV Omaha (ch 6)—Licensed to Chronicle Broadcasting Co. (see Cross-Ownership). Former owner: Meredith Corp. (see Group Ownership). Sale price: $9.15 million. FCC approved: May 27, 1975 [Changing Hands, June 2, 1975; For the Record, June 9, 1975]. Former call letters: WOW-TV. Note: original owner Radio Station WOW Inc. (Francis P. Matthews & associates) sold stn with WOW(AM) in 1951. Sale price: $2.525 million. FCC approved: September 26, 1951 [For the Record, October 1, 1951].

KSTF(TV) Scottsbluff (ch 10)—Licensed to Stauffer Communications. Former owner: Burke Broadcasting Co. of Cheyenne (see Group Ownership). (For details of sale see KYCU-TV Cheyenne.) FCC approved: July 8, 1986. Previous owner: Wyneco Communications Inc. (wholly owned subsidiary of Lamb Communications). Sale price: $9.7 million (part of a multi-stn deal, see KYCU-TV Cheyenne). FCC approved: October 14, 1983 [For the Record, November 7, 1983]. Note: Sold to Wyneco by Frontier Broadcasting Co. Sale price: $3 million (including KTVS(TV) Sterling, CO; KYCU-TV Cheyenne; & CP for KVRW(TV) Rawlins, WY). FCC approved: July 6, 1972 [*Broadcasting*, July 10, 1972].

KSNB-TV Superior (ch 4)—See KHGI-TV Kearney, NE.

Nevada

KVVU-TV Henderson-Las Vegas (ch 5)—Licensed to Meredith Corp. (see Group Ownership). Former owner: Carson Broadcasting Corp. (Johnny Carson, Herbert Kaufman & others). Sale price: $36 million. FCC approved: April 5, 1985. Previous owner: Nevada Independent Broadcasting Corp. (William H. Hemstadt & others). Sale price: $5.5 million. FCC approved: March 30, 1979 [*Broadcasting*, April 16, 1979]. Note: Founded in September 1967 by Nevada Communications Inc. (Charles Vanda). Nevada Communications Inc. sold CP in 1969 to Levin-Townsend Enterprises Inc. Sale price: $850,000. FCC approved: May 1, 1969 [For the Record, May 12, 1969]. Levin-Townsend sold stn to Nevada Independent Broadcasting Corp. in 1971. FCC approved: September 1, 1971 [*Broadcasting*, September 27, 1971].

KLAS-TV Las Vegas (ch 8)—Licensed to KLAS Inc. (owned by Landmark Communications Inc., see Cross-Ownership). Former owner: Summa Corp. (Howard R. Hughes estate). Sale price: $8 million. FCC approved: July 1978 [Changing Hands, July 17, 1978]. Original owner: Las Vegas Television Inc. (H.M. Greenspun & others). Sale price: $3.65 million. FCC approved: February 14, 1968 [For the Record, March 4, 1968]. Note: Founded by H.M. Greenspun & others in 1953. Greenspun increased his holdings to 67.525% by acquiring 44.755% from stockholder R. G. Jolley for $50,000 in 1957.

KTNV-TV Las Vegas (ch 13)—Licensed to WTMJ Inc., (owned by The (Milwaukee) Journal Co., see Group Ownership). Former owner: Channel 13 of Las Vegas Inc. (Arthur Powell Williams Family Group, 100%). Sale price: $13.5 million. FCC approved: June 29, 1979 [*Broadcasting*, July 16, 1979]. Former call letters: KSHO-TV. Note: Founded by Moritz Zenoff. Mr. Zenoff sold stn (with KBMI(AM) Henderson, NV) to Television Co. of America Inc. (Frank Ocarart, Albert Zugsmith, Arthur B. Hogan & John Feldmann) in 1956 for $200,000. FCC approved: November 29, 1956 [For the Record, December 29, 1956; December 10, 1956]. In 1957, Frank Oxarart & associates sold stn to Mervyn L. Adelson for $70,000. FCC approved: November 21, 1957 [For the Record, December 2, 1957]. In 1959 Mr. Adelson sold stn to Nevada Broadcasters Fund Inc. for $137,500. FCC approved: November 4, 1959 [For the Record, November 16, 1959]. In 1961 stn was transferred to Harry Wallerstein, receiver in bankruptcy. In 1965 the stn was denied a license renewal by the FCC. In 1967 Channel 13 of Las Vegas Inc. [Arthur Powell Williams (20%), Desert Broadcasting Inc. (20%), Ettlinger Broadcasting Corp. (20%), Clark County Communications Inc. (20%), & Talmac Inc. (20%)] was granted interim operating authority [*Broadcasting*, August 14, 1967]. In 1969 Talmac Inc. (now Channel 13 of Las Vegas Inc.) was granted a CP for Channel 13 in Las Vegas. FCC approved: April 16, 1969 [For the Record, April 28, 1969]. The Arthur Powell Williams Family Group acqured 100% control of Channel 13 of Las Vegas by buying out 50% share of the Ettlinger Group for $1.15 million in July 1974 [*Broadcasting*, July 29, 1974].

KBLR(TV) Paradise (ch 39)—Licensed to Summit Media Limited-Liability Co. (Scott Gentry, Bruce F. Becker, William O'Connell, et al.). Former owner: Rose Communications (Glenn Rose). Sale price: $1.5 million. FCC approved: 1993 [For the Record, September 20, 1993].

KCRL(TV) Reno (ch 4, now deleted)—Sunbelt Broadcasting Co. Former owner: Cord Foundation. Sale price: $24.45 million. FCC approved: September 13, 1989. Previous owner: Nevada Telecasting Corp. (Robert C. Fish). Note: Sale of control of permittee corporation to Ervin V. Willat for $500 [For the Record, April 21, 1958].

KTVN(TV) Reno (ch 2)—Licensed to Sarkes Tarzian Inc. Former owner: Lee Hirshland, et al. Sale price: $12.5 million. FCC approved: August 13, 1980.

New Hampshire

WNHT(TV) Concord (ch 21)—Licensed to New England Television. Former owner: NHTV 21 Inc. (The Flatley Company). Sale price: $1.5 million. FCC approved: November 1991 [Changing Hands, December 16, 1991]. Previous owner: Frances Shaine, et al. Sale price: $5 million. FCC approved: September 14, 1984.

WMUR-TV Manchester (ch 9)—Licensed to WMUR-TV Inc. (owned by Commercial Dispatch Publishing Co.). Former owner: United TV Co. of New Hampshire (owned by United Broadcasting Co.). Sale price: $5 million. FCC approved: October 14, 1981. Original owner: Radio Voice of New Hampshire Inc. (Francis P. Murphy). Sale price: $450,000. FCC approved: February 3, 1959 [For the Record, February 9, 1959].

WGOT(TV) Merrimack (ch 60)—Licensed to Paugus Television Inc. Former owner: Golden Triangle TV 60 Corp. Sale price: $1.35 million. FCC approved: January 6, 1989 [For the Record, January 23, 1989].

New Jersey

WOCN(TV) Atlantic City (ch 52, now deleted)—Licensed to David E. Mackay. Original owner: Matta Enterprises. Sale price: $10,446 (covering cost of securing CP). FCC approved: April 14, 1954 [For the Record, April 19, 1954].

WWAC(TV) Atlantic City (ch 53)—Licensed to Cellular Phone Centers Inc. (headed by David W. Allen & Harry R. Jenny Jr.). Former owner: Channel 53 Corp. (headed by William Gross). Sale price: $20,000. FCC approved: May 9, 1991 [For the Record, May 27, 1991]. Previous owners: Pennsylvania Pay TV Inc. (William & Leon Gross), preceded by Frank Syracusa, et al. Sale price of Penn.-Syracusa transaction: $200,000. FCC approved: September 16, 1985 [For the Record, March 4, 1985].

WKBS-TV Burlington (ch 48, now deleted)—Licensed to Field Communications Corp. (owned by Field Enterprises Inc., Chicago). Original owner: Kaiser Broadcasting Corp. (100%). Sale price: $42.62 million (including KBHK-TV San Francisco; WFLD-TV Chicago; WLVI-TV Cambridge, MA; & WKBD-TV Detroit). FCC approved: 1977.

WNJU-TV Linden (ch 47)—Licensed to Reliance Capital Group, L.P. Former owner: WNJU-TV Broadcasting Corp. [Jerry Perenchio, Alan D. (Bud) Yorkin, Norman Lear, et al]. Sale price: $70 million. FCC approved: December 3, 1986 [For the Record, November 10, 1986]. Previous owner: Columbia Pictures Industries Inc. Sale price: $6 million. FCC approved: December 26, 1979 [For the Record, January 14, 1979]. Previous owners: Henry P. Becton, Fairleigh S. Dickinson Jr., & others. Sale price: $8.1 million. FCC approved: September 9, 1970 [For the Record, September 21, 1970]. Note: Founded in 1965.

***WNET(TV) Newark (ch 13)**—Licensed to Educational Broadcasting Corp. {The National Educational Television (NET) network merged with Educational Broadcasting Corp. in 1970 [*Broadcasting*, July 6, 1970]}. Former call letters: WNDT(TV). Note: Founded in 1945 by Irving R. Rosenhaus & Frank Bremer as WATV(TV). Sold in 1958 to National Telefilm Assoc. (Elly Landau & associates) for $2.5 million stock transaction plus $988,000 in consultant fees & covenant not to compete (including WAAT-AM-FM). Sold in 1959 to National Theaters Inc. for $1.1 million in stock (including WNTA-AM-FM). Sold in 1961 as WNTA-TV to Educational Broadcasting Corp. for $6.2 million. FCC approved: October 25, 1961 [For the Record, November 6, 1961].

WWHT(TV) Newark (ch 68)—Licensed to Silver King Broadcasting (owned by Home Shopping Network Inc.) Former owner: Wometco WWHT Inc. (owned by KKR Associates). Sale price: $25 million (including WSNL-TV Smithtown, NY). FCC approved: September 18, 1986 [For the Record, August 25, 1986]. Former call letters: WBTB-TV. Previous owner: Blonder-Tongue Broadcasting [Issac S. Blonder & Ben H. Tongue (20% each);& Wometco, group owner (80%)]. (For details of sale see WTVJ(TV) Miami, FL.) FCC approved: July 20, 1977 [For the Record, August 1, 1977]. Note: Wometco interest acquired from Messrs. Blonder & Tongue for $1.7 million. Note: Atlantic Video Corp. sold the CP for WWRO to Blonder-Tongue in 1972 for $252,099. Blonder-Tongue Broadcasting Corp. [Isaac S. Blonder (80%) & Ben H. Tongue (20%)] was purchased from Blonder-Tongue Broadcasting Corp. [Issac S. Blonder & Ben H. Tongue (50% each)] for $60,000 for CP. FCC approved: August 12, 1974. Original call letters: WWRO(TV).

WXTV(TV) Paterson (ch 41)—Licensed to Univision. Former owner: Spanish International Communications Corp. Sale price: $301.5 million, comprising $75 million cash & remainder note (including KFTV(TV) Hanford, KMEX-TV Los Angeles, both CA; WLTV(TV) Miami, FL; & KWEX-TV San Antonio, TX.

WHSP(TV) Vineland (ch 65)—Licensed to Silver King Broadcasting (owned by Home Shopping Network Inc.). Former owner: Press Broadcast Co. (owned by *Asbury Park* (NJ) *Press*). Sale price: $23 million. FCC approved: December 1986 [For the Record, September 1, 1986]. Former call letters: WSJT(TV). Previous owner: Richard Milstead, trustee in bankruptcy. Sale price: $3 million. FCC approved: January 22, 1985 [For the Record, February 4, 1985]. Former call letters: WRBV(TV).

WMGM-TV Wildwood (ch 40)—Licensed to South Jersey Radio Inc. (Howard L. Green & D. Simmons). Former owner: Robert R. Nelson, et al. Sale price: $108,000 for 50% of stock. FCC approved: December 19, 1985 [For the Record, October 21, 1985]. Former call letters: WCMC-TV. Previous owner: Francis J. Matrangola. Sale price: $590,000 for CP (including WCMC-AM-FM). FCC approved: July 14, 1965 [For the Record, July 19, 1965].

New Mexico

KGGM-TV Albuquerque (ch 13)—Licensed to Lee Enterprises Inc. (see Group Ownership, Cross-Ownership). Former owner: New Mexico Broadcasting Co. Inc. Sale price: Constitutes purchase of remaining 58% of New Mexico Broadcasting stock, & includes satellite KBIM-TV Roswell, NM. FCC approved: September 16, 1991 [For the Record, September 30, 1991].

KNAT-TV Albuquerque (ch 23)—Licensed to Trinity Broadcasting of Arizona Inc. Former owner: Carson Communications Corp. [group of 18 stockholders headed by Johnny Carson, chmn, & Neil Simon, pres, (23.94% each)]. Sale price: $2.25 million. FCC approved: December 4, 1985 [For the Record, November 4, 1985]. Previous owner: New Mexico Visions Inc. (owned by Eddie Pena). Sale price: $2.875 million plus $830,000 for assumption of broadcast rights. FCC approved: July 23, 1982 [For the Record, August 9, 1982]. Former call letters: KLKK-TV.

KOAT-TV Albuquerque (ch 7)—Licensed to to KOAT Television Inc. (owned by Pulitzer Publishing Co., see Group Ownership). Former owner: WGAL Television Inc. (see Steinman Stations, Group Ownership). Sale price: $5 million. FCC approved: May 7, 1969 [For the Record, May 19, 1969]. Note: Founded in 1953. Sold by A.M. Caldwell, Walter Stiles & others in 1957 for $718,500 to Clinton D. McKinnon. In 1959 KOAT-TV & KVOA-TV Tucson, AZ, merged, & Mr. McKinnon became 40% owner of both stns. Both stns sold by Alvarado Television Co. in 1962 to Steinman for $3.25 million.

KOB-TV Albuquerque (ch 4)—Licensed to KOB-TV Inc. (owned by Hubbard Broadcasting Inc., see Group Ownership). Former owners: Time Inc. & Wayne Coy (each 50%). Sale price: $1.5 million (including KOB(AM)). FCC approved: March 13, 1957 [For the Record, March 18, 1957]. Note: Time Inc. & Mr. Coy purchased stns in May 1952 from T.M. Pepperday-Albuquerque *Journal* for $900,000 [For the Record, June 2, 1952].

KAVE-TV Carlsbad (ch 6)—Licensed to Marsh Media (Stanley Marsh III (50%), Michael C. Marsh (20%), Estelle Marsh Watlington (10%), Tom F. Marsh (10%), & Tom F. Marsh Special Trust (10%). Former owner: John B. Walton Jr. Sale price: $3 million (including KELP-TV El Paso). FCC approved: February 24, 1976 [For the Record, March 8, 1976]. Note: KAVE-TV was founded by Val Lawrence & associates. Bought by Edward P. Talbott, Nancy & John H. Battison in 1955 for $150,000. Mr. Talbott acquired full ownership in 1958 paying $43,500 for the Battisons' interests. John Deme & associates bought the stn in 1963 for the estate of Mr. Talbott for $168,000. Mr. Walton purchased the stn in 1966 for $326,425. FCC approved: September 7, 1966 [For the Record, September 19, 1966].

KVIO-TV Carlsbad (ch 6)—Licensed to Pulitzer Broadcasting Company. Former owner: Marsh Media of El Paso. Sale price: $1.75 million. FCC approved: December 27, 1992 [For the Record, January 18, 1993].

KVIH-TV Clovis (ch 12)—Licensed to Marsh Media Inc. Former owner: McAlister TV Enterprises (Bill B. McAlister & family). Sale price: $1.5 million. FCC approved: July 28, 1986 [For the Record, October 14, 1985]. Former call letters: KMCC-TV. Previous owner: Mel Wheeler Inc. (owned by Melvin L. Wheeler). Sale price: $658,000. FCC approved: March 23, 1979 [*Broadcasting*, April 16, 1979]. Former call letters: KFDW-TV. Note: Founded by Frank Lesley & Mae Strauss as KICA-TV in 1957. 50% sold to Texas Telecasting in 1959 for $10,000 & assumption of $170,000 in obligations. Bought by John H. Marshall & family in 1961 as KVER-TV for $295,600. Sold to Bass Broadcasting in 1964 for $350,000. FCC approved: January 22, 1964 [For the Record, February 3, 1964]. Sold to Mel Wheeler Inc. in 1976 for $480,000. FCC approved: October 6, 1976 [*Broadcasting*, October 25, 1976].

KOBF-TV Farmington (ch 12)—Licensed to KOB-TV Inc. (owned by Hubbard Broadcasting Inc., see Group Ownership). Former owner: Four States Television Inc., owned by Stephen Adams of Adams Communications (see Group Ownership). Sale price: $2.35 million. FCC approved: July 27, 1983 [For the Record, August 15, 1983]. Note: stn founded October 20, 1972 by Gerald R. Proctor et al Sold in 1977 to John R. Catsis et al. Purchased by Four States TV on January 30, 1981. Former call letters: KIVA-TV.

KHFT(TV) Hobbs (ch 29)—Licensed to Warren Electronics Systems Inc. Former owner: Hobbs Family Television Partnership. Sale price: assumption of debt for CP. FCC approved: September 25, 1989 [For the Record, October 16, 1989].

KZIA(TV) Las Cruces (ch 48)—Licensed to Lee Enterprises Inc. Former owner: Southwestern Broadcasting Co. Sale price: $440,000. FCC approved: February 26, 1993 [For the Record, March 15, 1993]. Former call letters: KASK-TV. Previous owner: Bayport Communications of New Mexico Inc. (owned by Roy E. Henderson). Sale price: $800,000. FCC approved: 1990. Previous owner: Las Cruces Full Power TV Inc. Sale price: $825,000. FCC approved: August 1987 [For the Record, June 15, 1987].

KBIM(TV) Roswell (ch 10)—Licensed to Lee Enterprises Inc. (see Group Ownership, Cross-Ownership). Former owner: New Mexico Broadcasting Co. Sale price: Constitutes purchase of remaining 58% of New Mexico Broadcasting stock, & includes KGGM-TV Albuquerque. FCC approved: September 16, 1991 [For the Record, September 30, 1991]. Previous owner: Holsum Inc. Sale price: $5 million. FCC approved: April 12, 1989 [For the Record, May 1, 1989].

KOBR-TV Roswell (ch 8)—Licensed to Stanley S. Hubbard Trust (Hubbard Broadcasting, see Group Ownership). Former owner: Caprock Telecasting Inc. Sale price: $2 million plus considerations. FCC approved: September 1983 [Changing Hands, September 5, 1983]. Former call letters: KSWS(TV). Note: Caprock purchased KSWS-TV & KCBD-TV Lubbock, TX, from KCBD Associates (subsidiary of the State-Record Co., a Columbia, SC-based nwspr publisher) for $10.75 million. Caprock already owned KBIM-TV Roswell, & the spin-off of KSWS-TV to Hubbard was part of the original deal. Founded by John A. Barnett in 1953. Sold by John A. Barnett estate (Frances Maye Barnett, Paul B. McEvoy & John A. Barnett Jr., executors) in 1968 to Bryant Radio & Television Inc. for $250,000 plus $234,375 in obligations. FCC approved: May 13, 1968 [For the Record, May 20, 1968]. Sold to State Telecasting Co. along with KCBD-TV Lubbock, TX, for $6 million. FCC approved: May 26, 1971 [*Broadcasting*, May 31, 1971].

KRNM-TV Roswell (ch 10, now deleted)—Licensed to New Mexico Telecasting Co. (Perry C. Maxwell, Penrod Toles & Clarence E. Hinkle). Original owner: William Sam Evans. Sale price: $10,000 for CP, plus assumption of obligations. FCC approved: February 15, 1961 [For the Record, February 27, 1961].

KFUR-TV Santa Fe (ch 11, now deleted)—Licensed to K&H TV Station (Milford Kay & Raymond F. Hayes). Original owner: Harrison M. Fuerst. Sale price: $2,700 for CP, for out-of-pocket expenses. FCC approved: March 1, 1961 [For the Record, March 6, 1961].

KKTO(TV) Santa Fe (ch 2)—Licensed to KGSW-TV Inc. Former owner: Coronado Communications Company. FCC approved: December 22, 1992 [For the Record, January 18, 1993].

New York

WNYT(TV) Albany (ch 13)—Licensed to Viacom Inc. (Viacom International Inc. merged with Arsenal Acquiring Corp., September 1987). Former owner: Sonderling Broadcasting Corp. (see Group Ownership). Sale price: merger between Viacom & Sonderling totalled $32 million (see *Broadcasting*, January 1, 1979). FCC approved: November 7, 1979. Former call letters: WAST(TV). Previous owner: Van Curler Broadcasting Corp. (Glen Alden Corp). Sale price: $8 million. FCC approved: November 6, 1968 [For the Record, November 11, 1968]. Note: Founded in 1954 by Stanley Warner Corp. & Colonel Harry Wilder & others. Left air in 1955 & resumed operation in 1956, when Stanley Warner Corp. bought 50% held by Wilder group for $425,000. Stanley Warner Corp. merged with Glen Alden Corp. in 1967. Former call letters: WTRI(TV).

WTEN(TV) Albany (ch 10)—Licensed to Young Broadcasting Inc. Former owner: Knight-Ridder Broadcasting. Sale price: $32 million (including WCDC(TV) Adams, MA). FCC approved: August 24. 1989 [For the Record, September 11, 1989]. Previous owner: Albany Television Inc. (see Poole Broadcasting in Group Ownership). Sale price: $49.63 million (including WCDC(TV) Adams, MA; WJRT-TV Flint, MI; & WPRI-TV Providence, RI). Former owner: Capital Cities Broadcasting Corp. (see Capital Cities Communications Inc., Group Ownership). Sale price: $19 million (including WCDC(TV) Adams, MA). FCC approved: February 24, 1971 [*Broadcasting*, March 1, 1971]. Note: Capital Cities purchased stn from original owners, Hyman Rosenblum & associates, in 1954. Sale price: $298,800 (with WROW-AM). FCC approved: November 3, 1954 [For the Record, November 8, 1954]. Former call letters: WROW-TV, WCDA(TV).

WXXA-TV Albany (ch 23)—Licensed to Heritage Broadcasting Group. Former owner: Albany TV-23 Inc. (Orion Pictures Corp., et al). Sale price: $10.1 million. FCC approved: September 12, 1986 [For the Record, August 11, 1986].

WOCD(TV) Amsterdam (ch 55)—Licensed to Cornerstone Television Inc. (owned by R. Russell Bixler). Former owner: Amsterdam Broadcasting Inc. (Louis J. Keam & family). Sale price: $375,000. FCC approved: May 8, 1992 [For the Record, June 1, 1992]. Previous owner: Beacon Broadcasting Inc. (William Kitchen). Sale price: $50,000 for CP. FCC approved: September 30, 1986 [For the Record, July 28, 1986].

WBNG-TV Binghamton (ch 12)—Licensed to Gateway Communications Inc. (see Group Ownership). Former owner: Triangle Publications Inc. (owned by Walter Annenberg). Sale price: $14.4 million (including WTAJ-TV Altoona & WLYH-TV Lancaster, both PA). FCC approved: September 1972 [*Broadcasting*, September 25, 1972]. Former call letters: WNBF-TV. Note: original owner Clark Associates Inc. (John C. Clark) sold stn (with WNBF) to Triangle in 1955 for $3 million. FCC approved: May 4, 1955 [For the Record, May 9, 1955].

WICZ-TV Binghamton (ch 40)—Licensed to Stainless Inc. [Henry J. Guzewicz (38.41%), et al]. Former owner: Binghamton Press Co. (Gannett Co. Inc., Rochester, NY). Sale price: $780,000. FCC approved: February 22, 1971 [For the Record, March 8, 1971]. Original call letters: WINR-TV. Note: Binghamton Press Co. purchased stn from original owner, Southern Tier Radio Service Inc., in 1957. Sale price: $165,000 (including WINR-AM). FCC approved: January 10, 1957 [For the Record, January 14, 1957].

WMGC-TV Binghamton (ch 34)—Licensed to Citadel Communications Co. Ltd. Former owner: Pinnacle Communications (Philip D. Marella, principal). Sale price: $5 million. FCC approved: August 6, 1986 [For the Record, July 7, 1986]. Previous owner: WBJA Inc. (Olive Lazare, Gerald T. Arthur & Jules Hessen). Sale price: $800,000. FCC approved: August 18, 1978 [Changing Hands, August 28, 1978]. Former call letters: WBJA-TV. Original owner: Alfred E. Anscombe & Associates. Sale price: $35,000 in cash, assumption of $656,000 in obligations (including WEPA-TV Erie, PA). FCC approved: August 17, 1966 [For the Record, August 29, 1966].

WBUF(TV) Buffalo (ch 17, now deleted)—Licensed to NBC. Original owner: WBUF-TV Inc. (Sherwin Grossman, Gary L. Cohen & others). Sale price: $312,500. FCC approved: September 21, 1955 [For the Record, September 29, 1955]. Stn went off the air in 1958.

WGRZ-TV Buffalo (ch 2)—Licensed to WGRZ License Corp. (owned by Smith Broadcasting). Former owner: WGRZ Television Corp (owned by General Cinema Corp.). Sale price: $56 million. FCC approved: July 31, 1986 [For the Record, April 21, 1986]. Previous owner: Taft Broadcasting Co. (see Group Ownership). Traded for WCIX(TV) Miami, FL. FCC approved: February 24, 1983. Former call letters: WGR-TV. Original owner: Transcontinent TV Corp. Sale price: $26.9 million (including WGR-AM-FM; WDAF-AM-FM-TV Kansas City, MO; & WNEP-TV Scranton, PA). FCC approved: February 19, 1964.

WIVB-TV Buffalo (ch 4)—Licensed to Buffalo Broadcasting Inc., (subsidiary of Howard Publications Inc., see Cross-Ownership). Former owner: Buffalo Evening News Inc. Sale price: $25.5 million. FCC approved: September 16, 1977 [For the Record, October 3, 1977]. Former call letters: WBEN-TV.

WKBW-TV Buffalo (ch 7)—Licensed to Queen City Broadcasting of New York. Former owner: Capital Cities Communications Inc. (see Group Ownership). Sale price: $65 million. FCC approved: November 14, 1985 [For the Record, September 30, 1985]. Previous owner: Rev. Clinton H. Churchill & group. Sale price: $14 million (including WKBW-AM-FM). FCC approved: August 1, 1961 [For the Record, August 14, 1961].

WNYB-TV Buffalo (ch 49)—Licensed to Aud Enterprises Inc. Former owner: TVX Buffalo Inc. (subsidiary of TVX Broadcast Group Inc.). Sale price: $4.9 million. FCC approved: August, 1987 [For the Record, August 3, 1987].

WUTV(TV) Buffalo (ch 29)—Licensed to Citadel Communications Corp. (see Group Ownership). Former owner: Whitehaven Entertainment Corp. (Herman Pease, 53.4%). Sale price: $15.2 million. FCC approved: September 12, 1984 [For the Record: July 23, 1984]. Original owner: Ultravision Broadcasting Co. Inc. Sale price: $3.5 million. FCC approved: 1977.

WWNY-TV Carthage (Watertown) (ch 7)—Licensed to Watertown/Carthage Television Corp. (Subsidiary of United Communication Corp., owned principally by Howard J. Brown). Former owner: Johnson Newspaper Corp. Sale price: $8.1 million. FCC approved: May 11, 1981 [For the Record, June 1, 1981].

WYDC(TV) Corning (ch 48)—Licensed to Cornerstone Television Inc. (see Group Ownership). Former owner: Dr. Robert Walker. Sale price: $0, assignment of CP was donation. FCC approved: August 31, 1992 [For the Record, September 21, 1992]. Previous owner: Rural New York Broadcasting. Sale price: $13,000 for CP. FCC approved: August 23, 1989 [For the Record, September 11, 1989].

WETM-TV Elmira (ch 18)—Licensed to WETM-TV Inc. (owned by Smith Broadcasting, see Group Ownership). Former owner: Times-Mirror Co. (see Group Ownership). Sale price: $79 million (including WHTM(TV) Harrisburg, PA, & WTSM(TV) Syracuse, NY). FCC approved: January 29, 1986 [For the Record, December 16, 1985]. Previous owner: Newhouse Broadcasting Co. Sale price: $82 million (including WAPI-TV Birmingham, AL; KTVI(TV) St. Louis, MO; WSYR-TV Syracuse & satellite WETM-TV (formerly WSYE-TV) Elmira, both NY; & WTPA(TV) Harrisburg, PA). FCC approved: March 27, 1980 [*Broadcasting*, March 31 & April 7, 1980].

WTZA(TV) (ch 62)—Licensed to WTZA-TV Associates Ltd. (Richard French Jr., president of Kingston Television Group Inc.). Former owner: WTZA-TV Associates (Edward Swyer, president of L.A. Swyer Realty & Management Co.). Sale price: $2.5 million for a 66% share. FCC approved: October 27, 1993 [For the Record, November 15, 1993].

WABC-TV New York (ch 7)—Licensed to Capital Cities/ABC Inc. Former owner: ABC Inc. (see Group Ownership). Sale price: $3.417 billion purchase of ABC Inc. FCC approved: November 14, 1985 [For the Record, July 15, 1985]. Note: This was change of ownership when ABC merged with United Paramount Theaters Inc. Original owner: American Broadcasting Co. Inc. FCC approved: February 9, 1953 [For the Record, February 16, 1953].

WNBC(TV) New York (ch 4)—Licensed to National Broadcasting Company (subsidiary of General Electric Company, see Group Ownership). Former owner: NBC (subsidiary of RCA Corp.). Sale price: $6.28 billion for RCA Corp. (including KNBC-TV Los Angeles; WMAQ-TV Chicago; WRC-TV Washington; WKYC-TV Cleveland; plus the network & radio stns & all other RCA properties. FCC approved: June 5, 1986. Former call letters: WNBC-TV.

WNYW(TV) New York (ch 5)—Licensed to Fox Television Stations Inc. (see Group Ownership). Former owner: Metromedia Inc. Sale price: $2.2 billion (including KTTV(TV) Los Angeles; WFLD-TV Chicago; KRLD-TV (now KDAF) Dallas; WCVB-TV Boston; & KRIV-TV Houston. FCC approved: November 14, 1986. Former call letters: WNEW-TV.

WOR-TV New York (ch 9)—Licensed to MCA Inc. Former owner: RKO General Inc. (see Group Ownership). Sale price: $387 million. FCC approved: November 1986. Previous owner: Bamberger Broadcasting Service Inc. (R.H. Macy Co.). Sale price: $4.5 million (including WOR-AM-FM) plus $315,000 per year for 25-year lease on studio & transmitter properties plus 10% interest in General Teleradio Inc. by R.H. Macy Co. FCC approved: January 17, 1952 [For the Record, January 21, 1952].

WPTZ(TV) North Pole (ch 57)—Licensed to Heritage Media, formerly Rollins Telecasting Inc., which merged with Heritage in March 1987 (see Group Ownership). Original owner: Carl F. Stohn Sr., Vincent S. Jerry, Joel H. Schier, Harry Schulman, Martin L. Schulman, Cyril Schulman & others. Sale price: $500,000. FCC approved: March 28, 1956 [For the Record, April 2, 1956]. Original call letters: WIRI(TV).

WTBY(TV) Poughkeepsie (ch 54)—Licensed to Trinity Broadcasting of New York Inc. (affiliated with noncommercial Trinity Broadcasting Network, see Group Ownership). Former owner: Family Television Inc. [closely held group owned by Evangelical Christian Corp. (35%) & eight others]. Sale price: $2.97 million plus assumption of $367,000 in leases. FCC approved: June 2, 1982. [For the Record, June 21, 1982]. Former call letters: WFTI-TV.

WHEC-TV Rochester (ch 10)—Licensed to Viacom Inc. (Viacom International Inc. merged with Arsenal Acquiring Corp., September 1987, see Group Ownership). Former owner: Broadcast Enterprises Network Inc. (Ragan Henry is controlling stockholder). Sale price: $24.5 million plus transfer of Viacom's KDIA(AM) Oakland, CA & WDIA(AM) Memphis to BENI. FCC approved: October 17, 1983 [For the Record, November 17, 1983]. Note: Stn founded November 1, 1953. FCC approved sale of stn from Gannett Co. to BENI June 7, 1978. (Sale was a spin-off of the Gannett-Combined Communications merger.) Sale price: $27 million.

WOKR(TV) Rochester (ch 13)—Licensed to Hughes Broadcasting Partners [owned by VS&A Communications Partners L.P., (55.8% class A stock) & Smith Barney Investors L.P., (29.5% class A stock)]. Former owners: WOKR Partners (owned by George N. Gillett Jr. & Edward W. Karrels). Sale price: $50 million. FCC approved: May 10, 1991 [For the Record, May 27, 1991]. Previous owners: Falmouth Broadacsting Corp. & Falmouth Communications, preceded by WOKR Partners. Sale price of Falmouth-WOKR transaction: $57.5 million. FCC approved: February 8, 1990. Previous owner: Post Corp. Sale price: $65 per share (including WEAU-TV Eau Claire, WI; WLUC-TV Marquette, MI; KTVO Ottumwa, IA; WLUK-TV Green Bay, WI; & two radio stns). FCC approved: June 14, 1984.

WROC-TV Rochester (ch 8)—Licensed to WROC Inc. (owned by Television Station Partners, see Group Ownership). Former owner: Ziff-Davis Corp. Sale price: $57 million (including WRDW-TV Augusta, GA; WEYI-TV Saginaw, MI; & WTOV-TV Steubenville, OH). FCC approved: January 18, 1983 [For the Record, February 7, 1983]. Note: Founded as WHAM-TV in 1949 by Stromberg-Carlson Co. Bought by Transcontinent TV Corp. for $5.6 million in 1956. Bought by Veterans Broadcasting Co. & WHEC Inc. for $6.5 million in 1961 (WHEC received full occupancy of ch 10, which it had shared with the then WVET-TV, & in return, Veterans Broadcasting became full owner of WROC-TV on ch 8). Sold February 10, 1965, to Veterans Broadcasting Co. (with WROC-AM-FM) for $7 million [For the Record, February 16, 1965]. Sold to Rust Craft Broadcasting of New York Inc. as part of $69 million deal (see *Broadcasting*, May 15, 1978). Sold to Ziff-Davis 1979. (For details of sale, see WTOV-TV Steubenville, OH.)

WUHF-TV Rochester (ch 31)—Licensed to ACT III Broadcasting of Rochester Inc. Former owner: Malrite TV of New York. Sale price: $12 million [For the Record, February 6, 1989]. FCC approved: January 23, 1989.

WMHX(TV) Schenectady (ch 45)—Licensed Mohawk-Hudson Council on Educational Television Inc. Former owner: Union Street Video Inc. Sale price: $1.8 million. FCC approved: July, 1987 [For the Record, June 22, 1987]. Former call letters: WUSV(TV).

WRGB(TV) Schenectady (ch 6)—Licensed to WRGB Broadcasting Inc. (owned by Freedom Newspapers Inc., see Cross-Ownership). Former owner: Universal Corp. (subsidiary of Forstmann Little & Co., New York). Sale price: $56 million. FCC approved: January 6, 1986 [For the Record, November 25, 1985]. Previous owner: General Electric Broadcasting Inc. (see Group Ownership). Sale price: $35 million. FCC approved: June 30, 1983 [For the Record, July 25, 1983]. Note: Stn founded November 6, 1939.

WSNL-TV Smithtown (ch 67)—Licensed to Silver King Broadcasting (owned by Home Shopping Network Inc.). Former owner: Wometco Broadcasting (owned by Kohlberg, Kravis, Roberts & Co.). Sale price: $25 million (including WWHT(TV) Newark, NJ). FCC approved: September 18, 1986 [For the Record, August 25, 1986]. Previous owner: Wometco Enterprises, 75%, (see Group Ownership), & Long Island Subscription Television, 25%, (principally owned by Universal Subscription Television, Burlingame, CA-based STV franchise holder for WQTV(TV) Boston; WGPR(TV) Detroit & KSTS-TV San Jose, CA). (See WTVJ(TV) Miami, FL.) Sold by Suburban Broadcasting Corp., publicly traded corporation (no other broadcast interests). Sale price: $3.6 million. FCC approved: November 18, 1980 [Changing Hands, November 24, 1980]. Previous owner: Suburban Broadcasting Corp. [Stanley R. Yarmuth, Burton I. Koffman & Christian Yegen (80%); Robert A. Rosen, David H. Polinger, et al (13%)]. Sale price: no financial consideration. FCC approved: March 31, 1976 [For the Record, April 19, 1976]. Note: former owner Suburban Broadcasting Corp. [Robert A. Rosen, David H. Polinger, et al (66%)] transferred stn in 1975 to Suburban Broadcasting Corp. [Messrs. Yarmuth, Koffman & Yegen (80%)]. FCC approved: February 24, 1975 [For the Record, March 10, 1975].

WFWY(TV) Syracuse (ch 43)—Licensed to Orion TV Broadcasting of Syracuse (Richard F. Shively & John B. Tupper). Former owner: Orion Pictures Corp. Sale price: $436,000. FCC approved: December 5, 1985 [For the Record, October 28, 1985].

WIXT(TV) Syracuse (ch 9)—Licensed to WIXT-TV Inc. (Barry A. Ackerley, principal owner). Former owner: Transcontinent Communications Corp. [WIXT Disposition Trust (51%), Larry Israel (34%), Steven J. Kumble (6.5%) & others). Sale price: $13.8 million. WIXT Disposition Trust is administered by former directors of Coca-Cola Bottling Co. of New York, which transferred its interest into trust after merging with Coca-Cola, Atlanta. Proceeds from sale went to former stockholders of Coca-Cola Bottling Co. of New York. FCC approved: April 16, 1982 [For the Record, May 10, 1982]. Note: W.R.G. Baker TV Corp. [W.R.G. Baker Inc. (40%), Six Nations Broadcasting Co. (20%), Onondaga Broadcasting Co. (18%), Salt City Broadcasting Co. (2%)] sold stn as WNYS-TV to The Outlet Co. in 1972 for $4.8 million. FCC approved: July 19, 1972 [*Broadcasting*, July 24, 1972]. Outlet sold WNYS-TV to Coca-Cola Bottling Co. of New York, Larry Israel, & others in 1977. Sale price: $11 million. [*Broadcasting*, November 28, 1977].

WSTM-TV Syracuse (ch 3)—Licensed to Federal Broadcasting Co. (see Group Ownership). Former owner: WSTM-TV Inc. (owned by Smith Broadcasting Co.). Sale price: $19.2 million. FCC approved: August 12, 1992 [For the Record, August 31, 1992]. Former owner: Times Mirror Co. (see Group Ownership). Sale price: $79 million (including WHTM(TV) Harrisburg, PA & WETM(TV) Elmira, NY). FCC approved: January 29, 1986 [For the Record, December 16, 1985]. Previous owner: Newhouse Broadcasting Co. Sale price: $82 million (including WAPI-TV Birmingham, AL; KTVI(TV) St. Louis, MO; WSTM-TV (formerly WSYR-TV) Syracuse & satellite WSYE-TV Elmira; both NY; & WTPA(TV) Harrisburg, PA). FCC approved: March 27, 1980 [*Broadcasting*, March 31 & April 7, 1980].

WSYT-TV Syracuse (ch 68)—Licensed to Encore Communications Inc. of Syracuse. Sale price: $7 million. FCC approved: June 8, 1990 [Changing Hands, April 2, 1990]. Former owner: Thomas J. Flatley.

WTVH(TV) Syracuse (ch 5)—Licensed to Granite Broadcasting Corp. (see Group Ownership). Former owner: Meredith Corp. (see Group Ownership). Sale price: $32 million (including KSEE(TV) Fresno, CA). FCC approved: August 9, 1993 [For the Record, August 30, 1993].

WKTV(TV) Utica (ch 2)—Licensed to Smith Television of NY Inc. [headed by Robert N. Smith (64%), Harron Communications (33%), David N. Fitz, William S. Reyner Jr., & Doris E. Shwedel (each 1%)]. Former owner: Harron Communications Corp. Sale price: $10 million [Changing Hands, April 22, 1991]. FCC approved: June 18, 1991 [For the Record, July 1, 1991]. Note: voting control was transferred to Margaret E. Harron, Paul F. Harron Jr., & Howard Gittis, trustees. FCC approved: October 26, 1979. Note: previously Margaret E. Harron had obtained voting control from Paul F. Harron. Original owners: Copper City Broadcasting Corp. (Myron J. Kallett, Penn-State Realty Co. & others). Sale price: $4 million (including WKAL(AM) Rome, NY) plus $100,000 for real estate & $300,000 over 10-year period as salary to W.T. McNeilly, one of transferers, as consultant. FCC approved: December 30, 1958 [For the Record, January 5, 1959].

WJCK(TV) Watertown (ch 50)—Licensed to Moreland Broadcast Associates. Former owner: Intercounty Communications Corp. Sale price: $100,000 for CP. FCC approved: January 16, 1986 [For the Record, December 2, 1985].

WWTI(TV) Watertown (ch 50)—Licensed to Desert Communications V Inc. Former owner: Watertown Television Corp. Sale price: no financial consideration; application was filed as result of debtor's plan of reorganization. FCC approved: August 18, 1992 [For the Record, September 7, 1992]. Former call letters: WNNY(TV). Previous owner: Moreland Broadcast Associates. Sale price: no financial consideration. FCC approved: June 22, 1990. Previous call letters: WFYF-TV.

North Carolina

WHNS(TV) Asheville (ch 21)—Licensed to Pappas Telecasting Inc. Former owner: Thomas Broadcasting Companies. Sale price: $206,000. FCC approved: July 27, 1979 [For the Record, August 20, 1979]. Former call letters: WANC-TV.

WLOS-TV Asheville (ch 13)—Licensed to Anchor Media Ltd. Former owner: Wometco Inc. (owned by Kohlberg, Kravis, Roberts & McDonnell) Sale price: $50 million. FCC approved: April 1987 [For the Record, March 3, 1987]. Previous owner: Wometco Enterprises. Sale price: over $1 billion for group (see WTVJ(TV) Miami, FL). FCC approved: 1984. Note: Wometco purchased an additional 35.2% interest for $277,940 from Charles A., Henry J. & Joe H. Britt, Julia L. Stamberger, & Harold K. Bennett. FCC approved: July 24, 1958 [For the Record, July 28, 1958].

WJZY(TV) Belmont (ch 46)—Licensed to Capitol Broadcasting Company Inc. Former owner: Metro-Crescent Communications Inc. Sale price: estimated $1.581 million in stock purchase agreement. FCC approved: November 1987. Note: Stn began operation March 1987.

WAAP(TV) Burlington (ch 16)—Licensed to Television Communications (Jack Rehburg). Former owner: KFG. Sale price: $2.8 million. FCC approved: November 20, 1985 [For the Record, October 14, 1985]. Former call letters: WRDG(TV).

WCCB(TV) Charlotte (ch 18)—Licensed to WCCB-TV Inc. (see Bahakel Broadcasting, Group Ownership). Former owner: Century Advertising Inc. (Dwight L. Phillips, Cecil J. Haines, Leonard Wilson Coppala & others). Sale price: $175,000. FCC approved: August 20, 1964 [For the Record, August 31, 1964]. Former call letters: WUTV(TV). Note: Founded by George W. Dowdy, Hugh Deadwyler & associates as WQMC(TV) in 1954. Transferred to Mr. Deadwyler for $4 & assumption of obligations totaling $150,000 in 1954. Transferred to receiver & back to Mr. Deadwyler in 1956. Sold by Mr. Deadwyler to Century Advertising in 1957 for $130,000 as WAYS-TV.

WSOC-TV Charlotte (ch 9)—Licensed to Carolina Broadcasting (owned by Cox Broadcasting Corp., see Group Ownership). Original owner: WSOC Broadcasting Co. [E.E. Jones (45%), R.S. Morris (21%), Hunter Marshall (20%), & others]. Sale price: $5.6 million (including WSOC-AM-FM). FCC approved: April 9, 1959 [For the Record, April 13, 1959].

WVGO-TV Charlotte (ch 36)—Licensed to Channel 36 Partners (Odyssey Partners, see Group Ownership). Former owner: Westinghouse Broadcasting Co. Sale price: $24 million. FCC approved: January 31, 1985. Former call letters: WPCQ-TV. Previous owner: Turner Broadcasting System. Sale price: $20 million. FCC approved: March 17, 1980. Former call letters: WRET-TV. Previous owner: Harold W. Twisdale, David L. Steel Sr. & others. Sale price: $1.22 million in liabilities. FCC approved: July 27, 1970 [For the Record, August 3, 1970]. Original call letters: WCTU-TV. Note: Founded in 1967.

WPTF-TV Durham (ch 39)—Licensed to F.S.F. Acquisition Corporation. Former owner: Durham Corporation (headed by F.P. Coley). Sale price: $3 million & 835,000 shares of stock. FCC approved: June 14, 1991 [For the Record, July 1, 1991]. Note: Sale transfer includes four NC radio stns, which will be transferred to various corporations.

WTVD(TV) Durham (ch 11)—Licensed to Capital Cities Communications Inc. (see Group Ownership). Original owner: Durham Broadcasting Enterprises Inc. Sale price: $1.41 million. FCC approved: May 24, 1957 [For the Record, June 3, 1957].

WKFT(TV) Fayetteville (ch 40)—Licensed to Delta Broadcasting Inc. [headed by Elbert M. Boyd (71.55%), Thomas Y. Baker III (23.85%) & Jerry W. Boyd (3.97%)]. Former owner: Ocie F. Murray, banckruptcy trustee for SJL Associates Ltd. Sale price: $1.4 million. FCC approved: March 20, 1991 [For the Record, April 8, 1991]. Previous owners: Central Carolina TV Inc., preceded by Derwood Gerwin, et al. Sale price of Central-Gerwin transaction: $5.17 million. FCC approved: March 22, 1985 [For the Record, April 8, 1985].

WFMY-TV Greensboro (ch 2)—Licensed to WFMY Television Corp. (subsidiary of Harte-Hanks Communications Corp., see Group Ownership). Former owner: Landmark Communications. Sale price: $19 million. FCC approved: October 29, 1976 [For the Record, November 22, 1976]. Note: WFMY Television Corp. was purchased from Mrs. Margaret A. Godbey (19.9%), Jefferson Standard Life Insurance Co. (19.9%), & others for $17,168,875 (including Greensboro *News & Record*). FCC approved: December 6, 1964.

WGGT(TV) Greensboro (ch 48)—Licensed to Atlantic Television Limited Partnership 1. Original owner: Guilford Telecasters Inc. Sale price: $11 million. FCC approved: June 7, 1985 [For the Record, March 25, 1985].

WLXI-TV Greensboro (ch 61)—Licensed to Radiant Life Ministries (owned by Garth W. Coonce). Former owner: Consolidated Broadcasting Corp. (Trinity Broadcasting Network, see Group Ownership). Sale price: $1.9 million. FCC approved: October 7, 1991 [For the Record, October 28, 1991]. Previous owner: Billy R. Satterfield. Sale price: $300,000. FCC approved: August 8, 1985 [For the Record, August 19, 1985]. Previous owner: Gary Smithwick & H. Powel. Sale price: $40,000. FCC approved: May 23, 1985 [For the Record, June 10, 1985].

WNCT-TV Greenville (ch 9)—Licensed to Roy H. Park Broadcasting Inc. (see Park Broadcasting in Group Ownership). Original owner: Carolina Broadcasting System Inc. (Earl McD. Westbrook & Associates). Sale price: $2.55 million (including 30% interest in WECT-TV Wilmington, NC). FCC approved: February 6, 1962 [For the Record, February 12, 1962].

WYDO(TV) Greenville (ch 14)—Licensed to KS Family Television Inc. (Frederic J. McCune). Former owner: Karl H. Stoll. Sale price: $4,000. FCC approved: August 4, 1992 [For the Record, November 9, 1992].

WHKY-TV Hickory (ch 14)—Licensed to the Long Family Partnership. Former owner: Catawba Valley Broadcasting Inc. (Edmund S. Long & family, 51%). Sale price: no financial consideration. FCC approved: June 5, 1991 [For the Record, June 24, 1991]. Original owner: Catawba Valley Broadcasting Inc. (Edmund S. Long & family 32%). Sale price: no financial consideration. FCC approved: August 26, 1976 [For the Record, October 11, 1976].

WGHP-TV High Point (ch 8)—Licensed to Great American Communications. Former owner: Taft Broadcasting (see Group Ownership). Sale price: $27 million. FCC approved: November 1991 [Changing Hands, November 18, 1991]. Previous owner: Gulf Broadcast Group (subsidiary of Gulf Life Co., see Group Ownership). Sale price: $755 million (including KTSP(TV) Phoenix; WTSP(TV) Tampa-St. Petersburg; KTXH(TV) Houston; & KTXA(TV) Arlington (Ft. Worth), TX). FCC approved: May 30, 1985 [For the Record, April 15, 1985]. Note: Harte-Hanks bought stn in June of 1978. Hanks in turn sold stn to Gulf. Previous owner: Southern Broadcasting Co. (Harte-Hanks subsidiary). Sale price: $24 million. FCC approved: June 16, 1978.

WFXI(TV) Morehead City (ch. 8)—Licensed to Ramon N. Redford Jr. & Ann T. Munden. Former owners: John W. Gainey III & Frederick J. McCune. Sale price: $43,636 (each sold 400 shares valued at $21,818). FCC approved: February 6, 1990.

WCTI-TV New Bern (ch 12)—Licensed to Lamco Communications Inc. (see Group Ownership). Former owner: Diversified Communications (Horace Hildreth Jr.). Sale price: $12.3 million. FCC approved: August 2, 1993 [For the Record, August 23, 1993]. Previous owner: Heritage Broadcasting [subsidiary of ICI Corp., Detroit (Mario Iacobelli, 80% & Robert Smith, 20%)]. Sale price: $22.5 million. FCC approved: February 24, 1986 [For the Record, January 6, 1986]. Previous owner: Malrite of North Carolina (see Malrite Communications, Group Ownership). Sale price: $9 million. FCC approved: June 7, 1983 [For the Record, June 27, 1983]. Note: founded as WNBE-TV in 1963 by Nathan Frank. He sold 50% to Harold H. Thomas that year for $60,000. Piedmont Television Corp. (Mr. Frank & Mr. Thomas) sold stn in 1969 to Continental TV Inc. for $960,000. FCC approved: April 15, 1969 [For the Record, May 5, 1969]. Sold to Malrite in 1976 for $2 million. FCC approved: October 14, 1976 [For the Record, November 1, 1976].

WJHF(TV) Raleigh (ch 22, now deleted)—Licensed to Springfield Television Broadcasting Corp. (see Group Ownership). Former owners: William H. White, Terry Sanford & Hugh Cannon (each 50%); Springfield Television (50%). Sale price: between $100,000 & $150,000 in stock. FCC approved: December 27, 1966 [For the Record, January 2, 1967].

WLFL(TV) Raleigh (ch 22)—Licensed to Television Corp. of Raleigh (owned by TVX Broadcast Group, see Group Ownership). Original owner: Family TV Corp. Sale price: $14.5 million. FCC approved: February 10, 1986 [For the Record, July 1, 1985].

WRAL(TV) Raleigh (ch 5)—Licensed to Capitol Broadcasting Co. Original owner: Aubrey H. Moore. Sale price: $655,168 for 7.39% of stock of Capitol (including WRAL-FM). FCC approved: February 20, 1985 [For the Record, March 4, 1985].

WPTF-TV Raleigh-Durham (ch 28)—Licensed to Durham Life Broadcasting Service Inc. (subsidiary of Durham Life Insurance Co.). Former owner: Triangle Telecasters Inc. Sale price: $2.27 million plus future payments not to exceed $800,000 based on stn's future performance over seven years. FCC approved: May 16, 1977 [For the Record, June 20, 1977]. Former call letters: WRDU-TV.

WRMY(TV) Rocky Mount (ch 47)—Licensed to Family Broadcasting Enterprises, owned by Robert J. Pelletier & Robert M. Chandler. Former owner: Victor Bruce Whitehead. Sale price: $100,000. FCC approved: November 25, 1991 [For the Record, December 16, 1991].

WITN-TV Washington (ch 7)—Licensed to American Family Corp. Former owner: North Carolina TV Inc. [Robertson family (62.5%), William S. Page (25%) & others). Sale price: $23.57 million. FCC approved: June 26, 1985. Original owners: H.W. Anderson & R.M. Fountain. Sale price: $121,840. FCC approved: September 23, 1955 [For the Record, October 3, 1955].

WECT(TV) Wilmington (ch 6)—Licensed to New Vision Television I Inc. (see New Vision Television Inc. in Group Ownership). Former owner: News-Press & Gazette Co. Sale price: $110 million. FCC approved: September 7, 1993 [For the Record, September 27, 1993]. Note: Part of multi-stn purchase (see KOLD-TV Tucson, AZ]. Previous owner: Atlantic Telecasting Corp. [Dan D. Cameron (42.86%), J.S. Brody (21.51%), Leo Brody (11.93%), Estate of J.W. Jackson (14.29%) & others]. Sale price: $30 million. FCC approved: November 21, 1986 [For the Record, October 6, 1986]. Original owner: Richard A. Dunlea & Louise M. Dunlea. Sale price: $153,850 for 60%. Mr. Cameron retained 40%. FCC approved: December 11, 1957 [For the Record, December 16, 1957]. Original call letters: WMFD-TV.

WWAY-TV Wilmington (ch 3)—Licensed to CLG Media of Seattle Inc. Former owner: Adams TV of Wilmington (Adams Communications Corp.). Sale price: assumption of liabilities arising from series of loan restructurings of CLG parent company Chrysler Capital (including KZOK-AM-FM Seattle, WA, & KHIH(AM) Boulder, CO). FCC approved: November 20, 1992 [For the Record, December 14, 1992]. Previous owner: Price Communications. Sale price: $26 million. FCC approved: July 15, 1988 [For the Record, August 15, 1988]. Previous owner: Clay Broadcasting Corp. (see Clay Communications Inc., Group Ownership). (For details of sale, see WAPT-TV Jackson, MS.) Previous owner: Cape Fear Telecasting Inc. (William G. Broadfoot Jr., Charles B. Britt & others). Sale price: $1.35 million. FCC approved: August 28, 1968 [For the Record, September 9, 1968]. Note: Founded by Cape Fear Telecasting Inc. in 1964.

WEOU(TV) Wilson (ch 30)—Licensed to Channel 30 Telecasters LP. Former owner: Wilson Telecasters Ltd. Sale price: no more than $100,000 for CP. FCC approved: March 3, 1986 [For the Record, December 16, 1985]. Former call letters: WWRD(TV).

WNRW-TV Winston-Salem (ch 45)—Licensed to Act III Broadcasting of Greensboro Inc. (Norman Lear, et al). Former owner: TVX Broadcast Group. Sale price: $11 million. FCC approved: December 17, 1986 [For the Record, November 17, 1986]. Previous owner: Good News Inc. (John L. Sims & family). Sale price: $1.56 million. FCC approved: August 19, 1980. Previous owner: Good News TV Network Inc. (nonprofit religious organization). Sale price: $698,000. FCC approved: September 17, 1979.

WXII(TV) Winston-Salem (ch 12)—Licensed to Pulitzer Broadcasting Co. (see Group Ownership). Former owner: Multimedia (see Group Ownership). Sale price: Part of a multi-stn deal in which Pulitzer traded KDSK-TV St. Louis, MO, for WXII-TV, WFBC-TV Greenville, SC, & $9 million. FCC approved: February 17, 1983 [For the Record, March 14, 1983]. Note: Sold to Multimedia by Triangle Broadcasting Corp. (Gordon Gray & family 100%). Sale price: $7.31 million. FCC approved: September 7, 1972 [For the Record, October 23, 1972]. Former call letters: WSJS-TV.

North Dakota

KXMB-TV Bismarck (ch 12)—Licensed to Bismarck Television Inc. (Chester Reiten, Lloyd R. Amoo & W.L. Hurley). Former owner: KXMB-TV Inc. (John Boler, pres). Sale price: $1.2 million. FCC approved: January 27, 1971 [For the Record, February 8, 1971].

KXMA-TV Dickinson (ch 2)—Licensed to Reiten Television. Former owner: Northern Plains Broadcasting. Sale price: $362,500 plus assumption of debt. FCC approved: December 4, 1984. Former call letters: KNDX(TV). Previous owner: Stanley Deck. Sale price: $950,000. FCC approved: April 22, 1983. Former call letters: KDIX-TV. Previous owner: Dickinson Radio Association. Sale price: $412,000 for 94.5% of company, which included KDIX(AM). FCC approved: 1966.

KTHI-TV Fargo (ch 11)—Licensed to Spokane Television Inc. (see Morgan Murphy Stations, Group Ownership). Former owner: Pembina Broadcasting Co. (see Fuqua Industries Stations, Group Ownership). Sale price: $1.49 million. FCC approved: January 22, 1969 [For the Record, February 3, 1969]. Previous owner: Polaris Corp. (See WTVW(TV) Evansville, IN, for details.) Original owner: North Dakota Broadcasting. Sale price: $390,000. FCC approved: 1962. Original call letters: KXGO-TV.

KVRR(TV) Fargo (ch 15)—Licensed to Fargo Broadcasting Inc. (owned by Curtis Squire Inc.). Former owners: Curtis Squire Inc. & John W. Boler. Sale price: $625,000 for Boler's 50% interest (including KNRR(TV) Pembina, ND, & KBRR(TV) Thief River Falls, MN). FCC approved: August 1987.

WDAY-TV Fargo (ch 6)—Licensed to WDAY-TV Inc. (Fargo Forum). Original owner: E.C. Reineke & wife (55.6%); N.D. Black Jr. & family (Fargo Forum) (35%); & others. Sale price: $900,000 for 55.6%. FCC approved: July 20, 1960 [For the Record, July 25, 1960].

KNOX-TV Grand Forks (ch 10, now deleted)—Licensed to Pembina Broadcasting Inc. (see Fuqua Industries Stations, Group Ownership). Original owner: Community Radio Corp. Sale price: $225,000. FCC approved: 1962.

KXMC-TV Minot (ch 13)—Licensed to KXMC-TV Inc. (Chester M. Reiten 55%). Former owner: KXMC-TV Inc. [Chester M. Reiten (40%), Lloyd R. Amoo (30%), W.L. Hurley (30%)]. Sale price: Transfer involved acquisition of stock from Security Pacific National Bank, executor of estate of Lloyd R. Amoo. FCC approved: July 31, 1974 [For the Record, August 19, 1974]. Note: Original owner North Dakota Broadcasting Co. sold 52.5% of KXMC-TV to KXMC-TV Inc. (Chester M. Reiten, Lloyd R. Amoo & W.L. Hurley) in 1959 for $1 million. FCC approved: October 21, 1959 [For the Record, November 2, 1959].

KCND-TV Pembina (ch 12, now deleted)—Licensed to McLendon Corp. (Gordon B. McLendon, pres). Former owner: Polaris Corp. Sale price: $850,000 for 68 months lease, with option to buy for additional $500,000. FCC approved: August 24, 1966. Note: Founded (with KTHI-TV Fargo) in 1959 by Harry Rice, Harry C. Lukkason & Associates. Sold to Polaris in 1962 for $675,200 (with KTHI-TV & KNOX-TV Grand Forks, ND). (See WTVW(TV) Evansville, IN, for 1965 sale of Polaris properties.)

KNRR(TV) Pembina (ch 12)—See KVRR(TV) Fargo, ND.

KXJB-TV Valley City (Fargo) (ch 4)—Licensed to Central Minnesota Television Co. [Thomas K. Barnstuble estate (53%), Joseph O. Perino & John McCarten (11% each) & others. Barnstuble interests are voted by Thomas K. Barnstuble Jr. & brother Bruce E]. Original owner: North Dakota Broadcasting Co. [John W. Boler (79%) & four others]. Sale price: $3.2 million. FCC approved: November 30, 1978 [For the Record & Changing Hands, December 18, 1978].

Ohio

WBNX-TV Akron (ch 55)—Licensed to Winston Broadcasting Inc. (owned by Grace Cathedral Inc.). Former owner: Rhema Television Corp. Sale price: assumption of liabilities. FCC approved: February 1987 [For the Record, January 19, 1987].

***WOUC-TV Cambridge (ch 44)**—Licensed to Ohio University. Original owner: Ohio Educational Television Network Commission. Sale price: no consideration. FCC approved: December 10, 1975 [For the Record, December 22, 1975].

WDLI(TV) Canton (ch 17)—Licensed to Trinity Broadcasting Network. Original owner: David Livingstone Foundation. Sale price: $4.5 million. FCC approved: March 5, 1986 [For the Record, September 23, 1985].

WOAC(TV) Canton (ch 67)—Licensed to Discovery Broadcasting of Ohio (owned by Glen H. Taylor, et al). Original owner: Canton 67 Ltd. Sale price: $5.8 million. FCC approved: June 20, 1985 [For the Record, May 13, 1985].

WLWT(TV) Cincinnati (ch 5)—Licensed to Channel 5 of Cincinnati Inc. (see Multimedia Broadcasting, Group Ownership). Original owner: Avco Broadcasting Corp. Sale price: $16.3 million. FCC approved: January 16, 1976 [For the Record, February 2, 1976].

WSTR-TV Cincinnati (ch 64)—Licensed to Abry Communications. Former owner: Channel 64 Joint Venture. Sale price: $8 million. FCC approved: September 22, 1989 [For the Record, October 9, 1989]. Previous owner: United Cable TV Corp. Sale price: $9.44 million. FCC approved: November 14, 1984. Former call letters WBTI(TV). Original owner: Buford TV. Sale price: $7 million. FCC approved: January 15, 1982. Original call letters: WIII(TV).

WCTF(TV) Cleveland (ch 19, now deleted)—Licensed to Zingale Broadcasting Co. (100% owned by Joseph T. Zingale). Original owner: Community Telecasters of Cleveland Inc. (Charles W. Steadman, pres, et al). Sale price: $180,976 for CP. FCC approved: October 25, 1973 [For the Record, November 5, 1973].

WHK-TV Cleveland (ch 19, now deleted)—Licensed to Metropolitan Broadcasting Corp. (formerly DuMont Broadcasting Corp.). Original owner: Cleveland *Plain Dealer* & *News*. Sale price: $700,000 (including WHK-AM-FM). FCC approved: April 16, 1958 [For the Record, April 21, 1958].

WJW-TV Cleveland (ch 8)—Licensed to WJW License Inc. (see SCI Television in Group Ownership). Former owner: Gillett Communications. Sale price: unknown. (See WAGA-TV Atlanta for details of sale). FCC approved: February 19, 1993 [For the Record, April 26, 1993]. Previous owner: KKR Associates (see Group Ownership). (See KCST-TV San Diego for details of sale.) Previous owner: Storer Broadcasting. Sale price: $1.98 billion (including KCST-TV San Diego; WAGA-TV Atlanta; WJBK-TV Detroit; WITI-TV Milwaukee; WSBK-TV Boston; & WTVG(TV) Toledo, OH. FCC approved: November 25, 1985. Former call letters: WJKW-TV. Original owner: Herbert Mayer. Sale price: $8.5 million (including KPTV(TV) Portland, OR, & Empire Coil Co., New Rochelle, NY). FCC approved: October 27, 1954 [For the Record, November 1, 1954]. Original call letters: WXEL(TV).

WKBF-TV Cleveland (ch 61, now deleted)—Licensed to Kaiser Broadcasting Co. [77.5% owned by Kaiser Broadcasting Corp. (see Group Ownership) & 22.5% by Field Communications Corp. (owned by Field Enterprises Inc., Chicago)]. Former owner: Kaiser Broadcasting Corp. Sale price: no financial consideration [merger of Kaiser Broadcasting Corp.'s five independent UHFs (including WKBF-TV) & Field Communications Corp.'s one independent UHF]. FCC approved: May 1973 [*Broadcasting*, May 14, 1973]. Note: Former owner Superior Broadcasting Corp. sold 50% of CP to Kaiser Broadcasting Corp. for $200,000 less expenses not to exceed $50,000 already incurred by Superior. Kaiser obtained the option to purchase 50% interest of Superior on certain terms & conditions. FCC approved: September 19, 1967 [For the Record, September 25, 1967]. Former call letters: WAFT-TV. Kaiser purchased the remaining 50% from Superior Broadcasting for $280,000 in 1972. FCC approved: August 14, 1972 [For the Record, September 4, 1972].

WKYC-TV Cleveland (ch 3)—Licensed to Multimedia Inc. (headed by Wilson C. Wearn, Walter E. Bartlett, Robert E. Hamby Jr. & Peter A. Lund). Former owner: NBC (see Group Ownership). Sale price: $65 million. FCC approved: December 24, 1990 [For the Record, January 14, 1991]. Previous owner: Westinghouse Broadcasting Co. (see Group Ownership). Sold as part of RCA Corp. to General Electric Co. for $6.28 billion. FCC approved: June 5, 1986. Former call letters: KYW-TV. Note: In exchange for NBC's Philadephia stns (with KYW-AM-FM), under FCC order. FCC approved: February 17, 1965 [For the Record, March 1, 1965]. Note: Founded as WNBK(TV) by NBC in 1948. Exchanged for Westinghouse's Philadelphia stns in 1955 plus $3 million to Westinghouse.

WQHS(TV) Cleveland (ch 61)—Licensed to Silver King Broadcasting Inc. Former owner: Channel Communications of Ohio Inc. (owned by NASCO Inc.). Sale price: $15 million. FCC approved: November 6, 1986 [For the Record, September 8,1986]. Former call letters: WCLQ-TV.

WCMH(TV) Columbus (ch 4)—Licensed to Outlet Communications Group (see Group Ownership). Previous owner: Rockefeller Group Inc. Sale price: $625 million (including WJAR-TV Providence, RI; KSAT-TV San Antonio, TX; KOVR-TV Stockton-Sacramento, CA; WCPX-TV Orlando, FL; & 4 radio stns). Former call letters: WCMH-TV. Former owner: The Outlet Co. Sale price: $332 million for group just listed. FCC approved: November 23, 1983. Original owner: Avco Broadcasting Corp. (see Group Ownership). Sale price: $16.1 million. FCC approved: December 22, 1975 [For the Record, January 12, 1976]. Original call letters: WLWC(TV).

WSYX(TV) Columbus (ch 6)—Licensed to Anchor Media Ltd. Former owner: Taft Broadcasting Co. (see Group Ownership). (Note: When Taft was reorganized, it could no longer hold Grandfather status for WTVN-TV Columbus & WKRC-TV Cincinnati, which had overlapping Grade B contours. Therefore licensee acquired the stn for no consideration.) Former call letters: WTVN-TV.

Original owners: Picture Waves Inc. (Edward Lamb). Sale price: $1.5 million. FCC approved: February 25, 1953 [For the Record, March 2, 1953].

WDTN(TV) Dayton (ch 2)—Licensed to Hearst Communications Corp. (see Group Ownership). Former owner: Grinnell Communications (wholly owned by trustees of Grinnell College, IA). Sale price: $49.9 million. FCC approved: July 16, 1981 [Changing Hands, August 10, 1981]. Original owner: Avco Broadcasting Corp. (subsidiary of Avco Corp.). Sale price: $12.9 million. FCC approved: April 28, 1976 [For the Record, May 10, 1976]. Original call letters: WLWD(TV).

WKEF(TV) Dayton (ch 22)—Licensed to KT Communications L.P. Former owner: Adams Communications. Sale price: $71.5 million. FCC approved: January 5, 1989 [For the Record, January 23, 1989]. Previous owner: Springfield Television Broadcasting Co. Sale price: $47.5 million (including WWLP(TV) Springfield, MA & KSTU(TV) Salt Lake City, UT). FCC approved: April 30, 1984. Previous owner: WONE-TV Inc. (Brush-Moore Newspapers). Sale price: $153,000 for CP. FCC approved: December 6, 1963 [For the Record, December 16, 1963]. Note: Brush-Moore Newspapers bought CP for then WONE-TV & WONE(AM) & WFIE(FM) in 1961 for $1.65 million. Stns were owned by Ronald Woodyard & Associates.

WRGT-TV Dayton (ch 45)—Licensed to Act III Broadcasting Inc. (principally owned by Norman Lear). Former owner: Greentree Associates (principally owned by Henry Posner Jr., Albert M. Holtz & Thomas D. Wright). Sale price: $22 million (including WVAH-TV Charleston, WV, & CP for ch 11 in Charleston, WV).

WEYE(TV) Hillsboro (ch 55)—Licensed to Gerald J. Robinson. Former owner: Gary Goone. Sale price: $130,000. FCC approved: June, 1987 [For the Record, March 30, 1987].

***WPTD-TV Kettering (ch 16)**—Licensed to University Regional Broadcasting. Former owner: Ohio Educational Television Network Commission. Sale price: no financial consideration. FCC approved: April 22, 1975 [For the Record, May 5, 1975]. Previous owner: Kittyhawk TV Corp. Sale price: $550,000 or higher of two appraised values. Note: WPTD-TV was a commercial stn when owned by Kittyhawk.

***WBGU-TV Lima (ch 27)**—Licensed to Bowling Green State University. Original owner: Ohio Educational Television Network Commission. FCC approved: November 17, 1976 [For the Record, December 13, 1976]. Note: Formerly ch 57.

WLIO(TV) Lima (ch 35)—Licensed to Lima Communications Corp. [Toledo Blade Co. (75%) & Midwestern Broadcasting Co. (25%)]. Original owner: WLOK Inc. (owned by Northwestern Ohio Broadcasting Corp.). Sale price: $1.5 million. FCC approved: January 19, 1972 [*Broadcasting*, January 24, 1972]. Former call letters: WIMA-TV.

WUAB(TV) Lorain (Cleveland) (ch 43)—Licensed to Cannell Communications Ltd. Former owner: Gaylord Broadcasting Co. (see Group Ownership). Sale price: $60 million. FCC approved: June 19, 1990. Original owner: United Artists Broadcasting Inc. (64%) & Kaiser Broadcasting Co. (36%). Sale price: $12.5 million. FCC approved: June 30, 1977 [For the Record, July 18, 1977].

WCEO(TV) Mansfield (ch 68)—Permitee: Channel 68 Corp. Original owner: Eagle Broadcasting Inc. Sale price: $112,011. FCC approved: February 11, 1986 [For the Record, December 16, 1985]. Former call letters: WLCH(TV).

***WMUB-TV Oxford (ch 14)**—Licensed to University Regional Broadcasting Inc. (consortium of Miami University, Wright State University & Central State University). Original owner: Trustees of Miami University. Sale price: no financial consideration. FCC approved: November 11, 1975 [For the Record, November 24, 1975].

WSWO-TV Springfield (ch 26, now deleted)—Licensed to Lester W. White. Former owner: Thomas T. Taggart, trustee in bankruptcy. Sale price: $452,184. FCC approved: June 1972 [*Broadcasting*, June 26, 1972].

WTJC(TV) Springfield (ch 26)—Licensed to Video Mall Communications Inc. [owned by Marvin D. Sparks (70%) Richard L. Woodby (15%) & John W. Elliott (15%)]. Former owner: Miami Valley Christian TV Inc. (headed by Sparks, Vernon Wilson, Homer Speece, Murray Ross, & William Koch). Sale price: $2 million (including WTLJ(TV) Muskegon, MI). FCC approved: January 15, 1991 [For the Record, February 4, 1991].

WTOV-TV Steubenville (ch 9)—Licensed to Television Station Partners (see Group Ownership). Former owner: Ziff Davis. Sale price: $57 million (including WRDW-TV Augusta, GA; WEYI-TV Saginaw, MI; & WROC-TV Rochester, NY). FCC approved: January 18, 1983 [For the Record, February 7, 1983]. Previous owner: Rust Craft. Part of $69 million deal with previously listed stns, WJKS-TV Jacksonville, FL, & WRCB-TV Chattanooga. FCC approved: May 10, 1978 [See *Broadcasting*, May 15, 1978]. Former call letters: WSTV-TV. Previous owner: Friendly Broadcast Group. Sold with KODE-TV Joplin, MO; WBOY-TV Clarksburg, WV; & WRCB-TV Chattanooga; & 2 radio stns in a stock transaction. FCC approved: 1962.

WNWO-TV Toledo (ch 24)—Licensed to Television Station Partners (see Group Ownership). Former owner: First National Bank of Boston, bankruptcy trustee. Sale price: $19.3 million. FCC approved: January 31, 1986. Former call letters: WDHO-TV. Previous owner: D.H. Overmyer Telecasting Co. (owned by The Overmyer Company Inc., debtor-in-possession). Original owner: D.H. Overmyer Telecasting Co. (owned by The Overmyer Company Inc.). Sale price: no financial consideration. FCC approved: February 25, 1976 [For the Record, March 15, 1976].

WTOL-TV Toledo (ch 11)—Licensed to Cosmos Broadcasting Co. (see Group Ownership). Original owners: Frazier Reams (60%), Morton Niepp (15%), Thomas S. Bretherton (15%), Glenn Reams (10%). Sale price: $12.35 million (including WTOL-AM-FM sold back to Reams group for $500,000). FCC approved: March 10, 1965 [For the Record, March 15, 1965].

WTVG(TV) Toledo (ch 13)—Licensed to WTVG Inc., owned by Media-Communications Partners Ltd. Former owner: WTVG Inc., owned by T. Anderson Lee, Jeffrey H. Lee, & Terry Lee. Sale price: $200.01 plus transfer of stock. FCC approved: December 3, 1991 [For the Record, January 6, 1992]. Previous owner: KKR Associates. Sale price: $65 million. FCC approved: June, 1987 [November 24, 1986]. Previous owner: Storer Broadcasting. Sale price: $1.98 billion (including WAGA-TV Atlanta; WJBK-TV Detroit; WJW-TV Cleveland; WITI-TV Milwaukee; & WSBK-TV Boston). FCC appproved: November 25, 1985. Former call letters: WSPD-TV. Note: WTVG(TV) divestiture by KKR required by FCC as condition of approval of sale, due to signal overlap with WJBK-TV.

WUPW(TV) Toledo (ch 36)—Licensed to Toledo Television Ltd. Partnership (gen ptnr, Independent Broadcasting Co.). Former owners: Arthur Dorfner, William C. Mitchell & Pamela Fruth. Sale price: $500,000 for 28%, raising Independent's share of stn from 42% to 70%. FCC approved: December 22, 1986 [For the Record, November 24, 1986].

WFMJ-TV Youngstown (ch 21)—Licensed to WFMJ Television Inc. (Mark A. Brown & Betty H. Brown Jagnow). Former owner: WFMJ Television Inc. Sale price: no cash consideration. FCC approved: July 14, 1993 [For the Record, August 2, 1993].

WKBN-TV Youngstown (ch 27)—Licensed to WKBN Broadcasting Corp. (wholly owned by W.P. Williamson Jr.). Note: Williamson increased holdings from 41% to 100% in purchase from Cleveland *Plain Dealer* & *News* for undisclosed sum in 1958.

WYTV(TV) Youngstown (ch 33)—Licensed to Benedek Broadcasting Corp. (owned by Richard Benedek). Previous owner: Adams Russell Co. (publicly traded corp based in Waltham, MA). Sale price: $9 million. FCC approved: April 15, 1983 [For the Record, May 16, 1983]. Note: Founded in 1957 by S.W. Townsend. Bought by Communications Industries Inc. in 1961 for $975,000 for 81.2% interest plus options. Purchased from Communications Industries by Adam Young & others for $1.05 million & other considerations [For the Record, February 15, 1965]. FCC approved: February 6, 1965. Sold to Adams-Russell in 1970.

Oklahoma

KTEN(TV) Ada-Ardmore (ch 10)—Licensed to United Broadcasting Ltd. (Tom L. Johnson). Former owner: Eastern Oklahoma TV Company (owned by Channel 10 Ltd. Partnership). Sale price: $7.98 million. FCC approved: September 30, 1992 [For the Record, November 9, 1992]. Previous owner: William Hoover. Sale price: $2.5 million. FCC approved: January 25, 1985.

KXII(TV) Ardmore (Sherman-Denslon, TX) (ch 12)—Licensed to M.N. (Buddy) Bostick. Former owner: Texoma Broadcasters Inc. Sale price: $14 million. FCC approved: October 30, 1986 [For the Record, September 29, 1986]. Original owner: John F. Easley estate. Sale price: $141,666. FCC approved: June 17, 1959 [For the Record, June 22, 1959].

KFOR-TV Oklahoma City (ch 4)—Licensed to Hughes Broadcasting Partners. Former owner: Palmer Communications. Sale price: undisclosed (including WHO-AM-TV & KLYF(FM), all Des Moines). FCC approved: November 1991 [Changing Hands, November 18, 1991]. Previous owner: KTVY Inc. (see Evening News Association, Group Ownership). Sale price: $160 million (including KOLD(TV) Tuscon, AZ, & WALA(TV) Mobile, AL). FCC approved: January 13, 1986 [For the Record, December 16, 1985]. Original owner: Gaylord Broadcasting Co. (see Group Ownership). Sale price: $22.5 million. FCC approved: October 29, 1975 [For the Record, November 17, 1975]. Former call letters: KTVY(TV). Original call letters: WKY-TV.

KGMC(TV) Oklahoma City (ch 34)—Licensed to Maddox Broadcasting Corp. Former owner: Oklahoma City Broadcasting Co. Sale price: $3.6 million. FCC approved: August 3, 1989 [For the Record, August 21, 1989]. Previous owner: Seraphim Corp. (owned by Beverly Hills Hotel Corp.), preceded by General Media Corp. (Earl Hickerson & 80 others). Sale price of Seraphim-General Media transaction: $5.2 million. FCC approved: February 16, 1983 [For the Record, March 7, 1983]. Note: Stn went on air October 28, 1979. Note: Oklahoma City owned 20% of stn before Seraphim-Oklahoma City sale, owned 100% after sale.

KOCB(TV) Oklahoma City (ch 34)—Licensed Superior Broadcasting Inc. (Albert M. Holtzand). Former owner: Oklahoma City Broadcasting Co. (Ted F. Baze, 100%). Sale price: $11 million (transfer of control). FCC approved: October 15, 1993 [For the Record, November 8, 1993].

KOCO-TV Oklahoma City (ch 5)—Licensed to Combined Communications Corp. (subsidiary of the Gannett Co., following merger in June 1979). (See KPNX-TV Phoenix.) Former owner: John E. Kirkpatrick, Dean A. McGee, Grayce B. Flynn estate, Leonard H. Savage & others. Sale price: $6.5 million. FCC approved: July 17, 1970 [For the Record, July 27, 1970]. Note: Founded in 1954. Cimarron TV Corp. (L.E. Caster & Ashley L. Robison) acquired stn (then KGEO-TV) in 1957 from Streets Electronics Inc. (P.R. Banta & others) for $2.5 million. Mr. Banta acquired 10% interest from Mr. Caster after transfer. Cimarron sold stn in 1961 to Capital City Investment Co. for $2.5 million. Capital City subsequently became Cimarron Television (Kirkpatrick group).

KOKH-TV Oklahoma City (ch 25)—Licensed to Channel 25 Acquisition Corp. (subsidiary of Heritage Media Corp.). Former owner: KOKH Acquisition Corp. (owned by George N. Gillett Jr., David Ramon & Stephen D. Spears). Sale price: $7 million. FCC approved: June 27, 1991 [For the Record, July 15, 1991]. Previous owner: Busse Broadcasting Corp. (owned by Lawrence A. Busse, James C. Ryan & Oscar David). Sale price: $7 million. FCC approved: December 28, 1990 [For the Record, January 21, 1991]. Previous owner: Pappas Telecasting of Oklahoma, preceded by KOLN Inc. (subsidiary of Busse Broadcasting). Sale price of Pappas-KOLN transaction: $9 million, plus assumption of liabilities up to $7 million. FCC approved: January 10, 1989. [For the Record, January 30, 1989]. Previous owner: Gillett Broadcasting, preceded by John Blair Co. (publicly owned & diversified). (For details of Gillett-Blair transaction, see KBSW-TV Salinas, CA.) Previous owner: Independent School District No. 89 of Oklahoma County. Sale price: $3.5 million. FCC approved: June 1979 [For the Record & Changing Hands, July 2, 1979]. Previous owner: Jack Ferris, who received license for cancellation of $100,000 of indebtedness in 1955. Note: Stn then left the air & the license was granted to the school system.

KTLC(TV) Oklahoma City (ch 43)—Licensed to Oklahoma Educational TV Authority Foundation (headed by Gene Rochelle & Carri A. Bell). Former owner: Heritage Media (formerly Rollins Telecasting, which merged with Heritage in March 1987). Sale price: $1.5 million. FCC approved: June 27, 1991 [For the Record, July 15, 1991]. Former call letters: KAUT(TV). Previous owner: Golden West Broadcasters (see Group Ownership). Sale price: $5.5 million. FCC approved: February 26, 1985 [For the Record, March 11, 1985]. Previous owner: Christian Broadcasting Co. of Oklahoma (nonprofit religious corporation, George Teagues, pres). Sale price: $60,000 for CP. FCC approved: January 24, 1980 [For the Record, February 11, 1980].

KWTV(TV) Oklahoma City (ch 9)—Licensed to Griffin Television Inc. (owned 100% by John T. Griffin). Former owner: Luther T. Dulaney & Ray J. Turner. Sale price: $200,000 plus ownership of all equipment owned by KWTV(AM). Dulaney & Turner sold their 50% interest to Griffin-Leake interests which already owned 50%. Note: In turn, they sold KATV(TV) Little Rock, AR, & KTUL-TV Tulsa, OK (all owned by Griffin-Leake) to Oklahoma City bankers for $3 million. FCC approved: January 20, 1964 [For the Record, January 27, 1964].

KVIJ-TV Sayre (ch 8)—Satellite of KVII-TV Amarillo, TX. Licensed to Marsh Media [Stanley Marsh III (50%), Michael C. Marsh (20%), Estelle Marsh Watlington (10%), Tom F. Marsh (10%), Tom F. Marsh Special Trust (10%)]. Former owner: Bass Broadcasting Co. Sale price: $300,000. FCC approved: December 19, 1975 [For the Record, January 12, 1976]. Former call letters: KFDO-TV. Original owner: Southwest Broadcasting Co. Sale price: $275,000. FCC approved: December 6, 1965 [For the Record, December 13, 1965]. Original call letters: KSWB(TV) (licensed to Elk City, OK).

KJRH(TV) Tulsa (ch 2)—Licensed to Scripps-Howard Broadcasting. Original owner: Central Plains Enterprises Inc. Sale price: $7 million. FCC approved: 1970.

KOKI-TV Tulsa (ch 23)—Licensed to Clear Channel Television Inc. Former owner: Tulsa 23 Ltd. Sale price: $6.075 million. FCC approved: February 7, 1990.

KOTV(TV) Tulsa (ch 6)—Licensed to KOTV Inc. (owned by Belo Broadcasting, see Group Ownership). Former owner: Corinthian Broadcasting Corp. Sale price: $41 million. (Transfer is part of a six stn deal totaling $606 million.) FCC approved: November 22, 1983 [For the Record, December 19, 1983]. Note: KOTV(TV) originally owned by Cameron TV Inc. (George Cameron) sold to Wrather-Alvarez interests for $2.5 million after FCC approved: July 30, 1952 [For the Record, August 4, 1952]. Wrather-Alvarez Inc. (J.D. Wrather, Mrs. Maizie Wrather & M.H. Alvarez) sold stn to Corinthian Television Corp. in 1954. Sale price: $4 million. FCC approved: May 14, 1954 [For the Record, May 24, 1954]. Stn was merged with Corinthian Broadcasting into Dun & Bradstreet Companies Inc. for stock valued at $137 million (including KHOU-TV Houston; WISH-TV Indianapolis; KXTV(TV) Sacramento, CA; WANE-TV Fort Wayne, IN; & two radio stns). FCC approved: April 14, 1971 [*Broadcasting*, April 19, 1971].

KTFO(TV) Tulsa (ch 41)—Licensed to Tulsa TV 41 (owned by Channel 41 Associates). Former owner: Green County Associates (Leonard Anderson). Sale price: transfer of interest for $500,000. FCC approved: August 23, 1989 [For the Record, September 11, 1989]. Former call letters: KGCT-TV. Previous owner: Green County Associates Ltd. & Satellite TV Systems. Sale price: $5 million. FCC approved: December 10, 1985.

KTUL-TV Tulsa (ch 8)—Licensed to Allbritton Communications Co. (see Group Ownership). Former owner: Leake TV Inc. (subsidiary of Leake Industries Inc.). Sale price: $80 million (including KATV(TV) Little Rock, AR). FCC approved: March 9, 1983. Note: Leake owns 80% of WSTE(TV) Fajardo, PR.

KWHB(TV) Tulsa (ch 47)—Licensed to KBJH Inc. [owned by LeSea Broadcasting (Lester Sumrall, et al)]. Former owner: Coit Drapery & Cleaners Inc. Sale price: $3.4 million. FCC approved: May 14, 1986 [For the Record, April 14, 1986]. Former call letters: KTCT(TV).

Oregon

***KOAB-TV Bend (ch 3)**—Licensed to Oregon Public Broadcasting (Charles J. Swindells). Former owner: State of Oregon (acting by & through the State Board of Higher Education). Sale price: no cash consideration. FCC approved: 1993 [For the Record, September 20, 1993]. Note: Part of multi-stn purchase (see KOAC-TV Corvallis, OR). Previous owner: Corvallis TV Cable Co. (wholly owned subsidiary of Liberty Communications Inc.). Sale price: $200,000. FCC approved: February 19, 1976 [For the Record, March 9, 1976]. Note: Formerly KVDO-TV was licensed to Salem. Original owner, Channel 3 Inc. (Harry E. Godsil, et al), sold stn in 1972 to Valley Broadcasters Inc. (owned by Liberty) for stock in Liberty equal to value of stockholders' investment in Channel 3 ($411,000) & certain liabilities ($190,000) to be retired. FCC approved: September 27, 1972 [*Broadcasting*, October 2, 1972].

KTVZ(TV) Bend (ch 21)—Licensed to Resort Broadcasting Inc. Former owner: Ponderosa Television Inc. [subsidiary of Sierra Cascade Communications Inc. (George R. Johnson)]. Sale price: $3.9 million. FCC approved: October 30, 1986 [For the Record, September 29, 1986]. Previous owners: J.L. DeArmond & John R. Dellenback. Sale price: $1.6 million. FCC approved: July 7, 1981 [Changing Hands, July 22, 1981]. Note: Sellers transferred their two-thirds interest in stns to Johnson. Sale price includes transfer of control of KTMT(FM) Medford, OR. Group also sold KTVL(TV) Medford, OR for $12.5 million (see KTVL(TV) Medford).

***KOAC-TV Corvallis (ch 7)**—Licensed to Oregon Public Broadcasting (Charles J. Swindells). Former owner: State of Oregon. Sale price: no cash consideration (including KOAC-AM Corvallis, KTVR-TV La Grande, KEPB-TV Eugene, KOAB-FM-TV Bend, KOPB-FM-TV Portland, KRBM-FM Pendleton, all OR). FCC approved: 1993 [For the Record, September 20, 1993]. Notes: In June 1993, the Oregon Legislative Assembly passed & the governor signed a bill which will abolish the Oregon Commission on Public Broadcasting & transfer all assets, rights, obligations & broadcast interests to a private nonprofit corporation, Oregon Public Broadcasting).

***KEPB-TV Eugene (ch 2)**—Licensed to Oregon Public Broadcasting (Charles J. Swindells). Former owner: State of Oregon. Sale price: no cash consideration. FCC approved: 1993 [For the Record, September 20, 1993]. Note: Part of multi-stn purchase (see KOAC-TV Corvallis, OR).

KEZI-TV Eugene (ch 9)—Licensed to Chambers Communication Corp. Original owner: Liberty Communication Inc. (see Group Ownership). Sale price: $18 million. FCC approved: August 10, 1983. Note: Stn founded December 19, 1960.

KMTR(TV) Eugene (ch 16)—Licensed to Robert W. Davis, et al. Previous owner: Joseph H. Gonyea, et al. Sale price: $1.13 million. FCC approved: January 16, 1984. Former call letters KMTR-TV.

KOTI(TV) Klamath Falls (ch 2)—Licensed to Oregon Broadcasting Co. (see Group Ownership). Original owner: W.D. Miller. Sale price: $30,000. FCC approved: May 16, 1956 [For the Record, May 28, 1956]. Original call letters: KFJI-TV.

***KTVR(TV) La Grande (ch 13)**—Licensed to Oregon Public Broadcasting (Charles J. Swindells). Former owner: State of Oregon (acting by & through State Board of Higher Education). Sale price: no cash consideration. FCC approved: 1993 [For the Record, September 20, 1993]. Note: Part of multi-stn purchase (see KOAC-TV Corvallis, OR). Previous owner: KTVB Inc. (George M. Davidson & family 100%). Sale price: $75,000. FCC approved: August 31, 1976 [For the Record, September 20, 1976].

KDRV(TV) Medford (ch 12)—Licensed to Sunshine TV Inc. [owned by Love Broadcasting Co. (principally owned by James S. Love, III, Jo Love Little, & Mary E. McMillan). Former owner: Sunshine Television Inc. Sale price: $7.5 million. FCC approved: September 1, 1987.

KSYS(TV) Medford (ch 8)—Licensed to Southern Oregon Education Co. (W. Boyce Stanard, pres; et al). Original owner: Liberty Television (joint venture of Liberty Communications Inc. & Siskiyou Broadcasters Inc.). Sale price: $48,000. FCC approved: July 20, 1973 [For the Record, August 6, 1973].

KTVL(TV) Medford (ch 10)—Licensed to Freedom Communications Inc. [subsidiary of Freedom Newspapers Inc. (C.H. Hoiles & family)]. Original owner: Sierra Cascade Communications Inc. Sale price: $12.5 million. FCC approved: July 7, 1981 [Changing Hands, July 27, 1981]. Note: Sellers also transferred two-thirds of KYVZ(TV) Bend, OR, for $1.6 million.

KGW-TV Portland (ch 8)—Licensed to King Holding Corp. (owned 50% each by Providence Journal Co. & Kelso Partners IV) Former owner: King Broadcasting Co. Sale price: $355 million. FCC approved: August 27, 1991 [For the Record, September 9, 1991]. Note: Part of multi-stn purchase. (See KING-TV Seattle).

KLOR(TV) Portland (ch 12, now deleted)—Licensed to Oregon TV Inc. Note: George Haggarty purchased stn for $1.79 million & combined its facilities with KPTV(TV) Portland. FCC approved: April 18, 1957 [For the Record, April 22, 1957].

KOIN-TV Portland (ch 6)—Licensed to KOIN-TV Inc. (see Lee Enterprises, Group Ownership). Former owners: Newhouse Broadcasting & M.M. Tonkin & Harvey Benson, trustees. Sale price: $27 million. FCC approved: 1977. Note: Samuel I. Newhouse purchased 50% interest in KOIN-AM-TV for $556,500 in 1954, later transferring the interest to the parent corporation.

***KOPB-TV Portland (ch 10)**—Licensed to Oregon Public Broadcasting (Charles J. Swindells). Former owner: State of Oregon. Sale price: no cash consideration. FCC approved: 1993 [For the Record, September 20, 1993]. Note: Part of multi-stn purchase (see KOAC-TV Corvallis, OR).

KPTV(TV) Portland (ch 12)—Licensed to Oregon TV Inc. (see Chris Craft Stations, Group Ownership). Former owner: George Haggarty. Sale price: $3.75 million. FCC approved: July 22, 1959 [For the Record, July 27, 1959]. Note: Founded by Herbert Mayer in 1952. Sold to Storer Broadcasting Co. in 1954 in $8.5 million package deal that included WXEL(TV) Cleveland (now WJW-TV) & Empire Coil Co., New Rochelle, NY. Storer sold stn to Mr. Haggarty in 1957 for $1.89 million.

KTDZ-TV Portland (ch 24)—Licensed to National Minority TV Inc. (nonprofit group of 15 TVs headed by Paul Crouch). Former owner: Greater Portland Broadcasting Corp. Sale price: $520,000 [Changing Hands, January 18, 1988].

KBSP-TV Salem (ch 22)—Licensed to Blackstar Communications Inc. (owned by John E. Oxendine, Kenneth O. Harria & Wesley S. Williams). Former owner: Silver King Broadcasting (owned by Home Shopping Network). Sale price: $5.135 million. FCC approved: February 18, 1988 [For the Record, February 29, 1988]. Former call letters: KHSP(TV). Previous owner: Emerald City Broadcasting Inc. Sale price: $5 million. FCC approved: July 1987 [For the Record, June 15, 1987]. Former call letters: KWVT(TV). Previous owner: Greater Williamette Vision Ltd. Sale price: $4.8 million. FCC approved: November 7, 1985. Former call letters: KECH-TV.

KEBN(TV) Salem (ch 32)—Licensed to Communications Programming Agency Inc. [owned by Glen A. & Beverly Chambers (40% each) & Ronna Scott (20%)]. Former owner: Willamette Valley Broadcasting Co. Ltd. Sale price: $800,000. FCC approved: July 17, 1991 [For the Record, August 5, 1991]. Former call letters: KUTF(TV).

Pennsylvania

WATM-TV Altoona (ch 23)—Licensed to Auburn Television Group Inc. Former owner: Evergreen Broadcasting Corp. (owned by Robert N. Smith & William S. Reyner Jr.). Sale price: $2.4 million. FCC approved: December 13, 1989. Former call letters: WWPC-TV. Former owner: John R. Powley. Sale price: $1.03 million. FCC approved: February 28, 1986. Former call letters: WOPC(TV).

WTAJ-TV Altoona (ch 10)—Licensed to Gateway Communications Inc. (80% owned by the Bergen Evening Record Corp., Hackensack, NJ). Former owner: Triangle Publications Inc. (owned by Walter Annenberg). Sale price: $14.4 million (including WBNG-TV Binghamton, NY & WLYH-TV Lancaster-Lebanon, PA). FCC approved: September 1972 [*Broadcasting*, September 25, 1972]. Former call letters: WFBG-TV. Note: Original owner, Gable Broadcasting Co., sold stn (with WFBG-AM) in 1956 to Triangle for $3.5 million. FCC aproved: January 11, 1956 [For the Record, January 16, 1956].

WEPA-TV Erie (ch 66, now deleted)—Licensed to Empire Television & Radio Inc. (see WBJA-TV Binghamton, NY).

WETG(TV) Erie (ch 66)—Licensed to Gannon University Broadcasting Inc. (David A. Rubino). Former owner: Gannon University Broadcasting Inc. (M. Daniel Henry). Sale price: no financial consideration. FCC approved: June 3, 1993 [For the Record, June 28, 1993].

WSEE-TV Erie (ch 35)—Licensed to NTG Inc. Former owner: Price Communications. Sale price: $120 million (including WZZM-TV Grand Rapids, MI, WAPT-TV Jackson, MS, & WNAC-TV Providence, RI). FCC approved: September 11, 1989 [For the Record, September 25, 1989]. Previous owner: Erie Broadcasting Partners. Sale price: $8.75 million. FCC approved: October, 1987 [Changing Hands, August 17, 1987]. Previous owner: SCS Comm. of Erie Inc. (subsidiary of MMT Sales Inc.). Sale price: $7.5 million. FCC approved: December 13, 1985 [For the Record, November 11, 1985]. Previous owner: Gillett Broadcasting. Sale price: $4.75 million. FCC approved: June 10, 1982. Original owners: Mead family of Erie (33%), which also owns Erie *Morning News* & *Times* & others. Sale price: $1.7 million. FCC approved: July 1978.

WPCB-TV Greensburg (ch 40)—Licensed to Cornerstone Television Inc. (owned by Western PA Christian Broadcasting Co.). Assignment is part of resolution of law suit. Former owner: Commercial Radio Institute. FCC approved: July 1978. Former call letters: WPFO-TV.

WHTM-TV Harrisburg (ch 27)—Licensed to Smith Broadcasting Group. Former owner: Times Mirror Co. (see Group Ownership). Sale price: $79 million (including WETM(TV) Elmira & WSTM(TV) Syracuse, both NY). FCC approved: January 29, 1986 [For the Record, December 16, 1985]. Previous owner: Newhouse Broadcasting Co. Sale price: $82 million [including WAPI-TV Birmingham, AL; KTVI(TV) St. Louis, MO; WSYR-TV Syracuse & satellite WSYE-TV Elmira, both NY; & WHTM-TV (formerly WTPA(TV)) Harrisburg, PA]. FCC approved: March 27, 1980. [*Broadcasting*, March 31 & April 7, 1980]. Original owner: Ronald E. Newhouse. FCC approved: November 17, 1954 [For the Record, November 22, 1954].

WJAC-TV Johnstown (ch 6)—Licensed to WJAC Inc. {owned 100% by Johnstown Tribune Publishing Co. [Alvin D. Schrott, Richard H. Mayer & Louis A. Pradt (60.2% jointly)]}. Former owner: WJAC Inc. {owned 100% by Johnstown Tribune Publishing Co. [Walter W. Krebs, special trustee of A.H. Walters estate (60.2%)]}. FCC approved: (involuntary transfer of control) August 16, 1974 [For the Record, September 2, 1974].

WPTJ(TV) Johnstown (ch 19)—Licensed to Leon A. Crosby (former pres & owner of KEMO-TV San Francisco). Former owner: Cover Broadcasting Inc. Sale price: $1.59 million. FCC approved: October 14, 1982. [*Broadcasting*, November 1, 1982]. Former call letters: WFAT-TV. Previous owner: Dominic Ciarimboli was appointed operating receiver of property of Cover Broadcasting by bankruptcy judge in U.S. district court. FCC approved: September 17, 1976 [For the Record, October 11, 1976]. Former call letters: WJNL-TV. Original call letters: WARD-TV. Note: former owner Rivoli Realty Co. [Margaret E. Gartland (38.7%), George D. Gartland (18%), Walter M. Thomas (14.3%), & others] sold stn in 1971 to Ben Werk Group of Canton, OH, for $575,000. FCC approved: March 17, 1971 [*Broadcasting*, March 22, 1971]. In 1972 stn, including WARD(AM), was sold to Cover Broadcasting Inc. (owned 100% by John E. Gelormino) for $886,593. FCC approved: July 19, 1972 [For the Record, August 21, 1972]. In 1975 stn, including WJNL-AM-FM, was transferred to Cover Broadcasting Inc., debtor-in-possession. FCC approved: August 11, 1976 [For the Record, September 1, 1975].

WLYH-TV Lancaster (ch 15)—Licensed to Gateway Communications Inc. (80% owned by the Bergen Evening Record Corp., Hackensack, NJ). Former owner: Triangle Publications Inc. (owned by Walter Annenberg). Sale price: $14.4 million (including WBNG-TV Binghamton, NY & WTAJ-TV Altoona, PA). FCC approved: September 1972 [*Broadcasting*, September 25, 1972]. Note: original owners [WLBR-AM-FM (52%) & Lebanon *News* (36%)] sold off-air stn to Triangle for $240,000. FCC approved: November 2, 1955 [For the Record, November 7, 1955] & May 2, 1957 [For the Record, May 6, 1957].

KYW-TV Philadelphia (ch 3)—Licensed to Westinghouse Broadcasting Co. (see Group Ownership). Former owner: NBC. Sale in exchange for Westinghouse's Cleveland stns (with KYW-AM), under FCC order. FCC approved: February 17, 1965 [For the Record, March 1, 1965]. Former call letters: WRCV-TV. Note: founded in 1948 as WPTZ(TV) by Philco Corp. Bought by Westinghouse in 1953 for $8.5 million. Exchanged for NBC's Cleveland stns & $3 million in 1955.

WCAU-TV Philadelphia (ch 10)—Licensed to CBS Inc. (see Group Ownership). Former owner: WCAU Inc. (Philadelphia *Bulletin*). Sale price: $15.6 million plus $4 million for land & real estate (including WCAU-AM-FM). FCC approved: July 31, 1958 [For the Record, August 4, 1958].

WGBS-TV Philadelphia (ch 57)—Licensed to Grant Broadcasting System. Former owner: Channel 57 Corp. (Leon S. Gross et al). Sale price: $30 million. FCC approved: April 24, 1985 [For the Record, March 18, 1985]. Former call letters: WWSG-TV.

WGTI(TV) Philadelphia (ch 23, now deleted)— Licensed to Seven Arts Broadcasting Inc. (owned by Seven Arts Associated Corp 100%). Former owner: Bernard Rappaport. Sale price: $14,202.66 for CP. FCC approved: July 5, 1967 [For the Record, July 17, 1967].

WPHL-TV Philadelphia (ch 17)—Licensed to Tribune Broadcasting Co. (see Group Ownership, Cross-Ownership). Former owner: WGHP Limited Partnership (owned by Dudley Taft & Randall E. Smith). Sale price: $19 million. FCC approved: November 1991 [Changing Hands, November 18, 1991]. Previous owner: WPHL-TV (owned by The Providence *Journal*, see Group Ownership). Sale price: $72 million. FCC approved: October 1987. Previous owner: AVC Corp. Sale price: $10 million plus 10 year consulting & non-competition agreement. FCC approved: November 16, 1978. Former call letters: WPCA-TV. Note: Founded in 1960 by Young People's Church of the Air (Donald B. Crawford). Left air in 1962. Sold to Philadelphia Television Broadcasting Co. (Aaron J. Katz & Leonard Stevens) in 1964 for $219,000 & returned to air in 1966.

WPVI-TV Philadelphia (ch 6)—Licensed to Capital Cities Communications Inc. (see Group Ownership). Former owner: Triangle Publications Inc. (owned by Walter H. Annenberg & family). Sale price: $110 million (including WFIL(AM) & WIOQ(FM); WNHC(AM), WPLR(FM), & WTNH-TV New Haven, CT; KFRE(AM), KFYE(FM) & KFSN-TV Fresno, CA; & television program syndication business). FCC approved: February 24, 1971 [*Broadcasting*, March 1, 1971]. Original call letters: WFIL-TV. Note: Contingent on sale was Capital Cities "spin-off" of WFIL(AM) & WIOQ(FM) (formerly WFIL-FM) Philadelphia; WNHC(AM) & WPLR(FM) (formerly WNHC-FM) New Haven, CT; & KFRE(AM), KFYE(FM) & KFRE-TV Fresno, CA to separate buyers for an aggregate sum of $14.45 million.

WTAF-TV Philadelphia (ch 29)—Licensed to TVX Broadcast Group (see Group Ownership). Former owner: Taft Broadcasting (see Group Ownership). (For details of sale, see KTXH(TV) Houston.) FCC approved: February 20, 1987. Original owners: William L. & Irwin C. Fox & Dorothy Kotin. Sale price: $1.4 million plus adjustments & assumptions of liabilities bringing price to an estimated $4.5 million. FCC approved: May 7, 1969 [For the Record, June 2, 1969]. Former call letters: WIBF-TV. Note: Founded by WIBF Broadcasting (Fox group) in May 1965.

KDKA-TV Pittsburgh (ch 2)—Licensed to Westinghouse Broadcasting Co. (see Group Ownership). Original owner: Allen B. DuMont Labs Inc. Sale price: $9.75 million. FCC approved: January 5, 1955 [For the Record, January 10, 1955]. Original call letters: WDTV(TV).

WENS(TV) Pittsburgh (ch 22, now deleted)—Licensed to Capital Communications Corp. (wholly-owned subsidiary of Springfield TV Broadcasting Corp). Original owners: Thomas P. Johnson & others. Sale price: 5,000 shares of Springfield TV Broadcasting Corp. (estimated $110,000) for CP. FCC approved: July 28, 1965 [For the Record, August 2, 1965].

WPGH-TV Pittsburgh (ch 53)—Licensed to Sinclair Broadcast Group Inc. [headed by brothers David D., J. Duncan, Robert E., & Frederick Smith (25% each)]. Former owner: Channel 53 Licensee Inc. (headed by Michael Finkelstein). Sale price: $55 million. FCC approved: June 21, 1991 [For the Record July 15, 1991]. Previous owner: LTB Corp (owned by Lorimar-Telepictures Corp, preceded by Meredith Corporation (see Group Ownership & Cross-Ownership). Sale price of LTB-Meredith transaction: $35 million. FCC approved: November 12, 1986 [For the Record, October 13, 1986]. Previous owner: Pittsburgh Telecasting Inc. [Leon Crosby (20%) & Stip Realty Inc. (80%)]. Sale price: $11.7 million. FCC approved: September 8, 1978 [Changing Hands, October 2, 1978]. Previous owner: Vincent M. Casey (receiver for U.S. Communications of Pittsburgh Inc.). Sale price: $100,000. FCC approved: December 12, 1973 [For the Record, December 31, 1973. Former call letters: WAND-TV. Note: Original owner, Agnes Jane Reeves Greer, sold CP (as WAND-TV) to D.H. Overmyer Communications Co. in 1965 for $28,000. FCC approved: July 28, 1965 [For the Record, August 2, 1965]. In 1967, 80% of CP (WECO-TV) was sold by D.H. Overmyer Communications Co. to U.S. Communications Corp. for $1 million (including CPs for KEMO-TV San Francisco; WMBO-TV Atlanta; WSCO-TV Newport, KY; & KJDO-TV Rosenberg, TX). FCC approved: December 8, 1967 [For the Record, December 18, 1967]. Original call letters: WKJF-TV.

WPTT(TV) Pittsburgh (ch 22)—Licensed to WPTT Inc. (headed by Edwin L. Edwards Sr. & Willette Edwards). Former owner: Commercial Radio Institute Inc. (headed by brothers David D., J. Duncan, Robert E., & Frederick Smith). Sale price: $7 million. FCC approved: June 21, 1991 [For the Record, July 15, 1991].

WPXI(TV) Pittsburgh (ch 11)—Licensed to WPXI Inc. (see Cox Broadcasting Corp., Group Ownership). Former owners: P-G Publishing Co. (Pittsburgh *Post-Gazette* & *Sun Telegraph*) & H. Kenneth Brennan family. Sale price: $20.5 million. FCC approved: November 20, 1964 [For the Record, November 30, 1964]. Former call letters: WIIC-TV. Note: previously, 50% of stn was sold to H. Kenneth Brennan & family by Pittsburgh Post-Gazette for $500,000 in 1957.

WTAE-TV Pittsburgh (ch 4)—Licensed to Hearst Corp. (see Group Ownership). Original owner: 50% interest owned by Earl F. Reed & Irwin D. Wolf Jr. & Group, along with Hearst Corp. Sale price: $10.6 million for 50% of Reed et al interest. FCC approved: August 1, 1962 [For the Record, August 6, 1962].

WNEP-TV Scranton (ch 16)—Licensed to New York Times Co. Former owner: NEP Communications Inc. (Thomas P. Shelburne, Catherine W. Shelburne, Thomas P. Shelburne III, et al). Sale price: $40 million. FCC approved: October 29, 1985 [For the Record, September 23, 1985]. Previous owner: NEP Communications Inc. [Thomas P. Shelburne (32.9%), Frank M. Henry (21.6%), Catherine W. Shelburne (21.9%), et al). Sale price: no financial consideration. Note: Thomas & Catherine (wife) Shelburne transferred some shares in the license to members of their immediate family for estate planning purposes. FCC approved: August 26, 1976 [For the Record, September 27, 1976]. WNEP-TV was formed by a merger of WARM-TV Scranton & WILK-TV Wilkes-Barre, both PA. Transcontinent TV Corp. bought a 60% interest in 1958, & William M. Scranton & associates purchased 20% each, in stock transaction considered to total $1.5 million. Transcontinent sold stn in 1964 to Taft Broadcasting Co. (see Group Ownership) for $26.9 million (including WGR-AM-FM-TV Buffalo, NY, & WDAF-AM-FM-TV Kansas City, MO). Taft sold stn in 1973 to NEP Communications for $3.9 million. FCC approved: November 1, 1973 [For the Record, November 26, 1973].

WYOU-TV Scranton (ch 22)—Licensed to Keystone Broadcasters (owned by Diversified Comm., see Group Ownership). Former owner: SB Television Corp. (owned by Southeast Capital). Sale price: $22.8 million. FCC approved: July 18, 1986 [Changing Hands, June 9, 1986]. Former call letters: WDAU-TV. Previous owner: Scranton Broadcasters Inc. Sale price: $12 million. FCC approved: July 27, 1984. Previous owner: WCAU Inc. (former 75% owner) Sale price: sold interest to Scranton Broadcasters Inc. FCC approved: May 27, 1959 [For the Record, June 8, 1959]. Note: WCAU Inc. (Philadelphia *Bulletin*, & former licensee WCAU-AM-TV Philadelphia) purchased 75% from Scranton Broadcasting Inc. (Mrs. M.E. Megargee & family) in 1956. Sale price: $650,000. FCC approved: October 18, 1956 [For the Record, October 22, 1956].

WBRE-TV Wilkes-Barre (ch 26)—Licensed to Adams TV of Wilkes-Barre Inc. Former owner: WBRE-TV Inc. {owned by Northeastern Television Investors [Martin Pompadur (60%) & Ralph Becker (40%)]. Sale price: $21 million [For the Record, July 10, 1989]. Previous owner: David M. Baltimore family. Sale price: $21 million. FCC approved: May 24, 1984.

WRAK-TV Williamsport (ch 36, now deleted)—Licensed to WGAL Inc. (WGAL-AM-FM-TV Lancaster, PA-Steinman Stations). Original owner: WRAK Inc. (Margaretta Steele & Associates). Sale price: $125,000 (including WRAK-AM-FM). FCC approved: February 7, 1957 [For the Record, February 11, 1957].

WNOW-TV York (ch 49, now deleted)—Licensed to WNOW Inc. (William F. Rust Jr. & Associates). Former owner: Morgan E. Cousler & Lowell W. Williams. Sale price: $255,000 (including WNOW(AM)). FCC approved: August 2, 1957 [For the Record, August 5, 1957].

WPMT-TV York (ch 43)—Licensed to Channel 43 Licensee Inc. Former owner: WYLP License Inc. Sale price: $13.47 million. FCC approved: March 30, 1990. Previous owner: Westport York Associates [Jonathan Hayes & Michael Rosenthal (50% each)]. Previous owner: Mohawk Broadcasting Ltd [owned by Cary W. Jones (13.5%), Kapuna Corp. (13.5%), & others]. Sale price: $13.85 million. FCC approved: September 12, 1986 [For the Record, August 11, 1986]. Previous owner: Susquehanna Broadcasting Co. (see Group Ownership). Sale price: $2 million. FCC approved: December 30, 1982 [For the Record, January 17, 1983]. Former call letters: WSBA-TV. Note: Stn went on air December 22, 1952.

Rhode Island

WJAR(TV) Providence (ch 10)—Licensed to Outlet Communications Group (see Group Ownership). Former owner: The Rockefeller Group. Sale price: $625 million (see WCMH(TV) Columbus, OH, for details). FCC approved: July 31, 1986. Previous owner: The Outlet Company. Sale price: $332 million (same properties sold to Wesray). FCC approved: November 23, 1983.

WNAC(TV) Providence (ch 64)—Licensed to NTG Inc. Former owner: Rhode Island Broadcasting Corp. (Price Communications Corp.). Sale price: $120 million (including WZZM-TV Grand Rapids, MI; WAPT-TV Jackson,

MS; & WSEE-TV Erie, PA). FCC approved: September 11, 1989 [For the Record, September 25, 1989]. Previous owner: Sudbrink Broadcasting. Sale price: $11.5 million [Changing Hands, March 21, 1988]. Previous owner: Providence Television Ltd. Partnership, debtor-in-possession. Sale price: $5.85 million. FCC approved: July 14, 1986 [For the Record, June 16, 1986]. Former call letters: WSTS(TV). Previous owner: Topcor Inc. Sale price: $2 million. FCC approved: December 9, 1983. Previous owner: Channel 16 of Rhode Island Inc. Sale price: $487,500 for CP. FCC approved: February 18, 1980.

WPRI-TV Providence (ch 12)—Licensed to Knight-Ridder Broadcasting. Former owner: Providence Television Inc. (see Poole Broadcasting Stations, Group Ownership). Sale price: $49.63 million (including WCDC(TV) Adams, MA; WJRT-TV Flint, MI; & WTEN(TV) Albany, NY). FCC approved: September 22, 1982. Previous owner: Capital Cities Broadcasting Corp. (see Capital Cities Communications Inc., Group Ownership). Sale price: $16.5 million. FCC approved: June 16, 1967 [For the Record, June 26, 1967]. Former call letters: WPRO-TV. Original owner: Cherry & Webb Broadcasting Co. Sale price: $6.5 million (including WPRO-AM-FM). FCC approved: 1959.

South Carolina

WAXA(TV) Anderson (ch 40)—Licensed to Mark III Broadcasting Co. (owned by Agronomics Inc.). Former owner: New South TV Corp. (owned by Frank Outlaw). Sale price: $200,000. FCC approved: December 28, 1982. Previous owner: William E. Hall. Sale price: $850,000. FCC approved: July 20, 1978.

WCBD-TV Charleston (ch 2)—Licensed to Charleston Television Inc. (Media General Telecommunications Inc., see Cross-Ownership). Former owner: State Record Co. (SC-based nwspr publisher which sold its three TV stns in 1983). Sale price: $8 million. FCC approved: November 8, 1982 [For the Record, January 24, 1983]. Previous owner: Reeves Telecom Corp. Sale price: $2 million. FCC approved: May 26, 1971 [*Broadcasting*, May 31, 1971]. Former call letters: WUSN-TV.

WCIV(TV) Charleston (ch 4)—Licensed to First Charleston Corp. (owned by Joseph Allbritton Communications). Former owner: Evening Star Broadcasting (Washington Star Communications). Sale price: $28.5 million (including WMAL-AM-FM-TV Washington & WLVA-AM-TV Lynchburg, VA). FCC approved: January, 1976. Original owner: First Charleston Corp. Sale price: $2.21 million plus assumption of $400,000 in obligations. FCC approved: October 5, 1966 [For the Record, October 10, 1966].

WCSC-TV Charleston (ch 5)—Licensed to Jefferson-Pilot Communications Co. (William E. Blackwell). Former owner: General Electric Capital Corp. Sale price: $15.5 million. FCC approved: September 3, 1993 [For the Record, September 27, 1993]. Previous owner: Crump Communications. Sale price: $250,000 & return to General Electric Capital Corp. for cancellation of Crump Communications' certificate representing 12,000 shares of prefered stock & warrant to purchase 376,200 shares of common stock. FCC approved: July 24, 1991 [For the Record, August 26, 1991]. Original owner: WCSC Inc. (owned by the John Rivers Family). Sale price: $60 million. FCC approved: September 1987 [Changing Hands, July 20, 1987].

WTAT-TV Charleston (ch 24)—Licensed to ACTV of Charleston SC Inc. [American Communications (80%) & Charleston Television Ltd. (20%)]. Former owner: Charleston Television Ltd. [Act III Broadcasting (principally owned by Norman Lear)]. Sale price: $5 million. FCC approved: September 14, 1989 [For the Record, October 2, 1989]. Previous owner: Charleston Community Television Ltd. Sale price: $4.821 million. FCC approved: October 1987 [Changing Hands, July 27, 1987].

WACH(TV) Columbia (ch 57)—Licensed to Elcom of South Carolina Inc. (see Ellis Communications in Group Ownership). Former owner: FCV Communications Inc. (owned by Walter K. Flynn, William J. Voute, E. Craig Coats Jr., Ronald M. Stuart, Murray Rosenblum). Sale price: $15 million, including WEVU(TV) Naples, FL. FCC approved: October 7, 1993 [For the Record, October 25, 1993]. Previous owner: Carolina Christian Broadcasting Inc. Sale price: $3.7 million. FCC approved: May 11, 1988. Former call letters: WCCT-TV.

WLTX(TV) Columbia (ch 19)—Licensed to Capital Communications Inc. (Lewis Broadcasting Corp.). Previous owner: Palmetto Radio Corp. (J.W. Lindau III, Irwin Kahn & W. Croft Jennings). Sale price: $3.98 million plus $112,500 for covenant not to compete for WNOK-AM-FM-TV. FCC approved: October 18, 1978 [For the Record, November 6, 1978). Former call letters: WNOK. Note: Lewis Broadcasting (J.C. Lewis) owns WJCL-FM-TV Savannah, GA & publishes *Journal-Record* weekly nwspr there.

WOLO-TV Columbia (ch 25)—Licensed to Columbia TV Broadcasters Inc. (see Bahakel Stations, Group Ownership). Former owner: First Carolina Corp. (Philip E. Pearce, Henry Sherrill, Edwin H. Cooper, Geddings H. Crawford, Richard Kennan & others). Sale price: $240,000. FCC approved: May 5, 1964 [For the Record, May, 1964].

WBTW(TV) Florence (ch 13)—Licensed to Spartan Radiocasting Co. (see Group Ownership). Former owner: Daily Telegraph Printing Co. Sale price: $36.75 million (including KIMT(TV) Mason City, IA). FCC approved: June 12, 1984. Previous owner: Jefferson Standard Broadcasting Co. Sale price: $4.55 million. FCC approved: February 28, 1968 [For the Record, March 11, 1968]. Note: Founded by Jefferson Standard Life Insurance Co. in 1954.

WFIL(TV) Florence (ch 21)—Licensed to Atlantic Media Group (C. Lenoir Sturkie). Former owner: Coastal Television Inc. (Ed Young). Sale price: no cash consideration for CP. FCC approved: July 30, 1993 [For the Record, August 23, 1993]. Previous owner: Tri-Star Communications. Sale price: $235,000 for CP. FCC approved: August 5, 1991 [For the Record, August 26, 1991]. Original owner: Magara Communications Corp. Sale price: $124,700 for CP. FCC approved: April 30, 1990.

WPDE(TV) Florence (ch 15)—Licensed to Diversified Communications. Former owner: Eastern Carolinas Broadcasting. Sale price: $14.5 million. FCC approved: June 27, 1985 [For the Record, June 3, 1985].

WYFF-TV Greenville (ch 4)—Licensed to Pulitzer Broadcasting Co. (see Group Ownership). Previous owner: Multimedia (see Group Ownership). Sale price: part of a multi-stn deal in which Pulitzer traded KSDK-TV St. Louis, MO for WFBC-TV (WYFF-TVs former call letters); WXII-TV Winston-Salem, NC; & $9 million. FCC approved: February 17, 1983 [For the Record, March 14, 1983]. Former call letters: WFBC-TV. Note: Stn founded December 31, 1953, by Southeastern Broadcasting Corp. Transferred to Multimedia in 1967.

WFVT(TV) Rock Hill (ch 55)—CP licensed to Family Fifty-Five Inc. Former owner: Rock Hill Broadcasting Corp. Sale price: $314,000. FCC approved: February 18, 1993 [For the Record, March 8, 1993].

South Dakota

KABY-TV Aberdeen (ch 9)— Licensed to New Vision Television I Inc. (see New Vision Television Inc. in Group Ownership). Former owner: South Dakota TV. Sale price: $110 million. FCC approved: September 7, 1993 [For the Record, September 27, 1993]. Note: Part of multi-stn purchase (see KOLD-TV Tucson, AZ). Previous owner: Forum Communications. Sale price: $9.25 million (including satellite KSFY-TV Sioux Falls & co-owned satellite KPRY-TV Lead, both SD). FCC approved: 1973. Previous owners: Gordon H. Ritz (41.5%), et al. Sale price: $2.25 million (including KSFY-TV Sioux Falls, SD). Former call letters: KCOO-TV. Original owner: John Boler. Sale price: $700,000. FCC approved: 1969.

KTTM(TV) Huron (ch 12)—Licensed to Independent Communications Inc. (owned by Jerry Noonan, E. C. Stangland, Thomas J. Whalen, Charles D. Poppen, Richard T. Devaney & Cal Neumeister). Former owner: Pacer TV of Huron Inc. (owned by Lyle R. Evans). Sale price: $40,000 for CP. FCC approved: December 18, 1990 [For the Record, January 7, 1991]. Former call letters: KIID-TV.

KIVV(TV) Lead-Deadwood (ch 5)—Licensed to Heritage Media. See KEVN-TV Rapid City, SD.

KDLT(TV) Mitchell (ch 5)—Licensed to Heritage Media. Former owner: Dakotaland Broadcasting Co. (owned by Sherwood Comer & Gilbert Moyle). Sale price: $15.5 million (including KEVN-TV Rapid City & satellite KIVV-TV Lead-Deadwood, both SD). FCC approved: August 14, 1985 [For the Record, June 3, 1985]. Previous owner: Gillett Broadcasting of South Dakota (owned by George Gillett, see Group Ownership). Sale price: $2 million plus $200,000 for covenant not to compete. FCC approved: May 12, 1982 [For the Record, May 31, 1982). Previous owner: Buford Television Inc. (see Group Ownership). Sale price: $1.5 million FCC approved: January 1978 [Changing Hands, January 30, 1978]. Previous owner: Mitchell Broadcasting Assn. Sale price: $775,000. FCC approved: 1972.

KPRY(TV) Pierre (ch 4)—See KSFY(TV) Sioux Falls, SD.

KEVN-TV Rapid City (ch 7)—Licensed to Heritage Media. (see Group Ownership). Former owner: Dakotaland Broadcasting. Sale price: $15.5 million (including KDLT(TV) Mitchell & satellite KIVV(TV) Lead-Deadwood, both SD). FCC approved: August 14, 1985 [For the Record, June 3, 1985].

KFXT(TV) Sioux Falls (ch 36)—Licensed to Jeffrey W. Hayzlett (dir, Minnesota Public Radio). Former owner: Kirkwood Broadcasting Inc. Sale price: $40,000 for CP. FCC approved: June 22, 1989 [For the Record, July 10, 1989].

KSFY-TV Sioux Falls (ch 13)—Licensed to New Vision Television I Inc. (see New Vision Television Inc. in Group Ownership). Former owner: South Dakota TV. Sale price: $110 million. FCC approved: September 7, 1993 [For the Record, September 27, 1993]. Note: Part of multi-stn purchase, including KPRY(TV) Pierre, SD (see KOLD-TV Tucson, AZ). Previous owner: Forum Communications Inc. (see Group Ownership). Sale price: $8 million (including satellites KABY(TV) Aberdeen & KPRY(TV) Pierre, both SD). FCC approved: November 15, 1985 [For the Record, October 7, 1985]. Original owner: KSOO-TV Inc. (Grodon H. Ritz, bd chmn, et al). Sale price: $2.25 million [including KCOO-TV (now KABY(TV)) Aberdeen, SD]. FCC approved: November 14, 1973 [For the Record, November 26, 1973]. Former call letters: KSOO-TV. Note: Morton H. Henkin, Thomas Barnstuble, Julius Hetland & others transferred 70% interest (with KSOO-AM) to Gordon Ritz, Wheelock Whitney, Mr. Henkin & others for $770,000 in 1965. FCC approved: August 23, 1965 [For the Record, August 30, 1965].

Tennessee

WDEF-TV Chattanooga (ch 12)—Licensed to Roy H. Park Broadcasting of Tenn. Inc. (see Park Broadcasting, Group Ownership). Former owners: Carter M. Parham & others. Sale price: $2.78 million (including WDEF(AM)). FCC approved: February 12, 1964 [For the Record, February 24, 1964].

WDSI-TV Chattanooga (ch 61)—Licensed to Pegasus Broadcast Televison Ltd. Former owner: D & K Broadcast Properties Ltd. Sale price: $21 million (including WDBD(TV) Jackson, MS). FCC approved: February 18, 1993 [For the Record, March 8, 1993]. Previous owner: WDSI Ltd. Partnership (M. Starr & L. Donatelli). Former owner: Group V Television Inc. (M & P Starr). Sale price: no financial consideration. FCC approved: March 19, 1985 [For the Record, April 8, 1985]. Previous owner: Prime Time Television Inc. [Roy Hess & David Smith (50% each)]. Sale price: $5 million. FCC approved: January 30, 1985. Original owner: WRIP Inc. (owned by Jay Sadow). Sale price: $1.5 million & a $500,000 consultancy agreement. FCC approved: January 18, 1983 [For the Record, February 7, 1983]. Note: Began operation as WRIP-TV January 24, 1972.

WRCB-TV Chattanooga (ch 3)—Licensed to Sarkes Tarzian Inc. (see Group Ownership). Former owner: Ziff Davis Broadcasting (subsidiary of Ziff Corp.). Sale price: $16 million. FCC approved: September 29, 1982 [For the Record, October 18, 1982]. Note: Ziff sold stn as part of its divesture from broadcasting [*Broadcasting*, July 26, 1982]. Previous owner: Rust Craft Broadcasting. Sale price: approx. $70 million (including WTOV-TV Steubenville, OH; WJKS-TV Jacksonville, FL; WRDW-TV Augusta, GA; & WEYI-TV Saginaw, MI). FCC approved: May 15, 1978. Former owners: Ramon G. & Helen H. Patterson (70%) & Follansbee Steel Co. (Jack & Louis Berkman) (30%). Sale price: $1.67 million for 70%. FCC approved: November 27, 1959 [For the Record, December 7, 1959]. Note: Founded by Ramon G. & Helen Patterson & Will Cummings. The Pattersons bought Mr. Cummings' 50% in 1956 for $87,000 plus assumption of $32,000 in obligations [For the Record, December 3, 1956]. Follansbee Steel Co. bought 30% interest in 1959 for $325,000.

WTVC(TV) Chattanooga (ch 9)—Licensed to WTVC Inc. (Freedom Newspapers, see Group Ownership). Former owner: Belo Broadcasting (see Group Ownership). Sale price: $24.5 million (including KFMD-TV Beaumont, TX). FCC approved: December 13, 1983 [For the Record, January 2, 1984]. Previous owner: Fuqua Industries Inc. Sale price: $19.5 million. FCC approved: June 13, 1980 [Changing Hands, June 30, 1980]. Note: Went on the air June 15, 1953, as WROM-TV Rome, GA. Original owner Dean Covington & Associates sold to Martin Theatres on October 31, 1957, for $722,500. Went dark December 5, 1957, moved to Chattanooga & resumed operation as WTVC(TV) on February 11, 1958. Then sold to Fuque (with WVTM(TV) Columbus, GA, plus 140 theaters) for $19 million in 1968.

WCTE(TV) Cookeville (ch 22)—Licensed to Upper Cumberland Broadcasting. Original owner: Tennessee State Board of Education. Sale price: no financial consideration. FCC approved: December 20, 1985 [For the Record, November 18, 1985].

WSJA(TV) Cookeville (ch 28)—Licensed to Dove Broadcasting Corp. Former owner: Sandra Lewis. Sale price: $5,000 for CP. FCC approved: September 1987.

WMTT(TV) Cookeville (ch 28)—Licensed to Inavision Broadcasting Inc. Former owner: Steve Sweeney. Sale price: $100,000. FCC approved: June 29, 1993 [For the Record, July 19, 1993].

WINT-TV Crossville (ch 20)—Licensed to WINT-TV Inc. (owned by Helen & John Cunningham). Former owner: Larry D. Hudson. Sale price: assumption of liabilities. FCC approved: February 20, 1985 [For the Record, March 4, 1985]. Note: Formerly broadcast on ch 60. Previous owners: Calvin C. Smith & John A. Cunningham. Sale price: $550,000, including consulting agreement & covenant not to compete. FCC approved: June 6, 1983. Former call letters: WCPT-TV. Previous owner: Edward M. Johnson. Sale price: $42,500. FCC approved: February 27, 1979.

WEMT(TV) Greeneville (ch 39)—Licensed to MaxEncore of Tri-Cities L.P. (John Trinder). Former owner: Television Marketing Group of Tri-Cities Inc. Sale price: $3 million. FCC approved: December 6, 1993 [For the Record, December 20, 1993]. Previous owner: East Tennessee Broadcasting Corp. (headed by Michael P. Thompson). Sale price: assumption of debt (including WMTU(TV) Jackson & WLMT(TV) Memphis, both TN). FCC approved: March 19, 1992 [For the Record, April 6, 1992]. Original owner: East Tennessee's Own Inc. (Jay & Eileen Austin). Sale price: $1.85 million [For the Record, October 16, 1989]. FCC approved: September 25, 1989. Former call letters: WETO-TV.

WPGD-TV Hendersonville (ch 50)—Licensed to Sonlight Broadcasting System Inc. (headed by Paul F. Crouch, pres., nonprofit Trinity Broadcasting). Former owner: Rel Way Ltd., Relcom Corp. & Texas Mineral Inc. Sale price: $2 million for CP (including WMPV-TV Mobile, AL, & WBUY Holly Springs, MS). FCC approved: July 27, 1989 [For the Record, August 14, 1989].

WBBJ-TV Jackson (ch 7)—Licensed to Jackson Telecasters Inc. (owned by Bahakel Broadcasting, see Group Ownership). Former owners: estate of Aaron B. Robinson & others (Dixie Broadcasting Co.). Sale price: $900,000. FCC approved: August 17, 1966 [For the Record, August 22, 1966].

WMTU(TV) Jackson (ch 16)—Licensed to Television Marketing Group of Jackson Inc. Former owner: Jackson Investment Corp. Sale price: assumption of debt (including WEMT(TV) Greeneville & WLMT(TV) Memphis, both TN). FCC approved: March 19, 1992 [For the Record, April 6, 1992]. Note: stn is satellite of WLMT(TV) Memphis.

WJHL-TV Johnson City (Bristol, VA-Kingsport, TN) (ch 11)—Licensed to Roy H. Park Broadcasting of Tri-Cities Inc. (see Park Broadcasting, Group Ownership). Former owner: W.H. Lancaster Sr. & Jr. Sale price: $2.5 million. FCC approved: June 8, 1964 [For the Record, June 15, 1964]. Note: Previously W.H. Lancaster Jr. Family acquired 45.4% interest in WJHL-AM-TV for $200,000 in 1956.

WATE-TV Knoxville (ch 6)—Licensed to Nationwide Communications Inc. (see Group Ownership). Former owner: Paul Mountcastle, W.H. Linebaugh & John A. Ayers, trustees (50%) & others. Sale price: $6.8 million (including WATE(AM)). FCC approved: April 8, 1965 [For the Record, April 19, 1965].

WBIR-TV Knoxville (ch 10)—Licensed to Multimedia Inc. (see Multimedia Broadcasting Co., Group Ownership). Former owner: Taft Broadcasting Co. Sale price: $3.25 million (including WBIR-AM-FM). FCC approved: November 16, 1960 [For the Record, November 21, 1960]. Note: Taft Broadcasting owned 30% of original stn, bought remaining 70% for $2.1 million in 1959 from Gilmore Nunn, Robert L. Ashe & John P. Hart.

WKCH(TV) Knoxville (ch 43)—Licensed to Elcom of Tennessee Inc. (owned by Ellis Communications, see Group Ownership). Former owner: Knoxville Family Television Inc. (owned by Media Central Inc., see Group Ownership). Sale price: $15 million. FCC approved: October 7, 1993 [For the Record, October 25, 1993]. Previous owner: Martha & Kent B. Dixon, et al. Sale price: $1.25 million. FCC approved: October 1, 1985 [For the Record, August 12, 1985]. Original owner: James Halsam. Sale price: $451,000 (transfer of control). FCC approved: June 25, 1985 [For the Record, June 3, 1985].

WKXT-TV Knoxville (ch 8)—Licensed to Knoxville Channel 8 Ltd., owned by Phipps Television of Tennessee Inc. Former owner: Knoxville Channel 8 Ltd., owned by John D. Engelbrecht & South Central Communications Corp. (see Group Ownership). Sale price: $5.77 million. FCC approved: June 9, 1992 [For the Record, June 29, 1992].

WTVK(TV) Knoxville (ch 26)—Licensed to South Central Communications. Original owner: TV Service of Knoxville Inc. [W.R. Tuley (80%), Harold Thomas (10%) & J. Horton Doughton (10%)]. Sale price: $300,000, including assumption of obligations not exceeding $216,500. FCC approved: July 28, 1954 [For the Record, August 2, 1954].

WJFB(TV) Lebanon (ch 66)—Licensed to James W. & Lorianne C. Owens. Former owner: Bryant Communications Inc. Sale price: $1.5 million. FCC approved: October 31, 1991 [For the Record, December 16, 1991].

WHBQ-TV Memphis (ch 13)—Licensed to Adams TV of Wilkes-Barre Inc. Sale price: $39 million. Former owner: South Jersey Radio Inc. FCC approved: January 11, 1990. Previous owner: Professional Broadcasters Group (owned by RKO General Inc., see Group Ownership), preceded by original owner Harding College. Sale price of Broadcasters-Harding transaction: $2.88 million (including WHBQ-AM). FCC approved: July 1, 1954 [For the Record, July 12, 1954].

WLMT(TV) Memphis (ch 30)—Licensed to Television Marketing Group of Memphis Inc. Former owner: West Tennessee Broadcasting Corp. Sale price: assumption of debt (including WEMT(TV) Greeneville & WMTU(TV) Jackson, both TN). FCC approved: March 19, 1992 [For the Record, April 6, 1992].

WMC-TV Memphis (ch 5)—Licensed to Elcom of Memphis Inc. (see Ellis Communications in Group Ownership). Former owner: Scripps-Howard Broadcasting. Sale price: $65 million, including WMC-AM-FM Memphis. FCC approved: October 7, 1993 [For the Record, October 25, 1993]. Previous owner: WMC Broadcasting (69% owned by Scripps-Howard). Sale included WMC-AM-FM & CP for WMCT-TV. FCC approved: 1961. Former call letters: WMCT-TV.

WPTY-TV Memphis (ch 24)—Licensed to Clear Channel Television Inc. (see Group Ownership). Former owner: WPTY-TV, a Ltd. Partnership, (owned by Chase Communications, see Group Ownership). Sale price: $21 million. FCC approved: March 26, 1992 [For the Record, April 13, 1992]. Previous owner: Precht Communications of Tennessee (Precht Communications Inc., Robert H. Precht & family, see Group Ownership). Sale price: $12.5 million. FCC approved: March 28, 1986 [For the Record, February 24, 1986]. Previous owner: Delta Television Corp. [Arthur E. Muth & Martin F. Connelly (80%); Robert K. Zelle (20%)]. Sale price: $11 million. FCC approved: July 23, 1984 [For the Record, August 13, 1984].

WREG-TV Memphis (ch 3)—Licensed to The New York Times Broadcasting Service Inc. (owned by New York Times Co., see Group Ownership). Former owner: Cowles Broadcasting Service Inc. (see Cowles Communications Inc., Group Ownership). Sale price: $10,966,410. FCC approved: August 18, 1971 [*Broadcasting*, August 23, 1971]. Original call letters: WREC-TV. Note: Cowles purchased stn from original owner, Hoyt Wooten, in 1963. Sale price: $8 million (including WREC-AM). FCC approved: April 23, 1963 [For the Record, May 6, 1963].

WHTN(TV) Murfreesboro (ch 39)—Licensed to Murfreesboro TV Corp. Former owner: Channel 39 Murfreesboro. Sale price: exchange of stock. FCC approved: August 2, 1985 [For the Record, June 24, 1985]. Former call letters: WFYZ(TV).

WKRN(TV) Nashville (ch 2)—Licensed to Young Broadcasting of Nashville Inc. Former owner: Knight-Ridder Broadcasting Inc. Sale price: $42 million. FCC approved: April 17, 1989 [For the Record, May 8, 1989]. Previous owner: General Electric Broadcasting Inc. (see Group Ownership). Sale price: $37 million. FCC approved: September 28, 1983 [For the Record, October 17, 1983]. Former call letters: WNGE-TV. Note: Louis Draughon purchased 33.3% owned by W.H. Criswell in 1956 for $250,000. Sold to General Electric by Louis Draughon group [Draughon (59.3%) & as trustee (14.8%); George J. Hearn Jr. (18.5%); & John D. Sprouse (7.4%)] for $9.7 million. FCC approved: April 6, 1966 [For the Record, April 18, 1966]. Previous to 1973, call letters were WSIX-TV & stn transmitted on ch 8.

WSMV-TV Nashville (ch 4)—Licensed to Cook Inlet Communications LP. Former owner: Gillett Broadcasting Co. of Tennessee Inc. (Gillett Broadcasting). Sale price: $125 million. FCC approved: April 17, 1989 [For the Record, May 8, 1989]. Previous owner: NLT Corp. Sale price: $38 million plus interest plus $4 million covenant not to compete. FCC approved: September 14, 1981 [Changing Hands, October 5, 1991]. Note: Seller retained co-located WSM-AM-FM. Former call letters: WSM-TV.

WTVF-TV Nashville (ch 5)—Licensed to Landmark Television Inc. (see Group Ownership, Cross-Ownership). Former owner: Channel Five Television Co. (owned by H&C Communications, see Group Ownership). Sale price: $46 million. FCC approved: September 12, 1991 [For the Record, September 30, 1991]. Previous owner: WLAC-TV Inc. (Thomas B. Baker Jr., A.G. Beaman & Trustees of American General Insurance Co.). Sale price: $15.75 million plus $3 million for real estate associated with stn. FCC approved: October 15, 1975 [For the Record, October 27, 1975]. Original call letters: WLAC-TV. Note: previously, 50% was acquired by T.B. Baker & A.G. Beaman for $200,000 from Life & Casualty Insurance Co., Nashville, in 1954. American General Insurance acquired working control of Life & Casualty in 1966.

WXMT(TV) Nashville (ch 30)—Licensed to TVX of Nashville Inc. (TVX Broadcast Group). Original owner: Soutwest MultiMedia Corp. Sale price: $5.8 million [Changing Hands, May 9, 1988]. Original call letters: WCAY(TV). Note: Stn began operation February 18, 1984.

WZTV-TV Nashville (ch 17)—Licensed to Act III Broadcasting. Former owner: Multimedia Broadcasting Co. Sale price: $14-15 million [Changing Hands, March 21, 1988]. Previous owner: Reel Broadcasting Co. Sale price: $6 million. FCC approved: December 14, 1979. Former call letters: WTLT(TV). Previous owner: Hudson Broadcasting. Sale price: $42,400 assumption of debts, plus lease agreement. FCC approved: September 30, 1975 [For the Record, October 20, 1975]. Original call letters: WMCV(TV). Note: Stn began operation August 5, 1968, & went off the air March 14, 1971 [*Broadcasting*, March 29, 1971]. Charles H. White, attorney, became owner of WMCV(TV) by commission grant of June 18, 1973. Mr. White, trustee in bankruptcy, sold stn to Hudson Broadcasting in 1974 for $25,000. FCC approved: July 31, 1974 [For the Record, August 12, 1974].

Texas

KRBC-TV Abilene (ch 9)—Licensed to Abilene Radio & TV Co. (see Group Ownership). Original owner: Mrs. Eva May Hanks. Sale price: $500,000 (including KRBC(AM)). FCC approved: September 16, 1953 [For the Record, September 28, 1953].

KTAB-TV Abilene (ch 32)—Licensed to Shamrock Broadcasting Co. (see Group Ownership). Former owner: International Broadcasting Corp. (privately traded corporation headed by principal stockholder Thomas K. Scallen, 15%). Sale price: $15.75 million. FCC approved: November 25, 1986 [For the Record, October 27, 1986]. Original owner: William Terry (50%) & 11 others. Sale price: $9 million ($7 million cash & $2 million note). FCC approved: July 30, 1984 [For the Record, August 13, 1984)].

KTHT(TV) Alvin (ch 67)—Licensed to Silver King Broadcasting (owned by Home Shopping Network Inc., see Group Ownership). Former owner: Four-Star Broadcasting Inc. (Harold V. Dutton, et al). Sale price: $15 million. FCC approved: October 30, 1986 [For the Record, September 29, 1986].

KAMR-TV Amarillo (ch 4)—Licensed to Canaan Communications Inc. (D.A. Canaan & Darrold A. Canaan Jr., together 95%). Former owner: Stauffer Publications Inc. (see Group Ownership). Sale price: $2.5 million. FCC approved: July 31, 1974 [For the Record, August 12, 1974]. Original call letters: KGNC-TV. Note: began operation in March 1953. Original owner Globe-News Publishing Co. sold stn, along with KGNC(AM) Amarillo & KFYO(AM) Lubbock, both TX, to the Roy N. Whittenburg Family in 1955 for $3.9 million [*Broadcasting*, June 27, 1955]. In 1966 stn (with KGNC-AM-FM) was sold to Stauffer Publications for $5.9 million. FCC approved: January 14, 1966. [For the Record, January 24, 1966].

KCIT(TV) Amarillo (ch 14)—Licensed to KCIT Acquisition Co. [headed by F. Lanham Lyne Jr. (50%), Martha Steed Lyne (25%), Peter D'Acosta (20%), & Charles R. Hart (5%)]. Former owner: Ralph C. Wilson Industries (headed by Ralph C. Wilson Jr., David N. Olsen, Jeffrey C. Littman, & P. Jane Wright). Sale price: $2.4 million.

Broadcasting & Cable Yearbook 1994
A-82

FCC approved: March 11, 1991 [For the Record, March 25, 1991].

KFDA-TV Amarillo (ch 10)—Licensed to Panhandle Telecasting Co. (joint venture of Ray Herndon & R.H. Drewry). Sale price: Lawton Cablevision Inc. acquired 50% interest from Midessa TV Trust for $3 million. FCC approved: October 4, 1976. Previous owner: Bass Broadcasting Co. [Perry R. Bass (51.58%), Bass Brothers Enterprises Inc. (39.96%), & others]. Sale price: $2.8 million. FCC approved: August 20, 1976 [For the Record, September 13, 1976]. Note: Founded by Wendell Mayes, C.C. Woodson, Gene Cagle & Charles B. Jordon. Sold to Texas State Network in 1954 for $525,000 (with KFDA(AM)). Sold to Bass Broadcasting Co. (owned by Perry R. Bass) in 1966 for $2.29 million in multiple-stn deal. FCC approved: February 2, 1966 [For the Record, February 7, 1966].

KJTV(TV) Amarillo (ch 14)—Licensed to Ralph Wilson Industries. Former owner: Ray Moran. Sale price: $1 million. FCC approved: January 7, 1985. Previous owner: Amarillo Family Television. Sale price: exchange of KRIZ(FM) Roswell, NM, plus $325,000. FCC approved: September 10, 1981 [For the Record, October 12, 1981]. Original owner: Gary L. Acker (see Group Ownership). Sale price: $624,000. FCC approved: May 20, 1980 [Changing Hands, June 16, 1980].

KVII-TV Amarillo (ch 7)—Licensed to Marsh Media Ltd. Sale price: $60,000 (license was transferred from partnership of Stanley Marsh III, Tom F. Marsh, Michael Marsh, John S. Tyler & Estelle Marsh Watlington, dba Marsh Media Ltd., to partnership of Stanley Marsh III, Tom F. Marsh, Michael Marsh & Estelle Marsh Watlington, dba Marsh Media Ltd.). FCC approved: November 8, 1972. [For the Record, December 4, 1972]. Note: founded by John L. McCarty & associates in 1957. Sold 78% to Southwest States Inc. (Trigg-Vaughn group) in 1958 for $136,052. Sold to John B. Walton Jr., (see Group Ownership) in 1963 for $1.25 million. Sold to Marsh Media in 1968 for $1.5 million. FCC approved: January 31, 1968 [For the Record, February 12, 1968].

KTXA(TV) Arlington (ch 21)—Licensed to Taft Broadcasting Co. Former owner: Gulf Broadcast Group (see Group Ownership), subsidiary of Gulf Life Co. Sale price: $755 million (including KTSP(TV) Phoenix, WTSP(TV) Tampa-St. Petersburg, KTXH(TV) Houston, & WGHP(TV) High Point, NC). FCC approved: May 30, 1985 [For the Record, April 15, 1985].

KCFP(TV) Austin (ch 54)—Licensed to 54 Broadcasting Inc. Original owner: Balcones Broadcasting Co. Sale price: assumption of liabilities & permit costs. FCC approved: March 26, 1992 [For the Record, April 20, 1992].

KTBC-TV Austin (ch 7)—Licensed to Argyle Television Inc. (see Argyle Television Holding Inc. in Group Ownership). Former owner: Times-Mirror Co. (see Group Ownership). Sale price: $335 million, including KDFW-TV Dallas as part of 4-station purchase. FCC approved: October 6, 1993 [For the Record, October 25, 1993]. Previous owner: Texas Broadcasting Corp. [Claudia T. (Lady Bird) Johnson, et al]. Sale price: $9 million. FCC approved: September 6, 1973 [For the Record, September 24, 1973].

KTVV(TV) Austin (ch 36)—Licensed to LIN Broadcasting Corp. (see Group Ownership). Original owner: Kingstip Communications Inc. (John R. Kingsberry, Henry B. Tippie & others). Sale price: $4.5 million (including KHFI-FM Austin, TX). FCC approved: May 2, 1979 [*Broadcasting*, May 7, 1979].

KVUE(TV) Austin (ch 24)—Licensed to Gannett Co. Inc. (see Group Ownership). Former owner: Evening News Association. Sale price: $717 million (including WDVM-TV Washington; WALA-TV Mobile, AL; KTVY(TV) Oklahoma City; KOLD-TV Tucson, AZ; & two radio stns). FCC approved: January 1986 [January 13, 1986]. Previous owner: Channel Twenty-Four Corp. [Tolbert Foster, Allan Shivers, W.E. Dyche Jr. & Edgar B. Younger (54.4%); R.B. & Bill B. McAlister & others (45.6%)]. Sale price: $13 million. FCC approved: September 8, 1978. Note: Ray A. Butler acquired CP in 1965 from Willard Deason for $500,000 & sold it to Channel Twenty-Four for $44,138. FCC approved: June 10, 1970 [*Broadcasting*, June 6, 1970].

KRTW(TV) Baytown (ch 57)—Licensed to Patriot Broadcasting Inc., owned by Bess Harrison. Former owner: Pray Inc., owned by Eldred Thomas. Sale price: $12.7 million. FCC approved: May 5, 1992 [For the Record, May 25, 1992].

KBMT(TV) Beaumont (ch 12)—Licensed to Texas Telecasting (Michael G. & Clongton McKinnon). Former owner: Liberty National Corp. (Oklahoma City). Sale price: $2.4 million. FCC approved: October 22, 1976 [For the Record, November 15, 1977]. Note: Sabine Broadcasting Co. (John Nichols, pres, et al) sold stn to Harbour Television Systems Inc. in 1973 for $3 million. FCC approved: September 28, 1973. Harbour Television Systems Inc. (owned 100% by Liberty National Corp.) was purchased from Harbour Television Systems Inc. [A.O. Banning (56%), William G. Hill Jr. (27%), et al) for release of debt obligation. FCC approved: February 11, 1976.

KFDM-TV Beaumont (ch 6)—Licensed to Freedom-TV Sub Inc. (Freedom Newspapers; see Group Ownership). Former owner: Belo Broadcasting (see Group Ownership). Sale price: $24.5 million (including WTVC(TV) Chattanooga). FCC approved: December 13, 1983 [For the Record, January 2, 1984]. Previous owner: Beaumont Broadcasting Corp. Sale price: $4.88 million for 100% of stock. FCC approved: 1969. Note: previously, 32.5% of stock sold to W.F. Hobby & Houston Post for $232,901 (1962).

KWAB(TV) Big Spring (ch 4)—Licensed to Midessa Television Co. (headed by R.H. Drewry). Former owner: James T. Taylor. Sale price: $4.85 million (with KTPX(TV) Odessa). FCC approved: September 9, 1991 [For the Record, September 23, 1991]. Previous owner: Grayson Enterprises Inc. Sale price: $3.21 million [including KMON-TV (now KTPX(TV) Odessa, TX]. FCC approved: April 21, 1980. Previous owner: W.D. Rogers. Sale price: $4 million [including KBLK-AM-TV & tangible assets of KPAR-TV (now KXTS(TV)) Sweetwater, TX].

KVEO(TV) Brownsville (ch 23)—Licensed to Valley Broadcasting Co. Former owner: Bankruptcy Trustee. Sale price: $7.6 million. FCC approved: August 31, 1984. Previous owner: Tierra del Sol Broadcasting.

KTFH(TV) Conroe (ch 49)—Licensed to Dupont Investment Group 85 Ltd. Former owner: Florence Coaxum. Sale price: no financial consideration for CP. FCC approved: June 22, 1989 [For the Record, July 10, 1989].

KIII-TV Corpus Christi (ch 3)—Licensed to Texas Television Inc. [Michael D. McKinnon (50%), Daniel McKinnon (25%), Clinton D. McKinnon (19%) & others]. Sale price: $171,720. FCC approved: July 1979. Note: Clinton formerly owned 80% with others. Previous owner: Dr. J.A. Garcia & associates (74%); Mr. McKinnon (3.8%); & others. Sale price: $48,000 for 74%. FCC approved: January 17, 1964 [For the Record, January 27, 1964]. Former call letters: KVDO-TV. Note: founded in 1956 by Gabriel Lazano & others. Sold to Dr. Garcia & associates in 1957 for $194,300, including obligations not to exceed $100,000.

KTLG(TV) Corpus Christi (ch 43, now deleted)—Licensed to Trinity Broadcasting Corp. (Barton R. & Gordon B. McLendon). Original owner: H.L. Hunt. Sale price: $5,608.21 (cost of securing CP). FCC approved: April 7, 1954 [For the Record, April 12, 1954].

KDAF(TV) Dallas (ch 33)—Licensed to Fox Television Stations Inc., (see Group Ownership). Former owner: Metromedia Inc. (For details of sale, see WNYW-TV New York.) Former call letters: KRLD-TV. Previous owner: National Business Network Inc. [Sheldon K. Turner & Nolando Hill (40% each) & others]. Sale price: $14.9 million. FCC approved: November 8, 1983 [For the Record, December 5, 1983]. Original call letters: KNBN-TV.

KDFW-TV Dallas (ch 4)—Licensed to Argyle Television Inc. (see Argyle Television Holding Inc. in Group Ownership). Former owner: KDFW-TV Inc. (owned by Times-Mirror Co., see Group Ownership). Sale price: $335 million, including KTBC-TV Austin, TX as part of 4-station purchase. FCC approved: October 6, 1993 [For the Record, October 25, 1993]. Previous owner: Times Herald Printing Co. Sale price: Stock transaction valued at $30 million (including KRLD-AM-FM). FCC approved: May 15, 1970 [*Broadcasting*, May 18, 1970]. Former call letters: KRLD-TV.

KDTX(TV) Dallas (ch 58)—Licensed to Trinity Broadcasting. Former owner: Metroplex Broadcasting Co. (Adam C. Powell III, et al). Sale price: $1.6 million for CP. FCC approved: May 6, 1986 [For the Record, March 31, 1986].

KXTX-TV Dallas (ch 39)—Licensed to CBN Continental Broadcasting Network, 100% owned by Christian Broadcasting Network Inc. (see Group Ownership). Former owner: KDTV Broadcasting Co. (100% owned by Doubleday Broadcasting Co., see Group Ownership). Sale price: donated by gift of stock valued at $2 million. FCC approved: November 9, 1973 [For the Record, December 3, 1973]. Original call letters: KDTV(TV). Note: Trigg-Vaughn Stations Inc. (Cecil L. Trigg & Jack C. Vaughn) sold stn to Doubleday Broadcasting in 1967 for $14,125,018 with KOSA-TV Odessa-Midland, KROD-AM-TV El Paso & KITE-AM-FM Terrell Hills-San Antonio, all TX; KRNO(AM) San Bernadino, CA; KHOW(AM) Denver; & KDEF-AM-FM Albuquerque. FCC approved: February 1, 1967 [For the Record, February 6, 1967].

WFAA-TV Dallas (ch 8)—Licensed to Belo Broadcasting Corp. (see Group Ownership). Original owner: Lacy-Potter TV Broadcasting Co. (Rogers Lacy & Tom Potter). Sale price: $575,000. FCC approved: March 6, 1950 [For the Record, March 13, 1950]. Original call letters: KBTV(TV).

KTRG-TV Del Rio (ch 10)—Licensed to Thomas Gilchrist (permittee). Former owner (permittee): Republic Broadcasting Co. Sale price: $10. FCC approved: 1993 [For the Record, September 20, 1993].

KCIK-TV El Paso (ch 14)—Licensed to Cristo Rey Corp. (control of Cristo Rey transferred from Missionary Radio Evangelism to Santa Fe Communications Inc. & affiliate, DeRance Inc. Controlling interest held by Harry G. John). Sale price: $600,000 & assumption of $2 million in liabilites. FCC approved: April 20, 1983 [For the Record, May 9, 1983]. Note: stn on air December 1978.

KDBC-TV El Paso (ch 4)—Licensed to KDBC-TV Inc. (owned by United Broadcasting Corp.). Former owner: El Paso Television Co. (owned by Evening Post Publishing). Sale price: $32 million. FCC approved: April 21, 1986 [For the Record, March 24, 1986]. Previous owner: Doubleday Broadcasting Inc. (see Group Ownership). Sale price: $5 million. FCC approved: 1974. Previous owners: Trigg-Vaughn Stations Inc. Sale price: $14,125,018 (including KROD(AM) El Paso, KOSA-TV Odessa-Midland, KITE-AM-FM Terrell Hills-San Antonio, & KDTV(TV) Dallas, all TX; KRNO(AM) San Bernadino, CA; KHOW(AM) Denver; & KDEF-AM-FM Albuquerque). FCC approved: February 1, 1967 [For the Record, February 6, 1967]. Original owner: El Paso *Times*. Sale price: $3.45 million (including KROD-AM-FM). FCC approved: 1959. Original call letters: KROD-TV.

KSCE(TV) El Paso (ch 38)—Licensed to Channel 38 Christian Television, owned by William S. Francis. Former owner: St. Clement's Episcopal Parish. Sale price: no financial consideration. FCC approved: November 19, 1991 [For the Record, December 9, 1991].

KTSM(TV) El Paso (ch 9)—Licensed to Tri-State Broadcasting Co. (owned by El Paso Community Foundation). Former owner: Ameritrust Texas N.A., Independent Executor of Estate of Karl O. Wyler Sr. Sale price: no financial consideration (including KTSM-AM-FM El Paso). FCC approved: March 16, 1992 [For the Record, April 6, 1992].

KVIA-TV El Paso (ch 13)—Licensed to Marsh Media [Stanley Marsh III (50%), Michael C. Marsh (20%), Estelle Marsh Watlington (10%), Tom F. Marsh (10%), Tom F. Marsh Special Trust (10%)]. Former owner: KELP Inc. (owned by John B. Walton Jr.). Sale price: $3 million (including satellite KAVE-TV Carlsbad, NM). FCC approved: February 24, 1976 [For the Record, March 8, 1976]. Former call letters: KELP-TV. Note: Founded by McLendon Investment Corp. as KILT-TV. Sold in 1957 to Norman E. Alexander & Joseph Harris for $750,000 (with KELP(AM)). Sold with KELP(AM) in 1966 to John B. Walton Jr. for $2.37 million. FCC approved: January 19, 1966 [For the Record, January 24, 1966].

KFWD(TV) Fort Worth (ch 52)—Licensed to HIC Broadcast Partners Ltd. Sale price: $3,000. Former owner: Interspan Communications Inc. Seller is headed by Ronald L. Ulloa. FCC approved: February 28, 1990.

KTVT(TV) Fort Worth (ch 11)—Licensed to Gaylord Broadcasting Co. (see Group Ownership). Former owner: Nafi Telecasting Corp. Sale price: $800,000 plus assumption of $3 million in liabilities. FCC approved: August 1, 1962 [For the Record, August 6, 1962]. Note: Founded by Texas State Network as KCJZ-TV. Sold in 1960 to Nafi Telecasting Corp. for $4 million.

KTXA(TV) Fort Worth (ch 21)—Licensed to TVX Broadcast Group (see Group Ownership). Former owner: Taft Broadcasting. (For details of sale, see KTXH(TV) Houston.) Previous owner: DAL-GBC Corp (see Gulf Broadcast Group, Group Ownership). (For details of sale, see KTSP-TV Phoenix.) FCC approved: May 30, 1985. Previous owner: Channel 21 Inc. (Sydney Shlenker & Milt Grant). Sale price: $65.92 million plus prorated bonus related to first year operating profit. FCC approved: December 11, 1984.

KXAS-TV Fort Worth (ch 5)—Licensed to North Texas Broadcasting Corp. (100% owned by LIN Broadcasting Corp., see Group Ownership). Original owner: Carter Publications Inc. (Amon G. Carter Foundation, & others). Sale price: $35 million. FCC approved: May 13, 1974.

[For the Record, May 27, 1974]. Original call letters: WBAP-TV.

KUVN(TV) Garland (ch 23)—Licensed to Univision Station Group Inc. Former owner: I Am Broadcasting Television Inc. Sale price: $5.2 million [Changing Hands, May 30, 1988]. Former call letters: KIAB-TV.

KTAQ(TV) Greenville (ch 47)—Licensed to Mike Simons. Former owner: A.B.W. Communications Inc. Sale price: $50,000 for CP. FCC approved: March 24, 1992 [For the Record, April 13, 1992]. Original owner: Bill Richard Wright. Sale price: $18,632 for CP. FCC approved: May 15, 1989 [For the Record, May 29, 1989].

KGBT(TV) Harlingen (ch 4)—Licensed to KGBT-TV Ltd Partnership (owned by Draper Communications). Former owner: Harbenito Broadcasting Co. Sale price: $25 million. FCC approved: February 7, 1986.

KHOU-TV Houston (ch 11)—Licensed to Gulf Television Corp. (see Belo Broadcasting, Group Ownership). Control of stn transferred from Corinthian Broadcasting Corp. Sale price: $342 million (part of six stn deal totaling $606 million which included KXTV(TV) Sacramento, CA; WISH-TV Indianapolis; KOTV(TV) Tulsa, OK; WVEC-TV Hampton, VA; & WANE-TV Fort Wayne, IN). FCC approved: November 17, 1983 [For the Record, December 19, 1983]. Note: Gulf Television Corp. (J.H. Whitney & Co.) purchased stn from original owner, Paul Taft & Associates, in 1956. Sale price: $4.25 million for 90% of stn. FCC approved: July 11, 1956 [For the Record, July 16, 1956]. Stn merged with Corinthian into Dun & Bradstreet Companies Inc. for stock valued at $132 million [along with four other TV stns, except KXTV(TV), listed above & two radio stns]. FCC approved: April 14, 1971 [*Broadcasting*, April 19, 1971].

KHTV(TV) Houston (ch 39)—Licensed to Gaylord Broadcasting Co.(see Group Ownership). Former owners: Max Jacob & Irvin Schlenker (40% each) & David Morris (20%). Sale price: $240,000 for 80% of CP. FCC approved: October 13, 1965. Former call letters: KNUZ-TV. Note: Gaylord acquired remaining 20% in 1966.

KPRC-TV Houston (ch 2)—Licensed to Channel Two Television Co. (owned by Houston Post Co.). Original owner: W. Albert Lee. Sale price: $740,000. FCC approved: May 23, 1950 [For the Record, May 29, 1950]. Original call letters: KLEE-TV.

KRIV(TV) Houston (ch 26)—Licensed to Fox Television Stations Inc. (see Group Ownership). Former owner: Metromedia Inc. (For details of sale, see WNYW-TV New York.) Original owner: Crest Communications. Sale price: $11 million. FCC approved: April 6, 1978. Original call letters: KDOG-TV.

KTRK-TV Houston (ch 13)—Licensed to Texas Media Holding Co. (owned by Capital Cities/ABC Inc., see Group Ownership). Former owner: Houston Consolidated Television Co. Sale price: $21.3 million. FCC approved: June 16, 1967 [For the Record, June 26, 1967].

KTXH(TV) Houston (ch 20)—Licensed to TVX Broadcast Group (see Group Ownership). Former owner: Taft Broadcasting Co. Sale price: $240 million (including WTAF-TV Philadelphia; WDCA-TV Washington; KTXA(TV) Fort Worth, TX; & WCIX(TV) Miami, FL). FCC approved: February 20, 1987 [For the Record, December 15, 1986]. Previous owner: HOU-GBS Corp. (see Gulf Broadcast Group, Group Ownership). Sale price: $755 million (including KTSP(TV) Phoenix; WTSP(TV) Tampa-St. Petersburg; WGHP(TV) High Point, NC; & KTXA(TV) Arlington (Ft. Worth), TX). FCC approved: April 2, 1985 [For the Record, April 15, 1985]. Previous owner: Channel 21 Inc. (Sydney Shlenker & Milt Grant). Sale price: $62 million plus prorated bonus related to first year operating profit. FCC approved: December 31, 1984.

KXYZ-TV Houston (ch 29, now deleted)—Licensed to Houston Broadcasting Corp. (Milton R. Underwood & Philip R. Neuhaus). Original owner: Glenn R. McCarthy. Sale price: $600,000 (including KXYZ(AM)). FCC approved: March 28, 1957 [For the Record, April 1, 1957].

KHSX(TV) Irving (ch 49)—Licensed to Silver King Broadcasting (owned by Home Shopping Network, see Group Ownership). Former owner: CELA Ltd (owned by Eldred Thomas). Sale price: $16.25 million. FCC approved: April, 1987 [For the Record, March 9, 1987]. Former call letters: KLTJ-TV.

KETK-TV Jacksonville (ch 56)—Licensed to Region 56 Network Inc. (subsidiary of Lone Star Broadcasting). Former owner: Texas American Broadcasting Ltd. (Carl Westcott, et al). Sale price: $7.45 million. FCC approved: September 25, 1989 [For the Record, October 9, 1989]. Previous owner: James R. Chapman, trustee in bankruptcy for Thomas Gilchrist. Sale price: $150,000 for CP. FCC approved: August 13, 1986 [For the Record, April 21, 1986]. Former call letters: KTRG(TV).

KGNS-TV Laredo (ch 8)—Licensed to Century Development Corporation. Former owner: Burke Broadcasting Co., (see Group Ownership). Sale price: $3.8 million. FCC approved: December, 1986. Previous owner: Gulf Coast Broadcasting Co. [Frank Smith (88%) & others]. Sale price: $3 million, including $325,000 covenant not to compete. FCC approved: October 28, 1983 [For the Record, November 21, 1983]. Note: Western Communications Inc. (see Donrey Media, Group Ownership) was purchased from Vidicon Industries of America (H.C. Avery Jr. & David H. Cole) for $190,000 (for CP). FCC approved: July 31, 1958. Former call letters: KHAD-TV. Sold to Gulf Coast for $1 million, plus $250 property lease. FCC approved: October 4, 1977 [For the Record, October 31, 1977].

KFXK-TV Longview (ch 51)—Licensed to Kamin Broadcasting Co.-Longview Ltd. Warwick Broadcasting Co. (owned by Edward C. Stanton). Former owner: Kamin Broadcasting/Longview L.P. (see Group Ownership) Sale price: consideration includes forgiveness of $200,000 loan to Kamin Broadcasting by Warwick Broadcasting, $60,000 consulting fee & other consideration. Existing general partners would have no further voting power. FCC approved: May 13, 1992 [For the Record, June 15, 1992].

KTHP(TV) Longview (ch 54, now deleted)—Licensed to Atkins Broadcasting. Former owner: Channel 54 Broadcasting. Sale price: $100,000 for CP. FCC approved: December 13, 1988 [For the Record, January 16, 1989].

KAMC(TV) Lubbock (ch 28)—Licensed to McAlister Television Enterprises (Bill B. & R.B. McAlister, 100%). Former owner: McAlister Television Enterprises (Tolbert Foster, Allan Shivers, et al). Sale price: McAlister's 41.6% interest in KVUE-TV Austin, TX. FCC approved: March 24, 1975 [For the Record, April 14, 1975]. Note: stn founded in 1968 by McAlister group (R.B. & Bill B McAlister, et al). Control transferred through issuance of new stock to Tolbert Foster, Allan Shivers, et al in 1970. Sale price: $200,000 for 54.4%. FCC approved: June 10, 1970 [For the Record, July 6, 1970]. Former call letters: KSEL-TV.

KCBD-TV Lubbock (ch 11)—Licensed to Caprock Telecasting Inc. (see Group Ownership). Previous owner: State Telecasting Co. Sale price: $10.75 million (including KSWS-TV Roswell, NM). FCC approved: August 12, 1983 [Changing Hands, September 5, 1983]. Note: stn founded May 10, 1953 by Bryant Radio & Television. Sold to State Telecasting Co. for $6 million (including KSWS-TV Roswell, N.M.). FCC approved: May 26, 1971 [*Broadcasting*, May 31, 1971].

KJTV Lubbock (ch 34)—Licensed to Ramar Communications Inc. Former owner: Troy Raymond Moran. Sale price: $1 million. FCC approved: January 7, 1985. Note: First station on this channel was founded by KB Co. in 1967. KB Co. (owned by Chester H. & Clarence L. Kissell) sold CP for KMXN-TV (now deleted) to Double H Corp. (W.B. Rushing & others) for $55,000. FCC approved: August 30, 1968 [For the Record, September 16, 1968]. Note: New stn began operation on ch 34 December 10, 1981.

KLBK-TV Lubbock (ch 13)—Licensed to BANAM Broadcasting Inc. Former owner: Charles Woods Television Corp. Sale price: assumption of debt (including KDEB(TV) Springfield, MO; WTVW(TV) Evansville, IN; & KARD(TV) West Monroe, LA). FCC approved: March 16, 1993 [For the Record, April 5, 1993]. Previous owner: Prima Inc. Sale price: undisclosed [control transferred from Robert Dudley (50% before, none after) to Charles Woods (50% before, 100% after)]. FCC approved: September 15, 1983 [For the Record, October 10, 1983]. Original owner: Texas Telecasting Inc. (W.D. Rogers & associates). Original call letters: KDUB-TV. Note: sold to Grayson Enterprises in 1961. Sale price: $3.8 million [including KEDY-TV (now KWAB(TV)) Big Spring, TX). FCC approved: October 18, 1961 [For the Record, October 23, 1961]. Grayson sold to Prima Inc. (Dudley & Woods) in 1980. Sale price: $11.1 million (including KTXS-TV Sweetwater, TX). FCC approved: March 27, 1980 [Changing Hands, April 7, 1980].

KTRE-TV Lufkin (ch 9)—Licensed to Civic Communications Corp. II. Former owner: Buford Television Inc. Sale price: $42 million (including KLTV(TV) Tyler, TX). [For the Record, March 6, 1989]. FCC approved: February 16, 1989. Original owner: R.W. Wortham Jr. & Associates. Sale price: $750,000 (including KTRE(AM)). FCC approved: July 18, 1962 [For the Record, July 23, 1962].

KMID-TV Midland (ch 2)—Licensed to Goltrin Communications Inc. Former owner: Telepictures Broadcasting Corp (owned by Lorimar-Telepictures Corp.). Sale price: $23 million (including KSPR(TV) Springfield, MO). FCC approved: February 12, 1988 [For the Record, February 29, 1988]. Former owner: Midessa TV Company. Sale price: $15 million. FCC approved: January 4, 1984.

KAEC(TV) Nacogdoches (ch 19, now deleted)—Licensed to Fredonia Broadcasting Corp. [Mrs. Jessie P. Cudlipp (40.3%), Albert E. Cudlipp (32.25%), & others]. Previous owner: G.P. Scoggins. Sale price: $4,500 for CP. FCC approved: August 20, 1965 [For the Record, August 30, 1965]. Note: Founded by Lee Scarborough in 1958. Sold to Mr. Scoggins in 1960 for $5,000 for CP. Former call letters: KTES(TV).

KMLM(TV) Odessa (ch 42)—Licensed to Prime Time Christian Broadcasting Inc. (headed by Albert O. Cooper, Tommie J. Cooper & Henry C. Wunsch). Former owner: National Minority TV Inc. (owned by Paul F. Crouch, Philip Aguilar, P. Jane Duff, Charlene Williams, & Matthew Crouch). Sale price: $650,000. FCC approved: February 27, 1991 [For the Record, March 18, 1991].

KOSA-TV Odessa (ch 7)—Licensed to Adams TV of Odessa Inc., owned by Paul A. Brissette (see Group Ownership). Former owner: Adams Communications Corp. (see Group Ownership). Sale price: Undisclosed (including WHOI(TV) Peoria, IL; WWLP(TV) Springfield, MA; WILX-TV Onondaga, MI; KAUZ-TV Wichita Falls, TX; WMTV(TV) Madison & WSAW-TV Wausau, both WI; & WTRF-TV Wheeling, WV). FCC approved: December 24, 1991 [For the Record, January 27, 1992]. Previous owner: Forward Communications of Texas Inc. (For details of sale, see WHOI(TV) Peoria, IL.) Previous owner: Doubleday Broadcasting Co. Sale price: $2.25 million. FCC approved: September 11, 1973 [For the Record, September 24, 1973]. Note: brothers Jack C. & Grady H. Vaughn bought 50% of stn from C.L. Trigg (retaining 40%), W.B. Stowe & Brooks L. Harman (each retained 5%). Sale price: $20,000 plus assumption of approximately $85,000 in liabilites. FCC approved: January 23, 1957 [For the Record, January 28, 1957]. Trigg-Vaughn Stations Inc. sold stn to Doubleday Broadcasting in 1967 for $14,125,018 with KROD(AM) El Paso, KITE-AM-FM Terrell Hills-San Antonio & KDTV(TV) Dallas, all TX; KRNO(AM) San Bernardino, CA; KHOW(AM) Denver; & KDEF-AM-FM Albuquerque. FCC approved: February 1, 1967 [For the Record, February 6, 1967].

KTPX(TV) Odessa (ch 9)—Licensed to Midessa Television Co. (headed by R.H. Drewry). Former owner: James T. Taylor (appointed receiver as MSP Television has defaulted on its loans). Sale includes KWAB(TV) Big Spring, TX. FCC approved: September 9, 1991 [For the Record, September 23, 1991]. Previous owner: MSP Television of Midland-Odessa (owned by Francis A. Martin III, James H. Smith, et al), preceded by Permian Basin Television Inc. [John B. Tupper & Richard F. Shively (22.84% each) & others]. Sale price of MSP-Permian transaction: $16.5 million (including satellite KWAB(TV) Big Spring, TX). FCC approved: November 19, 1985 [For the Record, October 21, 1985]. Previous owner: Grayson Enterprises Inc. (see KLBK-TV Lubbock, TX). Sale price: $3.2 million (including KWAB-TV Big Spring). FCC approved: March 27, 1980 [Changing Hands, April 7, 1980]. Former call letters: KMOM-TV. Previous owner: John B. Walton Jr. (see Group Ownership). Sale price: $530,000. FCC approved: February 12, 1969 [For the Record, February 17, 1969]. Former call letters: KVKM-TV. Note: Went on air December 1, 1958.

KJAC-TV Port Arthur (ch 4)—Licensed to Price Communications. Former owner: Clay Communications Inc. (see Group Ownership). (See WAPT(TV) Jackson, MS for details of sale.) Previous owner: Texas Goldcoast Television Inc. (Janet Gordon Jack, Gayle A. Gordon Brannon, Lynn G. Jones, Valerie G. Tucker & Robert H. Park). Sale price: $3 million. FCC approved: May 31, 1973 [For the Record, July 2, 1973]. Note: began operation October 22, 1957 as KPAC-TV jointly owned by Jefferson Amusement Co. & Port Arthur College. Port Arthur College sold its 50% to Jefferson Amusement Co. in 1965 for $1.5 million. FCC approved: November 15, 1965 [For the Record, November 22, 1965].

KLST(TV) San Angelo (ch 8)—Licensed to Jewell Television (owned by T.B. Lanford Stations, see Group Ownership). Former owner: Westex Television Co. [Big Spring Broadcasting Co. (88.8%), Houston H. & Edward H. Harte (0.58% each), & Bruce B. Meador (10%). Big Spring Broadcasting is owned 43.32% each by Messrs. Harte, plus 3.36% by A.L. Hall]. Sale price: $250,000. FCC approved: 1970. Note: founded in 1953 as KTXL-TV by A.D. Rust & B.P. Bludworth. Lewis O. Seibert acquired 25% from the founders in 1957 for $32,288 & obligations. Mr. Rust sold his remaining 25% to Roy H. Simmons in 1957 for $50,000. Big Spring Broadcasting Co. acquired 50% in 1959 for $31,487. Roy H. Simmons & B.P. Bludworth (25% each); & Big Spring Broadcasting Co. (50%) sold stn to Westex Television Co. in 1962. Sale price: $226,000 for 50%. FCC approved: December 5, 1962 [For the Record, December 10, 1962]. Former call letters: KCTV(TV).

KENS-TV San Antonio (ch 5)—Licensed to Harte-Hanks Television Inc. (see The Harte-Hanks Broadcasting Group, Group Ownership). Former owners: 63.17% owned by Frank G. Huntress Jr. & family & estate of late George W. Brackenridge. Sale price: $6.25 million for 63.17% (including KENS-AM). FCC approved: July 3, 1962 [For the Record, July 23, 1962]. Note: founded as KEYL(TV) by W.L. Pickens, R.L. Wheelock & H.H. Coffield. Sold in 1951 to Storer Broadcasting Co. for $1.05 million. In 1954 Storer sold these facilities to Express Pub Co. for $3.5 million. Former call letters: KGBS-TV.

***KLRN(TV) San Antonio (ch 9)**—Licensed to Alamo Public Telecommunications Council. Former owner: Southwest Texas Public Broadcasting. Sale price: no financial consideration. FCC approved: August 11, 1989 [For the Record, August 28, 1989].

KMOL-TV San Antonio (ch 4)—Licensed to United Television Inc., see Group Ownership). Former owner: Avco Broadcasting Corp. (see Group Ownership). Sale price: $9.3 million. FCC approved: September 17, 1975 [For the Record, October 6, 1975]. Note: National Jewish Hospital, Denver, originally held 24% interest; sold to Southland Industries in 1958. Original owners: WOAI-TV. Sale price: $1.14 million for 24%. Note: Southland Industries Inc. (Hugh Halff & family) sold to Avco Broadcasting in 1965. Sale price: $12 million, including WOAI(AM/FM). FCC approved: September 15, 1965 [For the Record, September 20, 1965].

KSAT-TV San Antonio (ch 12)—Licensed to H&C Communications Inc. Former owner: Wesray Communications Corp. Sale price: $153 million. FCC approved: April 29, 1986 [For the Record, March 24, 1986]. Previous owner: Rockefeller Group Inc. (For details of sale, see WCMH(TV) Columbus, OH.) Previous owner: Outlet Co. Sale price: $332 million for group (see WJAR-TV Providence, RI). FCC approved: November 23, 1983. Previous owner: Mission Telecasting Corp. (Jack & Bob Roth). Sale price: $10.5 million. FCC approved: November 22, 1967. Note: founded in 1957. Mission Broadcasting Co. increased holdings from 50% to 100% in 1964 when it purchased stock held by James Calvert, L.A. Douglas & others for $1.62 million. Former call letters: KONO-TV.

KVDA(TV) San Antonio (ch 60)—Licensed to Telemundo Group Inc. Former owner: David A. Davila. Sale price: $1.27 million. FCC approved: August 9, 1990.

KWEX-TV San Antonio (ch 41)—Licensed to Univision. Former owner: Spanish International Broadcasting Communications Corp. (see Group Ownership). (For details of sale, see WXTV(TV) Paterson, NJ.) Original owner: Raoul Cortez & associates. Sale price: $200,000. FCC approved: December 6, 1961 [For the Record, December 11, 1961]. Original call letters: KUAL-TV.

KTXS-TV Sweetwater (Abilene) (ch 12)—Licensed to Lamco Communications Inc. Former owner: SouthWest Multimedia Corp. (owned by Billy Goldberg & Lester Kamin). Sale price: $11.74 million. FCC approved: November 25, 1986 [For the Record, October 27, 1986]. Previous owner: Catclaw Communications Co. (W.M. Moore, owner). Sale price: $8 million. FCC approved: November 29, 1985 [For the Record, September 23, 1985]. Previous owner: Prima Inc. (Charles Woods, prin., see KLRK-TV Lubbock, TX). Sale price: $3.5 million. FCC approved: July 25, 1983 [For the Record, August 8, 1983]. Previous owner: Grayson Enterprises (Theodore Shanbaum, et al). Sale price: $11.79 million (including KLBK-TV Lubbock, TX). FCC approved: 1979. Original owner: A.R. Elam & Associates. Sale price: $625,000. FCC approved: 1966. Original call letters: KPAR-TV. Note: stn went on air January 30, 1956. (See KLBK-TV Lubbock, TX).

KCEN-TV Temple-Waco (ch 6)—Licensed to Channel 6 Inc. [owned by Frank W. Mayborn (95%) & C.A. Schultz (5%)]. Former owner: Bell Publishing Co. Sale price: $300,000. FCC approved: 1962.

KLTV(TV) Tyler (ch 7)—Licensed to Civic Communications Corp. II. Former owner: Buford Television Inc. Sale price: $42 million (including KTRE-TV Lufkin, TX). FCC approved: February 16, 1989 [For the Record, March 6, 1989]. Original owner: Lucille R. Lansing (who retained a 49% interest in stn). Sale price: $7,460.32 for 51%. FCC approved: March 20, 1957 [For the Record, March 25, 1957].

KAVU(TV) Victoria (ch 25)— Licensed to W. Russell Withers Jr. Former owner: PMV Inc. Sale price: $1 million. FCC approved: March 12, 1990. Previous owner: 1st Victoria National Bank. Previous owner: Community Broadcasting of Coastal Bend Inc. Sale price of Victoria-Community transaction: no financial consideration [For the Record, September 11, 1989]. FCC approved: August 29, 1989.

KVCT(TV) Victoria (ch 19)—Licensed to Victoria Communications Corp. (Dewey T. Acker 29.5%, et al). Original Owner: Guadalupe Valley Telecasting Co. (subsidiary of South Texas Telecasting). Sale price: $225,000. FCC approved: March 4, 1976 [For the Record, March 22, 1976]. Original call letters: KXIX(TV).

KANG-TV Waco (ch 34, now deleted)—Licensed to Texas Broadcasting Co. (LBJ Co.-KTBC-AM-TV Austin). Original owners: Central Texas TV Co. (Clyde Weatherby & associates). Sale price: $115,000 & assumption of $19,000 in obligations. FCC approved: December 2, 1954 [For the Record, December 13, 1954]. Note: CP cancelled in 1955 with physical facilites turned over to KWTX-TV Waco in return for 29% of that stn.

KCTF(TV) Waco (ch 34)—Licensed to Brazos Valley Public Broadcasting Foundation. Former owner: Central Texas College. Sale price: $80,000. FCC approved: December 6, 1993 [For the Record, December 20, 1993].

KWKT(TV) Waco (ch 44)—Licensed to SouthWest Multimedia Corp. (owned by Billy Goldberg & Lester Kamin). Former owner: Focus Broadcasting of Waco (owned by Jacqueline B. Frank & Pablo J. Simeson). Sale price: $536,900, plus assumption of $375,000 in notes. FCC approved: November 25, 1986 [For the Record, November 3, 1986].

KXXV(TV) Waco (ch 25)—Licensed to Shamrock Broadcasting Inc. (see Group Ownership). Former owner: Central Texas Broadcasting Company Ltd. Sale price: $15.535 million. FCC approved: October 1987 [Changing Hands, May 25, 1987].

WACO-TV Waco (ch 25, now deleted)—Licensed to WACO Radio Inc. [McHenry Tichenor (57%), James Cullen Looney (21%), & others]. Former owner: R.E. Lee Glasgow. Sale price: $825,000 for CP (including WACO-AM-FM). FCC approved: May 6, 1970 [For the Record, May 18, 1970].

KRGV-TV Weslaco (ch 5)—Licensed to Mobile Video Tapes Inc. (see Manship Stations, Group Ownership). Former owner: Kenco Enterprises Inc. (Bruce L. & John A. Kennedy). Sale price: $1,375,000 (including KRGV(AM)). FCC approved: January 28, 1964 [For the Record, February 3, 1964]. Note: founded by O.L. Taylor in 1954. 50% sold to LBJ Co. (now Texas Broadcasting Co.) in 1956 for $5,000 plus loan of $140,000. LBJ Co. purchased remaining 50% in 1958 for $100,000. Sold to Kenco Enterprises in 1961 for $1.4 million (with KRGV-AM).

KAUZ-TV Wichita Falls (ch 6)—Licensed to Adams TV of Wichita Falls Inc., owned by Paul A. Brissette (see Group Ownership). Former owner: Adams Communications Corp. (see Group Ownership). Sale price: Undisclosed (including WHOI(TV) Peoria, IL; WWLP(TV) Springfield, MA; WILX-TV Onondaga, MI; KOSA-TV Odessa, TX; WMTV(TV) Madison & WSAW-TV Wausau, both WI; & WTRF-TV Wheeling, WV). FCC approved: December 24, 1991 [For the Record, January 27, 1992]. Previous owner: Wichita Falls Telecasters II [Golden Broadcasting (80%) & White Fuel Corp. (20%)]. Sale price: $10.92 million. FCC approved: January 5, 1984. Previous owner: Wichita Falls Telecasters I [Wichita Falls Television (80%) & White Fuel Corp. (20%)]. Sale price: $4.64 million. FCC approved: May 1978. Note: stn was sold in 1974 by Bass Brothers Telecasters Inc. to Wichita Falls Telecasters I for $4.25 million. FCC approved: September 19, 1974 [For the Record, October 7, 1974]. Note: Founded in 1953. Sold in 1956 as KWFT-TV by E.H. Rowley & Kenyon Brown to Sidney A. Grayson, Nat Levine & others for $825,000. Grayson group sold stn (then KSYD-TV) to Paul Harron for $2.35 million in 1963. Mr. Harron sold KAUZ-TV to Bass Brothers Telecasters Inc. in 1968 for $3.1 million. FCC approved: April 12, 1968 [*Broadcasting*, April 15, 1968].

KFDX-TV Wichita Falls (ch 3)—Licensed to Price Communications. Former owner: Clay Communications Inc. (See WAPT-TV Jackson, MS for details of sale.) Original owner: Wichtex Radio & Television Co. [Darrold A. Cannan (44.97%), D.A. Cannan Jr. (15.5%), Howard H. Fry (8.6%), & others]. Sale price: $5 million. FCC approved: January 27, 1971 [For the Record, February 8, 1971].

Utah

***KUSU-TV Logan (ch 12, now deleted)**—Licensed to Utah State University of Agriculture & Applied Sciences. Original owner: Herschell & Reed Bullen & others. Sale price: $6,331 for expenses. FCC approved: November 8, 1960 [For the Record, November 14, 1960].

KOOG-TV Ogden (ch 30)—Licensed to Miracle Rock Church. Former owner: Ogden Television Inc. Sale price: $65,000. FCC approved: July 14, 1993 [For the Record, August 2, 1993].

KSTU(TV) Salt Lake City (ch 20)—Licensed to Fox Television Stations Inc. Former owner: MWT Ltd. Sale price: $41 million. FCC approved: February 16, 1990. Previous owner: Adams Communications Corp. Sale price: $30 million. FCC approved: September 1987. Previous owner: Springfield TV Corp. (For details of sale, see WWLP(TV) Springfield, MA.)

KTVX(TV) Salt Lake City (ch 4)—Licensed to United Television Inc. (subsidiary of Twentieth Century Film Corp.). Former owners: Screen Gems Broadcasting of Utah, subsidiary of Screen Gems Stations. Sale price: $11 million. FCC approved: August 12, 1975. [For the Record, September 1, 1975]. Former call letters: KCPX-TV. Note: founded by S.S. Fox & associates as KDYL-TV. Sold to Intermountain Broadcasting & TV Corp. [Time Inc. (80%) & G. Bennet Larson (20%)] in 1953 for $2.1 million (with KDYL-AM-FM). Sold to Columbia Pictures in 1959 for $3.1 million (with KCPX-AM-FM). Sold to Screen Gems Stations in 1963 for $2.4 million (with KCPX-AM-FM). FCC approved: January 23, 1963) [For the Record, January 28, 1963].

KUTV(TV) Salt Lake City (ch 2)—Licensed to KUTV Inc. (owned 80% by Ogden *Standard Examiner* & 20% by Communications Investment Corp., see Hatch Stations, Group Ownership). Original owners: Salt Lake City *Tribune* & Frank Carmen-Grant Wrathall interests. Sale price: $683,333. FCC approved: March 7, 1956 [For the Record, March 12, 1956].

KXIV(TV) Salt Lake City (ch 14)—Licensed to Larry H. Miller Communications Corp. Former owner: Skaggs Telecommunications Service Inc. Sale price: $1.725 million. FCC approved: February 12, 1993 [For the Record, March 15, 1993]. Previous owner: Don L. Skaggs. Sale price: $415,000. FCC approved: September 27, 1989 [For the Record, October 16, 1989].

Vermont

WVNY-TV Burlington (ch 22)—Licensed to Champlain Communications Corp., (owned by Citadel Communications Co., see Group Ownership). Former owners: International Television Corp. Sale price: $4.5 million. FCC approved: October 8, 1982. [For the Record, November 1, 1982]. Original owner: Vermont-New York Television Inc. [Jack L. Siegal (30%) & others] sold to International Television. Sale price: $1.23 million (including WEZF-FM Burlington, VT). FCC approved: April 17, 1974 [For the Record, May 6, 1974]. Note: Began operation in 1968. Stn went off air April 2, 1971, & went on air again September 17, 1971.

Virginia

WCYB-TV Bristol (ch 5)—Licensed to Appalachian Broadcasting Corp. (owned by DGH Corp.). Former owner: Starr Broadcasting Group Inc. Sale price: $8.61 million. FCC approved: March 17, 1977 [For the Record, March 28, 1977]. Previous owners: Robert H. Smith, J. Fey Rogers, Charles H. Gore & Harry M. Daniel. Sale price: $5.2 million. FCC approved: November 12, 1970.

WVIR-TV Charlottesville (ch 29)—Licensed to Waterman Broadcasting Co. Former owner: Virginia Broadcasting Corp. (Charles E. Echols, et al). Sale price: $8.69 million. FCC approved: October 30, 1986 [For the Record, September 29, 1986].

WPAJ(TV) Danville (ch 24)—Licensed to Danville Television Partnership (Caroline K. Powley, Melvin N. Eleazer). Former owner: Danville Communications (William R. Mouer). Sale price: $10,000. FCC approved: June 12, 1992 [For the Record, June 29, 1992].

***WNVT(TV) Goldvein (ch 53)**—Licensed to Central Virginia Educational Television Corp. (B.W. Spiller, pres). Original owner: Northern Virginia Educational Telecommunications Association (Robert D. Smith, VP & gen mgr). Sale price: $550,000. FCC approved: July 3, 1974 [For the Record, July 22, 1974].

WVEC-TV Hampton (ch 13)—Licensed to WVEC Television Inc. (owned by Belo Broadcasting, see Group Ownership). Former owner: Corinthian Broadcasting (a subsidiary of Dun & Bradstreet Companies). Sale price: $40 million (part of a six stn deal totaling $606 million, which included KHOU-TV Houston; KXTV(TV) Sacramento, CA; WISH-TV Indianapolis; KOTV(TV) Tulsa, OK; & WANE-TV Ft. Wayne, IN). FCC approved: November 28, 1983 [For the Record, December 19, 1983]. Previous owner: Thomas P. Chisman, et al. Sale price: $34 million. FCC approved: February 12, 1980. Note: stn founded September 15, 1953.

WHSV-TV Harrisonburg (ch 3)—Licensed to Benedek Broadcasting Inc. (see Group Ownership). Former owner: Worrell Broadcasting Inc. (owned by Worrell Newspapers Inc.). (For details of this sale, see WIFR(TV) Freeport, IL.) FCC approved: November 5, 1986 [For the Record, September 29, 1986]. Previous owner: Gilmore Broadcasting Corp. of Virginia (see Gilmore Broadcasting Corp., Group Ownership). Sale price: $3.15 million plus $100,000 covenant not to compete. FCC approved: January 15, 1976 [For the Record, February 2, 1976]. Former call letters: WSVA-TV. Note: founded by Frederick L. Allman in 1953. Sold to Transcontinent TV Corp. & Hamilton Shea jointly in 1956 for $560,000. Washington *Evening Star* bought 51% interest in 1959 for $700,000. Sold with WSVA-AM-FM in 1965 to Gilmore Broadcasting for $1.69 million. FCC approved: August 9, 1965 [For the Record, August 16, 1965].

WJPR(TV) Lynchburg (ch 21)—Licensed to Grant Broadcasting System II Inc. Former owner: Lynchburg-Roanoke TV Partners. Sale price: $5.5 million, including satellite stn WVFT(TV) Roanoke, VA. FCC approved: May 21, 1993 [For the Record, June 14, 1993]. Previous owner: Carney Communications of Virginia Inc. Sale price: $335,000 for CP. FCC approved: December 24, 1985 [For the Record, November 4, 1985].

WSET-TV Lynchburg (ch 31)—Licensed to WSET Inc. (owned by Joseph Allbritton Communications). Former owner: Evening Star Broadcasting (Washington Star Communications). Sale price: $28.5 million (including WLVA(AM) Lynchburg, VA; WMAL-AM-FM-TV Washington; & WCIV(TV) Charleston, SC). FCC approved: January 1976. Former call letters: WLVA-TV. Previous owners: Phillip P. Allen (25.56%), Champe C. Allen (25.56%) & others. Sale price: $1.25 million (including WLVA-AM-FM). FCC approved: August 23, 1965 [For the Record, August 30, 1965].

WACH-TV Newport News (ch 33, now deleted)—Licensed to United Broadcasting Co. of Eastern Virginia Inc. Original owners: Eastern Broadcasting Corp. (Russell A. Collins, receiver for John Doley & others). Sale price: $54,000 (including WACH(AM)). FCC approved: July 19, 1956 [For the Record, July 30, 1956].

WJCB(TV) Norfolk (ch 49)—Licensed to Tidewater Christian Comm. Former owner: William Geisler & D. Ruhe. Sale price: $117,975 for CP. FCC approved: March 22, 1985 [For the Record, April 8, 1985]. Former call letters: WUHX(TV).

WTKR-TV Norfolk (ch 3)—Licensed to Knight-Ridder Broadcasting. (see Group Ownership). Former owner: Landmark Communications. Sale price: $48.3 million. FCC approved: January 16, 1981 [Changing Hands, January 26, 1981].

WTVZ-TV Norfolk (ch 33)—Licensed to WTVZ Inc. Former owner: TVX of Nashville Inc. Sale price: $10.75 million. FCC approved: July 19, 1989 [For the Record, August 14, 1989].

WRIC-TV Petersburg (ch 8)—Licensed to Nationwide Communications Inc. (see Group Ownership). Former owner: Petersburg Television Corp. (Thomas G. Tinsley, et al). Sale price: $7.15 million (including WLEE(AM)). FCC approved: November 3, 1967 [For the Record, November 13, 1967]. Former call letters: WXEX-TV.

WAVY-TV Portsmouth (ch 10)—Licensed to WAVY TV Inc. (owned by LIN Broadcasting, see Group Ownership). Former owner: Tidewater Teleradio Inc. (J. Glen Taylor & others). Sale price: $8 million. FCC approved: March 27, 1968 [For the Record, April 11, 1968]. Note: founded in 1957 by Tidewater Teleradio Inc.

WGNT(TV) Portsmouth (ch 27)—Licensed to Centennial Communications Inc. (Raymond Bottom Jr.). Former owner: Christian Broadcasting Network. Sale price: $8.2 million. FCC approved: May 22, 1989 [For the Record, June 12, 1989]. Former call letters: WYAH-TV. Previous owner: Tim Brite Inc. (Temus R. Bright). Sale price: not disclosed for CP. Former call letters: WTOV-TV. Original owner: Commonwealth Broadcasting Corp. (E.L. Scott, Robert Wasdon, Jack Siegel). Sale price: $17,500 plus assumption of $78,000 in obligations. FCC approved: March 9, 1955 [For the Record, March 14, 1955].

WRLH(TV) Richmond (ch 35)—Licensed to Gillett Group Inc. Former owner: Times Mirror Broadcasting. Sale price: $200 million (including WMAR-TV Baltimore). FCC approved: October 31, 1986 [For the Record, July 21, 1986]. Previous owner: Television Corp. of Richmond. Sale price: $14.4 million. FCC approved: April 24, 1985 [For the Record, March 25, 1985].

WTVR-TV Richmond (ch 6)—Licensed to Roy H. Park Broadcasting of Virginia Inc. (see Park Broadcasting, Group Ownership). Previous owner: Wilbur M. Havens & associates. Sale price: $5 million (including WMBG(AM) & WCOD(FM)). FCC approved: October 13, 1965 [For the Record, October 25, 1965].

WWBT(TV) Richmond (ch 12)—Licensed to Jefferson-Pilot Broadcasting (see Group Ownership). Former owner: Larus Investing Co. Sale price: $5 million. FCC approved: 1968.

WDBJ-TV Roanoke (ch 7)—Licensed to WDBJ Television Inc.(South Bend *Tribune*, WBST-AM-FM-TV South Bend, IN). Former owner: Times-World Corp. (Roanoke *Times & World News*). Sale price: $8.2 million. FCC approved: October 29, 1969 [For the Record, November 10, 1969]. Note: Founded by Times-World Corp. in October 1965.

WSLS-TV Roanoke (ch 10)—Licensed to Roy H. Park Broadcasting of Roanoke Inc. (see Park Broadcasting, Group Ownership). Previous owner: Shenandoah Life Stations Inc. (Shenandoah Life Insurance Co., G. Frank Clement & others). Sale price: $7 million (including WSLS-AM-FM). FCC approved: September 10, 1969 [For the Record, September 22, 1969]. Note: founded in November 1952 by Shenandoah Life Insurance Co.

WVFT-TV Roanoke (ch 27)—Licensed to Grant Broadcasting System II Inc. Former owner: Family Group Ltd. [owned by Ian (Sandy) Wheeler, et al]. Sale price: $5.5 million, including WJPR(TV) Lynchburg, VA. FCC approved: May 21, 1993 [For the Record, June 14, 1993]. Previous owner: Roanoke Christian Broadcasting. Sale price: $500,000 for CP. FCC approved: April 28, 1986 [For the Record, March 24, 1986].

Washington

KVOS-TV Bellingham (Vancouver, BC) (ch 12)—Licensed to KVOS-TV Inc. (owned by Ackerly Communications Inc., see Group Ownership). Former owner: KKR Assoc. (see Group Ownership). Sale price: $26 million. FCC approved: June 5, 1985. Previous owner: KVOS TV Corp. (see Wometco Stations, Group Ownership). (For details of sale, see WTVJ(TV) Miami, FL.) Original owners: Rogan Jones & associates. Sale price: $3 million. FCC approved: March 29, 1961 [For the Record, April 3, 1961].

KEPR-TV Pasco (ch 19)—Licensed to Retlow Enterprises Inc. Former owner: NWG Broadcasting Corp. (For details of sale, see KLEW-TV Lewiston, ID.) FCC approved: November 25, 1986 [For the Record, October 27, 1986].

KNDU(TV) Richland (ch 25)—Licensed to Farragut Communications. Former owner: Columbia Empire Broadcasting Corp. (For details of sale, see KNDO(TV) Yakima, WA).

KHCV(TV) Seattle (ch 45)—Licensed to North Pacific International Television Inc. Former owner: Allen E. Hom. Sale price: no cash consideration for CP. FCC approved: November 3, 1992 [For the Record, November 23, 1992].

KING-TV Seattle (ch 5)—Licensed to King Holding Corp. (owned 50% each by Providence Journal Co. & Kelso Partners IV). Former owner: King Broadcasting Co. (see Group Ownership). Sale price: $355 million (including KGW-TV Portland, OR; KREM-TV Spokane, WA; KTVB(TV) Boise, ID; & KHNL(TV) Honolulu, KOOG(TV) Wailuku, & KHBC-TV Hilo, all HI). FCC approved: August 27, 1991 [For the Record, September 9, 1991]. Original owners: Radio Sale Corp. (P.K. Leberman). Sale price: $375,000. FCC approved: July 20, 1949 [For the Record, July 25, 1949]. Original call letters: KRSC-TV. Note: Hearst Corp. bought 25% interest in King Broadcasting Co. for $375,000 in 1951, which was repurchased for $450,000 by licensee in 1953.

KIRO-TV Seattle (ch 7)—Licensed to Bonneville Holding Co. (see Bonneville International Corp., Group Ownership). Former owner: Saul Haas & others. Sale price: $5 million for 50.2% of stn (including KIRO-AM-FM). FCC approved: December 17, 1963 [For the Record, December 23, 1963].

KAYU-TV Spokane (ch 28)—Licensed to Bingham Comunications Group. Former owner: KAYU-TV Partners Ltd. Sale price: $7.7 million. FCC approved: January 28, 1988 [For the Record, February 22, 1988].

KHQ-TV Spokane (ch 6)—Licensed to KHQ Inc. (James P. Cowles, William S. Cowles). Former owner: KHQ Inc. (William H. Cowles III, deceased). Sale price: no cash consideration, estate transfer. FCC approved: July 15, 1992 [For the Record, August 3, 1992].

KREM-TV Spokane (ch 2)—Licensed to King Holding Corp. (owned 50% each by Providence Journal Co. & Kelso Partners IV) Former owner: King Broadcasting Co. (see Group Ownership). Sale price: $355 million. FCC approved: August 27, 1991 [For the Record, September 9, 1991]. Note: part of multi-stn purchase. (See KING-TV Seattle). Former owner: Louis Wasmer. Sale price: $2 million (including KREM-AM-FM). FCC approved: September 26, 1957 [For the Record, October 7, 1957].

KSKN(TV) Spokane (ch 22)—Licensed to KSKN Inc. [owned by Melvin J. Querico (80%), Stephen Whitehead (10%) & William R. Romine (10%)]. Former owner: Whitehead Broadcasting Co. (headed by Whitehead & Romine). Sale price: undisclosed. FCC approved: February 15, 1991 [For the Record, March 11, 1991]. Previous owner: 22 Spokane Ltd Partnership (owned by Sun Continental Group), preceded by Broadcast Vision TV. Sale price of 22 Spokane-Broadcast Vision transaction: $880,000. FCC approved: November 27, 1985.

KXLY-TV Spokane (ch 4)—Licensed to Spokane TV Inc. (owned by Morgan Murphy Stations, see Group Ownership). Original owner: KELP-TV Corp. (Joseph Harris & Norman Alexander). Sale price: $3.25 million (including KXLY-AM-FM). FCC approved: January 17, 1963 [For the Record, January 22, 1963]. Note: Founded by E.B. Craney & Harry L. (Bing) Crosby. Sold in 1954 to KELP-TV Inc. for $1.7 million.

KCPQ-TV Tacoma (ch 13)—Licensed to Kelly Television Co. Former owner: Clover Park School District No. 400 (Harold Mulholland, pres). Sale price: $6.25 million. FCC approved: January 21, 1981. Previous owner: KTVW Inc. (Robert A. Banks, trustee in bankruptcy). Sale price: $378,000. FCC approved: September 9, 1975 [For the Record, September 29, 1975]. Former call letters: KTVW(TV). Note: original owners Carl E. & C.D. Haymond sold to estate of J. Elroy McCaw in 1954 for $300,000. FCC approved: September 15, 1954. [For the Record, September 20, 1954]. Sold to KTVW Inc. (Blaidon Mutual Investors Corp.) in 1972 for $863,407. FCC approved: June 21, 1972 [For the Record, July 17, 1972]. Original call letters: KMO-TV.

KSTW(TV) Tacoma (ch 11)—Licensed to Gaylord Broadcasting Co. (see Group Ownership). Original owner: Tribune Publishing Co. (James Bellamy, VP; & others). Sale price: $4.5 million. FCC approved: January 23, 1974 [For the Record, February 11, 1974]. Original call letters: KTNT-TV. Note: began operation in 1953.

KPDX(TV) Vancouver (ch 49)—Licensed to Cannell Communications Ltd. Former owner: Columbia River Television Inc. Sale price: $15 million. FCC approved: November 6, 1992 [For the Record, November 23, 1992].

KCWT-TV Wenatchee (ch 27)—Licensed to Bingham Communications Group Inc. (owned by Robert R. Bingham). Former owner: KCWT Ltd. Partnership, (owned by Jerry R. Martin, et al). Sale price: $2.3 million. FCC approved: November 10, 1986 [For the Record, September 1, 1986].

KIMA-TV Yakima (ch 29)—Licensed to Retlaw Enterprises Inc. Former owner: NWG Broadcasting Co. [John Noel Jr. (75%) & Rodger Noel (25%)]. (For details of sale, see KLEW-TV Lewiston, ID.) FCC approved: November 25, 1986 [For the Record, October 27, 1986]. Previous sale: $6.5 million (including KLEW-TV Lewiston, ID & KEPR-TV Pasco, WA). Previous sale: $187,500 plus approximately $266,000 assumption of debt. FCC approved: October 15, 1975 [For the Record, October 27, 1975]. Note: founded in July 1953 by Thomas C. Bostic, W.W. Talbot & Ralph Sundquist. KEPR-TV founded in December 1954 & KLEW-TV founded in December 1955. Haltom Corp. (Mr. Bostic) purchased 80% from Messrs. Talbot & Sundquist in 1962 for $900,000 with KIMA(AM), KEPR(AM), & KEPR-TV Pasco; KBAS-TV

Ephrata; both WA; & KLEW-TV Lewiston, ID. Later Haltom changed name to Cascade. Sold by Mr. Bostic, John H. Reber & others in 1969 for about $3 million worth of Filmways stock with KEPR-TV Pasco, WA & KLEW-TV Lewiston, ID. FCC approved: July 3, 1969 [For the Record, August 4, 1969]. Cascade Broadcasting Co. (Filmways Inc.) sold stn (with KLEW-TV Lewiston, ID & KEPR-TV Pasco, WA) to NWG Broadcasting Co. in 1972 for $1 million. FCC approved: August 30, 1972 [For the Record, September 18, 1972].

KNDO(TV) Yakima (ch 23)—Licensed to Columbia Empire Broadcasting Corp. Original owner: Ralph Tronsrud. Sale price: $194,229 (including purchase price of leased property). FCC approved: February 1, 1961 [For the Record, February 6, 1961].

West Virginia

WVVA(TV) Bluefield (ch 6)—Licensed to Quincy Newspapers Inc. (Thomas A. Oakley & family). Original owners: Daily Telegraph Printing Co. (Hugh I. Shott & family). Sale price: $8 million. FCC approved: April 9, 1979 [*Broadcasting,* April 23, 1979]. Former call letters: WHIS-TV.

WCHS-TV Charleston (ch 8)—Licensed to Heritage Media (formerly Rollins Telecasting Inc. which merged with Heritage in March 1987, see Group Ownership). Original owner: Tierney Co. Sale price: $3 million (including WCHS(AM)). FCC approved: September 28, 1960 [For the Record, October 10, 1960].

WVAH-TV Charleston (ch 11)—Licensed to Act III Broadcasting (principally owned by Norman Lear). Former owner: Greentree Associates. (For details of sale see WRGT-TV Dayton, OH.) Note: Act III Broadcasting returned license to FCC & switched to ch 11 from ch 23. (CP included in sale).

WBOY-TV Clarksburg (ch 12)—Licensed to WBOY-TV Inc. (Birney Imes Jr.). Former owner: Northern WV Television Broadcasting. Sale price: $750,000. FCC approved: November 5, 1976 [For the Record: November 15, 1976]. Note: founded by News Pub. Co. in 1956 as WBLK-TV. Sold to Rust Craft Broadcasting (then Friendly Stations Group) in 1957 for $250,000 (including WBLK(AM) & WPAR-AM-TV Parkersburg, WV). Northern West Virginia TV Broadcasting Co. (Marion R. Ascoli, principal stockholder, wife of Max Ascoli) was purchased from Rust Craft Broadcasting Co. (see Group Ownership) for $825,000 (with WBOY-AM).

WOWK-TV Huntington (ch 13)—Licensed to Gateway Communications Inc. (see Group Ownership). Former owner: WHTN-TV Inc. (owned by Reeves Telecom Corp. Sale price: $7.42 million. FCC approved: September 23, 1974 [For the Record, October 7, 1974].) Former call letters: WHTN-TV. Note: initially owned by Greater Huntington Theaters Corp. (S.J. Hyman & family). Sold to Cowles Broadcasting Co. in 1956 for $535,000 plus assumption of $100,000 in debts (with WHTN-AM-FM). Cowles Broadcasting sold stn to Reeves Telecom Corp. in 1960 for $1.92 million. FCC approved: December 22, 1960 [For the Record, January 2, 1961].

WSAZ-TV Huntington (ch 3)—Licensed to Lee Enterprises Inc. (see Group Ownership). Former owner: Capital Cities Broadcasting Corp. (see Capital Cities Communications Inc., Group Ownership). Sale price: $18 million. FCC approved: February 24, 1971 [*Broadcasting,* March 1, 1971]. Note: Founded by Huntington Publishing Co. in 1949. Sold to Goodwill Stations Inc. (G.A. Richards trusts, John F. Platt, Worth Kramer & others) in 1961 for $6.1 million (including WSAZ(AM)). Sold to Capital Cities Broadcasting Corp.in 1964 for $15.14 million (including WSAZ(AM) & WJR-AM-FM Detroit). FCC approved: July 29, 1964 [For the Record, August 10, 1964].

WTAP-TV Parkersburg (ch 15)—Licensed to Benedek Broadcasting Corp. (principally owned by A. Richard Benedek, see Group Ownership). Former owner: CMA Communications (George R. Abels, Sherman A. Grimm, et al). Sale price: $2.2 million. FCC approved: December 13, 1979. Previous owner: Broadcasting Services Inc. (R.L. Drake 100%). Sale price: $300,000. FCC approved: November 15, 1974 [For the Record, December 2, 1974]. Note: founded in 1953. Sold in 1955 by Frank Baer-Howard Chernoff group to Zanesville Publishing for $124,609. Sold in 1967 by Zanesville Publishing Co. to Broadcasting Services Inc. for $579,000 (including WTAP-AM-FM). FCC approved: November 2, 1967.

WDTV(TV) Weston (ch 5)—Licensed to Withers Broadcasting Co. of West Virginia (W. Russell Withers Jr. & William P. Brenton). Previous owner: Broadcast Industries of West Virginia Inc. (Broadcast Industries of New York Inc. 100%. William Grossman is pres of parent co.). Sale price: $600,000 [*Broadcasting,* April 16, 1973]. Note: founded as WJPB-TV in 1960 by J.P. Beacom, who sold 50% for $100,000 in same year to Thomas P. Johnson & George W. Elby. Messrs. Beacom, Johnson & Elby sold stn to Broadcast Industries of West Virginia Inc. in 1966 for $571,720. FCC approved: August 24, 1966 [For the Record, August 29, 1966].

WTRF-TV Wheeling (ch 7)—Licensed to Adams TV of Wheeling Inc., owned by Paul A. Brissette (see Group Ownership). Former owner: Adams Communications Corp. (see Group Ownership). Sale price: undisclosed (including WHOI(TV) Peoria, IL; WWLP(TV) Springfield, MA; WILX-TV Onondaga, MI; KOSA-TV Odessa & KAUZ-TV Wichita Falls, both TX; WMTV(TV) Madison & WSAW-TV Wausau, both WI; & WTRF-TV Wheeling, WV). FCC approved: December 24, 1991 [For the Record, January 27, 1992]. Previous owner: Forward Tele-Productions Inc. (owned by Wesray Communications Corp., see Group Ownership). (For details of sale, see WHOI(TV) Peoria, IL.) Previous owner: Forward Communications. Sale price: $95 million for group (for details of sale, see KOSA-TV Odessa, TX). FCC approved: August 16, 1984. Previous owner: WTRF-TV Inc. (Robert W. Ferguson, Albert V., Robert C., Raymond E. & Gordon C. Dix, see Dix Stations, Group Ownership). Sale price: $7.25 million (including WTRF-FM). FCC approved: February 28, 1969 [For the Record, March 10, 1969]. Note: Previous owner, Tri-City Broadcasting Co. (Thomas M. Bloch & W.L. Harris families, News Pub. Co.), sold 56.13% December 17, 1958 to Dix family for $1.684 million. Dix family already owned 30.96% of Tri-City Broadcasting.

Wisconsin

WXGZ(TV) Appleton (ch 32)—Licensed to Ace TV Corp. (see Group Ownership). Former owner: Appleton Acquisition Corp., owned by Martha D. Kent. Sale price: $505,000 plus 85% of the accounts receivable. FCC approved: August 3, 1992 [For the Record, August 31, 1992]. Former owner: Appleton Midwestern Television Ltd., debtor, owned by Richard D. Ellenberg. Sale price: $300,000 plus assumption of debt. FCC approved: March 27, 1992 [For the Record, April 20, 1992].

WEUX-TV Chippewa Falls (ch 48)—Licensed to Aries Telecommunications Corp. Former owner: Family Group Ltd. III. Sale price: $7.6 million (including WGBA(TV) Green Bay & WLAX(TV) La Crosse, both WI). FCC approved: April 9, 1991 [For the Record, April 22, 1991]. Previous owner: Krypton Broadcasting Corp. (headed by C.E. Feltner Jr.), preceded by Family Group Ltd. III. (principally owned by Ian Wheeler). Sale price for Krypton-Family transaction: $7 million (included WLAX(TV) & WGBA(TV)). FCC approved: May 17, 1989. [For the Record, June 12, 1989].

WEAU-TV Eau Claire (ch 13)—Licensed to Benedek Broadcasting of Wisconsin Inc. Former owner: Busse Broadcasting Corp. Sale price: $31 million. FCC approved: April 6, 1990. Previous owner: GNG Inc. (owned by Gillett Group, see Group Ownership), preceded by Appleton (WI) Post-Crescent Publishing Co. Sale price of GNG-Appleton transaction: $65 a share (including WLUC-TV Marquette, MI; KTVO(TV) Kirksville, MO; WOKR(TV) Rochester, NY; WLUK-TV Green Bay, WI; & 3 radio stns). FCC approved: June 14, 1984. Original owner: Morgan Murphy Stations. Sale price: $2.1 million. FCC approved: 1962 [For the Record, May 21, 1962].

WQOW-TV Eau Claire (ch 18)—Licensed to Wisconsin TV Network (owned by Tak Communications, see Group Ownership). Former owner: Liberty Broadcasting. Sale price: $22 million (including 3 other TV stns). (See WKOW-TV Madison, WI.) FCC approved: January 24, 1985.

WBAY-TV Green Bay (ch 2)—Licensed to Nationwide Communications Inc. (see Group Ownership). Original owners: Nobertine Fathers (religious community). Sale price: $5.73 million. FCC approved: December 27, 1974 [For the Record, January 13, 1975].

WFRV-TV Green Bay (ch 5)—Licensed to WFRV Television Inc. [owned by Midwest Radio-Television Inc. (descendants of W.J. & F.E. Murphy families)]. Former owner: Orion Broadcasting Corp. Sale price: $18.7 million (including WJMN-TV Escanaba, MI). FCC approved: August 14, 1981 [Changing Hands, August 31, 1981]. Note: Stn was one of four that were spun off to meet FCC ownership requirements & clear way for merger of Orion-Cosmos [*Broadcasting,* June 16, 1980].

Previous owners: S.N. Pickard & Associates. Sale price: $1.6 million. FCC approved: January 4, 1961 [For the Record, January 16, 1961].

WGBA(TV) Green Bay (ch 26)—Licensed to Aries Telecommunications Corp. Former owner: Family Group Ltd. III. Sale price: $7.6 million (including WLAX(TV) La Crosse & WEUX(TV) Chippewa Falls, both WI). FCC approved: January 14, 1991 [For the Record, February 4, 1991]. Previous owner: Krypton Broadcasting Corp. (headed by C.E. Feltner Jr.), preceded by Family Group Ltd. III (owned by Ian N. (Sandy) Wheeler). (For details of this transaction, see listing of WEUX-TV Chippewa Falls.) Original owner: TV-26 Inc. (Jerald D. Newman, et al). Sale price: $2.57 million & assumption of debt (including CP for WWQI(TV) LaCrosse, WI). FCC approved: September 27, 1985. Original call letters: WLRE-TV.

WLUK-TV Green Bay (ch 11)—Licensed to Burnham Broadcasting Company (see Group Ownership). Former owner: Gillett Group, preceded by WLUK Inc. (owned by the Appleton (WI) Post-Crescent Publishing Co.). Sale price of Gillett-WLUK transaction: $15.75 million plus assumption of debt. FCC approved: June 14, 1984. Previous owner: Morgan Murphy Stations. Sale price: $3.1 million (including WLUC-TV Marquette, MI). FCC approved: January 6, 1965 [For the Record, January 11, 1965]. Note: founded in 1957 as WMBV-TV Marinette, WI by William Walker & associates. Sold to Mr. Murphy & others in 1958 for $211,764 for 75% of stn & WMAM(AM).

WJNW(TV) Janesville (ch 57)—Licensed to Harish Puri. Former owner: Tri-M Communications Ltd. (Harry Monk). Sale price: $30,000 for CP. FCC approved: June 14, 1993 [For the Record, July 12, 1993].

WHKE(TV) Kenosha (ch 55)—Licensed to Lab Partners (headed by Dewayne Adamson). Former owner: LeSea Broadcasting (L. Sumrall, et al). Sale price: $1.35 million. FCC approved: July 29, 1992 [For the Record, August 24, 1992]. Previous owner: Midwest Broadcast Associates Inc. Sale price: $100,000 for CP. FCC approved: May 30, 1986 [For the Record, April 7, 1986]. Former call letters: WKRW-TV.

WKBT(TV) La Crosse (ch 8)—Licensed to Young Broadcasting Inc. Former owner: Backe Communications. (For details of sale, see WLNS-TV Lansing, MI.) Previous owner: Gross Telecasting. Sale price: $48 million (including WLNS-TV Lansing, MI). FCC approved: October 2, 1984. Previous owner: WKBH Television (La-Crosse *Tribune,* et al). Sale price: $4.9 million. FCC approved: 1969.

WLAX(TV) La Crosse (ch 48)—Licensed to Aries Telecommunications Corp. Former owner: Family Group Ltd. III. Sale price: $7.6 million (including WGBA(TV) Green Bay & WEUX(TV) Chippewa Falls, both WI). FCC approved: January 14, 1991 [For the Record, February 4, 1991]. Previous owner: Krypton Broadcasting Corp. (headed by C.E. Feltner Jr.), preceded by Family Group Ltd. III. (For details of this transaction, see WEUX(TV) Chippewa Falls, WI.)

WWQI(TV) La Crosse (ch 25)—See WGBA(TV) Green Bay.

WXOW-TV La Crosse (ch 19)—Licensed to Wisconsin TV Network Associates (owned by Tak Communications, see Group Ownership). (For details of acquisition, see WKOW-TV Madison, WI.)

WKOW-TV Madison (ch 27)—Licensed to Wisconsin TV Network (owned by Tak Communications). Former owner: Liberty Communications Inc. (Durwood L. Boyles & Donald E. Tykeson). Sale price: $22 million (including WQOW-TV Eau Claire, WXOW-TV La Crosse, & WAOW-TV Wausau, all WI). FCC approved: January 7, 1985. Previous owner: Horizons Communications Corp. (William Mulvey, Ed Wood & Jerry Feniger). Sale price: $8 million (including WXOW-TV La Crosse & WAOW-TV Wausau, both WI). FCC approved: September 1978 [Changing Hands, October 9, 1978]. Previous owner: Midcontinent Broadcasting Co. of Wisconsin Inc. (see BFR Stations, Group Ownership). Sale price: $3 million (including WAOW-TV Wausau & WXOW-TV La Crosse, both WI). FCC approved: September 9, 1970 [For the Record, September 28, 1970]. Note: WKOW-TV founded in 1953, was acquired by Midcontinent in 1960 for $925,000 from Stewart Watson, George W. Icke, E.C. Severson, B.W. Huiskamp & others. WAOW-TV was purchased by Midcontinent in 1964 for $34,439 from Walter A. Bamgardt & others, & went on the air in 1965. Midcontinent put WXOW-TV on the air in March 1970.

WMTV(TV) Madison (ch 15)—Licensed to Adams TV of Madison Inc., owned by Paul A. Brissette (see Group Ownership). Former owner: Adams Communications

Corp. (see Group Ownership). Sale price: undisclosed (including WHOI(TV) Peoria, IL; WWLP(TV) Springfield, MA; WILX-TV Onondaga, MI; KOSA-TV Odessa & KAUZ-TV Wichita Falls, both TX; WSAW-TV Wausau, WI; & WTRF-TV Wheeling, WV). FCC approved: December 24, 1991 [For the Record, January 27, 1992]. Previous owner: Forward TV Inc. (see Wesray Communications, Group Ownership). (For details of sale, see WHOI(TV) Peoria, IL.) Previous owner: Forward Communications. Sale price: $95 million (including group, see KOSA-TV Odessa, TX). FCC approved: August 16, 1984. Previous owners: Lee Radio Group (Lee P. Loomis). Sale price: $563,000. FCC approved: May 15, 1963 [For the Record, May 27, 1963]. Note: founded by Bartell TV Corp. Purchased by Lee Ruwitch, Gordon Sherman, Mitchell Wolfson & Sidney Meyer in 1957 for $350,000. Bought by Lee group in 1958 for $339,333.

WWRS(TV) Mayville (ch 52)—Licensed to TV-52 Inc. (Lyle R. Evans). Former owner (permittee): Estate of Wayne R. Stenz (Wayne R. Stenz 50%, Lyle R. Evans, 50%). Sale price: $850. FCC approved: April 15, 1993 [For the Record, May 3, 1993].

WCAN-TV Milwaukee (ch 24, now deleted)—Licensed to Field Communications Corp. (owned by Field Enterprises Inc.). Former owner: Lou Poller. Sale price: $35,000. FCC approved: December 21, 1966. Note: WCAN-TV has been dark since 1955. Lou Poller operated stn from 1953-1955 when he sold physical plant to CBS, which operated ch 18 Milwaukee with those facilities. (See WVTV(TV) Milwaukee.)

WCGV-TV Milwaukee (ch 24)—Licensed to B&F Broadcasting Inc. [owned by HR Broadcasting Corp. (Albert Krivin, Hal Gaba, Robin French, Hal Reach Studios)]. Former owner: Arlington Broadcast Group (Byron Lasky, et al). Sale price: $30.5 million (including WTTO(TV) Birmingham, AL). FCC approved: July 14, 1986 [For the Record, June 16, 1986]. Note: previously, Arlington Broadcast Group purchased additional 46% of stn, raising holdings to 66%, for $1 million. FCC approved: July 23, 1984.

WISN-TV Milwaukee (ch 12)—Licensed to Hearst Corp. (see Group Ownership). Original owner: Milwaukee Area Telecasting Corp. (permit granted to MATC after merger agreement among four applicants; other three were WEMP(AM) & WFOX(AM) Milwaukee; & Kolero Telecasting Inc.). Sale price: $2 million. FCC approved: March 2, 1955 [For the Record, March 14, 1955]. Original call letters: WTVW(TV).

WITI-TV Milwaukee (ch 6)—Licensed to WITI License Inc. (see SCI Television Inc. in Group Ownership). Former owner: Gillett Communications. Sale price: unknown. (See WAGA-TV Atlanta for details of sale). FCC approved: February 19, 1993 [For the Record, April 26, 1993]. Previous owner: WITI-TV Inc. (owned by KKR Assoc., see Group Ownership). (For details of sale see KCST-TV San Diego.) Previous owner: Storer Broadcasting Co. (For details of sale, see WJW-TV Cleveland.) Original owners: Independent TV Inc. (Sol J. Kahn). Sale price: $4.4 million. FCC approved: November 12, 1958 [*Broadcasting*, November 17, 1958].

WVTV(TV) Milwaukee (ch 18)—Licensed to Gaylord Broadcasting Co. (see Group Ownership). Former owner: Harold Sampson (43%), Bernard J. Sampson (43%), Herbert Wilk (9%), & Lawrence M. Turet (5%). Sale price: $500,000 plus $150,000 for covenant not to compete. FCC approved: March 23, 1966. Note: founded in 1953 as WOKY-TV by Gerald Bartell & family. Sold to CBS in 1954 for $350,000 & call letters changed to WXIX(TV). Sold to Gene Posner, Harold & Bernard J. Sampson & others in 1959 for $50,000 & call letters changed to WUHF(TV). Messrs. Sampson bought out Mr. Posner's 51% interest in 1962 for $1 & other valuable considerations.

WJFW-TV Rhinelander (ch 12)—Licensed to Northland Television Inc. [John W. Swain (11.2%), Jasper F. Williams (2.8%), & 32 others]. Original owner: Northland Television Inc. (Alvin E. O'Konski). Sale price: $912,588 (distress sale). FCC approved: April 20, 1979 [*Broadcasting*, May 7, 1979]. Former call letters: WAEO-TV.

KBJR-TV Superior (ch 6)—Licensed to RJR Communications Inc. [Robert J. Rich (60%) & Richard W. Pearson (10%)]. Original owners: Northwest Publications Inc. (owned by Ridder Publications Inc.). Sale price: $1.86 million. FCC approved: September 5, 1974 [For the Record, September 23, 1974]. Original call letters: WDSM-TV. Note: Founded in 1954.

WAOW-TV Wausau (ch 9)—Licensed to Wisconsin TV Network Associates (owned by Tak Communications). Former owner: Liberty Broadcasting. (For details of sale, see WKOW-TV Madison.) Previous owner: Horizon Communications. (For details of sale, see WKOW-TV Madison.) Original owner: Central Wisconsin TV Inc. Sale price: $34,439 for CP. FCC approved: 1964.

WSAW-TV Wausau (ch 7)—Licensed to Adams TV of Wausau Inc., (owned by Paul A. Brissette, see Group Ownership). Former owner: Adams Communications Corp. (see Group Ownership). Sale price: Undisclosed (including WHOI(TV) Peoria, IL; WWLP(TV) Springfield, MA; WILX-TV Onondaga, MI; KOSA-TV Odessa & KAUZ-TV Wichita Falls, both TX; WMTV(TV) Madison, WI; & WTRF-TV Wheeling, WV). FCC approved: December 24, 1991 [For the Record, January 27, 1992]. Previous owner: Forward Telecasting. (For details of sale, see WHOI(TV) Peoria, IL.) Original owner: Forward Communications Inc. Sale price: approx $95 million (including WHOI(TV) Peoria, IL; KCAU-TV Sioux City, IA; KOSA-TV Odessa, TX; WTRF-TV Wheeling, WV; WMTV(TV) Madison, WI; eight radio stns; & the Marshfield (WI) *New Herald* nwspr). FCC approved: August 16, 1984.

Wyoming

KGWC-TV Casper (ch 14)—Licensed to Stauffer Communications Inc. Former owner: Rocky Mountain Communications Inc. Sale price: $3.5 million [including satellites KOWY(TV) (now KGWL-TV) Lander & KWWY(TV) (now KGWR-TV) Rock Springs, both WY]. FCC approved: August 25, 1986 [For the Record, July 28, 1986]. Former call letters: KCWY-TV.

KTWO-TV Casper (ch 2)—Licensed to KTWO Corp (owned by Dix Communications). Former owner: Harriscope Broadcasting Corp. Sale price: $12.2 million (including KULR-TV Billings, MT). FCC approved: December 12, 1986 [For the Record, November 3, 1986]. Note: Harriscope increased its share of stn (and KTWO(AM)) from 60% to 100% by purchasing minority interest from Television Properties Inc. for $400,000 in 1964.

KGWN-TV Cheyenne (ch 5)—Licensed to Stauffer Communications Inc. Former owner: Burke Broadcasting Co. Sale price: $13 million (including satellites KSTF-TV Scottsbluff, NE & KTVS-TV Sterling, CO). FCC approved: July 8, 1986 [Changing Hands, March 3, 1986]. Former call letters: KYCU-TV. Previous owner: Wyneco Communications Inc. (wholly owned subsidiary of Lamb Communications. See Lamb Communications Inc., Group Ownership). Sale price: $9.7 million (part of a multi-stn deal including KTVS(TV) Sterling, CO & KSTF(TV) Scottsbluff, NE). FCC approved: October 14, 1983 [For the Record, November 7, 1983]. Former call letters: KFBC-TV. Note: sold to Wyneco by Frontier Broadcasting Co. Sale price: $3 million (including KTVS(TV) Sterling, CO; KSTF(TV) Scottsbluff, NE; & CP for KVRW(TV) Rawlins, WY). FCC approved: July 6, 1972 [*Broadcasting*, July 10, 1972].

KLWY(TV) Cheyenne (ch 27)—Licensed to Wyomedia Corp. Former owner: Mark R. Nalbone. Sale price: $100,000. FCC approved: December 4, 1991 [For the Record, January 6, 1992].

KGWL-TV Lander (ch 5)—Licensed to Stauffer Communications Inc. Former owner: Rocky Mountain Communications Inc. (For details of sale, see KGWC-TV Casper, WY.) Former call letters: KOWY(TV). Note: Satellite of KGWC-TV Casper.

KFNR(TV) Rawlins (ch 11)—Licensed to Rawlins Broadcasting Corp. (owned by First National Broadcasting Corp; Frederic Bauer, et al). Former owner: Rawlins Broadcasting Corp. (owned by Manuel A. Cantu & Continental Communications Systems Inc.). Sale price: $97,573. FCC approved: July 2, 1986 [For the Record, May 12, 1986]. Former call letters: KRWY-TV.

KVRW(TV) Rawlins (ch 11, now deleted)—Licensed to Wyneco Communications Inc. (a wholly owned subsidiary of Lamb Communications). Former owner: Frontier Broadcasting Co. Sale price: $3 million (including KTVS(TV) Sterling, CO; KSTF(TV) Scottsbluff, NE; & KYCU-TV Cheyenne. FCC approved: July 6, 1972 [*Broadcasting*, July 10, 1972].

KFNE(TV) Riverton (ch 10)—Licensed to Hi-Ho Broadcasting Co. of Wyoming. Former owner: Chief Washakie TV (Joseph P. Earnest & wife, Mildred, who also own KRTR(AM) Thermopolis, WY). Sale price: $700,000. FCC approved: February 28, 1980 [Changing Hands, March 17, 1980]. Former call letters: KFWY-TV, KWRB-TV.

KGWR-TV Rock Springs (ch 13)— Licensed to Stauffer Communications Inc. Former owner: Rocky Mountain Communications Inc. (Chrysostom Corp.). (For details of sale KGWC-TV Casper, WY.) [For the Record, July 28, 1986]. Former call letters: KWWY(TV). Note: Satellite of KGWC-TV Casper. Previous owner: Western Broadcasting Inc. (Gerald E. Devine & wife, Linda). Sale price: $150,000. FCC approved: February 28, 1982 [For the Record, March 25, 1982].

Guam

KUAM-TV Agana (ch 8)—Licensed to Micronesia Broadcasting Corp. (headed by Manuel A. Tenorio), transfer within company. FCC approved: February 8, 1991 [For the Record, March 4, 1991]. Note: Includes transfer of control of KUAM-AM-FM. Previous owner: Pacific Telestations Inc., preceded by Pacific Broadcasting Corp. [H. Scott Kilgore (65%) & Samuel N. Rubin (35%)]. Sale price of Pacific Telestations-Pacific Broadcasting transaction: $650,000. FCC approved: 1977. Previous owner: Phil Berg, et al. Sale price: $650,000. FCC approved: April 9, 1964 [For the Record, April 20, 1964].

Puerto Rico

***WELU(TV) Aguadilla (ch 32)**—Licensed to Healthy Christian Family Media Inc. (Norman O. Ganzalez). Former owner: Faith Pleases God Church. Sale price: $500,000. FCC approved: July 31, 1992 [For the Record, August 24, 1992].

WVEO(TV) Aguadilla (ch 44)—Licensed to Seglares Iglesia Catolica (Antonio Falco, Pres.). Former owner: Ginetta P. Pirallo. Sale price: $600,000. FCC approved: January 23, 1985 [For the Record, February 4, 1985].

WLII(TV) Caguas (ch 11)—Licensed to Estrella Brillante Ltd. [subsidiary of Malrite Communications Group Inc., 78% (see Group Ownership), Lucas Thomas Muniz, 20% & Milton Maltz, 2%]. Former owner: Teleonce Corp. (owned by Lorimar-Telepictures Corp., see Group Ownership). Sale price: $3 million (including WSUR-TV Ponce, PR). FCC approved: August 1, 1991. Previous owner: American Colonial Broadcasting Corp. Sale price: $6.12 million (including WSUR-TV Ponce, PR). FCC approved: July 22, 1985. Former call letters: WKBM-TV.

WUJA(TV) Caguas (ch 58)—Licensed to Caguas Educational TV Inc. Former owner: Faith Pleases God Church Corp. Sale price: $95,000. FCC approved: July 13, 1990.

WPRV-TV Fajardo (ch 13)—Licensed to WSTE-TV Inc. (owned by James C. Leake & Carmina Mendea, see Group Ownership). Original owners: Continental Broadcasting Corp. (William R. Anthony & others). Sale price: $60,000. FCC approved: March 26, 1959. Former call letters: WSTE(TV).

WVSN(TV) Humacao (ch 68)—Licensed to Tito Atiles Natal. Former owner: Bocanegra Girald Broadcasting Group (headed by Angel F. Bocanegra Girald). Sale price: $500,000. FCC approved: February 15, 1991 [For the Record, March 11, 1991].

WMGZ(TV) Mayaguez (ch 16, now deleted)—Licensed to Tele San Juan Inc. (See WTSJ(TV) San Juan, PR.)

WNJX-TV Mayaguez (ch 22, now deleted)—Licensed to United Hemisphere TV of Puerto Rico Inc. (See WUHT-TV San Juan, PR.)

WECN(TV) Naranjito (ch 64)—Licensed to Encuentro Christian Network Corp. Former owner: ART Broadcasting Corp. Sale price: $175,000. FCC approved: September 1987 [For the Record, April 13, 1987].

WLUZ-TV Ponce (ch 7)—Licensed to Ponce Television Corp. (owned by Malrite Communications, see Group Ownership). Former owner: Tele-Luz Washington Inc. (owned by Tele-Luz de P.R. Inc., Lucas Muniz, pres). Sale price: $1.3 million for 20%. FCC approved: September 27, 1985. Previous owner: United Artists Broadcasting of P.R. (see United Artists Stations, Group Ownership). Sale price: $1.8 million. FCC approved: December 21, 1978. Former call letters: WRIK-TV. Previous owner: Alfredo A. de Arellano III. Sale price: $6.1 million for 80.1% Note: founded in 1958. Alfredo C. Ramirez de Arellano del Valle acquired 61.67% for $338,919 in 1964, later increasing his holdings to

Television Ownership Transfers

82.23%. Mr. de Arellano, owner of 82.23%, acquired 17.77% from other stockholders & sold 80.1% to United Artists, retaining 19.9%. UA had four-year option to buy remaining interest for $1.5 million or certain multiple of stn profits. FCC approved: March 11, 1970 [For the Record, April 13, 1970].

WSTE(TV) Ponce (ch 7)—Licensed to Siete Grand Television Inc. (owned by Jerry B. & Esther M. Hartman). Former owner: Channel 7 Inc., owned by Malrite Communications Group Inc. (see Group Ownership). Sale price: $6 million. FCC approved: August 1, 1991 [For the Record August 26, 1991].

WSUR-TV Ponce (ch 9)—Licensed to Estrella Brillante Ltd. [subsidiary of Malrite Communications Group Inc., 78% (see Group Ownership), Lucas Thomas Muniz, 20% & Milton Maltz, 2%]. Former owner: Teleonce Corp. Sale price: $3 million (including WLII(TV) Caguas, PR). FCC approved: August 1, 1991 [For the Record, August 26, 1991]. Previous owner: American Colonial Broadcasting Corp. Sale price: $6.12 million (including WLII(TV) Caguas, PR). FCC approved: July 22, 1985.

WUHP-TV Ponce (ch 20, now deleted)—See WUHT-TV San Juan, PR.

WAPA-TV San Juan (ch 4)—Licensed to Commacq Inc. Former owner: SFN Companies. Sale price: $155 million (including WJBF(TV) Augusta, GA; WTVM(TV) Columbus, GA; KSCH-TV Stockton, CA; KCAP(AM), KZMT(FM) Helena, MT; & KVGO(AM) Missoula, MT). FCC approved: October 2, 1986 [Changing Hands, July 14, 1986]. Previous owner: WAPA-TV Broadcasting Corp. (see Dale G. Moore Stations, Group Ownership). (See WFTV(TV) Orlando for details of sale.) Previous owner: WAPA-TV Broadcasting Corp. (see Columbia Pictures Industries, Group Ownership). Sale price: $11 million, FCC approved: May 26, 1976 [For the Record, June 7, 1976] Note: founded by Jose Ramon Quinenes & associates. Sold in 1957 to Winston-Salem Broadcasting Co. & others for $320,000. Sold in 1962 to WAPA-TV Broadcasting Corp. for $1.5 million (including a one-third interest in WOLE-TV Aguadilla, P.R.). FCC approved: April 25, 1962 [For the Record, April 30, 1962].

WKAQ-TV San Juan (ch 2)—Licensed to TPR Television Inc. (principally owned by Anthony B. Cassara, Christopher D. Jennings & George A. Vandeman). Former owner: Telemundo of Puerto Rico Inc. Sale price: $160 million. FCC approved: January 30, 1989 [For the Record, February 13, 1989]. Previous owner: John Blair & Co. (see Group Ownership), preceded by Telemundo Inc. Sale price of Blair-Telemundo transaction: $55 million. FCC approved: August 9, 1983 [For the Record, August 29, 1983]. Note: Founded by Telemundo Inc. March 28, 1954. Telemundo Inc. retain control of co-located WKAQ-AM-FM under licensee name of El Mundo Broadcasting Corp.

WSJN(TV) San Juan (ch 24)—Licensed to JEM Communications (Multi-Media Television). Former owner: Multi-Media Communications Corp. FCC approved: June 20, 1986 [For the Record, September 30, 1985].

WTSJ(TV) San Juan (ch 8, now deleted)—Licensed to Tele San Juan Inc. (O. Roy Chalk). Previous owner: Julio Morales Ortiz & Clement L. Littauer. Sale price: $669,825 plus 27,000 shares of Trans-Carribean Airways stock & assumption of $245,372 in obligations (including WMGZ(TV) Mayaguez & WPSJ(TV) Ponce, both PR).

WUHT-TV San Juan (ch 30, now deleted)—Licensed to United Hemisphere TV of Puerto Rico Inc. [United Hemisphere Productions Inc. 100% (principals include Harry W. Bank, Sidney Pink & Art Merrill)]. Former owner: Iris Mieres Ayuso. Sale price: $200,000 for CP (including CPs for WUHM-TV Mayaguez & WUHP-TV Ponce, both PR). FCC approved: June 29, 1970 [For the Record, July 13, 1970]. Former call letters: WUHT-TV, WUHM-TV, & WUHP-TV were WITA-TV, WITB-TV, & WITP-TV, respectively.

Virgin Islands

WBNB-TV Charlotte Amalie (ch 10)—Licensed to Benedek Broadcasting Inc., (see Group Ownership). Former owner: Worrell Broadcasting Inc., (owned by Worrell Newspapers Inc.). (For details of this sale, see WIFR(TV) Freeport, IL.) FCC approved: November 5, 1986 [For the Record, September 29, 1986]. Previous owner: Island Teleradio Service Inc. (owned by District Communications [Theodore Ledbetter Jr. (9%), Cleveland L. Dennard (21.2%), Jeanus B. Parks Jr. (18.2%), Samuel C. Jackson (15.2%)]}. Sale price: $750,000. FCC approved: June 6, 1980 [Changing Hands, June 14, 1980]. Previous owner: Island Teleradio Service Inc. (owned by Federated Media Inc.). Sale price: $991,127. FCC approved: September 6, 1974 [For the Record, September 30, 1974]. Note: Began operation in 1961. Original owners Robert Moss, Robert Noble, Faye Russell & Kenneth Granger sold stn to Television Communications Corp. in 1970 for $750,100 [*Broadcasting*, May 11, 1970]. When Television Communications Corp. sold its cable TV business to Warner Communications Inc. in 1972, individual stockholders of Television Communications Corp. (formed into a company known as Federated Media Inc.) acquired WBNB-TV [*Broadcasting*, February 7, 1972].

WSVI-TV Christiansted (ch 8)—Licensed to Group III Broadcasting Inc. (owned by Commonwealth Corp.). Former owner: Antilles Broadcasting Corp. (Baraket Saleh, et al). Sale price: $4 million. FCC approved: December 22, 1986 [For the Record, November 24, 1986]. Previous owner: Peoples Broadcasting Corp. Sale price: $375,885. FCC approved: 1977. Previous owner: Quality Telecasting Corp. Sale price: $650,000. FCC approved: 1973.

WWCW(TV) Christiansted (ch 15, deleted)—Licensed to Cabarrus Television Corp. Former owner: W.C. White. Sale price: $40,000 for CP [For the Record, October 28, 1985].

1993 Station Sales

The following are 1993 radio and television station sales with transactions of $1 million and above. All transaction information is listed as reported in *Broadcasting & Cable* magazine's "Changing Hands" column and is current to December 1993. For more detail on television sales, see *Television Ownership Transfers* in this section.

Price: $335 million
Properties: KDFW-TV Dallas and KTBC-TV, Austin, Tex.
Seller: Times Mirror Co.
Buyer: Argyle Communications

Price: $204 million
Property: WHDH-TV, Boston
Seller: New England Television Corp.
Buyer: Sunbeam Television Corp.

Price: $165 million
Properties: KCCI-TV Des Moines, Iowa, and WESH(TV), Daytona Beach, Fla.
Seller: H & C Communications Inc.
Buyer: Pulitzer Broadcasting Co.

Price: $163 million
Property: WTVT(TV), Tampa, Fla.
Seller: GHTV Inc., subsidiary of Gillett Holdings Inc.
Buyer: SCI Television Inc.

Price: $110 million
Properties: KOLD-TV, Tucson, Ariz; WSAV-TV, Savannah, Ga.; WECT-TV, Wilmington, N.C.; WJTV-TV, Jackson, and WHLT-TV, Hattiesburg, both Miss.; KSFY-TV, Sioux Falls, satellites KPRY-TV, Pierre, and KABY-TV, Aberdeen, all S.D.
Seller: News Press and Gazette Co.
Buyer: New Vision Communications Inc.

Price: $105 million
Property: WKBD-TV, Detroit
Seller: Cox Enterprises Inc.
Buyer: Paramount Stations Group Inc.

Price: $60-80 million
Property: WATL(TV), Atlanta
Seller: Renaissance Communications
Buyer: Fox Broadcasting

Price: $65 million
Property: WMC-FM-TV, Memphis, Tenn.
Seller: Scripps Howard Broadcasting Co.
Buyer: Elcom of Memphis Inc.

Price: $60 million
Properties: WCGV-TV, Milwaukee, and WTTO-TV, Birmingham, Ala.
Seller: ABRY Communications
Buyer: Sinclair Broadcast Group Inc. (Edwin L. Edwards)

Price: $57 million
Property: WGMS-TV, Philadelphia
Seller: Combined Broadcasting Inc.
Buyer: FTS Philadelphia Inc.

Price: $50 million
Property: WYNY(FM), Lake Success, N.Y.
Seller: Westwood One Stations Group Inc.
Buyer: Broadcasting Partners Inc.

Price: $49 million
Properties: KTRH(AM)-KLOH(FM), Houston
Seller: Rusk Corp.
Buyer: KTRH License Corp., subsidiary of Evergreen Media

Price: $48 million
Property: KFBK(AM) and KGBY-FM, Sacramento, Calif.
Seller: Group W Radio Inc.
Buyer: Chancellor Communications Corp.

Price: $40 million
Property: KQLZ-FM, Los Angeles
Seller: Westwood One Inc.
Buyer: Viacom International

Price: $38.05 million
Property: WKYT-TV, Lexington, Ky., and WYMT-TV, Hazard, Ky.
Seller: Kentucky Central Television Co. (Don W. Stephens, rehabilitator of the licensee)
Buyer: Gray Communications Systems Inc. (John T. Williams)

Price: $37.395 million
Property: WVTV-TV, Milwaukee
Seller: WVTV Inc. (Abry Communications)
Buyer: WVTV Licensee Inc. (Edwin L. Edwards)

Price: $36 million
Property: KITN-TV, Minneapolis
Seller: Nationwide Communications
Buyer: Clear Channel Communications

Price: $34 million
Property: WKYT-TV, Lexington, Ky., and WYMT-TV, Hazard, Ky.
Seller: Don W. Stephens, rehabilitator for Kentucky Central Life Insurance Co.
Buyer: Gray Communications Systems Inc.

Price: $32 million
Properties: WTVH(TV), Syracuse, N.Y., and KSEE-TV, Fresno, Calif.
Seller: Meredith Corp.
Buyer: Granite Broadcasting Corp.

Price: $28 million
Property: WWBZ-FM, Chicago
Seller: Major Broadcasting of Chicago Inc.
Buyer: WWBZ License Corp.

Price: $25.65 million
Properties: WHYN-AM-FM, Springfield, Mass. and WWBB(FM), Providence, R.I.
Seller: Wilks-Schwartz Broadcasting
Buyer: Radio Equity Partners Ltd.

Price: $25 million
Property: WXXA-TV, Albany, N.Y.
Seller: Heritage Broadcasting Co. of New York
Buyer: McKee Communications

Price: $22 million
Properties: KFRC-AM-FM, San Francisco, Calif.
Seller: Subsidiary of Bedford Broadcasting
Buyer: Alliance Broadcasting

Property: KRBK-TV, Sacramento, Calif.
Seller: Koplar Communications of California Inc. (Edward J. Koplar)
Buyer: Pappas Telecasting of Sacramento (Harry J. Pappas)

Property: WJMN-FM, Boston
Seller: Ardman Broadcasting Corp. (Myer Feldman)
Buyer: Pyramid Broadcasting (Rich Balsaugh)

Price: $21 million
Property: WDBD(TV), Jackson, Miss.
Seller: D&K Broadcast Properties Ltd.
Buyer: Pegasus Broadcast Television Ltd.

Property: KALB-TV, Alexandria, La.
Seller: Lanford Telecasting Company Inc.
Buyer: Park Broadcasting of Louisiana Inc.

Price: $19.64 million
Property: WFYV-FM, Atlantic Beach, Fla., and WAPE-FM, Jacksonville, Fla.
Seller: Evergreen Media Corp. (Scott K. Ginsburg)
Buyer: Hirsch Holdings of Cleveland Inc. (Carl E. Hirsch)

Price: $19.5 million
Property: WJZE(FM), Washington
Seller: United Broadcasting Co.
Buyer: Colfax Communications

Price: $19 million
Property: WYAY(FM), Gainesville, Ga.
Seller: NewCity Communications
Buyer: Capital Cities/ABC

Price: $18.5 million
Property: WSSH-FM, Lowell, Mass.
Seller: Noble Broadcast Group
Buyer: Granum Communications Inc.

Price: $18 million
Properties: WNUA-FM, Chicago; WXKS(AM), Everett, Mass., and WXKS-FM, Medford, Mass.; WYXR-FM, Philadelphia; WPXY-AM-FM, Rochester, N.Y., and WHTT-AM-FM, Buffalo, N.Y.; WRFX-FM, Kannapolis, N.C.
Seller: KISS L.P. (Richard M. Balsbaugh)
Buyer: Vestar Equity Partners L.P. (Dan O'Connell and John Howard)

Price: $16 million
Property: KRXQ-FM, Sacramento, Calif.
Seller: Fuller-Jeffrey Broadcasting Co. (Robert F. "Doc" Fuller)
Buyer: Great American Communications Corp. (David Crowl)

Price: $15.625 million
Property: WHFS(FM), Annapolis, Md.
Seller: Duchossois Communications
Buyer: Liberty Broadcasting

Price: $15.5 million
Property: WCSC-TV, Charleston, S.C.
Seller: General Electric Capital Corp.
Buyer: Jefferson-Pilot Communications Co.

Price: $15 million
Property: WKCH-TV, Knoxville, Tenn.
Seller: FCVS Communications
Buyer: Elcom of Tennessee Inc.

Properties: WACH-TV, Columbia, S.C., and WEVU (TV), Naples, Fla.
Seller: FCVS Communications
Buyer: Elcom of South Carolina Inc.

Property: WCOL-AM-FM, Columbus, Ohio
Seller: Great Trails Broadcasting
Buyer: Nationwide Communications Inc.

Price: $14.2 million
Property: KKHI-AM-FM, San Francisco
Seller: Buckley Broadcasting Corp. (Richard Buckley)
Buyer: Group W Radio (Don Mason)

Price: $14 million
Properties: KFOX(FM), Redondo Beach, Calif. and KRZE-FM, Ontario, Calif.
Seller: Torrance Media Partners (KFOX) and Boulder Ridge Cable TV (KRZE-FM)
Buyer: Chagal Communications

Price: $13.5 million
Property: KSOL-FM, San Mateo (San Francisco), Calif.
Seller: Intercontinental Radio Inc.
Buyer: KSOL L.P.

Price: $13.25 million
Property: KVOA-TV, Tucson, Ariz.
Seller: H&C Communications Inc.
Buyer: KVOA Communications

Price: $13 million
Property: KKLQ-AM-FM, San Diego
Seller: Edens Broadcasting
Buyer: Par Broadcasting

Properties: WCOS-AM-FM, Columbia, S.C., and WHKZ(FM), Cayce, S.C.
Seller: U.S. Radio Ltd. and Universal Communications Corp.
Buyer: Benchmark Communications

Property: KDFC-AM-FM, San Francisco
Seller: Sundial Broadcasting Corp.
Buyer: Brown Organization

1993 Station Sales

Property: KNCI-FM, Sacramento, Calif.
Seller: Nationwide Communications
Buyer: EZ Communications

Price: $12.5 million
Property: WOLF-TV, Scranton, Pa.
Seller: Scranton TV Partners Ltd.
Buyer: Pegasus Broadcast Television

Price: $12.3 million
Property: WCTI(TV), New Bern, N.C.
Seller: Diversified Communications
Buyer: Lamco Communications

Price: $12.1 million
Properties: KBLA(AM), Santa Monica, Calif., and KNAC(FM), Long Beach, Calif.
Seller: Fred C. Sands
Buyer: Keymarket Communications

Price: $12 million
Property: KVI(AM)-KPLZ(FM), Seattle
Seller: Golden West Broadcasters
Buyer: Fisher Broadcasting

Property: KSNN-FM, Arlington, Tex.
Seller: KODZ License Corp.
Buyer: Armadillo Broadcasting L.P.

Property: KXRX-FM, Seattle
Seller: Shamrock Broadcasting Inc. (Bill Clark)
Buyer: Alliance Broadcasting Co. (John Hayes)

Price: $11.5 million
Property: WRIF-FM, Detroit
Seller: Great American Television and Radio Co. Inc. (David Crowl)
Buyer: Greater Media Inc. (Peter Bordes)

Price: $11 million
Property: KZVE(AM)-KXTN(FM), San Antonio
Seller: TK Communications
Buyer: Tichenor Media System

Properties: KONJ(AM)-KXTN(FM), San Antonio
Seller: TK Communications
Buyer: Tichenor Media System Inc.

Property: KSNN-FM, Dallas
Seller: Evergreen Media Corp.
Buyer: Alliance Broadcasting Co.

Property: KOCB(TV), Oklahoma City
Seller: Oklahoma City Broadcasting Co.
Buyer: Superior Broadcasting Inc.

Property: WCKT(FM), Fort Myers, Fla.
Seller: Sandab Communications of Fort Myers Ltd. (Stephen Seymour)
Buyer: Radio Equity Partners (George Sosson)

Price: $10 million
Property: WCOS-AM-FM, Columbia, S.C.
Seller: US Radio L.P.
Buyer: Benchmark Radio Acquisition Fund V L.P.

Property: WNUV-TV, Baltimore
Seller: WNUV TV-54 L.P., subsidiary of Abry Communications
Buyer: WNUV Licensee Inc. (Edwin L. Edwards)

Property: KVI(AM)-KPLZ-FM, Seattle
Seller: KPLZ Inc.
Buyer: Fisher Broadcasting Inc.

Price: $9.75 million
Properties: WRNL(AM)-WRXL(FM), Richmond, Va.
Seller: Capitol Broadcasting
Buyer: Clear Channel Communications

Price: $9.375 million
Property: WZZO-FM, Bethlehem, Pa.
Seller: Holt Media Group
Buyer: CRB Broadcasting of Pennsylvania

Price: $9.3 million
Property: WAKR(AM) and WONE-FM, Akron, Ohio
Seller: US Radio L.P. (Ragan A. Henry)
Buyer: Gordon-Thomas Communications Inc.

Price: $9.25 million
Property: WHP-TV, Harrisburg, Pa.
Seller: WHP Inc.
Buyer: WHP Television Ltd.

Price: $9 million
Property: WERQ-AM-FM, Baltimore
Seller: United Broadcasting Co./The Eaton Estate
Buyer: Radio One Inc.

Price: $8.5 million
Property: KTVQ-TV, Billings, Mont.
Seller: SJL of Montana Associates L.P. (George D. Lilly)
Buyer: KTVQ Communications Inc. (Peter Manigault)

Price: $8.4 million
Property: WCKN(AM)-WRZX(FM), Indianapolis
Seller: Win Communications Inc. of Indiana
Buyer: Broadcast Alchemy Ltd.

Price: $8.2 million
Property: KMST-TV, Monterey, Calif.
Seller: Retlaw Broadcasting Co.
Buyer: Harron Television Corp.

Price: $8 million
Property: WYAI-FM, La Grange, Ga.
Seller: NewCity Communications of Massachusetts Inc.
Buyer: WSB Inc.

Properties: WKSJ(AM), Prichard, Ala., and WKSJ-FM, Mobile, Ala.
Seller: Franklin Communications Partners L.P. (Morton I. Hamburg)
Buyer: WAVH-FM Inc. (Carl T. Robinson)

Price: $7.5 million
Property: KSSK-AM-FM, Honolulu
Seller: Coast Broadcasting Co.
Buyer: NewTex Communications

Property: KEBC-FM, Oklahoma City
Seller: Independence Broadcasting Co. (John Goodwill)
Buyer: Clear Channel Communications Inc.

Property: WRVF-FM, Upper Arlington, Ohio
Seller: Tri-City Radio L.P. (Alan Gray)
Buyer: Hirsch Holdings of Cleveland Inc. (Carl E. Hirsch)

Price: $7.1 million
Property: WAJC(FM), Indianapolis
Seller: Butler University
Buyer: Susquehanna Radio Corp.

Price: $7 million
Properties: KASP(AM), St. Louis, and WKBQ-FM, Granite City, Ill.
Seller: WKBQ License Corp. (Evergreen Media, Scott K. Ginsburg)
Buyer: Zimcor Inc. (Jerome R. Zimmer)

Property: WLZR-AM-FM, Milwaukee
Seller: Great American Television and Radio Co. Inc. (David H. Crowl)
Buyer: Saga Communications Inc. (Edward K. Christian)

Price: $6.5 million
Property: WDCG-FM, Durham, N.C.
Seller: Durham Herald Co. (James G. Alexander)
Buyer: Prism Radio Partners L.P. (William Phalan)

Price: $6.375 million
Properties: WWKY(AM)-WVEZ(FM), Louisville, Ky.
Seller: Wilks-Schwartz Southwest Broadcasting Inc.
Buyer: Prism Radio Partners Ltd.

Price: $6.3 million
Property: WAPI-AM-FM, Birmingham, Ala.
Seller: WAPI Inc., debtor-in-possession (Bernard S. Dittman)
Buyer: Dick Broadcasting Co.

Price: $6 million
Property: WPRO-AM-FM, Providence, R.I.
Seller: Capital Cities-ABC Inc.
Buyer: Tele-Media Broadcasting Co. of America

Property: WEZC(FM), Hickory, N.C.
Seller: Keymarket of Charlotte Inc.
Buyer: Trumper Communications of North Carolina Ltd.

Properties: KHOP(FM), Modesto, Calf. and KHOV(FM), Mariposa, Calf.
Seller: Fuller-Jeffrey Broadcasting Companies Inc.
Buyer: Citadel Communications Corp.

Property: WAKC-TV, Akron, Ohio
Seller: Group One Broadcasting L.P. (Roger Berk)
Buyer: ValueVision International Inc. (Robert Johander)

Property: WRMX-FM, Murfreesboro, Tenn.
Seller: Shores Broadcasting Co. and Nashville Partners L.P. (Richard E. Oppenheimer)
Buyer: South Central Communications Corp. (John D. Engelbrecht)

Price: $5.7 million
Property: WSYW(AM), Indianapolis, WSYW-FM, Danville, Ind., and WCBW-FM, Columbia, Ind.
Seller: Howard Warshaw and Miriam Warshaw (Continental Broadcast Group Inc.)
Buyer: Marvin B. Kosofsky

Price: $5.6 million
Property: WEZW-FM, Wauwatosa, Wis.
Seller: Multimedia Radio Inc. (Pat A. Servodidio)
Buyer: Heritage-Wisconsin Broadcasting Corp. (Paul W. Fiddick)

Price: $5.5 million
Property: WRRK(FM), Pittsburgh
Seller: WHYW Associates
Buyer: Saul Frischling

Property: WJPR(TV), Lynchburg, Va.
Seller: Roanoke-Lynchburg TV Acquisition Corp.
Buyer: Grant Broadcasting System II Inc.

Property: WFDF(AM)-WDZZ(FM), Flint, Mich.
Seller: McVay Broadcasting (Mike McVay)
Buyer: Connoisseur Communications Corp.

Price: $5.405 million
Properties: KONO(AM), San Antonio, and KONO-FM, Fredericksburg, Tex.
Seller: Genesis Broadcasting Inc. (Ralph H. Booth II)
Buyer: October Communications Group Inc. (John W. Barger)

Price: $5.4 million
Property: WTKK-TV, Manassas, Va.
Seller: National Capital Christian Broadcasting Inc.
Buyer: VVI Manassas Inc. (Robert L. Johander)

Price: $5.1 million
Property: WGY-AM-FM, Schenectady, N.Y.
Seller: Empire Radio Partners Ltd., debtor-in-possession
Buyer: Dame Media Consultants Inc.

Price: $5 million
Property: WROW-AM-FM, Albany, N.Y.
Seller: Radio Terrace of Albany Inc.
Buyer: Albany Broadcasting Co. Inc.

Property: WTXL-TV, Tallahassee, Fla.
Seller: ET Broadcasting Inc.
Buyer: Media Venture Management Inc.

Property: WHB(AM)-KUDL(FM), Kansas City, Mo.
Seller: Shamrock Broadcasting Inc.
Buyer: Apollo Radio of Kansas City Inc.

Property: WQKB-FM, New Kensington, Pa.
Seller: Signature Broadcasting
Buyer: EZ Communications

Property: KHIH-FM, Boulder, Colo.
Seller: CLG Media of Denver Inc.
Buyer: Salem Media of Colorado Inc.

Properties: WRXR-FM, Aiken, S.C., and CP for WKBG-FM, Martinez, Ga.
Seller: J&L Broadcasting Inc. (Jeff Wilks)
Buyer: Multi-Market Radio of Augusta Inc. (Michael G. Ferrel)

Property: WWKB(AM) and WKSE-FM, Buffalo, N.Y.
Seller: Price Communications Corp. (Robert Price)
Buyer: Keymarket Communications (Kerby Confer)

Price: $4.875 million
Property: KRLR-TV, Las Vegas (Frank E. Scott)
Seller: DRES Media Inc.
Buyer: Las Vegas Channel 21 Inc. (Michael J. Lambert)

Price: $4.75 million
Property: WEZY(FM), Lakeland, Fla.
Seller: Chapman S. Root Living Trust
Buyer: Paxson Enterprises

Price: $4.6 million
Property: WMFX-FM, St. Andrews, S.C.
Seller: BTMI Inc.
Buyer: Clyde G. Haehnle & Co., trustee for ORR 1 Inc.

1993 Station Sales

Price: $4.5 million
Property: WTAR(AM)-WLTY(FM), Norfolk, Va.
Seller: Landmark Communications Inc.
Buyer: Benchmark Communications

Property: WWMG(FM), Charlotte, N.C.
Seller: Voyager Communications Group
Buyer: The Dalton Group

Price: $4,429,510
Properties: WGTQ-TV Sault Ste. Marie, Mich. and WGTU-TV, Traverse City, Mich.
Seller: Scanlan Communications
Buyer: Scanlan Communications Inc.

Price: $4.4 million
Property: WDLP-TV, Miami, Fla.
Seller: New Miami Latino Broadcasting Corp. (William De La Pena)
Buyer: Christian Network Inc. (Jim West)

Price: $4.375 million
Property: WKFT-TV, Fayetteville, N.C.
Seller: Delta Broadcasting Inc. (Elbert M. Boyd Jr., T.Y. Baker, Jerry Boyd and Jim Regalia)
Buyer: Allied Communications Co. (Robert P. Holding III)

Price: $4.3 million
Property: WKLX(FM), Rochester, N.Y.
Seller: WKLX Inc.
Buyer: Heritage Media

Price: $4.25 million
Property: WPYR(FM), Memphis
Seller: Diamond Broadcasting
Buyer: Barnstable Broadcasting

Price: $4.2 million
Property: KYKZ-FM, Lake Charles, La.
Seller: Southwest TV and Radio Inc. (G. Russell Chambers)
Buyer: Louisiana Media Interests Inc. (John M. Borders)

Price: $4.1 million
Property: KDRV(TV), Medford, Ore.
Seller: Sunshine Television Inc.
Buyer: Soda Mountain Broadcasting Inc.

Price: $4.068 million
Properties: KYKS(FM), Lufkin, Tex., and KIXS(FM), Victoria, Tex.
Seller: Osburn-Reynolds Group
Buyer: Gulfstar Communications Inc.

Price: $4 million
Property: WRMM-AM-FM, Rochester, N.Y.
Seller: Atlantic Radio of New York Ltd.
Buyer: Stoner Broadcasting System Inc.

Property: WVKS(FM), Toledo, Ohio
Seller: Noble Broadcasting
Buyer: Keymarket Communications

Property: WSPD(AM)-WLQR(FM), Toledo, Ohio
Seller: Commonwealth Communications
Buyer: Keymarket Communications

Property: WAFX-FM, Norfolk, Va.
Seller: Radio Ventures I L.P.
Buyer: Saga Communications Inc.

Property: WBUF-FM, Buffalo, N.Y.
Seller: Lincoln Group Ltd. (Albert "Bud" Werheimer)
Buyer: Pyramid Broadcasting (Richard Balsbaugh)

Property: WAQS(AM) and WAQQ-FM, Charlotte, N.C.
Seller: Adams Radio of Charlotte Inc. (Lee W. Shubert, receiver)
Buyer: Pyramid East Corp. (Richard M. Balsbough)

Price: $3.95 million
Property: KLUP(AM)-KISS(FM), San Antonio
Seller: Lawrence S. Wexler, receiver for Radio Group of San Antonio Inc.
Buyer: KISS Radio of San Antonio Ltd.

Price: $3.9 million
Properties: KOWL(AM)-KRLT(FM), South Lake Tahoe, Calif.; KAAA(AM)- KZZZ(FM), Kingman, Ariz.; KZGL(FM), Cottonwood, Ariz.
Seller: Regency Communications
Buyer: The Park Lane Group

Price: $3.8 million
Property: KSRR-FM, San Antonio
Seller: Genesis Broadcasting Inc.
Buyer: Tichenor Media System Inc.

Property: WQTV(TV), Boston
Seller: Monitor Television Inc.
Buyer: Boston University

Price: $3,798,814
Property: KKRD(FM), Wichita, Kan.
Seller: KKRD Inc.
Buyer: New West Radio Inc.

Price: $3.75 million
Property: WKFM(FM), Syracuse, N.Y.
Seller: Wilks-Schwartz Broadcasting
Buyer: New-City Communications Inc.

Property: WICD-TV, Champaign, Ill.
Seller: Plains Television Partnership (Elenore Balaban)
Buyer: Guy Gannett Publishing Co. (Jean G. Hawley)

Price: $3.6 million
Property: WNVZ(FM), Norfolk, Va.
Seller: Wilks-Schwartz Broadcasting
Buyer: Max Radio Inc.

Price: $3,500,288
Property: KUKQ(AM)-KUPD(FM), Tempe, Ariz.
Seller: G&C Broadcasting Inc.
Buyer: Robert Fish

Price: $3.5 million
Property: KHFI-FM, Georgetown, Tex.
Seller: Rusk L.P.
Buyer: Clear Channel Communications

Properties: WGLD(AM), Greensboro, N.C., and WWWB(FM), High Point, N.C.
Seller: WGLD Inc.
Buyer: MHD Corp.

Properties: WHET(FM), Sturgeon Bay, Wis., and WOZZ(FM), New London, Wis.
Seller: Martin Communications
Buyer: Midwest Communications

Property: WJIM-AM-FM, Lansing, Mich.
Seller: Double L Broadcasting of Lansing Ltd.
Buyer: Liggett Broadcast Inc.

Property: KFIZ(AM)-WFON(FM), Fond du Lac, Wis.
Seller: Independence Broadcasting Wisconsin Corp.
Buyer: Lakeside Cablevision L.P.

Properties: WJQI(AM), Chesapeake, Va., and WJQI-FM, Virginia Beach, Va.
Seller: Radio WJQI Inc. (Aylett Coleman)
Buyer: Sunshine Wireless Company Inc. (Dan Cohen)

Property: KOQL-FM, Oklahoma City
Seller: Entercom (Joseph M. Field)
Buyer: NewMarket Media Corp. (Stephen Robertson and Pete Schulte)

Price: $3.4 million
Property: WZZU-FM, Burlington, N.C.
Seller: Villcom Broadcasting Inc.
Buyer: Prism Radio Partners L.P.

Price: $3.35 million
Property: KQLD-FM, New Orlean, La.
Seller: Beasley Broadcast Group
Buyer: New-Market Media Corp.

Price: $3.2 million
Properties: WSDR(AM)-WSSQ-FM, Sterling, Ill., and WZZT-FM, Morrison, Ill.
Seller: Sterling Radio Stations Inc.
Buyer: LH&S Communications Inc.

Property: WJMH-FM, Reidsville, N.C.
Seller: Beasley Broadcasting of Reidsville Inc. (George G. Beasley)
Buyer: Max Radio of The Triad Inc. (Larry Saunders)

Price: $3.1 million
Property: KRYS-AM-FM, Corpus Christi, Tex.
Seller: Corpus Christi Media Partners Ltd.
Buyer: Ranger Communications Co.

Price: $3 million
Property: WGBI-AM-FM, Scranton, Pa.
Seller: Megargee Co.
Buyer: Lackazerne Inc.

Property: KJRB(AM)-KEZE-FM, Spokane, Wash.
Seller: Apollo Radio Ltd.
Buyer: Citadel Communications Corp.

Property: KCAL(AM), Redlands, Calif.
Seller: Sarape Communications Inc.
Buyer: Redlands Radio Inc.

Property: WCKZ-FM, Gastonia, N.C.
Seller: Compass Media Group Inc.
Buyer: BPI Charlotte License Subsidiary Inc.

Properties: WGLD(AM), Greensboro, N.C., and WWWB-FM, High Point, N.C.
Seller: MHD Inc.
Buyer: Franklin Communications Partners L.P.

Property: WOKC-FM, Okeechobee, Fla.
Seller: Okeechobee Broadcasters Inc.
Buyer: Amaturo Group Ltd.

Property: WOKC(AM), Okeechobee, Fla.
Seller: Okeechobee Broadcasters Inc.
Buyer: Amaturo Group Ltd.

Property: KAAM(AM), Dallas
Seller: Bonneville International Corp. (Rodney Brady)
Buyer: Cardinal Communications Partners L.P. (Spence Kendrick)

Property: WEMT-TV, Greeneville, Tenn.
Seller: Chesapeake Bay Holding Co. (for Television Marketing Group of Tri-Cities Inc., Richard Davis)
Buyer: Max Encore of Tri-Cities L.P. (John Trinder)

Price: $2.925 million
Properties: KJOC(AM), Davenport, Iowa, and WXLP-FM, Moline, Ill.
Seller: Goodrich Broadcasting Inc. (Robert E. Goodrich)
Buyer: Connoisseur Communications Corp. (Jeffrey D. Warshaw)

Price: $2.825 million
Property: WGCB-AM-FM, Red Lion, Pa.
Seller: Red Lion Broadcasting Co. Inc.
Buyer: Thomas Harvey Moffit Sr.

Price: $2.78 million
Property: KXFX(FM), Santa Rosa, Calif.
Seller: Keffco Inc.
Buyer: Fuller-Jeffrey Broadcasting Corp.

Price: $2.75 million
Property: KATZ-AM-FM, St. Louis
Seller: Inter Urban Broadcasting of St. Louis Inc.
Buyer: Noble Broadcast of St. Louis Inc.

Price: $2.7 million
Property: KIOA-AM-FM, Des Moines, Iowa
Seller: Midwest Communications
Buyer: Saga Communications

Property: WOMI(AM)-WBKR(FM), Owensboro, Ky.
Seller: Owensboro Broadcasting Co.
Buyer: Tri-State Broadcasting

Property: WWFE(AM), Miami, Fla.
Seller: Jeanette E. Tavormina, Chapter 11 trustee for Todamerica Inc.
Buyer: Fenix Broadcasting Corp.

Property: WHKZ-FM, Cayce, S.C.
Seller: Universal Communications Corp.
Buyer: Benchmark Radio Acquisition Fund V L.P.

Property: KSET-FM, El Paso, Tex.
Seller: Dunn Broadcasting Inc.
Buyer: Magic Media Inc.

Price: $2,677,074
Property: WTCX-FM, Lakeville, Minn.
Seller: Southern Twin Cities Area Radio Inc. (J. Thomas Lijewski)
Buyer: 105 Inc. (James R. Cargill II)

Price: $2.625 million
Property: KMXI(FM), Lake Oswego, Ore.
Seller: Rogue Broadcasting Corp.
Buyer: BayCom Oregon Ltd.

Price: $2.6 million
Property: WKOC(FM), Elizabeth City, N.C.
Seller: Edge Broadcasting Co.
Buyer: Benchmark Radio Acquisition Fund IV Ltd.

Property: WBBO-FM, Forest City, N.C.
Seller: Rutherford County Radio Co. (Stella Trapp)
Buyer: AmCom Associates Inc. (George R. Francis Jr.)

1993 Station Sales

Price: $2.5 million
Property: WODL(FM), Birmingham, Ala.
Seller: Charles E. Giddens
Buyer: Birmingham Communications Inc.

Property: KMXX(FM), Killen, Tex.
Seller: Genesis Broadcasting Inc.
Buyer: The KLBJ Co.

Property: WTZA(TV), Kingston, N.Y.
Seller: WTZA-TV Associates
Buyer: WTZA-TV Associates Ltd.

Property: WMQX-AM-FM, Winston-Salem, N.C.
Seller: EBE Communications L.P.
Buyer: Max Radio of Greensboro Inc.

Properties: KIIZ-FM, Killeen, Tex., and KLFX(FM), Harker Heights, Tex.
Seller: Conner Communications and Mid-Texas Communications
Buyer: Sonance Killeen

Property: WHVK-FM, Tullahoma, Tenn.
Seller: Fortune Media Communications Inc.
Buyer: Tennessee Valley Radio Inc.

Property: KQBR-FM, Davis, Calif.
Seller: EZ Communications (Alan Box)
Buyer: Progressive Media Group Inc. (Ricky Tatum)

Price: $2.4 million
Property: WSLM-FM, Salem, Ind.
Seller: Don H. Martin
Buyer: Snowden Broadcasting of Louisville Inc.

Properties: WMMM-FM, Verona, Wis., and WYZM-FM, Waunakee, Wis.
Seller: Horizon Media Inc.
Buyer: Woodward Communications Inc.

Price: $2.35 million
Property: WNEU-FM, Eden, N.C.
Seller: WWMY-FM Broadcasting Inc. (SBM Industries Inc.)
Buyer: Voyager Communications V Inc. (Carl V. Venters Jr.)

Price: $2.3 million
Property: WIRL(AM) and WSWT-FM, Peoria, Ill.
Seller: Community Radio Inc.
Buyer: James D. Glassman

Price: $2.25 million
Property: KEYV(FM), Las Vegas
Seller: Unicom Broadcasting Inc.
Buyer: Broadcast Associates Inc.

Price: $2.23 million
Property: WCOA(AM)-WJLQ(FM), Pensacola, Fla.
Seller: BREM Broadcasting
Buyer: WKRG-TV Inc.

Price: $2.2 million
Property: KTGL(FM), Lincoln, Neb.
Seller: ERM Associates
Buyer: KTGL Corp.

Property: WKHI(FM), Ocean City, Md.
Seller: Baltimore Radio Show
Buyer: Benchmark Radio Acquisition Fund

Price: $2,153,788
Property: WJAC(AM)-WKYE-FM, Johnstown, Pa.
Seller: Winston Radio Corp.
Buyer: Michael F. Brosig

Price: $2.1 million
Property: WLQV(AM), Detroit
Seller: Detroit SRN Inc.
Buyer: Midwest Broadcasting Corp. Too

Price: $2.05 million
Properties: KHGI-TV, Kearney, Neb., KSNB-TV Superior, Neb., and KWNB-TV, Hays Center, Neb.
Seller: Girard Communications
Buyer: Fant Broadcasting

Price: $2 million
Property: WAVH(FM), Mobile, Ala.
Seller: Pourtales Holdings Inc.
Buyer: WESHAM Broadcasting Co.

Property: KQBR(FM), Davis, Calif.
Seller: KYLO Radio Inc.
Buyer: EZ Sacramento Inc.

Property: WGSN(AM)-WNMB(FM), North Myrtle Beach, S.C.
Seller: Ogden Broadcasting of South Carolina Inc.
Buyer: Ocean Drive Communications Inc.

Property: KKYK-FM, Little Rock, Ark.
Seller: Shepard Communications of Arkansas Inc.
Buyer: Signal Media of Arkansas Inc.

Property: WWAT-TV, Chillicothe, Ohio
Seller: Triplett and Associates (Marc S. Triplett)
Buyer: Fant Broadcasting Co. (Anthony J. Fant)

Property: WAQZ-FM, Cincinnati (Milford)
Seller: Plessinger Radio Group (Richard Plessinger)
Buyer: WAQZ Inc. (Charles Reynolds)

Property: WTWS-TV, New London, Conn.
Seller: R&R Media Corp.
Buyer: VVI New London Inc. (Robert L. Johander)

Price: $1.9 million
Property: WBRQ(FM), Cidra, P.R.
Seller: Radio Musical Inc.
Buyer: American National Broadcasting Corp.

Property: WXLT(FM), Baton Rouge
Seller: San-Dow Broadcasting
Buyer: Citywide Broadcasting

Properties: KYAK(AM)-KGOT(FM), Anchorage, and KIAK-AM-FM, Fairbanks, Alaska
Seller: Olympia Broadcasting
Buyer: Comco Broadcasting Inc.

Properties: WYRE(AM), Annapolis, Md., and WXZL(FM), Grasonville, Md.
Seller: Vision Broadcasting Co. Ltd. (Richard Winn)
Buyer: Sequel Broadcasting of Maryland Inc. (Jacob Einstein)

Price: $1,800,001
Property: WCEM(AM) and WCEM-FM, Cambridge, Md.
Seller: M. Belmont VerStandig Inc.
Buyer: MTS Broadcasting

Price: $1.8 million
Property: WAQZ-FM, Milford, Ohio
Seller: Richard L. Plessinger Sr.
Buyer: WAQZ Inc. (Charles Reynolds)

Price: $1.75 million
Property: KXOK-FM, St. Louis
Seller: WPNT Inc. (Saul Frischling)
Buyer: Crawford Broadcasting Co. (Don Crawford)

Price: $1.7 million
Property: KJUL(FM), North Las Vegas, Nev.
Seller: Carrigan Communications
Buyer: Eight Chiefs Inc.

Property: KTID-AM-FM, San Rafael, Calif.
Seller: Marin Broadcasting Co. (N. Arthur Astor)
Buyer: Mount Wilson FM Broadcasters Inc. (Saul Levine)

Property: KFMH-FM, Muscatine, Iowa
Seller: Flambo Broadcasting Inc. (John Flambo)
Buyer: Connoisseur Communications (Jeffrey D. Warshaw)

Price: $1.689 million
Property: WJTT-FM, Red Bank, Tenn.
Seller: Jettcom Inc. (James Brewer Sr., Jim Clemons and George Reed)
Buyer: Brewer Broadcasting of Chattanooga Inc. (James Brewer Sr., Vicki Brewer and James Brewer II)

Price: $1.65 million
Property: KTPK-FM, Topeka, Kan.
Seller: Topeka Broadcomm Inc. (Pierce McNally)
Buyer: Twenty First Century Broadcasting Inc. (Marvin H. Wilson)

Property: WYVN-TV, Martinsburg, W. Va.
Seller: Flying A Communications Inc. (Ralph D. Albertazzie)
Buyer: Green River Broadcasting of Martinsburg Inc. (William B. Ewing)

Property: KEEL(AM)-KITT-FM, Shreveport, La.
Seller: Multimedia Radio Inc. (Pat Servodidio)
Buyer: Progressive United Corp. (William R. Fry)

Price: $1.6 million
Properties: WCAW(AM)-WVAF(FM), Charleston, W. Va.
Seller: Franklin Communications Partners Ltd.
Buyer: West Virginia Radio Corp. of Charleston

Property: KAYI(FM), Muskogee, Okla.
Seller: Narragansett Radio Ltd.
Buyer: Renda Broadcasting Corp.

Property: WJRC(AM), Cincinnati
Seller: Great American Television and Radio Co. Inc.
Buyer: Jacor Broadcasting Corp.

Properties: WGLL-FM, Mercersburg, Pa., and WCBG(AM), Chambersburg, Pa.
Seller: Pennsylvania Radioroad Co.
Buyer: M. Belmont VerStandig Inc.

Property: KRZN(AM), Thornton, Colo.
Seller: Genesis Broadcasting Inc. (John L. Booth II)
Buyer: Jacor Broadcasting of Colorado Inc. (Randy Michaels)

Price: $1.5 million
Property: WLYV(AM)-WJLT(FM), Fort Wayne, Ind.
Seller: Fairfield Broadcasting Co.
Buyer: Sarkes Tarzian Inc.

Property: WYAM(FM), Hartselle, Ala.
Seller: Radio 106 Inc.
Buyer: Griffith Broadcasting Inc.

Property: KBLR(TV), Paradise, Nev.
Seller: Rose Communications
Buyer: Summit Media Limited-Liability Co.

Properties: WNOO(AM), Chattanooga, Tenn., and WFXS-FM, Soddy Daisy, Tenn.
Seller: Tennessee Communications L.P. (William H. Sanders)
Buyer: Pye Broadcasting Inc. (Lionel F. Pye Jr.)

Property: WZNS-FM, Dillon (Fayetteville, N.C.), S.C.
Seller: Metropolitan Broadcasters Associates (Steve Garchik)
Buyer: Beasley Broadcasting (George G. Beasley)

Price: $1.45 million
Properties: KIAK-AM-FM, Fairbanks, Alaska, and KYAK(AM)-KGOT(FM), Anchorage
Seller: KGOT Corp. and KQRZ Corp.
Buyer: Comco Broadcasting Inc.

Price: $1.44 million
Property: WVEM(FM) Springfield, Ill.
Seller: Dan Menghini
Buyer: Saga Communications of Illinois Inc.

Price: $1.4 million
Property: KNTA(AM), San Jose-Santa Clara, Calif.
Seller: Tamarack Communications Inc.
Buyer: Imperio Enterprises Inc.

Property: WADC(AM)-WHCM-FM, Parkersburg, W.Va.
Seller: Dailey Corp.
Buyer: Valley Communications Corp.

Property: WYGC-FM, Gainesville, Fla.
Seller: Gator Country Broadcasting Inc.
Buyer: Asterisk Communications Inc.

Price: $1.375 million
Property: WNSS(AM)-WEZG-FM, Syracuse, N.Y.
Seller: Syracuse Broadcasting Group
Buyer: The Radio Corp. (Ed Levine, Frank Toce, Robert Raide)

Price: $1.35 million
Property: KMND(AM)-KNFM(FM), Midland, Tex.
Seller: Dennis Elam, Chapter 11 trustee
Buyer: Midland-Odessa Broadcasting LC

Property: WJRX(FM), East Ridge, Tenn.
Seller: Sattler Broadcasting Inc.
Buyer: WDOD of Chattanooga Inc.

Property: KDMI-FM, Des Moines, Iowa
Seller: KDMI Inc.
Buyer: Stoner Broadcasting System Inc.

Property: WSYA-AM-FM, Montgomery, Ala.
Seller: U.S. Broadcasting L.P. (Douglas M. Grimm)
Buyer: Colonial Broadcasting Co. Inc. (David Coppock)

Price: $1,314,800
Property: WKAN(AM)-WLRT-FM, Kankakee, Ill.
Seller: Imagery Inc. (Suzanne S. Bergeron)
Buyer: STARadio Corp. (Jack Whitley, Howard Doss and Derek Parrish)

1993 Station Sales

Price: $1.3 million
Property: WIAI(FM), Danville, Ill.
Seller: Kickapoo Broadcasting Inc.
Buyer: I.A.I. Broadcasting

Property: KEZQ-FM, Little Rock, Ark.
Seller: Omni Communications
Buyer: GHB Broadcasting

Property: WJRX-FM, East Ridge, Tenn.
Seller: Sattler Broadcasting Inc.
Buyer: Radio Chattanooga Inc.

Property: KBFX-FM, Anchorage
Seller: TCT Communications Inc.
Buyer: Community Pacific Broadcasting Co. L.P.

Property: WMYA-FM, Cape Charles, Va.
Seller: WKSV Inc.
Buyer: Sinclair Communications

Price: $1.263 million
Property: KTZN(FM), Green Valley, Ariz.
Seller: Nova Communications Ltd.
Buyer: Arizona Lotus Corp.

Price: $1.226 million
Property: WYNU-FM, Milan, Tenn.
Seller: Andrew Jackson Broadcasting Corp., debtor-in-possession
Buyer: Ohio Broadcast Associates

Price: $1.25 million
Property: WAKB(FM), Wrens, Ga.
Seller: Advertisement Network Systems Inc.
Buyer: Davis Broadcasting

Property: WVIP-FM, Mount Kisco, N.Y.
Seller: VIP Broadcasting Corp.
Buyer: Impulse Broadcasting Corp.

Price: $1.21 million
Properties: WIOU(AM)-WZWZ(FM), Kokomo, Ind.
Seller: Caravelle Broadcast Group
Buyer: Mid-America Radio Group of Kokomo Inc.

Price: $1.2 million
Property: WKKW-FM, Clarksburg, W. Va.
Seller: Morton J. Victorson
Buyer: West Virginia Radio Corp.

Property: WOSO(AM), San Juan, P.R.
Seller: MCO Industries Inc.
Buyer: Sherman Broadcasting Corp.

Properties: WGUS(AM) North Augusta, S.C., and WGUS-FM, Augusta, Ga.
Seller: HVS Partners
Buyer: Benchmark Radio Acquisition Fund II L.P.

Property: KMXK-FM, Cold Spring-St. Cloud, Minn.
Seller: Gross Communications Corp.
Buyer: Andrew Hilger

Property: KRSP-FM, Salt Lake City
Seller: Holiday Broadcasting Co. (Ralph J. Carlson)
Buyer: KRSP Inc. (G. Craig Hanson)

Price: $1.175 million
Property: WMGR(AM)-WJAD(FM), Bainbridge, Ga.
Seller: Guardian Corp.
Buyer: Sabre Communications Inc.

Property: WHKX-FM, Lafayette (Tallahassee), Fla.
Seller: Marcus Communications
Buyer: Catamount Communications (Adam Levinson and David Parnigoni)

Price: $1.165 million
Property: WAIR(FM), Atlanta, Mich., and WTRV(FM), Leland, Mich.
Seller: W-Air Inc. and Grand Traverse Broadcasting Co.
Buyer: Northern Michigan Radio Inc.

Price: $1,156,872.12
Property: WKQB-FM Jackson, Miss.
Seller: WLIN Inc.
Buyer: Capstar Communications of Jackson Inc.

Price: $1.125 million
Property: KAKI(FM), Benton, Ark.
Seller: Bridges Broadcasting Service
Buyer: Southern Skies Corp.

Property: KONO(AM), San Antonio
Seller: Genesis Broadcasting Inc.
Buyer: Gillespie Broadcasting Co.

Price: $1.1 million
Properties: WANV(AM), Waynesboro, Va., and WANV-FM, Staunton, Va.
Seller: WANV Inc.
Buyer: WANV Ltd.

Property: KCTZ(TV), Bozeman, Mont.
Seller: Big Horn Communications Inc.
Buyer: KCTZ Communications Inc.

Property: WYNX(AM), Smyrna, Ga.
Seller: Hoffman Media Inc.
Buyer: GA-MEX Broadcasting Inc.

Property: WLOV-TV, West Point, Miss.
Seller: Love Communications Co.
Buyer: Lingard Broadcasting Corp.

Price: $1.06 million
Property: WVLR(FM), Lynchburg-Roanoke, Va.
Seller: L-R Radio Group Inc. (Robert Goyns)
Buyer: Virginia Network Inc. (Bruce Houston)

Price: $1.025 million
Property: WZNN(AM)-WWEM(FM), Rochester, N.H.
Seller: Bear Broadcasting Co. (Philip Urso)
Buyer: Precision Media Corp. (Timothy J.A. Montgomery)

Price: $1.003 million
Property: WCXL(FM), Kill Devil Hills, N.C.
Seller: Kill Devil Hills Communications Ltd.
Buyer: Ray-D-O Biz Inc.

Price: $1 million
Property: WBES-FM, Dunbar, W. Va.
Seller: Thomas Communications
Buyer: Ardman Broadcasting Corp. of West Virginia

Property: KRVR(FM), Davenport, Iowa
Seller: Community Radio Inc.
Buyer: K-River Broadcasting Inc.

Property: WGUS-AM-FM, Augusta, Ga.
Seller: HVS Partners
Buyer: Benchmark Communications

Property: KRZR(FM), Hanford-Fresno, Calif.
Seller: Louis C. DeArias, as receiver for KMGX Corp.
Buyer: NewTex Communications

Property: KBOQ-FM, Marina, Calif.
Seller: Model Associates Inc.
Buyer: Charlton Buckley

Property: WXBB(FM), Kittery, Me. (Portsmouth, N.H.)
Seller: Bear Broadcasting Co.
Buyer: Fuller-Jeffrey Broadcasting (Robert "Doc" Fuller)

Properties: WKPV-TV, Ponce, P.R., and WSJN-TV, San Juan, P.R.
Seller: Multi-Media Television Inc. (Franklin D. Lopez)
Buyer: Interstate General Properties (James J. Wilson)

40 Years of Station Transactions

Dollar volume of transactions approved by the FCC (Number of stations changing hands)

YEAR	RADIO ONLY	GROUPS*	TV ONLY	TOTAL
1954	$10,224,047 (187)	$26,213,323 (18)	$23,906,760 (27)	$60,344,130
1955	27,333,104 (242)	22,351,602 (11)	23,394,660 (29)	73,079,366
1956	32,563,378 (316)	65,212,055 (24)	17,830,395 (21)	115,605,828
1957	48,207,470 (357)	47,490,884 (28)	28,489,206 (38)	124,187,660
1958	49,868,123 (407)	60,872,618 (17)	16,796,285 (23)	127,537,026
1959	65,544,653 (436)	42,724,727 (15)	15,227,201 (21)	123,496,581
1960	51,763,285 (345)	24,648,400 (10)	22,930,225 (21)	99,341,910
1961	55,532,516 (282)	42,103,708 (13)	31,167,943 (24)	128,804,167
1962	59,912,520 (306)	18,822,745 (8)	23,007,638 (16)	101,742,903
1963	43,457,584 (305)	25,045,726 (3)	36,799,768 (16)	105,303,078
1964	52,296,480 (430)	67,185,762 (20)	86,274,494 (36)	205,756,736
1965	55,933,300 (389)	49,756,993 (15)	29,433,473 (32)	135,123,766
1966	76,633,762 (367)	28,510,500 (11)	30,574,054 (31)	135,718,316
1967	59,670,053 (316)	32,086,297 (9)	80,316,223 (30)	172,072,573
1968	71,310,709 (316)	47,556,634 (9)	33,588,069 (20)	152,455,412
1969	108,866,538 (343)	35,037,000 (5)	87,794,032 (32)	231,697,570
1970	86,292,899 (268)	1,038,465 (3)	87,454,078 (19)	174,785,442
1971	125,501,514 (270)	750,000 (2)	267,296,410 (27)	393,547,924
1972	114,424,673 (239)	0 (0)	156,905,864 (37)	271,330,537
1973	160,933,557 (352)	2,812,444 (4)	66,635,144 (25)	230,381,145
1974	168,998,012 (369)	19,800,000 (5)	118,983,462 (24)	307,781,474
1975	131,065,860 (363)	0 (0)	128,420,101 (22)	259,485,961
1976	180,663,820 (413)	1,800,000 (3)	108,459,657 (32)	290,923,477
1977	161,236,169 (344)	0 (0)	128,635,435 (25)	289,871,604
1978	331,557,239 (586)	30,450,000 (5)	289,721,159 (51)	651,728,398
1979	335,597,000 (546)	463,500,000 (52)	317,581,000 (47)	1,116,648,000
1980	339,634,000 (424)	27,000,000 (3)	534,150,000 (35)	876,084,000
1981	447,838,060 (625)	78,400,000 (6)	227,950,000 (24)	754,188,067
1982	470,722,833 (597)	0 (0)	527,675,411 (30)	998,398,244
1983	621,077,876 (669)	332,000,000 (10)	1,902,701,830 (61)	2,854,895,356
1984	977,024,266 (782)	234,500,000 (2)	1,252,023,787 (82)	2,118,056,053
1985	1,414,816,073 (1,558)	962,450,000 (218)	3,290,995,000 (99)	5,668,261,073
1986	1,490,131,426 (959)	1,993,021,955 (192)	2,709,516,490 (128)	6,192,669,871
1987	1,236,355,748 (775)	4,610,965,000 (132)	1,661,832,724 (59)	7,509,154,473
1988	1,841,630,156 (845)	1,326,250,000 (106)	1,779,958,042 (70)	4,947,838,198
1989	1,148,524,765 (663)	533,599,078 (40)	1,541,055,033 (84)	3,235,436,376
1990	868,636,700 (1,045)	411,037,150 (60)	696,952,350 (75)	1,976,626,100
1991	302,041,109 (547)	337,129,401 (212)	1,067,579,400 (83)	1,706,749,910
1992	684,863,272 (556)	375,569,895 (187)	1,441,205,936 (62)	2,501,639,103
1993	810,949,833 (615)	721,721,833 (213)	1,598,810,952 (94)	3,131,482,618
TOTAL	$15,319,634,379	$13,099,414,195	$22,490,029,441	$50,909,078,015

Note: Dollar volume figures represent total considerations reported for all transactions with exception of minority interest transfers in which control of stations did not change hands and stations sold as part of larger company transactions. Although all sales have been approved by the FCC, they may not necessarily have reached final closing. Prior to 1978, combined AM-FM facilities were counted as one station in computing total number of stations traded. Now AM-FM combinations are counted as two stations.

*Figures represent group deals involving combinations of radio and TV stations, multiple TV stations, or multiple radio stations. In 1985, mergers of large groups with collateral interests could not be evaluated, since individual stations were not broken out of larger sales.

Group Ownership

Listed here are individuals and companies with multiple station holdings. Included are all those controlling three or more radio stations and/or two or more television stations. FCC rules limit multiple ownership to 18 AM stations, 18 FM stations and 12 television stations, as long as the 12 TV stations don't reach more than 25% of the nation's television homes. UHFs are assessed for only half of a market's television homes. Group broadcasters may own up to 21 AM, 21 FM and 14 TV stations if three of the AM, three of the FM or two of the TV stations are controlled by minorities. Ownership of cable TV systems, as reported by these stations, is also listed. Unless otherwise noted, the first station listed is the group headquarters.

A

A&B Broadcasting Inc. Stns: 2 AM, 2 FM. KLMR(AM) & KSEC(FM) Lamar, Colo.; KFXX-FM Hugoton & KULY(AM) Ulysses, both Kan. Ownership: Lamar Food Stores Inc., 80%; Bill Arnold, 20%. Hqtrs: Box 890, Lamar, Colo. 81052. (719) 336-2206. FAX: (719) 336-7973.

ABRY Communications. Stns: 5 TV. WTTO(TV) Birmingham, Ala.; WNUV-TV Baltimore; KSMO-TV Kansas City, Mo.; WSTR-TV Cincinnati; & WCGV-TV Milwaukee. Ownership: A partnership. Hqtrs: 18 Newbury St., Boston 02116. (617) 859-2959. FAX: (617) 859-7205.

ABS Communications Inc. Stns: 1 AM, 4 FM. WRQN(AM) Bowling Green, Ohio; WROQ(AM) Anderson, S.C.; WKHK(FM) Colonial Heights & WSVS(AM)-WKIK(FM) Crewe, both Va. (All 100% owned.) Ownership: Kenneth A. Brown. Hqtrs: 4401 Waterfront Dr., Suite 110, Glen Allen, Va. 23060. (804) 270-9600.

AFLAC Broadcast Division. Stns: 7 TV. WAFF(TV) Huntsville, Ala.; WTVM(TV) Columbus & WTOC-TV Savannah, both Ga.; KWWL(TV) Waterloo, Iowa; WAFB(TV) Baton Rouge; KFVS-TV Cape Girardeau, Mo.; & WITN-TV Washington, N.C. Ownership: AFLAC Inc., 100%. Hqtrs: 1932 Wynnton Rd., Columbus, Ga. 31999. (706) 596-5053. FAX: (706) 596-5064.

Abilene Radio & TV Stations. Stns: 2 TV. KRBC-TV Abilene & KACB-TV San Angelo, both Tex. Ownership: Carol Cagle Trust, 33.34%. Hqtrs: 4510 S. 14th St., Abilene, Tex. 79605. (915) 692-4242. FAX: (915) 692-8265.

Ackerley Communications Inc. Stns: 1 AM, 1 FM, 5 TV. KGET(TV) Bakersfield & KCBA(TV) Salinas, both Calif.; KKTV(TV) Colorado Springs; WIXT(TV) Syracuse, N.Y.; KVOS-TV Bellingham & KJR(AM)-KLTX(FM) Seattle, both Wa. (All 100% owned.) Executives: William Ackerley, pres. Ownership: Barry Ackerley. Hqtrs: 800 5th Ave., Suite 3770, Seattle 98104. (206) 624-2888. FAX: (206) 623-7853.

Act III Broadcasting Inc. Stns: 8 TV. WUTV(TV) Buffalo & WUHF(TV) Rochester, both N.Y.; WNRW(TV) Winston-Salem, N.C.; WRGT-TV Dayton, Ohio; WTAT-TV Charleston, S.C.; WZTV(TV) Nashville; WRLH-TV Richmond, Va.; & WVAH-TV Charleston, W.Va. Executives: Richard Ballinger, pres; John F. DeLorenzo, exec VP. Ownership: Act III Communications Holdings L.P., Los Angeles, 35.53%; Prudential Insurance Co., 23.07%; General Motors Investment Management Corp., 10.46%; & T.C.W. Capital, 7.93%. Act III Communications Holdings L.P. owns 80.83% to elect directors. Act III Communications Holdings L.P. is owned 99% by Norman Lear & various wholly-owned S. corporations, & 1% by Act III Communications Holdings GP Inc., Los Angeles. (Note: S. corporation is a tax term.) Act III Communications Holdings GP Inc. is owned 100% by Norman Lear, Los Angeles. Hqtrs: 1999 Ave. of the Stars, 5th Fl., Los Angeles 90067. (310) 553-3636. FAX: (310) 553-3928.

Adventure Communications Inc. Stns: 4 AM, 5 FM. WSIC(AM) & WFMX(FM) Statesville, N.C.; WXVK(FM) Coal Grove, Ohio; WHHR(AM) & WFXH(FM) Hilton Head Island, S.C.; WHIS(AM)-WHAJ(FM) Bluefield & WKEE-AM-FM Huntington, both W.Va. (All 100% owned.) Ownership: Michael R. Shott. Hqtrs: 900 Bluefield Ave., Bluefield, W.Va. 24701. (304) 327-7114. FAX: (304) 325-7850.

Agpal Broadcasting Inc. Stns: 2 AM, 2 FM. KTIX(AM)-KWHT(FM) Pendleton & KZUS-AM-FM Toledo, both Ore. (All 100% owned.) Ownership: Andrew F. Harle, Cheryl L. Harle. Hqtrs: Box 456, Newport, Ore. 97365. (503) 265-5000. FAX: (503) 265-9576.

Air South Radio Inc. Stns: 2 AM, 3 FM. WKEA-FM Scottsboro, Ala.; WEPA(AM) Eupora, WFTO(AM)-WFTA(FM) Fulton & WLZA(FM) Starkville, all Miss. Executive: Olive E. Sisk, pres. Hqtrs: Box 249, Fulton, Miss. 38843. (601) 862-2233.

Airplay Broadcasting/Stay Tuned Broadcasting. Stns: 1 AM, 2 FM. WXRX(FM) Belvidere & WRRR(AM) Rockford, both Ill.; & WKHY(FM) Lafayette, Ind. (All 100% owned.) Hqtrs: 2830 Sandy Hollow Rd., Rockford, Ill. 61109. (815) 874-7861. FAX: (815) 874-2202.

All Pro Broadcasting Inc. Stns: 2 AM, 3 FM. KACE(FM) Inglewood, KAEV(FM) Lake Arrowhead & KCKC(AM) San Bernardino, all Calif.; WMCS(AM) Greenfield & WLUM-FM Milwaukee, both Wis. (All 100% owned.) Executives: Willie D. Davis, pres/CEO; Steven Sinicropi, exec VP. Ownership: Willie D. Davis, 66%; Northwestern Mutual Life Insurance, 33%. Hqtrs: 161 N. La Brea Ave., Inglewood, Calif. 90301. (310) 330-3100. FAX: (310) 410-7803.

Allbritton Communications Co. Stns: 5 TV. KATV(TV) Little Rock, Ark.; WJLA-TV Washington; KTUL(TV) Tulsa, Okla.; WCIV(TV) Charleston, S.C.; & WSET-TV Lynchburg, Va. (All 100% owned.) Executives: Joe L. Allbritton, chmn; Lawrence I. Herbert, pres; Marvin A. Shirley, exec VP. Cable TV: Newschannel 8, 7600 Boston Blvd., Springfield, Va. 22153. (See also Cross-Ownership, Sect. A.) Hqtrs: 800 17th St. N.W., Suite 301, Washington 20006. (202) 789-2130. FAX: (202) 822-6749.

Allegheny Mountain Network Stns. Stns: 4 AM, 6 FM. WOVU(FM) Clarendon, WKBI-AM-FM St. Marys & WTRN(AM)-WGMR(FM) Tyrone, all Pa.; 71% of WFRM-AM-FM Coudersport, WQRM(FM) Smethport & WNBT-AM-FM Wellsboro, all Pa. Ownership: Cary H. Simpson. Hqtrs: Box 247, Tyrone, Pa. 16686. (814) 238-0792. FAX: (814) 684-1220.

Alliance Broadcasting. Stns: 1 AM, 4 FM. KFRC-AM-FM San Francisco; WYCD(FM) Detroit; KSNN(FM) Arlington & KYNG(FM) Dallas, both Tex. (All 100% owned.) Note: Group has purchased KXRX(FM) Seattle, pending FCC approval. Hqtrs: 2121 N. California Blvd., Suite 690, Walnut Creek, Calif. 94596. (510) 256-4690. FAX: (510) 256-4695.

Altdoerffer Group. Stns: 2 AM, 2 FM. WRUN(AM) & WFRG-FM Utica, N.Y.; & WLAN-AM-FM Lancaster, Pa. Ownership: Sam Altdoerffer Sr., 40%; Frank Altdoerffer, 20%; John Altdoerffer, 20%; Sam Altdoerffer Jr., 20%. Hqtrs: 252 N. Queen St., Lancaster, Pa. 17603. (717) 295-9700. FAX: (717) 295-7329.

Amaturo Group Ltd. Stns: 2 AM, 5 FM. KOOJ(FM) Riverside & KFRG(FM) San Bernardino, both Calif.; WKGR(FM) Fort Pierce, Fla.; WRUS(AM) & WBVR(FM) Russellville, Ky.; KKMJ-FM Austin & KJCE(AM) Rollingwood, both Tex. Executive: Joseph C. Amaturo, gen ptnr. Hqtrs: 2929 E. Commercial Blvd., Penthouse C, Fort Lauderdale, Fla. 33308. (305) 776-7815.

Ambassador Media Corp. Stns: 3 TV. KPVI(TV) Pocatello & KKVI(TV) Twin Falls, both Idaho; & KJVI(TV) Jackson, Wyo. (All 100% owned.) Ownership: William Armstrong, Ellen Armstrong, Brian Hogen. Hqtrs: 425 E. Center, Pocatello, Idaho 83201. (208) 232-6666. FAX: (208) 233-6678.

AmCom General Corp. Stns: 1 AM, 2 FM. KRMD-AM-FM Shreveport, La.; & WJMZ-FM Anderson, S.C. (All 100% owned.) Executives: George R. Francis Jr., pres/CEO; E. Gray Payne, exec VP/CFO; Robert D. Herman, VP engrg. Ownership: George R. Francis Jr., 100%. Hqtrs: 84 Villa Rd., 3rd Fl., B-35, Greenville, S.C. 29615-3030. (803) 242-3800. FAX: (803) 271-2226.

American Broadcasting Systems. Stns: 4 AM, 6 FM. KVVA-FM Apache Junction & KVVA(AM) Phoenix, both Ariz.; KRKY(AM) Granby, KRKM(FM) Kremmling, KBCR(AM)-KSBT(FM) Steamboat Springs & KSKE-AM-FM Vail, all Colo.; WIXI(FM) Naples Park, Fla.; & KZTO(FM) Ottawa, Kan. Ownership: Ronald Shaffer, Tom Kearney. Hqtrs: 6209 N. K 61 Hwy., Hutchinson, Kan. 67502. (316) 669-8193. FAX: (316) 669-8199.

American Family Radio. Stns: 1 AM, 3 FM. WSEY(FM) Mount Morris, Ill.; WQST-AM-FM Forest & WAFR(FM) Tupelo, both Miss. Hqtrs: Box 2440, Tupelo, Miss. 38803. (601) 844-8888. FAX: (601) 844-9176.

American General Media. Stns: 5 AM, 5 FM. WYDE(AM) Birmingham, Ala.; KKAL(AM) Arroyo Grande, KERN-AM-FM Bakersfield & KZOZ(FM) San Luis Obispo, all Calif.; WWWG(AM) Rochester, N.Y.; WWTN(FM) Manchester, Tenn.; KKCL(FM) Lorenzo & KLLF(AM)-KWFS(FM) Wichita Falls, both Tex. (All 100% owned.) Ownership: Anthony S. Brandon, Lawrence Brandon, L. Rogers Brandon. Hqtrs: Box 2700, Bakersfield, Calif. 93303. (805) 328-0118. FAX: (805) 328-0190.

American Media Inc. Stns: 5 AM, 7 FM. KAHI(AM)-KHYL(FM) Auburn, KGGI(FM) Riverside & KMEN(AM) San Bernardino, all Calif.; WOCL(FM) De Land, Fla.; KTCJ(AM) & KTCZ-FM Minneapolis; WALK-AM-FM Patchogue, N.Y.; WUBE-AM-FM Cincinnati & WYGY(FM) Hamilton, both Ohio. Executives: Arthur Kern, chmn (San Francisco); Alan Beck, pres (Patchogue, N.Y.). Hqtrs: 50 Francisco St., Suite 490, San Francisco 94133. (415) 397-1000; 66 Colonial Dr., Patchogue, N.Y. 11772. (516) 475-5200.

American National Broadcasting. Stns: 1 AM, 2 FM. WBRQ(FM) Cidra, WPRA(AM) Mayaguez & WRPC(FM) San German, all P.R. (All 100% owned.) Ownership: Fernando Vigil & Miguel Maldonado. Hqtrs: Box 364701, San Juan, P.R. 00936-4701. (809) 720-7444. FAX: (809) 731-1000.

American Network Group Inc. Stns: 2 AM, 1 FM. WTMC(AM) Ocala, Fla.; WPTN(AM) & WGSQ(FM) Cookeville, Tenn. Executives: John Casey, chmm/CEO; Bob Williamson, pres; Mike McDonald, CFO; Kevin Moore, VP sls & mktg; Dan Gordon, VP net opns; Don Williams, VP sports opns. Ownership: John J. Casey, 29.61%. Note: American Network Group Inc. also operates Tennessee Radio Network, Tennessee AgriNet & South Carolina Network. Hqtrs: 621 Mainstream Dr., Suite 230, Nashville 37228. (615) 742-6100. FAX: (615) 742-6124.

American Radio Systems. Stns: 7 AM, 11 FM. WZMX(FM) Hartford, Conn.; KDMI(AM), KGGO-FM & KHKI(FM) Des Moines, Iowa; WDJX-AM-FM Louisville, Ky.; WHDH(AM), WRKO(AM) & WBMX(FM) Boston; WNBF(AM)-WHWK(FM) Binghamton, WYRK(FM) Buffalo, WCMF-AM-FM Rochester & WRMM-FM Rochester, all N.Y.; WMMX(FM) & WONE(AM)-WTUE(FM) Dayton, Ohio. Note: Group has purchased WNEZ(AM) & WRCH(FM) New Britain, Conn., subject to FCC approval. Executives: Steve Dodge, CEO; Tom Stoner, chmn of exec committee; David Pearlman, COO; Joseph Winn, CFO/co-COO. Hqtrs: 116 Huntington Ave., Boston 02116. (617) 375-8000. FAX: (617) 375-8080.

Americom. Stns: 3 AM, 4 FM. KODS(FM) Carnelian Bay, KEZL(FM) Fowler, KEYQ(AM) Fresno, KHTZ(AM) Truckee & KEYX(AM)-KFSO-FM Visalia, all Calif.; & KFBI(FM) Pahrump (Las Vegas), Nev. Executives: Tom Quinn, pres/CEO; Paul S. Almond, VP; Richard Nagler, VP. Hqtrs: 6255 Sunset Blvd., Suite 1901, Los Angeles 90028. (213) 465-7700. FAX: (213) 465-3635.

Americus Communications Corp. Stns: 2 AM, 2 FM. WBIZ-AM-FM Eau Claire & WSPO(AM)-WSPT(FM) Stevens Point, both Wis. (All 100% owned.) Ownership: Richard L. Muzzy. Hqtrs: Box 247, Stevens Point, Wis. 54481. (715) 342-1776. FAX: (715) 341-0000.

Anaheim Broadcasting Corp. Stns: 3 FM. KHQT(FM) Los Altos (San Jose), KCAL-FM Redlands (Riverside-San Bernardino) & KBZS(FM) San Diego, all Calif. Executive: Tim Sullivan, pres. Hqtrs: 1415 3rd St. Promenade, Suite 210, Santa Monica, Calif. 90401. (310) 394-1445. FAX: (310) 394-7299.

Anchor Baptist Broadcasting Association. Stns: 3 AM. WKJV(AM) Asheville, WGCR(AM) Pisgah Forest & WTYN(AM) Tryon, all N.C. (All 100% owned.) Hqtrs: Box 720, Pisgah Forest, N.C. 28768. (704) 884-9427. FAX: (704) 883-9427.

Annapolis Valley Radio Ltd. Stns: 4 AM, 2 FM. CKDY(AM) Digby, CKEN(AM) & CKWM-FM Kentville, CKAD(AM) Middleton, CKDY-FM-1 Weymouth & CFAB(AM) Windsor, all N.S. (All stns are located in Canada.) (All 100% owned.) Ownership: Neil H. MacMullen, pres, 100%. Hqtrs: Box 310, 29 Oakdene St., Kentville, N.S., Canada B4N 1H5. (902) 678-2111.

Apollo Radio Ltd. Stns: 1 AM, 5 FM. KUDL(FM) Kansas City, Kan.; KMXV(FM) Kansas City, Mo.; WEZL(FM) Charleston, S.C.; KKAT(FM) Ogden & KALL(AM)-KODJ(FM) Salt Lake City, both Utah. Ownership: George Castell, Terrence Elkes, Kenneth Gorman, William Stakelin. Hqtrs: 350 Park Ave., New York 10022. (212) 750-4530. FAX: (212) 750-4531.

Arctic Broadcasting Association. Stns: 1 AM, 2 FM. KYKD(FM) Bethel & KICY-AM-FM Nome, both Alaska. (All 100% owned.) Hqtrs: Box 820, Nome, Alaska 99762. (907) 443-2213. FAX: (907) 443-2344.

Ardman Broadcasting Corp. Stns: 2 AM, 8 FM. WIRA(AM) & WOVV(FM) Fort Pierce, Fla.; WJMN(FM) Boston & WCIB(FM) Falmouth, both Mass.; KKCJ(FM) Liberty, Mo.; WENZ(FM) Cleveland; & WOGY-FM Germantown, Tenn.; WBES-FM Dunbar & WVSR-AM-FM Charleston, both W.Va. Note: WJMN(FM) Boston has been sold, subject to FCC approval. Executives: Myer Feldman, pres. Ownership: Adrienne Arsht Feldman is the major stockholder in all stns except WJMN(FM). Hqtrs: 1250 Connecticut Ave. N.W., Suite 700, Washington 20036. (202) 637-9025. FAX: (202) 637-9195.

Argyle Television Holding Inc. Stns: 4 TV. WVTM-TV Birmingham, Ala.; KTVI(TV) St. Louis; KTBC-TV Austin & KDFW-TV Dallas, both Tex. (All 100% owned.) Ownership: Ibra Morales, Argyle Communications Partners L.P., DLJ Merchant Banking Partners L.P. Hqtrs: 100 N.E. Loop 410, Suite 1400, San Antonio, Tex. 78216. (210) 308-0800. FAX: (210) 308-6116.

Aries Telecommunications Corp. Stns: 3 TV. WEUX(TV) Chippewa Falls, WGBA(TV) Green Bay & WLAX(TV) La Crosse, all Wis. Ownership: Donald Clark. Hqtrs: Box 19099, Green Bay, Wis. 54307. (414) 494-2626.

Arso Radio Corp. Stns: 1 AM, 3 FM. WDSR(AM) & WNFB(FM) Lake City, Fla.; WIVA-FM Aguadilla & WPRM-FM San Juan, both P.R. (All 100% owned.) Executive: Jesus Soto, pres. Hqtrs: Box 3299, Lake City, Fla. 32056-3299. (904) 752-1340. FAX: (904) 755-9369.

Associated Broadcasters Inc. Stns: 3 TV. KVEO(TV) Brownsville, KPEJ(TV) Odessa & KWKT(TV) Waco, all Tex. (All 100% owned.) Ownership: Thomas R. Galloway Sr., 100%. Hqtrs: Drawer 3030, Lafayette, La. 70502. (318) 237-1142. FAX: (318) 237-1373.

Asterisk Inc. Stns: 3 AM, 4 FM. WTRS-AM-FM Dunnellon, WYGC(FM) Gainesville, WJOE(AM)-WKNB(FM) Port St. Joe & WAMR(AM)-WCTQ(FM) Venice, all Fla. (All 100% owned.) Ownership: Richard S. Ingham, 100%. Hqtrs: 1429 N. Federal Hwy., Office E, Fort Lauderdale, Fla. 33304. (305) 566-7559.

Astor Broadcast Group. Stns: 2 AM, 3 FM. KSPA(AM)-KOWF(FM) Escondido, KIKF(FM) Garden Grove & KTID-AM-FM San Rafael, all Calif. Note: KTID-AM-FM San Rafael, Calif. has been sold, subject to FCC approval. Executives: N. Arthur Astor, pres; Susan Burke, exec VP; Paul Sakrison, dir engrg. Ownership: N. Arthur Astor. Hqtrs: 1623 5th Ave., Bldg. D, San Rafael, Calif. 94901. (415) 456-1510. FAX: (415) 456-7261.

Athens Broadcasting Co. Inc. Stns: 1 AM, 3 FM. WVNN(AM)-WZYP(FM) Athens & WTXT(FM) Fayette, both Ala.; & WHVK(FM) Tullahoma, Tenn. Ownership: William E. Dunnavant, H.F. Dunnavant, Mary Martha Newby estate. Hqtrs: Box 389, Athens, Ala. 35611. (205) 830-8300. FAX: (205) 232-6842.

Atlantic Broadcasting Group. Stns: 1 AM, 2 FM. WZFX(FM) Whiteville, N.C.; WROV-FM Martinsville & WROV(AM) Roanoke, both Va. Ownership: David Weil. Note: WZFX(FM) is licensed to Joyner Communications Inc. WROV-FM & WROV(AM) are licensed to Lisa Broadcasting Inc. Hqtrs: Box 2063, Goldsboro, N.C. 27533. (919) 734-1111. FAX: (919) 734-0877.

Atlantic Morris Broadcasting Inc. Stns: 2 AM, 4 FM. WABT(FM) Dundee, Ill.; WCSO(FM) Portland & WLPZ(AM) Westbrook, both Me.; WKTU(FM) Ocean City, N.J.; WALL(AM) & WKOJ(FM) Middletown, N.Y. (All 100% owned.) Ownership: Saddle River Holdings Corp. Hqtrs: One Beach Plaza, Middletown, N.Y. 10940. (914) 343-4744. FAX: (914) 343-1633.

B

B & B Broadcasting. Stns: 4 AM, 4 FM. KEZJ-AM-FM & KLIX-AM-FM Twin Falls, Idaho; & KLAD-AM-FM Klamath Falls, Ore.; KBBO(AM) & KRSE(FM) Yakima, Wash. (All 100% owned.) Note: KEZJ(AM) Twin Falls, Idaho has been sold, subject to FCC approval. Ownership: George Broadbin, Robert Barron. Hqtrs: Box 1259, Twin Falls, Idaho 83303. (208) 733-7512.

BANAM Broadcasting Inc. Stns: 4 TV. WTVW(TV) Evansville, Ind.; KARD(TV) West Monroe, La.; KDEB-TV Springfield, Mo.; & KLBK-TV Lubbock, Tex. (All 100% owned.) Executive: Paula Garrett, pres. Hqtrs: 3000 E. Cherry St., Springfield, Mo. 65802. (417) 862-2727.

BCTV, a division of Westcom TV Group Ltd. Stns: 30 TV. CHAN-TV Vancouver, CHAN-TV-2 Bowen Island, CHAN-TV-5 Brackendale, CKTN-TV-1 Castlegar, CHAN-TV-1 Chilliwack, CHAN-TV-4 Courtenay, CKTN-TV-4 Creston, CISR-TV-1 Grand Forks, CHKM-TV Kamloops, CHKL-TV Kelowna, CKTN-TV-3 Nelson, CKKM-TV Oliver/Osoyoos, CITM-TV 100 Mile House, CHKL-TV-1 Penticton, CIFG-TV Prince George, CHKM-TV-1 Pritchard, CITM-TV-2 Quesnel, CHKL-TV-3 Revelstoke, CISR-TV Santa Rosa, CHAN-TV-3 Squamish, CKTN-TV-2 Taghum, CKTN-TV Trail, CHKL-TV-2 Vernon & CITM-TV-1 Williams Lake, CHAN-TV-6 Wilson Creek, all B.C. (All licensed to British Columbia Television Broadcasting System Ltd.); & CHEK-TV Victoria, CHEK-TV-5 Campbell River, CHEK-TV-4 Coal Harbour, CHEK-TV-3 Port Alberni, CHEK-TV-2 River Jordan & CHEK-TV-1 Sooke, all B.C. (All licensed to CHEK-TV Ltd.). (All stns are located in Canada.) Executives: D.M. Holtby, chmn of bd; R. Bremner, pres; F. Babich, VP sls; R. Gardner, VP progmg; T. Parsons, VP news; T. Negoro, VP engrg; W. Olson, VP fin & admin. Ownership: WIC Western International Communications Ltd. Hqtrs: Box 4700, Vancouver, B.C., Canada V6B 4A3. (604) 420-2288. FAX: (604) 421-9427.

BSP Broadcasting Inc. Stns: 2 TV. KCIT(TV) Amarillo & KJTL(TV) Wichita Falls, both Tex. Executives: Pete D'Acosta, pres; F. Lanham Lyne, VP. Ownership: F. Lanham Lyne, 75%; Pete D'Acosta, 20%. Hqtrs: 3800 Call Field Rd., Wichita Falls, Tex. 76308. (817) 691-1808. FAX: (817) 696-5766.

Bahakel Communications. Stns: 6 AM, 4 FM, 8 TV. WAKA(TV) Selma, Ala.; KILO(FM) Colorado Springs; WRSP-TV Springfield & WCCU(TV) Urbana, both Ill.; WBAK-TV Terre Haute, Ind.; KXEL(AM) & KOKZ(FM) Waterloo, Iowa; WLBJ(AM) Bowling Green, Ky.; WABG-AM-TV Greenwood, Miss.; WCCB(TV) Charlotte & WPET(AM)-WKSI(FM) Greensboro, both N.C.; WOLO-TV Columbia, S.C.; WDOD-AM-FM Chattanooga & WBBJ-TV Jackson, both Tenn.; & WWOD(AM) Lynchburg, Va. (All 100% owned). Executives: Cy N. Bahakel, pres; Lorraine Lancaster, sr VP; Cy N. Bahakel Jr., exec VP; Stephen Bahakel, asst VP radio division; Beverly Poston, VP; Rick Smith, controller; Amy Bahakel, dir of corporate promotions. Cable TV. Hqtrs: Box 32488, Charlotte, N.C. 28232. (704) 372-4434. FAX: (704) 335-9904.

Baker Family Stations. Stns: 12 AM, 3 FM. WOKT(AM) Cannonsburg, Ky.; WKDI(AM) Denton, Md.; WCXN(AM) Claremont, WSGH(AM) Lewisville, WNOW(AM) Mint Hill, New FM Oxford, WFTK(AM) Wake Forest & WXRI(FM) Winston-Salem, all N.C.; WBZI(AM) Xenia, Ohio; WKTR(AM) Earlysville, WCQR(AM) Fairlawn & WKGM(AM) Smithfield, all Va.; WAMN(AM) Green Valley & WBGS(AM)-WBYG(FM) Point Pleasant, both W.Va. Principal owns: Vernon H. Baker, Edward A. Baker, Virginia L. Baker. Hqtrs: Box 889, Blacksburg, Va. 24063. (703) 552-4252. FAX: (703) 951-5282.

Vernon R. Baldwin Inc. Stns: 3 AM, 4 FM. WWLT(AM)-WWXL-FM Manchester (50%) & WWAG(FM) McKee (50%), both Ky.; WCNW(AM) Fairfield (100%), WNLT(FM) Harrison (100%) & WRKG(AM)-WZLE(FM) Lorain (90%), all Ohio. Note: WWAG(FM) McKee, Ky. has been sold, subject to FCC approval. Ownership: Vernon R. Baldwin, pres. Note: Ermal Ison owns 50% of WWAG(FM). Johnny Wade Sloan owns 10% of WZLE(FM). Hqtrs: 8686 Michael Ln., Fairfield, Ohio 45014. (513) 829-7700. FAX: (513) 829-8687.

Barnstable Broadcasting Inc. Stns: 3 AM, 7 FM. WHOM(FM) Mt. Washington, N.H.; WGNA-AM-FM Albany & WHLI(AM)-WKJY(FM) Hempstead, both N.Y.; WSLR(AM) & WKDD(FM) Akron, Ohio; WWKL(FM) Harrisburg, Pa.; WGKX(FM) Memphis & WYKL(FM) Millington, both Tenn. (All 100% owned.) Executive: David S. Gingold, pres/COO. Ownership: Albert J. Kaneb, chmn/CEO, 100%. Hqtrs: Box 9042, 125 Technology Dr., Waltham, Mass. 02254. (617) 647-0608. FAX: (617) 647-2621.

Baton Broadcasting Inc. Stns: 20 TV. CTV affils: CKNY-TV North Bay, CJOH-TV Ottawa, CHBX-TV Sault Ste. Marie, CICI-TV Sudbury, CITO-TV Timmins & CFTO-TV Toronto, all Ont.; CIPA-TV Prince Albert, CKCK-TV Regina, CFQC-TV Saskatoon & CICC-TV Yorkton, all Sask. CBC affils: CHNB-TV North Bay, CHRO-TV Pembroke, CJIC-TV Sault Ste. Marie, CKNC-TV Sudbury & CFCL-TV Timmins, all Ont.; CKBI-TV Prince Albert & CKOS-TV Yorkton, both Sask. Independent stns: CFPL-TV London, CHWI-TV Wheatley & CKNX-TV Wingham, all Ont. (All stns are located in Canada.) Executives: Douglas Bassett, pres/CEO. Ownership: Telegram Corporation Ltd., 52.65%; Caisse de Depot Placement de Quebec, 11%; Ontario Municipal Employees Retirement Board, 10.04%. Hqtrs: Box 9, Station O, Toronto, Canada M4A 2M9. (416) 299-2000. FAX: (416) 299-2220.

Baton Rouge Broadcasting Co. and Transcontinental Broadcasting Co. Stns: 1 AM, 2 FM. WJBO(AM) & WFMF(FM) Baton Rouge; & KPRR(FM) El Paso, Tex. (All 100% owned.) Ownership: George Jenne & John Noland. Hqtrs: Box 496, Baton Rouge 70821. (504) 383-5271. FAX: (504) 388-0526.

BayCom Partners L.P. Stns: 1 AM, 2 FM. KSJX(AM) & KSJO(FM) San Jose, Calif.; & KKBK(FM) Lake Oswego, Ore. (All 100% owned.) Hqtrs: 50 Francisco St., Suite 257, San Francisco 94133. (415) 421-0680. FAX: (415) 421-0683.

Bayport Broadcast Group. Stns: 2 AM, 5 FM. KFRD(AM) Bellville, KHEN(FM) Caldwell, KLTR(FM) Franklin, KEZB(FM) Hempstead, KMIA(FM) Jasper, KMPQ(AM) Rosenberg-Richmond & KMPQ-FM Rosenberg, all Tex. (All 100% owned.) Note: Group also owns low power TV stns K05IL & K69FW Clear Lake City (Houston), Tex. Ownership: Roy E. Henderson, 100%. Hqtrs: Box 590209, Houston 77259. (713) 480-9992. FAX: (713) 286-1666.

Beacon Broadcasting Corp. Stns: 2 AM, 3 FM. WTHT(FM) Lewiston, Me.; WBNR(AM) Beacon, WMRV-AM-FM Endicott & WSPK(FM) Poughkeepsie, all N.Y. (All 100% owned.) Ownership: Alford H. Lessner, Robert E. Lessner & Robert A. Outer. Hqtrs: Box 511, Beacon, N.Y. 12508. (914) 831-8000. FAX: (914) 838-2109.

Bear Broadcasting Co. Stns: 2 AM, 2 FM. WXBB(FM) Kittery, Me.; WZNN(AM) & WWEM(FM) Rochester, N.H.; & WHIM(AM) Providence, R.I. Ownership: Natale L. Urso. Hqtrs: Box 325, Westerly, R.I. 02891. (401) 781-9979. FAX: (401) 596-6688.

Beasley Broadcast Group. Stns: 6 AM, 8 FM, 1 TV. KAAY(AM) Little Rock, Ark. (85%); KRTH(FM) Los Angeles (90%); WRXK-FM Bonita Springs (85%), WJHM(FM) Daytona Beach, WPOW(FM) Miami (50%) & WWCN(AM) North Fort Myers (85%), all Fla.; WGAC(AM) Augusta, Ga.; WBIG(AM) & WYSY-FM Aurora, Ill.; WYED(TV) Goldsboro (100%), WTSB(AM)-WKML(FM) Lumberton (85%) & WJMH(FM) Reidsville (100%), all N.C.; WTEL(AM) & WXTU(FM) Philadelphia (85%). Note: Group has bought WZNS(FM) Dillon, S.C., & sold KRTH(FM) Los Angeles & WYSY-FM Aurora, Ill., subject to FCC approval. Executives: George G. Beasley, chmn/CEO; Simon T, pres/COO; J. Peter Bardwick, exec VP; Bruce G. Beasley, VP opns; Caroline Beasley, VP fin; Marie Tedesco, controller. Principal own: George G. Beasley. Hqtrs: Suite 200, 3033 Riviera Dr., Naples, Fla. 33940. (813) 263-5000. FAX: (813) 434-8808.

Beck-Ross Communications Inc. Stns: 3 FM. WHCN(FM) Hartford, Conn.; WSNE(FM) Taunton, Mass. (Providence, R.I.); & WBLI(FM) Patchogue, N.Y. (All 100% owned.) Ownership: Partners are James E. Champlin, Martin F. Beck & George H. Ross. Hqtrs: Two Lincoln Ave., Rockville Centre, N.Y. 11570. (516) 764-8999. FAX: (516) 764-7759.

Steve Bellinger. See Prairieland Stations.

A.H. Belo Corp., Broadcast Division. Stns: 5 TV. KXTV(TV) Sacramento, Calif.; KOTV(TV) Tulsa, Okla.; WFAA-TV Dallas; KHOU-TV Houston; & WVEC-TV Hampton, Va. Executives: Robert W. Decherd, chmn; Ward L. Huey Jr., vice chmn/pres bcst division. Ownership: A.H. Belo Corp. (See also Cross-Ownership, Sect. A.) Cable TV. Hqtrs: Communications Center, Dallas 75265. (214) 977-6600. FAX: (214) 977-6603.

Benchmark Communications Radio. Stns: 6 AM, 12 FM. WKHI(FM) Bethany Beach & WDOV(AM)-WDSD(FM) Dover, both Del.; WXFG(FM) & WZNY(FM) Augusta, Ga.; WETT(AM) & WWFG(FM) Ocean City, Md.; WKOC(FM) Elizabeth City, N.C.; WHKZ(FM) Cayce, WCOS-AM-FM Columbia & WGUS(AM) North Augusta, both S.C.; WTAR(AM)-WLTY(FM) Norfolk, WVGO(FM) Richmond, WDCK(FM) Williamsburg & WNTW(AM)-WUSQ-FM Winchester, all Va. Note: Group also operates WFQX(FM) Front Royal, Va. under a loc mktg agreement. Hqtrs: 111 S. Calvert St., Suite

2700, Baltimore 21202. (410) 385-5249. FAX: (410) 752-1855.

Benedek Broadcasting Co. Stns: 9 TV. WIFR(TV) Freeport, Ill.; WBKO(TV) Bowling Green, Ky.; KDLH(TV) Duluth, Minn.; WTOK-TV Meridian, Miss.; KHQA-TV Hannibal, Mo. (Quincy, Ill.); WYTV(TV) Youngstown, Ohio; WHSV-TV Harrisonburg, Va.; WTAP-TV Parkersburg, W.Va.; & WBNB-TV Charlotte Amalie, V.I. Ownership: A. Richard Benedek, sole own. Hqtrs: 985 5th Ave., New York 10021. (212) 744-2333.

Benns Stns. Stns: 1 AM, 2 FM. WNUS(FM) Belpre, Ohio; WLTP(AM) Parkersburg & WDMX(FM) Vienna, both W.Va. Ownership: William E. Benns III. Hqtrs: c/o WDMX(FM), Box 5559, Vienna, W.Va. 26105. (304) 295-6070. FAX: (304) 295-4389.

L.S. Berger Stations. Stns: 3 AM, 2 FM, 1 TV. KHVH(AM) & KHHH(FM) Honolulu; KUAM-AM-FM-TV Agana, Guam; & WVUV(AM) Vailoa, American Samoa. Executive: Lawrence S. Berger, pres. Hqtrs: 1160 N. King St., Honolulu 96817. (808) 845-9902. FAX: (808) 845-9905.

Berkshire Group. Stns: 2 AM, 1 FM. WSBS(AM) Great Barrington & WNAW(AM)-WMNB(FM) North Adams, both Mass. Ownership: Donald A. Thurston, 100%. Hqtrs: Box 707, North Adams, Mass. 01247. (413) 663-6567.

Bible Broadcasting Network. Stns: 2 AM, 29 FM, plus 24 FM trans. WYFD(FM) Decatur, Ala.; KYFF(FM) Fort Smith & KYFB(FM) Pine Bluff, both Ark.; WYFB(FM) Gainesville, WYFO(FM) Lakeland & WYFE(FM) Tarpon Springs, all Fla.; WYFK(FM) Columbus, WYFZ(FM) Evans, WYFS(FM) Savannah, WAGW(FM)-WYFA(FM) Waynesboro & WYFW(FM) Winder, all Ga.; KYFW(FM) Wichita, Kan.; KYFE(FM) Alexandria, KYFI(FM) Lafayette & KYFL(FM) Monroe, all La.; WYFQ(AM) Charlotte, WYFL(FM) Henderson & WHPE-FM High Point, all N.C.; WYFV(FM) Cayce, WYFG(FM) Gaffney & WYFH(FM) North Charleston, all S.C.; WYFC(FM) Clinton & WYFN(AM) Nashville, both Tenn.; KYFA(FM) Amarillo, KYFT(FM) Lubbock & KYFS(FM) San Antonio, all Tex.; WYFJ(FM) Ashland, WYFT(FM) Luray & WYFI(FM) Norfolk, all Va.; & WYFY(FM) Fisher, W.Va. (All 100% owned.) Note: The following stns have been sold, pending FCC approval: WYFZ(FM) Evans & WAGW(FM) Waynesboro, both Ga. Ownership: non-profit, non-stock corporation. Hqtrs: Charlotte, N.C. 28241. (704) 523-5555.

Bick Broadcasting Co. Stns: 2 AM, 4 FM. KRRR(FM) Canton, KHMO(AM) Hannibal, KXKX(FM) Knob Noster, KICK-FM Palmyra & KSIS(AM)-KSDL(FM) Sedalia, all Mo. Executive: James E. Janes, pres. Ownership: Frank C. Bick, 46%; James P. Bick, 46%; James E. Janes, 8%. Hqtrs: Box 711, 119 N. 3rd St., Hannibal, Mo. 63401. (314) 221-3450. FAX: (314) 221-5331.

Big Horn Communications Inc. Stns: 1 AM, 1 FM, 4 TV. KSVI(TV) Billings, KCTZ(TV) Bozeman, KOUS-TV Hardin & KYUS-TV Miles City, all Mont.; & KZMQ-AM-FM Greybull, Wyo. Hqtrs: Box 23309, Billings, Mont. 59104. (406) 652-4743. FAX: (406) 652-6963.

Howard G. Bill Stations. Stns: 1 AM, 2 FM. KOLM(AM) & KWWK(FM) Rochester, Minn.; & WLJO(FM) La Crosse, Wis. Ownership: Howard G. Bill. Hqtrs: c/o KOLM(AM)-KWWK(FM), 1220 4th Ave. S.W., Rochester, Minn. 55902. (507) 288-1971. FAX: (507) 288-1520.

Birach Broadcasting Corp. Stns: 3 AM. WDMV(AM) Pocomoke City, Md.; WNZK(AM) Westland, Mich. (Detroit); & WWCS(AM) Canonsburg, Pa. (All 100% owned.) Note: WDMV(AM) Pocomoke City, Md. has a CP to change its city of license to Brinklow, Md. Ownership: Sima Birach, 100%. Hqtrs: 21700 Northwestern Hwy., Suite 1190, Southfield, Mich. 48075. (313) 557-3500. FAX: (313) 557-3241.

Black River Broadcasting. Stns: 3 AM, 2 FM. WMSA(AM) Massena (100%), WIBX(AM)-WLZW(FM) Utica & WTNY-AM-FM Watertown (100%), all N.Y. Ownership: David McCall, Richard Passanant & Donald Alexander. Hqtrs: c/o WTNY-AM-FM, 134 Mullin St., Watertown, N.Y. 13601. (315) 788-0790. FAX: (315) 788-4379.

Blackstar Communications Inc. Stns: 3 TV. WBSF(TV) Melbourne, Fla.; WBSX(TV) Ann Arbor, Mich.; & KBSP-TV Salem, Ore. Ownership: John E. Oxendine. Hqtrs: 1765 N St. N.W., Washington 20036. (202) 463-8040. FAX: (202) 463-8015.

Blade Communications Inc. Stns: 4 TV. KTRV(TV) Nampa, Idaho; WLFI-TV Lafayette, Ind.; WDRB-TV Louisville, Ky.; & WLIO(TV) Lima, Ohio. (All 100% owned.) Ownership: William Block, Paul Block Jr. estate. (See also Cross-Ownership, Sect. A, under Lima Communications Corp.) Cable TV. Hqtrs: 541 Superior St., Toledo, Ohio 43660. (419) 245-6000. Fax: (419) 245-6167.

Bloomington Broadcasting Corp. Stns: 4 AM, 7 FM. WJBC(AM) & WBNQ(FM) Bloomington, Ill.; WKLQ(FM) Holland (Grand Rapids), Mich.; WXLY(FM) North Charleston & WTCB(FM) Orangeburg (Columbia), both S.C.; WGOW(AM)-WSKZ(FM) Chattanooga, WOGT(FM) East Ridge, WJCW(AM)-WQUT(FM) Johnson City & WKIN(AM)-WKOS(FM) Kingsport, all Tenn. (All 100% owned.) Ownership: Timothy R. Ives, Davis U. Merwin. Hqtrs: Box 8, Bloomington, Ill. 61702. (309) 829-1221. FAX: (309) 827-8071.

Blount Communications Group. Stns: 3 AM. WFIF(AM) Milford, Conn.; WVNE(AM) Leicester, Mass.; & WARV(AM) Warwick, R.I. (All 100% owned.) Ownership: William A. Blount, Deborah C. Blount. Hqtrs: 19 Luther Ave., Warwick, R.I. 02886. (401) 737-0700. FAX: (401) 737-1604.

Bluefield Broadcasting Co. Inc. Stns: 1 AM, 2 FM. WBDY-AM-FM Bluefield & WBBY(FM) Cedar Bluff, both Va. (All 100% owned.) Ownership: George F. Barnes Jr., 50%; W. Curt Gillespie, 50%. Hqtrs: 900 Bluefield Ave., Bluefield, W.Va. 24701. (304) 327-7114. FAX: (304) 325-7850.

Bluegrass Broadcasting Co. Inc. Stns: 1 AM, 1 FM, 2 TV. WYMT-TV Hazard & WVLK-AM-FM & WKYT-TV Lexington, both Ky. (All 100% owned.) Ownership: Mid-Central Investment Co. Inc., 100%, which in turn is owned 100% by Kentucky Central Life Insurance Co. Hqtrs: Box 1559, Lexington, Ky. 40592. (606) 253-6524.

Bogue Chitto Communications Co. Stns: 2 AM, 2 FM. WBOX(AM) Bogalusa & WBOX-FM Varnado, both La.; WCHJ(AM) & WBKN(FM) Brookhaven, Miss. (All 100% owned.) Ownership: Thomas F. McDaniel. Hqtrs: Box 351, Columbia, Miss. 39429. (601) 731-2298. FAX: (601) 736-2617.

Boles Broadcasting. Stns: 2 AM, 2 FM. KSEL-AM-FM Portales, N.M.; & KPOS-AM-FM Post, Tex. (All 100% owned.) Executive: Steve Richey, prog dir. Ownership: James G. Boles. Hqtrs: Box 886, Portales, N.M. 88130. (505) 359-1759. FAX: (505) 359-0724.

Bonneville International Corp. Stns: 7 AM, 9 FM, 2 TV. KIDR(AM) & KPSN(FM) Phoenix; KBIG(FM) Los Angeles & KOIT-AM-FM San Francisco; WTMX(FM) Skokie, Ill. (Chicago); KCMO-AM-FM & KMBZ(AM)-KLTH(FM) Kansas City, Mo.; WMXV(FM) New York; KAAM(AM) & KZPS(FM) Dallas; KSL-AM-TV Salt Lake City; & KIRO-AM-FM-TV Seattle. Executive: Rodney H. Brady, pres. Ownership: Deseret Management Corp., which is 100% owned by the Corp. of the President of the Church of Jesus Christ of Latter-day Saints. Hqtrs: Box 1160, Broadcast House, Salt Lake City, Utah 84110. (801) 575-7500. FAX: (801) 575-7548.

Booth American Co. Stns: 4 AM, 7 FM. WZPL(FM) Greenfield (Indianapolis) & WRBR-FM South Bend, both Ind.; WIOG(FM) Bay City, WJLB(FM) Detroit & WSGW(AM) Saginaw, all Mich.; WSAI(AM)-WWNK-FM Cincinnati, WWWE(AM)-WLTF(FM) Cleveland & WTOD(AM)-WKKO(FM) Toledo, all Ohio. Principal owns: John L. Booth, Mrs. John L. Booth, John L. Booth II, Ralph H. Booth II. Cable TV. Other interests: Booth American Co. also owns 100% of Genesis Broadcasting Inc. (see listing). Hqtrs: 333 W. Fort St., Detroit 48226. (313) 965-3360. FAX: (313) 965-1160.

Bott Broadcasting. Stns: 5 AM, 3 FM. KCIV(FM) Mount Bullion, Calif.; WFCV(AM) Fort Wayne, Ind.; KCCV-FM Olathe & KCCV(AM) Overland Park, both Kan.; KSIV(AM) Clayton, Mo. (St. Louis); KQCV(AM) Oklahoma City & KABH(FM) Shawnee, both Okla.; & WCRV(AM) Collierville (Memphis), Tenn. (All 100% owned.) Ownership: Richard P. Bott. Hqtrs: 8801 E. 63rd St., Kansas City, Mo. 64133. (816) 353-7844. FAX: (816) 353-8228.

Brechner Management Co. Stns: 1 AM, 1 FM, 2 TV. KTKA-TV Topeka, Kan.; WMDT(TV) Salisbury, Md.; WKFI(AM) & WSWO(FM) Wilmington, Ohio. (All 100% owned.) Ownership: Marion Brechner, Berl Brechner. Hqtrs: Box 531103, Orlando, Fla. 32853-1103. (407) 423-4431. FAX: (407) 843-0704.

Brewer Broadcasting Corp. Stns: 3 AM, 2 FM. WTOT(AM) & WJAQ(FM) Marianna, Fla.; WHON(AM) Centerville, WQLK(FM) Richmond & WTCJ(AM) Tell City, all Ind. Ownership: estate of James R. Brewer, James L. Brewer, Maytha N. Brewer. Hqtrs: 409 Chestnut St., Suite A-154, Chattanooga 37402. (812) 547-2345. FAX: (812) 547-2346.

Brill Media Company Inc. Stns: 5 AM, 6 FM. KUAD-FM Windsor, Colo.; WOMI(AM) & WBKR(FM) Owensboro, Ky.; WEBC(AM)-WAVC(FM) Duluth & KQWB-FM Moorhead, both Minn.; KLIK(AM) & KTXY(FM) Jefferson City, Mo.; KQWB(AM) Fargo, N.D.; WIOV-FM Ephrata & WIOV(AM) Reading, both Pa. Ownership: Alan R. Brill. (See also Cross-Ownership, Sect. A.) Hqtrs: Box 3353, Evansville, Ind. 47732. (812) 423-6200.

Brissette Broadcasting Corp. Stns: 8 TV. WHOI(TV) Peoria, Ill.; WWLP(TV) Springfield, Mass.; WILX-TV Onondaga, Mich.; KOSA-TV Odessa & KAUZ-TV Wichita Falls, both Tex.; WTRF-TV Wheeling, W.Va.; WMTV(TV) Madison & WSAW-TV Wausau, both Wis. Ownership: Paul Brissette, chmn, 100%. Hqtrs: 1908 Royal Palm Way, Boca Raton, Fla. 33432. (407) 395-0494. FAX: (407) 750-0997.

Broadcasters Unlimited Inc. Stns: 1 AM, 3 FM. KKYR(AM) Texarkana, Ark.; KKYR-FM Texarkana, KNUE(FM) Tyler & KCKR(FM) Waco, all Tex. (All 100% owned.) Ownership: Don Chaney, Wade Ridley, Sam Roosth & Wilton Fair. Hqtrs: 3810 Brookside Dr., Tyler, Tex. 75701-9420. (903) 581-0606. FAX: (903) 509-4152.

Broadcasting Partners Inc. Stns: 2 AM, 5 FM. WVAZ(FM) Oak Park, Ill. (Chicago); WKQI(FM) Detroit; WYNY(FM) Lake Success, N.Y. (New York); WGIV(AM) Charlotte, WPEG(FM) Concord & WCKZ-FM Gastonia, all N.C.; & KSKY(AM) Dallas. Note: Group has purchased WMTG(AM) & WNIC(FM) Dearborn, Mich., subject to FCC approval. Executives: Perry J. Lewis, chmn; Barry Mayo, pres; Lee Simonson, exec VP. Hqtrs: 150 W. 55th St., New York 10019. (212) 581-3210.

Brown Broadcasting Co. Stns: 4 AM, 7 FM. KYNO(AM) & KJFX(FM) Fresno, KDFC(AM) Palo Alto, KQPT(FM) Sacramento, KXOA-AM-FM Sacramento, KPOP(AM)-KGB-FM San Diego & KDFC-FM-KKSF(FM) San Francisco, all Calif.; & KRWM(FM) Bremerton, Wash. Executives: Michael J. Brown, pres; Phil Melrose, pres radio division. Hqtrs: c/o The Brown Organization, 5700 Wilshire Blvd., Suite 480, Los Angeles, Calif. 90036-3659. (310) 274-8411. FAX: (213) 954-8940.

Buckley Broadcasting Corp. Stns: 5 AM, 8 FM. KNZR(AM) Bakersfield, KUBB(FM) Mariposa, KWAV(FM) Monterey, KLLY(FM) Oildale, KMGX(FM) San Fernando, KKHI-AM-FM San Francisco & KSEQ(FM) Visalia, all Calif.; WDRC-AM-FM Hartford, Conn.; WFBL(AM)-WSEN-FM Baldwinsville & WOR(AM) New York, both N.Y. Note: KKHI-AM-FM San Francisco has been sold, subject to FCC approval. Hqtrs: 166 W. Putnam Ave., Greenwich, Conn. 06830. (203) 661-4307. FAX: (203) 622-7341.

Bulmer Communications Group. Stns: 3 FM. WHZR(FM) Royal Center (Logansport), Ind.; WZOO-FM Edgewood (Ashtabula) & WHMQ(FM) North Baltimore (Findlay), both Ohio. Ownership: John A. Bulmer, 100%. Hqtrs: Box 289, Ashtabula, Ohio 44004-0289. (216) 964-3823. FAX: (216) 993-1025.

Paul Bunyan Network. Stns: 2 AM, 3 FM. WATZ-AM-FM Alpena, WBCM(FM) Boyne City & WTCM-AM-FM Traverse City, all Mich. (All 100% owned.) Ownership: Ross Biederman, 52.5%; William Kiker Estate, 16.25%; William McClay, 15%. Hqtrs: 314 E. Front St., Traverse City, Mich. 49684. (616) 947-7675. FAX: (616) 929-3988.

Burbach Broadcasting Group. Stns: 3 AM, 4 FM. WMRN-AM-FM Marion, Ohio; WMAJ(AM) & WBHV(FM) State College, Pa.; WXIL(FM) Parkersburg & WBBD(AM)-WEGW(FM) Wheeling, both W.Va. (All 100% owned.) Ownership: John L. Laubach Jr., Robert H. Burstein. Hqtrs: 2350 One PPG Place, Pittsburgh 15222. (412) 263-6725. FAX: (412) 263-6737.

Burnham Broadcasting Co. Stns: 7 TV. WALA-TV Mobile, Ala.; KBAK-TV Bakersfield, Calif.; KHAW-TV Hilo, KHON-TV Honolulu & KAII-TV Wailuku, all Hawaii; WVUE(TV) New Orleans; & WLUK-TV Green Bay, Wis. (All 100% owned.) Executive: Peter Blaise Desnoes, mgng gen ptnr. Ownership: Peter Blaise Desnoes, 44%; Larry Beck, 9%; Dean Buntrock, 9%; Peer Pedersen, 9%; Leonard Ring, 9%; Howard Warren, 9%; & others, 11%. Hqtrs: 980 N. Michigan Ave., Suite 1200, Chicago 60611. (312) 787-9800. FAX: (312) 787-3964.

Busse Broadcasting Corp. Stns: 3 TV. WWMT(TV) Kalamazoo, Mich.; KOLN(TV) Lincoln, Neb.; & WEAU-TV Eau Claire, Wis. (All 100% owned.) Executive: Lawrence A. Busse, pres. Hqtrs: 590 W. Maple St., Kalamazoo, Mich. 49008. (616) 388-8019. FAX: (616) 388-6089.

C

CBS Broadcast Group. Stns: 8 AM, 13 FM, 9 TV. KNX(AM)-KCBS-FM-TV Los Angeles & KCBS(AM)-KRQR(FM) San Francisco; WCIX(TV) Miami & WWRM(FM) Tampa, both Fla.; WBBM-AM-FM-TV Chicago; WARW(FM) Bethesda, Md. (Washington); WODS(FM) Boston; WWJ(AM)-WJOI(FM) Detroit & WJMN-TV Escanaba, both Mich.; KCCO-TV Alexandria & WCCO-AM-TV & WLTE(FM) Minneapolis, both Minn.; KMOX(AM) & KLOU(FM) St. Louis; WCBS-AM-FM-TV New York; WOGL-AM-FM & WCAU-TV Philadelphia; KTXQ(FM) Fort Worth & KKRW(FM) Houston; & WFRV-TV Green Bay, Wis. Note: Group has bought WSUN(AM)-WCOF(FM) St. Petersburg, Fla. & sold KTXQ(FM) Fort Worth, pending FCC approval. Group also plans to change the call letters of KLTR(FM) Houston to KKRW-FM. (For a listing of CBS divisions & executives, see index, section F.) Hqtrs: 51 W. 52nd St., New York, NY 10019. (212) 975-4321. FAX: (212) 975-4226.

CD Broadcasting Corp. Stns: 8 AM, 9 FM. KNUI-AM-FM Kahului, Hawaii; KKBJ-AM-FM Bemidji, KQHT(FM) Crookston, WWTC(AM) Minneapolis & KLGR-AM-FM Redwood Falls, all Minn.; KRRZ(AM), KIZZ(FM) & KZPR(FM) Minot, N.D.; KKAA(AM)-KQAA(FM) Aberdeen, KBHB(AM)-KRCS(FM) Sturgis & KJJQ(AM)-KKQQ(FM) Volga, all S.D. (All 100% owned.) Ownership: Christopher T. Dahl, 75%; Russell Cowels, 25%. Hqtrs: 724 First St. N., Minneapolis 55401. (612) 338-3300. FAX: (612) 338-4318.

CHET-5 Broadcasting. Stns: 1 AM, 2 FM. WDSP(FM) Arlington, WKNY(AM) Kingston & WDST(FM) Woodstock, all N.Y. Executives: Gary H. Chetkof, chmn/pres. Hqtrs: 118 Tinker St., Woodstock, N.Y. 12498. (914) 679-7266. FAX: (914) 679-5395.

CHUM Ltd. Stns: 13 AM, 10 FM, 6 TV. CIBQ(AM) Brooks, CKDQ(AM) Drumheller & CKSQ(AM) Stettler, all Alta.; CFUN(AM) & CHQM-FM Vancouver, B.C.; CIFX(AM) & CHIQ-FM Winnipeg, Man.; CKCW-TV Moncton & CKLT-TV Saint John, both N.B.; CJCH-AM-TV/CIOO-FM Halifax & CJCB-TV Sydney, both N.S.; CKVR-TV Barrie, CKKW(AM)-CFCA-FM Kitchener, CFRA(AM)-CKKL-FM Ottawa, CKPT(AM)-CKQM-FM Peterborough, CHUM-AM-FM & CITY-TV Toronto, CKLW-AM-FM & CKWW(AM)-CIMX-FM Windsor, all Ont.; & CKIS(AM) & CHOM-FM Montreal. (All stns are located in Canada.) Ownership: Allan Waters, controlling shareholder. Other interests: MuchMusic, MusiquePlus, Atlantic Satellite Network, CHUMCITY Productions, CHUM Satellite Business Music Network. Hqtrs: 1331 Yonge St., Toronto, Ont., Canada M4T 1Y1. (416) 925-6666. FAX: (416) 926-4042.

CLW Communications Group Inc. Stns: 2 AM, 1 FM. WHYD(AM) Columbus, Ga.; WSCW(AM) & WJYP(FM) South Charleston, W.Va. (All 100% owned.) Executive: Irv Daugherty, pres. Hqtrs: 6815 Shallowford Rd., Chattanooga 37421. (615) 894-6060. FAX: (615) 894-1055.

CRB Broadcasting Corp. Stns: 5 AM, 7 FM. WNLK(AM) & WEFX(FM) Norwalk, Conn.; WJBR-AM-FM Wilmington, Del.; WZZR(FM) Stuart, Fla.; WFAS-AM-FM White Plains, N.Y.; WAEB-AM-FM Allentown & WZZO(FM) Bethlehem, both Pa.; WTCR-FM Huntington & WTCR(AM) Kenova, both W.Va. (All 100% owned.) Ownership: Carter Burden. Hqtrs: Rm. 2930, 630 5th Ave., New York 10111. (212) 581-7550. FAX: (212) 969-9102.

CRISTA Broadcasting. Stns: 1 AM, 2 FM. KCIS(AM)-KCMS(FM) Edmonds & KLYN(FM) Lynden, both Wa. (All 100% owned.) Hqtrs: 19303 Fremont Ave. N., Seattle 98133. (206) 546-7350.

California Oregon Broadcasting Inc. Stns: 6 TV. KAEF(TV) Arcata, KFWU(TV) Fort Bragg & KRCR-TV Redding, all Calif.; KOTI(TV) Klamath Falls, KOBI(TV) Medford & KLSR-TV Roseburg, all Ore. (All 100% owned.) Other interests: Cable TV: Crestview Cable TV (systems in Oregon). Hqtrs: Box 5M, Medford, Ore. 97501. (503) 779-5555.

Cannell Communications L.P. Stns: 3 TV. WHNS(TV) Asheville, N.C.; WUAB(TV) Lorain, Ohio; & KPDX(TV) Vancouver, Wash. (All 100% owned.) Ownership: Saratoga II TV Corp., New York, gen ptnr; Cannell Communications Inc., Hollywood, gen ptnr; Stephen J. Cannell Productions Inc., Hollywood, limited ptnr; The Cannell Studios Inc., Hollywood, limited ptnr; William A. Schwartz, Atlanta, limited ptnr. Hqtrs: 400 Perimeter Ctr. Terr. N.E., Suite 975, Atlanta 30346. (404) 395-1004. FAX: (404) 395-1007.

Cape Fear Broadcasting. Stns: 1 AM, 3 FM. WFNC(AM)-WQSM(FM) Fayetteville, WGNI(FM) Wilmington & WMNX(FM) Wilmington, all N.C. (All 100% owned.) Ownership: Victor W. Dawson, Margaret Dawson Highsmith, Ann Cameron Highsmith. Hqtrs: 1890 Dawson St., Wilmington, N.C. 28403. (919) 763-6511. FAX: (919) 763-5926.

Capital Cities/ABC Broadcast Group. Stns: 9 AM, 9 FM, 8 TV. KFSN-TV Fresno, KABC-AM-TV/KLOS(FM) Los Angeles & KGO-AM-TV San Francisco, all Calif.; WMAL(AM) & WRQX(FM) Washington; WKHX(AM) Atlanta, WYAY(FM) Gainesville & WKHX-FM Marietta, all Ga.; WLS-AM-FM-TV Chicago; WJR(AM) & WHYT(FM) Detroit; KQRS-AM-FM Golden Valley, Minn.; WABC-AM-TV & WPLJ(FM) New York; WTVD(TV) Durham, N.C.; WPVI-TV Philadelphia; WBAP(AM)-KSCS(FM) Fort Worth & KTRK-TV Houston. Officers of Capital Cities/ABC Inc. are: Thomas S. Murphy, chmn of bd; John B. Fairchild, exec VP; Robert A. Iger, exec VP; John B. Sias, exec VP; Michael P. Mallardi, sr VP; Phillip J. Meek, sr VP; Ronald J. Doerfler, sr VP/CFO; Stephen A. Weisswasser, sr VP/gen counsel; James P. Arcara, pres Capital Cities-ABC Radio; Lawrence J. Pollock, pres owned stns; Don P. Bouloukos, pres owned radio stns-Group I; Norman S. Schrutt, pres owned radio stns-Group II; Robert O. Niles, VP/dir engrg owned TV stns; Philip R. Beuth, Paul L. Bures Jr., Robert O. Burton, James E. Duffy, Joseph M. Fitzgerald, John E. Frisoli, James Goldberg, Robert T. Goldman, Ann Maynard Gray, Christine Hikawa, Andrew E. Jackson, Patricia J. Matson, Jeffrey Ruthizer, all VPs; David J. Vondrak, VP/treas; Philip R. Farnsworth, sec; Allen J. Edelson, VP/controller/asst sec; David S. Loewith, VP, asst sec/asst controller. Capital Cities also owns Fairchild Publications Inc. (See also Cross-Ownership, Sect. A.) Ownership: Warren E. Buffett, beneficial holder of 18.71%; William S. Lasdon, 1.3%; David Minikin, 1.1%; publicly traded. Hqtrs: 77 W. 66th St., New York 10023. (212) 456-7777. FAX: (212) 456-7909.

Capital Kids' Radio Co. Stns: 4 AM. WITH(AM) Baltimore, WKDL(AM) Silver Spring & WKDB(AM) Towson, all Md.; & WKDV(AM) Manassas, Va. Ownership: Lawrence A. Kessner, Virginia S. Carson. Hqtrs: 8555 16th St., Suite 100, Silver Spring, Md. 20910. (301) 588-1050. FAX: (301) 588-2249.

Capitol Broadcasting Co. Inc. Stns: 2 FM, 2 TV. WWMX(FM) Baltimore; WJZY(TV) Belmont (Charlotte) & WRAL(FM) & WRAL-TV Raleigh, all N.C. (All 100% owned.) Note: Group has purchased WVRT(FM) Baltimore, subject to FCC approval. Ownership: James F. Goodmon, 65.56%; Ray H. Goodmon III, 31.13%. Capitol Broadcasting Co. Inc. also owns & operates the Capitol Radio Network, North Carolina News Network, Tobacco Radio Network, Capitol Satellite/Communications & Microspace Communications Corp. Hqtrs: Box 12000, Raleigh, N.C. 27605. (919) 821-8500.

Capstar Media of the Southeast Inc. Stns: 2 AM, 5 FM. WJDS(AM), WKTF(FM) & WMSI(FM) Jackson, Miss.; WMYI(FM) Hendersonville, N.C.; WSSL-FM Gray Court (Greenville) & WSSL(AM) Greenville, both S.C.; & WSIX-FM Nashville. Executives: Steve Hicks, pres. Ownership: Capstar Media of the Southeast Inc. is part of SFX Broadcasting Inc. (see listing). Hqtrs: 600 Congress, Suite 1270, Austin, Tex. 78701. (512) 477-7338. FAX: (512) 477-7389.

Cardinal Communications Inc. Stns: 2 AM, 2 FM. KWSL(AM) & KGLI(FM) Sioux City, Iowa; KSFT(AM) & KKJO(FM) St. Joseph, Mo. Ownership: S.A. McMaster Jr., John D. Daniels, Theodore H. Mahn. Hqtrs: 1113 Nebraska St., Sioux City, Iowa 51105. (712) 258-5595. FAX: (712) 252-2430.

Cariboo Central Interior Radio Inc. Stns: 12 AM, 5 FM. CFLD(AM) Burns Lake, CIFJ(AM) Fort St. James, CIFL(AM) Fraser Lake, CHLD(AM) Granisle, CKBV(AM) Hazelton, CHBV(AM) Houston, CKBX(AM)-CFFM-FM-1 100 Mile House, CJCI(AM) & CIRX-FM Prince George, CKCQ(AM)-CFFM-FM-2 Quesnel, CFBV(AM) Smithers, CIVH(AM)-CIBC-FM-1 Vanderhoof & CKWL(AM)-CFFM-FM Williams Lake, all B.C. (All stns are located in Canada.) Executive: Terry Shepherd, gen mgr. Ownership: R.A. East, 30%; S.W. Davis, 30%. Hqtrs: 1940 3rd Ave., Prince George, B.C., Canada V2M 1G7. (604) 564-2524. FAX: (604) 562-6611.

Carlson Communications International. Stns: 1 AM, 2 FM. KRJC(FM) Elko, Nev.; KRSP-FM Salt Lake City & KKDS(AM) South Salt Lake, both Utah. (All 100% owned.) Officers: Ralph J. Carlson, pres; Alan D. Hague, exec VP; R. Steve Carlson, sec/treas. Ownership: Ralph J. Carlson, 56%; Arthur W. Carlson, 34%. Hqtrs: Box 57760, Salt Lake City 84157. (801) 268-8181. FAX: (801) 266-1510.

Carolina Christian Broadcasting Inc. Stns: 4 TV. WATC(TV) Atlanta; KMCT-TV West Monroe, La.; WGGS-TV Greenville & WGSE(TV) Myrtle Beach, both S.C. (All 100% owned.) Ownership: James H. Thompson, 92%. Hqtrs: Box 1616, Greenville, S.C. 29602. (803) 244-1616. FAX: (803) 292-8481.

Carter Broadcasting Corp. Stns: 6 AM, 1 FM, 2 LPTV. WLOB(AM) Portland & WRUM(AM)-WWMR(FM) Rumford, both Me.; WROL(AM) Boston, WCRN(AM) Cherry Valley & WACE(AM) Chicopee, all Mass.; & WRIB(AM) Providence, R.I. LPTV: W45AL Portland, Me.; & W34BL Leicester, Mass. Ownership: Kenneth R. Carberry, 100%. Hqtrs: 20 Park Plaza, Suite 315, Boston 02116. (617) 423-0210. FAX: (617) 482-9305.

Cavaness Broadcasting Inc. Stns: 2 AM, 2 FM. KVOL(AM) Lafayette, KDEA(FM) New Iberia, KVOL-FM Opelousas & KXKW(AM) Tioga, all La. (All 100% owned.) Ownership: Roger W. Cavaness, Joel Cavaness, Dorothy Cavaness, Oran Vincent. Hqtrs: 123 E. Main St., Lafayette, La. 70501. (318) 233-1330. FAX: (318) 237-7733.

Cayuga/Northstar Radio Group. Stns: 4 AM, 5 FM. WTSV(AM) & WHDQ(FM) Claremont, N.H.; WKRT(AM)-WYYS(FM) Cortland, WNCQ-FM Morristown & WNCQ(AM)-WCIZ(FM) Watertown, all N.Y.; WNHV(AM) & WKXE-FM White River Junction, Vt. Ownership: J.D. Shapiro, B.G. Danziger & W.D. Goddard, principals. Hqtrs: Box 1230, Claremont, N.H. 03743. (603) 542-7735.

Century Broadcasting Corp. Stns: 1 AM, 2 FM. KYBG(AM) Aurora (Denver) & KYBG-FM Castle Rock (Denver), both Colo.; & WPNT-FM Chicago. Executives: George A. Collias, pres/CEO; Anthony C. Karlos, chmn; Richard J. Bonick Jr., exec VP. Hqtrs: 875 N. Michigan Ave., Chicago 60611. (312) 922-1000.

Chambers Communications Corp. Stns: 3 TV. KEZI(TV) Eugene, KDKF(TV) Klamath Falls & KDRV(TV) Medford, all Ore. (All 100% owned.) Executive: Carolyn Chambers, pres. Hqtrs: Box 7009, Eugene, Ore. 97401. (503) 485-5611. FAX: (503) 342-2695.

Chaparral Communications. Stns: 4 AM, 3 FM. KSGT(AM)-KMTN(FM) Jackson, KMER(AM) Kemmerer, KLDI(AM)-KRQU(FM) Laramie & KPOW(AM)-KLZY(FM) Powell, all Wyo. Ownership: Jerrold Lundquist. Hqtrs: Box 100, Jackson, Wyo. 83001. (307) 733-2120. FAX: (307) 733-7773.

Charisma Communications Group. Stns: 3 AM, 4 FM. WESE(FM) Baldwyn, WKOR-FM Columbus, WWZD(FM) New Albany, WKOR(AM)-WMSU(FM) Starkville, WPMX(AM) Tupelo & WTUP(AM) Tupelo, all Miss. (All 100% owned.) Executive: Terry Barber, VP-opns. Ownership: Donald R. DePriest, Sandra F. DePriest, Terry L. Barber. Hqtrs: Box 3300, Tupelo, Miss. 38803. (601) 842-1067. FAX: (601) 844-0725.

Charlottesville Broadcasting Corp. Stns: 2 AM, 1 FM. WINA(AM), WKAV(AM) & WQMZ(FM) Charlottesville, Va. Ownership: Laurence E. Richardson, Catharine G. Richardson, Colin Rosse. Box 498, 501 E. Main St., Charlottesville, Va. 22902. (804) 977-3030. FAX: (804) 977-3775.

Children's Broadcasting Corp. Stns: 6 AM. KCNW(AM) Fairway, Kan.; KYCR(AM) Golden Valley, Minn.; KTEK(AM) Alvin & KAHZ(AM) Fort Worth, both Tex.; WDCT(AM) Fairfax, Va.; & WYLO(AM) Jackson, Wis. Executives: Christopher Dahl, pres/CEO. Hqtrs: 724 First St. N., 4th Fl., Minneapolis 55401. (612) 338-3300. FAX: (612) 338-4318.

Chris Craft Industries Inc. Stns: 8 TV. KUTP(TV) Phoenix; KCOP(TV) Los Angeles & KBHK-TV San Francisco; KMSP-TV Minneapolis; WWOR-TV Secaucus, N.J.; KPTV(TV) Portland, Ore.; KMOL-TV San Antonio, Tex.; & KTVX(TV) Salt Lake City. Executives: Herbert J. Siegel, chmn/pres; Evan C. Thompson, VP/pres bcstg div; Bill Frank, exec VP; John C. Siegel, sr VP; William D. Siegel, sr VP; Laurence M. Kashdin, VP fin/controller; Brian Kelly, VP/gen counsel/sec; Joelen K. Merkel, treas. Hqtrs: 767 5th Ave., 46th Fl., New York 10153. (212) 421-0200. FAX: (212) 935-8462.

Christian Faith Broadcasting Inc. Stns: 1 FM, 2 TV. WLLA(TV) Kalamazoo, Mich.; WGGN(FM) Castalia & WGGN-TV Sandusky, both Ohio. Hqtrs: 3809 Maple Ave., Castalia, Ohio 44824. (419) 684-5311. FAX: (419) 684-5378.

Chronicle Broadcasting Co. Stns: 5 TV. KRON-TV San Francisco; KLBY(TV) Colby, KUPK-TV Garden City & KAKE-TV Wichita, all Kan.; & WOWT(TV) Omaha. (All 100% owned.) Executives: Amy McCombs, pres/CEO. Ownership: Chronicle Broadcasting Co. is subsidiary of Chronicle Publishing Co. (see Cross-Ownership, Sect. A). Cable TV. Hqtrs: 1001 Van Ness Ave., San Francisco 94109. (415) 441-4444. FAX: (415) 561-8069.

Citadel Communications Company Ltd., Coronet Communications Co. Stns: 5 TV. WOI-TV Ames & KCAU-TV Sioux City, both Iowa; KCAN(TV) Albion, Neb.; WMGC-TV Binghamton, N.Y.; & WVNY(TV) Burlington, Vt. Executive: Philip J. Lombardo, pres. Ownership: Philip J. Lombardo, mgng gen ptnr of Citadel Communications Company Ltd., also is pres & 100% owner of Lombardo Communications Inc., mgng gen ptnr & 80% owner of Coronet Communications Co., licensee of WHBF-TV Rock Island, Ill. Hqtrs: 17 Kraft Ave., Bronxville, N.Y. 10708. (914) 793-3400.

Citadel Communications Corp. Stns: 7 AM, 14 FM. KHOV(FM) Mariposa, KBEE(AM)-KATM(FM) Modesto & KHOP(FM) Modesto, all Calif.; KKFM(FM) Colorado Springs; KHEZ(FM) Caldwell, Idaho; KCTR-AM-FM Billings, KKBR(FM) Billings, KBOZ(AM)-KATH(FM) Bozeman & KBOZ-FM Livingston, all Mont.; KBUL(FM) Carson City & KROW(AM)-KNEV(FM) Reno, both Nev.; KLZX-AM-FM Salt Lake City; KGA(AM), KDRK-FM, KJRB(AM) & KEZE-FM Spokane, Wash. (All 100% owned.) Hqtrs: 1255 W. Baseline Rd., Suite 191, Mesa, Ariz. 85202. (602) 730-6663.

Civic Communication Corp. Stns: 3 TV. WLBT(TV) Jackson, Miss.; KTRE(TV) Lufkin & KLTV(TV) Tyler, both Tex. Ownership: Aaron E. Henry & Frank E. Melton. Hqtrs: Box 1712, Jackson, Miss. 39205. (601) 948-3333.

Clancy-Mance Communications. Stns: 3 AM, 4 FM. WTOJ(FM) Carthage, WDNY-AM-FM Dansville, WLKC(FM) Henderson, WCDO-AM-FM Sidney & WATN(AM) Watertown, all N.Y. (All 100% owned.) Ownership: Jack Clancy, David Mance. Hqtrs: 199 Wealtha Ave., Watertown, N.Y. 13601. (315) 782-1240.

Clarke Broadcasting Corp. Stns: 2 AM, 3 FM. KVRQ(FM) Atwater & KVML(AM)-KZSQ-FM Sonora, both Calif.; WGAU(AM) & WNGC(FM) Athens, Ga. (All 100% owned.) Ownership: H. Randolph Holder Sr. Hqtrs: 850 Bobbin Mill Rd., Athens, Ga. 30610. (706) 549-1340. FAX: (706) 546-0441.

Clear Channel Communications Inc. Stns: 14 AM, 15 FM, 9 TV. WPMI(TV) Mobile, Ala.; KTTU-TV Tucson, Ariz.; KLRT(TV) Little Rock, Ark.; WKCI(FM) Hamden, WAVZ(AM) New Haven & WELI(AM) New Haven, all Conn.; WAWS(TV) Jacksonville, WRBQ(AM) St. Petersburg & WRBQ-FM Tampa, all Fla.; KAAS-TV Salina & KQAM(AM)-KEYN-FM/KSAS-TV Wichita, both Kan.; WHAS(AM) & WAMZ(FM) Louisville, Ky.; WQUE-AM-FM New Orleans; KITN-TV Minneapolis; KTOK(AM)-KJYO(FM) Oklahoma City & KAKC(AM)-KMOD-FM-KOKI-TV Tulsa, both Okla.; WPTY-TV Memphis; KPEZ(FM) Austin, KTAM(AM)-KORA-FM Bryan, KHFI-FM Georgetown, KALO(AM)-KHYS(FM) Port Arthur, KQXT(FM) San Antonio, KZXS(AM) San Antonio & WOAI(AM)-KAJA(FM) San Antonio, all Tex.; WRVH(AM)-WRXL(FM) & WRVA(AM)-WRVQ(FM) Richmond, Va. (All 100% owned.) Note: Group manages the following stns, through loc mktg agreements: WYLD-AM-FM New Orleans; WMTU(TV) Jackson & WLMT(TV) Memphis, both Tenn. Executive: L. Lowry Mays, pres. Ownership: L. Lowry Mays, 22%; B.J. McCombs, 17%. Hqtrs: Box 659512, San Antonio, Tex. 78265. (210) 822-2828. FAX: (210) 822-2299.

Close Communications. Stns: 2 AM, 2 FM. WTVL-AM-FM Waterville, Me.; & WPNH-AM-FM Plymouth, N.H. Ownership: E.H. Close. Hqtrs: Box 1750, Keene, N.H. 03431. (603) 352-3691. FAX: (603) 357-2450.

Cobb Communications Inc. Stns: 6 AM, 2 FM. KLAM(AM) Cordova, KAKQ-AM-FM Fairbanks, KZXX(AM) Kenai, KVOK(AM)-KJJZ(FM) Kodiak, KSWD(AM) Seward & KVAK(AM) Valdez, all Alaska. Ownership: Thomas C. Tierney, pres, 100%. Note: Mr. Tierney also owns 100% of T.C.T. Communications Inc., licensee of KENI(AM) Anchorage. Hqtrs: 1777 Forest Park Dr., Anchorage 99517. (907) 272-7461. FAX: (907) 279-2112.

Cogeco Inc. Stns: 2 AM, 4 FM, 4 TV. CHLC(AM)-New FM Baie-Comeau, CFRP(AM) Forestville, CFGL-FM Laval, CJMF-FM Quebec, CFEI-FM St. Hyacinthe, CFKS-TV & CKSH-TV Sherbrooke, & CFKM-TV & CKTM-TV Trois-Rivieres, all Que. (All stns are located in Canada.) Executive: Louis Audet, pres. Ownership: Publicly traded. Controlled by Gestion Audem (Henri Audet & family). (See also Cross-Ownership, Sect. A.) Cable TV: Systems serving 427,900 subs. Hqtrs: One Place Ville-Marie, Suite 3636, Montreal, Que., Canada H3B 3P2. (514) 874-2600. FAX: (514) 874-2625.

Colfax Communications Inc. Stns: 1 AM, 4 FM. WBIG-FM & WGMS-FM Washington; WTEM(AM) Bethesda, Md.; KQQL(FM) Anoka & WBOB-FM Minneapolis, both Minn. Ownership: Equity Group Holdings (Steven Rales, Mitchell Rales). Hqtrs: 3033 Excelsior Blvd., Suite 300, Minneapolis 55416. (612) 924-2362. FAX: (612) 924-2310.

Colorado Farm-Ranch Radio Network. Stns: 2 AM, 2 FM. KSIR-AM-FM Brush & KRDZ(AM)-KATR-FM Wray, both Colo. Ownership: Robert D. Zellmer & Majorie M. Zellmer. Hqtrs: Box 2224, Greeley, Colo. 80632. (303) 353-6522.

Combined Broadcasting Inc. Stns: 3 TV. WBFS-TV Miami, Fla.; WGBO-TV Joliet, Ill.; & WGBS-TV Philadelphia. Note: WGBS-TV Philadelphia has been sold, pending FCC approval. Executives: Albert P. Krivin, chmn; Robert E. O'Connor, pres; Sharon Holloway, comptroller. Hqtrs: 16550 N.W. 52 Ave., Miami, Fla. 33014. (305) 621-3333. FAX: (305) 621-3844.

Commonwealth Broadcasting Co. Stns: 1 AM, 3 FM. KYXI(FM) Yuma, Ariz.; KMZQ-FM Henderson, Nev.; KRZY(AM) & KRST(FM) Albuquerque, N.M. (All 100% owned.) Note: Group also manages KOLT-FM Santa Fe, N.M., through a loc mktg agreement. Ownership: Dex Allen, Michael Thorsnes, Vince Bartolotta, John McGuire, Michael Padilla. Hqtrs: 2550 5th Ave., 11th Fl., San Diego 92103. (619) 236-9599. FAX: (619) 233-6517.

Communications Corp. Stns: 1 AM, 2 FM. KEZA(FM) Fayetteville, Ark.; KPEL(AM) & KTDY(FM) Lafayette, La. Ownership: Thomas R. Galloway, Michael B. Mitchell. Hqtrs: 1749 Bertrand Dr., Lafayette, La. 70506. (318) 233-6000.

Communications Properties Inc. Stns: 2 AM, 2 FM. WDBQ(AM) & KLYV(FM) Dubuque, Iowa; KATE(AM) & KCPI(FM) Albert Lea, Minn. Ownership: Philip T. Kelly, 100%. Hqtrs: 5490 Saratoga Rd., Dubuque, Iowa 52002. (319) 583-6475. FAX: (319) 583-4535.

Communicom Co. of America L.P. Stns: 3 AM. WWDJ(AM) Hackensack, N.J.; WZZD(AM) Philadelphia; & KSLR(AM) San Antonio, Tex. (All 100% owned.) Executives: Richard L. Kylberg Jr., pres. Ownership: CCA Inc., gen ptnr. Hqtrs: 4100 E. Mississippi Ave., Suite 1750, Denver 80222. (303) 759-8481. FAX: (303) 758-4964.

Community Pacific Broadcasting Company L.P. Stns: 2 AM, 3 FM. KBFX(FM) Anchorage & KKSD(AM)-KASH-FM Anchorage; KFIV(AM) & KJSN(FM) Modesto, Calif. (All 100% owned). Executives: David J. Benjamin, pres/CEO; Judy Peterson, controller. Hqtrs: 2511 Garden Rd., Bldg. A, Suite 104, Monterey, Calif. 93940. (408) 655-6350. FAX: (408) 655-6355.

Community Service Radio Group Stns: 5 AM, 6 FM. KSWM(AM) Aurora & KELE(FM) Mount Vernon, both Mo.; KWHW(AM)-KRKZ(FM) Altus & KWON(AM)-KYFM(FM) Bartlesville, both Okla.; KDNT(AM) Denton, KTXJ(AM)-KWYX(FM) Jasper, KIOL-FM Lamesa & KDXE(FM) Sulphur Springs, all Tex. Ownership: Galen O. Gilbert, Jesse Gilbert, Jimmy Young. Hqtrs: Box 492, Sulphur Springs, Tex. 75483. (903) 439-4985. FAX: (903) 439-4894.

Compass Radio Group. Stns: 3 AM, 3 FM. KOOL-AM-FM Phoenix; KCBQ-AM-FM San Diego; KFNS(AM) Wood River, Ill.; & KEZK-FM St. Louis. (All 100% owned.) Ownership: Bob Hughes, 50%; Jonathan Schwartz, 50%. Hqtrs: 9416 Mission Gorge Rd., Santee, Calif. 92071. (619) 286-1170. FAX: (619) 449-8548.

Confederation Tribes of Warm Springs. Stns: 3 FM. KTWS(FM) Bend, KTWI(FM) Warm Springs & noncommercial KWSO(FM) Warm Springs, all Ore. (All 100% owned.) Hqtrs: Box 489, Warm Springs, Ore. 97761. (503) 553-1968. FAX: (503) 553-3348.

Contemporary Communications. Stns: 1 AM, 4 FM. KWLT(FM) North Crossett, Ark. (51%); WDTL-AM-FM Cleveland (51%) & WKZB(FM) Drew (51%), both Miss.; & KOOZ(FM) Great Falls, Mont. (100%). Ownership: Larry G. Fuss, 100%. Hqtrs: Box 1787, Cleveland, Miss. 38732. (601) 846-1787. FAX: (601) 843-0494.

Contemporary Media Broadcasting Group. Stns: 2 AM, 4 FM. WBFX(AM), WBOW(AM) & WZZQ(FM) Terre Haute, Ind.; KFMZ(FM) Columbia, KBMX(FM) Eldon & KTDI(FM) Huntsville, all Mo. (All 100% owned.) Ownership: Mike Rice, 100%. Hqtrs: 235 Jungerman Rd., St. Peters, Mo. 63376. (314) 928-6569. FAX: (314) 928-6525.

Continental Broadcasting Ltd. Stns: 1 AM, 2 FM, 4 TV. KOVR(TV) Stockton, Calif.; KZSS(AM)-KZRR(FM) Albuquerque & KLSK(FM) Santa Fe, both N.M.; WLOS(TV) Asheville, N.C.; WSYX(TV) Columbus, Ohio; & WAXA(TV) Anderson, S.C. Executives: Benjamin Diesbach, pres; Patrick Murphy, CFO. Hqtrs: Carew Tower, 441 Vine St., Suite 3900, Cincinnati 45202. (513) 333-3000. FAX: (513) 333-3007.

Continental Television Network Inc. Stns: 3 TV. KWYB(TV) Butte, KTGF(TV) Great Falls & KTMF(TV) Missoula, all Mont. (All 100% owned.) Ownership: James M. Colla, William Cordingley, Al Donohue, Penny Adkins. Hqtrs: 118 6th St. S., Great Falls, Mont. 59405. (406) 761-8816. FAX: (406) 454-3484.

Cook Inlet Radio Partners L.P. Stns: 1 AM, 3 FM. WPGC-AM-FM Morningside, Md.; KBXX(FM) Houston; & KUBE(FM) Seattle. Note: WPGC-AM-FM Morningside, Md. has been sold, subject to FCC approval. Executives: Ben Hill, pres; Dale Williamson, VP fin & admin. Hqtrs: 6301 Ivy Ln., Suite 800, Greenbelt, Md. 20770. (301) 441-3332. FAX: (301) 982-0981.

Cordillera Communications Inc. Stns: 5 TV. KOAA-TV Pueblo, Colo.; KIVI(TV) Nampa, Idaho; KXLF-TV Butte, KRTV(TV) Great Falls & KPAX-TV Missoula, all Mont. Note: Group has purchased KTVQ(TV) Billings, Mont., subject to FCC approval. Executive: Travis O. Rockey, pres. (See Evening Post Publishing Co. under Cross-Ownership, Sect. A.) Hqtrs: 134 Columbus St., Charleston, S.C. 29403-4800. (803) 577-7111. FAX: (803) 937-5788.

Cornerstone TeleVision Inc. Stns: 3 TV. WOCD(TV) Amsterdam, N.Y.; WKBS-TV Altoona & WPCB-TV Greensburg, both Pa. Note: Group also owns low-power TV stn W50BF Sharon-Hermitage, Pa. (ch 50). Ownership: nonprofit. Hqtrs: Wall, Pa. 15148-1499. (412) 824-3930. FAX: (412) 824-5442.

Coshocton Broadcasting Co. Stns: 1 AM, 3 FM. WUFA(FM) Byesville, WTNS-AM-FM Coshocton & WKLM(FM) Millersburg, all Ohio. Ownership: Bruce Wallace, 100%. Hqtrs: 114 N. 6th St., Coshocton, Ohio 43812. (614) 622-1560. FAX: (614) 622-7940.

Cosmos Broadcasting Corp. Stns: 7 TV. WSFA(TV) Montgomery, Ala.; KAIT-TV Jonesboro, Ark.; WFIE-TV Evansville, Ind.; WAVE(TV) Louisville, Ky.; KPLC-TV Lake Charles, La.; WTOL-TV Toledo, Ohio; & WIS(TV) Columbia, S.C. (All 100% owned.) Executives: James R. Sefert, chmn; James M. Keelor, pres; G. Neil Smith, VP fin; Clyde W. Anderson, Conrad L. Cagle, J. Harold Culver, Guy W. Hempel, Ronald F. Loewen, Melbourne A. Stebbins, James D. Serra, VPs. Ownership: The Liberty Corp., Greenville, S.C. (Francis M. Hipp, W. Hayne Hipp & families, principals). Hqtrs: Box 789, Greenville, S.C. 29602. (803) 292-4370. FAX: (803) 292-4420.

Cottonwood Communications Corp. Stns: 1 AM, 2 FM. KPSA(AM) Alamogordo, KOKN(FM) Hobbs & KPSA-FM La Luz, all N.M. (All 100% owned.) Note: Group is seeking FCC approval to operate on two FM frequencies in the Alamogordo, N.M. area: On 103.7 mhz in Alamogordo, N.M. with 50 kw & on 92.7 mhz in La Luz, N.M. Ownership: Robert J. Flotte & Beverly R. Flotte, 100%. Note: Company also prints a mthy *Real Estate Showcase* magazine. Hqtrs: Box 720, Alamogordo, N.M. 88310. (505) 437-1505. FAX: (505) 437-5566.

Cox Broadcasting. Stns: 5 AM, 8 FM, 6 TV. WSB-AM-FM-TV Atlanta; WSOC-TV Charlotte, N.C.; WHQT(FM) Coral Gables, Fla.; KRRW(FM) Dallas; WHIO-AM-TV & WHKO(FM) Dayton, Ohio; WCKG(FM) Elmwood Park, Ill. (Chicago); KFI(AM) & KOST(FM) Los Angeles; WIOD(AM) & WFLC(FM) Miami; KTVU(TV) Oakland, Calif. (San Francisco); WFTV(TV) Orlando, Fla.; WPXI(TV) Pittsburgh; WSUN(AM) & WCOF(FM) St. Petersburg, Fla. Note: Group has bought WYAI(FM) La Grange, Ga., WYSY-FM Aurora, Ill. & KTXQ(FM) Fort Worth & sold WSUN(AM) & WCOF(FM) St. Petersburg, Fla., subject to FCC approval. Corporate officers: James C. Kennedy, chmn/CEO; John R. Dillon, sr VP/CFO; Timothy W. Hughes, VP human resources; John G. Boyette, VP/controller; Andrew A. Merdek, VP legal affrs/corporate sec. Broadcasting division officers: Nicholas D. Trigony, pres; Robert F. Neil, exec VP radio; Andrew S. Fisher, exec VP affils; Kevin P. O'Brien, exec VP independent group; Patrick J. Gmiter, VP mktg; Thomas E. McClendon, VP/dir rsch; John J. Rouse Jr., VP/controller; John F. Swanson, VP engrg. Cable TV: Cox Cable Communications. (See also Cox Enterprises Inc. under Cross-Ownership, Sect. A.) Hqtrs: Box

105357, Atlanta 30348. (404) 843-5000. FAX: (404) 843-5280.

Crain Broadcasting Co. Stns: 1 AM, 2 FM. WLVV(AM) Mobile, Ala.; WHLE(FM) Byhalia, Miss.; & KWTA(FM) Electra, both Tex. Note: Group has purchased KGRW(FM) Friona, Tex., subject to FCC approval. Executives: Albert L. Crain, pres; Jimmie Henderson, mgr Mobile, Ala. Ownership: Albert L. Crain. Hqtrs: 102 Brookhaven Dr., Columbia, Tenn. 38401. (615) 381-4511. FAX: (615) 381-4511.

Crawford Broadcasting Co. Stns: 6 AM, 5 FM. WDJC(FM) Birmingham, Ala.; KBRT(AM) Avalon (Los Angeles) & KCBC(AM) Riverbank, both Calif.; KLZ(AM) Denver; WYCA(FM) Hammond, Ind. (Chicago); WMUZ(FM) Detroit; WDCX(FM) Buffalo, WDCW(AM) Syracuse & WDCZ(FM) Webster, all N.Y.; KPHP(AM) Lake Oswego (Portland), Ore.; & KPBC(AM) Garland (Dallas), Tex. (All 100% owned.) Executive: Donald B. Crawford, pres. Ownership: Donald B. Crawford is sole own of all the stns except WMUZ(FM). WMUZ(FM) is owned by Donald B. Crawford & Dean A. Crawford. Hqtrs: Box 3003, Blue Bell, Pa. 19422. (215) 628-3500. FAX: (215) 628-0818.

Criswell Center for Biblical Studies. Stns: 1 AM, 5 FM. KSYE(FM) Frederick, Okla.; KAGN(FM) Abilene, KCBI-FM Dallas, KTDN(FM) Palestine & KCRN-AM-FM San Angelo, all Tex. (All 100% owned.) Hqtrs: 411 Ryan Plaza Dr., Arlington, Tex. 76011. (817) 792-3800.

The Cromwell Group Inc. Stns: 5 AM, 11 FM. WHQQ(FM) Charleston, WYDS(FM) Decatur, WFYR(FM) Elmwood, WMCI(FM) Mattoon, WVEL(AM)-WGLO(FM) Pekin & WSHY(AM)-WEJT(FM) Shelbyville, all Ill.; WLME(FM) Cannelton, Ind.; WKCM-AM-FM Hawesville & WBIO(FM) Philpot, both Ky.; WCTZ(AM) Clarksville, WQZQ(FM) Dickson (Nashville) & WHAL(AM)-WYCQ(FM) Shelbyville, all Tenn. (All 100% owned.) Ownership: Bayard H. Walters, pres, 100%. Hqtrs: Box 150846, Nashville 37215. (615) 361-7560. FAX: (615) 366-4313.

Crown Broadcasting Inc. Stns: 1 AM, 2 FM. KZXY-AM-FM Apple Valley, Calif.; & KTRR(FM) Loveland, Colo. Executive: Thomas P. Gammon, pres. Hqtrs: 8401 Old Courthouse Rd., Suite 140, Vienna, Va. 22182. (703) 506-0990. FAX: (703) 506-0992.

The Curators of the University of Missouri. Stns: 5 FM, 1 TV. KOMU-TV Columbia, Mo. (commercial TV stn) plus the following noncommercial FM stns: KBIA(FM) Columbia, KCUR-FM Kansas City, KMNR(FM) & KUMR(FM) Rolla, & KWMU(FM) St. Louis, all Mo. (All 100% owned.) Hqtrs: 6 Clark Hall, University of Missouri, Columbia, Mo. 65211. (314) 882-6205. FAX: (314) 884-4347.

Curtis Media Group. Stns: 6 AM, 5 FM. WBBB(AM)-WPCM(FM) Burlington (100%), WGBR(AM)-WKTC(FM) Goldsboro (100%), WEWO(AM)-WAZZ(FM) Laurinburg (100%), WPTF(AM) Raleigh (67%), WQDR(FM) Raleigh (100%), WTAB(AM)-WYNA(FM) Tabor City (84%) & WCPS(AM) Tarboro, all N.C. Ownership: Donald W. Curtis & others. Hqtrs: 3012 Highwoods Blvd., Raleigh, N.C. 27604. (919) 876-0674. FAX: (919) 790-6341.

D

Davis Broadcasting Inc. Stns: 2 AM, 3 FM. WTHB(AM)-WFXA-FM Augusta, WOKS(AM)-WFXE(FM) Columbus & WAKB(FM) Wrens, all Ga. Ownership: Gregory A. Davis, 76%. Hqtrs: 1115 14th St., Columbus, Ga. 31902-1998. (706) 576-3565. FAX: (706) 576-3683.

Davis-Goldfarb Co. Stns: 3 TV. KCPM(TV) Chico, Calif.; KSPR(TV) Springfield, Mo.; & KMID(TV) Midland, Tex. Ownership: John Davis, Joseph Goldfarb, Barbara E. Goldfarb. Hqtrs: 2121 Ave. of the Stars, Suite 2800, Los Angeles 90067. (310) 551-2288. FAX: (310) 286-9359.

DeDominicis Broadcasting. Stns: 2 AM, 2 FM. WNEZ(AM) & WRCH(FM) New Britain, Conn.; WBEU(AM) & WYKZ(FM) Beaufort, S.C. (All 100% owned.) Note: WNEZ(AM) & WRCH(FM) New Britain, Conn. have been sold, subject to FCC approval. Ownership: Enzo DeDominicis, 100%. Hqtrs: Box 507, WRCH-WNEZ, Radio Park, Farmington, Conn. 06034-0507. (203) 678-9100. FAX: (203) 678-7053.

Deer River Group. Stns: 1 AM, 2 FM. WFGL(AM) & WXLO-FM Fitchburg (Worcester), Mass.; & WIZN(FM) Vergennes (Burlington), Vt. Executives: Robin B. Martin, pres/CEO; Jay P. Williams Jr., COO. Ownership: Robin B. Martin, Jay P. Williams. Hqtrs: 2000 L St. N.W., Suite 200, Washington 20036. (202) 659-3331.

Delaware County Broadcasting Corp. Stns: 1 AM, 3 FM. WDHI(FM) Delhi, WIYN(FM) Deposit & WDLA-AM-FM Walton, all N.Y. (All 100% owned.) Ownership: Amos F. Finch, 50%; Myra A. Youmans, 50%. Hqtrs: Box 58, Walton, N.Y. 13856. (607) 865-4321. FAX: (607) 865-4189.

Demaree Media Inc. Stns: 3 AM, 5 FM. KOLZ(FM) Bentonville, KFAY(AM) Farmington (100%), KKEG(FM) Fayetteville (100%), KZNG(AM)-KQUS-FM Hot Springs (100%) & KWCK-AM-FM Searcy (65%), all Ark.; & KXUS(FM) Springfield, Mo. (100%). Executive: Levoy Patrick Demaree, pres. Ownership: Levoy Patrick Demaree, 89%; Reba Pearl Demaree, 10%; Charles Arnold Demaree, 1%. Hqtrs: Box 878, 1780 Holly St., Fayetteville, Ark. 72702. (501) 521-5566. FAX: (501) 521-0751.

Desert West Air Ranchers Corp. Stns: 3 FM. KFLX(FM) Kachina Village, KZLZ(FM) Kearny & KCDX(FM) San Carlos, all Ariz. (All 100% owned.) Ownership: Ted Tucker, 50%. Hqtrs: Box 36717, Tucson, Ariz. 85740. (602) 797-1008. FAX: (602) 797-1008.

Design Media Inc. Stns: 2 AM, 2 FM. WKEU(AM) & WQUL(FM) Griffin, Ga.; WQIS(AM) & WNSL(FM) Laurel, Miss. (All 100% owned.) Ownership: John C. Thomas, Leonard Bolton. Hqtrs: 3021 Sheffield Dr., Emmaus, Pa. 18049. (215) 965-8427.

Diamond Broadcasting Inc. Stns: 3 AM, 2 FM. WSBC(AM), WSCR(AM) & WXRT(FM) Chicago; KOMA(AM) & KRXO(FM) Oklahoma City. (All 100% owned.) Ownership: Daniel R. Lee, 100%. Hqtrs: 4949 W. Belmont Ave., Chicago 60641. (312) 777-1700. FAX: (312) 777-5031.

Dick Broadcasting Co. Stns: 3 AM, 6 FM. WJOX(AM) & WZRR(FM) Birmingham, Ala.; WKRR(FM) Asheboro & WKZL(FM) Winston-Salem, both N.C.; WGFX(FM) Gallatin, WIVK-AM-FM Knoxville & WKDA(AM)-WKDF(FM) Nashville, all Tenn. (All 100% owned.) Ownership: James A. Dick Sr., chmn; James Allen Dick Jr., pres; Marilyn M. Dick, Jeannette Dick Hundley, Emily Dick McAlister, C. Arthur Dick. Hqtrs: 6711 Kingston Pike, Knoxville, Tenn. 37919. (615) 588-6511. FAX: (615) 588-3725.

Dispatch Printing Co. Stns: 2 TV. WTHR(TV) Indianapolis; & WBNS-TV Columbus, Ohio. Executive: John Walton Wolfe, chmn. Ownership: Privately owned by Wolfe family, Columbus, Ohio. (See Cross-Ownership, Sect. A.) Hqtrs: 34 S. 3rd St., Columbus, Ohio 43216. (614) 461-5000. FAX: (614) 461-7588.

Dittman Group Inc. Stns: 2 AM, 2 FM. WAPI-AM-FM Birmingham & WABB-AM-FM Mobile, both Ala. Note: WAPI-AM-FM Birmingham, Ala. has been sold, subject to FCC approval. Ownership: Bernard S. Dittman. Hqtrs: 1551 Springhill Ave., Mobile, Ala. 36604. (205) 432-5572. FAX: (205) 438-4044.

Diversified Communications. Stns: 1 AM, 1 FM, 4 TV. WCJB(TV) Gainesville, Fla.; WABI-AM-TV & WYOU-FM Bangor, Me.; WYOU(TV) Scranton, Pa.; & WPDE-TV Florence, S.C. (All 100% owned.) Executives: Horace A. Hildreth Jr., pres; Garry H. Ritchie, pres bcst division. Ownership: Horace A. Hildreth Jr., Josephine H. Detmer, Anne Russell. (See Cross-Ownership, Sect. A.) Cable TV. Hqtrs: Box 7437, 5 Milk St., Portland, Me. 04112. (207) 774-5981. FAX: (207) 761-7915.

Dix Communications. Stns: 3 AM, 4 FM, 6 TV. WMMZ(FM) Ocala, Fla.; WTBO(AM) & WKGO(FM) Cumberland, Md.; KAAL(TV) Austin, Minn.; KULR-TV Billings & KFBB-TV Great Falls, both Mont.; WKVX(AM) & WQKT(FM) Wooster, Ohio; WRAD(AM) & WRIQ(FM) Radford, Va.; KTWO-TV Casper, KKTU(TV) Cheyenne & KRBQ(TV) Sheridan, all Wyo. Executives: A.E. Dix, pres; Robert C. Dix, TV div chmn; R. Victor Dix, David E. Dix, G. Charles Dix, VPs; Dale E. Gerber, controller. Ownership: Albert Dix, Robert C. Dix, R. Victor Dix, David E. Dix, Charles Dix. (See also Cross-Ownership, Sect. A.) Hqtrs: 212 E. Liberty St., Wooster, Ohio 44691. (216) 264-3511, (502) 227-4556. FAX: (216) 263-5013.

Double L Broadcasting. Stns: 2 AM, 2 FM. WIBA-AM-FM Madison & WMAD-AM-FM Sun Prairie, both Wis. (All 100% owned.) Executive: Lee Leicinger, pres. Hqtrs: Box 99, Madison, Wis. 53701. (608) 274-5450. FAX: (608) 274-5521.

Douglas Broadcasting Inc. Stns: 5 AM, 5 FM. KMAX(FM) Arcadia, KBAX(FM) Fallbrook, KEST(AM) San Francisco, KWIZ-FM Santa Ana, KAXX(FM) Ventura & KOBO(AM) Yuba City, all Calif.; WVVX(FM) Highland Park, Ill.; WNDZ(AM) Portage, Ind.; WNJR(AM) Newark, N.J.; & KGOL(AM) Humble, Tex. (All 100% owned.) Note: Group has purchased WBIV(AM) Natick, Mass., subject to FCC approval. Ownership: N. John Douglas, 100%. Hqtrs: 499 Hamilton Ave., Suite 140, Palo Alto, Calif. 94301. (415) 324-5888. FAX: (415) 688-1166.

Draper Communications Inc. Stns: 2 TV. WBOC-TV Salisbury, Md.; & KGBT-TV Harlingen, Tex. (Both 100% owned.) Ownership: Tom Draper, 60%; & others. Hqtrs: Box 2057, Salisbury, Md. 21801. (410) 749-1111. FAX: (410) 749-6098.

R.H. Drewry Group. Stns: 2 AM, 1 FM, 4 TV. KRHD-AM-FM Duncan & KSWO-AM-TV Lawton, both Oklahoma; KFDA-TV Amarillo, KWAB(TV) Big Spring & KWES-TV Odessa, all Tex. Ownership: R.H. Drewry owns 62.1% of KRHD-AM-FM & 69% of KSWO-AM-TV. KFDA-TV is a joint venture owned by Lawton Cablevision (50%), KSWD-TV (45%), KSWO(AM) (2 1/2%) & KRHD-AM-FM (2 1/2%). KWAB(TV) & KWES-TV are owned by KSWO Television Inc. (50%) & Lawton Cablevision Inc. (50%). Cable TV. Hqtrs: Box 708, Lawton, Okla. 73502. (405) 353-0820. FAX: (405) 355-7531.

Dudley Communications Corp. Stns: 2 TV. WXMI(TV) Grand Rapids, Mich.; & KTZZ-TV Seattle. (Both 100% owned.) Ownership: Robert L. Dudley, 40%; Richard D. Dudley, 38%; Nancy Dudley, 10%. Hqtrs: 500 3rd St., Suite 208-17, Wausau, Wis. 54401. (715) 848-1456. FAX: (715) 848-6189.

Dudman Communications Corp. Stns: 1 AM, 2 FM. WEZQ(FM) Bangor & WDEA(AM)-WWMJ(FM) Ellsworth, both Me. (All 100% owned.) Ownership: Helen Sloane Dudman, Janet Sloane Dudman, Martha Tod Dudman. Hqtrs: Box 1129, 68 State St., Ellsworth, Me. 04605. (207) 667-9555. FAX: (207) 667-2436.

Duhamel Broadcasting Enterprises. Stns: 1 AM, 1 FM, 4 TV. KDUH-TV Scottsbluff, Neb.; KHSD-TV Lead, KOTA-AM-TV Rapid City & KEZV(FM) Spearfish, all S.D.; & KSGW-TV Sheridan, Wyo. (All 100% owned.) Executives: William F. Duhamel, pres/gen mgr; Peter A. Duhamel, VP; Jacquelyn C. Duhamel, sec; Lois G. Duhamel, treas; Wes Haugen, natl sls mgr; Monte Loos, prog dir/film buyer. Ownership: William F. Duhamel & Jacquelyn C. Duhamel, 63%; Peter A. & Lois G. Duhamel, 37%. Cable TV. Hqtrs: Box 1760, Rapid City, S.D. 57709. (605) 342-2000.

Duke Broadcasting Corp. Stns: 1 AM, 2 FM. KBTM(AM), KFIN(FM) & KIYS(FM) Jonesboro, Ark. (All 100% owned.) Hqtrs: Box 1737, Jonesboro, Ark. 72403. (501) 932-8400. FAX: (501) 932-3814.

E

EZ Communications Inc. Stns: 3 AM, 10 FM. KQBR(FM) Davis & KRAK-AM-FM Sacramento, both Calif.; WEZB(FM) New Orleans; KSD-AM-FM & KYKY(FM) St. Louis; WMXC(FM) & WSOC-FM Charlotte, N.C.; WIOQ(FM) Philadelphia & WBZZ(FM) Pittsburgh; & KMPS-AM-FM Seattle. (All 100% owned.) Note: Group has purchased KNCI(FM) Sacramento, Calif., pending FCC approval. Executives: Arthur Kellar, chmn; Alan Box, pres; Ron Peele, VP/sec/treas. Hqtrs: 10800 Main St., Fairfax, Va. 22030. (703) 591-1000. FAX: (703) 934-1200.

Eagle Communications. Stns: 1 AM, 5 FM. KGGY(FM) Dubuque, Iowa; WGFG(FM) Branchville & WIGL(FM) Orangeburg, both S.C.; KAFX-AM-FM Diboll, Tex.; & WMGU(FM) Stevens Point, Wis. (All 100% owned.) Executive: John Hazlewood, gen mgr. Ownership: Tom Love, 100%. Hqtrs: Box 588, Lufkin, Tex. 75902. (409) 634-5596. FAX: (409) 639-5540.

Eagle Communications Group. Stns: 6 AM, 8 FM. KLOE(AM)-KKCI(FM) Goodland, KAYS(AM)-KHAZ(FM) Hays, KHOK(FM) Hoisington & KWBW(AM)-KHUT(FM) Hutchinson, all Kan.; KFEQ(AM) St. Joseph & KSJQ(FM) Savannah, both Mo.; KCOW(AM)-KAAQ(FM) Alliance, KQSK(FM) Chadron & KOOQ(AM)-KELN(FM) North Platte, all Neb. Ownership: Robert E. Schmidt, 100%. Cable TV. Hqtrs: Box 817, Hays, Kan. 67601. (913) 625-4000. FAX: (913) 625-8030.

Eagle Communications Inc. Stns: 3 TV. KTVM(TV) Butte, KCFW-TV Kalispell & KECI-TV Missoula, all Mont. (All 100% owned.) Note: Group also owns a low-power TV stn: K42BZ Bozeman, Mont. Ownership: Precht Communications Inc., 100% (Robert Precht, chmn of bd). Precht Television Associates Inc. owns KIEM-TV Eureka, Calif. Hqtrs: 340 W. Main, Missoula, Mont. 59802. (406) 721-2063. FAX: (406) 549-6500.

Eagle's Nest Inc. Stns: 2 AM, 1 FM. WELR-AM-FM Roanoke, Ala.; & WLAG(AM) La Grange, Ga. (All 100% owned.) Note: WLAG(AM) La Grange, Ga. & WELR-FM Roanoke, Ala. are operated as a combo in La Grange, Ga. Ownership: Jim Vice, 51%; Kay Vice, 49%. Hqtrs: Box 709, Roanoke, Ala. 36274. (205) 863-4139. FAX: (205) 863-2540.

Ellis Communications. Stns: 1 AM, 1 FM, 6 TV. WEVU(TV) Naples, Fla.; KAME-TV Reno; WUPW(TV) Toledo, Ohio; WACH(TV) Columbia, S,C.; WKCH-TV Knoxville & WMC-AM-FM-TV Memphis, both Tenn. (All 100% owned.) Ownership: Kelso & Co., U. Bertram Ellis Jr. Hqtrs: 3060 Peachtree Rd., Suite 930, Atlanta 30305. (404) 240-0924.

Emmet Broadcasting Co. Stns: 2 AM, 1 FM. WPTX(AM) & WMDM-FM Lexington Park, Md.; & WAGE(AM) Leesburg, Va. Ownership: Grenville Emmet III, Grenville Emmet IV, Patrick Emmet, Bradford Emmet, Samantha Emmet. Hqtrs: 711 Wage Dr., Leesburg, Va. 22075. (703) 777-1200. FAX: (703) 777-7431.

Emmis Broadcasting Corp. Stns: 5 FM. KPWR(FM) Los Angeles; WKQX(FM) Chicago; WENS(FM) Shelbyville, Ind.; KSHE(FM) Crestwood, Mo.; & WQHT(FM) New York. (All 100% owned.) Executive: Jeffrey H. Smulyan, chmn of bd. Ownership: Jeffrey H. Smulyan, 60%; Morgan Stanley-Cigna, 20%; Steven C. Crane, 10%. (See also Cross-Ownership, Sect. A.) Hqtrs: Gateway Plaza, 950 N. Meridian St., Suite 1200, Indianapolis 46204. (317) 266-0100.

Empire Radio Partners Ltd. Stns: 1 AM, 3 FM. WJYY(FM) Concord & WRCI(FM) Hillsboro, both N.H.; & WGY-AM-FM Schenectady, N.Y. (All 100% owned.) Note: FCC approved the sale of WJYY(FM) Concord & WRCI(FM) Hillsboro, both N.H., on July 2, 1993, but the transfer had not been completed as of Nov. 15, 1993. Ownership: Great Northeast Communications. Hqtrs: 1430 Balltown Rd., Schenectady, N.Y. 12309. (518) 381-4800. FAX: (518) 381-4855.

Entercom. Stns: 3 AM, 9 FM. KITS(FM) San Francisco; WKTK(FM) Crystal River (Gainesville-Ocala) & WYUU(FM) Safety Harbor (Tampa-St. Petersburg), both Fla.; KRXX-FM Minneapolis & KRXX(AM) Richfield (Minneapolis), both Minn.; KOQL(FM) Oklahoma City; WEEP(AM) Hampton twp (Pittsburgh), WDSY-FM Pittsburgh & WXRB(FM) Pittsburgh, all Pa.; KLDE(FM) Houston; & KMTT-AM-FM Tacoma, Wash. (Seattle). (All 100% owned.) Ownership: Joseph M. Field. Hqtrs: 100 Presidential Blvd., Suite 10, Bala-Cynwyd, Pa. 19004. (215) 667-1226. FAX: (215) 667-1326.

Enterprise Network. Stns: 3 AM, 2 FM. KGVW-AM-FM Belgrade, KURL(AM) Billings & KALS(FM) Kalispell, all Mont.; & KUYO(AM) Evansville, Wyo. Executives: Harold Erickson, pres; Bruce Erickson, exec VP. Hqtrs: Box 30455, Billings, Mont. 59107-0455. (406) 248-4990. FAX: (406) 248-6436.

Erin Communications Inc. Stns: 2 AM, 2 FM. WMNS (AM)-WMXO(FM) Olean & WLSV(AM)-WJQZ(FM) Wellsville, both N.Y. Ownership: John R. & Elaine A. Murphy. Hqtrs: 48 South Ridge Trail, Fairport, N.Y. 14450. (716) 372-6660. FAX: (716) 372-8700.

Eure Communications Inc. Stns: 1 AM, 2 FM. WCHV(AM)-WWWV(FM) Charlottesville & WXEZ(FM) Yorktown, both Va. (All 100% owned.) Ownership: William L. Eure, 51%; Sue S. Eure, 49%. Hqtrs: 4026 George Washington Hwy., Yorktown, Va. 23692. (804) 898-9494. FAX: (804) 898-9401.

Eureka Broadcasting Co. Stns: 2 AM, 1 FM. KINS(AM), KWSW(AM) & KEKA-FM Eureka, Calif. Hqtrs: 1101 Marsh Rd., Eureka, Calif. 95501. (707) 442-5744. FAX: (707) 444-3899.

Evangel Ministries Inc. Stns: 1 AM, 3 FM. WAAU(FM) Appleton, WSGC(AM) Kaukauna, WGNV(FM) Milladore & WEMI(FM) Neenah-Menasha, all Wis. (All 100% owned.) Hqtrs: 1909 W. 2nd St., Appleton, Wis. 54914. (414) 731-6310. FAX: (414) 749-0474.

Evergreen Media Corp. Stns: 4 AM, 6 FM. KKBT(FM) Los Angeles & KMEL(FM) San Francisco; WTOP(AM) & WASH(FM) Washington; WVCG(AM) Coral Gables, Fla.; WMVP(AM)-WLUP-FM & WWBZ(FM) Chicago; KTRH(AM) & KLOL(FM) Houston. Note: Group has bought KIOI(FM) San Francisco, pending FCC approval. Executives: Scott K. Ginsburg, chmn/CEO; James E. de Castro, pres/COO; Matthew E. Devine, treas/CFO. Hqtrs: 433 E. Las Colinas Blvd., Suite 1130, Irving, Tex. 75039. (214) 869-9020. FAX: (214) 869-3671.

F

Fairbanks Communications Inc. Stns: 3 AM, 2 FM. WJNX(AM) Fort Pierce, WRMF(FM) Palm Beach & WJNO(AM) West Palm Beach, all Fla.; WKOX(AM) & WCLB-FM Framingham, Mass. (Boston). Executives: Richard M. Fairbanks, pres; James C. Hilliard, exec VP; Roger Snowdon, VP fin; Richard Smart, VP engrg. Cable TV: Leadership Cablevision, Delray Beach, Fla. (including Gulf Stream. Ocean Ridge & Palm Beach County); Fairbanks Cable, Bright, Ind.; Dearborn Cablevision, Lawrenceburg, Ind. (including Aurora, Rising Sun & Dearborn County); Fairbanks Cable, Milan, Ind. (including Moores Hill); & Fairbanks Cable, Osgood, Ind. (including Versailles). Hqtrs: 1601 Belvedere Rd., No. 202E, West Palm Beach, Fla. 33406. (407) 838-4370. FAX: (407) 689-9957.

Faircom Inc. Stns: 1 AM, 2 FM. WFNT(AM) & WCRZ(FM) Flint, Mich.; & WHFM(FM) Southampton, N.Y. (All 100% owned.) Executives: Joel M. Fairman, pres; John E. Risher, VP Flint, Mich. Ownership: Officers & directors, 23.8%; balance publicly owned. Hqtrs: 333 Glen Head Rd., Old Brookville, N.Y. 11545. (516) 676-2644.

Fairmont Communications Corp. Stns: 3 AM, 4 FM. KIOI(FM) San Francisco; WMTG(AM) & WNIC(FM) Dearborn, Mich.; KKOB-AM-FM Albuquerque, N.M.; & WLAC-AM-FM Nashville. Note: KIOI(FM) San Francisco & WMTG(AM)-WNIC(FM) Dearborn, Mich. have been sold, subject to FCC approval. Executives: Frank Osborn, chmn (405 Lexington Ave., 54th Fl., New York 10174); Mark O. Hubbard, pres; Barry M. Wolper, sec/treas. Ownership: Osborn Communications Corp., 25% (see listing); Price Communications Corp., 25%; Citicorp Venture Capital, 25%; Prudential-Bache Interfunding Inc., 25%. Hqtrs: 430 Reading Rd., 4th Fl., Cincinnati 45202. (513) 421-6726. FAX: (513) 381-2691.

Family Broadcasting Company Inc. Stns: 3 TV. KTVC(TV) Cedar Rapids, Iowa; KKFT(TV) Fort Scott, Kan.; & KTVG(TV) Grand Island, Neb. Ownership: Jerry Montgomery, 48%; Donna Montgomery, 48%; Opal Montgomery, 1%; Karla Schmidt, 1%; Betty Harris, 1%; Peggy Kinder, 1%. Hqtrs: 1404 5th Ave. S.E., Altoona, Iowa 50009. (515) 967-6228.

Family Broadcasting Network. Stns: 3 FM. WGLV(FM) Hartford, WMNV(FM) Rupert & WGLY-FM Waterbury, all Vt. (All 100% owned.) Note: Group also owns low-power TV stn W39AS Burlington, Vt. (ch 39). Ownership: Alexander McEwing, 35%; Arthur & Jennie McEwing, 30%; & Canaan Foundation, 30%. Hqtrs: Box 150, Waterbury, Vt. 05676-0150. (802) 244-5683. FAX: (802) 244-5685.

Family Life Broadcasting System. Stns: 3 AM, 4 FM. KFLR-FM Phoenix & KFLT(AM) Tucson, both Ariz.; WUFN(FM) Albion, WUNN(AM) Mason, WUGN(FM) Midland & WUFL(AM) Sterling Heights, all Mich.; & KFLQ(FM) Albuquerque, N.M. (All 100% owned.) Ownership: All stns are owned by the Family Life Broadcasting System Inc. A nonprofit, noncommercial Christian organization. No individual stockholders. Hqtrs: Box 35300, Tucson, Ariz. 85740. (602) 742-6976. FAX: (602) 742-6979.

Family Stations Inc. Stns: 8 AM, 35 FM, 1 SW, 1 TV. WBFR(FM) Birmingham, Ala.; KPHF(FM) Phoenix; KHAP(FM) Chico, KECR-AM-FM El Cajon, KFNO(FM) Fresno, KEFR(FM) Le Grand, KFRN(AM) Long Beach, KEBR-FM North Highlands, KEBR(AM) Rocklin, KEDR(FM) Sacramento, KEAR(FM) San Francisco, KFTL(TV) Stockton & KPRA(FM) Ukiah, all Calif.; WCTF(AM) Vernon, Conn.; WJFR(FM) Jacksonville, WWFR(FM)/WYFR (shortwave) Okeechobee & WFTI-FM St. Petersburg, all Fla.; WFRC(FM) Columbus, Ga.; WJCH(FM) Joliet, Ill.; KDFR(FM) Des Moines & KYFR(AM) Shenandoah, both Iowa; WFSI(FM) Annapolis, Md.; WBMA(AM) Dedham, Mass.; WKDN-FM Camden, WPFR(FM) Netcong & WFME(FM) Newark, all N.J.; WFBF(FM) Buffalo, WFRH(FM) Kingston, WFRS(FM) Smithtown & WFRW(FM) Webster, all N.Y.; WCUE(AM) Cuyahoga Falls, WOTL(FM) Toledo & WYTN(FM) Youngstown, all Ohio; KQFE(FM) Springfield, Ore.; WEFR(FM) Erie & WFRJ(FM) Johnstown, both Pa.; WFCH(FM) Charleston, S.C.; KTXB(FM) Beaumont & KBTT(FM) Bridgeport, both Tex.; KUFR(FM) Salt Lake City; KARR(AM) Kirkland & KJVH(FM) Longview, both Wa.; & WMWK(FM) Milwaukee. (All 100% owned).) Note: Group has sold WBMA(AM) Dedham, Mass. & KBTT(FM) Bridgeport, Tex., pending FCC approval. Ownership: nonprofit corporation. Hqtrs: 290 Hegenberger Rd., Oakland, Calif. 94621. (415) 568-6200. FAX: (510) 633-7983.

Farmer Stations. Stns: 2 AM, 2 FM. KVAS(AM) Astoria (100%) & KCST-AM-FM Florence (80%), both Ore.; & KKEE(FM) Long Beach, Wash. (100%). Ownership: Charles Farmer, own. Hqtrs: 1490 Marine Dr., Astoria, Ore. 97103. (503) 325-6221.

Farragut Communications Inc. Stns: 2 TV. KNDU(TV) Richland & KNDO(TV) Yakima, both Wa. (Both 100% owned.) Hqtrs: Box 10028, Yakima, Wash. 98909. (212) 593-2626.

Fawcett Broadcasting Ltd. Stns: 9 AM. CKDR-6(AM) Atikokan, CKDR(AM) Dryden, CKDR-4(AM) Ear Falls, CFOB(AM) Fort Frances, CKDR-3(AM) Hudson, CKDR-1(AM) Ignace, CJRL(AM) Kenora, CKDR-5(AM) Red Lake & CKDR-2(AM) Sioux Lookout, all Ont. (All 100% owned.) (All stns are located in Canada.) Ownership: E.P. Fawcett, 100%. Hqtrs: Box 489, 242 Scott St., Fort Frances, Ont., Canada P9A 1G7. (807) 274-5341. FAX: (807) 274-8746.

Federal Broadcasting Co. Stns: 7 TV. WCFT-TV Tuscaloosa, Ala.; WTOM-TV Cheboygan, WLUC-TV Marquette & WPBN-TV Traverse City, all Mich.; WDAM-TV Laurel (Hattiesburg), Miss.; KTVO(TV) Kirksville, Mo. (Ottumwa, Iowa); & WSTM-TV Syracuse, N.Y. Ownership: Dale G. Rands, 17%; City of Detroit General Retirement Fund, 15%; City of Detroit Police & Fire Retirement Fund, 15%; Peter A. Kizer, 11%; Lawrence S. Jackier, 10%. Hqtrs: 1533 N. Woodward Ave., Suite 240, Bloomfield Hills, Mich. 48304. (313) 645-8930. FAX: (313) 645-8939.

Federated Media. Stns: 7 AM, 6 FM. WADM(AM)-WQHK-FM Decatur, WTRC(AM)-WLTA(FM) Elkhart & WQHK(AM)-WMEE(FM) Fort Wayne, all Ind.; WCUZ-AM-FM Grand Rapids & WQWQ(AM) Muskegon Heights, both Mich.; WCKY(AM) & WIMJ(FM) Cincinnati; KQLL-FM Owasso & KQLL(AM) Tulsa, both Okla. Executives: John F. Dille Jr., chmn; John F. Dille III, pres. (See also Cross-Ownership, Sect. A.) Hqtrs: Box 2500, Elkhart, Ind. 46515. (219) 295-2500.

The Findlay Publishing Co. Stns: 3 AM, 2 FM. WCSI(AM) & WKKG(FM) Columbus, Ind.; WFIN(AM)-WKXA-FM Findlay & WMOH(AM) Hamilton, both Ohio. (All 100% owned.) Executives: Edwin L. Heminger, chmn; Kurt P. Kah, pres; David P. Glass, dir bcst. (See Cross-Ownership, Sect. A.) Hqtrs: 701 W. Sandusky St., Findlay, Ohio 45840. (419) 422-5151. FAX: (419) 422-9337.

Fisher Broadcasting Inc. Stns: 1 AM, 2 TV. KATU(TV) Portland, Ore.; KOMO-AM-TV Seattle. (All 100% owned.) Note: Group has purchased KVI(AM) & KPLZ(FM) Seattle, pending FCC approval. Ownership: Fisher Companies Inc., Seattle. Hqtrs: 100 4th Ave. N., Seattle 98109. (206) 443-4000. FAX: (206) 443-4014.

The Formby Stations. Stns: 3 AM, 3 FM. KPAN-AM-FM Hereford, KSAM-AM-FM Huntsville & KTEM(AM)-KPLE(FM) Temple, all Tex. Ownership: KPAN-AM-FM (Clint Formby, 60%; Buddy Peeler, 40%), KSAM-AM-FM (Clint Formby, 50%; George Franz, 50%) & KTEM-KPLE (Clint Formby, 100%). Cable TV. Hqtrs: Drawer 1757, Hereford, Tex. 79045. (806) 364-1860. FAX: (806) 364-5814.

Forum Communications Co. Stns: 2 AM, 1 FM, 4 TV. KMMJ(AM) Grand Island, Neb.; KBMY(TV) Bismarck, WDAZ-TV Devils Lake, WDAY-AM-FM-TV Fargo & KMCY(TV) Minot, all N.D. Note: Group also manages KLRB(FM) Aurora, Neb. through a loc mktg agreement. Ownership: Forum Publishing Co. (William C. Marcil, pres). (See also Cross-Ownership, Sect. A.) Hqtrs: Box 2020, Fargo, N.D. 58107. (701) 235-7311. FAX: (701) 241-5406.

Forum Communications Inc. Stns: 2 AM, 2 FM. WQXC-AM-FM Otsego & WMSH-AM-FM Sturgis, both Mich. Executives: Robert Brink, pres; Bert Elzinga, Deborah Whiteman, VPs. Hqtrs: Box 980, Otsego, Mich. 49078. (616) 343-1717. FAX: (616) 692-6861.

Forus Communications. Stns: 2 AM, 1 FM. WAEC(AM) Atlanta; WVOA(FM) De Ruyter Twp & WSIV(AM) East Syracuse, both N.Y. Ownership: Simon Rosen, 50%; Lind Carl Voth, 50%. Hqtrs: 11300 4th St. N., St. Petersburg, Fla. 33716. (813) 576-0647. FAX: (813) 576-1841.

4-K Radio Inc. Stns: 3 AM, 3 FM. KORT-AM-FM Grangeville & KOZE-AM-FM Lewiston, both Idaho; KORD(AM) Pasco & KORD-FM Richland, both Wash. Executives: Michael R. Ripley, pres; Mrs. E.A. Hamblin, VP; Eric Peterson, sec. Ownership: Michael R. Ripley owns 13.3% of KORT-AM-FM & KOZE-AM-FM & 60% of KORD(AM) & KORD-FM. Hqtrs: Box 936, Lewiston, Idaho 83501. (208) 743-2502. FAX: (208) 743-1995.

4M Broadcasting Inc. Stns: 1 AM, 2 FM. WKAB(FM) Berwick & WAZL(AM)-WZMT(FM) Hazleton, both Pa. (All 100% owned.) Ownership: Robert J. Moisey, Janice Gans Moisey, Jennifer Moisey, Jeffrey Moisey. Cable TV. Hqtrs: Box 1259, Conyngham, Pa. 18219. (717) 759-3570. FAX: (717) 759-3438.

Forvest Broadcasting Corp. Stns: 4 AM, 3 FM. CIRK-FM Edmonton, Alta.; CKST(AM) Vancouver, B.C.; CKRC(AM) & CKLU-FM Winnipeg, Man.; CKCK(AM)-CKIT-FM Regina & CJWW(AM) Saskatoon, both Sask. (All stns are located in Canada.) Executive: Clinton C. Forster, COO. Hqtrs: #101-1199 W. Pender St., Vancouver, B.C., Canada V6E 2R1 (604) 669-7088. FAX: (604) 688-3367.

Fox Communications Co. Inc. Stns: 2 AM, 2 FM. KID-AM-FM Idaho Falls & KWIK(AM)-KPKY(FM) Pocatello, both Idaho. (All 100% owned.) Ownership: James W. & Helen Su Fox. Hqtrs: Box 998, Pocatello, Idaho 83204-0998. (208) 233-1133. FAX: (208) 232-1240.

Fox Television Stations Inc. Stns: 8 TV. KTTV(TV) Los Angeles; WTTG(TV) Washington; WATL(TV) Atlanta; WFLD(TV) Chicago; WNYW(TV) New York; KDAF(TV) Dallas & KRIV(TV) Houston; & KSTU(TV) Salt Lake City. Note: Group has purchased WGBS-TV Philadelphia, subject to FCC approval. Executives: Chase Carey, exec VP Fox Inc.; Mitchell Stern, exec VP/COO. Hqtrs: 5746 Sunset Blvd., Los Angeles 90028. (213) 856-1000. FAX: (213) 856-1981.

Frandsen Broadcasting Co. Stns: 3 AM, 3 FM. KECN(AM)-KLCE(FM) Blackfoot & KICN(AM) Idaho Falls, both Idaho; KLGN(AM)-KBLQ-FM Logan & KVYS(FM) St. George, both Utah. Note: Group has purchased KCVI(FM) Blackfoot, Idaho, pending FCC approval. Ownership: M. Kent Frandsen. Hqtrs: Box 570, Logan, Utah 84321. (801) 752-1390. FAX: (801) 752-1392.

Fraser Valley Broadcasters Ltd. Stns: 3 AM, 3 FM. CFVR(AM)-CFSR-FM Abbotsford, CKGO-FM-1 Boston Bar, CHWK(AM)-CKSR-FM Chilliwack & CKGO(AM) Hope, all B.C. (All 100% owned.) (All stns are located in Canada.) Ownership: William Coombes & Robert Singleton. Hqtrs: Box 386, Chilliwack, B.C., Canada V2P 6J7. (604) 795-5711. FAX: (604) 795-6643.

Freedom Newspapers Inc., Broadcast Division. Stns: 5 TV. WLNE(TV) New Bedford, Mass. (Providence, R.I.); WRGB(TV) Schenectady, N.Y.; KTVL(TV) Medford, Ore.; WTVC(TV) Chattanooga; & KFDM-TV Beaumont, Tex. (All 100% owned.) Executive: Alan J. Bell, pres. Cable TV: OCN (Orange County News Channel), a 24-hour loc news network, Santa Ana, Calif. (See also Cross-Ownership, Sect. A.) Hqtrs: Box 19549, Irvine, Calif. 92713-9549. (714) 253-2313. FAX: (714) 253-2349.

Friends Communications. Stns: 1 AM, 2 FM. WFPS(FM) Freeport, Ill.; WABJ(AM) & WQTE(FM) Adrian, Mich. Ownership: Michael Brooks, Chuck Brooks. Hqtrs: c/o WFPS(FM), Box 701, Freeport, Ill. 61032. (815) 235-7191.

Fuller Broadcasting Co. Stns: 1 AM, 2 FM. WKKR(FM) Auburn & WZMG(AM)-WMXA(FM) Opelika, both Ala. Executive: Gary Fuller, pres. Ownership: Gary Fuller, Laura Fuller. Hqtrs: Box 2329, Opelika, Ala. 36803. (205) 745-4656. FAX: (205) 749-1520.

Fuller-Jeffrey Broadcasting Companies Inc. Stns: 5 AM, 6 FM. KVVV(FM) Healdsburg (Santa Rosa), KSTE(AM) Rancho Cordova, KRCX(AM)-KRXQ(FM) Roseville (Sacramento) & KSRO(AM) Santa Rosa, all Calif.; KJJY-FM Ankeny & KKSO(AM) Des Moines, both Iowa; WIDE(AM)-WSTG(FM) Biddeford & WBLM(FM) Portland, both Me.; & WOKQ(FM) Dover, N.H. Note: Group has purchased KXFX(FM) Santa Rosa, Calif., subject to FCC approval. Ownership: Robert F. "Doc" Fuller, pres, 51%; J.J. Jeffrey, sr VP, 49%. Hqtrs: 8842 Quail Ln., Granite Bay, Calif. 95746. (916) 791-3522. FAX: (916) 791-4111.

J.W. Furr Stns. See Gulf Central Radio Network.

G

GHB Radio Group. Stns: 11 AM, 4 FM. WMGY(AM) Montgomery, Ala.; KURB-AM-FM Little Rock & KEZQ(FM) Sheridan, both Ark.; WYZE(AM) Atlanta & WEAM(AM) Columbus, both Ga.; WTIX(AM) New Orleans; WHVN(AM) Charlotte & WAME(AM) Statesville, both N.C.; WNAP(AM) Norristown, Pa.; WKXC-FM Aiken, WSLT(FM) Clearwater, WOLS(AM) Florence, WRIP(AM) Lake City & WAVO(AM) Rock Hill, all S.C. Officers: George H. Buck Jr., pres; June N. Phelps, VP; Jacob E. Bogan, sec/treas/COO, GHB Broadcasting Corp.; Helen J. Humphries, CFO, GHB Broadcasting; Joyce A. McIlwain, chief accountant. Ownership: GHB Broadcasting Corp. owns KURB-AM-FM, KEZQ(FM), WTIX(AM), WKXC-FM, WOLS(AM) & WRIP(AM). GHB of Clearwater Inc. owns WSLT(FM). The following stns are owned individually by George H. Buck Jr.: WMGY(AM), WYZE(AM), WEAM(AM), WHVN(AM), WAME(AM), WNAP(AM) & WAVO(AM). Hqtrs: 1776 Briarcliff Rd. N.E., Suite A, Atlanta 30306-2106. (404) 875-1110. FAX: (404) 875-1186.

GHTV Inc. Stns: 2 TV. KSBW(TV) Salinas & KSBY(TV) San Luis Obispo, both Calif. Ownership: GHTV Trust, Irving M. Pollack, trustee. Hqtrs: c/o GHTV Management Inc., 555 17th St., Suite 3300, Denver 80202. (303) 292-0045. FAX: (303) 292-9603.

GO Radio Inc. Stns: 3 AM, 2 FM. KWBG(AM) Boone, KSIB(AM)-KITR(FM) Creston & KQWC-AM-FM Webster City, all Iowa. Ownership: Glenn Olson, 100%. Hqtrs: Box 550, Webster City, Iowa 50595. (515) 832-1570.

GRK Productions Joint Venture. Stns: 2 TV. WGKI(TV) Cadillac & WGKU(TV) Vanderbilt, both Mich. (Both 100% owned.) Note: Group also owns low-power TV stn W40AY Traverse City, Mich. Executive: Gary R. Knapp, pres. Hqtrs: 7400 S. 45 Rd., Cadillac, Mich. 49601. FAX: (616) 775-1898.

Galesburg Broadcasting Co. Stns: 2 AM, 2 FM. WGIL(AM) & WAAG(FM) Galesburg, Ill.; KMCD(AM) & KIIK-FM Fairfield, Iowa. Note: KMCD(AM) & KIIK-FM Fairfield, Iowa have been sold, pending FCC approval. Hqtrs: 154 E. Simmons St., Galesburg, Ill. 61401. (309) 342-5131. FAX: (309) 342-0840.

Gannett Broadcasting (Division of Gannett Co. Inc.) Stns: 5 AM, 6 FM, 10 TV. KPNX(TV) Mesa, Ariz. (Phoenix); KIIS-AM-FM Los Angeles & KSDO(AM)-KCLX-FM San Diego; KUSA-TV Denver; WUSA(TV) Washington; WTLV(TV) Jacksonville & WDAE(AM)-WUSA-FM Tampa, both Fla.; WXIA-TV Atlanta; WGCI-AM-FM Chicago; WLVI-TV Cambridge, Mass. (Boston); KARE(TV) Minneapolis; WFMY-TV Greensboro, N.C.; KOCO-TV Oklahoma City; KVUE-TV Austin, KHKS(FM) Denton, KKBQ(AM) Houston & KKBQ-FM Pasadena, all Tex. Note: WLVI-TV Cambridge, Mass. has been sold, subject to FCC approval. Executives: Cecil L. Walker, pres/CEO; Ron Townsend, pres TV group; Gerry DeFrancesco, pres radio div; Daniel S. Ehrman Jr., VP fin & bus affrs; Leon Anglin, VP engrg. Radio division hqtrs: Gannett Radio, 6255 Sunset Blvd., 11th Fl., Los Angeles 90028. Ownership: Gannett Co. Inc. (John J. Curley, chmn/CEO; Douglas H. McCorkindale, vice chmn/CFO), Arlington, Va. (See also Gannett Co. under Cross-Ownership, Sect. A.) Broadcast hqtrs: 1100 Wilson Blvd., Arlington, Va. 22234. (703) 284-6760.

Guy Gannett Broadcasting Services Inc. Stns: 4 TV. WICS(TV) Springfield, Ill.; KGAN(TV) Cedar Rapids, Iowa; WGME-TV Portland, Me.; & WGGB-TV Springfield, Mass. Note: Group has purchased WICD(TV) Champaign, Ill., subject to FCC approval. Ownership: Privately held. (See Guy Gannett Communications under Cross-Ownership, Sect. A.) Hqtrs: Box 15277, One City Ctr., Portland, Me. 04101. (207) 780-9050. FAX: (207) 780-9355.

Gardiner Broadcast Partners Ltd. Stns: 1 AM, 5 FM. KZYR(FM) Avon, KSMT(FM) Breckenridge, KPKE(AM)-KKYY(FM) Gunnison, KIDN-FM Hayden & KSNO-FM Snowmass Village, all Colo. (All 100% owned.) Note: Group has purchased KRMH-AM-FM Leadville, Colo., subject to FCC approval. Ownership: Clifton H. Gardiner. Hqtrs: Box 5559, Avon, Colo. 81620. (303) 949-0140. FAX: (303) 949-0266.

Gateway Communications Inc. Stns: 4 TV. WBNG-TV Binghamton, N.Y.; WTAJ-TV Altoona & WLYH-TV Lancaster, both Pa.; & WOWK-TV Huntington, W.Va. Executives: Lamont T. Pinker, pres. Ownership: Macromedia Inc., 100%. (See also Cross-Ownership, Sect. A.) Hqtrs: Box 12, Johnson City, N.Y. 13790-0012. (607) 729-8812. FAX: (607) 797-6148.

Gaylord Broadcasting Co. Stns: 2 AM, 1 FM, 4 TV. WKY(AM) Oklahoma City; WSM-AM-FM Nashville; KTVT(TV) Fort Worth (Dallas) & KHTV(TV) Houston; KSTW(TV) Tacoma, Wash. (Seattle); & WVTV(TV) Milwaukee. (All 100% owned.) Executive: Tom Griscom, VP. Ownership: A division of Gaylord Entertainment Co. Hqtrs: 2806 Opryland Dr., Nashville 37214. (615) 889-6600. FAX: (615) 871-6944.

Gazette Broadcast Co. Stns: 3 AM, 3 FM. WCLO(AM)-WJVL(FM) Janesville, WBKV(AM)-WBWI-FM West Bend & WFHR(AM)-WWRW(FM) Wisconsin Rapids, all Wis. Executives: S.H. Bliss, pres; Robert S. Dailey, gen mgr; Charles A. Flynn, chief engr. Ownership: Sidney H. Bliss, majority stockholder. (See also Gazette Printing Co. under Cross-Ownership, Sect. A.) Hqtrs: One S. Parker Dr., Janesville, Wis. 53547. (608) 754-3311. FAX: (608) 752-4438.

Genesis Broadcasting Inc. Stns: 2 AM, 2 FM. KSMJ(AM) Sacramento & KSFM(FM) Woodland, both Calif.; KMJI(FM) Denver & KTLK(AM) Thornton, both Colo. (All 100% owned.) Ownership: Booth American Co. (see listing). Hqtrs: 5949 Sherry Ln., Suite 935, Dallas 75225. (214) 361-2932. FAX: (214) 987-2524.

Genesis Communications Inc. Stns: 2 AM. WLQY(AM) Hollywood, Fla.; & WNIV(AM) Atlanta. Note: Group operates WVNF(AM) Alpharetta, Ga. through a loc mktg agreement. Ownership: Bruce C. Maduri, Robert F. Sterling III, Joan Temple. Hqtrs: 2970 Peachtree Rd. N.W., 8th Fl., Atlanta 30305. (404) 365-0970. FAX: (404) 816-0748.

Gleason Marketing Services Inc. Stns: 2 AM, 2 FM. WTME(AM) Lewiston, WTBM(FM) Mexico, WOXO-FM Norway & WKTQ(AM) South Paris, all Me. (All 100% owned.) Ownership: Richard D. Gleason, 100%. Hqtrs: Box 72, 114 Main St., Norway, Me. 04268. (207) 743-5911. FAX: (207) 743-5913.

Global Television Network (CanWest Global System). Stns: 14 TV. CIII-TV-2 Bancroft, CIII-TV-55 Fort Erie, CIII-TV-7 Midland, CIII-TV-2 North Bay, CIII-TV-29 Oil Springs, CIII-TV-6 Ottawa, CIII-TV-4 Owen Sound, CIII-TV Paris, CIII-TV-27 Peterborough, CIII-TV-12 Sault Ste. Marie, CIII-TV-22 Stevenson, CIII-TV-11 Sudbury, CIII-TV-13 Timmins & CIII-TV-41 Toronto, all Ont. (All 100% owned.) (All stns are located in Canada.) Note: Call letters were provided by the Global Television Network, but could not be checked against CRTC sources. The North Bay, Ont. call letters appear to be incorrect. Ownership: Global Communications Ltd., 100%. Parent company: CanWest Global Communications Corp. Hqtrs: 81 Barber Greene Rd., Don Mills, Ont., Canada M3C 2A2. (416) 446-5311. FAX: (416) 446-5371.

Goetz Broadcasting Corp. Stns: 6 AM, 6 FM. WIXN-AM-FM Dixon, Ill.; WIAN(AM)-WJPD(FM) Ishpeming & WDMJ(AM) Marquette, both Mich.; WFAW(AM)-WSJY(FM) Fort Atkinson, WDLB(AM)-WLJY(FM) Marshfield, WRDB(AM)-WNFM(FM) Reedsburg & WOSX(FM) Spencer, all Wis. Executives: Nathan L. Goetz, pres; John H. Hackman, sr VP/COO. Ownership: Nathan L. Goetz, 60%; Robert W. Goetz, 40%. Hqtrs: Box 630, Marshfield, Wis. 54449. (715) 384-2191. FAX: (715) 387-3588.

Golden West Broadcasters. Stns: 2 AM, 2 FM. KLIT(FM) Glendale & KMPC(AM) Los Angeles, both Calif.; KVI(AM) & KPLZ(FM) Seattle. Note: KVI(AM) & KPLZ(FM) Seattle have been sold, subject to FCC approval. Executives: Gene Autry, chmn; Bill Ward, exec VP. Ownership: Gene Autry, 100%. Hqtrs: 5858 Sunset Blvd., Los Angeles 90028. (213) 460-5672. FAX: (213) 460-6621.

Golden West Broadcasting Ltd. Stns: 11 AM. CFXL(AM) Calgary & CHRB(AM) High River, both Alta.; CFAM(AM) Altona, CJRB(AM) Boissevain, CHSM(AM) Steinbach & CKMW(AM) Winkler-Morden, all Man.; CHOO(AM) Ajax & CHAM(AM) Hamilton, both Ont.; CHAB(AM) Moose Jaw, CJSN(AM) Shaunavon & CKSW(AM) Swift Current, all Sask. (All stns are located in Canada.) Executives: Elmer Hildebrand, pres; Ken Wiebe, comptroller; David Wiebe, mgr; Menno Friesen, sls mgr. (See also Cross-Ownership, Sect. A.) Hqtrs: Box 950, Altona, Man., Canada R0G 0B0. (204) 324-6464. FAX: (204) 324-8918.

The Goldman Group. Stns: 2 AM, 2 FM. WJTN(AM) & WWSE(FM) Jamestown, N.Y.; WVMT(AM) Burlington & WXXX(FM) South Burlington, both Vt. (All 100% owned.) Ownership: Simon Goldman & Paul Goldman. Hqtrs: Box 1139, Jamestown, N.Y. 14702-1139. (716) 487-1151. FAX: (716) 664-9326.

The Gomez Group. Stns: 2 AM, 1 FM. KABQ(AM) Albuquerque, N.M.; KQXX(FM) McAllen & KIRT(AM) Mission, both Tex. (All 100% owned.) Ownership: Edward L. Gomez, Dr. Severo Gomez, Vernon Gomez. Hqtrs: Box 4486, Albuquerque, N.M. 87196. (505) 243-1744.

Goodrich Broadcasting Inc. Stns: 3 AM, 6 FM. WXLP(FM) Moline, Ill.; KJOC(AM) Davenport, Iowa; WMMQ(FM) Charlotte, WVFN(AM)-WVIC-FM East Lansing, WODJ(FM) Greenville (Grand Rapids),

WSFN(AM)-WSNX-FM Muskegon & WMRR(FM) Muskegon Heights, all Mich. (All 100% owned.) Ownership: Robert Emmett Goodrich, 100%. Hqtrs: 3565 29th St. S.E., Grand Rapids, Mich. 49512. (616) 949-8760. FAX: (616) 949-8395.

Gowdy Family Limited Partnership. Stns: 2 AM, 2 FM. WCCM(AM) & WCGY(FM) Lawrence, Mass. (100%); KOWB(AM) (100%) & KCGY-FM (91%) Laramie, Wyo. Ownership: Curt Gowdy & Jerre Gowdy, 100%. Hqtrs: 33 Franklin St., Lawrence, Mass. 01840. (508) 682-5511. FAX: (508) 685-9500.

Grand Canyon Television Company Inc. Stns: 2 TV. KNAZ-TV Flagstaff & KMOH-TV Kingman, both Ariz. (Both 100% owned.) Executives: Dan J. Robbins, VP/gen mgr; David Franke, VP. Hqtrs: 2201 N. Vickey St., Flagstaff, Ariz. 86004. (602) 526-2232. FAX: (602) 526-8110.

Grande Radio Inc. Stns: 2 AM, 2 FM. KBKR(AM)-KKBC-FM Baker & KLBM(AM)-KUBQ(FM) La Grande, both Ore. (All 100% owned.) Hqtrs: Box 907, La Grande, Ore. 97850. (503) 963-4121.

Granite Broadcasting Corp. Stns: 6 TV. KSEE(TV) Fresno & KNTV(TV) San Jose, both Calif.; WEEK-TV Peoria, Ill.; WPTA(TV) Fort Wayne, Ind.; WTVH(TV) Syracuse, N.Y.; & KBJR-TV Superior, Wis. Executives: W. Don Cornwell, CEO; Stuart Beck, pres. Hqtrs: One Dag Hammarskjold Plaza, New York 10017. (212) 826-2530. FAX: (212) 826-2858.

Grant Broadcasting System II Inc. Stns: 2 TV. WJPR(TV) Lynchburg & WFXR-TV Roanoke, both Va. (Both 100% owned.) Hqtrs: Box 2127, Roanoke, Va. 24009. (703) 344-2127.

Gray Communications Systems Inc. Stns: 3 TV. KTVE(TV) El Dorado, Ark. (Monroe, La.); WJHG-TV Panama City, Fla.; & WALB-TV Albany, Ga. (All 100% owned.) Executive: John T. Williams, pres. Ownership: Bull Run Corp., Sandler & Assoc. (See also Cross-Ownership, Sect. A.) Hqtrs: Box 48, Albany, Ga. 31702-0048. (912) 888-9390. FAX: (912) 888-9374.

Great American Broadcasting. Stns: 5 AM, 11 FM, 6 TV. WBRC-TV Birmingham, Ala.; KTSP-TV Phoenix & KOPA(AM)-KSLX(FM) Scottsdale, both Ariz.; KSEG(FM) Sacramento, Calif.; KBPI-FM Denver; WXTB(FM) Clearwater & WTSP(TV) St. Petersburg, both Fla.; WKLS-FM Atlanta; WRIF(FM) Detroit; WDAF-AM-TV & KYYS(FM) Kansas City, Mo.; WGHP-TV High Point, N.C.; WKRQ(FM)-WKRC-TV Cincinnati & WTVN(AM)-WLVQ(FM) Columbus, both Ohio; KEX(AM) & KKRZ(FM) Portland, Ore.; & WLZR-AM-FM Milwaukee. Note: WRIF(FM) Detroit & WLZR-AM-FM Milwaukee have been sold, subject to FCC approval. Corporate offs: John P. Zanotti, pres/COO; Gregory C. Thomas, sr VP fin/CFO; William Baumann, sr VP planning & corporate dev; Anita L. Wallgren, VP/assoc gen counsel; Suzanne Cook, VP human resources; Leon Brown, VP TV engrg; Marcie Ersoff, VP TV news. Broadcast group: David Crowl, pres radio group; David Boylan, pres/gen mgr WGHP-TV; Perry Frey, pres/gen mgr WTVN(AM); Herndon Hasty, pres/gen mgr WDAF(AM) & KYYS(FM); Steve Mauldin, pres/gen mgr WTSP(TV); Craig Millar, pres & gen mgr WBRC-TV; Dave Milner, pres/gen mgr KEX(AM); William Moll, pres/gen mgr WKRC-TV; Edward Piette, pres/gen mgr WDAF-TV; Ronald Bergamo, VP/gen mgr KTSP-TV; James Bryant, VP/gen mgr WKRQ(FM); Thomas Connolly, pres/gen mgr WKLS-FM; Dan DiLoreto, VP/gen mgr WXTB(FM); Thomas Schurr, VP KSEG(FM); Clint Sly, VP/gen mgr WRIF(FM); Tom Sly, gen mgr KBPI-FM; Thomas Thon, pres/gen mgr WLVQ(FM); James Ary, VP; Jerry Kersting, VP bus affrs; Nick Miller, VP mktg. Ownership: Subsidiary of Great American Communications Co., a public company. Hqtrs: One E. 4th St., Cincinnati 45202. (513) 562-8000. FAX: (513) 721-8413.

Great Empire Broadcasting Inc. Stns: 5 AM, 5 FM. KFDI-AM-FM Wichita, Kan.; KWKH-AM-FM Shreveport, La.; KTTS-AM-FM Springfield, Mo.; WOW-AM-FM Omaha; & KVOO-AM-FM Tulsa, Okla. (All 100% owned.) Ownership: F.F. Mike Lynch, Michael D. Oatman, Harold Stuart. Hqtrs: Box 1402, Wichita, Kan. 67201. (316) 838-9141. FAX: (316) 838-3607.

Great Scott Broadcasting. Stns: 5 AM, 4 FM. WSSR (AM) & WZBH(FM) Georgetown, Del.; WTTM(AM) & WCHR(FM) Trenton, N.J.; WMBO(AM) & WPCX(FM) Auburn, N.Y.; WKST-FM Ellwood City, WKST(AM) New Castle & WPAZ(AM) Pottstown, all Pa. (All 100% owned.) Hqtrs: 224 Maugers Mill Rd., Pottstown, Pa. 19464. (215) 326-4000. FAX: (215) 326-4809.

Great Trails Broadcasting Corp. Stns: 1 AM, 1 FM, 2 TV. WFFT-TV Fort Wayne, Ind.; WHAG-TV Hagerstown, Md.; WING(AM) Dayton & WGTZ(FM) Eaton, both Ohio. Note: Group also operates WAZU(FM) Springfield, Ohio under a loc mktg agreement. Executives: Alexander J. Williams, pres/COO TV; David Macejko, VP/COO radio; Scot L. Freeman, CFO. Hqtrs: 717 E. David Rd., Dayton, Ohio 45429. (513) 294-3333. FAX: (513) 297-5223.

Greater Media Inc. Stns: 7 AM, 8 FM. KLSX(FM) Los Angeles & KRLA(AM) Pasadena, both Calif.; WWRC(AM) & WGAY(FM) Washington; WBCS(FM) & WMEX(AM)-WMJX(FM) Boston; WCSX(FM) Birmingham & WHND(AM) Monroe, both Mich.; WCTC(AM) & WMGQ(FM) New Brunswick, N.J.; WGSM(AM) Huntington & WMJC(FM) Smithtown, both N.Y.; WPEN(AM) & WMGK(FM) Philadelphia. Note: Group has purchased WRIF(FM) Detroit, pending FCC approval. Executives: Peter A. Bordes, chmn/CEO; Frank Kabela, pres; Tom Milewski, exec VP; Charles W. Banta, group VP radio; Walter Veth, group VP cable TV; John W. Zielinski, sr VP fin; Milford Smith, VP radio engrg; Robin Buss, VP bus affrs. Washington counsel: Schwartz, Woods & Miller. Cable TV. (See also Cross-Ownership, Sect. A.) Hqtrs: 2 Kennedy Blvd., East Brunswick, N.J. 08816. (908) 247-6161. FAX: (908) 247-0215.

Green Bay Broadcasting Co. Stns: 2 AM, 2 FM. KSDN-AM-FM Aberdeen, S.D.; WDUZ(AM) & WQLH(FM) Green Bay, Wis. (All 100% owned.) Executive: William C. Laird, pres. Hqtrs: Box 310, 810 Victoria St., Green Bay, Wis. 54305. (414) 468-4100. FAX: (414) 468-0250.

The Green Group. Stns: 4 AM, 3 FM, 2 TV. WECY-AM-FM Seaford, Del.; WMGM(FM) Atlantic City, WONZ(AM) Hammonton, WOND(AM) Pleasantville & WMGM-TV Wildwood, all N.J.; & WENY-AM-FM-TV Elmira, N.Y. Ownership: Howard L. Green, 50%; Donald M. Simmons, 50%. (See also South Jersey Radio Inc. under Cross-Ownership, Sect. A.) Hqtrs: 1601 New Rd., Linwood, N.J. 08221. (609) 641-1400.

The Griffin Group/Broadcast Division. Stns: 3 AM, 4 FM. WPOP(AM) & WYSR(FM) Waterbury, both Conn.; WPYX(FM) Albany, WTRY-FM Rotterdam & WTRY(AM) Troy, all N.Y.; WHJJ(AM) & WHJY(FM) Providence, R.I. Ownership: Merv Griffin, 100%. Hqtrs: Box 31-1410, Newington Branch, Hartford, Conn. 06131. (203) 666-1411. FAX: (203) 667-9079.

Group W. See Westinghouse Broadcasting Co.

Guardian Communications Inc. Stns: 5 AM. KFEL(AM) Pueblo, Colo.; WKDB(AM) Towson, Md.; KKIM(AM) Albuquerque, N.M.; WTSJ(AM) Cincinnati & WCCD(AM) Parma, both Ohio. Executives: Mark McNeil, pres; Richard David, VP. Ownership: Mark F. McNeil, Richard David. Hqtrs: Box 31440, Cincinnati 45231. (513) 931-8080. FAX: (513) 931-8108.

Gulf Central Radio Network. Stns: 2 AM, 2 FM. WJWF(AM)-WMBC(FM) Columbus & WFOR(AM)-WHER(FM) Hattiesburg, both Miss. Ownership: J.W. Furr. Hqtrs: Box 707, Columbus, Miss. 39703. (601) 328-1400. FAX: (601) 328-1421.

Gulf South Broadcasters Ltd. Stns: 2 AM, 2 FM, 1 SW. KKAY-FM Donaldsonville (25%), KGLA(AM) Gretna (10%), WRNO (shortwave) New Orleans (100%), KXOR(FM) Thibodaux (100%) & KKAY(AM) White Castle (25%), all La. Ownership: Joseph M. Costello III. Hqtrs: 4539 I-10 Service Rd., Metairie, La. 70002. (504) 889-2424. FAX: (504) 889-0602.

Guyann Corp. Stns: 2 AM, 2 FM. KFLG-AM-FM Bullhead City & KAFF-AM-FM Flagstaff, both Ariz. (All 100% owned.) Ownership: Guy Christian, 100%. Hqtrs: Box 1930, Flagstaff, Ariz. 86002. (602) 774-5231. FAX: (602) 779-2988.

H

H&C Communications Inc. Stns: 2 TV. KPRC-TV Houston & KSAT-TV San Antonio, both Tex. Note: Both stns have been sold, subject to FCC approval. Executive: James E. Crowther, pres. Ownership: Oveta Culp Hobby, William P. Hobby, Jessica H. Catto. Hqtrs: 3050 Post Oak Blvd., Suite 1330, Houston 77056. (713) 993-2500.

H & D Broadcast Group. Stns: 7 AM, 7 FM. WSUB(AM) & WQGN-FM Groton, Conn.; WKRS(AM) & WXLC(FM) Waukegan, Ill.; WFHN(FM) Fairhaven & WBSM(AM) New Bedford, both Mass.; WFPG-AM-FM Atlantic City, N.J.; WTLB(AM) & WRCK(FM) Utica, N.Y.; WBBW(AM) & WBBG(FM) Youngstown, Ohio; WSYB(AM) & WZRT(FM) Rutland, Vt. Executives: Joel M. Hartstone & Barry J. Dickstein. Hqtrs: 20 Stanford Dr., Farmington, Conn. 06032. (203) 678-7800. FAX: (203) 676-2439.

HGF Media Group. Stns: 4 AM, 5 FM, one low-power TV. WXKW(AM) Allentown, WMRE(AM) Hughesville, WLSH(AM) Lansford, WMPA(FM) Mansfield, WMHU(FM) Renovo, WFRY(FM) Salladasburg, WMGH-FM Tamaqua & WQXA-AM-FM York, all Pa. Note: WMPA(FM) Mansfield, Pa. has been sold, subject to FCC approval. Group also owns W09BI Williamsport, Pa., a low-power TV stn. Ownership: Harold G. Fulmer III, 100%. Hqtrs: Hotel Traylor, 15th & Hamilton Sts., Allentown, Pa. 18102. (215) 434-9511. FAX: (215) 435-8918.

HVS Partners. Stns: 2 AM, 6 FM. WLBW(FM) Fenwick Island, Del.; WHBT(AM), WHBX(FM) & WBGM-FM Tallahassee, Fla.; WQHQ(FM) Ocean City-Salisbury & WTGM(AM)-WLVW-FM Salisbury, both Md.; & WWQQ-FM Wilmington, N.C. (All 100% owned.) Ownership: Gisela Huberman & Thomas Schattenfield. Hqtrs: 8900 Harvest Square Ct., Potomac, Md. 20854. (301) 983-0098. FAX: (301) 983-4066.

Hall Communications Inc. Stns: 5 AM, 5 FM. WICH(AM) & WCTY(FM) Norwich, Conn.; WONN(AM) Lakeland & WPCV(FM) Winter Haven, both Fla.; WNBH(AM) & WCTK(FM) New Bedford, Mass.; WLPA(AM) & WROZ(FM) Lancaster, Pa.; WJOY(AM) & WOKO(FM) Burlington, Vt. Executives: Robert M. Hall, chmn/CEO; Arthur J. Rowbotham, pres; Richard P. Reed, exec VP; Ed Monskie, VP engrg; Evelyn Wolf, bus mgr; James Reed, VP news & progmg. Hqtrs: Cuprak Rd., Norwich, Conn. 06360. (203) 887-3511. FAX: (203) 886-7649.

Harriscope Corp. Stns: 2 TV. KWHY-TV (74%) Los Angeles; & WSNS(TV) Chicago (50%). Executives: Burt I. Harris, pres. Ownership: Burt I. Harris & Irving B. Harris. Hqtrs: 10960 Wilshire Blvd., Suite 1528, Los Angeles 90024. (310) 477-7724. FAX: (310) 477-9646.

He's Alive Inc. Stns: 5 FM. WLIC(FM) Frostburg & WAIJ(FM) Grantsville, both Md.; WRIJ(FM) Masontown & WRWJ(FM) Murrysville, both Pa.; & WKJL(FM) Clarksburg, W.Va. Ownership: Non-stock, nonprofit organization. Hqtrs: Box 540, Grantsville, Md. 21536. (301) 895-3292. FAX: (301) 895-3293.

Hearst Broadcasting Group. Stns: 3 AM, 3 FM, 6 TV. WBAL-AM-TV & WIYY(FM) Baltimore; WCVB-TV Boston; WDTN(TV) Dayton, Ohio; KMBC-TV Kansas City, Mo.; WISN-AM-TV & WLTQ(FM) Milwaukee; WTAE-AM-TV & WVTY(FM) Pittsburgh. Executives: John G. Conomikes, VP/gen mgr bcstg; David J. Barrett, deputy gen mgr bcstg. Ownership: All bcsting properties are 100% owned & operated by The Hearst Corp. WBAL-AM-TV & WIYY(FM), WCVB-TV, WDTN(TV), KMBC-TV, WISN-AM-TV-WLTQ(FM) & WTAE-AM-TV, WVTY(FM) licensed to The Hearst Corp. Cable TV networks & svcs: Arts & Entertainment Network (A&E) (a joint venture between The Hearst Corp., Capital Cities-ABC Inc. & NBC), ESPN Inc. (a one-fifth ownship), Hearst-ABC Video Services (a joint venture with Capital Cities-ABC Inc.), Lifetime Television (a joint venture between The Hearst Corp., Capital Cities-ABC Inc. & Viacom International Inc.) & New England Cable News (a joint venture between Hearst Broadcasting, Hearst Entertainment & Syndication & Continental Cablevision). (See The Hearst Corporation under Cross-Ownership, Sect. A.) Hqtrs: 959 8th Ave., New York 10019. (212) 649-2300. FAX: (212) 489-2314.

Heartland Communications Inc. Stns: 1 AM, 2 FM. WTCO(AM)-WCKQ(FM) Campbellsville & WTCO-FM Russell Springs, both Ky. Ownership: George E. Owen Jr. Hqtrs: Box 1053, Campbellsville, Ky. 42718. (502) 789-2401. FAX: (502) 789-1450.

Hedberg Broadcasting Group. Stns: 4 AM, 5 FM. KLGA-AM-FM Algona, KRIB(AM)-KLSS-FM Mason City, KUOO(FM) Spirit Lake & KAYL-AM-FM Storm Lake, all Iowa; KMRS(AM) & KKOK-FM Morris, Minn. Ownership: Paul C. Hedberg owns 100% of KRIB(AM)-KLSS-FM & KUOO(FM), 50% of KAYL-AM-FM, 16% of KMRS(AM) & KKOK-FM & 10% of KLGA-AM-FM. Mark P. Hedberg owns 90% of KLGA-AM-FM & 50% of KAYL-AM-FM. Hqtrs: Box 528, Spirit Lake, Iowa 51360. (712) 336-5800. FAX: (712) 336-1634.

Ragan Henry Broadcast Group Inc. Stns: 1 AM, 2 FM. WRZR(FM) Johnstown, Ohio; WDIA(AM) & WHRK(FM) Memphis. Ownership: Ragan Henry, Michael Driscoll, Sheila Weiss, Patricia Hussey. Ragan Henry owns 100% of U.S. Radio L.P. (see listing). Other interests: U.S. Radio II Inc. [licensee of KMGR(AM) Murray & KMXB(FM) Orem, both Utah], U.S. Radio IV Inc. [licensee of KCPX(AM) & KUMT(FM) Centerville, Utah] & Allur Communications Group Inc. [owner of WDZR(FM) Mount Clemens, Mich.; KJLA(AM) Independence, Mo.; WCMC(AM)-WZXL(FM) Wildwood, N.J.; & operator of KISF(AM) Lexington, Mo., under a loc mktg agreement]. Hqtrs: 1234 Market St., Suite 1940, Philadelphia 19107. (215) 563-2910.

Henry Broadcasting. Stns: 5 AM, 6 FM. KMJ(AM)-KSKS(FM) Fresno, KHTX(FM) Riverside, KRQC(AM)-KDON-FM Salinas & KRSO(AM) San Bernardino, all Calif.; KVOD(FM) Denver; KFAB(AM) & KGOR(FM) Omaha; KBBT(AM) & KUFO(FM) Portland, Ore. (All 100% owned.) Note: Group operates KBOQ(FM) Marina, Calif. under a loc mktg agreement. Ownership: Charlton H. Buckley, pres, 100%. Note: Henry Broadcasting Co. is 75% own of Henry Hawaii Broadcasting, licensee of KIKI-AM-FM Honolulu. Hqtrs: 2277 Jerrold Ave., San Francisco 94124. (415) 285-1133. FAX: (415) 285-3592.

The Herbort Stations. Stns: 2 AM, 2 FM. KBEN(AM) Carrizo Springs, KHER(FM) Crystal City & KVWG-AM-FM Pearsall, all Tex. Ownership: KBEN(AM) is licensed to Noelia S. Herbort, executrix. KHER(FM) is licensed to Acelga Broadcasting Inc. (owned 100% by Noelia Herbort). KVWG-AM-FM is licensed to Pearsall Broadcasters Inc. (Noelia Herbort, 70%; Betty Sifuentes, 30%). Hqtrs: Box 335, Carrizo Springs, Tex. 78834. (210) 876-2210. FAX: (210) 876-2210.

Heritage Broadcast Group Inc. Stns: 3 AM, 5 FM. WAAX(AM) & WQEN(FM) Gadsden, Ala.; WOLZ(FM) Fort Myers & WFKS(FM) Palatka, both Fla.; WWNC(AM) & WKSF(FM) Asheville, N.C.; KRKK(AM) & KQSW(FM) Rock Springs, Wyo. Executives: James T. Cullen Jr., chmn; Steven E. Humphries, pres. Hqtrs: 4210 Metro Pkwy., #315, Fort Myers, Fla. 33916. (813) 275-0095. FAX: (813) 275-3299.

Heritage Broadcasting Group. Stns: 3 TV. WWTV(TV) Cadillac & WWUP-TV Sault Ste. Marie, both Mich.; & WXXA-TV Albany, N.Y. Executive: Mario F. Iacobelli, pres. Hqtrs: Box 627, Cadillac, Mich. 49601. (616) 775-3478. FAX: (616) 775-3671.

Heritage Media Corp. Stns: 5 AM, 8 FM, 8 TV. WEAR-TV Pensacola, Fla.; KCFX(FM) Harrisonville & WRTH(AM)-WIL-FM St. Louis, both Mo.; WPTZ(TV) North Pole (Plattsburgh), WBBF(AM)-WBEE-FM Rochester & WKLX(FM) Rochester, all N.Y.; WOFX(FM) Fairfield, Ohio; KOKH-TV Oklahoma City; KKSN-FM Portland, Ore.; KIVV-TV Lead, KDLT(TV) Mitchell & KEVN-TV Rapid City, all S.D.; WNNE-TV Hartford, Vt.; KULL(AM) Seattle, KRPM-FM Tacoma & KKSN(AM) Vancouver, all Wa.; WCHS-TV Charleston, W.Va.; WEMP(AM) & WMYX(FM) Milwaukee. (All 100% owned.) Note: Group has purchased WEZW(FM) Wauwatosa, Wis. (Milwaukee), pending FCC approval. Executives: Jim Hoak, chmn; David Walthall, pres; Jack Robinette, pres TV group; Paul Fiddick, pres radio group. Ownership: James M. Hoak Jr. Hqtrs: One Galleria Tower, 13355 Noel Rd., Suite 1500, Dallas 75240. (214) 702-7380. FAX: (214) 702-7382.

The Heusser Group. Stns: 1 AM, 3 FM. KELF(FM) Camarillo (56%), KKDJ(FM) Fresno (100%) & KKZZ(AM) Santa Paula (56%), all Calif.; & KZHT(FM) Provo, Utah (56%). Ownership: Wallace A. Heusser, 100%. Hqtrs: 1525 E. Shaw Ave., Fresno, Calif. 93710. (209) 226-5991. FAX: (209) 226-1149.

Bennie E. Hewett Stations. Stns: 3 AM, 2 FM. WHOD-AM-FM Jackson, Ala.; WLBA(AM) Gainesville, WHFE(FM) Lakeland & WNGA(AM) Nashville, all Ga. (All 100% owned.) Ownership: Bennie Hewett. Hqtrs: 311 Green St. N.E., Suite 211, Gainesville, Ga. 30501. (404) 536-3890.

High Media Group. Stns: 1 AM, 2 FM. WCKU(FM) Nicholasville, Ky.; & WCYK-AM-FM Crozet, Va. Cable TV. Executive: Terry Kile, pres. Hqtrs: 1853 William Penn Way, Lancaster, Pa. 17601. (717) 293-4410. FAX: (717) 293-4416.

Hirsch Broadcasting Inc. Stns: 2 AM, 2 FM. WWRK-AM-FM Elberton & WWNS(AM)-WMCD(FM) Statesboro, both Ga. (All 100% owned.) Ownership: Nathan Hirsch. Hqtrs: Box 958, Statesboro, Ga. 30459. (912) 764-5446. FAX: (912) 764-8827.

Hoffman Communications/Hoffman Media Inc. Stns: 1 AM, 2 FM. WQCK(FM) Clinton, La.; WGGM(AM) & WDYL(FM) Chester, Va. (All 100% owned.) Executive: Hubert Hoffman, pres. Hqtrs: 2461 Eisenhower Ave., Alexandria, Va. 22331. (703) 960-4700, (804) 275-7697. FAX: (703) 960-1754.

Holt Broadcasting Service. Stns: 2 AM, 1 FM, 1 TV. WTWC(TV) Tallahassee, Fla.; WHSY-AM-FM Hattiesburg & WHNY(AM) McComb, both Miss. Executive: Charles W. Holt, chmn. Ownership: Charles W. Holt owns 100% of WHNY(AM); 80% of WTWC(TV); & 75.5% of WHSY-AM-FM. Robert N. Robinson owns 24.5% of WHSY-AM-FM & 20% of WTWC(TV). Hqtrs: Box 1978, Hattiesburg, Miss. 39403. (601) 545-1230. Fax: (601) 545-1243.

The Holt Corporations. Stns: 3 AM, 4 FM. WTKX-AM-FM Pensacola, Fla.; WOAD(AM) & WJMI(FM) Jackson, Miss.; KMXQ(FM) Socorro, N.M.; WKAP(AM) Allentown & WDLE(FM) Benton, both Pa. Ownership: Arthur H. Holt, I. Phyllis Holt. Hqtrs: Box 9595, Allentown, Pa. 18105. (215) 821-9085. FAX: (215) 821-9504.

The Home News Co. Stns: 2 AM, 1 FM, 1 TV. WKTP(AM) Jonesboro & WKPT-AM-TV & WTFM(FM) Kingsport, both Tenn. Note: Group also owns low-power TV stn W07BR Fort Myers, Fla. Executive: William M. Boyd, chmn.. Ownership: William M. Boyd & George Krouse Jr., Trustees U/A Est. by Hugh M. Boyd, c/o Simpson, Thatcher & Bartlett, 425 Lexington Ave., New York. (See also Cross-Ownership, Sect. A.) Hqtrs: 3601 Hwy. 66, Neptune, N.J. 08816. (908) 922-6000. FAX: (908) 246-3167.

Home Shopping Network Inc. See Silver King Communications Inc.

Hubbard Broadcasting Inc. Stns: 1 AM, 1 FM, 9 TV. WTOG(TV) St. Petersburg, Fla; KSAX(TV) Alexandria, WDIO-TV Duluth, WIRT(TV) Hibbing, KRWF(TV) Redwood Falls & KSTP-AM-FM-TV St. Paul (Minneapolis), all Minn.; KOB-TV Albuquerque, KOBF(TV) Farmington & KOBR(TV) Roswell, all N.M. Officers: Stanley S. Hubbard, chmn/pres/CEO; Gerald D. Deeney, VP/treas; Marvin L. Rosene, Stanley E. Hubbard II, Carlos Luis, Ralph J. Dolan, VPs; John Mayasich, VP/pres of radio stns; Harold C. Crump, VP/pres/gen mgr KSTP-TV; Ginny Hubbard Morris, VP/gen mgr KSTP(AM); Robert W. Hubbard, VP; Wallace J. Jorgenson, exec VP; C. Thomas Newberry, VP/controller; Kathryn Hubbard Rominski, sec; Constance L. Eckert, Marvin Rosenberg, asst secs. Stockholders: Stanley E. Hubbard Trust, 71%; Stanley S. Hubbard & Trust, 20%. Hqtrs: 3415 University Ave., St. Paul 55114. (612) 646-5555. FAX: (612) 642-4103.

Humber Valley Broadcasting Co. Stns: 6 AM, 4 FM. CFCB(AM) Corner Brook (AM stereo), CFLC-FM Churchill Falls (Labrador), CFDL-FM Deer Lake, CFLN(AM) Goose Bay (Labrador), CFNW(AM) Port au Choix, CFGN(AM) Port aux Basques, CFCV-FM St. Andrews, CFNN-FM St. Anthony, CFSX(AM) Stephenville & CFLW(AM) Wabush (Labrador), all Nfld. (All stns are located in Canada.) (All 100% owned.) Executives: Dr. Noel F. Murphy, pres; James R. O'Rourke, gen mgr; Roger Humber, stn mgr; Trent De Roche, gen sls mgr; Ed Hynes, news dir. Hqtrs: Box 570, Corner Brook, Nfld., Canada A2H 6H5. (709) 634-3111. FAX: (709) 634-4081.

I

Illinois Bible Institute Inc. Stns: 6 FM. WIBI(FM) Carlinville, WBGL(FM) Champaign, WRVY-FM Henry, WCIC(FM) Pekin & WSCT(FM) Springfield, all Ill.; & WCRT(FM) Terre Haute, Ind. (All 100% owned.) Executive: Richard C. Whitworth, dir of radio. Hqtrs: Box 140, Carlinville, Ill. 62626. (217) 854-4671. FAX: (217) 854-4610.

Imes Communications. Stns: 4 TV. WCBI-TV Columbus, Miss. (25%); WMUR-TV Manchester, N.H. (90%); KDBC-TV El Paso; & WBOY-TV Clarksburg, W. Va. (92.5%). (See also Imes Communications Group under Cross-Ownership, Sect. A.) Hqtrs: c/o Columbus Television Inc., Box 271, Columbus, Miss. 39703. (601) 327-4444. FAX: (601) 328-5222.

Independence Broadcasting Corp. Stns: 3 AM, 4 FM. KOEL-AM-FM Oelwein, Iowa; KSAL(AM) & KYEZ(FM) Salina, Kan.; KEBC(FM) Oklahoma City; WLIP(AM) & WIIL(FM) Kenosha, Wis. (All 100% owned.) Executives: John C. Goodwill, pres/CEO; Edward J. Hurley, VP/sec/treas. Hqtrs: 199 Ethan Allen Hwy, Ridgefield, Conn. 06877. (203) 431-6877. FAX: (203) 438-5358.

Independent Communications Inc. Stns: 2 TV. KTTM(TV) Huron & KTTW(TV) Sioux Falls, both S.D. (Both 100% owned.) Ownership: Robert Elmen, James Elmen, Charles Poppen. Hqtrs: Box 5103, Sioux Falls, S.D. 57117. (605) 338-0017. FAX: (605) 338-7173.

Infinity Broadcasting Corp. Stns: 8 AM, 14 FM. KROQ-FM Pasadena & KOME(FM) San Jose, both Calif.; WQYK-FM St. Petersburg & WQYK(AM) Seffner (St. Petersburg), both Fla.; WZGC(FM) Atlanta; WJJD(AM), WJMK(FM) & WUSN(FM) Chicago; WJFK(AM) & WLIF-FM Baltimore; WBCN(FM) & WZLX(FM) Boston; WOMC(FM) Detroit; WFAN(AM), WZRC(AM) & WXRK(FM) New York; WIP(AM) & WYSP(FM) Philadelphia; KVIL(AM) Highland Park, KVIL-FM Highland Park-Dallas & KXYZ(AM) Houston, all Tex.; & WJFK-FM Manassas, Va. (All 100% owned.) Note: Group has purchased KRTH(FM) Los Angeles & WPGC-AM-FM Morningside, Md., subject to FCC approval. Executive: Mel Karmazin, pres/CEO. Ownership: Mel Karmazin, 20%; Mike Wiener, co-chmn, 10%; Gerald Carrus, co-chmn, 10%. Hqtrs: 600 Madison Ave., New York 10022. (212) 750-6400.

James Ingstad Broadcasting Inc. Stns: 7 AM, 11 FM. KRUU(FM) Boone, KIAQ(FM) Clarion, KLKK(FM) Clear Lake, KRNQ(FM) Hampton & KGLO(AM)-KIAI(FM) Mason City, all Iowa; KNUJ(AM)-KXLP(FM) New Ulm, KRFO-AM-FM Owatonna, KNUJ-FM Sleepy Eye & KWAD(AM)-KKWS(FM) Wadena, all Minn.; KBYZ(FM) Bismarck, KLXX(AM) Bismarck-Mandan, KDDR(AM) Oakes & KOVC-AM-FM Valley City, all N.D. (All 100% owned.) Ownership: James Ingstad, pres, 100%. Hqtrs: 2501 13th Ave. S.W., Suite 201, Fargo, N.D. 58103. (701) 237-3775. FAX: (701) 280-0861.

Robert Ingstad Broadcast Properties. Stns: 3 AM, 4 FM. KKJQ(FM) Garden City & KBUF(AM) Holcomb, both Kan.; KQPR-FM Albert Lea & KWEB(AM)-KRCH(FM) Rochester, both Minn.; & KGFX-AM-FM Pierre, S.D. Ownership: Robert E. Ingstad, 100%. Hqtrs: Box 907, Valley City, N.D. 58072. (701) 845-1490. FAX: (701) 845-2903.

Tom Ingstad Broadcasting Group Stns: 4 AM, 7 FM. KEAG(FM) & KPXR(FM) Anchorage; KXIC(AM) & KKRQ(FM) Iowa City; KLTA(FM) Breckenridge, Minn.; KIMM(AM)-KGGG-FM Rapid City & KSOO(AM)-KPAT(FM) Sioux Falls, both S.D.; KIT(AM) & KATS(FM) Yakima, Wash. Executive: Tom Ingstad, pres. Hqtrs: Box 50005, Minneapolis, Minn. 55405. (612) 927-5566. FAX: (612) 927-5627.

Inner City Broadcasting. Stns: 2 AM, 3 FM. KBLX-AM-FM Berkeley, Calif.; WLIB(AM) & WBLS(FM) New York; & KSJL-FM San Antonio, Tex. (All 100% owned.) Executive: Pierre Sutton, chmn. Cable TV: Inner-Unity Cable, Queens, New York. Hqtrs: 801 2nd. Ave., New York 10017. (212) 661-3344. FAX: (212) 661-7409.

International Church of the Foursquare Gospel. Stns: 1 AM, 2 FM. KHIS-AM-FM Bakersfield & KFSG(FM) Los Angeles, both Calif. (All 100% owned.) Executives: Dr. John Holland, pres; Alan Bowles, stn mgr; Paul Gulino, opns dir; Richard Taylor, mus dir. Ownership: No stockholders. Religious, nonprofit corporation. Hqtrs: 1910 W. Sunset Blvd., Los Angeles 90026. (213) 483-5354. FAX: (213) 484-8304.

Interstate Broadcasting Systems Inc. Stns: 1 AM, 2 FM. KRDS(AM) Tolleson & KRDS-FM Wickenburg, both Ariz.; & KYMS(FM) Santa Ana, Calif. Ownership: Paul J. Toberty, Joyce K. Toberty. Hqtrs: 1740 W. Katella, Suite A, Orange, Calif. 92667. (714) 997-4436. FAX: (714) 997-8539.

J

JS Marketing & Communications. Stns: 2 AM, 2 FM. KMSL(AM)-KQDI-FM Great Falls & KYLT(AM)-KZOQ-FM Missoula, both Mont. (All 100% owned.) Executive: Dan Gittings, gen mgr, bcst division, JS Corp. Hqtrs: 2701 North Reserve, Missoula, Mont. 59806. (406) 728-5000. FAX: (406) 549-0503.

Jackson County Broadcasting Inc. Stns: 1 AM, 2 FM. WCJO(FM) Jackson & WYPC(AM)-WKOV-FM Wellston, both Ohio. (All 100% owned.) Ownership: Lewis E. Davis, Irene Kovalan, Steve Kovalan. Hqtrs: Box 606, 287 E. Main St., Jackson, Ohio 45640. (614) 286-3023. FAX: (614) 286-6679.

Jacor Communications Inc. Stns: 6 AM, 7 FM. KAZY(FM), KOA(AM) & KRFX(FM) Denver; WQIK-AM-FM Jacksonville & WFLA(AM)-WFLZ-FM Tampa, both Fla.; WGST(AM) & WPCH(FM) Atlanta; WLW(AM), WLWA(AM) & WEBN(FM) Cincinnati; & WMYU(FM) Sevierville (Knoxville), Tenn. (All 100% owned.) Note: Group has purchased WGUL(AM) Dunedin, Fla., subject to FCC approval. Executives: Randy Michaels, pres/co-COO; Robert L. Lawrence, co-COO; R. Christopher Weber, sr VP/CFO; Jon M. Berry, sr VP/treas. Cable TV: Telesat. Hqtrs: PNC Center, 201 E. 5th St., Suite 1300, Cincinnati 45202. (513) 621-1300. FAX: (513) 621-0090.

Group Ownership

Jefferson-Pilot Communications Co. Stns: 6 AM, 6 FM, 3 TV. KSON-AM-FM San Diego; KYGO-AM-FM Denver & KWMX-AM-FM Lakewood, both Colo.; WLYF(FM) Miami & WMRZ(AM) South Miami, both Fla.; WQXI(AM) Atlanta & WSTR(FM) Smyrna, both Ga.; WBT-AM-FM & WBTV(TV) Charlotte, N.C.; WCSC-TV Charleston, S.C.; & WWBT(TV) Richmond, Va. (All 100% owned.) Note: Group has purchased WMXJ(FM) Pompano Beach, Fla., subject to FCC approval. Executives: William E. Blackwell, pres. Ownership: Jefferson-Pilot Corp., 100%. Hqtrs: 100 N. Greene St., Greensboro, N.C. 27401. (919) 691-3000. FAX: (919) 691-3222.

The Jet Broadcasting Co. Stns: 1 AM, 2 FM, 1 TV. WHOT-AM-FM Youngstown, Ohio; WJET(FM) & WJET-TV Erie, Pa. Ownership: Myron Jones owns 85% of WHOT-AM-FM & 75% of WJET(FM) & WJET-TV. John Kanzius owns 15% of WHOT-AM-FM & 25% of WJET(FM) & WJET-TV. Hqtrs: 8455 Peach St., Erie, Pa. 16509. (814) 864-2400. FAX: (814) 868-3041.

Johnson Communications. Stns: 2 AM, 2 FM. KCMX-AM-FM Ashland (Medford), KTMT-FM Medford & KTMT(AM) Phoenix (Medford), all Ore. Ownership: Robert Johnson, Karen Johnson, Gary Johnson. Hqtrs: Box 159, Medford, Ore. 97501. (503) 779-1550. FAX: (503) 776-2360.

Johnson Communications Inc. Stns: 2 AM, 3 FM. KCAB(AM)-KWKK(FM) Dardanelle, KAMO-AM-FM Rogers & KCJC(FM) Russellville, all Ark. (All 100% owned.) Ownership: Dewey Johnson. Hqtrs: Box 1793, Springdale, Ark. 72765. (501) 756-9933. FAX: (501) 756-9933.

Johnson Enterprises Inc. Stns: 2 AM, 2 FM. KLEY(AM)-KWME(FM) Wellington & KKLE(AM)-KKWM(FM) Winfield, both Kan. Ownership: E. Gordon Johnson, Susan G. Johnson. Hqtrs: R.R. 3, Box 1AA, Wellington, Kan. 67152. (316) 326-3341. FAX: (316) 326-8512.

Jones-Eastern Radio Inc. Stns: 2 AM, 2 FM. WVBS(AM) Burgaw & WRSF(FM) Columbia, both N.C.; WUJM(AM) & WSSP(FM) Goose Creek (Charleston), S.C. (All 100% owned.) Note: Group has purchased WYFZ(FM) Evans & WAGW(FM) Waynesboro, both Ga., subject to FCC approval. Executives: C.J. Jones, pres/CEO; Carolyn S. Jones, sr VP; Don Powers, dir engrg. Ownership: C.J. Jones, 100%. Hqtrs: Box 1250, Evans, Ga. 30809. (706) 869-1313. FAX: (706) 869-9318.

Journal Communications Inc. See WTMJ Inc.

K

K to Z Ltd. Stns: 2 AM, 2 FM. KLNT(AM) & KCLN-FM Clinton, Iowa; & WGLR-AM-FM Lancaster, Wis. Ownership: Jack E. Kauffman & James L. Zimmermann. Hqtrs: 206 S. Sheridan St., Lancaster, Wis. 53813. (608) 723-7671. Fax: (608) 723-7674.

K-Z Radio Inc. Stns: 1 AM, 2 FM. KGUM(AM) & KZGZ(FM) Agana, Guam; & KPXP(FM) Garapan, Saipan, Northern Mariana Islands. (All 100% owned.) Ownership: Rex W. & Kathleen A. Sorensen. Hqtrs: Box GM, Agana, Guam 96910. (671) 477-5700. FAX: (671) 477-3982.

KWTX Broadcasting Co. Stns: 1 AM, 1 FM, 1 TV. KWTX-AM-FM-TV Waco, Tex. Stockholders of KWTX also own 50% of KBTX-TV Bryan, Tex. Ownership: M.N. Bostick, the LBJ Co., L.L. Sams & Sons Inc. Hqtrs: Box 2636, Waco, Tex. 76702. (817) 776-1330. FAX: (817) 751-1088.

KX Acquisition Limited Partnership. Stns: 2 TV. KXLT-TV Rochester & KXLI(TV) St. Cloud, both Minn. (Both 100% owned.) Executive: Richard Latora, pres. Ownership: KXLI Acquisition Corp., 100%. Hqtrs: 230 Park Ave., 7th Fl., New York 10169. (212) 551-9567.

KXOJ Inc. Stns: 1 AM, 3 FM. KEOJ(FM) Caney, Kan.; KEMX(FM) Locust Grove & KXOJ-AM-FM Sapulpa, both Okla. (All 100% owned.) Executive: Michael P. Stephens, pres. Hqtrs: Box 1250, Sapulpa, Okla. 74067. (918) 224-2620. FAX: (918) 224-4984.

David Keister Stns. Stns: 3 AM, 4 FM. WBWN(FM) Le Roy, Ill.; WIOU(AM)-WZWZ(FM) Kokomo, WBAT(AM) Marion, WKBV(AM)-WFMG(FM) Richmond & WCJC(FM) Van Buren, all Ind. Ownership: David Keister, principal own. Hqtrs: c/o Mid-America Radio Group, Box 1970, Martinsville, Ind. 46151. (317) 349-1485. FAX: (317) 342-3569.

Kelly Broadcasting Co. Stns: 2 TV. KCRA-TV Sacramento, Calif.; & KCPQ(TV) Tacoma, Wash. (Both 100% owned.) Ownership: KCRA-TV, licensed to Kelly Broadcasting Co., is owned by Kelly Television Co., 90% (partnership). KCPQ(TV), licensed to Kelly Television Co., is owned by Robert E. Kelly, 40%; Jon S. Kelly, 40%. Hqtrs: 3 Television Cir., Sacramento, Calif. 95814. (916) 446-3333. FAX: (916) 325-3731.

Key Broadcasting Inc. Stns: 8 AM, 9 FM. WIAI(FM) Danville & WVLN(AM)-WSEI(FM) Olney, both Ill.; WCVL(AM) & WIMC(FM) Crawfordsville, Ind.; WAIN-AM-FM Columbia, WHIC-AM-FM Hardinsburg, WFTG(AM)-WWEL(FM) London, WSIP-AM-FM Paintsville & WTCW(AM)-WXKQ(FM) Whitesburg, all Ky.; & WDBL-AM-FM Springfield, Tenn. (All 100% owned.) Note: Group has purchased WPRS(AM) & WACF(FM) Paris, Ill., subject to FCC approval. Ownership: Terry E. Forcht. Hqtrs: Drawer 1450, Corbin, Ky. 40702. (606) 528-9600. FAX: (606) 528-8487.

Key Chain Inc. Stns: 3 FM. WKRY(FM) Key West, WAVK(FM) Marathon & WFKZ(FM) Plantation Key, all Fla. (All 100% owned.) Ownership: Joel B. Day, pres; Brian Cobb, Julian Gonzalez & C.G. Day. Hqtrs: 93351 Overseas Hwy., Tavernier, Fla. 33070. (305) 852-9085. FAX: (305) 852-5586.

Keymarket Communications Stns: 4 AM, 4 FM. KNAC(FM) Long Beach & KBLA(AM) Santa Monica, both Calif.; WWL(AM) & WLMG(FM) New Orleans; WILK(AM) & WKRZ-FM Wilkes-Barre, Pa.; & WJCE(AM) & WRVR-FM Memphis. Note: Group has purchased WBEN(AM) & WMJQ(FM) Buffalo, N.Y., subject to FCC approval. Executives: Kerby E. Confer, chmn; Barry Drake, pres; Donald J. Alt, CFO; Lynn Deppen, chief engr. Ownership: Kerby E. Confer, 100%. Hqtrs: 2743 Perimeter Pkwy., Bldg. 100, Suite 250, Augusta, Ga. 30909. (706) 855-0555. FAX: (706) 855-1955.

Kimel Broadcast Group Inc. Stns: 2 AM, 2 FM. WSNO(AM)-WORK(FM) Barre & WWSR(AM)-WLFE(FM) St. Albans, both Vt. Ownership: John O. Kimel, David R. Kimel. Hqtrs: 102 Swanton Rd., St. Albans, Vt. 05478. (802) 524-2133. FAX: (802) 527-1450.

King Broadcasting Co. Stns: 6 TV. KHNL(TV) Honolulu & KOGG(TV) Wailuku, both Hawaii; KTVB(TV) Boise, Idaho; KGW-TV Portland, Ore.; KING-TV Seattle & KREM-TV Spokane, both Wa. Note: Group also owns a low power TV stn, K38AS Twin Falls, Idaho. Ownership: King Holding Corp. Cable TV. Hqtrs: 333 Dexter Ave. N., Seattle 98109. (206) 448-5555. FAX: (206) 448-3936.

Knight Quality Group Stations. Stns: 2 AM, 4 FM. WTAG(AM) & WSRS(FM) Worcester, Mass.; WGIR-AM-FM Manchester & WHEB(FM) Portsmouth, both N.H.; & WEZF(FM) Burlington, Vt. Ownership: Norman Knight, 100%. Cable TV. Hqtrs: 63 Bay State Rd., Boston 02215. (617) 262-1950. FAX: (617) 267-5160.

Koplar Communications Inc. Stns: 2 TV. KRBK-TV Sacramento, Calif.; & KPLR-TV St. Louis. (Both 100% owned.) Note: KRBK-TV Sacramento, Calif. has been sold, subject to FCC approval. Ownership: Koplar Enterprises Inc. Estate of Harold Koplar, 100%. Hqtrs: 4935 Lindell Blvd., St. Louis 63108. (314) 367-7211. FAX: (314) 454-6488.

Kramer Broadcasting Inc. Stns: 2 AM, 2 FM. WTOQ(AM)-WKPL(FM) Platteville & WPDR(AM)-WDDC(FM) Portage, both Wis. (All 100% owned.) Ownership: Edward Kramer, 100%. Hqtrs: Box 300, Portage, Wis. 53901. (608) 742-8833. FAX: (608) 742-1688.

Krypton Broadcasting Corp. Stns: 3 TV. WABM(TV) Birmingham, Ala.; WTVX(TV) Fort Pierce & WNFT(TV) Jacksonville, both Fla. (All 100% owned.) Ownership: C.E. Feltner Jr., 100%. Hqtrs: Box 664, Palm Beach, Fla. 33480. (407) 842-1558.

Kuiper Stns. Stns: 3 AM, 3 FM. WDOW-AM-FM Dowagiac, WFUR-AM-FM Grand Rapids, WKPR(AM) Kalamazoo & WQFN(FM) Walker, all Mich. Ownership: William E. Kuiper. Hqtrs: Box 1808, 399 Garfield S.W., Grand Rapids, Mich. 49501. (616) 451-9387. FAX: (616) 451-8460.

L

LIN Broadcasting Corp. Stns: 7 TV. WAND(TV) Decatur, Ill.; WANE-TV Fort Wayne & WISH-TV Indianapolis, both Ind.; WOOD-TV Grand Rapids, Mich.; KXAN-TV Austin & KXAS-TV Fort Worth, both Tex.; & WAVY-TV Portsmouth, Va. (All 100% owned.) Executives: Tom Alberg, pres/chmn; Gary R. Chapman, pres television group; Don Guthrie, VP fin; Roberta Katz, VP/gen coun-sel/sec. Ownership: Publicly owned corporation. Hqtrs: 5295 Carillon Point, Kirkland, Wash. 98033. (206) 828-1902. FAX: (206) 828-1900.

L.M. Communications Inc. Stns: 2 AM, 3 FM. WLXG(AM) Lexington (100%) & WGKS(FM) Paris (100%), both Ky.; WYBB(FM) Folly Beach, S.C. (100%); WCOZ(AM) & WKLC-FM St. Albans, W.Va. (40%). Executive: Lynn Martin, pres. Hqtrs: Box 11788, Lexington, Ky. 40578. (606) 233-1515. FAX: (606) 233-1517.

La Nueva KBOR Inc. Stns: 1 AM, 2 FM. KBOR(AM) Brownsville, KTJN(FM) Mercedes & KTJX(FM) Mission, all Tex. (All 100% owned.) Ownership: Edgar C. Trevino. Hqtrs: 1050 McIntosh, Brownsville, Tex. 78521. (210) 544-1600. FAX: (210) 544-0311.

Lackey Group. Stns: 2 AM, 1 FM. WSON(AM) Henderson & WHOP-AM-FM Hopkinsville, both Ky. Ownership: Henry G. Lackey owns 100% of WSON(AM). F. E. Lackey owns WHOP stns. Hqtrs: Box 418, Henderson, Ky. 42420. (502) 826-3923. FAX: (502) 827-6572.

Lamco Communications Inc. Stns: 1 AM, 1 FM, 3 TV. WCTI(TV) New Bern, N.C.; WYLC(TV) & WILQ(FM) Williamsport, Pa.; KTXS-TV Sweetwater, Tex.; & WCYB-TV Bristol, Va. Executive: Marshall R. Noecker, pres. Hqtrs: 460 Market St., Suite 312, Williamsport, Pa. 17701. (717) 323-2252. FAX: (717) 323-2298.

Landmark Communications Inc. Stns: 2 TV. Landmark Broadcast Division: KLAS-TV Las Vegas; & WTVF(TV) Nashville. Executives: Frank Batten, chmn Landmark Communications Inc.; John Wynne, pres. Ownership: Frank Batten owns controlling interest in Landmark Communications Inc. (See also Crossownership, Sect. A.) Cable TV: The Weather Channel & The Travel Channel, Atlanta (Michael Eckert, CEO). Hqtrs: Landmark Broadcast Division, Landmark Communications Inc., 150 W. Brambleton Ave., Norfolk, Va. 23510. (804) 446-2000. FAX: (804) 446-2489.

Lew Latto Group of Northland Radio Stations. Stns: 2 AM, 3 FM. KGPZ(FM) Coleraine, WAKX(FM) Duluth & WEVE-AM-FM Eveleth, all Minn.; & KXTP(AM) Superior, Wis. (All 100% owned.) Ownership: Lew Latto, 100%. Hqtrs: 419 W. Michigan St., Duluth, Minn. 55802. (218) 727-7271. FAX: (218) 727-7108.

Le Sea Broadcasting. Stns: 1 FM, 7 TV, 1 SW. KWHD(TV) Castle Rock, Colo.; KWHH(TV) Hilo, KWHE(TV) Honolulu & KWHM(TV) Wailuku, all Hawaii; WHRI (shortwave) & WHMB-TV Indianapolis & WHME(TV) & WHME-TV South Bend, both Ind.; & KWHB(TV) Tulsa, Okla. Executives: Lester Sumrall, chmn; Steve Sumrall, pres; Pete Sumrall, VP/gen mgr. Hqtrs: Box 12, South Bend, Ind. 46624. (219) 291-8200. FAX: (219) 291-9043.

Lee Enterprises Inc. Stns: 10 TV. KGUN(TV) Tucson, Ariz.; KHNL-TV Hilo, KGMB(TV) Honolulu & KGMV(TV) Wailuku, all Hawaii; KMTV(TV) Omaha; KRQE(TV) Albuquerque, KZIA(TV) Las Cruces & KBIM-TV Roswell, all N.M.; KOIN(TV) Portland, Ore.; & WSAZ-TV Huntington, W. Va. Executives: Lloyd G. Schermer, chmn; Richard D. Gottlieb, pres/CEO; Gary N. Schmedding, VP bcstg; Larry L. Bloom, VP fin/treas/CFO. (See also Cross-Ownership, Sect. A.) Hqtrs: 400 Putnam Bldg., 215 N. Main St., Davenport, Iowa 52801-1924. (319) 383-2100. FAX: (319) 323-9608.

Leighton Enterprises Inc. Stns: 2 AM, 3 FM. KYCK(FM) Crookston, KDLM(AM)-KKDL(FM) Detroit Lakes & KNSI(AM)-KCLD-FM St. Cloud, all Minn. (All 100% owned.) Executive: Al Leighton, pres. Hqtrs: Box 1458, St. Cloud, Minn. 56302. (612) 251-1450. FAX: (612) 251-8952.

Lesso Inc. Stns: 4 AM, 10 FM. KLLS(FM) Augusta, KXXX(AM)-KQLS(FM) Colby, KDGB(FM) Dodge City, KGNO(AM)-KOLS(FM) Dodge City, KEGS(FM) Emporia, KZLS(FM) Great Bend, KYUU(AM)-KSLS(FM) Liberal, KILS(FM) Minneapolis & KWLS(AM)-KGLS(FM) Pratt, all Kan.; & KXLS(FM) Alva, Okla. (All 100% owned.) Ownership: Larry Steckline. Hqtrs: 1632 S. Maize Rd., Wichita, Kan. 67209. (316) 721-8484. FAX: (316) 267-0521.

Lewis Broadcasting Corp. Stns: 1 AM, 2 FM, 3 TV. WLTZ(TV) Columbus, & WJCL-FM & WJCL(TV) Savannah, both Ga.; WZRX(AM) Jackson & WSTZ-FM Vicksburg, both Miss.; & WLTX(TV) Columbia, S.C. (All 100% owned.) Ownership: J.C. Lewis Jr., 100%. Hqtrs: Box 61268, 10001 Abercorn St., Savannah, Ga. 31406. (912) 925-0022. FAX: (912) 925-8621.

Liggett Broadcast Inc. Stns: 3 AM, 8 FM. KMGG(FM) Monte Rio (Santa Rosa), Calif.; WBCK(AM)-WBXX(FM) Battle Creek, WELL(AM) Battle Creek, WHNN(FM) Bay City (Saginaw), WFMK(FM) East Lansing, WLHT(FM) Grand Rapids, WJIM-AM-FM Lansing & WELL-FM Marshall, all Mich.; & WLQT(FM) Kettering, Ohio. Executives: Robert G. Liggett Jr., chmn; James A. Jensen, pres; Donald H. Layman, treas. Ownership: Robert G. Liggett Jr., 100%. Hqtrs: 160 E. Grand River Ave., Williamston, Mich. 48895. (517) 349-2040. FAX: (517) 349-4100.

The Lincoln Group Ltd. Stns: 2 AM, 3 FM. WBUF(FM) Buffalo & WHAM(AM)-WVOR-FM Rochester, both N.Y.; WSOM(AM) & WQXK(FM) Salem, Ohio. (All 100% owned.) Note: WBUF(FM) Buffalo, N.Y. has been sold, pending FCC approval. Ownership: Albert L. "Bud" Wertheimer, Albert Wertheimer, John A. Palvino. Hqtrs: 351 S. Warren St., Suite 600, Syracuse, N.Y. 13202. (315) 478-5030. FAX: (315) 478-0251.

Linder Broadcasting Group. Stns: 2 AM, 6 FM. KKSI(FM) Eddyville, Iowa; KKRC(FM) Granite Falls, KARP(FM) Glencoe, KTOE(AM) Mankato, KMHL(AM)-KKCK(FM) Marshall, KDOG(FM) North Mankato & KARL(FM) Tracy, all Minn. Ownership: Donald Linder, John Linder & Bruce Linder. Hqtrs: Box 1420, Mankato, Minn. 56001. (507) 345-4537. FAX: (507) 625-5364.

J.R. Livesay Group. Stns: 3 AM, 2 FM. WBAR(AM) Bartow, Fla.; WHOW-AM-FM Clinton & WLBH-AM-FM Mattoon, both Ill. Executives: J.R. Livesay, chmn. Ownership: J.R. Livesay owns 51% of WBAR, 53.34% of WHOW-AM-FM & 51% of WLBH-AM-FM. J.R. Livesay II (son of J.R. Livesay) owns 25% of WBAR, 14.86% of WHOW-AM-FM & 24.6% of WLBH-AM-FM. Shirley Herrington (daughter of J.R. Livesay) owns 10% of WBAR, 14.8% of WHOW-AM-FM & 10% of WLBH-AM-FM. Mrs. J.R. Livesay (wife of pres) owns 16.9% of WHOW-AM-FM. Hqtrs: Box 322, Mattoon, Ill. 61938. (217) 234-6464. FAX: (217) 234-6019.

Pirallo Lopez Stns. Stns: 4 AM, 2 FM. WMIA(AM) Arecibo, WLDI(FM) Bayamon, WAEL-FM Maricao, WAEL(AM) Mayaguez, WISO(AM) Ponce & WRAI(AM) San Juan, all P.R. Ownership: Ginette P. Pirallo, estate of Carlos M. Pirallo, Jose L. Pirallo, Carmen E. Pirallo, Lirio Pirallo. Hqtrs: 74 Mayaguez St., San Juan, P.R. 00917. (809) 763-0020. FAX: (809) 250-8005.

Lotus Communications Corp. Stns: 10 AM, 9 FM. KEKO(FM) Green Valley & KTKT(AM)-KLPX(FM) Tucson, both Ariz.; KGST(AM) Fresno, KWKW(AM) Los Angeles, KOXR(AM) Oxnard & KFSD-FM San Diego, all Calif.; WTAQ(AM) La Grange, Ill.; KENO(AM)-KOMP(FM) Las Vegas, KORK(AM)-KXPT(FM) Las Vegas, KHIT-FM Reno, KOZZ-AM-FM Reno & KHIT(AM) Sun Valley, all Nev.; KONE(FM) Lubbock & KZEP-AM-FM San Antonio, both Tex. Executives: Howard A. Kalmenson, pres; Jerry Roy, VP; William Shriftman, VP/treas; Lynden Williams, VP engrg. Hqtrs: 6777 Hollywood Blvd., Hollywood, Calif. 90028. (213) 461-8225.

Lovcom Inc. Stns: 3 AM, 2 FM. KFTM(AM) & KBRU(FM) Fort Morgan, Colo.; KBFS(AM) Belle Fourche, S.D.; & KROE-AM-FM Sheridan, Wyo. Executive: W.K. Love, pres. Hqtrs: Box N, Sheridan, Wyo. 82801. (307) 672-9003. FAX: (307) 674-5449.

M

M.B. Communications. Stns: 1 AM, 1 FM. WFLK(FM) Geneva & WYLF(AM) Penn Yan, both N.Y. (Both 100% owned.) Ownership: Russell S. Kimble. Note: Also owns 43% of WCGR(AM) & WLKA(FM) Canandaigua, N.Y. Hqtrs: 100 Main St., Penn Yan, N.Y. 14527. (315) 536-0850. FAX: (315) 536-3299.

M.M. Group Inc. Stns: 1 AM, 2 FM. WCSJ(AM) & WCFL(FM) Morris, Ill.; & WQTL(FM) Ottawa, Ohio. Note: WQTL(FM) Ottawa, Ohio has been sold, subject to FCC approval. Hqtrs: Robert J. Maccini, Receiver, 170 Westminster St., Suite 170, Providence, R.I. 02903. (401) 454-3130.

MacDonald Broadcasting Co. Stns: 4 AM, 4 FM. WATT(AM) & WWLZ(FM) Cadillac, WILS-AM-FM Lansing, WMBN-AM-FM Petoskey, & WSAM(AM) & WKCQ(FM) Saginaw, all Mich. Executives: Carolyn Ann MacDonald, CEO. Ownership: Carolyn MacDonald, Ken MacDonald Jr., Patricia Garber, Andrew Neale MacDonald. Hqtrs: Box 1776, Saginaw, Mich. 48605. (517) 752-8161. FAX: (517) 752-8102.

Magic Broadcasting Companies. Stns: 3 AM, 3 FM. WSYA-AM-FM Montgomery, Ala.; KTOM-AM-FM Salinas, Calif.; & WDEN-AM-FM Macon, Ga. (All 100% owned.) Ownership: Magic Broadcasting II Inc., 7%; Lishil Enterprises Ltd., 16%; Anne S. Reich 1977 Securities Trust, 14%; Anne S. Reich 1984 Revocable Trust, 14%. Note: Magic Broadcasting Companies controls U.S. Broadcasting L.P. & Magic Broadcasting II Inc. KTOM-AM-FM Salinas, Calif. is owned by KTOM Broadcasting Inc., gen ptnr (Donald G. McCoy, pres, 65%; Douglas M. Grimm, exec VP, 35%); California Broadcasting Investors Limited Partnership, limited ptnr. Hqtrs: WDEN-AM-FM, Box 46, Macon, Ga. 31297. (912) 745-3383. FAX: (912) 745-9693.

Mahaffey Enterprises Inc. Stns: 3 AM, 4 FM. KGGF(AM) & KUSN(FM) Coffeyville, Kan.; KRMS(AM)-KYLC(FM) Osage Beach, KTTR(AM)-KZNN(FM) Rolla & KZYQ(FM) St. James, all Mo. (All 100% owned.) Ownership: John B. Mahaffey, Fredna B. Mahaffey, Robert B. Mahaffey. Hqtrs: Box 4584, Springfield, Mo. 65808. (417) 883-9180.

Maine Radio and Television Co. Stns: 2 TV. KMEG(TV) Sioux City, Iowa; & WCSH-TV Portland, Me. (Both 100% owned.) Executive: Frederic L. Thompson, pres. Ownership: No stockholder owns more than 10%. Hqtrs: One Congress Sq., Portland, Me. 04101. (207) 828-6666. FAX: (207) 828-6630.

Malkan Broadcast Assoc. Stns: 1 AM, 3 FM. WIST(FM) Lobelville & WYNU(FM) Milan, both Tenn.; KEYS(AM) & KZFM(FM) Corpus Christi, Tex. Note: Group has purchased KNGV(FM) Kingsville, Tex., subject to FCC approval. Ownership: Arnold Malkan, Audrey Malkan. Hqtrs: Box 9757, Corpus Christi, Tex. 78469. (512) 883-3516. FAX: (512) 882-9767.

Malrite Communications Group Inc. Stns: 1 FM, 5 TV. WFLX(TV) West Palm Beach, Fla.; WXIX-TV Newport, Ky. (Cincinnati); WOIO(TV) Shaker Heights, Ohio (Cleveland); WJJZ(FM) Philadelphia; WLII(TV) Caguas & WSUR-TV Ponce, both P.R. Executives: Milton Maltz, chmn/CEO; John C. Chaffee Jr., pres/COO; Kevan A. Fight, VP/CFO; John M. Schohl, VP/sec/gen counsel; Nicholas M. Marra, controller/chief accounting off; Tom Bracanovich, VP engrg. Hqtrs: 800 Skylight Office Tower, 1660 W. 2nd St., Cleveland 44113-1454. (216) 781-3010. FAX: (216) 781-0869.

Manship Stns. Stns: 2 TV. WBRZ(TV) Baton Rouge; & KRGV-TV Weslaco, Tex. Ownership: WBRZ: C.P. Manship Jr., 29.57%; D.L. Manship, 22.30%. KRGV-TV jointly owned by the Messrs. Manship. (See also Cross-Ownership, Sect. A.) Hqtrs: Box 2906, Baton Rouge 70821. (504) 387-2222. FAX: (504) 336-2246.

Mark Media Group. Stns: 4 AM. WISE(AM) Asheville, WKYK(AM) Burnsville, WTZQ(AM) Hendersonville & WTOE(AM) Spruce Pine, all N.C. Executives: J. Ardell Sink, pres/CEO; Remelle Sink, exec VP/CFO; Michael Sink, VP/COO. Hqtrs: Box 607, Mark Group Bldg., 401 Sawmill Rd., Burnsville, N.C. 28714. (704) 682-6221; (800) 949-3798. FAX: (704) 682-6227.

Marlin Broadcasting Inc. Stns: 3 FM. WTMI(FM) Miami; WQRS(FM) Detroit; & WFLN-FM Philadelphia. Ownership: Howard P. Tanger, Alexander M. Tanger, Brenda R. Tanger. Hqtrs: 32 Fairfield St., Boston 02116. (617) 267-0515.

Mars Hill Broadcasting Co. Stns: 3 FM. WMHI(FM) Cape Vincent, WMHR(FM) Syracuse & WMHN(FM) Webster, all N.Y. (All 100% owned.) Ownership: Not-for-profit corporation. Hqtrs: 4044 Makyes Rd., Syracuse, N.Y. 13215. (315) 469-5051. FAX: (315) 469-4066.

Marsh Media. Stns: 3 TV. KVIH-TV Clovis, N.M.; KVII-TV Amarillo & KVIA-TV El Paso, both Tex. (All 100% owned.) Executive: James R. McCormick, CEO. Ownership: KVIH-TV & KVII-TV are owned by Stanley Marsh III, 99%; Estelle Marsh Watlington, 1%. KVIA-TV is owned by Stanley Marsh III, 25%; Stanley Marsh III Special Trust, 20%; Michael C. Marsh, 20%; Tom F. Marsh, 10%; Tom F. Marsh Special Trust, 10%; David L. Weir, 5%; Tom F. Marsh Family Trust No. 2, 4.5%; Micbael C. Marsh Family Trust No. 2, 4.5%; Estelle Marsh Watlington, 1%. Hqtrs: One Broadcast Ctr., Amarillo, Tex. 79101-4328. (806) 373-1787. FAX: (806) 371-7329.

Martin Broadcasting Inc. Stns: 5 AM. KZZB(AM) Beaumont, KSSQ(AM) Conroe, KRMY(AM) Killeen, KCHL(AM) San Antonio & KANI(AM) Wharton, all Tex. Executive: Darrell E. Martin, pres. Hqtrs: Box 419, Baytown, Tex. 77522. (713) 424-7000.

Martz Communications Group. Stns: 1 AM, 9 FM. WBPW(FM) Presque Isle, Me.; WODQ(FM) Baraga, WENL(FM) Gladstone, WZNL(FM) Norway & WKNW(AM)-WYSS(FM) Sault Ste. Marie, all Mich.; WYUL(FM) Chateaugay, N.Y.; KYWG(FM) Sarles, N.D.; WXMX(FM) Canaan, Vt.; & WFNL(FM) Sturgeon Bay, Wis. Executives: Timothy D. Martz, pres. Ownership: Timothy D. Martz, 90%. Hqtrs: 5595 Liberty Rd., Chagrin Falls, Ohio. 44022. (216) 498-1221.

Max Radio Inc. Stns: 1 AM, 4 FM. WJMH(FM) Reidsville & WMQX-AM-FM Winston-Salem, both N.C.; WWDE-FM Hampton & WNVZ(FM) Norfolk, both Va. Ownership: Max Media Inc. & Quad-C Inc., Charlottesville & Richmond, both Va. Hqtrs: 5501 Greenwich Rd., Suite 198, Virginia Beach, Va. 23462. (804) 499-9800. FAX: (804) 499-0034.

May Broadcasting. Stns: 3 AM, 3 FM. KKBZ(FM) Clarinda & KMA(AM) Shenandoah, both Iowa; KFOR(AM) & KFRX(FM) Lincoln, Neb.; WKTY(AM) & WSPL(FM) La Crosse, Wis. Ownership: Edward W. May Jr., gen ptnr, 25%; Edward W. May, limited ptnr, 12.5%; Eleanor J. May, limited ptnr, 12.5%; Annette M. Marra, limited ptnr, 25%; Karen L. Sislo, limited ptnr, 25%. Hqtrs: Box 960, Shenandoah, Iowa 51601. (712) 246-5270. FAX: (712) 246-5275.

Wendell Mayes Stations. Stns: 3 AM, 3 FM. KCRS-AM-FM Midland (100%), KSNY-AM-FM Snyder (32.5%), KAMG(AM) & KVIC(FM) Victoria (100%), all Tex. Principal own: Wendell Mayes Jr. Cable TV. Hqtrs: 1907 N. Lamar, Suite 200, Austin, Tex. 78705. (512) 477-6866. FAX: (512) 476-1879.

McClure Broadcasting. Stns: 2 AM, 3 FM. WCHK(AM)-WGST-FM Canton, WRCG(AM)-WCGQ(FM) Columbus & WMKS(FM) Macon, all Ga. Ownership: WCHK(AM)-WGST-FM & WRCG(AM)-WCGQ(FM) are owned by C.A. McClure, 90%; F.K. Brown, 10%. WMKS(FM) is owned by C.A. McClure, 65%. Hqtrs: Box 1537, Columbus, Ga. 31994. (706) 327-1217. FAX: (706) 596-4600.

McCoy Broadcasting Co. Stns: 2 AM, 4 FM. KPAY-AM-FM Chico, Calif.; KCCY(FM) & KDZA-FM Pueblo, Colo.; & KPNW-AM-FM Eugene, Ore. Executive: Craig McCoy, pres. Hqtrs: 4700 S.W. Macadam Ave., Portland, Ore. 97201. (503) 796-1070. FAX: (503) 796-0525.

McGraw Group Stations. Stns: 1 AM, 2 FM. WCDK(FM) Cadiz, Ohio; WELK(FM) Elkins & WEIR(AM) Weirton, both W.Va. Ownership: Richard H. McGraw, 50%; Karen G. McGraw, 50%. Hqtrs: 228 Randolph Ave., Elkins, W.Va. 26241. (304) 636-8800. FAX: (304) 636-8801.

McGraw-Hill Broadcasting Group. Stns: 4 TV. KERO-TV Bakersfield & KGTV(TV) San Diego, both Calif.; KMGH-TV Denver; & WRTV(TV) Indianapolis. (All 100% owned.) Executives: Edward T. Reilly Jr., pres; David Ingraham, sr VP fin, planning & admin. Ownership: McGraw-Hill Inc., 100%. (See Cross-Ownership, Sect. A.) Hqtrs: McGraw-Hill Inc., 1221 Ave. of the Americas, New York 10020. (212) 512-6457. FAX: (212) 512-2282.

McKinnon Broadcasting Co. Stns: 3 TV. KUSI-TV San Diego; KBMT(TV) Beaumont & KIII(TV) Corpus Christi, both Tex. Ownership: Michael McKinnon. Hqtrs: 800 N. Shoreline, Corpus Christi, Tex. 78401. (512) 884-3300. FAX: (512) 884-0718.

McNaughton Stns. Stns: 3 AM, 4 FM. WCRA(AM)-WCRC(FM) Effingham & WRMN(AM)-WJKL(FM) Elgin, both Ill.; WBEV(AM)-WXRO(FM) Beaver Dam & WYKY(FM) Columbus, both Wis. Ownership: WCRA & WCRC are owned by Joseph E. McNaughton, 55%; Mary Cecille Helmer, 13%; Jo Ann Mansfield, 13%; Eddie W. Howard, 10%. WRMN & WJKL are owned by Joseph E. McNaughton, 69%; Alexander McNaughton, 16%; Richard Jakle, 15%. WBEV & WXRO are owned by Kewanee Broadcasting Co. (WKEI-WJRE), 65%; John Klinger, 20%; & Richard Jakle, 15%. WYKY is owned by Beaver Dam Radio Inc. (See also Cross-Ownership, Sect. A.) Hqtrs: Box 568, 208 W. Jefferson, Effingham, Ill. 62401. (217) 342-4141. FAX: (217) 342-9315.

Media General Broadcast Group. Stns: 3 TV. WJKS(TV) Jacksonville & WFLA-TV Tampa, both Fla.; & WCBD-TV Charleston, S.C. (All 100% owned.) Executives: James A. Zimmerman, VP/opns; Edward H. Deichman Jr., VP/corporate controller; Richard W. Roberts, dir per; Russell H. Myerson, dir progmg; Ardell Hill, dir engrg. (See also Media General Inc. under Cross-Ownership, Sect. A.) Cable TV: Cablevision of Fredericksburg Inc., Fredericksburg, Va.; Media General Cable of Fairfax Inc., Chantilly, Va. Hqtrs: 905 E.

Jackson St., Tampa, Fla. 33602. (813) 228-8888. FAX: (813) 221-5787.

Media Ltd. Stns: 3 AM, 4 FM. KJNO(AM)-KTKU(FM) Juneau, KTKN(AM)-KGTW(FM) Ketchikan, KIFW(AM)-KSBZ(FM) Sitka & KMBQ(FM) Wasilla, all Alaska. Ownership: E. Roy Paschal, gen ptnr, 62.8%; U.S. Bank of Oregon, Trustee of The Jason S. Paschal Irrevocable Trust, limited ptnr, 33.7%; Jack Huff, limited ptnr, 3.5%. Hqtrs: 3161 Channel Dr., Suite 202, Juneau, Alaska 99801. (907) 586-3630. FAX: (907) 463-3685.

Mega Media Ltd. (The Super "C" Radio Network) Stns: 1 AM, 4 FM. KCHA-AM-FM Charles City, KCZQ(FM) Cresco, KCZE(FM) New Hampton & KCZY(FM) Osage, all Iowa. (All 100% owned.) Ownership: Jim Bernard Hebel. Hqtrs: 207 N. Main St., Charles City, Iowa 50616. (515) 228-1000. FAX: (515) 228-1200.

Mercury Broadcasting Company Inc. Stns: 1 AM, 1 FM, 2 TV. KASN(TV) Pine Bluff, Ark.; WJTC(TV) Pensacola, Fla.; KFON(AM) Austin & KEYI-FM San Marcos, both Tex. (All 100% owned.) Ownership: Van H. Archer III. Hqtrs: 115 E. Travis, Suite 1427, San Antonio, Tex. 78205. (210) 222-0973. FAX: (210) 222-0975.

Meredith Broadcasting Group, Meredith Corp. Stns: 5 TV. KPHO-TV Phoenix; WOFL(TV) Orlando, Fla.; WNEM-TV Bay City, Mich.; KCTV(TV) Kansas City, Mo.; & KVVU-TV Henderson, Nev. (All 100% owned.) Executive: Philip A. Jones, pres, Broadcasting Group. Meredith Broadcasting is an operating group of Meredith Corp., Des Moines, Iowa, which publishes *Better Homes & Gardens, Successful Farming* and consumer books. Hqtrs: 1716 Locust St., Des Moines, Iowa 50309-3023. (515) 284-3331. FAX: (515) 284-2393.

Merit Broadcasting Corp. Stns: 2 AM, 2 FM. KATA(AM) Arcata, KARZ(FM) Burney, KFMI(FM) Eureka & KNRO(AM) Redding, all Calif. (All 100% owned.) Executives: Jeff Martin, pres; Mike Martin, VP; Jane Martin, sec/treas. Hqtrs: Box 492890, Redding, Calif. 96049. (916) 243-2222.

MetroCities Communications Inc. Stns: 2 AM, 2 FM. WKYD(AM) & WWSF-FM Andalusia, Ala.; & WIBM-AM-FM Jackson, Mich. (All 100% owned.) Note: WKYD(AM) & WWSF-FM Andalusia, Ala. have been sold, pending FCC approval. Ownership: Henry Posner Jr. Cable TV. Hqtrs: 381 Mansfield Ave., Suite 500, Pittsburgh 15220. (412) 928-7700. FAX: (412) 928-7715.

Metroplex Communications Inc. Stns: 3 AM, 4 FM. WMTX-FM Clearwater (Tampa), WHYI(FM) Fort Lauderdale & WMTX(AM) Pinellas Park (Tampa), all Fla.; WWWS(AM) & WUFX(FM) Buffalo, N.Y.; WERE(AM) & WNCX(FM) Cleveland. Note: Group also manages WAXY(FM) Fort Lauderdale, Fla. through a loc mktg agreement. Executives: Norman Wain, chmn/CEO; Robert C. Weiss, pres/COO. Ownership: Norman Wain & Robert C. Weiss. Hqtrs: 1818 Ohio Savings Plaza, Cleveland 44114. (216) 566-8080. FAX: (216) 566-8142.

Meyer Broadcasting Co. Stns: 1 AM, 1 FM, 4 TV. KFYR-AM-TV & KYYY(FM) Bismarck, KQCD-TV Dickinson, KMOT(TV) Minot & KUMV-TV Williston, all N.D. (All 100% owned.) Executives: Judith Ekberg Johnson, pres/CEO. Ownership: Judith Ekberg Johnson, 51%; Nancy B. Ekberg, 16%; Marietta E. Turner, 16%; Margaret E. Hammerling, 16%. Hqtrs: Box 1738, Bismarck, N.D. 58502. (701) 223-0900.

Meyer Communications Inc. Stns: 2 AM, 5 FM. KFAL(AM)-KKCA(FM) Fulton (80%), KBOA(AM)-KTMO(FM) Kennett, KISF(FM) Lexington (80%) & KTXR(FM) Springfield (92.88%), all Mo.; & KATP(FM) Amarillo, Tex. (80%). Executive: Kenneth E. Meyer, pres. Ownership: Kenneth E. Meyer, 100%. Hqtrs: Box 3676, Springfield, Mo. 65808. (417) 862-3990. FAX: (417) 869-7675.

Michigan Communications Group. Stns: 1 AM, 2 FM. WPZX(FM) Big Rapids & WOAP(AM)-WMZX(FM) Owosso, both Mich. (All 100% owned.) Ownership: Russell C. Balch, Keith J. Rudolf. Hqtrs: 1415 Hatcher Crescent, Ann Arbor, Mich. 48103. (313) 665-3847.

Mid-America Gospel Radio. Stns: 4 AM. KXEG(AM) Tolleson, Ariz. (Phoenix); KQXI(AM) Arvada, Colo.; KXEN(AM) Festus-St. Louis, Mo.; & KSHY(AM) Cheyenne, Wyo. Ownership: Burt W. Kaufman, Dirk L. Hallemeier & George Spicer. Sales offices: 1817 N. 3rd St., Phoenix 85004. (602) 254-5001. FAX: (602) 254-5348. Central Accounting Agency: Box 8085, Mitchell, Ill. 62040.

Mid Atlantic Network. Stns: 3 AM, 3 FM. WFVA(AM)-WBQB(FM) Fredericksburg, WKCY-AM-FM Harrisonburg & WINC-AM-FM Winchester, all Va. Controlling ownship: John P. Lewis, David P. Lewis & Howard P. Lewis. Hqtrs: Box 3300, Winchester, Va. 22604. (703) 667-2224. FAX: (703) 722-3295.

Midcontinent Media Inc. Stns: 4 AM, 5 FM, 4 TV. KXLK(FM) Haysville & KFH(AM) Wichita, both Kan.; KDWB-FM Richfield & WDGY(AM) St. Paul, both Minn.; KDLO-TV Florence, KCLO-TV Rapid City, KPLO-TV Reliance, KELO-AM-FM-TV Sioux Falls & KDLO-FM Watertown, all S.D.; WTSO(AM) & WZEE(FM) Madison, Wis. Principals: N. L. Bentson, chmn, pres/CEO; Joe H. Floyd, exec VP/COO. Cable TV. Hqtrs: 7900 Xerxes Ave. S., Suite 1100, Minneapolis 55431-1108. (612) 844-2600. FAX: (612) 844-2660.

Midwest Communications Inc. Stns: 3 AM, 6 FM. WTBX(FM) Hibbing & WKKQ(AM) Nashwauk, both Minn.; KYNN(FM) Lincoln, Neb.; WGEE(AM)-WIXX(FM) Green Bay, WOZZ(FM) New London, WRIG(AM) Schofield, WGEE-FM Sturgeon Bay & WDEZ(FM) Wausau, all Wis. Ownership: D.E. Wright owns 92% of WTBX(FM), WKKQ(AM) & KYNN(FM), WGEE(AM) & WIXX(FM), WOZZ(FM) & WGEE-FM. D.E. Wright owns 100% of WRIG(AM) & WDEZ(FM). Hqtrs: Box 23333, Green Bay, Wis. 54305. (414) 435-3771.

Mid-West Family Stations. Stns: 9 AM, 15 FM. WNTA(AM) Rockford, WMAY(AM)-WNNS(FM) Springfield, WQLZ(FM) Taylorville & WKMQ(FM) Winnebago, all Ill.; WTKA(AM)-WQKL(FM) Ann Arbor, WCFX(FM) Clare, WCHT(AM)-WGLQ(FM) Escanaba, WIXC(FM) Essexville & WSJM(AM)-WIRX(FM) St. Joseph, all Mich.; KOSP(FM) Willard, Mo.; WEAQ(AM)-WIAL(FM) Eau Claire, WIZM-AM-FM La Crosse, WFDL(FM) Lomira, WTDY(AM)-WMGN(FM) Madison, WOSH(AM)-WMGV(FM) Oshkosh & WJJO(FM) Watertown, all Wis. Executive: William R. Walker, dir. Ownership: William R. Walker, Philip Fisher. Hqtrs: Box 253, Madison, Wis. 53701. (608) 273-3766. FAX: (608) 273-3588.

Midwest Television Inc. Stns: 2 AM, 2 FM, 4 TV. KFMB-AM-FM-TV San Diego; WCIA(TV) Champaign, WMBD-AM-TV/WKZW(FM) Peoria & WCFN(TV) Springfield, all Ill. (All 100% owned.) Ownership: August C. Meyer Jr., estate of August C. Meyer Sr. Hqtrs: Box 20, Champaign, Ill. 61824-0020. (217) 356-8333.

Midwestern Broadcasting Co. See Paul Bunyan Network.

Milliken Investment Corp. Stns: 2 AM, 1 FM. WVKV(AM) Hurricane & WSGB(AM)-WCKA(FM) Sutton, both W.Va. (All 100% owned.) Ownership: James S. Milliken, Jack C. Milliken, Teresa L. Milliken & Betty J. Milliken. Hqtrs: Box 1080, Hurricane, W.Va. 25526. (304) 562-9155.

Mitchell Broadcasting Co. Stns: 2 AM, 1 FM. KQKQ-FM Council Bluffs, Iowa; KOIL(AM) Bellevue & KKAR(AM) Omaha, both Neb. Ownership: John C. Mitchell. Hqtrs: 1001 Farnam, Omaha 68102. (402) 342-2000. FAX: (402) 346-5748.

Monarch Broadcasting Ltd. Stns: 7 AM, 1 FM, 2 TV. CJXX(AM) Grande Prairie, CKRX(AM) Lethbridge, CHAT-AM-TV Medicine Hat, CKRD(AM) Red Deer & CKTA(AM) Taber, all Alta.; CKMK(AM) Mackenzie, & CKPG-AM-TV & CIOI-FM Prince George, both B.C. (All stns are located in Canada.) Ownership: W.H. Yuill. Cable TV. Hqtrs: 361 First St. S.E., Medicine Hat, Alta., Canada T1A0A5. (403) 526-4529. FAX: (403) 526-4000.

Montrose Broadcasting Corp. Stns: 2 AM, 2 FM. WPGM-AM-FM Danville & WPEL-AM-FM Montrose, both Pa. (All 100% owned.) Ownership: No stock. Nonprofit, noncommercial licensee controlled by a bd of directors, none of whom own stock. Hqtrs: Box 248, Locust & High Sts., Montrose, Pa. 18801. (717) 278-2811. FAX: (717) 278-1442.

The Moody Bible Institute of Chicago. Stns: 4 AM, 13 FM. WMBV(FM) Dixons Mills, Ala.; WRMB(FM) Boynton Beach & WKES(FM) St. Petersburg, both Fla.; WAFS(AM) Atlanta; WMBI-AM-FM Chicago, WDLM-AM-FM East Moline & WGNR(FM) Monee, all Ill.; WIWC(FM) Kokomo, Ind.; WJSO(FM) Pikeville, Ky.; WGNB(FM) Zeeland, Mich.; WCRF(FM) Cleveland & WVMS(FM) Sandusky, both Ohio; WMBW(FM) Chattanooga; & KMBI-AM-FM Spokane, Wash. Hqtrs: 820 N. LaSalle St., Chicago 60610. (312) 329-4302. FAX: (312) 329-4468.

Morris Network Inc. Stns: 4 TV. WDHN(TV) Dothan, Ala.; KARK-TV Little Rock, Ark.; WMGT(TV) Macon & WVGA(TV) Valdosta, both Ga. (All 100% owned.) Ownership: Charles H. Morris & Alden Morris Maier. (See Morris Newspaper Corp. under Cross-Ownership, Sect. A.) Hqtrs: Box 8167, Savannah, Ga. 31412. (912) 233-1281. FAX: (912) 232-4639.

Mortenson Broadcasting Co. Stns: 4 AM, 3 FM. KLTT(AM) Brighton, Colo.; WCGW(AM) Nicholasville & WJMM-FM Versailles, both Ky.; WBGR(AM) Baltimore; WHLO(AM) Akron & WTOF-FM Canton, both Ohio; & WEMM(FM) Huntington, W. Va. Executive: Jack Mortenson, pres. Ownership: Jack Mortenson, 60%; Marianne Carter, 20%; R. Stan Mortenson, 20%; . Hqtrs: 3191 Nicholasville Rd., Suite 600, Lexington, Ky. 40503. (606) 245-1000. FAX: (606) 245-1600.

Mount Royal Broadcasting Inc./Metromedia CMR Inc. Stns: 2 AM, 2 FM. CIQC(AM)-CFQR-FM Montreal & CKVL(AM)-CKOI-FM Verdun, both Que. Ownership: CIQC(AM) & CFQR-FM are licensed to Mount Royal Broadcasting Inc. CKVL(AM) & CKOI-FM are licensed to Metromedia CMR Inc. (All stns are located in Canada.) Hqtrs: 1200 McGill College, Suite 300, Montreal, Que., Canada H3B 4G7. (514) 874-4040. FAX: (514) 393-4659.

Multi Media Television Inc. Stns: 2 TV. WKPV(TV) Ponce & WSJN-TV San Juan, both P.R. Note: Both stns have been sold, pending FCC approval. Ownership: Maria E. Rivera. Hqtrs: GPO Box 2556, San Juan, P.R. 00936.

Multimedia Broadcasting Co. Stns: 4 AM, 4 FM, 5 TV. WMAZ-AM-TV & WAYS(FM) Macon, Ga.; KEEL(AM) & KITT(FM) Shreveport, La.; KSDK(TV) St. Louis; WLWT(TV) Cincinnati & WKYC-TV Cleveland; WFBC-AM-FM Greenville & WORD(AM) Spartanburg, both S.C.; WBIR-TV Knoxville, Tenn.; & WEZW(FM) Wauwatosa, Wis. (Milwaukee). Note: KEEL(AM)-KITT(FM) Shreveport, La., & WEZW(FM) Wauwatosa, Wis. have been sold, subject to FCC approval. Executives: Pat Servodidio, pres: Greg Anderson, exec VP radio; James M. Hart, Leeann Lewis, Don McGouirk, Bill Scaffide, John Kueneke, Raymond Cal, James McLendon, James A. Clayton, VPs. (See also Cross-Ownership, Sect. A.) Cable TV. Hqtrs: 140 W. 9th St., Cincinnati 45202. (513) 352-5700. FAX: (513) 352-5969.

Morgan Murphy Stations (Evening Telegram). Stns: 1 AM, 1 FM, 5 TV. KTHI-TV Fargo, N.D.; KVEW(TV) Kennewick, KXLY-AM-FM-TV Spokane & KAPP(TV) Yakima, all Wa.; & WISC-TV Madison, Wis. Evening Telegram Co. owns 100% of KTHI-TV, KVEW(TV), KXLY-AM-FM-TV & KAPP(TV). Evening Telegram Co. owns 84.4% of WISC-TV, with an additional 15.2% of the stn held by Evening Telegram stockholders. (See also Cross-Ownership, Sect. A.) Hqtrs: Box 44965, Madison, Wis. 53744-4965. (608) 271-4321. FAX: (608) 271-1709.

N

NBC TV Stations Division. Stns: 6 TV. WNBC(TV) New York; WMAQ-TV Chicago; KCNC-TV Denver; KNBC-TV Los Angeles; WTVJ(TV) Miami; & WRC-TV Washington. (All 100% owned.) (For a listing of NBC divisions & executives, see section G.) Hqtrs: 30 Rockefeller Plaza, New York 10112. (212) 664-4444. FAX: (212) 664-5830.

NTV Network. Stns: 3 TV. KWNB-TV Hayes Ctr., KHGI-TV Kearney & KSNB-TV Superior, all Neb. (All 100% owned.) Ownership: Fant Broadcasting Company of Nebraska Inc. Other interests: WNAL-TV Gadsden, Ala. Hqtrs: Box 220, Kearney, Neb. 68848. (308) 743-2494. Fax: (308) 743-2644.

Narragansett Capital Inc. (Narragansett Radio L.P., Narragansett Television L.P.) Stns: 2 AM, 2 FM, 2 TV. WYNK-AM-FM Baton Rouge; KEZO-AM-FM Omaha; WPRI-TV Providence, R.I.; & WTKR-TV Norfolk, Va. (All majority controlled.) (See also Cross-Ownership, Sect. A.) Cable TV. Hqtrs: Fleet Center, 50 Kennedy Plaza, Providence, R.I. 02903. (401) 751-1700. FAX: (401) 751-1790.

Nationwide Communications Inc. (Nationwide Mutual Insurance Co). Stns: 3 AM, 11 FM, 3 TV. KVRY(FM) Mesa (Phoenix), Ariz.; KNCI(FM) Sacramento, Calif.; WOMX-AM-FM Orlando, Fla.; WPOC(FM) Baltimore; KXNO(AM) North Las Vegas & KLUC-FM Las Vegas, both Nev.; WGAR-FM Cleveland, WCOL-AM-FM Columbus & WNCI(FM) Columbus, all Ohio; WATE-TV Knoxville, Tenn.; KDMX(FM) Dallas & KHMX(FM) Houston; WRIC-TV Petersburg (Richmond), Va.; KISW(FM) Seattle; & WBAY-TV Green Bay, Wis. (All 100% owned.)

Note: KNCI(FM) Sacramento, Calif. has been sold, subject to FCC approval. Executives: Steve Berger, pres; Willard Hoyt, VP/treas; Benjamin D. McKeel, VP TV; Don Watkins, VP engrg; Joseph "Mickey" Franko, VP radio; Gordon E. McCutchan, sr VP/gen counsel/sec; Patricia L. Glassburn, asst treas; Joan Hamm, corporate comptroller. Hqtrs: One Nationwide Plaza, 27th Fl., Columbus, Ohio 43216. (614) 249-7676. FAX: (614) 249-6995.

Nebraska Rural Radio Association. Stns: 2 AM, 2 FM. KRVN-AM-FM Lexington & KNEB-AM-FM Scottsbluff, both Neb. (All 100% owned.) Hqtrs: Box 880, Lexington, Neb. 68850. (308) 324-2371. FAX: (308) 324-5786.

Neuhoff Broadcasting Corp. Stns: 2 AM, 2 FM. WDAN(AM)-WDNL(FM) Danville & WFMB-AM-FM Springfield, both Ill. Ownership: Geoffrey H. Neuhoff, 100%. Hqtrs: 3055 S. 4th St., Springfield, Ill. 62703. (217) 528-3033. FAX: (217) 528-5348.

New South Communications Inc. Stns: 2 AM, 3 FM. KMLB(AM) & KJLO-FM Monroe, La.; WSYE(FM) Houston & WALT(AM)-WOKK(FM) Meridian, both Miss. (All 100% owned.) Ownership: F.E. Holladay, 100%. Hqtrs: Box 5797, Meridian, Miss. 39302. (601) 693-2661. FAX: (601) 483-0826.

New Vision Television Inc. Stns: 8 TV. KOLD-TV Tucson, Ariz.; WSAV-TV Savannah, Ga.; WHLT(TV) Hattiesburg & WJTV(TV) Jackson, both Miss.; WECT(TV) Wilmington, N.C.; KABY-TV Aberdeen, KPRY-TV Pierre & KSFY-TV Sioux Falls, all S.D. (All 100% owned.) Executives: Bennett S. Smith, pres. Ownership: Bennett S. Smith, 33 1/3%; Jason Elkin, 33 1/3%; G. Woodward Stover II, 28 1/3%; & Brian W. Brady, 5%. Hqtrs: 5784 Lake Forest Dr., Suite 290, Atlanta 30328. (404) 256-4444. FAX: (404) 257-9517.

The New York Times Co. Stns: 1 AM, 1 FM, 5 TV. Broadcasting Group: WHNT-TV Huntsville, Ala.; KFSM-TV Fort Smith, Ark.; WQAD-TV Moline, Ill.; WQEW(AM) & WQXR-FM New York; WNEP-TV Scranton, Pa.; & WREG-TV Memphis. Executives: Arthur Ochs Sulzberger, chmn; Lance R. Primis, pres; Katharine P. Darrow, sr VP bcstg. Broadcasting group executives: C. Frank Roberts, group pres; Margaret T. Vyncke, group controller. (See also Cross-Ownership, Sect. A.) Hqtrs: 229 W. 43rd St., New York 10036. (212) 556-1234.

NewCap Broadcasting Ltd. Stns: 9 AM, 3 FM. CFCW(AM) Camrose & CKRA-FM Edmonton, both Alta.; CKXX(AM) Corner Brook, CKXD(AM) Gander, CKXG(AM) Grand Falls, CKXB(AM) Musgravetown & CJYQ(AM)-CKIX-FM St. John's, all Nfld.; CFDR(AM) & CFRQ-FM Dartmouth, N.S.; CJLB(AM) Thunder Bay, Ont.; & CHTN(AM) Charlottetown, P.E.I. (All stns are located in Canada.) Ownership: Newfoundland Capital Corp. Hqtrs: Box 1007, 45 Alderney Dr., Dartmouth, N.S., Canada B2Y 3Z7. (902) 464-1119. FAX: (902) 469-5077.

NewCity Communications Inc. Stns: 5 AM, 9 FM. WODL(FM) & WZZK-AM-FM Birmingham, Ala.; WEZN(FM) Bridgeport, Conn.; WDBO(AM) & WWKA(FM) Orlando, Fla.; WYAI(FM) La Grange, Ga.; WBBS(FM) Fulton & WSYR(AM)-WYYY(FM) Syracuse, both N.Y.; KRMG(AM) & KWEN(FM) Tulsa, Okla.; KKYX(AM) & KCYY(FM) San Antonio, Tex. Note: WYAI(FM) La Grange, Ga. has been sold, pending FCC approval. Executive: Richard A. Ferguson, pres. Ownership: Richard A. Ferguson, Jim Morley, Rich Reis. Hqtrs: 10 Middle St., Bridgeport, Conn. 06604. (203) 333-4800. FAX: (203) 367-9346.

Newfoundland Broadcasting Co. (NTV & OZ Networks) Stns: 9 FM, 22 TV. TV stns: CJAP-TV Argentia, CJON-TV-4 Bay Bulls, CJWB-TV Bonavista, CJBL-TV Cape Broyle, CJCV-TV-10 Clarenville, CJWN-TV Corner Brook, CJLW-TV-7 Deer Lake, CJFR-TV Fermeuse, CFFE-TV Ferryland, CJSG-TV Glenwood West, CJOX-TV Grand Bank, CJCN-TV Grand Falls, CJLT-TV LaScie, CJLN-TV Lawn, CJMA-TV-11 Marystown, CJRR-TV-11 Red Rocks, CJST-TV-13 St. Alban's, CJON-TV St. John's, CJSV-TV Stephenville, CJSC-TV Swift Current, CJON-TV-5 Tors Cove & CJND-TV Twillingate, all Nfld. Radio stns: CFOZ-FM Argentia, CJOZ-FM Bonavista, CJKK-FM Clarenville, CKOZ-FM Corner Brook, CHOS-FM Grand Falls (Rattling Brook), CIOZ-FM Marystown, CKSS-FM Red Rocks, CHOZ-FM St. John's & CIOS-FM Stephenville, all Nfld. (All stns are located in Canada.) Executives: G.W. Stirling, chmn; S.G. Stirling, pres; B. Vallis, gen mgr; D. Lawrence, mgr opns & prod; Doug Neal, dir engrg; Ted Gardner, sls mgr. Ownership: G.W. Stirling, 100%. Also owns a publication, *Herald TV Week.* Hqtrs: Box 2020, NTV-H.Q. Bldg., St. John's, Nfld., Canada A1C 5S2. (709) 722-5015. FAX: (709) 726-5107.

NewMarket Media Corp. Stns: 4 AM, 6 FM. WNOE-AM-FM New Orleans & KGTR(FM) Port Sulphur, both La.; WRXQ(FM) Olive Branch, Miss.; WSJS(AM) & WTQR(FM) Winston-Salem, N.C.; KXXY-AM-FM Oklahoma City; WREC(AM) & WEGR(FM) Memphis. Note: Group has purchased KOQL(FM) Oklahoma City, pending FCC approval. All of the stns have been sold to Radio Equity Partners, subject to FCC approval. Executives: Stephen L. Robertson, chmn/CEO; Peter M. Schulte, pres/COO. Ownership: Stephen L. Robertson, 50%; Peter M. Schulte, 50%. Hqtrs: Box 2080, Advance, N.C. 27006. (919) 998-0691. FAX: (919) 998-0694.

Newport Broadcasting Co. See Sudbury Services Inc.

Newsweb Corp. Stns: 2 TV. KTVJ(TV) Boulder, Colo.; & WPWR-TV Gary, Ind. (Chicago). (Both 100% owned.) Ownership: Fred Eychaner, 100%. Hqtrs: 1645 W. Fullerton Ave., Chicago 60614. (312) 975-0400.

Nicolet Broadcasting Inc. Stns: 2 AM, 3 FM. WBDK(FM) Algoma, WERL(AM)-WRJO(FM) Eagle River & WNBI(AM)-WCQM(FM) Park Falls, all Wis. Ownership: Mary Jo B. Utnehmer. Hqtrs: Box 309, Eagle River, Wis. 54521. (715) 479-4451. FAX: (715) 479-6511.

Nininger Stns. Stns: 3 AM, 4 FM. WKDQ(FM) Henderson (100%) & WKYX(AM)-WKYQ(FM) Paducah (100%), both Ky.; WXBQ-FM Bristol, Tenn. (92%); WXBQ(AM) Bristol, Va. (100%); & WQBE-AM-FM Charleston, W. Va. (100%). Ownership: W.L. Nininger. Hqtrs: WXBQ-FM, Box 1389, Bristol, Va. 24203. (703) 669-8112. FAX: (703) 669-0541.

Noalmark Broadcasting Corp. Stns: 4 AM, 7 FM. KELD(AM)-KIXB(FM) El Dorado, KISQ(FM) El Dorado, KKIX(FM) Fayetteville, KXOW(AM)-KLAZ(FM) Hot Springs & KISK(FM) Lowell, all Ark.; KYKK(AM) & KZOR(FM) Hobbs, N.M.; & KKTX-AM-FM Kilgore, Tex. (All 100% owned.) Ownership: William C. Nolan Jr., 65%; Edwin B. Alderson Jr., 35%. Hqtrs: 202 W. 19th St., El Dorado, Ark. 71730. (501) 862-7777. FAX: (501) 862-0203.

Noble Broadcast Group Stns: 7 AM, 8 FM. KBCO-AM-FM Boulder & KHOW-AM-FM Denver, both Colo.; KATZ-FM Alton, Ill.; WSSH(AM) Boston; KBEQ(AM) Blue Springs, KBEQ-FM Kansas City & KATZ(AM)-KMJM(FM) St. Louis, all Mo.; WVKS(FM) Toledo, Ohio; KYOK(AM) & KMJQ(FM) Houston; & XETRA-AM-FM Tijuana, Mexico. Executives: John Lynch, chmn/CEO; Frank DeFrancesco, exec VP/CFO; Dennis Ciapura, exec VP opns. Hqtrs: 4891 Pacific Hwy, San Diego 92110. (619) 291-8510. FAX: (619) 298-5949.

Nolan Broadcast Group. Stns: 1 AM, 2 FM. KAUS-AM-FM Austin & KEEZ-FM Mankato, both Minn. (All 100% owned.) Ownership: Phil Nolan, Kathleen Nolan (wife) & Mike Nolan (son). Hqtrs: Box 159, Austin, Minn. 55912. (507) 437-1480. FAX: (507) 437-7669.

Nor-Net Communications Ltd. Stns: 10 AM. CKBA(AM) Athabasca, CJCM(AM) Grand Centre, CKVH(AM) High Prairie, CHLW(AM) St. Paul, CKWA(AM) Slave Lake, CKKY(AM) Wainwright, CFOK(AM) Westlock & CJOI(AM) Wetaskiwin, all Alta.; CFNL(AM) Fort Nelson & CKNL(AM) Fort St. John, both B.C. (All stns are located in Canada.) Ownership: Marco Holdings Ltd., Len Novak. Hqtrs: Box 1800, Westlock, Alta., Canada T0G 2L0. (403) 349-4421. FAX: (403) 349-6259.

Northeast Broadcasting Company Inc. Stns: 1 AM, 2 FM. WHAV(AM) & WLYT(FM) Haverhill, Mass.; & WNCS(FM) Montpelier, Vt. (All 100% owned.) Ownership: Steven A. Silberberg, Jane N. Cole. Hqtrs: 288 S. River Rd., Bedford, N.H. 03110. (603) 668-9999. FAX: (603) 668-6470.

Northeast Communications Corp. Stns: 2 AM, 4 FM. WABK-AM-FM Gardiner, Me.; WMLY(FM) Conway, WFTN-AM-FM Franklin & WSCY(FM) Moultonborough, all N.H. (All 100% owned.) Ownership: Jeff Fisher, 44.5%; Chris Fisher, 17.5%; & Phil Fisher, 16.5%. Hqtrs: Radio Park, Babbit Rd., Franklin, N.H. 03235. (603) 934-2500.

Northern TV Inc. Stns: 2 AM, 2 FM, 2 TV. KBYR(AM), KNIK-FM, KTVA(TV) Anchorage & KCBF(AM), KXLR(FM), KTVF(TV) Fairbanks, both Alaska. Stockholders: A. G. Hiebert, 41.325%; & others. Hqtrs: 1007 W. 32nd Ave., Anchorage 99503. (907) 562-3456. FAX: (907) 562-0953.

Northstar Television Group Inc. Stns: 4 TV. WZZM-TV Grand Rapids, Mich.; WAPT(TV) Jackson, Miss.; WSEE-TV Erie, Pa.; & WNAC-TV Providence, R.I. Executives: Richard F. Appleton, pres; Frank D. Osborn, chmn; Barry M. Wolper, treas. Ownership: Osborn Communications Corp. (see listing), Desai Capital Management, Price Communications Corp. (see listing) & Bankers Trust Co. Hqtrs: 405 Lexington Ave., 54th Fl., New York 10174. (212) 697-2502. FAX: (212) 697-2249.

Northwest Television Inc. Stns: 4 TV. KBCI-TV Boise, Idaho; KCBY-TV Coos Bay, KVAL-TV Eugene & KPIC(TV) Roseburg (50%), all Ore. Executive: James W. Putney, VP. Ownership: Donald E. Tykeson Trust, 50.02%; Robert P. Booth, 19.52%; & 8 other stockholders. Hqtrs: Box 1313, Eugene, Ore. 97440. (503) 342-4961. FAX: (503) 342-7252.

Northwestern College Radio Network. Stns: 4 AM, 7 FM. KNWS-AM-FM Waterloo, Iowa; KDNI(FM) Duluth, KDNW(FM) Duluth & KTIS-AM-FM Minneapolis, all Minnesota; KFNW-FM Fargo & KFNW(AM) West Fargo, both N.D.; KNWC-AM-FM Sioux Falls, S.D.; & WNWC(FM) Madison, Wis. (All 100% owned.) Executives: Paul Ramseyer, VP radio; Harv Hendrickson, exec dir. Ownership: nonprofit organization. Northwestern College, St. Paul, is the owner & operator of the 11 radio licenses. Hqtrs: 3003 N. Snelling Ave., St. Paul, Minn. 55113-1599. (612) 631-5000. FAX: (612) 631-5010.

O

Omni Broadcasting Co. Stns: 1 AM, 2 FM. KIKV-FM Alexandria & KBUN(AM)-KBHP(FM) Bemidji, both Minnesota. (All 100% owned.) Ownership: Louis H. Buron Jr. & Mary Campbell. Hqtrs: Box 1656, Bemidji, Minn. 56601. (218) 751-4120. FAX: (218) 751-8091.

OmniAmerica Communications Inc. Stns: 2 AM, 7 FM. WFYV-FM Atlantic Beach & WAPE-FM Jacksonville, both Fla.; WHK(AM)-WMMS(FM) Cleveland, WMJI(FM) Cleveland, WLOH(AM)-WHOK(FM) Lancaster & WRVF(FM) Upper Arlington, all Ohio; & WYHY(FM) Lebanon, Tenn. (All 100% owned.) Ownership: Carl E. Hirsch, Dean Thacker, Anthony Ocepek. Hqtrs: 11111 Santa Monica Blvd., Suite 220, Los Angeles 90025. (310) 478-1111. FAX: (310) 445-4606.

Opus Media Group Inc. Stns: 2 AM, 4 FM. WSOK(AM) & WAEV(FM) Savannah, Ga.; KMYY(FM) Monroe, La.; WKXI(AM) & WTYX(FM) Jackson, Miss.; & WLVH(FM) Hardeeville, S.C. Executive: Raymond M. Quinn, pres. Hqtrs: 723 Lari Dawn, San Antonio, Tex. 78258. (210) 490-8360. FAX: (210) 490-5228.

Orr & Earls Broadcasting Inc. Stns: 2 AM, 2 FM. KOMC(AM) & KRZK(FM) Branson, Mo. (60%); WDLY(FM) Gatlinburg (50%) & WSEV(AM) Sevierville (50%), both Tenn. Executives: Charles C. Earls, chmn; Roderick W. Orr, pres. Ownership: Roderick W. Orr & Carol A. Orr, 40%; Charles C. Earls & Scottie S. Earls, 40%. Note: Orr & Earls Broadcasting Inc. also owns The Vacation Channel, a tourist info svc delivered on cable. Markets include Eureka Springs, Ark.; Breckenridge-Summit County, Colo.; & Branson, Mo. Also owns Branson RadioTours, a tour operation that markets trips through radio & TV stns. Based in Branson, Mo. Hqtrs: 202 Courtney St., Branson, Mo. 65616. (417) 334-6012. FAX: (417) 334-7141.

Osborn Communications Corp. Stns: 3 AM, 6 FM, 1 TV. WJSU-TV Anniston, Ala.; WBYB(FM) Brunswick, Ga. (Jacksonville, Fla.); WNDR(AM) & WNTQ(FM) Syracuse, N.Y.; WFXK(FM) Tarboro, N.C.; WAZU(FM) Springfield (Dayton), Ohio; WTJS(AM) & WTNV(FM) Jackson, Tenn.; WWVA(AM) & WOVK(FM) Wheeling, W.Va. Executives: Frank D. Osborn, pres; Barry M. Wolper, sr VP/treas; Ellen Strahs Fader, sr VP admin & corporate affrs; Matthew M. O'Connell, sr VP/gen counsel; Heather L. Short, sec. Ownership: Frank D. Osborn; Brentwood Associates; Spears, Benzak, Salomon & Farrell. Publicly held. Note: Osborn Communications Corp. also owns 70% of Osborn Healthcare Communications, 32% of Northstar Television Group Inc. (see listing) & 25% of Fairmont Communications Corp. (see listing). Hqtrs: 405 Lexington Ave., 54th Fl., New York 10174. (212) 697-2280. FAX: (212) 697-2249.

Osburn/Reynolds Group. Stns: 3 FM. KYKS(FM) Lufkin, KAGG(FM) Madisonville & KIXS(FM) Victoria, all Tex. (All 100% owned.) Ownership: Dick Osburn, 50%; Rusty Reynolds, 50%. Hqtrs: Box 2209, Lufkin, Tex. 75901. (409) 639-4455. FAX: (409) 632-5957.

Outlet Communications Inc. Stns: 2 TV. WCMH(TV) Columbus, Ohio; & WJAR(TV) Providence, R.I. (All 100% owned.) Executives: James G. Babb, chmn/pres/CEO. Ownership: management stockholders & ptnrs in Wesray Capital Corp. (all parties to Stockholders Agreement), 38.1%; Mutual Benefit Life Insurance Co., 32.6%; Gabelli Group Inc., 11.9%. Hqtrs:

23 Kennedy Dr., Cranston, R.I. 02920-4489. (401) 455-9200. FAX: (401) 455-9216.

Buck Owens Productions Inc. Stns: 2 AM, 2 FM, 1 TV. KCWW(AM) Tempe (Phoenix) & KNIX-FM Phoenix, both Ariz.; KCWR(AM) & KUZZ-FM-TV Bakersfield, Calif. Note: Group has purchased KTIE(FM) Bakersfield, Calif., subject to FCC approval. Executives: Alvis E. Owens Jr., pres; Michael L. Owens, VP; Mel Owens, sec. Hqtrs: 3223 Sillect, Bakersfield, Calif. 93308. (805) 326-1011. FAX: (805) 328-7503.

Owensboro on the Air Inc. Stns: 1 AM, 2 FM. WVJS(AM)-WSTO(FM) Owensboro & WEHR(FM) Shepherdsville, both Ky. Hqtrs: Box 1828, Owensboro, Ky. 42302. (502) 685-2991. FAX: (502) 685-7098.

P

PBMI Holdings Co. Stns: 2 AM, 2 FM. KGHL(AM)-KIDX(FM) Billings & KCAP(AM)-KZMT(FM) Helena, both Mont. (All 100% owned.) Ownership: Chris Brennan, CEO, major stockholder. Hqtrs: 144 Green Bay Rd., Winnetka, Ill. 60093. (708) 446-0580. FAX: (708) 446-0155.

Pacer Radio Packerland Inc. Stns: 3 FM. WHET(FM) Birnamwood, WEZR(FM) Brillion & KFKQ(FM) New Holstein, all Wis. Hqtrs: Box 1075, 1750 Freedom Rd., Green Bay, Wis. 54305-1075. (414) 687-1075. FAX: (414) 687-0710.

Pacific Northwest Broadcasting Corp. Stns: 2 AM, 3 FM. KBOI(AM)-KQFC(FM) Boise, KLCI(FM) Nampa & KSEI(AM)-KMGI(FM) Pocatello, all Idaho. Executive: Charles H. Wilson, pres. Cable TV. Hqtrs: Box 1280, Boise, Idaho 83701. (208) 336-3670. FAX: (208) 336-3734.

Pacifica Foundation Inc. dba Pacifica Radio. Stns: 6 FM. KPFA(FM) Berkeley, KPFB(FM) Berkeley & KPFK(FM) Los Angeles, all Calif.; WPFW(FM) Washington; WBAI(FM) New York; & KPFT(FM) Houston. (All noncommercial licenses.) Executives: Jack O'Dell, chmn; David Salniker, CEO; Bill Thomas, dir Pacifica Program Service-Radio Archives; Sandra Rosas, controller. Station gen mgrs: Marci Lockwood, actg gen mgr, KPFA-KPFB; Alan Fong, KPFK; Leon Collins, WPFW; Valerie Van Isler, WBAI; Barry Forbes, KPFT. Ownership: Public community radio. Hqtrs: 1929 Martin Luther King Jr. Way, Berkeley, Calif. 94704. (510) 843-0130. FAX: (510) 845-0289.

Palmer Communications Inc. Stns: 2 AM, 3 FM, 2 TV. WCVU(FM) & WNOG-AM-FM Naples, Fla.; WHO-AM-TV & KLYF(FM) Des Moines, Iowa; & KFOR-TV Oklahoma City. (All 100% owned.) Executives: William J. Ryan, pres/CEO; Robert G. Engelhardt, exec VP; M. Wayne Wisehart, VP/treas. Ownership: A trust created under the will of David D. Palmer. Hqtrs: 12800 University Dr., Suite 500, Fort Myers, Fla. 33907-5333. (813) 433-4350. FAX: (813) 433-8213.

Panache Broadcasting L.P. Stns: 1 AM, 2 FM. WTLC-AM-FM Indianapolis; & WWDB(FM) Philadelphia. Ownership: Charles D. Schwartz. Hqtrs: 166 E. Levering Mill Rd., Bala Cynwyd, Pa. 19004. (215) 668-4400.

Pappas Telecasting Companies. Stns: 2 TV. KMPH(TV) Visalia (Fresno), Calif.; & KPTM(TV) Omaha. (Both 100% owned.) Note: Group has purchased KRBK-TV Sacramento, Calif., pending FCC approval. Ownership: Harry J. Pappas. Hqtrs: 500 S. Chinowth Rd., Visalia, Calif. 93277. (209) 733-7800. FAX: (209) 627-5363.

Par Broadcasting. Stns: 2 AM, 2 FM. KGMG(AM)-KIOZ(FM) Oceanside & KOGO(AM)-KKLQ-FM, San Diego, both Calif. (All 100% owned.) Ownership: Leon Parma, Ernest Rady. Hqtrs: 5735 Kearney Villa Rd., San Diego 92123. (619) 560-5464. FAX: (619) 279-9553.

Paramount Stations Group. Stns: 7 TV. WDCA(TV) Washington; WKBD(TV) Detroit; WLFL(TV) Raleigh, N.C.; WTXF(TV) Philadelphia; KTXA(TV) Fort Worth, KTXH(TV) Houston & KRRT(TV) Kerrville, all Texas. (All 100% owned.) Executives: Anthony Cassara, pres; Ray Rajewski, VP/CFO; William Ferrari, controller. Ownership: Paramount Communications Inc., 100%. Hqtrs: c/o Paramount Pictures, 5555 Melrose Ave., Los Angeles 90038. (213) 956-8100.

Park Communications Inc. Stns: 11 AM, 11 FM, 9 TV. WBMG(TV) Birmingham, Ala.; WNLS(AM) & WTNT(FM) Tallahassee, Fla.; KWLO(AM) & KFMW(FM) Waterloo, Iowa; WTVQ-TV Lexington, Ky.; KALB-TV Alexandria, La.; KJJO-AM-FM St. Louis Park, Minn.; WPAT-AM-FM Paterson, N.J.; WHEN-AM-FM Syracuse & WUTR(TV) Utica, both N.Y.; WNCT-AM-FM-TV Greenville, N.C.; KWJJ-AM-FM Portland, Ore.; WNAX-AM-FM Yankton, S.D.; WDEF-AM-FM-TV Chattanooga & WJHL-TV Johnson City, both Tenn.; WTVR-AM-FM-TV Richmond & WSLS-TV Roanoke, both Va.; & KEZX-AM-FM Seattle. Executives: Dorothy D. Park, sec; Wright M. Thomas, pres/COO; W. Randall Odil, VP television; Rick A. Prusator, VP radio; Randel Stair, VP/controller. Ownership: (See also Cross-Ownership, Sect. A.) Hqtrs: Box 550, Ithaca, N.Y. 14851. (607) 272-9020.

The Park Lane Group. Stns: 4 AM, 6 FM. KZGL(FM) Cottonwood & KAAA(AM)-KZZZ(FM) Kingman, both Ariz.; KPPL(FM) Colusa, KVOY(AM) Mojave, KQMS(AM)-KSHA(FM) Redding, KOWL(AM)-KRLT(FM) South Lake Tahoe & KTPI(FM) Tehachapi, all Calif. Hqtrs: 750 Menlo Ave., Suite 340, Menlo Park, Calif. 94025. (415) 324-8464. FAX: (415) 324-3817.

The Jim Pattison Broadcast Group. Stns: 2 AM, 2 FM, 1 TV. CFJC-AM-TV & CIFM-FM Kamloops, CKBD(AM) & CJJR-FM Vancouver, both B.C. (All stns are located in Canada.) Ownership: The Jim Pattison Group. Hqtrs: CKBD(AM) & CJJR-FM, 1401 W. 8th Ave., Vancouver, B.C., Canada V6H IC9. (604) 731-6111 & (604) 731-7772.

Paxson Broadcasting. Stns: 6 AM, 7 FM. WAIA(FM) Callahan, WJRR(FM) Cocoa Beach, WNZS(AM) Jacksonville, WROO(FM) Jacksonville, WZNZ(AM) Jacksonville, WINZ(AM) Miami, WLVE(FM) Miami Beach, WZTA(FM) Miami Beach, WMGF(FM) Mount Dora, WWNZ(AM) Orlando, WHNZ(AM) Pinellas Park, WHPT(FM) Sarasota & WWZN(AM) Winter Park, all Fla. (All 100% owned.) Executives: Jim Bocock, pres. Ownership: Lowell W. Paxson, 100%. Note: Paxson Broadcasting also owns the Florida Radio Network. Hqtrs: 18401 N. U.S. 19, Clearwater, Fla. 34624. (813) 536-2211.

Pegasus Broadcast Television L.P. Stns: 5 TV. WDBD(TV) Jackson, Miss.; WWLF-TV Hazleton, WOLF-TV Scranton & WILF(TV) Williamsport, all Pa.; & WDSI-TV Chattanooga. (All 100% owned.) Ownership: Marshall W. Pagon, 100%. Hqtrs: 5 Radnor Corporate Ctr., Suite 454, Radnor, Pa. 19087. (215) 341-1809. FAX: (215) 341-1835.

Pegasus Broadcasting Inc. Stns: 2 TV. KSCH-TV Stockton, Calif.; & WAPA-TV San Juan, P.R. (Both 100% owned.) Executives: Michael L. Eskridge, pres Broadcast Management Services; Allan J. Gaherty, sr VP Broadcast Management Services. Ownership: General Electric Capital Corp., 100%. General Electric Capital Corp. is owned 100% by General Electric Financial Services Inc. Note: General Electric Financial Services Inc. is owned 100% by General Electric Co., Fairfield, Conn. General Electric Co. also owns NBC Holdings Inc., the parent corporation of National Broadcasting Co. Inc. (see listing for NBC TV Stations Division). Hqtrs: 2200 Fletcher Ave., Fort Lee, N.J. 07024. (201) 585-6453. FAX: (201) 585-6216.

Pelmorex Broadcasting Inc. Stns: 14 AM, 2 FM. CHVR-2(AM) Arnprior, CJNR(AM) Blind River, CKNR(AM) Elliot Lake, CKNS(AM) Espanola, CHOH(AM) Hearst, CHYK(AM) Kapuskasing, CKAP(AM) Kapuskasing, CHUR(AM) North Bay, CHVR(AM) Pembroke, CHVR-1(AM) Renfrew, CJQM-FM Sault Ste. Marie, CHYC(AM) Sudbury, CHNO(AM) & CJMX-FM Sudbury, CKOY(AM) Timmins & CJWA(AM) Wawa, all Ont. (All stns are located in Canada.) (All 100% owned.) Executive: Pierre L. Morrissette, pres & CEO. Ownership: Pelmorex Communications Inc. Note: Pelmorex also manages CHAS-FM Sault Ste. Marie, Ont. on behalf of Telemedia Communications Ontario Inc. Hqtrs: 186 Robert Speck Pkwy., Suite 200, Mississauga, Ont., Canada L4Z 3G1. (905) 566-9511. FAX: (905) 566-9696.

Pembrook Pines Inc. Stns: 4 AM, 2 FM. WABH(AM)-WVIN-FM Bath, WELM(AM)-WLVY(FM) Elmira, WACK(AM) Newark & WPIE(AM) Trumansburg, all N.Y. Executives: Robert J. Pfuntner, pres/CEO; Eugene A. Pfuntner, exec VP; Phebe Pfuntner, sec. Ownership: Robert J. Pfuntner, 100%. Company also owns Pembrook Pines Mass Media agency. Hqtrs: 1705 Lake St., Elmira, N.Y. 14901. (607) 733-5626. FAX: (607) 733-5627.

Peninsula Communications Inc. Stns: 1 AM, 2 FM. KGTL(AM)-KWVV-FM Homer & KPEN-FM Soldotna, both Alaska. (All 100% owned.) Ownership: David F. Becker, 50%; Eileen L. Becker, 50%. Hqtrs: Box 109, Homer, Alaska 99603. (907) 235-7551.

Pennsylvania Broadcasting Associates I, II, III. Stns: 4 AM, 4 FM. WHP(AM), WKBO(AM) & WRVV(FM) Harrisburg, WNTJ(AM)-WMTZ(FM) Johnstown & WRAK-AM-FM & WKSB(FM) Williamsport, all Pa. Note: FCC also approved group's purchase of WGY-AM-FM Schenectady, N.Y. on Oct. 28, 1993. Hqtrs: Box 6477, Harrisburg, Pa. 17112. (717) 540-9230. FAX: (717) 540-9326.

Perenchio Television Inc. Stns: 9 TV. KTVW-TV Phoenix; KFTV(TV) Hanford, KMEX-TV Los Angeles & KDTV(TV) San Francisco, all Calif.; WLTV(TV) Miami; WXTV(TV) Paterson, N.J.; KLUZ-TV Albuquerque, N.M.; KUVN(TV) Garland & KWEX-TV San Antonio, both Tex. Ownership: Perenchio Communications Inc., 80% voting stock; Univisa Inc., 10% voting stock; & Venevision International Ltd., 10% voting stock. Perenchio Communications Inc. is headed by A. Jerrold Perenchio. Hqtrs: 1901 Avenue of the Stars, Suite 680, Los Angeles 90067. (310) 556-7600. FAX: (310) 556-3568.

John H. Phipps Inc. Stns: 3 TV. WCTV(TV) Tallahassee (100%) & WPBF(TV) Tequesta (50%), both Fla.; & WKXT-TV Knoxville (70%), Tenn. Ownership: John H. Phipps is mgng ptnr of all the above stns. Hqtrs: Box 3048, Tallahassee, Fla. 32315. (904) 668-0842. FAX: (904) 668-0546.

Phoenix Holdings Inc. Stns: 2 AM, 2 FM. WELO(AM) & WZLQ(FM) Tupelo, Miss.; WVOL(AM) Berry Hill (Nashville) & WQQK(FM) Hendersonville (Nashville), both Tenn. Ownership: Samuel Howard. Hqtrs: Vanderbilt Plaza, 2100 W. End Ave., Suite 780, Nashville 37203. (615) 327-8755. FAX: (615) 327-8754.

Pikes Peak Broadcasting Co. Stns: 1 AM, 1 FM, 2 TV. KRDO-AM-FM-TV Colorado Springs & KJCT(TV) Grand Junction, both Colo. (All 100% owned.) Ownership: The Harry Hoth family. Hqtrs: Box 1457, Colorado Springs 80901. (719) 632-1515. FAX: (719) 475-0815.

Pillar of Fire Inc. Stns: 1 AM, 2 FM. KPOF(AM) Denver; WAWZ(FM) Zarephath, N.J.; & WAKW(FM) Cincinnati. (All 100% owned.) Ownership: No stockholders; non-profit corporation. (See also Cross-Ownership, Sect. A.) Hqtrs: Box 37, Weston Canal Rd., Zarephath, N.J. 08890. (908) 469-0991. FAX: (908) 271-1968.

Pilot Communications. Stns: 1 AM, 2 FM. WMME-AM-FM Augusta, Me.; & WAQX-FM Manlius, N.Y. (All 100% owned.) Ownership: James L. Leven, 100%. Hqtrs: 92 Whetton Rd., West Hartford, Conn. 06117. (203) 232-3004. FAX: (315) 472-1146; (203) 232-3004.

Pinnacle Broadcasting Co. Stns: 5 AM, 7 FM. WSOY-AM-FM Decatur, Ill.; WYNG-FM Evansville, Ind.; WDUR(AM)-WFXC(FM) Durham & WRNS-AM-FM Kinston, both N.C.; WYAV(FM) Conway, S.C.; KAMA(AM)-KAMZ(FM) El Paso & KLLL-AM-FM Lubbock, both Tex. (All 100% owned.) Ownership: Ballston Trust Services L.C. is trustee for the corporation. Hqtrs: 2505 N. Hwy 360, Suite 620, Grand Prairie, Tex. 75050-7801. (817) 649-0184, (817) 695-1739. FAX: (817) 649-1707.

Pioneer Communications. Stns: 2 AM, 1 FM. WKXO-AM-FN Berea & WEKY(AM) Richmond, both Ky. (All 100% owned.) Hqtrs: 128 Big Hill Ave., Richmond, Ky. 40475. (606) 623-1340. FAX: (606) 623-1439.

Plessinger Radio Group (R.L. Plessinger Holding Co.). Stns: 1 AM, 3 FM. WOYS(FM) Apalachicola, Fla.; WCVG(AM) Covington, Ky.; WAXZ(FM) Georgetown & WAQZ(FM) Milford, both Ohio. (All 100% owned.) Note: WAQZ(FM) Milford, Ohio has been sold, subject to FCC approval. Ownership: Richard L. Plessinger Sr., own. Hqtrs: 1591 Boyle Rd., Hamilton, Ohio 45013. (513) 863-0774. FAX: (513) 868-1779.

Pompadur-Becker Group. Stns: 6 TV. I. Martin Pompadur & Ralph E. Becker have interests in & are mgng gen ptnrs of Northeastern Television Investors, a Connecticut limited partnership, which owns WBRE-TV Wilkes-Barre, Pa. Principals have interests in Toledo Television Investors, a Connecticut limited partnership which owns WNWO-TV Toledo, Ohio. See also Television Station Partners, which owns WRDW-TV Augusta, Ga.; WEYI-TV Saginaw, Mich.; WROC-TV Rochester, N.Y.; & WTOV-TV Steubenville, Ohio. Note: I. Martin Pompadur has interests in ML Media Partners, which owns WREX-TV Rockford, Ill. & KATC(TV) Lafayette, La. Hqtrs: 321 Railroad Ave., Greenwich, Conn. 06830. (203) 622-7534. FAX: (203) 622-4876.

Ponce Broadcasting Corp. Stns: 3 AM, 1 FM. WLEY(AM) Cayey, WLEO(AM) & WZAR(FM) Ponce, & WKFE(AM) Yauco, all P.R. (All 100% owned.) Ownership: J.H. Conesa, pres, 22%; L.F. Sala, 26%; Catalina Scarano, 26%; J.G. Scarano, 26%. Other interests: a 26% interest in a 16 ch multiple multipoint distribution svc (MMDS) system. Hqtrs: GPO Box 7213, Ponce, P.R. 00732. (809) 840-3160. FAX: (809) 840-0049.

Post-Newsweek Stations Inc. Stns: 4 TV. WFSB(TV) Hartford, Conn.; WJXT(TV) Jacksonville & WPLG(TV) Miami, both Fla.; & WDIV(TV) Detroit. Note: Group has purchased KPRC-TV Houston & KSAT-TV San Antonio, both Tex., pending FCC approval. Executives: G. William Ryan, pres. Ownership: Post-Newsweek Stations is a subsidiary of the publicly traded Washington Post Co. (See also Cross-Ownership, Sect. A.) Cable TV: Post-Newsweek Cable. Hqtrs: 1150 15th St. N.W., Washington 20071. (202) 334-4600. FAX: (202) 334-4536.

Power Broadcasting Inc. Stns: 9 AM, 8 FM, 3 TV. CKBB(AM) Barrie, CIAM(AM) Cambridge, CKCB(AM) Collingwood, CJOY(AM)-CIMJ-FM Guelph, CFFX(AM)-CFMK-FM & CKWS-TV Kingston, CKDO(AM)-CKGE-FM Oshawa, CKRU(AM)-CKWF-FM & CHEX-TV Peterborough, all Ont.; CFVM(AM) Amqui, CHAU-TV Carleton, CJDM-FM Drummondville, CFEL-FM Montmagny, CFLP(AM)-CIKI-FM Rimouski & CFZZ-FM St. Jean-sur-Richelieu, all Que. (All stns are located in Canada.) (All 100% owned.) Ownership: Power Corporation of Canada, 100%. Hqtrs: 751, Square Victoria, Montreal, Que., Canada H2Y 2J3. (514) 286-7444. FAX: (514) 286-7464.

Prairieland Stations. Stns: 2 AM, 2 FM. WDZ(AM)-WDZQ(FM) Decatur & WIZZ(AM)-WSTQ(FM) Streator, both Ill. Ownership: Steve Bellinger. Hqtrs: 337 N. Water St., Decatur, Ill. 62523. (217) 423-9744. FAX: (217) 423-9764.

Precision Media Limited Partnership. Stns: 1 AM, 2 FM. WKSS(FM) Hartford-Meriden, Conn.; WMYF(AM) & WERZ(FM) Exeter (Portsmouth), N.H. Ownership: Frank Barsalona, Don Law, Timothy J.A. Montgomery. Hqtrs: 10 Columbus Blvd., Hartford, Conn. 06106. (203) 249-9577.

Premier Group. Stns: 2 AM, 1 FM. KITI(AM) Chehalis-Centralia & KEDO(AM)-KLYK(FM) Longview, both Wash. (All 100% owned.) Note: Group anticipates receiving a CP for a New FM at Winlock, Wash. & plans to use the call letters KITI-FM for the New FM. Ownership: Garry White, Rod Etherton. Hqtrs: 1133 Kresky, Centralia, Wash. 98531. (206) 736-1355. FAX: (206) 736-4761.

Press Broadcasting Inc. Stns: 1 AM, 2 FM, 1 TV. WKCF(TV) Clermont & WTKS(FM) Cocoa Beach, both Fla.; WBUD(AM) & WKXW(FM) Trenton, N.J. (All 100% owned.) Ownership: New Jersey Press Inc., 100%. New Jersey Press Inc. is owned by Jules Plangere Jr., 50%; Lass Family Trust, 50%. (See also Cross-Ownership, Sect. A.) Hqtrs: 3601 N.J. Hwy. 66, Neptune, N.J. 07753. (908) 922-2800. FAX: (908) 922-6326.

Prettyman Broadcasting. Stns: 3 AM, 6 FM. WXJN(FM) Lewes & WYUS(AM)-WAFL(FM) Milford, both Del.; WXCY(FM) Havre de Grace, WZJO(FM) Ocean Pines & WICO-AM-FM Salisbury, all Md.; WEPM(AM) & WKMZ(FM) Martinsburg, W.Va. Executives: William E. Prettyman Jr., pres; Alex Kolobielski, VP. Hqtrs: Box 909, Salisbury, Md. 21803. (410) 742-3212. FAX: (410) 548-1543.

Price Broadcasting Co. Stns: 2 AM, 2 FM. WOMG-AM-FM Columbia, S.C.; KCNR(AM) & KVRI(FM) Salt Lake City. Executives: John Price, pres; Martin G. Peterson, VP. Hqtrs: 35 Century Pkwy., Salt Lake City 84115. (801) 486-3911. FAX: (801) 485-0751.

Price Communications Corporation Stations. Stns: 3 AM, 3 FM, 3 TV. WBZT(AM) & WIRK-FM West Palm Beach, Fla.; WOWO(AM) Fort Wayne & WOWO-FM Huntington, both Ind.; KSNF(TV) Joplin, Mo.; WWKB(AM) Buffalo & WKSE(FM) Niagara Falls, both N.Y.; KJAC-TV Port Arthur & KFDX-TV Wichita Falls, both Tex. (All 100% owned.) Officers: Robert Price, pres; Kim I. Pressman, sr VP/treas; Alisa Diamond, VP/sec. Ownership: Robert Price, 2%. Publicly owned. (See also Cross-Ownership, Sect. A.) Hqtrs: 45 Rockefeller Plaza, New York 10020. (212) 757-5600. FAX: (212) 397-3755.

Providence Journal Broadcasting Corp. Stns: 4 TV. KMSB-TV Tucson, Ariz.; WHAS-TV Louisville, Ky.; KASA-TV Santa Fe, N.M.; & WCNC-TV Charlotte, N.C. (All 100% owned.) Executives: Jack C. Clifford, pres; John Hayes, VP TV. Ownership: Providence Journal Company. Firm is also engaged in cable TV (Colony Communications Inc.) & radio paging. Note: Providence Journal Co. and Kelso & Co., New York, own KHBC-TV Hilo, KHNL(TV) Honolulu & KOGG(TV) Wailuku, all Hawaii; KTVB(TV) Boise, Idaho; KGW-TV Portland, Ore.; KING-TV Seattle & KREM-TV Spokane, both Wa. Providence Journal Co. and Kelso & Co. also own a cable division (King Videocable Co.) consisting of 13 systems (222,000 subs) in four states. (See also Providence Journal Co. under Cross-Ownership, Sect. A.) Hqtrs: 75 Fountain St., Providence, R.I. 02902. (401) 277-7745. FAX: (401) 274-2076.

Pueblo Broadcasters Inc. Stns: 1 AM, 2 FM. KCSJ(AM), KNKN(FM) & KYZX(FM) Pueblo, Colo. Ownership: Marc Hand, Max Hand, Martin Hart. Hqtrs: 101 W. Main St., Pueblo, Colo. 81003. (719) 543-5900. FAX: (719) 543-7609.

Pulitzer Broadcasting Co. Stns: 1 AM, 1 FM, 10 TV. KTAR(AM) & KKLT(FM) Phoenix; WESH(TV) Daytona Beach, Fla.; KCCI-TV Des Moines, Iowa; WLKY-TV Louisville, Ky.; WDSU(TV) New Orleans; KETV(TV) Omaha; KOAT-TV Albuquerque & KOCT(TV) Carlsbad, both N.M.; WXII(TV) Winston-Salem, N.C.; WGAL(TV) Lancaster, Pa.; & WYFF(TV) Greenville, S.C. Executives: Michael Pulitzer, vice-chmn; Ken J. Elkins, pres/CEO. Ownership: Pulitzer Publishing Co., 100% (see also Cross-Ownership, Sect. A). Hqtrs: 101 S. Hanley Rd., Suite 1250, St. Louis 63105-3428. (314) 721-7335. FAX: (314) 721-5363.

Pyramid Broadcasting. Stns: 3 AM, 6 FM. WNUA(FM) Chicago; WXKS-AM-FM Medford, Mass.; WHTT-AM-FM Buffalo & WHTK(AM)-WPXY-FM Rochester, both N.Y.; WRFX(FM) Kannapolis, N.C.; & WYXR(FM) Philadelphia. Note: Group has purchased WJMN(FM) Boston, WBUF(FM) Buffalo, N.Y., & WAQS(AM)-WAQQ(FM) Charlotte, N.C., pending FCC approval. Executive: Richard M. Balsbaugh, CEO. Hqtrs: 99 Revere Beach Pkwy., Medford, Mass. 02155. (617) 396-1430. FAX: (617) 391-8367.

Q

Quality Broadcasting Inc. Stns: 2 AM, 1 FM. WBNM(AM)-WNEX-FM Gordon & WNEX(AM) Macon, both Ga. Ownership: Jim McAfee. Note: Quality Broadcasting of Tennessee owns WZDQ(FM) Humboldt & WQCR(AM) Jackson, both Tenn. Hqtrs: Box 7948, Macon, Ga. 31209. (912) 745-3301. FAX: (912) 742-2293.

Quincy Newspapers Inc. Stns: 1 AM, 1 FM, 5 TV. WGEM-AM-FM-TV Quincy, Ill.; WSJV(TV) Elkhart, Ind.; KTIV(TV) Sioux City, Iowa; KTTC(TV) Rochester, Minn.; & WVVA(TV) Bluefield, W.Va. Executives: F.M. Lindsay Jr., chmn; Thomas A. Oakley, pres. (See also Cross-Ownership, Sect. A.) Hqtrs: 130-138 S. 5th St., Quincy, Ill. 62301. (217) 223-5100.

R

R Group Communication. Stns: 3 TV. WYZZ-TV Bloomington, Ill.; WMCC(TV) Marion, Ind.; & WSMH(TV) Flint, Mich. (All 100% owned.) Executive: G.J. Robinson, pres. Hqtrs: 2250 Seymour Ave., Cincinnati 45212. (513) 351-9110. FAX: (513) 631-2666.

RP Companies Inc. Stns: 4 AM, 6 FM, 10 TV. KORG(AM) & KEZY(FM) Anaheim, Calif.; WICC(AM) Bridgeport & WEBE(FM) Westport, both Conn.; WRDW-TV Augusta & WRBL(TV) Columbus, both Ga.; WREX-TV Rockford, Ill.; WCKN(AM)-WRZX(FM) Indianapolis & WTWO(TV) Terre Haute, both Ind.; KATC(TV) Lafayette, La.; WEYI-TV Saginaw, Mich.; KQTV(TV) St. Joseph, Mo.; WROC-TV Rochester, N.Y.; WQAL(FM) Cleveland & WTOV-TV Steubenville, all Ohio; WBRE-TV Wilkes-Barre, Pa.; WMXN(FM) Norfolk, Va.; WFID(FM) Rio Piedras & WUNO(AM) San Juan, both P.R. [All 100% owned except for WRBL(TV) Columbus, Ga.; WTWO(TV) Terre Haute, Ind.; & KQTV(TV) St. Joseph, Mo. WFID(FM) & WUNO(AM) are 50% owned by RP entities, with the other 50% owned by Century Communications Corp.] Executives: I. Martin Pompadur, CEO. Note: Martin Pompadur supervises WRDW-TV, WEYI-TV, WROC-TV, WTOV-TV & WBRE-TV. Brian N. Byrnes supervises the management of the 5 TV stns owned by ML Media Opportunity Partners & ML Media Partners. George L. Sosson serves as pres of the radio division. Ownership: All of the radio stns except WMXN(FM) Norfolk, Va. are owned by ML Media Partners L.P. WMXN(FM) is owned by ML Media Opportunity Partners L.P. WRDW-TV, WEYI-TV, WROC-TV & WTOV-TV are owned by Television Station Partners L.P. (see listing). WRBL(TV), WTWO(TV) & KQTV(TV) are ownd by TCS Television Partners L.P., which is 51% owned by ML Media Opportunity Partners L.P. WREX-TV & KATC(TV) are owned by ML Media Partners L.P. WBRE-TV is owned by Northeastern Television Investors L.P. Cable TV: Owns majority of U.S. Cable Television Group L.P., operated by Cablevision Systems Corp. Operates systems in California, Maryland, North Carolina & Virginia under the name MultiVision Cable TV Corp. Owns 50% of a cable system in San Juan, P.R. operated by Century Communications Corp. Hqtrs: 321 Railroad Ave., Greenwich, Conn. 06830. (203) 622-4860. FAX: (203) 622-4873.

Radio Americas/Estereotempo Group. Stns: 3 FM. WIOB(FM) Mayaguez, WIOC(FM) Ponce & WIOA(FM) San Juan, all P.R. Ownership: Alfred R. de Arellano. Hqtrs: Box 13427, Santurce, P.R. 00908. (809) 721-4020. FAX: (809) 722-6740.

Radio Associates. Stns: 2 AM, 3 FM. KEWB(FM) Anderson (Redding) & KMIX-AM-FM Turlock (Modesto), both Calif.; WBCT(FM) Grand Rapids & WKZO(AM) Kalamazoo, both Mich. (All 100% owned.) Ownership: Jerry L. Miller, Kenneth V. Miller, Robert M. Salmon. Hqtrs: 3503 Greenleaf Blvd. #203, Kalamazoo, Mich. 49008. (616) 375-1800. FAX: (616) 375-1346.

Radio Cleveland Inc. Stns: 1 AM, 3 FM. WAID(FM)-WKDJ(FM) Clarksdale & WCLD-AM-FM Cleveland, both Miss. (All 100% owned.) Ownership: Homer Sledge Jr., pres, 11.11%; Kevin W. Cox, sec, 11.11%; Clint L. Webster, gen mgr, 11.11%. Hqtrs: Drawer 780, Cleveland, Miss. 38732. (601) 843-4091. FAX: (601) 843-9805.

Radio Equity Partners L.P. Stns: 1 AM, 2 FM. WHYN-AM-FM Springfield, Mass.; & WWBB(FM) Providence, R.I. Note: Group has purchased 10 radio stns from New-Market Media Corp. (see listing) & WCKT(FM) Lehigh Acres, Fla., pending FCC approval. Ownership: Limited partnership. Hqtrs: 40 Richards Ave., Norwalk, Conn. 06854. (203) 857-5602. FAX: (203) 857-5609.

The Radio Group. Stns: 4 AM, 4 FM. KCTO-AM-FM Columbia, KFNV-AM-FM Ferriday, KAPB-AM-FM Marksville & KMAR-AM-FM Winnsboro, all La. (All 100% owned.) Ownership: Tom D. Gay, 100%. Hqtrs: Box 1319, Columbia, La. 71418. (318) 649-7959.

Radio Management Associates Inc. Stns: 3 AM, 2 FM. WIKE(AM) Newport & WSTJ(AM)-WNKV(FM) St. Johnsbury, both Vt.; KEVA(AM) & KOTB(FM) Evanston, Wyo. (All 100% owned.) Note: Group also has time brokerage agreement for WMTK(FM) Littleton, N.H. Executive: Jim Epstein, pres/CEO. Ownership: Eric H. Johnson & Brent W. Lambert. Hqtrs: 175 Derby St., Suite 33, Hingham, Mass. 02043. (617) 749-0858.

Radio Music Box Co., L.C. Stns: 2 AM, 2 FM. KKYN-AM-FM & KVOP(AM)-KATX(FM) Plainview, Tex. (All 100% owned.) Ownership: Michael Fox, 50%; Donald A. Williams, 50%. Hqtrs: Box 147, 3218 Quincy, Plainview, Tex. 79072. (806) 293-2661. FAX: (806) 293-5732.

Radiomutuel Inc. Stns: 6 AM, 8 FM. CJAB-FM Chicoutimi, CJRC(AM) & CKTF-FM Gatineau, CKRS(AM) Jonquiere, CIMO-FM Magog, CJMS(AM) & CKMF-FM Montreal, CJRP(AM) & CHIK-FM Quebec City, CJMM-FM Rouyn, CKSM(AM) Shawinigan, CJTR(AM) & CIGB-FM Trois Rivieres, & CJMV-FM Val d'Or, all Que. (All 100% owned except for 50% owned CJMM-FM Rouyn & CJMV-FM Val d'Or, both Que.) (All stns are located in Canada.) Executive: Normand Beauchamp, pres. Hqtrs: 1717 Rene Levesque Blvd. E., Montreal, Que., Canada H2L 4E8. (514) 529-3210.

Radio-Nord Inc. Stns: 4 AM, 4 FM, 5 TV. CHPR-FM Hawkesbury, Ont.; CFGS-TV Ottawa/Hull, Que.; CHAD(AM) Amos, CHOT-TV Hull, CKLS(AM) La Sarre, CJLA-FM Lachute, CFEM-TV Rouyn, CKRN-AM-TV & CHLM-FM Rouyn, CHOA-FM Rouyn-Noranda & CKVD(AM) & CFVS-TV Val d'Or, all Que. (All stns are located in Canada.) Executive: Jean-Joffre Gourd, chmn. Hqtrs: 380 Murdoch, Noranda, Que., Canada J9X 1G5. (819) 762-0741. FAX: (819) 762-2280.

Radio One Broadcasting Inc. Stns: 5 AM, 5 FM. KQAD(AM) & KLQL(FM) Luverne, Minn.; KTTT(AM)-KKOT(FM) Columbus & KMEM(AM)-KLDZ(FM) Lincoln, both Neb.; KBRK-AM-FM Brookings & KIJV(AM)-KZNC(FM) Huron, both S.D. (All 100% owned.) Executives: Raymond A. Lamb, chmn; H. Roger Dodson, pres. Ownership: Raymond A. Lamb. Hqtrs: 1230 O St., Suite 311, Lincoln, Neb. 68508. (402) 476-3222. FAX: (402) 476-1300.

Radio-Quebec. Stns: 17 TV. CIVK-TV-1 Anse-aux-Gascons, CIVF-TV Baie Trinite, CIVK-TV Carleton, CIVP-TV Chapeau, CIVV-TV Chicoutimi, CIVK-TV-3 Gaspe, CIVB-TV-1 Grand Portage, CIVO-TV Hull, CIVM-TV Montreal, CIVK-TV-2 Perce, CIVQ-TV Quebec City, CIVB-TV Rimouski, CIVA-TV-1 Rouyn, CIVG-TV Sept-Iles, CIVS-TV Sherbrooke, CIVC-TV Trois-Rivieres & CIVA-TV Val d'Or, all Que. (All stns are located in Canada.) Executives: Francoise Bertrand, pres/CEO; Daniel Beauchesne, VP programs; Alain Dufour, VP admin & fin; Andre Beaudet, dir comm. Ownership: La Societe de radio-television du Quebec is a para-governmental organization. Its mandate is to manage an educ television net throughout the province of Quebec. Hqtrs: 1000, rue Fullum, Montreal, Que., Canada H2K 3L7. (514) 521-2424. TELEX 05-25808. FAX: (514) 873-7464.

Radio South Inc. Stns: 2 AM, 2 FM. WFFN(FM) Cordova, WARF(AM) Jasper & WTSK(AM)- WTUG(FM) Tuscaloosa, all Ala. Ownership: Houston L. Pearce, 50%; John T. Davis, 25%; Charles R. Wiggins, 25%. Hqtrs: 142 Skyland Blvd., Tuscaloosa, Ala. 35405. (205) 345-7200. FAX: (205) 349-1715.

Raven Broadcasting Corp. Stns: 1 AM, 2 FM. WMQA-AM-FM Minocqua & WZTT(FM) Rhinelander, both Wis. Ownership: Dave Raven, Gene Anderson, Bart Kellnhauser, Lane Ware, David Scholfield, John Kraft. Hqtrs: Box 96, 7380 Hwy. 51 S., Minocqua, Wis. 54548. (715) 356-9696. FAX: (715) 356-1977.

Rawlco Communications Ltd. Stns: 6 AM, 4 FM. CFFR(AM) Calgary, Alta.; CFGO(AM)-CJMJ-FM Ottawa & CISS-FM Toronto; CJNB(AM) North Battleford, CKBI(AM) Prince Albert, CJME(AM)-CIZL-FM Regina & CKOM(AM)-CFMC-FM Saskatoon, all Sask. (All stns are located in Canada.) Executives: Gordon Rawlinson, pres; Douglas E. Rawlinson, exec VP. Hqtrs: 2723 37th Ave. N.E., Calgary, Alta., Canada T1Y 5R8. (403) 291-0000. FAX: (403) 291-0037.

Ray-D-O Biz Inc. Stns: 1 AM, 2 FM. WQDK(FM) Ahoskie, WGAI(AM) Elizabeth City & WCXL(FM) Kill Devil Hills, all N.C. (All 100% owned.) Hqtrs: Box 1408, Elizabeth City, N.C. 27909. (919) 335-0856. FAX: (919) 335-2496.

Red River Broadcast Corp. Stns: 4 TV. KBRR(TV) Thief River Falls, Minn.; KVRR(TV) Fargo, KJRR(TV) Jamestown & KNRR(TV) Pembina, all N.D. (All 100% owned.) Note: Group also owns five low power TV stns: K26AC Bemidji, K54AT Brainerd, K18AI Grand Rapids & K05VI Park Rapids, all Minnesota; & K23AJ Devils Lake, N.D. (All 100% owned.) Ownership: Curtis Squire Inc., 100%. Myron Kunin owns 100% of Curtis Squire Inc. Hqtrs: Box 9115, 4015 9th Ave. S.W., Fargo, N.D. 58106. (701) 277-1515. FAX: (701) 277-1830.

Regional Group Inc. Stns: 2 AM, 2 FM. WKOP(AM) & WAAL(FM) Binghamton, N.Y.; WPIC(AM) & WYFM(FM) Sharon, Pa. (All 100% owned) Executives: Norman Volk, pres; Thomas Klein, VP/COO; Judith Lewis, VP admin. Hqtrs: 1965 Shenango Valley Fwy., Suite 3, Hermitage, Pa. 16148. (412) 983-1622. FAX: (412) 983-1669.

Regional Radio. Stns: 2 AM, 2 FM. KDGO(AM) Durango & KTRN(FM) Silverton, both Colo.; KENN(AM) & KRWN(FM) Farmington, N.M. Ownership: Kenny Kendrick, Bob Williams. Hqtrs: Box 1558, Farmington, N.M. 87499-1558. (505) 325-3541. FAX: (505) 327-5796.

Renaissance Communications Corp. Stns: 7 TV. KTXL(TV) Sacramento, Calif.; KDVR(TV) Denver & KFCT(TV) Fort Collins, both Colo.; WTIC-TV Hartford, Conn.; WDZL(TV) Miami; WXIN(TV) Indianapolis; & WPMT(TV) York, Pa. (All 100% owned.) Ownership: Michael Finkelstein; Warburg, Pincus Capital L.P. Hqtrs: One Fawcett Place, Suite 120, Greenwich, Conn. 06830. (203) 629-1888. FAX: (203) 629-9821.

Renda Broadcasting Corp.-Renda Radio Inc. Stns: 2 AM, 6 FM. WEJZ(FM) Jacksonville, Fla.; KHTT(FM) Muskogee, KMGL(FM) Oklahoma City & KBEZ(FM) Tulsa, all Okla.; WJAS(AM)-WSHH(FM) Pittsburgh & WECZ(AM)-WPXZ-FM Punxsutawney, both Pa. Ownership: Anthony F. Renda, 100%. Hqtrs: Renda Broadcasting Corp., Broadcast Plaza, Crane Ave., Pittsburgh 15220. (412) 531-9500. FAX: (412) 531-4068.

Reseau des Appalaches. Stns: 4 AM, 1 FM. CJAN(AM) Asbestos, CJLP(AM) Disraeli, CKLD(AM)-CFJO-FM Thetford Mines & CFDA(AM) Victoriaville, all Que. (All stns are located in Canada.) Executive: Francois Labbe, pres. Hqtrs: C.P. 69, Thetford Mines, Que., Canada G6G 5S3. (418) 335-7533. FAX: (418) 338-0386.

The Result Radio Group Stns: 3 AM, 3 FM, KBEW-AM-FM Blue Earth, KBRF(AM)-KZCR(FM) Fergus Falls & KAGE-AM-FM Winona, all Minnesota. Executive: Jerry Papenfuss, pres. Ownership: Jerry Papenfuss. Hqtrs: Box 5767, Winona, Minn. 55987. (507) 452-4000. FAX: (507) 452-9494.

Retlaw Broadcasting Co. Stns: 5 TV. KJEO(TV) Fresno, Calif.: KIDK(TV) Idaho Falls & KLEW-TV Lewiston, both Idaho; KEPR-TV Pasco & KIMA-TV Yakima, both Wa. (All 100% owned.) Executives: Benjamin Tucker, pres. Ownership: Lillian B. Disney, Diane Disney Miller. Hqtrs: Box 5455, Fresno, Calif. 93755. (209) 222-2411. FAX: (209) 222-5593.

River City Broadcasting. Stns: 1 FM, 5 TV. WTTV(TV) Bloomington & WTTK(TV) Kokomo, both Ind.; KDSM-TV Des Moines, Iowa; KPNT(FM) Ste. Genevieve & KDNL-TV St. Louis, both Mo.; & KABB(TV) San Antonio, Tex. (All 100% owned.) Ownership: Barry Baker, Larry Marcus, J. Patrick Michaels, others. Hqtrs: 1215 Cole St., St. Louis 63106. (314) 436-3030. FAX: (314) 259-5763.

F.W. Robbert Broadcasting Co. Inc. Stns: 3 AM, 1 SW. WVOG(AM) New Orleans; WITA(AM) Knoxville & WNQM(AM) & WWCR (shortwave) Nashville, all Tenn. (All 100% owned.) Note: WWCR Nashville uses three sw transmitters. Ownership: Fred P. Westenberger, 51%; Chris P. Westenberger, 9.75%; Fritz N. Westenberger, 9.75%; Lisa M. Westenberger, 9.75%; Eric M. Westenberger, 9.75%; George McClintock, 10%. Hqtrs: 2730 Loumor Ave., Metairie, La. 70001. (504) 831-6941. FAX: (504) 832-4039.

Roberts Broadcasting Inc. Stns: 2 AM, 2 FM. WJMS(AM) & WIMI(FM) Ironwood, Mich.; WJMT(AM) & WMZK(FM) Merrill, Wis. (All 100% owned.) Ownership: W. Donald Roberts Jr., 100%. Hqtrs: Box 39010, Sarasota, Fla. 34238. (813) 966-2287.

Rodgers Broadcasting Corp. Stns: 4 AM, 3 FM. WBML(AM) Macon, Ga.; WIFE(AM)-WCNB-FM Connersville & WMCB(AM)-WCBK-FM Martinsville, both Ind.; WOFR(AM) & WCHO-FM Washington Court House, Ohio. Ownership: David Rodgers, 100%. Hqtrs: Box 1577, Martinsville, Ind. 46151. (317) 342-3394.

Rollings Communications Companies. Stns: 1 AM, 5 FM. WZNX(FM) Arcola, WWDZ(FM) Danville, WZZP(FM) Kankakee, WUFI(AM)-WZNF(FM) Rantoul & WUBB(FM) Tuscola, all Ill. (All 100% owned.) Note: Group also operates WLTM(FM) Rantoul, Ill. through a loc mktg agreement. Ownership: Dale Rollings, Mark Rollings. Hqtrs: Box 882, Chesterfield, Mo. 63006. (314) 458-5595. FAX: (314) 458-1835.

Root Communications Stns: 2 AM, 2 FM, 1 TV. WNDB(AM)-WCFB(FM) Daytona Beach & WLKF(AM)-WEZY-FM Lakeland, both Fla.; & KMVT(TV) Twin Falls, Idaho. Note: FCC has approved the sale of WEZY-FM Lakeland, Fla., although the transfer has not been completed. Ownership: Root Communications, 100%. Hqtrs: Box 2860, Daytona Beach, Fla. 32120-2860. (904) 258-1235. FAX: (904) 253-3267.

Roper Broadcasting Inc. Stns: 1 AM, 2 FM. WHKR(FM) Rockledge & WITS(AM)-WCAC(FM) Sebring, both Fla. (All 100% owned.) Ownership: Robert T. Rowland, 35%; Gwendolyn G. Rowland, 35%; Valree A. Peralta, 10%; Douglas L. Peralta, 10%; & Robert T. Rowland Jr., 10%. Hqtrs: 2355 Pluckebaum Rd., Cocoa, Fla. 32922. (407) 639-1176. FAX: (407) 639-1027.

Roth Communications Stns: 4 AM, 4 FM. WCHY-AM-FM Savannah, Ga.; WKBF(AM) & WPXR-FM Rock Island, Ill.; WKPE-AM-FM Orleans, Mass.; WIPI(AM) & WODE-FM Easton, Pa. (All 100% owned.) Executive: Peter S. Crawford, exec VP/group mgr. Ownership: David A. Roth, M.D. Hqtrs: 3 Woodland Rd., Stoneham, Mass. 02180. (617) 662-4800. FAX: (617) 662-9675.

Rowland Family Radio. Stns: 3 FM. WGUF(FM) Marco, Fla.; WEGC(FM) Leesburg (Albany) & WBGA(FM) Waycross, both Ga. (All 100% owned.) Ownership: Marshall W. Rowland, Carol C. Rowland. Hqtrs: 253 Hwy. 82, Brunswick, Ga. 31525. (912) 267-7200. FAX: (912) 267-0908.

Rubber City Radio Group Inc. Stns: 1 AM, 2 FM. WAKR(AM)-WONE-FM Akron & WQMX(FM) Medina, both Ohio. (All 100% owned.) Ownership: Thomas Mandel. Hqtrs: 3610 W. Market St. #107, Akron, Ohio 44333. (216) 434-6499. FAX: (216) 666-6086.

Rusk Corp. Stns: 1 AM, 2 FM. KISS-FM San Antonio, KSMG(FM) Seguin (San Antonio) & KLUP(AM) Terrill Hills, all Tex. Ownership: Members of the Jones family. Note: Rusk Corp. also manages KHHT(FM) Killeen, Tex., through a loc mktg agreement. Hqtrs: 1200 Travis, Suite 725, Houston 77001. (713) 651-1691. FAX: (713) 630-3667.

S

SBC Technologies Inc. Stns: 1 AM, 2 FM. WACO-AM-FM Waco, Tex. (51%); & WVMX(FM) Stowe, Vt. (100%). Executives: Leonard J. Fassler, chmn; Gerald A. Poch, pres; Gerald M. LeBow, exec VP. Hqtrs: 700 Canal St., Stamford, Conn. 06902. (203) 357-1464. FAX: (203) 357-1531.

SCI Television Inc. Stns: 7 TV. WAGA-TV Atlanta, WSBK-TV Boston, WJW-TV Cleveland, WJBK-TV Detroit, WITI-TV Milwaukee, KNSD(TV) San Diego & WTVT(TV) Tampa, Fla. Ownership: Ronald Perelman, 51%. Hqtrs: 3200 Windy Hill Rd., Suite 1100-W, Marietta, Ga. 30067. (404) 955-0045. FAX: (404) 563-9600.

SFX Broadcasting Inc. Stns: 3 AM, 7 FM. KJQY(FM) San Diego; WJDS(AM), WKTF(FM) & WMSI(FM) Jackson, Miss.; WMYI(FM) Hendersonville, N.C.; WSSL-FM Gray Court (Greenville) & WSSL(AM) Greenville, both S.C.; WSIX-FM Nashville; KRLD(AM) Dallas & KODA(FM) Houston. Executives: Robert F.X. Sillerman, pres; R. Steven Hicks, Norm Feuer, sr exec VPs. Hqtrs: 600 Congress, Suite 1270, Austin, Tex. 78701. (512) 477-7338. FAX: (512) 477-7389.

SJL Broadcast Management Corp. Stns: 7 TV. KSNG(TV) Garden City, KSNC(TV) Great Bend, KSNT(TV) Topeka & KSNW(TV) Wichita, all Kan.; WJRT-TV Flint, Mich.; KTVQ(TV) Billings, Mont.; & KSNK(TV) McCook, Neb. Note: KTVQ(TV) Billings, Mont. has been sold, pending FCC approval. Group also manages KOAM-TV Pittsburg, Kan., & WTVG(TV) Toledo, Ohio. Executives: George D. Lilly, pres; Dave McCurdy, VP/sec. Also an office of SJL Broadcast Management Corp. at 633 Picacho Ln., Montecito, Calif. 93108. (805) 969-9278. Fax: (805) 969-2399. (George D. Lilly is located in Montecito, Calif. office.) Ownership: George D. Lilly, 100%. Hqtrs: Box 2557, Billings, Mont. 59103. (406) 256-0705. FAX: (406) 252-9144.

S & P Broadcasting Co. Stns: 2 AM, 3 FM. WALY(FM) Bellwood (Altoona), WCDL(AM)-WSGD(FM) Carbondale (Scranton-Wilkes-Barre), WWWD(FM) Jersey Shore (Williamsport) & WWPA(AM) Williamsport, all Pa. (All 100% owned.) Executives: Ronald K. Swanson, pres/CEO; Robert L. VanDerheyden Jr., VP/COO; Darrell L. Alva, VP mktg. Ownership: 100% owned by respective S & P limited partnerships. S & P Broadcasting is gen ptnr. S & P Broadcasting Co. (gen ptnr) owns in excess of 51% of each limited partnership. WALY(FM): S & P Broadcasting L.P. I. WCDL(AM) & WSGD(FM): S & P Broadcasting L.P. III. WWWD(FM) & WWPA(AM): S & P Broadcasting L.P. II. Hqtrs: One Montage Mountain Rd., Moosic, Pa. 18507. (717) 343-1214. FAX: (717) 343-0696.

STARadio Corp. Stns: 2 AM, 3 FM. KGRC(FM) Hannibal, Mo.; KMON-AM-FM Great Falls, Mont.; & WNXT-AM-FM Portsmouth, Ohio. Note: Group has purchased WKAN(AM) & WLRT(FM) Kankakee, Ill., pending FCC approval. Ownership: Howard A. Doss, Derek Parrish & Jack Whitley. Hqtrs: 8 State & Plaza, 433 S. 8th St., Quincy, Ill. 62301. (217) 224-4102. FAX: (217) 224-4133.

Saga Communications Inc. Stns: 8 AM, 13 FM. WIXY(FM)-WLRW(FM) Champaign, WYMG(FM) Jacksonville (Springfield) & WQQL(FM) Springfield, all Ill.; KIOA-AM-FM & KRNT(AM)-KSTZ(FM) Des Moines, Iowa; WGAN(AM)-WMGX(FM) Portland, WZAN(AM) Portland & WYNZ(FM) Westbrook, all Me.; WAQY(AM) East Longmeadow & WAQY-FM Springfield, both Mass.; WFEA(AM) & WZID(FM) Manchester, N.H.; WVKO(AM) & WSNY(FM) Columbus, Ohio; WNOR-AM-FM Norfolk, Va.; & WKLH(FM) Milwaukee. Note: Group has purchased WLZR-AM-FM Milwaukee, pending FCC approval. Executives: Edward K. Christian, pres/CEO; Steven Goldstein, exec VP/group prog dir; Norm McKee, VP/CFO. Ownership: Edward K. Christian, 68% of the voting stock. Hqtrs: 73 Kercheval, Suite 201, Grosse Pointe Farms, Mich. 48236. (313) 886-7070. FAX: (313) 886-7150.

Sainte Ltd. Stns: 4 TV. KNSO(TV) Merced, KCSO(TV) Modesto & KCVU(TV) Paradise, all Calif.; & KREN-TV Reno. (All 100% owned.) Note: Group also owns KBVU(TV) Eureka, Calif. (49% ownship with contract to purchase remaining 51%, subject to FCC approval), two low power TV stns (K09UF Morro Bay & KO7TA Santa Maria, both Calif.) & a CP for a low power TV stn on ch. 21 in Chico, Calif. Ownership: Chester Smith, gen ptnr, & Naomi Smith, gen ptnr, 54%; & other limited ptnrs. Hqtrs: Box 4159, Modesto, Calif. 95352. (209) 523-0777. FAX: (209) 523-0898.

Salem Communications Corp. Stns: 10 AM, 8 FM. KGER(AM) Long Beach (Los Angeles), KKLA(FM) Los Angeles, KDAR(FM) Oxnard (Ventura), KAVC(FM) Rosamond, KLFE(AM) San Bernardino, KFAX(AM) San Francisco & KPRZ(AM) San Marcos-Poway (San Diego), all Calif.; KRKS-FM Boulder, Colo.; WYLL(FM) Des Plaines, Ill. (Chicago); WEZE(AM) Boston; WMCA(AM) New York; WRFD(AM) Columbus-Worthington, Ohio; KPDQ-AM-FM Portland, Ore.; WPIT(AM) & WORD-FM Pittsburgh; WAVA(FM) Arlington, Va. (Washington); & KGNW(AM) Burien-Seattle,

Wash. Note: Group has purchased WPHY(AM) Philadelphia, subject to FCC approval. Ownership: Edward G. Atsinger III, pres/CEO, 50%; Stuart W. Epperson, chmn, 50%. Edward G. Atsinger III also owns a 50% interest in KGFT(FM) Pueblo, Colo., & 38% of KCHT(FM) Bakersfield & KKXX-FM Delano (Bakersfield), both Calif. Stuart W. Epperson also owns 50% of WPMH(AM) Portsmouth, Va. & 38% of KCHT(FM) Bakersfield & KKXX-FM Delano, both Calif. Hqtrs: 4880 Santa Rosa Rd., Suite 300, Camarillo, Calif. 93012. (805) 987-0400. FAX: (805) 482-8570.

Salter Broadcasting Co. of Delaware. Stns: 2 AM, 2 FM. WKKD-AM-FM Aurora, WRWC(FM) Rockton & WBEL(AM) South Beloit, all Ill. (All 100% owned.) Ownership: Corporation name is Salter Broadcasting Co. Hqtrs: Box C-1730, Aurora, Ill. 60507. (708) 898-6668. FAX: (708) 898-2463.

Sandusky Radio. Stns: 1 AM, 3 FM. KDKB(FM) Mesa, Ariz.; KEGL(FM) Fort Worth; KLSY-FM Bellevue & KIXI(AM) Seattle, both Wa. (All 100% owned.) Executives: David Rau, chmn. Ownership: Alice S. White trust. All 100% owned by the White & Rau families. (See also Sandusky Newspapers Inc. under Cross-Ownership, Sect. A.) Hqtrs: 601 California St., Suite 2260, San Francisco 94108. (415) 788-3161. FAX: (415) 788-3165.

Schurz Communications Inc. Stns: 2 AM, 2 FM, 4 TV. WAGT(TV) Augusta, Ga.; WASK-AM-FM Lafayette & WSBT-AM-TV & WNSN(FM) South Bend, both Ind.; KYTV(TV) Springfield, Mo.; & WDBJ(TV) Roanoke, Va. (All 100% owned.) Executives: Franklin D. Schurz Jr., pres; James M. Schurz, sr VP newspapers; E. Berry Smith, sr VP bcstg; Scott C. Schurz, VP; Mary Schurz, VP/sec; James G. Young Jr., treas. Cable TV. (See also Cross-Ownership, Sect. A.) Hqtrs: 225 W. Colfax Ave., South Bend, Ind. 46626. (219) 287-1001.

Scofield Broadcasting Co. Stns: 2 AM, 1 FM. KLPZ(AM) Parker, Ariz.; KEYZ(AM) & KYYZ(FM) Williston, N.D. (All 100% owned.) Ownership: Charles L. Scofield, 100%. Hqtrs: Box 2048, Williston, N.D. 58802. (701) 572-5371.

Sconnix Broadcasting Co. Stns: 4 AM, 6 FM. WMXJ(FM) Pompano Beach, Fla.; WLLR-FM East Moline & WLLR(AM) Moline, both Ill.; WIBC(AM) & WKLR(FM) Indianapolis; KFKF-FM Kansas City, Kan.; WBMD(AM) Baltimore & WQSR(FM) Catonsville, both Md.; & WLNH-AM-FM Laconia, N.H. Note: WMXJ(FM) Pompano Beach, Fla. has been sold, pending FCC approval. Ownership: Scott R. McQueen, Theodore E. Nixon & Randall T. Odeneal. Hqtrs: Tysons International Plaza, 1921 Gallows Rd., Suite 850, Vienna, Va. 22182. (703) 356-6000. FAX: (703) 790-1290.

Scripps Howard Broadcasting Co. Stns: 9 TV. KNXV-TV Phoenix; WFTS(TV) Tampa & WPTV(TV) West Palm Beach, both Fla.; WMAR-TV Baltimore; WXYZ-TV Detroit; KSHB-TV Kansas City, Mo.; WCPO-TV Cincinnati & WEWS(TV) Cleveland; & KJRH(TV) Tulsa, Okla. Executives: Charles E. Scripps, chmn of bd; Lawrence A. Leser, pres/CEO. Cable TV: Scripps Howard Cable Co. Ownership: The E.W. Scripps Co. Hqtrs: Box 5380, 312 Walnut St., 28th Fl., Cincinnati 45201. (513) 977-3000.

Seacoast Communications Group Inc. Stns: 2 AM, 1 FM. CKOV(AM)-CKLZ-FM Kelowna & CFAX(AM) Victoria, both B.C. (All stns are located in Canada.) Ownership: Melco Management Ltd., 87.45%. Note: Also owns Seacoast Sound, Victoria, B.C. (music & sound prod). Hqtrs: 825 Broughton St., Victoria, B.C., Canada V8W 1E5. (604) 386-1070. FAX: (604) 386-5775.

Seaton Stns. Stns: 2 AM, 2 FM, 1 TV. KMAN(AM) & KMKF(FM) Manhattan, Kan.; KHAS-TV Hastings, Neb.; KFYO(AM) & KZII-FM Lubbock, Tex. Ownership: Major stockholders are R.M. Seaton, Gladys D. Seaton, Edward L. Seaton, Donald R. Seaton, & others. (See also Cross-Ownership, Sect. A.) Hqtrs: Box 877, Coffeyville, Kan. 67337. (316) 251-2900.

Seaway Communications Inc. Stns: 2 TV. WVII-TV Bangor, Me.; & WJFW-TV Rhinelander, Wis. Executives: James L. Buckner, chmn; Bernard Chase, gen mgr; Herbert Harris, sec; Khamalow Beard, treas. Hqtrs: 371 Target Industrial Circle, Bangor, Me. 04401. (207) 945-6457. FAX: (207) 942-0511.

Seehafer Broadcasting Corp. Stns: 2 AM, 2 FM. WOMT(AM)-WQTC-FM Manitowoc & WXCO(AM)-WYCO(FM) Wausau, both Wis. (All 100% owned.) Ownership: Don Seehafer, 100%. Hqtrs: 3730 Mangin St., Manitowoc, Wis. 54220. (414) 682-0351.

Segue Communications Corp. Stns: 1 AM, 2 FM. KLXK(FM) Duluth & WQPM-AM-FM Princeton, both Minn. (All 100% owned.) Ownership: Paul Stagg, Susan Schmidgall, Mark Kleinschmidt. Hqtrs: Box 106, Princeton, Minn. 55371. (612) 389-1300. FAX: (612) 389-1359.

Seward County Broadcasting Co. Stns: 1 AM, 2 FM. KLDG(FM) & KSCB-AM-FM Liberal, Kan. Hqtrs: Box 3125, Liberal, Kan. 67905-3125. (316) 624-3891. FAX: (316) 624-9472.

Shamrock Broadcasting Inc. Stns: 7 AM, 12 FM, 2 TV. KMLE(FM) Chandler, Ariz.; KLAC(AM)-KZLA-FM Los Angeles, KABL(AM) Oakland, KNEW(AM) Oakland, KABL-FM San Francisco & KSAN-FM San Francisco, all Calif.; KXKL-AM-FM Denver; WFOX(FM) Gainesville, Ga.; WWWW-AM-FM Detroit; KFAN(AM) Minneapolis & KEEY-FM St. Paul; WHTZ(FM) Newark, N.J.; WWSW-AM-FM Pittsburgh; KTAB-TV Abilene, KZFX(FM) Lake Jackson & KXXV(TV) Waco, all Tex.; & KXRX(FM) Seattle. Note: KXRX(FM) Seattle has been sold, subject to FCC approval. Executives: Bill Clark, chmn; Martin Loughman, pres. Ownership: Roy E. Disney & family. Hqtrs: Box 7774, Burbank, Calif. 91510-7774. (818) 845-4444. FAX: (818) 845-9718.

Shamrock Communications Inc. Stns: 3 AM, 6 FM. WDIZ(FM) Orlando, Fla.; WTTR(AM) & WGRX(FM) Westminster, Md. (Baltimore); KMYZ-AM-FM Pryor (Tulsa), Okla.; WEJL(AM) & WEZX(FM) Scranton, Pa.; KUTZ(FM) Lampasas, Tex.; & WQFM(FM) Milwaukee. Principal owns: William R. Lynett, James J. Haggerty, Edward J. Lynett, George V. Lynett. (See also Cross-Ownership, Sect. A.) Hqtrs: 149 Penn Ave., Scranton, Pa. 18501. (717) 348-9108.

Shaw Radio. Stns: 3 AM, 5 FM. CHQT(AM)-CISN-FM Edmonton & CKGY(AM)-CIZZ-FM Red Deer, both Alta.; CKLG(AM) & CFOX-FM Vancouver, B.C.; CHAY-FM Barrie & CKDK-FM Woodstock, both Ont. (All stns are located in Canada.) (All 100% owned.) Ownership: Jim Shaw. Cable TV. Hqtrs: 10550 102nd St., Edmonton, Alta., Canada T5H 2T3. (403) 424-8800. FAX: (403) 426-6502.

Shepherd Group Stns: 5 AM, 4 FM. KAAN-AM-FM Bethany (100%), KREI(AM)-KTJJ(FM) Farmington (80%), KJCF(AM) Festus (80%), KJEL(AM)-KIRK(FM) Lebanon (100%) & KWIX(AM)-KRES(FM) Moberly (100%), all Mo. Executive: Jerrell A. Shepherd, pres. Hqtrs: Box 430, Moberly, Mo. 65270. (816) 263-5800. FAX: (816) 263-2300.

Sheridan Broadcasting Corp. Stns: 2 AM, 1 FM. WUFO(AM) Amherst, N.Y.; WYJZ(AM) & WAMO-FM Pittsburgh. Hqtrs: 411 7th Ave., Suite 1500, Pittsburgh 15219. (412) 456-4000. FAX: (412) 391-3559.

Shockley Communications Corp. Stns: 1 AM, 3 FM. KDAL-AM-FM Duluth, Minn.; WOLX-FM Baraboo (Madison) & WZTR(FM) Milwaukee, both Wis. Executives: Terry K. Shockley, pres; Sandra Shockley, VP; Dave Dunkin, group prog dir. Ownership: Terry & Sandy Shockley. Other interest: ProVideo, Madison, Wis. (production company). Hqtrs: 2306 W. Badger Rd., Madison, Wis. 53713. (608) 273-0077. FAX: (608) 273-2507.

Sigma Broadcasting Inc. Stns: 2 TV. KHOG-TV Fayetteville & KHBS(TV) Fort Smith, both Ark. (Both 100% owned.) Ownership: Bob Hernreich, 70%; Cindy Hernreich, 30%. Hqtrs: Box 4150, Fort Smith, Ark. 72914. (501) 783-4040. FAX: (501) 783-0550.

Silver King Communications Inc. Stns: 12 TV. KHSC-TV Ontario, Calif. (Los Angeles); WYHS-TV Hollywood (Miami) & WBHS-TV Tampa, both Fla.; WEHS-TV Aurora, Ill. (Chicago); WHSW-TV Baltimore; WHSH-TV Marlborough, Mass. (Boston); WHSE-TV Newark (New York) & WHSP-TV Vineland (Philadelphia), both N.J.; WHSI-TV Smithtown, N.Y.; WQHS-TV Cleveland; KHSH-TV Alvin (Houston) & KHSX-TV Irving (Dallas), both Tex.; plus low power TVs: W52BF Mobile, Ala.; K21CX Tucson, Ariz.; W24BF St. Petersburg, Fla.; W24AL Atlanta; W33AY Springfield, Ill.; K15DD Wichita, Kan.; K14IE New Orleans; K35CY Minneapolis; K26CR Kansas City & K21OD St. Louis, both Mo.; W60AI New York; W13BN Columbus, Ohio; K39CW Tulsa, Okla.; W56CM Knoxville, Tenn.; and W17BH Huntington, W. Va. Executives: Jeff McGrath, chmn; James M. Lawless, pres; Steven H. Grant, vice chmn/exec VP/CFP/CFO/treas; Chuck Bohart, exec VP dev; Michael Drayer, exec VP/gen counsel/sec; Al Evans, exec VP engrg; Joe Centorino, VP engrg; Joan Halfaker, VP/controller; Lia Hernandez, VP compliance. Ownership: Publicly held, traded on NASDAQ. Symbol: SKTV. Other interests: Telemation Inc. (production) located in Chicago, Denver and Ontario, Calif.; Home Shopping Network (satellite progmg for bcst & cable TV). Hqtrs: 12425 28th St. N., #300, St. Petersburg, Fla. 33716-1826. (813) 573-0339. FAX: (813) 572-1349.

Sinclair Broadcast Group Inc. Stns: 3 TV. WBFF(TV) Baltimore; WTTE(TV) Columbus, Ohio; & WPGH-TV Pittsburgh. Ownership: Smith brothers. Hqtrs: 2000 W. 41st St., Baltimore 21211. (410) 467-4545. FAX: (410) 467-5043.

Sinclair Communications Inc. Stns: 2 AM, 4 FM. KINE-FM Honolulu; WROX-FM Cape Charles, WCDX(FM) Mechanicsville, WNIS(AM) Norfolk & WGCV(AM)-WPLZ-FM Petersburg, all Va. Note: KINE-FM Honolulu has been sold, pending FCC approval. Executive: John L. Sinclair, pres. Cable TV: Owns 100% of AAA Cablecom in Benton County, Ark. Hqtrs: 9 Londonderry Cir., Danville, Ind. 46122. (317) 745-7368. FAX: (317) 745-2189.

Sisk Group. See Air South Radio Inc.

John Slatton Stations. Stns: 2 AM, 2 FM. WJBB-AM-FM Haleyville & WLAY-AM-FM Muscle Shoals, both Ala. (All 100% owned.) Ownership: John L. Slatton & Mrs. John L. Slatton, 100%. Hqtrs: Box 370, Haleyville, Ala. 35565. (205) 486-2277. FAX: (205) 486-3905.

Smith Broadcasting Group Inc. Stns: 11 TV. KCCN-TV Monterey & KEYT-TV Santa Barbara, both Calif.; KBSD-TV Ensign, KBSL-TV Goodland, KBSH-TV Hays & KWCH-TV Hutchinson, all Kan.; WETM-TV Elmira & WKTV(TV) Utica, both N.Y.; WATM-TV Altoona, WHTM-TV Harrisburg & WWCP-TV Johnstown, all Pa. Executives: Robert N. Smith, pres; David A. Fitz, exec VP. Smith Broadcasting Group Inc. owns controlling interest in Smith Broadcasting of California Inc., which owns 100% of KEYT-TV, & in Smith Television of New York Inc., which owns 100% of WETM-TV & WKTV(TV). Smith Broadcasting Group Inc. also owns controlling interest in Smith Acquisition Corp., which owns 100% of WHTM-TV. Smith Broadcasting Group owns a 51% controlling interest in Evergreen Broadcasting Corp., which owns WATM-TV Altoona & WWCP-TV Johnstown, both Pa. Smith Broadcasting Group owns 10% of Harron-Smith Television Partnership, which owns KCCN-TV, & 5% of KBSD-TV, KBSL-TV, KBSH-TV & KWCH-TV. Hqtrs: 127 El Paseo, Santa Barbara, Calif. (805) 965-0400; 3839 4th St. N., Suite 420, St. Petersburg, Fla. 33703. (813) 821-7900.

Lou Smith Ministries Inc. Stns: 5 FM. WJYB(FM) Breese, Ill.; WJYL(FM) New Washington, Ind.; KWND(FM) Springfield, Mo.; KABS(FM) Great Falls, Mont.; & WJYC(FM) Delhi Hills, Ohio. Note: Group also owns a FM translator on 104.7 mhz in New Albany, Ind. (Louisville, Ky.) & a low-power TV stn, W08CT New Albany, Ind. (ch 8). Ownership: Mary L. Smith, pres, 33 1/3%; David B. Smith, VP, 33 1/3%; John W. Smith Sr., 33 1/3%. Hqtrs: Box 1226, Jeffersonville, Ind. 47131. (812) 284-2600. FAX: (812) 282-4177.

Bob Smith Stations. Stns: 3 AM, 2 FM. WIMN(AM) Stillwater, Minn. (100%); WWIS-AM-FM Black River Falls (99%) & WIXK-AM-FM New Richmond (95%), both Wis. Ownership: Bob Smith, pres. Hqtrs: 125 E. 3rd St., New Richmond, Wis. 54017. (715) 246-2254. FAX: (715) 246-7090.

Sonlight Broadcasting Systems Inc. Stns: 5 TV. WMPV-TV Mobile & WMCF-TV Montgomery, both Ala.; WELF(TV) Dalton, Ga.; WBUY(TV) Holly Springs, Miss.; & WPGD(TV) Hendersonville, Tenn. (All 100% owned.) Ownership: nonprofit, no stock issued. Hqtrs: 120 Zeigler Cir. E., Mobile, Ala. 36608. (205) 633-2100. FAX: (205) 633-2174.

Sorenson Broadcasting Corp. Stns: 5 AM, 5 FM. KCUE(AM) & KWNG(FM) Red Wing, Minn.; KQDJ(AM) & KYNU(FM) Jamestown, N.D.; KCCR(AM)-KLXS-FM Pierre, KWAT(AM)-KIXX(FM) Watertown & KYNT(AM)-KKYA(FM) Yankton, all S.D. (All 100% owned.) Ownership: Dean P. Sorenson. Note: Dean P. Sorenson also owns 100% of KVFD(AM) & KUEL(FM) Fort Dodge, Iowa. Hqtrs: 604 N. Kiwanis Plaza, Sioux Falls, S.D. 57104. (605) 334-1117. FAX: (605) 338-0326.

South Central Communications Corp. Stns: 2 AM, 4 FM. WJPS(AM) & WIKY-FM Evansville, Ind.; WEZK-AM-FM Knoxville, WIMZ-FM Knoxville & WZEZ(FM) Nashville, all Tenn. (All 100% owned.) Note: Group also owns 10 low-power TV stns. John D. Engelbrecht & family, 100%. Hqtrs: Box 3848, Evansville, Ind. 47736. (812) 464-1150.

Southern Broadcasting Companies Inc. Stns: 3 AM, 5 FM. WPAP-FM Panama City & WWSD(AM)-WFHT(FM) Quincy, both Fla.; WGMG(FM) Crawford, WZOT(AM)-WTSH-FM Rockmart, WTSH(AM) Rome & WSNI(FM) Thomasville, all Ga. Note: Group has purchased WKNB(FM) Port St. Joe, Fla., subject to FCC approval. Group has applied to change the call letters of

WFHT(FM) Quincy, Fla. to WXSR-FM. Ownership: Paul Stone, 50%; Charles Giddens, 50%. Hqtrs: 3360 Capital Cir. N.E., Tallahassee, Fla. 32308. (904) 422-3107. FAX: (904) 422-0008.

Southern Communications Corp. Stns: 2 AM, 1 FM. WIWS(AM)-WCIR-FM Beckley & WHRD(AM) Huntington, both W.Va. Ownership: Ira W. Southern, Judy M. Southern. Hqtrs: 21 Airport Industrial Park, Beaver, W.Va. 25813. (304) 252-6452. FAX: (304) 255-1044.

Southern Minnesota Broadcasting Co. Stns: 3 AM, 5 FM. KROC-AM-FM Rochester & KYBA(FM) Stewartville, both Minn.; KKLS(AM)-KKMK(FM) Rapid City, KIKN(FM) Salem & KXRB(AM)-KKLS-FM Sioux Falls, all S.D. Hqtrs: 122 4th St. S.W., Rochester, Minn. 55902. (507) 286-1010. FAX: (507) 286-9370.

Southern Skies Corp. Stns: 1 AM, 3 FM. KMVK(FM) Benton & KSSN(FM) Little Rock, both Ark.; KZSN-FM Hutchinson & KZSN(AM) Wichita, both Kan. (All 100% owned.) Ownership: Jerry Atchley, 100%. Hqtrs: 8114 Cantrell Rd., Little Rock, Ark. 72207. (501) 227-9696. FAX: (501) 228-9547.

Southern Starr Broadcasting Group. Stns: 4 FM. KOLL(FM) Maumelle, Ark.; WPLR(FM) New Haven, Conn.; WGNE-FM Titusville, Fla.; & WKNN-FM Pascagoula, Miss. (All 100% owned.) Hqtrs: 99 Canal Ctr. Plaza, Suite 220, Alexandria, Va. 22314. (703) 683-8488. FAX: (703) 683-1496.

Southwestern Broadcasting Corp. Stns: 2 AM, 4 FM. KGOE(FM) Eureka, Calif.; KICA(AM) Clovis, N.M.; KLZK(FM) Brownfield, KICA-FM Farwell & KMUL(AM)-KKYC(FM) Muleshoe, all Texas. Ownership: Thomas Crane. Hqtrs: Box 7000, Clovis, N.M. 88101. (505) 762-6200. FAX: (505) 762-8800.

Spanish Broadcasting System Inc. Stns: 3 AM, 4 FM. KLAX-FM Long Beach & KXED(AM) Los Angeles, both Calif.; WCMQ-FM Hialeah (Miami), WZMQ(FM) Key Largo & WCMQ(AM) Miami Springs (Miami), all Fla.; WSKQ(AM) Newark, N.J.; & WSKQ-FM New York. Executives: Raul Alarcon Sr., chmn; Raul Alarcon Jr., pres/CEO; Jose Grimalt, exec VP. Ownership: Raul Alarcon Sr., Raul Alarcon Jr., Jose Grimalt. Hqtrs: 26 W. 56th St., New York 10019. (212) 541-9200. FAX: (212) 541-9236; (212) 541-8535.

Spartan Radiocasting Company Inc. Stns: 1 AM, 1 FM, 5 TV. WMBB(TV) Panama City, Fla.; WJBF(TV) Augusta, Ga.; KIMT(TV) Mason City, Iowa; WBTW(TV) Florence & WSPA-AM-FM-TV Spartanburg, both S.C. (All 100% owned.) Ownership: Walter J. Brown, 55.5%. Hqtrs: Box 1717, Spartanburg, S.C. 29304. (803) 576-7777. FAX: (803) 587-5425.

Spinks Group. Stns: 1 AM, 2 FM. WWHK(FM) Greenville & WLLS-AM-FM Hartford, both Ky. (All 100% owned.) Ownership: Hayward F. Spinks, 100%. Hqtrs: Hwy. 231 S., Spinks Shopping Ctr., Hartford, Ky. 42347. (502) 298-3268.

Spur Capital Inc. Stns: 1 AM, 2 FM. WSLI(AM) & WJDX(FM) Jackson, Miss.; & KVET-FM Austin, Tex. (All 100% owned.) Ownership: Don R. Kuykendall. Hqtrs: 301 Congress Ave., Suite 410, Austin, Tex. 78701. (512) 495-6495. FAX: (512) 495-6496.

Stainless Broadcasting Co. Stns: 2 TV. WICZ-TV Binghamton, N.Y.; & KTVZ(TV) Bend, Ore. (Both 100% owned.) Ownership: WICZ-TV is owned by Stainless Broadcasting Co. KTVZ(TV) is owned by Stainless Enterprises of Pennsylvania. Major stockholders: Henry J. Guzewicz, Richard J. Eberle. Hqtrs: 3rd & Montgomery Ave., North Wales, Pa. 19454. (215) 699-4871. FAX: (215) 699-9597.

Standard Broadcasting Corp. Stns: 6 AM, 6 FM. CFCN(AM)-CJAY-FM Calgary & CFRN(AM)-CFBR-FM Edmonton, both Alta.; CJSB(AM)-New FM Ottawa, CKTB(AM) & CHTZ-FM St. Catharines, & CFRB(AM), CKFM-FM & CFRX (shortwave) Toronto, all Ont.; CJAD(AM) & CJFM-FM Montreal. (All stns are located in Canada.) Ownership: Slaight Communications Inc., 100%. Hqtrs: 2 St. Clair Ave. W., 11th Fl., Toronto, Ont., Canada M4V 1L6. (416) 960-9911. FAX: (416) 323-6828.

Stansell Communications Inc. Stns: 1 AM, 2 FM. KLAK(FM) Durant, Okla.; KTBB(AM) & KTYL-FM Tyler, Tex. (All 100% owned.) Executives: Jim Stansell, pres/CEO; Bill Harrison, exec VP. Hqtrs: Box 7966, Dallas 75209-7966. (214) 528-4633. FAX: (903) 592-9923.

Star Radio. Stns: 1 AM, 2 FM. KBCN-FM Marshall & KERX(FM) Paris, both Ark.; & WLEE(AM) Richmond, Va. Note: Group has purchased KDEW-FM De Witt & KLRA-AM-FM England, both Ark., subject to FCC approval. Group also manages KTRI-FM Mansfield, Mo. through a loc mktg agreement. Hqtrs: 7450 Midlothian Pike, Richmond, Va. 23225. (804) 745-0300. FAX: (804) 745-7823.

Starcast Stations. Stns: 2 AM, 1 FM. WBHN(AM) Bryson City, N.C.; WKLP(AM) & WQZK-FM Keyser, W. Va. (All 100% owned.) Ownership: Jack Mullen I, William P. Kelly, Jack Mullen II, Curtis Durst. Hqtrs: Starcast Systems Inc., Box F, Keyser, W.Va. 26726. (304) 788-1662. FAX: (304) 788-1662.

StarCom Inc. Stns: 3 FM. KYRS(FM) Atwater, KKSR(FM) Sartell & WRSR(FM) Two Harbors, all Minn. Ownership: Dennis Carpenter, Sheldon Johnson. Hqtrs: 24 W. Division St., Waite Park, Minn. 56387. (612) 253-9600. FAX: (612) 255-5276.

Stauffer Communications Inc. Stns: 2 AM, 2 FM, 9 TV. KCOY-TV Santa Maria, Calif.; KTVS(TV) Sterling, Colo.; WIBW-AM-FM-TV Topeka, Kan.; KMIZ(TV) Columbia, Mo.; KSTF(TV) Scottsbluff, Neb.; KGNC-AM-FM Amarillo, Tex.; KGWC-TV Casper, KGWN-TV Cheyenne, KGWL-TV Lander & KGWR-TV Rock Springs, all Wyo. Executives: Frank H. Shepherd, pres/CEO (616 Jefferson, Topeka, Kan. 66607; 913-295-1111; FAX: 913-295-1144); Gerald N. Holley, VP bcstg (5600 S.W. 6th, Topeka, Kan. 66606; 913-272-3456). Ownership: John H. Stauffer, chmn, 616 Jefferson, Topeka, Kan. 66607. (913) 295-1111. (See also Cross-Ownership, Sect. A.) Stauffer Communications also owns the Kansas Agriculture Network, Topeka, Kan.; Kansas Information Network, Topeka, Kan.; Weathervue, Topeka, Kan.; Wildcat Sports Network, Topeka, Kan.; & the Kansas City Royals Radio Network, Kansas City, Mo. Hqtrs: 616 Jefferson, Topeka, Kan. 66607. (913) 295-1111. FAX: (913) 295-1144.

Stone Communications. Stns: 1 AM, 2 FM. WAIR(FM) Atlanta, WTRV(FM) Leland & WJML(AM) Petoskey, all Mich. (All 100% owned.) Ownership: Richard D. Stone, 100%. Hqtrs: 322 Bay St., Petoskey, Mich. 49770. (616) 348-2000. FAX: (616) 348-2092.

Straus Media Group. Stns: 3 AM, 3 FM. WCKL(AM)-WCTW(FM) Catskill & WELV(AM)-WWWK(FM) Ellenville, both N.Y.; & WFTR-AM-FM Front Royal, Va. Ownership: R. Peter Straus, Eric P. Straus, Jeanne H. Straus. (See also Cross-Ownership, Sect. A.) Hqtrs: 22 N. Main St., Ellenville, N.Y. 12428. (914) 647-5678. FAX: (914) 647-5008.

Studstill Broadcasting. Stns: 2 AM, 4 FM. WXRS-AM-FM Swainsboro, Ga.; WGLC-AM-FM Mendota, WZLC(FM) Oglesby & WXKO-FM Pana, all Ill. (All 100% owned.) Ownership: Owen L. Studstill Jr., Lamar Studstill, Doris Studstill, Cole Studstill. Hqtrs: WGLC-AM-FM, Box 88, Mendota, Ill. 61342. (815) 539-6751. FAX: (815) 539-5956.

Suburban Radio Group. Stns: 1 AM, 2 FM. WABZ-FM Albemarle & WEGO(AM) Concord, both N.C.; & WWFN(FM) Lake City, S.C. Ownership: Robert R. Hilker, 60%; William R. Rollins, 40%. Note: Robert R. Hilker & William R. Rollins each own 22.5% of WPIQ(AM) & WHJX-FM Brunswick, Ga. & 15% of WFXI(TV) Morehead City, N.C. Hqtrs: Box 888, Belmont, N.C. 28012. (704) 825-5272.

Sudbrink Broadcasting. Stns: 1 AM, 3 TV. WXTL(AM) Jacksonville Beach, Fla.; WTLK-TV Marietta, Ga.; WCEE(TV) Mount Vernon, Ill.; & WDKA(TV) Paducah, Ky. Note: WXTL(AM) Jacksonville Beach, Fla. has a CP to change its city of license to Baldwin, Fla. Ownership: Robert W. Sudbrink, Marion Sudbrink. Hqtrs: 2001 Palm Beach Lakes Blvd., Suite 303, West Palm Beach, Fla. 33409. (407) 684-7488. FAX: (407) 640-7699.

Sudbury Services Inc. & Newport Broadcasting Co. Stns: 5 AM, 4 FM. KLCN(AM)-KHLS(FM) Blytheville, KAWW-AM-FM Heber Springs, KHPA(FM) Hope, KNBY(AM)-KOKR(FM) Newport, KTPA(AM) Prescott & KSUD(AM) West Memphis, all Ark. Executive: Rob Hill, mgr of group opns. Ownership: Harold L. Sudbury Jr., Lydia Sudbury Langston, LaNeal Sudbury Salter. Cable TV: Blytheville TV Cable Co., Blytheville, Ark. Hqtrs: Box 989, Blytheville, Ark. 72315. (501) 762-2093. FAX: (501) 763-8459.

Summit Communications Group Inc. Stns: 3 AM, 4 FM. WAOK(AM) & WVEE(FM) Atlanta; WCAO(AM) & WXYV(FM) Baltimore; KJMZ(FM) Dallas & KHVN(AM) Fort Worth; & WRKS-FM New York. (All 100% owned.) Executives: James W. Wesley Jr., chmn/CEO; James M. Strawn, exec VP/sec; Nanette Allen, VP fin & admin; Roger P. Heffelfinger, VP/treas; Janice Benfield, asst sec. Broadcast division: Mary Catherine Sneed, exec VP radio. Cable division: Adrian Cox, exec VP/gen mgr. Ownership: Principally owned by trusts for the Gordon Gray family. Cable TV: In Georgia serving Atlanta, portions of Barrow County, Cherokee County, Cobb County, north Fulton County & the town of Woodstock; in North Carolina serving Bermuda Run, Clemmons, Davidson County, Forsyth County, Kernersville, Lewisville, Lexington, Rural Hall, portions of Stokes County, Thomasville & Winston-Salem. Hqtrs: 115 Perimeter Ctr. Pl., Suite 1150, Atlanta 30346. (404) 394-0707. FAX: (404) 394-9778.

Sunbrook Communications. Stns: 4 AM, 9 FM. KBLG(AM)-KRKX(FM) Billings, KYYA(FM) Billings, KAAR(FM) Butte, KXTL(AM)-KQUY-FM Butte, KXGF(AM)-KAAK(FM) Great Falls & KGRZ(AM)-KDXT(FM) Missoula, all Mont.; KYSN(FM) East Wenatchee, KXAA(FM) Rock Island & KEEH(FM) Spokane, all Wash. (All 100% owned.) Ownership: Larry Roberts, Edward Cooper, Alan Cooper, Centennial Business Development Fund. Other interests: Montana News Network (a rgnl radio network). Hqtrs: N. 1212 Washington, Suite 124, Spokane, Wash. 99201. (509) 326-9500. FAX: (509) 326-1560.

Sundance Broadcasting Inc. Stns: 4 AM, 4 FM. KOY(AM) Phoenix, KYOT-AM-FM Phoenix & KZON(FM) Phoenix; KIDO(AM) & KLTB(FM) Boise, Idaho; WOKY(AM) Milwaukee & WMIL(FM) Waukesha, both Wis. Executives: Michael D. Jorgenson, pres; David E. Reese, chmn. Hqtrs: Box 20920, Milwaukee 53220. (414) 545-5920. FAX: (414) 545-4069.

SunGroup Inc. Stns: 1 AM, 6 FM. WOWW(FM) Pensacola, Fla.; KMJJ-FM Shreveport, La.; KKSS(FM) Santa Fe, N.M.; KEAN-AM-FM Abilene, KKYS(FM) Bryan & KYKX(FM) Longview, all Tex. Executives: John W. Biddinger, chmn/treas; John E. Southwood Jr., VP fin/CFO; Bennett Scott Smith, VP/sec; James A. Reeder, VP radio. Ownership: publicly traded. Hqtrs: 9102 N. Meridian St., Suite 545, Indianapolis 46260. (317) 844-7425. FAX: (317) 844-7427.

Sunrise Broadcasting Corp. Stns: 3 AM, 5 FM. WQLS-AM-FM Ozark, Ala.; KISP(FM) Blair & KNCY-AM-FM Nebraska City, both Neb.; WGNY-AM-FM Newburgh, N.Y.; & WCKX(FM) London, Ohio. (All 100% owned.) Ownership: CVC Capital Corp. Hqtrs: 131 E. 62nd St., New York 10021. (212) 319-7210. FAX: (212) 832-5611.

Sunshine Wireless Company Inc. Stns: 1 AM, 2 FM. WKIS(FM) Boca Raton (Miami) & WQAM(AM) Miami, both Fla.; & WFOG(FM) Suffolk (Norfolk), Va. Hqtrs: 9881 Sheridan St., Hollywood, Fla. 33024. (305) 431-6200.

Susquehanna Radio Corp. Stns: 6 AM, 10 FM. KNBR(AM) & KFOG(FM) San Francisco; WNNX(FM) Atlanta; WFMS(FM) & WGRL(FM) Indianapolis; WRRM(FM) Cincinnati; WARM(AM) Scranton, WMGS(FM) Wilkes-Barre & WSBA(AM)-WARM-FM York, all Pa.; KLIF(AM) Dallas, KPLX(FM) Fort Worth & KRBE-AM-FM Houston; & WGH-AM-FM Newport News, Va. Note: Group also operates WBHT(FM) Mountaintop, Pa. under a loc mktg agreement. Executives: Louis J. Appell Jr., chmn; Arthur W. Carlson, pres; Larry Grogan, exec VP; Craig W. Bremer, gen counsel/sec; David E. Kennedy, sr VP; Charles T. Morgan, sr VP/dir engrg; Joe Barlek, VP/controller; Sue Krom, VP admin; Rick McDonald, VP progmg. Ownership: A subsidiary of Susquehanna Pfaltzgraff Co. Cable TV. Hqtrs: 140 E. Market St., York, Pa. 17401. (717) 852-2132.

Jimmy Swaggart Ministries. Stns: 2 AM, 1 FM. WLUX(AM) & KAFL(FM) Baton Rouge; & WJYM(AM) Bowling Green, Ohio. (All 100% owned.) Executives: Jimmy Swaggart, pres; Donnie Swaggart, VP; Frances Swaggart, sec/treas. Additional bd members: Clyde Fuller, Elizabeth Fuller. Jimmy Swaggart Ministries owns Starcom, a TV prod facility in Baton Rouge. Hqtrs: Box 262550, Baton Rouge 70821. (504) 768-8300. FAX: (504) 769-2244.

T

T.C.T. Communications Inc. See Cobb Communications Inc.

TGR Broadcasting Inc. Stns: 2 AM, 2 FM. KLFA(FM) King City (Salinas), KLOQ(AM) Merced, KTGE(AM) Salinas & KFMK(FM) Winton, all Calif. (All 100% owned.) Ownership: Hector Villalobos, Jose Villalobos, Carlos Moncada, Jose Moncada. Hqtrs: 548 E. Alisal St., Suite A, Salinas, Calif. 93905. (408) 757-1910. FAX: (408) 757-9582.

TK Communications Inc. Stns: 2 AM, 3 FM. WSRF (AM)-WSHE(FM) Fort Lauderdale & WHOO(AM)-WHTQ(FM) Orlando, both Fla.; & KLUV(FM) Dallas. (All 100% owned.) Executive: John F. Tenaglia, chmn, CEO.

Ownership: John F. Tenaglia, Robert K. Weary. Hqtrs: 110 S.E. 6th St., Suite 1601, Fort Lauderdale, Fla. 33301. (305) 525-8500. FAX: (305) 462-4949.

TM Multi-Regions Inc. Stns: 5 TV. CJPM-TV Chicoutimi, CFCM-TV Quebec City, CFER-TV Rimouski, CHLT-TV Sherbrooke & CHEM-TV Trois-Rivieres, all Que. (All stns are located in Canada.) Ownership: Tele-Metropole Inc., 100%. Hqtrs: Tele-4, 1000 Myrand Ave., Ste.-Foy, Que., Canada G1V 2W3. (418) 688-9330. FAX: (418) 681-4239.

TMZ Broadcasting Co. (dba Telemedia Broadcasting) Stns: 5 AM, 7 FM. WTAD(AM) & WQCY(FM) Quincy, Ill.; WEST(AM)-WLEV(FM) Easton, WQKK(FM) Ebensburg, WRKZ(FM) Hershey, WRSC(AM) State College & WQWK(FM) University Park, all Pa.; WLKW(AM)-WWLI(FM) & WPRO-AM-FM Providence, R.I. Executive: Ira Rosenblatt, VP of opns. Ownership: Robert E. Tudek, chmn, 50%; Everett I. Mundy, vice chmn, 50%. Cable TV. Hqtrs: Box 39, Bellefonte, Pa. 16823. (814) 355-8355. FAX: (814) 353-2072.

Tak Communications Inc. Stns: 3 FM, 6 TV. WTPX(FM) Fort Lauderdale, Fla.; KITV(TV) Honolulu; WKIO(FM) Urbana, Ill.; WGRZ-TV Buffalo, N.Y.; WUSL(FM) Philadelphia; WQOW-TV Eau Claire, WXOW-TV La Crosse, WKOW-TV Madison & WAOW-TV Wausau, all Wis. Hqtrs: 1355 Piccard Dr., Suite 350, Rockville, Md. 20850. (301) 921-8880. FAX: (301) 921-9396.

Talley Radio Stations. Stns: 2 AM, 2 FM. WSMI-AM-FM Litchfield, Ill.; & KBKB-AM-FM Fort Madison, Iowa. (All 100% owned.) Ownership: Hayward L. Talley. Hqtrs: Box 10, Litchfield, Ill. 62056. (217) 324-5921.

Sarkes Tarzian Inc. Stns: 1 AM, 3 FM, 2 TV. WGCL(AM)-WTTS(FM) Bloomington, WAJI(FM) Fort Wayne & WJLT(FM) Fort Wayne, all Ind.; KTVN(TV) Reno; & WRCB-TV Chattanooga. Ownership: Pat Tarzian, Tom Tarzian, Mary Tarzian. Hqtrs: Box 62, Bloomington, Ind. 47402. (812) 332-7251.

Tate Communications Inc. Stns: 1 AM, 2 FM. KMCK(FM) Siloam Springs, Ark.; KTEX(FM) Brownsville & KVJY(AM) Pharr, both Tex. Ownership: Harvey J. Tate, George Hochman. Hqtrs: Box 1808, Harlingen, Tex. 78551. (210) 423-5068. FAX: (210) 421-2582.

Taylor Broadcasting. Stns: 1 AM, 4 FM. WQBZ(FM) Fort Valley, Ga. (100%); WMDH-AM-FM New Castle, Ind. (67.5%); WTLZ(FM) Saginaw, Mich. (67.5%); & WIKS(FM) New Bern, N.C. (100%). Ownership: Stephen Taylor, 52%; Edward Taylor IV, 24%; Suzanne Taylor, 24%. Hqtrs: 598 W. Sandtown Rd., Marietta, Ga. 30064. (404) 421-1165.

Taylor Communications Inc. Stns: 1 AM, 4 FM. WIVY-FM Jacksonville, WXXL(FM) Leesburg & WEAT-AM-FM West Palm Beach, all Fla.; & WCOD-FM Hyannis, Mass. Ownership: John J. Taylor Jr., John J. Taylor III. Hqtrs: 11780 U.S. Hwy. 1, Suite 204, North Palm Beach, Fla. 33408. (407) 775-1777. FAX: (407) 694-8387.

Tel Lease Inc. Stns: 1 AM, 2 FM. WNRJ(AM)-WAHC(FM) Circleville & WWHT(FM) Marysville, both Ohio. Hqtrs: 2000 W. Henderson Rd., Suite 400, Columbus, Ohio 43220. (614) 442-2000.

Telemedia Communications Inc. Stns: 12 AM, 14 FM. CFBG-FM Bracebridge, CKSL(AM) & CIQM-FM London, CICZ-FM Midland, CFCH(AM) & CKAT-FM North Bay, CICX-FM Orillia, CHAS-FM Sault Ste. Marie, CJCS(AM) Stratford, CIGM(AM) & CJRQ-FM Sudbury, CKGB(AM) & CJQQ-FM Timmins, & CJCL(AM) Toronto, all Ont.; CJMT(AM) & CFIX-FM Chicoutimi, CKCH(AM) & CIMF-FM Hull, CKAC(AM) & CITE-FM Montreal, CITF-FM Quebec, CHLT(AM) & CITE-FM-1 Sherbrooke, CKTS(AM) Sherbrooke, & CHLN(AM) & CHEY-FM Trois Rivieres, all Que. (All stns are located in Canada.) Hqtrs: 50 Holly St., Toronto, Ont., Canada M4S 3B3. (416) 482-8600. FAX: (416) 482-9633.

Telemundo Group Inc. Stns: 7 TV. KVEA(TV) Corona & KSTS(TV) San Jose, both Calif.; WSCV(TV) Fort Lauderdale, Fla.; WNJU(TV) Linden, N.J.; KTMD(TV) Galveston & KVDA(TV) San Antonio, both Tex.; & WKAQ-TV San Juan, P.R. Executives: Saul P. Steinberg, chmn; Jose C. Cancela, pres stn group. Ownership: Reliance Group Holdings. Hqtrs: 1740 Broadway, New York 10019. (212) 492-5500. FAX: (212) 492-9498.

TeleSouth Communications. Stns: 2 AM, 2 FM. WVMI(AM)-WQID(FM) Biloxi & WKXG(AM)-WYMX(FM) Greenwood, both Miss. Ownership: Steve Davenport. Hqtrs: 6310 I-55 N., Jackson, Miss. 39211. (601) 957-1700. FAX: (601) 956-5228.

Television Station Partners. Stns: 4 TV. WRDW-TV Augusta, Ga.; WEYI-TV Saginaw, Mich.; WROC-TV Rochester, N.Y.; & WTOV-TV Steubenville, Ohio. (All 100% owned.) Executives: I. Martin Pompadur, mgng gen ptnr/CEO; Victor Kopko, CFO. Ownership: R K Companies is a gen ptnr. (See also Pompadur-Becker Group.) Hqtrs: 350 Park Ave., New York 10017. (212) 980-7110.

Tichenor Media System Inc. Stns: 7 AM, 6 FM. WIND(AM) Chicago & WOJO(FM) Evanston, both Ill.; KUNO(AM) Corpus Christi (26%), KBNA-AM-FM El Paso, KGBT(AM)-KIWW(FM) Harlingen, KLAT(AM) Houston, KSAB(FM) Robstown (26%), KCOR(AM)-KROM(FM) San Antonio & KXTN-AM-FM San Antonio, all Tex. Note: Group also operates KLTN(FM) Port Arthur, Tex. through a loc mktg agreement. Ownership: Over 90% owned by the Tichenor family (McHenry Tichenor, McHenry T. Tichenor, McHenry T. Tichenor Jr., Warren Tichenor, Jean T. Russell, Bill Tichenor, David Tichenor). Hqtrs: 100 Crescent Ct., Suite 1777, Dallas 75201. (214) 855-8882. FAX: (214) 855-8881.

Timm Enterprises. Stns: 4 AM, 5 FM. WVOJ(AM) Jacksonville, WOZN(FM) Key West (80%), WSGL(FM) Naples & WANM(AM)-WGLF(FM) Tallahassee, all Fla.; WDMG-AM-FM Douglas & WRCC-AM-FM Warner Robins, both Ga. Hqtrs: Box 1874, Tallahassee, Fla. 32302. (904) 224-4001. FAX: (904) 222-8688.

Tipple Communications Inc. Stns: 3 FM. KKLI(FM) Widefield (Colorado Springs), Colo.; KVLY(FM) Edinburg (McAllen) & KNCN(FM) Sinton (Corpus Christi), both Tex. Ownership: Henry B. Tippie (over 90%). Hqtrs: Box 26557, Austin, Tex. 78755. (512) 346-1800.

Tri State Broadcasting Co. Stns: 2 AM, 2 FM. WTVB(AM)-WNWN(FM) Coldwater & WHEZ(AM)-WFAT(FM) Portage (Kalamazoo), both Mich. Executive: Gary B. Mallemee, pres. Hqtrs: Box 1590, Coldwater, Mich. 49036. (517) 279-9767. FAX: (517) 279-9760.

Tribune Broadcasting Co. Stns: 3 AM, 3 FM, 7 TV. KTLA(TV) Los Angeles & KCTC(AM)-KYMX(FM) Sacramento, both Calif.; KEZW(AM) Aurora & KOSI(FM)-KWGN-TV Denver, both Colo.; WGNX(TV) Atlanta; WGN-AM-TV Chicago; WGNO(TV) New Orleans; WQCD(FM) & WPIX(TV) New York; & WPHL-TV Philadelphia. Note: Group has purchased WLVI-TV Cambridge, Mass., pending FCC approval. Group also operates Tribune Entertainment Co. based in Chicago & ChicagoLand Television, a rgnl news cable ch. Executives: James Dowdle, pres/CEO; Marc Schacher, VP progmg; Shaun Sheehan, VP Washington; Gerald W. Agema, VP opns/CFO; William Murray, dir info systems; George Babick, VP corporate dev; Richard Stone, VP Tribune Plus; Cynthia Vivian, dir human resources; Dennis J. FitzSimons, pres Tribune Television; Wayne Vriesman, VP radio group; Ira Goldstone, dir engrg. (See also Cross-Ownership, Sect. A.) Hqtrs: 435 N. Michigan Ave., Chicago 60611. (312) 222-3333.

Trinity Broadcasting Network. Stns: 1 AM, 1 FM, 11 TV. KPAZ-TV Phoenix; KTBN-TV Santa Ana, Calif. (Los Angeles); WHFT(TV) Miami; WHSG(TV) Monroe, Ga.; WCLJ(TV) Bloomington & WKOI(TV) Richmond, both Ind.; WTBY(TV) Poughkeepsie, N.Y.; WDLI(TV) Canton, Ohio; KTBO-TV Oklahoma City; KDTX-TV Dallas; KGHO(AM) Hoquiam, KGHO-FM Hoquiam-Aberdeen & KTBW-TV Tacoma, all Wa. Executive: Paul F. Crouch, pres. Ownership: nonprofit corporation. Hqtrs: 2442 Michelle Dr., Tustin, Calif. 92680; Box A, Santa Ana, Calif. 92711. (714) 832-2950. FAX: (714) 730-0657.

Tri-State Christian Television. Stns: 6 TV. WTCT(TV) Marion, Ill.; WINM(TV) Angola, Ind.; WAQP(TV) Saginaw & WTLJ(TV) Muskegon, both Mich.; WNYB-TV Buffalo, N.Y.; & WLXI-TV Greensboro, N.C. Note: Group also owns low power TV stns W66BD Fort Wayne, Ind. (ch 66); W54AE Paducah, Ky. (ch 54); W59CA Jackson (ch 59), W24BO Kalamazoo (ch 24) & W69BJ Lansing (ch 69), all Mich.; W59BV Rochester, N.Y. (ch 59). Ownership: nonprofit corporation. Hqtrs: Box 1010, Marion, Ill. 62959. (618) 997-9333. FAX: (618) 997-1859.

Trumper Communications Inc. Stns: 1 AM, 5 FM. WLAP(AM)-WMXL(FM) Lexington & WWYC(FM) Winchester, both Ky.; WEZC(FM) Hickory & WTDR(FM) Statesville (Charlotte), both N.C.; & KKCW(FM) Beaverton (Portland), Ore. Ownership: Jeffrey E. Trumper. Hqtrs: 900 Oakmont Ln., Suite 210, Westmont, Ill. 60559. (708) 789-0090. FAX: (708) 789-0102.

Tschudy Communications Corp. Stns: 1 AM, 3 FM. WBRJ(AM) & WEYQ(FM) Marietta, Ohio; WSKO(FM) Buffalo Gap, Va.; & WMQC(FM) Westover, W.Va. Ownership: Earl Judy Jr., 100%. Hqtrs: 15 Campbell St., Luray, Va. 22835. (703) 743-3000. FAX: (703) 743-3002.

Twin W Communications Co. Stns: 2 AM, 1 FM. KKFR(FM) Glendale & KFYI(AM) Phoenix, both Ariz.; & WCAR(AM) Livonia, Mich. (All 100% owned.) Ownership: Walter Wolpin, Fredric Weber. Hqtrs: 1600 Modern, Detroit 48203. (313) 865-3900. FAX: (313) 865-0010.

U

UNO Broadcasting Corp. Stns: 4 AM, 4 FM. KBLU(AM) & KTTI(FM) Yuma, Ariz.; WJOL(AM) & WLLI-FM Joliet, Ill.; KTOP(AM) & KDVV(FM) Topeka, Kan.; KKMY(FM) Orange (Beaumont) & KOLE(AM) Port Arthur, both Tex. Ownership: Robert J. Tezak, 100%. Hqtrs: 10 Joyce Rd., Joliet, Ill. 60435. (815) 744-8603. FAX: (815) 744-8602.

U.S. Radio L.P. Stns: 4 AM, 6 FM. WRAW(AM) & WRFY-FM Reading, Pa.; KJOJ(AM)-KKZR(FM) Conroe, KHEY-AM-FM El Paso & KJOJ-FM Freeport, both Tex.; WOWI(FM) Norfolk, WSVY(AM) Portsmouth & WQOK(FM) South Boston, all Va. Ownership: US Radio Group Inc., gen ptnr. Note: Ragan A. Henry owns 100% of US Radio Group Inc. Other interests: Ragan Henry Broadcast Group Inc. (see listing), U.S. Radio II Inc. [licensee of KMGR(AM) Murray & KMXB(FM) Orem, both Utah], U.S. Radio IV Inc. [licensee of KIDZ(FM) Brigham City & KCPX(AM)-KUMT(FM) Centerville, both Utah] & Allur Communications Group Inc. [owner of WDZR(FM) Mount Clemens, Mich.; KJLA(AM) Independence, Mo.; WCMC(AM) & WZXL(FM) Wildwood, N.J.; & operator of KISF(FM) Lexington, Mo. under a loc mktg agreement]. Hqtrs: 1234 Market St., Suite 1940, Philadelphia 19107. (215) 563-2910. FAX: (215) 563-9947.

United Communications Corp. Stns: 2 TV. KEYC-TV Mankato, Minn.; & WWNY-TV Carthage, N.Y. (Both 100% owned.) (See also Cross-Ownership, Sect. A.) Ownership: Howard J. Brown. Hqtrs: 1209 Orange St., Wilmington, Del. 19801. (414) 657-1000. FAX: (414) 657-5101.

United Television Inc. Stns: 5 TV. KUTP(TV) Phoenix; KBHK-TV San Francisco; KMSP-TV Minneapolis; KMOL-TV San Antonio, Tex.; & KTVX(TV) Salt Lake City. (All 100% owned.) Executives: Evan C. Thompson, pres/COO; Garth S. Lindsey, exec VP. Ownership: Chris-Craft Industries Inc., 50.3% (see listing). Hqtrs: 8501 Wilshire Blvd., Suite 340, Beverly Hills, Calif. 90211. (310) 854-0426. (310) 659-8121.

Universal Broadcasting Corp. Stns: 3 AM, 2 FM. KPPC(AM) Pasadena, Calif.; WCBW(FM) Columbia, Ill.; WSYW-FM Danville (Indianapolis) & WSYW(AM) Indianapolis, both Ind.; & WTHE(AM) Mineola, N.Y. Ownership: Marvin B. Kosofsky, Howard Warshaw & Miriam Warshaw. Howard & Miriam Warshaw are owns of Alchemy Communications Corp., which owns WKIX(AM) & WYLT(FM) Raleigh, N.C. Marvin B. Kosofsky owns 50% & Howard Warshaw owns 25% of Bursam Communications Corp., licensee of WVNJ(AM) Oakland, N.J. Marvin B. Kosofsky owns 14.1% of publicly traded Jacor Communications Inc., which owns KAZY(FM), KOA(AM) & KRFX(FM) Denver; WQIK-AM-FM Jacksonville & WFLA(AM)-WFLZ-FM Tampa, both Fla.; WGST(AM) & WPCH(FM) Atlanta; WLW(AM), WLWA(AM) & WEBN(FM) Cincinnati; & WMYU(FM) Sevierville (Knoxville), Tenn. West Coast offices: 3844 E. Foothill Blvd., Pasadena, Calif. 91107. (818) 577-1224. Corporate offices (Howard Warshaw, pres): 1086 Teaneck Rd., Teaneck, N.J. 07666. (201) 837-0400. FAX: (201) 837-9664.

University Broadcasting Co. Stns: 1 AM, 3 FM. KCOL(AM) & KIMN-FM Fort Collins, Colo.; WBWB(FM) Bloomington & WAZY(FM) Lafayette, both Ind. (All 100% owned.) Ownership: Heritage Venture Partners II. Hqtrs: 135 N. Pennsylvania St., Suite 2380, Indianapolis 46204. (317) 635-5696. FAX: (317) 635-5699.

V

Valu Broadcasting Inc. Stns: 1 AM, 2 FM. KVOE(AM)-KFFX(FM) Emporia & KFNF(FM) Oberlin, both Kan. Ownership: Steve Sauder. Hqtrs: Box 968, Emporia, Kan. 66801. (316) 342-1400. FAX: (316) 342-0804.

Carolyn G. Vance Group. Stns: 1 AM, 2 FM. KEEE(AM)-KJCS(FM) Nacogdoches & KISX(FM) Whitehouse, both Tex. Hqtrs: 1200 Briar Crest, Suite 4000, Bryan, Tex. 77802. (409) 779-1200. FAX: (409) 779-0248.

Broadcasting & Cable Yearbook 1994
A-115

VerStandig Broadcasting Stns: 3 AM, 3 FM. WCBG(AM) Chambersburg, WSRT(FM) Mercersburg & WHGT(AM)-WAYZ-FM Waynesboro, all Pa.; WSVA(AM) & WQPO(FM) Harrisonburg, Va. (All 100% owned.) Executive: John VerStandig, pres. Ownership: M.B. VerStandig Inc., Helen VerStandig, John VerStandig. Hqtrs: 4850 Connecticut Ave. N.W., Suite 103, Washington 20008. (202) 244-1422.

Viacom Broadcasting Inc. Stns: 3 AM, 11 FM, 5 TV. KXEZ(FM)-KYSR(FM) Los Angeles, KSRY(FM) San Francisco & KSRI(FM) Santa Cruz, all Calif.; WVIT(TV) New Britain, Conn.; WMZQ-FM Washington; WLIT-FM Chicago; KSLA-TV Shreveport, La.; WLTI(FM) Detroit; KMOV(TV) St. Louis; WNYT(TV) Albany, WLTW(FM) New York & WHEC-TV Rochester, all N.Y.; WCPT(AM) Alexandria, WMZQ(AM) Arlington & WCXR-FM Woodbridge, all Va.; KBSG(AM) Auburn, KNDD(FM) Seattle & KBSG-FM Tacoma, all Wa. Executives: Edward Horowitz, chmn/CEO; Francis P. Brady, sr VP/pres TV div; William R. Figenshu, sr VP/pres radio div; Kevin Reymond, sr VP/CFO. Ownership: Viacom International Inc. Cable TV: Viacom Cable. Hqtrs: 1515 Broadway, 40th Fl., New York 10036. (212) 258-7136. FAX: (212) 258-7154.

The Village Companies. Stns: 1 AM, 2 FM. WKQQ(FM) Lexington, Ky.; WZZU(FM) Burlington-Graham (Raleigh) & WCHL(AM) Chapel Hill, both N.C. (All 100% owned.) Ownership: James A. Heavner, 90%. (See also Cross-Ownership, Sect. A.) Hqtrs: Box 3300, Chapel Hill, N.C. 27515. (919) 968-4811. FAX: (919) 968-3748.

Visionary Related Entertainment Inc. Stns: 2 AM, 4 FM. KAOE(FM) Hilo, KKON(AM)-KAOY(FM) Kealakekua, KAOI(AM) Kihei, KDLX(FM) Makawao & KAOI-FM Wailuku, all Hawaii. Executive: John Detz, pres. Hqtrs: Box 15261, Santa Rosa, Calif. 95402. (707) 528-0339.

Voyager Communications. Stns: 3 AM, 4 FM. WMFR(AM)-WMAG(FM) High Point & WRDU(FM) Wilson (Raleigh-Durham), both N.C.; WOIC(AM)-WNOK-FM Columbia & WLWZ-AM-FM Easley (Greenville-Spartanburg), both S.C. (All 100% owned.) Ownership: Carl Venters, chmn; Jack McCarthy, pres; Fred Setzer & others. Hqtrs: 3201 Glenwood Ave., Suite 301, Raleigh, N.C. 27612. (919) 781-7333. FAX: (919) 781-7443.

W

WAMC/Northeast Public Radio. Stns: 6 FM. WAMQ(FM) Great Barrington, Mass.; WAMC(FM) Albany, WCAN(FM) Canajoharie, WAMK(FM) Kingston, WOSR(FM) Middletown & WANC(FM) Ticonderoga, all N.Y. (All 100% owned.) Ownership: Non-stock educ corporation. Hqtrs: 318 Central Ave., Albany, N.Y. 12206. (518) 465-5233. FAX: (518) 432-0991.

WDUN Radio Inc. Stns: 2 AM, 1 FM. WMJE(FM) Clarkesville, WDUN(AM) Gainesville & WGGA(AM) Gainesville, all Ga. (All 100% owned.) Ownership: John W. Jacobs III & John W. Jacobs Jr. Hqtrs: Box 10, 1102 Thompson Bridge Rd., Gainesville, Ga. 30503. (404) 532-9921. FAX: (404) 532-0506.

WENK Broadcast Group Inc. Stns: 2 AM, 3 FM. WWKF(FM) Fulton, Ky.; WTPR(AM)-WAKQ(FM) Paris, WAAT(FM) Tiptonville & WENK(AM) Union City, all Tenn. Ownership: Terry L. Hailey, pres; E.B. Tanner, Tom F. Elam, W.P. Burnett Jr., William H. Latimer III. Hqtrs: 1729 Nailling Dr., Union City, Tenn. 38261. (901) 885-1240. FAX: (901) 885-3405.

WESHAM Broadcasting Co. Stns: 1 AM, 3 FM. WAVH(FM) Mobile, WKSJ-FM Mobile & WKSJ(AM) Prichard, all Ala.; & WRKA(FM) St. Matthews (Louisville), Ky. Hqtrs: Box 160706, Mobile, Ala. 36616. (205) 343-1000. FAX: (205) 344-6006.

WIN Communications Inc. Stns: 4 AM, 6 FM. KORG(AM) & KEZY(FM) Anaheim, Calif.; WICC(AM) Bridgeport & WEBE(FM) Westport, both Connecticut; WCKN(AM) & WRZX(FM) Indianapolis; WQAL(FM) Cleveland; WMXN(FM) Norfolk, Va.; WFID(FM) Rio Piedras & WUNO(AM) San Juan, both P.R. [All 100% owned except for WFID(FM) & WUNO(AM).] Note: WCKN(AM) & WRZX(FM) Indianapolis have been sold, subject to FCC approval. Ownership: ML Media. Note: Century Communications owns 50% of WFID(FM) Rio Piedras & WUNO(AM) San Juan, both P.R. Cable TV. Hqtrs: 40 Richards Ave., Norwalk, Conn. 06854. (203) 857-5602.

WMRI Inc. Stns: 1 AM, 4 FM. WYEZ(FM) Bremen, WEZV-FM Brookston, WGOM(AM)-WMRI(FM) Marion & WLEZ(FM) Terre Haute (80%), all Ind. Hqtrs: Box 1538, Marion, Ind. 46952. (317) 664-7396. FAX: (317) 668-6767.

WPAY/WPFB Inc. Stns: 2 AM, 2 FM. WPFB-AM-FM Middletown & WPAY-AM-FM Portsmouth, both Ohio. Ownership: Ruth M. Braden & Douglas L. Braden, 100%. Hqtrs: 4505 Central Ave., Middletown, Ohio 45044. (513) 422-3625. FAX: (513) 424-9732.

WPNT Inc. Stns: 1 AM, 2 FM. KXOK-FM Florissant & KXOK(AM) St. Louis, both Mo.; & WLTJ(FM) Pittsburgh. (All 100% owned.) Ownership: Saul Frischling. Hqtrs: 1044 Northern Blvd., Suite 209, Roslyn, N.Y. 11576. (516) 621-1670. FAX: (516) 621-1697.

WSHN Inc. Stns: 2 AM, 2 FM. WSHN-AM-FM Fremont, WCMM(FM) Gulliver & WTIQ(AM) Manistique, all Mich. (All 100% owned.) Ownership: Stuart Noordyk. Hqtrs: Box 190, 517 N. Beebe St., Fremont, Mich. 49412. (616) 924-4700. FAX: (616) 924-4534.

WTMJ Inc. Stns: 2 AM, 3 FM, 3 TV. KQRC-FM Leavenworth, Kan.; WSYM-TV Lansing, Mich.; KTNV(TV) Las Vegas; WTMJ-AM-TV/WKTI(FM) Milwaukee & WSAU(AM)-WIFC(FM) Wausau, both Wis. (All 100% owned.) Ownership: Journal Communications Inc., 100%. (See also Cross-Ownership, Sect. A.) Hqtrs: 720 E. Capitol Dr., Milwaukee 53201. (414) 332-9611. FAX: (404) 223-5400.

Wabash Valley Broadcasting Corp. Stns: 1 AM, 1 FM, 3 TV. WFTX(TV) Cape Coral (Fort Myers-Naples market) & WOGX(TV) Ocala (Gainesville market), both Fla.; & WTHI-AM-FM-TV Terre Haute, Ind. (All 100% owned.) Executives: Chris Duffy, pres; John Newcomb, exec VP; Jim Borgioli, VP engrg. Ownership: Hulman & Co., 81.2%. Hqtrs: 401 Pennsylvania Pkwy., Suite 300, Indianapolis 46280. (317) 844-7484.

Walker Broadcasting. Stns: 3 AM, 2 FM. WBUG(AM) Amsterdam, WRWD(AM) Cornwall, WBUG-FM Fort Plain, WRWD-FM Highland & WBGG(AM) Saratoga Springs, all N.Y. Hqtrs: Box 570, Amsterdam, N.Y. 12010. (518) 843-1570.

Walton Co. Stns: 2 AM, 2 FM. WHTC(AM) & WKEZ(FM) Holland, Mich.; WHBL(AM) & WWJR(FM) Sheboygan, Wis. Ownership: Michael R. Walton, 100%. Hqtrs: 2100 Washington Ave., Sheboygan, Wis. 53081. (414) 458-2100.

Walton Stations. Stns: 3 AM, 3 FM. KKCS-AM-FM Colorado Springs; KBUY(AM) & KWES(FM) Ruidoso, N.M.; KDJW(AM) & KBUY-FM Amarillo, Tex. Ownership: John B. Walton, 100%. Hqtrs: Box 776, Kermit, Tex. 79745. (915) 586-3366. FAX: (915) 586-3958.

Warner Stations. Stns: 4 AM, 3 FM. KRLN-AM-FM Canon City, KSTR(AM) Grand Junction & KSTR-FM Montrose, all Colo.; KWBE(AM) Beatrice & KLIN(AM)-KEZG(FM) Lincoln, both Neb. Ownership: Norton E. Warner & Diana H. Warner. Hqtrs: 4343 O St., Lincoln, Neb. 68510. (402) 475-4567. FAX: (402) 797-1411.

Waterman Broadcasting Corp. Stns: 1 AM, 1 FM, 2 TV. WBBH-TV Fort Myers, Fla.; KTSA(AM) & KTFM(FM) San Antonio, Tex.; & WVIR-TV Charlottesville, Va. Ownership: Bernard Waterman. Hqtrs: Box 7578, Fort Myers, Fla. 33911-7578. (813) 939-2020. FAX: (813) 275-4294.

Webster Broadcasting. Stns: 2 AM, 3 FM. WMFL(AM) & WJPH(FM) Monticello, Fla.; KKHR(FM) Anson & KGDD(AM)-KBUS(FM) Paris, both Tex. (All 100% owned.) Executive: Suzy Dutton, exec VP. Hqtrs: 2303 S. Danville, Abilene, Tex. 79605. (915) 691-9898. FAX: (915) 691-9991.

West Group Broadcasting Corp. Stns: 1 AM, 2 FM. KIZN(FM) Meridian, Idaho; KFSB(AM) Joplin & KIXQ(FM) Webb City, both Mo. Note: Group operates KZMG(FM) New Plymouth, Idaho through a loc mktg agreement. Ownership: Paul Meacham & Richard M. Reider. Hqtrs: 2000 S. College Ave., Suite 305, Fort Collins, Colo. 80525. (303) 221-5758. FAX: (303) 221-0755.

West Virginia Radio Corp. Stns: 3 AM, 4 FM. WCAW(AM)-WVAF(FM) Charleston, WCHS(AM)-WKWS(FM) Charleston, WKKW-FM Clarksburg & WAJR(AM)-WVAQ(FM) Morgantown, all W.Va. (All 100% owned.) Ownership: John R. Raese, David A. Raese. (See also Cross-Ownership, Sect. A.) Hqtrs: 1251 Earl L. Core Rd., Morgantown, W.Va. 26505. (304) 296-0029. (304) 296-3876.

Westcoast Broadcasting Inc. Stns: 1 AM, 2 FM. KKJG(FM) San Luis Obispo & KJUG-AM-FM Tulare, both Calif. (All 100% owned.) Ownership: Larry W. Woods, 100%. Hqtrs: 717 N. Mooney Blvd., Tulare, Calif. 93274. (209) 686-2866. FAX: (209) 686-5265.

Westinghouse Broadcasting Co. (Group W). Stns: 9 AM, 7 FM, 5 TV. WJZ-TV Baltimore; WBZ-AM-TV Boston; WMAQ(AM) Chicago; WLLZ(FM) Detroit; KIKK-FM & KILT-AM-FM Houston; KFWB(AM) & KTWV(FM) Los Angeles; WINS(AM) & WNEW(FM) New York; KIKK(AM) Pasadena, Tex.; KYW-AM-TV & WMMR(FM) Philadelphia; KDKA-AM-TV Pittsburgh; KFBK(AM) & KGBY(FM) Sacramento, Calif.; KPIX(TV) San Francisco. Note: Group has bought KKHI-AM-FM San Francisco & sold KFBK(AM)-KGBY(FM) Sacramento, Calif., subject to FCC approval. Executives: Burton B. Staniar, chmn/CEO; Bill Korn, pres; Jonathan Klein, pres Group W television; Dan Mason, pres Group W radio; John Waugaman, exec VP Group W radio; Donald Mitzner, pres Group W Satellite Communications; Derk Zimmerman, pres Group W Productions; Robert E. Buenting Jr., VP/controller; John D. Moran, VP human resources & admin; Martin P. Messinger, VP/chief counsel; Gil Schwartz, VP communications. Ownership: Westinghouse Broadcasting Co. is a wholly owned subsidiary of Westinghouse Electric Corp. Also owns Group W Productions, Los Angeles (production & syndication); Group W VideoServices, Pittsburgh (tape duplication & uplink svcs); Group W Satellite Communications, Stamford, Conn. (satellite uplink & cable proging). Hqtrs: 888 7th Ave., New York 10106. (212) 307-3000.

Westwind Broadcasting Inc. Stns: 1 AM, 2 FM. KPUR(AM)-KLSF(FM) Amarillo & KPUR-FM Canyon, both Tex. Hqtrs: Box 7407, Amarillo, Tex. 79114. (806) 371-9797. FAX: (806) 371-9129.

Wheeler Broadcasting Inc. Stns: 2 AM, 3 FM. WJNR-FM Iron Mountain, Mich.; KWNO-FM Rushford & KWNO(AM) Winona, both Minn.; WTCH(AM) & WOWN(FM) Shawano, Wis. Ownership: Ray L. Wheeler, Bruce Grassman. Hqtrs: 2045 Fawn Ln., Green Bay, Wis. 54304. (414) 494-7708. FAX: (414) 494-7708.

Mel Wheeler Inc. Stns: 1 AM, 1 FM, 3 TV. WSIL-TV Harrisburg, Ill.; KRCG(TV) Jefferson City & KPOB-TV Poplar Bluff, both Mo.; WSLC(AM) & WSLQ(FM) Roanoke, Va. (All 100% owned.) Ownership: Mel Wheeler, 70%; Clark Wheeler, 10%; Leonard Wheeler, 10%; Steve Wheeler, 10%. Hqtrs: 1507 S. University Dr., No. 146, Fort Worth 76107-9501. (817) 338-4475.

Wilkerson Broadcasting Group. Stns: 2 AM, 1 FM. WLIL-AM-FM Lenoir City & WLIK(AM) Newport, both Tenn. Ownership: Arthur Wilkerson, 100%. Hqtrs: Box 340, Lenoir City, Tenn. 37771. (615) 986-7536. FAX: (615) 986-1716.

Williams County Broadcasting System Inc. Stns: 2 AM, 2 FM. WLKM-AM-FM Three Rivers, Mich.; WQCT(AM) & WBNO-FM Bryan, Ohio. (All 100% owned.) Executive: Carl L. Shipley, pres. Ownership: Carl L. Shipley, J. William Middendorf III. Hqtrs: Box 603, Bryan, Ohio 43506. (419) 636-3175. FAX: (419) 636-4570.

Willis Broadcasting Corp. Stns: 8 AM, 11 FM. WAYE(AM) Birmingham, Ala.; KMZX(FM) Lonoke, KFTH(FM) Marion & KLRG(AM) North Little Rock, all Ark.; WIMV(FM) Madison, Fla.; WTJH(AM) East Point, Ga.; WPZZ(FM) Franklin, Ind.; WBOK(AM) New Orleans; WJXN(AM) Jackson, WJXN-FM Utica & WJNS-FM Yazoo City, all Miss.; WCLN-FM Clinton, WSRC(AM) Durham, WMYK(FM) Moyock, WTNC(AM) Thomasville & WGTM(AM) Wilson, all N.C.; WKWQ(FM) Batesburg & WKSO(FM) Orangeburg, both S.C.; WSVY-FM Windsor, Va. (All 100% owned.) Note: WIMV(FM) Madison, Fla. has been exchanged for WVCA(FM) Selma, Ala., subject to FCC approval. Hqtrs: 645 Church St., Suite 400, Norfolk, Va. 23510. (804) 622-4600. FAX: (804) 624-6515.

Willis Family Broadcasting Corp. Stns: 7 AM, 1 FM. WESL(AM) East St. Louis, Ill.; WWCA(AM) Gary, Ind.; WGSP(AM) Charlotte & WBXB(FM) Edenton, both N.C.; WURD(AM) Philadelphia; WXSS(AM) Memphis; KDFT(AM) Ferris, Tex.; & WPCE(AM) Portsmouth, Va. Note: WWCA(AM) Gary, Ind. has a CP to change its city of license to East Chicago, Ind. Hqtrs: 645 Church St., Suite 400, Norfolk, Va. 23510. (804) 622-4600.

The Wireless Group Inc. Stns: 2 AM, 3 FM. WNWS(AM)-WTBG(FM) Brownsville, WNWS-FM Jackson & WTNE(AM)-WWEZ(FM) Trenton, all Tenn. Ownership: Carlton Veirs, pres, 50%; Lyle Reid, 50%. (See also Cross-Ownership, Sect. A.) Hqtrs: Box 198, Brownsville, Tenn. 38012. (901) 772-3700.

Group Ownership

The Wireless Works Inc. Stns: 2 AM, 3 FM. WIGS(AM)-WGIX-FM Gouverneur, WSLB(AM)-WPAC(FM) Ogdensburg & WZOZ(FM) Oneonta, all N.Y. (All 100% owned.) Ownership: Christopher B.T. Coffin, Patricia Tocatlian. Hqtrs: Box 239, Ogdensburg, N.Y. 13669. (315) 393-1100. FAX: (315) 393-6673.

Wisconsin Voice of Christian Youth Inc. Stns: 4 FM, 2 TV. KVCY(FM) Fort Scott, Kan.; KVCX(FM) Gregory, S.D.; WVCY(FM) & WVCY-TV Milwaukee, WSCO(TV) Suring & WVCX(FM) Tomah, all Wis. Hqtrs: 3434 W. Kilbourn, Milwaukee 53208. (414) 935-3000. FAX: (414) 935-3015.

Wisdom Stations. Stns: 1 AM, 2 FM. WAOV(AM)-WZDM(FM) Vincennes & WWBL(FM) Washington, both Ind. Ownership: Mark R. & Saundra K. Lange, 75%; David L. & Kimberly M. Crooks, 25%. Note: Mark R. & Saundra Lange own 100% of WZDM(FM) & 50% of WAOV(AM) & WWBL(FM). David L. & Kimberly M. Crooks own 50% of WAOV(AM) & WWBL(FM). Hqtrs: Box 242, Vincennes, Ind. 47591. (812) 882-6060. FAX: (812) 885-2604.

Withers Broadcasting Co. Stns: 3 AM, 3 FM, 6 TV. KREG-TV Glenwood Springs, KREX-TV Grand Junction, KREY-TV Montrose & KREZ-TV Durango, all Colo.; WMIX-AM-FM Mount Vernon, Ill.; KOKX-AM-FM Keokuk, Iowa; KAPE(AM) & KGMO(FM) Cape Girardeau, Mo.; KAVU-TV Victoria, Tex.; & WDTV(TV) Weston, W. Va. (All 100% owned.) Ownership: W. Russell Withers Jr., 100%. Hqtrs: Box 1508, Mount Vernon, Ill. 62864. (618) 242-3500. FAX: (618) 242-4444.

The Woodfin Group. Stns: 2 AM, 3 FM. WGSY(FM) Phenix City, Ala. (Columbus, Ga.); WGNE(AM) & WFSY(FM) Panama City, Fla.; WFXM-FM Forsyth (Macon) & WXKO(AM) Fort Valley (Macon), both Ga. (All 100% owned.) Ownership: B. Ken Woodfin, 60%; M. Hirsch, 40%. Hqtrs: Box 2127, Columbus, Ga. 31902. (706) 327-9955. FAX: (706) 327-5867.

Woodward Communications Inc. Stns: 2 AM, 2 FM. KDTH(AM) & KATF(FM) Dubuque, Iowa; WAPL-FM Appleton & WHBY(AM) Kimberly, both Wisconsin. (All 100% owned.) Executive: Susan F. Knaack, VP bcstg. (See also Cross-Ownership, Sect. A.) Hqtrs: Box 688, Dubuque, Iowa 52004. (319) 588-5611. FAX: (319) 588-5739.

The Word in Music. Stns: 4 FM. KBIQ(FM) Fountain, Colo.; KLTE(FM) Kirksville, Mo.; KSLT(FM) Spearfish, S.D.; & KTSL(FM) Medical Lake, Wash. Ownership: nonprofit bd of directors. Hqtrs: 1465 Kelly Johnson Blvd., Suite 202, Colorado Springs 80919. (719) 594-0009. FAX: (719) 531-6820.

World Radio Network Inc. Stns: 6 FM. KBNR(FM) Brownsville, KBNJ(FM) Corpus Christi, KEPX(FM) Eagle Pass, KVER(FM) El Paso, KBNL(FM) Laredo & KVMV(FM) McAllen, all Tex. Executives: Dr. Abe C. Van Der Puy, pres; Dr. Ben Cummings, VP/net dir; Mayra Harms, bus mgr; Stanley Swanson, net chief engr; Hernan Meneses, Spanish producer. Ownership: nonprofit corporation. Note: World Radio Network Inc. is affiliated with World Radio Missionary Fellowship Inc., which operates international shortwave missionary stn HCJB in Quito, Ecuador. Hqtrs: Box 3333, McAllen, Tex. 78502-3333. (210) 787-9700, (800) 275-5868. FAX: (210) 787-9783.

Wright Broadcasting Systems. Stns: 2 AM, 2 FM. KRPT-AM-FM Anadarko & KWEY-AM-FM Weatherford, both Okla. (All 100% owned.) Ownership: G. Harold Wright, 80%; Glenn Wright, 20%. Hqtrs: Box 587, Weatherford, Okla. 73096. (405) 772-5939. FAX: (405) 772-1590.

Wynne Broadcasting Company Inc. Stns: 1 AM, 2 FM. KFLS-FM Tulelake, Calif.; KFLS(AM) & KKRB(FM) Klamath Falls, Ore. (All 100% owned.) Ownership: Robert Wynne, Floyd Wynne, Barbara Wynne. Hqtrs: 1338 Oregon Ave., Klamath Falls, Ore. 97601. (503) 882-4656. FAX: (503) 884-2845.

Y

Yellowhead Broadcasting Ltd. Stns: 5 AM. CJYR(AM) Edson, CKYR-1(AM) Grande Cache, CIYR(AM) Hinton, CKYR(AM) Jasper & CFYR(AM) Whitecourt, all Alta. (All stns are located in Canada.) (All 100% owned.) Ownership: Ernest Mushtuk & Mel Lazarenko. Hqtrs: Box 6600, Edson, Alta., Canada T7E 1T9. (403) 723-4461. FAX: (403) 723-3765.

Young Broadcasting Inc. Stns: 7 TV. WTVO(TV) Rockford, Ill.; KLFY-TV Lafayette, La.; WCDC(TV) Adams, Mass.; WLNS-TV Lansing, Mich.; WTEN(TV) Albany, N.Y.; WKRN-TV Nashville; & WKBT(TV) La Crosse, Wis. (All 100% owned.) Ownership: Adam J. Young, 66%; Vincent J. Young, 33%. Hqtrs: 599 Lexington Ave., 47th Fl., New York 10022. (212) 688-5100. FAX: (212) 758-1229.

Z

Zia Broadcasting Co. Stns: 3 AM, 2 FM. KCLV-AM-FM Clovis, N.M.; KACT-AM-FM Andrews & KQTY(AM) Borger, both Tex. Ownership: Allsup's Convenience Stores Inc., 100%. Hqtrs: Box 1907, Clovis, N.M. 88101-1907. (505) 763-4401. FAX: (505) 769-2564.

Newspaper/Magazine Cross-Ownership with Broadcasting Stations

The following companies have interests in both broadcasting and newspaper or magazine publishing. Minority interests are indicated where information is available. In many instances stations and publications are owned by the same interests, but operations are entirely separate.

A state-by-state cross-reference list of broadcasting stations and the publishing companies or newspapers with which they are associated follows this listing.

A

Allbritton Communications Co. Hqtrs: 800 17th St., N.W., Suite 301, Washington 20006. (202) 789-2130. FAX: (202) 822-6749. Allbritton Communications publishes the *Enfield Press,* Enfield, Conn.; the *Longmeadow News,* Longmeadow, Mass.; the *Westfield Evening News,* Westfield, Mass.; & the *The Penny Saver,* Westfield, Mass. Stations: KATV(TV) Little Rock, Ark.; WJLA-TV Washington; KTUL(TV) Tulsa, Okla.; WCIV(TV) Charleston, S.C.; & WSET-TV Lynchburg, Va.

B

Bar-B Broadcasting Inc. Hqtrs: Box 390, El Campo, Tex. 77437. (409) 543-3303. FAX: (409) 543-0093. Fred V. Barbee Jr., 50% owner of the weekly *El Campo* (Tex.) *Leader-News,* owns 50% of Bar-B Broadcasting Inc., licensee of KULP(AM) El Campo, Tex. A. Richard Elam Jr., 50% owner of the *Leader-News,* owns 50% of KULP(AM).

A.H. Belo Corp. Hqtrs: Box 655237, Dallas 75265. (214) 977-8730. A.H. Belo Corp., publisher of *The Dallas Morning News,* & owner of Dallas-Fort Worth Suburban Newspapers Inc., owns KXTV(TV) Sacramento, Calif.; KOTV(TV) Tulsa, Okla.; WFAA-TV Dallas & KHOU-TV Houston; & WVEC-TV Hampton, Va.

Bonneville International Corp. Hqtrs: Box 1160, Salt Lake City 84110. (801) 575-7500. FAX: (801) 575-7548. Deseret Management Corp., which is 100% owned by the Corporation of the President of the Church of Jesus Christ of Latter-day Saints, owns the Deseret News Publishing Co., which publishes the Salt Lake City daily *Deseret News.* Deseret Management Corp. also owns Bonneville International Corp., which operates KMEO(AM) & KPSN(FM) Phoenix; KBIG(FM) Los Angeles & KOIT-AM-FM San Francisco, both Calif.; WTMX(FM) Skokie, Ill. (Chicago); KCMO-AM-FM & KMBZ(AM)-KLTH(FM) Kansas City, Mo.; WMXV(FM) New York; KAAM(AM) & KZPS(FM) Dallas; KSL-AM-TV Salt Lake City; & KIRO-AM-FM-TV Seattle.

Brill Media Company Inc. Hqtrs: Box 3353, Evansville, Ind. 47732. (812) 423-6200. FAX: (812) 428-4021. Brill Newspapers Inc. owns the *Alma* (Mich.) *Morning Sun* (daily) & *Reminder* (weekly); *Mt. Pleasant* (Mich.) *Morning Sun* (daily) & *Buyers Guide* (weekly); & weekly as follows: *Cadillac* (Mich.) *Buyer's Guide, Carson City* (Mich.) *Reminder, Edmore* (Mich.) *Advertiser, Gladwin* (Mich.) *Buyer's Guide, Hemlock* (Mich.) *Buyer's Guide* & the *Midland* (Mich.) *Buyer's Guide.* Stations: KUAD-FM Windsor, Colo.; WOMI(AM) & WBKR(FM) Owensboro, Ky.; WEBC(AM)-WAVC(FM) Duluth & KQWB-FM Moorhead, both Minn.; KLIK(AM) & KTXY(FM) Jefferson City, Mo.; KQWB(AM) Fargo, N.D.; WIOV-FM Ephrata & WIOV(AM) Reading, both Pa.

C

Calvary Inc. Hqtrs: 411 7th Ave., Pittsburgh 15219. (412) 562-5900. FAX: (412) 562-5936. Richard M. Scaife, publisher of the *Greensburg Tribune Review* in Greensburg, Pa., owns Calvary Inc., licensee of KQV(AM) Pittsburgh.

Capital Cities/ABC Inc. Hqtrs: 77 W. 66th St., New York 10023. (212) 456-7777. FAX: (212) 456-7909. Capital Cities/ABC Inc. owns:
Daily newspapers: *Milford Citizen* (evening & Sunday), Milford, Conn.; *Belleville News-Democrat* (morning & Sunday), Belleville, Ill.; *The Oakland Press* (all-day & Sunday), Pontiac, Mich.; *The Kansas City Star* (morning & Sunday), Kansas City, Mo.; *St. Louis Countian* (morning), St. Louis; *St. Louis Daily Record* (morning), St. Louis; *St. Peters Courier Post* (morning), St. Peters; *Albany Democrat-Herald* (evening), Albany, & *The Daily Tidings* (evening), Ashland, both Ore.; *The Times Leader* (morning), Wilkes-Barre, Pa.; & the *Fort Worth Star-Telegram* (morning, evening & Sunday).
Weekly newspapers: 69 weekly community newspapers in Connecticut, Illinois, Massachusetts, Michigan, Oregon, Pennsylvania & Rhode Island.
Shopping guides: 26 shopping guides in California, Connecticut, Kansas, Massachusetts, Missouri, Nevada, Oregon & Washington.
Fairchild Publications (New York): *Women's Wear Daily, Children's Business, Daily News Record, Footwear News, Golf Pro Merchandiser, HFD-Retailing Home Furnishings, Home Fashions, SportStyle, Supermarket News, W, W Fashion Life* (Europe) & Fairchild Books & Visuals.
Financial Services & Medical Group (New York). Institutional Investor (New York): *Institutional Investor-Domestic Edition, Institutional Investor-International Edition.* International Medical News Group: *Clinical Psychiatry News, Family Practice News, Internal Medicine News, Ob. Gyn. News, Pediatric News, Skin & Allergy News.* Mercury Publishing Services (Rockville, Md.).
Philatelic Publications (Albany, Ore.): *Stamp Collector, The Stamp Wholesaler.*
Diversified Publishing Group (New York). Chilton Publications (Radnor, Pa.): *Automotive Body Repair News, Automotive Industries, Automotive Marketing, Commercial Carrier Journal, Distribution, Electronic Component News, Energy User News, Food Engineering, Food Engineering International, Hardware Age, IMPO (Industrial Maintenance & Plant Operations), Industrial Safety & Hygiene News, Instrument & Automation News, Instrument & Control Systems, Jewelers' Circular-Keystone, Motor Age, Outdoor Power Equipment, Owner Operator, Product Design & Development, Review of Optometry.* Hitchcock Publishing Co. (Carol Stream, Ill.): *Assembly, Business Publishing, Heat Treating, Industrial Finishing, Iron Age, Metal Center News, Manufacturing Systems, Office Products Dealer, P.I. Quality, Quality.* Communications & Commodities Group (New York): *American Metal Market, CableVision, CED, Metal Pricing & Data, Multichannel News, Recycling Manager, Video Business, Video Software.* Chilton Enterprises (Radnor, Pa.): Chilton Book Co., Chilton Research Services, Professional Exposition Management Co. (Carol Stream, Ill.). Agricultural Group. Farm Progress Companies (Carol Stream, Ill.): *American Agriculturist, California Farmer, Colorado Rancher & Farmer, Dakota Wallaces Farmer, Farm Progress, Indiana Prairie Farmer, Kansas Farmer, Kentucky Prairie Farmer, Michigan Farmer, Minnesota Wallaces Farmer, Missouri Ruralist, Nebraska Farmer, Ohio Farmer, Oklahoma Farmer-Stockman, Pennsylvania Farmer, Prairie Farmer, Texas Farmer-Stockman, Wallaces Farmer, Wisconsin Agriculturist.* Miller Publishing (Minnetonka, Minn.): *Farm Futures, Feedstuffs & Tack 'n Togs Merchandising. Los Angeles Magazine* (Los Angeles). NILS Publishing Co. (Chatsworth, Calif.) Word Inc. (Dallas): Word Music, Word Publishing, Word Book & Record Clubs, Word Canada, Word United Kingdom, International Cassette Corp.
Other interests: Capital Cities also publishes *The Cable Connection* (Fort Worth) & *StarText* (Fort Worth). Homes Magazines: Gamer Publishing (Hartford, Conn.; Springfield, Mass.; R.I.), *The Oakland Press* (8 in southeastern Mich.), Mariner Newspapers (Springfield, Mass.), *Fort Worth Star-Telegram* (Tarrant County, Tex.) & *The Times-Leader* (Pa.).
Stations: KFSN-TV Fresno, KABC-AM-TV/KLOS(FM) Los Angeles & KGO-AM-TV San Francisco, all Calif.; WMAL(AM) & WRQX(FM) Washington; WKHX(AM) Atlanta, WYAY(FM) Gainesville & WKHX-FM Marietta, all Ga.; WLS-AM-FM-TV Chicago; WJR(AM) & WHYT(FM) Detroit; KQRS-AM-FM Golden Valley, Minn.; WABC-AM-TV & WPLJ(FM) New York; WTVD(TV) Durham, N.C.; WPVI-TV Philadelphia; WBAP(AM)-KSCS(FM) Fort Worth & KTRK-TV Houston.

Cedar Rapids Television Co. Hqtrs: 2nd Ave. at 5th St. S.E., Cedar Rapids, Iowa 52401. (319) 398-8422. FAX: (319) 398-8378. The Gazette Co., publisher of the *Cedar Rapids* (Iowa) *Gazette,* owns 100% of KCRG-AM-TV Cedar Rapids, Iowa.

Channel 6 Inc. Hqtrs: Box 6103, Temple, Tex. 76503. (817) 773-1633. (817) 770-0204. Anyse Sue Mayborn, owner of the *Temple* (Tex.) *Daily Telegram* & owner of the *Killeen* (Tex.) *Herald,* also owns KCEN-TV Temple, Tex.

Chronicle Publishing Co. Hqtrs: 901 Mission St., San Francisco 94103. (415) 777-1111. FAX: (415) 512-8196. The Chronicle Publishing Co., 100% owner of the *San Francisco Chronicle, The Pantagraph* in Bloomington, Ill. & the *Worcester Telegram & Gazette* in Worcester, Mass., also owns 100% of Chronicle Broadcasting Co. Stations: KRON-TV San Francisco; KLBY(TV) Colby, KUPK-TV Garden City & KAKE-TV Wichita, all Kan.; & WOWT(TV) Omaha.

Cogeco Inc. Hqtrs: One Place Ville-Marie, Suite 3636, Montreal, Que. Canada H3B 3P2. (514) 874-2600. FAX: (514) 874-2625. Cogeco Inc. owns 100% of Publications Dumont (1988) Inc., publisher of 34 wkly newspapers with a circ of 1 million copies wkly.
Stations: CHLC(AM)-New FM Baie-Comeau, CFRP(AM) Forestville, CFGL-FM Laval, CJMF-FM Quebec, CFEI-FM St. Hyacinthe, CFKS-TV & CKSH-TV Sherbrooke, & CFKM-TV & CKTM-TV Trois-Rivieres, all Que.

Cowles Publishing Co. Hqtrs: Review Tower, W. 999 Riverside, Spokane, Wash. 99210. (509) 459-5000. FAX: (509) 459-5482. Cowles Publishing Co., which owns 100% of the *The Spokesman-Review,* Spokane, Wash., owns 100% of KHQ Inc., licensee of KHQ-TV Spokane, Wash.

Cox Enterprises Inc. Hqtrs: 1400 Lake Hearn Dr. N.E., Atlanta 30319. (404) 843-5000. FAX: (404) 843-5777. Cox Enterprises Inc. owns *The Atlanta Journal & Constitution; Dayton Daily News* & *Springfield News-Sun,* both Ohio; & *Palm Beach Daily News, The Palm Beach Post* & *Palm Beach Life* (a magazine), all Fla.; & *Austin American-Statesman, Longview News-Journal, The Lufkin Daily News, The* (Nacogdoches) *Daily Sentinel* & *Waco Tribune-Herald,* all Tex.; *Grand Junction* (Colo.) *Daily Sentinel; Chandler Arizonan Tribune, The Gilbert Tribune, Mesa Tribune, Tempe Daily News Tribune* & the *The Yuma Daily Sun,* all Ariz. Stations: WSB-AM-FM-TV Atlanta; WSOC-TV Charlotte, N.C.; WHQT(FM) Coral Gables, Fla.; KRRW(FM) Dallas; WHIO-AM-TV & WHKO(FM) Dayton, Ohio; WCKG(FM) Elmwood Park, Ill. (Chicago); KFI(AM) & KOST(FM) Los Angeles; WIOD(AM) & WFLC(FM) Miami, Fla.; KTVU(TV) Oakland, Calif. (San Francisco); WFTV(TV) Orlando, Fla.; WPXI(TV) Pittsburgh; WSUN(AM) & WCOF(FM) St. Petersburg, Fla. Note: Group has bought WYAI(FM) La Grange, Ga., WYSY-FM Aurora, Ill. & KTXQ(FM) Fort Worth & sold WSUN(AM) & WCOF(FM) St. Petersburg, Fla., subject to FCC approval.

Cox Newspapers—See Cox Enterprises Inc.

Crain Broadcasting Inc., Hqtrs: Box 183E, Rt. 5, Big Pine Key, Fla. 33043. (305) 872-9100. FAX: (305) 872-8935. Gertrude R. Crain & family, who publish 22 trade magazines, including *Advertising Age,* own WWUS(FM) Big Pine Key, Fla.

D

D.W.S. Inc. Hqtrs: Box 3939, Champaign, Ill. 61826-3939. (217) 351-5300. FAX: (217) 351-5385. *The Champaign News-Gazette* has interlocking ownership with D.W.S. Inc., licensee of WDWS(AM) & WHMS-FM Champaign, Ill.

Daily News Broadcasting Co. Hqtrs: Box 930, Bowling Green, Ky. 42102. (502) 781-2121. FAX: (502) 842-0232. Owners of the *Park City Daily News,* Bowling Green, Ky., also control Daily News Broadcasting Co., licensee of WKCT(AM) & WDNS(FM) Bowling Green, Ky.

Delmarva Broadcasting Co. Hqtrs: Box 7492, 2727 Shipley Road, Wilmington, Del. 19803. (302) 478-2700. FAX: (302) 478-0100. *Lancaster Inteligencer-Journal* & *New Era,* Lancaster, Pa., have the same ownership (Steinman) as Delmarva Broadcasting Co. Stations (operated independently): WDEL(AM) & WSTW(FM) Wilmington, Del.

The Dispatch Printing Co. Hqtrs: 34 S. 3rd St., Columbus, Ohio 43215. (614) 461-5000. FAX: (614) 461-5058. Owns 100% of *The Columbus* (Ohio) *Dispatch, This Week* & *Ohio Magazine.* Stations: WBNS-AM-FM-TV Columbus, Ohio & WTHR(TV) Indianapolis.

Diversified Communications. Hqtrs: Box 7437, 5 Milk St., Portland, Me. 04112. (207) 774-5981. FAX: (207) 761-7915. Diversified Communications publishes *Na-*

tional *Fisherman*, *Seafood Business* & *Work Boat* magazines. Stations: WCJB(TV) Gainesville, Fla.; WABI-AM-TV & WYOU-FM Bangor, Me.; WYOU(TV) Scranton, Pa.; & WPDE-TV Florence, S.C.

Dix Communications. Hqtrs: 212 E. Liberty St., Wooster, Ohio 44691. (216) 264-1125. FAX: (216) 263-5013. Dix Newspapers: Frankfort, Ky. *State Journal*; *Alliance Review*, Ashland, Ky.; *Times Gazette*, Cambridge Jeffersonian, Defiance *Crescent News*, Kent-Ravenna *Record Courier*, & the Wooster *Daily Record*, all Ohio. Owned by the Dix family with WMMZ(FM) Ocala, Fla.; WTBO(AM) & WKGO(FM) Cumberland, Md.; KAAL(TV) Austin, Minn.; KULR-TV Billings & KFBB-TV Great Falls, both Mont.; WKVX(AM) & WQKT(FM) Wooster, Ohio; WRAD(AM) & WRIQ(FM) Radford, Va.; KTWO-TV Casper, KKTU(TV) Cheyenne & KRBQ(TV) Sheridan, all Wyo.

Donrey Media Group. Administrative Center: Box 17017, Fort Smith, Ark. 72917-7017. (501) 785-7810. FAX: (501) 785-9479. Donrey Media Group (Donald W. Reynolds, founder; Fred W. Smith, pres) publishes the following newspapers:
Arkansas: *Daily Siftings Herald*, Arkadelphia; *Southwest Times Record*, Fort Smith; *Pine Bluff Commercial*; *Northwest Arkansas Morning News*, Rogers; & the *Morning News*, Springdale. Non-daily newspaper: *Booneville Democrat*.
California: *Chico Enterprise-Record*, *Daily Democrat* (Woodland), *Hemet News*, *Inland Valley Daily Bulletin* (Ontario), *Lompoc Record*, *Mercury-Register* (Oroville), (Red Bluff) *Daily News*, *Redlands Daily Facts*, *Ukiah Daily Journal* & the *Vallejo Times-Herald*. Non-daily newspapers: *Fort Bragg Advocate-News* & the (Moreno Valley) *Valley Times*.
Hawaii: *Hawaii Tribune-Herald*, Hilo; & *West Hawaii Today*, Kailua-Kona.
Indiana: *Washington Times-Herald*.
Iowa: *Clinton Herald* & the *Oskaloosa Herald*.
Kentucky: *Glasgow Daily Times*.
Mississippi: *Picayune Item*.
Missouri: *Moberly Monitor-Index*.
Nevada: *Ely Daily Times*; & the *Las Vegas Review-Journal*.
New Mexico: *Alamogordo Daily News*.
North Carolina: *Asheboro Courier-Tribune*.
Oklahoma: *Altus Times*, *Bartlesville Examiner-Enterprise*, *Blackwell Journal-Tribune*, *Chickasha Daily Express*, *Claremore Daily Progress*, *Durant Daily Democrat*, *Frederick Daily Leader*, *Guthrie Daily Leader*, *Guymon Daily Herald*, *Henryetta Daily Free-Lance*, *Norman Transcript*, *Okmulgee Daily Times* & the *Pauls Valley Daily Democrat*. Non-daily newspaper: *Pawhuska Journal-Capital*.
Tennessee: (Columbia) *Daily Herald*.
Texas: *Athens Daily Review*, *Borger News-Herald*, (Cleburne) *Times-Review*, *Denison Herald*, *Gainesville Daily Register*, *Jacksonville Daily Progress*, *Kilgore News Herald*, *Sherman Democrat*, *Sweetwater Reporter* & the *Weatherford Democrat*. Non-daily newspaper: *Cedar Creek Pilot*, Gun Barrel City.
Washington: (Aberdeen) *Daily World*.
Other interests: Arkansas: Rogers Cable Vision; California: Vallejo Cable Vision; Oklahoma: Bartlesville Cable Vision, Blackwell Cable Vision & Guymon Cable Vision.
Station: KOLO-TV Reno, Nev.

Donze Communications Inc. Hqtrs: Box 428, Radio Hill, Ste. Genevieve, Mo. 63670. (314) 883-2980. Donze Communications Inc., 100% owner of the *Sun Times* in Perryville & Ste. Genevieve, both Mo., also owns 100% of KSGM(AM) Chester, Ill. & KBDZ(FM) Perryville, Mo.

William R. Dunaway. Hqtrs: c/o Mountain States Communications Inc., 310 E. Main, Aspen, Colo. 81611. William R. Dunaway, publisher of wkly *Aspen Times*, & *Times Daily* (five days a week), owns 44.69% of KGLN(AM) & KMTS(FM) Glenwood Springs, Colo.

Durham Herald Co. Hqtrs: 2828 Pickett Rd., Durham, N.C. 27705. (919) 419-6500. FAX: (919) 361-2552. Durham Herald Co., publisher of the *Chapel Hill Herald* & *Durham Herald-Sun*, both N.C., & owner of AdTrax Recording Studio, Durham, N.C., is licensee of WDNC(AM) & WDCG(FM) Durham, N.C.

E

Emmis Broadcasting Corp. Hqtrs: Gateway Plaza, 950 Meridian St., Suite 1200, Indianapolis 46204. (317) 266-0100. The publishing unit of Emmis Broadcasting Corp. publishes two magazines: *Atlanta Magazine* & *Indianapolis Monthly*. Stations: KPWR(FM) Los Angeles, WKQX(FM) Chicago; WENS(FM) Shelbyville, Ind.; KSHE(FM) Crestwood, Mo.; & WQHT(FM) New York.

Enterprise Publishing Co. Hqtrs: Box 1450, Brockton, Mass. 02403-1450. (508) 588-5000. FAX: (508) 586-7903. Enterprise Publishing Co. (*The Enterprise* in Brockton, Mass.) owns WBET(AM) & WCAV(FM) Brockton, Mass.

Evening Post Publishing Co. Hqtrs: 134 Columbus St., Charleston, S.C. 29403-4800. (803) 577-7111. Evening Post Publishing Co. owns 100% of *Aiken Standard*, Aiken, S.C.; *The Post & Courier*, Charleston, S.C.; *The Georgetown Times*, Georgetown, S.C.; *Kingstree News*, Kingstree, S.C.; & 60% of the *Buenos Aires Herald*, Buenos Aires, Argentina. Evening Post Publishing Co. also owns 100% of KOAA-TV Pueblo, Colo.; KIVI(TV) Nampa, Idaho; KXLF-TV Butte, KRTV(TV) Great Falls & KPAX-TV Missoula, all Mont. Note: Group has purchased KTVQ(TV) Billings, Mont., subject to FCC approval.

F

Fairchild Publications Inc.—See Capital Cities/ABC Inc.

Federated Media. Hqtrs: Box 2500, Elkhart, Ind. 46515. (219) 294-1661. John F. Dille Jr., 100% owner of *The Elkhart Truth*, Elkhart, Ind., also is chmn of Pathfinder Communications Corp., licensee of WTRC(AM)-WLTA(FM) Elkhart & WQHK(AM)-WMEE(FM) Fort Wayne, both Ind.; WCUZ-AM-FM Grand Rapids & WQWQ(AM) Muskegon Heights, both Mich.; WCKY(AM) & WIMJ(FM) Cincinnati. Truth Publishing Co., which publishes *The Elkhart Truth*, is licensee of KQLL-FM Owasso & KQLL(AM) Tulsa, both Okla. Federated Media also has ownership interests in WADM(AM) & WQHK-FM Decatur, Ind.

The Findlay Publishing Co. Hqtrs: 701 W. Sandusky St., Findlay, Ohio 45840. (419) 422-5151. FAX: (419) 422-2937. The Findlay Publishing Co. publishes the *Findlay* (Ohio) *Courier*. Stations: The Findlay Publishing Co. owns 100% of WCSI(AM) & WKKG(FM) Columbus, Ind.; WFIN(AM)-WKXA-FM Findlay & WMOH(AM) Hamilton, both Ohio.

Forum Communications Co. Hqtrs: Box 2020, Fargo, N.D. 58107. FAX: (701) 241-5487. Forum Communications Co., owner of the *Alexandria* (Minn.) *Press & Echo*; *Detroit Lakes Tribune* & *The Becker Co. Record*, Detroit Lakes, Minn.; the *Park Rapids* (Minn.) *Enterprise*; *The Wadena* (Minn.) *Pioneer Journal*; the *West Central Daily Tribune*, Willmar, Minn.; & *The* (N.D.) *Forum*, owns KMMJ(AM) Grand Island, Neb.; KBMY(TV) Bismarck, WDAZ-TV Devils Lake, WDAY-AM-FM-TV Fargo & KMCY(TV) Minot, all N.D. Note: Forum Communications Co. is the owner, not the publisher, of the newspaper properties.

Freedom Newspapers Inc. Hqtrs: Box 19549, 17666 Fitch, Irvine, Calif. 92713-9549. (714) 253-2313. FAX: (714) 253-2349. Freedom Newspapers Inc., publisher of 27 daily & 27 wkly newspapers in 13 states, & publisher of *World Trade* & *USA Exports* magazines, owns WLNE(TV) New Bedford, Mass. (Providence, R.I.); WRGB(TV) Schenectady (Albany-Schenectady-Troy market), N.Y.; KTVL(TV) Medford, Ore.; WTVC(TV) Chattanooga; KFDM-TV Beaumont, Tex.; & Orange County NewsChannel (OCN), a 24-hour cable news ch in Santa Ana, Calif.

The Free Lance-Star Publishing Co. Hqtrs: 616 Amelia St., Fredericksburg, Va. 22401. (703) 373-1500. FAX: (703) 373-8450. The Free Lance-Star Publishing Co., publisher of the *Fredericksburg* (Va.) *Free Lance-Star*, is licensee of WFLS-AM-FM Fredericksburg & WPLC(FM) Spotsylvania, both Va.

G

Gannett Co. Hqtrs: 1100 Wilson Blvd., Arlington, Va. 22234. (703) 284-6000. Gannett Co. is publisher of the following daily newspapers:
Arizona: *Tucson Citizen*, Tucson.
California: *Marin Independent Journal*, Marin county; *The Desert Sun*, Palm Springs; *Salinas Californian*, Salinas; *The San Bernardino County Sun*, San Bernardino; *The Stockton Record*, Stockton; & *Visalia Times-Delta*, Visalia.
Colorado: *Fort Collins Coloradoan*, Fort Collins.
Connecticut: *Norwich Bulletin*, Norwich.
Delaware: *The News Journal*, Wilmington.
Florida: *Florida Today*, Brevard county; *News-Press*, Fort Myers; & the *Pensacola News Journal*, Pensacola.
Georgia: *The Times*, Gainesville.
Hawaii: *Honolulu Advertiser*, Honolulu.
Idaho: *The Idaho Statesman*, Boise.
Illinois: *Commercial-News*, Danville; & the *Rockford Register Star*, Rockford.
Indiana: *Journal & Courier*, Lafayette; *Chronicle-Tribune*, Marion; & *Palladium-Item*, Richmond.
Iowa: *The Des Moines Register*, Des Moines; & the *Iowa City Press-Citizen*, Iowa City.
Kentucky: *The Courier-Journal*, Louisville.
Louisiana: *The News-Star*, Monroe; & *The Times*, Shreveport.
Michigan: *Battle Creek Enquirer*, Battle Creek; *The Detroit News*, Detroit; *Lansing State Journal*, Lansing; & the *Times Herald*, Port Huron.
Minnesota: *St. Cloud Times*, St. Cloud.
Mississippi: *Hattiesburg American*, Hattiesburg; & *The Clarion-Ledger*, Jackson.
Missouri: *The News-Leader*, Springfield.
Montana: *Great Falls Tribune*, Great Falls.
Nevada: *Reno Gazette-Journal*, Reno.
New Jersey: *The Courier-News*, Bridgewater; *Courier-Post*, Camden; & *The Daily Journal*, Vineland.
New York: *Press & Sun-Bulletin*, Binghamton; *Star-Gazette*, Elmira; *The Ithaca Journal*, Ithaca; *Niagara Gazette*, Niagara Falls; *Poughkeepsie Journal*, Poughkeepsie; *Democrat & Chronicle Times-Union*, Rochester; *The Saratogian*, Saratoga Springs; & the *Observer-Dispatch*, Utica.
New York (Gannett Suburban Newspapers): *The Daily Times*, Mamaroneck; *The Daily Argus*, Mount Vernon; *The Standard-Star*, New Rochelle; *The Citizen Register*, Ossining; *The Star*, Peekskill; *The Daily Item*, Port Chester; *The Daily News*, Tarrytown; *The Journal-News*, West Nyack-Rockland; *The Reporter Dispatch*, White Plains; & *The Herald Statesman*, Yonkers.
Ohio: *Chillicothe Gazette*, Chillicothe; *The Cincinnati Enquirer*, Cincinnati; *The News-Messenger*, Fremont; *The Marietta Times*, Marietta; & the *News Herald*, Port Clinton.
Oklahoma: *Muskogee Daily Phoenix*, Muskogee.
Oregon: *Statesman Journal*, Salem.
Pennsylvania: *Public Opinion*, Chambersburg; *The Reporter*, Lansdale; the *Valley News Dispatch*, Tarentum; & the *North Hills News Record*, Warrendale.
South Dakota: *Argus Leader*, Sioux Falls.
Tennessee: *The Jackson Sun*, Jackson; & *The Tennessean*, Nashville.
Texas: *El Paso Times*, El Paso.
Vermont: *The Burlington Free Press*, Burlington.
Washington: *The Bellingham Herald*, Bellingham; & *The Olympian*, Olympia.
West Virginia: *The Herald-Dispatch*, Huntington.
Wisconsin: *Green Bay Press-Gazette*, Green Bay; & the *Wausau Daily Herald*, Wausau.
Guam: *Pacific Daily News*, Agana.
Virgin Islands: *The Virgin Islands Daily News*, St. Thomas.
Note: Gannett Co., Arlington, Va., also publishes a natl daily newspaper, *USA Today*, & *USA Today Baseball Weekly* (wkly during the baseball season & every other week in the off-season).
Non-daily publications: non-daily publications in Connecticut, Florida, Georgia, Illinois, Iowa, Michigan, Mississippi, New Jersey, New York, Ohio, Oregon, Pennsylvania, Virginia & Washington.
Stations: KPNX(TV) Mesa, Ariz. (Phoenix); KIIS-AM-FM Los Angeles & KSDO(AM)-KCLX-FM San Diego; KUSA-TV Denver; WUSA(TV) Washington; WTLV(TV) Jacksonville & WDAE(AM)-WUSA-FM Tampa, both Fla.; WXIA-TV Atlanta; WGCI-AM-FM Chicago; WLVI-TV Cambridge, Mass. (Boston); KARE(TV) Minneapolis; WFMY-TV Greensboro, N.C.; KOCO-TV Oklahoma City; KVUE-TV Austin, KHKS(FM) Denton, KKBQ(AM) Houston & KKBQ-FM Pasadena, all Tex. Note: WLVI-TV Cambridge, Mass. has been sold, subject to FCC approval.

Guy Gannett Communications. Hqtrs: Box 15277, One City Center, Portland, Me. 04101. (207) 780-9050. FAX: (207) 828-8160. Guy Gannett Publishing Co. publishes *The Kennebec Journal*, Augusta, Me.; *The Portland Press Herald*, Portland, Me.; *The Maine Sunday Telegram*, Portland, Me.; & *The Central Maine Morning Sentinel*, Waterville, Me. The company also owns Minnesota Sun Publications. Stations: WICS(TV) Springfield, Ill.; KGAN(TV) Cedar Rapids, Iowa; WGME-TV Portland, Me. & WGGB-TV Springfield, Mass. Note: Group has purchased WICD(TV) Champaign, Ill., subject to FCC approval.

Gateway Communications Inc. Hqtrs: Box 12, Johnson City, N.Y. 13790. (607) 729-8996. FAX: (607) 797-6148. Macromedia Inc. (Malcolm A. Borg, chmn), publisher of the *The Record* in Bergen county, N.J., owns 100% of Gateway Communications Inc. (Lamont T. Pinker, pres), licensee of WBNG-TV Binghamton, N.Y., WTAJ-TV Altoona & WLYH-TV Lancaster, both Pa.; & WOWK-TV Huntington, W.Va.

Gazette Printing Co. Hqtrs: 1 S. Parker Dr., Box 5001, Janesville, Wis. 53547-5001. (608) 754-3311. FAX: (608) 754-8038. Gazette Printing Co., publisher of the *Ironwood* (Mich.) *Daily Globe*, the *Menominee* (Mich.) *Herald-Leader*, *The Delavan* (Wis.) *Enterprise* & *The Week* (in Delavan, Wis.), the *Janesville* (Wis.) *Gazette*, the *Marinette* (Wis.) *Eagle-Star* & the *Monroe* (Wis.) *Evening Times*, owns WCLO(AM)-WJVL(FM) Janesville, WBKV(AM)-WBWI-FM West Bend & WFHR(AM)-WWRW(FM) Wisconsin Rapids, all Wis.

Gleaner & Journal Publishing Co. Hqtrs: Box 309, Franklin, Ky. 42135. (502) 586-4481. FAX: (502) 586-6031. Gleaner & Journal Publishing Co., publisher of the wkly *Franklin Favorite*, is licensee of WFKN(AM) Franklin, Ky.

Golden West Broadcasting Ltd. Hqtrs: Box 950, Altona, Man. Canada R0G 0B0. (204) 324-6464. FAX: (204) 324-8918. The *Red River Valley Echo* in Altona, Man. has ownership with interests in Golden West Broadcasting Ltd. Golden West Broadcasting Ltd. operates the following stations: CFXL(AM) Calgary & CHRB(AM) High River, both Alta.; CFAM(AM) Altona, CJRB(AM) Boissevain, CHSM(AM) Steinbach & CKMW(AM) Winkler-Morden, all Man.; CHOO(AM) Ajax & CHAM(AM) Hamilton, both Ont.; CHAB(AM) Moose Jaw, CJSN(AM) Shaunavon & CKSW(AM) Swift Current, all Sask.

Gray Communications Systems Inc. Hqtrs: Box 48, Albany, Ga. 31703. (912) 888-9390. FAX: (912) 888-9374. Gray Communications publishes, through Albany Herald Publishing Co., *The Albany* (Ga.) *Herald.* Stations: WALB-TV Albany, Ga.; WJHG-TV Panama City, Fla., & KTVE(TV) El Dorado, Ark. (Monroe, La.). (All 100% owned.)

Greater Media Inc. Hqtrs: Box 1059, Two Kennedy Blvd., East Brunswick, N.J. 08816. (908) 247-6161. FAX: (908) 247-0215. Greater Media Inc. owns 98% of Sentinel Publishing Co. of East Brunswick, N.J., publisher of two wkly newspapers: *Sentinel* & *Suburban;* & 100% of Greater Monmouth Publishing Corp., publisher of the twice-wkly *News Transcript* of Freehold, N.J., & the wkly *Independent* of Middletown, N.J. Greater Media Inc. owns KLSX(FM) Los Angeles & KRLA(AM) Pasadena, both Calif.; WWRC(AM) & WGAY(FM) Washington; WBCS(FM) & WMEX(AM)-WMJX(FM) Boston; WCSX(FM) Birmingham & WHND(AM) Monroe, both Mich.; WCTC(AM) & WMGQ(FM) New Brunswick, N.J.; WGSM(AM) Huntington & WMJC(FM) Smithtown, both N.Y.; WPEN(AM) & WMGK(FM) Philadelphia. Note: Group has purchased WRIF(FM) Detroit, pending FCC approval.

H

Harte-Hanks Communications Inc. Hqtrs: Box 269, 200 Concord Plaza Dr., Suite 800, San Antonio, Tex. 78291. (512) 829-9000. FAX: (512) 829-9403.

Massachusetts: *The Arlington Advocate*, Arlington; *The Belmont Citizen-Herald*, Belmont; *Daily Transcript*, Dedham; *The Middlesex News*, Framingham; *The Needham Chronicle*, Needham; *The Newton Graphic*, Newton; *Parkway Transcript*, Roslindale; *Sudbury Town Crier*, Sudbury; *Wayland-Weston Town Crier*, Sudbury; *News Tribune*, Waltham; *The Watertown Sun*, Watertown; *The Wellesley Townsman*, Wellesley; *West Roxbury Transcript*, West Roxbury; & *The Winchester Star*, Winchester.

South Carolina: *Anderson Independent-Mail*, Anderson.

Texas: *Abilene Reporter-News*, Abilene; *The Allen American*, Allen; *Carrollton Chronicle*, Carrollton; *The Colony Leader*, Colony; *Coppell Gazette*, Coppell; *Corpus Christi Caller-Times*, Corpus Christi; Trademark Press Inc., Corpus Christi; *Farmers Branch Times*, Farmers Branch; *Lewisville Leader*, Lewisville; *The Mesquite News*, Mesquite; *Plano Star-Courier*, Plano; *San Angelo Standard-Times*, San Angelo; Harte-Hanks Graphics, San Antonio; & the *Wichita Falls Times Record News*, Wichita Falls.

Television group: KENS-TV San Antonio, Tex.

The Hearst Corporation. Hqtrs: 959 8th Ave., New York 10019. (212) 649-2000. Hearst newspapers are:

California: *San Francisco Examiner.*
Illinois: *Edwardsville Intelligencer.*
Michigan: *Huron Daily Tribune*, Bad Axe; & the *Midland Daily News.*
New York: *Albany Times Union.*
Texas: *Beaumont Enterprise, Houston Chronicle, Laredo Morning Times, Midland Reporter-Telegram, Plainview Daily Herald* & the *San Antonio Express-News.*
Washington: *Seattle Post-Intelligencer.*

Wkly newspapers: 2 weeklies in Mich. & 3 weeklies in Tex.

Hearst magazines: *Colonial Homes, Cosmopolitan, Country Living, Esquire, Good Housekeeping, Harper's Bazaar, House Beautiful, Motor Boating & Sailing, Popular Mechanics, Redbook, Sports Afield, Town & Country* & *Victoria.*

Overseas magazine activities: The National Magazine Company Ltd. publishes 11 magazines in the United Kingdom. Hearst Magazines International publishes more than 60 foreign editions under license in 11 languages & distributed in more than 80 countries.

Business publishing: *American Druggist, American Druggist Blue Book, Diversion, Electronic Engineers Master Catalog, Electronic Products Magazine, Floor Covering Weekly, Integrated Circuits Master Catalog*, Motor Books, Motor Crash Estimating Guides, *Motor Magazine*, Motor Professional Manuals, National Auto Research Publications, *Official Guide to Disneyland, Official Guide to Walt Disney World*, Retirement Advisors Inc.

Newspaper syndication & merchandise licensing: King Features Syndicate, North America Syndicate Inc., Cowles Syndicate Inc., King Features Licensing.

Stations: WBAL-AM-TV & WIYY(FM) Baltimore; WCVB-TV Boston; WDTN(TV) Dayton, Ohio; KMBC-TV Kansas City, Mo.; WISN-AM-TV & WLTQ(FM) Milwaukee; WTAE-AM-TV & WVTY(FM) Pittsburgh.

Herald Broadcasting Syndicate Inc. Hqtrs: One Norway St., Boston 02115. (617) 450-2000. FAX: (617) 787-6853. Herald Broadcasting Syndicate Inc., affiliated with *The Christian Science Monitor*, operates three international bcst stations: KHBI Saipan, The Marianna Islands; WCSN Scotts Corner, Me. (near Bangor, Me.); & WSHB Cypress Creek, S.C.

The Home News Co. Hqtrs: 35 Kennedy Blvd., East Brunswick, N.J. 08816. (908) 246-5500. FAX: (908) 937-6046. The Home News Co. publishes six wkly newspapers: *The Brookfield Journal*, Brookfield, *The Kent Good Times Dispatch*, Kent, *The Litchfield Enquirer*, Litchfield, *The Advertiser*, New Milford, & *The Washington Eagle*, Washington, all Conn.; *The Pawling Chronicle*, Pawling, & *The Putnam County Courier*, Putnam county, both N.Y. The Home News Co. also owns WKTP(AM) Jonesboro & WKPT-AM-TV & WTFM(FM) Kingsport, both Tenn.

Huntingdon Broadcasters Inc. Hqtrs: 400 Washington St., Huntingdon, Pa. 16652. (814) 643-3340. FAX: (814) 643-7379. The Joseph F. Biddle Publishing Co., Huntingdon, Pa. (publisher of *The Daily News, The Daily Herald* & *Mount Union Times*) owns 100% of Huntingdon Broadcasters Inc., licensee of WHUN(AM) & WLAK(FM) Huntingdon, Pa.

Huse Publishing Co.—See WJAG Inc.

I

Illini Media Co. Hqtrs: 57 E. Green St., Champaign, Ill. 61820. (217) 333-3733. FAX: (217) 244-6616. Illini Media Co. (a company affiliated with the University of Illinois) publishes the *Daily Illini*, a newspaper; *Technograph*, a magazine; & "Illio", a yearbook. Illini Media Co. also is licensee of WPGU(FM) Urbana, Ill.

Imes Communications Group. Hqtrs: Box 511, Columbus, Miss. 39703; 516 Main St., Columbus, Miss. 39702. (601) 328-2424. FAX: (601) 328-2424. Birney Imes Jr., publisher of the *Columbus* (Miss.) *Commercial Dispatch*, owns WCBI-TV Columbus, Miss. (25%); WMUR-TV Manchester, N.H. (90%); KDBC-TV El Paso; & WBOY-TV Clarksburg, W.Va. (92.5%).

J

Johnson County Broadcasters Inc. Hqtrs: Box 398, Warrensburg, Mo. 64093. (816) 747-9191. Avis Green Tucker, owner & operator of the *Daily Star-Journal* in Warrensburg, Mo., is a 95% owner of Johnson County Broadcasters Inc., licensee of KOKO(AM) Warrensburg, Mo. & 95% owner of KLMX(AM) Clayton, N.M.

Johnson Publishing Co. Hqtrs: 820 S. Michigan Ave., Chicago 60605. (312) 322-9200. FAX: (312) 322-0039. Johnson Publishing Co. publishes *Ebony, Jet* & *EM-Ebony Man* magazines. The company also produces syndicated TV programs: *Ebony/Jet Showcase* & *American Black Achievement Awards.* Johnson Publishing Co. also owns 100% of WJPC(AM) Chicago & WJPC-FM Lansing, both Ill., & WLOU(AM) Louisville, Ky.

Journal Communications Inc.—See WTMJ Inc.

K

KTTC Television Inc. Hqtrs: 601 First Ave. S.W., Rochester, Minn. 55902. (507) 288-4444. FAX: (507) 288-6324. Quincy Newspapers Inc., publisher of the *Quincy* (Ill.) *Herald-Whig*, owns KTTC(TV) Rochester, Minn.

L

La Salle County Broadcasting Corp. Hqtrs: Box 215, La Salle, Ill. 61301. (815) 223-3100. FAX: (815) 223-3095. Peter Miller, pres & 95% owner of Daily News-Tribune Inc., publisher of the *News Tribune*, also owns La Salle County Broadcasting Corp., licensee of WLPO(AM) & WAJK(FM) La Salle, Ill.

Landmark Communications Inc. Hqtrs: 150 W. Brambleton Ave., Norfolk, Va. 23510. (804) 446-2000. FAX: (804) 446-2489. Landmark Communications Inc. publishes daily newspapers as follows:

California: *The Daily Californian*, El Cajon.
Florida: *Citrus County Chronicle*, Inverness.
Kentucky: *News-Enterprise*, Elizabethtown.
Maryland: *Carroll County Times*, Westminster.
New Mexico: *Los Alamos Monitor*, Los Alamos.
North Carolina: *News & Record*, Greensboro.
Virginia: *The Virginian-Pilot*, & *The Ledger-Star*, Norfolk; *Roanoke Times & World-News*, Roanoke.

The Landmark Community Newspapers Inc., Shelbyville, Ky. division publishes three tri-weeklies, eight biweeklies, 18 weeklies, nine specialty publications & 24 shoppers & free newspapers in the states of Calif., Fla., Ill., Ind., Iowa, Ky., Md., Miss., N.M., Tenn. & Va.

The Landmark Classified Advertising Publications, Shelbyville, Ky. division publishes 17 photo guide & classified advertising publications in the states of Illinois, Michigan, Minnesota, Missouri, North Carolina, Ohio, Pennsylvania & South Carolina.

The Landmark Special Publications, Norfolk, Va. division publishes five free-distribution wkly newsprint magazines covering leisure-time activities in Florida, Louisiana, North Carolina & Virginia.

The Executive Productivity Systems Inc., Norfolk, Va. division distributes computers & related products coast-to-coast.

Landmark Communications Inc. owns 49.9% of Capital-Gazette Communications Inc., publisher of the daily *Annapolis Capital*, the twice-wkly *Maryland Gazette, Baltimore Magazine, Washingtonian Magazine* & non-daily newspapers in Bowie, Brooklyn & Crofton, all Md.

Cable TV progmg: The Weather Channel & The Travel Channel, Atlanta.

Stations: KLAS-TV Las Vegas; & WTVF(TV) Nashville.

Lee Enterprises Inc. Hqtrs: 215 N. Main St., Davenport, Iowa 52801. (319) 383-2100. FAX: (319) 323-9608. Lee Enterprises Inc. publishes:

Illinois: *Southern Illinoisan*, Carbondale; *Herald & Review*, Decatur; *Bicon*, Geneseo; & *Star-Courier*, Kewanee.

Iowa: *The Bettendorf News*, Bettendorf (weekly); *Quad City Times*, Davenport; *Globe-Gazette*, Mason City; *Muscatine Journal*, Muscatine; & *The Ottumwa Courier*, Ottumwa.

Minnesota: *Winona Daily News*, Winona.

Montana: *Billings Gazette*, Billings; *The Montana Standard*, Butte; *Independent Record*, Helena; & *Missoulian*, Missoula.

Nebraska: *The Lincoln Star*, Lincoln.

North Dakota: *Farm & Ranch Guide*, Bismarck; *The Bismarck Tribune*, Bismarck; & Dakota West Publishing Inc., Mandan.

Oregon: *Corvallis Gazette-Times*, Corvallis.

South Dakota: *The Rapid City Journal*, Rapid City.

Wisconsin: *La Crosse Tribune*, La Crosse; *Wisconsin State Journal*, Madison; & *The Racine Journal-Times*, Racine.

Other interests: Lee Enterprises publishes, directly or through its affils, 19 daily newspapers & 33 wkly & specialty publications; & manufactures graphic arts products for the newspaper industry through NAPP Systems Inc.

Stations: KGUN(TV) Tucson, Ariz.; KGMD-TV Hilo, KGMB(TV) Honolulu & KGMV(TV) Wailuku, all Hawaii; KMTV(TV) Omaha; KRQE(TV) Albuquerque, KZIA(TV) Las Cruces & KBIM-TV Roswell, all N.M.; KOIN(TV) Portland, Ore.; & WSAZ-TV Huntington, W.Va.

Lima Communications Corp. Hqtrs: 1424 Rice Ave., Lima, Ohio 45805. (419) 228-8835. FAX: (419) 229-7091. Blade Communications Inc., publisher of the *Toledo* (Ohio) *Blade* & *Pittsburgh Post-Gazette*, & with interests in the *Monterey Peninsula Herald*, owns 100% of KTRV(TV) Nampa, Idaho, WLFI-TV Lafayette, Ind. &

WDRB-TV Louisville, Ky., & 100% of Lima Communications Corp., licensee of WLIO(TV) Lima, Ohio.

Lorain County Printing & Publishing Co. Hqtrs: 225 East Ave., Elyria, Ohio 44035. (216) 329-7000. FAX: (216) 329-7272. *Chronicle-Telegram*, Elyria, & *Medina Gazette*, Medina, both Ohio, have ownership with interests in Elyria-Lorain Broadcasting Co., licensee of WEOL(AM) & WNWV(FM) Elyria, Ohio.

M

Manship Stations. Hqtrs: Box 2906, Baton Rouge 70821. (504) 387-2222. FAX: (504) 336-2246. *Baton Rouge Morning Advocate* & *Saturday & Sunday Advocate* have same ownership as WBRZ(TV) Baton Rouge & KRGV-TV Weslaco, Tex.

McGraw-Hill Broadcasting Group. Hqtrs: 1221 Ave. of the Americas, New York 10020. (212) 512-6457. FAX: (212) 512-2282. McGraw-Hill Inc., owner of the McGraw-Hill Broadcasting Group, publishes *Business Week* magazine & various trade publications. McGraw-Hill Broadcasting Group owns KERO-TV Bakersfield & KGTV(TV) San Diego, both Calif.; KMGH-TV Denver; & WRTV(TV) Indianapolis.

McNaughton Stations. Hqtrs: c/o WCRA(AM)-WCRC(FM), 208 W. Jefferson Ave., Effingham, Ill. 62401. Ownership (Joseph E. McNaughton & family) identified with *The Davis Enterprise, Fairfield Republic* & the *Placerville Mountain Democrat*, all Calif. Stations: WCRA(AM)-WCRC(FM) Effingham & WRMN(AM)-WJKL(FM) Elgin, both Ill. WBEV(AM)-WXRO(FM) Beaver Dam & WYKY(FM) Columbus, both Wis.

Media General Inc. Hqtrs: 333 E. Grace St., Richmond, Va. 23219. (804) 649-6000. FAX: (804) 649-6898. Media General Inc. is publisher of *The Tampa* (Fla.) *Tribune, Winston-Salem* (N.C.) *Journal* & the *Richmond* (Va.) *Times-Dispatch*. Media General also publishes *Virginia Business* (mthy).

Other interests: Fairfax Cable, Chantilly, Va.

Stations: Media General Inc. owns 100% of WJKS(TV) Jacksonville & WFLA-TV Tampa, both Fla.; & WCBD-TV Charleston, S.C.

Meredith Corp. Hqtrs: 1716 Locust St., Des Moines, Iowa 50309-3023. (515) 284-3000. The publishing group includes:

Magazines: *Better Homes & Gardens, Country America, Country Home, Craft & Wear, Cross Stitch & Country Crafts, Decorative Woodcrafts, Golf for Women, Ladies' Home Journal, Midwest Living, Successful Farming, Traditional Home, Weekend Woodworking Projects* & *WOOD*. Other magazine group products include *Better Homes & Gardens* (Australian edition), *Better Homes & Gardens* (Korean licensee) & Meredith Video Publishing.

The broadcasting group of Meredith Corp. operates KPHO-TV Phoenix; WOFL(TV) Orlando, Fla.; WNEM-TV Bay City, Mich.; KCTV(TV) Kansas City, Mo.; & KVVU-TV Henderson, Nev.

Miles City (Mont.) Star.—See Star Printing Co.

Milwaukee Courier Hqtrs: 3815 N. Teutonia Ave., Milwaukee 53206. (414) 445-2031. FAX: (414) 449-4872. Jerrel W. Jones, CEO & majority stockholder of Courier Publishing Co., publisher of the wkly *Milwaukee Courier*, owns 60% of Courier Communications Corp., licensee of WNOV(AM) Milwaukee.

Monroe Journal. Hqtrs: Box 826, 126 Hines St., Monroeville, Ala. 36461. (205) 575-3282. FAX: (205) 575-3283. William M. Stewart, publisher of the wkly *Monroe Journal*, is principal stockholder in Monroe Broadcasting Co., licensee of WMFC-AM-FM Monroeville, Ala.

Morgan Murphy Stations. Hqtrs: Box 44965, Madison, Wis. 53744-4965. (608) 271-4321. FAX: (608) 271-6111. Evening Telegram Co. publishes the *Evening Telegram* (Superior, Wis.) & owns 100% of the *Ashland Daily Press* (Ashland, Wis.) & the *Hibbing Tribune* (Hibbing, Minn.). Evening Telegram shareholders individually own the *Virginia/Mesabi Daily News* (Virginia, Minn.). Stations: KTHI-TV Fargo, N.D.; KVEW(TV) Kennewick, KXLY-AM-FM-TV Spokane & KAPP(TV) Yakima, all Wash.; & WISC-TV Madison, Wis.

Morris Newspaper Corp. Hqtrs: Box 8167, Savannah, Ga. 31412. (912) 233-1281. Owns 100% of the following newspapers:

California: *Ceres Courier, Colusa County Sun Herald, Manteca Bulletin, Newhall Signal* & the *Willows Journal*.

Georgia: *The Covington News; Coastal Courier*, Hinesville; *Savannah Penny-Savers; The Herald*, Rincon; & the *Statesboro Herald*.

Kansas: *Great Bend Tribune*.

South Carolina: *Camden Chronicle-Independent*& the *Florence News & Shopper*. (Both 80% owned.)

Tennessee: *Brentwood Journal*, Franklin; *Franklin Review-Appeal; Southern Standard*, McMinnville; *Merchants' Advocate*, Murfreesboro; *Murfreesboro Daily News Journal; Smithville Review;* & the *Rutherford Courier*, Smyrna.

Stations: WDHN(TV) Dothan, Ala.; KARK-TV Little Rock, Ark.; WMGT(TV) Macon & WVGA(TV) Valdosta, both Ga. (All 100% owned.)

Multimedia Inc. Hqtrs: Box 1688, Greenville, S.C. 29602. (803) 298-4373. FAX: (803) 298-4271. Multimedia Inc. publishes *The Advertiser*, Montgomery, Ala.; the *Baxter Bulletin*, Mountain Home, Ark.; *Moultrie* (Ga.) *Observer; Asheville Citizen-Times*, Asheville, N.C.; *Gallipolis Daily Tribune*, Gallipolis, & the *Daily Sentinel* & *Sunday Times-Sentinel*, Pomeroy-Middleport, both Ohio; *Greenville* (S.C.) *News* & *Piedmont;* the *Clarksville* (Tenn.) *Leaf-Chronicle; Music City News* & *The Gospel Voice*, both Nashville; *Staunton* (Va.) *Daily & Sunday News-Leader;* & the *Point Pleasant* (W. Va.) *Register*.

Other interests: Multimedia Cablevision, Wichita, Kan., operates 100 plus cable television systems in Illinois, Indiana, Kansas, North Carolina & Oklahoma & serves approximately 410,000 basic subscribers. Multimedia Entertainment, located at Rockefeller Plaza in New York City, produces & syndicates television progmg such as the Phil Donahue, Sally Jessy Raphael, Jerry Springer & Rush Limbaugh shows.

Stations: WMAZ-AM-TV & WAYS(FM) Macon, Ga.; KEEL(AM) & KITT(FM) Shreveport, La.; KSDK(TV) St. Louis; WLWT(TV) Cincinnati & WKYC-TV Cleveland; WFBC-AM-FM Greenville & WORD(AM) Spartanburg, both S.C.; WBIR-TV Knoxville, Tenn.; & WEZW(FM) Wauwatosa, Wis. (Milwaukee). Note: KEEL(AM) & KITT(FM) Shreveport, La. have been sold, subject to FCC approval.

N

Narragansett Capital Inc. Hqtrs: 900 Fleet Center, 50 Kennedy Plaza, Providence, R.I. 02903. (401) 751-1000. FAX: (401) 751-9340. Narragansett Capital Inc. owns the following newspapers:

Michigan: *Cassopolis Vigilant, Dowagiac Daily News, Edwardsburg Argus* & the *Niles Daily Star*.

Oklahoma: *Miami News Record*.

Texas: *Alice Echo News, Brownwood Bulletin, Stephenville Empire Tribune* & the *Waxahachie Daily Light*.

Stations: WYNK-AM-FM Baton Rouge; KEZO-AM-FM Omaha; WPRI-TV Providence, R.I.; & WTKR-TV Norfolk, Va.

The New York Times Co. Hqtrs: 229 W. 43d St., New York 10036. (212) 556-1234. The New York Times Co. is the publisher of *The New York Times, The Boston Globe* & (through its regional newspaper group) the following daily newspapers:

Alabama: *Times Daily*, Florence; *The Gadsden Times*, Gadsden; & *The Tuscaloosa News*, Tuscaloosa.

California: *Santa Barbara News-Press*, Santa Barbara; & *The Press-Democrat*, Santa Rosa.

Florida: *The Gainesville Sun*, Gainesville; *Lake City Reporter*, Lake City; *The Ledger*, Lakeland; *Daily Commercial*, Leesburg; *Ocala Star-Banner*, Ocala; *Palatka Daily News*, Palatka; & the *Sarasota Herald-Tribune*, Sarasota.

Kentucky: *The Messenger*, Madisonville.

Louisiana: *Houma Daily Courier*, Houma; *Daily World*, Opelousas; & the *Daily Comet*, Thibodaux.

Mississippi: *The Daily Corinthian*, Corinth.

North Carolina: *Times-News*, Hendersonville; *Lenoir News-Topic*, Lenoir; *The Dispatch*, Lexington; & the *Wilmington Morning Star*, Wilmington.

South Carolina: *Spartanburg Herald-Journal*, Spartanburg.

Tennessee: *State Gazette*, Dyersburg.

Regional non-dailies: *The News-Sun*, Avon Park, Fla.; *News-Leader*, Fernandina Beach, Fla.; *Marco Island Eagle*, Marco Island, Fla.; *The News-Sun*, Sebring, Fla.; *York County Coast Star*, Kennebunk, Me.; & *The Banner-Independent*, Booneville, Miss.

Note: The New York Times Co. also holds a half interest in the *International Herald Tribune* in Paris.

Magazine group (women's magazines): *Child, Decorating Remodeling, Family Circle, Family Circle Great Ideas* & *McCall's*.

Magazine group (sports & leisure magazines): *Cruising World, Golf Digest, Golf Digest Sverige* (Sweden), *Golf Illustrated Weekly* (United Kingdom), *Golf Shop Operations, Golf World* (United States), *Golf World* (United Kingdom), *Golf World Industry News, Sailing World, Snow Country, Tennis* & *Tennis Buyer's Guide*.

Broadcasting group: WHNT-TV Huntsville, Ala.; KFSM-TV Fort Smith, Ark.; WQAD-TV Moline, Ill.; WQEW(AM) & WQXR-FM New York; WNEP-TV Scranton, Pa.; & WREG-TV Memphis.

News Corp. Ltd.-News America Publishing Inc. Hqtrs: 1211 Ave. of the Americas, New York 10036. (212) 852-7000. FAX: (212) 852-7186. The News Corporation Ltd., owns the *Boston Herald* & the *New York Post*. (All 100% owned.) Stations: KTTV(TV) Los Angeles; WTTG(TV) Washington; WATL(TV) Atlanta; WFLD(TV) Chicago; WNYW(TV) New York; KDAF(TV) Dallas & KRIV(TV) Houston; & KSTU(TV) Salt Lake City.

O

Ogden Newspapers Inc. Hqtrs: 1500 Main St., Wheeling, W.Va. 26003. (304) 233-0100. FAX: (304) 233-0100. Owns daily newspapers in Florida, Iowa, Michigan, Minnesota, New York, Ohio, Pennsylvania, West Virginia & Wisconsin.

Stations: WTON-AM-FM Staunton, Va.; plus three low power TV stns: K28AE Fairmont & K22AE New Ulm, both Minn.; & W43AP Jamestown, N.Y.

P

Paducah Newspapers Inc. Hqtrs: Box 1197, Paducah, Ky. 42002-1197. (502) 442-8214. FAX: (502) 442-2096. Paducah Newspapers Inc., publisher of the *Paragould* (Ark.) *Daily Press, Russellville* (Ark.) *Courier-Democrat, Salem* (Ark.) *News*, (Searcy, Ark.) *Daily Citizen* & the *Paducah* (Ky.) *Sun*, is licensee of WPSD-TV Paducah, Ky.

Park Communications Inc. Hqtrs: Box 550, Ithaca, N.Y. 14851. (607) 272-9020. FAX: (607) 272-0980. Park Newspapers Inc. owns the following newspapers:

Arkansas: *Courier News, Sunday Courier News, Mail Call-Blythe Spirit*, Blytheville; *The Daily World, The Sunday World, Twin City Tribune/Advertiser*, Helena; *Osceola Times, The Missco Shopper Guide*.

Georgia: *The Houston Home Journal, Shoppers Extra*, Perry; *Daily Sun & Sunday Sun*, & *Houston County News-Rev-Up*, Warner Robins.

Idaho: *South Idaho Press, Minidoka County News, The News Review, Magic Valley Farmlines*, Burley; *The Wood River Journal*, Hailey.

Illinois: *Effingham Daily News, The Weekly Advertiser*, Effingham; *Macomb Daily Journal, Macomb Sunday Journal, Business News*, Macomb.

Indiana: *The Evening News, Clark County Journal, Golden Opportunities*, Jeffersonville; *The Pilot-News, Farm & Home News, Bourbon News-Mirror, The Bremen Enquirer, The Nappanee Advance News, Co-Pilot*, Plymouth; & *The News-Gazette, The News & Advertiser*, Winchester.

Iowa: *The Evening Sentinel, The Essex Independent, The Weekly Times*, Shenandoah.

Kentucky: *Menifee County News*, Frenchburg; *The Carlisle Mercury, Grayson County News-Gazette, The Grayson County Advertiser*, Leitchfield; *Sentinel-Echo, The Morehead News, Shopping News, The Sentinel Neighbor*, London; *Rock Castle Neighbor*, London/Somerset; *Logan Leader, News Democrat, Olive Hill Times, Grayson Journal-Enquirer, The Greenup County News, The Logan Advertiser*, Russellville; *The Commonwealth-Journal, McCreary County Record, Lake Cumberland Shopper*, Somerset.

Michigan: *Coldwater Daily Reporter, The Branch County Outdoors, The Sturgis Free Advisor*.

Minnesota: *The Pioneer, The Advertiser, The Mid-Week Advertiser*, Bemidji; *The American, The Blackduck Shopper*, Blackduck.

Nebraska: *Nebraska City News-Press*& *Tri-State Weekly Times*.

New York: *Albion Advertiser; St. Lawrence Plaindealer, Chatham Courier*, Canton; *The Register-Star, Columbia Views*, Hudson; *Union-Sun & Journal, Tri-County News*, Lockport; The Courier Observer, Massena; *The Journal-Register, Eastern Niagara Edition, TV Signals, Pennysaver*, Medina; *The Evening Sun, Chenango Shopper*, Norwich; *Advance News* (Sunday), *The Journal* (evening), *Rural News*, Ogdensburg.

North Carolina: *Citizen News-Record, News Outlook Shopping Guide*, Aberdeen; *News-Herald, Golden Opportunities* (quarterly), Ahoskie; *The Sampson Independent, Sunday Independent, Sampson County Shopping Guide & TV Schedule*, Clinton; *The Concord Tribune, The Tribune* (Sunday); *The Cabarrus Observer Nugget, The Edge*, Concord/Kannapolis; *Mecklenburg Gazette*, Davidson; *Eden Daily News, The Virginia Carolina Beacon*, Eden; *Bladen Daily Journal, The Southeastern Times*, Elizabethtown; *Enfield Progress, Southwest Halifax Advantage*, Enfield; *Gates County Index*, Gatesville; *The News-Messenger*, Hamlet; *North-*

ampton News, Jackson; *The Daily Independent,* Kannapolis; *The Robesonian, Robesonian Weekly, The Robeson Mid-Weekly,* Lumberton; *The McDowell News, McDowell Express,* Marion; *Mooresville Tribune, Shoppers Guide; The News Herald, The Sunday News Herald, The Burke County Observer,* Morganton; *Murfreesboro Advantage,* Murfreesboro; *Observer-News Enterprise, County News Enterprise-Maiden Times,* Newton; *Pinehurst Outlook* (mthy); *The North Carolina Beacon,* Research Triangle Park; *The Richmond County Daily Journal, The Journal Advantage,* Rockingham; *Commonwealth, Southeast Halifax Advantage,* Scotland Neck; *Statesville Record & Landmark, Sunday Record & Landmark, Landmark Observer,* Statesville; *The Valdese News,* Valdese.

North Dakota: *Devils Lake Daily Journal, The Country Peddler.*

Oklahoma: *Bixby Bulletin; Daily Ledger, Broken Arrow Weekly Ledger, Tri-Cities Shopper* (bi-wkly), Broken Arrow; *Hartshorne Sun; Jenks Journal; Mannford Eagle; News-Capital & Democrat, Southeast Oklahoma Shopping News,* McAlester; *Sand Springs Leader, Sand Springs Extra, Golden Opportunities* (quarterly) Sand Springs; & *The Sapulpa Daily Herald, Herald Extra.*

Pennsylvania: *Wayne Independent, The Wayne County Sunday,* Honesdale; *Lewisburg Daily Journal, The Milton Standard* & *The Central Penn Shopper,* Milton/Lewisburg.

Virginia: *The Journal Messenger, Suburban Virginia Times,* Manassas; & *The News-Virginian, The Rockfish Valley Buyers Guide, Shenandoah Shopper,* Waynesboro.

Stations: WBMG(TV) Birmingham, Ala.; WNLS(AM) & WTNT(FM) Tallahassee, Fla.; KWLO(AM) & KFMW(FM) Waterloo, Iowa; WTVQ-TV Lexington, Ky.; KALB-TV Alexandria, La.; KJJO-AM-FM St. Louis Park, Minn.; WPAT-AM-FM Paterson, N.J.; WHEN-AM-FM Syracuse & WUTR(TV) Utica, both N.Y.; WNCT-AM-FM-TV Greenville, N.C.; KWJJ-AM-FM Portland, Ore.; WNAX-AM-FM Yankton, S.D.; WDEF-AM-FM-TV Chattanooga & WJHL-TV Johnson City, both Tenn.; WTVR-AM-FM-TV Richmond & WSLS-TV Roanoke, both Va.; & KEZX-AM-FM Seattle.

Pillar of Fire Inc. Hqtrs: Box 37, Weston Canal Rd., Zarephath, N.J. 08890. Pillar of Fire Inc. publishes one religious periodical, a semi-mthy for the family (*Pillar of Fire*). Stations: KPOF(AM) Denver; WAWZ(FM) Zarephath, N.J.; & WAKW(FM) Cincinnati.

Ponca City Publishing Co. Hqtrs: Box 588, Ponca City, Okla. 74602. (405) 765-6607. FAX: (405) 762-6397. Ponca City Publishing Co., publisher of the *Ponca City* (Okla.) *News,* is licensee of WBBZ(AM) Ponca City, Okla.

The Post Co. Hqtrs: Box 2148, Idaho Falls, Idaho 83403. (208) 525-8888. FAX: (208) 522-1930. The Post Co. owns 100% of *The Post Register,* Idaho Falls, Idaho. The company also is licensee of KIFI-TV Idaho Falls, Idaho.

Post-Newsweek Stations Inc. Hqtrs: 1150 15th St. N.W., Washington 20071. (202) 334-4600. FAX: (202) 334-4536. The Washington Post Co. (parent company of Post-Newsweek Stations Inc.) publishes the *Washington Post,* the *Everett* (Wash.) *Herald, Newsweek magazine, Newsweek International* (New York), *Newsweek Japan* & *Newsweek Korea.* The Washington Post Co. also holds a 50% interest in the *International Herald Tribune* of Paris. Post-Newsweek stations: WFSB(TV) Hartford, Conn.; WJXT(TV) Jacksonville & WPLG(TV) Miami, both Fla.; & WDIV(TV) Detroit. Note: Group has purchased KPRC-TV Houston & KSAT-TV San Antonio, both Tex., pending FCC approval.

Press Broadcasting Co. (subsidiary of New Jersey Press Inc.) Hqtrs: Box 1550, 3601 Hwy 66, Neptune, N.J. 07753. (908) 922-2800. FAX: (908) 922-6326. New Jersey Press Inc., publisher of the *Asbury Park* (N.J.) *Press* (daily & Sunday), is parent company of Press Television Corp., licensee of WKCF(TV) Clermont, Fla., & Press Broadcasting Co., licensee of WTKS(FM) Cocoa Beach, Fla. & WBUD(AM)-WKXW(FM) Trenton, N.J.

Price Communications Corp. Hqtrs: 45 Rockefeller Plaza, New York 10020. (212) 757-5600. Owns *The New York Law Journal,* New York. Wkly newspapers include *National Law Journal,* New York & Washington.

Other interests include a Law Book Publishing Co., a National Legal Seminar & 20 nationally distributed newsletters. The company also owns Price Outdoor Media of Mid-Missouri, an outdoor advertising company, & has a 42.5% interest in Pri Cellular, a joint venture with Time-Warner Inc. in cellular telephone systems.

Stations: WBZT(AM) & WIRK-FM West Palm Beach, Fla.; WOWO(AM) Fort Wayne & WOWO-FM Huntington, both Ind.; KSNF(TV) Joplin, Mo.; WWKB(AM) Buffalo & WKSE(FM) Niagara Falls, both N.Y.; KJAC-TV Port Arthur & KFDX-TV Wichita Falls, both Tex.

Progressive Publishing Co. Hqtrs: Box 291, Clearfield, Pa. 16830. (814) 765-5051. FAX: (814) 765-5165. Progressive Publishing Co., publisher of the *Clearfield* (Pa.) *Progress,* owns 100% of Clearfield Broadcasters Inc., licensee of WCPA(AM) & WQYX(FM) Clearfield, Pa.

Providence Journal Co. Hqtrs: 75 Fountain St., Providence, R.I. 02902. (401) 277-7000. FAX: (401) 274-2076. The Providence Journal Co., publisher of the *Providence* (R.I.) *Journal-Bulletin,* owns 100% of KMSB-TV Tucson, Ariz.; WHAS-TV Louisville, Ky.; KASA-TV Santa Fe, N.M.; & WCNC-TV Charlotte, N.C. Note: Providence Journal Co. also owns & manages cable systems serving 770,000 subscribers in Calif., Fla., Idaho, Mass., Minn., N.Y., R.I., & Wash. under the names Colony, Copley/Colony, Dynamic, King Video & U.S. Cable. Providence Journal Co. owns 50%, with Kelso & Co., New York, of the following TV stns: KHBC-TV Hilo, KHNL(TV) Honolulu & KOGG(TV) Wailuku, all Hawaii; KTVB(TV) Boise, Idaho; KGW-TV Portland, Ore.; KING-TV Seattle & KREM-TV Spokane, both Wash.

Pulaski Broadcasting Co. Hqtrs: 104 S. 2nd St., Pulaski, Tenn. 38478. (615) 363-2505. FAX: (615) 363-8656. S. Hershal Lake, who owns 55% of Pulaski Publishing Inc. (newspaper publisher in Pulaski, Tenn.) & 60% of *The Carthage Courier,* Carthage, Tenn., owns 55% of WKSR(AM) & WINJ(FM) Pulaski, Tenn. Geraldine Lake, who owns 35% of Pulaski Publishing Inc. & 40% of *The Carthage Courier,* owns 45% of WKSR(AM) & WINJ(FM) Pulaski, Tenn.

Pulitzer Publishing Co. Hqtrs: 900 N. Tucker Blvd., St. Louis 63101. (314) 340-8000. Pulitzer Publishing Co. publishes the *St. Louis Post-Dispatch; Arizona Daily Star,* Tucson, Ariz.; *Daily Southtown,* Chicago; & Lerner Newspapers, Chicago. Stations: KTAR(AM) & KKLT(FM) Phoenix; WESH(TV) Daytona Beach, Fla.; KCCI-TV Des Moines, Iowa; WLKY-TV Louisville, Ky.; WDSU(TV) New Orleans; KETV(TV) Omaha; KOAT-TV Albuquerque & KOCT(TV) Carlsbad, both N.M.; WXII(TV) Winston-Salem, N.C.; WGAL(TV) Lancaster, Pa.; & WYFF(TV) Greenville, S.C.

Q

Quincy Newspapers Inc. Hqtrs: Box 909, Quincy, Ill. 62306. (217) 223-5100. FAX: (217) 223-5019. Quincy Newspapers Inc., publishers of the *Quincy* (Ill.) *Herald-Whig,* owns the *New Jersey Herald,* Newton, N.J. (100%), & the following stations: WGEM-AM-FM-TV Quincy, Ill. (95%); WSJV(TV) Elkhart (South Bend), Ind. (100%); KTIV(TV) Sioux City, Iowa (100%); KTTC(TV) Rochester, Minn. (100%); & WVVA(TV) Bluefield, W.Va. (100%).

R

Rusk (Tex.) Cherokeean-Herald. Hqtrs: Box 475, Rusk, Tex. 75785. (903) 683-2257. E.H. Whitehead, 52% owner of the wkly *Rusk* (Tex.) *Cherokeean-Herald,* is licensee & 100% owner of KTLU(AM) & KWRW(FM) Rusk, Tex.

S

Sandusky Newspapers Inc. Hqtrs: 601 California, Suite 2260, San Francisco 94108. (415) 788-3161. FAX: (415) 788-3165. Sandusky Newspapers Inc. publishes the *Sandusky* (Ohio) *Register,* the *Grand Haven* (Mich.) *Tribune, Norwalk* (Ohio) *Reflector,* the *Kingsport* (Tenn.) *Times* & *News* & the *Ogden* (Utah) *Standard-Examiner.* Stations: KDKB(FM) Mesa, Ariz.; KEGL(FM) Fort Worth; KLSY-FM Bellevue & KIXI(AM) Seattle, both Wash.

Schurz Communications Inc. Hqtrs: 225 W. Colfax Ave., South Bend, Ind. 46626. Schurz Communications publishes the following newspapers:

California: *Imperial Valley Press.*

Indiana: *Bedford Times-Mail, Bloomington Herald-Telephone* & *Herald-Times,* & *South Bend Tribune.*

Kentucky: *Danville Advocate-Messenger.*

Maryland: *Hagerstown Herald* & *Mail.*

Stations: WAGT(TV) Augusta, Ga.; WASK-AM-FM Lafayette & WSBT-AM-TV & WNSN(FM) South Bend, both Ind.; KYTV(TV) Springfield, Mo.; & WDBJ(TV) Roanoke, Va.

Scripps Howard. Hqtrs: 312 Walnut St., 28th Fl., Cincinnati 45201. (513) 977-3825. Scripps Howard newspapers are:

Daily newspapers: *Birmingham Post-Herald,* Birmingham, Ala.; *The Rocky Mountain News,* Denver; *The Naples Daily News,* Naples, Fla.; *The Stuart News,* Stuart, Fla.; *The Evansville Courier,* Evansville, Ind.; *The Kentucky Post,* Covington, Ky.; *The Albuquerque Tribune,* Albuquerque, N.M.; *The Cincinnati Post,* Cincinnati; *The Knoxville News-Sentinel,* Knoxville, Tenn.; *The Commercial Appeal,* Memphis; & the *El Paso Herald-Post,* El Paso, Tex.

Non-daily newspapers: *The Destin Log,* Destin, Fla.; *The Jensen Beach Mirror,* Jensen Beach, Fla.; *The Port St. Lucie Mirror,* Jensen Beach, Fla.; *Jupiter Courier Journal,* Jupiter, Fla.; & *The Stuart Mirror,* Stuart, Fla.

John P. Scripps Newspapers: Dailies—*Camarillo Daily News,* Camarillo, Calif.; *Monterey County Herald,* Monterey, Calif.; *Redding Record Searchlight,* Redding, Calif.; *San Luis Obispo Telegram-Tribune,* San Luis Obispo, Calif.; *Simi Valley Enterprise,* Simi Valley, Calif.; *Thousand Oaks News Chronicle,* Thousand Oaks, Calif.; *Tulare Advance-Register,* Tulare, Calif.; *Ventura County Star-Free Press,* Ventura, Calif.; *Watsonville Register-Pajaronian,* Watsonville, Calif.; & *The Sun,* Bremerton, Wash. Non-dailies: *The Cambrian,* Cambria, Calif.; & the *Morro Bay Sun-Bulletin,* Morro Bay, Calif.

Stations: KNXV-TV Phoenix; WFTS(TV) Tampa & WPTV(TV) West Palm Beach, both Fla.; WMAR-TV Baltimore; WXYZ-TV Detroit; KSHB-TV Kansas City, Mo.; WCPO-TV Cincinnati & WEWS(TV) Cleveland; & KJRH(TV) Tulsa, Okla.

Seaton Stations. Hqtrs: Box 877, Coffeyville, Kan. 67337. (316) 251-2900. Seaton Group of newspapers includes the *Manhattan Mercury* & the *Winfield Courier,* both Kan.; *Alliance Times-Herald* & the *Hastings Tribune,* both Neb.; *Deadwood Pioneer-Times, Lead Call* & the *Spearfish Queen City Mail,* all S.D.; & the *Sheridan* (Wyo.) *Press.* Stations: KMAN(AM) & KMKF(FM) Manhattan, Kan.; KHAS-TV Hastings, Neb.; KFYO(AM) & KZII-FM Lubbock, Tex.

Shamrock Communications Inc. Hqtrs: 149 Penn Ave., Scranton, Pa. 18503. Principals of Shamrock Communications Inc. also publish *The City Paper,* Baltimore; *The Pennysaver Press,* Owego, N.Y.; *The Scranton Times, The Tribune, The Sunday Times,* Scranton, Pa.; *The Pocono Shopper,* Stroudsburg, Pa.; *The Towanda Daily Review,* Towanda, Pa.; *The Farmers Friend,* Towanda, Pa.; *The Troy Pennysaver,* Troy, Pa.; & *The New Age-Examiner,* Tunkhannock, Pa. Stations: WDIZ(FM) Orlando, Fla.; WTTR(AM) & WGRX(FM) Westminster, Md. (Baltimore); KMYZ-AM-FM Pryor (Tulsa), Okla.; WEJL(AM) & WEZX(FM) Scranton, Pa.; KUTZ(FM) Lampasas, Tex.; & WQFM(FM) Milwaukee.

South Jersey Radio Inc. Hqtrs: 1601 New Road, Linwood, N.J. 08221. South Jersey Radio Inc. (Howard L. Green, pres) owns the wkly *Cape May* (N.J.) *Star* & *Wave* & 100% of the wkly *Ocean City* (N.J.) *Sentinel-Ledger.* Stations: WECY-AM-FM Seaford, Del.; WMGM(FM) Atlantic City, WONZ(AM) Hammonton, WOND(AM) Pleasantville & WMGM-TV Wildwood, all N.J.; & WENY-AM-FM-TV Elmira, N.Y.

Star Printing Co. Hqtrs: Box 700, 810 S. Haynes St., Miles City, Mont. 59301. (406) 232-7700. Star Printing Co., publisher of the *Miles City* (Mont.) *Star,* is licensee of KATL(AM) Miles City, Mont.

Stauffer Communications Inc. Hqtrs: 616 Jefferson, Topeka, Kan. 66607. (913) 295-1111. FAX: (913) 295-1261. Stauffer Communications Inc. is publisher of the *Glenwood Springs* (Colo.) *Post; Auburndale Star, Haines City Ridge Shopper, Haines City Herald, Lake Wales Highlander, Lake Wales Shopper, Shopper Publishing Group,* Lakeland, & the *Winter Haven News Chief,* all Fla.; *Topeka Capital-Journal, Arkansas City Traveler, Dodge City Daily Globe, Shoppers Weekly* (Dodge City), *Pittsburg Morning Sun, Newton Kansan* & *Cappers,* & *National Grit,* all Kan.; *Hillsdale Daily News* & the *Holland Sentinel,* both Mich.; *Brainerd* (Minn.) *Daily Dispatch; Blue Springs Examiner, Hannibal Courier-Post* & the *Independence Examiner,* all Mo.; *Grand Island Independent,* & *York News-Times,* all Neb.; *Ardmore Ardmoreite* & *Shawnee News-Star,* both Okla.; *Yankton* (S.D.) *Press & Dakotan;* & the *Oak Ridge Oak Ridger,* Oak Ridge, Tenn.

Other interests: Kansas City Royals Radio Network, Kansas Information Network, Kansas Agriculture Network, Wildcat Sports Network, Topeka, Kan. (100% ownership).

Stauffer Communications Inc. owns KCOY-TV Santa Maria, Calif.; KTVS(TV) Sterling, Colo.; WIBW-AM-FM-TV Topeka, Kan.; KMIZ(TV) Columbia, Mo.; KSTF(TV) Scottsbluff, Neb.; KGNC-AM-FM Amarillo, Tex.; KGWC-TV Casper, KGWN-TV Cheyenne, KGWL-TV Lander & KGWR-TV Rock Springs, all Wyo.

Stillwater Publishing Co. Hqtrs: Box 2288, Stillwater, Okla. 74076. (405) 372-5000. Stillwater Publishing Co., publisher of the *Stillwater* (Okla.) *News-Press,* is licensee of KSPI-AM-FM Stillwater, Okla.

Newspaper/Magazine Cross-Ownership

Straus Media Group. Hqtrs: 22 N. Main St., Ellenville, N.Y. 12428. (914) 647-5678. FAX: (914) 647-5008. Straus Media Group, owner of six wkly newspapers, also owns WCKL(AM)-WCTW(FM) Catskill & WELV(AM)-WWWK(FM) Ellenville, both N.Y.; & WFTR-AM-FM Front Royal, Va.

T

Times & News Publishing Co. Hqtrs: Box 3669, Gettysburg, Pa. 17325. (717) 334-1131. FAX: (717) 334-4243. Times & News Publishing Co., publisher of the *Gettysburg* (Pa.) *Times*, is licensee of WGET(AM) & WGTY(FM) Gettysburg, Pa.

Tribune Broadcasting Co. Hqtrs: 435 N. Michigan Ave., Chicago 60611. (312) 222-3333. FAX: (312) 329-0611. Same ownership as *Chicago Tribune*. Interlocking ownership with the following newspapers:
 California: *Escondido Times-Advocate* & the *Californian* (San Diego).
 Florida: *Fort Lauderdale Sun-Sentinel* & *The Orlando Sentinel*.
 Virginia: *Daily Press* (Newport News).
 Stations: KTLA(TV) Los Angeles & KCTC(AM)-KYMX(FM) Sacramento, both Calif.; KEZW(AM) Aurora & KOSI(FM)-KWGN-TV Denver, both Colo.; WGNX(TV) Atlanta; WGN-AM-TV Chicago; WGNO(TV) New Orleans; WQCD(FM) & WPIX(TV) New York; & WPHL-TV Philadelphia. Note: Group has purchased WLVI-TV Cambridge, Mass., subject to FCC approval.

Truth Publishing Co.—See Federated Media.

U

United Communications Corp. Hqtrs: 1209 Orange St., Wilmington, Del. 19801. United Communications owns the *Attleboro* (Mass.) *Sun-Chronicle* & the *Kenosha* (Wis.) *News*. Stations: KEYC-TV Mankato, Minn. & WWNY-TV Carthage (Watertown), N.Y.

V

Vidalia Communications Inc. Hqtrs: Box 900, Vidalia, Ga. 30474. (912) 537-9202. FAX: (912) 537-4477. Advance-Progress Newspaper Inc., publisher of the wkly *Vidalia Advance*, is part of the partnership of Vidalia Communications Inc., owner of WVOP(AM) & WTCQ(FM) Vidalia, Ga. Note: Vidalia Communications Inc. also has purchased WKTM(FM) Soperton, Ga., subject to FCC approval.

The Village Companies. Hqtrs: Box 3300, Chapel Hill, N.C. 27515. (919) 968-4811. FAX: (919) 942-2826. The Village Companies owns *The Village Advocate*, Chapel Hill, N.C.; & *The Triangle Pointer*, Chapel Hill, N.C. (Both 100% owned.) The Village Companies also owns University Directories, Village Printing, Mall Advocate, Village Sports & Print Shops. Stations: WKQQ(FM) Lexington, Ky.; WZZU(FM) Burlington-Graham (Raleigh-Durham) & WCHL(AM) Chapel Hill, both N.C.

W

WEEU Broadcasting Co. Hqtrs: 34 N. 4th St., Reading, Pa. 19601. (215) 376-7335. FAX: (215) 376-7756. Reading Eagle Co., publisher of the *Reading* (Pa.) *Times* (morning) & *Reading* (Pa.) *Eagle* (evening & Sunday), owns 51% of WEEU Broadcasting Co., licensee of WEEU(AM) Reading, Pa.

WEHCO Media Inc. Hqtrs: 115 E. Capitol, Little Rock, Ark. 72203. (501) 378-3400. W.E. Hussman Jr. publishes the following newspapers:
 Arkansas: *Camden News*, *El Dorado News-Times*, *Hot Springs Sentinel-Record*, (Little Rock) *Arkansas Democrat-Gazette* & the *Magnolia Banner-News*.
 Texas: *Texarkana Gazette*.
 Other interests: 14 cable systems serving Ark., Miss., Okla. & Tex.
 Stations: KAMD(AM) & KWEH(FM) Camden, Ark.; KCMC(AM) & KTAL-FM-TV Texarkana, Tex. (Shreveport, La.).

WJAG Inc. Hqtrs: Box 789, Norfolk, Neb. 68702. (402) 371-0780. E.F. Huse Jr., publisher of the *Norfolk* (Neb.) *Daily News* & the *Bellevue* (Neb.) *Leader*, & Mrs. E.F. Huse Jr. own controlling interest in WJAG(AM) & KEXL(FM) Norfolk, Neb.

WTMJ Inc. Hqtrs: 720 E. Capitol Dr., Milwaukee 53212. (414) 332-9611. FAX: (414) 223-5400. Journal Communications Inc., publisher of the morning *Milwaukee Sentinel* & evening *Milwaukee Journal*, owns 100% of WTMJ Inc., licensee of KQRC-FM Leavenworth, Kan., WTMJ-AM-TV & WKTI(FM) Milwaukee, & owner of WSYM-TV Lansing, Mich.; KTNV(TV) Las Vegas; WSAU(AM) & WIFC(FM) Wausau, Wis.

West Virginia Radio Corp. Hqtrs: 1251 Earl L. Core Rd., Morgantown, W.Va. 26505. (304) 296-0029. FAX: (304) 296-3876. *Morgantown Dominion-Post*, Morgantown, W.Va., is affiliated with Metronews Radio Network & West Virginia Radio Corp., owner of WCAW(AM)-WVAF(FM) Charleston, WCHS(AM)-WKWS(FM) Charleston, WKKW-FM Clarksburg & WAJR(AM)-WVAQ(FM) Morgantown, all W.Va.

The Wireless Group Inc. Hqtrs: 42 S. Washington, Brownsville, Tenn. 38012. (901) 772-1172. The Wireless Group Inc., which publishes the wkly *Brownsville* (Tenn.) *States-Graphic*, also owns WNWS(AM)-WTBG(FM) Brownsville & WTNE(AM)-WWEZ(FM) Trenton, both Tenn. Note: Group also has entered into a time brokerage agreement with Jackson Broadcasters L.P. to provide progmg & sales mgmt svcs for WVYG(FM) Jackson, Tenn.

Woodward Communications Inc. Hqtrs: 8th & Bluff Streets, Dubuque, Iowa 52001. (319) 588-5611. FAX: (319) 588-5739. Publisher of:
 Illinois: *Freeport Shopping News*, Freeport; *Network*, Peoria.
 Iowa: *Telegraph Herald*, Dubuque; *Eastern Iowa Shopping News*, Edgewood; *Oelwein-Wapsipinicon Shopping News*, Oelwein; *The Bremer County Independent*, Waverly; & *The Waverly Democrat*, Waverly. (All 100% owned.)
 Wisconsin: *Monroe Shopping News*, Monroe; *Grant, Iowa, Lafayette Shopping News*, Platteville; *Prairie du Chien Shopping News*, Prairie du Chien; & the *Richland Center Shopping News*, Richland Center. (All 100% owned.)
 Stations (Susan F. Knaack, VP bcstg): KDTH(AM) & KATF(FM) Dubuque, Iowa; WAPL-FM Appleton & WHBY(AM) Kimberly, both Wis. (All 100% owned.)

Z

J.H. Zerbey Newspapers Inc. Hqtrs: Box 209, 111 Mahantongo St., Pottsville, Pa. 17901. (717) 462-2759 (WMBT). FAX: (717) 462-3423 (WMBT). J.H. Zerbey Newspapers Inc., which owns 100% of the *Pottsville Republican* in Pottsville, Pa., also owns 100% of WMBT Broadcasting Inc., licensee of WMBT(AM) Shenandoah, Pa.

Broadcasting Stations Associated with Newspaper/Magazine Ownership

Note: The following stations have, in some form, interlocking ownership with newspapers or magazine publishing companies. To use this list, find the desired station, then locate the indicated company or newspaper in the accompanying directory, *Newspaper/Magazine Cross-Ownership,* for details.

United States

Alabama
WBMG(TV) Birmingham—Park Communications Inc.
WDHN(TV) Dothan—Morris Newspaper Corp.
WHNT-TV Huntsville—The New York Times Co.
WMFC-AM-FM Monroeville—*Monroe Journal*

Arizona
KNAZ-TV Flagstaff—Capitol Broadcasting Co.
KDKB(FM) Mesa—Sandusky Newspapers Inc.
KPNX(TV) Mesa—Gannett Co.
KMEO(AM) and KPSN(FM) Phoenix—Bonneville International Corp.
KNXV-TV Phoenix—Scripps Howard
KPHO-TV Phoenix—Meredith Corp.
KTAR(AM) and KKLT(FM) Phoenix—Pulitzer Publishing Co.
KGUN(TV) Tucson—Lee Enterprises Inc.
KMSB-TV Tucson—Providence Journal Co.

Arkansas
KAMD(AM) and KWEH(FM) Camden—WEHCO Media Inc.
KTVE(TV) El Dorado—Gray Communications Systems Inc.
KFSM-TV Fort Smith—The New York Times Co.
KARK-TV Little Rock—Morris Newspaper Corp.
KATV(TV) Little Rock—Allbritton Communications Co.

California
KERO-TV Bakersfield—McGraw-Hill Broadcasting Group
KFSN-TV Fresno—Capital Cities/ABC Inc.
KABC-AM-TV and KLOS(FM) Los Angeles—Capital Cities/ABC Inc.
KBIG(FM) Los Angeles—Bonneville International Corp.
KFI(AM) and KOST(FM) Los Angeles—Cox Enterprises Inc.
KIIS-AM-FM Los Angeles—Gannett Co.
KLSX(FM) Los Angeles—Greater Media Inc.
KPWR(FM) Los Angeles—Emmis Broadcasting Corp.
KTLA(TV) Los Angeles—Tribune Broadcasting Co.
KTTV(TV) Los Angeles—News Corp. Ltd.-News America Publishing Inc.
KBOQ(FM) Marina—Peoria Journal Star Inc.
KTVU(TV) Oakland—Cox Enterprises Inc.
KRLA(AM) Pasadena—Greater Media Inc.
KCTC(AM) and KYMX(FM) Sacramento—Tribune Broadcasting Co.
KXTV(TV) Sacramento—Belo Broadcasting Corp.
KGTV(TV) San Diego—McGraw-Hill Broadcasting Group
KSDO(AM) and KCLX-FM San Diego—Gannett Co.
KGO-AM-TV San Francisco—Capital Cities/ABC Inc.
KOIT-AM-FM San Francisco—Bonneville International Corp.
KRON-TV San Francisco—Chronicle Publishing Co.
KCOY-TV Santa Maria—Stauffer Communications Inc.
KOVR(TV) Stockton—McClatchy Newspapers

Colorado
KEZW(AM) Aurora—Tribune Broadcasting Co.
KSSS(AM) Colorado Springs—Peoria Journal Star Inc.
KMGH-TV Denver—McGraw-Hill Broadcasting Group
KOSI(FM) Denver—Tribune Broadcasting Co.
KPOF(AM) Denver—Pillar of Fire Inc.
KUSA-TV Denver—Gannett Co.
KWGN-TV Denver—Tribune Broadcasting Co.
KGLN(AM) and KMTS(FM) Glenwood Springs—William R. Dunaway
KOAA-TV Pueblo—Evening Post Publishing Co.
KVUU(FM) Pueblo—Peoria Journal Star Inc.
KTVS(TV) Sterling—Stauffer Communications Inc.
KUAD-FM Windsor—Brill Media Co. Inc.

Connecticut
WFSB(TV) Hartford—Post-Newsweek Stations Inc.

Delaware
WECY-AM-FM Seaford—South Jersey Radio Inc.
WDEL(AM) and WSTW(FM) Wilmington—Delmarva Broadcasting Co.

District of Columbia
WJLA-TV Washington—Allbritton Communications Co.
WMAL(AM) and WRQX(FM) Washington—Capital Cities/ABC Inc.
WTTG(TV) Washington—News Corp. Ltd.-News America Publishing Inc.
WUSA(TV) Washington—Gannett Co.
WWRC(AM) and WGAY(FM) Washington—Greater Media Inc.

Florida
WWUS(FM) Big Pine Key—Crain Broadcasting Inc.
WKCF(TV) Clermont—Press Broadcasting Co.
WTKS(FM) Cocoa Beach—Press Broadcasting Co.
WHQT(FM) Coral Gables—Cox Enterprises Inc.
WESH(TV) Daytona Beach—Pulitzer Publishing Co.
WCJB(TV) Gainesville—Diversified Communications
WJKS(TV) Jacksonville—Media General Inc.
WJXT(TV) Jacksonville—Post-Newsweek Stations Inc.
WTLV(TV) Jacksonville—Gannett Co.
WIOD(AM) and WFLC(FM) Miami—Cox Enterprises Inc.
WPLG(TV) Miami—Post-Newsweek Stations Inc.
WMMZ(FM) Ocala—Dix Communications
WDIZ(FM) Orlando—Shamrock Communications Inc.
WFTV(TV) Orlando—Cox Enterprises Inc.
WOFL(TV) Orlando—Meredith Corp.
WJHG-TV Panama City—Gray Communications Systems Inc.
WSUN(AM) and WCOF(FM) St. Petersburg—Cox Enterprises Inc.
WNLS(AM) and WTNT(FM) Tallahassee—Park Communications Inc.
WDAE(AM) and WUSA-FM Tampa—Gannett Co.
WFLA-TV Tampa—Media General Inc.
WFTS(TV) Tampa—Scripps Howard
WBZT(AM) and WIRK-FM West Palm Beach—Price Communications Corp.
WPTV(TV) West Palm Beach—Scripps Howard

Georgia
WALB-TV Albany—Gray Communications Systems Inc.
WATL(TV) Atlanta—News Corp. Ltd.-News America Publishing Inc.
WGNX(TV) Atlanta—Tribune Broadcasting Co.
WKHX(AM) Atlanta—Capital Cities/ABC Inc.
WSB-AM-FM-TV Atlanta—Cox Enterprises Inc.
WXIA-TV Atlanta—Gannett Co.
WAGT(TV) Augusta—Schurz Communications Inc.
WYAY(FM) Gainesville—Capital Cities/ABC Inc.
WYAI(FM) La Grange—Cox Enterprises Inc.
WMGT(TV) Macon—Morris Newspaper Corp.
WMAZ-AM-FM-TV Macon—Multimedia Inc.
WKHX-FM Marietta—Capital Cities/ABC Inc.
WKTM(FM) Soperton—Vidalia Communications Inc.
WVGA(TV) Valdosta—Morris Newspaper Corp.
WTCQ(FM) Vidalia—Vidalia Communications Inc.
WVOP(AM) Vidalia—Vidalia Communications Inc.

Hawaii
KGMD-TV Hilo—Lee Enterprises Inc.
KHBC-TV Hilo—Providence Journal Co.
KGMB(TV) Honolulu—Lee Enterprises Inc.
KHNL(TV) Honolulu—Providence Journal Co.
KGMV(TV) Wailuku—Lee Enterprises Inc.
KOGG(TV) Wailuku—Providence Journal Co.

Idaho
KTVB(TV) Boise—Providence Journal Co.
KIFI-TV Idaho Falls—The Post Co.
KIVI(TV) Nampa—Evening Post Publishing Co.
KTRV(TV) Nampa—Lima Communications Corp.

Illinois
WYSY-FM Aurora—Cox Enterprises Inc.
WDWS(AM) and WHMS-FM Champaign—D.W.S. Inc.
WICD(TV) Champaign—Guy Gannett Communications
KSGM(AM) Chester—Donze Communications Inc.
WFLD(TV) Chicago—News America Publishing Inc.
WGCI-AM-FM Chicago—Gannett Co.
WGN-AM-TV Chicago—Tribune Broadcasting Co.
WJPC(AM) Chicago—Johnson Publishing Co.
WKQX(FM) Chicago—Emmis Broadcasting Corp.
WLS-AM-FM-TV Chicago—Capital Cities/ABC Inc.
WCRA(AM) and WCRC(FM) Effingham—McNaughton Stations
WRMN(AM) and WJKL(FM) Elgin—McNaughton Stations
WCKG(FM) Elmwood Park—Cox Enterprises Inc.
WJPC-FM Lansing—Johnson Publishing Co.
WLPO(AM) and WAJK(FM) La Salle—La Salle County Broadcasting Corp.
WQAD-TV Moline—The New York Times Co.
WGEM-AM-FM-TV Quincy—Quincy Newspapers Inc.
WTMX(FM) Skokie—Bonneville International Corp.
WICS(TV) Springfield—Guy Gannett Communications.
WPGU(FM) Urbana—Illini Media Co.

Indiana
WCSI(AM) and WKKG(FM) Columbus—Findlay Publishing Co.
WADM(AM) and WQHK-FM Decatur—Federated Media
WSJV(TV) Elkhart—Quincy Newspapers Inc.
WTRC(AM) and WLTA(FM) Elkhart—Federated Media
WOWO(AM) Fort Wayne—Price Communications Corp.
WQHK(AM) and WMEE(FM) Fort Wayne—Federated Media
WOWO-FM Huntington—Price Communications Corp.
WRTV(TV) Indianapolis—McGraw-Hill Broadcasting Group
WTHR(TV) Indianapolis—The Dispatch Printing Co.
WASK-AM-FM Lafayette—Schurz Communications Inc.
WLFI-TV Lafayette—Lima Communications Corp.
WENS(FM) Shelbyville—Emmis Broadcasting Corp.
WSBT-AM-TV and WNSN(FM) South Bend—Schurz Communications Inc.

Iowa
KCRG-AM-TV Cedar Rapids—Cedar Rapids Television Co.
KGAN(TV) Cedar Rapids—Guy Gannett Communications.
KCCI-TV Des Moines—Pulitzer Publishing Co.
KDTH(AM) and KATF(FM) Dubuque—Woodward Communications Inc.
KTIV(TV) Sioux City—Quincy Newspapers Inc.
KWLO(AM) and KFMW(FM) Waterloo—Park Communications Inc.

Kansas
KLBY(TV) Colby—Chronicle Publishing Co.
KUPK-TV Garden City—Chronicle Publishing Co.
KQRC-FM Leavenworth—WTMJ Inc.
KMAN(AM) and KMKF(FM) Manhattan—Seaton Stations
WIBW-AM-FM-TV Topeka—Stauffer Communications Inc.
KAKE-TV Wichita—Chronicle Publishing Co.
KICT-FM Wichita—Peoria Journal Star Inc.

Kentucky
WKCT(AM) and WDNS(FM) Bowling Green—Daily News Broadcasting Co.
WFKN(AM) Franklin—Gleaner and Journal Publishing Co.
WKQQ(FM) Lexington—The Village Companies
WTVQ-TV Lexington—Park Communications Inc.
WDRB-TV Louisville—Lima Communications Corp.
WHAS-TV Louisville—Providence Journal Co.
WLKY-TV Louisville—Pulitzer Publishing Co.
WLOU(AM) Louisville—Johnson Publishing Co.
WOMI(AM) and WBKR(FM) Owensboro—Brill Media Company Inc.
WPSD-TV Paducah—Paducah Newspapers Inc.

Broadcasting Stations Associated with Cross-Ownership

Louisiana
KALB-TV Alexandria—Park Communications Inc.
WBRZ(TV) Baton Rouge—Manship Stations
WYNK-AM-FM Baton Rouge—Narragansett Capital Inc.
WDSU(TV) New Orleans—Pulitzer Publishing Co.
WGNO(TV) New Orleans—Tribune Broadcasting Co.
KEEL(AM) and KITT(FM) Shreveport—Multimedia Inc.

Maine
WABI-AM-TV and WYOU-FM Bangor—Diversified Communications
WGME-TV Portland—Guy Gannett Communications

Maryland
WBAL-AM-TV and WIYY(FM) Baltimore—The Hearst Corp.
WMAR-TV Baltimore—Scripps Howard
WTBO(AM) and WKGO(FM) Cumberland—Dix Communications
WTTR(AM) and WGRX(FM) Westminster—Shamrock Communications Inc.

Massachusetts
WBCS(FM) Boston—Greater Media Inc.
WCVB-TV Boston—The Hearst Corp.
WMEX(AM) and WMJX(FM) Boston—Greater Media Inc.
WBET(AM) and WCAV(FM) Brockton—Enterprise Publishing Co.
WLVI-TV Cambridge—Gannett Co.
WLNE(TV) New Bedford—Freedom Newspapers Inc.
WGGB-TV Springfield—Guy Gannett Communications.

Michigan
WNEM-TV Bay City—Meredith Corp.
WCSX(FM) Birmingham—Greater Media Inc.
WDIV(TV) Detroit—Post-Newsweek Stations Inc.
WJR(AM) and WHYT(FM) Detroit—Capital Cities/ABC Inc.
WRIF(FM) Detroit—Greater Media Inc.
WXYZ-TV Detroit—Scripps Howard
WCUZ-AM-FM Grand Rapids—Federated Media
WSYM-TV Lansing—WTMJ Inc.
WHND(AM) Monroe—Greater Media Inc.
WQWQ(AM) Muskegon Heights—Federated Media

Minnesota
KAAL(TV) Austin—Dix Communications
WEBC(AM) and WAVC(FM) Duluth—Brill Media Co. Inc.
KQRS-AM-FM Golden Valley—Capital Cities/ABC Inc.
KEYC-TV Mankato—United Communications Corp.
KARE(TV) Minneapolis—Gannett Co.
KQWB-FM Moorhead—Brill Media Co. Inc.
KTTC(TV) Rochester—Quincy Newspapers Inc.
KJJO-AM-FM St. Louis Park—Park Communications Inc.

Mississippi
WCBI-TV Columbus—Imes Communications Group
WONA-AM-FM Winona—*Columbus (Miss.) Commercial Dispatch*

Missouri
KMIZ(TV) Columbia—Stauffer Communications Inc.
KSHE(FM) Crestwood—Emmis Broadcasting Corp.
KLIK(AM) and KTXY(FM) Jefferson City—Brill Media Co. Inc.
KSNF(TV) Joplin—Price Communications Corp.
KCMO-AM-FM Kansas City—Bonneville International Corp.
KCTV(TV) Kansas City—Meredith Corp.
KMBC-TV Kansas City—The Hearst Corp.
KMBZ(AM) and KLTH(FM) Kansas City—Bonneville International Corp.
KSHB-TV Kansas City—Scripps Howard.
KBDZ(FM) Perryville—Donze Communications Inc.
KSDK(TV) St. Louis—Multimedia Inc.
KYTV(TV) Springfield—Schurz Communications Inc.
KOKO(AM) Warrensburg—Johnson County Broadcasters Inc.

Montana
KGHL(AM) and KIDX(FM) Billings—Standard Communications Inc.
KTVQ(TV) Billings—Evening Post Publishing Co.
KULR-TV Billings—Dix Communications
KXLF-TV Butte—Evening Post Publishing Co.
KFBB-TV Great Falls—Dix Communications
KRTV(TV) Great Falls—Evening Post Publishing Co.
KATL(AM) Miles City—Star Printing Co.
KPAX-TV Missoula—Evening Post Publishing Co.

Nebraska
KMMJ(AM) Grand Island—Forum Communications Co.
KHAS-TV Hastings—Seaton Stations
WJAG(AM) and KEXL(FM) Norfolk—WJAG Inc.
KETV(TV) Omaha—Pulitzer Publishing Co.
KEZO-AM-FM Omaha—Narragansett Capital Inc.
KMTV(TV) Omaha—Lee Enterprises Inc.
WOWT(TV) Omaha—Chronicle Publishing Co.
KSTF(TV) Scottsbluff—Stauffer Communications Inc.

Nevada
KVVU-TV Henderson—Meredith Corp.
KLAS-TV Las Vegas—Landmark Communications Inc.
KTNV(TV) Las Vegas—WTMJ Inc.
KOLO-TV Reno—Donrey Media Group

New Hampshire
WMUR-TV Manchester—Imes Communications Group

New Jersey
WONZ(AM) Hammonton—South Jersey Radio Inc.
WCTC(AM) and WMGQ(FM) New Brunswick—Greater Media Inc.
WPAT-AM-FM Paterson—Park Communications Inc.
WOND(AM) Pleasantville and WMGM(FM) Atlantic City—South Jersey Radio Inc.
WBUD(AM) and WKXW(FM) Trenton—Press Broadcasting Co.
WMGM-TV Wildwood—South Jersey Radio Inc.
WAWZ(FM) Zarephath—Pillar of Fire Inc.

New Mexico
KRQE(TV) Albuquerque—Lee Enterprises Inc.
KOAT-TV Albuquerque—Pulitzer Publishing Co.
KOCT(TV) Carlsbad—Pulitzer Publishing Co.
KLMX(AM) Clayton—Johnson County Broadcasters Inc.
KZIA(TV) Las Cruces—Lee Enterprises Inc.
KBIM-TV Roswell—Lee Enterprises Inc.
KASA-TV Santa Fe—Providence Journal Co.

New York
WBNG-TV Binghamton—Gateway Communications Inc.
WWKB(AM) Buffalo—Price Communications Corp.
WWNY-TV Carthage—United Communications Corp.
WCKL(AM) and WCTW(FM) Catskill—Straus Media Group
WELV(AM) and WWWK(FM) Ellenville—Straus Media Group
WENY-AM-FM-TV Elmira—South Jersey Radio Inc.
WGSM(AM) Huntington—Greater Media Inc.
WABC-AM-FM and WPLJ(FM) New York—Capital Cities/ABC Inc.
WMXV(FM) New York—Bonneville International Corp.
WNYW(TV) New York—News Corp. Ltd.-News America Publishing Inc.
WQCD(AM) and WPIX(TV) New York—Tribune Broadcasting Co.
WQEW(AM) and WQXR-FM New York—The New York Times Co.
WQHT(FM) New York—Emmis Broadcasting Corp.
WKSE(FM) Niagara Falls—Price Communications Corp.
WRGB(TV) Schenectady—Freedom Newspapers Inc.
WMJC(FM) Smithtown—Greater Media Inc.
WHEN-AM-FM Syracuse—Park Communications Inc.
WUTR(TV) Utica—Park Communications Inc.

North Carolina
WZZU(FM) Burlington-Graham—The Village Companies
WCHL(AM) Chapel Hill—The Village Companies
WCNC-TV Charlotte—Providence Journal Co.
WSOC-TV Charlotte—Cox Enterprises Inc.
WDNC(AM) and WDCG(FM) Durham—Durham Herald Co.
WTVD(TV) Durham—Capital Cities/ABC Inc.
WFMY-TV Greensboro—Gannett Co.
WNCT-AM-FM-TV Greenville—Park Communications Inc.
WXII(TV) Winston-Salem—Pulitzer Publishing Co.

North Dakota
KBMY(TV) Bismarck—Forum Communications Co.
WDAZ-TV Devils Lake—Forum Communications Co.
KQWB(AM) Fargo—Brill Media Co. Inc.
KTHI-TV Fargo—Morgan Murphy Stations
WDAY-AM-FM-TV Fargo—Forum Communications Co.
KMCY(TV) Minot—Forum Communications Co.

Ohio
WAKW(FM) Cincinnati—Pillar of Fire Inc.
WCKY(AM) and WIMJ(FM) Cincinnati—Federated Media
WCPO-TV Cincinnati—Scripps Howard
WLWT(TV) Cincinnati—Multimedia Inc.
WEWS(TV) Cleveland—Scripps Howard
WKYC-TV Cleveland—Multimedia Inc.
WBNS-AM-FM-TV Columbus—The Dispatch Printing Co.
WDTN(TV) Dayton—The Hearst Corp.
WHIO-AM-TV and WHKO(FM) Dayton—Cox Enterprises Inc.
WEOL(AM) and WNWV(FM) Elyria—Lorain County Printing & Publishing Co.
WFIN(AM) and WKXA-FM Findlay—The Findlay Publishing Co.
WMOH(AM) Hamilton—The Findlay Publishing Co.
WLIO(TV) Lima—Lima Communications Corp.
WKVX(AM) and WQKT(FM) Wooster—Dix Communications

Oklahoma
KVSO(AM) Ardmore—KVSO Broadcasting Co.
KOCO-TV Oklahoma City—Gannett Co.
KQLL-FM Owasso—Federated Media
WBBZ(AM) Ponca City—Ponca City Publishing Co.
KMYZ-AM-FM Pryor—Shamrock Communications Inc.
KSPI-AM-FM Stillwater—Stillwater Publishing Co.
KJRH(TV) Tulsa—Scripps Howard
KOTV(TV) Tulsa—Belo Broadcasting Corp.
KQLL(AM) Tulsa—Federated Media
KTUL(TV) Tulsa—Allbritton Communications Co.

Oregon
KTVL(TV) Medford—Freedom Newspapers Inc.
KGW-TV Portland—Providence Journal Co.
KOIN(TV) Portland—Lee Enterprises Inc.
KWJJ-AM-FM Portland—Park Communications Inc.

Pennsylvania
WTAJ-TV Altoona—Gateway Communications Inc.
WCPA(AM) and WQYX(FM) Clearfield—Progressive Publishing Co.
WIOV-FM Ephrata—Brill Media Co. Inc.
WGET-AM-FM Gettysburg—Times & News Publishing Co.
WHUN(AM) and WLAK(FM) Huntingdon—Huntingdon Broadcasters Inc.
WJAC-AM-FM-TV Johnstown—WJAC Inc.
WGAL-TV Lancaster—Pulitzer Publishing Co.
WLYH-TV Lancaster—Gateway Communications Inc.
WMGK(FM) Philadelphia—Greater Media Inc.
WPEN(AM) Philadelphia—Greater Media Inc.
WPHL-TV Philadelphia—Tribune Broadcasting Co.
WPVI-TV Philadelphia—Capital Cities/ABC Inc.
WPXI(TV) Pittsburgh—Cox Enterprises Inc.
WTAE-AM-TV and WVTY(FM) Pittsburgh—The Hearst Corp.
WEEU(AM) Reading—WEEU Broadcasting Co.
WIOV(AM) Reading—Brill Media Co. Inc.
WEJL(AM) and WEZX(FM) Scranton—Shamrock Communications Inc.
WNEP-TV Scranton—The New York Times Co.
WYOU(TV) Scranton—Diversified Communications
WMBT(AM) Shenandoah—J.H. Zerbey Newspapers Inc.

Rhode Island
WPRI-TV Providence—Narragansett Capital Inc.

South Carolina
WCBD-TV Charleston—Media General Inc.
WCIV(TV) Charleston—Allbritton Communications Co.
WPDE-TV Florence—Diversified Communications
WFBC-AM-FM Greenville—Multimedia Inc.
WYFF(TV) Greenville—Pulitzer Publishing Co.
WORD(AM) Spartanburg—Multimedia Inc.

South Dakota
WNAX-AM-FM Yankton—Park Communications Inc.

Broadcasting Stations Associated with Cross-Ownership

Tennessee

WNWS(AM) and WTBG(FM) Brownsville—The Wireless Group Inc.
WDEF-AM-FM-TV Chattanooga—Park Communications Inc.
WTVC(TV) Chattanooga—Freedom Newspapers Inc.
WJHL-TV Johnson City—Park Communications Inc.
WKTP(AM) Jonesboro—The Home News Co.
WKPT-AM-TV and WTFM(FM) Kingsport—The Home News Co.
WBIR-TV Knoxville—Multimedia Inc.
WREG-TV Memphis—The New York Times Co.
WTVF(TV) Nashville—Landmark Communications Inc.
WKSR(AM) and WINJ(FM) Pulaski—Pulaski Broadcasting Co.
WTNE(AM) and WWEZ(FM) Trenton—The Wireless Group Inc.

Texas

KGNC-AM-FM Amarillo—Stauffer Communications Inc.
KVUE-TV Austin—Gannett Co.
KFDM-TV Beaumont—Freedom Newspapers Inc.
KAAM(AM) and KZPS(FM) Dallas—Bonneville International Corp.
KDAF(TV) Dallas—News Corp. Ltd.-News America Publishing Inc.
KRRW(FM) Dallas—Cox Enterprises Inc.
WFAA-TV Dallas—Belo Broadcasting Corp.
KHKS(FM) Denton—Gannett Co.
KULP(AM) El Campo—Bar-B Broadcasting Inc.
KDBC-TV El Paso—Imes Communications Group
KEGL(FM) Fort Worth—Sandusky Newspapers Inc.
KTXQ(FM) Fort Worth—Cox Enterprises Inc.
WBAP(AM)-KSCS(FM) Fort Worth—Capital Cities/ABC Inc.
KHOU-TV Houston—Belo Broadcasting Corp.
KKBQ(AM) Houston—Gannett Co.
KPRC-TV Houston—Post-Newsweek Stations Inc.
KRIV(TV) Houston—News Corp. Ltd.-News America Publishing Inc.
KTRK-TV Houston—Capital Cities/ABC Inc.
KUTZ(FM) Lampasas—Shamrock Communications Inc.
KFYO(AM) and KZII-FM Lubbock—Seaton Stations
KKBQ-FM Pasadena—Gannett Co.
KJAC-TV Port Arthur—Price Communications Corp.
KTLU(AM) and KWRW(FM) Rusk—*Rusk* (Tex.) *Cherokeean*.
KENS-TV San Antonio—Harte-Hanks Communications Inc.
KSAT-TV San Antonio—Post-Newsweek Stations Inc.
KCEN-TV Temple—Channel 6 Inc.
KCMC(AM) and KTAL-FM-TV Texarkana—WEHCO Media Inc.
KRGV-TV Weslaco—Manship Stations
KFDX-TV Wichita Falls—Price Communications Corp.

Utah

KSL-AM-TV Salt Lake City—Bonneville International Corp.
KSTU(TV) Salt Lake City—News Corp. Ltd.-News America Publishing Inc.

Virginia

WFLS-AM-FM Fredericksburg—The Free Lance-Star Publishing Co.
WFTR-AM-FM Front Royal—Straus Media Group.
WVEC-TV Hampton—Belo Broadcasting Corp.
WSET-TV Lynchburg—Allbritton Communications Co.
WTKR-TV Norfolk—Narragansett Capital Inc.
WRAD(AM) and WRIQ(FM) Radford—Dix Communications
WTVR-AM-FM-TV Richmond—Park Communications Inc.
WDBJ(TV) Roanoke—Schurz Communications Inc.
WSLS-TV Roanoke—Park Communications Inc.
WPLC(FM) Spotsylvania—The Free Lance-Star Publishing Co.
WTON-AM-FM Staunton—Ogden Newspapers Inc.

Washington

KLSY-FM Bellevue—Sandusky Newspapers Inc.
KVEW(TV) Kennewick—Morgan Murphy Stations
KEZX-AM-FM Seattle—Park Communications Inc.
KING-TV Seattle—Providence Journal Co.
KIRO-AM-FM-TV Seattle—Bonneville International Corp.
KIXI(AM) Seattle—Sandusky Newspapers Inc.
KHQ-TV Spokane—Cowles Publishing Co.
KREM-TV Spokane—Providence Journal Co.
KXLY-AM-FM-TV Spokane—Morgan Murphy Stations
KAPP(TV) Yakima—Morgan Murphy Stations

West Virginia

WVVA(TV) Bluefield—Quincy Newspapers Inc.
WCAW(AM) and WVAF(FM) Charleston—West Virginia Radio Corp.
WCHS(AM) and WKWS(FM) Charleston—West Virginia Radio Corp.
WBOY-TV Clarksburg—Imes Communications Group.
WKKW-FM Clarksburg—West Virginia Radio Corp.
WOWK-TV Huntington—Gateway Communications Inc.
WSAZ-TV Huntington—Lee Enterprises Inc.
WAJR(AM) and WVAQ(FM) Morgantown—West Virginia Radio Corp.

Wisconsin

WAPL-FM Appleton—Woodward Communications Inc.
WBEV(AM) and WXRO(FM) Beaver Dam—McNaughton Stations
WYKY(FM) Columbus—McNaughton Stations
WCLO(AM) and WJVL(FM) Janesville—Gazette Printing Co.
WHBY(AM) Kimberly—Woodward Communications Inc.
WISC-TV Madison—Morgan Murphy Stations
WISN-AM-TV and WLTQ(FM) Milwaukee—The Hearst Corp.
WNOV(AM) Milwaukee—*Milwaukee Courier*
WQFM(FM) Milwaukee—Shamrock Communications Inc.
WTMJ-AM-TV and WKTI(FM) Milwaukee—WTMJ Inc.
WSAU(AM) and WIFC(FM) Wausau—WTMJ Inc.
WEZW(FM) Wauwatosa—Multimedia Inc.
WBKV(AM) and WBWI-FM West Bend—Gazette Printing Co.
WFHR(AM) and WWRW(FM) Wisconsin Rapids—Gazette Printing Co.

Wyoming

KGWC-TV Casper—Stauffer Communications Inc.
KTWO-TV Casper—Dix Communications
KGWN-TV Cheyenne—Stauffer Communications Inc.
KKTU(TV) Cheyenne—Dix Communications
KGWL-TV Lander—Stauffer Communications Inc.
KGWR-TV Rock Springs—Stauffer Communications Inc.
KRBQ(TV) Sheridan—Dix Communications

Canada

Alberta

CFXL(AM) Calgary—Golden West Broadcasting Ltd.
CHRB(AM) High River—Golden West Broadcasting Ltd.

Manitoba

CFAM(AM) Altona—Golden West Broadcasting Ltd.
CJRB(AM) Boissevain—Golden West Broadcasting Ltd.
CHSM(AM) Steinbach—Golden West Broadcasting Ltd.
CKMW(AM) Winkler-Morden—Golden West Broadcasting Ltd.

Ontario

CHOO(AM) Ajax—Golden West Broadcasting Ltd.
CHAM(AM) Hamilton—Golden West Broadcasting Ltd.

Quebec

CHLC(AM) and New FM Baie-Comeau—Cogeco Inc.
CFRP(AM) Forestville—Cogeco Inc.
CFGL-FM Laval—Cogeco Inc.
CJMF-FM Quebec—Cogeco Inc.
CFEI-FM St. Hyacinthe—Cogeco Inc.
CFKS-TV and CKSH-TV Sherbrooke—Cogeco Inc.
CFKM-TV and CKTM-TV Trois-Rivieres—Cogeco Inc.

Saskatchewan

CHAB(AM) Moose Jaw—Golden West Broadcasting Ltd.
CJSN(AM) Shaunavon—Golden West Broadcasting Ltd.
CKSW(AM) Swift Current—Golden West Broadcasting Ltd.

Section B
Radio

Table of Contents

Table of Contents	B-1
Key to Listings	B-2
Directory of Radio Stations in the United States and Canada	
United States	B-3
Canada	B-427
Miscellaneous Radio Services	B-449
U.S. AM Stations by Call Letters	B-451
U.S. FM Stations by Call Letters	B-460
Canadian AM Stations by Call Letters	B-473
Canadian FM Stations by Call Letters	B-474
Table of FM Allotments	B-475
College, University and School-Owned Radio	B-484
U.S. AM Stations by Frequency	B-486
U.S. FM Stations by Frequency	B-502
Canadian AM Stations by Frequency	B-525
Canadian FM Stations by Frequency	B-527
Radio Formats by State and Province	
Radio Formats Defined	B-529
Radio Formats by State	B-530
Radio Formats by Province	B-540
U.S. and Canadian Radio Programming Formats	B-542
Programming on Radio Stations in the United States and Canada	
Programming on Radio Stations in the United States	B-543
Programming on Radio Stations in Canada	B-571
Special Programming on Radio Stations in the United States and Canada	
Special Programming on Radio Stations in the United States	B-573
Special Programming on Radio Stations in Canada	B-589
Radio Market Statistics	
U.S. Radio Markets	B-591
U.S. Radio Markets: Arbitron Metro Survey Area Ranking	B-598
U.S. Radio Markets: Population Ranking	B-600
Growth of Radio Broadcasting Pre-Television 1922-1945	B-602
U.S. Radio Set Sales 1958-1992	B-603
Record of Station Growth Since Television Began	B-604
U.S. Radio Audiences	B-605

Key to Radio Listings

Radio listings include AM (amplitude modulation) and FM (frequency modulation) radio stations in the United States, its territories and Canada. All collected data for these listings include information current to January 1994. The following is a breakdown of a sample radio listing. The sample, WOF, is a co-owned AM/FM station. To use the radio key, see boldface numbers and corresponding explanations.

(1) WOF(AM)—(2) Oct 8, 1946: **(3)** 1000 khz; 1 kw-D, 250 w-N, DA-D. (L-KQSL) TL: N35 48 31 W121 43 28. (CP: 5 kw-U). **(3a)** Stereo. **(4)** Box 1000 (99999). (909) 555-1000. FAX: (909) 999-9999. **(5)** General Broadcasting Corp. (group owner; acq 7-20-69; $255,000 with co-located FM; **(5a)** FTR 2-12-83). **(6)** Net: ABC/E, AP, Mountain State Network. Rep: Jones & Company, Penn State. Format: MOR, C&W. Spec prog: Sp 3 hrs wkly. **(7)** John Jones, gen mgr; David Smith, chief engr. **(8)** Rates: $14; 13.50; 14; 12.50.

(1a) WOF-FM—(2) October 1959: **(9)** 101.1 mhz; 3 kw. Ant 300 ft. **(3a)** Stereo. **(10)** Dups AM 50%. Format: C&W. **(11)** WOF-TV affil. **(8)** Rates: $8.50; 7; 8.50; na.

(1) Station call letters as assigned by the Federal Communications Commission (FCC) or Canadian Radio-television and Telecommunications Commission (CRTC).

(1a) Station call letters for co-owned FM station. WOF-FM has the same ownership as WOF(AM), and the FM listing contains only information different from the AM. Co-owned AM and FM stations are always listed together, even when they have dissimilar call letters. In some instances FM may be listed first.

(2) Date station first went on air (regardless of subsequent ownership changes).

(3) Frequency in kilohertz; power and hours of operation. WOF operates with one kilowatt in daytime hours, 250 watts at night, and uses a directional antenna in daytime. Nighttime operation is limited to hours when dominant station KQSL is operating in daylight. TL refers to the geographical coordinates (longitude and latitude) of the transmitter. WOF holds a construction permit for five kilowatts power day and night.

(3a) WOF broadcasts in stereo.

(4) Address and zip code, telephone and FAX. Teletype Writer Exchange number may also be included.

(5) Licensee name and date of acquisition (if not original owner). If the licensee is a group owner—a company with several broadcast properties—it is so identified, as a group owner of which the licensee is a subsidiary. Details on group owners are listed in Section A. If the station has been sold and the sale information is available, it is recorded after the acquisition date, ie. acq. date; purchase price; FTR date.

(5a) FTR date. FTR refers to *Broadcasting & Cable* magazine's weekly "For the Record" column, where station sales are recorded as received from the FCC.

(6) Network, representative and programming. WOF national affiliates are ABC Entertainment Network and AP Network. The regional affiliate is Mountain State. The WOF national sales representative is Jones & Company and their regional sales representative is Penn State. The WOF program format is part middle-of-the-road, part country and western, with three hours weekly of special programming in Spanish. For radio format definitions, see page B-529.

(7) Key personnel.

(8) Advertising rates. This data indicates the prices the station charges for a one-minute spot, run 12-times-a-week during the following time slots: 6 a.m.-10 a.m.; 10 am.-3 p.m.; 3 p.m.-7 p.m.; 7 p.m.-midnight, respectively. If a time slot is not applicable, "na" replaces the rate.

(9) Frequency for WOF-FM is 101.1 megahertz, with 3 kilowatts of effective radiated power and an antenna height of 300 feet above average terrain. WOF-FM broadcasts in stereo (see **(3a)**).

(10) Programming. WOF-FM duplicates WOF(AM) programs 50% of the time and has a country and western format.

(11) Co-owned TV. WOF-TV has the same licensee as WOF-AM-FM.

Note: Listings for independent AM & FM stations follow the sample shown for WOF(AM).

An asterisk (*) preceding station call letters indicates noncommercial stations.

Directory of Radio Stations in the U.S.

Alabama

LAUREN A. COLBY
301-663-1086
COMMUNICATIONS ATTORNEY
Special Attention to
Difficult Cases

Alabaster

WGTT(AM)—Sept 28, 1981: 1500 khz; 1 kw-D. TL: N35 15 09 W86 49 14. Box 584, 800 Industrial Park Dr. (35007). (205) 664-1500; (205) 664-1515. Licensee: WGTT Inc. (acq 4-21-92; $17,500; FTR 5-11-92). Net: USA. Wash atty: Gardner, Carton & Douglas. Format: Great gospel. Target aud: 25 plus. ■ John Sides, pres, gen mgr, chief opns, progmg dir & mus dir; Dave Robinson, gen sls mgr & adv mgr; Clay Lemley, asst mus dir; Frank Giardina, chief engr.

Albertville

WAVU(AM)—1948: 630 khz; 1 kw-D, 28 w-N. TL: N34 14 28 W86 09 41. Hrs opn: 24. Box 190 (35950). (205) 878-8575. FAX: (205) 878-1051; (205) 878-2104. Licensee: Sand Mountain Broadcasting Service Inc. Net: NBC. Format: Southern gospel. News staff one. Target aud: 35 plus. ■ Pat M. Courington Jr., pres; Warren H. Penney, gen mgr; Ted McCreless, gen sls mgr; Barry Galloway, progmg dir; Jeff Allen, mus dir; Allen Taylor, news dir; Walt Howard, chief engr.

WQSB(FM)—Co-owned with WAVU(AM). 1948: 105.1 mhz; 100 kw. Ant 1,000 ft. TL: N34 09 27 W86 02 44. Stereo. Hrs opn: 24. Prog sep from AM. Net: NBC. Format: C&W. News staff one. Target aud: 25-54. ■ Dale Stallings, progmg dir. ■ Rates: $40; 38; 36; 32.

Alexander City

WTLM(AM)—May 31, 1947: 1050 khz; 1 kw-D. TL: N32 56 51 W85 59 17. Box 1640, Radio Road, Columbus, GA (31994). (404) 706-5100; (800) 445-4106. FAX: (404) 596-5115. Licensee: Solar Broadcasting Co. Inc. (acq 10-86; $1,720,000 with co-located FM; FTR 8-11-86). Wash atty: Haley, Bader & Potts. Format: Country. Target aud: 25-54; adults. ■ Allen M. Woodall, pres; Bonnie Woodall, vp; Jerry Katz, gen mgr; Judy Rivers, Ed Patie, gen sls mgrs; Judy Rivers, Ed Patie, natl sls mgrs; Al Jefreys, progmg dir.

WSTH-FM—Co-owned with WTLM(AM). Sept 30, 1949: 106.1 mhz; 100 kw. Ant 981 ft. TL: N32 45 33 W85 28 04. Stereo. Hrs opn: 24. Dups AM 100%. Box 1640, 1236 Broadway, Columbus GA (31901). Net: ABC, NBC. Rep: Katz. News staff one. ■ Jerry Katz, opns dir.

Aliceville

WCKO(FM)—See Carrollton.

Andalusia

WAAO-FM—Aug 24, 1987: 103.7 mhz; 3 kw. Ant 328 ft. TL: N31 20 27 W86 28 02. Stereo. Box 987, Hwy. 29 N. (36420). (205) 222-1166. Licensee: Companion Broadcasting Co. Net: AP. Wash atty: Miller & Fields. Format: Country. News progmg 7 hrs wkly. Target aud: General. ■ Betty S. Williams, pres & gen mgr; Jamey Williams, gen sls mgr; Lee Williams, prom mgr & progmg dir; Wayne Caylor, mus dir; Charles Grantham, chief engr. ■ Rates: $15; 9; 9; 9.

WKYD(AM)—Aug 12, 1946: 920 khz; 5 kw-D, 500 w-N, DA-N. TL: N31 19 05 W86 26 47. Box 8, Hwy. 84 E. (36420). (205) 222-0920. FAX: (205) 222-8641. Licensee: MetroCities Communications (group owner). Net: ABC/I, NBC Talknet, ABC, Unistar. Format: Btfl mus, news/talk. News staff one; news progmg 10 hrs wkly. Target aud: General; middle to upper class, mature adults, offices. Spec prog: Talk 20 hrs wkly. ■ Deane Johnson, pres; Ronald A. Hill, gen mgr; Audrey Moore, stn mgr, sls dir, news dir & pub affrs dir; E.Y. Mock, Gerald Wilson, chiefs engr. ■ Rates: $5; 5; 5; na.

WWSF-FM—Licensed to Andalusia. See Fort Walton Beach, Fla.

Anniston

WANA(AM)—August 1954: 1490 khz; 1 kw-U. TL: N33 41 15 W85 49 49. 115 W. 33rd St. (36202). (205) 237-1627. FAX: (205) 237-1628. Licensee: Anniston Radio Co. (acq 6-87; $115,000; FTR 8-24-87). Net: Ala Net. Format: Southern gospel. News progmg one hr wkly. Target aud: 18-70; relg people who like southern & Black gospel. Spec prog: Black 12 hrs, farm one hr wkly. ■ Joe Burney, pres, gen mgr, gen sls mgr, progmg dir & chief engr; Anthony Vickers, mus dir.

WDNG(AM)—July 1, 1957: 1450 khz; 1 kw-U. TL: N33 40 01 W85 50 56. Box 1450 (36202). (205) 236-8291. FAX: (205) 236-8292. Licensee: WDNG Inc. (acq 6-30-87; $500,000; FTR 7-6-87). Net: ABC TalkRadio, CBS, EFM. Format: News/talk. News staff one. Target aud: General. ■ J. Dark, pres & gen mgr; Teresa Goodman, sls dir; Rob Street, progmg dir; David Ford, news dir; Bob Crandell, chief engr. ■ Rates: $16; 11; 16; 11.

WHMA(AM)—1938: 1390 khz; 5 kw-D, 1 kw-N, DA-N. TL: N33 42 31 W85 51 14. Hrs opn: 19. Box 278 (36202); Williamson Commerce Ctr., Suite 8, 801 Noble St. (36201). (205) 237-8741. FAX: (205) 231-9414. Licensee: Sapphire Broadcasting Inc. Group owner: Crown Broadcasting Inc. (acq 11-13-89; $7,500,000 with co-located FM; FTR 11-13-89). Net: Unistar, NBC. Format: Country, Black. News staff one; news progmg 12 hrs wkly. Target aud: 25-54; those with upscale, mobile, discresionary incomes. Spec prog: Sports - football coverage: Jacksonville State University, Anniston; Alexandra High School. ■ Tom Gammon, pres; Thomas E. Williams, gen mgr; Mike Carter, opns mgr, progmg mgr & mus dir; Eva Gibson, natl sls mgr; Treva Reid, prom dir; Tracy Haynes, news dir; Paul McCain, chief engr.

WHMA-FM—Apr 1947: 100.5 mhz; 100 kw. Ant 1,141 ft. TL: N33 40 51 W85 48 56. Stereo. Hrs opn: 24. Wash atty: Arent, Fox, Kintner, Plotkin & Kahn. Format: Contemp country.

WSSY-FM—See Talladega.

DATABASES - MAILING LABELS

★ RADIO/TELEVISION US/CANADA
99.7% Deliverable - System Updated Daily
Over 25 Selection Options: Accurate Formats, Market Size, Station Audiences, States, Networks, Random Lists, Execs by Name, Secondary Formats, Ethnic Stations, Delete/Add Markets or Stations

★ DATABASE AUDITS
We Correct, Update and Maintain Your Database

★ RADIOSCAN
All US Radio on Your PC - Includes Powerful Software
Instant Station Data on Screen - Reports in 10 Seconds
Station Lists for Each of 585 Markets
Rolls Royce of all Radio Database Systems
Ideal for Syndicators, Networks, all Vendors
Reasonably Priced

The CENTER For RADIO INFORMATION
19 Market Street, Cold Spring, NY 10516
PH: (800) 359-9898   FAX: (914) 265-2715

Arab

WCRQ-FM—Nov 5, 1979: 92.7 mhz; 700 w. Ant 670 ft. TL: N34 21 03 W86 26 25. Stereo. Prog sep from AM. Box 568, Bldg. 981, N. Pkwy. (35016). (205) 586-9300. FAX: (205) 586-9301. Licensee: Roland Broadcasting Inc. ($546,000; FTR 7-5-93). Format: Adult contemp. News staff one; news progmg 3 hrs wkly. Target aud: 18-49. Spec prog: Gospel 5 hrs, relg 2 hrs. ■ Major Logan, gen mgr, progmg dir & mus dir; Bill Glass, opns mgr, sls dir & news dir. ■ Rates: $12; 10; 12; 10.

WRAB(AM)—Oct 25, 1961: 1380 khz; 1 kw-D. TL: N34 20 09 W86 28 07. Box 625, 311 S. Main St. (35016). (205) 586-4123. Licensee: Arab Broadcasting Co. Inc. (acq 12-87). Net: ABC/D. Format: Country, relg. ■ Kerry Rich, pres, gen mgr & gen sls mgr; Tim Maze, progmg dir & mus mgr; Archie Anderson, news dir; Steve King, chief engr.

Ashland-Lineville

WASZ(FM)—Oct 4, 1984: 95.3 mhz; 1 kw. Ant 541 ft. TL: N33 18 30 W85 50 58. Stereo. Box 395, Ashland (36251). (205) 354-4600. FAX: (205) 354-7224. Licensee: Perry Communications. Net: AP; Ala. Net. Format: C&W. Target aud: 18-54. Spec prog: Black 6 hrs wkly. ■ Robert A. Perry, pres; Al Haynes, gen mgr, gen sls mgr & news dir; Tommy Wood, opns dir.

Athens

WKAC(AM)—September 1964: 1080 khz; 5 kw-D. TL: N34 50 13 W86 58 28. Hrs opn: Sunrise-sunset. Box 1083, 2901 N. Jefferson (35611). (205) 232-6827. Licensee: Limestone Broadcasting Co. Net: CNN; Tobacco. Rep: Keystone (unwired net), Midsouth; Rgnl Reps. Format: Modern country. News progmg 6 hrs wkly. Target aud: 25-54; adults mid/upper income, blue/white collar. Spec prog: Farm 5 hrs wkly. ■ Keith A. Casey, pres, gen mgr & gen sls mgr; Kirk Harvey, prom mgr, progmg dir & mus dir; Suzanne Schrimsher, asst mus dir; Kennith A. Casey, chief engr. ■ Rates: $7.50; 7; 7.50; na.

WVNN(AM)—Nov 8, 1948: 770 khz; 10 kw-D, 250 w-N, DA-N. TL: N34 50 21 W86 55 44. Stereo. Hrs opn: 24. Box 389, 1717 Hwy. 72 E. (35611). (205) 232-3911; (205) 233-1414. FAX: (205) 220-1FAX. Licensee: Athens Broadcasting Co. Net: ABC/D, ABC TalkRadio; Ala. Net. Rep: Christal. Format: News/talk. News staff 4; news progmg 60 hrs wkly. Target aud: 25-64. Spec prog: Farm 2 hrs, gospel 3 hrs wkly. ■ Bill Dunnavant, pres; Mary Dunnavant, vp; Bill West, gen sls mgr; Rick Tyler, prom dir; Dave Stone, progmg dir; Michael Hayden, chief engr. ■ Rates: $20; 45; 20; 10.

WZYP(FM)—Co-owned with WVNN(AM). Oct 1, 1958: 104.3 mhz; 100 kw. Ant 1,115 ft. TL: N34 49 05 W86 44 16. Stereo. Hrs opn: 24. Prog sep from AM. Net: ABC/C. Format: CHR. News staff 3. Target aud: 18-49. ■ Cat Thomas, progmg dir; Dave Stone, news dir. ■ Rates: $125; 90; 100; 60.

Atmore

WASG(AM)—Nov 12, 1981: 550 khz; 25 kw-D, 144 w-N. TL: N31 00 26 W87 32 15. Stereo. Hrs opn: 24. 1210 S. Main St. (36502-2899). (205) 368-2511; (205) 368-5500. Licensee: Alabama Native American Broadcasting Co. (acq 8-14-92; $26,673 with co-located FM; FTR 8-31-92). Net: ABC/E, AP. Wash atty: Gardner, Carton & Douglas. Format: C&W, talk, farm. News staff one; news progmg 9 hrs wkly. Target aud: 18-54. Spec prog: American Indian one hr, Creek Indian one hr, Black one hr wkly. ■ Nathan Martin, chmn; Dale Gehman, pres, gen mgr & chief engr; William Reynolds, opns mgr; Jerry Gehman, gen sls mgr; Rick Dean, prom mgr, progmg dir & mus dir; Paul Reynolds, adv dir; Al Burns, news dir. ■ Rates: $15; 12.50; 14; 7.50.

WYDH(FM)—Co-owned with WASG(AM). June 28, 1991: 105.9 mhz; 3.7 kw. Ant 446 ft. TL: N31 00 26 W87 32 15. Stereo. Hrs opn: 24. Prog sep from AM. Net: ABC/E, AP. Format: Adult contemp. News progmg 18 hrs wkly. Spec prog: American Indian one hr, Black one hr, farm 5 hrs, gospel 12 hrs wkly. ■ Kim McKay, prom mgr, progmg dir & mus dir. ■ Rates: $15; 12.50; 14; 9.50.

WGCX(FM)—May 19, 1966: 104.1 mhz; 100 kw. Ant 1,555 ft. TL: N30 37 35 W87 38 50. Stereo. Hrs opn: 24. Box 1044, Mobile (36633); Bldg. B, Suite 201, 29000 Hwy. 98, Daphne (36526). (205) 626-9600. FAX: (205) 626-3352. Licensee: Wescom of Alabama Inc. (acq 10-3-88). Net: ABC/R. Rep: Eastman. Wash atty: Cohn & Marks. Format: AOR. News staff one; news progmg 5 hrs wkly. Target aud: 25-40. ■ Dale Matteson, pres; Timothy P. O'Connell, vp & gen mgr; Chris Kalifeh, gen sls mgr; Mark Sturcken, rgnl sls mgr; Andy Holt, progmg dir; Charlie Ocean, mus dir; Mike Leff, chief engr.

WGYJ(AM)—Dec 17, 1949: 1590 khz; 5 kw-D, 1 kw-N, DA-N. TL: N31 02 12 W87 29 42. 805 N. Main St. (36502); Box 10 (36504). (205) 368-9495. FAX: (205) 368-1946. Licensee: Maranatha Ministries Foundation Inc. (acq 10-31-88; $175,000; FTR 10-31-88). Net: USA, CBN. Format: Southern gospel. ■ John K. Mathis, pres, gen mgr & gen sls mgr. ■ Rates: $9; 9; 9; 8.

WYDH(FM)—Listing follows WASG(AM).

Attalla

WKXX(FM)—Licensed to Attalla. See Gadsden.

Auburn

WAUD(AM)—Dec 22, 1947: 1230 khz; 1 kw-U. TL: N32 37 47 W85 28 08. Hrs opn: 5:30 AM-midnight. Box 3387, 165 E. Magnolia (36831). (205) 887-3401. FAX: (205)

Broadcasting & Cable Yearbook 1994

Alabama Directory of Radio

887-7909. Licensee: Auburn Broadcasting & Communications Co. Inc. (acq 9-1-77). Net: ABC/I. Rep: Rgnl Reps. Format: Btfl mus, big band, jazz. Target aud: 25 plus; all adults. Spec prog: Farm 2 hrs, gospel 2 hrs, sports (call in) 10 hrs wkly. ■ Lewis A. Pick Jr., pres; Bob Sanders, gen mgr, gen sls mgr & mus dir; Rod Bramblett, news dir; Terry Harper, chief engr. ■ Rates: $12; 10.25; 11; 10.25.

***WEGL(FM)**—Apr 25, 1971: 91.1 mhz; 3 kw. Ant 190 ft. TL: N32 36 11 W85 29 12 (CP: Ant 214 ft.). Stereo. Hrs opn: 24. Auburn University, 116 Foy Union (36849-5231). (205) 844-4057; (205) 844-4061. FAX: (205) 844-4118. Licensee: Board of Trustees, Auburn Univ. Net: CNN, AP. Format: Rock-progsv. News staff one; news progmg 6 hrs wkly. Target aud: College students. Spec prog: Various specialty shows. ■ James V. Doyle Jr., gen mgr; Daphne Meeks, mktg dir; Laura Lewis, prom dir; Gene Toelle, progmg dir; Carl Ratliff, mus dir; Derek Roberts, Tom Feary, asst mus dirs; Catherine Perry, news dir; Jennifer Taylor, pub affrs dir; Brian Wingfield, chief engr.

WJHO(AM)—See Opelika.

WKKR(FM)—July 8, 1968: 97.7 mhz; 1.35 kw. Ant 476 ft. TL: N32 37 19 W85 30 05. Stereo. Hrs opn: 24. Box 2329, 915 Saugahatchee Lake Rd., Opelika (36803). (205) 745-4657. FAX: (205) 749-1520. Licensee: Fuller Broadcasting Co. (group owner; acq 2-1-85). Wash atty: Gardner, Carton & Douglas. Format: C&W. News staff 2. Target aud: 25-54. ■ Gary Fuller, pres & gen mgr; Roy Harrison, opns mgr & progmg dir; Clarence VanCure, gen sls mgr; Andy Burcham, news dir; Terry Harper, chief engr.

WZMG(AM)—See Opelika.

Bay Minette

WBCA(AM)—1958: 1110 khz; 10 kw-D. TL: N30 52 10 W87 46 09. Box 426, 720 S. White Ave. (36507). (205) 937-5596. Licensee: Gordon Earls Radio Inc. (acq 10-1-90; $165,000; FTR 10-22-90). Net: MBS, ABC/I; Ala. Net. Format: C&W. News staff one; news progmg 5 hrs wkly. Target aud: 18-64. ■ Gordon Earls, pres, stn mgr & gen sls mgr; Ted Allen, sls dir & progmg dir; Keith Hammond, mus dir & news dir. ■ Rates: $7.50; 7.50; 7.50; 7.50.

WFMI(FM)—May 15, 1993: 106.5 mhz; 7.3 kw. Ant 607 ft. TL: N30 49 34 W87 51 52. Suite 2, 1551 Springfield Ave., Mobile (36604). (205) 937-4106. FAX: (205) 432-9346. Licensee: Baldwin Broadcasting Company. Net: CBS. Wash atty: Jones, Waldo, Holbrook & McDonough. Format: Lite adult contemp, jazz. ■ Barry D. Wood, pres & gen mgr; William H. Phillips, stn mgr & progmg dir; Elizabeth Wright, opns mgr.

WNSP(FM)—Oct 1, 1964: 105.5 mhz; 2.6 kw. Ant 348 ft. TL: N30 49 34 W87 51 52 (CP: 1.9 kw, ant 410 ft.). Stereo. Hrs opn: 24. Box 339 (36507). (205) 937-9511. FAX: (205) 937-2012. Licensee: Faulkner-Phillips Media Inc. (acq 1987; $525,000). Net: CBS Spectrum, American Urban. Rep: Katz & Powell. Wash atty: Irwin Krasnow. Format: Urban contemp. News staff one; news progmg 10 hrs wkly. Target aud: 18-49. Spec prog: Jazz 3 hrs wkly. ■ James H. Faulkner, pres; Tim Camp, gen mgr & progmg dir.

Bessemer

WSMQ(AM)—June 1, 1950: 1450 khz; 1 kw-U. TL: N33 25 23 W86 57 17. Box 368 (35021); 3300 Jaybird Rd. (35020). (205) 428-0146. Licensee: Bessemer Radio Inc. (acq 9-1-88). Net: CNN. Wash atty: Larry Perry. Format: C&W. Target aud: 25 plus. ■ Betty Landau, pres; Jason Hook, opns mgr.

Birmingham

WAGG(AM)—1950: 1320 khz; 5 kw-D, 111 w-N. TL: N33 31 29 W86 47 10. 424 16th St. N. (35203). (205) 254-1820. FAX: (205) 254-1833. Licensee: Booker T. Washington Broadcasting (acq 2-76). Rep: D & R Radio. Format: Gospel. ■ Kirkwood R. Balton, pres; Charles Richardson, gen mgr; Walter Stuckey, opns mgr, progmg dir & mus dir; Rose Walker, gen sls mgr; Marie Pickett, prom mgr; Bennie Miles, news dir; Jay Mitchell, chief engr.

WENN-FM—Co-owned with WAGG(AM). Sept 15, 1969: 107.7 mhz; 100 kw. Ant 1,237 ft. TL: N33 43 52 W86 37 57. Format: Urban contemp. ■ Dave Donnell, progmg dir; Michael Starr, mus dir.

WAPI(AM)—1922: 1070 khz; 50 kw-D, 5 kw-N, DA-N. TL: N33 33 07 W86 54 40. Hrs opn: 24. Box 10888; (35205); 2146 Highland Ave. S. (35205). (205) 933-9274. FAX: (205) 933-2748. Licensee: WAPI Inc. Group owner: Dittman Group Inc. (acq 1-12-83; $4,000,000 with co-located FM; FTR 1-17-83). Net: NBC. Rep: Christal. Wash atty: Arent, Fox, Kintner, Plotkin & Kahn. Format: Nostalgia, MOR. Target aud: 35 plus. Spec prog: Sports talk 17 hrs wkly. ■ Bernard Dittman, pres; Bernie Barker, vp & gen mgr; Walter Berry, gen sls mgr; Betsy S. Jones, prom dir; Mark St. John, progmg dir; Scott Bohannon, mus dir; Bill Baron, news dir; Frank Giardina, chief engr. ■ Rates: $150; 100; 125; 80.

WAPI-FM—1947: 94.5 mhz; 100 kw. Ant 1,214 ft. TL: N33 29 26 W86 47 48. Stereo. Prog sep from AM. Net: ABC/C. Format: CHR. News staff one. Target aud: 18-34; General.

WATV(AM)—May 20, 1946: 900 khz; 1 kw-U. TL: N33 32 14 W86 50 16. Box 39054 (35208). (205) 780-2014. Licensee: Birmingham Ebony Broadcasting Inc. (acq 12-31-88). Net: ABC. Rep: Roslin. Format: Black urban. Target aud: 18 plus. ■ Erskine Faush Sr., pres, gen mgr & progmg dir; Shelley Stewart, vp & gen sls mgr; E. Ramsay, prom mgr; Ron January, mus dir.

WAYE(AM)—Aug 1, 1972: 1220 khz; 1 kw-D, 75 w-N. TL: N33 28 39 W86 50 57 (CP: TL: N33 28 41 W86 50 55). 836 Lomb Ave., S.W. (35211). (205) 786-9293. FAX: (205) 786-9296. Licensee: Birmingham Christian Radio Inc. Group owner: Willis Broadcasting Corp. (acq 8-20-87; $225,000; FTR 9-7-87). Format: Gospel. Target aud: 19 plus; loyal, mature & financially stable. ■ Bishop L. E. Willis, pres; Mel Fowler, gen mgr & prom mgr; Prince Yelder, progmg dir; John Walker, mus dir; Jimmie Jones, chief engr.

***WBFR(FM)**—1988: 89.5 mhz; 100 w. Ant 672 ft. TL: N33 29 02 W86 48 35. Suite 118, 244 Goodwin Crest Dr. (35209). (205) 942-3530. Licensee: Family Stations Inc. (group owner). Format: Relg. ■ David Pope, gen mgr.

***WBHM(FM)**—Dec 1976: 90.3 mhz; 32 kw. Ant 1214 ft. TL: N33 29 19 W86 47 58. Stereo. 650 11th St. S. (35294-4530). (205) 934-2606. FAX: (205) 934-5075. Licensee: Board of Trustees, University of Ala. Net: NPR, AP, APR. Format: Classical, news. News progmg 37 hrs wkly. Spec prog: Jazz 13 hrs, new age 12 hrs wkly. ■ Mike Morgan, gen mgr & stn mgr; Patrick Dorriety, opns mgr; Dick Deason, dev dir; Lisa Davis, progmg dir.

WCEO(AM)—March 25, 1953: 1260 khz; 5 kw-D, 44 w-N. TL: N33 31 29 W86 47 10 (CP: COL Homewood, 1 kw-N, DA-N). Suite G-1260, 244 Goodwin Crest Dr. (35209). (205) 942-8500. FAX: (205) 942-6578. Licensee: Broadcast Properties Inc. Net: CNN, BRN. Rep: McGavren Guild. Format: Talk. Target aud: 25-54; affluent professionals. ■ Berkley Frazier, gen mgr; Rick Stone, progmg dir; Jim Grey, chief engr.

WDJC(FM)—April 22, 1968: 93.7 mhz; 100 kw. Ant 1,007 ft. TL: N33 26 36 W86 52 50. Stereo. Box 59621 (35259); 2727 19th Place S. (35209). (205) 879-3324. Licensee: Kimtron Inc. Group owner: Crawford Broadcasting Co. Format: Relg, adult contemp, talk, gospel. News staff one; news progmg 15 hrs wkly. Target aud: 25-60; conservative middle income up/male & female. Spec prog: Southern quartet mus 4 hrs wkly. ■ Donald B. Crawford, pres; Larry Adcock, gen mgr & gen sls mgr; Wayne Morris, progmg dir; Ronnie Bruce, mus dir; Lester Hollans, news dir; Jerry Claybrook, chief engr. ■ Rates: $36; 34; 34; 34.

WENN-FM—Listing follows WAGG(AM).

WERC(AM)—May 25, 1925: 960 khz; 5 kw-U, DA-N. TL: N33 32 02 W86 51 07. 530 Beacon Pkwy. W., Suite 600 (35209). (205) 942-9600; (205) 942-4133. FAX: (205) 945-9013; (205) 942-2536. Licensee: Ameron Broadcasting Inc. (acq 8-90; $4.2 million; FTR 9-10-90). Net: ABC/I, NBC Talknet. Rep: McGavren Guild. Wash atty: Reed, Smith, Shaw & McClay. Format: News/talk. News staff 4; news progmg 45 hrs wkly. Target aud: 25-54. ■ Bill Thomas, CEO, pres & gen mgr; Donna Haggler, CFO; Andy Fisher, vp sls; Beverly Budd, sls dir; Judy Usher, natl sls mgr; Lisa Fields, prom dir; John Jenkins, vp progmg; Chris James, progmg dir; Dave Perry, news dir; Bob Newberry, engrg dir. ■ Rates: $175; 160; 165; 90.

WMJJ(FM)—Co-owned with WERC(AM). June 1, 1961: 96.5 mhz; 100 kw. Ant 1,027 ft. TL: N33 26 38 W86 42 10. Stereo. (acq 8-90; $16.5 million; FTR 9-10-90). Net: CBS, Spectrum. Format: Adult contemp. News progmg 4 hrs wkly. ■ Rates: $210; 200; 200; 100.

***WGIB(FM)**—1983: 91.9 mhz; 600 w. Ant 679 ft. TL: N33 29 02 W86 48 35. 1137 10th Pl. & 14th Ave. S. (35205). (205) 323-1516. FAX: (205) 323-2747. Licensee: Glen Iris Baptist School. Format: Educ, relg. ■ Jack LeGrand, pres & gen mgr; Steve Kluth, opns mgr.

WJLD(AM)—(Fairfield). 1942: 1400 khz; 1 kw-U. TL: N33 28 36 W86 53 01. Box 19123, Birmingham (35219). (205) 942-1776. FAX: (205) 942-4814. Licensee: Richardson Broadcasting Corp. (acq 10-87). Net: MBS, SMN, American Urban. Format: Urban contemp. ■ Gary R. Richardson, pres & gen mgr; Bob Freedman, gen sls mgr; Curtis Bell, mus dir; Leciel K. Hubbard, chief engr.

WJOX(AM)—Oct 15, 1947: 690 khz; 50 kw-D, 30 w-N. TL: N33 26 56 W86 55 18 (CP: 500 w-N, DA-N). 236 Goodwin Crest Dr. (35209). (205) 945-4646. FAX: (205) 942-8959. Licensee: Dick Broadcasting Corp. of Alabama. Group owner: Dick Broadcasting Co. (acq 1988). Net: CBS, CBS Spectrum. Format: Classic country. News staff 2. Target aud: 25-54. ■ Mike Hammond, gen mgr; Kerry Lambert, progmg dir; Keith Tela, chief engr.

WZRR(FM)—Co-owned with WJOX(AM). December 1975: 99.5 mhz; 100 kw. Ant 870 ft. TL: N33 26 28 W86 53 00 (CP: Ant 1,000 ft.). Prog sep from AM. Net: CBS Spectrum. Format: Classic rock. Target aud: 18-34. Spec prog: Jazz 3 hrs wkly.

***WJSR(FM)**—Aug 11, 1977: 91.1 mhz; 100 w. Ant 195 ft. TL: N33 39 07 W86 42 20. Stereo. Hrs opn: 7:30 AM-10 PM. 2601 Carson Rd. (35215). (205) 856-7702. FAX: (205) 853-0340. Licensee: Jefferson State Community College. Format: Adult contemp. ■ Charles S. Cobb Jr., gen mgr.

WLPH(AM)—See Irondale.

WMJJ(FM)—Listing follows WERC(AM).

WODL(FM)—June 1959: 106.9 mhz; 100 kw. Ant 1,150 ft. TL: N33 29 19 W86 47 58. Stereo. Hrs opn: 24. 530 Beacon Pkwy. W. (35209). (205) 942-7800. FAX: (205) 916-1150. Licensee: Birmingham Communications Inc. (acq 4-2-93; $2.5 million; FTR 4-19-93). Net: ABC, SMN. Rep: McGavren Guild. Wash atty: Wiley, Rein & Fielding. Format: Oldies. ■ Jerdan Bullard, gen mgr; John Henley, gen sls mgr; Brad Ellis, progmg dir; Troy Pennington, chief engr.

WSMQ(AM)—See Bessemer.

***WVSU-FM**—April 6, 1967: 91.1 mhz; 125 w. Ant 216 ft. TL: N33 27 57 W86 47 45. Stereo. Hrs opn: 17. Samford Univ., 800 Lakeshore Drive (35229). (205) 870-2877. FAX: (205) 870-2638. Licensee: Samford University. Net: ABC/FM, Alabama. Format: Jazz, relg. News progmg one hr wkly. Target aud: 20-35. Spec prog: Contemp Christian 17 hrs, oldies 4 hrs, electronic 3 hrs, blues 2 hrs, Cajun one hr wkly. ■ Dan Parker, gen mgr & gen sls mgr; Carol Guthrie, progmg dir; Ken Whetstone, mus dir; Grant Guffin, news dir; Jim Gray, chief engr.

WYDE(AM)—April 1, 1953: 850 khz; 50 kw-D, 1 kw-N, DA-2. TL: N33 37 25 W86 44 45. Suite G-1260, 244 Goodwin Crest Dr. (35209). (205) 942-5300. FAX: (205) 942-6578. Licensee: WYDE Inc. Group owner: American General Media (acq 3-86; $740,000; FTR 3-3-89). Net: USA. Format: Christian mus. ■ Berkley Frazer, gen mgr; Mike Wood, progmg dir; Jim Gray, chief engr.

WZRR(FM)—Listing follows WJOX(AM).

WZZK-FM—1948: 104.7 mhz; 100 kw. Ant 1,300 ft. TL: N33 29 02 W86 48 21. Stereo. 530 Beacon Pkwy. W., #300 (35209). (205) 916-1100. FAX: (205) 916-1151. Licensee: NewCity Communications of Alabama Inc. Group owner: NewCity Communications Inc. (acq 1980; grpsl; FTR 4-28-86). Net: AP. Rep: Katz. Format: Country. News staff 2; news progmg 10 hrs wkly. Target aud: 25-54. ■ Richard Ferguson, pres; Jerdan Bullard, vp & gen mgr; Jim Tice, opns mgr & progmg dir; John Henley, gen sls mgr; Despina Vodantis, prom dir; Todd Berry, mus dir; Don Daily, news dir; Troy Pennington, chief engr. ■ Rates: $400; 250; 270; 180.

WZZK(AM)—1927: 610 khz; 5 kw-D, 1 kw-N, DA-N. TL: N33 29 40 W86 52 30. Stereo. Dups FM 100%.

Boaz

WBSA(AM)—Oct 1, 1959: 1300 khz; 1 kw-D. TL: N34 12 50 W86 09 10. 1525 Wills Rd. (35957). (205) 593-4264. FAX: (205) 593-4265. Licensee: Good News Broadcasting Inc. (acq 5-21-92; $100,000; FTR 6-15-92). Format: Southern gospel. Target aud: General. ■ Kayron Guffey, pres; Mark Huber, vp, stn mgr & mus dir; Roger Watkins, gen mgr, adv dir, progmg dir, asst mus dir & news dir; Bill Seckbach, pub affrs dir; Earnest Stone, chief engr. ■ Rates: $5.75; 5.75; 5.75; na.

Brewton

WEBJ(AM)—Aug 1, 1947: 1240 khz; 1 kw-U. TL: N31 06 35 W87 03 36. Hrs opn: 6 AM-8 PM. Box 736, East St. Extension (36427-0736). (205) 867-5717; (205) 867-5718. Licensee: Brewton Broadcasting Co. (acq 10-1-86; $150,000). Net: AP. Wash atty: Gardner, Carton & Douglas. Format: MOR, C&W, news/talk. News staff one; news progmg 11 hrs wkly. Target aud: 25 plus; 40%

Stations in the U.S.

Alabama

Black, 75% female. Spec prog: Farm one hr, relg 9 hrs, gospel one hr, oldies 14 hrs wkly. ■ Gene Cashman, pres & news dir; Candy Smith, gen mgr, gen sls mgr, prom mgr, progmg dir & mus dir; Charles Johns, chief engr. ■ Rates: $5; 5; 5; 5.

WKNU(FM)—Aug 19, 1974: 106.3 mhz; 3 kw. Ant 300 ft. TL: N31 06 45 W87 01 19. Hrs opn: 5 AM-11 PM. Box 468, Ridge Rd., Rt. 6 (36427). (205) 867-4824; (205) 867-7003. FAX: (205) 867-7003. Licensee: Ellington Radio Inc. (acq 12-28-78). Net: ABC/D. Rep: Midsouth. Format: C&W. News staff one; news progmg 8 hrs wkly. Target aud: General. Spec prog: Farm 3 hrs wkly, relg 4 hrs wkly. ■ Hugh L. Ellington, pres, sls dir, adv dir & chief engr; Carol Ellington, gen mgr, gen sls mgr & adv mgr; Joe Ellington, prom mgr, progmg dir & progmg mgr; Rick Dease, mus dir; James Chauers, pub affrs dir. ■ Rates: $10; 10; 10; 10.

*WYJD(FM)—Oct 1, 1986: 90.9 mhz; 6 kw. Ant 479 ft. TL: N31 06 45 W87 01 19. Box 958, Jefferson Davis State Jr. College, Alco Dr. (36426). (205) 867-4832. Licensee: Jefferson Davis State Jr. College.

Bridgeport

WBTS(AM)—Sept 19, 1961: 1480 khz; 1 kw-D. TL: N34 56 34 W85 42 26. Box U (35740). (205) 495-2274. FAX: (205) 495-2274. Licensee: Bridgeport Broadcasting Co. Net: CBN, Sun. Format: C&W, gospel. ■ Roy C. McCloud, pres, gen mgr & chief engr; Mrs. Roy C. McCloud, gen sls mgr.

Brundidge

NEW FM—Not on air, target date unknown: 94.7 mhz; 1.26 kw. Ant 495 ft. One College Dr., Troy (36081). Licensee: Troy Broadcasting Corp.

Butler

WPRN(AM)—July 11, 1959: 1330 khz; 5 kw-D. TL: N32 06 02 W88 14 07. Box 664 (36904). (205) 459-3222. FAX: (205) 459-4140. Licensee: Butler Broadcasting Corp. (acq 1-75). Net: Ala. Net. Format: C&W. ■ Darryl Jackson, pres & gen mgr; George Vice, gen sls mgr; Steve O'Connor, mus dir; Henry Tyson, chief engr.

WQGL(FM)—Co-owned with WPRN(AM). Nov 20, 1978: 93.5 mhz; 3 kw. Ant 299 ft. TL: N32 06 02 W88 14 07. Stereo. Format: Country.

Calera

WBYE(AM)—Jan 12, 1958: 1370 khz; 1 kw-D. TL: N33 05 26 W86 46 37. Hrs opn: 6 AM-6 PM. Box 2005 (35040). (205) 668-1370. Licensee: WBYE Broadcasting Co. Inc. (acq 4-14-89; $100,754; FTR 4-24-89). Net: ABC/D; Alabama. Rep: Keystone (unwired net), Walker. Format: Country. Target aud: Adults. Spec prog: Black 9 hrs wkly. ■ Benjamin H. Franklin, pres & chief engr; James Tolbert, mus dir. ■ Rates: $10; 10; 10; na.

Camden

WCOX(AM)—Dec 11, 1968: 1450 khz; 1 kw-U. TL: N31 59 09 W87 17 17. Box 820 (36726). (205) 682-9898; (205) 682-4242. Licensee: Down Home Broadcasting (acq 4-8-91; $30,000; FTR 4-21-91). Rep: Keystone (unwired net). Format: Relg, Black. Target aud: Black 25 plus; the majority population of Wilcox County and the large population of the broadcast area. ■ William Powpey, pres; John McLemore, gen mgr. ■ Rates: $15; 12; 15; 12.

WYVC(FM)—Co-owned with WCOX(AM). 1990: 102.3 mhz; 6 kw. Ant 328 ft. TL: N31 57 14 W87 15 56. Hrs opn: 24. Format: Gospel, relg.

Carrollton

WRAG(AM)—1951: 590 khz; 1 kw-D. TL: N33 13 04 W88 05 48. Box 71, Hwy 17 (35447). (205) 367-8136. FAX: (205) 367-8689. Licensee: Vintage Broadcasting Corp. (acq 8-7-90; $100,200; FTR 8-7-90). Net: Ala. Net. Rep: Midsouth. Wash atty: Gammon & Grange. Format: Black, relg & gospel. News staff one. Target aud: General. Spec prog: Farm 2 hrs wkly. ■ Terry Fulton, pres; Bill Fancher, progmg dir & news dir; Olin Booth, chief engr.

WCKO(FM)—Co-owned with WRAG(AM). February 1970: 94.1 mhz; 99 kw. Ant 1,007 ft. TL: N33 14 04 W88 05 48. Stereo. Prog sep from AM. (acq 8-9-90; $660,100; FTR 8-27-90). Format: Oldies. News staff one. Target aud: General. ■ Kevin Webb, prom mgr; Bill Fancher, progmg dir.

Centre

WAGC(AM)—Nov 9, 1962: 1560 khz; 1 kw-D. TL: N34 07 41 W85 38 27. Box 602, U.S. Hwy 411 E. (35960). (205) 927-5353. Licensee: Radio Centre Inc. (acq 12-1-81). Net: USA. Format: Country. News staff one; news progmg 7 hrs wkly. Target aud: 25-55; working middle class, rural. Spec prog: Gospel 10 hrs, farm one hr wkly. ■ John C. Kelsey, pres; John Kelsey, gen mgr; Tony Griffin, progmg dir; Joan Laney, news dir; Emerson Blythe, chief engr. ■ Rates: $7; 6; 7; na.

WEIS(AM)—Sept 30, 1961: 990 khz; 1 kw-D, 30 w-N. TL: N34 09 10 W85 40 44. Hrs opn: 5 AM-10 PM. Box 297 477 S. Pratt St. (35960). (205) 927-5152; (205) 927-4232. FAX: (205) 927-8717. Licensee: Baker Enterprises Inc. (acq 9-8-83; $157,675; FTR 9-26-83). Format: C&W, southern gospel. ■ Jerry W. Baker, pres; Linda G. Baker, gen mgr; Darrell Baker, progmg dir & mus dir; Jerry Baker, news dir; Jim Davis, chief engr.

WRHY(FM)—Oct. 10, 1992: 105.9 mhz; 6 kw. Ant 150 ft. TL: N34 12 51 W85 46 20. Hrs opn: 24. Box 215 (35960); 839 W. Main St. (35960). (205) 523-1059; (205) 523-1060. FAX: (205) 523-WRHY. Licensee: Cherokee Broadcasting Corp. Wash atty: Smithwick & Belendiuk. Format: Soft adult contemp, title country mix. News progmg one hr wkly. Target aud: 25-54. Spec prog: Gospel 5, farm news one hrs wkly ■ Wynette R. Hayes, pres & gen mgr; Ken Stokes, progmg mgr. ■ Rates: $14; 10; 14; 8.

Centreville

WBIB(AM)—Dec 14, 1964: 1110 khz; 1 kw-D. TL: N32 58 01 W87 09 01. Box 217 (35042). (205) 926-4969. FAX: (205) 926-4969. Licensee: Rigdon Broadcasting Inc. (acq 11-1-83; $175,000; FTR 11-7-83). Net: ABC/C; Ala. Net. Rep: Keystone (unwired net). Format: C&W. ■ Ben David Rigdon, pres, gen mgr & gen sls mgr; Roy Weed, prom mgr, progmg dir & mus dir; Chris Johnson, chief engr.

Chickasaw

WDLT(FM)—Licensed to Chickasaw. See Mobile.

Citronelle

WHXT(FM)—June 25, 1989: 101.9 mhz; 2.07 kw. Ant 436 ft. TL: N31 02 32 W88 13 08 (CP: 102.1 mhz, 15.4 kw, ant 426 ft, TL: N31 05 04 W88 23 51). Stereo. Hrs opn: 24. Box 127, 101 Odom Rd. (36522); Box 2329, 915 Saugahatchee Lake Rd., Opelika (36803). (205) 866-5444. FAX: (205) 749-1520. Licensee: Lyn Communications. Format: Country. Target aud: 25-54. ■ David Allen, gen mgr; Michael Mott, progmg dir.

WZMG(AM)—See Opelika.

Clanton

WKLF(AM)—Nov 2, 1947: 980 khz; 1 kw-D. TL: N32 08 W86 40 49. Box 1820 (35045). (205) 755-0980. FAX: (205) 280-0980. Licensee: Southeastern Broadcasting Co. (acq 5-15-61). Net: Ala. Net. Rep: Keystone (unwired net). Format: Relg, farm. Spec prog: Black 3 hrs wkly. ■ James H. Dennis, pres & gen mgr; Piper Dennis, gen sls mgr; Robert King, progmg dir; Layle Sanford, mus dir; Ricky Tremel, news dir; Robert Williams, chief engr.

WEZZ(FM)—Co-owned with WKLF(AM). May 15, 1953: 97.7 mhz; 3 kw. Ant 245 ft. TL: N32 50 08 W86 40 49. Format: C&W. Spec prog: Black 5 hrs wkly.

Cordova

WFFN(FM)—June 22, 1987: 95.3 mhz; 2.2 kw. Ant 544 ft. TL: N33 50 42 W87 18 26. Stereo. 400 Third Ave., Jasper (35501). (205) 221-2222. FAX: (205) 384-6069. Licensee: Radio South Inc. (group owner). Format: C&W. ■ Sunny Posey, pres.

Cullman

WFMH(AM)—March 25, 1950: 1460 khz; 5 kw-D, 500 w-N, DA-N. TL: N34 10 44 W86 51 58. Box 280 (35056-0280). (205) 734-3271. Licensee: Voice of Cullman. Format: Adult contemp, country, gospel. ■ B.C. Eddins, gen mgr.

WFMH-FM—Aug 6, 1949: 101.1 mhz; 87 kw. Ant 330 ft. TL: N34 10 44 W86 51 58. Dups AM 100%

WKUL(FM)—September 1967: 92.1 mhz; 3 kw. Ant 155 ft. TL: N34 10 34 W86 50 30. Stereo. Box 803, 214 1st Ave. S.E. (35056). (205) 734-0183. FAX: (205) 739-2999. Licensee: Jonathan Christian Corp. (acq 3-1-77). Net: ABC/E. Format: Country. Target aud: 25-54. Spec prog: Farm 15 hrs wkly. ■ Don Mosley, pres & gen mgr; Ron Mosley, opns mgr, gen sls mgr & adv dir; Diane Hanks, dev mgr, mktg dir & Dusty Taylor, progmg dir; Grant Smith, mus dir; David Cooper, news dir; Art Ray, chief engr.

WXXR(AM)—October 1946: 1340 khz; 1 kw-U. TL: N34 11 40 W86 50 50. Box 968 (35056-0968). (205) 734-0207. FAX: (205) 734-8600. Licensee: Good Earth Broadcasting Inc. (acq 2-89; $62,000; FTR 2-6-89). Net: CNN, Unistar. Rep: T.N., Keystone (unwired net), Kost. Format: Oldies. News staff one; news progmg 9 hrs wkly. Target aud: 25-54; middle & upper income adults. Spec prog: Farm 2 hrs wkly. ■ Roger Myers, gen mgr; Randall Tucker, progmg dir.

Dadeville

WDLK(AM)—Aug 11, 1980: 1450 khz; 1 kw-U. TL: N32 50 56 W85 46 10. Hrs opn: 5 AM-10 PM. Box 188 (36853); Hwy 280, Jacksons Gap (36861). (205) 825-4222. FAX: (205) 825-4270. Licensee: Dale Broadcasting Inc. (acq 1-89; $185,000; FTR 1-30-89). Net: Ala. Net. Rep: Rgnl Reps. Format: Country. News staff one; news progmg 5 hrs wkly. Target aud: General. Spec prog: Gospel 20 hrs wkly. ■ Walter King, pres; Gary Burkett, gen mgr & sls dir; Angelle Patterson, opns mgr & progmg dir; Richard Daugherty, chief engr. ■ Rates: $4; 2; 3; 2.

WZLM(FM)—Co-owned with WDLK(AM). July 23, 1989: 97.3 mhz; 3 kw. Ant 328 ft. TL: N32 52 58 W85 49 16. Stereo. Prog sep from AM. Box 909, Hwy 280, Alexander City (35010). Net: ABC/D. Format: Adult contemp. News staff one; news progmg 5 hrs wkly. Target aud: 18-55. Spec prog: Gospel 3 hrs wkly. ■ Rates: $10; 8; 9; 6.60.

*WDVI(FM)—March 1, 1990: 88.7 mhz; 9 kw. Ant 328 ft. TL: N32 51 20 W85 46 31. Stereo. Hrs opn: 24. Box 284, Highway 49 N. (36853). (205) 825-6426. FAX: (205) 825-6626. Licensee: Tallapoosa County Broadcasting Inc. Net: USA. Wash atty: Bill Crispin. Format: Adult contemp, relg. News staff one. Target aud: 24 plus. ■ Donald Bailey, pres; Philip L. Williams, vp & gen mgr; Cassie Keyes, opns mgr & news dir; Richard Daugherty, chief engr.

WZLM(FM)—Listing follows WDLK(AM).

Daleville

WTKN(AM)—Oct 25, 1983: 1560 khz; 5 kw-D, 2.5 kw CH. TL: N31 16 35 W85 45 54. Box 81, Mark Donnell Rd. (36322). Licensee: News/Talk 1560 Inc. (acq 8-1-92). Format: News/talk. ■ Herbert R. Kraft, pres; Wyatt V. Cox, sr vp & gen mgr.

Decatur

WAJF(AM)—Oct 3, 1953: 1490 khz; 1 kw-U. TL: N34 35 14 W86 59 13. 1301 Central Pkwy. S.W. (35601). (205) 340-1490. FAX: (205) 351-1234. Licensee: Brainerd Broadcasting Inc. (acq 8-3-89). Net: MBS. Format: Talk. ■ Shirley Ludlow, gen mgr & gen sls mgr; John Nichols, progmg dir & mus dir; Jim Grey, chief engr.

WAVD(AM)—May 1935: 1400 khz; 1 kw-U. TL: N34 44 W86 59 28. Box 248 (35602-0248). (205) 353-0361. FAX: (205) 353-0363. Licensee: R&B Communications (acq 9-4-86; $228,000; FTR 8-4-86). Net: CBN. Rep: Riley. Format: Oldies. Target aud: 25-54. ■ Ronald W. Rose, pres, gen mgr & gen sls mgr; Jeff Ellis, prom mgr, progmg dir & mus dir; Brett Michaels, news dir.

WDRM(FM)—Listing follows WHOS(AM).

WHOS(AM)—October 1948: 800 khz; 1 kw-D, 215 w-N. TL: N34 35 51 W87 00 24. Hrs opn: 24. Box 789, 401 14th St., S.E. (35601). (205) 353-1810. FAX: (205) 355-8013. Licensee: Dixie Broadcasting Inc. Rep: Katz. Format: Country. News staff 3. Target aud: 25-54. ■ J. Mack Bramlett, gen mgr & chief engr; Mark J. Goodwin, gen sls mgr; Dan McClain, progmg dir & mus dir; Nathan Tate Sr., pub affrs dir. ■ Rates: $22; 17; 17; 8.

WDRM(FM)—Co-owned with WHOS(AM). September 1951: 102.1 mhz; 100 kw. Ant 981 ft. TL: N34 49 08 W86 44 19. Stereo. Hrs opn: 24. (acq 1976). ■ Rates: Same as AM.

WRSA(FM)—Nov 23, 1965: 96.9 mhz; 100 kw. Ant 1,010 ft. TL: N34 29 19 W86 37 08 Stereo. Hrs opn: 24. Box 4144, Huntsville (35802); Rt. 1, Box 497, Telephone Tower Rd., Lacey's Springs (35754). (205) 498-2634; (205) 350-9700. FAX: (205) 498-2791. Licensee: Paul R. Nielsen. Net: CBS. Format: Contemp btfl mus. News staff one; news progmg 20 hrs wkly. Target aud: 35 plus. ■ Allen Moore, opns dir, progmg dir & mus dir; Nancy Hofues, prom dir; Paul Peterson, news dir; John Hain, chief engr.

Broadcasting & Cable Yearbook 1994

***WYFD(FM)**—May 7, 1975: 91.7 mhz; 3 kw. Ant 300 ft. TL: N34 33 05 W87 03 56. Stereo. Box 482B, RR 9 (35603); 504 Meadowview Dr. (35603). (205) 353-7951. Licensee: Bible Broadcasting Network (group owner; acq 10-19-90; $75,000; FTR 11-12-90). Format: Relg, educ. ■ Lowell Davey, pres; Scott Beigle, stn mgr.

Demopolis

WXAL(AM)—Nov 9, 1947: 1400 khz; 1 kw-U. TL: N32 30 08 W87 00 24. Drawer X, U.S. Hwy. 80 E. (36732). (205) 289-1400. FAX: (205) 289-2156. Licensee: Edmonds Broadcasting Co. Inc. (acq 12-11-92; $316,776 with co-located FM; FTR 1-11-93). Net: MBS, Westwood One. Format: Country, Black gospel. News progmg 10 hrs wkly. Target aud: 25-54. ■ Hugh Edmonds, pres; Ellis Stewart, gen mgr & progmg dir; Derrick Robertson, chief engr.

WZNJ(FM)—Co-owned with WXAL(AM). 1975: 106.3 mhz; 3 kw. Ant 300 ft. TL: N32 20 08 W87 49 07 (CP: 106.5 mhz, 50 kw, ant 492 ft., TL: N32 20 40 W87 37 43). Stereo. Prog sep from AM. Format: Rock n' roll oldies. News progmg 4 hrs wkly. Target aud: 18-49.

Dixon's Mills

***WMBV(FM)**—Aug 15, 1988: 91.9 mhz; 62 kw. Ant 613 ft. TL: N32 07 45 W87 44 16. Stereo. Hrs opn: 24. Box 91.9 FM, Marengo Co. Rd. 30 (36736-0199). (205) 992-2425; (205) 992-2105. Licensee: Moody Bible Institute. Group owner: The Moody Bible Institute of Chicago (acq 3-31-88). Net: Moody, USA. Wash atty: Jeff Southmayd. Format: Relg. News progmg 10 hrs wkly. Target aud: 25-55; general. Spec prog: Financial 3 hrs, mental health 6 hrs, sports one hr wkly. ■ Robbie Moore, gen mgr; Tammy Sumerlin, progmg mgr; Bill Ralph, mus dir; Alan Kilgore, chief engr.

Dora

WPYK(AM)—Apr 1, 1982: 1010 khz; 5 kw-D. TL: N33 48 04 W87 06 42. Box 460 (35062); Route 2, Hwy. 78 E. Mile Marker 73, Cordova (35550). (205) 648-3242; (205) 384-6612. Licensee: Paul T. Johnson (acq 6-90). Net: Unistar. Format: Country, relg. News staff one; news progmg 14 hrs wkly. Target aud: General; community-oriented. ■ Paul T. Johnson, pres, gen mgr & prom mgr; Bill Purdue, opns mgr, progmg dir & mus dir; Bob Uptain, gen sls mgr; Ann Purdue, news dir; Jimmy Jones, chief engr. ■ Rates: $12; 12; 12; na.

Dothan

WAGF(AM)—Sept 29, 1932: 1320 khz; 1 kw-U, DA-N. TL: N31 14 56 W85 23 20. Suite M., 805 N. Oates St. (35056-0280). (205) 671-1753. FAX: (205) 677-6923. Licensee: James R. Wilson III (acq 8-13-92; $60,000; FTR 8-31-92). Format: Sports. ■ James Wilson, gen mgr.

WESP(FM)—Sept 1, 1989: 102.5 mhz; 6 kw. Ant 328 ft. TL: N31 13 39 W85 21 10. Stereo. Hrs opn: 24. Box 5707 (36302). (205) 671-1025. FAX: (205) 794-6155. Licensee: Broadcast Associates Inc. Format: Oldies. New progmg one hr wkly. Target aud: 35 plus. ■ Charles Chapman, pres; Richard Morgan, gen mgr & gen sls mgr; Ken Carlile, opns mgr; Allen Skipper, mus dir; Jeff Baxter, chief engr.

***WGTF(FM)**—September 1988: 89.5 mhz; 5.5 kw. Ant 213 ft. TL: N31 14 02 W85 26 02. 308 Westgate Parkway (36303). (205) 794-4770. Licensee: Dothan Community Educational Radio Inc. Net: Unistar. Format: Traditional Christian. ■ Jeff Blodgett, gen mgr.

WGZS(AM)—Not on air, target date unknown: 700 khz; 5 kw-D. TL: N31 12 03 W85 20 02. Box 936 (36301). Licensee: Holy Ground Broadcasting.

WJJN(FM)—1991: 101.3 mhz; 3 kw. Ant 328 ft. TL: N31 12 02 W85 20 12. Suite M-2, 805 N. Oates (36303). (205) 671-1753. Licensee: James Wilson III. Wash atty: Arter & Hadden. Format: Urban contemp. News staff one; news progmg 3 hrs wkly. Target aud: 25-54; African-American. ■ James R. Wilson III, CEO; Shae Wilson, gen mgr; Larry Steele, opns mgr, progmg dir & mus dir; Linda Davis, gen sls mgr; Fred Pendergast, rgnl sls mgr; Deborah Pearson, news dir; Harvey Luke, chief engr. ■ Rates: $30; 25; 30; 30.

WOOF-FM—Sept 18, 1964: 99.7 mhz; 100 kw. Ant 1,021 ft. TL: N31 15 07 W85 17 12. Stereo. Box 1427 (36302); 2518 Columbia Hwy. (36303). (205) 792-1149; (205) 793-2656. FAX: (205) 677-4612. Licensee: WOOF Inc. Net: MBS. Wash atty: Fisher, Wayland, Cooper & Leader. Format: Adult contemp. News staff 2; news progmg 3 hrs wkly. Target aud: 25-54; women 18-49 dominant. ■ Agnes W. Simpson, pres; Leigh Simpson, gen mgr; Hal Edwards, gen sls mgr; Leigh Simpson, Michael D. Holderfield, progmg dirs; John Daniel, news dir; Pat Sigmon, pub affrs dir; Michael D. Holderfield, chief engr. ■ Rates: $54; 51; 57; 18.

WOOF(AM)—Feb 17, 1947: 560 khz; 5 kw-D, 117 w-N. TL: N31 13 05 W85 21 10. Stereo. Prog sep from FM. Net: SMN. Rep: Roslin. Format: MOR. Target aud: 35 plus. Spec prog: Black gospel 14 hrs wkly.

***WRWA(FM)**—December 1985: 88.7 mhz; 50 kw. Ant 500 ft. TL: N31 12 30 W85 36 51. Stereo. Hrs opn: 6 AM-midnight. Wallace Hall, Troy State Univ. (36082). (205) 288-7311. Licensee: Troy State University. Net: NPR, APR. Format: Btfl mus, classical, news. News progmg 25 plus hrs wkly. Target aud: General. Spec prog: Jazz 5 hrs wkly. ■ John McVay, gen mgr, progmg mgr & mus dir; Steve Holmes, opns mgr & news dir; Pat Warner, pub affrs dir; John Brunson, chief engr.

WTVY-FM—Sept 20, 1968: 95.5 mhz; 100 kw. Ant 1,078 ft. TL: N31 15 16 W85 15 39. Stereo. Hrs opn: 24. Box 2088 (36302-2088). Scarlet Woods Bldg., 227 N. Foster-8th Fl. (36301). (205) 792-0047. FAX: (205) 793-3947. Licensee: Woods Communications Group Inc. (group owner). Net: ABC/D. Rep: Katz. Wash atty: Jack Kenkel. Format: Country. News staff one; news progmg 7 hrs wkly. Target aud: 25-54. Spec prog: Farm 10 hrs wkly. ■ Charles Woods, pres; Linda Prescott, gen mgr & gen sls mgr; Shannon O'Neal, prom mgr; David Sommers, progmg dir; Shannon O'Neil, mus dir; Andrea Boutwell, news dir; Oscar Lanman, chief engr. ■ Rates: $120; 95; 90; 45.

***WVOB(FM)**—Dec 8, 1988: 91.3 mhz; 2.5 kw. Ant 328 ft. TL: N31 10 57 W85 24 21. Hrs opn: 6 AM-10 PM. Box 1944 (36302); 2311 Hodgesville Rd. (36301). (205) 671-9862; (205) 793-3189. FAX: (205) 793-4344. Licensee: Bethany Bible College and Bethany Theological Seminary Inc. Net: USA. Format: Educ & relg. News staff one; news progmg 6 hrs wkly. Target aud: General; college students & religious community. ■ Dr. H.D. Shuemake, CEO, pres & gen mgr; Dr. Steve A. Shuemake, stn mgr; Keith Brady, prom dir & progmg mgr; Lynn Miley, news dir; Harvey Luke, engrg mgr; Charles T. Wooten, chief engr.

WWNT(AM)—Apr 30, 1947: 1450 khz; 1 kw-U. TL: N31 13 10 W85 22 14. 810 S. Oates St. (36301). (205) 671-0075. FAX: (205) 671-0091. Licensee: Dove Broadcasting (acq 6-10-83; $115,000; FTR 7-4-83). Format: Contemp Christian. ■ Lamar Trammell, pres; Larry Williams, gen mgr; Janet Williams, progmg dir; John Hubbard, chief engr. ■ Rates: $8; 8; 8; 4.

East Brewton

WAFN(FM)—Not on air, target date unknown: 95.7 mhz; 6 kw. Ant 328 ft. Box 88, Rt. 4, Atmore (36502). Licensee: Escambia Creek Indian Broadcasting Co.

Elba

WELB(AM)—Nov 16, 1958: 1350 khz; 1 kw-D. TL: N31 27 10 W86 04 00. Hrs opn: 11. 1800 Neil Grantham Dr. (36323). (205) 897-2216; (205) 897-2217. FAX: (205) 897-3694. Licensee: Elba Radio Co. (acq 3-4-76). Format: Oldies. News progmg 6 hrs wkly. Target aud: General. Spec prog: Gospel 12 hrs wkly. ■ William D. Holderfield, gen mgr & gen sls mgr; Darrell Holderfield, mus dir; Michael Holderfield, chief engr. ■ Rates: $3.80; 3.50; 3.80; na.

WZTZ(FM)—Co-owned with WELB(AM). Oct 1, 1986: 101.1 mhz; 640 w. Ant 682 ft. TL: N31 24 41 W85 57 32. Stereo. Hrs opn: 19. Prog sep from AM. Format: Hit country. ■ Jerome Jackson, progmg dir & mus dir. ■ Rates: $15.20; 13.20; 15.20; 13.20.

Enterprise

WDJR(FM)—July 1, 1968: 96.9 mhz; 100 kw. Ant 1,515 ft. TL: N31 17 54 W85 49 41 (CP: TL: N30 55 11 W85 44 30). Stereo. Box 9663, Dothan (36304). (205) 712-9233. FAX: (205) 712-0374. Licensee: Gulf South Communications Inc. (acq 7-9-92; $700,000; FTR 7-27-92). Format: Hot country. ■ Jay Joyce, gen mgr; Mitch English, progmg dir.

WKMX(FM)—Nov 27, 1974: 106.7 mhz; 100 kw. Ant 1,068 ft. TL: N31 24 41 W85 57 32. Stereo. Box 840 (36331); 100 N. Main St. (36330). (205) 347-2278. FAX: (205) 393-2141. Licensee: WKMX Inc. (acq 8-79). Net: ABC/C, AP. Format: Adult contemp. News progmg 2 hrs wkly. Target aud: 18-49; rgnl radio for Southeast Ala., North Fla. & Southwest Ga. Spec prog: Farm 2 hrs wkly. ■ Jones Wallace Miller, pres; Terry Duffie, gen mgr & gen sls mgr; Phil Thomas, opns mgr; Wendy Campbell-Sexton, prom mgr; John Erdlitz, progmg dir; Tim Godwin, mus dir; Joy Berry, news dir; Al Miller, chief engr.

Eufaula

WDMT(FM)—Mar 16, 1992: 97.9 mhz; 3 kw. Ant 328 ft. TL: N31 56 04 W85 12 27. 538 S. Randolph Ave. (36027). (205) 616-0097. FAX: (205) 687-3600. Licensee: Toole & Co. Format: Adult contemp, oldies. ■ DeVaugn Toole, gen mgr; Mary Toole, news dir.

WULA(AM)—1948: 1240 khz; 1 kw-U. TL: N31 54 30 W85 09 51. Box 531, Hwy. 431 S. (36072). (205) 687-2066; (205) 687-2067. Licensee: Lake Eufala Broadcasting Inc. (acq 8-15-85; $390,000 with co-located FM; FTR 4-22-85). Net: Unistar. Format: C&W. News progmg 2 hrs wkly. Target aud: 25-54. Spec prog: Farm 2 hrs, Black 3 hrs wkly. ■ Richard C. Snowdon, pres; Magdalene E. Snowdon, vp; Bob Smith, news dir; D. Johnson, Terry Harper, chiefs engr.

WULA-FM—1969: 92.7 mhz; 3 kw. Ant 328 ft. TL: N31 54 30 W85 09 51. Stereo. Prog sep from AM. Format: Adult contemp. Spec prog: Farm, Black. ■ Richard C. Snowdon, CEO. ■ Rates: $12; 12; 12; 12.

Eutaw

WQLW(FM)—August 1990: 104.3 mhz; 2.3 kw. Ant 370 ft. TL: N32 54 16 W87 50 09. Box 76, Rt. 3 (35462). (205) 345-4787; (205) 372-1041. FAX: (205) 345-4790. Licensee: Jim Lawson Communications Inc. (acq 3-27-93). Format: Black urban. ■ Jim Lawson, gen mgr.

Evergreen

WIJK(AM)—July 1, 1957: 1470 khz; 1 kw-D. TL: N31 26 29 W86 56 08. Box 350, Hwy 31 N. (36401). (205) 578-2780. FAX: (205) 578-3041. Licensee: Wolfe Broadcasting Corp. (acq 1-87). Net: ABC/D. Format: Gospel, talk. News staff 3; news progmg 20 hrs wkly. Target aud: 34-64. ■ Luther Upton, gen mgr.

WPGG(FM)—Co-owned with WIJK(AM). October 1982: 93.3 mhz; 50 kw. Ant 406 ft. TL: N31 26 29 W86 56 08 (CP: TL: N31 26 04 W86 56 07). Prog sep from AM. Format: Hot Country.

Fairfield

WJLD(AM)—Licensed to Fairfield. See Birmingham.

Fairhope

WABF(AM)—Aug 12, 1961: 1220 khz; 1 kw-D, 64 w-N, DA-D. TL: N30 30 38 W87 54 13. Box 1220 (36533); 460 S. Section St. (36532). (205) 928-2384; (205) 928-9228. Licensee: Jubilee Broadcasting Co. Inc. (acq 4-20-92; $350,000; FTR 5-11-92). Net: MBS; Ala. Net. Format: MOR, big band. News progmg 15 hrs wkly. Target aud: 40 plus. Spec prog: Farm one hr, Swap Shop 4 hrs, btfl mus 4 hrs wkly. ■ Morrow B. Garrison, chmn; John Ward Hinds Jr., pres, gen mgr & progmg mgr; B.G. Hinds, vp; Robbie Jones, prom mgr; Pete Hoffman, news dir & pub affrs dir; Charles Strozier, chief engr.

WBLX(AM)—Licensed to Fairhope. See Mobile.

WZEW(FM)—Aug 28, 1966: 92.1 mhz; 13.5 kw. Ant 449 ft. TL: N30 41 33 W88 02 29. Stereo. Hrs opn: 24. Box 2608, Mobile (36652-2608); Suite B-15, 107 St. Francis St., Mobile (36602). (205) 432-0102. FAX: (205) 432-0078. Licensee: WZEW Inc. (acq 6-19-89; $750,000; FTR 8-7-89). Net: CNN. Rep: Torbet. Format: Adult AOR. News staff one; news progmg 6 hrs wkly. Target aud: 25-44. Spec prog: Jazz 6 hrs wkly. ■ George O'Rear, pres & gen mgr; Glenn Sirten, opns mgr; Steve Gemignani, natl sls mgr & rgnl sls mgr; Catt Sirten, progmg dir; Linda Woodworth, mus dir; Caryn Fulda, news dir; Glenn Walters, chief engr. ■ Rates: $30; 30; 30; 20.

Fayette

WLDX(AM)—Sept 3, 1949: 990 khz; 1 kw-D, 42 w-N. TL: N33 41 06 W87 49 16. Box 189, 733 Columbus St. E. (35555). (205) 932-3318. Licensee: SIS Sound of Fayette Inc. (acq 9-86; $212,500; FTR 3-24-86). Net: ABC/I. Wash atty: Fletcher, Heald & Hildreth. Format: Country. News staff one; news progmg 14 hrs wkly. Target aud: 25-55; middle-income adults. ■ W.A. Grant Jr., pres; Eloise Thomley, gen mgr & gen sls mgr; Lana Bynum, prom mgr; Joe Jackson, progmg dir & mus dir; Carolyn Stough, news dir; Frank Giardina, chief engr. ■ Rates: $10; 10; 10; 8.

WTXT(FM)—Jan 29, 1977: 98.1 mhz; 100 kw. Ant 984 ft. TL: N33 34 31 W87 59 27 (CP: TL: N33 31 17 W87 51 38). Stereo. Hrs opn: 24. 1848 McFarland Ave., Northport (35476). (205) 333-9800. FAX: (205) 333-8834. Licensee: Tuscaloosa Broadcasting Co. (acq 6-89; $1.25 million; FTR 6-12-89). Net: NBC. Rep: Christal. Format: Contemp country. News staff one. Target aud: 25-54. ■ Bill Dunnavant, pres; Kim Woodworth, gen mgr, gen sls mgr & prom mgr; Russ Williams, progmg dir & mus dir; Dan Cates, news dir; David Boughn, chief engr. ■ Rates: $22; 22; 22; 18.

Florala

WKWL(AM)—Nov 3, 1979: 1230 khz; 1 kw-U. TL: N31 00 20 W86 19 53. Hrs opn: 6 AM-6 PM. Box 158, S. 6th St. (36442). (205) 858-6162; (205) 858-6132. Licensee: Florala Broadcasting Co. Inc. Net: USA. Format: Relg. News staff one; news progmg 15 hrs wkly. Target aud: General. Spec prog: Farm 2 hrs wkly. ■ J.C. Tew, pres; Annabel T. Zorn, gen mgr; Arthur Tew, gen sls mgr; Barbara Tew, progmg dir; George Scroggins, mus dir; Ey Mock, chief engr. ■ Rates: $2.70; 2.70; 2.70; na.

Florence

WBCF(AM)—1946: 1240 khz; 1 kw-U. TL: N34 47 02 W87 42 16. Stereo. Hrs opn: 24. Box 1316, 525 E. Tennessee St. (35630). (205) 764-8170; (205) 764-1240. FAX: (205) 764-1240. Licensee: Benny Carle Broadcasting (acq 8-11-77). Rep: Roslin. Wash atty: Rosenman & Colin. Format: MOR. News staff 2; news progmg 2 hrs wkly. Target aud: 25-54. Spec prog: "Golden Age of Radio" comedy & drama 7 hrs wkly. ■ Benny Carle, pres; Benjy Carle, gen mgr & gen sls mgr; Alan Counts, mus dir; Paul Kelly, chief engr.

WXFL(FM)—Co-owned with WBCF(AM). Feb 1992: 96.1 mhz; 2.45 kw. Ant 600 ft. TL: N34 40 24 W87 42 56. Stereo. Hrs opn: 24. Prog sep from AM. Format: Adult contemp. News progmg 10 hrs wkly. Target aud: 18-49.

*WBHL(FM)—Mar 20, 1988: 91.3 mhz; 30 kw. Ant 600 ft. TL: N34 40 24 W87 42 56. Stereo. Hrs opn: 5 AM-11 PM. Box IBC, 3625 Helton Rd. (35630). (205) 760-9191. Licensee: Tri-State Inspirational Broadcasting Inc. Net: ABC/D. Format: Easy lstng, relg. News progmg 15 hrs wkly. Target aud: 30 plus. Spec prog: Sports. ■ T. J. Hughes, pres; Ken McFall, gen mgr; Johnny Behel, opns mgr; Jim Lancaster, gen sls mgr; Mike McGee, progmg dir & mus dir; Jeff Vaughn, chief engr.

WQLT(FM)—Listing follows WSBM(AM).

WSBM(AM)—March 29, 1946: 1340 khz; 1 kw-U. TL: N34 47 50 W87 39 54. Stereo. Hrs opn: 24. Box 932, 624 S. Chestnut St. (35631). (205) 764-8121. FAX: (205) 764-8169. Licensee: Big River Broadcasting Corp. (acq 2-21-73). Net: ABC/E. Rep: Katz & Powell. Format: Urban contemp. News staff 2. ■ Knox Phillips, pres; Bill Thomas, gen mgr; Nick Martin, sls dir; Rocky Reich, gen sls mgr; Tim Turner, progmg dir; Paul Kelley, chief engr.

WQLT(FM)—Co-owned with WSBM(AM). May 29, 1967: 107.3 mhz; 100 kw. Ant 1,000 ft. TL: N34 40 24 W87 42 56. Stereo. Prog sep from AM. Net: ABC/C, ABC/FM. Format: Adult contemp. News staff 2. Target aud: 25-54. ■ Jerry Phillips, vp; Charlie Ross, opns dir & progmg dir; Rocky Reich, rgnl sls mgr.

WXFL(FM)—Listing follows WBCF(AM).

Foley

WHEP(AM)—May 31, 1953: 1310 khz; 1 kw-D. TL: N30 26 06 W87 41 00. Hrs opn: 6 AM-6 PM. Drawer 210, 20109 Hadley Rd. (36536). (205) 943-7131; (205) 943-5866. FAX: (205) 943-5866. Licensee: Stewart Broadcasting Co. Inc. (acq 5-1-61). Net: MBS. Format: MOR, talk. Target aud: 25 plus. Spec prog: Farm 2 hrs wkly. "The Trading Post" twice daily. ■ James E. Stewart, pres; Clark J. Stewart, gen mgr & gen sls mgr; Courtney Benjamin, vp mktg; James Alexander, vp prom; "Gator" Purvis, vp adv; Anne J. Stewart, vp progmg; Sean Dunlap, news dir; Robert Krueger, chief engr. ■ Rates: $7; 7; 7; na.

Fort Mitchell

WAGH(FM)—1988: 98.3 mhz; 3 kw. Ant 328 ft. TL: N32 21 48 W85 03 06. Box 9816, Columbus, GA (31908). (404) 568-9800. FAX: (706) 569-1686. Licensee: Minority Radio Associates Inc. Format: Urban contemp. News staff one. ■ Art Angell, gen mgr; Ed Harbison, gen sls mgr & progmg dir & news dir; Edgar Champagne, prom mgr; Darrell Jaye, mus dir; John Simmons, chief engr.

Fort Payne

WFPA(AM)—December 1949: 1400 khz; 1 kw-U. TL: N34 26 21 W85 42 09. Stereo. Hrs opn: 24. Box 155, 1210 Johnson St. E. (35967). (205) 845-2111; (205) 845-0024. FAX: (205) 845-0024. Licensee: PEPA Communications Inc. (acq 8-28-90; $200,000; FTR 8-20-90). Net: ABC/E, SMN. Format: Oldies, modern country. News staff one; news progmg 15 hrs wkly. Target aud: 25 plus. Spec prog: Southern gospel 18 hrs wkly. ■ Paul White, pres, gen mgr & chief engr; Wanda White, stn mgr & prom mgr; Campbell Smith, opns mgr & news dir; LeRoy Stancell, gen sls mgr; Terry Naper, progmg dir. ■ Rates: $8.50; 6.50; 8.50; 7.50.

WZOB(AM)—July 2, 1950: 1250 khz; 5 kw-U. TL: N34 26 23 W85 45 12. Hrs opn: 18. Box 748, Hwy. 35 W. (35967). (205) 845-2810. Licensee: Central Broadcasting Co. (acq 12-1-70). Net: CBS. Rep: T N; Dora-Clayton. Format: C-W. News staff one. Spec prog: Farm 2 hrs, gospel 5 hrs, relg 5 hrs wkly. ■ Peggy H. Kirby, pres; Dennis M. Kirby, gen mgr; Gloria Vogel, stn mgr & progmg dir; Doris Hobbs, gen sls mgr; Bill Mobbs, mus dir; Roland Walls, chief engr. ■ Rates: $12; 12; 12; 12.

Fort Rucker

WXUS(FM)—1991: 100.5 mhz; 3 kw. Ant 328 ft. TL: N31 19 38 W85 35 35 (CP: 2.8 kw, ant 476 ft.). 205 Walnut Dr., Enterprise (36330). (205) 598-3374. FAX: (205) 598-2362. Licensee: Sky Way Broadcasting Ltd. Format: Progsv country. ■ David Swaim, gen mgr.

Fruithurst

WCKS(FM)—Not on air, target date 1993: 102.7 mhz; 1.65 kw. Ant 630 ft. TL: N33 43 34 W85 27 22. FAX: (404) 574-7655. Licensee: Steven L. Gradick.

Gadsden

WAAX(AM)—Oct 18, 1947: 570 khz; 5 kw-D, 500 w-N, DA-N. TL: N33 58 45 W86 05 15. Box 517, 1716 Rainbow Dr. (35901). (205) 549-5229. FAX: (205) 543-3279. Licensee: Big Thicket Broadcasting Co. of Alabama Inc. Group owner: Heritage Broadcast Group (acq 4-15-84; $3,472,000 with co-located FM; FTR 4-16-84). Net: ABC/E. Format: C&W. Spec prog: Farm 6 hrs wkly. ■ Steve Humphries, pres; Mark Bass, gen mgr; Jim Pruett, progmg dir; Wayne Ball, mus dir; Dave Fitz, news dir.

WQEN(FM)—Co-owned with WAAX(AM). Oct 7, 1966: 103.7 mhz; 100 kw. Ant 1,080 ft. TL: N33 57 11 W86 13 00. Stereo. Prog sep from AM. Format: CHR. ■ Mark Bass, stn mgr; Rick Burgess, progmg dir; Keith Allen, mus dir.

WGAD(AM)—May 26, 1947: 1350 khz; 5 kw-D, 1 kw-N, DA-N. TL: N34 01 03 W86 05 15. Box 1350, 823 Forrest Ave. (35902). (205) 546-1611; (205) 547-9061. FAX: (205) 547-9062. Licensee: Coosa Broadcasting Co. (acq 10-10-57). Net: NBC; Ala. Net. Format: Adult contemp, news/talk, sports. News staff one; news progmg 16 hrs wkly. Target aud: 25 plus. Spec prog: Gospel 5 hrs wkly. ■ Ed Z. Carrell, pres, gen mgr & gen sls mgr; Archie Wade, progmg dir & news dir; Chuck Evans, mus dir; David Burgess, chief engr. ■ Rates: $18; 16; 18; 12.

WJBY(AM)—(Rainbow City). 1926: 930 khz; 5 kw-D, 500 w-N, DA-2. TL: N33 59 09 W86 02 15. Stereo. Hrs opn: 17. Box 930, 2725 Rainbow Dr., Gadsden (35902). (205) 442-1222; (205) 442-5369. FAX: (205) 442-1222. Licensee: Gadsden Broadcasting Co. Inc. (acq 3-78). Net: USA; Ala. Net. Rep: Midsouth. Format: Relg. News progmg 15 hrs wkly. Target aud: General. ■ Hinton Mitchem, pres; Gordon Henderson, vp; Joyce Henderson, gen mgr, opns mgr, gen sls mgr & adv mgr; Shirley Stephens, mktg mgr; Joyce Henderson, Mike Hooks, prom mgrs; Mike Hooks, progmg dir & mus dir; Bill Lowery, news dir; Claudia Stephens, pub affrs dir; Bill Morrow, chief engr. ■ Rates: $13; 10; 13; 8.

WKXX(FM)—(Attalla). Aug 31, 1991: 102.9 mhz; 1.1 kw. Ant 702 ft. TL: N33 58 28 W86 12 24. Hrs opn: 24. 100 Spurlock St., Rainbow City (35906). Box 8405, Gadsden (35902). (205) 442-3944. Licensee: Kerry Rich. Format: Country. Target aud: 12-49. ■ Kerry Rich, CEO & sls dir; Larry Logan, progmg dir; Ken Gray, news dir; Steve King, engrg dir.

WMGJ(AM)—Sept 11, 1985: 1240 khz; 1 kw-U. TL: N34 00 04 W86 01 48. 815 Tuscaloosa Ave. (35901). (205) 546-4434. FAX: (205) 546-9645. Licensee: Floyd L. Donald Broadcasting Co. Inc. Rep: Roslin. Format: Black, urban contemp. ■ Floyd L. Donald, gen mgr & prom mgr; Donna Wilson, gen sls mgr; Bill Morrow, chief engr.

WQEN(FM)—Listing follows WAAX(AM).

*WSGN(FM)—Feb 11, 1975: 91.5 mhz; 6.3 kw. Ant 520 ft. TL: N34 04 29 W86 01 11. Stereo. Box 227 (35999-0227). 1001 George Wallace Dr. (35999-9990). (205) 549-8439; (205) 549-8449. Licensee: Gadsden State Community College. Format: Classic rock, pub affrs. Spec prog: Jazz 19 hrs wkly. ■ Neil D. Mullin, gen mgr; Liz Patterson, progmg dir; Gil Brothers, chief engr.

Geneva

WGEA(AM)—Mar 17, 1953: 1150 khz; 1 kw-D, 50 w-N. TL: N31 01 21 W85 52 16. Box 339 (36340). (205) 684-7079. FAX: (205) 774-7979. Licensee: Shelley Broadcasting Co. (acq 10-26-87). Format: Gospel & Christian. Target aud: 30 plus. ■ Doc Parker, gen mgr; Jack Mizell, progmg dir; Osborn Henley, chief engr.

WRJM-FM—Co-owned with WGEA(AM). Sept 12, 1969: 93.5 mhz; 3 kw. Ant 225 ft. TL: N31 01 21 W85 52 16 (CP: 93.7 mhz; 50 kw, ant 443 ft.). Prog sep from AM. 409 E. Broad St., Geneva (36360). (800) 846-0937. Format: Easy lstng. Target aud: 30 plus. Spec prog: Big band 5 hrs, jazz 4 hrs, 50-60s oldies 11 hrs wkly. ■ Jack Mizell, gen mgr; Jim Powell, gen sls mgr.

Georgiana

WWGA(FM)—Not on air, target date unknown: 107.7 mhz; 6 kw. Ant 328 ft. TL: N31 37 50 W86 44 11. 4755 White Willow Lane, Orlando, FL (32808). Licensee: Sharon A. Seifert.

Glencoe

WGMZ(FM)—Not on air, target date unknown: 93.1 mhz; 1.55 kw. Ant 636 ft. TL: N33 57 15 W85 51 43. Box 459, Cropwell (35054). Licensee: Applachian Broadcasting Co.

Greenville

WGYV(AM)—Aug 18, 1948: 1380 khz; 1 kw-D. TL: N31 50 01 W85 52 16. Box 585 (36037). (205) 382-5444. Licensee: Butler Broadcasters (acq 7-16-82; $150,000; FTR 8-2-82). Net: Ala. Net. Rep: Rgnl Reps. Format: C&W. ■ Terry Golden, gen mgr; Les Taylor, progmg dir; Ken Hartman, news dir; Bob Luman, chief engr.

WKXN(FM)—Co-owned with WGYV(AM). July 18, 1977: 95.9 mhz; 3 kw. Ant 225 ft. TL: N31 50 43 W86 38 56 (CP: 4 kw, ant 296 ft.). Prog sep from AM. Box 369 (36037). (205) 382-6555. Licensee: WKXN Inc. Net: ABC/E; Ala. Net. Format: Adult contemp. ■ Terry Golden, pres & gen mgr; Mike Morris, stn mgr; Tracy Golden, news dir.

WQZX(FM)—Aug 19, 1985: 94.3 mhz; 1.75 kw. Ant 410 ft. TL: N31 54 40 W86 36 19. Stereo. 205 W. Commerce (36037). (205) 382-6633. Licensee: Haynes Broadcasting. Net: NBC. Format: C&W with crossover mix. Spec prog: Farm. ■ Fannie G. Haynes, pres; Kyle Haynes, gen mgr, progmg dir, mus dir & news dir; Robert E. Haynes, gen sls mgr.

Guntersville

WGSV(AM)—Apr 16, 1950: 1270 khz; 1 kw-D. TL: N34 18 31 W86 17 44. Box 220 (35976). (205) 582-8131. FAX: (205) 582-4347. Licensee: Guntersville Broadcasting Co. Net: ABC/C. Format: Adult contemp. ■ Lavell Jackson, pres; Kerry Jackson, gen mgr & opns mgr.

WTWX-FM—Co-owned with WGSV(AM). Aug 1, 1969: 95.9 mhz; 3 kw. Ant 300 ft. TL: N34 20 03 W86 16 57. (205) 582-4946. Net: ABC/FM. Format: C&W.

Haleyville

WJBB(AM)—Apr 1, 1949: 1230 khz; 1 kw-U, DA-1. TL: N34 14 00 W87 37 32. Hrs opn: 5 AM-midnight. Drawer 370, 807 Hwy. 5 N. (35565). (205) 486-2277; (205) 486-2278. FAX: (205) 486-3905. Licensee: Haleyville Broadcasting Co. Inc. Group owner: John Slatton Stations (acq 1951). Net: MBS. Rep: Rgnl Reps. Wash atty: Gardner, Carton & Douglas. Format: C&W. News staff one; news progmg 36 hrs wkly. Target aud: 25-55; professionals. Spec prog: Farm 3 hrs, gospel 5 hrs wkly. ■ John L. Slatton, pres & gen mgr; Pat Slatton, progmg dir; Chester Barber, chief engr.

WJBB-FM—July 14, 1979: 92.7 mhz; 3.9 kw. Ant 240 ft. TL: N34 14 00 W87 37 32 (CP: Ant 328 ft.). Stereo. Hrs opn: 5 AM-midnight. Prog sep from AM. Net: Moody. Target aud: 24-55.

Hamilton

WERH(AM)—Aug 24, 1950: 970 khz; 5 kw-D. TL: N34 07 01 W87 59 29. Box 1119 (35570). (205) 921-3481. FAX: (205) 921-7187. Licensee: Kate F. Fite (acq 4-1-58). Format: Country. Target aud: General. Spec prog: Farm, gospel. ■ Kate F. Fite, pres; James B. Fowler, gen mgr; Paul Kelly, chief engr.

Alabama

WERH-FM—Apr 1, 1968: 92.1 mhz; 3 kw. Ant 120 ft. TL: N34 07 01 W87 59 29. Stereo. Hrs opn: 5 AM-11 PM. Prog sep from AM. Format: Easy lstng, country.

Hanceville

WRJL(AM)—April 1986: 1170 khz; 460 w-D. TL: N34 04 28 W86 46 44. Hrs opn: Sunrise-sunset. 315 College Dr. N.E. (35077). (205) 352-9556. Licensee: Rojo Inc. (acq 11-2-90; $45,487; FTR 11-19-90). Format: Relg. Target aud: 25-54; homeowners with families. Spec prog: Farm one hr wkly. ■ Jo French, pres, gen mgr, sls dir, mus dir & engrg dir.

Hartselle

WHRT(AM)—Oct 1, 1956: 860 khz; 250 w-D, 17 w-N. TL: N34 07 01 W87 32 37. Hrs opn: 18. 923 Sparkman N.W. (35640). (205) 773-2558; (205) 351-2345. FAX: (205) 351-1234. Licensee: Dorsey Eugene Newman. Net: SMN. Format: Adult contemp. ■ Gene Newman, pres; Robert Newman, gen mgr, gen sls mgr & chief engr.

WTAK-FM—August 1992: 106.1 mhz; 6 kw. Ant 328 ft. TL: N34 28 54 W86 51 36. 200 Lime Quarry Rd., Madison (35758). (205) 340-1490. FAX: (205) 464-FAX1. Licensee: Griffith Broadcasting Inc. (acq 5-4-93; $1.5 million; FTR 5-24-93). Format: Classic rock, AOR. ■ Paul Buxton, gen mgr.

Hazel Green

WBXR(AM)—Dec 11, 1970: 1140 khz; 15 kw-D, DA. TL: N34 57 18 W86 38 32. Box 778, Fayetteville, TN (37334). (615) 433-7017. FAX: (615) 433-8282. Licensee: Low Country Corp. Inc. (acq 3-12-91; $10,000; FTR 3-25-91). Net: CNN. Format: Country. News staff one. ■ Marie Caldwell, gen mgr & gen sls mgr; Sue Brooks, prom mgr; Butch Menefee, progmg dir; Tim Lampert, news dir; Carl Sampieri, chief engr.

Hobson City

WHOG(AM)—Apr 15, 1991: 1120 khz; 500 w-D. TL: N33 36 50 W85 51 19. Hrs opn: Sunrise-sunset. Radio Bldg, 1330 Noble St., Suite 25, Anniston (36201). (205) 236-6484. Licensee: Hobson City Broadcasting Co. Rep: Clayton-Davis, Dora-Clayton. Format: Urban. Target aud: General. ■ Mark Hogan, gen mgr & gen sls mgr; Jeff Hogan, opns mgr, prom mgr, progmg dir, mus dir & chief engr.

Huntsville

WAHR(FM)—July 28, 1959: 99.1 mhz; 100 kw. Ant 984 ft. TL: N34 47 53 W86 38 24. Stereo. 2312 S. Memorial Pkwy. (35801). (205) 534-1666. FAX: (205) 534-1667. Licensee: W.A.H.R. Inc. (acq 8-24-62). Net: NBC. Rep: Torbet. Format: Adult contemp. News staff one. Target aud: 35-55. ■ Arnold Hornbuckle, pres; John Malone, prom mgr; Ted Cannon, progmg dir; Bonnie O'Brian, mus dir; Erika Lathon, news dir; Don Roden, chief engr.

WBBI(AM)—See Madison.

WBHP(AM)—May 23, 1937: 1230 khz; 1 kw-U. TL: N34 43 09 W86 35 42. Box 1230 (35807). (205) 534-3521. FAX: (205) 536-1329. Licensee: Radio WBHP Inc. Net: ABC/I. Rep: Katz. Format: Country. News progmg 30 hrs wkly. Target aud: General. Spec prog: Farm 6 hrs wkly. ■ W.H. Pollard Jr., pres, gen mgr, progmg dir & mus dir; Terry Stevens, news dir.

WEUP(AM)—Mar 20, 1958: 1600 khz; 5 kw-D, 500 w-N, DA-D. TL: N34 45 32 W86 38 35. Stereo. Box 11398 (35814); 2609 Jordan Lane N.W. (35806). (205) 837-9387. FAX: (205) 837-9404. Licensee: Hundley Batts. Net: American Urban. Rep: Rgnl Reps. Format: Urban contemp, relg. News progmg one hr wkly. Target aud: 18-34; adults. Spec prog: Jazz 2 hrs, community affrs one hr wkly. ■ Virginia Caples, gen mgr; Dee Handley, opns mgr; Hundley Batts, gen sls mgr; Steve Murry, progmg mgr & mus dir; Drew Morris, asst mus dir; John Hain, chief engr. ■ Rates: $20; 20; 20; 20.

*WJAB(FM)—May 9, 1991: 90.9 mhz; 100 kw. Ant 334 ft. TL: N34 47 09 W86 34 00. Stereo. Hrs opn: 24. Box 174, Normal (35762); 3409 Meridian St. (35811). (205) 851-5795; (205) 851-5861. FAX: (205) 859-5034. Licensee: Bd. of Trustees, Alabama A&M Univ. Net: NPR. Format: Jazz, blues. News progmg 5 hrs wkly. Spec prog: Black 3 hrs, oldies 3 hrs, reggae 4 hrs, Latin 2 hrs, gospel 5 hrs wkly. ■ Sam Matthews, stn mgr, dev dir, sls dir & adv dir; Ellen C. Washington, prom dir, progmg mgr & mus dir; Robert Drake, news dir; Oliver Dilliard, chief engr.

WLOR(AM)—June 1948: 1550 khz; 50 kw-D, 500 w-N, DA-2. TL: N34 44 36 W86 35 39. Unit 2, 3228 Bob Wallace (35805). (205) 539-4670. FAX: (205) 539-0318. Licensee: M.B. Associates. Format: Gospel. News progmg 2 hrs wkly. Target aud: General. ■ Milton Brown, gen mgr; Ed Gaines, progmg dir.

*WLRH(FM)—Oct 13, 1976: 89.3 mhz; 100 kw. Ant 810 ft. TL: N34 37 41 W86 30 59. Stereo. Hrs opn: 24. Univ. of AL-Huntsville, 4701 University Dr. (35899). (205) 895-9574. FAX: (205) 830-4577. Licensee: Alabama ETV Commission (acq 12-14-77). Net: APR, NPR. Format: Class, jazz, talk. News staff one; news progmg 40 hrs wkly. Target aud: General. ■ Jacob Walker, pres; Judy Stone, gen mgr; George Dickerson, stn mgr; Arlene Yedid, dev dir; Wayne Blackwell, progmg dir; David Brown, mus dir; Henry Hoffman, chief engr.

WNDA(FM)—Oct 6, 1960: 95.1 mhz; 50 kw. Ant 110 ft. TL: N34 42 56 W86 35 55. Stereo. Hrs opn: 24. 2407 9th Ave., S.W. (35805-4198). (205) 534-2433; (205) 534-2434. FAX: (205) 533-6265. Licensee: Wells Broadcasting Co. Inc. (acq 5-1-71; $95,000). Net: USA, CBN. Wash atty: Sam Miller. Format: Contemporary Christian music. News staff one; news progmg 22 hrs wkly. Target aud: 24-54; young adult, families. ■ Frederic E. Wells, pres & gen mgr; Mike Wilson, opns mgr & progmg dir; Frederic M. Wells, gen sls mgr; Mike Pawlowicz, prom mgr & news dir; Mike Pawlowicz, Dave Franklin, mus dirs; Jerome Hall, chief engr. ■ Rates: $16; 16; 16; 16.

*WOCG(FM)—March 1978: 90.1 mhz; 25 kw. Ant 230 ft. TL: N34 45 28 W86 39 44. Stereo. Hrs opn: 18. Oakwood Rd., N.W. (35896). (205) 726-7420. FAX: (205) 726-7409. Licensee: Oakwood College. Wash atty: Don Martin. Format: Inspirational MOR. Target aud: 18-55; college students, community people, professionals. ■ Benjamin Reaves, pres; Victoria L. Miller, gen mgr, opns mgr & dev dir; Jody Jones Stennis, progmg dir & mus dir; Henry Hoffman, chief engr.

WRSA(FM)—See Decatur.

WTAK(AM)—Oct 1, 1968: 1000 khz; 10 kw-D, DA. TL: N34 46 43 W86 39 16. Hrs opn: Sunrise-sunset. 200 Lime Quarry Rd. Madison (35758). (205) 772-9825. FAX: (205) 464-3291. Licensee: Gant Broadcasting Co. (acq 12-13-83; $400,000; FTR 2-14-83). Rep: Rgnl Reps. Format: Rock (AOR), classic rock. Target aud: General. Spec prog: Gospel 3 hrs wkly. ■ Parker Griffith, pres; Paul Buxton, gen mgr; Chris Cook, gen sls mgr; Kris Kelly, prom mgr; Tom Kelley, progmg dir; Teresa Taylor, mus dir; Don Roden, chief engr. ■ Rates: $32; 32; 32; na.

WTKI(AM)—November 1946: 1450 khz; 1 kw-U. TL: N34 43 30 W86 36 15. 3300 Holmes Ave. Huntsville (35816). (205) 533-1450. FAX: (205) 536-4349. Licensee: Jennings Enterprises Inc. (acq 8-7-92; $100,000; FTR 8-24-92). Net: SMN; Ala. Net. Rep: Roslin. Format: Talk. ■ Donn Jennings, pres; Fred Holland, gen mgr; Ben Small, progmg dir.

WZYP(FM)—See Athens.

Irondale

WLPH(AM)—Dec 5, 1960: 1480 khz; 5 kw-D. TL: N33 32 54 W86 39 56. Box 100067, Birmingham (35210). (205) 956-5470. Licensee: Alabama Religious Broadcasting Co. (acq 9-8-84). Format: Relg. News staff 4. Target aud: 40 plus. ■ Jim Lang, pres; Bill Frink, gen mgr; R.D. Eddy, progmg dir; Margaret Gallups, mus dir; Tom Arledge, chief engr.

Jackson

WHOD(AM)—June 1, 1950: 1230 khz; 1 kw-U. TL: N31 32 38 W87 52 30. Hrs opn: 5 AM-midnight. Box 518, 4428 Hwy. 43 N. (36545). (205) 246-4431; (205) 246-5581. FAX: (205) 246-5581. Licensee: Radio Station WHOD Inc. Group owner: Bennie E. Hewett Stations. Net: ABC/I. Format: Classic rock. News staff one. Target aud: 25-54; business minded, baby-boomers. ■ Benny Hewett, pres; Michelle Werther, gen mgr, gen sls mgr & prom mgr; Micheal Meadows, progmg dir; Melissa Sollie, news dir; Allen Kilgore, chief engr. ■ Rates: $20; 7.50; 10; 5.25.

WHOD-FM—Aug 1, 1964: 94.5 mhz; 19 kw. Ant 448 ft. TL: N31 29 51 W87 42 23. Hrs opn: 5 AM-midnight. Dups AM 99%. Net: ABC. News staff one; news progmg 2 hrs wkly. ■ Bennie Hewett, CEO; Michelle Werther, opns mgr; Micheal Meadows, mus dir. ■ Rates: Same as AM.

Jacksonville

*WLJS-FM—Sept 29, 1975: 91.9 mhz; 3 kw. Ant 246 ft. TL: N33 49 29 W85 45 49. Stereo. Box 3009, Self Hall, Jacksonville State U. (36265). (205) 782-5781. Licensee: Bd of Trustees-Jacksonville State Univ. Wash atty: Gardner, Carton & Douglas. Format: Contemporary hit, classic rock. News progmg 20 hrs wkly. Target aud: General. Spec prog: Adult contemp, classical. ■ Joe Langston, gen mgr; Mike Hathcock, chief engr.

Jasper

WARF(AM)—Mar 1, 1957: 1240 khz; 1 kw-U. TL: N33 48 54 W87 16 19. 400 3rd Ave. (35501). (205) 221-2222. FAX: (205) 384-6069. Licensee: Radio South Inc. (group owner; acq 6-1-65). Net: AP. Format: C&W. News staff one. ■ Sonny Posey, pres & gen sls mgr; Bill Watt, progmg dir; Barry Partilla, news dir.

WZBQ-FM—Listing follows WZPQ(AM).

WZPQ(AM)—Nov 2, 1946: 1360 khz; 1 kw-D, 42 w-N. TL: N33 49 12 W87 16 26. Stereo. Hrs opn: 14. Box 622, 409 9th Ave. (35501). (205) 384-3461; (205) 384-3221. FAX: (205) 384-3462. Licensee: SIS Sound Inc. (acq 10-1-86; $737,500 with co-located FM; FTR 3-24-86). Net: ABC/I. Rep: Torbet. Wash atty: Fletcher, Heald & Hildreth. Format: Adult contemp, oldies. News progmg 4 hrs wkly. Target aud: General. Spec prog: Gospel 6 hrs wkly. ■ W. A. Grant Jr., pres; Rick L. Jones, gen mgr & prom mgr; Joe Cook, gen sls mgr; John Whitmer, chief engr.

WZBQ-FM—Co-owned with WZPQ(AM). March 28, 1962: 102.5 mhz; 13 kw. Ant 2,028 ft. TL: N33 28 51 W87 24 03 (CP: 78.5 kw). Stereo. Prog sep from AM. Drawer 4, Flatwoods Rd., Tuscaloosa (35402). (205) 339-3700. FAX: (205) 339-3704. Format: Adult contemp. News staff one; news progmg 3 hrs wkly. ■ Walter Grant, gen mgr; Teddy Katz, gen sls mgr; Sammy Watson, prom dir; Jim Suite, mus dir.

Lanett

WRLD(AM)—May 1944: 1490 khz; 1 kw-U. TL: N32 52 26 W85 11 32. Hrs opn: 5 AM-midnight. Box 312, West Point, GA (31833); 602 Cherry Dr. (36863). (205) 644-1179. FAX: (205) 644-1490. Licensee: Alford M. Pearce (acq 6-14-90; FTR 7-2-90). Net: ABC/I; Ga. Net. Wash atty: Gardner, Carton & Douglas. Format: Oldies. News staff one; news progmg 9 hrs wkly. Target aud: 18-55. Spec prog: Gospel 17 hrs wkly. ■ Al Pearce, pres, gen mgr & news dir; Randy Shears, gen sls mgr; Linda Pearce, prom mgr; D. Buchannan, progmg dir; Bradley Smith, mus dir; Phil Kitchens, chief engr. ■ Rates: $8; 6; 8; 4.

Langdale

*WEBT(FM)—Jan 17, 1986: 91.5 mhz; 380 w. Ant 85 ft. TL: N32 48 15 W85 10 43. 2615 64th Blvd., Valley (36854). (205) 756-6923. Licensee: Langdale Educational Broadcasting Foundation. Format: Educ, relg. ■ Sanford Chose, pres & gen mgr.

Lexington

WKNI(AM)—Feb 20, 1981: 620 khz; 5 kw-D, 99 w-N. TL: N34 58 37 W87 22 10. Box 188 (35645). (205) 229-6262. Licensee: Country Boy Communications Inc. (acq 12-26-91; $85,009; FTR 1-13-92). Net: SMN. Format: Sports, talk. ■ Eugene Hutchens, gen mgr; Jerry Thompson, stn mgr.

Linden

WINL(FM)—Not on air, target date unknown: 98.5 mhz; 100 kw. Ant 817 ft. TL: N32 07 34 W87 44 02. 300 Monsanto Rd., Anniston (36201). Licensee: Radio Communications Inc. (acq 10-28-90 $125,000; FTR 11-12-90).

WNPT-FM—Dec 19, 1990: 102.9 mhz; 40 kw. Ant 551 ft. TL: N32 27 40 W87 34 50. Stereo. Hrs opn: 24. Box 2787 (35403); 229 Third St., Northport (35476). Licensee: Linden Radio Joint Venture. Format: Classical, rhythm & blues Target aud: 24-54; mature business audience. ■ Ellis J. Parker, pres; Cornelius Frisson, gen mgr.

Lineville

WZZX(AM)—1967: 780 khz; 5 kw-D. TL: N33 17 04 W85 47 24. Box 395, Ashland (36251). (205) 354-4600. FAX: (205) 354-7224. Licensee: Robert A. Perry (acq 6-20-86; $82,715.43; FTR 5-12-86). Net: NBC. Format: Southern gospel, country. ■ Robert A. Perry, pres; Al Haynes, gen mgr; Tommy Wood, progmg dir & mus dir; Hugh O'Neil, chief engr.

Livingston

WSLY(FM)—See York.

WYLS(AM)—See York.

Stations in the U.S. Alabama

Madison

WBBI(AM)—Mar 29, 1983: 730 khz; 1 kw-D, 123 w-N. TL: N34 41 46 W86 44 19. Stn currently dark. 200 Main St. (35758). (205) 461-7373. FAX: (205) 461-0393. Licensee: Phoenix Capital Corp. (acq 11-30-87). Format: Headline news. ■ Carl Sampieri, pres & gen mgr.

Marion

WAJO(AM)—Dec 8, 1951: 1310 khz; 5 kw-D. TL: N32 38 04 W87 17 48. Drawer 930 (36756). (205) 683-6168. Licensee: Marion Radio Inc. (acq 6-86; $115,000; FTR 6-30-86). Net: Tobacco, Ala. Net. Format: Urban contemp. ■ Elizah Rollins III, gen mgr.

WJAM-FM—Co-owned with WAJO(AM). Not on air, target date unknown: 97.3 mhz; 3.71 kw. Ant 419 ft. TL: N32 20 21 W87 23 24.

Millbrook

WMCZ(FM)—Not on air, target date unknown: 97.1 mhz; 3 kw. Ant 328 ft. TL: N32 25 58 W86 20 07. 648 S. Perry St., Montgomery (36104,). Box 2231, Montgomery (36102). (205) 262-2323. FAX: (205) 263-3483. Licensee: Clinton Enterprises Inc. (acq 4-5-93; $155,000; FTR 4-26-93). ■ Tamara Eubanks, stn mgr.

Mobile

WABB(AM)—November 1948: 1480 khz; 5 kw-U, DA-N. TL: N30 43 11 W88 04 16. Box 2148 (36652); 1551 Springhill Ave. (36604). (205) 432-5572. FAX: (205) 438-4044. Licensee: WABB Inc. Group owner: Dittman Group Inc. Net: NBC Talknet, SMN. Rep: Christal. Format: Div. News staff 2; news progmg 8 hrs wkly. Target aud: 18-49. ■ Bernard Dittman, pres & gen mgr; Kelly Bell, gen sls mgr; Dusty Hayes, prom mgr; James Sansing, progmg dir & chief engr; Kathy Richardson, news dir.

WABB-FM—Feb 5, 1973: 97.5 mhz; 100 kw. Ant 1,644 ft. TL: N30 41 20 W87 49 49 (CP: Ant 1,551 ft.). Stereo. Prog sep from AM. Net: ABC/FM. Format: Top-40. News progmg 4 hrs wkly. ■ Leslie Fram, progmg dir; Lee Chestnut, mus dir.

WAVH(FM)—Dec 5, 1964: 96.1 mhz; 100 kw. Ant 1,342 ft. TL: N30 41 20 W87 49 49. Stereo. Hrs opn: 24. Suite 405, Riverview Plaza, 63 S. Royal St. (36602); 1135 E. Cross St., Pensacola, FL (32513). (205) 344-9900; (904) 469-9636. FAX: (205) 433-9604. Licensee: Franklin Communications Partners LP. Group owner: WESHAM Broadcasting Co. (acq 7-1-93; $2 million; FTR 8-9-93). Rep: D & R Radio. Format: Oldies. News staff one; news progmg 15 hrs wkly. Target aud: 25-54 (core 35-44); front edge baby boomers. ■ Wayne Gardner, vp, gen mgr & rgnl sls mgr; Scott O'Brien, progmg dir & mus dir; Glenn Walters, chief engr. ■ Rates: $45; 40; 45; 30.

WBHY(AM)—Dec 9, 1943: 840 khz; 10 kw-D. TL: N30 45 50 W88 06 36. Box 1328, (36633); 2621-B Ralston Rd. (36606). (205) 473-8488; (205) 770-9249. FAX: (205) 473-8854. Licensee: Goforth Media Inc. (acq 4-11-86). Net: CBN. Wash atty: Fletcher, Heald & Hildreth. Format: Christian progmg/talk. Target aud: 34-64; Christians. ■ Wilbur Goforth, pres & gen mgr; Steve Riggs, exec vp & vp engrg; Stephen Goforth, vp, vp opns, progmg dir & mus dir; Tommy Hodge, sls dir; Jean Williams, prom mgr.

***WBHY-FM**—Mar 20, 1992: 88.5 mhz; 50 kw. Ant 624 ft. TL: N30 40 56 W87 49 41. Stereo. Hrs opn: 24. Prog sep from AM. (205) 473-8007; (205) 473-8080. (acq 6-27-90 $150,000; FTR 7-30-90.) Net: USA. Format: Contemp Christian music. News progmg 7 hrs wkly. Target aud: 18-34; young adults. ■ Wilbur Goforth, CEO; Evelyn Young, dev dir; Stephen Goforth, vp progmg; Alice Chateau, asst mus dir.

WBLX(AM)—(Fairhope). Apr 22, 1965: 660 khz; 22.5 kw-D, 850 w-N, DA-N. TL: N30 42 27 W88 03 55 (CP: 1550 khz; 22 kw-N, non DA-N). Hrs opn: 24. Box 1967, Mobile (36633). 1204 Dauphin St., Mobile (36604). (205) 432-7609. FAX: (205) 432-2054. Licensee: April Broadcasting (acq 7-23-90; grpsl; FTR 8-13-90). Net: SMN, ABC. Rep: D & R Radio. Format: R&B. News staff one. Target aud: 25 plus; Black adults. Spec prog: Black gospel, sports 12 hrs wkly. ■ Phil Giordano, CEO; Jon Smith, pres; David Clark, vp & gen mgr; Lee Clear, gen sls mgr; Blaine Kelly, natl sls mgr & prom mgr; James Simon, mus dir; Pat Trenier, pub affrs dir; Dana Walters, chief engr.

WBLX-FM—April 1976: 92.9 mhz; 98 kw. Ant 1,555 ft. TL: N30 37 35 W87 38 50. Stereo. Prog sep from AM. (Acq 7-23-90; grpsl; FTR 8-13-90). Net: ABC. Format: Urban contemp. Target aud: 12 plus; primarily Black women, 18-34.

WDLT(FM)—(Chickasaw). 1980: 98.3 mhz; 6 kw. Ant 300 ft. TL: N30 44 14 W88 08 02 (CP: 40 kw, ant 550 ft.). Stereo. Hrs opn: 24. Box 180426, Mobile (36618-0426). (205) 380-9098. FAX: (205) 380-9029. Licensee: United Broadcasting Inc. (acq 5-11-92; $879,000; FTR 6-1-92). Net: Unistar. Rep: Katz & Powell. Format: Soft adult contemp. Target aud: 25-54. ■ Tom Wilson, pres & chief engr; Guy Keiting, progmg dir.

WGOK(AM)—Nov 21, 1958: 900 khz; 1 kw-D, 381 w-N, DA-2. TL: N30 42 27 W88 03 55. Stereo. Box 1425 (36633). (205) 432-8661. FAX: (205) 432-1921. Licensee: Roberds Broadcasting Inc. (acq 10-1-77). Rep: Roslin. Format: Urban contemp. News staff one. Target aud: 18-54; Black adults. ■ Dickie Roberds, pres & gen sls mgr; Irene Johnson Ware, stn mgr.

***WHIL-FM**—Aug 29, 1974: 91.3 mhz; 100 kw. Ant 245 ft. TL: N30 41 47 W88 08 15 (CP: Ant 994 ft., TL: N30 40 55 W87 49 41). Stereo. Hrs opn: 5 AM-1 AM. Box 160326 (36616); 4000 Dauphin St. (36608). (205) 460-2395. FAX: (205) 460-2773. Licensee: Spring Hill College. Net: APR, AP. Wash atty: Dow, Lohnes & Albertson. Format: Class. News progmg 10 hrs wkly. Target aud: 35 plus. ■ Jeffrey R. Stoll, gen mgr; Rhoda Baldwin, dev dir; Charlie Smoke, progmg dir; Barry Little, chief engr.

WKRG(AM)—1946: 710 khz; 1 kw-D, 500 w-N. TL: N30 43 13 W88 03 34. Box 160587 (36616); 555 Broadcast Dr. (36606). (205) 479-5555. FAX: (205) 479-3418. Licensee: WKRG-TV Inc. (acq 1956). Net: ABC TalkRadio, CBS, MBS. Rep: Katz. Wash atty: Leventhal, Senter & Lerman. Format: News/talk, sports. News staff 3. Target aud: 25 plus. ■ D.H. Long Jr., pres; T.W. Diamond, stn mgr; Gary Smith, gen sls mgr; Mary Booth, prom mgr; Mike Malone, progmg dir; Bill Farris, news dir; Tom Brown, chief engr.

WKRG-FM—Oct 16, 1947: 99.9 mhz; 100 kw. Ant 1,755 ft., TL: N30 41 20 W87 49 49. Stereo. Prog sep from AM. TWX: 810-741-4263. Format: Adult contemp. News staff 4. Target aud: 25-54. ■ Jack Gorday, gen sls mgr; Greg Gordon, progmg dir; Rich Freeman, mus dir; Mary Booth, news dir; Jim Richardson, chief engr. ■ WKRG-TV affil.

WKSJ(AM)—See Prichard.

WKSJ-FM—Apr 12, 1971: 94.9 mhz; 100 kw. Ant 410 ft. TL: N30 35 36 W87 39 40 (CP: Ant 1,554 ft., TL: N30 37 35 W87 38 50). Stereo. Box 160706 (36616); Suite 504, 917 Western American Cir. (36609). (205) 344-9900. FAX: (205) 344-3525. Licensee: Franklin Communications Partners L.P. Group owner: WESHAM Broadcasting Co. (acq 7-16-92; FTR 8-3-92). Net: ABC/E. Rep: Banner. Format: Contemp country. News staff 3. ■ Ken Johnson, pres; Wayne Gardner, gen mgr; Bill Roth, gen sls mgr; Scott Johnson, progmg dir; Jef Funk, mus dir; Michael Sloan, news dir; Glenn Walters, chief engr.

WLPR(AM)—(Prichard). Dec 31, 1986: 960 khz; 5 kw-U, DA-N. TL: N30 45 50 W88 06 36. Stereo. Hrs opn: 24. 3325 Crestwood Dr., Semmes (36575-5443). (205) 473-8488. Licensee: Mobile Broadcast Service Inc. Net: SMN. Wash atty: Brown, Finn, Nietert. Format: Big band. News progmg 13 hrs wkly. Target aud: 35 plus. ■ Howard L. Smith (owner), pres; Howard L. Smith, gen mgr. ■ Rates: $5; 5; 6; 5.

WLVV(AM)—Feb 7, 1930: 1410 khz; 5 kw-U, DA-N. TL: N30 40 52 W88 00 02. 1263 Battleship Pkwy., Stanish Fort (36527). Licensee: Albert L. Crain (acq 4-26-91; $25,000; FTR 5-6-91). Net: American Urban. Rep: Katz & Powell. Format: MOR. News staff one. Target aud: 18-44; Black. ■ Jimmy Henderson, gen mgr.

WMOB(AM)—Jan 25, 1961: 1360 khz; 5 kw-D, 212 w-N, DA-2. TL: N30 41 26 W88 01 33. Box 63, 200 Addsco Rd. Causeway (36601). (205) 432-1360. Licensee: Buddy Tucker Enterprises (acq 4-84; $395,000; FTR 4-9-84). Format: Relg. ■ Theodore Tucker, pres & gen mgr; A.J. Crawford, opns mgr.

***WTOH(FM)**—September 1974: 105.9 mhz; 10 w. Ant 290 ft. TL: N30 41 48 W88 08 15 (CP: Ant 327 ft.). 4000 Dauphin St. (36608). (205) 460-2392. Licensee: Spring Hill College. Format: Progsv. ■ Varnell Lee, stn mgr.

Monroeville

WMFC(AM)—April 1952: 1360 khz; 1 kw-D. TL: N31 30 51 W87 17 55. Box 645, 820 Pineville Rd. (36460). Box 641 (36461). (205) 575-3281; (205) 575-4061. FAX: (205) 575-3280. Licensee: Monroe Broadcasting Co. Inc. Net: ABC/I. Format: Country. Target aud: 25-54. ■ W.M. Stewart, pres; David Stewart, vp; David Stewart, Judy Chamblin (admin ass't), gen mgrs; Misty Armstrong, gen sls mgr; Carol Casey, progmg dir & mus dir; Jim DeWitt, news dir; Alan Kilgore, chief engr. ■ Rates: $9; 7.25; 9; 5.25.

WMFC-FM—December 1965: 99.3 mhz; 3 kw. Ant 328 ft. TL: N31 30 51 W87 17 55 (CP: 50 kw, ant 492 ft.). Stereo. Hrs opn: 5 AM-midnight. Dups AM 100%. Target aud: General. ■ Rates: Same as AM.

WYNI(AM)—Dec 6, 1982: 930 khz; 5 kw-D, 48 w-N. TL: N31 29 40 W87 21 29. 201 Office Park (36460). (205) 575-9966. Licensee: Hub City Broadcasting Corp. Net: NBC. Format: Adult contemp. ■ Harold Harris, pres, gen mgr, mus dir & chief engr; Vivian Tuberville, vp; Margie Daniels, gen sls mgr; Jerry Daniel, news dir.

Montgomery

WACV(AM)—Jan 16, 1939: 1170 khz; 10 kw-D, 1 kw-N, DA-2. TL: N32 27 16 W86 17 21. Hrs opn: 24. Box 1669 (36102). (205) 244-1170. Licensee: Montgomery Broadcast Properties Ltd. (acq 5-26-93; $125,000; FTR 6-14-93). Net: CBS. Format: News, talk, sports. News staff 3. Target aud: 25 plus. Spec prog: Farm 5 hrs wkly. ■ Charles Woods, CEO; Brent Markwell, gen mgr; Betty Szerzo, stn mgr & gen sls mgr; Fred Thompson, opns dir; Don Markwell, progmg dir; Ed Davies, news dir.

WBAM-FM—Jan 1, 1961: 98.9 mhz; 100 kw. Ant 1095 ft. TL: N32 24 11 W86 11 48. Stereo. 4740 Radio Rd. (36116). (205) 288-0150. FAX: (205) 281-4081. Licensee: Deep South Broadcasting Co. (acq 9-22-78). Rep: Christal. Format: Oldies. ■ Robert G. Brennan, vp & gen mgr; Neil Smith, gen sls mgr; Fred Leemhuis, progmg dir; Mike Wascher, news dir; Tom Jones, chief engr.

WHHY-FM—Jan 9, 1962: 101.9 mhz; 100 kw. Ant 1,200 ft. TL: N32 29 33 W86 08 50 (CP: TL: N32 24 11 W86 11 48). Stereo. 3435 Norman Bridge Rd. (36105); Box 250210 (36125-0210). (205) 264-2288. FAX: (205) 834-9102. Licensee: Thomas Duddy, Receiver (acq 3-93). Net: ABC/C, AP. Rep: McGavren Guild Radio. Wash atty: Scott Johnson. Format: Hot adult contemp. News staff 2; news progmg 5 hrs wkly. Target aud: 18-40. ■ Robert N. Robinson, CEO; Ann Collister, pres & gen mgr; Bob Robinson, Jr., gen sls mgr; Bill Thomas, progmg dir; Karen Rite, prom mgr & mus dir; Blake Scott, news dir; Charles Grider, chief engr.

WHHY(AM)—Apr 30, 1930: 1440 khz; 5 kw-D, 1 kw-N, DA-N. TL: N32 18 24 W86 13 40 (CP: TL: N32 24 11 W86 11 48). Dups FM 75%.

***WLBF(FM)**—Apr 4, 1984: 89.1 mhz; 100 kw. Ant 537 ft. TL: N32 24 13 W86 11 50. Stereo. Hrs opn: 24. Box 210789 (36121); 381 Mendel Pkwy. E. (36117). (205) 271-8900. FAX: (205) 260-8962. Licensee: Montgomery Educ Radio Inc. Net: Moody, USA. Wash atty: Southmayd & Miller. Format: Educ, relg, MOR. News progmg 14 hrs wkly. Target aud: General. ■ D.G. Markwell, pres; Carolyn Snow, CFO; Jonn Albritton, vp; Alex Saks, gen mgr & progmg dir; Bob Crittenden, mus dir & pub affrs dir; Larry Wilkins, chief engr.

WLNE-FM—Dec 1, 1990: 96.1 mhz; 4.5 kw. Ant 820 ft. TL: N32 21 32 W86 19 57 (CP: 900 w, ant 820 ft., TL: N32 22 03 W86 15 42). Stereo. Hrs opn: 24. Box 21073 (36121); 4101 A-Wall St. (36106). (205) 244-0961. FAX: (205) 279-9563. Licensee: Montgomery Broadcast Properties Ltd. Net: USA. Rep: Banner. Format: Soft adult contemp. Target aud: 25-54. ■ Al Stroh, pres & gen mgr; Brenda Stroh, vp.

WLWI(AM)—1953: 740 khz; 50 kw-D, 73 w-N, DA-2. TL: N32 18 39 W86 17 25. Box 4999, (36195). (205) 240-9274. FAX: (205) 240-9219. Licensee: Colonial Broadcasting Co. Inc. (acq 2-22-85; $500,000). Net: MBS, NBC. Rep: Katz. Wash atty: Gardner, Carton & Douglas. Format: Standards, MOR, sports. News staff 3; news progmg 12 hrs wkly. Target aud: 35 plus. ■ David Coppock, CEO, pres & gen mgr; Robert Lowder, chmn; Mike Holley, CFO; Bill Cameron, opns mgr; Rick Brown, gen sls mgr; Tana Jackson, news dir; Larry Wilkins, chief engr. ■ Rates: $30; 20; 25; 10.

WLWI-FM—July 15, 1969: 92.3 mhz; 100 kw. Ant 1,095 ft. TL: N32 24 13 W86 11 50 (CP: TL: N32 24 11 W86 11 48). Stereo. Prog sep from AM. (acq 12-77). Net: MBS. Rep: Katz. Format: Country. News staff 3; news progmg 3 hrs wkly. Target aud: 25-54. ■ Rick Brown, stn mgr; Carson James, progmg dir & mus dir; Larry Wilkins, vp engrg. ■ Rates: $125; 85; 100; 55.

WMGY(AM)—June 1, 1946: 800 khz; 1 kw-D, 193 w-N. TL: N32 24 48 W86 17 25. Hrs opn: 6 AM-midnight. 2305 Upper Wetumpka Rd. (36107-1345). (205) 834-3710. FAX: (205) 269-5953. Licensee: WMGY Radio Inc. Group owner: GHB Radio Group (acq 7-75). Net: USA. Format: Southern gospel. News progmg 7 hrs wkly. Target aud: 35 plus. Spec prog: Black 15 hrs, sports 6 hrs wkly. ■ Greg Holtan, gen mgr.

Alabama

WSYA(AM)—May 8, 1953: 950 khz; 1 kw-U, DA-N. TL: N32 26 23 W86 15 49. Box 5000 (36103); 330 Madison Ave. (36104). (205) 832-4295. FAX: (205) 834-1117. Licensee: U.S. Broadcasting Ltd. Partnership. Group owner: Magic Broadcasting Companies (acq 8-14-87). Net: Unistar. Rep: Torbet. Wash atty: Latham & Watkins. Format: Adult contemp. News staff 2. Target aud: 25-49. ■ Don McCoy, pres; Douglas Grimm, exec vp & gen mgr; Kim Narmour, gen sls mgr; Mickey Coulter, progmg dir; Leigh Hutchens, news dir; Tom Jones, chief engr. ■ Rates: $50; 50; 50; na.

WSYA-FM—July 9, 1961: 103.3 mhz; 100 kw. Ant 1,007 ft. TL: N32 24 48 W86 17 25 (CP: TL: N32 24 11 W86 11 48). Stereo. Dups AM 100%. News staff one; news progmg 5 hrs wkly. Target aud: 25-54; adults.

*WVAS(FM)—June 15, 1984: 90.7 mhz; 25 kw. Ant 308 ft. TL: N32 29 31 W86 08 48 (CP: 80 kw, ant 347 ft., TL: N32 21 58 W86 17 40). Stereo. Hrs opn: 18 Mon-Fri, 24 Sat-Sun. Box 371, Alabama State Univ. (36101-0271). (205) 293-4287; (205) 293-4306. Licensee: Alabama State Univ. (acq 6-83). Net: ABC/FM, Westwood One. Wash atty: Wilkes, Artis, Hedrick & Lane. Format: Jazz. ■ Dr. C.C. Baker, pres; John F. Knight Jr., gen mgr; Candy Caper, progmg dir; Carol Stephens, mus dir; Robb Taylor, news dir.

WXVI(AM)—May 1947: 1600 khz; 5 kw-D, 1 kw-N, DA-2. TL: N32 23 40 W86 17 21. Box 4280 (36104); one WCOV Ave. (36111). (205) 263-3459. FAX: (205) 288-5414. Licensee: Capital Communications. Net: American Urban. Rep: Roslin. Format: Black. ■ David Woods, gen mgr; Linda Moorer, mus dir; Phil Witt, chief engr.

Moody

WURL(AM)—October 1984: 760 khz; 1 kw-D. TL: N33 35 13 W86 28 18. 732 N. Pine Hill Rd., Birmingham (35217). (205) 699-9875; (205) 849-9586. Licensee: Bill Davison Evangelistic Assn. (acq 9-89; $175,000; FTR 10-2-89). Net: USA. Format: Gospel. Target aud: General. ■ William J. Davison, pres; William J. Davison Sr., gen mgr & gen sls mgr; Bill Bell, progmg dir & mus dir; Ben Franklin, chief engr. ■ Rates: $6; 6; 6; 6.

Moulton

WHIY(AM)—Dec 11, 1963: 1190 khz; 2.5 kw-D. TL: N34 28 55 W87 18 04. Box 307, 13471 Court St. (35650). (205) 974-0681. Licensee: Moulton Broadcasting Co. Inc. (acq 1-27-68). Net: USA. Rep: T N, Midsouth; Rgnl Reps. Format: Contemp country & classic rock oldies. News staff one. Target aud: 22-54. Spec prog: Farm 6 hrs wkly. ■ Ray Wallace, pres, gen mgr, gen sls mgr & vp adv; Carol Towry, adv dir; Teddy Wallace, progmg dir, mus dir & news dir; Kenneth Casey, chief engr. ■ Rates: $13.80; 13.80; 13.80; 13.80.

WXKI(FM)—Co-owned with WHIY(AM). Sept 1, 1991: 103.1 mhz; 6 kw. Ant 328 ft. TL: N34 32 07 W87 13 31. Stereo. Hrs opn: 20. (205) 974-0682. ■ Ray Wallace, Carol Towry, adv mgrs.

Muscle Shoals

WBCF(AM)—See Florence.

WLAY(AM)—Jan 15, 1933: 1450 khz; 1 kw-U. TL: N34 45 29 W87 40 08. Stereo. Box 220, 520 E. 2nd St. (35660). (205) 383-2525. FAX: (205) 381-1450. Licensee: Slatton-Quick Co., Inc. (group owner). Net: MBS. Wash atty: M. Scott Johnson. Format: C&W. News staff 2. Target aud: 18-54. ■ John L. Slatton, pres; Jim Smith, gen mgr; Gary Murdock, opns mgr; Mark Allen, gen sls mgr; Pat Sanders, news dir; Jeff Vaughn, chief engr. ■ Rates: $48; 36; 48; 30.

WLAY-FM—Oct 28, 1964: 105.5 mhz; 530 w. Ant 743 ft. TL: N34 40 24 W87 42 56. Stereo. Dups AM 95%. 520 E. 2nd St. (35661). Format: Country. ■ Jerry Knight, gen mgr.

*WQPR(FM)—November 1987: 88.7 mhz; 20 kw. Ant 430 ft. TL: N34 34 40 W87 46 54. Stereo. Hrs opn: 24. Box 870370, Suite 297, Reese Pfifer Hall, Tuscaloosa (35487). (205) 348-6644. FAX: (205) 348-6648. Licensee: Board of Trustees University of Alabama. Net: APR, NPR. Wash atty: Arter & Hadden. Format: Class, jazz, news/info. News staff 2; news progmg 5 hrs wkly. Spec prog: Bluegrass, blues, folk 5 hrs, new age 20 hrs wkly. ■ Anthony Dean, gen mgr; Daryl Fletcher, opns mgr; Kathy Henslee, dev mgr; Gina Carter, prom mgr & pub affrs dir; Roger Duvall, progmg dir; Jack Massey, mus dir; Glenda Webb, news dir; David Baughn, chief engr.

WSBM(AM)—See Florence.

WXFL(FM)—See Florence.

Northport

WLXY(FM)—Not on air, target date unknown: 100.7 mhz; 6 kw. Ant 328 ft. TL: N33 17 42 W87 40 06. Box 1020 (35476). (205) 333-1007. FAX: (205) 339-8771. Licensee: Warrior Broadcasting Inc. (acq 3-15-91; FTR 4-8-91). ■ Jimmy Shaw, gen mgr.

Oneonta

WCRL(AM)—July 29, 1952: 1570 khz; 2.5 kw-D. TL: N33 57 16 W87 28 20. Box 490 (35121). (205) 625-3333. FAX: (205) 625-5433. Licensee: Blount County Broadcasting Service (acq 3-55). Net: MBS. Format: Adult contemp. ■ L.D. Bentley Jr., pres; Danny Bentley, gen mgr & gen sls mgr; Wayne Shaddix, mus dir; Tom Baty, chief engr.

WKLD(FM)—Co-owned with WCRL(AM). July 12, 1968: 97.7 mhz; 4 kw. Ant 480 ft. TL: N33 56 52 W86 29 01 (CP: 6 kw, ant 262 ft.). Dups AM 100%.

Opelika

WJHO(AM)—June 3, 1940: 1400 khz; 1 kw-U. TL: N32 38 13 W85 24 23. Box 710 (36803); 223 S. Ninth St. (36801). (205) 745-6484. FAX: (205) 749-0088. Licensee: Sun Broadcasting Co. Inc. (acq 12-27-91; $50,000; FTR 1-14-91). Net: MBS. Ala. Net. Format: News/talk. News staff one. ■ Bud Smith, progmg dir & news dir.

WKKR(FM)—See Auburn.

WMXA(FM)—Listing follows WZMG(AM).

WZMG(AM)—Aug 12, 1968: 1520 khz; 5 kw-D, DA. TL: N32 39 13 W85 25 25. Box 2329, 915 Saugahatchee Lake Rd. (36803). (205) 745-4656. FAX: (205) 749-1520. Licensee: Fuller Broadcasting Co. Inc. (group owner; acq 2-1-85). Wash atty: Gardner, Carton & Douglas. Format: Black, urban contemp. ■ Gary Fuller, pres & gen mgr; Clarence Van Cure, gen sls mgr; Charlie Pruitt, progmg dir; Amy Burcham, news dir; Terry Harper, engrg mgr. ■ Rates: $14.12; 11.77; 12.94; na.

WMXA(FM)—Co-owned with WZMG(AM). July 1, 1991: 96.7 mhz; 730 w. Ant 682 ft. TL: N32 37 34 W85 19 18. (Acq 11-30-93; $650,000; FTR 11-8-93). Format: Light rock, adult contemp, classic rock. ■ Randy Brothers, gen sls mgr; Alisa Riley, progmg dir.

Opp

WAMI(AM)—Dec 12, 1952: 860 khz; 1 kw-D, 47 w-N. TL: N31 18 54 W86 15 45. Stereo. Box 169, N. Main (36467). (205) 493-3588. FAX: (205) 493-3589. Licensee: Opp Broadcasting Co. Inc. Net: ABC. Format: Country. News progmg 14 hrs wkly. Target aud: 25-45; agricultural & garment industry workers. Spec prog: Gospel 15 hrs wkly. ■ Louis Johnson, pres; Bill Smith, gen mgr & news dir; Sam Dozier, gen sls mgr; Karen Mathews, progmg dir; Mike Glisson, mus dir; Robert Page, chief engr. ■ Rates: $5; 5; 5; 3.

WAMI-FM—Nov 9, 1973: 102.3 mhz; 3.4 kw. Ant 230 ft. TL: N31 18 54 W86 15 45. Stereo. Dups AM 100%.

*WJIF(FM)—Not on air, target date unknown: 91.9 mhz; 380 w. Ant 164 ft. TL: N31 15 50 W86 13 26. S.W. Corner Hwy 52 & Folsom St. (36467). Licensee: Opp Educational Broadcasting Foundation.

WOPP(AM)—Sept 19, 1980: 1290 khz; 2.5 kw-D, 500 w-N, DA-2. TL: N31 17 27 W86 13 51. Hrs opn: 5 AM-10 PM. Box 560, 1101 Cameron Rd. (36467). (205) 493-4545; (205) 303-8835. FAX: (205) 493-4546. Licensee: E & R Broadcasting Inc. (acq 8-87). Net: Westwood One. Rep: Rgnl Reps. Wash atty: Roy F. Perkins. Format: Progsv C&W, oldies mix. News staff one; news progmg 16 hrs wkly. Target aud: 19-58; progressive & highly localized. Spec prog: Farm 4 hrs, Black 2 hrs, gospel 19 hrs wkly. ■ Ronnie L. Boothe, pres & chief engr; Robert H. Boothe Jr., gen mgr & news dir; Ruth T. Boothe, stn mgr & sls dir; Joe Adams, opns mgr, rgnl sls mgr & adv dir; Robert Boothe, natl sls mgr & progmg dir; Irvin Judd, prom mgr; Cris Anderson, mus dir; Daryel Baxley, asst mus dir; Irving Judd, pub affrs dir. ■ Rates: $10; 9; 10; 9.

Orange Beach

WXAH(FM)—Not on air, target date unknown: 105.7 mhz; 6 kw. Ant 328 ft. TL: N30 17 45 W87 33 42. 417 Ledgewood Dr., Gulf Shore (36542). Licensee: Pleasure Island Broadcasting Inc.

Oxford

WOXR(AM)—April 1956: 1580 khz; 2.5 kw-D, 22 w-N. TL: N33 26 55 W86 03 54. Box 3770, 90 Friendship Rd. (36203). (205) 835-1580. FAX: (205) 831-1500. Licen-

see: Woodard Broadcasting Co. (acq 5-62). Format: Easy lstng. ■ Jimmy E. Woodard, pres; Harry Mabry, gen mgr; Bill Giddins, gen sls mgr; Chris Wright, progmg dir & mus dir; Hugh O'Neal, chief engr. ■ Rates: $18; 18; 18; 18.

WVOK(FM)—Co-owned with WOXR(AM). Feb 19, 1990: 97.9 mhz; 280 kw. Ant 1,082 ft. TL: N33 37 21 W85 52 22. Stereo. Hrs opn: 19. Prog sep from AM. Format: Adult contemp. ■ George Salmon, gen mgr; Don Ward, mus dir. ■ Rates: Same as AM.

Ozark

WOAB(FM)—Listing follows WOZK(AM).

WOZK(AM)—May 3, 1953: 900 khz; 1 kw-D, 78 w-N. TL: N31 27 19 W85 40 58. Box 911 (36360). (205) 774-5600. Licensee: Ozark Broadcasting Corp. Format: Adult contemp. ■ Howard Pierce, gen mgr; Howard Parrish Jr., progmg dir & chief engr.

WOAB(FM)—Co-owned with WOZK(AM). July 9, 1967: 104.9 mhz; 2.5 kw. Ant 275 ft. TL: N31 27 19 W85 40 53. Prog sep from AM. Format: C&W.

WQLS(AM)—April 1968: 1200 khz; 10 kw-D. TL: N31 28 40 W85 41 07 (CP: N31 23 46 W85 33 01). 331 Ross Clark Cir., Dothan (36303). (205) 671-1234. FAX: (205) 792-5180. Licensee: Sunrise Broadcasting of Alabama Inc. Group owner: Sunrise Broadcasting Corp. (acq 6-21-90; with co-located FM; FTR 7-16-90). Net: CNN. Format: News/talk. News staff one; news progmg 20 hrs wkly. Target aud: 25-64. Spec prog: Gospel 12 hrs wkly. ■ Robert Maines, vp, gen mgr, prom mgr, progmg dir & news dir; Bob De Felice, gen sls mgr; Neil Riddle, chief engr.

WQLS-FM—Oct 5, 1968: 103.9 mhz; 3 kw. Ant 328 ft. TL: N31 26 25 W85 33 49 (CP: 6 kw, TL: N31 23 46 W85 30 01). Stereo. Hrs opn: 24. Dups AM 10%. Box 5629, Dothan (36362). (205) 792-5180. Net: CNN, Moody, NBC. Format: Easy lstng, talk. News staff one; news progmg 15 hrs wkly. Spec prog: Gospel 8 hrs, jazz 4 hrs, oldies 6 hrs wkly.

Pell City

WFHK(AM)—Jan 7, 1956: 1430 khz; 5 kw-D. TL: N33 35 10 W86 19 35. Box 608 (35125). (205) 338-1430. FAX: (205) 338-2238. Licensee: St. Clair Broadcasting System (acq 10-1-76). Net: ABC/D; Ala Net. Format: C&W. ■ Lamar Williamson, pres & gen mgr; Betty Williamson, gen sls mgr; Steve Teller, mus dir; Hugh O'Neal, chief engr.

Phenix City

WGSY(FM)—Licensed to Phenix City. See Columbus, Ga.

WPNX(AM)—Licensed to Phenix City. See Columbus, Ga.

WSTH(AM)—See Columbus, Ga.

Piedmont

WPID(AM)—June 1953: 1280 khz; 1 kw-D, 84 w-N. TL: N33 55 50 W85 35 00. Hrs opn: 6 AM-10 PM. Box 227, 412 Cedartown Hwy. (36272). (205) 447-9096; (205) 447-9743. Licensee: Piedmont Communications Co. (acq 6-15-84; $125,000). Net: MBS, Unistar; Ala. Net. Format: Adult contemp, oldies. News progmg 2 hours wkly. Target aud: 25-55. ■ Jimmy Kennedy, gen mgr & stn mgr; Andy Kennedy, gen sls mgr; Sherry Kennedy, progmg dir; James Hudson, chief engr. ■ Rates: $6.50; 6.50; 6.50; 6.50.

Prattville

WXFX(FM)—August 1977: 95.1 mhz; 50 kw. Ant 492 ft. TL: N32 28 01 W86 24 15. Stereo. Hrs opn: 24. Box 604, Suite 9, Pratt Plaza Mall (36067). (205) 365-0393. FAX: (205) 365-4992. Licensee: Downs Broadcasting Inc. (acq 1-82; $675,000; FTR 3-1-82). Rep: Torbet. Format: Classic rock. Target aud: 25-54; upscale adults, two pay check households. ■ Paul H. Downs, pres; Harold Rowe, gen mgr; Kelly Dickey, prom mgr; Keith Mitchell, progmg dir; Scott Hamilton, mus dir.

Priceville

WJRA(AM)—August 1986: 1310 khz; 1 kw-D. TL: N34 32 32 W86 54 14. Rt. 2, Box 71, Decatur (35603). (205) 353-4060. Licensee: Abercrombie Broadcasting Corp. (acq 8-86). Format: Southern gospel. Target aud: 25-65. ■ Emmett Ferguson, pres, gen mgr & mus dir; James Norris, opns mgr.

Prichard

WKSJ(AM)—June 13, 1966: 1270 khz; 5 kw-D, 103 w-N. TL: N30 44 44 W88 05 40. Box 160706, Mobile (36616). (205) 344-9900. FAX: (205) 344-3525. Licensee: Franklin Communications Partners L.P. Group owner: WESHAM Broadcasting Co. (acq 7-16-92; grpsl; FTR 8-3-92). Net: ABC/E. Rep: Banner. Format: Country. ■ Kenneth S. Johnson, pres; Wayne Gardner, gen mgr; Bill Roth, gen sls mgr; Scott Johnson, progmg dir; Michael P. Sloan, news dir; Glenn Walters, chief engr.

WKSJ-FM—See Mobile.

WLPR(AM)—Licensed to Prichard. See Mobile.

Rainbow City

WJBY(AM)—Licensed to Rainbow City. See Gadsden.

Rainsville

WVSM(AM)—May 16, 1967: 1500 khz; 1 kw-D. TL: N34 29 56 W85 50 34. Hrs opn: Sunrise-sunset. Box 339, Hwy. 75 N. (35986). (205) 638-2137. FAX: (205) 638-4237. Licensee: Sand Mountain Advertising Co. Inc. Format: Southern country gospel. News staff 4; news progmg 9 hrs wkly. Target aud: General. ■ Mark Huber, pres, gen mgr, progmg dir & mus dir; Kayron Guffey, vp; Ruth Huber, gen sls mgr; Glenn Martin, asst mus dir; Robert Gay, chief engr. ■ Rates: $7.50; 7.50; 7.50; 7.50.

Red Bay

WRMG(AM)—June 29, 1968: 1430 khz; 1 kw-D. TL: N34 24 51 W88 08 11 (CP: 3 kw-D). Box 656 (35582). (205) 356-4458. Licensee: Redmont Broadcasting Corp. Format: C&W. ■ Maurice Fikes, pres; Keith Ledbetter, gen mgr.

Reform

WTID(FM)—May 7, 1991: 101.7 mhz; 23.37 kw. Ant 727 ft. TL: N33 13 48 W87 50 50. Box 1197, Flatwoods Rd., Northport (35476). (205) 333-1200. FAX: (205) 333-0100. Licensee: Kudzu Broadcasting. Format: Classic rock. Target aud: 25-44. ■ Doug McCain, gen mgr, progmg dir & mus dir; Jeff Baxter, chief engr.

Roanoke

WELR(AM)—April 1954: 1360 khz; 1 kw-D. TL: N33 09 45 W85 22 30. Box 709, 705 N. Main St. (36274). (205) 863-4139. FAX: (205) 863-2540. Licensee: Eagle's Nest Inc. (group owner; acq 10-15-88). Net: ABC/I; Ala Net. Wash atty: Gardner, Carton & Douglas. Format: Southern gospel. ■ Jim Vice, pres & gen mgr; Kay Vice, opns mgr & prom mgr; Bernard Fuller, progmg dir & mus dir. ■ Rates: $8; 7; 7; na.

WELR-FM—Feb 14, 1969: 102.3 mhz; 3 kw H, 1.25 kw V. Ant 436 ft. TL: N33 13 49 W85 24 37 (CP: 9 kw, and 544 ft.). Stereo. Hrs opn: 24. Prog sep from AM. Net: ABC. Format: Country. ■ Don Strength, progmg dir & mus dir. ■ Rates: $14; 12; 12; 8.

Robertsdale

WXWY(AM)—March 1, 1985: 1000 khz; 1 kw-D. TL: N30 32 10 W87 42 55. Box 578 (36567). (205) 947-2346. Licensee: Opal Carrol Coley. Net: CNN. Format: Country, relg, Southern gospel. News staff one; news progmg 2 hrs wkly. ■ Gordon Coley, gen mgr, gen sls mgr & news dir; Angela Lambert, prom mgr & mus dir; Opal Coley, progmg dir; Michael Schwartz, chief engr. ■ Rates: $6.50; 6; 6.50; na.

Rogersville

WFIX(FM)—Not on air, target date unknown: 93.9 mhz; 2.25 kw. Ant 531 ft. TL: N34 51 52 W87 23 43. c/o WKNI, Box 620, Lexington (35648). (205) 229-6262. Licensee: Country Boy Communications Inc. (acq 1-12-93; FTR 2-8-93). ■ Dave Hammonds, gen mgr.

Russellville

WJRD(AM)—May 29, 1949: 920 khz; 1 kw-D, 43 w-N. TL: N34 30 50 W87 42 55. Box 518, Drawer 518, Underwood Rd. (35653). (205) 332-0214; FAX: (205) 331-WJRD. Licensee: SIS Sound of Russellville Inc. (acq 6-4-86; $125,000; FTR 3-24-84). Net: Ala. Net. Format: Country. News progmg 9 hrs wkly. Target aud: 25-60. Spec prog: Black gospel 4 hrs, relg 10 hrs wkly. ■ W. A. Grant, pres; Judy Horton, stn mgr & gen sls mgr & mus dir; Paul Kelly, chief engr. ■ Rates: $6.25; 6.25; 6.25; 6.25.

WKAX(AM)—Apr 3, 1974: 1500 khz; 1 kw-D. TL: N34 31 42 W87 42 41. 112 Washington Ave. (35653). (205) 332-6104. Licensee: Ron Underwood (acq 10-24-90; $50,000; FTR 11-19-90). Net: SMN. Format: Southern Gospel. News staff one; news progmg 10 hrs wkly. Target aud: 21-54. Spec prog: Black 4 hrs wkly. ■ Ron Underwood, pres, gen sls mgr & prom mgr; Ron Underwood (owner), gen mgr; Al Gray, sls dir, progmg dir & mus dir.

WSHK(FM)—Oct 1, 1986: 97.7 mhz; 4.5 kw. Ant 321 ft. TL: N34 34 23 W87 40 19 (CP: 3.5 kw, ant 429 ft., N34 35 44 W87 40 47). Stereo. Hrs opn: 24. Box 9797, Muscle Shoals (35662). (205) 389-9700. FAX: (205) 389-9702. Licensee: James Michael Self (acq 7-90; $10,000; FTR 7-16-90). Format: CHR. ■ James Michael Self, pres & gen mgr; Jeff Vaughn, chief engr.

Scottsboro

WKEA-FM—Nov 3, 1965: 98.3 mhz; 6 kw. Ant 531 ft. TL: N34 34 50 W85 47 30. Box 966, Rt. 4 John T. Reid Pkwy. (35768). (205) 259-2341. FAX: (205) 574-2156. Licensee: KEA Radio Inc. Net: ABC/E. Format: Country. News staff one; news progmg 2 hrs wkly. Target aud: 25-54. Spec prog: Farm one hr, relg 4 hrs wkly. ■ Ronald H. Livengood, CEO, pres & gen mgr; Brian Blankenship, prom mgr; Jennifer Griffin, adv dir; Rick Rivera, progmg dir; Jeff Scott, mus dir; Rick Malone, news dir; Brian Keith, pub affrs dir; David Kennamer, chief engr. ■ Rates: $14; 11; 14; 11.

WWIC(AM)—June 13, 1950: 1050 khz; 1 kw-D, 101 w-N. TL: N34 40 23 W86 03 11. Box 759, 815 W. Willow St. (35768). (205) 259-1050. FAX: (205) 574-6397. Licensee: Kenneth Thomson, Deborah Thomson and Ron Dykes (acq 8-89). Net: MBS. Format: C&W. ■ Kenneth Thompson, pres & gen mgr; Greg Bell, opns mgr, gen sls mgr, prom mgr, progmg dir & mus dir; Ernie Stone, chief engr.

WZCT(AM)—June 11, 1952: 1330 khz; 5 kw-D, 38 w-N. TL: N34 42 07 W86 00 15. Hrs opn: 24. 2002 E. Willow St. (35768); Drawer A (35768). (205) 259-1313; (205) 574-1330. Licensee: Bonner and Carlile Enterprises (acq 2-28-90). Net: SMN, CNN. Format: Oldies. News progmg 14 hrs wkly. Target aud: 25-54; male/female boomers. ■ Donald H. Wray, gen mgr; Becky Lewis, opns mgr; Linda Wray, gen sls mgr & mktg dir; Donald Wray, progmg mgr.

Selma

WALX(FM)—Listing follows WMRK(AM).

WDXX(FM)—Listing follows WHBB(AM).

WHBB(AM)—Nov 11, 1935: 1490 khz; 1 kw-U. TL: N32 26 02 W87 00 40. Hrs opn: 24. Box 1055 (36702); 505 Lauderdale St. (36701). (205) 875-3350. FAX: (205) 875-4254. Licensee: Broadsouth Communications Inc. Group owner: GMX Corp. (acq 7-24-92; $400,000; with co-located FM; FTR 8-17-92). Net: ABC/I; Ala Net. Rep: Rgnl Reps. Format: Classic rock, oldies. News staff one; news progmg 13 hrs wkly. Target aud: 25-54. Spec prog: Black 18 hrs, farm 10 hrs wkly. ■ Glenn Hutton, gen mgr & gen sls mgr; Steven McLamb, news dir; Jeff Tharp, chief engr. ■ Rates: $18; 12; 15; 10.

WDXX(FM)—Co-owned with WHBB(AM). September 1965: 100.1 mhz; 50 kw. Ant 288 ft. TL: N32 26 02 W87 00 40. Stereo. Hrs opn: 24. Prog sep from AM. Format: Country. News staff 2; news progmg 5 hrs wkly. ■ Carolyn Wilbourne, prom mgr; George Henry, progmg dir & mus dir. ■ Rates: $25; 15; 20; 12.

WMRK(AM)—Dec 19, 1946: 1340 khz; 1 kw-U. TL: N32 25 31 W86 59 47. Persimmon Tree Rd. (36701). (205) 875-9360. FAX: (205) 875-1340. Licensee: Alexander Broadcasting Co. Inc. Net: CNN. Format: Easy lstng, light AC. News staff one. Target aud: 25-49. ■ Scott Alexander, pres, gen mgr & chief engr; Betty Alexander, mus dir.

WALX(FM)—Co-owned with WMRK(AM). Dec 12, 1973: 100.9 mhz; 50 kw. Ant 492 ft. TL: N32 21 40 W86 52 28. Stereo. Prog sep from AM. Format: CHR, adult contemp. Target aud: 18-40. ■ Scott Alexander, mus dir.

WTQX(AM)—May 19, 1956: 1570 khz; 5 kw-D, 43 w-N. TL: N32 26 03 W87 02 43. One Valley Creek Circle (36701). (205) 872-1570; (205) 872-7111. Licensee: Bob Carl Bailey (acq 3-14-79). Format: Black, div. News staff one; news progmg 50 hrs wkly. Target aud: 21-65. Spec prog: Gospel. ■ Bob Carl Bailey, pres & gen mgr; Allen Taylor, stn mgr, gen sls mgr, mktg progmg dir & chief engr; Francine Jiles, sls dir, mus dir, news dir & pub affrs dir. ■ Rates: $12; 12; 12; 12.

WVCA(FM)—Not on air, target date Summer 1993: 105.9 mhz; 50 kw. Ant 485 ft. TL: N32 17 14 W86 14 38. Suite 400, 645 Church St., Norfolk, VA (23510-2809). (804) 624-6500. Licensee: FM 103 Corp. (acq 3-8-91; FTR 4-1-91).

Sheffield

WBTG(AM)—Nov 6, 1963: 1290 khz; 1 kw-D, 79 w-N. TL: N34 46 27 W87 40 14. Box 518, 1605 Gospel Rd. (35660). (205) 383-1290; (205) 383-1063. FAX: (205) 381-6801. Licensee: Slatton & Associates (acq 12-17-87). Net: CBN. Format: Contemp Christian. News staff one; news progmg 18 hrs wkly. Target aud: 18-35; conservative, mainstream family audience. ■ Paul Slatton, pres & gen mgr; Gerald Broadrick, gen sls mgr; Michael Simon, prom mgr; Chad Payne, progmg dir; Jacky Ward, mus dir; Lincoln Hughes, news dir.

WBTG-FM—July 2, 1969: 106.3 mhz; 6 kw. Ant 682 ft. TL: N34 40 24 W87 42 56 (CP: 22.1 kw, ant 738 ft., TL: N34 59 49 W87 48 13). Stereo. Hrs opn: 5 AM-midnight. Prog sep from AM. (205) 381-6800. (acq 1-17-78). Net: USA. Format: Relg, gospel. News staff one; news progmg 12 hrs wkly. Spec prog: Farm one hr wkly. ■ Brenda Holman, news dir; Chad Payne, chief engr. ■ Rates: $22; 22; 22; 22.

Stevenson

WVSV(FM)—June 13, 1977: 101.7 mhz; 940 w. Ant 490 ft. TL: N34 49 41 W85 45 54 (CP: 531 w., ant 603 ft.). Stereo. Rte. 3, Box 66A (35772). (205) 437-7442. FAX: (205) 437-2249. Licensee: Lynn Ltd. (acq 7-83; $32,025; FTR 10-3-83). Format: Mod country. ■ George Guess, pres & gen mgr.

Sulligent

WVSA(AM)—See Vernon.

Sumiton

WRSM(AM)—June 27, 1978: 1540 khz; 1 kw-D. TL: N33 45 50 W87 03 47. Box 100, Hull Rd. (35148). (205) 648-3241. Licensee: Sumiton Broadcasting Co. Inc. Format: C&W. Spec prog: Farm one hr wkly. ■ T. Herb Steadman, gen mgr & gen sls mgr; Sara Steadman, progmg dir & mus dir.

Sylacauga

WAWV(FM)—Listing follows WYEA(AM).

WFEB(AM)—March 1945: 1340 khz; 1 kw-U. TL: N33 10 16 W86 13 57. Hrs opn: 19. Box 358, 1209 Millerville Hwy. (35150). (205) 245-3050; (205) 245-3281. Licensee: Alabama Broadcasting Inc. Net: MBS. Rep: Carpenter; Rgnl Reps. Wash atty: Gardner, Carton & Douglas. Format: Oldies. News staff 3; news progmg 17 hrs wkly. Target aud: 25-54. Spec prog: Gospel 6 hrs wkly. ■ Nerine C. Carr, pres; Bruce C. Carr, gen mgr; Lloyd Ross, gen sls mgr; Michael Cannon, progmg dir, mus dir & news dir; Hugh O'Neal, chief engr. ■ Rates: $11; 9; 11; 9.

WYEA(AM)—May 16, 1948: 1290 khz; 1 kw-D, 50 w-N. TL: N33 11 15 W86 14 06. Box 629, One Motes Rd. (35150). (205) 249-4263; (205) 249-4500. Licensee: W.O. Powers (acq 7-30-93; with co-located FM; FTR 8-23-93). Net: Ala. Net. Format: Christian. Target aud: General. ■ John Bodiford, gen mgr; John Vogel, stn mgr & progmg dir; Jimmy Abrams, gen sls mgr; Steve Lowery, mus dir. ■ Rates: $5.25; 5.25; 5.25; 4.25.

WAWV(FM)—Co-owned with WYEA(AM). Dec 20, 1959: 98.3 mhz; 2.7 kw. Ant 502 ft. TL: N33 12 23 W86 13 54. Stereo. (205) 245-4354. Format: Top-30 and oldies from 60s through 80s. News staff one. ■ John Bodiford, gen mgr, prom mgr & progmg dir; Suzanne Moore, opns mgr; Dennis Tyler, mus dir; Chris Weber Jr., news dir. ■ Rates: $8.50; 8.50; 8.50; 6.

Talladega

WEYY-FM—Nov 10, 1972: 92.7 mhz; 250 w. Ant 870 ft. TL: N33 24 42 W86 12 20 (CP: 400 w.). Stereo. Drawer 329 (35160); 34915 Alabama Hwy. 21 (35160). (205) 362-8890. FAX: (205) 362-3440. Licensee: Jacobs Broadcast Group Inc. (acq 9-16-92; $570,000; FTR 10-19-92). Format: Modern country. ■ James H. Jacobs, pres & gen mgr; Hugh O'Neal, chief engr.

WNUZ(AM)—1945: 1230 khz; 1 kw-U. TL: N33 25 16 W86 07 13. Hrs opn: 5 AM- midnight. 101 Fort Lashley Ave. (35160). (205) 362-1230; (205) 362-1231. Licensee: Radio Alabama Inc. (acq 6-1-59). Format: Top-40/CHR. ■ Charles Osbom, pres, gen mgr, gen sls mgr, progmg dir & news dir; Charles Whatley, chief engr.

Alabama

WSSY-FM—April 4, 1990: 97.5 mhz; 910 w. Ant 574 ft. TL: N33 25 49 W86 04 52. Stereo. Hrs opn: 24. Drawer 1270 (35160). (205) 761-9779. FAX: (205) 761-9700. Licensee: Stroh Communications Corp. Format: Adult contemp, classic hits. News staff one; news progmg 40 hrs wkly. Target aud: 25-54. ■ Allan G. Stroh, pres; Rick Robinson, gen mgr; Teresa Henry, sls dir; Richard Jacks, progmg dir; John Yuhas, mus dir; Dave Richards, news dir; Tom Jones, chief engr.

Tallassee

WACQ(AM)—June 30, 1979: 1130 khz; 1 kw-D. TL: N32 33 22 W85 52 17. Rt. 4, Box 12 (36078). (205) 283-6888. FAX: (205) 283-2152. Licensee: Tiger Broadcasting Co. Inc. (acq 3-9-92; $50,000 with co-located FM; FTR 3-30-92). Net: SMN. Format: Adult contemp. Spec prog: Farm one hr wkly. ■ Terry Daughtry, pres; Fred Randall Hughey, gen mgr & gen sls mgr; Windel Jay, progmg dir; Terry Harper, chief engr.

WACQ-FM—(Tuskegee). Oct 29, 1992: 99.9 mhz; 2.95 kw. Ant 466 ft. TL: N32 26 24 W85 48 15.

WTLS(AM)—June 1, 1954: 1300 khz; 1 kw-D. TL: N32 33 27 W85 55 03. Stereo. 1702 Gilmer Ave. (36078). (205) 283-6565. FAX: (205) 283-6565. Licensee: Ned Nile Butler Sr. Net: Ala. Net. Format: Oldies, C&W. Spec prog: Farm 6 hrs wkly. ■ Ned Butler, pres, news dir & chief engr; Betty Butler, gen mgr, gen sls mgr & progmg dir.

Thomasville

WJDB(AM)—July 16, 1956: 630 khz; 1 kw-D. TL: N31 52 58 W87 44 42. Box 219, 2211 Hwy. 43 S. (36784). (205) 636-4438. FAX: (205) 636-4439. Licensee: Griffin Broadcasting Corp. (acq 1-4-91; $375,000 with co-located FM; FTR 1-28-91). Net: CBS; Ark. Radio Net. Format: Country. News staff one; news progmg 10 hrs wkly. Target aud: General. Spec prog: Rush Limbaugh 15 hrs, Black 8 hrs wkly. ■ Ivey Griffin, pres & dev dir; Deborah Griffin, sr vp, mktg dir, prom dir & pub affrs dir; Tom Orr, gen sls mgr; George Rivers, progmg dir & mus dir; Steve Christian, news dir; Alan Kilgore, chief engr. ■ Rates: $8.24; 7.06; 8.24; 7.06.

WJDB-FM—Nov 2, 1972: 95.5 mhz; 3 kw. Ant 300 ft. TL: N31 52 58 W87 44 42 (CP: 9.6 kw, ant 525 ft.). Stereo. Dups AM 100%. News staff one; news progmg 11 hrs wkly. Target aud: General.

Trinity

WAZK(FM)—Oct 4, 1992: 92.5 mhz; 3.1 kw. Ant 423 ft. TL: N34 42 36 W87 04 54. Stereo. Hrs opn: 24. Rt. 10, Box 64A, Decatur (35603). (205) 544-7635. Licensee: Radio 92 Inc. (acq 3-20-92). Format: Classic Rock. News progmg 6 hrs wkly. Target aud: 25-44.

Troy

WTBF(AM)—Feb 25, 1947: 970 khz; 5 kw-D, 500 w-N, DA-N. TL: N31 50 04 W85 56 00. Hrs opn: 6 AM-10 PM. Box 747, One College Dr. (36081-0747). (205) 566-0300. FAX: (205) 566-0810. Licensee: Troy Broadcasting Corp. Net: MBS. Format: Country. News progmg 20 hrs wkly. Target aud: 35 plus. Spec prog: Farm 17 hrs wkly. ■ Asa Dudley, gen mgr & news dir; Joe Gilchrist, opns mgr & chief engr; Jim Roling, gen sls mgr; Doc Kirby, progmg dir & mus dir. ■ Rates: $12; 8; 9; 8.

*****WTSU(FM)**—March 1, 1977: 89.9 mhz; 100 kw. Ant 560 ft. TL: N32 03 33 W86 01 22. Stereo. Hrs opn: 6 AM-midnight. Wallace Hall, Troy State University (36082). (205) 670-3100. FAX: (205) 670-3199. Licensee: Troy State University. Net: NPR, APR. Format: Class, btfl mus, news. News progmg 25 plus hrs wkly. Target aud: General. Spec prog: Jazz 5 hrs wkly. ■ John McVay, gen mgr, progmg mgr & mus dir; Steve Holmes, opns mgr & news dir; Pat Warner, pub affrs dir; John Brunson, chief engr.

WZHT(FM)—Feb 28, 1973: 105.7 mhz; 100 kw. Ant 1,847 ft. TL: N31 58 32 W86 09 46. Stereo. Box 4420, Montgomery (36103); 648 S. Perry St., Montgomery (36104). (205) 262-2323. FAX: (205) 263-3483. Licensee: Capital Communications. Group owner: New South Communications (acq 1-91). Net: ABC. Rep: McGavren Guild. Format: Urban. News staff one. ■ Ronald W. Eubanks, pres & gen mgr; Arnessa Maddox, gen sls mgr; Mildred Perryman, prom mgr; Monica May, progmg dir & mus dir; Tanya Scott, news dir; Barry Walters, chief engr.

Trussville

WWBR(FM)—Not on air, target date unknown: 105.9 mhz; 1 kw. Ant 561 ft. TL: N33 36 41 W86 39 19. 413 Chickasaw Ln. (35173). Licensee: Stanton Broadcasting Corp.

Tuscaloosa

WACT(AM)—September 1958: 1420 khz; 5 kw-D, 108 w-N. TL: N33 10 30 W87 33 18. Box 020126 (35402-0126); 3900 11th Avenue (35401). (205) 349-3200; (205) 752-9228. FAX: (205) 752-9269. Licensee: Taylor Broadcasting (group owner; acq 10-25-89; $2,250,000 with co-located FM; FTR 11-13-89). Net: AP. Rep: Roslin. Format: Religious (southern gospel). Target aud: 35 plus. ■ Thomas J. Lich, pres & gen mgr; Lynn C. Woods, stn mgr; Johnny Price, gen sls mgr; Laurie Ray, prom mgr; Eric Adams, progmg dir; Shane Collins, mus dir; Bryan Keith, pub affrs dir; Bruce Albright, chief engr.

WACT-FM—June 1, 1966: 105.5 mhz; 1.5 kw. Ant 400 ft. TL: N33 10 30 W87 33 18 (CP: 6 kw). Stereo. Dups AM 20%. Format: Country. Target aud: 25 plus.

WFFX(FM)—Listing follows WTNW(AM).

WSPZ(AM)—Oct 10, 1936: 1150 khz; 5 kw-D, 1 kw-N, DA-N. TL: N33 15 02 W87 36 35. Drawer 4 (35402). (205) 339-3700. FAX: (205) 339-3704. Licensee: GMC Broadcasting Inc. (acq 12-1-76). Format: CHR. News staff one. ■ W. A. Grant Jr., pres; Walter Grant, gen mgr; Rick Jones, vp opns; Jan Jefferies, progmg dir; Scott Sands, mus dir; Susan Sanderson, news dir; David Baughn, chief engr.

WTNW(AM)—Dec 23, 1946: 1230 khz; 1 kw-U. TL: N33 12 05 W87 32 00. Box 2000 (35403). (205) 758-5523. FAX: (205) 752-9696. Licensee: Alabama Universal Corp. (acq 11-20-92; $1 million with co-located FM; FTR 12-14-92). Rep: Eastman. Format: Easy lstng. News staff one; news progmg 5 hrs wkly. Target aud: 40 plus; upscale, affluent. Spec prog: Relg one hr wkly. ■ Warren Kirk, gen mgr; Ron Michaels, opns mgr & progmg dir; Keith LaCaste, gen sls mgr; Mike Neighbors, news dir; Bill Moats, chief engr.

WFFX(FM)—Co-owned with WTNW(AM). 1952: 95.7 mhz; 100 kw. Ant 410 ft. TL: N33 12 05 W87 32 00 (CP: Ant 981 ft., TL: N33 03 15 W87 32 57). Stereo. Prog sep from AM. Net: ABC, CNN. Wash atty: Dick Bodorff. Format: Adult contemp.

WTSK(AM)—February 1958: 790 khz; 5 kw-D, 36 w-N. TL: N33 11 17 W87 35 23. 142 Skyland Blvd. (35405). (205) 345-1415. FAX: (205) 349-1715. Licensee: Radio South Inc. (group owner; acq 7-77). Rep: Banner. Format: Rhythm & blues. ■ Houston L. Pearce, pres; Voncile Pearce, gen mgr & gen sls mgr; Kimberly Essex, news dir; Sonny Posey, chief engr.

WTUG(FM)—Co-owned with WTSK(AM). March 1979: 92.9 mhz; 6 kw. Ant 328 ft. TL: N33 05 40 W87 29 58. Stereo. Prog sep from AM. Net: American Urban. Format: Urban contemp. ■ Al Brown, progmg dir & mus dir.

*****WUAL-FM**—Jan 4, 1982: 91.5 mhz; 100 kw. Ant 523 ft. TL: N33 05 40 W87 24 47. Stereo. Hrs opn: 24. Box 870370, 7 Bryce Lawn (35487). (205) 348-6644. FAX: (205) 348-6648. Licensee: Board of Trustees of the U. of Alabama. Net: APR, NPR. Wash atty: Arter & Hadden. Format: Class, jazz, news/talk. News staff 2; news progmg 5 hrs wkly. Spec prog: Bluegrass, blues, folk 5 hrs, new age 20 hrs wkly. ■ Anthony Dean, gen mgr; Daryl Fletcher, opns mgr; Kathy Henslee, dev mgr; Gina Carter, prom mgr & pub affrs dir; Roger Duvall, progmg dir; Jack Massey, mus dir; Glenda Webb, news dir; David Baughn, chief engr.

*****WVUA-FM**—Sept 7, 1972: 90.7 mhz; 160 w. Ant 142 ft. TL: N33 12 33 W87 32 57. Stereo. Box 870152 (35487-0152). (205) 348-6461. FAX: (205) 348-2754. Licensee: Board of Trustees, U. of Alabama. Format: Alternative News progmg 5 hrs wkly. Target aud: 18-25; high school & college students. Spec prog: Christian 3 hrs, hardcore 3 hrs, blues 3 hrs, heavy metal 4 hrs, reggae 3 hrs wkly. ■ Loy Singleton, gen mgr; Frank Petit, chief engr.

WWPG(AM)—Dec 10, 1951: 1280 khz; 5 kw-D, 500 w-N, DA-N. TL: N33 13 07 W87 34 05. Box 2787 (35403); 229 3rd St., Northport (35476). (205) 758-3311; (205) 758-9678. FAX: (205) 349-4824. Licensee: Lawson of Tuscaloosa Inc. (acq 3-17-93; $160,000; FTR 4-5-93). Net: NBC, NBC Talknet, Westwood One. Wash atty: Taylor, Smith & Parker. Format: Rhythm & blues, gospel. News staff one; news progmg 6 hrs wkly. Target aud: 24-54; mature business audience. Spec prog: Jazz 2 hrs wkly. ■ Ellis J. Parker, pres & gen mgr; B.C. Frison, stn mgr.

Tuscumbia

WVNA(AM)—Apr 5, 1955: 1590 khz; 5 kw-D, 1 kw-N, DA-N. TL: N34 45 24 W87 36 35. Box 447, 509 N. Main St. (35674); Box 748, Florence (35630). (205) 383-3500. FAX: (205) 383-2727. Licensee: Elton H. Darby (acq 1956). Net: ABC TalkRadio, CBS, NBC Talknet, AP, MBS. Rep: Katz. Format: News/talk, sports. News staff 3; news progmg 60 hrs wkly. Target aud: 25-64. Spec prog: Atlanta Braves Network, local talk shows & sport shows. ■ M. D. Bedford, pres & gen mgr; Jim Jackson, stn mgr, prom dir & progmg dir; Jan Moore, opns mgr; Greg Thronton, gen sls mgr; Bill Erwin, news dir; Mary Ann Tidwell, pub affrs dir; Carl Samperi, chief engr.

WVNA-FM—May 2, 1962: 100.3 mhz; 100 kw. Ant 245 ft. TL: N34 45 24 W87 41 10 (CP: TL: N34 40 24 W87 42 56). Stereo. Hrs opn: 24. Prog sep from AM. Net: NBC. Format: CHR, adult contemp, rock hybrid. News staff 2; news progmg 60 hrs wkly. Target aud: 18-34. ■ John Lyons, progmg dir; Jim Jackson, mus dir.

WZZA(AM)—July 4, 1972: 1410 khz; 500 w-D, 51 w-N. TL: N34 42 29 W87 41 35. 1570 Woodmont Dr. (35674). (205) 381-1862. Licensee: Muscle Shoals Broadcasting (acq 1-9-78). Rep: Midsouth. Format: Black, relg, urban contemp. News progmg 15 hrs wkly. Target aud: General; Black; all age groups. ■ Bob Carl Bailey, pres, gen mgr, gen sls mgr, prom mgr & adv mgr; Odessa Bailey, opns mgr, mus dir & pub affrs dir; Tori C. Bailey, asst mus dir; Paul Kelly, chief engr. ■ Rates: $12.50; 12.50; 12.50; 6.25.

Tuskegee

WACQ-FM—Licensed to Tuskegee. See Tallassee.

WBIL(AM)—July 1, 1952: 580 khz; 500 w-D, 139 w-N. TL: N32 22 36 W85 39 28. Box 666 (36083). (205) 727-2100. FAX: (205) 727-2969. Licensee: All Channel TV Service Inc. (acq 8-75). Format: Urban contemp. News staff one. ■ George H. Clay, pres; Jesse Caldwell, gen sls mgr; Costee McNair, progmg dir; Denise Hicks, news dir; Terry Harper, chief engr.

WBIL-FM—July 12, 1975: 95.9 mhz; 3 kw. Ant 320 ft. TL: N32 22 36 W85 39 28 (CP: 4.32 kw, ant 377 ft.). Stereo. Dups AM 100%.

Uniontown

WVFG(FM)—Not on air, target date unknown: 107.5 mhz; 1.45 kw. Ant 469 ft. TL: N32 22 05 W87 26 29. Box 116, Enterprise (36331). Licensee: James Wilson III (acq 12-30-92; $5,000; FTR 1-25-93).

Valley

WUAF(FM)—Not on air, target date unknown: 98.1 mhz; 3 kw. Ant 328 ft. TL: N32 55 12 W85 13 04. 608 S. 4th St., Lanett (36863). Licensee: Pearce Broadcasting Partnership.

Valley Head

WQRX(AM)—Feb 10, 1986: 870 khz; 10 kw-D. TL: N34 33 20 W85 37 12. Stereo. Hrs opn: Sunrise-sunset. Box 309, 870 Jeff Cook Dr. (35989). (205) 635-6284. FAX: (205) 635-6285. Licensee: Cook Communications Inc. Net: Unistar. Format: Adult contemp. Spec prog: Alabama "Crimson Tide" football & basketball games. ■ Jeff Cook, pres; Joyce Hamilton, gen mgr & gen sls mgr; Johnny Allen, vp adv; Karen Cook, progmg dir; Charles Jolley, news dir.

Vernon

WVSA(AM)—July 4, 1966: 1380 khz; 5 kw-D, 39 w-N. TL: N33 47 45 W88 07 03. Box 630 (35592). (205) 695-9191. Licensee: Lamar County Broadcasting Co. Inc. Format: C&W, gospel. ■ Joel Camp, pres, gen mgr & mus dir; Karan Riffle, prom mgr; Tommy Knight, chief engr.

WJEC(FM)—Co-owned with WVSA(AM). April 1, 1991: 106.5 mhz; 6 kw. Ant 328 ft. TL: N33 51 15 W88 01 55. Format: Adult contemp. ■ Joel Camp, gen mgr.

Warrior

WLBI(FM)—Not on air, target date unknown: 98.7 mhz; 6 kw. Ant 328 ft. TL: N33 49 09 W86 51 23. 651 Arkadelphia Rd. (35180). (205) 590-0805. FAX: (205) 590-0809. Licensee: Teresa B. Lowry. ■ Theresa Lowry, gen mgr; Mike Tracy, gen sls mgr.

Wetumpka

WAPZ(AM)—Oct 2, 1954: 1250 khz; 5 kw-D, 80 w-N. TL: N32 29 06 W86 12 25. Rt. 6, Box 43 (36092). (205) 567-2251. Licensee: J&W Promotions Inc. (acq 9-1-84; $235,000; FTR 7-23-84). Format: Relg. ■ Johnny Roland, pres; Clarence E. Stewart Jr., gen mgr; Walter Ellis, progmg dir & mus dir.

Winfield

WKXM(AM)—Aug 23, 1965: 1300 khz; 5 kw-D, 30 w-N. TL: N33 55 52 W87 48 36. Box 608, Hwy. 78 (35594). (205) 487-3261. FAX: (205) 487-4693; (205) 487-4653. Licensee: Harper-Mainord Broadcasting (acq 12-30-91; $365,000 with co-located FM; FTR 1-27-92). Format: Country. ■ Maxine Harper, pres; Jack Mainord, vp & gen mgr.

WKXM-FM—1991: 105.9 mhz; 2.5 kw. Ant 410 ft. TL: N34 01 53 W87 48 06.

York

WYLS(AM)—November 1970: 670 khz; 4.8 kw-D. TL: N32 31 24 W88 15 28. 11474 U.S. Hwy. 11 (36925). (205) 392-5234. FAX: (205) 392-5234. Licensee: William B. Grant. Net: NBC. Format: MOR & memories. News staff one; news progmg 15 hrs wkly. Target aud: Mature adults. ■ William B. Grant, pres, gen mgr & chief engr; Tim Craddock, progmg dir & news dir.

WSLY(FM)—Co-owned with WYLS(AM). September 1976: 104.9 mhz; 50 kw. Ant 492 ft. TL: N32 16 54 W88 15 28 Stereo. Prog sep from AM. Format: Urban contemp. News staff one; news progmg 10 hrs wkly. Target aud: 18-54. ■ Tim Craddock, progmg dir.

Alaska

Anchorage

KABN(AM)—(Long Island). Oct 20, 1993: 830 khz; 10 kw-U. TL: N61 34 05 W149 43 21 (CP: 840 khz; 10 kw-U). Stereo. Hrs opn: 24. ARB Inc., Suite 625, 1255 Post St., San Francisco, CA (94109); 3/4 mile S.E. Parks Hwy. & Big Lake Rd. at M.P. 51.5, Big Lake (99652). (907) 892-8300; (415) 441-3377. Licensee: Chester Coleman (acq 11-15-91; $38,510). Net: ABC. Wash atty: David Tillotson. Format: Adult contemp, div, news/talk. News staff 3; news progmg 20 hrs wkly. Target aud: 18-49; "Mat-Su Valley" adults, mass appeal. Spec prog: KABN Trap Line, local sports, Iditarod Trail-Dogsled Race. ■ Chester Coleman, pres & gen mgr; Marlo Holmes, chief opns; Seymour Schafer, progmg dir; Anita Martini, mus dir; Merry Melodies, asst mus dir; Remington Noble, news dir; Anita Hill, pub affrs dir; "Julio" Titsup, chief engr. ■ Rates: $22; 19; 22; 16.

KXDZ(FM)—Co-owned with KABN(AM). Sept 1, 1987: 103.1 mhz; 6 kw. Ant 328 ft. TL: N61 09 56 W149 49 34. Stereo. Hrs opn: 24. (Acq 5-4-93; $85,000; FTR 5-24-93). Format: Adult contemp. Target aud: 18-49. KYES(TV) affil. ■ Rates: $25; 20; 25; 20.

***KANH(FM)**—Not on air, target date unknown: 90.3 mhz; 100 kw. Ant 195 ft. Box 93330, Suite 507, 2525 C St. (99509). Licensee: Koahnic Broadcast Corp.

KASH-FM—Listing follows KKSD(AM).

***KATB(FM)**—June 1985: 89.3 mhz; 4.9 kw. Ant 643 ft. TL: N61 05 53 W149 41 04 (CP: ant 344 ft., TL: N61 07 32 W149 42 46). Stereo. Hrs opn: 24. Box 210389 (99521); 6401 E. Northern Lights Blvd. (99504). (907) 333-5282. FAX: (907) 333-9851. Licensee: Christian Broadcasting Inc. Net: Moody. Wash atty: Russell C. Powell. Format: Relg. Target aud: 25-49; women. ■ Jerry L. Prevo, pres; Michael D. Murray, exec vp & gen mgr; Allan Woosley, progmg dir. ■ Rates: $19; 19; 19; 19.

KBFX(FM)—Oct 1, 1978: 100.5 mhz; 25 kw. Ant 178 ft. TL: N61 11 52 W149 52 31. Stereo. Licensee: Community Pacific Broadcasting Company LP (acq 1993; $1.3 million; FTR 9-13-93). Format: Classic rock. ■ David Benjamin, pres; John Ruby, gen mgr; Lisa Mounds, prom mgr; Devon Mitchell, progmg mgr. ■ Rates: $56; 56; 56; 28.

KBRJ(FM)—Listing follows KHAR(AM).

KBYR(AM)—1948: 700 khz; 10 kw-U. TL: N61 12 25 W149 55 20. Hrs opn: 24. Suite 12, 501 W. International Airport Rd. (99518); 1007 W. 32nd Ave. (99503). (907) 562-4200; (907) 562-3456. FAX: (907) 561-4688; (907) 562-0953. Licensee: Northern TV Inc. (group owner; acq 8-16-65). Net: CBS, BRN, Mutual. Rep: Eastman; Art Moore. Format: Talk, sports, news. News progmg 30 hrs wkly. Target aud: 25-54. ■ A. G. Hiebert, CEO; Julie Guy, pres; Craig Bennett, gen mgr; Bob Dehn, opns dir, progmg dir & mus dir; Jan Andrews, gen sls mgr; Steve MacDonald, news dir; Jennifer Summers, pub affrs dir; Duane Millsap, chief engr. ■ Rates: $18; 15; 18; 9.

KNIK-FM—Co-owned with KBYR(AM). Sept 15, 1960: 105.3 mhz; 25 kw. Ant 265 ft. TL: N61 11 33 W149 54 01 (CP: 44.5 kw). Stereo. Hrs opn: 24. Prog sep from AM. (907) 561-4200; (907) 561-5645. Net: CBS. Format: Jazz, new age. News progmg 9 hrs wkly. Target aud: 25 plus; educated, affluent, professional suburbanites. KTVA-TV affil. ■ Rates: $25; 22; 25; 12.

KEAG(FM)—1987: 97.3 mhz; 100 kw. Ant 593 ft. TL: N61 25 22 W149 52 20. Suite 800, 3700 Woodland Dr. (99517). (907) 243-3141. FAX: (907) 279-9797; (907) 248-3758. Licensee: Ingstad Alaska Broadcasting Inc. Group owner: Tom Ingstad Broadcasting Group (acq 11-30-93; $285,000; FTR 12-20-93). Format: Classic hits. ■ Jim Markum, pres; Don Nordin, gen mgr & gen sls mgr; Brian Roberts, progmg dir; Paula Price, mus dir; Rosie Mills, news dir; Marlow Holmes, chief engr.

AMERICAN RADIO BROKERS, INC.
MOST TRUSTED NAME IN MEDIA BROKERAGE
CHESTER P. COLEMAN / PRESIDENT
FOR THE BEST STATIONS FOR SALE FROM THIS AREA
CALL — 415 / 441-3377
1255 POST STREET / SUITE 625 / SAN FRANCISCO, CA 94109

KENI(AM)—May 2, 1948: 550 khz; 5 kw-U. TL: N61 12 25 W149 55 20. 1777 Forest Park Dr. (99517). (907) 272-7461. FAX: (907) 279-2112. Licensee: TCT Communications Inc. (acq 5-17-89). Net: ABC/I, ABC TalkRadio, MBS, NBC Talknet. Rep: D & R. Wash atty: Haley, Bader & Potts. Format: Talk. News staff 2; news progmg 3 hrs wkly. Target aud: 25-54. ■ Tom Tierney, pres & gen mgr; Dan Larson, gen sls mgr; Jerry Ritter, news dir; Van Craft, chief engr. ■ Rates: $35; 35; 28; 17.

KFQD(AM)—1924: 750 khz; 50 kw-U. TL: N61 08 13 W149 50 06. Stereo. 9200 Lake Otis Parkway (99507). (907) 344-9622. Licensee: Pioneer Broadcasting Co. Inc. (acq 8-1-62). Net: ABC/E. Rep: McGavren Guild. Format: Adult contemp. News staff 2; news progmg 15 hrs wkly. Target aud: 25-54; higher income, mostly female. ■ Elizabeth Clapp, CEO; Matthew N. Clapp Jr., pres; Louis Wright, CFO; Dennis Bookey, gen mgr; Scott Smith, gen sls mgr; Kathy Egan, prom mgr; Michael Rogers, progmg dir; Mark Guy, news dir; Jay White, chief engr.

KWHL(FM)—Co-owned with KFQD(AM). Sept 18, 1982: 106.5 mhz; 100 kw. Ant -89 ft. TL: N61 08 13 W149 50 06. Stereo. Prog sep from AM. Format: Rock (AOR). News staff one; news progmg 6 hrs wkly. Target aud: 18-44; medium income adults, mostly men. ■ Phill Remick, progmg dir; Loren Dixon, mus dir.

KGOT(FM)—Listing follows KYAK(AM).

KHAR(AM)—Jan 7, 1961: 590 khz; 5 kw-U. TL: N61 07 12 W149 53 43. Stereo. 11259 Tower Rd. (99515). (907) 522-1515. FAX: (907) 349-3299. Licensee: Alaska Broadcast Communications Inc. (acq 2-23-93; $800,000 with co-located FM; FTR 3-15-93). Net: AP. Rep: Roslin, Tacher. Wash atty: Haley, Bader & Potts. Format: MOR, easy listening. News progmg 3 hrs wkly. Target aud: 35 plus; white collar, professional, upper-income demo. ■ Roy Pastal, pres; Steve Rhyner, gen mgr; Lisa Hester, gen sls mgr; Cary Carringan, progmg dir; Terry Straight, mus dir; Walter Sorton, chief engr.

KBRJ(FM)—Co-owned with KHAR(AM). November 1966: 104.1 mhz; 55 kw. Ant 61 ft. TL: N61 07 12 W149 53 43. Stereo. Prog sep from AM. Format: Hot new country. Target aud: 25-49; active adult country listeners involved in career & family.

KKSD(AM)—May 10, 1975: 1080 khz; 10 kw-U. TL: N61 07 12 W149 53 43. Suite 208, 1300 E. 68th St. (99518). (907) 522-1515. FAX: (907) 349-6801. Licensee: Community Pacific Broadcasting Co. L.P. (group owner; acq 11-15-82; $1,106,750; FTR 11-1-82). Net: ABC/E. Rep: Major Mkt. Format: News. ■ David J. Benjamin, pres; Andrew Lohman, gen mgr; Steve Hood, gen sls mgr; Steve Chapman, progmg dir; Eddie Maxwell, mus dir; Mike Ford, news dir; Terry Reynolds, chief engr. ■ Rates: $48; 42; 48; 28.

KASH-FM—Co-owned with KKSD(AM). Dec 1, 1985: 107.5 mhz; 100 kw. Ant 1,014 ft. TL: N61 09 53 W149 41 05. Stereo. Prog sep from AM. Format: Country. Target aud: 25-54. ■ Rates: $38; 34; 36; 20.

KLEF(FM)—Sept 16, 1988: 98.1 mhz; 25 kw. Ant -85 ft. TL: N61 11 17 W149 52 57. Hrs opn: 19. Suite 290, 3601 C St. (99503). (907) 561-5556. Licensee: Chinook Concert Broadcasters Inc. (acq 6-87; FTR 6-8-87). Rep: CMBS; Tacher. Format: Class. Target aud: 25-64; highly educated, affluent adults. ■ Rick Goodfellow, chmn, vp & sls dir; Timothy Tullis, opns mgr; Dr. Jan Ingram, progmg mgr; Derek Edmondson, chief engr. ■ Rates: $28; 28; 28; 20.

KNIK-FM—Listing follows KBYR(AM).

KPXR(FM)—Feb 1, 1973: 102.1 mhz; 25 kw. Ant 174 ft. TL: N61 20 10 W149 30 46 (CP: 24.54 kw, ant -157 ft.). Stereo. 3700 Woodland Dr., No. 800 (99517). (907) 243-3141. FAX: (907) 243-3291. Licensee: Ingstad Alaska Bcstng Inc. Group owner: Tom Ingstad Broadcasting Group (acq 9-22-86; $650,000; FTR 7-28-86). Format: CHR. ■ Tom Ingstad, pres; Don Nordin, gen mgr; Jay Perry, gen sls mgr; Jason Palmer, progmg dir; Marlo Homes, chief engr.

***KRUA(FM)**—Feb 14, 1992: 88.1 mhz; 155 w. Ant 292 ft. TL: N61 07 32 W149 42 46. Hrs opn: 7 AM-1 AM. 3211 Providence Dr. (99508). (907) 786-1098. Licensee: Univ. of Alaska-Anchorage. Wash atty: Wilkinson, Barker, Knauer & Quinn. Format: Progsv. News staff 3. Target aud: General. ■ Suzi Pearson, stn mgr; Ken Bodensteiner, prom mgr; John Fisher, mus dir; Geoff Camps, asst mus dir; Ellen Lockyer, news dir; Ibrahim Khan, pub affrs dir; Ron Zastrow, engrg dir.

***KSKA(FM)**—Aug 15, 1978: 91.1 mhz; 36 kw. Ant 126 ft. TL: N61 11 25 W149 48 16 (CP: Ant 189 ft.). Stereo. Hrs opn: 24. 4101 Univ. Dr. (99508). (907) 561-1161. FAX: (907) 561-8035. Licensee: Aurora Community Broadcasting Inc. Net: NPR, AP. Format: In-depth news, jazz, classical. News staff 2. Target aud: Adults. Spec prog: Sp 3 hrs wkly. ■ Diane Heard, gen mgr; Shonti Elder, opns mgr; Nancy K. Baer, dev dir; Bede Trantina, progmg dir; Robert Howk, news dir; James Haack, chief engr.

KWHL(FM)—Listing follows KFQD(AM).

KXDZ(FM)—Listing follows KABN(AM).

KYAK(AM)—July 15, 1967: 650 khz; 50 kw-U. TL: N61 09 58 W149 49 34. Hrs opn: 24. Suite 200, 500 L St. (99507). (907) 272-5945. Licensee: Comco Broadcasting Inc. (group owner; acq 5-21-93; grpsl; FTR 6-14-93). Net: MBS. Rep: Christal. Format: Modern country. News staff one; news progmg 5 hrs wkly. Target aud: 25-64. ■ Garry Donovan, gen mgr; Prudy Bowman, gen sls mgr; Sezy Grew, prom dir; Darryl Webster, progmg dir & mus dir; Roxy Lenix, news dir; Erick Coleman, chief engr. ■ Rates: $19; 17; 18; 15.

KGOT(FM)—Co-owned with KYAK(AM). Sept 15, 1975: 101.3 mhz; 26 kw. Ant -66 ft. TL: N61 09 58 W149 49 34. Stereo. Hrs opn: 24. Prog sep from AM. (907) 563-3555. Net: MBS. Format: Contemp hit. News progmg 2 hrs wkly. Target aud: 12-17, 18-49; teens, adults. ■ Sezy Grew, progmg dir; Darryl Webster, mus dir. ■ Rates: $38; 35; 36; 30.

KYMG(FM)—Jan 1, 1989: 98.9 mhz; 100 kw. Ant 499 ft. TL: N61 25 22 W149 52 20. Stereo. Hrs opn: 24. Suite 200, 500 L St. (99501). (907) 272-5945. FAX: (907) 272-5055. Licensee: Comco Broadcasting Inc. Net: AP. Rep: Banner. Wash atty: Becker & Finerfrock. Format: Adult contemp. News staff one; news progmg 4 hrs wkly. Target aud: 25-49; mostly women. Spec prog: Relg one hr wkly. ■ Gary Donovan, pres & gen mgr; John Roberts, progmg dir & mus dir; Tim Wolston, news dir; Erik Cuhlmann, chief engr.

Barrow

***KBRW(AM)**—Dec 22, 1975: 680 khz; 10 kw-U. TL: N71 15 24 W156 31 32. Hrs opn: 24. Box 109, 1695 Okpik St. (99723). (907) 852-6811. FAX: (907) 852-7941. Licensee: Silakkuagvik Communications Inc. Net: APR, AP; Alaska Pub. Wash atty: Schwartz, Woods & Miller. Format: Div, news. News staff one; news progmg 24 hrs wkly. Target aud: General. Spec prog: Eskimo 15 hrs, classical 2 hrs, jazz 6 hrs, relg 7 hrs, Filipino 2 hrs wkly. ■ Edith Nashoalook, pres; Don Rinker, gen mgr; Isaac Tuckfield, opns dir; Kim Pigg, dev mgr; Stephen Hamlin, progmg dir; David Dean, mus dir; Earl Finkler, news dir.

Bethel

KYKD(FM)—Sept 12, 1983: 100.1 mhz; 3 kw. Ant 76 ft. TL: N60 48 20 W161 47 14. Stereo. Box 820, Nome (99762). (907) 443-2213. FAX: (907) 443-2344. Licensee: Arctic Broadcasting Association (group owner; acq 5-8-87; $10,000; FTR 5-25-87). ■ John McBride, stn mgr.

***KYUK(AM)**—May 13, 1971: 640 khz; 10 kw-U. TL: N60 46 57 W161 53 00. Pouch 468, 640 Radio St. (99559). (907) 543-3131. FAX: (907) 543-3130. Licensee: Bethel Broadcasting Inc. Net: APR, NPR; Alaska Pub. Format: Bi-lingual talk/div mus, public info, Yupik Eskimo. News staff 5; news progmg 28 hrs wkly. Target aud: General. Spec prog: Class 4 hrs, country 4 hrs wkly. ■ Andrew Guy, pres; John McDonald, gen mgr; Jennifer Duford, dev dir; Peter Twitchell, progmg dir; Rhonda McBride, news dir; Joe Seibert, chief engr. ■ *KYUK-TV affil.

Chevak

***KCUK(FM)**—1990: 88.1 mhz; 150 w. Ant 75 ft. TL: N61 31 46 W165 35 20 (CP: 6 kw, ant 78 ft). 98S KSDY Way (99563). (907) 858-7014. FAX: (907) 858-7328. Licensee: Kashunamiut School District. Format: Country, rock 'n roll. ■ Peter Tuluk, gen mgr.

College

KSUA(FM)—Sept 6, 1984: 103.9 mhz; 3 kw. Ant 120 ft. TL: N64 51 32 W147 49 41. Stereo. Univ. of Alaska, 307 Constitution Hall, Fairbanks (99775). (907) 474-7054; (907) 474-5782. FAX: (907) 474-7054. Licensee: Student Media Inc. Rep: Major Mkt. Format: AOR, progsv. Target aud: 18-34. ■ Erick Glos, gen mgr; Chris McElfresh, opns dir; Matt Schantzen, progmg dir; Lee Santono, chief engr. ■ Rates: $15; 12; 15; 8.

Cordova

KLAM(AM)—May 1953: 1450 khz; 250 w-U. TL: N60 32 20 W145 45 35. Box 60, One Forrestry Way (99574). (907) 424-3796. FAX: (907) 424-3737. Licensee: TCT Communications Inc. Group owner: Cobb Communications Inc. (acq 6-12-90; grpsl; FTR 7-2-90). Net: ABC. Rep: Alaska Radio/TV Sls. Wash atty: Haley, Bader & Potts. Format: Ecclectic, AC, country, oldies. News staff one; news progmg 3 hrs wkly. Target aud: General. ■ Tom Tierney, pres; J. R. Lewis, gen mgr, gen sls mgr, progmg dir & mus dir; Leslie Lewis, prom mgr. ■ Rates: $7.50; 7.50; 7.50; 7.50.

Dillingham

***KDLG(AM)**—July 22, 1975: 670 khz; 10 kw-U. TL: N59 02 43 W158 27 07. Hrs opn: 18. Box 670, 670 Seward St. (99576). (907) 842-5281. FAX: (907) 842-5645. Licensee: Dillingham City School District. Net: NPR; Alaska Pub. Format: Adult contemp, country, rock. News staff one; news progmg 20 hrs wkly. Spec prog: Yupik one hr wkly. ■ Carol Schroeder, pres; K.C. Jackson (acting), gen mgr; K.C. Jackson, gen sls mgr; Clifford Tubbs, progmg dir; Bob King, news dir; Rob Carpenter, chief engr.

KPVV(FM)—Not on air, target date unknown: 99.1 mhz; 6 kw. Ant 167 ft. TL: N59 02 31 W158 31 19. Airport Rd. (99576). Licensee: McCormick Broadcasting.

Eagle River

KFFR(AM)—Dec 25, 1986: 1020 khz; 10 kw-U, DA-N. TL: N61 29 03 W149 45 52. Suite 212, 13135 Old Glenn Hwy. (99577). (907) 696-1020. FAX: (907) 694-1027. Licensee: Prevailing Word Broadcasting Inc. (acq 2-10-92; $100,000; FTR 3-2-92). Wash atty: Peter Gutmann. Format: Contemp Christian. ■ Stuart Back, gen mgr.

Fairbanks

KAKQ(AM)—Sept 12, 1983: 1300 khz; 5 kw-U. TL: N64 51 49 W147 45 06. Suite A, 3000 A St., Anchorage (99503). Licensee: Cobb Communications Inc. (group owner; acq 4-12-91; FTR 4-29-91). Format: Talk. ■ Ed Parsons, gen mgr.

KAKQ-FM—Apr 4, 1981: 101.1 mhz; 25 kw. Ant 131 ft. TL: N64 54 53 W147 38 54. Stereo. 3504 Industrial Ave. (99701). (907) 452-5299. FAX: (907) 452-5329. Licensee: North Country Wireless Inc. Group owner: Cobb Communications Inc. (acq 11-1-91; $600,000). Net: Unistar, Westwood One. Rep: McGavren Guild. Format: Adult contemp. News progmg 3 hrs wkly. Target aud: 25-34; working families & adults. ■ Tom Tierney, pres & gen mgr; Jay Lewis, gen sls mgr; Kevin Marsh, progmg dir & mus dir; Willie Forgue, chief engr.

KCBF(AM)—1948: 820 khz; 50 kw-U. TL: N64 51 49 W147 45 06. Hrs opn: 24. 3528 International Way (99701). (907) 452-5121. FAX: (907) 452-5120. Licensee: Northern Television Inc. (group owner; acq 8-16-65). Net: CBS, SMN. Rep: Katz & Powell; Art Moore.Format: Oldies. News staff one; news progmg 4 hrs wkly. Target aud: 35-54. ■ Henry Hove, pres; Jerry Bever, gen mgr & gen sls mgr; Tina O'Shea, opns mgr & progmg dir; Chuck Hinde, news dir; Lester Secrest, chief engr.

KXLR(FM)—Co-owned with KCBF(AM). July 1989: 95.9 mhz; 3 kw. Ant 7 ft. TL: N64 51 49 W147 45 06 (CP: 25 kw). Stereo. Hrs opn: 24. Prog sep from AM. (acq 5-8-90; $56,900; FTR 7-16-90). Format: Oldies, classic rock. Target aud: 25-49. ■ KTVF(TV) affil.

KFAR(AM)—1939: 660 khz; 10 kw-U. TL: N64 52 09 W147 49 20. 1060 Aspen St. (99709). (907) 451-5910. FAX: (907) 451-5999. Licensee: Borealis Broadcasting Inc. (acq 9-8-81; $675,000; FTR 9-28-81). Net: ABC Talk-Radio, AP, NBC Talknet. Rep: Katz. Wash atty: Fisher, Wayland, Cooper & Leader. Format: All news/talk. News staff one. Target aud: 25 plus. Spec prog: Gospel 2 hrs wkly. ■ L.F. Delong, pres; Terry Walley, gen mgr, prom mgr & progmg dir; Hugh Smith, gen sls mgr; Charles Beck, chief engr.

KWLF(FM)—Co-owned with KFAR(AM). Oct 31, 1987: 98.1 mhz; 25 kw. Ant -7 ft. TL: N64 52 38 W147 48 46 (CP: 28 kw). Stereo. Prog sep from AM. Net: SMN. Format: CHR. Target aud: 18 plus; general.

KIAK(AM)—Sept 18, 1972: 970 khz; 5 kw-U. TL: N64 52 48 W147 40 29. Hrs opn: 24. Box 73410, 546 Ninth Ave. (99701). (907) 457-1921. FAX: (907) 457-2128. Licensee: Comco Broadcasting Inc. (group owner; acq 5-21-93; grpsl; FTR 6-14-93). Net: MBS. Rep: Christal. Format: News, sports. News staff one; news progmg 8 hrs wkly. Target aud: 25-54. ■ Gary Donovan, pres; Peter Van Nort, gen mgr; Pete Hutton, gen sls mgr; Monte Bowen, news dir; David Castor, chief engr.

KIAK-FM—Sept 21, 1983: 102.5 mhz; 26.3 kw. Ant 1,626 ft. TL: N64 52 48 W147 40 29. Stereo. Format: Modern country. ■ Peter Van Nort, progmg dir. ■ Rates: $18; 10; 15; 6.

KSUA(FM)—See College.

***KUAC(FM)**—Sept 20, 1962: 104.7 mhz; 10.5 kw. Ant 440 ft. TL: N64 54 42 W147 46 30. Stereo. Hrs opn: 20. Box 755620, Univ. of Alaska-Fairbanks (99775-5620). (907) 474-7491. Licensee: Univ. of Alaska-Fairbanks. Net: NPR. Wash atty: Cohn & Marks. Format: Div, classical, news/talk. News staff 3; news progmg 32 hrs wkly. Target aud: General. Spec prog: Jazz 15 hrs, folk 10 hrs, blues 4 hours, new age 3 hrs wkly. ■ Joan K. Wadlow, chmn; Bruce L. Smith, gen mgr; Scott Diseth, stn mgr; Kara Metty, dev dir; Sandra Chaffin, mus dir; Ann Thomsen, news dir; Tom McGrane, engrg dir; John Reisinger, chief engr. ■ *KUAC-TV affil.

***KUWL(FM)**—Oct 10, 1985: 91.5 mhz; 380 w. Ant 48 ft. TL: N64 52 05 W147 39 48. Stereo. Hrs opn: 24. Box 70339 (99707); 270 Fairhill (99712). (907) 457-5895; (907) 457-2091. Licensee: Fairbanks Educ Broadcasting Foundation. ■ Jack L. Benson, pres.

KWLF(FM)—Listing follows KFAR(AM).

KXLR(FM)—Listing follows KCBF(AM).

Fort Yukon

KZPA(AM)—Sept 30, 1993: 900 khz; 5 kw-U. TL: N66 33 24 W145 12 04. Box 50, E. 3rd Ave. (99740). (907) 662-8255. Licensee: Gwandak Public Broadcasting Inc. Format: Div. ■ Marilyn Savage, gen mgr.

Galena

KIYU(AM)—July 4, 1986: 910 khz; 5 kw-U. TL: N64 41 18 W156 43 29. Hrs opn: 6 AM-midnight. Box 165, Tiger Fwy. (99741). (907) 656-1488. FAX: (907) 656-1734. Licensee: Big River Public Broadcasting Corp. Net: NPR; Alaska Pub. Format: Country, oldies, rock. News staff one; news progmg 35 hrs wkly. Target aud: General. Spec prog: Jazz 4 hrs, Sp 3 hrs, Alaska native 2 hrs, gospel 3 hrs wkly. ■ Mike Spindler, pres; Robert Sommer, gen mgr.

Glennallen

KCAM(AM)—Apr 16, 1964: 790 khz; 5 kw-U. TL: N62 06 52 W145 32 07. Hrs opn: 24. Box 249, Mile 187 Glenn Hwy. (99588). (907) 822-3434. FAX: (907) 822-3761. Licensee: Northern Light Network (acq 2-25-92). Net: Moody, Skylight, USA. Format: Relg. News progmg 28 hrs wkly. Target aud: General. Spec prog: Amer Indian one hr, class 5 hrs, gospel 19 hrs wkly. ■ Carlyle Callis, pres; George Reichman, stn mgr & mus dir; Dan Callaway, sls dir & news dir; Scott Yahr, progmg dir; Dan Zachary, chief engr. ■ Rates: $10.50; 10.50; 10.50; 9.

Haines

***KHNS(FM)**—Oct 4, 1980: 102.3 mhz; 3 kw. Ant -1,220 ft. TL: N59 13 06 W135 25 29. Stereo. Hrs opn: 18. Box 1109, One Chilkat Ctr. for the Arts (99827). (907) 766-2020; (907) 766-2021. FAX: (907) 766-2022. Licensee: Lynn Canal Broadcasting. Net: NPR; Alaska Pub. Wash atty: Arter & Hadden. Format: Div, adult contemp, CHR. News staff 2; news progmg 21 hrs wkly. Target aud: General. Spec prog: Black 4 hrs, class 14 hrs, C&W 17 hrs, folk 6 hrs, gospel 3 hrs, jazz 5 hrs wkly. ■ Linda McCormick, chmn; Barnaby Dow, gen mgr & dev mgr; Joanne Waterman, opns mgr; John Hedrick, progmg dir; Steve Williams, news dir; Bruce Whittington, chief engr.

Homer

***KBBI(AM)**—Aug 4, 1979: 890 khz; 10 kw-U. TL: N59 40 14 W151 26 38. Hrs opn: 5:30 AM-midnight. 3913 Kachemak Way (99603). (907) 235-7721. FAX: (907) 235-2357. Licensee: Kachemak Bay Broadcasting Inc. Net: APR, NPR, AP; Alaska Pub. Format: Div, news. News staff 2; news progmg 35 hrs wkly. Target aud: General. Spec prog: Class 20 hrs, C&W 4 hrs wkly. ■ Will Peterson, gen mgr; Joan Stempniak, opns mgr; David Anderson, dev dir; Kathy Steberl, progmg dir; Joe Gallagher, news dir; Scott Morton, chief engr.

KGTL(AM)—Feb 11, 1981: 620 khz; 5 kw-U. TL: N59 41 03 W151 37 51. Box 109 (99603); 66140 Diamond Ridge Rd. (99603). (907) 235-6000. Licensee: Peninsula Communications Inc. (group owner). Net: CNN. Format: Soft hits, adult contemp. News progmg 14 hrs wkly. Target aud: 35 plus; professionals. ■ David F. Becker, pres, gen mgr & chief engr; Glenn Hermann, gen sls mgr. ■ Rates: $17.50; 13; 13; 11.50.

KWVV-FM—Co-owned with KGTL(AM). Sept 22, 1979: 103.5 mhz; 100 kw. Ant 1,150 ft. TL: N59 41 03 W151 37 51. Stereo. Prog sep from AM. Net: AP. Wash atty: Southmayd & Miller. Format: Adult contemp. News progmg 14 hrs wkly. Target aud: 18-34. ■ Dave Webb, prom mgr; Tim White, progmg dir & news dir. ■ Rates: Same as AM.

Houston

KADX(FM)—Not on air, target date 1994: 94.3 mhz; 6 kw. Ant 262 ft. TL: N61 34 05 W149 43 21. Stereo. Hrs opn: 24. Cathedral Hill Hotel Office Bldg., 1255 Post St., Suite 625, San Francisco, CA (94109). Licensee: Chester P. Coleman dba American Radio Brokers Inc. Format: Full service. News staff 4; news progmg 10 hrs wkly. Target aud: 25-44; general. Spec prog: Hawaiian 2 hrs wkly. ■ Chester P. Coleman, pres. ■ KYES(TV) affil.

Juneau

KINY(AM)—May 28, 1935: 800 khz; 10 kw-D, 5 kw-N. TL: N58 18 05 W134 26 26. Stereo. Hrs opn: 24. #2, 1107 W. 8th St. (99801). (907) 586-1800. FAX: (907) 586-3266. Licensee: Alaska-Juneau Communications Inc. Net: ABC/I. Rep: Katz. Format: Adult contemp. News staff one; news progmg 4 hrs wkly. Target aud: General. ■ Dennis W. Egan, pres & gen mgr; Kelly Peres, opns mgr; Dan King, gen sls mgr; Guy James, prom dir & progmg dir; Charlie Gray, engrg dir.

KSUP(FM)—Co-owned with KINY(AM). Dec 1, 1984: 106.3 mhz; 10 kw. Ant -1,007 ft. TL: N58 18 05 W134 26 26. Stereo. Hrs opn: 24. Prog sep from AM. (907) 586-1063. Net: ABC/R. Format: Classic & contemp rock. ■ Ron Davis, progmg dir.

KJNO(AM)—Oct 19, 1952: 630 khz; 5 kw-D, 1 kw-N. TL: N58 19 47 W134 28 17. 3161 Channel Dr. No. 2 (99801). (907) 586-3630. FAX: (907) 463-3685. Licensee: Media Ltd. (group owner; acq 1-3-91; grpsl; FTR 1-21-91). Net: CNN. Rep: Tacher. Wash atty: Haley, Bader & Potts. Format: Adult contemp. Target aud: 25-54. ■ Roy Paschal, pres; Jill Paschal, vp; Steve Rhyner, gen mgr & stn mgr; Gary Buell, opns mgr; Michelle Shaw, gen sls mgr; Bob Wegner, progmg dir & mus dir; Ken Eklund, chief engr. ■ Rates: $36; 30; 36; 24.

KTKU(FM)—Co-owned with KJNO(AM). July 9, 1984: 105.1 mhz; 3.84 kw. Ant -1,057 ft. TL: N58 19 47 W134 28 17. Stereo. Prog sep from AM. Licensee: Juneau Broadcasters Inc. Net: ABC/FM. Format: Contemp hit.

KSUP(FM)—Listing follows KINY(AM).

KTKU(FM)—Listing follows KJNO(AM).

***KTOO(FM)**—Jan 27, 1974: 104.3 mhz; 1.4 kw. Ant -1,016 ft. TL: N58 18 04 W134 25 21. Stereo. Hrs opn: 5 AM-1 AM. 224 4th St. (99801). (907) 586-1670. FAX: (907) 586-3612. Licensee: Capital Community Broadcasting Inc. Net: NPR, APR; Alaska Pub. Wash atty: Schwartz, Woods & Miller. Format: Class, div, news. News staff 3;

Stations in the U.S.   Alaska

news progmg 48 hrs wkly. Target aud: General. Spec prog: Class 17 hrs, folk 6 hrs, Sp one hr, Alaska native one hr wkly. ■ Bill Legere, pres & gen mgr; Lori Brotherton, vp; James Waste, stn mgr; Susan Fitzgerald, opns mgr; Ron Clarke, dev dir; Toby Tobiason, progmg dir; Jeff Brown, mus dir; John Greely, news dir; Jack McKain, chief engr. ■ KTOO-TV affil.

Kenai

*KCZP(FM)—Not on air, target date unknown: 91.9 mhz; 4.9 kw. Ant 72 ft. TL: N60 34 03 W151 07 25. Box 2111 (99611). Licensee: Pickle Hill Public Broadcasting Inc.

KPEN-FM—See Soldotna.

KSRM(AM)—See Soldotna.

KWHQ-FM—Nov 18, 1976: 100.1 mhz; 3 kw. Ant 260 ft. TL: N60 30 49 W151 11 19. Stereo. Hrs opn: 24. HC 2, Box 853, Mile 16.5 K-Beach Rd., Soldotna (99669). (907) 283-9430; (907) 283-5811. FAX: (907) 283-9177. Licensee: KSRM Inc. Net: SMN. Rep: Tacher. Wash atty: Pepper & Corazzini. Format: Contemp hit. Target aud: 18-34; young movers & shakers. ■ John C. Davis, pres & gen mgr; Tom Farrell, opns dir & progmg dir; Jim Wolverton, gen sls mgr; Doug Johnson, prom mgr; Jim Hein, news dir; Kim Graham, pub affrs dir; Bill Glynn, chief engr. ■ Rates: $27.50; 25; 22; na.

KZXX(AM)—1985: 980 khz; 1 kw-U. TL: N60 34 02 W151 07 57. Hrs opn: 24. 6672 Spur Hwy. (99611). (907) 283-3051. FAX: (907) 283-3051. Licensee: Cobb Communications Inc. (group owner; acq 6-12-90; grpsl; FTR 7-2-90). Net: Alaska Radio Net. Rep: D & R Radio. Wash atty: Haley, Bader & Potts. Format: Class rock. News staff one. Target aud: 18-45; baby boomers. ■ Thomas C. Tierney, pres; Brent Elkington, stn mgr & progmg dir; Ron Clement, rgnl sls mgr; Jerry Ritter, news dir; Van Craft, chief engr. ■ Rates: $8; 8; 8; 6.

Ketchikan

KGTW(FM)—Listing follows KTKN(AM).

*KRBD(FM)—May 1976: 105.9 mhz; 15 kw. Ant -105 ft. TL: N55 20 20 W131 37 21. Stereo. 123 Stedman (99901). (907) 225-9655. Licensee: Rainbird Community Broadcasting Corp. Net: NPR, APR; Alaska Pub. Format: Div. News staff 2; news progmg 36 hrs wkly. Target aud: General. Spec prog: Class 11 hrs, C&W 14 hrs, folk 10 hrs, jazz 10 hrs, tribal topics one hr wkly. ■ Marty West, gen mgr; Robert Walsh, progmg dir; Carolyn Minor, news dir; Chuck LaKaytis, engrg mgr.

KTKN(AM)—1942: 930 khz; 5 kw-D, 1 kw-N. TL: N55 20 22 W131 38 12. Hrs opn: 5 AM-midnight. 526 Stedman St. (99901). (907) 225-2193. FAX: (907) 225-0444. Licensee: Gateway Broadcasting Co., Inc. Group owner: Alaska Broadcast Communications, Inc. Net: ABC/I, Unistar. Rep: Tacher. Wash atty: Haley, Bader & Potts. Format: MOR, info. News staff one; news progmg 20 hrs wkly. Target aud: 37 plus. ■ Jack Emmerson, gen mgr & gen sls mgr; Brandon Simms, progmg dir; Ken Ecklund, chief engr. ■ Rates: $36; 32; 36; 25.

KGTW(FM)—Co-owned with KTKN(AM). November 1987: 106.7 mhz; 4 kw. Ant -308 ft. TL: N55 20 22 W131 38 12. Stereo. Hrs opn: 5 AM-midnight. Prog sep from AM. Net: Unistar. Format: Classic rock. Target aud: 12-35. ■ Rates: Same as AM.

Kodiak

KJJZ(FM)—Listing follows KVOK(AM).

*KMXT(FM)—June 1, 1976: 100.1 mhz; 3 kw. Ant 3 ft. TL: N57 47 41 W152 23 28. Stereo. Hrs opn: 18. 718 Mill Bay Rd. (99615). (907) 486-3181. Licensee: Kodiak Public Broadcasting Corp. (acq 10-2-75). Net: NPR, APR. Wash atty: Larry Miller. Format: Div, news. News staff 2; news progmg 5 hrs wkly. Spec prog: Filipino 2 hrs, Aleut/Yupik, Native American one hr, Sp one hr wkly. ■ Cecelia Esparza, pres; Kellie K. Law, gen mgr; Rod O'Conner, opns dir; Diane Schunk, dev dir & prom mgr; Charlene Parent, progmg dir; Cindy Moffit, mus dir; Rhonda Lichtwark, news dir; Joe Stevens, chief engr.

KVOK(AM)—Nov 7, 1974: 560 khz; 1 kw-U. TL: N57 48 36 W152 20 54. Box 708 (99615). (907) 486-5159. FAX: (907) 486-3044. Licensee: TCT Communications Inc. Group owner: Cobb Communications Inc. (acq 6-14-90; with co-located FM; FTR 7-2-90). Net: ABC/I. Format: Adult contemp. ■ Frank Townsend, gen mgr & gen sls mgr; Tim Moffet, progmg dir & mus dir.

KJJZ(FM)—Co-owned with KVOK(AM). 1987: 101.1 mhz; 3.1 kw. Ant 46 ft. TL: N57 48 36 W152 20 54. Dups AM 100%.

Kotzebue

*KOTZ(AM)—March 1973: 720 khz; 10 kw-U. TL: N66 50 22 W162 34 05. Box 78 (99752). (907) 442-3434. FAX: (907) 442-2292. Licensee: Kotzebue Broadcasting Inc. Net: AP; Alaska Pub. Format: Div. News staff 2. Target aud: 90% rural Eskimo, 10% white-collar caucasian. Spec prog: Class 4 hrs wkly. ■ Linda Joule, pres; Robert Rawls, gen mgr; Wes Goodwin, progmg dir; David Calechman, mus dir; Bill Murray, news dir; Pierre Lonewolf, chief engr.

Long Island

KABN(AM)—Licensed to Long Island. See Anchorage.

McGrath

*KSKO(AM)—July 1, 1981: 870 khz; 10 kw-U. TL: N62 55 57 W155 31 07. Hrs opn: 18. Rebroadcasts KIYU(AM) Galena 70%. Box 70 (99627). (907) 524-3001. FAX: (907) 524-3436. Licensee: Kuskokwim Public Broadcasting. Net: APR, AP; Alaska Pub. Format: Div, country. News staff one; news progmg 21 hrs wkly. Target aud: General. Spec prog: American Indian one hr, blues 3 hrs, oldies 6 hrs, jazz 3 hrs, classical 2 hrs, relg 3 hrs, kids progmg one hr wkly. ■ Andy Alexandrou, pres; Susan Braine, gen mgr; Amie Hind, opns dir; Betsy McGuire, progmg dir & mus dir; Doug Letch, news dir.

Naknek

KAKN(FM)—May 1987: 100.9 mhz; 3 kw. Ant 338 ft. TL: N58 44 33 W156 58 39. Stereo. Hrs opn: 6 AM- midnight. Box 0214 (99633). (907) 246-7492. Licensee: Bay Broadcasting Co. Net: AP, CBN. Format: Easylstng, relg, country. News staff one; news progmg 15 hrs wkly. Target aud: General; mobile town/village population and commercial fishermen. ■ Curtis Nestegard, pres & gen mgr; Jewel Nestegard, CFO; Jim Phelps, vp; Joe Duray, stn mgr, gen sls mgr, adv dir, progmg dir & news dir; Wesley Foster, mus dir; Roberta Frost, pub affrs dir; Bill Gentile, chief engr. ■ Rates: $16; 16; 16; 12.75.

Nenana

KIAM(AM)—June 28, 1985: 630 khz; 5 kw-D, 2.2 kw-N. TL: N64 29 26 W165 19 12. Box 474 (99760). (907) 832-5426. FAX: (907) 832-5450. Licensee: Voice for Christ Ministries. Net: USA. Format: Relg. ■ Robert Eldridge, pres; Brian Anderson, stn mgr; Tim Zook, chief engr.

Nome

KICY(AM)—Apr 17, 1960: 850 khz; 10 kw-U. TL: N64 29 16 W165 19 12. Box 820 (99762). (907) 443-2213. FAX: (907) 443-2344. Licensee: Arctic Broadcasting Association (group owner). Net: CBS, ABC. Wash atty: Pepper & Corazzini. Format: Adult contemp, relg. News progmg 20 hrs wkly. Target aud: 18-34. Spec prog: Eskimo 11 hrs, Russian 6 hrs wkly. ■ Kathy Erickson, pres; Steve Dawson, gen mgr; John McBride, stn mgr & gen sls mgr; Dan Smith, prom mgr; Marilynn McCrackin, mus dir. ■ Rates: $28; 26; 26; 22.

KICY-FM—Sept 11, 1977: 100.3 mhz; 84 w. Ant 40 ft. TL: N64 30 04 W165 24 39. Stereo. Prog sep from AM. News progmg 6 hrs wkly. Target aud: 18-34. Spec prog: Class 2 hrs wkly. ■ John McBride, gen mgr; Laura Smith, mus dir. ■ Rates: Same as AM.

*KNOM(AM)—July 14, 1971: 780 khz; 10 kw-U. TL: N64 29 16 W165 17 58. Hrs opn: 20. Box 988, 262 E. 3rd Ave. (99762). (907) 443-5221. FAX: (907) 443-5757. Licensee: Catholic Bishop of Northern Alaska. Net: AP; Alaska Pub. Wash atty: Wilkinson, Barker, Knauer & Quinn. Format: Div. News staff 2; news progmg 30 hrs wkly. Target aud: General. Spec prog: Class 8 hrs, top-40 12 hrs, relg 15 hrs wkly. ■ Michael J. Kaniecki, pres; Thomas A. Busch, gen mgr & dev dir; John Albers, progmg dir; Craig Jones, mus dir; Kathy Clark, news dir; Michelle Thompson, pub affrs dir; Timothy Cochran, chief engr.

*KNOM-FM—May 17, 1993: 96.1 mhz; 88 w. Ant -138 ft. TL: N64 29 56 W165 23 56. Stereo. Hrs opn: 20. Dups AM 100%.

North Pole

KJNP(AM)—Oct 11, 1967: 1170 khz; 50 kw-D, 21 kw-N. TL: N64 45 34 W147 19 26. Box 0 (99705). (907) 448-2216. FAX: (907) 488-5246. Licensee: Evangelistic Alaska Missionary Fellowship. Net: AP. Format: C&W, relg. Spec prog: Russian 11 hrs, Athabaskan Indian 2 hrs, Eskimo one hr wkly. ■ Donald L. Nelson, pres; Genevieve L. Nelson, vp; Roger Skold, gen mgr & news dir; Beverly Olson, progmg dir; Eric Nichols, chief engr.

KJNP-FM—Oct 11, 1977: 100.3 mhz; 25 kw. Ant 1,570 ft. TL: N64 52 44 W148 03 10. Stereo. Dups AM 36%. ■ KJNP-TV affil.

Petersburg

*KFSK(FM)—September 1977: 100.9 mhz; 2 kw. Ant -482 ft. TL: N56 48 55 W132 57 12. Stereo. Box 149 (99833). (907) 772-3808. FAX: (907) 772-9296. Licensee: Narrows Broadcasting Corp. Net: APR, AP; NPR; Alaska Pub. Format: News, public affairs, lite rock. News staff 2. ■ Linda Bunge, pres; Matt Holmes, gen mgr; Deb Boettcher, progmg dir; Sonja Oyler, mus dir; John Back, news dir.

KRSA(AM)—Sept 24, 1982: 580 khz; 5 kw-U, DA-1. TL: N56 40 23 W132 55 00. Hrs opn: 24. Box 650 (99833). (907) 772-3891. FAX: (907) 772-4538. Licensee: Northern Light Network (acq 2-20-92). Net: AP. Format: Relg, country. News progmg 20 hrs wkly. Target aud: General. Spec prog: Class 5 hrs, oldies 5 hrs, gospel 2 hrs, jazz one hr wkly. ■ Carlyle Callis, pres; Don Johnson, stn mgr, natl sls mgr, progmg mgr & mus dir; John Mosher, news dir; Dan Zachary, chief engr. ■ Rates: $16.50; 15; 16.50; 11.50.

St. Paul Island

*KUHB(FM)—July 4, 1985: 91.9 mhz; 3 kw. Ant 56 ft. TL: N57 07 14 W170 16 45. Stereo. Pribilof School District (99660). (907) 546-2254. FAX: (907) 546-2367. Licensee: Pribilof School District. Net: NPR. Format: C&W, AOR, oldies. ■ Alicia Misikin, gen mgr.

Sand Point

*KSDP(AM)—Mar 2, 1983: 840 khz; 1 kw-U. TL: N55 21 06 W160 28 02. Box 328 (99661). (907) 383-5737. FAX: (907) 383-5737. Licensee: Aleutian Peninsula Broadcasting Inc. Net: NPR, APR. Format: Div. Target aud: General. ■ Ruth M. Farrens, gen mgr.

Seward

KSWD(AM)—November 1948: 950 khz; 1 kw-U. TL: N60 06 51 W149 26 44. Hrs opn: 24. Box 405, 611 4th Ave. (99664). (907) 224-3456. FAX: (907) 224-3247. Licensee: Cobb Communications Inc. (group owner; acq 6-12-90; grpsl; FTR 7-2-90). Net: ABC. Rep: D & R Radio. Wash atty: Haley, Bader & Potts. Format: Oldies. Target aud: General. Spec prog: Relg 4 hrs wkly. ■ John Ruby, gen mgr; Paul Wonder, stn mgr, opns mgr, progmg dir & mus dir; Van Craft, chief engr. ■ Rates: $8; 8; 8; 6.

Sitka

*KCAW(FM)—Feb 19, 1982: 104.7 mhz; 5 kw. Ant -612 ft. TL: N57 03 13 W135 21 07. Stereo. 2B Lincoln St. (99835). (907) 747-5877; (907) 747-5879. FAX: (907) 747-5977. Licensee: Raven Radio Foundation. Net: NPR, APR; Alaska Pub. Format: Div, news. News staff one; news progmg 34 hrs wkly. Spec prog: Indian 3 hrs wkly. ■ Rich McClear, CEO; Lily Herwald, CFO; Ken Fate, gen mgr; Clint Daniels, dev dir; Jake Schumacher, progmg dir & mus dir; Lisa Numberger, news dir; Bill Prendergast, chief engr.

KIFW(AM)—September 1949: 1230 khz; 1 kw-U. TL: N57 03 27 W135 20 02. Hrs opn: 5 AM-12 AM. Box 299, 611 Lake St. (99835). (907) 747-6626. FAX: (907) 747-8455. Licensee: Media Ltd. (group owner; acq 1-3-91; grpsl; FTR 1-21-91). Net: ABC/I. Rep: Tacher. Wash atty: Haley, Bader & Potts. Format: MOR, oldies, news/talk. News progmg 60 hrs wkly. Target aud: 35 plus; mature adults. Spec prog: Relg 5 hrs wkly. ■ Roy Paschal, pres; Steve Rhyner, sr vp; Geoffrey A. Brandt, stn mgr; Betty Conklin, opns mgr & prom mgr; John DeTemple, gen sls mgr, progmg dir, mus dir & news dir; Ken Eklund, chief engr. ■ Rates: $32; 30; 32; 22.

KSBZ(FM)—Co-owned with KIFW(AM). Oct 18, 1990: 103.1 mhz; 3 kw. Ant 144 ft. TL: N57 03 27 W135 20 02. Stereo. Hrs opn: 12. Prog sep from AM. Net: Unistar. Format: Classic rock, contemp hit. Target aud: 18-34; young adults. ■ Roy Paschal, chmn.

Soldotna

KAZO(FM)—Listing follows KSLD(AM).

KPEN-FM—Dec 1, 1984: 101.7 mhz; 25 kw. Ant 239.5 ft. TL: N60 30 40 W151 16 12. Stereo. Box 109, Homer (99603). (907) 262-6000; (907) 283-7451. FAX: (907) 235-6683. Licensee: Peninsula Communications Inc. (group owner). Net: AP. Format: Country. Target aud: 25-54. ■ David F. Becker, pres, gen mgr & chief engr; Tim White, opns mgr, progmg mgr & news dir; Glenn Hermann, sls dir & gen sls mgr; David Webb, prom mgr. ■ Rates: $17.50; 13; 13; 11.50.

KSLD(AM)—Apr 6, 1985: 1140 khz; 10 kw-U. TL: N60 31 26 W151 03 23. Stereo. 374 Lover's Lane (99669). (907) 262-8700. FAX: (907) 262-8722. Licensee: King Broadcasters (acq 4-9-91; $283,000 with co-located FM; FTR 4-29-91). Net: SMN. Rep: D & R Radio. Wash atty: Haley, Bader & Potts. Format: Oldies. News staff one. Target aud: 25-54; General. ■ Sally Hoskins, pres; Ron Holloway, gen mgr & stn mgr; Dan Donovan, progmg dir; Al Jones, chief engr. ■ Rates: $8; 8; 8; 6.

KAZO(FM)—Co-owned with KSLD(AM). Not on air, target date unknown: 96.5 mhz; 10 kw. Ant 259 ft. TL: N60 31 26 W151 03 23.

KSRM(AM)—Sept 27, 1967: 920 khz; 5 kw-U. TL: N60 30 49 W151 11 19. Hrs opn: 24. HC 2, Box 852, Mile 16.5 K-Beach Rd. (99669). (907) 283-5811; (907) 283-5959. FAX: (907) 283-9177. Licensee: KSRM Inc. (acq 4-72). Net: ABC/E, ABC/I, SMN. Rep: Tacher. Wash atty: Pepper & Corazzini. Format: Adult contemp, news/talk. News staff one; news progmg 2 hrs wkly. Target aud: 18-54. ■ John C. Davis, pres & gen mgr; Tom Farrell, opns mgr & progmg dir; Jim Heim, dev dir & news dir; Jim Wolverton, gen sls mgr; Doug Johnson, prom mgr; Bill Glynn, chief engr. ■ Rates: $25; 25; 25; na.

Talkeetna

*KTNA(FM)—Feb 1993: 88.5 mhz; 1.9 kw. Ant 62 ft. TL: N62 19 05 W150 17 52. Stereo. Hrs opn: 24. Box 300, 2nd Ave. (99676). (907) 733-1700. Licensee: Talkeetna Community Radio Inc. Format: Eclectic, news/talk. News staff one; news progmg 15 hrs wkly. Target Aud: Rural Alaskans. Spec prog: Class 10 hrs, jazz 5 hrs, classic rock 5 hrs, world beat 5 hrs, blues 5 hrs, light rock 5 hrs, American Indian 2 hrs, reggae 2 hrs, teen-age 3 hrs wkly. ■ Sandy Norberg, progmg mgr; Sharon Delsack, mus dir; Kathy Sullivan, news dir; Michael Vaughan, engrg dir.

Unalakleet

KNSA(AM)—Not on air, target date unknown: 930 khz; 2.5 kw-U. TL: N63 53 17 W160 41 29. No. 32 Airport Heights (99684). (907) 624-3101. Licensee: Unalakleet Broadcasting Inc. ■ Henry Ivanoff, gen mgr.

Unalaska

KIAL(AM)—Sept 1, 1978: 1450 khz; 50 w-U, DA-1. Hrs opn: 24. Box 181 (99685-9999). (907) 581-1888. Licensee: Unalaska Community Broadcasting. Net: NPR. Format: Div, classic rock. News staff one; news progmg 4 hrs wkly. Spec prog: News 14 hrs, rock 8 hrs, relg 4 hrs, country 4 hrs, Black 4 hrs, gospel 2 hrs wkly. ■ Cregan Newhouse, pres & gen mgr; Joy Mendoza, dev mgr; Robert Duncan, progmg mgr.

Valdez

*KCHU(AM)—Aug 3, 1986: 770 khz; 9.7 kw-U. TL: N61 06 40 W146 15 39. Box 467, 128 Pioneer Dr. (99686). (907) 835-4665. FAX: (907) 835-2847. Licensee: Terminal Radio Inc. (acq 10-84; $250,000; FTR 10-8-84). Net: NPR, APR, AP; Alaska Pub. Format: Div. News staff 2; news progmg 40 hrs wkly. Target aud: General. ■ Eric Neilsen, pres; James Winchester, gen mgr; Dave Perkins, vp progmg; Greg Williams, news dir.

KVAK(AM)—January 1983: 1230 khz; 1 kw-U. TL: N61 07 16 W146 15 25. Box 367 (99686). (907) 835-2405. Licensee: Cobb Communications Inc. (group owner; acq 10-18-90; $205,000; FTR 11-5-90). Net: ABC/I. Format: Adult contemp. ■ Thomas C. Tierney, pres; Pat Lynn, gen mgr.

KVLD(AM)—Not on air, target date unknown: 1400 khz; 1 kw-D, 250 w-N. c/o 6712 Old Dominion Dr., McLean, VA (22101). Licensee: Prince William Sound Broadcasters.

Wasilla

KMBQ(FM)—Mar 15, 1985: 99.7 mhz; 51 kw. Ant -187 ft. TL: N61 38 03 W149 26 25. Stereo. Box 871526 (99687). (907) 373-0222. FAX: (907) 376-1575. Licensee: KMBQ Corp. Group owner: Alaska Broadcast Communications Inc. (acq 5-8-92; $175,000; FTR 6-1-92). Net: NBC, AP. Format: Adult contemp. News progmg 11 hrs wkly. Target aud: 25-54; mid-upper class suburbanites & farm community. ■ J. J. McCartney, gen mgr; J.J. McCartney, gen sls mgr, prom mgr, progmg dir, mus dir & chief engr.

Wrangell

*KSTK(FM)—July 2, 1977: 101.7 mhz; 3 kw. Ant -294 ft. TL: N56 27 14 W132 22 54. Stereo. Box 1141, 202 St. Michael's (99929). (907) 874-2345. FAX: (907) 874-2392. Licensee: Wrangell Radio Group Inc. Net: APR, ABC/C; Alaska Pub. Format: Div. News staff 2; news progmg 20 hrs wkly. Target aud: General. Spec prog: Class 4 hrs, country 16 hrs, jazz 8 hrs, Indian 4 hrs wkly. ■ George M. Bell, pres; Liz Peterman, gen mgr; Dawn Hutchinson, progmg dir; Dixie Hutchinson, mus dir; Matt Miller, news dir.

Arizona

Ajo

KTTZ(FM)—Not on air, target date unknown: 98.3 mhz; 3 kw. Ant 69 ft. TL: N32 23 35 W112 52 15. Box 36717, Tucson (85740). (602) 797-1008. Licensee: Desert West Air Ranchers Corp. (acq 10-19-89). ■ Ted Tucker (owner), pres.

Apache Junction

KVVA-FM—July 1, 1973: 107.1 mhz; 2.5 kw. Ant 405 ft. TL: N33 26 48 W111 37 32 (CP: 25 kw, ant 312 ft.). Stereo. Suite 8, 1641 E. Osborne Rd., Phoenix (85016). (602) 266-2005. Licensee: American Broadcasting Systems Inc. Group owner: Steamboat Springs Broadcasting Inc. (acq 1-30-92; $6.9 million with KVVA(AM) Phoenix; FTR 2-24-92). Net: CRC. Rep: Lotus. Wash atty: Cohn & Marks. Format: Sp. ■ Ron Shaffer, pres; Bob Feinman, gen mgr; Richard Torres, opns mgr; Yolanda Rascon, prom mgr; Luis Trujillo, progmg dir; Gilberto Romo, mus dir; Angel Torres, news dir; Ed Knight, chief engr.

Arizona City

KONZ(FM)—Apr 13, 1985: 106.3 mhz; 3 kw. Ant 298 ft. TL: N32 50 04 W111 38 15 (CP: 3.4 kw, ant 440 ft., TL: N32 37 43 W111 34 09). 7401 W. Camelback, Phoenix (85033). (602) 622-1360. Licensee: Arizona City Broadcasting Corp. (acq 7-20-90; $605,000; FTR 8-13-90). Format: Modern rock. ■ G.A. Gamblin, gen mgr; Kevin Curran, opns dir; Kathy Lawrence, gen sls mgr; John Clay, progmg dir.

Benson

KAVV(FM)—April 1983: 97.7 mhz; 630 w. Ant 590 ft. TL: N31 54 19 W110 27 08. Stereo. Box 18899, Tucson (85731-8899). (602) 586-2397; (602) 882-9797. Licensee: Stereo 97 Inc. Net: UPI. Format: C&W. Target aud: 25-49. Spec prog: Relg 3 hrs wkly. ■ Jack Lotsof, pres; Paul S. Lotsof, gen mgr, stn mgr, progmg dir, mus dir & chief engr.

Bisbee

KWCD(FM)—Oct 12, 1979: 92.3 mhz; 51 w. Ant 2,217 ft. TL: N31 28 52 W109 57 30. Stereo. 2300 Busby Dr., Sierra Vista (85635). (602) 458-9631. FAX: (602) 458-4317. Licensee: G.C.S. Broadcasting Company Inc. (acq 7-6-93; $350,000; FTR 8-2-93). Format: C&W. News staff one; news progmg one hr wkly. Target aud: 18-45; financially secure adults & military personnel. ■ Sam Young, pres, gen mgr, opns mgr & gen sls mgr; Paul Moden, progmg dir; Jason Bacon, chief engr. ■ Rates: $13.50; 13.50; 13.50; 11.50.

Buckeye

KMJK(FM)—Not on air, target date unknown: 106.9 mhz; 6 kw. Ant 305 ft. TL: N33 27 01 W112 35 58. 5220 N. Seventh St., Phoenix (85022). (602) 386-7196. Licensee: Arthur A. Mobley (acq 3-1-91; FTR 3-25-91). ■ Arthur A. Mobley, gen mgr.

Bullhead City

KBAS(AM)—Nov 15, 1981: 1490 khz; 1 kw-U. TL: N35 05 10 W112 07 40. 2332 Hwy. 95 (86442). (602) 763-5227. Licensee: Green River Broadcasting Corp. (acq 7-91; $1,284,000 with KWAZ(FM) Needles, CA; FTR 7-29-91). Net: SMN. Format: C&W. Target aud: 45 plus. ■ R. Michael Flynn, gen mgr & gen sls mgr; Don Howard, opns dir; Patti Todd, prom mgr; Mike Van Acker, progmg mgr; Gary Thompson, news dir; Art Crane, chief engr. ■ Rates: $15; 10; 15; 10.

KFLG(AM)—Oct 1, 1978: 1000 khz; 5 kw-D. TL: N35 10 10 W114 38 02 (CP: 1 kw-D). 1343 Hancock Rd. (86442). (602) 763-2100. Licensee: The Guyann Corp. (group owner; acq 10-15-87). Net: ABC. Format: Country. News staff one; news progmg 3 hrs wkly. Target aud: 24 plus;

upper demographics. ■ Guy Christian, pres; Tamie Phillips, gen mgr; Darrell Stevens, prom dir & progmg dir; Tom Sherman, mus dir; Doug Wood, news dir; Art Crane, chief engr.

KFLG-FM—Jan 7, 1976: 102.7 mhz; 53 kw. Ant 2,408 ft. TL: N35 14 56 W114 44 37. Stereo. Hrs opn: 24. Prog sep from AM. Net: ABC. Format: Country. Target aud: 18 plus; active adults.

Casa Grande

KFAS(AM)—Listing follows KKER(FM).

KKER(FM)—Apr 8, 1976: 105.5 mhz; 1.9 kw. Ant 362 ft. TL: N32 49 27 W111 42 09 (CP: 50 kw, ant 492 ft.). Stereo. Suite 1, 177 W. Cottonwood Lane (85222). (602) 836-7779. FAX: (602) 836-2040. Licensee: Arizona Radio Players Inc. (acq 9-88; $550,000; with co-located AM; FTR 9-5-88). Format: Contemp country. News staff one; news progmg one hr wkly. Target aud: General; 18 plus. Spec prog: Sports 7 hrs wkly. ■ Wayne Cook, gen mgr & sls dir; Joaquin Haro, progmg dir & news dir. ■ Rates: $13; 12.50; 13; 11.75.

KFAS(AM)—Co-owned with KKER(FM). Not on air, target date unknown: 1260 khz; 1 kw-D.

KWLL(AM)—Not on air, target date unknown: 1460 khz; 2.5 kw-D, 1 kw-N. 2136 Elm St., Radio City, SD (57701). Licensee: Grand Broadcasting of Arizona.

Cave Creek

KCCF(AM)—Not on air, target date unknown: 1100 khz; 25 kw-D, 1 kw-N, DA-2. TL: N33 51 05 W112 01 56. c/o Cave Creek Broadcasting Co., 10410 Windsor View Dr., Potomac, MD (20854). Licensee: Cave Creek Broadcasting Co.

Chandler

KMLE(FM)—Licensed to Chandler. See Phoenix.

Claypool

KIKO-FM—Licensed to Claypool. See Miami.

Clifton

KCUZ(AM)—Licensed to Clifton. See Safford.

KJJJ(FM)—Oct 1, 1986: 102.1; 2.8 kw. Ant 2221 ft. TL: N32 53 22 W109 19 24. Stereo. 857 S. Hwy. 70, Safford (85541); Box 231, Safford (85541). (602) 428-1020. FAX: (602) 428-6818. Licensee: Rick L. Murphy (acq 11-90). Net: SMN. Format: Adult contemp. ■ Rick L. Murphy, pres; Rex Jensen, stn mgr; Nick Fiore, progmg dir.

Colorado City

KCCA(FM)—Not on air, target date unknown: 107.1 mhz; 6.1 kw. Ant -327 ft. TL: N37 05 42 W113 11 12. Box 711 (86021). Licensee: Uzona Broadcasting Co. (acq 4-2-91; FTR 4-22-91).

Coolidge

KAZR(FM)—Feb 25, 1981: 103.9 mhz; 3 kw. Ant 300 ft. TL: N33 02 16 W111 30 59. Stereo. Hrs opn: 24. Box 1437, Coolidge Pima Industria Pk., 103 E. Evans (85228). Licensee: Chriscom Inc. (acq 6-10-91; $380,000; FTR 7-1-91).

KCKY(AM)—Nov 19, 1964: 1150 khz; 5 kw-D, 1 kw-N, DA-2. TL: N33 00 27 W111 32 54. Hrs opn: 18. Box 6, 13968 N. Harmony Rd. (85228); Box 22, Chandler (85244). (602) 723-5448; (602) 963-9290. FAX: (602) 723-5961. Licensee: Grande Voz Inc. (acq 6-1-79). Net: MBS. Format: Sports/talk. News staff one; news progmg 7 hrs wkly. Target aud: General. ■ Tom Petersen, gen mgr & gen sls mgr; Ken Byers, opns dir & progmg dir; Bill Oostenburg, news dir & chief engr.

Cortaro

KEVT(AM)—Not on air, target date unknown: 1030 khz; 10 kw-D, 1 kw-N, DA-2. TL: N32 20 30 W111 04 13. 4547 E. Malvern St., Tucson (85711). Licensee: Statewide Broadcasters Inc.

Cottonwood

KVRD(AM)—Dec 20, 1964: 1600 khz; 1 kw-D. TL: N34 43 15 W109 31 45. Box 187 (86326). (602) 634-2286; (800) 473-KVRD. FAX: (602) 634-0583. Licensee: KVRD Inc. (acq 6-7-79). Net: AP, SMN. Wash atty: B. Jayu Baraff. Format: Big band. News staff one; news progmg 4 hrs wkly. Target aud: Mature adults. ■ Richard Dehnert, pres & gen mgr; Joy Anderson, opns dir &

progmg dir; Jackie Bessler, gen sls mgr; Mark Bachman, news dir; Scott Braden, chief engr. ■ Rates: $10; 10; 10; na.

KVRD-FM—July 1991: 105.7 mhz; 3 kw. Ant 672 ft. TL: N34 41 15 W112 07 02. Format: Contemp country. News staff one; news progmg one hr wkly. Target aud: General. ■ Richard Dehnert, CEO, pres & gen mgr; Scott Braden, engrg dir. ■ Rates: $12; 12; 12; 8.

KZGL(FM)—August 1983: 95.9 mhz; 3 kw. Ant 203 ft. TL: N34 45 35 W112 06 48 (CP: 5 kw, ant 2,499 ft., TL: N34 41 14 W112 07 00). Stereo. Box 10, 830 S. Sixth St., Suite 2B (86326). (602) 634-3693. FAX: (602) 634-8481. Licensee: Park Lane Regency Radio Inc. Group owner: The Park Lane Group (acq 6-7-93; grpsl; FTR 6-21-93). Rep: D & R Radio. Format: Adult contemp. News staff 2; news progmg 7 hrs wkly. Target aud: 18-49. ■ Gary Hershey, gen mgr & gen sls mgr; Rich Creeger, progmg dir; Jennifer Wafford, news dir; Dave Rose, chief engr.

Douglas

KAPR(AM)—Mar 8, 1958: 930 khz; 2.5 kw-D. TL: N31 22 08 W109 31 45. Hrs opn: 6 AM-sunset. Rt. 2, Box 243 (85607); 2950 N. Washington Ave (85607). (602) 364-4467. FAX: (602) 364-5277. Licensee: Unicom Communications Inc. (acq 8-13-86; $230,000 with co-located FM; FTR 5-5-86). Net: CNN. Format: Sp. Target aud: General; Spanish speaking. Spec prog: Farm 2 hrs wkly. ■ Dave Tucker, gen mgr; Salvador Ocano, stn mgr & gen sls mgr; Patty Navares, adv dir & mus dir; J. Alvin Williams, chief engr. ■ Rates: $8.90; 8.90; 8.90; na.

KKRK(FM)—Co-owned with KAPR(AM). March 15, 1979: 95.3 mhz; 3 kw. Ant 210 ft. TL: N31 22 08 W109 31 45. Stereo. Hrs opn: 5 AM-midnight. (602) 364-4495. Format: Adult contemp.

KDAP(AM)—1946: 1450 khz; 1 kw-U. TL: N31 21 18 W109 31 45. Box 1179, 2031 N. G Avenue (85608). (602) 364-3484; (602) 364-3485. FAX: (602) 364-3483. Licensee: KDAP Inc. (acq 9-1-84; $215,000; FTR 8-6-84). Format: Sp. News staff one. Target aud: General; local Hispanic & Mexican residents. ■ Dr. William Sandy, pres; Howard Henderson, gen mgr & gen sls mgr; Luis Aguilar, progmg dir & mus dir; Rick Mize, chief engr. ■ Rates: $11.20; 11.20; 11.20; 11.20.

KDAP-FM—Nov 15, 1990: 96.5 mhz; 3 kw. Ant 30 ft. TL: N31 21 18 W109 33 06. Stereo. Hrs opn: 24. Prog sep from AM. Licensee: Howard Henderson. Format: Country. News staff one. Target aud: General. ■ Jane Callison, prom mgr; Michael Burtch, news dir. ■ Rates: Same as AM.

KKRK(FM)—Listing follows KAPR(AM).

Flagstaff

KAFF(AM)—Oct 15, 1963: 930 khz; 5 kw-D, 50 w-N. TL: N35 11 26 W111 40 37. Hrs opn: 5 AM-midnight. Box 1930 (86002); One Mile W. Hwy. 66 (86001). (602) 774-5231; (602) 774-5233. TWX: (602) 779-2988. Licensee: Guyann Inc. Group owner: Guyann Corp. (acq 9-1-88). Net: ABC/I. Wash atty: Haley, Bader & Potts. Format: Country. News staff 2 Target aud: 25-54. ■ Guy Christian, CEO, pres & gen mgr; Ken Brown, stn mgr; Kathy Kelly, prom mgr; Ken Noble, progmg dir; Tim Stokes, mus dir; Joe Cox, news dir; John Swett, chief engr. ■ Rates: $37.40; 37.40; 37.40; 26.60.

KAFF-FM—October 1968: 92.9 mhz; 100 kw. Ant 1,512 ft. TL: N34 58 07 W111 30 24. Stereo. Hrs opn: 24. Dups AM 100%.

KCLS(AM)—Aug 8, 1950: 600 khz; 5 kw-D, 500 w-N, DA-N. TL: N35 11 47 W111 40 28. Suite 400, 305 E. Main St., Mesa (85201). Licensee: TVNA Ltd. (acq 1993; $20,000; FTR 9-13-93). Net: UPI. Format: Full svc adult contemp. ■ Charles Goyette, pres & gen mgr; Anthony DeFazio, gen sls mgr; John Koger, progmg dir; Kimberly Ott, mus dir; Jon Swett, chief engr.

KFLX(FM)—(Kachina Village). Spring 1994: 105.1 mhz; 1.0 kw. Ant 1,968 ft. TL: N35 14 26 W111 35 48. Stereo. Hrs opn: 24. Box 36717, Tucson (85740). (602) 797-1008. Licensee: Desert West Air Ranchers Corp. Wash atty: Arent, Fox, Kintner, Plotkin & Kahn. ■ Ted Tucker, pres.

***KJTA(FM)**—Not on air, target date unknown: 89.9 mhz. 5712 Massachusetts Ave., Bethesda, MD (20816). Licensee: Joy Public Broadcasting Corp.

KMGN(FM)—1975: 93.9 mhz; 100 kw. Ant 1,509 ft. TL: N34 58 08 W111 30 28. Stereo. 2615 N. 4th St., No. One (86004); Box 3421 (86003). (602) 526-5765. FAX: (602) 779-4477. Licensee: Northland Broadcasting Inc. (acq 6-86; $580,000; FTR 3-10-86). Net: AP, CNN. Rep: Katz. Wash atty: Cohn & Marks. Format: Adult contemp. News staff one; news progmg 4 hrs wkly. Target aud: 25-54; upscale, educated, regional audience. ■ Pete Forester, pres & gen mgr; Paul Lancaster, progmg dir; Theresa Kelley, news dir; Jon Swett, chief engr.

***KNAU(FM)**—Nov 24, 1970: 88.7 mhz; 100 kw. Ant 1,549 ft. TL: N34 57 40 W111 31 00. Stereo. Hrs opn: 19. Box 5764 (86011); Rm. 140, College of Creative Arts Northern Arizona Univ. (86011). (602) 523-5628. FAX: (602) 523-6202. Licensee: Northern Arizona University. Net: AP, NPR. Wash atty: Schwartz, Woods & Miller. Format: News & info, class. News staff one; news progmg 29 hrs wkly. Target aud: 25-54. Spec prog: Opera 3 hrs wkly. ■ John Stark, stn mgr; John Burk, progmg mgr; Duart Martin, mus dir; Dave Riek, news dir & pub affrs dir.

KVNA(AM)—1958: 690 khz; 1 kw-D, 500 w-N, DA-2. TL: N35 10 16 W111 41 59 (CP: 10 kw-D). Hrs opn: 24. 2690 Huntington Dr. (86004). (602) 526-2700. FAX: (602) 774-5852. Licensee: The Voice of Northern Arizona Ltd. Partnership (acq 7-9-86). Net: NBC, Westwood One, SMN. Format: Oldies. News staff one; news progmg one hr wkly. Target aud: 25-54. Spec prog: Sp 4 hrs, sports 12 hrs wkly. ■ Richard Herman, pres; Diane DeArmond, gen mgr; Lori Morris, gen sls mgr; Rich Malone, prom mgr, progmg dir & mus dir; Bob Hardy, news dir; Jon Swett, chief engr. ■ Rates: $252; 228; 204; 180.

KVNA-FM—Jan 15, 1988: 97.5 mhz; 100 kw. Ant 1,509 ft. TL: N34 58 06 W111 30 28. Stereo. Hrs opn: 24. Prog sep from AM. Net: SMN. Format: CHR. Target aud: 18-34. ■ Rates: $276; 252; 228; 204.

Glendale

KKFR(FM)—Licensed to Glendale. See Phoenix.

KNNS(AM)—Licensed to Glendale. See Phoenix.

KTWC(FM)—Licensed to Glendale. See Tempe.

Globe

KIKO(AM)—See Miami.

KJAA(AM)—1971: 1240 khz; 1 kw-U. TL: N33 22 51 W110 45 25. Hrs opn: 24. Box 1161 (85502); 1240 S. Saguaro Dr. (85501). (602) 425-8185; (602) 425-8186. FAX: (602) 425-3947. Licensee: Gila Co. Broadcasting Co. Inc. (acq 5-6-89; $111,000; FTR 6-26-89). Net: CBS. Format: Country, talk, sports. News staff one; news progmg 3 hrs wkly. Target aud: 24-54. Spec prog: Sp 10 hrs, Apache 3 hrs wkly. ■ Gene Pearsall, pres & gen mgr; Rebecca Chant, gen sls mgr; Pat Pearsall, news dir; J.E. Thayer, chief engr. ■ Rates: $9; 9; 9; 9.

KRXS-FM—Not on air, target date April 1994: 97.3 mhz; 490 w. Ant 3,418 ft. TL: N33 17 37 W110 50 09. Stereo. Hrs opn: 24. Box 1660, 1221 Monroe St. (85502); 1730 E. Indigo St., Mesa (85203). (602) 969-7707; (602) 425-5063. FAX: (602) 969-7707. Licensee: Linda C. Potyka. Wash atty: Mullin, Rhyne, Emmons & Topel. Format: Adult contemp, news, classic rock. News staff one; news progmg 12 hrs wkly. Target aud: General. ■ Linda C. Potyka, gen mgr; Michael Miller, sls dir; Richard Potyka, mktg mgr & engrg dir; Linda Potyka, mus dir. ■ Rates: $15; 12; 8; 5.

KZRX(FM)—Sept 25, 1980: 100.3 mhz; 15 kw. Ant 2,047 ft. TL: N33 17 21 W110 49 45. Stereo. 7401 W. Camelback Rd., Phoenix (85033-1499). (602) 266-1360. FAX: (602) 846-0985. Licensee: G.G. International Ltd. (acq 11-91; $750,000; FTR 11-18-91). Net: SMN. Rep: Roslin. Format: Hard rock. Target aud: 25-54; upscale, well-educated, affluent adults. ■ Sandy Gamblin, gen mgr; Kevin Curran, opns mgr; Kathy Lawrence, gen sls mgr; Scott Mc Dougal, chief engr.

Green Valley

KEKO(FM)—Feb 20, 1983: 92.1 mhz; 50 kw. Ant 600 ft. TL: N32 00 11 W110 47 49 (CP: 50 kw, ant 492 ft.). Stereo. Hrs opn: 24. 1920 W. Copper Place, Tucson (85745). (602) 622-6711. FAX: (602) 622-6711. Licensee: Arizona Lotus Corp. Group owner: Lotus Communications Corp. (acq 5-10-93; $1.263 million; FTR 5-31-93). Rep: Eastman. Format: Adult contemporary. Target aud: 25 plus. ■ Howard Kalmenson, pres; Tony Schabietello, gen mgr; Blake Williams, chief engr.

KGMS(FM)—Licensed to Green Valley. See Tucson.

KGVY(AM)—Licensed to Green Valley. See Tucson.

Holbrook

KDJI(AM)—October 1955: 1270 khz; 5 kw-D, 130 w-N. TL: N34 53 55 W110 11 30. Hrs opn: 6 AM-midnight. Box 430, 250 N. Broadcast Lane (86025). (602) 524-3994. FAX: (602) 524-3995. Licensee: Navajo Broadcasting Co. Inc. (acq 1965). Net: MBS, Jones Satellite Audio. Rep: Keystone (unwired net); Gillis.Wash atty: Haley, Bader & Potts. Format: Oldies, news. News staff one; news progmg 10 hrs wkly. Target aud: 25-54; professionals and baby boomers. Spec prog: Sports 10 hrs, farm 8 hrs wkly. ■ Roy Roberts, pres, gen mgr, gen sls mgr, vp progmg & mus dir; Jay B. Williams, vp; Robert Shelley, prom mgr, news dir & pub affrs dir; Keith Gardner, chief engr. ■ Rates: $9.90; 9.90; 9.90; 7.60.

KZUA(FM)—Co-owned with KDJI(AM). Dec 6, 1993: 92.1 mhz; 3 kw. Ant 328 ft. TL: N34 52 25 W110 09 56. Stereo. Hrs opn: 24. Prog sep from AM. Net: Unistar, CNN. Format: Country music full svc. News staff one; news progmg 2 hrs wkly. Target aud: 25-54; today's western lifestyle. ■ Vera Adair, mus dir.

Kachina Village

KFLX(FM)—Licensed to Kachina Village. See Flagstaff.

Kearny

KZLZ(FM)—Licensed to Kearny. See Tucson.

Kingman

KAAA(AM)—Oct 7, 1949: 1230 khz; 1 kw-U. TL: N35 11 48 W114 01 18. Box 3939, 2534 Hualapai Mountain Rd. (86402). (602) 753-2537. FAX: (602) 753-1551. Licensee: Park Lane Regency Radio Inc. Group owner: The Park Lane Group (acq 6-7-93; grpsl; FTR 6-21-93). Net: ABC/I. Wash atty: Cohn & Marks. Format: News/talk. News staff 2; news progmg 28 hrs wkly. Target aud: General; 25 plus. Spec prog: Sports. ■ Richard D. Singer, vp & gen mgr; Shay Givens, gen sls mgr; Mike Runge, progmg dir; Michael Lyon, news dir; Lisa Baxter, pub affrs dir; Dave Rose, chief engr. ■ Rates: $18; 15; 18; 10.

KZZZ(FM)—Co-owned with KAAA(AM). Dec 6, 1974: 94.7 mhz; 46 kw. Ant 2,492 ft. TL: N35 06 40 W113 53 08. Stereo. Hrs opn: 24. Prog sep from AM. Net: ABC/FM. Format: Adult contemp. Target aud: 25-54; professionals. ■ Jodie Brooks, progmg dir; Bob Mitchell, mus dir. ■ Rates: $28; 24; 24; 20.

KGMN(FM)—Feb 14, 1984: 99.9 mhz; 360 w. Ant 761 ft. TL: N35 11 43 W114 06 51 (CP: 930 w., ant 2,896 ft., TL: N35 06 37 W133 52 55). Stereo. 812 E. Beale St. (86401). (602) 753-9100. FAX: (602) 753-1978. Licensee: New West Broadcasting Systems Inc. Net: AP. Format: Country. ■ Lowell Patton, gen mgr; Ken Campbell, opns mgr & progmg dir; Rita Johnson, gen sls mgr; Deana Campbell, prom mgr; Art Crane, chief engr.

KRCY(FM)—Nov 1990: 105.9 mhz; 17 kw. Ant 3,060 ft. TL: N35 06 48 W113 53 00. 1984 Hwy. 95 Bullhead City (86430). (602) 855-1051. FAX: (602) 763-2290. Licensee: Hualapai Broadcasters Inc. Net: SMN. Format: Oldies rock. ■ Chris Sarros, pres & gen mgr; Rick Murphy, vp; Chris Rolando, stn mgr; Brian Calkins, news dir.

KZZZ(FM)—Listing follows KAAA(AM).

Lake Havasu City

KBBC(FM)—Listing follows KFWJ(AM).

KFWJ(AM)—Sept 23, 1970: 980 khz; 1 kw-D, 53 w-N. TL: N34 29 41 W114 20 59. Hrs opn: 24. 2001 Industrial Blvd. (86403). (602) 855-4098; (602) 453-5222. FAX: (602) 855-5395. Licensee: London Bridge Broadcasting Inc. Net: AP, APR. Wash atty: Arent, Fox, Kintner, Plotkin & Kahn. Format: MOR, nostalgia, oldies. News staff one; news progmg 12 hrs wkly. Target aud: 35-64. ■ Lee Shoblom, pres, gen mgr & progmg dir; Terry Watt, sr vp, vp opns & pub affrs dir; Linda Mattus, opns mgr; Ron Nickle, gen sls mgr; Chris Want, mus dir; Larry Rogers, chief engr. ■ Rates: $14.25; 13.25; 14.25; 13.25.

KBBC(FM)—Co-owned with KFWJ(AM). Sept 9, 1974: 101.1 mhz; 100 kw. Ant 988 ft. TL: N34 39 26 W114 20 42. Stereo. Hrs opn: 24. Prog sep from AM. (602) 855-4099. Format: CHR. News staff one; news progmg 5 hrs wkly. Target aud: 18-34. ■ Michael Jones, mktg mgr & adv mgr. ■ Rates: $12.75; 10.75; 12.75; 9.25.

***KNLB(FM)**—July 1983: 91.1 mhz; 1.15 kw. Ant 452 ft. TL: N34 29 10 W114 13 06. Stereo. Hrs opn: 24. 510 N. Acoma Blvd. (86403). (602) 855-9110. FAX: (602) 453-2588. Licensee: New Life Christian School. Net: USA. Wash atty: Arent, Fox, Kintner, Plotkin & Kohn. Format: Relg. News progmg 8 hrs wkly. Target aud: General. ■ Richard D. Tatham, pres; Coy Sawyer, stn mgr, opns mgr & progmg dir; David Curl, mus dir; Art Crane, chief engr.

KZUL-FM—1986: 105.1 mhz; 280 kw. Ant 426 ft. TL: N34 32 54 W114 11 37 (CP: 280 w., ant 2,302 ft.). Stereo. Box 1866 (86405). (602) 855-1051. FAX: (602) 855-7996.

Broadcasting & Cable Yearbook 1994
B-17

Licensee: Mad Dog Wireless Inc. Net: CNN, Unistar. Format: Adult contemp. News staff one; news progmg 3 hrs wkly. Target aud: 25-54. ■ Rick Murphy, pres; Steve Greeley, vp & gen mgr; Steve Reno, progmg dir. ■ Rates: $22.50; 21; 22.50; 21.

Marana

KOHT(FM)—Oct 1, 1984: 98.3 mhz; 3 kw. Ant 200 ft. TL: N32 27 09 W111 05 09. Stereo. Hrs opn: 24. 889 W. El Puente Ln., Tucson (85713). (602) 623-6429. FAX: (602) 622-2680. Licensee: Cactus Broadcasting Ltd. (acq 8-89). Net: CRC, CBS Hispanic Radio Ntwk. Rep: Lotus. Format: Sp. News staff one; news progmg 4 hrs wkly. Target aud: 18-49; Spanish, contemp, white collar adults. ■ Frank Lazarus, vp & gen mgr; Rick Verdugo, mktg dir; Mario Celis, progmg dir, mus dir & news dir; Joe Kirby, chief engr.

Mesa

KDKB(FM)—(Mesa-Phoenix). Apr 20, 1968: 93.3 mhz; 100 kw. Ant 1,538 ft. TL: N33 20 04 W112 03 36. Stereo. 1167 W. Javelina, Mesa (85210). (602) 897-9300. FAX: (602) 491-8482. Licensee: Mesa Radio Inc. Group owner: Sandusky Radio (acq 1977). Rep: Christal. Format: AOR. News staff one. ■ Norman Rau, pres; Chuck Artigue, gen mgr; Lisa Moore-Plant, gen sls mgr; Fred Pandrok, prom mgr; Tim Maranville, progmg dir; Lane Segal, news dir; Ray Thomson, chief engr.

KFNN(AM)—Licensed to Mesa. See Phoenix.

***KJZZ(FM)**—(Phoenix). 1951: 91.5 mhz; 96 kw. Ant 1,607 ft. TL: N33 19 58 W112 03 53. Stereo. Hrs opn: 24. 1435 S. Dobson Rd., Mesa (85202). (602) 834-5627. Licensee: Maricopa County Community College District. Net: NPR, APR. Format: Contemp jazz, news. News staff 4; news progmg 50 hrs wkly. Target aud: 25-54. ■ Carl Matthusen, vp & gen mgr; Scott Williams, progmg dir; Bill Shedd, mus dir; Laura Carlson, news dir; Dennis Gilliam, chief engr.

KVRY(FM)—1967: 104.7 mhz; 100 kw. Ant 1,550 ft. TL: N33 20 04 W112 03 35. Stereo. Hrs opn: 24. Box 5159 (85211); 727 S. Extension (85210). (602) 964-4000. FAX: (602) 898-8583. Licensee: Nationwide Communications Inc. Group owner: Nationwide Mutual Insurance Co. (acq 3-85; grpsl). Net: AP. Rep: McGavren Guild. Wash atty: Fletcher, Heald & Hildreth. Format: Adult contemp. News staff one; news progmg 7 hrs wkly. Target aud: 25-49; women. ■ Steve Berger, pres; Mickey Franko, vp; Wayne Walker, gen mgr; Susan Karis, sls dir; Cathy Burau, natl sls mgr; Bill Knoop, mktg dir & prom dir; Gordon Nobriga, prom mgr & pub affrs dir; Steve Elliott, progmg dir; Dave Cooper, mus dir; Robert Reymont, engrg dir; Patrick Williams, chief engr.

KXAM(AM)—1946: 1310 khz; 5 kw-D, 500 w-N, DA-N. TL: N33 26 23 W111 50 09. Stereo. Hrs opn: 24. Suite 540, 6900 E. Camelback, Scottsdale (85251). (602) 423-1310. FAX: (602) 423-3867. Licensee: Embee Broadcasting Inc. (acq 9-25-90). Wash atty: Hogan & Hartson. Format: MOR. News staff one; news progmg 5 hrs wkly. Target aud: 45 plus; mature adults. ■ Byron Gerson, pres; Geoff Hammond, gen mgr; Dave Teller, progmg dir & mus dir; Dave Dixson, chief engr.

Mesa-Phoenix

KDKB(FM)—Licensed to Mesa-Phoenix. See Mesa.

Miami

KIKO(AM)—June 13, 1958: 1340 khz; 1 kw-U. TL: N33 24 41 W110 50 17. Stereo. Hrs opn: 19. 4501 Broadway (85539); for UPS: 401 Broadway, Claypool (85532). (602) 425-4471; (602) 254-9142. FAX: (602) 425-9393. Licensee: Willard Shoecraft (acq 7-1-88; FTR 11-9-87). Net: ABC/I. Rep: Gillis. Wash atty: Fisher, Wayland, Cooper & Leader. Format: Adult contemp, sports. News staff 2; news progmg 8 hrs wkly. Target aud: 21-70; 2,200 industrial/blue collar in 3 copper mines, highest hourly wage earners in Arizona. Spec prog: Sp 6 hrs wkly. ■ Willard Shoecraft, CEO, gen mgr, vp mktg, vp prom & vp adv; John Libynski, progmg dir; Jon Caravella, mus dir; Tom Twynam, news dir; Rudy Petracci, chief engr.

KIKO-FM—(Claypool). Aug 1, 1991: 106.1 mhz; 6 kw. Ant 297 ft. TL: N33 24 23 W110 48 18. Stereo. Hrs opn: 18. Licensee: Claypool Broadcasting Co. (acq 8-1-91). Format: "Format 41," Unistar. News staff one; news progmg 6 hrs wkly. Target aud: 24-55; as programmed with "Format 41."

KQSS(FM)—March 30, 1987: 98.3 mhz; 3 kw. Ant -380 ft. TL: N33 24 30 W110 48 14. Stereo. Hrs opn: 24. Box 292 (85539); 502 McKinney, Globe (85531). (602) 425-7186. Licensee: William D. Taylor. Net: USA. Format: Country. News staff one; news progmg 5 hrs wkly. Target aud: 25-54; males & females. ■ Bill Taylor, chmn, vp & sls dir; Richard Potyka, chief engr.

Morenci

KCUZ(AM)—See Safford.

Nogales

KLCR(FM)—June 1978: 98.3 mhz; 215 w. Ant 228 ft. TL: N31 23 17 W110 55 38. Stereo. Hrs opn: 6 AM-midnight. Suite 6, 67 E. Baffert (85621-9748). (602) 761-1954. FAX: (602) 761-3251. Licensee: Matthews Broadcasting (acq 5-1-88). Rep: Gillis. Format: Adult contemp. News progmg one hr wkly. Target aud: 25-45; two-income young family. Spec prog: Jazz 4 hrs, AOR 5 hrs, alternative rock 4 hrs wkly. ■ Jim Matthews, pres; Patrick Busby, stn mgr & progmg dir; Dean Adams, opns dir & pub affrs dir; Lori Barrett, sls dir; Steve Parkman, engrg dir. ■ Rates: $15; 15; 15; 10.

Oracle

KLQB(FM)—December 1984: 103.1 mhz; 900 w. Ant 502 ft. TL: N32 37 07 W110 47 20. Stereo. Box 26040, Tuscon (85726). Licensee: Golden State Broadcasting Corp. (acq 7-2-87; $750,000; FTR 6-8-87). ■ Laurie Weisert, pres; Jim Wood, gen mgr; Bill Mortimer, opns mgr; John Fouts, gen sls mgr; John Varga, chief engr.

Oro Valley

KRKN(FM)—April 28, 1992: 97.5 mhz; 3 kw. Ant 299 ft. TL: N32 23 28 W111 01 48 (CP: Ant -13 ft.). Suite 201, 2761 N. Country Club., Tuscon (85716). (602) 326-8788. FAX: (602) 325-3057. Licensee: Maloney Broadcasting Inc. (acq 6-5-92). Format: Classic rock. ■ Tom Hassey, pres.

KVOI(AM)—Sept 23, 1953: 690 khz; 250 w-D, DA. TL: N32 15 11 W110 57 44. 3222 S. Richey Blvd., Tucson (85713-5453). (602) 790-2440. FAX: (602) 790-2937. Licensee: Good News Broadcasting. Wash atty: Wray Fitch. Format: Teaching & talk. News staff one. Spec prog: Gospel 3 hrs wkly. ■ Doug Martin, pres & gen mgr; Phil Thompson, progmg dir; Adam Calwell, news dir; Frank Fergosa, chief engr. ■ Rates: $15; 12; 12; na.

Page

KPGE(AM)—May 15, 1971: 1340 khz; 1 kw-U. TL: N36 45 23 W111 27 32. Hrs opn: 5 AM-midnight. Box CC, 91 Seventh Ave. (86040). (602) 645-8181. FAX: (602) 645-3341. Licensee: Lake Powell Communications Inc. (acq 7-1-91; with co-located FM; FTR 6-17-91). Net: ABC/I. Format: Country. News staff one; news progmg 15 hrs wkly. Target aud: 25-54. Spec prog: Phoenix Cardinals football. ■ Dan Brown, gen mgr; Ted Jenne, gen sls mgr; Lance Newman, progmg dir; Beth Russler, news dir; Brian Wheeler, chief engr.

KXAZ(FM)—Co-owned with KPGE(AM). Sept 22, 1980: 93.5 mhz; 1.15 kw. Ant 480 ft. TL: N36 46 42 W111 25 46. Stereo. Hrs opn: 24. Prog sep from AM. Format: Adult contemp.

Paradise Valley

KXLL(FM)—Not on air, target date unknown: 105.9 mhz; 1 kw. 5529 E, Sapphire Ln. (85253). Licensee: Scottsdale Talking Machine/Wireless.

Parker

KLPZ(AM)—Sept 7, 1974: 1380 khz; 2.5 kw-D, 58 w-N. TL: N34 09 14 W114 17 15. Hrs opn: 24. 816 6th St. (85344). (602) 669-9274. FAX: (602) 669-9300. Licensee: Scofield Broadcasting Co. (group owner; acq 4-1-83). Net: ABC/E, Jones Satellite Audio. Format: Country. News staff 2; news progmg 2 hrs wkly. Target aud: 35-55; male. Spec prog: Rush Limbaugh 15 hrs, farm one hr wkly. ■ Charles Scofield, pres; Pennie Dickinson, gen mgr & gen sls mgr; Shawn Bannister, progmg dir & mus dir; Rick Fine, news dir; Art Crane, chief engr.

***KWFH(FM)**—November 1984: 90.1 mhz; 180 w. Ant 1,010 ft. TL: N34 07 22 W114 12 40. Stereo. Hrs opn: 24. 401 15th St. (85344). (602) 669-5683. Licensee: Desert View Baptist Church. Net: Moody. Format: Relg. Target aud: General. ■ Kelley Tetzlaff, chmn; Gary Covert, opns mgr; Louie Marsh, progmg dir & mus dir; Art Crane, chief engr.

Payson

KMOG(AM)—Nov 1, 1983: 1420 khz; 2.5 kw-D, 500 w-N, DA-N. TL: N34 16 00 W111 18 54. HCR Box 44-A, (85541). (602) 474-5214. Licensee: Farrell Enterprises (acq 12-19-89; FTR 1-8-90). Net: ABC/C, Ariz. Net. Format: Country. News staff one; news progmg 11 hrs wkly. Target aud: 25-54; working adults. ■ Mike Farrell, pres & gen mgr; Blane Kimball, gen sls mgr & prom mgr; Kermit Jones, progmg dir & mus dir; Randy Roberson, news dir; Roy Barnes, chief engr. ■ Rates: $11; 7; 11; 6.

KRIM(FM)—July 4, 1984: 104.3 mhz; 100 kw. Ant 1,023 ft. TL: N34 25 48 W111 30 16 (CP: Ant 1,164 ft.). Stereo. Box 104.3, 200 W. Fronteir #P (85547-2579). (602) 474-0822. FAX: (602) 474-0970. Licensee: Pleasant Valley Broadcasting Corp. (acq 6-30-88). Net: AP. Rep: Katz & Powell. Format: Country. News staff 2; news progmg 6 hrs wkly. Target aud: 25-60. Spec prog: Relg one hr wkly. ■ Jeffrey R. Morris, pres; Marilynn Van Wagner, gen mgr, opns dir & gen sls mgr; Dan Basinski, rgnl sls mgr & prom mgr; Monica Sheble, mktg mgr; Tom Vorce, mus dir, news dir & pub affrs dir. ■ Rates: $25; 20; 25; 10.

ARB AMERICAN RADIO BROKERS, INC.
MOST TRUSTED NAME IN MEDIA BROKERAGE
CHESTER P. COLEMAN / PRESIDENT
FOR THE BEST STATIONS FOR SALE FROM THIS AREA
CALL — 415/441-3377
1255 POST STREET / SUITE 625 / SAN FRANCISCO, CA 94109

Phoenix

KASA(AM)—Jan 6, 1967: 1540 khz; 10 kw-D, DA. TL: N33 22 36 W112 05 25. 1445 W. Baseline Rd. (85041). (602) 276-4241; (602) 276-5272. FAX: (602) 276-8119. Licensee: KASA Radio Hogar Inc. (acq 8-26-92; $475,000; FTR 9-14-92). Wash atty: Cohn & Marks. Format: Relg. Target aud: General. ■ Moses Herrera, pres & opns mgr; Blanca Cineros, gen sls mgr. ■ Rates: $12; 12; 12; 12.

KBAQ(FM)—Not on air, target date unknown: 89.5 mhz; 3910 E. Washington St. (85034). Licensee: Maricopa County Community College.

KCWW(AM)—(Tempe). June 23, 1960: 1580 khz; 50 kw-U, DA-N. TL: N33 27 22 W111 50 01. Stereo. Box 3174, Tempe (85280); 600 E. Gilbert Dr., Tempe (85281). (602) 966-6236. Licensee: Buck Owens Production Co. Inc. Group owner: Buck Owens Productions Inc. (acq 6-25-67). Rep: Katz. Format: Traditional country. News staff 2; news progmg 4 hrs wkly. Target aud: 35-54. ■ Buck Owens, pres; Michael L. Owens, vp & gen mgr; Dave Nicholson, opns mgr; Bob Podolsky, gen sls mgr; Barbara Maack, prom dir; Larry Daniels, progmg mgr; Buddy Owens, mus dir; Darlene Dixon, asst mus dir; Larry Clark, news dir; Nancy Weaver, pub affrs dir; Bob Van Buhler, chief engr.

KNIX-FM—Co-owned with KCWW(AM). Sept 1, 1969: 102.5 mhz; 98 kw. Ant 1,620 ft. TL: N33 19 58 W112 03 53. Stereo. Prog sep from AM. Format: Country. News staff 3. Target aud: 25-54. ■ Patty Kincaid, mktg dir; R.J. Curtis, progmg dir; Nancy Weaver, pub affrs dir.

KEDJ(FM)—See Sun City.

KESZ(FM)—July 1982: 99.9 mhz; 100 kw. Ant 1,670 ft. TL: N33 20 02 W112 03 40. Stereo. Suite A300, 5555 N. 7th St. (85013). (602) 207-9999. FAX: (602) 207-3177. Licensee: Media America Corp. (acq 3-21-91; $10.4 million; FTR 4-15-91). Net: Unistar, AP. Rep: Banner. Format: Adult contemp. Spec prog: Jazz 4 hrs wkly. ■ Jerry Ryan, gen mgr; Patty Graham, gen sls mgr; Kristen Brassel, prom mgr; Mike Del Rosso, progmg dir; Amy Maliga, mus dir; Jay Bretlinger, chief engr.

***KFLR-FM**—December 1985: 90.3 mhz; 2.2 kw. Ant 354 ft. TL: N33 26 09 W112 06 35 (CP: 28.31 kw, ant 1,555 ft., TL: N33 20 02 W112 03 04). Stereo. 702 E. Thunderbird (85022-5310). (602) 978-0903. FAX: (602) 548-8089. Licensee: Family Life Broadcasting System (group owner). Format: Relg. Spec prog: Sp one hr wkly. ■ Warren Bolthouse, pres; Alan Cook, gen mgr; Jon Couch, mus dir; George Tanner, news dir; Jim Nelson, chief engr.

KFNN(AM)—(Mesa). November 1962: 1510 khz; 10 kw-D. TL: N33 23 30 W111 50 16. 4800 N. Central Ave., Phoenix (85012). (602) 241-1510. FAX: (602) 241-1540. Licensee: CRC Broadcasting Co. Inc. (acq 1988). Net: BRN. Wash atty: Sidley & Austin. Format: News/talk, business news, investment advice. News staff 3; news progmg 84 hrs wkly. Target aud: 30 plus; upscale, investment-oriented professionals & entrepreneurs; decision makers. ■ Ronald E. Cohen, pres, gen mgr & vp progmg; Matt Ganis, opns mgr, progmg dir & news dir; Mike Loebel, gen sls mgr; Dave Dickson, chief engr. ■ Rates: $50; 30; 40; na.

KFYI(AM)—1940: 910 khz; 5 kw-U, DA-N. TL: N33 32 00 W112 07 18. Hrs opn: 24. 631 N. 1st Ave. (85003). (602) 258-6161. FAX: (602) 252-9563. Licensee: The Broadcast Group Inc. Group owner: Twin W Communications Co. (acq 1-4-82; grpsl; FTR 11-30-81). Net: NBC, AP, MBS, UPI. Rep: D & R Radio. Wash atty: Hogan & Hartson. Format: News/talk. News staff 7. Target aud: General. ■ Fred Weber, CEO, exec vp & gen mgr; Walter Wolpin, pres; Mike Bama, gen sls mgr & natl sls mgr; Christine Dennison, prom dir; Barry Young, progmg dir; Ron Kilgore, news dir; Gary Wachter, chief engr.

KKFR(FM)—(Glendale). Co-owned with KFYI(AM). Dec 19, 1979: 92.3 mhz; 100 kw. Ant 1,646 ft. TL: N33 20 00 W112 03 46. Stereo. Prog sep from AM. Format: CHR. Target aud: 18-49. ■ Fred Weber, CFO.

KHEP(AM)—1956: 1280 khz; 2.5 kw-D, 230 w-N. TL: N33 29 32 W112 08 28. Hrs opn: 24. Suite 720, 100 W. Clarendon Ave. (85013). (602) 234-1280. Licensee: Christian Communications Inc. (acq 1957). Net: USA. Wash atty: Wilkinson, Barker, Knauer & Quinn. Format: Inspirational. Target aud: 25 plus; families, female, educated. Spec prog: Sp 5 hrs wkly. ■ Herm Gebert, vp & gen mgr; Will Ray, progmg dir; Bob Thornburg, chief engr.

KIDR(AM)—Feb 1, 1958: 740 khz; 1 kw-D, 292 w-N, DA-2. TL: N33 21 55 W112 06 30. Stereo. Hrs opn: 24. 3719 N. 32nd Ave. (85017). (602) 279-5577. FAX: (602) 230-2781. Licensee: Bonneville Holding Co. (group owner; acq 11-21-91; with co-located FM). Rep: Group W. Format: Easy listening. News staff one. Target aud: 25-54. ■ Barbara Dean, vp & gen mgr; Michael Mallace, gen sls mgr; Joel Gray, progmg dir; Allen Cook, news dir.

KPSN(FM)—Co-owned with KIDR(AM). October 1964: 96.9 mhz; 100 kw. Ant 1,560 ft. TL: N33 20 03 W112 03 36. Stereo. Hrs opn: 24. Format: Oldies.

***KJZZ(FM)**—Licensed to Phoenix. See Mesa.

KKFR(FM)—Listing follows KFYI(AM).

KKLT(FM)—Listing follows KTAR(AM).

KMLE(FM)—(Chandler). Apr 18, 1980: 107.9 mhz; 100 kw. Ant 1,735 ft. TL: N33 20 03 W112 03 43. Stereo. Suite 244, 645 E. Missouri, Phoenix (85012). (602) 264-0108. FAX: (602) 230-2116. Licensee: Shamrock Broadcasting Inc. (group owner). Net: AP. Rep: Eastman. Wash atty: Leventhal, Senter & Lerman. Format: Country. News staff 2. Target aud: 25-54. Spec prog: "Camel Views" one hr wkly. ■ Bill Clark, pres; Bruce Blevins, gen mgr; Donn Seidholz, gen sls mgr; Sean Holly, prom mgr; Alan Sledge, progmg dir; H. G. Listiak, news dir; Eric B. Schecter, chief engr.

***KNAI(FM)**—Licensed to Phoenix. See Keene, Calif.

KNIX-FM—Listing follows KCWW(AM).

KNNS(AM)—(Glendale). 1946: 1360 khz; 5 kw-D, 1 kw-N, DA-N. TL: N33 30 30 W112 13 03 (CP: TL: N33 31 05 W112 10 55). Stereo. Hrs opn: 24. 7401 W. Camelback Rd., Phoenix (85033). (602) 266-1360. FAX: (602) 846-0985. Licensee: Resource Media Inc. (acq 4-3-90). Net: MBS. Rep: CMBS. Wash atty: Dow, Lohnes & Albertson. Format: Sports. News staff one; news progmg 35 hrs wkly. Target aud: 45 plus. Spec prog: Jewish 2 hrs, relg one hr, Ger 2 hrs wkly. ■ Steven Taslitz, pres; Sandy Gamblin, gen mgr; Kevin Curran, opns mgr; Don Walker, gen sls mgr; Dawn Noci, progmg dir; Joe Groves, news dir; Jay Brentlinger, chief engr.

KOOL(AM)—June 1947: 960 khz; 5 kw-U, DA-N. TL: N33 39 12 W111 55 39 (CP: TL: N33 41 34 W112 00 09). 2196 E. Camelback Rd. (85016). (602) 956-9696. FAX: (602) 468-0325. Licensee: Compass Radio of Phoenix Inc. Group owner: Compass Radio Group (acq 4-23-93; grpsl; FTR 5-10-93). Net: SMN. Rep: D & R Radio. Format: Oldies. Target aud: 25-54. ■ Brian Bieler, gen mgr; Bruce Olson, gen sls mgr; Jima Peterson, prom mgr; Tom Peake, Brian Beazer, progmg dirs; Tom Peake, Brian Beazer, mus dirs; Chan Martinez, pub affrs dir; Jay Brentlinger, Gary Blau, chief engrs.

KOOL-FM—May 1956: 94.5 mhz; 100 kw. Ant 1,655 ft. TL: N33 20 02 W112 03 42. Stereo. Prog sep from AM. ■ Shelly Jamison, news dir.

KOY(AM)—October 1921: 550 khz; 5 kw-D, 1 kw-N. TL: N33 23 17 W112 00 22. Hrs opn: 24. 840 N. Central Ave. (85004). (602) 258-8181. FAX: (602) 420-9916; (602) 440-6530. Licensee: Sundance Broadcasting Inc. (group owner; acq 7-2-93; $7 million with co-located FM; FTR 8-2-93). Net: Unistar, CNN. Rep: Christal. Format: Nostalgia, MOR. News staff 2. Target aud: 45-65. Spec prog: Relg 2 hrs wkly. ■ Michael Jorgenson, pres & gen mgr; Jim Trapp, opns dir; Paul Talbot, sls dir; Norine Mihajlovich, natl sls mgr; Juliet Peters, mktg dir; Roger Heinrich, news dir; Dee Dee Sturr, pub affrs dir; John Baker, chief engr.

KYOT-FM—Co-owned with KOY(AM). Oct 31, 1963: 95.5 mhz; 96 kw. Ant 1,570 ft. TL: N33 20 06 W112 03 39. Stereo. Hrs opn: 24. Prog sep from AM. Format: Rhythm & Rock. News staff one. Target aud: 30-50. ■ Jim Trapp, progmg dir.

***KPHF(FM)**—December 1991: 88.3 mhz; 22.5 kw. Ant 997 ft. TL: N33 45 37 W112 05 29. Hrs opn: 7:30 PM-4:30 AM. c/o 290 Hegenberger Rd., Oakland CA (94621). (602) 583-1420; (800) 543-1495. Licensee: Family Stations Inc. (group owner). Format: Relg. ■ Harold Camping, pres; Thad McKinney, gen mgr; Charles Conn, opns mgr.

KPHX(AM)—June 10, 1958: 1480 khz; 1 kw-D, 500 w-N, DA-2. TL: N33 24 02 W112 06 28 (CP: 5 kw-D). 824 E. Washington St. (85034). (602) 257-1351. FAX: (602) 256-0741. Licensee: Continental Broadcasting Corp. (acq 2-80; $650,000; FTR 2-18-80). Rep: Caballero. Format: Sp. ■ Jose Molina, pres; Freddy Morales, vp & gen mgr; Patricio Barraza, gen sls mgr; Juan Antonio Garcez, progmg dir; Rene Boeta, news dir; James Clark, chief engr.

KPSN(FM)—Listing follows KIDR(AM).

KRDS(AM)—See Tolleson.

KSUN(AM)—Aug 27, 1954: 1400 khz; 1 kw-U. TL: N33 23 23 W111 59 52. 714 N. Third St. (85004). (602) 252-0030. FAX: (602) 252-4211. Licensee: Fiesta Radio Inc. (acq 10-86; $600,000; FTR 12-8-86). Rep: Caballero. Format: Adult contemp. Target aud: 19-45. ■ Pedro Marquez, pres; Gloria Cavazos, gen mgr; Jose Mario Gonzales, prom mgr & progmg dir; Greg Perez, mus dir; Javier Acosta, news dir; Dave Dixon, chief engr.

KTAR(AM)—June 21, 1922: 620 khz; 5 kw-U, DA-N. TL: N33 28 44 W112 00 06. Hrs opn: 24. 301 W. Osborn Rd. (85013). (602) 274-6200. FAX: (602) 266-3858; (602) 265-9941. Licensee: Pulitzer Broadcasting Co. (group owner; acq 4-1-79). Net: ABC/I, AP, Wall Street, CBS. Rep: Group W. Wash atty: Verner, Liipfert, Bernhard, McPherson & Hand. Format: News/talk. News staff 10; news progmg 50 hrs wkly. Target aud: 35 plus; listeners who listen to the radio for information. ■ Jim Taszarek, vp & gen mgr; Kirk Nelson, gen sls mgr; Jack Nietzel, prom mgr; Marc McCoy, progmg dir; Jeff Scott, news dir; Dean Kannes, chief engr.

KKLT(FM)—Co-owned with KTAR(AM). July 1, 1960: 98.7 mhz; 100 kw. Ant 1,680 ft. TL: N33 20 00 W112 03 48. Stereo. Hrs opn: 24. Prog sep from AM. FAX: (602) 266-6838; (602) 260-5483. Format: Adult contemp. News staff one; news progmg 2 hrs wkly. Target aud: 25-54; listeners who enjoy soft contemporary music. ■ Marc McCoy, opns dir; Carol Kannes, gen sls mgr; Jack Nietzel, prom dir; Roger Thomas, progmg dir.

KVRY(FM)—See Mesa.

KVVA(AM)—Nov 23, 1949: 860 khz; 1 kw-U, DA-N. TL: N33 24 16 W112 07 24. Suite 8, 1641 E. Osborn Rd. (85016). (602) 266-2005. Licensee: American Broadcasting Systems Inc. Group owner: American Broadcasting Systems (acq 1-30-92; $6.9 million with KVVA-FM Apache Junction; FTR 2-24-92). Rep: Lotus. Format: Sp. Target aud: General; Hispanic. ■ Ron Shaffer, pres; Bob Feinman, gen mgr; Richard Torres, gen sls mgr; Yolanda Rascon, prom mgr; Luis Trujillo, progmg dir; Gilberto Romo, mus dir; Angel Torres, news dir; Ed Knight, engrg mgr.

KXAM(AM)—See Mesa.

KXEG(AM)—See Tolleson.

KYOT(AM)—May 1949: 1230 khz; 1 kw-U. TL: N33 26 09 W112 06 35. Suite 135, 840 N. Central Ave. (85004); Box 353 (85001). (602) 258-8181. FAX: (602) 420-9961; (602) 440-6530. Licensee: Sundance Broadcasting of Wisconsin Inc. Group owner: Sundance Broadcasting Inc. (acq 4-6-92; $5 million with co-located FM; FTR 4-27-92). Net: AP, MBS. Rep: Major Mkt. Wash atty: Koteen & Naftalin. Format: Adult contemp. Target aud: 25-64. ■ Mike Jorgenson, pres & gen mgr; Paul Talbot, sls dir; Norine Mahojlovich, natl sls mgr; Juliet Peters, mktg dir; Jim Trapp, progmg dir; John Baker, chief engr.

KYOT-FM—Listing follows KOY(AM).

KZON(FM)—Co-owned with KYOT(AM). July 5, 1964: 101.5 mhz; 100 kw. Ant 1,740 ft. TL: N33 19 52 W112 03 46. Stereo. Prog sep from AM. Format: Eclectic. Target aud: 25-54. ■ Jim Trapp, adv dir; Erika Smith, mus dir.

KZRX(FM)—See Globe.

Pinetop

***KKGL(FM)**—Not on air, target date unknown: 106.7 mhz; 100 kw. Ant 1,023 ft. TL: N34 12 20 W109 56 26. Box 880. Gallup, NM (87301). Licensee: D&M Communications Inc.

Prescott

KAHM(FM)—Listing follows KYCA(AM).

***KGCB(FM)**—Not on air, target date unknown: 90.9 mhz; 55 kw. Ant 2,486 ft. Box 11274, Phoenix (85061). Licensee: Grand Canyon Broadcasters Inc.

KIHX-FM—See Prescott Valley.

KNOT(AM)—June 22, 1957: 1450 khz; 1 kw-U. TL: N34 32 42 W112 26 46. Hrs opn: 18. Box 151 (86302); 116 S. Alto (86301). (602) 445-6880. FAX: (602) 445-6852. Licensee: Payne-Prescott Broadcasting Corp. (acq 9-25-80; $420,000; FTR 6-1-81). Net: ABC/E. Format: Country. Target aud: 25-54. ■ William F. Payne, pres & gen mgr; Paul Hurt, progmg dir; Doreen Conti, news dir; Bill Kafka, chief engr.

KNOT-FM—Nov 11, 1977: 99.1 mhz; 6 kw. Ant 200 ft. TL: N34 34 29 W112 28 45. Stereo. Prog sep from AM. Net: ABC. Wash atty: Peper, Martin, Jensen, Maichal & Hetlage. News staff 2; news progmg 3 hrs wkly. ■ William F. Payne, gen sls mgr.

KYCA(AM)—August 1940: 1490 khz; 1 kw-U. TL: N34 33 03 W112 27 45. Hrs opn: 6 AM-midnight. Box 1631 (86302); 500 Henry St. (86301). (602) 445-1700. Licensee: Southwest Broadcasting Corp. (acq 9-25-70). Net: CBS, NBC Talknet, MBS. Rep: Gillis. Wash atty: Cohn & Marks. Format: News/talk. News staff 4; news progmg 20 hrs wkly. Target aud: 35-64. ■ Lou Silverstein, pres & gen mgr; Jason Zinzuletta, opns mgr; Chris Harmon, news dir; Al Hartzell, chief engr. ■ Rates: $12; 8; 10; 8.

KAHM(FM)—Co-owned with KYCA(AM). Sept 9, 1981: 102.1 mhz; 45 kw. Ant 2,551.8 ft. TL: N34 32 27 W112 25 40. Stereo. Hrs opn: 6 AM-midnight. Prog sep from AM. Box 2529 (86302); 510 Henry St. (86301). (602) 445-7800. Licensee: Southwest FM Broadcasting Co. Format: Easy lstng. ■ Lou Silverstein, stn mgr; Nancy Silverstein, opns dir & mus dir. ■ Rates: Same as AM.

Prescott Valley

KDTK(FM)—Not on air, target date unknown: 98.3 mhz; 875 w. Ant 2,526 ft. 6745 N. Chapultepec Circle, Tucson (85715). Licensee: Mic Rathje.

KIHX-FM—Sept 1, 1985: 106.7 mhz; 3.7 kw. Ant 1,627 ft. TL: N34 29 25 W112 32 00. Stereo. Hrs opn: 24. Box 26523, 8201 Jacque Dr. (86312). (602) 775-5277; (800) 264-5449. FAX: (602) 775-4188. Licensee: Prescott Valley Broadcasting Co Inc. Net: AP. Wash atty: David Tillotson. Format: Light rock, oldies. News staff 2; news progmg 18 hrs wkly. Target aud: 30 plus; middle to upper income professionals. Spec prog: Jazz 2 hrs wkly. ■ Sanford B. Cohen, pres, gen mgr & gen sls mgr; Terry Pollack Cohen, exec vp; Belinda Wofford, opns mgr; Allison Flannery, natl sls mgr; Tina Falco, mus dir; Juli Haas, news dir; Mona Gauthier, pub affrs dir; Dave Baron, chief engr.

KWDS(AM)—June 28, 1986: 1130 khz; 1 kw-D. TL: N34 37 46 W112 18 56. Box 27030 (86312); Deliveries only: 8000 E. Hwy. 69 (86314). (602) 775-4930. FAX: (602) 776-8214. Licensee: Oasis International Communications (acq 4-29-91; $70,500; FTR 5-20-91). Net: SMN, USA; Ariz. Net. Format: Soft adult contemp. News staff one; news progmg 5 hrs wkly. Target aud: 25-54; upscale adults. Spec prog: Class one hr, comedy one hr, big band/dixieland 5 hrs wkly. ■ Clifton W. Glasgow, gen mgr & chief engr; Bob Miller, gen sls mgr; Patrick Frisch, news dir. ■ Rates: $12; 10; 10.50; na.

Quartzsite

KBUX(FM)—Nov 1988: 94.3 mhz; 205 w. Ant -161 ft. TL: N33 40 58 W114 13 59. Stereo. Hrs opn: 24. Box 1, 16031 Camel Dr. (85346). (602) 927-5111. Licensee: Buck Burdette. Format: Btfl mus, country, oldies. Target aud: Retired. ■ Buck Burdette, gen mgr; Maude J. Burdette, gen sls mgr. ■ Rates: $10; 10; 10; na.

Safford

KATO(AM)—May 5, 1961: 1230 khz; 1 kw-U. TL: N32 49 30 W109 45 30. Drawer L (85548); 3335 W. 8th St. (85546). (602) 428-1230. FAX: (602) 428-1311. Licensee: McMurray Communications Inc. (acq 12-17-92; $10,000 with co-located FM; FTR 2-1-93). Net: AP, Unistar. Format: Oldies. News staff 7; news progmg 5 hrs wkly. Target aud: 25-54. ■ Bud McMurray, pres; Tom

Arizona

Armshaw, gen mgr & gen sls mgr; Reed Richins, progmg dir & chief engr; Tim Walters, news dir.

KXKQ(FM)—Co-owned with KATO(AM). Aug 11, 1979: 94.1 mhz; 100 kw. Ant -320 ft. TL: N32 49 30 W109 45 30. Stereo. Prog sep from AM. Format: Country.

KCUZ(AM)—(Clifton). July 31, 1969: 1490 khz; 1 kw-U. TL: N33 02 30 W109 17 40. Hrs opn: 24. Box 1330, Safford (85548-1330). 301 B. Hwy. 70E, Safford (85546). (602) 428-0916. FAX: (602) 428-5396. Licensee: Wick Broadcasting Co. (acq 2-14-84; grpsl; FTR 1-16-84). Net: MBS, SMN. Format: Adult contemp. News staff one; news progmg 7 hrs wkly. Target aud: 25-54. Spec prog: Relg 2 hrs, loc talk 8 hrs wkly. ■ Frank H. Newell, pres; Bob Jones, gen mgr; Jonathan Wolff, opns mgr, progmg dir & news dir; Steve Nunn, rgnl sls mgr; J.I. McClelland, chief engr.

KFMM(FM)—(Thatcher). Co-owned with KCUZ(AM). Dec 7, 1981: 99.1 mhz; 50 kw. Ant 2,280 ft. TL: N32 53 22 W109 19 23. Stereo. Prog dups AM 90%. News progmg 2 hrs wkly. Spec prog: Talk 8 hrs wkly.

KXKQ(FM)—Listing follows KATO(AM).

Sahuarita

KQTL(AM)—Oct 12, 1985: 1210 khz; 10 kw-D, 1 kw-N, DA-N. TL: N32 02 04 W110 56 45. Box 1511, Tucson (85702). (602) 628-1200. FAX: (602) 326-4927. Licensee: El Saguarito Broadcasting Co. Rep: Caballero. Format: Sp. ■ Raul Gamez, gen mgr & gen sls mgr; Bertha Gallego, progmg dir & news dir; Peter Trowbridge, chief engr.

St. Johns

KQZE(FM)—Not on air, target date unknown: 95.7 mhz; 91 kw. Ant 1,161 ft. TL: N34 15 06 W109 35 06. Box 795 (85936). Licensee: Plateau Communications Inc.

San Carlos

KCDX(FM)—Not on air, target date unknown: 103.7 mhz; 3 kw. Ant 298 ft. Box 36717, Tucson (85740). Licensee: Desert West Air Ranchers Corp. (group owner).

Scottsdale

KOPA(AM)—1956: 1440 khz; 5 kw-D. TL: N33 29 00 W111 56 25 (CP: N33 28 43 W111 56 24). 4601 N. Scottsdale Rd. (85251). (602) 941-1007. FAX: (602) 941-2997. Licensee: Great American Television and Radio Company Inc. (group owner; acq 4-7-92; $11,406,240 with co-located FM; FTR 5-4-92). Format: Classic hits. News staff one. ■ Reid Reiker, gen mgr; Dana Baudin, gen sls mgr; Nancy Stevens, prom mgr & progmg dir; Jeannie Sidello, progmg dir & mus dir; Bob Bell, news dir; Gary Jacques, chief engr.

KSLX(FM)—Co-owned with KOPA(AM). Aug 1, 1969: 100.7 mhz; 100 kw. Ant 1,847 ft. TL: N33 19 53 W112 03 47. Stereo. Dups AM 100%.

Sedona

KAZM(AM)—Nov 1, 1974: 780 khz; 5 kw-D, 250 w-N, DA-N. TL: N34 51 38 W111 49 10. Stereo. Hrs opn: 24. Box 1525, 3400 W. Hwy. 89A (86339). (602) 282-4154; (602) 634-0712. FAX: (602) 282-2230. Licensee: Tabback Broadcasting Co. Original Owner. Net: AP. Format: MOR, Phoenix contemp hit, News/talk. News staff 2; news progmg 8 hrs wkly. Target aud: 25 plus; retired, affluent, professional or tourist related. ■ Joseph P. Tabback, pres & gen mgr; C.J. Sells, vp sls; Larry Barwick, progmg dir; Theresa Tabback, mus dir; John Hutchinson (night), Brad Miller (day), news dirs; John Swett, chief engr. ■ Rates: $25; 25; 25; 7.

KQST(FM)—May 1, 1984: 100.1 mhz; 500 w. Ant 751 ft. TL: N34 52 26 W111 40 47 (CP: 102.9 mhz, 100 kw, ant 1,427 ft., TL: N34 58 07 W111 30 28). Stereo. Hrs opn: 6 AM-midnight. Box 1966 (86336); 2545 W. 89-A (86336). (602) 282-2111; (602) 282-6874. Licensee: Linda M. Melton (acq 10-28-92; $500,000; FTR 11-30-92). Wash atty: Borsari & Kump. Format: Easy contemp & natural sound mix, adult contemp. Target aud: 24-59. Spec prog: Jazz 15 hrs, new age 10 hrs, relg 5 hrs, big band 4 hrs, Univ. of Arizona football wkly. ■ Alma C. Gilbert, pres & gen mgr; Ralph L. Borkman, vp & vp engrg; Jack Cornelius, stn mgr; Richard "Dick" B. Gilbert, opns dir, prom dir, adv dir & pub affrs dir; Gary R. Gilbert, progmg dir. ■ Rates: $12; 12; 12; 12.

KSED(FM)—Spring 1993: 107.5 mhz; 98.4 kw. Ant 1,463 ft. TL: N34 58 07 W111 30 22. Stereo. Hrs opn: 24. Box 347 (86336). (602) 282-0720. Licensee: Red Rock Communications Ltd. (acq 3-18-93; $100,000; FTR 4-

12-93). Net: Unistar. Wash atty: Arent, Fox, Kintner, Plotkin & Kahn. Format: Special blend. Target aud: 25-55; middle-aged retired. ■ Peggy Durham, pres & gen mgr; David Kessel, progmg dir; Jon Swett, chief engr.

Show Low

KRFM(FM)—Listing follows KVSL(AM).

KVSL(AM)—July 6, 1968: 1450 khz; 1 kw-U. TL: N34 16 00 W110 20 10. 300 E. Savage St. (85901). (602) 537-2921; (602) 537-2922. FAX: (602) 537-2922. Licensee: KBW Assoc. Inc. (acq 9-1-74). Net: ABC/E. Format: C&W. News progmg 4 hrs wkly. Target aud: down to earth hard workers. Spec prog: Farm 2 hrs wkly. ■ Hugh Williams, pres, gen mgr & chief engr; Sandy Keele, adv mgr; Jeanne Nix, mus dir.

KRFM(FM)—Co-owned with KVSL(AM). July 1, 1983: 96.5 mhz; 100 kw. Ant 994 ft. TL: N34 12 20 W109 56 26. Stereo. Prog sep from AM. Net: ABC/E. Format: Adult contemp. Target aud: 15-55; discriminating adults.

KVWM(AM)—May 17, 1957: 970 khz; 5 kw-D, 114 w-N. TL: N34 13 14 W110 01 49. Box 970 (85901). (602) 537-2345. FAX: (602) 537-3991. Licensee: Peak Broadcasting Co. Format: Adult contemp. News staff one. ■ Gary Woodworth, gen mgr & news dir; Dorothy L. Woodworth, progmg dir; Michael Woodworth, chief engr.

KVWM-FM—Sept 13, 1964: 93.5 mhz; 3 kw. Ant 150 ft. TL: N34 13 14 W110 01 49 (CP: 25 kw). Dups AM 100%.

Sierra Vista

KKYZ(FM)—February 1993: 101.7 mhz; 3 kw. Ant 299 ft. TL: N31 33 59 W110 13 57. Box 3037 (85635). (602) 378-2282; (602) 622-4204. Licensee: Ana L. Zumuano.

KNXN(AM)—June 20, 1980: 1470 khz; 2.5 kw-D, 39 w-N. TL: N31 32 53 W110 14 54. Hrs opn: Sunrise-11:30 PM. Park Professional Bldg, Suite B-8, 2700 E. Fry Blvd (85635). (602) 459-1470; (602) 459-7351. Licensee: Blue Horizon Investments Inc. dba Blue Horizon Broadcasting (acq 1991). Net: ABC/I, Unistar. Format: Top 40. News staff one; news progmg 5 hrs wkly. Target aud: 35 plus; upper-income. ■ Ed Nunez, pres, gen mgr, opns mgr & gen sls mgr; Steve Thomas, progmg dir, news dir & pub affrs dir; Rick Mize, chief engr. ■ Rates: $90; 84; 84; 84.

KTAN(AM)—March 1957: 1420 khz; 1.5 kw-D, 500 w-N, DA-N. TL: N31 32 47 W110 16 29. Box 2770 (85636); 2300 Busby Dr. (85635). (602) 458-4313. FAX: (602) 458-4317. Licensee: GCS Broadcasting Inc. (acq 4-18-90; $875,000 with co-located FM; FTR 5-7-90). Net: AP. Wash atty: Jay Babbiff. Format: Country. News staff 2; news progmg 20 hrs wkly. Target aud: 25-54. Spec prog: Swinging years of big band 4 hrs wkly. ■ Sam Young, pres; Mike Maffia, prom mgr; Paul Michaels, progmg dir; Darrell Wilson, mus dir; Ginger Ashford, news dir; Jason Bacon, chief engr.

KZMK(FM)—Co-owned with KTAN(AM). September 1973: 100.9 mhz; 3 kw. Ant -46 ft. TL: N31 32 47 W110 16 29. Stereo. Prog sep from AM. Format: Adult contemp.

KWCD(FM)—See Bisbee.

KZMK(FM)—Listing follows KTAN(AM).

South Tucson

KMRR(AM)—Licensed to South Tucson. See Tucson.

KXEW(AM)—Licensed to South Tucson. See Tucson.

Springerville-Eager

KRVZ(AM)—June 11, 1982: 1400 khz; 1 kw-U. TL: N34 08 17 W109 16 10. Box 1069 (85938); 1367 E. Main St. (85938). (602) 333-2080. Licensee: Double Z Enterprises Inc. (acq 4-25-91; $130,000 with co-located FM; FTR 5-13-91). Net: SMN; Ariz. Net. Format: C&W. News staff one. ■ Theodore M. Barbone, pres, gen mgr & gen sls mgr; Desmond Barry, stn mgr; Pamela Schoolcraft, opns dir, mus dir & news dir; Joan Hill, pub affrs dir; Mike Malo, chief engr.

KQAZ(FM)—Co-owned with KRVZ(AM). July 15, 1984: 101.7 mhz; 3 kw. Ant -97 ft. TL: N34 08 17 W109 16 10 (CP: 1.1 kw). Stereo. Prog sep from AM. Net: AP. Format: MOR.

Sun City

KEDJ(FM)—Mar 7, 1975: 106.3 mhz; 3.5 kw. Ant 882 ft. TL: N33 36 05 W112 17 31. Stereo. 7401 W. Camelback Rd., Phoenix (85033). (602) 266-1360. FAX: (602) 846-0985. Licensee: Resource Media Inc. (acq 4-3-90; grpsl; FTR 12-25-89). Net: NBC. Rep: CMBS. Wash atty: Dow,

Lohnes & Albertson. Format: Modern rock. News staff one. ■ Steven Taslitz, pres; Kevin Curran, opns mgr; Kathy Lawrence, gen sls mgr; John Clay, progmg dir; Mary Ziehl, news dir.

Tempe

KCWW(AM)—Licensed to Tempe. See Phoenix.

KNIX-FM—See Phoenix.

KTWC(FM)—(Glendale). December 1993: 103.5 mhz; 52 kw. Ant 2,428 ft. TL: N33 35 30 W112 34 55. Stereo. 5555 N. 7th Ave., Phoenix (85013). (602) 207-3850. FAX: (602) 207-3859. Licensee: Newmountain Broadcasting Corp. Wash atty: Bechtel & Cole. ■ Don Jerome, pres; Roy Track, Rose Martinez, vps; Bob Jerome, vp engrg.

KUKQ(AM)—Apr 16, 1960: 1060 khz; 5 kw-D, 500 w-N, DA-N. TL: N33 21 43 W111 58 03. Hrs opn: 24. 1900 W. Carmen (85283). (602) 838-0400. FAX: (602) 820-8469. Licensee: Robert Fish (acq 1993; $3,500,288 with co-located FM; FTR 9-6-93). Rep: Banner. Format: Alternative music. News staff one. Target aud: 18-34 males. ■ Bob Fish, vp; Jim Seemiller, progmg dir; Del Hull, news dir; Mike Malo, chief engr.

KUPD-FM—Co-owned with KUKQ(AM). April 1960: 97.9 mhz; 100 kw. Ant 1,620 ft. TL: N33 19 57 W112 03 53. Stereo. Prog sep from AM. Wash atty: Wiley, Rein & Fielding. Format: AOR.

Thatcher

KFMM(FM)—Licensed to Thatcher. See Safford.

Tolleson

KRDS(AM)—Jan 23, 1961: 1190 khz; 5 kw-D, 250 w-N, DA-2. TL: N33 26 42 W112 15 54. Hrs opn: 24. Suite 206, 8611 N. Black Canyon Hwy., Phoenix (85021). (602) 995-9555; (602) 247-1053. FAX: (602) 995-3390. Licensee: Interstate Broadcasting Systems Inc. (group owner; acq 12-81). Wash atty: Latham & Watkins. Format: Talk, adult contemp Christian. News progmg 30 hrs wkly. Target aud: 18-44; young families. ■ Paul Toberty, pres; Mike Hamelton, gen mgr; Don Woodward, opns mgr & mus dir; Randy White, prom mgr; Dave Frazier, progmg dir; Jim Clark, chief engr. ■ Rates: $32; 32; 32; 32.

KXEG(AM)—Dec 12, 1962: 1010 khz; 1 kw-D, 250 w-N. TL: N33 26 46 W112 12 24 (CP: 7.5 kw-D, DA-D). Suite 202, 1817 N. 3rd St., Phoenix (85004). (602) 254-5001. FAX: (602) 254-5348. Licensee: Radio Property Ventures Inc. Group owner: Mid-America Gospel Radio (acq 9-15-86). Format: Christian mus & progs. ■ George Spicer, gen mgr; Jess Spurgin, stn mgr; Richard Dugan, opns mgr; Phillip W. French, natl sls mgr; Jim Clark, chief engr.

Tuba City

***KGHR(FM)**—Nov 27, 1991: 91.5 mhz; 100 w. Ant -82 ft. TL: N36 08 00 W123 13 111. Stereo. Hrs opn: 6 AM-10 PM. Box 160, Greyhills High School, Warrior Dr. (86045). (602) 283-6271, ext 177. FAX: (602) 283-6271, ext 163. Licensee: Tuba City High School Board Inc. Format: Div. country, reggae. Target aud: 12-34. Spec prog: Pub affrs 5 hrs, American Indian 20 hrs wkly. ■ Stu Schader, gen mgr.

KTBA(AM)—1980: 1050 khz; 5 kw-D, 5.2 w-N. TL: N36 07 54 W111 14 59. Box 1050, Cemetary Rd. (86045). (602) 283-5776. Licensee: Western Indian Ministries Inc. (group owner; acq 1980). Format: Relg. Target aud: 25-54; Christian families. Spec prog: Navajo & Hopi 28 hrs wkly. ■ Larry Harper, pres; Jim Maiorano, gen mgr; L. Thomas, progmg dir; Wesley Little, mus dir; Bill Hurne, chief engr.

Tucson

KCRZ(FM)—Not on air, target date unknown: 107.5 mhz; 14.5 kw. Ant 3,526 ft. TL: N32 24 54 W110 42 56. c/o Tucson Community Broadcasting Inc., 2509 N. Campbell Ave. #342 (85719). Licensee: Tucson Community Broadcasting Inc.

KCUB(AM)—August 1929: 1290 khz; 1 kw-U. TL: N32 16 37 W110 58 50 (CP: 5 kw-D). Hrs opn: 24. Box 50006 (85703). (602) 887-1000. Licensee: Rex Broadcasting Corp. (acq 6-68). Net: SMN. Rep: Katz. Format: Country. News staff one. Target aud: 25-54. ■ Jim Slone, pres & gen mgr; Jamie Slone, exec vp; Keith Samuels, gen sls mgr; Mary Slone, prom mgr; Erik Foxx, progmg dir; Phil Williams, mus dir; Dan Gates, news dir; Bob Malsbury, chief engr.

KIIM-FM—Co-owned with KCUB(AM). March 1954: 99.5 mhz; 90 kw. Ant 2,037 ft. TL: N32 14 56 W111 06 59. Stereo. Prog sep from AM. (acq 10-1-83; $2,650,000; FTR 10-10-83). ■ Jamie Slone, vp; Mary Slone, prom dir; Phil Williams, news dir.

***KFLT(AM)**—October 1976: 830 khz; 50 kw-D, 1 kw-N, DA-N. TL: N32 26 39 W111 05 27. Box 36868 (85740); Suite 102, 7355 N. Oracle (85740). (602) 797-3700; (800) 797-3700. Licensee: Family Life Broadcasting System (group owner; acq 10-86; $125,000; FTR 4-14-86). Net: Moody. Format: Relg. News staff one; news progmg 15 hrs wkly. Target aud: 25-45; Christian families. Spec prog: Sp one hr wkly. ■ Warren Bolthouse, pres; Alan Cook, stn mgr; Jon Couch, mus dir; Rob Daniels, news dir; Jim Nelson, chief engr.

KGMS(FM)—(Green Valley). Oct 21, 1990: 97.1 mhz; 1.65 kw. Ant 500 ft. TL: N31 54 39 W111 02 38 (CP: 3 kw). Stereo. Hrs opn: 24. 3222 S. Richey Ave., Tucson (85713). (602) 880-5467; (602) 790-2440. Licensee: Good Music Inc. (acq 3-11-90; $637,756; FTR 4-1-91). Wash atty: Wray Fitch. Format: Christian hit radio. News staff one. Target aud: 18-35. ■ Doug Martin, pres & mktg dir; Phil Thompson, opns mgr, progmg dir, mus dir & pub affrs dir; Lorri Puckett, gen sls mgr, rgnl sls mgr & adv dir; Wendi Myers, prom dir; Adam Colewell, news dir; Frank Fergosa, chief engr.

KGVY(AM)—(Green Valley). Sept 23, 1981: 1080 khz; 1 kw-D. TL: N31 55 34 W110 59 45. Hrs opn: 5:55 AM-sunset. Box 767 (85622); 3147 E. Pima St., Tucson (85716). (602) 625-0700. FAX: (602) 648-0275. Licensee: Crystal Sets Inc. Net: APR. Rep: Katz & Powell. Wash atty: Semmes & Semmes. Format: Big Band, MOR. News staff one; news progmg 13 hrs wkly. Target aud: 50 plus; mature, well educated, higher income, retired. Spec prog: Jazz. ■ Joe Crystall, pres, gen mgr, gen sls mgr & pub affrs dir; Martha Crystall, CFO & dev dir; Judith Williams, vp; Bonnie Crystall, opns mgr & adv dir; Bonnie Leigh, rgnl sls mgr & mktg dir; B.L. Crystall, prom dir; Lance Freeman, progmg dir; Dan Baldwin, mus dir; Mort Beach, asst mus dir; Chris Tall, news dir; Charles Sellman, chief engr. ■ Rates: $25; 25; 25; na.

KIIM-FM—Listing follows KCUB(AM).

KJYK(AM)—Jan 1957: 1490 khz; 1 kw-U. TL: N32 14 56 W110 55 29. Hrs opn: 24. 3438 N. Country Club (85716). (602) 795-1490. FAX: (602) 327-2260. Licensee: Behan Broadcasting LLC (acq 1-1-93; $4 million with co-located FM; FTR 12-14-92). Net: ABC. Rep: Major Mkt. Format: CHR. News progmg 2 hrs wkly. Target aud: 12-24; teens, young adults. ■ Dennis Behan, pres; Doug Michaelis, CFO; Laury Browning, vp & gen mgr; Kevin O'Brien, gen sls mgr; Tammy Hutchison, prom mgr; Bruce St. James, progmg mgr; Jowcol Gilchrist, asst mus dir; John Decker, chief engr.

KKLD(FM)—Co-owned with KJYK(AM). Apr 11, 1973: 94.9 mhz; 97 kw. Ant 1,952 ft. TL: N32 14 56 W111 06 59. Stereo. Hrs opn: 24. Prog sep from AM. Format: Adult contemp. Target aud: 25-54. ■ Bobby Rich, progmg mgr; Lisa McDaniel, mus dir.

KLPX(FM)—Listing follows KTKT(AM).

KMRR(AM)—(South Tucson). 1957: 1330 khz; 2 kw-D, 5 kw-N, DA-N. TL: N32 18 51 W110 50 17. Box 35367, Tucson (85740-5367). (602) 888-9292. Licensee: Golden State Broadcasting Corp. (acq 9-10-82). Net: SMN. Rep: Republic. Format: Big band. News staff one. Target aud: 35-64. ■ Bob Kellogg, progmg dir; Bill Mortimer, news dir; John Varga, chief engr.

KNST(AM)—Oct 1, 1958: 790 khz; 5 kw-D, 500 w-N. TL: N32 14 54 W111 00 30. Suite 200, 4400 E. Broadway (85711). (602) 323-9400. FAX: (602) 327-9384. Licensee: Prism Radio Partners Ltd. (group owner; acq 1-25-93; $4.5 million with co-located FM; FTR 2-15-93). Net: ABC/I, ABC TalkRadio, Moody, Wall Street. Rep: McGavren Guild. Format: News/talk, sports. News staff 5; news progmg 25 hrs wkly. Target aud: 35 plus. ■ Mike Shields, gen mgr; Bob Lee, progmg dir.

KRQQ(FM)—Co-owned with KNST(AM). Feb 1, 1971: 93.7 mhz; 91 kw. Ant 2,030 ft. TL: N32 14 56 W11 06 57. Stereo. Prog sep from AM. Format: CHR, top 40. Target aud: 18-54. ■ Mark Todd, progmg dir.

KOHT(FM)—See Marana.

KRQQ(FM)—Listing follows KNST(AM).

KSAZ(AM)—1990: 580 khz; 5 kw-D, 500 w-N, DA-N. TL: N32 17 36 W110 53 40 (CP: COL Marana; 1 kw-N. TL: N32 27 18 W111 16 54). 6831 E. Grant Rd. (85715). Licensee: Owl Broadcasting and Development Inc. (acq 4-89; $1,050,000; FTR 5-1-89). Net: ABC. ■ Phyllis Ehlinger, pres & gen mgr.

KTKT(AM)—December 1949: 990 khz; 10 kw-D, 1 kw-N, DA-2. TL: N32 15 19 W111 00 32. 1920 W. Copper St. (85745). (602) 622-6711. FAX: (602) 624-3226. Licensee: Arizona Lotus Corp. Group owner: Lotus Communications Corp. (acq 1973). Net: CNN, Unistar. Rep: D & R Radio. Format: All news. News staff one; news progmg 164 hrs wkly. Target aud: 25-54; professionals & managers. Spec prog: Black one hr, relg 2 hrs wkly. ■ Howard Kalmenson, pres; Michael Madigan, gen mgr; Tony Schavietello, gen sls mgr; Mike Rapp, progmg dir & news dir; Bob Malsbury, chief engr.

KLPX(FM)—Co-owned with KTKT(AM). June 1, 1967: 96.1 mhz; 93 kw. Ant 90 ft. TL: N32 17 23 W111 01 06 (CP: 96.5 kw, ant 1,952 ft., TL: N32 14 56 W111 06 59). Stereo. Prog sep from AM. (acq 6-79). Format: AOR. News staff one. Target aud: 18-44. ■ Larry Miles, prom mgr; Larry Snider, progmg dir & mus dir.

KTUC(AM)—July 10, 1926: 1400 khz; 1 kw-U. TL: N32 08 43 W110 53 38 (CP: TL: N32 14 56 W110 55 29). Suite 201, 2761 N. Country Club Rd. (85716). (602) 326-8788. Licensee: KTUC Inc. (acq 5-21-92). Net: CBS, NBC Talknet, MBS. Rep: Roslin. Format: All news/talk, sports. News staff 2; news progmg 15 hrs wkly. Target aud: General; college educated, upper income, politically active male and female. ■ Tom Hassey, pres & gen mgr; Tom Johnson, gen sls mgr; Jim Hassey, mktg dir & prom mgr; Mike Gabrielson, progmg dir; John Macko, news dir; Adrienne Brawley, pub affrs dir; Frank Fregoso, chief engr. ■ Rates: $40; 40; 35; 25.

KTZR(AM)—Feb 27, 1947: 1450 khz; 1 kw-U. TL: N32 12 04 W110 56 48. Stereo. 2475 N. Jackrabbit Dr. (85745). (602) 670-1450. FAX: (602) 670-1601. Licensee: Radio Pantera Inc. (acq 3-11-91; $975,000; FTR 3-25-91). Format: Spanish. ■ Heberto Garcia, CEO; Franciso Garcia, pres; Isaac Ruiz, gen mgr & stn mgr; Rufino Cantu Jr., opns dir, prom dir, progmg dir & mus dir; Felipe De Jesus-Celis, asst mus dir & pub affrs dir; Martin Del Campo, news dir; Paul Howe, chief engr.

***KUAT(AM)**—Oct 7, 1968: 1550 khz; 50 kw-D. TL: N32 22 21 W111 05 52. Univ. of Ariz. (85721). (602) 621-7548. FAX: (602) 621-9105. Licensee: Arizona Board of Regents. Net: NPR, UPI, APR. Format: News, jazz. Spec prog: Sp 5 hrs, Indian one hr wkly. ■ Don Burgess, gen mgr; Edward Kupperstein, stn mgr; Sharon McCormick, prom mgr; Steve Hahn, mus dir; Thomas Machamer, news dir; Tom Boone, chief engr.

***KUAT-FM**—May 19, 1975: 90.5 mhz; 12.5 kw. Ant 3,580 ft. TL: N32 24 55 W110 42 54. Stereo. Hrs opn: 24. Prog sep from AM. Net: APR, Concert Music Net., UPI. Format: Class. News progmg 7 hrs wkly. Target aud: 35 plus. ■ *KUAT-TV affil.

***KUAZ(FM)**—Apr 27, 1992: 89.1 mhz; 3 kw. Ant 10 ft. TL: N32 22 21 W111 05 52. Hrs opn: 5 AM- midnight. KUAT Communications Group/KUAZ Univ. of Arizona (85721). (602) 621-7548. Licensee: Arizona Board of Regents for Benefit of the Univ. of Arizona. Format: Jazz, pub affrs. News staff 4; news progmg 38 hrs wkly. Target aud: General. Spec prog: Sp 6 hrs wkly ■ Edward Kupperstein, stn mgr; Sharon McCormick, prom dir; Edward Kesterson, progmg dir; Steve Hahn, mus dir; Tom Machamer, news dir; Ron Stewart, engrg dir.

KUDO(FM)—Not on air, target date unknown: 104.1 mhz; 3 kw. Ant 46 ft. 711 N. Banff Ave. (85748). Licensee: F.E.M. Ray Inc.

KVOI(AM)—See Oro Valley.

KWFM(AM)—Aug 10, 1963: 940 khz; 5 kw-D, 1 w-N, DA-2. TL: N32 12 04 W111 01 02. 2100 N. Silverbell Rd. (85745). (602) 623-7556. FAX: (602) 729-1019. Licensee: Prism Radio Partners Ltd. (group owner; acq 1-25-93; $4 million with co-located FM; FTR 2-15-93). Rep: Major Mkt. Format: Oldies. ■ Mike Shields, gen mgr; Debbie Wagner, gen sls mgr; Sunny Turner, prom mgr; Andy Beaubien, progmg dir & mus dir; Jack Baty, news dir; Bill Croghan, chief engr.

KWFM-FM—May 18, 1970: 92.9 mhz; 90 kw. Ant 2,037 ft. TL: N32 14 56 W111 06 59. Stereo. Prog dups AM 100%.

***KXCI(FM)**—Dec 17, 1983: 91.3 mhz; 335 w. Ant 3,641 ft. TL: N32 24 54 W110 42 56. Stereo. 220 S. 4th Ave. (85701). (602) 623-1000. FAX: (602) 882-5820. Licensee: Foundation for Creative Broadcasting. Format: Jazz, eclectic. Spec prog: Black 10 hrs, C&W 6 hrs, Ger 2 hrs, American Indian one hr wkly. ■ Jow Lowrey, gen mgr; Sherry Landry, opns mgr; David Barber, progmg dir; Stephany Friez, pub affrs dir; Jim Brady, chief engr.

KXEW(AM)—(South Tucson). May 10, 1963: 1600 khz; 1 kw-U, DA-N. TL: N32 11 48 W110 59 01 (CP: 2.5 kw-D). 889 W. El Puente Ln., Tucson (85753). (602) 623-6429. FAX: (602) 622-2680 Licensee: Cactus Broadcasting (acq 11-81; $1,325,000; FTR 10-5-81). Net: CRC. Rep: Lotus. Format: Sp. News staff one; news progmg 4 hrs wkly. Target aud: 25-54; blue collar Hispanic. ■ Frank Lazarus, pres, gen mgr, gen sls mgr & prom dir; Josue Rojas, progmg dir & news dir; Joe Kirby, chief engr. ■ Rates: $50; 50; 50; 35.

KZLZ(FM)—(Kearny). Aug 31, 1991: 105.3 mhz; 50 kw. Ant 492 ft. TL: N32 49 38 W110 34 12. Stereo. Hrs opn: 24. Box 36717, Tucson (85740). (602) 322-9988. Licensee: Desert West Air Ranchers Corp. (acq 9-3-88). Wash atty: Arent, Fox, Kintner, Plotkin & Kahn. Format: Sp. Target aud: General. ■ Ted Tucker, chmn & vp.

Tusayan

KSGC(FM)—Not on air, target date unknown: 92.1 mhz; 1.6 kw. Ant 335 ft. TL: N35 58 14 W112 07 53. Box 3346, Grand Canyon (86023). (602) 638-9552. Licensee: Tusayan Broadcasting Co. ■ Jason Cook, gen mgr.

Whiteriver

***KNNB(FM)**—Sept 11, 1982: 88.1 mhz; 630 w. Ant 600 ft. TL: N33 45 47 W109 57 39. Stereo. Hrs opn: 18. Box 310, Hwy. 73, Skill Center Rd. (85941); Box 700 (85941). (602) 338-5229; (602) 338-5211. FAX: (602) 338-1744. Licensee: Apache Radio Broadcasting Corp. Format: Div, educ. News staff one; news progmg 3 hrs wkly. Target aud: 15-60. Spec prog: Apache 8 hrs wkly. ■ Phoebe L. Nez, gen mgr; Lynn Key, dev dir & chief engr; Patrick James, progmg dir; Maybelline Lee, mus dir; Udell Opah, asst mus dir.

Wickenburg

KMEO(FM)—Listing follows KTIM(AM).

KRDS-FM—Dec 2, 1983: 105.3 mhz; 6 kw. Ant -1,364 ft. TL: N34 11 32 W112 45 13. Stereo. Hrs opn: 24. Prog dups KRDS(AM) Tolleson 85%. Suite 206, 8611 N. Black Canyon Hwy., Phoenix (85021); Box 369 (85358). (602) 995-9555; (602) 247-1053. FAX: (602) 995-3390. Licensee: Interstate Broadcasting Systems Inc. (group owner; acq 12-90; FTR 10-29-90). Net: USA. Wash atty: Latham & Watkins. Format: Adult contemp, Christian. News progmg 2 hrs wkly. Target aud: 18-44; young families. ■ Paul Toberty, pres; Keith Passon, gen mgr & gen sls mgr; Mike Adams, prom mgr; Don Woodard, progmg dir; Dave Frazier, mus dir; Jim Clark, chief engr. ■ Rates: $35; 26; 35; 24.

KTIM(AM)—Jan 27, 1968: 1250 khz; 350 w-D, 202 w-N. TL: N33 55 32 W112 47 38. Hrs opn: 24. Drawer Y, 801 W. Wickenburg Way (85390). (602) 684-7804; (602) 254-6644. FAX: (602) 684-7805. Licensee: Circle S. Broadcasting Co. Inc. (acq 1990). Format: Country. ■ Harold R. Shumway, pres & gen mgr; Sharon Shumway, opns mgr & pub affrs dir; Mike Shumway, rgnl sls mgr; Cindy Rowland, prom dir & news dir. ■ Rates: $15; 15; 15; 15.

KMEO(FM)—Co-owned with KTIM(AM). January 1993: 93.7 mhz; 1.4 kw. Ant 659 ft. Hrs opn: 24. ■ Sharon Shumway, opns dir. ■ Rates: $25; 25; 25; 25.

Willcox

KHIL(AM)—Dec 2, 1959: 1250 khz; 5 kw-D, 196 w-N. TL: N32 16 00 W109 49 58. Box 1250 (85643). (602) 384-4626. Licensee: William Konopnicki (acq 9-23-92; $32,500; FTR 11-2-92). Net: USA. Format: C&W. ■ Rex K. Jensen, pres; Glenn R. Nelson, gen mgr; Jeff Hazleton, progmg dir & news dir.

KWCX(FM)—Co-owned with KHIL(AM). July 8, 1976: 98.3 mhz; 3 kw. Ant 57 ft. TL: N32 16 00 W109 49 58. Stereo. Format: CHR. ■ Candi Carper, progmg dir & news dir.

Williams

KVTF(FM)—Not on air, target date unknown: 96.7 mhz; 1 kw. Ant 804 ft. TL: N35 14 36 W112 09 55. c/o Box 36717, Tucson (85740). Licensee: Jana Tucker (group owner).

KYET(AM)—Aug 17, 1992: 1180 khz; 10 kw-U. TL: N35 15 38 W112 10 55. 138 W. Bill Williams Ave. (86046). (602) 635-5938. Licensee: Szoelloesi Broadcasting Company Inc. Format: Music of the 30s, 40s & 50s, easy lstng. ■ Crystal A. Szoelloesi, pres; Mary Ribant, gen mgr.

Arkansas

Window Rock

KHAC-FM—Not on air, target date unknown: 103.1 mhz; 3 kw. TL: N35 39 17 W109 02 01. Drawer F (86515). Licensee: Western Indian Ministries Inc.

KTNN(AM)—Feb 26, 1986: 660 khz; 50 kw-U, DA-N. TL: N35 53 41 W109 08 29. Box 2569 (86515). (602) 871-2666. FAX: (602) 871-3479. Licensee: The Navajo Nation (acq 1-86). Net: NBC, AP. Format: Country. ■ Roy Hubbell, gen mgr; Michael Moore, gen sls mgr & progmg dir; Roy Tracy, mus dir; Ernie Muruelito, chief engr.

KWRK(FM)—Co-owned with KTNN(AM). Not on air, target date unknown: 96.1 mhz; 94 kw. Ant 328 ft. TL: N35 33 36 W109 06 30. Box 308 (86515).

Winslow

KINO(AM)—Dec 18, 1962: 1230 khz; 1 kw-U. TL: N35 02 15 W110 43 00. Drawer K (86047). (602) 289-3364. FAX: (602) 289-3366. Licensee: Sunflower Communications (acq 1-15-77). Net: CBS. Format: Country. News progmg 14 hrs wkly. Target aud: General. ■ Loy Engelhardt, gen mgr; Steve Adams, gen sls mgr; John Abrahamsen, progmg dir & mus dir; Jeff Budka, pub affrs dir. ■ Rates: $7.75; 7.75; 7.75; 7.75.

Yuma

*KAWC(AM)—July 11, 1970: 1320 khz; 1 kw-D, 147 w-N. TL: N32 41 10 W114 29 38. Hrs opn: 6 AM-9 PM. Box 929 (85366); 9500 S. Ave., 8E (85366). (602) 344-7690; (602) 344-4210. FAX: (602) 344-7730. Licensee: Arizona Western College. Net: NPR. Format: Varied. Target aud: General. Spec prog: Sp 15 hrs, class 13 hrs, Black 3 hrs wkly. ■ Frank Preciado, gen mgr, progmg dir & mus dir; Mary Reynolds, prom mgr; Greg Gardner, news dir; John Gaboury, chief engr.

*KAWC-FM—Not on air, target date unknown: 88.9 mhz; 3 kw. Ant 75 ft. TL: N32 41 10 W114 29 38. Stereo. Hrs opn: 6 AM-10 PM. Prog dups AM 25%. Format: Class, jazz, news.

KBLU(AM)—March 1940: 560 khz; 1 kw-U, DA-N. TL: N32 43 25 W114 38 39. Box 5609 (85366); 1320 S. Fourth Ave. (85364). (602) 782-4355. TWX: (602) 782-7237. Licensee: Uno Broadcasting Corp. (group owner; acq 3-28-89). Net: Unistar. Rep: Torbet. Format: Oldies. News staff one; news progmg 3 hrs wkly. Target aud: 25-54; yuppies. Spec prog: Farm 6 hrs wkly. ■ Bob Tezak, pres; Steve Lewis, gen mgr; Jane Mullen, gen sls mgr; Michael Stanhope, progmg dir; Richard Davis, chief engr.

KTTI(FM)—Co-owned with KBLU(AM). Nov 6, 1970: 95.1 mhz; 25 kw. Ant 96.5 ft. TL: N32 42 42 W114 38 58 (CP: 100 kw, ant 1,256 ft., TL: N32 40 25 W114 20 12). Stereo. Prog sep from AM. Format: Country.

*KCFY(FM)—March 1992: 88.1 mhz; 3 kw. Ant 239 ft. TL: N32 38 31 W114 33 34. 2690 S. Third Ave. (85364). (602) 341-9730. FAX: (602) 341-9099. Licensee: The Voice of International Christian Evangelism Inc. Format: Adult contemp Christian. ■ Donna Myers, gen mgr.

KEZC(AM)—Dec 11, 1950: 1400 khz; 1 kw-U. TL: N32 39 06 W114 39 00. Hrs opn: 24. Box 228 (85366); 228 699 S. Ave B (85366-0228). (602) 782-4321; (602) 782-3544. FAX: (602) 343-1710. Licensee: Magnamedia Inc. (acq 3-1-71). Net: ABC/I. Rep: Katz & Powell. Wash atty: Booth, Freret & Imlay. Format: Adult contemp, news. News staff one; news progmg 60 hrs wkly. Target aud: 35 plus. Spec prog: Farm one hr wkly. ■ Jim Stowe, pres & gen mgr; Colby Girard, sls dir; Kim Johnson, news dir. ■ Rates: $30; 25; 30; 23.

KJOK(FM)—Co-owned with KEZC(AM). Aug 20, 1972: 93.1 mhz; 100 kw. Ant 80 ft. TL: N32 39 06 W114 39 00. Stereo. Hrs opn: 24. Prog sep from AM. Net: SMN. Rep: Katz & Powell. Format: CHR. News staff one; news progmg one hr wkly. Target aud: 25-49. ■ Rates: Same as AM.

KTTI(FM)—Listing follows KBLU(AM).

KYXI(FM)—Sept 5, 1986: 100.9 mhz; 3 kw. Ant 274 ft. TL: N32 38 31 W114 33 34 (CP: Ant 1,075 ft.). Stereo. 755 W. 28th St. (85364). (602) 344-4980; (602) 726-9101. FAX: (602) 344-4983. Licensee: Commonwealth Broadcasting of Northern California. Group owner: Commonwealth Broadcasting Co. Rep: Katz. Format: Adult contemp. Target aud: 25-54. ■ Dex Allen, chmn; Keith Lewis, gen mgr; Sheila Booth, sls dir; John Schofield, progmg dir; Robert Lucero, pub affrs dir; Richard Nix, chief engr. ■ Rates: $26; 26; 26; 12.

Arkansas

Arkadelphia

KDEL-FM—Listing follows KVRC(AM).

*KSWH(FM)—Sept 25, 1969: 91.1 mhz; 10 w. Ant 70 ft. TL: N34 07 32 W93 03 48. Stereo. Box 7536, Henderson State Univ. (71923). (501) 246-5511. Licensee: Henderson State University. Format: Contemp hit. Target aud: 18-35; college community. ■ Williams Atkins, gen mgr; Stuart Thomas, prom dir; Mike Cromier, progmg dir & mus dir; Genie Marrero, news dir.

KVRC(AM)—Sept 25, 1947: 1240 khz; 1 kw-U. TL: N34 06 39 W93 03 01. Box 40, 1100 S. Third (71923). (501) 246-4561. Licensee: Graham Broadcasting Inc. (acq 8-12-86; $500,000 with co-located FM; FTR 6-24-86). Format: C&W. Target aud: General. ■ Eddie Graham, pres, gen mgr, progmg dir & chief engr.

KDEL-FM—Co-owned with KVRC(AM). June 12, 1977: 100.9 mhz; 3 kw. Ant 95 ft. TL: N34 06 39 W93 03 01. Stereo. Prog sep from AM. Format: Adult contemp. ■ Eddie Graham, adv dir & vp progmg; Steve Thomas, mus dir; Jerry Westmoreland, news dir. ■ Rates: $9; 7; 8; 6.

KYXK(FM)—See Gurdon.

Ashdown

KARQ(FM)—May 25, 1985: 92.1 mhz; 2.8 kw. Ant 305 ft. TL: N33 41 56 W94 07 24. Stereo. Hrs opn: 24. Box 705, 335 Keller (71822). (501) 898-3624. FAX: (501) 898-6435. Licensee: Bunyard Broadcasting Inc. (acq 5-7-90; $380,000; FTR 5-28-90). Format: Country. News staff one; news progmg 7 hrs wkly. Target aud: General. Spec prog: Relg 4 hrs wkly. ■ Jay Bunyard, pres; Loren Hinton Jr., gen mgr, gen sls mgr & mus dir; Steve Pearce, prom mgr, progmg dir & news dir; Sonny Graham, chief engr. ■ Rates: $12; 6; 6; 6.

KHSP-FM—May 19, 1972: 103.9 mhz; 2.65 kw. Ant 354 ft. TL: N33 36 06 W94 04 38 (CP: 5.1 kw). 1323 College Dr., Texarkana, TX (75503). (903) 793-1109. FAX: (903) 794-4717. Licensee: Beat of His Heart Broadcasting (acq 8-13-90; grpsl; FTR 9-3-90). Format: Adult contemp., christian mus. News staff one. ■ Jay Calhoun, gen mgr & progmg dir; Warren Cullom, chief engr.

Augusta

KABK-FM—Licensed to Augusta. See Mayflower.

Bald Knob

KABK-FM—See Mayflower.

KAPZ(AM)—Aug 18, 1980: 710 khz; 250 w-D, DA. TL: N35 16 32 W91 33 39. Box 1488, Searcy (72143). (501) 268-0596. Licensee: John Paul Capps. Format: Contemp country. Spec prog: Farm 3 hrs wkly. ■ John Paul Capps, pres & gen mgr; Bob Allen, mus dir; Ron Price, news dir; Dale Johnson, chief engr.

KKSY(FM)—Co-owned with KAPZ(AM). Oct 15, 1984: 107.1 mhz; 3 kw. Ant 298 ft. TL: N35 17 29 W91 40 24. Dups AM 100%.

Barling

KOLX(FM)—Sept 1, 1987: 94.5 mhz; 3 kw. Ant 193.52 ft. TL: N35 19 38 W94 17 59. Stereo. Hrs opn: 24. 1912 Church St. (72923). (501) 484-9864. FAX: (501) 484-7813. Licensee: Hendren-McChristian Communications. (group owner; acq 6-9-92; $1.2 million; grpsl; FTR 6-29-92). Format: Gospel. ■ Dale Sexton, gen mgr; Michael Kaufman, gen sls mgr & progmg dir; Ken Ecklund, chief engr.

Batesville

KAAB(AM)—August 1980: 1130 khz; 1 kw-D, DA. TL: N35 16 32 W91 38 21 (CP: 20 w-N). 453 Batesville Blvd. (72501). (501) 793-4196. FAX: (501) 793-5222. Licensee: Maggie Inc. Net: Ark. Net. Rep: Broadcast Reps. Format: Relg. Spec prog: Farm 5 hrs wkly. ■ John R. Grace, pres; Gary Bridgeman, gen mgr, gen sls mgr, progmg dir & mus dir; Jack Oyler, chief engr.

KBTA(AM)—June 30, 1950: 1340 khz; 1 kw-U. TL: N35 44 40 W91 38 16. Hrs opn: 18. Box 2077 (72503); 1740 Chaney Dr. (72501). (501) 793-3861. FAX: (501) 793-4437. Licensee: White River Valley Broadcasters Inc. (acq 12-31-75). Net: ABC/E, AP. Format: Country. News staff 2; news progmg 22 hrs wkly. Target aud: 18 plus. ■ Andy Vinson, pres & gen sls mgr; Brent Wayne, progmg dir & news dir; Dale Johnson, chief engr. ■ Rates: $4.50; 4.50; 4.50; 4.50.

KZLE(FM)—Co-owned with KBTA(AM). March 3, 1982: 93.1 mhz; 100 kw. Ant 984 ft. TL: N35 53 27 W91 44 01. Stereo. Prog sep from AM. Format: Country. News progmg 3 hrs wkly. Target aud: 24 plus. ■ Andy Vinson, opns mgr; Chris Knight, prom mgr; David Paul, mus dir. ■ Rates: $12; 12; 12; 12.

Beebe

KPIK(FM)—June 22, 1991: 101.5 mhz; 6 kw. Ant 328 ft. TL: N35 11 26 W91 54 45. Hrs opn: 24. 1206 N. Main (72012). (501) 882-1015; (501) 882-3331. FAX: (501) 882-3332. Licensee: KPIK Communications Inc. Format: Adult contemp. News progmg 3 hrs wkly. Target aud: 25-54. Spec prog: Sports, gospel. ■ Judi Davis, CEO & gen mgr; Ron Davis, chief engr. ■ Rates: $8; 7; 8; 6.

Bella Vista

KBVA(FM)—November 1991: 106.5 mhz; 37 kw. Ant 567 ft. TL: N36 18 21 W94 27 29. Rt. 5, Hwy. 72 E., Gravette (72736). (800) 467-1065. FAX: (501) 787-6116. Licensee: Gayla Joy Hendren. Format: Variety. ■ Gayla Joy Hendren, pres & gen mgr.

KJEM(AM)—See Bentonville-Bella Vista.

Bellefonte

KNWA(AM)—1986: 1600 khz; 5 kw-D, 50 w-N. TL: N36 14 49 W93 05 06. Box 850, Harrison (72601). (501) 741-1402. FAX: (501) 741-9702. Licensee: Harrison Radio Station Inc. Net: ABC/C. Format: Rock. ■ Tom Arnold, gen mgr; Allan Scott, progmg dir; Glenn Rowe, chief engr.

Benton

KEWI(AM)—June 26, 1953: 690 khz; 250 w-D, 73 w-N. TL: N34 31 57 W92 34 16. Hrs opn: 6 AM-midnight. Box 1169, 115 West South (72015). (501) 778-6677; (501) 778-5394. Licensee: Bernard Bottenberg (acq 8-26-92; $7,500; FTR 9-14-92). Net: USA, UPI. Format: Talk, news, sports. News staff one; news progmg 10 hrs wkly. Target aud: 25-54 plus; all income levels, male & female. ■ Bernard Bottenberg, gen mgr, stn mgr & gen sls mgr; Charlie Bottenberg, opns mgr & chief engr; Ron Stailey, prom dir, progmg dir, news dir & pub affrs dir. ■ Rates: $14; 12; 10; 7.

KGKO(AM)—April 1963: 850 khz; 1 kw-D. TL: N34 30 30 W92 32 42. 202 E. Cross (72015). (501) 778-8257. FAX: (501) 778-1073. Licensee: Bridges Broadcasting Service (acq 1-10-67). Net: CNN, Unistar. Format: MOR, adult standards. Target aud: 45 plus. ■ Preston Bridges, pres, gen mgr, stn mgr & gen sls mgr; Jeff Hunt, news dir. ■ Rates: $15; 15; 15; na.

KMVK(FM)—Jan 1, 1979: 106.7 mhz; 16 kw. Ant 866 ft. Stereo. Hrs opn: 24. 8114 Cantrell Rd., Little Rock (72207); Box 76, Little Rock (72203-0096). (501) 227-9696; (501) 433-1993. FAX: (501) 228-9547. Licensee: Southern Skies Corp. (group owner; acq 6-8-93; $1.125 million; FTR 6-28-93). Rep: Katz. Wash atty: Miller & Miller. Format: Young country. Target aud: 18-34. ■ Jerry Atchley, chmn & pres; Jay Werth, gen mgr; Joanne Scott, vp opns; Paul Massey, sls dir; Michelle Carney, prom dir; Ken Wall, progmg dir & mus dir; Tom Rusk, chief engr.

Bentonville

KAMO(AM)—See Rogers.

KAMO-FM—See Rogers.

KESE(FM)—See Seligman, Mo.

Stations in the U.S. — Arkansas

KOLZ(FM)—Nov 7, 1983: 98.3 mhz; 10.5 kw. Ant 339 ft. TL: N36 23 11 W94 10 07 (CP: Ant 499 ft.). Stereo. Hrs opn: 24. Box 878, 1780 Holly St., Fayetteville (72702). (501) 521-5566. FAX: (501) 521-0751. Licensee: Demaree Media Inc. (group owner; acq 6-23-86; $425,000; FTR 2-12-90). Format: Oldies. Target aud: 25-54. Spec prog: Class 2 hrs wkly. ■ Bret Hash, gen mgr.

Bentonville-Bella Vista

KJEM(AM)—Feb 5, 1979: 1190 khz; 2.5 kw-D. TL: N36 23 17 W94 11 42. Hrs opn: Sunrise-sunset. 216 N. Main St. (72712). (501) 273-9039. Licensee: Jem Broadcasting Co. Inc. Net: USA. Format: Big band, relg. News staff one; news progmg 7 hrs wkly. Target aud: 35 plus. ■ Elvis L. Moody, pres & gen mgr.

Berryville

KTHS(AM)—February 1958: 1480 khz; 5 kw-D, 64 w-N. TL: N36 21 42 W93 33 40. Hrs opn: 6 AM-8:30 PM. Box 191, No.1 Radio Dr. (72616). (501) 423-2147. FAX: (501) 423-2146. Licensee: KTHS/KSCC Inc. (acq 7-2-82). Net: ABC/E. Format: Modern country. Spec prog: Farm 15 hrs wkly. ■ Tom Earls, pres & gen mgr; Carroll Autry, gen sls mgr; Jim Earls, progmg dir; Linda Boyer, news dir.

KTHS-FM—Dec 19, 1974: 107.1 mhz; 3.6 kw. Ant 627 ft. TL: N36 20 45 W93 29 17. Stereo. Hrs opn: 24. Dups AM 100%. News staff one; news progmg 10 hrs wkly. Target aud: General. ■ Jim Earls, vp & progmg dir.

Blytheville

KLCN(AM)—1922: 910 khz; 5 kw-D, 85 w-N. TL: N35 55 27 W89 52 18. Box 989 (72316). (501) 762-2093. FAX: (501) 703-8459. Licensee: Sudbury Services Inc. Group owner: Sudbury Svcs Inc. & Newport Broadcasting Co. Format: Div. ■ Harold L. Sudbury Jr., pres; Ed White, stn mgr; Fred Chamber, gen sls mgr.

KHLS(FM)—Co-owned with KLCN(AM). 1948: 96.3 mhz; 100 kw. Ant 450 ft. TL: N35 55 27 W89 52 18 (CP: Ant 351 ft., TL: N35 38 27 W89 56 54). Stereo. Prog sep from AM. Format: C&W.

Booneville

KEZU(FM)—Nov 1, 1981: 104.7 mhz; 50 kw. Ant 492 ft. TL: N35 11 01 W94 07 44. Stereo. Suite 105, 9001 Rogers Ave., Fort Smith (72903). (501) 452-0105. FAX: (501) 484-7808. Licensee: Westark Broadcasting Co. (acq 1-23-92). Format: EZ listing/light AC. News staff one; news progmg 10 hrs wkly. Target aud: 34 plus. Spec prog: Jazz 2 hrs, relg 5 hrs wkly. ■ Eldon Coffman, pres; Larry Tate, gen mgr; Judy Sorrell, gen sls mgr; Dave Earnhart, progmg mgr.

Brinkley

KBRI(AM)—Oct 25, 1959: 1570 khz; 250 w-D, 44 w-N. TL: N34 52 02 W91 12 04. Hrs opn: 6 AM-10 PM. Box 44, Hwy. 70 W. (72021). (501) 734-1570. Licensee: Tri-Country Broadcasting. Net: AP; Ark. Net. Format: Adult contemp. News staff one. Target aud: General. ■ John E. Harper, gen mgr; Joey Rodgers, progmg dir; Frances Harper, news dir; Ray Loewy, chief engr. ■ Rates: $5.59; 5.59; 5.59; na.

KQMC-FM—Co-owned with KBRI(AM). October 1969: 102.3 mhz; 3 kw. Ant 190 ft. TL: N34 52 02 W91 12 04. Stereo. Dups AM 15%. Format: Great American country. ■ Rates: Same as AM.

Cabot

KYXZ(AM)—Nov 16, 1980: 1350 khz; 2.5 kw-D, 73 w-N. TL: N34 59 59 W92 01 41. Box 724, Capitol City Radio Center (72023-0724). (501) 843-5661. FAX: (501) 843-8189. Licensee: Hall Broadcasting Inc. (acq 9-23-91; $100,000 with co-located FM; FTR 10-14-91). Net: CBN. Wash atty: Cohn & Marks. Format: Contemp Christian. Target aud: 18-49. ■ Phil Hall, chmn, pres & gen mgr; Robert Tindle, opns dir & vp engrg; Christy Hall, vp sls; Nicole Beam, progmg dir; Dave McKaye, news dir.

KLPQ(FM)—Co-owned with KYXZ(AM). May 1993: 102.5 mhz; 3 kw. Ant 328 ft. TL: N34 55 22 W92 00 32. Stereo. Hrs opn: 24. Prog sep from AM. Suite 1025, 6929 JFK Blvd., Little Rock (72116). Format: Classic rock. Target aud: 25-49. ■ Christy Hall, exec vp.

Camden

KAMD(AM)—June 19, 1946: 910 khz; 5 kw-D, 500 w-N, DA-2. TL: N33 36 00 W92 49 07 (CP: 1 kw-N, 125 w-N). Box 957 (71701). (501) 836-5091. FAX: (501) 836-8196. Licensee: Camden Radio Inc. Net: MBS. Format: C&W. News staff one. Target aud: 18 plus. Spec prog: Black 5 hrs, gospel 19 hrs wkly. ■ Walter Hussman Jr., pres; Bill Snearly, stn mgr; Greg Arnold, mus dir & news dir. ■ Rates: $8.50; 8.50; 8.50; 6.50.

KWEH(FM)—Co-owned with KAMD. Dec 1, 1968: 97.1 mhz; 39 kw. Ant 190 ft. TL: N33 35 13 W92 49 42. Stereo. Dups AM 100%. 113 Madison St. (71701). (501) 836-8197.

*KCAC(FM)—June 11, 1990: 89.5 mhz; 250 w. Ant 161 ft. TL: N33 34 31 W92 49 55. Stereo. Hrs opn: 6 AM-2 PM. 327 Stewart St. (71701). (501) 836-5289; (501) 836-4917. Licensee: Camden Career Center. Net: ABC. Wash atty: Cohn & Marks. Format: Top-40. Target aud: 25 & under. ■ Steve Taylor, gen mgr & engrg dir; Todd Parker, opns mgr & progmg dir; Jake Spivey, sls dir & adv dir; Jenny Smith, prom mgr; Dianna Harcrow, mus dir. ■ Rates: $5; 5; 5; 5.

KCXY(FM)—Sept 28, 1987: 95.3 mhz; 1 kw. Ant 500 ft. TL: N33 30 14 W92 48 38. Stereo. Hrs opn: 24. Box 956, 133 Washington S.W. (71701). (501) 836-9567. FAX: (501) 836-9500. Licensee: Y95 Radio Inc. Net: ABC/D; Ark. Radio Net. Wash atty: Mark Fields. Format: C&W. News staff one; news progmg 15 hrs wkly. Target aud: 25-54. ■ Gary D. Terrell, pres & gen mgr; Craig Taylor Dale, opns mgr, prom mgr & progmg dir; Monte Lyons, Patt Free-Walker, gen sls mgrs; Kevin Cunningham, mus dir; Susan Graham, news dir; Ray Lowey, chief engr. ■ Rates: $9.25; 8.50; 9.25; 8.

KOSG(AM)—Aug 8, 1963: 1450 khz; 1 kw-U. TL: N33 33 49 W92 50 37. 214 Van Buren St. (71701). (501) 836-8200. FAX: (501) 836-8400. Licensee: Hi-Top Broadcasting Inc. (acq 6-29-92; $10; FTR 7-20-92). ■ J. Howard Rogers, pres; Fred Hill, gen mgr.

KWEH(FM)—Listing follows KAMD.

Cave City

*KZIG(FM)—Jan 1, 1981: 89.9 mhz; 3.3 kw. Ant 351 ft. TL: N35 57 07 W91 32 58. Stereo. Box 190, Hwy. 167 (72521). (501) 283-5331. FAX: (501) 283-5394. Licensee: Cave City Schools. Net: USA. Format: Relg, educ, div. News staff one; news progmg 15 hrs wkly. Target aud: General. ■ Becky Sisk, gen mgr; Dave Fisher, progmg dir; Dale Johnson, chief engr.

Cherokee Village

KFCM(FM)—May 18, 1981: 100.9 mhz; 3 kw. Ant 298 ft. TL: N36 16 29 W91 30 18. Stereo. Hrs opn: 24. Box 909, FM 101 Rd., Hardy (72525). (501) 856-3249. Licensee: KFCM Inc. (acq 11-29-89; $174,500; FTR 12-18-89). Net: CBS. Format: Nostalgia, news. News staff 3; news progmg 25 hrs wkly. Target aud: 35 plus. ■ James Bragg, pres & gen mgr; Ruth Bragg, gen sls mgr; Beth McEntire, adv dir; Ken Loggains, progmg dir & news dir; Dale Johnson, chief engr. ■ Rates: $12; 10; 11; 8.

Clarendon

KXRC(FM)—Not on air, target date unknown: 107.3 mhz; 3 kw. Ant 321 ft. TL: N34 37 19 W91 22 46. 4004 Clay Dr., Jonesboro (72401). Licensee: B&H Broadcasting Co.

Clarksville

*KGMR(FM)—August 1985: 91.7 mhz; 380 w. Ant -39 ft. TL: N35 28 02 W93 31 10. 2246 W. Main (72830). (501) 754-7976. FAX: (501) 754-7978. Licensee: Clarksville Educational Broadcasting Foundation. Net: USA. Format: Christian mus, news. ■ Jack E. Glaze, gen mgr.

KLYR(AM)—Mar 18, 1957: 1360 khz; 500 w-D, 98 w-N. TL: N35 28 21 W93 29 28. Hrs opn: 16. Box 188 (72830). (501) 754-3092. Licensee: Randall P. Forrester. (acq 11-81; $31,816; FTR 11-9-81). Format: C&W. News progmg 12 hrs wkly. Target aud: General. Spec prog: Relg 8 hrs wkly. ■ Randy Forrester, gen mgr; Jay Davis, gen sls mgr; Myron Been, mus dir; Jim Alexander, chief engr. ■ Rates: $12.14; 12.14; 12.14; 7.43.

KLYR-FM—1974: 92.7 mhz; 3 kw. Ant 292 ft. TL: N35 29 38 W93 32 21. Hrs opn: 16. Dups AM 90%. Target aud: General. ■ Rates: Same as AM.

KXIO(FM)—April 1991: 106.9 mhz; 5.9 kw. Ant 112 ft. TL: N35 33 07 W93 24 33. Box 37 (72830). (501) 754-2076. Licensee: J.L. Richardson. Format: Adult contemp. ■ J. L. Richardson (owner), pres.

LAUREN A. COLBY
301-663-1086
COMMUNICATIONS ATTORNEY
Special Attention to Difficult Cases

Clinton

KGFL(AM)—Oct 1, 1977: 1110 khz; 5 kw-D. TL: N35 33 30 W92 27 32. Box 33 (72031). (501) 745-4474. FAX: (501) 745-5160. Licensee: Weber-King Radio. Format: News/talk. News staff one; news progmg 3 hrs wkly. Target aud: 35 plus.

KHPQ(FM)—Co-owned with KGFL(AM). Dec 23, 1982: 92.1 mhz; 3 kw. Ant 571 ft. TL: N35 40 44 W92 30 30. Stereo. Dups AM 100%. Net: Jones Satellite Audio. ■ Sid King, gen mgr.

Conway

KCON(AM)—Nov 13, 1950: 1230 khz; 1 kw-U. TL: N35 04 23 W92 27 36. Box 1406 (72033). (501) 327-6032. FAX: (501) 327-6033. Licensee: KCON Broadcasting Co. (acq 8-1-80). Net: ABC/D; Arkansas. Rep: Broadcast Reps. Format: Adult contemp. ■ Madge W. Clayton, pres; Monty Rowell, gen mgr; Mark Mauney, gen sls mgr; Mike Woodrum, news dir; Dan Wynn, chief engr.

KFCA(AM)—May 26, 1961: 1330 khz; 500 w-D, 64 w-N. TL: N35 06 00 W92 26 41. Box 1266 (72032). (501) 327-6611. Licensee: Creative Media Inc. (acq 6-3-82; $205,000; FTR 6-21-82). Net: NBC. Format: Country. Spec prog: Farm 6 hrs wkly. ■ Michael D. Harrison, pres, gen mgr & progmg dir; Elaine Harrison, prom mgr; Tom Rusk, chief engr.

KTOD-FM—Co-owned with KFCA(AM). April 1984: 92.7 mhz; 3 kw. Ant 282 ft. TL: N35 06 46 W92 24 42. Dups AM 75%. Net: MBS.

*KHDX(FM)—May 1973: 93.1 mhz; 8 w. Ant 59 ft. TL: N35 06 01 W92 26 29. Stereo. Hendrix College (72032). (501) 450-1312. FAX: (501) 450-1200. Licensee: Hendrix College. Net: Ark. Net. Format: Div, progsv, jazz. ■ Allison Lightwine, gen mgr; Eduardo Akins, progmg dir.

KMJX(FM)—June 1, 1967: 79 kw. Ant 1,053 ft. TL: N34 47 53 W92 29 33. Stereo. Hrs opn: 24. 11011 Anderson Dr., Little Rock (72212). (501) 224-6500. FAX: (501) 224-6596. Licensee: Magic Broadcasting of Little Rock Inc. (acq 12-31-90; $3.15 million). Net: ABC/R. Wash atty: Arent, Fox, Kintner, Plotkin & Kahn. Format: Contemp. News staff one; news progmg 3 hrs wkly. Target aud: 18-49. ■ Richard B. Booth, pres & gen mgr; John Signaigo, gen sls mgr; Sharon Anderson, prom mgr; Tom Wood, progmg dir; David Allen Ross, mus dir; Bill Downs, news dir; Tom Rusk, chief engr.

KTOD-FM—Listing follows KFCA(AM).

*KUCA(FM)—Oct 10, 1966: 91.3 mhz; 5 kw. Ant 346 ft. TL: N35 02 55 W92 27 49. Hrs opn: 5 AM-midnight. Univ. of Central Arkansas (72035). (501) 450-5555. Licensee: University of Central Arkansas. Format: News, info, children's progmg. News staff one; news progmg 35 hrs wkly. Target aud: 35 plus; post graduates, educated adults. Spec prog: Class 4 hrs, radio theater 6 hrs, acoustic 12 hrs wkly. ■ Shawn Fulper-Smith, progmg dir; Richard Franck, engrg dir.

Corning

KCCB(AM)—Feb 19, 1959: 1260 khz; 1 kw-D. TL: N36 24 00 W90 35 05. Box 398, 711 Pearl (72422). (501) 857-6646. Licensee: Shields-Adkins Broadcasting Inc. (acq 11-10-93; $186,670 with co-located FM; FTR 11-29-93). Rep: Keystone (unwired net). Format: Country. News progmg 20 hrs wkly. Target aud: General. ■ Eulis W. Cochran, pres; Bob Cochran, gen mgr; Doll Cochran, progmg dir; Terri Lee, mus dir; Scott Key, news dir; Larry Caldwell, chief engr.

KBKG(FM)—Co-owned with KCCB(AM). Sept 15, 1983: 93.5 mhz; 3 kw. Ant 138 ft. TL: N36 24 00 W90 35 05. Stereo. Prog sep from AM. Net: ABC. Format: Adult contemp, C&W. ■ Eulis W. Cochran, CEO; Bob Cochran, gen sls mgr; Doll Cochran, vp progmg. ■ Rates: $3; 3; 3; 3.

Crossett

KAGH(AM)—January 1951: 800 khz; 250 w-D. TL: N33 08 05 W91 56 49. Box 697 (71635). (501) 364-2181. Licensee: Ashley County Broadcasters Inc. (acq 8-1-69). Net: Ark. Net. Format: Country. ■ W. Barry Medlin, pres, gen mgr & chief engr; Russ Miller, progmg; Charlie Park, news dir.

KAGH-FM—Mar 16, 1967: 104.9 mhz; 3 kw. Ant 275 ft. TL: N33 08 05 W91 56 49. Dups AM 80%.

Danville

KDYC(FM)—Not on air, target date unknown: 105.5 mhz; 1.9 kw. Ant 581 ft. Apt. 425, 6726 S. Peoria, Tulsa, OK (74136). Licensee: Susan Lynn Adair.

Dardanelle

KCAB(AM)—Mar 24, 1964: 980 khz; 5 kw-D. TL: N35 13 02 W93 10 08. Box 2350, Russellville (72801). (501) 968-6816. FAX: (501) 968-2946. Licensee: Johnson Communications Inc. (acq 5-21-93; $270,000 with co-located FM; FTR 6-14-93). ■ Dewey Johnson, pres.

KWKK(FM)—Jan 26, 1966: 102.3 mhz; 200 w. Ant 1,227 ft. TL: N35 13 41 W93 15 20.

KWXT(AM)—October 1987: 1490 khz; 1 kw-U. TL: N35 13 08 W93 07 38. 701 E. Main, Russellville (72801). (501) 968-1337. FAX: (501) 968-1337. Licensee: George V. Domerese (acq 9-2-92; $60,000; FTR 9-21-92). Format: Country. ■ Tim Domerese, gen mgr.

De Queen

KDQN(AM)—Aug 1, 1956: 1390 khz; 500 w-D. TL: N34 01 57 W94 19 43. Box 311 (71832). (501) 642-2446. FAX: (501) 642-2442. Licensee: Jay W. Bunyard, Anne W. Bunyard (acq 6-15-83; $475,000 with co-located FM; FTR 7-4-83). Net: Ark. Net. Format: Country. ■ Jay Bunyard, pres & gen mgr; Steve Cole, gen sls mgr; Gerald Nix, progmg dir; Sonny Grams, chief engr.

KDQN-FM—Oct 6, 1978: 92.7 mhz; 3 kw. Ant 220 ft. TL: N34 01 57 W94 19 43. Stereo. Dups AM 40%.

Dermott

KGPL(AM)—Jan 1, 1980: 1110 khz; 10 kw-D, DA. TL: N33 31 32 W91 27 35. Stereo. 537 W. Gaines, Monticello (71655). (501) 367-8528. FAX: (501) 367-8527. Licensee: KXSA Radio Inc. Net: ABC/D; Ark. Net. Format: Contemp country. ■ P.Q. Gardner, pres & gen mgr; Ed Davis, gen sls mgr; Ross Carpenter, progmg mgr & mus dir; Norman Mason, chief engr.

KXSA-FM—Co-owned with KGPL(AM). Aug 24, 1924: 103.1 mhz; 5.5 kw. Ant 328 ft. TL: N33 31 56 W91 34 28. Dups AM 100%.

Dumas

KDDA(AM)—April 21, 1966: 1560 khz; 500 w-D. TL: N33 53 27 W91 31 38. Box 720, Highway 54 W. (71639). (501) 382-5606. FAX: (501) 382-6369. Licensee: Alan W. Eastham, Mrs. T.W. Eastham & Thomas O. Graves. Net: ABC/D, Unistar; Ark. Radio Net. Format: Country. News staff one. Target aud: 25-49. Spec prog: Black 5 hrs, farm 6 hrs wkly. ■ Alan W. Eastham, pres; Craig Eastham, gen mgr; Hal Gaves, mus dir; Thomas Graves, chief engr. ■ Rates: $7; 7; 7; 7.

KXFE(FM)—Co-owned with KDDA(AM). Sept 1, 1980: 107.1 mhz; 2.75 kw. Ant 160 ft. TL: N33 53 27 W91 31 38 (CP: 106.9 mhz, 25 kw, and 268 ft.). Stereo. ■ Rates: Same as AM.

El Dorado

*KBSA(FM)—December 1987: 90.9 mhz; 3 kw. Ant 581 ft. TL: N33 16 19 W92 42 12. One University Place, Shreveport, LA (71115). (800) 552-8502. Licensee: Board of Supervisors of Louisiana State Univ. and A&M College. Format: Class, jazz & news. ■ Catherine Fraser, gen mgr; Jean Hardman, mktg dir; Mary Masten, vp progmg; Rod Mathew, chief engr.

KBYB(FM)—May 12, 1984: 96.1 mhz; 100 kw. Ant 288 ft. TL: N33 16 51 W92 39 25. Stereo. Hrs opn: 24. Box 1624, 115 Christian Dr. (71731). (501) 862-9696. FAX: (501) 862-7727. Licensee: KIXK Inc. (acq 3-18-86). Format: Country. News staff one; news progmg 2 hrs wkly. Target aud: 18-34. ■ Charles R. Shinn, pres; Jim Lewis, stn mgr; Patt Free-Walker, sls dir; Craig Taylor Dale, prom dir & progmg dir; Kevin Cunningham, mus dir; Susan Graham, news dir; Gary Terrell, chief engr. ■ Rates: $13; 11; 13; 9.

KDMS(AM)—May 8, 1950: 1290 khz; 5 kw-D, 106 w-N. TL: N33 12 27 W92 41 10. 1904 W. Hillsboro (71730). (501) 863-5121. FAX: (501) 863-6221. Licensee: El Dorado Broadcasting Co. (acq 7-8-87; $950,000 with co-located FM; FTR 4-6-87). Net: SMN. Format: Golden oldies. ■ Rosh Partridge, pres & gen mgr; Brandt Heisner, opns mgr; Rick Finch, gen sls mgr; Kevin Davis, progmg dir; Shelly Garner, news dir.

KLBQ(FM)—Co-owned with KDMS(AM). Dec 23, 1963: 99.3 mhz; 2.95 kw. Ant 298 ft. TL: N33 12 27 W92 41 10 (CP: 98.7 mhz, 14 kw). Stereo. Prog sep from AM. Net: ABC/C. Format: Top-40, adult contemp. ■ Norm Mason, chief engr.

KELD(AM)—Oct 17, 1935: 1400 khz; 1 kw-U. TL: N33 12 43 W92 39 48. Stereo. Hrs opn: 24. 2525 Northwest Ave. (71730). (501) 863-6127; (501) 862-1400. FAX: (501) 863-4555. Licensee: Noalmark Broadcasting Corp. (group owner; acq 7-73). Net: Daynet, CNN; Ark. Radio Net. Rep: Target; Broadcast Reps Inc. Format: News/talk. News staff one; news progmg 20 hrs wkly. Target aud: General. ■ William C. Nolan Jr., pres; Edwin Anderson, exec vp; Bob Parks, vp & gen mgr; Dan Murphy, opns dir; Leanne Arndt, sls dir; Don Travis, news dir. ■ Rates: $8; 8; 8; 8.

KIXB(FM)—Co-owned with KELD(AM). Dec 9, 1963: 103.1 mhz; 100 kw. Ant 571 ft. TL: N33 13 20 W92 55 28. Stereo. Hrs opn: 24. Prog sep from AM. (501) 864-0103. Format: Country. News progmg 15 hrs wkly. Target aud: 18-54. ■ William Nolan, CEO; Dan Murphy, progmg dir; J.B. Billingly, mus dir. ■ Rates: $13; 13; 13; 13.

KISQ(FM)—Sept 29, 1993: 93.3 mhz; 8.5 kw. Ant 426 ft. TL: N33 13 46 W92 37 32. Stereo. Hrs opn: 24. 2525 Northwest Ave. (71730). (501) 864-0093. FAX: (501) 863-4555. Licensee: Noalmark Broadcasting Corp. (group owner; acq 1-8-93; $10,000; FTR 3-29-93). Rep: Target Radio. Format: CHR. News staff one; news progmg 15 hrs wkly. Target aud: General. ■ William C. Nolan, pres; Edwin Anderson, exec vp; Bob Parks, vp & gen mgr; Dan Murphy, opns dir & progmg dir; Leanne Arndt, sls dir; John West, mus dir. ■ Rates: $11.80; 11.80; 11.80; 11.80.

KIXB(FM)—Listing follows KELD(AM).

KLBQ(FM)—Listing follows KDMS(AM).

England

KLRA(AM)—Aug 31, 1979: 1530 khz; 250 w-D. TL: N34 32 45 W91 59 04 (CP: COL Scott, 500 w-D). Box 218 (72046). (501) 378-0965. Licensee: Diamond State Broadcasting Inc. Net: Ark. Net., Prog Farm. Format: Contemp country. Spec prog: Farm 5 hrs wkly. ■ Charlotte Price, pres, gen mgr & gen sls mgr; Vic Hart, prom mgr & mus dir; Calvin Rollings, chief engr.

KLRA-FM—Sept 26, 1988: 96.5 mhz; 3 kw. Ant 148 ft. TL: N34 32 45 W91 59 04 (CP: 5 kw). Dups AM 95%.

Eudora

KRVF(FM)—Not on air, target date unknown: 101.5 mhz; 3 kw. Ant 328 ft. TL: N33 10 28 W91 16 45. Box 865, Lake Providence, LA (71254). Licensee: Eudora Broadcasters Inc.

Eureka Springs

KTCN(FM)—May 13, 1985: 100.9 mhz; 1.1 kw. Ant 531 ft. TL: N36 22 49 W93 44 53. Stereo. Hrs opn: 6 AM-10 PM. Box 81, Hwy 23 S. (72632). (501) 253-9079. FAX: (501) 253-9863. Licensee: New Life Evangelistic Center Inc. (acq 11-23-92; $90,000; FTR 12-14-92). Net: ABC/D; Arkansas. Format: Relg. News staff one; news progmg 20 hrs wkly. Target aud: 35 plus; upper income and retired. Spec prog: Class 10 hrs, 50/60s 2 hrs wkly. ■ Larry Rice, pres, progmg dir & mus dir; Mike Conway, gen mgr & gen sls mgr; Chris Rice, prom mgr; Bob Hickman, chief engr. ■ Rates: $12; 11; 12; 11.

Fairfield Bay

KFFB(FM)—Dec 31, 1981: 106.1 mhz; 50 kw. Ant 500 ft. TL: N35 45 22 W92 14 49. Stereo. Hrs opn: 24. Box 1050, 548 Dave Creek Pkwy. (72088). (501) 884-6812; (800) 356-5106. FAX: (501) 884-6814. Licensee: Robert & Rosemary Holiday (acq 8-12-85; $475,000; FTR 6-3-85). Net: SMN. Wash atty: Haley, Bader & Potts. Format: MOR. News staff one; news progmg 8 hrs wkly. Target aud: 35 plus; middle & upper-middle class. ■ Robert W. Holiday, pres; Rosemary Holiday, gen mgr.

Farmington

KFAY(AM)—Dec 15, 1946: 1030 khz; 10 kw-D, 1 kw-N, DA-2. TL: N36 06 34 W94 10 59. Stereo. Hrs opn: 24. Box 878, 1780 Holly St., Fayetteville (72703). (501) 442-9859. FAX: (501) 521-0151. Licensee: Demaree Media Inc., debtor in possession (group owner; acq 9-5-75). Net: AP. Rep: Banner. Format: News/talk. News staff 6; news progmg 20 hrs wkly. Target aud: 25-64; general. ■ L. Patrick Demaree, pres; Brett Hash, gen mgr; Stephen Johns, gen sls mgr; Kelly Lewis, prom mgr; Matt Fincher, progmg dir & mus dir; Ken Ecklund, vp engrg; Les Carter, chief engr. ■ Rates: $25; 24; 25; 22.

Fayetteville

*KBHG(FM)—Not on air, target date unknown: 89.3 mhz; 5 kw. Ant 1,155 ft. 1150 W. King St., Cocoa, FL (32922). Licensee: National Christian Network Inc.

KEZA(FM)—Sept 6, 1983: 107.9 mhz; 99 kw. Ant 1,259 ft. TL: N35 51 12 W94 01 33. Stereo. Suite 600, First Place, 112 W. Center St., Springdale (72764). (501) 750-4108. FAX: (501) 751-8636. Licensee: Communications Corp. (group owner). Format: Adult contemp. Target aud: 25-54. Spec prog: Jazz, oldies. ■ Thomas Galloway, pres; Dale Daniels, gen mgr; Susan Parker, gen sls mgr; Chip Arledge, progmg dir; Rich Kelly, mus dir; Chuck Barrett, news dir; Doyle Garner, chief engr. ■ Rates: $30; 35; 30; 20.

KKEG(FM)—Oct 16, 1964: 92.1 mhz; 1.15 kw. Ant 459 ft. TL: N36 03 55 W94 12 24 (CP: 26.5 kw, ant 328 ft.). Stereo. Hrs opn: 24. Box 878, 1780 Holly St. (72703). (501) 521-5566. FAX: (501) 521-0751. Licensee: Demaree Media Inc. (group owner; acq 2-2-76). Net: AP. Rep: Roslin. Format: AOR, classic rock. News staff one. Target aud: 18-49. ■ L. Patrick Demaree, pres; Brett Hash, vp; Marsha Johnson, stn mgr; Steve Johns, gen sls mgr; Matt Fincher, progmg dir; Les Carter, chief engr. ■ Rates: $30; 28; 30; 24.

KKIX(FM)—Oct 1, 1966: 103.9 mhz; 100 kw. Ant 510 ft. TL: N36 01 17 W94 13 04. Stereo. Hrs opn: 24. Box 104 (72702). (501) 521-0104. Licensee: Noalmark Broadcasting Corp. (group owner; acq 5-1-83; $475,500; FTR 5-2-83). Rep: Katz. Wash atty: Leventhal, Senter & Lerman. Format: Country. News staff 2; news progmg 3 hrs wkly. Target aud: 25-54. ■ Doug Whitman, sr vp & gen mgr; Jeff Wood, gen sls mgr; Leny Fox, progmg dir; Jess Smith, news dir; Zeb Huffmaster, chief engr. ■ Rates: $150; 125; 135; 90.

KOFC(AM)—June 10, 1957: 1250 khz; 1 kw-D, 62 w-N. TL: N36 04 29 W94 11 00. Hrs opn: 17. Box 550 (72702). (501) 443-2900. FAX: (501) 443-2978. Licensee: William B. Disney (acq 12-11-87; $95,000; FTR 6-22-87). Net: USA. Format: Relg. News progmg 8 hrs wkly. Target aud: 35 plus; traditional Christian families. ■ William B. Disney, pres; Robert Johnson, opns mgr & chief engr; Stan Hines, gen sls mgr & news dir; Jeff Clandy, progmg dir & mus dir. ■ Rates: $6; 5; 5; 4.

*KUAF(FM)—Jan 15, 1973: 91.3 mhz; 60 kw. Ant 1,105 ft. TL: N35 51 12 W94 01 33. Stereo. Hrs opn: 24. 747 W. Dickson St. No. 2 (72701-5023). (501) 575-2556. FAX: (501) 575-7575. Licensee: Board of Trustees, Univ. of Arkansas. Net: NPR. Format: News, class, jazz. News staff one. Spec prog: Folk 4 hrs, big band 2 hrs wkly. ■ Rick Stockdell, gen mgr; P.J. Robowski, mus dir; Kyle Kellams, asst mus dir; Norman McChristian, chief engr.

Fordyce

KBJT(AM)—Aug 1, 1959: 1570 khz; 1 kw-D, 11 w-N. TL: N33 48 17 W92 26 07. 303 Spring St. (71742). (501) 352-7137. FAX: (501) 352-7139. Licensee: KBJT Inc. (acq 9-1-77). Format: C&W, news. News staff one; news progmg 20 hrs wkly. Target aud: General. Spec prog: Gospel 11 hrs wkly. ■ Gary Coates, pres & gen mgr; Gregory Scott, news dir. ■ Rates: $8; 8; 8; 8.

KQEW(FM)—Co-owned with KBJT(AM). Feb 23, 1982: 101.7 mhz; 3 kw. Ant 289 ft. TL: N33 48 17 W92 26 07. Stereo. Prog sep from AM. Format: C&W. News progmg 6 hrs wkly. Target aud: General. ■ Rates: Same as AM.

Forrest City

KXJK(AM)—Apr 29, 1949: 950 khz; 5 kw-D, 500 w-N. TL: N34 58 53 W90 51 27. Stereo. Hrs opn: 6 AM-10 PM. Box 707, 501 E. Broadway (72335). (501) 633-1252. FAX: (501) 633-9500. Licensee: Forrest City Broadcasting Co. Inc. Net: ABC/D; Ark. Radio Net. Rep: Dora-Clayton; Midsouth, Broadcast Reps. Wash atty: Gene Smith. Format: Adult contemp, oldies, news. News staff 2; news progmg 24 hrs wkly. Target aud: General. Spec prog: Farm 16 hrs wkly. ■ William Fogg, gen mgr & chief engr;

Richard Benson, opns mgr & gen sls mgr; Janet Benson, prom mgr; Tom Holbrook, adv dir; Rob Johnson, mus dir; Mark Kumming, news dir; Martha Farrell, pub affrs dir. ■ Rates: $13; 13; 13; 13.

KBFC(FM)—Co-owned with KXJK(AM). Sept 22, 1960: 93.5 mhz; 25 kw. Ant 340 ft. TL: N34 51 17 W90 55 02. Stereo. Hrs opn: 6 AM-10 PM. Prog sep from AM. Format: Modern country. News progmg 4 hrs wkly. ■ Rob Johnson, progmg dir; Tom Holbrook, mus dir. ■ Rates: Same as AM.

Fort Smith

KBBQ-FM—Listing follows KFPW(AM).

KBSY(FM)—See Poteau, Okla.

KFDF(AM)—See Van Buren.

KFPW(AM)—July 27, 1930: 1230 khz; 1 kw-U, DA-1. TL: N35 23 11 W94 21 44. Stereo. Hrs opn: 6 AM-12 AM. Box 303 (72902); 314 N. Greenwood (72901). (501) 783-5379. FAX: (501) 785-2638. Licensee: George T. Hernriech Broadcast (acq 5-7-88). Net: SMN. Rep: Major Market, Broadcast Reps Inc. Format: Big band, oldies, easy listening. News staff 2; news progmg 13 hrs wkly. Target aud: 35 plus; affluent. Spec prog: Sp 6 hrs wkly. ■ George Hernriech, pres; Gordon Brown, gen mgr, progmg dir & mus dir; Margie Cole, gen sls mgr & prom mgr; Brad Cason, news dir. ■ Rates: $12; 10; 12; 8.

KBBQ-FM—Co-owned with KFPW(AM). July 27, 1978: 100.7 mhz; 50 kw. Ant 459 ft. TL: N35 13 32 W94 20 29. Stereo. Prog sep from AM. Format: Golden oldies. News progmg 7 hrs wkly. Target aud: 25-64. ■ Larry Fridde, engrg mgr. ■ Rates: $18; 18; 18; 12.

KFSA(AM)—Feb 13, 1947: 950 khz; 1 kw-D, 500 w-N, DA-2. TL: N35 25 58 W94 28 13. Stereo. Box 488, 601 N. Greenwood (72902). (501) 782-9125. FAX: (501) 782-9127. Licensee: Fred H. Baker Sr. (acq 11-5-81; $297,000; FTR 11-30-81). Net: ABC/I, ABC/E. Rep: Katz & Powell. Format: Southern gospel. Target aud: General. ■ Fred H. Baker Sr., pres; Gary A. Keifer, gen mgr & gen sls mgr; Jerry Lynch, natl sls mgr; David J. Burdue, progmg dir & mus dir; Dale L. Davenport, chief engr. ■ Rates: $12; 10; 12; 8.

KISR(FM)—Co-owned with KFSA(AM). Aug 13, 1971: 93.7 mhz; 100 kw. Ant 1,250 ft. TL: N35 31 22 W94 23 32. Stereo. Hrs opn: 24. Box 3100, 605 N. Greenwood (72913). (501) 785-2526. Licensee: Stereo 93 Inc. Net: ABC/FM. Format: CHR. News staff one. Target aud: 18-39. ■ Fred Baker Jr., gen mgr & progmg dir; Scott Kramer, prom mgr & mus dir; Ray Zorback, news dir; Dale Davenport, engrg dir. ■ Rates: $22; 20; 22; 18.

KLSZ-FM—See Van Buren.

KMAG(FM)—Listing follows KWHN(AM).

KTCS(AM)—March 1956: 1410 khz; 1 kw-D. TL: N35 16 40 W94 22 35. Box 6321 (72906). (501) 646-6151. FAX: (501) 646-3509. Licensee: Big Chief Broadcasting Co. (acq 1961). Net: UPI. Format: C&W. News staff one. ■ Bill Harper, pres; Lee Young, gen mgr & gen sls mgr; Mac Remington, progmg dir; Greg Andrews, news dir.

KTCS-FM—Aug 15, 1964: 99.9 mhz; 100 kw. Ant 1,919 ft. TL: N35 04 20 W94 40 50. Stereo. Dups AM 100%.

KWHN(AM)—Nov 22, 1947: 1320 khz; 5 kw-U, DA-N. TL: N35 24 36 W94 21 30. Hrs opn: 24. 423 Garrison Ave. (72901). (501) 782-8888. FAX: (501) 785-5946. Licensee: Fort Smith FM Inc. (acq 7-11-89; $1.2 million with co-located FM). Net: ABC. Wash atty: Bryan, Cave, McPheeters & McRoberts. Format: Southern gospel. News staff 2; news progmg 2 hrs wkly. Target aud: 25-54. ■ Al Germond, pres; Del Williams, gen mgr & natl sls mgr; Tony Montgomery, gen sls mgr & rgnl sls mgr; Robert Huston, progmg dir, mus dir & news dir; Jimmy Poole, chief engr.

KMAG(FM)—Co-owned with KWHN(AM). Dec 31, 1964: 99.1 mhz; 100 kw. Ant 1,968 ft. TL: N35 09 56 W93 40 53. Stereo. Hrs opn: 24. Prog sep from AM. Format: Country. News staff 2. ■ Mark Scott, progmg dir.

***KYFF(FM)**—Not on air, target date unknown: 89.7 mhz; 1 kw. Ant 387 ft. Box 1818, Chesapeake, VA (23327). Licensee: Bible Broadcasting Network Inc.

KZBB(FM)—See Poteau, Okla.

Glenwood

KWXI(AM)—May 12, 1980: 670 khz; 5 kw-D. TL: N34 19 32 W93 33 27. Box S, Reggie Jones Plaza (71943). (501) 356-2151. FAX: (501) 356-2151. Licensee: Caddo Broadcasting Co. Net: NBC, Sun. Format: Country. News progmg 30 hrs wkly. Target aud: 34-54; affluent professionals. Spec prog: Consumer talk. ■ Tom Nichols, pres; Polly Nichols, gen mgr; Wilma Eldridge, progmg dir; Doyce Golden, chief engr.

KWXE(FM)—Co-owned with KWXI(AM). Nov 18, 1991: 104.5 mhz; 3 kw. Ant 328 ft. TL: N34 18 38 W93 32 04. Stereo. Hrs opn: 6 AM-midnight. Dups AM 100%.

Greenwood

KPBI(AM)—June 29, 1979: 1510 khz; 2.5 kw-D. TL: N35 15 00 W94 17 20. Suite 201, 523 Garrison Ave., Fort Smith (72901); Box 573, Fort Smith (72902). (501) 785-4600. FAX: (501) 785-4844. Licensee: Pharis Broadcasting Inc. Group owner: Bill & Karen Pharis. Format: Gospel. Target aud: 18-49. ■ John Wilhelm, gen mgr; Mike Vaughn, progmg dir; Marty Houston, news dir.

KZKZ-FM—December 1981: 106.3 mhz; 1.7 kw. Ant 433 ft. TL: N35 13 43 W94 15 45. Stereo. 6420 S. Zero St. (72903). (501) 646-6700. FAX: (501) 646-1373. Licensee: Family Communications Inc. (acq 5-11-93; FTR 6-7-93). Format: Contemp Christian. ■ Dave Burdue, progmg dir & mus dir; Keith Osteman, chief engr.

Gurdon

KYXK(FM)—December 1984: 92.7 mhz; 3 kw. Ant 298 ft. TL: N33 56 42 W93 10 43. Stereo. Box 149 (71743). (501) 353-2927. Licensee: PGR Communications Inc. Format: C&W. ■ Phil Robken, pres.

Hamburg

KHMB(FM)—Not on air, target date unknown: 99.5 mhz; 3 kw. Ant 328 ft. 1207 Louisa St., Rayville, LA (71269). Licensee: Kenneth W. Diebel.

Hampton

KKOL(FM)—Nov 26, 1984: 107.1 mhz; 3 kw. Ant 298 ft. TL: N33 32 23 W92 34 59. Box 1066 (71744). (501) 798-4107. Licensee: Southern Arkansas Radio Co. Format: Relg. ■ Wayne F. Brewies, pres & gen mgr; Ray Loy, chief engr.

Hardy

KOOU(FM)—Oct 4, 1993: 104.7 mhz; 6 kw. Ant 199 ft. TL: N36 18 17 W91 24 38. Hrs opn: 24. Box 480 (72542). (501) 856-2178; (501) 856-2188. FAX: (501) 856-4001. Licensee: John W. Shields. Format: Oldies. News progmg 6 hrs wkly. Target aud: General. ■ John W. Shields, pres & gen mgr. ■ Rates: 9; 9; 9; 6.

KSRB(AM)—Oct 6, 1976: 1570 khz; 1 kw-D. TL: N36 18 50 W91 16 41. Hrs opn: 6 AM-sunset. Box 486, Rt. 3 (72542). (501) 856-2179; (501) 856-2188. FAX: (501) 856-4001. Licensee: Kool Radio Inc. (acq 11-5-92; $30,000). Format: Oldies. News progmg 6 hrs wkly. Target aud: General. ■ John W. Shields, pres; Larry Caldwell, chief engr. ■ Rates: $7; 7; 7; na.

Harrison

KCWD(FM)—1982: 96.1 mhz; 3 kw. Ant 295 ft. TL: N36 16 36 W93 05 27 (CP: 8 kw, ant 1,191 ft.). Stereo. Hrs opn: 24. Box 850, 600 S. Pine (72601). (501) 741-1402. FAX: (501) 741-9702. Licensee: Harrison Radio Station Inc. Net: ABC/E. Format: C&W. ■ Tom Arnold, gen mgr; Scott Larson, progmg dir; Dave Almond, chief engr.

KHOZ(AM)—Sept 28, 1946: 900 khz; 1 kw-D. TL: N36 14 35 W93 06 43. Hrs opn: 24. Box 430, One Radio Ave. (72601). (501) 741-2302. FAX: (501) 741-3299. Licensee: Omni Communications Inc. (acq 5-12-92; $12,000 with co-located FM; FTR 6-1-92). Net: CBS. Format: MOR. News staff one. Target aud: General. Spec prog: Talk 12 hrs wkly. ■ W. J. Wheeler, gen mgr; Zettie Johnson, stn mgr; Bill Boswell, opns mgr & news dir; Linda Choate, gen sls mgr; Marc Williams, progmg dir; John Saxon, chief engr.

KHOZ-FM—Mar 25, 1963: 102.9 mhz; 100 kw. Ant 981 ft. TL: N36 26 11 W93 14 43. Stereo. Hrs opn: 24. Prog sep from AM. Format: Country. Target aud: 25-54. ■ Bob Mitchell, progmg dir; Jerry Bowman, mus dir; John Saxon, engrg dir.

Heber Springs

KAWW(AM)—July 15, 1967: 1370 khz; 1 kw-D. TL: N35 29 10 W92 02 05. Hrs opn: 6 AM-midnight. Box 324, 422 W. Main St. (72543). (501) 362-5663. FAX: (501) 362-5864. Licensee: Newport Broadcasting Co. Group owner: Sudbury Svcs Inc. & Newport Broadcasting Co. Net: Ark. Radio Net. Format: C&W, news/talk. News staff one; news progmg 7 hrs wkly. Target aud: 25-65. Spec prog: Gospel 14 hrs wkly. ■ Harold L. Sudbury, pres; David J. Lee, gen mgr, prom mgr & progmg dir; Layne Tubbs, gen sls mgr; Paul Headden, news dir; Dale Johnson, chief engr.

KAWW-FM—Sept 1, 1972: 96.7 mhz; 3 kw. Ant 328 ft. TL: N35 27 26 W92 02 11 (CP: 100.7 mhz, 50 kw). Stereo. Hrs opn: 5 AM-midnight. Prog sep from AM.

Helena

KFFA(AM)—Nov 19, 1941: 1360 khz; 1 kw-U, DA-N. TL: N34 31 39 W90 37 48. Box 430, 1360 Radio Dr. (72342). (501) 338-8361. FAX: (501) 338-8332. Licensee: Delta Broadcasting Inc. (acq 3-80; $445,000; FTR 3-10-80). Net: MBS; Prog Farm. Rep: Keystone (unwired net). Format: C&W, blues. News progmg 25 hrs wkly. Target aud: 25-54. Spec prog: Farm 12 hrs wkly, Black 4 hrs wkly. ■ Jim Howe, pres & gen mgr; Amy Treat, gen sls mgr.

KCRI-FM—Co-owned with KFFA(AM). 1972: 103.1 mhz; 6 kw. Ant 328 ft. TL: N34 31 39 W90 37 46 (CP: 13 kw, ant 318 ft.). Stereo. (acq 5-84; grpsl; FTR 5-7-84). Net: MBS. Format: Adult contemp. News progmg 15 hrs wkly. ■ Jim Howe, gen sls mgr.

Hope

KHPA(FM)—Apr 21, 1977: 104.9 mhz; 3 kw. Ant 298 ft. TL: N33 43 10 W93 29 07. Stereo. Box 424 (71801). (501) 777-8868; (510) 777-8869. FAX: (501) 777-8888. Licensee: Newport Broadcasting Co. Group owner: Sudbury Svcs Inc. & Newport Broadcasting Co. Format: Country. News staff one; news progmg 4 hrs wkly. ■ Harold L. Sudbury Jr., pres & chief engr; Rob Hill, gen mgr; Richard Haycox, gen sls mgr; Mark Hobson, progmg dir; John McCoy, news dir.

KXAR(AM)—Dec 12, 1947: 1490 khz; 700 w-U. TL: N33 41 20 W93 35 55 (CP: 690 w-U). Box 320, Hwy 29 at I-30 (71801). (501) 777-3601. FAX: (501) 777-3535. Licensee: KdD Inc. (acq 6-20-88). Net: ABC/D; Ark. Radio Net. Rep: Katz & Powell. Format: Country. News staff 2. Target aud: Double-income stable adult households. Spec prog: Farm 6 hrs, bluegrass 2 hrs wkly. ■ Bill Hoglund, pres & gen mgr; Mark Kieth, Rob Hoffman, progmg dirs; Mark Kieth, news dir; Norm Mason, chief engr.

KXAR-FM—Dec 31, 1984: 101.7 mhz; 3 kw. Ant 295 ft. TL: N33 41 20 W93 35 55. Stereo. Hrs opn: 24. Prog sep from AM. (501) 777-5747. Format: Urban contemp. Target aud: 12-54; young, Black adults. ■ W.A. Griffin, progmg dir.

Hot Springs

***KALR(FM)**—May 1989: 91.5 mhz; 1 kw. Ant 282 ft. TL: N34 37 31 W93 00 37 (CP: 3 kw, ant 485 ft.). 304 Applied Life Dr. (71909). (501) 623-6748. Licensee: Applied Life Educational Broadcasting Foundation. Format: Adult contemp Christian. News staff one; news progmg 7 hrs wkly. Target aud: 18-45. ■ Timothy Lee Brooks, pres; John C. Thomas, gen mgr.

KBHS(AM)—March 10, 1953: 590 khz; 5 kw-D, 500 w-N. TL: N34 27 19 W93 58 45. Box 6021 (71902). (501) 623-6661; Licensee: J&A Inc. (acq 9-8-93; FTR 9-27-93). Net: USA. Format: Country. Spec prog: Gospel 4 hrs, poetry one hr wkly. ■ George Donley, pres; Robby Swinney, opns mgr & progmg dir; Buddy McLellan, chief engr.

KLAZ(FM)—Listing follows KXOW(AM).

KLXQ(FM)—June 18, 1965: 96.7 mhz; 2.6 kw. Ant 320 ft. TL: N34 32 01 W93 03 24 (CP: 940 kw, ant 807 ft.). Box 160 (71951-0160). (501) 525-9700. Licensee: Kellstrom Broadcasting Inc. (acq 1-13-93; $300,000; FTR 2-2-93). Net: USA. Format: Adult contemp. ■ Jim Kellstrom, gen mgr.

KQUS-FM—Listing follows KZNG(AM).

***KSBC(FM)**—Mar 20, 1984: 90.1 mhz; 5 kw. Ant 785 ft. TL: N34 33 56 W93 05 03. Stereo. Hrs opn: 24. Box 2771, 600 Garland Ave. (71914). (501) 624-4455. Licensee: Central Arkansas Christian Broadcasting Inc. Net: Moody. Format: Educ. ■ James E. Gill Jr., CEO & gen mgr.

KXOW(AM)—Oct 6, 1966: 1420 khz; 5 kw-D, 87 w-N. TL: N34 27 19 W93 03 26. Box 1739 (71902); 208 Buena Vista Rd. (71913). (501) 525-1301. FAX: (501) 525-4344. Licensee: Noalmark Broadcasting Corp. (group owner; grpsl, including co-located FM). Net: MBS. Rep: Target. Format: Btfl mus. News staff one; news progmg 2 hrs wkly. Target aud: 35 plus; upscale, high-income residents & business people. ■ Eddie Tarpley, gen mgr & gen sls mgr; Phil O'Brien, progmg dir; Jack Ihrie, news dir; Buddy McLelland, chief engr.

KLAZ(FM)—Co-owned with KXOW(AM). October 1971: 105.9 mhz; 95 kw. Ant 994 ft. TL: N34 30 19 W93 05 06. Stereo. Prog sep from AM. (501) 525-4600. Format: Adult contemp. News staff one; news progmg 2 hrs wkly. Target aud: 18-49.

KYXK(FM)—See Gurdon.

KZNG(AM)—Jan 1, 1953: 1340 khz; 1 kw-U. TL: N34 29 43 W93 01 27. Box Q, 600 Main St. (71902). (501) 623-1340; (501) 521-5566. FAX: (501) 623-4069. Licensee: Demaree Media Inc., debtor in possession (group owner; acq 6-23-86; $1 million with co-located FM; FTR 4-14-86). Rep: Republic. Format: Oldies. ■ L. Patrick Demaree, pres; Jim Kellstrom, gen mgr.

KQUS-FM—Co-owned with KZNG(AM). Feb 7, 1969: 97.5 mhz; 100 kw. Ant 860 ft. TL: N34 24 11 W93 07 13. Stereo. Prog sep from AM. Net: ABC/I. Format: C&W. ■ Todd Woerpel, gen sls mgr; Darin Ray, progmg dir; Chuck Sullivan, news dir; Norm Laramee, chief engr.

Hoxie

KHOX(FM)—Jan 20, 1988: 105.3 mhz; 6 kw. Ant 156 ft. TL: N36 02 24 W90 59 11. Hrs opn: 6 AM-1 AM. 311 S.W. Andrews (72433). (501) 886-1350. Licensee: Mitchell Broadcasting Co. Format: Country, classic rock, top-40. News staff one; news progmg 6 hrs wkly. ■ Dennis Mitchell, gen mgr, gen sls mgr, mus dir, news dir & chief engr.

Huntsville

KREB(FM)—1955: 95.9 mhz; 3 kw. Ant 295 ft. TL: N36 00 33 W93 42 01. Box 878, Fayetteville (72702). (501) 738-2405. Licensee: Vekony Communications Inc. (acq 6-4-93; $100,000; FTR 6-28-93).

Jacksonville

KDDK(FM)—Sept 29, 1969: 100.3 mhz; 44.2 kw. Ant 1,369 ft. TL: N34 47 57 W92 29 29. Stereo. Hrs opn: 24. Box 100, Little Rock (72203); 314 Main St., North Little Rock (72214). (501) 372-7740. FAX: (501) 372-7787. Licensee: Galaxy Broadcasting Ltd. (acq 5-11-90; $3.25 million). Rep: McGavren Guild. Wash atty: Muller, Rhyne, Emmons & Topel. Format: Young country. News staff one. Target aud: 18-49. ■ Wally Tucker, gen mgr; Ted Jones, stn mgr; Stephanie Sherwin, gen sls mgr; Steve Drake, progmg mgr & mus dir; Len Day, news dir & pub affrs dir; Carr Stalnaker, chief engr. ■ Rates: $70; 65; 60; 25.

Jonesboro

***KASU(FM)**—May 17, 1957: 91.9 mhz; 100 kw. Ant 692 ft. TL: N35 53 24 W90 40 26. Stereo. Hrs opn: 24. Box 2160, Arkansas State U., 104 Cooley (72467). (501) 972-3070. FAX: (501) 972-3828. Licensee: Arkansas State Univ. Net: APR, AP, NPR. Format: Class, news. News staff one; news progmg 40 hrs wkly. Target aud: General. Spec prog: Farm 7 hrs, jazz 4 hrs wkly. ■ John Mangieri, pres; Richard Carvell, gen mgr; Laura Johnson, stn mgr, dev dir, prom mgr & progmg mgr; Marty Scarbrough, mus dir; Greg Chance, news dir; Jimmie Rushing, chief engr.

KBTM(AM)—Mar 15, 1930: 1230 khz; 1 kw-U. TL: N35 50 27 W90 39 44. Box 1737 (72403). (501) 935-5597. FAX: (501) 932-3814. Licensee: Duke Entertainment (acq 10-25-93; $1.75 million with co-located FM; FTR 11-8-93). Net: Ark. Net. Format: Talk. News staff one. ■ Clyde Bass, gen mgr.

KJBR(FM)—Co-owned with KBTM(AM). 1947: 101.9 mhz; 100 kw. Ant 1,059 ft. TL: N35 57 14 W90 41 41. Stereo. Prog sep from AM. Box 9375 (72403-0400). (501) 935-5598. Format: CHR. ■ Craig Yancey, stn mgr.

KDEZ(FM)—Nov 21, 1986: 100.3 mhz; 3 kw. Ant 230 ft. TL: N35 51 17 W90 43 40 (CP: 3.06 kw, ant 459 ft., TL: N35 54 26 W 90 41 38). Stereo. Suite 2010, 1720 Caraway Rd. (72401). (501) 933-8800. FAX: (501) 933-0403. Licensee: TM Jonesboro Inc. (acq 2-21-92; $10 and assumption of debt; FTR 3-16-92). Format: CHR. News staff one; news progmg one hr wkly. Target aud: 18-49. Spec prog: Relg one hr wkly. ■ Bill Thomas, pres; LaDawn Fuhr, gen mgr; Phil Stevens, progmg dir; Brett Hall, mus dir; Kirk Harnack, chief engr.

KFIN(FM)—Mar 4, 1974: 107.9 mhz; 100 kw. Ant 600 ft. TL: N35 47 56 W90 44 31. Stereo. Drawer 1737, 403 W. Parker Rd. (72403). (501) 932-1079. Licensee: Duke Broadcasting Corp. (acq 5-1-78). Net: CNN. Wash atty: Latham & Watkins. Format: Contemp country. News staff one; news progmg 9 hrs wkly. Target aud: 25-54; broad demographics. Spec prog: Farm 13 hrs wkly. ■ Larry A. Duke, CEO & pres; Mike Todd, CFO; Clyde Bass, vp & stn mgr; Christy Ellison, natl sls mgr; Lynetta Pilkinton, prom mgr; Dana Daniels, progmg dir; Wayne Hoffman, news dir; Bob Owens, vp engrg. ■ Rates: $73; 67; 73; 60.

KJBR(FM)—Listing follows KBTM(AM).

KNEA(AM)—Sept 20, 1950: 970 khz; 1 kw-D, 41 w-N. TL: N35 51 17 W90 43 40. Hrs opn: 16. 603 W. Matthews (72401). (501) 932-8381. FAX: (501) 932-6397. Licensee: John J. Shields Inc. (acq 7-5-88; $435,000). Net: Ark. Radio Net. Format: Gospel, relg. News staff 5. Target aud: General. Spec prog: Farm 6 hrs wkly. ■ Paul R. Boden, pres & gen mgr; Mia D. Boden, stn mgr; Paula Carter, gen sls mgr & prom mgr; Phillip Sweet, progmg dir, mus dir & news dir; Bob Snearly, chief engr. ■ Rates: $12; 12; 12; 12.

Lake Village

KEGT(FM)—Not on air, target date unknown: 103.5 mhz; 6 kw. Ant 328 ft. TL: N33 16 56 W91 13 02. 233 Rose St., Greenville, MS (38701). Licensee: Lula May Stone.

KUUZ(FM)—July 30, 1977: 95.9 mhz; 6 kw. Ant 328 ft. TL: N33 20 07 W91 07 33. Stereo. Box 1794, Greenville, MS (71730). (601) 332-0025. FAX: (601) 332-0038. Licensee: DBR Communications Inc. (acq 9-89; $90,000; FTR 9-25-89). ■ Wayne Bennett, gen mgr.

Little Rock

KAAY(AM)—Dec 20, 1924: 1090 khz; 50 kw-U, DA-N. TL: N34 46 20 W92 13 30. Suite One, 7123 I-30 (72209-3165). (501) 661-1090. FAX: (501) 562-9188. Licensee: Beasley Broadcasting of Arkansas Inc. Group owner: Beasley Broadcast Group (acq 6-16-87; $2,650,000; FTR 5-11-87). Format: Relg, southern gospel. Spec prog: Sp 2 hrs wkly. ■ George Beasley, pres; Dianne McArthur, gen mgr; Jim White, opns mgr; Bert McArthur, gen sls mgr; Scott Taylor, mus dir; Ken Moyer, news dir; Felix McDonald, chief engr.

***KABF(FM)**—Sept 31, 1984: 88.3 mhz; 91 kw. Ant 777 ft. TL: N34 47 31 W92 28 38. Stereo. 1501 Arch St. (72202). (501) 372-6119. Licensee: Arkansas Broadcasting Foundation. Format: Black, jazz, div. News staff one; news progmg 12 hrs wkly. Target aud: General; low-moderate income & politically disenfranchised. Spec prog: Blues 20 hrs, gospel 20 hrs, country 18 hrs, women 3 hrs, Sp 2 hrs, folk 6 hrs, American Indian 2 hrs wkly. ■ Ron Garner, stn mgr; Clyde Phillips, mus dir; Tom Rusk, chief engr.

KARN(AM)—1928: 920 khz; 5 kw-U, DA-N. TL: N34 46 20 W92 09 30. Box 4189 (72214); 4021 W. 8th St. (72204). (501) 661-7500. Licensee: Snider Corp. (acq 2-10-72). Net: CBS; Ark. Radio Net. Rep: Katz. Format: News/talk. News staff 9. ■ Ted L. Snider, pres; Neal Gladner, vp & gen mgr; Judith Anderson, gen sls mgr; Tracy Allen, progmg dir; Lee Clinton, chief engr.

KBIS(AM)—1925: 1010 khz; 10 kw-D, 5 kw-N, DA-N. TL: N34 46 10 W92 09 30. Stereo. 2400 Cottondale Ln. (72202). (501) 664-9410. FAX: (501) 664-5871. Licensee: Signal Media of Arkansas (acq 4-1-81; $2,300,000; FTR 2-16-81). Net: NBC, NBC Talknet, AP, Daynet, Sun, MBS, Westwood One. Rep: Christal. Wash atty: Winston & Strawn. Format: Sports & talk. News staff one. Target aud: 25-54. ■ Philip Jonsson, pres & gen mgr; Janet W. Hill, Jane Wasson, CFOs; Hal Smith, stn mgr, gen sls mgr & natl sls mgr; Tracy Carrington, prom dir; B. Jay Kaplan, progmg dir; Bill Powell, news dir; Susan Vail, pub affrs dir; Norm Laramee, chief engr. ■ Rates: $20; 20; 20; 20.

KHLT(FM)—Co-owned with KBIS(AM). Oct 26, 1960: 94.1 mhz; 100 kw. Ant 1,601 ft. TL: N34 47 56 W92 29 41. Stereo. Prog sep from AM. (acq 4-30-85; $2,750,000; FTR 3-11-85). Net: AP. Format: Adult contemp. News staff one; Target aud: 25-54; women. ■ Mark Pollitt, mus dir.

KDDK(FM)—See Jacksonville.

KHLT(FM)—Listing follows KBIS(AM).

KIPR(FM)—See Pine Bluff.

KITA(AM)—October 1956: 1440 khz; 5 kw-D, 240 w-N. TL: N34 42 46 W92 16 48. 723 W. 14th St. (72202). (501) 375-1440. FAX: (501) 375-0947. Licensee: Kita Ltd. (acq 6-28-84; $675,000; FTR 4-30-84). Format: Relg. Target aud: 25-54; primarily women. Spec prog: Black 19 hrs wkly. ■ Gary Vaile, gen mgr & gen sls mgr; Ulysses Robinson, progmg dir; Erin Green, mus dir & news dir; Tom Rusk, chief engr. ■ Rates: $10; 8; 10; 6.

KJBN(AM)—1946: 1050 khz; 1 kw-D, 19 w-N. TL: N34 45 57 W92 17 39. 1521 Main St., North Little Rock (72114). (501) 375-1050. FAX: (501) 374-0703. Licensee: Joshua Ministries and Community Development Corp. (acq 8-26-92; $250,000; FTR 9-21-92). Net: CNN. Format: Motivational/informational. Target aud: Career-oriented people. Spec prog: CNN News/Sports. ■ Earl Watson, gen mgr; Talmidge Harbison, prom mgr & progmg dir; Tom Rusk, chief engr.

KKYK-FM—1967: 103.7 mhz; 100 kw. Ant 1,510 ft. TL: N34 47 55 W92 29 58. Stereo. TCBY Tower, Suite 3104, 425 W. Capitol (72214). (501) 378-0104. FAX: (501) 375-4487. Licensee: Signal Media of Arkansas Inc. (acq 10-26-93: $2 million; FTR 11-8-93). Format: CHR. News progmg 4 hrs wkly. Target aud: 18-49. ■ John Shepard, pres; Dennis Moore, vp; Bill Presley, vp opns & mus dir; Charlie Pride, sls dir; Craig O'Neill, progmg dir; Lauri Allen, news dir; Dave Graves, chief engr.

***KLRE-FM**—February 1973: 90.5 mhz; 40 kw. Ant 265 ft. TL: N34 40 29 W92 19 04. Stereo. Hrs opn: 24. 2801 S. University (72204). (501) 569-8485. FAX: (501) 569-8491. Licensee: Little Rock School District & University of Arkansas. Net: Beethoven. Wash atty: Cohn & Marks. Format: Classical. ■ Regina Dean, gen mgr; Edwin Zoch, opns mgr; Mary Bea Gross, dev dir & mktg dir; Ben Fry, news dir & pub affrs dir; Tom Rusk, chief engr.

KLRG(AM)—See North Little Rock.

KMJX(FM)—See Conway.

KSSN(FM)—1966: 95.7 mhz; 92 kw. Ant 1,663 ft. TL: N34 47 57 W92 29 29. Stereo. Hrs opn: 24. Box 96 (72203); 8114 Cantrell Rd. (72207). (501) 227-9696. FAX: (501) 228-9547. Licensee: Southern Skies Corp. (group owner). Net: ABC/E. Rep: Katz. Wash atty: Bryan, Cave, McPheeters & McRoberts. Format: Contemp country. News staff one; news progmg 3 hrs wkly. Target aud: 25-54. ■ Jerry Atchley, chmn & pres; Jay Werth, gen mgr; Joanne Scott, vp opns; Paul Massey, sls dir; Michelle Carney, prom dir; Joe Logan, progmg dir; Sherry Westbrook, mus dir; Rhonda Atwood, news dir; Tom Rusk, chief engr.

***KUAR(FM)**—Sept 16, 1986: 89.1 mhz; 100 kw. Ant 882 ft. TL: N34 47 50 W92 29 26. Stereo. Hrs opn: 24. 2801 S. University (72204). (501) 569-8485. FAX: (501) 569-8491. Licensee: Little Rock School District & Univ. of Arkansas. Net: NPR. Wash atty: Cohn & Marks. Format: Classical, news/talk. Spec prog: Jazz 10 hrs wkly. ■ Regina N. Dean, gen mgr; Edwin Zoch, opns mgr; Mary Bea Gross, dev dir & mktg dir; Ben Fry, news dir & pub affrs dir; Tom Rusk, chief engr.

KURB(AM)—1929: 1250 khz; 2.5 kw-D, 1.2 kw-N, DA-2. TL: N34 42 05 W92 13 02. Hrs opn: 24. Suite 768, 1501 N. University (72207). (501) 661-0150. FAX: (501) 661-1562. Licensee: GHB of Little Rock Inc. Group owner: GHB Radio Group (acq 12-17-90; $1.65 million with co-located FM; FTR 1-7-91). Rep: D & R Radio. Format: Hot adult contemp. News staff one. Target aud: 25-54. ■ Jake Bogan, CEO; Randy Bush, gen mgr & natl sls mgr; Todd Curtis, gen sls mgr; Randy Cain, progmg dir; Kevin Miller, mus dir; Charles Davis, news dir; Tom Rusk, chief engr.

KURB-FM—July 7, 1972: 98.5 mhz; 99 kw. Ant 1,286 ft. TL: N34 47 56 W92 29 44. Stereo. Hrs opn: 24. Dups AM 100%.

KYFX(FM)—Aug 14, 1992: 99.5 mhz; 3 kw. Ant 312 ft. TL: N34 46 10 W92 21 22. 610 Plaza W. Bldg. (72205). (501) 666-5899. FAX: (501) 666-9699. Licensee: Nameloc Broadcasting. Format: New adult contemp. ■ Loretta Lever, pres.

Lonoke

KMZX(FM)—June 1982: 106.3 mhz; 2.5 kw. Ant 354 ft. TL: N34 46 30 W91 53 33 (CP: 50 kw, ant 492 ft.). Church St., Suite 400, Norfolk, VA (23510). (804) 624-6500. FAX: (804) 624-6515. Licensee: Lonoke Broadcasting Corp. Group owner: Willis Broadcasting Corp. (acq 1-90; $445,000; FTR 1-22-90). ■ L.E. Willis, pres; Don Michaels, progmg dir.

Lowell

KISK(FM)—June 30, 1992: 101.9 mhz; 50 kw. Ant 708 ft. TL: N36 26 28 W93 58 22. Stereo. Hrs opn: 24. Box 102, Fayetteville (72702). (501) 442-0102. Licensee: Noalmark Broadcasting Corp. (acq 11-16-92; $425,000 FTR 12-7-92). Wash atty: Dow, Lohnes, & Albertson. Format: CHR. News staff 2; news progmg one hr wkly. Target aud: 18-44. ■ Doug Whitman, sr vp & gen mgr; Jeff Wood, gen sls mgr; Rich Walton, progmg dir; Jess Smith, news dir; Zeb Huffmaster, chief engr. ■ Rates: $50; 40; 45; 25.

KKIP(AM)—Not on air, target date unknown: 1440 khz; 1 kw-D, 79 w-N. TL: N36 11 07 W93 59 27. Box 933, Bentonville (72712). Licensee: Tim Hutchinson (acq 3-28-90; $25,000; FTR 4-16-90).

Magnolia

KVMA(AM)—April 1948: 630 khz; 1 kw-D. TL: N33 17 59 W93 13 57. Box 430, 131 S. Jackson (71753). (501) 234-5862. FAX: (501) 234-5865. Licensee: Magnolia Broadcasting Co. Net: ABC/D; Ark. Net. Wash atty: Borsari & Assoc. Format: C&W. News progmg 8 hrs wkly. Target aud: General. Spec prog: Farm 2 hrs wkly. ■ Ken W. Sibley, pres, gen mgr, progmg dir & mus dir; Dan Gregory, prom mgr; Houston Taylor, news dir; Charles Price, chief engr. ■ Rates: $12; 6; 9; 6.

KVMA-FM—1968: 107.9 mhz; 100 kw. Ant 351 ft. TL: N33 17 59 W93 13 57. Stereo. Hrs opn: 24. Prog sep from AM. Net: SMN. Format: Adult contemp.

KZHE(FM)—See Stamps.

Malvern

KBOK(AM)—August 1951: 1310 khz; 1 kw-D. TL: N34 22 25 W92 49 52. 1402 Hwy. 270 N. (72104). (501) 332-6981. Licensee: Malvern Broadcasting Co. (acq 6-1-58). Net: ABC/D; Ark. Net. Format: C&W. News staff 2. Target aud: General. ■ Kermit L. Richardson, pres, gen mgr & sls dir; Larry Mann, gen sls mgr, mus dir & news dir; Pat Brandon, prom mgr; June Richardson, progmg dir; Andy Andersen, chief engr. ■ Rates: $7; 7; 7; 7.

KBOK-FM—April 1989: 93.3 mhz; 5.8 kw. Ant 215 ft. TL: N34 22 25 W92 49 52. Stereo. Dups AM 100%. ■ Larry Mann, sls dir; June Richardson, progmg dir.

KISI(FM)—Apr 1, 1991: 101.5 mhz; 6 kw. Ant 318 ft. TL: N34 23 32 W92 52 27. Stereo. Hrs opn: 24. 212 S. Main St. (72104). (501) 337-9000. FAX: (501) 337-9000. Licensee: Lyons Communications Inc. (acq 3-5-93); $125,000; FTR 3-29-93). Wash atty: Fletcher, Heald & Hildreth. Format: Easy listening. News progmg 10 hrs wkly. Target aud: 35 plus. ■ Donald C. Harbour, pres & gen mgr; Irma B. Harbour, vp; Billie Gregory, gen sls mgr; Jennifer Broyles, prom mgr. ■ Rates: $10; 8; 10; 6.

Mammoth Spring

KALM(AM)—See Thayer, Mo.

KAMS(FM)—Jan 1, 1956: 95.1 mhz; 100 kw. Ant 650 ft. TL: N36 32 58 W91 33 05. Stereo. Hrs opn: 24. Box 193 (72554); N. Hwy. 63, Thayer, MO (65791). (417) 264-7211; (417) 264-7063. FAX: (417) 264-7212. Licensee: Ozark Radio Network Inc. Net: ABC/D. Rep: Keystone (unwired net). Wash atty: Richard J. Hays, Jr. Format: Super country. News staff one; news progmg 11 hrs wkly. Target aud: General. ■ Shawn Neathery Marhefka, pres; Robert Eckman, gen mgr, gen sls mgr, prom mgr & adv mgr; Lynn Hobbs, stn mgr; Dave Watson, opns mgr & progmg dir; Mike Crase, prom dir & news dir; Harold Robertson, Chris Skaggs, mus dirs; Dan Hickinbotham, pub affrs dir; Bill Martin, chief engr. ■ Rates: $10.30; 10.30; 10.30; 10.30.

Marianna

KZOT(AM)—Sept 25, 1961: 1460 khz; 500 w-D, DA. TL: N34 44 46 W90 47 44. Box 2870, West Helena (72390). (501) 572-9506. Licensee: Raymond and L.T. Simes II (acq 1-28-93; $4,000; FTR 2-15-93). Net: Ark. Net. Format: Gospel. Spec prog: Black 12 hrs, farm 7 hrs wkly. ■ Raymond Simes, stn mgr; Michelle Albin, gen sls mgr; Tom Hale, progmg dir; Harold Baker, chief engr.

KAKJ(FM)—Co-owned with KZOT(AM). Not on air, target date 1994: 105.3 mhz; 6 kw. Ant 100 ft. Hrs opn: 24. Rebroadcasts KCLT(FM) West Helena 65%. Format: Black, urban contemp, relg. ■ Raymond Simes, pres; Elaine Simes, opns mgr; Val Jackson, natl sls mgr; Larry Evans, vp prom; Eddie Murphy, mus dir; L.T. Simes, news dir; Ray Lowery, chief engr.

Marion

KFTH(FM)—February 1986: 107.1 mhz; 3 kw. Ant 328 ft. TL: N35 09 23 W90 05 46. 2265 Central Ave., Memphis TN (38104). (901) 272-3004. FAX: (901) 272-0747. Licensee: Big Ben Communications Inc. Group owner: Willis Broadcasting Corp. Format: Contemp Inspirational. ■ Chuck Woodson, gen mgr & gen sls mgr; Paul Anthony, progmg dir; Jerry Campbell, chief engr.

Marked Tree

KXHW(FM)—Not on air, target date unknown: 93.7 mhz; 3 kw. Ant 288 ft. TL: N35 32 22 W90 26 35. Licensee: B & H Broadcasting Co. (acq 11-30-92; $10,000; FTR 12-21-92).

Marshall

KBCN-FM—Apr 25, 1983: 104.3 mhz; 100 kw. Ant 820 ft. TL: N35 52 17 W92 39 10 (CP: Ant 1,016 ft.). Stereo. Country Music Communications Inc., 100 Fall Creek Dr., Branson, MO (65616). (501) 448-3637; FAX: (501) 448-3645. Licensee: Country Music Communications Inc. Group owner: Star Radio (acq 4-30-93; $450,000; FTR 5-24-93). Format: C&W. ■ Ellek Seymour, gen mgr; Jim Screws, chief engr.

KCGS(AM)—May 24, 1975: 960 khz; 5 kw-D. TL: N35 54 56 W92 38 20. Box 368 (72650). (501) 448-5566. FAX: (501) 448-5384. Licensee: Rex Elliott (acq 9-22-83). Net: USA. Format: Relg. News staff 2; news progmg 10 hrs wkly. Target aud: General. ■ Rex Elliott, pres; Trisch De Priest, gen mgr & progmg dir; Ray Loey, chief engr. ■ Rates: $5; 5; 5; 5.

Maumelle

KOLL(FM)—1971: 94.9 mhz; 96 kw. Ant 1,843 ft. TL: N34 26 31 W92 13 03. Stereo. Hrs opn: 24. 11101 Anderson Dr., Little Rock (72212). (501) 225-9595. FAX: (501) 228-9875. Licensee: Southern Starr of Arkansas. Group owner: Southern Starr Broadcasting Group (acq 12-88; $250,000; FTR 12-26-88). Net: Unistar. Rep: McGavren Guild. Format: Oldies. News progmg 5 hrs wkly. Target aud: 25-54; Baby boomers. ■ Bob Long, CEO; Manuel Rodriquez, pres; Bill Motter, CFO; Dic Booth Magic Broadcasting, gen mgr; Jean Woods, stn mgr; Jim Hunt, gen sls mgr; Michael Langley, progmg dir; Billy St. James, pub affrs dir.

NEW FM—Not on air, target date unknown: 96.9 mhz; 3 kw. Ant 328 ft. 9628 Woodford Dr., Little Rock (72209). Licensee: Lake Maumelle FM Associates.

Mayflower

KABK-FM—(Augusta). Aug 27, 1979: 97.7 mhz; 3 kw. Ant 298 ft. TL: N35 18 45 W91 28 24. Stereo. 128 Hwy. 895, Mayflower (72106). (501) 985-0880. FAX: (501) 985-0260. Licensee: Harvey Fritts (acq 11-5-91; $150,000; FTR 11-30-92). Format: C&W.

McGehee

KVSA(AM)—June 29, 1953: 1220 khz; 1 kw-D, 40 w-N. TL: N33 33 39 W91 23 06. Box 110 (71653). (501) 222-4200. Licensee: Southeast Arkansas Broadcasters Inc. Rep: Keystone (unwired net). Format: Div. Spec prog: Farm 5 hrs wkly. ■ Abbott F. Kinney, pres & gen mgr; James S. Hunt, chief engr.

Mena

KENA(AM)—Feb 1950: 1450 khz; 1 kw-U. TL: N34 34 23 W94 14 55. Box 1450 (71953). (501) 394-1450. FAX: (501) 394-1459. Licensee: Ouachita Communications Inc. (acq 12-3-87). Net: ABC/I. Rep: Keystone (unwired net). Format: Country. News staff one; news progmg 10 hrs wkly. Target aud: 18 plus; industrial & agricultural workers, retirees, tourists & professionals. ■ Edward W. Stevenson, pres, gen mgr & prom mgr; Chris Daniel, sls dir & chief engr; Bevonna Williams, progmg dir; Grant Gieger, mus dir; Dwight Douglas, news dir.

KENA-FM—Nov 25, 1969: 101.7 mhz; 3 kw. Ant 298 ft. TL: N34 34 23 W94 14 55 (CP: 102.1 mhz, 25.1 kw). Format: Country.

KOUA(FM)—Not on air, target date unknown: 96.3 mhz; 47.18 kw. Ant 1,314 ft. TL: N34 36 40 W94 16 20. Rt 2, Box 384-B (71953). Licensee: Skyline Radio Inc. (acq 5-5-93; FTR 5-24-93).

Monticello

KGPL(AM)—See Dermott.

KHBM(AM)—Apr 1955: 1430 khz; 1 kw-D, 30 w-N, 500 w-PSSA. TL: N33 36 18 W91 47 14. Hrs opn: 5:30 AM-10 PM. Box 446, Midway Route (71655). (501) 367-6854. FAX: (501) 367-9564. Licensee: Midway Broadcasting Co. (acq 6-1-84; $400,000; FTR 4-23-84). Net: ABC/D; Ark. Radio Net. Format: Adult contemp, news. News progmg 10 hrs wkly. Target aud: General. Spec prog: Farm 5 hrs, relg 6 hrs wkly. ■ Truman Hamilton, pres & gen mgr; Ray Dawson, vp, news dir & chief engr; Carol Dawson, gen sls mgr. ■ Rates: $8.50; 7.50; 6.75; 6.75.

KHBM-FM—Sept 1, 1967: 93.5 mhz; 3.2 kw. Ant 341 ft. TL: N33 36 18 W91 47 14. Stereo. Hrs opn: 24. Dups AM 100%. Wash atty: Fletcher, Heald & Hildreth. ■ Rates: Same as AM.

KXSA-FM—See Dermott.

Morrilton

KVOM(AM)—Dec 25, 1952: 800 khz; 250 w-D, 42 w-N. TL: N35 09 32 W92 46 13. Box 541 (72110). (501) 354-2484. FAX: (501) 354-5629. Licensee: Morrilton Broadcasting Co. Format: C&W. ■ Stanton Willis, pres & gen mgr; Harold Nichols, gen sls mgr.

KVOM-FM—1981: 101.7 mhz; 3 kw. Ant 226 ft. TL: N35 09 32 W92 46 13. Dups AM 100%.

Mountain Home

*__KCMH(FM)__—June 28, 1988: 91.5 mhz; 400 w. Ant 420 ft. TL: N36 16 17 W92 25 20. Stereo. Hrs opn: 24. Box 93, 1015 B Hwy. 62 E. (72653). (501) 425-2525. Licensee: Christian Broadcasting Group of Mountain Home Inc. Net: Moody. Format: Educ, relg. News progmg 9 hrs wkly. Target aud: General. ■ Earl Hagar, pres; Howard Amey, stn mgr; Carl Albright, vp opns; Melva Derrickson, opns mgr; Howard Amey, Carl Albright, chiefs engr.

KKTZ(FM)—Oct 25, 1985: 107.5 mhz; 100 kw. Ant 656 ft. TL: N36 12 18 W92 11 40. Stereo. Drawer 930, 1322 Bradley Dr. (72653). (501) 425-5100. FAX: (501) 424-2137. Licensee: MAC Partners (acq 3-31-93; $300,000; FTR 4-19-93). Net: SMN. Format: Adult contemp, all sports. News staff 2; news progmg 7 hrs wkly. Target aud: Females 25-54. ■ Stuart Brunner, pres, gen mgr & gen sls mgr; Dave Almond, opns mgr & chief engr; Roger Lowery, prom mgr & progmg mgr; Tom Phillips, progmg dir & mus dir; Ben McDade, news dir.

KPFM(FM)—June 6, 1984: 105.5 mhz; 33.4. Ant 590 ft. TL: N36 20 55 W92 24 01 Stereo. Box 930, 1322 Bradley Dr. No. one (72653). (501) 425-6022. FAX: (501) 424-2137. Licensee: Mountain Home Radio Station Inc. (acq 1-85; $260,789.71; FTR 1-21-85). Net: NBC. Format: Country. News staff one; news progmg 15 hrs wkly. Target aud: 24-64; females with families. ■ Morgan Dowdy, pres; Stewart Brunner, gen mgr & gen sls mgr; Dave Almond, opns mgr, mus dir & chief engr; Roger Lowery, prom mgr & progmg dir; Ben McDade, news dir.

KTLO(AM)—May 30, 1953: 1240 khz; 1 kw-U. TL: N36 20 43 W92 23 40. Hrs opn: 24. Box C (72653). (501) 425-3101. FAX: (501) 424-4314. Licensee: Mountain Home Broadcasting Corp. (acq 9-75). Net: ABC/E. Format: Country. News staff 3; news progmg 11 hrs wkly. Target aud: 18-55; general. ■ John Ahrens, pres; Bob Knight, gen mgr; Brad Haworth, opns mgr, progmg dir & mus dir; Danny Ward, gen sls mgr; Jim Bodenhamer, news dir; Ken Wilkens, chief engr.

KTLO-FM—Jan 11, 1971: 98.3 mhz; 1.4 kw. Ant 420 ft. TL: N36 20 55 W92 23 59. Stereo. Prog sep from AM. Net: ABC/I; Ark. Net. Format: Stardust. Target aud: 40 plus.

Mountain View

KWOZ(FM)—Dec 1, 1981: 103.3 mhz; 100 kw. Ant 987 ft. TL: N35 47 06 W91 57 44. Stereo. Box 53, 103 Peabody (72560). (501) 269-4306. FAX: (501) 269-4308. Licensee: Mountain View Broadcasting Corp. Net: SMN. Format: C&W. ■ Gary Bridgeman, stn mgr; Karen Owens, sls dir.

Murfreesboro

KMTB(FM)—May 18, 1983: 95.3 mhz; 3 kw. Ant 298 ft. TL: N34 05 44 W93 41 31 (CP: 99.5 mhz, 20.5 kw, ant 358 ft.). Stereo. Hrs opn: 24. Box 907 (71958); Box 95, 120 N. Main St., Nashville (71852). (501) 845-1195. FAX: (501) 845-1767. Licensee: Penn-Lee Broadcasting Inc. (acq 2-26-93; $178,500; FTR 3-15-93). Format: C&W. Spec prog: Gospel 4 hrs wkly. ■ Greg Bobo, pres & gen mgr; John Gosney, progmg mgr; John Sheldon, news dir; Norm Mason, chief engr. ■ Rates: $6; 6; 6; 5.25.

Nashville

KBHC(AM)—May 1959: 1260 khz; 500 w-D. TL: N33 55 45 W93 51 01. 1513 S. 4rth St. (71852). (501) 845-3601. Licensee: Ann Gathright (acq 5-73). Net: Ark. Net. Rep: Keystone (unwired net). C&W, relg. ■ Pete Gathright, gen mgr; Ann Gathright, gen sls mgr; Rick Castleberry, progmg dir & chief engr; Rick Jeffers, mus dir; Brent Pinkerton, news dir.

KNAS(FM)—Co-owned with KBHC(AM). Feb 14, 1977: 105.5 mhz; 3 kw. Ant 85 ft. TL: N33 55 45 W93 51 01. Stereo. Prog sep from AM. Format: Adult contemp.

Arkansas

Newark

*KLLN(FM)—Jan 1, 1985: 90.9 mhz; 4 kw. Ant 456 ft. TL: N35 43 25 W91 26 40. Highway 233 (72562). (501) 799-8693. Licensee: Newark Public School. Format: Southern gosp. ■ Fred Ahlborn, gen mgr; Al Deeter, progmg dir; Dale Johnson, chief engr.

Newport

KNBY(AM)—Oct 12, 1949: 1280 khz; 1 kw-D, 87 w-N. TL: N35 36 38 W91 15 02. Box 520 (72112). (501) 523-5891. FAX: (501) 523-5893. Licensee: Newport Broadcasting Co. Group owner: Sudbury Svcs Inc. & Newport Broadcasting Co. Net: AP. Format: C&W. ■ Harold Sudbury, pres; Dale Gardner, gen mgr & gen sls mgr; Heath Shelby, progmg dir; Dale Johnson, chief engr.

KOKR(FM)—Co-owned with KNBY(AM). Sept 1, 1966: 100.7 mhz; 4.1 kw. Ant 220 ft. TL: N35 36 38 W91 15 02 (CP: 35 kw, ant 548 ft.). Stereo. Prog sep from AM. Format: CHR.

North Crossett

KWLT(FM)—Not on air, target date Spring 1994: 102.7 mhz; 25 kw. Ant 328 ft. TL: N33 12 58 W91 55 42. Stereo. Box 1787, Cleveland, MS (38732). (601) 846-1787. FAX: (601) 843-0494. Licensee: South Ark Broadcasting Inc. Group owner: Contemporary Communications. Format: Adult contemp. News progmg 2 hrs wkly. Target aud: General. ■ Larry G. Fuss, pres; Brian K. Medlin, gen mgr.

North Little Rock

KLRG(AM)—Apr 15, 1946: 1150 khz; 5 kw-D, 1 kw-N, DA-N. TL: N34 45 53 W92 11 51. 200 S. Arch St., Little Rock (72201). (501) 374-4574. Licensee: Willis Broadcasting Corp. (group owner; acq 3-22-90). Net: MBS. Rep: Katz & Powell. Format: Gospel, Black, relg. ■ Katrina Turner, gen mgr; Ken Peterson, progmg dir; Greg Harris, mus dir; Tracy Gates, chief engr. ■ Rates: $26; 22; 26; 18.

KZQA(FM)—Not on air, target date unknown: 101.1 mhz; 3 kw. Ant 328 ft. TL: N34 49 52 W92 19 18. North Little Rock Bcstg Ltd., 121 Dexter Road (72116). Licensee: North Little Rock Broadcasting Ltd.

Osceola

KOSE(AM)—Oct 11, 1949: 860 khz; 1 kw-D, 20 w-N. TL: N35 29 16 W89 58 57. Box 248 (72370). (501) 563-2641. FAX: (501) 563-3401. Licensee: Pollack Broadcasting Co. (acq 10-1-85; $400,000; FTR 8-12-85). Net: ABC/D; Ark. Radio Net. Rep: Roslin, Midsouth. Format: Solid gold rock & roll. News staff one; news progmg 6 hrs wkly. Target aud: 24-55; middle-class, blue/white collar workers. Spec prog: Black 6 hrs, farm 5 hrs wkly. ■ William H. Pollack, pres; Craig Konn, gen mgr & gen sls mgr; Bob Abel, opns mgr & progmg dir; Mike Wilson, news dir; Rob Herron, chief engr.

KAFW(FM)—Co-owned with KOSE(AM). Not on air, target date unknown: 107.3 mhz; 3 kw. Ant 223 ft. 509 S. Walnut St. (72370).

Ozark

KDYN(AM)—Feb 5, 1969: 1540 khz; 500 w-D. TL: N35 29 16 W93 48 43. Hrs opn: Sunrise-sunset. Box 1086 (72949). (501) 667-4567. FAX: (501) 667-5214. Licensee: Ozark Communications Inc. (acq 9-15-85). Net: ABC/I; Ark. Radio Net. Format: Contemp country. ■ Jerry V. Dietz, pres, gen mgr & gen sls mgr; Marc Dietz, progmg dir & news dir.

KDYN-FM—Oct 2, 1980: 96.7 mhz; 1.6 kw. Ant 400 ft. TL: N35 29 10 W93 53 29. Stereo. Dups AM 100%.

Paragould

KDRS(AM)—Jan 1, 1947: 1490 khz; 1 kw-U. TL: N36 02 56 W90 27 44. Box 117 (72451); 400 Tower Dr. (72450). (501) 236-7627; (501) 972-5032. FAX: (501) 239-4583. Licensee: SAS Communications Inc. (acq 6-89; $450,000 with co-located FM; FTR 6-26-89). Net: CBS; Prog Farm. Rep: Keystone (unwired net), Midsouth. Wash atty: F. Joseph Brinig. Format: Country. News progmg 7 hrs wkly. Target aud: Those with spendable income. Spec prog: Farm 10 hrs, relg 8 hrs wkly. ■ Jim Adkins, pres, gen mgr, gen sls mgr, prom mgr & progmg dir; Bob Hendricks, mus dir & news dir; Larry Caldwell, chief engr. ■ Rates: $15; 12; 15; 10.

KLQZ(FM)—Co-owned with KDRS(AM). March 5, 1983: 107.1 mhz; 1.9 kw. Ant 410 ft. TL: N36 01 48 W90 35 49. Stereo. Dups AM 98%. Net: CBS. ■ Rates: Same as AM.

KDXY(FM)—Oct 4, 1971: 104.9 mhz; 3 kw. Ant 277 ft. TL: N36 00 52 W90 31 47. Stereo. Hrs opn: 24. Box 1106, 3804 Linwood Dr. (72451). (501) 239-8588; (501) 932-5400. FAX: (501) 239-3030. Licensee: North Arkansas Radio Inc. (acq 8-4-84). Net: ABC/D. Rep: Roslin. Wash atty: Eugene T. Smith. Format: Adult contemp, oldies. News staff one; news progmg 6 hrs wkly. Target aud: 25-49; adults who prefer light current hits & oldies. ■ Bill Little, pres; Trey Stafford, gen mgr; Ron Roe, progmg dir & news dir; Tom J. Hill, chief engr. ■ Rates: $15; 15; 15; 15.

KLQZ(FM)—Listing follows KDRS(AM).

Paris

KERX(FM)—May 1981: 95.3 mhz; 6 kw. Ant 571 ft. TL: N35 18 06 W93 45 40. c/o Star Radio, 7450 Midlothian Pike, Richmond, VA (23225). (501) 963-6593. Licensee: Max H. Pearson. Group owner: Star Radio (acq 10-18-93; $42,000; FTR 11-8-93). Net: AP, SMN. Format: Country. News staff one. Target aud: General.

Piggott

KTEI(FM)—Oct 15, 1983: 105.5 mhz; 6 kw. Ant 298 ft. TL: N36 19 47 W90 06 58. Stereo. Hrs opn: 24. Box 569, Kennett, MO (63857); Box 299 (72454). (314) 888-5333; (314) 888-1540. FAX: (314) 888-5333. Licensee: KBXM Inc. (acq 10-86; $240,000; FTR 9-15-86). Net: SMN. Format: Progsv country. News staff one; news progmg 5 hrs wkly. Target aud: 18-55; young adults, young professionals, farmers. Spec prog: Farm 5 hrs wkly. ■ Gary Wilcoxson, pres; Mick Vandiver, gen mgr; Larry Warbritton, gen sls mgr & prom mgr; Buck Harrison, progmg dir & mus dir; Jason Willis, news dir; Palmer Johnson, chief engr.

Pine Bluff

*KCAT(AM)—April 1963: 1340 khz; 1 kw-U. TL: N34 12 47 W92 01 53. Box 8808 (71611). (501) 534-5001. Licensee: J.B. Scanlon (acq 4-62). Format: Urban contemp, relg, news. Target aud: 18-55. ■ J.B. Scanlon, gen mgr & chief engr; George Gatewood, progmg dir; Robert Holmes, mus dir; R.D. Robinson, news dir.

KCLA(AM)—Jan 16, 1947: 1400 khz; 1 kw-U. TL: N34 11 33 W92 02 42. Box 1004 (71613); 3601 Apple (71603). (501) 535-7883. FAX: (501) 535-7953. Licensee: KCLA Inc. (acq 6-21-68). Net: Ark. Net. Format: Country. News staff one; news progmg 5 hrs wkly. Target aud: 35 plus; lower to middle income. ■ Harley Cox, pres; Floyd Donald, gen mgr.

KZYP(FM)—Co-owned with KCLA(AM). Nov 1, 1984: 99.3 mhz; 3 kw. Ant 200 ft. TL: N34 11 33 W92 02 42. Stereo. Prog sep from AM. Format: Urban contemp. News staff one; news progmg one hr wkly. Target aud: 25-45; middle to upper income.

KIPR(FM)—1963: 92.3 mhz; 100 kw. Ant 938 ft. TL: N34 22 12 W92 10 07. Stereo. 415 N. McKinley, Suite 920, Little Rock (72205-3022). (501) 663-0092. FAX: (501) 664-9201. Licensee: Cornerstone Broadcasting (acq 12-31-84). Format: Urban contemp. News progmg 3 hrs wkly. Target aud: 18-44. ■ Calvin G. Arnold, vp; Gordon Heiges, gen mgr; Joe Booker, progmg dir.

KOTN(AM)—Mar 12, 1934: 1490 khz; 1 kw-U. TL: N34 13 15 W91 58 20. Hrs opn: 24. 920 Commerce Rd. (71601). (501) 534-8978. Licensee: University of Arkansas Board of Trustees. Net: ABC/E, MBS; Ark. Net. Format: Adult contemp. Target aud: 25-54; agri oriented men & women. Spec prog: Farm 6 hrs wkly. ■ Dawn Deane, opns dir; Michael Morgan, mus dir; Marinelle Howard, news dir. ■ Rates: $18; 12; 14; 7.

KPBA(AM)—Aug 19, 1960: 1270 khz; 5 kw-D. TL: N34 10 25 W92 00 30. 4006 Old Warren Rd. (71603). (501) 534-6848. Licensee: Family Time Ministries Inc. (acq 1-24-91; $20,000; FTR 2-11-91). Format: Black, gospel. Target aud: General; Black. ■ Amir Khan, pres; Maurice Ficklin, exec vp & gen mgr; Cal Rollins, chief engr. ■ Rates: $9; 9; 9; 9.

KPBQ-FM—Dec 23, 1991: 101.3 mhz; 25 kw. Ant 328 ft. TL: N34 15 13 W92 03 58. Stereo. Box 7096 (71611). (501) 535-1241. FAX: (501) 535-1272. Licensee: Colon Johnston (acq 10-16-90; $60,000; FTR 11-5-90). Format: Country. News staff 4. Target aud: 12-60. ■ Colon Johnston, pres. ■ Rates: $10; 10; 10; 10.

*KUAP(FM)—February 1994: 89.7 mhz. 6 kw Ant 285 ft. TL: N34 14 33 W92 01 02. Fine Arts Bldg. 1200 N. University (77601); KOTN 920 Commerce Rd. (71601). (501) 534-8978; (501) 543-8946; (501) 534-8911. FAX: (501) 543-8011. Licensee: Board of Trustees of Univ. of Arkansas. Format: Educational. ■ Eva McGee, chmn; Dawn Deane, opns dir.

*KYFB(FM)—Not on air, target date unknown: 91.1 mhz; 1 kw. Ant 200 ft. TL: N34 17 15 W92 02 02. Bible Broadcasting Network, Charlotte, NC (28241-7300). (704) 523-5555. Licensee: Bible Broadcasting Network (group owner).

KZYP(FM)—Listing follows KCLA(AM).

Pocahontas

KPOC(AM)—Nov 15, 1950: 1420 khz; 1 kw-D. TL: N36 16 36 W90 57 18. Box 508 (72455). (501) 892-5234. FAX: (501) 892-2576. Licensee: Scott Media Services (acq 6-15-84). Net: ABC/D; Ark. Net. Format: C&W, adult contemp. News staff one. Target aud: 25-54; general. Spec prog: Farm 10 hrs wkly. ■ W.W. Scott, pres; Timothy Scott, gen mgr & progmg dir; Larry Caldwell, chief engr. ■ Rates: $10.75; 9.50; 10.75; 9.50.

KPOC-FM—Apr 25, 1969: 103.9 mhz; 3 kw. Ant 145 ft. TL: N36 16 36 W90 57 18. Dups AM 100%.

Prairie Grove

KDAB(FM)—Dec 19, 1992: 94.9 mhz; 21 kw. Ant 761 ft. TL: N35 51 00 W94 23 00. Stereo. Hrs opn: 24. Box 949, 118 E. Buchanan (72753). Licensee: Vinewood Communications. Net: USA. Format: Southern gospel mus. News progmg 2 hrs wkly. Target aud: 30 plus; listeners who like positive, inspirational progs. ■ Joe Hart, Cheryl Hart, CEOs. ■ Rates: $72; 72; 72; 72.

Prescott

KHPA(FM)—See Hope.

KTPA(AM)—Dec 1, 1959: 1370 khz; 1 kw-D, 49 w-N. TL: N36 20 04 W94 10 41. Box 734 (71857). (501) 887-2638. FAX: (501) 777-8888. Licensee: Newport Broadcasting Co. Group owner: Sudbury Services Inc. & Newport Broadcasting Co. (acq 5-14-66). Net: UPI; Ark. Radio Net. Format: Country. ■ Harold Sudbury, pres; Rob Hill, gen mgr & stn mgr; Mark Hobson, progmg dir; John McCoy, news dir; Warren Collum, chief engr.

Rogers

KAMO(AM)—Sept 16, 1954: 1390 khz; 1 kw-D, DA. TL: N36 20 04 W94 10 41. 4001 W. Walnut (72756). (501) 636-4611; (501) 751-8800. FAX: (501) 631-6902. Licensee: Johnson Communications Inc. (acq 5-4-93; $600,000 with co-located FM; FTR 5-24-93). Net: ABC. Format: Country. News progmg 7 hrs wkly. Target aud: 25-54. ■ Dewey Johnson, pres, gen mgr & chief engr; Randy Jordan, gen sls mgr; Vickie Johnson, prom dir; Mitchell Johnson, progmg dir & mus dir. ■ Rates: $24; 20; 22; 16.

KAMO-FM—1971: 94.3 mhz; 5.2 kw. Ant 709 ft. TL: N36 26 30 W93 58 26. Stereo. Hrs opn: 24. Dups AM 100%. Rep: Katz & Powell. ■ Rates: $28; 25; 28; 24.

KURM(AM)—Nov 10, 1979: 790 khz; 5 kw-D, 500 w-N, DA-N. TL: N36 18 10 W94 06 47. Hrs opn: 5 AM-11 PM. 212 N. 2nd. St. (72756). (501) 636-7979. FAX: (501) 631-9711. Licensee: KERM Inc. Net: CBS. Format: Div. Spec prog: Farm 10 hrs wkly. ■ Kermit Womack, pres; Steve Womack, gen mgr; Renne Peachy, progmg dir; Mark Barron, news dir; Jim Alexander, chief engr.

Russellville

KARV(AM)—Feb 25, 1947: 610 khz; 1 kw-D, 500 w-N, DA-2. TL: N35 17 56 W93 09 09. Hrs opn: 24. Box 190, 201 W. 2nd (72801). (501) 968-6105. FAX: (501) 967-5278. Licensee: KERM Inc. (acq 10-22-92; $250,000; FTR 11-23-92). Net: CBS, NBC Talknet. Format: News, weather, sports, MOR. News staff 4; news progmg 38 hrs wkly. Target aud: 35 plus; affluent adults. Spec prog: Farm 5 hrs wkly. ■ Kermit Wolmack, pres; Bill Stevens, gen sls mgr; Johnny Story, progmg dir; John Storu, news dir; J. Alexander, chief engr. ■ Rates: $27; 18; 21; 12.

KCJC(FM)—Sept 29, 1985: 100.9 mhz; 6 kw. Ant 295 ft. TL: N35 17 37 W93 10 39. Stereo. Box 2350, Amy Lyn Pl. (72801). (501) 968-6816. FAX: (501) 968-2946. Licensee: Johnson Communications Inc. (acq 2-26-90; $485,400; FTR 3-12-90). Format: Christian mus. News staff one; news progmg 10 hrs wkly. Target aud: 29-54.

*KMTC(FM)—June 1987: 91.1 mhz; 360 w. Ant -62 ft. TL: N35 18 11 W93 08 42. Box 570, 805 Dike Rd. (72811-0570). (501) 967-7400. Licensee: Russellville Educational Broadcasting Foundation. Net: USA. Format: Christian adult contemp. News progmg one hr wkly. Target aud: 25-55. ■ Tom Underhill, gen mgr; Jim Gray, gen sls mgr & progmg mgr; Anthony Bucci, mus dir; Jim Alexander, chief engr.

*KXRJ(FM)—Apr 3, 1989: 91.9 mhz; 100 w. Ant -92 ft. TL: N35 17 47 W93 08 18. Hrs opn: Noon-midnight. Arkansas Tech. Univ., Hwy. 7 N. (72801). (501) 968-0641. Licensee: Arkansas Tech University. Format: Div, class, progsv. News progmg 10 hrs wkly. Target aud: General. Spec prog: Educ, jazz 15 hrs wkly. ■ John Gale, pres; La Nell Thompson, opns dir & news dir; George Cotton, chief engr.

Salem

KCAB(AM)—See Dardanelle.

KSAR(FM)—September 1977: 95.9 mhz; 2.5 kw. Ant 325 ft. TL: N36 22 51 W91 49 28. Stereo. Box 458 (72576). (501) 895-2665. FAX: (501) 895-4088. Licensee: Bragg Broadcasting Inc. (acq 12-1-87). Net: ABC/E; Ark. Radio Net. Format: Country, info. News progmg 21 hrs wkly. Target aud: 35 plus. Spec prog: Farm 4 hrs wkly. ■ James Bragg, pres & gen mgr; Ruth Bragg, gen sls mgr; Ken Loggains, progmg dir; Dale Johnson, chief engr. ■ Rates: $12; 10; 10; 8.

Searcy

KAPZ(AM)—See Bald Knob.

KKSY(FM)—See Bald Knob.

KWCK(AM)—Aug 25, 1951: 1300 khz; 5 kw-D, 30 w-N. TL: N35 15 27 W91 43 49. Box 1300, 100 E. Arch St. (72143). (501) 268-7123. FAX: (501) 279-2900. Licensee: Class Inc. Group owner: Demaree Media Inc. (acq 1-1-88). Net: AP, CNN. Format: C&W, agri & news. Spec prog: Farm 10 hrs wkly. ■ Alan Risener, pres, gen mgr & progmg dir; Brent Scott, mus dir; Ken Simmons, news dir & chief engr.

KWCK-FM—April 1971: 99.9 mhz; 50 kw. Ant 492 ft. TL: N35 26 50 W91 56 52. Stereo. Dups AM 95%. Spec prog: Farm 3 hrs wkly.

Sheridan

KEZQ(FM)—Nov 1, 1984: 102.9 mhz; 50 kw. Ant 488 ft. TL: N34 25 08 W92 22 17. Stereo. Hrs opn: 24. Suite 768, 1501 N. University, North Little Rock (72207). (501) 661-0150. Licensee: GHB Broadcasting Group owner: GHB Radio Group (acq 6-7-93; $1.3 million; FTR 6-28-93). Wash atty: Smithwick & Belendiuk. Format: Soft adult contemp. News staff one; news progmg 2 hrs. Target aud: 25-54. ■ Randy Bush, gen mgr; Todd Curtis, gen sls mgr; Mark Hyatt, progmg dir. ■ Rates: $40; 32; 36; 24.

KGHT(AM)—Mar 15, 1982: 880 khz; 220 w. TL: N34 41 36 W92 18 21 (D), N34 18 21 W92 23 06 (N). 10000 Warden Rd., North Little Rock (72120). (501) 985-0880. FAX: (501) 985-0260. Licensee: Country Broadcasting Inc. Format: Southern gospel. Spec prog: Farm 10 hrs, relg 5 hrs wkly. ■ Harvey Fritts, pres & gen mgr; Jerry Venable, progmg dir; Felix McDonald, chief engr.

Sherwood

KMTL(AM)—Oct 31, 1983: 760 khz; 10 kw-D. TL: N34 49 34 W92 12 19. 2808 E. Kiehl Ave., North Little Rock (72116). (501) 835-1554. Licensee: Sherwood Broadcasting Co. Format: Relg. ■ George Domerese, gen mgr; Jack Knight, progmg dir; Gary Lee, mus dir; Chester Pierce, chief engr.

KOUN(FM)—Not on air, target date unknown: 102.1 mhz; 2 kw. Ant 571 ft. TL: N34 44 38 W92 16 32. 22836 MacFarlane Dr., Woodlane Hills, CA (91364). Licensee: Sherwood Broadcasting of Arkansas.

Siloam Springs

*KLRC(FM)—Oct 1, 1981: 101.1 mhz; 3.1 kw. Ant 459 ft. TL: N36 11 25 W94 33 55. Stereo. Hrs opn: 18. John Brown Univ, 2000 W. University (72761). (501) 524-7101; (501) 524-3131. Licensee: John Brown University. Net: USA. Format: Contemp Christian. News progmg 2 hrs wkly. Target aud: 18-34. Spec prog: Jazz 15 hrs wkly. ■ George Ford, pres; Mike Flynn, gen mgr; Rick Sparks, progmg dir.

KMCK(FM)—1947: 105.7 mhz; 100 kw. Ant 410 ft. TL: N36 11 25 W94 33 55 (CP: Ant 476 ft., TL: N36 11 07 W94 17 49). Stereo. Suite 125, 280 N. College, Fayetteville (72701). (501) 521-5128. FAX: (501) 521-4968. Licensee: Tate Communications Inc. (group owner; acq 6-89). Net: AP. Rep: D & R Radio. Format: CHR. Target aud: 18-49; contemporary adults. ■ Harvey Tate, pres; George Hochman, gen mgr; Pat McQuaid, gen sls mgr; Terry Long, prom mgr & news dir; Dan Hentschel, progmg dir; Mike Chase, mus dir; Doyle Garner, chief engr.

KUOA(AM)—Apr 12, 1923: 1290 khz; 5 kw-D. TL: N36 11 25 W94 33 55. Box 3145 JBU, (72761). (501) 524-3154. Licensee: KUOA Inc. (acq 3-15-33). Net: CNN. Format: C&W. News staff one. ■ George Ford, pres; Carl McQuay, gen mgr; Ken Flory, gen sls mgr; Carl Tolbert, news dir; Norman McChristian, chief engr.

Springdale

KQXK(AM)—July 15, 1966: 1590 khz; 2.5 kw-D, 58 w-N. TL: N36 12 21 W94 07 11. 1180 W. Sunset Ave. (72764). (501) 756-0105; (501) 750-4108. FAX: (501) 751-8636. Licensee: Westark Broadcasting. Format: Oldies. ■ Eldon Coffman, pres; Dale Daniels, gen mgr & opns mgr; Dave Felker, gen sls mgr; Tom Browne, progmg dir & mus dir; Chuck Barrett, news dir.

KBEV(FM)—Co-owned with KQXK(AM). Sept 19, 1968: 104.9 mhz; 1 kw. Ant 479 ft. TL: N36 10 48 W94 05 07 (CP: 2.75 kw). Stereo. Prog sep from AM. Format: CHR. ■ Jerry Patton, stn mgr.

Stamps

KZHE(FM)—October 1980: 100.5 mhz; 50 kw. Ant 500 ft. TL: N33 26 01 W93 27 49. Stereo. Hrs opn: 24. 909 E. Main St., Magnolia (71753-3708). (501) 234-7790. Licensee: A-1 Communications Inc. (acq 5-20-92; $85,000; FTR 6-8-92). Net: SMN. Format: Country. Target aud: 25-54. Spec prog: Gospel 8 hrs wkly. ■ Troy Alphin, pres; Sharon Alphin, vp; Dave Sehon, gen mgr, stn mgr & opns mgr; Gwenna McClellan, gen sls mgr; Norm Mason, chief engr.

Stuttgart

KWAK(AM)—May 15, 1948: 1240 khz; 1 kw-U. TL: N34 29 27 W91 33 45. Hrs opn: 18. Box 907, 1818 S. Buerkle (72160). (501) 673-1595. Licensee: Arkansas County Broadcasters Inc. Net: ABC/I; Prog Farm. Format: Country, talk, information. Target aud: General. Spec prog: Farm 6 hrs wkly. ■ Bobby Caldwell, pres; Scott Siler, stn mgr, gen sls mgr & progmg dir; Sanji Levi, mus dir; Jerry Prince, news dir; Sandy Sandine, chief engr. ■ Rates: $16; 16; 16; 16.

KXDX(FM)—Co-owned with KWAK(AM). Dec 15, 1987: 105.5 mhz; 3 kw. Ant 325 ft. TL: N34 25 52 W91 26 08. Stereo. Dups AM 15%. Format: Adult contemp. News progmg 18 hrs wkly. ■ Rates: Same as AM.

Texarkana

KCMC(AM)—See Texarkana, Tex.

KKYR(AM)—Nov 15, 1951: 790 khz; 1 kw-D, 500 w-N, DA-N. TL: N33 22 30 W94 01 00. Hrs opn: 24. 2324 Arkansas Blvd. (75502). (501) 772-3771. Licensee: Broadcasters Unlimited Inc. (acq 6-89) $1.1 million with co-located FM; FTR 6-12-89). Net: AP. Rep: Banner. Format: Modern country. News staff one. Target aud: General. ■ Don R. Chaney, pres; Craig D. Reininger, gen mgr; Ed Torres, gen sls mgr; Larry Kent, progmg dir.

KKYR-FM—See Texarkana, Tex.

KTWN(AM)—See Texarkana, Tex.

KTWN-FM—June 11, 1968: 107.1 mhz; 2.9 kw. Ant 479 ft. TL: N33 25 45 W94 07 11. Stereo. Hrs opn: 24. 303 W. Broad, Texarkana, TX (75501). (903) 793-4671. FAX: (903) 794-5236. Licensee: KATQ Radio Inc. Net: ABC/E. Format: Adult contemp. News staff one; news progmg 3 hrs wkly. Spec prog: Farm 2 hrs, gospel 2 hrs wkly. ■ John H. Bell, pres & gen mgr; Floyd Bell, vp; Hazel E. Bell, news dir.

KUKB(FM)—Not on air, target date unknown: 106.3 mhz; 3 kw. Ant 328 ft. TL: N33 22 39 W93 56 38. 131 Chestnut St., Camden, TN (38320). Licensee: State Line Broadcasting Co. Inc.

Trumann

KWEZ(FM)—February 1991: 106.7 mhz; 6 kw. Ant 328 ft. TL: N35 44 51 W90 37 49. Stereo. Hrs opn: 24. Box 1199, 517 Southwest Dr., Jonesboro (72401). (501) 935-3279. FAX: (501) 935-7035. Licensee: Eagle Communications Inc. (group owner: acq 6-17-92; $250,000; FTR 7-6-92). Format: Country. ■ Doug Mould, gen mgr; Mark Ford, mus dir & news dir; Larry Caldwell, chief engr.

Van Buren

KAYR(AM)—Sept 6, 1979: 1060 khz; 500 w-D, DA. TL: N35 25 36 W94 18 11. 190 Cloverleaf Plaza (72956). (501) 474-3422. FAX: (501) 474-2869. Licensee: LKR Communications Inc. Format: Easy lstng. News staff one.

Larry Ruth, gen mgr; Don Jones, mus dir & chief engr; Ken Mitchell, news dir.

KLSZ-FM—Co-owned with KAYR(AM). May 22, 1983: 102.7 mhz; 3 kw. Ant 295 ft. TL: N35 26 39 W94 22 04 (CP: 11.83 kw, ant 476 ft., TL: N35 26 55 W94 32 06). Stereo. Box 5084, Fort Smith (72913). Format: Adult contemp.

KFDF(AM)—Nov 24, 1958: 1580 khz; 1 kw-D, 45 w-N. TL: N35 25 58 W94 19 47. Hrs opn: 24. 523 Garrison Ave. Fort Smith (72901). Box 573 Fort Smith (72902-0573). (501) 288-0040; (501) 785-4600. FAX: (501) 785-4484. Licensee: Broadcasters Inc. Format: Relg. Target aud: General. ■ William Pharis, CEO & pres; Karen Pharis, exec vp; John Wilhelm, gen mgr; Mike Vaughn, stn mgr, progmg dir & mus dir; Todd Roberts, news dir; Nancy Rowland, pub affrs dir; Willard Matten, Stuart Roland, chiefs engr.

KLSZ-FM—Listing follows KAYR(AM).

Waldron

KRWA-FM—May 18, 1982: 103.1 mhz; 3 kw. Ant 298 ft. TL: N34 51 44 W94 04 26 (CP: Ant 304 ft.). Stereo. Box 909, 115 Parker Ave. (72958). (501) 637-2199. Licensee: Cole Thomas Broadcasting Corp. (acq 6-5-92). Net: Ark. Radio Net. Format: C&W, relg. Spec prog: Farm 5 hrs wkly. ■ Joe McKinley, pres; Marty Starkey, mus dir.

Walnut Ridge

KRLW(AM)—June 29, 1951: 1320 khz; 1 kw-D. TL: N36 03 58 W90 56 24. Hrs opn: 24. Box 30, Hwy. 412 E. (72476). (501) 886-6666. Licensee: Voices Unlimited Inc. (acq 3-1-85). Net: CNN, Jones Satellite Audio. Format: Country, news/talk. News progmg 20 hrs wkly. Target aud: 25 plus. Spec prog: Relg 9 hrs wkly. ■ Lance Brown, vp, gen mgr & progmg dir; Stephanie Eagan, mus dir; Larry Caldwell, chief engr. ■ Rates: $8; 8; 6; 6.

KRLW-FM—Mar 27, 1977: 106.3 mhz; 3 kw. Ant 328 ft. TL: N36 03 58 W90 56 24 Stereo. Hrs opn: 24. Prog dups AM 100%. ■ Rates: Same as AM.

Warren

KWRF(AM)—August 1953: 860 khz; 250 w-D, 55 w-N. TL: N33 37 59 W92 03 51. Hrs opn: 24. 1255 N. Myrtle, (71671). (501) 226-2653; (501) 226-2654. FAX: (501) 226-2508. Licensee: Jimmy L. Sledge and Gwen Sledge (acq 4-12-91; $125,000 with co-located FM; FTR 5-6-91). Net: AP, SMN; Ark. Radio Net. Format: C&W. News staff one; news progmg 10 hrs wkly. Target aud: General. Spec prog: Gospel 8 hrs wkly. ■ Jimmy Sledge, pres, gen mgr, gen sls mgr, mus dir & progmg dir; Gwen Sledge, vp opns; Allen Wiese, news dir. ■ Rates: $6.75; 6.75; 6.75; 6.75.

KWRF-FM—June 21, 1976: 105.5 mhz; 3 kw. Ant 250 ft. TL: N33 37 59 W92 03 51. Hrs opn: 24. Dups AM 100%. ■ Gwen Sledge, exec vp. ■ Rates: Same as AM.

West Helena

KCLT(FM)—Dec 17, 1984: 104.9 mhz; 3 kw. Ant 328 ft. TL: N34 30 56 W90 40 13. Stereo. Hrs opn: 24. Box 2870, 307 Hwy. 49B (72390). (501) 572-9506; (501) 572-3796. FAX: (501) 572-1845. Licensee: West Helena Broadcasters Inc. (acq 8-8-84). Format: Black, urban contemp. Spec prog: Gospel 15 hrs wkly. ■ Alford Billingsley, pres; Raymond Simes, gen mgr & gen sls mgr; Lee Gary, progmg dir & mus dir; L.T. Simes, news dir; Ray Lowery, chief engr.

KCRI-FM—See Helena.

KJIW(AM)—Nov 21, 1988: 1600 khz; 1 kw. TL: N34 30 52 W90 38 18. 204 Moore St., Helena (72342). (501) 338-2700. Licensee: Elijah Mondy Jr. (acq 1988). Format: Relg. News staff 2; news progmg 8 hrs wkly. Target aud: Adults; baby-boomers. ■ Elijah Mondy, gen mgr.

KJIW-FM—Jan 5, 1989: 94.5 mhz; 6 kw. Ant 250 ft. TL: N34 30 52 W90 38 18. Dups AM 100%.

West Memphis

KSUD(AM)—Dec 1, 1961: 730 khz; 250 w-U, DA-N. TL: N35 08 31 W90 08 05. Hrs opn: 24. 102 N. 5th St. (72301); Box 3696, Memphis, TN (38103). (501) 735-6622. FAX: (501) 735-6646. Licensee: Newport Broadcasting Co. Group owner: Sudbury Services Inc. & Newport Broadcasting Co. Format: Christian, adult contemp, MOR. Target aud: 25-54; family types. ■ Harold L. Sudbury, pres; Harold Penn, gen mgr & gen sls mgr; Ed Blackburn, progmg dir, mus dir & news dir; Tom Hill, chief engr. ■ Rates: $18; 18; 18; 18.

California | Directory of Radio

White Hall

KWDA(FM)—Not on air, target date unknown: 104.5 mhz; 3 kw. Ant 328 ft. TL: N34 14 54 W92 02 08. c/o 1309 Bailey Dr. Pine Bluff (71601). Licensee: Bayou Broadcasting Inc.

Wrightsville

KYTN(FM)—Not on air, target date unknown: 107.7 mhz; 3 kw. Ant 328 ft. TL: N34 36 24 W92 14 17 (CP: 50 kw, ant 312 ft.). 723 W. 14th St., Little Rock (72202). (501) 433-1077. FAX: (501) 375-0947. Licensee: Wrightsville Communications Co. Inc. Format: Contemp Christian. ■ Garry Vaile, gen mgr; Gordon Stephen, opns mgr.

Wynne

KWYN(AM)—Sept 28, 1956: 1400 khz; 1 kw-U. TL: N35 15 21 W90 47 49. Hrs opn: 18. Box 789, Hwy. 64 W. (72396). (501) 238-8141; (501) 238-8142. FAX: (501) 238-5997. Licensee: East Arkansas Broadcasters Inc. Net: NBC. Format: Talk, C&W, Information. Target aud: General. Spec prog: Farm 6 hrs wkly. ■ Bobby Caldwell, CEO & gen mgr; Steve Chapman, sls dir & mktg dir; Steve Gadberry, progmg dir & mus dir; Lindell Staggs, news dir; Dan Winn, chief engr. ■ Rates: $20; 20; 20; 20.

KWYN-FM—May 15, 1969: 92.5 mhz; 25 kw. Ant 328 ft. TL: N35 11 59 W90 43 23. Stereo. Hrs opn: 18. Dups AM 10%. Format: Adult contemp, talk. ■ Steve Gadberry, opns dir. ■ Rates: Same as AM.

Yellville

KCTT-FM—1986: 97.7 mhz; 2.45 kw. Ant 331 ft. TL: N36 15 39 W92 41 42 (CP: 50 kw, ant 381 ft.). Stereo. Box 100, 112 N. Berry (72687). (501) 449-4001; (501) 449-4002. FAX: (501) 449-4001. Licensee: Glen B. Adams dba A&J Broadcasting Co. Inc. (acq 6-5-92; no charge (gift); FTR 6-22-92). Format: Traditional country. Spec prog: Folk 10 hrs wkly. ■ Glen Adams, CEO, vp opns & vp sls; Lindalu Duren, progmg dir & mus dir. ■ Rates: $7; 7; 7; 7.

California

WILLIAM A. EXLINE, INC
MEDIA BROKERS
CONSULTANTS

4340 Redwood Highway
Suite F 230
San Rafael, California 94903
TEL (415) 479-3484
• FAX (415) 479-1574

Alameda

KJAZ(FM)—Licensed to Alameda. See San Francisco.

Alisal

KTOM-FM—See Salinas.

Alturas

KCNO(AM)—June 4, 1951: 570 khz; 5 kw-D, 200 w-N. TL: N41 30 07 W120 30 01 (CP: 5 kw-U, DA-N). Box 570 (96101). (916) 233-3570. FAX: (916) 233-5570. Licensee: KCNO Inc. (acq 5-16-59). Net: Unistar, USA, ABC/E, NBC Talknet. Wash atty: Cohn & Marks. Format: News/talk, relg. News staff one; news progmg 3 hrs wkly. Target aud: General. Spec prog: Farm one hr wkly. ■ R.L. Hansen, pres; W.H. Hansen, gen mgr; Carol Irwin, opns mgr, gen sls mgr, prom mgr & progmg dir; Charlie Chrighton, mus dir & news dir; Dan Frey, chief engr. ■ Rates: $18; 12; 18; 8.

KYAX(FM)—Co-owned with KCNO(AM). Dec 4, 1990: 94.5 mhz; 100 kw. Ant 106 ft. TL: N41 33 50 W120 24 55 (CP: 52 kw, ant -78 ft.). Hrs opn: 14. Prog sep from AM. Net: SMN. Format: C&W. News progmg 17 hrs wkly. Target aud: General. ■ Bill Hansen, Dan Frey, Carol Irwin, dev dirs; Bill Hansen, sls dir & gen sls mgr. ■ Rates: $20; 12; 18; 10.

AMERICAN RADIO BROKERS, INC.
MOST TRUSTED NAME IN MEDIA BROKERAGE
CHESTER P. COLEMAN / PRESIDENT
FOR THE BEST STATIONS FOR SALE FROM THIS AREA
CALL — 415/441-3377
1255 POST STREET / SUITE 625 / SAN FRANCISCO, CA 94109

Anaheim

KORG(AM)—May 18, 1959: 1190 khz; 10 kw-D, 1.3 kw-N, DA-2. TL: N33 56 42 W117 51 44. Hrs opn: 24. 1190 E. Ball Rd. (92805). (714) 776-1190. FAX: (714) 774-1631. Licensee: ML Media Partners. Group owner: WIN Communications Inc. (acq 9-18-89); $15,125,000 with co-owned FM; FTR 10-9-89). Net: AP. Format: Talk, Korean, Arabic. Target aud: Specialized ethnic groups. Spec prog: Vietnamese 2 hrs, gospel, relg, Pol, Sp wkly. ■ I. Martin Pompadur, CEO; George Sosson, pres; Miles Sexton, vp & gen mgr; Lou Salatino, opns mgr; Dawn McKahan, gen sls mgr.

KEZY(FM)—Co-owned with KORG(AM). Apr 16, 1961: 95.9 mhz; 2.4 kw. Ant 328 ft. TL: N33 49 50 W117 48 39. Stereo. Prog sep from AM. Net: ABC/C. Wash atty: Wiley, Rein & Fielding. Format: Adult Top-40. News staff one; news progmg 5 hrs wkly. Target aud: 18-49. Spec prog: Flagship station for NHL's Mighty Ducks. ■ April Whitney, prom mgr; Chris Cox, progmg dir; Tammy Trujillo, news dir; Mark Moceri, chief engr.

Anderson

KEWB(FM)—Mar 20, 1983: 94.7 mhz; 4.2 kw. Ant 1,565 ft. TL: N40 39 06 W122 31 32. Stereo. 1538 Market St., Redding (96099); Box 994424, Redding (96001). (916) 243-5392. Licensee: Radio Associates Inc. (group owner; acq 9-89; $850,000; FTR 9-25-89). Rep: D & R Radio. Wash atty: Arent, Fox, Kintner, Plotkin & Kahn. Format: Country. Target aud: 18-49. ■ Ken Miller, chmn; Roy Leffel, vp & gen mgr; Tony Roberts, prom dir; Gary Moore, progmg dir; Clark Taylor, mus dir. ■ Rates: $18; 18; 18; 18.

Angwin

*KCDS(FM)—May 20, 1961: 89.9 mhz; 794 w. Ant 3,010. TL: N38 40 09 W122 37 53. Stereo. Hrs opn: 24. Broadcast Center (94508). (707) 965-7141. FAX: (707) 965-6390. Licensee: Howell Mountain Broadcasting Co. Inc. Format: Relg. Target aud: General; 35-49. ■ John McVay, pres; Jennifer Schooley-Acting, gen mgr & opns mgr; John Geli, mus dir; Jared Getz, chief engr.

Apple Valley

KAPL(AM)—Jan 26, 1991: 1550 khz; 5 kw-D, 500 w-N, DA-N. TL: N34 32 12 W117 09 22. 13470 Manhasset Rd., #1 (92308); Box 3666 (92307). (619) 247-1111. FAX: (619) 247-0884. Licensee: KAPL Broadcasting, Inc. (acq 7-21-92). Net: SMN. Format: Oldies. News staff one. Target aud: 35-54. An upscale affluent audience dominating the 35-54 demographic. Spec prog: UCLA sports 4 hrs, Maverick's baseball (minor league) 16 hrs, relg 4 hrs wkly. ■ Michael Norris, vp, gen mgr, dev mgr, gen sls mgr & mktg mgr; Gary A. Wilson, opns dir, prom dir, progmg dir, mus dir & news dir; Elizabeth J. Hunsicker, rgnl sls mgr. ■ Rates: $15; 15; 15; 10.

KZXY(AM)—June 5, 1954: 960 khz; 5 kw-D, 400 w-N, DA-2. TL: N34 31 00 W117 13 35. Rebroadcasts KIXA-FM Lucerne Valley 100%. Box 5002, Victorville (92393); Suite 17, 12370 Hesperia Rd., Victorville (92392). (619) 241-1313. FAX: (619) 241-0205 Licensee: Ruby Broadcasting Inc. Group owner: Crown Broadcasting Inc. (acq 4-1-88; $1,700,000 with co-located FM; FTR 1-4-88). Format: Country. News staff 2; news progmg 18 hrs wkly. Target aud: 18-54. ■ Jeff Salkin, gen mgr.

KZXY-FM—May 17, 1968: 102.3 mhz; 3 kw. Ant 53 ft. TL: N34 31 00 W117 13 35 (CP: 6 kw, ant 328 ft.). Stereo. Prog sep from AM. Net: CNN. Format: Adult Contemp. Target aud: 25-54.

Arcadia

KMAX(FM)—Dec 3, 1960: 107.1 mhz; 3 kw. Ant 240 ft. TL: N34 10 51 W118 01 38 (CP: Ant -44 ft.). Suite 130, 3350 Electronic Dr., Pasadena (91107). (213) 681-2486. Licensee: Douglas Broadcasting Inc. (group owner; acq 1-23-89); grpsl; FTR 1-23-89). Format: Black, Spanish. ■ N. John Douglas, pres; Linda Johnson-Hayes, gen mgr; Bob Gourley, progmg dir; Reginald Utley, mus dir; Fred Folmer, chief engr. ■ Rates: $90; 90; 90; 90.

Arcata

KATA(AM)—Nov 15, 1957: 1340 khz; 1 kw-U. TL: N40 51 12 W124 05 00. Drawer 1139 (95521). (707) 822-7223. Licensee: Merit Broadcasting Corp. (group owner; acq 10-88). Net: MBS, ABC/I. Rep: Christal. Format: Solid gold. News staff one; news progmg 14 hrs wkly. Target aud: 25-54; upscale adults. Spec prog: San Francisco Giants baseball, San Jose Sharks. ■ Mike Martin, gen mgr & gen sls mgr; Dave Roble, progmg dir; Rick Michaels, mus dir; Evonne Morrow, news dir; Hubert Reed, chief engr. ■ Rates: $15; 15; 15; 12.

*KHSU-FM—October 1960: 90.5 mhz; 9 kw. Ant 1,490 ft. TL: N40 43 36 W123 58 19. Stereo. Hrs opn: 24. Humboldt State University (95521). (707) 826-4807. FAX: (707) 826-6082. Licensee: Humboldt State Univ. Net: NPR, APR. Calif. Pub. Format: Div, news. News progmg 28 hrs wkly. Target aud: 25 plus. Spec prog: Class 18 hrs, folk 15 hrs, jazz 15 hrs wkly. ■ Jill L. Paydon, gen mgr; Rick Culbertson, opns mgr; Leira V. Satlof, dev dir & prom mgr; Ron Ockert, progmg dir; Brooks Otis, mus dir; Sharon Fennell, pub affrs dir; Mark Miller, chief engr.

KXGO(FM)—1970: 93.1 mhz; 93 kw. Ant 1,640 ft. TL: N40 43 36 W123 58 19. Stereo. 215 4th St. Eureka (95501). (707) 445-8104. FAX: (707) 445-3906. Licensee: Westar Broadcasting Group, L & D (acq 10-1-91). Rep: Katz & Powell. Format: Contemp, classic rock. News staff 3. Target aud: 12-54; upscale adults. ■ Howard M. Holzapfel, CEO; Howard M. Holzapfel, exec vp; G.M. Holzapfel, vp sls; Carlos Casarez, sls dir; Dana Hall, progmg dir; Mark Householter, chief engr.

Arnold

KAGV(FM)—Not on air, target date unknown: 95.9 mhz; 500 w. Ant 334 ft. Box 708, Twain Harte (95383). Licensee: Clear Mountain Air Broadcasting Co.

KCFA(FM)—Not on air, target date unknown: 106.1 mhz. 910 w. Ant 840 ft. Licensee: Central Valley Broadcasting Co. (acq 10-29-93; $24,000; FTR 11-15-93).

Arroyo Grande

KKAL(AM)—Licensed to Arroyo Grande. See San Luis Obispo.

Atascadero

KIQO(FM)—May 19, 1979: 104.5 mhz; 5.6 kw. Ant 1,410 ft. TL: N35 21 38 W120 39 21. Stereo. Hrs opn: 24. Drawer 6028 (93423). (805) 466-6511. FAX: (805) 466-5362. Licensee: Garry & Virginia Brill (acq 9-1-84). Net: SMN. Rep: W.R.B.S. Wash atty: Jim Gammon. Format: Oldies. Target aud: 25-55. ■ Virginia Brill, Garry Brill, CEOs; Garry Brill, gen mgr; Eddie Trent, opns dir & progmg dir; Del McCulley, gen sls mgr; Bill Bordeaux, chief engr. ■ Rates: $30; 25; 30; 20.

Atherton

*KCEA(FM)—June 2, 1979: 89.1 mhz; 100 w. Ant -216 ft. TL: N37 27 41 W122 10 30 (CP: Ant 5 ft.). Stereo. Box 2385, Menlo Park (94026); 555 Middle Field Dr. (94027). (415) 321-6049; (324) 324-8936. Licensee: Menlo Atherton High School. Format: Big band. Target aud: General. ■ G. Frank Spinetta, gen mgr; Mark Strathdee, progmg dir & mus dir.

Atwater

KVRQ(FM)—Not on air, target date unknown: 92.5 mhz; 6 kw. Ant 328 ft. TL: N37 16 42 W120 37 33. Stereo. Hrs opn: 24. 20445 Johnny Ave., Sonora (95370). (209) 533-9272. Licensee: Clarke Broadcasting Corp. (group owner). Rep: Katz & Powell. Wash atty: Leventhal, Senter & Lerman. ■ H. Randolph Holder, pres.

Auberry

KSLK(FM)—July 12, 1992: 105.1 mhz; 590 w. Ant 1,902 ft. TL: N 37 04 25 W119 25 52. Suite 203, 320 W. Bedford,

Fresno (93711). (209) 261-1110. FAX: (209) 261-1133. Licensee: 105 Mountain Air Inc. Format: Easy listening. ■ Robert Eurich, pres & gen mgr.

Auburn

KAHI(AM)—Nov 13, 1957: 950 khz; 5 kw-D, 4.2 kw-N, DA-2. TL: N38 51 28 W121 01 39. Suite 120, 1230 High St. (95603). (916) 885-5636. FAX: (916) 885-0166. Licensee: National Radio Partners Ltd. Group owner: American Media Inc. (acq 8-7-92; grpsl, including co-located FM; FTR 8-24-92). Net: SMN. Rep: Eastman. Format: Country. News staff one. Target aud: 25-54. ■ John Davison, gen mgr; Bob Patrick, gen sls mgr; Dan Songer, progmg dir.

KHYL(FM)—Co-owned with KAHI(AM). Dec 21, 1961: 101.1 mhz; 36.3 kw. Ant 577 ft. TL: N38 51 28 W121 01 39. Stereo. Prog sep from AM. 2435 Marconi Ave., Sacramento (95821). (916) 974-0290. FAX: (916) 974-0802. Net: AP. Wash atty: Crowell & Moring. Format: Oldies. ■ John Felt, gen sls mgr; Steve Dini, prom dir; Brian Chase, progmg dir; Ric Santos, mus dir; Mike Reynolds, news dir.

Avalon

KBRT(AM)—June 1, 1952: 740 khz; 10 kw-D, DA. TL: N33 21 36 W118 56 51. Stereo. 3183 D Airway Ave., Costa Mesa (92626). (714) 754-4450. FAX: (714) 754-0735. Licensee: Kierton Inc. Group owner: Crawford Broadcasting Co. (acq 5-21-80). Format: Relg, talk. Target aud: General. ■ Donald Crawford, pres; Todd Stickler, opns mgr; Ed Personius, gen sls mgr; Sue Koska, prom dir; Ann Harrison, progmg dir; Gary Bloodworth, chief engr.

***KISL(FM)**—Not on air, target date unknown: 88.7 mhz; 100 w. Ant -732 ft. TL: N33 20 36 W118 19 16. c/o Ann Marshall, 209 Metropole Ave. (90704). (213) 510-0928. Licensee: Community Services Dept., City of Avalon.

KRCI(FM)—Not on air, target date unknown: 92.7 mhz; 3 kw. Ant 161 ft. TL: N33 21 00 W118 21 05. 333 Weymouth Ave., San Pedro (90731). Licensee: Catalina Radio, a Calif. L.P.

Avenal

KAAX(FM)—Not on air, target date unknown: 105.7 mhz; 915 w. Ant 597 ft. Suite A, 12550 Brookhurst St., Garden Grove (92640). Licensee: Avenal Educational Services Inc.

Baker

KBXY(FM)—Not on air, target date unknown: 94.9 mhz; 15.5 kw. Ant 417 ft. 13260 Winona Rd., Apple Valley (92308). Licensee: Desert Broadcasting G.P. ■ Tom Gammon, CEO; Steve Stephenson, exec vp; Jeff Salkin, stn mgr; B.J. Kelly, opns dir & progmg dir; Pamela Brian, mus dir.

KIXF(FM)—Mar 1, 1994: 101.5 mhz; 4.6 kw. Ant 1,289 ft. TL: N35 26 00 W115 55 25. Stereo. Hrs opn: 24. Rebroadcasts KIXW(FM) Lenwood 100%. Box 5002, 12370 Hesperia Rd., #17, Victorville (92392). (619) 241-1313. FAX: (619) 241-0205. Licensee: Turquoise Broadcasting Inc. (acq 7-8-92; $40,000; FTR 7-27-92). Net: SMN. Wash atty: Roberts & Eckard. Format: Country. News staff one. Target aud: 25-54; interstate travelers to Las Vegas & Laughlin, Nevada. Spec prog: Hourly traffic report to service interstate travelers. ■ Thomas P. Gammon, CEO; Steve Stephenson, exec vp; B. J. Kelly, opns dir, progmg dir & mus dir; Jeff Salkin, natl sls mgr; Diana Rice, news dir; Pam Bryan, pub affrs dir; Joe Talbot, chief engr. ■ Rates: $50; 40; 50; 30.

Bakersfield

KAFY(AM)—October 1946: 970 khz; 1 kw-D, 5 kw-N, DA-2. TL: N35 27 00 W118 56 48. Hrs opn: 24. 230 Truxton Ave. (93301). (805) 324-4411. FAX: (805) 327-9459. Licensee: Barro Broadcasting Corp. (acq 6-1-87). Net: UPI, CBS. Rep: Caballero. Format: Spanish. News staff one; news progmg 7 hrs wkly. Target aud: 18-54; Hispanic. ■ Mary Helen Barro, pres, gen mgr & prom mgr; Robert Perez, gen sls mgr; Jorge Diaz, progmg dir & news dir; Terry Gaiser, chief engr. ■ Rates: $30; 28; 30; 27.

KBID(AM)—February 1958: 1350 khz; 1 kw-D, 33 w-N. TL: N35 21 00 W119 58 58. Suite 23, 1626 19th St. (93301). (805) 861-1350. FAX: (805) 861-0334. Licensee: Southpaw Communications Inc. (acq 10-16-91; $170,000; FTR 11-4-91). ■ Kevin Rush, gen mgr; Bob Watt, progmg dir; Jennifer O'Conner, news dir.

KCHT(FM)—Nov 1991: 99.3 mhz; 6 kw. Ant 154 ft. TL: N35 21 07 W118 57 29. Stereo. Hrs opn: 24. Box 10176 Suite 280, 1100 Mohawk St. (93309). (805) 322-9929. Licensee: Grapevine Radio Inc. (acq 7-16-93; $650,000; FTR 8-9-93). Format: Hot adult contemp. ■ Allan B. Hammerel, gen mgr.

KCWR(AM)—October 1946: 550 khz; 5 kw-U, DA-N. TL: N35 20 25 W118 56 14. Stereo. 3223 Sillect Ave. (93308). (805) 326-1011. FAX: (805) 328-7503. Licensee: Buck Owens Productions Inc. (group owner; acq 1986). Net: AP. Rep: Katz. Format: Country. News staff 2. Target aud: 25-54. ■ Buck Owens, pres; Mel Owens Jr., gen mgr; Richard Trejo, gen sls mgr; Jerry Hufford, prom mgr; Evan Bridwell, progmg dir & mus dir; Mark Howell, news dir; Terry Gaiser, chief engr.

KUZZ-FM—Co-owned with KCWR(AM). 1968: 107.9 mhz; 5.8 kw. Ant 1,358 ft. TL: N35 26 20 W118 44 23 (CP: 6 kw, ant 1,365 ft., TL: N35 26 20 W118 44 24). Stereo. Dups AM 100%.

KERN(AM)—Jan 3, 1932: 1410 khz; 1 kw-U. TL: N35 21 07 W118 56 48. Hrs opn: 24. Box 2700, Suite 134, 1400 Easton Dr. (93309). (805) 328-1410; (805) 326-1410. FAX: (805) 328-0873. Licensee: Brandon Communications Inc. Group owner: American General Media (acq 5-1-75). Net: ABC/I, NBC Talknet, AP, Sun. Rep: Christal. Format: News/talk. News staff 3; news progmg 30 hrs wkly. Target aud: 25-54. Spec prog: Farm one hr, religious one hr wkly. ■ Anthony S. Brandon, pres; Roger Brandon, exec vp; Roger Fessler, gen mgr; Pat Garrett, opns dir; Larry Gregg, opns mgr; Tami Turner, prom dir; Larry Gregg, Pat Garrett, progmg dirs; John Windover, news dir; Terry Gaiser, chief engr.

KERN-FM—1948: 94.1 mhz; 4.5 kw. Ant 1,312 ft. TL: N35 26 20 W118 44 23. Stereo. Hrs opn: 24. Prog sep from AM. Format: Oldies.

KGEO(AM)—Jan 1, 1946: 1230 khz; 1 kw-U. TL: N35 20 53 W119 00 33. Stereo. Box 260 (93302); 207 Truxton Ave. (93301). (805) 631-1230. FAX: (805) 327-0786. Licensee: Rogers Brandon (acq 12-9-92; $1.75 million with co-located FM; FTR 1-4-93). Net: CNN. Rep: McGavren Guild. Wash atty: Cohn & Marks. Format: Oldies. ■ Rogers Brandon, gen mgr; Aricia Leighton, prom mgr; Bill Curtis, progmg dir; Steve Mull, chief engr.

KGFM(FM)—Co-owned with KGEO(AM). October 1964: 101.5 mhz; 4.8 kw. Ant 1,280 ft. TL: N35 26 20 W118 44 23. Stereo. Format: Easy lstng. ■ Walter Powers, mus dir.

KHIS(AM)—1959: 800 khz; 250 w-D, 21.25 w-N. TL: N35 20 41 W118 59 01 (CP: 1 kw-D, 440 w-N, DA-2. TL: N35 20 44 W118 59 33). 521 H St. (93304). (805) 327-0631. FAX: (805) 327-0633. Licensee: International Church of the Foursquare Gospel (group owner; acq 1-4-77). Format: Relg, MOR/contemp. ■ Alan Bowles, gen mgr; Scott Williams, opns mgr; Steve Mull, chief engr.

KHIS-FM—Aug 24, 1963: 96.5 mhz; 50 kw. Ant 550 ft. TL: N35 29 08 W118 53 19. Stereo. Prog sep from AM.

KIWI(FM)—Listing follows KWAC(AM).

KKBB(FM)—(Shafter). Mar 3, 1978: 97.7 mhz; 3 kw. Ant 328 ft. TL: N35 26 32 W119 15 38. Stereo. Hrs opn: 24. Suite 230, 5055 California Ave., Bakersfield (93309). (805) 326-8000. FAX: (805) 326-0937. Licensee: KCI Radio Partners Ltd. (acq 6-21-90). Rep: Eastman. Wash atty: Pepper & Corazzini. Format: AOR/classic rock. News staff one; news progmg 5 hrs wkly. Target aud: 25-44; adults over 25, rock listeners who prefer classic rock to new music. Spec prog: Blues one hr wkly. ■ Ken Kohl, pres & gen mgr; Todd Brown, vp sls & gen sls mgr; Mary Ann Escondon, prom mgr; Steve Stevens, progmg dir; Jerry Garris, chief engr. ■ Rates: $35; 35; 35; 25.

KKXX-FM—See Delano.

KNZR(AM)—1933: 1560 khz; 10 kw-U, DA-1. TL: N35 18 30 W119 02 09. Hrs opn: 24. 3651 Pegasus Dr. (93308); Box 80658 (93380). (805) 393-1900. Licensee: Buckley Broadcasting Corp. (group owner; acq 1-25-90; $1 million; FTR 2-19-90). Net: CBS, CNN. Rep: Farmakis, D & R Radio. Wash atty: Fisher, Cooper, Wayland & Leader. Format: News, talk, farm. News staff 6; news progmg 75 hrs wkly. Target aud: 35-60. ■ Richard Buckley, pres; Randy Warwick, gen mgr; Susi Klassen, rgnl sls mgr; Robert Lang, progmg dir; Woody Chaves, news dir; Rick Hunt, chief engr. ■ Rates: $24; 24; 24; 8.

***KPRX(FM)**—Feb 28, 1987: 89.1 mhz; 12 kw. Ant 500 ft. TL: N35 29 10 W118 53 20. Suite 101, 3437 W. Shaw Ave., Fresno (93711). (800) 275-0764; (209) 275-0764. FAX: (209) 275-2202. Licensee: White Ash Broadcasting Inc. Net: NPR. Format: Class, news & info. ■ Mariam Stephanian, gen mgr; Dave Smith, opns mgr; Jim Meyer, progmg dir; Steve Mull, chief engr.

KRAB(FM)—(Green Acres). Oct 1, 1991: 106.3 mhz; 3.9 kw. Ant 410 ft. TL: N35 28 17 W119 01 38. Hrs opn: 24. Suite 123, 3701 Pegasus Dr., Bakersfield (93308). (805) 392-1100. FAX: (805) 392-0793. Licensee: Double D Broadcasting. Format: AOR. ■ Doug Shackett, gen mgr; Diana Burton, natl sls mgr & rgnl sls mgr; Chris Squires, progmg dir; Bruce Wayne, mus dir; Anne Kelly, pub affrs dir; Paul Kleinkramer, chief engr. ■ Rates: $26; 26; 26; 22.

KSUV-FM—See McFarland.

KTIE(FM)—Mar 21, 1990: 107.1 mhz; 6 kw. Ant 164 ft. TL: N35 22 08 W119 00 14. Hrs opn: 24. 3223 Sillect Ave. (93308). (805) 326-1001. FAX: (805) 328-7503. Licensee: Buck Owens Production Company Inc. July 27, 1993: Format: Country. ■ Buck Owens, CEO; Mel Owens Jr., gen mgr, opns mgr & dev mgr; Richard Trejo, gen sls mgr & mktg mgr; Jerry Hufford, prom dir; Evan Bridwell, progmg dir & mus dir; Terry Gaiser, chief engr.

***KTQX(FM)**—Apr 14, 1989: 90.1 mhz; 3 kw. Ant 128 ft. TL: N35 24 29 W118 58 08. 1111 Fulton Mall, Fresno (93721). (209) 486-5174. FAX: (209) 264-9309. Licensee: Radio Bilingue Inc. Format: Bilingual. ■ Hugo Morales, exec vp.

KUZZ-FM—Listing follows KCWR(AM).

KWAC(AM)—1954: 1490 khz; 1 kw-U. TL: N35 24 07 W119 02 45. Stereo. Hrs opn: 24. 5200 Standard St. (93308). (805) 327-9711. FAX: (805) 327-0797. Licensee: KMAP Inc. (acq 1961). Rep: Lotus. Format: Sp. Target aud: General. ■ Edward R. Hopple, pres; Mike Allen, gen mgr; Pat Ryan, stn mgr; Ramon Garza, opns mgr & progmg dir; Lola Bautista, mus dir; Manolo Martinez, news dir; Bob Turner, chief engr.

KIWI(FM)—Co-owned with KWAC(AM). Dec 15, 1985: 92.1 mhz; 6 kw. Ant 269 ft. TL: N35 22 08 W119 00 14. Stereo. Hrs opn: 24. Prog sep from AM. (805) 325-5494. ■ Eddie Leon, opns dir, progmg dir & mus dir; Pat Ryan, vp sls; Lydia Vernon, prom mgr.

KZPM(AM)—Not on air, target date unknown: 1100 khz; 5 kw-D, 1 kw-N. TL: N35 23 16 W118 52 45. No. 103, 1227 Del Prado Blvd., Cape Coral, FL (33904). Licensee: Jerry J. Collins.

Banning

KMET(AM)—1948: 1490 khz; 1 kw-U. TL: N33 55 49 W116 55 20. Suite 100, 5005 LaMart Dr., Riverside (92507). (909) 684-9992. FAX: (909) 787-9987. Licensee: KOLA Inc. Group owner: Frederick R. Cole. Net: ABC/C. Rep: Banner. ■ Frederick R. Cote, pres; John Lego, gen mgr & gen sls mgr; Perry Passage, progmg dir & news dir; Clayton Creekmore, chief engr. ■ Rates: $50; 45; 50; 45.

Barstow

KDUC(FM)—Listing follows KSZL(AM).

KIQQ(AM)—Sept 29, 1960: 1310 khz; 5 kw-D, 118 w-N, DA-1. TL: N34 54 51 W117 00 59. Hrs opn: 24. 11920 Hesperia Rd., Hesperia (92345). (619) 244-2000. Licensee: Eneida Orchard (acq 10-30-89; $775,000; FTR 6-26-89). Net: AP, MBS. Wash atty: Arent, Fox, Kintner, Plotkin & Kahn. Format: Adult contemp, news/talk. ■ Eneida Orchard, pres & gen mgr. ■ Rates: $12; 12; 12; 12.

KRXV(FM)—See Yermo.

KSZL(AM)—June 25, 1986: 1230 khz; 1 kw-U. TL: N34 54 44 W117 01 39. Stereo. Box 250, 29000 Radio Rd. (92311). (619) 256-2121. FAX: (619) 256-5090. Licensee: First American Communications Corp. (acq 9-65; $300,000 with co-located FM; FTR 9-23-85). Net: ABC/D. Rep: Katz & Powell. Format: Contemp and traditional country. News staff 2; news progmg 12 hrs wkly. Target aud: 25 plus. Spec prog: Relg one hr wkly. ■ Steven Hess, vp & gen mgr; Richard Korzuch, gen sls mgr; Paul Bachman, progmg dir; Bryan Golbel, news dir; Dave Rose, chief engr.

KDUC(FM)—Co-owned with KSZL(AM). June 4, 1986: 94.3 mhz; 4.6 kw. Ant 783 ft. TL: N34 58 15 W117 02 22. Stereo. Prog sep from AM. Format: CHR, adult contemp. News staff one; news progmg 7 hrs wkly. Target aud: 12-44.

KXXZ(FM)—Not on air, target date unknown: 95.9 mhz; 4.4 kw. Ant 781 ft. TL: N34 58 15 W117 02 21. Stereo. Hrs opn: 24. Box 1209, 1581 W. Main St. (92311). (619) 256-6695; (619) 256-5996. FAX: (619) 256-1913. Licensee: Hub Broadcasting Inc. Format: AOR. Target aud:

California

18-45. ■ Ed A. Belsky, CEO & gen mgr; Brad Sobel, vp opns; Bob Wellman, gen sls mgr; Cindy West, mus dir.

Bayside

*KZPN(FM)—Apr 15, 1992: 91.5 mhz; 125 w. Ant 823 ft. TL: N40 49 32 W124 00 05. Hrs opn: 24. 2803 Greenwood Heights Rd., Kneeland (95549); Box 915, Bayside (95524). (707) 444-8006; (707) 444-8727. Licensee: Community of Humboldt Educational Enhancement Radio Service. Format: Class, news, educ. News progmg 42 hrs wkly. Target aud: All ages; right-brained, high I.Q. cosmopolitans, learning disabled, alternative thinkers. Spec prog: Jazz 6 hrs, drama 4 hrs, science 3 hrs, relg 3 hrs, farm 2 hrs wkly. ■ Monica L. Olsen, CEO, stn mgr, opns dir & news dir; Rev. John K. Rogers, chmn & vp opns; Dr. Robert A. Wallace, mus dir; Lee Olsen, Tom Williams, engrg dirs.

Berkeley

*KALX(FM)—July 1967: 90.7 mhz; 500 w. Ant 778 ft. TL: N37 52 40 W122 14 44. Stereo. 2311 Bowditch St. (94720). (510) 642-1111. Licensee: The Regents of the Univ. of Calif. Format: Progsv, educ, div. News progmg 4 hrs wkly. ■ Sandra Wasson, gen mgr & progmg mgr; Xandy Buckner, dev mgr & adv mgr; Rick Arroyo, prom mgr; Anthony Bonet, mus dir; Kavita Menon, news dir; Tom Mannarelli, pub affrs dir; Steve Hawes, chief engr.

KBLX(AM)—May 22, 1922: 1400 khz; 1 kw-U. TL: N37 50 58 W122 17 44. Hrs opn: 24. 601 Ashby Ave. (94710); Suite 507, 6475 Christie Ave, Emeryville (94608). (510) 848-7713. FAX: (510) 658-0894. Licensee: Inner City Broadcasting Corp. of Berkeley. Group owner: Inner City Broadcasting (acq 1979). Net: UPI. Rep: D & R Radio. Format: Adult contemp. Target aud: 25-54. ■ Harvey Stone, pres & gen mgr; Barry Rose, gen sls mgr; Rhonda Amoe, natl sls mgr; Judy Kaneko, prom dir; Kevin Brown, progmg dir; Ken Glaser, mus dir; Dorothy Reed, news dir; Paul Marks, chief engr.

KBLX(FM)—Apr 29, 1949: 102.9 mhz; 50 kw. Ant 1,290 ft. TL: N37 41 20 W122 26 07. Stereo. Hrs opn: 24. Dups AM 100%.

*KPFA(FM)—April 1949: 94.1 mhz; 59 kw. Ant 1,330 ft. TL: N37 51 55 W122 13 12. Stereo. Hrs opn: 24. 1929 Martin Luther King Jr. Way (94704). (510) 848-6767. Licensee: Pacifica Foundation. Group owner: Pacifica Foundations Inc. dba Pacifica Radio. Wash atty: Haley, Bader & Potts. Format: Div mus & pub affrs. News staff 4; news progmg 11 hrs wkly. Spec prog: Sp 10 hrs, jazz 20 hrs, class 20 hrs, C&W 20 hrs, Black 20 hrs, folk 10 hrs, women's 10 hrs wkly. ■ Marci Lockwood, gen mgr & dev dir; Jim Bennett, opns mgr; Michelle Flannery, mus dir; Mark Mericle, Aileen Alfandary, news dirs; Philip Maldari, Chuy Varela, pub affrs dirs.

*KPFB(FM)—Co-owned with KPFA(FM). February 1954: 89.3 mhz; 460 w-H. Ant -98 ft. TL: N37 52 20 W122 16 18. Dups KPFA(FM) except for pub affrs and special events progmg. Format: Div, educ.

Beverly Hills

KJQI(AM)—October 1947: 1260 khz; 5 kw-U, DA-2. TL: N34 14 58 W118 27 15. Hrs opn: 24. 14800 Lassen St., Mission Hills (91345). (310) 478-5540. FAX: (310) 478-4189. Licensee: Mount Wilson FM Broadcasters Inc. (acq 11-20-92; $2.5 million; FTR 12-14-92). Net: NBC Talknet, AP, MBS. Rep: D & R Radio. Wash atty: Fisher, Wayland, Cooper & Leader. Format: News/talk. News staff 6; news progmg 22 hrs wkly. Target aud: 35 plus. ■ Saul Levine, pres; Robert Turner, chief engr.

Big Bear City

KBHR(FM)—Not on air, target date unknown: 93.3 mhz; 3 kw. Ant 299 ft. TL: N34 14 32 W116 51 57. Suite 121, 1666 Gateway Blvd., Los Angeles (90064). Licensee: Parallel Communications L.P. (acq 5-22-92).

Big Bear Lake

KTOT(FM)—May 1, 1975: 101.7 mhz; 90 w. Ant 1,500 ft. TL: N34 12 47 W116 51 59. Stereo. Hrs opn: 6 AM-10 PM. Box 2810, 575 Pine Knot Blvd. (92315-2810). (909) 866-3434. Licensee: Mountain Broadcasting Company Inc. (acq 6-67). Wash atty: David Tillotson. Format: Talk & country. ■ Vernon E. Thompson, pres.

KBBV(AM)—Co-owned with KTOT(FM). Nov 1, 1964: 1050 khz; 250 w-D, DA. TL: N34 14 53 W116 53 20 (CP: 500 w-D). Stn currently dark.

Big Pine

KRHU(FM)—Not on air, target date unknown: 93.3 mhz; Box 1284, Mammoth Lakes (93546). Licensee: David & Mary Digerness.

Bishop

KBOV(AM)—Apr 1, 1953: 1230 khz; 1 kw-U. TL: N37 20 44 W118 23 43. Box 757 (93515); S. Highway 395 (93514). (619) 873-6324; (619) 873-5427. FAX: (619) 872-2639. Licensee: Great Country Broadcasting Inc. (acq 8-6-81; $104,000; FTR 8-24-81). Net: ABC/E, SMN. Rep: W.R.B.S. Format: MOR. News staff one; news progmg 15 hrs wkly. Target aud: General. ■ John W. Young, pres, gen mgr, gen sls mgr, progmg dir & chief engr; John E. Dailey, news dir.

KIBS(FM)—Co-owned with KBOV(AM). Nov 1, 1974: 100.7 mhz; 1 kw. Ant 2,960 ft. TL: N37 25 00 W118 11 00. Stereo. Prog sep from AM. (acq 12-28-84). Net: SMN. Format: C&W. ■ Joe Fiorella, mus dir.

Blythe

KJMB(FM)—April 1975: 100.3 mhz; 36.4 kw. Ant 57 ft. TL: N33 37 16 W114 35 28. Stereo. Hrs opn: 24. 681 N. 4th St. (92225). (619) 922-7143. FAX: (619) 922-2844. Licensee: Blythe Radio Inc. Net: USA. Format: Adult contemp. ■ Jim Mayson, pres; Jim Morris, gen mgr. ■ Rates: $18; 18; 18; 18.

Brawley

KROP(AM)—Licensed to Brawley. See El Centro.

KSIQ(FM)—Licensed to Brawley. See El Centro.

KWST(FM)—April 4, 1988: 94.5 mhz; 50 kw. Ant 254 ft. TL: N32 48 27 W115 32 18. Stereo. Hrs opn: 24. Box 1018, El Centro (92244); 626 Main St., El Centro (92243). (619) 352-2277. FAX: (619) 352-1430. Licensee: Brawley Broadcasting Co. Net: NBC. Format: Country. Target aud: 25-54. ■ Cal Mandel, chmn, vp, sls dir & mus dir; Lois Mandel, progmg dir; Frank Lokey, news dir; Dean Imhof, chief engr.

LAUREN A. COLBY
301-663-1086
COMMUNICATIONS ATTORNEY
Special Attention to Difficult Cases

Buena Park

*KBPK(FM)—July 6, 1970: 90.1 mhz; 20 w. Ant 130 ft. TL: N33 51 35 W118 00 53. 321 E. Chapman Ave., Fullerton (92634). (714) 992-7419. Licensee: Buena Park School District. Format: Adult contemp, Top-40, educ. ■ Jim Bain, gen mgr.

Burbank

KRCK(AM)—Licensed to Burbank. See Los Angeles.

Burney

KARZ(AM)—Licensed to Burney. See Redding.

KAVA(AM)—Aug 13, 1967: 1450 khz; 1 kw-U, DA-1. TL: N40 52 32 W121 39 42. Hrs opn: 5 AM-10 PM. 37185 Park Ave. (96013). (916) 335-4515. Licensee: Thomas & Essie L. Collins (acq 11-1-76). Net: ABC/I. Rep: Katz & Powell. Format: Country. News staff 8; news progmg 7 hrs wkly. Target aud: 24-55. ■ Tom Collins, pres & chief engr; Mark Collins, gen mgr & opns mgr. ■ Rates: $12; 10; 12; 7.

*KIBC(FM)—Nov 15, 1985: 90.5 mhz; 412 w. Ant 1,321 ft. TL: N40 52 29 W121 46 15. Box 1717 (96013). (916) 335-5422. Licensee: Burney Educational Broadcasting Foundation. Format: Educ. ■ Wayne Hennessey, gen mgr.

*KNCA(FM)—July 1992: 89.7 mhz; 2.28 kw. Ant 1,465 ft. TL: N40 52 30 W121 46 14. Stereo. Southern Oregon State College, 1250 Siskiyou Blvd., Ashland, OR (92520). (503) 552-6301. FAX: (503) 552-6773. Licensee: State of Oregon Board of Higher Education. Net: APR, NPR. Wash atty: Arter & Hadden. Format: Jazz, new age, news. News staff one. Target aud: General. ■ Ronald Kramer, gen mgr; Keith Henty, opns dir; Paul Westhelle, dev dir; John Baxter, progmg dir; Pat Daly, mus dir; Annie Hoy, news dir; John Holt, engrg mgr.

Calexico

KICO(AM)—Apr 6, 1946: 1490 khz; 1 kw-U. TL: N32 41 58 W115 30 10. Hrs opn: 5 AM-10:30 PM. Box 232, 695 N. Hwy. 111 (92231). (619) 357-1490. FAX: (619) 357-4168. Licensee: Cal-Mex Broadcasting Co. Inc. (acq 10-15-91; $90,000; FTR 11-4-91). Rep: Caballero. Format: Sp. Target aud: 28-50; adult Hispanic. ■ Eduardo Medal, gen mgr. ■ Rates: $13; 13; 13; 13.

KQVO(FM)—Co-owned with KICO(AM). March 1984: 97.7 mhz; 3 kw. Ant 305 ft. TL: N32 40 48 W115 25 36. Stereo. Hrs opn: 24. (619) 357-5055. FAX: (619) 357-4176; (619) 357-4968. Rep: Lotus Hispanic. Format: Adult contemp, Sp. News progmg 6 hrs wkly. Target aud: 25-54; females.

*KUBO(FM)—1989: 88.7 mhz; 3 kw. Ant 272 ft. TL: N32 47 57 W115 30 12. Box 71, El Centro (92243). (619) 337-8051. FAX: (619) 337-8519. Licensee: Radio Bilingue Inc. Format: Bilingual talk & music. ■ Raul Silva, gen mgr & gen sls mgr.

Camarillo

KELF(FM)—Aug 15, 1972: 95.9 mhz; 5 kw. Ant 813 ft. TL: N34 06 47 W119 03 34 Stereo. Hrs opn: 24. Box 5596, Ventura (93003); Suite 2-M, 2284 S. Victoria, Ventura (93003). (805) 656-3696. FAX: (805) 644-4257. Licensee: Golden Bear Broadcasting Inc. Group owner: The Heusser Group (acq 12-21-88; grpsl; FTR 5-7-90). Rep: Katz Hispanic. Format: Spanish. Target aud: 25-54. ■ Wallace A. Heusser, pres; Cindy Shipe, gen mgr.

*KMRO(FM)—Jan 19, 1987: 90.3 mhz; 4.43 kw. Ant 1,250 ft. TL: N34 24 47 W119 11 10. Stereo. Hrs opn: 18. Suite 28, 2310 Ponderosa Dr. (93010). (805) 482-4797. Licensee: The Assoc. for Community Education Inc. Format: Relg, Sp. ■ Phil Guthrie, pres; Joe Gonzales, CFO; Mary Guthrie, gen mgr; Eric Mark, progmg dir; Scott Horner, chief engr.

Cambria

KOTR(FM)—Oct 1, 1984: 94.9 mhz; 25 kw. Ant 328 ft. TL: N35 31 26 W121 03 40. Stereo. Hrs opn: 24. 840 Sheffield St. (93428). (805) 927-5021. FAX: (805) 927-0235. Licensee: Central Coast Community Broadcasting Inc. Net: NBC. Format: AOR. Target aud: 25-54; male. ■ Bruce W. Howard, CEO & gen mgr; Joy Howard, opns mgr; Warren Flaschen, natl sls mgr & rgnl sls mgr; Diane Randazzo, vp prom; Mike Shaw, vp progmg; Mathew Lawton, asst mus dir; Tom Hughes, chief engr.

Canyon Country

KBET(AM)—June 1989: 1220 khz; 1 kw-D, 500 w-N, DA-2. TL: N34 27 55 W118 24 08. Stereo. Hrs opn: 24. 27565 Sierra Hwy. (91351). Licensee: Saddleback Broadcasting Inc. (acq 12-13-91; $330,000). Net: Unistar; CNN. Format: Oldies. News staff one. Target aud: General; 25-54. ■ Carl Goldman, CEO; Laurie Irons, opns dir; Chip Ehrhardt, vp sls; A.J. Morgan, news dir; Curt Hemming, chief engr. ■ Rates: $35; 25; 25; 12.

Capitola

KMBY(AM)—Dec 2, 1977: 1540 khz; 10 kw-U, DA-2. TL: N36 58 50 W121 54 44 (CP: 10 kw-U, DA-1; TL: 36 52 08N 121 46 59W). 8 Harris Ct., Suite B-4, Monterey (93940). (408) 655-4100. FAX: (408) 655-1710. Licensee: KMBY Inc. (acq 8-1-89). Rep: Banner. Format: Alternative rock. Target aud: 18-34; males/females of Generation X. ■ Stephen Adams, pres, gen mgr & adv dir; Rich Berlin, opns dir; Kim Bryant, gen sls mgr; Debbie Howitt, mktg mgr; C.J. Morgan, prom dir; Tim Kelly, progmg dir; Jim Petruchi, chief engr. ■ Rates: $20; 20; 20; 20.

Carlsbad

KKOS(FM)—Aug 22, 1965: 95.9 mhz; 3.3 kw. Ant 305 ft. TL: N33 09 09 W117 15 33. Stereo. Hrs opn: 24. Box 949 (92018). (619) 729-5945. FAX: (619) 729-7067. Licensee: Tri-Cities Broadcasting Inc. (acq 9-75). Format: Adult contemp. ■ Jeffrey Chandler, pres & gen mgr; Todd Palmer (local), rgnl sls mgr; Ron Lane, progmg dir.

Carmel

KRML(AM)—Dec 25, 1957: 1410 khz; 500 w-D, 16 w-N. TL: N36 32 22 W121 54 13 (CP: 2.5 kw-D, 2 kw-N). Box 22440, Bldg. 25, Carmel Rancho Rd. (93922). (408) 624-6431. FAX: (408) 625-5598. Licensee: Wisdom Broadcasting Co. Inc. (acq 12-5-85). Rep: A/D Sales. Format:

Jazz. Target aud: 25-65. Spec prog: Blues one hr wkly. ■ Gilbert Wisdom, pres, gen mgr & gen sls mgr; Johnny Adams, progmg dir & mus dir; Ernesto Herrera, chief engr. ■ Rates: $20; 15; 20; 15.

KVOQ(FM)—Dec 4, 1993: 95.5 mhz; 1.05 kw. TL: N36 33 10 W121 47 17. Suite C-150, 2511 Garden Rd., Monterey (93940). (408) 656-9550. Licensee: J & M Broadcasting Co. Format: Class. ■ Terry W. Gillingham, stn mgr.

KXDC-FM—Apr 29, 1971: 101.7 mhz; 800 w. Ant 590 ft. TL: N36 33 12 W121 47 05. Stereo. Hrs opn: 24. 551 Foam St., Monterey (93940); Box 1799, Monterey (93942). (408) 647-1017. FAX: (408) 655-3009. Licensee: Joaquin Financial Group (acq 8-1-91; grpsl; FTR 1-30-89). Rep: Katz & Powell. Format: Progsv, adult contemp/NAC. News staff one; news progmg 3 hrs wkly. Target aud: 25-54; High income, active achievers. ■ Jim Heidebrecht, pres; Russ Cornelius, gen mgr; Jim Seagull, progmg dir; Mike Blankenbecler, chief engr.

Carmel Valley

KIEZ(AM)—July 10, 1989: 540 khz; 10 kw-D, 500 w-N, DA-2. TL: N36 39 38 W121 32 29 (CP: 50 kw-D, 500 w-N, DA-2). Stereo. Hrs opn: 24. Suite 202, 1188 Padre Dr., Salinas (93901). (408) 758-5400; (408) 758-5625. FAX: (408) 758-5446. Licensee: Jaime Bonilla Valdez (acq 3-31-93; $840,000 with co-located KKLF[FM] Gonzales; FTR 4-19-93). Wash atty: James P. Riley. Format: Oldies, MOR. News staff one; news progmg 4 hrs wkly. Target aud: 35 plus; adults. ■ Jose Diaz, pres, gen mgr, gen sls mgr & prom mgr; Gary Beacham, chief engr. ■ Rates: $30; 30; 30; 15.

Carmichael

KFIA(AM)—Jan 11, 1979: 710 khz; 10 kw-D, 250 w-N, DA-2. TL: N38 43 12 W121 14 09 (CP: 25 kw-D, 500 w-N, TL: N38 52 57 W121 15 07). 5705 Marconi Ave. (95608). (916) 485-7710. Licensee: Olympic Broadcasters Inc. Format: Relg. ■ Douglas Kahle, pres; Jamie Clark, vp & gen mgr; F. Guy Coleman, opns mgr & gen sls mgr; Kevin Manna, progmg dir; Ray Curtis, news dir; Bill Emanuel, chief engr.

Carnelian Bay

KODS(FM)—Licensed to Carnelian Bay. See Reno, Nev.

Carpinteria

KSBL(FM)—June 1, 1981: 101.7 mhz; 310 w. Ant 810 ft. TL: N34 27 55 W119 40 37. Stereo. 1330 Cacique St. Santa Barbara (93013). (805) 966-1755. FAX: (805) 564-4489. Licensee: Michael Reichert. Group owner: Great Electric Communications Inc. Format: Adult contemp. ■ Michael Reichert, gen mgr; Andy Whatley, gen sls mgr; John Quimby, progmg dir; J.D. Strahler, chief engr.

Cartago

KWTY(FM)—November 1989: 102.9 mhz; 2 kw. Ant -1,787 ft. TL: N36 19 16 W118 10 22. Stereo. Box 773, Big Pine (93513). Licensee: Michael L. Benson. Format: Talk. News progmg 7 hrs wkly. Target aud: General. ■ Mark Miller, chief engr. ■ Rates: $1; 1; 1; 1.

Cathedral City

KWXY(AM)—Oct 4, 1964: 1340 khz; 1 kw-U. TL: N33 48 07 W116 27 44. Hrs opn: 5:30 AM-midnight. KWXY Broadcast Centre, 68700 Dinah Shore Dr., Palm Springs (92263). (619) 328-1104. FAX: (619) 328-7814. Licensee: Glen Barnett Inc. Rep: Katz & Powell. Format: Btfl mus. News staff one; news progmg 7 hrs wkly. Target aud: 35 plus; affluent adults. Spec prog: Canadian news 2 hrs wkly. ■ Glen Barnett, pres, progmg dir & chief engr; Estelle Layton, exec vp; Larry Collins, opns mgr; Lou Faust, sls dir; Fred Barton, news dir. ■ Rates: $30; 30; 30; 25.

KWXY-FM—Jan 19, 1969: 98.5 mhz; 50 kw. Ant 499 ft. TL: N33 51 55 W116 26 10. Stereo. Hrs opn: 5:30 AM-midnight. Dups AM 100%. ■ Rates: Same as AM.

Central Valley

KNNN(FM)—Oct 26, 1989: 99.3 mhz; 5.3 kw. Ant 328 ft. TL: N40 33 46 W122 27 07. 1326 Market St., Redding (96001). (916) 241-4141. FAX: (916) 241-4183. Licensee: Shasta Lake (acq 10-89; $475,000; FTR 10-16-89). Format: Adult contemp. News staff one. Target aud: 25-54. Spec prog: Jazz 3 hrs wkly. ■ Jerry Martin, opns dir; Kelly Schmid, natl sls dir; Bob Williams, progmg dir; Kathy Vance, news dir.

Ceres

***KBES(FM)**—unknown: 89.5 mhz; 30 w-H. Ant 135 ft. TL: N37 35 21 W120 57 23 (CP: 150 w-H, ant 131 ft.). Box 4116, Modesto (95352). (209) 537-0933. Licensee: Bet Nahrain Inc.

KLOC(AM)—Sept 15, 1963: 920 khz; 2.5 kw-U, DA-2. TL: N37 35 49 W121 04 15. Box 542, Modesto (95353). (209) 521-5562. Licensee: Clock Broadcasting Inc. (acq 4-7-81; $500,000; FTR 3-30-81). Rep: Lotus. Format: Contemp Sp. ■ Mike Sturtevant, pres & gen mgr; Victor A. Salazar, progmg dir; Alicia Urena, news dir; Jerry Moore, chief engr.

Chester

KCMT(FM)—Apr 6, 1989: 98.9 mhz; 25 kw. Ant 2,417 ft. TL: N40 14 00 W121 01 11. Stereo. Hrs opn: 24. Box 11370, 395 Main St., Quincy (95971). (916) 258-4300. Licensee: Ralph E. Wittick (acq 6-90; $175,000; FTR 7-2-90). Net: ABC. Format: Adult contemp. News staff 3; news progmg 28 hrs wkly. Target aud: 18-54; general. Spec prog: Relg one hr wkly. ■ Ralph Wittick, gen mgr; Laurie Wann, gen sls mgr; Tom Moore, progmg dir & mus dir; Steve Rice, chief engr. ■ Rates: $11; 9.75; 11; 9.75.

Chico

***KCHO(FM)**—Apr 22, 1969: 91.7 mhz; 7.71 kw. Ant 1,219 ft. TL: N39 57 30 W121 42 48. Stereo. Calif. State Univ. (95929-0500). (916) 898-5896. FAX: (916) 898-4348. Licensee: Calif. State U, Chico Foundation Net: APR, NPR. Wash atty: Cohn & Marks. Format: Class, jazz, news/info. News progmg 37 hrs wkly. Target aud: General. ■ Jack Brown, gen mgr; Mike Birdsill, opns dir & chief engr; Louise Philippi, dev dir, mktg dir & prom mgr; Joe Oleksiewicz, progmg dir & pub affrs dir.

KFMF(FM)—Feb. 1, 1974: 93.9 mhz; 2 kw. Ant 1,128 ft. TL: N39 56 46 W121 43 17. Stereo. Hrs opn: 24. Box 266 (95927); 1459 Humboldt Rd. (95928). (916) 343-8461. FAX: (916) 343-0243. Licensee: Nova Broadcasting (acq 7-90; $2.1 million; FTR 8-6-90). Rep: Christal. Format: Rock/AOR. News staff one; news progmg one hr wkly. Target aud: 18-44. ■ Jeff Kragel, gen mgr; Karen Ulsh, opns dir; Jim Dowd, sls dir; Lisa Kelly, vp prom; Marty Griffin, progmg dir & mus dir; Dan Barnett, news dir; Terry Green, chief engr. ■ Rates: $65; 55; 35; 25.

***KHAP(FM)**—Not on air, target date unknown: 88.3 mhz; 12 kw. Ant 285 ft. TL: N39 42 37 W121 40 45. Box 7573 (95927-7573). (916) 891-3550. Licensee: Family Stations Inc. (group owner). Format: Relg. ■ Pat Roy, gen mgr.

KHSL(AM)—Apr 17, 1935: 1290 khz; 5 kw-U, DA-N. TL: N39 44 00 W121 44 10. Stereo. Box 489 (95927). (916) 893-8926; (916) 342-1290. FAX: (916) 893-8937. Licensee: Golden Empire Broadcasting Co. (group owner; acq 1939). Net: CBS. Rep: Eastman. Wash atty: Haley, Bader & Potts. Format: Country. News staff one; news progmg 3 hrs wkly. Target aud: 25 plus; mature. ■ Hugh McClung, pres; Russell Pope, sr vp & engrg mgr; Dino Corbin, gen mgr; G.V. Smith, stn mgr; Ron Woodward, opns mgr; Phil Papeman, gen sls mgr; Christine Lardner, prom mgr; John Antonelli, progmg dir & mus dir; Dori McKay, news dir; Chrissy Lee, pub affrs dir. KHSL-TV affil. ■ Rates: $15; 15; 15; 13.

KHSL-FM—See Paradise.

KKXX(AM)—See Paradise.

KPAY(AM)—September 1949: 1060 khz; 10 kw-D, DA-2. TL: N39 42 38 W121 47 20. 2654 Cramer Ln. (95928). (916) 345-0021. FAX: (916) 345-1060. Licensee: McCoy Broadcasting Co. (acq 7-91; $4.1 million grpsl; FTR 7-15-91). Net: MBS. Rep: Katz. Format: Adult contemp. ■ Craig McCoy, pres; Dave Brower, gen mgr; Veronica Carter, news dir; Dan Butner, chief engr.

KPAY-FM—Nov 16, 1972: 95.1 mhz; 8.7 kw. Ant 1,171 ft. TL: N39 56 46 W121 43 17. Stereo. Prog sep from AM. Format: Easy lstng.

KPPL(FM)—(Colusa). September 1986: 107.5 mhz; 28 kw. Ant 600 ft. TL: N39 17 17 W122 20 02. Stereo. Suite J, 2525 Dominic Dr., Chico (95928); 437 Market St., Colusa (95932). (916) 458-8851. FAX: (916) 894-0302. Licensee: The Park Lane Group (group owner; acq 9-4-92; $2.5 million; FTR 10-19-92). Rep: McGavern Guild. Format: Soft adult contemp. News staff one; news progmg one hr wkly. Target aud: 24-48. ■ Jim Levy, CEO; Mel Dolezal, gen mgr; Paul Martin, progmg dir; Dave Redmund, chief engr.

***KZFR(FM)**—July 6, 1990: 90.1 mhz; 6.3 kw. Ant 587 ft. TL: N39 48 25 W121 37 35. Box 3173 (95927). (916) 895-0706; (916) 895-0131. Licensee: Golden Valley Community Broadcasters. Format: Eclectic. News progmg 8 hrs wkly. Spec prog: Black 3 hrs, farm one hr, folk 8 hrs, gospel 3 hrs, jazz 10 hrs, sp 6 hrs, children 5 hrs, Environmnt news one hr, peace issues one hr wkly. ■ Lee Edwards, chmn & gen mgr; Dan Robles, progmg dir; Evan Carlos, mus dir; Keleigh Nolan, pub affrs dir; Terry Green, chief engr.

KZZP(FM)—See Paradise.

China Lake

KSSI(FM)—Not on air, target date unknown: 102.7 mhz; 3 kw. Ant -22 ft. TL: N35 39 06 W117 40 58. 531 S. Erin, Ridgecrest (93555). Licensee: Sound Enterprises.

Chowchilla

KXDA(FM)—Not on air, target date unknown: 93.3 mhz; 2.95 kw. Ant 335 ft. TL: N37 13 01 W120 11 57. c/o KLVR(FM), 2290 Airport Blvd., Santa Rosa (95403). (707) 528-9236. Licensee: Educational Media Foundation (acq 6-14-93; $100,000; FTR 7-5-93). ■ Richard Jenkins, pres & gen mgr.

Chualar

***KHDC(FM)**—June 28, 1981: 90.9 mhz; 3 kw. Ant 195 ft. TL: N36 32 54 W121 26 34. Stereo. 161 S. Main St., Salinas (93901). (408) 757-8039. FAX: (408) 757-9854. Licensee: California Human Development Corp. (acq 11-86; $70,000; FTR 5-12-86). Format: Multi-lingual, div. ■ Candio Morales, gen mgr; Delia Saldivar, progmg dir & news dir; Mike Bankenbecler, chief engr.

Claremont

***KSPC(FM)**—February 1956: 88.7 mhz; 3 kw. Ant -265 ft. TL: N34 05 38 W117 42 35. Stereo. Pomona College, Thatcher Music Bldg., 340 N. College Ave. (91711-6340). (909) 621-8157. Licensee: Pomona College. Format: Alternative rock, div. News progmg 4 hrs wkly. Target aud: General. Spec prog: Class 12 hrs, jazz 12 hrs, Pol 3 hrs, reggae 6 hrs, blues 3 hrs, experimental 3 hrs, pub affrs 3 hrs, old-time radio 3 hrs, variety show one hr wkly. ■ Johannes Aaerbout, gen mgr; Erica Tyron, stn mgr; Aaron Lawn, dev dir; Larissa Mohamadi, prom dir; Anne-Marie Davidson, progmg dir; Mark Zepp, mus dir; Ann Oelschlager, news dir; Tina Briones, pub affrs dir; John Artal, chief engr.

KTSJ(AM)—See Pomona.

Clovis

KOQO(AM)—May 2, 1977: 790 khz; 5 kw-D, 2.5 kw-N, DA-2. TL: N36 50 39 W119 41 13. 4928 E. Clinton, Fresno (93727). (209) 454-7713. FAX: (209) 454-7721. Licensee: J & C Equinox XX L.P. (acq 11-10-92; $2.055 million with KOQO[FM] Fresno; FTR 12-7-92). Net: CNN. Rep: Caballero. Wash atty: Haley, Bader & Potts. Format: Sp, banda, ranchero. News progmg 8 hrs wkly. Target aud: 18-49; Hispanic adults. ■ Dwight Case, CEO; Ed Prince, pres & gen mgr; Armando Diaz, progmg dir; Raphael Bautista, asst mus dir; Scott Dean, chief engr.

Coachella

KCLB(AM)—1954: 970 khz; 5 kw-D, 1 kw-N, DA-2. TL: N33 41 12 W116 09 34. 1694 Sixth St. (92236). (619) 398-0693. FAX: (619) 398-2739. Licensee: Coachella Valley Broadcasting Co. (acq 8-2-93; $1,000 with co-located FM; FTR 8-23-93). Net: UPI. Rep: Katz. Format: Latin contemp hits. Target aud: 18-49. ■ Susan Gorges, gen mgr; Gene Abraham, stn mgr & gen sls mgr; JJ Jefferies, progmg dir & progmg mgr; Ron Striker, mus dir; John Ostrom, news dir; Joe Hanigan, chief engr.

KCLB-FM—Sept 1, 1960: 93.7 mhz; 26.5 kw. Ant 640 ft. TL: N33 44 07 W116 13 27. Stereo. Prog sep from AM. (619) 398-2171. Format: AOR. Target aud: 18-54. ■ Melvin Albanez, progmg dir.

Coalinga

KKFO(AM)—Aug 9, 1950: 1470 khz; 500 w-D, 30 w-N. TL: N36 08 40 W120 20 13. 152 E. Elm Ave. (93210). (209) 935-1470. Licensee: Coalinga Broadcasting (acq 1993). Format: Country. ■ William Zawilla, pres; Ann R. Zawilla, vp & gen mgr; Jim Barker, mus dir; Stanley Allen, news dir.

KNGS(FM)—Co-owned with KKFO(AM). Not on air, target date unknown: 100.1 mhz; 3 kw. Ant -312 ft. TL: N36 08 40 W120 20 13. c/o William L. Zawilla, Suite A, 12550 Brookhurst, Garden Grove (92640). (714) 636-5040.

Columbia

KAGF(FM)—Not on air, target date unknown: 98.9 mhz; 300 w. Ant 440 ft. Box 1001 (95310). Licensee: Gold Country Radio.

Colusa

KKCY(FM)—May 1990: 103.1 mhz; 135 w. Ant 1,964 ft. TL: N39 12 21 W121 49 11. Stereo. Hrs opn: 24. Box 7568, Chico (95927). (916) 342-2200; (916) 458-5558. FAX: (916) 342-2260. Licensee: Phoenix Broadcasting Inc. (acq 12-30-91; $390,000; FTR 1-20-92). Net: ABC/D. Rep: Katz. Wash atty: Kaye, Scholer, Fierman, Hays & Handler. Format: Country. News staff one; news progmg 7 hrs wkly. Target aud: 18-64. Spec prog: Sp one hr wkly. ■ Gary Katz, pres; C. Suzanne Morgan, stn mgr; Jan Baker, sls dir; E. Jay Lemmons, vp engrg.

KPPL(FM)—Licensed to Colusa. See Chico.

Compton

KJLH-FM—April 1965: 102.3 mhz; 3 kw. Ant 300 ft. TL: N33 59 52 W118 21 32 (CP: 2.88 kw, ant 338 ft.). Stereo. Hrs opn: 24. 3847 Crenshaw Blvd., Los Angeles (90008). (213) 299-5960. FAX: (213) 290-1284. Licensee: TAXI Productions Inc. (acq 6-79). Net: ABC/FM. Rep: Roslin. Wash atty: Arent, Fox, Kintner, Plotkin & Kahn. Format: Urban contemp. News staff 2; news progmg 6 hrs wkly. Target aud: 18-49; African-American audience. Spec prog: Black, relg 7 hrs, gospel 7 hrs wkly. ■ Stevland Morris, CEO; Karen Slade, vp & gen mgr; Al Ward, natl sls mgr; Cheryl Womack, rgnl sls mgr; Irma Malina, prom dir; Bill Durkes, progmg dir; Carl Nelson, news dir; Jacquie Stephens, pub affrs dir; Barry Clark, chief engr.

AMERICAN RADIO BROKERS, INC.
MOST TRUSTED NAME IN MEDIA BROKERAGE
CHESTER P. COLEMAN / PRESIDENT
FOR THE BEST STATIONS FOR SALE FROM THIS AREA
CALL — 415 / 441-3377
1255 POST STREET / SUITE 625 / SAN FRANCISCO, CA 94109

Concord

KKIS(AM)—Not on air, target date Sept 1, 1994: 1480 khz; 500 w-U. Stn is currently dark. c/o A.R.B. Inc/SFO, Cathederal Hill Hotel Office Bldg., Suite 625, 1255 Post St. (94109). Licensee: Concord Area Broadcasting Corp. (acq 3-1-86; $714,000; FTR 1-13-86). Wash atty: David Tillotson. ■ Chester P. Coleman, chmn; Joseph Buerry, pres.

*****KVHS(FM)**—May 16, 1969: 90.5 mhz; 410 w. Ant 450 ft. TL: N39 01 49 W122 00 04. Stereo. 1101 Alberta Way (94521). (510) 682-5847; (510) 687-5847. Licensee: Clayton Valley High School. Format: Educ, AOR. Target aud: 12-24; teens & young adults. ■ Tom Wilson, gen mgr; Richard Platt, Shawn Blumenfeld, opns dirs; Heather Simmons, Kevin Beard, progmg dirs; Chris Gaeden, chief engr.

Copperopolis

KREL(FM)—Not on air, target date unknown: 105.5 mhz; 1 kw. Ant 781 ft. Suite 100, 1656 N. California Blvd., Walnut Creek (94596). Licensee: Threshold Communications.

Corcoran

KLCZ-FM—Not on air, target date unknown: 102.3 mhz; 17.5 kw. Ant 380 ft. TL: N36 09 03 W119 28 23. Licensee: Radio Corcoran Inc.

Corning

KCEZ(FM)—Apr 8, 1988: 100.7 mhz; 50 kw. Ant 272 ft. TL: N39 53 17 W122 37 38. Stereo. Hrs opn: 24. Box 7568, Chico (95927). (916) 342-2200. FAX: (916) 342-2260. Licensee: Phoenix Broadcasting Inc. Wash atty: Kaye, Scholer, Fierman, Hays & Handler. Format: Oldies. News staff one. Target aud: 25-54. Spec prog: Spanish one hr wkly. ■ Gary Katz, pres; Jerrie Rindahl, gen mgr; E. Jay Lemmons, vp engrg.

Corona

KWRM(AM)—1948: 1370 khz; 5 kw-D, 2.5 kw-N, DA-2. TL: N33 52 52 W117 32 33. Hrs opn: 24. Box 100, 210 Radio Rd. (91720). (714) 737-1370. FAX: (714) 735-9572. Licensee: Major Market Stations Inc. Rep: Lotus. Wash atty: Handy & Carey. Format: Sp. News staff 2; news progmg 20 hrs wkly. Target aud: 18-49; young hispanic adults. ■ Jim Hanemaayer, exec vp; Gem O'Brien, gen mgr; Victor Ramirez, sls dir; Jorge Godinez, progmg dir; Juan Jose Ramirez, mus dir; Sergio Ramirez, news dir; Maria Hernandez, pub affrs dir; Dick Vosper, chief engr.

Costa Mesa

KOJY(AM)—October 1990: 540 khz; 25 kw-D, 400 w-N, DA-3. TL: N34 31 13 W116 56 24 (CP: 25 kw-D, 240-N, DA-3). Stereo. 1500 Cotner Ave., Los Angeles (90025). (310) 478-5540. FAX: (310) 478-4189. Licensee: Mt. Wilson FM Broadcasters Inc. Format: Btfl music.

Cottonwood

KTCD(AM)—Not on air, target date unknown: 1200 khz; 10 kw-D, 2.5 kw-N, DA-2. TL: N40 24 03 W122 03 09. Box 700, Folsom (95630). Licensee: Sundance Radio Corp.

Crescent City

KCRE-FM—Listing follows KFVR(AM).

KFVR(AM)—July 1950: 1310 khz; 1 kw-D. TL: N41 45 34 W124 09 49. Box 1089 (95531). (707) 464-9561. FAX: (707) 464-8758. Licensee: Pelican Bay Broadcasting Corp. (acq 1-17-91; $442,500 with co-located FM; FTR 2-4-91). Net: CNN. Format: Adult contemp. Target aud: 25-54. ■ Rene Shanle Hutzell, progmg dir; Martin Kelly, news dir.

KCRE-FM—Co-owned with KFVR(AM). Mar 21, 1980: 94.3 mhz; 3 kw. Ant -275 ft. TL: N41 45 34 W124 09 49 (CP: 6.2 kw). Stereo. Format: Adult contemp.

KPOD(AM)—Dec 5, 1959: 1240 khz; 1 kw-U. TL: N41 45 42 W124 11 33 (CP: TL: N41 45 35 W124 11 28). Box 1915, 825 Mason Mall (95531). (707) 464-3183. FAX: (707) 465-6703. Licensee: William E. Stamps Sr. (group owner; acq 6-21-83; $369,685; FTR 5-9-83). Net: AP, ABC. Format: Country. ■ William E. Stamps Sr., gen mgr & progmg dir; Teresa Throop, stn mgr; Pati Stamps, dev dir; Susan Smith, sls dir; Michelle Smith, vp mktg; Jerry Mann, prom dir & mus dir; Dwight Gregory, news dir; Ron Simpson, engrg mgr.

KPOD-FM—(Crescent North). January 1989: 97.9 mhz; 6 kw. Ant 310 ft. TL: N41 45 34 W124 11 28 (CP: 25 kw, ant -144 ft.). Stereo. Hrs opn: 24. Dups AM 100%. (707) 464-3183. Wash atty: Cohn & Marks. ■ William E. Stamps, gen mgr; Jim Thompson, natl sls mgr; Michelle Smith, pub affrs dir.

Crescent North

KPOD-FM—Licensed to Crescent North. See Crescent City.

Cupertino

*****KKUP(FM)**—May 15, 1972: 91.5 mhz; 200 w. Ant 2,294 ft. TL: N37 06 40 W121 50 36. Stereo. Hrs opn: 24. Box 820 (95015). (408) 253-6000. Licensee: Assurance Sciences Foundation Inc. Format: Div, educ. Target aud: General. Spec prog: Brazilian 2 hrs, African 3 hrs, class 4 hrs, gospel 2 hrs, country 11 hrs, jazz 9 hrs, Indian 3 hrs, R&B 19 hrs, Sp 3 hrs, folk 12 hrs, reggae 15 hrs, public affairs 13 hrs, Latin American 8 hrs wkly. ■ Al Calame, gen mgr; David Stafford, progmg dir; Mike Meyer, mus dir; Patti McKay, news dir; Patti Mckay, pub affrs dir; Dave Barnett, chief engr.

Davis

*****KDVS(FM)**—Jan 1, 1968: 90.3 mhz; 5 kw. Ant 150 ft. TL: N38 32 30 W121 45 15. Stereo. Hrs opn: 24. 14 Lower Freeborn Hall (95616). (916) 752-0728. FAX: (916) 752-8548. Licensee: Regents of the Univ. of California. Format: Freeform var, jazz, Black. News staff one; news progmg 5 hrs wkly. Target aud: General. Spec prog: Class 2 hrs, Sp 5 hrs, C&W 3 hrs wkly, American Indian 2 hrs, folk 9 hrs, gospel 3 hrs, blues 10 hrs, international 20 hrs. ■ Kali Akono, gen mgr; Gabriella Burlando, sls dir; Aimee O'Brien, Allen Campos, progmg dirs; Joey Patel, mus dir; Colby Mancasda, asst mus dir; Jennifer Gleason, news dir; Bob Sheppard, pub affrs dir; Greg Knipstein, Jeff McKnight, chiefs engr.

KQBR(FM)—February 1979: 105.5 mhz; 2.96 kw. Ant 462 ft. TL: N38 39 26 W121 43 12. Stereo. Suite 210, 1260 Lake Blvd. (95616). (916) 387-5086. FAX: (916) 387-5086. Licensee: EZ Sacramento Inc. Group owner: EZ Communications Inc. (acq 6-22-93; $2 million; FTR 7-19-93). Format: New adult contemp. ■ Ricky Tatum, pres & gen mgr; Chip Morgan, chief engr.

Delano

KCHJ(AM)—Dec 1, 1951: 1010 khz; 5 kw-D, 1 kw-N, DA-2. TL: N35 48 40 W119 19 18. Hrs opn: 24. 5200 Standard St., Bakersfield (93308). (805) 327-9711; (805) 725-9411. FAX: (805) 327-0797. Licensee: KCHJ Inc. Net: CRC. Rep: Lotus. Wash atty: Borsari & Paxson. Format: Sp. News staff 2; news progmg 5 hrs wkly. Target aud: 18 plus; Spanish audience. Spec prog: Filipino 3 hrs wkly. ■ Jean G. Johnes, pres & vp progmg; Charles H. Johnes, gen mgr & chief engr; Pat Ryan, stn mgr; Barbara Hienen, vp opns; Mike Allen, vp sls; Eddie Leon, mus dir. ■ Rates: $12; 12; 12; 10.

KDNO(FM)—November 1968: 98.5 mhz; 50 kw. Ant 499 ft. TL: N35 42 46 W118 47 22. Stereo. 1305 Glenwood (93215). (805) 725-2345. FAX: (805) 725-2609. Licensee: Tape Networks Inc. (acq 10-74). Format: Sacred mus, talk. ■ Richard Palmquist, pres & opns mgr; Barton Buhtz, mus dir.

KKXX-FM—Oct 2, 1986: 105.3 mhz; 50 kw. Ant 547 ft. TL: N35 30 53 W119 03 41. Stereo. Suite 280, 1100 Mohawk St., Bakersfield (93309). (805) 322-9929. TWX: (805) 322-9239. Licensee: Grapevineradio Inc. Rep: Dupretti. Wash atty: Wiley, Rein & Fielding. Format: CHR. News staff one; news progmg 2 hrs wkly. Target aud: 18-44. Spec prog: Altv 3 hrs wkly. ■ Edward G. Atsinger III, pres; Allan B. Hammerel, gen mgr; Wayne Stephens, gen sls mgr; Gina Davis, prom dir; Ken Richards, progmg dir; Kathy Kaylin, news dir; Rick Caldwell, chief engr.

Desert Center

KZAL(FM)—Not on air, target date unknown: 105.5 mhz; 58 w. Ant 1,965 ft. TL: N33 39 15 W115 27 00. Stereo. Box 1866, Lake Havasu City, AZ (86403). Licensee: Desert Broadcasting Corp. ■ Wolfram J. Dochtermann, pres.

Desert Hot Springs

KUTE(AM)—Not on air, target date unknown: 880 khz; 3 w-D, 900 w-N, DA-2. TL: N33 54 55 W116 28 40. Suite 100, 5005 La Mart Dr., Riverside (92507). (714) 684-9992. Licensee: K-IV Broadcasting Corp. (acq 10-1-92; $14,000; FTR 11-16-92).

Dinuba

KRDU(AM)—Dec 26, 1946: 1130 khz; 5 kw-D, 6.2 kw-N, DA-2. TL: N36 29 03 W119 15 57. 597 N. Alta Ave. (93618). (209) 591-1130. FAX: (209) 591-5250. Licensee: Radio Dinuba Co. Net: AP. Wash atty: Fletcher, Heald & Hildreth. Format: Relg. News staff one; news progmg 7 hrs wkly. Target aud: 18-65. ■ Dave L. Hofer, pres, gen sls mgr, prom mgr & progmg dir; Donna Hofer, gen mgr; Mike Klassen, news dir; Richard Dahlquist, chief engr. ■ Rates: $11; 11; 11; 11.

KJOI(FM)—Co-owned with KRDU(AM). June 5, 1975: 98.5 mhz; 19 kw. Ant 820 ft. TL: N36 38 15 W118 56 35. Stereo. Hrs opn: 24. Prog sep from AM. Rep: Major Mkt. Target aud: 25-54; women 32-49. ■ Scott Mosely, gen mgr.

Earlimart

KNKD(FM)—Not on air, target date unknown: 93.5 mhz; 3 kw. Ant 328 ft. Suite A, 12550 Brookhurst St., Garden Grove (92640). Licensee: Earlimart Educational Foundation Inc.

East Porterville

KOJJ(FM)—Dec 1, 1989: 100.5 mhz; 1.5 kw. Ant 465 ft. TL: N36 02 37 W118 56 08 (CP: 6.8 kw). Suite 3, 165 North D, Porterville (93257). (209) 782-1005. FAX: (209) 782-8497. Licensee: Azia's Entertainment Inc. (acq 10-15-93; $275,000; FTR 11-8-93). Net: Unistar, CNN. Format: Urban Contemp. Target aud: 25-40. ■ Ledoria Johnson, Shelby Johnson, presdts; Gireg Mack, gen mgr; Debra Fenley, gen sls mgr; Antonio Fernandez, prom mgr; Victor Gallardo, progmg dir.

El Cajon

KECR(AM)—1955: 910 khz; 5 kw-U, DA-2. TL: N32 53 38 W116 55 35. 312 W. Douglas Ave. (92020). (619) 442-4414. Licensee: Family Stations Inc. (group owner; acq 6-9-92). Format: Relg. ■ Sandra Hess, stn mgr; Dick Warren, chief engr.

KECR-FM—1961: 93.3 mhz; 2 kw. Ant 1,850 ft. TL: N32 41 45 W116 56 10 (CP: 1.8 kw, ant 1,885 ft.). Stereo.

El Centro

Spec prog: Sp 7 hrs wkly. ■ Patrick Roy, gen mgr & chief engr.

KAMP(AM)—June 21, 1958: 1430 khz; 1 kw-U. TL: N32 48 27 W115 32 18. Stereo. Hrs opn: 24. Box 1018 (92244); 626 Main St. (92243). (619) 352-2277. FAX: (619) 352-1430. Licensee: KAMP Radio Inc. (acq 11-86). Rep: Hugh Wallace, Riley. Format: Adult contemp, oldies. Target aud: 25-49. ■ Cal Mandel, pres, gen mgr, gen sls mgr, progmg dir & mus dir; Lois Mandel, opns dir; Frank Lokey, news dir; Dean Imhof, chief engr.

KGBA-FM—See Holtville.

KICO(AM)—See Calexico.

KROP(AM)—(Brawley). November 1946: 1300 khz; 1 kw-D, 500 w-N. TL: N33 40 40 W115 31 16. Hrs opn: 24. Box 238, 120 S. Plaza (92227). (619) 344-1300. FAX: (619) 344-1763. Licensee: Stodelle Broadcasting Corp. (acq 9-75). Net: ABC/I. Rep: Torbet. Wash atty: Miller & Miller. Format: C&W. News staff one; news progmg 15 hrs wkly. Target aud: 25-54. Spec prog: Farm 18 hrs, sports 7 hrs wkly. ■ Stephen Stodelle, pres & gen mgr; Alan Stelmach, gen sls mgr; Noel Kelly, progmg dir; Chris Olivarez, mus dir; John Clark, news dir; Clif Glasgow, chief engr. ■ Rates: $22; 21; 22; 20.

KSIQ(FM)—(Brawley). Co-owned with KROP(AM). Sept 10, 1981: 96.1 mhz; 50 kw. Ant 270 ft. TL: N33 30 30 W115 31 28. Stereo. Hrs opn: 24. Prog sep from AM. Net: ABC/I. Rep: Torbet. Format: CHR. News staff one; news progmg 7 hrs wkly. Target aud: 18-34; female 60%, male 40%. Spec prog: Syndicated top 40 countdown, hot mix, dance mix. ■ Dan Watson, progmg dir & mus dir. ■ Rates: Same as AM.

KXO(AM)—January 1927: 1230 khz; 1 kw-U. TL: N32 46 34 W115 32 58. Box 140 (92244). (619) 352-1230. Licensee: KXO Inc. (acq 1961). Net: NBC, ABC, CBS; Calif. Farm. Rep: Katz & Powell. Format: Adult contemp, oldies. Target aud: 18-54. Spec prog: Farm 7 hrs wkly. ■ Gene Brister, pres & gen mgr; Caroll Buckley, vp, gen sls mgr, prom mgr, progmg dir & mus dir; Richard Sampson, chief engr. ■ Rates: $15; 14; 15; 14.

KXO-FM—Aug 2, 1976: 107.5 mhz; 25.5 kw. Ant 155 ft. TL: N32 46 35 W115 32 58. Stereo. Prog sep from AM. Format: Adult contemp. Target aud: 25-49.

El Cerrito

*****KECG(FM)**—Sept 1979: 88.1 mhz; 10 w. Ant 130 ft. TL: N37 54 30 W122 17 39. Stereo. Hrs opn: 24. 540 Ashbury Ave. (94530). (510) 525-0234. Licensee: Richmond Unified School District. Net: USA. Format: Div. News progmg 5 hrs wkly. Target aud: General. Spec prog: Jazz, gospel 5 hrs, Sp 3 hrs, Laotion 2 hrs, Filipino 2 hrs wkly. ■ Paul Daniels, gen mgr; Philip H. Morgan Jr., stn mgr.

Ellwood

KCQR(FM)—Licensed to Ellwood. See Santa Barbara.

Escondido

KSPA(AM)—June 1958: 1450 khz; 1 kw-U. TL: N33 07 11 W117 07 07. Suite 212, 1523 E. Valley Pkwy. (92027). (619) 745-8511. FAX: (619) 745-5828. Licensee: North County Broadcasting Corp. Group owner: Astor Broadcast Group (acq 9-15-87; $3,000,000 with co-owned FM; FTR 6-29-87). Format: Adult contemp, big band, MOR. Target aud: 35-64. ■ Arthur Astor, pres; Michael Means, gen mgr; Kim Cooper, mus dir; Mark McKay, pub affrs dir; Paul Sakrison, chief engr.

KOWF(FM)—Co-owned with KSPA(AM). July 1966: 92.1 mhz; 3 kw. Ant 1,024 ft. TL: N33 06 39 W117 09 13. Stereo. Format: C&W. News progmg 2 hrs wkly. Target aud: 25-54; adults in North San Diego County. ■ Norman Barton, progmg dir.

Essex

KHWY(FM)—May 1, 1991: 98.9 mhz; 7.4 kw. Ant 1,073 ft. TL: N34 52 50 W115 04 05. Hrs opn: 24. Rebroadcasts KRXV(FM) Yermo 100%. Box 255606, #5, 12381 Wilshire Blvd., Los Angeles (90025). Licensee: KRXV, Inc. Wash atty: Hogan & Hartson. Format: Adult contemp. News staff one; news progmg 28 hrs wkly. Target aud: 35 plus; travelers on I-40 & I-15 and 250,000 residents on the Mojave Desert. ■ Howard B. Anderson, CEO, chmn & pres; Patricia C. Cookus, CFO; Timothy B. Anderson, vp; Kirk M. Anderson, vp sls; Jess Collins, natl sls mgr; Lance Todd, progmg dir; Keith Hayes, pub affrs dir.

Eureka

KAJK(AM)—See Fortuna.

KATA(AM)—See Arcata.

KEKA-FM—Nov 1, 1983: 101.5 mhz; 100 kw. Ant 3,200 ft. TL: N40 25 12 W124 05 00. Stereo. 1101 Marsh Rd. (95501). (707) 442-5744. Licensee: Eureka Broadcasting (acq 12-13-90; $430,189; FTR 1-7-91). Net: ABC. Rep: Katz. Format: Modern C&W. Target aud: 25-54. ■ Hugo Papstein, gen mgr.

KFMI(FM)—1973: 96.3 mhz; 30 kw. Ant 1,580 ft. TL: N40 43 36 W123 58 18 (CP: 100 kw). Stereo. Drawer 1139, 890 S. G Street, Arcata (95521). (707) 822-7223. Licensee: Merit Broadcasting Corp. (group owner; acq 10-88; $690,000; FTR 10-31-88). Net: ABC/FM, AP. Rep: Cristal. Format: Hot adult contemp. News staff one; news progmg 3 hrs wkly. ■ Jeffrey B. Martin, pres; Michael J. Martin, vp; Michael Martin, gen mgr & gen sls mgr; Dave Roble, progmg dir; Rick Michaels, mus dir; Evonne Morrow, news dir; Hubert Reed, chief engr. ■ Rates: $20; 20; 20; 18.

KGOE(FM)—Not on air, target date unknown: 105.5 mhz; 28 kw. Ant 1,588 ft. TL: N40 43 52 W123 57 06. Rebroadcasts KGO(AM) San Francisco. Radio Station KGOE(FM), 600 5th St. (95501). (707) 442-2000. FAX: (707) 442-2011. Licensee: Southwestern Pacific Broadcasting Corp (acq 10-17-91; $30,000 for CP; FTR 11-11-91). Format: News/talk. ■ Judy Clark, gen mgr.

KINS(AM)—January 1946: 980 khz; 5 kw-D, 500 w-N, DA-N. TL: N40 48 05 W124 07 31. Hrs opn: 24. 1101 Marsh Rd. (95501). (707) 442-5744. Licensee: Eureka Broadcasting Co. (acq 3-1-58). Net: CBS, NBC Talknet, AP, Wall Street. Rep: Katz. Format: News/talk. News staff 2; news progmg. Target aud: 35 plus; upscale, educated. ■ Hugo Papstein, pres, gen mgr, gen sls mgr & progmg dir; Chris Long, news dir; Mark Householter, chief engr.

KRED(AM)—May 12, 1933: 1480 khz; 5 kw-D, 1 kw-N. TL: N40 44 28 W124 12 05. 5640 S. Broadway (95501). (707) 443-1621. FAX: (707) 443-6848. Licensee: Hoff Broadcasting. Net: SMN. Rep: Art Moore. Format: Country. Target aud: 25-54. ■ James Hoff, pres; Dan Hoff, gen mgr; Kathy Murphy, gen sls mgr.

KRED-FM—Dec 17, 1979: 92.3 mhz; 25 kw. Ant 1,544 ft. TL: N40 43 37 W123 58 25. Stereo. Prog sep from AM. (707) 443-5072. Format: Adult contemp.

KWSW(AM)—Dec 20, 1979: 790 khz; 5 kw-D, 112 w-N. TL: N40 48 09 W124 08 20. 1101 Marsh Rd. (95501). (707) 442-5744. Licensee: Eureka Broadcasting Co. Inc. (acq 11-30-92; $105,000; FTR 12-21-92). Net: NBC. Rep: Katz. Format: Adult standard. Target aud: 35 plus; existing & graying baby boomers with discretionary income. Spec prog: Sp one hr wkly. ■ Hugo Papstein, pres, gen mgr, gen sls mgr, progmg dir & news dir. ■ Rates: $11; 10; 10; 7.

KXGO(FM)—See Arcata.

Fairfield

KUIC(FM)—See Vacaville.

Fallbrook

KBAX(FM)—Nov 22, 1977: 107.1 mhz; 3 kw. Ant 300 ft. TL: N33 23 01 W117 11 20. Stereo. Hrs opn: 24. 131 E. Fig St. (92028). (619) 731-5229. Licensee: Douglas Broadcasting Inc. (group owner; acq 10-9-91; $1.25 million; FTR 10-28-91). Net: AP. Wash atty: Cohn & Marks. Format: Christian. News staff one. Target aud: 25-54; female, professional, educated baby boomers, students & homemakers. ■ John Douglas, CEO; Linda Johnson-Hayes, vp, gen mgr, stn mgr & gen sls mgr; Bob Gorley, progmg dir; Fred Fulcom, chief engr.

Felton

KHIP(FM)—Not on air, target date unknown: 93.7 mhz; 656 w. Ant 492 ft. 734 Marnell Ave., Santa Cruz (95065). Licensee: Benedek-Dewey Partnership.

Ferndale

KAJK-FM—Apr 1, 1993: 99.3 mhz; 3.6 kw. Ant 407 ft. TL: N40 24 58 W124 12 11. Stereo. Hrs opn: 24. 337 W. 15th St., Eureka (95501). (707) 445-3699. FAX: (707) 445-3787. Licensee: M. Keith Allgood. Wash atty: Rosenman & Colin. Format: Adult contemp. News staff one; news progmg 3 hrs wkly. Target aud: 25-54; upscale adults. ■ M. Keith Allgood, gen mgr; Patty Bryant, prom dir; Brian Kelly, progmg dir & news dir; Mark Householter, chief engr. ■ Rates: $14; 12; 14; 10.

Folsom

KIOQ(AM)—Jan 25, 1985: 1030 khz; 50 kw-D, 1 kw-N. TL: N38 41 40 W121 06 39. c/o KWOD-FM, 801 K St., 27th Floor, Sacramento (95814); 6430 Sunset Blvd., Los Angeles (90028). (916) 448-5000. FAX: (916) 448-1655. Licensee: Royce International Broadcasting Co. (acq 10-22-93; $43,000; FTR 11-8-93). Format: News/talk. ■ Edward R. Stoltz, pres.

Ford City

KZPE(FM)—Not on air, target date unknown: 102.1 mhz; 3 kw. Ant 33 ft. TL: N35 07 59 W119 29 55. Suite A, 12550 Brookhurst St., Garden Grove (92640). Licensee: Ford City Broadcasting.

Fort Bragg

KDAC(AM)—June 1948: 1230 khz; 1 kw-U. TL: N39 26 35 W123 46 48. Box 1248, 31380 Sherwood Rd. (95437). (707) 964-3250. FAX: (707) 964-8704. Licensee: Paul D. Clark (acq 2-18-92; FTR 3-16-92). Net: AP. Format: Country. ■ Charles Stone, pres, gen sls mgr & progmg dir; Paul Clark, gen mgr; Joe Wagner, chief engr.

KLLK-FM—Feb 19, 1991: 96.7 mhz; 3.7 kw. Ant 420 ft. TL: N39 27 53 W123 19 27. Stereo. Hrs opn: 5 AM-midnight. Rebroadcasts KLLK (AM) Willits 100%. 12 W. Valley St., Willits (95490); 1260 Main St. #4, Fort Bragg (95437). (707) 459-1250; (707) 961-9670. FAX: (707) 459-1251. Licensee: The Henry Radio Co. Wash atty: Haley, Bader and Potts. Format: New rock. News progmg 8 hrs wkly. Target aud: 18-49; adults who enjoy a progressive mix of modern rock music. Spec prog: New age 2 hrs wkly. ■ Brian J. Henry, gen mgr & opns mgr; Cherie France, mus dir.

KOZT(FM)—Dec 5, 1981: 95.3 mhz; 3.1 kw. Ant 468 ft. TL: N39 24 24 W123 44 04. Stereo. Hrs opn: 24. 124 E. Laurel St. (95437). (707) 964-7277. FAX: (707) 964-9536. Licensee: California Radio Partners (acq 12-1-90; $350,000; FTR 12-17-90). Net: Westwood One. Wash atty: Pepper & Corrazini. Format: Classic Rock. News staff one; news progmg one hr wkly. Target aud: 25-49; affluent, educated consumers. ■ Tom Yates, CEO; Vicky Watts, chmn & CFO; Bill Rett, chief engr.

KPMO(AM)—See Mendocino.

KSAY(FM)—November 1988: 98.5 mhz; 3.4 kw. Ant 448 ft. TL: N39 28 03 W123 45 34. Stereo. Hrs opn: 24. Box 2269, 684 C S. Main St. (95437). (707) 964-5729. Licensee: Axell Broadcasting. Net: Unistar, CNN. Format: Adult contemp. News progmg 9 hrs wkly. Target aud: 25-54; upscale consumers. Spec prog: Sp 6 hrs wkly. ■ Wade Axell, gen mgr; Tom Driggers, chief engr. ■ Rates: $9; 7; 9; 4.

Fortuna

KAJK(AM)—Oct 31, 1966: 1090 khz; 10 kw-D. TL: N40 33 30 W124 07 24. Hrs opn: Sunrise-sunset. Box 1090, 3560 Hillras Way (95540). (707) 725-9363. Licensee: M. Keith Allgood (acq 8-1-85). Wash atty: Rosenman & Colin. Format: Adult contemp. News progmg 2 hrs wkly. Target aud: 25-54. ■ M. Keith Allgood, gen mgr; Patty Bryant, prom dir; Keith Allgood, news dir; Mark Householter, chief engr. ■ Rates: $14; 12; 14; 12.

Fowler

KEZL(FM)—Nov 7, 1980: 96.7 mhz; 22 kw. Ant 348 ft. TL: N36 41 39 W119 43 57. Stereo. Suite 124, 4991 E. McKinley, Fresno (93727). (209) 251-8614. FAX: (209) 251-3347. Licensee: Americom II (group owner: acq 7-2-92; $1 million; FTR 7-27-92). Rep: Katz & Powell. Format: Adult contemp, jazz. Target aud: 25-54. ■ Karl Krass, gen mgr; Mark Kallen, gen sls mgr; J. Weiden Heimer, progmg dir; Steve Weber, chief engr.

KRGO(AM)—July 1, 1962: 1220 khz; 250 w-D. TL: N36 39 46 W119 40 18 (CP: 1210 khz; 10 kw-D, 370 w-N, DA-D TL: N36 41 39 W119 43 57). Suite 126, 2736 Divisadero, Fresno (93721). (209) 223-1220. Licensee: Ka-Carr Communications Inc. Format: Hispanic. ■ Ray Carrasco, gen mgr.

Frazier Park

KNOB(AM)—Not on air, target date unknown: 1050 khz; 10 kw-D, DA. TL: N35 01 28 W118 55 05. Box 250028, Los Angeles (90025). Licensee: Anita L. Levine.

Freedom

KPIG(FM)—Dec 1, 1987: 107.5 mhz; 2.85 kw. Ant 336 ft. TL: N36 50 06 W121 42 22. Stereo. Suite 16, 110 Main St., Watsonville (95076). (408) 722-9000. FAX: (408) 722-7548. Licensee: Radio Ranch. Format: Country, rock. News staff one; news progmg 5 hrs wkly. Target aud: 25-54. ■ Laura Hopper, pres; Leo Kesselman, gen mgr; Ed Monroe, stn mgr; Rick Melzig, chief engr.

Fremont

KBRG(FM)—January 1961: 104.9 mhz; 3 kw. Ant 300 ft. TL: N37 35 06 W121 59 08. Stereo. 2905 S. King Rd., San Jose (95122). (408) 274-1170. FAX: (408) 274-1818. Licensee: Excel Communications (acq 8-28-86; $2,875,000; FTR 5-19-86). Rep: Katz. Format: Adult contemp, Sp. ■ Chris Marks, vp; Athena Marks, gen mgr.

***KOHL(FM)**—Sept 23, 1974: 89.3 mhz; 145 w. Ant 407 ft. TL: N37 32 00 W121 54 35. Stereo. Hrs opn: 24. 43600 Mission Blvd. (94539). (510) 659-6221. FAX: (510) 659-6001. Licensee: Fremont-Newark Community College Dist. Format: Contemp hit. News progmg one hr wkly. Target aud: 18-34. Spec prog: Big band-jazz 4 hrs, city council 4 hrs wkly. ■ Robert Dochterman, gen mgr & chief engr; Matt Graf, prom mgr; Tomas Briseno, progmg dir; Matthew Karl, news dir.

AMERICAN RADIO BROKERS, INC.
MOST TRUSTED NAME IN MEDIA BROKERAGE
CHESTER P. COLEMAN / PRESIDENT
FOR THE BEST STATIONS FOR SALE FROM THIS AREA
CALL — 415/441-3377
1255 POST STREET / SUITE 625 / SAN FRANCISCO, CA 94109

Fresno

KAGZ(FM)—Not on air, target date unknown: 99.3 mhz; 3 kw. Ant 328 ft. 521 N. Circle Dr. (93704). Licensee: John E. Ostlund.

KBIF(AM)—Nov 17, 1947: 900 khz; 1 kw-D, 500 w-N, DA-N. TL: N36 41 30 W119 40 46. 2811 N. Wishon (93704). (209) 222-0900. FAX: (209) 222-1573. Licensee: Cascade Broadcasting Corp. (acq 11-19-75). Net: USA. Format: Relg. ■ David M. Jack, pres & gen mgr; Linda Lopez, gen sls mgr & prom mgr; Mark Mayfield, progmg dir; Tony Donato, news dir; James Moore, chief engr.

KBOS-FM—(Tulare). 1965: 94.9 mhz; 16.4 kw. Ant 847 ft. TL: N36 38 15 W118 56 35. Stereo. (209) 237-9361. Licensee: CenCal Broadcasting Inc. (acq 9-16-92; $1.4 million with KBOS(AM) Fresno; FTR 10-19-92). Net: CBS. Format: CHR. Target aud: 12-34. ■ Charlie Scott, opns mgr.

KCIV(FM)—See Mount Bullion.

KEYQ(AM)—Oct 14, 1957: 980 khz; 500 w-D, 48 w-N. TL: N36 44 28 W119 51 12. Suite 124, 4991 E. McKinley (93727). (209) 251-8614. FAX: (209) 251-3347. Licensee: Americom (group owner; acq 3-16-67). Net: CRC. Format: Nostalgia/talk. Target aud: 40 plus. ■ Karl Crass, gen mgr; Mark Kallen, gen sls mgr & prom mgr; Mike Bushey, progmg dir; Steve Weber, chief engr.

***KFCF(FM)**—June 9, 1975: 88.1 mhz; 2.4 kw. Ant 1,900 ft. TL: N37 04 23 W119 25 51. Stereo. Hrs opn: 24. Rebroadcasts KPFA(FM) Berkeley 85%. Box 4364 (93744); 1526 N. West Ave. (93728). (209) 233-2221. Licensee: Fresno Free College Foundation. Wash atty: David Tillotson. Format: News, pub affrs, mus. News progmg 12 hrs wkly. Target aud: General; intelligent, discerning, questioning. Spec prog: Southeast Asian Languages one hr (Cambodian), American Indian 2 hrs, Black 20 hrs, classical 10 hrs, folk 20 hrs, gospel 3 hrs, jazz 20 hrs, Sp 5 hrs, reggae 3 hrs wkly. ■ Doug Noll, pres; Randi Stephens, sls dir; Rych Withers, prom dir, mus dir & pub affrs dir; Rand Stover, progmg dir; Rand L. Stover, chief engr.

KFIG(AM)—January 1938: 1430 khz; 5 kw-U, DA-1. TL: N36 50 49 W119 40 46. Box 4265 (93744). (209) 268-8801. FAX: (209) 268-1289. Licensee: Headliner Radio Inc. (acq 9-24-91; $2,116,640 with co-located FM; FTR 10-14-91). Net: AP. Rep: Torbet. Format: Oldies. News staff one. Target aud: 25 plus. ■ Ron Ostlund, pres, gen mgr & progmg dir; Diane Ostlund, stn mgr & gen sls mgr; Joe Garcia, opns mgr, mus dir & news dir; Scott Dean, chief engr. ■ Rates: $40; 40; 40; 30.

KSXY(FM)—Co-owned with KFIG(AM). 1963: 101.1 mhz; 50 kw. Ant 310 ft. TL: N36 44 10 W119 47 13 (CP: 10 kw, ant 1,076 ft.). Stereo. Dups AM 50%. Format: Adult contemp.

***KFNO(FM)**—Feb 12, 1992: 90.3 mhz; 1.35 kw. Ant 1,971 ft. TL: N37 04 26 W119 25 52. 706 W. Herndon Ave., Fresno (93650). (510) 568-6200. Licensee: Family Stations Inc. (group owner). Format: Relg. ■ Harold Camping, pres; Larry Millikin, gen mgr.

KFRE(AM)—1937: 940 khz; 50 kw-U, DA-2. TL: N36 50 49 W119 39 46. 999 N. Van Ness Ave. (93728). (209) 441-7600. FAX: (209) 441-7606. Licensee: EBE Communications Ltd. (acq 9-89). Net: ABC/I. Format: Country. News staff 2; news progmg 2 hrs wkly. Target aud: 25-54. ■ Al Grosby, pres & gen mgr; Rita Walls, gen sls mgr; Jerry Lee, prom mgr, progmg dir & mus dir; Dick Carr, news dir; Hal Torosian, chief engr.

KNAX(FM)—Co-owned with KFRE(AM). March 15, 1948: 97.9 mhz; 2.07 kw. Ant 1,987 ft. TL: N36 44 09 W119 47 59. Stereo. Prog sep from AM. (acq 8-88; $4,000,000; FTR 9-5-88). Format: Contemp country. News staff 2; news progmg 2 hrs wkly. Target aud: 25-54. ■ Brian Anthony, prom dir; Mike Brady, progmg dir; Ron Foster, news dir.

***KFSR(FM)**—Oct 30, 1982: 90.7 mhz; 2.55 kw. Ant 66 ft. TL: N36 48 42 W119 44 43. Stereo. Hrs opn: 24. California State Univ.-Fresno, 5201 N. Maple (93740-0046). (209) 278-2598. Licensee: California State Univ. Fresno. Format: Jazz, altv rock. News progmg 2 hrs wkly. Target aud: General. Spec prog: Blues 18 hrs, reggae 3 hrs, new age 6 hrs, soul 8 hrs wkly. ■ James R. Wilson, gen mgr; Kevin Adler, stn mgr; Ed Bore, prom mgr; Paul Sanders, progmg dir; Brent Batty, mus dir; George Constantin, news dir; Jason Terada, pub affrs dir; R.L. Stover, chief engr.

KGST(AM)—1949: 1600 khz; 5 kw-U, DA-N. TL: N36 29 20 W119 19 33. Suite 121, 1900 Mariposa Mall (93721). (209) 266-9901. FAX: (209) 266-0771. Licensee: Lotus Communications Inc. Group owner: Lotus Communications Corp. (acq 8-1-85; $1,764,000; FTR 4-22-85). Net: CBS Hispanic. Rep: Lotus. Format: Sp. Target aud: 18 plus. ■ Howard Kalmenson, pres; Daniel Crotty, gen mgr; Hector Padilla, progmg dir; Stella Romo, news dir; Randy Stover, chief engr.

KIRV(AM)—Oct 1, 1962: 1510 khz; 10 kw-D. TL: N36 42 36 W119 50 06. Suite 142, 3636 N. First St. (93726). (209) 225-1050. FAX: (209) 225-1052. Licensee: New Life Enterprises Inc. (acq 1-9-75). Net: CBN. Format: Christian. ■ Jim Patterson, pres.

KJFX(FM)—Listing follows KYNO(AM).

KJOI(FM)—See Dinuba.

KKDJ(FM)—Dec 8, 1979: 105.9 mhz; 2.4 kw. Ant 1,960 ft. TL: N37 04 23 W119 25 51. Stereo. Hrs opn: 24. Suite 200, 1525 E. Shaw Ave. (93710-8003). (209) 226-5991. FAX: (209) 226-1149. Licensee: Pacific Quadracasting Inc. Group owner: The Heusser Group. Net: NBC the Source. Rep: D & R Radio. Format: Modern rock. Target aud: 25-49. ■ Wallace A. Heusser, pres & gen mgr; Cris DeHart, gen sls mgr; Brian Moore, prom mgr; Don Parker, progmg dir; Sat Bisla, mus dir; Michael Bennett, pub affrs dir; Randy Stover, chief engr.

KKTR(AM)—June 26, 1953: 1340 khz; 1 kw-U. TL: N36 45 51 W119 47 08. 2020 E. McKinley Ave. (93703). (209) 265-4232. FAX: (209) 266-6943. Licensee: CenCal Broadcasting Inc. (acq 9-16-92; $1.4 million with KBOS-FM Tulare; FTR 10-19-92). Net: CBS, SMN. Rep: CBS Radio. Format: Talk. Target aud: 18-49. ■ Steve Miller, pres; John Brocks, vp; Charlie Scott, opns dir.

KMJ(AM)—June 1925: 580 khz; 5 kw-U. TL: N36 41 37 W120 03 16. Hrs opn: 24. Box 70002 (93744); 1110 E. Olive (93728). (209) 233-9393. FAX: (209) 266-3714. Licensee: Henry Broadcasting (group owner; acq 11-87; $5.5 million with co-located FM; FTR 11-9-87). Net: NBC, NBC Talknet. Rep: Katz. Format: News/talk. News staff 13; news progmg 44 hrs wkly. Target aud: 25-64. Spec prog: Farm 6 hrs, sports 8 hrs, old time radio 7 hrs wkly. ■ Charlton Buckley, pres; Al Smith, gen mgr; Chris Pacheco, gen sls mgr; John Broeske, progmg dir; Roy Isom, news dir; Joe Mauk, chief engr.

KSKS(FM)—Co-owned with KMJ(AM). 1946: 93.7 mhz; 68 kw. Ant 1,912 ft. TL: N37 04 44 W119 25 47. Stereo. Prog sep from AM. (acq 8-88; $5,100,000; FTR 9-5-88). Format: Modern country. ■ Chris Pacneco, sls dir; Dave Taylor, progmg dir.

KNAX(FM)—Listing follows KFRE(AM).

KOQO(AM)—See Clovis.

KOQO-FM—Mar 15, 1948: 101.9 mhz; 2.25 w. Ant 1,948 ft. TL: N37 04 25 W119 25 52. Box 25095 (93729); 1590 Alluvial, Clovis (93612). (209) 454-7713. FAX: (209) 454-7714. Licensee: Dwight Case (acq 11-10-92; $2.055 million with KOQO(AM) Clovis; FTR 12-7-92). Rep: McGavren Guild. Format: Sp. Target aud: 12-34. ■ Victor Menina, pres; Ron G. Flores, stn mgr; Armando Diaz, progmg dir; Scott Dean, chief engr.

KRZR(FM)—See Hanford.

***KSJV(FM)**—July 4, 1980: 91.5 mhz; 16 kw. Ant 870 ft. TL: N35 38 15 W118 56 35. Stereo. Hrs opn: 24. Suite 700, 111 Fulton Mall (93721). (209) 486-5174. FAX: (209) 264-9309. Licensee: Radio Bilingue Inc. Format: Ethnic, bilingual, Latino. News staff 5; news progmg one hr wkly. Target aud: 16-60; Latino. Spec prog: Jazz 19 hrs, Black 3 hrs, folk 4 hrs, Filipino one hr, Hmong 4 hrs wkly. ■ Hugo Morales, CEO; Keith Frady, opns dir; Samuel Orozco, progmg dir & news dir; Steve Weber Jr., chief engr.

KSKS(FM)—Listing follows KMJ(AM).

KSXY(FM)—Listing follows KFIG(AM).

KTHT(FM)—Jan 6, 1962: 102.7 mhz; 50 kw. Ant 500 ft. TL: N36 49 07 W119 30 33. Stereo. Hrs opn: 24. 2775 E. Shaw (93710). (209) 294-1234. FAX: (209) 294-0240. Licensee: KOSO Inc. (acq 8-15-84; $2,650,000; FTR 6-18-84). Rep: Christal. Wash atty: Haley, Bader & Potts. Format: Adult contemp. News staff one; news progmg 20 hrs wkly. Target aud: 25-54; women. ■ Mark Douglas, gen mgr; Kim Walker, sls dir; Art Farkas, progmg dir; Jenifer Music, news dir & pub affrs dir; Steve Webber, chief engr. ■ Rates: $58; 54; 56; 16.

***KVPR(FM)**—Oct 15, 1978: 89.3 mhz; 2.45 kw. Ant 1,890 ft. TL: N37 04 25 W119 25 52. Stereo. Suite 101, 3437 W. Shaw Ave. (93711). (209) 275-0764. FAX: (209) 275-2202. Licensee: White Ash Broadcasting Inc. Net: NPR. Format: Class, jazz, news. ■ Mariam Stepanian, pres & gen mgr; Jim Meyers, progmg dir; Scott Dean, chief engr.

KXEX(AM)—September 1962: 1550 khz; 5 kw-D, 2.5 kw-N, DA-2. TL: N36 46 14 W119 55 20. Box 12223, (93777); 2247 W. Church (93706). (209) 233-8803. FAX: (209) 233-8871. Licensee: Atlas Broadcasting Inc. Format: Sp. News staff one. Target aud: 18-49. ■ Tami Sonder, gen mgr & stn mgr; Carlos Coronel, progmg dir & mus dir; Moses Ochoa, news dir.

KYNO(AM)—October 1947: 1300 khz; 5 kw-D, 1 kw-N, DA-N. TL: N36 46 14 W119 45 00. Hrs opn: 24. 2125 N. Barton (93703). (209) 255-8383. FAX: (209) 453-1313. Licensee: Brown Broadcasting Co. (group owner). Net: CNN, Unistar. Rep: Banner. Format: Oldies. Target aud: 25-54; male. ■ Phil Melrose, pres; Mary Lou Gunn, gen mgr; Liz Balestrieri, gen sls mgr; Dave Case, progmg dir & chief engr; Steven Dodge, news dir.

KJFX(FM)—Co-owned with KYNO(AM). May 15, 1970: 95.7 mhz; 17.5 kw. Ant 850 ft. TL: N36 56 55 W119 29 09. Stereo. Prog sep from AM. Format: Top-40, classic rock. News staff one. Target aud: 18-34. ■ David Moore, prom mgr & progmg dir.

Garberville

KBEY(FM)—Not on air, target date unknown: 104.7 mhz; 50 kw. Ant 2,650 ft. TL: N40 07 15 W123 41 27. 940 California Ave., Palo Alto (94306). Licensee: Joseph P. Milliken.

***KMUD(FM)**—May 28, 1987: 91.1 mhz; 200 w. Ant 2,483 ft. TL: N40 07 15 W123 41 27 (CP: 178 w, ant 2,490 ft.). Hrs opn: 24. Box 135, Redway (95560); 971 Redwood Dr., Garberville (95540). (707) 923-2513; (707) 923-3911. FAX: (707) 923-2501. Licensee: Redwood Community Radio Inc. Format: Eclectic. News staff one; news progmg 5 hrs wkly. Target aud: General; diverse local. Spec prog: Black 3 hrs, ethinic one hr, class 4 hrs, country 6 hrs, farm one hr, jazz 6 hrs, Sp 2 hrs, American Indian one hr, call-in talk 7 hrs, children 3 hrs wkly. ■ Jack Maguire, chmn; Simon Frech, gen mgr & stn mgr; Pamela Parsons, opns mgr; Michael Brennan, adv mgr; Michael Jacinto, progmg dir; Georgia Long, mus dir; Michael Davis, asst mus dir; Estelle Fennell, news dir.

KWEO(FM)—Not on air, target date unknown: 103.7 mhz; 7.64 kw. Ant 2,647 ft. 11608 Blossomwood Ct., Moorpark (93021). Licensee: Brett E. Miller.

Garden Grove

KIKF(FM)—June 21, 1961: 94.3 mhz; 3 kw. Ant 245 ft. TL: N33 46 52 W117 53 34. Stereo. Hrs opn: 24. 2 City Blvd East, Suite 183, Orange (92668). (714) 835-1300. FAX: (714) 937-1262. Licensee: Orange Broadcasting Corp. Group owner: Astor Broadcast Group (acq 7-21-76). Net: AP. Wash atty: Cohn & Marks. Format: Modern country. News staff one; news progmg 4 hrs wkly. Target aud: 25-54. ■ N. Arthur Astor, pres; Michael Means, vp; Paul Sakrison, vp opns & vp engrg; Mary Stanley, sls dir; Liz Pennington, prom mgr & news dir; Craig Powers, progmg dir.

George

KATJ(FM)—June 29, 1989: 100.7 mhz; 260 w. Ant 1,548 ft. TL: N34 36 38 W117 17 18 Stereo. Box 1428, Suite 190, 15494 Palmdale Rd., Victorville (92392). (619) 245-2212. FAX: (619) 245-8012. Licensee: Island Broadcasting Assoc. L.P. (acq 12-21-90; grpsl; FTR 1-14-91). Net: CNN. Rep: Katz. Wash atty: Cohn & Marks. Format: Country. News staff one. ■ Scott Brody, pres; Linda Griggs, stn mgr. ■ Rates: $24; 20; 22; 12.

Gilroy

KAZA(AM)—September 1957: 1290 khz; 5 kw-D, DA. TL: N37 09 48 W121 38 28. No. 355, 2980 Stevens Creek Blvd., San Jose (95128). (408) 984-1290. FAX: (408) 985-9322. Licensee: Radio Fiesta Corp. (acq 5-14-73). Rep: Caballero. Format: Sp. ■ Albert S. Rodriquez, pres & gen sls mgr; Albert S. Rodriquez Jr., progmg dir; Filiberto Arteaga, mus dir & news dir; John Higdon, chief engr.

KUFX(FM)—Jan 1, 1970: 94.5 mhz; 1.23 kw. Ant 2,535 ft. TL: N37 06 39 W121 50 37. Hrs opn: 24. 1589 Schallenberger Rd., San Jose (95131). (408) 297-5977. FAX: (408) 297-0359. Licensee: KOOL Communications Inc. (acq 2-13-91; 4.5 million; FTR 3-4-91). Rep: D & R Radio. Format: Classic rock. News staff one; news progmg 4 hrs wkly. Target aud: 25-54. ■ Martin Loughman, pres; Mike Jackson, gen mgr; Don Girdner, gen sls mgr; Corrine Perri, rgnl sls mgr; Kristen Mealiffe, mktg dir & prom dir; Larry Sharp, progmg dir; Scott Mitchell, mus dir; Lisa Adams, news dir; Jim Duncan, chief engr.

Glendale

KIEV(AM)—1931: 870 khz; 10 kw-D, 1 kw-N, DA-2. TL: N34 08 13 W118 13 34 (CP: 15 kw-D). Stereo. Hrs opn: 24. 5900 San Fernando Rd. (91202-2797). (213) 245-2388; (818) 244-8483. FAX: (213) 245-5438. Licensee: Southern Calif. Broadcasting Co. (acq 6-1-61). Net: AP, CNN. Wash atty: Haley, Bader & Potts. Format: News/talk. News progmg 35 hrs wkly. Target aud: 35 plus; general. Spec prog: Irish one hr, Jewish one hr wkly. ■ Fred Beaton, chmn, gen mgr & natl sls mgr; Ron Beaton, pres & gen sls mgr; Bill Lobb, prom mgr; Dick Sinclair, progmg dir; George Putnam, news dir; Harold Williams, chief engr.

KLIT(FM)—March 1951: 101.9 mhz; 2.4 kw. Ant 2,848 ft. TL: N34 13 26 W118 03 45. Stereo. 5858 Sunset Blvd., Los Angeles (90028). (213) 464-5483. FAX: (213) 467-5483. Licensee: Golden West Broadcasters (group owner; acq 12-85). Rep: Banner. Wash atty: Irving Gastfreund. Format: Adult contemp. News staff one; news progmg 4 hrs wkly. Target aud: 25-54. ■ Gene Autry, chmn; Bill Ward, vp; Michelle Billy, sls dir; Robert Lyles, prom dir & adv dir; Scott O'Neil, progmg dir; Chris Downing, chief engr.

Goleta

KMGQ(FM)—Jan 30, 1982: 106.3 mhz; 365 w. Ant 879 ft. TL: N34 27 55 W119 40 38 (CP: 245 w, ant 827 ft.). Stereo. 1221 Chapala, Santa Barbara (93101). (805) 962-8700. Licensee: Channel Islands Broadcasting Inc. (acq 1-28-93; $1.5 million with KIST(AM) Santa Barbara; FTR 2-15-93). Rep: CBS Radio. Format: Adult contemp. News staff one; news progmg 4 hrs wkly. Target aud: 25-54. Spec prog: Jazz 13 hrs wkly. ■ Jennifer Van Donge, gen mgr & gen sls mgr; Jill Riveria, natl sls mgr; Jennifer Quinlan, prom dir; Joni Caryl, progmg dir; Nancy Newcomer, Michael Creek, mus dirs; Dick Williams, news dir; Doug Allen, chief engr.

Gonzales

KKLF(FM)—Oct. 25, 1990: 104.3 mhz; 6 kw. Ant 328 ft. N36 33 26 W121 22 46. Stereo. Hrs opn: 24. Suite 202, 1188 Padre Dr., Salinas (93901). (408) 758-5400; (405) 758-5625. FAX: (408) 758-5446. Licensee: Central Coast Communications Inc. (acq 3-31-93; $840,000 with KIEZ(AM) Carmel Valley; FTR 4-19-93) Wash atty: Jim Riley. Format: Contemp Christian. News staff one; news progmg 5 hrs wkly. Target aud: 25-49. ■ Jose Diaz, pres & gen mgr.

KKMC(AM)—Sept 22, 1984: 880 khz; 10 kw-D, 1 kw-N, DA-2. TL: N36 33 48 W121 26 04 (CP: COL: Del Rey Oaks, 50 kw-D, 2.5 kw-N). Hrs opn: 18. Suite 501, No. 8 E. Alisal St., Salinas (93901). (408) 424-5562. FAX: (408) 424-6437 Licensee: Monterey County Broadcasters Inc. Net: USA, IBN. Format: Relg. News progmg 7 hrs wkly. Target aud: 25 & up; family oriented. Spec prog: Sp 3 hrs, teen talk 10 hrs wkly. ■ Carl J. Auel, pres; John N. Dick, gen mgr; Lorraine Dick, gen sls mgr; Ronald Warren, chief engr. ■ Rates: $15; 15; 12; 12.

Grass Valley

KJFA(FM)—Not on air, target date unknown: 99.3 mhz; 3 kw. Ant 325 ft. TL: N39 16 29 W121 00 35. Box 2269, Fort Bragg (95473). (707) 964-5729. Licensee: Wade Axell.

KNCO(AM)—Oct 1, 1978: 830 khz; 5 kw-U. TL: N39 12 52 W121 00 55. Hrs opn: 19. Suite A, 1255 E. Main St. (95945). (916) 272-3424. FAX: (916) 272-2872. Licensee: Nevada County Broadcasters Inc. Net: ABC/I. Rep: Gillis. Wash atty: Fletcher, Heald & Hildreth. Format: News/talk. News staff 3; news progmg 30 hrs wkly. Target aud: 25-54; adults of western Nevada County. Spec prog: Christian 8 hrs wkly. ■ Barbara Juneau, chmn; Steven E. Brock, pres & gen mgr; Jay Cooper, vp, gen sls mgr & prom mgr; Jim Kerr, opns mgr & progmg dir; Steve Brock, news dir; Doug Tao, chief engr. ■ Rates: $24; 21; 21; 18.

KNCO-FM—Sept 7, 1982: 94.3 mhz; 290 w. Ant 980 ft. TL: N39 14 44 W120 57 52. Stereo. Hrs opn: 20. Prog sep from AM. Net: ABC/E. Format: Country. News staff one; news progmg 2 hrs wkly. Target aud: 25-55; adults of western Nevada County. ■ Rates: $20; 16; 16; 14.

Green Acres

*****KAXL(FM)**—Not on air, target date unknown: 88.3 mhz; 360 w. Ant 325 ft. TL: N35 23 02 W119 06 46 (CP: 21.14 kw, 328 ft.). 10130 Rosedale Hwy. (93308). Licensee: Skyride Unlimited Inc. (acq 7-8-91; $4,000 (CP); FTR 7-29-91).

KRAB(FM)—Licensed to Green Acres. See Bakersfield.

Greenfield

KSEA(FM)—Not on air, target date unknown: 107.9 mhz; 50 kw. Ant 492 ft. TL: N36 19 50 W121 10 16. Suite 1004, 818 W. 7th St., Los Angeles (90017). Licensee: Troposphere Broadcasting L.P.

KSUR-FM—Aug 7, 1989: 99.5 mhz; 50 kw. Ant 492 ft. TL: N36 27 51 W121 17 52 (CP: 30 kw, ant 640 ft.). 1514 Moffett St., Salinas (93905); 1500 Cotner Ave., Los Angeles (90025). (310) 478-5540. FAX: (310) 478-4189. Licensee: Mount Wilson FM Broadcasters. Rep: CMBS. Format: Country. ■ Saul Levine, pres; Douglas Brown, progmg dir; Bob Turner, chief engr.

Groveland

*****KXSR(FM)**—May 1992: 91.7 mhz; 6.9 kw. Ant 1,027 ft. TL: N37 47 38 W120 06 40. Rebroadcasts KXPR-FM, Sacramento. Suite B, 3416 American River Dr., Sacramento (95864). (916) 278-6011. Licensee: California State Univ., Sacramento. Format: Class & info.

Grover City

KIXT-FM—July 4, 1984: 107.3 mhz; 4.2 kw. Ant 807 ft. TL: N35 06 25 W120 30 57. Stereo. Box 1400, San Luis Obispo (93406). (805) 544-1400. FAX: (805) 543-0787. Licensee: R&L Broadcasters Inc. (acq 3-11-92). Format: Hot country. News staff one; news progmg 35 hrs wkly. Target aud: 18-44; emphasis on 25-34 year olds. ■ Guy Hackman, pres & gen mgr; Kyle Ronemus, gen sls mgr; Eric Shade, progmg dir & mus dir; Bill Bordeaux, chief engr. ■ Rates: $25; 22; 25; 18.

Guadalupe

KIDI(FM)—Not on air, target date unknown: 105.5 mhz; 160 w. Ant 1,342 ft. TL: N34 53 54 W120 35 28. Licensee: Spanish TV 59 (acq 11-23-92; $325,000; FTR 12-21-92).

Gualala

KWAN(FM)—Not on air, target date unknown: 100.5 mhz; 6 kw. Ant 669 ft. TL: N38 49 33 W123 34 12. c/o Box 200, The Sea Ranch (95497). Licensee: Gerhard J. Hanneman, Ph.D.

Hanford

KAFN(FM)—Not on air, target date unknown: 94.5 mhz; 3 kw. Ant 100 ft. 100 Robideaux Rd., Aptos (95003). Licensee: Hanford FM Radio.

KIGS(AM)—Feb 1, 1948: 620 khz; 1 kw-D, DA-N. TL: N36 19 37 W119 33 58. Hrs opn: 24. 6165 Hwy. 198 (93230). (209) 582-0361. FAX: (209) 582-3981. Licensee: P & C Broadcasting (acq 7-15-90). Rep: Lotus. Wash atty: Allan E. Aronowitz. Format: Portugese. News progmg 35 hrs wkly. Target aud: 18-49. ■ Tony Vieira, gen mgr, gen sls mgr, prom mgr & progmg dir; Moises Ochoa, news dir; Marv Sawyer, chief engr. ■ Rates: $22; 18; 22; 12.

KMPH-FM—September 1976: 107.5 mhz; 20.3 kw. Ant 784 ft. TL: N36 38 12 W118 56 34. Stereo. 5087 E. McKinley Ave., Fresno (93727). (209) 255-5000. FAX: (209) 252-4522. Licensee: KMPH NewsRadio, a California L.P. (acq 9-7-93; $950,000; FTR 9-27-93). Net: SMN. Rep: Eastman. Wash atty: Fisher, Wayland, Cooper & Leader. Format: 24 hr news. Target aud: 18-34. ■ J.R. Rowten, pres; Roger Gadley, news dir.

KRZR(FM)—Dec 24, 1976: 103.7 mhz; 50 kw. Ant 499 ft. TL: N36 33 36 W119 45 20. Stereo. Hrs opn: 24. 1765 N. Fine, Fresno (93727). (209) 252-8994. FAX: (209) 252-7466. Licensee: Bob Sherman (acq 1993; $950,000; FTR 9-13-93). Net: AP. Rep: Christal. Wash atty: Peter O'Connell. Format: Album oriented rock. News progmg one hr wkly. Target aud: 18-34; young adult. ■ Curtis Johnson, news dir.

Hayward

*****KCRH(FM)**—Apr 10, 1981: 89.9 mhz; 19 w. Ant -135 ft. TL: N37 38 23 W122 06 16. 25555 Hesperian Blvd. (94545). (510) 786-6954. FAX: (510) 782-9315. Licensee: Chabot College/Las Positas Community College District. Format: CHR. News progmg one hr wkly. Target aud: General; 17-35. Spec prog: Instructional one hr, pub affrs 5 hrs wkly. ■ Rick Strauss, gen mgr & chief engr.

Healdsburg

KVVV(FM)—Licensed to Healdsburg. See Santa Rosa.

Hemet

KHSJ(AM)—Apr 10, 1959: 1320 khz; 500 w-D, 300 w-N, DA-2. TL: N33 44 59 W116 59 53. Hrs opn: 24. 2615 W. Devonshire (92545); 28190 Rancho California Rd., Temecula (92590). (909) 925-9000; (909) 699-6989. FAX: (909) 699-9293. Licensee: 2588 Newport Corp. (acq 1-20-75). Net: MBS, Sun; Calif. Agri-Radio. Rep: W.R.B.S. Format: News/talk, sports, MOR. News staff one; news progmg 21 hrs wkly. Target aud: General. Spec prog: Sports, medicine. ■ H. Kandy Rohde, pres; Jerry Regier, gen mgr; Kristine Turner, opns mgr & prom dir; Joe Talbott, chief engr. ■ Rates: $18; 18; 18; 18.

KHYE(FM)—Co-owned with KHSJ(AM). Nov 9, 1963: 105.7 mhz; 170 w. Ant 1,023 ft. TL: N33 44 59 W116 59 53. Stereo. Hrs opn: 24. Prog sep from AM. Suite 1330, 26111 Ynez, Temecula (92591). FAX: (714) 658-0385. Net: ABC/C. Format: Country. News progmg 14 hrs wkly.

Hesperia

KVVQ(AM)—Feb 1, 1990: 910 khz; 700 w-D, 500 w-N, DA-2. TL: N34 23 19 W117 23 29. Stereo. Hrs opn: 24. 11920 Hesperia Rd. (92345). (619) 244-2000. Licensee: Kenneth B. Orchard. Net: AP, MBS. Wash atty: Arent, Fox, Kintner, Plotkin & Kahn. Format: MOR, news, talk, sports. News staff 4; news progmg 40 hrs wkly. Target aud: 40 plus. Spec prog: Los Angeles Dodgers. ■ Ken Orchard, pres & chief engr; Brad Orchard, gen mgr; John Berry, news dir. ■ Rates: $14; 14; 14; 14.

Hollister

KMPG(AM)—1966: 1520 khz; 5 kw-D, DA-2. TL: N36 50 16 W121 25 01. Hrs opn: 14. Box 1414, 1330 Nash Rd. (95023). (408) 637-7476. FAX: (408) 637-4031. Licensee: Adela Martinez and Rafel Meza (acq 6-1-93; $550,000; FTR 6-28-93). Net: SIS. Rep: Lotus. Format: Sp. News staff one. Target aud: General. ■ Scott Killgore, pres; Gilberto De Leon, gen mgr, gen sls mgr, prom mgr & progmg dir; Maco Antonio Nova, mus dir & news dir; Mike Blankenbecker, chief engr. ■ Rates: $28; 28; 28; na.

KMXZ(FM)—1979: 93.5 mhz; 116 w. Ant 1,519 ft. TL: N36 46 31 W121 28 27. Stereo. Suite 201, One Robar Center, Salinas (93901). (408) 757-2977. FAX: (408) 757-1386. Licensee: KHIP Partners (acq 9-89; $1,860,284; FTR 9-25-89). Format: Urban contemp. Target aud: 18-49. ■ Connie Sutherland, CFO; Gary R. Weinstein, vp & gen mgr; Linda Roberts, opns dir; Jerry O'Hara, sls dir; Christopher Lance, progmg mgr; Stephen Davis, news dir; Skip Bushell, chief engr.

Holtville

KGBA-FM—Aug 8, 1983: 100.1 mhz; 3 kw. Ant 298 ft. TL: N32 48 10 W115 29 53. Box 238 (92250); Studio, 605 State St., El Centro (92243). (619) 352-9860. FAX: (619) 352-1883. Licensee: The Voice of International Christian Evangelism Inc. (acq 11-1-86; $350,000; FTR 9-15-86). Wash atty: Miller & Miller. Format: Relg, Sp. News progmg 3 hrs wkly. Target aud: 30-60; adult family Christian conservatives. Spec prog: Cantonese 4 hrs wkly. ■ Alberto Lozano, pres; Frederick McCormick, sr vp; Ruth Ann Lozano, opns dir & mus dir; Richard L. Nix, chief engr.

Hoopa

*KIDE(FM)—December 1980: 91.3 mhz; 195 w. Ant -1,560 ft. TL: N41 03 51 W123 41 05 (CP: 305 w). Stereo. Box 1220 (95546). (916) 625-4245. Licensee: Hoopa Valley Telecommunications Corp. Format: Div. Spec prog: Hoopa Indian language, history & culture 20 hrs wkly. ■ Frank Starky, gen mgr; Matt Moore, progmg dir.

Idyllwild

KATY-FM—Dec 1, 1989: 101.3 mhz; 1.15 kw. Ant 731 ft. TL: N33 46 05 W116 44 01. Stereo. Hrs opn: 24. Box 1468, Hemet (92546); Suite H, 43613 Florida Ave., Hemet (92544). (909) 927-8099. FAX: (909) 927-1083. Licensee: Kay Sadlier-Gill. Net: SMN. Wash atty: Brown, Finn & Nietert. Format: Adult contemp. News staff one; news progmg 9 hrs wkly. Target aud: 25-49; affluent, upward, mobile. ■ Katy Gill, pres & gen mgr; David Carson, stn mgr & gen sls mgr; Charles Marquiss, opns progmg & news dir; Tony Smith, natl sls dir; David Petrik, chief engr.

Imperial

KMXX(FM)—Sept 17, 1980: 99.3 mhz; 3 kw. Ant 200 ft. TL: N32 51 44 W115 33 41. Stereo. Hrs opn: 24. 626 Main St., El Centro (92243-2920). (619) 352-2277. FAX: (619) 352-1430. Licensee: Brawley Broadcasting Co. (acq 11-5-92; $400,000; FTR 11-30-92). Net: CRC. Rep: Katz Hispanic. Format: Adult contemp, Sp. Target aud: 19-49. ■ Cal Mandel, gen mgr & mus dir.

Independence

KDAY(FM)—Not on air, target date unknown: 106.3 mhz; 3 kw. Ant -1,617 ft. TL: N36 50 00 W14 17. 532 N. Edwards St. (93526). Licensee: Ms. Bennett Kessler (acq 3-14-91; FTR 4-1-91).

Indio

KBZT(AM)—1946: 1400 khz; 1 kw-U. TL: N33 43 37 W116 15 10. Stereo. Hrs opn: 24. Box 956, La Quinta (92253); 41-945 Boardwalk, STC, Palm Desert (92260). (619) 568-6830. FAX: (619) 568-3984. Licensee: Pennino Broadcasting Corp. (acq 3-5-90; $650,000; FTR 2-5-90). Net: CNN, Unistar. Rep: Caballero. Format: Sp. News staff one; news progmg 7 hrs wkly. Target aud: General. ■ Jeannette Banoczi, pres; Jack Banoczi, gen mgr; Mark Wright, stn mgr & sls dir; Kathy Banas, prom dir; Barry O'Connor, chief engr.

KCLB(AM)—See Coachella.

KCLB-FM—See Coachella.

KCMJ-FM—April 13, 1984: 92.7 mhz; 3 kw. Ant 298 ft. TL: N33 47 45 W116 13 19. Stereo. Hrs opn: 24. Box 1626, Palm Springs (92263). (619) 320-6818. Licensee: Claridge Broadcasting Corp. Rep: McGavren Guild. Format: Adult contemp. News staff one; news progmg 2 hrs wkly. Target aud: 25-44. ■ Morris Bergreen, pres; Ed Groppo, gen mgr, opns mgr & natl sls mgr; Scott Kiner, mktg dir; Gary Demaroney, progmg dir & news dir; Bill Watson, chief engr. ■ Rates: $30; 30; 30; 20.

*KCRY(FM)—Not on air, target date unknown: 89.3 mhz; 775 w. Ant 590 ft. TL: N33 48 05 W116 13 27. 1900 Pico Blvd., Santa Monica (90405). Licensee: Santa Monica Community College.

KLCX(FM)—Mar 1993: 102.3 mhz; 600 w. Ant 587 ft. TL: N33 48 07 W116 13 29. Hrs opn: 24. Suite K, 77622 Country Club Dr., Palm Desert (92211). Licensee: Mirage Broadcasting Corp. (acq 2-4-91; FTR 2-25-91). Wash atty: Waysdorf & Van Bergh. Format: Classic rock. News staff one; news progmg 3 hrs wkly. Target aud: 25-45. ■ Andrew Reimer, CEO; Ty Stevens, pres & gen mgr; Bill Obian, opns mgr; Barry Gorfine, natl sls mgr; Don James, prom mgr; Jeff Michaels, news dir; Barry O'Connor, engrg dir.

Inglewood

KACE(FM)—1959: 103.9 mhz; 1.65 kw. Ant 390 ft. TL: N34 00 24 W118 21 52. Stereo. 161 N. LaBrea Ave. (90301). (310) 330-3100. Licensee: All Pro Broadcasting Inc. (group owner; acq 3-77). Net: AP; CBS, Unistar. Rep: Katz & Powell. Format: Adult contemp, ethnic. Target aud: 25-44; women, 60% African-American, 30% Hispanic. ■ Willie Davis, pres; Ann McCullom, gen mgr; Elston Buther, gen sls mgr; Tracey F. Riley, prom dir; Rich Guzman, progmg dir; Antoinette Russell, mus dir; Isidra Person-Lynn, news dir; David Petrik, chief engr. ■ Rates: $150; 125; 140; 110.

KTYM(AM)—Feb 14, 1958: 1460 khz; 5 kw-D, 500 w-N, DA-2. TL: N34 00 24 W118 21 52. 6803 West Blvd. (90302). (213) 678-3731. Licensee: Trans America Broadcasting Corp. Wash atty: Miller & Miller. Format: Div, relg. News staff 2; news progmg 2 hrs wkly. Target aud: 18-54. Spec prog: Gospel 15 hrs, Ger 2 hrs, It 4 hrs, Sp one hr, Armenian 3 hrs, Hungarian one hr, Japanese one hr, Croatian one hr, Serbian one hr, Lithuanian one hr, Pol one hr, Fr one hr wkly. ■ A.J. Williams, CEO & pres; Gerardo Borrego, vp & gen mgr; Claire T. Honovich, gen sls mgr; Bobby A. Howe, progmg dir & pub affrs dir; Gary Wayne, mus dir & news dir; Paul M. Wiren, chief engr. KAIL(TV) affil. ■ Rates: $18; 16.50; 18; 16.50.

Irvine

*KUCI(FM)—Oct 1, 1969: 88.9 mhz; 25 w. Ant 100 ft. TL: N33 38 38 W117 50 34 (CP: 200 w, ant -10 ft.). Box 4362 (92716-4362). (714) 856-6868. Licensee: Regents of the University of Calif. Format: Div. Spec prog: Class 5 hrs, jazz 20 hrs, Black 14 hrs, folk 6 hrs wkly. ■ Sonja Tanner, gen mgr; Dana Watanabe, chief engr.

Jackson

KNGT(FM)—Aug 16, 1973: 94.3 mhz; 230 w. Ant 1,100 ft. TL: N38 20 24 W120 43 13. Stereo. Box 609 (95642). (209) 223-0241; (209) 754-3745. Licensee: Gold Country Communications Inc. (acq 11-83; $600,000; FTR 11-28-83). Net: ABC/D. Rep: Radio Time. Format: Adult contemp. ■ Laurence G. Rutter, chmn & gen mgr; James Guidi, opns dir; Judy Hotchkiss, gen sls mgr; Jim Guidi, progmg dir; David Eisenhauer, news dir; Sue Duncan, pub affrs dir.

Johannesburg

KRAJ(FM)—March 1990: 103.9 mhz; 1.5 kw. Ant 1,322 ft. TL: N35 28 39 W117 41 58. Hrs opn: 24. 203 Panamint, Ridgecrest (93555). (619) 371-1700. FAX: (619) 371-1824. Licensee: Robert Adelman. Net: SMN. Format: Hot adult contemp. News staff one. Target aud: 25-49. ■ Robert Adelman, pres & gen mgr; Sue Avery, stn mgr & gen sls mgr; D.A. Collins, progmg dir.

Joshua Tree

KHWX(FM)—Not on air, target date unknown: 92.1 mhz; 6 kw. Ant 328 ft. 8646 Syracuse Rd., Lucerne Valley (92356). Licensee: Desert Willow Broadcasters.

Julian

KBNN(FM)—Oct 23, 1991: 100.1 mhz; 48 w. Ant 1,857 ft. TL: N33 06 07 W116 34 41 (CP: ant 2,221 ft., TL: N33 09 33 W116 36 53). Hrs opn: 24. Box 1947, Ramona (92065); Box 450, Santa Ysabel (92070). (619) 788-1001; (619) 765-1001. FAX: (619) 788-3200. Licensee: Nuevo Communications Inc. Wash atty: Cohn & Marks. Format: Soft adult contemp, local news. News staff 2. Target aud: 25-54; upscale affluence. ■ Andrew G. Smith, pres, gen mgr, opns mgr, prom dir & news dir; Marie Singer, vp; Harold Schachter, gen sls mgr.

Keene

*KNAI(FM)—(Phoenix, Ariz.). Oct. 23, 1991: 88.3 mhz; 22.5 kw. Ant 997 ft. TL: N33 35 47 W112 05 29. Stereo. Hrs opn: 4 AM-7:30 PM. ST *KPHF(FM). Box 62, Natl Farm Workers Serv. Ctr. Hqtrs., 29700 Woodford - Tehachap Rd., Keene, CA (93531); Box 759, KNAI Studio, 12227 N.W. Grand Ave., El Mirage (85335). (805) 822-5571. Licensee: National Farm Workers Service Center. Format: Sp - community pub affrs, mus & info progmg. Target aud: General; Sp farm workers & laborers. ■ Paul Chavez, chmn; Martin Orosco, gen mgr & progmg mgr; Anthony Chavez, opns dir. ■ Rates: $12; 12; 12; 12.

Kerman

KTAA(FM)—Apr 16, 1990: 94.3 mhz; 3 kw. Ant 328 ft. TL: N36 44 29 W120 05 08. 15260 Church Ave. (93630). (209) 846-8888. FAX: (209) 846-5333. Licensee: Barnard Broadcasting. Rep: Roslin. Wash atty: Haley, Bader & Potts. Format: Sp. News progmg 14 hrs wkly. Target aud: 18-34. ■ Eduardo Chavez, gen mgr & stn mgr; Bacilio Maciel, chief engr.

Kernville

KCNQ(FM)—November 1985: 102.5 mhz; 130 w. Ant 1,230 ft. TL: N35 37 21 W118 26 16. Stereo. Hrs opn: 24. Box 3434, 3630 Golden Spur St. Lake Isabella (93240). (619) 379-5636. FAX: (619) 379-5638. Licensee: Lake Isabella Broadcasting Inc. (acq 2-15-89). Net: ABC/I. Rep: Gillis. Format: C&W. News staff one; news progmg 18 hrs wkly. Target aud: General. Spec prog: Relg one hr wkly. ■ Ray Klotz, pres, gen mgr, gen sls mgr, progmg dir & chief engr; Robert Pinney, news dir. ■ Rates: $12.60; 11.35; 11.35; 8.75.

King City

KLFA(FM)—1981: 93.9 mhz; 5.4 kw. Ant 719 ft. TL: N36 22 48 W121 12 57. Stereo. Hrs opn: 24. 548 E. Alisal St., Suite A, Salinas (93905). (408) 757-1910. FAX: (408) 757-9582. Licensee: Tigre Radio Corporation. Group owner: TGR Broadcasting Inc. Rep: Caballero. Format: Sp. Target aud: General. ■ Hector Villalobos, chmn & vp; D. Wayne Wollard, chief engr. ■ Rates: $35; 35; 35; 15.

KRKC(AM)—Sept 21, 1958: 1490 khz; 1 kw-U. TL: N36 13 34 W121 07 26. Box B, 1134 Broadway (93930). (408) 385-5421. FAX: (408) 385-0635. Licensee: Radio Del Rey (acq 9-2-82; $270,000; FTR 9-13-82). Net: CNN. Rep: Hugh Wallace, Farmakis. Wash atty: Pepper & Corazzini. Format: Country. News staff one. Target aud: General. Spec prog: Farm 10 hrs, sports 9 hrs wkly. ■ Bill Gittler, pres & gen mgr; Bill Graff, gen sls mgr & progmg dir; Harold Fuller, news dir; Ron Warren, chief engr.

KRKC-FM—Jan 30, 1989: 102.1 mhz; 2.6 kw. Ant 1,820 ft. TL: N35 57 06 W121 00 03. Stereo. Prog sep from AM. Format: Adult contemp, Sp. Target aud: 18-49. ■ Bill Gittler, gen sls mgr; Michael Davis, progmg dir; Bill Graff, mus dir.

Kings Beach

*KXKB(FM)—Not on air, target date unknown: 89.9 mhz; 2.7 kw-H. Ant 715 ft. TL: N39 15 39 W120 04 25. Suite B, 3416 American River Dr., Sacramento (95864). Licensee: California State Univ. Sacramento. Format: Jazz, news, info. ■ Phil Corriveau, pres; Mark Jones, opns mgr; Susan Kelley, dev dir; Charles Starzynski, progmg dir; Gary Vercelli, mus dir; Jeff Browne, engrg dir.

Kingsburg

KJET(FM)—1991: 106.3 mhz; 6 kw. Ant 436 ft. TL: N36 27 45 W119 36 00 (CP: 3.296 kw, ant 397 ft.). Stereo. Hrs opn: 24. Suite 9, 1425 N. Market Blvd., Sacramento (95834). (707) 528-9236; (916) 928-1515. FAX: (916) 928-0888. Licensee: K-Jet Inc. (acq 10-21-91). Format: Contemp Christian. ■ Dick Jenkins, gen mgr; Johnnie Ray, progmg dir & mus dir.

La Jolla

KIFM(FM)—See San Diego.

La Quinta

KUNA(FM)—Aug 1, 1987: 96.7 mhz; 650 w. Ant 578 ft. TL: N33 48 08 W116 13 30. Stereo. Hrs opn: 24. Box 956 (92253); 41-945 Boardwalk St., Palm Desert (92260). (619) 568-6830. FAX: (619) 568-3984. Licensee: Pennino Broadcasting Corp. Net: CNN. Format: Sp. News staff one; news progmg 25 hrs wkly. Target aud: 40-64. ■ J.R. Banozci, pres; Jack Bonoczi, gen mgr; Mark Wright, stn mgr & sls mgr; Jose Arrieta, opns mgr; Kathy Banas, vp prom; Barry O'Connor, chief engr.

Lake Arrowhead

KAEV(FM)—June 1978: 103.9 mhz; 38 w. Ant 2,538 ft. TL: N34 13 50 W117 14 00 (CP: 190 w, ant 1,751 ft.). Stereo. Hrs opn: 24. Box 2565, San Bernardino (92406); 740 W. 4th St., San Bernardino (92410). (909) 882-2575. TWX: (909) 888-7302. Licensee: All Pro Broadcasting Inc. (group owner; acq 9-10-92; $5 million with KCKC[AM] San Bernardino; FTR 9-28-92). Rep: D & R Radio. Format: Urban adult contemp. News staff one; news progmg 5 hrs wkly. Target aud: 25-49. ■ Willie Davis, pres; Sheila Brown, gen mgr; Bill McNaulty, opns mgr; Ed Reynolds, gen sls mgr & adv mgr; Pete Parsons, progmg dir, mus dir & news dir; Mark Sadacca, chief engr.

Lake Isabella

KVLI(AM)—July 15, 1977: 1140 khz; 1 kw-D. TL: N35 38 20 W118 28 22. Hrs opn: Sunrise-sunset. Drawer T, 4120 Barlow Dr. (93240). (619) 379-4146; (619) 379-3648. FAX: (619) 379-3649. Licensee: KVLI Inc. Net: MBS, ABC, SMN. Rep: W.R.B.S. Wash atty: Dennis Corbitt. Format: Easy lstng. News progmg 10 hrs wkly. Target aud: 50 plus; mature. ■ John M. Ridenour, pres & chief engr; Janet C. Ridenour, vp, gen mgr & gen sls mgr; Becky Foster, progmg dir. ■ Rates: $15; 15; 15; na.

KVLI-FM—Oct 29, 1992: 104.5 mhz; 200 w. Ant 1,260 ft. TL: N35 37 21 W118 26 16. Stereo. Hrs opn: 24. Dups FM 100%. ■ Rates: $15; 15; 15; 7.50.

Lakeport

KNTI(FM)—Oct 21, 1984: 99.5 mhz; 2.5 kw. Ant 1,920 ft. TL: N39 07 50 W123 04 32. Stereo. Hrs opn: 24. 75 4th St. (95453); 169-A Mason St., Ukiah (95482). (707) 263-1551; (707) 459-4141. FAX: (707) 263-0614; (707) 468-8795. Licensee: Evans Broadcasting Service Inc. Net: MBS. Rep: Jerry Evans. Format: Adult contemp. News staff one; news progmg 8 hrs wkly. Target aud: 25-54. Spec prog: Sp 3 hrs, new adult contemp 3 hrs wkly. ■ Jerry Evans, CEO, chmn, gen mgr & gen sls mgr; Ray Oresco, opns dir & vp progmg; Courtney Fox, news dir & pub affrs dir; Nick Thill, chief engr. ■ Rates: $22.50; 22.50; 22.50; 18.

KXBX(AM)—June 17, 1966: 1270 khz; 500 w-D, 97 w-N. TL: N39 00 50 W122 53 39. Box 759, 2626 S. Main St. (95453). (707) 263-6113. FAX: (707) 263-0939. Licensee: North Country Communications Inc. (acq 7-90; $550,000 with co-located FM; FTR 8-13-90). Net: UPI. Format: MOR, nostalgia. News staff one; news progmg 4 hrs wkly. Target aud: 40 plus; retirees. ■ Bill Groody, pres; Geraldine Groody, vp; Gregg Allan, opns mgr; Rose Byerly, gen sls mgr; Paul Reading, news dir; Bill Rett, chief engr.

KXBX-FM—Aug 31, 1984: 98.3 mhz; 3 kw. Ant 300 ft. TL: N39 02 54 W122 45 59. Stereo. Prog sep from AM. Format: Adult contemp.

Lancaster

KAVL(AM)—Sept 8, 1950: 610 khz; 1 kw-D, 500 w-N, DA-2. TL: N34 42 22 W118 10 36. Stereo. Hrs opn: 24. 2501 W. Ave. I (93536). (805) 942-1121. FAX: (805) 723-5512. Licensee: Antelope Broadcasting Co. Inc. Net: AP, Westwood One. Format: Oldies, news/talk. News staff 2. Target aud: 25-54. Spec prog: Kings hockey, Raiders football, Dodgers baseball. ■ Ron Carter, pres; Larry Thornhill, gen mgr; Rich Bultman, natl sls mgr; Zack Taylor, progmg dir; Rob Baumgartner, mus dir; Bill Browning, news dir; Bruce Gary, chief engr.

KGMX(FM)—Listing follows KHJJ(AM).

KHJJ(AM)—August 1956: 1380 khz; 1 kw-D, DA. TL: N34 42 43 W118 10 34. Hrs opn: 24. Box 1152, 44748 N. Elm Ave. (93534). (805) 948-7521. FAX: (805) 942-1817. Licensee: Eric Chandler Ltd. (acq 9-89; $3,000,000 with co-located FM; FTR 9-25-89). Net: NBC. Rep: Banner. Wash atty: Keck, Mahin & Cate. Format: News/talk. News staff 3. Target aud: General. ■ Bob Geddes, chmn; Tom Miserndino, pres; Rudy Patino, CFO; Jeff Apregan, vp; Catherine Moreau, gen mgr; Lloyd Heaney, gen sls mgr; Andy Viera, progmg dir; Maelii Bauer, news dir; Scott Blake, chief engr. ■ Rates: $42; 37; 42; 32.

KGMX(FM)—Co-owned with KHJJ(AM). Oct 28, 1970: 106.3 mhz; 3 kw. Ant 210 ft. TL: N34 44 41 W118 07 30. Stereo. Hrs opn: 24. Licensee: Eric Chandler Communications of the Antelope Valley. Format: Adult contemp. Target aud: 24-54. ■ Jeff Ryan, progmg dir; Sue Freeman, pub affrs dir. ■ Rates: Same as AM.

KUTY(AM)—See Palmdale.

Le Grand

***KEFR(FM)**—Jan 11, 1985: 89.9 mhz; 1.8 kw. Ant 2,142 ft. TL: N37 32 01 W120 01 50. Stereo. Box 52, 13161 Jefferson St., (95333). (209) 389-4659; (209) 389-4020. FAX: (209) 389-0215. Licensee: Family Stations Inc. (group owner). Format: Educ, relg. Target aud: General. ■ Harold Camping, pres; Larry Milliken, stn mgr; Craig Husebos, progmg mgr; Kevin McGill, pub affrs dir; Greg Richards, chief engr.

Lemoore

KJOP(AM)—Dec 23, 1963: 1240 khz; 1 kw-U. TL: N36 18 47 W119 43 51. 15279 Hanford Armona Rd. (93245). (209) 584-5242. FAX: (209) 584-0310. Licensee: Goodwill Broadcasting Co. (acq 12-7-90; $376,942; FTR 12-31-90). Rep: Lotus. Format: Sp. ■ Jesus Larios, gen mgr; Federico Gomez, progmg dir.

Lenwood

KGXY(FM)—Not on air, target date unknown: 96.9 mhz; 1 kw. Ant 810 ft. 13260 Winona Rd., Apple Valley (92308). Licensee: Desert Broadcasting G.P.

KIQQ-FM—Not on air, target date unknown: 104.9 mhz; 1.078 kw. Ant 466 ft. TL: N34 51 20 W117 02 57. Stereo. Hrs opn: 24. 11920 Hesperia Rd., Hesperia (92345). (619) 244-2000. Licensee: Eneida Orchard. Net: AP. Format: Adult contemp. News staff 2. Target aud: 25-49. ■ Eneida Orchard, pres.

KIXW(FM)—Not on air, target date unknown: 107.3 mhz; 440 w. Ant 771 ft. TL: N34 58 13 W117 02 19. c/o 8401 Old Courthouse Rd. #140, Tysons Corner, VA (22180). Licensee: Turquoise Broadcasting Inc. (acq 5-18-92; $32,500 for CP; FTR 6-8-92).

Lindsay

KZPO(FM)—Not on air, target date unknown: 103.3 mhz; 528 w. Ant 751 ft. TL: N36 14 45 W119 03 37. Suite A, 12550 Brookhurst St., Garden Grove (92640). Licensee: Lindsay Broadcasting (acq 1-28-91; FTR 2-18-91).

Livermore

KKIQ(FM)—May 1969: 101.7 mhz; 4.5 kw. Ant 382 ft. TL: N37 35 42 W121 39 42. Stereo. Hrs opn: 24. 7901 Stoneridge Dr. #525, Pleasanton (94588). (510) 455-4500. FAX: (510) 416-1211. Licensee: Tri-Valley Broadcasters Inc. (acq 2-81). Net: AP. Wash atty: Fletcher, Heald & Hildreth. Format: Adult contemp. News staff one; news progmg 28 hrs wkly. Target aud: 25-54; high income & highly educated adults. ■ Helen L. Pedotti, chmn; Jack Chunn, pres & gen mgr; Jim Hampton, opns dir & progmg dir; Avi Strugo, sls dir; Mark Davis, prom mgr; Julie DePish, mus dir; Debra Mark, news dir; John Buckham, chief engr. ■ Rates: $60; 55; 60; 20.

Livingston

KNTO(FM)—Nov 1, 1984: 95.9 mhz; 3 kw. Ant 305 ft. TL: N37 18 57 W120 43 20. Stereo. Box 248, 416 Main St. (95334). (209) 394-3344. FAX: (209) 394-8043. Licensee: All American Broadcasting Co. (acq 2-3-93; $198,000; FTR 3-8-93). Rep: Lotus. Format: Spanish adult contemp. ■ Nelson Gomez, pres; Adele Garcia, progmg dir & news dir; Chet Hughes, chief engr.

Lodi

KCVR(AM)—1946: 1570 khz; 5 kw-D, 34 w-N, DA-2. TL: N34 09 18 W121 17 39 (CP: 500 w-N TL: N38 05 10 W121 12 57). Box 7871 Stockton (95267). (209) 333-8165. FAX: (209) 951-5025. Licensee: Front Line Communications Inc. (acq 6-6-91; $675,000 with co-located FM; FTR 6-24-91). Rep: Lotus. Format: Sp. ■ Mike Murphy, gen mgr; Carmen Torres, prom mgr & news dir; Jose Berumen, progmg dir & mus dir; Alan Graft, chief engr.

KWIN(FM)—Co-owned with KCVR(AM). Dec 24, 1959: 97.7 mhz; 3 kw. Ant 300 ft. TL: N38 03 05 W121 15 05. Stereo. Prog sep from AM. Rep: Major Mkt. Format: Contemp hit. ■ Bob Lewis, progmg dir; Ken Carr, mus dir; Greg Fox, news dir.

Loma Linda

***KSGN(FM)**—See Riverside.

Lompoc

KBOX(FM)—Licensed to Lompoc. See Santa Maria.

KCLL(AM)—Aug 8, 1958: 960 khz; 500 w-U, DA-N. TL: N34 38 47 W120 30 37 (CP: TL: N34 58 47 W120 27 13). Hrs opn: 24. Box 596 (93438); Suite D, 107 N.H. (93436). (805) 736-3496. Licensee: Green-Gold Broadcasting Inc. (acq 8-91). Net: SMN. Rep: Farmakis. Wash atty: Miller & Fields. Format: Oldies. News staff one; news progmg 2 hrs wkly. Target aud: 25-54; Spec prog: Farm 3 hrs wkly. ■ Randolph Johnston, pres & gen mgr; Rachel De LaRosa, opns mgr; Dale Williams, chief engr. ■ Rates: $16; 16; 16; na.

KLOM(AM)—Nov 2, 1962: 1330 khz; 1 kw-D, DA. TL: N34 37 56 W120 28 40. Stn currently dark. Box 697 (93438). Licensee: Dorsey Broadcasting Inc. (acq 8-1-84; $225,000). ■ Terry Dorsey, pres; Terry Dorsey II, gen mgr.

KRQK(FM)—Listing follows KTME(AM).

KTME(AM)—May 25, 1963: 1410 khz; 500 w-D, 77 w-N, DA-2. TL: N34 39 46 W120 23 03. Hrs opn: 24. Suite 102, 3070 Skyway Dr., Santa Maria (93454). (805) 922-3312; (805) 735-5656. FAX: (805) 922-1974. Licensee: Padre Serra Communications Inc. (acq 6-22-93; $450,000 with co-located FM; FTR 7-12-93). Net: Unistar. Rep: D & R Radio. Format: Nostalgia, MOR, adult contemp. News staff one. Target aud: 25-44. Spec prog: Lampoc High School football. ■ Andres Vergan, gen mgr & gen sls mgr; Ismel Antonio Leyba, opns dir & prom dir; Tom Hughes, chief engr.

KRQK(FM)—Co-owned with KTME(AM). Dec 18, 1979: 100.3 mhz; 3.65 kw. Ant 863 ft. TL: N34 44 24 W120 26 42. Stereo. Hrs opn: 24. Prog sep from AM. Format: Adult rock. Target aud: 18-49. ■ Ismel Antonio Leyba, progmg dir.

Long Beach

***KFRN(AM)**—March 1924: 1280 khz; 1 kw-U, DA-D. TL: N33 47 54 W118 14 47. Hrs opn: 24. 105 Linden Ave. (90802). (310) 435-0103. FAX: (310) 435-0104. Licensee: Family Stations Inc. (group owner; acq 9-19-77). Net: Family Stations. Format: Relg. Family spectrum. ■ Harold Camping, pres; Scott Smith, vp; Frederick Whiteman, gen mgr & stn mgr; Craig Hulsebos, progmg dir & news dir; David Oh, pub affrs dir; Robert Vetter, engrg mgr; Frederick C. Whiteman, chief engr.

KGER(AM)—1926: 1390 khz; 5 kw-D, 3.6 w-N, DA-2. TL: N33 53 30 W118 11 03. Hrs opn: 24. Box 7126, 3759 Atlantic Ave. (90807). (310) 427-7907; (714) 995-1390. Licensee: Salem Media of California. Group owner: Salem Communications Corp. (acq 12-31-86). Format: Relg, pub affrs. Target aud: 35 plus; mature audience. Spec prog: Black 8 hrs wkly. ■ Edward G. Attsinger, pres; Jay Davis, gen mgr & progmg dir; Norm Olsen, opns mgr; LaVoy Marquez, Norm Olsen, prom dirs; David Olson, Anne Hisey, asst mus dirs; Richard Navarro, pub affrs dir; William Sheets, chief engr. ■ Rates: $45; 45; 45; 45.

KLAX-FM—Apr 22, 1949: 97.9 mhz; 50 kw. Ant 390 ft. TL: N34 00 24 W118 21 52. Stereo. 5700 Sunset Blvd., Los Angeles (90028). (213) 466-3001. FAX: (213) 466-8259. Licensee: Spanish Broadcasting System of Florida Inc. Group owner: Spanish Broadcasting System Inc. (acq 2-87). Rep: SBS. Format: Sp. ■ Raul Alarcon Jr., chmn; Jose Grimalt, sr vp; Alfredo Rodriguez, gen mgr; Bob Williams, gen sls mgr; Fidel Fausto, progmg mgr & mus dir; Jorge Garcia, news dir; Fernanda Valdibia, pub affrs dir; Fred Holub, chief engr.

***KLON(FM)**—Jan 3, 1950: 88.1 mhz; 8 kw. Ant 430 ft. TL: N33 48 00 W118 09 45. Stereo. Hrs opn: 24. 1288 N. Bellflower Blvd. (90815-4198); (310) 985-5566. Licensee: Calif. State Univ., Long Beach Foundation (acq 6-18-81; $15,000; FTR 4-27-81). Net: AP Radio. Wash atty: Fletcher, Herald & Hildreth. Format: Jazz, info. News staff 8; news progmg 10 hrs wkly. Target aud: 25-64; educated, opinion leaders, jazz and music lovers. ■ Morton M. Winston, chmn; Rick Lewis, pres; Sharon Weissman, gen mgr; Russell Olevsky, vp dev, dev dir & mktg dir; Scott Willis, progmg dir; Nick Roman, news dir; Ron Thompson, engrg mgr. ■ Rates: $100; 75; 100; 50.

KNAC(FM)—August 1961: 105.5 mhz; 1.5 kw. Ant 403 ft. TL: N33 51 29 W118 13 22. Stereo. Suite P-280, 100 Oceangate Blvd. (90802). (310) 437-0366. FAX: (310) 436-8718. Licensee: Keymarket Communications (acq 10-25-93; $12.1 million with KBLA[AM] Santa Monica; FTR 11-8-93). Net: ABC/FM, Unistar. Format: Pure rock. Target aud: 18-34; male adults. Spec prog: Pub affrs 3 hrs, heavy metal 2 hrs, local 2 hrs wkly. ■ Gary Price, pres & gen mgr; John Squyres, stn mgr; Bill Banks, opns dir; Bryan Schock, progmg dir; Cindy Scull, mus dir; Bob Conger, chief engr.

Los Altos

***KFJC(FM)**—Dec 4, 1959: 89.7 mhz; 250 w. Ant 1,845 ft. TL: N37 19 14 W122 08 29. Stereo. Hrs opn: 24. 12345 El Monte Rd. (94022). (415) 949-7260; (415) 941-2500. FAX: (415) 948-1085. Licensee: Foothill Community College Board of Trustees. Format: Free form, eclectic. News progmg 8 hrs wkly. Target aud: 8-80 years of age; psychedelic speed freaks, radicals and other social outcasts. Spec prog: Blues 4 hrs, reggae 8 hrs, country/bluegrass 8 hrs, jazz 10 hrs, urban 4 hrs, soundtracks 3 hrs, surf one hr wkly. ■ Steve Taiclet, gen mgr; Robert "Doc" Pelzel, opns dir; Kathryn Ortiz, dev dir; Steve Guiliotis, sls dir; Nina Price, mktg dir; Russ Kent, prom dir; Amacker Bulliwinker, Richard Hester, progmg dirs; Alan Lowe, mus dir; Jason Biggs, asst mus dir; Grant Waldron, news dir; Mark Herbert, pub affrs dir; Eric Weaver, chief engr.

KHQT(FM)—Oct 17, 1960: 97.7 mhz; 1.65 kw. Ant 433 ft. TL: N37 18 27 W122 05 36 (CP: 3.2 kw). Stereo. Suite 201, 2860 Zanker Rd., San Jose (95134). (408) 943-

California Directory of Radio

0770. FAX: (408) 943-1589. Licensee: San Jose Broadcast Corp. (acq 1-1-88). Rep: D & R Radio. Format: CHR. News progmg one hr wkly. Target aud: 18-49. ■ Tim Sullivan, pres; Dayton Phillips, gen mgr; Krista Coutts, prom mgr; Bob Perry, progmg dir; Peter Manrequiz, mus dir; Phil Moore, chief engr.

AMERICAN RADIO BROKERS, INC.
MOST TRUSTED NAME IN MEDIA BROKERAGE
CHESTER P. COLEMAN / PRESIDENT
FOR THE BEST STATIONS FOR SALE FROM THIS AREA
CALL — 415/441-3377
1255 POST STREET / SUITE 625 / SAN FRANCISCO, CA 94109

Los Angeles

KABC(AM)—Nov 15, 1929: 790 khz; 5 kw-U, DA-N. TL: N34 01 40 W118 22 20. 3321 S. La Cienega Blvd. (90016). (310) 840-4912. Licensee: KABC-AM Radio Inc. Group owner: Capital Cities/ABC Broadcast Group (acq 6-86; grpsl; FTR 7-15-85). Format: Talk. News staff 3; news progmg 30-40 hrs wkly. Target aud: 35 plus; upscale, affluent, college educated. ■ George Green, pres & gen mgr; Bob K, opns mgr; Dina Silverman, gen sls mgr; Shelly Wagner, mktg dir & prom dir; Norm Avery, chief engr.

KLOS(FM)—Co-owned with KABC(AM). Dec 30, 1947: 95.5 mhz; 68 kw. Ant 2,920 ft. TL: N34 13 37 W118 03 58. Stereo. Prog sep from AM. (310) 840-4836. Net: ABC/FM. Format: AOR. ■ Bill Sommers, gen mgr; Tom Roe, gen sls mgr; Ken Anthony, progmg dir.

KACE(FM)—See Inglewood.

KALI(AM)—See San Gabriel.

KBIG(FM)—Feb 15, 1959: 104.3 mhz; 105 kw. Ant 2,950 ft. TL: N34 13 36 W118 03 59. Stereo. 7755 Sunset Blvd. (90046). (213) 874-7700. FAX: (213) 874-4276. Licensee: Bonneville International Corp. (group owner; acq 3-11-69). Net: UPI, AP. Rep: CBS Radio. Format: Adult contemp. Target aud: 25-54. ■ Rodney Brady, CEO; Bruce Reese, exec vp; Kari J. Winston, sr vp & vp; Steve Oshin, gen sls mgr; Bonnie Baker, natl sls mgr; Rosemary Matuz, prom dir; Rob Edwards, vp progmg; Dave Verdery, mus dir; Dennis Martin, chief engr.

KBLA(AM)—See Santa Monica.

KBRT(AM)—See Avalon.

KCBS-FM—Listing follows KNX(AM).

KFI(AM)—Apr 16, 1922: 640 khz; 50 kw-U. TL: N33 52 48 W118 00 48. 610 S. Ardmore (90005). (213) 385-0101. FAX: (213) 251-3170. Licensee: KFI Inc. Group owner: Cox Broadcasting (acq 6-1-73). Net: AP. Rep: Christal. Format: Talk. News staff 7; news progmg 25 hrs wkly. Target aud: 25-54. ■ Howard Neal, vp & gen mgr; Leon Clark, gen sls mgr; Bill Lewis, mktg dir & prom mgr; Mark A. Thomas, news dir.

KOST(FM)—Co-owned with KFI(AM). Oct 9, 1957: 103.5 mhz; 12.5 kw. Ant 3,100 ft. TL: N34 13 34 W118 03 55. Prog sep from AM. (213) 251-3128. Format: Adult contemp. ■ Duncan Payton, prom mgr; Jhani Kaye, progmg dir; Kim Amidon, mus dir.

KFSG(FM)—1949: 96.3 mhz; 54 kw. Ant 479 ft. TL: N34 05 05 W118 12 10. Stereo. Hrs opn: 24. Suite 480, 1910 W. Sunset Blvd. (90026). (213) 483-5374. FAX: (213) 413-3824. Licensee: Foursquare Radio. Group owner: International Church of the Foursquare Gospel. Net: AP. Format: Contemp Christian music & programs. Target aud: 25-49. ■ John Holland, pres; Alan Bowles, gen mgr, stn mgr & progmg dir; Paul Gulino, rgnl sls mgr; Margaret Beatty, mus dir; Glynn Covington, engrg dir; George Riggs, chief engr.

KFWB(AM)—Mar 25, 1925: 980 khz; 5 kw-U. TL: N34 04 11 W118 16 35. Hrs opn: 24. 6230 Yucca St. (90028). (213) 462-5392. FAX: (213) 871-4670; (213) 871-4679. Licensee: Westinghouse Broadcasting Co. Inc. (group owner; acq 2-28-66). Net: ABC, CNN, AP. Wash atty: Steve Hildebrandt. Format: News. News staff 60; news progmg 168 hrs wkly. Target aud: 25-54. ■ Chris Claus, vp & gen mgr; Tim Pehlman, gen sls mgr; Greg Tantum, progmg dir; Dick Rudman, chief engr.

KGFJ(AM)—1926: 1230 khz; 1 kw-U. TL: N34 02 15 W118 16 35. 1100 S. LaBrea Ave. (90019). (213) 930-9090. FAX: (213) 930-9056. Licensee: East-West Broadcasting Inc. (acq 10-86; $4,500,000; FTR 9-22-86). Rep: Roslin. Format: Oldies. Spec prog: Black 16 hrs wkly. ■ Bill Shearer, gen mgr; Theresa Price, gen sls mgr; Shirley Jackson, prom mgr; Don Tracy, progmg dir; John Morris, mus dir & chief engr; J.L. Martinez, news dir.

KIEV(AM)—See Glendale.

KIIS(AM)—1927: 1150 khz; 5 kw-U, DA-N. TL: N34 05 05 W118 12 10. Stereo. 6255 Sunset Blvd. (90028). (213) 466-8381. Licensee: Eleven-Fifty Corp. Group owner: Gannett Broadcasting (acq 5-79). Rep: McGavren Guild. Format: Top-40. Target aud: 18-34. ■ Marc S. Kaye, pres & gen mgr; Mil Yuc Tse, CFO; Roy Laughlin, gen sls mgr; Luz Erdman, natl sls mgr; Charlie Rahilly, rgnl sls mgr; Karen Lamas-Tobin, vp mktg; Mona Lapides, prom dir; Jeff Wyatt, Gwen Roberts (asst), progmg dirs; Brian Bridgman, mus dir; Vic Jacobs, news dir; Michael Callaghan, chief engr.

KIIS-FM—1948: 102.7 mhz; 8 kw. Ant 2,960 ft. TL: N34 13 36 W118 03 57. Stereo. Dups AM 100%.

KKBT(FM)—Dec 29, 1948: 92.3 mhz; 43 kw. Ant 2,910 ft. TL: N34 13 36 W118 03 57. Stereo. 6735 Yucca St., Hollywood (90028-4691). (213) 466-9566. FAX: (213) 466-2592; Licensee: Evergreen Media Corp. (group owner; acq 5-15-89; $55,000,000; FTR 4-10-89). Rep: McGavren Guild. Format: Urban contemp. News staff one; news progmg 10 hrs wkly. Target aud: 25-49; female. ■ Craig Wilbraham, gen mgr; Blake Mendenhall, gen sls mgr; Keith Naftaly, progmg dir; Harold Austin, mus dir; Terry Grieger, chief engr.

KKGO-FM—Feb 18, 1959: 105.1 mhz; 18 kw. Ant 2,900 ft. TL: N34 13 45 W118 04 04. Stereo. 1500 Cotner (90025). (310) 478-5540. FAX: (310) 478-4189. Licensee: Mt. Wilson FM Broadcasters Inc. Net: AP. Rep: CMBS. Wash atty: Cohen & Marks. Format: Classical. ■ Saul Levine, pres & gen mgr; J. Handman, gen sls mgr; Bob Wennersten, progmg dir; Robert Turner, chief engr.

DATABASES - MAILING LABELS
★ RADIO/TELEVISION US/CANADA
99.7% Deliverable - System Updated Daily
Over 25 Selection Options: Accurate Formats, Market Size, Station Audiences, States, Networks, Random Lists, Execs by Name, Secondary Formats, Ethnic Stations, Delete/Add Markets or Stations.
★ DATABASE AUDITS
We Correct, Update and Maintain Your Database
★ RADIOSCAN
All US Radio on Your PC - Includes Powerful Software
Instant Station Data on Screen - Reports in 10 Seconds
Station Lists for Each of 585 Markets
Rolls Royce of all Radio Database Systems
Ideal for Syndicators, Networks, all Vendors
Reasonably Priced
The CENTER For RADIO INFORMATION
19 Market Street, Cold Spring, NY 10516
PH: (800) 359-9898 FX: (914) 265-2715

KKHJ(AM)—Apr 13, 1922: 930 khz; 5 kw-U, DA-N. TL: N34 02 26 W118 22 18. Stereo. 5724 Hollywood Blvd., Hollywood (90028). (213) 461-9300. FAX: (213) 461-9946. Licensee: Liberman Broadcasting Inc. (group owner; acq 3-27-90). Rep: Caballero. Wash atty: Wiley, Rein & Fielding. Format: Spanish. News staff one. Target aud: 18-49. ■ Jose Liberman, pres & gen mgr; Ernesto Degali, news dir; James Blakey, chief engr.

KKLA(FM)—1985: 99.5 mhz; 30 kw. Ant 669 ft. TL: N34 09 50 W118 11 46 (CP: 10.7 kw, ant 2,880 ft.). Stereo. Suite 550, 701 N. Grand, Glendale (91203). (818) 956-5552. FAX: (818) 551-1110. Licensee: Salem Communications Corp. (group owner). Format: Relg. ■ Ken Gaines, gen mgr & progmg dir; Jim Tinker, opns mgr & pub affrs dir; Terry Fahy, gen sls mgr; Mark Pallock, chief engr.

KLAC(AM)—1924: 570 khz; 5 kw-U, DA-N. TL: N34 04 11 W118 11 36. Stereo. Hrs opn: 24. 6th Fl., 4000 W. Alameda Ave., Burbank (91510). (818) 842-0500. Licensee: Shamrock Holdings Inc. Group owner: Shamrock Broadcasting Inc. (acq 6-15-93; with co-located FM; FTR 7-5-93). Net: AP. Rep: Eastman. Format: Country. News staff 3. Target aud: 35-54. Spec prog: Sports. ■ J.D. Freeman, vp & gen mgr; Nancy Leichter, sls dir; Robert Novak, mktg dir; Gene Bridges, progmg dir; Lisa Puzo, mus dir; Dean Sander, news dir; Ron Blassnig, chief engr.

KZLA-FM—Co-owned with KLAC(AM). Aug 7, 1957: 93.9 mhz; 18.5 kw horz, 16 kw vert. Ant 3136 ft. TL: N34 13 57 W118 04 13. Stereo. Prog sep from AM. Box 7806 (91510-7806). Format: Country. ■ R.J. Curtis, progmg dir.

KLIT(FM)—See Glendale.

KLOS(FM)—Listing follows KABC(AM).

KLSX(FM)—1954: 97.1 mhz; 29.5 kw. Ant 2,998 ft. TL: N34 09 50 W118 11 46. Stereo. 3580 Wilshire Blvd. (90010). (213) 383-4222. Licensee: Greater Media Inc. (group owner; 9-6-79). Rep: Major Mkt. Format: Classic rock. ■ Allen Chlowitz, gen mgr; Jan Kopic, natl sls mgr; Scott Segelbaum, prom mgr; Warren Williams, mus dir; David Ping, chief engr.

KLVE(FM)—Listing follows KTNQ(AM).

KMPC(AM)—Feb 18, 1927: 710 khz; 50 kw-D, 10 kw-N, DA-N. TL: N34 10 24 W118 24 24. 5858 Sunset Blvd. (90078). (213) 464-5482. FAX: (213) 467-5483; TWX: 910-321-4412. Licensee: Golden West Broadcasters (group owner; acq 12-52). Net: NBC, AP. Rep: Banner. Wash atty: Irving Gastfreund. Format: Sports. News staff 4; news progmg 9 hrs wkly. Target aud: General. ■ Gene Autry, pres; Bill Ward, gen mgr; John Felz, opns mgr; Michele Billy, gen sls mgr; Robert Lyles, prom dir & adv dir; Len Weiner, progmg dir; Chris Downing, chief engr.

KNX(AM)—Sept 10, 1920: 1070 khz; 50 kw-U. TL: N33 51 35 W118 20 56. Stereo. Hrs opn: 24. 6121 Sunset Blvd. (90028). (213) 460-3000. FAX: (213) 460-3114; (213) 460-3352. Licensee: CBS Inc. Group owner: CBS Broadcast Group (acq 9-36). Net: CBS. Rep: CBS Radio. Format: News. News staff 40. Target aud: General. ■ George Nicholaw, vp & gen mgr; Michael J. Masterson, gen sls mgr; Fred Bergendorff, prom dir; Robert Sims, news dir; Steve Smith, pub affrs dir; Michael Smith, chief engr.

KCBS-FM—Co-owned with KNX(AM). 1948: 93.1 mhz; 54 kw. Ant 5,000 ft. TL: N34 13 57 W118 04 18. Stereo. Hrs opn: 24. Prog sep from AM. (213) 460-3293. FAX: (213) 463-9270. Net: CBS Spectrum. Format: All rock n' roll oldies, music from 70s, early 80s. News staff one; news progmg 3 hrs wkly. Target aud: 35-54. ■ Lawrence Tisch, CEO; Dave Van Dyke, gen mgr; Brad West, gen sls mgr; Kim Kelly, mktg dir, prom dir & adv dir; Tommy Edwards, progmg dir; Billy Sabatini, mus dir; Linda Lambert, news dir & pub affrs dir; Michael Smith, engrg dir.

KOST(FM)—Listing follows KFI(AM).

***KPFK(FM)**—July 26, 1959: 90.7 mhz; 112 kw. Ant 2,830 ft. TL: N34 13 45 W118 04 03. Stereo. Hrs opn: 24. 3729 Cahuenga Blvd. W., North Hollywood (91604). (818) 985-2711. Licensee: Pacifica Foundation. Group owner: Pacifica Foundation Inc. dba Pacifica Radio. Wash atty: Haley, Bader & Potts. Format: Progsv. News staff one; news progmg 11 hrs wkly. Target aud: General. Spec prog: Black 17 hrs, class 14 hrs, folk 10 hrs, jazz 12 hrs, Sp 11 hrs, rock 16 hrs, arts 13 hrs, women 4 hrs, children 2 hrs, pub affrs 4 hrs, spiritual 33 hrs wkly. ■ David Salniker, chmn; Clifford Roberts, stn mgr; Lucia Chappelle, progmg dir; Pablo Garcia, chief engr.

KPPC(AM)—See Pasadena.

KPWR(FM)—Dec 20, 1956: 105.9 mhz; 72 kw. Ant 770 ft. TL: N34 09 50 W118 11 45. Stereo. Suite 850, 2600 W. Olive Ave., Burbank (91505). (818) 953-4200. FAX: (818) 848-0961. Licensee: KPWR Inc. Group owner: Emmis Broadcasting (acq 1-84; grpsl; FTR 1-30-84). Rep: D & R Radio. Format: CHR. ■ Doyle Rose, pres & gen mgr; Marie Kordus, gen sls mgr; John Boyle, prom mgr; Rick Cummings, progmg dir; Michelle Mercer, mus dir; Monica Brooks, news dir; Tom Koza, chief engr.

KRCK(AM)—(Burbank). January 1986: 1500 khz; 50 kw-D, 14 kw-N, DA-2. TL: N34 16 09 W118 20 31. Stereo. Hrs opn: 24. c/o KWOD-FM, 801 K St., 27th Floor, Sacramento (95814); 6430 Sunset Blvd., Los Angeles (90028). (916) 448-5000. FAX: (916) 448-1655. Licensee: Royce International Broadcasting Co. Rep: D & R Radio. Wash atty: Hogan & Hartson. Format: AOR. Target aud: 18-49; mass appeal. ■ Edward R. Stolz II, pres, gen mgr, natl sls mgr & chief engr; Alex Cosper, progmg dir; Jeff Jensen, news dir.

KRLA(AM)—See Pasadena.

KRTH(FM)—1941: 101.1 mhz; 51 kw. Ant 3,130 ft. TL: N34 13 38 W118 04 00 (CP: 53.6 kw). Stereo. 5901 Venice Blvd. (90034). (213) 937-5230. FAX: (213) 936-3427; TWX: 510-101-2454. Licensee: GRADH-102 Group owner: Beasley Broadcast Group (acq 7-27-89). Net: AP. Rep: Banner. Format: Oldies. Target aud: 25-64. ■ George Beasley, pres; Patrick Duffy, vp & gen mgr; Peggy Schiavo, vp sls; Karen Sanchez, natl sls mgr; Howard Freshman, vp mktg & vp prom; Mike Phillips, progmg dir; Corbett Brattin, news dir; Bob Kanner, chief engr.

KTNQ(AM)—1925: 1020 khz; 50 kw-U, DA-2. TL: N34 02 00 W117 59 00. Stereo. Box 1140, Holly & Vine Plaza, Suite 200, 1645 N. Vine St., Hollywood (90028). (213) 465-3171; (213) 465-8466. FAX: (213) 461-9973. Licensee: KTNQ/KLVE Inc. (acq 7-27-92). Net: UPI. Rep: Caballero. Format: Sp. ■ Carl Parmer, pres, gen mgr & stn

Broadcasting & Cable Yearbook 1994
B-40

mgr; Julio Omano, natl sls mgr; Bill Beadles, prom mgr; Adrian Lopez, progmg dir; Antonio Gonzales, news dir; Bob Moore, chief engr.

KLVE(FM)—Co-owned with KTNQ(AM). May 2, 1959: 107.5 mhz; 29.5 kw. Ant 3,100 ft. TL: N34 13 44 W118 04 02. Stereo. Prog sep from AM. Format: Sp.

KTWV(FM)—Mar 7, 1961: 94.7 mhz; 58 kw. Ant 2,835 ft. TL: N34 13 29 W118 03 47. Stereo. Hrs opn: 24. Box 4310 (90078); Wilton Bldg. 5th Fl., 5746 Sunset Blvd. (90028). (213) 466-9283. FAX: (213) 469-0210. Licensee: Group W Radio Inc. Group owner: Westinghouse Broadcasting Co. (acq 12-89; grpsl; FTR 12-11-89). Rep: Group W. Format: New adult contemp. News staff one. Target aud: 25-54. ■ Christopher J. Claus, vp; Jack Hutchison, vp sls; Dick Warshaw, natl sls mgr; Mary Griswold (Research), mktg dir; Bonny Chick, prom mgr; Christine Brodie, progmg dir; Ralph Stewart, mus dir; Paul Crosswhite, news dir & pub affrs dir; Richard Rudman, engrg mgr; Bob Leembruggen, chief engr.

*****KUSC(FM)**—1946: 91.5 mhz; 17 kw. Ant 2922 ft. TL: N34 12 48 W118 03 41. Stereo. Hrs opn: 24. Box 77913 (90007-0913). 3716 S. Hope St. (90007). (213) 743-5872. FAX: (213) 743-5853. Licensee: Univ. of Southern California. Net: APR. Wash atty: Brining & Bernstein. Format: Class. News progmg 9 hrs wkly. Target aud: 35 plus. Spec prog: Jazz one hr, Sp 2 hrs, multi-ethnic 2 hrs wkly. ■ Wallace A. Smith, pres & gen mgr; Bill Kappelman, vp opns; Maryanne Horton, dev dir; Lyle C. Henry, engrg dir; Jim Sensenbach, chief engr.

KWKW(AM)—Apr 14, 1931: 1330 khz; 5 kw-U, DA-N. TL: N34 01 10 W118 20 42. Suite 400, 6777 Hollywood Blvd. (90048). (213) 466-8111. FAX: (213) 461-7347. Licensee: Lotus Communications Corp. (group owner; acq 2-13-89). Format: La Mexicana. ■ Jim Kalmenson, gen mgr.

KXED(AM)—Sept 22, 1952: 1540 khz; 50 kw-D, 10 kw-N, DA-2. TL: N34 04 43 W118 11 05. Stereo. 5700 Sunset Blvd. (90028). (213) 466-3001. FAX: (213) 466-8259. Licensee: Spanish Broadcasting System of California Group owner: Spanish Broadcasting System Inc. (acq 12-84). Format: Sp. ■ Jose Grimalt, pres; Gabriel Grimalt, stn mgr; Jack McVeigh, gen sls mgr; George Garcia, news dir; Fernanda Baldibia, pub affrs dir; Fred Holub, chief engr.

KXEZ(FM)—June 1, 1957: 100.3 mhz; 5.3 kw. Ant 3,005 ft. TL: N34 13 37 W118 03 58. Stereo. Suite 250, 3500 W. Olive, Burbank (91505). (818) 955-7000. FAX: (818) 953-7759. Licensee: Viacom International Inc. Group owner: Viacom Broadcasting Inc. (acq 6-3-93; $40 million; FTR 6-21-93). Net: NBC the Source. Rep: D & R Radio. Format: Adult contemp. Target aud: 18-49. ■ Bob Griffith, gen mgr; Des Phelan, gen sls mgr; Phil Gonzalez, prom dir; Dave Beasing, progmg dir; David Green, chief engr.

*****KXLU(FM)**—February 1957: 88.9 mhz; 3 kw. Ant 12 ft. TL: N33 58 16 W118 24 56. Stereo. 7101 W. 80th St. (90045). (310) 338-2866. FAX: (310) 338-5959. Licensee: Loyola Marymount Univ. Board of Trustees Net: AP. Format: Div. educ. News staff one; news progmg 3 hrs wkly. Spec prog: Jazz 11 hrs, Black 8 hrs, Por one hr, Sp 24 hrs wkly. ■ Ed Sandstrom, gen mgr; John Miller, chief engr.

KYSR(FM)—June 30, 1954: 98.7 mhz; 75 kw. Ant 1,180 ft. TL: N34 07 08 W118 23 30. Stereo. Hrs opn: 24. Suite 250, 3500 W. Olive, Burbank (91505). (818) 955-7000. FAX: (818) 953-7759. Licensee: Viacom Broadcasting Inc. (group owner; acq 1-3-90; $100.5 million; FTR 1-22-90). Rep: Torbet. Format: Adult contemp. Target aud: 25-49. Spec prog: Pub affrs 2 hrs wkly. ■ Robert Griffith, vp & gen mgr; R. Desmond Phelan, gen sls mgr; Dan de Percin, natl sls mgr; Jodie Marabella, rgnl sls mgr; Phil Gonzalez, prom mgr; Penny Tucker, news dir; Barbara Shaw, pub affrs dir; David Greene, chief engr.

KZLA-FM—Listing follows KLAC(AM).

Los Banos

KHTN(FM)—1966: 104.7 mhz; 50 kw. Ant 495 ft. TL: N37 11 29 W120 32 03. Stereo. Hrs opn: 24. 1723 N. St., Merced (95340). (209) 383-7900. FAX: (209) 383-5849. Licensee: Exelor Communications Inc. (acq 3-27-91; $700,000; FTR 4-15-91). Rep: Katz & Powell. Format: Adult contemp. Target aud: 25-45; women. ■ Jim Wilkinson, stn mgr.

KLBS(AM)—May 1961: 1330 khz; 500 w-D, 5 kw-N, DA-N. TL: N37 05 51 W120 49 51. Stereo. 401 Pacheco Blvd. (93635). (209) 826-0578. FAX: (209) 826-1906. Licensee: Ethnic Radio Los Banos Inc. (acq 5-82). Format: Por, Sp. Spec prog: Farm 5 hrs, relg 8 hrs. ■ Batista Vieira, pres; J.J. Encarnacao, gen mgr; Caroline Cota, opns mgr; Maria Vacas, progmg dir.

KQLB(FM)—November 1992: 106.9 mhz; 6 kw. Ant 328 ft. TL: N36 55 35 W120 50 42. 401 Pacheco Blvd. (93635). (209) 827-0101. FAX: (209) 826-1906. Licensee: VLB Broadcasting Inc. (acq 12-26-91). Format: Country. ■ J.J. Encancacao, gen mgr; Carolina Cota, opns mgr.

Los Gatos

KRTY(FM)—July 9, 1966: 95.3 mhz; 880 w. Ant 860 ft. TL: N37 12 17 W121 56 56. Stereo. Box 995, San Jose (95108). (408) 293-8030. FAX: (408) 293-6124; (408) 995-0823. Licensee: KRTY Ltd. (acq 2-93; $3.31 million; FTR 1-18-93). Rep: Major Mkt. Format: Country. News staff one. Target aud: 25-54. ■ Bob Kieve, pres; Greg Herpin, gen mgr & gen sls mgr; Stuart Hinkle, natl sls mgr; Terry Rust, rgnl sls mgr; Julie Stevens, prom dir & progmg dir; Russ Rayburn, prom mgr; Tony Michaels, mus dir; Rosana Madigal, pub affrs dir; John Higdon, chief engr. ■ Rates: $125; 125; 125; 40.

Los Osos-Baywood Park

KSTT-FM—1987: 101.1 mhz; 4.86 kw. Ant 1,506 ft. TL: N35 21 38 W120 39 21 (CP: 3.4 kw, ant 1,685 ft.). Hrs opn: 24. Suite 110, 51 Zaca Ln., San Luis Obispo (93401). (805) 545-0101. FAX: (805) 541-5303. Licensee: Stratosphere Broadcasting (acq 8-89; $1,300,000; FTR 9-5-89). Rep: Katz & Powell. Format: Soft adult contemp. News staff one; news progmg 5 hrs wkly. Target aud: 25-54. ■ Don Shore, gen mgr & natl sls mgr; Dave Reichart, gen sls mgr; David Atwood, progmg dir; Tom Lynch, news dir; Paul Kleinkramer, chief engr. ■ Rates: $30; 30; 30; 20.

Lucerne Valley

KIXA(FM)—Not on air, target date unknown: 106.5 mhz; 150 w. TL: N34 23 08 W117 03 25. Rasa Communications Corp., 11671 Locust Lane, Apple Valley (93208). Licensee: Rasa Communications Corp.

Ludlow

KDUQ(FM)—Not on air, target date unknown: 105.7 mhz; 1.8 kw. Ant 590 ft. TL: N34 42 21 W116 12 38. Box 250, Barstow (92311). Licensee: First American Communications.

Madera

KHOT(AM)—Dec 31, 1956: 1250 khz; 1.5 kw-D, 1 kw-N, DA-2. TL: N36 57 58 W120 02 06. Hrs opn: 24. Box 112, Fresno (93707). (209) 268-2625. FAX: (209) 268-2850. Licensee: KZFO Broadcasting Inc. (acq 10-22-93; $775,000 with co-located FM; FTR 11-8-93). Rep: Katz Hispanic. Format: Sp. News staff one; news progmg 30 hrs wkly. Target aud: 25-54. ■ John Boydstun, pres; Edward Distel, gen mgr; Imelda Puentes, asst mus dir; Scott Dean, chief engr. ■ Rates: $40; 40; 40; 32.

KXMX(FM)—Co-owned with KHOT(AM). Sept 30, 1974: 92.1 mhz; 25 kw. Ant 312 ft. TL: N36 57 58 W120 02 06. Stereo. Prog sep from AM. Net: UPI. Format: Adult contemp. Target aud: 18-49. ■ J.M. Hayes, CFO; Gil Garcia, opns mgr; Edward C. Distel, gen sls mgr. ■ Rates: Same as AM.

KMMM(FM)—October 1992: 107.3 mhz; 3 kw. Ant 328 ft. TL: N36 55 11 W120 07 03. 211 E. 6th St. (93638). (209) 673-7374. FAX: (209) 673-3502. Licensee: Madera FM Association. Format: Sp. ■ Pat Ryan, gen mgr; Manuel Jimenez, stn mgr.

KXMX(FM)—Listing follows KHOT(AM).

Magalia

*****KWXP(FM)**—Jan 1, 1993: 88.3 mhz; 1.45 kw. Ant 1,184 ft. TL: N39 57 45 W121 42 52. Hrs opn: 24. c/o 2290 Airport Blvd., Santa Rosa (95403). (707) 528-9236. FAX: (707) 528-9246. Licensee: Educational Media Foundation. Wash atty: Fishland, Wayland, Cooper & Leader. Format: Contemp Christian. Target aud: 25-35; Judaeo-Christian female. ■ Richard Jenkins, pres & gen mgr; David Pierce, progmg dir & mus dir.

Mammoth Lakes

KMMT(FM)—Apr 3, 1973: 106.3 mhz; 55 w. Ant 2,158 ft. TL: N37 37 40 W119 01 56. Stereo. Box 1284 (93546). (619) 934-8888. FAX: (619) 934-2429. Licensee: Mammoth Mountain F.M. Associates Inc. Net: MBS. Format: Adult contemp. News progmg 2 hrs wkly. Target aud: 18-45; active, athletic, affluent adults. Spec prog: Jazz 3 hrs, classic rock 5 hrs wkly. ■ David A. Digemess, pres, gen mgr, progmg dir & chief engr; Jim Rey, opns dir; Michael Drake, news dir.

Manteca

KVFX(FM)—Jan 15, 1979: 96.7 mhz; 3 kw. Ant 328 ft. TL: N37 43 45 W121 11 49. Stereo. Hrs opn: 24. Suite D-41, 1620 N. Carpenter Rd., Modesto (95351). (209) 521-9797. FAX: (209) 521-9844. Licensee: Cal Valley Radio L.P. (acq 11-87; $1,200,000; FTR 11-30-87). Rep: Banner. Wash atty: Mullins, Rhyne, Emmons & Topel. Format: Classic rock. Target aud: 25-54. ■ William H. Johnson Jr., pres & gen mgr. ■ Rates: $45; 45; 45; 30.

Marina

KBOQ-FM—Apr 6, 1982: 92.7 mhz; 6.9 kw. Ant 567 ft. TL: N36 33 12 W121 47 05. Stereo. Hrs opn: 24. 6 AM-midnight. Box 81460, Salinas (93912); 55 Plaza Cir., Salinas (93901). (408) 422-5363. FAX: (408) 375-0967. Licensee: Model Associates Inc. (acq 1-88; $2.98 million; FTR 11-16-87). Rep: D & R Radio. Format: Rock. ■ A. William Lee, pres; Susan Koza, gen sls mgr; Laura Cardinale, prom mgr; Eugene Kingdon, mus dir; Jerry Lewine, chief engr.

Mariposa

KHOV(FM)—Not on air, target date unknown: 103.9 mhz; 71 w. Ant 2,047 ft. TL: N37 32 00 W120 01 29. Stereo. Suite 700, 3401 Dale Rd., Modesto (95356). (209) 572-0104. Licensee: Citadel Communications Corp. (group owner; acq 7-30-93; $6 million; FTR 8-23-93). Rep: Christal. ■ Larry Wilson, pres; Scott Mahalick, vp & gen mgr; Bruno Lometti, gen sls mgr; Randy Rose, progmg dir; Chris Haggin, mus dir; Dave Holmes, news dir & pub affrs dir; Jerry Moore, engrg mgr.

KUBB(FM)—July 4, 1977: 96.3 mhz; 1.9 kw. Ant 2,112 ft. TL: N37 32 00 W120 01 29. Stereo. Hrs opn: 24. Box 429, 1735 Canal St., Merced (95341); 1024 J. Street, Modesto (95354). (209) 723-8461. Licensee: Buckley Broadcasting of Monterey. Group owner: Buckley Broadcasting Corp. (acq 7-1-85; $640,000; FTR 5-20-85). Net: Unistar. Rep: McGavren Guild. Wash atty: Martin Leader. Format: Country. News staff one; news progmg 2 hrs wkly. Target aud: 25-54. Spec prog: Farm 2 hrs wkly. ■ Julie Campbell, vp & gen mgr; Sandra Osborne, opns mgr & mus dir; Sharon Cresswell, gen sls mgr; Ken Warren, chief engr.

Marysville

KKCY(FM)—See Colusa.

KMYC(AM)—1940: 1410 khz; 5 kw-D, 1 kw-N, DA-2. TL: N39 08 18 W121 33 15. Hrs opn: 24. 6 AM-midnight. Box 631, 1605 Simpson Lane (95901). (916) 742-5555. FAX: (916) 741-3758. Licensee: River Cities Radio L.P. (acq 5-1-79). Format: Sports. News staff one. Target aud: 18 plus; general. Spec prog: Indian/Punjabi 2 hrs wkly. ■ Jeffrey D. Holden, gen mgr; Kenton Lee, rgnl sls mgr; Pam Roberts, progmg dir; Jim Naylor, mus dir; Tim White, chief engr. ■ Rates: $15; 15; 15; 5.

KRFD-FM—Co-owned with KMYC(AM). 1947: 99.9 mhz; 1.74 kw. Ant 2,181 ft. TL: N39 12 20 W121 49 10. Stereo. Hrs opn: 24. Prog sep from AM. Format: Progressive, AOR. Target aud: 25-49; men. ■ Jim Naylor, mus dir; David Rosenthal, news dir; Karen Marie, pub affrs dir. ■ Rates: $45; 45; 45; 20.

KOBO(AM)—See Yuba City.

KUBA(AM)—See Yuba City.

KXCL(FM)—See Yuba City.

McFarland

KSUV-FM—July 11, 1989: 102.9 mhz; 21 kw. Ant 383 ft. TL: N35 38 40 W119 16 08. Stereo. Hrs opn: 24. Suite 102, 3701 Pegasus Dr., Bakersfield (93308). (805) 393-0103. Licensee: Caballero, Caballero, Caballero. Rep:

California

Caballero. Format: Sp. ■ Eduardo Caballero, pres; Richard Keating, gen mgr; Frances C. Torres, opns mgr; Denny Jackson, rgnl sls mgr; Juan Jose Hernandez, progmg dir.

KSUV(AM)—Sept 1, 1970: 1590 khz; 500 w-D, 490 w-N, DA-2. Ant 180 ft. TL: N35 38 40 W119 16 08 (CP: 750 khz, 3 kw-D, 600-N, DA-2, TL: N35 23 55 W118 54 00). Dups FM 100%. Licensee: Caballero Radio West Inc. Format: Sp. News progrm 2 hrs wkly. Target aud: 18-49.

Mendocino

KPMO(AM)—Nov 16, 1966: 1300 khz; 5 kw-D, 77 w-N. TL: N39 20 33 W123 46 51. 14200 Prairie Way (95460). (707) 964-5307. FAX: (707) 964-3299. Licensee: Anderson Broadcasting Inc. (acq 8-12-82; $424,900 with co-located FM; FTR 8-16-82). Net: Sun. Rep: Katz & Powell. Format: News/talk. Target aud: 30 & up. Spec prog: Relg 2 hrs wkly. ■ George Anderson, pres, gen mgr & gen sls mgr; Tom Driggers, chief engr. ■ Rates: $10; 10; 10; na.

KMFB(FM)—Co-owned with KPMO(AM). June 26, 1967: 92.7 mhz; 3 kw. Ant 165 ft. TL: N39 20 33 W123 46 51. Stereo. Dups AM less than 5%. Format: Adult contemp, rock (AOR). News staff one. Target aud: 25-44. ■ Steve Starr, prom mgr; Nora Mitchell, mus dir; Fred Colby, news dir. ■ Rates: $12; 12; 12; na.

Merced

KABX-FM—Listing follows KYOS(AM).

***KAMB(FM)**—Nov 6, 1967: 101.5 mhz; 50 kw. Ant 390 ft. TL: N37 27 59 W120 14 09 (CP: 16.8 kw, ant 846 ft.). Stereo. Hrs opn: 24. 90 E. 16th St. (95340). (209) 723-1015. FAX: (209) 723-1945. Licensee: Central Valley Broadcasting Inc. Net: Moody, USA. Wash atty: Jim Riley. Format: Contemp Christian. News progmg 5 hrs wkly. Target aud: 25-49; Christian adults in central Calif. ■ Eric Bettencourt, pres; Richard L. Grant, stn mgr; Tim Land, opns dir, progmg dir & news dir; Mark Murdock, prom mgr & pub affrs dir; Bill Ronning, asst mus dir.

KFIE(FM)—May 14, 1989: 106.3 mhz; 2.95 kw. Ant 476 ft. TL: N37 25 34 W120 26 23 (CP: 2.5 kw). 1360 W. 18th St. (95340). (209) 723-5420. FAX: (209) 723-7254. Licensee: Merced Communications. Format: Sp. Target aud: 25-54; upscale professionals. ■ Barbara Harris, gen mgr; Charles Hughes, chief engr.

KHTN(FM)—See Los Banos.

KLOQ(AM)—Feb 26, 1956: 1580 khz; 1 kw-D, 297 w-N. TL: N37 17 31 W120 26 03. 705 W. Main St. (95340). (209) 722-1520. FAX: (209) 722-6166. Licensee: KGGE Broadcasting. Group owner: TGR Broadcasting Inc. Net: MBS. Rep: Katz. Format: Sp. ■ Carlo Moncado, pres; Hector Villovos, gen mgr; Steve Pacheco, chief engr.

KUBB(FM)—See Mariposa.

KXDE(FM)—Not on air, target date unknown: 107.7 mhz; 3 kw. Ant 328 ft. TL: N37 22 05 W120 27 10. 16 Main St., Sturbridge, MA (01566). Licensee: John Neuhoff (acq 3-30-92; $5,000 for CP; FTR 4-20-92).

KYAJ(FM)—Not on air, target date unknown: 94.1 mhz; 3 kw. Ant 328 ft. TL: N37.17 05 W120 24 09. Suite 9, 2201 Barrington St., Bakersfield (93309). Licensee: Mali Broadcasting.

KYOS(AM)—October 1936: 1480 khz; 5 kw-U, DA-N. TL: N37 22 30 W120 27 37. Box 717 (95341); 1744 G St. (95340). (209) 723-2191. FAX: (209) 383-2950. Licensee: Merced Radio Partners L.P. (acq 1-30-89; $1.75 million with co-located FM; FTR 1-30-89). Net: ABC/I, MBS. Rep: Christal. Format: News/talk. News staff one; news progmg 20 hrs wkly. Target aud: 25-54. Spec prog: Farm 5 hrs wkly. ■ Edward G. Hoyt Jr., pres & gen mgr; Pat Mullins, stn mgr; Brian Griffey, gen sls mgr; Marlene Messler, rgnl sls mgr; Jenny West, progmg dir; A.J. Presto, news dir. ■ Rates: $32; 26; 32; 21.

KABX-FM—Co-owned with KYOS(AM). Dec 18, 1975: 97.5 mhz; 50 kw. Ant 490 ft. TL: N37 22 31 W120 27 37. Stereo. Prog sep from AM. (209) 723-2193. Rep: Christal. Format: Oldies. ■ Brian Elder, progmg dir.

Middletown

KRSH(FM)—Not on air, target date unknown: 98.7 mhz; 3 kw. Ant 213 ft. 1812 Trinity No. 220, Walnut Creek (94546). Licensee: Wine Country Radio.

Mission Viejo

***KSBR(FM)**—May 7, 1979: 88.5 mhz; 620 w. Ant 600 ft. TL: N33 30 10 W117 36 06. Stereo. 28000 Marguerite Pkwy. (92692). (714) 582-5727. Licensee: Saddleback Community College District. Net: AP. Format: Jazz. Spec prog: Latin 4 hrs, blues 4 hrs, reggae 4 hrs, electronic 4 hrs, ragtime 2 hrs, folk 2 hrs wkly. ■ Greg Bishop, pres; Mark Schiffelbein, gen mgr; Terry Wedel, progmg mgr; Dawn Kamber, news dir.

Modesto

***KADV(FM)**—Nov 1988: 90.5 mhz; 1.5 kw. Ant 141 ft. TL: N37 36 26 W120 57 26. Stereo. Hrs opn: 24. Box 1312 (95353); 1204 Wallin Way, Ceres (95351-4825). (209) 537-1201; (209) 537-7059. FAX: (209) 537-7225. Licensee: Modesto Adventist Academy. Wash atty: Don Martin. Format: Educ, relg, class. News progmg 2 hrs wkly. Target aud: 45 plus. ■ Gaylord Boyer, pres; Donald Cowper, prom mgr, progmg dir & news dir; Marvin Bort, mus dir.

KATM(FM)—Listing follows KBEE(AM).

KBEE(AM)—1951: 970 khz; 1 kw-U, DA-2. TL: N37 41 28 W120 57 11. Stereo. Suite 135, 1581 Cummins Dr. (95358). (209) 523-7556. Licensee: Citadel Communications Corp. (group owner; acq 5-18-92; $12.5 million grpsl, including co-located FM; FTR 6-8-92). Net: ABC, CBS. Rep: Eastman. Format: MOR, sports. Target aud: 35 plus. ■ Larry Wilson, pres; Scott G. Mahalick, vp, gen mgr & stn mgr; Greg Edwards, opns dir, progmg dir & mus dir; Bruno Lometti, gen sls mgr; Mary Barr, prom dir; Ryn Stephens, news dir; Jerry Moore, chief engr. ■ Rates: $25; 25; 25; 15.

KATM(FM)—Co-owned with KBEE(AM). 1948: 103.3 mhz; 50 kw. Ant 500 ft. TL: N37 34 30 W121 21 13. Stereo. Prog sep from AM. Rep: Eastman. Format: Country. Target aud: 25-64; mass appeal. ■ Ed Hill, progmg dir. ■ Rates: $85; 85; 85; 38.

KCIV(FM)—See Mount Bullion.

KFIV(AM)—1950: 1360 khz; 5 kw-D, 1 kw-N, DA-2. TL: N37 39 52 W120 57 00 (CP: 950 w-N). Box 1360 (95353). (209) 545-5585. FAX: (209) 545-5587. Licensee: Community Pacific Broadcasting Co. L.P. (group owner; acq 10-1-82). Net: CNN, MBS. Rep: Major Mkt. Format: News/talk. News staff one. ■ David J. Benjamin, pres; Gary Halladay, exec vp & gen mgr; Rick Myers, gen sls mgr; Wilson Nersee, progmg dir; Tim St. Martin, news dir; Steve Minshall, chief engr.

KJSN(FM)—Co-owned with KFIV(AM). July 4, 1977: 102.3 mhz; 6 kw. Ant 300 ft. TL: N37 40 47 W120 55 28. Stereo. Prog sep from AM. Box 3408 (95353). Format: Adult contemp. Target aud: 25-49. ■ Rob Carlson, mus dir.

KHOP(FM)—1949: 104.1 mhz; 50 kw. Ant 500 ft. TL: N37 39 10 W121 28 38. Stereo. Hrs opn: 24. Suite 700, 3401 Dale Rd. (95356). (209) 572-0104. FAX: (209) 572-1931. Licensee: Citadel Communications Corp. (group owner; acq 10-1-93). Rep: Christal. Format: Rock (AOR). News staff one; news progmg 5 hrs wkly. Target aud: 25-49; baby boomers who grew up with rock & roll. ■ Larry Wilson, pres; Scott Mahalick, vp & gen mgr; Bruno Lometti, gen sls mgr; Randy Rose, progmg dir; Chris Haggin , mus dir; Dave Holmes, news dir & pub affrs dir; Jerry Moore, engrg dir.

KJSN(FM)—Listing follows KFIV(AM).

KLOC(AM)—See Ceres.

***KMPO(FM)**—January 1984: 88.7 mhz; 2 kw. Ant 1,500 ft. TL: N37 32 00 W120 01 29. Stereo. Hrs opn: 24. Suite 700, 1111 Fulton Mall, Fresno (93721). (209) 486-5174; (209) 498-6956. FAX: (209) 264-9309. Licensee: Radio Bilingue Inc. Format: Bilingual/Sp. News staff 5; news progmg one hrs wkly. Target aud: 16 plus; Latinos. Spec prog: Black 3 hrs, folk 4 hrs, Hmong 3 hrs, Filipino one hr wkly. ■ Hugo Morales, CEO; Keith Frady, opns dir; Steve Weber Jr., chief engr.

KOSO(FM)—(Patterson). June 6, 1966: 93.1 mhz; 2.95 kw. Ant 1,791 ft. TL: N37 30 14 W121 22 22. Stereo. Hrs opn: 24. 2121 Loncey Dr., Modesto (95355). (209) 551-1306. Licensee: KOSO Inc. Group owner: Space Com (acq 11-1-79). Net: AP. Rep: Katz. Format: Adult contemp. News staff one; news progmg 5 hrs wkly. Target aud: 25-54. ■ Jim Krebsbach, vp & gen mgr; Max Miller, opns mgr & progmg dir; Jerri Matoza, sls dir; Donna Miller, prom mgr; Tony Miranda, mus dir; Carol Benson, news dir; Perri Lancer, pub affrs dir; Brad Johnson, chief engr. ■ Rates: $50; 40; 50; 15.

KTRB(AM)—June 18, 1933: 860 khz; 50 kw-D, 10 kw-N, DA-3. TL: N37 42 32 W120 43 27. Stereo. 1192 Norwegian Ave. (95350). (209) 526-8600. FAX: (209) 578-3568. Licensee: The Pete Pappas Co. (acq 12-17-86). Net: NBC, NBC Talknet. Rep: Banner. Format: Country. News staff 2; news progmg 6 hrs wkly. Target aud: 25 & up. Spec prog: Pub affrs 2 hrs, legal affrs one hr wkly. ■ Bessie Pappas, gen mgr; Pete Culver, stn mgr.

Mojave

KAVS(FM)—May 1966: 97.7 mhz; 3 kw. Ant 145 ft. TL: N34 58 45 W118 10 02 (CP: Ant 300 ft.). Stereo. Hrs opn: 24. 2501 W Ave. I, Lancaster (93536). (805) 942-1121. FAX: (805) 723-5512. Licensee: Antelope Broadcasting Co. Net: Westwood One. Format: CHR. News staff one. Target aud: 18-34; active adults. ■ Ron Carter, pres; Lawrence R. Thornhill, gen mgr; Rich Bultman, natl sls mgr; Zack Taylor, progmg dir; Rob Dejai, mus dir; Jamie Lee, news dir; Candace Harrison, pub affrs dir; Bruce Gary, chief engr.

KTPI(FM)—See Tehachapi.

KVOY(AM)—May 1, 1958: 1340 khz; 1 kw-U. TL: N35 02 23 W118 08 57. 190 Sierra Court, B-2, Palmdale (93550). (805) 274-1031. FAX: (805) 274-1017. Licensee: The Park Lane Group (group owner; acq 3-20-92; $1.82 million with KTPI(FM) Tehachapi; FTR 4-13-92). Net: ABC/E. Rep: Christal. Format: Nostalgia, talk. Target aud: 25-54. Spec prog: Sp 8 hrs wkly. ■ Tom Caulkims, gen mgr & gen sls mgr; Joe Waldmen, progmg dir.

Monte Rio

KMGG(FM)—Licensed to Monte Rio. See Santa Rosa.

Montecito

KJEE(FM)—Not on air, target date unknown: 92.9 mhz; 363 w. Ant 827 ft. 2440 Murrell, Santa Barbara (93109). Licensee: James Evans.

KNZS(AM)—Not on air, target date unknown: 880 khz; 780 w-D, 220 w-N, DA-D. TL: N34 26 58 W119 35 48. c/o Jerry J. Collins, 25485 Boots Rd., Monterey (93940). (408) 372-8383. Licensee: Jerry J. Collins. ■ Jerry J. Collins, pres.

Margret Haney
GRAHAM-HANEY
Media Brokers/Consultants
2995 WOODSIDE ROAD, WOODSIDE, CA 94062
TEL: 415/325-5552, FAX: 415/325-5556

Monterey

KBOQ-FM—See Marina.

KIDD(AM)—1955: 630 khz; 1 kw-U, DA-2. TL: N36 41 28 W121 48 00. Hrs opn: 24. Box 1799 (93942); 551 Foam St. (93940). (408) 647-1017. FAX: (408) 655-3009. Licensee: Joaquin Financial Group (acq 8-1-91; $1.1 million; with co-located FM; FTR 8-5-91). Net: Unistar. Rep: Katz & Powell. Format: Big band. News staff one; news progmg one hr wkly. Target aud: 35-64; high-income, active achievers. ■ Jim Heidebrecht, pres; Robert Meester, vp; Russ Cornelius, gen mgr; Jim Seagull, progmg mgr; Carl Willeford, chief engr.

KMBY-FM—See Seaside.

KNRY(AM)—October 1935: 1240 khz; 1 kw-U. TL: N36 36 56 W121 53 53. Hrs opn: 24. 651 Cannery Row (93940). (408) 373-1234. FAX: (408) 373-1255. Licensee: KNRY Inc. (acq 8-19-92; FTR 9-7-92). Net: CNN, MBS, CBS. Wash atty: Haley, Bader & Potts. Format: Talk, sports. Spec prog: Gospel 6 hrs wkly. ■ David Wagenvourd, pres; Keith Moon, gen mgr, prom dir & adv dir; Abel Manley, news dir; Carl Willeford, chief engr. ■ Rates: $40; 30; 40; 25.

KOCN(FM)—See Pacific Grove.

KTOM(AM)—See Salinas.

KTOM-FM—See Salinas.

KWAV(FM)—Oct 14, 1961: 96.9 mhz; 18 kw. Ant 2,450 ft. TL: N36 32 05 W121 37 14. Stereo. Box 1391 (93942). (408) 649-0969. FAX: (408) 649-3335. Licensee: Buckley Broadcasting Corp. of Monterey. Group owner: Buckley Broadcasting Corp. (acq 5-1-80; $700,000; FTR 3-17-80). Net: AP. Rep: D & R. Format: Adult contemp. News staff one; news progmg 2 hrs wkly. Target aud: 18-54; women. ■ Richard Buckley, pres; Kathy Baker, sr vp; Sue Clark, sls dir; Jane Holladay, prom mgr; Bernie Moody, progmg dir & mus dir; Debi McCallister, news dir; Ken Warren, chief engr. ■ Rates: $65; 55; 55; 40.

Stations in the U.S.   California

Moraga

*KSMC(FM)—Sept 22, 1977: 89.5 mhz; 800 w. Ant 95 ft. TL: N37 50 25 W122 06 36. Stereo. Box 3223, St. Mary's College (94575). (510) 376-1242. Licensee: Associated Students of St. Mary's College of Calif. Format: Class, educ. Target aud: 15-30; young, urban & willing to experiment. Spec prog: Relg 3 hrs wkly. ■ Tom Lacher, gen mgr; Phil Gomes, prom dir; John Ryan, adv dir & pub affrs dir; Alan Sartirana, mus dir; Marc Tamo, Ryan Cone, asst mus dirs; Sean Vergho, news dir; Ed Tywoniak, chief engr.

Moreno Valley

KHPY(AM)—1989: 1530 khz; 10 kw-D, DA-3. TL: N34 00 42 W117 11 03. Box 909 (92556); 24490 Sunnymead Blvd., #215 (92553). (909) 247-5479. FAX: (909) 247-2790; TELEX: (909) 247-2790. Licensee: KHPY Hispanic Radio Corp. (acq 4-30-92; $1 million; FTR 5-11-92). Net: CRC. Wash atty: Fletcher, Heald & Hildreth. Format: Sp. News staff 2; news progmg 48 hrs wkly. Target aud: General. ■ Humberto Luna, pres; Ruben Chavez Jr., vp & gen mgr; Miguel A. Arenas, stn mgr & vp prom; Lucy Chavez, opns mgr & pub affrs dir; Juan M. Garcia, vp progmg & mus dir; Erika Morales, news dir; John Cooper, chief engr. ■ Rates: $22; 22; 22; na.

Morgan Hill

KSQQ(FM)—Dec 1990: 96.1 mhz; 530 w. Ant 781 ft. TL: N37 10 03 W121 34 20 (CP: 1 kw). Suite 220, 16360 Monterey Rd. (95037). (408) 778-9696. FAX: (408) 778-9602. Licensee: Coyote Communications Inc. Format: Ethnic. ■ Batista Vieira, pres & gen mgr; Peter Mieuli, vp; David Williams, chief engr.

Morro Bay

KBAI(AM)—Feb 4, 1974: 1150 khz; 5 kw-U, DA-N. TL: N35 21 36 W120 49 26. Box 1150 (93443). (805) 772-2263. FAX: (805) 772-2264. Licensee: KROZ Productions Inc. (acq 7-1-93; $360,000 with co-located FM; FTR 7-26-93). Net: SMN, Jones Satellite Audio. Format: Stardust, big band, swing. News progmg 10 hrs wkly. Target aud: 35 plus; mature adults with buying power. ■ Roz Roboff, CEO, vp opns, progmg dir & mus dir; Warren Lilly, exec vp; Bob Fox, gen mgr; Jim Bell, asst mus dir; Val Grant, news dir; Teresa DeSanits, pub affrs dir; Bill Bordeaux, chief engr. ■ Rates: $16; 14; 18; 12.

KWWV(FM)—May 1, 1991: 99.7 mhz; 220 w-H, 210 w-V. Ant 1,633 ft. TL: N35 21 37 W120 39 18. Hrs opn: 24. Box 1150, 325 Pacific St. (93442). (805) 772-2263. Wash atty: Gary Swartz. Format: Adult contemp. Target aud: 25-54; mature buyers. ■ Roz Roboff, CEO; Bob Fox, pres, gen mgr & vp sls. ■ Rates: $18; 14; 16; 12.

Mount Bullion

KCIV(FM)—April 24, 1989: 99.9 mhz; 1.85 kw. Ant 2,099 ft. TL: N37 32 00 W120 01 29. Suite 1, 1031 15th St., Modesto (95354). (209) 524-8999. FAX: (209) 524-9088. Licensee: Bott Communications Inc. Group owner: Bott Broadcasting. Format: Relg. News staff 5. Target aud: 25-54; Christian family audience. ■ Richard P. Bott, pres; Lee Fenicle, gen mgr.

Mount Shasta

KEDY(FM)—Listing follows KWSD(AM).

*KNSQ(FM)—Not on air, target date unknown: 88.1 mhz; 2.28 kw. Ant 2,385 ft. TL: N41 20 46 W122 11 42 (CP: 5 kw, and 890 ft.). Jefferson Public Radio, 1250 Siskiyou Blvd., Ashland, OR (97520). (503) 552-6301. Licensee: Oregon State Board of Education (acq 3-1-91; FTR 4-1-91). ■ Ronald Kramer, gen mgr.

KWSD(AM)—June 12, 1947: 620 khz; 1 kw-D. TL: N41 19 09 W122 18 35. Box 448 (96067). (916) 926-2124. FAX: (916) 926-3425. Licensee: Shasta Cascade Broadcasting Corp. Net: CBS. Format: Hot adult contemp. ■ David H. Rees, pres & chief engr; David Rees Jr., gen mgr & gen sls mgr; Harry Blackwell, progmg dir.

KEDY(FM)—Co-owned with KWSD(AM). Nov 26, 1977: 95.3 mhz; 3 kw. Ant -1,300 ft. TL: N41 19 09 W122 18 35 (CP: Ant 157 ft., TL: N41 17 20 W122 14 25). Prog sep from AM. Net: CBS. Format: Adult contemp, golden oldies.

Mountain Pass

KHYZ(FM)—April 1980: 99.5 mhz; 10 kw. Ant 1,710 ft. TL: N35 29 27 W115 33 27. Stereo. Hrs opn: 24. Box 25606, Suite 105, 12381 Wilshire Blvd., Los Angeles (90025). (310) 820-4628. FAX: (310) 826-7866. Licensee: KRXV Inc. Net: AP. Rep: Banner, Gillis. Wash atty: Hogan & Hartson. Format: Adult contemp. News staff one; news progmg 16 hrs wkly. Target aud: 35 plus; travelers & loc communities. ■ Howard B. Anderson, pres; Tim Anderson, gen mgr; Jack Spring, stn mgr; Kirk M. Anderson, natl sls mgr; Lance Todd, progmg dir; Keith Hayes, news dir.

Mountain View

*KSFH(FM)—1974: 90.5 mhz; 10 w. Ant 100 ft. TL: N37 22 09 W122 05 00. 1885 Miramonte Ave. (94040). (415) 968-1213. Licensee: St. Francis High School of Mountain View, Calif. Inc. Format: Modern, AOR. ■ Steve Martin, pres.

Napa

KVON(AM)—Nov 17, 1947: 1440 khz; 5 kw-D, 1 kw-N, DA-2. TL: N38 16 47 W122 18 06. Hrs opn: 24. 1124 Foster Rd. (94558). (707) 252-1440. FAX: (707) 226-7544. Licensee: Young Radio Inc. (group owner; acq 9-1-70). Net: ABC/E, AP, MBS. Rep: Christal. Format: News/talk. News staff 3; news progmg 30 hrs wkly. Target aud: 35 plus. Spec prog: Sp 5 hrs, farm 3 hrs wkly. ■ Thomas L. Young, CEO, pres & gen mgr; Barry Martin, opns dir & progmg dir; George Carl, gen sls mgr; Faeli Schwartz, rgnl sls mgr; Henry Mulak, news dir; Mike Martindale, chief engr. ■ Rates: $30; 30; 25; 20.

KVYN(FM)—See St. Helena.

Needles

KTOX(AM)—October 1952: 1340 khz; 1 kw-U. TL: N34 51 10 W114 37 19. Box 738 (92363); Rt. 4, Box 30, Old Hwy. US 66 W. (92363). (619) 326-2101; (800) 753-KTOX. FAX: (619) 326-5733. Licensee: Coburn Communications Corp. (acq 12-29-88). Net: CBS. Format: News/talk, sports. Target aud: 18 plus. ■ Maurice W. Coburn, gen mgr; Andy Ward, stn mgr, sls dir, progmg dir & news dir. ■ Rates: $9, 8.25, 9, 6.75.

KWAZ(FM)—May 1984: 97.9 mhz; 2.8 kw. Ant 1,571 ft. TL: N35 02 06 W114 22 09 (CP: 29.5 kw). Stereo. Suite C, 244 G. St. (92363). (619) 326-5060. Licensee: Green River Broadcasting Corp. (acq 7-91; $1,284,000 with KBAS(AM) Bullhead City, AZ; FTR 7-29-91). Net: AP. Format: Adult contemp. ■ R. Michael Flynn, gen mgr & gen sls mgr; Don Howard, opns mgr; Patti Todd, prom dir; Mike Van Acker, progmg dir; Gary Thompson, news dir; Art Cane, chief engr. ■ Rates: $20; 15; 20; 15.

Nevada City

*KVMR(FM)—July 17, 1978: 89.5 mhz; 1.96 kw. Ant 980 ft. TL: N39 14 47 W120 57 48. Stereo. Box 1327, 325 Spring St. (95959). (916) 265-9073. Licensee: Nevada City Community Broadcast Group (acq 7-11-89; $32,000; FTR 5-29-89). Format: Div, rock. News progmg 2 hrs wkly. Spec prog: Class 8 hrs, jazz 16 hrs, country 4 hrs, Black 4 hrs, folk 10 hrs, blues 5 hrs, gospel 2 hrs, reggae 4 hrs, Celtic 3 hrs, children 3 hrs wkly. ■ S.D. Ramsey, gen mgr; Bruce Doan, opns mgr & chief engr; Phyllis Kunin-Glasco, dev dir; George Parsons, mus dir.

Newport Beach

KBJZ(FM)—Jan 31, 1964: 103.1 mhz; 2.57 kw. Ant 322 ft. TL: N33 37 55 W117 56 15. Stereo. Suite 303, 2043 Westcliff Dr. (92660). (714) 548-6277; (310) 458-1031. FAX: (714) 548-6856. Licensee: Kelsho Radio Group Inc. (acq 2-15-91; grpsl; FTR 3-11-91). Format: Jazz ■ Bonnie Stone, gen mgr; John Paoli, chief engr.

North Highlands

*KEBR-FM—Feb 21, 1992: 89.3 mhz; 3.1 kw-V. Ant 354 ft. TL: N38 42 38 W121 28 54. Stereo. Hrs opn: 24. 3108 Fulton Ave., Sacramento (95821). (916) 481-8191. FAX: (916) 481-0410. Licensee: Family Stations Inc. (group owner). Format: Relg. ■ Harold Camping, pres; Peggy Renschler, opns mgr & progmg dir; Scott L. Smith, vp dev; Donald Perkins, chief engr.

Northridge

*KCSN(FM)—November 1963: 88.5 mhz; 52 w. Ant 2,128 ft. TL: N34 21 13 W118 24 57. Stereo. Hrs opn: 24. 18111 Nordhoff St. (91330). (818) 885-3090. Licensee: California State University Northridge. Net: APR, NPR, AP. Wash atty: Arter & Hadden. Format: Class. News staff one; news progmg 12 hrs wkly. Target aud: 35 plus; middle/upper middle-class, well educated. Spec prog: German 3 hrs, Jewish 3 hrs, bluegrass 5 hrs, Dixieland 2 hrs, old time radio 3 hrs wkly. ■ Dr. Blenda Wilson, chmn; Dr. Linda Bain, pres; Teresa Rogers, gen mgr; Tessa Marshall, dev dir & prom mgr; Jared Kliger, progmg dir; Keith Goldstein, news dir; Michael Worrall, chief engr.

Oakdale

KDJK(FM)—Mar 11, 1985: 95.1 mhz; 29.5 kw. Ant 633 ft. TL: N37 47 34 W120 31 08 (CP: 16 kw, ant 876 ft., TL: N37 49 39 W120 34 03). Stereo. Hrs opn: 24. 570 Armstrong Way (95361). (209) 847-9510. FAX: (209) 847-4848. Licensee: Goldrush Broadcasting Inc. Rep: Eastman. Wash atty: Fletcher, Heald & Hildreth. Format: AOR. News staff one; news progmg 3 hrs wkly. Target aud: 18-49. Spec prog: Jazz 2 hrs, blues 2 hrs wkly. ■ Joe L. Gross, pres, gen mgr & chief engr; L. Ann Gross, opns dir; Catrina Osburn Lunderburg, sls dir; Sherie Grazatto, prom mgr; Beaver Brown, progmg dir; Jeff Riedel, mus dir; Steve Ramirez, news dir.

Oakhurst

KAAT(FM)—Nov 1, 1982: 107.1 mhz; 280 w. Ant 1,070 ft. TL: N37 25 08 W119 44 04. Stereo. Hrs opn: 24. Box 1912, 40356 Oak Park Way (93644). (209) 683-5107. FAX: (209) 683-5488. Licensee: California Sierra Corp. Net: USA, Jones Satellite Audio. Wash atty: Gammon & Grange. Format: Light rock, adult contemp, big band. ■ Larry W. Gamble, CEO & stn mgr; Sylvia A. Gamble, pres; Bonnie Martucci, vp opns; Elise Jara, rgnl sls mgr; Lisa Youngblood, vp prom; Randy Stover, chief engr.

KTNS(AM)—Co-owned with KAAT(FM). 1988: 1090 khz; 500 w-D. TL: N37 18 07 W119 36 47. Hrs opn: Sunrise-sunset. Net: USA, Jones Satellite Audio. Format: Adult contemp, big band. Target aud: 25-49. ■ Mac Pilkington, gen sls mgr.

Oakland

KABL(AM)—1925: 960 khz; 5 kw-U, DA-1. TL: N37 49 40 W122 18 53. 1025 Battery St., San Francisco (94111-1201). (415) 788-5225. FAX: (415) 981-2930. Licensee: Shamrock Broadcasting Co. (group owner; acq 7-29-93). Rep: Christal. Format: Easy lstng. ■ Bill Clark, pres; Eddie Esserman, vp & gen mgr; Julie Kahn, gen sls mgr; Gerry McCracken, progmg dir; Dennis Gooch, chief engr.

KABL-FM—See San Francisco.

KDIA(AM)—July 1922: 1310 khz; 5 kw-U, DA-1. TL: N37 49 27 W122 19 10. 384 Embarcadero W., 3rd Fl. (94607); Box 29498 (94604). (510) 251-1400. FAX: (510) 251-2110. Licensee: Willie L. Brown Jr. (acq 4-28-92; $1.6 million; FTR 11-2-92). Net: ABC. Rep: Katz & Powell. Format: Rhythm & blues. News staff 2. Target aud: 25-54; adults. Spec prog: Gospel 20 hrs wkly. ■ Willie L. Brown Jr., pres; Elihu Harris, exec vp; Priscilla Watts, gen mgr; Bill Daisa, gen sls mgr; Camille Tompkins, rgnl sls mgr; Nichole Freeman, prom dir; Bob Jones, progmg dir; Bob Sherwood, news dir; Keith Davidson, chief engr. ■ Rates: $80; 80; 80; 45.

KNEW(AM)—July 2, 1921: 910 khz; 5 kw-U, DA-N. TL: N37 53 42 W122 19 29. Hrs opn: 24. Box 7448, San Francisco (94120); Suite 200, 750 Battery St. (94111). (415) 291-0202. TWX: (415) 395-9886. Licensee: Shamrock Holdings Inc. Group owner: Shamrock Broadcasting Inc. (acq 6-4-93; grpsl; FTR 6-21-93). Net: AP. Rep: McGavern Guild. Format: Country. News staff 2. Target aud: 25-54. ■ Eddie Esserman, vp & gen mgr; Lee Logan, opns dir; Julie Kahn, gen sls mgr; Marlene Augustine, prom mgr; Richard Ryan, mus dir; Dick Garcia, news dir; Dennis Gooch, chief engr.

Oceanside

KIOZ(FM)—Jan 20, 1962: 102.1 mhz; 10 kw. Ant 980 ft. TL: N33 12 53 W117 11 15. Stereo. Hrs opn: 24. Suite G, 5735 Kearny Villa Rd., San Diego (92123); 2952 Oceanside Blvd. (92054). (619) 560-5464; (619) 757-1321. FAX: (619) 560-0742. Licensee: Par Broadcasting Co. (acq 1-83; $3.17 million with co-located FM; FTR 12-20-82). Rep: Torbet. Wash atty: Chris Smallwood. Format: AOR. Target aud: 18-34; upscale, well educated. ■ Steve Jacobs, gen mgr; Al Peterson, vp opns; Rory Charitan, gen sls mgr; Jeff Lynch, natl sls mgr; Chris Ryan, mktg dir; Scott Jacobs, prom dir; Greg Stevens, progmg dir; Peg Pollard, mus dir; Shannon Leder, pub affrs dir; Dick Warren, chief engr.

KGMG(AM)—Co-owned with KIOZ(FM). July 4, 1956: 1320 khz; 9.5 kw, DA-1. Ant 299 ft. TL: N33 12 08 W117 36 46. (92123). Format: MOR. News staff one. Target aud: 35 plus; mature, educated adults. Spec prog: Big band 4 hrs wkly. ■ Chris Vaccaro, opns mgr.

Oildale

KLLY(FM)—January 1985: 95.3 mhz; 12.5 kw. Ant 394 ft. TL: N35 27 55 W119 01 04. Stereo. Hrs opn: 24. Box 80658, 3561 Pegasus, Bakersfield (93308). (805) 393-1900. Licensee: Buckley Broadcasting Corp. of California. Group owner: Buckley Broadcasting Corp. (acq 12-86; $1.3 million; FTR 11-10-86). Rep: D & R Radio. Format: Adult contemp. ■ Richard D. Buckley Jr., pres; Randy Warwick, gen mgr; Susi Klassen, gen sls mgr; Doug Fleniken, adv mgr; Russ Davidson, progmg dir. ■ Rates: $40; 40; 40; 18.

Ojai

KKUR(FM)—Licensed to Ojai. See Oxnard.

Ontario

KNSE(AM)—1946: 1510 khz; 10 kw-D, 1 kw-N, DA-2. TL: N34 05 41 W117 36 46. 8729 E. 9th St., Rancho Cucamonga (91730). (909) 981-8893. FAX: (909) 981-2032. Licensee: Coronado Four-County Broadcasting Inc. (acq 9-81; $1.1 million; FTR 9-21-81). Rep: Lotus. Format: Sp. ■ Tom Castro, pres; Francisco Oaxaca, vp; Malu Hernandez, progmg dir; Humberto Hernandez, news dir & gen mgr.

KREA(FM)—1967: 93.5 mhz; 3 kw. Ant -165 ft. TL: N34 10 35 W117 34 27. Stereo. Box 3520 (91761-1030); Suite C-200, 3602 Inland Empire Dr. (91764). (213) 389-1000. Licensee: Chagal Broadcasting (acq 7-14-93; $4.2 million; FTR 8-2-93). Format: Korean. ■ Kelli Charleston, gen mgr; John Artal, chief engr.

Orange

KPLS(AM)—Jan 13, 1992: 830 khz; 2.5 kw-D, 1 kw-N, DA-N. TL: N33 49 43 W117 38 22. 1592-1 N. Batavia (92667). (714) 282-8300. FAX: (714) 282-8409. Licensee: Orange County Broadcasting Corp. Format: Children's progmg. ■ Daniell Villanuva Jr., pres; Brad Lusk, gen mgr; Larry Morton, chief engr.

Orange Cove

KMAK(FM)—Oct 27, 1990: 100.3 mhz; 72 w. Ant 2,073 ft. TL: N36 44 45 W119 16 58. Stereo. Hrs opn: 24. Box 5, 1921 Bauder St., Selma (93662); 640 Park Blvd., Orange Cove (93646). (209) 626-7922. FAX: (209) 896-1631. Licensee: Richard B. Smith. Net: USA. Wash atty: Arent, Fox, Kintner, Plotkin & Kahn. Format: Contemp Christian music with ministry. News progmg 10 hrs wkly. Target aud: general. ■ Richard Smith, pres, gen mgr & chief engr; Ken Johnson, prom mgr; Tim Land, progmg dir & news dir; William Ronning, mus dir.

Orcutt

KGDP(AM)—Licensed to Orcutt. See Santa Maria.

Orland

KXHM(FM)—January 1994: 106.7 mhz; 25 kw. Ant 56 ft. TL: N39 53 17 W122 37 38. Hrs opn: 24. 1620 Oak Park Ave., Chico (95928). (916) 895-3365. Licensee: Tri Counties Broadcast Group Inc. (acq 1-13-92). Wash atty: Brown, Nietert, & Kaufman. ■ Edward Abramson, pres.

Oroville

KORV(AM)—Aug 4, 1962: 1340 khz; 1 kw-U. TL: N39 30 34 W121 35 55. Hrs opn: 5:45 AM-12:05 AM. Box 1340 (95966); Suite B, 2854-B Olive Hwy. (95966). (916) 533-1340; (916) 533-3700. FAX: (916) 533-1349. Licensee: Oroville Radio Inc. (acq 4-1-73). Net: ABC/I. Wash atty: Booth, Freret & Imlay. Format: Classic hits, adult contemp, local news/sports. News staff one; news progmg 10 hrs wkly. Target aud: 35-55; young adults developing their lifestyles & working couples. ■ Vernon H. Uecker, pres & gen mgr; Bill Thibault, progmg dir & mus dir; Michael McGauley, news dir; David Logasa, pub affrs dir; James E. Walley, chief engr. ■ Rates: $16; 15; 16; 15.

KEWE(FM)—Co-owned with KORV(AM). July 6, 1979: 97.7 mhz; 6 kw. Ant 160 ft. TL: N39 30 18 W121 18 35 (CP: 1.5 kw, ant 1,276 ft.). Stereo. Hrs opn: 5:45 AM-12:05 AM. Prog sep from AM. (916) 533-3700; (916) 533-1349. Net: ABC/E. Format: Big band, btfl mus, jazz. News progmg 11 hrs wkly. Target aud: 35 plus; retired, established adults; investors, financially secure. ■ Margaret J. David, CEO; Alice M. Uecker, CFO; Bill Thibault, opns dir; Vernon H. Uecker, vp sls; Dave Logasa, progmg dir; Janet Munn, pub affrs dir.

Oxnard

KBBY(AM)—See Ventura.

KCAQ(FM)—Sept 27, 1958: 104.7 mhz; 2.85 kw. Ant 1,580 ft. TL: N34 20 53 W119 20 07. Stereo. Box 1520, (93034); Suite 270, 1701 Pacific Ave. (93033). (805) 483-1000. FAX: (805) 483-6555. Licensee: Greater Pacific Radio Exchange Inc. (acq 1-1-88). Rep: McGavren Guild. Wash atty: Leibowitz & Spencer. Format: CHR. News staff one. Target aud: 12-49. ■ Harold A. Frank, pres; B.J. Young, vp; Tim Curtin, opns dir; Heather Draugh, prom mgr; Rooster Rhodes, progmg dir; Lucy Barragan, mus dir; Tony Chelsey, news dir.

***KCRU(FM)**—Not on air, target date unknown: 89.1 mhz; 200 w. Ant 853 ft. TL: N34 06 47 W119 03 34. 1900 Pico Blvd., Santa Monica (90405). Licensee: Santa Monica Community College District.

KDAR(FM)—Oct 28, 1974: 98.3 mhz; 3 kw. Ant 240 ft. TL: N34 13 44 W119 10 16 (CP: 790 w, ant 902 ft.). Stereo. Hrs opn: 24. Box 5626 (93031); Suite 1500, 500 Esplanade Dr. (93030). (805) 485-8881; (805) 656-5327. FAX: (805) 656-5330. Licensee: ATEP Radio Inc. Group owner: Salem Communications Corp. Format: Christian talk & music. News progmg 2 hrs wkly. Target aud: 25-54; upscale adults with large families. ■ Stuart Epperson, chmn; Ed Atsinger, pres; Jeff Crabtree, gen mgr & pub affrs dir; Terri Price, gen sls mgr, mktg mgr & adv mgr; Carl Peetz, progmg dir & mus dir; Mat Mitchell, asst mus dir; Mark Pallock, chief engr.

KELF(FM)—See Camarillo.

KKUR(FM)—(Ojai). Jan 4, 1972: 105.5 mhz; 100 w. Ant 1,358 ft. TL: N34 20 57 W119 20 07 (CP: 327 w). Stereo. Hrs opn: 24. 6150 Olivas Park Dr., Ventura (93003); (805) 656-6300. FAX: (805) 644-1966. Licensee: Buena Ventura Inc. (acq 11-3-92; $725,000; FTR 11-30-92). Net: AP. Rep: Banner. Format: Hot adult contemp. News staff one; news progmg 3 hrs wkly. Target aud: 25-49; fun, upscale, classy adults. ■ Marilyn Woods, gen mgr; Gil Furillo, gen sls mgr; Teri Hannan, prom mgr; Tim Curtin, adv mgr; Kevin Brooks, progmg mgr; Perry Van Houten, mus dir; Jennifer Quinlan, news dir; Rovolio Bayulot, engrg mgr. ■ Rates: $40; 35; 40; 30.

KKZZ(AM)—See Santa Paula.

KOXR(AM)—June 11, 1955: 910 khz; 5 kw-D, 1 kw-N, DA-2. TL: N34 16 58 W119 07 36. 418 W. Third St. (93030). (805) 487-0444. FAX: (805) 487-0444. Licensee: Lotus Oxnard Corp. Group owner: Lotus Communications Corp. (acq 12-1-70). Rep: Lotus. Format: Sp. Target aud: 25-54. ■ Howard A. Kalmenson, pres; Gines Guillen, gen mgr; Julio Maclovio Madaleno, prom dir; Marco Antonio Del Castillo, progmg dir & news dir; John Cooper, chief engr.

KVEN(AM)—See Ventura.

KXBS(FM)—See Santa Paula.

KXLM(FM)—Not on air, target date unknown: 102.9 mhz; 5.5 kw. Ant 112 ft. TL: N34 14 12 W119 12 11. #140, 250 Citrus Grove Ln. (93030). Licensee: Kext Broadcasters Inc.

Pacific Grove

***KAZU(FM)**—Oct 1, 1977: 90.3 mhz; 4.2 kw. Ant 341 ft. TL: N36 33 12 W121 47 05 (CP: TL: N36 33 09 W121 47 17). Stereo. Hrs opn: 20. Box 210, 176 Forest Ave. (93950). (408) 375-7275. FAX: (408) 375-0235. Licensee: Monterey Bay Public Broadcasting Foundation Inc. Format: Rock, blues, div, eclectic. News progmg 3 hrs wkly. Target aud: General; 25-49. Spec prog: Country 6 hrs, women's 6 hrs, gospel 5 hrs, folk 6 hrs, class 3 hrs, African 3 hrs, Caribbean 3 hrs, oldies 5 hrs wkly. ■ Marty Manson, pres; Rebecca Little, gen mgr; Nenita Arrellano, opns mgr; Antonette Gozoch, dev mgr; Peter Williams, progmg dir; Ace Lopez, mus dir; Mike Blankenbecler, chief engr. ■ Rates: $15; 15; 15; 15.

KOCN(FM)—Apr 10, 1977: 104.9 mhz; 1.8 kw. Ant 593 ft. TL: N36 33 09 W121 47 17 (CP: 105.1 mhz; 4.2 kw, ant 790 ft., TL: N36 30 38 W121 43 57). Stereo. Box KOCN, 121 Sloat Ave. (93950). (408) 375-2242. FAX: (408) 373-4268. Licensee: C.R. Pasquier Properties Inc. (acq 7-86; $1 million). Net: MBS, Unistar. Rep: Torbet. Format: Lite adult contemp. News staff one. Target aud 25-54; at work, double income households. ■ Roger P. Pasquier, pres; Cheryl J. Pasquier, vp; Mark Carbonaro, opns mgr; David Mars, progmg dir; Jim Vernon, news dir; Carl Wiliford, chief engr. ■ Rates: $45; 55; 45; 25.

Palm Desert

KEZN(FM)—Nov 28, 1977: 103.1 mhz; 640 w. Ant 590 ft. TL: N33 51 58 W116 25 56. Stereo. 72-915 Parkview Dr. (92260); Box 291 (92261). (619) 340-9383. FAX: (619) 340-5756. Licensee: Classic Broadcasting Inc. Net: Unistar. Rep: Torbet. Wash atty: Booth & Freret. Format: Adult contemp. News staff one. Target aud: 25-64. ■ Paul Posen, pres & gen mgr; Tera Lane, adv mgr; Jon Bruce, progmg dir; Willi Rose, news dir & pub affrs dir; Ken Warren, chief engr. ■ Rates: $22; 22; 22; 22.

***KHCS(FM)**—Not on air, target date unknown: 91.7 mhz; 2.5 kw. Ant 328 ft. TL: N33 41 25 W116 17 14 (CP: 681 w, ant 574 ft.). 13600 S. Prairie Ave., Hawthorne (90250). Licensee: Prairie Avenue Gospel Center.

Palm Springs

KCMJ(AM)—Feb 12, 1946: 1140 khz; 10 kw-D, 2.5 kw-N, DA-2. TL: N33 51 39 W116 28 20. Stereo. Box 1626 (92263). (619) 320-6818. FAX: (619) 320-1493. Licensee: Westminster Broadcasting Corp. (acq 9-1-61). Net: CBS. Rep: McGavren Guild. Format: Mod country, news, talk. News staff one; news progmg 2 hrs wkly. Target aud: 35-65. Spec prog: Farm 5 hrs wkly. ■ Morris Bergreen, pres; Ed Groppo, gen mgr, mktg mgr & adv mgr; Bruce Johnson, gen sls mgr; Kidd Carson, prom mgr; Gary DeMaroney, progmg dir; Bill Watson, chief engr. ■ Rates: $20; 20; 20; 10.

KDES(AM)—Oct 29, 1956: 920 khz; 5 kw-D, 1 kw-N, DA-2. TL: N33 51 29 W116 29 39. Stereo. Box 2745 (92263). (619) 325-1211. FAX: (619) 325-8163. Licensee: Tourtelot Broadcasting Co. (acq 11-9-71). Net: Unistar. Rep: D & R Radio. Format: Oldies. News staff one; news progmg 3 hrs wkly. Target aud: 25-54. ■ Joseph L. Tourtelot, pres; Joseph V. Tourtelot, vp & gen mgr; Donn Shelton, gen sls mgr; Kory Scott, prom mgr; Danny Fox, progmg dir; Kayla Stone, news dir; Barry O'Connor, chief engr. ■ Rates: $14; 14; 14; 14.

KDES-FM—Feb 10, 1963: 104.7 mhz; 42 kw. Ant 540 ft. TL: N33 51 56 W116 26 04. Stereo. Wash atty: Hogan & Hatson.

KPLM(FM)—Jan 24, 1983: 106.1 mhz; 50 kw. Ant 391 ft. TL: N33 52 14 W116 13 39. Stereo. Hrs opn: 24. Box 1825 (92263). (619) 320-4550. FAX: (619) 320-3037. Licensee: R Group Broadcasting Corp. (acq 4-28-86). Rep: Katz. Wash atty: Koteen & Naftalin. Format: Lite contemp. Target aud: 25-54. ■ Arthur Rivkin, chmn; Jim Keye, gen mgr; Todd Marker, sls dir; Al Gordon, progmg dir; Ed Craig, chief engr. ■ Rates: $35; 40; 35; 20.

***KPSC(FM)**—April 1978: 88.5 mhz; 3 kw. Ant 266 ft. TL: N33 52 14 W116 13 39. Stereo. Hrs opn: 24. Box 77913, Los Angeles (90007-0913). (213) 743-5872. FAX: (213) 743-5853. Licensee: University of Southern California (acq 9-9-86). Net: APR. Wash atty: Brinig & Bernstein. Format: Class. News progmg 9 hrs wkly. Target aud: 35 plus; general. Spec prog: Jazz one hr, Sp 2 hrs, ethnic 2 hrs wkly. ■ Wallace A. Smith, pres & gen mgr; Bill Kappelman, vp & engrg dir; Larry Mayer, opns mgr; Maryanne Horton, dev dir; Lyle Henry, chief engr.

KPSI(AM)—1969: 1450 khz; 1 kw-U. TL: N33 48 02 W116 30 25. Hrs opn: 24. 2100 E. Tahquitz Canyon Way (92262). (619) 325-2582; (619) 320-8255. FAX: (619) 322-3562. Licensee: KPSI Radio Corp. Net: ABC/I, ABC TalkRadio, Daynet, BRN. Rep: Christal. Wash atty: Cohn & Marks. Format: News/talk. News staff 2; news progmg 5 hrs wkly. Target aud: 25 plus; upscale, informed, involved adults. ■ Rozene Supple, pres; Ric Supple, CFO; Terry Masters (aka Bob Clark), gen mgr; Scott Crisman, opns mgr; Kirk Gregory, gen sls mgr & natl sls mgr; Gregg Aratin, rgnl sls mgr; Mike Keane, prom dir; Paul Johnson, progmg dir; Mike Meenan, news dir & pub affrs dir; Steve Karwan, chief engr.

KPSI-FM—June 1980: 100.5 mhz; 25 kw. Ant 121 ft. TL: N33 56 44 W116 24 34. Stereo. Prog sep from AM. (619) 323-1005. Format: CHR. Spec prog: American Top-40, Rick Dee's Weekly Top 40, Newspage (pub affrs). ■ Roger Douglas, mus dir.

KWXY(AM)—See Cathedral City.

KWXY-FM—See Cathedral City.

Palmdale

KUTY(AM)—August 1957: 1470 khz; 5 kw-U, DA-2. TL: N34 39 55 W118 00 40. Stereo. Hrs opn: 24. Q-9, 570 East Ave. (93550). (805) 947-3107. FAX: (805) 272-5688. Licensee: Fontana Steel Inc. (acq 7-8-81; $400,000; FTR 7-27-81). Rep: Lotus. Wash atty: Arent, Fox, Kintner, Plotkin & Kahn. Format: Sp. News staff 2; news progmg 20 hrs wkly. Target aud: 18-49; homeowners, married couples with discretionary income. ■ P. Dale

Ware Ph.D., vp, gen mgr & natl sls mgr; Patricia G. Ware, opns mgr; Art Furtado (local), rgnl sls mgr; Emmett Harrington, prom dir; Pepe Delgado, progmg dir & mus dir; Rob Marinko, news dir; Pierre Luissi, chief engr.

Palo Alto

KDFC(AM)—1947: 1220 khz; 5 kw-D, 147 w-N. TL: N37 29 04 W122 08 04. Hrs opn: 24. 2822 Van Ness Ave., San Francisco (94109). (415) 441-5332. FAX: (415) 441-0890. Licensee: Brown Broadcasting Corp. Rep: CBS. Format: Class. ■ David Kendrick, gen mgr; Erick Steinberg, stn mgr; K. Tyler Phelps, opns dir; Linda Frame, gen sls mgr; William O'Connell, progmg dir; Tim Posar, chief engr.

KDFC-FM—See San Francisco.

*KZSU(FM)—See Stanford.

Paradise

KHSL-FM—Oct 15, 1983: 103.5 mhz; 1.61 kw. Ant 1250 ft. TL: N39 48 25 W121 37 35 Stereo. Box 489, Chico (95927); 3490 Silver Bell Rd., Chico (95926). (916) 872-9270. FAX: (916) 893-8937. Licensee: KRIJ Partners. Net: SMN. Rep: Eastman. Wash atty: Haley, Bader & Potts Format: Country. News staff one; news progmg 6 hrs wkly. Target aud: 25-54; active. ■ Rick Ramirez, pres; Gary Weinstein, exec vp & gen mgr; Sharon Bonds, stn mgr; Dori McKay, pub affrs dir; Roger Daeschner, chief engr. ■ Rates: $16; 16; 16; 14.

KKXX(AM)—September 1960: 930 khz; 1 kw-D, 37 w-N. TL: N39 43 37 W121 40 45 (CP: 500 w-N). Box 2020 (95967). (916) 877-3872. Licensee: Butte Broadcasting Co. (acq 12-21-66). Format: Talk, relg. ■ Carl J. Auel, pres; Ron Warkentin, gen mgr & news dir; Sarah Warkentin, mus dir; Don Perkins, chief engr.

KZZP(FM)—June 4, 1977: 96.7 mhz; 3 kw. Ant 328 ft. TL: N39 47 01 W121 40 37. Stereo. Box 7950, Chico (95927); 407 W. 9th St., Chico (95928). (916) 893-4797. FAX: (916) 895-3740. Licensee: Paradise Broadcasting Inc. (acq 12-20-79). Format: Hot adult contemp. ■ Steve Berger, pres; Mickey Franko, vp; M. Wayne Walker, gen mgr; Susan Karis, gen sls mgr; Kathy Buran, rgnl sls mgr; Bill Knoop, prom mgr; Steve Elliot, progmg dir; Jon Zellner, mus dir; Kathy Hart, news dir; Don Watkins, vp engrg; Robert Rexmont, engrg dir; Todd Clark, chief engr.

Pasadena

KAZN(AM)—Sept 12, 1942: 1300 khz; 5 kw-D, 1 kw-N, DA-2. TL: N34 09 38 W118 04 46. Stereo. Hrs opn: 20. 800 Sierra Madre Villa Ave. (91107); Box 70068 (91117). (213) 388-1300; (818) 351-4301. FAX: (818) 351-4204. Licensee: Pan Asia Broadcasting, Inc. (acq 6-24-91; $7.5 million; FTR 7-15-91). Wash atty: Haley, Bader & Potts. Format: Asian languages. News progmg 7 hrs wkly. Target aud: Asian; Chinese, Tagalog, Thai, Vietnamese. ■ Edward A. Kim, chmn & pres; Gary Pinckard, chief engr.

KMAX(FM)—See Arcadia.

*KPCC(FM)—September 1957: 89.3 mhz; 680 w. Ant 2,922 ft. TL: N34 13 35 W118 03 58. Stereo. 1570 E. Colorado Blvd. (91106). (818) 585-7000. FAX: (818) 585-7916. Licensee: Pasadena Area Community College District Board of Trustees. Net: NPR. Format: Div. News staff one; news progmg 41 hrs wkly. Target aud: 18-49. Spec prog: Black one hr, Sp 6 hrs, German 5 hrs, Greek 2 hrs, Polish one hr, class 3 hrs, country 2 hrs wkly. ■ Rod Foster, gen mgr; Kaye Adler, dev dir; Larry Mantle, progmg dir; Rene Engel, mus dir; Fred Johnson, asst mus dir; Zoe Walrond, news dir; Beth Cooper, pub affrs dir; Larry Teffeteller, chief engr.

KPPC(AM)—December 1924: 1240 khz; 250 w-U. TL: N34 08 47 W118 08 18. 3844 E. Foothill Blvd. (91106). (818) 577-1240. Licensee: KPPC Inc. Group owner: Universal Broadcasting Corp. (acq 2-84). Format: Inspirational, ethnic. ■ Linda Johnson Hayes, gen mgr; Mark Pombey, progmg dir & chief engr.

KRLA(AM)—Feb 7, 1942: 1110 khz; 50 kw-D, 20 kw-N, DA-2. TL: N34 06 50 W117 59 51. Stereo. 3580 Wilshire Blvd., Los Angeles (90010). (213) 383-4222. FAX: (213) 386-3649. Licensee: Greater Media Inc. (group owner; acq 2-3-85). Rep: Major Mkt. Format: Oldies. ■ Allan D. Chlowitz, gen mgr; Jan Kopic, gen sls mgr; Shelly Harada, prom mgr; Mike Wagner, progmg dir; Ruth Collander, pub affrs dir; David Ping, chief engr.

KROQ-FM—1974: 106.7 mhz; 5 kw. Ant 2,000 ft. TL: N34 11 47 W118 15 30. Box 10670, Burbank (91510); 3500 W. Olive Ave., Burbank (91505). (818) 567-1067. FAX: (818) 520-1329. Licensee: Infinity Broadcasting of Los Angeles Inc. Group owner: Infinity Broadcasting Corp. (acq 8-15-86). Format: Rock (AOR). ■ Tony Berardini, sr vp; Trip Reeb, gen mgr; Andy Uris, gen sls mgr; Stacie Siefert, prom dir; Kevin Weatherly, progmg dir; Boyd "Doc" Britton, news dir; Scott Mason, chief engr.

Paso Robles

KDDB(FM)—Listing follows KPRL(AM).

KPRL(AM)—Oct 1, 1946: 1230 khz; 1 kw-U. TL: N35 39 15 W120 40 52. Box 7 (93447). (805) 543-6818. FAX: (805) 238-5332. Licensee: Dellar Broadcasting Co. (acq 8-3-81; $1 million with co-located FM: FTR 8-10-90). Net: ABC/I, CBS. Rep: D & R Radio. Wash atty: Haley, Bader & Potts. Format: News, sports, talk. News staff 2; news progmg 30 hrs wkly. Target aud: 25 plus. ■ Mrs. Lincoln Dellar, pres; Kathy Signorelli, gen mgr; Kevin Will, opns mgr & progmg dir; Ron Fisher, news dir; Bill Bordeaux, chief engr. ■ Rates: $18; 18; 18; na.

KDDB(FM)—Co-owned with KPRL(AM). Nov 20, 1972: 92.5 mhz; 17 kw. Ant 760 ft. TL: N35 38 45 W120 44 16 (CP: 4.8 kw, ant 1,428 ft.). Stereo. Hrs opn: 24. Prog sep from AM. (805) 543-5332. FAX: (805) 543-8950. Format: Country. News staff one; news progmg 12 hrs wkly. Target aud: 18 plus. Spec prog: Public affairs. ■ Joe McMahon, gen mgr; Kathy Signorelli, stn mgr; Tom Keffuney, opns mgr; J.C. Stevens, progmg dir; Diana Caine, news dir. ■ Rates: Same as AM.

KTBG(FM)—Not on air, target date unknown: 103.1 mhz; 1.2 kw. Ant 722 ft. 685 E. California, Pasadena (91106). Licensee: Andy J. Fakas (acq 7-8-93; $22,500; FTR 8-2-93).

Patterson

KZMS(FM)—Not on air, target date unknown: 97.1 mhz; 145 w. Ant 164 ft. 3090 Goodwin Ave., Redwood City (94061). Licensee: J.B. Broadcasting Inc.

KOSO(FM)—Licensed to Patterson. See Modesto.

Pebble Beach

*KSPB(FM)—Sept 22, 1978: 91.9 mhz; 1 kw. Ant 485 ft. TL: N36 35 11 W121 55 21. Box 657 (93953). (408) 626-5374 EXT. 68; (408) 626-5374. FAX: (408) 625-5208. Licensee: Robert Louis Stevenson School. Format: Progsv. Spec prog: Black 18 hrs, oldies 4 hrs, reggae 2 hrs, hard rock 2 hrs wkly. ■ Ernie DeKine, stn mgr; Mike Beck, progmg dir; Alex Tang, mus dir.

Petaluma

KTOB(AM)—Jan 10, 1950: 1490 khz; 1 kw-U. TL: N35 39 15 W120 40 52. Hrs opn: 19. 12 E. Washington St. (94952). (707) 766-9996. Licensee: Petaluma Broadcasting Corp. ($20,000; FTR 8-23-93). Net: Unistar. Format: Adult contemp. Target aud: 35-49. ■ Dave Devoto, pres; Dan Hess, gen mgr; Ken Carpenter, progmg dir; George McManus, news dir.

Philo

*KZYX(FM)—Oct 1989: 90.7 mhz; 3.41 kw. Ant 1,686 ft. TL: N39 01 22 W123 31 17. Box one (95466). (707) 895-2324. FAX: (707) 895-2451. Licensee: Mendocino County Public Broadcasting. Net: NPR. Format: Div. News staff one; news progmg 27 hrs wkly. Target aud: General. Spec prog: Black 8 hrs, class 14 hrs, folk 8 hrs, gospel 2 hrs, jazz 11 hrs, blues 3 hrs. ■ Dianne Hering, prom dir; Nicole Sawaya, progmg dir; Joseph Leon, news dir; Ron O'Brien, chief engr.

Pismo Beach

KWBR(FM)—Dec 7, 1974: 95.3 mhz; 4.2 kw. Ant 390 ft. TL: N35 09 24 W120 38 11. Stereo. Hrs opn: 24. Suite 229, 1303 Grand Ave, Arroyo Grande (93420). (805) 473-2778. FAX: (805) 473-2438. Licensee: Maverick Broadcasting Co. (acq 11-21-89). Rep: Eastman. Wash atty: Fisher, Wayland, Cooper & Leader. Format: AOR. News staff one; news progmg one hr wkly. Target aud: 18-34. Spec prog: Talk one hr wkly. ■ Chad Elison, gen mgr; Jeffrey Lind, gen sls mgr; John Bowman, prom dir; Dianna Smart, progmg dir & news dir; John Mackey, mus dir; Paul Kleinkramer, chief engr. ■ Rates: $30; 27; 30; 20.

Pittsburg

KATD(AM)—September 1949: 990 khz; 5 kw-D, DA-2. TL: N38 04 49 W121 50 33. 1251 Monument Blvd., Concord (94520). (510) 827-9900. FAX: (510) 674-1980. Licensee: People's Radio Inc. Net: UPI. Format: Adult contemp. ■ Joe Buerry, gen mgr; Jay Michaels, progmg dir; Mike Martindale, chief engr.

Placerville

KZSA(FM)—Dec 9, 1982: 92.1 mhz; 1.41 kw. Ant 446 ft. TL: N38 43 07 W120 47 40 (CP: Ant 472 ft.). Stereo. Suite 17, 4050 Flying C Rd., Cameron Park (95682). (916) 676-5996. Licensee: KZSA Broadcasting Inc. Net: BRN. Format: Sp, news/talk. News staff one. Target aud: 25-54. ■ Rates: $65; 50; 65; 35.

Pomona

KMNY(AM)—May 12, 1947: 1600 khz; 5 kw-U, DA-N. TL: N34 01 48 W117 43 35. 2300 S. Mills (91766). (909) 627-1600. FAX: (909) 465-1517. Licensee: Money Radio Inc. Format: Bus news & talk. News staff 6. Target aud: 30 plus; money oriented. ■ Buz Schwartz, CEO, gen mgr & opns dir; Vera Gold, exec vp & gen sls mgr; Margaret Melanie, progmg mgr; Amy Kremer, news dir; Rudy Agus, chief engr. ■ Rates: $150; 150; 150; 100.

KTSJ(AM)—Dec 23, 1960: 1220 khz; 250 w-U, DA-2, 1000 w. TL: N34 01 11 W117 43 03 (CP: 930 w-D). Hrs opn: 20. Box 847, Claremont (91711-0847). (909) 621-0884. FAX: (9090 621-0351. Licensee: American Sunrise Communications (acq 8-1-80). Net: USA, Moody. Format: Relg. News staff one; news progmg 7 hrs wkly. Target aud: 24-64. Spec prog: Sp 15 hrs wkly. ■ John Boyd, pres; Paul Johnson, opns dir; Cauhudemoc Ageuilar, progmg dir; Jose Martinez, mus dir; John Artal, vp engrg. ■ Rates: $16; 16; 16; 16.

Port Hueneme

KCAQ(FM)—See Oxnard.

KTRO(AM)—July 1958: 1520 khz; 10 kw-D, 1 kw-N, DA-2. TL: N34 10 02 W119 08 02. Box 1520, Oxnard (93034); Suite 270, 1701 Pacific Ave., Oxnard (93033). (805) 483-1000. FAX: (805) 483-6555. Licensee: Greater Pacific Radio Exchange Inc. (acq 1-1-88). Rep: Katz. Wash atty: Leibowitz & Spencer. Format: Sp. News staff one. Target aud: 18-49. ■ Harold A. Frank, pres & gen mgr; B.J. Young, stn mgr & opns dir; Tim Curtin, sls dir; Lloyd Maxwell, prom mgr; Jose Luis Pedroza, progmg dir; Abel Perez, mus dir; Alfredo Tristan, news dir; Al Taddeo, chief engr.

Porterville

KTIP(AM)—1947: 1450 khz; 1 kw-U. TL: N36 05 44 W119 03 10. 1616 N. Newcomb (93257). (209) 784-1450. FAX: (209) 784-2482. Licensee: Double M Broadcasting Inc. (acq 2-11-91; $91,453 with co-located FM; FTR 2-25-91). Net: AP. Format: Easy lstng, adult contemp. News staff 2; news progmg 10 hrs wkly. Target aud: 35 plus. ■ Bob Athey, gen mgr & progmg dir; Linda Burl, gen sls mgr; John Quinlan, news dir; Bill Piotter, chief engr.

KIOO(FM)—Co-owned with KTIP(AM). Aug 1, 1972: 99.7 mhz; 24 kw. Ant 690 ft. TL: N36 06 26 W119 01 45. Stereo. Prog sep from AM. (209) 781-5100. Format: Adult top tracks. News staff one; news progmg one hr wkly. Target aud: 25-44; active adults, upscale & mobile. Spec prog: Jazz 5 hrs wkly.

Prunedale

*KLVM(FM)—Feb 28, 1986: 89.7 mhz; 54 w. Ant 1,907 ft. TL: N36 45 22 W121 30 05. Stereo. Rebroadcasts KLVR(FM) Santa Rosa 90%. 8145 Prunedale N. Rd. (93907). (408) 663-6022. FAX: (408) 663-5110. Licensee: Prunedale Educational Assoc. Format: Light contemp Christian mus. Target aud: 20-49. ■ E.L. Moon, pres & gen mgr; Skip Bushell, chief engr.

Quincy

KNLF(FM)—Not on air, target date unknown: 103.1 mhz; 3 kw. Ant -499 ft. TL: N39 58 03 W120 53 34. Box 117, 440 Lawrence (95971). (916) 283-4144. Licensee: New Life Broadcasting. Net: CBN, USA. Format: Relg. ■ Ron Trumbo, pres.

KPCO(AM)—Aug 16, 1963: 1370 khz; 5 kw-D, 500 w-N, DA-2. TL: N39 56 54 W120 53 54. Hrs opn: 24. Box 11370, 395 Main St. (95971). (916) 283-1370. Licensee: Ralph W. Wittick (acq 12-24-74). Net: CBS Spectrum. Format: AM only- Unistar Satellite 40's-70's. News staff one. Format aud: General. Spec prog: Relg one hr wkly. ■ Ralph Wittick, pres, gen mgr & gen sls mgr; Lindsay Miller, prom mgr & vp progmg. ■ Rates: $11; 9.75; 11; 9.75.

KQNC(FM)—May 25, 1983: 101.9 mhz; 1.85 kw. Ant 2,115 ft. TL: N40 03 36 W120 54 46. Stereo. 1575 Delucchi Lane, Reno, NV (89502). (702) 828-8240. FAX: (702) 828-8246. Licensee: Olympic Broadcasters Inc. (acq 8-14-87). Format: Adult contemp. Spec prog: Class 5 hrs wkly. ■ Magda Martinez, gen mgr.

KSPY(FM)—Not on air, target date Summer 1994: 100.3 mhz; 3 kw. Ant -495 ft. TL: N39 58 03 W120 53 34. 1548 El Camino, Stockton (95209); Box 77766, Stockton (95267). (209) 946-7900. FAX: (209) 946-7902. Licensee: John K. LaRue.

Rancho Cordova

KSTE(AM)—Apr 19, 1990: 650 khz; 25 kw-D, 1 kw-N, DA-2. TL: N38 28 46 W121 16 34. Box 417250, Sacramento (95841). (916) 334-6500. FAX: (916) 349-0407. Licensee: Fuller-Jeffrey Broadcasting Corp. (acq 12-9-92; $1 million; FTR 1-4-93). Rep: Torbet. Format: Talk. News staff 4; news progmg 15 hrs wkly. Target aud: 25-54. ■ Robert Fuller, pres; Drew Houghton, CFO; J.J. Jeffrey, sr vp; David Burke, vp & gen mgr; Michael Espinosa, opns mgr; Donna Reed, gen sls mgr; Rick Stewart, news dir; Jay Rose, chief engr. ■ Rates: $120; 75; 75; 40.

Red Bluff

KALF(FM)—1978: 95.7 mhz; 7 kw. Ant 1,265 ft. TL: N39 55 03 W122 40 12. Stereo. Hrs opn: 24. Box 7950, Suite F, 312 Otterson, Chico (95927). (916) 343-5253. FAX: (916) 343-5491. Licensee: McNulty Broadcasting Corp. (acq 11-87). Rep: Katz & Powell. Wash atty: Smithwick & Belendiuk. Format: Country. News staff one; news progmg 10 hrs wkly. Target aud: 25-54. ■ Charles Wilkinson, CEO, vp opns, & engrg dir; Laura Wilkinson, pres, gen mgr, vp sls & vp mktg; Lisa Hamilton, rgnl sls mgr & adv mgr; Randy Chapman, vp progmg, mus dir & engrg mgr; Russ Matthews, news dir; Mark Amone, pub affrs dir.

KBLF(AM)—1946: 1490 khz; 1 kw-U. TL: N40 11 28 W122 12 54. Stereo. Box 1490, 20639 W. Walnut St. (96080). (916) 527-1490. FAX: (916) 527-3525. Licensee: Night Hawk Communications Inc. (acq 1993; $135,000; FTR 9-13-93). Net: AP, ABC/I. Format: Oldies, news/talk. News staff 2; news progmg 15 hrs wkly. Target aud: 25 plus. Spec prog: Farm 5 hrs, Sp 4 hrs wkly. ■ Greg Crawford, pres, mktg mgr & progmg dir; Anne Crawford, vp opns; Jennifer Martin, sls dir. ■ Rates: $12; 12; 12; 12.

KZAP(FM)—November 1985: 102.7 mhz; 12 kw. Ant 1,017 ft. TL: N40 15 46 W122 05 37. c/o California Radio Inc., 1525 E. Shaw Ave., Fresno (93710). Licensee: McCarthy Wireless Inc. (acq 4-1-93; $326,000; FTR 4-19-93). Rep: D & R Radio. Format: Adult contemp.

Redding

KARZ(FM)—(Burney). May 1985: 106.1 mhz; 100 kw. Ant 2,000 ft. TL: N40 54 21 W121 49 38. Stereo. Hrs opn: 24. Box 492890, Redding (96049); Suite C, 4352 Caterpillar Rd., Redding (96003). (916) 243-2222. FAX: (916) 243-2321. Licensee: Merit Broadcasting Corp. (group owner). Rep: Christal. Wash atty: Grif Johnson. Format: Adult contemp. News staff 2. Target aud: 25-54; upscale. ■ Jeff Martin, chmn; Mike Martin, vp; Jane Martin, vp opns; Trish Eversale, opns mgr; Kathryn Mincer, sls dir; John Butler, prom dir; Gary Moore, progmg dir; George Newcom, news dir; Jim Bremer, chief engr.

KNRO(AM)—Co-owned with KARZ(FM). Nov 26, 1936: 600 khz; 1 kw-U. TL: N40 37 13 W122 19 56. Hrs opn: 24. Prog sep from FM. (916) 243-2222. (acq 1977). Format: News/talk. News staff 6; news progmg 24 hrs wkly. Target aud: 25 plus; upscale, informed adults. ■ Jeff Martin, pres & adv dir; Mike Martin, exec vp; George Newcom, progmg dir; Nick Bais, news dir; Jim Bremer, pub affrs dir & engrg dir.

KEWB(FM)—See Anderson.

***KFPR(FM)**—Not on air, target date unknown: 88.9 mhz; 1.3 kw. Ant 1,499 ft. First and Normal, Chico (95929). Licensee: Univ. Foundation, California State Univ., Chico.

KLXR(AM)—August 1956: 1230 khz; 1 kw-U. TL: N40 33 14 W122 22 53. Suite 104, 5000 Bechilli Ln. (96002). (916) 241-5597. FAX: (916) 223-3434. Licensee: Redding Radio Corp. (acq 5-20-93; $94,900; FTR 6-14-93). Format: Full svc. ■ Frank Jolle, pres & gen mgr; Ron Davis, gen sls mgr; Jim Anderson, prom mgr; Jim Stevens, progmg dir; Kelly Frost, mus dir; Bud Foster, news dir; Bob Belongie, chief engr.

KNCQ(FM)—Oct 29, 1985: 97.3 mhz; 28 kw. Ant 3,569 ft. TL: N40 36 10 W122 38 58. Stereo. 1588 Charles Dr. (96003-1459). (916) 244-9700. FAX: (916) 244-9707. Licensee: McCarthy Wireless Inc. Rep: D & R Radio. Format: Contemp country. ■ Craig C. McCarthy, chmn & pres; Steve Thomas, sls dir; Gary Popejoy, prom mgr, progmg dir & mus dir; Paul Bryan, news dir; Mike Johnson, chief engr.

KNRO(AM)—Listing follows KARZ(FM).

KQMS(AM)—Sept 14, 1954: 1400 khz; 1 kw-U. TL: N40 33 33 W122 19 42. Box 1400 (96049). (916) 221-1400. FAX: (916) 221-6653. Licensee: Park Lane Redding Radio Inc. Group owner: The Park Lane Group (acq 10-21-92; $1.36 million with co-located FM; FTR 11-26-92). Net: NBC, NBC Talknet. Rep: McGavren Guild. Format: News/talk. ■ James Levy, pres; John Anthony, gen mgr & stn mgr; Brett Bonner, progmg dir.

KSHA(FM)—Co-owned with KQMS(AM). Sept 1, 1981: 104.3 mhz; 100 kw. Ant 1,560 ft. TL: N40 39 14 W122 31 12. Stereo. Prog sep from AM. Format: Adult contemp. ■ Dennis Kennedy, progmg dir.

KRDG(AM)—June 1958: 1330 khz; 5 kw-D. TL: N40 31 27 W122 22 15 (CP: 5 kw-U, DA-2; TL: N40 29 07 W122 13 14). Stereo. Suite 9, 1425 N. Market Blvd, Sacramento (95834). (916) 928-1515. FAX: (916) 928-0888. Licensee: Prather-Breck Broadcasting of Redding (acq 1-1-87). Net: CBS. Format: Contemp Christian. ■ Jeff Prather, pres & gen mgr; Paul Brawn, chief engr.

KSHA(FM)—Listing follows KQMS(AM).

***KVIP(AM)**—Jan 4, 1970: 540 khz; 2.5 kw-D, 17 w-N. TL: N40 32 36 W122 21 21 (CP: TL: N40 37 25 W122 16 49). Hrs opn: 24. Box 492727 (96049-2727). 1139 Hartnell Ave. (96002). (916) 222-4455. Licensee: Pacific Cascade Communications Corp. (acq 12-69). Net: Moody, USA. Format: Inspirational, Christian. News progmg 14 hrs wkly. Target aud: General. ■ David L. Morrow, vp; Tom Woods, gen mgr, prom mgr & pub affrs dir; Ted Hering, progmg dir; Paul Brown, chief engr.

***KVIP-FM**—Oct 19, 1975: 98.1 mhz; 30 kw. Ant 1,710 ft. TL: N40 36 10 W122 38 58. Stereo. Hrs opn: 24. Format: Inspirational, Christian. ■ Ted Hering, mus dir.

Redlands

KCAL(AM)—April 1954: 1410 khz; 5 kw-D, 4 kw-N, DA-N. TL: N34 04 08 W117 12 06. Hrs opn: 24. Box 3390, 29800 Greenspot Rd., Highland (92373-0997). (909) 825-5020. Licensee: Redlands Radio Inc. (acq 1993; $3 million; FTR 9-13-93). Rep: Lotus. Format: Sp. News staff 2. Target aud: 18-49. ■ Bob Ridzak, pres; Jorge Hercules, progmg dir; Enrique Mayans, mus dir; Onleia Martinez, news dir.

KCAL-FM—1965: 96.7 mhz; 1.75 kw. Ant 377 ft. TL: N34 11 51 W117 17 10. Stereo. Suite 101, 1940 Orange Tree Ln. (92374). (909) 793-3554. FAX: (909) 798-6627. Licensee: Anaheim Broadcasting Corp. (group owner). Format: Adult rock. Target aud: 16-30. ■ Jeff Parke, gen mgr; Glen Watson, gen sls mgr; Rick Shaw, progmg dir; M.J. Matthews, mus dir; Tiffany Angelo, news dir; Clayton Creekmore, chief engr.

***KUOR-FM**—October 1966: 89.1 mhz; 35 w. Ant 2,781 ft. TL: N34 03 35 W117 09 45. Stereo. Hrs opn: 24. Box 3080 (92373); 1200 E. Colton Ave. (92374). (909) 792-0721; (909) 792-0951. FAX: (909) 793-2029. Licensee: Univ. of Redlands. Net: AP. Format: Jazz, gospel, adult contemp. News progmg 2 hrs wkly. Target aud: 25-49; educated, professional. Spec prog: German one hr, big band 5 hrs, polka 6 hrs, reggae 4 hrs wkly. ■ William Bruns, gen mgr; Scott Sterl, gen sls mgr; Dana Carson, progmg dir, news dir & pub affrs dir; Mitch McClellan, mus dir; Joel Bump, chief engr.

Redondo Beach

KFOX(FM)—Aug 4, 1961: 93.5 mhz; 3 kw. Ant 175 ft. TL: N33 48 16 W118 22 02. Stereo. 123 Torrance Blvd. (90277). (310) 374-9796. FAX: (310) 318-2578. Licensee: Chagal Communications (acq 7-14-93; $9.8 million; FTR 8-2-93). Format: Talk/information. ■ Paul Wilson, gen mgr.

Ridgecrest

KLOA(AM)—Dec 11, 1956: 1240 khz; 250 w-U. TL: N35 37 24 W117 41 10 731 N. Balsam St. (93555). (619) 375-8888. Licensee: Roy William Mayhugh (acq 1-4-89). Format: News/talk, sports. ■ Roy Mayhugh, pres, gen mgr & chief engr.

KLOA-FM—1979: 104.9 mhz; 750 w. Ant one ft. TL: N35 37 24 W117 41 10. Stereo. Prog sep from AM. Format: Country.

KZIQ(AM)—Apr 7, 1974: 1360 khz; 1 kw-D, 38 w-N. TL: N35 36 58 W117 38 35. Hrs opn: 24. 121 W. Ridgecrest Blvd. (93555). (619) 384-1360. FAX: (619) 375-4614. Licensee: James & Donna Knudsen (acq 9-30-91; $250,000 with co-located FM; FTR 10-28-91). Net: ABC/E. Rep: W.R.B.S. Wash atty: Pepper & Corazzini. Format: Country gospel. News staff one; news progmg 11 hrs wkly. Target aud: 25-54; educated adults with high disposable income. ■ James L. Knudsen, pres; Ken Fish, gen mgr & stn mgr; Todd E. Landen, vp opns; Donna L. Knudsen, vp sls, progmg dir & mus dir; David Grayson, news dir.

KZIQ-FM—Jan 1, 1978: 92.7 mhz; 1.5 kw. Ant 1,296 ft. TL: N33 36 58 W117 38 35. Stereo. Hrs opn: 24. Prog sep from AM. Net: Unistar. Format: Lite adult contemp. News progmg 2 hrs wkly. Spec prog: Ski reports, road conditions. ■ Donna L. Knudsen, stn mgr & gen sls mgr; Todd E. Landen, opns mgr; Tim Nixon, chief engr.

Rio Dell

KRVD(FM)—Not on air, target date unknown: 107.1 mhz; 3 kw. Ant 535 ft. TL: N40 30 34 W124 06 30. 96 Dyer Ave., Collinsville, CT (06022). Licensee: Douglas C. Turnbull.

Rio Vista

***KRVH(FM)**—Nov 7, 1972: 101.5 mhz; 10 w. Ant 60 ft. TL: N38 09 17 W121 41 48. 410 South 4th (94571). (707) 374-6336. FAX: (707) 374-6810. Licensee: River Delta Unified School District. Format: Contemp hit, educ. Target aud: Teen-age, young adult. ■ Albert P. Eaton, gen mgr; Jared Cox, stn mgr; Robert Gillaspie, opns dir; Joanna Davis, progmg dir.

Riverbank

KCBC(AM)—Apr 5, 1987: 770 khz; 50 kw-D, 1 kw-N, DA-2. TL: N37 47 51 W120 53 01. Stereo. Hrs opn: 24. 10948 Cleveland Ave., Oakdale (95361). (209) 847-7700. Licensee: Kiertron Inc. (acq 12-30-92; $1 million; FTR 1-25-93). Format: News/talk, relg. News staff one; news progmg 25 hrs wkly. Target aud: 25-49. ■ Don Crawford, pres; Frank Fremciosi, stn mgr; Rick Woodruff, vp opns; Daryl Peavy, vp sls; Rich Woodruff, vp mktg; Dave Whittaker, mus dir; Steve Minshall, chief engr. ■ Rates: $30; 25; 30; 18.

Riverside

KDIF(AM)—Nov 15, 1941: 1440 khz; 1 kw-U. TL: N34 01 37 W117 21 27. Hrs opn: 24. 1465 A. Spruce St. (92507). (909) 784-4210. Licensee: Hispanic Radio Broadcasters. Net: UPI. Rep: Katz. Wash atty: Haley, Bader & Potts. Format: Spanish. News progmg 7 hrs wkly. Target aud: 18-49; Hispanic young adults. ■ Gilberto Esquivel, gen mgr; Rudy Bravo, gen sls mgr; Omar Lainez, prom mgr & progmg dir; Hector DeCoronado, news dir; John Batterson, chief engr.

KFRG(FM)—See San Bernardino.

KGGI(FM)—Jan 23, 1965: 99.1 mhz; 2.55 kw. Ant 1,843 ft. TL: N34 14 04 W117 08 24. Stereo. Box 991 (92502); #200, 2001 Iowa Ave. (92507). (909) 684-1991; (909) 431-5991. Licensee: Sanriver Radio Inc. Group owner: American Media Inc. (acq 9-2-87). Net: ABC FM. Rep: McGavren Guild. Wash atty: Lathan & Watkins. Format: Top-40. ■ David Presher, gen mgr; Rachel Roe, natl sls mgr; Rachel Roe, Paul Petrilli, rgnl sls mgrs; Gina Davis, prom mgr; Carmy Ferreri, progmg dir; Ali Jordan-Guilbert, pub affrs dir; Dave Wolfe, chief engr. ■ Rates: $140; 140; 140; 90.

KHTX(FM)—Mar 17, 1959: 97.5 mhz; 68 kw. Ant 1,571 ft. TL: N33 57 57 W117 17 21. Stereo. Hrs opn: 24. Box 50005, San Bernardino (92412); Suite 302, 1950 S. Sunwest Ln., San Bernardino (92408). (909) 384-9750. FAX: (909) 884-5844. Licensee: Henry Broadcasting (group owner). Rep: Eastman. Format: Country. News staff one; news progmg 2 hrs wkly. Target aud: 25-54. ■ Charlton Buckley, pres; Jeff Salgo, vp & gen mgr; Jan Jefferies, opns mgr & progmg dir; Bob Wood, gen sls mgr; Robert Fontaine, prom mgr; Bryan Jackson, mus dir; Caroline Gracie, news dir; Stew Berger, pub affrs dir; Joe Mauk, chief engr.

KOOJ(FM)—1959: 92.7 mhz; 3 kw. Ant 298 ft. TL: N34 11 51 W117 17 09. Stereo. Suite 315, 900 E. Washington (92324). (909) 824-5005. FAX: (909) 825-0441. Licensee: Amaturo Group Ltd. (group owner; acq 1-6-93; $3.25 million; FTR 2-1-93). Net: Internet. Rep: Major Mkt. Format: Hot country. News staff one; news progmg 4 hrs wkly. Target aud: 25-54; families. ■ Richard McIntosh, gen mgr; Ed Reynolds, gen sls mgr; Dave Clark, progmg dir & mus dir.

KPRO(AM)—June 22, 1957: 1570 khz; 5 kw-D, 194 w-N, DA-2. TL: N33 55 54 W117 23 47. Hrs opn: 24. 7351 Lincoln Ave. (92504). (909) 688-1570; (909) 824-9292. FAX: (909) 688-7009. Licensee: Olive L. Sherban (acq 1957). Net: MBS. Rep: Hugh Wallace, Inc. Format: Relg. Target aud: General. ■ Ollie Sherban, pres; Ronnie Olenick, vp; Valorie Stitely, stn mgr, opns mgr & gen sls mgr; Robert Johnston, progmg dir; Dennis Brougher, mus dir; Bill Elledge, chief engr. ■ Rates: $18; 18; 18; 12.

***KSGN(FM)**—January 1970: 89.7 mhz; 3 kw. Ant 300 ft. TL: N34 11 51 W117 17 10. Stereo. Hrs opn: 24. 11498 Pierce St. (92505). (714) 687-5746. FAX: (714) 785-2288. Licensee: KSGN Inc. Net: USA. Wash atty: Hamel & Park. Format: Relg, Christian educ. News progmg 12 hrs wkly. Target aud: General; Christians & church-goers. ■ Lee McIntyre, CEO, pres & mktg dir; Dale McCune, chmn; Bruce Potterton, CFO, gen mgr & engrg dir; John Parrish, vp dev; Jon Foreman, sls dir & chief engr; Jackie Neff, mktg mgr, prom mgr & news dir; Dawn Hibbard, progmg dir, mus dir & pub affrs dir.

***KUCR(FM)**—October 1966: 88.3 mhz; 750 w. Ant 291 ft. TL: N33 58 11 W117 17 50. Stereo. Univ. of Calif. (92521). (909) 787-3737. FAX: (909) 787-3240. Licensee: The Regents of the Univ. of California. Format: Div, alternative rock. Spec prog: Black 18 hrs, class 14 hrs, jazz 6 hrs wkly. ■ Louis Van Den Berg, gen mgr; Bill Elledge, chief engr.

Rocklin

KEBR(AM)—July 27, 1988: 1210 khz; 5 kw-D, 500 w-N, DA-D. TL: N38 27 46 W121 07 49. Hrs opn: 24. 3108 Fulton Ave., Sacramento (95821). (916) 481-8191. FAX: (916) 481-0410. Licensee: Family Stations Inc. (group owner). Format: Relg. Target aud: General. ■ Harold Camping, pres; Scott L. Smith, vp; Peggy Renschler, stn mgr, opns mgr & pub affrs dir; Don Perkins, chief engr.

Rohnert Park

KRPQ(FM)—Mar 4, 1986: 104.9 mhz; 340 w. Ant 915 ft. TL: N38 23 32 W122 39 54. Hrs opn: 24. Suite 202, 6640 Redwood Dr. (94928). (707) 584-1058. FAX: (707) 584-7944. Licensee: Sunrise Broadcasting Co. Ltd. Wash atty: Fletcher, Heald & Childreth. Format: Contemp country. Target aud: 25-54. ■ Ronald E. Castro, pres, progmg dir & chief engr; Gary Steel, gen sls mgr.

Rohnerville

KQEX(FM)—May 15, 1992: 100.5 mhz; 200 w. Ant 1,722 ft. TL: N40 30 03 W124 17 10 (CP: COL: Fortuna, CA, 100.3 mhz, 800 w, ant 1,686 ft.). 1713 Main St., Fortuna (95540). (707) 725-3408. FAX: (707) 725-3408. Licensee: North Star Communications. Format: Soft adult contemp. ■ Steven Hastings, gen mgr; Steve Parlato, stn mgr & gen sls mgr.

Rosamond

KAVC(FM)—Mar 1, 1985: 105.5 mhz; 3 kw. Ant 328 ft. TL: N34 51 03 W118 09 22. Stereo. Box 2069, Suite 201, 43301 N. Division, Lancaster (93536). (805) 945-0873. Licensee: Oasis Radio Inc. Group owner: Salem Communications Corp. (acq 4-10-86). Format: Christian, talk. News progmg 4 hrs wkly. ■ Edward G. Atsinger III, CFO; Dan Craig, stn mgr; Andy Waits, opns mgr; Heather Welch, sls dir; Mark Pallock, chief engr.

KLKX(FM)—Sept 1, 1993: 93.5 mhz; 3 kw. Ant 207 ft. 570 East Ave., Palmdale (93550). (805) 947-3107. FAX: (805) 272-5688. Licensee: Waremar Communications Inc. (Rosamond Radio). Net: Katz & Powell. Wash atty: Arent, Fox, Kintner, Plotkin & Kahn. Format: Classic rock, news. News progmg 20 hrs wkly. Target aud: 25-49; baby boomers, homeowners, married couples with disposable income. ■ P. Dale Ware, pres, CFO & progmg dir; Salvador D. Martinez, vp & natl sls mgr; Patricia G. Ware, opns mgr; Art Furtado, rgnl sls mgr; Emmett Harrington, prom dir; Kevin Barrett, mus dir; Rob Marinko, news dir; Pierre Luissi, chief engr.

Roseville

KRCX(AM)—Apr 1, 1968: 1110 khz; 5 kw-D, 500 w-N, DA-2. TL: N38 44 22 W121 12 48. Box 417250, Sacramento (95841). (916) 349-1100. FAX: (916) 349-0407. Licensee: Fuller-Jeffrey Broadcasting of the Sacramento Valley. Group owner: Fuller-Jeffrey Broadcasting Companies Inc. (acq 1-1-84; FTR 12-19-83). Net: CNN. Rep: Caballero. Format: Sp. ■ Robert F. Fuller, pres; Drew Houghton, CFO; J.J. Jeffrey, sr vp; David Burke, vp & gen mgr; Bob Breck, gen sls mgr & prom mgr; Jose Reynoso, progmg dir; Armando Botello, news dir; Jay Rose, chief engr. ■ Rates: $75; 65; 70; 50.

KRXQ(FM)—Licensed to Roseville. See Sacramento.

Sacramento

KCBC(AM)—See Riverbank.

KCTC(AM)—April 1945: 1320 khz; 5 kw-U, DA-2. TL: N38 42 42 W121 19 44. Stereo. Hrs opn: 24. 2225 19th St. (95818). (916) 441-5272. FAX: (916) 446-4142. Licensee: Tribune Sacramento Radio Inc. Group owner: Tribune Broadcasting Co. (acq 8-15-78). Net: Unistar. Rep: Christal. Format: Nostaglia, sports. Target aud: 35 plus. ■ Doug Stewart, pres & gen mgr; Mike Shores, opns mgr; Mike Knox, gen sls mgr & natl sls mgr; Roy Kingi, prom dir; Mike Shopes, progmg dir; Charlie Weiss, news dir; James Balcom, chief engr.

KYMX(FM)—Co-owned with KCTC(AM). 1947: 96.1 mhz; 50 kw. Ant 476 ft. TL: N38 38 09 W121 33 11. Stereo. Hrs opn: 24. Prog sep from AM. (916) 441-5282. Format: Soft adult contemp. Target aud: 25-54.

***KEDR(FM)**—1992: 88.3 mhz; 50 kw-V. Ant 472 ft. TL: N38 26 58 W121 04 24. Stereo. Hrs opn: 24. 3108 Fulton Ave. (95821). (916) 481-8191. FAX: (916) 481-0410. Licensee: Family Stations Inc. (group owner). Format: Relg. ■ Harold Camping, pres; Scott L. Smith, vp; Peggy Renschler, gen mgr & opns mgr.

KFBK(AM)—1922: 1530 khz; 50 kw-U, DA-2. TL: N38 50 54 W121 28 58. Suite 200, 1440 Ethan Way (95825). (916) 929-5325. TWX: (910) 367-0296. Licensee: Westinghouse Broadcasting Co. (group owner; acq 10-1-87). Net: AP, ABC/I, ABC TalkRadio, CNN. Rep: Group W. Format: News/talk. News staff 26; news progmg 60 hrs wkly. ■ James Thompson, pres; Rick Eytcheson, gen mgr; Jan Shay, gen sls mgr; Susan Rivieccio, natl sls mgr; Joyce Krieg, prom mgr; Betsy Braziel, progmg dir; Dale Harry, chief engr.

KGBY(FM)—Co-owned with KFBK(AM). 1946: 92.5 mhz; 50 kw. Ant 499 ft. TL: N38 42 26 W121 28 33. Stereo. Prog sep from AM. Format: Adult contemp. ■ Melonie Polka, prom mgr; Jeff Sattler, progmg dir; Vince Garcia, mus dir.

KFIA(AM)—See Carmichael.

KGBY(FM)—Listing follows KFBK(AM).

KJAY(AM)—May 23, 1963: 1430 khz; 500 w-D, DA. TL: N38 29 39 W121 32 47. 5030 S. River Rd., West Sacramento (95691); 217 Breckenwood Way, Sacramento (95864). (916) 371-5101; (916) 972-0262. Licensee: Jack L. Powell (acq 12-1-65). Wash atty: Lester Spillane. Format: Black, relg, talk. News progmg 2 hrs wkly. Target aud: 25-64. Spec prog: It one hr, Ger 2 hrs, Indian 2 hrs, jazz 5 hrs, big band 5 hrs wkly. ■ Jack L. Powell, CEO, pres, gen mgr & gen sls mgr; Jerry Sieber, vp opns; Trudi Powell, prom mgr & mus dir; Tif Powell, vp progmg & news dir; Alan Graft, chief engr. ■ Rates: $27; 27; 27; na.

KNCI(FM)—Nov 1, 1959: 98.5 mhz; 50 kw. Ant 500 ft. TL: N38 38 35 W121 05 51 (CP: TL: N38 38 53 W121 05 51). Stereo. Hrs opn: 24. Box 15985 (95852-1985); 298 Commerce Circle (95815-4212). (916) 925-3700. FAX: (916) 925-8898. Licensee: Nationwide Communications Inc. (group owner; acq 3-15-85). Rep: McGavren Guild. Wash atty: Fletcher, Heald & Hildreth. Format: Country. News staff one. Target aud: 25-40; males. Spec prog: Blues one hr wkly. ■ Steve Berger, pres; Thomas Weidle, gen mgr; Gordon Pirie, gen sls mgr; Bob Young, progmg dir; Chris Davis, news dir; Kent Randles, chief engr.

KQPT(FM)—October 1958: 100.5 mhz; 115 w-H, 105 w-V. Ant 380 ft. TL: N38 38 30 W121 05 25. Stereo. Hrs opn: 24 280 Commerce Cir. (95815). (916) 923-6800. FAX: (916) 646-3418. Licensee: The Brown Organization (acq 9-25-92; $7 million; FTR 3-8-93). Rep: CBS Spot. Wash atty: Pierson, Ball. Format: Album alternative. News staff one; news progmg 3 hrs wkly. Target aud: 25-54; upscale professionals. ■ Willet H. Brown, CEO; Michael J. Brown, chmn; Phil MelRose, pres; John Geary, gen mgr; Don Daniels, opns dir; Dave Strout, sls dir; Jim Donohue, natl sls mgr; Nancy Willson, rgnl sls mgr; Gina Stassi, prom dir; David Anderson, mus dir; Mick Rush, chief engr. ■ Rates: $200; 150; 150; 150.

KRAK(AM)—November 1926: 1140 khz; 50 kw-U, DA-2. TL: N38 23 34 W121 11 51. Box 60408 (95860). (916) 923-9200. FAX: (916) 923-9212. Licensee: Professional Broadcasting Inc. Group owner: EZ Communications Inc. (acq 11-86). Net: AP. Rep: Katz. Format: Modern country. News progmg 10 hrs wkly. Target aud: 35-44. Spec prog: Farm 4 hrs wkly. ■ Chuck Goldmark, sr vp; Bruce Cambern, gen sls mgr; Larry Pareigis, progmg dir; Bruce Hirsh, chief engr.

KRAK-FM—Feb 21, 1960: 105.1 mhz; 50 kw. Ant 500 ft. TL: N38 38 31 W121 05 25. Stereo. Prog sep from AM. Spec prog: Farm 5 hrs wkly. ■ Hal Murray, progmg dir; Mike Remy, news dir.

KRXQ(FM)—(Roseville). June 1970: 93.7 mhz; 25 kw. Ant 324 ft. TL: N38 43 12 W121 14 09 (CP: Ant 328 ft.). Stereo. Suite 100, 5345 Madison Ave., Sacramento (95841). (916) 334-7777. FAX: (916) 334-0822. Licensee: Fuller-Jeffrey Broadcasting of Greater Sacramento. Group owner: Fuller-Jeffrey Broadcasting Companies Inc. (acq 1-1-84; grpsl; FTR 12-19-83). Rep: Torbet. Format: AOR. News progmg 2 hrs wkly. Target aud: 18-34. ■ Robert F. Fuller, pres; Michael L. John, gen mgr; Jim Eaton, gen sls mgr; John Nelson, prom mgr; Judy McNutt, progmg dir; Pamela Roberts, mus dir; Jerry Susoeff, chief engr. ■ Rates: $300; 200; 200; 175.

KSAC(AM)—1938: 1240 khz; 1 kw-U. TL: N38 35 17 W121 28 05. Hrs opn: 24. 1021 Second St. (95814). (916) 446-2294. FAX: (916) 443-1240. Licensee: Jonsson Communications Corp. (group owner; acq 9-1-78). Net: NBC, CBS. Rep: Katz & Powell. Format: Sports. Target aud: 25-54; sports fans. ■ Kenneth A. Jonsson, pres; Jim W. Ross, CFO; Donald Early, stn mgr; Richard W. Irwin, opns mgr & chief engr; Jeff Kramer, prom mgr; Michael Kramer, pub affrs dir. ■ Rates: $36; 36; 36; 32.

KSEG(FM)—1959: 96.9 mhz; 50 kw. Ant 500 ft. TL: N38 38 54 W121 28 40. Stereo. 620 Bercut Dr. (95814). (916) 446-5769. FAX: (916) 446-3588. Licensee: Great American Television and Radio Co. Group owner: Great American Broadcasting (acq 12-30-88). Rep: Christal. Format: Classic rock. News staff one; news progmg 5 hrs wkly. Target aud: 18-49. ■ Tom Schurr, vp; Dave Everingham, gen sls mgr; Zendy Solero, prom mgr; Jeff McMurray, progmg dir; J. Walker, mus dir; Kat Maudru, news dir; Martin Ashley, chief engr. ■ Rates: $150; 150; 150; 85.

KSFM(FM)—Listing follows KSMJ(AM).

KSMJ(AM)—1952: 1380 khz; 5 kw-U, DA-2. TL: N38 33 19 W121 10 51. 1750 Howe Ave. (95825). (916) 920-1025. FAX: (916) 929-5341. Licensee: Genesis Broadcasting Inc. (group owner). Net: SMN. Rep: Major Mkt. Wash atty: Wiley, Rien & Fielding. Format: Oldies. ■ John Booth, pres; Jerry McKenna, vp & gen mgr; Stephen C. Cottingim, gen sls mgr; Shannon Anderson, mktg dir, prom dir & adv dir; Les Tracy, progmg dir; Le Marr Carr, mus dir; Tina Macuha, news dir; Chip Morgan, chief engr.

KSFM(FM)—(Woodland). Co-owned with KSMJ(AM). Feb 4, 1961: 102.5 mhz; 50 kw. Ant 500 ft. TL: N38 35 20 W121 43 30. Stereo. Net: ABC/C. Format: Contemp. News staff 2. Target aud: 12-44. ■ Chuck Field, opns dir & mus dir; David Ferguson, progmg dir.

KWOD-FM—Apr 1, 1957: 106.5 mhz; 50 kw. Ant 410 ft. TL: N38 38 30 W121 05 25. Stereo. Hrs opn: 24. 801 K St., 27th Floor (95814). (916) 448-5000. FAX: (916) 448-1655. Licensee: Royce International Broadcasting Corp. Net: ABC/FM, CBS Spectrum. Rep: D & R Radio. Wash atty: Hogan & Hartson. Format: Progressive modern rock. News staff 2; news progmg 6 hrs wkly. Target aud: 18-49; contemp mass appeal. ■ Edward R. Stolz II, pres; Robert Endsley, mktg dir; Alex Cosper, progmg dir; Jeff Jensen, news dir; Brian Endsley, pub affrs dir. ■ Rates: $300; 300; 300; 225.

***KXHV(FM)**—January 1993: 89.7 mhz; 300 w-V. Ant 89 ft. TL: N38 31 52 W121 22 54 (CP: Ant 85 ft.). c/o Sacramento High School, 2315 34th St. (95817). (916) 454-6236. FAX: (916) 454-6823. Licensee: Sacramento City Unified School District. Format: Eclectic ■ Douglas Peckhman, gen mgr.

***KXJZ(FM)**—June 1991: 88.9 mhz; 50 kw. Ant 500 ft. TL: N38 16 25 W121 30 11. Stereo. Hrs opn: 24. Suite B, 3416 American River Dr. (95864). (916) 485-5977. FAX: (916) 487-3348. Licensee: California State University, Sacramento. Net: NPR. Wash atty: Cohn & Marks. Format: Jazz, news & information. News staff 4; news progmg 35 hrs wkly. Target aud: General. Spec prog: World music 10 hrs wkly. ■ Phil Corriveau, pres & gen mgr; Mark Jones, opns mgr; Cynthia Wills, dev dir; Charles Starzynski, progmg dir; Gary Vercelli, mus dir; Jeff Browne, chief engr.

KXOA(AM)—Aug 1, 1945: 1470 khz; 5 kw-D, 1 kw-N, DA-2. TL: N38 35 30 W121 27 47. 280 Commerce Circle (95815-4212). (916) 923-6800. FAX: (916) 646-3418. Licensee: The Brown Organization. Group owner: Brown Broadcasting Co. (acq 12-19-87). Rep: CBC Spot. Format: Oldies Target aud: 25-54. ■ Michael Brown, CEO & chmn; Philip Melrose, pres; John Geary, gen mgr; Don Daniels , opns dir; Dave Strout, sls dir; Jim Donohue, Nancy Willson, natl sls mgrs; Lizann Hunt, prom mgr; Ken Hunt, news dir; Mick Rush, chief engr.

KXOA-FM—Aug 1, 1945: 107.9 mhz; 50 kw. Ant 403 ft. TL: N38 42 38 W121 28 54. Stereo. Prog sep from AM. Rep: CBS Spot. Format: Adult contemp. News staff one. Target aud: 25-44. ■ Phil Brooks, mus dir.

***KXPR(FM)**—October 1964: 90.9 mhz; 50 kw. Ant 500 ft. TL: N38 42 38 W121 28 54. Stereo. Hrs opn: 24. Suite B, 3416 American River Dr. (95864). (916) 485-5977. FAX: (916) 487-3348. Licensee: California State University, Sacramento. Net: NPR. Wash atty: Cohn & Marks. Format: Class, info. News staff 4; news progmg 17 hrs wkly. Target aud: General. ■ Phil Corriveau, pres & gen mgr; Mark Jones, opns mgr; Cynthia Wills, dev dir; Charles Starzynski, progmg dir; Jeff Browne, chief engr.

***KYDS(FM)**—Jan 24, 1979: 91.5 mhz; 410 w. Ant 108 ft. TL: N38 36 33 W121 21 38. 4300 El Camino Ave. (95821). (916) 971-7453. Licensee: San Juan Unified School District. Format: Variety. ■ Warner Sargent, gen mgr.

KYMX(FM)—Listing follows KCTC(AM).

KZSA(FM)—See Placerville.

St. Helena

KVYN(FM)—Nov 1976: 99.3 mhz; 3 kw. Ant 1,200 ft. TL: N38 25 34 W122 19 33. Stereo. 1124 Foster Rd., Napa (94558). (707) 252-1440. Licensee: Young Radio Inc. Rep: Christal. Wash atty: Lester Spillane. Format: Adult contemp. News staff 4. Target aud: 25-45. ■ Thomas L. Young, pres & gen mgr; George Carl, sls dir; Faeli Schwartz, prom mgr; Barry Martin, progmg dir; Gareth Nicholas, mus dir; Henry Mulak, news dir; Mike Martindale, chief engr. ■ Rates: $35; 35; 30; 25.

Salinas

KCTY(AM)—July 17, 1963: 980 khz; 1 kw-D, 247 w-N, DA-2. TL: N36 42 32 W121 36 46. Hrs opn: 24. Box 1939 (93902); Suite 201, 517 S. Main St. (93901). (408) 757-5911. FAX: (408) 757-9764. Licensee: KCTY AM & KRAY FM Inc. (acq 1976). Rep: Lotus. Wash atty: Brown, Finn & Nietert. Format: Sp. Target aud: General. ■ Robert B. Dahlstrom, pres & gen mgr; A.L. Trevino, stn mgr; Rachel Ybarra, opns mgr; Robert Dahlstrom, gen sls mgr; Vincente Romero Jr., progmg mgr; Jose Valenzuela, news dir; Vincente Romero Jr, pub affrs dir.

KRAY-FM—Co-owned with KCTY(AM). Dec 5, 1977: 103.5 mhz; 3 kw. Ant -134 ft. TL: N36 42 32 W121 36 46 (CP: 2.5 kw, ant 512 ft.). Stereo. Hrs opn: 24. Prog sep from AM. Format: Latino contemp. ■ Robert Dahlstrom, mktg mgr & prom mgr.

KDON-FM—Listing follows KRQC(AM).

***KHDC(FM)**—See Chualar.

KNRY(AM)—See Monterey.

KRAY-FM—Listing follows KCTY(AM).

KRQC(AM)—1947: 1460 khz; 5 kw-U, DA-1. TL: N36 52 11 W121 49 05. Box 81460 (93912). (408) 422-5363. FAX: (408) 758-1890. Licensee: Henry Broadcasting Co. Group owner: Henry Broadcasting (acq 5-86). Rep: Christal. Format: AOR. Target aud: 18-49. ■ Charlton Buckley, pres; Al Smith, gen mgr; Jamie Hiatt, progmg dir; Wayne Woollard, chief engr.

KDON-FM—Co-owned with KRQC(AM). December 1959: 102.5 mhz; 18.5 kw. Ant 2,270 ft. TL: N36 45 20 W121 30 00. Stereo. Prog sep from AM. 55 Plaza Circle (93901). Format: Contemp hit. News staff one.

KTGE(AM)—July 4, 1963: 1570 khz; 500 w-D. TL: N36 41 49 W121 37 22 (CP: 5 kw-D, 500 w-N, DA-2. TL: N36 39 38 W121 32 29). 548 E. Alisal (93905). (408) 757-1910. FAX: (408) 757-9582. Licensee: TGR Broadcasting Inc. (group owner; acq 1987). Rep: Katz. Format: Sp, news/talk. News staff one. ■ Hector Vinlobos, pres; Larry Wrathall, gen sls mgr; Alex Lucas, progmg dir & mus dir; Juan Gonzales, news dir.

KTOM(AM)—Sept 27, 1947: 1380 khz; 5 kw-U, DA-2. TL: N36 41 49 W121 37 22. Hrs opn: 24. Box 81380, 933 N. Main St. (93906). (408) 422-7484. FAX: (408) 422-5544. Licensee: California Broadcasting Co. Group owner: Magic Broadcasting Companies (acq 5-11-90; $6.25 million with co-located FM; FTR 6-4-90). Net: ABC/E. Rep: Katz. Wash atty: Anderson, Kill, Olick & Oshinsky. Format: C&W. News staff one; news progmg 11 hrs wkly. Target aud: 25-54. ■ Donald McCoy, pres; Douglas Grimm, vp; Caren Petrullo, gen mgr & gen sls mgr; Bob Sherry, stn mgr; Johnny Morgan, progmg dir; Keith Medlian, mus dir; Kimberley Monari, news dir; Mike Blankenbecler, chief engr.

KTOM-FM—Sept 16, 1964: 100.7 mhz; 910 w. Ant 2,575 ft. TL: N36 32 05 W121 37 14 (CP: 1.4 kw, ant 2,385 ft.). Stereo. Dups AM 100%.

KWAV(FM)—See Monterey.

San Bernardino

KCKC(AM)—Oct 15, 1947: 1350 khz; 5 kw-D, 500 w-N, DA-2. TL: N34 05 37 W117 17 57. Hrs opn: 24. Box 2565 (92406); 740 W. 4th St. (92410). (909) 882-2575. FAX: (909) 888-7302. Licensee: All Pro Broadcasting Inc. (group owner; acq 9-10-92; $5 million with KAEV(FM) Lake Arrowhead; FTR 9-28-92). Net: ABC/I. Rep: D & R Radio. Format: News/talk. News staff one; news progmg 7 hrs wkly. Target aud: 25-49; baby boomers. ■ Willie Davis, pres; Bill McNulty, gen mgr, gen sls mgr & progmg dir; Betsy Niece, prom mgr; Pete Parsons, news dir; Mark Sadacca, chief engr.

KFRG(FM)—August 1974: 95.1 mhz; 50 kw. Ant 489 ft. TL: N34 11 51 W117 17 10. Stereo. Suite 315, 900 E. Washington St. (92324). (909) 825-9525. FAX: (909) 825-0441. Licensee: The Tremont Group Ltd. Group owner: Amaturo Group Ltd. (acq 5-25-90; $8 million; FTR 6-11-90). Format: Country. Target aud: 25-54. ■ Richard McIntosh, gen mgr; Charles Harrigan, progmg dir; Don Jeffrey, mus dir; Richard Lee, news dir; Dave Toups, chief engr.

KHTX(FM)—See Riverside.

KLFE(AM)—August 1947: 1240 khz; 1 kw-U. TL: N34 04 55 W117 18 17. Hrs opn: 24. 992 Inland Center Dr. (92408). (909) 885-6555. FAX: (909) 381-9563. Licensee: Inland Radio Inc. Group owner: Salem Communications Corp. (acq 8-25-86). Net: USA. Format: Christian talk. News progmg 2 hrs wkly. Target aud: 30 plus. ■ Joe Gonzalez, gen mgr; Mike Gilbert, gen sls mgr; Lance White, progmg dir; Mark Sedaka, chief engr. ■ Rates: $38; 38; 38; 38.

KMEN(AM)—1947: 1290 khz; 5 kw-U, DA-2. TL: N34 07 27 W117 17 57. Hrs opn: 24. Box 1290, 2001 Iona Ave., Riverside (92507). (909) 684-1991. FAX: (909) 274-4949. Licensee: Sanriver Radio Inc. Group owner: American Media Inc. (acq 7-31-87). Net: CBS, AP. Rep: McGavren Guild. Format: Adult contemp. ■ David Presher, gen mgr; Connie Ferreri, opns dir; Paul Petrilli, natl sls mgr; Mike Karsting, prom dir; Mike Marino, mus dir; Dave Wolfe, chief engr. ■ Rates: $30; 30; 30; 20.

KOLA(FM)—June 15, 1959: 99.9 mhz; 29.5 kw. Ant 1,663 ft. TL: N33 57 55 W117 16 59. Stereo. Suite 101, 1940 Orange Tree Ln., Redlands (92374). (909) 684-9992. Licensee: KOLA Inc. (acq 12-22-65). Net: ABC/R. Rep: Banner. Format: Rock 'n roll, oldies. News progmg 8 hrs wkly. Target aud: 25-54. ■ Jeff Park, gen mgr; Glen Watson, gen sls mgr; Mark Markley, prom mgr; Rick Shaw, progmg dir; Paul La Voight, mus dir; Clayton Creekmore, chief engr.

KRSO(AM)—1929: 590 khz; 1 kw-U, DA-2. TL: N34 04 18 W117 17 50. Hrs opn: 24. Box 50005 (92412); Suite 302, 1950 S. Sunwest Lane (92408). (909) 384-9750. FAX: (909) 884-5844. Licensee: Henry Broadcasting (group owner). Net: Unistar; Rep: Eastman. Format: MOR. News staff one; news progmg 14 hrs wkly. Target aud: 35-64. ■ Charlton Buckley, pres; Jeff Salgo, vp & gen mgr; Jan Jefferies, opns mgr & progmg dir; Bob Wood, gen sls mgr; Katie Nagy, prom dir; Caroline Gracie, news dir; Stew Berger, pub affrs dir; Joe Mauk, chief engr.

***KVCR(FM)**—December 1953: 91.9 mhz; 900 w. Ant 1,605 ft. TL: N33 57 57 W117 17 05. Stereo. Hrs opn: 19. 701 S. Mt. Vernon Ave. (92410). (714) 888-6511, ext. 1305. FAX: (714) 381-4604. Licensee: San Bernardino Community College Dist. Net: NPR, APR. Wash atty: Tierney & Swift. Format: Educ. Target aud: General. Spec prog: Jazz, new age 15 hrs wkly. ■ Thomas Little, vp & gen mgr; Steve Ward, opns mgr, prom mgr & progmg dir; David Hinman, dev mgr; Jerry Alexander, mus dir; Sonny Belvin, Bill Eason, asst mus dirs; Roger Funk, chief engr. ■ *KVCR-TV affil.

San Clemente

KWVE(FM)—Nov 16, 1971: 107.9 mhz; 50 kw. Ant 500 ft. TL: N33 25 52 W117 35 47. Stereo. Hrs opn: 24. 1644 N. El Camino Real (92672). (714) 492-9800. Licensee: Calvary Chapel of Costa Mesa Inc. (acq 4-15-85). Format: Relg. News staff one. Target aud: General. Spec prog: Children's 3 hrs wkly. ■ Charles W. Smith, pres; Robert M. Cadman, gen mgr, adv dir & progmg dir; Mike Stephens, opns mgr & progmg mgr; Jan Runyon, gen sls mgr & adv mgr; Lisa Oswald, mus dir; Laura Poore, news dir; Keith Peters, pub affrs dir; Tom Koza, chief engr. ■ Rates: $50; 35; 50; 35.

San Diego

KBAX(FM)—See Fallbrook.

KBZS(FM)—Mar 6, 1960: 94.9 mhz; 21.8 kw. Ant 710 ft. TL: N32 50 21 W117 14 57. Stereo. Suite 350, 9191 Town Centre Dr. (92122). (619) 452-9595. FAX: (619) 452-8087. Licensee: San Diego Broadcasting Corp. Group owner: Anaheim Broadcasting Corp. (acq 9-18-91; $10.1 million; FTR 10-7-91). Rep: Banner. Format: Adult contemp. News staff one; news progmg one hr wkly. Target aud: 25-54; women. ■ Tim Sullivan, gen mgr; Bob Lueke, gen sls mgr; Lori Ello, prom dir; John Buffaloe, chief engr.

KCBQ(AM)—1946: 1170 khz; 50 kw-D, 1.5 kw-N, DA-2. TL: N32 50 23 W116 59 31. Stereo. Hrs opn: 24. Rebroadcasts KOOL(AM) Phoenix, AZ 98%. 9416 Mission Gorge Rd., Santee (92071). (619) 286-1170; (619) 570-1170. FAX: (619) 449-8548; (619) 258-2771. Licensee: Compass Radio of San Diego Inc. Group owner: Compass Radio Group (acq 4-23-93; grpsl; FTR 5-10-93). Net: AP, SMN. Wash atty: Fisher, Wayland, Cooper & Leader Format: Hits of the 50s and early 60s. Target aud: 35-64; baby boomers that grew up in the 50s & early 60s. ■ Bob Hughes, CEO & gen mgr; Jonathan Schwartz, CFO & exec vp; Pat Hughes, vp; Bob Ferro, sls dir; Diane Smith, gen sls mgr; Mark Nicholoson, natl sls mgr; Kim Leeds, prom dir; Mike Aiken, prom mgr; Rich Brother Robbin, progmg dir; Brian Beazer, mus dir; Don Mitchinson, pub affrs dir; Bill Lipis, chief engr.

KCBQ-FM—1954: 105.3 mhz; 29 kw. Ant 620 ft. TL: N32 50 17 W117 14 56. Stereo. Hrs opn: 24. Prog dups AM 100%. Box 1053 (92112). ■ Bob Ferro, vp sls; Jeff Stewart, mus dir.

KCLX-FM—Listing follows KSDO(AM).

KECR(AM)—See El Cajon.

KECR-FM—See El Cajon.

KFMB(AM)—May 19, 1941: 760 khz; 50 kw-U, DA-N. TL: N32 50 32 W117 01 29 (CP: TL: N32 50 36 W117 01 28). Stereo. Hrs opn: 24. Box 85888, 7677 Engineer Rd. (92111). (619) 292-7600. FAX: (619) 279-7676. Licensee: Midwest Television Inc. (group owner; acq 4-1-64). Net: CBS. Rep: McGavren Guild. Wash atty: Covington & Burling. Format: Full svc adult contemp. News staff 10. Target aud: 25-54. ■ August C. Meyer Jr., CEO; Arnold T. Kleiner, pres; Paul Palmer, vp; Bill Stairs, opns mgr; Peter Hallisay, gen sls mgr; ELizabeth Wold, prom mgr; Dave Sniff, asst mus dir; Cliff Albert, news dir; Maria Velasquez, pub affrs dir; Miguel Rountree, engrg mgr; John Weigard, chief engr.

KFMB-FM—Sept 21, 1959: 100.7 mhz; 30 kw-H, 26.5 kw-V. Ant 620 ft. TL: N32 50 17 W117 14 56 (CP: 38.4 kw, ant 536 ft.). Stereo. FAX: (619) 279-3380. Net: AP. Format: Hot adult contemp. ■ Peter Hallisay, natl sls mgr; Kelly Oden, prom mgr; Gene Knight, progmg dir & mus dir. ■ KFMB-TV affil.

KFSD-FM—1949: 94.1 mhz; 100 kw. Ant 640 ft. TL: N33 50 21 W117 14 57. 1540 6th Ave. (92101). (619) 239-9091. FAX: (619) 236-0269. Licensee: San Diego Lotus Corp. (acq 4-8-92). Rep: D & R Radio. Format: Class. News staff one; news progmg 2 hrs wkly. Target aud: 25 plus; well-educated. ■ Howard Kalmenson, pres; Hal Rosenberg, gen mgr; Debra McLaren, prom mgr & mus dir; Kingsley McLaren, progmg dir; Mike Tosch, chief engr. ■ Rates: $150; 150; 150; 150.

KGB-FM—Listing follows KPOP(AM).

KIFM(FM)—Feb 4, 1960: 98.1 mhz; 28 kw. Ant 640 ft. TL: N32 50 17 W117 14 56. Stereo. Suite 470, 3655 Nobel Dr. (92122). (619) 587-9800. FAX: (619) 587-0254. Licensee: KIFM Broadcasting Ltd. (acq 4-1-89). Rep: CBS Radio. Format: Jazz, new age, new adult contemp. News staff one; news progmg 2 hr wkly. Target aud: 25-54; upscale adults. ■ Bruce Walton, pres & gen mgr; Scotty Morache, gen sls mgr; Mark Costa, natl sls mgr; Leslie O'Neal, mktg dir & prom dir; Bob O'Connor, vp progmg; Tony Schondel, mus dir; Eric J. Chambers, pub affrs dir; Mike Tosch, chief engr.

KJQY(FM)—1965: 103.7 mhz; 36 kw. Ant 580 ft. TL: N32 50 21 W117 14 57. Stereo. Suite 1200, 625 Broadway (92101). (619) 238-1037. FAX: (619) 238-6157. Licensee: SFX Broadcasting. Group owner: SFX Broadcasting Inc. (acq 10-7-92; grpsl; FTR 11-16-92). Rep: Major Mkt. Format: Adult contemp. Target aud: 35-54. ■ Mike Kenney, vp & gen mgr; Jessie Bullett, opns mgr; Jim Verissimo, gen sls mgr; Andrea Goodrich, natl sls mgr; Holli Traeumer, mktg mgr, prom mgr & adv mgr; Jessie Bullet, progmg dir; Phil Wells, chief engr.

KKLQ(AM)—1926: 600 khz; 5 kw-U, DA-1. TL: N32 43 17 W117 04 11. Suite 204, 8525 Gibbs Dr. (92123). (619) 565-6006. FAX: (619) 279-9553. (619) 569-7510. Licensee: Par Broadcasting. (group owner; acq 1993; $13 million; with co-located FM). Rep: Christal. Format: Top-40/CHR. ■ Bob Bolinger, vp & gen mgr; Bobby Salvato, gen sls mgr; Tracy Johnson, Jo Jo Kincaid (asst), progmg dirs; Tom Gjerdrum, mus dir; Chuck Fritsch, news dir; Tom Cox, chief engr.

KKLQ-FM—June 26, 1960: 106.5 mhz; 7.4 kw. Ant 1,074 ft. TL: N32 43 17 W117 04 11. Stereo. Dups AM 100%.

***KPBS-FM**—Sept 12, 1960: 89.5 mhz; 1.77 kw. Ant 1,902 ft. TL: N32 41 47 W116 56 07. Stereo. Hrs opn: 24. 5164 College Ave. (92182). (619) 594-8100. FAX: (619) 265-6478. Licensee: San Diego State Univ. Net: APR, NPR. Wash atty: Bryan, Cave, Mcpheeters & McRoberts. Format: News/talk. News staff 6. ■ Doug Myrland, gen mgr; Craig Dorval, stn mgr; Flo Rogers, opns dir; Bruce Bauer, dev dir; Stephanie Bergsma, dev mgr; Deanna Martin-Mackey, prom dir; Patricia Finn, adv dir; Karen Kish, news dir; Chris Durso, chief engr.

KPOP(AM)—July 14, 1922: 1360 khz; 5 kw-D, 1 kw-N. TL: N32 43 49 W117 05 01. 7150 Engineer Rd. (92111). (619) 292-1360. FAX: (619) 571-6069. Licensee: KGB Inc. Group owner: Brown Broadcasting Co. Net: NBC. Rep: CBS Radio. Format: MOR. Target aud: 45-64. ■ Phil Melrose, pres; Tom Baker, gen mgr; Bob Iafrate, gen sls mgr; Clark Ryan, progmg dir; John Barcroft, chief engr.

KGB-FM—Co-owned with KPOP(AM). 1956: 101.5 mhz; 50 kw. Ant 500 ft. TL: N32 43 49 W117 05 01. Stereo. Prog sep from AM. Format: Classic rock (AOR). Target aud: 18-49. ■ Scott Chatfield, prom mgr; Clark Ryan, progmg dir & mus dir; Shelly Dunn, news dir.

KSDO(AM)—October 1947: 1130 khz; 10 kw-U, DA-2. TL: N32 51 04 W117 57 51. Hrs opn: 24. KSDO Bldg., 5050 Murphy Canyon Rd. (92123). (619) 278-1130. Licensee: Pacific & Southern Co. Group owner: Gannett Broadcasting (acq 4-21-87). Net: ABC/I, AP. Rep: Group W. Format: News, talk. News staff 25. Target aud: 25-54. ■ Michael Shields, pres; Susan Hoffman, vp & gen mgr; Sherry Toennies, prom mgr; Kelly Wheeler, progmg dir; May Ayala, news dir; Jack Rabbell, chief engr.

KCLX-FM—Co-owned with KSDO(AM). May 20, 1963: 102.9 mhz; 32 kw. Ant 616 ft. TL: N32 41 48 W116 56 10. Stereo. Hrs opn: 24. Prog sep from AM. Format: Classic rock. Target aud: 25-44. ■ Keith Miller, prom dir; Jack Silver, progmg dir.

***KSDS(FM)**—December 1951: 88.3 mhz; 830 w. Ant 170 ft. TL: N32 48 19 W117 10 09. Stereo. Hrs opn: 18. 1313 12th Ave. (92101). (619) 230-2522. FAX: (619) 230-2063. Licensee: San Diego Community College. Format: Jazz. News staff one; news progmg 7 hrs wkly. Target aud: 18-55. ■ James Dark, gen mgr; Hope W. Shaw, stn mgr; John Hilderbrand, opns dir; Mary Surrenting, dev mgr; Toni Sisti, progmg dir; Larry Quick, chief engr.

KSON(AM)—1946: 1240 khz; 1 kw-U. TL: N32 41 40 W117 07 17. Stereo. Suite 710, 1615 Murray Canyon Rd. (92108). (619) 299-1240. FAX: (619) 299-1240. Licensee: Jefferson-Pilot Communications Co. (group owner; acq 2-7-85). Rep: Banner. Format: Country. News staff one. Target aud: 25-54. ■ Mike Stafford, vp, gen mgr & gen sls mgr; Mike Shepard, opns dir & progmg dir; Steve Sapp, prom mgr; Nick Upton, mus dir; Jack Smith, news dir; John Buffaloe, chief engr.

KSON-FM—Jan 15, 1964: 97.3 mhz; 50 kw. Ant 442 ft. TL: N32 43 13 W117 04 14 (CP: 7.4 kw, ant 1,074 ft.). Stereo. Dups AM 100%. Format: Country.

KURS(AM)—November 1, 1992: 1040 khz; 9.5 kw-D, 4.5 kw-N, DA-2. TL: N32 54 21 W116 55 40. 296 H St., Suite 300, Chula Vista (91910). (619) 425-2132. FAX: (619) 427-5887. Licensee: Quetzal Bilingual Communications Inc. Format: Sp. ■ Mateo R. Camarillo, pres; Jose Mireles, gen mgr; David G. Martinez, gen sls mgr.

KYXY(FM)—1960: 96.5 mhz; 41 kw. Ant 540 ft. TL: N33 52 00 W116 25 29. Stereo. 8033 Linda Vista Rd. (92111). (619) 571-7600. FAX: (619) 571-0326. Licensee: Parker Broadcasting Co. (acq 2-15-78). Rep: D & R Radio. Format: Adult contemp. Target aud: 25-54. ■ Dan Carelli, pres & gen mgr; Jim Higgins, gen sls mgr; Jean Meade, prom mgr; Sonny West, progmg dir; Mark Blackwell, mus dir; Lee McGowan, chief engr.

XETRA(AM)—(Tijuana, Mexico). 1934: 690 khz; 50 kw-U, DA-2. Hrs opn: 24. 4891 Pacific Hwy., San Diego, CA (92110). (619) 291-9191. FAX: (619) 294-2916. Licensee: Noble Broadcast of San Diego. Group owner: Noble Broadcast Group (acq 3-12-78). Net: Unistar. Rep: Major Mkt. Format: All sports radio. Target aud: 25-54; men. ■ Mike Glickenhaus, gen mgr; Jim Votaw, gen sls mgr; Dawn Gallagher, mktg dir; Doug Stewart, prom dir; Howard Freedman, vp progmg; Bill Eisenhamer, chief engr.

XETRA-FM—(Tijuana, Mexico). 1978: 91.1 mhz; 100 kw. Ant 1,000 ft. Stereo. Hrs opn: 24. Wash atty: Haley, Bader & Potts. Format: Modern AOR. News staff one. Target aud: 18-49; Very active, college educated, above mkt average income, single. ■ Kevin Stapleford, vp opns; Rob Quinn, natl sls mgr; Robin Rockwell, prom dir & pub affrs dir; Mike Halloran, progmg dir & mus dir; Jeff Prescott, news dir; Bill Eisenhamer, engrg mgr.

92.5 THE FLASH

XHRM-FM—(Tijuana, Mexico). January 1981: 92.5 mhz; 50 kw. Ant 650 ft. Stereo. Hrs opn: 24. Suite A, 2434 Southport Way, National City, CA (91950). (619) 336-4900. FAX: (619) 336-4925. Licensee: The Rivas Kaloyan Family. Rep: Koteen & Naftalin. Format: Adult alternative. News staff one; news progmg 3 hrs wkly. Target aud: 18-49. ■ Louis Rivas Kaloyan, pres; Chuck Howard, exec vp & gen mgr; David Duron, vp sls; Lee Weiman, rgnl sls mgr; Dwight Arnold, vp mktg, vp prom & mus dir; Mike Garner, prom mgr; Sherman Cohen, vp progmg; Kelli Clugue, asst mus dir; Steve Sellman, chief engr. ■ Rates: $200; 200; 200; 100.

San Fernando

KMGX(FM)—Nov 14, 1958: 94.3 mhz; 3 kw. Ant 95 ft. TL: N34 17 03 W118 28 17. Stereo. 14800 Lassen St., Mission Hills (91345). (818) 894-9191. FAX: (818) 893-0581. Licensee: Buckley Communications Inc. Format: Adult contemp. News progmg one hr wkly. Target aud: 25-54; general. ■ Yvonne Guardado, opns dir. ■ Rates: $60; 40; 60; 35.

San Francisco

KABL(AM)—See Oakland.

KABL-FM—July 17, 1958: 98.1 mhz; 100 kw. Ant 940 ft. TL: N37 51 04 W122 29 49. Stereo. 1025 Battery St. (94111-1201). (415) 788-5225. FAX: (415) 981-2930. Licensee: Shamrock Broadcasting Co. (group owner; acq 7-79). Rep: Christal. Format: Easy lstng. ■ Eddie Esserman, vp & gen mgr; Julie Kahn, gen sls mgr; Gerry McCracken, progmg dir; Dennis Gooch, chief engr.

***KALW(FM)**—Mar 20, 1941: 91.7 mhz; 1.9 kw. Ant 920 ft. TL: N37 45 17 W122 26 44. Stereo. Hrs opn: 20. 2576 Harrison St. (94110-2720). (415) 695-5740. Licensee: San Francisco Unified School District. Net: APR, NPR. Wash atty: Arter & Hadden. Format: Div, educ, news/talk. News progmg 68 hrs wkly. Target aud: General; news & info oriented lstnrs. Spec prog: Black 2 hrs, jazz 5 hrs, American Indian 2 hrs, folk 3 hrs, Cantonese 3 hrs, classical 2 hrs wkly. ■ Jerry Jacob, gen mgr; William Helgeson, opns mgr; Dave Evans, chief engr.

KBRG(FM)—See Fremont.

KCBC(AM)—See Riverbank.

KCBS(AM)—April 1909: 740 khz; 50 kw, DA-2. TL: N38 08 23 W122 31 45. One Embarcadero Center (94111). (415) 765-4000. FAX: (415) 765-4146. Licensee: CBS Inc. Group owner: CBS Broadcast Group (acq 12-16-49). Net: CBS. Format: News. Target aud: 25-54. ■ Frank Oxarart, gen mgr; Steve DiNardo, gen sls mgr; Lin Galliani, natl sls mgr; Jesse Waters, prom mgr; Ed Cavagnaro, progmg dir & news dir; Shingo Kamada, chief engr.

KRQR(FM)—Co-owned with KCBS(AM). Feb 1, 1948: 97.3 mhz; 82 kw. Ant 1,100 ft. TL: N37 50 57 W122 29 56. Stereo. Hrs opn: 24. Prog sep from AM. (415) 765-4097. FAX: (415) 765-4084. Licensee: CBS Inc. Net: CBS Spectrum. Rep: CBS Radio. Format: Classic rock. Target aud: 18-54. ■ Don Marion, vp & gen mgr; Bob York, opns dir; Patrick Corr, opns mgr; Tim Roesler, gen sls mgr; Marcie Mills, natl sls mgr; Denise St. Louis, prom mgr; John McCrae, progmg dir; Zeb Norris, mus dir; Liz St. John, news dir & pub affrs dir; Shingo Kamada, chief engr.

KDFC-FM—Sept 1, 1947: 102.1 mhz; 33 kw. Ant 1,050 ft. TL: N37 50 57 W122 29 56. 77 Madison Ln., 3rd Fl. (94108). (415) 788-2022. FAX: (415) 956-4177. Licensee: The Brown Organization. Group owner: Brown Broadcasting Co. (acq 1993; $13 million with KDFC[AM] Palo Alto). Rep: CBS. Format: Classical. Target aud: 25-54; educated, upscale. ■ Michael Brown, chmn; Phil Melrose, pres; Denis Brumm, CFO; Tyler Phelps, opns dir & mus dir; Linda Frame, gen sls mgr; Jennifer Mangiantini, natl sls mgr; Tom Hypfensperger, rgnl sls mgr; Bill O'Connell, progmg dir.

KDIA(AM)—See Oakland.

***KEAR(FM)**—1958: 106.9 mhz; 80 kw. Ant 1,120 ft. TL: N37 50 58 W122 29 56. Stereo. 290 Hegenberger Rd., Oakland (94621-1436). (415) 626-3010. Licensee: Family Stations Inc. (group owner; acq 1958). Format: Relg. Target aud: General. ■ Harold Camping, gen mgr; Matthew Pearce, stn mgr; Anthony Serredia, chief engr.

KEST(AM)—1926: 1450 khz; 1 kw-U. TL: N37 46 41 W122 23 16. Hrs opn: 24. Suite 6500, 185 Berry St. (94107). (415) 978-5378. FAX: (415) 978-5380. Licensee: Douglas Broadcasting Inc. (group owner; acq 12-27-88; grpsl; FTR 1-23-89). Format: European & Asian languages, talk, new age. News staff one; news progmg 6 hrs wkly. Target aud: 25 plus. Spec prog: Greek 5 hrs, Ger 3 hrs, gospel 5 hrs, It one hr, Pol one hr, relg 24 hrs, Sp one hr, Chinese 5 hrs, Korean 15 hrs, Japanese 5 hrs, Filipino 5 hrs, Vietnamese 5 hrs, Hindi 8 hrs, Samoan one hr wkly. ■ John N. Douglas, pres; Alan P. Schultz, vp & gen mgr; Bob Stewart, rgnl sls mgr; Tom Johnson, progmg dir; Carole Jennings, news dir; Ernest Herrerra, chief engr. ■ Rates: $95; 95; 95; 95.

KFAX(AM)—1925: 1100 khz; 50 kw-U, DA-1. TL: N37 37 56 W122 07 49. Hrs opn: 24. Box 8125, Fremont (94537); 39138 Fremont Blvd., 3rd Fl., Fremont (94538). (510) 713-1100. FAX: (510) 505-1448. Licensee: Golden Gate Broadcasting Co. Inc. Group owner: Salem Communications Corp. (acq 9-1-84). Format: Christian teaching/talk. Target aud: 35 plus. Spec prog: Black 8 hrs, gospel 4 hrs wkly. ■ Robert Dunker, gen mgr; Richard Kennedy, gen sls mgr; Craig Guglielmetti, progmg dir; Leonard Harris, chief engr.

KFOG(FM)—Listing follows KNBR(AM).

KFRC(AM)—Sept 24, 1924: 610 khz; 5 kw-U. TL: N37 50 58 W122 17 44. Stereo. 500 Washington St. (94111). (415) 986-6100. FAX: (415) 391-9576. Licensee: Alliance Broadcasting California. Group owner: Alliance Broadcasting (acq 6-3-93; $20.15 million with co-located FM; FTR 6-21-93). Net: MBS. Rep: Katz. Format: Oldies. Target aud: 35-64. ■ David Bramnick, vp & gen mgr; Sharon Warren, gen sls mgr; Mark Arnold, mktg mgr; J. Paul Emerson, news dir; Phil Lerza, chief engr.

KFRC-FM—1949: 99.7 mhz; 45 kw. Ant 1,299 ft. TL: N37 41 15 W122 26 04 (CP: 40 kw, ant 1,299 ft.). Stereo. (415) 391-9970. Format: Oldies. Target aud: 25-54.

KGO(AM)—Jan 8, 1924: 810 khz; 50 kw-U, DA-1. TL: N37 31 39 W122 06 05. 900 Front St. (94111-1450). (415) 954-8100. FAX: (415) 391-2795. Licensee: Capital Cities/ABC Inc. Group owner: Capital Cities/ABC Broadcast Group (acq 1986). Net: ABC/I. Rep: Banner. Wash atty: Wilmer, Cutler & Pickering. Format: News/talk. News staff 24; news progmg 40 hrs wkly. Target aud: General; 25-54. ■ Michael Luckoff, pres & gen mgr; Ken Beck, opns dir; Bill Bacigalupi, gen sls mgr; Rose TenEyck, natl sls mgr; Bill Rose (local), rgnl sls mgr; Darcy Provo, mktg dir; Ken Berry, news dir; Allison Hodges, pub affrs dir; Bruce Schirmer, chief engr.

Margret Haney
GRAHAM-HANEY
Media Brokers/Consultants
2995 WOODSIDE ROAD, WOODSIDE, CA 94062
TEL: 415/325-5552, FAX: 415/325-5556

KIOI(FM)—Oct 27, 1957: 101.3 mhz; 125 kw. Ant 1,160 ft. TL: N37 41 24 W122 26 13 (CP: TL: N37 41 15 W122 26 01). Stereo. 700 Montgomery St. (94111). (415) 956-5101. FAX: (415) 397-5101. Licensee: Bay Broadcasting Corp. Group owner: Fairmont Communications Corp. (acq 10-1-83). Net: AP. Format: Adult contemp. ■ Gary Taylor, vp & gen mgr; Peter O'Brien, gen sls mgr; Linda Clark, prom mgr; Bob Lawrence, progmg dir; Angela Perelli, mus dir; John Evans, news dir.

KIQI(AM)—1957: 1010 khz; 10 kw-D, 500 w-N, DA-2. TL: N37 49 33 W122 18 39 (CP: COL: Sunnyvale; 25 kw-D, 10 kw-N, DA-1). 2601 Mission St. (94110). (415) 648-8800. FAX: (415) 695-1015. Licensee: Oro Spanish Broadcasting Co. Rep: Caballero. Format: Sp. ■ Rene De La Rosa, pres & gen mgr; Michael Sher, gen sls mgr; Carlos DeMarty, progmg dir; Paul Maltez, mus dir; Luis Quintanilla, news dir.

KITS(FM)—June 1, 1964: 105.3 mhz; 15 kw. Ant 1,200 ft. TL: N37 41 20 W122 26 07. Stereo. Suite 300, 730 Harrison (94107). (415) 512-1053. FAX: (415) 777-0608. Licensee: Entercom (group owner; acq 6-6-69). Format: Modern rock. ■ Pat McNally, vp; Mike Brandt, sls dir; Gabby Medecki, prom mgr; Richard Sands, progmg dir; Steve Masters, mus dir; Lori Thompson, news dir; Harry Osibin, pub affrs dir; John Scherer, chief engr.

KJAZ(FM)—(Alameda). Aug 1, 1959: 92.7 mhz; 1.8 kw. Ant 370 ft. TL: N37 47 54 W122 24 59 (CP: Ant 400 ft.). Stereo. 1131 Harbor Bay Pkwy., Alameda (94502). (510) 769-4800. Licensee: KJAZ Inc. (acq 1980; $1.4 million). Net: MBS. Rep: Katz & Powell. Format: Jazz. Target aud: 25-54. ■ Corey Mason, pres & gen mgr; Georgia Frazier, gen sls mgr; Denise Culver-Nelson, prom mgr; Bob Parlocha, progmg dir & mus dir; Doug Irwin, chief engr. ■ Rates: $125; 125; 125; 125.

KKHI(AM)—1947: 1550 khz; 10 kw-U, DA-2. TL: N37 31 49 W122 16 29. Stereo. 335 Powell St. (94102). (415) 986-2151. Licensee: Buckley Broadcasting Corp. (group owner). Net: Unistar. Rep: D & R Radio. Wash atty: Fisher, Wayland, Cooper & Leader. Format: Classical. News progmg one hr wkly. Target aud: 35 plus; affluent, home-owning, highly educated, business professionals. Spec prog: UCLA football & basketball. ■ Richard Buckley, CEO; Bruce Beebe, gen mgr; Lou Sinclair, opns mgr & chief engr; Len Mattson, gen sls mgr; Marita Dorenbecher, prom mgr; Bill Lueth, progmg dir. ■ Rates: $125; 125; 125; 125.

KKHI-FM—1959: 95.7 mhz; 6.9 kw. Ant 1,500 ft. TL: N37 41 23 W122 26 12. Stereo. Dups AM 100%. ■ Victor Ledin, progmg dir. ■ Rates: Same as AM.

KKSF(FM)—Nov 3, 1947: 103.7 mhz; 7.8 kw. Ant 1,470 ft. TL: N37 45 20 W122 27 05. Stereo. Hrs opn: 24. 3rd Fl., 77 Maiden Ln. (94108). (415) 788-2022. FAX: (415) 956-4177. Licensee: The Brown Organization (group owner; acq 6-87). Rep: Banner. Format: Adult contemp, jazz/fusion, new age. News progmg 5 hrs wkly. Target aud: 25-49. ■ Dave Kendrick, gen mgr; Susan Pfeifer, prom mgr; Steve Feinstein, progmg dir; Dore Stein, mus dir; Dave McQueen, news dir; Tim Pozar, chief engr. ■ Rates: $250; 250; 250; 175.

KLOK(AM)—See San Jose.

KMEL(FM)—Nov 30, 1960: 106.1 mhz; 69 kw. Ant 1,290 ft. TL: N37 41 24 W122 26 13. Stereo. 55 Francisco St. (94133). (415) 391-1061. FAX: (415) 392-7044. Licensee: Evergreen Media Corp. of San Francisco. Group owner: Evergreen Media Corp. (acq 7-22-92; $44 million; FTR 8-3-92). Rep: Christal. Format: CHR. ■ Richard Kelly, pres; Katie Eyerly, mktg dir; Dave Shakes, progmg dir; Joe Arbagey, mus dir; Joalen Huthchison, pub affrs dir; Dave Sherbourne, chief engr.

KNBR(AM)—1922: 680 khz; 50 kw-U. TL: N37 31 49 W122 16 29. 55 Hawthorne St. (94105). (415) 995-6800. Licensee: Susquehanna Broadcasting Co. Group owner: Susquehanna Radio Corp. (acq 5-24-89; $17.5 million; FTR 6-12-89). Net: ABC. Rep: Eastman. Format: Sports. News staff 3; news progmg 8 hrs wkly. Target aud: 25-54. Spec prog: Gardening, health, real estate, home improvement, computers, food, Hollywood entertainment. ■ Tony Salvadore, vp & gen mgr; Bob Agnew, opns mgr & progmg dir; Doug Sterne, gen sls mgr; Dave Shapiro, natl sls mgr; Joe Bayliss, Kari Fulton, rgnl sls mgrs; Isabelle Lemon, prom mgr; Mark Provost, news dir; Bill Ruck, chief engr.

KFOG(FM)—Co-owned with KNBR(AM). March 1, 1963: 104.5 mhz; 7.9 kw. Ant 1,454 ft. TL: N37 45 20 W122 27 05. Stereo. Prog sep from AM. Format: Adult alternative rock. News staff one; news progmg 4 hrs wkly. ■ Dwight Walker, stn mgr; Mark Silverstein, rgnl sls mgr; Jude Heller, prom mgr; Paul Marszalek, progmg dir; Rosalie Howarth, mus dir; Peter Finch, news dir; Bill Ruck, engrg mgr.

KNEW(AM)—See Oakland.

***KOHL(FM)**—See Fremont.

KOIT(AM)—1926: 1260 khz; 5 kw-D, 1 kw-N. TL: N37 42 59 W122 23 38. 400 2nd St., No. 300 (94107-1402). (415) 777-0965. FAX: (415) 826-0965. Licensee: Bonneville Holding Co. Group owner: Bonneville International Corp. Net: AP, UPI. Rep: Torbet. Format: Adult contemp. News staff one. Target aud: 25-54; upscale adults who earn an average of $30,000. ■ Charles R. Tweedle, vp & gen mgr; Valerie Howard, gen sls mgr; Alan Hotlen, progmg dir; Vickie Jenkins, news dir & pub affrs dir; Randy Pugsley, chief engr.

KOIT-FM—1959: 96.5 mhz; 33 kw. Ant 1,410 ft. TL: N37 45 20 W122 27 05. Dups AM 100%.

***KPOO(FM)**—April 1971: 89.5 mhz; 270 w. Ant 540 ft. TL: N37 47 33 W122 24 52. Stereo. Box 425000 (94142); 1329 Divisadero St. (94115). (415) 346-5373. FAX: (415) 346-5173. Licensee: Poor Peoples' Radio Inc. Format: Div. ■ Terry Collins, pres; Joe Rudolph, gen mgr; Jerome Parson, progmg dir & mus dir; Harrison Chastang, news dir; Dave Billeci, chief engr.

***KQED-FM**—June 1969: 88.5 mhz; 110 w. Ant 1,270 ft. TL: N37 41 23 W177 26 12. Stereo. Hrs opn: 24. 2601 Mariposa St. (94110). (415) 553-2129. TWX: (910) 372-6609. Licensee: KQED Inc. Net: NPR, APR. Format: All news. News staff 9; news progmg 160 hrs wkly. Target aud: General. ■ Mary Bitterman, chmn; Jo Anne Wallace, gen mgr; Monty Carlos, opns mgr; Raul Ramirez, news dir; Fred Krock, chief engr. ■ KQED(TV), KQEC(TV) affil.

KRQR(FM)—Listing follows KCBS(AM).

KSAN-FM—March 12, 1958: 94.9 mhz; 35 kw. Ant 1,290 ft. TL: N37 41 22 W122 26 10. Stereo. Suite 200, 750 Battery St. (94111). (415) 291-0202. FAX: (415) 395-9886. Licensee: Shamrock Holdings Inc. Group owner: Shamrock Broadcasting Inc. (acq 6-4-93; grpsl; FTR 6-21-93). Net: AP. Rep: McGavren Guild. Format: Country. News staff one. Target aud: 25-54. ■ Eddie Esserman, vp & gen mgr; Julie Kahns, gen sls mgr; Marlene Augustine, prom mgr; Lee Logan, progmg dir; Richard Ryan, mus dir; Betsy O'Connor, news dir; Dennis Gooch, chief engr.

KSFO(AM)—Aug 1, 1925: 560 khz; 5 kw-U, DA-N. TL: N37 44 44 W122 22 40. 300 Broadway (94133). (415) 398-5600. FAX: (415) 931-5464. Licensee: First Broadcasting Co. (acq 10-91; $13 million with co-located FM; FTR 11-4-91). Net: AP, CNN, NBC Talknet, MBS. Rep: Major Mkt. Format: Talk radio. News staff 4. Target aud: 25-54. ■ Ronald Unkefer, pres; Bob Vistocky, vp & gen mgr; Ali Shepherd, gen sls mgr; Michelle Falo, natl sls mgr; Susan Reynolds, prom mgr; Robert Hamilton, progmg dir; Dave Henderson, news dir; Marilyn Sandifur, pub affrs dir; Chuck Waltman, chief engr.

KYA(FM)—Co-owned with KSFO(AM). February 1959: 93.3 mhz; 50 kw. Ant 492 ft. TL: N37 43 27 W122 07 07. Stereo. Dups AM 85%. Rep: Major Mkt. Format: Oldies.

KSRY(FM)—Dec 10, 1959: 98.9 mhz; 6 kw. Ant 1,143 ft. TL: N37 45 20 W122 27 05. Stereo. Hrs opn: 24. Suite 404, 642 Harrison St. (94107). (415) 512-9999. Licensee: Viacom Broadcasting Inc. (group owner; acq 7-12-90; $15.5 million). Net: NBC. Rep: Katz. Format: Hot adult contemp (superstars of the 80s and 90s). News staff one; Target aud: 18-54. ■ Bruce Raven-Stark, vp & gen mgr; Lynne Simon, gen sls mgr; Rick Love, progmg dir; Dred Scott, news dir; Ted Minnard, chief engr.

***KUSF(FM)**—April 1964: 90.3 mhz; 3 kw. Ant 300 ft. TL: N37 46 34 W122 26 54. Stereo. Hrs opn: 24. 2130 Fulton St. (94117-1080). (415) 386-5873. FAX: (415) 386-6469. Licensee: University of San Francisco (acq 1973). Format: Alternative music, div, educ. Target aud: College educated, affluent, multicultural. Spec prog: Chinese 9 hrs, class 6 hrs, relg 5 hrs, jazz 3 hrs, French 2 hrs, Turkish 2 hrs, It one hr, Pol one hr, Armenian one hr, Finnish one hr, Irish one hr wkly. ■ Steve Runyon, gen mgr; Robert Barone, dev mgr; Justin Boland, prom mgr; Kate Ingram, progmg dir; Jim Heffeman, mus dir; Bill Ruck, chief engr.

KYA(FM)—Listing follows KSFO(AM).

San Gabriel

KALI(AM)—1942: 1430 khz; 5 kw-U, DA-2. TL: N34 07 10 W118 04 57. 5723 Melrose Ave., Hollywood (90038). (213) 466-6161. FAX: (213) 466-9021. Licensee: Tele Broadcasters of California Inc. (acq 2-57). Net: AP. Format: Sp. ■ Gerald Hroblak, pres; Raul Ortal, gen mgr; Gary Mercer, opns mgr; Tom Bell, gen sls mgr; Jose Reyes, progmg dir; Frank Calderon, news dir; Rick Sunt, chief engr.

San Jacinto

KWRP(FM)—Sept 23, 1990: 96.1 mhz; 60 w. Ant 1,502 ft. TL: N33 49 45 W116 57 10. Hrs opn: 24. 188 E. Main St. (92583); Box 637 (92581). (909) 654-1961; (909) 487-5977. FAX: (909) 654-3992. Licensee: H.S.C. Radio Inc. Verry Hartline. Net: USA. Format: Easy lstng. News progmg 15 hrs wkly. Target aud: 25 plus. ■ Jerry Hartline, CEO, pres, gen mgr & natl sls mgr; Judy Whitson, gen sls mgr; Bill Hoadley, prom mgr, progmg dir & mus dir; Luther Pillow, chief engr.

San Jose

KARA(FM)—See Santa Clara.

KAZA(AM)—See Gilroy.

KBAY(FM)—Listing follows KKSJ(AM).

KEZR(FM)—July 3, 1967: 106.5 mhz; 50 kw. Ant 430 ft. TL: N37 21 43 W121 45 23. Stereo. Box 2337 (95109); 95 S. Market St. (95113). (408) 287-5775. FAX: (408) 293-3341. Licensee: Alta Broadcasting Co. (acq 8-9-76). Rep: Christal. Format: Adult contemp. News staff 2; news progmg 2 hrs wkly. Target aud: 18-49. Spec prog: Jazz 5 hrs wkly. ■ Jame Levitt, chmn; John F. Levitt, pres & gen mgr; Debi Covello, gen sls mgr; Doris Blakes, prom dir; Bill Stedman, progmg dir; Michael Bennett, news dir; Ethel Santiago, pub affrs dir; Mike Stockwell, chief engr. ■ Rates: $125; 125; 125; 60.

KFAX(AM)—See San Francisco.

KHQT(FM)—See Los Altos.

KKSF(FM)—See San Francisco.

KKSJ(AM)—June 21, 1947: 1370 khz; 5 kw-U, DA-2. TL: N37 23 10 W121 53 55. Stereo. Hrs opn: 24. Box 6616 (95150); 399 N. 3rd St., Campbell (95008). (408) 370-1370. FAX: (408) 364-4545. Licensee: United Broadcasting Co. Net: UPI. Rep: Major Mkt. Format: Nostalgia. News staff 2. Target aud: 35 plus. ■ Steve Snell, gen mgr & progmg dir; Frank Angelino, gen sls mgr; Bill Holmberg, natl sls mgr; Lisa Kreisler, news dir; John Higdon, chief engr.

KBAY(FM)—Co-owned with KKSJ(AM). March 4, 1963: 100.3 mhz; 14.5 kw. Ant 2,580 ft. TL: N37 06 40 W121 50 34. Stereo. Hrs opn: 24. Prog sep from AM. (408) 370-7377. Format: Soft adult contemp. News staff 2. ■ Bob Kohtz, progmg dir & mus dir. ■ Rates: $145; 115; 115; 40.

***KLEL(FM)**—May 17, 1977: 89.3 mhz; 100 w. Ant -539 ft. TL: N37 12 59 W121 50 39. 6677 Camden Ave. (95120). (408) 268-6343. Licensee: San Jose Unified School District. Format: Rock (AOR). Spec prog: Educ 5 hrs wkly. ■ Joe Lobue, gen mgr; Bill Brooks, chief engr.

KLIV(AM)—1946: 1590 khz; 5 kw-U, DA-N. TL: N37 19 45 W121 51 23. Hrs opn: 24. Box 995 (95108); 750 Story Rd. (95122). (408) 293-8030. FAX: (408) 293-6124. Licensee: Empire Broadcasting Corp. (acq 7-1-67). Net: CNN. Wash atty: Rosenman & Colin. Format: News. News staff 6. Target aud: General. ■ Robert S. Kieve, pres; Vincent Lopopolo, gen mgr & chief engr; Carolyn Gray, gen sls mgr; Jane McMillan, progmg dir & news dir.

KLOK(AM)—Oct 19, 1946: 1170 khz; 50 kw-D, 5 kw-N, DA-2. TL: N37 18 41 W121 48 58. Hrs opn: 24. 2905 S. King Rd. (95122). (408) 274-1170. FAX: (408) 274-1170; TWX: (910) 338-0233. Licensee: Metro Mix Inc. (acq 6-16-92; $6.06 million; FTR 7-6-92). Net: CRC; Rep: Katz Radio. Format: Sp, news/talk. News staff 5; news progmg 30 hrs wkly. Target aud: 25-59. ■ Chris Marks, exec vp & vp mktg; Athena Marks, vp & gen mgr; Jeffery Liberman, stn mgr & natl sls mgr; Mary Hernandez, gen sls mgr; Martha Garza, rgnl sls mgr; Angela Zepeda, mktg dir, prom dir & news dir; Guillermo Prince, progmg dir & mus dir; Jim Philips, chief engr.

KNTA(AM)—(Santa Clara). Dec 18, 1964: 1430 khz; 1 kw-U, DA-1. TL: N37 23 54 W121 53 35 (CP: 1 kw-N). Hrs opn: 24. Box 631, San Jose (95150). (408) 244-1430. FAX: (408) 244-0824. Licensee: Imperio Enterprises Inc. (acq 7-7-93; $1.4 million; FTR 8-2-93). Rep: Lotus. Wash atty: Koteen & Naftlin. Format: Sp. News staff one; news progmg 14 hrs wkly. Target aud: 23-34; Hispanic. ■

Genaro Guizar, pres; Gene Hogan, gen mgr & gen sls mgr; Cindy Leon-Valdez, opns dir; Javier Marcias, mus dir; Ervin Higueros, news dir. ■ Rates: $65; 55; 65; 50.

KOME(FM)—July 1, 1959: 98.5 mhz; 12.5 kw. Ant 880 ft. TL: N37 12 17 W121 56 56. Stereo. Hrs opn: 24. Plaza W., Suite 3, 3031 Tisch Way (95128). (408) 985-9800. FAX: (408) 296-8962; (408) 985-8675. Licensee: The Audio House Inc. Group owner: Infinity Broadcasting Corp. (acq 5-1-73). Net: NBC the Source. Rep: Torbet. Wash atty: Leventhal, Senter & Lerman. Format: AOR. ■ Mel Karmazin, pres; Jim Hardy, gen mgr; Rich Kahn, gen sls mgr; David Wohlman, prom mgr; Ron Nenni, progmg dir; Stephen Page, mus dir; Bob Lilley, news dir; Marla Davies, pub affrs dir; John Higdon, chief engr.

KSJO(FM)—Listing follows KSJX(AM).

***KSJS(FM)**—Feb 22, 1963: 90.7 mhz; 1 kw. Ant -186 ft. TL: N37 20 09 W121 53 04 (CP: 2.5 kw, ant 393 ft.). Stereo. Calif. State Univ. San Jose, One Washington Square (95192-0094). (408) 924-4548; (408) 924-4545. FAX: (408) 928-1018. Licensee: San Jose State University. Format: Jazz, alternative. News staff 3; news progmg 2 hrs wkly. Target aud: 18-34; students. Spec prog: Black 6 hrs, Sp 5 hrs, women one hr, poetry 2 hrs, Vietnamese one hr wkly. ■ Mike Adams, pres; Pol VanRhee, gen mgr; Palle Madsen, asst mus dir; Marie Capuyan, news dir; Alesia Beischoff, pub affrs dir; Gary Ashby, chief engr.

KSJX(AM)—June 24, 1948: 1500 khz; 10-kw-D, 5 kw-N, DA-2. TL: N37 21 28 W121 52 17. 1420 Koll Circle (95112). (408) 453-5400. FAX: (408) 452-1330. Licensee: BayCom San Jose L.P. Group owner: BayCom Partners L.P. (acq 10-91; $5.5 million with co-located FM; FTR 11-4-91). Net: BRN. Rep: Katz. Format: International. News staff 2. Target aud: 25-54; managerial, professional, homeowners. ■ Jack McSorley, CEO; Edgar P. Canty, CFO; John A. Sutherland, gen mgr; Eric N. Stenberg, gen sls mgr; Marty Wright, prom mgr; Dana Jang, progmg dir & mus dir; Paul Tonelli, news dir; Dick Cownie, pub affrs dir; David Williams, chief engr.

KSJO(FM)—Co-owned with KSJX(AM). December 1946: 92.3 mhz; 50 kw. Ant 464 ft. TL: N37 12 33 W121 46 30. Stereo. Prog sep from AM. Net: ABC/R. Rep: McGavren Guild. Format: AOR. Target aud: 18-49; active adults. ■ John N. Stenberg, gen mgr.

San Luis Obispo

***KCBX(FM)**—July 25, 1975: 90.1 mhz; 5.3 kw. Ant 1,420 ft. TL: N35 21 38 W120 39 21. Stereo. 4100 Vachell Ln. (93401). (805) 781-3020. Licensee: KCBX Inc. Net: NPR. Wash atty: Cohn & Marks. Format: Classical, jazz, news. News progmg 103 hrs wkly. Target aud: General. Spec prog: Folk 15 hrs wkly. ■ Frank Lanzone, pres & gen mgr; Hank Hadley, opns mgr; Paul Severtson, dev dir & mktg mgr; Guy Rathbun, progmg dir; Chris O'Connell, mus dir; William Miller, chief engr.

***KCPR(FM)**—1968: 91.3 mhz; 2 kw. Ant -350 ft. TL: N35 17 58 W120 40 26. Stereo. Hrs opn: 24. Graphic Arts, Room 201, California Polytechnic State Univ. (93407). (805) 756-5277. Licensee: California Polytechnic State Univ. Format: College alternative rock. News progmg 4 hrs wkly. Target aud: General; Cal Poly students, San Luis Obispo community. Spec prog: Black 8 hrs, class 3 hrs, jazz 3 hrs, city council 4 hrs, reggae 3 hrs, Sp 3 hrs, public affrs 5 hrs, metal 3 hrs, blues 3 hrs, hardcore 2 hrs, sound tracks 2 hrs wkly. ■ Clark Farrell, gen mgr; Miles Stegall, mktg dir; David Welch, Jeanne Acceturo, prom dirs; Amy Hummel, progmg dir; James Paasche, mus dir; Jodi Ross, Cecilia Hastings, news dirs; Rob Wilhoite, pub affrs dir; Rosalie Pham, chief engr.

KGLW(AM)—Dec 13, 1949: 1340 khz; 1 kw-U. TL: N35 15 07 W120 40 24. Box 170, Arroyo Grande (93421); 1025 Grand Ave., Arroyo Grande (93420). (805) 544-5289; (805) 481-1804. Licensee: RocGlo Communications (acq 12-16-91; $25,000; FTR 2-17-92). Net: ABC/E. Rep: Republc. Format: News/talk, info. Target aud: 35 plus; People who are concerned about the world and their community. Spec prog: Holistic medicine, new age talk, drama, suspense, comedy. ■ Glo Rivera, pres & gen mgr; Edward Rivera, exec vp; Cathy Riddle, opns mgr; Rocky Rivera, chief engr. ■ Rates: $14; 14; 12; na.

KIID(AM)—Feb 6, 1960: 1400 khz; 1 kw-U. TL: N35 15 51 W120 39 56. Box 1400 (93406). (805) 544-1400. Licensee: San Luis Obispo Broadcasting L.P. (acq 9-9-86). Rep: Katz. Format: Country. ■ Eric Shade, progmg dir.

KSLY-FM—Co-owned with KIID(AM). December 1959: 96.1 mhz; 5.6 kw. Ant 1,410 ft. TL: N35 21 38 W120 39 21. Stereo. Dups AM 83.5%. (805) 543-9400. Format: Top-40. ■ Jonathan Harte, progmg dir; Dean Clarke, mus dir; Bill Bordeaux, chief engr.

KIQO(FM)—See Atascadero.

KIXT-FM—See Grover City.

KJDJ(AM)—Feb 8, 1988: 1030 khz; 2.5 kw-D, 700 w-N. TL: N35 17 58 W120 40 24. Suite 107, 1160 Marsh St. (93401). (805) 922-3312. FAX: (805) 922-1974. Licensee: Jaime Bonilla Valdez (acq 12-16-92; $155,000; FTR 1-11-93). ■ Mateo Camarillo, pres; Ismael Antonio Leyva, progmg dir.

KKAL(AM)—(Arroyo Grande). June 29, 1962: 1280 khz; 5-kw-D, 2.5 kw-N, DA-2. TL: N35 08 33 W120 31 10. Box 987, San Luis Obispo (93406-0987). (805) 781-2750. FAX: (805) 473-2890. Licensee: KZOZ Radio Inc. Group owner: American General Media (acq 6-89; grpsl; FTR 6-19-89). Net: MBS. Format: Sports. News staff one; news progmg 2 hrs wkly. Target aud: 18-49. ■ Joe McMahon, gen mgr; Dave Garrison (local), rgnl sls mgr; Autumn Cornwell, prom mgr; Rick Andrews, progmg mgr; Bill Bordot, chief engr.

KZOZ(FM)—Co-owned with KKAL(AM). 1962: 93.3 mhz; 29.5 kw. Ant 1,470 ft. TL: N35 21 38 W120 39 21. Stereo. Prog sep from AM. Format: Classic rock, AOR. ■ Joe McMahon, vp & gen mgr; Autumn Cornwell, prom dir; Rick Andrews, progmg dir.

KKJG(FM)—Jan 1, 1984: 98.1 mhz; 3.6 kw. Ant 1,624 ft. TL: N35 21 37 W120 39 18. Stereo. 396 Buckley Rd. (93401). (805) 541-8798. Licensee: Westcoast Broadcasting Inc. (group owner; acq 5-1-92; $800,000; FTR 5-25-92). Rep: D & R Radio. Format: Adult contemp. Spec prog: Jazz 2 hrs, Christian 3 hrs wkly. ■ Wayne Foster, gen mgr; John Katz, progmg dir & mus dir.

KSLY-FM—Listing follows KIID(AM).

KVEC(AM)—May 1937: 920 khz; 1 kw-D, 500 w-N. TL: N35 17 58 W120 40 24. Hrs opn: 24. 1329 Chorro St. (93401-4005). (805) 543-8830. FAX: (805) 781-2568. Licensee: Chorro Communications Inc. (acq 9-27-89; $300,000; FTR 10-16-89). Net: ABC/I, CNN. Rep: Roslin. Format: News/talk, sports, business. News staff 3; news progmg 45 hrs wkly. Target aud: 24-54; affluent decision & newsmakers, sports fans, business owners, retired folks. Spec prog: Paul Harvey, Success Stories, Financial Fitness, Senior Focus, Motor Mouths. ■ Frank Sheahan, pres; Dan Clarkson, stn mgr, gen sls mgr & progmg dir; John Christopher, news dir; Larry James, pub affrs dir; Bill Bordieax, chief engr. ■ Rates: $16; 14; 13; 13.

KZOZ(FM)—Listing follows KKAL(AM).

San Marcos

KPRZ(AM)—1986: 1210 khz; 20 kw-D, 5 kw-N, DA-2. TL: N33 04 12 W117 11 35. Hrs opn: 24. Suite 201, 1635 S. Rancho Santa Fe Rd. (92069-5158). (619) 471-1177. FAX: (619) 471-2256. Licensee: Radio 1210 Inc. Group owner: Salem Communications Corp. Format: Christian talk. News progmg 2 hrs wkly. Target aud: 25-54. Spec prog: Sp 13 hrs wkly. ■ Edward G. Astinger III., pres; Ron Walters, gen mgr & stn mgr; Monica Murray, opns mgr, prom dir & pub affrs dir; Tom Levine, gen sls mgr; Roger Marsh, progmg dir; David Manzi, mus dir; Bruce Johnson, news dir; Doug Schleutker, engrg dir. ■ Rates: $50; 40; 45; 35.

San Mateo

***KCSM(FM)**—October 1964: 91.1 mhz; 14 kw. Ant 330 ft. TL: N37 32 12 W122 20 02. 1700 W. Hillsdale Blvd. (94402). (415) 574-6427. Licensee: San Mateo County Community College District. Net: NPR. Format: Big band, jazz, news. News progmg 10 hrs wkly. Target aud: General. Spec prog: Blues 5 hrs, bluegrass 5 hrs wkly. ■ David Hosley, gen mgr; Anne Weitzel, stn mgr; Dick Conte, prom dir & mus dir; Melanie Berzon, progmg dir; Claire Mack (community affrs), pub affrs dir; Bill Fox, engrg mgr. ■ *KCSM-TV affil.

KOFY(AM)—1948: 1050 khz; 50 kw-D, 10 kw-N, DA-2. TL: N37 39 02 W122 09 08 Stereo. Hrs opn: 24. 2500 Marin St., San Francisco (94407). (415) 692-0129. Licensee: Pacific FM Inc. (acq 1-1-86). Rep: Lotus. Format: Sp. Target aud: 25-54. ■ James Gabbert, pres; Michael Lincoln, exec vp; Bill Gilreath, gen mgr; Sue Metzer, gen sls mgr; Karen Provenza, prom dir; Ignacio Alvarez, progmg dir; Carole Fertick, news dir; John Perry, engrg dir.

KSOL(FM)—September 1963: 107.7 mhz; 8.9 kw. Ant 1,162 ft. TL: N37 41 20 W122 26 07. Stereo. 55 Green St., 2nd Fl. San Francisco (94111-1412). (415) 391-1077. Licensee: KSOL L.P. (acq 9-21-93; $13.5 million; FTR 10-11-93). Net: AP. Rep: Major Mkt. Format: CHR. ■ Scott Fey, sr vp & vp; Sue Bell, sls dir; Rick Thomas, progmg dir; Michael Martin, mus dir; Bob Fuller, chief engr.

San Rafael

***KSRH(FM)**—May 1, 1980: 88.1 mhz; 10 w. Ant 66 ft. TL: N37 58 16 W122 30 47. Hrs opn: 9 AM-3 PM. AR 101, 185 Mission Ave. (94941). (415) 457-5314; (415) 457-5774. FAX: (415) 457-5314. Licensee: San Rafael High School District. Format: Div, Black. News progmg 5 hrs. Target aud: 12-29. Spec prog: Fr one hr wkly. ■ Donovan Hughes, gen mgr & stn mgr; Brandon Grundy, mus dir.

KTID(AM)—May 1947: 1510 khz; 1 kw-D. TL: N38 01 38 W122 31 13. Bldg. D., 1623 Fifth Ave. (94901). (415) 456-1510. FAX: (415) 456-7261. Licensee: Marin Broadcasting Co. Group owner: Astor Broadcast Group (acq 7-21-83; $1.4 million with co-located FM; FTR 8-8-83). Net: UPI. Format: Adult contemp. ■ N. Arthur Astor, pres; Susan E. Brice, vp; Carl Walker, gen mgr; Larry Ickes, progmg dir; Paul Sakrison, chief engr.

KTID-FM—June 1, 1961: 100.9 mhz; 480 w. Ant 798 ft. TL: N37 58 49 W122 31 39. Stereo. Prog sep from AM.

Santa Ana

KWIZ(AM)—Nov 26, 1926: 1480 khz; 5-kw-U, DA-2. TL: N33 45 06 W117 54 36. 3101 W. Fifth St. (92703). (714) 554-5000. FAX: (714) 554-9362; TWX: (910) 595-1126. Licensee: Liberman Broadcasting Inc. (group owner; acq 1-88; $6.25 million with co-located FM; FTR 1-4-88). Net: CNN, AP. Rep: Torbet. Format: Sp. ■ Jose Liberman, pres; Andy Mars, rgnl sls mgr.

KWIZ-FM—1947: 96.7 mhz; 3 kw. Ant 200 ft. TL: N33 48 08 W117 47 43 (CP: Ant 206 ft.). Stereo. Suite 130, 3350 Electronic Dr., Pasadena (91107). (213) 681-2486. Licensee: Radio KWIZ Partners L.P. Group owner: Douglas Broadcasting Inc. (acq 1-17-92; $8.75 million; FTR 2-17-92). Format: International. Spec prog: Vietnamese. ■ John Douglas, CEO; Linda Johnson-Hayes, vp & gen mgr; Bob Gourley, opns mgr & progmg dir; Jeff Farmer, sls dir & mktg dir; Fred Folmer, engrg dir.

KYMS(FM)—Feb 6, 1980: 106.3 mhz; 3 kw. Ant 130 ft. TL: N33 45 21 W117 51 16 (CP: Ant 203 ft., TL: N33 45 21 W117 51 17). Stereo. Suite 106, 1748 W. Katella, Orange (92667). (714) 633-2020; (714) 633-1063. FAX: (714) 744-KYMS. Licensee: Interstate Broadcasting Systems. Group owner: Interstate Broadcasting Systems Inc. (acq 1-81). Format: Contemp Christian. News staff one; news progmg one hr wkly. Target aud: 18-44. ■ Paul Toberty, pres; Kent Bagdascar, gen mgr & gen sls mgr; Gary Parkhurst, progmg dir, mus dir & news dir; Peter Bruins, chief engr.

Santa Barbara

KCQR(FM)—(Ellwood). Feb 6, 1989: 94.5 mhz; 1 kw. Ant 3,000 ft. TL: N34 31 32 W119 57 28. Hrs opn: 24. Suite E-9, 4141 State St., Santa Barbara (93110). (805) 964-7670. FAX: (805) 683-2753. Licensee: South Coast Broadcasting Inc. Rep: Banner. Wash atty: Fisher, Wayland, Cooper & Leader. Format: Quality classic rock. Target aud: 25-44; baby boomers. Spec prog: Blues one hr, reggae one hr wkly, folk 2 hrs wkly. ■ Sue Romaine, pres & gen mgr; Greg Bryce, vp; Traci Claussen, gen sls mgr; David Hefferman, prom dir & pub affrs dir; Tom Van Sant, progmg dir; Chuck Hastings, chief engr. ■ Rates: $50; 50; 50; 30.

***KCSB-FM**—November 1964: 91.9 mhz; 620 w. Ant 2,910 ft. TL: N34 31 31 W119 57 29 (CP: Ant 1,879 ft.). Stereo. UCEN, Room 3185 A (93106). (805) 893-3757. Licensee: Regents of the Univ. of California Format: Alternative, div. Spec prog: Black 20 hrs, Sp 12 hrs, jazz 10 hrs, blues 6 hrs, C&W 2 hrs, class 4 hrs wkly. ■ David Gardner, pres; Christina Guzy, gen mgr; Eric Lewis, prom dir; Monica Lopez, progmg dir; Marie Guinto, Dave Helm, mus dirs; Stephanie Adrouny, Mylinh Le, news dirs; Bamby Levy, pub affrs dir; Chuck Hastings, chief engr.

KDB(FM)—Feb 14, 1960: 93.7 mhz; 12.5 kw. Ant 870 ft. TL: N34 27 58 W119 40 37. Stereo. 23 W. Micheltorena St. (93101). (805) 966-4131. Licensee: Pacific Broadcasting Co. Rep: CMBS. Wash atty: Fletcher, Heald & Hildreth. Format: Class. Target aud: General; affluent, influential, active. ■ Bob Scott, gen mgr, sls dir, progmg dir & mus dir; Ran Bullard, engrg dir. ■ Rates: $37; 37; 37; 37.

***KFAC(FM)**—July 1985: 88.7 mhz; 12 kw. Ant 866 ft. TL: N34 27 55 W119 40 37. Stereo. Hrs opn: 24. Box 77913, Los Angeles (90007-0913). (213) 743-5872. FAX: (213) 743-5853. Licensee: Univ. of Southern California. Net: APR. Wash atty: Brinig & Bernstein. Format: Class. News progmg 9 hrs wkly. Target aud: 35 plus. Spec prog:

Sp 2 hrs, multi-ethnic 2 hrs wkly. ■ Wallace Smith, pres & gen mgr; Bill Kappelman, vp opns; Lyle Henry, chief engr.

KHTY(FM)—Listing follows KTMS(AM).

KIST(AM)—1946: 1340 khz; 1 kw-U. TL: N34 25 09 W119 41 54 (CP: 675 w-U). Stereo. 1221 Chapala (93101). (805) 962-7800. FAX: (805) 965-6001. Licensee: Channel Islands Broadcasting Inc. (acq 1-28-93; $1.5 million with KMGQ(FM) Goleta; FTR 2-15-93). Rep: CBS Radio. Format: Oldies. News staff one; news progmg 4 hrs wkly. Target aud: 25-54. ■ Mike Micassio, Dan Prodanovich, gen mgrs; Jennifer Van Donge, gen sls mgr; Jill Rivera, natl sls mgr; Karin Kasnoff, prom dir; Joni Caryl, progmg dir; Nancy Newcomer, Steve Bauer, mus dirs; Dick Williams, news dir; Chuck Hasting, chief engr.

KKSB(AM)—March 1961: 1290 khz; 500 w-D, 122 w-N. TL: N34 25 07 W119 41 10. Stereo. Hrs opn: 24. Box 40309 (93140). (805) 568-1444; (407) 283-6871. FAX: (805) 564-4489; (407) 283-6871. Licensee: Joyce C. Erway (acq 1973). Format: Country. Target aud: 18 plus. ■ Guy Erway, gen mgr, vp sls, mktg mgr, prom mgr & news dir; Joyce C. Erway, stn mgr. ■ Rates: $30; 20; 30; 15.

KMGQ(FM)—See Goleta.

KQSB(AM)—Aug 11, 1962: 990 khz; 5 kw-D, 500 w-N, DA-2. TL: N34 28 15 W119 40 33. Stereo. Hrs opn: 24. 5360 Hollister (93111). (805) 967-4511; (805) 967-5050. FAX: (805) 683-5893. Licensee: Seaview Broadcasting Inc. (acq 10-4-92; $450,000; FTR 11-23-92). Net: MBS. Format: Talk. News staff 2; news progmg 4 hrs wkly. Target aud: 25 plus; upscale adults. ■ David Perry, exec vp & gen mgr; Mark St. James, opns dir; Sandy Lupouski, gen sls mgr; Bob Burger, rgnl sls mgr; Sabrina Davies, prom mgr; Ran Bullard, chief engr.

KRUZ(FM)—Aug 8, 1961: 103.3 mhz; 105 kw. Ant 2,980 ft. TL: N34 31 30 W119 57 10. Stereo. Hrs opn: 24. 800 Miramonte Dr. (93109). (805) 963-1831. Licensee: The Schuele Org. Inc. (acq 5-21-71). Rep: Katz. Format: Easy lstng. ■ Carl L. Schuele, pres & gen mgr; Dorothy L. Schuele, vp; Albert B. Sturges, gen sls mgr; Randall Chase, progmg dir; Dirk Pinter, mus dir; Mark Waters, news dir; Chuck Hastings, chief engr.

KSBL(FM)—See Carpinteria.

KSPE(AM)—April 1926: 1490 mhz; 1 kw-U. TL: N34 24 57 W119 41 10. Stereo. Hrs opn: 24. KSPE Bldg., 331 N. Milpas St. F. (93103). (805) 965-1490. Licensee: Spectacular Broadcasting Inc. (acq 1-30-91; $302,000; FTR 2-18-91). Rep: Lotus. Wash atty: Fletcher, Heald & Hildreth. Format: Sp, news/talk. News staff one; news progmg 50 hrs wkly. Target aud: 16-65; Hispanic. ■ Richard C. Marsh, CEO & gen mgr; Jim Farr, vp & vp sls; Marlene Huddy, opns dir; Gerardo Lorenz, prom dir, vp progmg, progmg dir & mus dir; Pepe De Marco, news dir & pub affrs dir; Ransom Bullard, chief engr. ■ Rates: $26; 26; 26; 23.

KTMS(AM)—Oct 31, 1937: 1250 khz; 2.5 kw-D, 1 kw-N, DA-2. TL: N34 25 06 W119 49 05. Box 4458 (93140); 1330 Cacique St. (93103). (805) 966-1755. FAX: (805) 564-4489. Licensee: Pinnacle Communications Inc. (acq 3-88). Net: ABC TalkRadio, ABC/I, NBC Talknet, CNN. Rep: D & R Radio. Wash atty: Reed, Shaw & McClay. Format: News/talk. News staff 9; news progmg 28 hrs wkly. Target aud: 25 plus. ■ Leslie R. Carroll, pres; Lou Hebert, gen mgr; John Strahler, chief engr.

KHTY(FM)—Co-owned with KTMS(AM). Sept 1, 1957: 97.5 mhz; 17.5 kw. Ant 2,920 ft. TL: N34 31 31 W119 57 29. Prog sep from AM. Net: ABC/FM. Format: CHR. Target aud: 18-34; mass appeal. ■ Abigail Bonell, prom mgr; Steve Gunner, progmg dir & mus dir.

KTYD(FM)—Aug 11, 1972: 99.9 mhz; 34 kw. Ant 1,278 ft. TL: N34 28 15 W119 40 33. Stereo. Hrs opn: 24. Box 62110 (93160); 5360 Hollister Ave. (93111). (805) 967-4511. FAX: (805) 964-4430. Licensee: Criterion Media Group Inc. (acq 2-22-93; $1.3 million; FTR 3-8-93). Rep: McGavren Guild. Wash atty: Wiley, Rein & Fielding. Format: AOR. News staff one; news progmg 3 hrs wkly. Target aud: 18-49; upscale adults. Spec prog: Public affairs one hr. ■ David Perry, pres, vp, gen mgr & progmg dir; Sandy Lipowski, gen sls mgr; Sabine Davies, mktg mgr & prom mgr; Paul Cavagh, mus dir; John Palmenteri, news dir; Doug Allen, chief engr. ■ Rates: $125; 110; 120; 100.

Santa Clara

KARA(FM)—Sept 25, 1964: 105.7 mhz; 50 kw. Ant 500 ft. TL: N37 21 32 W121 45 22. Stereo. Hrs opn: 24. Box 995, San Jose (95108). (408) 293-8030. FAX: (408) 293-6124. Licensee: Empire Broadcasting Corp. (acq 7-1-72; $470,000). Rep: Major Mkt. Wash atty: Rosenman & Colin. Format: Adult contemp. News staff 5; news progmg 2 hrs wkly. Target aud: 25-54. ■ Robert S. Kieve, pres; Vincent A. Lopopolo, vp; Joanne Kilmartin, sls dir; Jodie Gonzalez, prom mgr; John McLeod, progmg dir; Mike Danberger, mus dir; Jane McMillan, news dir; Rosana Madrigal, pub affrs dir; Vince Lopopolo, chief engr.

KLIV(AM)—See San Jose.

KNTA(AM)—Licensed to Santa Clara. See San Jose.

***KSCU(FM)**—July 1, 1978: 103.3 mhz; 30 w. Ant 179 ft. TL: N37 20 53 W121 56 25. Stereo. Hrs opn: 20. Box 1207, Santa Clara University (95053); 500 El Camino Real 3207 (95053-3707). (408) 554-4413; (408) 248-5728. FAX: (408) 554-5544. Licensee: President and Board of Trustees of Santa Clara Univ. Format: Modern alternative rock w/specialty program. News progmg 2 hrs wkly. Target aud: 16-30; young adults who like modern music. Spec prog: Sports 2 hrs, interview one hr, rap 6 hrs, blues 12 hrs, techno 5 hrs wkly. ■ Tesin Uy, gen mgr; Victoria Schneider, dev dir; Diane Liu, prom dir; Desmond Crisis, mus dir; Lisa Larkin, news dir; Arthur Leberman, chief engr. ■ Rates: $33; 29; 33; 29.

Santa Cruz

***KFER(FM)**—Not on air, target date unknown: 89.9 mhz; 200 w. Ant 26 ft. TL: N37 00 459 W121 58 25. Box 13 (95063). Licensee: Santa Cruz Educational Broadcasting Foundation.

KMBY(AM)—See Capitola.

KSCO(AM)—Sept 21, 1947: 1080 khz; 10 kw-D, 5 kw-N, DA-2. TL: N36 57 43 W121 58 51. 2300 Portola Dr. (95062). (408) 475-1080. FAX: (408) 475-2967. Licensee: Zwerling Broadcasting System Ltd. (acq 1-31-91; $600,000; FTR 12-31-90). Net: CNN. Rep: McGavren Guild. Format: News/talk. ■ Michael L. Zwerling, pres; Dick Little, gen mgr & news dir; Rich Cornett, chief engr.

KSRI(FM)—Sept 2, 1961: 99.1 mhz; 1.1 kw. Ant 2,487 ft. TL: N37 06 40 W121 50 34. Stereo. Hrs opn: 24. Suite 404, 642 Harrison St., San Francisco (94107). (415) 512-9999. FAX: (415) 243-0384. Licensee: Viacom Broadcasting Inc. (group owner; acq 6-22-90; $5.75 million; FTR 7-30-90). Net: ABC/C. Rep: Katz. Format: Adult contemp, classic rock. News staff one; news progmg 4 hrs wkly. Target aud: 25-54. ■ Bruce Raven-Stark, vp & gen mgr; Lyne Simon, gen sls mgr; Rick Love, progmg dir; Scott Miller, news dir; Ted Minnard, chief engr.

***KUSP(FM)**—Apr 14, 1972: 88.9 mhz; 860 w. Ant 3,750 ft. TL: N36 32 05 W121 37 14 (CP: 1.25 kw, ant 2,496 ft.). Stereo. Hrs opn: 24. Box 423 (95061); 203 8th Ave. (95062). (408) 476-2800; (800) 695-KUSP. FAX: (408) 476-2802. Licensee: Pataphysical Broadcasting Foundation. Net: NPR, APR. Wash atty: Haley, Bader & Potts. Format: Eclectic. News staff 2; news progmg 41 hrs wkly. Spec prog: Black 20 hrs, folk 10 hrs, Sp 2 hrs wkly. ■ Louie X. Heinrich, chmn; John Henry Ledwith, vp; Marcia Kraus, gen mgr; Peter Troxell, dev dir, prom dir & adv dir; Dale Owen, sls dir; Johnny Simmons, mus dir & news dir; Spencer Critchley, pub affrs dir; Ray Dasher, chief engr. ■ Rates: $24; 15; 24; 15.

***KZSC(FM)**—August 1974: 88.1 mhz; 1.36 kw. Ant 350 ft. TL: N37 00 10 W122 03 05. Stereo. KZSC, UCSC (95064). (408) 459-0111. Licensee: Regents of Univ. of California. Format: Div. News progmg 40 hrs wkly. Target aud: College age through late 30s. Spec prog: Black 15 hrs, class 6 hrs, C&W 4 hrs, jazz 19 hrs, Portuguese 2 hrs, alternative lifestyle 2 hrs, Sp 6 hrs, soul 10 hrs, women's 5 hrs, Native American 2 hrs, Central American 2 hrs wkly. ■ Maggie O'Grady, gen mgr; L'Cinda Scott-McCall, mus dir; John Thorton, chief engr.

Santa Margarita

KWSP(FM)—July 21, 1986: 106.1 mhz; 950 w. Ant 1,467 ft. TL: N35 21 38 W120 39 21. Stereo. Hrs opn: 24. Box 3610, San Luis Obispo (93403). (805) 541-1212; (805) 438-3221. FAX: (805) 438-3608. Licensee: Hance Communications (acq 1-1-89; $1.26 million; FTR 1-16-89). Format: Easy lstng. News staff 2; news progmg 6 hrs wkly. Target aud: 35 plus; upscale homeowners. ■ Tom Hansen, chmn & vp; Chrys Barnes, gen mgr, sls dir & prom mgr; Bill Benica, progmg dir, mus dir & news dir; Paul Kleinkramer, chief engr. ■ Rates: $20; 15; 15; 15.

Santa Maria

KBOX(FM)—(Lompoc). Dec 24, 1968: 104.1 mhz; 5.7 kw. Ant 710 ft. TL: N34 43 50 W120 26 01. Stereo. Hrs opn: 24. Box 518, Santa Maria (93456). (805) 735-7656. FAX: (805) 735-3760. Licensee: Broadcast Management Consultants Inc. (acq 12-86). Rep: D & R Radio. Wash atty: Hogan & Hartson. Format: Adult contemp. News staff one. Target aud: 25-54. ■ Clifford M. Hunter, pres & gen mgr; Mark Stevens, opns mgr; Emily Heavner, gen sls mgr; Jim Foley, chief engr.

KGDP(AM)—(Orcutt). July 4, 1987: 660 khz; 10 kw-D, 1 kw-N, DA-2. TL: N34 57 04 W120 22 38. Suite 501, 3070 Skyway Dr., Santa Maria (93455). (805) 928-7707. FAX: (805) 922-8582. Licensee: Radio Representatives Inc. Net: AP, CNN. Format: Christian. Target aud: 35-65. ■ Sherwood Patterson, pres, gen mgr & progmg dir; Sam Jackson, prom mgr; Norwood J. Patterson, chief engr.

KIXT-FM—See Grover City.

KKAL(AM)—See San Luis Obispo.

KSBQ(AM)—Sept 1, 1961: 1480 khz; 1 kw-D, 61 w-N. TL: N34 57 02 W120 29 22. 212 W. Carmen Lane (93454). (805) 922-1777. FAX: (805) 922-9345. Licensee: Los Padres Broadcasting Corp. (acq 11-1-80). Net: ABC/D. Rep: Lotus. Format: Spanish. Target aud: 18-49; adults. ■ Pat Cooney, gen mgr; Alberto Leon, progmg dir; Dale Williams, chief engr.

KSMA(AM)—1946: 1240 khz; 1 kw-U. TL: N34 57 02 W120 29 27. Box 1240 (93456). (805) 925-2582. FAX: (805) 928-1544. Licensee: Bayliss Broadcasting Co. (acq 7-1-80; $1.4 million with co-located FM; FTR 6-2-80). Net: CBS, CBS Spectrum. Rep: Torbet. Format: News/talk. ■ Alice R. Bayliss, pres & gen mgr; C. Townshend, progmg dir; Doug Nelson, mus dir; Steve Southwick, news dir; Dennis Bornholft, chief engr.

KSNI-FM—Co-owned with KSMA(AM). 1960: 102.5 mhz; 17.5 kw. Ant 774 ft. TL: N34 50 08 W120 24 06. Stereo. Prog sep from AM. Format: Contemp country.

KTAP(AM)—June 10, 1962: 1600 khz; 470 w-D. TL: N34 58 48 W120 27 12. 200 Glenridge Ave., Los Gatos (95030); 104 W. Chapel St. (93454). (805) 928-4334. FAX: (805) 934-2765. Licensee: Leo Kesselman (acq 2-11-91; $300,000; FTR 2-25-91). Net: MBS. Rep: Katz. Wash atty: Mark Van Burgh. Format: Adult contemp, Sp. News staff one; news progmg 4 hrs wkly. Target aud: General. Spec prog: Filipino 3 hrs wkly. ■ Irene Escalante, gen mgr; Ed Carcary, gen sls mgr; Armondo Cuellar, progmg dir; Carlos Zunigia, news dir; Dale Williams, chief engr. ■ Rates: $22; 15; 22; 5.

KUHL(AM)—April 1946: 1440 khz; 5 kw-D, 1 kw-N, DA-N. TL: N34 59 02 W120 027 10. Box 1964 (93456); 211 E. Fessler (93455). (805) 922-7727. FAX: (805) 349-0265. Licensee: Blackhawk Communications Inc. (acq 11-18-91; $1,145,653 with co-located FM; FTR 12-9-91). Net: ABC/I, ABC TalkRadio, NBC Talknet. Format: News/talk. News staff 5; news prog 25-40 hrs wkly. Target aud: 35-64; upscale news & sports listeners. ■ Roger Blaemier (Owner), pres.

KXFM(FM)—Co-owned with KUHL(AM). 1959: 99.1 mhz; 1.8 kw. Ant 1,905 ft. TL: N34 54 37 W120 11 08. Stereo. Format: Adult contemp. News staff 5; news progmg 2 hrs wkly. Target aud: 18-49; contemp, active adults.

KZOZ(FM)—See San Luis Obispo.

Santa Monica

KAJZ(FM)—Dec 22, 1960: 103.1 mhz; 3 kw. Ant 265 ft. TL: N34 00 53 W118 22 50. Stereo. Hrs opn: 24. 1425 Fifth St. (90401-2498). Ste 303, 2043 Westcliff Dr., Newport Beach (92660). (310) 458-1031; (714) 548-6277. FAX: (310) 393-2443; (714) 548-6856. Licensee: Brentwood Communications Ltd. (acq 2-15-91; $5.25 million; grpsl; FTR 3-11-91). Format: Adult contemp. Target aud: 25-54; upscale adults in Los Angeles' Westside. ■ Bonnie Stone, gen mgr; Mimi Klein, stn mgr; Andrea Siegel, gen sls mgr; Christine Tondelli, natl sls mgr; Alison Horn, prom dir; Manon Hennessey, progmg dir; John Paoli, engrg dir.

KBLA(AM)—1947: 1580 khz; 50 kw-U, DA-2. TL: N34 05 08 W118 15 24. Stereo. 1700 N. Alvarado St., Los Angeles (90026). (213) 665-1580. FAX: (213) 660-1507. Licensee: Keymarket Communication (acq 10-25-93; $12.1 million with KNAC[FM] Long Beach; FTR 11-8-93). Net: ABC/C. Format: Korean. ■ Ron Thompson, vp, gen mgr & gen sls mgr; Ron Russ, chief engr.

***KCRW(FM)**—Jan 1, 1946: 89.9 mhz; 6.9 kw. Ant 1,110 ft. TL: N34 07 08 W118 23 30. Stereo. 1900 Pico Blvd. (90405). (310) 450-5183. Licensee: Santa Monica College District (acq 8-3-76). Net: NPR, APR. Format: Eclectic, news. Spec prog: Reggae, African, contemp, jazz, Latino, drama. ■ Ruth Seymour, gen mgr; Mitchell Harding, opns dir; Jacqueline Des Lauriers, prom mgr; Chris Douridas, mus dir; John Huntley, chief engr.

Santa Paula

KKZZ(AM)—1948: 1400 khz; 1 kw-U. TL: N34 19 48 W119 05 31. Stereo. Suite 2-M, 2284 S. Victoria Ave., Ventura (98003). (805) 656-3696. FAX: (805) 644-4257. Licensee: Golden Bear Broadcasting of Ventura Inc. Group owner: The Heusser Group (acq 4-11-90; grpsl; FTR 5-7-90). Rep: McGavren Guild. Format: Music from the 40s, 50s and 60s. News staff one. Target aud: 25-54. ■ Wallace A. Heusser, pres; B.J. Young, gen mgr; Cynthia Shipe, stn mgr; Tom Spence, opns mgr, progmg dir & news dir; Tim Curtin, gen sls mgr; Lloyd Maxwell, prom dir; Les Nelson, mus dir; Al Taddeo, chief engr.

KXBS(FM)—Oct 4, 1976: 96.7 mhz; 87 w. Ant 1,500 ft. TL: N34 19 33 W119 02 18. Stereo. Hrs opn: 24. Suite 230, 5200 Valentine Rd., Ventura (93003). (805) 644-6800. FAX: (805) 644-6181. Licensee: KXBS Broadcasting Company (acq 10-11-91; $775,000; FTR 11-4-91). Rep: CBS Spot. Format: Classic rock. ■ Peter Daradics, CEO & pres; Scotty Johnson, opns dir, progmg dir & mus dir; Dan Carter, gen sls mgr; Jim West, prom mgr; Doug Allan, chief engr. ■ Rates: $20; 15; 20; 13.

Santa Rosa

***KBBF(FM)**—May 30, 1973: 89.1 mhz; 1 kw. Ant 2,770 ft. TL: N38 39 23 W122 36 54. Box 7189 (95407). (707) 545-8833. FAX: (707) 545-6244. Licensee: Bilingual Broadcasting Foundation Inc. Format: Educ, Spanish. ■ Phillipe Garza, gen mgr; Gregorio Sarinana, progmg dir, mus dir & news dir; Tom Oja, chief engr.

***KLVR(FM)**—Oct 15, 1982: 91.9 mhz; 1.25 w. Ant 2,988 ft. TL: N38 40 09 W122 50 24. Stereo. Hrs opn: 24. 2288 Airport Blvd. (95403). (707) 528-9236. FAX: (707) 528-9246. Licensee: Educational Media Foundation (acq 1986). Wash atty: Fisher, Wayland, Cooper & Leader. Format: Contemp Christian. Target aud: 25-35; Judaeo-Christian females. ■ Richard Jenkins, pres & gen mgr; David Pierce, prom dir & progmg dir; Johnny Ray, mus dir.

KMGG(FM)—(Monte Rio). Nov 20, 1977: 97.7 mhz; 250 w. Ant 1,122 ft. TL: N38 29 08 W123 02 05. Stereo. Hrs opn: 24. Suite 3, 3535 Industrial Dr., Santa Rosa (95403). (707) 578-0977. FAX: (707) 578-1736. Licensee: Southcom Inc. Group owner: Liggett Broadcast Inc. (acq 1-1-86). Format: Oldies. Target aud: 25-54. ■ Robert G. Liggett, pres; Kent Bjugstad, gen mgr; Pat Gallagher, opns mgr; Sandy Loyko, prom mgr; Paul Siebert, chief engr.

KMXN(AM)—Dec 7, 1958: 1150 khz; 5 kw-D, 500 w-N, DA-2. TL: N38 27 14 W122 39 31. Hrs opn: 6 AM-11 PM. Suite A, 499 Humboldt St. (95404). Licensee: First Down Promotions Inc. (acq 3-12-92; $25,000; FTR 4-6-92). Format: Christian talk, Spanish mus. News staff one. Target aud: 20 plus; Christian adults. Spec prog: Ger 2 hrs, Portuguese 2 hrs wkly. ■ John Paye, pres; Thomas Driggers, gen mgr, opns mgr, dev mgr, progmg dir & chief engr; Ken Inlow, sls dir, mktg dir & adv dir; Doug Griffin, progmg mgr, mus dir & pub affrs dir. ■ Rates: $20; 20; 14; 14.

***KRCB-FM**—September 1993: 91.1 mhz; 180 w. Ant 2150 ft. TL: N38 44 25 W122 50 46. Stereo. Hrs opn: 24. 5850 Labath Ave., Rohnert Park (94928). (707) 585-8522. Licensee: Rural California Broadcasting Corp. Net: NPR, APR. Format: Class, progressive, news/talk. News staff one; news progmg 15 hrs wkly. Target aud: General. ■ Nancy Dobbs, CEO, pres, gen mgr & stn mgr; Gary Lester, chmn; Una Glass, CFO; Lucy Alexander, vp; Steve O'Niell, vp opns; John Moorhead, vp dev & vp sls; Tim Tattan, vp prom, vp progmg & mus dir; Paul Froug, pub affrs dir; Larry Stratton, vp engrg.

KRRS(AM)—Apr 1, 1962: 1460 khz; 1 kw-D, 33 w-N, DA-2. TL: N38 22 38 13 W122 43 39. Stereo. Box 2277 (95405); Suite 104 B., 1410 Neotomas Ave. (95405). (707) 545-1460. FAX: (707) 545-0112. Licensee: Moon Broadcasting Corp. (acq 1993; $400,000; FTR 9-6-93). Net: CRC. Rep: Caballero. Format: Sp. News staff one. Target aud: 25-54; contemporary Hispanic families. ■ Rene Meza, gen mgr; Baltezar Gouzman, opns dir. ■ Rates: $30; 30; 30; 18.

KSRO(AM)—May 1937: 1350 khz; 5 kw-U, DA-N. TL: N38 26 22 W122 44 51. 1410 Neo-Thomas Ave. (95405). (707) 545-0100. Licensee: Fuller-Jeffrey Broadcasting of Santa Rosa. Group owner: Fuller-Jeffrey Broadcasting Companies Inc. (acq 5-5-89). Net: NBC, ABC Talk-Radio. Rep: D & R Radio. Format: News/talk. News staff 8; News progmg 20 hrs wkly. Target aud: 35-64. ■ Robert F. Fuller, pres; Jim Kefford, vp & gen mgr; Jim Keyford, gen sls mgr; Jose Diaz, progmg dir; Sue McGuire, news dir; Randy Wells, chief engr.

KVVV(FM)—(Healdsburg). Co-owned with KSRO(AM). Dec 21, 1979: 92.9 mhz; 2.3 kw. Ant 1,800 ft. TL: N38 45 45 W122 50 24. Stereo. Format: CHR. News staff one; news progmg 3 hrs wkly. Target aud: 18-44.

KXFX(FM)—Dec 23, 1974: 101.7 mhz; 2.2 kw. Ant 1,056 ft. TL: N38 30 31 W122 39 41. Stereo. Box 2158, 1410 Neotomas Ave. (95405). (707) 543-0100. Licensee: KEFFCO Inc. Rep: Eastman. Wash atty: Pepper & Corazzini. Format: AOR, classic rock. News progmg 2 hrs wkly. Target aud: General. Spec prog: Jazz 5 hrs wkly. ■ James Kefford, gen mgr; J.R. Lorenzon, rgnl sls mgr; Liz Kelly, prom mgr; Jose Diaz, progmg dir; Sue McGuire, news dir; Randy Wells, chief engr. ■ Rates: $55; 55; 55; 40.

KZST(FM)—Apr 18, 1971: 100.1 mhz; 6 kw. Ant 240 ft. TL: N38 25 07 W122 40 33. Stereo. Hrs opn: 24. Box 100 (95402); 3392 Mendocino Ave. (95403). (707) 528-4434. FAX: (707) 527-8216. Licensee: Redwood Empire Stereocasters. Rep: McGavren Guild. Wash atty: Haley, Bader & Potts. Format: Adult contemp. News staff 2. Target aud: 25-54. ■ Gordon Zlot, chmn; Tom Skinner, vp & gen sls mgr; Tom Nelson, sls dir; Greg Hoffer, prom mgr; Brent Farris, progmg dir; Rob Singleton, news dir; Paul Siebert, chief engr.

Seaside

KLMY(FM)—Not on air, target date unknown: 103.5 mhz; 3 kw. Ant 328 ft. 1141 Fremont Blvd. (93955). Licensee: The Dunlin Group.

KMBY-FM—Nov 22, 1972: 107.1 mhz; 1.85 kw. Ant 587 ft. TL: N36 33 12 W121 47 05 Stereo. #8 Harris Ct., Monterey (93940). (408) 655-4100. FAX: (408) 655-1710. Licensee: KMBY Inc. (acq 8-1-89). Net: NBC the Source. Rep: Banner. Format: AOR. Target aud: 25-34. ■ Stephen M. Adams, gen mgr; Rich Berlin, chief opns; Kim Bryant, gen sls mgr; Debbie Hewitt, mktg dir; C.J. Morgan, prom dir; Tim Kelly, progmg dir; Milan Alnas, mus dir; Jim Petrucci, chief engr. ■ Rates: $50; 50; 50; 25.

Shafter

KKBB(FM)—Licensed to Shafter. See Bakersfield.

***KLOD(FM)**—Not on air, target date unknown: 90.9 mhz; 50 kw. Ant 86 ft. Suite 204, 35225 Ave. A, Yucaipa (92399). Licensee: Shepard Communications Inc.

KXHA(FM)—Not on air, target date unknown: 104.3 mhz; 3 kw. Ant 308 ft. TL: N35 25 10 W119 11 54. Box 1468, Hemet (92343). Licensee: Pioneer Broadcasting Co.

Shingle Springs

KSSJ(FM)—May 1, 1989: 101.9 mhz; 4.1 w. Ant 827 ft. TL: N38 37 51 W120 51 22 (CP: 50 kw, 475 ft, N38 53 55 W120 57 06). Stereo. 5707 Marconi Ave., Carmichael (95608). (916) 485-9100. Licensee: Olympic Broadcasters Inc. (acq 11-29-90; $400,000; FTR 12-17-90). Wash atty: Cohn & Marks. Format: New adult contemp, jazz. News progmg 10 hrs wkly. ■ Douglas Kahle, pres; Jamie Clark, vp & gen mgr; Bruce Pollock, gen sls mgr; Mike Martis, mktg dir; Bob Stephenson, progmg dir; Rich Green, chief engr.

Shingletown

KCFM(FM)—Not on air, target date Spring 1994: 105.3 mhz; 10 kw. Ant 1,056 ft. TL: N40 29 54 W121 53 25. Stereo. Hrs opn: 24. Box 1921, Chico (95927). (916) 898-6896. Licensee: Michael Robert Birdsill. Format: Adult contemp. Target aud: 25-54. ■ Michael Robert Birdsill, chmn, vp & sls dir; Bo Jive, progmg dir & mus dir; Sparks McHenry, chief engr.

Simi Valley

KWNK(AM)—Sept 21, 1984: 670 khz; 5 kw-D, 1 kw-N. TL: N34 191 0W 118 42 58. Hrs opn: 24. #700, 6633 Fallbrook Ave., West Hills (91307). (818) 887-1855. Licensee: Valley Radio 670 Ltd. Wash atty: Miller & Miller. Format: Sports. Target aud: 25-49; upscsale, primarily men. ■ M.A. Cabranes, gen mgr; William A. Cabranes, gen sls mgr; William Manning, vp progmg; Rick Joyce, news dir; Ulises Pier Luisi, chief engr. ■ Rates: $75; 50; 75; 30.

Soledad

KLUE(FM)—Oct 1, 1991: 106.3 mhz; 6 kw. Ant 1,720 ft. TL: N36 22 48 W121 12 57. Stereo. Hrs opn: 17. 1725 Siskiyou Dr., Salinas (93906); 519 Broadway, King City (93906). (408) 678-0711. FAX: (408) 385-1985. Licensee: Ralin Broadcasting Corp. (acq 7-27-92; FTR 8-17-92). Wash atty: Fletcher, Heald & Hildreth. Format: Classic rock. Target aud: 18-44. ■ Reinaldo Rodriguez, pres & stn mgr; Linda McGuire Mauras, vp; Linda Mcguire Mauras, gen mgr; Dan Mauras, mus dir; Ronald Warren, chief engr.

KSUR(AM)—1992: 700 khz; 2.5 kw-D, 700 w-N. TL: N36 27 51 W121 17 52. Suite 1, 1514 Moffett St., Salinas (93905). (408) 757-9950. FAX: (408) 757-9980. Licensee: Mount Wilson FM Broadcasters Inc. Format: Classical. ■ Sylvia Avila, gen mgr.

Solvang

KSYV(FM)—Sept 22, 1982: 96.7 mhz; 3 kw. Ant -51 ft. TL: N34 36 30 W120 08 42. Stereo. Hrs opn: 24. 1693 Mission Dr. (93463). (805) 688-5798. Licensee: Pacific Coast Broadcasting Co. Inc. Net: AP. Format: Adult contemp. Target aud: 24-54. ■ William O. Reelfs, chmn, pres & sls dir; Pat Leahy, progmg dir & news dir; Joel Saxberg, chief engr.

Sonora

***KTUO(FM)**—1979: 99.1 mhz; 35 w. Ant -150 ft, TL: N37 59 22 W120 23 05 (CP: 93.5 mhz). 430 N. Washington St. (95370). (209) 532-5511, ext. 168. Licensee: Sonora Union High School Board of Trustees. Format: Educ, top 40. News progmg 5 hrs wkly. Target aud: 15-20; students. ■ Bix Beeman, gen mgr.

KVML(AM)—1949: 1450 khz; 1 kw-U. TL: N38 00 30 W120 21 45. 342 S. Washington (95370). (209) 533-1450. Licensee: Clarke Broadcasting Corp. (group owner; acq 12-86; with co-located FM; FTR 10-6-86). Net: ABC/I. Rep: Katz & Powell. Wash atty: Leventhal, Senter & Lerman. Format: Country. News staff 2; news progmg 15 hrs wkly. Target aud: general; 25 plus. Spec prog: Relg 3 hrs wkly. ■ H. Randolph Holder, pres & gen mgr; Karen Nicholson, gen sls mgr; Rich Allen, progmg dir; Loree Sorrick, mus dir; Betty S. Martin, news dir; Dave Remund, chief engr. ■ Rates: $14.50; 14.50; 14.50; 14.50.

KZSQ-FM—Co-owned with KVML(AM). Oct 3, 1973: 92.7 mhz; 380 w. Ant 1,289 ft. TL: N38 00 30 W120 21 45. Stereo. Prog sep from AM. Format: Adult contmep. News progmg 7 hrs wkly. Target aud: 25-54. Spec prog: Jazz 13 hrs wkly. ■ Frank Shaw, mus dir. ■ Rates: Same as AM.

Soquel

KBOQ(AM)—Not on air, target date unknown: 1200 khz; 25 kw-D, 1 kw-N, DA-N. TL: N36 51 53 W121 47 28. c/o 100 Robideaux Rd., Aptos (95003). Licensee: Soquel Broadcasting Co.

South Lake Tahoe

KGLE-FM—Apr 12, 1966: 102.9 mhz; 1 kw. Ant 2,794 ft. TL: N39 09 15 W119 52 55. 1960 Idaho, Carson City, NV (89701). (916) 884-8000. Licensee: Dwight Millard (acq 11-1-93; $150,000; FTR 11-15-93). Format: Easy lstng. Target aud: 25-54. ■ Craig Swope, gen mgr.

KOWL(AM)—November 1956: 1490 khz; 1 kw-U. TL: N38 56 34 W119 57 25. Hrs opn: 24. Box 15460, 2435 Venice Dr. (96150). (916) 541-6681. FAX: (916) 541-4822. Licensee: Park Lane Regency Radio Inc. Group owner: The Park Lane Group (acq 6-7-93; grpsl; FTR 6-21-93). Net: ABC/I. Format: Adult contemp. News staff one; news progmg 12 hrs wkly. Target aud: 18-54. Spec prog: Sp 4 hrs wkly. ■ Rich Robinson, gen mgr; Stan Pierce, progmg dir & mus dir; Terry Laird, news dir; Dean Adrakias, pub affrs dir; Bill Kingman, chief engr.

KRLT(FM)—Co-owned with KOWL(AM). June 23, 1976: 93.9 mhz; 6 kw. Ant -190 ft. TL: N38 57 38 W119 56 26. Stereo. Hrs opn: 24. Dups AM 100%. Net: ABC/D.

KTHO(AM)—Mar 17, 1963: 590 khz; 2.5 kw-D, 500 w-N, DA-N. TL: N38 55 00 W119 57 46. Hrs opn: 24. Box AM (96156). (916) 542-5800. FAX: (916) 544-0119. Licensee: Grayghost Communications Inc. (acq 1-11-93; $450,000; FTR 2-1-93). Net: CBS, MBS. Wash atty: Keck, Mahin & Cate. Format: News/talk, adult contemp. News staff one; news progmg 20 hrs wkly. Target aud: 25-54. ■ Terry Hill, pres; Dick McKee, gen mgr; Dave Carr, progmg dir; Rick Roach, mus dir; Terry Laird, news dir; Kevin Finnegan, chief engr. ■ Rates: $24; 24; 24; 15.

Stanford

***KZSU(FM)**—Oct 10, 1964: 90.1 mhz; 500 w. Ant -10 ft. TL: N37 24 42 W122 10 41. Stereo. Box B, Memorial Auditorium, Serra St. (94309). (415) 725-4868. Licensee: Trustees of Leland Stanford Jr. University. Wash atty: Crowell & Moring. Format: Div, educ, jazz. Spec

California

prog: Black 18 hrs, Latin 6 hrs wkly. ■ Pat Dote, gen mgr; Chanel Wheeler, vp prom; Dan Rosenberg, vp progmg; Mike Howes, mus dir; Sonya Cranford, news dir; Carlos Diaz, pub affrs dir; Mark Lawrence, chief engr.

Stockton

*KCJH(FM)—Feb 24, 1975: 90.1 mhz; 26 kw. Ant 230 ft. TL: N37 57 10 W121 17 11. Stereo. Box 8744, 9019 W. Lane (95210). (209) 477-3690. Licensee: Christian Life College. Net: USA. Wash atty: Dick Helmick. Format: Gospel, MOR. Target aud: 25-45. Spec prog: Black 6 hrs wkly. ■ Dr. Dan Segraves, vp; Shirley Garner, gen mgr; Sherrie Woodward, vp prom; Brent Regnart, progmg dir; Scott Osborne, mus dir; Allan Graft, chief engr.

KEXX(FM)—See Tracy.

KFMR(FM)—Jan 24, 1980: 100.1 mhz; 6 kw. Ant 285 ft. TL: N38 01 21 W121 16 03. Stereo. 1120 N. San Joaquin St. (95202). (209) 462-5367. FAX: (209) 462-7959. Licensee: Carson Group Inc. Rep: Eastman. Format: Modern country. News progmg one hr wkly. Target aud: 25-54. ■ Susan Carson, chmn & stn mgr; Arthur Morrison, vp opns & progmg dir; Joann Stewart, vp dev; Valerie Hubbard, sls dir; Joann Stuart, prom mgr; Tim Whyte, chief engr.

KHOP(FM)—See Modesto.

KJAX(AM)—1947: 1280 khz; 1 kw-U, DA-N TL: N37 58 58 W121 13 46 (D), N37 58 55 W121 13 44 (N). Stereo. Hrs opn: 24. Box 201075 (95201). (209) 948-5569. FAX: (209) 464-9999. Licensee: Joseph Gamble Stations Inc. (acq 9-53). Rep: Christal. Format: News/talk. ■ Joel Gamble, vp & gen mgr; Al Wilson, stn mgr; Ken Thompson, gen sls mgr; Alan Graft, chief engr.

KJOY(FM)—Co-owned with KJAX(AM). June 15, 1968: 99.3 mhz; 2.35 kw. Ant 330 ft. TL: N38 01 21 W121 16 03. Stereo. Prog sep from AM. 110 N. El Dorado (95202). Format: Adult contemp. ■ Joel Gamble, exec vp; Bill Jeffries, progmg dir; Candy Stevens, mus dir.

*KSJC-FM—Apr 1, 1972: 89.5 mhz; 18.6 w. Ant 106 ft. TL: N37 59 46 W121 19 03. Stereo. 5151 Pacific Ave. (95207). (209) 474-5525. Licensee: San Joaquin Delta Jr. College District. Format: Var, educ, pub affrs. News staff 2; news progmg 10 hrs wkly. Target aud: Multi-ethnic, multi-lingual. Spec prog: Sp 10 hrs, foreign language/ethnic 3 hrs, Vietnamese one hr wkly. ■ Dr. E.B. Horton, CEO; Dr. Donald Bennett, vp; John W. Peterson, gen mgr; David Alexander, stn mgr & chief engr.

KSTN(AM)—November 1949: 1420 khz; 5 kw-D, 1 kw-N, DA-2. TL: N37 55 32 W121 14 44. Hrs opn: 24. 2171 Ralph Ave. (95206). (209) 948-5786. Licensee: San Joaquin Broadcasting Co. Net: ABC. Rep: Roslin. Format: CHR. News staff one; news progmg 20 hrs wkly. Target aud: 18-40. Spec prog: Farm 3 hrs, relg 5 hrs wkly. ■ Knox LaRue, pres, stn mgr & progmg mgr; John Hampton, mus dir.

KSTN-FM—1962: 107.3 mhz; 8.1 kw. Ant 1,610 ft. TL: N37 49 17 W121 46 49. Prog sep from AM. Net: CRC. Format: Sp. News progmg 10 hrs wkly. Target aud: General. Spec progmg Portuguese 14 hrs wkly. ■ Angela Dinamit, progmg dir; Danny Correa, mus dir.

*KUOP(FM)—Sept 22, 1947: 91.3 mhz; 7 kw. Ant 1,220 ft. TL: N37 28 48 W121 21 02. Stereo. Hrs opn: 24. 3601 Pacific Ave. (95211). (209) 946-2582; (209) 946-2379. Licensee: University of the Pacific. Net: NPR. Wash atty: Henry E. Crawford Format: Jazz, classical, news/talk. News staff one; news progmg 41 hrs wkly. Target aud: 25-49; professionals, educators, administrators. Spec prog: Folk/bluegrass 12 hrs, blues 14 hrs, progsv 8 hrs, reggae/world 6 hrs, urban contemp 6 hrs, oldies 3 hrs, Latin jazz 3 hrs wkly. ■ Dennis L. Easter, stn mgr, progmg dir & mus dir; Scott Mearns, opns dir & chief engr; Bridget Parks, dev dir, sls dir & mktg dir; Jeff Crawford, asst mus dir; Jack Thomas, news dir & pub affrs dir.

KWG(AM)—Nov 22, 1921: 1230 khz; 900 w-U. TL: N37 57 34 W121 15 28. 6820 Pacific Ave. (95207). (209) 476-1230. Licensee: Silverado Broadcasting Co. (group owner; acq 7-27-92; grpsl; FTR 8-17-92). Net: MBS. Rep: Katz. Format: Oldies. News staff one; news progmg 2 hrs wkly. Target aud: 25-54. ■ John W. Winkel, pres & gen mgr; Bill Jeffries, opns dir; Dora Ruiz, rgnl sls mgr; Matt Foor, progmg mgr; Dirk Kooyman, news dir; Chrys Frazier, pub affrs dir; Barry Cole, chief engr.

KWIN(FM)—See Lodi.

Sun City

KWXH(FM)—Not on air, target date unknown: 92.9 mhz; 370 w. TL: N33 37 25 W117 12 02. Box 8484 (92380). Licensee: Suncom Ltd., A California L.P.

Susanville

KJDX(FM)—Listing follows KSUE(AM).

KKLC(FM)—Not on air, target date unknown: 96.3 mhz; 25 kw. Ant 328 ft. TL: N40 27 21 W120 35 18. Stn currently dark. Box 159, Fayetteville, GA (30214). Licensee: Dale S. Ganske (acq 7-17-92; $100; FTR 8-10-92).

KSUE(AM)—Apr 22, 1948: 1240 khz; 1 kw-U. TL: N402 343 W120 3732. 3015 Johnstonville Rd. (96130). (916) 257-2121; (916) 257-8255. FAX: (916) 257-6955. Licensee: Sierra Broadcasting Corp. Net: MBS, AP. Wash atty: Pepper & Corrazini. Format: Full svc, oldies. News staff 2; news progmg 25 hrs wkly. Target aud: 35-54. Spec prog: Farm 2 hrs, religious 3 hrs wkly. ■ Rod Chambers, pres & gen mgr; Hugh Hardaway, opns dir & progmg dir; Keith Volberg, news dir; Mark Steele, pub affrs dir; Jack Watkins, chief engr. ■ Rates: $14; 12.50; 12.50; 7.50.

KJDX(FM)—Co-owned with KSUE(AM). Aug 19, 1976: 93.3 mhz; 100 kw. Ant 1,155 ft. TL: N40 27 13 W120 34 14. Stereo. Dups AM 15%. Format: Hot country. News staff one; news progmg 25 hrs wkly. Target aud: 25-64. Spec prog: Farm 3 hrs wkly. ■ Rates: $12.50; 10.50; 10.50; 10.50.

Sutter Creek

KMAT(FM)—Not on air, target date unknown: 101.7 mhz; 1.25 kw. Ant 515 ft. TL: N38 20 53 W120 41 00. c/o Susan E. Turgetto, 23 Eureka Terr. (95685). Licensee: Sutter Creek Broadcasting (acq 2-11-93; $32,500; FTR 3-8-93).

KNGT(FM)—See Jackson.

Taft

KMYX(AM)—Mar 16, 1948: 1310 khz; 1 kw-D, 45 w-N. TL: N35 08 46 W119 28 11. Suite 300, 333 Palmer Dr., Bakersfield (93309). (805) 834-4000. FAX: (805) 834-8842. Licensee: Adelman Communications Inc. (acq 9-2-93; $322,000 with co-located FM; FTR 9-27-93). Net: SMN. Format: Big band. News progmg 14 hrs wkly. Target aud: 35 plus. ■ Pete Elieff, gen mgr; Dave Dart, progmg dir & news dir; Joy Wolf, mus dir; Chris Compton, chief engr.

KMYX-FM—June 1986: 103.9 mhz; 3 kw. Ant 300 ft. TL: N35 07 09 W119 27 34 (CP: Ant 328 ft.). Stereo. Dups AM 100%. ■ Rates: Same as AM.

Tahoe City

KRZQ-FM—Licensed to Tahoe City. See Reno, Nev.

Tehachapi

KTPI(FM)—Jan 8, 1982: 103.1 mhz; 3 kw. Ant 580 ft. TL: N35 04 30 W118 22 08 (CP: 1.9 kw, ant 577 ft.). Stereo. Suite B-2, 190 Sierra Ct., Palmdale (93550). (805) 274-1031. FAX: (805) 274-1017. Licensee: The Park Lane Group (group owner; acq 3-20-92; $1.82 million with KVOY(AM) Mojave; FTR 4-13-92). Net: ABC/E. Rep: Christal. Format: Country. News staff one; news progmg 2 hrs wkly. Target aud: 25-54. ■ Jim Levy, CEO; Tom Caulkins, gen mgr; Joe Waldman, progmg dir; Tia Laird, mus dir; J.B. Brown, chief engr.

Temecula

*KRTM(FM)—Jan 1, 1989: 88.9 mhz; 3 kw. Ant -151 ft. TL: N33 30 35 W117 09 30. 27645 Jefferson (92590). (909) 694-0866. FAX: (909) 308-1414. Licensee: Penfold Communications Inc. Format: Adult Contemp. ■ Dennis Ross, gen sls mgr.

Templeton

KXER(AM)—Not on air, target date unknown: 1060 khz; 1 kw-U. TL: N35 33 53 W120 39 52. Suite A, 12550 Brookhurst St., Garden Grove (92640). (714) 636-5040. Licensee: William L. Zawila. ■ William L. Zawila, pres.

Thousand Oaks

*KCLU(FM)—Not on air, target date unknown: 88.3 mhz; 1.2 kw. Ant 535 ft. TL: N34 14 03 W118 52 41. 60 W. Olsen Rd. (91360). (805) 493-3474. Licensee: California Lutheran Univ. Format: Educ. ■ Art Lopez, stn mgr.

*KCPB(FM)—Dec 4, 1979: 91.1 mhz; 4.9 kw. Ant 1,280 ft. TL: N34 24 47 W119 11 10. Stereo. Hrs opn: 24. Box 77913, Los Angeles (90007-0913). (213) 743-5872. FAX: (213) 743-5853. Licensee: University of Southern Calif. (acq 3-17-82). Net: APR. Wash atty: Brinig & Bernstein. Format: Class. News progmg 9 hrs wkly. Target aud: 35 plus. Spec prog: Jazz one hr, Sp 2 hrs, multi-eth-

Directory of Radio

nic 2 hrs wkly. ■ Wallace A. Smith, pres & gen mgr; Bill Kappelman, vp opns; Maryanne Horton, dev dir; Lyle Henry, chief engr.

KCTQ(AM)—Sept 20, 1971: 850 khz; 500 w-D, 250 w-N, DA-2. TL: N34 12 07 W118 49 47. 1000 Business Center Circle, Newbury Park (91320). (805) 499-9971. Licensee: Buenaventura Communications Inc. (acq 10-3-91; $300,000; FTR 10-28-91). Net: AP. Format: Kids radio. ■ Rick Lemmo, gen mgr; Steve Hess, gen sls mgr; Pierre Ulisyes, chief engr.

KNJO(FM)—Apr 1, 1963: 92.7 mhz; 560 w. Ant 630 ft. TL: N34 09 53 W118 54 08. Stereo. Hrs opn: 24. 3721 E. Thousand Oaks Blvd. (91362). (805) 497-8511. Licensee: Flagship Communications Co. Inc. (acq 7-24-92; $1.1 million; FTR 8-17-92). Wash atty: Pepper & Corazzinni. Format: Adult contemp, soft hits. News staff one. Target aud: 25-54 ■ Darry Sragow, chmn; Edward Krovitz, vp & gen mgr; Mike Matthews, opns mgr; Al Kane, rgnl sls mgr; Cindy Phillips, prom dir; Doug Eldred, progmg dir; Ned Skaff, news dir & pub affrs dir; Pierg Pierlussi, engrg mgr.

Thousand Palms

KNWZ(AM)—Dec 7, 1963: 1270 khz; 5 kw-D, 750 w-N, DA-2. TL: N33 51 04 W116 23 36. Box 12700, Palm Desert (92255); Suite 200, 74-923 Hovley Ln. (92260). (619) 346-1270. FAX: (619) 341-6885. Licensee: Country Club Communications Inc. (acq 9-15-88). Net: MBS, NBC, AP, CNN, NBC Talknet, Unistar, Westwood One. Rep: W.R.B.S. Format: News/talk. News staff 8. Target aud: 25 plus. ■ William S. Hart Sr., pres; John Wilks, gen mgr. ■ Rates: $26; 26; 26; 26.

KPSL(AM)—November 14, 1992: 1010 khz; 3.6 kw-D, 400 w-N, DA-2. TL: N33 50 35 W116 25 39. Stereo. Hrs opn: 24. 303 N. Indian Canyon, Palm Springs (92263). (619) 323-5775. FAX: (619) 320-6702. Licensee: Vista Communications Corp. Rep: CMBS, Hugh Wallace. Wash atty: Haley, Bader & Potts. Format: Talk. Spec prog: Relg 17 hrs wkly. ■ Milt Jones, pres; Judy Gilliard, gen mgr; Dan Fritz, progmg dir; Berry O'Connor, chief engr. ■ Rates: $35; 30; 35; 30.

KVYZ(FM)—Not on air, target date unknown: 94.7 mhz; 630 w. Ant 581 ft. TL: N33 52 07 W116 25 58. 10601 Wilshire Blvd., 1604, Los Angeles (90024). Licensee: Rochlis-Johnson Partnership.

Tracy

KEXX(FM)—Co-owned with KWG(AM). Dec 14, 1966: 100.9 mhz; 6 kw. Ant 328 ft. TL: N37 37 32 W121 23 58. Stereo. News progmg one hr wkly.

Truckee

KHTZ(AM)—Licensed to Truckee. See Reno, Nev.

Tulare

KBOS-FM—Licensed to Tulare. See Fresno.

KGEN(AM)—1957: 1370 khz; 1 kw-D, 136 w-N. TL: N36 10 51 W119 19 44. Hrs opn: 24. Box 2040, 323 E. San Joaquin (93275). (209) 686-1370; (209) 685-1370. FAX: (209) 685-1394. Licensee: KGEN (acq 7-16-85). Wash atty: Linda Eckard. Format: Sp. Target aud: General. ■ Rolando Collantez, gen mgr; Margarita Hernandez, adv mgr; Robert Dahlquist, chief engr. ■ Rates: $25; 25; 25; 15.

KJUG(AM)—Licensed to Tulare. See Visalia.

KJUG-FM—Licensed to Tulare. See Visalia.

Tulelake

KFLS-FM—Not on air, target date unknown: 96.5 mhz; 1.78 kw. Ant 2,132 ft. Box 1450, 1338 Oregon Ave., Klamath Falls, OR (97601). Licensee: Wynne Broadcasting Co. Inc.

Turlock

*KCSS(FM)—Aug 13, 1975: 91.9 mhz; 151 w. Ant 112 ft. TL: N37 31 35 W120 51 25. Hrs opn: 20. C-108, 801 W. Monte Vista Ave. (95382). (209) 667-3900. Licensee: Calif. State College, Stanislaus. Format: Div, jazz, new age. Target aud: 25-54. Spec prog: Black 12 hrs, class 6 hrs, jazz 3, soul 10 hrs wkly. ■ George Xenox, gen mgr; John Caie, chief engr.

KMIX(AM)—October 1949: 1390 khz; 5 kw-U, DA-2. TL: N37 31 48 W120 41 37. 4043 Geer Rd., Houghson (95326). (209) 883-0433. FAX: (209) 883-4433. Licensee: Radio Associates Inc. Group owner: Radio Associates (acq 1986). Format: C&W. ■ Robert M. Salmon, pres; Karen Wolff, stn mgr; Jim Dorman, progmg dir; Bryant Smith, chief engr.

KMIX-FM—Mar 3, 1978: 98.3 mhz; 1.6 kw. Ant 390 ft. TL: N37 34 46 W120 50 48 (CP: 2 kw). Stereo. Dups AM 25%.

Twain Harte

KKBN(FM)—Oct 19, 1985: 93.5 mhz; 258 w. Ant 1,630 ft. TL: N38 03 49 W120 14 47. Stereo. Hrs opn: 24. Box 708, Suite K, 22960 Vantage Pointe Dr. (95383). (209) 586-1988; (209) 586-1990. FAX: (209) 509-1111. Licensee: Clear Mountain Air Broadcasting Co. Net: CBS, MBS. Wash atty: Fisher, Wayland, Cooper & Leader. Format: Adult contemp. News staff one; news progmg 3 hrs wkly. Target aud: 24-54; general. Spec prog: Jazz 4 hrs wkly. ■ Sylvia B. Leutz, stn mgr, natl sls mgr, prom mgr & news dir; Donald E. Leutz Jr., opns dir, progmg dir, mus dir & chief engr. ■ Rates: $14; 14; 14; 14.

Twentynine Palms

KCDZ(FM)—July 15, 1989: 107.7 mhz; 3 kw. Ant 328 ft. TL: N34 09 15 W116 11 50. Stereo. 6448 Hallee, No.5, Joshua Tree (92252). (619) 366-8471. FAX: (619) 366-2976. Licensee: Morongo Basin Broadcasting Corp. Net: AP. Wash atty: Richard Becker. Format: Adult contemp. News staff 2; news progmg 10 hrs wkly. Target aud: 25-54; baby boomers. ■ Cynthia M. Daigneault, pres, gen mgr & gen sls mgr; Gary Daigneault, progmg dir & news dir; Les Taylor, mus dir; Barry O'Conner, chief engr.

KDHI(AM)—Apr 3, 1961: 1250 khz; 1 kw-D, 120 w-N. TL: N34 08 11 W116 10 07. Box 908, 68474 Twentynine Palms Hwy. (92277). (619) 362-4264; (619) 365-4111. FAX: (619) 362-4463. Licensee: Three D Radio Inc. (acq 6-9-92; $70,000; with co-located FM; FTR 6-29-92). Net: ABC/D. Format: Full service. News staff 4; news progmg 15 hrs wkly. Target aud: 35 plus. ■J. Duane Hoover, pres; Cynthia Truitt, gen mgr, gen sls mgr, natl sls mgr & rgnl sls mgr; Dorothy Hopko, opns dir; Cythia Truitt, vp prom; Michelle Hammontree, mus dir; Jim Parker, chief engr. ■ Rates: $12; 10; 12; 8.

KQYN(FM)—Co-owned with KDHI(AM). Apr 1, 1965: 95.7 mhz; 19 kw. Ant 200 ft. TL: N34 09 17 W116 12 04 (CP: 20 kw, ant 229 ft.). Stereo. Hrs opn: 24. Prog sep from AM. Net: Westwood One. Rep: Gillis. Format: Rock 'n roll. Target aud: 18-34. ■ Rates: Same as AM.

Ukiah

***KPRA(FM)**—1988: 89.5 mhz; 710 w. Ant 1,135 ft. TL: N39 07 01 W123 13 54. 25 Oak Knoll Rd. (95482). (707) 468-8802. Licensee: Family Stations Inc. (group owner; acq 2-3-86). Format: Relg. ■ Mike Fenton, opns mgr; Tom Driggers, chief engr.

KQPM(FM)—February 1989: 105.9 mhz; 2.9 kw. Ant 2,017 ft. TL: N39 09 00 W123 12 30. Hrs opn: 24. Box 838 (95482). (707) 468-5336. Licensee: North Country Communications Inc. (acq 5-21-93; $810,000; FTR 6-14-93). Format: Country. ■ Bill Groody, pres; Bill Rhett, chief engr.

KUKI(AM)—Oct 1, 1950: 1400 khz; 1 kw-U. TL: N39 10 03 W123 13 02. 1400 Kuki Lane (95482). (707) 463-5868. FAX: (707) 463-5852. Licensee: Ukiah Broadcasting Corp. (acq 3-22-92; $465,000 with co-located FM; FTR 1-27-92). Net: CBS, ABC/D. Rep: Gillis. Wash atty: Pepper & Corazzini. Format: News/talk. News staff 2; news progmg 25 hrs wkly. Target aud: 25 plus. ■ Keith Bussman, pres; Mark Williamson, opns mgr; Annie Huntley, gen sls mgr; Brian West, news dir. ■ Rates: $18; 15; 18; 12.

KUKI-FM—Oct 16, 1974: 103.3 mhz; 2.7 kw. Ant 1,840 ft. TL: N39 19 36 W123 16 12 (CP: Ant 1,837 ft.). Stereo. Prog sep from AM. Format: C&W. News staff 2; news progmg 7 hrs wkly. Target aud: 25-54. ■ Mark Williamson, Annie Huntley, prom dirs; Tove Sorensen, mus dir; Jo-Lee V., pub affrs dir. ■ Rates: Same as AM.

KWNE(FM)—1968: 94.5 mhz; 2.15 kw. Ant 2,053 ft. TL: N39 07 50 W123 04 32. Stereo. Hrs opn: 24. Box 1056, 2397 N. State St. (95482). (707) 462-1451; (707) 462-0945. FAX: (707) 462-4670. Licensee: Broadcasting Corp of Mendocino County (acq 10-1-78). Net: ABC/C. Rep: Katz & Powell. Format: Adult contemp, CHR. News staff one; news progmg 12 hrs wkly. Target aud: 18-54. Spec prog: Jazz one, farm one hr wkly. ■ Guilford Dye, pres & gen mgr; Mike Spencer, stn mgr & gen sls mgr; Gudrun Dye, vp & prom mgr; Bill Steele, progmg dir; Zach Williams, mus dir. ■ Rates: $25; 22; 25; 13.

Vacaville

KUIC(FM)—Nov 1, 1968: 95.3 mhz; 4.3 kw. Ant 280 ft. TL: N38 17 56 W121 59 54 (CP: 594 w, ant 1,948 ft., TL: N38 23 48 W122 06 03). Stereo. Hrs opn: 24. KUIC Plaza, 600 E. Main St. (95688). (707) 446-0200. Licensee: Quick Broadcasting Inc. (acq 5-1-83; $1.5 million; FTR 4-18-83). Net: AP. Wash atty: Ginsburg, Feldman & Bress. Format: Adult contemp. News progmg 5 hrs wkly. Target aud: General; middle class, professionals. ■Andy Santamaria, CEO, pres & gen mgr; Harry Benton, chmn; Carol Benton, vp; Steve Bise, opns mgr; John Edwards, gen sls mgr; Dina Johnson, prom mgr; Andrew Reed, mus dir; Drew Sanser, news dir; Alan McCarthy, chief engr. ■ Rates: $74; 74; 74; 38.

Vallejo

KXBT(AM)—Aug 1, 1947: 1190 khz; 1 kw-D. TL: N38 07 04 W122 15 24. 3267 Sonoma Blvd. (94590). (707) 644-8944. Licensee: North Bay Broadcasters Inc. (acq 10-12-93; $50,000; FTR 10-25-93). Format: Oldies, news. News progmg 5 hrs wkly. Target aud: 25-54. Spec prog: Relg 5 hrs, Portuguese one hr wkly. ■ Andy Santamaria, pres; Stefan Ponek, gen mgr & stn mgr; Kevin Kel, prom dir; Eric Brown, progmg dir; Jay Lloyd, news dir.

Ventura

KAXX(FM)—Nov 1989: 107.1 mhz; 280 w. Ant 872 ft. TL: N34 18 10 W119 13 45 (CP: 420 w). Stereo. Hrs opn: 24. Box 6395, (93006-6395); Suite 190, 4882 McGrath St. (93003). (805) 644-5151. Licensee: KAXX Inc. (acq 1-31-92). Format: Soft adult contemp. ■ Jim Sylvester, chmn, gen mgr & sls dir; Donna Sylvester, progmg dir & news dir.

KBBY(AM)—June 1, 1947: 1590 khz; 5 kw-U, DA-2. TL: N34 1412 W119 1211. 6150 Olivas Park Dr. (93003). (805) 656-6300. FAX: (805) 644-1966. Licensee: Buena Ventura Inc. (acq 10-24-89; $6.7 million with co-located FM; FTR 11-13-89). Net: SMN. Rep: Katz. Format: Oldies, adult contemp. News staff one; news progmg 2 hrs wkly. Target aud: 18-54. ■ George Duncan, pres; Marilyn Woods, vp & gen mgr; Gail Furillo, gen sls mgr; Perry Van Houten, progmg dir.

KBBY-FM—Dec 27, 1962: 95.1 mhz; 10.8 kw. Ant 925 ft. TL: N34 14 12 W119 12 11. Prog sep from AM. Net: Unistar. Format: Adult contemp. Target aud: 18-54. ■ Bill Lee, progmg dir.

KCAQ(FM)—See Oxnard.

KELF(FM)—See Camarillo.

KHAY(FM)—Listing follows KVEN(AM).

KKZZ(AM)—See Santa Paula.

KTRO(AM)—See Port Hueneme.

KVEN(AM)—March 1948: 1450 khz; 1 kw-U. TL: N34 15 39 W119 14 28. Box 699 (93002); 3897 Market St. (93003). (805) 642-8595; (800) 367-5429. FAX: (805) 656-5838. Licensee: KVEN Broadcasting Corp. (acq 10-65). Net: ABC/E, NBC Talknet, AP. Rep: Radio Time. Wash atty: Erwin Krasnow. Format: News/talk. News staff 4; news progmg 45 hrs wkly. Target aud: 25 plus; affluent, educated, professional with above average income. ■ Robert L. Fox, CEO & chmn; David Loe, pres & gen mgr; Bob Adams, opns mgr; Cynthia Ginn, gen sls mgr; David Ciniero, prom mgr; Rich Gualano, progmg dir; Doug Drigot, news dir; Jerry Lewine, chief engr. ■ Rates: $36; 28; 36; 28.

KHAY(FM)—Co-owned with KVEN(AM). Jan 1, 1962: 100.7 mhz; 13.1 kw. Ant 1,210 ft. TL: N34 20 55 W119 19 57. Stereo. Prog sep from AM. Net: AP. Format: C&W. Target aud: 18-54. ■ Mark Hill, opns mgr, progmg dir & mus dir; Charley Parker, prom dir. ■ Rates: $61; 48; 61; 48.

KXBS(FM)—See Santa Paula.

Victorville

KATJ(FM)—See George.

KCIN(AM)—Sept 1, 1961: 1590 khz; 500 w-D, 135 w-N. TL: N34 32 15 W117 18 42. Hrs opn: 24. Box 1428 (92393); Suite 190, 15494 Palmdale Rd. (92392). (619) 245-2212. FAX: (619) 245-8012. Licensee: Island Broadcasting Assoc. L.P. (acq 12-20-90; grpsl; FTR 1-14-91). Net: ABC/E. Rep: Katz. Wash atty: Cohn & Marks. Format: Adult standards. News staff 2. ■ Scott Brody, pres; Linda Griggs, stn mgr. ■ Rates: $12; 10; 11; 6.

***KHMS(FM)**—Not on air, target date unknown: 88.5 mhz; 55 w. Ant 2,994 ft. TL: N34 32 15 W117 18 42. c/o Faith Communications Corp., 2201 S. 6th St., Las Vegas, NV (89104). Licensee: Faith Communications Corp. (acq 4-5-91; FTR 4-22-91).

KVVQ-FM—Aug 18, 1980: 103.1 mhz; 95 w. Ant 1,424 ft. TL: N34 36 45 W117 17 31 (CP: 310 w, ant 1,401 ft.). Stereo. Hrs opn: 24. 11920 Hesperia Rd., Hesperia (92345). (619) 244-2000. FAX: (619) 244-1198. Licensee: Kenneth B. Orchard. Net: AP. Format: Adult contemp. News staff 2. Target aud: 18-54. ■ Ken Orchard, chmn; Brad Orchard, vp; Kelly Orchard, prom mgr; Scott Orchard, progmg dir; John Barry, news dir. ■ Rates: $20; 20; 20; 20.

***KXRD(FM)**—Dec 1993: 89.5 mhz; 1.25 kw. Ant 1,410 ft. TL: N34 36 44 W117 17 27. Hrs opn: 24. Box 1000, 35225 Ave. A #204, Yucaipa (92399). Licensee: Shepherd Communications Inc. Format: Relg. News progmg 2 hrs wkly. Target aud: 18-34. ■ Jon E. Fugler, CEO; David Ferry, chmn; Candace Andrews, CFO; Christie Reasons, dev dir; Terry Taylor, sls dir; Don Carson, progmg mgr; Noonie Fugler, mus dir; Mark Sadocca, chief engr.

KZXY(AM)—See Apple Valley.

KZXY-FM—See Apple Valley.

Visalia

***KARM(FM)**—1990: 89.7 mhz; 1 kw. Ant 810 ft. TL: N36 38 10 W118 56 32. 1300 S. Woodland Dr. (93277). (209) 627-5276. FAX: (209) 625-9774. Licensee: Harvest Broadcasting Co. Format: Relg traditional, inspirational. ■ Nora A. Peppers, gen mgr; Chuck O'Dell, opns dir; Randy Stoller, chief engr.

***KDUV(FM)**—Jan 1, 1992: 88.9 mhz; 1 kw. Ant 2,647 ft. TL: N36 17 14 W118 50 17. 130 N. Kelsey, Suite H-1 (93291). (209) 651-4111. Licensee: Community Educational Broadcasting Inc. Format: Christian hit radio. ■ Bob Peart, gen mgr; Robert Croft, opns dir; Joe Croft, progmg dir.

KEYX(AM)—January 1948: 1400 khz; 1 kw-U. TL: N36 21 14 W119 17 02. 3232 S. Mooney Blvd. (93277); Suite 124, 4991 E. McKinley, Fresno (93727). (209) 733-1400; (209) 251-8614. FAX: (209) 251-3347. Licensee: Americom II. Group owner: Americom (acq 4-16-85). Rep: McGavren Guild. Format: Golden oldies. Target aud: 25-49. ■ Tom Quinn, pres; Karl F. Crass, gen mgr; Mark Kallen, gen sls mgr; Art Nugent, prom mgr; Michael Bushey, progmg dir; Steve Weber, chief engr.

KFSO-FM—Co-owned with KEYX(AM). Sept 1, 1951: 92.9 mhz; 18.5 kw-H, 17 kw-V. Ant 820 ft. TL: N36 38 10 W118 56 33 (CP: 17.5 kw, ant 853 ft., TL: N36 38 10 W118 56 34). Stereo. Prog sep from AM. Format: Oldies. ■ Michael Bushey, prom mgr & mus dir.

KGYU(FM)—Not on air, target date unknown: 96.1 mhz; 4.8 kw. Ant 358 ft. TL: N36 21 59 W119 10 46. 7179 N. Van Ness, Fresno (93711). Licensee: New Visalia Broadcasting Inc.

KJUG(AM)—(Tulare). Aug 1, 1946: 1270 khz; 5 kw-D, 1 kw-N, DA-N. TL: N36 13 10 W119 18 51. 717 N. Mooney Blvd., Tulare (93274). (209) 686-2866. FAX: (209) 686-5265. Licensee: Westcoast Broadcasting Inc. (group owner; acq 5-1-81). Format: Country. News staff 2; news progmg 7 hrs wkly. Target aud: 25-49. Spec prog: Farm 5 hrs wkly. ■ Larry W. Woods, pres; Wayne B. Foster, gen mgr; John A. Katz, opns mgr, prom mgr & progmg mgr; Kelly Fiscus, sls dir; Larry Santiago, mus dir; Darrin Cantrell, news dir; Scott Dean, chief engr.

KJUG-FM—(Tulare). May 6, 1965: 106.7 mhz; 1.2 kw. Ant 6,100 ft. TL: N36 17 08 W118 50 17. Stereo. Prog dups AM 90%.

KSEQ(FM)—October 1984: 97.1 mhz; 17 kw. Ant 777 ft. TL: N36 38 08 W118 56 32. Stereo. 617 W. Tulare Ave. (93277). (209) 627-9710. FAX: (209) 627-1590. Licensee: Buckley Broadcasting of Monterey. Group owner: Buckley Broadcasting Corp. (acq 12-87). Rep: McGavren Guild. Wash atty: Martin Leader. Format: Adult contemp. News staff one. Target aud: 25-54. ■ Rick Buckley, pres; Ray McCarty, vp & gen mgr; Charlie T. Wolff, opns dir & progmg dir; Clint Showalter, sls dir; Annette Christophe, news dir; Ken Warren, chief engr. ■ Rates: $35; 30; 35; 22.

Vista

KCEO(AM)—Nov 3, 1967: 1000 khz; 2.5 kw-D, 500 w-N, DA-2. TL: N33 13 59 W117 16 09. 550 Laguna Dr., Carlsbad (92083). (619) 729-5945. Licensee: Tri-Cities Broadcasting (acq 11-15-85). Net: ABC/D, MBS. Format: News/talk. News staff 3; news progmg 20 hrs wkly. Target aud: 35 plus. ■ Jeffrey Chandler, pres & gen mgr; Todd Palmer, gen sls mgr; Melanie Gascoyne, natl sls mgr; John Van Zante, progmg dir; Kurt Williams, news dir; Ken Crabtree, chief engr.

Walnut

*KSAK(FM)—Jan 10, 1974: 90.1 mhz; 3.5 w. Ant 460 ft. TL: N34 02 53 W117 51 43 (CP: Ant 410 ft.). 1100 N. Grand Ave. (91789). (909) 595-5725. Licensee: Mount San Antonio Community College District. Format: Variety rock. Target aud: 18-25; students. Spec prog: Comedy, nostalgia, jazz, new releases. ■ John Randall, pres; Phillip S. Markell, gen mgr & opns mgr.

Walnut Creek

*KCEQ(FM)—Sept 23, 1988: 100.5 mhz; 10 w. Ant 250 ft. TL: N37 52 35 W122 04 52. Stereo. Hrs opn: 7 AM-10 PM Mon-Fri. 1200 Pleasant Hill Rd., Lafayette (94549). (510) 935-2600. Licensee: Acalanes High School, Acalanes Union High (acq 1981; $3,800). Format: Black, classic rock. News progmg one hr wkly. Target aud: General; high school students. Spec prog: Heavy metal one hr, oldies 3 hrs, modern rock one hr, rap 4 hrs wkly. ■ Adam Winig, pres; Wendell Pleis, gen mgr; Jon Schiller, gen sls mgr; Jason Lechner, mktg dir; Nick Cosenza, prom mgr; Ryan O'Shea, progmg dir; Dean Paetzold, asst mus dir; Matt Ward, vp engrg.

KZWC(FM)—Dec 10, 1959: 92.1 mhz; 3 kw. Ant 89 ft. TL: N37 53 59 W122 05 38. Stereo. Suite 200, 14530 Willow Pass Rd., Concord (94520). (510) 825-9000. FAX: (510) 825-9000. Licensee: KZWC Broadcasting Inc. (acq 8-10-93; $850,000; FTR 9-6-93). Format: Sp. ■ Carlos Duharte, vp.

Wasco

KERI(AM)—May 17, 1950: 1180 khz; 50 kw-D, 10 kw-N, DA-2. TL: N35 34 17 W119 19 26. Hrs opn: 24. #205, 110 S. Montclair St., Bakersfield (93309). (805) 832-3100; (805) 758-1133. FAX: (805) 832-3164. Licensee: KWSO Inc. Net: USA. Format: Family talk, relg. News staff one; news progmg 11 hrs wkly. Target aud: 35-55; women. Spec prog: Sp 13 hrs wkly. ■ Don Bevilacqua, pres & gen mgr; Michael McCutchan, stn mgr & prom mgr; Terri Blankenship, prom dir; Michael Thomas, progmg dir & mus dir; Mark Heffernan, news dir; George Miller, pub affrs dir; Terry Geiser, chief engr. ■ Rates: $16.25; 16.25; 16.25; 16.25.

Weed

KWHO(FM)—November 1983: 102.3 mhz; 5.5 kw. Ant 1,437 ft. TL: N41 21 12 W122 15 35. Stereo. Hrs opn: 24. Box 1023, 113 E. Alma (96094). (916) 926-5946. FAX: (916) 926-0830. Licensee: Tristar Broadcasting Corp. Inc. (acq 6-16-92; $360,000; FTR 7-6-92). Net: ABC/I. Format: Modern country. News staff one; news progmg 6 hrs wkly. Target aud: 25-54. Spec prog: Nostalgia 2 hrs wkly. ■ Tom Erickson, pres, gen mgr, prom mgr & progmg dir; Tony Spada, mus dir; Mike Anthony, news dir; Joe Mauk, chief engr. ■ Rates: $6; 6; 6; 6.

West Covina

KGRB(AM)—Sept 25, 1963: 900 khz; 500 w-D, DA. TL: N34 0154 W117 5606. 108 N. McCadden Place, Los Angeles (90004). (213) 686-0300. Licensee: Robert Burdette & Assoc. Inc. Format: Big band. ■ Robert Burdette, pres, gen mgr, gen sls mgr, prom mgr & progmg dir.

KMQA-FM—Nov 18, 1957: 98.3 mhz; 2.3 w. Ant 328 ft. TL: N34 01 22 W117 56 15. Suite 650, 6430 Sunset Blvd., Los Angeles (90028). (213) 468-2355. FAX: (213) 468-2371. Licensee: El Dorado Communications Inc. (acq 12-30-92; $3.25 million; FTR 1-25-93). Rep: Caballero. Format: Contemp Sp. ■ Chris Nevil, gen mgr; Humberto Hernandez, stn mgr; Tom Bell, gen sls mgr.

Willits

KLLK(AM)—Aug 5, 1985: 1250 khz; 5.4 kw-D, 2.7 kw-N, DA-2. TL: N39 23 58 W123 19 20. Hrs opn: 5 AM-midnight. 12 West Valley St. (95490); 1260 N. Main St., Fort Bragg (95437). (707) 459-1250; (707) 961-9670. FAX: (707) 459-1251. Licensee: Henry Radio Co. Wash atty: Haley, Bader & Potts. Format: New rock. News progmg 8 hrs wkly. Target aud: 18-49; adults who like a progressive mix of modern rock music. Spec prog: New age 2 hrs wkly. ■ Brian J. Henry, gen mgr; Cherie France, mus dir.

Willows

KIQS(AM)—Dec 29, 1961: 1560 khz; 250 w-D. TL: N39 31 44 W122 10 09. Box 7, 118 W. Sycamore (95988). (916) 934-4654. FAX: (916) 934-4656. Licensee: KIQS Inc. (acq 9-72). Net: ABC. Rep: Radio Time. Wash atty: Jerold Miller. Format: Sp. News progmg 12 hrs wkly. Target aud: General. Spec prog: Farm 2 hrs wkly. ■ Anthony Rusnak, pres, gen sls mgr, prom mgr & adv mgr; Peggy Rusnak, progmg dir, mus dir & news dir; Gary Martin, chief engr. ■ Rates: $6.65; 6.65; 6.65; 6.65.

KIQS-FM—Sept 1, 1983: 105.5 mhz; 5.4 kw. Ant 140 ft. TL: N39 31 44 W122 10 09. Stereo. Hrs opn: 16. Dups AM 27%. Spec prog: Farm 3 hrs wkly. ■ Peggy Rusnak, pub affrs dir.

Windsor

KEZD(AM)—Not on air, target date unknown: 1580 khz; 700 w-D, DA. TL: N38 23 58 W122 47 22. Stereo. Hrs opn: 24. 502 Avenida Sevilla, Apt. D, Laguna Hills, CA (92653-3847). Licensee: Edith H. Owens (acq 7-9-93; FTR 8-2-93). ■ Edith H. Owens, gen mgr.

Winton

KFMK(FM)—Not on air, target date unknown: 98.7 mhz; 4.4 kw. Ant 384 ft. TL: N37 22 31 W120 27 37. 548 E. Alisal St., Salinas (93905). (408) 757-1910. Licensee: TGR Broadcasting Inc. (group owner; acq 5-17-90; $55,000; FTR 6-18-90). ■ Carlos Moncada, pres; Hector Villaiobos, gen mgr.

Woodlake

KFCL-FM—Not on air, target date unknown: 104.1 mhz; 17 kw. Ant 853 ft. TL: N36 38 12 W118 56 34. c/o Ionosphere Broadcasting, 818 W. 7th St., Suite 1004, Los Angeles (90017). Licensee: Ionosphere Broadcasting Ltd.

Woodland

KSFM(FM)—Licensed to Woodland. See Sacramento.

KSMJ(AM)—See Sacramento.

Yermo

KRXV(FM)—April 1980: 98.1 mhz; 1.1 kw. Ant 2,280 ft. TL: N34 59 43 W116 50 15. Stereo. Hrs opn: 24. Box 25606, #105, 12381 Wilshire Blvd., Los Angeles (90025). (310) 820-4628. FAX: (310) 826-7866. Licensee: KHWY Inc. (Group owner). Net: AP. Wash atty: Hogan & Hartson. Format: Adult contemp. News staff one; news progmg 28 hrs wkly. Target aud: 35 plus; travellers on I-15 & I-40 & loc communities. ■ Howard B. Anderson, CEO, chmn & pres; Patricia C. Cookus, CFO; Timothy B. Anderson, vp; Kirk M. Anderson, gen sls mgr; Jess Collins, natl sls mgr; Lance Todd, progmg dir; Keith Hayes, news dir. ■ Rates: $50; 50; 50; 50.

KYHT-FM—Not on air, target date unknown: 105.3 mhz; 560 w. Ant 1,037 ft. TL: N34 48 30 W116 41 01. 2501 West Ave. I, Lancaster (93534). Licensee: Antelope Broadcasting Co. Inc. ■ Ron Carter, pres; Larry Thomhill, gen mgr; Rich Bultman, natl sls mgr; Zach Taylor, progmg dir; Rob Dejai, mus dir; Candace Harrison, pub affrs dir.

Yountville

KRKL(AM)—Not on air, target date unknown: 840 khz; 2.5 kw-D, 250 w-N, DA-D. TL: N38 29 50 W122 23 05 (D), N38 21 55 W122 22 25 (N). 1290 Jefferson St., Napa (94559). Licensee: Heritage Communications.

Yreka

KSYC(AM)—July 27, 1947: 1490 khz; 1 kw-U. TL: N41 43 28 W122 39 00. 316 Lawrence Lane (96097). (916) 842-4158. FAX: (916) 842-7635. Licensee: Dalmatian Enterprises Inc. (acq 4-1-74). Net: SMN. Calif. Agri-Radio. Wash atty: David Tillotson. Format: C&W. News staff one; news progmg 11 hrs wkly. Target aud: 25-54. Spec prog: Weekday farm shows. ■ Gary Hawke, pres, gen mgr & gen sls mgr; Cherri Hawke, progmg dir; Cheri Hawke, mus dir; Jeff Sherman, chief engr. ■ Rates: $18; 18; 18; 16.

KYRE(FM)—Co-owned with KSYC(AM). June 1, 1983: 97.7 mhz; 1.4 kw. Ant 2,364 ft. TL: N41 43 28 W122 37 46. Stereo. Prog sep from AM. Net: Unistar. Format: Adult contemp. Target aud: 18-49. ■ Rates: Same as AM.

Yuba City

KMYC(AM)—See Marysville.

KOBO(AM)—June 1953: 1450 khz; 500 w-U. TL: N39 08 07 W121 36 41 (CP: 1 kw-N). 463 Palora Ave. Yuba City (95991). (916) 674-8505. Licensee: KOBO Radio Grande Inc. (acq 5-26-92). Net: ABC/I, ABC TalkRadio. Rep: Frederick Smith, Gillis. Format: News, talk. Spec prog: East Indian 3 hrs wkly. ■ Rigoberto Fuentes, gen mgr; Jason W. Fine, progmg dir; Larry Cooper, news dir.

KUBA(AM)—January 1948: 1600 khz; 5 kw-D, 2.5 kw-N, DA-N. TL: N39 06 00 W121 39 18. Hrs opn: 19. Drawer 232 (95992). (916) 673-1600. FAX: (916) 673-4768. Licensee: Ridge L. Harlan (acq 1-83; 775,000; Net: NBC; Calif. Agri-Radio, Calif. Farm. Rep: Katz & Powell. Wash atty: Koteen & Naftalin. Format: Mod country, news. News staff 2; news progmg 15 hrs wkly. Target aud: 25-64. Spec prog: Farm 4 hrs, Punjabi Indian 4 hrs, gospel 2 hrs, relg one hr wkly. ■ Ridge L. Harlan, pres; Robert R. Harlan, gen mgr; Dave Bear, opns mgr, progmg dir, mus dir & chief engr; R.J. Blount, gen sls mgr; David Petersen, prom dir; Chris Gilbert, news dir. ■ Rates: $15; 12.50; 15; 10.50.

KXCL(FM)—Co-owned with KUBA(AM). Nov 8, 1974: 103.9 mhz; 510 w. Ant 2,024 ft. TL: N39 12 20 W121 49 10. Stereo. Hrs opn: 20. Prog sep from AM. Format: Adult contemp. News staff 2; news progmg 3 hrs wkly. Target aud: 25-49; female office workers. Spec prog: Sp 3 hrs wkly. ■ Dave Bear, opns dir; R.J. Blount, gen sls mgr; Moe Howard, progmg dir & mus dir; Briggs Moor, asst mus dir. ■ Rates: $18; 17; 18; 11.

Yucaipa

*KLRD(FM)—July 15, 1986: 90.1 mhz; 300 w. Ant 1,024 ft. TL: N34 02 19 W116 57 09. Hrs opn: 24. Box 1000, Suite 204, 35225 Ave. A (92399). (909) 790-1848. Licensee: Shepherd Commmunications Inc. Net: USA. Wash atty: Fisher, Wayland, Cooper & Leader. Format: Contemp Christian. News progmg 7 hrs wkly. Target aud: 18-34; Christians. ■ David R. Ferry, chmn; Candace Andrews, CFO & gen mgr; Christie Reasons, vp dev; Terry Taylor, sls dir; Don Carson, progmg mgr; Noonie Fugler, mus dir; Mark Sadacca, chief engr. ■ Rates: $40; 30; 40; 30.

Yucca Valley

KROR(FM)—August 1988: 106.9 mhz; 4 kw. Ant 1,371 ft. TL: N34 04 55 W116 20 32. Stereo. Hrs opn: 19. Suite E, 58923 Business Center Dr. (92284-7311). (619) 365-0891. FAX: (619) 365-7792. Licensee: Corinthians XIII Broadcasting Co. Inc. Net: USA. Wash atty: Miller & Fields. Format: Country. News progmg 21 hrs wkly. Target aud: 25-45; urban middle class. ■ John J. Davis, pres & gen mgr; Deanne C. Davis, vp, progmg dir & mus dir; Cheryl King, gen sls mgr.

Colorado

Alamosa

KALQ-FM—Listing follows KGIW(AM).

*KASF(FM)—1967: 90.9 mhz; 1 kw. Ant 105 ft. TL: N37 28 20 W105 52 39. Stereo. Hrs opn: 19. c/o Adams State College (81102). (719) 589-7871. FAX: (719) 589-7522. Licensee: Adams State College. Format: Div, prog, rock. Target aud: Students; college-aged with diverse interests. Spec prog: Class 4 hrs, Black 20 hrs, jazz 4 hrs, world beat 6 hrs, new age 4 hrs, country 2 hrs wkly. ■ Jack Morris, pres; Rob Moeny, gen mgr & stn mgr; Carla Arnold, progmg mgr; Tatlana Giles, mus dir; Laurence Paverd, asst mus dir; Susan McKenna, news dir.

KGIW(AM)—Feb 27, 1929: 1450 khz; 1 kw-U. TL: N37 28 20 W105 51 13. Hrs opn: 6 AM-11 PM. Box 179 (81101); 292 Santa Fe. (81101). (719) 589-6644. FAX: (719) 589-0993. Licensee: Dale K. Burns. Group owner: Community Broadcasting (acq 1964). Net: ABC/I. Format: C&W, information. News staff one; news progmg 25 hrs wkly. Target aud: 18-60. Spec prog: Sp 6 hrs, farm 6 hrs wkly. ■ Dale K. Burns, pres; Marilyn Burns, exec vp; Neil J. Hammer, gen mgr; Helen Lozoya, gen sls mgr; Rosalie Maestas, prom dir; Alan Spears, progmg dir; Ron Loven, news dir; John Skinner, chief engr. ■ Rates: $12; 12; 12; 12.

KALQ-FM—Co-owned with KGIW(AM). June 26, 1969: 93.5 mhz; 2.8 kw. Ant 130 ft. TL: N37 28 20 W105 51 13. Stereo. (719) 589-6645. Net: MBS. Format: Adult contemp. ■ Patsy Garcia, opns mgr.

*****KRZA(FM)**—Oct 26, 1985: 88.7 mhz; 5 kw. Ant 2,393 ft. TL: N36 51 32 W106 00 28. Stereo. Box 1660, 528 9th St. (81101). (719) 589-9057. FAX: (719) 589-9258. Licensee: Equal Representation of Media Advocacy Corp. Net: NPR. Format: News, jazz, class. Spec prog: Sp 14 hrs, Latin American 3 hrs wkly. ■ Arnold Salazar, pres; Greg Shade, progmg dir; Robert Crow, chief engr.

Arvada

KQXI(AM)—Jan 9, 1962: 1550 khz; 10 kw-D, 166 w-N. TL: N39 40 02 W104 59 57 (CP: 10 kw-U, DA-N, TL: N39 38 48 W105 00 26). Hrs opn: 6AM-10PM. 2700 S. Platte River Dr., Englewood (80110). (303) 783-0880. FAX: (303) 783-0602. Licensee: BDG Enterprises Inc. Group owner: Mid-America Gospel Radio (acq 9-15-86; grpsl; FTR 8-16-86). Net: USA. Format: Relg, sports. News progmg 2 hrs wkly. Target aud: 25-44; Adults. ■ Scott Alexander, gen mgr; Frank Trueblood, opns mgr; Philip French, natl sls mgr; Paul Montoya, chief engr. ■ Rates: $50; 30; 50; 30.

Aspen

*****KAJX(FM)**—July 7, 1987: 91.5 mhz; 380 w-H, 370 w-V. Ant -987 ft. TL: N39 11 48 W106 48 14. Stereo. Hrs opn: 24. 307 J AABC (81611). (303) 925-6445. Licensee: Aspen Public Radio. Net: NPR, APR. Format: Class, jazz, news. News staff one; news progmg 50 hrs wkly. Target aud: General; Aspen residents and tourists. Spec prog: Bluegrass, folk 4 hrs wkly. ■ Sy Coleman, pres; Bill Capps, dev dir; Barry Smith, progmg dir.

KPVW(FM)—Not on air, target date unknown: 107.1 mhz; 470 w. Ant 804 ft. TL: N39 13 15 W106 48 44. Box 3884 (81612). Licensee: Aspen FM Inc.

KRKE(AM)—Mar 4, 1964: 1260 khz; 5 kw-D. TL: N39 12 28 W106 51 15. Stereo. Stn currently dark. 421-B A.A.B.C. (81611). (303) 925-7383. Licensee: Gardiner Broadcast Partners Ltd. (group owner; acq 4-1-91; $800,000; FTR 4-15-91). ■ David Laughner, gen mgr.

KSNO-FM—See Snowmass Village.

KSPN-FM—Feb 14, 1970: 97.7 mhz; 3 kw. Ant 54 ft. TL: N39 13 33 W106 50 00. Stereo. Hrs opn: 24. 225 N. Mill (81611). (303) 925-5776. FAX: (303) 925-1142. Licensee: Moss Entertainment Corp. (acq 6-91; $900,000). Net: AP. Rep: Christal. Wash atty: Rosenman & Colin. Format: AOR. News staff one; news progmg 6 hrs wkly. Target aud: 25-49; affluent, well educated people who live in resort areas. ■ Charley Moss, pres; Lynn Scott, gen mgr, gen sls mgr & mktg mgr; Gary Whipple, opns mgr & progmg dir; Peter Jaycox, sls dir; Rachel Gold, prom dir; Peter J. Cox, adv dir; Steve Cole, mus dir; Margie Shafer, news dir; Bill Humphreys, chief engr. ■ Rates: $30; 25; 30; 15.

Aurora

KEZW(AM)—1954: 1430 khz; 5 kw-U, DA-N. TL: N39 12 28 W104 55 46. Stereo. Hrs opn: 24. Suite B131, 10200 E. Girard Ave., Denver (80231). (303) 696-1714. FAX: (303) 696-0522. Licensee: Tribune Denver Radio Inc. Group owner: Tribune Broadcasting Co. (acq 11-25-92; $19.5 million with KOSI(FM) Denver; FTR 12-7-92). Net: SMN. Rep: Banner. Format: Nostalgia, big band, MOR. Target aud: 35 plus; general. ■ Samuel "Skip" Weller, exec vp & gen mgr; David Juris, gen sls mgr; Jeff Schatz, rgnl sls mgr; Sheryl Sheafor, prom dir; Rick Crandall, progmg dir & mus dir; Steve Hamilton, pub affrs dir; Rodger Tighe, chief engr.

KOSI(FM)—See Denver.

KYBG(AM)—Licensed to Aurora. See Denver.

Avon

KZYR(FM)—Dec 24, 1984: 103.1 mhz; 1.5 kw. Ant 459 ft. TL: N39 38 08 W106 26 46. Stereo. Hrs opn: 24. Box 5559, 0082 Beaver Creek Blvd. (81620). (303) 949-0140. FAX: (303) 949-0266. Licensee: Gardiner Broadcast Partners Ltd. (group owner; acq 8-9-91; $550,000; FTR 6-10-91). Net: UPI. Wash atty: Cole, Raywid & Braverman. Format: Rock/AOR. News staff 2. Target aud: 18-54. ■ Clifton H. Gardiner, CEO; Ruth Jones, gen mgr; Sandy Van Devienter, opns dir; Kim Jones, vp sls; Kaylen Wells, prom dir; Tony Mauro, progmg dir; Jackie Selby, mus dir; Gail Cameron-Britt, news dir; Marty Hijmans, engrg dir. ■ Rates: $19; 19; 19; 8.

Basalt

KVYT(FM)—Not on air, target date unknown: 106.1 mhz; 1.4 kw-H, 1.35 kw-V. Ant 338 ft. TL: N39 21 11 W107 05 36. c/o 1885 Ponder Heights Dr., Colorado Springs (80906). Licensee: Caren Lacy.

Boulder

KBCO(AM)—Nov 14, 1973: 1190 khz; 5 kw-D. TL: N39 57 54 W105 14 05. Stereo. Hrs opn: 24. 8975 E. Kenyon, Denver (80237). (303) 444-5600. FAX: (303) 449-3057. Licensee: Noble Broadcast of Colorado Inc. (group owner; acq 10-26-87; $27.25 million with co-located FM; FTR 10-26-87). Rep: Major Mkt. Wash atty: Haley, Bader & Potts. Format: Adult AOR. News staff 3; news progmg 3 hrs wkly. Target aud: 25-44. Spec prog: Jazz 3 hrs wkly. ■ John Lynch, pres; Dino Ianni, vp & gen mgr; Mary Rawlins, sls dir; Cheryl Holbeck, natl sls mgr; Kate Culligan, mktg dir & prom dir; Doug Clifton, progmg dir; Ginger Havlat, mus dir; Steve Chavis, news dir & pub affrs dir; Craig Roberts, chief engr. ■ Rates: $300; 300; 300; 175.

KBCO-FM—Oct 1, 1955: 97.3 mhz; 100 kw. Ant 1,541 ft. TL: N39 54 48 W105 17 32. Stereo. Dups AM 100%. ■ Dennis Constantine, opns mgr; Mary Rawlins, gen sls mgr. ■ Rates: Same as AM.

KBOL(AM)—Feb 15, 1947: 1490 khz; 1 kw-U. TL: N40 01 42 W105 15 06. Hrs opn: 6 AM-midnight. Box 146 (80306); 3085 Blurr St. (80301). (303) 444-1490. Licensee: Acorn Broadcasting Co. Inc. (acq 6-3-92; $225,000; FTR 7-20-92). Net: ABC/I. Format: Adult contemp, news/talk, sports. News staff one. Target aud: 25 plus; Boulder county residents. ■ Gordon Francis, pres, gen mgr & chief engr; Melanie Francis, vp; Roy Plumisto, rgnl sls mgr; Kelly Oliver, progmg dir; Tony Kindelspire, mus dir; Susan St. James, news dir. ■ Rates: $24.50; 19.50; 24.50; 15.

*****KGNU(FM)**—May 22, 1978: 88.5 mhz; 1.3 kw. Ant 215 ft. TL: N39 59 32 W105 09 10. Stereo. Hrs opn: 24. Box 885 (80306). (303) 449-4885. Licensee: Boulder Community Broadcast Association Inc. Net: APR, NPR; Colo. Pub. Wash atty: Haley, Bader & Potts. Format: Div. News staff one; news progrm 30 hrs wkly. Target aud: General. Spec prog: Black 7 hrs, folk 20 hrs, gospel 2 hrs, Sp 3 hrs, Amer Ind one hr, jazz 15 hrs, class 13 hrs, C&W 3 hrs wkly. ■ Marty Durlin, gen mgr; Scott Wilson, dev dir; Paul Metters, mus dir; Sam Fuquia, news dir; Erik Seville, chief engr.

KLMO(AM)—See Longmont.

KRKS-FM—Mar 15, 1971: 94.7 mhz; 100 kw. Ant 984 ft. TL: N40 04 19 W105 21 14. Stereo. 7880 E. Berry Place, Englewood (80111). (303) 779-8797. FAX: (303) 740-9019. Licensee: Salem Media of Colorado Inc. Group owner: Salem Communications Corp. (acq 12-15-93; $5 million; FTR 11-15-93). Format: The Wave. ■ John Irwin, gen mgr; Richard Puter, progmg dir.

Breckenridge

KSMT(FM)—Sept 12, 1975: 102.3 mhz; 3 kw. Ant -230 ft. TL: N39 29 44 W106 01 44. Stereo. Hrs opn: 24. Box 7069 (80424). (303) 453-2234. Licensee: Gardiner Broadcasting Inc. Group owner: Gardiner Broadcast Partners Ltd. (acq 5-15-91; $750,000; FTR 6-3-91). Net: AP. Format: Adult rock. News progmg 12 hrs wkly. Target aud: 18-44; upscale adults, heavy ski industry and outdoor industry consumers. Spec prog: Class 4 hrs, jazz 3 hrs wkly. ■ C.J. Pattons, gen mgr; Tony Mauro, opns mgr & progmg dir; Jay Foley, mus dir; Paul Pettit, chief engr.

Breen

KLLV(AM)—Sept 19, 1984: 550 khz; 1.8 kw-D, 80 w-N. TL: N37 11 02 W108 04 54. 14780 Hwy. 140 (81326-9775). (303) 259-5558. Licensee: Daystar Radio Ltd. Format: Inspirational. News progmg 2 hrs wkly. Target aud: General. ■ D. Jansen, pres; E. Harper, vp; Dave Williaims, gen mgr; J. Alexander, chief engr.

Brighton

KLTT(AM)—Apr 26, 1956: 800 khz; 1 kw-D, DA. TL: N40 01 41 W104 49 21 (CP: 2.5 kw-D, 200 w-N, TL: N39 41 06 W105 04 05). Suite 300, 2150 W. 29th Ave., Denver (80211). (303) 458-8579; (303) 433-8000. Licensee: KLZ Radio Inc. Format: Christian, Country. Target aud: 24-55; General. Spec prog: Black 2 hrs wkly. ■ Donald B. Crawford, pres; Donald B. Crawford, Jr., vp; Joy Mandel, progmg dir; Chris Alexander, chief engr. ■ Rates: $30; 24; 30; 22.

WILLIAM A. EXLINE, INC

MEDIA BROKERS
CONSULTANTS

*4340 Redwood Highway
Suite F 230
San Rafael, California 94903*

TEL **(415) 479-3484**

• *FAX* **(415) 479-1574**

Brush

KJYY(FM)—Not on air, target date unknown: 106.3 mhz; 3 kw. Ant 75 ft. TL: N40 15 39 W103 38 15. c/o Douglas C. Turnbull, 12 Smith Ave., Ware, MA (01082). Licensee: Douglas C. Turnbull.

KSIR(AM)—Aug 1, 1977: 1010 khz; 10 kw-D, 20 w-N. TL: N40 15 39 W103 38 15. Hrs opn: 5 AM-10 PM. 231 Main St., Fort Morgan (80701); Box 707 (80723). (303) 842-5005. Licensee: New Directions Media Inc. Group owner: Colorado Farm & Ranch Broadcasters (acq 4-1-90; with co-located FM; FTR 4-16-90). Net: ABC/I. Format: C&W. News staff one. Target aud: Farmers, ranchers. Spec prog: Farm 16 hrs wkly. ■ Robert D. Zellmer, pres, gen mgr & chief engr; Majorie Zellmer, vp; Terry Tobinson, progmg dir; Jim Bernhardt, news dir.

KSIR-FM—1978: 107.1 mhz; 100 kw. Ant 935 ft. TL: N40 16 24 W104 06 16. Net: ABC/D. Spec prog: Sp 3 hrs wkly.

Buena Vista

KDMN(AM)—Aug 22, 1986: 1450 khz; 1 kw-U. TL: N38 49 07 W106 09 01. Box 429 (81211). (719) 395-6000. Licensee: Alpine Broadcasting Corp. (acq 3-21-90; $32,0000; FTR 3-09-90). Net: SMN. Format: C&W. ■ Joe Frack, gen mgr.

Burlington

KNAB(AM)—July 11, 1967: 1140 khz; 1 kw-D. TL: N39 17 28 W102 15 45. Box 516, 17534 County Rd. No. 49 (80807). (719) 346-8600; (719) 346-5566. FAX: (719) 346-8656. Licensee: KNAB Inc. (acq 9-6-91). Net: ABC/I. Rep: Eastman, Art Moore. Wash atty: Fletcher, Heald & Hildreth. Format: Country, farm. News progmg 15 hrs wkly. Target aud: 18 plus. ■ Bette Bailly, pres, gen mgr & chief engr; Glen R. Viehmeyer, gen sls mgr; Charles Barnes, prom dir; progmg dir & mus dir; Jeremy Current, news dir.

KNAB-FM—Mar 7, 1980: 104.1 mhz; 50.7 kw. Ant 358 ft. TL: N39 17 41 W102 15 37. Stereo. Hrs opn: 24. Net: ABC. Format: Adult contemp, agriculture.

Canon City

KRLN(AM)—Aug 15, 1947: 1400 khz; 1 kw-U. TL: N38 27 35 W105 13 26. 1615 Central (81212). (719) 275-7488. Licensee: KRLN Inc. Group owner: Warner Stns. (acq 1-1-65). Net: CBS. Rep: Katz & Powell, Art Moore. Format: Oldies, news. News staff one. Target aud: 25-54; two income families and older discretionary income. ■ Norton Warner, pres; Ed Norden, Peggy Hitchcock, gen mgrs; Peggy Hitchcock, gen sls mgr; Ed Norden, news dir; Dick Romine, chief engr. ■ Rates: $13.80; 11.80; 13.80; 11.80.

KRLN-FM—June 1, 1975: 103.9 mhz; 3 kw. Ant 520 ft. TL: N38 27 35 W105 13 26. Stereo. Prog sep from AM. Net: Unistar. Format: Country. Target aud: 25-60. ■ Ed Norden, stn mgr; Peggy Hitchcock, adv mgr. ■ Rates: Same as AM.

Carbondale

***KDNK(FM)**—Apr 15, 1983: 90.5 mhz; 215 w. Ant 2,798 ft. TL: N39 25 35 W107 22 48. Hrs opn: 6 AM-1 AM (M-F)/7 AM-1 AM (Sat & Sun). Box 1388, 417 Main St. (81623). (303) 963-0139; (303) 963-2976. Licensee: Carbondale Community Access Radio Inc. Net: NPR. Wash atty: Haley. Bader & Potts. Format: Div, educ, news. News progmg 21 hrs wkly. Spec prog: Blues 12 hrs, class 10 hrs, bluegrass-country 10 hrs, jazz 17 hrs, Sp 2 hrs, folk 10 hrs wkly. ■ Julie Ross, gen mgr; Missy Bowen, opns mgr, mus dir & news dir; Cynthia Lindsay, gen sls mgr; Jim McDonald, chief engr. ■ Rates: $80; 45; 80; 35.

Castle Rock

KYBG-FM—Feb 26, 1978: 92.1 mhz; 820 w. Ant 613 ft. TL: N39 25 39 W104 52 00. Stereo. Suite 550, 9351 Grant St., Thornton (80229-4360). (303) 252-1090. FAX: (303) 451-0303. Licensee: Century Broadcasting Corp. (group owner; acq 8-21-87; $1.4 million; FTR 4-20-87). Rep: Roslin. Wash atty: Wiley, Rein & Fielding. Format: News/talk. Target aud: 25-54; upscale men. ■ George A. Collias, pres; Richard Bonick, exec vp; Ron Jamison, vp & vp progmg; John Vigil, opns mgr; Fritz Stahmer, gen sls mgr; Bridgette Papineau, prom mgr; Jeff Pinkerton, chief engr. ■ Rates: $75; 75; 100; 50.

Colorado Springs

KCCY(FM)—See Pueblo.

KCMN(AM)—Feb 9, 1964: 1530 khz; 1 kw-D. TL: N38 49 08 W104 46 32. Suite 218, 5050 Edison (80915). (719) 570-1530. FAX: (719) 570-1007. Licensee: KCMN Inc. (acq 1-1-88). Net: CNN, Unistar. Format: Big band. Target aud: 50 plus. ■ Chip Lusko, pres & gen mgr; Tron Simpson, vp opns & progmg dir; Kent Bagdasar, gen sls mgr; Ray Uberecken, vp engrg.

***KEPC(FM)**—Feb 15, 1957: 89.7 mhz; 7.88 kw. Ant -273 ft. TL: N38 45 42 W104 47 11. Stereo. Hrs opn: 24. 5675 S. Academy Blvd. (80906). (719) 540-7489. Licensee: Pikes Peak Community College. Format: Maximum var. News progmg 5 hrs wkly. Target aud: General. ■ Maryjane A. Paulson, pres; Kurt Grow, gen mgr, progmg dir, mus dir, news dir & pub affrs dir; Dennis Shawl, chief engr.

KHII(FM)—See Security.

KIKX-FM—See Manitou Springs.

KILO(FM)—Jan 21, 1966: 93.9 mhz; 83 kw. Ant 2,110 ft. TL: N38 44 44 W104 51 43. Stereo. Box 2080 (80901); 1805 E. Cheyenna Rd. (80906). (719) 634-4896. Licensee: Bahakel Communications (group owner; acq 8-14-84). Rep: Eastman. Format: AOR. News staff one. ■ Lou Mellina, gen mgr; Rich Hawk, stn mgr & progmg dir; Rob Culbert, prom mgr; Allan White, mus dir; Steve Rayan, news dir; John Gray, chief engr.

KKCS(AM)—Dec 15, 1956: 1460 khz; 5 kw-D, 500 w-N, DA-N. TL: N38 49 36 W104 44 30. Hrs opn: 24. Box 39102 (80949); Suite 200, 5145 Centennial Blvd. (80919). (719) 594-9000. FAX: (719) 594-9006. Licensee: Walton Stations of Colorado Inc. Group owner: Walton Stations (acq 10-15-82). Rep: Torbet. Wash atty: Cohn & Marks. Format: Hot country. ■ John B. Walton, pres; Bob Gourley, gen mgr; Jerry Grant, gen sls mgr; Chrissy Adsit, prom dir; Charlie Cassidy, progmg dir; Dave Shepel, mus dir; Gwen Rhea, news dir; Mel Rauh, chief engr.

KKCS-FM—Jan 28, 1967: 101.9 mhz; 79 kw. Ant 2,178 ft. TL: N38 44 40 W104 51 43. Stereo. Format: Country. Spec prog: Gospel 3 hrs wkly. ■ Jeff Haynie, dev mgr; Bruce Erickson, rgnl sls mgr; Shane Farris, pub affrs dir; Melvyn Rauh, engrg dir.

KKFM(FM)—1958: 98.1 mhz; 72 kw. Ant 2,300 ft. TL: N38 44 36 W104 51 44. Stereo. Penthouse Suite, 411 Lakewood Circle (80910). (719) 596-5536. FAX: (719) 596-6718. Licensee: Citadel Communications Corp. (group owner; acq 1-86; $2.5 million; FTR 8-16-82). Net: ABC/R. Rep: Christal. Format: Classic rock. ■ Fritz Beesemyer, pres; Bob Proffitt, gen mgr; Jeff Schatz, gen sls mgr; Mark Goldberg, news dir; Tom Beattie, chief engr.

KKLI(FM)—(Widefield). Mar 23, 1987: 106.3 mhz; 1.6 kw. Ant 2,224 ft. TL: N38 44 41 W104 51 46. Stereo. Hrs opn: 24. 2175 S. Academy Circle, Colorado Springs (80909). (719) 596-1000. FAX: (719) 573-1000. Licensee: Tippie Communications Colo. (group owner; acq 7-88; $1.25 million; FTR 6-20-88). Rep: Torbet. Format: Adult contemp. News staff one; news progmg 4 hrs wkly. Target aud: women 25-54; family-oriented, educated, upscale women. ■ Henry B. Tippie, pres; Joe Panico, exec vp; Henry B. Tippie II, gen mgr; Dan Cowen, opns mgr & progmg dir; Ron Mitchell, gen sls mgr; Judy Penny, rgnl sls mgr; Greg Allen, prom mgr; Sharon Green, mus dir; Mark Goldberg, news dir; Dan Remy, chief engr. ■ Rates: $54; 52; 47; 10.

***KRCC(FM)**—Oct 2, 1951: 91.5 mhz; 1 kw. Ant 2,103 ft. TL: N38 44 43 W104 51 42. Stereo. Hrs opn: 24. 912 N. Weber St. (80903). (719) 473-4801. Licensee: Colorado College. Net: NPR. Wash atty: Haley, Bader & Potts. Format: Div, jazz, news. News progmg 42 hrs wkly. Target aud: 25-44; males. Spec prog: Celtic 5 hrs, new age 6 hrs wkly. ■ Mario B. Valdes, gen mgr; Sharon Marrs, gen sls mgr; Lyn Akers, prom mgr; Jeff Bieri, mus dir; Dan Remy, chief engr.

KRDO(AM)—March 1947: 1240 khz; 1 kw-U. TL: N38 49 42 W104 50 15. Box 1457 (80901); 3 S. Seventh St. (80905). (719) 632-1515. FAX: (719) 520-9374. Licensee: Pikes Peak Broadcasting Co. (group owner). Net: ABC/I. Rep: D & R Radio. Wash atty: Fletcher, Heald & Hildreth. Format: New country. ■ Harry Hoth Jr., chmn; Patti Hoth, pres; Neil O. Klockziem, gen mgr; John Savidge, natl sls mgr; John Savidge (local), rgnl sls mgr; Tom Grinewich, prom dir; Lee Stewart, progmg mgr; Bruce Slusher, news dir; Charles Upton, chief engr.

KRDO-FM—Oct 1, 1969: 95.1 mhz; 96 kw. Ant 2,010 ft. TL: N38 44 47 W104 51 37. Stereo. Format: Today's soft favorites. ■ KRDO-TV affil.

KSPZ(FM)—Listing follows KVOR(AM).

***KTLF(FM)**—Feb 27, 1989: 90.5 mhz; 1.2 kw. Ant 2,050 ft. TL: N38 44 40 W104 51 37. Stereo. Hrs opn: 24. Suite A, 1802 Chapel Hills Dr. (80920). (719) 593-0600. Licensee: Education Communications of Colorado Springs Inc. Format: Relg. News staff one; news progmg 12 hrs wkly. Target aud: 25-49. ■ Dr. Ron Johnson, chmn; Larry Walters, opns mgr; Fred Carrell, dev mgr; Laura Davis, mus dir; Dan Remy, chief engr.

KTWK(AM)—March 1955: 740 khz; 3.3 kw-D, 1.5 kw-N, DA-2. TL: N39 05 02 W104 42 41. Dups KVUU(FM) Pueblo 100%. Suite 150, 2864 S. Circle Dr. (80906). (719) 579-0880. Licensee: KVUU-KSSS Inc. (acq 1-13-93; with KVUU(FM) Pueblo; FTR 2-8-93). Net: MBS. Rep: McGavren Guild. Format: National talk shows. ■ Greg Sher, pres & gen mgr; Libby Vogel, gen sls mgr; Jim Arthur, progmg dir & mus dir; Paul Richards, news dir; Joel Belik, chief engr.

KVOR(AM)—Sept 22, 1922: 1300 khz; 5 kw-D, 1 kw-N. TL: N38 48 46 W104 48 51. Stereo. Suite 150, 2864 S. Circle Dr. (80906-4180). (719) 527-1300. FAX: (719) 771-9336. Licensee: Springs Radio Inc. (acq 6-90; $3.25 million with co-located FM; FTR 6-25-90). Net: CBS, Wall Street, ABC TalkRadio, CNN. Rep: Katz. Format: News, talk, sports. News staff 3; News progmg 50 hrs wkly. Target aud: General; Spec prog: Air Force football & basketball, Denver Broncos & Nuggets coverage. ■ Greg Sher, gen mgr & sls dir; Jim Arthur, progmg dir; Joel Belik, chief engr.

KSPZ(FM)—Co-owned with KVOR(AM). Feb 1, 1960: 92.9 mhz; 53 kw. Ant 2,130 ft. TL: N38 44 44 W104 51 39. Stereo. Net: Unistar. Rep: Katz. Format: Oldies. Target aud: 25-54. ■ Randy Hill, progmg dir.

KWYD(AM)—June 22, 1957: 1580 khz; 10 kw-D. TL: N38 43 11 W104 43 16. Box 5668 (80931); S. Hwy 85-off Willow Spr. Rd. (80911). (719) 392-4219. FAX: (719) 392-3307. Licensee: Patrick Communications II (acq 5-87; $200,000; FTR 6-22-87). Wash atty: Peper, Martin, Jensen, Maichel & Hetlage. Format: Relg, talk. News staff one; news progmg 2 hrs wkly. Target aud: General. Spec prog: Seniors one hr wkly. ■ Edward J. Patrick, pres; Rick Martin, gen mgr & gen sls mgr; Jody Ilett, prom mgr; John Boles, progmg dir, mus dir & news dir; Mel Rouh, chief engr.

Commerce City

KMVP(AM)—Not on air, target date unknown: 670 khz; 2.5 kw-D, 1 kw-N, DA-N. TL: N39 57 21 W104 42 00 (CP: TL: N39 57 21 W104 43 40). 161 N. LaBrea, Inglewood, CA (90301). (310) 330-3123. Licensee: KMVP Inc. ■ Cliff Gill, vp.

Cortez

KISZ-FM—Sept 28, 1978: 97.9 mhz; 100 kw. Ant 1,360 ft. TL: N37 21 48 W108 09 00. Stereo. Hrs opn: 20. 653 W. Broadway, Farmington, NM (87401); Box 740 (81321). (505) 327-1098; (303) 565-3409. FAX: (505) 327-2020. Licensee: Explorer Communications Inc. (acq 4-85). Net: ABC/R. Rep: Art Moore. Wash atty: Verner, Liipfert, Bernhard, McPherson & Hand. Format: AOR, alt rock. Target aud: 18-49; young sophisticated adults. ■ James F. Hoffman, pres & gen sls mgr; Adam Savage, progmg dir; Andy Taylor, mus dir; Jim Burt, chief engr. ■ Rates: $24; 24; 24; 14.

KRTZ(FM)—Listing follows KVFC(AM).

***KSJD(FM)**—July 1990: 91.5 mhz; 145 w. Ant -417 ft. TL: N37 21 10 W108 26 07. Stereo. Hrs opn: 24. 33057 Hwy. 160, Mancos (81328). (303) 565-8457. FAX: (303) 565-8457. Licensee: Basin Area Voc-Technical School. Format: Rock, alternative. News staff one. Target aud: 16-30; college level. Spec prog: Relg one hr wkly. ■ Anthony Valdez, gen mgr.

KVFC(AM)—Feb 27, 1955: 740 khz; 1 kw-D, 250 w-N, DA-N. TL: N37 20 58 W108 32 29. Hrs opn: 18. 2402 Hawkins (81321). (303) 565-6565. FAX: (303) 565-8567. Licensee: DeLane Broadcasting Inc. Format: Top-40. Target aud: 18-54; young adults. Spec prog: Classic rock 6 hrs, comedy 2 hrs wkly. ■ William Beasley, gen mgr.

KRTZ(FM)—Co-owned with KVFC(AM). December 1981: 98.7 mhz; 27 kw. Ant 2,900 ft. TL: N37 13 10 W108 48 26. Stereo. Licensee: DeLane Broadcasting Inc (acq 10-2-85). Net: ABC/E. Rep: Eastman, Intermountain Net. Format: Country. News staff one. Spec prog: Ute Indian one hr wkly. ■ William E. Beasley, stn mgr; Lan DeGeneres, gen sls mgr; Tim Webb, progmg dir; Steve Rose, mus dir; Marc Wondra, news dir; John Morton, chief engr.

Craig

KRAI(AM)—1948: 550 khz; 5 kw-D, 500 w-N, DA-N. TL: N40 32 45 W107 31 52. Hrs opn: 19. Box 65 (81625); 1111 W. Victory Way (81626). (303) 824-6574; (303) 824-2601. FAX: (303) 879-3677. Licensee: Wild West Radio Inc. (acq 5-89). Net: CNN, Unistar. Rep: Intermountain Net., Eastman; Art Moore.Format: Country. News progmg 12 hrs wkly. Target aud: 25-54. Spec prog: Farm one hr wkly. ■ Frank R. Hanel Jr., pres, gen mgr, gen sls mgr & chief engr; Tammie Hanel, stn mgr; Brad Thomas, progmg dir; Mike Wainz, mus dir.

KRAI-FM—April 1976: 93.7 mhz; 100 kw. Ant 980 ft. TL: N40 34 35 W107 36 29. Stereo. Prog sep from AM. Format: Adult contemp. News progmg 2 hrs wkly. Target aud: 18-49. Spec prog: Oldies from the 60s & 70s 9 hrs wkly.

Crested Butte

***KBUT(FM)**—Dec 20, 1986: 90.3 mhz; 250 w. Ant -667 ft. TL: N38 52 19 W106 58 44. Stereo. Hrs opn: 18. Box 308, 801 Butte Ave. (81224). (303) 349-5225; (303) 349-7444. Licensee: Crested Butte MNT Educational Radio Inc. Net: NPR. Format: Div. ■ Bonnie Chlipala, stn mgr; Glenda W. Harper, sls dir; Jackie Scalzo, progmg dir; Jim Michael, mus dir; Rich Driscoll, chief engr.

Deer Trail

KTMG(AM)—July 16, 1983: 1370 khz; 5 kw-D, 160 w-N, DA-2. TL: N39 37 09 W104 01 40. Hrs opn: Dawn-dusk. Drawer A, 7th & Cedar (80105). (303) 769-4401; (303) 769-4402. FAX: (303) 769-4787. Licensee: Edmond A. Marshall (acq 2-23-93; $150,000; FTR 3-15-93). Rep: Roslin, Art Moore. Format: Country & agriculture. Spec prog: Farm, news, and market reports. ■ Ed Marshall, pres & gen mgr; Todd Marshall, gen sls mgr; Trent Marshall, progmg dir & news dir; Bill Harris, chief engr.

Delta

KDTA(AM)—Jan 14, 1955: 1400 khz; 1 kw-U. TL: N38 45 38 W108 05 28. Box 452, 461 Palmer St. (81416). (303) 874-4411; (303) 874-4412. Licensee: Blink Communications (acq 10-19-92; $24,000; FTR 11-23-92). Net: ABC/E, Unistar. Format: Country. News staff one; news progmg 10 hrs wkly. Target aud: 25-65. Spec prog: Sp 3 hr, farm one hr, Ger one hr, Pol one hr wkly. ■ Brad Link, pres & gen mgr; H.K. Swindler, mus dir.

KKLY(FM)—December 1980: 95.1 mhz; 100 kw. Ant 969 ft. TL: N38 52 40 W108 13 30. Stereo. Hrs opn: 24. Box 2450, Grand Junction (81502); Suite 430, 715 Horizon Dr. (81506). (303) 241-7070. FAX: (303) 245-5858. Licensee: Monument Broadcasters (acq 5-88). Net: Unistar. Rep: Intermountain Net, Eastman; Art Moore. Wash atty: Fletcher, Heald & Hildreth. Format: Adult contemp. News staff one; news progmg 6 hrs wkly. Target aud: 25-54; female. Spec prog: Acoustic Sun 6 hrs wkly. ■ James G. Spehar, gen mgr; Robert St. John, opns mgr & progmg dir; Pat Ralston, gen sls mgr; Tim Davis, news dir; Ted Wetzel, chief engr.

Denver

KAZY(FM)—June 19, 1962: 106.7 mhz; 100 kw. Ant 987 ft. TL: N39 43 59 W105 14 12. Stereo. Hrs opn: 24. Suite 1300, 1380 Lawrence (80204). (303) 893-3699. FAX: (303) 534-7625. Licensee: Z-C Radio Acquisition Group owner: Jacor Communications Inc. (acq 6-9-93; $5.5 million; FTR 6-28-93). Net: ABC/R. Format: AOR. Target aud: Men 25-34. ■ Don Howe, vp & gen mgr; Mark Remington, gen sls mgr; Rosemary Bennett, natl sls mgr; Mike DePriest, mktg dir & prom dir; Shauna Moran, mktg mgr & prom mgr; Lois Todd, mus dir; Tim Dunbar, news dir & pub affrs dir; Jack Lambiotte, chief engr.

KBNO(AM)—June 5, 1954: 1220 khz; 1 kw-D, 17 w-N. TL: N39 40 02 W104 59 57 (CP: TL: 39 39 34 W105 00 44). Suite 100, 2727 Bryant St. (80211-4154). (303) 292-5266. FAX: (303) 433-1330. Licensee: Colorado Communications Corp. (acq 11-6-90; $250,000; FTR 11-19-90). Net: SIS. Rep: Katz. Wash atty: Fisher, Wayland, Cooper & Leader. Format: Sp contemp. News staff one; news progmg 60 hrs wkly. Target aud: 18-49. ■ Zee Ferrufino, pres; Frank Ponce, CFO; Manuel Tarango, progmg mgr, news dir & pub affrs dir; Armando Hernandez, mus dir; Gunther Auerbach, chief engr. ■ Rates: $47; 43; 44; 34.

KBPI-FM—June 21, 1965: 105.9 mhz; 100 kw. Ant 900 ft. TL: N39 43 59 W105 14 12. Stereo. One Tabor Ctr., Suite 2300, 1200 17th St. (80202). (303) 534-6200. FAX: (303) 592-2399. Licensee: Great American Broadcasting (group owner; acq 12-12-89; $9.75 million; FTR 1-8-90). Rep: Banner. Wash atty: Koteen & Naftlin. Format: AOR. News staff one; news progmg 5 hrs wkly. Target aud: 18-34. ■ Dave Crowl, pres; Tom Sly, vp & gen mgr; Bill Betts, opns mgr & progmg dir; Todd Metz, gen sls mgr; Kelly Williams, vp prom; Roger Beaty, news dir; Jeff Garrett, chief engr.

***KCFR(FM)**—November 1970: 90.1 mhz; 50 kw. Ant 910 ft. TL: N39 43 49 W105 14 59. Stereo. Hrs opn: 24. 2249 S. Josephine St. (80210). (303) 871-9191. Licensee: Public Broadcasting of Colorado Inc. FTR 10-28-91). Net: NPR; Colo. Pub. Format: Class, news. News staff 7; news progmg 50 hrs wkly. Target aud: General. ■ Max Wycisk, gen mgr; Patricia Prevost, dev dir & gen sls mgr; Sandra James, prom mgr; Ed Trudeau, progmg dir; Monika Vischer, mus dir; Michael Rudeen, news dir; Robert Hensler, chief engr.

KCUV(AM)—See Englewood.

KEZW(AM)—See Aurora.

KHOW(AM)—1925: 630 khz; 5 kw-U, DA-2. TL: N39 54 36 W104 54 50. Stereo. 8975 E. Kenyon Ave. (80237). (303) 694-6300. FAX: (303) 779-8094. Licensee: Noble Broadcast San Diego Group (acq 12-29-92; traded with co-located FM in exchange for KNDD(FM) Seattle; FTR 1-25-93). Net: MBS. Rep: Banner. Format: Adult contemp. Target aud: 25-54. ■ Dino Ianni, gen mgr; Mary Rawlings, gen sls mgr; Kate Culligan, prom mgr; Tom Harper, progmg dir; Craig Roberts, chief engr.

KHOW-FM—Co-owned with KHOW(AM). March 31, 1968: 95.7 mhz; 100 kw. Ant 725 ft. TL: N39 43 59 W105 14 10. Stereo. Prog sep from AM. Format: Soft adult contemp. Target aud: 25-54; General. ■ Jamie Kartak, progmg mgr.

KJME(AM)—Jan 1, 1954: 1390 khz; 5 kw-D, DA. TL: N39 39 29 W105 00 49. Stereo. 828 Santa Fe Dr. (80204). (303) 623-1390. Licensee: Jo-Mor Communications (acq 5-90; $350,000; FTR 5-21-90). Format: Sp. ■ Andres Neidig, pres; Carmen Garcia, gen mgr; Mary Aragon, gen sls mgr; Tony Guerrero, progmg dir; Tim Cutforth, chief engr.

KKYD(AM)—Mar 4, 1956: 1340 khz; 1 kw-U. TL: N39 39 34 W105 00 44 (CP: TL: N39 41 01 W105 00 25). Hrs opn: 24. 7075 W. Hampden Ave. (80227). (303) 989-1340. Licensee: Kids Airwaves Ltd. (acq 1993; $800,000; FTR 9-13-93). Format: Children's radio. ■ Marc Hand, gen mgr.

KLTT(AM)—See Brighton.

KLZ(AM)—Mar 10, 1922: 560 khz; 5 kw-U, DA-1. TL: N39 50 36 W104 57 14. Hrs opn: 24. Suite 400, 2150 W. 29th Ave. (80211). (303) 433-5500. Licensee: Donald B. Crawford (acq 6-30-92; $1.5 million; FTR 7-20-92). Format: Adult contemp. Target aud: 18-34. ■ Donald B. Crawford, vp, gen mgr & natl sls mgr; Kathi Baerns, prom mgr; Bill MacCormick, progmg dir & mus dir; Toni Lyn, news dir; K.C. O'Brien, chief engr.

KMJI(FM)—Aug 1, 1959: 100.3 mhz; 100 kw. Ant 331 ft. TL: N39 41 06 W105 04 05 (CP: Ant 1,705 ft., TL: N39 54 48 W105 17 32). Stereo. Suite 210, 5350 S. Roslyn St., Englewood (80111). (303) 741-5654. FAX: (303) 220-7527. Licensee: Genesis Broadcasting Inc. (group owner; acq 2-88). Net: AP. Rep: Christal. Format: Lite Rock. Target aud: 25-54; leans slightly towards women. Spec prog: Pub affrs 2 hrs wkly. ■ Gail Shaw, gen mgr; Brenda Zellequiette, gen sls mgr; Ann Millison, mktg dir; Dave Ward, progmg dir & mus dir; Nancy Richards, news dir; Bill Harris, chief engr.

KNUS(AM)—1941: 710 khz; 5 kw-U, DA-1. TL: N39 57 19 W104 51 01. 5800 W. Alameda Ave., Lakewood (80226). (303) 935-7171. FAX: (303) 572-6217. Licensee: Boulder Broadcasting Corp. (acq 3-1-89; $1.5 million; FTR 3-20-89). Format: News/talk. News staff 3 Target aud: 35-64.

KOA(AM)—Dec 15, 1924: 850 khz; 50 kw-U. TL: N39 30 22 W104 45 57. Hrs opn: 24. 1380 Lawrence St., Suite 1300 (80204). (303) 893-8500; (303) 892-4800. FAX: (303) 892-4700. Licensee: Jacor Broadcasting of Colorado Inc. Group owner: Jacor Communications Inc. (acq 6-87; $20 million with co-located FM; FTR 6-22-87). Net: ABC/E, ABC/I, CBS. Rep: Eastman. Format: News/talk, sports. Target aud: 25-54. ■ Lee Larsen, vp & gen mgr; Dick Carlson, gen sls mgr; Ken Marks, prom mgr; Kris Olinger, progmg dir; Jerry Bell, news dir; Jan Chadwell, chief engr.

KRFX(FM)—Co-owned with KOA(AM). June 1, 1961: 103.5 mhz; 100 kw. Ant 1,045 ft. TL: N39 43 50 W105 14 07. Stereo. Prog sep from AM. (303) 893-0103. Format: Classic hits. Target aud: 25-54. ■ Don Howe, vp & gen mgr; Jack Evans, opns mgr; Mark Remington, gen sls mgr; Jerry Bell, news dir; Jack Lambiotte, chief engr.

KOSI(FM)—Mar 3, 1968: 101.1 mhz; 100 kw. Ant 1,624 ft. TL: N39 43 45 W105 14 06. Stereo. Hrs opn: 24. Suite B-131, 10200 E. Girard Ave. (80231). (303) 696-1714. FAX: (303) 696-0522. Licensee: Tribune Denver Radio Inc. Group owner: Tribune Broadcasting Co. (acq 11-25-92; $19.5 million with KEZW[AM] Aurora; FTR 12-7-92). Rep: Banner. Format: Light adult contemp. Target aud: 25-54. ■ Samuel "Skip" Weller, vp, gen mgr & gen sls mgr; Sheryl Sheafor, prom mgr; Scott Taylor, progmg dir; Steve Hamilton, mus dir; Rodger Tighe, chief engr.

***KPOF(AM)**—Mar 9, 1927: 910 khz; 5 kw-D, 1 kw-N. TL: N39 50 47 W105 01 59. 3455 W. 83rd Ave., Westminster (80030). (303) 428-0910. Licensee: Pillar of Fire Corp. Group owner: Pillar of Fire Inc. Net: AP, Moody. Format: Relg. Target aud: Mature adults & families. Spec prog: Classical 16 hrs, Greek one hr, Ger one hr, Sp one hr, Arabic one hr wkly. ■ Donald J. Wolfram, pres & news dir; Dr. Robert B. Dallenbach, vp & gen mgr; Rich Morthland, opns dir & prom mgr; Barry Blue, progmg dir & mus dir; Ray L. Rogers, chief engr.

KQXI(AM)—See Arvada.

KRFX(FM)—Listing follows KOA(AM).

KRKS(AM)—Aug 1, 1953: 990 khz; 5 kw-D, 390 w-N, DA-N. TL: N39 41 06 W105 04 05. Hrs opn: 24. 6535 W. Jewell Ave. (80232). (303) 922-5511. Licensee: KRKS General Partnership (acq 5-22-54). Net: USA. Format: Relg. Target aud: 25 plus. ■ Roger Anderson, pres; Jack H. Pelon, gen mgr, gen sls mgr & progmg dir; Dick Puter, opns mgr & news dir; Jan Chadwell, chief engr. ■ Rates: $28; 28; 28; na.

KTLK(AM)—See Thornton.

***KUVO(FM)**—Aug 29, 1985: 89.3 mhz; 26 kw. Ant 910 ft. TL: N39 43 49 W105 14 59. Stereo. Hrs opn: 24. Box 11111, 2246 Federal (80211). (303) 480-9272; (303) 477-0021. FAX: (303) 477-0474. Licensee: Denver Educ Broadcasting. Net: NPR, APR. Wash atty: Haley, Bader & Potts. Format: Jazz, bilingual. News staff one; news progmg 20 hrs wkly. Target aud: 25-49. Spec prog: Sp 15 hrs wkly. ■ Florence Hernandez-Ramos, pres & gen mgr; Tina Lujan, dev dir; Carlos Lando, progmg dir; Denise Washington-Blomberg, news dir. ■ Rates: $35; 25; 35; 15.

KVOD(FM)—Oct 2, 1959: 99.5 mhz; 100 kw. Ant 279 ft. TL: N39 41 01 W105 00 25 (CP: Ant 1,311 ft.). Stereo. Hrs opn: 24. 1601 W. Jewell Ave. (80223). (303) 936-3428; (303) 935-9950. FAX: (303) 936-0572. Licensee: Henry Broadcasting (group owner; acq 12-83; $6.6 million; FTR 1-02-84). Net: CMBS. Rep: Katz. Format: Class. News progmg 4 hrs wkly. Target aud: 35-64; upscale, educated. ■ Charlton Buckley, pres; Pam Kenny, gen mgr, stn mgr, sls dir & gen sls mgr; Gabrielle Cardwell, natl sls mgr; Robin Fountain, prom mgr; Jim Conder, progmg dir; John Samson, mus dir; Brad Hart, chief engr. ■ Rates: $100; 80; 90; 65.

***KWBI(FM)**—See Morrison.

KWMX-FM—See Lakewood.

KXKL(AM)—May 15, 1948: 1280 khz; 5 kw-U, DA-2. TL: N39 36 05 W104 58 49. Suite 1100, 1560 Broadway (80202). (303) 832-5665. FAX: (303) 832-7000. Licensee: Shamrock Broadcasting Inc. (group owner; acq 7-20-87). Rep: Katz. Format: Oldies. ■ Bill Sauer, gen mgr; Julie Silver, natl sls mgr; Sky Walker, progmg dir; Chris Hoffman, mus dir; Brooke Belson, news dir; Ted Nahil, chief engr.

KXKL-FM—Dec 1, 1956: 105.1 mhz; 100 kw. Ant 1,200 ft. TL: N39 36 00 W105 12 35 (CP: Ant 1,168 ft.). ■ Bob Zuroweste, gen mgr.

KYBG(AM)—(Aurora). Sept 12, 1972: 1090 khz; 50 kw-D, 500 w-N, DA-2. TL: N39 39 53 W104 39 24. Stereo. 9351 Grant St., Thornton (80222). (303) 832-1090. Licensee: Century Broadcasting Corp. (group owner; acq 9-85; $1,778,000; FTR 5-13-85). Net: CBS, MBS, NBC, Wall Street. Rep: Katz. Wash atty: Wiley, Rein & Fielding. Format: Sports/talk. News staff 6; news progmg 115 hrs wkly. Target aud: 25-64; affluent, managerial men. ■ George A. Collias, pres; Ron Jamison, vp & gen mgr; John Vigil, opns mgr; Fritz Stahmer, gen sls mgr; Teresa Metz, prom mgr; Steve Gramzy, progmg dir; Laurie White, news dir; Cindy Jamison, pub affrs dir; Jeff Pinkerton, chief engr. ■ Rates: $100; 75; 100; 50.

KYGO(AM)—July 4, 1922: 950 khz; 5 kw-U, DA-1. TL: N39 52 30 W104 56 00. Stereo. Hrs opn: 24. 1095 S. Monaco Pkwy. (80224). (303) 321-0950. FAX: (303) 321-3383. Licensee: Jefferson Pilot Communications Co. (group owner). Net: Unistar. Rep: CBS. Format: Country. Target aud: 35-64. Spec prog: Black one hr, Sp one hr wkly. ■ William Blackwell, pres; Robert Call, vp & gen mgr; Steve Price, gen sls mgr; Randy Weinner, natl sls mgr; Mark Etchason, prom mgr; Chuck St. John, progmg dir; Jennifer Page, mus dir; Doug Olipra, news dir; Brad Hart, chief engr.

KYGO-FM—Dec 1, 1953: 98.5 mhz; 100 kw. Ant 1,820 ft. TL: N39 40 35 W105 29 09. Stereo. Hrs opn: 24. Prog sep from AM. Target aud: 25-54. ■ John St. John, progmg dir; Kelly Ford, news dir.

Dillon

KHTH(AM)—June 30, 1987: 1130 khz; 5 kw-D. TL: N39 29 52 W106 03 11. Box 2148 (80435). (303) 468-2353. Licensee: Alameda Enterprises Inc. (acq 6-2-93; $75,000; FTR 6-21-93). Format: Talk. ■ Robin G. Theobald, pres; Mikol Hess, stn mgr; Wayne Hastings, gen sls mgr.

Durango

KDGO(AM)—Apr 18, 1958: 1240 khz; 1 kw-U. TL: N37 18 17 W107 51 10. Suite 308, 1315 Main St. (81301). (303) 247-1240. FAX: (303) 247-1771. Licensee: Regional Radio Inc. Group owner: Regional Radio (acq 10-22-92; $85,000; FTR 11-23-92). Net: CBS, CBS Spectrum. Format: Oldies. ■ Kenny Kendricks, pres; Randy Clock, gen mgr; Jarred Ewi, opns mgr.

***KDUR(FM)**—1975: 91.9 mhz; 225 w. Ant -447 ft. TL: N37 16 31 W107 52 00. Stereo. Fort Lewis College, 1000 Rim Dr. (81301). (303) 247-7261. FAX: (303) 247-7628. Licensee: Fort Lewis College. Net: UPI. Format: Div. Spec prog: Class 9 hrs, jazz 6 hrs, C&W 3 hrs, Native American Folk 3 hrs, new age 3 hrs, blues 3 hrs wkly. ■ Tami Graham, gen mgr.

KIQX(FM)—Oct 15, 1982: 101.3 mhz; 100 kw. Ant 439 ft. TL: N37 15 45 W107 54 07. Stereo. Box X (81302). (303) 259-4444. FAX: (303) 259-4450. Licensee: Four Corners Communications Co. Ltd. (acq 11-86; $1.35 million; FTR 9-15-86). Net: ABC/D. Wash atty: Akin, Gump, Hauer & Feld, L.P. Format: Adult contemp. News staff 2; new progmg 5 hrs wkly. Target aud: 25-49; mainstream business & professionals & families. Spec prog: Rockies baseball. ■ Harold L. Green, pres & gen mgr; Carolyn Green, stn mgr & gen sls mgr; Gary Shannon, progmg dir & mus dir; Bruce Anderson, news dir & chief engr. ■ Rates: $16; 11.50; 10.50; 7.

KIUP(AM)—Dec 10, 1935: 930 khz; 5 kw-D, 1 kw-N, DA-N. TL: N37 13 45 W107 51 49. Hrs opn: 19. Drawer P (81302). (303) 247-4464. Licensee: Fordstone Inc. (acq 6-1-80; $1.55 million with co-located FM; FTR 5-26-80). Net: CBS, MBS. Rep: Art Moore, Eastman, Intermountain Net. Wash atty: Reed, Smith, Shaw & McClay. Format: Full svc, MOR, news/talk. News staff one; news

Colorado Directory of Radio

progmg 5 hrs wkly. Target aud: 35-64. Spec prog: Class 2 hrs, Sp 3 hrs, jazz 4 hrs, sports 4 hrs wkly. ■ Gerald R. Ford, pres; Leonard K. Firestone, exec vp; John M. Mackley, vp & gen mgr; Dave Bray, progmg dir; Gene Shirley, mus dir; Jodi Cartwright, news dir; John Morton, chief engr.

KRSJ(FM)—Co-owned with KIUP(AM). Dec 4, 1972: 100.5 mhz; 100 kw. Ant 200 ft. TL: N37 15 46 W107 53 45. Stereo. Hrs opn: 19. Prog sep from AM. Net: ABC/I. Format: C&W. Target aud: 25 plus. Spec prog: Sports 4 hr wkly.

KWXA(FM)—Not on air, target date unknown: 99.7 mhz; 16 kw. Ant 879 ft. TL: N37 19 59 W107 49 13. 247 Pine Ridge Loop Licensee: Caren Lacy.

Eagle

KQMT(FM)—Apr 16, 1984: 101.5 mhz; 36 kw. Ant 2,210 ft. TL: N39 44 18 W106 47 58. Stereo. Hrs opn: 24. 1000 Lionsridge Loop, Vail (81657). (303) 476-7444. FAX: (303) 476-8211. Licensee: Mountain High Communications Inc. (acq 12-24-91; $500,000; FTR 1-27-92). Wash atty: Arter & Hadden. Format: Adult contemp. News staff one; news progmg 4 hrs wkly. Target aud: 25-63; affluent locals & tourists. ■ Patricia Kaplan, pres & gen mgr; Lulu Garton, sls dir & prom mgr; Rand Frangillo, progmg dir & mus dir; Kyle Troxel, news dir; John Chidester, chief engr. ■ Rates: $32; 22; 32; 15.

Englewood

KCUV(AM)—1951: 1150 khz; 5 kw-D, 1 kw-N, DA-2. TL: N39 36 18 W104 50 25. Suite 700, 1580 Lincoln, Denver (80203). (303) 861-1156. FAX: (303) 861-1158. Licensee: RMF Broadcasting. Format: Sp, talk. News progmg 5 hrs wkly. Target aud: 25-54. ■ Nina Torrez, gen mgr; Pearl O'Reilly, opns mgr; Roberta Gaytan, progmg dir; Tino Pacheco, pub affrs dir.

Estes Park

KRKI(AM)—Aug 19, 1967: 1470 khz; 1 kw-D. TL: N40 20 15 W105 31 36. Box 2677, 131 Stanley Ave. (80517). (303) 586-9555. FAX: (303) 586-9561. Licensee: Trail Broadcasting Co. Inc. (acq 4-1-91; $180,000; FTR 4-22-91). Net: SMN. Format: Adult contemp, oldies. ■ Steve Coffin, gen mgr & chief engr; David Cazpp, news dir.

Fort Collins

KCOL(AM)—Mar 1, 1947: 1410 khz; 1 kw-U, DA-N. TL: N40 35 34 W105 06 18 (CP: 5 kw-D, DA-2). 1612 LaPorte Ave. (80521). (303) 482-5991. FAX: (303) 482-5994. Licensee: University Broadcasting Co. (group owner; acq 9-28-90; with co-located FM; FTR 10-15-90). Net: ABC/I. Rep: Eastman, Art Moore. Format: News/talk. News progmg 35 hrs wkly. Target aud: 35-54; educated, affluent, professional. ■ Arthur A. Angotti, pres; Gary Krahn, stn mgr; Randy Keim, progmg dir.

KIMN-FM—Co-owned with KCOL(AM). July 27, 1975: 107.9 mhz; 100 kw. Ant 470 ft. TL: N40 40 50 W104 56 32. Stereo. Prog sep from AM. Format: CHR. News staff one. Target aud: 18-34; upscale, affluent, professional. ■ Patrick Kay, progmg dir.

***KCSU-FM**—Sept 20, 1964: 90.5 mhz; 10 kw. Ant -355 ft. TL: N40 36 00 W105 09 21. Stereo. Hrs opn: 24. Lory Student Center, Colorado State Univ. (80523). (303) 491-7611. FAX: (303) 491-7612. Licensee: Colo. State Board of Agriculture. Net: NPR, APR. Wash atty: Arter & Hadden. Format: News, AAA (adult-alternative-acoustic), rock. News staff 2; news progmg 35 hrs wkly. Target aud: General; upscale, well-educated, 20-50. Spec prog: Folk 10 hrs, gospel 3 hrs, reggae 3 hrs wkly. ■ William Hurt, gen mgr; Kellie Straub, dev dir & adv dir; Kimi Price, mktg mgr; Deni La Rue, prom dir & progmg dir; Bob Terrill, mus dir; Sandy Campbell, news dir; Andy Wurtz, engrg mgr. ■ Rates: $10; 10; 10; 5.

KIIX(AM)—(Wellington). Jan 12, 1959: 600 khz; 5 kw-D, 500 w-N, DA-2. TL: N40 39 00 W105 02 51. Box 2047, Fort Collins (80522); Suite 211, 1611 S. College, Fort Collins (80525). (303) 484-5449. FAX: (303) 484-5451. Licensee: U.S. Media Colorado Ltd. (acq 12-31-86). Net: NBC, NBC Talknet. Rep: McGavren Guild. Format: Oldies, big band, news/talk. News staff 2; news progmg 9 hrs wkly. Target aud: 35 plus. Spec prog: Farm 2 hrs, relg one hr, sports/talk 7 hrs wkly. ■ Micheal Kassner, pres; Stu Haskell, gen mgr & gen sls mgr; Wyatt Thompson, progmg dir & news dir; Jim Mross, chief engr. ■ Rates: $50; 50; 50; 50.

KTCL(FM)—Co-owned with KIIX(AM). September 1965: 93.3 mhz; 100 kw. Ant 1,328 ft. TL: N40 32 57 W105 11 49. Stereo. Licensee: U.S. Media Colorado L.P. (acq 12-31-86). Format: Freeform, progsv, alt. News staff 2. Target aud: 18 plus. Spec prog: Blues 2 hrs, jazz 2 hrs, new age 3 hrs, comedy one hr, loc bands one hr, reggae 2 hrs wkly. ■ John Hayes, progmg dir; Mary Moses, mus dir. ■ Rates: Same as AM.

KIMN-FM—Listing follows KCOL(AM).

KTCL(FM)—Listing follows KIIX(AM).

Fort Morgan

KFTM(AM)—May 22, 1949: 1400 khz; 1 kw-U. TL: N40 15 31 W103 51 07. Box 430 (80701). (303) 867-5674. FAX: (303) 867-3485. Licensee: Lovcom Inc. (acq 12-1-78). Net: SMN. Rep: Art Moore. Format: Country. News staff one; news progmg 6 hrs wkly. Target aud: General. Spec prog: Sp 4 hrs wkly. ■ Kim Love, pres; Deborah Quick, gen mgr & gen sls mgr; Roger Morgan, mus dir; Bruce Faulkner, chief engr.

KBRU(FM)—Co-owned with KFTM(AM). May 1, 1968: 101.7 mhz; 3 kw. Ant 135 ft. TL: N40 15 31 W103 51 07. Stereo. Prog sep from AM. Format: Country.

KSIR(AM)—See Brush.

Fountain

KBIQ(FM)—Sept 25, 1992: 96.1 mhz; 140 w. Ant 1,978 ft. TL: N38 44 47 W104 51 37. Stereo. Hrs opn: 24. Suite 340, 1465 Kelly Johnson Blvd., Colorado Springs (80920). (719) 531-9696. (719) 531-9697. Licensee: The Word In Music Inc. (group owner; acq 2-5-92; FTR 3-2-92). Format: Adult Christian contemp. News staff one. Target aud: 25-44. ■ Mark Pluimer, pres; Linda Tiernan, gen mgr; Jon Hull, progmg dir; Dave Masters, mus dir; Dan Remy, chief engr. ■ Rates: $20; 15; 18; 14.

Frisco

KYSL(FM)—May 27, 1988: 92.1 mhz; 290 w. Ant 1,050 ft. TL: N39 33 22 W106 06 53. Stereo. Hrs opn: 24. Box 27, 719A Ten Mile Dr. (80443). (303) 668-0292; (303) 668-3666. FAX: (303) 668-3667. Licensee: Krystal Broadcasting Inc. Net: SMN. Rep: Art Moore. Format: Adult contemp. News staff one; news progmg 8 hrs wkly. Target aud: 25-49; upscale adults. ■ Ann Penny Ogden, pres; Marilyn Hogan, gen mgr, gen sls mgr, progmg dir & mus dir; Jeff Valenteen, news dir & pub affrs dir; Paul Pettit, chief engr. ■ Rates: $20; 18; 20; 16.

Fruita

KEKB(FM)—Licensed to Fruita. See Grand Junction.

Glenwood Springs

***KDRH(FM)**—Not on air, target date unknown: 91.9 mhz; 220 w. Ant 788 ft. Suite 103, 207 Basalt Center Cir., Basalt (81621). Licensee: Valley Christian Radio Inc.

KGLN(AM)—May 14, 1950: 980 khz; 1 kw-D, 225 w-N. TL: N39 33 10 W107 19 48. Box 1028 (81601). (303) 945-9124. FAX: (303) 945-5409. Licensee: Colorado West Broadcasting Inc. (acq 6-93). Net: CNN. Format: Oldies, rock. News progmg 2 hrs wkly. Target aud: 45 plus. ■ John Tindall, pres & gen mgr; Dave Johnson, gen sls mgr, prom mgr, progmg dir & news dir. ■ Rates: 26; 26; 26; 19.

KMTS(FM)—Co-owned with KGLN(AM). June 6, 1977: 92.7 mhz; 3 kw. Ant -301 ft. TL: N39 32 36 W107 17 49 (CP: 6.2 kw, ant -233 ft.). Stereo. Prog sep from AM. Net: ABC/I. Format: Country. News staff one; news progmg 10 hrs wkly. Target aud: 25-50. ■ Dave Johnson, opns dir, prom dir & adv dir; John Tindale, progmg dir; Gabe Chenowith, chief engr.

Granby

KRKY(AM)—July 3, 1986: 930 khz; 4.5 kw-D. TL: N40 02 26 W105 56 11. Hrs opn: 24. Box 1030 (80446). (316) 669-8193. Licensee: Granby Broadcasting Systems Inc. Group owner: American Broadcasting Systems (acq 9-3-93; $250,000 with KRKM[FM] Kremmling; FTR 9-27-93). Net: SMN. Format: Local country. News staff one. Target aud: General. ■ Tom Palmer, gen mgr & gen sls mgr. ■ Rates: $15; 15; 15; na.

KSPN-FM—See Aspen.

Grand Junction

KBKL(FM)—Not on air, target date unknown: 107.9 mhz; 100 kw. Ant 1,305 ft. TL: N39 04 00 W108 44 41. c/o Robert Reichard, 2978 N. Charlotte St., Gilbertsville, PA (19525). Licensee: Jan-DI Broadcasting Inc. (acq 2-12-93; $225,000; FTR 3-8-93).

***KCIC(FM)**—Mar 4, 1979: 88.5 mhz; 450 w. Ant -431 ft. TL: N39 04 38 W108 30 38. Stereo. 3102 E Rd. (81504). (303) 434-8391. Licensee: Pear Park Baptist Schools. Format: Educ, relg. Spec prog: Class 14 hrs wkly. ■ Charles Hendrickson, gen mgr; Glenn Gardner, progmg dir; Mrs. Harlan Larsen, mus dir.

KEKB(FM)—(Fruita). May 24, 1984: 99.9 mhz; 79 kw. Ant 1,380 ft. TL: N39 03 56 W108 44 52. Stereo. 315 Kennedy, Grand Junction (81501). (303) 243-3699. FAX: (303) 243-0567. Licensee: Jan-Di Broadcasting Co. Rep: Banner, Art Moore. Format: Country. News staff one; news progmg 6 hrs wkly. Target aud: 25-54. ■ Jan Maynard, pres; Dick Maynard, gen mgr; Mike Flewelling, opns mgr; M. Miller, gen sls mgr; Ed Chandler, progmg dir & mus dir; Steve Heller, news dir; Mike Shafer, chief engr.

KEXO(AM)—Feb 29, 1948: 1230 khz; 1 kw-U. TL: N39 05 41 W108 34 41. Hrs opn: 24. Box 2450 (81502); Suite 430, 715 Horizon Dr. (81506). (303) 243-1230. FAX: (303) 245-5858. Licensee: Monument Broadcasters (acq 5-21-88). Net: Unistar, CNN. Rep: Intermountain Net, Eastman; Art Moore.Wash atty: Fletcher, Heald & Hildreth. Format: Oldies. News staff one; news progmg 18 hrs wkly. Target aud: 25-54. ■ Jim Spehar, gen mgr; Robert St. John, opns dir; Pat Ralston, gen sls mgr; Rick Lawrence, progmg dir; Jim Davis, news dir; Ted Wetzel, chief engr.

***KJOL(FM)**—Apr 24, 1982: 90.3 mhz; 1.5 kw. Ant 1,296 ft. TL: N30 03 57 W108 44 48. Stereo. 1206 Ute Ave. (81501). (303) 243-4361. FAX: (303) 242-1309. Licensee: Colorado Christian University (acq 2-86). Net: Moody, USA. Format: Christian MOR/easy contemp. Target aud: General; 35-55. Spec prog: Sp 2 hrs wkly. ■ Ken Andrews, stn mgr; Scott McIntire, progmg dir & mus dir; Al Stewart, chief engr.

KJYE-FM—Listing follows KNZZ(AM).

KMKE(FM)—Not on air, target date unknown: 104.3 mhz; 100 kw. Ant 1,296 ft. 2712 Caribbean Dr. (81506). Licensee: Blackridge Broadcasters Inc.

***KMSA(FM)**—Feb 20, 1975: 91.3 mhz; 500 w. Ant -382 ft. TL: N39 04 40 W108 33 09. Stereo. 1175 Texas Ave. (81502). (303) 248-1240. FAX: (303) 248-1199. Licensee: Mesa College. Format: Progsv, diversified, rock (AOR). News staff 2; news progmg 10 hrs wkly. Target aud: General. Spec prog: Black 9 hrs, folk 3 hrs, jazz 10 hrs wkly. ■ Ray Keift, pres; Gerald Weaver, sr vp; Jerry Moorman, vp; Eric Watson, stn mgr & pub affrs dir; "Koz" Kozmicky, opns dir; Mike Hull, sls dir; Tanya Smith, prom dir; "Tramp" Stires, mus dir; Fristi Davis, asst mus dir; Valarie Sukovaty, news dir; Norm Price, chief engr.

KNZZ(AM)—May 1, 1926: 1100 khz; 50 kw-D, 10 kw-N, DA-N. TL: N38 57 02 W108 25 11. Stereo. Hrs opn: 24. 1360 E. Sherwood Dr. (81501). (303) 241-9230. FAX: (303) 245-7551. Licensee: MBC Grand Broadcasting, Inc. (acq 8-30-89). Net: CBS, ABC TalkRadio, Daynet. Rep: Eastman; Target.Format: News/talk, sports. News staff one; news progmg 44 hrs wkly. Target aud: 25 plus; upscale adults. ■ Richard C. Dean, pres; Jim TerLouw, gen mgr; Joe Wethington, opns mgr; Bill Jones, news dir; Dwight Morgan, chief engr. ■ Rates: $20; 20; 20; 10.

KJYE-FM—Co-owned with KNZZ(AM). May 1, 1960: 92.3 mhz; 100 kw. Ant 1,378 ft. TL: N39 04 00 W108 44 41. Stereo. Hrs opn: 24. Prog sep from AM. Format: Easy lstng. News staff one; news progmg 8 hrs wkly. Target aud: 35 plus. ■ Rates: Same as AM.

***KPRN(FM)**—April 1985: 89.5 mhz; 10 kw. Ant 1,191 ft. TL: N39 03 57 W108 44 45 (CP: Ant 1,233 ft.). Stereo. Hrs opn: 18. Suite A116, 1048 Independent Ave. (81505). (303) 241-5776. FAX: (303) 245-8176. Licensee: Public Broadcasting of Colorado Inc. Public Radio Inc. Net: NPR; Colo. Pub. Wash atty: Arter & Hadden. Format: Class, news. News staff one; news progmg 28 hrs wkly. Target aud: 25 plus. Spec prog: Jazz. ■ Max Wycisk, gen mgr; Marsha Thomas, stn mgr; Ed Trudeau, progmg dir; Mike Ruden, news dir; Bob Hensler, chief engr.

KQIL(AM)—May 13, 1961: 1340 khz; 1 kw-U. TL: N39 05 35 W108 35 51. Stereo. Box 340, 421 Glenwood Ave. (81502). (303) 245-9000. FAX: (303) 245-7000. Licensee: Airwaves Communications Inc., debtor-in-possession (acq 8-89; $1,300,000 with co-located FM; FTR 9-18-89). Net: NBC. Format: Country. News staff 2. Target aud: General; 35 plus. ■ Dave Onstead, pres & gen mgr; Wayne Phillips, exec vp; Terry Jacobs, prom dir; Rick James, progmg dir; Rick Steele, news dir; Norm Price, chief engr. ■ Rates: $22; 22; 22; 18.

KQIX-FM—Co-owned with KQIL(AM). Nov 1, 1973: 93.1 mhz; 100 kw. Ant -95 ft. TL: N39 05 35 W108 35 51. Stereo. Prog sep from AM. Rep: Christal. Wash atty: Denise Moline. Format: Adult contemp/CHR. ■ Terry Jacobs, prom dir; Tamera Markley-Seipp, prom mgr; Charlie Michaels, progmg dir; Glenn Robbin, mus dir.

KSTR(AM)—June 19, 1957: 620 khz; 5 kw-U. TL: N39 07 35 W108 38 13. Hrs opn: 24. 660 Rood Ave. (81501). (303) 242-5787. FAX: (303) 245-6585. Licensee: First Star Corp. Group owner: Warner Stns. (acq 5-1-85; grpsl; FTR 4-1-85). Net: ABC, MBS. Rep: McGavren Guild. Format: News, talk. News staff 2; news progmg 30 hrs wkly. Target aud: 35 plus; mature adult audience seeking reliable news presentation. ■ Brad Legget, gen mgr; Ken Pilling, progmg mgr; Ken Bench, news dir; Ken James, chief engr.

Greeley

KFKA(AM)—May 21, 1921: 1310 khz; 5 kw-D, 1 kw-N, DA-N. TL: N40 21 56 W104 43 56. Hrs opn: 5 AM-midnight. Box K, 820 11th Ave. (80632). (303) 356-1310. FAX: (303) 356-1314. Licensee: Weld Broadcasting Co. Inc. (acq 3-15-91; $405,000; FTR 4-1-91). Net: MBS, NBC Talknet. Rep: Eastman; Target. Format: News/talk. News staff 2; news progmg 25 hrs wkly. Target aud: 35-65; community-minded, active people. Spec prog: German one hr, relg 4 hrs wkly. ■ Joe Tennessen, pres, gen mgr & gen sls mgr; Ann Weigle, opns mgr; Eldon Thomas, natl sls mgr & rgnl sls mgr; Mike Rice, prom dir & progmg dir; Bob Bernd, news dir; Larry Selzle, chief engr. ■ Rates: $27; 14; 18; 14.

KGLL(FM)—Dec 25, 1975: 96.1 mhz; 100 kw. Ant 660 ft. TL: N40 38 34 W104 49 08. Stereo. 5125 S. College, Fort Collins (80525). (303) 223-0435. FAX: (303) 223-3857. Licensee: Duchossois Wall Communications Co. of Colorado Inc. Group owner: Duchossois Communications Co. (acq 3-15-91; $525,000; FTR 4-1-91). Format: Country. ■ Gary Buchanan, gen mgr; Randy Robbins, opns mgr.

KGRE(AM)—Aug 24, 1948: 1450 khz; 1 kw-U. TL: N40 26 15 W104 43 25. Box 1199 (80632). (303) 356-1450. Licensee: Keith M. Ashton Sr. (acq 2-21-91; $275,000; FTR 3-11-91). Format: Country. Target aud: Farmers & ranchers. ■ Keith Ashton Sr., gen mgr; Joanne Salser, gen sls mgr.

***KUNC-FM**—Jan 1, 1967: 91.5 mhz; 100 kw. Ant 570 ft. TL: N40 38 34 W104 49 08. Stereo. Univ. of Northern CO (80639). (303) 351-2915. FAX: (303) 351-1780. Licensee: Univ. of Northern CO. Net: NPR, APR. Format: Div, news. News staff one; news progmg 50 hrs wkly. Target aud: General. ■ Neil Best, stn mgr & progmg dir; Bruce Clement, dev dir; Julie Amacher, mus dir; Jim Beers, news dir; Ron Bailer, chief engr.

KZDG(FM)—June 1967: 92.5 mhz; 57 kw. Ant 1,237 ft. TL: N40 05 47 W104 54 04. Stereo. Suite 600, 9351 Grant St., Thornton (80229). (303) 451-6700; (303) 451-6100. FAX: (303) 451-1773. Licensee: Premiere Radio Networks Inc. (acq 1-21-93; $3.55 million; FTR 2-8-93). Rep: Katz & Powell. Wash atty: Brown, Finn & Nietert. Format: Country. News staff one. Target aud: 25-54. ■ Lee Jamison, gen mgr; Greg Hoffman, gen sls mgr; John Holiday, progmg dir & mus dir; Paul Montoya, chief engr. ■ Rates: $75; 75; 75; 75.

Gunnison

KKYY(FM)—Listing follows KPKE(AM).

KPKE(AM)—Aug 23, 1960: 1490 khz; 1 kw-U. TL: N38 33 57 W106 55 32. 113 E. Georgia (81230). (303) 641-5000. FAX: (303) 641-3846. Licensee: Gardiner Broadcast Partners Ltd. (group owner; acq 3-31-92; $105,000 with co-located FM; FTR 4-27-92). Net: UPI. Format: AOR. News staff one; news progmg 3 hrs wkly. Target aud: 18-49. Spec prog: Sports 10 hrs wkly. ■ Clifton H. Gardiner, CEO; Kim Jones, vp sls; Shiela Thackaberry, gen sls mgr; Marty Hijmans, chief engr. ■ Rates: $8; 8; 8; 5.

KKYY(FM)—Co-owned with KPKE(AM). 1980: 98.3 mhz; 3 kw. Ant 304 ft. TL: N38 31 22 W106 54 28. Prog dups AM 100%. ■ Rates: Same as AM.

KVLE(FM)—Apr 18, 1980: 102.3 mhz; 3 kw. Ant 200 ft. TL: N38 33 53 W106 55 38. Stereo. Box 805, 1445 N. Hwy 135 (81230). (303) 641-3225. Licensee: High Country Communications Inc. (acq 8-6-84; FTR 8-13-84). Net: CBS. Rep: Art Moore. Format: Contemp country. ■ Marty Weyl, gen mgr; Dale Dixon, progmg dir. ■ Rates: $12; 10; 12; 8.

***KWSB-FM**—Jan 26, 1968: 91.1 mhz; 135 w. Ant 304 ft. TL: N38 31 22 W106 54 28. Stereo. Hrs opn: 18. Taylor Hall, Western State College (81231). (303) 943-3033; (303) 943-7048. FAX: (303) 943-7069. Licensee: Western State College of Colorado. Net: AP. Format: AOR. News progmg 2 hrs wkly. Target aud: College students & under 25. Spec prog: Class 3 hrs, jazz 3 hrs, reggae one hr, blues one hr, sixties one hr wkly. ■ Jim Gelwicks, gen mgr; John Talbert, stn mgr; Scott Mathews, opns dir; Todd Peede, dev dir; Torrie Hansen, prom dir; Kip Hall, progmg dir; Craig Parker, mus dir; Brett Reinherdt, Steve Inke, news dirs.

Hayden

KIDN-FM—Feb 15, 1985: 95.9 mhz; 1.8 kw. Ant 1181 ft. TL: N40 25 46 W107 05 34. Stereo. Suite One, 29587 W. Hwy. 40, Steamboat Springs (80487). (303) 870-0900. FAX: (303) 870-0300. Licensee: Gardiner Broadcast Partners Ltd. (group owner; acq 12-23-91; $275,000; with co-located FM; FTR 2-3-92). Net: UPI. Format: Rock. News staff one. Target aud: 21-54. Spec prog: Farm one hr, oldies 8 hrs wkly. ■ Clifton Gardiner, CEO & pres; Greg Magness, stn mgr; Kim Jones, vp sls; Dwight H. Gayer, prom mgr. ■ Rates: $12; 12; 12; 8.

Ignacio

***KSUT(FM)**—June 9, 1976: 91.3 mhz; 425 w. Ant 18 ft. TL: N37 05 51 W107 37 32. Stereo. Hrs opn: 20. Rebroadcasts KGLP(FM) Gallup, N.M. 90%. Box 737 (81137). (303) 563-0255. Licensee: Kute Inc. Net: NPR, APR. Format: News/info, music blend. News progmg 30 hrs wkly. Target aud: 24 plus; public radio audience. Spec prog: American Indian, classical 10 hrs, folk 7 hrs, jazz 5 hrs wkly. ■ Eddie Box Jr., pres; Carlos Sena, gen mgr; Scott Henning, chief opns; Beth Warren, dev mgr; Steve Rauworth, progmg mgr; Stasia Lanier, mus dir.

Johnstown

KHNC(AM)—January 1993: 1360 khz; 500 w-D, 450 w-N, DA-2. TL: N40 23 11 W104 54 19. Stereo. Box 430, 39 S. Parish (80534). (303) 587-5175. Licensee: Donald A. and Sharon A. Wiedeman. Format: Conservative news/talk. ■ Alan Wayne, progmg mgr.

Kremmling

KRKM(FM)—Nov 1, 1987: 106.3 mhz; 300 w. Ant 1,096 ft. TL: N40 00 18 W106 26 57. Stereo. Box 1030, Granby (80446). (316) 669-8193. Licensee: Granby Broadcasting Systems Inc. Group owner: American Broadcasting Systems (acq 9-3-93; $250,000 with KRKY[AM] Granby; FTR 9-27-93). Net: SMN. Format: Adult contemp. ■ Tom Palmer, gen mgr & gen sls mgr. ■ Rates: $15; 15; 15; na.

La Junta

KBZZ(AM)—July 23, 1937: 1400 khz; 1 kw-U. TL: N37 59 14 W103 34 01. Box 485 (81050). (719) 384-5456. Licensee: Broadcast Management Services Inc. (acq 5-27-92; $550,000 with co-located FM; FTR 6-15-92). Net: SMN. Format: Adult contemp. ■ Paul Coates, pres, vp, stn mgr & mus dir; Joe Konicek, chief engr.

KBLJ(FM)—Co-owned with KBZZ(AM). Aug 28, 1974: 92.1 mhz; 3 kw. Ant 300 ft. TL: N37 59 15 W103 34 02. Stereo. Prog sep from AM. Format: C&W.

Lakewood

KWMX(AM)—Jan 8, 1955: 1600 khz; 5 kw-U, DA-N. TL: N39 39 20 W105 04 28. 1095 S. Monaco Pkwy. Denver (80224). (303) 321-0950. FAX: (303) 333-2987. Licensee: Jefferson-Pilot Communications Co. (group owner; acq 11-24-92; $6.1 million with co-located FM; FTR 12-14-92). Net: ABC/R. Rep: Katz. Format: CHR. ■ Bob Call, pres & gen mgr; Steven Price, gen sls mgr; John Peake, progmg dir; Robbyn Hart, news dir; Brad Hart, chief engr.

KWMX-FM—July 9, 1966: 107.5 mhz; 100 kw. Ant 670 ft. TL: N39 41 45 W105 09 54. Stereo. Dups AM 100%.

Lamar

KLMR(AM)—December 1948: 920 khz; 5 kw-D, 500 w-N, DA-N. TL: N38 06 53 W102 37 16. Box 890 (81052). (719) 336-2206. FAX: (719) 336-7973. Licensee: A & B Broadcasting Inc. (acq 4-1-86). Net: ABC/I, MBS. Rep: Katz. Format: Traditional country. News staff one; news progmg 14 hrs wkly. Target aud: General. Spec prog: Farm 19 hrs, Sp 3 hrs wkly. ■ F.B. Becquet, pres; Bill Arnold, vp, gen mgr & gen sls mgr; Bill Flesher, opns mgr & progmg dir; Randy Troyer, news dir; Chuck Springer, chief engr.

KSEC(FM)—Co-owned with KLMR(AM). November 1978: 93.3 mhz; 100 kw. Ant 498 ft. TL: N38 02 10 W102 35 58. Stereo. Dups AM 10%. Net: CBS. Format: Contemp country. Target aud: 25-49.

KVAY(FM)—Aug 5, 1991. 105.7 mhz; 100 kw. Ant 545 ft. TL: N38 06 44 W102 57 37 (CP: Ant 479 ft.). Stereo. Box 1176, Suite 203, 224 S. Main (81052). (719) 336-8734. FAX: (719) 336-5977. Licensee: Bauer Properties. Net: AP. Wash atty: Leventhal, Senter & Lerman. Format: Country. News staff one. Target aud: 25-55. Spec prog: Sp 6 hrs wkly. ■ Larry E. Bauer, gen mgr, stn mgr & gen sls mgr; Chris Bauer, opns mgr, progmg mgr & mus dir; Wayne Cook, news dir; Steve Watson, chief engr. ■ Rates: $16; 16; 16; 16.

Leadville

KRMH(AM)—Nov 4, 1960: 1230 khz; 1 kw-U. TL: N39 14 51 W106 17 57. 121 Alsace Way, Colorado Springs (30906). Licensee: Phoenix Broadcasting (acq 10-85; $130,000; FTR 10-21-85). Net: Unistar. Format: Country. ■ Mike Lowery, pres & gen mgr.

KRMH-FM—Nov 29, 1985: 93.5 mhz; 3 kw. Ant 300 ft. TL: N39 14 51 W106 17 57. Stereo. Format: Adult contemp.

Littleton

KDKO(AM)—Aug 22, 1957: 1510 khz; 10 kw-D, 1.3 kw-N, DA-2. TL: N39 33 08 W105 02 00. 2559 Welton St., Denver (80205). (303) 295-1225. FAX: (303) 295-1521. Licensee: Peoples Wireless Inc. (acq 1-89; $900,000; FTR 1-23-89). Format: Urban contemp, Black. ■ Jim Walker, gen mgr & progmg dir; George Martinez, mus dir; Jim Walker, Jon Bowman, news dirs; Paul Montoya, chief engr.

Longmont

***KCDC(FM)**—September 1975: 90.7 mhz; 100 w. Ant 270 ft. TL: N40 14 24 W105 03 19. Stereo. 1200-A S. Sunset St. (80501-6595). (303) 776-4696; (303) 772-3333. Licensee: St. Vrain Valley School District. Format: Adult contemp. ■ George N. Baskos, gen mgr; James R. Boynton Sr., stn mgr.

KLMO(AM)—December 1949: 1060 khz; 10 kw-D, 100 w-N (500 w-CH). TL: N40 11 28 W105 07 35. Hrs opn: 15. Box 799, 614 Kimbark St. (80501). (303) 776-2323; (303) 449-3224. Licensee: W.G. & L.J Stewart, Partnership (acq 11-86). Net: ABC/D. Rep: Hugh Wallace. Format: Country. News staff one; news progmg 20 hrs wkly. Target aud: 30-60; news & sports listeners. Spec prog: Sp one hr, farm one hr wkly. ■ William G. Stewart, pres & gen mgr; Jim McDonald, opns mgr & chief engr; L.J. Stewart, sls dir & prom mgr; G. Stewart, gen sls mgr; Bob Shriver, rgnl sls mgr & adv dir; Mike Gillespie, progmg dir; Becky Palsmior, mus dir; W. Stewart, news dir. ■ Rates: $25; 16; 25; 16.

KQKS(FM)—September 1964: 104.3 mhz; 5.4 kw. Ant 1,433 ft. TL: N39 54 48 W105 17 32 (CP: 58.3 kw, ant 1,214 ft.). Stereo. Suite 550, 9351 Grant St., Thornton (80229). (303) 427-7700. Licensee: Western Cities Broadcasting Inc. (acq 12-86). Format: CHR. ■ Ron Jamieson, gen mgr; Bert Guillion, gen sls mgr; Chris Davis, progmg dir; Stephanie Stevens, news dir; Jeff Pinkerton, chief engr.

Loveland

KLOV(AM)—Jan 21, 1955: 1570 khz; 1 kw-D. TL: N40 23 31 W105 05 51. Box 8509, 1576 W. First St. (80537). (303) 667-1570. Licensee: RGW Communications Inc. (acq 12-14-90; $78,000; FTR 1-7-91). Net: MBS. Rep: Katz & Powell. Wash atty: John Bankson. Format: Oldies, adult contemp. News staff one; news progmg 15 hrs wkly. Target aud: 35 plus. Spec prog: Polka 3 hrs, big band 3 hrs, relg 6 hrs, Larry King 18 hrs wkly. ■ William Green, pres; Sara Weir, gen mgr & mktg dir; Bill Smith, prom mgr, progmg dir & mus dir; Michael Rayl, news dir; Ron Hink, chief engr.

KTRR(FM)—Feb 5, 1966: 102.5 mhz; 50 kw. Ant 410 ft. TL: N40 27 19 W104 55 25. Stereo. 5125 S. College, Fort Collins (80525). (303) 223-0435. FAX: (303) 223-3857. Licensee: ONYX Broadcasting Inc. Group owner: Crown Broadcasting Inc. (acq 4-1-88). Rep: Katz & Powell. Format: Adult contemp. Target aud: 25-54. ■ Gary Buchanan, gen mgr; Ron Barnhardt, gen sls mgr; Randy Robbins, mus dir; Quinn Morrison, chief engr.

Manitou Springs

***KCME(FM)**—Sept 1, 1979: 88.7 mhz; 16 kw. Ant 2,070 ft. TL: N38 44 42 W104 51 39. Stereo. Stn currently dark. 68 Minnehaha Ave. (80829). Licensee: Cheyenne Mt. Public Broadcast House Inc. ■ John Stevens, gen mgr & stn mgr.

KIKX-FM—May 1952: 102.7 mhz; 100 kw. Ant 2,000 ft. TL: N38 44 47 W104 51 37. Stereo. Hrs opn: 24. Box 39102 (80949); Suite 1027, 5145 Centennial Blvd., Colorado Springs (80919). (719) 599-5800. FAX: (719) 594-9006. Licensee: Wiskes-Abaris Communications KIIQ (acq 8-90; $4.73 million; FTR 8-6-90). Rep: Torbet. Format: Country. News progmg one hr wkly. Target aud: 18-54. ■ Bob Gourley, gen mgr; Jerry Grant, vp sls & vp adv; Chrissy Adsit, vp mktg & vp prom; Tom Fricke, vp progmg; Melvin Rauh, vp engrg.

KXRE(AM)—November 1956: 1490 khz; 500 kw-U. TL: N38 51 43 W104 55 32. Box 255, Evergreen (80439). Licensee: Quetzal Communications Corp. (acq 7-6-93; FTR 8-2-93). ■ Jack Higgins, pres.

Monte Vista

KSLV(AM)—February 1954: 1240 khz; 1 kw-U. TL: N37 36 10 W106 08 58. Hrs opn: 5 AM-midnight. Box 631, 109 Adams St. (81144). (719) 852-3581. FAX: (719) 852-3583. Licensee: San Luis Valley Broadcasting Inc. (acq 4-1-79). Net: ABC/D. Wash atty: Cohn & Marks. Format: Country. News staff one; news progmg 6 hrs wkly. Target aud: 25-54. Spec prog: Sp 10 hrs, farm 2 hrs, gospel 6 hrs wkly. ■ Robert Gourley, pres; Gerald Vigil, gen mgr; Karl Keller, gen sls mgr; Damian Arellano, mus dir; Linda Pacheco, news dir; Mel Raugh, chief engr.

KSLV-FM—1986: 95.3 mhz; 3 kw. Ant 89 ft. TL: N37 36 10 W106 08 58. Stereo. Hrs opn: 5 AM-midnight. Prog sep from AM. Format: Adult contemp. News progmg 2 hrs wkly. Target aud: 25-55.

Montrose

KKXK(FM)—Listing follows KUBC(AM).

KSTR-FM—Apr 10, 1980: 96.1 mhz; 100 kw. Ant 1,099 ft. TL: N38 52 40 W108 13 33. Stereo. 660 Rood Ave., Grand Junction (81501). (303) 242-5787. Licensee: First Star Corp. Group owner: Warner Stns. (acq 5-1-85). Net: Unistar, Westwood One. Rep: McGavren Guild. Format: Classic rock. News staff 2; news progmg 15 hrs wkly. Target aud: 25-54; adults seeking oldies music presentation. ■ Norton E. Warner, pres; Brad Legette, gen mgr; Ken Pillind, opns mgr & mus dir; Ken Bench, news dir; Ken Pellin, chief engr.

KUBC(AM)—Sept 25, 1947: 580 khz; 5 kw-D, 1 kw-N, DA-N. TL: N38 25 32 W107 52 57. Hrs opn: 24. Box 970 (81402); 2018 S. Townsend Ave. (81401). (303) 249-4546. FAX: (303) 249-2229. Licensee: Woodland Communications Corp. (acq 4-1-88). Net: CNN. Rep: Art Moore, Intermountain Net, Eastman. Wash atty: Haley, Bader & Potts. Format: Oldies, Interstate Radio network. News staff one; news progmg 4 hrs wkly. Target aud: 18-54. Spec prog: Gospel 2 hrs, relg 2 hrs wkly. ■ J. Stephen Glasmann, pres & gen mgr; Lee Preston, opns mgr, prom mgr, progmg dir & mus dir; Jim Chaplin, gen sls mgr; Dave Segal, news dir; Derek Sever, pub affrs dir; Norm Price, chief engr. ■ Rates: $14; 12; 14; 10.

KKXK(FM)—Co-owned with KUBC(AM). December 1976: 94.1 mhz; 31.5 kw. Ant 1,748 ft. TL: N38 20 16 W107 38 23. Stereo. Hrs opn: 5:30 AM-1 AM. Prog sep from AM. Net: SMN. Format: C&W. Spec prog: Farm 2 hrs wkly. ■ Wes Smith, opns mgr & progmg mgr. ■ Rates: $20; 16; 18; 12.

Monument

KCBR(AM)—July 20, 1986: 1040 khz; 4.6 kw-D. TL: N39 04 27 W104 52 05 (CP: 1.9 kw-D, TL: N38 49 08 W104 46 32). Stereo. Hrs opn: Sunrise-sunset. Box 1385, Suite 208, 5050 Edison Ave. (80915). (719) 570-1530. Licensee: Chip Lusko & Kent Bagdasar Partners (acq 6-14-91; $3,000; FTR 7-1-91). Net: BRN. Format: All news, business news. Target aud: 25-54; 70% male, upper-middle income or higher. ■ Kent Bagdasar, gen mgr; Tron Simpson, opns mgr, prom mgr & vp progmg; Mark Skalberg, gen sls mgr.

Morrison

***KWBI(FM)**—Mar 27, 1971: 91.1 mhz; 100 kw. Ant 1,184 ft. TL: N39 36 00 W105 12 35. Stereo. Hrs opn: 24. 16075 W. Belleview Ave. (80465). (303) 697-5924. FAX: (303) 697-5944. Licensee: Colorado Christian University. Net: UPI, AP. Format: Relg. News staff one; news progmg 3 hrs wkly. Target aud: 30-55. ■ Dr. Ronald Schmidt, pres; Roy Hanschke, stn mgr; Mike Brinks, opns dir; Shelly Frohs, prom dir; Al Hodges, progmg dir; Clint Holden, mus dir; Dick Schroeder, news dir; Al Stewart, chief engr.

Oak Creek

KFMU-FM—Sept 22, 1975: 104.1 mhz; 1.4 kw. Ant 1,073 ft. TL: N40 14 10 W106 52 30. Stereo. Hrs opn: 24. Box 772850, 2955 Village, Steamboat Springs (80477). (303) 879-5368; (800) 748-1844, (CO only). FAX: (303) 879-5843. Licensee: KFMU Limited Partnership (acq 6-23-82; $729,000; FTR 7-12-82). Net: NBC the Source. Rep: McGavren Guild. Wash atty: William Freedman. Format: Progsv, adult contemp. News staff 2; news progmg 10 hrs wkly. Target aud: 21-54. Spec prog: Jazz 2 hrs wkly. ■ Ronald E. Tarrson, CEO; Ward S. Holmes, gen mgr; Mike Huston, rgnl sls mgr; Brian Harvey, prom dir & asst mus dir; Glenn Roberts, progmg dir; John Hewitt, news dir; Linda Timberg, pub affrs dir; Jon Renaud, chief engr. ■ Rates: $16; 16; 16; 12.

Ouray

KURA(FM)—June 16, 1986: 105.7 mhz; 3.1 kw. Ant -20 ft. TL: N38 01 22 W107 40 12 (CP: 7 kw, ant -23 ft.). Stereo. Hrs opn: 6 AM-midnight. Box 560, Ridgway (81432). (303) 626-5234. FAX: (303) 626-5800. Licensee: San Juan Broadcasting Inc. (acq 1-28-93; FTR 2-22-93). Net: Moody, USA, Sun. Format: Country crossover/ adult contemp. Target aud: General. Spec prog: Sp one hr wkly. ■ Rob Hunter, pres; Steve LaMontia, John O'Haganward, gen mgrs; Russ Austin, progmg dir; Tim Cutforth, chief engr.

Pagosa Springs

KRQS(FM)—May 1, 1986: 106.3 mhz; 160 w. Ant 1,280 ft. TL: N37 11 32 W107 05 55 (CP: 255 w). Stereo. Box 840 (81147). (303) 264-2121. FAX: (303) 264-5739. Licensee: Pagosa Communications Inc. (acq 5-89). Net: NBC, ABC/E, ABC TalkRadio. Rep: Art Moore. Format: Country. News progmg 10 hrs wkly. Target aud: Adults. Spec prog: Gospel 3 hrs, country nostalgia 3 hrs wkly. ■ Harvey L. Twite, gen mgr, prom mgr & news dir; Jefferson Cox, gen sls mgr; Debbie Steele, mus dir; John Morton, chief engr. ■ Rates: $12; 8; 6; na.

KPAG(AM)—Co-owned with KRQS(FM). Aug 27, 1975: 1400 khz; 1 kw-U. TL: N37 15 24 W107 01 06. Dups FM 85%. Net: NBC, ABC/E.

Paonia

***KVNF(FM)**—Oct 5, 1979: 90.9 mhz; 3 kw. Ant -171 ft. TL: N38 52 20 W107 39 45. Stereo. Hrs opn: 18. Box 538, 213 Grand Ave. (81428). (303) 527-4866. Licensee: North Fork Valley Public Radio Inc. (acq 1-27-78). Net: NPR. Format: Div. Spec prog: Class 15 hrs, jazz 17 hrs, blues 3 hrs, C&W 5 hrs, new age 6 hrs, Sp 2 hrs, folk 6 hrs, gospel 3 hrs wkly. ■ Phil Egidi, chmn; Dottie Talmage, gen mgr; Rita Clagett, mktg dir; Jeff Reynolds, progmg dir; Candy Pennetta, mus dir; Felix Belmont, pub affrs dir; Alan Greagor, chief engr.

Pueblo

KCCY(FM)—Aug 23, 1975: 96.9 mhz; 100 kw. Ant 320 ft. TL: N38 21 32 W104 58 13. 106 W. 24th St. (81003). (719) 545-2080. FAX: (719) 543-9898. Licensee: McCoy Broadcasting Co. (acq 10-31-86; $1.82 million; FTR 8-5-85). Rep: McGavren Guild. Format: C&W. ■ Craig McCoy, pres; Olene Greenwood, vp, gen mgr, natl sls mgr & rgnl sls mgr; Gary Dall, gen sls mgr; Margaret Thornberg, prom mgr; Dave Moore, progmg dir; Kevin Hayes, mus dir; Dan Thomas, news dir & chief engr; Billy Kidd, pub affrs dir.

KCSJ(AM)—1947: 590 khz; 1 kw-U, DA-N. TL: N38 21 30 W104 38 13. Hrs opn: 24. Box 236, First and Main St. (81003). (719) 543-5900. FAX: (719) 543-7609. Licensee: Max Hand, Martin Hart, et al. (acq 8-26-93; $26,625; grpsl; FTR 11-22-93). Net: CBS, NBC Talknet, MBS. Rep: Eastman, Target. Wash atty: Cliff Harrington. Format: News/talk, sports. News staff 6; news progmg 41 hrs wkly. Target aud: 35-64; upscale. ■ Mark O. Hand, pres; Ken Salazar, vp; Lorri Froehlich, stn mgr & gen sls mgr; Robert Moore, opns mgr & progmg dir; Norm Smith, chief engr.

KNKN(FM)—Co-owned with KCSJ(AM). November 1979: 107.1 mhz; 50 kw. Ant 338 ft. TL: N38 17 48 W104 38 47. Stereo. Box 236 (81002). (719) 543-5900. FAX: (719) 543-7609. Licensee: Pueblo Broadcasters (acq 12-9-92; $174,000; FTR 1-4-93). Format: Country. News staff 6; news progmg 7 hrs wkly. Target aud: 35-64; upscale. ■ Lorri Froehlich, gen mgr; Jay Diamond, opns mgr.

KDZA-FM—March 3, 1987: 107.9 mhz; 100 kw. Ant 239 ft. TL: N37 56 40 W104 59 56. Stereo. 106 W. 24th (81003). (719) 545-2080. Licensee: McCoy Broadcasting Co. (group owner; acq 5-26-93; $500,000; FTR 6-21-93). Format: Oldies. ■ Craig McCoy, pres; Olene Greenwood, gen mgr; Gary Dall, gen sls mgr; Dan Thomas, news dir & chief engr.

***KERP(FM)**—June 1986: 91.9 mhz; 600 w. Ant 472 ft. TL: N38 22 23 W104 33 42. Stereo. Hrs opn: 24. Box 2460 (81004); 2102 S. Prarie (81004). (719) 561-8784. Licensee: Colorado Broadcasting Foundation Inc. Net: Moody. Format: Christian, educ. Target aud: General. ■ Ralph Arnold, pres; Merle Arnold, vp, stn mgr & progmg dir; Harv Smith, chief engr.

KFEL(AM)—August 1956: 970 khz; 3.2 kw-D, 184 w-N. TL: N38 15 57 W104 40 44. Hrs opn: 6 AM-9 PM. 4411 Goodnight Ave. (81005). (719) 561-4884. Licensee: Guardian Communications Inc. (group owner; acq 5-90; grpsl; FTR 5-21-90). Net: USA, Moody. Format: Christian radio, adult contemp. Target aud: 25 plus. Spec prog: Country gospel 4 hrs wkly. ■ Mark McNeil, pres; Iva Rafferty, gen mgr; Mike Lee, opns mgr & mus dir; Norm Smith, chief engr.

KGFT(FM)—Mar 31, 1988: 100.7 mhz; 13.5 kw. Ant 2,086 ft. TL: N38 44 42 W104 51 39 (CP: 72.4 kw, ant 2,217 ft., TL: N38 44 44 W104 51 39). Stereo. Suite 340, 6760 Corporate Dr., Colorado Springs (80919). (719) 531-5438. FAX: (719) 531-5588. Licensee: Falcon Media Inc. (group owner; acq 7-30-92; $950,000; FTR 8-17-92). Net: AP. Format: Contemp Christian. News staff one; news progmg 4 hrs wkly. Target aud: 18-34; males. ■ Ed Atsinger, pres; Dick Bruso, gen mgr & progmg dir; Larry Myers, gen sls mgr; Jennifer Bell, mus dir; Art Pemberton, chief engr.

KGHF(AM)—February 1928: 1350 khz; 5 kw-D, 1 kw-N, DA-N TL: N38 18 29 W104 38 24. Stereo. Box 293 (81002). (719) 542-5570. FAX: (719) 542-0429. Licensee: Martec Broadcasting Corp. Net: NBC. Rep: Torbet, Art Moore. Format: Oldies. ■ Paul T. Jones, pres; Ace Balch, chief engr.

KILO(FM)—See Colorado Springs.

KKMG(FM)—Jan 1, 1967: 98.9 mhz; 100 kw. Ant 1,715 ft. TL: N38 44 32 W104 51 41 (CP: 56 kw, ant 2,299 ft.). Stereo. Hrs opn: 24. Suite 2, 411 Lakewood Cir., Colorado Springs (80910). (719) 596-5536. Licensee: Whale Communications Inc. (acq 6-83; $650,000; FTR 5-9-83). Rep: Torbet. Wash atty: Cohn & Marks. Format: CHR, urban contemp, Black. ■ Mikeal Dixon, chmn; Gary Goodell, pres; Joel Belik, gen mgr & chief engr; Diana Barnes, prom mgr; Carolyn Barnes, adv dir; Scooter B. Stevens, progmg dir; Pete May, mus dir; Robin Lynne, news dir.

KKPC(AM)—Dec 29, 1947: 1230 khz; 1 kw-U. TL: N38 16 38 W104 39 13. 3426 N. Elizabeth (81008). (719) 549-3200. Licensee: Pueblo Community College (acq 12-29-92; $120,000; FTR 1-25-93). Format: Contemp hit. News staff 2. Target aud: 18-34. ■ Lee Douglas, stn mgr; Norman Smith, chief engr.

KNKN(FM)—Listing follows KCSJ(AM).

KRMX(AM)—1958: 690 khz; 250 w-D, 24 w-N. TL: N38 17 48 W104 38 47. Stereo. Hrs opn: 16. 2829 Lowell Ave. (81003). (719) 545-2883; (719) 545-1364. Licensee: Ventana Enterprises Inc. (acq 9-20-91). Format: Sp/bilingual. Target aud: General; Hispanic, families, working class. ■ Jerry De La Cruz, gen mgr, mktg dir & pub affrs dir; Diane Young, gen sls mgr & mus dir; Jair Isaza, asst mus dir; Al Magril, news dir; Harvey Smith, chief engr.

KRRU(AM)—June 1963: 1480 khz; 1 kw-D, DA. TL: N38 18 56 W104 37 03. 4211 N. Elizabeth St. (81008). (719) 542-4277. FAX: (719) 542-4278. Licensee: Quetzel Communications Corp. (acq 11-4-92; $140,000; FTR 11-23-92). Format: Sp. ■ Gail Wallace pres; David Wallace, pres; Oscar Evarra, gen mgr.

***KTSC-FM**—October 1970: 89.5 mhz; 9.8 kw. Ant 165 ft. TL: N38 18 38 W104 34 40. Stereo. Univ. of Southern Colorado, 2200 Bonforte Blvd. (81001). (719) 549-2822. FAX: (719) 549-2120. Licensee: Univ. of Southern Colorado. Format: Jazz, AOR. ■ Sam Lovato, stn mgr.

KVUU(FM)—1976: 99.9 mhz; 87.4 kw. Ant 2,200 ft. TL: N33 44 47 W104 51 37. Stereo. Suite 150, 2864 S. Circle Dr., Colorado Springs (80906). (719) 542-5888. Licensee: KVUU-KSSS Inc. (acq 1-13-93; with KSSS(AM) Colorado Springs; FTR 2-8-93). Rep: McGavren Guild. Wash atty: Kaye, Scholer, Fierman, Hays & Handler. Format: Adult contemp. News staff 2. Target aud: 25-54; upscale adults. ■ Terry Robinson, CEO & gen mgr; Greg Sher, gen sls mgr; Dan Jackson, prom mgr; Rick Morgan, progmg mgr & mus dir; John Anderson, news dir; Fred Periquet, chief engr.

KYZX(FM)—1993: 104.5 mhz; 50 kw. Ant 344 ft. TL: N38 21 28 W104 38 17. Box 236 (81002). (719) 543-5900. FAX: (719) 543-7609. Licensee: Max Hand, Martin Hart, et al. (acq 8-26-93; $26,625; grpsl; FTR 11-22-93). Format: Adult contemp. ■ Marc Hand, gen mgr; Lorri Froehlich, stn mgr.

Stations in the U.S.

Rifle

KKGD(AM)—June 9, 1967: 810 khz; 1 kw-D. TL: N39 32 55 W107 46 10. Stn currently dark. Box 1210, 400 Seventh St. S., #2000 (81650). Licensee: Canterbury Broadcasting Co. (acq 7-20-93; FTR 8-23-93). Net: ABC/I. ■ Lee Ann Canterbury, gen mgr.

KZKS(FM)—Not on air, target date unknown: 105.3 mhz; 1.8 kw. Ant 1,275 ft. TL: N39 43 10 W107 54 56. Stereo. Licensee: Western Media Inc. (acq 1-18-91; $36,380 with co-located AM; FTR 2-4-91).

Rocky Ford

KHUG(FM)—May 1966: 95.9 mhz; 2.6 kw. Ant 85 ft. TL: N38 02 05 W103 43 13. Stereo. Stn currently dark. Box 632 (81067). Licensee: Lovcom Inc. (acq 12-1-91). ■ Kim Love, pres.

Salida

KVRH(AM)—Dec 10, 1948: 1340 khz; 1 kw-U. TL: N38 31 55 W106 00 54. Hrs opn: 6 AM-10 PM. 7600 County Rd. 120 (81201). (719) 539-2575. FAX: (719) 539-4851. Licensee: All Heart Radio Inc. (acq 9-23-59). Net: AP. Rep: Katz & Powell. Format: Light adult contemp & country. News staff one; news progmg 7 hrs wkly. Target aud: General; 25-54. Spec prog: Class 3 hrs, relg 4 hrs wkly. ■ William J. Murphy, pres, gen mgr & gen sls mgr; Michael Kerrigan, progmg dir & mus dir; Patrick Lee, news dir; Bill Freeman, chief engr. ■ Rates: $10; 10; 10; 9.50.

KVRH-FM—1971: 92.1 mhz; 5.8 kw. Ant -655 ft. TL: N38 30 26 W106 01 22. Stereo. Hrs opn: 6 AM-10 PM. Dups AM 100%.

Security

KHII(FM)—Apr 8, 1973: 105.5 mhz; 409 w. Ant 2,230 ft. TL: N38 44 40 W104 51 41. Stereo. Hrs opn: 24. Box 1055, Colorado Springs (80901). (719) 578-1055. FAX: (719) 578-1092; (719) 520-9374. Licensee: Optima Communications Inc. (acq 1989). Net: Jones Satellite Audio. Wash atty: Mullin, Rhyne, Emmons & Topel. Format: Contemp Country. News progmg 14 hrs wkly. Target aud: 25-54; middle America. ■ J.B. McCoy III, pres; James R. Bond Jr., CFO; Edward L. Klimek, vp; Neal Klockziem, gen mgr; John Savidge, gen sls mgr; Lee Stewart, progmg dir; Bruce Slusher, news dir; Joe Reed, chief engr. ■ Rates: $23; 21; 23; 13.

Silverton

KTRN(FM)—Not on air, target date unknown: 103.7 mhz; 26 kw-H. Ant -582 ft. 1906 Brenwood Dr., Farmington, NM (87401). Licensee: Kenneth B. Kendrick.

Snowmass Village

KSNO-FM—April 1985: 103.9 mhz; 3 kw. Ant 328 ft. TL: N39 14 51 W106 55 13. Stereo. Hrs opn: 12. 421 AABC No. 8, Aspen (81611-3551). (303) 925-7383. FAX: (303) 920-4668. Licensee: Gardiner Broadcast Partners Ltd. (group owner; acq 4-1-91; FTR 4-15-91). Net: SMN. Rep: Katz & Powell. Wash atty: Haley, Bader & Potts. Format: AOR. News staff one; news progmg 16 hrs wkly. Target aud: 25-54. ■ Clifton Gardiner, pres; David Laughren, gen mgr; Tony Mauro, news dir; Marty Hijsmans, chief engr.

Steamboat Springs

KBCR(AM)—Aug 1, 1976: 1230 khz; 1 kw-U. TL: N40 29 19 W106 50 57. Box 774050 (80477). (303) 879-2270. FAX: (303) 879-1404. Licensee: American Broadcasting Systems (10-87; $900,000 with co-lcoated FM; FTR 10-26-87). Net: ABC/I. Rep: Mountain. Format: Adult contemp. ■ Tom Palmer, gen mgr; Tom Widdon, gen sls mgr; Scott Ramsey, progmg dir & mus dir; John Larson, news dir.

KSBT(FM)—Co-owned with KBCR(AM). July 25, 1974: 96.7 mhz; 870 w. Ant 510 ft. TL: N40 27 43 W106 51 02. Stereo. Dups AM 100%.

KFMU-FM—See Oak Creek.

Sterling

KNNG-FM—Listing follows KSTC(AM).

KPMX(FM)—Aug 19, 1983: 105.5 mhz; 3 kw. Ant 300 ft. TL: N40 37 04 W103 10 40. Stereo. 415 N. 5th St. (80751-3316). (303) 522-4800. FAX: (303) 522-3997. Licensee: BBG Enterprises Inc. (acq 10-29-81). Net: SMN. Rep: Target. Format: Adult contemp. ■ Russel Silvey, pres & chief engr; Darren Kreis, news dir.

KSTC(AM)—Jan 3, 1925: 1230 khz; 1 kw-U. TL: N40 37 04 W103 10 31. Hrs opn: 24. Box 830 (80751). (303) 522-1607. FAX: (303) 522-1322. Licensee: KSTC Inc. (acq 7-1-77). Net: ABC/I. Rep: Intermountain Net, Eastman, Art Moore. Format: C&W. News staff one; news progmg 12 hrs wkly. Target aud: General; country music oriented people of all ages. Spec prog: Farm 10 hrs wkly. ■ Ray Lockhart, pres; Richard Paye, gen mgr; Don Gilbert, progmg dir & mus dir; Dave Allen, news dir; Bob Cook, chief engr.

KNNG-FM—Co-owned with KSTC(AM). Feb 8, 1974: 104.7 mhz; 100 kw. Ant 500 ft. TL: N40 34 57 W103 01 56 (CP: 1.8 kw, ant 424 ft.). Stereo. Hrs opn: 24. Prog sep from AM. (303) 522-1609. Format: Adult contemp. News staff one. Target aud: General; the non-country contemp listener. ■ Rates: $19.80; 19.80; 19.80; 18.

Strasburg

KAGM(FM)—Not on air, target date unknown: 102.3 mhz; 6 kw. Ant 328 ft. TL: N39 36 32 W104 19 27. 2349 Paris St., Aurora (80010). Licensee: Lenora Alexander.

Telluride

***KOTO(FM)**—October 1975: 91.7 mhz; 2.35 kw. Ant -187 ft. TL: N37 55 59 W107 49 59. Stereo. Box 1069, 207 N. Pine St. (81435). (303) 728-4334. Licensee: San Miguel Educational Fund (acq 7-22-86). Net: NPR. Format: Free form. News staff one; news progmg 12 hrs wkly. Target aud: General; community. Spec prog: Class 9 hrs, country 12 hrs, jazz 9 hrs, blues 7 hrs; drama 3 hrs wkly. ■ Barbara Betts, pres; Cindy Obrand, gen mgr; Ben Kerr, progmg dir; Joan May, mus dir; Jon Kovash, news dir.

KRYD(FM)—Not on air, target date Summer 1994: 104.9 mhz; 100 kw. Ant -75 ft. TL: N37 55 59 W107 49 59. Box 2764 (81435). Licensee: Rocky III Investments Inc.

Thornton

KTLK(AM)—May 30, 1987: 760 khz; 5 kw-D, 1 kw-N, DA-2. TL: N39 36 18 W104 50 25. Suite 1300, 1380 Lawrence, Denver (80204). (303) 893-8500. FAX: (303) 595-0850. Licensee: Jaycor Broadcasting of Colorado Inc. Net: AP. Format: Talk. News staff one. ■ Lee Larsen, gen mgr; Dick Carlson, gen sls mgr; Ken Marks, mktg dir; Jerry Bell, progmg dir; Jan Chadwell, chief engr.

Trinidad

KCRT(AM)—May 21, 1946: 1240 khz; 250 w-U. TL: N37 08 45 W104 30 42. Hrs opn: 6 AM-10 PM. 100 Fisher Dr. (81082). (719) 846-3355. FAX: (719) 846-4711. Licensee: Phillips Broadcasting Inc. (acq 3-30-92; $235,000 with co-located FM; FTR 4-20-92). Net: ABC/I, AP. Rep: Art Moore, Eastman. Format: Country. News staff one; news progmg 15 hrs wkly. Target aud: General. Spec prog: Farm one hr, relg 5 hrs wkly. ■ Anita Phillips, pres & vp opns; Lory Phillips, gen mgr & gen sls mgr; Sandra Chavez, stn mgr & chief opns; David Phillips, mktg dir, vp progmg & mus dir; Rob Campbell, (asst) mus dir; Dave Phillips, news dir & pub affrs dir; Robert Herrera, Lory Phillips (asst), chiefs engr. ■ Rates: $6.50; 6; 6; 4.50.

KCRT-FM—August 1981: 92.7 mhz; 3 kw. Ant 150 ft. TL: N37 08 45 W104 30 42 (CP: 92.5 mhz, 15 kw, ant 1,020 ft.). Stereo. Hrs opn: 6 AM-10 PM. Prog sep from AM. Format: Country. Target aud: 25-42. ■ Rates: $12; 10; 10; 8.

Vail

KSKE(AM)—July 25, 1983: 610 khz; 5 kw-D, 217 w-N. TL: N39 34 47 W106 24 54. Hrs opn: 6 AM-6 PM. Box 1610 (81658-1610). (303) 949-7070. FAX: (303) 949-6386. Licensee: American Broadcasting Systems Inc. (group owner; acq 10-8-92; $1.3 million with co-located FM; FTR 11-2-92). Format: Country, hot adult contemp. News staff one. Target aud: 25-49; affluent, well educated people residing in resort areas. ■ Ron Crider, pres; Chris Vail, gen mgr & gen sls mgr; Danny T. Morris, progmg dir; Becky Thoreson, news dir; Tim Long, chief engr. ■ Rates: $3; 3; 3; na.

KSKE-FM—1975: 104.7 mhz; 100 kw. Ant 451 ft. TL: N39 38 08 W106 24 46 (CP: Ant 783 ft.). Stereo. Dups AM 100%.

Walsenburg

KSPK(FM)—March 1985: 102.3 mhz; 17 kw. Ant 377 ft. TL: N37 37 39 W104 49 17. Stereo. Hrs opn: 24. 516 Main (81089). (719) 738-3636. FAX: (719) 738-2010.

Connecticut

Licensee: Mainstreet Broadcasting Co. of Colorado Inc. (acq 9-12-90; $275,000; FTR 10-8-90). Net: SMN, ABC. Format: Local & state sports. News staff one; news progmg 3 hrs wkly. Target aud: 24-59; upwardly mobile, two-income families. ■ Mark Bossert, pres, gen mgr & gen sls mgr; J.J. Valentine, progmg dir; Paul Richards, mus dir; Paul Bossert, chief engr. ■ Rates: $10; 10; 10; 6.

Wellington

KIIX(AM)—Licensed to Wellington. See Fort Collins.

Widefield

KKLI(FM)—Licensed to Widefield. See Colorado Springs.

Windsor

KUAD-FM—May 31, 1975: 99.1 mhz; 100 kw. Ant 657 ft. TL: N40 38 34 W104 49 08. Stereo. 600 Main St. (80550). (303) 493-1170. FAX: (303) 686-7491. Licensee: Northern Colorado Radio Inc. Group owner: Brill Media Company Inc. (acq 11-10-88). Rep: Banner. Wash atty: Dow, Lohnes & Albertson. Format: Country. News staff one; news progmg 3 hrs wkly. Target aud: 25-54; upscale country listeners, 60% women. ■ Alan Brill, pres; Dan Conway, gen mgr & gen sls mgr; Scott James, prom mgr; Brian Gary, progmg dir; Art Opperman, mus dir; Todd Harding, news dir; Ron Bailor, chief engr.

KVVS(AM)—Apr 12, 1969: 1170 khz; 1 kw-D. TL: N40 27 46 W104 54 47. Hrs opn: Sunset-sundown. Box 698 1300 Carousel Dr., #211 (80550). (303) 686-7709; (303) 686-1170. FAX: (303) 686-7700. Licensee: Sanchez Velasco Corp. (acq 3-19-85). Rep: Caballero. Wash atty: Fisher, Wayland, Cooper & Leader. Format: Sp. News progmg 5 hrs wkly. Target aud: 18-54; general. Spec prog: pub affrs. ■ Veronica Sanchez-Velasco, CEO, pres, gen mgr, gen sls mgr & prom mgr; Antonio J. Velasco, vp, progmg dir, mus dir & news dir; Quinn Morrison, chief engr.

Winter Park

KRKM(FM)—See Kremmling.

Wray

KRDZ(AM)—Jan 11, 1978: 1440 khz; 5 kw-D, 200 w-N. TL: N56 04 00 W102 11 25. Hrs opn: 5 AM-10 PM. Box 466, 32992 Highway 34 (80758). (303) 332-4171. Licensee: New Directions Media Inc. (group owner; acq 9-26-87). Net: ABC/D; Brownfield. Format: Farm, adult contemp, C&W. News progmg 10 hrs wkly. Target aud: Farmers & ranchers. Spec prog: Focus on family 3 hrs, relg 4 hrs, Rush Limbaugh 15 hrs wkly. ■ Bob Zellmer, pres, gen mgr & chief engr; Marjorie Zellmer, vp; Robb Zellmer, stn mgr & opns mgr; Bruce Palmrose, news dir.

KATR-FM—Co-owned with KRDZ(AM). Sept 1, 1983: 98.3 mhz; 3 kw. Ant 331 ft. TL: N40 04 56 W102 11 25 (CP: 50 kw, ant 300 ft.). Stereo. 804 S. Ash (80759).

Connecticut

Ansonia

WADS(AM)—May 8, 1956: 690 khz; 1 kw-D, 33 w-N, DA-2. TL: N41 20 48 W73 06 56. Box 110, 361 E. Main St. (06401). (203) 735-4606. FAX: (203) 734-9239. Licensee: Jack Silva and Manuel B. Santos (acq 6-1-89; $550,000; FTR 5-29-89). Net: AP. Format: Adult contemp, Portuguese, Sp. News staff one; news progmg 15 hrs wkly. Target aud: 25 plus. Spec prog: Pol 14 hrs, Irish one hr, travel one hr, top hits 4 hrs wkly. ■ Manuel Santos, pres; Mario Sousa, gen mgr; John DeGennaro, gen sls mgr; Sharon Lydem, prom mgr; Kevin Copeland, progmg dir; Ed Flynn, mus dir; John Cannon, news dir; Terry Smith, chief engr.

Berlin

***WERB(FM)**—Jan 12, 1979: 97.3 mhz; 27.5 w. Ant 95 ft. TL: N41 37 18 W72 45 13. Stereo. Berlin H.S., Media Center, 139 Patterson Way (06037). Licensee: Berlin Board of Education. ■ Gerald Havel, gen mgr.

Bloomfield

WRDM(AM)—February 1964: 1550 khz; 5 kw-D, 2.4 kw-N, DA-2. TL: N41 51 47 W72 44 01. Hrs opn: 6 AM-6 PM. 886 Maple Ave., Hartford (06114). (203) 956-4225. FAX: (203) 956-6834. Licensee: Living Communications of Connecticut (acq 7-2-93; $275,000; FTR 8-2-93). Net:

USA, Moody. Format: Ethnic. News progmg 2 hrs wkly. Target aud: 25-44; married women, college educated, with children. Spec prog: Gospel 2 hrs wkly. ■ Lucio Ruzzier, pres; Gaetano Leone, gen mgr; Walter Martinez, gen sls mgr, adv mgr & progmg dir; William Newton, mktg mgr; Salvatore Minniti, chief engr.

Bridgeport

WCUM(AM)—September 1941: 1450 khz; 1 kw-U. TL: N41 12 40 W73 11 28. 1862 State St. (06605). (203) 335-1450. FAX: (203) 331-9378. Licensee: Radio Cumbre Broadcasting Inc. (acq 4-89; $550,000; FTR 4-24-89). Wash atty: Adam Eisgrau. Format: Sp, news/talk. News staff 2; news progmg 14 hrs wkly. Target aud: General; 25 plus. ■ Pablo De Jesus Colon Hijo, pres & gen mgr; Migdalia Ramos Colon, vp; C. Falcon, gen sls mgr; Jose Angel Colon, progmg dir, mus dir & news dir; Rev. Moises Mercedes, pub affrs dir; Kevin Plumb, chief engr. ■ Rates: $360; 312; 360; 286.

WDJZ(AM)—Apr 30, 1977: 1530 khz; 5 kw-D, DA. TL: N41 10 09 W73 13 14. 513 Boston Ave. (06610). (203) 576-6518; (203) 723-0678. FAX: (203) 723-7813. Licensee: Candido D. Carrelo (acq 4-6-92; $200,000; FTR 4-27-92). Format: Sp & Portuguese. Target aud: 35 plus. ■ Cany Carrelo, gen mgr; Celeste Rodriguez, progmg dir; Thomas G. Osenkowsky, chief engr.

WEZN(FM)—Oct 24, 1960: 99.9 mhz; 27.6 kw. Ant 669 ft. TL: N41 16 46 W73 11 09. Stereo. 10 Middle St. (06604). (203) 366-9321. FAX: (203) 336-9988. Licensee: Katz Broadcasting of Conn. Group owner: NewCity Communications Inc. (acq 4-86; grpsl; FTR 4-28-86). Rep: Katz. Format: Adult contemp. News staff one. Target aud: 25-54. ■ Richard A. Ferguson, pres; James Morley, gen mgr; John Ryan, gen sls mgr; Regina Thompson, prom mgr; Bill White, progmg dir; Bob Michaels, news dir; Dom Bordonaro, chief engr. ■ Rates: $175; 175; 175; 55.

WICC(AM)—1926: 600 khz; 1 kw-D, 500 w-N, DA-2. TL: N41 09 36 W73 09 53. Stereo. Hrs opn: 24. 2 Lafayette Sq. (06604-6000). (203) 366-6000. FAX: (203) 384-0600. Licensee: WICC Associates. Group owner: WIN Communications Inc. (acq 1989; $6.25 million). Net: AP; Rep: Banner. Wash atty: Wiley, Rein & Fielding. Format: Full svc adult contemp, talk. News staff 6; news progmg 25 hrs wkly. Target aud: 25-54. ■ Vince Cremona, vp & gen mgr; Curt Hansen, vp opns, opns mgr, vp progmg & progmg dir; Jeff Ketcham, vp sls & gen sls mgr; Megan O'Connell, prom mgr; Tim Quinn, news dir & pub affrs dir; Ed Butler, chief engr. ■ Rates: $150; 135; 150; 75.

***WPKN(FM)**—Oct 10, 1963: 89.5 mhz; 10 kw. Ant 550 ft. TL: N41 16 43 W73 11 08 (CP: Ant 482 ft.). Stereo. 244 University Ave. (06601). (203) 576-4895. Licensee: WPKN Inc. (acq 4-16-92; $10 and programming/education facilities exchange; FTR 5-11-92). Format: Div. Spec prog: Class 2 hrs, Sp 4 hrs wkly. ■ Harry Minot, gen mgr.

Bristol

WPRX(AM)—October 1948: 1120 khz; 1 kw-D, 500 w-N, DA-N. TL: N41 39 29 W72 56 51. Box 297, 1021 Farmington Ave. (06011-0297). (203) 582-1120. Licensee: Connecticut Communications House II Inc. (acq 8-25-87). Net: MBS, Daynet, BRN; Conn. Net. Format: Talk, local sports. News staff 2. Target aud: 25 plus. Spec prog: Fr 2 hrs, relg 3 hrs, Pol 8 hrs, Sp 6 hrs wkly. ■ Susan P. Huber, exec vp, vp opns & pub affrs dir; Steve Markoski, news dir; Terry Smith, chief engr. ■ Rates: $15; 12; 15; na.

Brookfield

WINE(AM)—May 9, 1966: 940 khz; 1 kw-D, 4 w-N. TL: N41 29 35 W73 25 47. Federal Rd. (06813); Box 95, Danbury (06804). (203) 775-1212. FAX: (203) 775-6452. Licensee: Danbury Broadcasting Inc. (acq 5-12-92; $3.35 million with co-located FM; FTR 6-1-92). Net: ABC/I, CNN. Rep: Eastman. Wash atty: Haley, Bader & Potts. Format: CNN headline news/talk. News staff 3. Target aud: 35-54. ■ Gary Starr, pres; Tom Pronlipi, gen sls mgr; Tim Sheehan, progmg dir; Pat Scully, news dir; Patrick Carlone, chief engr.

WRKI(FM)—Co-owned with WINE(AM). July 14, 1957: 95.1 mhz; 50 kw. Ant 500 ft. TL: N41 29 35 W73 25 47. Stereo. Format: AOR. ■ John F. Fullam, vp & gen mgr; Robert Mordente, gen sls mgr; Ray Graham, progmg dir.

Danbury

WDAQ(FM)—Listing follows WLAD(AM).

***WFAR(FM)**—July 19, 1981: 93.3 mhz; 18 w. Ant 210 ft. TL: N41 23 44 W73 25 24. Stereo. 78 Liberty St. (06810). (203) 748-0001. Licensee: Danbury Community Radio Inc. Format: Educ, Portuguese. News staff 2; news progmg 10 hrs wkly. Spec prog: It one hr, East Indian one hr wkly. ■ David Abrantes, pres & gen mgr; Antonio Botelho, vp; Helena Abrantes, opns mgr.

WINE(AM)—See Brookfield.

WLAD(AM)—October 1947: 800 khz; 1 kw-D, 287 w-N. TL: N41 22 27 W73 26 47. Stereo. Hrs opn: 24. 198 Main St. (06810). (203) 744-4800. Licensee: Berkshire Broadcasting Corp. Net: MBS, BRN. Rep: D & R Radio. Wash atty: Cohn & Marks. Format: Full svc adult contemp. News staff 5. Target aud: General. ■ James B. Lee Jr., pres; Irving J. Goldstein, vp & gen mgr; Wayne Leland, gen sls mgr; Dennis Lamar, news dir; Thomas Osenkowsky, chief engr.

WDAQ(FM)—Co-owned with WLAD(AM). December 1953: 98.3 mhz; 1.3 kw. Ant 460 ft. TL: N41 22 27 W73 26 47. Stereo. Prog sep from AM. Format: Hot adult contemp. Target aud: 25-54. ■ Bill Trotta, progmg dir; Ryan Carrington, mus dir.

WREF(AM)—See Ridgefield.

WRKI(FM)—See Brookfield.

***WXCI(FM)**—Feb 10, 1973: 91.7 mhz; 1.2 kw. Ant 205 ft. TL: N41 23 44 W73 25 24. Stereo. Hrs opn: 6 AM-2 AM. Student Center, 181 White St. (06810). (203) 792-8666; (203) 797-4461. FAX: (203) 744-6826. Licensee: Western Connecticut State Univ. Board of Trustees. Net: AP. Format: New wave. News progmg 3 hrs wkly. Target aud: 14-25. Spec prog: Club music 3 hrs, jazz 3 hrs, reggae 2 hrs, new age 3 hrs, metal 3 hrs wkly. ■ Melissa Wasik, gen mgr; Amy DiCesare, mktg dir; Ron Lewis, prom dir; Ed Biebel, progmg dir; Dave Lieb, mus dir; Al Robinson, news dir; Kevin Haddad, pub affrs dir; Brad Paynter, chief engr.

East Lyme

WXZR(FM)—Not on air, target date unknown: 98.7 mhz. 3.8 kw. Ant 236 ft. 919 Pequot Ave., New London (06320). Licensee: Margaret O. Pescatello.

Enfield

WPKX(FM)—July 1990: 97.9 mhz; 2.22 kw. Ant 528 ft. TL: N42 05 05 W72 42 14. 1655 Main St., Springfield, MA (01103). (413) 732-5353. FAX: (413) 732-7851. Licensee: Multi-Market Radio of Springfield Inc. (acq 4-16-93; grpsl; FTR 5-3-93). Format: Contemp country. ■ Mike Ferrel (owner), CEO.

Fairfield

***WSHU(FM)**—February 1964: 91.1 mhz; 12.5 kw. Ant 595 ft. TL: N41 16 46 W73 11 09. Stereo. 5151 Park Ave. (06432). (203) 371-7989. FAX: (203) 371-7991. Licensee: Sacred Heart University Inc. (acq 1-5-90). Net: NPR, APR, Beethoven. Format: Class. Spec prog: Folk, western swing 2 hrs wkly. ■ George Lombardi, gen mgr & chief engr; Suzanne Bona, progmg dir; Tom Kuser, news dir.

***WVOF(FM)**—Sept 1, 1970: 88.5 mhz; 100 w. Ant 35 ft. TL: N41 09 32 W73 15 35. Stereo. Box R, Campus Ctr., Fairfield Univ., N. Benson Rd. (06430). (203) 254-4111. FAX: (203) 254-1253. Licensee: Fairfield University. Format: Div. News progmg 4 hs wkly. Spec prog: Class 8 hrs, jazz 10 hrs, Black 12 hrs, Sp 12 hrs, C&W 3 hrs, Polish 3 hrs, Irish 2 hrs, Hungarian 2 hrs, Ger 2 hrs, Jewish 2 hrs, It one hr, Slovak 2 hrs wkly. ■ Bridgette Kelleher, gen mgr; Steve Berg, progmg dir; Gina Sata, mus dir; Lynn Marchetti, news dir; Tom Osenkowski, chief engr.

Greenwich

WGCH(AM)—Sept 14, 1964: 1490 khz; 1 kw-U. TL: N41 01 37 W73 37 59. Stereo. 1490 Dayton Ave. (06830). (203) 869-1490. Licensee: Greenwich Broadcasting Corp. Net: AP, Unistar. Wash atty: Cohn & Marks. Format: Full svc adult contemp. News staff 4; news progmg 23 hrs wkly. Target aud: 35-60; very upscale, active, athletic, community-minded. Spec prog: High school sports 6 hrs, educational one hr, talk 4 hrs wkly. ■ Clark Burgard, CEO & pres; John T. Becker, chmn; Bernedette Salvatore, prom mgr; George Wright, mus dir; James A. Thompson, news dir; Frank Hajdu, chief engr.

Groton

WSUB(AM)—July 26, 1958: 980 khz; 1 kw-D. TL: N41 23 05 W72 04 13. Suite One, 100 Fort Hill Rd. (06340). (203) 446-1980. FAX: (203) 446-0294. Licensee: H & D Media L.P. (acq 6-12-92; with co-located FM). Net: AP, Daynet. Format: News/talk. News staff 2. Target aud: 25-49; professionals that have an income of $40,600. ■ Mike Tapoo, gen mgr; Frank Carolano, progmg dir; Dave Marrero, news dir; Frank Doremus, chief engr.

WQGN-FM—Co-owned with WSUB(AM). 1971: 105.5 mhz; 3 kw. Ant 275 ft. TL: N41 23 05 W72 04 13. Stereo. Format: CHR. News staff one; news progmg 15 hrs wkly. Target aud: 18-34. ■ Jody Morris, prom mgr; Chuck Davis, progmg dir & mus dir.

Guilford

***WGRS(FM)**—Not on air, target date Jan 1994: 91.5 mhz; 2 kw. Ant 82 ft. TL: N41 17 19 W72 39 32. Stereo. Hrs opn: 5 AM-midnight. Rebroadcasts WMNR (FM) Monroe 100%. 1014 Monroe Tpke., Monroe (06468). (203) 268-9667. Licensee: Monroe Board of Education (acq 3-23-92; $31,524 for CP; FTR 4-13-92). Format: Class. Spec prog: Big band 8 hrs, folk 2 hrs, new age one hr, Broadway one hr wkly. ■ Kurt Anderson, gen mgr, progmg dir & mus dir; Carol Babina, stn mgr & dev dir; Jane Stadler, opns dir.

Hamden

WAVZ(AM)—See New Haven.

WKCI(FM)—Co-owned with WAVZ(AM). Feb 10, 1969: 101.3 mhz; 10 kw. Ant 1,070 ft. TL: N41 25 23 W72 57 06. Stereo. 495 Benham St. (06514). (203) 245-8814. (acq 7-24-92). Rep: McGavren Guild. Format: Top-40. ■ Faith Zila, vp & gen mgr; Pete Cosenva, progmg dir.

***WQAQ(FM)**—February 1973: 88.3 mhz; 16 w. Ant -82 ft. TL: N41 25 10 W72 53 41. Stereo. Hrs opn: 18. Box 59, Quinnipiac College, 555 New Rd. (06518). (203) 288-5251, ext. 8355. FAX: (203) 288-8098. Licensee: Quinnipiac College. Net: AP. Format: CHR, AOR, news/talk. News progmg 20 hrs wkly. Target aud: 18-30. Spec prog: Relg 4 hrs, polka 4 hrs wkly. ■ Dawn LeVasseur, gen mgr; Bart N. Miller, opns mgr; Leslie Smith, progmg dir; R.J. Vilardi, mus dir; Todd Yacovone, news dir. ■ Rates: $na; 30; 30; 30.

WXCT(AM)—July 17, 1960: 1220 khz; 1 kw-D, 320-N, DA-1. TL: N41 22 32 W72 55 54. Stereo. Hrs opn: 24. 473 Denslow Hill Rd. (06514). (203) 288-8282. FAX: (203) 248-1466. Licensee: Milstar Broadcasting Corp. Rep: Lotus. Format: Hispanic. News staff one; news progmg 14 hrs wkly. Target aud: Hispanic. ■ Marty Wilson, pres, gen mgr, gen sls mgr & progmg dir; Wanda DeLeon, news dir; Jackie Talavera, pub affrs dir; Robert Radil, chief engr. ■ Rates: $45; 40; 45; 25.

Hartford

WCCC-FM—June 7, 1960: 106.9 mhz; 23 kw. Ant 730 ft. TL: N41 47 51 W72 47 52. Stereo. Hrs opn: 24. ■ Milt Aninger, vp sls.

WDRC(AM)—Dec 10, 1922: 1360 khz; 5 kw-U, DA-N. TL: N41 48 45 W72 41 44. Stereo. 869 Blue Hills Ave., Bloomfield (06002). (203) 243-1115. FAX: (203) 286-8257. Licensee: Buckley Broadcasting Corp. of Connecticut. Group owner: Buckley Broadcasting Corp. (acq 8-1-59). Net: AP, Unistar. Format: MOR. ■ Richard D. Buckley, pres; Wayne G. Mulligan, vp & gen mgr; Gram Winters, opns mgr; Ron Pell, gen sls mgr; Frank Holler, progmg dir; Kim Zachary, news dir; Lee Steele, chief engr.

WDRC-FM—1936: 102.9 mhz; 19.5 kw. Ant 810 ft. TL: N41 33 44 W72 50 40. Stereo. Dups AM 10%. Net: AP. Format: Oldies. ■ Wayne G. Mulligan, stn mgr; Frank Holler, progmg mgr.

WHCN(FM)—1939: 105.9 mhz; 16 kw. Ant 867 ft. TL: N41 33 47 W72 50 42. Stereo. Hrs opn: 24. 1039 Asylum Ave. (06105). (203) 247-1060. FAX: (203) 549-5075. Licensee: WHCN Inc. Group owner: Beck-Ross Communications Inc. (acq 8-74). Net: ABC/R. Rep: Christal. Format: AOR. ■ Boyd E. Arnold, exec vp & gen mgr; Gordon Weingarth, vp sls & gen sls mgr; Anette Babek, prom mgr; Bob Bittens, vp progmg & progmg dir; Pam Brooks, mus dir; Maurice Miner, news dir; Rick Walsh, vp engrg & chief engr.

***WJMJ(FM)**—Oct 18, 1976: 88.9 mhz; 7.2 kw. Ant 580 ft. TL: N41 45 09 W72 59 40. Stereo. Hrs opn: 24. St. Thomas Seminary, Bloomfield (06002). (203) 242-8800; (203) 562-7889. Licensee: St. Thomas Seminary. Net: ABC/I. Wash atty: Haley, Bader & Potts. Format: Btfl mus, class, educ, jazz. News staff one; News progmg 10 hrs wkly. Target aud: 40-65; working, middle-class, family group. Spec prog: Foreign one hr wkly. ■ Archbishop Daniel A. Cronin, pres; John L. Ellinger, gen mgr; Fred Swanson, progmg dir & news dir; Ivor Hugh, mus dir; John Ramsey, chief engr.

WKND(AM)—See Windsor.

WKSS(FM)—June 1947: 95.7 mhz; 16.5 kw. Ant 880 ft. TL: N41 33 41 W72 50 39. Stereo. Hartford Sq. N., 10 Columbus Blvd., Hartford (06106-1944). (203) 249-9577. FAX: (203) 522-7567. Licensee: Precision Media L.P. (group owner; acq 9-89). Net: AP; Conn. Radio Net. Format: CHR. News staff one; news progmg 3 hrs wkly. Target aud: 18-34. ■ Timothy Montgomery, vp & gen mgr; Jeremy Savage, opns dir & pub affrs dir; Debra F. Gould, natl sls mgr; Karen Kintner, rgnl sls mgr; Larry Hryb, prom mgr; Jay Beau Jones, progmg dir; Kandy Klutch, asst mus dir; Robin King, news dir; John Ramsey, chief engr.

WLAT(AM)—See Manchester.

WNEZ(AM)—See New Britain.

WPOP(AM)—July 1935: 1410 khz; 5 kw-U, DA-2. TL: N41 41 35 W72 45 30. Hrs opn: 24. Box 31-1410, Newington Branch (06131); 345 E. Cedar St., Newington (06111). (203) 666-1411. FAX: (203) 667-9079. Licensee: Greater Conn. Broadcasting Inc. Group owner: The Griffin Group/Broadcast Division (acq 9-12-86). Net: AP, ABC/I. Rep: D & R Radio. Wash atty: Arent, Fox, Kintner, Plotkin & Kahn. Format: News/talk/info. News staff 8; news progmg 25 hrs wkly. Target aud: 35-54. ■ Merv Griffin, pres; Albert B. Pellegrino, vp & gen mgr; Dean Pagani, opns mgr & news dir; Bob Lang, sls dir; Frank Clifford, chief engr.

***WQTQ(FM)**—November 1974: 89.9 mhz; 63 w. Ant 86 ft. TL: N41 47 47 W72 41 42. Weaver High School, 415 Granby St. (06112). (203) 722-8661. Licensee: Hartford Board of Education. Net: UPI. Format: Educ, urban contemp. ■ Paul Robertson, gen mgr; Connie Coles, progmg dir; Michael Leclair, chief engr.

WRCH(FM)—See New Britain.

***WRTC-FM**—February 1958: 89.3 mhz; 350 w-H. Ant 62 ft. TL: N41 44 48 W72 41 32. Stereo. Hrs opn: 24. c/o Trinity College, 300 Summit St. (06106). (203) 297-2450; (203) 297-2439. FAX: (203) 297-2257. Licensee: Trustees of Trinity College. Format: Div, Black. Target aud: 15 plus. Spec prog: Class 4 hrs, gospel 6 hrs, West Indian 6 hrs, Pol 3 hrs, Portuguese 8 hrs, Sp 6 hrs wkly. ■ Pat West, stn mgr; Clair Pingel, mus dir; Charles Henry Smith, chief engr.

WTIC(AM)—Feb 10, 1925: 1080 khz; 50 kw-U, DA-N. TL: N41 46 39 W72 48 19. Stereo. Hrs opn: 24. One Financial Plaza (06103). (203) 522-1080. FAX: (203) 549-3431; TWX: 710-425-0133. Licensee: Ten Eighty Corp. Group owner: Chase Communications Inc. (acq 3-8-74). Net: CBS. Rep: Group W. Format: Full svc news/talk. News progmg 30 hrs wkly. Target aud: 35-59; intelligent, mature men & women. ■ Gary Zenobi, vp & gen mgr; James Principi, gen sls mgr; Vincent Turco, natl sls mgr; Jack Mitchell, prom mgr; Paul Douglas, progmg dir; Tom Ray, chief engr.

WTIC-FM—Feb 5, 1940: 96.5 mhz; 20 kw. Ant 810 ft. TL: N41 46 27 W72 48 20. Stereo. Hrs opn: 24. Prog sep from AM. Net: CBS. Format: Contemp hit. News progmg 8 hrs wkly. Target aud: 18-34; intelligent, spirited, youthful adults. ■ Steve Salhany, prom mgr; Paul Cannon, progmg dir; Dana Lundon, mus dir; John Elliott, news dir.

***WWUH(FM)**—See West Hartford.

WWYZ(FM)—See Waterbury.

WYSR(FM)—See Waterbury.

WZMX(FM)—1939: 93.7 mhz; 16 kw. Ant 869 ft. TL: N41 33 41 W72 50 39. Stereo. Ten Executive Drive, Farmington (06032). (203) 677-6700. FAX: (203) 677-6799. Licensee: American Radio Systems License Corp. Group owner: American Radio Systems (acq 9-15-93; FTR 10-4-93). Rep: Katz. Wash atty: Wiley, Rein & Fielding. Format: Adult contemp. Target aud: 25-54; adults in Hartford and New Haven. ■ Steven Dodge, CEO; David Pearlman, pres; Jodi Long, gen sls mgr; Herb Crowe, progmg dir; Debra Daigle, news dir; Gene Faultus, chief engr.

Ledyard

WBMW(FM)—Dec 24, 1992: 106.5 mhz; 6 kw. Ant 514 ft. TL: N41 27 44 W72 01 27. Stereo. Hrs opn: 24. Box 357 (06339). (203) 464-1065. FAX: (203) 464-8143. Licensee: Redwolf Broadcasting Corp. Net: USA, Unistar. Wash atty: Smithwick & Belendiuk. Format: Adult contemp. News staff one. Target aud: 20-49. ■ John J. Fuller, pres & chief engr; Arthur V. Belendiuk, vp. ■ Rates: $28; 18; 28; 15.

Litchfield

WZBG(FM)—July 8, 1992: 97.3 mhz; 3 kw. Ant 328 ft. TL: N41 48 08 W73 09 50. Box 1497, Litchfield Commons, 49 Commons Dr. (06759). Licensee: Local Girls & Boys Broadcasting Corp. Net: CBS. Wash atty: Erwin Krasnow. Format: News/information, adult contemp. News staff 3. Target aud: 25-54. ■ Susan Saint James, chmn; Virginia Mortara, pres; Dick Ebersol, exec vp; Jennifer L. Warner, gen mgr & sls dir; Karen Kobylenski, opns mgr; Sharon Berman, progmg dir & mus dir; Jeffrey Zeiner, news dir; Frank Jankowicz, chief engr. ■ Rates: $25; 15; 20; 5.

Manchester

WLAT(AM)—May 18, 1958: 1230 khz; 1 kw-U. TL: N41 46 34 W72 33 27. Hrs opn: 24. 905 Wethersfield Ave., Hartford (06114). (203) 296-1230. FAX: (203) 296-4204. Licensee: Jeffrey P. Dressler (acq 11-30-90; $125,000; FTR 12-17-90). Wash atty: Hogan & Hartson. Format: Sp. News staff 2; news progmg 12 hrs wkly. Target aud: 18-45; Spanish community of greater Hartford area. ■ Jeffrey Dressler, pres; Mercedes Chinchilla, gen mgr; Frank Pingroee, chief engr.

Meriden

WMMW(AM)—1946: 1470 khz; 2.5 kw-U, DA-N. TL: N41 33 14 W72 48 07. Hrs opn: 24. 900 E. Main St. (06450). (203) 634-1470; (203) 235-5747. Licensee: AM Radio Inc. (acq 12-30-86; $500,000; FTR 12-1-86). Net: SMN. Rep: Roslin. Wash atty: Miller & Fields. Format: MOR. Target aud: 28 plus; middle income, grass roots America. Spec prog: Pol one hr, relg 4 hrs wkly. ■ Anthony Pescatello, pres & gen mgr; Jeffrey Pescatello, gen sls mgr; Phil Callan, mus dir; Frank Jankewicz, chief engr.

***WPKT(FM)**—June 11, 1978: 90.5 mhz; 18.5 kw-H, 13.5 kw-V. Ant 823 ft-H, 817 ft-V. TL: N41 33 42 W72 50 41. Stereo. Hrs opn: 24. Box 260240, 240 New Britain Ave. Hartford (06126-0240). (203) 527-0905. Licensee: Connecticut Public Broadcasting Inc. Net: NPR, APR. Format: Class, news, info. Spec prog: Jazz 8 hrs wkly. ■ Jerry Franklin, pres; John Berky, vp & stn mgr; Gordon Shelp, opns dir; Steve Futernick, vp dev; Donna Collins, vp mktg; Kim Grehn, progmg dir; John Nowacki, mus dir.

Middlefield

***WPKT(FM)**—See Meriden.

Middletown

WCNX(AM)—Dec 12, 1948: 1150 khz; 2.5 kw-D, 46 w-N. TL: N41 11 33 W72 37 13. Hrs opn: 5 AM-midnight. Box 359, 777 River Rd. (06457). (203) 347-2565. FAX: (203) 347-7704. Licensee: Radio Middletown Inc. (acq 12-1-93; FTR 12-20-93). Net: Conn. Radio Net. Format: News/talk. News staff 2; news progmg 33 hrs wkly. Target aud: 25-54. Spec prog: Pol one hr. ■ Edward J. Creem Jr., pres, gen mgr & news dir; Scott R. Baecker, vp & gen sls mgr; John Parks, opns mgr; John G. Eppler, chief engr.

***WESU(FM)**—September 1939: 88.1 mhz; 1.5 kw. Ant 38 ft. TL: N41 33 16 W72 39 30. Stereo. Wesleyan Station (06459). (203) 347-0050. Licensee: Wesleyan Broadcast Association. Format: AOR, jazz, div. News progmg 5 hrs wkly. Target aud: General. Spec prog: Class 2 hrs, country 2 hrs, blues 10 hrs, gospel 6 hrs, oldies 2 hrs, new age 2 hrs, reggae 10 hrs, metal 5 hrs wkly. ■ Jacob Bricca, pres & gen mgr; Yoshi Matsumuto, chief engr.

***WIHS(FM)**—Oct 11, 1969: 104.9 mhz; 3 kw. Ant 300 ft. TL: N41 30 18 W72 39 32. Hrs opn: 24. 1933 S. Main St. (06457). (203) 346-3846. FAX: (203) 347-1049. Licensee: Connecticut Radio Fellowship Inc. Net: AP, USA. Format: Christian. ■ Alfred C. Thyberg, pres & gen mgr; Halena Sajko, mus dir; Paul Kretschmer, pub affrs dir; Geri Gerard, chief engr.

Milford

WADS(AM)—See Ansonia.

WFIF(AM)—Sept 4, 1965: 1500 khz; 5 kw-D, DA. TL: N41 11 33 W73 06 05. Hrs opn: Sunrise-sunset. 90 Kay Ave. (06460). (203) 878-5915. Licensee: K.W. Dolmar Broadcasting Co. Inc. (acq 4-82; $425,000; FTR 1-19-81). Net: USA, CBN. Format: Christian. Target aud: General. Spec prog: Black 15 hrs wkly. ■ William Blount, pres & gen mgr; Dave Young, vp & vp opns; Lou Gallucci, gen sls mgr & prom mgr; Willie Barnett, mus dir; Eleanor Hubbard, pub affrs dir; Terry Smith, chief engr.

Monroe

***WMNR(FM)**—Jan 31, 1974: 88.1 mhz; 5.0 kw. Ant 403 ft. TL: N41 19 08 W73 15 13. Stereo. Hrs opn: 5 AM-midnight. 1014 Monroe Tpke. (06468). (203) 268-9667. Licensee: Monroe Board of Education. Format: Class. Spec prog: Big band 8 hrs, folk 2 hrs, new age one hr, Broadway one hr wkly. ■ Kurt Anderson, gen mgr, progmg dir & mus dir; Carol Babina, stn mgr & dev dir; Jane Stadler, opns dir.

Naugatuck

WFNW(AM)—Feb 26, 1961: 1380 khz; 5 kw-D, 500 w-N, DA-2. TL: N41 30 35 W73 03 20. Stereo. 46 Mallane (06770). (203) 723-0678. FAX: (203) 723-9920. Licensee: Candido Dias Carrelo (acq 6-90; $350,000; FTR 6-25-90). Format: Sp, Portugese. ■ Emanuel Ramile, pres; Emilo Emello, gen mgr; Gene Faltus, chief engr.

New Britain

***WFCS(FM)**—Oct 17, 1972: 97.9 mhz; 50 w. Ant 160 ft. TL: N41 41 36 W72 45 49. Stereo. Hrs opn: 24. Student Center, 1615 Stanley St. (06050). (203) 223-6767. Licensee: Trustees of Central Connecticut State College. Net: ABC/I. Format: Alternative. News staff 7; news progmg 15 hrs wkly. Target aud: 14-50. Spec prog: Class 2 hrs, blues 2 hrs, jazz 4 hrs wkly. ■ Chris Kraft, gen mgr; Rob Garbowski, prom mgr; Ruth Lofbowski, progmg dir; Sean Nelligan, mus dir.

WNEZ(AM)—May 20, 1949: 910 khz; 5 kw-U, DA-N. TL: N41 42 58 W72 48 38. Stereo. Hrs opn: 24. Box 507, 130 Birdseye Rd., Farmington (06034). (203) 678-9100. FAX: (203) 677-5483. Licensee: Radio Corp. of Hartford Group owner: DeDominicis Broadcasting (acq 12-29-77). Net: Unistar, CNN. Rep: Eastman. Wash atty: Arent, Fox, Kintner, Plotkin & Kahn. Format: News. Target aud: 35-54; males. ■ Enzo DeDominicis, pres; Ronald Roy, vp & gen mgr; Allan Camp, opns mgr & progmg mgr; Ronald Ray, gen sls mgr; Nunzia DeDominicis, natl sls mgr & rgnl sls mgr; Michael Stacy, prom mgr; Kathy Wyler, news dir; Joanne Tacinelli, pub affrs dir; Bobby Gray, chief engr.

WRCH(FM)—Co-owned with WNEZ(AM). July 1, 1968: 100.5 mhz; 7.5 kw. Ant 1,250 ft. TL: N41 42 13 W72 49 57. Stereo. Hrs opn: 24. Prog sep from AM. Format: Adult contemp. News staff one; news progmg 24 hrs wkly. Target aud: 25-54; women. ■ Kathy Wyler, pub affrs dir.

WRYM(AM)—August 1946: 840 khz; 1 kw-D. TL: N41 41 15 W72 43 46. 1056 Willard Ave., Newington (06111). (203) 666-5646. FAX: (203) 666-5647. Licensee: Hartford County Broadcasting Corp. (acq 8-61). Rep: Caballero. Format: Sp. News staff 4; news progmg 8 hrs wkly. Target aud: General, Spanish. Spec prog: Pol 5 hrs wkly. ■ Sylvia Sodokoff, pres; Barry A. Kursman, vp, gen mgr & gen sls mgr; Omar Augilera, progmg dir; Tom Cawett, chief engr. ■ Rates: $35; 35; 35; 35.

New Canaan

***WSLX(FM)**—1975: 91.9 mhz; 10 w-H. Ant 518 ft. TL: N41 11 32 W73 29 46 (CP: 19 w-V, ant 171 ft.). Stereo. Box 1148, 377 N. Wilton Rd. (06840). (203) 966-5612. Licensee: St. Luke's Foundation. Format: Class, div. ■ Matt Kaishian, chief opns.

New Fairfield

WMJV-FM—See Patterson, N.Y.

New Haven

WAVZ(AM)—September 1947: 1300 khz; 1 kw-U, DA-N. TL: N41 17 16 W72 56 48. Hrs opn: 24. (06473). (203) 248-4012. FAX: (203) 777-7246. Licensee: Clear Channel Communications (acq 12-18-92; $10 with WKCI(FM); FTR 1-11-93). Net: ABC/I. Rep: McGavren Guild. Format: Z-rock. News staff one. Target aud: 18-34. ■ Faith Zilg, gen mgr; Pete Cosenza, progmg dir; Mike McGowan, mus dir; Carolyn Foxx, news dir; Fred Santor, chief engr.

WELI(AM)—October 1935: 960 khz; 5 kw-U, DA-N. TL: N41 22 14 W72 56 15. Stereo. Box 85 (06501); 495 Benham St., Hamden (06514). (203) 281-9600. FAX: (203) 281-7640. Licensee: Clear Channel Radio Licenses Inc. (group owner; acq 8-5-85). Net: AP. Rep: McGavren-Guild. Format: Adult contemp. Target aud: 18 plus. ■ L. Lowry Mays, pres; Stan Shields, gen mgr; David Bradford, gen sls mgr; Chuck Gross, progmg dir; Jay McCormick, mus dir; Sandy St. Pierre, news dir; Fred Santore, chief engr.

WKCI(FM)—See Hamden.

WNHC(AM)—1944: 1340 khz; 1 kw-U. TL: N41 17 32 W72 57 12. 112 Washington Ave., North Haven (06473). (203) 234-1340. FAX: (203) 239-6712. Licensee: Willis Communications. Net: MBS; Conn. Radio Net. Rep: Katz. Format: Adult Urban contemp, news. Spec prog: Sp one hr wkly. ■ Edith Willis, pres & gen mgr; Will Mebane Jr., gen sls mgr; Stan Boston, progmg dir; Lenny Green, mus dir; Roger Vann, news dir; Winn Sutter, chief engr.

WPLR(FM)—1944: 99.1 mhz; 14.1 kw. Ant 950 ft. TL: N41 25 23 W72 57 06. Stereo. 1191 Dixwell Ave., Hamden (06514). (203) 287-9070. FAX: (203) 287-8997. Licensee: General Communicorp Inc. Group owner: Southern Starr Broadcasting Group (acq 9-83). Rep: Eastman. Format: AOR. ■ Robert E. Long, CEO; William Motter, CFO; Manuel V. Rodriguez, exec vp & gen mgr; Richard Wolf, gen sls mgr; Dona Goodman, natl sls mgr; Samuel Tilery, prom mgr; John Griffin, progmg dir; Pam Landry, mus dir; Marylee Raila, news dir; Matt Valleau, chief engr.

WXCT(AM)—See Hamden.

WYBC-FM—Mar 9, 1959: 94.3 mhz; 1.2 kw. Ant 122 ft. TL: N41 18 49 W72 55 53 (CP: 1.78 kw, ant 325 ft., TL: N41 20 58 W72 58 27). Stereo. Hrs opn: 24. Box WYBC, Yale Station, 165 Elm St. (06520). (203) 432-4118. FAX: (203) 432-4117. Licensee: Yale Broadcasting Co. Format: Urban contemp, progsv rock. News progmg 10 hrs wkly. Target aud: Urban and college age listeners. Spec prog: Irish 2 hrs, gospel 8 hrs, jazz 8 hrs, folk 3 hrs wkly. ■ David Flynn, pres & gen mgr; Stanley Puzycki, gen sls mgr; Wayne Schmidt, prom dir; Seong An, progmg dir; Lucy Carrone, news dir; Clif Mills, chief engr.

New London

*****WCNI(FM)**—1974: 91.1 mhz; 490 w. Ant 169 ft. TL: N41 22 53 W72 06 28 (CP: 262 w, ant 200 ft.). Stereo. Box 4972, Connecticut College, 270 Mohegan Ave. (06320). (203) 439-2853; (203) 439-2850. Licensee: Connecticut College Broadcast Association Inc. Format: Rock. Target aud: General; we go for all musical audiences except pop. Spec prog: Black 3 hrs, class 6 hrs, folk 9 hrs, gospel 3 hrs, jazz 9 hrs, Pol 3 hrs, Sp 3 hrs, women's 3 hrs wkly. ■ Steve Keefe, pres & gens dir; Jonathan Morris, gen mgr; Dave Skalka, prom mgr; Taylor Hubbard, progmg dir; Emma Scioli, mus dir; Todd Renschler, asst mus dir; Charles Sammons, pub affrs dir; Stephen Keefe, chief engr.

WNLC(AM)—Sept 13, 1936: 1510 khz; 10 kw-D, 5 kw-N, DA-2. TL: N41 22 38 W72 10 02. Hrs opn: 5 AM-midnight. Box 1031 (06320); 90 Foster Rd., Waterford (06385). (203) 442-5328. FAX: (203) 442-6532. Licensee: Andross Communications (acq 3-3-89; $5.2 million with co-located FM; FTR 2-26-90). Net: CBS, CNN; Conn. Net. Rep: McGavren Guild. Format: News. News staff 2; news progmg 133 hrs wkly. Target aud: 30 plus; affluent, upscale. Spec prog: It one hr, relg 3 hrs, country 2 hrs wkly. ■ Ross Elder, pres; Andy Russell, gen mgr; Bernie Daigle, gen sls mgr; Joanne Gregory, news dir. ■ Rates: $36; 26; 36; 18.

WTYD(FM)—Co-owned with WNLC(AM). Jan 1, 1970: 100.9 mhz; 3 kw. Ant 328 ft. TL: N41 16 27 W72 08 29. Stereo. Hrs opn: 24. Prog sep from AM. Format: Light adult contemp. News progmg 2 hrs wkly. Target aud: 25-54. ■ Rick Joseph, opns mgr. ■ Rates: $54; 42; 54; 32.

WQGN-FM—See Groton.

WSUB(AM)—See Groton.

WTYD(FM)—Listing follows WNLC(AM).

Norwalk

WNLK(AM)—1948: 1350 khz; 1 kw-D, 500 w-N, DA-N. TL: N41 06 54 W73 26 06 (CP: 2.5 kw-D). 148 E. Ave (06851). (203) 838-5566. FAX: (203) 854-5116. Licensee: CRB of Norwalk. Group owner: CRB Broadcasting Corp. (acq 7-89; $5 million with co-located FM; FTR 8-14-89). Net: CNN. Rep: Christal. Format: MOR. News staff 2. Target aud: General; upscale, affluent. ■ Cindy McCurdy, vp & gen mgr; Susan Farquhar, prom mgr; Mike Lee, progmg dir; Frank Marro, news dir; Clif Mills, chief engr.

WEFX(FM)—Co-owned with WNLK(AM). 1966: 95.9 mhz; 3 kw. Ant 299 ft. TL: N41 06 54 W73 26 06. Stereo. Prog sep from AM. Format: Classic rock.

Norwich

WCTY(FM)—Listing follows WICH(AM).

WICH(AM)—September 1946: 1310 khz; 5 kw-U, DA-2. TL: N41 33 10 W72 04 34. Hrs opn: 24. Box 551, Cuprak Rd. (06360). (203) 887-3511. FAX: (203) 886-7649. Licensee: WICH Inc. Group owner: Hall Communications Inc. (acq 7-1-65). Net: MBS; Conn. Net. Rep: D & R Radio. Wash atty: Arent, Fox, Kintner, Plotkin & Kahn. Format: Full svc. News staff 3. Target aud: 35 plus. Spec prog: Pol one hr wkly. ■ Robert M. Hall, chmn; Richard P. Reed, pres; James J. Reed, gen mgr; John London, stn mgr; Karen Dole, opns dir & pub affrs dir; Stu Bryer, progmg dir; Bryan Lee, news dir; Roger Arnold, chief engr.

WCTY(FM)—Co-owned with WICH(AM). May 1968: 97.7 mhz; 1.9 kw. Ant 410 ft. TL: N41 28 28 W72 06 14. Stereo. Hrs opn: 24. Prog sep from AM. Net: ABC/FM. Format: Country. Target aud: 25-54. ■ James J. Reed, progmg dir.

*****WNPR(FM)**—Oct 17, 1981: 89.1 mhz; 5.1 kw. Ant 590 ft. TL: N41 31 11 W72 10 04. Stereo. Hrs opn: 24. Rebroadcasts WPKT(FM) Meriden 100%. Box 260240, 240 New Britian Ave., Hartford (06240-0240). (203) 527-0905. Licensee: Connecticut Public Broadcasting Inc. Net: NPR, APR. Format: Class, news & info. News progmg 21 hrs wkly. Target aud: General. ■ Jerry Franklin, pres; John Berky, vp & stn mgr; Gordon Shelp, opns dir; Donna Collins, vp mktg; John Nowacki, mus dir; Jay Whitsett, engrg dir; Joe Zareski, chief engr.

Old Saybrook

WLIS(AM)—Sept 27, 1956: 1420 khz; 5 kw-D, 500 w-N, DA-N. TL: N41 19 38 W72 23 21. Drawer W (06475). (203) 388-3546. FAX: (203) 388-2931. Licensee: Del Raycee (acq 8-20-87; $900,000; FTR 8-31-87). Net: ABC/I; Conn. Net. Format: Soft & easy favorites. News staff one; news progmg 22 hrs wkly. Target aud: 25-64. Spec prog: Class 2 hrs, jazz 2 hrs wkly. ■ Ida Raycee, pres; Del Raycee, gen mgr; Bob Muscatel, opns mgr; David Thom, progmg dir; Brian May, news dir; John McGuire, chief engr. ■ Rates: $25; 23; 25; 19.

Putnam

WINY(AM)—May 3, 1953: 1350 khz; 5 kw-D, 70 w-N. TL: N41 54 10 W71 53 43. Stereo. Box 231, 45 Pomfret St. (06260). (203) 928-2721. FAX: (203) 928-7878. Licensee: Gerardi Broadcasting Corp. (acq 3-27-89). Net: AP; Conn. Radio Net. Wash atty: Miller & Fields. Format: Adult contemp. News staff 3; news progmg 13 hrs wkly. Target aud: 25 plus. Spec prog: Talk 10 hrs wkly. ■ Michael J. Gerardi, pres, gen mgr & gen sls mgr; Gary Osbrey, progmg dir & mus dir; Cara Landi, news dir; Steve Jurczyk, chief engr. ■ Rates: $31; 27; 31; 18.25.

Ridgefield

WREF(AM)—Mar 15, 1985: 850 khz; 2.5 kw. TL: N41 17 27 W73 29 16. Stereo. Hrs opn: 24. Box 1085, 165 Danbury Rd. (06877-0842). (203) 438-1211. FAX: (203) 431-8473. Licensee: Ridgefield Broadcasting Corp. (acq 3-15-85). Net: NBC. Wash atty: Wilkes, Artis, Hedrick & Lane. Format: MOR, jazz, news. News staff 2; news progmg 8 hrs wkly. Target aud: 35 plus; upscale adults. Spec prog: It 3 hrs, jazz 5 hrs wkly. ■ Dennis Jackson, CEO & chief engr; William E. Hoover, stn mgr & vp sls; Jonathan Becker, vp mktg; Bob Lasprogato, vp progmg; Michele Donofrio, news dir. ■ Rates: $35; 30; 30; 20.

Salisbury

WKZE-FM—Sept 1, 1992: 98.1 mhz; 1.8 kw. Ant 604 ft. TL: N41 58 35 W73 31 27. Stereo. Hrs opn: 5 AM-midnight. 67 Main St., Sharon (06069). (203) 364-5800. FAX: (203) 364-0129. Licensee: Tri-State Broadcasting Inc. (acq 4-27-93; $350,000; FTR 3-1-93). Net: CNN. Wash atty: Fisher, Wayland, Cooper & Leader. Format: Div. News staff 2; news progmg 15 hrs wkly. Target aud: 25-54. ■ Stan Gurell, pres; Ira Howard Levy, exec vp; Dr. Pamela Chassin, vp & gen mgr; Dale Jones, vp opns, progmg dir & news dir; Drew Wilder, vp sls; Louise Coogan, pub affrs dir; David Groth, chief engr.

Sharon

WKZE(AM)—Dec 23, 1986: 1020 khz; 2.5 kw-D. TL: N41 58 35 W73 31 27. Stereo. Hrs opn: Sunrise-sunset. Box 1020, 67 Main St. (06069). (203) 364-5800. FAX: (203) 364-0129. Licensee: Tri-State Broadcasting Inc. (acq 3-22-92; $500,000; FTR 2-17-92). Net: AP; Conn. Radio Net. Wash atty: Fisher, Wayland, Cooper & Leader. Format: Country. News staff 2. Target aud: 25-54. ■ Stan Gurell, pres; Ira Levy, exec vp; Pamela Chassin, gen mgr; Dale Jones, vp opns & news dir; Drew Wilder, vp sls; Chuck Johnson, mus dir.

WQQQ(FM)—Jan 28, 1993: 103.3 mhz; 1.5 kw. Ant 640 ft. TL: N41 55 03 W73 33 32. Stereo. Hrs opn: 24. 19 Boas Lane, Wilton (06897-1301). Box 446, 333 Main St., Lakeville (06039). (203) 435-3333; (203) 435-0103. FAX: (203) 435-3333; (203) 438-1211. Licensee: Radio South Burlington Inc. Net: NBC. Wash atty: Cohn & Marks. Format: Adult contemp, MOR, talk. Target aud: Upscale adults. ■ Dennis Jackson, CEO & chief engr; Marshall Miles, gen mgr; William A. Hoover, vp sls. ■ Rates: $25; 30; 30; 20.

Shelton

*****WRXC(FM)**—1977: 90.1 mhz; 100 w. Ant 343 ft. TL: N41 21 43 W73 06 48. Stereo. Hrs opn: 5 AM-midnight. Rebroadcasts WMNR (FM) Monroe 100%. 1014 Monroe Turnpike, Monroe (06468). (203) 268-9667. Licensee: Monroe Board of Education. Format: Class. Spec prog: Big band 8 hrs, folk 2 hrs, new age one hr, Broadway one hr wkly. ■ Kurt Anderson, gen mgr, progmg dir & mus dir; Carol Babina, stn mgr & dev dir; Jane Stadler, opns dir.

Somers

*****WDJW(FM)**—Oct 6, 1986: 105.3 mhz; 9.2 w. Ant -58 ft. TL: N41 57 43 W72 27 51. Somers High School, 9th District Rd. (06071). (203) 749-2501; (203) 749-0719. FAX: (203) 627-9697. Licensee: Somers High School. Format: AOR, top-40. Target aud: General. ■ Peter Stone, pres & gen mgr.

South Kent

*****WGSK(FM)**—Dec 25, 1987: 90.1 mhz; 150 w. Ant -124 ft. TL: N41 40 32 W73 28 54. Box 90 (06785). (203) 927-0049. Licensee: South Kent School. Format: Div, country, big band. News progmg 16 hrs wkly. Target aud: 55 plus; elderly persons needing security of memories and information. Spec prog: Folk 4 hrs, Broadway musicals 4 hrs, live drama one hr wkly. ■ Hamilton O'Hara, gen mgr & progmg dir; Mary Grusauski, mus dir; Charles A. Parrish, chief engr.

Southington

WNTY(AM)—Sept 2, 1969: 990 khz; 2.5 kw-D, DA. TL: N41 34 59 W72 53 01. 440 Old Turnpike Rd. (06489). (203) 628-0311. FAX: (203) 276-9940. Licensee: WNTY Associates (acq 1978). Net: CNN, Unistar. Rep: Katz, New England. Format: Adult contemp. ■ George W. Stevens, pres, gen mgr & progmg dir; Norma E. Stevens, gen sls mgr; Tom Osenkowski, chief engr.

Stamford

*****WEDW-FM**—Feb 17, 1992: 88.5 mhz; 2 kw-H, 1.8 kw-V. Ant 302 ft. TL: N41 02 49 W73 31 36. Stereo. 307 Atlantic St. (06901). (203) 965-0440. FAX: (203) 965-0447. Licensee: Connecticut Public Broadcasting Inc. ■ Jerry Franklin, pres; Lynn Latman, stn mgr; Gordon Shelp, opns dir; Donna Collins, vp mktg; Joe Zareski, chief engr.

WKHL(FM)—Oct 18, 1947: 96.7 mhz; 3 kw. Ant 328 ft. TL: N41 02 49 W73 31 36. Stereo. Century Plaza N., 100 Prospect St., 2nd Fl. (06901). (203) 327-1400. FAX: (203) 359-9907. Licensee: Q Broadcasting Inc. Rep: Katz. Format: Oldies. Target aud: 25-54; upscale. ■ Bob Marrone, progmg dir.

WSTC(AM)—Co-owned with WKHL(FM). Sept 18, 1941: 1400 khz; 1 kw-U. TL: N41 02 49 W73 31 36. Stereo. Prog sep from FM. Licensee: Q Broadcasting Inc. (acq 6-5-92; $4.15 million; with co-located FM; FTR 6-29-92). Net: ABC/I, NBC Talknet, AP, Wall Street, Conn. Net. Rep: Katz. Wash atty: Sidley & Austin. Format: Adult contemp, news/talk. News staff 5; news progmg 22 hrs wkly. Target aud: 35-64. ■ Richard Brescia, gen mgr; Charles Ponger, sls dir; Rick Patron, progmg dir.

Stonington

WVVE(FM)—November 1981: 102.3 mhz; 3 kw. Ant 298 ft. TL: N41 24 23 W71 50 15 (CP: Ant 328 ft.). Stereo. Box 97, Mystic (06355). (203) 599-2214. FAX: (203) 599-3568. Licensee: Shoreline Communications Inc. (acq 6-19-84; $800,000; FTR 3-26-84). Net: AP. Rep: D & R Radio. Format: Good time oldies/The Wave. News staff 2; news progmg 5 hrs wkly. Target aud: 21-54. ■ David J. Quinn, pres & gen mgr; Karen A. Quinn, vp & vp sls; Robert E.P. Elmer III, gen sls mgr; Kevin O'Connor, prom mgr & progmg dir; Bill Haberman, news dir; Richard Williams, chief engr.

Storrs

*****WHUS(FM)**—1956: 91.7 mhz; 3.16 kw. Ant 360 ft. TL: N41 48 48 W72 15 33. Stereo. Box U-8R, 2110 Hillside Rd. (06269-3008). (203) 486-4007. FAX: (203) 486-2955. Licensee: Board of Trustees, Univ. of Conn. Net: AP. Format: Div. Spec prog: Sp 3 hrs wkly. ■ John Murphy, gen mgr; Dan Cohen, opns mgr; Ruth Zelanski, Dan Tedesco, mus dirs; Lauren Pozucek, news dir.

Torrington

WSNG(AM)—Jan 29, 1948: 610 khz; 1 kw-D, 500 w-N, DA-2. TL: N41 45 28 W73 03 06. Hrs opn: 17. Box 657, 8 Church St. (06790). (203) 489-4181. FAX: (203) 496-8262. Licensee: Consumer Service Radio Inc. (acq 9-23-88; $815,000). Net: CBS. Wash atty: Erwin Krasnow. Format: Full svc adult contemp. News staff 3; news progmg 25 hrs wkly. Target aud: 25-54. Spec prog: Call-in program one hr wkly. ■ Jay Sheldon, gen mgr & progmg dir; Kevin Cooper, chief engr.

Vernon

***WCTF(AM)**—Nov 21, 1982: 1170 khz; 1 kw-D, DA. TL: N41 52 38 W72 28 43 (CP: 2.5 kw-D). 13 Park St. (06066). (203) 871-2526. Licensee: Family Stations Inc. (group owner; acq 1-86; $136,000; FTR 9-23-85). Format: Relg. ■ Harold Camping, pres; Scott L. Smith, vp; Donald White Jr., gen mgr.

Wallingford

***WWEB(FM)**—Nov 10, 1976: 89.9 mhz; 10 w. Ant 230 ft. TL: N41 27 34 W72 48 48. Box 788, Choate Rosemary Hall Foundation (06492). (203) 269-7722. Licensee: Choate Rosemary Hall Foundation. Format: AOR. Target aud: High school students. Spec prog: Class 2 hrs, C&W 2 hrs wkly. ■ Chris Davies, gen mgr.

Waterbury

WATR(AM)—June 15, 1934: 1320 khz; 5 kw-D, 1 kw-N, DA-2. TL: N41 32 12 W73 01 52. One Broadcast Ln. (06706). (203) 755-1121. FAX: (203) 574-3025. Licensee: WATR Inc. Net: CBS. Rep: Banner. Format: MOR, talk. News staff 2; news progmg 15 hrs wkly. Target aud: 35-64. Spec prog: Pol 2 hrs wkly. ■ B. Preston Gilmore, pres; Steve Gilmore, gen mgr; Barbara Davitt, gen sls mgr; Tom Chute, progmg dir; Gregg Little, news dir; Mark Gilmore, chief engr.

WWYZ(FM)—Co-owned with WATR(AM). Aug 1, 1961: 92.5 mhz; 17.8 kw. Ant 879 ft. TL: N41 33 43 W72 50 41. Stereo. Hrs opn: 24. Prog sep from AM. 151 New Park Ave., Hartford (06106). (203) 755-3111; (203) 247-1102. FAX: (203) 233-1280. Licensee: WWYZ Inc. Net: Unistar. Format: Country. News staff 2; news progmg 5 hrs wkly. Target aud: 25-54. ■ Steve Gilmore, stn mgr; Steven Peters, prom mgr; Dale Carter, progmg dir; John Saville, mus dir; Elizabeth McGuire, news dir; Ken Stiles, chief engr.

WWCO(AM)—1946: 1240 khz; 1 kw-U. TL: N41 33 59 W73 03 23. Stereo. Hrs opn: 20. Ramada Inn., One Schraffts Dr. (06705). (203) 755-9926. FAX: (203) 753-8729. Licensee: Mattatuck Communications Inc. (acq 7-14-93; $75,000; FTR 8-9-93). Net: CNN. Format: Classic oldies. News staff one; news progmg 3 hrs wkly. Target aud: 25-54. Spec prog: Gospel 2 hrs, It 2 hrs, Pol one hr wkly. ■ Thomas W. Coffey, gen mgr; Robert W. Somerville, sls dir; Wally Mann, prom mgr; Tim Clark, progmg mgr; Lou Morton, news dir; Tom Cawett, chief engr. ■ Rates: $25; 20; 25; 15.

WWYZ(FM)—Listing follows WATR(AM).

WYSR(FM)—Dec 25, 1967: 104.1 mhz; 50 kw. Ant 859 ft. TL: N41 33 41 W72 50 39. Stereo. Hrs opn: 24. Box 31-1410, Hartford (06131); 345 E. Cedar St., Newington (06111). (203) 666-1411. FAX: (203) 667-9079. Licensee: Greater Connecticut Broadcasting Inc. Group owner: The Griffin Group/Broadcast Division (acq 9-12-86). Rep: D & R Radio. Wash atty: Arent, Fox, Kintner, Plotkin & Kahn. Format: Adult contemp. Target aud: 25-54. ■ Merv Griffin, pres; Larry Cohen, CFO; Albert B. Pellegrino, exec vp & gen mgr; Steve Wiersman, opns mgr & progmg dir; Bob Lang, gen sls mgr; Annette Grella, prom mgr; Steve Weirsman, mus dir; Frank Clifford, chief engr.

West Hartford

WCCC(AM)—1947: 1290 khz; 490 w-D. TL: N41 47 48 W72 47 50. 243 S. Whitney St. (06105). (203) 233-4426. FAX: (203) 232-6511. Licensee: Greater Hartford Communications Corp. (acq 4-1-70). Net: ABC/C, NBC the Source, Westwood One. Rep: D & R Radio. Format: Rock/AOR. News staff 2; news progmg 10 hrs wkly. Target aud: 18-49; adults listening for newest rock/mix of classic rock. Spec prog: Entertainment/reviews 10 hrs, news/talk 10 hrs wkly. ■ Sy Dresner, pres; Milt Aninger, gen mgr, stn mgr & gen sls mgr; Ron Dresner, vp mktg, vp prom & prom mgr; Ted Sellers, progmg dir; Phil Marlowe, mus dir; Diane Novak, news dir; Art Ginsberg, vp engrg.

WRYM(AM)—See New Britain.

***WWUH(FM)**—July 15, 1968: 91.3 mhz; 1 kw. Ant 520 ft. TL: N41 46 26 W72 48 20. Stereo. Hrs opn: 24. Rebroadcasts WWEB(FM) Wallingford, 65%. Univ. of Hartford, Gray Ctr., 200 Bloomfield Ave. (06117). (203) 768-4703. Licensee: University of Hartford. Format: Jazz, folk, alternative. News progmg 2 hrs wkly. Target aud: General. Spec prog: Black 10 hrs, class 20 hrs, It 3 hrs, Portuguese 3 hrs, Sp 3 hrs, new age 4 hrs, pub affrs 20 hrs, bluegrass 7 hrs, Asian one hr, Pol 3 hrs, Lithuanian 2 hrs, jewish one hr, gay/lesbian one hr wkly. ■ John N. Ramsey, pres, gen mgr, engrg dir & chief engr; Art Green, opns dir; Susan Mullis, dev dir, mktg dir, prom dir & prom mgr; Tom Aparo, sls dir; Nick Vukasinovic, progmg dir; Gina Gunn, mus dir; Adena Chernosky, asst mus dir; Mike DeRosa, news dir.

West Haven

***WNHU(FM)**—1973: 88.7 mhz; 1.7 kw. Ant 150 ft. TL: N41 17 29 W72 57 40. Stereo. Hrs opn: 6 AM-2 AM. Maxcy Hall, 300 Orange Ave. (06516). (203) 934-8888. Licensee: University of New Haven Inc. Net: AP. Wash atty: Dow, Lohnes & Albertson. Format: Alternative, big band, black. News progmg 12 hrs wkly. Target aud: General. Spec prog: Jazz 12 hrs, Sp 12 hrs, folk 6 hrs, Irish 5 hrs, metal 9 hrs, class 18 hrs, gospel 5 hrs wkly. ■ Bruce Avery, gen mgr; Jennifer Ryan, stn mgr; Robin Andreoli, prom dir; Monica Moore, progmg dir; Sharon Walsh, mus dir; Jay McAnany, news dir; Dr. David Morris, pub affrs dir; Tom Osenkowsky, chief engr.

Westport

WEBE(FM)—Sept 1, 1962: 107.9 mhz; 50 kw. Ant 383 ft. TL: N41 10 14 W73 11 05. Stereo. Hrs opn: 24. 2 Lafayette Sq., Bridgeport (06604-6000). (203) 333-9108. FAX: (203) 333-9107. Licensee: WEBE Associates. Group owner: WIN Communications Inc. (acq 1987). Rep: Banner. Wash atty: Wiley, Rein & Fielding. Format: Adult contemp. News staff one; news progmg 3 hrs wkly. Target aud: 25-54; upscale females. Spec prog: Talk one hr wkly. ■ Vince Cremona, vp & gen mgr; Curtis Hansen, opns mgr & vp progmg; Jefferson H. Ketcham, vp sls; Megan O'Connell, prom dir; Tim Quinn, news dir; Ed Butler, chief engr. ■ Rates: $175; 175; 175; 75.

WMMM(AM)—Apr 15, 1959: 1260 khz; 1 kw-D, DA. TL: N41 07 44 W73 23 20. Stereo. Hrs opn: 6 AM-7 PM. Box 511, 163 Main St. (06881). (203) 226-9666; (203) 335-9185. FAX: (203) 227-2087. Licensee: Minuteman Broadcasting Inc. (acq 2-87). Net: USA. Rep: Roslin. Format: Oldies. News staff one; news progmg 6 hrs wkly. Target aud: 35 plus; white collar, college-educated, affluent. Spec prog: "Successful Living", It 7 hrs, Sp 7 hrs wkly. ■ Robert A. Graham, pres; Mark S. Graham, vp, progmg dir & news dir; Walter Broadhurst, gen mgr; Beth Olmsted, pub affrs dir; Cliff Mills, chief engr. ■ Rates: $30; 25; 30; na.

***WWPT(FM)**—1975: 90.3 mhz; 330 w. Ant 110 ft. TL: N41 10 19 W73 19 43. Stereo. Staples High School, 70 North Ave. (06880). (203) 226-9978; (203) 365-7669. Licensee: Board of Education, Town of Westport. Format: Free form. News progmg 2 hrs wkly. Target aud: 14-24; youth. Spec prog: Slovak 3 hrs wkly. ■ Stephanie Erman, gen mgr; Charles Bartonek, progmg dir; Erin Donavan, news dir.

Willimantic

***WECS(FM)**—Feb 6, 1982: 90.1 mhz; 421 w. Ant 380 ft. TL: N41 41 00 W72 12 59. 83 Windham St. (06226). (203) 456-2164. Licensee: Eastern Connecticut State University. Format: Div. Spec prog: Class 15 hrs, jazz 12 hrs wkly. ■ John L. Zatowski, gen mgr & chief engr.

WILI(AM)—Oct 1957: 1400 khz; 1 kw-U. TL: N41 42 54 W72 11 23. Stereo. Hrs opn: 24. Box 496 (06226); 720 Main St. (06226). (203) 456-1111. FAX: (203) 456-9501. Licensee: Nutmeg Broadcasting Co. (acq 5-59). Net: ABC/D, MBS, SMN, ABC/E. Wash atty: Miller & Miller. Format: Full svc adult contemp, news/talk. News staff 2; news progmg 10 hrs wkly. Target aud: 35 plus; local residents. Spec prog: Pol 2 hrs, Ukrainian one hr, relg 2 hrs wkly. ■ Michael C. Rice, pres; David M. Evan, vp & gen mgr; Colin K. Rice, vp opns; Donna M. Evan, gen sls mgr; Gordon Smith, prom dir; Wayne Norman, progmg dir & mus dir; Mike Morrissette, news dir; Craig Mellon, chief engr. ■ Rates: $35; 32; 35; 20.

WILI-FM—June 16, 1975: 98.3 mhz; 1.05 kw. Ant 525 ft. TL: N41 41 00 W72 12 59. Stereo. Hrs opn: 24. Prog sep from AM. (acq 11-24-85). Format: CHR. News staff one; news progmg 6 hrs wkly. Target aud: 22-44; college students, young married couples, young families. Spec prog: News interview one hr wkly. ■ Colin K. Rice, prom dir; David M. Evan, progmg dir & mus dir. ■ Rates: $36; 34; 36; 34.

Windsor

WKND(AM)—May 4, 1961: 1480 khz; 500 w-D, DA. TL: N41 51 10 W72 40 43. 544 Windsor Ave. (06095). (203) 688-6221. FAX: (203) 688-0711. Licensee: Hartcom Inc. (acq 7-12-81; $500,000 FTR 4-20-81). Format: Black contemp. News staff 2; news progmg 8 hrs wkly. Target aud: Greater Hartford's minority population. Spec prog: Jazz 3 hrs wkly. ■ John F. Merchant, pres; Marion Anderson, gen mgr; Eddie Jordan, prom mgr; James Johnson, progmg dir & mus dir; Lloyd Wimbush, news dir; M. Terry Smith, chief engr.

Delaware

Bethany Beach

WKHI(FM)—1974: 95.9 mhz; 6 kw. Ant 299 ft. TL: N38 30 06 W75 10 07 (CP: 6 kw, ant 328 ft.). Stereo. Box 758, 5700 Coastal Hwy., Ocean City, MD (21842). (410) 723-6505. FAX: (410) 723-6508. Licensee: R. Akin & Banking Services Corp. Group owner: Benchmark Communications Radio. Rep: Banner. Format: CHR. Target aud: 18-54. Spec prog: Reggae one hr, oldies 7 hrs wkly. ■ Chris Walus, gen mgr; Doug Weldon, stn mgr; Bonnie Jones, gen sls mgr; Jack Dawack, progmg dir; Danny Ocean, mus dir.

Christiana

***WXHL(FM)**—Not on air, target date unknown: 89.1 mhz; one w-H, 1.2 kw-V. Ant 67 ft. 179 Christiana-Stanton Rd., Newark (19702). Licensee: World Revivals Inc.

Dover

WDOV(AM)—1948: 1410 khz; 5.4 kw, DA-2. TL: N39 12 03 W75 33 13. Hrs opn: 24. Drawer B (19903); Denny's Rd. & N. Dupont Hwy. (19901). (302) 674-1410. FAX: (302) 674-8621. Licensee: Benchmark Radio Acquisiton Fund L.P. Group owner: Benchmark Communications Radio (acq 1993; with co-located FM; FTR 9-13-93). Net: Unistar, CNN. Rep: Torbet. Format: News/talk. News staff 2; news progmg 162 hrs wkly. Target aud: 25-54. ■ Christopher John Walus, gen mgr; Martha Burns, gen sls mgr; Marc Fisher, progmg dir; Dennis Jones, news dir; Bruce Rogers, pub affrs dir; Bob Reinhart, chief engr.

WDSD(FM)—Co-owned with WDOV(AM). 1956: 94.7 mhz; 50 kw. Ant 377 ft. TL: N39 12 03 W75 33 55. Stereo. Prog sep from AM. (302) 734-5816. (302) 674-2049. Net: Unistar. Rep: Torbet. Wash atty: Latham & Watlins. Format: Country. News staff 2; news progmg 8 hrs wkly. Target aud: general. ■ Sky Phillips, progmg dir; Donna Cavender, mus dir. ■ Rates: $85; 80; 85; 40.

WKEN(AM)—Aug 2, 1957: 1600 khz; 5 kw-D, 1 kw-N, DA-2. TL: N39 10 11 W75 33 13. Box 553 (19903-0553). Walker Rd. (19901). (302) 674-1234. FAX: (302) 674-5407. Licensee: First State Broadcasting Inc. (acq 9-20-90; FTR 10-8-90). Net: ABC/E. Format: Oldies. News staff 2. Spec prog: Black one hr wkly. ■ Joseph Farley, pres; Mike Mennit, gen mgr; John Vincent, progmg dir; Ray Santini, chief engr.

***WRTX(FM)**—Spring 1994: 91.7 mhz; 708 w-H. Ant 279 ft. TL: N39 11 30 W75 33 46. Stereo. Hrs opn: 24. 100 Ennenberg Hall, 13th & Diamond Sts., Philadelphia, PA (19122). (215) 204-8405. FAX: (215) 204-4870. Licensee: Temple Univ. of the Commonwealth. System of Higher Educ. Net: NPR, AP; Radio Pa. Wash atty: Arent, Fox, Kintner, Plotkin & Kahn. Format: Jazz. News staff 2; news progmg 15 hrs wkly. Target aud: 25-49. Spec prog: Caribbean 4 hrs, Sp 4 hrs wkly. ■ W. Theodore Eldredge, gen mgr; Tobias Poole, opns mgr & chief engr; Valorie Jarrell, dev dir & sls dir; Monika Morris, prom dir; Bill Clark, progmg dir; Kim Berry, mus dir; Audrey Foltz, news dir. ■ Rates: $75; 50; 75; 50.

Fenwick Island

WLBW(FM)—Not on air, target date unknown: 92.1 mhz; 3 kw. Ant 328 ft. 936 Heron Dr., Bethaney Beach (19930). Licensee: HVS Partners (acq 12-2-93; $130,000; FTR 12-20-93).

Georgetown

WSSR(AM)—June 23, 1951: 900 khz; 10 kw-D, one w-N, DA-1. TL: N38 42 31 W75 24 25. Stereo. Hrs opn: 6 AM-midnight. 701 N. Dupont Hwy. (19947). (302) 856-2567. FAX: (302) 856-6839. Licensee: Great Scott Broadcasting Ltd. Group owner: Great Scott Broadcasting. Wash atty: Cohn & Marks. Format: Big band. Target aud: 25-54; mature adults. Spec prog: Relg 6 hrs wkly. ■ Faye Scott, pres; Laura Mitchell, gen mgr.

WZBH(FM)—Co-owned with WSSR(AM). July 4, 1969: 93.5 mhz; 11.5 kw. Ant 550 ft. TL: N38 31 24 W75 17 55 (CP: 11.2 kw, ant 485 ft.). Hrs opn: 24. Prog sep from AM. Format: Adult oriented rock. Target aud: Adults; baby boomers. ■ Cory Gallant, prom mgr; Septh Michaels, progmg dir; Billy Warner, mus dir; Terry Dalton, chief engr.

Laurel

WDNO(FM)—Nov 19, 1991: 95.3 mhz; 6 kw. Ant 328 ft. TL: N38 30 12 W75 39 39. Stereo. Hrs opn: 24. 109 Central Ave. (19956). (302) 875-4444; (302) 875-3196. Licensee: Dennis O' Neal. Format: Adult contemp. News progmg 6 hrs wkly. Target aud: 25-49. ■ Dennis O'Neal, pres & gen mgr; David Parks, stn mgr, opns mgr, mktg dir, prom dir & progmg dir; Darryl Forsythe, sls dir; Chris Handy, mus dir & pub affrs dir; Bruce Blanchard, engrg dir. ■ Rates: $16; 14; 16; 12.

Lewes

WXJN(FM)—June 1, 1991: 105.9 mhz; 6 kw. Ant 341 ft. TL: N38 38 36 W75 13 00. Stereo. Hrs opn: 24. Box 193, 1550-F Savanna Rd. (19958). (302) 645-9008. FAX: (302) 645-9535. Licensee: Prettyman Broadcasting Co. c/o Radio Station WICO & WICO-FM (group owner; acq 7-28-92; $150,000; FTR 8-17-92). Format: Country. ■ Bruce Collier, gen mgr; Stevie Prettyman, rgnl sls mgr; Doug Hall, progmg dir; Kathy Linkous, news dir; Tom Ringer, engrg dir; Greg Michaels, chief engr. ■ Rates: $25; 20; 25; 18.

Milford

WAFL(FM)—May 19, 1973: 97.7 mhz; 6 kw. Ant 328 ft. TL: N38 55 39 W75 29 20. Stereo. Box 808, Milford-Harrington Rd. (19963). (302) 422-7575; (302) 424-1234. FAX: (302) 422-3069. Licensee: Prettyman Broadcasting Co. (group owner; acq 6-28-85; $1.5 million with co-located AM; FTR 5-20-85). Net: CBS, Westwood One. Rep: Katz & Powell. Wash atty: Dow, Lohnes & Albertson. Format: Adult contemp. News staff 2; news progmg 12 hrs wkly. Target aud: 18-54; active, affluent adults in central & southern Delaware. Spec prog: Southern gospel 2 hrs wkly. ■ Alex Kolobielski, vp & gen mgr; Kelly Suramey, prom mgr; Joyce Hooper, progmg dir & pub affrs dir; Jeff Farrow, mus dir; Joe Furghum, news dir; Tom Ringer, chief engr.

WYUS(AM)—Co-owned with WAFL(FM). 1953: 930 khz; 500 w-D, 100 w-N, DA-1. TL: N38 55 39 W75 29 20. Hrs opn: 6 AM-midnight. Prog sep from FM. (302) 422-2428. Net: CBS, American Urban. Format: Talk. News staff 2; news progmg 12 hrs wkly. Target aud: 35 plus; affluent adults in central & southern Delaware. Spec prog: Farm 2 hrs, relg 10 hrs, Sp 6 hrs wkly. ■ Joe Scott, progmg dir; A.J. Jackson, pub affrs dir.

WXPZ(FM)—Nov 5, 1990: 101.3 mhz; 3 kw. Ant 328 ft. TL: N38 51 21 W75 29 02. Stereo. Hrs opn: 24. Box K, County Rd. 626 (19963). (302) 424-1013. FAX: (302) 424-2358. Licensee: Samson Communications Inc. Net: CBN, Moody, USA. Wash atty: Gammon & Grange. Format: Adult contemp, relg. News staff one; news progmg 7 hrs wkly. Target aud: General; women aged 25-49. ■ William T. Sammons Jr., pres & gen mgr; Denise Harper, opns mgr, progmg dir & mus dir; Jay Waddell, gen sls mgr; Jason Sharp, prom dir; Terry Dalton, chief engr. ■ Rates: $22; 12; 14; 12.

WYUS(AM)—Listing follows WAFL(FM).

Newark

WNRK(AM)—Aug 17, 1964: 1260 khz; 1 kw-D, 42 w-N, DA-2. TL: N39 38 39 W75 41 33. Box 8152 (19714). (302) 737-5200. Licensee: ARC Broadcasting. (acq 10-8-84; $500,000; FTR 7-16-84). Net: MBS, AP. Format: MOR. ■ Alfred R. Campagnone, pres & gen mgr; Jim Hicks, opns mgr; Tim Qualles, gen sls mgr; Dave Schmidt, chief engr.

***WVUD(FM)**—Oct 4, 1976: 91.3 mhz; 1 kw. Ant 135 ft. TL: N39 41 26 W75 45 23. Stereo. Univ. of Delaware, Perkins Student Center (19716). (302) 831-2701. Licensee: University of Delaware. Net: AP. Format: Progsv, div, educ. News progmg 2 hrs wkly. Target aud: General. Spec prog: Class 10 hrs, Black 10 hrs, jazz 15 hrs, folk 15 hrs, gospel 2 hrs, big band 3 hrs, bluegrass 5 hrs, oldies 6 hrs, Sp 2 hrs, nostalgia one hr wkly. ■ Chuck Tarver, stn mgr; Rich McGuire, chief engr.

Ocean View

WRKE(FM)—Jan 12, 1986: 101.7 mhz; 3 kw. Ant 328 ft. TL: N38 29 20 W75 12 01. Stereo. Rt. One, Box 24 (19970). (302) 539-2600. FAX: (302) 539-5815. Licensee: Q-Tone Broadcasting Corp. (acq 12-13-88; $1.29 million; FTR 1-23-89). Net: NBC. Format: Top-40. ■ Tony Quartarone, vp & gen mgr; Janet Mena, opns mgr; Manuel Mena, mus dir; Jim Morgan, news dir; John Bisset, chief engr.

Rehoboth Beach

WGMD(FM)—Sept 21, 1975: 92.7 mhz; 3 kw. Ant 300 ft. TL: N38 42 05 W75 11 58. Stereo. Hrs opn: 24. No. 288, County Rd., Lewes (19958); Box 530 (19971). (302) 945-2050. FAX: (302) 945-3781. Licensee: Resort Broadcasting Co. (acq 7-25-80). Format: Adult contemp, news/talk. News staff 2; news progmg 16 hrs wkly. Target aud: 35 plus. Spec prog: Big band 8 hrs, farm 2 hrs, jazz 2 hrs, relg 2 hrs wkly. ■ Marie Moulinier, gen sls mgr, prom dir & adv dir; Rich Hancock, progmg dir, mus dir & news dir; Art Curley, pub affrs dir.

Seaford

WECY(AM)—1955: 1280 khz; 1 kw-D, 250 w-N. TL: N38 37 03 W75 35 09 (CP: 840 w-D, 211 w-N). 1039 S. Dual Highway (19973). (302) 629-6636. FAX: (302) 628-0983. Licensee: South Jersey Radio Inc. (acq 8-1-91). Net: Unistar, CNN. Format: Hybred AC. News staff 2; news progmg 7 hrs wkly. Target aud: 18-49; active, affluent. Spec prog: Cruisin' with the Classics 6 hrs wkly. ■ Howard Green, pres; Frank Bradley, gen mgr & gen sls mgr; Bill Grayston, progmg dir & pub affrs dir; John Rogers, mus dir; Dave Layton, news dir; Mark Moss, engrg dir. ■ Rates: $24; 22; 24; 21.

WECY-FM—February 1972: 98.3 mhz; 3 kw. Ant 328 ft. TL: N38 36 47 W75 35 12. Stereo. Prog dups AM 100%.

Selbyville

WSBL(FM)—March 1993: 97.9 mhz; 3 kw. Ant 328 ft. TL: N38 25 20 W75 08 23. Hrs opn: 24. Box 379, 55 W. Church St. (19975-0379). (302) 436-9725. FAX: (302) 436-9726. Licensee: Anchor Broadcasting Ltd. (group owner; acq 1-25-91; FTR 4-8-91). Wash atty: Cohen/Berfield. Format: Hot country. News progmg one hr wkly. Target aud: 25-40; seasonal, beach residents & local urban/farm. ■ Herman F. Stamps, CEO & mktg dir; Crystal Layton, stn mgr, sls dir & gen sls mgr; Bruce Blanchard, chief opns; Ken Gogh, mus dir; Greg Davis, pub affrs dir. ■ Rates: $25; 25; 25; 25.

Smyrna

WYHH(FM)—1993: 92.9 mhz; 1.7 kw. Ant 377 ft. TL: N39 16 08 W75 31 28. Rebroadcasts WDOV(AM) Dover 100%. Drawer B, c/o Radio Station WDOV, Dover (19903). (302) 674-1410. Licensee: Kent County Radio L.P. Format: News/talk. ■ Guy Vanderlek, gen mgr.

Wilmington

WDEL(AM)—1922: 1150 khz; 5 kw-U, DA-2. TL: N39 48 54 W75 31 47. Stereo. Hrs opn: 24. Box 7492, 2727 Shipley Road (19803). (302) 478-2700. FAX: (302) 478-0100. Licensee: Delmarva Broadcasting Co. Inc. (acq 9-12-89). Net: AP, Wall Street, Westwood One, CNN, Unistar. Rep: Eastman. Wash atty: Hogan & Hartson. Format: News/talk. News staff 10; news progmg 53 hrs wkly. Target aud: 25 plus. Spec prog: Farm one hr wkly. ■ C. Robert Taylor, CEO & pres; Julian "Pete" H. Booker, vp & gen mgr; Bob Mercer, opns mgr, progmg dir & news dir; Cynthia Morgan, gen sls mgr; Kate String, prom mgr; Carlotta Bradley, pub affrs dir; George Moyer, chief engr.

WSTW(FM)—Co-owned with WDEL(AM). 1950: 93.7 mhz; 50 kw. Ant 490 ft. TL: N39 48 57 W75 31 31. Stereo. Hrs opn: 24. Prog sep from AM. Net: AP. Format: Hot adult contemp. News staff 4; news progmg 20 hrs wkly. Target aud: 25-54. Spec prog: Relg 2 hrs, public affrs one hr wkly. ■ Mike Sommers, progmg dir; Mike Rossi, mus dir.

WILM(AM)—Oct 1, 1923: 1450 khz; 1 kw-U. TL: N39 43 46 W75 33 07. Hrs opn: 24. Box 1990 (19899); 1215 French St. (19801). (302) 656-9800. FAX: (302) 655-1450. Licensee: Delaware Broadcasting Co. (acq 1949). Net: CBS, MBS, Wall Street. Rep: Savalli. Format: News, talk & info. News staff 25; news progmg 168 hrs wkly. Target aud: 25 plus. ■ Sally V. Hawkins, pres & gen mgr; E.B. Hawkins, exec vp, vp sls & gen sls mgr; Allan R. Loudell, progmg mgr; Fred W. Hosier, news dir; John Watson, pub affrs dir; Larry Radka, chief engr.

WJBR-FM—January 1957: 99.5 mhz; 50 kw. Ant 499 ft. TL: N39 50 03 W75 31 25. Stereo. Hrs opn: 24. Box 7230 (19810); 3001 Philadelphia Pike, Claymont (19703). (302) 791-4110. FAX: (302) 791-9669. Licensee: CRB Broadcasting of Delaware Inc. Group owner: CRB Broadcasting Corp. (acq 9-7-85). Net: Unistar. Rep: Katz. Wash atty: Fisher, Wayland, Cooper & Leader. Format: Adult contemp. News staff 2. Target aud: 25-54. ■ Henry Stein, CEO; Bruce Freidman, CFO; Jay Sterin, vp & gen mgr; Doug Welldon, opns mgr; Greg Sweet, Ken Brown, gen sls mgrs; Michael Waite, prom mgr, progmg dir & mus dir; Valorie Mack, news dir; Joe Robinson, pub affrs dir.

WJBR(AM)—Apr 21, 1947: 1290 khz; 2.5 kw-U. TL: N39 44 03 W75 31 44. Hrs opn: 24. Dups FM 100%. (acq 6-85; $4.3 million with co-located FM; FTR 6-17-85).

WJIC(AM)—(Salem, N.J.). Sept 1, 1966: 1510 khz; 2.5 kw-D, DA. TL: N39 34 58 W75 27 39. Box 132, 81 Woodstown Rd., Salem, NJ (08079). (609) 935-1510. FAX: (609) 935-1515. Licensee: PJF Broadcasting Inc. (acq 7-1-78). Net: ABC/C. Format: C&W, news/talk. News staff 2; news progmg 3 hrs wkly. Target aud: 18-54 plus. ■ Gloria Jennings, pres & gen mgr; Benjamin Ferguson, vp & chief engr; Cathy Townsend, prom mgr; Adam Gaynor, progmg dir; Gene Ryan, news dir. ■ Rates: $16; 12; 14; na.

***WMPH(FM)**—October 1969: 91.7 mhz; 100 w. Ant 143 ft. TL: N39 46 23 W75 30 25. Stereo. Hrs opn: 6 AM-11 PM. 5201 Washington St. Ext. (19809). (302) 762-7125; (302) 762-7199. FAX: (302) 762-7042. Licensee: Brandywine School District. Format: Rock, dance, news/talk. News staff one; news progmg 2 hrs wkly. Target aud: 17-30; high school & college students. Spec prog: Relg 4 hrs wkly. ■ Dr. Carl Smith, CEO; Jack Vinokur, chmn; Tom Lapinski, pres; Clint Dantinne, gen mgr, gen sls mgr & prom mgr; John Whitton, stn mgr & mktg mgr; Dave Bradley, opns dir; Rob Fioretti Jr., opns mgr, progmg dir & mus dir; Larry Nicholson, dev dir; Steve Welch, news dir & pub affrs dir; Warren Racine, chief engr.

WSTW(FM)—Listing follows WDEL(AM).

District of Columbia

Washington

WABS(AM)—See Arlington, Va.

***WAMU(FM)**—Oct 23, 1961: 88.5 mhz; 50 kw. Ant 500 ft. TL: N38 56 09 W77 05 33. Stereo. Hrs opn: 24. The American Univ., 4400 Massachusetts Ave. N.W. (20016-8082). (202) 885-1030. Licensee: American Univ. Net: NPR, APR. Format: News/talk, bluegrass. News staff 4; news progmg 39 hrs wkly. Target aud: 25-54. Spec prog: Vintage radio 4 hrs, country 4 hrs, jazz 5 hrs wkly. ■ F. Kim Hodgson, gen mgr; Kay Tuttle, dev dir; Laura Forman, prom dir; Steve Palmer, progmg dir; William Troop, news dir; Mike Byrnes, chief engr.

WARW(FM)—See Bethesda, Md.

WASH(FM)—Listing follows WTOP(AM).

WAVA(FM)—(Arlington, Va.). Aug 1, 1948: 105.1 mhz; 50 kw. Ant 500 ft. TL: N38 53 44 W77 08 04 (CP: 41 kw, ant 541 ft.). Stereo. 5232 Lee Hwy., Arlington, VA (22207). (703) 534-0320. Licensee: Beltway Media Partners (acq 2-13-92; $20 million; FTR 11-18-91). Net: Unistar. Wash atty: Fletcher, Heald & Hildreth. Format: Adult contemp Christian, talk. News staff 2; news progmg 4 hrs wkly. Target aud: 25-54. ■ David Ruleman, gen mgr; Tom Moyer, gen sls mgr; Heidi Lesko, prom mgr; Fred Gleason, chief engr.

WBIG-FM—1948: 100.3 mhz; 40 kw-H, 38 kw-V. Ant 323 ft. TL: N38 57 17 W77 00 17 (CP: 36 kw, ant 574 ft., TL: N38 53 44 W77 08 04). Stereo. 11300 Rockville Pike (20852). (301) 468-1800. FAX: (301) 468-0491. Licensee: Radio 100 of Maryland L.P. Group owner: Colfax Communications Inc. (acq 3-9-93; $19.5 million; FTR 3-29-93). Net: ABC/FM. Rep: McGavren Guild. Format: Oldies. News staff one; news progmg one hr wkly. Target aud: 25-49; Professional, college, upscale. ■ Steve Goldstein, pres; Catherine Maloy, gen mgr.

WCPT(AM)—(Alexandria, Va.). Dec 10, 1945: 730 khz; 5 kw-D, 20 w-N. TL: N38 44 41 W77 05 57. Stereo. 510 King St., Alexandria, VA (22314). (703) 683-3000. FAX: (703) 549-3960. Licensee: Viacom Broadcasting Inc.

(group owner; acq 10-21-93; with co-located FM; FTR 11-8-93). Net: Unistar. Rep: Group W. Wash atty: Steven & Hildebrand. Format: CNN Headline News. News staff 2; news progmg 160 hrs wkly. Target aud: 25-54. Spec prog: Jewish one hr wkly. ■ Cordel Weaver, vp; William Sherard, Charlie Ochs, gen mgrs; Jerry Lyons, opns mgr; Mark Lapidus, mktg dir; Steve Kosbav, progmg dir; Tom Grooms, news dir; John Diamantis, Tom Shadliek, chiefs engr.

WCXR-FM—(Woodbridge, Va.). Co-owned with WCPT(AM). Dec 25, 1958: 105.9 mhz; 28 kw. Ant 648 ft. TL: N38 52 28 W77 13 24. Stereo. Prog sep from AM. Format: Classic rock. ■ Val Parker, prom mgr.

WCTN(AM)—See Potomac-Cabin John, Md.

WCXR-FM—Listing follows WCPT(AM).

WDCT(AM)—See Fairfax, Va.

***WDCU(FM)**—May 8, 1982: 90.1 mhz; 6.8 kw. Ant 450 ft. TL: N38 57 44 W77 01 36 (CP: 50 kw). Stereo. Hrs opn: 24. Bldg. 38, Rm. A-03, 4200 Connecticut Ave. N.W. (20008). (202) 282-7588. FAX: (202) 282-3096. Licensee: Univ of District of Columbia (acq 3-80; FTR 3-25-80). Net: NPR. Format: Jazz. Target aud: 25-44; upscale. Spec prog: Sp 2 hrs, African/Caribbean 2 hrs, oldies 3 hrs, blues 2 hrs, relg 3 hrs, gospel 11 hrs wkly. ■ Edith B. Smith, gen mgr; Vickie Johnson, mktg dir; Debbie A. Kwei, prom mgr; Wylie Rollins, progmg dir; Ted Sims, chief engr.

***WETA-FM**—Apr 19, 1970: 90.9 mhz; 75 kw. Ant 448 ft. TL: N38 53 30 W77 07 55. Stereo. Hrs opn: 24. 3700 S. Four Mile Run, Arlington, VA (22206-2304); Box 2626, Washington, DC (20013). (703) 998-2790. Licensee: Greater Washington Educational Telecommunications Assn. Inc. Net: NPR, APR. Wash atty: Dow, Lohnes & Albertson. Format: Class, news. News progmg 15 hrs wkly. Target aud: General; educated adults. Spec prog: Folk 7 hrs wkly. ■ Sharon Rockerfeller, CEO; David Maxwell, chmn; Sharon Rockefeller, pres; Lin Lloyd, CFO; Neil Mahrer, exec vp; Tom Livingston, sr vp & gen mgr; Cynthia Cotton, opns mgr; Mike Soper, vp dev; Lin Terrell, dev dir; Elise Adde, vp prom; Mary Stewart, prom mgr; Marilyn Cooley, mus dir; Joe Davis, chief engr. ■ WETA-TV affil.

WFAX(AM)—(Falls Church, Va.). September 1948: 1220 khz; 5 kw-D, 100 w-N. TL: N38 52 47 W77 10 18. Hrs opn: 6 AM-8:30 PM. 161-B Hillwood Ave., Falls Church, VA (22046-2983). (703) 532-1220. FAX: (703) 533-7572. Licensee: Newcomb Broadcasting Corp. Format: Relg. News staff one; news progmg 3 hrs wkly. Target aud: 34-54. Spec prog: Black 3 hrs, It one hr, Sp one hr, Greek one hr wkly. ■ Doris N. Newcomb, pres; Mitchell A. Miller, gen mgr & gen sls mgr; Henry Stewart, prom mgr & chief engr; Roy C. Martin, progmg dir & mus dir; R.C. Woolfenden, news dir; Sue Thompson, pub affrs dir. ■ Rates: $25; 25; 25; na.

WGAY(FM)—Listing follows WWRC(AM).

WGMS-FM—September 1948: 103.5 mhz; 44 kw. Ant 518 ft. TL: N38 56 09 W77 05 33. Stereo. Suite #905, 11300 Rockville Pike, Rockville, MD (20852). (301) 468-1800. FAX: (301) 468-0491. Licensee: Classical Acquisition Partnership. Group owner: Colfax Communications Inc. Net: Mutual News. Rep: D & R Radio. Format: Class. Target aud: Adults 25-54; affluent, educated, young professionals. ■ Catherine Meloy, gen mgr; Amy Michaels, gen sls mgr; Michele Abballe, mktg dir; Susan Dedeyan, prom dir; Mary Kading, progmg dir; Jim Allison, mus dir; Chil Leyh, chief engr.

***WGTS-FM**—See Takoma Park, Md.

WHUR-FM—Dec 10, 1971: 96.3 mhz; 24 kw. Ant 669 ft. TL: N38 57 01 W77 04 47. Stereo. Hrs opn: 24. 529 Bryant St. N.W. (20059). (202) 806-3500. FAX: (202) 806-3522. Licensee: Howard University Bd. of Trustees. Net: CBS Spectrum. Rep: D & R Radio. Format: Urban adult contemporary. News staff 3; news progmg 7 hrs wkly. Target aud: 25-44. Spec prog: Gospel 14 hrs, Caribbean 6 hrs wkly. ■ Dr. Franklyn G. Jenifer, pres; Millard J. Watkins III, gen mgr; Ellis Terry, opns mgr; Jeanette Tyce, gen sls mgr; Alaina Moss, mktg dir & prom dir; Hector Hannibal, progmg dir; Pamela Hall, mus dir; John Thomas, chief engr.

WILC(AM)—See Laurel, Md.

WINX(AM)—See Rockville, Md.

WJFK-FM—(Manassas, Va.). April 8, 1968: 106.7 mhz; 22.5 kw-H, 18.5 kw-V. Ant 731 ft. TL: N38 52 28 W77 13 24 (CP: 22 kw, ant 745 ft.). Stereo. Hrs opn: 24. Box 3649, Georgetown Station, Washington, DC (20007). (703) 691-1900. FAX: (703) 385-0189. Licensee: Infinity Broadcasting of Washington D.C. Inc. Group owner: Infinity Broadcasting Corp. (acq 10-86; $13 million; FTR 9-22-86). Net: ABC/R, NBC the Source. Rep: Torbet. Format: Personality, jazz. News staff 2; news progmg 3 hrs wkly. Target aud: men 18 plus. ■ Ken Stevens, gen mgr; Jeremy Coleman, opns mgr; Alan Leinwand, gen sls mgr; Jeff Shrinsky, natl sls mgr; Tammy Sacks, prom dir; Cerphe Colwell, progmg dir; Buzz Burbank, news dir; Mike Elston, pub affrs dir; Dan Ryson, chief engr.

WKDL(AM)—(Silver Spring, Md.). Dec 7, 1946: 1050 khz; 1 kw-D, 43 w-N. TL: N39 00 50 W77 01 46. Hrs opn: 24. Suite 100, 8555 16th St., Silver Spring, MD (20910). (301) 588-1050. FAX: (301) 587-9267. Licensee: Capital Kids' Radio Co. (acq 12-28-92; $650,000; FTR 1-25-93). Net: Children's Radio Net. Format: Children's music & features. News progmg 4 hrs wkly. Target aud: 4-12; children & parents. ■ Virginia Carson, CEO; Lawrence Kessner, pres; David D. Eppler, sr vp; Joan Schultz, gen mgr; Michael Kelly, opns mgr; Charlene Meyer, prom dir; Kenneth Curtis, progmg dir. ■ Rates: $75; 50; 75; 50.

WKYS(FM)—Aug 1, 1947: 93.9 mhz; 24 kw. Ant 707 ft. TL: N38 56 24 W77 04 54. Stereo. Hrs opn: 24. 4001 Nebraska Ave. N.W. (20016). (202) 686-9300. FAX: (202) 686-2028. Licensee: Albimar Communications (acq 12-10-88). Rep: D & R Radio. Wash atty: Latham & Watkins. Format: Urban contemp. Target aud: 25-54; upscale Black adults. ■ Skip Finley, CEO, pres & gen mgr; Rick Boland, CFO; Mary Ellen Nunes, vp; Jeffrey Myers, gen sls mgr; Jill Godfrey, natl sls mgr; Bart Horton, rgnl sls mgr; Peggy Miley, mktg dir; Scott Jantzen, prom dir; Barbara Prieto, progmg dir; John Irving, news dir; Alma Brown, pub affrs dir; Bob Clinton, chief engr.

WMAL(AM)—Oct 12, 1925: 630 khz; 5 kw-U, DA-2. TL: N39 00 55 W77 08 30. Stereo. 4400 Jennifer St. N.W. (20015). (202) 686-3100. Licensee: WMAL Inc. Group owner: Capital Cities/ABC Broadcast Group (acq 3-5-77). Net: ABC/I. Rep: Katz. Format: News/talk. ■ Tom Bresnahan, pres & gen mgr; Jim Gallant, opns mgr; Zemira Jones, gen sls mgr; Amy Rosen, prom mgr; John Butler, news dir; Don Culp, chief engr.

WRQX(FM)—Co-owned with WMAL(AM). May 15, 1948: 107.3 mhz; 34 kw. Ant 602 ft. TL: N38 57 01 W77 04 47. Stereo. Prog sep from AM. Net: ABC/C. Format: Hot adult contemp. ■ Jim Robinson, pres & gen mgr; Jeff Boden, gen sls mgr; John Quinn, prom mgr; Lorrin Palagi, progmg dir; Linda Silver, mus dir; Barbara Britt, news dir.

WMDO(AM)—See Wheaton, Md.

WMMJ(FM)—See Bethesda, Md.

WMOM(AM)—See La Plata, Md.

WMZQ(AM)—See Arlington, Va.

WMZQ-FM—Sept 1968: 98.7 mhz; 50 kw. Ant 490 ft. TL: N38 53 12 W77 12 05. Stereo. Hrs opn: 24. 5513 Connecticut Ave. N.W. (20015). (202) 362-8330. FAX: (202) 966-6279. Licensee: Viacom Broadcasting Inc. (group owner; acq 3-28-90). Rep: Christal. Format: C&W. News staff one. Target aud: 25-54. ■ Charlie Ochs, vp & gen mgr; Gary McCartie, opns mgr & progmg dir; Nancy Bryant, gen sls mgr; Vasco Bramao, natl sls mgr; Janie Floyd, prom mgr; Mac Daniels, mus dir; Kim Leslie, news dir & pub affrs dir; Thomas Shedlick, chief engr.

WNTL(AM)—See Indian Head, Md.

WOL(AM)—1924: 1450 khz; 1 kw-U. TL: N38 54 16 W77 00 25. 400 H St. N.E. (20002). (202) 675-4800. Licensee: Almic Broadcasting Inc. (acq 10-3-80). Net: ABC/E. Format: Contemporary, Jazz. Spec prog: Talk 20 hrs wkly. ■ Alfred Liggins, pres; Ed Turner, gen mgr; Tony Washington, gen sls mgr; Emma O'Neal, prom dir; Lawrence Jones, progmg dir; Jim Allen, news dir; Carl Gorham, chief engr.

***WPFW(FM)**—Feb 28, 1977: 89.3 mhz; 50 kw. Ant 410 ft. TL: N38 56 09 W77 05 33. Stereo. Hrs opn: 24. 702 H St. N.W. (20001-3794). (202) 783-3100. FAX: (202) 783-3106. Licensee: Pacifica Foundation Inc. Group owner: Pacifica Radio. Wash atty: Haley, Bader & Potts. Format: Jazz, news/talk, world music. News progmg 7 hrs wkly. Target aud: 25-55. Spec prog: Comedy 3 hrs, oldies 3 hrs, youth issues 2 hrs, women 3 hrs, poetry one hr wkly. ■ Phil Watson, gen mgr; Askia Muhammad, news dir.

WPGC(AM)—See Morningside, Md.

WPGC-FM—See Morningside, Md.

WRQX(FM)—Listing follows WMAL(AM).

WTEM(AM)—See Bethesda, Md.

WTOP(AM)—Sept 25, 1926: 1500 khz; 50 kw-U, DA-2. TL: N39 02 30 W77 02 45. 3400 Idaho Ave. N.W. (20016). (202) 895-5000. FAX: (202) 895-5140. Licensee: Washington Radio Associates L.P. Group owner: Chase Communications Inc. (acq 1-6-92; grpsl; FTR 2-19-90). Net: CBS. Rep: Group W. Wash atty: Latham & Watkins. Format: All news. News staff 25. Target aud: General. ■ R. Thomas McKinley, exec vp & gen mgr; Mark O'Brien, sls dir; Melissa Huston, natl sls mgr; Terry Lowe-Edwards, prom dir; Hal Brown, progmg dir & news dir; Melvin Chase, pub affrs dir; David Garner, chief engr.

WASH(FM)—Co-owned with WTOP(AM). 1948: 97.1 mhz; 26 kw. Ant 690 ft. TL: N38 57 21 W77 04 57. Stereo. Prog sep from AM. (202) 895-5080. FAX: (202) 895-5105. Rep: Group W. Format: Adult contemp. News staff one. Target aud: General. ■ Steve Streit, progmg dir; Kate Ryan, news dir; Dave Garner, chief engr.

WUST(AM)—1949: 1120 khz; 20 kw-D, 3 kw-CH. TL: N38 54 15 W77 09 54. 2131 Crimmins Ln., Falls Church, VA (22043). (703) 532-0400. FAX: (703) 532-5033. Licensee: New World Radio Inc. (acq 10-26-92; $1.15 million; FTR 8-24-92). Format: Multi-cultural, informational. ■ Allen Pendleton, gen mgr; Ray Andrewson, opns mgr.

WWDC(AM)—1941: 1260 khz; 5 kw-U, DA-2. TL: N38 59 59 W77 03 27. 8750 Brookville Rd., Silver Spring, MD (20910-1801). (301) 587-7100. FAX: (301) 587-0225. Licensee: Capitol Broadcasting Co. (acq 9-75). Net: Unistar. Rep: Christal. Format: Big band, sports. ■ Goff Lebhar, pres & gen mgr; Jeff Hedges, gen sls mgr; Shryl Whighan, prom mgr; Dave Brown, progmg dir; Bill Scanlon, mus dir; Joe Doniger, news dir; Pat Malley, chief engr.

WWDC-FM—1947: 101.1 mhz; 22.5 kw. Ant 760 ft. TL: N38 59 59 W77 03 27. Stereo. Prog sep from AM. Format: Rock/AOR. ■ Jeff Hedges, stn mgr; Dave Brown, progmg dir.

WWRC(AM)—Aug 1, 1923: 980 khz; 50 kw-D, 5 kw-N, DA-2. TL: N38 57 43 W76 58 24. WRC World Bldg., 8121 Georgia Ave, Silver Spring, MD (20910). (301) 587-4900. FAX: (301) 589-9461. Licensee: Greater Washington Radio Inc. Group owner: Greater Media Inc. (acq 9-1-84; $3.6 million; FTR 7-30-84). Net: NBC. Rep: Major Mkt. Format: Talk. News staff 5; news progmg 16 hrs wkly. Target aud: 25-54. ■ Frank Kabela, pres; Dick Rakovan, gen mgr; Peter Laufer, opns mgr; Diane Earley, natl sls mgr; Dick Eury (local), rgnl sls mgr; George Papagiannis, progmg dir; Peter Laufon, news dir; Kevin McNamara, chief engr.

WGAY(FM)—Co-owned with WWRC(AM). 1960: 99.5 mhz; 21 kw. Ant 780 ft. TL: N38 57 49 W77 06 18 (CP: 21.8 kw, ant 751 ft.). Prog sep from AM. Format: Easy lstng/btfl music. Target aud: 25-54. ■ Bob Moke, progmg dir.

WXTR-FM—See Waldorf, Md.

WYCB(AM)—1978: 1340 khz; 1 kw-U. TL: N38 55 04 W77 01 27 (CP: TL: N38 51 50 W76 54 38). Suite 1030, 1025 Vermont Ave., N.W. (20005). (202) 737-6400. FAX: (202) 638-3027. Licensee: Broadcast Holdings Inc. (acq 3-8-90; $150,000; FTR 4-2-90). Net: American Urban. Format: Contemp, gospel. ■ Karen Jackson, gen mgr & gen sls mgr; Winston Chaney, progmg dir & news dir; Roger Default, chief engr.

Florida

LAUREN A. COLBY
301-663-1086
COMMUNICATIONS ATTORNEY
Special Attention to Difficult Cases

Apalachicola

WOYS(FM)—July 1988: 100.9 mhz; 5.4 kw. Ant 344 ft. TL: N29 43 57 W84 53 24. Box 527, Eastpoint (32328). (904) 670-8450. Licensee: Richard L. Plessinger Sr. Group owner: Plessinger Radio Group (R.L. Plessinger Holding Co.) (acq 11-16-89; $10,000; FTR 12-19-88). Net: ABC/E. Format: Adult contemp. News staff one. Target aud: General. ■ Richard L. Plessinger Sr., gen mgr; Michael Allen, prom mgr; Jerry Proctor, progmg dir; Ted Mosteller, chief engr.

Apopka

WTLN(AM)—May 4, 1964: 1520 khz; 5 kw-D, DA. TL: N28 39 08 W81 29 40. Box 607000, Orlando (32860-7000). 400 W. Lake Brantley, Altamonte Springs (32714). (407) 682-9494. FAX: (407) 682-7005. Licensee: Alton Rainbow Corp. Format: Relg, Southern Gospel. ■ Thomas H. Moffit Sr., pres; Thomas H. Moffit Jr., gen mgr & gen sls mgr; William J. Bloomer III, opns mgr; Dean O'Neal, mus dir; Jim Hoge, chief engr.

WTLN-FM—Sept 1, 1968: 95.3 mhz; 6 kw. Ant 315 ft. TL: N28 39 08 W81 29 40. Prog sep from AM. (Acq 6-18-92). Format: Relg, MOR. Spec prog: Talk 17 hrs wkly.

Arcadia

WKGF(AM)—Sept 3, 1955: 1480 khz; 1 kw-D, 155 w-N. TL: N27 13 43 W81 51 28. Hrs opn: 6 AM midnight. Box 632, 201 W. Ashbury St. (33821). (813) 494-2427; (813) 494-2525. FAX: (813) 494-9444. Licensee: Dakos Broadcasting (acq 1993). Net: USA. Format: Contemp Christian. Target aud: 24-44; upscale adults. Spec prog: Black 7 hrs, gospel 5 hrs wkly. ■ Dr. William N. Dakos, pres; G.W. "Gibby" Sullivan, gen mgr, stn mgr, gen sls mgr, prom mgr & progmg dir; Jeri Sullivan, mus dir; Dick Parrish, chief engr. ■ Rates: $7.25; 6.85; 7.25; 6.50.

WKGF-FM—March 7, 1977: 98.3 mhz; 2 kw. Ant 400 ft. TL: N27 11 01 W81 56 57 (CP: 25 kw). Stereo. Dups AM 100%. Box 794, 201 W. Asbury St. (33821). ■ Rates: Same as AM.

Atlantic Beach

WFYV-FM—March 10, 1980: 104.5 mhz; 100 kw. Ant 984 ft. TL: N30 16 34 W81 33 53. Stereo. 9090 Hogan Rd., Jacksonville (32216). (904) 641-1055. FAX: (904) 641-3297. Licensee: Evergreen Media Corp. of Atlantic Beach Group owner: Evergreen Media Corp. (acq 2-18-93; $8 million; FTR 3-8-93). Net: AP. Rep: McGavren Guild. Format: AOR. News staff one; news progmg 3 hrs wkly. Target aud: 18-49; male oriented. ■ Mark Schartz, pres & gen mgr; Rich Rectanus, gen sls mgr; Carol Royer, prom mgr; Jim Knight, news dir.

WNCM(AM)—Jan 30, 1958: 1600 khz; 5 kw-D, 90 w-N. TL: N30 19 30 W81 25 42. 2361 Cortez Rd., Jacksonville (32246). (904) 641-9626. FAX: (904) 645-9626. Licensee: New Covenant Educational Ministries Inc. (acq 1-16-92; $27,500; FTR 2-10-92). Net: USA. Rep: Bennett. Format: Talk. Spec prog: Korean one hr wkly. ■ Wiley Tomlinson, pres; Calvin Grabau, gen mgr & progmg dir; Jerry Smith, chief engr.

Auburndale

WTWB(AM)—Oct 10, 1956: 1570 khz; 5 kw-D, TL: N28 04 32 W81 49 19. Box 7 (33823). (813) 967-1570. Licensee: WTWB Radio Station Inc. (acq 11-14-91). Net: ABC/E. Format: Southern gospel. ■ L.M. Hughey, pres; Richard W. Boyce, gen mgr, gen sls mgr & progmg dir; Dale Wade, mus dir & news dir; Mike Stukey, chief engr. ■ Rates: $5.50; 5.50; 5.50; na.

Avon Park

WKHF(AM)—Oct 1, 1970: 1390 khz; 1 kw-D, 770 w-N. TL: N27 37 08 W81 29 27. Hrs opn: 6 AM-10 PM. Box 632, Arcadia (33821). (813) 494-2427. Licensee: Pearl Lee (acq 7-92). Format: Contemp Christian. News staff 3; news progmg 12 hrs wkly. Target aud: 30-54; upscale adults. ■ G.W. "Gibby" Sullivan, gen mgr; James M. Fuchs, gen sls mgr; David Womack, prom mgr & news dir; Charles Castle, chief engr. ■ Rates: $7.25; 6.85; 7.25; 6.50.

WWOJ(FM)—August 1982: 106.3 mhz; 2.25 kw. Ant 370 ft. TL: N27 33 37 W81 29 36 (CP: 4.6 kw, ant 370 ft.). Stereo. 3750 U.S. 27 N., Sebring (33870). (813) 382-1063. FAX: (813) 382-1982. Licensee: Highlands Media Co. Inc. (acq 8-85; $300,000; FTR 5-20-85). Net: NBC. Wash atty: Leibowitz & Spencer. Format: Country. News staff 2; news progmg 7 hrs wkly. Target aud: 25 plus. Spec prog: Bluegrass 2 hrs, relg 3 hrs wkly. ■ James M. Johnson, pres & chief engr; Duane McConnell, vp; Karen Sasnow, stn mgr; John Meder, sls dir; J.J. Kale, progmg dir; Barry Foster, news dir.

Baker

*WTJT(FM)—May 1987: 90.1 mhz; 5 kw. Ant 253 ft. TL: N30 49 21 W86 42 41. Box 187 (32531). (904) 537-2009. FAX: (904) 537-4663. Licensee: Okaloosa Public Radio Inc. Net: USA. Format: Christian. ■ Robert Williamson, gen mgr; Randy Henry, chief engr.

Baldwin

WXQL(FM)—July 30, 1992: 105.7 mhz. Stereo. 3147 Waller St., Jacksonville (32205). (904) 387-2820. FAX: (904) 387-1705. Licensee: Peaches Broadcasting Ltd. ■ Fred Matthews, pres & gen mgr.

Bartow

WBAR(AM)—Sept 28, 1953: 1460 khz; 1 kw-D, 155 w-N. TL: N27 54 34 W81 51 29. Box 820, 1355 Maple Ave. (33830). (813) 533-9227. Licensee: WBAR Radio Inc. Group owner: J.R. Livesay Group (acq 9-1-79). Net: UPI. Format: Country, gospel. Target aud: General. ■ Ray Livesay, pres; Elmer White, gen mgr; Paul Rebmann, engrg mgr.

WWBF(AM)—Sept 16, 1969: 1130 khz; 2.5 kw-D, 500 w-N. TL: N27 54 34 W81 49 35. Stereo. Hrs opn: 24. 1130 Radio Rd. (33830). (813) 533-0744. FAX: (813) 533-8546. Licensee: Thomas N. Thornburg (acq 1-27-84; $220,000; FTR 2-6-84). Net: MBS; Fla. Net. Format: Oldies. News staff one; News progmg 10 hrs wkly. Target aud: 35-54; affluent adults. Spec prog: Sports. ■ Thomas N. Thornburg, pres, gen mgr & gen sls mgr; Susan E. Thornburg, stn mgr & pub affrs dir; Jeffrey A. Thornburg, progmg dir, mus dir & chief engr. ■ Rates: $10; 10; 10; 10.

Belle Glade

WSWN(AM)—Oct 7, 1947: 900 khz; 1 kw-D, 26 w-N. TL: N26 42 54 W80 40 58. Box 1505, 2001 State Rd. 715 (33430). (407) 996-2063. FAX: (407) 996-1852. Licensee: Seminole Broadcasting Co. (acq 1954). Net: ABC/C, Florida's Radio Net. Format: Relg, urban contemp, Black. Target aud: 25-54. ■ M.B. Rivers, pres; Vern Thacker, gen mgr; Phil Haire, gen sls mgr; Joe Fisher, progmg dir; Rick Rieke, chief engr.

WBGF(FM)—Co-owned with WSWN(AM). May 31, 1965: 93.5 mhz; 3 kw. Ant 285 ft. TL: N26 42 56 W80 40 58. Stereo. Prog sep from AM. Net: ABC. Format: Soft hits. News staff one. ■ Jim Tafuri, progmg dir.

Beverly Hills

WXOF(FM)—Not on air, target date unknown: 97.1 mhz; 2.5 kw. Ant 354 ft. TL: N28 53 38 W82 26 39. Box 880 (32665). Licensee: Heart of Citrus Inc.

Big Pine Key

WWUS(FM)—Sept 22, 1980: 104.7 mhz; 100 kw. Ant 443 ft. TL: N24 39 38 W81 25 10. Stereo. Hrs opn: 24. Box 183E, Rt. 5 (33043). (305) 872-9100. FAX: (305) 872-8930. Licensee: Crain Broadcasting Inc. (acq 1-11-85; $450,000; FTR 1-7-85). Net: CNN. Wash atty: Haley, Bader & Potts. Format: Adult contemp. News staff one. Target aud: 30-50. Spec prog: Island music 4 hrs wkly. ■ Rance Crain, pres; Bob Soos, gen mgr; Gene Michaels, stn mgr & chief engr; Chris Todd, prom mgr; Steve Miller, progmg dir; Bill Becker, news dir. ■ Rates: $15; 15; 15; 15.

Blountstown

WYBT(AM)—Sept 8, 1962: 1000 khz; 1 kw-D. TL: N30 27 15 W85 02 32. 269 Kelley (32424). (904) 674-5101. FAX: (904) 674-1586. Licensee: Blountstown Communications (acq 6-26-86; $103,000; FTR 4-14-86). Format: Classic country. Spec prog: Gospel & relg 15 hrs wkly. ■ Harry S. Hagen, pres; Kathy Hagen, progmg dir.

WPHK(FM)—Co-owned with WYBT(AM). Dec 18, 1968: 102.3 mhz; 3 kw. Ant 185 ft. TL: N30 27 15 W85 02 32. Stereo. Prog sep from AM. Format: Adult contemp. Spec prog: Black 12 hrs wkly. ■ Harry S. Hagen, gen mgr.

Boca Raton

WKIS(FM)—Licensed to Boca Raton. See Miami.

WSBR(AM)—April 1965: 740 khz; 2.5 kw-D, 940 w-N, DA-2. TL: N26 20 06 W80 15 55. Suite 200, 6699 N. Federal Hwy. (33487). (407) 997-0074. FAX: (407) 997-0476. Licensee: SMH Broadcasting. Net: ABC/E, CBS. Format: Business news/talk, sports. ■ Bob Morensy, gen mgr; Laura Delosreyes, stn mgr; Arthur Hendragon, opns mgr; Bill Wheatley, gen sls mgr; Rick Rieke, chief engr.

Bonifay

WTBB(FM)—Apr 23, 1983: 97.7 mhz; 3 kw. Ant 298 ft. TL: N30 41 57 W85 37 17 (CP: 91 kw, ant 1,006 ft.). Suite 21, 8317 W. Hwy 98, Panama City (32407). (904) 233-6606. FAX: (904) 233-1541. Licensee: Group M. Communications Inc. (acq 8-20-92; $682,405; FTR 9-14-92). Format: Adult contemp. ■ Christopher Murray, stn mgr.

Bonita Springs

WRXK-FM—Sept 1, 1974: 96.1 mhz; 100 kw. Ant 1,122 ft. TL: N26 26 53 W81 48 54. Stereo. Box 9600, Estero (33928). (813) 495-2100. FAX: (813) 992-8165. Licen-

see: Beasley Broadcasting of Western Florida Inc. Group owner: Beasley Broadcast Group (acq 8-12-86). Net: ABC/R. Rep: Katz. Format: AOR. Target aud: 18-49. ■ George G. Beasley, pres; Webster A. James, vp; Bruce Simel, gen mgr; Brad Beasley, progmg dir; Tony Baladjay, news dir; Richard Gallow, chief engr.

Boynton Beach

*WRMB(FM)—April 15, 1979: 89.3 mhz; 100 kw. Ant 500 ft. TL: N26 31 07 W80 10 17. Stereo. Hrs opn: 24. 1511 W. Boynton Beach Blvd. (33436). (407) 737-9762. Licensee: Moody Bible Institute of Chicago (group owner). Net: Moody. Format: Ed, relg. Target aud: General. ■ Joseph Stowell, pres; Michael L. Bingham, stn mgr; Diana Heyden, mus dir; Ken Senes, news dir; Chuck Conlon, chief engr.

*WXEL(FM)—See West Palm Beach.

WYFX(AM)—Jan 23, 1973: 1040 khz; 25 kw-D, 1.2 kw-N, DA-2. TL: N26 28 26 W80 12 11. Stereo. Hrs opn: 24. 400 Gulfstream Blvd., Delray Beach (33444). (407) 265-1040; (407) 737-1040. FAX: (407) 278-1040. Licensee: Beach Broadcasting Corp. Inc. (acq 6-81; $426,000; FTR 8-10-81). Rep: Katz & Powell. Wash atty: Borsari & Paxton. Format: Urban contemp, gospel. News staff one. Target aud: 25-54. Spec prog: Black adult. ■ Gary Lewis, pres; Carol Schroepfer, exec vp; Gary Dean, sls dir; Mike James, progmg dir & mus dir; Rick Rieke, chief engr.

Bradenton

WDUV(FM)—October 1963: 103.3 mhz; 100 kw. Ant 649 ft. TL: N27 32 42 W82 34 28. Stereo. Hrs opn: 24. Box 240 (34206). (813) 749-1420. Licensee: Sunshine State Broadcasting Co. Inc. Net: MBS. Rep: Christal. Format: Easy lstng. ■ Robert R. Nelson, pres; Robert W. Nelson, vp & gen mgr; Judy Johnson, gen sls mgr; Bob Keehn, pub affrs dir; Rob Lankton, chief engr.

WISP(FM)—See Holmes Beach.

*WJIS(FM)—1989: 88.1 mhz; 100 kw. Ant 397 ft. TL: N27 07 54 W82 23 29. 6469 Parkland Dr., Sarasota (34243). (813) 753-0401. FAX: (813) 753-2963. Licensee: WJIS FM Radio (acq 8-17-89; grpsl; FTR 9-11-89). Format: Christian/inspirational. ■ James Campbell, pres; Cindy Carr, prom mgr; Jeff MacFarlane, progmg dir & mus dir; Tim Nixon, news dir; Rodger Roth, chief engr.

Brandon

WBDN(AM)—February 1988: 760 khz; 10 kw-D, 1 kw-N, DA-2. TL: N28 01 30 W82 17 01. 214 Cook St. (33511). (813) 684-9922. FAX: (813) 685-1652. Licensee: Asti Broadcssting (acq 5-86; grspl; FTR 5-5-86). Net: UPI, Sun. Format: News/talk. News staff 6; news progmg 72 hrs wkly. Target aud: 35-54 plus. ■ Carla O'Donell, gen mgr; Billy Apgar, opns mgr.

Brooksville

WWJB(AM)—Oct 11, 1958: 1450 khz; 1 kw-U. TL: N28 33 20 W82 22 34. Hrs opn: 24. Box 1507 (34605); Hernando Sq., 55 W. Fort Dade Ave. (34601). (904) 796-7469; (904) 796-0141. FAX: (904) 796-5074. Licensee: Hernando Broadcasting Co. (acq 3-1-82; FTR 4-5-82). Net: ABC/I. Rep: Dora-Clayton. Wash atty: Gardner, Carton & Douglas. Format: Full serv MOR. News staff 2. Target aud: 25 plus. ■ Steve Manuel, pres, gen mgr & chief engr; Bob Haa, opns mgr & news dir; Chad Lewis, prom mgr; Glynn Vagts, progmg dir & mus dir. ■ Rates: $14; 14; 14; na.

Callahan

WAIA(FM)—Licensed to Callahan. See Jacksonville.

WELX(AM)—Not on air, target date unknown: 1160 khz; 5 kw-D, 250 w-N, DA-D. TL: N30 34 47 W87 17 18. Stn currently dark. c/o 988 Spyglass Ct., Roseville, CA (95678). (916) 677-1873. Licensee: Spanish Broadcasting of America Inc. (acq 3-24-93; $11,160; FTR 4-12-93). ■ Jane A. Filler, gen mgr.

Callaway

WDRK(FM)—Feb 1990: 103.5 mhz; 100 kw. Ant 475 ft. TL: N30 03 18 W85 18 09 (CP: Ant 423 ft.). Stereo. 6906 W. Hwy. 98, Panama City Beach (32404). (904) 234-8858. FAX: (904) 234-6592. Licensee: Millblack Inc. Format: Pure rock & roll. ■ Jimmy Vinyard, gen mgr; John Stuart, opns mgr.

Cantonment

WKGT(AM)—Licensed to Cantonment. See Pensacola.

Stations in the U.S.   Florida

Cape Coral

WXKB(FM)—1975: 103.7 mhz; 50 kw. Ant 273 ft. TL: N26 38 19 W82 01 35 (CP: 100 kw, ant 981 ft.). Stereo. Suite 102, 3440 Marina Town Ln., Ft. Myers (33903). (813) 997-2103. FAX: (813) 997-8960. Licensee: WRCC Partners (acq 2-16-83; $1.55 million; FTR 3-7-83). Format: CHR News staff one. Target aud: General. ■ Rates: $30; 25; 30; 20.

Cedar Creek

*****WKSG(FM)**—Not on air, target date unknown: 89.5 mhz; 3 kw. Ant 91 ft. 1688 Yellowstone, Cocoa (32922). Licensee: Cedar Creek Public Radio Inc.

Cedar Key

WVNM(FM)—Not on air, target date unknown: 102.7 mhz; 25 kw. Ant 328 ft. TL: N29 12 24 W83 00 51. Rt. One, Box 905, c/o Karen Marie Voyles, Newberry (32669-9743). Licensee: Ronald J. Linder. Group owner: Linder Broadcasting Group (acq 7-2-93; $15,000; FTR 8-2-93).

Century

WKGT-FM—July 1989: 105.1 mhz; 6 kw. Ant 328 ft. TL: N30 52 09 W87 20 18. Suite 27, 312 E. Nine Mile Rd., Pensacola (32514). FAX: (904) 474-0709. Licensee: Ziffle Broadcasting Co. (acq 2-1-89; $625,000; FTR 2-13-89). ■ Jack Hixon, gen mgr.

Chattahoochee

WTCL(AM)—Nov 1, 1963: 1580 khz; 5 kw-D. TL: N30 40 14 W84 50 08 (CP: 10 kw-D, 500 w-N, DA-N). P.O. Box 157 (32324). (904) 663-2323. Licensee: Lighthouse Broadcasting of New Jersey (acq 5-12-88). Net: USA; Florida Radio Net. Format: Oldies, relg, urban contemp. News progmg 5 hrs wkly. Target aud: General. ■ Betty Williams, pres & gen mgr; Romeo Pete, progmg dir. ■ Rates: $7; 5; 7; na.

WUMG(FM)—Not on air, target date unknown: 105.3 mhz; 6 kw. Ant 328 ft. TL: N30 49 27 W84 48 52. Box 735, Rt. One, Camilla, GA (31730). Licensee: Chattahoochee Broadcast Assocs.

Chiefland

WLQH(AM)—June 6, 1968: 940 khz; 1 kw-D. TL: N29 31 00 W82 53 11. Stereo. Box 99 (32626). (904) 493-4011. FAX: (904) 493-9943. Licensee: White Construction Co. Inc. Net: AP. Format: C&W. Spec prog: Relg 9 hrs wkly. ■ Luther White, pres; Norma W. Schossler, gen mgr; Richard Bailey, gen sls mgr; Donna Stacy, mus dir; Bill Schossler, chief engr.

WLQH-FM—Not on air, target date unknown: 97.3 mhz; 6 kw. Ant 328 ft. TL: N29 31 00 W82 53 11.

*****WTBH(FM)**—1988: 91.5 mhz; 3 kw. Ant 233 ft. TL: N29 27 35 W82 53 53. Stereo. Rt. 2, Box 497 (32626). (904) 493-2650. Licensee: Long Pond Baptist Church. Format: Relg, southern gospel. News staff one. ■ Ron Cason, pres.

Chipley

WBGC(AM)—April 10, 1956: 1240 khz; 1 kw-U. TL: N30 46 19 W85 33 31. 901 S. Blvd. (32428). (904) 638-0234. Licensee: Homer L. Rhoden Sr. (acq 12-11-91). Net: Florida Radio Net. Rep: Keystone (unwired net). Format: Div. ■ Homer Rhoden, pres, gen mgr & mus dir; Dan Solomon, opns mgr, gen sls mgr, prom mgr & progmg dir; Charles P. Wooten, chief engr.

Christmas

WORL(AM)—1986: 650 khz; 10 kw-D, DA. TL: N28 32 21 W80 58 26. Box 214186, Sacramento, CA (95821). (916) 481-8191. Licensee: Floyco Inc. ■ Carl J. Auel, pres.

Clearwater

WLVU(AM)—See Dunedin.

WMTX-FM—Aug 19, 1963: 95.7 mhz; 100 kw. Ant 607 ft. TL: N27 52 00 W82 37 27. Stereo. Hrs opn: 24. Suite 500, 18167 U.S. Hwy. 19 N. (34624). (813) 536-9600. FAX: (813) 536-6000. Licensee: Metroplex Communications Inc., an Ohio Corp. Group owner: Metroplex Communications Inc. (acq 2-5-92; no financial consideration; FTR 2-24-92). Net: AP. Wash atty: Jim Weitzman. Format: Adult contemp. News staff one. Target aud: 18-49; upwardly mobile adults. ■ Jon Pinch, pres & gen mgr;

Kevin Malone, gen sls mgr; Kirsten Leigh Rivrio, prom mgr; Mason Dixon, progmg dir; Rico Blanco, mus dir; Pat Brooks, news dir; Ben Umberger, chief engr.

BECKERMAN ASSOCIATES
Media Brokers—Consultants
14001 MIRAMAR AVENUE
MADEIRA BEACH, FLORIDA 33708
TELEPHONE (813) 391-2824

WTAN(AM)—June 1948: 1340 khz; 1 kw-U. TL: N27 57 49 W82 24 14. Hrs opn: 24. 200 Pierce Blvd. (34616). (813) 447-9826. FAX: (813) 447-7709. Licensee: Drenik Communications Inc. (acq 10-15-90; $750,000; FTR 10-22-90). Format: Greek, relg, Sp. News staff 2; news progmg 12 hrs wkly. Target aud: 25-45; Greek community. Spec prog: Big band 6 hrs wkly. ■ Virginia C. Nikitakis, pres & gen sls mgr; George Nikitakis, vp & gen mgr; Ted Drettakis, chief engr.

WXTB(FM)—Dec 1, 1967: 97.9 mhz; 100 kw. Ant 649 ft. TL: N28 02 34 W82 40 16 (CP: Ant 580 ft.). Stereo. Suite 550, 2 Corporate Dr. (34622). (813) 572-9808. Licensee: Great American Television & Radio Co. Group owner: Great American Broadcasting (acq 12-26-89; $20 million; FTR 2-12-90). Net: ABC/R. Rep: Banner. Format: AOR. News staff one; news progmg 2 hrs wkly. Target aud: Men 18-49. Spec prog: Pub affrs 4 hrs wkly. ■ Daniel DiLoreto, gen mgr; Barry Levin, gen sls mgr; Mike Oliviero, prom mgr; Greg Mull, progmg dir; Ted Cannarozzi, mus dir; John Wolf, news dir; Scott Miller, chief engr.

WYUU(FM)—See Safety Harbor.

Clewiston

WAFC(AM)—Feb 16, 1988: 590 khz; 930 w-D, 470 w-N. TL: N26 43 47 W80 54 45. Hrs opn: 24. Box 2109, 116 Commercio (33440). (813) 983-6106. FAX: (813) 983-6109. Licensee: Glades Media Co. Wash atty: Leibowitz & Spencer. Format: International Sp. Target aud: General; adult Hispanics male & female. ■ Robert Castellanos, gen mgr & gen sls mgr; Gail Castellanos, opns mgr; Francisco Arredomdo, progmg dir; Jim Johnson, chief engr.

WAFC-FM—July 2, 1979: 106.3 mhz; 1.5 kw. Ant 460 ft. TL: N26 42 35 W80 54 00. Stereo. Hrs opn: 24. Prog sep from AM. Net: NBC; Florida's Radio Net. Rep: Midsouth. Format: Mod country. News staff one; news progmg 3 hrs wkly. Spec prog: Farm one hr, relg 5 hrs wkly. ■ Gail Castellanos, news dir.

Cocoa

WLRQ-FM—Listing follows WWHL(AM).

*****WMIE(FM)**—December 1984: 91.5 mhz; 20 kw-H, 19 kw-V. Ant 98 ft. TL: N28 21 21 W80 44 47. Stereo. Hrs opn: 24. Box 493 (32923); Box 1510, 1150 W. King St. (32922). (407) 632-1000; (407) 632-1510. Licensee: National Christian Network. Format: Contemp Christian. Target aud: 18-49. ■ Raymond A. Kassis, pres; Thomas C. Shaw, gen mgr & progmg dir; Ed Huffman, chief engr.

WRFB(AM)—January 1952: 860 khz; 1 kw-D, 121 w-N. TL: N28 21 08 W80 45 37. Hrs opn: 24. Box 561270, Rockledge (32926-1270). 200 S. Burnett Rd. (32926). (407) 631-6827. FAX: (407) 631-6866. Licensee: Brevard Broadcasting Inc. (acq 3-1-93; $90,000; FTR 10-11-93). Format: News/talk. Target aud: active "on the go" adults. ■ Keith Walker, gen mgr; Steve Curry, progmg dir.

WWBC(AM)—July 1965: 1510 khz; 1 kw-D. TL: N28 21 30 W80 42 38 (CP: COL: Rockledge, 770 khz, 1 kw-D, 480 w-N, DA-2, TL: N28 20 05 W80 46 56). 1150 W. King St. (32922). (407) 632-1510. Licensee: Astro Enterprises (acq 3-1-76). Format: Relg. ■ Ray Kassis, pres & gen mgr; Thomas Shaw, opns mgr & mus dir; Ed Huffman, chief engr.

WWHL(AM)—Oct 4, 1957: 1350 khz; 1 kw-U. DA-N. TL: N28 21 58 W80 45 08. Stereo. 2405 Broadcast Ct. (32922). (407) 636-4411. FAX: (407) 636-4380. Licensee: Ezy Comm Inc. (acq 4-4-82; $1,050,000 with co-located FM; FTR 4-12-82). Net: AP, Wall Street; Fla. Net. Rep: Eastman. Format: Soft AC. News staff one. ■ Tanya Klepper, gen mgr; Jim Faires, gen sls mgr; Barbara Bell, news dir; Russ Martin, chief engr.

WLRQ-FM—Co-owned with WWHL(AM). June 15, 1967: 99.3 mhz; 1.2 kw. Ant 500 ft. TL: N28 16 42 W80 42 03 (CP: 50 kw, ant 492 ft.). Stereo. Prog sep from AM. Format: News.

Cocoa Beach

WJRR(FM)—July 19, 1962: 101.1 mhz; 100 kw. Ant 1,598 ft. TL: N28 34 51 W81 04 32. Stereo. Suite 401, 2500 Maitland Center Pkwy., Maitland (32751). (407) 660-1011. FAX: (407) 660-0329. Licensee: Paxson Enterprises Inc. Group owner: Paxson Broadcasting (acq 2-18-93; $6.7 million; FTR 3-8-93). Net: AP. Rep: Republic. Format: AOR. News staff one; news progmg 2 hrs wkly. Target aud: 18-34; men. ■ Lowel W. Paxson, pres; Jenny Sue Rhoades, gen mgr; John Frost, opns mgr & progmg dir; Deonne Darden, gen sls mgr; Deborah Magnuson, natl sls mgr; Judi Pearl, prom mgr; Steve Robertson, mus dir; Dave Riley, news dir; Dave Murray, chief engr.

WTKS(FM)—Licensed to Cocoa Beach. See Orlando.

WXXU(AM)—June 22, 1959: 1300 khz; 5 kw-D, 1 kw-N, DA-2. TL: N28 20 38 W80 46 06. 1801 Clark Rd., Orlando. (32818). (407) 632-1300. FAX: (407) 578-1734. Licensee: Rama Communications Inc. (acq 10-13-93; $950,000 with WXTO[AM] Winter Garden; FTR 11-8-93). Net: CRC. Wash atty: Cohn & Marks. Format: Sp. News staff one. Target aud: 25-54. Spec prog: French 9 hrs, gospel 12 hrs wkly. ■ Mathew B. Hoffman, pres; J.D. Ricci, gen mgr; Pedro F. Sanchez, progmg dir; Jay Wagner, chief engr.

Coleman

WFRK(AM)—Aug 24, 1985: 1320 khz; 500 w-D, 60 w-N. TL: N28 47 58 W81 59 50. c/o 193 E. Bergen Pl., Red Bank, NJ (07701). Licensee: Starett Media Corp. Format: Oldies. News staff 2. Target aud: 25-49. ■ John W. Bussanick, pres & gen mgr; John Michaels, gen sls mgr; Tim Downs, progmg dir; Cindy Dickey, news dir; Bruce Mattson, chief engr.

Coral Cove

WVFE(FM)—Not on air, target date unknown: 107.9 mhz; 3 kw. Ant 328 ft. TL: N27 11 23 W82 28 25. 235 Hunt Club Blvd., Longwood (32774). (407) 682-7104. FAX: (407) 682-7144. Licensee: Coral Cove FM Partnership (acq 3-11-91; FTR 4-1-91). Wash atty: Denise Moline. ■ Richard L. Vega, CEO.

Coral Gables

WHQT(FM)—Nov 15, 1958: 105.1 mhz; 100 kw. Ant 1,049 ft. TL: N25 57 59 W80 12 33 (CP: Ant 1,007 ft.). Stereo. 1401 N. Bay Causeway, Miami (33141). (305) 759-4311. FAX: (305) 758-5683. Licensee: WIOD Inc. Group owner: Cox Broadcasting (acq 12-28-92; FTR 1-11-93). Rep: Christal. Wash atty: Dow, Lohnes & Albertson. Format: Urban adult contemp. News staff one; news progmg 7 hrs wkly. Target aud: 18-49. ■ Robert Green, pres & gen mgr; Jeff Clark, gen sls mgr; John Lynch, natl sls mgr; Curt Steier, mktg dir; Kurt Steier, mktg mgr; Tony Kidd, progmg dir; Lisa Campbell, pub affrs dir; Mitch Wein, chief engr.

WRHC(AM)—1963: 1550 khz; 10 kw-D, 500 w-N, DA-2. TL: N25 44 36 W80 18 52 (CP: 1560 khz, 50 kw-D, 4.4 kw-N. TL: N25 51 25 W80 20 42). Hrs opn: 24. 330 S.W. 27th Ave. 2nd F., Miami (33135). (305) 643-1121; (305) 541-3300. FAX: (305) 642-6224. Licensee: WRHC Broadcasting Corp. (acq 3-23-93; FTR 4-5-93). Rep: Lotus. Wash atty: Schwartz, Woodsand & Miller. Format: Sp, news/talk. ■ Carlos G. Carreras, chmn; Anna M. Vidal, vp; George Rodriguez, gen mgr; Lazaro Ascencio, news dir; Edwardo Rodriguez, engrg dir.

WVCG(AM)—Feb 18, 1949: 1080 khz; 50 kw-D, 20 kw-N, DA-2. TL: N25 44 53 W80 32 47. Suite 203, 2100 Salzedo Centre (33134). (305) 445-1080. FAX: (305) 445-7754. Licensee: WVCG License Corp. Group owner: Evergreen Media Corp. (acq 2-25-83). Format: Religious. ■ Scott K. Ginsburg, pres; Matthew B. Rowe, gen mgr & gen sls mgr; John Latzteo, rgnl sls mgr & prom mgr; Roberto Hernandez, progmg mgr; Ron Streeter, chief engr.

*****WVUM(FM)**—May 1968: 90.5 mhz; 365 w. Ant 175 ft. TL: N25 43 02 W80 16 48. Stereo. Hrs opn: 24. Box 248191, Univ. Ctr. #204, 1306 Stanford Dr. (33124). (305) 284-3131; (305) 284-5786. FAX: (305) 284-3132. Licensee: WVUM Inc. Net: AP. Wash atty: Cohen, Dippell & Everist. Format: Alt mus. News progmg 3 hrs wkly. Target aud: High school, college students, young adults. Spec prog: Jazz 3 hrs, Pub Affrs 2 hrs, Heavy Metal 3 hrs, Sports 5 hrs, Blues 3 hrs, Black 3 hrs, Relg 6 hrs wkly. ■ Dr. Paul Driscoll, CEO; Dr. William Butler, pres; Dr. Robert J. Dubord, CFO; Nikki Tominac, gen mgr; Jonathan Bell, prom dir; Jason Gordon, progmg dir; Mary Koma, mus dir; Lisa Huriash, news dir; Gregory Szeto, engrg dir; Roy Pressman, chief engr.

Crawfordville

WAKU(FM)—Not on air, target date unknown: 94.1 mhz; 6 kw. Ant 328 ft. Box 1181 (32326). Licensee: Dash Communications Inc.

Crestview

WAAZ-FM—Listing follows WJSB(AM).

WCNU(AM)—April 8, 1948: 1010 khz; 10 kw-D, 84 w-N. TL: N30 42 36 W86 34 19. Stn currently dark. 4980 S. Ferdon Blvd. (32536). (904) 682-1010. Licensee: Ashley Norman Davis Jr. (acq 12-26-90; $150,000; FTR 1-14-91). ■ Shelby L. Atkins, chief engr.

WJSB(AM)—Sept 15, 1954: 1050 khz; 5 kw-D. TL: N30 45 56 W86 35 06 (CP: 3.1 kw-D, 500 w-N, DA-N, TL: N30 46 00 W86 35 08). Box 267 (32536). End of W. First St. (32536). (904) 682-3040; (904) 962-4623. FAX: (904) 682-5232. Licensee: Crestview Broadcasting Co. (acq 8-1-70). Net: CBS. Format: C&W, MOR. ■ James T. Whitaker, pres, gen mgr & chief engr; Dutch Van, gen sls mgr; Sallie Stapleton, prom mgr; Betty Whitaker, progmg dir; Joe Cin, news dir.

WAAZ-FM—Co-owned with WJSB(AM). July 15, 1965: 104.9 mhz; 3 kw. Ant 275 ft. TL: N30 45 56 W86 35 06 (CP: 104.7 mhz, 50 kw, ant 492 ft. TL: N30 46 01 W86 35 07). Dups AM 30%. Format: C&W.

Cross City

WDFL(AM)—November 1985: 1240 khz; 1 kw-U. TL: N29 36 35 W83 08 03. Hrs opn: 24. Box 2220, Horseshoe Beach Rd. (32628). (904) 498-0304. FAX: (904) 498-0304. Licensee: Women in Florida Broadcasting Inc. (acq 2-23-90; $245,677; FTR 3-19-90). Net: CNN. Format: Country. Spec prog: Relg 5 hrs wkly. ■ Duane McConnell, pres; James M. Johnson, vp & chief engr; Jerry Prater, gen mgr; Ray Stanfield, gen sls mgr. ■ Rates: $7; 7; 7; 7.

WDFL-FM—Nov 16, 1987: 106.3 mhz; 4.5 kw. Ant 184 ft. TL: N29 24 07 W83 08 10. Stereo. Prog dups AM 100%. ■ Avis Asbell, mktg mgr.

Crystal River

WKTK(FM)—Feb 13, 1976: 98.5 mhz; 100 kw. Ant 1,332 ft. TL: N29 15 32 W82 34 03. Stereo. 1440 N.E. Waldo Rd., Gainesville (32601). (904) 377-0985. FAX: (904) 377-1884; (904) 377-4436. Licensee: Entertainment Communications Inc. Group owner: Entercom (acq 11-13-86; $3.6 million; FTR 7-21-86). Wash atty: Cohn & Marks. Format: Adult contemp. News staff one; news progmg 6 hrs wkly. Target aud: 25-54. ■ Joseph Field, pres; Jack Donlevie, Gene Levin, David Field, sr vps; Gary Granger, vp, gen sls mgr; Bill McFarland (local), sls mgr; Mark Granger, rgnl sls mgr; Rosey Moreno, prom mgr; Briton Jon Rice, progmg dir & mus dir; John Boyer, news dir & pub affrs dir; Garrett Wood, chief engr.

WXCV(FM)—See Homosassa Springs.

*****WXJC(FM)**—November 1992: 91.9 mhz; 3 kw. TL: N28 47 50 W82 32 58. 6831 Holiday St., Homosassa (34446). (904) 621-0402. Licensee: Christian Family Cinema Inc. Format: Christian. ■ Peter Swartz, gen mgr & stn mgr.

Cypress Gardens

WHNR(AM)—Licensed to Cypress Gardens. See Winter Haven.

Dade City

WBSB(FM)—Sept 3, 1993: 96.1 mhz; 3.8 kw. Ant 413 ft. Suite 200, 1415 S. Highway 301 (33525). (904) 523-9696. FAX: (904) 523-9610. Licensee: Dade City Broadcasting Inc. Format: Adult contemp. ■ David M. Zeplowitz, pres; Marianne Vorhies, gen mgr; Steve Michaels, opns mgr; Dave Terry, chief engr.

WDCF(AM)—December 1954: 1350 khz; 1 kw-D, 500 w-N, DA-N. TL: N28 20 04 W82 11 23. 37905 WDCF Dr. (33525-5735). (904) 567-5683; (904) 567-1350. FAX: (904) 567-5532. Licensee: Collins Communications Group Inc. (acq 3-14-93; $85,000; FTR 5-3-93). Net: SMN; Fla. Net. Format: Country, news. News progmg 10 hrs wkly. Target aud: 25 plus; basic country demographics. Spec prog: Interview shows 16 hrs, farm 2 hrs, relg

6 hrs, gospel 6 hrs, Sp 3 hrs wkly. ■ Edward L. Collins, pres; Jeff Collins, gen mgr; Jay Price, vp opns; Juliann Schrader, gen sls mgr; Lori Collins, progmg dir, mus dir, news dir & pub affrs dir; Paul Rebmann, chief engr. ■ Rates: $9; 7; 8; 5.

Davie

WAVS(AM)—Aug 21, 1970: 1170 khz; 5 kw-D, 250 w-N, DA-N. TL: N26 04 39 W80 13 03. Hrs opn: 24. 4124 S.W. 64th Ave. (33314). (305) 584-1170. TWX: 305-581-6441. Licensee: Radio WAVS Inc. (acq 8-83; $388,000; FTR 8-1-83). Format: Caribbean. News staff one. Target aud: General; West Indians/Dade, Broward, Palm Beach Counties, Bahamas. Spec prog: Black. ■ Dr. Roy H. Bresky, pres; Ray A. Hooper, gen mgr; Winsome Charlton, prom mgr; Winston Barnes, progmg dir & news dir; Ralph Chambers, chief engr. ■ Rates: $50; 50; 50; 30.

Daytona Beach

WCFB(FM)—Listing follows WNDB(AM).

WELE(AM)—See Ormond Beach.

WGNE-FM—(Titusville). September 1968: 98.1 mhz; 50 kw. Ant 462 ft. TL: N28 50 54 W80 51 44. Stereo. Hrs opn: 24. 340 S. Beach St., Daytona Beach (32114). (904) 239-9836. FAX: (904) 239-9898. Licensee: Southern Starr L.P. Group owner: Southern Starr Broadcasting Group (acq 11-26-91; $3.5 million; FTR 12-16-91). Rep: Banner. Wash atty: Walker, Bordelon, Hamlin, Theriot & Hardy. Format: Country. News staff one; news progmg 2 hrs wkly. Target aud: 25-54. ■ Robert Long, pres; Bill Motter, CFO; Bob Lima, gen mgr & gen sls mgr; Bob Mello, rgnl sls mgr; Jim King, prom mgr & progmg dir; Diane Kaeppel, adv mgr; Ron Jones, mus dir; Jennifer Jones, news dir & pub affrs dir; Harold Utter, chief engr. ■ Rates: $75; 50; 60; 35.

WJHM(FM)—Nov 1, 1967: 101.9 mhz; 28 kw. Ant 1,584 ft. TL: N28 55 16 W81 19 09. Stereo. Suite 4200, 37 Skyline Dr., Lake Mary (32746). (407) 333-0073. FAX: (407) 333-2342. Licensee: Augusta Broadcasters Inc. Group owner: Beasley Broadcast Group (acq 10-87; $9.2 milion; FTR 10-12-87). Net: AP. Format: Urban contemp. ■ Dave Donahue, pres, gen mgr & stn mgr; Lee Cutler, gen sls mgr; Duff Lindsey, progmg dir; Cedric Hollywood, mus dir; Ovie Loman, chief engr.

WMFJ(AM)—April 16, 1935: 1450 khz; 1 kw-U. TL: N29 13 30 W81 01 30. 4295 Ridgewood, Port Orange (32127). (904) 767-6000. Licensee: Weeks Broadcasting (acq 2-5-65). Net: UPI, CBN. Format: Relg. Target aud: General. ■ Robert M. Weeks, pres; Dick Van Zandt, gen mgr; Ken Young, prom mgr, progmg dir & mus dir; Bill Leisner, chief engr. ■ Rates: $13; 13; 13; 13.

WNDB(AM)—April 1948: 1150 khz; 1 kw-U, DA-N. TL: N29 14 06 W81 04 19. Hrs opn: 24. 220 S. Ridgewood Ave. (32114). (904) 257-1150. FAX: (904) 239-0966. Licensee: Chapman S. Root 1982 Living Trust (group owner; acq 10-20-92; grpsl; FTR 11-23-92). Net: ABC, Daynet, CBS, NBC Talknet, MBS; Rep: Torbet. Wash atty: Dow, Lohnes & Albertson. Format: News/talk. News staff 2. Target aud: General; 25-64. ■ Charles T. Cohoon, pres; Wally Ranck, gen sls mgr; Bill Wathen, news dir; Phil Angley, chief engr. ■ Rates: $60; 50; 50; 20.

WCFB(FM)—Co-owned with WNDB(AM). March 1947: 94.5 mhz; 100 kw. Ant 1,500 ft. TL: N28 58 55 W81 27 18. Stereo. Hrs opn: 24. Prog sep from AM. Format: Adult contemp.

WPUL(AM)—See South Daytona.

WROD(AM)—1947: 1340 khz; 1 kw-U. TL: N29 11 19 W81 00 28. Box 991 (32115); 103 Wilder Blvd. (32114). (904) 253-0000. FAX: (904) 255-3178. Licensee: La Paz Broadcasting Inc. (acq 4-10-86; $1.2 million; FTR 3-3-86). Net: ABC/I, Unistar, Sun. Rep: Rgnl Reps. Wash atty: Putbeese, Hunsokee & Ruddy. Format: Big band, oldies. News staff 2; news progmg 4 hrs wkly. Target aud: 50 plus; senior community. ■ Anthony Welch, pres & gen mgr; Shirley H. Welch, exec vp; James Underwood, gen sls mgr; Catherine Welch, prom mgr & progmg dir; Prince Andrew, mus dir; Bill Mathews, asst mus dir; Bob Edwards, news dir; Bill Leisner, chief engr. ■ Rates: $40; 40; 40; 30.

WWBH(AM)—See New Smyrna Beach.

De Land

WOCL(FM)—July 10, 1967: 105.9 mhz; 100 kw. Ant 1,650 ft. TL: N28 55 16 W81 19 09. Stereo. Hrs opn: 24. Suite 305, 2101 State Rd. 434, Longwood (32779). (407) 682-2121. FAX: (407) 682-2902; Licensee: Mid-Florida Radio Inc. Group owner: American Media Inc. (acq 2-86).

Rep: Christal. Wash atty: Latham & Watkins. Format: Oldies. News staff one. ■ Gary Eaves, gen mgr; Michael Gowick, gen sls mgr; Melissa Richards-Druley, prom mgr; Scott Sherwood, progmg dir & mus dir; Frank Lasko, news dir; Mike Sprysenski, chief engr.

WXVQ(AM)—Sept 10, 1948: 1490 khz; 1 kw-U. TL: N29 00 58 W81 17 10. 220 E. Hubbard Ave. (32721). (904) 734-9386; (904) 734-9361. Licensee: Green Broadcast Group Inc. (acq 11-8-91; $175,000; FTR 12-2-91). Net: ABC/I, Sun; Fla. Net. Format: News/talk, community affrs, sports. ■ Rick Green, pres & gen mgr; EJ Dunkley, adv dir; Al Everson, news dir; Harold Utter, chief engr. ■ Rates: $15; 15; 15; 15.

WYND(AM)—Dec 7, 1956: 1310 khz; 5 kw-D, 95 w-N. TL: N28 59 57 W81 17 55. 316 E. Taylor Rd. (32724). (904) 734-1310. Licensee: Buddy Tucker Association Inc. (acq 12-30-86; $255,000; FTR 12-1-86). Format: Christian, music, talk. ■ Buddy Tucker, gen mgr; Harold Utter, chief engr.

DeFuniak Springs

WGTX(AM)—Mar 1, 1956: 1280 khz; 5 kw-D. TL: N30 42 41 W86 06 25. Stn currently dark. Box 627, 2nd & Bruce Ave. (32433). (904) 892-3158. Licensee: Sonic Enterprises Inc. (acq 3-8-93; $450,000 with co-located FM; FTR 3-29-93). ■ Art Dees, gen mgr.

WLGH(FM)—Co-owned with WGTX(AM). November 1974: 103.1 mhz; 2.6 kw. Ant 350 ft. TL: N30 43 19 W86 07 27 (CP: 50 kw, ant 482 ft.). Stereo. Prog sep from AM. Box 747, Niceville, AL (32578). (904) 729-1031. Format: Adult contemp. News staff one; news progmg 20 hrs wkly. Target aud: 18-54. ■ M. Scott McAda, gen mgr; Trena McNulty, gen sls mgr.

WZEP(AM)—1955: 1460 khz; 5 kw-D, 186 w-N. TL: N30 43 43 W86 07 03. Hrs opn: 5 AM-7 PM. Box 627, 449 N. 12th St. (32433). (904) 892-3158; (800) 881-1460. FAX: (904) 892-9675. Licensee: Walton County Broadcasting Inc. (acq 6-1-93; $60,000; FTR 2-2-93). Net: Florida's Radio Net. Format: Full-svc news/talk, country, MOR. News staff one; news progmg 29 hrs wkly. Target aud: 25 plus; the 60% of our county with 85% of the money. Spec prog: Gospel 8 hrs wkly. ■ Arthur F. Dees, pres & gen mgr; Martha K. Dees, vp; Marty Dees, stn mgr; M. Scott McAda, gen sls mgr; Ed Curtis, progmg dir & mus dir; Ron Kelley, news dir; Charles Wooten, chief engr.

Delray Beach

WDBF(AM)—February 1952: 1420 khz; 5 kw-D, 500 w-N, DA-2. TL: N26 27 22 W80 05 58. Box 1420, 2710 W. Atlantic Ave. (33447). (407) 278-1420. FAX: (407) 278-1898. Licensee: Quality Broadcasting Corp. (acq 7-65). Net: CBS, UPI. Format: Big band, America's Gold. News staff one. Spec prog: Black 4 hrs, jazz 10 hrs wkly. ■ Vic Knight, pres, gen mgr & gen sls mgr; Jeff Rudolph, stn mgr; Bruce Hamilton, opns mgr & news dir; Ted Knight, progmg dir & mus dir; Mario Lipari, chief engr.

Destin

WBZR(AM)—Not on air, target date unknown: 1120 khz; 1 kw-D. TL: N30 30 34 W86 28 34. 2001 N. Mercy Dr., Orlando (32808). Licensee: Willie J. Martin.

WMMK(FM)—Sept 24, 1981: 92.1 mhz; 25 kw. Ant 279 ft. TL: N30 23 08 W86 24 52. Stereo. 755 Legion Drive (32541). (904) 837-0101. FAX: (904) 837-7621. Licensee: Emerald Coast Radio Corp. (acq 7-25-92). Net: NBC. Rep: Roslin. Format: C&W. ■ Rick Anderson, gen mgr; Sam Faulk, opns mgr; P. Norden, gen sls mgr; Skip Davis, progmg dir & mus dir; Gerald Wilson, chief engr. ■ Rates: $34; 28; 34; 22.

Dogwood Lakes Estate

*****WJED(FM)**—Jan 15, 1992: 91.1 mhz; 700 w. Ant 180 ft. TL: N30 51 34 W85 47 45. Stereo. Box 1944, Bethany Bible College, Dothan, AL (36302); Box 537, Bonifay (32425). (904) 547-9405; (904) 671-9862. FAX: (205) 793-4344. Licensee: Bethany Bible College & Bethany Theological Seminary Inc. Net: USA. Format: Educ, relg, Southern & country gospel. News progmg 3 hrs wkly. Target aud: General; college students & religious community. ■ Dr. H.D. Shuemake, CEO & gen mgr; Dr. Steve Shuemake, pres & stn mgr; Sylvia Green, progmg dir & mus dir; Linda Martin, asst mus dir.

Dunedin

WGUL(AM)—Licensed to Dunedin. See Tampa.

WLVU(AM)—1955: 1470 khz; 5 kw-D, 500 w-N. TL: N28 03 24 W82 44 16. 2625 County Rd. 95, Palm Harbor

(34684). (813) 786-1723. Licensee: Pasco Pinellas Broadcasting (acq 2-1-86; grpsl; FTR 12-9-85). Rep: D & R Radio. Format: Ethnic, diversified. Spec prog: Ger 15 hrs, Irish one hr, It 15 hrs, GR one hr, Pol one hr, relg one hr wkly. ■ Walter Solarz, opns mgr; Manny Depina, progmg dir.

Dunellon

WTRS-FM—Mar 11, 1969: 102.3 mhz; 3 kw. Ant 300 ft. TL: N29 11 16 W82 23 39 (CP: 50 kw, ant 489 ft.). Stereo. 3357 Southwest 7th St., Ocala (34474). (904) 732-9877. FAX: (904) 622-6675. Licensee: Asterisk Inc. Format: Country. ■ John Rutledge, gen mgr & gen sls mgr; Tommy Rockwell, progmg dir; Tanya Ragin, pub affrs dir; Lee Freshwater, chief engr.

WTRS(AM)—Mar 11, 1969; 920 khz; 500 w-D. TL: N29 01 52 W82 27 05. Stn currently dark. Net: ABC/E; Fla. Net.

Eatonville

WHBS(AM)—Licensed to Eatonville. See Orlando.

Eau Gallie

WGGD-FM—See Melbourne.

WMEL(AM)—See Melbourne.

WMMB(AM)—See Melbourne.

WTAI(AM)—See Melbourne.

Edgewater

WEDG(FM)—Not on air, target date unknown: 93.1 mhz; 3 kw. Ant 328 ft. TL: N28 54 52 W80 53 48. 136 Heritage Cir., Ormond Beach (32074). Licensee: Edge Broadcasting Inc. (acq 3-3-93; $132,000; FTR 3-22-93).

Englewood

WENG(AM)—Nov 15, 1964: 1530 khz; 1 kw-D. TL: N26 57 55 W82 19 15. Hrs opn: Sunrise-sunset. Box 2908 (34295-2908). (813) 474-3231. FAX: (813) 475-2205. Licensee: Murray Broadcasting Co. (acq 8-4-93; $165,000; FTR 8-23-93). Net: ABC/A. Fla. Net. Wash atty: Pepper Corazzini. Format: Listener participation, talk, info, news. News staff one; news progmg 12 hrs wkly. Target aud: 35 plus; securely established, financially independent. ■ John H. Murray, pres; Michael Anthony, vp & gen mgr; Matt DuBois, sls dir; Don Doepker, rgnl sls mgr; Scott Holcomb, pub affrs dir; Perley Tribou, chief engr. ■ Rates: $17; 13; 15; 10.

*WSEB(FM)—May 1989: 91.3 mhz; 62 kw-H, 60 kw-V. Ant 282 ft. TL: N26 51 48 W87 17 54. Stereo. Hrs opn: 24. Suite C4-2, 517 Paul Morris Dr. (34223). (813) 475-9732. FAX: (813) 473-1797. Licensee: Suncoast Educational Broadcasting Corp. Format: Relg, news/talk, educ. Target aud: 35 plus; Christian families. ■ Wallis C. Metts, pres; John P. Higgins, gen mgr; Garry Clark, mus dir; Paul Wolf, chief engr.

Eustis

WKIQ(AM)—June 1955: 1240 khz; 1 kw-U. TL: N28 50 19 W81 41 46. Hrs opn: 24. Box 1448, Sanford (32772). (407) 322-1400. Licensee: J & V Communications Inc. (acq 11-6-92; $75,000; FTR 11-30-92). Net: ABC/D, MBS, SMN; Florida's Radio Net. Format: Music, talk. Spec prog: Sp. Sunday mornings. ■ John Torrado, pres; Frank Vaught, gen mgr; Bob Green, stn mgr; Frank Strnad, chief engr.

WLBE(AM)—See Leesburg.

Fernandina Beach

*WNLE(FM)—Oct 6, 1985: 91.7 mhz; 38 kw. Ant 167 ft. TL: N30 37 20 W81 31 48. Stereo. Hrs opn: 17. c/o Rt. 2, Box 705-A, Blackrock Rd. & A1A, Yule (32097), (904) 277-2256; (904) 261-4818. FAX: (904) 261-2349. Licensee: Nassau Baptist College. Net: USA. Wash atty: Jeff Southmayd. Format: Christian, relg, southern gospel. News progmg 11 hrs wkly. Target aud: General. ■ Larry Montgomery, CEO & pres; Carlos Chapman, gen mgr, sls dir, prom mgr & pub affrs dir; Sarah Chapman, mus dir; Robert Moughten, chief engr.

WQAI(AM)—1955: 1570 khz; 5 kw-D. TL: N30 41 03 W81 27 30. 707 Dade St. (32034). (904) 277-0630. FAX: (904) 277-0506. Licensee: North East Florida Radio Inc. (acq 1-26-93; $133,136; FTR 2-15-93). Format: First Coast Country. ■ Charley White, gen mgr; George Spurlock, opns mgr & news dir; Tom Lowe, gen sls mgr; Jim Lawson, prom mgr; Marvin Sigers, chief engr.

Five Points

WCJX(FM)—Not on air, target date unknown: 106.5 mhz; 3 kw. Ant 328 ft. TL: N30 14 40 82 40 11. Box 1479, Cross City (32628). Licensee: Carol Jean Lamons.

Fort Lauderdale

*WAFG(FM)—1973: 90.3 mhz; 3 kw. Ant 280 ft. TL: N26 11 48 W80 06 45. Stereo. 5555 N. Federal Highway (33308). (305) 776-7705. Licensee: Westminster Academy. Net: USA. Format: Easy lstng, Christian. ■ Kenneth Wackes, pres; Mildred Wettich, gen mgr; Ched Kieler, chief engr.

WAXY(FM)—July 1960: 105.9 mhz; 100 kw. Ant 1,048 ft. TL: N25 59 34 W80 10 27. Stereo. 1975 E. Sunrise Blvd. (33304). (305) 463-9299. FAX: (305) 522-1441. Licensee: GRADH-105 Inc. Group owner: Ackerley Communications Inc. ($21 million). Net: AP. Format: Oldies. ■ Tammy Moye, stn mgr.

WEXY(AM)—See Wilton Manors.

WFTL(AM)—Sept 16, 1946: 1400 khz; 1 kw-U. TL: N26 09 13 W80 10 11. Box 100819 (33310); 2100 N.W. 21st Ave. (33311). (305) 485-4111. Licensee: Tri-Talk Radio, L.C. Net: CNN. Format: Talk. News staff one; 25 plus. ■ Paul Bronstein, chmn; Dolores King, stn mgr; Lew Krone, gen sls mgr; Steve Kane, progmg dir; Jim Sorenson, chief engr.

WHYI-FM—July 31, 1960: 100.7 mhz; 100 kw. Ant 928 ft. TL: N25 59 34 W80 10 27 (CP: 1,007 ft, TL: N25 57 59 W80 12 33). 1975 E. Sunrise Blvd. (33004). (305) 463-9299. FAX: (305) 522-1441. Licensee: Metroplex Communications Inc., an Ohio Corp. Group owner: Metroplex Communications Inc. (acq 2-5-92; FTR 2-24-92). Rep: McGavren Guild. Format: Christian. ■ Norman Wain, pres; Julie Wilson, mktg dir; Rob Roberts, progmg dir; Al Chio, mus dir; Howard Quinton, chief engr.

WMXJ(FM)—See Pompano Beach.

WRBD(AM)—See Pompano Beach.

WSHE(FM)—Listing follows WSRF(AM).

WSRF(AM)—1955: 1580 khz; 10 kw-D, 5 kw-N, DA-2. TL: N26 04 54 W80 13 34. 3000 SW 60th Ave. (33314). (305) 581-1587. FAX: (305) 581-1301. Licensee: T-K Communications Inc. (group owner; acq 12-79). Rep: Eastman. Format: Relg. Spec prog: Gr 2 hrs, Greek 10 hrs, It 12 hrs wkly. ■ John Tenaglia, pres; Gary S. Lewis, vp & gen mgr; Mark Krieger, gen sls mgr; Ernesto Gladden, progmg dir; Max Sitero, chief engr.

WSHE(FM)—Co-owned with WSRF(AM). Oct 17, 1959: 103.5 mhz; 100 kw. Ant 1,007 ft. TL: N25 57 59 W80 12 33. Stereo. (305) 587-1035. Format: AOR.

WTPX(FM)—Aug 15, 1962: 106.7 mhz; 100 kw. Ant 984 ft. TL: N25 59 34 W80 10 27. Stereo. Hrs opn: 24. 2100 N.W. 21st Ave. (33311); Box 5333 (33310). (305) 484-8107; (305) 621-8107. FAX: (305) 739-7251. Licensee: TAK Communications (group owner; acq 11-87; $34 million; FTR 11-30-87). Rep: D & R Radio. Format: Adult contemp. News staff one. Target aud: 25-54; women & adults. ■ Richard K. Penn, pres & gen mgr; Fran Yacovone, natl sls mgr; Mike Breahl, rgnl sls mgr; Debra Towsley, prom mgr; Jere Sullivan, progmg dir; Jodi Stewart, pub affrs dir; Jim Sorensen, chief engr.

WWNN(AM)—See Pompano Beach.

Fort Myers

*WAYJ(FM)—October 1987: 88.7 mhz; 50 kw. Ant 400 ft. TL: N26 19 00 W81 47 13 (CP: 100 kw, ant 620 ft.). Stereo. Hrs opn: 24. Box 61275, Suite 202, 1860 Boy Scout Dr. (33907). (813) 936-1929. Licensee: Southwest Florida Community Radio Inc. Net: USA. Wash atty: Gammon & Grange. Format: Contemp Christian. News staff one; news progmg one hr wkly. Target aud: 18-34. ■ Bob Augsburg, pres & gen mgr; Bill Scott, stn mgr & gen sls mgr; Steve Dees, prom dir; Johnnie Hale, progmg dir.

WCKT(FM)—See Lehigh Acres.

WCRM(AM)—Aug 22, 1964: 1350 khz; 1 kw-D, 150 w-N. TL: N26 37 31 W81 50 29 (CP: 5 kw-D). Hrs opn: 19. 3448 Canal St. (33916). (813) 334-1350. FAX: (813) 332-5183. Licensee: Manna Christian Missions Inc. (acq 6-89). Net: USA. Wash atty: Schwartz, Woods & Miller. Format: Spanish, English. News staff one; news progmg 5 hrs wkly. Target aud: General. ■ Salvador Santana, gen mgr; Katherine Santana, prom dir; David Lopez, mus dir; Enrique Martinez, news dir; Paul Wolfe, chief engr.

WCVU(FM)—See Naples.

WDCQ(AM)—(Pine Island Center). Feb 20, 1986: 1200 khz; 10 kw-D, 2.5 kw-N. TL: N26 42 52 W82 02 46. Stereo. Hrs opn: 24. Barnett Bank Bldg. Suite 502, 12381 S. Cleveland Ave., Fort Myers (33907). (813) 278-1212. FAX: (813) 278-0423. Licensee: Network Properties of America Ltd. (acq 8-1-90; $800,000; FTR 7-30-90). Net: ABC/I, BRN, NBC Talknet; Florida's Radio Net. Rep: Banner. Wash atty: Latham & Watkins. Format: Talk. News staff 3. Target aud: 35 plus; listeners with buying power. Spec prog: Auto, real state, stock exchange. ■ Steve Gilbert, sr vp & gen mgr; Chris Fanella, opns dir; Larry Kent, gen sls mgr; Joe Routte, news dir; Paul Wolf, chief engr.

WHEW(FM)—Listing follows WMYR(AM).

WINK(AM)—March 1, 1940: 1240 khz; 1 kw-U. TL: N26 37 28 W81 49 52. Box 331, 1412 Jackson St. (33902). (813) 337-2346. FAX: (813) 334-4329. Licensee: Fort Myers Broadcasting Co. Net: CBS, MBS, Daynet. Rep: McGavren Guild. Wash atty: Leibowitz & Spencer. Format: News, talk. News staff 2; news progmg 38 hrs wkly. Target aud: 35-64. Spec prog: Information hr wkly. ■ Edward McBride, pres; Joseph C. Schwartzel, vp; Robert Grissinger, stn mgr; Wayne Simons, gen sls mgr; Carol White, progmg dir; Brian Burns, news dir; Galen Hassinger, chief engr.

WINK-FM—Oct 10, 1964: 96.9 mhz; 100 kw. Ant 1,322 ft. TL: N26 38 40 W081 52 10. Stereo. Prog sep from AM. Format: Adult contemp. News staff 2; news progmg 8 hrs wkly. Target aud: 25-54; females. ■ Bob Grissinger, progmg dir & mus dir. ■ WINK-TV affil.

*WJYO(FM)—1988: 91.5 mhz; 3 kw. Ant 285 ft. TL: N26 30 18 W81 51 14. 6469 Parkland Dr., Sarasota (34243). (813) 275-6868. FAX: (813) 753-2963. Licensee: Radio Training Network Inc. (acq 1-23-92; $375,000; FTR 2-17-92). Format: Contemp Christian. ■ Greg Francis mgr; Bill Martin, progmg dir.

WMYR(AM)—Nov 11, 1952: 1410 khz; 5 kw-U, DA-N. TL: N26 37 23 W81 51 18. Box 216 (33902). Licensee: Robert Hecksher. Format: Country. ■ Robert Hecksher, gen mgr & chief engr; Kathleen Hecksher, gen sls mgr; Simon Train, progmg dir.

WHEW(FM)—Co-owned with WMYR(AM). Dec 2, 1969: 101.9 mhz; 100 kw. Ant 1,020 ft. TL: N26 25 23 W81 37 07. Stereo. Prog sep from AM. (813) 332-2102. Format: Country. ■ Robert Hecksher, progmg dir.

WOLZ(FM)—January 1970: 95.3 mhz; 97 kw. Ant 453 ft. TL: N26 37 25 W82 06 56. Stereo. Suite 315, 4210 Metro Pkwy. (33916). (813) 275-0095. FAX: (813) 275-3299. Licensee: Heritage Broadcast Group Inc. (group owner). Rep: D & R Radio. Format: Oldies. News staff one. Target aud: 25-54; general. ■ James T. Cullen Jr., chmn; Steven E. Humphries, pres & gen mgr; Marty Berger, opns mgr; Marshall Zotara, gen sls mgr; Staci Chase, news dir; Mark Skinner, chief engr.

WRXK-FM—See Bonita Springs.

*WSFP-FM—Sept 12, 1983: 90.1 mhz; 100 kw. Ant 813 ft. TL: N26 48 54 W81 45 44. Stereo. Hrs opn: 24. Re-broadcasts WUSF(FM) Tampa 85%. 8111 College Parkway (33919). (813) 432-5580 Licensee: University of South Florida. Net: NPR, APR; Fla. Pub. Wash atty: Cohn & Marks. Format: Class, jazz, news & info. News staff 2; news progmg 28 hrs wkly. Target aud: 24 plus. ■ JoAnn Urofsky, stn mgr; Barney Boque, dev mgr; Jill Erickson, prom mgr; Michael Crane, progmg dir; Valerie Alker, news dir; Earl Carron, chief engr.

Fort Myers Beach

WJBX(FM)—1983: 99.3 mhz; 50 kw. Ant 476 ft. TL: N26 30 18 W81 51 14. Stereo. Suite 258-263, 12993 S. Cleveland Blvd., Fort Myers (33907). Licensee: Schefflera Inc. (acq 5-13-92; $1.55 million; FTR 6-1-92). Rep: Eastman. Wash atty: Leventhal, Senter & Lerman. Format: Classic rock. Target aud: 25-54. Spec prog: Sunday Night Blues Jam 5 hrs wkly. ■ John R. Linn, pres & gen mgr; Mike Linn, gen sls mgr; Jennifer Vaughn, prom dir, news dir & pub affrs dir; Dick Tyler, progmg dir.

Fort Myers Villas

WSUV(FM)—July 31, 1991: 106.3 mhz; 6 kw. Ant 266 ft. TL: N26 30 18 W81 51 14. Suite 258 S. Cleveland Ave. (33907). (813) 275-9980. (813) 275-5611. Licensee: Jerry Bellairs. Group owner: Sunshine Broadcasting Inc. Net: Unistar. Wash atty: Peter Tannenwald. Format: Adult contemp. Target aud: 25-54; middle to upper scale. ■ Jerry Bellairs, pres & gen mgr; Vivian Bellairs, vp opns; Dean Tyler, progmg dir; Paul Wolf, vp engrg. ■ Rates: $50; 30; 30; 30.

Fort Pierce

WIRA(AM)—May 18, 1946: 1400 khz; 1 kw-U. TL: N27 26 07 W80 21 41. Box 3032 (34948); 706 N. 7th St. (34950). (407) 464-1400. FAX: (407) 461-7089. Licensee: Ardman Broadcasting Corp. of Florida. Group owner: Ardman Broadcasting Corp. (acq 1993; FTR 9-13-93). Net: NBC, NBC Talknet, Unistar; Fla. Net. Format: Adult contemp. Spec prog: Creole 2 hrs wkly. ■ Steve Lipa, gen mgr; Ed Burfield, mus dir; Scott Tanner, chief engr.

WOVV(FM)—Co-owned with WIRA(AM). Oct 30, 1969: 95.5 mhz; 100 kw. Ant 981 ft. TL: N27 07 20 W80 23 21. Stereo. Prog sep from AM. Net: Unistar. Format: CHR. Target aud: 18-49; active, contemporary. Spec prog: Black one hr wkly. ■ M.J. Kalli, progmg dir.

***WJFP(FM)**—Not on air, target date unknown: 91.1 mhz; 6 kw. Ant 157 ft. 1150 W. King St., Cocoa (32922). Licensee: Black Media Works Inc.

WJNX(AM)—Dec 24, 1952: 1330 khz; 5 kw-D, 1 kw-N, DA-2. TL: N27 27 20 W80 22 02. Hrs opn: 24. 1500 N. Flagler (33401). (407) 464-1330. Licensee: Fairbanks Communications Inc. (group owner; acq 2-21-91; $365,000; FTR 3-11-91). Net: ABC/E, Westwood One. Rep: Katz & Powell. Format: News/talk. News progmg 20 hrs wkly. Target aud: 25-54. Spec prog: Relg 7 hrs wkly. ■ George Mills, gen mgr; Warren Chiavaroli, gen sls mgr; John Picano, prom mgr; Francis Sherwood, chief engr.

WKGR(FM)—May 1, 1961: 98.7 mhz; 100 kw. Ant 1,381 ft. TL: N27 07 20 W80 23 21. Stereo. Suite 101, 3223 Commerce Pl., West Palm Beach (33407). (407) 686-9505. FAX: (407) 489-0157. Licensee: Amaturo Group Ltd. (group owner; acq 9-90; $11.6 million; FTR 9-3-90). Rep: D & R Radio. Format: Classic rock. News staff one. Spec prog: Black one hr, farm one hr, relg one hr wkly. ■ Jeff Sleete, gen mgr; Rad Messick, progmg dir & mus dir; Peg Browning, news dir; Chris Hicks, chief engr.

WOVV(FM)—Listing follows WIRA(AM).

***WQCS(FM)**—April 1982: 88.9 mhz; 100 kw. Ant 436 ft. TL: N27 25 17 W80 21 23. Stereo. 3209 Virginia Ave. (34981). (407) 462-4744. FAX: (407) 462-4743. Licensee: Indian River Community College. Net: NPR, AP, APR. Format: Class. ■ Jim Holmes, gen mgr; George Dyer, opns mgr; Tina Burr, mus dir; Jill Roberts, news dir; Mike Gerley, chief engr.

Fort Walton Beach

WFSH(AM)—See Valparaiso-Niceville.

WFTW(AM)—Nov 20, 1953: 1260 khz; 2.5 kw-D. TL: N30 24 49 W86 37 40 (CP: 1 kw-D. TL: N30 24 51 W86 37 40). Box 2347, 225 N.W. Hollywood Blvd. (32549). (904) 243-7676. FAX: (904) 664-0203. Licensee: Holladay Broadcasting Co. Inc. (acq 1993; $1 million with co-located FM; FTR 9-20-93). Net: AP; Florida. Format: News/talk. ■ Clay Holladay, pres; Georgia Edmiston, gen mgr; Zoe Rawley, gen sls mgr; Rick Zurick, progmg dir; Bruce Campbell, chief engr.

WKSM(FM)—Co-owned with WFTW(AM). May 28, 1965: 99.3 mhz; 3 kw. Ant 171 ft. TL: N30 24 49 W86 37 40 (CP: 99.5 mhz, 50 kw, ant 449 ft, TL: N30 24 51 W86 37 40). Stereo. Prog sep from AM. Format: Rock. ■ Scratch Malone, opns mgr & progmg dir; Jane Trepagnier, gen sls mgr; Steve O'Day, prom mgr; Rick Allen, mus dir; Dave Mackenzie, news dir; Neil Fox, pub affrs dir. ■ Rates: $28; 28; 28; 15.

WJUS(FM)—Not on air, target date unknown: 96.5 mhz; 98 kw. Ant 984 ft. TL: N30 45 04 W86 42 38 (CP: Ant 666 ft.). Juanina Inc., 17 Racetrack Rd. (32548). Licensee: Juanina Inc.

WKSM(FM)—Listing follows WFTW(AM).

WNUE(AM)—1956: 1400 khz; 1 kw-U. TL: N30 25 26 W86 38 22. 281 W. Miracle Strip Pkwy. (32548); 118 Wright Pkwy. (32548). (904) 664-0242. Licensee: Triple B Broadcasting Corp. (acq 9-90; $10,000; FTR 9-24-90). Net: UPI. Rep: Busby. Format: Sports. ■ Jerry D. Braswell, pres; David Hedrick, gen mgr.

***WPSM(FM)**—July 1, 1985: 91.1 mhz; 383 w. Ant 120 ft. TL: N30 25 14 W86 36 43. Stereo. Hrs opn: 24. Box 1474 (32549); 13 Kelly Ave. (32548). (904) 244-7667. FAX: (904) 244-3068; (904) 244-7667. Licensee: Fort Walton Beach Educ Broadcasting Corp. Net: USA. Format: Adult contemp, Christian. News staff one; news progmg 14 hrs wkly. Target aud: 25-55; young to middle-age adult Christians. ■ L.M. Thome, pres; Terry K. Thome, gen mgr; Dale Riddick, progmg dir; Bruce Campbell, chief engr.

WWSF-FM—(Andalusia, Ala.). July 1950: 98.1 mhz; 89 kw. Ant 1,090 ft. TL: N30 59 14 W86 43 08. Stereo. Suite 5, 38 Miracle Strip Pkwy. S.W., Ft. Walton Beach, FL (32548). (904) 664-2400. FAX: (904) 664-2552. Licensee: MetroCities Communications (group owner). Rep: Christal. Wash atty: Wiley, Rein, Fielding. Format: CHR. News staff one. Target aud: 18-44; young adults & couples, persons in "age of acquisition." ■ Deane Johnson, pres; Ronald A. Hill, gen mgr; Gwen Allegretto, gen sls mgr; Lisa Captain, prom dir; Tim Kincaid, progmg dir & mus dir; Cheryl Adams, asst mus dir, news dir & pub affrs dir; Gerald Wilson, chief engr. ■ Rates: $30; 28; 28; 20.

Gainesville

WAJD(AM)—May 31, 1961: 1390 khz; 5 kw-D, 51 w-N. TL: N29 39 56 W82 17 26. 7120 S.W. 24th Ave. (32607). (904) 331-2200. FAX: (904) 331-0401. Licensee: Gillen Broadcasting Corp. (acq 9-22-87; $1.9 million; with co-located FM; FTR 8-17-87). Net: AP. Rep: Banner. Format: CHR. Target aud: 12-49. ■ Douglas J. Gillen, pres; Barry Sides, gen sls mgr; Jeri Banta, progmg dir; Wayne Irwin, chief engr. ■ Rates: $40; 35; 40; 20.

WYKS(FM)—Co-owned with WAJD(AM). May 4, 1970: 105.5 mhz; 3 kw. Ant 266 ft. TL: N29 37 52 W82 25 18. Dups AM 100%.

WEAG-FM—(Starke). Feb 28, 1978: 106.3 mhz; 1.35 kw. Ant 495 ft. TL: N29 55 50 W82 06 16. Stereo. Hrs opn: 24. 1421 S. Water St. (32091). (904) 964-5001. Licensee: Dickerson Broadcasting Inc. (acq 1-29-84). Format: Modern country. News progmg 5 hrs wkly. Target aud: 25-54. ■ Ruth Dickerson, gen mgr; Chuck Kramer, opns mgr.

WEAG(AM)—(Starke). Feb 23, 1957: 1490 khz; 650 w-U. TL: N29 55 50 W82 06 16. Stereo. Hrs opn: 24. Dups FM 100%. News progmg 5 hrs wkly.

WFEZ(FM)—See Williston.

WGGG(AM)—February 1948: 1230 khz; 1 kw-U. TL: N29 40 56 W82 24 48. 900 N.W. 8th Ave. (32601). (904) 376-1230. FAX: (904) 376-2666. Licensee: Gator Broadcasting Corp. (acq 10-23-86; $500,000; FTR 6-10-85). Format: Talk. ■ Mike Jurian, gen mgr; Michael Jurian, gen sls mgr; Mike Jurain, progmg dir; Tim McGuire, chief engr.

***WJLF(FM)**—Aug 26, 1991: 91.7 mhz; 2 kw. Ant 400 ft. TL: N29 38 34 W82 25 13. Stereo. Hrs opn: 24. 2925 N.W. 39th Ave. (32605). (904) 374-4941; (904) 373-WJLF. Licensee: First Assembly of God. Net: USA. Wash atty: Wiley, Rein & Fielding. Format: Contemp Christian. News progmg 21 hrs wkly. Target aud: 18-49. ■ A.L. Lastinger, chmn; Michael Perry, stn mgr & gen sls mgr; Daryl Taylor, progmg dir; Robin Levy, mus dir; George Perdue, chief engr.

WKTK(FM)—See Crystal River.

WLUS(AM)—October 1954: 980 khz; 5 kw-D, 166 w-N. TL: N29 37 26 W82 17 19. Box 1068 (32602). (904) 372-2528. FAX: (904) 372-2520. Licensee: Eagle Broadcasting Co. (acq 10-88; $407,000 FTR 10-31-88). Net: AP. Rep: Roslin. Format: MOR. ■ Jim Brown, gen mgr; Jim Brand, progmg dir; George Fogle, chief engr.

WRUF(AM)—1928: 850 khz; 5 kw-U, DA-N. TL: N29 38 34 W82 25 13. Box 14444, University of Florida (32604); 3200 Wiemer Hall (32611). (904) 392-0771. FAX: (904) 392-0519. Licensee: Board of Regents of the Univ. of Florida. Net: CBS, NBC Talknet, CNN Radio; Fla. Net. Wash atty: Irwin, Campbell, Bell. Format: News/talk. News staff 3; news progmg 54 hrs wkly. Target aud: 25-60; adults, middle-to-upper income. Spec prog: Black 4 hrs wkly. ■ Bob Clarke, vp, dev dir, sls dir, mktg dir & prom dir; Tom Krynski, opns mgr, progmg mgr & news dir; Don Rice, chief engr.

WRUF-FM—1948: 103.7 mhz; 100 kw. Ant 768 ft. TL: N29 42 34 W82 23 40. Stereo. Prog sep from AM. Net: ABC/R. Format: AOR, classic rock. News staff 3; news progmg 7 hrs wkly. Target aud: 18-49. Spec prog: Black one hr, progsv 2 hrs wkly. ■ Harry Guscott, stn mgr; David Singer, prom dir.

***WUFT-FM**—Sept 27, 1981: 89.1 mhz; 100 kw. Ant 771 ft. TL: N29 42 34 W82 23 40. Stereo. Hrs opn: 24. 2206 Weimer Hall, Univ. of Florida (32611). (904) 392-5200. FAX: (904) 392-5731. Licensee: Board of Regents, Univ. of Florida. Net: NPR. Wash atty: Schwartz, Wood & Miller. Format: Class, jazz, public. News staff 3; news progmg 15 hrs wkly. Target aud: General. ■ Richard A. Lehner, gen mgr; Henri Pensis, stn mgr; Susan Wagner, prom mgr; Bill Beckett, progmg dir; Richard Drake, mus dir; Cindy Hosbein, news dir; Manis Samons, chief engr. ■ WUFT-TV affil.

WWLO(AM)—January 1990: 1430 khz; 2.5 kw-D. TL: N29 37 26 W82 17 19. Suite 204 E, 1601 Belvedere Rd., W. Palm Beach FL (33406); Suite 3, 102 NE 10th Ave. (32601). (904) 377-5656. FAX: (904) 399-1925. Licensee: Gainesville Broadcasters. Wash atty: Irwin, Campbell & Grove. Format: Black. ■ Carl J. Auel, pres; Willy Martin, gen mgr.

***WYFB(FM)**—Aug 4, 1985: 90.5 mhz; 100 kw. Ant 679 ft. TL: N29 52 08 W82 12 04 (CP: 96.81 kw). Stereo. Hrs opn: 24. Rt. 2, Box 1012, Keystone Heights (32656). (904) 473-7077; (904) 377-0636. Licensee: Bible Broadcasting Network. (group owner). Net: Bible Bcstg Net, USA. Format: Relg. News progmg 12 hrs wkly. Target aud: General. ■ Lowell Davey, pres; Robert Reed, stn mgr & pub affrs dir; Leo Galetta, chief opns; Vic Gregory, progmg dir; Harold Richards, progmg mgr; Hal Mashburn, chief engr.

WYGC(FM)—May 1, 1982: 100.9 mhz; 3 kw. Ant 300 ft. TL: N29 38 02 W82 18 50. Stereo. Box 5069 (32602); Suite C-3, 4424 N.W. 13th St. (32609). (904) 375-1317. FAX: (904) 375-6961. Licensee: Asterisk Communications Inc. Group owner: Asterisk Inc. (acq 10-4-93; $1.4 million; FTR 10-25-93). Net: ABC/E. Rep: McGavren Guild. Format: C&W. News staff one. ■ Mel Clark, gen mgr; Nancy Keeney, progmg dir & news dir; Mark Skinner, chief engr.

WYKS(FM)—Listing follows WAJD(AM).

WYOC(FM)—(High Springs). Jan 31, 1984: 104.9 mhz; 1.6 kw. Ant 450 ft. TL: N29 49 16 W82 34 28. Stereo. Hrs opn: 24. Box 1646, 305. N.E. 21st St., (32643). (904) 454-3666. Licensee: Santa Fe Wireless Inc. (acq 12-12-90; $800,000; FTR 11-26-90). Net: Unistar, CNN. Rep: P.M.C. Rgnl Reps. Wash atty: Larry Perry. Format: Oldies. News progmg 4 hrs wkly. Target aud: 25-54. ■ Beth Kenney, pres & gen mgr; Tom Kenney, gen sls mgr; Keith Conway, progmg dir; Kyle Magrill, chief engr. ■ Rates: $25; 20; 25; 10.

Goulds

WRTO(FM)—February 1976: 98.3 mhz; 1.1 kw. Ant 462 ft. TL: N25 32 24 W80 28 07 (CP: 100 kw, ant 1,627 ft.). Stereo. 2960 Coral Way, Miami (33145). (305) 445-4040. FAX: (305) 529-6631. Licensee: License Corporation Number Two. Net: UPI. Format: Latin/tropical, Hispanic. ■ Charlie Fernandez, vp & gen mgr.

Green Cove Springs

WJBT(FM)—1978: 92.7 mhz; 6 kw. Ant 300 ft. TL: N30 04 12 W81 38 50 (CP: 1.3 kw, ant 497 ft.). Stereo. Suite 1, 9454 Phillips Hwy. (32256). (904) 292-0811. FAX: (904) 292-0434. Licensee: UNC Media of Jacksonville Inc. (acq 12-2-91; with WZAZ(AM) Jacksonville). Net: CBS Spectrum. Format: Urban contemp. Target aud: 12-54; the young and the-young-at-heart. ■ Connie Balthrop, pres; Bruce Demps, gen mgr & gen sls mgr; Shaun Freeland, prom mgr; Gary Young, progmg dir; Nate Bell, mus dir; Brandy Shannon, news dir; Jerry Smith, chief engr.

Gretna

WGWD(FM)—Oct 2, 1989: 93.3 mhz; 3 kw. Ant 328 ft. TL: N30 33 24 W84 36 05 (CP: 6 kw). Stereo. Hrs opn: 24. Box 919, 100A N. Adams, Quincy (32351). (904) 627-7086. FAX: (904) 627-3422. Licensee: De Col Inc. (acq 9-18-91; $75,000; FTR 10-7-91). Net: USA. Format: Country. News progmg 21 hrs wkly. Target aud: 25-54. Spec prog: Black 20 hrs wkly. ■ Monte Bitner, gen mgr & gen sls mgr; Billy Rachels, progmg dir; Jimmy Devane, chief engr. ■ Rates: $10; 8; 10; 8.

Haines City

WLVF(AM)—Sept 9, 1960: 930 khz; 500 w-D, DA. TL: N28 04 52 W81 38 23. 110 W. Scenic Hwy. (33844). (813) 422-9583. Licensee: Landmark Baptist Church. Format: Conservative gospel. ■ Jeff Cruse, gen mgr & progmg dir; Bruce Johnson, mus dir.

***WLVF-FM**—April 11, 1986: 90.3 mhz; 800 w. Ant 265 ft. TL: N28 09 28 W81 37 34 (CP: 3 kw, ant 200 ft.). Stereo. (acq 7-90; FTR 7-16-90). Format: Relg. Spec prog: Southern gospel 18 hrs wkly.

Havana

WMLO(FM)—1986: 104.9 mhz; 47 kw. Ant 494 ft. TL: N30 35 11 W84 14 11. Stereo. Hrs opn: 24. 1401 Maclay Commerce Dr., Tallahassee (32312); Box 4069, Tallahassee (32315). (904) 668-6600. FAX: (904) 668-9995. Licensee: Ed Winton (acq 5-1-87). Net: Wall Street. Rep: Eastman. Wash atty: Michael Jankowski. Format: Mello adult contemp. News staff one; news progmg 21 hrs wkly. Target aud: 35-64. Spec prog: U. of Georgia football 3 hrs wkly. ■ Ed Winton, pres & gen sls mgr; Bill Dutcher, gen mgr; Lance Winton, opns dir & news dir; Roger Craig, mktg mgr; Charles Kinney, chief engr. ■ Rates: $24; 24; 24; 19.

Hernando

WRZN(AM)—June 1989: 720 khz; 10 kw-D, 250 w-N, DA-N. TL: N28 55 21 W82 22 21. 3988 N. Roscoe Rd. (34442). (904) 726-7221; (904) 732-7200. FAX: (904) 726-3172. Licensee: Management and Marketing Synergy Inc. Net: SMN. Wash atty: Leibowitz & Spencer. Format: Big band, MOR. News progmg 6 hrs wkly. Target aud: 45 plus. Spec prog: Rebroadcast WFLA-TV (Tampa) local news 4 hrs wkly. ■ Franklin Watson, pres & gen mgr. ■ Rates: $18; 12; 15; 6.

Hialeah

WCMQ-FM—Dec 22, 1969: 92.3 mhz; 31 kw. Ant 617 ft. TL: N25 46 29 W80 11 19. Stereo. 1001 Ponce De Leon, Coral Gables (33134). (305) 444-9292. FAX: (305) 461-4951. Licensee: Spanish Broadcasting System of Florida Inc. Group owner: Spanish Broadcasting System Inc. (acq 12-22-86; grpsl; FTR 9-29-86). Rep: Major Mkt. Format: Adult contemp Sp. News staff 10. ■ Victor Aleman, gen mgr; Thomas Garcia Fuste, news dir; Ralph Chambers, chief engr.

WRFM(AM)—Licensed to Hialeah. See Miami.

High Springs

WYOC(FM)—Licensed to High Springs. See Gainesville.

Holiday

WLVU-FM—1979: 106.3 mhz; 3 kw. Ant 300 ft. TL: N28 16 51 W82 42 52. Stereo. 6214 Springer Dr., Port Richey (34668). (813) 845-1063. Licensee: Pasco Pinellas Broadcasting (acq 2-1-86; grpsl; FTR 12-9-85). Rep: D & R Radio. Format: Adult standards. ■ Frank Ferreri, gen mgr; Susan Campbell, gen sls mgr; Larry Pugliese, prom mgr.

Holly Hill

***WAPN(FM)**—October 1985: 91.5 mhz; 1.8 kw. Ant 300 ft. TL: N29 15 06 W81 02 53. Hrs opn: 24. Box 311, Daytona Beach (32125); 1508 State Ave. (32117). (904) 677-4272. FAX: (904) 673-3715. Licensee: Public Radio Inc. Format: Gospel word & praise, adult contemp, Black. Target aud: General. Spec prog: Sp 4 hrs wkly. ■ Gordon C. Lund, pres, gen mgr, gen sls mgr & mus dir; Earlyne Lund, prom mgr, progmg dir & news dir; Shane Stanton, chief engr.

Hollywood

WLQY(AM)—April 1953: 1320 khz; 5 kw-U, DA-2. TL: N26 01 53 W80 16 42. Suite 102-B, 11645 Biscayne Blvd., Miami (33181-3138). (305) 776-9899. Licensee: Genesis Communications Inc. (group owner; acq 5-21-88). Format: Relg, Sp. News staff one; news progmg one hr wkly. Target aud: 35 plus; female. Spec prog: Haitian, Jamaican. ■ Bruce Maduri, pres; Sandra Herzberg, gen mgr; Rick Santos, stn mgr, vp opns & opns dir; Rick Rieke, chief engr.

Holmes Beach

WISP(FM)—Jan 27, 1992: 98.7 mhz; 3 kw. Ant 328 ft. TL: N27 27 49 W82 35 32. Stereo. Hrs opn: 24. Suite 904, 1605 Main St., Sarasota (34236). Licensee: Alpalm Broadcasting Corp. (acq 1-2-92; $2.3 million; FTR 1-27-92). Net: CNN. Wash atty: Pepper & Corazzini. Format: Soft adult contemp. Target aud: 25 plus; professional, educated, upscale audience. Spec prog: Jazz 3 hrs wkly. ■ Norman Alpert, pres; David Alpert, vp & gen mgr; John Sanders, rgnl sls mgr; Jack Evans, news dir; Doug Lindberg, pub affrs dir; Al Baxa, chief engr.

Homestead

WOIR(AM)—Nov 4, 1957: 1430 khz; 5 kw-D, 500 w-N, DA-N. TL: N25 27 09 W80 30 57. 100 Blair Rd., Oyster Bay, NY (11771). (305) 245-8408. Licensee: Continental Broadcasting Corp. Format: Spanish. ■ Aurelio Duque Estrada, opns mgr; Frank Huerta, progmg dir; Jose A. Marques, news dir; Charles Dreher, chief engr.

WXDJ(FM)—1986: 95.7 mhz; 100 kw. Ant 982 ft. TL: N25 32 24 W80 28 07 (CP: 23.5 kw, ant 1,683 ft.). Stereo. Suite 1000, 3191 Coral Way, Miami (33145). (305) 447-9595. FAX: (305) 448-4735. Licensee: New Age Broadcasting Inc. (acq 12-1-87; $8.1 million; FTR 10-19-87). Rep: Lotus. Wash atty: Wiley, Rein & Fielding. Format: Spanish. News progmg 4 hrs wkly. Target aud: 12 plus; all Hispanic groups. ■ Kymm Abrahamson, gen mgr; Maggie Rodriquez, gen sls mgr; Pio Ferro, progmg dir.

Homosassa Springs

WXCV(FM)—March 1983: 95.3 mhz; 3 kw. Ant 410 ft. TL: N28 53 14 W82 31 39 (CP: 2.8 kw, ant 339 ft.). Stereo. Hrs opn: 24. Box 1408, 9244 W. Fort Island Trail, Crystal River (34429). (904) 795-9595; (904) 563-0953. FAX: (904) 795-7220. Licensee: Westwind Broadcasting Inc. Net: AP. Format: Adult contemp. News staff one; news progmg 7 hrs wkly. Target aud: 25-54. Spec prog: Jazz 7 hrs, oldies 6 hrs wkly. ■ Bruce Snow, pres; Alan Chatman, gen mgr & gen sls mgr; Christine Stuart, prom dir & news dir; Chris Howard, progmg dir. ■ Rates: $21; 19; 21; 18.

Immokalee

WZOR(AM)—Oct 14, 1964: 1490 khz; 1 kw-U. TL: N26 25 27 W81 26 32. 2105 W. Immokalee Dr. (33934). (813) 657-6262. Licensee: HAB Communications Systems Inc. (acq 8-21-89; $210,000; FTR 9-11-89). Format: Sp, urban contemp. Spec prog: French 3 hrs wkly. ■ Ed Lozeme, gen mgr.

Indian Rocks Beach

***WKES(FM)**—See St. Petersburg.

***WXYB(AM)**—May 11, 1963: 1520 khz; 1 kw-D, DA. TL: N27 50 26 W82 46 10 (CP: 600 w, TL: N27 50 45 W82 46 21). 27873 US 19 N., Clearwater (34621). (813) 725-5555; (813) 725-5552. FAX: (813) 724-1229. Licensee: ASA Broadcasting Inc. (acq 5-24-93; $31,000; FTR 6-14-93). Format: Ethnic, Greek, International. ■ Sotrios Agelatos, pres & gen mgr; Darlyne Agelatos, opns dir; Angelo Agelatos, progmg dir; John Stortz, chief engr.

Inglis

WAVQ(FM)—March 1, 1994: 104.3 mhz. 6 kw. Ant 329 ft. Stereo. Hrs opn: 24. 3507-A Van Tassel, Amarillo, TX (79121). Licensee: West Coast Radio. Wash atty: Gardner, Carton & Douglas. Format: Btfl music. News staff one; news progmg 10 hrs wkly. Target aud: 25-54; adults. ■ Lu Lacy, CEO, chmn, pres, CFO & gen mgr; Mark Whisenhunt, stn mgr; David Bell, opns mgr; Tim Guentz, engrg mgr.

Inverness

WINV(AM)—Sept 1, 1965: 1560 khz; 5 kw-D, 500 w-N. TL: N28 50 30 W82 22 16. Stereo. 1541 S. Hillock Terrace (34452). (904) 726-1560. FAX: (904) 637-3223. Licensee: WINV Inc. (acq 3-22-89). Net: USA. Wash atty: Michael Wilhelm. Format: News/talk. News staff one; news progmg 20 hrs wkly. Target aud: 25-65. ■ Robert G. Webb, pres & gen mgr; Karen Webb, gen sls mgr; Becky Webb, prom dir; Jerry Webb, progmg dir & news dir; Dave Tarry, chief engr. ■ Rates: $10; 8; 10; 5.

***WWUA(FM)**—Not on air, target date unknown: 90.1 mhz; 4.5 kw. Ant 354 ft. TL: N28 52 09 W82 26 47. R.R. 1, Box 888, Webster (33597). Licensee: Alkalodge Inc.

Jacksonville

WAIA(FM)—(Callahan). June 1, 1983: 93.3 mhz; 50 kw. Ant 462 ft. TL: N30 33 22 W81 33 13 Stereo. Hrs opn: 24. 8386 Bay Meadows Rd., Suite 107, Jacksonville (32256). (904) 636-0507. FAX: (904) 636-0533. Licensee: Paxson Jacksonville License L.P. Group owner: Paxson Broadcasting (acq 1993). Rep: Banner. Format: Classic rock. Target aud: 18-45. ■ Bud Paxson, CEO; Jim Bocock, pres; Linda Byrd, gen mgr & gen sls mgr; John Richards, opns mgr; Dea Sims, mktg dir; Craig Williams, progmg dir; Charlie Chase, news dir; Kyle Dickson, chief engr.

WAPE-FM—April 1949: 95.1 mhz; 100 kw. Ant 460 ft. TL: N30 17 09 W81 44 52. Stereo. 9090 Hogan Rd. (32216). (904) 642-1055. FAX: (904) 641-3297. Licensee: Evergreen Media Corp of Jacksonville. Group owner: Evergreen Media Corp. Rep: Christal. Format: CHR. ■ Mark Schwartz, pres & gen mgr; Rich Rectanus, gen sls mgr; Rick Everett, prom mgr; Jeff McCartney, progmg dir; Damon Cox, mus dir; Marge Fizzy, news dir; Jim Henry, chief engr.

***WAYR(AM)**—See Orange Park.

WCGL(AM)—1948: 1360 khz; 5 kw-D. TL: N30 16 33 W81 38 12. 70 Sherwood Sq. (32208). (904) 766-9955. FAX: (904) 765-9214. Licensee: JBD Communications Inc. (acq 12-27-89; $510,000; FTR 1-15-90). Net: American Urban. Rep: Katz & Powell. Format: Relg. ■ Deborah Maiden, pres & gen mgr; Freddie Rhoades, progmg dir; Kelvin Postdale, news dir; Jerry Smith, chief engr.

WCRJ(AM)—Nov 18, 1976: 1530 khz; 50 kw-D, DA. TL: N30 21 50 W81 44 54. Stereo. 5900 Picketville Rd. (32205). (904) 786-9088. Licensee: Country Radio Jacksonville Inc. (acq 9-2-93; $500,000; FTR 9-27-93). Format: Country/Auction Radio Network. News staff one; news progmg 10 hrs wkly. Target aud: General. ■ Glen Black, CEO; Nick Durbano, pres; Neil Lintor, dev dir; Jim Hughes, gen sls mgr; Lee Shannon, progmg dir & mus dir; Bob Dillehay, vp engrg.

WEJZ(FM)—1949: 96.1 mhz; 100 kw. Ant 984 ft. TL: N30 19 22 W81 38 34. Stereo. 1896 Corporate Square Blvd. (32216). (904) 727-9696. FAX: (904) 721-9322. Licensee: Renda Broadcasting Corp. (group owner; acq 6-90; grpsl; FTR 6-25-90). Rep: Katz. Format: Soft adult contemp. News staff one. Target aud: 35-54; office, home and in-the-car audience. ■ Tony Renda, pres; Larry O. Garrett, gen mgr; Doug Berle, gen sls mgr; Sandy Carr, prom dir; Ron Foster, progmg dir & mus dir; Jim Byard, news dir & pub affrs dir; Dick Jones, chief engr.

WHJX-FM—(Brunswick, Ga.). Sept 1, 1966: 101.5 mhz; 100 kw. Ant 239 ft. TL: N31 08 40 W81 34 56 (CP: Ant 1,463 ft.). Stereo. Suite One, 10592 E. Balmoral Circle, Jacksonville, FL (32218). (904) 696-1015. FAX: (904) 696-1011. Licensee: Eagle Broadcasting Inc. (acq 6-22-89; $4.8 million with co-located AM; FTR 7-10-89). Format: Urban contemp. ■ Jim Jerrels, vp & gen mgr; Mark Shands, opns mgr; Phil Tuck, chief engr.

WIVY-FM—November 1965: 102.9 mhz; 100 kw. Ant 984 ft. TL: N30 16 34 W81 33 53. Stereo. Hrs opn: 24. Suite 200, 3101 University Blvd. S. (32216). (904) 721-9111. FAX: (904) 725-9103. Licensee: J.J. Taylor Companies Inc. Group owner: Taylor Communications Inc. (acq 6-1-88; $8,130,000; FTR 5-2-88). Rep: Major Mkt. Wash atty: Leibowitz & Spencer. Format: Adult contemp. News staff one; news progmg 7 hrs wkly. Target aud: 25-49. Spec prog: Jazz 14 hrs wkly. ■ John J. Taylor Jr., CEO; John Taylor III, pres; Henri Desplaines, CFO; Paul Levesque, exec vp; John D. Hunt, gen mgr; Paul Rogers, gen sls mgr; Frank Celebre, natl sls mgr; Rhoda Bohrer, rgnl sls mgr; Larry Kahn, vp mktg; Donna LePre, prom mgr; Kris Abrahams, progmg dir; Shannon West, mus dir; Susan Shaw, news dir & pub affrs dir; Paul Christenson, engrg dir. ■ Rates: $135; 110; 120; 70.

WJAX(AM)—Listing follows WKTZ-FM.

WJBT(FM)—See Green Cove Springs.

***WJCT-FM**—Apr 17, 1972: 89.9 mhz; 100 kw. Ant 835 ft. TL: N30 16 53 W81 34 15. Stereo. 100 Festival Park Ave. (32202). (904) 353-7770. FAX: (904) 358-6331. Licensee: WJCT Inc. Net: APR, NPR; Fla. Pub. Format: Classical, jazz, news. ■ Gene Napier, pres; Raymond Hickman, stn mgr. ■ WJCT-TV affil.

***WJFR(FM)**—Sept 15, 1987: 88.7 mhz; 8 kw. Ant 380 ft. TL: N30 16 53 W81 34 15. Stereo. 2611 WERD Radio Dr. (32204). (904) 389-9088. Licensee: Family Stations Inc. Format: Relg. Target aud: Conservative Christians. ■ Harold Camping, pres; Mike Lewis, stn mgr; Craig Hulsebos, progmg dir; Ron Long, chief engr.

WJXR(FM)—(Macclenny). September 1978: 92.1 mhz; 25 kw. Ant 328 ft. TL: N30 17 54 W82 00 55 Stereo. Hrs opn: 24. Box One, Jacksonville (32234). (904) 259-2292. FAX: (904) 358-2265. Licensee: WJXR Inc. (acq 1-8-85; $335,000; FTR 2-4-85). Net: ABC/D. Rep: Roslin. Wash atty: Rothman & Gordon. Format: Country. News staff one; news progmg 7 hrs wkly. Target aud: 25-54; middle class & upscale families. Spec prog: Farm one hr, bluegrass one hr wkly. ■ Gregory G. Perich, pres & gen mgr; Larry Edwards, opns mgr & progmg dir; Bonnie Thompson, gen sls mgr; Sarah Perich, prom mgr; Doc Anthony, mus dir; Hank Jilek, pub affrs dir; Jerry Smith, chief engr. ■ Rates: $35; 25; 30; 20.

WKQL(FM)—Listing follows WOKV(AM).

***WKTZ-FM**—Feb 8, 1973: 90.9 mhz; 50 kw. Ant 500 ft. TL: N30 16 36 W81 33 47. Stereo. 5353 Arlington Expwy. (32211). (904) 743-2400. Licensee: Jones College (acq 2-7-86). Net: MBS. Format: Btfl mus. News progmg 9 hrs wkly. Target aud: 40 plus; mature adults. ■ Jack H. Jones, pres; Wayne Mashburn, gen mgr; Bill Thomas, gen sls mgr; Tom Buetow, progmg dir; Richard Jones, chief engr.

WJAX(AM)—Co-owned with WKTZ-FM. 1958: 1220 khz; 1 kw-D, 37 w-N. TL: N30 19 30 W81 34 15. Stereo. Dups FM 100%.

***WNCM-FM**—Mar 16, 1984: 88.1 mhz; 1 kw. Ant 500 ft. TL: N30 16 36 W81 33 57. Stereo. Hrs opn: 24. 2361 Cortez Rd. (32246). (904) 641-9626. FAX: (904) 645-

9626. Licensee: New Covenant Educ Ministries. Net: UPI. Format: Christian contemp. ■ Pastor Wiley Tomlinson, pres; Calvin Grabau, gen mgr, vp progmg & mus dir; Bernie Gonzalez, pub affrs dir; Jerry Smith, chief engr.

WNZS(AM)—November 1925: 930 khz; 5 kw-U, DA-N. TL: N30 17 09 W81 44 52. Suite 107, 8386 Baymeadows Rd. (32256). (904) 636-0507. FAX: (904) 636-0533. Licensee: Paxson Broadcasting of Jacksonville Inc. Group owner: Paxson Broadcasting. Net: NBC. Rep: Banner. Format: Sports. Target aud: 25-49. ■ Bud Paxson, CEO; Jim Bocock, pres; Linda Byrd, gen mgr & gen sls mgr; John Richards, opns mgr; Dea Sims, mktg dir; Leigh Hutchins, prom dir; Van Page, progmg dir; Dee Davenport, news dir; Kyle Dickson, chief engr.

WOKV(AM)—Dec 9, 1933: 600 khz; 5 kw-D, 5.4 kw-N, DA-N. TL: N30 18 00 W81 45 34. Hrs opn: 24. Box 6877 (32236); 6869 Lennox Ave. (32205). (904) 783-3711. FAX: (904) 786-1529. Licensee: Phalen & Associates Inc. (acq 6-18-92; $3.75 million; with co-located FM; FTR 7-13-92). Net: ABC TalkRadio, CBS, NBC Talknet, Wall Street, CNN, Mutual; Fla. Net. Rep: Major Mkt. Format: News/talk, sports. Target aud: 25-54. ■ Bill Phalan, pres; Jeff Dorf, vp; Dave Josserand, gen mgr; Mike Johnson, gen sls mgr; Gayle Hart, prom mgr; Mike Darwart, progmg dir; John Buckley, news dir; Craig Kopcho, chief engr.

WKQL(FM)—Co-owned with WOKV(AM). July 1, 1969: 96.9 mhz; 98 kw. Ant 1,014 ft. TL: N30 16 34 W81 33 53. Stereo. Prog sep from AM. Format: Oldies. Target aud: 25-54. ■ Dave Michaels, opns mgr; Yvonne Anderson, mus dir.

WPDQ(AM)—November 1925: 690 khz; 50 kw-D, 10 w-N, DA-N. TL: N30 18 27 W81 56 28. Hrs opn: 24. 6869 Lenox Ave. (32205). (904) 783-3711. Licensee: Prism Radio Partners L.P. (acq 10-22-93; $400,000; FTR 11-8-93). Net: ABC/I. Wash atty: Cohn & Marks. ■ Bill Phalan, pres; Dave Jossarand, gen mgr.

WQIK(AM)—1945: 1320 khz; 5 kw-U, DA-N. TL: N30 17 50 W81 44 35. Stereo. 5555 Radio Ln. (32205). (904) 388-7711; (904) 384-0859. Licensee: Jacor Broadcasting of Florida Inc. Group owner: Jacor Communications Inc. (acq 6-1-04). Net: ABC/E. Rep: Eastman Radio. Format: Country. News staff 3; news progmg 13 hrs wkly. Target aud: 25-54. ■ Randy Michaels, pres; Les Samuels, vp & gen mgr; Buc Weatherby, gen sls mgr; Kaye Jewell, prom mgr; Lee Rogers, progmg dir; Larry Stevens, mus dir; Tim McGuire, news dir; Jim Godbold, pub affrs dir; Mike Hagans, chief engr.

WQIK-FM—September 1964: 99.1 mhz; 100 kw. Ant 1,050 ft. TL: N30 16 34 W81 33 53. Stereo. Hrs opn: 24. Format: Country. News progmg 8 hrs wkly. Target aud: 18-54.

WROO(FM)—May 9, 1977: 107.3 mhz; 100 kw. Ant 705 ft. TL: N30 21 48 W81 45 09. Stereo. Suite 107, 8386 Baymeadows Rd. (32256). (904) 636-0507. FAX: (904) 636-0533. Licensee: Paxson Broadcasting of Jacksonville Inc. Group owner: Paxson Broadcasting (acq 7-22-91; $3.5 million; FTR 8-5-91). Net: CBS. Format: Country. News staff one. Target aud: 25-49. ■ Bud Paxson, CEO; Jim Bocock, pres; Linda Byrd, gen mgr & gen sls mgr; John Richards, opns mgr & progmg dir; Dea Sims, mktg dir; Leigh Hutchins, prom dir; Bobby Knight, mus dir; Dee Davenport, news dir & pub affrs dir; Kyle Dickson, chief engr.

WROS(AM)—July 1955: 1050 khz; 5 kw-D, DA. TL: N30 21 14 W81 44 21. 5590 Rio Grande Ave. (32254). (904) 353-1050. Licensee: The Rose of Jacksonville (acq 6-1-85; $525,000; FTR 4-1-85). Format: Relg. Target aud: 25-65; Christians. ■ Elwyn V. Hall, gen mgr & vp sls; Dean Hall, vp opns, sls dir, vp adv & vp progmg; Jeremy Methin, opns dir & progmg mgr; Rags Hall, opns mgr & adv mgr; M.L. Brinkley, gen sls mgr; Rosemary Dawkins, natl sls mgr; Nicole Ellis, adv dir; Dr. Dan Allen, progmg dir; Chicky Cain, mus dir; Jerry Smith, chief engr.

WVOJ(AM)—Jan 1, 1969: 970 khz; 500 w-U, DA-1. TL: N30 23 08 W81 40 04. 2427 University Blvd. N. (32211). (904) 743-6970. Licensee: WBOM Inc. Group owner: Timm Enterprises (acq 7-1-74). Net: CBN. Format: Relg, news/talk, sports. News progmg 8 hrs wkly. Target aud: General. ■ Bruce Timm, pres; Marilyn Buckner, gen mgr & gen sls mgr; Jim Colling, progmg dir; Jim Collins, mus dir & pub affrs dir; Dick Boekeloo, chief engr. ■ Rates: $10; 10; 10; 10.

WXTL(AM)—See Jacksonville Beach.

WZAZ(AM)—July 4, 1950: 1400 khz; 1 kw-U. TL: N30 19 43 W81 41 42. Stereo. Suite One, 9454 Philips Hwy. (32256). (904) 292-0811. FAX: (904) 292-0434. Licensee: UNC Media of Jacksonville Inc. Group owner: UNC Media Group Ltd. (acq 12-2-91; $2,025,000 with WJBT[FM] Green Cove Springs; FTR 1-6-92). Net: CBS Spectrum. Rep: Roslin. Format: Black. News staff 2; news progmg 5 hrs wkly. Target aud: 25-54; adult Black listeners. ■ Connie Balthrop, pres; Bruce Demps, gen mgr & gen sls mgr; Shawn Freeland, prom mgr; Gary Young, progmg dir; Nate Bell, mus dir; Brandy Shannon, news dir; Jerry Smith, chief engr.

WZNZ(AM)—August 1942: 1460 khz; 5 kw-U, DA-N. TL: N30 19 40 W81 44 49. Stereo. Suite 107, 8386 Baymeadows Rd. (32256). (904) 636-0507. FAX: (904) 636-0533. Licensee: Paxson Enterprises Inc. Group owner: Paxson Broadcasting (acq 1993; $5.6 million; FTR 10-19-92). Net: CNN. Rep: Banner. Format: News. News staff one. news progmg 2 hrs wkly. Target aud: 12-34; heavy teen & male. ■ Bud Paxson, CEO; Jim Bocock, pres; Linda Byrd, gen mgr & gen sls mgr; John Richards, opns mgr; Dea Sims, mktg dir; Van Page, progmg dir; Rose Imperato, news dir; Robert Dillehay, chief engr.

Jacksonville Beach

WXTL(AM)—1946: 1010 khz; 10 kw-D, DA. TL: N30 17 42 W81 33 11. Box 16658, Jacksonville (32216). 10055 Beach Blvd. (32216). (904) 641-1010. FAX: (904) 646-4539. Licensee: Sudbrink Broadcasting of Jacksonville Inc. Group owner: Sudbrink Broadcasting (acq 10-85; $436,250; FTR 8-5-85). Net: USA. Format: Relg. News progmg 2 hrs wkly. Target aud: 25 plus. ■ Robert W. Sudbrink, chmn; Hal Gore, pres; Wes Howard, gen mgr; John Newman, opns dir & prom mgr.

Jensen Beach

WHLG(FM)—Dec 10, 1980: 102.3 mhz; 3 kw. Ant 300 ft. TL: N27 12 53 W80 15 24. Stereo. Hrs opn: 24. 1000 N.W. Alice Ave., Stuart (34994). (407) 692-1000. FAX: (407) 692-2231. Licensee: Genevieve H. Glascock (acq 12-10-80). Net: AP. Wash atty: Kaye, Scholer, Fierman, Hays & Handler. Format: Easy lstng. News progmg 17 hrs wkly. Target aud: 35-64. ■ Genevieve H. Glascock, pres & gen mgr; Patricia Larschau, vp; Patricia A. Larschan, gen sls mgr; Barbra Clifton, prom mgr; Barry Marsh, progmg dir; Robert N. Hurley, mus dir; Tom Teter, news dir; Dane Goode, pub affrs dir; Robert L. Statham, chief engr.

Jupiter

WMLZ(AM)—Not on air, target date unknown: 1000 khz. 1260 W. Third St., Riviera Beach (33404). Licensee: Jupiter Broadcasting Corp.

WADY(FM)—Co-owned with WMLZ(AM). Not on air, target date unknown: 99.5 mhz; 3 kw. Ant 328 ft.

WTRU(FM)—Oct 15, 1971: 99.5 mhz; 3 kw. Ant 315 ft. TL: N26 56 22 W80 07 04. Stereo. 500 N. Delaware Blvd. (33458). (407) 744-6398. FAX: (407) 744-0915. Licensee: Taylor Broadcast Group. Format: Sp. ■ Robert B. Taylor, pres; Jamie Garza, gen mgr.

Key Colony Beach

WKKB(FM)—Not on air, target date unknown: 105.5 mhz; 50 kw. Ant 276 ft. TL: N24 42 25 W81 06 17. c/o Sombrero Marina, 35 Sombrero Blvd., Marathon (33050). Licensee: Richard L. Silva.

Key Largo

WZMQ(FM)—Jan 20, 1990: 103.9 mhz; 6 kw. Ant 150 ft. TL: N25 05 29 W80 26 37 (CP: 50 kw, ant 239 ft., TL: N21 01 35 W80 30 30). Stereo. 1001 Ponce De Leon, Coral Gables (33134). (305) 444-9292. Licensee: Spanish Broadcasting System of Florida Inc. Group owner: Spanish Broadcasting System Inc. (acq 7-12-89; $114,000; FTR 7-31-89). Format: Adult contemp, Sp. ■ Raul Alarcon Jr., pres; Jose Grimalt, gen mgr; Claudia Puig, gen sls mgr; Victor Aleman, prom mgr; Gilda Miros, progmg dir; Elio Oliva, news dir; Charles Dreher, chief engr.

Key West

WAIL(FM)—Listing follows WKWF(AM).

WEOW(FM)—Listing follows WKIZ(AM).

WIIS(FM)—June 1978: 107.1 mhz; 3 kw. Ant 200 ft. TL: N24 33 18 W81 48 07. Stereo. Hrs opn: 24. 517 Eaton St. (33040). (305) 292-1133; (305) 292-1071. FAX: (305) 292-6936. Licensee: White Broadcasting (acq 9-91; $400,000; FTR 5-21-90). Format: Hot adult contemp. News staff one; news progmg 5 hrs wkly. Target aud: 25-54; professional men and women. Spec prog: Oldies 5 hrs, talk 5 hrs, blues one hr, latin music 3 hrs wkly. ■ J. Larry White, CEO; Connie Rice, pres, gen mgr, gen sls mgr & prom dir; George Murphy, vp; Donna Brown, opns mgr; Mark Davids, progmg dir & mus dir. ■ Rates: $15; 15; 15; 11.

***WJIR(FM)**—December 1986: 90.9 mhz; 390 w. Ant 121 ft. TL: N24 33 07 W81 47 53 (CP: 3 kw, ant 105 ft.). Stereo. Hrs opn: 24. 1209 United St. (33040). (305) 294-9547; (305) 296-5773. Licensee: Key West Educational Broadcasting (acq 12-15-85). Format: Relg, educ, adult contemp. News progmg 12 hrs wkly. Target aud: General. ■ Ernest DeLoach, stn mgr; Bill Hopper, opns mgr; Paul Hitchock, chief engr.

WKIZ(AM)—Feb 2, 1959: 1500 khz; 250 w-U, DA-1. TL: N24 34 01 W81 44 54. Stereo. Stock Island, 5016 Fifth Ave. (33040). (305) 294-2523. FAX: (305) 296-0358. Licensee: Fotosonic of Florida Inc. (acq 5-90; $2,050; FTR 5-21-90). Net: CBS. Rep: Roslin. Format: Oldies. ■ Todd Swofford, gen mgr; Timothy Lee, progmg dir; Ian Hutchson, chief engr.

WEOW(FM)—Co-owned with WKIZ(AM). February 1967: 92.5 mhz; 100 kw. Ant 600 ft. TL: N24 40 35 W81 30 41. Stereo. Prog sep from AM. Format: Rock Top-40. ■ Melody Agliardo, gen mgr; Bill Bravo, progmg dir.

WKRY(FM)—Nov 17, 1985: 93.5 mhz; 31.5 kw. Ant 1,148 ft. TL: N24 34 19 W81 44 25. Hrs opn: 24. 3820 N. Roosevelt Blvd. (33040). (305) 296-2435. FAX: (305) 296-1155. Licensee: Key Chain Inc. (group owner; acq 6-13-86). Format: Soft adult contemp, jazz. News staff 2; news progmg 8 hrs wkly. Target aud: 25 plus; affluent, upscale, culturally supportive. Spec prog: Class, Sp 2 hrs wkly. ■ Joel B. Day, pres; Kim Combs, gen mgr, gen sls mgr & adv mgr; Vicki Roush, mktg mgr; Bruce Peterson, prom dir; Gary Branson, progmg dir, news dir & pub affrs dir; Simon Hendrix, mus dir; Bill Smiley, chief engr. ■ Rates: $20; 15; 20; 12.

WKWF(AM)—October 1945: 1600 khz; 500 w-U. TL: N24 34 30 W81 44 01. Hrs opn: 24. Box 16899, Rocky River, OH (44116). Licensee: Spottswood Family Trust (acq 7-23-93; with co-located FM; FTR 8-23-93). ■ Joe Landon, vp; Connie Rice, gen mgr & gen sls mgr; Chuck Higbee, progmg dir; Mark Thorne, chief engr.

WAIL(FM)—Co-owned with WKWF(AM). December 1978: 99.5 mhz; 100 kw. Ant 991 ft. TL: N24 39 25 W81 32 18 (CP: ant 239 ft.). Stereo. Hrs opn: 24. Prog sep from AM. 21010 Center Ridge Rd., Rocky River, OH (44116). ■ Rich Johnston, progmg dir; Mark Thorne, news dir.

WOZN(FM)—January 1986: 98.7 mhz; 100 kw. Ant 300 ft. TL: N24 34 42 W81 44 49. Stereo. Hrs opn: 24. 3710 N. Roosevelt Blvd. (33040). (305) 293-9898. FAX: (305) 293-9654. Licensee: Key West Communications Inc. Group owner: Timm Enterprises (acq 3-12-85). Wash atty: Donald E. Ward. Format: AOR. News progmg one hr wkly. Target aud: 24-55; military, baby boomers & largest income holders. Spec prog: Armed Forces news one hr. ■ B.F.J. Timm, pres; Roger Leeper, gen mgr, gen sls mgr & adv mgr; Dano Amann, progmg dir & mus dir; Kim Alexander, pub affrs dir. ■ Rates: $18; 18; 18; 18.

WSKP(FM)—Not on air, target date unknown: 107.9 mhz; 100 kw. Ant 472 ft. TL: N24 39 08 W81 32 04. c/o CSJ Investments Inc., 1401 Duval St. (33040). Licensee: CSJ Investments Inc.

***WUNW(FM)**—Not on air, target date unknown: 90.1 mhz; 6.1 kw. TL: N24 33 18 W81 48 07. Box 2252, Boca Raton (33486). Licensee: Key West Public Radio Inc.

Kissimmee

WFIV(AM)—April 1965: 1080 khz 10 kw-D, DA. TL: N28 20 35 W81 20 22. Drawer 555519 (32855); 1080 Country Blvd. (34741). (407) 847-4422. Licensee: Edward C. Allmon dba Radio, Florida Broadcasters. Net: USA. Format: C&W. Spec prog: Farm 7 hrs, Creole 5 hrs, Sp 5 hrs wkly. ■ Edward C. Allmon, pres & gen sls mgr; Edward Allmon, gen mgr; Linden Campbell, chief engr.

WMJK(AM)—Oct 23, 1978: 1220 khz; 1 kw-D. TL: N28 19 27 W81 23 44. Hrs opn: 6 AM-6 PM. 5770 W. Irlo Bronson Hwy. (34746). (407) 397-2993. FAX: (407) 397-2978. Licensee: Kissimmee Broadcasting Corp. Inc. Net: AP, UPI, Sun, NBC, USA, Fla. Net. Format: Tourist Info. Target aud: tourists. ■ Rick Naney, pres; Mark Rosenbauer, gen mgr & news dir; Susan Blake, sls dir; Mark Ryan, progmg mgr; Jay Wagoner, chief engr. ■ Rates: $20; 20; 20; na.

La Belle

WKZY(FM)—Dec 16, 1978: 92.1 mhz; 3 kw. Ant 299 ft. TL: N26 39 13 W81 21 16. Stereo. Hrs opn: 24. Box 460, 329 S. Main St. (33935-0189). (813) 675-2700; (813) 675-2941. FAX: (813) 675-6060. Licensee: Omega Broadcasting Corp. (acq 8-15-88; $550,000; FTR 8-22-

88). Net: SMN. Rep: Katz & Powell. Format: Country. News staff one; news progmg 14 hrs wkly. Target aud: 25-54. Spec prog: Farm one hr, gospel 3 hrs, relg one hr wkly. ■ Stan Karas, pres; Katherine Santana, gen mgr; Paul Wolf, chief engr.

Lafayette

WHKX(FM)—Licensed to Lafayette. See Tallahassee.

Lake City

WDSR(AM)—May 6, 1946: 1340 khz; 1 kw-U. TL: N30 09 20 W82 38 14. Box 3299 (32056); 3507 S. Marion St. (32055). (904) 752-1340; (904) 752-9436. FAX: (904) 755-9369. Licensee: Arso Radio Corp. (group owner; acq 5-1-89). Net: NBC, NBC Talknet; Fla. Agrinet. Format: News/talk, sports. Spec prog: Black 2 hrs wkly. ■ Jesus Soto, pres; Larry Edwards, gen mgr; Chris Brand, progmg dir; Luis Soto, chief engr.

WNFB(FM)—Co-owned with WDSR(AM). May 28, 1969: 94.3 mhz; 50 kw. Ant 492 ft. TL: N30 07 44 W82 52 49. Stereo. Prog sep from AM. Net: NBC. Format: Adult contemp.

WGRO(AM)—Nov 14, 1958: 960 khz; 500 w-D, 1 kw-N, DA-N. TL: N30 11 47 W82 40 48 (CP: 1 kw-U, DA-N). Hrs opn: 6 AM-midnight Mon-Sat, 7 AM-11 PM Sun. Rt. 13, Box 318 (32055). (904) 752-0960. FAX: (904) 752-9861. Licensee: WGRO Radio Inc. (acq 11-75). Net: MBS; Florida. Rep: Bolton. Format: MOR, oldies. ■ Bob Hendrickson, gen mgr; Scott Burns, progmg dir; Mark Schumucker, chief engr.

WNFB(FM)—Listing follows WDSR(AM).

***WOLR(FM)**—Sept 11, 1986: 91.3 mhz; 18 kw-V. Ant 285 ft. TL: N30 02 56 W82 48 44. Box 667, Rt. 2 (32055). (904) 935-3300; (800) 450-9286. Licensee: WOLR 91.3 FM Inc. (acq 6-25-93; $75,000; FTR 7-19-93). Format: Adult contemp Christian. ■ Gordon Lund, pres & gen mgr; Shelly M. Lund, vp.

Lake Placid

WWTK(AM)—1989: 730 khz; 500 w-D, 340 w-N, DA-1. TL: N27 24 25 W81 25 56. Hrs opn: 24. 3750 U.S. 27 N., Sebring (33870). (813) 382-1063. FAX: (813) 382-1982. Licensee: Highlands Media Co. Inc. (acq 3-86; $10,000; FTR 3-31-86). Net: NBC, ABC, MBS, Daynet. Wash atty: Leibowitz & Spencer. Format: News/talk. News staff one. Spec prog: Gospel 5 hrs, Hatian one hr wkly. ■ James M. Johnson, pres; Duane McConnell, vp; Karen Sasnow, stn mgr; John Meder, sls dir; J.J. Kale, progmg dir; Barry Foster, news dir; James Johnson, chief engr. ■ Rates: $22; 19; 22; 12.

Lake Wales

WIPC(AM)—July 1951: 1280 khz; 1 kw-D, 500 w-N, DA-N. TL: N27 55 30 W81 36 16. Hrs opn: 24. 630 Mtn. Lake Cutoff Rd. (33853-7854). (813) 676-9179. Licensee: Seggi Broadcasting Corp. of Florida Inc. (acq 5-13-93; $245,000; FTR 5-31-93). Net: Sun; Florida. Rep: Dora-Clayton. Format: Positive country. News staff one; news progmg 126 hrs wkly. Target aud: General. Spec prog: Sp 6 hrs, Black 2 hrs, relg 5 hrs wkly. ■ Cecil Underwood, gen mgr & stn mgr. ■ Rates: $16; 16; 16; 10.

Lake Worth

WLVS(AM)—May 1, 1959: 1380 khz; 1 kw-D, 500 w-N. TL: N26 37 23 W80 04 20. Hrs opn: 6 AM-9 PM. 1939 7th Ave. N., (33461). (407) 585-5533; (407) 585-1380. FAX: (407) 585-0131. Licensee: Gold Coast Broadcasting Co. Net: CBN. Rep: MidSouth. Format: Relg, Southern gospel. Spec prog: Finnish 4 hrs, Haitian 14 hrs wkly. ■ Sam Phillips, pres; Eugene Tognacci Sr., gen mgr & gen sls mgr; Kelly Lynn, mus dir & pub affrs dir; Rick Rieke, chief engr.

Lakeland

***WCIE-FM**—May 20, 1975: 91.1 mhz; 100 kw. Ant 500 ft. TL: N28 04 46 W82 02 27. Stereo. Hrs opn: 24. 777 Carpenters Way (33804). (813) 859-1477. FAX: (813) 859-5424. Licensee: Evangel Christian School Inc. Net: AP. Wash atty: James Gammon. Format: Adult hit radio, Christian. News staff one; news progmg 12 hrs wkly. Target aud: 18-55; dayparted to teens, retirees, midrange. ■ Karl D. Strader, pres; Joe Perez, vp & gen mgr; Rick Thomas Elmhorst, stn mgr; Kevin MacKenzie, mus dir; Rick Thomas, news dir; Jack Collins, chief engr.

WEZY-FM—Sept 11, 1967: 94.1 mhz; 100 kw. Ant 430 ft. TL: N27 59 56 W81 53 16 (CP: Ant 1,601 ft., TL: N27 37 56 W82 07 01). Stereo. Hrs opn: 24. Prog sep from AM. Licensee: Paxson Enterprises (group owner; acq 3-29-93; $4.75 million; FTR 4-12-93). Format: Easy lstng. News staff one. Target aud: 35 plus; middle-upper income adults, skews heavier female. ■ Bob Crews, opns mgr & mus dir; Joey Austin, prom dir. ■ Rates: $59; 63; 56; 53.

WLKF(AM)—1936: 1430 khz; 5 kw-D, 1 kw-N. TL: N28 02 27 W81 56 08. Hrs opn: 24. Box 827, 1412 E. Lime St. (33802). (813) 682-4191. FAX: (813) 682-3143. Licensee: Chapman S. Root 1982 Living Trust (group owner; acq 10-20-83; grpsl; FTR 11-23-92). Net: ABC/E, NBC Talknet, Sun, Daynet; Fla. Net, Agri-Net. Rep: Banner. Wash atty: Dow, Lohnes & Albertson. Format: News/Talk. News progmg 15 hrs wkly. Target aud: 25 plus; middle to upper income adults. ■ Charlie Cohoon, pres; LeRoy Bradley, gen mgr & gen sls mgr; Joey Austin, prom mgr; Bob Crews, progmg dir & news dir; Paul Rebmann, chief engr. ■ Rates: $20; 30; 20; 11.

WONN(AM)—Sept 15, 1949: 1230 khz; 1 kw-U. TL: N28 02 23 W81 57 39. Hrs opn: 24. Box 2038 (33806); 404 W. Lime St. (33801). (813) 682-8184. FAX: (813) 683-2409. Licensee: Hall Communications Inc. (group owner; acq 10-1-81; $2 million with co-located FM; FTR 8-10-81). Net: NBC. Rep: D & R Radio. Wash atty: Arent, Fox, Kintner, Plotkin & Kahn. Format: MOR. News staff one; news progmg 20 hrs wkly. Target aud: 35 plus. Spec prog: Relg 2 hrs wkly. ■ Robert M. Hall, chmn; Arthur J. Rowbotham, pres & gen mgr; Dick Goleno, opns mgr & progmg dir; Nancy Cattarius, rgnl sls mgr; Debbie Hogan, prom mgr & pub affrs dir; John Bond, news dir; Rodger Roth, chief engr.

WPCV(FM)—(Winter Haven). Co-owned with WONN(AM). 1962: 97.5 mhz; 100 kw. Ant 1,017 ft. TL: N28 07 35 W81 33 03. Stereo. Hrs opn: 24. Prog sep from AM. (407) 297-1201. Net: NBC. Format: Country. News staff one; news progmg 4 hrs wkly. Target aud: 25-54. ■ Tunie Moss, prom dir; Jack Robertson, mus dir.

WWAB(AM)—September 1957: 1330 khz; 1 kw-D. TL: N28 02 40 W81 58 28. Box 65 (33802); 1203 Chase St. (33801). (813) 682-2998. Licensee: WWAB Inc. (acq 1-16-73). Net: Natl Black. Format: Talk. News progmg 7 hrs wkly. Target aud: 18-49. Spec prog: Gospel 6 hrs wkly. ■ Hugh R. Hughes, pres & gen mgr; Jerry Hughes, progmg dir & mus dir; Hugh Hughes, chief engr.

***WYFO(FM)**—March 1988: 91.9 mhz; 25 kw-H, 23 kw-V. Ant 328 ft. TL: N27 56 35 W81 54 45. 2176 Hwy. 540 A (33813). (813) 648-5516. Licensee: Bible Broadcasting Network (group owner; acq 9-21-89; $200,000; FTR 10-16-89). Format: MOR, Christian, educational. ■ Hank Crull, stn mgr.

Largo

WRFA(AM)—May 29, 1972: 820 khz; 50 kw-D, 1 kw-N, DA-2. TL: N27 54 30 W82 46 51. Hrs opn: 5 AM-midnight. 800 8th Ave. S.E. (34641-2900). (813) 581-9424; (813) 581-7800. FAX: (813) 584-4805. Licensee: Largo Broadcasting Co. Net: USA. Format: Relg. Target aud: 35 plus. ■ Vernon Cross, stn mgr; Jeannie O'Brien, gen sls mgr; David Graycheck, mus dir; Shannon Murdock, chief engr. ■ Rates: $45; 45; 45; 20.

Lecanto

***WLMS(FM)**—September 1992: 88.3 mhz; 3.8 kw. Ant 259 ft. TL: N28 52 55 W82 31 30. Box 18081, Tampa (33679). (813) 823-5346. FAX: (813) 282-3580. Licensee: Bishop of the Diocese of St. Petersburg. Format: Relg. ■ Tom Derzypolski, gen mgr.

Leesburg

WHOF(AM)—See Wildwood.

WLBE(AM)—August 1949: 790 khz; 5 kw-D, 1 kw-N, DA-N. TL: N28 49 00 W81 46 45. Hrs opn: 24. Drawer 490799 (34749); 32916 Radio Rd. (34788). (904) 787-7900. FAX: (904) 787-1402. Licensee: WLBE 790 Inc. Net: NBC, Fla. Net. Rep: Dora Clayton. Format: MOR, big band. News progmg 25 hrs wkly. Target aud: 45 plus. Spec prog: Black 3 hrs, farm 3 hrs, gospel 4 hrs, Pol 2 hrs wkly. ■ Ben Griffen, pres; Merrill Isaacson, gen mgr; Dick Ravenhill, progmg dir; Bill Gephart, news dir; Frank Strad, chief engr. ■ Rates: $8.25; 8.25; 8.25; 8.25.

WQBQ(AM)—Sept 12, 1962: 1410 khz; 5 kw-D, 90 w-N. TL: N28 47 13 W81 53 26. Stereo. 10401-328 Hwy. 441. (34788). (904) 787-1410. FAX: (904) 787-4446. Licensee: WQBQ Radio Corp. (acq 8-88; $500,000; FTR 8-8-88). Net: ABC, CBS, ARN. Format: Country. News staff one; news progmg 4 hrs wkly. Target aud: 25 plus; emphasis on 35-65. ■ Jeff Harper, gen mgr; Don Connelly, chief engr.

WXXL(FM)—Feb 12, 1969: 106.7 mhz; 100 kw. Ant 800 ft. TL: N28 33 31 W81 35 38 (CP: Ant 823 ft.). Stereo. 337 S. N. Lake Blvd., Altamonte Springs (32701). (407) 339-1067. Licensee: J.J. Taylor Companies Inc. Group owner: Taylor Communications Inc. (acq 10-10-89; $12 million; FTR 10-23-89). Rep: Major Mkt. Format: CHR. News staff one. Target aud: 18-34. Spec prog: Alternative 6 hrs wkly. ■ Joe Taylor, chmn; John Taylor, pres; Hank Desplaines, CFO; Paul Lavesque, exec vp; Randall L. Rahe, gen mgr; Robin Smith, sls dir; Frank Celebre, natl sls mgr; Rhoda Bohrer, rgnl sls mgr; Larry Kahn, vp mktg; Dave Deemer, prom dir; Adam Cook, progmg dir; Larry Dee, mus dir; Deborah Smurava, news dir; Ken Skok, chief engr. ■ Rates: $120; 100; 120; 90.

Lehigh Acres

WCKT(FM)—Jan 1, 1976: 107.1 mhz; 15.5 kw. Ant 732 ft. TL: N26 32 02 W81 41 04. Stereo. Hrs opn: 24. 4048 Evans Ave., #308, Fort Myers (33901). (813) 275-5107. FAX: (813) 275-4669. Licensee: Sandab Communications of Fort Myers Ltd. (acq 7-19-89; $3 million; FTR 8-7-89). Net: Katz Radio Net. Rep: Banner. Format: Continuous country. ■ R. Scott Frothingham, gen mgr; Gator Michaels, prom dir; Rick McGee, progmg dir; Doc Daily, mus dir; Dave Barry, news dir; Paul Wolf, chief engr.

WWCL(AM)—April 29, 1970: 1440 khz; 5 kw-D, 1 kw-N, DA-2. TL: N26 36 05 W81 33 30. Box 51137, Fort Myers (33905). (813) 368-3939. Licensee: Dwyer Broadcasting Inc. (acq 1-1-79). Format: Hispanic. ■ Castro Resendiz, gen sls mgr; Patrick Deisch, chief engr.

Live Oak

WQHL(AM)—June 16, 1949: 1250 khz; 1 kw-D, 83 w-N. TL: N30 17 14 W82 57 56. Hrs opn: 19. Box 130, 1305 E. Helvenston St. (32060). (904) 362-1250; (904) 364-3500. FAX: (904) 364-3504. Licensee: Day Communications Inc. (acq 9-88). Net: ABC/E; Fla. Net. Wash atty: Pepper & Corazzini. Format: Oldies, talk. News staff 2; news progmg 12 hrs wkly. Target aud: General. Spec prog: Gospel 7 hrs, relg 6 hrs wkly. ■ George R. Day Jr., pres; N. Shannon Day, gen mgr; Jack Hall, gen sls mgr; Dean Blackwell, vp prom; Wayne Latrell, progmg dir; Marion Catalano, mus dir; John Koch, news dir; Mark Schmucker, chief engr.

WQHL-FM—October 1973: 98.1 mhz; 50 kw. Ant 367 ft. TL: N30 17 14 W82 57 56. Stereo. Hrs opn: 24. Prog sep from AM. Net: ABC/I. Format: Country. Spec prog: Gosp 2 hrs, relg 2 hrs wkly. ■ Rates: $12; 12; 12; 12.

Macclenny

WJXR(FM)—Licensed to Macclenny. See Jacksonville.

Madison

WMAF(AM)—Dec 6, 1956: 1230 khz; 1 kw-U. TL: N30 28 23 W83 26 09. Box 621, Country Club Rd. (32340). (904) 973-6333. Licensee: Billy G. Walker (acq 12-6-72). Net: NBC. Rep: Keystone (unwired net). Format: Southern gospel, country gospel. Spec prog: Black 21 hrs wkly. ■ Billy G. Walker, pres; Gail Walker, gen mgr; Bob Hantson, progmg dir; Paul Wilkins, chief engr.

Marathon

WAVK(FM)—Oct 15, 1984: 106.3 mhz; 3 kw-H. Ant 112 ft. TL: N24 43 44 W81 02 05. Stereo. 11399 Overseas Hwy. (33050). (305) 743-3434. FAX: (305) 743-9091. Licensee: Key Chain Inc. (group owner; acq 4-18-86). Net: SMN. Rep: Torbet. Format: Adult contemp. Spec prog: Talk/call-in one hr wkly. ■ Joel B. Day, pres; Shannon L. Smiley, gen mgr & gen sls mgr; Betty Frey, progmg dir; Dewey Acker, news dir; William Smiley, chief engr.

WFFG(AM)—April 7, 1962: 1300 khz; 2.5 kw-U, DA-1. TL: N24 41 28 W81 06 30. Box 488, One Boer Key (33050). (305) 743-5563. FAX: (305) 743-9441. Licensee: The Great Marathon Radio Co. (acq 11-5-90; grpsl; FTR 11-26-90). Net: ABC/I. Format: Country, talk. ■ Joseph Nascone, pres; James McGerry, opns mgr; Charley Miller, news dir; Richard Crosby, chief engr. ■ Rates: $12; 12; 12; 12.

WGMX(FM)—Co-owned with WFFG(AM). December 1976: 94.3 mhz; 3 kw. Ant 160 ft. TL: N24 41 28 W81 06 30 (CP: 3.1 kw). Stereo. Hrs opn: 24. (305) 743-5563. Licensee: The Great Marathon Radio Co. (acq 11-5-90; grpsl; FTR 11-26-90). Format: Adult contemp. ■ James McGerry, stn mgr. ■ Rates: Same as AM.

Marco

WAVV(FM)—May 30, 1987: 101.1 mhz; 100 kw. Ant 981 ft. TL: N26 10 57 W81 34 32. Stereo. Hrs opn: 24. 11800

Florida Directory of Radio

Tamiami Trail East, Naples (33962); 1400 Royal Palm Sq. Blvd, Fort Myers (33919). (813) 775-9288. FAX: (813) 793-7000. Licensee: Alpine Broadcasting Corp. (group owner; acq 4-84; $95,000; FTR 4-23-84). Net: AP. Rep: Torbet. Format: Modern, easy lstng. News progmg 8 hrs wkly. Target aud: 25 plus; an economically qualified audience that is somewhat more affluent. Spec prog: Jazz 3 hrs wkly. ■ Norman R. Alpert, pres & gen mgr; Kenny Lamb, opns mgr; Robin Craig, sls dir; Norman R. Albert, progmg dir; Bob Berry, news dir & pub affrs dir; Al Baxa, chief engr. ■ Rates: $55; 60; 55; 45.

WGUF(FM)—1990: 92.7 mhz; 4.1 kw. Ant 328 ft. TL: N26 01 50 W81 38 33. Stereo. Hrs opn: 24. Suite 204, 5101 E. Tamiami Trail, Naples (33962). (813) 793-4100. FAX: (813) 793-1444. Licensee: Rowland Gulf Radio Inc. Group owner: Rowland Family Radio. Net: ABC/E. Rep: Katz & Powell. Format: Btfl mus. News progmg 7 hrs wkly. Target aud: 35 plus; affluent Collier County residents. ■ Marshall W. Rowland Sr., pres; Stephen Rowland, gen mgr; Rick Rowland, opns mgr, progmg dir & engrg mgr.

Marco Island

WNOG-FM—See Naples.

WODX(AM)—Jan 1, 1975: 1480 khz; 1 kw-U, DA-2. TL: N25 59 30 W81 37 30. 599 S. Collier Blvd. (33937). (813) 394-5353. Licensee: Marco Island Broadcasting Inc. (acq 6-15-92; $70,000; FTR 7-6-92). Net: ABC/I. Format: Soft gold. ■ Terry Lee, gen mgr; Paul Martin, chief engr.

Marianna

WBNF(FM)—Dec 5, 1993: 93.3 mhz; 3 kw. Ant 328 ft. TL: N30 45 47 W85 13 52. Stereo. Hrs opn: 24. Box 777, 2725 Jefferson (36446). (904) 482-2131. FAX: (904) 526-3687. Licensee: Jackson Radio Ltd. Format: Classic rock. News staff one; news progmg one hr wkly. Target aud: 25-54. ■ Rates: $10; 8.50; 10; 6.50.

WJAQ(FM)—Listing follows WTOT(AM).

***WJNF(FM)**—June 1985: 91.1 mhz; 383 w. Ant 154 ft. TL: N30 48 12 W85 11 48. Box 450 (32447-0450). (904) 526-4477. Licensee: Marianna Educational Broadcasting Foundation. Net: USA, Moody. Format: Relg. News staff 2; news progmg 9 hrs wkly. Target aud: Families. ■ Jack Hollis, pres; Shellie Hollis, gen mgr & mktg dir; Michelle Whitfield, prom mgr; Charles Wooten, chief engr.

WTOT(AM)—Sept 24, 1958: 980 khz; 1 kw-D, 500 w-N. TL: N30 47 01 W85 15 18. Box 569, Suite A, 4376 Lafayette St. (32446). (904) 482-3046. Licensee: Brewer Broadcasting Corp. (group owner; acq 1976). Net: NBC. Format: Black, R&B. News staff one; news progmg 6 hrs wkly. Target aud: General; mornings audience-18 to 54, evening audience-12 plus. ■ James L. Brewer, pres; Lina M. Parish, gen mgr; Bill Collins, gen sls mgr; Don Moore, news dir; Charles Wooten, chief engr. ■ Rates: $18; 7.60; 7.60; 7.60.

WJAQ(FM)—Co-owned with WTOT(AM). Sept 1, 1964: 100.9 mhz; 2.5 kw-H. Ant 331 ft. TL: N30 47 01 W85 15 18. Stereo. Prog sep from AM. Net: NBC. Format: Country. ■ Rates: $18; 9.60; 9.60; 9.60.

WTYS(AM)—1948: 1340 khz; 1 kw-U. TL: N30 45 49 W85 13 52. Box 777 (32447); 2725 Jefferson (32446). (904) 482-2131. FAX: (904) 526-3687. Licensee: William F. Dunkle III, receiver (acq 3-1-86). Net: ABC/I, USA; Florida's Radio Net. Format: Talk/news. News staff one; news progmg 7 hrs wkly. Target aud: 25-54; female. Spec prog: Black 4 hrs, farm one hr, gospel 11 hrs wkly. ■ W.F. Dunkle III, pres, gen mgr & gen sls mgr; Tom O'Brien, progmg dir; Jeanette Vickery, news dir.

Mary Esther

WYZB(FM)—May 1986: 105.5 mhz; 6 kw. Ant 328 ft. TL: N30 24 42 W86 37 14. Stereo. Box 489, 217 Page Bacon Rd. #11 (32569). (904) 243-2323. FAX: (904) 243-6806. Licensee: Holladay Broadcasting Co. Inc. Format: Oldies. News staff one. Target aud: 25-54. ■ Clay Holladay, pres; Georgia Edmiston, gen mgr; Rick Zurick, opns mgr & progmg dir; Jud Robertson, gen sls mgr; Steve O'Day, prom mgr; Shari Flowers, news dir; Bruce Campbell, chief engr. ■ Rates: $30; 30; 30; 14.

Mayo

***WGSG(FM)**—1991: 89.5 mhz; 2.5 kw-H, 20 kw-V. Ant 249 ft. TL: N30 02 30 W83 07 45. Stn currently dark. Box 644 (32066). (904) 294-2525. Licensee: True Concepts of Levy County Inc. ■ Frank Ellerker, gen mgr.

Melbourne

WAOA(FM)—Listing follows WTAI(AM).

WCIF(FM)—Jan 1, 1980: 106.3 mhz; 3 kw. Ant 230 ft. TL: N28 04 40 W80 39 26. Stereo. Box 366 (32901); 702 E. New Haven Ave (32902). (407) 725-9243. Licensee: First Baptist Church Inc. Format: Relg. ■ Lee J. Martinez, gen mgr; Curt Parrish, chief engr.

***WFIT(FM)**—April 1975: 89.5 mhz; 2.35 kw. Ant 112 ft. TL: N28 03 51 W80 37 25. Stereo. 150 W. University Blvd. (32901-6988). (407) 768-8000, ext. 8140. FAX: (407) 984-8461. Licensee: Florida Institute of Technology. Net: AP. Format: Contemp jazz. Spec prog: Class 3 hrs wkly. ■ David Kelshaw, gen mgr; Rob Selkow, progmg dir; Mike Hurley, chief engr.

WGGD-FM—Listing follows WMMB(AM).

WMEL(AM)—Jan 4, 1956: 920 khz; 5 kw-D, 1 kw-N, DA-2. TL: N28 08 11 W80 41 20. Stereo. Box 361318 (32934); 1800 Turtlemound Rd. (32934). (407) 254-2282. Licensee: Twin Towers Broadcasting Inc. (acq 7-21-93; $350,000; FTR 8-9-93). Format: Classic Talk. ■ John Harper, pres & gen mgr.

WMMB(AM)—1947: 1240 khz; 1 kw-U. TL: N28 04 40 W80 35 55. Hrs opn: 24. 2221 Front St. (32901). (407) 723-1240. FAX: (407) 725-6821. Licensee: City Broadcasting Co. Inc. (acq 12-19-86; $2.2 million with co-loacted FM; FTR 11-10-86). Net: MBS, ABC/I; Fla. Net. Rep: Torbet. Wash atty: Robert A. DePont. Format: MOR. News staff 3; news progmg 4 hrs wkly. Target aud: 35 plus. ■ David P. Franco, pres & gen mgr; Larry Brewer, opns dir & progmg dir; John Intelisano, gen sls mgr; Neal Stein, news dir; Jon Roberts, chief engr.

WGGD-FM—Co-owned with WMMB(AM). Dec 25, 1965: 102.3 mhz; 3 kw. Ant 250 ft. TL: N28 04 40 W80 35 55. Stereo. Hrs opn: 24. Prog sep from AM. Net: MBS, SMN. Format: Oldies. News progmg one hr wkly. Target aud: 25-54. ■ Ken Holliday, progmg dir.

WTAI(AM)—March 8, 1968: 1560 khz; 5 kw-D. TL: N28 07 40 W80 42 29. Hrs opn: 6 AM-7 PM. Suite 301, 1775 W. Hibiscus Blvd. (32901). (407) 984-1000. FAX: (407) 724-1565. Licensee: Silicon East Communications Partnership (acq 2-84; $846,000 with co-located FM; FTR 2-6-84). Net: ABC TalkRadio, CBS, EFM. Rep: McGavren Guild. Wash atty: Erwin Krasnaw. Format: News/talk. News staff 2. Target aud: General. Spec prog: Gospel 2 hrs, relg 3 hrs wkly. ■ Jeffrey C. Kimmel, gen mgr; John Roberts, opns mgr & chief engr; Jeffrey C. Roberts, gen sls mgr; Wayne West, news dir; Dan Deaton, pub affrs dir. ■ Rates: $25; 20; 20; na.

WAOA(FM)—Co-owned with WTAI(AM). Nov 9, 1972: 107.1 mhz; 100 kw. Ant 500 ft. TL: N28 08 14 W80 42 11. Stereo. Prog sep from AM. Format: CHR. News progmg 2 hrs wkly. Target aud: 18-49; young adults of Melbourne. ■ Dan Deaton, progmg dir; Michael W. Lowe, mus dir. ■ Rates: $75; 65; 65; 35.

Merritt Island

WWBC(AM)—See Cocoa.

Mexico Beach

WEBZ(FM)—Nov 28, 1990: 99.3 mhz; 50 kw. Ant 519 ft. TL: N30 00 21 W85 20 36. Stereo. Hrs opn: 24. c/o WGNE-WFSY, Box 759, Panama City (32402). (904) 769-4499. FAX: (904) 769-6164. Licensee: Woodfin Broadcasting Inc. (acq 7-2-93; $250,000; FTR 8-2-93). Wash atty: Lucas, McGowan, Nace & Gutierrez. Format: Adult contemp, div. Target aud: 30 plus; professional adults. ■ Blane A. Woodfin, pres; Patsy Sellers, gen mgr. ■ Rates: $10; 10; 10; 10.

Miami

WAQI(AM)—1939: 710 khz; 50 kw-U, DA-2. TL: N25 58 07 W80 22 44. 2960 Coral Way (33145). (305) 445-4040. FAX: (305) 529-6631. Licensee: Viva America Media Group. Format: Sp, news/talk, entertainment. ■ Amancio Victor Suarez, chmn; Charles Fernandez, pres; Amancio J. Suarez, exec vp & chief opns; Armando Perez Roura, gen mgr; Enrique Landin, gen sls mgr; Tomas Regalado, news dir; Carlos Fernandez, chief engr.

WAXY(FM)—See Fort Lauderdale.

WCMQ(AM)—(Miami Springs). May 18, 1958: 1210 khz; 25 kw-D, 2.5 kw-N, DA-2. TL: N25 54 00 W80 21 49. Stereo. 1411 Coral Way, Miami (33145). (305) 444-9292. FAX: (305) 856-8812. Licensee: Spanish Broadcasting System of Florida Inc. Group owner: Spanish Broadcasting Systems Inc. (acq 11-86; grpsl; FTR 9-29-86). Rep: Major Mkt. Format: Sp adult contemp, MOR. ■ Raul Alarcon Jr., pres; Victor Aleman, opns mgr; Teri Vila, gen sls mgr; Mari Mayoral, natl sls mgr; Carmen Azcuy, progmg dir & mus dir; Ralph Chambers, chief engr.

WCMQ-FM—See Hialeah.

***WDNA(FM)**—June 10, 1980: 88.9 mhz; 2.3 kw. Ant 710 ft. TL: N25 32 24 W80 28 07. Stereo. Hrs opn: 22. Box 558636, 4848 S.W. 74 Ct. (33255). (305) 662-8889. FAX: (305) 662-1975. Licensee: Bascomb Memorial Broadcasting Foundation Inc. (acq 1971). Wash atty: Haley, Bader & Potts. Format: Jazz, Sp. News progmg 3 hrs wkly. Target aud: General; minorities. Spec prog: Black 2 hrs, folk 5 hrs, Fr 2 hrs, Pakistani 2 hrs, East Indian 3 hrs, Haitian 8 hrs, Arabic 2 hrs, reggae 4 hrs wkly. ■ Margarita Pelleya, stn mgr; Evan Chern, pub affrs dir; Ray Ball, chief engr.

WEDR(FM)—May 18, 1963: 99.1 mhz; 100 kw. Ant 926 ft. TL: N25 57 30 W80 12 44 (CP: TL: N25 57 59 W80 12 33). Stereo. 3790 N.W. 167th St. (33054). (305) 623-7711. FAX: (305) 624-2736. Licensee: WEDR Inc. Rep: McGavren-Guild. Wash atty: Smithwick & Belendiuk. Format: R&B. ■ Andrew J. Guest, pres; Jerry Rushin, vp & gen mgr; James Thomas, progmg dir & mus dir; Rick Reike, chief engr.

WFBA(AM)—Not on air, target date unknown: 990 khz; 5 kw-U. TL: N25 50 34 W80 25 12. 2333 Brickell Ave. (33129). Licensee: Community Broadcasters Inc.

WFLC(FM)—Listing follows WIOD(AM).

WHYI-FM—See Fort Lauderdale.

WINZ(AM)—1946: 940 khz; 50 kw-D, 10 kw-N. TL: N25 57 36 W80 16 13. 4330 N.W. 207th Dr. (33055); 194 N.W. 187th St. (33169). (305) 654-9494; (305) 624-6397 (NEWS ROOM). FAX: (305) 621-4934; (305) 623-1309 (NEWS ROOM). Licensee: Paxson Enterprises of Miami L.P. Group owner: Paxson Broadcasting (acq 2-20-92; $18.3 million; grpsl). Net: CBS, CNN, AP. Rep: Katz. Format: News, sports. News progmg 88 hrs wkly. Target aud: 35-64; upscale, professional, managerial adults. ■ Powell W. Paxson, chmn; James Bocock, pres; Dean Goodman, vp & gen mgr; Ronna Fink-Woulfe, Janice Banken, gen sls mgrs; Mary Corso, natl sls mgr; Dan Weiss, Toni Shreffler, prom mgrs; Peter Bolger, progmg dir & pub affrs dir; Elaine Ettorre, news dir; Roy Pressman, engrg mgr; Jim Leifer, chief engr.

WIOD(AM)—Jan 19, 1926: 610 khz; 10 kw-U, DA-N. TL: N25 50 58 W80 09 18. Stereo. 1401 N. Bay Causeway (33141). (305) 759-4311. FAX: (305) 757-7516. Licensee: WIOD Inc. Group owner: Cox Broadcasting (acq 1-19-26). Rep: Christal. Format: News/talk. News staff 10. Target aud: 25-64. ■ Robert Green, vp & gen mgr; Jeff Clark, gen sls mgr; John Lynch, natl sls mgr; Kurt Steier, prom mgr; Gary Bruce, progmg dir; Tom Hopkins, news dir; Mitch Wein, chief engr.

WFLC(FM)—Co-owned with WIOD(AM). July 20, 1951: 97.3 mhz; 100 kw. Ant 800 ft. TL: N25 57 30 W80 12 44. Stereo. Prog sep from AM. Format: Adult contemp. Target aud: 25-54. ■ Fleetwood Gruver, progmg dir.

WKAT(AM)—See North Miami.

WKIS(FM)—Listing follows WQAM.

***WLRN-FM**—February 1949: 91.3 mhz; 100 kw. Ant 652 ft. TL: N25 58 48 W80 11 47. Stereo. 172 N.E. 15th St. (33132). (305) 995-2204. FAX: (305) 995-2299. Licensee: School Board of Dade County Fla. Net: NPR, APR, SMN. Format: Jazz, div. News progmg 41 hrs wkly. Target aud: General; well educated, moderate to high income bracket. Spec prog: Class 12 hrs, Sp 3 hrs, Haitian 3 hrs wkly. ■ Don MacCullough, gen mgr; Roger R. Kobzina, stn mgr; Joseph E. Cooper, progmg dir; Edward Bell III, mus dir; Peter Dom, chief engr. ■ *WLRN-TV affil.

WLYF(FM)—Dec 23, 1970: 101.5 mhz; 100 kw. Ant 810 ft. TL: N25 57 59 W80 12 44. Stereo. Hrs opn: 24. 20450 N.W. Second Ave. (33169). (305) 653-8811. Licensee: Jefferson Pilot Communications. Group owner: (acq 10-23-85). Format: Soft adult contemp. ■ Dennis Collins, gen mgr; Rick Charnack, gen sls mgr; Larry Travers, progmg dir; Rob Sidney, mus dir; John Morris, chief engr.

***WMCU(FM)**—Aug 24, 1970: 89.7 mhz; 100 kw. Ant 981 ft. TL: N25 32 24 W80 28 07 (CP: Ant 1,502 ft.). Stereo. Hrs opn: 24. Suite 600, 330 Biscayne Blvd. (33162). (305) 953-1155. FAX: (305) 953-1117. Licensee: Trinity Evangelical Divinity School (acq 7-8-91; FTR 7-29-91). Net: USA, AP. Wash atty: Dow, Lohnes & Albertson. Format: Educ, Christian. News staff one. Target aud: 25-54. ■ Steve James, gen mgr; Dwight Taylor, opns mgr, progmg dir & mus dir; Earl Lewis, prom dir; Sandra Furnell, news dir; Bill Coppage, chief engr.

WMRZ(AM)—See South Miami.

WOCN(AM)—Dec 22, 1956: 1450 khz; 1 kw-U. TL: N25 50 24 W80 11 20. Hrs opn: 24. 350 N.E. 71 St., (33138). (305) 759-7280. FAX: (305) 759-2276. Licensee: Minority Broadcasters Inc. (acq 6-26-84). Rep: Lotus. Wash atty: Akin, Gump, Strauss, Haver & Feld. Format: Sp, news, talk. Target aud: General. ■ Pablo Vega, pres; Sebastian Vega, vp; Richard Vega, gen mgr, gen sls mgr & progmg dir; Eusebio Sanchez, mus dir; Harolo Solis, asst mus dir; Miguel Triay, chief engr.

WPOW(FM)—June 15, 1985: 96.5 mhz; 100 kw. Ant 1,007 ft. TL: N25 57 59 W80 12 33. Stereo. 20295 N.W. 2nd Ave. (33169). (305) 653-6796. FAX: (305) 770-1456. Licensee: Beasley-Reed Broadcasting of Miami Inc. Group owner: Beasley Broadcast Group (acq 4-86). Net: NBC. Format: CHR. ■ George Beasley, pres; Greg Reed, vp & gen mgr; Matthew Bell, gen sls mgr; Frank Walsh, progmg dir; John Rogers, mus dir; Louie Aguirre, news dir; Greg Strickland, chief engr.

WQAM(AM)—May 1921: 560 khz; 5 kw-D, 1 kw-N. TL: N25 44 36 W80 09 14. Stereo. Hrs opn: 24. 9881 Sheridan St., Hollywood (33024). (305) 431-6200; (305) 621-4300. FAX: (305) 437-2466. Licensee: Sunshine Wireless Co. Inc. (group owner; acq 9-23-85; $2,850,000; FTR 7-1-85). Net: NBC. Wash atty: Winston & Strawn. Format: Oldies, sports, talk. News staff 2; news progmg 8 hrs wkly. Target aud: 25-54; males. Spec prog: Relg 4 hrs wkly. ■ Dan N. Cohen, pres; Jeffrey D. Greenhawt, vp & gen mgr; Ray Perry, natl sls mgr; Mark Freedman (local), Carol Bowen, rgnl sls mgrs; Brooks Alsbrook, prom mgr; Stu Opperman, progmg dir; Dave Lamont, news dir; Cheryl Mizell, pub affrs dir; George Corso, chief engr.

WKIS(FM)—(Boca Raton). Co-owned with WQAM. October 1965: 99.9 mhz; 100 kw. Ant 986 ft. TL: N25 59 34 W80 10 27. Stereo. Hrs opn: 24. Prog sep from AM. 9881 Sheridan St., Hollywood (33024). Format: Country. News staff one; news progmg 2 hrs wkly. Target aud: 25-54. ■ Bob McKay, progmg dir; Darlene Evans, mus dir.

WQBA(AM)—1947: 1140 khz; 50 kw-D, 10 kw-N, DA-2. TL: N25 45 46 W80 29 03. 2828 Coral Way (33145). (305) 441-2073. FAX: (305) 445-8908. Licensee: SRN Texas Inc. (acq 9-90; FTR 9-3-90). Rep: Eastman, Caballero. Format: Sp news, talk, entertainment. ■ Herb Levine, vp & gen mgr; Evette M. Davidson, stn mgr; Thomas Martinez, gen sls mgr; Omar Fernandez, prom mgr; Oscar Haza, news dir; Miquel Triay, chief engr.

WQBA-FM—June 7, 1974: 107.5 mhz; 95 kw-H, 80 kw-V. Ant 1,007 ft. TL: N25 57 59 W80 12 33. Stereo. Prog sep from AM. Format: Sp adult contemp. ■ Maria Elena Llansa, gen sls mgr; Tony Campos, prom mgr; Maria Cristina Ruiz, progmg dir.

WRFM(AM)—(Hialeah). Dec 1, 1987: 830 khz; 1 kw-U, DA-2. TL: N25 46 22 W80 25 16. Stereo. Hrs opn: 24. Suite 3-E, 8080 W. Flagler St., Miami (33144). (305) 264-1100; (305) 266-0200. FAX: (305) 266-9919. Licensee: Interamerican Broadcasting Inc. (acq 6-22-92). Net: CBS. Format: Sp. News staff 5; news progmg 18 hrs wkly. Target aud: General; adult 25-49. Spec prog: Sports. ■ Adib Eden Jr., CEO, pres, gen mgr & progmg dir; Morton R. Goudiss, Alberto Sabina, Jorge Cunill, vps; Dayton Saballos, chief opns; Damaso Santana, vp sls; Alberto Sabina, vp mktg; Grace Amador, vp prom; Elisabeth Eden, mus dir; Frank Huertas, news dir; Sofia Montiel, pub affrs dir; Greg Strom, chief engr. ■ Rates: $75; 55; 75; 45.

WRHC(AM)—See Coral Gables.

WSBH(AM)—See Miami Beach.

WSHE(FM)—See Fort Lauderdale.

WSUA(AM)—June 20, 1969: 1260 khz; 5 kw-U, DA-2. TL: N25 46 23 W80 25 17. 2100 Coral Way (33145). (305) 285-1260. FAX: (305) 858-5907. Licensee: Howard Broadcasting Corp. (acq 12-3-93; FTR 12-20-93). Rep: Caballero. Format: Sp lite contemp. ■ Howard Premer, pres; Alberto Diaz, gen mgr & gen sls mgr; Sam Stoddard, chief engr. ■ Rates: $50; 50; 50; 50.

WTMI(FM)—Nov 1, 1960: 93.1 mhz; 96 kw. Ant 1,040 ft. TL: N25 57 59 W80 12 33. Stereo. 3225 Aviation Ave. (33133). (305) 856-9393. FAX: (305) 854-0783. Licensee: Marlin Broadcasting Inc. (group owner; acq 3-71). Rep: CMBS. Format: Class, jazz. News staff one; news progmg 2 hrs wkly. Target aud: 25-64; upscale, educated adults. ■ Howard P. Tanger, pres; Allen Stieglitz, vp & gen mgr; Scott Schwartz, gen sls mgr; Lyn Farmer, progmg dir; Ken Martin, mus dir; Eric Goodman, news dir; Greg Strickland, chief engr.

WTPX(FM)—See Fort Lauderdale.

***WVUM(FM)**—See Coral Gables.

WWFE(AM)—July 1989: 670 khz; 50 kw-D, 2.5 kw-N, DA-2. TL: N25 51 27 W80 28 52. Stereo. Box 351625, 2381 W. Flagler St. (33135). (305) 642-4422. FAX: (305) 541-9528. Licensee: Fenix Broadcasting Corp. (acq 6-22-93; $2.7 million; FTR 7-12-93). Net: UPI. Wash atty: Mullin, Rhyne, Emmons & Topel. Format: Sp, news/talk. News progmg 27 hrs wkly. Target aud: 25-54. ■ Emilio M. Milian, pres; Emilio M. Milian III, gen mgr; Mr. Menendez, chief engr. ■ Rates: $80; 60; 70; 40.

WZTA(FM)—See Miami Beach.

Miami Beach

WLVE(FM)—July 1, 1968: 93.9 mhz; 96 kw. Ant 1,006 ft. TL: N25 57 59 W80 12 33 (CP: 100 kw-H, 82 kw-V). Stereo. 194 N.W. 187th St., Miami (33169). (305) 654-9494. FAX: (305) 654-9090. Licensee: Paxson Enterprises Inc. Group owner: Paxson Broadcasting (acq 2-18-93; $14 million; FTR 3-8-93). Rep: Torbet. Wash atty: Wiley, Rein & Fielding. Format: New adult contemp, jazz. Target aud: 25-54. ■ Jim Bocock, pres; Dean Goodman, exec vp & gen mgr; Rich McMillan, opns mgr & progmg dir; Mary Corso, natl sls mgr; Dan Weiss, prom mgr; Joanne Rice, news dir; Roy Pressman, chief engr.

WSBH(AM)—1949: 1490 khz; 1 kw-U. TL: N25 46 10 W80 08 11. 814 First St. (33139). (305) 672-1100. FAX: (305) 673-1199. Licensee: Margolis Broadcasting Co. Ltd. (acq 1985). Rep: Katz & Powell. Wash atty: Pepper & Corazzini. Format: Talk. News staff one; news progmg 3 hrs wkly. Target aud: 25 plus; mature Black, self-motivated. Spec prog: Sp 10 hrs, Fr 10 hrs, Jewish 2 hrs wkly, Haitian. ■ Edward Margolis, pres & gen mgr; Maximo Gomez, vp & vp opns; Pat Reeves-Moore, gen sls mgr; Barry Stephens, progmg dir; Dwayne King, mus dir; Delphine Hannah, pub affrs dir; Richard Van Hook, chief engr. ■ Rates: $65; 56; 65; 40.

WZTA(FM)—1961: 94.9 mhz; 100 kw. Ant 1,007 ft. TL: N25 46 29 W80 11 19. Stereo. 194 N.W. 187th St., Miami (33169). (305) 654-9494. FAX: (305) 654-9090. Licensee: Paxson Miami License L.P. Group owner: Paxson Broadcasting (acq 11-91; $18.3 million; grpsl; FTR 12-3-91). Net: Westwood One. Rep: Katz. Format: Classic Rock. Target aud: 25-34; yuppies. ■ Bud Paxson, pres; Dean Goodman, gen mgr; Rona Fink, gen sls mgr; Mary Corso, natl sls mgr; Toni Shreffler, prom mgr; Neal Mirsky, progmg dir; Mike Lyons, mus dir; Roy Pressman, chief engr.

Miami Springs

WCMQ(AM)—Licensed to Miami Springs. See Miami.

Micanopy

WRRX(FM)—Sept 7, 1985: 97.7 mhz; 3.2 kw. Ant 305 ft. TL: N29 32 08 W82 19 17 (CP: 2.6 kw, ant 495 ft.). Stereo. 900 N.W. 8th Ave., Gainesville (32601). (904) 376-1230. FAX: (904) 376-2666. Licensee: Gator Broadcasting Co. Group owner: American Communications and Television Inc. (acq 10-86). Net: NBC the Source. Rep: Christal. Wash atty: David Oxenford. Format: Classic rock. News progmg 2 hrs wkly. Target aud: 18-54; male. ■ David Gregg, pres; Michael Jurian, gen mgr, progmg dir & mus dir; Donna Lubrano, stn mgr. ■ Rates: $35; 29; 35; 26.

Milton

WEBY(AM)—1978: 1330 khz; 5 kw-D, 79 w-N. TL: N30 37 12 W87 01 21. Stereo. 133 Ward Basin Rd. (32583). (904) 623-1330. FAX: (904) 994-2103. Licensee: No. One Radio Inc. (acq 1985). Net: ABC/I. Format: News/talk. ■ H. Byrd Mapoles, pres & gen mgr; Dave Johnston, opns mgr; Dave Johnson, news dir; Byrd Mapoles, chief engr.

WECM(AM)—Dec 18, 1957: 1490 khz; 1 kw-U. TL: N30 37 30 W87 02 54. Hrs opn: 6 AM-midnight. 703 Berryhill Rd. (32570); 1207 Hamilton Bridge Rd. (32570). (904) 623-1490; (904) 623-8618. FAX: (904) 623-5444. Licensee: Faith Communications (acq 3-20-90; $75,000; FTR 3-9-90). Net: USA. Format: Christian. News progmg 12 hrs wkly. Target aud: General. ■ Mac Johnson, gen mgr; John C. Gunton, chief opns, gen sls mgr, progmg dir, mus dir & news dir; Dave Walkden, chief engr. ■ Rates: $5.75; 4.75; 5.75; 3.75.

***WEGS(FM)**—Oct 15, 1985: 91.7 mhz; 2 kw. Ant 300 ft. TL: N30 37 29 W87 05 08. Stereo. 1836 Olive Rd., Pensacola (32514). (904) 474-1223. FAX: (904) 494-2234. Licensee: Florida Public Radio Inc. Format: Contemp Christian. ■ Randy Henry, pres; Dave Talley, gen mgr; Robert Smith, progmg dir.

***WTGF(FM)**—Not on air, target date unknown: 90.5 mhz. (904) 994-3747. Licensee: Faith Bible College Inc.

WXBM-FM—Apr 28, 1964: 102.7 mhz; 100 kw. Ant 1,328 ft. TL: N30 35 18 W87 33 16. Stereo. 1687 Quintet Rd., Pace (32571). (904) 994-5357. FAX: (904) 994-7191. Licensee: June Broadcasting Inc. (acq 11-23-92; $4.5 million; FTR 12-14-92). Net: MBS. Rep: Katz. Format: Modern country. ■ Lou Mahacek, pres & gen mgr; Truman Conley, gen sls mgr; Dan Sommers, progmg dir & mus dir; Ballard Fore, chief engr.

Mims

WPGS(AM)—May 5, 1986: 840 khz; 250 w-D. TL: N28 44 17 W80 52 52. Stereo. Hrs opn: Sunrise-sunset. Box 2069, Titusville (32781); 3910 S. Washington Ave., Titusville (32780). (407) 383-1000. Licensee: WPGS Radio Inc. (acq 3-93; $65,000; FTR 3-29-93). Net: UPI. Format: Nostalgia, div, talk. News progmg 12 hrs wkly. Target aud: over 45; upscale NASA employees & the local retirement community. Spec prog: Talk show one hr, gospel 4 hrs wkly. ■ Ed Schiflett, exec vp; Joe Bryan, gen mgr; Ed Shiflett, vp prom & vp engrg; John Rowland, chief engr. ■ Rates: $7; 6; 7; na.

Monticello

WJPH(FM)—May 1989: 101.9 mhz; 6 kw. Ant 249 ft. TL: N30 31 58 W83 52 17. 2303 S. Denville, Abiline, TX (79605). (915) 691-9898. FAX: (915) 691-9991. Licensee: Webster Broadcasting Inc. Group owner: Webster Broadcasting (acq 5-7-92; $200,000 with co-located AM; FTR 5-25-92). Net: CBS. Format: MOR. ■ Jack Hyden, pres; Vic Aderhold, vp, gen mgr & gen sls mgr; Ray Matthews, progmg dir & mus dir.

WMFL(AM)—Co-owned with WJPH(FM). Not on air, target date unknown: 1090 khz; 1 kw-D. TL: N30 31 54 W83 52 11. Format: Country. Spec prog: Farm 2 hrs wkly.

Mount Dora

WBGB(AM)—July 31, 1974: 1580 khz; 5 kw-D. TL: N28 48 57 W81 38 52. Box 655, New Albany, IN (47151). (812) 941-1570. Licensee: Cross Country Communications Inc. (acq 8-12-93; $30,000; FTR 8-30-93). ■ George Zarris, gen mgr.

WMGF(FM)—1966: 107.7 mhz; 100 kw. Ant 1,584 ft. TL: N28 55 16 W81 19 09. Stereo. Hrs opn: 24. Suite 401, 2500 Maitland Center Pkwy., Maitland, (32751). (407) 298-5510. Licensee: Paxson Broadcasting of Orlando. Group owner: Paxson Broadcasting (acq 2-18-93; $5.6 million with WWZN[AM] Winter Park; FTR 3-8-93). Net: AP. Rep: Banner. Format: Soft adult contemp. News staff one; news progmg 2 hrs wkly. Target aud: 25-54; working women. ■ Lowel "Bud" W. Paxson, pres; Jenny Sue Rhoades, gen mgr; John Frost, opns mgr & progmg mgr; Deonne Darden, gen sls mgr; Deborah Magnuson, natl sls mgr; Judi Pearl, prom mgr; Joe Casey, mus dir; Regan Smith, news dir; Dave Murray, chief engr.

Naples

WCVU(FM)—Listing follows WNOG(AM).

WNOG(AM)—Oct 14, 1954: 1270 khz; 5 kw-D, 1.9 kw-N, DA-2. TL: N26 15 26 W81 40 33. Hrs opn: 24. 333 Eighth St. (33940). (813) 263-4600. FAX: (813) 263-6525. Licensee: Palmer Communications Inc. (group owner; acq 6-68). Net: ABC TalkRadio, CBS, NBC Talknet, MBS. Rep: Christal. Format: News/talk. News progmg 24 hrs wkly. Target aud: 35 plus. ■ William J. Ryan, pres; James M. Keating, gen mgr; Todd Olson, sls dir; Donna Gibala, prom dir; Marvin Durant, progmg dir; Carl Loveday, news dir; Peter Spalvins, chief engr. ■ Rates: $40; 40; 45; 30.

WNOG-FM—Dec 1, 1971: 93.5 mhz; 3 kw. Ant 299 ft. TL: N26 07 21 W81 43 22 (CP: 2.2 kw, ant 381 ft.). Stereo. Hrs opn: 24. 333 8th St. S. (33940). (813) 263-4600. FAX: (813) 263-6525. Licensee: Palmer Communications Inc. (group owner; acq 7-23-93; $865,311; FTR 8-23-93). Net: Unistar. Format: News/talk. News staff one; news progmg 15 hrs wkly. Target aud: 25-54. ■ James M. Keating, gen mgr.

WCVU(FM)—Co-owned with WNOG(AM). May 8, 1962: 94.5 mhz; 100 kw. Ant 1,049 ft. TL: N26 20 26 W81 42 48. Prog sep from AM. Format: Soft adult contemp. Target aud: 35 plus. Spec prog: Relg 4 hrs wkly. ■ Joseph Ademy, gen sls mgr; John Conrad, progmg dir. ■ Rates: $40; 40; 40; 40.

WSGL(FM)—May 10, 1980: 103.1 mhz; 2 kw. Ant 384 ft. TL: N26 07 34 W81 43 18. Stereo. Suite 211, 2500 Airport Rd. (33962). (813) 793-1031. FAX: (813) 793-7329. Licensee: Sterling Communications Corp. Group owner: Timm Enterprises. Rep: Banner. Format: Adult contemp, oldies. News staff one. Target aud: 25-54. ■ Joe Landon, gen mgr; Nick Caplan, progmg dir; Paul Martin, chief engr.

Florida

*WSOR(FM)—1989: 90.9 mhz; 36 kw. Ant 909 ft. TL: N262026 W814322. 940 Tarpon St., Fort Myers (33916-1198). (813) 334-1393. FAX: (813) 334-0596. Licensee: Southwest Florida Educational Corp. (acq 2-16-89; $400,000; FTR 3-6-89). Net: USA. Format: MOR, inspirational. News staff one. Target aud: 40 plus. ■ Bill Simon, gen mgr & progmg dir; Ron Maxwell, mus dir; Dave Coffman, chief engr.

*WSRX(FM)—August 1988: 89.5 mhz; 550 w. Ant 249 ft. TL: N260721 W814322. 2634 E. Tamiami Tr. (33962). (813) 775-8950. FAX: (813) 774-1775. Licensee: Youth Foundation of America Inc. (acq 2-3-92; $117,114; FTR 2-24-92). Format: Christian. ■ Bruce Graham, gen mgr; Sean Davis, progmg dir.

Naples Park

WIXI(FM)—Oct 22, 1987: 105.5 mhz; 950 w. Ant 584 ft. TL: N26 19 00 W81 47 13. Stereo. 3337 Tamiami Trail N., Naples (33940). (813) 262-1000. FAX: (813) 649-0555. Licensee: Naples Communications Systems Inc. Group owner: American Broadcasting Systems (acq 4-19-93; $3 million; FTR 5-17-93). Net: SMN. Rep: Torbet. Format: Big band. ■ Stephen Wodlinger, gen mgr & gen sls mgr; Bill Thompson, progmg dir; Jack Spiess, chief engr.

New Port Richey

WGUL-FM—Licensed to New Port Richey. See Tampa.

*WLPJ-FM—Apr 10, 1985: 91.5 mhz; 2.7 kw. Ant 185 ft. TL: N28 16 41 W82 43 06 (CP: 25 kw, ant 390 ft, TL: N28 23 30 W82 36 45). Stereo. Box 10, Suite 109, 8410 U.S. 19 (34673). (813) 848-9150. FAX: (813) 848-1233. Licensee: Showem Inc. Format: Relg, talk, adult contemp. ■ Andrew Stamat, pres; Bill Carlin, gen mgr; Bob Liebel, chief engr.

WPSO(AM)—Oct 31, 1963: 1500 khz; 250 w-D. TL: N28 15 32 W82 43 54. 27873 U.S. Hwy. N. 19, Clearwater (34621). (813) 848-8161; (813) 725-5552. FAX: (813) 724-1229. Licensee: AKMA Broadcast Network Inc. (acq 1993; $250,000; FTR 9-13-93). Net: ABC TalkRadio; Florida. Format: Talk/greek. News staff one; news progmg 35 hrs wkly. Target aud: 35 plus. Spec prog: Pol 2 hrs wkly. ■ Sum Angelatos, gen mgr; Glen Adkins, progmg dir & mus dir; Angelos Angelatos, chief engr.

New Smyrna Beach

*WJLU(FM)—Sept 7, 1989: 89.7 mhz; 5 kw. Ant 328 ft. TL: N29 00 32 W80 58 27. Stereo. Hrs opn: 24. 4295 Ridgewood Ave., Port Orange (32129). (904) 427-9000. FAX: (904) 760-7107. Licensee: Cornerstone Community Radio Inc. Net: USA, Moody, Skylight. Wash atty: J. Geoffrey Bentley. Format: Relg. News progmg 18 hrs wkly. Target aud: General; families. ■ Richard Van Zandt, pres & gen mgr; Arthur Gregg, exec vp; Dick Reed, vp mktg; Ken Young, mus dir; Barbara Cram, pub affrs dir; Bill Leisner, chief engr.

WSBB(AM)—1950: 1230 khz; 1 kw-U. TL: N29 01 57 W80 55 03. Box 130 (32170); 175 N. Causeway (32169). (904) 428-9091. FAX: (904) 428-7835. Licensee: T.K. Radio Inc. (acq 10-7-91; $50,000; FTR 10-28-91). Net: MBS. Format: MOR. Target aud: General. Spec prog: Jazz one hr, Polish one hr, relg 5 hrs wkly. ■ Brian E. Tolby, pres; Marilyn Timmer, gen sls mgr; Bob Belz, progmg dir; Jim Bryan, news dir; James Tillis, chief engr. ■ Rates: $12; 10; 12; 8.

WWBH(AM)—Feb 1, 1962: 1550 khz; 1 kw-D, 84 w-N. TL: N29 00 48 W80 54 50. Box 1700 (32170). (904) 427-1550. FAX: (904) 423-3290. Licensee: Pelican Broadcasting Inc. (acq 11-16-87). Net: Sun; Fla. Net. Rep: Dora Clayton. Format: New/ talk. ■ Bob Belz, pres, gen mgr; progmg dir & news dir.

Newberry

WNFQ(FM)—Not on air, target date unknown: 100.5 mhz; 11 kw. Ant 492 ft. TL: N29 48 42 W82 42 31. 2912 N.W. 62nd Ter., Gainesville (32606-6486). Licensee: Newberry Broadcasting Corp.

Niceville

WNCV(FM)—Not on air, target date unknown: 100.3 mhz; 3 kw. Ant 328 ft. TL: N30 29 20 W86 25 16. 618 St. Martin Cove (32578). Licensee: Century 100 Broadcasting Inc.

North Fort Myers

WWCN(AM)—Dec 17, 1983: 770 khz; 10 kw-D, 1 kw-N, DA-2. TL: N26 46 30 W81 50 51. Stereo. 20125 S. Tamiami Trail, Estero (33928). (813) 597-3696. Licensee: Beasley Radio Co. Group owner: Beasley Broadcast Group (acq 12-16-87). Net: SMN. Format: Hard rock. ■ George Beasley, pres; Maureen Knorr, gen mgr; Brad Beasley, progmg dir; Richard Gallo, chief engr.

North Miami

WKAT(AM)—November 1937: 1360 khz; 10 kw-D, 1 kw-N. TL: N25 44 36 W80 09 14. 13499 Biscayne Blvd. (33181). (305) 949-9528. FAX: (305) 944- 4788. Licensee: Howard Broadcasting Corp. (acq 9-23-86; $2 million; FTR 8-25-86). Wash atty: Bob Healey. Format: Spanish. Target aud: 30-50. Spec prog: Relg 2 hrs, Caribbean 10 hrs, Haitian 10 hrs, oldies 3 hrs, talk 3 hrs wkly. ■ Howard Premer, pres; Arnie Premer, gen mgr; Ilene Premer, prom mgr; Sam Stoddard, chief engr. ■ Rates: $50; 50; 50; 30.

Ocala

*WHIJ(FM)—Mar 30, 1990: 88.1 mhz; 1.25 kw. Ant 394 ft. TL: N29 14 17 W82 07 17. Stereo. Hrs opn: 18. 814 N.E. 2nd St. (34470). (904) 351-8810. FAX: (904) 351-8917. Licensee: Marion Community Radio Inc. Net: USA. Format: Relg. Target aud: 20-50. ■ Brad Dinkins, pres; Mark Okus, gen mgr.

WMFQ(FM)—Listing follows WOCA(AM).

WMMZ(FM)—Nov 7, 1960: 93.7 mhz; 100 kw. Ant 1,348 ft. TL: N29 16 06 W82 04 51. Stereo. Box 70229, 3602 N.E. 20th Pl. (34470). (904) 622-5600. FAX: (904) 622-7822. Licensee: Ocala Broadcasting Corp. Group owner: Dix Communications (acq 7-1-86). Format: Hot adult contemp. News staff one. Target aud: 25-44; young families, working people. ■ David Dix, pres; Chris R. Corson, gen mgr; Chris R. Colson, gen sls mgr; Bill McCown, progmg dir; Mark Moralis, news dir. ■ Rates: $45; 35; 45; 30.

WMOP(AM)—Dec 18, 1953: 900 khz; 5 kw. TL: N29 14 17 W82 07 17. Stereo. Hrs opn: 5:45 AM-10 PM. Box 3930, 343 N.E. First Ave., (34478-3930). (904) 732-2010; (904) 732-3368. FAX: (904) 732-6261. Licensee: WMOP Broadcasting Inc. (acq 11-5-93; $200,000; FTR 11-29-93). Net: AP. Rep: Dora Clayton; Midsouth. Format: C&W. News staff 2; news progmg 3 hrs wkly. Target aud: 35 plus. Spec prog: Farm one hr wkly. ■ Richard F. Kirk, pres, progmg dir, mus dir & news dir; Carol Carpenter, gen mgr, stn mgr & gen sls mgr; Joan Becker, prom mgr; Bill Boyer, chief engr. ■ Rates: $18; 18; 18; na.

WOCA(AM)—May 1957: 1370 khz; 5 kw-D. TL: N29 12 04 W82 09 07. Hrs opn: 6 AM-7 PM. Box 1056 (34478); 1515 E. Silver Springs Blvd. (32670). (904) 732-8000; (904) 732-2442. FAX: (904) 732-2144. Licensee: Robert M. Hauck (acq 12-6-93; $453,334 with co-located FM; FTR 12-20-93). Net: ABC/D, Daynet. Format: News/talk. News staff one; news progmg 16 hrs wkly. Target aud: 35 plus. ■ Robert M. Hauck, pres & gen mgr; Tishia Morgan, vp; Fred Petty, opns mgr; Clyde Moeller, chief engr. ■ Rates: $30; 24; 30; 20.

WMFQ(FM)—Co-owned with WOCA(AM). July 11, 1977: 92.9 mhz; 50 kw. Ant 476 ft. TL: N29 04 45 W82 05 35. Stereo. Hrs opn: 24. Prog sep from AM. Box 2092 (34478). (904) 732-2442. Format: MOR. News staff one; news progmg 10 hrs wkly.

WTMC(AM)—1939: 1290 khz; 5 kw-D, 1 kw-N, DA-N. TL: N29 11 51 W82 10 57. Hrs opn: 24. 3621 N.W. 10th St. (34475). (904) 629-1290. FAX: (904) 629-2139. Licensee: The American Network Group Inc. (acq 11-23-92; $250,000; FTR 12-14-92). Net: NBC; S.E. Agri. Format: News, sports. News staff one; news progmg 20 plus hrs wkly. Target aud: 35 plus. Spec prog: Farm 5 hrs, gospel 4 hrs, relg 4 hrs wkly. ■ Larry Whitler, opns mgr; Clyde Moeller, engrg dir. ■ Rates: $12; 10; 12; 9.

WWGO(FM)—(Silver Springs). Feb 1, 1991: 95.5 mhz; 3 kw. Ant 340 ft. TL: N29 16 55 W82 02 50. Stereo. Hrs opn: 24. 3343 E. Silver Springs Blvd., Ocala, (34470). (904) 622-9550. FAX: (904) 622-4449. Licensee: Stoehr Communications Corporation. Net: SMN. Format: Oldies. Target aud: 25-54. ■ Robert D. Stoehr, pres & gen mgr; Betty L. Stoehr, exec vp & stn mgr; Don Connelly, vp opns, opns mgr & chief engr; Duke Roberts, vp progmy; Steve Mack, news dir. ■ Rates: $30; 28; 30; 24.

Ocoee

WUNA(AM)—Oct 25, 1962: 1480 khz; 1 kw-D, 71 w-N. TL: N28 33 27 W81 32 29. Stereo. 749 S. Bluford Ave. (34761). (407) 656-9823. FAX: (407) 656-2092. Licensee: Ephrain Archilla-Roig (acq 2-83; $400,000; FTR 2-28-83). Net: CBN; Fla. Net. Format: Sp contemp. News staff one. ■ William A. Masi, pres; Juan Nieves, gen mgr; Herb Cruise, gen sls mgr; Ovil Naveis, prom mgr & progmg dir; Dale Moudy, chief engr.

Okeechobee

WOKC(AM)—Feb 6, 1962: 1570 khz; 1 kw-D, 14 w-N. TL: N27 12 59 W80 49 53. Hrs opn: 6 AM-11 PM. Box 1247 (34973); 3101 Hwy 441 S. (34974). (813) 763-3181; (813) 763-6829. FAX: (813) 763-6036. Licensee: Okeechobee Broadcasters Inc. Net: Florida's Radio Net. Wash atty: John M. Spencer. Format: Top 40 Hispanic dance music. News staff one; news progmg 10 hrs wkly. Target aud: Spanish-speaking (Mexican farm workers). ■ Charles C. Castle, pres; William A. Stokes, vp & gen mgr; Barbara Ann Stokes, gen sls mgr; Al Stokes, prom mgr & chief engr; Richard Stokes, progmg dir & mus dir; Jeff Gunstein, news dir.

WOKC-FM—July 4, 1965: 103.1 mhz; 3 kw. Ant 321 ft. TL: N27 12 59 W80 49 53. Stereo. Hrs opn: 17. Prog sep from AM. Net: NBC. Format: Mod Country. News staff one; news progmg 12 hrs wkly. Target aud: General. ■ Al Stokes, opns mgr, mktg mgr & adv mgr; Heath Schoenseld, mus dir; Jeff Gunstein, pub affrs dir.

*WWFR(FM)—1988: 91.7 mhz; 20 kw. Ant 299 ft. TL: N27 07 20 W80 23 21 (CP: 3 kw, ant 291 ft.). Stereo. Hrs opn: 24. Box 277 (34973-0277). (813) 763-5454. FAX: (813) 763-8867. Licensee: Family Stations Inc. (group owner). Format: Relg. Target aud: General. ■ Harold Camping, pres & exec vp; Scott Smith, vp; Ed Dearborn, gen mgr, chief opns & chief engr.

Olviedo

NEW AM—Not on air, target date unknown: 880 khz. C 82nd St., Urb El Retiro Quebradillas, PR (00742). Licensee: Seminole Broadcasting.

Orange Park

*WAYR(AM)—May 28, 1960: 550 khz; 5 kw-D, 500 w-N, DA-1. TL: N30 04 21 W81 47 24. Hrs opn: 24. 2500 Russell Rd., Green Cove Springs (32043-9492). (904) 272-1111; (904) 284-2500. Licensee: Good Tidings Trust Inc. Net: Moody, VCY America. Format: Relg. News staff one; news progmg 5 hrs wkly. Target aud: General. ■ Jerry King, pres; Dick Weer, opns dir, dev dir, prom dir, progmg dir & mus dir; Mary Mitchell, news dir; Jim Asher, pub affrs dir; Hal Mashburn, chief engr.

Orlando

WAJL(AM)—See Pine Castle-Sky Lake.

WDBO(AM)—May 24, 1924: 580 khz; 5 kw-U, DA-N. TL: N28 37 12 W81 24 34. 4192 John Young Parkway (32804). (407) 295-5858. FAX: (407) 291-4879. Licensee: NewCity Communications of Fla. Inc. Group owner: NewCity Communications Inc. (acq 8-8-86; grpsl; FTR 4-28-86). Net: ABC/I, NBC Talknet. Rep: Katz. Format: Adult contemp, news/talk. ■ Dick Ferguson, pres; Richard A. Reis, gen mgr; Steve Holbrook, opns mgr; Bill Hendrich, gen sls mgr; Mike Krupa, natl sls mgr; Denise Dillman, prom mgr; Paul Duckworth, progmg dir; Marsha Taylor, news dir; Tom Bohannon, chief engr.

WWKA(FM)—Co-owned with WDBO(AM). April 24, 1952: 92.3 mhz; 100 kw. Ant 1,380 ft. TL: N28 36 08 W81 05 37 (CP: 97.6 kw). Stereo. Prog sep from AM. (407) 298-9292. Format: Country. ■ Mike James, prom mgr; Scott St. James, mus dir; Gary Anstaett, news dir.

WDIZ(FM)—July 1, 1971: 100.3 mhz; 100 kw. Ant 1,597 ft. TL: N28 36 08 W81 05 37. Suite 2150, 2180 W. State Rd. 434, Longwood (32779). (407) 682-7676. FAX: (407) 682-5297. Licensee: Shamrock Communications Inc. (group owner; acq 3-71). Net: ABC/R. Rep: Major Mkt. Format: AOR. News staff one; news progmg 2 hrs wkly. Target aud: 18-49. ■ Bill Lynett, CEO; Tom Owens, gen mgr; Bill Bromley, gen sls mgr & adv mgr; Mick Dolan, prom mgr; Tim Travis, mus dir; Carole Dedman, news dir; Lou Mueller, chief engr. ■ Rates: $150; 150; 150; 80.

WGTO(AM)—See Pine Hills.

WHBS(AM)—(Eatonville). 1957: 1270 khz; 5 kw-U, DA-N. TL: N28 34 03 W81 25 38. Box 5724, Winter Park (32793); One Purliue Pl., Suite 219, Winter Park (32792). (407) 671-7023. Licensee: Rumbaut & Associates Inc., receiver for S.E. Broadcasting Inc. (acq 7-15-92). Net:

CBS Hispanic. Format: News/talk, music, Sp. News staff 2; news progmg 20 hrs wkly. Target aud: 25-54; affluent men and women. ■ Anibal Torres Sr., CEO; Anibal Torres Jr., pres, gen mgr & vp sls; Hector Torres, exec vp; Edwin Ayola, stn mgr; Magaly Rodriguez, progmg mgr; Homan Machuca, news dir.

WHOO(AM)—Listing follows WHTQ(FM).

WHTQ(FM)—1952: 96.5 mhz; 100 kw. Ant 1,600 ft. TL: N28 34 51 W81 04 32. Stereo. One Radio WHOO Rd. (32808). (407) 295-3990. FAX: (407) 295-3999. Licensee: TK Communications Inc. (group owner; acq 6-10-87; $12 million with co-located AM; FTR 6-22-87). Net: NBC the Source. Rep: Eastman. Format: AOR. News progmg 2 hrs wkly. Target aud: 18-49. ■ Frank Tenore, vp & gen mgr; J.T. Stevens, progmg dir; Joe Finger, news dir; Roger Parker, chief engr.

WHOO(AM)—Co-owned with WHTQ(FM). Dec 5, 1947: 990 khz; 50 kw-D, 5 kw-N, DA-2, 10 kw non-DA-CH. TL: N28 34 28 W81 27 48. Stereo. Prog sep from FM. Format: Class rock, div, Caribbean. News staff one; news progmg 4 hrs wkly. Target aud: 25-49. Spec prog: Combination of relg & special interests.

***WMFE-FM**—July 14, 1980: 90.7 mhz; 100 kw. Ant 731 ft. TL: N28 36 08 W81 05 37. Stereo. Hrs opn: 24. 11510 E. Colonial Dr. (32817-4699). (407) 273-2300. FAX: (407) 273-8462. Licensee: Community Communications Inc. Net: APR, NPR. Format: Class, news, info. News staff 5; news progmg 45 hrs wkly. Target aud: 35 plus; well-educated, executive, professional, upper-income. Spec prog: New instrumental 4 hrs wkly. ■ Stephen M. Steck, chmn & pres; Malcolm B. Wall, exec vp; Ben Hardcastle, vp dev; JaWanda Thacker, prom mgr; Dale Spear, vp progmg; Robert B. Peterson III, progmg mgr; David Glerum, mus dir; Dave Pignanelli, news dir; Steve Fluker, chief engr. ■ Rates: $120; 83; 120; 83.

WMGF(FM)—See Mount Dora.

WMMO(FM)—Aug 19, 1990: 98.9 mhz; 38 kw. Ant 439 ft. TL: N28 32 23 W81 22 46. Stereo. Hrs opn: 24. Suite 2240, 200 S. Orange Ave. (32801). (407) 422-9890. FAX: (407) 423-9666. Licensee: GCI Orlando Inc. Group owner: Granum Communications Inc. (acq 11-21-91; $8.15 million; FTR 12-16-91). Rep: Eastman. Wash atty: Bring & Bernstein. Format: Adult contemp. News staff one. ■ Mark Warlaumont, gen mgr; Ellen Johnson, gen sls mgr; Jim Stout, prom mgr; Cary Pall, progmg dir; Lisa Miller, mus dir; Winifred King, news dir & pub affrs dir; Steve Fluker, chief engr.

WOMX(AM)—Apr 1, 1940: 950 khz; 5 kw-U, DA-N. TL: N28 32 08 W81 26 55. Hrs opn: 24. Box 8105, 1801 Lee Rd., Suite 270, Winter Park (32789). (407) 629-5105. FAX: (407) 647-6515. Licensee: Nationwide Communications Inc. (acq 9-15-82; $6,665,000 with co-located FM; FTR 8-16-82). Net: AP. Rep: McGavren Guild. Wash atty: Fletcher, Heald & Hildreth. Format: Adult contemp. News staff one; news progmg 4 hrs wkly. Target aud: 25-44; female. ■ Steve Berger, pres; Mickey Franko, vp; Rick Weinkauf, gen mgr; Dennis Frawley, gen sls mgr; Greg Otte, mktg dir & prom mgr; Pat Paxton, progmg dir; Rick Stone, mus dir; Sue Schelle, pub affrs dir; Jeff Keith, chief engr.

WOMX-FM—Aug 15, 1967: 105.1 mhz; 95 kw. Ant 1,309 ft. TL: N28 36 17 W81 05 13. Stereo. Hrs opn: 24. Prog dups AM 100%. ■ Erica Lee, news dir.

WPCV(FM)—See Lakeland.

WRMQ(AM)—Oct 21, 1985: 1140 khz; 4.1 kw-D. TL: N28 30 42 W81 14 09. Stereo. Suite 253, Semoran Blvd, Castleberry (32707). (407) 830-0800. FAX: (407) 260-6100. Licensee: Q Broadcasting. Net: CNN. Rep: Caballero. Wash atty: Roy F. Perkins. Format: Sp. News staff 3. Target aud: 25-54. ■ George M. Arroyo, pres, gen mgr & chief engr; Esperanza T.M. Lezcano, gen sls mgr; Paul Gamane, prom mgr; George Mier, progmg dir; Lolita Ayala, mus dir. ■ Rates: $26; 26; 26; 26.

WTKS(FM)—(Cocoa Beach). May 8, 1962: 104.1 mhz; 100 kw. Ant 1,609 ft. TL: N28 34 51 W81 04 32. Stereo. Hrs opn: 24. Suite 100, 600 Courtland St., Orlando (32804). (407) 628-4104. FAX: (407) 628-5872. Licensee: Press Broadcasting Company Inc. (acq 5-6-93; $5.01 million; FTR 4-12-93). Net: AP. Rep: McGavren Guild. Format: Talk. News staff 3; news progmg 6 hrs wky. Target aud: 25-54. ■ E. Donald Lass, CEO; Jules L. Plangere, chmn; Robert E. McAllan, pres; Alfred D. Colantoni, CFO; Mark Lass, vp; Richard Boemer, opns mgr; Karen Kjos, gen sls mgr; Joe Addalia, chief engr.

WTRR(AM)—See Sanford.

***WUCF-FM**—Jan 30, 1978: 89.9 mhz; 7.9 kw. Ant 160 ft. TL: N28 36 00 W81 12 05. Stereo. Hrs opn: 24. Box 162199 (32816-2199). (407) 823-3689; (407) 823-2133. FAX: (407) 823-6364. Licensee: University of Central Florida. Net: AP. Format: Progsv rock, class, jazz. News progmg 3 hrs wkly. Spec prog: Fr one hr, It one hr, Sp 3 hrs, Indian one hr, blues 2 hrs, bluegrass 3 hrs, Irish one hr, folk 2 hrs, new age 3 hrs wkly. ■ John Hitt, pres; Jose Maunez-Cuadra, gen mgr; Rafael Gonzalez, gen sls mgr; Mike Hidalgo, chief engr.

WWKA(FM)—Listing follows WDBO(AM).

WWNZ(AM)—1947: 740 khz: 50 kw-U, DA-2. TL: N28 28 53 W81 39 43. 3500 W. Colonial (32808). (407) 661-1900. Licensee: Paxson Broadcasting of Orlando L.P. Net: CBS, CNN. Rep: Christal. Format: News. News staff 8; news progmg 80 hrs wkly. Target aud: 25-54. ■ Bud Paxson, CEO; Jim Bocock, pres; Jim Bocock, Jenney Sue Rhoades, gen mgrs; Jim Poling, opns dir & progmg dir; David Murray, chief opns; Deonne Darden, gen sls mgr; Judi Pearl, prom mgr; Wayne Trout, news dir; Dave Murray, chief engr.

WWZN(AM)—See Winter Park.

WXTO(AM)—See Winter Garden.

WXXL(FM)—See Leesburg.

Ormond Beach

WELE(AM)—Aug 1, 1957: 1380 khz; 5 kw-D, 2.5-N, DA-2. TL: N29 16 09 W81 04 54. 432 S. Nova Rd. (32074). (904) 677-4122. FAX: (904) 677-4123. Licensee: Wings Communications (acq 9-90; $175,000; FTR 9-24-90). Net: NBC. Format: Christian talk. Target aud: General; mature, interested adults in Christian teaching & current events. ■ F. Douglas Wilhite, pres & gen mgr; Sean Hughes, opns dir & gen sls mgr; Doug Wilhite II, progmg dir, news dir & pub affrs dir; Ovie Loman, chief engr. ■ Rates: $15; 10; 15; na.

Ottawa

***NEW FM**—Not on air, target date unknown: 88.9 mhz; 3 kw. Ant 459 ft. 2596 State Rd. 44, New Smyrna Beach (32168). Licensee: Cornerstone Community Radio Inc.

Oviedo

WONQ(AM)—Nov 21, 1992: 1030 khz; 10 kw-D, 500 w-N, DA-2. TL: N28 40 31 W81 10 01. Hrs opn: 24. Suite 253, 1033 N. Semoran Blvd., Casselberry (32707). (407) 830-0800; (407) 331-1030. Licensee: Florida Broadcasters. Rep: Caballero. Wash atty: Roy F. Perkins. Format: Sp. ■ George M. Arroyo, pres & gen mgr; Renee Dwyer, prom mgr; George Mier, progmg dir & mus dir; Paul Gamache, news dir; Esperenza T. Arroyo, chief engr.

Palatka

***WAEQ(FM)**—Not on air, target date unknown: 91.9 mhz; 3 kw. Ant 151 ft. 3111 St. Johns Ave. (32177). Licensee: Putnam Radio Ministries Inc.

WFKS(FM)—Dec 13, 1973: 99.9 mhz; 100 kw. Ant 1,201 ft. TL: N29 31 08 W81 19 02. Stereo. 801 W. Granada Blvd., Ormand Beach (32174). (904) 672-9210. FAX: (904) 677-2252. Licensee: Beachside East Broadcasting Inc. Group owner: Heritage Broadcast Group Inc. (acq 6-20-86; $8.5 million; FTR 5-19-86). Format: CHR. News staff one. ■ Tom Panucci, gen mgr; Joseph Russo, gen sls mgr; J.J. Duling, Chris Earl Philips, progmg dirs; Russ Smith, mus dir; Scott Harris, news dir; Mark Skinner, chief engr.

WIYD(AM)—Feb 14, 1947: 1260 khz; 1 kw-D, 500 w-N, DA-N. TL: N29 38 23 W81 38 26. Hrs opn: 5:45 AM-10 PM. Box 918, 900 River St. (32178-0918). (904) 325-4556. FAX: (904) 328-5161. Licensee: Hall Broadcasting Co. (acq 2-14-57; $100,000). Net: ABC/C; Fla. Radio Net. Format: C&W. Spec prog: Black 5 hrs wkly. ■ Ronald G. Tumlin, pres, sls dir & adv mgr; Suzanne Tumlin, gen mgr; Mary Makie, gen sls mgr; Bob Henry, prom mgr, progmg dir & mus dir; Joe Munroe, chief engr.

WPLK(AM)—1957: 800 khz; 1 kw-D, 334 w-N. TL: N29 37 40 W81 34 35 (CP: TL: N29 39 07 W81 35 32). Stereo. Hrs opn: 18. Box 335, 1501 Reid St. (32078). (904) 325-5800. FAX: (904) 328-8725. Licensee: Radio Palatka Inc. (acq 7-90; $180,000; FTR 7-9-90). Net: NBC; Fla. Net. Format: Country. News staff one; news progmg 2 hrs wkly. Target aud: General. ■ Janice Register, pres; Wayne Bullock, gen mgr & gen sls mgr; Byron King, prom mgr; Bill Meetze, progmg dir; George Duck, mus dir, news dir & chief engr. ■ Rates: $10; 8; 8; na.

Palm Bay

***WEJF(FM)**—Not on air, target date unknown: 90.3 mhz; 2 kw. Ant 295 ft. TL: N28 02 54 W80 40 34. Licensee: Palm Bay Public Radio Inc.

***WWIA(FM)**—Not on air, target date unknown: 88.5 mhz; 1 kw-V. Ant 98 ft. TL: N28 02 54 W80 40 34. Stereo. 100 Emerson Dr. N.W. (32907). (407) 768-2601. Licensee: Victory Christian Academy. Target aud: Christian. ■ L. Mark Ostrander, pres; Cliff Lethbridge, gen mgr.

Palm Beach

WJNO(AM)—See West Palm Beach.

WPBR(AM)—1941: 1340 khz; 1 kw-U. TL: N26 36 41 W80 02 17 (CP: TL: N26 33 26 W80 04 20). Box 1340, Lake Worth (33460-1340). (407) 582-7401. FAX: (407) 582-9254. Licensee: PBR Communications Inc. (acq 1-6-88). Net: Moody, NBC, Daynet. Format: News, talk. News staff one; news progmg 14 hrs wkly. Target aud: 35-64. Spec prog: Financial 9 hrs, medical 8 hrs, Jewish 3 hrs wkly. ■ Arnold Lampert, pres; Al Kahan, gen mgr.

WRMF(FM)—1957: 97.9 mhz; 100 kw. Ant 1,350 ft. TL: N26 34 37 W80 14 32. Box 189, West Palm Beach (33402). (407) 838-4300. FAX: (407) 838-4257. Licensee: Fairbanks Communications Inc. (group owner). Format: Adult contemp. ■ Richard M. Fairbanks, pres; George Mills, vp & gen mgr; Russ Morley, progmg dir & mus dir; Dick Lucas, chief engr.

Palm City

***WCNO(FM)**—April 1, 1990: 89.9 mhz; 100 kw. Ant 613 ft. TL: N27 07 20 W80 23 21. 177 S.W. Monterey Rd. S.W., Stuart (34994). (407) 221-1100. Licensee: National Christian Network Inc. Format: Christian, adult contemp. ■ Tom Craton, gen mgr; Tom Chorley, progmg dir & mus dir; Ray Kassis, chief engr.

Palmetto

WBRD(AM)—October 1957: 1420 khz; 2.5 kw-D, 1 kw-N, DA-2. TL: N27 32 42 W82 34 28. Stereo. Hrs opn: 24. Box 1038, Bradenton (34206). (813) 749-1420. FAX: (813) 747-3523. Licensee: Sunshine State Broadcasting Co. Net: ABC/I, ABC TalkRadio. Rep: Christal. Format: Talk. ■ Robert R. Nelson, pres; Robert W. Nelson, vp & gen mgr; Judy Johnson, gen sls mgr; Rob Lankton, chief engr.

Panama City

WEBZ(FM)—See Mexico Beach.

***WFSW(FM)**—Not on air, target date unknown: 89.1 mhz; 100 kw. Ant 403 ft. 2561 Pottsdamer St., Tallahassee (32310). Licensee: The Board of Regents of State of Florida.

WFSY(FM)—Listing follows WGNE(AM).

WGNE(AM)—April 1940: 590 khz; 1.7 kw-D, 2.5 kw-N, DA-N. TL: N30 10 20 W85 36 49. Stereo. Box 759 (32402). (904) 769-6163. FAX: (904) 769-6164. Licensee: The Woodfin Group (group owner; acq 9-26-86; $3.07 million; with co-located FM; FTR 6-2-86). Rep: Torbet. Format: Btfl mus. ■ Ken Woodfin, pres; Randy Sheffield, vp; Patsy Sellers, gen mgr & stn mgr; Jim Dooley, progmg dir & mus dir; Charlie Wooten, chief engr.

WFSY(FM)—Co-owned with WGNE(AM). October 1971: 98.5 mhz; 100 kw. Ant 1,090 ft. TL: N30 30 41 W85 29 24. Stereo. Prog sep from AM. Net: Mutual. Format: Classic hits of 60s, 70s, & 80s. News staff one. Target aud: 25-54. ■ David Nolin, mus dir.

WILN(FM)—Apr 11, 1985: 105.9 mhz; 50 kw. Ant 406 ft. TL: N30 10 44 W85 46 55. Stereo. Hrs opn: 24. Box 1790 (32402); Suites 20-21, 8317 W. Hwy 98, Panama City Beach (32407). (904) 233-6606. FAX: (904) 233-1541. Licensee: BayMedia Inc. Rep: Banner. Wash atty: Frank A. Woods. Format: CHR. News staff one; news progmg 2 hrs wkly. Target aud: 18-49. ■ James Broaddus II, pres; Bertie S. Broaddus, vp; Chris Murray, gen mgr; Charlie Doggett, sls dir; Todd Shannon, progmg dir & mus dir; Dain Weister, news dir. ■ Rates: $50; 40; 50; 30.

***WJTF(FM)**—Not on air, target date unknown: 89.9 mhz; 100 kw. Ant 105 ft. TL: N30 10 05 W85 40 30. c/o Joy Public Broadcasting Corp., 341 S. Washington, Lancaster, WI (53813). (608) 723-7888. Licensee: Joy Public Broadcasting Corp. (acq 5-4-93; $11,000; FTR 5-24-93).

***WKGC-FM**—October 1964: 90.7 mhz; 100 kw. Ant 336 ft. TL: N30 13 05 W85 51 16. Stereo. 5230 W. Hwy. 98 (32401). (904) 769-5241. FAX: (904) 872-3836. Licensee: Gulf Coast Community College. Net: NPR; Fla. Pub. Format: Class, jazz, news. Spec prog: Black 6 hrs wkly. ■ Robert McSpadden, pres; Lester Spencer, gen mgr; Jean Warren, dev dir & prom dir; Wallace Crawford, progmg dir; Brenton Peacock (reporter), news dir; Gil Halstead, pub affrs dir; Charles T. Wooten, chief engr.

WLTG(AM)—Dec 11, 1949: 1430 khz; 5 kw-U, DA-2. TL: N30 09 38 W85 43 43 (CP: TL: N30 09 55 W85 35 19). Box 15635 (32406); Suite B, 3216 W. Hwy. 390 (32405). (904) 784-9873. FAX: (904) 784-6908. Licensee: Hour Group Broadcasting Inc. (acq 1-9-91; $212,219; FTR 1-28-91). Format: News/talk, sports, info. Target aud: General. Spec prog: Black gospel 6 hrs wkly. ■ John Gay, gen mgr; Pamela Kidwell, sls dir; Michael Bailey, progmg dir & chief engr; Vincent Childs, news dir; Leia Scofield, pub affrs dir.

WPAP-FM—March 30, 1967: 92.5 mhz; 100 kw. Ant 930 ft. TL: N30 22 05 W85 12 24. Stereo. Hrs opn: 24. Caller Box 2288 (32402); 1834 Linsen Ave. (32405). (904) 769-1408. FAX: (904) 769-0659. Licensee: Southern Broadcasting Co. Group owner: Southern Broadcasting Companies Inc. (acq 10-12-90; grpsl; FTR 11-5-90). Net: NBC. Rep: McGavren Guild. Format: Mod country. Target aud: 25-54. ■ Paul C. Stone, pres; Lyn Hindsman, vp & gen mgr; Pat Quirk, sls dir; Reed Kinney, chief engr.

WPFM(FM)—September 1963: 107.9 mhz; 100 kw. Ant 781 ft. TL: N30 26 00 W85 24 51. Stereo. 69096 W. Hwy. 98 (32407). (904) 234-8858. FAX: (904) 234-6592. Licensee: Milback Inc. (acq 10-26-92; $600,000; FTR 11-23-92). Format: CHR. News progmg 2 hrs wkly. Target aud: 18-49; active lifestyle, young adult audience. ■ Jimmy Vineyard, gen mgr; Bob Zinn, rgnl sls mgr; Kelly Mc Kann, progmg dir; Mike Stone, mus dir; Charles Wooten, chief engr.

WYOO(FM)—(Springfield). Mar 2, 1993: 101.3 mhz; 5.2 kw. Ant 267 ft. TL: N30 12 12 W85 36 57. Stereo. Hrs opn: 24. Box 15635, Panama City (32406); Suite B, 3216 W. Hwy. 390, Panama City (32405). (904) 784-9873. Licensee: Tideline Broadcasting Inc. Net: CNN. Wash atty: Richard J. Hayes Jr. Format: News/talk. News progmg 28 hrs wkly. Target aud: General; educated, upscale. Spec prog: Sports 8 hrs wkly. ■ Randall R. Wahlberg, pres; John Gay, gen mgr; Pamela Kidwell, gen sls mgr; Mike Bailey, progmg dir. ■ Rates: $50; 50; 50; 30.

Panama City Beach

WFSY(FM)—See Panama City.

***WKGC(AM)**—June 25, 1965: 1480 khz; 500 w-D, 87 w-N. TL: N30 10 33 W85 48 03. Hrs opn: 6 AM-9 PM. 5230 W. Hwy. 98, Panama City (32401). (904) 769-5241. FAX: (904) 872-3836. Licensee: Gulf Coast Community College (acq 12-1-72). Net: NPR. Format: News, progressive. News progmg 25 hrs wkly. Target aud: General; college students & older high school students. Spec prog: Folk 2 hrs, educ 8 hrs wkly. ■ Robert McSpadden, pres; Lester Spencer, gen mgr; Paula Weaver, stn mgr & opns mgr; Brian Parsley, mus dir; Charles Wooten, chief engr.

WPCF(AM)—Sept 23, 1958: 1290 khz; 270 w-D, 1 kw-N. TL: N30 10 44 W85 46 55. Box 4398, Panama City (32401); 1111 Laurie Ave. (32407). (904) 234-3128. Licensee: Winstanley Broadcasting (acq 1-21-71). Net: CBN. Format: Relg. News progmg 10 hrs wkly. Target aud: 25-54; 66% female, 33% male. ■ C. K. Winstanley, pres; W. H. Underwood, vp & gen mgr; Mary Kate Underwood, gen sls mgr; Frank Mooney, prom mgr, progmg dir & mus dir; John Osgoode, news dir; Charlie Wooten, chief engr.

WPCF-FM—June 1988: 100.1 mhz; 1.7 kw. Ant 413 ft. TL: N30 10 44 W85 46 55 (CP: 25 kw, ant 233 ft., TL: N30 10 45 W85 42 05). Stereo. Format: Adult contemp Christian.

Pennsuco

***WFHQ(FM)**—Not on air, target date unknown: 88.3 mhz; 3 kw. Ant 167 ft. Box 660506, Miami Springs (33266). Licensee: Hispanic Educational System Inc.

Pensacola

WBSR(AM)—Sept 1, 1946: 1450 khz; 1 kw-U. TL: N30 25 44 W87 14 27. Box 8057, c/o WMEZ(FM) (32505-0057). (904) 432-3723. FAX: (904) 433-7932. Licensee: Easy Media Inc. (acq 3-22-85; $330,000; FTR 2-25-85). Rep: Torbet. Format: Easy listening. Target aud: 35-54. ■ Frederic T. C. Brewer, pres, gen mgr & progmg dir; Jane Lewis, opns mgr; Sam Trent, vp sls.

WMEZ(FM)—Co-owned with WBSR(AM). Nov 11, 1960: 94.1 mhz; 100 kw. Ant 1,328 ft. TL: N30 35 18 W87 33 16. Stereo. Prog sep from AM. (904) 432-4775. Licensee: Frederic T.C. Brewer (acq 7-1-65). Net: ABC/FM, ABC/D. Format: Light hits, soft AC. Target aud: 25-54. ■ Gene Pfalzer, vp, gen sls mgr & chief engr.

WCOA(AM)—Feb 3, 1926: 1370 khz; 5 kw-U, DA-N. TL: N30 26 57 W87 15 46. Box 12487 (32573); 6565 N. W St. (32505). (904) 478-6011. FAX: (904) 478-3971. Licensee: Brem Broadcasting (acq 1-31-91; $2.23 million with co-located FM; FTR 2-18-91). Net: ABC/I, Moody, NBC Talknet. Rep: McGavren Guild. Format: Adult contemp, talk, news. News staff 4; news progmg 28 hrs wkly. Target aud: 25-54. Spec prog: Relg 6 hrs wkly. ■ Darrell Tate, gen mgr; Dave Pauloc, gen sls mgr; Greg Gordon, progmg dir; Don Priest, news dir; Dave Kiker, chief engr.

WJLQ(FM)—Co-owned with WCOA(AM). Sept 1, 1965: 100.7 mhz; 100 kw. Ant 1,555 ft. TL: N30 37 35 W87 38 50. Stereo. Prog sep from AM. Net: ABC/C. Format: Contemp hit. Target aud: 25-44. ■ Mark Dagwell, progmg dir.

WKGT(AM)—(Cantonment). December 1955: 1090 khz; 8.6 kw-D. TL: N31 00 22 W87 16 42. Suite 27, 312 E 9 Mile Rd., Pensacola (32514). Licensee: Ann T. Goodrich (acq 9-23-93; $100,000; FTR 10-11-93). ■ Jerry Wayne Spencer, pres.

WMEZ(FM)—Listing follows WBSR(AM).

WOWW(FM)—Nov 10, 1976: 107.3 mhz; 100 kw. Ant 1,407 ft. TL: N30 42 20 W87 19 00. Stereo. Hrs opn: 24. Box 2788, 4220 N. Davis Hwy. (32503). (904) 434-7388. FAX: (904) 433-7107. Licensee: SunMedia Inc. Group owner: SunGroup Inc. (acq 1-1-90; $5 million). Net: Unistar. Rep: McGavern Guild. Wash atty: Wiley, Rein & Fielding. Format: Country. News staff 2; news progmg 15 hrs wkly. Target aud: 25-54. ■ John W. Biddinger, pres; Mike McGough, vp & gen mgr; Paula Petersen, opns mgr; Mike Bates, gen sls mgr; Gary Coleman, mus dir; Dave Kiker, chief engr. ■ Rates: $80; 47; 60; 28.

***WPCS(FM)**—June 22, 1971: 89.5 mhz; 100 kw. Ant 1,328 ft. TL: N30 35 18 W87 33 16. Stereo. Box 18000 (32523). (904) 478-8480. FAX: (904) 494-6738. Licensee: Pensacola Christian College. Net: ABC/FM. Format: Relg, educ. ■ Dr. Arlin Horton, stn mgr; Paul Stimer, opns mgr; Joel Mullenix, progmg dir; R.D. Bowman, chief engr.

WRNE(AM)—November 1957: 980 khz; 2.5 kw-D, 1 kw-N, DA-2. TL: N30 29 08 W87 05 01. Stereo. Hrs opn: 24. Suite 27, 312 E. Nine Mile Rd. (32514). (904) 478-6000. FAX: (904) 484-8080. Licensee: Media One Communications Inc. (acq 11-15-90; FTR 11-19-90). Net: SMN. Wash atty: Tim Brady. Format: Urban contemp, gospel-Hispanic. News staff one; news progmg 5 hrs wkly. Target aud: 25-54; minorities. Spec prog: Gospel, talk, Sp. ■ Robert Hill, pres; Wayne G. Sharpe, gen mgr; Mark Anthony, prom dir; Sonny Dee, progmg dir; Bob Sheher, chief engr.

WSWL(AM)—October 1956: 790 khz; 1 kw-D. TL: N30 27 18 W87 14 22. Box 8127, 4151 N. Pace Blvd. (32505). (904) 433-1141. Licensee: Gerald D. Schroeder (acq 4-1-81). Net: CNN. Wash atty: Gary Smithwick. Format: Talk. ■ Gerald Schroeder, pres & gen mgr; Don Schroeder, gen sls mgr, progmg dir & news dir; Bob Schehr, chief engr. ■ Rates: $25; 20; 24; 14.

WTKX(AM)—1947: 1230 khz; 1 kw-U. TL: N30 25 57 W87 13 07. 2070 N. Palafox (32501). (904) 438-7543. FAX: (904) 432-1466. Licensee: Holt Communications Corp. Group owner: The Holt Corporations (acq 1986; grpsl; FTR 10-27-86). Rep: D & R Radio. Format: Oldies. Target aud: 25-54. ■ Arthur Holt, pres; Howard Seaton, gen mgr; Mike Strummer, progmg dir; Dave Kiker, chief engr.

WTKX-FM—1971: 101.5 mhz; 100 kw. Ant. 633 ft. TL: N30 37 29 W87 05 08. Stereo. Hrs opn: 24. Prog sep from AM. 111 N. Baylen St. (32501). (904) 934-4636. Format: AOR. Target aud: 18-49; General. ■ J.J. Waters, gen sls mgr; Linda Jacobsen, prom mgr; Mike Strummer, mus dir.

***WUWF(FM)**—January 1981: 88.1 mhz; 100 kw. Ant 617 ft. TL: N30 24 09 W86 59 35. Stereo. Hrs opn: 24. 11000 University Pkwy. (32514). (904) 474-2327. FAX: (904) 474-3283. Licensee: Board of Regents of Florida, Univ. of Western Florida. Net: APR, NPR; Fla. Pub. Format: Class, jazz, pub affrs. News staff 2; news progmg 34 hrs wkly. Target aud: General. Spec prog: Folk, new acoustic. ■ Patrick Crawford, gen mgr; Walt Gillette, dev dir; Carol Lege, prom dir; Rebecca Baltas, progmg dir; Steve Tortorici (class), John Macdonnell (jazz), mus dirs; Phil Burger, news dir; Danny Wester, chief engr.

WVTJ(AM)—Nov 1, 1959: 610 khz; 500 w-D, 142 w-N. TL: N30 26 52 W87 15 30. Hrs opn: 16. 2800 Hollywood Ave. (32505); Box 17446 (32522). (904) 438-1605. FAX: (904) 438-9983. Licensee: Cathedral of Praise Ministries Inc. (acq 1-15-92; $83,500; FTR 2-10-92). Net: UPI, USA. Format: Relg, gospel. Target aud: 18-64. ■ Franklin Walden, pres; Steve Williams, sr vp, gen mgr, gen sls mgr, prom mgr & mus dir; Shawn Taylor, pub affrs dir; Carl Foster, chief engr. ■ Rates: $10; 8; 10; 8.

WXBM-FM—See Milton.

Perry

WPRY(AM)—1953: 1400 khz; 1 kw-U. TL: N30 07 43 W83 35 27 (CP: TL: N30 06 42 W83 34 03). Box 779, One Broadcast Pl. (32347). (904) 584-2972. FAX: (904) 584-4616. Licensee: RAHU Broadcasting Co. (acq 1-15-89; $550,000 with co-located FM; FTR 1-30-89). Net: SMN. Format: Country. News staff 2; news progmg 4 hrs wkly. Target aud: 18 plus. Spec prog: Black 2 hrs wkly. ■ Don W. Hughes, vp & gen mgr; Don Hughes, gen sls mgr & news dir; Amy Hughes, progmg mgr & mus dir.

WNFK(FM)—Co-owned with WPRY(AM). December 1989: 105.5 mhz; 2.45 kw. Ant 345 ft. TL: N30 07 36 W83 36 28. Stereo. Prog sep from AM. (904) 584-2972. Format: Contemp hit.

Pine Castle-Sky Lake

WAJL(AM)—Jan 28, 1977: 1190 khz; 5 kw-D. TL: N28 27 58 W81 22 30. Box 547068, Orlando (32854). (407) 841-9255. FAX: (407) 841-8094. Licensee: Daystar Ministries Inc. (acq 2-24-93; $350,000; FTR 3-15-93). Format: Contemp Christian. ■ Jason Linkous, gen mgr; Scott Fallows, natl sls mgr; Al Chubb, progmg dir; Ray Hanna, chief engr.

Pine Hills

WGTO(AM)—Sept 9, 1955: 540 khz; 50 kw-U, DA-2. TL: N28 07 57 W81 43 16. Stereo. Hrs opn: 24. 821 Marshall Farms Rd., Ocoee (34761). (407) 656-5440. FAX: (407) 656-5492. Licensee: Florida Media Inc. Net: Unistar, MBS. Wash atty: Liebowitz & Spencer. Format: Talk. Target aud: 18-49; adults. Spec prog: Univ. of Florida football & basketball; Motor Racing Network broadcasts. ■ Terry Mason, gen mgr; Keith Feeney, opns dir; Mark C. Edwards, sls dir; Jeff Allen, progmg dir; Jay Waggoner, chief engr. ■ Rates: $65; 65; 50; 40.

Pine Island Center

WDCQ(AM)—Licensed to Pine Island Center. See Fort Myers.

Pinellas Park

WHNZ(AM)—Nov 12, 1966: 570 khz; 5 kw-U, DA-2. TL: N28 12 40 W82 31 46. Suite 318, 11300 4th St. N., St. Petersburg (33716). (813) 577-7131. FAX: (813) 578-2477. Licensee: Paxson Broadcasting of Tampa L.P. Group owner: Paxson Broadcasting (acq 10-24-91; $6.4 million with WHPT[FM] Sarasota; FTR 11-25-91). Net: CNN, CBS, MBS; Fla. Net. Rep: Banner. Format: News/talk, sports. News staff 6. Target aud: Adults. ■ Lowell W. Paxson, CEO; James B. Bocock, pres; Drew M. Rashbaum, gen mgr; Jeff Messerman, gen sls mgr; Rose E. Bogier, prom mgr; Rich Carey, progmg dir; Matthew Hilk, news dir; Dave Glenn, chief engr.

WMTX(AM)—Licensed to Pinellas Park. See Tampa.

Plant City

WFNS(AM)—July 1949: 910 khz; 5 kw-U, DA-1. TL: N27 59 26 W82 12 31. Hrs opn: 24. 7201 E. Hillborough, Tampa (33610). (813) 620-9100. FAX: (813) 621-5874. Licensee: Harmon Communications Inc. (acq 10-87; $850,000; FTR 10-12-87). Net: CBS. Wash atty: Baraff, Koerner, Olender & Hochberg. Format: Sports/talk & play-by-play. Target aud: 25-54; active, male sports enthusiasts. ■ Elvin Harmon, pres; Brent Harmon, gen mgr; Dave Pecchia, gen sls mgr; Jennifer Farina, prom dir; Norm Hale, progmg dir; Mark Guthrie, chief engr. ■ Rates: $30; 25; 30; 15.

Plantation Key

WCTH(FM)—July 1969: 100.3 mhz; 100 kw. Ant 440 ft. TL: N24 57 30 W80 34 30. Stereo. Box 1360, 81990 Overseas Hwy., Islamorada (33036). (305) 664-1003. Licensee: Sounds of Service Inc. Net: Jones Satellite Audio. Format: Soft hits. Target aud: 30-54; residents and tourists. ■ M.B. Rivers, pres; Fred J. Webb, gen mgr & gen sls mgr; Duke Rollins, opns dir; Duke Rollins, progmg dir; Kevin Smith, news dir; Chuck Dreher, chief engr. ■ Rates: $20; 18; 20; 18.

WFKZ(FM)—Jan 2, 1984: 103.1 mhz; 6 kw. Ant 250 ft. TL: N25 01 35 W80 30 30. 93351 Overseas Hwy., Tavemier (33070). (305) 852-9085. FAX: (305) 852-5586. Licensee: Key Chain Inc. (group owner; acq 6-13-86). Net: AP. Format: Adult contemp. News progmg 8 hrs wkly. Target aud: 21-49; adults, active, community interest, expendable income. ■ Joel B. Day, chmn & pres; Jack Niedbalski, vp, gen mgr, stn mgr & gen sls mgr; K.C. Stuart, vp opns, opns dir, progmg dir & mus dir; Bill Smiley, chief engr. ■ Rates: $18; 18; 18; 14.

Pompano Beach

WMXJ(FM)—1960: 102.7 mhz; 100 kw. Ant 1,007 ft. TL: N25 57 59 W80 12 33. Stereo. 20450 N.W. 2nd Ave., Miami (33169). (305) 653-8811. FAX: (305) 923-5183. Licensee: Tampa Bay Broadcasting Inc. Group owner: Sconnix Broadcasting Co. (acq 6-26-87). Format: Oldies. ■ Dennis Collins, vp; James Butler, gen mgr.

WRBD(AM)—1959: 1470 khz; 5 kw-D, 2.5 kw-N, DA-2. TL: N26 10 46 W80 13 15. 4431 Rock Island Rd., Fort Lauderdale (33319). (305) 731-4800. FAX: (305) 739-7917. Licensee: WRBD Inc. (acq 10-29-92; $202,000; FTR 11-23-92). Net: Natl Black, American Urban. Format: Black. Spec prog: Jazz 4 hrs, relg 6 hrs, reggae 5 hrs, blues 6 hrs wkly. ■ Kevin Hemmings, gen sls mgr; James Thomas, progmg dir & mus dir; Rick Ricky, chief engr.

WWNN(AM)—1959: 980 khz; 5 kw-D, 1 kw-N, DA-D. TL: N26 14 26 W80 10 07. 6699 N. Federal Hwy., Boca Raton (33487). (407) 997-0074. FAX: (407) 997-0476. Licensee: HMS Broadcasting Inc. (acq 6-4-92; $1.8 million; FTR 6-22-92). Net: Winners News Net. Wash atty: Jason Shrinsky. Format: Motivation/self help. News progmg 8 hrs wkly. Target aud: 25-54; baby boomers weaned on the electronic media as an information source. Spec prog: Winners News Network. ■ Howard Goldsmith, pres; Bob Morenzy, gen mgr; Arthur Pendragon, progmg dir; Rick Rieke, chief engr.

Port Charlotte

WEEJ(FM)—Oct 1, 1976: 100.1 mhz; 100 kw. Ant 450 ft. TL: N26 52 11 W82 10 36. Stereo. Hrs opn: 24. Suite 56, 3151 Cooper St., Punta Gorda (33950). (813) 639-1112. FAX: (813) 637-6187. Licensee: Kneller Broadcasting of Charlotte County Inc. (acq 1-1-93; $1.5 million; FTR 1-18-93). Net: CNN. Wash atty: Kaye, Scholer, Fierman, Hays & Handler. Format: Oldies. News staff one; news progmg 20 hrs wkly. Target aud: 25-54. ■ Harold M. Kneller Jr., CEO, pres & gen mgr; Janet G. Kneller, exec vp; Ray Deluna Jr., opns dir; Steve Johnson, sls dir; Janet Kneller, prom dir; Lisa Hoffman, news dir; Harold Kneller, chief engr.

WKII(AM)—Nov 19, 1986: 1090 khz; 4.5 kw-D, 2.5 kw-N. TL: N26 54 40 W82 02 12 (D), N27 05 49 W82 08 58 (N) (CP: COL: Solana, 1070 khz, 3.1 kw-D, 260 w-N, TL: N26 54 40 W82 02 12). Stereo. Hrs opn: 24. Suite 56, 3151 Cooper St., Punta Gorda (33950). (813) 639-1112; (813) 337-1112. FAX: (813) 637-6187. Licensee: Kneller Broadcasting of Charlotte County Inc. Net: CNN, Unistar; Florida's Radio Net. Rep: Roslin. Wash atty: Kaye, Scholar, Fierman, Hays & Handler. Format: MOR. News staff one; news progmg 2 hrs wkly. Target aud: 35 plus. Spec prog: Texas Rangers baseball, relg 4 hrs wkly. ■ Harold M. Kneller Jr., pres, gen mgr & chief engr; Raymond Deluna, opns dir; Steve Johnson, gen sls mgr & prom mgr; Hal Kneller, progmg dir; Lisa Hoffman, news dir. ■ Rates: $23; 18; 21; 14.

***WVIJ(FM)**—July 26, 1987: 91.7 mhz; 380 w. Ant 130 ft. TL: N26 58 48 W82 04 03 (CP: 3.6 kw, ant 328 ft.). Stereo. 3279 Sherwood Rd. (33980). (813) 624-5000. FAX: (813) 625-5364. Licensee: Port Charlotte Educational Broadcasting Foundation Inc. Format: Ed, relg. Target aud: 35 plus. ■ Daniel P. Kolenda Jr., pres & gen mgr.

Port Richey

WLVU-FM—See Holiday.

Port St. Joe

WJOE(AM)—Listing follows WKNB(FM).

WKNB(FM)—August 1977: 94.5 mhz; 100 kw. Ant 991 ft. TL: N29 49 09 W85 15 34. Stereo. Hrs opn: 24. 3101 W. Hwy. 98, Panama City (32401). (904) 785-9549; (904) 785-9595. FAX: (904) 785-9292. Licensee: Asterisk Inc. (group owner; acq 6-1-87; $1,825,000 with co-located AM; FTR 4-20-87). Format: Country. Target aud: 25 plus; adults. Spec prog: Relg 5 hrs wkly. ■ Fred Ingham, pres; Joan J. Demeter, gen mgr; Ed Cousins, progmg dir; T.J. Cruz, pub affrs dir; Lee Freshwater, chief engr.

WJOE(AM)—Co-owned with WKNB(FM). Nov 7, 1956: 1080 khz; 1 kw-D. TL: N29 47 05 W85 17 28. Stn currently dark.

WMTO(FM)—March 12, 1990: 93.5 mhz; 1.3 kw. Ant 659 ft. TL: N29 49 09 W85 15 34 (CP: 14.5 kw, ant 669 ft.). Box 13622, Mexico Beach (32410). (904) 648-8700. FAX: (904) 648-8892. Licensee: Skylo Inc. (acq 7-9-93; $246,000; FTR 8-2-93). Format: Adult contemp. News staff one. ■ Donald G. McCoy, gen mgr.

Port St. Lucie

WPSL(AM)—Oct 26, 1985: 1590 khz; 5 kw-D, 64 w-N. TL: N27 18 28 W80 18 26. Hrs opn: 24. 8245 Business Park Dr. (34952). (407) 340-1590; (407) 879-4200. FAX: (407) 340-3245. Licensee: Port St. Lucie Broadcasters Inc. (acq 4-12-93; $200,000; FTR 4-26-93). Net: MBS. Florida's Radio Net. Format: News/talk. News staff one; news progmg 4 hrs wkly. Target aud: 25-55; established families. Spec prog: It 2 hrs wkly. ■ Carol Wyatt, CEO & pres; Greg Wyatt, vp & gen mgr; Walter Heinrich, stn mgr & vp sls; Mike Kerley, chief engr. ■ Rates: $16; 20; 16; na.

Punta Gorda

WCCF(AM)—Sept 15, 1961: 1580 khz; 1 kw-D, 122 w-N, DA-2. TL: N26 53 37 W82 03 01 (CP: 710 w). 4810 Deltona Dr. (33950-1929). (813) 639-1188. FAX: (813) 639-6742. Licensee: Intermart Broadcasting Southwest Florida Inc. (acq 11-20-92; with co-located FM; FTR 12-14-92). Net: Sun. Format: News, talk. Target aud: 45 plus. ■ James Martin, pres; Michael Moody, gen mgr & opns mgr; David Ayres, progmg dir; Barry Smith, chief engr. ■ Rates: $15; 15; 15; 10.

WIKX(FM)—Co-owned with WCCF(AM). Sept 1, 1970: 92.9 mhz; 50 kw. Ant 361 ft. TL: N26 53 37 W82 03 03. Stereo. Hrs opn: 24. Prog sep from AM. Net: ABC/E. Format: Light adult contemp. News progmg 10 hrs wkly. Target aud: 25-54. ■ Rates: $23; 23; 23; 11.

Quincy

WXSR(FM)—December 1966: 101.5 mhz; 50 kw. Ant 476 ft. TL: N30 31 08 W84 27 04. Suite E, 3360 Capital Circle N.E., Tallahassee (32308). (904) 877-1014. FAX: (904) 878-5900. Licensee: Broad Based Communications Inc. Group owner: Southern Broadcasting Companies Inc. (acq 5-24-93; $775,000 with co-located AM; FTR 6-14-93). Format: Urban contemp. ■ Sharon Walker, gen mgr; Dan Murray, progmg dir & mus dir; Clyde Scott, chief engr.

WWSD(AM)—Co-owned with WXSR(FM). March 15, 1948: 1230 khz; 1 kw-U. TL: N30 34 55 W84 35 59. ■ Sharon Walker, gen mgr.

Riviera Beach

WOLL(FM)—Licensed to Riviera Beach. See West Palm Beach.

WPOM(AM)—Aug 17, 1959: 1600 khz; 5 kw-D, 4.7 kw-N, DA-2. TL: N26 44 55 W80 08 02. Stereo. Hrs opn: 24. 6667 42nd Terrace N., West Palm Beach (33407). (407) 844-6200. FAX: (407) 840-0061. Licensee: Riviera Communications (acq 6-85). Net: Natl Black, CRC. Rep: Roslin. Format: Gospel. News staff 2; news progmg 30 hrs wkly. Target aud: Local Blacks & Hispanics. Spec prog: Sp. ■ Ron Leonard, gen mgr; Robert Huntley, gen sls mgr; Hurcucles Aikens, prom mgr; Damon Ware, progmg dir; Robert Charles, mus dir & news dir. ■ Rates: $40; 30; 40; 20.

Rock Harbor

WKLG(FM)—Nov 1, 1984: 102.1 mhz; 50 kw. Ant 250 ft. TL: N25 05 29 W80 26 37. Stereo. Box 457, 99344 U.S. Hwy. One, Key Largo (33037). (305) 451-2085; (305) 245-9731. FAX: (305) 451-5005. Licensee: WKLG Inc. Net: Fla Net, Agribuisness Net. Format: Modern Country. ■ Douglas G. LaRue, pres & gen mgr; David W. Freeman, vp. ■ Rates: $35; 35; 35; 15.

Rockledge

WHKR(FM)—Nov 25, 1989: 102.7 mhz; 50 kw. Ant 492 ft. TL: N28 35 03 W80 50 56. Stereo. Hrs opn: 24. 2355 Plackebaum Rd., Cocoa (32922); Box 7010, Rockledge (32955). (407) 639-1176. FAX: (407) 639-1027. Licensee: Roper Broadcasting Inc. (group owner; acq 7-90; FTR 7-9-90). Net: AP. Rep: Eastman. Wash atty: Pepper & Corazzini. Format: Modern country. News staff 2; news progmg 6 hrs wkly. Target aud: 25-54. Spec prog: Pub svc one hr wkly. ■ Robert Rowland, chmn, pres & gen mgr; Doug Peralta, gen sls mgr; Bob Thomas, progmg dir; Mark Lander, mus dir; Valree Peralta, news dir; Jay Wagoner, chief engr.

Royal Palm Beach

WLVJ(AM)—April 1987: 640 khz; 25 kw-D, 8.2 w-N, DA-2. TL: N26 45 34 W80 22 11 (CP: 1 kw-D, DA-N. TL: N26 44 14 W80 16 23). Hrs opn: 24. Suite 204E, 1601 Belvedere Rd., West Palm Beach (33406). (407) 688-9585. FAX: (407) 688-9601. Licensee: South Florida Radio Inc. Net: IBN, USA, Ambassador. Format: Relg, talk. News progmg 4 hrs wkly. Target aud: 25-55; middle-aged, married Christians with children. ■ Carl J. Auel, pres; Stanley W. Bowman, gen mgr & progmg mgr; Ken Vaughn, opns mgr & pub affrs dir; Bruce Wells, gen sls mgr; Keith Betts, chief engr. ■ Rates: $36; 24; 36; 18.

WOEQ(AM)—February 1991: 1190 khz; 1 kw-U, DA-N. TL: N26 44 14 W80 16 23. Hrs opn: 18. Suitc 111E, 4833 Okeechobee Blvd., West Palm Beach (33417). (407) 687-9350; (407) 687-9345. FAX: (407) 687-3398. Licensee: George M. Arroyo (acq 5-87; $75,000; FTR 5-11-87). Net: UPI. Rep: Caballero. Wash atty: Roy F. Perkins. Format: Sp. News staff 2; news progmg 20 hrs wkly. Target aud: 25-54. ■ George M. Arroyo, pres; Josefina Rodriquez, opns dir; Lissette Diaz, gen sls mgr & rgnl sls mgr; Davis Estavez, progmg dir; David Estavez, mus dir. ■ Rates: $26; 26; 26; 26.

Safety Harbor

WYUU(FM)—October 1983: 92.5 mhz; 50 kw. Ant 489 ft. TL: N27 50 33 W82 48 52 (CP: 6 kw, ant 453 ft.). Stereo. Suite 200, 9721 Executive Center Dr., St. Petersburg (33702). (813) 579-1925. FAX: (813) 579-9111. Licensee: Entertainment Communications Inc. Group owner: Entercom (acq 8-12-85). Format: Oldies. ■ Joseph M. Field, pres; Stephen Godofsky, vp & gen mgr; Dennis Anderson, opns mgr; Joe Corbett, gen sls mgr; Mike Gority, chief engr.

St. Augustine

WAOC(AM)—December 1953: 1420 khz; 4 kw-D, 460 w-N. TL: N29 51 00 W81 19 50. 567 Lewis Point Rd Ext. (32086). (904) 797-4444. FAX: (904) 797-3446. Licensee: Ariel Broadcasting Inc. (acq 7-1-85). Net: ABC/I. Format: Country, talk. News staff one; news progmg 20 hrs wkly. Target aud: General. Spec prog: Black 3 hrs wkly. ■ Kenneth Stein, pres & gen mgr; Eileen Rowe, prom mgr; Jim Shannon, news dir. ■ Rates: $14; 11.50; 14; 9.

***WAYL(FM)**—Not on air, target date unknown: 91.9 mhz; 3 kw. Ant 328 ft. Box 2, Ramey, PR (00604). Licensee: Ocala Radio Ministries Inc.

***WFCF(FM)**—Not on air, target date unknown: 88.5 mhz; 6 kw. Ant 141 ft. 74 King St. (32084). Licensee: Flagler College.

WFOY(AM)—July 7, 1936: 1240 khz; 1 kw-U. TL: N29 54 26 W81 18 51. Hrs opn: 24. Box 3847, One Radio Rd. (32085). (904) 829-3416. FAX: (904) 829-8051. Licensee: Shull Broadcasting Co., Inc. (acq 4-84). Net: NBC, CBS, NBC Talknet, MBS; Florida. Wash atty: Dow, Lohnes & Albertson. Format: Adult music and talk. News staff one; news progmg 15 hrs wkly. Target aud: 35 plus; affluent, mature adults. Spec prog: University of Florida football & basketball. ■ Douglas D. Shull, pres, gen mgr & vp prom; Irv Feldman, opns dir; Mac Davis, gen sls mgr; David Shull, progmg dir & mus dir; Al Brennan, news dir; Parks Boone, chief engr. ■ Rates: $24; 26; 24; 12.

WSOS(FM)—July 17, 1982: 94.1 mhz; 19 kw. Ant 377 ft. TL: N29 55 05 W81 23 26. Stereo. Hrs opn: 24. 2715 Stratton Blvd. (32095-0823). (904) 824-0833; (904) 824-0834. FAX: (904) 825-0105. Licensee: WSOS-FM Inc. (acq 5-90; $1.62 million; FTR 5-21-90). Net: NBC. Wash atty: McFadden, Evans & Sill. Format: Adult contemp, news. News staff one. Target aud: 25-54. Upscale audience. Spec prog: Relg 2 hrs wkly. ■ Zoe Roseman, pres; Bob Walke, opns dir; Wayne Sims, opns mgr; Gina Haggar, gen sls mgr; Steve Elliott, progmg dir & news dir; Doug L. Schwartz, mus dir; Alan Alsobrook, chief engr. ■ Rates: $32; 28; 32; 28.

WSTF(FM)—August 1965: 97.9 mhz; 50 kw. Ant 482 ft. TL: N30 06 14 W81 28 11. Stereo. Hrs opn: 24. Suite 107, 8386 Baymeadows Rd., Jacksonville (32256). (904) 636-0507; (904) 733-2321. FAX: (904) 636-7971. Licensee: Todd Communications Inc. (acq 1-8-92; $1.2 million; FTR 1-27-92). Format: Class hits, adult contemp, oldies. News staff one; news progmg one hr wkly. Target aud: Women & men 34-44; 44 yr old women. ■ Devon Paxson, pres; Hank Doyle, stn mgr; Hank Dole, opns mgr, progmg dir & mus dir; Linda Byrd, gen sls mgr; Maggy McDaniel, rgnl sls mgr; Dea Sims, prom dir; Odette Hench, news dir & pub affrs dir; Kyle Dickson, engrg dir; Richard Clemons, chief engr. ■ Rates: $40; 30; 30; 20.

Florida   Directory of Radio

St. Augustine Beach

WKLN(AM)—Oct 15, 1986: 1170 khz; 1 kw-D. TL: N29 55 05 W81 23 26. Box 5102, St. Augustine (32085:). 2121 U.S. Hwy. One S., St. Augustine (32086). (904) 794-0200. FAX: (904) 794-0018. Licensee: Visitor Information Radio of Florida. Format: News. Target aud: General. ■ Rates: $10; 10; 10; na.

St. Petersburg

WCOF(FM)—1958: 107.3 mhz; 100 kw. Ant 649 ft. TL: N27 51 24 W82 37 26. Stereo. Suite 300, 877 Executive Ctr. Dr. W., St. Petersburg (33702). (813) 576-6090. FAX: (813) 577-9276. Licensee: WWRM Inc. Group owner: Cox Broadcasting. Net: CBS. Rep: CBS Radio Reps. Format: Greatest hits of the 70s. ■ Todd Leiser, gen mgr.

WFLA(AM)—See Tampa.

WFLZ-FM—See Tampa.

*WFTI-FM—June 1988: 91.7 mhz; 3 kw. Ant 282 ft. TL: N27 46 15 W82 38 19. Stereo. Hrs opn: 24. 360 Central Ave., #1240 (33701). (813) 823-1140. Licensee: Family Stations Inc. (group owner; acq 11-19-88). Format: Relg. News progmg 9 hrs wkly. Target aud: General. ■ Bob Barnes, gen mgr & pub affrs dir; Roz Clark, chief engr.

WHPT(FM)—See Sarasota.

*WKES(FM)—July 1, 1961: 101.5 mhz; 100 kw. Ant 1,358 ft. TL: N27 50 32 W82 15 46. Stereo. Hrs opn: 24. Box 8888 (33738). (813) 391-9994. FAX: (813) 397-6425. Licensee: Moody Bible Institute (group owner; acq 1977). Net: Moody. Wash atty: Southmayd & Miller. Format: Relg, ed. News progmg 14 hrs wkly. Target aud: General; 25 plus. ■ Dr. Joseph Stowell III, pres; Robert Neff, vp; Dick Florence, stn mgr, opns dir, opns mgr & progmg dir; Michael Gleichman, news & pub affrs dir; John Stortz, chief engr.

WQYK-FM—May 1958: 99.5 mhz; 100 kw. Ant 984 ft. TL: N27 56 50 W82 27 35. Stereo. Hrs opn: 24. Box 20087 (33742); Duval Bldg., 9450 Koger Blvd. (33702). (813) 576-6055. FAX: (813) 577-1324. Licensee: Infinity Broadcasting Corp. of Florida (group owner; acq 12-1-86; FTR 10-6-86). Rep: Katz. Wash atty: Leventhal, Senter & Lerman. Format: Contemp country. News staff 2; news progmg 6 hrs wkly. Target aud: 25-54. Spec prog: Sports, Tampa Bay Bucs football. ■ Jay Miller, gen mgr; David Hutchinson, gen sls mgr; Lori Moon, prom dir; Beecher Martin, progmg dir; Jay Roberts, mus dir; Rita Ciccarello, news dir; Frank Berry, chief eng.

WRBQ(AM)—1939: 1380 khz; 5 kw-U, DA-N. TL: N27 52 15 W82 37 03. Hrs opn: 24. 5510 W. Gray St., Tampa (33609). (813) 287-1047. FAX: (813) 289-9999. Licensee: Clear Channel Radio Licenses Inc. (acq 7-24-92). Net: ABC/FM. Rep: McGavren Guild. Format: Urban adult contemp. News staff 6. Target aud: 25-54. Spec prog: Gospel 2 hrs wkly. ■ L. Lowery Mays, chmn; Mark Mays, exec vp; David F. Manning, vp & gen mgr; Valerie Hawkins, gen sls mgr; Teddi Lewis, natl sls mgr; Pat George, prom dir; Brian Thomas, progmg dir & mus dir; Roger Schulman, news dir; Lou Facenda, chief engr. ■ Rates: $20; 50; 50; 50.

WRBQ-FM—See Tampa.

WRMD(AM)—May 5, 1950: 680 khz; 1 kw-D. TL: N27 51 24 W82 37 26. 2700 W. Martin Luther King Blvd., Tampa. (33607). (813) 870-6680. FAX: (813) 877-4466. Licensee: ZGS Broadcasting of Tampa Inc. (acq 1-18-91; $200,000; FTR 2-4-91). Net: Wall Street. Format: Sp adult contemp. ■ Mark Jorgensen, CEO; Matthew Rodiguez, gen mgr; Carlos Beralta, progmg dir; Art Karmgard, chief engr.

WSUN(AM)—Nov 1, 1927: 620 khz; 5 kw-D, 5.4 kw-N, DA-N. TL: N27 52 37 W82 35 26. Stereo. Hrs opn: 24. Suite 300, 877 Executive Ctr. Dr. W. (33702). (813) 576-1073. FAX: (813) 576-8098. Licensee: WWRM Inc. Group owner: Cox Broadcasting (acq 7-1-90). Net: CBS. Rep: D & R Radio. Format: Country classics. ■ Todd Leiser, vp & gen mgr; Tom Paleveda, opns mgr & progmg dir; Richard Turkheimer, gen sls mgr & natl sls mgr; Dave Solinske, chief engr.

WWRM(FM)—(Tampa) Co-owned with WSUN(AM). 1958: 94.9 mhz; 100 kw. Ant 649 ft. TL: N27 51 24 W82 37 26. Stereo. (Acq 7-1-88). Format: Soft adult contemp. Target aud: 35-54. ■ Read Shepherd, news dir.

WUSA-FM—See Tampa.

WWRM(FM)—Listing follows WSUN(AM).

St. Petersburg Beach

WRXB(AM)—1957: 1590 khz; 5 kw-D, 1 kw-N, DA-2. TL: N27 44 03 W82 41 08. Suite 206B 1700 34th St. S. (33711). (813) 327-9792. FAX: (813) 321-3025. Licensee: Rolyn Communications (acq 12-75). Net: ABC/C, Natl Black. Format: Adult contemp, urban contemp. Target aud: 23-54; urban contemporary. Spec prog: Jazz 15 hrs wkly. ■ J. Eugene Danzey, pres & gen mgr; V. Garner, vp opns; Michael E. Danzey, gen sls mgr & prom mgr; Rob Simone, progmg mgr & mus dir; Steve Zagony, chief engr.

Sanford

WTRR(AM)—May 20, 1947: 1400 khz; 1 kw-U. TL: N28 48 04 W81 15 06. Hrs opn: 24. Box 1448 (32772-1448). (407) 322-1400. FAX: (407) 330-7571. Licensee: J & V Communications Co. (acq 6-5-92; $300,000; FTR 6-22-92). Net: SMN; Florida. Format: Music & talk. Target aud: General; 21 plus. Spec prog: Relg 3 hrs wkly. ■ Frank Vaught, gen mgr, stn mgr, adv dir & progmg dir; Michelle Dewey (loc), rgnl sls mgr; Frank Strnad, chief engr. ■ Rates: $12; 12; 12; 6.

Sanibel

WRWX(FM)—1994: 98.5 mhz; 2.6 kw. Ant 490 ft. TL: N26 32 01 W82 04 50. 19172 Cypress View Dr., Ft. Myers (33912). (813) 267-3206. Licensee: Ruth Communications Corp. ■ Ruth H. Ray, pres.

Santa Rosa Beach

WWAV(FM)—April 3, 1985: 102.3 mhz; 3 kw. Ant 328 ft. TL: N30 22 31 W86 21 39. Stereo. Suite 108, 1234 Airport Rd., Destin (32541). (904) 654-5102. FAX: (904) 654-5387. Licensee: Emerald Coast Communications Inc. (acq 12-1-88; $1.65 million; FTR 1-16-89). Format: Adult contemp. ■ Ray Quinn, pres; Jack Jernigan, gen mgr; Roger Harrison, progmg dir & mus dir; Charlie Wooten, chief engr.

Sarasota

*WAYG(FM)—Not on air, target date unknown: 89.1 mhz; 50 kw. Ant 462 ft. TL: N27 06 00 W82 22 19. Suite 202, 1860 Boyscout Dr., Ft. Myers (33907). Licensee: Southwest Florida Community Radio Inc.

WBRD(AM)—See Palmetto.

WHPT(FM)—1973: 102.5 mhz; 100 kw. Ant 1,776 ft. TL: N27 29 08 W82 32 00. Stereo. Suite 318, 11300 4th St. N., St. Petersburg (33716). (813) 577-7131. FAX: (813) 578-2477. Licensee: Paxson Broadcasting of Tampa L.P. Group owner: Paxson Broadcasting (acq 10-24-91; $6.4 million with WHNZ[AM] Pinellas Park; FTR 11-18-91). Rep: Banner. Format: Adult contemp, AOR. ■ Lowell W. Paxson, CEO; James B. Babcock, pres; Drew N. Rashbaum, gen mgr; Jeff Messerman, gen sls mgr.

WISP(FM)—See Holmes Beach.

WKXY(AM)—May 23, 1949: 930 khz; 5 kw-D, 2.5 w-N, DA-2. TL: N27 21 19 W82 22 54. 2500 10th St. (34237). (813) 366-4422; (813) 955-1193. Licensee: Sarasota Broadcasting Co. Net: MBS, Westwood One. Format: News/talk. Target aud: 25-54. ■ A.G. Fernandez, pres; Charles Fernandez, gen mgr & gen sls mgr; Charlie Lawrence, progmg dir; Tony William, mus dir; Tony W. Fernandez, chief engr.

*WKZM(FM)—Oct 21, 1974: 105.5 mhz; 3 kw. Ant 180 ft. TL: N27 19 25 W82 27 40 (CP: Ant 328 ft., TL: N27 16 30 W82 28 54). Hrs opn: 24. Box 7627 (34278-7627); 1004 Ponder Ave. (34232). (813) 377-3163. FAX: (813) 377-8575. Licensee: Christian Fellowship Mission Inc. Format: Inspirational, educ. News progmg 14 hrs wkly. Target aud: General. ■ Lowell A. Brubaker, gen mgr & progmg dir; Roy S. Mazelin, chief engr.

WQSA(AM)—Jan 1, 1961: 1220 khz; 1 kw-D, 600 w-N, DA. TL: N27 19 27 W82 29 47. Hrs opn: 24. Box 7700, 1111 Beneva Rd. (34232). (813) 366-0424. Licensee: Horizon Communications Ltd. (acq 10-83; $547,500; FTR 10-10-83). Net: ABC/D. Rep: Savalli. Format: Div. News staff 2; news progmg 25 hrs wkly. Target aud: 35 plus. Spec prog: relig 5 hrs, Pol one hr wkly. ■ Myron Thomas, gen mgr; Kristie Thomas, opns mgr & progmg dir; Pete Schafhausen, news dir; James Grant, chief engr.

WSPB(AM)—Dec 7, 1939: 1450 khz; 1 kw-D. TL: N27 20 12 W82 34 25. Stereo. Hrs opn: 24. Box 2618, 1713 Ken Thompson Pkwy. (34236). (813) 388-2966. FAX: (813) 388-3720. Licensee: Sarasota Bay Broadcasting Co. (acq 7-90; $400,000; FTR 7-23-90). Net: Concert Music Net. Rep: Concert Music. Format: Classical. Target aud: 35-64; General. Spec prog: Sp one hr wkly. ■ Richard Harris, pres; David Bishop, gen mgr; Connie McCrea, gen sls mgr; Cynthia Bishop, mktg dir & prom dir.

WSRZ-FM—June 30, 1965: 106.3 mhz; 3 kw. Ant 280 ft. TL: N27 20 12 W82 34 25. Stereo. 1713 Ken Thompson Pkwy. (34266). (813) 388-3936. FAX: (813) 388-3720. Licensee: Sarasota FM Inc. (acq 8-27-86; $2.4 million; FTR 7-7-86). Format: Oldies. ■ Bill Burns, gen sls mgr; Scott Chase, mus dir.

WTMY(AM)—Dec 2, 1961: 1280 khz; 2.5 kw-D, 340 w-N, DA-2. TL: N27 21 21 W82 29 13. 2101 Hammock Pl. (34235). (813) 365-0521. FAX: (813) 955-9062. Licensee: Pana Media of Sarasota Inc. Net: BRN. Format: Moneytalk, healthtalk, Sp. News progmg one hr wkly. Target aud: 38 plus; affluent, wealth & health oriented in addition to hispanics. Spec prog: Spanish radio bcstg-simulcast selected cable access channel 4-BLAB-TV programs, gospel. ■ Howard Goldsmith, pres; Robert Morency, vp; T. Michael Craft, gen mgr & gen sls mgr; Melanie Ripley, prom mgr; Roy "Bud" Smith, progmg dir; Frank Pineiro, mus dir; Roy Smith, pub affrs dir; Ed Allen, chief engr. ■ Rates: $25; 20; 22; 15.

Sebring

WCAC(FM)—Listing follows WITS(AM).

WITS(AM)—Nov 24, 1959: 1340 khz; 1 kw-U. TL: N27 28 06 W81 27 03. Hrs opn: 24. Box 871, 2411 U.S. 27 S. (33870). (813) 385-5151. FAX: (813) 385-5511. Licensee: Roper Broadcasting Inc. (group owner; acq 12-12-86; $940,404.81; FTR 11-10-86). Net: Unistar. Wash atty: Pepper & Corazzini. Format: Big band. News staff one; news progmg 5 hrs wkly. Target aud: 55 plus; retired, upscale senior citizens. ■ Robert T. Rowland Sr., pres; Robert Young, gen mgr & gen sls mgr; Celeste Chung, prom mgr; J.P. Proctor, progmg dir & mus dir; Marc Valero, news dir; Charles Castle, chief engr. ■ Rates: $11; 9; 11; 7.

WCAC(FM)—Co-owned with WITS(AM). July 1967: 105.5 mhz; 3 kw. Ant 178 ft. TL: N27 28 06 W81 27 03 (CP: Ant 328 ft.). Stereo. Prog sep from AM. (813) 385-5152. Format: Oldies. Target aud: 25-54; upscale adults. ■ Jim Ziegler, sls dir; Mark Valero, mus dir. ■ Rates: Same as AM.

WJCM(AM)—May 22, 1950: 960 khz; 5 kw-D, 1 kw-N, DA-1. TL: N30 29 W31 25 18. Hrs opn: 24. Box 1766, 4124 Cemetery Rd. (33870). (813) 385-7140. Licensee: WJCM Inc. (acq 8-1-79). Net: ABC/I, Jones Satellite Audio; Fla. Net. Rep: Rgnl Reps. Wash atty: Booth, Freret & Imlay. Format: Soft hits of yesterday & today. News progmg 6 hrs wkly. Target aud: 35-64; mature, affluent. ■ Kay Eshleman, pres & gen mgr; Don Ray, opns mgr; Steve Brown, vp sls; James Kowalski, progmg dir & chief engr. ■ Rates: $16; 14; 15; 7.

WKHF(AM)—See Avon Park.

WWOJ(FM)—See Avon Park.

WWTK(AM)—See Lake Placid.

Seffner

WQYK(AM)—Licensed to Seffner. See Tampa.

Silver Springs

WWGO(FM)—Licensed to Silver Springs. See Ocala.

Solana

WMMY(FM)—Not on air, target date unknown: 105.3 mhz; 3 kw. Ant 328 ft. TL: N26 50 41 W82 02 15. 455 38th Court, Vero Beach (32962). Licensee: West Florida Media Inc.

South Daytona

WPUL(AM)—June 13, 1957: 1590 khz; 1 kw-D. TL: N29 09 16 W81 01 20. Box 4010, 2598 S. Nova Rd. (32121). (904) 767-1131; (904) 756-1590. FAX: (904) 724-7510. Licensee: PSI Communications Inc. (acq 2-1-89; $250,000; FTR 1-23-89). Net: American Urban. Format: Jazz, blues. News staff one; news progmg 3 hrs wkly. Target aud: General. ■ Charles W. Cherry, pres; Charles W. Cherry Sr., gen mgr; Cloe Sears, progmg dir; Cleo Sears, mus dir; Harold Utter, chief engr.

South Miami

WMRZ(AM)—Sept 15, 1947: 790 khz; 25 kw-U, DA-N. TL: N25 46 25 W80 38 13 (CP: 780 khz; 50 kw-D, 10 kw-N). Stereo. Hrs opn: 24. 20450 N.W. 2nd Ave., Miami (33169). (305) 653-8811. FAX: (305) 652-5385. Licensee: Jefferson-Pilot Communications Co. (group owner; acq 10-23-85; $4 million; FTR 7-29-85). Format: Time Brokerage Entertainment & Talk. News progmg 35 hrs wkly. Target aud: 35-64. ■ Dennis P. Collins, vp & gen mgr; Donald Keams, opns mgr; Richard A. Chamack, gen sls mgr; Leanne Sarkisian, prom mgr; Naomi Wright, news dir; John Morris, chief engr.

Springfield

WRBA(FM)—June 1986: 95.9 mhz; 50 kw. Ant 300 ft. TL: N30 12 12 W85 36 57. 2316 W. 23rd St., Panama City (32405). (904) 769-2299. FAX: (904) 763-5489. Licensee: Styles Broadcasting Co. Inc. (acq 12-19-89; $1 million; FTR 1-8-90). Net: Unistar, CNN. Rep: Roslin. Wash atty: Mullin, Rhyne, Emmons & Topel. Format: Adult comtemp. News progmg 2 hrs wkly. Target aud: 25-49; females. ■ Thomas A. DiBacco, pres & gen mgr; Steve King, opns mgr, progmg dir & mus dir; Darrell Johnson, gen sls mgr; Kim E. Styles, prom mgr; Emily Evans, news dir; Charles Wooten, chief engr. ■ Rates: $30; 30; 30; 30.

WYOO(FM)—Licensed to Springfield. See Panama City.

Starke

WEAG(AM)—Licensed to Starke. See Gainesville.

WEAG-FM—Licensed to Starke. See Gainesville.

***WTLG(FM)**—1982: 88.3 mhz; 7 kw. Ant 285 ft. TL: N29 54 34 W82 06 02. Stereo. Hrs opn: 7 AM-8 PM. Box 1258, 163 W. Jefferson at Clarke (32901). (904) 964-9854. Licensee: Starke Christian Educational Radio & TV. Net: Moody. Format: Southem gospel, light contemp. Target aud: General. ■ Rev. Ben Bryant, pres; Billye Seratt, gen mgr; Charles Noble, progmg dir; Hal Mashburn, chief engr.

Stuart

WSTU(AM)—Dec 9, 1954: 1450 khz; 1 kw-U. TL: N27 12 53 W80 15 24. Hrs opn: 24. 1000 N.W. Alice Ave. (34994). (407) 692-1000. FAX: (407) 692-2231. Licensee: Genevieve H. Glascock. Net: ABC/I, AP; Fla. Net. Wash atty: Kaye, Scholer, Fierman, Hays & Handler. Format: Adult contemp. Target aud: 25-54. ■ Genevieve H. Glascock, pres & gen mgr; Barry Marsh, opns mgr & progmg dir; Patricia A. Larschan, gen sls mgr; Barbra Clifton, prom mgr; Ron Donovan, mus dir; Tom Teter, news dir; Robert Statham, chief engr.

WZZR(FM)—Dec 24, 1964: 92.7 mhz; 50 kw. Ant 571 ft. TL: N27 16 07 W80 17 19. Stereo. Drawer 0093, Port St. Lucie (34985). (407) 335-9300. FAX: (407) 335-3291. Licensee: CRB of Florida Inc. Group owner: CRB Broadcasting Corp. (acq 7-1-87; $3.5 million; FTR 6-22-87). Format: AOR. News staff one. ■ Charles DiToro, gen mgr; Larry Kindel, gen sls mgr; Richard Dickerson, progmg dir; Mike Lee, mus dir; Mike Kerley, chief engr.

Summerland Key

WPIK(FM)—December 1991: 102.5 mhz; 50 kw. Ant 413 ft. TL: N24 40 35 W81 30 41. Stereo. Hrs opn: 24. Box 4202499 (33042). Licensee: Theresa P. Parrish. Format: Mod Country. Target aud: 28-54. Spec prog: Relg one hr, swap shop 2 hrs, country currents one hr, veterans report one hr, all requests 5 hrs wkly. ■ James J. Parrish, CEO & gen mgr; Theresa Parrish, pres; Damon Collins, opns mgr; Nancy Tunick, mus dir; Nancy Tinick, news dir; Richard Farkas, chief engr.

Sunrise

***WKPX(FM)**—Feb 14, 1983: 88.5 mhz; 3 kw. Ant 100 ft. TL: N26 10 38 W80 15 23. Stereo. Hrs opn: 12 (15 Tues). 8000 N.W. 44th St. (33351). (305) 572-1321. FAX: (305) 572-1344. Licensee: School Board of Broward County. Wash atty: Pepper & Corazzini. Format: Modern rock. Target aud: 15-35; people interested in alternative progmg. Spec prog: Black 6 hrs, reggae 5 hrs, jazz 3 hrs, blues 3 hrs, folk rock 3 hrs wkly. ■ Robert Hankerson, gen mgr; Jo Anne Boggus, stn mgr; Warren Exmore, chief engr.

Tallahassee

***WAMF(FM)**—November 1976: 90.5 mhz; 1.6 w-V. Ant 167 ft. TL: N30 25 49 W84 17 27. Stereo. Hrs opn: 7 AM-1AM. Florida A&M Univ., 314 Tucker Hall (32307); Box 6202 (32314). (904) 599-3083; (904) 599-3084. Licensee: Florida A&M Univ., Board of Regents. Format: Black, div, jazz. Target aud: General. ■ Dr. John O. Omachonu, gen mgr; Ramona Jackson, progmg dir; jeffrey St. Arromand, mus dir; Phillip Keirstead, news dir; Robert Lloyd, chief engr.

WANM(AM)—August 1974: 1070 khz; 10 kw-D. TL: N30 25 38 W84 14 43. Box 10174 (32302). (904) 222-1070. FAX: (904) 561-3645. Licensee: WANM Inc. Group owner: Timm Enteprises. Net: CNN. Rep: Banner. Format: News. Spec prog: Relg 6 hrs wkly. ■ B.F.J. Timm, pres; Charles Kinney, chief engr.

WGLF(FM)—Co-owned with WANM(AM). December 1967: 104.1 mhz; 100 kw. Ant 1,359 ft. TL: N30 27 09 W84 00 50. Stereo. Hrs opn: 24. Prog sep from AM. 1310 Paul Russell Rd. (32301). (904) 878-1104. FAX: (904) 877-1040. Licensee: Tallahassee Broadcasting Co. Group owner: Timm Enteprises. Format: AOR. ■ Bill Marriott, gen mgr.

WBGM-FM—Listing follows WHBT(AM).

WCVC(AM)—Nov 5, 1953: 1330 khz; 5 kw-D. TL: N30 29 03 W84 17 13. 117 1/2 Henderson Rd. (32312). (904) 386-1330. Licensee: WCVC Inc. (acq 10-4-85; $500,000; FTR 8-12-85). Format: Relg. Target aud: 25-54. ■ Wendell Borrink, pres, gen mgr, gen sls mgr & progmg dir; Gwen Hall, mus dir; Lee Cardice, chief engr.

***WFSQ(FM)**—May 1954: 91.5 mhz; 100 kw. Ant 662 ft. TL: N30 21 29 W84 36 39. Stereo. Hrs opn: 24. Public Bcst. Ctr., 1600 Red Barber Plaza (32310). (904) 487-3086. FAX: (904) 487-3293. Licensee: The Board of Regent of Florida Acting For and On Behalf of Florida State Univ. Net: NPR, APR; Fla. Pub. Wash atty: Bryan, Cave, McPheeters & McRoberts. Format: Classical. News progmg one hr wkly. Target aud: 35 plus; highly educated. ■ Madison Hodges, CEO; Caroline Austin, stn mgr & progmg dir; Roy Hardman, opns mgr; Marc Gaspard, mus dir; Sally Spencer, news dir; Andrew Hanus, chief engr. ■ WFSU-TV affil.

***WFSU-FM**—Oct 14, 1990: 88.9 mhz; 95 kw. Ant 1,243 ft. TL: N30 40 13 W83 56 26. Stereo. Hrs opn: 24. Public Broadcast Center, 1600 Red Barber Plaza (32310). (904) 487-3086. FAX: (904) 487-3293. Licensee: The Board of Regents of Florida Acting For and on Behalf of Florida State University. Net: NPR, APR; Fla. Pub. Wash atty: Bryan, Cave, McPheeters & McRoberts. Format: All news. News staff 9. Target aud: 35-54; highly educated. ■ Madison Hodges, gen mgr; Caroline Austin, stn mgr; Ray Hardman, opns mgr; Sally Spener, news dir; Andy Hanus, chief engr.

WGLF(FM)—Listing follows WANM(AM).

WHBT(AM)—Aug 6, 1959: 1410 khz; 5 kw-D, 39 w-N. TL: N30 29 35 W84 17 00. Box 3168 (32315); 109B Ridgeland Rd. (32312). (904) 385-1156. FAX: (904) 224-8329. Licensee: HVS Partners (group owner; acq 7-12-89). Net: ABC/C, ABC, SMN. Rep: Katz. Format: Gold Soul. News staff one. Target aud: 25-54. Spec prog: Classic hits 5 hrs, jazz 4 hrs wkly. ■ Gisela Huberman, pres; Jon Hill, gen mgr; Victor Duncan, opns dir; Jim Bowman, chief engr.

WBGM-FM—Co-owned with WHBT(AM). July 15, 1962: 98.9 mhz; 100 kw. Ant 390 ft. TL: N30 29 35 W84 16 55. Stereo. Dups AM 100%.

WHBX(FM)—June 28, 1982: 96.1 mhz; 3 kw. Ant 300 ft. TL: N30 27 46 W84 18 04 (CP: 37 kw, ant 479 ft.). Stereo. Hrs opn: 24. 109B Ridgeland Rd. (32312-1906). (904) 385-6512. FAX: (904) 224-8329. Licensee: HVS Partners (acq 1-14-93; $2.7 million with WLVW-FM Salisbury, MD; FTR 2-15-93). Net: SMN. Rep: Katz. Wash atty: Arent, Fox, Kintner, Plotkin & Kahn. Format: Adult urban contemp. Target aud: 25-54. ■ Jon A. Hill, gen mgr; Victor Duncan, opns mgr; Larry Wright, rgnl sls mgr; Jay Creswell, progmg mgr; Jim Bowman, chief engr. ■ Rates: $24; 23; 24; 22.

WHKX(FM)—(Lafayette). Dec 17, 1989: 99.9 mhz; 3 kw. Ant 328 ft. TL: N30 20 59 W84 17 13 (CP: 50 kw, ant 492 ft., TL: N30 20 59 W84 17 13). Unit B, 2320 N. Monroe St., Tallahassee (32303). (904) 422-2100. FAX: (904) 422-3299. Licensee: Catamount Communications (acq 11-30-93; $1.175 million; FTR 12-20-93). Format: Adult contemp. ■ David Parnigoni, gen mgr; Tommy High, stn mgr; Linda Presley, gen sls mgr; Charlie Wooten, chief engr.

WMLO(FM)—See Havana.

WNLS(AM)—Oct 15, 1946: 1270 khz; 5 kw-U, DA-N. TL: N30 25 38 W84 19 46. Bldg E-200, 325 John Knox Rd. (32303). (904) 386-6143. Licensee: Park Broadcasting of Florida Inc. Group owner: Park Communications Inc. (acq 10-1-92; $2.65 million with co-located FM; FTR 9-21-92). Net: MBS, NBC Talknet. Rep: Christal. Format: News/talk. News staff one. Target aud: 25-54. Spec prog: Florida State Univ. sports. ■ David A. Lowe, gen mgr; Judy Powell Bailey, gen sls mgr; Valerie Stewart, prom dir; Ronald Ebben, progmg dir; Ronald J. Ebben, news dir; Leo Barfield, chief engr.

WTNT(FM)—Co-owned with WNLS(AM). July 24, 1967: 94.9 mhz; 100 kw. Ant 840 ft. TL: N30 34 43 W84 15 49. Stereo. Prog sep from AM. Net: ABC/I. Format: Country. ■ Tim Mercer, progmg dir; Bill Kelly, mus dir.

WRZK(FM)—May 1992: 106.1 mhz; 3 kw. Ant 328 ft. TL: N30 28 37 W84 20 07. Hrs opn: 24. Suite 203, 1020 E. Lafayette St. (32301). Licensee: Southeast Broadcasters Inc. Format: Rock/AOR. ■ John Summers, gen mgr; Jeff Hom, mus dir. ■ Rates: $45; 41; 45; 38.

WSNI(FM)—(Thomasville, Ga). 1971: 107.1 mhz; 100 kw. Ant 981 ft. TL: N30 43 55 W84 08 45. Stereo. Hrs opn: 24. Suite D, 3360 Capital Cir. N.E., Tallahassee, FL (32308). (904) 422-3107. FAX: (904) 422-0008. Licensee: Southern Broadcasting Companies (group owner). Net: NBC. Rep: McGavren Guild. Wash atty: Gary Smithwick. Format: Good time oldies. News staff one; news progmg 5 hrs wkly. Target aud: 25-54. ■ Paul Stone, CEO, chmn & pres; Charles Giddens, vp & mktg dir; LaNeal Evans, gen sls mgr & adv mgr; Sharon Walker, prom mgr; Bob Walker, progmg dir; Tim Bryant, news dir; Clyde Scott, chief engr. ■ Rates: $45; 40; 45; 20.

WTAL(AM)—1935: 1450 khz; 1 kw-U. TL: N30 26 20 W84 15 30. Hrs opn: 24. Box 3885 (32315). (904) 656-1450. FAX: (904) 877-5199. Licensee: Radio Florida Inc. (acq 10-80; $480,000; FTR 10-6-80). Net: CBS, Daynet, ABC Talkradio. Rep: Roslin. Wash atty: Bosari & Paxson. Format: News/talk. News staff 4; news progmg 21 hrs wkly. Target aud: 25-54; educated, intelligent, affluent. ■ Rick Warren, pres, gen mgr & gen sls mgr; Jennifer Warren, opns mgr & prom dir; John Matthews, news dir; James Ravencraft, chief engr. ■ Rates: $16; 14; 16; 14.

WTNT(FM)—Listing follows WNLS(AM).

WUMX(FM)—May 12, 1976: 103.1 mhz; 3 kw. Ant 300 ft. TL: N30 29 43 W84 13 51 (CP: 3.3 kw). Stereo. Box 13549 (32317); 3000 Olson Rd. (32308). (904) 386-5141. FAX: (904) 422-1897. Licensee: Dolcom Inc. (acq 2-5-91; $761,450; FTR 2-25-91). Rep: Major Market. Format: Adult contemp. ■ Howard B. Dolgoff, pres, gen mgr & gen sls mgr; Denver Lee, progmg dir & mus dir; Rick Flagg, news dir; Ray Chamberlain, chief engr.

***WVFS(FM)**—September 1987: 89.7 mhz; 272 w. Ant 170 ft. TL: N30 26 22 W84 17 29 (CP: 2.7 kw-V, ant 174 ft.). 420 Diffenbaugh Bldg, Florida State Univ. (32306). (904) 644-3871. FAX: (904) 644-8642. Licensee: Board of Regents on behalf of Florida State Univ. ■ Lee Stepino, gen mgr; Lindee Morgan, progmg dir.

Tampa

WAMA(AM)—1961: 1550 khz; 10 kw-D, 222 w-N. TL: N27 55 16 W82 23 41. Hrs opn: 18. 5203 N. Armenia Ave. (33603). (813) 875-0086; (813) 879-8600. FAX: (813) 871-2871. Licensee: Efrain Archilla-Roig (group owner; acq 8-28-86; $750,000; FTR 5-12-86). Net: AP. Rep: Caballero. Wash atty: Hopkins & Sutter. Format: Sp, adult contemp. News staff one; news progmg 18 hrs wkly. Target aud: 18 plus. ■ Efrain Archilla-Roig, pres, gen mgr & gen sls mgr; Silvia C. Abreu, prom mgr, progmg dir, mus dir & news dir; Arthur Karmgard, chief engr. ■ Rates: $35; 35; 35; 35.

***WBVM(FM)**—May 27, 1986: 90.5 mhz; 100 kw. Ant 958 ft. TL: N27 49 09 W82 14 26. Stereo. Box 18081 (33679); 3816 Morrison Ave. (33629). (813) 289-8040. FAX: (813) 282-3580. Licensee: The Bishop of the Diocese of St. Petersburg. Net: CNN. Format: Btfl mus, Catholic educ. News progmg 4 hrs wkly. Target aud: 55 plus; mature listeners. Spec prog: Black 4 hrs, Greek one hr, Pol one hr, pre-teen 4 hrs, teens 4 hrs. ■ Tom Derzypolski, gen mgr; Dennis M. O'Shey, chief engr.

WCOF(FM)—See St. Petersburg.

WDAE(AM)—May 15, 1922: 1250 khz; 5 kw-U, DA-1. TL: N28 00 41 W82 29 53. 504 Reo St. (33609). (813) 289-0455. FAX: (813) 289-8884. Licensee: Combined Communications Corp. Group owner: Gannett Broadcasting (acq 4-87). Net: ABC/I. Rep: McGavren Guild. Format: Adult contemp. News staff 2; news progmg 3 hrs wkly. Target aud: 25-54. ■ Jay Cook, pres & gen mgr;

Broadcasting & Cable Yearbook 1994
B-85

Nick Puddicolbe, gen sls mgr; Kris Boyd, prom mgr; Joe Montione, progmg dir; Johnny Williams, mus dir; Lloyd Berg, chief engr.

WUSA-FM—Co-owned with WDAE(AM). November 1947: 100.7 mhz; 100 kw. Ant 600 ft. TL: N28 02 21 W82 39 21. Stereo. Hrs opn: 24. Dups AM 95%. (Acq 6-30-80).

WFLA(AM)—1924: 970 khz; 5 kw-U, DA-2. TL: N28 01 14 W82 36 34. 4002A Gandy Blvd. (33611). (813) 839-9393. FAX: (813) 831-4475; (813) 837-0300. Licensee: Jacor Broadcasting of Tampa Bay Inc. Group owner: Jacor Communications Inc. (acq 5-29-88). Net: ABC/I. Rep: Eastman. Wash atty: Hogan & Hartson. Format: News/talk. News staff 17; news progmg 21 hrs wkly. Target aud: 25-54. ■ David Reinhart, vp & gen mgr; Gabe Hobbs, opns mgr & progmg dir; Chuck Deskins, sls dir; Jim Beard, gen sls mgr; Tom Doyle, rgnl sls mgr; Arlana Vincent, prom mgr; Don Richards, news dir; Wilson Welch, chief engr.

WFLZ-FM—Co-owned with WFLA(AM). 1948: 93.3 mhz; 99 kw. Ant 1,358 ft. TL: N27 50 32 W82 15 46. Stereo. Prog sep from AM. Format: CHR. Target aud: 18-49. ■ Darcel Schouler, prom mgr; Marc Chase, progmg dir.

WGUL(AM)—(Dunedin). Nov 21, 1959: 860 khz; 2 kw-D, 1.5 kw-N, DA-2. TL: N27 59 55 W82 42 01. 7623 Little Rd., #100, New Port Richey (34654-5526). (813) 849-2285. FAX: (813) 841-7903. Licensee: Gulf Atlanti Media Corp. (acq 5-7-86). Net: MBS. Format: Music of your life. Target aud: 35 plus. Spec prog: It one hr wkly. ■ Carl J. Marcocci, pres; Steve Schurdell, gen mgr & gen sls mgr; Dan Henry, progmg dir; Paul Mueller, chief engr.

WGUL-FM—(New Port Richey). Sept 19, 1969: 105.5 mhz; 3 kw. Ant 255 ft. TL: N28 15 32 W82 43 54 (CP: 6 kw, 285 ft.). Stereo. Dups AM 100%. Licensee: WGUL-FM Inc., debtor in posession.

WHPT(FM)—See Sarasota.

***WMNF(FM)**—Sept 14, 1979: 88.5 mhz; 70 kw. Ant 520 ft. TL: N27 49 04 W82 14 31. 1210 E. Martin Luther King Jr. Ave. (33603). (813) 238-8001. FAX: (813) 237-4259. Licensee: The Nathan B. Stubblefield Foundation. Format: Div. Spec prog: Black, Jewish, gospel, polka, reggae, blues, pop, big band, new wave. ■ Greg Muffelman, gen mgr; Randy Wynne, progmg dir.

WMTX(AM)—(Pinellas Park). November 1948: 1040 khz; 5 kw-D, 500 w-N, DA-N. TL: N27 50 50 W82 46 21. Suite 500, 18167 U.S. 19 N., Clearwater (34624). (813) 536-9600. FAX: (813) 536-6000. Licensee: Metroplex Communications Inc., an Ohio Corp. Group owner: Metroplex Communications Inc. (acq 2-5-92; FTR 2-24-92). Net: AP. Format: Oldies. ■ Jon Pinch, pres & gen mgr; Kirsten Leigh, prom mgr; Pat Brooks, news dir; Ben Umberger, chief engr.

WMTX-FM—See Clearwater.

WQBN(AM)—(Temple Terrace). 1956: 1300 khz; 5 kw-D, 1 kw-N, DA-2. TL: N28 03 44 W82 19 44. 3825 W. Henderson Blvd, Suite 100, Tampa (33629). (813) 281-0013. FAX: (813) 286-7422. Licensee: WTYM Radio Inc. (acq 1-87; $550,000; FTR 12-1-86). Net: AP. Rep: Katz. Format: Sp. News staff one; news progmg 20 hrs wkly. Target aud: 25 plus; those fluent in Sp. ■ Frank S. Detillio, pres, gen mgr & gen sls mgr; Carlos Alberto, progmg dir & mus dir; Mario Quevedo, news dir; Bill Brown, chief engr.

WQYK(AM)—(Seffner). Nov 7, 1960: 1010 khz; 50 kw-D, 5 kw-N, DA-2. TL: N27 59 25 W82 15 06. Stereo. Hrs opn: 24. Box 20087, St. Petersburg (33742); 9450 Koger Blvd., St. Petersburg (33702). (813) 576-6055. FAX: (813) 577-1324; (813) 797-3333. Licensee: Infinity Broadcasting Corp. of Florida (group owner; acq 11-21-87). Net: AP. Rep: Katz. Wash atty: Leventhal, Senter & Lerman. Format: Country. News staff one; news progmg 6 hrs wkly. Target aud: 25-54. Spec prog: Sports 20 hrs wkly. ■ Jay Miller, gen mgr; Dave Hutchinson, gen sls mgr; Lori Moon, prom dir; Beecher Martin, progmg dir; Jay Roberts, mus dir; Rita Ciccarello, news dir; Frank Berry, chief engr.

WRBQ-FM—1954: 104.7 mhz; 100 kw. Ant 555 ft. TL: N27 56 50 W82 27 35. Stereo. Net: ABC/FM, AP. Format: Hot country hits. News staff 2. Target aud: 18-49.

WSUN(AM)—See St. Petersburg.

WTIS(AM)—1946: 1110 khz; 10 kw-D, DA. TL: N27 52 26 W82 37 53. 311 112th Ave. N.E., St. Petersburg (33716). (813) 576-2234. FAX: (813) 577-3814. Licensee: WTIS(AM) Inc. (acq 12-13-89; $1.7 million; FTR 1-1-90). Format: Relg, ethnic. Target aud: 25-54; women. Spec prog: Sp one hr wkly. ■ Ron Roseman, pres; Edward Roseman, exec vp; Zoe Roseman, vp; Bob Walke, gen mgr & progmg dir; Norm Swenson, prom mgr & news dir; Art Karmgard, chief engr.

WTMP(AM)—(Temple Terrace). 1954: 1150 khz; 5 kw-D, 2.5 kw-N, DA-2. TL: N28 03 49 W82 18 43. 5207 Washington Blvd., Tampa (33619-3437). (813) 620-1300; (813) 622-6611. FAX: (813) 628-0713. Licensee: Broadcap of Florida Inc. (acq 8-14-92; $670,000; FTR 8-31-92). Net: American Urban. Rep: D & R Radio. Format: Urban contemp. Target aud: 20-54; Black adults. Spec prog: Gospel 20 hrs wkly. ■ Chris Turner, CEO & gen mgr; John Oxendine, pres; Victor Brown, CFO; Marion Brown, rgnl sls mgr; Lawrence Hires, prom mgr; Doc Jordon, progmg dir & mus dir; Ed Pendino, chief engr.

WUSA-FM—Listing follows WDAE(AM).

***WUSF(FM)**—September 1963: 89.7 mhz; 100 kw. Ant 820 ft. TL: N27 50 53 W82 15 48. Hrs opn: 24. 4202 E. Fowler Ave., WRB 219 (33620-6870). (813) 974-4890; (813) 974-2075. FAX: (813) 974-5016. Licensee: Board of Regents of South Florida. Net: NPR, APR; Fla. Pub. Wash atty: Cohen & Marks. Format: Class, jazz, news/info. News staff 6; news progmg 28 hrs wkly. Target aud: General. ■ Dr James B. Heck, gen mgr; John Young, stn mgr; Wende Sherwood, opns mgr; Evelyn Massaro, dev mgr; Gerald Leonard, sls dir; Connie McDonnell, prom mgr; Mike Crain, progmg dir; Mary Diana, mus dir; Patricia Kemp, news dir; Michael O'Shea, chief engr. ■ *WUSF-TV affil.

WWRM(FM)—Licensed to Tampa. See St. Petersburg.

WXTB(FM)—See Clearwater.

Tarpon Springs

***WYFE(FM)**—June 14, 1988: 88.9 mhz; 50 kw. Ant 500 ft. TL: N28 24 07 W82 36 30. Stereo. Suite One, 16310 U.S. Hwy. 19, Hudson (34667). (813) 862-9323. Licensee: Bible Broadcasting Network (group owner; acq 8-11-89). Format: Relg. News staff one. Target aud: General; Christians. ■ Lowell C. Davey, pres; Jeff Tenny, gen mgr; David Fuller, stn mgr; Ron Muffley, chief engr.

Temple Terrace

WQBN(AM)—Licensed to Temple Terrace. See Tampa.

WTMP(AM)—Licensed to Temple Terrace. See Tampa.

Titusville

WAMT(AM)—Nov 20, 1957: 1060 khz; 10 kw-D, 5 kw-N, DA-2. TL: N28 39 47 W80 55 17. Box 1060 FL (32781). (407) 264-1060. Licensee: Radio Brevard Inc. (acq 12-16-92; $265,000; FTR 1-11-93). Format: Oldies.

WGNE-FM—Licensed to Titusville. See Daytona Beach.

WORL(AM)—See Christmas.

***WPIO(FM)**—Oct 19, 1975: 89.3 mhz; 10 kw Ant 300 ft. TL: N28 34 49 W80 51 00. Stereo. 505 Josephine St. (32796). (407) 267-3000. FAX: (407) 264-9370. Licensee: Florida Public Radio Inc. Format: Inspirational mus, pub affrs. ■ Randy Henry, pres & gen mgr; Larry Linkous, progmg dir; Archie Shetler, mus dir & chief engr.

Trenton

WCWB-FM—February 1988: 101.7 mhz; 3 kw. Ant 328 ft. TL: N29 36 40 W82 51 14. Stereo. Hrs opn: 24. Box 1197, Radio Rd. (32693). (904) 463-1345; (904) 463-1344. FAX: (904) 463-6920. Licensee: Florida Radio Partners Inc. (acq 9-14-93; $250,000; FTR 10-11-93). Net: NBC. Format: Country. News progmg 7 hrs wkly. Target aud: 25 plus; working class and professionals. Spec prog: Gospel, bluegrass, oldies, farm 2 hrs wkly. ■ R. W. Kulz, gen mgr; Gerald Boutwell, gen sls mgr, prom mgr & news dir; Suzanne Ames, mktg dir; Jesse Miller, mus dir; Darin Janeczko, pub affrs dir; R.W. Kulz, chief engr. ■ Rates: $12.75; 12.75; 12.75; 7.50.

Valparaiso-Niceville

WFSH(AM)—November 1958: 1340 khz; 1 kw-U. TL: N30 30 34 W86 28 34. Box 308, Valparaiso (32580). (904) 678-2141. FAX: (904) 678-6843. Licensee: Bayou Communications (acq 12-1-83). Net: USA. Format: Big band, oldies. Target aud: 35 plus. ■ Red Gilson, pres, gen mgr & news dir; Jim Allen, progmg dir & mus dir; John Lacey, chief engr.

Venice

WAMR(AM)—Feb 1, 1960: 1320 khz; 5 kw-D, 1 kw-N, DA-2. TL: N27 06 20 W82 24 01. 282 N. Auburn Rd. (34292). (813) 484-2636. FAX: (813) 488-4159. Licensee: Asterisk Inc. (group owner; acq 1-18-88). Net: NBC, NBC Talknet, Daynet; Florida. Rep: Katz & Powell. Format: News/talk. News staff one; news progmg 20 hrs wkly. Target aud: 25-54; active, upscale, affluent. Spec prog: Sports. ■ Fred Ingham, pres; Dave McClure, gen mgr & gen sls mgr; Lenore Leopold, prom dir; John Brooks, mus dir; Lee Freshwater, chief engr.

WCTQ(FM)—Co-owned with WAMR. March 1, 1974: 92.1 mhz; 6 kw. Ant 300 ft. TL: N27 06 20 W82 24 01. Stereo. Prog sep from AM. Net: NBC, ABC/I, MBS. Format: Country. Target aud: 25-54; upwardly mobile, affluent. ■ John Brooks, progmg dir.

Vero Beach

***WAOJ(FM)**—Not on air, target date unknown: 90.5 mhz; 3 kw. Ant 90 ft. 1990 25th St. (32960). Licensee: School Board of Indian River County, Florida.

WAVW(FM)—May 29, 1986: 101.7 mhz; 1.48 kw. Ant 471 ft. TL: N27 32 46 W80 22 08. Box 39 (32961). (407) 567-1055. FAX: (407) 595-0214. Licensee: Media VI (acq 9-89; $2,100,000; FTR 9-18-89). Format: Country. ■ James Pagano, gen mgr; Neal Stannard, news dir; Joseph Buneta, chief engr.

WAXE(AM)—May 1954: 1370 khz; 1 kw-D. TL: N27 36 01 W80 23 33. Box 39 (32961). (407) 567-1055. FAX: (407) 595-0214. Licensee: Media IV (acq 10-3-89). Format: Big band. ■ James J. Pagano, pres; Jan Wallag Pagano, gen sls mgr; Neal Burnett, news dir; Craig Jerome, chief engr.

WGYL(FM)—Listing follows WTTB(AM).

WQOL(FM)—Sept 1, 1979: 103.7 mhz; 50 kw. Ant 476 ft. TL: N27 33 21 W80 22 08. Stereo. 2024 U.S. One S.E. (32962). (407) 567-7700. FAX: (407) 569-7662. Licensee: Treasure Coast Media Inc. (acq 8-29-89). Format: Oldies. ■ Wayne Dillos, gen mgr & stn mgr.

***WSCF-FM**—Feb 1, 1990: 91.9 mhz; 15.5 kw. Ant 305 ft. TL: N27 38 10 W80 27 59. 6767 20th St. (32966). (407) 569-0919. FAX: (407) 562-4892. Licensee: Central Educational Broadcasting Inc. (acq 2-15-89). Net: USA. Format: Contemp Christian. ■ Jon Hamilton, gen mgr & progmg dir; Paul Tipton, mus dir; William Narramon, chief engr.

WTTB(AM)—June 7, 1954: 1490 khz; 1 kw-U. TL: N27 37 12 W80 25 01. 1235 16th St. (32960). (407) 567-0937. FAX: (407) 562-4747. Licensee: Sandab Communications L.P. II. (group owner; acq 12-18-91; $4,445,000 grpsl, including co-located FM; FTR 1-13-92). Net: ABC TalkRadio, CBS, MBS, NBC Talknet; Florida. Rep: Christal. Format: Talk, news. News staff 2; news progmg 120 hrs wkly. Target aud: General. ■ Geoff Carter, chief engr.

WGYL(FM)—Co-owned with WTTB(AM). November 1970: 93.7 mhz; 50 kw. Ant 475 ft. TL: N27 36 04 W80 23 33. Stereo. Dups AM 10%. Format: Easy listening. News staff 2. Target aud: 35 plus. Spec prog: Jazz 4 hrs wkly. ■ Gregory Bone, pres & gen mgr; Max Hopkins, opns mgr; Joe Bonota, chief engr.

WWDO(FM)—Not on air, target date unknown: 99.7 mhz; 50 kw. Ant 321 ft. TL: N27 46 38 W80 27 17. 4700 39th Ave. (32967). Licensee: Vero Beach Communcations Inc.

Watertown

WQLC(FM)—Oct 6, 1990: 102.1 mhz; 9.0 kw. Ant 531 ft. TL: N30 13 58 W82 48 18. Rt. 13, Box 318, Lake City (32055). (904) 755-4102; (800) 241-1021. FAX: (904) 752-9861. Licensee: Louis D. Bolton II. Wash atty: Tharrington, Smith & Hargrove. Format: Country. Target aud: 18-54. ■ L.D. Bolton II, CEO; Bob Hendrickson, pres & gen mgr; Scott Burns, stn mgr & chief opns; Bob Hnedrickson, vp sls. ■ Rates: $8.75; 8.75; 8.75; 5.25.

Wauchula

WAUC(AM)—Jan 7, 1958: 1310 khz; 5 kw-D, 500 w-N, DA-2. TL: N27 31 48 W81 49 08. Hrs opn: 6AM-midnight. Box 908, S. Florida Ave. (33873). (813) 773-5008; (813) 773-9282. Licensee: Marlene Ayala (acq 5-20-93; $50,000; FTR 6-7-93). Net: Florida. Format: Mexican. Target aud: 35-54. ■ Chay Gonzales, gen mgr.

West Palm Beach

***WAYF(FM)**—Not on air, target date unknown: 88.1 mhz; 50 kw. Ant 417 ft. TL: N26 47 59 W80 04 33. Licensee: Southwest Florida Community Radio Inc.

WBZT(AM)—July 15, 1947: 1290 khz; 5 kw-U, DA-N. TL: N26 37 55 W80 07 07. 4763 10th Ave. N., Lake Worth (33463). (407) 965-9211. Licensee: Atlantic Broadcast-

Stations in the U.S.   Georgia

ing Corp. Group owner: Price Communications Corp. Stns. (acq 10-1-83; $7 million with co-located FM; FTR 10-3-83). Net: ABC/E, AP. Rep: D & R Radio. Format: News/talk, sports. Spec prog: Miami Heat, Miami Hurricanes, NBA Playoffs, MLB Playoffs/World Series. ■ Lee K. Strasser, gen mgr & gen sls mgr; Sandy DeRaffele, prom mgr; Marie Turner, progmg mgr; Doug Campbell, chief engr.

WIRK-FM—Co-owned with WBZT(AM). Aug 1, 1965: 107.9 mhz; 100 kw. Ant 340 ft. TL: N26 43 32 W80 03 04 (CP: Ant 535 ft.). Stereo. Prog sep from AM. Format: Country. ■ Sandy DeRaffele, prom dir; Ron Brooks, progmg dir.

WEAT(AM)—1948: 850 khz; 5 kw-D, 1 kw-N, DA-2. TL: N26 38 28 W80 05 09. 2406 S. Congress Ave. (33406). (407) 965-5500. Licensee: J.J. Taylor Companies Inc. Group owner: Taylor Communications Inc. (acq 12-29-86; $13 million with co-located FM; FTR 11-3-86). Rep: D & R Radio. Wash atty: Liebowitz & Spencer. Format: Easy lstng. Target aud: 55 plus. ■ John J. Taylor III, pres; Jim Connor, gen mgr; Jeanne Ryan, gen sls mgr; Cinde Everett Martin, mktg dir; Les Howard, progmg dir; Bert Brown, chief engr.

WEAT-FM—Aug 30, 1969: 104.3 mhz; 100 kw. Ant 1,273 ft. TL: N26 34 37 W80 14 32. Stereo. Format: Soft adult contemp. Target aud: 25-54. ■ Joseph J. Taylor Jr., CEO; Henri Des Plaines, CFO; Paul Levesque, exec vp; Les Howard, progmg dir.

WIRK-FM—Listing follows WBZT(AM).

WJNO(AM)—July 31, 1936: 1230 khz; 1 kw-U. TL: N26 43 36 W80 03 03. 1500 N. Flagler Dr. (33401). (407) 838-4300. FAX: (407) 838-4357. Licensee: Fairbanks Communications Inc. (group owner; acq 7-12-79). Net: CBS, AP, Wall Street. Rep: Banner. Format: News, talk. ■ Richard M. Fairbanks, pres; George Mills, vp & gen mgr; Debbie McLean, gen sls mgr; Robbie Hartsock, natl sls mgr; Christie Geltz, prom mgr; John Picano, progmg dir; Jim Edwards, news dir; Dick Lucas, chief engr.

WKGR(FM)—See Fort Pierce.

WOLL(FM)—(Riviera Beach). 1971: 94.3 mhz; 1.26 kw. Ant 480 ft. TL: N26 47 58 W80 04 35 (CP: 1.38 kw). 100 W. Blue Heron Blvd. (33404). (407) 842-4616. FAX: (407) 863-3406. Licensee: Lappin Communications Inc. (acq 11-82; $1,625,000; FTR 11-15-82). Net: NBC. Rep: Republic. Format: Adult contemp. Target aud: 25-54. ■ Tom Haymond, gen mgr; Jeff Thomas, natl sls mgr; Lindy Rome, prom mgr; J.J. Duling, progmg dir.

WRLX(FM)—Dec 13, 1975: 92.1 mhz; 3 kw. Ant 365 ft. TL: N26 44 58 W80 04 04 (CP: 7.2 kw, ant 498 ft.). Stereo. 1016 N. Dixie Hwy. (33401). (407) 835-0700. FAX: (407) 838-4378. Licensee: Pearl Broadcasting Inc. (acq 7-7-78). Net: AP. Rep: Eastman. Format: Easy listening. News staff one; news progmg 4 hrs wkly. Target aud: 25-54; upscale professionals. ■ George Mills, Roberta Kenny (asst), gen mgrs; Russ Morley, opns mgr; JoAnne Coblentz, sls dir; Tony Bonbini, gen sls mgr; Nancy Nicol, prom mgr; Paul Dunn, progmg dir; Rick Reike, chief engr.

***WXEL(FM)**—Nov 24, 1969: 90.7 mhz; 25 kw. Ant 350 ft. TL: N26 34 37 W80 14 32. Stereo. Drawer 6607 (33405); 3401 S. Congress Ave., Boynton Beach (33426). (407) 737-8000. FAX: (407) 369-3067. Licensee: South Florida Public Telecommunications Inc. Net: NPR; Fla. Pub. Wash atty: Schwartz, Woods & Miller. Format: Class, news & info. News staff 2; news progmg 40 hrs wkly. Target aud: General; career oriented men and women, ages 35 plus (news & info); ages 45 plus music progmg. ■ Mary Souder, pres, gen mgr & stn mgr; Stan Salony, opns mgr; Phil DiComo, dev mgr; John LaBonnicia, gen sls mgr; Kevin Petrich, progmg dir & mus dir; Andres Avello, news dir; Ed Murphy, chief engr.

WYFX(AM)—See Boynton Beach.

Wildwood

WHOF(AM)—Sept 1987. 640 khz; 830 w-D, 980 w-N. TL: N28 51 19 W81 58 12. Stereo. Hrs opn: 6 AM-midnight. Box 237, CR 466A (34785). (904) 748-6164. FAX: (904) 748-0359. Licensee: Walker Heart of Florida Broadcasting Inc. (acq 5-15-93; FTR 11-23-92). Format: Relg/talk. Target aud: 18 plus; General. ■ Keith Walker, gen mgr; Joseph A. Ruggiero, opns mgr & gen sls mgr; Johnny Jackson, progmg dir & mus dir.

Williston

WFEZ(FM)—July 1, 1983: 101.3 mhz; 3.5 kw. Ant 433 ft. TL: N29 25 04 W82 32 58. Stereo. Hrs opn: 24. Suite 1738, 3390 Peachtree Rd. N.E., Atlanta, GA (30326). (404) 237-2570. Licensee: Bogie Broadcasting Co. (acq 5-15-92; $130,000; FTR 6-8-92). Format: Urban adult contemp. ■ Moe Negrin, pres & gen mgr.

Wilton Manors

WEXY(AM)—June 1963: 1520 khz; 3.5 kw-D, 250 w-N, DA-N. TL: N26 10 26 W80 09 27. 412 W. Oakland Park Blvd., Fort Lauderdale (33311). (305) 561-1520. FAX: (305) 561-9830. Licensee: Celebrities Inc. (acq 6-77). Format: Relg. ■ Juno Beattie, pres & gen mgr; Doug De Vos, opns mgr & rgnl sls mgr; Henry Green, progmg dir; Jerome Jenkins, mus dir; Gregory Strom, chief engr.

Windermere

WUNA(AM)—See Ocoee.

Winter Garden

WXTO(AM)—Jan 1, 1958: 1600 khz; 5 kw-U, DA-2. TL: N28 34 06 W81 31 09. Hrs opn: 24. 1801 Clark Rd., Orlando (32818). (407) 291-1395. FAX: (407) 578-1734. Licensee: Rama Communications Inc. (acq 10-13-93; $950,000 with WXXU[AM] Cocoa Beach; FTR 11-8-93). Net: CRC. Wash atty: Cohn & Marks. Format: Spanish. News staff one. Target aud: 25-54. Spec prog: French 9 hrs, gospel 12 hrs wkly. ■ Jose D. Ricci, gen mgr & news dir; Diana Cordero, progmg dir; Jay Wagoner, chief engr.

Winter Haven

WHNR(AM)—(Cypress Gardens). Nov 29, 1958: 1360 khz; 5 kw-D, 2.5 kw-N, DA-2. TL: N28 01 16 W81 42 02. Hrs opn: 6 AM-midnight. Box 7742, 1505 Dundee Rd., Winter Haven (33883). (813) 299-1141; (813) 299-1360. FAX: (813) 299-5702. Licensee: Florida Community Radio Inc. (acq 3-8-90; $300,000; FTR 3-12-90). Net: ABC/I. Florida Radio Net. Format: News, info, big band. News staff one; news progmg 20 hrs wkly. Target aud: 55 plus. Spec prog: Relg 5 hrs wkly. ■ B.J. Nielson, gen mgr & gen sls mgr; Terry Lombardi, prom mgr; Tony Verity, mus dir; Jim Greenfield, news dir; Jim Sweeney, pub affrs dir; Jeff Thomburg, chief engr. ■ Rates: $19; 16; 19; 16.

WLKF(AM)—See Lakeland.

WPCV(FM)—Licensed to Winter Haven. See Lakeland.

WSIR(AM)—Feb 14, 1947: 1490 khz; 1 kw-U. TL: N28 00 50 W81 45 02. Hrs opn: 24. 665 Lake Howard Dr. S.W. (33880-2577). (813) 294-4111; (813) 425-3411. Licensee: William Mark Histed. Group owner: Histed Media Group (acq 3-6-90; $230,000; FTR 4-2-90). Format: CHR. News progmg 5 hrs wkly. Target aud: 21-55; young & middle-aged adults. Spec prog: Black 6 hrs, gospel 6 hrs, Sp 6 hrs, Haitian 2 hrs wkly. ■ William M. Histed, CEO, pres & news dir; Robert Cubero, gen mgr & stn mgr; W. Richard Bingaman, opns mgr, gen sls mgr & progmg mgr; Frank Clark, dev mgr, mktg mgr & prom mgr; Robert Histed Sr., mus dir; Carole M. Histed, pub affrs dir; Jeff Thonberg, engrg mgr. ■ Rates: $15; 12; 15; 12.

Winter Park

WLOQ(FM)—1966: 103.1 mhz; 2.65 kw. Ant 351 ft. TL: N28 36 32 W81 23 17. Stereo. Box 2085, 170 W. Fairbanks Ave. (32789). (407) 647-5557. FAX: (407) 647-4495. Licensee: Gross Communications Corp. (group owner; acq 1977). Rep: Banner. Wash atty: Pepper & Corazzini. Format: Jazz. Target aud: 25-49; white collar/professionals. ■ Herbert Paul Gross, pres; John Gross, gen mgr; M.F. Kershner, gen sls mgr; Steve Huntington, progmg dir; Bob Church, mus dir; Joe Frances, news dir & pub affrs dir; Tom Bohannon, chief engr.

***WPRK(FM)**—Dec 10, 1952: 91.5 mhz; 1.32 kw. Ant 89 ft. TL: N28 35 40 W81 20 07. Stereo. Hrs opn: 24. Box 2746, Rollins College, 1000 Holt Ave. (32789-4499). (407) 646-2624; (407) 646-2241. FAX: (407) 646-1560; (407) 646-2445. Licensee: Rollins College. Format: Class, progsv. News progmg 2 hrs wkly. Target aud: General; non-traditional classical and/or rock listeners. Spec prog: Relg one hr wkly. ■ Drew Williams, gen mgr; Joe Beck, stn mgr; Carla Borsoi, dev dir; Mark Snyder, mktg dir; Lisa Blanning, prom dir; Julian Gonzalez, progmg dir; Mario Gonzalez, Carlos Pinto, mus dirs; Kline Stephens, chief engr.

WWZN(AM)—September 1954: 1440 khz; 5 kw-D, 1 kw-N, DA-N. TL: N28 35 18 W81 22 35. Stereo. Hrs opn: 24. Suite 407, 2500 Maitland Ctr. Pkwy., Maitland (32751). (407) 660-1011. FAX: (407) 661-1940. Licensee: Paxson Enterprises Inc. Group owner: Paxson Broadcasting (acq 2-18-93; $5.6 million with WMGF[FM] Mount Dora; FTR 3-8-93). Net: CNN, Unistar. Rep: Major Mkt. Wash atty: James Weitzman. Format: Sports. Target aud: 25-64; upscale. ■ Jenny Sue Rhoades, gen mgr; David Elliott, prom mgr; Chris Persaud, progmg dir; Jym Buss, news dir; David Kreitzer, chief engr. ■ Rates: $100; 95; 100; 20.

Zephyrhills

WPAS(AM)—May 9, 1962: 1400 khz; 1 kw-U. TL: N28 16 54 W82 12 30. Hrs opn: 6 AM-10 PM. Suite 200-A, 1415 S. Hwy. 301, Dade City (33525). (904) 523-9696. FAX: (904) 523-9610. Licensee: Big Z Broadcasting Inc. (acq 2-1-89; $335,000; FTR 1-23-89). Net: NBC. Format: MOR. Target aud: 25 plus. Spec prog: CHR 10 hrs wkly. ■ David M. Zeplowitz, pres & gen mgr; Bobbee Camp, progmg dir; Dave Terry, chief engr.

Zolfo Springs

WZZS(FM)—Not on air, target date unknown: 106.9 mhz; 6 kw. Ant 328 ft. TL: N27 21 59 W81 47 52. 6800 Fleetwood Rd. P 539, McLean, VA (22101). Licensee: Teddy Bear Communications Inc.

Georgia

LAUREN A. COLBY
301-663-1086
COMMUNICATIONS ATTORNEY
Special Attention to Difficult Cases

Adel

WBIT(AM)—Mar 19, 1957: 1470 khz; 1 kw-D, 350 w-N. TL: N31 08 15 W83 23 41. Hrs opn: 24. Suite 11, 1203 W. 4th St. (31620). (912) 896-4571. FAX: (912) 896-4710. Licensee: Williams Investment Co. (acq 11-1-90; $164,148 with co-located FM; FTR 11-5-90). Net: NBC; Ga. Net. Wash atty: Pepper & Corrazini. Format: Southern gospel, Black gospel, MOR contemp. News staff one; news progmg 12 hrs wkly. Target aud: General. Spec prog: Black 2 hrs wkly. ■ Ron Hester, gen mgr; Bettye Joiner, gen sls mgr & mus dir; Wink DeVane, prom mgr; C.H. Fletcher, chief engr. ■ Rates: $7; 7; 7; 7.

WDDQ(FM)—Co-owned with WBIT(AM). Oct 1979: 92.1 mhz; 3 kw. Ant 300 ft. TL: N31 08 15 W83 23 41 (CP: 4.2 kw, ant 390 ft, N31 08 22 W83 20 57). Stereo. Hrs opn: 24. Prog sep from AM. Format: Tourist Information Radio. Target aud: 18-50. ■ Ron Hester, adv mgr & progmg mgr. ■ Rates: $4; 4; 4; 4.

Albany

WALG(AM)—1940: 1590 khz; 5 kw-D, 1 kw-N, DA-2. TL: N31 37 19 W84 09 09. Hrs opn: 24. Box 2407, 400 Dunbar Ln. (31703). (912) 436-7233. FAX: (912) 888-6018. Licensee: K-Country Inc. (acq 7-15-93; with co-located FM; FTR 7-19-93). Net: ABC, ARN; Southern Radio. Rep: Katz, Eastman. Format: News/talk, sports. Target aud: General. ■ Robert Brooks, CEO; Robert Brooks Jr., pres; Bob Roddy, vp & gen mgr; Richard Cobb, natl sls dir; Kurt Baker, prom mgr; Steve Preston, progmg dir; Steve Selby, news dir; Al Crumpton, pub affrs dir; Buddy Green, chief engr.

WKAK(FM)—Co-owned with WALG(AM). Dec 17, 1972: 101.7 mhz; 3 kw. Ant 300 ft. TL: N31 37 15 W84 09 11. Stereo. Prog sep from AM. Format: Country. ■ Dotti Davis, opns mgr & progmg dir; Steve Preston, news dir.

WANL(AM)—July 10, 1962: 1250 khz; 1 kw-D, 53 w-N. TL: N31 37 00 W84 09 32. 2804 N. Jefferson St. (31701). (912) 436-0544. FAX: (912) 436-0544. Licensee: Lifeline Radio Corporation (acq 1-1-86; $300,000; FTR 11-4-85). Net: NBC. Format: Relg. ■ Jimmy Keyton, pres; Sherry Jackson, gen mgr.

***WGNP(FM)**—July 12, 1990: 90.7 mhz; 3 kw. Ant 328 ft. TL: N31 38 42 W84 21 15. Hrs opn: 16. 2724 Ledo Rd. (31707). (912) 883-6620. Licensee: Lamad Ministries Inc. (acq 7-89). Format: Relg. News progmg 4 hrs wkly. Target aud: 35 plus. ■ C. Wm. Eidenire, pres.

WGPC(AM)—1933: 1450 khz; 1 kw-U. TL: N31 34 55 W84 11 58. Stereo. 2011 Gillionville Rd. (31707). (912) 883-6500. FAX: (912) 883-1450. Licensee: Albany Broadcasting Co. (acq 1-1-58). Net: CBS; Ga. Net. Wash atty: Fletcher, Heald & Hildreth. Format: Full svc radio-light adult. News progmg 20 hrs wkly. Target aud: 25 plus;

middle to upper income. ■ L. M. George, pres, gen mgr & gen sls mgr; John Green, chief engr. ■ Rates: $16.50; 15; 15; 15.

WGPC-FM—Feb 22, 1963: 104.5 mhz; 100 kw. Ant 981 ft. TL: N31 32 57 W84 00 19. Stereo. Hrs opn: 24. Dups AM 100%. Wash atty: Fletcher, Heald & Hildreth. News progmg 20 hrs wkly.

WJIZ-FM—Listing follows WJYZ(AM).

WJYZ(AM)—November 1952: 960 khz; 5 kw-D, DA. TL: N31 37 06 W84 10 33. Stereo. 2700 N. Slappy Blvd. (31702). (912) 436-0112. FAX: (912) 436-8985. Licensee: Keys Communications Group Inc. (acq 11-15-91; $2,541,000 with co-located FM; FTR 3-16-92). Net: MBS. Rep: D & R Radio. Format: Solid gold. Spec prog: Farm 10 hrs wkly. ■ Brady Keys Jr., pres; Cecillia Morris, gen mgr; Ben St. Hollywood, progmg dir & mus dir; Betty Green, chief engr.

WJIZ-FM—Co-owned with WJYZ(AM). January 1965: 96.3 mhz; 100 kw. Ant 469 ft. TL: N31 39 20 W84 10 30. Stereo. Prog sep from AM. Box 5226 (31706); 506 W. Ogelthorpe Blvd. (31701). (912) 883-5397. FAX: (912) 439-7239. Net: American Urban Radio. Format: Urban contemp. ■ John Draper, gen mgr; Norm Miller, progmg dir; Adrian Guyton, mus dir.

WKAK(FM)—Listing follows WALG(AM).

WSGY(FM)—(Tifton). 1975: 100.3 mhz; 100 kw. Ant 1,100 ft. TL: N31 25 49 W83 45 22 (CP: Ant 1,005 ft.). Stereo. Box 1466, Tifton (31793); 200 John Howard Way, Tifton (31794). (912) 436-9100; (912) 382-1100. FAX: (912) 382-1234. Licensee: WWGS/WCUP Partnership. Group owner: Kelsey Broadcasting Corp. Net: ABC/E, ABC/FM, Westwood One. Rep: Rgnl Reps. Wash atty: Bechtel & Cole. Format: Country. News progmg 2 hrs wkly. Target aud: 25-49. ■ Jon Peterson, pres; Scott Davis, gen mgr; Ron Jones, stn mgr; Jim Jacobs, progmg dir; Jeff Flynt, chief engr. ■ Rates: $25; 22; 25; 20.

***WUNV(FM)**—1990: 91.7 mhz; 3 kw. Ant 328 ft. TL: N31 40 20 W84 03 27. Stereo. 1540 Stewart Ave. S.W., Atlanta (30310). (404) 756-4730. FAX: (404) 756-4088. Licensee: Georgia Public Telecommunications Commission. Net: APR, NPR. Format: Class, jazz. News staff 10; news progmg 27 hrs wkly. Target aud: 35 plus; professional, college educated. Spec prog: Big band, drama. ■ Richard E. Ottinger, pres; Frank Bugg, vp; Bill Bergeron, gen mgr; Norman Bemelmans, progmg dir; Al Korn, chief engr.

Alma

WULF(AM)—October 1957: 1400 khz; 1 kw-U. TL: N31 31 50 W82 27 45. Box K, Radio Station Rd. (31510). (912) 632-4411. FAX: (912) 632-8996. Licensee: Sunbelt Media Inc. (acq 2-25-93; $352,552 with co-located FM; FTR 3-15-93). Net: NBC; Ga. Net. Format: Country, adult contemp. News staff one; news progmg 40 hrs wkly. Target aud: General. Spec prog: Farm 2 hrs wkly. ■ Robert Williams, pres; Freddy Willis, gen mgr, gen sls mgr & progmg dir; Bob Sass, news dir; Larry D. Ring, chief engr.

WKXH-FM—Co-owned with WULF(AM). May 14, 1987: 104.3 mhz; 1.9 kw. Ant 397 ft. TL: N31 36 26 W82 32 46 (CP: 2.1 kw, ant 387 ft.). Stereo. Dups AM 100% News staff one; news progmg 6 hrs wkly. Target aud: General.

Alpharetta

WVNF(AM)—Aug 25, 1986: 1400 khz; 1 kw-U. TL: N34 03 49 W84 16 34. Licensee: Milton Broadcasting Inc.

Americus

WDEC(AM)—July 5, 1947: 1290 khz; 1 kw-D, 31 w-N. TL: N32 04 30 W84 14 20. Box 1307, 605 McGarrah St. (31709). (912) 924-1290. FAX: (912) 928-3579. Licensee: Sumter Broadcasting Co. (acq 1994; with co-located FM). Net: SMN. Rep: Dora-Clayton. Format: Black, heart & soul, classic R&B. News staff one; news progmg 7 hrs wkly. Target aud: General. Spec prog: Jazz 5 hrs wkly. ■ R.E. Lashley Jr., pres & chief engr; Steve Lashley, gen mgr; Al Crumpton, prom mgr & news dir; John Bell, progmg dir & mus dir.

WDEC-FM—Sept 12, 1964: 94.3 mhz; 3 kw. Ant 180 ft. TL: N32 04 30 W84 14 20. Stereo. Prog sep from AM. Net: SMN. Rep: Dora-Clayton. Format: Country. Spec prog: Black 5 hrs, farm one hr wkly.

WISK(AM)—Aug 28, 1962: 1390 khz; 5 kw-D. TL: N32 04 51 W84 15 20. Hrs opn: Sunrise-sunset. Box 727, Georgia Hwy. 30 W. (31709). (912) 924-1390; (912) 924-6500. Licensee: Sumter Broadcasting Co. Inc. Net: MBS; Ga. Net. Format: Country. News staff one. Target aud: 19-65. ■ Robert E. Lashley Jr., pres & gen mgr; Steve Lashley, vp, gen sls mgr & chief engr; Thurston Clary, progmg dir; Donnie McCrary, mus dir & news dir.

WISK-FM—September 1973: 98.7 mhz; 25 kw. Ant 302 ft. TL: N32 04 51 W84 15 20. Stereo. Hrs opn: 6 AM-midnight. Prog sep from AM. (912) 924-6500. Rep: Rgnl Reps.

Ashburn

WFFM(FM)—December 1989: 105.7 mhz; 6 kw. Ant 328 ft. TL: N31 41 17 W83 38 38. Box 72 (31714). (912) 567-0252. Licensee: Wade Keck and Dawn Acree (acq 9-30-93; $120,000; FTR 10-18-93). Format: Adult contemp. News staff one. ■ Carolyn Segers, gen mgr.

WNNQ(AM)—May 27, 1961: 1570 khz; 1 kw-D, 31 w-N. TL: N31 41 22 W83 38 37. Box 7350 (31793). Licensee: Dawn M. Lott (acq 9-1-80; $250,000; FTR 10-6-80). ■ Aubrey Smith, gen mgr.

Athens

WALR(FM)—January 1964: 104.7 mhz; 100 kw. Ant 981 ft. TL: N33 51 56 W83 49 34. Stereo. 209 CNN Center, Atlanta (30303). (404) 688-0068. FAX: (706) 688-4262. Licensee: Ring Radio Co. (acq 4-24-89). Wash atty: Fletcher, Heald & Hildreth. Format: Urban contemp. Spec prog: Gospel 2 hrs wkly. ■ Rob Huntley, gen mgr; Lindsay Neal, prom mgr; Mike Watkins, progmg dir & mus dir; Ted Ronneburger, chief engr. ■ Rates: $150; 130; 140; 120.

WBKZ(AM)—(Jefferson). Sept 15, 1984: 880 khz; 5 kw-D. TL: N34 00 52 W83 27 11. Box 88, Athens (30603); 548 Hawthorn Ave., Athens (30606). (706) 548-8800. FAX: (706) 549-8800. Licensee: Brown Broadcasting System Inc. (acq 9-29-93; $270,000; FTR 10-18-93). Net: Mutual. Format: Gospel, urban, oldies. ■ Stan Carter, pres & gen sls mgr; Jim Rhinehart, gen mgr; Dan Davis, chief engr.

WGAU(AM)—May 1, 1938: 1340 khz; 1 kw-U. TL: N33 56 28 W83 24 13. Stereo. Hrs opn: 24. 850 Bobbin Mill Rd. (30610). (706) 549-1340. FAX: (706) 546-0441. Licensee: Clarke Broadcasting Corp. (group owner; acq 8-56). Net: CBS, MBS, NBC Talknet, Unistar. Rep: Dora-Clayton. Wash atty: Leventhal, Senter & Lerman. Format: News/talk. News staff 5. Target aud: 25-54 plus; educated, middle- & upper-income, news & information-oriented. Spec prog: Exclusive rights for all Univ. of Georgia sports. ■ H. Randolph Holder Jr., pres; Clementi Holder, vp; Larry England, gen mgr & stn mgr; Richard A. Mattocks, gen sls mgr; Matt Caesar, progmg dir; Mike Wooten, news dir; Dan Davis, chief engr. ■ Rates: $17; 17; 17; 17.

WNGC(FM)—Co-owned with WGAU(AM). May 1948: 95.5 mhz; 100 kw. Ant 1,268 ft. TL: N34 05 02 W83 19 18. Stereo. Hrs opn: 24. Prog sep from AM. Net: NBC. Format: Country. Target aud: 25-54. blue collar to executive, modern country music lovers. Spec prog: Gospel 2 hrs wkly. ■ K.B. Travis, mus dir. ■ Rates: $42.75; 34; 42.75; 34.

***WMSL(FM)**—October 1987: 88.9 mhz; 1.35 kw. Ant 328 ft. TL: N33 54 25 W83 29 35. Stereo. Hrs opn: 24. Box 8003, 585 Prince Ave. (30603). (706) 549-8000. FAX: (706) 353-1991. Licensee: Prince Avenue Christian School. Net: USA, Moody. Wash atty: Haley, Bader & Potts. Format: Christian easy lstng. News progmg 11 hrs wkly. Target aud: 25-54; General. ■ James Hutto, gen mgr & mus dir; Nick Kimmel, mktg dir; Dan Davis, chief engr.

WNGC(FM)—Listing follows WGAU(AM).

WPUP(FM)—(Royston). Dec 1, 1988: 103.7 mhz; 25 kw. Ant 328 ft. TL: N34 16 50 W83 07 09. Stereo. Hrs opn: 24. 255 S. Milledge Ave., Athens (30605). (706) 549-6222. Licensee: Athena Broadcasting (acq 1-1-90; $700,000). Format: CHR, alt rock, new rock. News staff 2; Target aud: 18-24. ■ Hugh Christian, pres & gen mgr; Julie Irby, stn mgr; Mark Haddon, gen sls mgr; Allen Tibbetts, progmg dir; Brian Thomas, mus dir. ■ Rates: $16; 14; 16; 14.

WRFC(AM)—May 1, 1948: 960 khz; 5 kw-D, 2.5 kw-N, DA-N. TL: N33 59 58 W83 26 00. Stereo. Hrs opn: 24. 255 S. Milledge Ave. (30605-1045). (706) 549-6222. Licensee: AM 96 Inc. (group owner; acq 12-31-83; $350,000; FTR 5-2-83). Net: ABC/I, ESPN. Format: Adult contemp, news/talk, sports. News staff 4. Target aud: 25-54; community-minded adults. Spec prog: Oldies 6 hrs, sports 12 hrs, talk 12 hrs wkly. ■ Hugh Christian, pres & gen mgr; Mark Haddon, gen sls mgr; Allen Tibbetts, progmg dir; Penny Walls, news dir; Steve Splitt, chief engr. ■ Rates: $16; 14; 16; 14.

***WUGA(FM)**—Aug 28, 1987: 91.7 mhz; 3 kw. Ant 328 ft. TL: N33 55 13 W83 14 46. Stereo. Hrs opn: 24. Ga. Ctr. for Continuing Ed. (30602). (706) 542-9842. FAX: (706) 542-6718. Licensee: Georgia Public Telecommunications Commission. Net: APR, AP, NPR; Peach State Public Radio. Format: Classical, jazz, news. News staff one. Target aud: General. Spec prog: Folk 6 hrs, new age 10 hrs, drama 6 hrs, children 4 hrs wkly. ■ Richard E. Ottinger, pres; Gene Craven, gen mgr & progmg dir; June Sparks, prom mgr; Robb Holmes, mus dir; Mary Kay Mitchell, news dir; Phil Allen, chief engr.

***WUOG(FM)**—Oct 16, 1972: 90.5 mhz; 9.5 kw. Ant 180 ft. TL: N33 57 00 W83 22 02 (CP: 26 kw, ant 179 ft., TL: N33 56 59 W83 22 58). Stereo. Tate Student Center (30602). (706) 542-7100. FAX: (706) 542-0351. Licensee: Univ. of Georgia. Net: Ga. Net. Format: Progsv. News progmg 4 hrs wkly. Students & faculty of Univ. of Georgia & Athens area residents. Spec prog: Folk 2 hrs, jazz 6 hrs, dance/rap 4 hrs, country 2 hrs, blues 2 hrs, hardcore 2 hrs, garage 2 hrs, local 3 hrs wkly. ■ Marianne Gouge, gen mgr; Heather Wagner, prom mgr; Josh Houk, mus dir; Brian Morrow, asst mus dir; Jennifer Wargula, Mark Bullock, news dirs; Wilbur Harrington, chief engr.

Atlanta

***WABE(FM)**—Sept 13, 1948: 90.1 mhz; 100 kw. Ant 955 ft. TL: N33 45 35 W84 20 07 (CP: 95.9 kw). Stereo. Hrs opn: 24. 740 Bismark Rd. N.E. (30324). (404) 827-8900. Licensee: Board of Education of the City of Atlanta. Net: NPR. Wash atty: Schwartz, Woods, Miller. Format: News, class. News staff 2. Target aud: 25-60 plus; upscale, news advocates, classical enthusiasts. Spec prog: Jazz 11 hrs wkly. ■ Reva Ezell, stn mgr & pub affrs dir; Earl Johnson, opns mgr; Bernice Chandler, sls dir; Eric Weston, prom mgr; Lois Reitzes, progmg mgr & mus dir; Mike Bucki, news dir; Duncan Pearson, chief engr. ■ *WPBA(TV) affil.

WAEC(AM)—1947: 860 khz; 5 kw-D. TL: N33 47 27 W84 25 23 (CP: 500 w-N, TL: N33 43 45 W84 19 19). Suite 14, 1465 Northside Dr. (30318). (404) 355-8600. FAX: (404) 355-4156. Licensee: Forus Communications (group owner; acq 4-5-82). Format: Contemp Christian. ■ Don Stone, gen mgr, gen sls mgr, prom mgr & news dir; Ken Rogers, progmg dir; George Pass, chief engr.

WAFS(AM)—Mar 17, 1922: 920 khz; 5 kw-D, 1 kw-N. TL: N33 48 35 W84 21 23. Suite 600, 1447 Peachtree St. N.E. (30309). (404) 888-0920. Licensee: Moody Bible Institute of Chicago (group owner; acq 8-18-89; $2,300,000; FTR 9-5-89). Net: Moody; USA; AP. Format: Relg. News staff one; news progmg 6 hrs wkly. Target aud: General. ■ Dr. Joseph Stowell, pres; Dennis Shere, sr vp; Robert Neff, vp; Joseph Emert, gen mgr; Charles Burge (asst), stn mgr; DeLain Robins, news dir; Robert Lipscomb, chief engr.

WAOK(AM)—Mar 15, 1954: 1380 khz; 5 kw-U, DA-N. TL: N33 45 36 W84 28 45 (CP: 4.2 kw-N). Suite 1000, 120 Ralph McGill Blvd. (30365-6901). (404) 898-8900. FAX: (404) 898-8934. Licensee: Summit-Atlanta Broadcasting Corp. Group owner: Summit Communications Group Inc. (acq 1-1-88; $11.4 million with co-located FM; FTR 2-29-88). Net: ABC, MBS. Rep: McGavren Guild. Format: Gospel. Target aud: 25-64. ■ James Wesley, CEO & pres; Mary Catherine Sneed, exec vp; Rick Mack, vp & gen mgr; Glenn Way, gen sls mgr; Joe Libios, prom mgr; Connie Flint, progmg dir; Lenair Holton, mus dir; Felicia Church, news dir; Sidney Daniels, chief engr.

WVEE(FM)—Co-owned with WAOK(AM). July 1, 1948: 103.3 mhz; 100 kw. Ant 1,022 ft. TL: N33 45 35 W84 20 07. Stereo. Net: NBC the Source. Format: Urban contemp. Target aud: 18-49. ■ Tony Brown, progmg dir.

***WCLK(FM)**—Apr 10, 1974: 91.9 mhz; 2.5 kw. Ant 300 ft. TL: N33 44 56 W84 24 26. Stereo. 111 James P. Brawley Dr. S.W. (30314). (404) 880-8273. FAX: (404) 880-8869. Licensee: Clark Atlanta Univ. Net: NPR, APR; SECA. Format: Jazz. News staff 2; news progmg 13 hrs wkly. Target aud: 25-49. Spec prog: Gospel 17 hrs, reggae 3 hrs, blues 3 hrs, oldies 3 hrs wkly. ■ Thomas W. Cole Jr., pres; Reggie Hicks, gen mgr; Deborah Strahorn, mktg dir; Bobby Jackson, progmg dir; Tony Phillips, news dir; Bill Burson, chief engr.

WCNN(AM)—(North Atlanta). Dec 4, 1967: 680 khz; 60 kw-D, 10 kw-N, DA-2. TL: N33 57 42 W84 15 48. Hrs opn: 24. 209 CNN Center, Atlanta (30303). (404) 688-0068. FAX: (404) 688-4262. Licensee: Ring Radio Co. (acq 6-15-81). Net: Unistar, CNN. Rep: Banner. Format: News, sports. News staff 4; news progmg 130 hrs wkly. ■ Bob Huntley, gen mgr; Charles Smithgall III., stn mgr; Randy Blake, opns mgr; Karen Lang, prom mgr; Edgar Treiguts, pub affrs dir; Ted Ronneburger, chief engr.

WFOM(AM)—See Marietta.

WFTD(AM)—See Marietta.

WGKA(AM)—Sept 1, 1955: 1190 khz; 10 kw-D. TL: N33 48 35 W84 21 14. Stereo. Hrs opn: Sunrise-sunset. Box 52128 (30355). (404) 231-1190. Licensee: WGKA Inc. (acq 3-5-76). Rep: CMBS. Format: Class. Target aud: 25-64. Spec prog: Ger one hr, Greek one hr, It one hr wkly. ■ Eathel Holley, pres & gen mgr; Dianne Watson, stn mgr. ■ Rates: $55; 55; 55; 45.

WGST(AM)—April 7, 1988: 640 khz; 50 kw-D, 1 kw-N, DA-2. TL: N33 45 43 W84 27 29. Suite 400, 550 Pharr Rd. N.W. (30363). (404) 233-0640. FAX: (404) 237-5856. Licensee: Jacor Broadcasting of Atlanta. Group owner: Jacor Communications Inc. (acq 4-85; $20 million; FTR 4-29-85). Net: ABC, CBS, MBS, AP. Format: News/talk. Target aud: 25-54. ■ John Hogan, vp & gen mgr; Steve Yonlios (local), rgnl sls mgr; Arnie Katinsky, prom mgr; Eric Seidel, progmg dir; David Joy, mus dir; Pete Konenkamp, news dir; Mike Lawing, chief engr.

WPCH(FM)—Co-owned with WGST(AM). Feb 18, 1962: 94.9 mhz; 100 kw. Ant 984 ft. TL: N33 48 27 W84 20 26. Stereo. Prog sep from AM. (404) 261-9500. Net: CBS. Format: Contemp easy lstng. News staff one; news progmg 6 hrs wkly. Target aud: 25-64. ■ Vance Dillard, progmg dir; Susan Andrews, news dir; Jim Gantner, chief engr.

WGUN(AM)—Licensed to Atlanta. See Tucker.

WIGO(AM)—Nov 20, 1965: 1340 khz; 1 kw-U. TL: N33 44 56 W84 24 26. Hrs opn: 24. Suite 520, 2001 Martin Luther King Jr. Dr. S.W. (30310). (404) 752-5460. FAX: (404) 752-5564. Licensee: Allied Media of Georgia (acq 11-14-90; grpsl; FTR 12-3-90). Format: Black, news/talk. News staff 2; news progmg 10 hrs wkly. Target aud: 25-64; Black adults. ■ Ron Sailor, CEO, pres & gen mgr; T.S. Woods, opns mgr; Marcita Ford, gen sls mgr; Charmaine Coachman, mktg mgr; Yao Seidu, progmg dir; Carlos Beck, news dir; George Pass, chief engr. ■ Rates: $60; 40; 40; na.

***WJSP-FM**—(Warm Springs). Feb 3, 1985: 88.1 mhz; 100 kw. Ant 975 ft. TL: N32 51 08 W84 42 04. Stereo. Hrs opn: 6 AM-midnight. 1540 Stewart Ave. S.W., Atlanta (30310). (404) 756-4730. FAX: (404) 756-4713. Licensee: Georgia Public Telecommunications Commission. Net: NPR, APR. Format: News, class. News staff 3; news progmg 35 hrs wkly. Target aud: 35-54. Spec prog: Jazz. ■ Richard Ottinger, CEO; Frank Bugg, exec vp; Bill Bergeron, gen mgr & progmg dir; Norman Bemelmans, opns dir; Edith Bonde, prom mgr; James Argroves, news dir; Bill Burson, engrg mgr.

WKHX(AM)—July 1, 1938: 590 khz; 5 kw-U, DA-N. TL: N33 49 34 W84 18 56 (CP: 4.5 kw-N, DA-2). Suite 101, 360 Interstate N. (30339). (404) 955-0101. FAX: (404) 953-4612. Licensee: Capital Cities/ABC Communications Inc. Group owner: Capital Cities/ABC Broadcast Group (acq 5-17-85; $6,850,000; FTR 6-3-85). Rep: Republic. Format: Personality country. Target aud: 25-54; general. ■ Norman Schrutt, pres; Norm Schrutt, gen mgr; Neil McGinley, opns mgr; Diane Dalton Verzijl, gen sls mgr; Andy Guzman, prom dir; Deborah Richards, news dir; Bill Massey, chief engr.

WKHX-FM—(Marietta). November 1960: 101.5 mhz; 99 kw. Ant 968 ft. TL: N33 48 27 W84 20 26. Stereo. ■ Verners J. Ore, pres; Norm Schrutt, gen mgr; Neil McGinley, opns mgr & progmg dir; Bob French, gen sls mgr; Andy Guzman, prom dir; Johnny Gray, mus dir; Deborah Richards, news dir; Bill Massey, chief engr.

WKLS-FM—Dec 2, 1960: 96.1 mhz; 99 kw. Ant 984 ft. TL: N33 48 27 W84 20 26. Stereo. 1800 Century Blvd. (30345). (404) 325-0960. FAX: (404) 325-8715. Licensee: Great American TV and Radio Co. Inc. Group owner: Great American Broadcasting. Net: NBC the Source. Rep: Katz. Format: AOR. News staff one. Target aud: 18-34; primarily male. ■ Tom Connolly, vp & gen mgr; Alan Rothenberg, gen sls mgr; Mark Cooper, prom dir; Michael Hughes, progmg dir; Lisa Sturgis, mus dir; Beth Kepple, news dir; Michelle Monroe, pub affrs dir; Bob Helbush, chief engr.

WNIV(AM)—1948: 970 khz; 5 kw-D, 39 w-N. TL: N33 48 35 W84 21 14. 2970 Peachtree Rd. N.W. (30305). (404) 365-0970. FAX: (404) 816-0748. Licensee: Genesis Communications Inc. (group owner; acq 5-88). $630,000). Net: CBN. Format: Relg, talk. News staff one; news progmg one hr wkly. Target aud: 25-49. ■ Bruce Maduri, CEO, pres & gen mgr; Robert F. Sterling III, CFO; Steve Barrett, stn mgr; Ron Theus, vp opns, prom mgr & progmg dir; Monica DeMuth, sls dir; Laila Walker, prom dir; John Young, mus dir; Susan King, news dir; Tom Taylor, chief engr. ■ Rates: $50; 40; 50; 30.

WNNX(FM)—November 1963: 99.7 mhz; 100 kw. Ant 1,032 ft. TL: N33 46 57 W84 23 20. Stereo. Suite 500, 3405 Piedmont Rd. N.E. (30305). (404) 266-0997. FAX: (404) 364-5855. Licensee: Susquehanna Radio Corp. (group owner; acq 2-28-74). Rep: D & R Radio. Format: Modem rock. ■ Brian Philips, opns mgr & prom dir; Amy Henry, prom mgr; Sean Demory, mus dir; Vic Jester, chief engr.

WPCH(FM)—Listing follows WGST(AM).

WQXI(AM)—October 1947: 790 khz; 5 kw-D, 1 kw-N, DA-N. TL: N33 48 42 W84 21 13. Stereo. 3350 Peachtree Rd. N.E. (30326); One Capital City Plaza (30326). (404) 261-2970. FAX: (404) 365-9026. Licensee: Jefferson Pilot Communications Co. (group owner; acq 3-1-74). Net: AP, UPI. Format: Adult contemp. ■ Clarke R. Brown Jr., pres & gen mgr; Mark Kanov, gen sls mgr; Alan Hennes, prom mgr; Lee Chestnut, progmg dir; Rob Stadler, news dir; Tom Giglio, chief engr.

***WRAS(FM)**—Jan 18, 1971: 88.5 mhz; 100 kw. Ant 436 ft. TL: N33 41 04 W84 17 23. Stereo. Hrs opn: 24. Box 4048, Univ. Plaza, Georgia State Univ. (30303). (404) 651-2240. Licensee: Georgia State Univ. Net: ABC/D; Ga. Net. Format: Progressive. News progmg 6 hrs wkly. Target aud: 18-34. Spec prog: Big band one hr, class 3 hrs, reggae 4 hrs, blues 2 hrs, world beat 3 hrs, new age 3 hrs, jazz 2 hrs, rap/hip-hop/house 4 hrs wkly. ■ Cecily Walker, gen mgr; Claire Roberts, opns mgr; Sandy Fein, prom mgr; Julie Hoyt, progmg dir; Dusty Fohs, David Hill, mus dirs; Chip Davis, news dir; Butch Foster, chief engr.

***WREK(FM)**—Apr 1, 1968: 91.1 mhz; 40 kw. Ant 340 ft. TL: N33 46 41 W84 24 22. Stereo. Hrs opn: 24. Georgia Tech. Univ., 165 Eighth St. N.W. (30332). (404) 894-2468. FAX: (404) 853-3066. Licensee: Radio Communications Board, Georgia Institute of Technology. Net: Ga. Net. Format: Div, progsv. Target aud: General. Spec prog: Jazz 15 hrs, class 8 hrs, rap 2 hrs, experimental 4 hrs, ambient 10 hrs wkly. ■ Leigh Martin, gen mgr; John Selbie, opns mgr; Anne Turner, progmg dir; Mike Ferrigno, Steve Lefcart, Marcus DeShon, mus dirs; Steve Bowling, chief engr.

***WRFG(FM)**—July 15, 1973: 89.3 mhz; 24.5 kw. Ant 150 ft. TL: N33 44 56 W84 24 26 (CP: 100 kw, 279 ft.). Stereo. Hrs opn: 24. 1083 Austin Ave. N.E. (30307). (404) 523-3471. Licensee: Radio Free Georgia Broadcasting Foundation Inc. Wash atty: Haley, Bader & Potts. Format: Community, div. News progmg 3 hrs wkly. Target aud: 18-45; socially conscious African-Americans. Spec prog: Country 7 hrs, women 5 hrs, punk/new wave/rap 6 hrs, reggae 20 hrs, Indian 3 hrs, Sp 5 hrs, interview 9 hrs, poetry 4 hrs, R&B 2 hrs, class 2 hrs, world mus 6 hrs, jazz 18 hrs, bluegrass 10 hrs wkly. ■ Paul Willams, pres; Phil Graitcer, vp; Tom Davis, gen mgr & stn mgr; Skip Marshall, chief engr.

WSB(AM)—March 15, 1922: 750 khz; 50 kw-U. TL: N33 50 43 W84 15 12. 1601 W. Peachtree St. N.E. (30309). (404) 897-7500. FAX: (404) 897-7525. Licensee: WSB Inc. Group owner: Cox Broadcasting Inc. Net: AP. Rep: Christal. Wash atty: Dow, Lohnes & Albertson. Format: News/talk. News staff 9; news progmg 34 hrs wkly. Target aud: 25-54. ■ Marc W. Morgan, vp & gen mgr; James C. Prain, gen sls mgr; Susan Corley, natl sls mgr; Lisa Fernald, mktg mgr; Greg Moceri, progmg mgr; Ron Wilson, chief engr.

WSB-FM—Nov 10, 1944: 98.5 mhz; 100 kw. Ant 919 ft. TL: N33 45 35 W84 20 07. Stereo. Prog sep from AM. Format: Adult contemp. ■ Maria Taylor, mktg mgr; Phil LoCascio, progmg mgr. ■ WSB-TV affil.

WSTR(FM)—See Smyrna.

WTJH(AM)—See East Point.

WVEE(FM)—Listing follows WAOK(AM).

WWEV(AM)—See Cumming.

WYAI(FM)—See La Grange.

WYZE(AM)—June 1957: 1480 khz; 5 kw-D, 44 w-N. TL: N33 43 25 W84 22 08. 1111 Boulevard S.E. (30312). (404) 622-7802. FAX: (404) 622-6767. Licensee: GHB Broadcasting Inc. Group owner: GHB Radio Group. Net: Ga. Net. Format: Black gospel. ■ George H. Buck Jr., pres; Neelie Reese, sls dir; Regina Slaughter, prom mgr, progmg dir & mus dir; Skip Marshall, chief engr.

WZGC(FM)—Sept 1, 1965: 92.9 mhz; 100 kw. Ant 910 ft. TL: N33 45 34 W84 23 19. Stereo. Hrs opn: 24. Suite 593, 1100 Johnson Ferry Rd. N.E. (30342). (404) 851-9393. FAX: (404) 843-3541. Licensee: Infinity Broadcasting Corp. (group owner; acq 12-18-92; grpsl; FTR 1-25-93). Rep: D & R Radio. Format: Classic rock. News staff one; news progmg 2 hrs wkly. Target aud: 25-49; upscale baby boomers; male skew. ■ David Meszaros, gen mgr; Mark Penneta, gen sls mgr; Cheryl Kiewit, natl sls mgr; Scott Keithley, prom mgr; Mike O'Connor, Mark Bradley (asst), progmg dirs; Marcia Shipley, news dir; Linda Neils, pub affrs dir; Dick Byrd, chief engr.

Augusta

***WACG-FM**—June 2, 1970: 90.7 mhz; 25 kw. Ant 400 ft. TL: N33 24 15 W81 50 19. Stereo. Augusta College (30904-2200). (706) 737-1661. FAX: (706) 737-1773. Licensee: Georgia Public Telecommunications Commission (acq 4-87). Net: APR, NPR. Format: Class. Target aud: 18 plus; upscale, professional, educated, affluent. ■ Alan Cooke, gen mgr.

WBBQ-FM—March 1955: 104.3 mhz; 100 kw. Ant 1,003 ft. TL: N33 36 41 W81 56 30. Stereo. Hrs opn: 24. Box 2066 (30903-2066). 1305 Geogia Ave., North Augusta, SC (29841). (803) 279-6610. FAX: (803) 279-0220. Licensee: Savannah Valley Broadcasting Co. Net: ABC/C. Rep: Eastman. Format: CHR, heavy local news. News staff 8; news progmg 7 hrs wkly. Target aud: General. ■ George G. Weiss, chmn; E. B. Florie, pres, gen mgr & gen sls mgr; Ken Freeman, vp & chief engr; Dick Shannon, prom mgr; Bruce Stevens, progmg dir & mus dir; Jim DeFontes, news dir. ■ Rates: $150; 125; 125; 50.

WBBQ(AM)—Jan 12, 1947: 1340 khz; 1 kw-U. TL: N33 27 46 W82 00 29. Hrs opn: 24. Dups FM 100%. ■ Rates: Same as FM.

WFAM(AM)—March 10, 1952: 1050 khz; 5 kw. TL: N33 27 21 W81 56 20. Hrs opn: 19. 552 Laney-Walker Ext. (30901). (706) 722-6077. FAX: (706) 722-7066. Licensee: Family Broadcasters Inc. (acq 5-1-86; $150,000; FTR 2-17-86). Net: USA. Format: Relg, southern gospel. News progmg 2 hrs wkly. Target aud: General. Spec prog: Sp one hr wkly. ■ J. R. McClure, pres; Rob McClure, gen mgr; Mark Woodard, stn mgr & progmg dir; Bob Halverson, gen sls mgr; Jim Cook, chief engr. ■ Rates: $8.50; 8; 8.50; 6.

WFXA-FM—July 11, 1968: 103.1 mhz; 3 kw. Ant 299 ft. TL: N33 30 00 W81 56 03. Stereo. Prog sep from AM. Box 1584 (30903). (803) 279-2330. FAX: (803) 279-8149. Licensee: Davis Broadcasting Inc. (Columbus) Net: ABC/FM. Format: Urban contemp. News staff one. ■ Greg Davis, pres; Bill Yeager, gen mgr; Richard Burkeen, gen sls mgr; Carroll Redd, progmg dir & news dir; Robert Taylor, mus dir; Walter Brumbeloe, chief engr.

WTHB(AM)—Co-owned with WFXA-FM. May 1960: 1550 khz; 5 kw-D. TL: N33 30 00 W81 56 03. Prog sep from FM. (Acq 7-24-92). Net: American Urban. Rep: Torbet. Format: News/talk.

WGAC(AM)—1940: 580 khz; 5 kw-D, 1 kw-N, DA-N. TL: N33 30 41 W82 04 44. Box 211045 (30917). (706) 863-5800. FAX: (706) 860-9343. Licensee: Beasley Broadcasting of Augusta Inc. (group owner; acq 5-19-92; assumption of debt; FTR 6-8-92). Net: CBS; Ga. Net. Rep: Rgnl Reps. Format: Sports, news, talk. News staff 2; news progmg 25 hrs wkly. Target aud: 35-65. Spec prog: Farm 4 hrs, military 3 hrs wkly. ■ Duane Hargrove, gen mgr; Austom Rhodes, progmg dir; Austin Rhodes, news dir; Earl Welsh, chief engr.

WGOR(FM)—See Martinez.

***WGPH(FM)**—(Vidalia). 1988: 91.5 mhz; 50 kw. Ant 387 ft. TL: N31 14 02 W82 28 52. Stereo. Hrs opn: 24. 3213 Huxley Dr., Augusta (30909-3128). (706) 733-8201. Licensee: Augusta Radio Fellowship. Net: Moody. Format: Christian. Target aud: General. ■ C. T. Barinowski, pres; Jim Screws, chief engr.

WGUS(AM)—(North Augusta, S.C). July 30, 1958: 1380 khz; 5 kw-D, 710 w-N, DA-2. TL: N33 29 17 W81 56 46. Hrs opn: 24. Building 200, Suite 105, 2743 Perimeter Pkwy., Augusta, GA (30909). (706) 855-4000. FAX: (706) 868-4440. Licensee: Benchmark Radio Acquisition Fund II L.P. (acq 10-27-93; $1.2 million with co-located FM; FTR 11-15-93). Net: ABC. Rep: Katz. Wash atty: Tom Schattenfield. Format: Country. News staff one; news progmg 7 hrs wkly. Target aud: 25-54; traditional country listeners. ■ David A. Trusty, gen mgr; Mary Liz Nolan, vp opns; Elizabeth O. Norris, sls dir; Jon Brewster, natl sls mgr; Lisa Bryant, prom mgr; John Patrick, progmg dir; Brian Ainsley, mus dir; Earl Welsh, chief engr.

WXFG(FM)—Co-owned with WGUS(AM). Nov 11, 1967: 102.3 mhz; 1.5 kw. Ant 666 ft. TL: N33 26 15 W82 05 27. Stereo. Hrs opn: 24. Prog sep from AM. Format: Contemp hit. Target aud: 18-44. ■ Kevin Barrett, progmg dir.

WKXC-FM—See Aiken, S.C.

WKZK(AM)—See North Augusta, S.C.

***WLPE(FM)**—Nov 17, 1984: 91.7 mhz; 1.35 kw. Ant 479 ft. TL: N33 36 42 W81 56 30. Stereo. Hrs opn: 24. 3213

Georgia

Huxley Dr. (30904). (706) 733-8201. Licensee: Augusta Radio Fellowship Institute Inc. Net: Moody. Format: Relg. ■ C. T. Barinowski, pres & chief engr.

WRDW(AM)—July 1930: 1480 khz; 5 kw-U, DA-N. TL: N33 31 02 W82 00 30. Stereo. 1480 Eisenhower Dr. (30904). (706) 667-8001. FAX: (706) 667-8001. Licensee: Advertisement Network Systems (acq 4-12-91; grpsl; FTR 5-6-91). Net: NBC, Natl Black. Rep: Katz & Powell. Format: Urban contemp. News staff one; news progmg 4 hrs wkly. Target aud: 18-49; well educated. ■ April Beard, gen mgr, progmg dir & mus dir; Lee Beard, gen sls mgr; Earl Welch, chief engr.

WRXR-FM—See Aiken, S.C.

WTHB(AM)—Listing follows WFXA-FM.

WXFG(FM)—Listing follows WGUS(AM).

WYFA(FM)—(Waynesboro). Aug 1, 1991: 107.1 mhz; 6 kw. Ant 328 ft. TL: N33 10 42 W81 59 24. Stereo. Hrs opn: 24. 1388 Old Wagnesboro Rd. (30830). (706) 554-3942. Licensee: Bible Broadcasting Network Inc. (group owner; acq 8-26-92; $225,000; FTR 9-21-92). Format: Relg. ■ John C. Lung, pres & gen sls mgr; Jason Padget, gen mgr; James Borrone, opns dir; Ken Ringgold, chief engr. ■ Rates: $35; 44; 35; 22.

WZNY(FM)—Mar 10, 1952: 105.7 mhz; 100 kw. Ant 1,168 ft. TL: N33 25 15 W81 50 19. Stereo. Hrs opn: 24. Bldg. 200, Suite 105, 2743 Perimeter Pkwy. (30909). (706) 855-4000. FAX: (706) 868-4440. Licensee: Benchmark Radio Acquisition Fund II. Group owner: Benchmark Communications Radio (acq 8-7-91; $4.6 million). Net: AP, Unistar, ABC. Rep: Torbet. Format: Adult contemp. News staff one; news progmg 3 hrs wkly. Target aud: 25-54. ■ Joe Mathias, pres; David A. Trusty, gen mgr; John Patrick, opns dir & progmg dir; Eugene Chambers, gen sls mgr; Jon Brewster, natl sls mgr; Lisa Bryant, prom dir; Mary Liz Nolan, news dir; Earl Welsh, chief engr. ■ Rates: $70; 56; 62; 25.

Austell

WAOS(AM)—Apr 16, 1968: 1600 khz; 5 kw-D. TL: N33 48 34 W84 39 25. Box 746, 5815 Westside Rd. (30001). (404) 944-6684. FAX: (404) 944-9794. Licensee: La Favorita Inc. (acq 1-24-90). Net: CRC. Rep: Caballero. Format: Sp. News progmg 2 hrs wkly. Target aud: 18 plus; Hispanics in metro Atlanta & northeast Ga. ■ Samuel Zamarron, pres, gen mgr & progmg dir; Garciela Zamarron, gen sls mgr & prom mgr; Aubrey Smith, news dir; Bill Loudermilk, chief engr.

WXEM(AM)—(Buford). Dec 12, 1957: 1460 khz; 5 kw-D. TL: N34 07 15 W83 58 35. Box 746, Austell-Atlanta (30001). (404) 944-0900. FAX: (404) 944-9794. Licensee: La Favorita Inc. (acq 6-12-91; $120,000; FTR 7-1-91). Format: Spanish. News progmg 12 hrs wkly. Target aud: Hispanic. ■ Samuel Zamarron, pres, gen mgr, prom mgr, progmg dir & mus dir; Garciela Zamarron, gen sls mgr; John Moore, chief engr.

Bainbridge

WJAD(FM)—Dec 20, 1967: 97.3 mhz; 100 kw. Ant 1,200 ft. TL: N31 09 12 W84 32 42. Hrs opn: 24. Box 706, 1609 Shotwell St. (31717). (912) 246-1650. FAX: (912) 248-0975. Licensee: Sabre Communications Inc. (acq 6-11-93; $1.175 million with co-located AM; FTR 6-28-93). Net: ABC/C. Rep: Banner. Format: Adult contemp. Target aud: 18-49. ■ Tom Love, gen mgr; Jan Whitaker, sls dir; John Dawson, progmg dir & mus dir; Clyde Scott, chief engr. ■ Rates: $39; 37; 39; 34.

WMGR(AM)—Co-owned with WJAD(FM). Aug 17, 1947: 930 khz; 5 kw-D, 500 w-N. TL: N30 54 25 W84 33 02. Hrs opn: 18. Prog sep from FM. Net: ABC/I. Format: Oldies, news/talk. Target aud: 30 plus. Spec prog: Sports 15 hrs wkly. ■ Walt Hardy, gen sls mgr.

Barnesville

WBAF(AM)—July 23, 1966: 1090 khz; 1 kw-D. TL: N33 03 13 W84 08 07. 645 Forsyth St. (30204). (404) 358-1090. Licensee: Barnesville Broadcasting Inc. Net: NBC; Ga. Net. Wash atty: Reddy, Begley & Martin. Format: C&W, relg. News progmg 7 hrs wkly. Spec prog: Local 5 hrs wkly. ■ Charles Waters, pres, gen mgr, gen sls mgr & prom mgr; Ken Green, progmg dir & news dir; Gene Ray, mus dir & chief engr. ■ Rates: $4; 4; 4; na.

Baxley

WUFE(AM)—December 1954: 1260 khz; 5 kw-D TL: N31 48 00 W82 24 40. Hrs opn: 6 AM-sunset. Box 389 (31513). (912) 367-3000. FAX: (912) 367-9779. Licensee: South Georgia Broadcasters (acq 1-19-82; $240,000; FTR 2-8-82). Net: ABC/E. Wash atty: Fletcher, Heald & Hildreth. Format: Relg. News staff one; news progmg 10 hrs wkly. Target aud: General. ■ Al Graham, pres, progmg dir & pub affrs dir; Peggy C. Miles, gen mgr, gen sls mgr & prom mgr; Brack Haynes, news dir; Larry D. Ring, chief engr. ■ Rates: $5.50; 5.50; 5.50; na.

WBYZ(FM)—Co-owned with WUFE(AM). July 1983: 94.5 mhz; 100 kw. Ant 1,014 ft. TL: N31 47 10 W82 27 03. Stereo. Net: ABC/I. Format: Country. Target aud: 20-55; those with buying power. ■ Peggy C. Miles, adv mgr; J.D. Graham, mus dir. ■ Rates: $9.50; 9.50; 9.50; 9.50.

Blackshear

WGIA(AM)—March 10, 1961: 1350 khz; 5 kw-D. TL: N31 18 44 W82 14 00. Drawer 619, 245 E. Main St. (31516). (912) 449-3442. FAX: (912) 449-1266. Licensee: Christian Media Network Inc. (acq 7-18-87). Net: USA, CBN. Rep: William Cook Adv. Format: Contemp Christian. News staff one; news progmg one hr wkly. Target aud: General; families. Spec prog: Black 10 hrs, farm 10 hrs wkly. ■ Joe Chalk, pres, gen mgr & progmg dir; Clay B. Miller, stn mgr & mus dir; James McKinnen, sls dir.

WKUB(FM)—Dec 1, 1979: 105.1 mhz; 25 kw. Ant 308 ft. TL: N31 15 49 W82 17 30. Stereo. Hrs opn: 24. Box 112, Highway 84 W. (31516); Box 1472, Waycross (31502). (912) 449-3391. FAX: (912) 449-6284. Licensee: Mattox-Guest Broadcasting Inc. (group owner). Net: SMN; Ga. Net. Rep: Dora-Clayton. Wash atty: Pepper & Corazzini. Format: Country. News progmg 4 hrs wkly. Target aud: 25 plus. ■ G. Troy Mattox, pres, gen mgr & chief engr; Jim Miller, gen sls mgr; Ray Williamson, progmg dir. ■ Rates: $11; 11; 11; na.

Blakely

WBBK(AM)—Oct 22, 1959: 1260 khz; 1 kw-D. TL: N31 21 11 W84 56 50. Stn currently dark. c/o WCEH(AM)-WQSY(FM), Box 489, Hawkinsville (31036). (912) 892-9061. FAX: (912) 892-9063. Licensee: Jerry D. Braswell (acq 1-30-91; $120,000 with co-located FM; FTR 2-18-91). ■ Jay Braswell, gen mgr.

WBBK-FM—November 1984: 93.5 mhz; 3 kw. Ant 328 ft. TL: N31 20 03 W84 50 21. Stereo. Stn currently dark.

Blue Ridge

WPPL(FM)—1971: 103.9 mhz; 3 kw. Ant 300 ft. TL: N34 52 02 W84 20 03 (CP: 6 kw, ant 256 ft.). Box 938 (30513). (706) 632-9775. FAX: (706) 632-5922. Licensee: Fannin County Broadcasting Co. Net: Ga. Net. Format: Country. ■ Robert P. Schwab, Sr., pres & gen sls mgr; Barry Newman, gen mgr, progmg dir & mus dir; Kenneth Ferguson, chief engr.

Bolingbroke

WDBS(FM)—Not on air, target date unknown: 102.1 mhz; 3 kw. Ant 328 ft. Box 300 (31004). Licensee: Joseph I. Kendrick.

Boston

WTUF(FM)—July 18, 1988: 106.3 mhz; 3 kw. Ant 328 ft. TL: N30 47 40 W83 46 54 (CP: 2.4 kw, ant 495 ft., TL: N30 49 05 W83 40 35). Stereo. Hrs opn: 6 AM-midnight. Box 129, Thomasville (31799). (912) 225-1063. Licensee: Boston Radio Co. Rep: Rgnl Reps. Format: Town & Country 25 plus, 75% classic country. Target aud: 18-65. Spec prog: Gospel 7 hr wkly. ■ Len Robinson, pres & gen mgr; Richard Harris, opns mgr, sls dir & chief engr; Gary Stevens, progmg dir & mus dir.

Bostwick

WMOQ(FM)—Not on air, target date unknown: 92.3 mhz; 3 kw. Ant 328 ft. 1081 N. Cherokee Rd., Social Circle (30275). Licensee: Bostwick Broadcasting Group Partners.

Bremen

WGMI(AM)—October 1957: 1440 khz; 2.5 kw-D. TL: N33 42 56 W85 09 34. Hrs opn: 24. 613 Tallapoosa St. (30110). (706) 537-0840. Licensee: Winfred Garner Ministries Inc. (acq 11-10-93; $150,000; FTR 11-29-93). Wash atty: Christopher Smallwood. Format: Relg, Southern gospel. News staff one; news progmg varies. Target aud: General. ■ Horace Garner, stn mgr; Scott Garner, progmg dir. ■ Rates: $5; 5; 5; na.

Broxton

WULS(FM)—Not on air, target date unknown: 103.7 mhz; 6 kw. Ant 328 ft. TL: N31 33 26 W82 52 10. Licensee: Roundtree-Carver Enterprises.

Brunswick

WBGA(FM)—(Waycross). Oct 10, 1971: 102.5 mhz; 100 kw. Ant 980 ft. TL: N31 09 13 W81 58 00. Stereo. Hrs opn: 24. 253 Hwy. 82, Brunswick (31525). (912) 267-1025. FAX: (912) 264-5462. Licensee: Rowland Radio Inc. Group owner: Rowland Family Radio (acq 1986; $800,000). Net: NBC. Rep: Roslin. Wash atty: Gary Smithwick. Format: Country. Target aud: 25-54. ■ Marty Rowland, pres, vp & stn mgr; Jim Squires, gen sls mgr; Jim Scott, progmg dir & mus dir; Dick Boekeloo, chief engr. ■ Rates: $16; 12; 16; 9.

WBYB(FM)—Nov 8, 1965: 100.7 mhz; 36 kw. Ant 1,463 ft. TL: N30 49 17 W81 44 13. Stereo. Hrs opn: 24. Suite 612, 435 Clark Rd., Jacksonville, FL (32218). (904) 776-0884; (912) 638-8420. FAX: (904) 764-6560. Licensee: Nelson Broadcasting Corp. Group owner: Osborn Communications Corp. Net: USA. Wash atty: Haley, Bader & Potts. Format: Contemp Christian, talk. Target aud: 29-54; women. ■ Rebecca Langlois, gen mgr; Mike Stevens, progmg dir, mus dir & pub affrs dir; Robert Dillehay, chief engr. ■ Rates: $30; 30; 30; 30.

WGIG(AM)—March 5, 1949: 1440 khz; 5 kw-D, 1 kw-N, DA-N. TL: N31 10 07 W81 32 14. 117 Marina Dr., St. Simons Island (31522). (912) 634-0674. FAX: (912) 634-6037. Licensee: Stewart Broadcasting Corp. Net: CBS; Ga. Net. Format: News/talk, sports. News staff one. ■ Wayne Stewart, vp; Judy Stewart, stn mgr; John Gregory, progmg dir.

WHFX(FM)—(Waycross). June 3, 1972: 103.3 mhz; 100 kw. Ant 1,100 ft. TL: N31 15 42 W82 19 26 (CP: TL: N31 09 22 W81 58 19). Stereo. Box 430, Brunswick (31521); Suite 150, 120 Darien Hwy., Brunswick (31525). (912) 264-1033. FAX: (912) 264-1033. Licensee: Teletronics Inc. Format: Adult contemp. Target aud: 25-54. ■ James Rivers, gen mgr & gen sls mgr; Doug Hayden, progmg dir & mus dir. ■ Rates: $18; 15; 18; 10.

WHJX-FM—Licensed to Brunswick. See Jacksonville, Fla.

WMOG(AM)—June 1940: 1490 khz; 1 kw-U. TL: N31 09 55 W81 28 28 (CP: 600 w-U, TL: N31 09 42 W81 28 28). Box 100, 4 Torras Causeway (31521). (912) 265-5980. FAX: (912) 265-3661. Licensee: Lee M. Mitchell (acq 1-28-92; with co-located FM). Net: ABC/I. Rep: Roslin. Format: MOR, news/talk. News staff 3; news progmg 20 hrs wkly. Target aud: 35 plus. Spec prog: Black 8 hrs, class one hr wkly. ■ Alexander "Sandy" Tharpe, gen mgr; Julie Andrew, gen sls mgr; Collins Knighton, progmg dir & mus dir; Dick Boekeloo, chief engr. ■ Rates: $21; 11; 14; 8.

WMOG-FM—(St. Simons Island). Jan 1, 1990: 92.7 mhz; 6 kw. Ant 340 ft. TL: N31 09 55 W81 28 28. Stereo. Hrs opn: 24. Prog sep from AM. Net: Unistar. Format: Adult contemp. Target aud: 24-45. ■ Rates: $18; 14; 17; 8.

WPIQ(AM)—Sept 1, 1966: 790 khz; 500 w-D, 115 w-N, DA-2. TL: N31 08 40 W81 34 56. 7515 Hwy. 303 (31525). (912) 264-9977. FAX: (912) 264-9991. Licensee: Eagle Broadcasting Inc. Net: USA. Format: Inspirational Christian. ■ Larry Dean Hickerson, gen mgr.

WSEG(FM)—Not on air, target date unknown: 104.1 mhz; 6 kw. Ant 328 ft. 612 King Cotton Row (31525). Licensee: CGB Inc.

***WWIO(FM)**—Feb 28, 1993: 89.1 mhz; 7 kw. Ant 135 ft. TL: N31 11 19 W81 28 10. 1540 Stewart Ave. S.W. Atlanta (30310). (404) 756-4730. FAX: (404) 756-4088. Licensee: Georgia Public Telecommunication Commission. Net: NPR. ■ Susan Westfall, stn mgr.

WYNR(FM)—See Darien.

Buford

WLKQ(FM)—Jan 1, 1970: 102.3 mhz; 3.3 kw. Ant 400 ft. TL: N34 07 15 W83 58 35. Stereo. Hrs opn: 24. Box 48465, Atlanta (30362). (404) 932-1102. FAX: (404) 932-0988. Licensee: Lake Radio Inc. (acq 5-21-87). Net: MBS; Ga. Net. Wash atty: Kenkel & Associates. Format: Oldies. News staff 2; news progmg 6 hrs wkly. Target aud: 35-54; upper-middle class professionals. ■ Robert P. Joseph, pres; Al Garner, rgnl sls mgr; Mark Joseph, progmg dir & mus dir; John Moore, engrg dir. ■ Rates: $26; 21; 24; 14.

WXEM(AM)—Licensed to Buford. See Austell.

Byron

***WPWB(FM)**—1988: 90.5 mhz; 16.5 kw. Ant 453 ft. TL: N32 40 56 W83 22 11. Stereo. 3213 Huxley Dr., Augusta (30909). (706) 733-8201. Licensee: Augusta Radio Fellowship Institute Inc. Net: Moody. Format: Christian. ■ C. T. Barinowski, pres.

Cairo

WGRA(AM)—October 1949: 790 khz; 1 kw-D. TL: N30 54 08 W84 14 03. Box 120, U.S. 84 W. (31728). (912) 377-4392. Licensee: Lovett Broadcasting Enterprises Inc. (acq 1-84; $450,000; FTR 4-23-84). Net: NBC; Ga. Net. Rep: Rgnl Reps. Format: Country, gospel. News staff 3; news progmg 12 hrs wkly. Target aud: 30 plus; mainly women. Spec prog: Black 6 hrs wkly. ■ Wendell Lovett, pres & gen mgr; Jeffery Lovett, stn mgr, opns mgr, progmg dir, mus dir & news dir; Jerry White, vp sls; Valerie Bomar, vp mktg; Jenny Rouse, vp prom; Jim Ravencraft, chief engr. ■ Rates: $8; 7.50; 7.00; na.

WSLE(FM)—Co-owned with WGRA(AM). June 1983: 102.3 mhz; 3 kw. Ant 300 ft. TL: N30 56 49 W84 08 07. Stereo. Prog sep from AM. (912) 228-4970. (Acq 4-9-91; $510,000; FTR 4-29-91). Format: Adult contemp. News staff one; news progmg 15 hrs wkly. Target aud: 35 plus. ■ Jeff Lovett, pres. ■ Rates: $7; 6.50; 6.75; 6.

Calhoun

WEBS(AM)—Nov 1, 1966: 1110 khz; 250 w-D. TL: N34 29 15 W84 55 00. Box 1299, 427 S. Wall St. (30703). (706) 629-2238. FAX: (706) 629-7092. Licensee: Radio WEBS Inc. (acq 7-1-80). Net: NBC, Unistar. Format: Oldies, adult contemp. News staff one. Target aud: 18-52. Spec prog: Black 2 hrs wkly. ■ Ken D. Payne, pres, gen mgr, gen sls mgr & news dir; Carolyn Glaze, opns mgr; Kevin Casey, progmg & mus dir; Phil Baker, chief engr. ■ Rates: $10; 9.50; 10; na.

WJTH(AM)—June 16, 1977: 900 khz; 1 kw-D, 266 w-N. TL: N34 27 40 W84 53 44. Hrs opn: 6 AM-10 PM. Box 1119, 329 Richardson Rd. S.E. (30701). (706) 629-6397. FAX: (706) 629-8463. Licensee: Cherokee Broadcasting Co. Net: ABC/I; Ga. Net. Rep: Rgnl Reps. Format: C&W, loc news & info. News staff 2; news progmg 4 hrs wkly. Target aud: General. Spec prog: Farm one hr, gospel 2 hrs, urban 16 hrs wkly. ■ Sam Thomas, gen mgr; Keith Thomas, stn mgr, progmg dir, mus dir & news dir; Helen Jane McDonald, gen sls mgr; Philip M. Baker, chief engr. ■ Rates: $11; 10; 11; 8.

Camilla

WQVE(FM)—April 1977: 105.5 mhz; 6 kw. Ant 300 ft. TL: N31 18 51 W84 12 18. Stereo. Hrs opn: 24. Box 434, U.S. 19 S. (31730). (912) 294-0010. FAX: (912) 294-0010. Licensee: Mitchell Broadcasting Inc. (acq 10-87). Net: Ga. Net. Rep: Rgnl Reps. Format: Urban contemp. Spec prog: Farm 10 hrs, Gospel 8 hrs wkly. ■ Ron Allen, gen mgr & progmg mgr; Jimmy Rogers, chief engr.

Canton

WGST-FM—Aug 1, 1964: 105.7 mhz; 50 kw. Ant 492 ft. TL: N34 16 06 W84 29 50. Stereo. Hrs opn: 24. Box 231 (30114). (404) 233-0640; (404) 524-5316. FAX: (404) 237-5856. Licensee: Cherokee Broadcasting Co. Inc. Group owner: McClure Broadcasting. Net: ABC/D. Format: C&W. Target aud: 25-54; Atlanta. ■ Bob Houghton, gen mgr; Eric Feidel, progmg dir; Mike Lawing, chief engr.

WCHK(AM)—Co-owned with WGST-FM. April 11, 1957: 1290 khz; 5 kw-D, 500 w-N, DA-N. TL: N34 15 08 W84 27 49. Box 1290 (30114). Net: Ga. Net. Format: News/talk, gospel. News staff 2; news progmg 35 hrs wkly. Target aud: 35 plus; residents of Cherokee and Pickens counties. ■ Byron L. Dobbs, pres & pub affrs dir; Bob Potter, mktg mgr, prom mgr & adv prog dir; Jon Gresham, progmg mgr, mus dir & news dir.

Carrollton

WBTR-FM—1964: 92.1 mhz; 580 w. Ant 635 ft. TL: N33 33 54 W85 01 02. Stereo. Box 569 (30117). (706) 832-9685. FAX: (706) 832-9686. Licensee: Carroll County Media Inc. (acq 6-93; $950,000; FTR 4-26-93). Net: Ga. Net. Format: Country. News staff one; news progmg 3 hrs wkly. Target aud: 25-49. Spec prog: Black 5 hrs wkly. ■ Jim Martin, vp & gen mgr; Jeff Davis, progmg dir.

WLBB(AM)—Jan 7, 1947: 1100 khz; 1 kw-D. TL: N33 36 34 W85 05 13. Hrs opn: Sunrise-sunset. Box 890, 1558 Hwy. 27 N. (30117). (404) 832-7041. FAX: (404) 832-2593. Licensee: West Georgia Broadcasting Inc. (acq 8-19-81). Format: Contemp country. News staff one; news progmg 8 hrs wkly. Target aud: 35 plus; mature audience. Spec prog: Farm one hr, relg 12 hrs wkly. ■ Leonard "Kip" Carter, pres; Jack Witcher, vp; Mary Ann Myers, opns mgr; Mitch Gray, mus dir; Ken Childs, news dir; Mike Mallory, chief engr. ■ Rates: $11; 11; 11; na.

WPPI(AM)—Nov 19, 1975: 1330 khz; 500 w-D. TL: N33 34 17 W85 03 02. Box 710 (30117). (706) 832-1330. Licensee: Radio Carrollton (acq 6-30-76). Net: NBC. Format: Country. ■ Bill Johnson, pres; Gordon Staples, gen mgr & gen sls mgr; Kevin Sanders, progmg dir & mus dir; Tom Kocourek, chief engr.

***WWGC(FM)**—Feb 19, 1973: 90.7 mhz; 500 w. Ant 494 ft. TL: N33 33 50 W85 01 04. Stereo. Hrs opn: 18. West Georgia College (30118). (706) 836-6731; (706) 836-6732. Licensee: West Georgia College. Format: Div. Target aud: General; students and area residents. Spec prog: Black 6 hrs, class 5 hrs, jazz 6 hrs, news/talk one hr wkly. ■ Rhett Turnipseed, gen mgr & progmg dir; Trevor Head, opns mgr; Kyle Berry, mus dir; Chris Cochran, news dir; Michael Mallory, chief engr.

Cartersville

WBHF(AM)—July 17, 1946: 1450 khz; 1 kw-U. TL: N34 09 31 W84 48 45. Box 190 (30120). (404) 382-3000. FAX: (404) 387-1248. Licensee: Frier Broadcasting Co. (acq 1972). Net: MBS. Format: Top-40. ■ Lee Burger, gen mgr & progmg dir; Seth Hopkins, news dir; Phil Baker, chief engr.

***WCCV(FM)**—Jan 24, 1983: 91.7 mhz; 910 w. Ant 537 ft. TL: N34 11 35 W84 45 31. Stereo. Box 1000 (30120-1000). (404) 387-0917. Licensee: Immanuel Educational Broadcasting Inc. Format: Relg. ■ Ed Tuten, pres & gen mgr; Jane Tuten, vp & opns mgr; Denise Barnette, mus dir; Chris Clayton, chief engr.

WYXC(AM)—Sept 21, 1961: 1270 khz; 500 w-U. TL: N34 12 34 W84 47 49. 1410 Hwy. 411 N.E. (30120). (404) 382-1270. FAX: (404) 386-7350. Licensee: Empire Radio Ltd. (acq 4-1-81; $242,000; FTR 5-4-81). Net: CBS. Format: Country. News staff one; news progmg 8 hrs wkly. Target aud: 25-55. Spec prog: Farm 5 hrs, Black 2 hrs wkly. ■ Julia N. Frew, pres & gen mgr; John P. Frew, chief engr. ■ Rates: $7; 7; 7; 7.

Cedartown

WGAA(AM)—1941: 1340 khz; 1 kw-U. TL: N34 02 06 W85 15 04. Box 167 (30125); 413 Lakeview Dr. (30125). (404) 748-1340. Licensee: Broadcast South Inc. (acq 10-86; $460,000; FTR 8-25-86). Net: NBC; Ga. Net. Wash atty: Dows, Lohnes & Albertson. Format: Country. News staff one; news progmg 5 hrs wkly. Target aud: General. Spec prog: College football, farm 2 hrs wkly. ■ Connie Thumma, gen mgr, gen sls mgr, progmg dir & mus dir; Jennifer Leifheit, news dir & pub affrs dir.

***WJCK(FM)**—Not on air, target date unknown: 88.3 mhz; 6 kw. Ant 328 ft. TL: N34 04 11 W85 14 48. Box 1000, Cartersville (30120-1000). Licensee: Immanuel Educational Broadcasting Inc. Format: Relg. ■ Ed Tuten, pres & gen mgr; Jane Tuten, vp & opns mgr; Denise Barnette, mus dir; Chris Clayton, chief engr.

Chatsworth

WQMT(FM)—Nov 13, 1976: 98.9 mhz; 3 kw. Ant 299 ft. TL: N34 45 29 W84 43 59 (CP: 950 w, ant 813 ft., TL: N34 44 34 W84 42 46). Hrs opn: 24. Box 808, 716 S. Thorton Ave., Dalton (30722-0808). (706) 278-9950. FAX: (706) 272-7966. Licensee: Cohutta Broadcasting Co. Inc. Net: ABC/I, Motor Racing Net; Ga. Net. Format: Country. News staff one. Target aud: General. ■ Annice Trevitt, pres; Paul Fink, gen mgr; Paul Roberts, opns mgr; Steve Sommers, mus dir; Janine Ellison, news dir; Phil Baker, chief engr.

Chauncey

WQIL(FM)—Not on air, target date unknown: 101.3 khz; 50 kw. Ant 492 ft. TL: N32 21 37 W83 08 28. Box 157, Eastman (31023). Licensee: Chauncey Broadcasting Inc.

Clarkesville

WCHM(AM)—December 1989: 1490 khz; 1 kw-U. TL: N34 36 27 W83 32 15. Hrs opn: 6 AM-midnight. Box 468, W. Waters St. (30523). (706) 754-6272. FAX: (706) 754-8621. Licensee: Joshua Communications Inc. (acq 6-10-92; $90,000; FTR 6-29-92). Net: NBC. Wash atty: Chris Reynolds. Format: News/talk, information. News staff one; news progmg 12 hrs wkly. Target aud: 40 plus. Spec prog: Gospel, relg 5 hrs wkly. ■ Scott Mote, pres, gen mgr, gen sls mgr, progmg dir & chief engr; Bill Knowles, news dir & pub affrs dir. ■ Rates: $7; 6; 7; 6.

WMJE(FM)—1989: 102.9 mhz; 16 kw. Ant 413 ft. TL: N34 29 05 W83 38 24. Stereo. Hrs opn: 24. Box 10, 1102 Thompson Bridge Rd., Gainesville (30503). (706) 532-9921. FAX: (404) 532-0506. Licensee:

WDUN Radio Inc. (acq 3-19-92). Net: AP, Unistar. Format: Soft hits. Target aud: 25-54; females with a median age of 41. ■ John W. Jacobs III, pres; Joel Williams, opns mgr; Jean Pethel, gen sls mgr; Bill Maine, progmg dir; Gary Smith, chief engr. ■ Rates: $10; 7; 8; 5.

Claxton

WCLA(AM)—July 20, 1958: 1470 khz; 1 kw-D, 260 w-N. TL: N32 10 12 W81 53 56. Hrs opn: 6 AM-11 PM. Box 427, 316 N. River St. (30417). (912) 739-3035. FAX: (912) 739-0050. Licensee: The Evans County Broadcasting Co. Net: SMN; Ga. Net. Rep: Rgnl Reps. Format: Country. ■ W. Don Sports, pres & chief engr. ■ Rates: $6; 6; 6; na.

WCLA-FM—Sept 15, 1972: 107.1 mhz; 3 kw. Ant 195 ft. TL: N32 10 12 W81 53 56 (CP: 107.3 mhz, 25 kw, ant 328 ft., TL: N32 10 01 W81 54 07). Stereo. Dups AM 100%. ■ Rates: Same as AM.

Clayton

WGHC(AM)—June 28, 1961: 1370 khz; 2.5 kw-D. TL: N34 51 41 W83 24 25. Box 1149 (30525). (706) 782-4251. Licensee: Richard J. Turner Jr. (acq 8-90; FTR 8-27-90). Net: AP, UPI; Ga. Net. Format: Gospel. ■ Dr. Richard J. Turner, pres & gen mgr; Jan Lundsford, progmg dir; Jan Lunsford, mus dir; Larry Smith, news dir; Dan Davis, chief engr.

WQXJ(FM)—Co-owned with WGHC(AM). 1989: 104.1 mhz; 480 w. Ant 817 ft. TL: N34 52 23 W83 22 35. Prog sep from AM. (706) 782-6816. Format: Lite adult contemp.

Cleveland

WCGX(FM)—1989: 101.9 mhz; 6 kw. Ant 410 ft. TL: N34 33 49 W83 38 26. Stereo. 340 Jesse Jewel Pkwy., Gainesville (30501); Box 1318, Gainesville (30503). (404) 536-8003. FAX: (404) 534-2614. Licensee: Allied Media of Georgia (acq 6-27-91; grpsl; FTR 7-15-91). Net: CBS. Format: Adult contemp, oldies. News staff 4; news progmg one hr wkly. Target aud: 21-48. ■ Rates: $24; 22; 24; 20.

WRWH(AM)—Sept 27, 1958: 1350 khz; 1 kw-D. TL: N34 35 11 W83 46 01. Hrs opn: 6 AM-sunset. Box 181, Hood St. (30528). (706) 865-3181. FAX: (706) 865-0421. Licensee: Newsic Inc. (acq 5-17-89). Net: NBC; Ga. Net. Wash atty: Reddy, Begley & Martin. Format: Country, gospel. Target aud: 35 plus. ■ Dean Dyer, pres, gen mgr, gen sls mgr, progmg dir & news dir; Bonnie Dyer, prom mgr & mus dir; Bob Bierman, chief engr. ■ Rates: $8.95; 8.75; 8.95; na.

Cochran

***WDCO-FM**—Feb 4, 1985: 89.7 mhz; 100 kw. Ant 1,010 ft. TL: N32 28 11 W83 15 17. Stereo. Hrs opn: 18. 1540 Stewart Ave. S.W., Atlanta (30310). (912) 934-2220. FAX: (912) 934-2250. Licensee: Georgia Public Telecommunications Commission. Net: NPR, APR. Format: Class, jazz, news/talk. ■ Richard E. Cramer, opns mgr; Richard Augusta, mktg mgr; Edith Bonde, prom mgr; Norman Bemelmans, progmg mgr; Anna Marie Hartman, pub affrs dir; Al Korn, chief engr.

WVMG(AM)—July 4, 1965: 1440 khz; 1 kw-D. TL: N32 24 43 W83 21 42. Box 570 (31014). (912) 934-4548. Licensee: Heartland Broadcasting Co. Inc., trustee in bankruptcy (acq 7-17-87). Format: Country. ■ Charlie Hill, pres & gen mgr; Martha Sharer, gen sls mgr; Jim Simmons, chief engr.

WVMG-FM—July 4, 1968: 96.7 mhz; 3 kw. Ant 319 ft. TL: N32 24 43 W83 21 42. Stereo. Prog sep from AM. Format: Country, relg.

Columbus

WCGQ(FM)—Listing follows WRCG(AM).

WEAM(AM)—December 1954: 1580 khz; 2.3 kw-D, 1 kw-N, DA-N. TL: N32 27 55 W85 01 22. Hrs opn: 20. Box 766 (31902); 1714 E. 280 Bypass, Phenix City, AL (36867). (205) 298-1590; (205) 298-1580. FAX: (205) 298-7800. Licensee: Muscogee Broadcasting. Group owner: GHB Radio Group (acq 1980). Net: USA. Wash atty: Reddy, Begley & Martin. Format: Black relg. Target aud: General. Spec prog: Jazz one hr wkly. ■ George H. Buck Jr., pres, gen mgr & gen sls mgr; Angel Anderson, progmg dir; Tom Jones, chief engr.

***WFRC(FM)**—June 14, 1985: 90.5 mhz; 8.5 kw. Ant 248 ft. TL: N32 27 37 W85 00 30. Stereo. 1010 7th Place, Phenix City, AL (36867). (205) 291-0399. Licensee: Family Stations Inc. (group owner). Format: Relg. Spec prog: Call-in 8 hrs wkly. ■ Harold Camping, pres; James Copp, stn mgr.

WFXE(FM)—Listing follows WOKS(AM).

WGSY(FM)—(Phenix City, Ala). March 4, 1971: 100.1 mhz; 6 kw. Ant 328 ft. TL: N32 30 42 W85 00 41. Stereo. Box 2127, 1015 Peachtree Dr., Columbus, GA (31902). (404) 327-9955. Licensee: Ken Woodfin. Group owner: The Woodfin Group (acq 11-86; $1,635,000). Rep: Torbet. Wash atty: Miller & Fields. Format: Adult contemp. News staff one. Target aud: 25-54; women, 30-44. ■ Ken Woodfin, CEO & chmn; David McManus, vp opns & progmg dir; Jan Plemmons, sls dir; Jan Woodfin-Drew, prom mgr; David Nolan, mus dir; Frank McLemore, vp engrg. ■ Rates: $50; 45; 45; 30.

WHYD(AM)—1947: 1270 khz; 5 kw-D. TL: N32 26 16 W85 01 10. Hrs opn: 17. Box 1704 (31902); Box 1804, 5th St. S., Phenix City, AL (36869). FAX: (205) 297-4485. Licensee: CLW Communications Group Inc. (group owner; acq 1-4-77). ■ Spiros Zodhiates, pres.

***WJSP-FM**—See Atlanta.

WOKS(AM)—March 2, 1959: 1340 khz; 1 kw-U. TL: N32 27 07 W84 58 25. Box 1998 (31902-1998). (706) 576-3565. FAX: (706) 576-3683. Licensee: Davis Broadcasting Inc. (Columbus) (acq 7-24-92). Net: American Urban, Natl Black. Rep: Katz. Format: Black. News staff one. ■ Gregory Davis, pres & gen mgr; Phillip March, progmg dir; Pat Key, news dir.

WFXE(FM)—Co-owned with WOKS(AM). Sept 22, 1969: 104.9 mhz; 6 kw. Ant 289 ft. TL: N32 27 37 W85 00 30. Stereo. Prog sep from AM. Net: ABC/FM. Format: Urban contemp.

WPNX(AM)—(Phenix City, Ala). 1951: 1460 khz; 5 kw-D, 1 kw-N, DA-N. TL: N32 29 50 W85 00 20. Stereo. 1826 Wynnton Rd., Columbus, GA (31906); Box 687 (31902). (706) 576-3000. FAX: (706) 576-3010. Licensee: JRM Broadcasting Inc. (acq 12-7-85; $300,000; FTR 1-7-85). Net: SMN. Rep: McGavren Guild. Format: Oldies. News staff 3; news progmg 3 hrs wkly. Target aud: 25 plus. ■ Jim Martin, pres & gen mgr; Jerry Northington, gen sls mgr; Frank McLemore, chief engr.

WVRK(FM)—Co-owned with WPNX(AM). Nov 16, 1946: 102.9 mhz; 100 kw. Ant 1,521 ft. TL: N32 19 25 W84 46 46. Stereo. Prog sep from AM. Licensee: M&M Partnership (acq 5-31-86; $3,250,000; FTR 4-7-86). Net: Unistar, ABC/R. Format: AOR. News progmg 2 hrs wkly. ■ Brad Hardin, progmg dir; Dean Grindle, mus dir.

WRCG(AM)—May 10, 1928: 1420 khz; 5 kw-U, DA-N. TL: N32 29 52 W85 02 48. Box 1537 (31902-1537). (706) 324-0338. FAX: (706) 396-4600. Licensee: WGBA Inc. Group owner: McClure Broadcasting (acq 1-1-77). Net: CBS, ABC/I. Rep: Christal. Format: Big band, MOR, news/talk. Spec prog: Farm 3 hrs wkly. ■ C.A. McClure, pres; Joe McClure, gen mgr; Fran Malphrus, gen sls mgr; Scott Miller, progmg dir; Doug Kellett, news dir; Charlie Harrell, chief engr.

WCGQ(FM)—Co-owned with WRCG(AM). July 15, 1966: 107.3 mhz; 100 kw. Ant 1,011 ft. TL: N32 27 59 W85 03 23. Stereo. (706) 327-1217. Net: ABC/C. Format: Top-40. ■ Lee McCard, progmg dir.

WSTH(AM)—August 1940: 540 khz; 5 kw-D, 500 w-N, DA-N. TL: N32 27 08 W85 03 18. Stereo. Box 1640 (31902); 1236 Broadway St. (31901). (706) 596-5100. FAX: (706) 596-5115. Licensee: Solar Broadcasting Co. Inc. Net: ABC/E, NBC. Rep: McGavren Guild. Wash atty: Michael Bader. Format: Southern Gospel. News progmg 5 hrs wkly. Target aud: 25-54. ■ Allen Woodall, pres; Bonnie Woodall, vp; Jerry Katz, gen mgr & opns mgr; Ed Papie, gen sls mgr & prom mgr; Johnny O, progmg dir; Al "Bubba" Jeffreys, mus dir; Kristie Lee, news dir; John Simmons, chief engr.

WSTH-FM—See Alexander City, Ala.

***WTJB(FM)**—Dec 15, 1984: 91.7 mhz; 30 kw. Ant 300 ft. TL: N32 27 28 W84 53 08. Stereo. Hrs opn: 6 AM-midnight. Wallace Hall, Troy State Univ., Troy, AL (36082). (205) 670-3268. FAX: (205) 670-3272. Licensee: Troy State Univ. Net: NPR, APR. Format: Class, jazz, news. News progmg 25 plus hrs wkly. Target aud: General. Spec prog: Jazz 5 hrs wkly. ■ John McVay, gen mgr, progmg mgr & mus dir; Steve Holmes, opns mgr & news dir; Pat Warner, pub affrs dir; John Brunson, chief engr.

WVRK(FM)—Listing follows WPNX(AM).

***WYFK(FM)**—July 1987: 89.5 mhz; 50 kw. Ant 439 ft. TL: N32 40 03 W84 57 19. Stereo. 75 Raymond Dr., Cataula (31804). (706) 322-1980. Licensee: Bible Broadcasting Network (group owner). Format: Relg. News staff 2; news progmg 24 wkly. Target aud: General. ■ Lowell Davey, pres; Mark Andrews, gen mgr; Harold Richards, prom mgr, progmg dir & mus dir; David Fuller, chief engr.

Commerce

WJJC(AM)—June 27, 1957: 1270 khz; 5 kw-D. TL: N34 12 57 W83 26 09. Hrs opn: 6 AM-sunset. Box 379, 153 Little St. (30529). (706) 335-3155; (706) 335-2902. Licensee: WJJC Broadcasting Inc. (acq 1979). Net: NBC; Ga. Net. Rep: Rgnl Reps. Format: Country, relg, news. News progmg 30 hrs wkly. Target aud: 25-55. Spec prog: Farm 2 hrs wkly. ■ Herb Hattaway, gen mgr & gen sls mgr; Linda Bourroughs, progmg mgr; Keith Parnell, mus dir; Grady Cooper, news dir; Bill Carlson, pub affrs dir & chief engr. ■ Rates: $9; 9; 9; 9.

Conyers

WPBS(AM)—November 1979: 1050 khz; 1 kw-D, 266 w-N. TL: N33 40 48 W84 01 44. Hrs opn: 24. 1381 Rockbridge Rd. (30207). (404) 483-1000. FAX: (404) 903-6030. Licensee: Midway Holiness Church Inc. (acq 3-17-93; $85,000; FTR 4-5-93). Net: USA; Ga. Net. Rep: Rgnl Reps. Wash atty: Latham & Watkins Format: MOR, Black, relg. News staff one; news progmg 10 hrs wkly. Target aud: 25-49; females. Spec prog: Relg 6 hrs wkly. ■ Jerry Williams, gen mgr; Eric Janzen, opns mgr & mus dir; Julian Clark, chief engr. ■ Rates: $17; 13; 17; 13.

Coosa

WSRM(FM)—Not on air, target date unknown: 95.3 mhz; 3 kw. Ant 328 ft. TL: N34 11 41 W85 20 55. 32 Saddle Mountain Rd., Rome (30161). Licensee: Jean M. Gradick.

Cordele

WUWU(AM)—Oct 7, 1940: 1490 khz; 1 kw-U. TL: N31 57 26 W83 46 08. Stereo. Box 460, 910 20th Ave. E. (31015). (912) 276-0306. Licensee: Radio Cordele Inc. (acq 3-9-92; $350,000 with co-located FM; FTR 4-6-92). Net: NBC. Format: Relg. News staff 2. Target aud: General. ■ Jim Jennings, gen mgr; Ray Walsh, prom mgr, progmg dir, mus dir & news dir; Don Jones, chief engr.

WKKN(FM)—Co-owned with WUWU(AM). Feb 22, 1969: 98.3 mhz; 3 kw. Ant 300 ft. TL: N31 57 26 W83 46 08. Stereo. Prog sep from AM. Net: NBC. Format: Country.

Cornelia

WCON(AM)—March 28, 1953: 1450 khz; 1 kw-U. TL: N34 30 57 W83 32 20. Hrs opn: 24. Box 100, 540 N. Main St. (30531). (706) 778-2241. FAX: (706) 778-0576. Licensee: Habersham Broadcasting Co. (acq 2-1-61). Net: ABC/E; Ga. Net. Format: MOR, gospel, country. Target aud: Adults. ■ Bobbie C. Foster, pres & gen mgr; John C. Foster, vp; Ted Taylor, news dir; Boyd M. Anderson, chief engr. ■ Rates: $9; 8; 9; 7.

WCON-FM—March 27, 1965: 99.3 mhz; 50 kw. Ant 808 ft. TL: N34 31 24 W83 40 46. Stereo. Hrs opn: 24. Dups AM 55%. Format: Country. News staff one. Target aud: 18 plus. Spec prog: Gospel 10 hrs wkly.

Covington

WGFS(AM)—Oct 9, 1946: 1430 khz; 5 kw-D, 250 w-N. Ant 199 ft. TL: N33 36 25 W83 53 15. Stereo. Box 869, 1151 Hendricks St. (30209). (404) 786-1430; (404) 786-1431. FAX: (404) 784-9892. Licensee: Radio Covington Inc. (acq 6-16-89; $200,000; FTR 7-3-89). Net: CBS; Ga. Net. Wash atty: Mullin, Rhyne, Emmons & Topel. Format: MOR. News staff one; news progmg 20 hrs wkly. Target aud: General. Spec prog: Relg 14 hrs wkly. ■ J. Charles Elder, pres; G. Christopher Elder, vp & gen mgr; Susan Fuller, opns mgr; Andrea Hammond, gen sls mgr; Susan J. Fuller, news dir; George Hawk, chief engr. ■ Rates: $6.10; 5.80; 5.50; 5.

Crawford

WGMG(FM)—April 1990: 102.1 mhz; 6 kw. Ant 328 ft. TL: N33 55 18 W83 14 14. 1137 Cedar Shoals Dr., Athens (30605). (706) 369-7301; (706) 369-1021. FAX: (706) 369-7518. Licensee: New Broadcast Investment Properties. Group owner: Southern Broadcasting Companies Inc. Format: Adult contemp. News staff one; news progmg 7 hrs wkly. Target aud: General; 18-49. ■ Paul Stone, pres; Charles Giddens, vp; Sanders Hickey, gen mgr; John Drake, opns mgr, progmg dir & mus dir; Angela Noles, gen sls mgr; Bill Jervis, news dir; Cheri Mohr, pub affrs dir; Phil Baker, chief engr. ■ Rates: $27; 24; 27; 16.

Cumming

WMLB(AM)—1962: 1170 khz; 5 kw-D. TL: N34 10 41 W84 09 23. 1107 Atlanta Hwy. (30130). (404) 887-3136. FAX: (404) 887-3333. Licensee: Lanier Broadcasting Inc. (acq 4-10-89; $150,000; FTR 4-24-89). Net: ABC/E; Ga. Net. Format: Relg, country. News staff one; news progmg 15 hrs wkly. Target aud: General. ■ Jeff Hilliard, gen mgr; Jon Gresham, news dir; Phil Baker, chief engr.

WWEV(AM)—(Decatur). July 19, 1958: 1420 khz; 1 kw-D, DA. TL: N33 47 13 W84 14 53. Box 248, Cumming (30130). (404) 577-9150. FAX: (404) 781-5003. Licensee: Curriculum Development Foundation Inc. (acq 3-30-92; $150,000; FTR 4-20-92). Format: Relg, educ, news. Target aud: General; conservative Christians.

***WWEV-FM**—Dec 5, 1981: 91.5 mhz; 8.9 kw. Ant 960 ft. TL: N34 14 13 W84 09 36. Stereo. Format: Contemp Christian mus. News progmg 6 hrs wkly. Target aud: 18-49; the family unit. ■ Paul L. Walker, pres; N. Barry Holt, gen mgr; Larry Grover, mus dir; Marty Passmore, chief engr.

Cuthbert

WCUG(AM)—Dec 1, 1971: 850 khz; 500 w-D. TL: N31 46 26 W84 50 16. Box 348 (31740). (912) 732-3725. Licensee: Mullis Communications Inc. Net: Ga. Net. Format: Country. Spec prog: Black 4 hrs, farm 8 hrs wkly. ■ N. Scott Mullis, gen mgr & progmg dir.

Dahlonega

WDGR(AM)—March 1, 1982: 1210 khz; 10 kw-D. TL: N34 31 45 W84 00 23. Box 1210, (30533). (706) 864-4477. Licensee: Gold City Broadcasting Inc. (acq 8-25-92; $120,000; FTR 9-14-92). Net: NBC; Ga. Net. Rep: Southern. Format: Country, bluegrass, gospel. ■ Phil Castleberry, pres & gen mgr; Sandy Griffith, chief engr.

Dalton

WBLJ(AM)—April 8, 1940: 1230 khz; 1 kw-U. TL: N34 45 23 W84 57 02. Hrs opn: 24. Box 809 (30722). (706) 278-3300. FAX: (706) 226-1408. Licensee: North Georgia Radio Inc. (acq 1-1-60). Net: MBS; Ga. Net. Format: Adult contemp, oldies, news. News staff 2; news progmg 28 hrs wkly. Spec prog: Relg mus, Sp 2 hrs wkly. ■ Werner Wortsman, pres; Sam Lake, opns mgr & progmg mgr; Barbara Wilson, gen sls mgr, prom mgr & adv mgr; Diane Pearson, natl sls mgr; Clarence Graham, Barbara Wilson (gospel), mus dirs; Lisa Elders, news dir; Phil Baker, chief engr. ■ Rates: $23; 13; 16; 13.

WLSQ(AM)—Oct 1, 1954: 1430 khz; 2.5 kw-D, 72 w-N. TL: N34 47 22 W84 57 05. Stereo. Hrs opn: 24. Box 1284 (30722); 104 S. Pentz St. (30720). (706) 278-5511; (706) 226-1422. FAX: (706) 278-9917. Licensee: Radio Center Dalton Inc. (acq 10-15-85). Net: CBS, BRN, Sun. Rep: Rgnl Reps. Format: News/talk. News staff 3; news progmg 30 hrs wkly. Target aud: 25-45. ■ Gilbert H. Watts Jr., pres; Paul Fink, gen mgr; Paul Roberts, opns mgr; Bill Seaton, news dir; Jane Harrell, pub affrs dir; Phil Langston, chief engr. ■ Rates: $22; 18; 22; 10.

WTTI(AM)—June 17, 1965: 1530 khz; 10 kw-D, DA (CH). TL: N34 47 09 W85 02 40. Box 216 (30722); 562 Deck Dr., Rocky Face (30740). (706) 673-7141. FAX: (706) 673-4420. Licensee: Pye Wilson Broadcasting. Net: CNN. Format: Christian. News staff one; news progmg 8 hrs wkly. Target aud: 25-54; families, with emphasis on parents. ■ Devona Poe, gen mgr; C. W. Queen, chief opns, progmg mgr & news dir; Freda Atkins, gen sls mgr & prom mgr; Mitchell Hughes, mus dir & pub affrs dir; Phil Langstar, chief engr. ■ Rates: $10; 8; 10; na.

Darien

WYNR(FM)—May 13, 1993: 107.7 mhz; 50 kw. Ant 403 ft. TL: N31 10 09 W81 32 14. 117 Marina Dr., St. Simons Island (31522). (912) 634-1077. Licensee: Stewart Broadcasting Corp. Net: ABC/E. Rep: Rgnl Reps. Wash atty: Steve Simpson. Format: Country. News staff one; news progmg 4 hrs wkly. Target aud: General; 25 plus. ■ Kyle Bragg, progmg dir. ■ Rates: $10; 8; 10; 6.

Decatur

WPCH(FM)—See Atlanta.

WWEV(AM)—Licensed to Decatur. See Cumming.

WXLL(AM)—Aug 11, 1964: 1310 khz; 500 w-D. TL: N33 46 22 W84 16 55. 3333 Covington Dr. (30032). (404) 288-3200; (404) 288-7283. Licensee: L W & M Watson Audio Enterprises (acq 10-87). Format: Black, relg. News progmg 5 hrs wkly. Target aud: 25-65; college-age, professionals, senior citizens. ■ Margery J. Watson, pres & gen mgr; William Thompson, gen sls mgr & news dir; Wendy Watson, progmg dir; Elder Leroy Watson, chief engr. ■ Rates: $15; 10; 15; na.

Dock Junction

WXMK(FM)—May 1, 1991: 105.9 mhz; 6.2 kw. Ant 489 ft. TL: N31 10 09 W81 32 14. Hrs opn: 24. 108 Benedict Rd., Brunswick (31520). (912) 261-1000; (912) 261-1059 (REQUEST). FAX: (912) 265-8391. Licensee: Southland Radio Inc. Wash atty: Pepper & Corazzini. Format: Adult top-40, CHR. ■ Lorraine M. Wiggins, CEO, gen mgr & gen sls mgr; L. J. Smith, progmg dir.

Donalsonville

WSEM(AM)—Feb 12, 1963: 1500 khz; 1 kw-D. TL: N31 04 26 W84 52 47. Box 87 (31745). (912) 524-5123. FAX: (912) 524-2265. Licensee: Seminole Broadcasting Co. (acq 3-1-71). Net: Ga. Net. Rep: T N. Format: Southern gospel, religious, news. Target aud: 25-65 plus. ■ Gilbert Kelley, pres & gen mgr; Grace Kelley, gen sls mgr; Gil Kelley Jr., progmg dir & news dir; Charles Wooten, chief engr.

WGMK(FM)—Co-owned with WSEM(AM). Sept 1, 1980: 106.3 mhz; 3 kw. Ant 350 ft. TL: N31 04 26 W84 52 47. Box 236 (31745). (912) 524-5124. Licensee: Merchant Broadcasting Co. Net: SMN. Format: Adult contemp. ■ Gil Kelly Jr., pres, gen mgr & prom mgr.

Douglas

WDMG(AM)—March 1947: 860 khz; 5 kw-U, DA-N TL: N31 30 26 W82 48 46 (CP: TL: N31 30 23 W82 49 10). 620 E. Ward St. (31533). (912) 384-3250. FAX: (912) 383-8552. Licensee: WDMG Inc. Group owner: Timm Enpterises. Net: Unistar. Rep: Dora Clayton, T N. Format: Adult contemp. Spec prog: Farm 20 hrs, Black 3 hrs wkly. ■ B.F.J. Timm, pres; Roy Jones, gen mgr; John Higgs, stn mgr & news dir; Roy L. Jones Jr., gen sls mgr; Maureen Morgan, prom mgr; Don Talbot, chief engr.

WDMG-FM—April 7, 1978: 99.5 mhz; 51 kw. Ant 200 ft. TL: N31 32 12 W82 57 49 (CP: Ant 157 ft.). Dups AM 90%. Format: Country, MOR.

WOKA(AM)—Dec 10, 1962: 1310 khz; 1 kw-D. TL: N31 31 24 W82 52 22. Box 471 (31533). (912) 384-8153. FAX: (912) 384-6323. Licensee: Coffee County Broadcasters (acq 1971). Net: NBC. Format: Country, adult contemp, relg. Target aud: General. ■ Pierre Mitchell, pres; Lauren N. Nobles, gen mgr, mus dir & news dir; Robert Mason, progmg dir; E.F. Mitchell III, chief engr. ■ Rates: $6; 6; 6.

WOKA-FM—July 1971: 106.7 mhz; 100 kw. Ant 295 ft. TL: N31 31 24 W82 52 22. Dups AM 25%. (912) 384-2956. Format: Country. ■ Grady Seawright, gen mgr.

Douglasville

WDCY(AM)—Apr 4, 1964: 1520 khz; 2.5 kw-D. TL: N33 45 48 W84 44 28. Hrs opn: 7:30 AM-7 PM. Suite B, 8451 S. Chrokee Blvd. (30134). (404) 920-1520. FAX: (404) 949-0448. Licensee: Word Christian Broadcasting Inc. (acq 3-25-93); $95,000; FTR 4-12-93). Wash atty: Fletcher, Heald & Hildreth. Format: Gospel. News staff one. Target aud: 25-54. Spec prog: Southern gospel. ■ Ken Johns, gen mgr. WSB-TV affil. ■ Rates: $18; 14; 18; na.

Dublin

WKKZ(FM)—Apr 4, 1967: 92.7 mhz; 50 kw. Ant 417 ft. TL: N32 31 21 W82 54 00. Stereo. Hrs opn: 24. Box 967 (31040). Glenwood Rd. (31021). (912) 272-9270. FAX: (912) 275-3592. Licensee: Kirby Broadcasting Co. (acq 7-31-80). Rep: Dora-Clayton. Format: Hot adult contemp. ■ Mike Kirby, pres, gen mgr & gen sls mgr; Steve O'Neal, progmg dir & mus dir; Clinton Branch, chief engr.

WMLT(AM)—Jan 12, 1945: 1330 khz; 5 kw-D, 500 w-N, DA-N. TL: N32 33 50 W82 52 00. Box 130 (31040). (912) 272-4422. FAX: (912) 275-4657. Licensee: State Broadcasting Co. Inc. ABC/E; Ga. Net. Rep: Rgnl Reps. Format: Adult contemp, top country. Target aud: 25-54. Spec prog: Farm 6 hrs wkly. ■ C. Wayne Dowdy, pres; Jamie Holt, gen mgr; Anne M. Everly, gen sls mgr; Steve Lawfon, progmg dir & mus dir; Yvonne Lamb Castillo, news dir; Jim Slasen, chief engr.

WQZY(FM)—Co-owned with WMLT(AM). 1978: 95.9 mhz; 3 kw. Ant 298 ft. TL: N32 33 51 W82 52 18 (CP: 88 kw, ant 1,023 ft.). Stereo. Net: ABC/C; Ga. Net. Format: Top-40. Target aud: 18-34.

WXLI(AM)—Mar 16, 1958: 1230 khz; 1 kw-U. TL: N32 31 21 W82 54 00. Box 967 (31040). (912) 272-4282. FAX: (912) 275-2557. Licensee: Laurens County Broadcasting Co. (acq 4-7-61). Net: CBS. Rep: Dora-Clayton. Format: Country. ■ Peggy Kirby, pres; Mike Kirby, gen mgr & gen sls mgr; Steve O'Neal, progmg dir; LaJean Hall, news dir; Clinton Branch, chief engr.

East Point

WMLD(AM)—Not on air, target date unknown: 1160 khz; 10 kw-D, 400 w-N, DA-2. TL: N33 41 34 W84 30 07. c/o Darrell Spann, 1760 Cedar Grove Drive, Connally (30327). Licensee: Darrell Spann.

WTJH(AM)—December 1949: 1260 khz; 5 kw-D. TL: N33 41 47 W84 28 29. 2146 Dodson Dr. (30364). (404) 344-2233. FAX: (404) 346-0647. Licensee: Radio Station WTJH. Group owner: Willis Broadcasting Corp. Rep: Walter Brickhouse. Format: Inspirational. ■ Bishop L. E. Willis Sr., pres; Silas Buchanan Jr., gen mgr, gen sls mgr & news dir; Rhodell Lewis, prom mgr, progmg dir & mus dir; Skip Marshall, chief engr.

Eastman

WUFF(AM)—Sept 1, 1961: 710 khz; 2.5 kw-D. TL: N32 13 35 W83 13 10. Box 4097 (31023). (912) 374-3437. Licensee: Farnell O'Quinn. Net: NBC. Format: Country. Spec prog: Black 5 hrs wkly. ■ Farnell O'Quinn, pres; Gene Rogers, gen mgr & gen sls mgr; Clark Parkerson, chief engr.

WUFF-FM—1976: 97.5 mhz; 2 kw. Ant 371 ft. TL: N32 13 35 W83 13 10 (CP: 97.5 mhz, 4.6 kw, ant 364 ft.). Stereo. Prog sep from AM.

Eatonton

WKVQ(AM)—Dec 15, 1966: 1520 khz; 1 kw-D. TL: N33 19 19 W83 25 03. Box 3965, 869 Church St. (31024); Box 266, 107 Boggs St., Lexington (30648). (706) 485-8792; (706) 743-3410. FAX: (706) 743-3652. Licensee: Dennis Peter Helmreich (acq 7-24-92; $125,000; FTR 8-3-92). Net: MBS; Ga. Net. Format: Modern country. Target aud: General. ■ Dennis Peter Helmreich, pres & gen mgr; Brian Pilkington, opns mgr, gen sls mgr & news dir; Wayne Welch, prom mgr; George B. Peters Jr., progmg dir & mus dir; Dan Davis, chief engr. ■ Rates: $7; 7; 7; 7.

Elberton

WWRK(AM)—1946: 1400 khz; 1 kw-U. TL: N34 06 45 W82 52 52. Box 638 (30635). (706) 283-1400. FAX: (706) 283-8710. Licensee: Willie Palmer of Radio Elberton Inc. (acq 10-26-93; $260,000 with co-located FM; FTR 11-8-93). Format: Country. ■ Mickey Palmer, gen mgr; Mel Stovall, gen sls mgr; Scott Smith, progmg dir & mus dir; Larry Nixon, chief engr.

WWRK-FM—1973: 92.1 mhz; 3 kw. Ant 299 ft. TL: N31 04 45 W82 55 16. Dups AM 15%. Box 638 (30635). (706) 283-1400. FAX: (706) 283-8710. Format: Country. ■ Mikey Palmer, gen mgr; Mel Stovall, gen sls mgr; Scott Smith, progmg dir & mus dir; Larry Nixon, chief engr.

Ellijay

WLJA(AM)—May 10, 1978: 1560 khz; 1 kw-D. TL: N34 42 14 W84 28 35. Box 545, Tabor St. (30540). (706) 276-2016. FAX: (706) 635-1018. Licensee: Lee Broadcasting Co. Inc. (acq 7-85; $10,000; FTR 7-1-85). Net: CNN. Format: MOR. ■ Della L. Rucker, pres & gen mgr; Bobbi Rucker, gen sls mgr.

WLJA-FM—Nov 1, 1985: 93.5 mhz; 5.2 kw. Ant 272 ft. TL: N34 42 49 W84 30 50. Dups AM 100%.

Evans

WYFZ(FM)—November 1991: 92.3 mhz; 3 kw. Ant 328 ft. TL: N33 35 25 W82 13 52. Box 1250 (30809). (706) 869-1313. Licensee: Bible Broadcasting Network Inc. (acq 3-6-91; FTR 3-25-91). ■ Bruce Nickel, stn mgr.

Fitzgerald

WBHB(AM)—Oct 8, 1946: 1240 khz; 1 kw-U. TL: N31 42 23 W83 15 40. Box 100, 601 W. Roanoke Dr. (31750). (912) 423-2077. FAX: (912) 423-8313. Licensee: Harper Broadcasting Inc. (acq 9-1-92; $20,000; FTR 9-21-92). Net: NBC, Westwood One. Format: Adult contemp. News staff 2; news progmg 20 hrs wkly. Target aud: General. Spec prog: Black 4 hrs, farm 6 hrs, gospel 10 hrs wkly. ■ Harold Harper, pres; Mike Roberts, stn mgr & dev dir & news dir; John Puckett, opns dir & progmg dir; Buddy Green, chief engr. ■ Rates: $7; 6; 7; 5.

WRDO(FM)—1991: 96.9 mhz; 6 kw. Ant 328 ft. TL: N31 44 33 W83 14 41. Hrs opn: 24. Box 988, 351 Bowens Mill Hwy. (31750). (912) 423-7661. FAX: (912) 423-6717. Licensee: Gralean Broadcasting Co. Inc. Net: USA. Wash atty: Roy Perkins. Format: Classic oldies. News staff one. Target aud: 25-55; baby boomers. Spec prog: Gospel 6 hrs wkly. ■ Margaret Graham, CEO; Jeanna Tillery, chmn; Howard Jordan, CFO.

WSIZ(AM)—See Ocilla.

Folkston

WOKF(FM)—Nov 1989: 92.5 mhz; 6 kw. Ant 324 ft. TL: N30 43 45 W81 56 21 (CP: Ant 328 ft.). Stereo. Hrs opn: 24. Box 777 104 N. 1st St. (31537). (912) 496-3511; (912) 496-3512. FAX: (912) 496-3116. Licensee: Jack R. Mays (acq 9-15-89). Net: NBC; Ga. Net. Rep: Rgnl Reps. Wash atty: Stan Emert. Format: Modern country. News staff one. Target aud: General. Spec prog: Gospel 5 hrs wkly. ■ Jack R. Mays, pres & news dir; Michelle Lloyd, gen mgr, stn mgr, sls dir & pub affrs dir; Bean Bodine, progmg dir, progmg mgr & mus dir; Dick Boekeloo, chief engr. ■ Rates: $10; 9; 10; 8.

Forsyth

WFXM-FM—Nov 22, 1973: 100.1 mhz; 3 kw. Ant 209 ft. TL: N32 58 31 W83 52 11 (CP: 2 kw, ant 574 ft., TL: N32 55 41 W83 52 37). Stereo. 369 Second St., Macon (31201). (912) 742-2505. FAX: (912) 742-8299. Licensee: Middle Georgia Broadcasting Inc. Format: Urban contemp. ■ Albert Smith, gen mgr; Patricia Glass, gen sls mgr; George Threatt, progmg dir; Valerie Beebe, news dir; Richard Hamilton, chief engr.

Fort Gaines

*****WJWV(FM)**—Feb 28 1993: 90.9 mhz; 85 kw. Ant 267 ft. TL: N31 36 16 W85 02 02. 1540 Stewart Ave. S.W., Atlanta (30310). (404) 756-4700. FAX: (404) 756-4088. Licensee: Georgia Public Telecommunication Commission (group owner). Format: Classical, news & info. ■ Bill Bergeron, gen mgr.

Fort Valley

*****WJTG(FM)**—March 1, 1989: 91.3 mhz; 100 kw. Ant 459 ft. TL: N32 41 27 W83 51 45. Stereo. Hrs opn: 24. 1110 Richardson Mill Rd. (31030). (912) 738-9191. FAX: (912) 825-9911. Licensee: Joy Public Broadcasting Corp. Net: UPI. Format: Gospel. Target aud: General. ■ Wally Vander Zwaag, gen mgr, progmg dir & mus dir; Jerry Arthur, chief engr.

WQBZ(FM)—Licensed to Fort Valley. See Macon.

WVVY(FM)—Licensed to Fort Valley. See Macon.

WXKO(AM)—June 1951: 1150 khz; 1 kw-D, 60 w-N. TL: N32 34 34 W83 54 17. Hrs opn: 24. Box 1150 (31030). (912) 825-5547; (912) 922-5920. FAX: (912) 825-5548. Licensee: Middle Georgia Broadcasting Inc. Group owner: The Woodfin Group (acq 6-6-91; $693,000 with co-located FM; FTR 6-24-91). Net: SMN; Ga. Net. Wash atty: Julien Freret. Format: Gospel, R&B. News staff one; news progmg 10 hrs wkly. Target aud: 25 plus; Black. ■ Ken Woodfin, pres, gen mgr & gen sls mgr; George Threatt, progmg dir & mus dir; Richard Hamilton, chief engr.

Gainesville

*****WBCX(FM)**—1977: 89.1 mhz; 835 w. Ant 544 ft. TL: N34 19 01 W83 49 45. Brenau University (30501). (404) 718-0555. FAX: (404) 287-7021. Licensee: Brenau University. Format: Easy lstng. ■ Larry Aldridge, gen mgr; Gary Smith, chief engr.

WDUN(AM)—April 2, 1949: 550 khz; 5 kw-D, 2.5 kw-N, DA-N. TL: N34 20 11 W83 47 41. Stereo. Box 10, 1102 Thompson Bridge Rd. (30503). (404) 532-9921. FAX: (404) 532-0506. Licensee: WDUN Radio Inc. (acq 9-83; $750,000; FTR 9-5-83). Net: ABC/I, MBS; Ga. Net. Format: News/talk, sports. News staff 6; news progmg 24 hrs wkly. Target aud: 25-65. ■ John W. Jacobs Jr., chmn; John W. Jacobs III, pres, gen mgr & gen sls mgr; Joel M. Williams, opns mgr & progmg dir; Jean Pethel, rgnl sls mgr; Ken Stanford, news dir; Gary Smith, chief engr. ■ Rates: $27; 19; 20; 17.

WFOX(FM)—Nov 1, 1965: 97.1 mhz; 97 kw. Ant 1,571 ft. TL: N34 07 32 W83 51 31. Stereo. Hrs opn: 24. Suite 797, 2000 RiverEdge Pkwy., Atlanta (30328). (404) 953-9369. FAX: (404) 955-5483. Licensee: Shamrock Broadcasting Inc. (group owner; acq 1983). Rep: Group W. Format: Oldies. News staff one. Target aud: 25-54. ■ Bill Clark, chmn; Marty Loughman, pres; Clancy Woods, gen mgr; Roger Stallard, gen sls mgr; Tim Johnson, prom

Georgia

mgr; Dennis Winslow, progmg dir; Mark Bell, mus dir; Greg Black, news dir; Randy Mullinax, chief engr.

WGGA(AM)—Oct 10, 1941: 1240 khz; 1 kw-U. TL: N34 19 01 W83 49 45. Stereo. Hrs opn: 24. 1102 Thompson Bridge Rd. N.E. (30503). (404) 532-9921. FAX: (404) 532-0506. Licensee: WDUN Radio Inc. (acq 4-20-93; $360,000; FTR 5-10-93). Net: CBS, Sun. Rep: Rgnl Reps. Format: Adult contemp, oldies, news/talk. News staff 2; news progmg 31 hrs wkly. Target aud: 25-54; middle, upper income adults. ■ Jay Jacobs, gen mgr; Joel Williams, prom mgr; Tom Israel, progmg dir; Brian Rothel, mus dir; Gary Smith, chief engr. ■ Rates: $15; 12; 15; 10.

WKZD(AM)—(Murrayville). Nov 1, 1986: 1330 khz; 1 kw-D. TL: N34 22 16 W83 56 47. Box 2255, Gainesville (30503); 1864 Thompson Bridge Rd., Gainesville (30501). (706) 531-1330. Licensee: Georgia Mountain Communications. Net: CNN. Format: Adult contemp. News staff one. Target aud: General. Spec prog: Sp 4 hrs wkly. ■ David Puckett, pres & gen mgr; Kathleen Bearden, prom mgr; Sam Davis, progmg dir; Carol McAboy, mus dir; Dave Stewart, news dir. ■ Rates: $9; 9; 9; 9.

WLBA(AM)—Jan 26, 1957: 1130 khz; 10 kw-D. TL: N34 16 45 W83 46 33. Hrs opn: Sunrise-sunset. Box 2849, 311 Green St. N.E., Suite 211 (30503). (404) 532-6331; (404) 536-890. FAX: (404) 532-3828. Licensee: WLBA Inc. Group owner: Bennie E. Hewett Stns. Net: NBC, Unistar. Format: Sp. ■ Bennie Hewett, pres & gen mgr; Sam Zamarron, vp sls; Gracie Zamarron, vp prom.

WMJE(FM)—See Clarkesville.

WYAY(FM)—Apr 3, 1949: 106.7 mhz; 99 kw. Ant 1,400 ft. TL: N34 07 32 W83 51 31. Stereo. Simulcasts WYAI(FM) La Grange. Suite 900, 200 Galleria Pkwy., Atlanta (30339). (404) 955-0106. FAX: (404) 956-0498. Licensee: Capital Cities/ABC Inc. Group owner: Capital Cities/ABC Broadcast Group (acq 7-30-93; $19 million; grpsl; FTR 8-23-93). Format: Country. Target aud: 25-54. ■ Norm Schratt, pres & gen mgr; Sally Appel, Diane Dalton, gen sls mgrs; Bill Bear, natl sls mgr; Andy Guzman, prom mgr; B.J. Williams, Sandy Carroll, news dirs; John Bridges, Charlie Nuttleman, chiefs engr.

Garden City

WNMT(AM)—June 6, 1968: 1520 khz; 1 kw-D. TL: N32 05 08 W81 10 16. Box 7042 (31408). (912) 964-8124; (912) 354-4601. Licensee: Woods & Watkins. Format: Div. ■ Chris Watkins, pres; M.E. Watkins, opns mgr & progmg dir; Martin Fogel, chief engr.

Glennville

WKIG(AM)—June 25, 1961: 1580 khz; 1 kw-D. TL: N31 55 58 W81 55 24. Box 98, 226 E. Bolton St. (30427). (912) 654-3580. FAX: (912) 654-3580. Licensee: Tattnall County Broadcasting Co. (acq 5-30-68). Net: NBC. Format: Southern gospel. ■ Don P. Cobb, pres; Judy W. Cobb, gen mgr & stn mgr. ■ Rates: $6.65; 6.65; 6.65; 6.65.

WKIG-FM—Nov 18, 1977: 106.3 mhz; 3 kw. Ant 300 ft. TL: N32 00 27 W81 54 51. Stereo. Format: Adult contemp. ■ Judy W. Cobb, gen sls mgr. ■ Rates: Same as AM.

Gordon

WBNM(AM)—Sept 1, 1969: 1120 khz; 10 kw-D, 2.5 kw-CH. TL: N32 50 59 W83 28 38. Box 7948, Macon (31209). (912) 745-3301. FAX: (912) 742-2293. Licensee: Quality Broadcasting Inc. (acq 4-1-85). Net: BRN; Ga. Net. Format: Business news. Target aud: Upper class bus people. ■ Wayne Sawyer, gen mgr.

WNEX-FM—Co-owned with WBNM(AM). March 30, 1976: 107.1 mhz; 2.25 kw. Ant 541 ft. TL: N32 51 43 W83 21 56. Stereo. Hrs opn: 24. Prog sep from AM. (Acq 11-19-91; $200,000; FTR 12-16-91). Format: Big band, jazz. Target aud: Middle & upper class Georgians.

Gray

WWIQ(FM)—Not on air, target date unknown: 96.5 mhz; 1.99 kw. Ant 414 ft. TL: N32 59 03 W83 33 16. 2361 Kensington Rd., Macon (31211). (912) 744-0047. Licensee: IQ Radio Network Inc. Format: Classic rock. ■ Robert Connelly, gen mgr.

Grayson

WPLO(AM)—Licensed to Grayson. See Lawrenceville.

Greensboro

WDDK(FM)—July 12, 1980: 103.9 mhz; 3 kw. Ant 299 ft. TL: N33 34 54 W83 10 27 (CP: Ant 328 ft., TL: N33 28 29 W83 14 46). Hrs opn: 24. 1271-B E. Broad St. (30642). (706) 453-4140. Licensee: Briarpatch Radio Inc. (acq 2-26-90; $300,000; FTR 2-26-90). Net: ABC; Ga. Net. Wash atty: Venable, Baeijer, Howard & Civiletti. Format: Adult contemp, oldies. News progmg 4 hrs wkly. Target aud: 24-29. Spec prog: Relg 6 hrs wkly. ■ Chip Lyness, vp & gen mgr; Craig Andrews, progmg dir; Jim Nicholson, mus dir; Steve Splitt, engrg dir. ■ Rates: $12; 12; 12; 10.

Griffin

WHIE(AM)—Dec 15, 1952: 1320 khz; 5 kw-D, 83 w-N. TL: N33 14 30 W84 18 17. Drawer G (30224). (404) 227-9451. Licensee: Telerad Inc. (acq 1957). Rep: Ochs. Format: Country, talk. ■ Fred L. Watkins, pres, gen mgr & gen sls mgr; Bonnie Pfrogner, mus dir & news dir; Sydney Daniel, chief engr.

WKEU(AM)—1933: 1450 khz; 1 kw-U. TL: N33 14 25 W84 14 54. Box 997, 1000 Memorial Dr. (30224). (404) 227-5507. FAX: (404) 229-2291. Licensee: Design Media Inc. (group owner). Net: ABC/E; Ga. Net. Rep: Rgnl Reps. Format: Adult contemp. News staff 2; news progmg 32 hrs wkly. Target aud: 25 plus. ■ Leonard Bolton, pres & gen mgr; Joe Beail, stn mgr; Barry Clark, gen sls mgr; Pete Owen, progmg dir.

WQUL(AM)—Co-owned with WKEU(AM). March 8, 1966: 97.7 mhz; 4.4 kw. Ant 380 ft. TL: N33 14 25 W84 14 54. Stereo. Prog sep from AM. Net: SMN. Format: Solid gold hits.

Hahira

WSHF(AM)—Not on air, target date unknown: 810 khz; 2.5 kw-D. TL: N30 52 25 W83 15 07. Box 3135, Valdosta (31604). (912) 242-1636. FAX: (912) 242-9645. Licensee: Anne White. Format: Adult contemp (Gold hits 60s, 70s). ■ Deidre White, gen mgr.

Harlem

WCHZ(FM)—Not on air, target date unknown: 95.1 mhz; 6 kw. Ant 328 ft. TL: N33 31 34 W82 15 55. Box 14698, Augusta (30919-0698). (706) 650-1122. FAX: (706) 650-0610. Licensee: GMR Broadcasting Inc. (acq 8-3-92; $38,000; FTR 8-24-92). Format: Alternative. ■ Tom Ptak, pres; Frank Cupsidas, gen mgr.

Hartwell

WKLY(AM)—Sept 5, 1947: 980 khz; 1 kw-D, 140 w-N. TL: N34 21 28 W82 58 35 (CP: 149 w-N). Hrs opn: 15. Box 636, Bowersville Hwy. (30643). (706) 376-2233. FAX: (706) 376-3100. Licensee: WKLY Broadcasting Co. (acq 11-18-89; $200,000; FTR 12-19-88). Net: Ga. Net. Format: Country, gospel, relg. News staff 2; news progmg 18 hrs wkly. Target aud: 30 plus; middle class, working adults. ■ Edward Hicks, pres; Frances Hicks, vp, gen sls mgr & adv mgr; Bryan Hicks, gen mgr, stn mgr & mktg mgr; Bruce Hicks, dev mgr, prom mgr & mus dir; E. Harris Brown, progmg dir & asst mus dir; Mike Atkins, news dir; Frances Hicks, Bryan Hicks, pub affrs dirs; Daniel L. Davis, chief engr. ■ Rates: $13.53; 13.53; 13.53; 13.53.

Hawkinsville

WCEH(AM)—Dec 11, 1952: 610 khz; 500 w-D, 128 w-N. TL: N32 16 50 W83 26 37. Stereo. Hrs opn: 24. Box 489, Hwy. 341 S. (31036). (912) 892-9061. FAX: (912) 892-9063. Licensee: Tri County Broadcasting Co. Inc. Net: ABC/I, MBS, Sun; Ga. Net. Format: News, talk, sports. News staff 2; news progmg 30 hrs wkly. Target aud: 25 plus; male skewed, info oriented adults. Spec prog: Farm 5 hrs, relg 6 hrs wkly. ■ James D. Popwell Sr., pres; Dave Hedrick, vp & stn mgr; Jerry "Jay" D. Braswell, gen mgr & gen sls mgr; Bill Boys, mus dir; Thomas K. Kirk, news dir & pub affrs dir; James Popwell Jr., chief engr. ■ Rates: $9; 6.75; 9; 5.

WQSY(FM)—Co-owned with WCEH(AM). Sept 26, 1968: 103.9 mhz; 25 kw. Ant 255 ft. TL: N32 16 50 W83 26 31 (CP: 25 kw, ant 500 ft.). Stereo. Prog sep from AM. Net: ABC/E. Format: Adult contemp, MOR, oldies. News staff 2; news progmg 16 hrs wkly. Target aud: 35-64; adults, female oriented. Spec prog: Talk 15 hrs, sports 10 hrs wkly. ■ Rates: $12.50; 9.25; 12.50; 7.

Hazlehurst

WVOH(AM)—Sept 6, 1962: 920 khz; 500 w-D, 39 w-N. TL: N31 51 15 W82 34 00. Stereo. Box 757 (31539). (912) 375-4511. Licensee: Jeff Davis Broadcasters Inc. Net: NBC. Format: C&W, gospel. Spec prog: Farm 2 hrs wkly. ■ John Hulett, pres, gen mgr & gen sls mgr; Wilbur Heath, prom mgr & progmg dir; Ronnie Williams, mus dir; Bruce Bostwick, news dir; Jim Kleg, chief engr.

WVOH-FM—Dec 9, 1975: 93.5 mhz; 3 kw. Ant 320 ft. TL: N31 51 15 W82 34 00. Dups AM 50%. Format: Country.

Helen

WHEL(FM)—Dec 6 1993: 105.1 mhz; 1.68 kw. Ant 613 ft. Box 256, Bruckenstrasse at Edelweiss (30545). (706) 878-1425. Licensee: Helen Broadcasters Inc. Format: Oldies. ■ Judith A. Breese, stn mgr.

Hinesville

WGML(AM)—Dec 9, 1958: 990 khz; 250 w-D, 76 w-N. TL: N31 51 01 W81 36 04. Box 615 (31313-4303). (912) 368-3399; (912) 369-6930. Licensee: Bullie Broadcasting Corp. (acq 11-14-91; FTR 12-2-91). Format: Gospel, relg. ■ Marie Logan, gen mgr & progmg dir.

WSKX(FM)—Aug 2, 1982: 92.3 mhz; 50 kw. Ant 482 ft. TL: N31 41 37 W81 23 27. Stereo. Hrs opn: 24. Box 1280, 404 S. Main St. (31313). (912) 368-9258. FAX: (912) 368-5526. Licensee: TCB Broadcasting Inc. (acq 7-91; $300,000; FTR 7-29-91). Rep: Rgnl Reps. Wash atty: Roy F. Perkins Jr. Format: Urban contemp. News progmg 2 hrs wkly. Target aud: 18-34; Ft. Stewart. Spec prog: Relg 6 hrs, Sp 2 hrs wkly. ■ Ray Bilbrey, pres, gen mgr, gen sls mgr & chief engr; Ralph Trapnell, CFO; Billie Clanton, sr vp; Bubba Chavez, opns dir & progmg dir; Xavier Cruz, sls dir; Lady Charie, mus dir; Arlene Frennier, pub affrs dir. ■ Rates: $20; 20; 20; 12.

Hogansville

WEIZ(FM)—Sept 3, 1992: 97.5 mhz; 3 kw. Ant 394 ft. TL: N33 03 54 W84 57 23. Stereo. Hrs opn: 24. Box 1114, 603 Greenville St, La Grange (30241). (706) 882-9699; FAX: (706) 882-0421. Licensee: T. Wood & Assocs. Inc. Wash atty: L.J. Bernard. Format: Adult contemp, oldies. News staff 2; news progmg 20 hrs wkly. Target aud: 30-64; non-country listeners. ■ L.A. Tony Wood, CEO & pres; Tom Golden, stn mgr; Elizabeth Dukes, sls dir. ■ Rates: $11.50; 11.50; 9.50; 9.50.

WMXY(AM)—Aug 12, 1985: 720 khz; 10 kw-D. TL: N33 03 53 W84 57 21 (CP: 7.97 kw-D). Box 1114, LaGrange (30240). (706) 882-9699. FAX: (706) 882-0421. Licensee: Tharpe Communications Inc. Format: Black urban. News staff one. Target aud: Blacks 24 plus. ■ L.A. "Tony" Wood, pres & gen mgr; Judy Childs, news dir.

Homerville

WBTY(FM)—December 1980: 105.5 mhz; 3 kw. Ant 312 ft. TL: N31 02 04 W82 51 50. Stereo. Intersection of Ga. Rts. 168 & 37 (31634). Licensee: Southern Broadcasting & Investments (acq 3-9-90; $100,000; FTR 4-30-90). Net: NBC. Format: Oldies Target aud: General. ■ Nancy K. Strickland, pres, gen mgr & gen sls mgr; A.M. Anderson, chief engr.

Irwinton

WVKX(FM)—Not on air, target date unknown: 103.7 mhz; 3 kw. Ant 328 ft. TL: N32 52 48 W83 11 07. Box 88, c/o WBKZ(AM), Athens (30603). Licensee: Wilkinson Broadcast (acq 8-10-92; $60,000; FTR 8-31-92). ■ Stan Carter, gen mgr.

Jackson

WJGA-FM—April 24, 1967: 92.1 mhz; 2.15 kw. Ant 374 ft. TL: N33 16 37 W83 57 59. Stereo. Box 3878, Brownlee Rd. (30233). (404) 775-3151. FAX: (404) 957-9915. Licensee: Donald W. Earnhart (acq 8-90; $600,000; FTR 8-27-90). Rep: Keystone (unwired net); Rgnl Reps. Wash atty: Miller & Fields. Format: Adult contemp, Black. News progmg 20 hrs wkly. Target aud: General. ■ Don Earnhart, pres & gen mgr; Susanne Earnhart, sls dir; Don Jones, chief engr. ■ Rates: $9; 9; 9; 9.

Jefferson

WBKZ(AM)—Licensed to Jefferson. See Athens.

Jeffersonville

WMGB(FM)—Sept 27, 1993: 93.7 mhz; 50 kw. Ant 490 ft. TL: N32 54 49 W83 29 47. Stereo. Hrs opn: 24. Box 351, 503 Magnolia St., (31044); Box 995, 544 Mulberry St., Macon (31202). (912) 755-0937; (912) 749-1905. Licensee: A.L.P. L.P. Wash atty: Lawrence J. Bernard. Format: CHR. Target aud: 18-34. ■ Al Parker, CEO & stn mgr; Joe Meredith, chief opns. ■ Rates: $25; 25; 25; 25.

Jesup

WIFO-FM—Listing follows WLOP(AM).

WLOP(AM)—July 12, 1949: 1370 khz; 5 kw-D, 36 w-N. TL: N31 36 06 W81 56 00. Box 647, Hwy. 84 W. (31545). (912) 427-3711. FAX: (912) 427-3712. Licensee: Jesup Broadcasting Corp. (group owner; acq 9-17-90). Net: ABC/I; Ga. Net., Tobacco. Rep: Rgnl Reps. Format: Country. News staff 2; news progmg 18 hrs wkly. Target aud: General. Spec prog: Farm 10 hrs, gospel 10 hrs wkly. ■ Charles Hubbard Jr., pres, gen mgr, gen sls mgr, prom mgr & progmg dir; Jim NESmith, mus dir; Bob Morgan, news dir; James Cote, chief engr. ■ Rates: $15.29; 15.29; 15.29; 15.29.

WIFO-FM—Co-owned with WLOP(AM). July 1, 1968: 105.5 mhz; 3 kw. Ant 300 ft. TL: N31 36 06 W81 56 00. Stereo. Dups AM 20%. Format: Adult contemp. News staff 2; news progmg 18 hrs wkly. Target aud: General. Spec prog: Black 4 hrs, farm 10 hrs wkly. ■ Rates: Same as AM.

***WLPT(FM)**—1988: 88.3 mhz; 30 kw. Ant 239 ft. TL: N31 41 23 W81 52 21. Stereo. 3213 Huxley Dr., Augusta (30909-3128). (706) 722-6681; (706) 733-8201. Licensee: Georgia Radio Fellowship. Net: Moody. Format: Christian. Target aud: General. ■ C. T. Barinowski, pres; Jim Screws, chief engr.

Kingsland

WKBX(FM)—February 23, 1987: 106.3 mhz; 3 kw. Ant 330 ft. TL: N30 48 04 W81 40 43. Stereo. Hrs opn: 24. Box 2525, 111 N. Grove Blvd. (31548). (912) 729-6106; (912) 729-5229. FAX: (912) 729-4106. Licensee: Radio Kings Bay Inc. (acq 7-1-89; $1 million; FTR 5-29-89). Net: Ga. Net. Rep: Rgnl Reps. Wash atty: Lowenthal, Landau, Fischer & Bring. Format: Country. News staff one; news progmg one hr wkly. Target aud: 18-54; contemporary country audience. ■ James Steele, pres, gen mgr & vp engrg; Wendy Steele, exec vp; Doug Vaught, gen sls mgr; Bruce O'Connell, progmg mgr, news dir; John Fleury, pub affrs dir. ■ Rates: $15; 12; 15; 9.

La Fayette

WQCH(AM)—November 1954: 1590 khz; 5 kw-D. TL: N34 42 57 W85 16 06. Box 746, Warthen St., (30728). (706) 638-3276. Licensee: Radix Broadcasting Inc. (acq 6-1-88). Net: NBC, Ga. Net. Rep: Rgnl Reps. Format: Country. News staff one; news progmg 8 hrs wkly. Target aud: 25 plus. Spec prog: Farm 2 hrs wkly. ■ Rich Gwyn, gen mgr; Joan Butler, news dir. ■ Rates: $9.50; 8.10; 9.50; na.

La Grange

WELR-FM—See Roanoke, Ala.

WLAG(AM)—May 1, 1941: 1240 khz; 1 kw-U. TL: N33 02 24 W85 01 27. Hrs opn: 24. Rebroadcasts WELR-FM Roanoke, Ala. 95%. Box 1429 (30241); 304 Broome St. (30240). (404) 845-1023; (800) 239-6516. FAX: (404) 882-0041; (205) 863-2540. Licensee: Eagle's Nest Inc. (group owner; acq 4-3-92; $10; FTR 4-27-92). Net: NBC. Format: Country. News staff one; news progmg 4 hrs wkly. Target aud: 25-54; general. Spec prog: Black one hr, gospel 3 hrs, relg 2 hrs wkly. ■ Don Strength, gen mgr, progmg dir & mus dir; Jim Vice, stn mgr, gen sls mgr & adv mgr; Kay Vice, opns mgr; Carol Cobb, news dir; Ted Ronnenberger, chief engr. ■ Rates: $10; 8; 10; 7.

***WOAK(FM)**—June 11, 1984: 90.9 mhz; 3.4 kw. Ant 299 ft. TL: N32 57 57 W84 59 08. 1921 Hamilton Rd. (30241). (706) 884-2950. FAX: (706) 882-4200. Licensee: Oakside Christian School. Net: USA. Format: Ed, relg. ■ Dr. Ralph Taylor, gen mgr; Deena Brand, progmg dir.

WTRP(AM)—Jan 9, 1953: 620 khz; 1 kw-D, 127 w-N. TL: N33 03 33 W85 01 40. 806 New Franklin Rd. (30241). (706) 884-8611; (706) 884-9877. FAX: (706) 884-8612. Licensee: Thompson Broadcasting Co. (acq 3-1-87). Net: MBS. Rep: Rgnl Reps. Format: News/talk, sports. News staff one; news progmg 28 hrs wkly. Target aud: General. Spec prog: Black gospel, southern gospel 5 hrs wkly. ■ V. Larry Thompson Sr., pres; Michael Thompson, gen mgr, stn mgr & progmg dir; Red Jones, gen sls mgr; David Bell, news dir; Ted Ronneburger, chief engr. ■ Rates: $9; 7.95; 6; 5.

WYAI(FM)—Sept 1, 1947: 104.1 mhz; 60 kw. Ant 1,217 ft. TL: N33 24 43 W84 50 03. Stereo. Simulcasts WYAY(FM) Gainesville. Suite 900, 200 Galleria Pkwy., Atlanta (30339). (404) 955-0106. FAX: (404) 956-0498. Licensee: New City Broadcasting Inc. Group owner: NewCity Communications Inc. (acq 6-21-89) Rep: McGavren Guild. Format: Country. Target aud: 25-54. ■ Norm Schrutt, gen mgr; Diane Dalton, gen sls mgr; Andy Guzman, prom mgr; Neil McGinley, progmg dir; Johnny Gray, mus dir; Sandra Carroll, news dir; Charlie Nettleman, chief engr.

Lakeland

WHFE(FM)—Not on air, target date 1994: 105.9 mhz; 6 kw. Ant 328 ft. TL: N31 04 55 W83 10 47. Stereo. Suite 211, 311 Green St. N.E., Gainesville (30501). Licensee: Bennie E. Hewett. Group owner: Bennie E. Hewett Stns. ■ Bennie E. Hewett, pres.

Lawrenceville

WPLO(AM)—(Grayson). Jan 7, 1959: 610 khz; 1.5 kw-D, 225 w-N. TL: N33 57 11 W83 58 15. Stereo. Hrs opn: 6 AM-midnight. Box 246, 239 Ezzard St., Lawrenceville (30245). (404) 962-4848. FAX: (404) 962-4864. Licensee: C.L. Nash and Norris J. Nash (acq 5-18-92; $125,000; FTR 6-8-92). Net: NBC Talknet, Motor Racing Net; Ga. Net. Format: Country. News staff 2; news progmg 5 hrs wkly. Target aud: 25-54; middle to upper income. Spec prog: Gospel 6 hrs wkly. ■ Lamar Nash, pres; Len Anthony, stn mgr, vp opns & vp adv; Bobby Johnson, gen sls mgr; Kurt Andrews, progmg dir & mus dir; Dennis Wayne, news dir; Julian Clark, chief engr. ■ Rates: $22; 14; 17; 10.

Leesburg

WEGC(FM)—October 1989: 103.5 mhz; 12.5 kw. Ant 460 ft. TL: N31 39 09 W84 05 20. Suite 501, 235 Roosevelt Ave., Albany (31701). Licensee: Rowland Albany Radio Inc. Group owner: Rowland Family Radio. Format: Oldies. Target aud: 25-54. ■ Marshall W. Rowland Sr., CEO; Brian M. Rowland, gen mgr; Beth Smith, sls dir; Brian Rowland, prom mgr & progmg mgr; Buddy Green, engrg mgr. ■ Rates: $15.50; 13.50; 14.50; 10.50.

Louisville

WPEH(AM)—Sept 10, 1960: 1420 khz; 1 kw-D, 159 w-N. TL: N33 00 48 W82 23 33. Hrs opn: 6 AM-midnight. Box 425, 1442 Middleground Rd. (30434). (912) 625-7248. Licensee: Peach Broadcasting Co. Inc. Net: MBS; Ga. Net. Wash atty: Fletcher, Heald & Hildreth. Format: Modern country. News progmg 11 hrs wkly. Target aud: General. ■ Ottis G. Stephens, pres, gen mgr & gen sls mgr; Sue Stephens, prom mgr; Wendell F. Stephens, progmg dir, news dir & chief engr; John D. Reid, mus dir. ■ Rates: $6; 6; 6; 6.

WPEH-FM—May 6, 1971: 92.1 mhz; 3 kw. Ant 296 ft. TL: N33 00 48 W82 23 33. Dups AM 100%. Format: Country. Target aud: 25 plus. ■ Rates: Same as AM.

Lumpkin

WKCN(FM)—Nov 6, 1993: 99.3 mhz; 50 kw. Ant 492 ft. TL: N32 09 25 W85 05 51. Stereo. Hrs opn: 24. 1353 13th Ave., Columbus (31901). (706) 596-9000. FAX: (706) 660-4634. Licensee: Radio Lumpkin Inc. Wash atty: Fletcher, Heald & Hildreth. Format: New hot country. Target aud: 18-49. ■ Wayne Bishop, pres & gen mgr; Dave Kelley, opns mgr; Susan Breazeale, gen sls mgr; Chad King, mus dir; Charlie Harrell, chief engr. ■ Rates: $45; 35; 45; 35.

Lyons

WBBT(AM)—March 12, 1959: 1340 khz; 1 kw-U. TL: N32 12 50 W82 19 51. Hrs opn: 18. Box 111, 901 N. Victory Dr. (30436). (912) 526-8122; (912) 526-6333. FAX: (912) 526-8123. Licensee: Thompson Radio Broadcasting Co. Inc. (acq 5-2-88). Net: NBC; Ga. Net. Wash atty: Gary S. Smithwick. Format: MOR, 50s, 60s, 70s & 80s hits. News staff 2; news progmg 20 hrs wkly. Target aud: General. Spec prog: Farm 6 hrs wkly. ■ Harry H. Thompson, pres, gen mgr & chief engr; Michael P. Thompson, stn mgr & gen sls mgr; Sonia Peterson, prom mgr; Earl Averett, progmg dir & mus dir; Tony DeLoach, news dir. ■ Rates: $5; 5; 5; 5.

WLYU(FM)—Co-owned with WBBT(AM). Jan 1, 1989: 100.9 mhz; 3 kw. Ant 328 ft. TL: N32 06 48 W82 23 52. Stereo. Hrs opn: 24. Prog sep from AM. Net: CNN. Format: Country. News staff 3; news progmg 8 hrs wkly. Target aud: General. ■ Peggy Spikes, prom mgr & mus dir.

Macon

WAYS(FM)—Listing follows WMAZ(AM).

WBML(AM)—Oct 15, 1940: 900 khz; 2 kw-D, 145 w-N. TL: N32 50 58 W83 36 06. Box 6298 (31208-6298); 735 Reese St. (31201). (912) 743-5453. FAX: (912) 743-5475. Licensee: David Rodgers. Group owner: Rogers Broadcasting Group. Net: CNN. Rep: Gates. Format: Relg. News progmg 3 hrs wkly. Target aud: 35 plus. ■ David A. Rogers, pres; Orvil Nichols, gen mgr & gen sls mgr; Michael Mimbs, progmg dir & mus dir; John Timms, chief engr.

WCOP(AM)—See Warner Robins.

WDDO(AM)—Nov 25, 1957: 1240 khz; 1 kw-U. TL: N32 50 18 W83 39 02. Box 900 (31202). (912) 745-3375. FAX: (912) 742-8061. Licensee: Piedmont Communications Corp. (acq 12-1-76). Net: Natl Black, MBS. Rep: Christal. Format: Black gospel. ■ Fred L. Newton, pres & gen mgr; Willie Collins, progmg dir & mus dir; Laura Worth, news dir.

WPEZ(FM)—Co-owned with WDDO(AM). Oct 19, 1973: 107.9 mhz; 100 kw. Ant 690 ft. TL: N32 45 12 W83 33 46. Stereo. Prog sep from AM. (912) 746-6286. Net: Unistar. Format: Adult contemp. ■ Oscar Leverette, stn mgr & progmg dir; Jim Franklin, mus dir.

WDEN(AM)—Aug 1967: 1500 khz; 1 kw-D. TL: N32 48 47 W83 37 36. Box 46, 173 First St. (31297). (912) 745-3383. FAX: (912) 745-9693. Licensee: U.S. Broadcasting L.P. Group owner: Magic Broadcasting Companies (acq 10-87; $6 million with co-located FM; FTR 8-31-87). Net: NBC. Rep: McGavren Guild. Format: Gospel. News staff one. Target aud: 25-54. ■ Donald G. McCoy, pres; Douglas M. Grimm, exec vp & gen mgr; Leigh Hurd, gen sls mgr; Tommy Martin, prom mgr; Gerry Marshall, progmg dir; Laura Starling, mus dir; Ken Mann, news dir; John Timms, chief engr.

WDEN-FM—June 10, 1968: 105.3 mhz; 100 kw. Ant 777 ft. TL: N32 53 48 W83 32 05. Stereo. Hrs opn: 24. Wash atty: Latham & Watkins. Format: Country. ■ Tommy Martin, opns dir; Ken Mann, pub affrs dir. ■ Rates: $110; 100; 100; 50.

WKXK(AM)—November 1948: 1280 khz; 5 kw-D, 99 w-N. TL: N32 48 16 W83 36 16. 2525 Pio Nono Ave. (31206-3162). (912) 781-1063. FAX: (912) 781-6711. Licensee: Taylor Communications Corp. Rep: Banner. Wash atty: Pepper & Corazzini. Format: Sports. Target aud: 18-49. ■ Selman Krenin, pres; Gary Burrell, CFO; Jim Fain Jr., stn mgr & rgnl sls mgr; Bill Lamb, opns mgr & chief engr.

WMAZ(AM)—Oct 30, 1922: 940 khz; 50 kw-D, 10 kw-N, DA-N. TL: N32 53 06 W83 43 50. Stereo. Hrs opn: 24. Box 5008, 1314 Gray Hwy. (31213). (912) 752-9494; (912) 752-0940. FAX: (912) 752-1339. Licensee: Multimedia Inc. Group owner: Multimedia Broadcasting Co. Net: ABC/D, Unistar. Rep: Katz. Wash atty: Dow, Lohnes & Albertson. Format: News/talk, sports. News staff 2; news progmg 40 hrs wkly. Target aud: 40 plus; upscale, college educated, household income $50K plus. Spec prog: Relg 4 hrs wkly. ■ Jim McLendon, vp & gen mgr; Hal Sutton, opns dir; Jess Branson, rgnl sls mgr; Julie Muller, prom mgr; J.D. Sommers, progmg dir; Kenny Burgamy, news dir; M.T. Grabowski, pub affrs dir; Jerry Dowd, chief engr.

WAYS(FM)—Co-owned with WMAZ(AM). Feb 17, 1947: 99.1 mhz; 100 kw. Ant 648 ft. TL: N32 45 10 W83 33 32. Stereo. Hrs opn: 24. Prog sep from AM. (912) 752-9999; (912) 646-0000. Net: ABC/FM. Format: Oldies. News staff one; news progmg 4 hrs wkly. Target aud: 25-54; female/male split-median age 37. ■ Nancy Larson, rgnl sls mgr; Scott Tyler, mus dir. ■ WMAZ-TV affil.

WMKS(FM)—August 1992: 92.3 mhz; 3 kw. Ant 328 ft. TL: N32 46 26 W83 38 15. 3083 Pio Nono Ave. (31206). (912) 784-9230. FAX: (912) 784-1974. Licensee: Radio Macon Inc. (acq 1-13-92; $20,000 for CP; FTR 2-10-92). Format: Country. ■ Randy Sheffield, gen mgr; Jim West, progmg dir.

WNEX(AM)—April 1945: 1400 khz; 1 kw-U. TL: N32 51 07 W83 39 12. Box 7948 (31209). (912) 745-3301. FAX: (912) 742-2293. Licensee: Quality Broadcasting Inc. (acq 11-19-91). Net: NBC. Format: Talk. ■ Jim Macafee, pres; Wayne Sawyer, gen mgr; Bob Davis, progmg dir & mus dir; Dave Stewart, chief engr.

WPEZ(FM)—Listing follows WDDO(AM).

WQBZ(FM)—(Fort Valley). Apr 6, 1981: 106.3 mhz; 50 kw. Ant 426 ft. TL: N32 45 31 W83 44 49. Stereo. Hrs opn: 24. 2525 Pio Nono Ave., Macon (31206-3162). (912) 781-1063; (912) 825-0106. FAX: (912) 781-6711. Licensee: Taylor Broadcasting of Macon Inc. Group owner: Taylor Broadcasting (acq 3-26-90; $3 million; FTR 4-16-90). Net: Unistar. Rep: Banner. Wash atty: Pepper & Corazzini. Format: AOR. Target aud: 18-49. ■ Stephen J. Taylor, pres; Curtis T. Jones, vp, gen mgr & gen sls mgr; Nathan Hale, opns mgr & progmg dir; Jim Fain Jr., rgnl sls mgr; Bill Lamb, chief engr.

Georgia

WRCC(AM)—See Warner Robins.

WRCC-FM—See Warner Robins.

WVVY(FM)—(Fort Valley). March 3, 1993: 97.9 mhz; 10.5 kw. Ant 499 ft. TL: N32 34 12 W83 45 26. Stereo. Hrs opn: 24. 2525 Pio Nono Ave., Macon (31206-3162). (912) 781-1063; (912) 825-0106. FAX: (912) 781-6711. Licensee: Taylor Communications Corp. (acq 12-2-92; $1 million with WKXK[AM] Macon; FTR 12-21-92). Net: SMN; Ga. Net. Rep: Banner. Wash atty: Pepper & Corrazzini. Format: Adult contemp. News staff one; news progmg 14 hrs wkly. Target aud: 18 plus. ■ Edward L. Taylor, chmn; Selman Kremer, pres; Gary Burnell, CFO; Jim Fain Jr., gen mgr & stn mgr; Bill Lamb, opns mgr & chief engr; Judy Murrel, gen sls mgr; Jim Fain Jr.(local), rgnl sls mgr; Doris Studstill, prom mgr; Wright Peavy, progmg dir; Jim Landis, mus dir. ■ Rates: $8.75; 8; 8.75; 4.75.

Madison

WYTH(AM)—June 1955: 1250 khz; 1 kw-D. TL: N33 34 45 W83 28 40. Hrs opn: 6 AM-sunset. Drawer 635 (30650). (706) 342-1250. FAX: (706) 342-1752. Licensee: Central Georgia Broadcasting Co. (acq 9-1-59). Net: NBC; Ga. Net. Format: Var, country. News staff one; news progmg 15 hrs wkly. Target aud: General. Spec prog: Farm 15 hrs, class one hr, Black 13 hrs, talk 15 hrs wkly. ■ James F. Small Jr., pres, gen mgr, progmg dir & pub affrs dir; Russell Brooks, engrg mgr; Paul Paschal, chief engr. ■ Rates: $6; 6; 6; 6.

Manchester

WFDR(AM)—June 1957: 1370 khz; 1 kw-D. TL: N32 53 14 W84 35 54. Box 510, Hwy. 190, Scenic Heights (31816). (706) 846-3115. FAX: (706) 846-2425. Licensee: Provident Broadcasting Co. (acq 8-81; $790,000 with co-located FM; FTR 9-7-81). Net: USA. Rep: Rgnl Reps. Format: Relg, Black. Target aud: General. Spec prog: Farm 15 hrs, class one hr, Black 13 hrs wkly. ■ Jim Campbell, pres; Rick Davison, gen mgr & gen sls mgr; Rod Hampton, prom mgr, progmg dir & mus dir; Frank McLemore, chief engr.

WVFJ-FM—Co-owned with WFDR(AM). 1967: 93.3 mhz; 100 kw. Ant 1,250 ft. TL: N32 50 40 W84 37 25. Stereo. Dups AM 50%. Format: Relg. News progmg one hr wkly. Target aud: 18-54. ■ Barbara Harrison, news dir.

Marietta

WFOM(AM)—Oct 13, 1946: 1230 khz; 1 kw-U. TL: N33 55 38 W84 30 08. Suite 1-1230, 1033 Franklin Rd. (30067-8004). (404) 419-0935. Licensee: Toccoa Falls College Inc. (acq 10-21-91; $300,000; FTR 11-11-91). Format: Adult contemp, Christian. ■ Chuck Powell, stn mgr; Bob Bierman, chief engr.

WFTD(AM)—Nov 14, 1955: 1080 khz; 10 kw-D, DA. TL: N34 01 25 W84 40 04. Hrs opn: Sunrise-sunset. 744 Roswell St. (30060). (404) 424-9850. Licensee: Pnuema Foundation (acq 10-87; $240,000; FTR 10-26-87). Net: Skylight, USA. Format: Relg. News progmg 6 hrs wkly. Target aud: 35-55; predominantly female Christians, family oriented homemakers. ■ Nelson L. Price, pres; Rocky L. Payne, gen mgr; George Pass, chief engr.

*****WGHR(FM)**—Oct 7, 1981: 102.5 mhz; 16.5 w. Ant 250 ft. TL: N33 56 26 W84 31 13. Hrs opn: 24. 1100 S. Marietta Pkwy. (30060). (404) 528-7354; (404) 528-7300. FAX: (404) 528-7409. Licensee: Southern College of Technology. Format: Free form, college. Target aud: 18-24; college students, general. Spec prog: Techno/trance, punk, metal. ■ Jon McAleek, gen mgr; David Conrad, opns mgr & chief engr; Shawn Moseley, prom mgr; Shawn Moseley, Gerald Holmes, Harold Thompson, mus dirs; Stephen Wishart, asst mus dir; Bill Greve, news & pub affrs dir.

WKHX-FM—Licensed to Marietta. See Atlanta.

Martinez

WGOR(FM)—May 31, 1984: 93.9 mhz; 25 kw. Ant 328 ft. TL: N33 26 17 W82 05 19. Stereo. Box 211045, 124 N. Bellair Rd., Evans (30809). (706) 855-9494. FAX: (706) 868-1594. Licensee: CSRA Broadcasters Inc. (acq 11-10-92; $810,000; FTR 11-30-92). Net: CNN. Format: Oldies. ■ Duane Hargarve, gen mgr.

WKBG(FM)—Not on air, target date unknown: 107.7 mhz; 50 kw. Ant 492 ft. TL: N33 38 35 W82 19 50. c/o WRXR-FM, 753 Broad St. Augusta (30901). (706) 722-9696. Licensee: Kennedy Broadcasting Inc.

McDonough

WKKP(AM)—Apr 2, 1979: 1410 khz; 2.5 kw-D. TL: N33 25 47 W84 07 52. Hrs opn: 6 AM-8:10 PM. Box 351, 12 N. Cedar St. (30253). (404) 957-0208. FAX: (404) 957-0279. Licensee: Henry County Radio Co. Inc. (acq 3-30-92; $65,000; FTR 4-20-92). Net: NBC; Ga. Net. Rep: Rgnl Reps. Format: MOR. News progmg 20 hrs wkly. Target aud: General. Spec prog: Farm one hr, relg 5 hrs wkly. ■ Richard A. Moore, pres; Don Earnhardt, gen mgr; Tom Lynde, opns mgr; George Pass, chief engr.

*****WMVV(FM)**—Not on air, target date unknown: 90.7 mhz; 11 kw. Ant 300 ft. TL: N32 22 58 W84 05 16. Stereo. 1738 Fairview Rd., Stockbridge (30281). (404) 474-1313. Licensee: Mount Vernon Baptist Church of Henry County Inc. Format: Relg. ■ Terry Rainey, pres; Emery Hamilton, gen mgr.

McRae

WYIS(AM)—July 27, 1957: 1410 khz; 1 kw-D. TL: N32 03 25 W82 51 56. Box 1410, Hwy. 341 S. (31055). (912) 868-5611. FAX: (912) 868-5611. Licensee: WDAX Inc. Net: ABC/I. Rep: Rgnl Reps. Format: Country. News staff one. Target aud: 25-50; mature, wage earners. Spec prog: Black 4 hrs, gospel 10 hrs wkly. ■ Richard C. Bailey, pres; Ken Howard, gen mgr & gen sls mgr; Jamie Hussey, progmg dir, mus dir & news dir; Jim Slawson, chief engr.

WYSC(FM)—Co-owned with WYIS(AM). Aug 3, 1979: 95.3 mhz; 3 kw. Ant 289 ft. TL: N32 03 25 W82 51 56. Prog sep from AM. Format: CHR.

Metter

WMAC(AM)—Dec 22, 1961: 1360 khz; 1 kw-D. TL: N32 23 56 W82 02 36. Box 238 (30439). (912) 685-2136. Licensee: Radio Metter Inc. Format: Adult contemp, oldies. ■ Jimmy Page, pres & gen mgr; Lou Phil Kitchens, opns mgr; Chuck Merrion, progmg dir; Jim Slauslen, chief engr.

WHCG(FM)—Co-owned with WMAC(AM). Aug 1, 1971: 103.7 mhz; 3 kw. Ant 299 ft. TL: N32 23 56 W82 02 36. Prog sep from AM. Format: Adult contemp, oldies.

Midway

WGCO(FM)—Licensed to Midway. See Savannah.

Milan

WMCG(FM)—1982: 104.9 mhz; 3 kw. Ant 600 ft. TL: N32 07 16 W83 16 05 (CP: 38.5 kw, ant 548 ft.). Stereo. Hrs opn: 24. Box 1060; 115 First St., Rochelle (31079). (912) 365-7788. FAX: (912) 365-7799. Licensee: Tel-Dodge Broadcasting. Net: ABC/E. Rep: T N. Format: Country. Target aud: 25-54. Spec prog: Farm one hr wkly. ■ Jim Ball, gen mgr; Dick Merrill, chief engr.

Milledgeville

WKGQ(AM)—March 6, 1975: 1060 khz; 1 kw-D. TL: N33 05 45 W83 11 36. Box 832, 131 W. Hancock St. (31061); Studios, 156 Lake Laurel Rd. (31061). (912) 453-9406; (912) 453-2123. FAX: (912) 453-3298. Licensee: Good Medicine Radio, Ga. Inc. (acq 2-18-92; $185,000 with WSKS[AM] Sparta; FTR 3-9-92). Net: CNN, Daynet. Rep: Southern. Format: News/talk. News staff one; news progmg 70 hrs wkly. Target aud: 25 plus. ■ Frank Copsidas Jr., pres; Cheryl Hackett, gen mgr & opns mgr; Rodney Hilloway, progmg dir; Dan Davis, chief engr. ■ Rates: $9; 11; 9; 9.

WKZR(FM)—Listing follows WMVG(AM).

WLRR(FM)—July 24, 1990: 100.7 mhz; 3 kw. Ant 328 ft. TL: N33 06 50 W83 13 08. 185 Ivey-Weaver Rd. (31061). (912) 453-1007. FAX: (912) 453-1007. Licensee: Preston W. Small.

WMVG(AM)—March 29, 1946: 1450 khz; 1 kw-U. TL: N33 04 58 W83 15 01. Hrs opn: 5:45 AM-midnight. Box 519, 1250 W. Charlton St. (31061). (912) 452-0586. FAX: (912) 452-5886. Licensee: WMVG Inc. Net: ABC/I. Rep: Rgnl Reps. Format: Adult contemp, news/talk. News staff one; news progmg 25 hrs wkly. Target aud: 25 plus. Spec prog: Black 4 hrs wkly. ■ Dale Van Cantfort, pres & gen mgr; Scott MacLeod, opns mgr & progmg dir; Chase Allen, news dir; Ed Discher, chief engr. ■ Rates: $17; 17; 17; 10.

WKZR(FM)—Co-owned with WMVG(AM). June 30, 1966: 102.3 mhz; 3.3 kw. Ant 300 ft. TL: N33 04 58 W83 15 01. Stereo. Prog sep from AM. Format: Country. ■ Rates: Same as AM.

*****WXGC(FM)**—August 1975: 88.9 mhz; 38 w. Ant 110 ft. TL: N33 04 44 W83 13 55. Box 3124, Georgia College (31061). (912) 453-4101. FAX: (912) 453-4102. Licensee: Georgia College (acq 8-75). Format: Top 40. Spec prog: Jazz 12 hrs, class 7 hrs wkly. ■ Laurel Townsend, gen mgr; Michelle Rader, progmg dir; Keenan Foster, mus dir; Patrick Davis, news dir; Richard Hamilton, chief engr.

Millen

WMKO(FM)—Dec 4, 1989: 94.9 mhz; 14.5 kw. Ant 400 ft. TL: N32 43 57 W81 51 43. Stereo. Hrs opn: 24. Box 1129 (30442); Crossroads Executive Park, 115 Northside Dr., W., Statesboro (30458). (912) 982-5695; (912) 489-2086. FAX: (912) 982-5562. Licensee: Tommy Cooper, receiver (acq 4-23-92). Net: ABC; Ga. Net., Tobacco. Wash atty: Hamel & Park. Format: Country. News staff one; news progmg 8 hrs wkly. Target aud: General. Spec prog: Farm 10 hrs wkly. ■ Brian Tolby, gen sls mgr; Tommy Cooper, prom mgr; Rick Pittman, mus dir; R.F. Burns, chief engr. ■ Rates: $10; 9; 10; 8.

Monroe

WKUN(AM)—Feb 4, 1971: 1580 khz; 1 kw-D. TL: N33 48 37 W83 42 01. Hrs opn: 6 AM-10 PM. Box 649, 204 W. Spring St. (30655). (404) 267-6558. Licensee: Community Broadcasting Co. Inc. Format: C&W. Spec prog: Farm 10 hrs wkly. ■ Grace Morris, pres & gen mgr; June Carr, gen sls mgr; John Still, progmg dir & news dir; Dan Davis, chief engr.

Montezuma

WMNZ(AM)—Nov 29, 1961: 1050 khz; 250 w-D, 42 w-N. TL: N32 17 58 W84 01 34 (CP: TL N32 17 53 W84 02 02). Box 511 (31063). (912) 472-8386. Licensee: Macon County Broadcasting Co. Format: C&W, MOR, gospel. ■ William E. Blizzard Jr., pres, gen mgr, gen sls mgr, prom mgr & news dir; Danny Blizzard, progmg dir & mus dir.

WLML(FM)—Co-owned with WMNZ(AM). Not on air, target date 1994: 95.1 mhz; 6 kw. Ant 157 ft. TL: N32 17 53 W84 02 02. Format: Country, sports.

Morrow

WSSA(AM)—November 1956: 1570 khz; 5 kw-D, 58 w-N. TL: N33 36 05 W84 18 40. Box 831, 2424 Old Rex Morrow Rd. (30260). (404) 361-8843. Licensee: Wings Radio Co. Inc. (acq 5-10-82; $85,000; FTR 5-10-82). Net: USA. Format: Relg, talk. News staff one. Target aud: 24-55. ■ F. Douglas Wilhite, pres & gen mgr; Sean Hughes, opns mgr; Jay F. Springs, gen sls mgr; John Lee, mus dir. ■ Rates: $18; 18; 18; 18.

Moultrie

WMGA(AM)—September 1939: 580 khz; 900 w-D, 250 w-N, DA-N. TL: N31 12 20 W83 46 45 (CP: COL Riverside, GA). Box 1380, U.S. Hwy. 319 N. (31776). (912) 985-0580. FAX: (912) 890-8609. Licensee: Radio Moultrie Inc. (acq 7-86; $400,000; FTR 6-2-86). Net: CBS. Format: Adult contemp, talk. News staff one; news progmg 17 hrs wkly. Target aud: 30 plus; middle & upper income. Spec prog: Farm 10 hrs, loc news 4 hrs, relg 5 hrs wkly. ■ G. Christopher Elder, gen mgr; Eric Rowan, stn mgr, chief opns, gen sls mgr & prom dir; Sonja Heinze, news dir; A.M. Anderson, chief engr.

WMTM(AM)—Nov 10, 1953: 1300 khz; 5 kw-D. TL: N31 12 54 W83 47 13. Stereo. Hrs opn: 6 AM-sundown. Box 788, WMTM Rd. (31776). (912) 985-1300. FAX: (912) 890-0905. Licensee: Colquitt Broadcasting Co. Net: ABC TalkRadio, MBS; S.E. Agri. Rep: Rgnl Reps. Wash atty: Smithwick & Belendiuk. Format: Country, gospel. News staff one. Target aud: General. Spec prog: Farm 16 hrs wkly. ■ Douglas J. Turner, pres & chief engr; Donnie Turner, gen mgr, sls dir, adv dir, progmg dir & news dir; Lee Redmond, mus dir. ■ Rates: $6.35; 6.35; 6.35 6.35.

WMTM-FM—Nov 17, 1964: 93.9 mhz; 100 kw. Ant 555 ft. TL: N31 12 54 W83 47 13. Stereo. Hrs opn: 6 AM-midnight. Prog sep from AM. Net: MBS. Format: Country. Target aud: General. ■ Donnie Turner, opns mgr, mktg mgr & prom mgr. ■ Rates: $6.35; 6.35; 6.35; 6.35.

Mountain City

WALH(AM)—May 1, 1986: 1340 khz; 1 kw-U. TL: N34 56 16 W83 23 27. Box F (30562). (706) 746-2256. Licensee: W.L. Savage/Hugh H. Walden, gen partners & Valley Communications Corp. Wash atty: Hamel & Park. Format: Country, bluegrass, gospel. News staff one; news progmg 5 hrs wkly. Target aud: 30-50; blue collar. Spec prog: Farm 2 hrs wkly. ■ W.L. Savage, pres, gen mgr, gen sls mgr & news dir; Loraine Savage, progmg dir; W.P. Franklin, mus dir; E.O. Holden, chief engr. ■ Rates: $4.25; 4.25; 4.25; na.

Murrayville

WKZD(AM)—Licensed to Murrayville. See Gainesville.

Nashville

WJYF(FM)—Licensed to Nashville. See Tifton.

WNGA(AM)—1960: 1600 khz; 1 kw-D. TL: N31 12 07 W83 13 18. Hrs opn: 12. 311 Green St. N.E., Suite 211, Gainesville (30501). (912) 686-2001. Licensee: Bennie E. Hewett. Group owner: Bennie E. Hewett Stns. Format: Country. News staff one. ■ Bennie E. Hewett, pres.

Newnan

WCOH(AM)—December 1947; 1400 khz; 1 kw-U. TL: N33 21 53 W84 48 42. 154 Boone Dr. (30263). (404) 253-4636. FAX: (404) 251-8260. Licensee: Newnan Broadcasting Co. Inc. (acq 11-85; $300,000; FTR 11-11-85). Net: MBS. Ga. Net. Wash atty: Miller & Miller. Format: Country. News staff 2; news progmg 10 hrs wkly. Target aud: 25-54. ■ Dallas M. Tarkenton II, pres; Stephen D. Tarkenton, gen mgr; Nadine Richardson, opns mgr; Jim Martin, gen sls mgr; Brad Myers, prom mgr; Richard Mann, mus dir; Tom Corker, news dir; Tom Taylor, chief engr.

WMKJ(FM)—Licensed to Newnan. See Peachtree City.

WNEA(AM)—April 18, 1962; 1300 khz; 1 kw-D. TL: N33 22 31 W84 47 08. Box 1213 (30264); 8 Madison St. (30263). (404) 253-4711. Licensee: Radio Newnan Inc. Net: NBC; Ga. Net. Format: Country. News progmg 14 hrs wkly. Target aud: 18-64. Spec prog: Gospel 15 hrs wkly. ■ Eathel Holley, pres; Harlan Parks, gen mgr, gen sls mgr & progmg mgr. ■ Rates: $6; 6; 6; 6.

North Atlanta

WCNN(AM)—Licensed to North Atlanta. See Atlanta.

Ochlocknee

WJEP(AM)—June 4, 1984; 1020 khz; 10 kw-D. TL: N30 54 00 W83 59 55. Box 90, Thomasville (31799). (912) 228-5683. FAX: (912) 436-0544. Licensee: Lifeline Ministries Inc. (acq 8-18-83). Net: UPI. Format: Adult contemp, MOR, Christian. Spec prog: Black 2 hrs, southern gospel 3 hrs wkly. ■ J.W. Keyton Jr., pres & gen mgr; Jeffery Davis, progmg dir; Clyde Scott, chief engr.

Ocilla

WKAA(FM)—December 1983; 97.7 mhz; 1.8 kw. Ant 400 ft. TL: N31 31 37 W83 20 07 (CP: Ant 393 ft.). Suite 322, Myon Complex, Tifton (31794). (912) 386-5679. Licensee: Harper Broadcasting Corp. (acq 10-15-91; $205,000; FTR 11-4-91). Format: Country. ■ Mike Roberts, gen mgr.

WLPF(FM)—December 1993; 98.5 mhz; 4.3 kw. Ant 361 ft. TL: N31 38 01 W83 14 49. Box 12155, Augusta (30914). (800) 926-4669. Licensee: Clarence T. Barinowski (acq 11-17-92; $55,000; FTR 12-7-92). ■ Clarence Barnowski, pres.

WSIZ(AM)—March 14, 1961; 1380 khz; 5 kw-D. TL: N31 37 42 W83 14 53 (CP: TL: N31 33 01 W83 14 49). Box 585 (31774). Licensee: Ben Hill-Irwin Broadcasting Corp. (acq 12-30-92; $11,500; FTR 1-25-93). ■ Joe Rogers, pres & chief engr; Virginia Rogers, gen mgr & gen sls mgr; Bennie Spiers, progmg dir & news dir; Michael Day, mus dir.

Omega

WTIF-FM—Not on air, target date unknown; 107.5 mhz; 1.8 kw. Ant 400 ft. TL: N31 27 17 W83 33 37. Box 968, Tifton (31793). (912) 382-1340. Licensee: Omega Broadcasting Corp. (acq 2-22-93; $280,000; FTR 3-15-93). Format: Country. ■ Ron Griffin, gen mgr.

Peachtree City

WMKJ(FM)—(Newnan). 1948; 96.7 mhz; 1 kw. Ant 545 ft. TL: N33 26 22 W84 42 42. Stereo. Box 2547, Peachtree City (30609). (404) 577-4850. FAX: (404) 251-8260. Licensee: South Metro Broadcasting Co. Inc. (acq 11-87). Format: Adult contemp. News staff one; news progmg 5 hrs wkly. Target aud: 25-54. ■ Jim Martin, adv dir; Richard Mann, progmg dir; Tom Corker, news dir; Tom Taylor, chief engr.

Pelham

WQVE(FM)—See Camilla.

Perry

WPGA(AM)—1955; 980 khz; 5 kw-D, 270 w-N. TL: N32 26 40 W83 45 00. Stereo. Hrs opn: 6 AM-midnight. Drawer 980, 404 Gen. Hodges Blvd. (31069). (912) 987-2980. FAX: (912) 987-7595. Licensee: Radio Perry Inc. (acq 1960). Net: Ga. Net. Format: Oldies. News staff 2; news progmg 6 hrs wkly. Target aud: General. Spec prog: Farm 2 hrs, relg 6 hrs wkly. ■ Lowell L. Register, pres; Janice Register, gen mgr; John Lynn, gen sls mgr; Phil Clark, progmg dir; Len Register, chief engr.

WPGA-FM—May 3, 1966; 100.9 mhz; 3 kw. Ant 345 ft. TL: N32 33 20 W83 44 14. Stereo. Hrs opn: 24. Prog sep from AM. Net: ABC/C. Format: Adult contemp. News staff one. ■ Chuck Wallace, mus dir. ■ WPGA-TV affil.

Quitman

WSFB(AM)—Nov 19, 1955; 1490 khz; 1 kw-U. TL: N30 46 51 W83 34 30. Box 632 (31643). (912) 263-4373. Licensee: R.B.H. Broadcasting Co. Inc. (acq 11-1-61). Format: Country. ■ William F. Hoopes, pres & gen mgr; David White, progmg dir & mus dir.

WSTI-FM—Sept 12, 1986; 105.3 mhz; 3 kw. Ant 300 ft. TL: N30 48 45 W83 31 18. Stereo. Box 5286, Valdosta (31603). (912) 247-7568. Licensee: Orb Communications Inc. (acq 4-22-93; $515,215; FTR 5-10-93). Format: Adult contemp. Spec prog: Farm 5 hrs wkly. ■ Bob Harrison, pres & gen mgr; Nikki Fawcett, opns mgr; Brian Kelly, progmg dir; C.H. Fletcher, chief engr.

Reidsville

WTNL(AM)—June 25, 1976; 1390 khz; 500 w-D. TL: N32 05 14 W82 07 47. Box 69 (30453). (912) 557-3777. Licensee: WRBX/WTNL Inc. ($35,000 with co-located FM; FTR 2-15-93). Format: Southern gospel. ■ Dan Brown, gen mgr.

WRBX(FM)—Co-owned with WTNL(AM). Not on air, target date unknown: 104.1 mhz; 3 kw. Ant 187 ft. TL: N32 05 14 W82 07 47. Hrs opn: 6 AM-11 PM. Dups AM 100%.

Richmond Hill

WRHQ(FM)—May 13, 1991; 105.3 mhz; 11 kw. Ant 485 ft. TL: N32 02 52 W81 07 26. Stereo. Hrs opn: 24. Box 1150, Number 4, Fords Village (31324). (912) 756-3111; (912) 234-1053. FAX: (912) 756-4689. Licensee: Richmond Hill Broadcasting. Group owner: Thoroughbred Communications. Wash atty: Verner, Liipfert, Bernhard, McPherson & Hand. Format: Rock, adult contemp. News progmg 2 hrs wkly. Target aud: 25-44; affluent. ■ Jerry Rogers, pres, gen mgr & gen sls mgr; Dennis Eversoll, vp, opns dir & chief engr; Beth Brantley, prom dir; Lisa Macolly, adv mgr; Bill Owen, progmg dir; Lyndy Branner, news dir & pub affrs dir. ■ Rates: $18; 18; 18; 8.

Ringgold

WSGC-FM—March 1989; 101.9 mhz; 650 w. Ant 702 ft. TL: N34 58 11 W85 05 10. Box 91189, Chattanooga, TN (37412). (706) 937-4653. Licensee: Battlefield Broadcasting Radio Inc. (acq 9-1-93; $250,000; FTR 9-27-93). Format: Oldies. ■ Marshall Brandy, pres & gen mgr.

Rockmart

WTSH-FM—Feb 28, 1972; 107.1 mhz; 3 kw. Ant 300 ft. TL: N34 00 14 W85 03 22 (CP: 45 kw, ant 518 ft.). Box 6008, Rome (30162). (706) 291-9496. Licensee: Broadcast Investment Assoc. Net: NBC. Format: Country. ■ Bobby Price, gen mgr.

WZOT(AM)—Aug 28, 1959; 1220 khz; 5 kw-D, 150 w-N. TL: N34 00 14 W85 03 22. Box 520 (30153). (404) 684-7848. Licensee: Broadcast Investment Assoc. Group owner: Southern Broadcasting Companies Inc. (acq 1-15-88). Net: NBC; Ga. Net. Format: Southern gospel. News staff one; news progmg 8 hrs wkly. Target aud: 18-45. ■ Bobby Price, gen mgr.

Rome

WKCX(FM)—May 22, 1965; 97.7 mhz; 3.3 kw. Ant 790 ft. TL: N34 14 00 W85 14 02 (CP: 18 kw). Stereo. Hrs opn: 24. Box 1546 (30162); 710 Turner McCall Blvd. (30161). (706) 291-9766. FAX: (706) 291-9706. Licensee: Briar Creek Broadcasting. Net: MBS. Format: Adult contemp. News staff one; news progmg 10 hrs wkly. Target aud: 18-54; family-oriented active in the community. ■ A. Mills Fitzner, pres, gen mgr & mus dir; Tom Barclay, stn mgr; Robert Smyth, sls dir; Ed McIntyre, news dir; Phil Baker, chief engr. ■ Rates: $21; 19; 19; 17.

WLAQ(AM)—1947; 1410 khz; 1 kw-U, DA-N. TL: N34 15 43 W85 12 22. Box 228 (30162-0228). (706) 232-7767. FAX: (706) 295-9225. Licensee: Cripple Creek Broadcasting Co. (acq 4-1-87). Net: CBS, MBS. Rep: Southern. Format: Talk, sports, news. News staff one. ■ Randy Davis, pres, gen mgr & news dir; Cal Owens, progmg dir; Andy Walker, chief engr.

WQTU(FM)—Listing follows WRGA(AM).

WRGA(AM)—November 1929; 1470 khz; 5 kw-U, DA-N. TL: N34 18 05 W85 09 19. Hrs opn: 24. Box 1187, Broadcast Center, 104 E. 6th Ave. (30161). (706) 291-9742. FAX: (706) 291-7155. Licensee: McDougald Broadcasting Corp. (acq 8-2-77). Net: ABC/E; Ga. Net. Rep: Rgnl Reps. Wash atty: Fletcher, Heald & Hildreth. Format: News/talk, country. News staff 3; news progmg 20 hrs wkly. Target aud: General. ■ Michael H. McDougald, pres; Leeta McDougald, exec vp & gen mgr; Randy Quick, progmg dir; Don Briscar, mus dir; Doug Walker, news dir; Phil Baker, chief engr. ■ Rates: $19.50; 17.50; 19.50; 17.50.

WQTU(FM)—Co-owned with WRGA(AM). May 2, 1966; 102.3 mhz; 6 kw. Ant 804 ft. TL: N34 14 02 W85 13 50 (CP: 1.1 kw, ant 745 ft.). Stereo. Hrs opn: 24. Prog sep from AM. (706) 295-1023. Format: Adult contemp. News progmg 6 hrs wkly. Target aud: 25-54. Spec prog: Black 3 hrs wkly. ■ Rates: $19.50; 17.50; 19.50; 17.50.

WROM(AM)—Dec 26, 1946; 710 khz; 1 kw-D. TL: N34 15 30 W85 09 15. Hrs opn: Sunrise-sunset. Box 5031, 1105 Calhoun Ave. (30161-5031). (706) 234-7171. FAX: (706) 234-8043. Licensee: Promiseland Communications Inc. (acq 10-11-93). Net: Moody. Wash atty: Maupin & Taylor. Format: Gospel, talk. News staff one; news progmg 14 hrs wkly. Target aud: 45 plus. ■ Roy Taylor, pres & gen mgr; Dathon Sorrow, progmg dir; Phil Baker, chief engr. ■ Rates: $12; 10; 10; 10.

WTSH(AM)—Aug 1, 1962; 1360 khz; 500 w-D, 150 w-N. TL: N34 16 15 W85 11 00. Hrs opn: 6 AM-11 AM. Box 6008 (30162); 20 John Davenport Dr. (30161). (706) 291-9496. FAX: (706) 234-7107. Licensee: Broadcast Investment Assoc. Group owner: Southern Broadcasting Companies Inc. (acq 1-15-88). Net: NBC, Unistar. Format: Country. News staff one. Target aud: 25-54. Spec prog: Black 4 hrs wkly. ■ Paul Stone, CEO; Robert Price, gen mgr; Kris Cantrell, gen sls mgr; Bobby Green, vp adv & mus dir. ■ Rates: $10; 10; 10; na.

Rossville

WLMX(AM)—Nov 11, 1958; 980 khz; 500 w-D. TL: N34 58 03 W85 18 00. Hrs opn: Sunrise-sunset. Box 989, Chattanooga, TN (37401); 203 Ellis Rd. (30741). (706) 861-1050. FAX: (706) 861-5547. Licensee: Wicks Radio L.P. (acq 3-11-93; $6.9 million with co-located FM; FTR 4-12-93). Net: CNN. Rep: Eastman. Format: News. News staff one. Target aud: 25-54. ■ D. Rex Tackett, pres & gen mgr; Mariann M. Tackett, gen sls mgr & natl sls mgr; Bill Burkett, progmg dir & mus dir; Robin Parks, news dir; Parks Hall, chief engr.

WLMX-FM—June 8, 1966; 105.5 mhz; 3 kw. Ant 270 ft. TL: N35 02 55 W85 15 10 (CP: 2.7 kw, ant 344 ft.). Stereo. Prog sep from AM. Format: Adult contemp.

Royston

WBIC(AM)—January 1971; 810 khz; 250 w-D. TL: N34 16 50 W83 07 09. Hrs opn: Sunrise-sunset. 431 Turner St. (30662). (706) 245-6101. Licensee: Athena Broadcasting (acq 12-89; $700,000 with co-located FM; FTR 12-4-89). Net: Ga. Net. Format: Oldies, gospel. News staff one; news progmg 7 hrs wkly. Target aud: General. ■ Hugh Christian, pres; Julie Irby, gen mgr & gen sls mgr; Don Nestor, progmg dir & news dir; Joe Massey, mus dir & pub affrs dir; Steve Split, chief engr.

WPUP(FM)—Licensed to Royston. See Athens.

St. Mary's

WECC(AM)—Oct 15, 1985; 1190 khz; 2.5 kw-D. TL: N30 45 48 W81 36 40. Box 1190, 2101 Hwy. 40 E. (31558). (912) 882-3000. FAX: (912) 882-9322. Licensee: Lois V. Casey. Net: USA, ABC/E. Rep: Rgnl Reps. Format: Relg. News staff one; news progmg 15 hrs wkly. Target aud: General. Spec prog: Black 4 hrs wkly. ■ Paul Hafer, gen mgr; Vickie Hafer, prom mgr. ■ Rates: $4; 4; 4; na.

St. Simons Island

WBYB(FM)—See Brunswick.

WGIG(AM)—See Brunswick.

WHJX-FM—See Jacksonville, Fla.

WMOG-FM—Licensed to St. Simons Island. See Brunswick.

Sandersville

WSNT(AM)—May 11, 1956: 1490 khz; 1 kw-U. TL: N32 58 23 W82 48 34. Box 150, 312 Morningside Dr. (31082). (912) 552-5182. FAX: (912) 237-2011. Licensee: Radio Station WSNT Inc. Net: NBC; Tobacco. Format: Relg, country. ■ Francis Brazzell, pres; Capers Brazzell, gen mgr; Maria Smith, stn mgr & progmg dir; Roy Thompson, sls dir & prom mgr; Barbara Graves, gen sls mgr; Michael Howell, mus dir; Curtis Parsons, news dir; James Slawson, chief engr. ■ Rates: $8; 8; 8; 6.

WSNT-FM—1975: 99.9 mhz; 3 kw. Ant 184 ft. TL: N32 58 23 W82 48 34. Stereo. Hrs opn: 6 AM-midnight. Dups AM 100%. ■ Rates: Same as AM.

Savannah

WAEV(FM)—Listing follows WSOK(AM).

WBMQ(AM)—Dec 29, 1939: 630 khz; 5 kw-U, DA-N. TL: N32 03 51 W81 00 52. Box 876 (31498); One Riverview Rd. (31410). (912) 897-1529. FAX: (912) 897-4047. Licensee: Radio Southeast (acq 4-1-88). Net: CBS, NBC Talknet, Daynet. Rep: Katz. Format: News/talk. News progmg 16 hrs wkly. Target aud: 35 plus. ■ Bill McCormick, pres; John Ade, gen mgr; Don Scott, opns dir; Mark Blake, progmg dir; Jay Sisson, mus dir; Sharon McDonald, news dir; Marty Foglia, chief engr.

WIXV(FM)—Co-owned with WBMQ(AM). April 24, 1972: 95.5 mhz; 100 kw. Ant 900 ft. TL: N32 03 30 W81 20 20. Stereo. Prog sep from AM. Format: AOR. News staff one; news progmg 2 hrs wkly. Target aud: 18-49. ■ Mark Blake, progmg dir.

WCHY(AM)—Oct 15, 1929: 1290 khz; 5 kw-U, DA-N. TL: N32 05 26 W81 08 55. Stereo. Box 1247 (31402); 245 Alfred St. (31408). (912) 964-7794. FAX: (912) 964-9414. Licensee: Roth Broadcasting of Savannah. Group owner: Roth Communications (acq 11-2-87). Net: ABC/E. Rep: Christal. Wash atty: Kaye, Scholer, Fierman, Hayes & Handler. Format: Contemp country. News staff one; news progmg 7 hrs wkly. Target aud: 25-54. ■ Dennis Jones, gen mgr; Dave Gibson, gen sls mgr; Shannon Burns, progmg dir; Zack Taylor, mus dir; Debbie Bolton, news dir; Marty Foglia, chief engr. ■ Rates: $65; 60; 60; 35.

WCHY-FM—Nov 29, 1946: 94.1 mhz; 100 kw. Ant 1,320 ft. TL: N32 03 14 W81 21 01. Stereo. Dups AM 100%.

WEAS(AM)—Oct 6, 1950: 900 khz; 5 kw-D, 157 w-N. TL: N32 05 13 W81 05 35 (CP: TL: 32 04 30 W81 04 16). Box 23268 (31403). (912) 234-7264. FAX: (912) 233-7247. Licensee: WEAS Inc. Format: Sports, talk. News staff one. ■ M.B. Rivers, pres; Eric Anderson, gen mgr; Linda Patgette, gen sls mgr; Mark Waters, progmg dir; John Jackson, news dir; Dennis Eversoll, chief engr.

WEAS-FM—August 1967: 93.1 mhz; 100 kw. Ant 310 ft. TL: N32 05 13 W81 05 35 (CP: 81.3 kw, ant 981 ft., TL: N32 02 48 W81 20 27). Stereo. Prog sep from AM. Box 23268 (31403). (912) 234-7264. FAX: (912) 233-7247. Licensee: WEAS, Inc. Format: Urban contemp. ■ M.B. Rivers, pres; Floyd Blackwell, progmg dir.

WGCO(FM)—(Midway). 1974: 98.3 mhz; 100 kw. Ant 1,047 ft. TL: N31 36 45 W81 21 37. Stereo. Hrs opn: 24. Suite 201-F, 401 Mall Blvd., Savannah (31406); Box 1134, Brunswick (31521). (912) 351-9830; (912) 634-0983. FAX: (912) 352-4821; (912) 638-1733. Licensee: Intermart Broadcasting Georgia Coast Inc. Group owner: InterMart Broadcasting Corp. (acq 11-16-88; $1,200,000; FTR 12-19-88). Net: MBS, Unistar. Rep: Eastman. Wash atty: Smithwick & Belenduik, P.C. Format: Oldies. News staff one; news progmg 2 hrs wkly. Target aud: 25-54; yuppies. ■ Jim Martin Jr., pres; Robert A. Angel, vp & gen mgr; Jim Tapley, prom dir; Bill Young, progmg dir; Jennifer Chaffman, pub affrs dir; Dick Boekeloe, chief engr. ■ Rates: $30; 30; 30; 20.

***WHCJ(FM)**—Aug 18, 1975: 90.3 mhz; 6 kw. Ant 100 ft. TL: N32 01 23 W81 03 24. Box 20484 (31404). (912) 356-2399. FAX: (912) 356-2996. Licensee: Savannah State College. Net: UPI. Format: Jazz, educational, relg. Target aud: 17-65; interested in jazz, reggae, blues & gospel. ■ Theron "Ike" Carter, gen mgr; Ursula Yvette Boyd, progmg dir & pub affrs dir; Stephen A. Bess, mus dir; Natasha Beckett, news dir; Marty Foglia, chief engr.

WIXV(FM)—Listing follows WBMQ(AM).

WIZA(AM)—Aug 14, 1946: 1450 khz; 1 kw-U. TL: N32 04 12 W81 06 41. 1601 Whitaker St. (31401). (912) 236-9926. FAX: (912) 236-3832. Licensee: Inter Urban Broadcasting Co. (acq 9-30-86; $156,000; FTR 7-28-86). Net: SMN. Format: Lite contemp. ■ Wilhemina Manning, gen mgr; Dennis Eversoll, chief engr.

WJCL-FM—June 18, 1972: 96.5 mhz; 100 kw. Ant 1,232 ft. TL: N32 03 30 W81 20 20. Stereo. Hrs opn: 24. Box 61268 (31420). (912) 925-0022. FAX: (912) 925-8621. Licensee: Lewis Broadcasting Corp. (group owner). Net: Unistar. Rep: D & R Radio. Format: Hot Country. News staff one. Target aud: 25-54. ■ J. Curtis Lewis, pres; J. Fred Pierce, vp; Raleigh Neal, stn mgr; Charlie Solomon, opns mgr; Mike Allen, gen sls mgr; Beth Kelley, prom dir; Kelli Richards, progmg dir; Jay Morgan, mus dir; Wallace Tidwell, chief engr. WJCL-TV affil. ■ Rates: $43; 43; 43; 18.

WNMT(AM)—See Garden City.

WSGA(AM)—May 1956: 1400 khz; 1 kw-U. TL: N32 04 18 W81 04 47. Hrs opn: 24. Box 8247 (31412); Bank South Centre, 7 E. Congress St. (31401). (912) 233-8807. TWX: 912-233-4487. Licensee: Gulf Atlantic Media of Georgia, d.i.p. (acq 7-13-88; with co-located FM). Net: CNN. Rep: McGavren Guild. Format: News/talk. News staff one; news progmg 168 hrs wkly. Target aud: 18 plus; general. ■ Carl J. Marocci, CEO; Steve Schurdell, gen sls mgr; Terry Welsh, prom dir; David Allen, progmg dir; Keli Reynolds, mus dir; Sally Taylor, pub affrs dir; Dennis Eversoll, chief engr. ■ Rates: $40; 40; 40; 25.

WZAT(FM)—Co-owned with WSGA(AM). Oct 19, 1971: 102.1 mhz; 100 kw. Ant 1,328 ft. TL: N32 03 30 W81 20 20. Prog sep from AM. Net: ABC/C, ABC/R. Rep: McGavren Guild. Format: CHR. ■ Brady McGraw, progmg dir; Ray Williams, mus dir.

WSOK(AM)—October 1946: 1230 khz; 1 kw-U. TL: N32 04 20 W81 04 35. Box 727 (31402); 24 W. Henry St. (31401). (912) 232-3322. FAX: (912) 232-6144. Licensee: Thomas C. Birch & Raymond M. Quinn Opus Media Group (acq 2-12-90; grpsl; FTR 3-5-90). Net: American Urban. Rep: Banner. Format: Black. News staff one. ■ Raymond Quinn, CEO; Thomas C. Birch, chmn; Daniel N. Gorby, gen mgr; Walt Rosen, sls dir; Jay Bryant, progmg dir; Mark Taylor, news dir; Marty Foglia, chief engr.

WAEV(FM)—Co-owned with WSOK(AM). Feb 4, 1969: 97.3 mhz; 100 kw. Ant 1,000 ft. TL: N32 03 30 W81 20 20. Stereo. Prog sep from AM. (912) 232-0097. Net: Unistar, ABC. Format: Adult contemp. Target aud: 25-54; affluent. ■ Raymond Quinn, pres; Paige Grady, rgnl sls mgr; Jeff Roper, progmg mgr; Jim Hipps, news dir; Marty Foglia, engrg dir.

***WSVH(FM)**—April 20, 1981: 91.1 mhz; 100 kw. Ant 1,068 ft. TL: N32 03 32 W81 17 57. Stereo. Hrs opn: 24. 409 E. Liberty St. (31401). (912) 238-0911; (800) 673-7332. Licensee: Georgia Public Telecommunications Commission. Net: APR, NPR; Ga. Pub. Format: Class, news. News staff one; news progmg 28 hrs wkly. Target aud: 25 plus; thinking people who enjoy alternative progmg. Spec prog: Folk 3 hrs wkly. ■ Richard E. Ottinger, pres; Susan G. Westfall, gen mgr; Susan Curry Brun, opns mgr; Carroll Baker, chief engr.

***WYFS(FM)**—Nov 1, 1986: 89.5 mhz; 100 kw. Ant 630 ft. TL: N32 04 04 W81 21 17. Stereo. Rt. One, Box 358, Bloomingdale (31302-9338). (912) 748-0031. Licensee: Bible Broadcasting Network (group owner). Net: AP. Format: Educ, relg. Target aud: General; Christian progmg for the entire family. ■ Lowell Davey, pres; Tex Robertson, gen mgr; Harold Richards, mus dir & news dir; Ron Muffley, chief engr.

WZAT(FM)—Listing follows WSGA(AM).

Smithville

WZIQ(FM)—Not on air, target date unknown: 106.9 mhz; 6 kw. Ant 328 ft. TL: N31 59 54 W84 12 59. c/o 3017 Piedmont Rd. N.E., Atlanta (30305). (404) 262-7511. Licensee: IQ Radio Network. Format: Classic rock. ■ Donald Jones, pres.

Smyrna

WAZX(AM)—March 1962: 1550 khz; 50 kw-D, 500 w-N, DA-2. TL: N33 53 29 W84 31 19. Hrs opn: 24. 2460 Atlanta Rd. (30080). (404) 436-6171. FAX: (404) 436-0100. Licensee: GA-MEX Broadcasting Inc. (acq 7-29-93; $1.1 million; FTR 8-23-93). Net: CBN. Format: Sp. Target aud: 35-54. ■ Bernie Eisenstein, pres; Javier Macias, gen mgr; Caroline Bailey, opns mgr; Jose McDonald, gen sls mgr; Jesus Ybanez, progmg dir & mus dir; Daniel King, news dir; John York, chief engr.

WSTR(FM)—May 1966: 94.1 mhz; 100 kw. Ant 910 ft. TL: N33 45 34 W84 23 19. Penthouse, 3350 Peachtree Rd., Atlanta (30326). (404) 261-2970. FAX: (404) 365-9026. Licensee: Jefferson Pilot Communications Co. (group owner; acq 3-1-74). Net: AP. Rep: Banner. Format: Hot adult contemp. ■ Mark Kanov, gen mgr; Tony Novia, opns mgr; Dave Kabakoff, gen sls mgr; Alan Hennes, prom mgr; Lee Chestnut, progmg dir & mus dir; Rob Stadler, news dir; Tom Giglio, chief engr.

Soperton

WKTM(FM)—Nov 23, 1982: 101.7 mhz; 3 kw. Ant 300 ft. TL: N32 25 31 W82 33 26 (CP: 106.1 mhz, 6 kw). Stereo. Box 900, Vidalia (30474). (912) 537-9202. Licensee: Vidalia Communications Corp. (acq 2-26-93; $110,000; FTR 3-15-93). ■ John Ladson, pres.

Sparta

WMGZ(FM)—Feb 8, 1988: 97.7 mhz; 3 kw. Ant 328 ft. TL: N33 13 36 W83 03 09 (CP: 6 kw). Stereo. Hrs opn: 24. Box 832; Sales Office, Milledgeville (31061); Studios, 156 Lake Laurel Rd., Milledgeville (31061). (912) 453-9406; (912) 453-2123. FAX: (912) 453-3298. Licensee: Good Medicine Radio Georgia Inc. (acq 2-18-92; $185,000 with WKGQ(AM) Milledgeville; FTR 3-9-92). Format: CHR. News staff one; news progmg 4 hrs wkly. Target aud: 18-49. ■ Frank Copsidas Jr., pres; Cheryl Hackett, gen mgr & prom dir; Cherly Hackett, opns mgr; Dan Davis, chief engr. ■ Rates: $13; 10.50; 13.50; 10.50.

Statesboro

WMCD(FM)—Listing follows WWNS(AM).

WPTB(AM)—April 4, 1976: 850 khz; 1 kw-U, DA-N. TL: N32 28 02 W81 50 07. Box 289 (30458). (912) 764-6621. FAX: (912) 764-6622. Licensee: T.C. Communications Inc. (acq 1-5-87; $150,000; FTR 12-1-86). Net: Southern Radio. Rep: Dora-Clayton. Format: Southern gospel. News staff one; news progmg 7 hrs wkly. Target aud: General. Spec prog: Black 4 hrs, farm 3 hrs wkly. ■ Thomas Cowan, pres, gen mgr & chief engr; Bill Kent, prom mgr, progmg dir & news dir.

WUUF(FM)—Not on air, target date unknown: 102.9 mhz; 25 kw. Ant 328 ft. TL: N32 26 43 W81 58 05. c/o Pamela H. Hodges, 110 Sherwood Ct. (30458). Licensee: Pamela H. Hodges.

***WVGS(FM)**—1975: 91.9 mhz; 1 kw. Ant 161 ft. TL: N32 25 32 W81 46 58. Stereo. Box LB 8016, Georgia Southern Univ. (30460). (912) 681-0877; (912) 681-5525; (912) 681-5507. Licensee: Board of Regents, University System of Georgia. Format: New music, punk, Indies. Spec prog: Jazz 5 hrs, reggae 3 hrs wkly. ■ Dr. Russell Dewey, gen mgr.

WWNS(AM)—Dec 1, 1946: 1240 khz; 1 kw-U. TL: N32 27 21 W81 46 27. Hrs opn: 24. Box 958, 561 E. Olliff St. (30458). (912) 764-5446. FAX: (912) 764-8827. Licensee: Radio Statesboro Inc. (acq 6-1-80; $790,000; FTR 5-26-80). Net: CBS; Ga. Net., Tobacco. Rep: T N. Wash atty: Fletcher, Heald & Hildreth. Format: News/talk, sports. News staff one. Target aud: 25-54. Spec prog: Farm 12 hrs wkly. ■ Nate Hirsch, pres & gen mgr; Buddy Horne, progmg dir, mus dir & news dir; Scott Pendergraft, chief engr. ■ Rates: $12; 10; 12; 8.

WMCD(FM)—Co-owned with WWNS(AM). May 1, 1967: 100.1 mhz; 50 kw. Ant 300 ft. TL: N32 27 21 W81 46 27. Stereo. Hrs opn: 24. Prog sep from AM. (912) 764-5448. Format: Adult contemp, classic rock. Target aud: 18-45. ■ Nate Hirsch, stn mgr; Buddy Horne, mus dir. ■ Rates: $12; 12; 12; 12.

Summerville

WGTA(AM)—Aug 27, 1950: 950 khz; 5 kw-D, 140 w-N. TL: N34 27 53 W85 21 12. Hrs opn: 18. Box 200, State Hwy. 100 (30747). (706) 857-2466. FAX: (706) 857-2466. Licensee: Tri-State Broadcasting Co. Net: AP. Wash atty: Cordon & Kelly. Format: C&W. News staff one; news progmg 15 hrs wkly. Target aud: 18 plus. Spec prog: Relg 12 hrs wkly. ■ William B. Farrar, pres & gen mgr; Deborah Gilleland, gen sls mgr; Margaret Dillard, progmg dir; Aleta Kellett, mus dir; David Daniel, news dir; Philip Baker, chief engr. ■ Rates: $6; 5; 6; 4.50.

Swainsboro

WJAT(AM)—Jan 1, 1950: 800 khz; 1 kw-D, 500 w-N. TL: N32 35 08 W82 21 42. Hrs opn: 5 AM-1 AM. Box 289 (30401); 1000 W. Moring St. (30401). (912) 237-2011. FAX: (912) 237-2011. Licensee: Radio Station WJAT Inc.

(acq 1-1-77). Net: ABC/D. Rep: T N. Wash atty: Borsari & Paxson. Format: Country. News progmg 5 hrs wkly. Target aud: 25 plus; general. Spec prog: Farm 5 hrs, gospel 10 hrs, Black gospel 5 hrs wkly. ■ Frances M. Brazzell, pres; Capers Brazzell, vp; Barry Stewart, stn mgr; Charlie Fri, progmg dir & mus dir; James W. Slawson, chief engr. ■ Rates: $9.75; 9.75; 9.75; 8.

WJAT-FM—Dec 18, 1966: 98.1 mhz; 3 kw. Ant 285 ft-H, 280 ft-V. TL: N32 35 08 W82 21 42. Stereo. Net: MBS. Rep: Rgnl Reps. Format: CHR. Spec prog: Oldies 10 hrs, Black 10 hrs wkly. ■ Rates: Same as AM.

WXRS(AM)—March 10, 1978: 1590 khz; 2.5 kw-D, 25 w-N. TL: N32 33 25 W82 20 29. Hrs opn: 24. Box 1590, Halls Bridge Rd. (30401). (912) 237-1590; (912) 237-0104. FAX: (912) 237-3559. Licensee: Lacom Communications Inc. Group owner: Studstill Broadcasting (acq 10-28-91; $448,773 with co-located FM). Format: Black. News staff 3; news progmg 10 hrs wkly. Spec prog: Gospel 14 hrs wkly. ■ Owen L. Studstill, pres; Melinda M. Studstill, gen mgr & gen sls mgr; Lee Studstill, prom mgr; Jeff Wiggens, news dir & chief engr. ■ Rates: $5; 4; 5; 3.

WXRS-FM—Aug 2, 1982: 100.5 mhz; 3 kw. Ant 300 ft. TL: N32 34 52 W82 23 14. Stereo. Hrs opn: 24. Prog sep from AM. Format: C&W. News staff 3; news progmg 10 hrs wkly. ■ Rates: $7; 6; 7; 5.

Sylvania

WSYL(AM)—Dec 1, 1955: 1490 khz; 1 kw-U. TL: N32 43 51 W81 37 04. Box 519 (30467). (912) 564-7461; (912) 564-2212. FAX: (912) 564-7462. Licensee: Shirley Mahaffey. Net: SMN Ga. Net., Tobacco. Rep: Rgnl Reps. Format: Real Country. News staff 2; news progmg 7 hrs wkly. Target aud: 35-65; affluent. Spec prog: Farm 10 hrs wkly. ■ Shirley Mahaffey, gen mgr & gen sls mgr; Scott Kidd, stn mgr, progmg dir & mus dir; Mac Mahaffey, news dir; Jim Taylor, vp engrg. ■ Rates: $14.66; 12.97; 14.66; 12.97.

WZBX(FM)—Co-owned with WSYL(AM). Sept 6, 1991: 106.5 mhz; 6 kw. Ant 328 ft. TL: N32 43 53 W81 37 03. Box 519 (30467). (912) 564-7461. FAX: (912) 564-7462. Licensee: Shirley Mahaffey. Format: Country. ■ Shirley Mahaffey, gen mgr; Scott Kidd, stn mgr.

Sylvester

WVYF(FM)—Jan 27, 1993: 106.1 mhz; 3 kw. Ant 328 ft. TL: N31 30 15 W83 55 46. c/o K&B Broadcasting Co. Inc., 105 Dunbar Cir. (31791). (912) 776-9565. Licensee: K&B Broadcasting Co. Inc. (acq 9-23-93: FTR 10-18-93). Format: Adult contemp. ■ Karen Barnard, pres; Rick Seigers, gen mgr.

Tallapoosa

WKNG(AM)—Sept 1, 1977: 1060 khz; 5 kw-D. TL: N33 44 06 W85 15 08. Box 626, Hwy. 78, Golf Course Rd. (30176). (404) 574-7655; (404) 836-1060. FAX: (404) 749-1060. Licensee: WKNG Inc. Net: ABC; Ga. Net. Wash atty: O'Connor & Hannan. Format: C&W. Target aud: 25-54. ■ Steven L. Gradick, pres & gen mgr. ■ Rates: $11.95; 11.95; 11.95; 11.95.

Tennille

WJFL(FM)—Not on air, target date unknown: 99.9 mhz; 6 kw. Ant 328 ft. Box 314, McRae (31055). Licensee: Broadcast Media Co.

Thomaston

WSFT(AM)—May 26, 1947: 1220 khz; 1 kw-D. TL: N32 52 08 W84 19 16. Box 689 (30286). (706) 647-5421. Licensee: Upson Broadcasting Co. Inc. Net: NBC; Ga. Net. Rep: Rgnl Reps. Format: C&W. Spec prog: Black 12 hrs, farm 2 hrs wkly. ■ Claude Thames, pres & gen sls mgr; Bill Chapman, mus dir; John Thames, news dir & chief engr. ■ Rates: $6.50; 6.50; 6.50; 6.50.

WTGA(AM)—Nov 1, 1962: 1590 khz; 500 w-D, 25 w-N. TL: N32 53 45 W84 18 10. 208 S. Center St. (30286). (706) 647-7121. Licensee: Radio Georgia Inc. (acq 1972). Net: ABC/I. Format: C&W. Spec prog: Black 4 hrs wkly. ■ David L. Piper, pres, gen mgr & progmg dir; John Davis, chief engr.

WTGA-FM—Nov 15, 1982: 95.3 mhz; 3 kw. Ant 290 ft. TL: N32 51 49 W84 25 10. Prog sep from AM. Format: Country. ■ Dave Piper, gen mgr.

Thomasville

WHGH(AM)—Dec 15, 1987: 840 khz; 10 kw-D. TL: N30 47 54 W83 56 22. Box 2218, Hwy. 19 S. at Pallbearer Rd. (31799). (912) 228-4124. FAX: (912) 225-9508. Licensee: H.G.H. Investment Corp. Net: Natl Black. Format: Urban contemp. Target aud: 12 plus; Blacks. ■ Moses Gross, pres & news dir; Lamar Thomas, mus dir; James Devane, chief engr.

WPAX(AM)—Dec 27, 1922: 1240 khz; 1 kw-U. TL: N30 50 10 W83 59 19. Stereo. Hrs opn: 6 AM-midnight. Box 129, 117 Remington Ave. (31799). (912) 226-1240; (912) 226-1241. FAX: (912) 226-1361. Licensee: LenRob Inc. (acq 10-85). Net: CBS; Ga. Net. Rep: Rgnl Reps. Wash atty: Miller & Fields. Format: MOR, news. News staff one; news progmg 20 hrs wkly. Target aud: 40 plus; mature with disposable income. Spec prog: Farm 2 hrs, class 5 hrs, gospel 6 hrs, relg 3 hrs wkly. ■ Len Robinson, pres & gen mgr; Steve Love, progmg dir; Mark Brannan, news dir; Richard Harris, chief engr. ■ Rates: $11.75; 11.75; 11.75; 11.75.

WSNI(FM)—Licensed to Thomasville. See Tallahassee, Fla.

WSTT(AM)—1947: 730 khz; 5 kw-D, 27 w-N. TL: N30 48 50 W84 00 48. c/o Radio Station WTAL, 1812 E. Park Ave., Tallahassee, FL (32301); Box 3885 (32315). (912) 228-7302. Licensee: Malren Broadcasting Inc. (acq 4-6-92; $30,000; FTR 4-27-92). Net: CBS. Format: News/talk. ■ Paul Stone, pres; Rick Warren, gen mgr & gen sls mgr; Jennifer Warren, progmg dir.

Thomson

WTHO-FM—Feb 22, 1971: 101.7 mhz; 3 kw. Ant 300 ft. TL: N33 28 21 W82 30 00. Stereo. Box 900, 788 Cedar Rock Rd. N.W. (30824). (706) 595-5122; (706) 556-0485. FAX: (706) 595-3021. Licensee: Camellia City Communications Inc. (acq 2-5-93; $110,000 with co-located AM; FTR 3-1-93). Net: NBC; Ga. Net. Rep: Rgnl Reps. Wash atty: Covington & Burling. Format: C&W. News staff one; news progmg 2 hrs wkly. Target aud: 25-54. Spec prog: Farm 3 hrs, gospel one hr, relg 2 hrs, bluegrass 2 hrs wkly. ■ Mike Wall, pres, gen mgr & chief engr; Bill McConnell, adv mgr; Roy Grice, progmg mgr; Steve Ferguson, mus dir; Lisa Kitchens, news dir & pub affrs dir. ■ Rates: $15.85; 10.30; 12; 6.65.

WTWA(AM)—Co-owned with WTHO-FM. Jan 10, 1948: 1240 khz; 1 kw-U. TL: N33 28 20 W82 31 02. Hrs opn: 19. Prog sep from FM. (706) 595-1561. Net: MBS; Ga. Net. Format: Adult contemp. Target aud: 35 plus. ■ Steve Ferguson, progmg mgr. ■ Rates: $12; 8.45; 10.30; 6.15.

Tifton

***WABR-FM**—December 1973: 91.1 mhz; 30 kw. Ant 249 ft. TL: N31 29 30 W83 31 49. Box 8, 1540 Steward Ave. S.W., Atlanta (30310). (912) 386-3964; (404) 756-4730. Licensee: Georgia Public Telecommunications Commission. Net: NPR. Format: News, classical. ■ Dr. A.W. Bergeron, gen mgr.

WJYF(FM)—Listing follows WTIF(AM).

***WPLH(FM)**—January 1988: 103.1 mhz; 29 w-H. Ant 177 ft. TL: N31 28 51 W83 31 38. Stereo. Box 8 (31794). (912) 386-7158; (912) 386-3255. Licensee: Abraham Baldwin Agriculture College (acq 4-1-88). Net: Peach State Public Radio. Format: Variety progmg. ■ Tom Call, gen mgr.

WSGY(FM)—Licensed to Tifton. See Albany.

WTIF(AM)—1957: 1340 khz; 1 kw-U. TL: N31 28 16 W83 29 12. Box 968 (31793); 104 E. 7th St. (31794). (912) 382-1340. FAX: (912) 386-8658. Licensee: Tifton Broadcasting Corp. (acq 3-5-92; $600,000 with co-located FM; FTR 3-30-92). Net: CBS, MBS. Format: Country. News staff one; news progmg 15 hrs wkly. Target aud: 18 plus. Spec prog: Farm 5 hrs wkly. ■ Ronald D. Griffin, pres & gen mgr; Ron Yontz, vp; David Haire, opns dir & news dir; Linda Tucker, gen sls mgr; K.C. Edwards, progmg dir; Clyde Scott, chief engr.

WJYF(FM)—(Nashville). Co-owned with WTIF(AM). Nov 26, 1986: 95.3 mhz: 1.2 kw. Ant 500 ft. TL: N31 10 18 W83 21 57. Stereo. Hrs opn: 24. Prog sep from AM. Format: Soft adult comtemp. News staff one; news progmg one hr wkly. Target aud: 30 plus.

WWGS(AM)—1946: 1430 khz; 5 kw-D, 1 kw-N, DA-N. TL: N31 27 23 W83 33 39. Hrs opn: 6 AM-midnight. Box 1466 (31793); 200 John Howard Way (31794). (912) 382-1430. FAX: (912) 382-1234. Licensee: WWGS/WCUP Partnership. Group owner: Kelsey Broadcasting Corp. (acq 3-1-81; $1,175,000 with co-located FM; FTR 2-16-81). Net: NBC Talknet, ABC/I, Westwood One. Rep: Rgnl Reps. Wash atty: Bechtel and Cole. Format: News, information. Spec prog: Relg 6 hrs wkly. ■ Jon Peterson, pres; Scott Davis, gen mgr; Ron Jones, stn mgr; Jim Jacobs, progmg dir; Jeff Flynt, chief engr. ■ Rates: $10; 8; 10; 8.

Toccoa

WLET(AM)—May 1, 1941: 1420 khz; 5 kw-D. TL: N34 35 23 W85 19 11. Hrs opn: 6 AM-6 PM. 423 Prather Bridge Rd. (30577). (404) 886-2191. Licensee: Sonic Broadcasting (acq 12-4-90; $2,050,000 with co-located FM; FTR 12-18-89). Rep: Rgnl Reps. Wash atty: Verner, Liipfert, Bernhard, McPherson & Hand. Format: Oldies, news/talk. News staff one; news progmg 10 hrs wkly. Target aud: 35 plus; Stephens County residents seeking news & community information. Spec prog: Black one hr, gospel 8 hrs, country 4 hrs wkly. ■ Gene Mark, pres; Kerry Fink, gen mgr; Gene Bollinger, stn mgr & progmg dir; Woody Bollinger, opns mgr, adv mgr & mus dir; Greg Oliver, news dir; Ted McCall, chief engr. ■ Rates: $8; 6.50; 6.50; na.

WLET-FM—November 1947: 106.1 mhz; 100 kw. Ant 1,132 ft. TL: N34 43 46 W83 29 29. Stereo. Hrs opn: 24. Prog sep from AM. Wachouia Ctr., Suite 525, 340 Jewell Pkwy., Gainesville (30501). (404) 534-8106. FAX: (404) 534-2614. Rep: Rgnl Reps. Format: Adult contemp. News staff one; news progmg 10 hrs wkly. Target aud: 25-54; adults with disposable income. Spec prog: Gospel. ■ Tim Johnston, stn mgr & gen sls mgr; Noelle Stettner, progmg dir; DeAnna Martin, mus dir; Bruce Martin, pub affrs dir.

WNEG(AM)—April 21, 1956: 630 khz; 500 w-D. TL: N34 34 15 W83 19 35. Hrs opn: 6 AM-local sunset. Box 907, 100 Boulevard (30577). (404) 886-3131; (404) 886-3132. FAX: (404) 886-7033. Licensee: Stephens County Broadcasting Co. Inc. Net: AP; Ga. Net. Rep: Roslin. Wash atty: Bryan, Cave, McPheeter & McRoberts. Format: MOR. News staff one; news progmg 18 hrs wkly. Target aud: General; adult working class. Spec prog: Black 3 hrs, farm one hr wkly. ■ Roy E. Gaines, pres & gen mgr; Ken Brady, gen sls mgr; Gaynelle Thomason, progmg dir; Connie Gaines, mus dir; Lamar Ramey, news dir; Thomas Shockley, chief engr. WNEG-TV affil. ■ Rates: $7; 7; 7; na.

Toccoa Falls

***WRAF-FM**—Sept 4, 1980: 90.9 mhz; 100 kw. Ant 564 ft. TL: N34 35 57 W83 21 55. Stereo. Hrs opn: 24. Box 780, Toccoa Falls College (30598). (404) 886-1912; (404) 886-5816. FAX: (404) 886-0690. Licensee: Toccoa Falls College. Net: Moody, ARN, USA. Wash atty: Wiley, Rein & Fielding. Format: Relg. Target aud: General; families. ■ Paul L. Alford, CEO, pres & gen mgr; James I. Piper, stn mgr; Joe Barker, opns mgr; Bob Biermann, chief opns & chief engr; Lillian Cash, mus dir.

Trenton

WADX(AM)—April 4, 1982: 1420 khz; 2.5 w-D, 112 w-N. TL: N34 51 43 W85 29 59. Hrs opn: 6 AM-6 PM. Box 829 (30752). (706) 657-7594; (404) 298-1658. FAX: (706) 398-1658. Licensee: RA-AD of Trenton Inc. Net: NBC. Format: Country, news, talk. News staff one; news progmg 2 hrs wkly. Target aud: 40 plus; locals. Spec prog: Relg 6 hrs, gospel 17 hrs wkly. ■ Herbert Adcox, pres; Audrey Clark, gen sls mgr; Phil Patton, chief engr. ■ Rates: $8; 6; 5; na.

WBDX(FM)—Co-owned with WADX(AM). 1989: 102.7 mhz; 500 w. Ant 817 ft. TL: N34 53 56 W85 26 38 (CP: 318 w, ant 1,374 ft.). Prog sep from AM. Eastgate Mall, Suite G-30, 5600 Braineard Rd., Chattanooga, TN (37411). (615) 899-5111. FAX: (615) 899-1776. Format: Adult contemp. Target aud: 18-49. ■ Doug Fisher, gen mgr; Rick Gross, prom mgr; Joe Cook, progmg dir; Parks Hall, chief engr. ■ Rates: $16; 14; 16; 12.

Trion

WATG(FM)—Not on air, target date unknown: 95.7 mhz; 600 w. Ant 699 ft. TL: N34 28 10 W85 17 48. Box 200, Summerville (30747). (706) 857-2466. FAX: (706) 857-3652. Licensee: Tri-State Broadcasting Co. Wash atty: Cordon & Kelly. Format: Adult contemp, oldies. Target aud: 18 plus. ■ William B. Farrar, CEO.

Tucker

WGUN(AM)—(Atlanta). July 1947: 1010 khz; 50 kw-D, 300 w-N. TL: N33 41 55 W84 17 23. Hrs opn: 24. 2901 Mountain Industrial Blvd., Tucker (30084). (404) 491-1010. FAX: (404) 491-3019. Licensee: Dee Rivers Group. Format: News/talk, sports. News staff 3. Target aud: 18-56; working class. ■ Dick Schroeder, gen mgr; Howard Ebo, gen sls mgr; Mark McKinnon, progmg mgr; Laura Dietz, news dir; Preston Mobley, pub affrs dir; George Pass, chief engr. ■ Rates: $50; 40; 50; na.

Unadilla

WAFI(FM)—Not on air, target date unknown: 103.5 mhz; 6 kw. Ant 328 ft. 100 Wexford Place, Athens (30606). Licensee: Tarkenton Broadcasting Co. Inc.

Valdosta

WAAC(FM)—Listing follows WGOV(AM).

WAFT(FM)—Nov 25, 1971: 101.1 mhz; 100 kw. Ant 558 ft. TL: N30 51 50 W83 23 39. Stereo. Hrs opn: 24. Box 338, Morven Rd. (31603-0338). (912) 244-5180. FAX: (912) 242-8808. Licensee: Christian Radio Fellowship Inc. Net: USA, Moody. Format: Relg. News progmg 3 hrs wkly. Target aud: General. ■ Bill Tidwell, pres & chief engr. ■ Rates: $4.50; 4.50; 4.50; 4.50.

WFVR(AM)—Nov 3, 1951: 910 khz; 5 kw-U, DA-N. TL: N30 52 21 W83 20 36. Florida Welcome Center, 4908-6 N.W. 34th St., Gainesville, FL (32605). (904) 376-4442. Licensee: Florida Welcome Station Inc. Net: NBC. Format: Tourist info. ■ Robert Saunders (owner), CEO; C. H. Fletcher, gen sls mgr & chief engr.

WGOV(AM)—1939: 950 khz; 5 kw-D, 1 kw-N, DA-N. TL: N30 48 09 W83 21 17. Hrs opn: 24. Box 1207 (31603); Hwy. 84 W. (31601). (912) 242-4513; (912) 244-9590. Licensee: WGOV Inc. Group owner: Des Rivers Group. Net: ABC/R. Rep: Rgnl Reps. Format: Urban contemp. News staff one; news progmg 3 hrs wkly. Target aud: 18-45; Blacks. Spec prog: Gospel 14 hrs wkly, oldies 10 hrs wkly. ■ M. B. Rivers, pres; Jay Clark, gen mgr & gen sls mgr; Harvey Moore, prom mgr; Mike Mink, mus dir; Chuck Preston, news dir; Clyde Scott, chief engr. ■ Rates: $13; 11; 13; 9.

WAAC(FM)—Co-owned with WGOV(AM). 1968: 92.9 mhz; 100 kw. Ant 509 ft. TL: N30 48 13 W83 21 20. Stereo. Prog sep from AM. Net: ABC/E. Format: Country. News staff one; news progmg 3 hrs wkly. Target aud: 25-54. Spec prog: Gospel 4 hrs wkly. ■ Robert Whitt, opns dir, progmg dir & mus dir; Tod Edwards, prom dir; Jim Morgan, adv dir; Jack Ryan, pub affrs dir. ■ Rates: $35; 32; 35; 25.

WJEM(AM)—August 1955: 1150 khz; 5 kw-D. TL: N30 50 49 W83 14 14. Box 5883, Wazerau Hwy. (31603); Hwy. 84 E. (31601). (912) 241-9797. Licensee: WJEM Inc. (acq 3-9-92; $401,382; FTR 3-30-92). Net: NBC, Unistar. Rep: Roslin. Format: Gospel. News staff 2; news progmg 10 hrs wkly. Target aud: 25-54; people interested in hometown progmg. Spec prog: Loc news remotes. ■ Cedric Carthern (owner), CEO.

WQPW(FM)—September 1977: 95.7 mhz; 35.9 kw. Ant 606 ft. TL: N30 50 11 W83 17 56. Stereo. Hrs opn: 24. Box 1327 (31603); 1001 W. Gordon St. (31601). (912) 244-8642. FAX: (912) 242-7620. Licensee: Metro Media Broadcasting Inc. (acq 2-81; $340,000; FTR 3-16-81). Wash atty: Borsari & Paxson. Format: Adult contemp. News staff 14. Target aud: 18-44. ■ Harrison Cooper, pres & gen mgr; John Rodrigues, opns mgr, gen sls mgr & prom mgr; John Byrd, mus dir; Lynn Morgan, news dir; Robert Combs, chief engr. ■ Rates: $28; 26; 28; 22.

WVLD(AM)—Sept 3, 1959: 1450 khz; 1 kw-U. TL: N30 50 11 W83 17 56. Hrs opn: 24. Box 1529 (31603); 1001 W. Gordon St. (31601). (912) 242-4821. FAX: (912) 242-7620. Licensee: Valdosta Media Service Inc. (acq 1-81; $400,000). Net: CBS, MBS. Wash atty: Borsari & Paxson. Format: Oldies, news/talk. News progmg 10 hrs wkly. Target aud: 35 plus. Spec prog: Gospel 2 hrs wkly. ■ Harrison Cooper, pres, gen mgr, prom mgr, mus dir & news dir; Robert Combs, opns dir, prom dir & chief engr; John Rodriguez, sls dir; Robert LaFore, progmg dir. ■ Rates: $10; 8; 10; 6.

***WVVS(FM)**—July 26, 1971: 90.9 mhz; 5.3 kw. Ant 68 ft. TL: N30 50 50 W83 17 26. Stereo. Box 142, VFU Student Union, 1500 N. Patterson (31698). (912) 333-5661; (912) 333-7313. Licensee: Valdosta State College. Format: Progsv, rock. Target aud: 18-25; students of VSC, education through young adults, and beyond. Spec prog: Folk 3 hrs, jazz 6 hrs, blues 3 hrs, dance 3 hrs, death rock 3 hrs, heavy metal 3 hrs, urban contemp 3 hrs, punk 3 hrs, new age 3 hrs wkly. ■ Chris Waldrop, gen mgr; Mitch Long, opns mgr; Chris Shriver, mus dir; Matt Fry, chief engr.

***WWET(FM)**—December 1989: 91.7 mhz; 185 w. Ant 236 ft. TL: N30 50 23 W83 16 39. 1540 Stewart Ave. S.W., Atlanta (30310). (404) 756-4730. Licensee: Georgia Public Telecommunications Commission. Format: Class, news, pub affrs. ■ Dr. A.W. Bergeron, gen mgr.

WWRQ(FM)—Feb 1, 1992: 107.7 mhz; 3 kw. Ant 243 ft. TL: N30 49 32 W83 16 59. 5-A Al Brooks Dr. (31601). (912) 247-1077. Licensee: Albert Leon Brooks. Format: Classic rock. ■ Logan Birdsong, stn mgr.

WYZK(FM)—June 1985: 96.7 mhz; 3 kw. Ant 300 ft. TL: N30 50 10 W83 12 40 (CP: 50 kw, ant 492 ft, TL: N30 48 37 W83 31 19). Stereo. Box 5406 (31603); 704 N. Ashly St. (31601). (912) 333-0755. FAX: (912) 333-0286. Licensee: CDJ Inc. (acq 7-1-91; FTR 7-22-91). Format: C&W. Target aud: 18-49. ■ Lloyd Kilday, gen mgr.

Vidalia

WBBT(AM)—See Lyons.

***WGPH(FM)**—Licensed to Vidalia. See Augusta.

WLYU(FM)—See Lyons.

WTCQ(FM)—Listing follows WVOP(AM).

WVOP(AM)—Dec 2, 1946: 970 khz; 5 kw-D. TL: N32 13 12 W82 26 13. Stereo. Box 900, 1501 Mt. Vernon Rd. (30474). (912) 537-9202. FAX: (912) 537-4477. Licensee: Vidalia Communications Corp. Net: ABC/I; Ga. Net. Rep: Rngl Reps. Format: Goldies, news, sports. News staff 2. Target aud: 25-54. Spec prog: Pub affairs 2 hrs, relg 8 hrs wkly. ■ John Ladson, pres; Zack Fowler, stn mgr; Bill Boyd, opns mgr; Johnny Winge, gen sls mgr; Judie Turner, prom mgr; Ed Johnson, progmg dir; Dennis Eversoll, chief engr.

WTCQ(FM)—Co-owned with WVOP(AM). March 5, 1969: 97.7 mhz; 6 kw. Ant 300 ft. TL: N32 13 12 W82 26 13. Stereo. Prog sep from AM. Net: ABC/C; Ga. Net. Rep: Regl Reps. Format: AC. Target aud: 18-34. ■ Johnny Winge, rgnl sls mgr; Bill Boyd, progmg dir.

Vienna

WWWN(AM)—Nov 17, 1979: 1550 khz; 1 kw-D, 23 w-N. TL: N32 07 44 W83 47 46. Hwy. 41 N. (31092). (912) 268-1550. Licensee: Dooly-Crisp Communications Corp. Net: Ga. Net. Format: C&W. ■ Jack Powers, gen mgr, gen sls mgr, progmg dir & chief engr; Betty Powers, mus dir.

Warm Springs

***WJSP-FM**—Licensed to Warm Springs. See Atlanta.

Warner Robins

WCOP(AM)—Oct 13, 1954: 1350 khz; 5 kw-D, 500 w-N, DA-N. TL: N32 37 00 W83 39 00. Stereo. Hrs opn: 5:30 AM-midnight. Box 2127, 1350 Radio Loop (31099). (912) 923-3416. FAX: (912) 923-3416. Licensee: Toccoa Falls College (acq 7-3-85; $140,000; FTR 6-10-85). Net: USA. Format: Christian. Spec prog: Sp, East Indian. ■ Paul Alford, pres; Bill Bruton, gen mgr; Bill Best, gen sls mgr; Joyce Hutcherson, prom dir. ■ Rates: $11; 11; 11; 11.

WRCC(AM)—Aug 15, 1966: 1600 khz; 2.5 kw-D, 500 w-N, DA-N. TL: N32 38 19 W83 38 33. Hrs opn: 18. Box 5051, 2052 Watsen Blvd. (31099). (912) 922-2222; (912) 922-2223. FAX: (912) 929-4487. Licensee: Televiewers Inc. Net: Jones Satellite Audio; Ga. Net. Rep: Dora-Clayton. Wash atty: Don Ward. Format: Country, relg. News progmg 3 hr wkly. Target aud: 21-54. Spec prog: Relg 2 hrs wkly. ■ Bruce Tim, Jan Tim, presdts; Vernon Arnold, gen mgr; Janiz Arnold, gen sls mgr & vp prom; Harvey V. Arnold, progmg dir; Shirley Jones, mus dir; Donovon Jones, engrg dir. ■ Rates: $21; 21; 21; na.

WRCC-FM—August 1969: 101.7 mhz; 2.5 kw. Ant 350 ft. TL: N32 38 19 W83 38 33 (CP: 4.9 kw). Stereo. Hrs opn: 24. Prog sep from AM. Net: NBC, Format: Adult contemp. News progmg one hr wkly. Target aud: 21-54. Spec prog: Relg 12 hrs, American Indian 2 hrs, farm 3 hrs wkly. ■ Bruce F. Timm, CEO & CFO; Jan Timm, vp; Janiz Arnold, vp sls; Vernon Arnold, natl sls mgr & rgnl sls mgr; Donavon Jones, vp engrg. ■ Rates: $21; 21; 21; 21.

WYIQ(FM)—Not on air, target date unknown: 102.5 mhz; 6 kw. Ant 328 ft. TL: N32 33 20 W83 44 14. Suite 200, 3017 Piedmont Rd. N.E., Atlanta (30305). Licensee: Genesis Broadcasting Corp.

Washington

WLOV-FM—June 1, 1970: 100.1 mhz; 2.4 kw. Ant 321 ft. TL: N33 43 50 W82 43 10. Stereo. Hrs opn: 24. 823 Berkshire Dr. (30673). (706) 678-2125. FAX: (706) 678-1925. Licensee: Ptak Broadcasting Co. (acq 11-2-90; $355,000 with co-located AM; FTR 11-19-90). Net: SMN. Format: Pure Gold. Target aud: 25-54; baby boomers. ■ Tom Ptak, chmn & pres; Betty Davis, vp sls; Mike Wall, vp engrg. ■ Rates: $7; 5.50; 6.50; 4.50.

WLOV(AM)—Sept 1, 1955: 1370 khz; 1 kw-D. TL: N33 43 50 W82 43 10. Prog sep from FM. Net: SMN; Ga. Net. Format: News/talk. News staff one; news progmg 5 hrs wkly. ■ Rodney Holloway, gen mgr; Jan Vandiver, stn mgr; Greg Scott, news dir; Dan Davis, chief engr. ■ Rates: Same as FM.

Waycross

WACL(AM)—July 1, 1951: 570 khz; 5 kw-D, 1 kw-N, DA-N. TL: N31 15 42 W82 19 26. Box 858, 528 Memorial Dr. (31502). (912) 283-4660. FAX: (912) 283-4661. Licensee: Teletronics Inc. Net: ABC/C. Rep: Tobacco. Format: Southern gospel. Target aud: 25-60. ■ Bill Parker, gen sls mgr; Jim Rivers, progmg dir & mus dir; Knox Carreker, chief engr.

WAYX(AM)—Oct 12, 1936: 1230 khz; 1 kw-U. TL: N31 12 51 W82 22 47. Box 1982 (31502); 1600 Carswell Ave. (31501). (912) 285-1711; (912) 285-8962. FAX: (912) 285-7636. Licensee: GHI Inc. (acq 9-1-92; $115,000 FTR 9-21-92). Net: SMN. Format: Music of the 50s, 60s and 70s (soft hits). ■ Wayne G. Johnson, gen mgr; Lew Essick, progmg dir.

WBGA(FM)—Licensed to Waycross. See Brunswick.

WHFX(FM)—Licensed to Waycross. See Brunswick.

WKUB(FM)—See Blackshear.

WWUF(FM)—Jan 25, 1986: 97.7 mhz; 3 kw. Ant 310 ft. TL: N31 11 05 W82 15 24. 701 Carlswell St. (31503); 701 Carswell Ave. (31501). (912) 283-2229. FAX: (912) 285-9797. Licensee: Joann Brehm (acq 1-25-86). Rep: Keystone (unwired net). Format: Classic rock. Target aud: 16-45; mainly female & bus offices. ■ Tim Chisolm, pres; Rick Ward, gen mgr; Rcik Ward, gen sls mgr; Steve Summers, progmg dir; Dick Buckaloo, chief engr.

***WXVS(FM)**—December 1985: 90.1 mhz; 79 kw-H, 71 kw-V. Ant 918 ft. TL: N31 13 17 W82 34 24. 1540 Stewart Ave. S.W., Atlanta (30310). (404) 756-4730. FAX: (404) 756-4088. Licensee: Georgia Public Telecommunications Commission. Format: Div. ■ Richard E. Ottinger, pres; Frank Bugg, vp; A. W. Bergeron, stn mgr.

Waynesboro

***WAGW(FM)**—1975: 100.9 mhz; 6 kw. Ant 279 ft. TL: N33 05 15 W82 02 17. Stereo. Hrs opn: 24. 1388 Old Lanesboro Rd. (30830). (706) 554-3942. Licensee: Bible Broadcasting Network (group owner; acq 7-85; $300,000; FTR 7-15-85). Format: Relg. News staff one. Target aud: General; family. ■ Jason Padgett, gen mgr.

WBRO(AM)—October 1954: 1310 khz; 1 kw-D. TL: N33 06 14 W81 59 11. Stereo. Hrs opn: 6 AM-midnight. Box 509, Hwy 56 N. (30830). (404) 554-7459. FAX: (404) 554-7459. Licensee: P.A.S.T. Inc. (acq 10-1-90; $45,000, FTR 10-22-90). Net: NBC. Rep: T N. Format: Urban contemp, relg, Black. Target aud: 12-55; general. ■ Gilbert Banks, chmn; Ron Thomas, stn mgr & progmg dir.

WYFA(FM)—Licensed to Waynesboro. See Augusta.

West Point

WPLV(AM)—August 1958: 1310 khz; 1 kw-D. TL: N32 53 42 W85 09 32 (CP: TL: N32 53 48 W85 09 24). 705 4th Ave. (31833). (706) 645-1310. Licensee: Radio Valley Inc. Net: ABC/E; Keystone (unwired net). Format: Country. ■ C. Jim Murphy, pres & gen mgr; Janice Horne, progmg dir; Susie Britt, mus dir; Jim Weldon, chief engr.

WCJM(FM)—Co-owned with WPLV(AM). July 18, 1966: 100.9 mhz; 1.85 kw. Ant 235 ft. TL: N32 53 42 W85 09 32 (CP: 6 kw, ant 177 ft., TL: N32 53 48 W85 09 24). Net: Ala. Net., Ga. Net. Format: Country. ■ Jim Murphy, gen mgr.

WRLD(AM)—See Lanett, Ala.

Winder

WIMO(AM)—Nov 4, 1952: 1300 khz; 1 kw-D, 59 w-N. TL: N33 58 22 W83 42 40. Box 1300 (30680). (404) 867-1300. Licensee: Cooper Broadcasting Network Inc. (acq 2-1-93; $200,000; FTR 4-12-93). Net: ABC/E; Ga. Net. Format: Country, gospel. News progmg 6 hrs wkly. Target aud: General. Spec prog: Relg 14 hrs wkly. ■ Lewis J. Cooper, pres; Jean Cooper, vp; Steve Thompson, gen mgr, gen sls mgr & news dir; Larry Brewer, progmg dir & mus dir; Dedra Blakley, pub affrs dir; Dan Davis, chief engr. ■ Rates: $7.50; 7.50; 7.50; 3.75.

***WYFW(FM)**—December 1987: 89.5 mhz; 530 w. Ant 130 ft. TL: N33 59 32 W83 45 15. Stereo. Hrs opn: 24. 496 Atlanta Hwy. (30680). (404) 867-8133. Licensee: Bible Broadcasting Network Inc. (group owner; acq 6-24-93; $104,000; FTR 6-28-93). Net: USA. Format: Relg, MOR. News progmg 7 hrs wkly. Target aud: 35-44. ■ Lowell Daerly, pres; John Murphy, stn mgr; Jerry Kuhn, chief engr.

Stations in the U.S.

Woodbine

WCGA(AM)—June 15, 1987: 1100 khz; 10 kw-D. TL: N30 55 54 W81 42 31. Box 280 E., Rt. 9, St. Simons Island (31522). (912) 638-1176; (912) 638-5611. Licensee: Cox Broadcast Group Inc. Format: News/talk. News progmg 7 hrs wkly. Target aud: General; males 18 plus. ■ J. Wesley Cox, pres & gen mgr; Burwell A. Russell Cox, gen sls mgr; Richard Burguet, prom mgr; Deirdre R. Cox, progmg dir; Jessica D.C. Cox, mus dir; Wes Cox, news dir. ■ Rates: $9; 8.50; 9; na.

Wrens

WAKB(FM)—June 10, 1979: 96.9 mhz; 1 kw. Ant 489 ft. TL: N33 16 21 W82 25 32 (CP: 750 w, ant 1,364 ft.). Stereo. 2316 Millers Pond Rd. (30833). (706) 547-0963. Licensee: Gregory A. Davis. Group owner: Davis Broadcasting Inc. (acq 6-25-93; $1.25 million; FTR 8-2-93). Format: Urban contemp. News staff one; news progmg 4 hrs wkly. ■ Gregory Davis, gen mgr; Carroll Redd, progmg dir.

Wrightsville

WDBN(FM)—May 27, 1986: 107.5 mhz; 3 kw. Ant 295 ft. TL: N32 42 24 W82 43 08. Box 130, Dublin (31040). (912) 864-1829. FAX: (912) 275-4657. Licensee: Johnson County Broadcasters Inc. (acq 5-29-89; $160,000; FTR 5-29-89). Net: NBC. Format: Hot adult contemp. ■ Jamie Holt, gen mgr; Jim Slawson, chief engr.

Young Harris

WZCM(AM)—May 1984: 770 khz; 750 w-D. TL: N34 56 26 W83 51 13. Box 860, Young Marris (30582). (706) 379-3168; (706) 379-9770. FAX: (706) 379-3169. Licensee: Young Harris Broadcasting Corp. (acq 12-23-85). Net: SMN. Format: Country, relg. News progmg 10 hrs wkly. Spec prog: Farm one hr wkly. ■ Matthew Miller, pres; Stan Raymond, gen mgr; Rebecca St. John, progmg dir.

Hawaii

WILLIAM A. EXLINE, INC
MEDIA BROKERS CONSULTANTS

4340 Redwood Highway
Suite F 230
San Rafael, California 94903
TEL (415) 479-3484
• FAX (415) 479-1574

Aiea

KGMZ(FM)—September 1992: 107.9 mhz; 100 kw-H, 79 kw-V. Ant 1,965 ft. TL: N21 23 51 W158 06 01. Suite 376, 2153 N. King St., Honolulu (96819). (808) 841-7600. FAX: (808) 847-2855. Licensee: KTSS-FM Inc. (acq 3-30-92). Format: Contemp. ■ Casey Stangl, gen mgr; Kimo Akane, opns mgr.

Eleele

KUAI(AM)—June 30, 1965: 720 khz; 5 kw-U. TL: N21 53 37 W159 33 27. Hrs opn: 5 AM-midnight. Box 720, 4469 Waialo Rd. (96705). (808) 335-3171. FAX: (808) 335-3834. Licensee: American Islands Broadcasting Corp. Net: MBS. Format: Adult contemp. News progmg 21 hrs wkly. Target aud: 25-65; local long-time residents, blue & white collar. Spec prog: Hawaiian 5 hrs, jazz 4 hrs wkly. ■ William G. Dahle, pres & gen mgr; J. Robertson, gen sls mgr; Reggie De Roos, progmg dir; Michael Friedlander, chief engr. ■ Rates: $20; 16; 17; 14.

Haiku

KUAU(AM)—Not on air, target date 1994: 1570 khz; 1 kw-D, 500 w-N. TL: N20 54 37 W156 17 15 (CP: 50 kw-U). 490 Ulumalu Rd. (96708); Box 565, Kuau (96779). (808) 572-5534. FAX: (808) 572-5534. Licensee: Latitude 21 Broadcasting. Wash atty: Baraff, Koerner, Olender & Hochberg. ■ Richard Miller, CEO.

Haliimaile

KPMW(FM)—Not on air, target date unknown: 105.5 mhz; 6 kw. Ant 295 ft. TL: N20 42 32 W156 21 33. Licensee: Rey-Cel Broadcasting L.P.

Hilo

KAHU(AM)—October 1986: 1060 khz; 1 kw-U. TL: N19 41 48 W155 03 05. Box 4727, KANI Communications Inc. (96720). (808) 959-2056. FAX: (808) 959-4507. Licensee: KANI Communications (acq 4-6-90). Format: Hawaiian mus. Spec prog: Hawaiian culture & language. ■ Frederick Baker Jr., gen mgr; Hauuani Baker, stn mgr; Jeremy Storm, chief engr.

KAOE(FM)—Sept 20, 1992: 92.7 mhz; 16 kw. Ant -157 ft. TL: N19 41 48 W155 03 05. Box 5544 (96720). (808) 959-8446. Licensee: Visionary Related Entertainment Inc. (group owner; acq 11-1-91; $55,000). Format: AOR. Target aud: 25-54. ■ John Detz, pres; David Hoffman, gen sls mgr; Jack Gist, prom dir; Milan Leggett, chief engr.

KFSH(FM)—Aug 3, 1985: 97.1 mhz; 40 kw. Ant -124 ft. TL: N19 45 33 W155 08 33. Stereo. Hrs opn: 5 AM-10:30 PM. 47 Punahoa St. (96720); 75-5851 Kuakini Hwy., Kailua-Kona (96740). (808) 935-7434; (808) 326-7228. FAX: (808) 329-2387. Licensee: The University of the Nations (acq 1987). Net: CBN. Format: Relg, adult contemp. News staff one; news progmg 8 hrs wkly. Target aud: 25-45. Spec prog: Class 3 hrs wkly. ■ Loren Cunningham, pres; David B. Hall, gen mgr; David Boyd, dev dir; Jeremy Storm, chief engr. ■ Rates: $10; 9; 10; 9.

KHLO(AM)—April 1, 1950: 850 khz; 5 kw-U. TL: N19 44 11 W155 02 07. Hrs opn: 24. 913 Kanoelehua (96720). (808) 935-1952. FAX: (808) 935-0396. Licensee: Ling Hing Mui Inc. (acq 3-5-90; $180,000; FTR 3-19-90). Format: Country, talk. News staff 2; news progmg 7 hrs wkly. Target aud: 25-54. ■ Philip L. Brewer, pres; David Fransen, stn mgr; Terry Conners, gen sls mgr; Pat Springer, prom mgr; Rod Pacheco, news dir; Jeremey Storm, chief engr. ■ Rates: $12; 12; 12; 12.

KHWI(FM)—Listing follows KIPA(AM).

KIPA(AM)—Sept 10, 1947: 620 khz; 10 kw-U. TL: N19 51 03 W155 05 09. Hrs opn: 24. Box 1602 (96721); 688 Kinoole St. (96720). (808) 935-6858. FAX: (808) 969-7949. Licensee: Big Island Broadcasting Co. Ltd. (acq 1967). Net: NBC, NBC Talknet. Format: Div, MOR, talk. News staff 2. Target aud: 35 plus. Spec prog: Filipino 7 hrs, Japanese 8 hrs wkly. ■ Buddy Gordon, pres, gen mgr & gen sls mgr; Melvin Medeiros, progmg dir & mus dir; Chris Loos, news dir; Allan Roycroft, chief engr.

KHWI(FM)—Co-owned with KIPA(AM). December 1988: 100.3 mhz; 74 kw. Ant -515 ft. TL: N19 50 19 W155 06 43. Stereo. Hrs opn: 24. Prog sep from AM. Net: SMN. Format: Classic rock, oldies. Target aud: 25-49.

KKBG(FM)—Aug 5, 1980: 97.9 mhz; 35 kw-H, 29.5 kw-V. Ant -240 ft. TL: N19 44 11 W155 01 48. 913 Kanoelehua (96720). (808) 961-0651. FAX: (808) 935-0396. Licensee: Brewer Broadcasting Corp. (acq 3-30-82; $205,000; FTR 4-19-82). Format: Adult contemp. ■ Philip L. Brewer, pres; Jeanine Atebara, gen mgr & stn mgr; Pat Springer, prom mgr; David Fransen, progmg dir; Ken Styles, mus dir; Rod Pacheco, news dir; Army Curtis, chief engr. ■ Rates: $25; 23; 25; 23.

KPUA(AM)—1936: 670 khz; 10 kw-U. TL: N19 47 02 W155 05 25 (CP: 50 kw-U, DA-N). Stereo. Hrs opn: 24. 1145 Kilauea Ave. (96720). (808) 935-5461. FAX: (808) 935-7761. Licensee: New West Broadcasting Corp. (acq 5-18-92; $370,000 with co-located FM; FTR 6-8-92). Net: AP, CBS, Westwood One, MBS. Wash atty: Dan Alpert. Format: MOR, news/talk, sports. News staff 3; news progmg 22 hrs wkly. Target aud: 25 plus; upscale adults with interest in news. Spec prog: Sports, Japanese 6 hrs wkly. ■ John Leonard, pres, gen mgr & gen sls mgr; Ken Hupp, stn mgr & progmg dir; Christopher Leonard, sls dir & mktg mgr; Gavin Michael, prom dir; Jonathan Masaki, news dir & pub affrs dir; Jeff Ward, chief engr. ■ Rates: $25; na; 15; 12.

KWXX-FM—Co-owned with KPUA(AM). Dec 16, 1984: 94.7 mhz; 100 kw. Ant -330 ft. TL: N19 43 02 W155 08 13. Stereo. Hrs opn: 24. Prog sep from AM. Net: AP, Westwood One, CBS Spectrum. Format: Hot adult contemp, Hawaiian. News staff one; news progmg 3 hrs wkly. Target aud: 25 plus; upscale adults. Spec prog: Contemp Hawaiian 20 hrs, reggae 20 hrs. ■ Skylark Rossetti-Ota, gen mgr & adv dir; Chris Leonard, gen sls mgr; Desiree' Douglas, asst mus dir. ■ Rates: $25; 18; 25; 16.

KPVS(FM)—Not on air, target date unknown: 95.9 mhz; 50 kw. Ant 230 ft. Hrs opn: 24. Box 38, Carlisle, PA (17013); Box 10780 (96721). Licensee: Pacific View Broadcasting. Wash atty: Cohen & Berfield. Format: Adult contemp. ■ Jon Gardner, vp & vp opns. ■ Rates: $22; 11; 22; 11.

KWXX-FM—Listing follows KPUA(AM).

Honolulu

KAIM(AM)—Aug 31, 1956: 870 khz; 50 kw-U, DA-1. TL: N21 10 56 W157 13 27 (CP: TL: N21 28 41 W157 58 23). 3555 Harding Ave. (96816). (808) 735-2424. FAX: (808) 735-2428. Licensee: Billy Graham Evangelistic Association (acq 2-4-91; with co-located FM; FTR 2-18-91). Wash atty: Fisher, Wayland, Cooper & Leader. Format: Relg. News staff one. ■ Del Gibbs, gen mgr; Vicki Akisada, gen sls mgr; Jack Waters, progmg dir & mus dir; Ken Wooley, chief engr. ■ Rates: $12; 12; 12; na.

KAIM-FM—Nov 1, 1953: 95.5 mhz; 100 kw. Ant -23 ft. TL: N21 17 08 W157 48 08 (CP: 99 kw, ant 1,988 ft., TL: N21 23 42 W158 05 55). Stereo. Dups AM 25%.

KAUI(FM)—(Kekaha). Not on air, target date May 1994: 103.3 mhz; 85 kw. Ant 810 ft. TL: N21 58 16 W159 42 46. Suite 376, 2153 N. King St., Honolulu (96819). (808) 841-7600. FAX: (808) 847-2855. Licensee: Stangle Broadcasting Inc. (group owner; acq 6-90; $4,500; FTR 6-4-90). Format: Rock. ■ Casey Stangl, pres.

KCCN(AM)—Nov 1, 1966: 1420 khz; 5 kw-U. TL: N21 19 26 W157 52 47. Suite 400, 900 Fort St. (96813). (808) 536-2728. FAX: (808) 536-2528. Licensee: KCCN Broadcasting Co. Inc. (acq 9-82). Net: UPI. Rep: Katz. Format: Traditional Hawaiian music. News staff one. ■ B.J. Glascock, pres; Jan Glascock, vp; Michael Kelly, gen sls mgr; Rhoda Kihikihi, prom mgr; Farden Akui, progmg dir; Kimann Chung, news dir; Ralph Wilson, chief engr.

KCCN-FM—May 21, 1990: 100.3 mhz; 100 kw-H, 81 kw-V. Ant 1,965 ft. TL: N21 23 51 W158 06 01. Prog sep from AM. Format: Contemp Hawaiian music.

KGU(AM)—May 11, 1927: 760 khz; 10 kw-U. TL: N21 17 41 W157 51 49. Suite 376, 2153 N. King St. (96819). (808) 841-7600. FAX: (808) 847-2855. Licensee: KGU Partners Ltd. (acq 7-87). Net: ABC/E, ABC TalkRadio, CBS, CBS Spectrum. Rep: Banner. Format: Talk/news, sports. News staff 6; news progmg 49 hrs wkly. Target aud: General. ■ Charles J. Givens, pres; Casey Stangl, gen mgr; Kimo Akane, opns mgr & progmg dir; John Kelleher, gen sls mgr; Gregory Skaltsas, prom dir; Jill Kuramoto, news dir; Steven Morris, pub affrs dir.

KHHH(FM)—Listing follows KHVH(AM).

KHNR(AM)—1946: 650 khz; 10 kw-U. TL: N21 17 28 W157 50 20 (CP: DA-1, TL: N21 28 41 W157 58 20). 850 Richards St. (96813). (808) 533-0065. FAX: (808) 528-5467. Licensee: Coral Communications Corp. (acq 10-28-91; $375,000 for CP; FTR 11-18-91). Format: News. ■ Ron Burley, gen mgr.

***KHPR(FM)**—Nov 13, 1981: 88.1 mhz; 27 kw. Ant 2,000 ft. TL: N21 24 03 W158 06 10. Stereo. Hrs opn: 24. 738 Kaheka St. (96814). (808) 955-8821. FAX: (808)-942-5477. Licensee: Hawaii Public Radio. Net: APR, AP, NPR. Wash atty: Bryan & Cave. Format: Class, news, info. News staff 3; news progmg 35 hrs wkly. Target aud: General. Spec prog: Pacific Island. ■ Al Hulsen, pres & progmg dir; Mark Wagner, opns dir; Teppi Waxman, mktg dir; Alan Bruin, mus dir; Scott Kim, news dir.

KHVH(AM)—March 18, 1957: 990 khz; 5 kw-U. TL: N21 17 59 W157 51 33. Hrs opn: 24. 1160 N. King St. (96817). (808) 845-9902. FAX: (808) 842-1457; (808) 845-9905. Licensee: KHVH Inc. Group owner: L.S. Berger Stations (acq 7-31-73). Net: ABC/I, NBC, MBS. Rep: D & R Radio. Wash atty: Reed, Smith, Shaw & McClay. Format: News/talk. News staff 12; news progmg 168 hrs wkly. Target aud: General. Spec prog: Sports, 49ers, Giants baseball, Portland Trail Blazers. ■ Lawrence S. Berger, pres; Bob Bowen, gen mgr; Bill Morse, opns mgr, progmg

Broadcasting & Cable Yearbook 1994

dir & news dir; Gary Thomas, sls dir & prom dir; Don Porter, chief engr. ■ Rates: $27.50; 15; 20; 15.

KHHH(FM)—Co-owned with KHVH(AM). July 4, 1988: 98.5 mhz; 100 kw. Ant -968 ft. TL: N21 18 49 W157 51 43. Stereo. Hrs opn: 24. Prog sep from AM. (808) 842-1360. Format: News, talk. Target aud: General; upscale, white collar, college educated. ■ Gary Thomas, mktg dir; Bill Morse, adv dir, mus dir & pub affrs dir. ■ Rates: Same as AM.

***KIFO(AM)**—(Pearl City). May 2, 1990: 1380 khz; 6.1 kw-U. TL: N21 26 18 W157 59 29. Hrs opn: 24. Suite 101, 738 Kaheka, Honolulu (96814). (808) 955-8821. Licensee: Hawaii Public Radio (acq 11-89; $525,000; FTR 11-13-89). Net: NPR, APR, AP. Wash atty: Bryan, Cave,McPheeters & McRoberts. Format: News/talk. News staff 3; news progmg 84 hrs wkly. Target aud: General. Spec prog: Pacific Island 2 hrs wkly.

KIKI(AM)—April 1951: 830 khz; 10 kw-U. TL: N21 19 26 W157 52 32. Stereo. Medi Five Bldg., 345 Queen St., Suite 601 (96813). (808) 531-4602; (808) 545-3447. FAX: (808) 531-4606; (808) 531-5454. Licensee: Henry Hawaii Broadcasting. Group owner: Henry Broadcasting (acq 12-30-88; $4.1 million with co-located FM; FTR 1-16-89). Net: Unistar. Rep: Christal. Format: Oldies, talk. News staff one. Target aud: 25-54. ■ Charlton Buckley, pres; Lee Coleman, gen mgr; David Chapman, opns mgr; Michol Klabo, gen sls mgr; Lori Flores, prom dir; Jeff Hunter, progmg dir; Danielle Tucker, news dir; Jerry Varoujean, chief engr.

KIKI-FM—Feb 14, 1979: 93.9 mhz; 100 kw. Ant -144 ft. TL: N21 19 26 W157 52 32. Stereo. Prog sep from AM. Rep: Christal. Format: CHR. News staff one. Target aud: 18-49. adults. ■ David Chapman, pub affrs dir.

KINE-FM—November 1988: 105.1 mhz; 100 kw. Ant 1,948 ft. TL: N21 23 51 W158 06 01. Stereo. Suite 400, 900 Fort St. (96813-4812). (808) 524-7100. Licensee: RLS Radio Inc. (acq 12-88; $51,000; FTR 12-19-88). Rep: Major Mkt. Format: Contemp Hawaiian. Target aud: 25-44. ■ Michael Kenney, gen mgr. ■ Rates: $55; 45; 55; 41.

*KIPO-FM—1989: 89.3 mhz; 3.3 kw. Ant 1,968 ft. TL: N21 24 03 W158 06 10. Stereo. Hrs opn: 24. 738 Kaheka St. (96814). Net: APR, NPR, AP. Wash atty: Bryan Cave. Format: News/info, jazz, international music. News staff 3; news progmg 50 hrs wkly. Target aud: General. ■ Al Hulsen, pres & progmg dir; Mark Wagner, opns dir; Teppi Waxman, mktg dir; Alan Bunin, mus dir; Scott Kim, news dir.

KISA(AM)—April 24, 1973: 1540 khz; 5 kw-D. TL: N21 19 27 W157 52 47. 904 Kohou St., Suite 204 (96817). (808) 841-4555. FAX: (808) 841-4855. Licensee: Manayan Ventures Inc. (dba KISA Radio) (acq 4-24-73). Format: Filipino-American, adult contemp, contemp hit. Target aud: 25-54; Filipino adults. ■ Rick Manayan, pres, gen mgr & gen sls mgr; Lynn Mata, progmg dir; Amelia Casamina, news dir; Ralph Wilson, chief engr.

***KKUA(FM)**—(Wailuku). April 15, 1988: 90.7 mhz; 7 kw. Ant 5,533 ft. TL: N20 42 41 W156 15 26. Hrs opn: 24. Rebroadcasts KHPR(FM) Honolulu, 100%. 738 Kaheka St., Honolulu (96814). (808) 955-8821. FAX: (808) 942-5477. Licensee: Hawaii Public Radio. Net: APR, AP, NPR; HPR. Wash atty: Bryan Cave. Format: Class, news, info. News staff 3: news progmg 35 hrs wkly. Target aud: General. Spec prog: Pacific Island 2 hrs wkly. ■ Al Hulsen, pres & progmg dir; Mark Wagner, opns dir; Leslie Allen, dev dir; Pat Avery, sls dir; Teppi Waxman, mktg dir; Alan Bruin, mus dir; Scott Kim, news dir.

KLHT(AM)—1946: 1040 khz; 5 kw-U. TL: N21 17 08 W157 48 08. Hrs opn: 24. 1190 Nuuanu (96817). (808) 524-1040. FAX: (808) 524-0998. Licensee: Calvary Chapel of Honolulu (acq 5-85). Format: Relg. Target aud: General. ■ William Stonebraker, pres; Derald Skinner, gen mgr, gen sls mgr, prom mgr & progmg dir; Jim Neuman, mus dir; Ralph Wilson, chief engr.

KNDI(AM)—July 11, 1960: 1270 khz; 5 kw-U. TL: N21 19 26 W157 52 47. 1734 S. King St. (96826). (808) 946-2844. FAX: (808) 947-3531. Licensee: KNDI Radio (acq 12-16-86). Format: Relg, ethnic. Spec prog: Por 3 hrs, Okinawan 2 hrs, Chinese 6 hrs, Samoan 12 hrs wkly. ■ Leona Jona, gen mgr; Harvey Winestin, opns mgr; Ralph Wilson, chief engr.

KOHO(AM)—December 1959: 1170 khz; 5 kw-U. TL: N21 17 08 W157 48 08. 2696 Waiwai Loop, Rm. 205 (96819). (808) 836-1551. Licensee: Cosmopolitan Broadcasting Corp. (acq 9-8-61). Format: Japanese language. News staff one. ■ Ikuko Tomita, gen mgr & gen sls mgr; Maggie Tateishi, prom mgr; Ralph Wilson, chief engr.

KORL(FM)—March 1, 1993: 99.5 mhz; 100 kw. Ant -386 ft. TL: N21 18 02 W157 51 53. Stereo. Hrs opn: 24. Box 841421, Houston, TX (77284). (713) 890-5943. Licensee: Coral Communications Corp. (acq 12-15-92; $117,000; FTR 1-11-93). ■ Roger Agnew, gen mgr; Jacqueline S. Agnew, stn mgr.

KPOI-FM—Mar 6, 1962: 97.5 mhz; 83 kw. Ant 46 ft. TL: N21 17 41 W157 51 49. Stereo. The Dillingham Bldg., 741 Bishop St. (96813). (808) 524-7100. Licensee: Kilohana Broadcasting Inc. (acq 11-21-86; $2.6 million; FTR 5-5-86). Rep: Banner. Wash atty: Haley, Bader & Potts. Format: New rock. News staff one. Target aud: 18-49. ■ Charles Cotton, pres; Michael Vassar, vp, gen mgr & gen sls mgr; Bill Gillman, prom mgr; Kerry Gray, progmg dir; Chris Rowe, mus dir; Charlene Espina, news dir. ■ Rates: $80; 68; 68; 50.

KQMQ(AM)—May 14, 1947: 690 khz; 10 kw-U. TL: N21 17 41 W157 51 49. Stereo. Hrs opn: 24. Suite 1193, 711 Kapiolani Blvd. (96813). (808) 591-9369. FAX: (808) 591-9349. Licensee: Desert Communication II Inc. (acq 5-4-93; with co-located FM; FTR 5-24-93). Rep: Katz. Wash atty: Wilkinson, Barker, Knauer & Quinn. Format: CHR. Target aud: 18-34. ■ Ronnie Hope, gen mgr; Alan Yamamoto, gen sls mgr; Jeff Kind, prom dir; Kriss Hart, mus dir; Candice Cruise, news dir; Michael Heilman, chief engr. ■ Rates: $125; 70; 65; 30.

KQMQ-FM—Oct 1, 1967: 93.1 mhz; 54 kw. Ant -119 ft. TL: N21 17 46 W157 50 36. Stereo. Dups AM 100%. ■ Rates: Same as AM.

KRTR-FM—See Kailua.

KSSK(AM)—1929: 590 khz; 7.5 kw-U. TL: N21 19 26 W157 52 32. Suite 208, 1505 Dillingham Blvd. (96817). (808) 841-8300. FAX: (808) 841-9219. Licensee: New-Tex Communications (acq 10-25-93; $7.5 million with KSSK-FM Walpahu; FTR 11-8-93) Rep: Eastman. Wash atty: Ginsburg, Feldman & Bress. Format: Adult contemp, personalities. News progmg 12 hrs wkly. Target aud: 30-60. ■ Ray Barnett, gen mgr; Suzi Mechler, opns dir; Mimi Beams, gen sls mgr; Dave Lancaster, progmg dir; Erika Engle, news dir; Dale Machado, chief engr.

KSSK-FM—See Waipahu.

***KTUH(FM)**—Jan 1, 1969: 90.3 mhz; 100 w. Ant -62 ft. TL: N21 18 14 W157 49 22. Stereo. Suite 202, 2445 Campus Rd. (96822). (808) 956-7431. FAX: (808) 956-5271. Licensee: University of Hawaii. Format: Div. News staff one; news progmg one hr wkly. Target aud: 18-59; college age, Island of Oahu. Spec prog: Jazz 21 hrs, international music 5 hrs, Hawaiian 6 hrs, reggae 9 hrs, class 18 hrs, rap 3 hrs wkly. ■ Drew Hartnett, gen mgr; Shawn Casey, prom mgr; Pat Louie, progmg dir; Kimo Nichols, mus dir; Eve Brandt, asst mus dir; Kawika Liu, news dir; Jim Knoubuhl, pub affrs dir; Dale Machado, chief engr.

KULA(AM)—March 1992: 1460 khz; 5 kw-U. TL: N21 19 26 W157 52 32. Stereo. c/o KKGO-FM, 1500 Cotner Ave., Los Angeles, CA (90025). Licensee: Mount Wilson FM Broadcasters. ■ Saul Levine, pres.

KUMU-FM—Sept 1, 1967: 94.7 mhz; 100 kw. Ant 78 ft. TL: N21 17 09 W157 50 19. Stereo. 441 N. Nimitz Hwy. (96817). (808) 531-4511. Licensee: John Hutton Corp. (acq 8-16-71). Rep: Banner. Format: Easy listening. 25-54. Target aud: 25-54. ■ John H. Weiser Jr., pres; Jeff Coelho, exec vp, gen mgr & gen sls mgr; George Rudolph, stn mgr & mus dir; Paul Miller, news dir; Ernie Nearman, chief engr.

KUMU(AM)—Mar 1, 1963: 1500 khz; 10 kw-U. TL: N21 17 08 W157 48 08. Hrs opn: 24 Dups FM 100%.

KWAI(AM)—Jan 21, 1972: 1080 khz; 5 kw-U. TL: N21 17 41 W157 51 49. Hrs opn: 24. 1088 Bishop, Suite 204 (96813). (808) 522-5100. FAX: (808) 522-5105. Licensee: Radio Hawaii Inc. (acq 2-85). Format: News/talk, financial. News staff 3; news progmg 72 hrs wkly. Target aud: 25-64; general. Spec prog: Tongan 8 hrs, Samoan 10 hrs, relg 4 hrs, health 12 hrs, sports 3 hrs, Iranian one hr wkly. ■ Sam Wagenvoord, pres & gen mgr; Barry Wagenvoord, vp opns & dev dir; Lloyd Ray, prom mgr; Gloria May, progmg dir & news dir; Ralph Wilson, chief engr.

KZOO(AM)—Oct 18, 1963: 1210 khz; 1 kw-U. TL: N21 17 59 W157 51 33 (CP: N21 17 41 W157 51 49). 250 Ward Ave. (96814). (808) 593-2880. FAX: (808) 595-0083. Licensee: Polynesian Broadcasting Inc. (acq 4-1-67). Format: Japanese & Eng. ■ Noboru Furuya, pres; Yoshio Sato, gen mgr; Mure Kimi, news dir; Ralph Wilson, chief engr.

Kahaluu

KLEO(FM)—Not on air, target date unknown: 106.1 mhz; 3 kw. Ant -2,585 ft. TL: N19 35 31 W155 58 23. c/o Brewer Broadcasting Corp., 913 Kanoelehua, Hilo (96720). (808) 961-0651. Licensee: Brewer Broadcasting Corp. (acq 6-5-92; $75,000; FTR 6-29-92).

Kahului

KAOI(AM)—(Kihei). Oct 11, 1979: 1110 khz; 5 kw-U. TL: N20 47 30 W156 28 21. Stereo. Box 38, Kahului (96732). (808) 244-9145. Licensee: Visionary Related Entertainment Inc. (group owner; acq 7-21-90; grpsl; FTR 6-18-90). Format: Talk, sports. Target aud: 25-54. Spec prog: Jazz 10 hrs, Hawaiian 15 hrs wkly. ■ John Detz, pres & gen mgr; Jack Gist, progmg dir; Bill Best, news dir; Alex Kowalski, chief engr.

KAOI-FM—(Wailuku). June 1974: 95.1 mhz; 100 kw. Ant 1,227 ft. TL: N20 38 12 W156 23 24. Stereo. Hrs opn: 24. Prog sep from AM. FAX: (808) 244-8247. (acq 8-1-90; $650,000; FTR 8-20-90). Format: Rock. News staff one; news progmg 5 hrs wkly. Target aud: General. ■ Jack Gist, mus dir; Milan Leggett, chief engr.

KNUI(AM)—Sept 14, 1962: 900 khz; 5 kw-U. TL: N20 47 30 W156 28 21. Hrs opn: 24. 311 Ano St. (96732). (808) 877-5566. FAX: (808) 871-0666. Licensee: CD Broadcasting Corp. (group owner; acq 8-90; $1.6 million with co-located FM; FTR 8-13-90). Net: ABC/E. Format: Oldies. News staff one; news progmg 14 hrs wkly. Target aud: 35-54. Spec prog: Filipino 12 hrs wkly. ■ Christopher T. Dahl, pres; Greg Everett, gen mgr; Pamela Tsutsui, gen sls mgr; Cliff Arquette, progmg dir; Greg Howard, news dir; Earl Tolley, chief engr.

KNUI-FM—June 22, 1984: 99.9 mhz; 100 kw. Ant -540 ft. TL: N20 47 30 W156 28 21. Format: Adult contemp. News progmg 6 hrs wkly.

Kailua

KRTR-FM—Oct 9, 1978: 96.3 mhz; 75 kw. Ant 2,120 ft. TL: N21 19 49 W157 45 24. Stereo. Pali Palms Plaza, 970 N. Kalaheo (96734). (808) 254-3596. FAX: (808) 254-3299. Licensee: Ohana Broadcasting Inc. (acq 3-16-93; $1.25 million; FTR 4-12-93). Rep: Republic. Format: Adult contemp. Spec prog: Hawaiian 4 hrs wkly. ■ Austin Vali, stn mgr; Linda Vali, gen sls mgr; Patrick Leonard, mktg dir & prom mgr; Mahlon Moore, progmg dir & mus dir; Jane Pascual, news dir; Clayton Caughill, chief engr.

Kailua-Kona

KLUA(FM)—1991: 93.9 mhz; 5.3 kw. Ant 2,831 ft. TL: N19 43 15 W155 55 16. Stereo. 74-5605 Luhia St. B7 (96740). (808) 329-8688. FAX: (808) 329-7244. Licensee: Sirius Communications Inc. ■ James Fakas, gen mgr.

Kaneohe

KBLZ(FM)—Not on air, target date unknown: 104.3 mhz; 69.4 kw-H, 68.8 kw-V. Ant 209 ft. TL: N21 19 49 W157 45 24. Licensee: Kaneohe Radio Inc.

Kawaihae

KWYI(FM)—Not on air, target date 1994: 106.9 mhz; 5.5 kw. Ant 341 ft. TL: N19 53 09 W155 39 28. Box 6540, Kamuela (96743). (808) 885-9866. FAX: (808) 885-6480. Licensee: Colin H. Naito.

Kealakekua

KKON(AM)—October 1963: 790 khz; 5 kw-U. TL: N19 31 10 W155 55 08. Hrs opn: 24. Box 845 (96750). (808) 323-2200. FAX: (808) 323-3186. Licensee: Visionary Related Entertainment Inc. (group owner; acq 1-16-92; $405,000 with co-located FM; FTR 2-10-92). Format: Adult contemp. Target aud: 25-54; general. ■ John Detz, pres; Mark Taylor, gen sls mgr & progmg mgr; Sharon Bonini, mus dir; Becky Summers, news dir; Stan Tomyl, chief engr.

KAOY(FM)—Co-owned with KKON(AM). Nov 11, 1982: 101.5 mhz; 6 kw. Ant 2,052 ft. TL: N19 31 10 W155 55 08. Stereo. Prog sep from AM. Format: AOR. Target aud: 18-49.

Kekaha

KAUI(FM)—Licensed to Kekaha. See Honolulu.

Kihei

KAOI(AM)—Licensed to Kihei. See Kahului.

Lahaina

KLHI-FM—May 1984: 101.1 mhz; 100 kw. Ant 745 ft. TL: N20 41 27 W156 22 07. Stereo. 840 Wainee St. (96761). (808) 667-5544. FAX: (808) 667-2765. Licensee: Dale J. Parsons, Jr. (acq 4-91). Net: Unistar. Format: Oldies-based adult contemp, some Hawaiian. News progmg 14 hrs wkly. Target aud: 25-49. Spec prog: Children 2 hrs wkly. ■ Dale J. Parsons, Jr., pres; Ginny Parsons, gen mgr; Audrey Dougherty, opns mgr; Glenn Vares, gen sls mgr; Earl Tolley, chief engr. ■ Rates: $10; 7; 8; 5.

KPOA(FM)—October 1984: 93.5 mhz; 1.4 kw. Ant 1,305 ft. TL: N20 50 43 W156 54 04 (CP: 346 w, ant 2,421 ft.). Stereo. Suite 215, 505 Front St. (96761). (808) 667-9110; (808) 667-9221. FAX: (808) 661-8850. Licensee: Lahaina Broadcasting Co. Ltd. Wash atty: Kenkel & Assoc. Format: Hawaiian, jazz. ■ Chuck Bergson, pres & gen mgr; Al Pokipala, sls dir; Ken Harris, Chuck Kaupu, progmg dirs; George Paoa, mus dir; Alex Kowalski, chief engr. ■ Rates: $15; 12; 15; 12.

Lanai City

KONI(FM)—Nov 1, 1993: 104.7 mhz; 50 kw. Ant 2,447 ft. TL: N20 48 23 W156 52 01. Suite C-318, 300 Ohukai Rd., Kihei (96753). (808) 875-8866. FAX: (808) 875-8870. Licensee: Ivan N. Dixon III. Format: Adult contemp. ■ Ivan Dixon, CEO; Bernard Clark, gen mgr.

Lihue

KFMN(FM)—March 7, 1988: 96.9 mhz; 100 kw. Ant 400 ft. TL: N21 59 54 W159 25 35. Stereo. Hrs opn: 24. Box 1566 (96766-5566). (808) 246-1197; (808) 246-9797. FAX: (808) 246-9697. Licensee: FM 97 Associates (acq 6-7-88; $600,000). Wash atty: Mullin, Rhyne, Emmons & Topel. Format: Adult contemp. News staff one; news progmg 4 hrs wkly. Target aud: 25-54; island residents & visitors. ■ Dianne Mikami, gen mgr & prom dir; Steven Y.S. Choi, sls dir; Jason Yotsuda, progmg dir; John Wada, mus dir; Russel Wada, chief engr. ■ Rates: $30; 30; 30; 22.

KQNG(AM)—1939: 570 khz; 1 kw-U. TL: N21 59 33 W159 24 24. Box 1748, KQNG Radio Bldg., 4271 Halenani St. (96766). (808) 245-9527. FAX: (808) 245-3563. Licensee: Sanchez Communications Corp. (acq 6-26-91; $1.5 million with co-located FM; FTR 7-15-91). Net: AP. Rep: Torbet/Select. Format: Oldies. News staff one; news progmg 7 hrs wkly. Target aud: 25-54; those with spendable income. Spec prog: Country 5 hrs, Filipino 12 hrs wkly. ■ Rodney Sanchez, gen mgr; M.B. Melamed, gen sls mgr; Consuelo Cruz, prom mgr; Lee Cataluna, news dir; Ernie Nearman, chief engr. ■ Rates: $29; 25; 29; 23.

KQNG-FM—Oct 17, 1983: 93.5 mhz; 100 kw. Ant 226 ft. TL: N21 59 33 W159 24 24. Stereo. Dups AM 38%. Format: CHR. Target aud: 18-49. ■ Ed Kanoi, progmg dir. ■ Rates: Same as AM.

Makawao

KDLX(FM)—Dec 31, 1980: 94.3 mhz; 3 kw. Ant -22 ft. TL: N20 50 48 W156 19 35. Stereo. Hrs opn: 24. Box 28, Kahului (96732). (808) 244-9145. Licensee: Visionary Related Entertainment Inc. (group owner; acq 6-9-93; $265,000; FTR 6-28-93). Format: Country. ■ John Detz, pres & gen mgr; David Hoffman, sls dir; Jack Gist, progmg dir; Alex Kowalski, chief engr.

Pearl City

***KIFO(AM)**—Licensed to Pearl City. See Honolulu.

KUPU(FM)—Not on air, target date unknown: 101.9 mhz; 100 kw. Ant 1,948 ft. TL: N21 23 51 W158 06 01. c/o Paul Yang, 685 E. California Blvd., Pasadena, CA (91106). Licensee: Paul Yang (acq 7-90; $232,394; FTR 7-23-90).

Poipu

KSRF(FM)—Not on air, target date unknown: 95.9 mhz; 1.13. kw. Ant 738 ft. 34001 Granada Dr., Dana Point, CA (92629). Licensee: Lu Ann Chida Lane and William A. Lane.

Princeville

KBQB(FM)—Not on air target date unknown: 98.9 mhz; 100 kw. Ant -53 ft. TL: N22 12 25 W159 23 27. North Shore Radio, Suite 105, 435 S. Lafayette Park Pl., Los Angeles, CA (90057). Licensee: North Shore Radio Inc.

Pukalani

KMVI-FM—June 15, 1984: 98.3 mhz; 3 kw. Ant -546 ft. TL: N20 42 19 W156 21 54 (CP: 50 kw, ant 101 ft.). 250 Waiehu Beach Rd., Wailuku (96793). (808) 242-6611. FAX: (808) 244-8017. Licensee: Brian Obie Broadcasting. Format: Adult contemp. News staff one. ■ Brian Obie, pres; Ronald Vaught, vp & gen mgr; Ron Vaught, gen sls mgr; Brendon Freitas, progmg dir & news dir; Earl Talley, chief engr.

Volcano

KKOA(FM)—Not on air, target date unknown: 107.7 mhz; 3 kw. Ant 207 ft. TL: N19 29 08 W155 16 17. Box 367 (96785). Licensee: Li Hing Mui Inc. (acq 11-18-92; $51,163; FTR 12-14-92).

Wailuku

KAOI-FM—Licensed to Wailuku. See Kahului.

***KKUA(FM)**—Licensed to Wailuku. See Honolulu.

KMVI(AM)—March 17, 1947: 550 khz; 5 kw-U. TL: N20 53 29 W156 29 23. 250 Waiehu Beach Rd. (96793). (808) 242-6611. FAX: (808) 244-8017. Licensee: Obie Broadcasting (acq 8-80; $1 million; FTR 8-11-80). Format: Adult contemp, Hawaiian. News staff one. Spec prog: Japanese 6 hrs, Filipino 11 hrs wkly. ■ Brian Obie, pres; Ronald Vaught, vp & gen mgr; Brendon Freitas, progmg dir & news dir; Earl Talley, chief engr. ■ KMVI-TV affil.

KMVI-FM—See Pukalani.

Waipahu

KDEO(AM)—Sept 20, 1950: 940 khz; 10 kw-U. TL: N21 26 43 W158 03 49. 94-1088 Farrington Hwy. (96797). (808) 671-2851. FAX: (808) 671-4701. Licensee: Loew Broadcasting Corp. (acq 4-84; $402,000; FTR 4-2-84). Net: MBS. Format: C&W. Spec prog: Samoan one hr wkly. ■ Robert M. Loew, pres & gen mgr; Cary Hayashikawa, gen sls mgr; Norm Winter, progmg dir; Ralph Wilson, chief engr.

KDEO-FM—Nov 23, 1988: 102.7 mhz; 61 kw. Ant 1,893 ft. TL: N21 23 49 W158 05 58. Stereo. Dups AM 95%.

KSSK-FM—Dec 30, 1976: 92.3 mhz; 100 kw. Ant 1,630 ft. TL: N21 23 49 W158 05 58 (CP: Ant 1,950 ft.). Stereo. Suite 208, 1505 Dillingham Blvd., Honolulu (96817). (808) 841-8300. FAX: (808) 841-9219. Licensee: New-Tex Communications (acq 10-25-93; $7.5 million with KSSK[AM] Honolulu; FTR 11-8-93). Rep: Eastman. Wash atty: Ginsburg, Feldman & Bress. Format: Adult contemp. Target aud: 18-34. ■ Ray Barnett, gen mgr; Bill logan, opns dir; Scott Mackenzie, prom mgr; Michael Shishido, progmg dir; Dale Machado, chief engr.

Idaho

LAUREN A. COLBY
301-663-1086
COMMUNICATIONS ATTORNEY
Special Attention to Difficult Cases

American Falls

KOUU(FM)—Not on air, target date unknown: 104.1 mhz; 3 kw. Ant 328 ft. TL: N42 45 24 W112 48 38. c/o Dobson, Goss, Rones & Dahl, 906 Olive St., St. Louis, MO (63101). Licensee: Dobson, Goss, Rones & Dahl.

Blackfoot

***KCVI(FM)**—Not on air, target date unknown: 101.5 mhz; 100 kw. Ant 1512 ft. TL: N43 30 03 W112 39 43. 8603 Buckingham Ln., Kansas City, MO (64138). Licensee: Richard P. Bott II.

KECN(AM)—November 1951: 690 khz; 1 kw-D, 43 w-N. TL: N43 10 70 W112 22 10. Box 699 (83221). (208) 785-1400. FAX: (208) 785-0184. Licensee: Western Communications Inc. (acq 1-1-75). Net: CNN. Format: All news. News staff one. ■ Jim T. Burgoyne, gen mgr; Keith Walker, gen sls mgr; Russ Novak, progmg dir; Carl Watkins, chief engr.

KLCE(FM)—Co-owned with KECN(AM). Oct 15, 1975: 97.3 mhz; 100 kw. Ant 1,512 ft. TL: N43 30 03 W112 39 43. Stereo. Prog sep from AM. Rep: McGavren Guild. Format: Adult contemp. Target aud: 18-49. ■ Blake Macintosh, mus dir.

WILLIAM A. EXLINE, INC

MEDIA BROKERS
CONSULTANTS

4340 Redwood Highway
Suite F 230
San Rafael, California 94903
TEL (415) 479-3484
• FAX (415) 479-1574

Boise

KBOI(AM)—May 1, 1947: 670 khz; 50 kw-U, DA-N. TL: N43 25 44 W116 19 43. Stereo. Hrs opn: 24. Box 1280 (83701); 1419 W. Bannock (83702). (208) 336-3670. FAX: (208) 336-3734. Licensee: KBOI Inc. Group owner: Pacific Northwest Broadcasting Corp. (acq 1-27-75). Net: ABC/I. Rep: Katz. Format: Adult contemp. Target aud: 25-54. Spec prog: Farm 3 hrs wkly. ■ Charles H. Wilson, pres; Al Vuylsteke, vp & gen mgr; Bob Rosenthal, natl sls mgr; Larry Doss, progmg dir; Bill Scott, news dir; Bill Frahm, chief engr.

KQFC(FM)—Co-owned with KBOI(AM). Nov 1, 1960: 97.9 mhz; 47 kw. Ant 2,499 ft. TL: N43 45 12 W116 06 08 (CP: 58kw). Stereo. Prog sep from AM. Format: Country. ■ Paul Wilson, progmg dir.

***KBSU(AM)**—Dec 4, 1955: 730 khz; 15 kw-D, 500 w-N, DA-2. TL: N43 34 13 W116 20 45. 1910 University Dr. (83725). (208) 385-3663. Licensee: Idaho State Board of Education (Boise State University) (acq 12-30-91; donation; FTR 1-20-92). Format: Div, educ, Sp. Spec prog: Fr 2 hrs, American Indian one hr wkly. ■ James V. Paluzzi, gen mgr.

***KBSU-FM**—Jan 16, 1977: 90.3 mhz; 19 kw. Ant 2,637 ft. TL: N43 35 41 W116 08 39. Stereo. Hrs opn: 24. Licensee: Boise State Univ. (acq 12-30-91). Net: APR, NPR. Wash atty: Dow, Lohnes & Albertson. Format: Classical, new age. News staff 3; news progmg 100 hrs wkly. ■ Paul Kjellander, stn mgr; David Lentz, opns mgr; Carolyn Sinnard, dev dir; Samantha Wright, mus dir; Jyl Hoyt, pub affrs dir; Ralph Hogan, chief engr.

KBXL(FM)—See Caldwell.

KCIX(FM)—(Garden City). Jan 1, 1985: 105.9 mhz; 50 kw. Ant 2,700 ft. TL: N43 45 18 W116 05 52. Stereo. 5257 Fairview Ave., Boise (83706). (208) 376-6666. Licensee: Contemporary Media Corp. Net: AP. Rep: McGavren Guild. Format: Adult contemp. ■ Kip Guth, pres & gen mgr; Don Jennings, opns mgr; David Levi, gen sls mgr; Cindy Lee, prom mgr; Larry Gebert, news dir; Lee Eichelberger, chief engr.

KFXD(AM)—See Nampa.

KGEM(AM)—1945: 1140 khz; 10 kw, DA-N. TL: N43 35 54 W116 15 14 (CP: 50 kw-D). Stereo. 5601 Cassia St. (83705). (208) 344-3511. FAX: (208) 336-3264. Licensee: Boise Viking Associates L.P. (acq 12-87; $2.1 million with co-located FM; FTR 11-2-87). Net: Unistar. Rep: Major Mkt Radio. Wash atty: Haley, Bader & Potts. Format: Original hits of the 40s, 50s and 60s. Target aud: 35 plus. ■ Bruce Johnson, pres; Ken Koch, gen mgr; Lynda Johnson, gen sls mgr; Terry Petersen, prom mgr; Bryan Michaels, progmg mgr; Roger Iverson, news dir; Mark McGaha, chief engr.

KJOT(FM)—Co-owned with KGEM(AM). 1979: 105.1 mhz; 43 kw. Ant 2,570 ft. TL: N43 45 19 W116 06 52 (CP:

52.5 kw, ant 2,570 ft.). Stereo. Format: AOR. News progmg 3 hrs wkly. 25-49.

KHEZ(FM)—See Nampa.

KIDO(AM)—Nov 9, 1928: 630 khz; 5 kw-U, DA-2. TL: N43 30 57 W116 19 49 (CP: TL: N43 30 56 W116 19 43). Box 63 (83707); Suite 570, 1109 Main St. (83702). (208) 344-6363; (208) 384-5483. FAX: (208) 385-9064. Licensee: Sundance Broadcasting Inc. (group owner; acq 5-2-79). Net: ABC, NBC, NBC Talknet. Rep: Christal. Format: News/talk. Target aud: 35-64; managerial, professional, affluent. ■ Michael D. Jorgenson, pres; Dick Lumenello, gen mgr; John Sheftic, gen sls mgr; John Duane, progmg dir; Lee Eichelberger, chief engr.

KLTB(FM)—Co-owned with KIDO(AM). Nov 2, 1979: 104.3 mhz; 52 kw. Ant 2,574 ft. TL: N43 45 18 W116 05 52. Stereo. Prog sep from AM. Format: Classic oldies. News staff 2; news progmg 10 hrs wkly. Target aud: 25-54; affluent, managerial, professional. ■ Dick Lumenello, natl sls mgr; Jack Armstrong, mktg dir & progmg dir; Gene Hayes, news dir.

KIZN(FM)—Aug 1, 1968: 92.3 mhz; 44 kw. Ant 2,500 ft. TL: N43 45 19 W116 05 52. Stereo. Hrs opn: 24. 9400 Fairview Ave. (83704-8101). (208) 378-9200. FAX: (208) 375-2707. Licensee: W.G. Boise Ltd. Group owner: West Group Broadcasting (acq 9-10-91; $650,000). Rep: Banner. Format: Country. News staff one. Target aud: 25-54. ■ Michael Baer, gen mgr; Ken Boesen, progmg dir; Dan Valley, mus dir; Mac Magaha, chief engr. ■ Rates: $38; 32; 32; 19.

KJOT(FM)—Listing follows KGEM(AM).

KKIC(AM)—Apr 8, 1961: 950 khz; 5 kw-D, 35 w-N. TL: N43 37 14 W116 17 57. Box 4489 (83711). (208) 322-3437. Licensee: Northwest Broadcasting Inc. (acq 7-78). Net: ABC/E. Format: Country. Spec prog: Farm 5 hrs wkly. ■ Steve Sumner, pres & gen mgr.

KLTB(FM)—Listing follows KIDO(AM).

KQFC(FM)—Listing follows KBOI(AM).

KSPD(AM)—April 29, 1959: 790 khz; 1 kw-D. TL: N43 33 57 W116 20 13. 1477 S. Five Mile Rd. (83709). (208) 377-3790; (208) 466-0110. Licensee: KSPD Inc. (3-24-83; $200,000; FTR 4-18-83). Net: Moody. Rep: Savalli. Format: Christian, talk. Target aud: 18-54. ■ Lee Schafer, pres, gen mgr & gen sls mgr; Scott Riggan, progmg dir; Lee Eichelberger, chief engr.

KZMG(FM)—(New Plymouth). March 17, 1982: 93.1 mhz; 50 kw. Ant 2,630 ft. TL: N43 45 19 W116 05 52. 7272 Potomac, Boise (83704). (208) 375-9300. Licensee: PTI Broadcasting Inc. Rep: D & R Radio. Format: Top 40. ■ Mike Baer, gen mgr.

Bonners Ferry

KBFI(AM)—Sept 1, 1977: 1450 khz; 1 kw-U. TL: N48 41 20 W116 20 04. Box X, 305 First St. (83805). (208) 267-5593. FAX: (208) 267-7293. Licensee: Radio Bonners Ferry. Net: ABC/C. Format: Adult contemp, country. News progmg one hr wkly. Target aud: General. Spec prog: Class 3 hrs, Farm 2 hrs wkly. ■ Michael Cockrill, gen mgr.

KRBF(FM)—Co-owned with KBFI(AM). Not on air, target date unknown: 92.1 mhz; 3 kw. Ant 63 ft.

Burley

KBAR(AM)—Aug 31, 1946: 1230 khz; 1 kw-U. TL: N42 32 05 W113 48 54. Stereo. 1841 W. Main (83318). (208) 678-2244. Licensee: Mini-Cassia Broadcasting Inc. (acq 8-21-84). Net: ABC/I. Rep: Intermountain. Format: MOR. ■ Richard Huizinga, gen mgr; Gerald Thaxton, progmg dir & chief engr; Mark Maier, news dir.

KZDX(FM)—Co-owned with KBAR(AM). Feb 15, 1975: 99.9 mhz; 25 kw. Ant 2,460 ft. TL: N42 20 07 W113 36 17. Stereo. Prog sep from AM. Net: ABC/FM. Format: CHR.

Caldwell

KBGN(AM)—Oct 5, 1960: 1060 khz; 10 kw-D. TL: N43 43 13 W116 31 58. 3303 E. Chicago (83605). (208) 459-3635. Licensee: Nelson M. Wilson & Karen E. Wilson (acq 8-25-89; $188,000; FTR 9-11-89). Net: USA. Format: Inspirational, Christian. Target aud: General. Spec prog: Sp 5 hrs wkly. ■ Nelson M. Wilson, gen mgr & chief engr; Don Dutton, opns dir & news dir; Karen Wilson, sls dir.

KBXL(FM)—Feb 22, 1961: 94.1 mhz; 40 kw. Ant 2,574 ft. TL: N43 45 14 W116 06 08. Stereo. 1477 S. Five Mile Rd., Boise (83709). (208) 377-3790. Licensee: KSPD Inc. (acq 4-26-89; $200,000; FTR 7-10-89). Format: Relg. Target aud: 25-54. ■ Lee Schafer, pres, gen mgr & gen sls mgr; Scott Riggan, progmg dir & mus dir; Lee Eichelberger, chief engr.

KCID(AM)—1947: 1490 khz; 1 kw-U. TL: N43 39 51 W116 38 10. Hrs opn: 16. Box 1175, 921 Cleveland Blvd. (83605). (208) 459-3608. FAX: (208) 459-1490. Licensee: Twin Cities Broadcasting Co. (acq 9-13-93; $118,200 with co-located FM; FTR 10-4-93). Net: AP. Rep: Farmakis. Wash atty: Dow, Lohnes & Albertson. Format: Adult contemp. Target aud: 35-64; agricultural & business families. Spec prog: Sp 4 hrs, farm 16 hrs wkly. ■ Dale G. Peterson, pres, gen mgr, gen sls mgr & prom mgr; Carl Follick, opns dir, progmg dir & mus dir; Sam Bass, news dir & pub affrs dir; Lee Eichelberger, chief engr. ■ Rates: $16; 16; 16; 16.

KCID-FM—Dec 1, 1983: 107.1 mhz; 3 kw. Ant 365 ft. TL: N43 39 51 W116 38 10. Stereo. Hrs opn: 16. Prog sep from AM. Format: Country. Target aud: General. Spec prog: Farm 4 hrs wkly.

KHEZ(FM)—Licensed to Caldwell. See Nampa.

***KTSY(FM)**—Oct 14 1990: 89.5 mhz; 8.3 kw. Ant 2,601 ft. TL: N43 45 18 W116 05 52 (CP: Ant 2,594 ft.). Stereo. Hrs opn: 24. 16115 S. Montana Ave. (83605). (208) 459-5879; (208) 887-0895. FAX: (208) 459-3144. Licensee: Southern Idaho Corp. Net: USA, AP. Wash atty: Donald Martin. Format: Contemp Christian mus. News progmg 4 hrs wkly. Target aud: 25-45. ■ Stephen L. McPherson, CEO; Russell Johnson, chmn; Michael Agee, gen mgr & progmg dir; John Runkle, chief engr.

Chubbuck

KRCD(AM)—1981: 1490 khz; 1 kw-U. TL: N42 55 38 W112 30 03. Hrs opn: 24. Box Z, 811 W. Cedar (Rear) Pocatello. (83206). (208) 232-0010. Licensee: Good Times Inc. Rep: Katz & Powell. Wash atty: Barry Wood. Format: News/talk News progmg 15 hrs wkly. Target aud: 35-55. Spec prog: Sp 4 hrs wkly. ■ Thomas W. Mathis, pres & gen mgr; Joyce M. Mathis, vp. ■ Rates: $6; 5; 6; 3.

KRSS(FM)—Nov 10, 1984: 98.5 mhz; 150 w. Ant 1,350 ft. TL: N42 55 15 W112 20 40 (CP: 98.5 mhz, 6.24 kw). Stereo. 5147 Whitacker Rd., Pocatello (83202). (208) 237-1425. FAX: (208) 237-7271. Licensee: Calvary Chapel of Costa Mesa Inc. (acq 9-23-91; $103,500; FTR 10-14-91). Format: Christian. Target aud: General. Spec prog: Sp 4 hrs wkly. ■ Chuck Smith, pres; Ty Orr, CFO; Lewis Phelps, stn mgr; Nick Davidson, chief engr.

Coeur d'Alene

KCDA(FM)—Licensed to Coeur d'Alene. See Spokane, Wash.

KETB(FM)—Not on air, target date unknown: 102.3 mhz; 340w. Ant 764 ft. TL: N47 39 50 W116 53 57. Stereo. Rt. 1, Box 215-6, St. Anthony (83445). Licensee: Communications Group Inc.

KKCH-FM—Listing follows KVNI(AM).

KVNI(AM)—Nov 1, 1946: 1080 khz; 10 kw-D, 1 kw-N, DA-N. TL: N47 36 57 W116 43 07. Hrs opn: 24. Box 308, First & Lakeside (83814). (208) 664-9271. FAX: (208) 667-0945. Licensee: North Idaho Broadcasting Co. (acq 8-12-91). Net: NBC. Rep: Eastman; Art Moore. Wash atty: Reddy, Begley & Martin. Format: Adult contemp, news/talk. News staff 2. Target aud: 25 plus. Spec prog: Farm one hr wkly. ■ B. Todd Hagadone, pres; Joe Stanosch, vp & gen mgr; Jim Richmond, gen sls mgr; Dick Haugen, progmg dir; Kevin Hagen, news dir; Steve Franko, chief engr. ■ Rates: $18; 16; 18; 14.

KKCH-FM—(Hayden). Co-owned with KVNI(AM). Nov 1, 1991: 94.5 mhz; 100 kw. Ant 1,883 ft. TL: N47 39 34 W116 57 48. Stereo. Hrs opn: 24. Prog sep from AM. Format: Hot adult contemp. Target aud: 24-54. ■ Beau Tyler, progmg dir. ■ Rates: $28; 24; 20; 16.

Cottonwood

***KNWO(FM)**—Not on air, target date unknown: 90.1 mhz; 250 w. Ant 612 ft. 382 Murrow Communications Center, Pullman, WA (99164). Licensee: Washington State University.

Eagle

KIDH(AM)—Not on air, target date July 1, 1994: 1000 khz; 10 kw-D, DA. TL: N43 41 50 W116 24 16. Suite 285, 967 E. Park Blvd., Boise (83706-6700). (208) 368-9717; (208) 467-1990. FAX: (805) 528-1982. Licensee: Radio Representatives Inc. Format: Relg, talk. ■ Norwood J. Patterson., pres; Sherwood Patterson, vp & gen mgr.

KRVG(FM)—Not on air, target date unknown: 107.9 mhz; 1.1 kw. Ant 2,585 ft. TL: N43 45 18 W116 05 52. 5000 Joe Ln., Nampa (83651). Licensee: Eagle Broadcasting Inc.

Emmett

KJHY(FM)—Mar 12, 1973: 101.9 mhz; 57 kw. Ant 2,532 ft. TL: N43 48 18 W116 05 52. Stereo. Box 4489, Boise (83711). (208) 322-3437. Licensee: Radio Broadcasting Inc. (acq 2-19-85; $450,000; FTR 3-11-85). Format: Jazz, easy lstng. ■ Steve Sumner, pres & gen mgr.

Garden City

KCIX(FM)—Licensed to Garden City. See Boise.

Gooding

KRXR(AM)—1992: 1480 khz; 1 kw-D. TL: N42 54 54 W114 42 41. Box 545 (83330). (208) 934-8630. FAX: (208) 934-8630. Licensee: Arlis E. and Marlin O. Tranmer (acq 4-15-92). Format: Country. ■ Arlis Tramner, gen mgr; Thomas R. Atkinson, progmg mgr.

Grangeville

KORT(AM)—Oct 8, 1954: 1230 khz; 1 kw-U. TL: N45 55 52 W116 07 50. Box 510 (83530). (208) 983-1230. FAX: (208) 983-2744. Licensee: 4-K Radio Inc. (group owner; acq 6-1-71). Net: ABC/C. Rep: Major Mkt. Format: Today's C&W. Spec prog: Farm 2 hrs wkly. ■ Mike Ripley, pres; Melinda Alley, gen mgr, opns mgr, gen sls mgr & progmg dir; Brian Danner, mus dir; Paul Carpenter, Mia Carlson, news dirs; David Forsman, chief engr.

KORT-FM—Dec 1, 1979: 92.7 mhz; 362 w. Ant 2,352 ft. TL: N45 51 48 W116 07 24. Stereo. Prog sep from AM. Format: C&W.

Hailey

KSKI-FM—See Sun Valley.

Hayden

KKCH-FM—Licensed to Hayden. See Coeur d'Alene.

Idaho Falls

KFTZ(FM)—May 24, 1986: 103.3 mhz; 50 kw. Ant 581 ft. TL: N43 32 34 W111 53 07. Stereo. 1190 Lincoln (83401). (208) 523-3722. FAX: (208) 525-2575. Licensee: Eagle Rock Broadcasting Co. Inc. Net: NBC The Source. Format: CHR. ■ Kim Lee, pres & gen mgr; Rich Summers, opns dir, progmg dir & news dir; Jerry Williamson, gen sls mgr; Don Larsen, chief engr. ■ Rates: $22; 22; 22; 22.

KICN(AM)—Sept 10, 1960: 1260 khz; 5 kw-D, 64 w-N. TL: N43 31 15 W111 59 33. 765 S. Woodruff (83402). (208) 785-1400. FAX: (208) 785-0184. Licensee: Western Communications Inc. (acq 5-90; $55,000; FTR 6-18-90). Net: CNN. Format: All news. News staff 6. Target aud: 35 plus; upscale, mature adults

KID(AM)—1928: 590 khz; 5 kw-D, 1 kw-N, DA-N TL: N43 33 35 W111 55 15. 1655 S. Woodruff (83404). (208) 524-5900. FAX: (208) 522-9690. Licensee: Fox Communications Corp. (acq 5-21-93; $700,000 with co-located FM; FTR 6-14-93). Net: CBS, ARN, Sun. Rep: Banner, Art Moore, Target. Wash atty: Pepper & Corrazini. Format: News/talk. News staff one; news progmg 34 hrs wkly. Target aud: 25-54; upscale decision-making professionals. Spec prog: Farm 18 hrs wkly. ■ Jim Fox, pres; Mike Hudson, gen mgr; Steve Powers, opns dir; Darin Rankin, chief engr.

KID-FM—May 1, 1965: 96.1 mhz; 100 kw. Ant 1,500 ft. TL: N43 29 51 W112 39 50. Stereo. Prog sep from AM. Format: Lite adult contemp. News progmg 3 hrs wkly.

KOSZ-FM—Not on air, target date unknown: 105.5 mhz. 5152 N. Santa Monica, Whitefish, WI (53217). Licensee: SPH Associates.

KUPI(AM)—Nov 9, 1957: 980 khz; 5 kw-D, 1 kw-N, DA-2. TL: N43 31 23 W112 00 36. Stereo. 854 Lindsay Blvd. (83402). (208) 522-1101. FAX: (208) 522-6110. Licensee: Kupi Broadcasting Co. (acq 9-1-91; $1,300,000 with co-located FM). Net: ABC/I. Rep: Eastman, Intermountain Net. Wash atty: Haley, Bader & Potts. Format: Oldies. News staff 2. ■ Ray E. Groth, pres; Michael Groth, vp; James C. Garshow, gen sls mgr; Dennis Carlson, gen sls mgr; Phyllis Kerr, prom dir; Phillip Moon, progmg dir; Gary Marvin, mus dir; John Balginy, news dir; Marv Hepworth, chief engr.

KUPI-FM—Aug 16, 1975: 99.1 mhz; 100 kw. Ant 1,513 ft. TL: N43 32 33 W111 53 04. Stereo. Prog sep from AM.

Stations in the U.S. Idaho

Net: ABC/E. Format: Country. ■ Phil Boone, progmg dir; Gary Marvin, mus dir.

Jerome

KART(AM)—August 1956: 1400 khz; 1 kw-U. TL: N42 43 51 W114 32 17. 47 N. 100 West (83338). (208) 324-8181. FAX: (208) 324-7124. Licensee: KART Broadcasting Co. (acq 9-1-64). Net: Unistar. Rep: IMN, Eastman, Art Moore. Format: C&W. News staff one; news progmg 3 hrs wkly. Target aud: 25 plus. Spec prog: Sp 3 hrs wkly. ■ Al Lee, pres & chief engr; Kent Lee, gen mgr & gen sls mgr; Lamont Summers, progmg dir & mus dir; Carla Cunha, news dir.

KMVX(FM)—Co-owned with KART(AM). August 1970: 102.9 mhz; 100 kw. Ant 760 ft. TL: N42 43 54 W114 25 04. Stereo. Prog sep from AM. Rep: Art Moore. Format: CHR. Target aud: 18-34; females 31 plus. ■ Lamont Summers, chief opns.

Ketchum

KRMR(FM)—Not on air, target date unknown: 104.7 mhz; 155 w. Ant 1,922 ft. TL: N43 38 36 W114 23 49. Licensee: Idaho Broadcasting Consortium Inc. (acq 10-1-92; $7,500; FTR 11-2-92).

Lewiston

KATW(FM)—Oct 2, 1986: 101.5 mhz; 100 kw. Ant 848 ft. TL: N46 27 38 W117 01 00. Stereo. Hrs opn: 24. Suite 302, 301 D St. (83501). (208) 743-6564. FAX: (208) 746-6397. Licensee: Woodcom Inc. (acq 1-1-90). Net: CBS. Rep: Eastman/Intermountain, Target. Wash atty: Arter & Hadden. Format: Adult contemp, oldies. News staff one; news progmg 4 hrs wkly. Target aud: 25-54. Spec prog: Jazz 3 hrs wkly; CBS Sports. ■ Mark Bolland, CEO, pres & gen mgr; Bob Sammons, gen sls mgr; Jeff Walker, prom dir; Don Kelly, progmg mgr; Bob McKoy, mus dir. ■ Rates: $30; 20; 25; 15.

KCLK-FM—See Clarkston, Wash.

***KLHS-FM**—October 1967: 88.9 mhz; 155 w. Ant 810 ft. TL: N46 24 38 W117 00 54. 1114 Ninth Ave. (83501). (208) 743-5557. FAX: (208) 746-7724. Licensee: David S. Case. Format: Rock. ■ Cheryl Flory, gen mgr.

KMOK(FM)—Listing follows KRLC(AM).

KOZE(AM)—Oct 6, 1955: 950 khz; 5 kw-D, 1 kw-N, DA-2. TL: N46 23 32 W117 02 03. Stereo. Hrs opn: 24. Box 936 (83501). (208) 743-2502. FAX: (208) 743-1995. Licensee: 4-K Radio Inc. (group owner; acq 6-1-71). Net: ABC/E, SMN. Rep: Major Mkt. Format: Oldies. News staff 2. Target aud: 25-54. Spec prog: Farm 2 hrs wkly. ■ Michael R. Ripley, pres; Paul Carpenter, news dir; David Forsman, chief engr.

KOZE-FM—Jan 17, 1961: 96.5 mhz; 25 kw. Ant 741 ft. TL: N46 27 48 W117 00 01. Stereo. Hrs opn: 24. Prog sep from AM. Net: ABC/C. Format: AOR. Target aud: 18-49. ■ Jay McCall, progmg dir. ■ Rates: $18; 18; 18; na.

KRLC(AM)—March 1935: 1350 khz; 5 kw-D, 1 kw-N, DA-N. 805 Stewart Ave. (83501). (208) 743-1551. Licensee: Ida-Vend Inc. (acq 11-1-81). Net: AP. Rep: Katz & Powell, Eastman. Format: Country. News staff 2; news progmg 10 hrs wkly. Target aud: 25-54. Spec prog: Farm 5 hrs, radio auction 2 hrs wkly. ■ Robert Prasil, pres & gen mgr; Melva Prasil, stn mgr; William Cooper, gen sls mgr; Steve Small, prom mgr, progmg dir & mus dir; John Thomas, news dir; Kelly Wayne, pub affrs dir; Steve Franco, chief engr. ■ Rates: $16; 15; 16; 13.

KMOK(FM)—Co-owned with KRLC(AM). March 1983: 106.9 mhz; 99 kw. Ant 1,230 ft. TL: N46 27 33 W117 02 18. Stereo. Prog sep from AM. Net: AP. Format: Adult top 40. News progmg 3 hrs wkly. Target aud: 18-34. ■ Aaron Taylor, vp progmg. ■ Rates: Same as AM.

McCall

***KBSM(FM)**—Jan 20, 1991: 91.7 mhz; 220 w. Ant 1,912 ft. TL: N45 00 38 W116 07 53. Stereo. BSU Radio, 1910 Univ. Dr., Boise (83725). (208) 385-3663. FAX: (208) 344-6631. Licensee: Idaho State Board of Education. Net: APR, NPR. Format: Classical, jazz, news. News staff 2; news progmg 60 hrs wkly. Target aud: General. ■ James Paluzzi, gen mgr; Paul Kjellander, stn mgr; Ralph Hogan, chief engr.

KMCL(AM)—Oct 15, 1965: 1240 khz; 500 w-D, 1 kw-N. TL: N44 54 45 W116 07 42. Stn currently dark. Box 813, 100 N. 3rd (83638). (208) 634-4777. FAX: (208) 634-3059. Licensee: Idaho Heartland Broadcasting Inc. ■ Buzz McCabe, opns mgr; Jan McIntosh, gen sls mgr.

KMCL-FM—Oct 22, 1990: 101.1 mhz; 3.9 kw. Ant 1,873 ft. TL: N44 45 54 W116 11 54. Stereo. Hrs opn: 24. Box 813, 100 N. 3rd (83638). (208) 634-4777. FAX: (208) 634-3059. Licensee: Idaho Heartland Broadcasting Inc. Net: SMN. Rep: Eastman/IMN, Art Moore, Target. Wash atty: Putbrese, Hunsaker & Ruddy. Format: Adult contemp, country. News staff one; news progmg 5 hrs wkly. Target aud: 25-54; upper-middle class to white collar, young families & students. Spec prog: Bus one hr, relg one hr wkly; sports & entertainment. ■ Nancy Gentry, pres; Lorry Peck, exec vp, gen mgr, opns mgr, gen sls mgr & progmg dir. ■ Rates: $14; 10; 14; 6.

Montpelier

KVSI(AM)—July 20, 1965: 1450 khz; 1 kw-U. TL: N42 18 54 W111 18 38. Box 340 (83254). (208) 847-1450. FAX: (208) 847-1451. Licensee: Tri-State Broadcasting Co. (acq 11-1-68). Net: ABC/I. Rep: Sandeberg-Glenn. Format: Country. Spec prog: Farm 4 hrs, relg 2 hrs wkly.

Moscow

KQQQ(AM)—See Pullman, Wash.

***KRFA-FM**—Sept 1, 1963: 91.7 mhz; 1.45 kw. Ant 1,009 ft. TL: N46 40 54 W116 58 13. Stereo. Murrow Communications Center, Washington State Univ., Pullman (99164-2530); KRFA Bldg., Univ. of Idaho (83843). (509) 335-6500; (208) 885-6020. FAX: (509) 335-3772. Licensee: Washington State Univ. (acq 7-1-84). Net: NPR, APR. Format: Class, news. News staff one; news progmg 37 hrs wkly. Target aud: General. Spec prog: Folk, jazz. ■ Dennis Haarsager, gen mgr; Jean Palmquist, stn mgr & progmg dir; Jerry Miller, opns mgr; Elizabeth Carroll, dev dir; Barbara Hanford, dev mgr; Dale Harrison, news dir; John Gray, engrg dir.

KRPL(AM)—May 20, 1947: 1400 khz; 1 kw-U. TL: N46 44 47 W117 01 06. Hrs opn: 24. Box 8849, 1114 N. Almon (83843). (208) 882-2551. FAX: (208) 883-3571. Licensee: KRPL Inc. (acq 9-24-87; $454,109 with co-located FM; FTR 10-12-87). Net: ABC/D. Rep: McGavren Guild. Wash atty: Haley, Bader & Potts. Format: Oldies. News staff one; news progmg 12 hrs wkly. Target aud: 25-54. Spec prog: Farm 4 hrs, relg 2 hrs wkly. ■ Dennis Deccio, pres, gen mgr & gen sls mgr; Gary Cummings, opns mgr; Sandy Murphy, prom mgr; Steve Heller, progmg dir; Larry Ayer, chief engr. ■ Rates: $23; 22; 23; 21.

KZFN(FM)—Co-owned with KRPL(AM). Feb 24, 1973: 106.1 mhz; 62.1 kw. Ant 921 ft. TL: N46 40 51 W116 58 26. Stereo. Hrs opn: 24. Prog sep from AM. Net: ABC/D. Format: CHR. News staff one; news progmg 5 hrs wkly. Target aud: 25-54. ■ Steve Shannon, progmg dir & mus dir. ■ Rates: $24; 23; 24; 22.

***KUOI-FM**—November 1968: 89.3 mhz; 50 w. Ant -92 ft. TL: N46 43 43 W117 00 11. Stereo. Hrs opn: 24. Student Union Bldg., Univ. of Idaho (83844). (208) 885-6433. Licensee: Univ. of Idaho. Format: Var/div. News staff 3; News progmg 2 hrs wkly. Target aud: General; alternative music listeners. Spec prog: Black 3 hrs, C&W one hr, class 3 hrs, Sp 2 hrs, Indian 2 hrs wkly. ■ Keith Hamby, stn mgr; Tabitha Simmons, dev mgr; Lisa Cole, progmg dir & mus dir; Frank Lockwood, news dir; Jeff Kimberling, chief engr.

KZFN(FM)—Listing follows KRPL(AM).

Mountain Home

KLVJ(AM)—March 20, 1962: 1240 khz; 1 kw-U. TL: N43 09 03 W115 42 26. Box 704, 1795 Canyon Ct. Rd. (83647). (208) 587-8424. Licensee: William Konopnicki (group owner; acq 9-23-92; $78,000 with co-located FM; FTR 11-2-92). Format: Classic rock. News staff one; news progmg one hr wkly. Target aud: General. Spec prog: Rush Limbaugh 15 hrs, Sp 5 hrs wkly. ■ Jack Jensen, pres & gen sls mgr; Brian Mobley, progmg dir; Rockwell Smith, chief engr.

KLVJ-FM—1982: 99.1 mhz; 100 kw. Ant -1,400 ft. TL: N43 12 29 W115 34 19. Stereo. Hrs opn: 24. Dups AM 100%. Format: Classic rock.

Nampa

KANR(AM)—Nov 1, 1962: 1340 khz; 1 kw-U. TL: N43 32 58 W116 24 38. 5257 Fairview Ave., Boise (83706). (208) 376-6666. FAX: (208) 323-7918. Licensee: Contemporary Media Corp. (acq 11-20-86; $166,000; FTR 7-28-86). Rep: McGavren Guild. Format: News. ■ Kip Guth, pres & gen mgr; Don Jennings, opns mgr; Dan Melvin, gen sls mgr; David Levi, natl sls mgr; Cindy Lee, prom mgr; Kimberly Van Scoy, news dir; Lee Eichelberger, chief engr.

KFXD(AM)—May 17, 1920: 580 khz; 5 kw-U, DA-N. TL: N43 33 35 W116 24 02. Box 107, Boise (83701); 455 W. Amity Rd., Meridian (83642). (208) 888-4321. FAX: (208) 888-2841. Licensee: Doubledee Broadcast Group (acq 6-4-86). Net: CNN, BRN, Sun, MBS, CBS, ABC. Rep: Eastman, Art Moore. Format: News, business, talk, sports. Target aud: 25-54. ■ David Obenauf, CEO, chmn, pres & gen mgr; Alex Krisik, CFO; Margo Obenauf, vp; Chris Brewer, progmg dir. ■ Rates: $10; 8; 8; 5.

KFXD-FM—Jan 10, 1975: 94.9 mhz; 49 kw. Ant 2,692 ft. TL: N43 45 18 W116 05 52. Stereo. Prog sep from AM. Rep: IMN, Eastman; Art Moore. Format: Adult contemp. Target aud: Women. ■ Rates: $29; 26; 26; 22.

KHEZ(FM)—(Caldwell). Sept 28, 1982: 103.3 mhz; 54 kw. Ant 2,525 ft. TL: N43 45 18 W116 05 52. Stereo. Hrs opn: 24. Suite 120, 3050 N. Lake Harbor Ln., Boise (83703). (208) 384-1033. FAX: (208) 343-2103. Licensee: Citadel Communications Corp. (group owner; acq 5-18-92; $12.5 million grpsl; FTR 6-8-92). Net: NBC. Rep: Eastman. Wash atty: Fletcher, Heald & Hildreth. Format: Easy lstng. News staff one; news progmg one hr wkly. Target aud: 25-54; upscale, white collar. Spec prog: Class 2 hrs, jazz 4 hrs wkly. ■ Larry Wilson, CEO, chmn, pres & exec vp; Stewart Stanek, sr vp; Greg Williamson, gen mgr, opns dir, gen sls mgr, progmg dir & mus dir; Lee Eichelberger, chief engr. ■ Rates: $20; 25; 23; 18.

KLCI(FM)—February 1977: 96.9 mhz; 44 kw. Ant 2,520 ft. TL: N43 45 19 W116 05 52. Stereo. Hrs opn: 24. Box 1280, Boise (83701); 1419 W. Bannock, Boise (83702). (208) 336-3670. FAX: (208) 336-3734. Licensee: Pacific Northwest Broadcasting Corp. (group owner; acq 3-2-93; $475,000; FTR 3-29-93). Format: Classic rock. Target aud: 25-44. ■ Charles H. Wilson, pres; Al G. Vuylstene, vp & gen mgr; Bob Rosenthal, gen sls mgr; Paul Wilson, progmg dir; Bill Frahm, chief engr.

New Plymouth

KZMG(FM)—Licensed to New Plymouth. See Boise.

Orofino

KLER(AM)—Oct 15, 1958: 1300 khz; 5 kw-D, 1 kw-U, DA-N. TL: N46 28 41 W116 14 34. Box 32 (83544). (208) 476-5702. Licensee: Central Idaho Broadcasting (acq 12-7-92; $75,000 with co-located FM; FTR 1-4-93). Net: ABC/C. Rep: Radio Time, Major Mkt. Format: Adult contemp. News staff one; news progmg one hr wkly. Target aud: General; family or logging industry-federal employee workers. ■ Jeff Jones, gen mgr & gen sls mgr; Mike Benson, mus dir; Paul Carpenter, news dir; David Forsman, chief engr. ■ Rates: $7; 7; 7; 7.

KLER-FM—Sept 20, 1979: 95.3 mhz; 100 w. Ant 750 ft. TL: N46 28 45 W116 14 15. Stereo. Prog sep from AM. Box 3110, Upper Fords Creek Rd. (83544). (208) 476-5703. Format: C&W. ■ Jeff Jones, opns mgr; Monica Jones, mktg mgr. ■ Rates: Same as AM.

Pocatello

KMGI(FM)—Listing follows KSEI(AM).

KPKY(FM)—Listing follows KWIK(AM).

KRCD(AM)—See Chubbuck.

KRSS(FM)—See Chubbuck.

KSEI(AM)—Sept 23, 1926: 930 khz; 5 kw-U, DA-N. TL: N42 57 44 W112 29 50. Box 40 (83204). (208) 233-2121. FAX: (208) 234-0105. Licensee: Pacific Northwest Broadcasters Inc. Group owner: Pacific Northwest Broadcasting Corp. (acq 8-83; $1.35 million; with co-located FM; FTR 8-1-83). Net: MBS. Rep: Katz. Format: Adult contemp. Spec prog: Farm one hr wkly. ■ Charles H. Wilson, pres; Frank Nuding, gen mgr & gen sls mgr; Paul Wilson, progmg dir; Greg Licht, news dir.

KMGI(FM)—Co-owned with KSEI(AM). April 1, 1978: 102.5 mhz; 100 kw. Ant 1,023 ft. TL: N42 51 57 W112 30 46 (CP: Ant 1,036 ft.). Prog sep from AM. Format: Classic rock.

KWIK(AM)—September 1946: 1240 khz; 1 kw-U. TL: N42 55 14 W112 27 17. Stereo. Hrs opn: 24. Box 998, 259 E. Center St. (83201). (208) 233-1133; (208) 232-0950. FAX: (208) 232-1240. Licensee: KWIK Inc. (acq 10-1-77; $650,000; $150,000 non-competitive agreement). Net: ABC/I. Rep: Torbet; Art Moore. Wash atty: Pepper & Corazzini. Format: C&W. News staff one; news progmg 5 hrs wkly. Target aud: 45 plus. Spec prog: Farm 3 hrs, gospel 2 hrs, relg one hr, American Indian one hr wkly. ■ James W. Fox, pres, gen mgr & gen sls mgr; Steve Brekke, vp opns & vp progmg; Patty Tea, opns mgr

Idaho

& progmg mgr; Mike Hudson, vp sls; Tim Pressy, mktg dir & prom dir; Gary Shockley, vp adv, progmg dir & news dir; Ron Price, engrg dir.

KPKY(FM)—Co-owned with KWIK(AM). Aug 18, 1975; 94.9 mhz; 100 kw. Ant 1,004 ft. TL: N42 52 26 W112 30 47. Stereo. Prog sep from AM. Licensee: James W. Fox. Net: ABC/C. Format: CHR. News staff one; news progmg one hr wkly. Target aud: General; 35 plus. Spec prog: Gospel 2 hrs wkly. ■ Deb Burns, prom dir; Mike Hudson, vp adv; J.D. Kelly, progmg mgr & news dir; Rick Ryan, mus dir; Su Fox, pub affrs dir.

KZBQ(AM)—Dec 20, 1956: 1290 khz; 1 kw-D. TL: N42 57 28 W112 25 46. Stereo. Box 97, 436 N. Main (83204). (208) 234-1290. FAX: (208) 234-9451. Licensee: Idaho Wireless Corp. (acq 3-86; $325,000 with co-located FM; FTR 12-9-85). Rep: Eastman, Intermountain-Tacher. Format: Contemp country. ■ Paul E. Anderson, pres, gen mgr & progmg dir; Lauren McCarther, chief engr.

KZBQ-FM—Dec 27, 1969; 93.7 mhz; 100 kw. Ant 984 ft. TL: N42 51 57 W112 30 46. Stereo. Dups AM 100%.

Preston

KACH(AM)—Sept 4, 1948: 1340 khz; 1 kw-U. TL: N42 07 45 W111 51 00. Box 1340, 1133 E. Glendale Rd. (83263). (208) 852-1340. Licensee: Zeldon A. & Mary Lynne Nelson (acq 3-21-89). Format: Country. News progmg 12 hrs wkly. Target aud: 18-54; general. Spec prog: Farm. ■ Mike Adams, gen mgr & gen sls mgr; Todd Adams, progmg dir. ■ Rates: $10.50; 10.50; 10.50; 10.50.

KACH-FM—Not on air, target date unknown: 96.7 mhz; 105 w. Ant 226 ft. TL: N47 07 45 W111 51 00. Box 1340, 1133 E. Glendale Rd. (83263). (208) 852-1340. Licensee: Zeldon Nelson. Format: Country.

Rexburg

KADQ(FM)—Aug 18, 1975: 94.3 mhz; 3 kw. Ant 315 ft. TL: N43 48 56 W111 45 28 (CP: 25 kw, ant 295 ft.). Stereo. Hrs opn: 24. Box 66, 90 S. 1st W. (83440). (208) 356-7323. Licensee: Ted W. Austin Jr. (acq 1987). Net: Unistar, USA. Rep: Katz & Powell, Tacher. Format: Adult contemp. News staff one; news progmg 2 hrs wkly. Target aud: 18-49. Spec prog: LDS Christian 6 hrs wkly. ■ Ted W. Austin Jr., pres; Dave Plourde, gen mgr & news dir; Marvin Frandsen, sls dir & prom mgr. ■ Rates: $11; 9; 10; 8.

***KRIC(FM)**—Nov 13, 1972: 100.5 mhz; 75 kw. Ant 403 ft. TL: N43 43 16 W111 56 30. Stereo. Ricks College (83460-0115). (208) 356-2907. FAX: (208) 356-2911. Licensee: Ricks College. Net: APR, NPR. Format: Class. News staff one; news progmg 29 hrs wkly. ■ Steven Bennion, pres; John A. Haeberle, gen mgr; Ernie Reidelbach, gen sls mgr; Ernie Riedelbach, adv dir; LaMar Barrus, progmg dir; Mark L. Bailey, news dir; Richard Harker, chief engr.

KRXK(AM)—January 1951: 1230 khz; 1 kw-U. TL: N43 50 50 W111 47 03. Box 458 (83440). (208) 356-3651. FAX: (208) 356-8585. Licensee: Communicast Consultants Inc. (acq 2-10-92; $115,000 with co-located FM; FTR 3-2-92). Net: ABC/I, Unistar, Intermountain. Rep: IMN; Target.Format: Country. News staff one; news progmg 10 hrs wkly. Target aud: 25-54. ■ David Grow, pres; Jeff Harris, gen sls mgr, progmg dir, mus & news dir; April Harris, prom mgr; Don Larson, chief engr.

KRXK-FM—Jan 17, 1986: 98.1 mhz; 3 kw. Ant 299 ft. TL: N43 48 55 W111 46 09 (CP: 25 kw, ant 276 ft.). Stereo. Dups AM 100%. ■ Jeff Harris, mktg dir; Don Larson, engrg dir.

***KWBH(FM)**—Not on air, target date unknown: 91.5 mhz; 100 w-H. Ant -39 ft. Ricks College (83460). Licensee: Ricks College Corp.

Rupert

KBBK(AM)—Oct 12, 1955: 970 khz; 2.5 kw-D. TL: N42 37 08 W113 39 31 (CP: 900 w-N, DA-N). TL: N42 36 10 W113 43 21). Rt. 2, Box 349A (83350). (208) 436-4757. Licensee: Tri-Market Radio Broadcasters (acq 9-24-93; $700,000 with co-located FM; FTR 10-11-93). Net: MBS. Rep: Hopewell, Moore. Format: C&W. Spec prog: Sp. ■ Charlie Michaels, gen mgr.

KKMV(FM)—Co-owned with KBBK(AM). Dec 5, 1978: 92.5 mhz; 53 kw. Ant 2,466 ft. TL: N42 37 08 W113 39 31 (CP: 3 kw, ant 205 ft.). Prog sep from AM. Format: CHR.

St. Anthony

KIGO(AM)—July 10, 1966: 1400 khz; 1 kw-U. TL: N43 58 23 W111 39 28. 365 E. 3rd N. (83445). Licensee: Fremont Broadcasting Co. Inc. (acq 10-1-92; FTR 11-2-92). ■ Ernie Riedelbach, pres & gen mgr; Jim McDaniel, mus dir & news dir; Gordon Black, chief engr.

St. Maries

KOFE(AM)—Mar 1, 1970: 1240 khz; 1 kw-D, 500 w-N. TL: N47 19 14 W116 32 50. Hrs opn: 24. 1525 Main Ave. (83861). (208) 245-4559. Licensee: Terry C. Duffey (acq 3-10-86; $107,000; FTR 12-9-85). Net: ABC, SMN. Rep: Tacher. Format: C&W. News staff 2; news progmg 9 hrs wkly. Target aud: General. Spec prog: Farm 2 hrs, local sports 3 hrs wkly. ■ Terry Duffy, gen mgr; Jeff Pugh, chief engr. ■ Rates: $8; 8; 8; 8.

Salmon

KSRA(AM)—March 1, 1959: 960 khz; 1 kw-D. TL: N45 11 02 W113 52 12. 315 Hwy. 93 N. (83467). (208) 756-2218. FAX: (208) 756-2098. Licensee: Renee Smith. Net: ABC/I. Format: C&W, MOR. Spec prog: Farm 4 hrs, class one hr wkly. ■ Renee Smith, pres, gen mgr & progmg dir; Leo Marshall, gen sls mgr; Jenifer Smith, mus dir; Blair Smith, vp engrg.

KSRA-FM—September 1979: 92.7 mhz; 1.5 kw. Ant -880 ft. TL: N45 11 02 W113 52 12. Stereo. Dups AM 100%.

Sandpoint

KJDE(FM)—Not on air, target date unknown: 102.5 mhz; 3 kw. Ant 177 ft. TL: N48 15 22 W116 30 46. Stereo. c/o Kennedy Broadcasting Inc., 3555 Marthas Ln., Vero Beach, FL (32967). Licensee: Kennedy Broadcasting Inc. (acq 4-23-91; $2,000; FTR 5-20-91).

KPND(FM)—Listing follows KSPT(AM).

KSPT(AM)—Mar 23, 1949: 1400 khz; 1 kw-U. TL: N48 18 16 W116 32 32. 334 N. First Ave. (83864). (208) 263-2179. FAX: (208) 265-5440. Licensee: Blue Sky Broadcasting Inc. (acq 5-4-83; $250,000; FTR 5-30-85). Net: SMN. Rep: Tacher. Format: Country. Target aud: 25 plus. Spec prog: Sports 6 hrs, relg 2 hrs wkly. ■ Kim Benefield, pres, gen mgr, progmg dir & mus dir; David Broughton, gen sls mgr; Bill Gott, chief engr.

KPND(FM)—Co-owned with KSPT(AM). May 19, 1980: 95.3 mhz; 1 kw. Ant -430 ft. TL: N48 15 22 W116 30 46 (CP: 3 kw, ant -385 ft.). Dups AM 5%. Net: SMN. Format: Adult contemp.

Soda Springs

KBRV(AM)—Sept 22, 1957: 790 khz; 5 kw-D. TL: N42 38 30 W111 36 40. Box 777, 81 S. Main (83276). (208) 547-4012. FAX: (208) 547-3775. Licensee: Douglas R. Mathis (acq 4-10-92; with co-located FM). Format: Adult contemp. ■ Doug Mathis, gen mgr.

KFIS(FM)—Co-owned with KBRV(AM). Sept 10, 1982: 100.1 mhz; 3 kw. Ant -174 ft. TL: N42 38 30 W111 36 40. Stereo. Dups AM 100%.

Sun Valley

KECH-FM—Nov 21, 1988: 95.3 mhz; 435 w. Ant 2,168 ft. TL: N43 39 42 W114 24 07. Hrs opn: 24. Box 2158, 221 Northwood Way-300B (83340). (208) 726-5324. FAX: (208) 726-5459. Licensee: Wood River Communications Inc. (acq 9-29-93; $215,000; FTR 10-18-93). Net: CBS Spectrum. Format: Classic rock. News staff one; news progmg 6 hrs wkly. Target aud: 30-49; baby boomers with above average income. Spec prog: Jazz 5 hrs wkly. ■ Chris Haugh, pres; Larry Mott, gen mgr, mktg mgr, prom mgr & adv mgr; Jeff Ballou, progmg dir; Jim King, mus dir; Stacey Nesmann, news dir; Frank Vetsch, chief engr. ■ Rates: $17; 17; 17; 17.

KSKI-FM—Aug 3, 1977: 103.7 mhz; 51.8 w. Ant 1,905 ft. TL: N43 38 36 W114 23 49. Stereo. Box 1340, Hailey (83333). (208) 788-4504. FAX: (208) 788-4444. Licensee: Silver Creek Communications Inc. (acq 12-7-89; grpsl; FTR 12-25-89). Net: Intermountain. Rep: Conrac, Intermountain, Leisure Market. Format: Adult contemp. ■ Stanley McCammon, vp; Melinda McKee, gen mgr; Charles Bernstein, gen sls mgr; Frank Vetsch, chief engr.

***KWRV(FM)**—July 29, 1993: 91.9 mhz; 100 w. Ant -512 ft. TL: N43 40 59 W114 22 52. 45 E. 7th St., Saint Paul, MN (55101). (612) 290-1500. FAX: (612) 290-1260. Licensee: Minnesota Public Radio. Net: APR, Minn. Pub. Format: Class. ■ William Kling, pres; Dennis Hamilton,

vp; Anne Hovland, vp dev; Ginger Sisco, vp mktg; Vic Bremer, vp progmg; Ralph Hornberger, engrg dir.

Twin Falls

KART(AM)—See Jerome.

***KAWZ(FM)**—Apr 13, 1988: 89.5 mhz; 3 kw. Ant 328 ft. TL: N42 33 25 W114 28 18 (CP: 11.6 kw). Stereo. Hrs opn: 6 AM-midnight. Box 271 (83303); 241 Main Ave., W. (83301). (208) 734-4357. Licensee: Calvary Chapel of Twin Falls Inc. Net: CBN, USA. Format: Relg, Christian, AOR. Target aud: General; Christians & non-Christians. ■ Mike Kestler, pres & gen mgr; Dan Romans, stn mgr, progmg mgr & mus dir.

***KBSW(FM)**—May 15, 1989: 91.7 mhz; 1.95 kw. Ant 492 ft. TL: N42 43 48 W114 25 06. Stereo. Hrs opn: 24. Boise State Univ., 1910 University Dr., Boise (83725). (208) 385-3663. FAX: (208) 344-6631. Licensee: Idaho State Board of Education. Net: APR, NPR. Format: Div, news, info, class. News staff 3; news progmg 100 hrs wkly. Spec prog: Jazz 20 hrs. ■ James V. Paluzzi, gen mgr; Paul Kjellander, stn mgr; Kevin O'Connor, mus dir; Ralph Hogan, chief engr.

***KCIR(FM)**—Dec 12, 1982: 90.7 mhz; 20 kw. Ant 2,519 ft. TL: N42 20 07 W113 36 17. 1446 Filer Ave. E. (83301). (208) 734-5777. Licensee: Faith Communications Corp. (acq 9-29-82). Net: USA. Format: Christian educ, relg. News progmg 5 hrs wkly. Target aud: 25-49; adults with families. Spec prog: Children 2 hrs wkly. ■ Jack Franch, pres; Duane Luchsinger, gen mgr; Chris Staley, progmg dir & mus dir; Tim Hunt, chief engr.

KEZJ-FM—Mar 15, 1977: 95.7 mhz; 50 kw. Ant 670 ft. TL: N42 43 45 W114 24 55. Stereo. Box 1259, 415 Park Ave. (83301). (208) 733-7512. Licensee: B&B Broadcasting (group owner; acq 12-31-87). Net: ABC/I. Format: Country. News staff one; news progmg 17 hrs wkly. Target aud: 25-54. Spec prog: Farm 5 hrs wkly. ■ Jerre Fender, progmg dir & mus dir; Kelly Klaas, news dir.

KEZJ(AM)—1946: 1450 khz; 1 kw-U. TL: N42 32 36 W114 28 14. Stn currently dark. ■ Terry Tario, gen mgr.

KLIX(AM)—Dec 12, 1946: 1310 khz; 5 kw-D, 2.5 kw-N, DA-N. TL: N42 33 30 W114 26 40. Box 1259, 415 Park Ave. (83301). (208) 733-1310. FAX: (208) 733-7525. Licensee: B & B Broadcasting (group owner; acq 3-23-93; $652,000 with co-located FM; FTR 4-12-93). Net: ABC/I, CNN. Format: News, talk. Spec prog: Farm 2 hrs wkly. ■ George R. Broadbin, pres; Terry Tario, gen mgr & gen sls mgr; Jerre Fender, opns mgr & progmg dir; Kelly Klaas, chief engr.

KLIX-FM—June 15, 1974: 96.5 mhz; 100 kw. Ant 130 ft. TL: N42 33 05 W114 30 59. Stereo. Prog sep from AM. Net: SMN. Format: Adult gold.

KMVX(FM)—See Jerome.

KTFI(AM)—October 1928: 1270 khz; 5 kw-D, 1 kw-N. TL: N42 33 30 W114 32 00. Box 2820, Hwy. 30 W. (83303). (208) 733-3381. FAX: (208) 733-4196. Licensee: Veis Communications Inc. (acq 7-15-88). Net: AP, SMN. Format: Adult standards, MOR. News staff 2; news progmg 13 hrs wkly. Target aud: 35 plus. Spec prog: Farm 3 hrs, relg 5 hrs, sports 3 hrs wkly. ■ Terry Veis, pres, gen mgr, progmg dir & mus dir; Walt Ross, gen sls mgr; Carol Stephens, news dir; Kelly Carlson, chief engr.

Wallace

KSQA(FM)—Not on air, target date unknown: 100.7 mhz; 75 kw. Ant 2,240 ft. TL: N47 33 44 W115 50 32. Hrs opn: 24. Box 24, Osburn (83849). (208) 753-0601. Licensee: Sam Widge Advtg. L.P.

KWAL(AM)—May 1938: 620 khz; 1 kw-U, DA-N. TL: N47 30 290 W116 00 17. Box U, Osburn (83849). (208) 752-1141. FAX: (208) 753-5111. Licensee: Silver Valley Broadcasters (acq 1-1-73). Net: ABC/I. Rep: Sandeberg-Glenn, Art Moore. Format: C&W. ■ Paul E. Robinson, pres & gen mgr; George White, gen sls mgr; Larry Crigger, progmg dir; John Davis, mus dir; Don McPeak, chief engr.

Weiser

KWEI(AM)—December 1947: 1260 khz; 1 kw-D, 60 w-N. TL: N44 14 00 W116 57 18. Box 791, 556 Hwy. S. 95 (83672). (208) 549-2241. Licensee: Treasure Valley Broadcasting Co. (acq 7-10-87). Format: Sp. News staff 2; news progmg 10 hrs wkly. Target aud: 35-65; mass appeal. Spec prog: News/talk. ■ Randy Williamson, pres, gen mgr & prom mgr; Ed Miller, chief engr.

KWEI-FM—March 1984: 99.3 mhz; 3 kw. Ant -185 ft. TL: N44 14 00 W116 57 18 (CP: 99.5 mhz, 8.3 kw, ant 2,585 ft.). Stereo. Prog sep from AM. Net: SMN. Format: Contemp country. News progmg 15 hrs wkly. Target aud: 25-54; mostly city folks or agri.

Illinois

LAUREN A. COLBY
301-663-1086
COMMUNICATIONS ATTORNEY
Special Attention to Difficult Cases

Aledo

WRMJ(FM)—June 12, 1979: 102.3 mhz; 3 kw. Ant 300 ft. TL: N41 12 29 W90 46 10. Stereo. Hrs opn: 24. Box 187, 2104 S.E. Third St. (61231). (309) 582-5666. Licensee: Western Illinois Broadcasting Co. (acq 8-83; $200,000; FTR 8-1-83). Net: ABC/D. Brownfield. Wash atty: Baraff, Koerner, Olender & Hochberg. Format: Country. News progmg 20 hrs wkly. Target aud: 25-54; adults & elderly in rural area. Spec prog: Relg 3 hrs wkly. ■ John Hoscheidt, gen mgr, gen sls mgr & adv mgr; Mike Robinson, progmg dir; Jim Taylor, news dir; Carl Stratton, chief engr. ■ Rates: $9.75; 8.45; 8.45; 7.15.

Alton

KATZ-FM—September 1961: 100.3 mhz; 50 kw. Ant 482 ft. TL: N38 55 44 W90 13 03. Stereo. Hrs opn: 24. Box 4888, St. Louis, MO (63110). (314) 361-1108. FAX: (314) 367-2297. Licensee: Noble Broadcast of St. Louis Inc. Group owner: Noble Broadcast Group (acq 3-16-93; $2.75 million with KATZ[AM] St. Louis; FTR 4-5-93). Net: ABC/C. Format: New jazzy adult contemp. News staff 2; news progmg 7 hrs wkly. Spec prog: Relg 2 hrs wkly, Black. ■ Linda O'Conner, gen mgr; Chuck Atkins, opns dir; Steve Mosier, gen sls mgr; Ken Keys, prom dir; Keith Antoine, progmg dir; Darryl Eason, mus dir; John O'Day, news dir; Darryl McQuinn, chief engr.

WBGZ(AM)—1948: 1570 khz; 1 kw-D, 74 w-N. TL: N38 55 44 W90 13 03. Hrs opn: 24. Box 615, Suite 162, 1900 Homer Adams Pkwy. (62002). (618) 465-3535. Licensee: Metroplex Communications Inc. (acq 7-20-84; $200,000; FTR 8-27-84). Net: USA, UPI, Sun. Format: News/talk. News staff 2; news progmg 20 hrs wkly. Target aud: General. ■ Clyde Jones, pres; Sam Stemm, gen mgr; Jim Scanlan, news dir; Bob Hoffman, chief engr. ■ Rates: $20; 18; 20; 10.

Anna

WRAJ(AM)—Jan 10, 1957: 1440 khz; 500 w-D, 109 w-N. TL: N37 26 45 W89 15 00. Box 606, 202 N. Main (62906). (618) 833-2148. FAX: (618) 833-2149. Licensee: Union Broadcasting Inc. (acq 7-21-80; $300,000 with co-located FM; FTR 8-11-80). Net: ABC/E, AP. Format: Gospel. ■ Benjamin Stratemeyer, pres; Dan Mohler, gen mgr, gen sls mgr & progmg dir; Debbi Allison, mus dir; Tim Meehan, news dir; Craig Bradley, chief engr.

WRAJ-FM—Jan 13, 1958: 92.7 mhz; 3 kw. Ant 290 ft. TL: N37 26 45 W89 15 00 (CP: 96.5 mhz, 20 kw, ant 780 ft.). Stereo. Prog sep from AM. Format: C&W.

Arlington Heights

WCBR-FM—Licensed to Arlington Heights. See Chicago.

Arthur

WKJR(FM)—See Mattoon.

Auburn

WCVS-FM—See Springfield.

Aurora

WAUR(AM)—(Sandwich). May 1986: 930 khz; 2.5 kw-D, 2.2 kw-N, DA-2. TL: N41 36 26 W88 27 11 (CP: 4.2 kw-N). Hrs opn: 24. 52 W. Downer Pl., Aurora (60506); One Broadcast Center, Plano (60545). (708) 896-9300. FAX: (708) 552-9300. Licensee: Nelson Broadcasting Co. Net: ABC/E. Format: Oldies, full svc. Target aud: 25-54. Spec prog: Farm 15 hrs wkly. ■ Larry Nelson, pres; Dean Abbott, opns mgr; Beth Abbott, gen sls mgr; Sarah Churness, prom mgr; Jenny Nelson, mus dir;

Doug Booth, news dir; Lane Lindstrom, chief engr. ■ Rates: $28; 20; 25; 20.

WBIG(AM)—Dec 13, 1938: 1280 khz; 1 kw-D, 500 w-N, DA-2. TL: N41 46 10 W88 14 44. Hrs opn: 24. Box 2010 (60507); 620 Eola Rd. (60504). (708) 851-4600. FAX: (708) 851-6225. Licensee: Midwest Broadcasting of Chicago Inc. Group owner: Beasley Broadcast Group (acq 10-86; $3,185,000 with co-located FM; FTR 5-18-87). Wash atty: Latham & Watkins. Format: Adult contemp. News staff one; news progmg 6 hrs wkly. Target aud: 25-54; professional, upscale, suburbanites with children. Spec prog: Relg 6 hrs wkly. ■ George Beasley, pres; Frank D. DiMatteo, vp & gen mgr; David Sonefeld, gen sls mgr; Wendy Van Loon, prom mgr; Ken Anderson, progmg dir; Mary Lawrentz, pub affrs dir. ■ Rates: $75; 75; 75; 50.

WYSY-FM—Co-owned with WBIG(AM). 1965: 107.9 mhz; 22.5 kw. Ant 734 ft. TL: N41 47 43 W87 59 07 (CP: 21.2 kw, ant 761 ft.). Stereo. Hrs opn: 24. Dups AM 100%. (708) 851-9108. Net: AP. Target aud: 25-54; suburban Chicago.

WKKD(AM)—Sept 21, 1960: 1580 khz; 250 w-D, 200 w-N, DA-2. TL: N41 46 12 W88 16 03. Stereo. Hrs opn: 24. Box C-1730, 1880 Plain Ave., (60507). (708) 898-1580; (708) 898-6668. FAX: (708) 898-2463. Licensee: WFVR Inc. Group owner: Salter Broadcasting Co. of Delaware. Net: USA. Format: Oldies, news, sports. News staff one; news progmg 10 hrs wkly. Target aud: 18 plus. Spec prog: Sp 3 hrs, relg 8 hrs wkly. ■ Shelly S. Johnson, pres; William H. Baker, exec vp & gen mgr; Bob Coyne, gen sls mgr; David Beckman, progmg dir & mus dir; Jeff Blanton, news dir; Chuck Ingle, chief engr. ■ Rates: $12; 12; 12; 6.

WKKD-FM—Feb 12, 1961: 95.9 mhz; 3 kw. Ant 338 ft. TL: N41 26 12 W88 16 03. Stereo. Hrs opn: 24. Prog sep from AM. 1884 Plain Ave. (60505). (708) 898-6668; (708) 357-9590. Licensee: WKKD, Inc. Format: Oldies. News staff one; news progmg 5 hrs wkly. Target aud: 25-54; suburban Chicago adults. Spec prog: Relg 2 hrs wkly. ■ Dave Beckman, progmg mgr; Dave Fischer, asst mus dir. ■ Rates: $32; 32; 32; 20.

WYSY-FM—Listing follows WBIG(AM).

Ava

WXAN(FM)—Jan 11, 1982: 103.9 mhz; 3 kw. Ant 675 ft. TL: N37 51 19 W89 28 06. Stereo. Hrs opn: 24. Box 213A, Rt 2, Ava Rd. (62907). (618) 426-3308; (618) 426-3309. FAX: (618) 426-3310. Licensee: Harold and Carlene Lawder. Net: USA, Moody. Tribune, Ill. Net. Format: Relg. 10 hrs wkly. Target aud: General; Christians and family-oriented listeners. Spec prog: Farm 2 hrs, sports 5 hrs wkly. ■ Harold Lawder, pres; Doug Apple, gen mgr, gen sls mgr & progmg dir; Carolyn Cremeens, mus dir; Rick Jones, pub affrs dir; Joe Bellis, chief engr. ■ Rates: $7.70; 7; 7.70; 7.

Beardstown

WRMS(AM)—Nov 1, 1959: 790 khz; 500 w-D, DA. TL: N40 00 13 W90 23 49. 108 E. Main St. (62618). (217) 323-1790. Licensee: Conner Family Broadcasting Inc. (acq 3-87). Net: ABC/C. Format: Adult contemp. ■ John Conner, gen mgr; Lyn Stoutamayer, chief engr.

WRMS-FM—1976: 94.3 mhz; 3 kw. Ant 300 ft. TL: N40 04 45 W90 25 58 (CP: 6 kw). Dups AM 100%.

Belleville

WFXB(FM)—See East St. Louis.

WIBV(AM)—July 13, 1947: 1260 khz; 5 kw-U, DA-2. TL: N38 27 28 W89 57 43. Hrs opn: 24. Box A, 3199 S. Illinois (62222); Box 511111, St Louis, MO (63151). (618) 233-5000; (314) 241-1260. FAX: (618) 234-5515. Licensee: Belleville Broadcasting Inc. (acq 12-19-88; $600,000; FTR 1-16-89). Net: MBS, NBC. Format: News/talk. News staff one; news progmg 20 hrs wkly. Target aud: 35 plus; affluent, well educated, business & professional. Spec prog: Black one hr, farm 3 hrs wkly. ■ Emert Wyss, pres; William Kniesly, vp & gen mgr; J.C. Hall, opns mgr; Tom Calhoun, progmg dir; Bill Reeker, news dir. ■ Rates: $35; 90; 35; 25.

Belvidere

WXRX(FM)—Feb 27, 1971: 104.9 mhz; 4 kw. Ant 333 ft. TL: N42 19 21 W88 57 15. Stereo. Box 7180, 2830 Sandy Hollow Rd., Rockford (61109). (815) 874-7861. FAX: (815) 874-2202. Licensee: Airplay Broadcasting Corp. Group owner: Airplay Broadcasting/Stay Tuned Broadcasting (acq 7-10-89; $1,350,000). Net: NBC the Source. Rep: Katz. Wash atty: Fisher, Wayland, Cooper

& Leader. Format: Classic AOR. News staff one; news progmg 2 hrs wkly. Target aud: 18-49. ■ Robert E. Rhea Jr., pres; David McAley, vp & gen mgr; Rich Fruin, gen sls mgr; Sky Drysdale, prom mgr; Tim Crull, progmg dir; Linda Lampert, news dir; Greg Stephens, chief engr.

Benton

WQRL(FM)—Oct 1, 1973: 106.3 mhz; 12.5 kw. Ant 328 ft. TL: N37 55 51 W88 40 52 (CP: Ant 459 ft.). Stereo. Hrs opn: 24. Box 818, Wood Bldg., Suite 506 (62812). (618) 435-8100. FAX: (618) 435-8102. Licensee: Dana Communications Corp. (acq 4-28-92; $250,000; FTR 5-18-92). Net: CBS Spectrum. Format: Country. News staff 2; news progmg 15 hrs wkly. Target aud: 25-49; adults & young adults preferring new country. Spec prog: Farm 3 hrs wkly. ■ Dana Withers, pres & gen mgr; Gregg A. Buickel, opns mgr, progmg dir & mus dir; Jazz Jackson, asst mus dir; Edward Ness, news dir; Kevin Potter, chief engr. ■ Rates: $15; 12; 15; 12.

Bethalto

WFUN-FM—April 1991: 95.5 mhz; 6 kw. Ant 328 ft. TL: N38 49 09 W90 00 53. Stereo. Hrs opn: 24. Box 141, 412 E. Bethalto Dr. (62010). (618) 377-0427; (314) 291-9386. Licensee: Bethalto Broadcasting Corp. (acq 10-24-91). Format: Children's progmg. Target aud: General. ■ Bob Howe, pres; Reed Hale, gen mgr; Lisa Tinsley, vp opns & vp progmg; Pat Clark, mus dir; Bob Marshall, vp engrg. ■ Rates: $45; 20; 30; 15.

Bloomington

WBNQ(FM)—Listing follows WJBC(AM).

WBWN(FM)—See Le Roy.

*WESN(FM)—1972: 88.1 mhz; 120 w. Ant 98 ft. TL: N40 29 28 W88 59 37. Stereo. Box 2900 (61701). (309) 556-2634. Licensee: Illinois Wesleyan Univ. Net: APR. Format: Div. progmg: Black 18 hrs, class 6 hrs, jazz 6 hrs wkly. ■ Brian Murphy, gen mgr; Bob Coleman, stn mgr; Eric Person, progmg dir; Marta Conlon, mus dir; Mike Bove, chief engr.

WIHN(FM)—See Normal.

WJBC(AM)—1925: 1230 khz; 1 kw-U. TL: N40 27 32 W89 00 38. Box 8 (61702). (309) 829-1221. Licensee: Twin Cities Broadcasting Corp. Group owner: Bloomington Broadcasting Corp. (acq 1956). Net: ABC/I. Rep: McGavren Guild. Wash atty: Reddy, Begley & Martin. Format: MOR. Spec prog: Farm 13 hrs wkly. ■ Richard D. Johnson, pres & gen mgr; Don Munson, vp & opns mgr; William Pitcher, gen sls mgr; Christine Ellenberger, prom mgr; Dan Swaney, progmg dir; Bones Bach, mus dir; Marc Magliari, news dir; Larry Shoel, chief engr.

WBNQ(FM)—Co-owned with WJBC(AM). 1947: 101.5 mhz; 50 kw. Ant 460 ft. TL: N40 27 32 W89 00 38. Stereo. Prog sep from AM. Format: Top-40. Spec prog: Farm one hr wkly. ■ Tim O. Ives, stn mgr; Keith Palmgren, gen sls mgr; Scott Robins, progmg dir; Scott Laughlin, mus dir.

Brookport

WRIK(AM)—October 1987: 750 khz; 500 w-D. TL: N37 08 31 W88 38 58. 105 W. Fifth, Metropolis (62960). (618) 524-3698. FAX: (618) 564-3202. Licensee: Samuel K. Stratemeyer. Format: Talk. ■ Samuel Stratemeyer, gen mgr; Michael Reineking, progmg dir; Craig Bradley, chief engr.

Bushnell

WLMD(FM)—Aug 1992: 104.7 mhz; 3 kw. Ant 328 ft. TL: N40 32 52 W90 26 25. Rebroadcasts WLRB(AM) Macomb 100%. 119 W. Carroll, Macomb (61455). (309) 772-9232. Licensee: Larry Derry (acq 10-31-91; $20,801 for CP; FTR 11-18-91). Net: ABC/D. Format: Country. News staff 2; news progmg 15 hrs wkly. Target aud: General. Spec prog: Farm 6 hrs, relg one hr wkly. ■ Don Sharp, gen mgr & gen sls mgr; Rick Bulger, opns mgr; Becky Weaver, natl sls mgr; Tim Crowley, news dir; Rick Fess, chief engr. ■ Rates: $20; 20; 20; na.

Cairo

WKRO(AM)—Jan 8, 1942: 1490 khz; 1 kw-U. TL: N37 02 36 W89 11 02. Hrs opn: 24. Box 311, Hwy. 51 N. (62914). (618) 734-1490. FAX: (618) 734-0884. Licensee: Roger Price (acq 10-1-93). Net: ABC/D; Brownfield. Format: C&W, oldies. News staff one; news progmg 6 hrs wkly. Target aud: 25-54. Spec prog: Gospel 12 hrs wkly. ■ Roger Price, pres, gen mgr, stn mgr & gen sls mgr; R.J. Price, prom dir & mus dir; Danny Mack, progmg dir; William T. Crain, news dir; Joe L. Bellis, chief engr. ■ Rates: $9; 9.50; 8.65; 6.90.

Illinois Directory of Radio

Canton

WBYS(AM)—Oct 5, 1947: 1560 khz; 250 w-D. TL: N40 32 43 W90 01 08. Hrs opn: 6 AM-local sunset. Box 600, 1000 E. Linn St. (61520). (309) 647-1560. FAX: (309) 647-1563. Licensee: Fulton County Broadcasting Co. Net: ABC/I; Tribune, Ill. Net. Wash atty: Putbrese & Hunsaker. Format: Div. News staff 2; news progmg 20 hrs wkly. Target aud: 25-54; community-oriented with above average income. ■ Charles E. Wright, CEO, pres & gen mgr; Kevin Stephenson, gen sls mgr & prom mgr; Leon Groover, progmg dir; Dean Cramer, mus dir; Phil Miller, news dir; Rick Fess, chief engr. ■ Rates: $14.50; 11.70; 11.70; na.

WBYS-FM—Oct 7, 1968: 98.3 mhz; 3 kw. Ant 265 ft. TL: N40 32 43 W90 01 08. Stereo. Hrs opn: 5:30 AM-midnight. Dups AM 30%. Format: Div, sports. News progmg 25 hrs wkly. Target aud: 25-54; community & sports oriented. ■ Rates: $14.50; 11.70; 11.70; 8.15.

Carbondale

WCIL(AM)—Nov 14, 1946: 1020 khz; 1 kw-D. TL: N37 43 31 W89 15 25. Hrs opn: Sunrise-sunset. Box 700, 211 W. Main (62903). (618) 457-8114. FAX: (618) 457-6556. Licensee: The McRoy Corp. (acq 7-1-77). Net: ABC/I, SMN; Tribune. Format: MOR. News staff 2; news progmg 10 hrs wkly. Target aud: 35 plus. Spec prog: Farm one hr wkly. ■ Paul H. McRoy, pres; Charlotte McRoy, vp; Dennis Lyle, gen mgr, stn mgr, gen sls mgr, prom mgr & adv mgr; Rich Bird, progmg dir; Joey Helleny, news dir; Shannon Collins, chief engr.

WCIL-FM—July 1968: 101.5 mhz; 50 kw. Ant 430 ft. TL: N37 43 31 W89 15 25. Stereo. Hrs opn: 24. Prog sep from AM. Net: ABC/C. Format: Top-40. Target aud: 12 plus. ■ Tony Waitekus, opns dir, progmg dir & mus dir; Dennis Lyle, sls dir, prom dir & adv dir; Joey Helleny, pub affrs dir.

***WSIU(FM)**—Sept 15, 1958: 91.9 mhz; 50 kw. Ant 299 ft. TL: N37 42 29 W89 14 05. Stereo. Hrs opn: 5 AM-1 AM. 1048 Comm. Bldg., Southern Illinois Univ.-Carbondale (62901). (618) 453-4343. FAX: (618) 453-6186. Licensee: Board of Trustees, Southern Ill. Univ. Net: NPR, APR. Wash atty: Cohn & Marks. Format: Class, jazz, news. News staff 2; news progmg 36 hrs wkly. Target aud: 35-64; highly educated, upper income, socially conscious. Spec prog: New age 4 hrs, opera 4 hrs, big band 4 hrs, folk 3 hrs, Broadway one hr, American Indian one hr, Black one hr wkly. ■ Lee D. O'Brien, CEO & gen mgr; Jerry Parks, CFO; Tom Godell, stn mgr & progmg dir; Mike Zelten, opns mgr; Yana Davis, dev mgr; Gillian Martin, mus dir; Tony Donley, asst mus dir; Jay Pearce, news dir; Jerry Kline, chief engr. ■ WSIU-TV affil.

WTAO(FM)—See Murphysboro.

Carlinville

WCNL(FM)—Dec 8, 1990: 95.9 mhz; 6 kw. Ant 325 ft. TL: N39 14 25 W89 54 26. Stereo. Hrs opn: 24. Box 166, #55 Carlinville Plaza (62626). (217) 854-3131. FAX: (217) 854-3416. Licensee: Carlinville Broadcasting Corp. Group owner: Miller Media Group. Net: SMN. Wash atty: Fisher, Wayland, Cooper & Leader. Format: Contemp country. News staff one; news progmg 16 hrs wkly. Target aud: 25-64. Spec prog: Farm 6 hrs, high school sports 3 hrs wkly. ■ Randal J. Miller, pres; Chip Douglas Mosley, gen mgr & progmg dir; Greg Blevins, stn mgr. ■ Rates: $15.25; 13.25; 15.25; 6.75.

***WIBI(FM)**—Sept 30, 1975: 91.1 mhz; 43 kw. Ant 370 ft. TL: N39 20 58 W89 48 16. Stereo. Hrs opn: 24. Box 140, Lake Williamson (62626). (217) 854-4800. FAX: (217) 854-4610. Licensee: Ill. Bible Institute (group owner). Net: UPI. Wash atty: Gammon & Grange. Format: Educ, relg. Target aud: 25-49. ■ Ernest J. Moen, pres; Richard Whitworth, gen mgr; Paul Anthony, progmg dir; Jana Garner, mus dir; Robert Miller, chief engr.

Carmi

WROY(AM)—Dec 13, 1948: 1460 khz; 1 kw-D, 85 w-N. TL: N38 04 54 W88 12 04. Hrs opn: 24. Box 400, 101 N. Church St. (62821). (618) 382-4161; (618) 382-2345. FAX: (618) 382-4162. Licensee: Carmi Broadcasting Co. Net: AP. Rep: Savalli. Format: Oldies. News staff 2; news progmg 25 hrs wkly. Target aud: 35 plus; general. Spec prog: Farm 6 hrs wkly. ■ Rebecca Drone, pres; Roger Swan, gen mgr & gen sls mgr; Irma Dennis, progmg dir; Scott Mareing, mus dir; Bob Miller, news dir; Frank Hertel, chief engr. ■ Rates: $13; 11; 13; 10.

WRUL(FM)—Co-owned with WROY(AM). 1951: 97.3 mhz; 50 kw. Ant 496 ft. TL: N38 04 54 W88 12 04. Stereo. Hrs opn: 24. Prog sep from AM. Net: SMN. Format: Country. News progmg 8 hrs wkly. Target aud: General. ■ Rates: $16; 14; 16; 13.

Carrier Mills

***WBVN(FM)**—Jan 8, 1990: 104.5 mhz; 3 kw. Ant 328 ft. TL: N37 46 25 W88 44 20. Stereo. Hrs opn: 17. Box 1126, New Rt. 13 E., Marion (62959). (618) 997-1500. FAX: (618) 997-3194. Licensee: Kenneth and Jane Anderson. Format: Contemp Christian. Target aud: 18-45; general. ■ Ken Anderson, pres, gen mgr & progmg dir; Mark Miles, prom mgr; Patti Thurmond, mus dir; Jeff Oestreick, chief engr.

Carterville

WXLT(FM)—Not on air, target date unknown: 95.1 mhz; 6 kw. Ant 279 ft. TL: N37 50 03 W89 01 37. Licensee: M.P. Broadcasting.

Carthage

WCAZ(AM)—1922: 990 khz; 1 kw-D, 9 w-N. TL: N40 24 30 W88 12 04. 84 S. Madison (62321). (217) 357-3128. Licensee: Reality Plus Corp. (acq 6-22-92; $850,000; with co-located FM; FTR 7-6-92). Net: UPI. Format: Farm, C&W. ■ Dan Bryan, pres & gen mgr; Chuck Porter, progmg dir & chief engr.

WCAZ-FM—Nov 1, 1978: 92.1 mhz; 25 kw. Ant 328 ft. TL: N40 16 45 W91 17 41. Prog sep from AM. Format: Oldies, contemp hit.

Casey

WCBH(FM)—Sept 19, 1988: 104.3 mhz; 11.2 kw. Ant 495 ft. TL: N39 16 24 W87 55 39. Hrs opn: 24. Box 250, 8 W. Main St. (62420). (217) 932-4900. FAX: (217) 932-4487. Licensee: Casey Broadcast Group Inc. Rep: Roslin. Format: Adult contemp. ■ M.N. Sholar, pres; Dick Hunicut, gen mgr; Steve Hamm, chief engr.

WKZI(AM)—Dec 14, 1963: 800 khz; 250 w-U. TL: N39 18 16 W87 58 17. Hrs opn: 24. Box 8, 6 E. Colorado Ave. (62420). (217) 932-4051. Licensee: Word Power Inc. (acq 5-4-93; $152,400; FTR 5-24-93). Net: Moody. Format: Christian. News progmg 17 hrs wkly. Target aud: General; Christians. ■ Paul Dean Ford, pres, gen mgr, gen sls mgr, news dir & chief engr; Eleanor Jean Ford, progmg dir & mus dir.

Centralia

WILY(AM)—Aug 15, 1946: 1210 khz; 1 kw-D. TL: N38 34 44 W89 06 46. Box 528, 302 S. Poplar (62801). (618) 532-6404. FAX: (618) 532-6653. Licensee: Centralia Radio Communications Inc. (acq 9-30-91; $450,000 with co-located FM; FTR 10-28-91). Net: ABC/I, CNN; Brownfield. Wash atty: Wiley, Rein & Fielding. Format: News, info. News staff 3; news progmg 60 hrs wkly. Target aud: 25-54. ■ James Warner, pres; Toni White, gen sls mgr; Erik Decker, progmg dir.

WRXX(FM)—Co-owned with WILY(AM). Dec 24, 1964: 95.3 mhz; 3 kw. Ant 217 ft. TL: N38 34 44 W89 06 46. Stereo. Prog sep from AM. Net: CNN; Brownfield. Format: Classic rock. Target aud: 18-49. ■ Rates: $24.50; 22.50; 22.50; 20.50.

Champaign

WBCP(AM)—See Urbana.

***WBGL(FM)**—Oct 31, 1982: 91.7 mhz; 20 kw. Ant 500 ft. TL: N40 09 09 W88 06 56. Stereo. Hrs opn: 24. 2108 W. Springfield St. (61821). (217) 359-8232. FAX: (217) 359-7374. Licensee: Illinois Bible Institute Inc. (group owner). Net: USA. Format: Educ, relg. News staff one. Target aud: 25-44. ■ Ernest Moen, pres; Dick Whitworth, gen mgr; Stephen Young, stn mgr & progmg dir; Doug Hannah, mus dir; George Howe, chief engr.

WDWS(AM)—Jan 24, 1937: 1400 khz; 1 kw-U. TL: N40 05 04 W88 14 53. Stereo. Hrs opn: 24. Box 3939, 2301 S. Neil (61826). (217) 351-5300. FAX: (217) 351-5385. Licensee: D.W.S. Inc. Net: CBS, MBS; Ill. Net., Tobacco. Rep: Christal. Format: News/talk. News staff 5; news progmg 26 hrs wkly. Target aud: General. Spec prog: Farm 10 hrs wkly. ■ Marajen S. Chinigo, pres; Jim Turpin, gen mgr; Dave Burns, gen sls mgr; Jim Manley, prom mgr; R.L. Atterberry, progmg dir; Robin Neal, news dir; Gene Barnert, chief engr. ■ Rates: $55; 50; 37.50; 35.

WHMS-FM—Co-owned with WDWS(AM). 1949: 97.5 mhz; 50 kw. Ant 358 ft. TL: N40 05 04 W88 14 53. Stereo. Hrs opn: 24. Prog sep from AM. Format: Light rock. News progmg 10 hrs wkly. Target aud: 25-54. ■ Keath Edwards, progmg dir. ■ Rates: Same as AM.

***WEFT(FM)**—Sept 21, 1981: 90.1 mhz; 10 kw. Ant 135 ft. TL: N40 10 51 W88 19 04. Stereo. Hrs opn: 6 AM-2 AM. 113 N. Market St. (61820-4004). (217) 359-9338. Licensee: Prairie Air Inc. Net: NPR, APR. Wash atty: Haley, Bader & Potts. Format: Div, progsv, jazz. News progmg 10 hrs wkly. Target aud: General. Spec prog: American Indian one hr, Black 8 hrs, class one hr, country 5 hrs, blues 10 hrs, folk 10 hrs, pub affrs 5 hrs, Sp 3 hrs wkly. ■ Linda Neuman, gen mgr; Clark Jackson, opns dir & chief engr; Clark Jackson, Linda Neuman, progmg dirs; Paul Mueth, pub affrs dir. ■ Rates: $10; 10; 15; 10.

WHMS-FM—Listing follows WDWS(AM).

***WILL(AM)**—See Urbana.

***WILL-FM**—See Urbana.

WIXY(FM)—June 1, 1992: 100.3 mhz; 12.9 kw. Ant 453 ft. TL: N40 00 58 W88 06 42. 2603 W. Bradley Ave. (61821). (217) 355-2222. FAX: (217) 355-9494. Licensee: Saga Communications of Illinois Inc. Group owner: Saga Communications Inc. (acq 11-4-92; $250,000; FTR 11-30-92). ■ Dale Weber, gen mgr.

WKIO(FM)—See Urbana.

WLRW(FM)—January 1963: 94.5 mhz; 50 kw. Ant 400 ft. TL: N40 07 32 W88 17 29 (CP: Ant 492 ft.). Stereo. 2603 W. Bradley (61821). (217) 352-4141. FAX: (217) 352-1256. Licensee: Saga Communications (group owner; acq 10-86; grpsl; FTR 7-7-86). Net: ABC/E. Rep: Katz. Format: CHR. Target aud: 18-49. ■ Dale Weber, gen mgr; Karen Cochrane, gen sls mgr; Gina Elliott, prom mgr; Mike Blakemore, progmg dir; Steve Grzanich, news dir.

WLTM(FM)—See Urbana.

***WPCD(FM)**—Jan 1978: 88.7 mhz; 3.3 kw. Ant 290 ft. TL: N40 07 32 W88 17 29. Stereo. Parkland College, 2400 W. Bradley Ave. (61821). (217) 351-2450. Licensee: Parkland College Community College District No. 505. Net: AP. Format: Educ, oldies, AOR. News staff one; news progmg 8 hrs wkly. Target aud: General. Spec prog: Country 5 hrs, alt 12 hrs, news 8 hrs, jazz 6 hrs wkly. ■ Dan Hughes, gen mgr, progmg dir & mus dir; Tom McDonnell, news dir & pub affrs dir; Richard Furr, chief engr.

WPGU(FM)—See Urbana.

WUFI(AM)—(Rantoul). Feb 1, 1963: 1460 khz; 500 w-D, DA. TL: N40 18 37 W88 12 54. Hrs opn: 24. 400 N. Broadway Ave., Urbana (61801). (217) 367-1195. FAX: (217) 367-3291. Licensee: Rollings Communications of Illinois Inc. Group owner: Rollings Communications Inc. (acq 6-27-88; with co-located FM). Rep: Banner. Format: News/talk. News staff 3. Target aud: General. ■ Mark Rollings, pres & gen mgr; Scott Schwritzer, opns dir; Rick LeCompte, gen sls mgr; Scott Black, prom dir; Cheri Preston, news dir; Greg Stephens, chief engr.

WZNF(FM)—(Rantoul). Co-owned with WUFI(AM). March 15, 1972: 95.3 mhz; 3 kw. Ant 425 ft. TL: N40 13 05 W88 06 55. Stereo. Hrs opn: 24. Prog sep from AM. Net: NBC the Source. Wash atty: Rosenman & Colin. Format: Classic rock, AOR. News staff one. Target aud: 18-49. ■ Harry Gregor, gen mgr; Rick LeCompte, natl sls mgr; Dale Holden, engrg dir.

Charleston

WEIC(AM)—Dec 10, 1954: 1270 khz; 1 kw-D, 500 w-N, DA-3. TL: N39 30 18 W88 12 54. Hrs opn: 19. RR 2, Box 185A (61920). (217) 345-2148. FAX: (217) 348-7036. Licensee: Com-Stat Communications Inc. (acq 10-19-83; $650,000 with co-located FM; FTR 11-7-83). Rep: Group W. Format: C&W. Spec prog: Farm 8 hrs wkly. ■ Stephen H. Garman, pres & gen mgr; Gary Lee, stn mgr; Steve Hamm, chief engr. ■ Rates: $14; 12; 14; 10.

***WEIU(FM)**—July 1, 1985: 88.9 mhz; 4 kw. Ant 166 ft. TL: N39 28 43 W88 10 21. Stereo. Hrs opn: 8 AM-midnight. Eastern Illinois Univ. (61920). (217) 581-6116. FAX: (217) 581-6650. Licensee: Eastern Illinois Univ. Net: CNN. Wash atty: Cohn & Marks. Format: Rock, jazz, class. News progmg 5 hrs wkly. Target aud: General. Spec prog: Black 3 hrs, C&W 3 hrs, big band 3 hrs, new age 3 hrs, news & public affairs 5 hrs wkly. ■ John L. Beabout, gen mgr; Joe Heumann, stn mgr; Eric Larson, dev dir & mktg dir; Gaye Harrison, prom mgr; Elaine Fine, mus dir; Susan Kaufman, news dir; Ron Amyx, chief engr.

WHQQ(FM)—Oct 1, 1965: 92.1 mhz; 2.2 kw. Ant 140 ft. TL: N39 30 18 W88 12 54. Stereo. Hrs opn: 19. Box 789, Matton (61938). (217) 348-9292. Licensee: The Cromwell Group Inc. of Ill. Group owner: The Cromwell Group Inc. (acq 1993). Net: SMN. Rep: Roslin. Wash atty: Arent, Fox, Kintner, Plotkin & Kahn. Format: Adult contemp.

News staff one. Target aud: 25-54; yuppies. ■ Terry Weinacht, gen mgr.

Chester

KPNT(FM)—See Ste. Genevieve, Mo.

KSGM(AM)—July 5, 1947: 980 khz; 1 kw-D, 500 w-N, DA-N. TL: N37 51 24 W89 49 44. Box 428, Ste. Genevieve, MO (63670). (314) 883-2980. Licensee: Donze Communications Inc. (acq 6-20-89; $200,000; FTR 7-10-89). Net: MBS, NBC, Learfield Data. Wash atty: Reddy, Begley & Martin. Format: Country, news/talk. News staff 3; news progmg 15 hrs wkly. Target aud: General; adults. Spec prog: Farm 2 hrs, relg 6 hrs wkly. ■ Elmo L. Donze, pres, gen mgr & chief engr; Bob Scott, gen sls mgr & progmg dir; Brian Snider, mus dir; Art Schwent, news dir. ■ Rates: $10; 10; 10; 10.

DATABASES - MAILING LABELS

★ RADIO/TELEVISION US/CANADA
99.7% Deliverable - System Updated Daily
Over 25 Selection Options: Accurate Formats, Market Size, Station Audiences, States, Networks, Random Lists, Execs by Name, Secondary Formats, Ethnic Stations, Delete/Add Markets or Stations

★ DATABASE AUDITS
We Correct, Update and Maintain Your Database

★ RADIOSCAN
All US Radio on Your PC - Includes Powerful Software
Instant Station Data on Screen - Reports in 10 Seconds
Station Lists for Each of 585 Markets
Rolls Royce of all Radio Database Systems
Ideal for Syndicators, Networks, all Vendors
Reasonably Priced

The CENTER For RADIO INFORMATION
19 Market Street, Cold Spring, NY 10516
PH: (800) 359-9898 FX: (914) 265-2715

Chicago

WBBM(AM)—Nov 14, 1923: 780 khz; 50 kw-U. TL: N41 59 32 W88 01 36. 630 N. McClurg Ct. (60611). (312) 944-6000. Licensee: CBS Inc. Group owner: CBS Broadcast Group (acq 1931). Net: CBS, AP. Format: News. ■ Steve Carver, vp & gen mgr; Val Carolin, gen sls mgr; Barbara DiGuido, prom mgr; Chris Berry, progmg dir & news dir; Mark Williames, chief engr.

WBBM-FM—Dec 7, 1941: 96.3 mhz; 6.2 kw. Ant 1,174 ft. TL: N41 53 56 W87 37 23 (CP: 4.2 kw, ant 1,554 ft.). Stereo. Prog sep from AM. Net: CBS. Format: CHR. ■ Thomas Matheson, vp & gen mgr; Thad Gentry, mktg dir & prom mgr; Todd Cavanah, progmg dir; Eric Bradley, mus dir; Karen Hand, news dir.

WBEE(AM)—See Harvey.

***WBEZ(FM)**—1942: 91.5 mhz; 8.3 kw. Ant 1,180 ft. TL: N41 53 56 W87 37 23. Stereo. Hrs opn: 24. 105 W. Adams (60603). (312) 460-9150. FAX: (312) 460-9318. Licensee: The WBEZ Alliance Inc. (acq 9-7-90; FTR 10-1-90). Net: NPR. Wash atty: Arter & Hadden. Format: Jazz, pub affrs, talk. News staff 3. Target aud: General; people who want to know about the world around them. ■ Carole R. Nolan, CEO, pres & gen mgr; Allan J. Arlow, chmn; Ted Madaj, CFO; Tony Judge, gen sls mgr; Gloria Ciaccio, mktg mgr; Torey Malatia, vp progmg; Dayna Calderon, mus dir; Cheryl Corley, news dir; Alfred Antlitz, vp engrg; Joseph DiFranco, chief engr.

***WBHI(FM)**—Sept 9, 1973: 90.7 mhz; 7 w. Ant 55 ft. TL: N41 44 55 W87 43 13. 3939 W. 79th St. (60652). (312) 535-2199; (312) 535-2180. FAX: (312) 535-2165. Licensee: Bogan High School. Format: Div, educ, news. Target aud: General. ■ John R. Higgins, stn mgr; Richard R. Renik, engrg dir.

WCBR-FM—(Arlington Heights). March 10, 1960: 92.7 mhz; 3 kw. Ant 299 ft. TL: N42 07 50 W87 58 59. Stereo. 120 W. University Dr., Arlington Heights (60004-1892). (708) 255-5800. FAX: (708) 255-0129. Licensee: Darrell Peters Productions Inc. (acq 9-14-82; $550,000; FTR 9-13-82). Format: Adult contemp, blues. News staff one. Target aud: 18-49. Spec prog: Pub affrs 2 hrs, news 4 hrs wkly. ■ Darrel L. Peters, pres; Alaine Peters, gen mgr & stn mgr; Jeff Fritz, gen sls mgr; Tim Disa, progmg mgr; Gary Horn, chief engr.

WCFJ(AM)—See Chicago Heights.

WCGO(AM)—See Chicago Heights.

WCKG(FM)—See Elmwood Park.

WCRW(AM)—July 1926: 1240 khz; 1 kw-U (ST WEDC & WSBC). TL: N41 58 53 W87 46 20. 5625 N. Milwaukee (60646). (312) 763-8250. Licensee: WCRW Inc. (acq 11-63). Net: UPI. Rep: Caballero. Format: Ethnic & Sp. Target aud: General. ■ Leona Peterson, gen mgr; Frank McCoy, chief engr.

***WCRX(FM)**—July 29, 1975: 88.1 mhz; 100 w. Ant 150 ft. TL: N41 52 22 W87 38 52. Hrs opn: 7 AM-midnight. 600 S. Michigan Ave. (60605). (312) 663-1693. FAX: (312) 663-5204. Licensee: Columbia College (acq 10-5-82). Wash atty: Dow, Lohnes & Albertson. Format: Urban contemp. Target aud: 12-24; ethnic. ■ Karen Cavaliero, gen mgr; Brett J. Johnson, chief engr.

***WCYC(FM)**—Dec 1, 1969: 90.5 mhz; 8 w. Ant 56 ft. TL: N41 20 26 W87 43 05 (CP: 17 w, ant 85 ft.). 2801 S. Ridgeway Ave. (60623). (312) 762-9292. FAX: (312) 762-1677. Licensee: Chicago Boys & Girls Clubs Educational Corp. Format: Dance oriented urban contemp. ■ Bob Bucaro, gen mgr.

WEDC(AM)—1926: 1240 khz; 1 kw-U (ST WCRW & WSBC). TL: N41 58 53 W87 46 20. Hrs opn: 11. 5475 N. Milwaukee Ave. (60630). (312) 631-0700; (312) 792-1240. Licensee: Foreign Language Broadcasts Inc. (acq 1964). Format: Sp, news/talk, ethnic. News staff one; news progmg 13 hrs wkly. Target aud: Spanish. Spec prog: Greek one hr, It one hr, Pol 7 hrs, Russian one hr, Ukranian one hr wkly. ■ Roman Pucinski, chmn; Jim Keithley, gen mgr; Carmen Castro, stn mgr, progmg dir, mus dir, news dir & chief engr.

WFMT(FM)—Dec 13, 1951: 98.7 mhz; 16 kw. Ant 1,170 ft. TL: N41 53 56 W87 37 23. Stereo. Hrs opn: 24. 3 Illinois Center, 303 E. Wacker Dr. (60601). (312) 565-5000. FAX: (312) 565-5169. Licensee: Chicago Educational Television Assn. (acq 3-5-70). Rep: D & R Radio. Wash atty: Schwartz, Woods & Miller. Format: Class. News progmg 7 hrs wkly. Target aud: 25-54; upscale, professional, college educated, upper income adults. Spec prog: Folk 4 hrs, drama 2 hrs, talk 5 hrs, comedy one hr wkly. ■ Daniel J. Schmidt, sr vp & gen mgr; Raymond Nordstrand, dev dir; Jim Barker, sls dir & gen sls mgr; Jon Kavanaugh, prom mgr; Norman Pellegrini, progmg dir; Dennis Moore, mus dir; Gordon Carter, engrg mgr. WTTW(TV) affil. ■ Rates: $175; 140; 175; 125.

WGCI(AM)—1924: 1390 khz; 5 kw-U, DA-2. TL: N41 44 13 W87 42 00. Suite 600, 332 S. Michigan Ave. (60604). (312) 427-4800. FAX: (312) 427-7410. Licensee: Pacific and Southern Co. Inc. Group owner: Gannett Broadcasting (acq 4-63). Rep: McGavren Guild. Format: Oldies. ■ Marv Dyson, pres & gen mgr; Darryll J. Green, stn mgr; Maynard Grossman, vp sls; Bill Ryan, natl sls mgr; Rosalie Bucci, mktg dir & prom dir; Shean Ross, progmg dir; Vic Clemans, mus dir; Jeff Andrews, chief engr.

WGCI-FM—Dec 11, 1958: 107.5 mhz; 33 kw. Ant 600 ft. TL: N41 52 57 W87 38 15. Stereo. Prog sep from AM. Format: Urban contemp. ■ Elroy Smith, progmg mgr.

WGN(AM)—June 1, 1924: 720 khz; 50 kw-U. TL: N42 00 42 W88 02 07. 435 N. Michigan Ave. (60611). (312) 222-4700. FAX: (312) 222-5165. Licensee: Tribune Broadcasting Co. (group owner). Net: ABC/I. Rep: Christal. Format: Div, MOR, news/talk. News staff 16; news progmg 42 hrs wkly. Target aud: General; people with ears and a mind in between them. Spec prog: Cubs, Bears, DePaul play-by-play. ■ James C. Dowdle, pres; Wayne Vriesman, exec vp; Dan Fabian, vp & gen mgr; Denise Palmer, stn mgr; Lori Brayer, opns dir; Kenton Morris, dev dir; Robert D. Starr, sls dir; Jim Herrmann, mktg dir & prom mgr; Tisa LaSorte, progmg dir; John Tondelli, mus dir; Dave Ellsworth, news dir; Robert Manewith, pub affrs dir; James J. Carollo, chief engr. ■ WGN-TV affil.

***WHPK-FM**—Mar 15, 1968: 88.5 mhz; 100 w. Ant 121 ft. TL: N41 47 40 W87 35 55. Stereo. Hrs opn: 24. 5706 S. University Ave. (60637-1514). (312) 702-8289. Licensee: The Univ. of Chicago. Format: Div, educ, jazz. News progmg 5 hrs wkly. Spec prog: Classical 10 hrs, country one hr, reggae 8 hrs, salsa 3 hrs, African one hr, Haitian 3 hrs, Israeli one hr, Irish one hr, Calypso 3 hrs, Black one hr, folk 6 hrs wkly. ■ Kevin Esterling, stn mgr; Will Mollard, sls dir; Chris Holmes, progmg dir; Rob Shraeder, mus dir; Lee Onus, asst mus dir; Greta Nathan, news dir; James Hatt, pub affrs dir; Greg Lane, chief engr.

WIND(AM)—1927: 560 khz; 5 kw-U, DA-2. TL: N41 33 54 W87 25 11. 3rd Fl., 625 N. Michigan Ave. (60611). (312) 751-5560. FAX: (312) 664-2472. Licensee: Tichenor Radio of Chicago Inc. Group owner: Tichenor Media Systems (acq 8-14-87). Rep: Katz. Format: Sp mus. News staff 5; news progmg 8 hrs wkly. Target aud: 18-49; Mexican. ■ McHenry Tichenor, pres; Charles J. Brooks, vp & gen mgr; Juan Montenegro, gen sls mgr; Luisa Torres, vp progmg; Margarita Vasquez, mus dir; Luis De Gonzalez, news dir; Morton Campbell, pub affrs dir; Donald Jeffers, chief engr. ■ Rates: $98; 98; 98; 88.

WJJD(AM)—Oct 13, 1924: 1160 khz; 50 kw-D, 5 kw-N, DA-2. TL: N42 02 30 W87 51 57. Suite 1200, 180 N. Michigan Ave. (60601). (312) 977-1800. FAX: (312) 977-1859; (312) 855-1043. Licensee: Infinity Broadcasting Corp of Illinois. Group owner: Infinity Broadcasting Corp. (acq 7-23-84). Net: Unistar. Rep: Katz. Format: MOR, talk. News staff one. Target aud: 35-64. ■ Mel Karmazin, CEO & pres; Harvey Pearlman, vp & gen mgr; Barb Larson, gen sls mgr; Vince Perez, natl sls mgr; Doug Bensing, Marssie Mencotti, mktg dirs; Gary Price, progmg dir; Rick Patton, mus dir; John Humi, chief engr.

WJMK(FM)—Co-owned with WJJD(AM). Jan 2, 1961: 104.3 mhz; 4.1 kw. Ant 1,575 ft. TL: N41 52 44 W87 38 10. Stereo. Prog sep from AM. Rep: Katz. Format: Oldies. Target aud: 25-54. ■ Harvey Pearlman, stn mgr; Kevin Robinson, progmg dir.

WJPC(AM)—May 1922: 950 khz; 1 kw-D, 5 kw-N, DA-N. TL: N41 38 29 W87 33 14. 820 S. Michigan Ave. (60605). (312) 322-9400. FAX: (708) 895-1458. Licensee: Johnson Publishing Co. (acq 5-29-73). Net: Natl Black. Format: Rap. Target aud: 25-54. ■ Linda Johnson-Rice, pres; Charles Mootry, gen mgr; Lillian Y. Terrell, opns mgr; Gerald Scrutchions, chief engr.

***WKKC(FM)**—1975: 89.3 mhz; 250 w. Ant 112 ft. TL: N41 46 15 W87 37 48. Stereo. Kennedy-King College, 6800 S. Wentworth Ave. (60621). (312) 602-5313. FAX: (312) 602-5245. Licensee: Kennedy-King College. Format: Urban contemp, educ. Target aud: 15-50. ■ Dean Genus, gen mgr; Kevin Brown, stn mgr.

WKQX(FM)—1948: 101.1 mhz; 6 kw. Ant 1,710 ft. TL: N41 53 56 W87 37 23. 1700 Merchandise Mart Plaza (60654). (312) 527-8348. FAX: (312) 527-5682. Licensee: Emmis Broadcasting Corp. of Chicago. Group owner: Emmis Broadcasting Corp. Rep: D & R Radio. Format: Adult contemp. ■ Chuck Hillier, gen mgr; Val Maki, gen sls mgr; Chris Marsh, mktg mgr; Bill Gamble, progmg dir; Mary Shuminas, mus dir; Dave McBride, news dir; Joel Hodroff, chief engr.

WLIT-FM—Apr 7, 1958: 93.9 mhz; 4 kw. Ant 1,581 ft. TL: N41 52 44 W87 38 10. Stereo. Suite 1135, 150 N. Michigan Ave. (60601). (312) 329-9002. Licensee: Viacom Broadcasting Inc. (group owner; acq 3-1-82; $8 million; FTR 1-25-82). Rep: Christal. Format: Adult contemp. News staff one; news progmg 2 hrs wkly. Target aud: 25-54; affluent adults. ■ Philip L. Redo, vp & gen mgr; Kathleen Cahill, gen sls mgr; Julie Murphy, natl sls mgr; Terry O'Brien (local), rgnl sls mgr; Mark Edwards, progmg dir; Maryann Meyers, news dir; Blane Webster, chief engr.

WLS(AM)—Apr 12, 1924: 890 khz; 50 kw-U. TL: N41 33 21 W87 50 54. Stereo. 190 N. State St. (60601). (312) 984-0890; (312) 984-5333. FAX: (312) 984-5305. Licensee: Capital Cities/ABC Inc. Group owner: Capital Cities/ABC Broadcast Group (acq 6-86; grpsl; FTR 7-15-85). Net: ABC/D, ABC/E. Rep: Banner. Format: Talk. News staff 4; news progmg 43 hrs wkly. Target aud: 35-64; listeners involved in Chicago news & community affairs. ■ Tom Tradup, pres & gen mgr; Drew Hayes, opns dir & progmg dir; Steve Lichtenfels, gen sls mgr; Mark Stough, rgnl sls mgr; Roe Conn, prom mgr; Diana Bodkins, pub affrs dir; Warren Shulz, chief engr.

WLS-FM—Apr 1, 1949: 94.7 mhz; 4.4 kw. Ant 1,535 ft. TL: N41 53 56 W87 37 23. Stereo. Dups AM 100%. News staff one. Target aud: 18-34. ■ Carl Fromme-Hegewisch, pub affrs dir. ■ WLS-TV affil.

WLUP-FM—Listing follows WMVP(AM).

***WLUW(FM)**—Sept 19, 1978: 88.7 mhz; 100 w. Ant 230 ft. TL: N42 00 04 W87 39 36. Stereo. Hrs opn: 24. 820 N. Michigan Ave. (60611). (312) 915-6558; (312) 915-6566. FAX: (312) 915-7095. Licensee: Loyola Univ. of Chicago. Net: ABC/I; Ill. Net. Format: Dance radio, contemp. News progmg 8 hrs wkly. Target aud: 18-24; young adults, university age. Spec prog: Sp 4 hrs, community 12 hrs wkly. ■ Tony Compton, gen mgr; Jim Lemon, stn mgr; Rob Creighton, progmg dir; Joanna Manning, news dir.

WMAQ(AM)—April 1922: 670 khz; 50 kw-U. TL: N41 56 01 W88 04 23. Stereo. NBC Tower, 455 N. Cityfront Plaza (60611). (312) 670-6767. FAX: (312) 245-6143; (312) 245-6162. Licensee: Group W Radio Subsidiary Inc. Group owner: Westinghouse Broadcasting Co. (acq 3-1-88). Net: NBC, CNN, AP; Ill. News Net. Rep: Group W. Format: All news. News staff 50; news progmg 168 hrs wkly. Target aud: General. Spec prog: Sports (White Sox and Chicago Bulls Flagship). ■ Rick Starr, vp & gen mgr; Weezie Kramer, gen sls mgr; Marna Spizz, natl sls mgr; Julie Roberts, mktg mgr & prom mgr; Jim Frank, progmg mgr; Margaret Bryant, chief engr.

329-4468. Licensee: The Moody Bible Institute of Chicago (group owner). Net: Moody. Format: Relg, educ, Sp. News staff one. Target aud: General. Spec prog: Children 7 hrs wkly. ■ Dr. Joseph Stowell, pres; John Maddex, gen mgr & progmg dir; Jim Marshall, mus dir; Monte Larrick, news dir & pub affrs dir; Robert Caithamer, chief engr.

***WMBI-FM**—July 25, 1960: 90.1 mhz; 100 kw. Ant 440 ft. TL: N41 55 35 W88 00 22. Stereo. Dups AM 100%.

WMVP(AM)—June 25, 1926: 1000 khz; 50 kw-U, DA-2. TL: N41 49 04 W87 59 17. 875 N. Michigan Ave. (60611). (312) 447-5270. FAX: (312) 440-9896. Licensee: Evergreen Media Corp. (group owner; acq 4-87). Rep: Major Mkt. Wash atty: Latham & Watkins. Format: Sports. News staff 2; news progmg 70 hrs wkly. Target aud: 25-54. ■ Scott Ginsberg, pres; Lawrence J. Wert, gen mgr; Cheryl Esken, gen sls mgr; Cindy Gatziolis, vp mktg; Greg Solk, progmg dir; Eneyda Rodriguez, pub affrs dir; Tom Knauss, chief engr.

WLUP-FM—Co-owned with WMVP(AM). 1942: 97.9 mhz; 6 kw. Ant 1,710 ft. TL: N41 53 56 W87 37 23. Stereo. Hrs opn: 24. FAX: (312) 440-9377. Format: Personality oriented rock. News staff 2. Target aud: 18-49. ■ Lawrence J. Wert, vp; Dave Logan, progmg dir.

WNIB(FM)—July 9, 1955: 97.1 mhz; 8.4 kw. Ant 1,196 ft. TL: N41 53 08 W87 37 15. Stereo. Hrs opn: 24. 1140 W. Erie (60622). (312) 633-9700. FAX: (312) 633-9710. Licensee: Northern Illinois Broadcasting Co. Format: Class. ■ William C. Florian, pres; Sonia Florian, vp & gen mgr; Steve Adler, natl sls mgr; Ron Ray, progmg dir.

WNUA(FM)—March 9, 1959: 95.5 mhz; 8.3 kw. Ant 1,174 ft. TL: N41 53 56 W87 37 23. Stereo. 444 N. Michigan Ave. (60611). (312) 645-9550. FAX: (312) 645-9645. Licensee: Pyramid West L.P. Group owner: Pyramid Broadcasting (acq 6-87). Rep: D & R Radio. Format: Adult contemp, jazz. News staff 2. Target aud: 25-54. ■ John Gehron, gen mgr; Ralph Sherman, gen sls mgr; Tracey Thomas-Knox, mktg mgr; Lee Hansen, progmg dir; Michael Fischer, mus dir; Charlie Myerson, news dir; Bill Maylone, chief engr.

WOJO(FM)—See Evanston.

WOPA(AM)—December 1988: 1200 khz; 10 kw-D, 1 kw-N, DA-2. TL: N41 42 14 W87 35 47. Stereo. Hrs opn: 24. 509 W. Roosevelt Rd. (60607). (312) 738-1200. FAX: (312) 738-5618. Licensee: CID Broadcasting Inc. Rep: Caballero, McGavren Guild. Wash atty: Fisher, Wayland, Cooper & Leader. Format: Sp. News staff 4; news progmg 10 hrs wkly. Target aud: Urban Spanish. ■ Arthur R. Velasquez, chmn, pres & gen mgr; Joanne Velasquez, Edward J. Fanning, vps; Edward J. Fanning, vp opns, vp sls, vp mktg & vp prom; Mark B. Kritz, natl sls mgr; Angie Staujrianos, prom dir; Mary Moreira, progmg dir; Ezequiel Banda, news dir; John McGuinnes, chief engr. ■ Rates: $80; 65; 80; 50.

***WOUI(FM)**—June 1974: 88.9 mhz; 10 w. Ant 90 ft. TL: N41 50 04 W87 37 43. Stereo. Hrs opn: 12. 3300 S. Federal St. (60616). (312) 567-3087; (312) 567-3080. FAX: (312) 567-3224. Licensee: Ill. Institute of Technology. Format: Black, div, progsv. Target aud: 15-35; college & young urban community. Spec prog: Folk 3 hrs, jazz 9 hrs wkly. ■ Hugo Prill, gen mgr; Larry Todd, chief engr.

WPNT-FM—1947: 100.3 mhz; 8.3 kw. Ant 1,174 ft. TL: N41 53 56 W87 37 23. Stereo. #3201, Suite 1510, 875 N. Michigan Ave. (60611). (312) 440-3100. FAX: (312) 440-0587. Licensee: Century Chicago Broadcasting Ltd. Group owner: Century Broadcasting. Rep: Eastman. Format: Adult contemp. ■ George Collias, pres; Bill Bungerotn, gen mgr; Sheila Mulcahey, gen sls mgr; Denise Hart, adv dir; Michael Spearas, progmg dir; Eric Stallone, news dir; Dave Dybas, chief engr.

WSBC(AM)—1925: 1240 khz; 1 kw-U (ST WCRW & WEDC). TL: N41 56 18 W87 45 05. 4949 W. Belmont Ave. (60641). (312) 282-9722. Licensee: Diamond Broadcasting Inc. (group owner). Format: Ethnic. Spec prog: Pol 11 hrs, Hindi-Pak 6 hrs, Ukrainian one hr, Irish one hr, Sp 18 hrs, Russian one hr, gospel 2 hrs wkly. ■ Daniel R. Lee, pres; Roy J. Bellavia, gen mgr, gen sls mgr & progmg dir; Mark Nielson, chief engr.

WXRT(FM)—Co-owned with WSBC(AM). 1959: 93.1 mhz; 6.7 kw. Ant 1,310 ft. TL: N41 53 56 W87 37 23. Stereo. Prog sep from AM. (312) 777-1700. Net: CBS. Format: Adult rock. ■ Seth Mason, exec vp; Harvey Wells, gen mgr; Michael Damsky, gen sls mgr & natl sls mgr; Terri Gidwitz, mktg dir; Eugene Cacub, prom mgr; Norman Winer, progmg dir; Neil Parker, news dir.

WSCR(AM)—1941: 820 khz; 5 kw-D. TL: N41 56 18 W87 45 05. Stereo. 4949 Belmont Ave. (60641). (312) 777-1700. Licensee: Diamond Broadcasting Inc. (acq 1-2-92). Rep: CBS Radio. Format: Sports, talk. Target aud: 25-54; males. ■ Daniel Lee, pres; Seth Mason, exec vp; Harvey Wells, gen mgr; Michael Damsky, gen sls mgr; Teri Girwitz, mktg dir; Dave Karwowski, prom dir; Ron Gleason, progmg dir; Mark Nielsen, chief engr.

***WSSD(FM)**—Sept 15, 1987: 88.1 mhz; 10 w. Ant 100 ft. TL: N41 52 22 W87 38 52. Stereo. 11026 S. Wentworth (60628). (312) 928-8800. FAX: (312) 928-9292. Licensee: Lakeside Communications Inc. Format: Community svc. ■ Bill Tyson, gen mgr; Vernon Winstead, stn mgr.

WUSN(FM)—1940: 99.5 mhz; 8.3 kw. Ant 1,174 ft. TL: N41 53 56 W87 37 23. Stereo. 875 N. Michigan Ave. (60611). (312) 649-0099. Licensee: Infinity Broadcasting Corp. (group owner; acq 12-18-92; grpsl; FTR 1-25-93). Net: Unistar. Rep: Torbet. Format: Country. Target aud: 25-64. ■ Stephen D. Ennen, gen mgr; Steven Gobel, gen sls mgr; J.D. Spangler, progmg dir; Tricia Biondo, mus dir; Lee Ann Protter, news dir; Bob Larson, chief engr.

WWBZ(FM)—November 1957: 103.5 mhz; 4.3 kw. Ant 1,548 ft. TL: N41 52 44 W87 38 10. Stereo. Suite 3750, 875 N. Michigan (60611). (312) 861-8100. FAX: (312) 440-9143. Licensee: WWBZ License Corp. (acq 11-12-93; $28 million; FTR 11-29-93). Net: Unistar. Rep: Republic. Format: AOR. ■ Larry Wert, gen mgr; Ed Coile, gen sls mgr; John Edwards, progmg dir; Kevin Lewis, mus dir.

WXRT(FM)—Listing follows WSBC(AM).

***WZRD(FM)**—July 8, 1974: 88.3 mhz; 100 w. Ant 76 ft. TL: N41 58 56 W87 43 07. 5500 N. St. Louis Ave. (60625). (312) 583-4050. Licensee: Northeastern Illinois Univ. Format: Div, educ. News progmg 12 hrs wkly. Target aud: General. ■ Var Strid, stn mgr; Glenn Herman, chief engr.

Chicago Heights

WCFJ(AM)—Aug 15, 1963: 1470 khz; 1 kw-U, DA-2. TL: N41 25 29 W87 38 27. Hrs opn: 24. 1000 Lincoln Highway, Ford Heights (60411). (708) 758-8600. FAX: (708) 758-8602. Licensee: Liberty Temple Full Gospel Church Inc. Format: Christian adult contemp. Target aud: General; 18-44. ■ Darryl Chavrs, gen mgr. ■ Rates: $20; 20; 20; 20.

WCGO(AM)—Aug 29, 1959: 1600 khz; 1 kw-D, 23 w-N, DA-2. TL: N41 31 05 W87 35 11. 3313 Chicago Rd. (60411). (708) 756-6100. FAX: (708) 756-6698. Licensee: South Cook Broadcasting Inc. Net: CNN. Format: Adult contemp, Sp. News staff 2. Target aud: General. ■ Anthony V. Santucci, pres & gen mgr; William G. Biendorff, gen sls mgr; Tony D. Santucci, progmg dir & mus dir; Ted Field, news dir; Pete Van Milligan, chief engr. ■ Rates: $27; 27; 27; 15.

WEMG-FM—See Crete.

Chillicothe

WQEZ(FM)—May 16, 1977: 94.3 mhz; 3 kw. Ant 300 ft. TL: N40 49 48 W89 29 54 (CP: 1.3 kw). Stereo. Suite 2, 4541 N. Prospect Rd., Peoria Heights (61614). (309) 688-8022. FAX: (309) 688-9346. Licensee: Peoria Satellite Radio Corp. Net: SMN. Rep: Katz & Powell. Format: Z Rock. Target aud: General; affluent adults. ■ William Bro, pres; Jerry Scott, gen mgr; Candy Scott, gen sls mgr; Denise Kline, natl sls mgr; Dale Bargmann, chief engr.

Christopher

WUEZ(FM)—Dec 25, 1990: 103.5 mhz; 6 kw. Ant 328 ft. TL: N37 55 55 W88 57 28. Second Flr., 200 N. Park Ave., Herrin (62948). (618) 942-7722. FAX: (618) 942-7550. Licensee: Brandt Broadcasting Inc. Format: Easy lstng. ■ Clyde Crawford, pres & gen mgr; Forrest Richardson, chief engr.

Cicero

WCEV(AM)—Oct 1, 1979: 1450 khz; 1 kw-U (ST WVON). TL: N41 49 57 W87 42 40. Hrs opn: one PM-10 PM M-F, one PM-8:30 PM Sat, 5 AM-10 PM Sun. 5356 W. Belmont Ave., Chicago (60641-4103). (312) 282-6700; (312) 777-1450, STUDIO. FAX: (312) 282-5930. Licensee: Migala Communications Corp. Format: Ethnic. News progmg 7 hrs wkly. Target aud: Adult ethnic Americans. Spec prog: Pol 23 hrs, Polka 5 hrs, gospel 7 hrs, Lithuanian 10 hrs, Croatian 3 hrs, Ukranian 4 hrs, Irish 2 hrs, Czechoslovak 2 hrs, Greek 5 hrs, Slovenian one hr, Macedonian one hr, Haitian one hr wkly. ■ Joseph Migala, pres & gen mgr; George Migala, stn mgr; Herman Rowe, gen sls mgr & prom mgr; Lucyna Migala, progmg dir & news dir; Frank McCoy, chief engr. ■ Rates: $55; 55; 55; 55.

WLUP-FM—See Chicago.

WVON(AM)—1979: 1450 khz; 1 kw-U (ST WCEV). TL: N41 49 57 W87 42 20. 3350 S. Kedzie Ave., Chicago (60623). (312) 247-6200. Licensee: Midway Broadcasting Corp. Format: Black, urban contemp. ■ Wesley W. South, pres & gen mgr; Eddie Thomas, gen sls mgr; Pervis Spann, prom mgr; Melody Spann, progmg dir; Tom Berry, chief engr.

Clinton

WHOW(AM)—Aug 1, 1947: 1520 khz; 5 kw-D, 1 kw-CH. TL: N40 05 43 W88 57 51. Hrs opn: Sunrise-sunset. R.R. 2, Box 117-M (61727). (217) 935-2161. FAX: (217) 935-9600. Licensee: Cornbelt Broadcasting Co. Group owner: J.R. Livesay Group (acq 9-50). Net: UPI. Format: C&W. Spec prog: Farm 10 hrs, relg 15 hrs wkly. ■ J.R. Livesay, pres & chief engr; J.R. Livesay Jr., vp; Betty Gross, gen mgr; Charlie Johnson, mus dir; Bill Ward, news dir. ■ Rates: $16.40; 11; 11; 11.

WHOW-FM—Dec 15, 1975: 95.9 mhz; 3 kw. Ant 300 ft. TL: N40 05 43 W88 57 51. Stereo. Hrs opn: 6 AM-midnight. Prog sep from AM. Format: Easy lstng. Spec prog: Farm 6 hrs wkly. ■ Rates: Same as AM.

Coal City

WKBM(FM)—Feb 8, 1991: 100.7 mhz; 1.4 kw. Ant 482 ft. TL: N41 17 39 W88 10 15. Stereo. Hrs opn: 24. 32401 S. Rt. 53, Wilmington (60481). (815) 476-5855. FAX: (815) 476-1007. Licensee: Barden Broadcasting of Coal City. Net: SMN. Wash atty: Cohn & Marks. Format: Oldies. News staff 2; news progmg 8 hrs wkly. Target aud: 25-54; affluent young adults. Spec prog: Gospel/relg 8 hrs wkly. ■ Don Barden, pres; Ken Kramer, CFO & vp; Ralph Sherman, gen mgr & gen sls mgr; Jon Knepper, opns mgr; Vicki Fundator Crawford, news dir; Art Reis, chief engr. ■ Rates: $12; 10; 10; 8.

Columbia

WCBW(FM)—Feb 15, 1964: 104.9 mhz; 11.5 kw. Ant 480 ft. TL: N38 34 24 W90 19 30. Stereo. Hrs opn: 24. Suite 201, 4121 Union, St. Louis, MO (63129). (314) 487-1006. FAX: (314) 487-4148. Licensee: WCBW Inc. Group owner: Universal Broadcasting Corp. (acq 1-80). Format: Adult contemp Christian. Target aud: 25-49; women and their families. ■ Howard Warshaw, pres; Gregory Lhamon, gen mgr & gen sls mgr; Greg Cassidy, progmg dir & mus dir; Margaret Cox, pub affrs dir; Dave Obergoenner, chief engr. ■ Rates: $45; 27; 40; 25.

Crest Hill

WCCQ(FM)—Licensed to Crest Hill. See Joliet.

Crete

WEMG-FM—Sept 5, 1965: 102.3 mhz; 3 kw. Ant 299 ft h, 295 ft v. TL: N41 18 53 W87 37 11. Stereo. 12844 S. Halsted St. Chicago (60628). (708) 946-2226. Licensee: Word of Faith Fellowship Inc. (acq 9-30-93; $800,000; FTR 10-18-93). Net: CNN, Sun. Format: Gospel. News staff one; news progmg 3 hrs wkly. Target aud: General. ■ Rickey Singleton, pres & gen mgr. ■ Rates: $27; 27; 27; 18.

Crystal Lake

WAIT(AM)—Oct 1, 1965: 850 khz; 2.5 kw-D, DA. TL: N42 15 30 W88 21 48. 8600 Rt. 14 (60012). (815) 459-7000. FAX: (815) 459-7027. Licensee: Pride Communications Ltd. (acq 5-31-91; $2.2 million with co-located FM; FTR 6-24-91). Format: MOR. News staff one; news progmg 2 hrs wkly. Target aud: 35 plus; mature adults. Spec prog: Ger one hr, Serbian one hr, polka 4 hrs wkly. ■ Jim Hooker, gen mgr; Paul Klocek, gen sls mgr.

WZSR(FM)—See Woodstock.

Danville

WDAN(AM)—October 1938: 1490 khz; 1 kw-U. TL: N40 08 58 W87 37 35. 1501 N. Washington (61832). (217) 442-1700. FAX: (217) 431-1489. Licensee: Neuhoff Broadcasting Corp. (group owner; acq 8-15-90; with co-located FM; FTR 4-30-90). Net: CBS Spectrum, NBC Talknet; Ill. News Net. Rep: McGavren Guild. Format: News/talk, sports, MOR. News staff one; news progmg 12 hrs wkly. Target aud: 25-54. Spec prog: Farm 5 hrs wkly. ■ Geoff Neuhoff, pres; Mike Hulvey, gen mgr; Scott Eisenhauer, Tom Barnes, prom mgrs; Scott Eisenhauer, Tom Barnes, progmg dirs; Bill Pickett, news dir; Don Russel, chief engr. ■ Rates: $25; 20; 20; 16.

WDNL(FM)—Co-owned with WDAN(AM). May 1967: 102.1 mhz; 50 kw. Ant 380 ft. TL: N40 08 58 W87 37 35. Stereo. Hrs opn: 24. Prog sep from AM. Net: Unistar,

Westwood One. Format: Adult contemp. News progmg 2 hrs wkly. Target aud: 18-49. ■ Scott Eisenhauer, sls dir; Tom Barnes, mus dir. ■ Rates: $30; 27; 27; 20.

WIAI(FM)—March 2, 1970: 99.1 mhz; 50 kw. Ant 500 ft. TL: N40 08 52 W87 46 20. 4 N. Vermilion St. (61832). (217) 443-5500. FAX: (217) 443-6308. Licensee: I.A.I. Broadcasting Inc. (acq 3-26-93; $1.3 million; FTR 4-12-93). Net: NBC. Rep: D & R Radio. Format: Contemp country. News staff 2; news progmg 2 hrs wkly. Target aud: 25 plus. Spec prog: Farm report 10 hrs wkly. ■ Terry Forcht, pres; R. Brent Marlin, gen mgr, gen sls mgr, natl sls mgr & adv mgr; Randy Jones, progmg dir & mus dir; Linda Bolton, news dir; Alan Woodrum, chief engr. ■ Rates: $37; 29; 37; 21.

WITY(AM)—Nov 24, 1953: 980 khz; 1 kw-U, DA-2. TL: N40 04 42 W87 38 19. Box 142, Hegeler Lane (61832). (217) 446-1312. Licensee: Vermilion Broadcasting Corporation (acq 1981). Net: ABC/I. Wash atty: Donald E. Ward. Format: Talk, MOR. Target aud: 35 plus; general. Spec prog: Jazz 2 hrs wkly. ■ Allan M. Thomann, gen mgr; Dennis Hughes, opns mgr; Brad Schofield, sls dir & pub affrs dir; Walt Jenkins, mus dir; David Dixson, news dir; Stu Toft, chief engr.

WLLR-FM—See East Moline.

WWDZ(FM)—November 1992: 94.9 mhz; 6 kw. Ant 328 ft. TL: N40 10 40 W87 28 55. Hrs opn: 24. 3100 N. Vermilion (61832). (217) 443-2700. FAX: (217) 443-3298. Licensee: Rollings Communications of Danville Inc. Group owner: Rollings Communications Co. (acq 4-12-91; FTR 5-6-91). Net: NBC the Source. Rep: Banner. Format: AOR. News progmg 5 hrs wkly. Target aud: 18-49. ■ Mark Rollings, pres; Doug Quick, gen mgr.

De Kalb

WDEK(FM)—Listing follows WLBK(AM).

WDKB(FM)—Aug 13, 1990: 94.9 mhz; 3 kw. Ant 328 ft. TL: N41 56 58 W88 53 33. 2201 N. 1st St. (60115). (815) 758-0950; (815) 758-4926. FAX: (815) 758-6226. Licensee: De Kalb County Radio Ltd. Net: ABC. Wash atty: Besozzi & Gavin. Format: Adult contemp. News staff one; news progmg 15 hrs wkly. Target aud: 25-54; adults with moderate to upper incomes. Spec prog: Relg one hr wkly. ■ Tana S. Knetsch, pres; Jim Day, gen mgr, gen sls mgr & prom mgr; Tom Gaines, progmg dir & mus dir; Julie Mann, news dir; Michael McCarthy, chief engr.

WLBK(AM)—Dec 7, 1947: 1360 khz; 1 kw-D. TL: N41 56 18 W88 45 03. Hrs opn: 5:30 AM-8 PM. 711 N. 1st St. (60115). (815) 758-8686. Licensee: De Kalb Radio Studios Inc. (acq 8-30-65). Net: AP. Wash atty: Koteen & Naftalin. Format: Full svc. News staff 3; news progmg 21 hrs wkly. Target aud: General. Spec prog: Farm 12 hrs wkly. ■ Jerome F. Cerny, pres; Dianne Leifheit, gen mgr; Ken Huske, gen sls mgr; Mark Charvat, progmg dir; Dick Kliesch, news dir; Bob Senne, chief engr.

WDEK(FM)—Co-owned with WLBK(AM). Dec 17, 1961: 92.5 mhz; 20 kw. Ant 495 ft. TL: N41 52 33 W88 45 16. Stereo. Hrs opn: 24. Prog sep from AM. Format: CHR. News progmg 5 hrs wkly. Target aud: 18-35. ■ Dave Bavido, progmg dir; Keith Bansemer, mus dir.

*WNIJ(FM)—See Rockford.

*WNIU(FM)—October 1954: 89.5 mhz; 50 kw. Ant 421 ft. TL: N42 00 55 W89 00 07. Stereo. Hrs opn: 5 AM-midnight. NIU Broadcast Center, 801 N. First St. (60115); Riverfront Museum Park, 711 N. Main St., Rockford (61103). (815) 753-9000; (815) 961-8000. FAX: (815) 753-9938; (815) 963-5374. Licensee: Northern Illinois Univ. Net: APR, NPR. Wash atty: Arter & Hadden. Format: Class. News staff 3; news progmg one hr wkly. Target aud: General. Spec prog: Folk 4 hrs wkly. ■ Michael Lazar, gen mgr; Bill Drake, opns dir; Elaine Harrington, dev dir; Eric Hradecky, mus dir; Lester Graham, Todd Mundt (asst), news dirs; Robin Cross, chief engr.

Decatur

WDZ(AM)—March 17, 1921: 1050 khz; 1 kw-U. TL: N39 48 54 W89 00 05. 337 N. Water St. (62523). (217) 423-9744. FAX: (217) 423-9764. Licensee: Prairieland Broadcasters. Group owner: Prairieland Stations (acq 1-1-64). Net: ABC/C. Format: Adult contemp, talk/sports. ■ Bernie Brobst, gen mgr; Andra Lee, progmg dir; Bob Wille, chief engr.

WDZQ(FM)—Co-owned with WDZ(AM). Nov 1, 1976: 95.1 mhz; 50 kw. Ant 500 ft. TL: N39 37 36 W89 04 49. Stereo. Prog sep from AM. Rep: Eastman. Format: Modern country. Spec prog: Farm 8 hrs wkly. ■ Brian Shimmel, gen sls mgr; John Mellon, progmg dir.

*WJMU(FM)—Mar 10, 1971: 89.5 mhz; 1 kw. Ant 95 ft. TL: N39 50 30 W88 58 29 (CP: 1.66 kw). Stereo. Hrs opn: 7 AM-1 AM. 1184 W. Main St. (62522). (217) 424-6377; (217) 424-6369. FAX: (217) 424-3993. Licensee: Millikin Univ. Net: USA. Format: Div. Target aud: 20 plus; students, surrounding community. Spec prog: Classical 2 hrs, blues 3 hrs, jazz 3 hrs wkly. ■ Dr. Curtis McCray, pres; Jimm Seaney, gen mgr.

WSOY-FM—November 1946: 102.9 mhz; 54 kw. Ant 495 ft. TL: N39 52 40 W88 56 30. Stereo. Hrs opn: 24. Box 2350 (62524); 1100 E. Pershing Rd. (62526). (217) 877-5371. FAX: (217) 877-8777. Licensee: Ballston Trust Services L.C. Group owner: Pinnacle Broadcasting Co. (acq 12-22-92; grpsl; FTR 1-18-93). Net: CBS; Ill. Net. Rep: Eastman. Format: Adult contemp. News staff 4; news progmg 45 hrs wkly. Target aud: 18-34. ■ Orv Graham, gen mgr; Terry McCarthy, gen sls mgr; Sean Streaty, news dir; Frank Konwinski, chief engr.

WSOY(AM)—1925: 1340 khz; 1 kw-U. TL: N39 52 40 W88 56 30. Hrs opn: 24. Prog sep from FM. Format: Full svc. Target aud: 25 plus. Spec prog: Farm 17 hrs wkly. ■ Lynn McClure, progmg dir.

WYDS(FM)—Not on air, target date unknown: 93.1 mhz; 6 kw. Ant 328 ft. TL: N39 48 35 W88 59 31. c/o Howard G. Bill, Suite 507, 625 19th St. N.W., Rochester, MN (55901). Licensee: WEJT Inc. (acq 4-9-93; $750,000; FTR 5-3-93).

Deerfield

WEEF(AM)—See Highland Park.

WVVX(FM)—See Highland Park.

Des Plaines

WYLL(FM)—Dec 3, 1971: 106.7 mhz; 50 kw. Ant 299 ft. TL: N42 08 10 W87 58 55. Stereo. Hrs opn: 24. Suite 400, 25 Northwest Point, Elk Grove Village (60007). (708) 956-5030. FAX: (708) 956-5040. Licensee: Greater Chicago Radio Inc. Group owner: Salem Communications Corp. (acq 2-90; $9,250,000; FTR 2-26-90). Format: Christian talk. News progmg 2 hrs wkly. Target aud: 25-54; upscale adults. ■ Philip Bandy, gen mgr; Ron Turner, opns mgr; Roy Wikoff, gen sls mgr; Suzanne Murdoch, news dir; Carl Gluck, chief engr.

Dixon

WIXN(AM)—July 1961: 1460 khz; 1 kw-D, DA. TL: N41 49 38 W89 29 11. Hrs opn: 24. 1460 S. College Ave. (61021). (815) 288-3341. FAX: (815) 284-1017. Licensee: Farm Belt Radio Inc. Group owner: Goetz Broadcasting Corp. Net: ABC/I. Wash atty: Miller & Fields. Format: Adult contemp, news. News staff 2; news progmg 14 hrs wkly. Target aud: 25-54. Spec prog: Farm 11 hrs wkly. ■ Nathan L. Goetz, pres; Jack Hackman, sr vp; Allan L. Knickrehm, stn mgr & gen sls mgr; Scott M. Trentadue, vp adv; Steve Marco, progmg dir; Mark Baker, mus dir & chief engr; Danette Dallgas-Frey, news dir.

WIXN-FM—Sept 1, 1965: 101.7 mhz; 6 kw. Ant 300 ft. TL: N41 49 29 W89 29 51. Stereo. Hrs opn: 24. Prog sep from AM. Net: ABC/E; Goetz Farm Net., Free Enterprise Radio Net. Format: Country. News staff 2; news progmg 10 hrs wkly. Target aud: 25-54. ■ Al Knickrehm, gen mgr.

Downers Grove

*WDGC-FM—Feb 28, 1969: 88.3 mhz; 250 w. Ant 130 ft. TL: N41 48 16 W88 00 44. 4436 Main St. (60515). (708) 852-0404, ext. 319. Licensee: High School District No. 99, Dupage County. Format: Div. Spec prog: Community affairs 6 hrs wkly. ■ Laura Fraisier, gen mgr; Stacey Urvan, stn mgr.

Dundee

WABT(FM)—June 8, 1967: 103.9 mhz; 3 kw. Ant 299 ft. TL: N42 06 20 W88 22 46 (CP: 2.55 kw, ant 321 ft., TL: N46 06 21 W88 27 37). Stereo. Hrs opn: 24. Box 249 (60118); Suite 213, 211 W. Main, Carpentersville (60110). (708) 551-3450. FAX: (708) 551-9065. Licensee: Atlantic Morris Broadcasting Inc. (group owner). Wash atty: Hogan & Hartson. Format: Adult rock n' roll. Target aud: 18-49. ■ Don Schwartz, vp; Sue Schmitz, gen mgr; Tony Brinati, gen sls mgr; Cara Stern, progmg dir. ■ Rates: $47; 47; 47; 17.

DuQuoin

WDQN(AM)—1951: 1580 khz; 250 w-D. TL: N38 02 19 W89 14 32. Box 190 (62832). (618) 542-3894. FAX: (618) 542-4514. Licensee: Marianne Showalter (acq 4-21-71). Net: ABC/E. Rep: Devney. Format: Adult contemp. ■ Greg G. Showalter, gen mgr & gen sls mgr; Gordon Showalter, progmg dir; Jeff Proffitt, news dir; Jim Schobert, chief engr.

WDQN-FM—Sept 1, 1969: 95.9 mhz; 3 kw. Ant 320 ft. TL: N38 02 19 W89 14 32. Dups AM 90%. Format: MOR, div.

East Moline

*WDLM(AM)—April 3, 1960: 960 khz; 1 kw-D, 102 w-N, DA-2. TL: N41 24 57 W90 23 54. Box 149 (61244). (309) 234-5111. FAX: (309) 234-5114. Licensee: Moody Bible Institute of Chicago. (group owner). Format: Relg. ■ Lane D. Morgan, gen mgr; Glenn Rogerson, chief engr.

*WDLM-FM—Jan 20, 1980: 89.3 mhz; 100 kw. Ant 500 ft. TL: N41 32 52 W90 28 30. Dups AM 75%.

WLLR-FM—Feb 23, 1976: 101.3 mhz; 50 kw. Ant 500 ft. TL: N41 37 10 W90 17 41. Stereo. Corp. E, Suite 12, 1910 E. Kimberly Rd., Davenport, IA (52807). (319) 355-5331; (319) 359-9557. FAX: (319) 359-8524. Licensee: Mississippi Valley Broadcasting Inc. Group owner: Sconnix Broadcasting Co. (acq 1-1-83). Rep: Katz. Format: Modern country. News staff one; news progmg 6 hrs wkly. Target aud: 25-54; contemp, upscale adults. Spec prog: Pub affrs 6 hrs, farm one hr wkly. ■ Larry R. Rosmilso, vp & gen mgr; Scott Bitting, gen sls mgr; Jim O'Hara, prom mgr & progmg dir; Ron Evans, mus dir; Nick Linberg, news dir; Jeff Cantrill, chief engr. ■ Rates: $75; 55; 65; 25.

East St. Louis

WESL(AM)—Aug 1, 1934: 1490 khz; 1 kw-U, DA-2. TL: N38 37 16 W90 09 36. Stereo. 149 S. 8th St. (62201). (618) 271-1490. FAX: (618) 875-0600. Licensee: Willis Family Broadcasting Inc. (group owner; acq 3-4-92; $1 million grpsl; FTR 3-28-92). Net: American Urban. Rep: Katz & Powell. Format: Gospel. News progmg 7 hrs wkly. Target aud: 23-55. ■ L. E. Willis, pres & gen mgr; Frank Davis, stn mgr & gen sls mgr; Rev. Larry Brown, progmg dir & mus dir; Deborah Powell, news dir; Bettye Robinson, pub affrs dir; J.C. Hall, chief engr.

WFXB(FM)—June 6, 1965: 101.1 mhz; 44 kw. Ant 525 ft. TL: N38 45 11 W90 07 09. Stereo. 1215 Cole St. St. Louis, MO (63106). (314) 436-3030. FAX: (314) 259-5789. Licensee: River City Broadcasting Corp. (acq 10-86). Rep: Torbet. Wash atty: Haley, Bader & Potts. Format: Adult rock. News progmg 3 hrs wkly. Target aud: 25-49. Spec prog: Jazz 6 hrs wkly. ■ Richard Stein, Edward J. Murray, gen mgrs; Pat Crocker, gen sls mgr; Ken Anthony, progmg dir; Scott Clifton, chief engr.

Edwardsville

WRYT(AM)—Nov 20, 1987: 1080 khz; 500 w-D, DA. TL: N38 47 58 W89 57 45 (CP: 250 w-N, DA-2, TL: N38 38 30 W89 57 45). 9 Cougar Rd. (62025). (618) 692-9798. FAX: (618) 692-9801. Licensee: Horizon Broadcasting Corp. (acq 10-29-92; $200,000; FTR 11-23-92). Net: SMN; Ill. News Net. Format: Big band. News staff one; news progmg 9 hrs wkly. Target aud: 35 plus. ■ Robert E. Howe, pres; Tom Lauher, gen mgr & pub affrs dir; Kim Paris, news dir. ■ Rates: $17; 14; 17; na.

*WSIE(FM)—Sept 4, 1970: 88.7 mhz; 50 kw. Ant 500 ft. TL: N38 47 06 W89 59 10. Stereo. Hrs opn: 24. Box 1773, Communications Bldg., S.I.U.E. (62026). (618) 692-2228. FAX: (618) 692-2233. Licensee: Board of Trustees, Southern Illinois Univ. Net: NPR, APR; Ill. Pub. Wash atty: Dow, Lohnes & Albertson. Format: Jazz. News staff one; news progmg 20 hrs wkly. Target aud: 25-49; adults seeking a sophisticated alternative. Spec prog: New age 16 hrs, blues one hr wkly. ■ Roy Gerritsen, gen mgr & progmg dir; Scott Heinemeier, mus dir; Jim Bafaro, news dir; David Caires, chief engr.

Effingham

WBFG(FM)—Oct 4, 1982: 97.7 mhz; 3 kw. Ant 300 ft. TL: N39 07 20 W88 38 31. Stereo. Box 278 (62401). (217) 347-5518. Licensee: Premier Broadcasting Inc. (acq 11-3-93; $380,000; FTR 11-22-93). Net: ABC/D. Format: Relg. Spec prog: Farm 15 hrs wkly. ■ Olen Evans, pres, gen mgr & progmg dir; Debi Evans, prom mgr & mus dir; Steve Hamm, chief engr.

WCRA(AM)—June 8, 1947: 1090 khz; 1 kw-D. TL: N39 06 26 W88 33 44. Box 568, 208 W. Jefferson (62401). (217) 342-4141. Licensee: Effingham Broadcasting Co. Group owner: McNaughton Stns. ■ Joseph McNaughton, pres; E.W. Howard, vp, gen mgr & gen sls mgr; Glen Roley, progmg dir; Mark Turner, news dir. ■ Rates: $20.50; 18.50; 18.50; 18.50.

WCRC(FM)—Co-owned with WCRA(AM). June 14, 1963: 95.7 mhz; 50 kw. Ant 480 ft. TL: N39 06 26 W88 33 44. Stereo. Hrs opn: 24. Dups AM 10%. Format: C&W.

Eldorado

WEBQ-FM—April 1972: 102.3 mhz; 3 kw. Ant 296 ft. TL: N37 49 14 W88 27 11. Stereo. 701 S. Commercial, Harrisburg (62946). (618) 252-6307. FAX: (618) 252-2366. Licensee: Turner Communications Inc. (acq 6-90; grpsl; FTR 7-9-90). Net: Sun. Format: Adult contemp. ■ David Bard, gen mgr; Cathy Horton, progmg dir & mus dir; Bob Romonosky, chief engr.

Elgin

***WEPS(FM)**—1950: 88.9 mhz; 740 w. Ant 100 ft. TL: N42 02 17 W88 16 15. Hrs opn: 6. 355 E. Chicago St. (60120). (708) 888-5048. Licensee: Board of Education, Union School District 46. Format: Div. Target aud: Parents of students in school district. Spec prog: Class 3 hrs, jazz 6 hrs, community affrs 3 hrs, educ 13 hrs wkly. ■ Eleanor P. MacKinney, stn mgr; Carolyn Brandes, progmg dir; Don E. Tuttle, chief engr.

WJKL(FM)—Listing follows WRMN(AM).

WRMN(AM)—1949: 1410 khz; 1 kw-D, 500 w-N, DA-N. TL: N42 00 21 W88 17 55. 14 Douglas Ave. (60120). (708) 741-7700. Licensee: Elgin Broadcasting Co. Group owner: McNaughton Stations (acq 1952). Net: MBS, NBC Talknet. Wash atty: Blair, Joyce & Silva. Format: News/talk. News staff 3; news progmg 45 hrs wkly. Target aud: General. Spec prog: Sp 10 hrs wkly. ■ Richard Jakle, CEO, pres & gen mgr; Brad Bohlen, opns mgr & progmg dir; Evan Gordon, gen sls mgr; Ken Kosek, news dir; Harold Cattron, chief engr.

WJKL(FM)—Co-owned with WRMN(AM). September 1960: 94.3 mhz; 6 kw. Ant 350 ft. TL: N42 02 43 W88 15 35. Stereo. Hrs opn: 24. Prog sep from AM. Net: MBS. Format: Adult contemp. Target aud: 25-49.

Elmhurst

WKDC(AM)—Oct 10, 1974: 1530 khz; 500 w-D, DA. TL: N41 52 03 W87 55 07. Stereo. Box 1530, 130 N. York (60126). (708) 530-1530. Licensee: DuPage Broadcasting Inc. Format: Big band, jazz, MOR. Target aud: 45 plus; affluent adults. Spec prog: It 6 hrs, Greek one hr, relg one hr wkly. ■ Frank Blotter, pres; Kevin Horan, stn mgr, progmg dir & mus dir; Rob Quarles, pub affrs dir; Frank McCoy, chief engr. ■ Rates: $45; 45; 45; na.

***WRSE-FM**—Dec 7, 1962: 88.7 mhz; 100 w. Ant 95 ft. TL: N41 53 46 W87 56 45. Stereo. Hrs opn: 1 PM-1 AM. 190 Prospect Ave. (60126). (708) 617-3220; (708) 279-4100. FAX: (708) 617-3393. Licensee: Board of Trustees, Elmhurst College. Format: Progsv, rock. Target aud: General. Spec prog: Jazz one hr, Black one hr, class one hr wkly. ■ Brian O'Keefe, gen mgr; Paul Ohde, stn mgr.

Elmwood

WFYR(FM)—Aug 2, 1993: 97.3 mhz; 23.5 kw. Ant 338 ft. TL: N40 46 22 W89 44 50. Stereo. Hrs opn: 24. Box 383, Pekin (61555). (309) 346-2134; (309) 673-9595. Licensee: Rainbow Broadcasting Corp. Wash atty: Reddy, Begley & Martin. Format: Country. Target aud: 18-49. ■ Jerald L. Scott, pres & chief engr; Candace K. Scott, exec vp; Bayard H. Walters, vp; James E. MacFarlane, gen mgr; Susan Thompson, gen sls mgr; Steve Larson, progmg dir.

Elmwood Park

WCKG(FM)—1947: 105.9 mhz; 4.2 kw. Ant 1,575 ft. TL: N41 52 44 W87 38 10. Stereo. Suite 1040, 150 N. Michigan Ave., Chicago (60601). (312) 781-7300. FAX: (312) 443-1516. Licensee: WCKG Inc. Group owner: Cox Broadcasting (acq 1-10-84; $9 million; FTR 12-19-83). Rep: Katz. Format: Classic rock. ■ Michael Disney, vp & gen mgr; Debbie Morel, gen sls mgr; Michael Dirkx, prom mgr; Tom Daniels, mus dir; Randi Blake, news dir; John Valenta, chief engr.

Elsah

***WTPC(FM)**—Dec 1, 1970: 105.3 mhz; 17 w. Ant 210 ft. TL: N38 56 52 W90 20 57. Stereo. Merrick Wing, Principia College (62028). (618) 374-4934. Licensee: Principia College Communications (acq 3-5-90). Net: UPI, AP. Format: Alternative rock. News progmg 4 hrs wkly. Target aud: College students. Spec prog: Class 3 hrs, jazz 3 hrs, hardcore 3 hrs, dance rock 3 hrs, new age 3 hrs, female artists 3 hrs wkly. ■ Peter Goodrich, gen mgr; Naomi Bate, progmg dir; Ralph Drancato, chief engr.

Eureka

WCRI(FM)—1989: 98.5 mhz; 3 kw. Ant 328 ft. TL: N40 44 20 W89 16 13. Stereo. Hrs opn: 6 AM-10:30 PM. 103 N. Major (61530). (309) 467-5555. Licensee: Woodford County Radio Inc. Net: AP. Format: MOR. News progmg 20 hrs wkly. Target aud: General; county residents. Spec prog: Farm 16 hrs, big band 6 hrs, nostalgia 5 hrs wkly. ■ Michael L. Stanton, pres; Mary S. Stanton, opns mgr. ■ Rates: $7; 7; 7; 7.

Evanston

WKTA(AM)—1953: 1330 khz; 5 kw-D, 17 w-N, DA-1. TL: N42 08 23 W87 53 09. Hrs opn: 24. 4320 Dundee Rd., Northbrook (60062). (708) 498-3350. Licensee: Polnet Communications Ltd. (acq 5-5-86; $1.6 million; FTR 2-17-86). Net: Sun, USA. Wash atty: Gardner, Carton & Douglass. Format: News/talk. News progmg 5 hrs wkly. Target aud: General; English speaking audience ages 18-54. Spec prog: Ger 4 hrs, Serbian 12 hrs, Russian one hr wkly. ■ Walter K. Kotaba, pres; Kent D. Gustafson, gen mgr; Mike Czark, opns mgr; Bruce Goldberg, sls dir; Zophia Orqvec, gen sls mgr; Dave Dybas, chief engr. ■ Rates: $45; 45; 45; 45.

***WNUR-FM**—May 8, 1950: 89.3 mhz; 7.2 kw. Ant 100 ft. TL: N42 03 12 W87 40 33. Stereo. Hrs opn: 24. Basement, 1905 Sheridan Rd. (60208-2260). (708) 491-7101; (708) 491-2234. FAX: (708) 467-2058. Licensee: Northwestern Univ. Format: Alt radio. Target aud: General. Spec prog: Class 3 hrs, reggae 4 hrs, blues 3 hrs, C&W 5 hrs, folk 4 hrs, poetry readings one hr, metal 2 hrs, jazz one hr wkly. ■ David H. Zarefsky, pres; Dana Hirsch, gen mgr; Jeremy Lehrer, opns mgr; Jeff Staack, dev mgr; Matt Walters, prom dir; David Sack, progmg dir; Shane Graham, mus dir; Bryal Gilmer, news dir; Brian Wilson, pub affrs dir; Tony Tonlai, chief engr.

WOJO(FM)—1946: 105.1 mhz; 6.2 kw. Ant 1,174 ft. TL: N41 53 56 W87 37 23 (CP: 8.4 kw). Stereo. 3rd Floor, 625 N. Michigan Ave., Chicago (60611-3110). (312) 649-0105. FAX: (312) 664-2472. Licensee: WOJO Radio Inc. Group owner: Tichenor Media System Inc. (acq 12-19-86). Rep: Katz. Format: Spanish contemp hit. News staff 5; news progmg 60 hrs wkly. Target aud: 18-35; international/Mexican. ■ Mac Tichenor Jr., pres; Jim Pagliai, gen sls mgr; Martha Muniz, prom mgr; Alberto Augusto, progmg dir; Fernando Jaramillo, mus dir; Luis De Gonzalez, news dir; Don Jeffers, chief engr. ■ Rates: $122; 122; 122; 104.

WONX(AM)—1947: 1590 khz; 1 kw-D, 2.5 kw-N, DA-N. TL: N42 01 20 W87 42 43 (CP: 3.5 kw-D, DA). 2100 Lee St. (60202). (708) 475-1590. FAX: (708) 475-1592. Licensee: Kovas Communications Inc. (acq 12-1-75). Format: Ethnic, Sp. Target aud: General. Spec prog: Relg 2 hrs, Greek 2 hrs, Indian 7 hrs, Assyrian 3 hrs, Persian one hr, Arabic one hr, Haitian 3 hrs wkly. ■ Frank Kovas, pres; Ken Kovas, gen mgr, mus dir & chief engr; Don Munn, opns mgr, progmg dir, news dir & pub affrs dir; Judy Selby, gen sls mgr. ■ Rates: $30; 20; 30; 15.

Fairfield

WFIW(AM)—Aug 21, 1953: 1390 khz; 1 kw-D, 87 w-N. TL: N38 22 46 W88 19 33. Hrs opn: 5 AM-midnight. Box 310, Hwy. 15 E. (62837). (618) 842-2159. FAX: (618) 847-5907. Licensee: Wayne County Broadcasting Co. Net: ABC/D, EIB, Daynet; Ill. Farm. Rep: Rgnl Reps. Format: Modern country, news/talk. News staff one; news progmg 22 hrs wkly. Target aud: 45 plus; small town rural, business, farm, older adults. Spec prog: Farm 16 hrs wkly. ■ Thomas S. Land, chmn; David H. Land, pres, gen mgr, gen sls mgr & progmg dir; Margaret H. Land, vp; Len Wells, news dir; Kirk Wallace, chief engr. ■ Rates: $16; 16; 16; 8.

WFIW-FM—1965: 104.9 mhz; 3.4 kw. Ant 273 ft. TL: N38 22 46 W88 19 33. Stereo. Hrs opn: 5 AM-midnight. Dups AM 20%. Format: Adult contemp, oldies. News progmg 16 hrs wkly. Target aud: 25-49; small town rural, young, middle age, business, farm. Spec prog: Farm 12 hrs wkly. ■ David H. Land, vp opns & sls dir; Len Wells, asst mus dir. ■ Rates: Same as AM.

Farmer City

WZRO(FM)—Oct 1, 1983: 98.3 mhz; 3 kw. Ant 300 ft. TL: N40 16 54 W88 32 00. Stereo. 407 N. Main (61842). (309) 928-9876. Licensee: Potomac Broadcasting Inc. (acq 2-1-88). Net: SMN. Format: C&W. News progmg 5 hrs wkly. Target aud: 25-54; reach city, suburbs and rural listeners in east central Illinois. Spec prog: Gospel, farm 5 hrs, sports 5 hrs wkly. ■ Sharon C. Johnson, pres; Robert E. Johnson, stn mgr.

Farmington

WZKT(FM)—Not on air, target date unknown: 96.5 mhz; 4.1 kw. Ant 381 ft. TL: N40 40 11 W89 53 34. c/o Robert M. Mason, 1943 Greenview, Northbrook (60062). Licensee: Robert M. Mason.

Flora

WNOI(FM)—May 21, 1971: 103.9 mhz; 3.3 kw. Ant 300 ft. TL: N38 40 42 W88 29 14. Stereo. Hrs opn: 24. Box 368, 12th & N. Olive (62839). (618) 662-8331. FAX: (618) 662-2407. Licensee: H&R Communications Inc. (acq 10-16-88). Net: SMN. Format: Adult contemp. News staff one; news progmg 12 hrs wkly. Target aud: General. ■ Steven S. Lovellette, pres; Randy W. Poole, gen mgr; Brenda Whitehead, gen sls mgr; Randy Poole, progmg dir; Bill Thompson, news dir; Kirk Wallace, chief engr. ■ Rates: $9.50; 9.50; 9.50; 9.50.

Flossmoor

***WHFH(FM)**—January 1965: 88.5 mhz; 1.5 kw. Ant 92 ft. TL: N41 32 43 W87 41 30. Stereo. Hrs opn: 14. 999 Kedzie Ave. (60422). (708) 798-9434. FAX: (708) 799-3142. Licensee: Community High School District No. 233. Net: AP. Format: Div. News progmg 4 hrs wkly. Target aud: Teens-Adult. Spec prog: News/Talk one hr, sports talk one hr, live sports 4 hrs wkly. ■ Robert Comstock, pres & gen mgr; Brad Peterson, stn mgr; Tom Gunderson, opns dir; P.J. Burt, sls dir; Joel Moweray, mus dir; Joe Tatti, asst mus dir; Karen Collins, news dir; Emily Feinstein, pub affrs dir; Tom Sauch, chief engr.

Freeport

WFPS(FM)—Nov 1, 1970: 92.1 mhz; 3 kw. Ant 300 ft. TL: N42 19 41 W89 43 32. Stereo. Box 701, (61032). (815) 235-7191. Licensee: Friends Communications Inc. (acq 6-15-89). Net: NBC. Format: Adult contemp. News staff one; news progmg 15 hrs wkly. Target aud: 25-49. ■ Michael Brooks, pres; Kim Grimes, gen mgr & gen sls mgr; Bill Johnson, opns mgr & prom mgr; Jim Douglas, progmg dir & mus dir; Brad Hart, news dir; Carl Plaster, chief engr.

WFRL(AM)—Oct 28, 1947: 1570 khz; 5 kw-D, 500 w-N, DA-2. TL: N42 18 45 W89 35 38. Hrs opn: 24. Box 810, 834 N. Tower Rd. (61032). (815) 235-4113. FAX: (815) 235-9377. Licensee: Stateline Broadcasting Inc. (acq 10-23-91; $900,000 with co-located FM; FTR 11-18-91). Net: CBS; Tribune, Ill. Farm, Ill. News. Rep: McGavren Guild. Format: Adult contemp. News staff 2; news progmg 24 hrs wkly. Target aud: 35 plus. Spec prog: Farm 15 hrs wkly. ■ Tom Imhoff, gen mgr; Michael Weif, progmg dir; Christine Stukenburg, news dir; Carl Plaster, chief engr.

WXXQ(FM)—Co-owned with WFRL(AM). April 11, 1965: 98.5 mhz; 50 kw. Ant 450 ft. TL: N42 18 45 W89 35 38. Stereo. Hrs opn: 24. Prog sep from AM. Format: CHR. Target aud: 18-35. Spec prog: Farm 7 hrs wkly.

Galena

WJOD(FM)—February 1989: 107.5 mhz; 6 kw. Ant 328 ft. TL: N42 24 02 W90 23 55. Stereo. Box 276, 527 Bouthillier St. (61036). (815) 777-2555. Licensee: JDC Communications Inc. Net: CNN, Unistar. Format: Country. ■ Bruce Salzman, gen mgr; Scott Meyer, gen sls mgr; Ken Peiffer, progmg dir.

Galesburg

WAAG(FM)—Listing follows WGIL(AM).

WAIK(AM)—1957: 1590 khz; 5 kw-D, 50 w-N, DA-2. TL: N40 57 43 W90 18 30. Hrs opn: 6 AM-10 PM. Box 431 (61401); 235 E. Main St. (61402). (309) 342-3161. FAX: (309) 342-0199. Licensee: Northern Broadcast Group Inc. (acq 6-15-93; $600,000 with co-located FM; FTR 5-3-93). Net: ABC/I. Wash atty: Semmes, Bowen & Semmes Format: Big Band. News staff 3; news progmg 24 hrs wkly. Target aud: 25 plus. Spec prog: Talk 10 hrs, loc sports 10 hrs, relig 6 hrs wkly. ■ Michael McCulloch, pres & gen mgr; Meg Self, opns dir; Bill Hungate, gen sls mgr; Lisa Martin, prom dir & pub affrs dir; Chris Postin, progmg dir; David Klockenga, news dir. ■ Rates: $9.50; 8; 9.50; 4.50.

WGBQ(FM)—Co-owned with WAIK(AM). Jan 17, 1979: 92.7 mhz; 3 kw. Ant 355 ft. TL: N40 57 43 W90 18 30. Stereo. Hrs opn: 24. Prog sep from AM. (309) 342-7193. Net: ABC/R. Format: Adult contemp. News staff 3; news progmg 18 hrs wkly. Target aud: 18-34. Spec prog: Loc sports 10 hrs wkly. ■ Rates: Same as AM.

Broadcasting & Cable Yearbook 1994
B-112

WGIL(AM)—June 12, 1938: 1400 khz; 1 kw-U. TL: N40 56 36 W90 20 39. Hrs opn: 24. Box 1227, 154 E. Simmons (61402-1227). (309) 342-5131. FAX: (309) 342-0840. Licensee: Galesburg Broadcasting Co. (group owner). Net: MBS. Format: MOR, talk, farm. News staff 3. Target aud: General. ■ Jon Raymond, gen mgr; Terry Cavanaugh, news dir; Jennifer McCarthy, news dir; Wally Boller, chief engr. ■ Rates: $16.50; 16.50; 16.50; 16.50.

WAAG(FM)—Co-owned with WGIL(AM). Dec 15, 1966: 94.9 mhz; 50 kw. Ant 350 ft. TL: N40 56 36 W90 20 39. Stereo. Hrs opn: 24. Prog sep from AM. Format: Country. Spec prog: Farm 5 hrs wkly. ■ Brian Hamline, mus dir. ■ Rates: $18; 18; 18; 18.

*WVKC(FM)—April 12, 1961: 90.7 mhz; 1 kw. Ant 98 ft. TL: N40 56 46 W90 22 11. Box K154, Knox College (61401). (309) 343-9940. Licensee: Knox College. Net: MBS. Format: Div. Spec prog: Black 6 hrs, jazz 15 hrs, class 18 hrs wkly. ■ John Barstad, Peter Birk, gen mgrs; Roger Lunden, chief engr.

Geneseo

WGEN(AM)—Nov 7, 1963: 1500 khz; 250 w-D. TL: N41 26 23 W90 09 18. Hrs opn: 14. Box 67, 1003 S. Oakwood (61254). (309) 944-4633; (309) 944-2222. FAX: (309) 944-2200. Licensee: Coleman Broadcasting Co. (acq 3-1-90; $481,900; FTR 4-2-90). Net: ABC/E; Tribune. Wash atty: Baraff, Koerner, Olender & Hochberg. Format: Adult contemp, community, country. News staff one; news progmg 13 hrs wkly. Target aud: 25 plus; community oriented adults. Spec prog: Big band 5 hrs wkly, all-nite sportstalk. ■ Roger H. Coleman, pres & gen mgr; Jeri Johnson, prom dir; Ann McKay, progmg dir & mus dir; Richard Kinney, news dir; Andy Andressen, chief engr. ■ Rates: $12.50; 10; 8.50; 6.

WGEN-FM—Jan 12, 1977: 104.9 mhz; 3.3 kw. Ant 280 ft. TL: N41 25 47 W90 16 34. Stereo. Hrs opn: 24 Format: Adult contemp, farm, sports. ■ Rates: Same as AM.

Geneva

WFXW(AM)—Nov 11, 1961: 1480 khz; 1 kw-D, 500 w-N, DA-2. TL: N41 54 25 W88 17 43. Hrs opn: 24. 1215 E. Fern Ave., Saint Charles (60174-4425). (708) 232-6464; (708) 232-1480 (STUDIO LINE). FAX: (708) 513-1101. Licensee: Valley Communications Inc. (acq 8-17-88). Net: ABC/E, AP. Format: Adult Comtemp, big band, oldies. News staff 2; news progmg 10 hrs wkly. Target aud: 35-65. Spec prog: Ger 4 hrs, relg 4 hrs, news/talk 15 hrs wkly. ■ Louis Pignatelli, pres; Don Oberbillig, gen mgr & gen sls mgr; P.J. Harrigan, progmg dir & mus dir; Jon Morgan, asst mus dir & chief engr; Geoff Gillette, news dir; John Czech, pub affrs dir. ■ Rates: $35; 30; 30; 15.

Gibson City

WGCY(FM)—Nov 28, 1983: 106.3 mhz; 3 kw. Ant 292 ft. TL: N40 34 01 W88 20 41. Stereo. Hrs opn: 6 AM-midnight. Box 192, 607 S. Sangamon Ave. (60936). (217) 784-8661. FAX: (217) 784-8677. Licensee: F & G Broadcasting Inc. (acq 12-30-86; $225,000 FTR 11-24-86). Net: AP, USA. Format: Btfl mus. News staff one. Target aud: 35 plus. ■ Fred McCullough, pres; Gary McCullough, gen mgr & gen sls mgr; Jill Doran, news dir; Greg Stephens, chief engr. ■ Rates: $8.25; 8.25; 8.25; 8.25.

Girard

WCVS-FM—See Springfield.

Glen Ellyn

*WDCB(FM)—July 5, 1977: 90.9 mhz; 5 kw. Ant 300 ft. TL: N41 50 36 W88 05 00. Stereo. Hrs opn: 19. College of DuPage, 22nd St. & Lambert Rd. (60137). (708) 858-5196. FAX: (708) 858-5173. Licensee: College of DuPage. Net: APR, AP, UPI; Ill. Pub. Wash atty: Cohn & Marks. Format: Div, jazz. News staff 2; news progmg 13 hrs wkly. Target aud: General. Spec prog: Class 6 hrs, college classes 18 hrs, folk 2 hrs, gospel 2 hrs, bluegrass 3 hrs, blues 3 hrs, big band 2 hrs, reggae 2 hrs wkly. ■ Sidney Fryer, gen mgr; Scott Wager, stn mgr & opns mgr; Clarice Nickols, chief opns; Ken Scott, dev mgr & prom mgr; MaryPat LaRue, progmg dir & Erv Jezek, mus dir; Scot Witt, news dir; John Valenta, chief engr.

Glenview

*WMWA(FM)—Jan 13, 1979: 88.5 mhz; 100 w. Ant 100 ft. TL: N42 04 30 W87 49 23. Stereo. 74 Park Dr. (60025). (708) 998-9556. Licensee: Midwestern Academy of the New Church. Format: Class, educational. Target aud: 30 plus; college educated. Spec prog: Relg 2 hrs, high school sports 8 hrs wkly. ■ Robert Henderson, gen mgr; Gary Schroeder, chief engr.

Godfrey

*WLCA(FM)—1974: 89.9 mhz; 1.4 kw. Ant 112 ft. TL: N38 57 00 W90 11 38. Rev. 18. 5800 Godfrey Rd. (62035). (618) 466-3411. Licensee: Lewis and Clark Community College. Net: USA. Format: Progrv, rock (AOR). ■ Kent Scheffel, gen mgr; Dave Caires, chief engr.

Golconda

WDXR-FM—Nov 22, 1990: 94.3 mhz; 3.1 kw. Ant 449 ft. TL: N37 14 04 W88 29 48. Stereo. Hrs opn: 24. Box 2250, One Executive Blvd., Paducah, KY (42002-2250). (502) 443-1000; (502) 443-1757. FAX: (502) 442-1000. Licensee: Mason-Dixon Broadcasting Co. (acq 9-3-91; $20,300 with WDXR(AM) Paducah, KY; FTR 8-5-91). Net: SMN. Wash atty: Sadowski. Format: Traditional country. News staff one; news progmg 5 hrs wkly. Target aud: 30-65. Spec prog: Relg 2 hrs wkly. ■ David J. Emerson, pres & stn mgr; Emily Brown, Rhouda Dalton (asst), opns mgrs; Randy Scheiding, sls dir; Emily Brown, prom dir & news dir; Row Alvey, engrg mgr. ■ Rates: $15; 10; 12; 7.

Granite City

WGNU(AM)—Licensed to Granite City. See St. Louis, Mo.

WKBQ(AM)—Licensed to Granite City. See St. Louis, Mo.

Greenville

WGEL(FM)—Dec 20, 1984: 101.7 mhz; 3 kw. Ant 300 ft. TL: N38 48 11 W89 20 56. Stereo. Hrs opn: 24. 309 W. Main (62246). (618) 664-3300. FAX: (618) 664-1221. Licensee: Bond Broadcasting (acq 6-1-85; $170,000; FTR 6-10-85). Net: USA. Format: Country. News staff one; news progmg 19 hrs wkly. Target aud: 25-64. Spec prog: Farm 19 hrs wkly. ■ John Kennedy, pres, gen mgr, gen sls mgr, mktg mgr & adv mgr; Eleanor Kennedy, progmg dir; John Goldsmith, mus dir & news dir; John King, chief engr. ■ Rates: $13; 11; 13; 11.

*WGRN(FM)—Sept 26, 1966: 89.5 mhz; 300 w. Ant 206 ft. TL: N38 53 43 W89 24 30. Stereo. Hrs opn: 18. 315 E. College Ave. (62246). (618) 664-1840. FAX: (618) 664-1373. Licensee: Greenville College Educational Broadcasting Foundation Inc. Format: Christian hit radio. Target aud: 16-24. ■ Cary Holman, gen mgr; Jim Broni, stn mgr; Mike Blaha, prom dir; Jeff Jordan, adv mgr; Marcus White, progmg dir; Kimberly Engstrom, mus dir; Joanne Hunt, pub affrs dir; John Killinger, engrg mgr.

Harrisburg

WEBQ(AM)—September 1923: 1240 khz; 1 kw-U. TL: N37 43 03 W88 32 37. 701 S. Commercial St. (62946). (618) 252-6307. FAX: (618) 252-2366. Licensee: Turner Communications Inc. (acq 6-90; grpsl; FTR 7-9-90). Net: NBC. Format: Country. Spec prog: Farm 6 hrs wkly. ■ Dave Bard, gen mgr & adv mgr; Cathy Horton, progmg dir & mus dir; Bob Romonosky, chief engr.

WOOZ-FM—September 1947: 99.9 mhz; 32 kw. Ant 650 ft. TL: N37 36 45 W88 52 03. Stereo. Box 2228, 1025 E. Main St., Carbondale, (62902). (618) 549-3243. FAX: (618) 549-2455. Licensee: Zimmer Communications Inc. (acq 7-19-89). Wash atty: Fletcher, Heald & Hildreth. Format: Country. News staff one. Target aud: 18-49. ■ Jerry Zimmer, CEO & vp; Bruce Welker, gen mgr; Ron Covert, sls mgr; Wayne Kelly, prom dir & progmg dir. ■ Rates: $37; 33; 37; 20.

Harvard

WMCW(AM)—1955: 1600 khz; 500 w-D, 19 w-N. TL: N42 26 07 W88 36 39. Stereo. Hrs opn: 5 AM-10 PM. Box 786, 67 N. Ayer (60033). (815) 943-3100. FAX: (815) 943-5120. Licensee: Mitchell Broadcasting Co. (acq 7-1-82; FTR 6-21-82). Net: NBC. Format: Adult contemp, news. News staff 2; news progmg 12 hrs wkly. Target aud: General. Spec prog: Farm 6 hrs wkly. ■ Forrest Mitchell, pres; Mianne Mitchell Nelson, vp; Dave Nelson, gen mgr; Paul Zack, gen sls mgr; Doug Cartland, progmg dir; Todd Allen, news dir; Steve Paska, pub affrs dir.

Harvey

WBEE(AM)—1955: 1570 khz; 1 kw-D, 500 w-N, DA-2. TL: N41 36 14 W87 40 45. Hrs opn: 24. 15700 Campbell Ave. (60426-2881). (708) 331-7840. FAX: (708) 333-2560. Licensee: Mariner Broadcasters Inc. (acq 8-1-87; FTR 6-29-87). Format: Jazz, blues. Target aud: 18-64; affluent Americans. ■ Charles R. Sherrell II, pres; Cari D. Farley, gen mgr; Jacqueline Neal, opns dir; Davita Shipp, mus dir; Jerome Burdeau, chief engr. ■ Rates: $95; 85; 95; 45.

Havana

WDUK(FM)—Feb 27, 1970: 99.3 mhz; 3 kw. Ant 300 ft. TL: N40 18 43 W90 03 19. 901 N. Promenade (62644). (309) 543-3331. Licensee: Illinois Valley Radio (acq 3-5-73). Net: Ill. Farm. Format: MOR, C&W. Target aud: General. Spec prog: Farm 8 hrs wkly. ■ Edwin Stimpson, pres, gen mgr, progmg dir, mus dir & news dir. ■ Rates: $3.70; 3.70; 3.70; 3.70.

Henry

WRVY-FM—July 30, 1990: 100.5 mhz; 3 kw. Ant 328 ft. TL: N41 04 32 W89 21 10. Stereo. Hrs opn: 5:30 AM-11 PM. c/o Radio Station WCIC(FM), 3263 Court St., Pekin (61554). (309) 353-9191. FAX: (309) 353-1141. Licensee: Illinois Bible Institute (group owner; acq 4-5-93; FTR 4-26-93). Format: Contemp Christian. ■ Dave Brooks, stn mgr.

Herrin

WDDD(AM)—See Johnston City.

WJPF(AM)—Aug 28, 1940: 1340 khz; 1 kw-U. TL: N37 50 03 W89 01 37 (CP: 770 w-U). Hrs opn: 24. Box 550, N. Rt. 148 (62948). (618) 942-2181. FAX: (618) 988-8111. Licensee: Egyptian Broadcasting Co. (acq 5-26-88). Net: ABC TalkRadio, NBC Talknet, Westwood One; Ill. News Net. Format: News/talk. News staff 3; news progmg 10 hrs wkly. Target aud: 35 plus; mature, middle-income wage earners. ■ Robert A. Ferrari, pres, gen mgr & opns director; Kerry J. Baichtal, gen sls mgr; Scott Davenport, progmg dir; Ray Gruny, news dir; Jason Sullivan, pub affrs dir; Jon Brookmyer, chief engr. ■ Rates: $10; 9; 9.50; 6.

WVZA(FM)—Not on air, target date unknown: 92.7 mhz; 6 kw. Ant 325 ft. TL: N37 49 47 W89 08 19. c/o Herrin Broadcasting Inc., 2279 Springs Landing Blvd., Longwood, FL (32779). Licensee: Wayne E. Tate (acq 8-3-93; $135,000; FTR 8-23-93).

Highland

WINU(AM)—Dec 2, 1963: 880 khz; 1 kw-D, DA. TL: N38 45 23 W89 39 18 (CP: 1.7 kw-D, 160 w-N, DA-2). Hrs opn: 5 AM-10 PM. Box 303 (62249). (618) 654-7521. Licensee: Progressive Broadcasting Corp. (acq 4-2-91; $170,000). Net: ABC/D; Brownfield. Wash atty: James Edmundson. Format: Contemp, news, sports. News staff one; news progmg 18 hrs wkly. Target aud: General; mature adults. Spec prog: Farm 3 hrs, Ger one hr wkly. ■ Jack E. Chor, pres, gen mgr & mus dir; Phoebe J. Morris, opns dir; Ken Monken, news dir. ■ Rates: $12; 12; 12; 12.

Highland Park

WEEF(AM)—Aug 15, 1963: 1430 khz; 1 kw-D, 29 w-N, DA. TL: N42 10 53 W87 57 05. 210 Skokie Valley Rd. (60035). (708) 831-5440. Licensee: Winston AM Radio Inc. (acq 1-1-84). Wash atty: Dow, Lohnes & Albertson. Format: It, Greek. Target aud: General; ethnic. Spec prog: Assyrian, Jewish, East Indian, Romanian, Russian, music/talk. ■ Gordon H. Winston, pres; Myra M. Winston, stn mgr; Chris Bagat, progmg dir.

WVVX(FM)—Aug 15, 1963: 103.1 mhz; 3 kw. Ant 241 ft. TL: N42 09 24 W87 48 20. 210 Skokie Valley Rd. (60035). (708) 831-5250. Licensee: Douglas Broadcasting Inc. (group owner; acq 4-16-92; $3.7 million; FTR 5-4-92). Format: Ger, heavy metal, Korean. Spec prog: Pol 8 hrs, Sp 10 hrs, Romanian 4 hrs, Iranian 6 hrs, Greek 5 hrs, Latvian one hr, Russian one hr, Armenian one hr wkly. ■ N. John Douglas, pres; Bill Paar, vp & gen mgr; Sarah Fell, opns dir; David Bolander, opns mgr; Beverly Rosenstein, pub affrs dir; Frank McCoy, chief engr.

Hillsboro

WXAJ(FM)—Not on air, target date unknown: 99.7 mhz; 50 kw. Ant 492 ft. TL: N39 20 14 W89 32 04. Rt. 5, Box 110, Centralia (62801). Licensee: Benjamin L. Stratemyer.

Hinsdale

*WHSD(FM)—Dec 6, 1970: 88.5 mhz; 200 w. Ant 131 ft. TL: N41 47 25 W87 55 11. Stereo. Hrs opn: 3 PM-10 PM. Hinsdale Central High School, 55th & Grant Sts. (60521). (708) 887-1340. FAX: (708) 887-1362. Licensee:

Illinois Directory of Radio

Hinsdale High School District 86. Format: Progsv. Target aud: General. ■ Harry Priester, chief engr.

Hoopeston

WHPO(FM)—May 29, 1979: 100.9 mhz; 3 kw. Ant 280 ft. TL: N40 28 36 W87 41 36. Stereo. Box 55, 627 N. Market (60942). (217) 283-7744. FAX: (217) 283-6090. Licensee: Hoopeston Radio Inc. (acq 5-1-84). Net: AP. Format: Country. News staff one; news progmg 6 hrs wkly. Target aud: 25 plus; rural middle class. Spec prog: Sp one hr, gospel 7 hrs wkly. ■ Richard Stipp, pres, gen mgr & sls dir; John Clark, mktg dir; Becky Buss, progmg dir & mus dir; Johnny McCrory, news dir & pub affrs dir; Don Russell, chief engr. ■ Rates: $15; 12; 14; 10.

Jacksonville

WJIL(AM)—November 1961: 1550 khz; 1 kw-D, 10 w-N, DA-2. TL: N39 43 20 W90 11 43. Hrs opn: 6 AM-midnight. Box 1065, E. Morton Rd. (62651). (217) 245-5119. FAX: (217) 245-1596. Licensee: Morgan County Broadcasting Co. Inc. (acq 5-1-93; including co-owned FM). Net: ABC/I, Tribune. Format: Country, talk. News staff one; news progmg 9 hrs wkly. Target aud: General. Spec prog: Farm 8 hrs wkly. ■ B.D. Hunter, pres; David Comstock, gen mgr; Scott Lambie, opns mgr & mus dir; Marcy Nolan, natl sls mgr, rgnl sls mgr & mktg mgr; Shannon Aosey, news dir; Tom Howerton, chief engr.

WJVO(FM)—(South Jacksonville). Co-owned with WJIL(AM). Sept 1, 1986: 105.5 mhz; 6 kw. Ant 340 ft. TL: N39 43 20 W90 11 43. Stereo. Hrs opn: 24. Prog sep from AM. Format: Classic rock. News progmg 4 hrs wkly. Target aud: 25-49. Spec prog: Folk 3 hrs wkly. ■ Marcy Nolan, adv dir; Dave Comstock, progmg dir; Brett Hunter, mus dir.

WLDS(AM)—Dec 9, 1941: 1180 khz; 1 kw-D. TL: N39 44 06 W90 11 50. Hrs opn: Sunrise-sunset. Box 1180, E. Old State Rd. (62651). (217) 245-7171; (217) 243-2800. FAX: (217) 245-7171, ext. 56. Licensee: Jerdon Broadcasting (acq 8-1-89; $650,000; FTR 6-5-89). Net: CBS; Ill. News Net. Rep: Katz. Wash atty: Kaye, Scholer, Fierman, Hays & Handler. Format: Adult contemp, news/talk. News staff 3; news progmg 23 hrs wkly. Target aud: 35 plus; business & professional people, farmers & housewives. Spec prog: Farm 20 hrs wkly. ■ Jerry Symons, vp & gen mgr; Donald Hamilton, vp & gen sls mgr; Richard Smith, prom dir; Marty Megginson, prom mgr; Tim Thomson, progmg dir; Perry Brown, progmg mgr; Gary Ballard, mus dir; Gary Scott, news dir; Jeff Squibb, pub affrs dir; Terry Poe, chief engr. ■ Rates: $41; 32; 37; na.

WYMG(FM)—Licensed to Jacksonville. See Springfield.

Jerseyville

WJBM(AM)—Oct 11, 1959: 1480 khz; 500 w-D, 32 w-N, DA-2. TL: N39 06 46 W90 18 43. 1010 Shipman Rd. (62052). (618) 498-2185. FAX: (618) 498-9830. Licensee: Gary Brown (acq 10-31-91; $180,000; FTR 12-2-91). Net: ABC/D; Brownfield. Rep: Roslin. Format: Country, oldies, news. News staff 5; news progmg 23 hrs wkly. Target aud: 25 plus; general market through retirement. Spec prog: Farm 18 hrs, gospel 12 hrs, sports 13 hrs, relg 3 hrs wkly. ■ Gary Brown (Owner), pres; Shirley Scott, prom mgr; Craig Baalman, progmg dir & mus dir; Alan Ringhausen, news dir; Gary Brown, chief engr. ■ Rates: $13; 12; 9; 9.

WKKX(FM)—Oct 10, 1967: 104.1 mhz; 50 kw. Ant 500 ft. TL: N38 51 36 W90 18 38. Stereo. Hrs opn: 24. 111 W. Port Plaza, St. Louis, MO (63146). (314) 878-1040. FAX: (314) 878-1564. Licensee: Zimmer Broadcasting (acq 9-13-91). Rep: Banner. Format: Contemp country. News staff one; news progmg 2 hrs wkly. Target aud: 25-54; families with children, singles. Spec prog: Heartland Issues one hr, Today's Issues one hr, Public Agenda one hr wkly. ■ Jerry Zimmer, pres; Bill Viands, gen mgr; Joe Rusch, gen sls mgr; John Pace, rgnl sls mgr; Mike Stoehner, prom mgr; Tom Bradley, progmg dir; Susan Benson, mus dir; George Depper, news dir & pub affrs dir; Bob Hoffman, chief engr. ■ Rates: $125; 65; 85; 25.

Johnston City

WDDD(AM)—July 1, 1979: 810 khz; 250 w-U, DA-N. TL: N37 51 14 W88 52 12. Stereo. Hrs opn: 24. Box 127, One Broadcast Ctr., Marion (62959). (618) 997-8123. Licensee: 3-D Communications Corp. Net: NBC. Format: Country. News staff 3; news progmg 10 hrs wkly. Target aud: 25 plus. ■ Dutch Doelitzsch, pres, gen mgr, progmg dir & chief engr; Jerry Crouse, stn mgr & gen sls mgr; Pat Benton, opns mgr; Tracy McSherry, mus dir; Steve Land, Ken Smith, news dirs.

Joliet

WCCQ(FM)—(Crest Hill). Jan 28, 1976: 98.3 mhz; 3 kw. Ant 300 ft. TL: N41 27 55 W88 07 33. 1520 N. Rock Run Dr., Joliet (60435). (815) 729-4400. FAX: (815) 729-4444. Licensee: CHB Venture. Net: SMN. Wash atty: Winston & Strawn. Format: C&W. ■ Robert Channick, pres & gen mgr; Leonard Frisaro, gen sls mgr; Roy Gregory, prom dir & progmg dir; Lane Lindstrom, chief engr. ■ Rates: $38; 36; 36; 33.

***WCSF(FM)**—Sept 5, 1988: 88.7 mhz; 100 w. Ant 108 ft. TL: N41 31 58 W88 05 54. Stereo. Hrs opn: Mon.-Fri., 7 AM-2 AM. 500 N. Wilcox St, (60435). (815) 740-3425; (815) 740-3214. Licensee: College of St. Francis. Format: Rock, contemp hit. Target aud: 18-45; males. Spec prog: Black 2 hrs, jazz 2 hrs, talk 4 hrs, requests 4 hrs, classic rock 4 hrs wkly. ■ Robert Zak, gen mgr; Dave Frieberg, progmg dir & mus dir; Scott Scheuber, pub affrs dir.

***WJCH(FM)**—April 25, 1986: 91.9 mhz; 50 kw. Ant 460 ft. TL: N41 24 55 W88 16 19. Stereo. Hrs opn: 24. 13 Fairlane Dr. (60435). (815) 725-1331. Licensee: Family Stations Inc. (group owner). Format: Relg. Spec prog: Class 2 hrs wkly. ■ Harold Camping, pres & gen mgr; John Rorvik, stn mgr & pub affrs dir; Craig Hulsebos, progmg dir; Phyllis Johnston, mus dir; Greg Stephens, chief engr.

WJOL(AM)—1924: 1340 khz; 1 kw-U. TL: N41 32 10 W88 03 15. Hrs opn: 24. Box 430, 601 Walnut St. (60434). (815) 726-4761. FAX: (815) 726-0357. Licensee: UNO Broadcasting Corp. (group owner; acq 10-4-87). Net: ABC/I. Rep: Katz & Powell. Wash atty: Arent, Fox, Kintner, Plotkin & Kahn. Format: Adult contemp, news/talk. News staff 4; news progmg 40 hrs wkly. Target aud: 35 plus. ■ Robert Tezak, pres; Jack Daly, gen mgr; Ed Morris, opns dir & chief engr; Jody Sebby, sls dir; Tony Ray, progmg dir; Derrick Brown, mus dir; Randy Bunger, news dir.

WLLI-FM—Co-owned with WJOL(AM). Feb 6, 1960: 96.7 mhz; 3 kw. Ant 300 ft. TL: N41 32 10 W88 03 15. Stereo. Hrs opn: 24. Prog sep from AM. Net: ABC/FM. Format: Adult rock. Target aud: 21-36.

WJTW(FM)—Apr 17, 1960: 93.5 mhz; 3 kw. Ant 259 ft. TL: N41 32 18 W88 05 35. Stereo. Suite 209, 2455 Glenwood Ave. (60435). (815) 729-9596. FAX: (815) 729-9623. Licensee: New Horizons Communications Co. (acq 9-30-85; $450,000; FTR 9-3-85). Format: Adult contemp. News staff one. Target aud: 25-54. ■ Terry Knust, gen mgr; Bill Guertin, gen sls mgr; Rob Martini, progmg dir & mus dir; Sandy Friend, news dir.

WLLI-FM—Listing follows WJOL(AM).

WWHN(AM)—April 10, 1964: 1510 khz; 1 kw-D. TL: N41 30 50 W88 03 10. Stereo. 240 E. 103rd St., Chicago, (60628). (312) 928-7070. FAX: (312) 928-6441. Licensee: Hawkins Braodcasting Co. (acq 12-89; $250,000; FTR 12-4-89). Format: Gospel. News progmg 5 hrs wkly. Target aud: 18-54; affluent adults. Spec prog: Sp one hr wkly. ■ Raymond J. Hawkins, pres; Tomelia Hawkins, vp, gen mgr & news dir; Karen L. Fletcher, opns dir; Tim Jones, dev mgr; Hattie Herbert, prom mgr; Karen Fletcher, progmg dir; Fran Kane, asst mus dir; Frank McCoy, chief engr. ■ Rates: $50; 50; 50; 50.

Kankakee

WBUS(FM)—Jan 5, 1962: 99.9 mhz; 50 kw. Ant 500 ft. TL: N91 18 04 W87 49 35. Stereo. Hrs opn: 24. Box 999, 292 N. Convent, Bourbonnais (60914). (815) 933-9287. FAX: (815) 933-8696. Licensee: Gene Milner Broadcasting Co Inc. (acq 3-17-84; $1.2 million; FTR 4-2-84). Format: CHR. News staff one. Target aud: 18-49. ■ Jacqueline A. Milner, pres & gen mgr; Kathy Gagliano, gen sls mgr; Mickey Milner, progmg dir; Robert King, chief engr.

WKAN(AM)—June 1, 1947: 1320 khz; 1 kw-D, 500 w-N, DA-N. TL: N41 08 08 W87 49 10. Hrs opn: 24. 2 Dearborn Sq. (60901). (815) 935-9555. FAX: (815) 935-9593. Licensee: Imagery Inc. (acq 9-10-86). Net: AP. Format: Adult contemp. News staff 2; news progmg 20 hrs wkly. Target aud: 35 plus. Spec prog: Farm 10 hrs wkly. ■ Susanne S. Bergeron, pres; Gary G. Wright, gen mgr; Lawrence Timpe, opns dir & progmg dir; Edgar Munday, news dir; Donald Kerouac, chief engr. ■ Rates: $31.75; 31.75; 31.75; 9.50.

WLRT(FM)—Co-owned with WKAN(AM). Sept 21, 1986: 92.7 mhz; 3 kw. Ant 300 ft. TL: N41 07 22 W87 53 35. Stereo. Hrs opn: 24. Prog sep from AM. Format: Country. Target aud: 25-49. ■ Larry Timpe, opns mgr. ■ Rates: Same as AM.

***WONU(FM)**—1966: 89.7 mhz; 35 kw. Ant 431 ft. TL: N41 09 24 W87 52 16. Stereo. Box 592, Olivet Nazarene University (60901). (815) 939-5330. FAX: (815) 939-5087. Licensee: Olivet Nazarene University. Net: CNN. Wash atty: Miller & Miller P.C. Format: Relg. Target aud: 25-54. ■ Dr. John Bowling, pres; Bill DeWees, gen mgr; Carl Fletcher, opns mgr, mktg mgr & progmg mgr; Brian Dishon, prom mgr; Kim Elridge, adv mgr; Tajhia Lynn, mus dir; Jeffrey Scott, news dir; Maria Bar, pub affrs dir; Don Kerovac, chief engr.

***WTKC(FM)**—June 1, 1992: 91.1 mhz; 1.75 kw. Ant 305 ft. TL: N41 09 24 W87 52 16. Hrs opn: 24. Box 464, Bourbonnais (60914); Suite 1, 1711 Rt. 50, (60914). (815) 935-7390. FAX: (815) 935-5169. Licensee: Kankakee Community College. Format: Educ, tourism. Target aud: General; travelers in northern Ill. ■ Jeannine Crooks, gen mgr.

WZZP(FM)—Oct 22, 1992: 95.1 mhz; 3 kw. Ant 328 ft. TL: N41 04 39 W87 45 22. 32 Briarcliff Professional Ctr, Bourbonnais (60914). (815) 933-9545. FAX: (815) 933-3291. Licensee: Rollings Communications of Kankakee Inc. (acq 12-31-92; $90,000; FTR 1-25-93). Format: Classic rock. ■ Mark Rollings, pres; Hy Farbman, stn mgr.

Kewanee

WKEI(AM)—Sept 11, 1952: 1450 khz; 500 w-D, 1 kw-N. TL: N41 13 37 W89 56 08. Box 266, 133 E. Division St. (61443). (309) 853-4471; (309) 853-4472. Licensee: Miller Broadcast Co. Inc. (acq 10-1-87). Net: ABC/D. Format: MOR, news/talk, adult contemp. News staff one; news progmg 10 hrs wkly. Target aud: 30-75. Spec prog: Farm 20 hrs, relg 10 hrs wkly. ■ Gary Petersen, gen mgr & adv mgr; Kathy Neubert, progmg dir; Dave Stone, news dir; Milton Nicholas Jr., chief engr.

WJRE(FM)—Co-owned with WKEI(AM). May 20, 1966: 92.1 mhz; 3 kw. Ant 300 ft. TL: N41 13 37 W89 56 08. Stereo. Prog sep from AM. Format: Adult contemp Target aud: 25 plus. ■ Gary Petersen, stn mgr; Kathy Neubert, opns dir.

La Grange

***WLTL(FM)**—Jan 5, 1968: 88.1 mhz; 180 w. Ant 138 ft. TL: N41 48 45 W87 52 51. Stereo. Hrs opn: 7 AM-10 PM. 100 S. Brainard Ave. (60525). (708) 482-9585; (708) 579-6408. Licensee: Lyons Township High School. Format: Community affrs & variety rock. News progmg 10 hrs wkly. Target aud: General; young adults 14-35. Spec prog: Sports 5 hrs, news & views 10 hrs wkly. ■ Kathleen Singletary, gen mgr & progmg dir; Dennis Strecker, chief engr.

WTAQ(AM)—October 1950: 1300 khz; 5 kw-D, 500 w-N, DA-2. TL: N41 46 36 W87 51 44 (CP: 4 kw-N. TL: N41 40 29 W87 45 45). 6012 S. Pulaski Rd., Chicago (60629). (312) 284-8184. FAX: (312) 284-8134. Licensee: Illinois Lotus Corp. Group owner: Lotus Communications Corp. (acq 5-85; $1,650,000; FTR 6-10-85). Format: Sp. ■ Mario Limon, gen mgr; Mike Mazurski, natl sls mgr; Jose Alaniz, progmg dir; Andy Weiss, chief engr.

La Salle

WLPO(AM)—Nov 16, 1947: 1220 khz; 1 kw-D, 500 w-N, DA-2. TL: N41 18 14 W89 05 44. Box 215 (61301). (815) 223-3100. FAX: (815) 223-3095. Licensee: La Salle County Broadcasting Corp. (acq 8-1-49). Net: NBC, NBC Talknet. Format: MOR, news/talk. News staff 2; news progmg 27 hrs wkly. Target aud: 30 plus. Spec prog: Farm 10 hrs wkly. ■ Peter Miller II, pres; Peter Miller III, gen mgr & prom mgr; Joseph D. Hogan, progmg dir, mus dir & news dir; Stephen C. Vogler, chief engr.

WAJK(FM)—Co-owned with WLPO(AM). Dec 4, 1964: 99.3 mhz; 11 kw. Ant 500 ft. TL: N41 18 15 W89 05 46. Stereo. Prog sep from AM. Format: Adult contemp. News staff one; news progmg 5 hrs wkly. Target aud: 18-40; females. ■ John Spencer, progmg dir & mus dir.

Lake Forest

***WMXM(FM)**—Sept 10, 1973: 88.9 mhz; 300 w. Ant 100 ft. TL: N42 15 00 W87 49 45. Stereo. Hrs opn: 18. Durand Commons, Basement, 555 N. Sheridan Rd. (60045). (708) 735-5220. Licensee: Lake Forest College Board of Trustees. Format: Div, classic rock, progsv. News staff 2; news progmg 5 hrs wkly. Target aud: 18-25; students. Spec prog: Black 6 hrs, class 3 hrs, gospel 3 hrs, jazz 6 hrs wkly. ■ Brad Swanson, gen mgr; April Lorez, Rachael Ellis, prom dirs; Fred Stanley, Kate Evelyn, progmg dirs; Jim Gubbins, Adam Yoffee, mus dirs; Dan Faber, Hillary Keaver, news dirs; Dan Faber, pub affrs dir; Blaise Miadeck, chief engr.

Lansing

WJPC-FM—Aug 28, 1961: 106.3 mhz; 2 kw. Ant 397 ft. TL: N41 34 44 W87 32 46. 2915 Bernice Rd. (60438). (708) 895-1400. Licensee: Illiana FM Broadcasters Inc. (acq 10-16-70). Format: Black oldies. Target aud: 25-54. Spec prog: Jazz 15 hrs, Sp 12 hrs wkly. ■ Linda Johnson-Rice, pres; Lillian Y. Terrell, opns mgr; Al Greer, progmg dir & mus dir; Gerald Scruthions, chief engr.

Lawrenceville

WAKO(AM)—June 9, 1959: 910 khz; 500 w-D, 59 w-N, DA-2. TL: N38 43 23 W87 39 13. Hrs opn: 5 AM-midnight. Box 210, Hwy. 250 E. (62439). (618) 943-3354. FAX: (618) 943-4173. Licensee: Lawrenceville Broadcasting Co. Inc. (acq 5-31-73). Net: AP, Westwood One, MBS. Format: Adult contemp. News staff one; news progmg 12 hrs wkly. Target aud: 20-60; young adults through middle age groups. ■ Stuart K. Lankford, pres; Dave Dascit, opns dir; David Dasch, progmg dir; Steve Anderson, news dir. ■ Rates: $12; 12; 12; 12.

WAKO-FM—Mar 1965: 103.1 mhz; 6 kw. Ant 328 ft. TL: N38 43 23 W87 39 13. Stereo. Hrs opn: 19. Dups AM 90%. ■ Rates: Same as AM.

Le Roy

WBWN(FM)—Oct 15, 1979: 104.1 mhz; 25 kw. Ant 299 ft. TL: N40 24 35 W88 46 26 (CP: 104.1 mhz, 50 kw, ant 492 ft., TL: N40 27 34 W88 32 46). Stereo. 1303 Morrissey Dr., Bloomington (61701). (309) 663-1041. Licensee: McLean County Broadcasters Inc. Group owner: David Keister Stations (acq 4-23-87). Net: USA. Format: Country. News staff one.

Lincoln

WESZ(FM)—Listing follows WPRC(AM).

***WLNX(FM)**—Jan 28, 1974: 88.9 mhz; 225 w. Ant 68 ft. TL: N40 09 23 W89 21 40. Hrs opn: Noon-midnight. 300 Keokuk St. (62656). (217) 735-3495. Licensee: Lincoln Univ. Group owner: Lincoln College Board of Trustees. Format: New wave Top 40. News progmg 2 hrs wkly. Target aud: 15-35; college, high school students. Spec prog: Relg 4 hrs wkly. ■ Loyd Kirby, gen mgr; Ron Bluhm, chief engr.

WPRC(AM)—April 1951: 1370 khz; 1 kw-D, 35 w-N. TL: N40 08 24 W89 23 10. Box 190, 800 S. Postville Dr. (62656). (217) 735-2337. Licensee: L&M Broadcasting Co. Inc. (acq 8-90; $390,000 with co-located FM; FTR 9-3-90). Net: CNN. Format: C&W. News staff one; news progmg 14 hrs wkly. Target aud: General. Spec prog: Farm 10 hrs wkly. ■ Steve Lovellette, pres; Jon Walsh, gen mgr; Jeff Benjamin, progmg dir; Jim Ash, news dir. ■ Rates: $14; 12; 12; 10.

WESZ(FM)—Co-owned with WPRC(AM). May 10, 1971: 100.1 mhz; 3 kw. Ant 200 ft. TL: N40 08 24 W89 23 10. Dups AM 40%. Format: Adult contemp. News progmg 9 hrs wkly. Target aud: 25-54. ■ Rates: Same as AM.

Litchfield

WSMI(AM)—Nov 2, 1950: 1540 khz; 1 kw-D. TL: N39 10 21 W89 34 14. Box 10, E. Rt. 16 (62056). (217) 324-5921. FAX: (217) 532-2431. Licensee: Talley Broadcasting Corp. Group owner: Talley Radio Stations. Net: MBS. Rep: Banner. Format: Farm, C&W, news. News staff 3; news progmg 13 hrs wkly. ■ Hayward L. Talley, pres, gen mgr & natl sls mgr; Brian Talley, vp opns & chief engr; Mike Niehaus, rgnl sls mgr; Kevin Talley, prom mgr; Terry Todt, progmg dir; Chuck Sebastian, mus dir; Eric Sipos, pub affrs dir.

WSMI-FM—Mar 5, 1960: 106.1 mhz; 50 kw. Ant 500 ft. TL: N39 15 21 W89 36 48. Stereo. Dups AM 15%. Net: MBS. Rep: Banner. Format: Adult contemp, rock, news. ■ Brian Talley, vp & stn mgr; Tom Allman, mus dir.

Lockport

***WLRA(FM)**—November 1972: 88.1 mhz; 250 w. Ant 95 ft. TL: N41 36 06 W88 04 51. Stereo. Hrs opn: 24. Box 528, Rte 53, Lewis University, Romeoville (60441). (815) 838-0500, ext. 881. FAX: (815) 838-9456. Licensee: Lewis University. Format: Educ, div. News progmg 2 hrs wkly. Target aud: 13-30; college bound or post-college. Spec prog: Black 15 hrs, class 6 hrs, jazz 15 hrs, sports 15 hrs, talk 10 hrs wkly. ■ John P. Carey, pres; Steve L. Gordan, gen mgr; Edward C. Tennant Jr., opns mgr; Jason Brenski, progmg dir; Richard Murphy, mus dir; Renee Szymonick, news dir; John D. Freberg, chief engr.

Loves Park

***WGSL(FM)**—Mar 28, 1988: 91.1 mhz; 4 kw. Ant 400 ft. TL: N42 19 18 W89 00 42. Stereo. 5375 Pebble Creek Trail, Rockford (61111). (815) 654-1200. FAX: (815) 282-7779. Licensee: Christian Life Center School. Net: USA. Format: Relg. News staff one; news progmg 11 hrs wkly. Target aud: 35-50; older families. ■ Don Gladden, gen mgr; Ron Tietsort, opns mgr; Randy Adams, mus dir; Cindy Swanson, news dir; Joe McCaw, chief engr.

WLUV(AM)—Sept 29, 1962: 1520 khz; 500 w-D TL: N42 19 48 W89 04 58. Box 2616 (61131); 2272 Elmwood Rd., Rockford (61103). (815) 877-9588. FAX: (815) 877-9649. Licensee: Loves Park Broadcasting Co. Net: ABC/I. Format: Country, sports. News progmg 10 hrs wkly. Target aud: 25-60; blue collar workers. Spec prog: Farm 6 hrs, polka 6 hrs wkly. ■ Angelo Joseph Salvi, pres, gen mgr, gen sls mgr, prom mgr & progmg dir.

WLUV-FM—Mar 25, 1964: 96.7 mhz; 3 kw. Ant 300 ft. TL: N42 19 48 W89 04 58. Stereo. Format: Country, sports, Black. Spec prog: Polka 6 hrs, Sp one hr wkly. ■ G. LaMeyer, gen mgr. ■ Rates: Same as AM.

Lynnville

WEAI(FM)—Nov 15, 1989: 107.1 mhz; 6 kw. Ant 328 ft. TL: N39 37 16 W90 15 28. Stereo. Hrs opn: 5 AM-midnight. Box 1180, E. Old State Rd., Jacksonville (62651). (217) 245-7171; (217) 243-2800. FAX: (217) 245-7171, ext. 56. Licensee: Jerdon Broadcasting. Wash atty: Kaye, Scholer, Fierman, Hays & Handler. Format: Classic hits. News staff 3; news progmg 6 hrs wkly. Target aud: 20-40; young adults. ■ Jerry Symons, vp & gen mgr; Don Hamilton, vp & gen sls mgr; Richard Smith, prom dir; Tim Thomson, progmg dir; Gary Scott, news dir; Perry Brown, pub affrs dir; Terry Poe, chief engr. ■ Rates: $35; 28; 35; 25.

Macomb

***WIUM(FM)**—May 23, 1956: 91.3 mhz; 50 kw. Ant 485 ft. TL: N40 25 40 W90 40 58. Stereo. Hrs opn: 24. 429 Memorial Hall, Western Illinois Univ. (61455). (309) 298-2424; (309) 298-1873. FAX: (309) 298-2133. Licensee: Western Illinois Univ. Net: NPR, APR; Ill. Pub. Wash atty: Cohn & Marks. Format: Class, news. News staff 2; news progmg 45 hrs wkly. Target aud: General. Spec prog: Folk/blues 7 hrs, jazz 5 hrs wkly. ■ Dorie Gain, gen mgr; Ken Thermon, opns mgr; Debra Miller, dev dir; Julie Stacker (asst), prom mgr; Jeff Holtz, mus dir; William Wheelhouse, news dir; Don Johnson, pub affrs dir; James Sticklen, chief engr.

***WIUS(FM)**—Feb 1, 1982: 88.3 mhz; 120 w. Ant 83 ft. TL: N40 27 47 W90 41 00. Stereo. Memorial Hall 307, Western Ill. Univ. (61455). (309) 298-3218. Licensee: Western Illinois Univ. Wash atty: Cohns & Marks. Format: Progsv new music. News progmg 2 hrs wkly. Target aud: 18-30. Spec prog: Black 16 hrs wkly. ■ Rebecca Stekl, pres & stn mgr; Ken Thermon, progmg dir.

WJEQ(FM)—February 1983: 102.7 mhz; 25 kw. Ant 269 ft. TL: N40 29 00 W90 38 19. Stereo. 1506 E. Jackson St. (61455). (309) 833-2121. FAX: (309) 836-3291. Licensee: Central Illinois Broadcasting (acq 6-14-89). Net: AP; Ill. News Net. Format: Classic Rock. News staff one; news progmg 10 hrs wkly. Target aud: 25-54. ■ Bruce Foster, pres; Nancy Foster, gen mgr; Cyndi Helling, opns mgr; Mark Bretsch, gen sls mgr; Chris Smith, progmg dir & mus dir; Bill Horrell, news dir; Jon Symmonds, chief engr. ■ Rates: $15; 15; 15; 10.

WKAI(FM)—Listing follows WLRB(AM).

WLRB(AM)—July 4, 1947: 1510 khz; 1 kw-D. TL: N40 29 50 W90 40 30. Box 250, 119 W. Carroll (61455). Licensee: Sharp Broadcasting Co. (acq 1985). Net: ABC; INN, Brownfield. Format: Country. News staff 2; news progmg 9 hrs wkly. Target aud: General. Spec prog: Farm 6 hrs wkly. ■ Don Sharp, gen mgr & gen sls mgr; Rick Bulger, opns mgr; Becky Weaver, natl sls mgr; Tim Crowley, news dir. ■ Rates: $20; 20; 20; 14.50.

WKAI(FM)—Co-owned with WLRB(AM). June 6, 1966: 100.1 mhz; 3.08 kw. Ant 463 ft. TL: N40 26 57 W90 42 22. Stereo. Hrs opn: 24. (309) 833-5561. (Acq 9-27-85; $175,000; FTR 8-12-85). Net: ABC/D; Brownfield. Format: CHR. News staff 2; news progmg 5 hrs wkly. Target aud: 18-49. ■ Don Sharp, pres; Rick Bulger, progmg dir & mus dir.

Mahomet

WHZT(FM)—Dec 15, 1990: 105.9 mhz; 1.25 kw. Ant 512 ft. TL: N40 13 27 W88 17 56. Suite 205, 313 N. Mattis, Champaign (61821). (217) 355-1059. FAX: (217) 355-8466. Licensee: Adlai Stevenson IV (acq 12-30-92; $225,000; FTR 2-1-93). Net: SMN. Format: CHR. ■ Doug Jean, gen mgr; Guy Webb, opns mgr; Greg Sutter, progmg dir.

Marion

WDDD(AM)—See Johnston City.

WDDD-FM—Nov 22, 1970: 107.3 mhz; 50 kw. Ant 500 ft. TL: N37 45 15 W88 56 05. Stereo. Hrs opn: 24. Box 127, One Broadcast Center, (62959). (618) 997-8123. Licensee: 3-D Communications Corp. Net: NBC. Format: Country. News staff 3; news progmg 10 hrs wkly. Target aud: 25 plus. ■ Dutch Doelitzsch, pres, gen mgr, progmg dir & chief engr; Jerry Crouse, stn mgr & gen sls mgr; Pat Benton, opns mgr; Tracy McSherry, mus dir; Steve Land, Ken Smith (sports), news dirs.

WGGH(AM)—Sept 24, 1949: 1150 khz; 5 kw-D, DA. TL: N37 43 47 W88 53 44. Box 340, Old Rt. 13 E. (62959). (618) 993-8102; (618) 997-2307. Licensee: Vine Broadcasting Inc. (acq 4-7-92; $380,000; FTR 6-09-92). Format: Christian. Spec prog: Farm 2 hrs wkly. ■ Johnny Gomaz, pres; Elaine Gomez, gen mgr, prom mgr & progmg mgr; Marcia Raubach, gen sls mgr; Steve Sine, news dir.

Marseilles

WKOT(FM)—March 1992: 96.5 mhz; 3 kw. Ant 328 ft. TL: N41 18 40 W88 49 07. Stereo. Hrs opn: 24. 3000 N. Columbus, Ottawa (61350); 32401 S. Rt. 53, Wilmington (60481). (815) 434-4000; (815) 476-5855. FAX: (815) 434-4055; (815) 476-1007. Licensee: Barden Broadcasting of Coal City Inc. (acq 1-30-90; $30,000; FTR 3-5-90). Net: SMN. Format: Oldies. News staff one; news progmg 8 hrs wkly. Target aud: 35-54. ■ Don H. Barden, pres; Ken Kramer, vp; Ralph Sherman, gen mgr & gen sls mgr; Pat Bridges, stn mgr & natl sls mgr; Jon Knepper, opns mgr & rgnl sls mgr; Chris Johnson, news dir; Art Reis, chief engr.

Marshall

WMMC(FM)—Oct 2 1989: 105.9 mhz; 2.8 kw. Ant 338 ft. TL: N39 21 38 W 87 47 31 (CP: 3.3 kw, ant 295 ft.). Stereo. Hrs opn: 20. Stn currently dark. Box 10 (62441). Licensee: Illini Broadcasting Inc. (acq 3-9-93; $3,100; FTR 3-29-93). ■ Joyce McDaniel, pres, gen mgr & progmg dir; John McDaniel, gen sls mgr & chief engr.

Mattoon

WKJR(FM)—(Sullivan). Dec 19, 1974: 106.3 mhz; 7.3 kw. Ant 312 ft. TL: N39 37 49 W88 30 28 (CP: 9.5 kw, ant 528 ft.). Stereo. Rt 2, Box 199 (61951). (217) 728-2028. FAX: (217) 728-2028. Licensee: Superior Broadcasting Inc. (acq 11-15-82; $310,000; FTR 11-15-82). Net: CNN, Unistar, ABC/D; Brownfield. Format: Country. Target aud: 25-54. ■ Jay Martin, pres & gen mgr; Tracey Greathouse, progmg dir & news dir; John Sullivan, chief engr.

WLBH(AM)—Nov 26, 1946: 1170 khz; 5 kw-D, DA. TL: N39 31 05 W88 33 48. Hrs opn: 6 AM-7 PM. Box 1848, N. Rt. 45 (2 miles) (61938-1848). (217) 234-6464; (217) 345-2526. FAX: (217) 234-6019. Licensee: Mattoon Broadcasting Co. Group owner: J.R. Livesay Group. Net: UPI. Rep: Katz & Powell. Format: Farm, news/talk, C&W. News staff 2; news progmg 20 hrs wkly. Target aud: General. Spec prog: Jazz one hr, gospel 5 hrs, relg 5 hrs wkly. ■ J.R. Livesay, chmn; J.R. Livesay II, pres & gen mgr; Pat Martin, natl sls mgr; Marc Nichols, news dir & pub affrs dir. ■ Rates: $46; 34; 46; na.

WLBH-FM—Aug 1949: 96.9 mhz; 50 kw. Ant 500 ft. TL: N39 31 02 W88 22 13. Stereo. Hrs opn: 5:45 AM-midnight. Prog sep from AM. Format: Btfl mus, news, big band. News progmg 18 hrs wkly. Spec prog: Farm 9 hrs wkly. ■ Rates: $46; 34; 46; 22.

***WLKL(FM)**—Jan 20, 1975: 89.9 mhz; 1.3 kw. Ant 203 ft. TL: N39 25 07 W88 22 55. Stereo. 5001 Lakeland Blvd. (61938). (217) 235-3231. FAX: (217) 258-6459. Licensee: Community College District 517 Lake Land College. Format: Adult contemp, rock. ■ Ken Beno, gen mgr; Carroll Livesay, chief engr.

WMCI(FM)—Aug 24, 1989: 101.3 mhz; 3 kw. Ant 318 ft. TL: N39 31 39 W88 21 23 (CP: 6 kw). Stereo. Hrs opn: 24. Box 789, Suite 201, 1632 Broadway Ave. (61938). (217) 235-5624. FAX: (217) 235-6624. Licensee: The Cromwell Group Inc of Illinois. Group owner: The Cromwell Group Inc. Net: MBS. Wash atty: Pepper & Corrazini. Format: Country. News staff one; news progmg 20 hrs wkly. Target aud: 25-54. Spec prog: Farm 5 hrs wkly. ■ Bayard H. Walters, pres; Terry Weinacht, gen mgr; Jeff Owens, gen sls mgr; Renee Fonner, prom dir; Bub McCullough, progmg dir & mus dir; Jo Gordon, asst mus dir; Andy Dahl, news dir & pub affrs dir; Steve Hamm, chief engr. ■ Rates: $16; 12; 14; 6.

McLeansboro

WMCL(AM)—Jan 26, 1968: 1060 khz; 2.5 kw-D, DA. TL: N38 06 16 W88 33 48. Box 46 A, Rt. 1, Hwy. 142 W. (62859). (618) 643-2311. FAX: (618) 643-3299. Licensee: Liberty Radio Inc. (group owner; acq 5-1-92; grpsl; FTR 5-25-92). Net: Unistar. Format: Country. News staff one; news progmg 14 hrs wkly. Target aud: 25-54; agricultural community. ■ James Glassman, pres; T. Christopher Gullett, vp & gen mgr; Danny Johnson, progmg dir; Duane Kubicki, news dir; Jeff Oestreich, chief engr. ■ Rates: $14; 14; 14; na.

Mendota

WGLC(AM)—Sept 1, 1964: 1090 khz; 250 w-D. TL: N41 34 58 W89 07 33. Box 88, 4162 E. Third Rd. (61342). (815) 539-6751. FAX: (815) 539-5956. Licensee: Mendota Broadcasting Inc. Group owner: Studstill Broadcasting (acq 4-8-88). Net: ABC/D. Format: Country. News staff one. Target aud: 30-55. Spec prog: Farm 5 hrs wkly. ■ Owen L. Studstill, pres; Cole Studstill, gen mgr; Judy Miller, gen sls mgr; Lee Studstill, progmg dir; Larry Psonak, news dir; Del Dayton, chief engr.

WGLC-FM—Sept 1, 1965: 100.1 mhz; 6 kw. Ant 328 ft. TL: N41 32 16 W89 06 25. Stereo. Hrs opn: 24. Dups AM 100%. Wash atty: Booth, Freret & Imlay.

Metropolis

WMOK(AM)—Feb 4, 1951: 920 khz; 1 kw-D, 73 w-N. TL: N37 09 13 W88 42 30. Stereo. Hrs opn: 17. Box 720, 339 Fairgrounds Rd. (62960). (618) 524-9209. Licensee: WMOK Inc. (acq 2-82; $204,000; FTR 2-11-82). Format: Country. News staff one. Target aud: General. Spec prog: Relg 5 hrs wkly. ■ Gary Kidd, pres, gen mgr & gen sls mgr; Michele Kidd, stn mgr; Greg Leath, prom dir; Steve Bunyard, progmg dir & mus dir; Ken Thurmond, news dir; Todd Bryant, pub affrs dir; Joe Bellis, chief engr.

WREZ(FM)—Co-owned with WMOK(AM). Dec 12, 1988: 105.5 mhz; 6 kw. Ant 328 ft. TL: N37 10 25 W88 42 29. Stereo. Hrs opn: 24. Prog sep from AM. Box 7501, Paducah, KY (42002). (618) 524-1055; (502) 442-1055. Format: Light adult contemp. Target aud: 25-54. ■ Greg Leath, opns dir, progmg dir & mus dir.

WRIK-FM—July 11, 1984: 98.3 mhz; 1.3 kw. Ant 456 ft. TL: N37 08 32 W88 39 01. Stereo. Box 32 (62960); Box 9105, Paducah, KY (42002-9105). (618) 524-3698. FAX: (618) 564-3202. Licensee: Sun Media Inc. Format: CHR with AOR. ■ Samuel K. Stratemeyer, pres & gen mgr; Craig Bradley, progmg dir, mus dir & chief engr.

Moline

WLLR(AM)—1946: 1230 khz; 1 kw-U. TL: N41 28 54 W90 31 49. Hrs opn: 24. Corp East, Suite 12, 1910 E. Kimberly Rd., Davenport, IA (52807). (309) 764-6727; (319) 355-5331. FAX: (319) 359-8524. Licensee: Mississippi Valley Broadcasting Inc. Group owner: Sconnix Broadcasting Co. (acq 10-1-84; $400,000; FTR 7-23-84). Rep: Katz. Format: Country. News staff one; news progmg 6 hrs wkly. Target aud: 25-54; upscale/comtemporary. Spec prog: Pub affrs 4 hrs, farm one hr wkly, sports. ■ Larry R. Rosmilso, vp & gen mgr; Joanne Brown, opns mgr; Scott Bitting, gen sls mgr; Jim O'Hara, prom mgr & progmg dir; Ron Evans, mus dir; Nick Linborg, news dir; Jeff Cantrill, chief engr. ■ Rates: $75; 60; 65; 35.

WXLP(FM)—Nov 22, 1970: 96.9 mhz; 50 kw. Ant 499 ft. TL: N41 20 16 W90 22 46. Stereo. 1229 Brady St., Davenport, IA (52803). (319) 326-2541. FAX: (319) 326-1819. Licensee: Goodrich Broadcasting Inc. (group owner; acq 4-9-87). Net: Unistar. Rep: Katz. Format: AOR. News progmg 2 hrs wkly. Target aud: 18-49. ■ Bob Goodrich, pres; David Bevins, gen mgr; Steve Watt, gen sls mgr; Dan Burich, prom dir; Ray Sherman, progmg dir; Steve Gunner, mus dir; Larry Timmons, chief engr.

Monee

***WGNR(FM)**—Not on air, target date unknown: 88.9 mhz. 820 N. La Salle Dr., Chicago (60610). Licensee: The Moody Bible Institute of Chicago (group owner). ■ Joseph M. Stowell, CEO & pres; Dennis Shere, sr vp; Robert Neff, vp; J. Scott Keegan, gen mgr, stn mgr & progmg dir; Scott Curtis, mus dir; James Klopfenstein, chief engr.

Monmouth

WRAM(AM)—May 1957: 1330 khz; 1 kw-D, 50 w-N, DA-2. TL: N40 56 59 W90 34 19. Hrs opn: 6 AM-6 PM. Box 885, 55 Public Square (61462). (309) 734-9452; (309) 734-2111. FAX: (309) 734-3276. Licensee: KCD Enterprises Inc. (acq 2-1-86; $325,000; FTR 12-2-85). Net: CBS; Tribune, Ill. News Net. Wash atty: Lauren Colby. Format: Country. News staff 3; news progmg 20 hrs wkly. Target aud: General; adult, mature. Spec prog: Farm 18 hrs wkly. ■ Kevin Potter, pres & gen mgr; Dan Nolan, opns mgr & progmg dir; Pat Terpening, gen sls mgr; Dorea Potter, prom mgr; Tom Peterson, mus dir; Randy Van, news dir; Jim Lee, pub affrs dir; Jim Davies, chief engr. ■ Rates: $13; 13; 13; na.

WMOI(FM)—Co-owned with WRAM. Dec 6, 1967: 97.7 mhz; 3.36 kw. Ant 439 ft. TL: N40 53 25 W90 36 31. Stereo. Hrs opn: 5:30 AM-10 PM. Prog sep from AM. (Acq 7-27-82). Format: Adult contemp. Spec prog: Farm 8 hrs wkly. ■ Jim Lee, mus dir. ■ Rates: $13; 13; 13; 11.

Monticello

WCZQ(FM)—Jan 18, 1972: 105.5 mhz; 3 kw. Ant 300 ft. TL: N40 02 52 W88 34 22. Stereo. Hrs opn: 24. Box 105 (61856). (217) 762-2588. FAX: (217) 762-2589. Licensee: Mumbles Corp. (acq 4-11-91; $200,000; FTR 5-6-91). Net: Unistar. Rep: Torbet. Format: Country. Target aud: 25-45; upscale suburban. Spec prog: Farm 11 hrs wkly. ■ Bernard Brobst, gen mgr; John Rhea, stn mgr; Roy J. Kleven, chief engr.

Morris

WCFL(FM)—Listing follows WCSJ(AM).

WCSJ(AM)—Jan 15, 1964: 1550 khz; 250 w-D, 6 w-N. TL: N41 20 20 W88 25 20. Hrs opn: 24. M.B.T.C., Suite 403, 1802 N. Division St. (60450). (815) 942-0022. FAX: (815) 942-3346. Licensee: Robert J. Maccini, receiver. Group owner: M.M. Group Inc. (acq 4-13-93; with co-located FM). Net: MBS, ABC; Tribune, Ill. Farm. Format: Adult contemp, news, info. News staff 2; news progmg 20 hrs wkly. Target aud: 25 plus; community oriented. Spec prog: Farm 20 hrs wkly. ■ Bill Badurski, pres & gen mgr; Randy Ness, vp progmg; Lou Anne Lenzie, progmg dir & mus dir; Jenny Glick, news dir.

WCFL(FM)—Co-owned with WCSJ(AM). April 16, 1990: 104.7 mhz; 50 kw. Ant 496 ft. TL: N41 21 17 W88 29 55. Stereo. Hrs opn: 24. Prog sep from AM. (815) 942-1048. Format: Oldies-60s & 70s only. News progmg 3 hrs wkly. Target aud: 25-54; white/blue collar professionals who love the 60s & 70s. Spec prog: Farm 15 hrs wkly. ■ Stacy Karonis, prom dir; Rafe Sampson, progmg dir; Len O'Kelly, mus dir; Randy Ness, engrg mgr.

WJDK(FM)—Not on air, target date unknown: 103.1 mhz; 3 kw. Ant 328 ft. TL: N41 17 35 W88 20 04. 109 Sherwood Place (60450). Licensee: DMR Media Inc.

Morrison

WZZT(FM)—Apr 10, 1991: 95.1 mhz; 3 kw. Ant 328 ft. TL: N41 50 16 W89 55 29. Box 658, Sterling (61081). (815) 772-3995. FAX: (815) 625-6940. Licensee: WZZT Inc. (acq 3-20-92; $349,000; FTR 4-13-92). Format: Adult contemp. ■ Jack Stower, gen mgr & opns mgr; Casey Kelly, gen sls mgr.

Morton

WTAZ(FM)—Nov 28, 1976: 102.3 mhz; 6 kw. Ant 300 ft. TL: N40 38 27 W89 24 33. Hrs opn: 24. 332 Detroit Ave. (61550). (309) 263-0102; (309) 693-0102. FAX: (309) 263-2915. Licensee: Morton-Washington Broadcasting Co. Net: ABC TalkRadio, NBC Talknet, Daynet, MBS. Rep: Katz & Powell. Wash atty: Arent, Fox, Kintner, Plotkin & Kahn. Format: Talk, sports, news. News staff one; news progmg 3 hrs wkly. Target aud: 18 plus; active, affluent males. Spec prog: Relg 3 hrs wkly. ■ Richard J. Parker, opns mgr & progmg dir; Wayne R. Ulrich, gen sls mgr; Richard A. Draeger, news dir; Neil Burk, chief engr. ■ Rates: $14; 12; 14; 12.

Mt. Carmel

WRBT(FM)—Listing follows WYER(AM).

***WVJC(FM)**—July 23, 1973: 89.1 mhz; 50 kw. Ant 330 ft. TL: N38 26 29 W87 45 26. Stereo. Hrs opn: 7 AM-10 PM. 2200 College Dr. (62863). (618) 262-8989; (618) 262-8641, ext. 3209. FAX: (618) 262-7317. Licensee: Illinois Eastern Community Colleges. Net: AP. Wash atty: Arent, Fox, Kintner, Plotkin & Kahn. Format: Div, educ, rock. Target aud: General. ■ James L. Cox, gen mgr; Robert Effland, chief engr.

WYER(AM)—Dec 1, 1948: 1360 khz; 500 w-D, 20 w-N. TL: N38 26 58 W87 46 12. Hrs opn: 5 AM- midnight. Box 490, N. Cherry St. (62863). (618) 263-6567. FAX: (618) 263-3220. Licensee: River Valley Radio Inc. (acq 6-19-89; with co-located FM; FTR 6-5-89). Net: AP, NBC. Format: Country. News staff 2. Target aud: General. Spec prog: Farm 5 hrs wkly. ■ Scott J. Fenneman, pres, gen mgr & sls dir; Mary Jo Wagener, opns mgr; Charles Wilson III, chief engr.

WRBT(FM)—Co-owned with WYER(AM). Nov 28, 1960: 94.9 mhz; 50 kw. Ant 425 ft. TL: N38 23 57 W87 47 18. Stereo. Prog sep from AM. Suite 202, 220 N.W. 4th St., Evansville, IN (47708). (812) 422-0223. Format: Classic rock. Target aud: 18-49.

Mount Morris

WSEY(FM)—Not on air, target date unknown: 95.7 mhz; 2.7 kw. Ant 495 ft. TL: N42 04 09 W89 27 01. Box 9089 Downers Grove (60515). Licensee: American Family Association Inc. (acq 11-5-93; $10,000; FTR 11-29-93).

Mt. Vernon

WMIX(AM)—1947: 940 khz; 5 kw-D, 1.5 kw-N, DA-2. TL: N38 21 15 W89 00 29. Hrs opn: 24. Box 1508, 3501 Broadway (62864). (618) 242-3500. FAX: (618) 242-4444. Licensee: Withers Broadcasting Co. of Illinois. Group owner: Withers Broadcasting Co. (acq 5-30-73). Net: MBS, Westwood One. Rep: D & R Radio. Format: Adult contemp, talk. News staff 2; news progmg 15 hrs wkly. Target aud: 25 plus. Spec prog: Farm 18 hrs wkly. ■ W. Russell Withers Jr., pres; Lee Crawford, gen mgr; Brad Meyer, sls dir; Tom Sheldon, progmg dir; Doug Schmidt, mus dir; Tom Marlow, news dir; Kay Hamil, pub affrs dir; Kevin Potter, chief engr. ■ Rates: $30; 30; 30; 25.

WMIX-FM—1946: 94.1 mhz; 50 kw. Ant 550 ft. TL: N38 22 14 W88 55 20. Stereo. Hrs opn: 24. Prog sep from AM. Net: Unistar, MBS. Rep: D & R Radio. Format: C&W. Spec prog: Farm 12 hrs wkly. ■ Doug Schmidt, progmg dir; Tom Marlow, pub affrs dir. ■ Rates: Same as AM.

Mt. Zion

WXFM(FM)—October 1984: 99.3 mhz; 1.15 kw. Ant 495 ft. TL: N39 48 35 W88 59 31. Stereo. 120 Wildwood (62549). (217) 864-4141. Licensee: Technicom Inc. Format: Adult popular. News progmg 5 hrs wkly. Target aud: Free spending, affluent adults. ■ Mary Ellen Burns, pres & gen mgr; Linda Davis, gen sls mgr; Jack Strong, chief engr. ■ Rates: $25; 25; 25; 25.

Murphysboro

WINI(AM)—Sept 15, 1954: 1420 khz; 420 w-D, 500 w-N, DA-N. TL: N37 45 30 W89 14 02. Hrs opn: 5:30 AM-11 PM. 1601 N. 14th St. (62966); 308 W. Walnut St., Carbondale (62901). (618) 684-2128; (618) 529-5763. Licensee: Radio Station WINI (acq 7-27-68). Net: Sun, UPI. Wash atty: Eugene T. Smith. Format: News/talk. News progmg 22 hrs wkly. Target aud: 25-59. Spec prog: Relg 6 hrs wkly. ■ Nancy Engel, opns mgr & progmg mgr; Duane Crites, gen sls mgr; Dale W. Adkins, chief engr.

WTAO(FM)—August 1972: 105.1 mhz; 25 kw. Ant 308 ft. TL: N37 45 15 W89 19 14. Stereo. Hrs opn: 24. Box 1477, Carbondale (62903); Rt. 5, Fiddlers Ridge Rd., Murphysboro (92966). (618) 687-1779. FAX: (618) 687-3933. Licensee: Liberty Radio Inc. (group owner; acq 5-1-92; grpsl; FTR 5-25-92). Net: Unistar. Rep: Christal. Format: Rock. News progmg 3 hrs wkly. Target aud: 18-49. ■ James Glassman, pres; T. Christopher Gullett, vp, gen mgr & gen sls mgr; Tom Miller, opns mgr; Lester St. James, progmg dir & mus dir; Jeff Oestreich, chief engr. ■ Rates: $18.25; 18.25; 18.25; 10.50.

Naperville

WBIG(AM)—See Aurora.

WKKD-FM—See Aurora.

***WONC(FM)**—July 1, 1968: 89.1 mhz; 3.9 kw. Ant 98 ft. TL: N41 46 45 W88 08 25. Stereo. Hrs opn: 6 AM-2 AM (Mon-Fri), 8 AM-2 AM (Sat-Sun). Box 3063, 30 N. Brainard St. (60566-7063). (708) 420-3437. FAX: (708) 420-6206. Licensee: North Central College. Format: Rock (AOR). Target aud: General. Spec prog: Relg 4 hrs wkly. ■ John Madormo, gen mgr; Dave Monahan, opns mgr; Andi Leisman, prom dir; Steve Rogers, progmg dir; Keith Carlson, mus dir; Donna Moeller, asst mus dir; Chad Mitchell, news dir; Eric Zapchenk, pub affrs dir; John Valenta, chief engr.

Nashville

WNSR(FM)—Not on air, target date unknown: 104.7 mhz; 3 kw. Ant 328 ft. TL: N38 20 38 W89 20 59. Licensee: Dana K. Withers (acq 1-16-92; $60,000; FTR 2-10-92).

Newton

WIKK(FM)—May 4, 1992: 103.5 mhz; 25 kw. Ant 328 ft. TL: N38 59 23 W88 11 19. Stereo. Hrs opn: 5 AM-midnight. Box 304, Hwy. 33 W., Newton (62448). (618) 783-8000. FAX: (618) 783-4040. Licensee: S. Kent Lankford. Net: MBS. Format: Soft country, light AC, oldies. News staff one; news progmg 15 hrs wkly. Target aud: 25-54. ■ S. Kent Lankford, CEO, mktg mgr & chief engr; Mike Brady, stn mgr, gen sls mgr, prom mgr & adv mgr; Chris Stevens, mus dir; April Burry, news dir. ■ Rates: $12; 12; 12; 12.

Normal

WBNQ(FM)—See Bloomington.

***WGLT(FM)**—Feb 4, 1966: 89.1 mhz; 2.3 kw. Ant 141 ft. TL: N40 30 33 W89 00 00 (CP: 25 kw, ant 377 ft., TL: N40 28 46 W89 03 12). Stereo. Hrs opn: 18. 8910 Illinois State University (61790-8910). (309) 438-2255. FAX: (309) 438-7870. Licensee: Illinois State University. Net: NPR. Format: Jazz, blues, pub affrs. News staff 3; news progmg 40 hrs wkly. Target aud: 25-44. ■ Bruce Bergethon, gen mgr; Kathryn Carter, dev dir; Chuck Miller, progmg dir; Marke Boon, mus dir; Mike McCurdy, news dir.

WIHN(FM)—Dec 21, 1973: 96.7 mhz; 6 kw. Ant 410 ft. TL: N40 28 34 W89 02 02. Stereo. Hrs opn: 24. Box 610, Bloomington (61702-0610); 1309 S. Center St. (61761). (309) 888-4496. FAX: (309) 452-9677. Licensee: Bell-Mason Communications (acq 10-1-83; $700,000; FTR 10-3-83). Net: ABC; Ill. News Net. Rep: Christal. Wash atty: Putbrese, Hunsaker, Ruddy. Format: Oldies. News staff one; news progmg 9 hrs wkly. Target aud: 25-54. ■ Edwin R. Neaves, gen mgr & stn mgr; Christine Knight, gen sls mgr; John Sparx, prom mgr; Pat Walston, progmg dir; Tony Jordan, news dir & chief engr. ■ Rates: $27; 29; 27; 28.

Norris City

***WZJW(FM)**—Not on air, target date unknown: 90.1 mhz; 19 kw-V. Ant 295 ft. TL: N37 56 17 W88 24 03. Hrs opn: Stn currently dark. 905 High St., Eldorado (62930). Licensee: Voice of Calvary Ministries.

Oak Park

WPNA(AM)—Oct 7, 1950: 1490 khz; 1 kw-U. TL: N41 52 52 W87 47 38. Hrs opn: 24. Box 3878 (60303); 408 S. Oak Park Ave. (60302). (708) 848-8980; (708) 524-9762. FAX: (708) 848-9220. Licensee: Alliance Communications Inc. (acq 5-1-87). Format: Ethnic, Polish. News progmg one hr wkly. Target aud: General. Spec prog: Gospel 9 hrs, relg one hr, Sp 10 hrs, Irish 7 hrs, Ukranian 4 hrs, Lithuanian 4 hrs, Arabic 2 hrs, blues 8 hrs wkly. ■ Edward J. Moskal, pres; Margaret Sas, gen mgr; Bob Suwalski, chief opns; Jerry Obrecki, gen sls mgr; Len Petrulis, news dir; David Dybas, chief engr. ■ Rates: $38; 36; 38; 32.

WVAZ(FM)—Oct 17, 1950: 102.7 mhz; 6 kw. Ant 1,170 ft. TL: N41 53 56 W87 37 23 (CP: 9 kw). Stereo. Hrs opn: 24. Suite 250, 800 S. Wells St., Chicago (60607). (312) 360-9000. FAX: (312) 360-9070. Licensee: Broadcasting Partners Inc. (acq 6-10-88; grpsl; FTR 6-20-88). Net: UPI. Rep: Banner. Format: Black adult contemp. News staff 2; news progmg one hr wkly. Target aud: 25-54; Black adults. Spec prog: Gospel 4 hrs, pub affrs 2 hrs wkly. ■ Perry L. Lewis, Lee Simonson (vice), chrs; Barry Mayo, pres & gen mgr; Nathan W. Pearson Jr., CFO; Ron Atkins, opns mgr; Chris Wilson, gen sls mgr; Morris Freeman, natl sls mgr; Kristin Hartman (local), rgnl sls mgr; Merry Green, prom mgr; Maxx Myrick, mus dir; John Bortowski, chief engr.

Oglesby

WZLC(FM)—February 1993: 102.1 mhz; 1.35 kw. TL: N41 18 05 W88 57 11. 726 First St., La Salle (61301). (815) 539-6751. FAX: (815) 224-3162. Licensee: Doris A. Studstill. Group owner: Studstill Broadcasting. Format: Country. ■ Doris A. Studstill, gen mgr; Tyler Haze, progmg dir; Larry Psonac, news dir.

Olney

***WPTH(FM)**—July 1992: 88.1 mhz; 133 w. Ant 203 ft. TL: N38 41 50 W88 02 15. 817 Orchard Dr. (62450). (618) 863-2765. Licensee: Olney Voice of Christian Faith Inc. Format: Christian talk, music. ■ Dr. Thomas E. Benson, pres & gen mgr; Ron James, vp.

WSEI(FM)—Listing follows WVLN(AM).

***WUSI(FM)**—Nov. 1, 1992. 90.3 mhz; 25 kw. Ant 472 ft. TL: N38 50 18 W88 07 46. Hrs opn: 5 AM-1 AM. Box 430, (62450); Southern Illinois Univ. Communications Bldg., Rm. 1048, Carbondale (62901). (618) 754-3335. FAX: (618) 453-6186. Licensee: Southern Illinois Univ. (group owner). Net: NPR, APR. Wash atty: Cohn & Marks. Format: Class, jazz, news. News progmg 36 hrs wkly. Target aud: 35-64; highly educated, upper income, socially conscious. Spec prog: Big Band 3 hrs, opera 4 hrs, new age 4 hrs, Broadway one hr wkly. ■ Lee O'Brian, gen mgr; Jerri Uffelman, prom mgr; Jerry Kline, chief engr.

WVLN(AM)—Nov 11, 1947: 740 khz; 250 w-D, 7 w-N. TL: N38 42 00 W88 04 53. Box L, Radio Tower Rd. (62450). (618) 393-2156. FAX: (618) 392-4536. Licensee: V.L.N. Broadcasting Inc. Group owner: Key Broadcasting Inc. (acq 7-21-87; $1,120,000 with co-located FM; FTR 6-8-87). Net: CNN; Ill. Farm, Hometown Radio. Rep: Rgnl Reps. Format: Country. News staff one; news progmg 30 hrs wkly. Spec prog: Farm 10 hrs wkly. ■ Terry E. Forcht, pres; Mike Lowe, gen mgr, vp sls & vp adv; Ed Ballinger, vp prom; Mike Shipman, mus dir; Mark Weiler, news dir; Steve Hamm, chief engr. ■ Rates: $20; 18; 20; 16.

WSEI(FM)—Co-owned with WVLN(AM). 1953: 92.9 mhz; 50 kw. Ant 552 ft. TL: N38 42 00 W88 04 49. Stereo. Prog sep from AM. Format: Adult contemp. News staff one; news progmg 30 hrs wkly. Target aud: 25-54. ■ Mike Lowe, Linda Loudermelt, vps; Mike Lowe, stn mgr; Ed Ballinger, opns dir; Doug Stewart, news dir; Marla Galloway, pub affrs dir. ■ Rates: Same as AM.

Ottawa

WCMY(AM)—March 5, 1952: 1430 khz; 500 w-D, 38 w-N. TL: N41 20 53 W88 48 15. Hrs opn: 24. 216 W. Lafayette (61350). (815) 434-6050. Licensee: Virginia Broadcasting Corp. Net: AP, MBS. Format: Adult contemp, news/talk. News staff 3; news progmg 35 hrs wkly. Target aud: 25 plus. Spec prog: Farm 9 hrs wkly. ■ Richard E. Fister, pres; Dan Parker, vp & gen mgr; Eve Mazon, gen sls mgr; Jay LeSeure, progmg dir; Jim French, news dir. ■ Rates: $24.50; 22.50; 22.50; 21.50.

WRKX(FM)—Co-owned with WCMY(AM). Sept 1, 1964: 95.3 mhz; 3 kw. Ant 200 ft. TL: N41 23 03 W88 51 15. Stereo. Net: SMN. Format: Adult contemp. ■ Rates: Same as AM.

Pana

WXKO-FM—May 5, 1977: 100.9 mhz; 6 kw. Ant 290 ft. TL: N39 22 19 W89 04 51. Stereo. Hrs opn: 24. Box 465 (62557). (217) 562-3949. FAX: (217) 562-3945. Licensee: Southeastern Video Inc. Group owner: Studstill Broadcasting (acq 1-31-89; $150,000; FTR 2-13-89). Net: SMN. Wash atty: Julian Freret. Format: Country. News staff one; news progmg 6 hrs wkly. Target aud: 25-54; general. ■ Lamar Studstill, pres; Lee Studstill, gen mgr; Cole Studstill, stn mgr & prom mgr; Dee Carroll, gen sls mgr; Cole Weathers, progmg dir & mus dir; Todd Fultz, news dir; Del Dayton, chief engr. ■ Rates: $7; 7; 7; 5.

Paris

WPRS(AM)—1951: 1440 khz; 1 kw-D, 250 w-N. TL: N39 36 21 W87 43 35. Stereo. Hrs opn: 24. Box 367 (61944). (217) 465-6336. FAX: (217) 466-1408. Licensee: Paris Broadcasting Corp. Net: ABC/E. Format: MOR. News staff one. Target aud: General. Spec prog: Farm 6 hrs wkly. ■ Adlai C. Ferguson Jr., pres; William J. Brown, gen mgr, gen sls mgr & progmg dir. ■ Rates: $18; 18; 18; 18.

WACF(FM)—Co-owned with WPRS(AM). 1952: 98.5 mhz; 50 kw. Ant 500 ft. TL: N39 36 21 W87 43 35. Stereo. Prog sep from AM. Format: C&W. News staff one; news progmg 14 hrs wkly. Target aud: 18-55 plus. ■ Rates: Same as AM.

Park Ridge

***WMTH(FM)**—May 22, 1960: 90.5 mhz; 100 w. Ant 103 ft. TL: N42 02 14 W87 51 30. 2601 W. Dempster St. (60068). (708) 692-8484; (708) 825-4484, ext. 4652. Licensee: Board of Education, School Dist. No. 207. Net: UPI. Format: Eclectic. Spec prog: Class 4 hrs, jazz 2 hrs wkly. ■ William R. Mitchell, gen mgr.

Paxton

WPXN(FM)—Oct 1, 1984: 104.9 mhz; 3 kw. Ant 298 ft. TL: N40 27 11 W88 06 11. Hrs opn: 5 AM-midnight. 361 N. Railroad Ave. (60957). (217) 379-4333. FAX: (217) 379-4304. Licensee: Paxton Broadcasting Corp. (acq 7-84). Net: ABC/D; Brownfield. Rep: Roslin. Wash atty: Borsari & Paxson. Format: Oldies. News staff one; news progmg 8 hrs wkly. Target aud: 25-49. Spec prog: Farm 10 hrs wkly. ■ Dan Daugherity, gen mgr & gen sls mgr; Joel Cluver, stn mgr; Kevin Scott, mus dir; Keith Ayers, news dir. ■ Rates: $8; 6; 6; 6.

Pekin

***WBNH(FM)**—January 1989: 88.5 mhz; 4.3 kw. Ant 524 ft. TL: N40 38 38 W89 32 38. Stereo. 700 S. Capital St. (61555). (309) 347-8850. FAX: (309) 346-8101. Licensee: Central Illinois Radio Fellowship Inc. Net: Moody. Wash atty: Southmayd & Simpson. Format: Relg. Target aud: General. ■ Bubie C. Goodman Jr, pres & gen mgr; Scott Krus, stn mgr; Donald L. Markley, chief engr.

***WCIC(FM)**—Nov 2, 1983: 91.5 mhz; 35 kw. Ant 338 ft. TL: N40 33 24 W89 34 04. Stereo. Hrs opn: 24. 3263 Court St. (61554). (309) 353-9191. FAX: (309) 353-1141. Licensee: Illinois Bible Institute. Group owner: Illinois Bible Institute Inc. Format: Educ, relg. News progmg 2 hrs wkly. Target aud: 25-49. ■ Ernest J. Moen, pres; Dave Brooks, stn mgr; Chuck Pryor, progmg dir & mus dir; Ron Bluhm, chief engr.

WGLO(FM)—Listing follows WVEL(AM).

WVEL(AM)—April 21, 1948: 1140 khz; 5 kw-D, 3.2 kw-CH. TL: N40 36 08 W89 37 32. 2400 W. Nebraska Ave., Peoria (61604); 28 S. Fourth St., Pekin (61554). (309) 673-9500; (309) 346-2134. Licensee: Lenk Broadcasting Co. Inc. Group owner: The Cromwell Group Inc. (acq 10-22-86; with co-located FM). Net: CBN. Format: Relg, Black. News staff one. Target aud: General. ■ Bayard H. Walters, pres; James E. MacFarlane, vp & gen mgr; Watt Harriston, chief engr.

WGLO(FM)—Co-owned with WVEL(AM). Nov 18, 1971: 95.5 mhz; 25 kw. Ant 620 ft. TL: N40 36 23 W89 32 20. Stereo. Prog sep from AM. Rep: D & R Radio. Format: Adult contemp, oldies. News staff 2. Target aud: 25-49. ■ Sue Thompson, gen sls mgr; Steve Larson, progmg dir.

WXCL-FM—1973: 104.9 mhz; 3 kw. Ant 328 ft. TL: N40 38 34 W89 32 28. Stereo. Box 180, Peoria (61650). (309) 685-5975. FAX: (309) 685-7150. Licensee: Kelly Communications Inc. (group owner). Net: Unistar. Rep: Banner. Format: Modern country. News staff 2. Target aud: 25-54. ■ Bill Early, vp & gen mgr; Joyce Powell, gen sls mgr; Dale Van Horn, progmg dir; Kimber Bennett, news dir; Neil Burke, chief engr.

Peoria

WBGE(FM)—November 1992: 92.3 mhz; 6 kw. Ant 148 ft. TL: N40 43 32 W89 33 52. 516 W. Main (61606). (309) 637-2923. FAX: (309) 688-9346. Licensee: B&G Broadcasting Inc. ■ Joyce Banks, pres; Garry Moore, gen mgr.

***WCBU(FM)**—January 1970: 89.9 mhz; 50 kw. Ant 650 ft. TL: N40 37 44 W89 34 12. Stereo. 1501 W. Bradley Ave. (61625). (309) 677-3690. FAX: (309) 677-3462. Licensee: Bradley Univ. Net: NPR. Format: Class, news. ■ Joel Hartman, gen mgr; Frank Thomas, stn mgr; Laura Garfinkel, opns mgr; Terry Solomonson, mus dir; Keith Turcot, chief engr.

***WECU(FM)**—Not on air, target date unknown: 88.5 mhz; 4.3 kw. Ant 495 ft. TL: N40 38 34 W89 32 38. 700 First National Bank Bldg. (61602). Licensee: William H. Christison (acq 3-10-92).

WGLO(FM)—See Pekin.

WIRL(AM)—1947: 1290 khz; 5 kw-U, DA-2. TL: N40 37 24 W89 35 27. Stereo. Box 3335 (61612); 22484 Grosenbach Rd., Washington (61571). (309) 694-6262. FAX: (309) 694-2233. Licensee: Community Service Radio Inc. (acq 4-30-92; grpsl). Net: ABC/E. Rep: Christal. Format: Adult contemp, news/talk, oldies. News staff one; news progmg 30 hrs wkly. Target aud: 25-54. ■ Jim Glassman, pres; Henry Baltanz, gen mgr; Lee Malcolm, prom mgr & progmg dir; Mike Throop, news dir; Mark Hill, chief engr.

WSWT(FM)—Co-owned with WIRL(AM). 1964: 106.9 mhz; 50 kw. Ant 480 ft. TL: N40 43 22 W89 30 40. Stereo. Prog sep from AM. Net: ABC/R. Format: Adult contemp. Target aud: 25-64. Spec prog: Relg 3 hrs wkly. ■ Randy Rundle, progmg dir.

WKZW(FM)—Listing follows WMBD(AM).

WMBD(AM)—1927: 1470 khz; 5 kw-U, DA-2. TL: N40 34 23 W89 32 04 (CP: TL: N40 34 22 W89 32 00). Stereo. Hrs opn: 24. 3131 N. University St. (61604). (309) 688-3131. FAX: (309) 686-8650. Licensee: Midwest Televi-

Illinois

sion Inc. (group owner; acq 7-60). Net: CBS. Rep: Katz. Wash atty: Covington & Burling. Format: Adult contemp/full svc. Spec prog: Farm 15 hrs wkly. ■ Gene C. Robinson, vp & gen mgr; Lindsay Wood Davis, stn mgr; Joell Estes, gen sls mgr; Greg Batton, progmg dir; Paul Baumgartner, chief engr. WMBD-TV affil. ■ Rates: $50; 40; 50; 40.

WKZW(FM)—Co-owned with WMBD(AM). 1947: 93.3 mhz; 41 kw. Ant 548 ft. TL: N40 38 07 W89 32 19. Stereo. Prog sep from AM. Rep: Katz. Format: CHR. ■ Scott Wheeler, progmg dir; Gene Stern, mus dir. ■ Rates: Same as AM.

WPEO(AM)—1946: 1020 khz; 1 kw-D. TL: N40 41 53 W89 31 31. 1708 Highview Rd. (61611); Box One (61650). (309) 698-9736. Licensee: Pinebrook Foundation Inc. (acq 1-6-70). Net: USA. Wash atty: Jones, Waldo, Holbrook & McDonough. Format: Relg. Target aud: 25 plus. ■ Richard T. Crawford, pres; Robert Ulrich, gen mgr; Linda Butler, opns mgr, prom mgr & pub affrs dir; Ken Smith, gen sls mgr; Neil Burk, chief engr. ■ Rates: $15; 15; 15; na.

WQEZ(FM)—See Chillicothe.

WSWT(FM)—Listing follows WIRL(AM).

WVEL(AM)—See Pekin.

WWCT(FM)—May 14, 1972: 105.7 mhz; 38 kw. Ant 581 ft. TL: N40 38 34 W89 32 28. Stereo. 1111 Main St. (61606). (309) 674-2000. FAX: (309) 676-8426. Licensee: Central Illinois Broadcasting Co. (acq 12-23-83). Net: NBC The Source. Rep: D & R Radio. Format: AOR. ■ Bruce T. Foster, pres & gen mgr; Michael Rea, gen sls mgr; Rob Seligmann, prom mgr; Rick Hirschmann, progmg dir; Jamie Markley, mus dir; John Lamb, news dir; Neil Burk, chief engr.

WXCL(AM)—Feb 8, 1960: 1350 khz; 1 kw-U, DA-2. TL: N40 35 41 W89 35 40. Box 180 (61650). (309) 685-5975. FAX: (309) 685-7150. Licensee: Kelly Communications Inc. (group owner; acq 11-86; $1.4 million with co-located FM; FTR 9-29-86). Net: ABC/D. Rep: Banner. Format: Traditional country. News staff 2. Target aud: 25-54. ■ Bob Kelly, pres; Bill Early, vp & gen mgr; Shawn McCrudden, opns mgr; Joyce Powell, Dan Dermody, gen sls mgrs; Roger Wiggs, prom dir; Dale Van Horn, progmg dir; Buck Stevens, mus dir; Kimber Bennett, news dir & pub affrs dir; Neil Burke, chief engr.

Peru

WLRZ(FM)—March 15, 1970: 100.9 mhz; 1.15 kw. Ant 518 ft. TL: N41 17 32 W78 07 58. Stereo. Box 73, 3905 Progress Blvd. (61354). (815) 224-2100. FAX: (815) 224-2066. Licensee: Starved Rock Radio Project Inc. (acq 8-28-85). Format: Classic rock. News staff one. Spec prog: Class 5 hrs wkly. ■ Thomas N. Spaight, pres, mus dir & chief engr; Sandy Taylor, gen sls mgr; Doug Shaunessy, news dir.

WXAN(FM)—See Ava.

Petersburg

WLUJ(FM)—March 1987: 97.7 mhz; 6 kw. Ant 328 ft. TL: N40 00 05 W89 41 49. Stereo. Hrs opn: 24. Box 500, Hwy. 97 S. (62675). (217) 632-2266. Licensee: Richard L. Van Zandt. Net: USA, Moody. Format: Relg. ■ Richard Van Zandt, gen mgr; Howard Fouks, stn mgr, prom mgr & progmg mgr; Steve Miller, mus dir & news dir; Wayne Childers, chief engr.

Pittsfield

WBBA(AM)—Dec 1, 1954: 1580 khz; 250 w-D, 15 w-N. TL: N39 34 53 W90 47 52. Stereo. Hrs opn: 24. Box 150 (62363). (217) 285-2157; (217) 285-2158. FAX: (217) 285-4006. Licensee: Starlight Corp. (acq 2-23-93; $268,000 with co-located FM; FTR 3-15-93). Net: SMN; Brownfield, Ill. Farm. Format: Oldies, info, news. News staff 2; news progmg 7 hrs wkly. Target aud: General. Spec prog: Farm 10 hrs, gospel 3 hrs, relg 3 hrs, local sports 6 hrs wkly. ■ Larry Hanna, pres; Ray Hanna, exec vp; David Fuhler, gen mgr, gen sls mgr & prom mgr; Debbie Conner, rgnl sls mgr & adv mgr; Bob Schote, progmg dir & mus dir; Kim Martin, news dir; Glen Hopkins, chief engr. ■ Rates: $12; 12; 10; 3.

WBBA-FM—Aug 1, 1966: 97.5 mhz; 10 kw. Ant 300 ft. TL: N39 34 53 W90 47 52. Stereo. Hrs opn: 24. Dups AM 100%. Format: Country, news. ■ Rates: Same as AM.

***WIPA(FM)**—Jan 4 1993: 89.3 mhz; 50 kw. 492 ft. TL: N39 43 25 W90 41 09. Stereo. Hrs opn: 5 AM-1 AM (Mon-Fri), 6 AM-3 AM (Sat), 6 AM-midnight (Sun). Rebroadcasts WSSU(FM) Springfield 100%. Sangamon State Univ., Springfield (62794-9243). (217) 786-6516.

Licensee: Sangamon State University. Format: News, classical, jazz.

Plano

WSPY(FM)—Jan 19, 1974: 107.1 mhz; 1.5 kw. Ant 466 ft. TL: N41 39 55 W88 34 34. Stereo. One Broadcast Ctr. (60545). (708) 552-7018; (708) 552-1000. FAX: (708) 552-9300. Licensee: Nelson Enterprises Inc. Net: ABC/E. Format: Full-svc adult contemp. News staff 2. Target aud: 25-54. Spec prog: Farm 18 hrs wkly. ■ Larry Nelson, pres & gen mgr; Beth Abbott, gen sls mgr; Dean Abbott, progmg dir; Doug Booth, news dir.

Polo

WLLT(FM)—Dec 12, 1989: 107.7 mhz; 1.35 kw. Ant 476 ft. TL: N41 53 52 W89 36 20. 260 Illinois Rt. 2, Dixon (61021). (815) 284-1077. Licensee: Sauk Valley Broadcasting Co. Format: Soft adult contemp. ■ Bob Thomas Burns, gen mgr.

Pontiac

WPOK(AM)—Aug 1, 1966: 1080 khz; 1 kw-D, DA. TL: N40 52 31 W88 36 11. 315 N. Mill St. (61764). (815) 844-6101. Licensee: Livingston County Broadcasters Inc. (acq 7-21-81; $304,500 with co-located FM; FTR 6-22-81). Net: CBS. Format: Hits of the 40s, 50s and 60s. News staff one; news progmg 4 hrs wkly. Target aud: 45 plus. Spec prog: Farm 16 hrs wkly. ■ Collins Miller, pres; Marc Edwards, prom mgr & progmg dir; Linda Fry, mus dir; Roy Frankenhof, news dir; Lane Lindstrom, chief engr.

WJEZ(FM)—Co-owned with WPOK(AM). July 1969: 97.3 mhz; 3 kw. Ant 500 ft. TL: N40 52 31 W88 36 11. Stereo. Hrs opn: 24. Prog sep from AM. Format: Lite adult contemp. News staff one. Target aud: 25-54.

Princeton

WZOE(AM)—Oct 25, 1961: 1490 khz; 1 kw-U. TL: N41 21 08 W89 28 05. Hrs opn: 24. Box 69, Broadcast Ctr., S. Main St. (61356). (815) 875-8014. Licensee: WZOE Inc. (acq 11-1-73). Net: MBS. Format: News/talk. Spec prog: Farm 15 hrs wkly. ■ Steve Samet, pres & gen mgr; Barry Martell, opns dir & progmg dir; Greg HalBleib, news dir.

WZOE-FM—July 1, 1980: 98.1 mhz; 6 kw. Ant 300 ft. TL: N41 21 49 W89 23 36. Stereo. Prog sep from AM. Format: Adult contemp.

Quincy

KGRC(FM)—See Hannibal, Mo.

***WGCA-FM**—Sept 20, 1987: 88.5 mhz; 40 kw. Ant 449 ft. TL: N39 58 18 W91 19 42. Stereo. Box 467 (62306). (217) 223-7700. FAX: (217) 224-0447. Licensee: Great Commission Broadcasting Corp. Net: CBN, USA. Format: Relg, adult contemp, CHR. Target aud: 25-45. ■ Bruce Rice, stn mgr; Jim Taylor, opns mgr & progmg dir; John T. Ingraham IV, chief engr.

WGEM(AM)—Jan 1, 1948: 1440 khz; 5 kw-D, 1 kw-N, DA-2. TL: N39 58 47 W91 19 27. Stereo. Box 80, 513 Hampshire (62301). (217) 228-6600. FAX: (217) 228-6670; TWX: 910-246-3209. Licensee: Quincy Broadcasting Co. Net: ABC/I, NBC Talknet; Tribune, Ill. News, Ill. Farm. Rep: Banner. Format: News/talk. News staff 18; news progmg 35 hrs wkly. Target aud: 25-54; general. ■ Ralph Oakley, vp & gen mgr; Jeff Dorsey, opns mgr; Pamela Hale, gen sls mgr; Don Hale, mktg dir; Becky Cramblit, prom mgr; Les Sachs, news dir; Jim Martens, chief engr.

WGEM-FM—1947: 105.1 mhz; 27.5 kw. Ant 500 ft. TL: N39 57 03 W91 19 54. Stereo. Hrs opn: 20. Prog sep from AM. Net: ABC/E; Miss. Net. Rep: Banner. Wash atty: Wilkinson, Barker, Knauer and Quinn. Format: Country, farm. ■ Thomas A. Oakley, pres. ■ WGEM-TV affil.

WQCY(FM)—Listing follows WTAD(AM).

***WQUB(FM)**—April 1974: 90.3 mhz; 10 kw. Ant 417 ft. TL: N39 56 23 W91 23 11 (CP: TL: N39 58 44 W91 18 33). Stereo. 1800 College Ave. (62301). (217) 228-5409. FAX: (217) 228-5473. Licensee: Quincy University Corp. Net: NPR. Wash atty: Wilkinson, Barker, Knauer & Quinn. Format: Div, classical, news. News progmg 29 hrs wkly. Target aud: General. Spec prog: Jazz 7 hrs, new age one hr, folk 2 hrs, blues 2 hrs wkly. ■ Harry Speckman, stn mgr; Matt Zeni, progmg dir.

WTAD(AM)—July 25, 1925: 930 khz; 5 kw-D, 1 kw-N, DA-N. TL: N39 53 31 W91 25 25. Box 731 (62306); WCU Bldg., 510 Maine St. (62301). (217) 228-2800. FAX: (217) 228-1031. Licensee: Tele-Media Broadcasting Co.

of Quincy. Group owner: TMZ Broadcasting Co. (acq 2-13-89; grpsl; FTR 2-27-89). Net: CBS, MBS. Rep: McGavren Guild. Format: Adult contemp, news/talk. Target aud: 25-54; general. Spec prog: Farm. ■ Steve Boll, opns mgr; Bob Gough, news dir; Bob Kratz, chief engr. ■ Rates: $70; 50; 35; 20.

WQCY(FM)—Co-owned with WTAD(AM). 1948: 99.5 mhz; 27 kw. Ant 750 ft. TL: N39 58 22 W91 19 54. Stereo. Prog sep from AM. Net: ABC/FM. Format: CHR. News staff 2; news progmg 7 hrs wkly. Target aud: 18-44; general. ■ Simon Will, progmg dir. ■ Rates: $40; 30; 40; 30.

Ramsey

***WJLY(FM)**—Nov 21, 1990: 93.3 mhz; 3 kw. Ant 328 ft. TL: N39 08 06 W89 06 02. Stereo. Hrs opn: 15. R.R. 2, Box 51A (62080). (618) 423-2082. FAX: (618) 423-2082. Licensee: Henry J. Voss. Net: Moody. Wash atty: Southmayd, Simpson & Miller. Format: Christian. News progmg 14 hrs wkly. Target aud: General; Christians of all denominations and interested non-Christians. ■ Henry Voss, pres & chief engr; Dan Voss, gen mgr; Richard Wheeler, stn mgr & opns mgr.

Rantoul

WLTM(FM)—Licensed to Rantoul. See Urbana.

WUFI(AM)—Licensed to Rantoul. See Champaign.

WZNF(FM)—Licensed to Rantoul. See Champaign.

River Grove

***WRRG(FM)**—Mar 10, 1975: 88.9 mhz; 100 w. Ant 128 ft. TL: N41 54 56 W87 50 12. 2000 5th Ave. (60171). (708) 456-0300, ext. 462. Licensee: Triton College. Format: CHR, urban contemp. News progmg 2 hrs wkly. Target aud: 18-34. ■ Mark West, opns mgr & chief engr; Chris Moran, progmg mgr.

Robinson

WTAY(AM)—Jan 9, 1956: 1570 khz; 250 w-D. TL: N39 00 29 W87 46 41. Box 245, Rt. 33 W. (62454). (618) 544-2191. FAX: (618) 544-3621. Licensee: Ann Broadcasting Corp. Net: AP; Brownfield. Rep: Walton. Format: Adult contemp. Spec prog: Farm 12 hrs, C&W 12 hrs wkly. ■ Ernest W. Patton, pres; Jerry F. Tye, gen mgr; Roger D. Reynolds, mus dir; Greg Jackson, news dir; Todd Seaney, chief engr.

WTAY-FM—Jan 4, 1963: 101.7 mhz; 1.45 kw. Ant 449 ft. TL: N39 00 29 W87 46 41. Stereo. Dups AM 100%.

Rochelle

WRHL(AM)—Sept 16, 1966: 1060 khz; 250 w-D, DA. TL: N41 55 24 W89 03 30. Box 177 (61068). (815) 562-7001. FAX: (815) 562-7002. Licensee: Rochelle Broadcasting Co. Inc. (acq 10-11-70). Net: Ill. Farm. Format: MOR, modern country. ■ David Van Drew, gen mgr; Doug Moorehead, mus dir; Jeffrey Leon, news dir; Roger L. Belke, chief engr.

WRHL-FM—Oct 5, 1973: 102.3 mhz; 3 kw. Ant 180 ft. TL: N41 55 24 W89 03 30. Dups AM 100%.

Rock Falls

WSDR(AM)—See Sterling.

Rock Island

WKBF(AM)—Feb 16, 1925: 1270 khz; 5 kw-U, DA-N. TL: N41 29 40 W90 28 00. Box 3100 (61204); 225 18th St. (61201). (309) 786-1800. Licensee: Roth Broadcasting of Quad Cities Inc. Group owner: Roth Communications (acq 3-16-87). Net: CBS. Rep: McGavren Guild. Format: C&W. Target aud: 25-54. Spec prog: Farm 9 hrs wkly. ■ Dennis Lamme, gen mgr; Terry Simmons, progmg dir; Max Molleston, news dir; Andy Anderson, chief engr.

WPXR-FM—Co-owned with WKBF(AM). October 1947: 98.9 mhz; 39 kw. Ant 900 ft. TL: N41 19 40 W90 22 47. Stereo. Prog sep from AM. Format: CHR. Target aud: 18-49.

***WVIK(FM)**—Feb 25, 1963: 90.3 mhz; 31 kw. Ant 1,096 ft. TL: N41 32 52 W90 28 29. Stereo. Hrs opn: 24. Augustana College (61201). (309) 794-7500. FAX: (309) 794-1236. Licensee: Augustana College. Net: NPR, Ill. Pub. Wash atty: Dow, Lohnes & Albertson. Format: Class, news. News staff 2. Target aud: General. Spec prog: Jazz 9 hrs wkly. ■ Don Wooten, gen mgr; Lowell Dorman, stn mgr; Herb Trix, Kai Swenson, news dirs; Christopher Downs, chief engr.

Rockford

*WFEN(FM)—Aug 25, 1992: 88.3 mhz; 5.4 kw. Ant 325 ft. TL: N42 21 51 W89 08 15 (CP: 1.6 kw, ant 581 ft.). 4700 S. Main St. (61102). (815) 964-9336. FAX: (815) 964-0550. Licensee: Faith Academy (acq 10-2-91; FTR 10-28-91). Format: Lite contemp Christian. ■ Fred Scholl, gen mgr.

WKMQ(FM)—See Winnebago.

WLUV(AM)—See Loves Park.

*WNIJ(FM)—April 28, 1991: 90.5 mhz; 50 kw. Ant 367 ft. TL: N42 00 55 W89 00 07. Stereo. Hrs opn: 5 AM-midnight. NIU Broadcast Center, 801 N. First St., DeKalb (60115); Riverfront Museum Park, 711 N. Main St. (61103). (815) 753-9000; (815) 961-8000. FAX: (815) 753-9938; (815) 963-5374. Licensee: Northern Illinois Univ. Net: APR, NPR. Wash atty: Arter & Hadden. Format: Jazz, news, pub affrs. News staff 3; news progmg 52 hrs wkly. Target aud: General. Spec prog: New age 3 hrs, blues 4 hrs wkly. ■ Michael Lazar, gen mgr; Bill Drake, opns dir; Elaine Harrington, dev dir; John Hill, mus dir; Lester Graham, Todd Mundt (asst), news dirs; Robin Cross, chief engr.

*WNIU(FM)—See DeKalb.

WNTA(AM)—Dec 1, 1964: 1150 khz; 1 kw-D, 60 w-N, DA-2. TL: N42 17 28 W88 58 56. Hrs opn: 24. 1901 Reidfarm Rd. (61111). (815) 877-3075. FAX: (815) 877-3286. Licensee: Midwest FM Inc. Group owner: Mid-West Family Stations (acq 9-17-86). Net: ABC, NBC, CNN. Rep: Christal. Wash atty: Fisher, Wayland, Cooper & Leader. Format: News/talk. News staff 4. Target aud: 25-54; upscale professional. ■ Rory Fraley, pres, gen mgr & mktg dir; Blake Patton, opns mgr; Sara Christianson, gen sls mgr; Mark Mayhew, prom dir, progmg dir & news dir; Fred Merkel, chief engr. ■ Rates: $29; 24; 26; 15.

WQFL(FM)—May 2, 1974: 100.9 mhz; 3 kw. Ant 300 ft. TL: N42 19 17 W89 00 47. Stereo. 5375 Pebble Creek Trail (61111). (815) 654-1200. Licensee: Quest for Life Inc. (acq 6-80; $590,000 FTR 6-2-80). Net: UPI. Format: Christian Contemporary Music. News staff one; one hr wkly. Target aud: 25-44; female dominant, educated, upscale & middle class. ■ Don Gladden, gen mgr; Jim Beeler, prom dir & progmg dir; Randy Adams, mus dir; Cindy Swanson, news dir; Joe McCall, chief engr.

WROK(AM)—1923: 1440 khz; 5 kw-D, 270 w-N, DA-D. TL: N42 16 50 W89 02 16. Stereo. Box 6186 (61125); 3901 Brendenwood Rd. (61107). (815) 399-2233. FAX: (815) 399-8148. Licensee: Nolte Communications Inc. (acq 10-1-63). Net: ABC/D, NBC Talknet. Rep: McGavren Guild. Wash atty: Wiley, Rein & Fielding. Format: New/talk. News staff 5; news progmg 13 hrs wkly. Target aud: 35 plus. ■ Lucille Nolte, CEO; John A. Nolte, pres & gen mgr; Adlai Rust, exec vp & mktg dir; David W. Salisbury, vp; Bob Elliott, stn mgr; Ted Schulz, natl sls mgr; Charlie Stone, progmg dir; Ken De Coster, news dir; Greg Dahl, chief engr. ■ Rates: $59; 44; 46; 19.

WZOK(FM)—Co-owned with WROK(AM). 1949: 97.5 mhz; 50 kw. Ant 235 ft. TL: N42 16 50 W89 02 16 (CP: Ant 429 ft.). Stereo. Prog sep from AM. Format: Adult contemp. Target aud: 25-34. ■ Tom Garrett, mus dir. ■ Rates: $62; 56; 59; 31.

WRRR(AM)—Dec 24, 1953: 1330 khz; 1 kw-D, 91 w-N, DA-2. TL: N42 13 32 W89 02 47. Box 7180 (61126); 2830 Sandy Hollow Rd. (61109). (815) 874-7861. FAX: (815) 874-2207. Licensee: Airplay Broadcasting Corp. Group owner: Airplay Broadcasting/Stay Tuned Broadcasting (acq 7-10-89; $1.35 million; FTR 7-24-89). Net: SMN. Rep: Katz. Wash atty: Fisher, Wayland, Cooper & Leader. Format: Stardust. Target aud: 35 plus. ■ Robert E. Rhea Jr., pres; David W. McAley, vp & gen mgr; Rich Fruin, gen sls mgr; Bob Schuman, news dir.

WRWC(FM)—See Rockton.

WXRX(FM)—See Belvidere.

WZOK(FM)—Listing follows WROK(AM).

Rockton

WRWC(FM)—March 1963: 103.1 mhz; 1.5 kw. Ant 525 ft. TL: N42 22 02 W89 05 13. Stereo. Hrs opn: 24. Box 345 (61072). (815) 624-2603. FAX: (815) 624-7777. Licensee: WRWC Inc. Group owner: Salter Broadcasting Co. of Delaware. Net: MBS. Rep: Katz & Powell. Format: Adult contemp. ■ John G. Weitzel, pres & gen mgr; Patty Rinehart, gen sls mgr; Rick West, progmg dir; Steve Chapman, mus dir; Charles Ingle, chief engr. ■ Rates: $38; 44; 38; 25.

Rushville

WKXQ(FM)—May 1, 1985: 96.7 mhz; 3 kw. Ant 328 ft. TL: N40 08 20 W90 39 26 (CP: 6 kw). Stereo. Hrs opn: 5 AM-midnight. Box 196, 123 N. Liberty (62681). (217) 322-3396; (800) 745-9636. Licensee: Larry and Cathy Price (acq 3-18-92; $225,000; FTR 4-13-92). Net: CNN. RFD, Ill., INN. Rep: Walton. Wash atty: Reddy, Begley & Martin. Format: Oldies. News staff one; news progmg 12 hrs wkly. Target aud: 18-54. Spec prog: Relg 6 hrs, farm 6 hrs wkly. ■ L. K. (Bud) Price, gen mgr; Kevin B. Sager, opns dir, progmg dir & pub affrs dir; Cathy M. Price, sls dir & gen sls mgr; Bob Utter, prom mgr; Bill Lovekamp, mus dir; Wanda Coy, news dir; Dwayne Davis, chief engr.

Salem

WJBD(AM)—Dec 16, 1956: 1350 khz; 430 w-D, 60 w-N. TL: N38 37 56 W88 55 02. Hrs opn: 24. Box 70, 310 W. McMackin St. (62881); 104 S. Elm, Centralia (62801). (618) 548-2000; (618) 532-9600. FAX: (618) 548-2079. Licensee: Virginia Broadcasting Corp. (acq 8-90; $800,000 with co-located FM; FTR 9-3-90). Net: NBC; Ill. News Net. Format: Adult contemp, news, talk. News staff 3; news progmg 30 hrs wkly. Target aud: General. Spec prog: Farm 4 hrs, relg 6 hrs wkly. ■ Dick Fister, pres; Bruce Kropp, vp opns, progmg dir & news dir; Doris Baker, vp sls; Kurt Wallace, mus dir.

WJBD-FM—June 1, 1972: 100.1 mhz; 1.5 kw. Ant 450 ft. TL: N38 33 45 W88 59 57. Stereo. Hrs opn: 24. Dups AM 95%. Format: Adult contemp, news. Spec prog: Farm 4 hrs wkly.

Sandwich

WAUR(AM)—Licensed to Sandwich. See Aurora.

Savanna

WCCI(FM)—Nov 7, 1971: 100.3 mhz; 25 kw. Ant 450 ft. TL: N42 07 49 W90 08 24. Stereo. Box 310, 316 Main (61074). (815) 273-7757. FAX: (815) 273-2760. Licensee: Carroll County Communications Inc. (acq 9-1-76). Net: ABC/D. Wash atty: Rine & Coran, P.C. Format: New hit country. News staff one. Target aud: 25-54. ■ John Miller, pres, gen mgr & gen sls mgr; Edward F. Bock, vp; Ann E. Murphy, stn mgr; Leslie Smith, progmg dir & mus dir; Mark Schoening, news dir. ■ Rates: $9; 9; 9; 9.

Shelbyville

WSHY(AM)—Nov 24, 1972: 1560 khz; 500 w-D, 2.1 w-N, DA. TL: N39 24 05 W88 49 00. Box 139, 2000W S. 5th St. (62565). (217) 774-2146. FAX: (217) 774-5765. Licensee: Cromwell Group Inc. of Illinois. Group owner: The Cromwell Group Inc. (acq 8-1-89; $320,000 with co-located FM; FTR 7-31-89). Net: SMN. Wash atty: Pepper & Corazzini. Format: Oldies. News staff one. Target aud: 25-54. Spec prog: Farm 5 hrs, big band 4 hrs wkly. ■ Bayard Walters, pres; J. Kevin Hughey, stn mgr, progmg dir & news dir; Rodney Schoonover, chief engr.

WEJT(FM)—Co-owned with WSHY(AM). Dec 31, 1969: 105.1 mhz; 13 kw. Ant 459 ft. TL: N39 35 39 W88 50 44. Stereo. Prog sep from AM. Box 70, Suite C, 410 N. Water, Decatur (62523). (217) 428-4487. FAX: (217) 428-4501. Rep: D & R Radio. Format: Oldies, adult contemp. News progmg 5 hrs wkly. Target aud: 25-54; baby boomers. ■ Joel Fletcher, gen mgr; Chris Bullock, prom mgr & mus dir.

Skokie

WTMX(FM)—Aug 18, 1961: 101.9 mhz; 4.2 kw. Ant 1,561 ft. TL: N41 52 44 W87 38 10. Stereo. Hrs opn: 24. 8833 Gross Point Rd. (60077). (708) 677-5900. FAX: (708) 677-9666. Licensee: Bonneville International Corp. (group owner; acq 8-70). Rep: McGavren Guild. Format: Adult contemp. News staff one. ■ Drew Horowitz, gen mgr; Chuck Williams, gen sls mgr; Barry James, progmg dir; Mark West, mus dir; Barry Keefe, news dir; Ron Turner, chief engr.

South Beloit

WBEL(AM)—Licensed to South Beloit. See Beloit, Wis.

South Jacksonville

WJVO(FM)—Licensed to South Jacksonville. See Jacksonville.

Sparta

WHCO(AM)—February 1955: 1230 khz; 1 kw-U. TL: N38 07 25 W89 43 20. Box 255, Hwy. 154-W (62286); 47 W. Maine, Mascoutah (62258). (618) 443-2121; (618) 566-2280. FAX: (618) 443-2280. Licensee: Hirsch Communication Engineering Corp. Net: ABC/D; Ill. Farm, Brownfield. Format: Adult contemp, farm, news. Target aud: 25-55. Spec prog: Country 10 hrs, relg 20 hrs wkly. ■ Jack L. Scheper, pres & gen mgr; John Scheper II, gen sls mgr; Kay Joiner, progmg dir; Andrew Zepeda, mus dir; Mike Arnold, news dir; Mike Hoefft, chief engr. ■ Rates: $40; 35; 30; 30.

Spring Valley

WAIV(FM)—December 1993: 103.3 mhz; 2.5 kw. Ant 118 ft. TL: N41 17 32 W89 07 58. Box 103 (61362-0103). (815) 663-0103. Licensee: Illinois Valley Radio. Format: Info, public svc.

Springfield

WCVS-FM—(Virden). May 10, 1982: 96.7 mhz; 6 kw. Ant 328 ft. TL: N39 38 26 89 39 24. Stereo. Hrs opn: 24. Box 296 (62690); Box 2989, 3055 S. 4th, Springfield (62703). (217) 528-3033; (217) 528-9287. FAX: (217) 528-5348. Licensee: Virden Broadcasting Corp. Net: SMN. Wash atty: Pepper & Corazzini. Format: Oldies. News staff one. Target aud: 25-54. ■ Randal J. Miller, pres & chief engr; Kevin O'Dea, gen mgr; Phil Voth, sls dir. ■ Rates: $27; 25; 27; 14.50.

WDBR(FM)—Listing follows WTAX(AM).

WFMB(AM)—1922: 1450 khz; 1 kw-U. TL: N39 45 36 W89 39 05. Hrs opn: 24. Box 2989 (62708); 3055 S. 4th St. (62703). (217) 528-3033. FAX: (217) 528-5348. Licensee: Neuhoff Broadcasting Corp. (group owner; acq 12-27-88; $4.25 million with co-located FM; FTR 1-23-89). Net: ABC/I. Rep: McGavren Guild. Format: C&W, sports. News staff 2; news progmg 5 hrs wkly. Target aud: 25-54; upscale professionals. ■ Geoffrey H. Neuhoff, pres; Kevin O'Dea, gen mgr; Phil Voth, gen sls mgr; Bob Grayson, progmg dir; John Harris, news dir; Mac Krueger, chief engr.

WFMB-FM—July 1965: 104.5 mhz; 43 kw. Ant 465 ft. TL: N39 45 36 W89 39 05. Stereo. Prog sep from AM. Net: ABC/D. Format: Country. News progmg 2 hrs wkly. Professional adults. ■ John Spalding, mus dir.

WMAY(AM)—Oct 15, 1950: 970 khz; 1 kw-D, 500 w-N, DA-2. TL: N39 51 42 W89 32 32. 502 S. Allen, Spaulding (62561). (217) 629-7077. FAX: (217) 629-7952. Licensee: WMAY Inc. Group owner: Mid-West Family Stations (acq 12-7-76). Net: NBC, CNN, FNN. Rep: D & R Radio. Wash atty: Fisher, Wayland, Cooper & Leader. Format: News, oldies. News staff 4. Target aud: 25-64. ■ Thomas M. Kushak, pres & gen mgr; Paul Layendecker, opns dir; Marilyn Kushak, vp sls & vp mktg; Danny Russel, mus dir; Greg Man Froi, chief engr.

WNNS(FM)—Co-owned with WMAY(AM). Nov 1, 1980: 98.7 mhz; 50 kw. Ant 500 ft. TL: N39 41 59 W89 46 55. Stereo. Prog sep from AM. Format: Lite rock. ■ Kellie Michaels, progmg dir; Ashley Blake, mus dir.

*WQNA(FM)—Aug 31, 1979: 88.3 mhz; 3 kw. Ant 80 ft. TL: N39 43 03 W89 37 35. Stereo. Hrs opn: 8 AM-4 PM. 2201 Toronto Rd. (62707). (217) 529-5431. FAX: (217) 529-7861. Licensee: Capital Area Vocational Center. Net: ABC/FM. Wash atty: Fisher Wayland. Format: Div. News progmg 2 hrs wkly. Target aud: 13-18; high school students. ■ J.G. Reynolds, chmn; Jim Grimes, gen mgr, progmg dir & news dir; Jerry Schneider, opns dir; H.J. Dunn, chief engr.

WQQL(FM)—Nov 15, 1993: 101.9 mhz; 50 kw. Ant 300 ft. TL: N39 42 39 W89 38 42. Stereo. Hrs opn: 24. 1030 Durkin Dr. (62704). (217) 546-9000. FAX: (217) 546-4388. Licensee: Saga Communications of Illinois Inc. Group owner: Saga Communications Inc. (acq 9-10-93; $1.44 million; FTR 10-4-93). Rep: Katz. Wash atty: Smith & Belenduik. Format: Oldies. News progmg 2 hr wkly. Target aud: 25 plus; upscale educated adults. ■ Ed Christian, CEO; Norm McKee, CFO; Kevin Mashek, gen mgr; Simon Mulverhill, gen sls mgr; Randi West, prom dir; Patrick Walston, progmg dir; Paul Figge, engrg dir.

*WSCT(FM)—Not on air, target date unknown: 90.5 mhz; 850 w. Ant 617 ft. TL: N39 45 37 W89 39 06. Box 140, R.R. 3, Lake Williamson, Carlinville (62626). (217) 854-4671. Licensee: Illinois Bible Institute.

*WSSU(FM)—Jan 3, 1975: 91.9 mhz; 50 kw. Ant 524 ft. TL: N39 47 00 W89 26 46. Stereo. Hrs opn: 5 AM-1 AM (Mon-Fri), 6 AM-3 AM (Sat), 6 AM-midnight (Sun). Sangamon State Univ. (62794-9243). (217) 786-6516. FAX: (217) 786-6527. Licensee: Sangamon State Univ. Net: NPR, UPI, APR. Wash atty: Dow, Lohnes & Albertson. Format: News, classical, jazz. News staff 3; news progmg 45 hrs wkly. ■ Robert Gordon, gen mgr; Jeanne Urbanek, dev dir; Bradley Swanson, progmg dir; Karl Scroggin, mus dir; Richard Bradley, news dir.

WTAX(AM)—1930: 1240 khz; 1 kw-U. TL: N39 47 36 W89 36 18. Box 2759, 712 S. Dirksen (62703). (217) 753-5400. Licensee: Lakeshore Communications Corp. (acq 12-6-89; $4 million; with co-located FM; FTR 12-25-89). Net: ABC TalkRadio, Moody, CBS; Tribune. Rep: Christal. Format: News, sports, talk. News staff 4; news progmg 43 hrs wkly. Target aud: 30 plus. Spec prog: Farm 16 hrs wkly. ■ Thomas Bookeu, pres; Jerry Schnacke, gen mgr; Chris Schnacke, gen sls mgr; Tim Schweizer, news dir; Glenn Hopkins, chief engr.

WDBR(FM)—Co-owned with WTAX(AM). April 1948: 103.7 mhz; 50 kw. Ant 320 ft. TL: N39 47 36 W89 36 18. Prog sep from AM. Format: CHR. News progmg 6 hrs wkly. Target aud: General; 18-49. ■ Jim Moore, progmg dir; Lisa Crocker, mus dir.

WYMG(FM)—(Jacksonville). March 1948: 100.5 mhz; 50 kw. Ant 500 ft. TL: N39 39 40 W89 55 18. Stereo. 1030 Durkin Dr., Springfield (62704). (217) 546-9000. FAX: (217) 546-4388. Licensee: SAGA Communications Inc. (group owner; acq 10-1-86). Rep: Katz. Format: AOR. Target aud: 18-49. Spec prog: Jazz 2 hrs, comedy one hr wkly. ■ Ed Christian, pres; Kevin Maschek, gen mgr; Simon Mulverhill, gen sls mgr; Randi West, prom mgr; Bryan Jeffries, progmg dir; Keef Fulgham, mus dir; Paul Figge, chief engr.

Sterling

WSDR(AM)—Aug 21, 1949: 1240 khz; 500 w-D, 1 kw-N. TL: N41 48 59 W89 40 13. Box 658, 3101 Freeport Rd. (61081). (815) 625-3400. FAX: (815) 625-6940. Licensee: L.H.& S. Communication Inc. with co-located FM). Net: CBS, MBS; III. Net. Rep: Christal. Format: News/talk. News staff 5. Target aud: 35 plus. Spec prog: Farm 16 hrs, Sp 2 hrs wkly. ■ Larry E. Sales, chmn; Jack Stower, gen mgr; Casey Kelly, gen sls mgr; Pete Herrick, progmg dir; Mark Morris, news dir.

WSSQ(FM)—August 1966: 94.3 mhz; 6 kw. Ant 309 ft. TL: N41 51 06 W89 42 38. Stereo. Prog sep from AM. Licensee: LH&S Communications Inc. (acq 9-9-93; FTR 10-4-93). Net: Unistar, Westwood One. Format: Adult contemp. Target aud: 18-35.

Streator

WIZZ(AM)—Sept 26, 1953: 1250 khz; 500 w-D, 100 w-N, DA-D. TL: N41 09 30 W88 50 13. Hrs opn: 15. Box 377, Rt. 23 N. (61364). (815) 672-2947. FAX: (815) 673-1833. Licensee: Streator Broadcasting Co. Group owner: Prairieland Stations. Net: ABC/E. Format: Oldies, talk. News staff 2; news progmg 14 hrs wkly. Target aud: 25 plus. ■ Stephen P. Bellinger, pres; Richard C. Huckaba, gen mgr; Phil Ahearn, gen sls mgr; Ted Weber, progmg dir; Jim Selle, news dir.

WSTQ(FM)—Co-owned with WIZZ(AM). Sept 15, 1964: 97.7 mhz; 3 kw. Ant 328 ft. TL: N41 10 49 W88 52 06. Stereo. Prog sep from AM. Format: Country. ■ Rates: $12; 12; 12; na.

Sullivan

WKJR(FM)—Licensed to Sullivan. See Mattoon.

Summit

***WARG(FM)**—Jan 1976: 88.9 mhz; 500 w. Ant 98 ft. TL: N41 46 36 W87 48 17. Stereo. 7329 W. 63rd St. (60501). (708) 728-3222. FAX: (708) 728-3155. Licensee: Community High School Dist. No. 217. Format: Alt, new music, rap. Spec prog: World beat, metal music. ■ Pamela Konkol, gen mgr.

Sycamore

WDEK(FM)—See De Kalb.

WLBK(AM)—See De Kalb.

WSQR(AM)—June 11, 1981: 1560 khz; 250 w-D. TL: N42 00 24 W88 40 40. 801 N. 1st St. (60115). (815) 753-1278. Licensee: Hometown Communications Inc. Net: UPI. Rep: Robert's. Format: Alternative rock. News progmg 5 hrs wkly. Spec prog: Farm 3 hrs wkly. ■ Larry S. Weatherford, pres & gen mgr; Gregory Clark, opns mgr; Len Watson, chief engr.

Taylorville

WQLZ(FM)—December 1967: 92.7 mhz; 2.7 kw. Ant 300 ft. TL: N39 32 28 W89 16 36. Stereo. Hrs opn: 18. 502 S. Allen, Spaulding (62561). (217) 629-7707. FAX: (217) 629-7952. Licensee: Long Nine Inc. Group owner: Mid-West Family Stations (acq 2-3-93; $1 million; FTR 2-22-93). Wash atty: Fisher, Wayland, Cooper & Leader. Format: Mainstream rock. News staff one; news progmg 3 hrs wkly. Target aud: 18-34. ■ Tom Kushak, pres & gen mgr; Vince Richards, progmg dir; Todd Ellis, Johnny Walker, mus dirs; Greg Manfroi, chief engr. ■ Rates: $15.25; 13.25; 15.25; 13.25.

WTIM(AM)—1952: 1410 khz; 1 kw-D, 63 w-N, DA-1. TL: N39 32 38 W89 16 36. Hrs opn: 19. Box 169 (62568-0169). (217) 824-9846. FAX: (217) 824-3301. Licensee: Miller Communications Inc. (acq 10-22-92; $85,000; FTR 11-23-92). Net: CNN; Brownfield. Format: News/talk. News staff one; news progmg 25 hrs wkly. Target aud: 35 plus. Spec prog: Farm 7 hrs, relg 4 hrs wkly. ■ Randall J. Miller, pres & gen mgr; Matt McLemore, opns mgr; Jeremy Sweigart, news dir & pub affrs dir.

Teutopolis

WAES(FM)—Not on air, target date unknown: 102.3 mhz; 6 kw. Ant 100 ft. Box 566, Effingham (62401). Licensee: John W. Kirby.

Tuscola

WUBB(FM)—Sept 30, 1970: 93.5 mhz; 3 kw. Ant 148 ft. TL: N39 47 58 W88 17 20 (CP: 6 kw, ant 284 ft.). Stereo. 400 N. Broadway, Urbana (61801). (217) 367-1195. FAX: (217) 367-3291. Licensee: Rollings Communications of Tuscola Inc. Group owner: Rollings Communications Companies (acq 10-8-93; $30,000; FTR 11-1-93). Format: Country. ■ Mark Rollings, gen mgr; Scott Sweitzer, opns mgr.

Urbana

WBCP(AM)—1948: 1580 khz; 250 w-D, 10 w-N. TL: N40 07 32 W88 17 29. Box 1023, 822 Pioneer, Champaign (61820). (217) 359-1580. FAX: (217) 359-1583. Licensee: WBCP Inc. (acq 12-89; $135,000; FTR 1-4-89). Net: American Urban. Format: Urban contemp. ■ Lonnie Clark, pres; Robert Jackson, gen sls mgr; James Shepherd, progmg dir; Sam Britten, mus dir; Alan Wolfe, chief engr.

***WILL(AM)**—Mar 28, 1922: 580 khz; 5 kw-D, DA-D. TL: N40 04 53 W88 14 18. Hrs opn: 5 AM-10 PM (Mon-Thu), 5 AM-11 PM (Fri-Sun). 228 Gregory Hall, 810 S. Wright St. (61801). (217) 333-0850. FAX: (217) 333-7151. Licensee: Univ. of Illinois. Net: NPR, APR. Wash atty: Dow, Lohnes & Albertson. Format: News info. News staff 14; news progmg 115 hrs wkly. Target aud: 25-60; educated, upper middle income, professionals. Spec prog: Farm 7 hrs wkly. ■ Donald P. Mullally, gen mgr; Dan Simeone, stn mgr; Deborah Day, dev dir; Terry Bush, mktg dir; Alex Ashlock, progmg dir; Bill Raack, news dir; Ed West, chief engr.

***WILL-FM**—Sept 1, 1941: 90.9 mhz; 105 kw. Ant 850 ft. TL: N40 06 00 W88 13 27. Stereo. Hrs opn: 24. Prog sep from AM. Format: Class. News progmg 2 hrs wkly. Target aud: 35-70. Spec prog: Folk one hr, jazz 10 hrs, new age one hr wkly. ■ Nancy Stagg, progmg dir & mus dir. ■ *WILL-TV affil.

WKIO(FM)—Dec 4, 1967: 92.5 mhz; 3 kw. Ant 145 ft. TL: N40 06 42 W88 14 26 (CP: 20 kw, ant 370 ft.). Stereo. 505 S. Locust, Champaign (61820). (217) 352-1040. FAX: (217) 356-3330. Licensee: WKIO Inc. Group owner: Tak Communications Inc. (acq 1978). Net: Unistar. Rep: Eastman. Format: Oldies. ■ Jeff Balding, gen mgr; Mike Haile, opns mgr & progmg dir; Tom Difilipo, gen sls mgr; Steve Hamm, chief engr.

WLRW(FM)—See Champaign.

WLTM(FM)—(Rantoul). Jan 1993: 96.1 mhz; 3.8 kw. Ant 403 ft. TL: N40 12 27 W88 17 56. Stereo. 400 N. Broadway, Urbana (61801). (217) 367-1195. FAX: (217) 367-3291. Licensee: WLTM Inc. Format: Adult contemp. ■ Jay Martin, gen mgr; John Sullivan, chief engr.

WPGU(FM)—Apr 17, 1967: 107.1 mhz; 3 kw. Ant 235 ft. TL: N40 06 34 W88 14 06. Stereo. Hrs opn: 24. 204 E. Peabody Dr., Champaign (61820-6923). (217) 333-2016. FAX: (217) 244-3001. Licensee: Illini Media Co. Net: ABC/R. Wash atty: Fisher, Wayland, Cooper & Leader. Format: Modern rock. News progmg 7 hrs wkly. Target aud: 18-34. ■ William Berry, chmn; Bradley Fuhr, gen mgr; Andy Worthington, stn mgr; Stacey Keefe, mktg mgr & prom mgr; Neela Marnell, progmg dir; Zac Repking, mus dir; John Rastino, asst mus dir; Mike Keeney, news dir; Bryan Holloway, engrg mgr; Mike Williams, chief engr. ■ Rates: $26; 29; 29; 26.

Vandalia

WPMB(AM)—Dec 9, 1963: 1500 khz; 250 w-D. TL: N38 57 30 W89 07 27. Box 100, 232 S Fourth St. (62471). (618) 283-2325. Licensee: Midwest Communications Corp. (acq 11-14-83; $342,500 with co-located FM; FTR 11-14-83). Net: ABC/D; Tribune, Ill. News Net. Rep: Bruce Schneider. Format: MOR. News staff one; news progmg 6 hrs wkly. Target aud: General. Spec prog: Farm 4 hrs wkly. ■ Don Hecke, pres; Tom Wright, gen mgr; Marietta Dickson, gen sls mgr; Dan Michel, progmg dir & mus dir; Mark Turner, news dir.

WKRV(FM)—Co-owned with WPMB(AM). May 28, 1974: 107.1 mhz; 3 kw. Ant 165 ft. TL: N38 57 30 W89 07 27. Stereo. Dups AM 5%. Format: CHR. Target aud: 20-45.

Vernon Hills

WNVR(AM)—Mar 1, 1988: 1030 khz; 500 w-D. TL: N42 12 40 W87 57 41. Hrs opn: 9 AM-5 PM. 4320 Dundee Rd., Northbrook (60062). (708) 498-3350. Licensee: Poinet Communications Ltd. (acq 12-23-92; $495,000; FTR 1-25-93). Net: BRN. Wash atty: Gardner, Carton & Douglass. Format: Pol. News progmg 9 hrs wkly. Target aud: General; non-English speaking audience ages 18-54. Spec prog: Ger 4 hrs, Russian one hr wkly. ■ Walter K . Kotaba, pres; Kent D. Gustafson, gen mgr; Mike Czark, opns mgr & mus dir; Bruce Goldberg, sls dir; Zophia Orqvec, gen sls mgr; Dave Dybas, chief engr. ■ Rates: $60; 60; 60; 60.

Virden

WCVS-FM—Licensed to Virden. See Springfield.

Watseka

WGFA-FM—March 2, 1962: 94.1 mhz; 26 kw. Ant 405 ft. TL: N40 47 48 W87 45 11. Stereo. Hrs opn: 24. R.R. 4, Box 100 (60970-9300). (815) 432-4955. FAX: (815) 432-4957. Licensee: Iroquois County Broadcasting Co. Net: ABC/E; Tribune. Rep: Keystone (unwired net). Wash atty: Bosari & Paxson. Format: Adult contemp, div, classic rock. News staff one; news progmg 12 hrs wkly. Target aud: General. Spec prog: Farm 20 hrs, business 2 hrs, sports 20 hrs wkly. ■ R. A. Martin, CEO & pres; Maggie Martin, exec vp, gen mgr, gen sls mgr & prom mgr; Ron Hunt, prom mgr; Patricia McGill, adv mgr; Ron Hunt, progmg dir & mus dir; Carl Gerdovich, news dir. ■ Rates: $21; 20; 20; 19.

WGFA(AM)—Sept 1, 1961: 1360 khz; 1 kw-D, DA. TL: N40 47 48 W87 45 11. Format: Adult contemp, btfl music, classic rock. Target aud: General. Spec prog: Class one hr, relg 3 hrs, big band 2 hrs, talk one hr wkly. ■ Rates: Same as FM.

Waukegan

WKRS(AM)—Sept 25, 1949: 1220 khz; 1 kw-D, DA. TL: N42 20 59 W87 52 53. 3250 Belvidere Rd. (60085). (708) 336-7900. Licensee: H & D Entertainment Inc. (acq 6-11-92; with co-located FM). Net: ABC/D. Format: News/talk. News staff 4; news progmg 40 hrs wkly. Target aud: General. ■ Hal Coxon, gen mgr; Nick Farella, opns mgr; Larry Leafblad, gen sls mgr; Lisa Tribley, prom mgr; Jan Johnson, progmg dir; Jeff Pearce, chief engr.

WXLC(FM)—Co-owned with WKRS(AM). May 1963: 102.3 mhz; 3 kw. Ant 322 ft. TL: N42 20 59 W87 52 53. Stereo. Prog sep from AM. Format: Rock (AOR). News progmg 6 hrs wkly. Target aud: 25-39. ■ Lisa Tribley, prom mgr; Nick Farella, progmg dir; Chuck Summers, mus dir.

West Frankfort

WFRX(AM)—May 2, 1951: 1300 khz; 1 kw-D. TL: N37 53 04 W88 55 44. Box 128 (62896). (618) 932-6615. FAX: (618) 932-3094. Licensee: Pyramid Radio Broadcasting & TV Co. Format: MOR, sports. News staff one; news progmg 20 hrs wkly. Target aud: Adult. ■ Gobel Patton, pres; Art Smith, gen mgr; Ron Clem, news dir; Forrest Richardson, chief engr. ■ Rates: $10; 10; 10; 10.

WFRX-FM—Mar 14, 1972: 97.7 mhz; 3 kw. Ant 205 ft. TL: N37 53 04 W88 55 44. Hrs opn: 6 AM-10 PM. Prog sep from AM. Format: MOR, news & sports. Target aud: Adult. Spec prog: Illinois football & basketball, Chicago Cubs, White Sox, Bulls & Bears. ■ Rates: Same as AM.

Wheaton

*WETN(FM)—Feb 27, 1962: 88.1 mhz; 250 w. Ant 140 ft. TL: N41 52 09 W88 05 56. Stereo. Wheaton College (60187). (708) 752-5074. FAX: (708) 752-5286. Licensee: Trustees of Wheaton College. Format: Div. Target aud: General. ■ Stuart Johnson, gen mgr; Scott Miraldi, mus dir.

Wilmington

WDND(FM)—Sept 29, 1980: 105.5 mhz; 3 kw. Ant 275 ft. TL: N41 17 13 W88 14 23. Stereo. Box 119 (60481). (815) 458-2141. Licensee: DBC Broadcasting Inc. (acq 4-29-82; $160,000 FTR 5-17-82). Format: Hot adult contemp. ■ Donald T. Burgeson, pres, gen mgr, gen sls mgr & news dir; Chris Kelly, progmg dir; Bob MacKay, mus dir; Lane Lindstrom, chief engr.

Winnebago

WKMQ(FM)—1971: 95.3 mhz; 1.25 kw. Ant 512 ft. TL: N42 17 26 W89 09 51. Stereo. Hrs opn: 24. 1901 Reidfarm Rd., Rockford (61114). (815) 877-3075. FAX: (815) 877-3286. Licensee: Midwest FM Inc. Group owner: Mid-West Family Stations (acq 9-17-86). Format: Oldies. News staff 3; news progmg 3 hrs wkly. Target aud: 25-54. ■ Rory Fraley, gen mgr; Blake D. Patton, opns mgr, progmg dir & mus dir; Sara Christianson, gen sls mgr; Chuck Diamond, prom mgr; Mark Mayhew, news dir; Fred Merkel, chief engr. ■ Rates: $55; 47; 50; 24.

Winnetka

*WNTH(FM)—1961: 88.1 mhz; 100 w. Ant 105 ft. TL: N42 05 40 W87 43 07. Stereo. 385 Winnetka Ave. (60093). (708) 446-4090. Licensee: New Trier Township Board of Educ. (acq 1961). Format: Div. ■ Timothy Kraemer, stn mgr; Robert Wittenberg, opns dir; Dominique Johnson, adv dir; Matthew Friedman, progmg dir; Mark Lunkenheimer, Kara Cobb, mus dirs; Matthew Gomberg, chief engr.

Wood River

KFNS(AM)—Oct 5, 1961: 590 khz; 1 kw-U, DA-2. TL: N38 55 43 W90 05 08. Suite 304, 7711 Carondelet, St. Louis, MO (63105-3385). (314) 727-2160. FAX: (314) 727-7696. Licensee: Compass Radio of St. Louis Inc. Group owner: Compass Radio Group (acq 4-23-93; grpsl; FTR 5-10-93). Rep: D & R Radio. Format: All sports radio. Target aud: Men 25-54. ■ Joe Cariffe, vp & gen mgr; Bob Burch, opns mgr; Mike Jennewein, gen sls mgr; Ruth Medina, prom mgr; Sam Caputa, chief engr. ■ Rates: $100; 100; 100; 28.

Woodlawn

WDML(FM)—Not on air, target date unknown: 106.9 mhz; 3 kw. Ant 328 ft. TL: N38 21 29 W89 05 56. Box 1591, Volunteer Broadcasting of Ill., Mt. Vernon (62864). Licensee: Volunteer Broadcasting of Illinois.

Woodstock

WZSR(FM)—May 24, 1974: 105.5 mhz; 3 kw. Ant 429 ft. TL: N42 15 30 W88 21 48. Stereo. 8600 Rt. 14, Crystal Lake (60012). (815) 459-7000. FAX: (815) 459-7027. Licensee: Pride Communications (acq 8-01-91). Format: Contemp hit. News staff one; news progmg one hr wkly. Target aud: 18-49. Spec prog: Jazz 5 hrs wkly. ■ Jim Hooker, gen mgr; Thor Kolner, progmg dir; Stew Cohen, news dir.

Zion

WKGA(AM)—Sept 19, 1967: 1500 khz; 250 w-D, DA. TL: N42 27 18 W87 54 01. Suite 105, 3567B Grand Ave., Gurnee (60031). (708) 336-7606. Licensee: North Shore Broadcasting Group Inc. (acq 4-90; $175,000; FTR 4-23-90). Format: Sp. Target aud: 18-40; middle class hispanic. Spec prog: Gospel 6 hrs wkly. ■ Robert Jeffers, pres; Scott Bremner, vp & gen mgr. ■ Rates: $25; 25; 25; 15.

WNIZ-FM—1962: 96.9 mhz; 50 kw. Ant 500 ft. TL: N42 30 36 W87 53 11. Stereo. 2700 Sheridan Rd. (60099). (708) 746-1484; (312) 633-9700. Licensee: Northern Illinois Broadcasting Co. Format: Class. ■ William C. Florian, pres; Sonia Florian, gen mgr; Charles E. King, opns mgr & chief engr; Steve Adler, gen sls mgr; Ron Ray, progmg dir.

Indiana

Alexandria

WAXT(FM)—Sep 3, 1980: 96.7 mhz; 2.3 kw. Ant 367 ft. TL: N40 10 38 W85 40 23. Stereo. Hrs opn: 24. Box 610, Anderson (46015). (317) 644-7791. FAX: (317) 641-2383. Licensee: Triplett Broadcasting Co. of Indiana Inc. (acq 1980). Format: Country. News staff 2; news progmg 14 hrs wkly. Target aud: 25-54. ■ Marc Triplett, pres; James A. Mougeotte, vp; Sam Graves, gen mgr; Chad Niccum, vp opns & vp progmg; Ronda Farmer, mus dir; Ron Estep, chief engr. ■ Rates: $20.10; 20.10; 20.10; 20.10.

Anderson

WHBU(AM)—April 1923: 1240 khz; 1 kw-U. TL: N40 06 17 W85 40 45. Box 610, Suite 105, 1106 Meridian Plaza (46015). (317) 644-7791. FAX: (317) 641-2383. Licensee: Anderson Communications. Net: CBS, NBC Talknet; Net Ind. Rep: Roslin, Rgnl Reps. Wash atty: Roy Perkins. Format: Talk. News staff one; news progmg 40 hrs wkly. Target aud: 25-54. Spec prog: Cincinnati Reds, Chicago White Sox, Indiana Pacers, Indianapolis Colts, Purdue Sports, Indy 500, NASCAR Motor Racing Net. ■ Marc Triplett, pres; Sam Graves, gen mgr; Chad Niccum, opns mgr & progmg mgr; Ronda Farmer, mus dir; Andy Zirkle, news dir; Ron Estep, chief engr.

WHUT(AM)—Listing follows WXXP(FM).

WQME(FM)—Nov 29 1990: 98.7 mhz; 6 kw. Ant 328 ft. TL: N40 03 43 W85 42 34. Stereo. Hrs opn: 6 AM-midnight Sun-Th, 6AM-2 AM F-Sat. 1100 E. 5th St. (46012). (317) 641-4349. FAX: (317) 641-3851. Licensee: Anderson University Inc. Net: CNN. Wash atty: Arent, Fox, Kinter, Plotkin & Kahn. Format: Contemp Christian. News progmg 8 hrs wkly. Target aud: 25-54. Spec prog: Relg 15 hrs wkly. ■ Donald Boggs, gen mgr; Gary Brummitt, stn mgr; David Harness, gen sls mgr; Jason Whiteaker, chief engr. ■ Rates: $12.50; 12.50; 12.50; 12.50.

WXXP(FM)—Sept 11, 1973: 97.9 mhz; 50 kw. Ant 489 ft. TL: N40 03 43 W85 42 34. Stereo. 2000 W. 53rd (46013). (317) 644-1255. FAX: (317) 644-1775. Licensee: Anderson Radio G.P. (acq 4-30-91; 1.5 million with co-located AM; FTR 6-3-91). Net: ABC/D. Format: Adult contemp. ■ Gary Todd, pres; Scott Todd, gen mgr, progmg dir & mus dir; T.J. Meyers, news dir; David Hood, chief engr.

WHUT(AM)—Co-owned with WXXP(FM). 1946: 1470 khz; 1 kw-D, 35 w-N. TL: N40 03 43 W85 42 37. Net: ABC/I. Format: MOR. News staff 2; news progmg 20 hrs wkly. Target aud: 45 plus; older professionals, civic leaders, conservative adults.

Angola

*WEAX(FM)—September 1979: 88.3 mhz; 920 w. Ant 151 ft. TL: N41 37 53 W85 00 37. Stereo. Stewart Hall, W. Park Ave. (46703-1750). (219) 665-3314; (219) 665-7310. FAX: (219) 665-4292. Licensee: Tri-State Univ. Format: Classic rock, AOR, heavy metal. News staff one; news progmg 10 hrs wkly. Target aud: 16-30; general. Spec prog: Class 4 hrs, Black 2 hrs, jazz 2 hrs wkly. ■ Christopher J. Hicks, gen mgr; Leann Pierce, sls dir & vp prom; Shawn McGrath, progmg dir; Robert Elliott, mus dir; Steve Vruckel, news dir; Chris Baker, chief engr.

WLKI(FM)—July 15, 1974: 100.3 mhz; 2.05 kw. Ant 393 ft. TL: N41 40 51 W85 00 05. Stereo. Box 999, 2655 N. S.R. 127 (46703). (219) 665-9554. FAX: (219) 665-9064. Licensee: Lake Cities Broadcasting Corp. Net: ABC/FM. Format: Hot adult contemp. News staff one; news progmg 7 hrs wkly. Target aud: 25-49; adults with youthful outlook, skews female. ■ Thomas R. Andrews, pres & gen mgr; Bill Kerner, vp; Carter Snider, gen sls mgr; Garry Osborn, progmg dir; Andy St. John, mus dir; Brook Steed, news dir; Chris Arnaut, chief engr.

Attica

WBQR(FM)—Apr 1990: 95.7 mhz; 4.1 kw. Ant 387 ft. TL: N40 22 09 W87 08 59. Stereo. 106 Mill St. (47918). (317) 762-2534. Licensee: Attica Community Radio Corp. Format: Soft adult contemp, talk. News staff one; news progmg 16 hrs wkly. Target aud: 24-55. Spec prog: Folk, jazz, relg, big band, local sports, bluegrass 2 hrs, local talent 3 hrs wkly. ■ Bruce Quinn, chief engr; Gerald Quinn, gen sls mgr. ■ Rates: $7.50; 7.50; 7; 6.

Auburn

WIFF(AM)—Sept 3, 1968: 1570 khz; 500 w-D, 151 w-N, DA-2. TL: N41 20 01 W85 03 08. Hrs opn: 17. 5446 CR 29 (46706). (219) 925-1055. Licensee: C.P. Broadcasters Inc. Net: USA. Rep: Rgnl Reps. Wash atty: Lauren Colby. Format: Jazz, new age. News staff one; news progmg 5 hrs wkly. Target aud: 25-54; upscale. Spec prog: Relg 15 hrs wkly. ■ Wayne H. Paradise, pres & chief engr; Dennis Hackett, gen mgr; Phil Haberkorn, news dir.

WGTB(FM)—Co-owned with WIFF(AM). April 10, 1967: 102.3 mhz; 3 kw. Ant 300 ft. TL: N41 20 01 W85 03 08. Stereo. Hrs opn: 20. Prog sep from AM. ■ John Vance, progmg dir.

Aurora

WSCH(FM)—Oct 29, 1970: 99.3 mhz; 1.15 kw. Ant 525 ft. TL: N38 57 55 W84 56 51. Stereo. 6857 Salem Ridge Rd. (47001). (812) 438-2777. Licensee: Dearborn County Broadcasters Inc. Net: CNN. Format: C&W. Spec prog: Farm 3 hrs wkly. ■ John W. Schuler, pres, gen mgr & gen sls mgr; Barbara Schuler, mus dir; Chris Mchenry, news dir. ■ Rates: $9.25; 9.25; 9.25; 9.25.

Austin

WJAA(FM)—1991: 96.3 mhz; 3 kw. Ant 328 ft. TL: N38 50 39 W85 49 26. 1531 W. Tipton St., Seymour (47274). (812) 523-3343. FAX: (812) 523-5116. Licensee: Midland Media Inc. (acq 6-28-91; $15,000; FTR 7-22-91). ■ Robert Becker, gen mgr; Tracy Becker, gen sls mgr.

WJLR(FM)—Dec 1993: 92.7 mhz; 3.9 kw. Ant 400 ft. TL: N38 50 30 W85 46 52. Stereo. Hrs opn: 24. Box 1236, Seymour (47274). (812) 522-5483. FAX: (812) 793-2582. Licensee: Austin Radio. Format: Contemp christian. News staff one; news progmg 21 hrs wkly. Target aud: 25-49; professional, family oriented Christians.

Batesville

WRBI(FM)—May 14, 1977: 103.9 mhz; 1.95 kw. Ant 360 ft. TL: N39 13 22 W85 15 28. Stereo. Hrs opn: 24. 133 S. Main St., (47006). (812) 934-5111. FAX: (812) 934-2765. Licensee: ARS Broadcasting Corp. (acq 6-1-83; $180,000; FTR 5-2-83). Net: MBS. Rep: Rgnl Reps. Format: C&W. Spec prog: Farm 5 hrs wkly. ■ Alan R. Schriber, pres; Ronald E. Green, vp, gen mgr & vp mktg; Renee Day, progmg dir; Bryan Kelly, news dir. ■ Rates: $12.50; 12.50; 12.50; 9.40.

Battle Ground

WIIZ(FM)—March 11, 1993: 98.7 mhz; 4.4 kw. Ant 384 ft. TL: N40 29 57 W86 52 25. Hrs opn: 24. 190 Professional Ct., Lafayette (47905). (317) 447-9870; (317) 448-9111. FAX: (317) 449-3299. Licensee: Wizard Broadcasting Inc. (acq 3-24-92; $112,995; FTR 4-13-92). Format: New age, progsv, rock. News staff one; news progmg 3 hrs wkly. Target aud: 18-44; young, well educated, high income. Spec prog: Black 3 hrs, jazz 4 hrs wkly. ■ Mick Brooks, CEO, pres, CFO & gen mgr; Juan Montegro, chmn; Buzz Fitzgerald, opns dir & progmg dir; Diana Waltz, gen sls mgr; Virginia Leahy, prom dir; Shaun Campbell, mus dir; Diane Shook, pub affrs dir; Kim Hearst, Alex Keddie, chiefs engr. ■ Rates: $21; 18; 20; 12.

Bedford

WBIW(AM)—October 1948: 1340 khz; 1 kw-U. TL: N38 52 23 W86 28 34. Hrs opn: 24. Box 1307, 424 Heltonville Rd. (47421). (812) 275-7555. FAX: (812) 279-8046. Licensee: Ad-Venture Media Inc. (acq 1-30-89; $1 million with co-located FM; FTR 1-30-89). Net: ABC, Brownfield; Tribune. Rep: Rgnl Reps. Wash atty: Reed, Smith, Shaw & McClay. Format: Modern country, news, talk. News staff two; news progmg 8 hrs wkly. Target aud: 25 plus; general, male & female, balanced. Spec prog: Farm 3 hrs wkly, sports, weather. ■ Dean Spencer, pres & gen mgr; Barbara Spencer, gen sls mgr; Laura Duncan, progmg dir; Myron Rainey, mus dir; Bill Silvers, news dir; Vance Lockenour, chief engr.

WQRK(FM)—Co-owned with WBIW(AM). Oct 1, 1975: 105.5 mhz; 2 kw. Ant 400 ft. TL: N38 54 29 W86 28 28. Stereo. Hrs opn: 24. Prog sep from AM. (812) 333-1050; (812) 279-5746. Net: ABC, Unistar, SMN; Tribune. Rep: Rgnl Reps. Format: Classic hits. News staff 2; news progmg 8 hrs wkly. Target aud: 18-45; upscale adults. Spec prog: Jazz 4 hrs wkly. ■ William Browning, gen sls mgr; Laura Duncan, prom mgr & progmg dir; Gary Parker, news dir.

Beech Grove

WNTS(AM)—Dec 10, 1956: 1590 khz; 5 kw-D, 500 w-N, DA-3. TL: N39 44 21 W86 05 26 (night), N39 44 21 W86 05 29 (day). Hrs opn: 5:30 AM-midnight. 4800 E. Raymond St., Indianapolis (46203). (317) 359-5591. Licensee: S & M Broadcasting Co. (acq 4-15-74). Net: USA. Wash atty: Gardner, Carton & Douglas. Format: Relg. Target aud: 25-54. ■ Samuel W. Smulyan, pres; James S. Wilson, gen mgr; Nancy Wilson, pub affrs dir.

Berne

*****WRJV(FM)**—Not on air, target date unknown: 91.1 mhz; 25 kw. Ant 100 ft. Box 347 (46711). Licensee: Faith Christian Academy.

WZBD(FM)—Aug 27, 1993: 92.7 mhz; 2.05 kw. Ant 394 ft. TL: N40 46 15 W85 56 05. Hrs opn: 5 AM-10 PM. Box 4050, Graber Insurance, U.S. 27 N. (46711). (219) 589-9300; (219) 589-9927. FAX: (219) 589-8045. Licensee: Robert Alan Weaver. Net: MBS.

Bicknell

WUZR(FM)—Licensed to Bicknell. See Vincennes.

Bloomfield

WBHQ(FM)—Not on air, target date 1994: 101.1 mhz; 3 kw. Ant 300 ft. TL: N39 02 19 W86 50 08. Stereo. Rt. 2, Box 344, West Baden (47469). (812) 936-9450. Licensee: W.G. & Catherine Willis dba Willtronics Broadcasting Co. Wash atty: Fisher, Wayland, Cooper & Leader. Format: Modern country. ■ Col. W.G. Willis, CEO, gen mgr, gen sls mgr & chief engr; Catherine Willis, CFO.

Bloomington

WBWB(FM)—July 17, 1978: 96.7 mhz; 1.65 kw. Ant 439 ft. TL: N39 09 46 W86 28 21. Stereo. Box 7797 (47407). (812) 336-8000. FAX: (812) 336-7000. Licensee: University Broadcasting Co. (group owner; acq 1-89; grpsl; FTR 1-23-89). Rep: Christal. Wash atty: Haley, Bader & Potts. Format: Hot A/C. News staff one. Target aud: 18-49. ■ Art Angotti, pres; Davis Nathan, gen mgr; Jerilyn Kennedy, gen sls mgr; Tony Manes, prom dir & progmg dir; Jon Callahan, news dir. ■ Rates: $38; 34; 34; 18.

*****WFHB(FM)**—December 1992: 91.3 mhz; 2.5 kw. Ant 266 ft. TL: N39 01 55 W86 36 33. Hrs opn: 9. Box 1973 (47402); 108 W. 4th St. (47404). (812) 323-1200. FAX: (812) 323-0320. Licensee: Bloomington Community Radio Inc. Format: Div, news, public affairs. Target aud: Children, parents, teens, students & seniors. ■ Lisa Sorg, mus dir.

*****WFIU(FM)**—Sept 30, 1950: 103.7 mhz; 34 kw. Ant 590 ft. TL: N39 08 32 W86 29 43. Stereo. Hrs opn: 24. Radio-TV Center, Indiana Univ. (47405). (812) 855-1357; (812) 855-2664. FAX: (812) 855-0729. Licensee: Trustees of Indiana Univ. Net: AP, NPR. Format: Class, jazz, news. News staff one; news progmg 7 hrs wkly. Target aud: General. ■ Don Agostino, gen mgr; Judy Witt, Marla Keller, dev dirs; Christina Kuzmych, progmg dir; Catherine Lasocki, mus dir; Margaret Jospeh, news dir; Bradley Howard, chief engr. ■ WTIU(TV) affil.

WGCL(AM)—March 11, 1949: 1370 khz; 5 kw-D, 500 w-N, DA-2. TL: N39 11 25 W86 38 02 (CP: 1 kw-N). Hrs opn: 24. 400 One City Centre (47401). (812) 332-3366. FAX: (812) 331-4570. Licensee: Sarkes Tarzian Inc. (group owner). Net: ABC/E. Rep: Banner. Format: News/talk. Target aud: 30 plus. Spec prog: Sports. ■ Tom Tarzino, CEO; Geoffrey Vargo, pres; Thomas Hunt, gen mgr; Linda Clay, gen sls mgr; Pam Thrash, prom mgr; Chris Dorej, progmg dir; Tom Stein, news dir; Marc Antonetti, chief engr. ■ Rates: $30; 30; 25; 10.

WTTS(FM)—Co-owned with WGCL(AM). Jan 7, 1960: 92.3 mhz; 37 kw. Ant 1,090 ft. TL: N39 24 27 W86 08 52. Stereo. Hrs opn: 24. Prog sep from AM. 5948 N. College Ave, Indianapolis (46220). (317) 726-0923. FAX: (317) 479-3161. Format: Adult rock. News staff one. Target aud: 25-49. Spec prog: Blue Sunday 2 hrs, overeasy 3 hrs, acoustic show & brave new world 4 hrs wkly. ■ Linda Clay, sls dir; Pam Thrash, prom dir; Rich Anton, vp progmg; John McCue, mus dir; Kirk Ardery, news dir; Mike Rabey, engrg dir. ■ Rates: $40; 50; 50; 35.

Bluffton

WNUY(FM)—Dec 10, 1963: 100.1 mhz; 2.6 kw. Ant 351 ft. TL: N40 44 50 W85 10 21. Stereo. Hrs opn: 24. Box 321, 118 S. Main (46714). (219) 824-2804; (219) 824-5883. FAX: (219) 824-2805. Licensee: Wells County Radio Corp. (acq 4-10-86). Format: Adult contemp. News staff one; news progmg 3 hrs wkly. Target aud: 25-49; professional women. Spec prog: Relg 4 hrs wkly. ■ Joe Shanley, gen mgr; Rob Caylor, stn mgr, progmg dir & mus dir; Rick Elwell, gen sls mgr & prom dir; Mike Peters, chief engr. ■ Rates: $16; 16; 16; 16.

Boonville

WBNL(AM)—Sept 10, 1950: 1540 khz; 250 w-D. TL: N38 03 58 W87 16 27. Box 270 (47601). (812) 897-2080. Licensee: Boonville Broadcasting Co. Net: Network Ind. Format: Automated country. ■ Norman Hall, pres & gen mgr; Larry Swietzer, gen sls mgr & news dir; Artie Hinsley, chief engr.

WBNL-FM—Dec 19, 1967: 107.1 mhz; 3 kw. Ant 185 ft. TL: N38 03 58 W87 16 27. Prog sep from AM. Format: Adult contemp.

Brazil

WSDM(AM)—1959: 1130 khz; 500 w-D. TL: N39 30 43 W87 08 19. Box 650 (47834). (812) 446-2507. FAX: (812) 446-1250. Licensee: Equity One Media Partners (acq 7-26-90; $350,000 with co-located FM; FTR 8-6-90). Net: CNN. Rep: Rgnl Reps. Wash atty: Julian Feret. Format: News. News staff one. Target aud: General. Spec prog: Farm 10 hrs wkly. ■ Mike Petersen, gen mgr; Ryan Michaels, news dir; Mike Rabey, chief engr. ■ Rates: $15; 14; 15; na.

WSDM-FM—Nov 13, 1973: 97.7 mhz; 6 kw. Ant 300 ft. TL: N39 30 43 W87 08 19. Stereo. Prog sep from AM. White Rock Rd. (47834). Net: SMN. Format: Pure gold. News staff one. Target aud: 25-54. ■ Rates: $15; 14; 15; 12.

Bremen

WYEZ(FM)—Mar 1, 1993: 96.9 mhz; 2.99 kw. Ant 462 ft. TL: N41 26 37 W86 01 18. Suite 203, 3900 Edison Lakes Pkwy., Mishawaka (46545). (219) 273-9690. FAX: (219) 277-9692. Licensee: WMRI Inc. (group owner). Net: ABC. Format: Easy listening. ■ Mike Day, vp; Paul Grant, gen mgr; Rich Coolman, opns dir; Bob Miller, mus dir; Paul Dixon, engrg dir. ■ Rates: $20; 15; 20; 10.

Brookston

WEZV-FM—Apr 16, 1967: 95.3 mhz; 1.15 kw. Ant 520 ft. TL: N40 40 57 W86 51 34 (CP: 2.3 kw, ant 505 ft.). Stereo. Hrs opn: 24. Box 2771, 2655 Yeager Rd., West Lafayette (47906). (317) 497-9530. FAX: (317) 497-9495. Licensee: Bomar Broadcasting Co. Lafayette (acq 3-14-91; $525,000; FTR 4-1-91). Net: ABC. Wash atty: Verner, Liipfert, Bernhard, McPherson & Hand. Format: Jazz, MOR, new age. News staff one; news progmg 14 hrs wkly. Target aud: 35 plus; affluent, educated & upscale. ■ Frank Bove, pres; Mike Day, vp; Doug Kern, gen mgr; Bob Miller, mus dir. ■ Rates: $22; 25; 22; 17.

Brownsburg

WQFE(FM)—March 23, 1992: 101.9 mhz; 2.5 kw. Ant 252 ft. TL: N39 49 07 W86 22 40. Stereo. Hrs opn: 24. 733 N. Green St. (46112). (317) 852-9119. FAX: (317) 852-8018. Licensee: Quinn Broadcasting Inc. Net: USA, Ind. Net. Format: Easy listening, big band. News staff one; news progmg 12 hrs wkly. Target aud: 45 plus. Spec prog: Sports/talk. ■ Helen Sparks Quinn (owner), CEO; Stephen Ross, gen mgr; Dale Edwards, opns dir; Burt James, sls dir; Kim Seals, prom dir; John Marer, news dir; Irma White, pub affrs dir; Niles Geboe, chief engr. ■ Rates: $35; 28; 31; 20.

Cannelton

WLME(FM)—July 1990: 105.7 mhz; 2.2 kw. Ant 371 ft. TL: N37 55 33 W86 43 19 (CP: 12.5 kw, ant 466 ft.). Stereo. Hrs opn: 24. Box 335, Tell City (47586). (502) 927-8121. FAX: (812) 547-8121. Licensee: Hancock Communications. Group owner: The Cromwell Group Inc. Net: Kentuckry News Net. Format: Country. News staff one; news progmg 10 hrs wkly. Target aud: 25-54; general. Spec prog: Sports 6 hrs wkly. ■ Bayard H. Walters, pres; Bob Munson, gen mgr; Todd Ellis, gen sls mgr; Pat Michael, progmg dir.

Carmel

*****WHJE(FM)**—September 1963: 91.3 mhz; 400 w. Ant 100 ft. TL: N39 58 45 W86 07 10. Stereo. Hrs opn: 24. 520 E. Main St. (46032). (317) 571-4055; (317) 846-7721, ext. 1460. FAX: (317) 571-4066. Licensee: Carmel Clay Schools. Net: AP. Format: CHR. Target aud: 12 plus. ■ Scott M. Gregg, gen mgr; Thomas Allebrandi, chief engr.

Centerville

WHON(AM)—Licensed to Centerville. See Richmond.

Charlestown

WHOX(FM)—Not on air, target date unknown: 104.3 mhz; 3 kw. Ant 328 ft. TL: N38 28 55 W85 37 33. R.R. One, Box 231B, c/o WUZR(FM), Vincennes (47591). Licensee: Media Five Corp.

Chesterton

*****WDSO(FM)**—November 1976: 88.3 mhz; 413 w. Ant 180 ft. TL: N41 36 43 W87 03 41. Stereo. Chesterton High School, 651 W. Morgan Ave. (46304). (219) 926-4700; (219) 926-2151, ext. 229. FAX: (219) 926-4387; (219) 926-7603. Licensee: Duneland School Corp. Format: Rock. News progmg 6 hrs wkly. Target aud: General. Spec prog: Class one hr, specialty rock 8 hrs wkly. ■ James Cavallo, gen mgr; Brent Barber, stn mgr & chief engr; Michele Stipanovich, opns mgr.

Churubusco

WKQM(FM)—Not on air, target date unknown: 96.3 mhz; 3 kw. TL: N41 11 26 W85 11 13 (CP: 6.7 kw, ant 554 ft., TL: N41 06 13 W85 10 44). c/o Radio Station WGL-AM-FM, 2000 Lower Huntington Rd., Fort Wayne (46819). (219) 747-1511. Licensee: Robert M. Peters. ■ Frank Kovas, gen mgr.

Clinton

WAXI(FM)—See Rockville.

Columbia City

WDJB(FM)—Oct 13, 1968: 106.3 mhz; 1.55 kw. Ant 400 ft. TL: N41 06 25 W85 21 34. Stereo. 6112 Constitution Dr. Fort Wayne (46804). (219) 436-9223. FAX: (219) 436-2068. Licensee: IRP Inc. (acq 12-8-89). Rep: Banner. Wash atty: Leventhal, Senter & Lerman. Format: Contemp hit top-40. Target aud: 12-34. Spec prog: Public affairs. ■ Daniel F. Dudley, vp & gen mgr; Ashley Dressel, gen sls mgr; John O'Rourke, prom mgr, mus dir & progmg dir.

*****WJHS(FM)**—Aug 12, 1985: 91.5 mhz; 2.65 kw. Ant 219 ft. TL: N41 10 04 W85 29 41. Stereo. 600 N. Whitley St. (46725). (219) 248-8915; (219) 244-6136, ext. 212. FAX: (219) 244-4099; (219) 244-5610. Licensee: Whitley County Consolidated Schools Board of Control. Net: AP. Format: Div. Target aud: General. Spec prog: Sports events. ■ Robert D. Thomas, stn mgr.

Columbus

WCSI(AM)—1950: 1010 khz; 500 w-D, 19 w-N. TL: N39 11 05 W85 57 17. Stereo. Hrs opn: 24. Box 709, 3212 Washington St. (47203). (812) 372-4448; (812) 376-4744. FAX: (812) 372-1061. Licensee: White River Broadcasting Co. Group owner: Findlay Publishing Co. Inc. (acq 11-1-57). Net: AP, MBS, AgriAmerica. Rep: Rgnl Reps. Format: News, talk, weather. News staff 2. Target aud: 25-54. ■ Edwin L. Heminger, chmn; Kurt P. Kah, pres; David P. Glass, vp; Tasha Kah, opns mgr & gen sls mgr; Rick Reed, prom mgr; Darren Tandy, progmg dir & pub affrs dir; Leslie Behrman, news dir; Jerry Mathis, chief engr.

WKKG(FM)—Co-owned with WCSI(AM). 1958: 101.5 mhz; 50 kw. Ant 492 ft. TL: N39 11 05 W85 57 17. Stereo. Prog sep from AM. Net: AP. Format: Country. News staff 2. Target aud: 25-54. ■ Steve Lee, progmg dir.

WRZQ-FM—See Greensburg.

WWWY(FM)—Jan 30, 1975: 104.9 mhz; 6 kw. Ant 300 ft. TL: N39 11 09 W85 57 37. Stereo. Box 487, 1333 Washington (47202). (812) 372-9933. FAX: (812) 372-9935. Licensee: Mid-State Media Inc. (acq 6-85; $391,000; FTR 6-3-85). Net: ABC/D. Format: Oldies, classic hits. News staff 2; news progmg 12 hrs wkly. Target aud: 25-54; upscale adults. Spec prog: Farm 2 hrs, new age 3 hrs wkly. ■ Scott E. Goodwin, pres & gen mgr; Dennis Rediker, opns mgr; Diane Johnson, sls dir; Mark Webber, news dir; Jim Walker, chief engr. ■ Rates: $22.80; 22.80; 22.80; 22.80.

Connersville

WIFE(AM)—Apr 5, 1948: 1580 khz; 250 w-ND. TL: N39 38 18 W85 08 54. Hrs opn: 18. Box 619, 406 Central Ave. (47331). (317) 825-6411; (317) 825-8561. Licensee: Rodgers Broadcasting Corp. (group owner; acq 8-88; grpsl; FTR 8-29-88). Net: AG America. Format: Country. News staff one; news progmg 10 hrs wkly. Target aud:

25-54; affluent, middle-aged country listeners. Spec prog: Farm 6 hrs, relg 6 hrs wkly. ■ David A. Rodgers, pres; John Trine, gen mgr; Rick Bemius, opns mgr & mus dir; Steve Frey, gen sls mgr; John White, news dir; Mike Peacock, chief engr. ■ Rates: $19; 19; 19; 19.

WCNB-FM—Co-owned with WIFE(AM). Feb 27, 1948: 100.3 mhz; 28 kw. Ant 275 ft. TL: N39 38 18 W85 08 54 (CP: 50 kw, ant 436 ft., TL: N39 38 15 W85 08 45). Stereo. Dups AM 100%. ■ Steve Frey, adv mgr. ■ Rates: Same as AM.

Corydon

WGZB-FM—June 20, 1988: 96.5 mhz; 3 kw. Ant 200 ft. TL: N38 12 52 W86 01 00. Stereo. Suite 400, 981 S. Third St., Louisville, KY (40203). (502) 581-9798. FAX: (502) 581-9795. Licensee: Power Communications Inc. Format: Urban contemp. ■ Rod Burbridge, gen mgr.

WOCC(AM)—May 22, 1964: 1550 khz; 250 w-D. TL: N38 11 26 W86 08 00. Box 503 (47112); 211 N. Capitol Ave. (812) 738-9622. Licensee: Radio Corydon Inc. (acq 11-5-90; $5,000; FTR 11-19-90). Net: CNN. Rep: Rgnl Reps. Format: Country. Target aud: 25-54. ■ Donnie Butler, pres; Mike Wix, exec vp; Gerald Schlatter Jr., gen mgr & news dir; Jill Waganer, gen sls mgr; Joe Pollack, chief engr. ■ Rates: $84; 84; 84; na.

Covington

WCDV(FM)—June 1, 1982: 103.1 mhz; 3 kw. Ant 300 ft. TL: N40 08 46 W87 27 15. Stereo. Hrs opn: 24. Box 67, 30 N. Vermilion, Danville, IL (61834); 820 Railroad St. (47932). (217) 443-4004; (317) 793-4823. FAX: (317) 793-4644. Licensee: Benton-Weatherford Broadcasting Inc. of Indiana (acq 7-12-85; $325,000; FTR 6-3-85). Rep: Roslin. Wash atty: Borsari & Paxson. Format: Adult contemp, oldies. News staff one; news progmg 10 hrs wkly. Target aud: 25-54. ■ Larry Weatherford, pres & opns dir; Rhea Benton-Weatherford, gen mgr; Greg Green, stn mgr & gen sls mgr; G.E. Holycross, progmg mgr; Chuck Sergent, mus dir; Tom Johnson, news dir; Jeff Stapleton, pub affrs dir; George Dudich, engrg dir; Len Watson, chief engr. ■ Rates: $12; 12; 12; 10.

***WFOF(FM)**—June 17, 1984: 90.3 mhz; 19 kw. Ant 265 ft. TL: N40 09 08 W87 27 58. Stereo. Hrs opn: 24. Box 227, 610 3rd St. (47932). (317) 793-4088. Licensee: Doxa Inc. Format: Relg. ■ Ray McDaniel, pres; Ogle Snider, gen mgr.

Crawfordsville

WCVL(AM)—Dec 12, 1964: 1550 khz; 250 w-U, DA-N. TL: N40 03 54 W86 56 00. Box 603, 1801 N. 200 W. (47933). (317) 362-8200. Licensee: C.V.L. Broadcasting Inc. Group owner: Key Broadcasting Inc. (acq 1986). Net: ABC/I. Rep: Rgnl Reps. Format: Country. News staff one. Target aud: General; local. Spec prog: Farm 5 hrs wkly. ■ Terry Forcht, pres; Dick Munro, gen mgr & gen sls mgr; Guy Mitchell, progmg dir; Mark Robbins, news dir. ■ Rates: $25; 14; 14; 10.

WIMC(FM)—Co-owned with WCVL(AM). June 1, 1974: 103.9 mhz; 1.35 kw. Ant 500 ft. TL: N40 08 05 W86 54 12. Stereo. Prog sep from AM. Format: Adult contemp. Target aud: 25-49.

WNDY(FM)—Aug 13, 1953: 106.3 mhz; 3 kw. Ant 77 ft. TL: N40 02 19 W86 54 22. Stereo. 301 W. Wabash Ave. (47933). (513) 745-3000. Licensee: Wabash College Radio (acq 10-22-64). Format: Top-40. Spec prog: Jazz 8 hrs, class 8 hrs, Black 3 hrs wkly. ■ Horace Turner, pres; Dr. James King, gen mgr; Chris May, gen sls mgr; Mike Bancroft, prom mgr; Mark Walker, progmg dir; Dave Mares, mus dir; Darrel Fletcher, news dir.

Crown Point

WWJY(FM)—Nov 10, 1972: 103.9 mhz; 3 kw. Ant 330 ft. TL: N41 19 24 W87 21 22. Stereo. 10200 S. Broadway (46307). (219) 738-2221. FAX: (219) 663-2634. Licensee: M & M Broadcasters Inc. (acq 3-2-93; $600,000; FTR 3-22-93). Net: MBS; Network Indiana. Wash atty: Roddy & Martin. Format: Easy adult contemp. Target aud: 25-54. ■ John Meyer, pres & mus dir; Roger Knautz, gen mgr & progmg dir; Marty Wielgus, stn mgr; Tula Kalleres, gen sls mgr; Paul Anderson, news dir; Harold Snure, chief engr.

Danville

WSYW-FM—Jan 10, 1975: 107.1 mhz; 883 w. Ant 604 ft. TL: N39 48 06 W86 34 24. Stereo. Hrs opn: 24. 8203 Indy Ct., Indianapolis (46214). (317) 271-9799. FAX: (317) 273-1507. Licensee: Universal Broadcasting of Indiana Inc. Group owner: Universal Broadcasting Corp. (acq 8-8-79). Rep: CMBS. Wash atty: Putbrese & Hunsaker. Format: Class. Target aud: 35-64; very upscale, professional mgmt credentials. ■ Howard Warshaw, pres; Ernest Caldemone, gen mgr; Jim Bricker, rgnl sls mgr; Matt Miles, progmg mgr & mus dir; Peter Meisel, pub affrs dir; Wayne Miller, chief engr. ■ Rates: $25; 25; 25; 25.

Decatur

WQHK-FM—Nov 8, 1966: 105.1 mhz; 2 kw. Ant 397 ft. TL: N40 49 14 W84 55 12 (CP: 13.4 kw, ant 449 ft.). Stereo. 2915 Maple Rd., Fort Wayne (46816). (219) 447-5511. FAX: (219) 447-7546. Licensee: Jam Communications Inc. Format: Contemp country. ■ Tony Richards, gen mgr; Kevin Meek, sls dir; Ed Didier, chief engr. ■ Rates: $14; 12; 14; 10.

WADM(AM)—Co-owned with WQHK-FM. Not on air, target date Unknown: 1540 khz; 250 w-D. TL: N40 49 14 W84 55 12. Hrs opn: Stn currently dark. (acq 1-5-93; $350,000 with co-located FM; FTR 1-25-93). Net: AgriAmerica.

Delphi

WNJY(FM)—May 24, 1989: 102.9 mhz; 1.2 kw. Ant 515 ft. TL: N40 40 18 W86 41 44. Stereo. Hrs opn: 24. Box 500, 701 N. Main, Monticello (47960-0500); Box 569, 215 S. Washington St. (46923-0569). (219) 583-2569; (317) 564-2569. FAX: (219) 583-8363. Licensee: Whitecar Regional Broadcasting Co. Net: MBS, NBC, Unistar, Westwood One; AgriAmerica, Tribune. Wash atty: Miller & Fields. Format: Oldies, farm. News staff 2; news progmg 17 hrs wkly. Target aud: 25 plus; highly educated, affluent. Spec prog: Gospel 7 hrs, jazz 3 hrs, big band 3 hrs wkly. ■ William Deibel, pres, gen mgr, gen sls mgr & prom mgr; Rex Fausett, progmg dir, mus dir & pub affrs dir; Steve Tyler, news dir; Steve Truex, chief engr. ■ Rates: $16; 12.30; 12.30; 12.30.

Earl Park

WIBN(FM)—Oct 15, 1983: 98.1 mhz; 25 kw. Ant 328 ft. TL: N40 34 22 W87 27 42. Stereo. Box 25, Oxford (47971). (317) 385-2373. Licensee: IBN Broadcasting Inc. (acq 11-8-85). Format: Adult contemp. ■ Sidney P. Thompson, pres & gen mgr.

Elkhart

***WAUS(FM)**—See South Bend, Ind.

WFRN(AM)—March 16, 1956: 1270 khz; 5 kw-D, 1 kw-N, DA-2. TL: N41 37 18 W85 57 37. Box 307 (46515). (219) 875-5166. FAX: (219) 875-6662. Licensee: Progressive Broadcasting System Inc. Net: MBS. Format: Relg. News staff 2. Target aud: 25-54. Spec prog: Farm 5 hrs wkly. ■ Edwin Moore, gen mgr; Dewey Moede, gen sls mgr; Doug Smith, vp progmg. ■ Rates: $10; 10; 10; 4.

WFRN-FM—June 10, 1963: 104.7 mhz; 50 kw. Ant 488 ft. TL: N41 37 18 W85 57 37. Stereo. ■ Doug Smith, progmg dir; Wendell Tyler, mus dir. ■ Rates: $40; 35; 35; 20.

WLTA(FM)—Listing follows WTRC(AM).

WTRC(AM)—Nov 18, 1931: 1340 khz; 1 kw-U. TL: N41 40 28 W85 56 51. Hrs opn: 5 AM-midnight. Box 699, 58096 CR 7 S. (46515). (219) 293-5611. Licensee: Pathfinder Communications Corp. Group owner: Federated Media. Net: NBC, NBC Talknet, Unistar. Rep: Christal. Format: Adult contemp, news/talk. News staff 2; news progmg 21 hrs wkly. Target aud: 35-64; Elkhart County residents. ■ John Dille III, pres; Dick Rhodes, gen mgr; Brad Williams, gen sls mgr; Allen Strike, progmg dir; Tom Rogers, news dir; Ed Schmidt, chief engr. ■ Rates: $50; 30; 30; 15.

WLTA(FM)—Co-owned with WTRC(AM). Apr 1, 1947: 100.7 mhz; 15 kw. Ant 910 ft. TL: N41 36 58 W86 11 38. Stereo. One Edison Center, Suite 200, 237 Edison Rd., Mishawaka (46545). (219) 258-5483. Rep: Christal. Format: lite adult contemp. News staff one. Target aud: 25-54. Spec prog: Relg 2 hrs wkly. ■ Steven Kline, gen mgr; Gene Walker, opns mgr; Bob Maxwell, prom dir; Keith Wright, progmg dir. ■ Rates: $35; 35; 35; 20.

***WVPE(FM)**—May 1972: 88.1 mhz; 10 kw. Ant 400 ft. TL: N41 36 20 W86 12 46 (CP: 10.5 w, ant 554 ft., TL: N41 36 59 W86 11 43). Stereo. 2424 California Rd. (46514). (219) 262-5660. FAX: (219) 262-5700. Licensee: Elkhart Community Schools Corp. Net: APR. Format: Jazz. News progmg 13 hrs wkly. Spec prog: Blues 5 hrs, folk 9 hrs, new age 5 hrs wkly. ■ Tim Eby, gen mgr; Tim Miller, opns mgr; Jim Biddle, mus dir; Robin Alexander, news dir; Charles Pitts, chief engr.

WZOW(FM)—See Goshen.

Ellettsville

WGCT(FM)—Not on air, target date unknown: 105.1 mhz; 6 kw. Ant 328 ft. TL: N39 11 32 W86 41 46. Box 7797, Bloomington (47407). (812) 335-1051. FAX: (812) 336-7000. Licensee: Katieco Inc. Net: Jones Satellite Audio. Wash atty: Haley, Bader & Potts. ■ Katie Williams, pres; Davis Nathan, stn mgr; Jerilyn Kennedy, gen sls mgr; Rick Evans, progmg mgr; Jon Callahan, pub affrs dir.

Elwood

WIVM(FM)—July 1964: 101.7 mhz; 3 kw. Ant 328 ft. TL: N40 16 33 W85 51 44. Stereo. Hrs opn: 24. Box 101, RR 3 County Line Rd. (46036). (317) 552-5043; (317) 552-0506. Licensee: Phoenix Broadcasting Corp. (acq 7-2-92; $80,000; FTR 7-6-92). Net: Net. Ind., AgriAmerica. Rep: Rgnl Reps. Format: AOR. News staff one. Target aud: 25-54; adult buying public. ■ Joel Schneider, pres; Steve Dunham, gen mgr, stn mgr, gen sls mgr, mktg mgr & prom mgr; Jay Wallace, opns mgr & progmg dir; Keith Mason, mus dir; Leland Franklin, pub affrs dir; Shawn Mattingly, chief engr. ■ Rates: $16; 16; 16; 13.

Evansville

WGBF-FM—See Henderson, Ky.

WIKY-FM—Listing follows WJPS(AM).

WJPS(AM)—1935: 1400 khz; 1 kw-U. TL: N37 56 17 W87 31 51. Stereo. Hrs opn: 24. Box 3848, (47736). (812) 424-8284. FAX: (812) 426-7928. Licensee: South Central Communications Corp. (group owner; acq 11-81). Net: Unistar. Rep: Katz. Wash atty: Bryan McCaue. Format: Oldies. News staff 3; news progmg 2 hrs wkly. Target aud: 25-49; general. ■ John D. Engelbrecht, pres; Terry Bond, gen mgr; Mark Steele, prom dir; Brenda Whitney, progmg dir & mus dir; Randy Wheeler, news dir. ■ Rates: $25; 25; 25; 25.

WIKY-FM—Co-owned with WJPS(AM). Aug 28, 1948: 104.1 mhz; 39 kw. Ant 580 ft. TL: N37 59 21 W87 35 48. Stereo. 1162 Mt. Auburn Rd. (47720). (Acq 1948). Format: Adult contemp. News staff 3; news progmg 14 hrs wkly. Target aud: 25-54; females, workplace. Spec prog: Farm 17 hrs wkly. ■ Mark Baker, vp progmg. ■ Rates: $104; 95; 60; 38.

***WNIN-FM**—Feb 1, 1982: 88.3 mhz; 45 kw. Ant 510 ft. TL: N38 01 27 W87 21 43 (CP: ant 492 ft.). Stereo. Hrs opn: 24. 405 Carpenter St. (47708). (812) 423-2973. FAX: (812) 428-7548. Licensee: S.W. Indiana Public Broadcasting Inc. Net: APR, NPR. Wash atty: Dow, Lohnes & Albertson. Format: Class, news. News progmg 20 hrs wkly. Target aud: General. ■ David L. Dial, pres & gen mgr; Herb Wilbum, stn mgr; Carolyn McClintock, vp dev; David Roden, progmg dir & mus dir; Trish Muse, news dir; Jerry Kissinger, chief engr.

***WPSR(FM)**—September 1957: 90.7 mhz; 14 kw. Ant 130 ft. TL: N38 01 45 W87 34 42. Stereo. Hrs opn: 7 AM-10 PM. 5400 First Ave. (47710). (812) 465-8241. FAX: (812) 465-8241. Licensee: Evansville Vanderburg School Corp. (acq 9-57). Net: IBS, UPI. Format: Div, educ. News progmg 3 hrs wkly. Target aud: General. ■ Michael H. Reininga, gen mgr, stn mgr, dev dir & prom dir; Sue Holland, progmg dir; Frank Hertal, chief engr.

WRBT(FM)—See Mt. Carmel, Ill.

***WSWI(AM)**—Aug 6, 1947: 820 khz; 250 w-D. TL: N37 57 53 W87 40 06. Radio Center, 8600 University Blvd. (47712). (812) 464-1836. FAX: (812) 464-1960. Licensee: Univ. of Southern Indiana (acq 11-3-81). Net: AP. Format: Modern rock. News staff one; news progmg 10 hrs wkly. Target aud: 18-54; loc students, faculty and community members. Spec prog: Broadway musicals one hr, oldtime drama 2 hrs, big band 3 hrs, soul/rap 3 hrs, class 10 hrs wkly. ■ Wayne Rinks, gen mgr; Holly Geibel, news dir; Frank Hertel, chief engr.

***WUEV(FM)**—Apr 1, 1951: 91.5 mhz; 6.1 kw. Ant 150 ft. TL: N37 58 24 W87 31 48. Stereo. Hrs opn: 21. 1800 Lincoln Ave. (47722). (812) 479-2022. Licensee: Univ. of Evansville. Net: AP; Network Indiana. Format: Div. ■ Leonard Clark, gen mgr & opns mgr; Phillip Bailey, chief engr.

WVHI(AM)—Oct 31, 1948: 1330 khz; 5 kw-D, 1 kw-N, DA-N. TL: N38 03 12 W87 35 40. Box 3636 (47735). (812) 425-2221. Licensee: Geyer Broadcasting Inc. (acq 10-1-64). Format: Relg, adult contemp. Target aud: General. ■ Wayne W. Geyer, pres; Sally Carr, gen mgr; Kevin Barnett, progmg dir; Steve Chapman, mus dir; Sharyl Harper, news dir; Ralph Turpin, chief engr. ■ Rates: $14.50; 14.50; 14.50; 14.50.

WWOK(AM)—Nov 22, 1923: 1280 khz; 5 kw-D, 1 kw-N, DA-N. TL: N37 59 53 W87 28 33. Stereo. Hrs opn: 24. Box 297 (47702). (812) 477-8811. FAX: (812) 474-1492. Licensee: Aiken Communications Corp. (acq 5-9-87). Net: Unistar, CNN. Rep: Banner. Wash atty: Fisher, Wayland, Cooper & Leader. Format: MOR. News staff one; news progmg 6 hrs wkly. Target aud: 35-64; affluent, mature. ■ Larry Aiken, pres & gen mgr; Mike Bevers, gen sls mgr; Lisa Yockey, prom dir; Tony Couch, mus dir; Dan Egierski, news dir; Steve Chandler, chief engr. ■ Rates: $32; 26; 30; 20.

WYNG-FM—Dec 22, 1964: 105.3 mhz; 50 kw. Ant 480 ft. TL: N38 04 47 W87 36 36. Stereo. Box 2777 (47728); 1133 Lincoln Ave. (47714). (812) 425-4226. FAX: (812) 421-0005. Licensee: Ballston Trust Services L.C. Group owner: Pinnacle Broadcasting Co. (acq 12-22-92; FTR 1-25-93). Net: Unistar. Rep: Eastman. Format: Modern country. News staff one; news progmg 5 hrs wkly. Target aud: 25-54. ■ Philip D. Marella, pres; John Bowen, vp & gen mgr; Ron Eberhart, gen sls mgr; Dave Kennedy, prom mgr & progmg mgr; K.C. Todd, mus dir; Jim Bretz, news dir; Marty Hensley, chief engr.

Fort Branch

***WBGW(FM)**—July 20, 1990: 101.5 mhz; 1 kw. Ant 561 ft. TL: N38 10 45 W87 29 13. Stereo. Hrs opn: 24. Box 4164, Evansville (47724); c/o 5708 Spring Lake Dr., Evansville (47710). (812) 768-5550; (812) 423-2786. FAX: (812) 768-5552. Licensee: Music Ministries Inc. Net: Moody, USA. Format: Relg. News progmg 12 hrs wkly. Target aud: General. ■ Donald C. Chagle, pres; Floyd E. Turner, gen mgr & chief engr.

Fort Wayne

WAJI(FM)—August 1959: 95.1 mhz; 39 kw. Ant 680 ft. TL: N41 06 13 W85 11 28. Stereo. Hrs opn: 24. 6th Floor Medical Center, Suite 600, 347 W. Berry (46802). (219) 423-3676. FAX: (216) 422-5266. Licensee: Sarkes Tarzian Inc. (group owner). Rep: Katz. Format: Adult contemp of 70s, 80s & today. News staff one. Target aud: 25-54. ■ Candace A. Wendling, pres & gen mgr; Daryl McIntire, gen sls mgr; Janine Grover, prom mgr; Lee Tobin, progmg dir; Barb Richards, mus dir; Carrie Wellman, news dir; Jack Didier, chief engr.

***WBCL(FM)**—Jan 8, 1976: 90.3 mhz; 50 kw. Ant 499 ft. TL: N41 06 13 W85 11 46. Stereo. Hrs opn: 24. 1025 W. Rudisill Blvd. (46807). (219) 745-0576. FAX: (219) 745-2001. Licensee: Taylor University Inc. (acq 6-24-92; FTR 7-20-92). Format: Relg. ■ Char Binkley, gen mgr; Jeff Carlson, prom mgr & chief engr; Scott Tsuleff, mus dir; Jim Stanley, news dir.

***WBNI-FM**—June 15, 1978: 89.1 mhz; 34 kw. Ant 604 ft. TL: N41 06 25 W85 11 46 (CP: TL: N41 06 13 W85 11 28). Stereo. Hrs opn: 24. Rebroadcasts WBKE (FM) N. Manchester 50%. Box 8459 (46898-8459); 2000 N. Wells St. (46808). (219) 423-1629. FAX: (219) 424-3706. Licensee: Public Broadcasting of Northeastern Indiana Inc. (acq 1-15-82). Net: APR, AP, NPR. Wash atty: Bosari & Paxson. Format: Class, jazz, news & info. News staff one; news progmg 22 hrs wkly. Target aud: 25 plus. Spec prog: Black 3 hrs wkly. ■ J.C. Heithalls, pres; Andrew Candor, vp; Bruce R. Haines, gen mgr & progmg dir; J. Michael Venable, opns mgr; Carol Ver Wiebe, dev dir; Janice Furtner, mus dir; Dan Drayer, news dir; Mike Peters, chief engr.

WBTU(FM)—(Kendallville). Dec 16, 1964: 93.3 mhz; 50 kw. Ant 450 ft. TL: N41 23 55 W85 15 08. Stereo. Hrs opn: 24. 2100 Goshen Rd., Fort Wayne (46808). (219) 482-9288. FAX: (219) 482-8655. Licensee: Fort Wayne Media Ltd. Group owner: Fort Wayne Media Ltd. (acq 1-1-87). Net: MBS, Unistar. Format: Country. Target aud: 18-54; upscale, young audience. ■ Dick Young, stn mgr; Mitch Mahan, progmg dir & mus dir; Jenette Heller, news dir. ■ Rates: $62; 62; 62; 26.

WFCV(AM)—June 17, 1968: 1090 khz; 1 kw-D, DA. TL: N41 05 00 W85 04 33. 909 Coliseum Blvd. (46805). (219) 423-2337. FAX: (219) 423-6355. Licensee: Bott Broadcasting (group owner; acq 5-1-80). Net: USA. Format: Relg, news/talk. Target aud: 35-64; family oriented, mature. ■ Richard P. Bott, pres; Kathy McClish, opns mgr; Dale Gerke, sls dir.

WFWI(FM)—March 4, 1993: 92.3 mhz; 1.9 kw. Ant 400 ft. TL: N41 06 33 W85 11 44 (CP: 2.7 kw, ant 482 ft.). Suite 220, 3400 Coliseum Blvd. E. (46805). (219) 484-1923. FAX: (219) 483-1923. Licensee: Edgewater Radio Inc. Format: Soft adult contemp. ■ Steve Avellone, gen mgr.

WGL(AM)—Jan 24, 1924: 1250 khz; 2.5 kw-D, 1.4 kw-N, DA-2. TL: N41 01 16 W85 09 46. 2000 Lower Huntington Rd. (46819). (219) 747-1511. FAX: (219) 747-1511. Licensee: Kovas Communications (acq 9-1-81). Net: APR, CNN, EFM, MBS. Format: News/talk. News staff one. Target aud: 25 plus. ■ Frank Kovas, pres; Connie Kovas, vp; Mary Kain, vp prom & news dir; Paul Phillips, asst mus dir; Mike Peters, chief engr.

WJLT(FM)—Aug 24, 1970: 101.7 mhz; 3 kw. Ant 328 ft. TL: N41 04 58 W85 04 22. Stereo. 347 W. Berry, Suite 600 (46802). (219) 423-3676. FAX: (219) 422-5266. Licensee: Sarkes Tarzian Inc. (group owner; acq 2-16-93; FTR 3-8-93). ■ Candace Wendling, gen mgr; Lee Tobin, mus dir. ■ Rates: $35; 35; 35; 25.

***WLAB(FM)**—Aug 23, 1976: 88.3 mhz; 1.45 kw. Ant 100 ft. TL: N41 06 48 W85 06 47 (CP: 7 kw, ant 341 ft., N41 05 58 W85 08 43). Stereo. 6600 N. Clinton St. (46825). (219) 483-8236. FAX: (219) 482-7707. Licensee: The Indiana District, Lutheran Church-Missouri Synod Inc. (acq 4-24-87). Format: Contemp Christian. News staff one; news progmg one hr wkly. Target aud: 18-65 plus. ■ Jim Zix, gen mgr & chief engr; Melissa Etnyre, progmg dir & pub affrs dir.

WLYV(AM)—Mar 28, 1948: 1450 khz; 1 kw-U. TL: N41 04 14 W85 07 10. Stereo. c/o Michael B. Glinter, 8506 Bradshaw, Lenexa, KS (66215). (913) 894-1833. Licensee: Fort Wayne Gospel Broadcasting Co. (acq 7-14-93; $45,000; FTR 8-9-93). Net: Unistar. Rep: Banner. Format: Country, gospel. Target aud: 25-54. Spec prog: Sports-Chicago Bears, Cubs, White Sox, Bulls. ■ Mike Glinter, pres.

WMEE(FM)—Listing follows WQHK(AM).

WOWO(AM)—Mar 31, 1925: 1190 khz; 50 kw-U, DA-N. TL: N40 59 47 W85 21 06. Stereo. Hrs opn: 24. 203 W. Wayne St. (46802). (219) 424-2400. FAX: (219) 422-2673. Licensee: Wayne Broadcasting Corp. Group owner: Price Communications Corp. Stations (acq 11-1-82; $6 million; FTR 10-4-82). Net: CBS. Rep: McGavren Guild. Format: Full service adult contemp. News staff 5. Target aud: 25-54. ■ Gina Maxwell, vp & gen mgr; Christine Kennedy, prom mgr; Gary Noe, progmg dir; Curt Miller, news dir; Eric Culp, chief engr.

WQHK(AM)—November 1947: 1380 khz; 5 kw-U, DA-2. TL: N41 00 10 W85 05 50. Stereo. 2915 Maples Rd. (46816). (219) 447-5511. FAX: (219) 447-7546. Licensee: Pathfinder Communications Corp. Group owner: Federated Media. Net: ABC. Rep: Christal. Format: C&W. ■ Tony Didier, gen mgr; Kevin Meek, gen sls mgr; Jeanette Reese, mktg dir & prom dir; Scott Miller, news dir.

WMEE(FM)—Co-owned with WQHK(AM). Feb 5, 1965: 97.3 mhz; 26 kw. Ant 689 ft. TL: N41 06 42 W85 11 43. Stereo. Format: Top-40, CHR, adult contemp. ■ Jeff Davis, progmg dir.

WXKE(FM)—May 6, 1976: 103.9 mhz; 3 kw. Ant 380 ft. TL: N41 06 31 W85 09 56. Stereo. Hrs opn: 24. 2541 Goshen Rd. (46808). (219) 484-0580. Licensee: Taylor Broadcast Group. Rep: D & R Radio. Format: AOR. News staff one; news progmg 3 hrs wkly. Target aud: 18-44; Woodstock generation, young adult rockers. ■ Robert B. Taylor, pres; David Riethmiller, gen mgr & prom mgr; Jeff Archer, gen sls mgr; Rick West, progmg dir; Buzz Maxwell, mus dir; Liz Thatcher, news dir; Greg Gibbons, chief engr. ■ Rates: $88; 88; 65; 50.

Frankfort

WILO(AM)—Nov 23, 1953: 1570 khz; 250 w-U. TL: N40 16 40 W86 29 07. Box 545 (46041). (317) 659-3338. Licensee: Kaspar Broadcasting Co. Inc. (acq 10-1-59). Net: AP. Rep: Rgnl Reps. Format: Country. Spec prog: Farm 12 hrs wkly. ■ V.J. Kaspar, pres & gen mgr; R.B. Kaspar, gen sls mgr.

WSHW(FM)—Co-owned with WILO(AM). Sept 14, 1962: 99.7 mhz; 50 kw. Ant 460 ft. TL: N40 25 14 W86 24 47. Stereo. Prog sep from AM. (317) 452-9955. Format: Adult contemp. Spec prog: Farm 8 hrs wkly.

Franklin

***WFCI(FM)**—Oct 15, 1960: 89.5 mhz; 1 kw. Ant 140 ft. TL: N39 24 29 W86 08 52. Stereo. Hrs opn: 9 AM-midnight. Franklin College of Indiana, Shirk Hall (46131). (317) 738-8200; (317) 738-8197. FAX: (317) 738-8233. Licensee: Franklin College of Indiana. Format: College, alt rock. News progmg 3 hrs wkly. Target aud: 18-24; college & high school students. ■ Ted Madden, gen mgr; Krona Lanham, prom mgr; Kevin Aides, progmg dir; Charles D. Sears, chief engr.

WPZZ(FM)—Dec 15, 1961: 95.9 mhz; 3 kw. Ant 300 ft. TL: N39 30 49 W86 04 07. Stereo. 645 Industrial Dr. (46131-9617). (317) 736-4040. FAX: (317) 736-7998. Licensee: FM 96 Corporation. Group owner: Willis Broadcasting Corp. (acq 7-1-88). Net: SMN, American Urban. Rep: Rgnl Reps. Format: Inspirational. Spec prog: Jazz 10 hrs wkly. ■ Levi Willis Bishop, pres; Tina Willis, gen mgr.

French Lick

WFLQ(FM)—April 12, 1983: 100.1 mhz; 6 kw. Ant 300 ft. TL: N38 35 41 W86 36 48. Stereo. Hrs opn: 6 AM-midnight. Box 100 (47432). (812) 936-9100. FAX: (812) 936-9495. Licensee: W.G. Willis dba Willtronics Broadcasting. Net: SMN. Wash atty: Fisher, Wayland, Cooper & Leader. Format: Country. News staff one; news progmg 11 hrs wkly. Target aud: 25 plus. Spec prog: Farm 3 hrs, relg 6 hrs wkly. ■ William Gerald Willis, CEO, pres, gen mgr, gen sls mgr & chief engr; Jim Ingalls, mus dir; Eric Hickman, news dir. ■ Rates: $9.50; 8.50; 9.50; 7.50.

Gary

***WGVE(FM)**—January 1954: 88.7 mhz; 2.1 kw. Ant 91 ft. TL: N41 33 15 W87 19 05. 1800 E. 35th Ave. (46409). (219) 962-7571. FAX: (219) 962-6269. Licensee: Gary Community School Corp. Format: Educ, pub affrs, reading svc for the blind. Spec prog: Class 16 hrs wkly. ■ Vernon Williams, gen mgr & progmg dir; Joe McMillan, chief engr.

WLTH(AM)—Nov 5, 1950: 1370 khz; 1 kw-D, 500 w-N, DA-N. TL: N41 32 22 W87 18 00. Box 2300 (46409). (219) 884-9409. FAX: (219) 980-0483. Licensee: Lorenzo P Butler II (acq 11-6-89; $900,000; FTR 11-27-89). Net: NBC, CNN. Format: News, talk, sports. News staff one. ■ Pluria Marshall, gen mgr & gen sls mgr; Jesse Coopwood, progmg dir & mus dir; Jim Ragonesse, news dir; Joseph McMillon, chief engr. ■ Rates: $55; 55; 55; 55.

WWCA(AM)—Dec 7, 1949: 1270 khz; 1 kw-U, DA-1. TL: N41 31 38 W87 22 36 (CP: COL: East Chicago, Ind., 2.5 kw-U, DA-1, TL: N41 31 38 W87 22 41). 545 Broadway (46402-1983). (219) 886-9171. FAX: (219) 886-3684. Licensee: Willis Family Broadcasting Inc. (group owner; acq 3-4-92; grpsl; FTR 3-28-92). Format: Relg. ■ L. E. Willis Sr., pres; Chuck Mansker, gen mgr & gen sls mgr; Kevin L. Ford, progmg dir; Quintete McDuffy, chief engr.

Goshen

***WGCS(FM)**—Oct 2, 1958: 91.1 mhz; 7.4 kw. Ant 65 ft. TL: N41 33 47 W85 49 39. Stereo. Goshen College (46526). (219) 535-7488. Licensee: Goshen College Broadcasting Corp. Format: Div, educ, class. News progmg 5 hrs wkly. Target aud: General. Spec prog: Sp 5 hrs wkly. ■ Bill Frisbie, gen mgr; Jay Carlin, chief engr.

WKAM(AM)—1954: 1460 khz; 2.5 kw-D, 500 w-N, DA-N. TL: N41 35 24 W85 48 56. Box 497 (46526-0497). (219) 533-1460. FAX: (219) 534-3698. Licensee: Northern Indiana Broadcasters. Net: Sun; Network Indiana. Rep: Rgnl Reps, Katz & Powell. Format: Adult contemp. News staff one. Target aud: 30-65; mature, family oriented, goal oriented. ■ John Carpenter, gen mgr; Brent Randall, gen sls mgr; Dan Eckelbarger, prom mgr & progmg dir; Ernie Ferland, news dir; Bob Henning, chief engr. ■ Rates: $12; 10; 12; 10.

WZOW(FM)—Co-owned with WKAM. Jan 17, 1977: 97.7 mhz; 2.9 kw. Ant 482 ft. TL: N41 36 04 W85 55 41 Stereo. Hrs opn: 24. Prog sep from AM. Drawer 967, Elkhart (46515). (219) 674-4330; (219) 294-1896. FAX: (219) 294-1722. Net: SMN. Rep: Katz & Powell; Rgnl Reps.Format: Classic rock. News staff one; news progmg 20 hrs wkly. Target aud: 25-54; baby boomers. ■ Lynn Bradley, gen mgr & gen sls mgr; Jim Callahan, progmg dir & mus dir.

Granger

WRBR-FM—See South Bend.

Greencastle

***WGRE(FM)**—Apr 25, 1949: 91.5 mhz; 115 w. Ant 160 ft. TL: N39 39 16 W86 51 40. Stereo. Center for Contemporary Media, 609 S. Locust (46135). (317) 658-4642. Licensee: DePauw Univ. Net: AP. Format: Alternative. News progmg 11 hrs wkly. Target aud: 18-25; college campus & local community. Spec prog: Jazz 3 hrs wkly. ■ Jeff McCall, pres & gen mgr; Debbie Bernsee, opns mgr; Brian Hatton, prom dir; Cyndi Schoolcraft, progmg dir; Kaia Van Dam, mus dir; Andy Slipher, asst mus dir; Ryan Smith, news dir; Shawna Delaney, pub affrs dir; Greg Stephan, chief engr.

WJNZ(FM)—May 16, 1966: 94.3 mhz; 3 kw. Ant 165 ft. TL: N39 39 38 W86 53 34. Stereo. Hrs opn: 5 AM-midnight. Box 494, Rt. 6, Dunbar Hill (46135). (317) 653-9717. FAX: (317) 653-6677. Licensee: Radio Greencastle Inc. (acq 5-77). Net: SMN; Net. Ind., Tribune. Format: Adult contemp, loc news, sports. News staff one; news progmg 37 hrs wkly. Target aud: General. Spec prog: Farm 5 hrs wkly. ■ Jinsie S. Bingham, pres, gen mgr, opns mgr, gen sls mgr & prom mgr; Brad Hudson, stn mgr; Mike Mitchell, mus dir; Hilary Gordon, news dir; Alan Homsher, chief engr. ■ Rates: $11; 9.75; 10; 9.

Greenfield

WZPL(FM)—June 1, 1962: 99.5 mhz; 12.5 kw. Ant 991 ft. TL: N39 46 03 W86 00 12. Stereo. Suite 1060, 3500 De Pauw Blvd., Indianapolis (46268). (317) 899-9999. FAX: (317) 337-2434. Licensee: WZPL Inc. Group owner: Booth American Co. (acq 11-86; $13 million; FTR 10-20-86). Net: AP. Rep: D & R Radio. Format: Adult contemp. News staff one. ■ Roger Ingram, gen mgr; Gary Hoffman, progmg dir; Julie Patterson, news dir; Don Payne, chief engr.

Greensburg

WTRE(AM)—July 1, 1968: 1330 khz; 500 w-D, 41 w-N, DA-2. TL: N39 19 41 W85 30 06. Hrs opn: 18. Box 487, 1217 W. Park Rd. (47240). (812) 663-3000. Licensee: WTRE Inc. (acq 3-31-76). Net: ABC/D; Network Ind. Format: Country, div, news/talk. News staff one; news progmg 24 hrs wkly. Target aud: 25 plus. Spec prog: Farm 10 hrs, relg 3 hrs wkly. ■ Keith Reising Jr., pres; Sandy Biddinger, stn mgr & news dir; Gene McCoy, sls dir; Jere Schoettmer, gen sls mgr; Chip Martz, progmg dir; Robert Hawkins, chief engr.

WRZQ-FM—Co-owned with WTRE(AM). December 1962: 107.3 mhz; 41.8 kw. Ant 531 ft. TL: N39 14 13 W85 34 00. Stereo. Hrs opn: 24. Radio Building, 825 Washington St., Columbus (47201). (812) 379-1077. FAX: (812) 378-4359. Format: Adult contemp. News progmg 4 hrs wkly. Target aud: 18-49. ■ Keith Reising Jr., gen mgr.

Greenwood

WGGR(FM)—Not on air, target date unknown: 106.1 mhz; 3 kw. Ant 328 ft. TL: N39 42 42 W86 08 45. Licensee: Greater Greenwood Broadcasting L.P.

Hammond

WJOB(AM)—1928: 1230 khz; 1 kw-U. TL: N41 35 46 W87 28 42. 6405 Olcott (46320). (219) 844-1230; (312) 375-4220. Licensee: Colby Broadcasting Corp. (acq 2-23-60). Wash atty: Wilmer, Cutler & Pickering. Format: MOR, news/talk. News staff 10; news progmg 17 hrs wkly. Target aud: 25-49; general. Spec prog: Sports, Pol 2 hrs, relg 2 hrs, Greek one hr wkly. ■ Julian Colby, pres; Judith Grambo, gen mgr; Michael Fray, gen sls mgr; John Baranowski, progmg dir; Jerry Siska, news dir; Gordon Boss, chief engr.

WYCA(FM)—Sept 14, 1959: 92.3 mhz; 50 kw H, 44 kw V. Ant 492 ft. TL: N41 37 50 W87 31 40. Stereo. Hrs opn: 24. 6336 Calumet Ave. (46324). (219) 933-4455; (708) 957-0105; (312) 734-4455. Licensee: Crawford Broadcasting Co. (group owner; acq 9-14-59). Format: Relg. Target aud: 18-49; young adult Christian. Spec prog: Black 10 hrs wkly. ■ Donald Crawford, pres; Taft Harris, stn mgr, gen sls mgr & mus dir; Tracie Reynolds, progmg dir; Henry Renken, chief engr.

Hartford City

WWWO(FM)—Feb 26, 1965: 93.5 mhz; 3.04 kw. Ant 456 ft. TL: N40 25 16 W85 25 40. Stereo. Hrs opn: 24. 5216 Bradburn Dr., Muncie (47304). (317) 289-9500. Licensee: Viking Communications Inc. (acq 10-88). Net: NBC, Unistar. Rep: Rgnl Reps. Format: Adult contemp. News staff one. Target aud: 25-54. ■ Bernie Kvale, pres & gen mgr; Rick Stephens, gen sls mgr; Sean Mattingly, progmg dir & engrg mgr; Mike Haston, news dir. ■ Rates: $34; 29; 34; 24.

Howe

***WHWE(FM)**—May 1, 1970: 89.7 mhz; 100 w. Ant 68 ft. TL: N41 43 32 W85 25 30. Box 247 (46746). (219) 562-2131. FAX: (219) 562-3678. Licensee: Howe Military School. Format: Educ. ■ Dave Marsett, gen mgr.

***WQKO(FM)**—Not on air, target date unknown: 91.9 mhz; 3 kw. Ant 298 ft. 6200 E State Rd. 120 (46746). Licensee: Maranatha Radio.

Huntingburg

WBDC(FM)—Licensed to Huntingburg. See Jasper.

Huntington

WOWO-FM—Sept 1, 1965: 103.1 mhz; 3 kw. Ant 298 ft. TL: N40 55 33 W85 23 15. Stereo. Hrs opn: 24. Rebroadcasts WOWO(AM) Fort Wayne 100%. 203 W. Wayne, Ft. Wayne (46802). (219) 424-2400. FAX: (219) 422-2673. Licensee: Huntington Broadcasting Corp. Group owner: Price Communications Corp. Stations (acq 3-85). Net: CBS. Rep: McGavren Guild. Format: Full service oldies. News staff 5. Target aud: 25-54. ■ Gina Maxwell, vp & gen mgr; Christine Kennedy, prom mgr; Gary Noe, progmg dir; Curt Miller, news dir; Eric Culp, chief engr. ■ Rates: $70; 60; 60; 25.

WPDJ(AM)—May 25, 1957: 1300 khz; 500 w-D, DA. TL: N40 52 31 W85 28 27 (CP: 250 w-D, DA). Hrs opn: 24. Box 367, 1600 E. Taylor St. (46750). (219) 358-0718; (219) 356-0069. FAX: (219) 358-0718. Licensee: Williams Radio Inc. (acq 11-2-90; $60,000; FTR 11-19-90). Format: Div. News staff one; news progmg 3 hrs wkly. Target aud: General. ■ William Dinkins, gen mgr, opns dir, sls dir & progmg dir; Ruby Thompson, stn mgr & opns mgr; Jean Rouse, news dir.

***WVSH(FM)**—Jan 1, 1950: 91.9 mhz; 920 w. Ant 110 ft. TL: N40 53 32 W85 30 38. 450 McGahn St. (46750). (219) 356-2019. FAX: (219) 358-2210. Licensee: Huntington County Community School Corp. Net: Network Indiana. Format: Contemporary hit. ■ William Walker Jr., gen mgr; Randy Cress, chief engr.

Indianapolis

***WBDG(FM)**—Sept 13, 1965: 90.9 mhz; 400 w. Ant 78 ft. TL: N39 47 05 W86 17 27. Stereo. 1200 N. Girls School Rd. (46214). (317) 244-9234. Licensee: Metropolitan School District of Wayne Township. Format: Rock (AOR). Spec prog: Jazz 7 hrs, rap 5 hrs, progsv 5 hrs wkly. ■ Paul Mendenhall, gen mgr; Jack Tiller, chief engr.

WBRI(AM)—Mar 10, 1964: 1500 khz; 5 kw-D, DA. TL: N39 52 14 W86 05 17. 4802 E. 62d St. (46220). (317) 255-5484. FAX: (317) 255-4452. Licensee: Radio One-Five-Hundred Inc. Group owner: American Bible Radio (acq 1963). Net: USA, Moody. Rep: Salem Radio Reps. Wash atty: Kaye, Scholer, Fierman, Hays & Handler. Format: Christian talk & info. News staff 2. Target aud: 35 plus. ■ Douglas D. Kahle, pres; Gary Arnold, vp & gen mgr; Debi Coughenour, prom mgr; Dave White, progmg dir; Tony Silva, mus dir; Bill Donnella, news dir; Max Turner, chief engr. ■ Rates: $40; 30; 40; 25.

WCKN(AM)—1923: 1430 khz; 5 kw-U, DA-N. TL: N39 50 17 W86 11 53. Stereo. Hrs opn: 24. 6161 Fall Creek Rd. (46220). (317) 257-7565. FAX: (317) 254-9619. Licensee: WIN Communications Inc. of Indiana. Group owner: WIN Communications Inc. (acq 7-22-86). Net: ABC/I. Rep: Banner. Format: Country. News staff one; news progmg 18 hrs wkly. Target aud: 25-54. ■ Christopher J. Wheat, pres & gen mgr; Lee Anne Brooks, vp & gen sls mgr; Barry Donovan, prom dir; Lara Szekendi, prom mgr; Scott Jameson, progmg dir & mus dir; Eileen Wooster, news dir; Kevin Van Wyk, chief engr.

WRZX(FM)—Co-owned with WCKN(AM). May 15, 1964: 103.3 mhz; 18 kw. Ant 850 ft. TL: N39 53 43 W86 12 04. Stereo. Format: Classic rock.

***WEDM(FM)**—Sept 14, 1970: 91.1 mhz; 180 w. Ant 180 ft. TL: N39 47 29 W85 59 53. Stereo. Hrs opn: 24. c/o Walker Career Ctr., 9651 E. 21st St. (46229). (317) 899-2000; (317) 899-6801. FAX: (317) 895-2155. Licensee: Metropolitan School District of Warren Township. Net: UPI. Format: CHR. News progmg 3 hrs wkly. Target aud: General; Warren Township residents. ■ Daniel J. Henn, stn mgr; Mike Rabey, chief engr.

WFBQ(FM)—Listing follows WNDE(AM).

WFMS(FM)—March 17, 1957: 95.5 mhz; 13 kw. Ant 1,000 ft. TL: N39 46 03 W86 00 12. Stereo. 8120 Knue Rd. (46250). (317) 842-9550. FAX: (317) 577-3361. Licensee: Radio Indianapolis Inc. Group owner: Susquehanna Radio Corp. (acq 11-20-72). Rep: Eastman. Format: Modern country. ■ Arthur W. Carlson, pres; Monte Maupin-Gerard, gen mgr; Charlie Morgan, opns mgr & mktg mgr; Jennifer Skjodt, gen sls mgr; Kevin Mason, progmg dir; J.D. Cannon, mus dir; Kevin Freeman, news dir; Max Turner, chief engr.

***WFYI-FM**—Oct 1, 1954: 90.1 mhz; 10 kw. Ant 560 ft. TL: N39 53 59 W86 12 01. Stereo. Hrs opn: 24. 1401 N. Meridian St. (46202). (317) 636-2020; (317) 633-7409. FAX: (317) 633-7418. Licensee: Metropolitan Indianapolis Public Broadcasting Inc. (acq 12-1-86). Net: APR, NPR. Format: Classical, news. News progmg 41 hrs wkly. Target aud: 25-54. Spec prog: Jazz 4 hrs, blues 5 hrs wkly. ■ Lloyd Wright, pres; Douglas Dillon, stn mgr; Jeanelle Adamak, vp dev; Daina Chamness, mktg mgr; Sharon Gamble, prom mgr; Vicki Wright, pub affrs dir; Paul Tyler, vp engrg; George Fowler, chief engr. ■ WFYI-TV affil.

WGRL(FM)—Sep 25, 1950: 104.5 mhz; 40 kw. Ant 492 ft. TL: N30 50 25 W86 10 34. Stereo. Hrs opn: 24. 8120 Knue Rd. (46250). (317) 842-9550. FAX: (317) 921-1996. Licensee: Indianapolis Radio License Co. Group owner: Susquehanna Radio Corp. (acq 10-7-93; $7,150,000; FTR 11-8-93). Net: AP, NPR, APR. Wash atty: Haley, Bader & Potts. Format: Hit country. News staff one. Target aud: 18 plus. Spec prog: Ger 2 hrs, reggae one hr, Sp one hr, Irish one hr, international contemp 4 wkly. ■ Arthur Carlson, pres; Monte Maupin Gerard, vp & gen mgr; Sam McGuire, progmg dir; Mark Roberts, mus dir; Max Turner, chief engr.

WHHH(FM)—Oct 28, 1991: 96.3 mhz; 770 w. Ant 656 ft. TL: N39 46 11 W86 09 26 (CP: 640 w, ant 715 ft.). Stereo. Hrs opn: 24. 6264 La Paz Trial (46268). (317) 293-9600. Licensee: Shirk Inc. (acq 8-91). Net: CNN. Format: Contemp hits. Target aud: 18-49. ■ William S. Poorman, pres & gen mgr; Bill Shirk, stn mgr; Liz Poorman, opns mgr; Mike Davidson, gen sls mgr; Scott Wheeler, progmg dir; Carl Frye, mus dir; Kim Hurst, chief engr. ■ Rates: $50; 50; 50; 40.

WIBC(AM)—1938: 1070 khz; 50 kw-D, 10 kw-N, DA-2. TL: N39 57 21 W86 21 30. Stereo. 9292 N. Meridian St. (46260). (317) 844-7200. FAX: (317) 846-1081. Licensee: Horizon Broadcasting Inc. Group owner: Sconnix Broadcasting Co. (acq 7-2-87). Net: NBC Talknet. Rep: D & R Radio. Format: MOR. Spec prog: Farm 12 hrs wkly. ■ Tom Durney, vp & gen mgr; Ed Lennon, opns mgr & progmg dir; Dennis Logston, gen sls mgr; Pam Cohen, prom mgr; Dave Reynold, news dir; Norm Beaty, chief engr.

WKLR(FM)—Co-owned with WIBC(AM). Dec 5, 1960: 93.1 mhz; 12.5 kw. Ant 1,023 ft. TL: N39 46 03 W86 00 12. Stereo. Prog sep from AM. (317) 843-9300. Format: Classic oldies. ■ Simon Jeffries, stn mgr; Vic Olson, gen sls mgr; Beth Bueltman, prom mgr; Roy Laurence, progmg dir; Cindy Wine, news dir.

***WICR(FM)**—Aug 20, 1962: 88.7 mhz; 2.5 kw. Ant 1,000 ft. TL: N39 53 59 W86 12 02. Stereo. Hrs opn: 24. Buxton Hall, 1400 E. Hanna Ave. (46227). (317) 788-3280. FAX: (317) 788-3490. Licensee: Univ. of Indianapolis. Net: APR; Network Indiana. Wash atty: John C. Pellegrin. Format: Div. Spec prog: Indian one hr wkly. ■ Benjamin Lantz, pres; Edward W. Roehling, gen mgr; Stacy Thorne, prom mgr; Brant Douglas, mus dir; Adina Carr, news dir; John Lyzott, chief engr.

***WJEL(FM)**—Sept 3, 1975: 89.3 mhz; 125 w. Ant 180 ft. TL: N39 54 34 W86 07 39. Stereo. Hrs opn: 7:30 AM-9:30 PM. 1901 E. 86th St. (46240). (317) 259-5278. Licensee: Metropolitan School District of Washington Township. Net: ABC/D. Format: CHR. ■ John R. King, gen mgr; Robert L. Hendrix, progmg dir; Mike Rabey, chief engr.

WKLR(FM)—Listing follows WIBC(AM).

WNDE(AM)—Oct 23, 1924: 1260 khz; 5 kw-U, DA-N. TL: N39 51 54 W86 03 43. 6161 Fall Creek Rd. (46220). (317) 257-7565. FAX: (317) 253-6501. Licensee: Broadcast Alchemy Inc. (acq 10-14-91; $54 million grpsl, including co-located FM; FTR 10-14-91). Net: MBS. Rep: Katz. Format: Sports/talk. News progmg 12 hrs wkly. Target aud: 25-54. Spec prog: Indiana Pacers, Indianapolis Ice, Cincinnati Reds, World Series, Indianapolis 500, Indianapolis Colts. ■ Christopher Wheat, pres & gen mgr; Marty Bender, opns mgr; Lee Anne Brooks, gen sls mgr; Jody Stumpe, prom dir; Pam Ferrin, progmg dir; Ace Cosby, mus dir; Kristi Lee, news dir; Dan Mettler, chief engr.

WFBQ(FM)—Co-owned with WNDE(AM). Nov 26, 1959: 94.7 mhz; 52 kw. Ant 850 ft. TL: N39 53 59 W86 12 02 (CP: 47 kw, ant 892 ft., TL: N39 53 20 W86 12 07). Stereo. Hrs opn: 24. Prog sep from AM. Net: NBC the Source. Format: AOR.

***WRFT(FM)**—June 6, 1978: 91.5 mhz; 130 w. Ant 180 ft. TL: N39 40 39 W86 00 58. Stereo. 6215 S. Franklin Rd. (46259). (317) 862-6646; (317) 862-6649. FAX: (317) 862-7262. Licensee: Franklin Township Community School Corp. Format: Educ, MOR. ■ Lori Schlahach, gen mgr.

WRZX(FM)—Listing follows WCKN(AM).

WSYW(AM)—May 15, 1963: 810 khz; 250 w-D. TL: N39 43 32 W86 11 08. 8203 Indy Ct. (46214). (317) 271-9799. FAX: (317) 273-1507. Licensee: Continental Broadcasting Co. Inc. Group owner: Universal Broadcasting Corp. (acq 11-22-84; $300,000; FTR 9-24-84). Net: UPI, ABC/D. Rep: CMBS. Format: Class. Target aud: 25-54. ■ Ernest Caldemone, vp & gen mgr. ■ Rates: $21; 21; 21; 21.

WTLC(AM)—July 27, 1941: 1310 khz; 5 kw-D, 1 kw-N, DA-N. TL: N39 43 08 W86 10 33. Hrs opn: 24. 2255 Hawthorne Ln. (46218). (317) 351-1310. FAX: (317) 924-9684. Licensee: Panache Broadcasting L.P. (group owner; acq 3-87; grpsl; FTR 10-20-86). Net: CBS, ABC. Rep: Major Mkt. Format: Black. Target aud: 35 plus. Spec prog: Gospel 18 hrs wkly. ■ Chuck Schwartz, pres; Paul Major, gen mgr; John Emerson, opns mgr; Russ Dodge, gen sls mgr; King Ro, progmg dir; Lang Sturgeon, chief engr.

WTLC-FM—Jan 22, 1968: 105.7 mhz; 50 kw. Ant 445 ft. TL: N39 48 01 W86 04 39. Stereo. 2126 N. Meridian St. (46202). (317) 923-1456. Format: Urban contemp. Spec prog: Jazz 14 hrs, gospel 14 hrs wkly. ■ Amos Brown, stn mgr; Vicki Buchanon, progmg dir & mus dir.

WTPI(FM)—Oct 15, 1984: 107.9 mhz; 22 kw. Ant 762 ft. TL: N39 53 43 W86 12 04. Stereo. Hrs opn: 24. 3135 N. Meridian St. (46208). (317) 925-1079. FAX: (317) 921-3676. Licensee: MyStar Communications Corp. (acq 1-29-90). Rep: Torbet. Wash atty: Pepper & Corrazzini. Format: Soft adult contemp. News staff 2. Target aud: 25-54. Spec prog: Sp one hr wkly. ■ Tim Medland, exec vp; Alex Keddie, opns dir & engrg dir; Jody Veldkamp, rgnl sls mgr; Linda Retz, prom dir; Gary Havens, progmg dir & mus dir; Kelly Vaughn, news dir. ■ Rates: $125; 125; 125; 60.

WXLW(AM)—August 1948: 950 khz; 5 kw-D, 117 w-N, DA-2. TL: N39 51 05 W86 14 39. Box 68920 (46268-0920); 6264 La Pas Trail (46268). (317) 293-9600. FAX: (317) 328-3870. Licensee: Shirk Inc. (acq 11-30-74). Net: CNN. Format: Relg, news. Target aud: General. Spec prog: Gospel 5 hrs wkly. ■ William S. Poorman, pres; Liz Poorman, vp, opns mgr & progmg dir; Ed Sears, gen mgr; Mike Davidson, gen sls mgr; Lisa Boyer, prom mgr; Jut Rutter, chief engr.

WZPL(FM)—See Greenfield.

Jasper

WBDC(FM)—(Huntingburg). Dec 22, 1975: 100.9 mhz; 3.3 kw. Ant 300 ft. TL: N38 22 26 W86 56 21 (CP: 25 kw, ant 530 ft., TL:N38 12 31 W86 54 00). Stereo. Hrs opn: 24. Box 1009, Central Bldg., 201 W. 6th St., Jasper (47547-1009); Box 330, 501 Old State Rd. Huntingburg (47542-0330). (812) 683-4144; (812) 634-9232. FAX: (812) 683-5891. Licensee: Dubois County Broadcasting, Inc. Net: AP, MBS, Interstate. Wash atty: Miller & Miller. Format: Country. News progmg 10 hrs wkly. Target aud: 18-54. Spec prog: Farm 5 hrs, relg 5 hrs, sports 6 hrs wkly. ■ Paul Knies, pres & gen mgr; Terry Seitz, stn mgr & sls dir; Charlie Wayne, progmg dir & mus dir; Jim Anderson, news dir; Dave Ferguson, chief engr. ■ Rates: $16; 16; 16; 16.

WITZ-FM—Nov 1, 1954: 104.7 mhz; 50 kw. Ant 490 ft. TL: N38 21 02 W86 56 26. Stereo. Box 167, 1978 S. WITZ Rd. (47547-0167). (812) 482-2131. FAX: (812) 482-9609. Licensee: Jasper On The Air Inc. Net: AP, ABC/D; AgriAmerica, Net. Ind., Farm Service Radio. Rep: Rgnl Reps. Wash atty: Barnes & Thornburg. Format: Adult contemp. News progmg 12 hrs wkly. Target aud: 18-54. Spec prog: Paul Harvey 3 hrs wkly. ■ G. Earl Metzger, pres & gen mgr; Gene Kuntz, opns mgr; Bob Boyles, gen sls mgr; Walt Ferber, progmg dir; Jim Baugh, news dir; Jerry Eckerle, chief engr. ■ Rates: $26.55; 24.05; 26.55; 22.15.

WITZ(AM)—July 4, 1948: 990 khz; 1 kw-D. TL: N38 21 02 W86 56 26. Stereo. Dups FM 100%.

Jeffersonville

WQMF(FM)—Apr 25, 1974: 95.7 mhz; 34 kw. Ant 580 ft. TL: N38 09 21 W85 55 11. Stereo. 4010 Dupont Circle, Louisville, KY (40207). (502) 896-4400. FAX: (502) 896-1496. Licensee: Otting Broadcasting Inc. (acq 3-86; $5 million; FTR 3-10-86). Rep: Eastman. Format: AOR. ■ John Page Otting, pres & gen mgr; Kevin Otting, gen sls mgr; Gary Guthrie, progmg dir; Duke Meyer, mus dir; Bernadine Barney, news dir; Kirk Wesley, chief engr.

WXVW(AM)—June 26, 1961: 1450 khz; 1 kw-U. TL: N38 17 41 W85 45 07. Hrs opn: 24. Box 726, 213 Magnolia Ave. (47130); Box 1897, Louisville, KY (40201). (812) 283-3577. FAX: (812) 285-5060. Licensee: Sunnyside Communications Inc. (acq 8-14-81; $600,000 FTR 8-24-81). Net: SMN. Rep: Savalli; Rgnl Reps. Wash atty: Barry Wood. Format: 50s and 60s rock 'n roll. News staff one. Target aud: 35 plus; mature. ■ Charles J. Jenkins, pres, gen mgr & gen sls mgr; Betty Kelley, prom mgr; Ron Chilton, progmg dir; Bob McIntosh, news dir; Steve Petty, chief engr. ■ Rates: $27; 27; 27; 27.

Kendallville

WAWK(AM)—Nov 9, 1955: 1140 khz; 250 w-D. TL: N41 27 16 W85 15 48. 931 East Ave. (46755). (219) 347-2400. FAX: (219) 347-2524. Licensee: Northeast Indiana Broadcasting Inc. Format: Oldies. News staff one. Target aud: 25-54. ■ Don Moore, pres, vp & gen mgr; Steve Smith, progmg dir; Mike Shultz, news dir; Dan Lash, chief engr.

WBTU(FM)—Licensed to Kendallville. See Fort Wayne.

Knightstown

***WKPW(FM)**—Sept 7, 1993: 90.7 mhz; 400 w. TL: N39 46 08 W85 31 05. 11410 N. State Rd. 140 (46148). (317) 345-9070. Licensee: New Castle Area Vocational School. Format: Top-40, oldies, country. ■ Mike York, gen mgr.

Knox

WKVI(AM)—June 30, 1969: 1520 khz; 250 w-D. TL: N41 19 20 W86 36 17 (CP: 1.8 kw-D). Box 10, 400 W. Culver Rd. (46534). (219) 772-6241. FAX: (219) 772-5920. Licensee: Kankakee Valley Broadcasting Co. Inc. Net: AP. Format: Classic hits. ■ Ted Hayes, gen mgr; Tim Price, gen sls mgr; William Beaver, progmg dir; Ed Hasherl, news dir; Paul Stage, chief engr.

WKVI-FM—July 21, 1969: 99.3 mhz; 3 kw. Ant 303 ft. TL: N41 19 20 W86 36 17. Stereo. Prog sep from AM. Format: Country.

Kokomo

WIOU(AM)—July 16, 1948: 1350 khz; 5 kw-D, 1 kw-N, DA-2. TL: N40 25 00 W86 06 49. Hrs opn: 24. Box 2208 (46904-2208); 671 E. 400 South (46902). (317) 453-1212. FAX: (317) 455-3882. Licensee: Mid-America Broadcast Group (acq 3-24-93; $1.21. million with co-located FM; FTR 4-12-93). Net: CNN. Rep: Katz & Powell. Format: Classic oldies. News staff 2; news progmg 9 hrs wkly. Target aud: 25-54. Spec prog: Rush Limbaugh 15 hrs wkly. ■ Dave Poyhloer, vp; Bill Eldridge, gen sls mgr; Dennis Bergendorf, progmg dir; Curt Alexander, news dir; Chip Longshore, chief engr. ■ Rates: $43; 40; 43; 24.

WZWZ(FM)—Co-owned with WIOU(AM). Nov 20, 1964: 92.7 mhz; 3 kw. Ant 298 ft. TL: N40 28 18 W86 09 52. Stereo. Hrs opn: 24. Prog sep from AM. Format: Hot adult contemp. News staff 2; news progmg 2 hrs wkly. Target aud: 18-44. ■ Rob Rupe, progmg dir. ■ Rates: $45; 42; 45; 25.

***WIWC(FM)**—Not on air, target date unknown: 91.7 mhz; 2.1 kw. Ant 299 ft. TL: N40 36 00 W86 18 08. 820 N. Lasalle Dr., Chicago, IL (60610). (312) 329-4000. Licensee: The Moody Bible Institute of Chicago (group owner).

WWKI(FM)—Oct 21, 1962: 100.5 mhz; 50 kw. Ant 480 ft. TL: N40 27 04 W86 02 12. Stereo. Hrs opn: 24. 519 N. Main St. (46901-4661). (317) 459-4191. FAX: (317) 456-1111; (317) 456-1112. Licensee: Shepard Communications (acq 7-86; $3.9 million). Net: ABC/D. Network Indiana. Rep: Roslin, Rgnl Reps. Wash atty: Wiley, Rein & Fielding. Format: Country. News staff 3; news progmg 13 hrs wkly. Target aud: 25-54. ■ Dick Lange, vp & gen mgr; Mike Christopher, gen sls mgr; Dave Broman, progmg dir; Jerry Hoffman, news dir; Jim Schroeder, chief engr. ■ Rates: $47; 41; 41; 31.

WZWZ(FM)—Listing follows WIOU(AM).

La Porte

WLOI(AM)—1948: 1540 khz; 250 w-D. TL: N41 37 55 W86 45 43. Hrs opn: Sunrise-sunset. 902 1/2 Lincolnway (46350). (219) 362-6144; (800) 877-2894. FAX: (219) 872-8986. Licensee: La Porte County Broadcasting Company, Inc. (acq 1955). Net: ABC; Net. Ind., Tribune. Rep: Rgnl Reps. Wash atty: Wiley, Rein & Fielding. Format: Big band, MOR, news. News staff one; news progmg 26 hrs wkly. Target aud: 35 plus. Spec prog: Farm 8 hrs wkly. ■ Kenneth S. Coe, pres, gen mgr & gen sls mgr; Norma Sabie, prom mgr; Dennis Siddall, progmg dir & mus dir; Stan Maddux, news dir; Frank McCoy, chief engr. ■ Rates: $23; 21; 23; 21.

WCOE(FM)—Co-owned with WLOI(AM). Jan 23, 1964: 96.7 mhz; 3 kw. Ant 265 ft. TL: N40 37 55 W86 45 43. Stereo. Hrs opn: 24. Prog sep from AM. (219) 362-5290; (219) 874-9881. Net: ABC/C. Format: Country. News staff 2; news progmg 19 hrs wkly. Target aud: 35-54; upper income, middle-aged. Spec prog: Farm 8 hrs wkly. ■ Kenneth S. Coe, adv mgr. ■ Rates: $21; 19; 21; 19.

Lafayette

WASK(AM)—1942: 1450 khz; 1 kw-U. TL: N40 24 08 W86 50 59. Box 7880 (47903); 3575 McCarty Ln. (47905). (317) 447-2186. FAX: (317) 448-4452. Licensee: Schurz Communications Inc. (group owner; acq 1-28-91; $8.25 million with co-located FM; FTR 1-28-91). Net: NBC, NBC Talknet, AP, Westwood One, Unistar; Tribune. Rep: Banner, Rgnl Reps. Format: Adult contemp. News staff 6; news progmg 15 hrs wkly. Target aud: 35 plus; affluent, well-educated adults. Spec prog: Farm 2 hrs wkly. ■ Hal M. Youart, pres & gen mgr; John Trent, vp sls & gen sls mgr; Natlie Bake, mktg dir; Keith Harris, prom mgr, progmg dir & mus dir; Max Showalter, news dir; George Williamson, chief engr.

WASK-FM—Sept 28, 1964: 105.3 mhz; 50 kw. Ant 375 ft. TL: N40 24 08 W86 50 59. Stereo. Prog sep from AM. Net: ABC/E, AP. Format: Modern country. News progmg 12 hrs wkly. Target aud: 25-54. Spec prog: Farm 3 hrs wkly. ■ Don Riley, progmg dir.

WAZY(FM)—March 1965: 96.5 mhz; 50 kw. Ant 500 ft. TL: N40 23 02 W87 07 55. Stereo. Hrs opn: 24. Box 1410 (47902). (317) 474-1410. FAX: (317) 474-3442. Licensee: University Broadcasting Co. (group owner; acq 10-86; $2 million; FTR 9-22-86). Net: ABC; Purdue Sports Network. Rep: Christal. Wash atty: Haley, Bader & Potts. Format: Adult CHR. News staff one; news progmg 4 hrs wkly. Target aud: 18-49. ■ Arthur Angotti, pres; Michael Wild, gen mgr; Fred Stuart, opns mgr; Wally Leavitt, gen sls mgr; C.J. Ryan, prom mgr; Jason Dean, mus dir; Jane Kingseed, news dir; Michael Gay, chief engr. ■ Rates: $32; 27; 32; 25.

WCFY(AM)—Nov 28, 1959: 1410 khz; 1 kw-D, 65 w-N, DA-1. TL: N40 21 38 W86 52 38. Hrs opn: 24. 108 Beck Ln. (47905). (317) 474-4436. FAX: (317) 474-5845. Licensee: First Assembly of God, Lafayette Indiana Inc. (acq 7-4-84; $135,000; FTR 5-7-84). Format: Adult contemp, Christian mus. News progmg 3 hrs wkly. Target aud: 25-49. ■ Greg Hackett, pres; Parris S. Foxworthy, gen mgr, progmg dir & mus dir; Larae Meyer, gen sls mgr; Stevan W. Speheger, chief engr. ■ Rates: $12.50; 11; 12.50; 6.

***WJEF(FM)**—Feb 7, 1972: 91.9 mhz; 250 w. Ant 100 ft. TL: N40 23 52 W86 52 26. Stereo. Hrs opn: 7:15 AM-3:15 PM. 1801 S. 18th St. (47905); 2300 Cason St. (47904). (317) 449-3400, ext. 257, 258. FAX: (317) 449-3413. Licensee: Lafayette School Corp. Format: Oldies. News progmg 6 hrs wkly. Target aud: General. ■ Tina Overly-Hilt, (asst) opns dir.

WKHY(FM)—Jan 1, 1970: 93.5 mhz; 6 kw. Ant 282 ft. TL: N40 23 13 W86 58 10. Stereo. Hrs opn: 24. Box 7093, 711 N. Earl Ave. (47903). (317) 448-1566. FAX: (317) 448-1348. Licensee: Stay Tuned Broadcasting Corp. Group owner: Airplay Broadcasting/Stay Tuned Broadcasting (acq 8-31-92; $1.78 million; FTR 10-5-92). Net: AP. Rep: Katz. Wash atty: Fisher, Wayland, Cooper & Leader. Format: Classic rock & roll. News staff one. Target aud: 18-49; adults that are active, mobile & moderately affluent. ■ Eric F. McCart, gen mgr, gen sls mgr & natl sls mgr; Dan Anderson, prom dir; Mike Morgan, progmg dir & mus dir; Kate Walker, news dir; Mike Rabey, chief engr.

Lafayette Township

***WCYT(FM)**—Not on air, target date unknown: 91.1 mhz; 1 kw. Ant 541 ft. 4510 Homestead Rd., Fort Wayne (46804). Licensee: Southwest Allen County Schools.

Lagrange

WYPI(FM)—Not on air, target date unknown: 105.5 mhz; 3 kw. Ant 328 ft. TL: N41 39 48 W85 27 46. c/o WLKI(FM), Box 999, Angola (46703). (219) 665-9554. Licensee: Lake Cities Broadcasting Corp. (acq 7-14-93; $26,000; FTR 8-9-93). ■ Thomas R. Andrews, pres & gen mgr.

Lebanon

WIRE(FM)—May 28, 1967: 100.9 mhz; 3 kw. Ant 300 ft. TL: N39 57 35 W86 26 46. Hrs opn: 5:30 AM-midnight. Box 227, 722 W. Pearl St. (46052). (317) 482-4427. Licensee: Boone County Broadcasters Inc. (acq 7-1-92). Net: ABC. Format: Modern country. News staff 2; news progmg 12 hrs wkly. Target aud: General. Spec prog: Farm 12 hrs wkly. ■ John R. Dotas, pres, gen mgr, opns mgr & progmg dir; Helen J. Dotas, vp & prom mgr; Charolette Copelano, gen sls mgr; Norm Beaty, chief engr. ■ Rates: $18; 14; 16; 10.

Ligonier

WLNB(FM)—June 10, 1991: 102.7 mhz; 3 kw. Ant 328 ft. TL: N41 29 02 W85 35 43. Stereo. Hrs opn: 19. 514 W. Union St. (46767); 206 S. Main St., Kendallville (46755). (219) 894-3662. FAX: (219) 894-4212. Licensee: Summit Radio Inc. Group owner: Summit Communications Group Inc. (acq 7-2-93; $284,550; FTR 8-2-93). Net: USA. Format: Adult contemp. News progmg 9 hrs wkly. Target aud: 25-54. Spec prog: Farm one hr, relig 3 hrs, Sp one hr, country 3 hrs, oldies 6 hrs wkly. ■ Dan Caskey, gen sls mgr; Sally Kaufman, news dir. ■ Rates: $12; 12; 12; 12.

Linton

WBTO(AM)—Oct 10, 1953: 1600 khz; 500 w-D, 32 w-N. TL: N39 03 57 W87 11 19. RR 3, Box 394A (47441-9756). (812) 847-4474. Licensee: Greene Country Broadcasting Corp. (acq 12-12-79). Net: MBS; Tribune. Rep: Rgnl Reps. Format: Big band, MOR, talk. ■ Mike McDaniel, pres, gen mgr & chief engr.

WQTY(FM)—Co-owned with WBTO-AM. Sept 14, 1970: 93.3 mhz; 12 kw. Ant 475 ft. TL: N39 00 46 W87 22 23. Stereo. Prog sep from AM.

Logansport

WSAL(AM)—Feb 24, 1949: 1230 khz; 1 kw-U. TL: N40 45 16 W86 18 40. Hrs opn: 24. Box 719 (46947). (219) 722-4000. Licensee: Logansport Radio Corp. (acq 12-11-85; $850,000; FTR 11-4-85). Net: Unistar. Format: C&W. News staff 2; news progmg 14 hrs wkly. Target aud: General. Spec prog: Farm 10 hrs wkly. ■ John P. Jenkins, CEO & pres; Andy Eubank, gen mgr; Tim Kiesling, opns mgr & progmg mgr; Dick Prescott, news dir; Steve Waldron, chief engr.

WLHM(FM)—Co-owned with WSAL(AM). May 11, 1965: 102.3 mhz; 3 kw. Ant 300 ft. TL: N40 45 16 W86 18 40. Hrs opn: 24. Prog sep from AM. Format: Adult contemp. News staff 2. Target aud: General. ■ Andy Eubank, vp; Tim Kiesling, progmg dir & mus dir.

Lowell

WZVN(FM)—Nov 24, 1972: 107.1 mhz; 1.29 kw. Ant 499 ft. TL: N41 21 09 W87 24 12. 6405 Olcott, Hammond (46320); 8105 Georgia, Merrillville (46410). Licensee: Gracol Broadcasting Corp. (acq 4-87). Net: SMN. Wash atty: Wilmer, Cutler & Pickering. Format: Adult contemp. News staff 2; news progmg 10 hrs wkly. Target aud: 25-45. ■ Judith Grambo, pres; Diane Grambo, gen mgr & gen sls mgr; Jerry Siska, news dir; Gordon Boss, chief engr.

Madison

WIKI(FM)—See Carrollton, Ky.

WORX(AM)—Mar 1956: 1270 khz; 1 kw-D, 58 w-N, DA-2. TL: N38 44 28 W85 21 41. Box 95, 1224 E. Telegraph Hill Rd. (47250). (812) 265-3322. FAX: (812) 273-5509. Licensee: Dubois County Broadcasting Inc. Net: AP, USA, Tribune. Rep: Rgnl Reps. Format: Adult contemp, news. News staff one; news progmg 7 hrs wkly. Target aud: General. Spec prog: Farm 3 hrs, relg 6 hrs wkly. ■ Paul Knies, pres; Bill Potter, gen mgr; Todd Hunt, mus dir; Paul Voris, news dir; James Gray, chief engr. ■ Rates: $19; 19; 19; 10.

WORX-FM—Mar 1950: 96.7 mhz; 3 kw. Ant 320 ft. TL: N38 44 30 W85 21 41. Stereo. Dups AM 100%. ■ Rates: Same as AM.

Marion

WBAT(AM)—June 7, 1947: 1400 khz; 1 kw-U. TL: N40 33 40 W85 41 30. Box 839, 120 N. Miller Ave. (46952). (317) 664-6239. Licensee: Mid-America Radio Group. Group Owner: David Keister Stations (acq 12-88; grpsl; FTR 12-19-88). Net: CBS. Format: Adult contemp. News staff 3. Target aud: 25-54. ■ David Keister, pres; David G. Poehler, gen mgr; James F. Brunner, gen sls mgr; Mark Metzner, progmg dir & mus dir; Tim Rush, news dir; Warren Arnett, chief engr.

WGOM(AM)—May 11, 1955: 860 khz; 1 kw-D, 500 w-N, DA-2. TL: N40 33 12 W85 38 45. Stereo. Box 1538, 820 S. Pennsylvania St. (46952). (317) 664-7396; (317) 664-9466. FAX: (317) 668-6767. Licensee: WMRI Inc. (group owner; acq 1-1-66). Net: ABC/E. Format: Adult contemp, talk. News staff one. Target aud: 25-54. ■ Frank Bove, pres; Michael Day, vp & gen mgr; Rich Coolman, opns mgr; Mark Allison, news dir; Paul Dixon, chief engr. ■ Rates: $15; 12; 15; 10.

WMRI(FM)—Co-owned with WGOM(AM). Dec 19, 1948: 106.9 mhz; 50 kw. Ant 499 ft. TL: N40 35 52 W85 39 21. Stereo. Prog sep from AM. Format: Easy lstng. ■ Bob Miller, mus dir. ■ Rates: $40; 40; 40; 20.

Martinsville

WMCB(AM)—Apr 18, 1967: 1540 khz; 500 w-D. TL: N39 24 31 W86 25 10. Box 1577, 1639 Burton Ln. (46151). (317) 342-3394. Licensee: Rodgers Broadcasting Corp. (group owner; acq 12-88; grpsl; FTR 8-29-88). Net: USA; Network Indiana, Tribune. Format: C&W. News staff 2. Target aud: 25-54. Spec prog: Farm one hr wkly. ■ David Rodgers, pres & gen mgr; James Conner, gen sls mgr; David Stanley, progmg dir; Mark Jaynes, news dir.

WCBK-FM—Co-owned with WMCB(AM). Oct 15, 1968: 102.3 mhz; 3 kw. Ant 300 ft. TL: N39 26 18 W86 27 54. Stereo. Dups AM 95%.

Michigan City

WEFM(FM)—Sept 15, 1966: 95.9 mhz; 3 kw. Ant 230 ft. TL: N41 42 58 W86 51 47. Stereo. 1903 Springland Ave. (46360). (219) 879-8201. FAX: (219) 879-8202. Licensee: Mich. City FM Broadcasters (acq 8-68). Net: USA; Net. Ind, Mich News Network. Rep: Katz & Powell. Format: Oldies. ■ Thomas Burns, pres & stn mgr; Howard Dybedock, chief engr.

WIMS(AM)—Aug 10, 1947: 1420 khz; 5 kw-U, DA-2. TL: N41 40 26 W86 55 58. 685 E. County Rd. 1675 North (46360). (219) 874-9467. FAX: (219) 874-2464. Licensee: M&M Broadcasting Inc. (acq 12-88; $880,000; FTR 12-5-88). Net: CNN. Rep: Rgnl Reps. Format: News, adult contemp, sports. News staff 3; news progmg 15 hrs wkly. Target aud: 30 plus; general. Spec prog: Polish 3 hrs wkly. ■ Dan Lynch, gen mgr & gen sls mgr; Elizabeth Sobkowiak, prom mgr; Chuck Van Cure, progmg dir & mus dir; Bill Cromer, news dir; Robert Shilling, chief engr. ■ Rates: $20; 14; 16; 14.

Mitchell

WWEG(FM)—Aug 17 1991: 102.5 mhz; 6 kw. Ant 282 ft. TL: N38 38 16 W86 27 11. Hrs opn: 17. 609 W. Main St. (47446). (812) 275-7555. FAX: (812) 279-8046. Licensee: Mitchell Community Broadcast Co. (acq 2-26-92; $8,000 for CP; FTR 3-16-92). Net: Moody, USA. Format: Relg. Target aud: General. ■ Dean Spencer (owner), CEO; Dean Spencer, gen mgr.

Monticello

WMRS(FM)—March 1989: 107.7 mhz; 4.4 kw. Ant 131 ft. TL: N40 45 03 W86 48 17. Hrs opn: 24. Dups WBQR-FM (Attica) 100%. Rt. 5, Box 12 (47960). (219) 583-8933; (219) 583-8121. Licensee: Gerald N. Quinn (acq 1-15-91; FTR 2-11-91). Net: USA. Format: Oldies, div, talk. News progmg 20 hrs wkly. Target aud: 25-60; motivated, intelligent, diverse. Spec prog: Class one hr, folk 2 hrs, gospel 3 hrs, big band 4 hrs, bluegrass 2 hrs wkly. ■ Gerald Quinn, Laura Page, stn mgrs; Laura Page, opns mgr; Bruce Quinn, dev dir, progmg dir, mus dir & chief engr; Helen Quinn, sls dir; Kevin Page, pub affrs dir. ■ Rates: $15; 15; 15; 12.

Mt. Vernon

WPCO(AM)—Aug 21, 1955: 1590 khz; 500 w-D, 35 w-N. TL: N37 56 03 W87 55 42. 601 Upton Rd. (47620). (812) 838-4484. FAX: (812) 838-6434. Licensee: Posey County Broadcasting Corp. (acq 7-6-83; $185,000; FTR 8-15-83). Format: Country. News staff one; news progmg 21 hrs wkly. Target aud: 25 plus; local county. Spec prog: Farm 5 hrs wkly. ■ Ann Nussel, pres & gen mgr; Trey Duncan, progmg dir; Mike Warren, news dir; Bill Nussel, chief engr.

WBLZ(FM)—Co-owned with WPCO(AM). August 1992: 106.9 mhz; 2 kw. Ant 295 ft. TL: N37 56 03 W87 55 35. Format: CHR.

Muncie

***WBST(FM)**—Sept 12, 1960: 92.1 mhz; 3 kw. Ant 300 ft. TL: N40 12 48 W85 27 36. Stereo. Hrs opn: 24. Ball State Univ. (47306-0550). (317) 285-5888. FAX: (317) 285-9278. Licensee: Ball State Univ. Net: APR, NPR. Format: Class, jazz, news & information. News staff 2; news progmg 33 hrs wkly. Target aud: General. ■ Joe Misiewicz, gen mgr; Stewart Vanderwilt, stn mgr; Cynthia McCabe, sls dir; Steven Turpin, progmg mgr; John Althardt, news dir; Robert Mittendorf, chief engr.

WERK(AM)—Feb 14, 1965: 990 khz; 250 w-D, 2 w-N, DA-1. TL: N40 06 54 W85 22 02. 8510 S. State Rd. 3, (47302). FAX: (317) 286-3493. Licensee: American Home Town Radio Corp. (acq 9-91; $670,000). Rep: Roslin; Rgnl Reps. Wash atty: Harris, Beach & Wilcox. Format: Oldies, contemp Christian, talk. News staff one; news progmg 7 hrs wkly. Target aud: 25-54; upscale adults & families, professional & blue collar. Spec prog: Play-by-play sports. ■ Chris Cage Caggiano, pres; Lisa Beard, news dir; Paul Dixon, chief engr. ■ Rates: $13; 13; 13; na.

WERK-FM—Jan 16, 1986: 104.9 mhz; 3 kw. Ant 328 ft. TL: N40 09 19 W85 25 48. Stereo. Hrs opn: 24. Box 2426 (47307-0426). Format: Oldies. ■ Tom Simpson, gen sls mgr; Lee Strayer, prom dir; Phil Dashler, progmg dir; Bill Patterson, chief engr. ■ Rates: $20; 20; 20; 8.

WLBC(AM)—November 1926: 1340 khz; 1 kw-U. TL: N40 09 42 W85 22 41. 800 E. 29th St. (47302). (317) 288-4403. FAX: (317) 288-0429. Licensee: DRMS Communications Inc. (acq 5-29-87). Format: Adult contemp. News staff 2. Target aud: 25-54. ■ Jeff Weller, gen mgr & gen sls mgr; Steve Linden, progmg dir; Tracy Ball, news dir; Jeff Goode, chief engr. ■ Rates: $42; 23; 26; 16.

WLBC-FM—October 1947: 104.1 mhz; 50 kw. Ant 420 ft. TL: N40 09 38 W85 22 42. Stereo. Prog sep from AM. Net: CBS. Rep: Eastman Radio. Format: Adult contemp, oldies.

WMDH-FM—See New Castle.

***WWDS(FM)**—1978: 90.5 mhz; 10 w. Ant 169 ft. TL: N40 16 42 W85 20 52. Stereo. 3400 E. State Rd. 28 (47303). (317) 288-5597. Licensee: Delaware Community School Corp. Format: Adult contemp. ■ Jerry L. Jones, stn mgr.

***WWHI(FM)**—1950: 91.5 mhz; 310 w. Ant 79 ft. TL: N40 09 45 W85 22 45. 1601 E. 26th St. (47302). (317) 747-5339. Licensee: South Side High School, Muncie Community Schools. Format: Educ. ■ James F. Bailey, gen mgr; Sonya Paul, progmg dir.

Nappanee

WLRX(FM)—Dec 16, 1991. 95.7 mhz; 1.4 kw. Ant 500 ft. TL: N41 24 43 W86 01 51. Stereo. Hrs opn: 24. Box 370, 12478 N. 950 W. (46550). Licensee: North Central Broadcasting Inc. (acq 12-2-91). Format: Adult comtemp. News staff one; news progmg 10 hrs wkly. Target aud: 35-70; secretaries, bankers, etc. ■ Marilyn S. Cobb, pres; James W. Cobb, exec vp, gen mgr & stn mgr.

Nashville

WVNI(FM)—Not on air, target date unknown: 95.1 mhz; 1.6 kw. Ant 636 ft. TL: N39 13 39 W86 25 05. Licensee: Brown County Broadcasters Inc.

New Albany

***WNAS(FM)**—May 28, 1949: 88.1 mhz; 2.85 kw. Ant 3 ft. TL: N38 17 56 W85 48 45. 1020 Vincennes St. (47150). (812) 949-4272. FAX: (812) 949-6926. Licensee: New Albany-Floyd County Consolidated School Corp. Format: Educ, top-40. Spec prog: Fr one hr, Ger one hr, farm one hr, jazz 2 hrs, class one hr, C&W 2 hrs wkly. ■ Lee Kelly, gen mgr; Pete Boyce, chief engr.

WZCC(AM)—June 15, 1949: 1570 khz; 1 kw-D, 412 w-N. TL: N38 18 27 W85 47 49 (CP: 1.5 kw-D, 233 w-N, TL: N38 19 40 W85 46 56). Box 655 (47151). (812) 941-1570. FAX: (812) 944-7782. Licensee: Cross Country Communications Inc. (acq 10-26-92; $175,500; FTR 11-23-92). Format: Southern gospel. ■ George Zarris, gen mgr; Olympus Zarris, progmg dir.

New Carlisle

WGTC(FM)—July 2 1991: 102.3 mhz; 2 kw. Ant 397 ft. TL: N41 43 38 W86 24 30. Stereo. Hrs opn: 24. Suite 310, 3371 Cleveland Rd. Ext., South Bend (46628). (219) 271-9482; (219) 674-5577. FAX: (219) 271-0494. Licensee: Summit Radio Inc. Net: ABC/D. Rep: Banner. Format: Modern country. News staff one; news progmg 2 hrs wkly. Target aud: 25-54. Spec prog: Country gospel 2 hrs wkly. ■ Jim Leep, pres, gen mgr & gen sls mgr; John Vance, stn mgr; Peggy Neer, natl sls mgr; Doug Montgomery, John Vance, progmg dirs; Robin Rock, mus dir; Kelli Thompson, news dir & pub affrs dir; Roland Ernest, chief engr. ■ Rates: $44; 38; 44; 28.

New Castle

WMDH(AM)—Nov 14, 1960: 1550 khz; 250 w-U, DA-2. TL: N39 55 57 W85 24 24. Box 690, 1134 W. St. Rd. 38 (47362). (317) 529-2600. FAX: (317) 529-1688. Licensee: WTL Indiana Inc. Group owner: Taylor Broadcasting (acq 8-90; $2.6 million; with co-located FM; FTR 9-10-90). Net: AP; Net. Ind. Rep: Rgnl Reps. Wash atty: Pepper & Corazinni. Format: Adult contemp, classic hits, country. News staff 2; news progmg 8 hrs wkly. Target aud: 49 plus. Spec prog: Farm 2 hrs wkly. ■ Jack Lich, pres & gen mgr; Steve Brown, opns mgr & chief engr; Karen Schuman, gen sls mgr; Dawn Miller, prom mgr; Bob Richards, progmg dir; Mike Lees, mus dir; Kevin Lee, news dir.

WMDH-FM—Aug 6, 1947: 102.5 mhz; 50 kw. Ant 500 ft. TL: N40 03 18 W85 23 05. Stereo. Prog sep from AM. (317) 282-7539. FAX: (317) 289-6034. Net: AP. Format: C&W. Target aud: 25-49; upper middle class. Spec prog: Farm one hr wkly.

New Haven

WJFX(FM)—April 1990: 107.9 mhz; 3 kw. Ant 57 ft. TL: N41 04 37 W84 57 47. 5936 E. State Blvd., Fort Wayne (46815). (219) 493-9239. FAX: (219) 749-5151. Licensee: Allen County Broadcasting L.P. Rep: Interep. Wash atty: John Tierney. Format: Urban contemp hit. ■ Louis Dinwiddie, pres & gen mgr; Hugh Roberts, gen sls mgr; Ange Canessa, progmg dir; Jack Diddier, chief engr. ■ Rates: $60; 42; 60; 30.

New Washington

*****WJYL(FM)**—Not on air, target date January 1994: 88.3 mhz; 1 kw. Ant 272 ft. Stereo. Hrs opn: 24. Box 1226, WCTV Building, 120 W. Court Ave., Jeffersonville (47130). (812) 284-2600. FAX: (812) 282-4177. Licensee: Lou Smith Ministries Inc. Net: CBN. Format: Urban contemp (Christian). Target aud: 18-34. Spec prog: Gospel. ■ Mary L. Smith, CEO & pres; John W. Smith Sr., chmn; David B. Smith, CFO.

Newburgh

WGAB(AM)—March 5, 1984: 1180 khz; 670 w-D. TL: N37 57 16 W87 25 07. 1180 Maple Ln. (47630). (812) 451-2422. FAX: (812) 451-2422. Licensee: Newburgh Broadcasting Corp. Net: Daynet, Unistar. Format: Talk. News progmg 7 hrs wkly. Target aud: General. Spec prog: Relg 5 hrs wkly. ■ Don Davis, pres, gen mgr & gen sls mgr; Jeff Davis, opns mgr; Nick P. Davis, prom mgr; Linda Davis, progmg dir; Tony Ormond, news dir; Russ Vail, pub affrs dir; Frank Hertel, chief engr. ■ Rates: $13; 13; 13; na.

WJPS-FM—Co-owned with WGAB(AM). Feb. 11, 1991: 106.1 mhz; 6 kw. Ant 328 ft. TL: N37 57 16 W87 25 07. Stereo. Hrs opn: 24. Rebroadcasts WJPS(AM) Evansville 95%. Box 3848, 1162 Mt. Auburn Rd., Evansville (47736). (812) 424-8284. FAX: (812) 426-7928. Rep: Katz. Format: Oldies. Target aud: 25-54. ■ Terry Bond, stn mgr; Brenda Whitney, progmg dir; Randy Wheeler, news dir; Lee Thompson, chief engr.

Noblesville

WXTZ(FM)—Not on air, target date unknown: 93.9 mhz; 10789 Downing St., Carmel (46032). Licensee: Weiss Broadcasting of Noblesville.

North Manchester

*****WBKE-FM**—May 1967: 89.5 mhz; 3 kw. Ant 80 ft. TL: N41 00 40 W85 45 45. Stereo. Hrs opn: 24. Box 88, Manchester College, 604 College Ave. (46962). (219) 982-5272. FAX: (219) 982-6868. Licensee: Manchester College. Format: Div. News staff one; news progmg 10 hrs wkly. Target aud: General. Spec prog: Class 10 hrs, Black 2 hrs, jazz 5 hrs, relg 2 hrs, Sp one hr, classic rock 6 hrs, AOR 6 hrs, top 40/rap 10, alt 7 hrs wkly. ■ Julie Cutlip, stn mgr; Walter Patton, gen sls mgr & pub affrs dir; Vanessa Miller, prom dir; Jennifer Dumond, progmg dir; Chris Smith, mus dir; Keith Roberts, news dir; J. Randy Cress, chief engr.

North Vernon

WKRP(AM)—Jan 8, 1955: 1460 khz; 1 kw-D, 92 w-N. TL: N38 59 46 W85 39 02. Stereo. Box 46 (47265). 5775 N. Highway 7, Scipio (47273). (812) 392-2710; (812) 392-2579. FAX: (812) 392-2605. Licensee: ARS Broadcasting Corp. (acq 1-6-93; $909,291 with co-located FM; FTR 2-1-93). Net: SMN. Rep: SMN. Format: MOR. News staff one; news progmg 7 hrs wkly. Target aud: 35-64; mature, affluent. Spec prog: Farm 5 hrs, relg 9 hrs wkly. ■ Alan R. Schriber, pres; Ron Green, vp; Sue King, stn mgr & gen sls mgr; Joe Ammerman, progmg dir; Brad Sheldon, news dir; Pete Boyce, chief engr. ■ Rates: $15; 15; 15.

WINN(FM)—Co-owned with WKRP(AM). March 19, 1963: 106.1 mhz; 50 kw. Ant 486 ft. TL: N39 04 02 W85 42 10. Stereo. Prog sep from AM. Box 669, Columbus (47202). (812) 378-0106. Format: CHR.

Notre Dame

*****WSND-FM**—Sept 17, 1962: 88.9 mhz; 3.4 kw. Ant 361 ft. TL: N41 36 20 W86 12 46. Stereo. Office of Student Activities, LaFortune Student Center (46556). (219) 631-7308. FAX: (219) 631-8139. Licensee: Voice of the Fighting Irish Inc. Format: Class. ■ Adele M. Lanan, gen mgr & progmg dir; Brian Hoover, chief engr.

Paoli

WSEZ(AM)—Dec 7, 1963: 1560 khz; 250 w-D. TL: N38 32 25 W86 28 42. Hrs opn: 6 AM-6 PM. Box 26 (47454). (812) 723-4484. FAX: (812) 723-4966. Licensee: Indiana Patoka Development Corp. (acq 3-24-87). Net: Network Ind. Rep: Rgnl Reps. Format: Btfl mus. News staff one; news progmg 7 hrs wkly. Target aud: General. Spec prog: Farm 7 hrs wkly. ■ Sharon Reynolds, pres & gen mgr; Imujean Apple, gen sls mgr; Todd Edwards, mktg mgr & chief engr; Johnny Henderson, Todd Edwards, mus dirs; Dave Dedrick, news dir.

WUME-FM—Co-owned with WSEZ(AM). September 1972: 95.3 mhz; 3 kw. Ant 300 ft. TL: N38 32 25 W86 28 42. Stereo. Hrs opn: 24. Prog sep from AM. Net: SMN. Format: Adult contemp. News progmg 9 hrs wkly. ■ Johnny Henderson, progmg dir. ■ Rates: $12; 10; 12; 8.

Pendleton

*****WEEM(FM)**—Nov 1, 1971: 91.7 mhz; 1.2 kw. Ant 154 ft. TL: N39 59 52 W85 44 07. Stereo. One Arabian Dr. (46064). (317) 778-2161, ext. 236; (317) 778-2161, ext. 238. Licensee: South Madison Community School Corp. Format: Oldies, educ. Spec prog: High school sports 10 hrs, Sp 5 hrs wkly. ■ Reggie Laconi, pres; Stephen M. Cherry, gen mgr & mus dir; Kip Golden, sls dir; Steve Cherry, prom dir; Carole Johnson, progmg dir; Ron Estep, chief engr.

Peru

WARU(AM)—Sept 12, 1954: 1600 khz; 1 kw-D. TL: N40 45 53 W86 02 26. Hrs opn: 6 AM-10 PM. Box 1010 (46970). (317) 473-4448. FAX: (317) 473-4449. Licensee: WCDB Inc. (acq 4-2-93; $300,000; FTR 4-26-93). Net: CNN; Tribune, Agri-Net. Rep: Rgnl Reps. Format: Oldies. News staff one; news progmg 20 hrs wkly. Target aud: 30-50. Spec prog: Relg 10 hrs, big band 2 hrs wkly. ■ David L. Vitek, pres; Joe Vlery, news dir; Erica Vitek, pub affrs dir; Steve Truex, chief engr. ■ Rates: $9.45; 9.45; 9.45; 9.45.

WARU-FM—Apr 5, 1965: 98.3 mhz; 3 kw. Ant 43 ft. TL: N40 45 53 W86 02 26. Stereo. Licensee: Wabash Peru Broadcasting Co. Inc. Format: Classic rock.

Petersburg

WFPC(FM)—Oct 8, 1984: 102.3 mhz; 3 kw. Ant 321 ft. TL: N38 30 33 W87 17 28. Stereo. Box 538, Hwy. 57 S. (47567). (812) 354-9923. FAX: (812) 354-6601. Licensee: Pike Broadcasting Corp. (acq 4-27-84). Net: Unistar. Rep: Rgnl Reps. Format: C&W. News staff one; news progmg 9 hrs wkly. Target aud: General. ■ George R. Tevault, pres; Linda L. Padgett, gen mgr; David Foster, mus dir; Mike Voyles, chief engr. ■ Rates: $13.80; 12.60; 13.80; 11.30.

Plainfield

WXIR(FM)—Aug 16, 1964: 98.3 mhz; 3 kw. Ant 300 ft. TL: N39 45 33 W86 22 30. Stereo. Hrs opn: 24. 4802 E. 62 St., Indianapolis (46220). (317) 255-5484. FAX: (317) 255-4452. Licensee: Radio One Five Hundred (acq 10-80; $800,000; FTR 10-6-80). Net: Moody, USA. Wash atty: Jason Shrinsky. Format: Contemp Christian mus. News staff 2; news progmg 20 hrs wkly. Target aud: 24-54. ■ Douglas Kahle, pres; Gary Arnold, vp & gen mgr; Dick Sickles, rgnl sls mgr; David White, progmg dir; Tony Silva, mus dir; Bill Donnella, news dir; Nancy Toumey, pub affrs dir; Max Turner, chief engr. ■ Rates: $35; 30; 40; 25.

Plymouth

WTCA(AM)—Aug 18, 1964: 1050 khz; 250 w-U, DA-2. TL: N41 19 06 W86 18 41. 112 W. Washington St. (46563). (219) 936-4096. FAX: (219) 936-6776. Licensee: Community Service Broadcasters, Inc. Wash atty: Reddy, Begley & Martin. Format: Memories, older music of the 40s, 50s & 60s, oldies. News staff one; news progmg 12 hrs wkly. Target aud: 25-65. Spec prog: Farm 11 hrs wkly. ■ Kenneth E. Kunze, pres & gen mgr & chief engr; James Bottorff, vp sls & vp mktg; Kathy Bottorff, vp prom; Tymm Nelson, mus dir; James Kunze, news dir & vp engrg.

WNZE(FM)—Co-owned with WTCA(AM). July 20, 1966: 94.3 mhz; 3 kw. Ant 240 ft. TL: N41 19 06 W86 18 41. Stereo. Prog sep from AM. Net: Unistar. Format: Super country. ■ James Kunze, stn mgr, prom dir & chief engr; Jack Swart, gen sls mgr.

Portage

WNDZ(AM)—May 13, 1987: 750 khz; 2.5 kw-D, DA. TL: N41 33 49 W87 09 18. 2576 Portage Mall (46368). (219) 763-2750. Licensee: Douglas Broadcasting Inc. (group owner; acq 4-16-92; $2 million; FTR 5-4-92). Format: Relg, div, Pol. News staff one; news progmg 5 hrs wkly. Target aud: General. Spec prog: Ger 2 hrs, gospel 2 hrs, Serbian 2 hrs, Lithuanian 4 hrs, Bosnian one hr, Indian 3 hrs wkly. ■ John Douglas, pres; Bill Paar, gen mgr; John Young, opns mgr & mus dir; Mark Sodetz, progmg mgr; Diana Kapnas, pub affrs dir; Frank McCoy, chief engr. ■ Rates: $31; 31; 31; na.

Portland

WPGW(AM)—Jan 14, 1951: 1440 khz; 500 w-D, 35 w-N, DA-1. TL: N40 26 10 W85 00 56. Box 1440 (47371). (219) 726-8780. FAX: (219) 726-4311. Licensee: WPGW Inc. (acq 8-1-74). Net: MBS; ABN, AgriAmerica. Rep: Rgnl Reps. Format: Adult contemp. Target aud: General. ■ Robert A. Weaver, pres & gen mgr; Betty Stone, prom mgr. ■ Rates: $7.70; 7.70; 7.70; 7.70.

WPGW-FM—May 19, 1975: 100.9 mhz; 3 kw. Ant 180 ft. TL: N40 26 14 W85 01 02. Stereo. Dups AM 18%. Format: Country. Target aud: General. ■ Rates: $7.15; 7.15; 7.15; 7.15.

Princeton

WRAY(AM)—Dec 16, 1950: 1250 khz; 1 kw-D, 59 w-N. TL: N38 21 25 W87 35 25. Box 8, 1900 W. Broadway (47670). (812) 386-1250. FAX: (812) 386-6249. Licensee: Princeton Broadcasting Co. Inc. Net: CNN. Format: Adult contemp. News staff 3. Target aud: 25-54. ■ Richard Lankford, pres & news dir; Stephen R. Lankford, gen mgr; Stephen Lankford, opns mgr, gen sls mgr & progmg dir; Lynn Davis, prom mgr; Rodger Beard, mus dir; Harold S. Bass, chief engr.

WRAY-FM—May 15, 1960: 98.1 mhz; 50 kw. Ant 420 ft. TL: N38 21 25 W87 35 25. Stereo. Dups AM 100%.

WSJD(FM)—Not on air, target date unknown: 100.5 mhz; 3 kw. Ant 328 ft. 4314 Cherry Ct., Evansville (47715). Licensee: Randolph V. Bell.

Rensselaer

WLQI(FM)—Listing follows WRIN(AM).

*****WPUM(FM)**—Sept 6, 1977: 90.5 mhz; 10 w. Ant 190 ft. TL: N40 55 12 W87 09 27. Hrs opn: 7 AM-2 AM. Box 651, St. Joseph's College (47978). (219) 866-6905. FAX: (219) 866-4497. Licensee: St. Joseph's College (acq 8-1-76). Format: Rock. News progmg one hr wkly. Target aud: 18-34; men. ■ Brian K. Simmons, gen mgr.

WRIN(AM)—Sept 14, 1963: 1560 khz; 1 kw-D, (500 w-CH). TL: N40 57 41 W87 09 07. Box D (47978). (219) 866-5105; (219) 866-4104. FAX: (219) 866-5104. Licensee: Brothers Broadcasting Corp. (acq 6-18-86). Net: ABC/D; AgriAmerica. Rep: Rgnl Reps. Format: Country, loc info. News staff one; news progmg 12 hrs wkly. Target aud: 30 plus. Spec prog: Farm 12 hrs, gospel 2 hrs, relg 10 hrs wkly. ■ John Balvich, pres & gen mgr; Dave Galt, gen sls mgr & prom mgr; Bob Burt, progmg dir; Matt Raters, news dir; Steve Truex, chief engr.

WLQI(FM)—Co-owned with WRIN(AM). 1973: 97.7 mhz; 3.3 kw. Ant 300 ft. TL: N40 58 14 W87 09 10. Stereo. Hrs opn: 24. Prog sep from AM. Net: ABC/D, Jones Satellite Audio; Tribune. Wash atty: Cohn & Marks. Format: Adult contemp. Target aud: 25 plus. Spec prog: Farm 15 hrs wkly.

Richmond

*****WECI(FM)**—September 1964: 91.5 mhz; 400 w. Ant 106 ft. TL: N39 49 22 W84 54 39. Stereo. Drawer 45, Earlham College (47374). (317) 962-3541. Licensee: Earlham College. Net: AP. Format: Div, classical, classic rock. Spec prog: Jazz 16 hrs, new age 2 hrs, oldies 3 hrs, bluegrass/folk 20 hrs, new rock 12 hrs, Black 4 hrs wkly. ■ Luke Clippinger, gen mgr; Morgan Coe, progmg dir; Rebekah Cole, mus dir; Andrew Graham, chief engr.

Stations in the U.S.   **Indiana**

WFMG(FM)—Listing follows WKBV(AM).

WHON(AM)—(Centerville). Feb 17, 1964: 930 khz; 500 w-D, 114 w-N, DA-2. TL: N39 53 33 W84 56 09. Hrs opn: 24. Box 1647, Tingler Rd., Richmond (47374). (317) 962-1595. FAX: (317) 966-4824. Licensee: Brewer Broadcasting Corp. (group owner; acq 3-10-66). Net: MBS. Rep: Rgnl Reps. Format: Easy listening, news/talk. News staff one; Target aud: 35 plus. ■ James R. Brewer, pres; Dave Strycker, gen mgr; Pete Lyons, gen sls mgr; Jim Thomas, progmg dir; Bill O'Hara, news dir; Dave Gill, chief engr. ■ Rates: $13; 12; 13; 12.

WQLK(FM)—Co-owned with WHON(AM). Oct 15, 1973: 96.1 mhz; 50 kw. Ant 350 ft. TL: N39 53 33 W84 56 09. Stereo. Hrs opn: 24. Prog sep from AM. Net: NBC the Source. Format: Classic hits. News staff 2. Target aud: 25-45. ■ Bill O'Hara, progmg dir. ■ Rates: $28; 26; 28; 26.

WKBV(AM)—Sept 27, 1926: 1490 khz; 1 kw-U. TL: N39 49 30 W84 55 50. Box 1646, 2301 W. Main St. (47374). (317) 962-6533. Licensee: Mid-America Radio Group Inc. Group owner: David Keister Stns (acq 12-19-88; grpsl; FTR 12-19-88). Net: ABC/I. Rep: Eugene Gray. Format: MOR, news/talk. News staff 3. Target aud: 25-54. Spec prog: Farm 4 hrs wkly. ■ Jeff Hancock, gen mgr; Dennis Daily, prom mgr; progmg dir & mus dir; Steve Cox, news dir.

WFMG(FM)—Co-owned with WKBV(AM). Dec 17, 1960: 101.3 mhz; 50 kw. Ant 280 ft. TL: N39 49 30 W84 55 50. Stereo. Prog sep from AM. Format: Mus intensive adult contemp. Target aud: 18-44. Spec prog: Relg 4 hrs wkly. ■ Jeff Hancock, stn mgr; Mike Rabey, chief engr.

WQLK(FM)—Listing follows WHON(AM).

*****WVXR(FM)**—Dec 24, 1988: 89.3 mhz; 4.2 kw. Ant 187 ft. TL: N39 52 08 W84 47 47. Stereo. Rebroadcasts WVXU(FM) Cincinnati 100%. 3800 Victory Pkwy., Cincinnati, OH (45207). (513) 745-3738. Licensee: Xavier Univ. Net: APR, AP, NPR, CNN; Ohio Public Network. Format: Var/div, jazz, news/talk. News progmg 34 hrs wkly. Target aud: General; intelligent listeners who enjoy alt progmg. Spec prog: Class 5 hrs, business 8 hrs wkly. ■ Dr. James C. King, gen mgr; George Zahn, opns dir & progmg dir; Jo Strauss, dev dir; Mike Boberg, prom mgr; Mark Keefe, mus dir; Lorna Jordan, news dir; Jay Crawford, chief engr.

Rising Sun

WSCH(FM)—See Aurora.

Roanoke

WGL-FM—1991: 94.1 mhz; 6 kw. Ant 340 ft. TL: N40 58 51 W85 16 48. 2000 Lower Huntington Rd., Fort Wayne (46819). (219) 747-1511. Licensee: Frank S. Kovas (acq 9-14-92; $100,000; FTR 10-19-92). Format: News/talk, sports. ■ Frank Kovas, pres; Connie Kovas, gen mgr.

Rochester

WROI(FM)—Aug 29, 1971: 92.1 mhz; 4.3 kw. Ant 240 ft. TL: N41 03 02 W86 15 39. Stereo. Hrs opn: 5 AM-midnight. 100 W. Ninth St., Suite 306 (46975). (219) 223-6059. FAX: (219) 223-2238. Licensee: Bair Communications Inc. (acq 1-21-92; $225,000; FTR 1-19-92). Net: SMN. Rep: Rgnl Reps. Wash atty: John Pellegrin. Format: Adult contemp. News staff one; news progmg 20 hrs wkly. Target aud: 25-54; baby boomers. Spec prog: Farm 10 hrs, big band 2 hrs, relg 6 hrs wkly. ■ Tom Bair, pres & gen mgr; Ryan Showley, opns dir; Jack Allen, news dir; Chip Longshore, chief engr. ■ Rates: $10; 10; 10; 8.

Rockville

WAXI(FM)—Aug 1977: 104.9 mhz; 1.5 kw. Ant 400 ft. Stereo. Hrs opn: 6 AM-midnight. Box 20 (47872); R.R. 4, Box 144A (47872). (317) 569-2026; (317) 832-2166. FAX: (317) 569-2027. Licensee: Covered Bridge Broadcasting Ltd. (acq 8-1-83; FTR 8-15-83). Net: NBC, SMN. AgriAmerica. Rep: Rgnl Reps. Format: Big band, MOR. News staff one; news progmg 13 hrs wkly. Target aud: 35 plus; active. Spec prog: Farm 5 hrs, gospel 2 hrs, relg 4 hrs wkly. ■ Robert Rouse, pres; Sharon Rouse, vp; Bill Cook, gen mgr; Dennis Porter, news dir; Don Mier, chief engr. ■ Rates: $9.75; 9.75; 9.75; 9.75.

Royal Center

WHZR(FM)—Oct 16, 1989: 103.7 mhz; 6 kw. Ant 328 ft. TL: N40 48 43 W86 21 56. Stereo. Box 103, 1302 E. Broadway, Logansport (46947); Box 289, Corp. Headquarters, Ashtabula, OH (44004). (219) 732-1037. FAX: (219) 739-1037. Licensee: Bulmer Communications of Logansport Inc. Group owner: Bulmer Communications Group. Format: CHR. News staff one. Target aud: 18-49; mass appeal. ■ John A. Bulmer, pres; Karl Hess, vp; Milt Hess, gen mgr.

Rushville

WRCR(FM)—Aug 5, 1971: 94.3 mhz; 740 w. Ant 550 ft. TL: N39 42 22 W85 29 34. Stereo. 102 N. Perkins St. (46173). (317) 932-3983. FAX: (317) 938-1916. Licensee: Quantum Broadcasting Corp. (acq 1-1-88). Net: ABC/D. Rep: Rgnl Reps, IRMA. Format: Oldies, adult contemp, news/talk. News staff 2; news progmg 8 hrs wkly. Target aud: 35 plus. Spec prog: Farm 10 hrs wkly. ■ Louis U. Disinger, pres, gen mgr, opns dir, progmg dir & engrg dir; Kevin Stone, gen sls mgr; Mike Wardwell, rgnl sls mgr & prom mgr; Kevin Green, mus dir & news dir; Horce Smith, chief engr. ■ Rates: $11; 11; 11; 11.

Salem

WKJK(FM)—1962: 98.9 mhz; 50 kw. Ant 300 ft. TL: N38 35 59 W86 05 17 (CP: Ant 492 ft., TL: N38 21 56 W85 58 55). Stereo. Hrs opn: 18. Licensee: Snowden Broadcasting of Louisville Inc. (acq 1993; $2.4 million; FTR 9-13-93). Format: Div. News progmg 30 hrs wkly. Target aud: 18-65. Spec prog: Relg, gospel, bluegrass, live sports, talk. ■ Jim Snowden, pres.

FARM STATIONS
WSLM - WSLM - CH 17-TV
P.O. Box 385, Salem, IN 47167
PHONES - (812) 883-5750, 2797

WSLM(AM)—Feb 14, 1953: 1220 khz; 5 kw-D, 384 w-N, DA-2. TL: N38 36 55 W86 05 10. Hrs opn: 16. Box 385, Hwy. 60 E., Radio Ridge (47167). (812) 883-5750; (812) 883-2797. FAX: (812) 883-5202. Licensee: Don H. Martin. Net: AgriAmerica, Network Ind., Tribune. Rep: Rgnl Reps. Wash atty: B. Jay Baraff. Format: Farm, C&W, gospel. News staff 5; news progmg 12 hrs wkly. Target aud: 21-70. ■ Don H. Martin, pres & gen mgr; J.R. Martin, stn mgr, prom mgr, progmg dir & chief engr; Elmo Brough, gen sls mgr; Becky L. Martin, adv dir; David Stuart, mus dir; Rick Martin, news dir. ■ Rates: $25; 20; 25; 20.

WSLM-FM—1992: 97.9 mhz; 3 kw. Ant 220 ft. TL: N38 38 07 W86 10 37. Stereo. Hrs opn: 18. Dups AM 50%. FAX: (812) 883-2797. Format: News, farm markets. Target aud: 18-65. Spec prog: Relg, country, live sports, talk. ■ Don H. Martin, adv mgr; David Stuart, progmg dir. ■ Rates: Same as AM.

Scottsburg

WMPI(FM)—Dec 16, 1966: 100.9 mhz; 3 kw. Ant 300 ft. TL: N38 37 12 W85 45 15. Stereo. Box 270, 22 E. McClain Ave. (47170). (812) 752-5612. FAX: (812) 752-2345. Licensee: D. R. Rice Broadcasting Inc. Net: ABC/D. Rep: Rgnl Reps. Format: C&W. News progmg 14 hrs wkly. Target aud: 25-54. ■ Donald R. Rice, pres; Raymond Rice, gen mgr; Thomas W. Culi, gen sls mgr; Jay Alan, prom mgr; Rob Davis, progmg dir & asst mus dir; Jay Allan, mus dir; Steve Woodruff, chief engr. ■ Rates: $13.50; 13.50; 13.50; 11.50.

Seelyville

WAGD(FM)—Not on air, target date unknown: 95.9 mhz; 6 kw. Ant 100 ft. Christian Center Assembly of God Inc., 9400 Wabash Ave., Terre Haute (47803). Licensee: Radio Ministries Board of Victory.

Seymour

WZZB(AM)—Nov 4, 1949: 1390 khz; 1 kw-D, 74 w-N. TL: N38 58 23 W85 53 20. Hrs opn: 24. Box 806, 1534 Ewing St. (47274). (812) 522-1390. FAX: (812) 522-9541. Licensee: SCI Broadcasting Inc. (acq 11-2-89; $600,000 with co-located FM; FTR 11-20-89). Net: SMN; AgriAmerica, NetworkIndiana. Rep: Rgnl Reps. Format: Oldies, news. News staff one; news progmg 17 hrs wkly. Target aud: 25 plus; community oriented. Spec prog: Farm 2 hrs wkly. ■ Charles J. Jenkins, pres; Blair Trask, vp, gen mgr & gen sls mgr; Greg Fish, opns dir & mus dir; Robert Shippee, news dir. ■ Rates: $20; 20; 20; 20.

WQKC(FM)—Co-owned with WZZB(AM). Feb 23, 1961: 93.7 mhz; 25 kw. Ant 699 ft. TL: N38 58 22 W86 10 03. Stereo. Hrs opn: 24. Prog sep from AM. Format: Country. Target aud: General. ■ Greg Fish, progmg dir; Robert Shippee, pub affrs dir. ■ Rates: Same as AM.

Shelbyville

WENS(FM)—Nov 6, 1964: 97.1 mhz; 23 kw. Ant 739 ft. TL: N39 46 02 W86 01 51. Stereo. Hrs opn: 24. 950 N. Meridian, Suite 1297, Indianapolis (46204). (317) 266-9700. FAX: (317) 634-1618. Licensee: Emmis Broadcasting Corp. (group owner; acq 6-81). Rep: McGavren Guild. Wash atty: Gardner, Carton & Douglas. Format: Adult contemp. News staff one. Target aud: 25-49. ■ Jeffrey H. Smulyan, pres; Christine Woodward-Duncan, vp & gen mgr; Donna Dwyer Pitz, gen sls mgr; Lori Ballard, natl sls mgr; Todd Alexander, prom dir; Chuck Knight, progmg dir; Ann Craig, news dir & pub affrs dir; Bob Hawkins, chief engr. ■ Rates: $135; 135; 135; 60.

WOOO(AM)—Jan 14, 1961: 1520 khz; 1 kw-D, 250 w-N, DA-2. TL: N39 33 25 W85 46 18. Box 338 (46176); 2356 N. Morristown Rd. (46176). (317) 398-9757. FAX: (317) 392-3292. Licensee: ARS Broadcasting. Format: Country. News staff one. ■ Alan R. Shriver, pres; Ron Green, gen mgr; Wayne Thomas, stn mgr & news dir; Jerry Willis, gen sls mgr; Mark Gravely, progmg dir; Ken Owens, chief engr.

South Bend

*****WAUS(FM)**—(Berrien Springs, Mich). 1971: 90.7 mhz; 50 kw. Ant 492 ft. TL: N41 57 42 W86 21 02. Stereo. Hrs opn: 24 Campus Center, Andrew Univ., Berrien Springs, MI (49104). (616) 471-3400. Licensee: Andrews Broadcasting Corp. Net: APR. Wash atty: Donald E. Martin, P.C. Format: Class, news. News progmg 25 hrs wkly. Target aud: 35 plus; listeners with interest in classical music. Spec prog: Relg 10 hrs wkly. ■ Richard Lesher, chmn; Michael Wiist, gen mgr; Brian Darrough, opns dir; Waverly Tyson, dev dir; Brenda Zarska, progmg dir & mus dir.

*****WETL(FM)**—Nov 17, 1958: 91.7 mhz; 3 kw. Ant 200 ft. TL: N41 37 24 W86 14 15. Stereo. 635 S. Main St. (46601). (219) 282-4076. FAX: (219) 282-4122. Licensee: South Bend Community School Corp. (acq 11-17-58). Format: Educ, instructional. Target aud: Students in the South Bend Community Schools & the community at large. ■ Joanne Bendall, stn mgr; Jerry V. Limbert, progmg dir; Allen Wujcik, chief engr.

WHME(FM)—Jan 1968: 103.1 mhz; 3 kw. Ant 300 ft. TL: N41 36 11 W86 12 51. Hrs opn: 24. Box 12 (46624); 61300 S. Ironwood Rd. (46614). (219) 291-8200. FAX: (219) 291-9043. Licensee: Lester Sumrall Evangelistic Assn. Group owner: LeSea Broadcasting. Wash atty: Gardner, Carton & Douglas. Format: Adult contemp Christian. News progmg 3 hrs wkly. Target aud: 24-36; women, homemakers & adult males. ■ Dr. Lester Sumrall, chmn; Steve Sumrall, pres; Peter Sumrall, vp, gen mgr, vp opns & vp sls; Jim Veldhuis, stn mgr, progmg dir & mus dir; Fran Wright, dev mgr & mktg mgr; Craig Wallin, natl sls mgr; Anna Riblet, rgnl sls mgr; Dar Monosmith, chief engr. ■ Rates: $19; 17; 19; 16.

WIWO(AM)—Dec 22, 1947: 1580 khz; 1 kw-D, 500 w-N, DA-N. TL: N41 41 09 W86 09 53. Hrs opn: 5 AM-midnight. 1129 N. Hickory Rd. (46615). (219) 234-1580; (219) 287-8255. FAX: (219) 287-8375. Licensee: Times Communications Inc. (acq 5-20-93; $27,000; FTR 6-14-93). Net: MBS, BRN; Format: Talk, sports. News staff one; news progmg 5 hrs wkly. Target aud: 35 plus. Spec prog: Black 2 hrs, gospel 2 hrs, Pol 7 hrs wkly. ■ William Dobslaw, pres & gen sls mgr; Michael Shannon, gen mgr, opns mgr, prom dir & progmg dir; Larry Humphrie, chief engr. ■ Rates: $25; 20; 23; 16.

WLTA(FM)—See Elkhart.

WNDU(AM)—1944: 1490 khz; 1 kw-U. TL: N41 41 38 W86 13 50. Hrs opn: 24. Box 1616 (46634). (219) 631-1616. FAX: (219) 631-1630; TWX: 810-229-2594. Licensee: Michiana Telecasting Corp. (acq 9-55). Net: ABC/I. Rep: McGavren Guild. Format: Oldies. Target aud: 25-54. Format: Hungarian one hr, Sp one hr wkly. ■ Jim Behling, pres & gen mgr; Melissa Collins, prom mgr; Elliot Crooke, news dir; George Molnar, chief engr.

WNDU-FM—1962: 92.9 mhz; 12.5 kw. Ant 800 ft. TL: N41 36 20 W86 12 45. Stereo. Hrs opn: 24. Prog sep from AM. Format: Contemp hit. Target aud: 18-49; women. ■ WNDU-TV affil. ■ Rates: $65; 60; 65; 40.

WNSN(FM)—Listing follows WSBT(AM).

WRBR-FM—1965: 103.9 mhz; 3 kw. Ant 328 ft. TL: N41 41 53 W86 09 20. Stereo. Unit 12, 6910 N. Maine, Granger (46530-9681). (219) 271-5550. FAX: (219) 271-

Broadcasting & Cable Yearbook 1994
B-129

5555. Licensee: Booth Broadcasting Co. Group owner: Booth American Co. (acq 1969). Rep: Major Mkt. Format: Oldies. News staff one; news progmg 2 hrs wkly. Target aud: 25-54; affluent, older people. ■ Vince Ford, vp, gen mgr & gen sls mgr; Bob Henning, prom mgr, progmg dir, mus dir & chief engr; Dale Reese, news dir.

WSBT(AM)—Apr 1922: 960 khz; 5 kw-U, DA-2. TL: N41 37 00 W86 13 01. 300 W. Jefferson Blvd. (46601). (219) 233-3141. TWX: 810-299-2500. Licensee: WSBT Inc. Group owner: Schurz Communications Inc. (acq 9-24-76). Net: CBS. Rep: Katz. Format: News/talk, sports. Target aud: 35-54. Spec prog: Farm 3 hrs, Hungarian one hr, Sp one hr wkly. ■ Jim Freeman, pres; Jack Swart, stn mgr & natl sls mgr; Sally Brown, rgnl sls mgr; Mary Firtl, prom mgr; Rob Poulin, progmg dir; Bill Crafton, news dir; Chris Thornton, chief engr.

WNSN(FM)—Co-owned with WSBT(AM). Aug 1, 1962: 101.5 mhz; 13 kw. Ant 970 ft. TL: N41 37 00 W86 13 01. Stereo. Prog sep from AM. Format: Adult contemp. ■ Rob Poulin, mus dir. ■ WSBT-TV affil.

***WUBS(FM)**—Not on air, target date unknown: 89.7 mhz; 1.5 kw. TL: N41 40 51 W86 15 34. Box 3931 (46619). Licensee: Interfaith Christian Union Inc.

WUBU(FM)—Not on air, target date unknown: 106.3 mhz; 3 kw. Ant 292 ft. TL: N41 44 11 W86 17 19. 3565 29th St. S.E., Kentwood, MI (49508). (616) 949-8760. Licensee: Focus Radio Inc. (acq 12-30-92; $300,000; FTR 1-25-93).

WZOW(FM)—See Goshen.

South Whitley

WLZQ(FM)—Dec 2, 1992: 101.1 mhz; 6 kw. Ant 328 ft. TL: N41 04 42 W85 31 20. Stereo. Hrs opn: 24. Box 2020, Warsaw (46581). (219) 268-2500. Licensee: Larko Communications. Net: SMN. Wash atty: James R. Cooke. Format: Hot AC. News staff one. Target aud: 25-44. ■ Chris Larko, CEO & gen mgr; Susan Derr, stn mgr. ■ Rates: $14; 12; 14; 5.

Spencer

WSKT(FM)—Sept 15, 1983: 92.7 mhz; 1 kw. Ant 480 ft. TL: N39 15 18 W86 51 51. Stereo. 201 N. VanDalia Ave. (47460). (812) 829-9393. FAX: (812) 829-9747. Licensee: Spencer Communications Inc. (acq 4-22-92; no financial consideration; FTR 5-18-92). Net: SMN. Format: C&W. Spec prog: Relg 6 hrs wkly. ■ Reggie Johnson, stn mgr; Katie Williams, gen sls mgr; Tony Kale, progmg dir & news dir; Tom Mulvahill, chief engr.

Sullivan

WNDI(AM)—Oct 7, 1963: 1550 khz; 250 w-D. TL: N39 04 32 W87 23 57. R.R. 5, Box 19B, Hwy. 54 E. (47882). (812) 268-6322. FAX: (812) 268-6575. Licensee: Antrosiek Inc. (acq 10-5-90; with co-located FM; FTR 10-29-90). Net: CNN. Format: Country. News staff one; news progmg 24 hrs wkly. Target aud: 24-54. Spec prog: Farm 6 hrs wkly. ■ Arthur F. Stanley, pres & gen mgr. ■ Rates: $10; 10; 10; 10.

WNDI-FM—Aug 10, 1982: 95.3 mhz; 3 kw. Ant 150 ft. TL: N39 05 36 W87 26 38. Dups AM 100%. ■ Rates: Same as AM.

Syracuse

WAWC(FM)—May 31, 1991: 103.5 mhz; 3 kw. Ant 328 ft. TL: N41 22 57 W85 41 35. Stereo. Hrs opn: 24. 10129 N. 800 E. (46567). (219) 457-8181; (219) 457-7126. FAX: (219) 457-4488. Licensee: William Andrew Dixon. Net: USA. Format: Adult contemp. News staff one; news progmg 5 hrs wkly. Target aud: 25-54. Elkart, Noble & Kosciusko residents. Spec prog: Business news 5 hrs, relg 4 hrs wkly. ■ William Andrew Dixon, gen mgr & gen sls mgr; Cathy Williams, opns dir; John Dixon, mktg mgr; Lori Dixon, prom dir; Bill Dixon, progmg dir & news dir; Jeremy Van Lue, mus dir; Bob Densmore, chief engr. ■ Rates: $10.50; 10.50; 10.50; 4.50.

Tell City

WTCJ(AM)—Feb 1, 1948: 1230 khz; 1 kw-U. TL: N37 56 16 W86 45 28. Hrs opn: 5 AM-midnight. Box 397, Hwy. 66 (47586). (812) 547-2345. FAX: (812) 547-2346. Licensee: Maytha N. Brewer. Group owner: Brewer Broadcasting Corp. Net: Unistar. Rep: Rgnl Reps. Format: Adult contemp. News staff one. Target aud: 25-54; community-oriented listeners. Spec prog: Gospel 6 hrs wkly. ■ Maytha N. Brewer, pres; Jay Brewer, gen mgr, gen sls mgr & chief engr; Tim Merkley, mus dir; Dave Allen, news dir & pub affrs dir. ■ Rates: $6.85; 6.85; 6.85; 6.85.

Terre Haute

WBFX(AM)—June 15, 1927: 1230 khz; 250 w-U, DA-2. TL: N39 29 23 W87 25 04. Stereo. Hrs opn: 24. Box 35, 1341 Ohio St. (47807). (812) 232-5034. FAX: (812) 234-4383. Licensee: Contemp Media Inc. Group owner: Contemporary Media Broadcasting Group (acq 5-1-82; $750,000 with co-located FM; FTR 3-29-82). Net: ABC/I. Rep: Christal, Rgnl Reps. Wash atty: Rosenman & Colin. Format: AOR. News staff 3; news progmg 20 hrs wkly. Target aud: 35-64; general. Spec prog: Farm 6 hrs wkly. ■ Mike Rice, pres; Ken Brown, gen mgr; Robert Cox, sls dir; Tom Lisella, progmg dir; Taylor Brown, news dir; Gerald Probst, chief engr.

WZZQ(FM)—Co-owned with WBFX(AM). Sept 28, 1967: 107.5 mhz; 27.5 kw. Ant 670 ft. TL: N39 30 14 W87 26 37. Stereo. Hrs opn: 24. Net: ABC/R. Rep: Christal. News staff 3; news progmg 5 hrs wkly. Target aud: 18-49. ■ Ben Jacobs, progmg dir; Danny Wayne, mus dir.

WBOW(AM)—1993: 640 khz; 1 kw, DA-N. TL: N39 29 21 W87 25 11. Stereo. Hrs opn: 24. 1341 Ohio St. (47807). (812) 232-5034. FAX: (812) 234-4383. Licensee: Contemporary Media Inc. Group owner: Contemporary Media Broadcasting Group. Net: ABC/I. Rep: Christal. Format: Sports, info. Target aud: Adults. ■ Mike Rice, pres; Janet Cox, CFO; Ken Brown, gen mgr; R.C. Cox, gen sls mgr; Gary Kern, news dir; Gerry Probst, chief engr.

***WCRT(FM)**—January 1992: 88.5 mhz; 550 w. Ant 308 ft. TL: N39 30 14 W87 26 37. 2108 W. Springfield, Champagne, IL (61821). (217) 359-8232. Licensee: Illinois Bible Institute. Format: Contemp Christian. ■ Steven Young, stn mgr.

***WISU(FM)**—Sept 13 1964: 89.7 mhz; 13.5 kw. Ant 512 ft. TL: N39 30 26 W87 31 50. Stereo. Hrs opn: Noon-midnight. Dreiser Hall, Indiana State Univ., 217 N. 6th St. (47809). (812) 237-3248; (812) 237-3252. FAX: (812) 237-3241. Licensee: Indiana State Univ. Board of Trustees. Wash atty: Crowell. Format: Jazz, urban contemp. News progmg 4 hrs wkly. Target aud: 25-50; young professionals. Spec prog: Blues 10 hrs wkly. ■ John Moore, pres; David Sabaini, gen mgr & stn mgr; Timothy Blocksom, opns mgr; James Chesebro, vp dev; Kathleen Hansen, mus dir; Andy Heavilin, news dir; Don Mier, chief engr.

WJSH(AM)—May 23, 1958: 1300 khz; 500 w-D. TL: N39 28 01 W87 25 34. Hrs opn: 6 AM-10 PM. Suite 509, 721 Wabash Ave. (47807). (812) 232-1300. Licensee: Cardinal Broadcasting Inc. (acq 10-15-91; $17,000; FTR 11-4-91). Rep: Katz & Powell. Format: Adult comtemp, big band, oldies. News progmg one hr wkly. Target aud: 35 plus. ■ Ron Mott, gen mgr; Rick James, gen sls mgr; Paulette Tauber, prom dir; Dennis Roberts, progmg dir; John Connelly, chief engr. ■ Rates: $17; 12; 12; 12.

WLEZ(FM)—Sept 11, 1962: 102.7 mhz; 50 kw. Ant 500 ft. TL: N39 32 54 W87 24 36. Stereo. 1072 Windsor Rd. (47802). (812) 299-4343. FAX: (812) 299-4608. Licensee: Bomar Broadcasting Inc. (acq 8-91; FTR 9-9-91). Rep: Katz. Format: CHR. News staff one; news progmg 2 hrs wkly. Target aud: 18-49; young professionals. ■ Jim Ganley, gen mgr & prom mgr; Rich Coolman, progmg dir; Bob Miller, mus dir; Dick Purlee, news dir; Paul Dixon, chief engr.

WMGI(FM)—June 13, 1960: 100.7 mhz; 50 kw. Ant 500 ft. TL: N30 27 22 W87 28 50. Stereo. Box 3190 (47803); US 40 W., West Terre Haute (47885). (812) 533-2141. FAX: (812) 533-0513. Licensee: Bright Tower Communications Inc. (acq 7-16-85). Net: CBS Spectrum. Rep: Eastman. Format: Adult contemp. News staff one. Target aud: 25-54. ■ Donald E. Foster, pres; Paula J. Phillips, gen mgr; Marvin R. Phillips, gen sls mgr; Bob Day, progmg dir; Bryan Thomas, mus dir; Dave Taylor, news dir; Harold Wesley, chief engr.

***WMHD-FM**—1981: 90.5 mhz; 160 w-H. Ant 79 ft. TL: N41 28 37 W87 19 33 (CP: 700 w-V, ant 348 ft., TL: N39 30 14 W87 26 37). Box 14, 5500 Wabash Ave. (47803). (812) 877-8350; (812) 877-8441. Licensee: Rose Hulman Institute of Technology. Net: USA. Format: Educ, AOR. News progmg 9 hrs wkly. Target aud: General; local. Spec prog: Class 2 hrs, jazz one hr, reggae 2 hrs, bluegrass one hr, blues one hr, contemp Christian 4 hrs wkly. ■ David Piker, gen mgr.

WTHI(AM)—Jan 6, 1948: 1480 khz; 5 kw-D, 1 kw-N, DA-2. TL: N39 30 02 W87 23 10. Hrs opn: 24. Box 1486 (47808). (812) 232-9481. FAX: (812) 234-0089. Licensee: Hulman & Co. Group owner: Wabash Valley Broadcasting Corp. (acq 7-13-92; grpsl; FTR 11-2-92). Net: MBS; Network Indiana, AgriAmerica. Rep: Katz. Wash atty: Dow, Lohnes & Albertson. Format: News/talk. News staff 2. Target aud: 25 plus. ■ G. Christopher Duffy, pres; John Newcomb, exec vp; David L. Liston, vp & gen mgr; Barry Kent, opns dir & progmg dir; Tony Clark, gen sls mgr; Frank Rush, progmg mgr; Martin Plascak, news dir; Jim Borgioli, vp engrg; Dan Watson, chief engr.

WTHI-FM—Oct 1948: 99.9 mhz; 50 kw. Ant 494 ft. TL: N39 27 57 W87 24 12. Stereo. Hrs opn: 24. Prog sep from AM. Net: MBS. Format: Country. ■ G. Christopher Duffy, CEO; Steve Hall, mus dir. ■ WTHI-TV affil.

WWVR(FM)—See West Terre Haute.

WZZQ(FM)—Listing follows WBFX(AM).

Union City

WBNN(AM)—Not on air, target date unknown: 1030 khz; 330 kw-D, DA. TL: N40 11 32 W84 47 58. 400 Alleghany St., Blackburg, VA (24063). Licensee: Union City Radio.

***WPER(FM)**—Not on air, target date unknown: 88.9 mhz; 4.1 kw. TL: N40 11 32 W84 47 58. Box 889, Blacksburg, VA (24063). Licensee: Positive Alternative Radio Inc. ■ Vernon H. Baker, gen mgr.

Valparaiso

WAKE(AM)—Nov 4, 1964: 1500 khz; 1 kw-D, DA. TL: N41 26 36 W87 02 54. Hrs opn: 6 AM-6 PM. 2755 Sager Rd. (46383). (219) 462-6111. Licensee: Porter County Broadcasting Corp. Net: ABC/C; Indian Net. Wash atty: Miller & Fields. Format: Loc news, talk & info. News staff 2; news progmg 21 hrs wkly. Target aud: 30 plus; community oriented, middle to middle-upper class. ■ Len Ellis, chmn; Leigh Ellis, pres & gen mgr; Richard Harlan, gen sls mgr; Tod Allen, prom mgr, progmg dir & mus dir; James J. Pinkerton, news dir; Carl Fletcher, chief engr. ■ Rates: $20.30; 18.35; 20.30; na.

WLJE(FM)—Co-owned with WAKE(AM). Oct 6, 1967: 105.5 mhz; 1.25 kw. Ant 513 ft. TL: N41 31 28 W87 01 08. Stereo. (219) 462-8125. Net: ABC/D. Format: Country. News progmg 7 hrs wkly. Target aud: 25-55; family, middle income. ■ Jim Heath, progmg dir & mus dir. ■ Rates: $26; 19.50; 26; na.

WNWI(AM)—Dec 31, 1965: 1080 khz; 250 w-D. TL: N41 28 20 W87 04 30. Box 1130, One Center St. (46384). (219) 462-2158. Licensee: Northwestern Indiana Radio Co. Inc. Net: AP. Rep: Keystone (unwired net), Rgnl Reps. Format: Adult contemp/flex. Spec prog: Class 2 hrs, Serbian one hr wkly. ■ G. Edward Hershman, pres; Mickey Hershman, gen sls mgr; Marv Walters, progmg dir; Ed Lee, news dir; D.E. Wiggins, chief engr.

***WVUR-FM**—Sept 25, 1966: 95.1 mhz; 36 w. Ant 125 ft. TL: N41 27 57 W87 02 29. Stereo. Hrs opn: 24. Valparaiso Univ., Box 31, 816 Union St. (46383). (219) 464-6673. FAX: (219) 464-5491. Licensee: Valparaiso University Association Inc. Net: AP. Format: Rock. News staff 2; news progmg 8 hrs wkly. Target aud: 18-34. Spec prog: Classical 3 hrs, jazz 3 hrs, urban contemp 3 hrs, metal 3 hrs, classic rock 3 hrs, blues 3 hrs, new age 3 hrs, big band 3 hrs wkly. ■ Kat Sanderson, gen mgr; Kim Gleason, Nikki Brillhart, gen sls mgrs; Nikkie Brillhart, prom mgr; Jarett Millar, progmg dir; Chad Bailey, mus dir; John Anderson, news dir; Johnny Heintz, chief engr.

Van Buren

WCJC(FM)—Aug 28, 1989: 99.3 mhz; 3 kw. Ant 328 ft. TL: N40 40 01 W85 37 50. Stereo. Box 839, 120 N. Miller Ave., Marion (46952). (317) 664-6239. Licensee: Mid-America Radio Group Inc. Group owner: David Keister Stations (acq 12-19-88; grpsl; FTR 12-19-88). Net: SMN. Format: Country. News staff 2 Target aud: 25-54; consumer-oriented modern country fans. Spec prog: Relg 3 hrs wkly. ■ David Keister, pres; David G. Poeler, gen mgr; James F. Brunner, gen sls mgr; Mark Metzner, progmg dir; Tim Rush, news dir; Warren Arnett, chief engr.

Versailles

WXCH(FM)—Nov 15, 1984: 103.1 mhz; 3 kw. Ant 328 ft. TL: N39 10 38 W85 17 00. Stereo. 6857 Salem Ridge Rd., Aurora (47001). (812) 438-2777. Licensee: Dearborn County Broadcasters Inc. (acq 3-23-92; $85,000; FTR 4-13-92). Format: Country. ■ John Schuler, gen mgr.

Vevay

WKID(FM)—Sept 6, 1974: 95.9 mhz; 2.7 kw. Ant 480 ft. TL: N38 50 12 W85 01 48. Hrs opn: 24. 118 W. Main St. (47043). (812) 427-9590. FAX: (812) 427-2492. Licensee: Raydell Media Group Inc. (acq 11-13-92; $32,146; FTR 12-14-92). Net: ABC/E; Ky. Net. Format: Country. News staff one; news progmg 7 hrs wkly. Target aud: 25-49. Spec prog: Farm 8 hrs, talk 2 hrs, high school

Stations in the U.S. Iowa

sports 12 hrs wkly. ■ Dell Hubbard, pres; Carlos P. Gray, gen sls mgr; Mike Burdette, news dir. ■ Rates: $8.25; 6.25; 7.25; 5.25.

Vincennes

WAOV(AM)—Oct 22, 1940: 1450 khz; 1 kw-U. TL: N38 42 26 W87 29 42. Hrs opn: 24. Box 2000, Executive Inn, One Executive Blvd. 6th Fl. (47591). (812) 882-6060. FAX: (812) 885-2604. Licensee: Old Northwest Broadcasting Inc. Group owner: Wisdom Stations (acq 9-28-93; $250,000 with WWBL[FM] Washington; FTR 10-18-93). Net: CBS. Rep: Savalli, Rgnl Reps. Format: News, talk, sports. News staff 2; news progmg 56 hrs wkly. Target aud: 25 plus. ■ David L. Crooks, pres & gen sls mgr; Mark R. Lange, gen mgr; Mike Cady, progmg dir; Lisa Midkiff, news dir; Jim Evans, chief engr.

WFML(FM)—May 16, 1965: 96.7 mhz; 3 kw. Ant 377 ft. TL: N38 42 26 W87 29 42. Stereo. Hrs opn: 24. Box 2213, 1200 N. 2nd (47591). (812) 885-5830; (812) 886-9696. FAX: (812) 882-2237. Licensee: The Vincennes University Foundation (acq 8-29-86). Net: ABC/D; Network Indiana, AgriAmerica. Format: Contemp country. ■ Phil Smith, gen mgr & progmg dir; Steve McClure, chief engr. ■ Rates: $11.56; 11.56; 11.56; 11.56.

WUZR(FM)—(Bicknell). June 4, 1991: 105.7 mhz; 3 kw. Ant 292 ft. TL: N38 43 47 W87 24 44 (CP: 1.8 kw, ant 426 ft.). Stereo. Hrs opn: 24. Box 2412, R.R. 1, Box 231 B (47591). (812) 324-2200. FAX: (812) 324-9023. Licensee: Media Five Corp. (acq 1-91). Net: SMN. Wash atty: Haley, Bader & Potts. Format: Pure gold. News staff one. Target aud: 25-54. Spec prog: Local news, high school sports, Indianapolis Colts football. ■ Keith A. Doades, pres, gen mgr & sls dir; William McAdams, progmg dir & news dir. ■ Rates: $12; 12; 12; na.

***WVUB(FM)**—Dec 7, 1970: 91.1 mhz; 50 kw. Ant 500 ft. TL: N38 39 06 W87 28 37. Stereo. Davis Hall No. 64, Vincennes Univ. (47591-5201). (812) 885-5354. FAX: (812) 882-2237. Licensee: Board of Trustees for Vincennes Univ. Net: NPR, AP. Format: Easy lstng. Spec prog: Jazz 4 hrs wkly. ■ Phillip M. Summers, pres; T. Mack Seed, stn mgr; Scott Hockman, progmg dir; John David Szink, Ed Thurman (asst), news dirs; Tony Cloud, pub affrs dir; Michael Murphy, chief engr.

WZDM(FM)—September 1988: 92.1 mhz; 2 kw. Ant 400 ft. TL: N38 43 18 W87 33 37. Stereo. Hrs opn: 24. Box 242, Executive Inn, one Executive Blvd 6th FL (47591). (812) 882-6060. FAX: (812) 885-2604. Licensee: The Original Co. Inc. Group owner: Wisdom Stations. Format: Adult contemp. News staff one; news progmg 10 hrs wkly. Target aud: 25-54; upscale. ■ Mark R. Lange, pres & gen mgr; Dave Crooks, gen sls mgr; Dave Young, progmg dir; Lisa Midkiff, news dir; Jim Evans, chief engr.

Wabash

WAYT(AM)—November 1971: 1510 khz; 250 w-D. TL: N40 47 11 W85 49 19. 1360 S. Wabash St. (46992). (219) 563-1161. Licensee: Conway Communications Corp. (acq 9-17-76). Net: AP, MBS. Rep: Rgnl Reps. Format: Adult contemp, country variety. News staff one; news progmg 12 hrs wkly. Target aud: 25-54. Spec prog: Gospel 6 hrs wkly. ■ Sandra Schram, pres; Roderick Schram, gen mgr, gen sls mgr, prom mgr, progmg dir & mus dir; Bob Ferguson, asst mus dir; Alice Greene, news dir & pub affrs dir; Brian Walsh, chief engr. ■ Rates: $7.50; 9; 8.50; na.

WKUZ(FM)—April 1, 1965: 95.9 mhz; 3 kw. Ant 150 ft. TL: N40 50 00 W85 87 11. Stereo. Hrs opn: 18. Box 342, Red Apple Inn, 111 W. Market St. (46992). (219) 563-4111; (219) 563-4425. FAX: (219) 563-4425. Licensee: Upper Wabash Broadcasting Corp. Net: USA, AgriAmerica, Net. Ind. Format: Adult contemp. News staff one; news progmg 10 hrs wkly. Target aud: 25-54; men & women, families with children. Spec prog: Big band 3 hrs, C&W 13 hrs, farm 5 hrs wkly. ■ Sara Adams, pres; Paul Adams, gen mgr, mktg mgr, prom mgr, adv mgr & chief engr; Charles Adams, opns mgr, progmg dir, mus dir & news dir. ■ Rates: $8.50; 8.50; 8.50; 8.50.

WWIP(FM)—July 1, 1993: 105.9 mhz; 3 kw. Ant 318 ft. TL: N40 47 11 W85 49 19. Hrs opn: 5 AM-1 AM. 1360 S. Wabash (46992). Licensee: Conaway Communications Corp. Format: Adult contemp, contemp hit. Target aud: 18-54. Spec prog: Jazz 2 hrs, alternative college 3 hrs wkly. ■ Roderick E. Schram, gen mgr.

Warsaw

WRSW(AM)—1951: 1480 khz; 1 kw-D, 500 w-N. TL: N41 13 21 W85 50 17. Hrs opn: 4:55 AM-midnight. Box 1448, Times Building, Market & Indiana Sts. (46581-1448). (219) 267-3115; (219) 267-3071. FAX: (219) 267-7784. Licensee: WRSW Broadcasting Inc. Net: AP; AgriAmerica, Tribune. Format: MOR. News staff one; news progmg 18 hrs wkly. Target aud: General; adults. Spec prog: Farm 11 hrs, Sp 2 hrs wkly. ■ M.R. Williams, gen mgr; Harvey J. Miller, gen sls mgr & prom mgr; Ladonna Odell, progmg dir; Mike Rees, mus dir; Roger Grossman, news dir; Andrew Farmer, chief engr. ■ Rates: $23; 21; 23; 21.

WRSW-FM—1948: 107.3 mhz; 50 kw. Ant 293 ft. TL: N41 13 21 W85 50 17. Stereo. Dups AM 30%. Format: Adult contemp. Target aud: General; affluent adults. Spec prog: Sp 2 hrs wkly. ■ M.R. Williams, pres; Harvey J. Miller, stn mgr; Andrew Farmer, opns dir; Roger Grossman, dev dir. ■ Rates: Same as AM.

Washington

WAMW(AM)—Jan 1955: 1580 khz; 500 w-D, DA-D. TL: N38 39 04 W87 09 55. 102 E. Main (47501). (812) 254-6761. FAX: (812) 254-6761. Licensee: Greene Electronics. Net: USA. Format: Southern country gospel. News staff one; news progmg 8 hrs wkly. Target aud: 30 plus; those with gospel music interest. ■ William A. Greene, gen mgr & chief engr; Jim Ritterskamp, gen sls mgr; Zane Rudnik, prom mgr, progmg dir & news dir. ■ Rates: $5; 5; 5; na.

WAMW-FM—Nov 20, 1989: 107.9 mhz; 3 kw. Ant 328 ft. TL: N38 38 47 W87 16 47. Stereo. Hrs opn: 5 AM-midnight. Prog sep from AM. Net: NBC; AgriAmerica, Network Indiana. Format: Adult contemp. News progmg 10 hrs wkly. Target aud: 35 plus. Spec prog: Relg 7 hrs, farm 2 hrs wkly. ■ William A. Greene, stn mgr & vp engrg; Zane Rudnik, vp progmg & mus dir. ■ Rates: $10; 10; 10; 6.75.

WWBL(FM)—February 1948: 106.5 mhz; 50 kw. Ant 340 ft. TL: N38 39 04 W87 09 55 (CP: 35 kw, ant 581 ft., TL: N38 39 05 W87 09 52). Stereo. Hrs opn: 24. 3 1/2 E. Van Tress St. (47501); Box 2000, One Executive Blvd., Vincennes (47591). (812) 254-4300; (812) 882-6060. FAX: (812) 886-1468; (812) 885-2604. Licensee: Old Northwest Broadcasting Inc. Group owner: Wisdom Stations (acq 10-93; $250,000 with WAOV[AM] Vincennes; FTR 10-18-93). Rep: Rgnl Reps. Format: Country. News staff one; news progmg 10 hrs wkly. Target aud: 25-54. Spec prog: Farm 15 hrs wkly. ■ David L. Crooks, pres & gen mgr; Brad Deetz, progmg dir; Jim Evans, chief engr.

West Lafayette

***WBAA(AM)**—Apr 4, 1922: 920 khz; 5 kw-D, 1 kw-N, DA-N. TL: N40 20 29 W86 53 01. Purdue Univ., 1740 Elliott Hall of Music (47907-1740). (317) 494-5920. FAX: (317) 496-1542. Licensee: Purdue Univ. Net: NPR. Format: Classical, jazz, news/talk. Spec prog: Black one hr, mixed nationality one hr wkly. ■ Dan Skinner, gen mgr, dev mgr & progmg dir; David Bunte, mus dir; Colleen Condron, news dir; Frank Dudgeon, pub affrs dir; Maurice Mogridge, chief engr.

***WBAA-FM**—February 1993 101.3 mhz; 5 kw. Ant 358 ft. TL: N40 17 50 W86 54 05. (Acq 2-22-91; FTR 3-25-91). ■ Caryl Matthews, mus dir.

WEZV-FM—See Brookston.

WGLM(FM)—June 15, 1992: 106.7 mhz; 6 kw. Ant 328 ft. TL: N40 31 20 W86 58 57. Hrs opn: 24. 2700-A Kent Ave. (47906). Licensee: KVB Broadcasting. Net: CNN. Format: Adult contemp. News staff one; news progmg 8 hrs wkly. Target aud: 25-54. ■ Kelly Busch, gen mgr, stn mgr, sls dir & mktg dir; Dan McKay, prom dir, progmg dir & mus dir; Jean Shannon, news dir; Michael Vitale, pub affrs dir.

***WHPL(FM)**—Sept 10, 1993: 89.9 mhz; 100 w. Ant 328 ft. TL: N40 17 50 W86 54 05. Box 2721 (47906). (317) 463-9475. Licensee: Von Tobel Foundation Inc. Format: Relgious. ■ John T. Johnson, gen mgr.

West Terre Haute

WWVR(FM)—Jan 20, 1967: 105.5 mhz; 3.3 kw. Ant 314 ft. TL: N39 27 15 W87 28 18. Hrs opn: 6 AM-midnight. Box 207, 3438 W. Larimer Dr. (47885). (812) 533-1663. Licensee: United Broadcasting Co Inc. Net: USA. Wash atty: Miller & Fields. Format: Relg. News progmg 6 hrs wkly. Target aud: 35-64. Spec prog: Black 6 hrs wkly. ■ Howard E. Huey, pres & gen sls mgr; Betty S. Huey, gen mgr, prom mgr, adv dir & progmg dir; Mike Varvel, chief engr.

Westport

***WKLO(FM)**—Not on air, target date May 1993: 91.5 mhz; 14.55 kw. Ant 305 ft. TL: N39 11 16 W85 40 50. Stereo. Hrs opn: 24. 725 E. North St., Greensburg (47240); Box 147 (47283). (812) 663-8413. Licensee: Good Shepherd Radio Inc. Net: Skylight. Wash atty: Fisher, Wayland, Cooper & Leader. Format: Contemp Christian. Target aud: 30-80; Christians. ■ Ruth Bausback, chmn & mus dir; Joe Bausback, opns dir; Bill Leak, dev dir; Tammy Leak, mktg dir; Teresa Buell, prom dir; Ralph Haines, engrg dir; Jim Hawkins, chief engr.

Winamac

WOTD(FM)—Not on air, target date unknown: 100.1 mhz; 3 kw. Ant 300 ft. Box 989, C/O Balvich Monticello (47960). Licensee: Brothers Broadcasting Corp. (acq 10-85; grpsl; FTR 10-28-85). Rep: Rgnl Reps. Format: Loc info, sports. Spec prog: Farm 10 hrs, class 5 hrs, C&W 5 hrs wkly. ■ Thomas F. Jurek, pres.

Winchester

WZZY(FM)—May 1967: 98.3 mhz; 3 kw. Ant 300 ft. TL: N40 05 23 W84 56 13. Stereo. Hrs opn: 24. Box 427, 213-1/2 S. Main, (47394). (317) 584-2800; (317) 874-2536. Licensee: Winchester Radio Inc. (acq 9-1-86). Net: USA; AgriAmerica. Rep: Rgnl Reps. Format: CHR, adult contemp, rock. News staff one; news progmg 10 hrs wkly. Target aud: 12-55; adult. Spec prog: Farm 10 hrs, sports 10 hrs, relg 5 hrs wkly. ■ E.R. Miller, pres & gen sls mgr; E.C. Miller, gen mgr, stn mgr & opns dir; Jeff Robinson, progmg dir. ■ Rates: $12; 12; 12; 10.

Iowa

Albia

KLBA(AM)—November 1979: 1370 khz; 500 w-D, 128 w-N, DA-2. TL: N41 00 34 W92 43 46. 201 S. Main (52531). (515) 932-2112. Licensee: H&H Broadcasting Corp. (acq 3-84; $75,000 FTR 3-5-84). Net: ABC/E; Brownfield, Tribune. Rep: Keystone (unwired net). Wash atty: Fisher, Wayland, Cooper & Leader. Format: Memory music. News progmg 6 hrs wkly. Target aud: General; 35-50. ■ John R. Hallstrom, pres & gen mgr; Louise Hallstrom, gen sls mgr; Bob Williams, progmg dir; Concheta Lanpher, news dir; Don DeBoef, chief engr. ■ Rates: $4.50; 4.50; 4.50; 3.

KLBA-FM—Not on air, target date unknown: 96.7 mhz; 25 kw. Ant 328 ft.

Algona

KLGA(AM)—1956: 1600 khz; 5 kw-D, 500 w-N, DA-2. TL: N43 03 52 W94 18 13. Hrs opn: 24. Box 160, 2102 80th Ave. (50511). (515) 295-2475. FAX: (515) 295-3851. Licensee: Kossuth County Broadcasting L.C. Group owner: Hedberg Broadcasting Group (acq 2-26-93; $550,000 with co-located FM; FTR 4-12-93). Net: ABC; Radio Iowa. Rep: Farmakis. Wash atty: Bryan, Cave, McPheeters, McRoberts. Format: Adult contemp. News staff one; news progmg 44 hrs wkly. Target aud: 25-54. Spec prog: Farm, news, weather. ■ Mark Hedberg, pres; Bob Ketchum, gen mgr; Al Lauck, progmg dir; Bob Jennings, news dir; Mike Hendrickson, chief engr.

KLGA-FM—Aug 17, 1970: 92.7 mhz; 50 kw. Ant 226 ft. TL: N43 04 05 W94 12 08. Hrs opn: 6 AM-10:30 PM. Dups AM 100%.

Ames

KASI(AM)—1948: 1430 khz; 1 kw-D, 32 w-N. TL: N42 02 15 W93 41 21. Hrs opn: 5:30 AM-11 PM. Box 728, 415 Main St. (50010). (515) 232-1430. Licensee: Ames Broadcasting Co. (acq 6-1-85). Net: ABC. Format: Oldies. News staff 2; news progmg 25 hrs wkly. Target aud: 25 plus. ■ Betty Baudler, pres & gen mgr; J.D. Stites, gen sls mgr; Kenn McCloud, progmg dir; Rich Fellingham, news dir.

KCCQ(FM)—Co-owned with KASI(AM). June 20, 1968: 107.1 mhz; 3 kw. Ant 300 ft. TL: N42 02 15 W93 41 21. Stereo. Prog sep from AM. Format: CHR. Target aud: 18-40. ■ Kenn McCloud, opns dir.

KEZT(FM)—June 2, 1967: 104.1 mhz; 100 kw. Ant 1,026 ft. TL: N41 54 09 W93 54 15 (CP: Ant 1,009 ft.). Stereo. Box 1642, 2825 E. 13th St. (50010). (515) 232-0104. FAX: (515) 232-0835. Licensee: Bunce Broadcasting Co. (acq 10-75). Rep: Masla. Format: Lite contemp. ■ Robert D. Bunce, pres & gen mgr; Sandy Wybomy, stn mgr, opns mgr & prom mgr; George Wylie, news dir; Bob Pink, chief engr.

***KUSR(FM)**—Apr 17, 1970: 91.5 mhz; 200 w. Ant 100 ft. TL: N42 01 24 W93 39 00. Stereo. Hrs opn: 24. 1199 Friley Hall, Iowa State Univ. (50012). (515) 294-4332. FAX: (515) 294-8093. Licensee: Residence Broadcasting Services Inc. Format: Div. News progmg 10 hrs wkly.

Target aud: 18-25; Iowa State Univ. students. Spec prog: Btfl mus, Black, classic rock, jazz, new age, AOR, urban contemp. ■ Michael Hand, gen mgr; Rian Harkins, opns dir; Jenny Howes, mktg dir; Kelly Henderson, prom dir; Don Bennett, progmg dir; Brian Thompson, mus dir; Erich Grubert, news dir; Mike Jenkins, pub affrs dir; Abraham Schlott, chief engr.

***WOI(AM)**—1922: 640 khz; 5 kw-D, 1 kw-N, DA-N. TL: N41 59 34 W93 41 27. Hrs opn: 19. 204 Communicatons Bldg., Iowa State Univ. (50011). (515) 294-2025. FAX: (515) 294-1544; TWX: 910-520-1152. Licensee: Iowa State Univ. Net: AP, NPR, APR. Wash atty: Dow, Lohnes & Albertson. Format: News/talk, jazz. News staff 3; news progmg 40 hrs wkly. Target aud: General. Spec prog: Folk 6 hrs wkly. ■ Dr. Martin Jischke, pres; Rick Lewis, gen mgr; Catherine E. Watkins, dev dir; David Knippel, chief engr.

***WOI-FM**—July 1, 1949: 90.1 mhz; 100 kw. Ant 1,490 ft. TL: N41 48 33 W93 36 53. Stereo. Hrs opn: 24. Prog sep from AM. Format: Class. News staff 3; news progmg 12 hrs wkly. Spec prog: Folk 4 hrs, jazz 18 hrs wkly.

Anamosa

KLEH(AM)—Sept 14, 1979: 1290 khz; 500 w-D, 22 w-N DA-2. TL: N42 06 00 W91 15 22. Hrs opn: 6 AM-10:15 PM. Box 488, Hwy. 64 E. (52205). (319) 462-4384. Licensee: Missouri Valley Productions Inc. (acq 11-8-85; FTR 9-30-85). Rep: Farmakis. Format: C&W. Spec prog: Farm 5 hrs wkly. ■ Lanier Korsmeyer, pres & progmg dir; Janet Blair, gen sls mgr; Carla Jesse, mus dir.

Ankeny

KJJY-FM—Licensed to Ankeny. See Des Moines.

KMXD(FM)—1991: 106.3 mhz; 3 kw. Ant 328 ft. TL: N41 40 45 W93 35 46. 1549 N.E. 66th Ave., Des Moines (50313-1236). (515) 289-2000. FAX: (515) 289-1324. Licensee: V.O.B. Inc.

Asbury

KIKR(FM)—Not on air, target date unknown: 103.3 mhz; 25 kw. Ant 328 ft. TL: N42 34 19 W90 30 55. 876 Arrowhead Cir., Sun Prairie, WI (53590). Licensee: Tri-State Broadcasting.

Atlantic

KJAN(AM)—September 1950: 1220 khz; 250 w-D, 86 w-N. TL: N41 25 16 W95 00 22. Box 389, N. Olive St. (50022). (712) 243-3920. Licensee: Wireless Communications Corp. (acq 1-13-88; FTR 11-16-87). Net: ABC/E. Format: MOR. News staff one; news progmg 24 hrs wkly. Target aud: General. Spec prog: Farm 12 hrs wkly. ■ J.C. Van Ginkel, chmn; Merlyn Christensen, pres & gen sls mgr; Alan W. Hazelton, gen mgr; Jim Field, progmg dir & news dir; John Scheffler, mus dir; Scott Williams, chief engr. ■ Rates: $18; 10; 10; 10.

KXKT(FM)—April 8, 1966: 103.7 mhz; 100 kw. Ant 1,246 ft. TL: N41 23 53 W95 28 17. Stereo. 1108 Douglas, Omaha, NE (68102). (402) 345-2526. FAX: (402) 345-3652. Licensee: Valley Broadcasting Inc. (acq 8-30-89; $5,575,000; FTR 9-18-89). Net: AP. Rep: Banner. Format: Country. News staff 2. Target aud: General. ■ Robert H. Dean, pres & gen mgr; Mark Evans, opns mgr; Cathy Roach, gen sls mgr; Roger Olson, news dir; Richard Dennis, chief engr.

Belle Plaine

KNJS(FM)—Not on air, target date unknown: 95.5 mhz; 6 kw. Ant 328 ft. TL: N41 51 44 W92 08 33. Suite 3F, c/o 50 Park Terrace E., New York, NY (10034). Licensee: Cynthia A. Siragusa.

Bettendorf

KQCS(FM)—July 7, 1984: 93.5 mhz; 3.3 kw. Ant 300 ft. TL: N41 35 59 W90 24 33. Stereo. Hrs opn: 24. 5315 Tremont Ave., Davenport (52807-2640). (319) 391-0712. FAX: (319) 391-0620. Licensee: Eternity Broadcasting (acq 12-90). Net: CNN. Wash atty: Hunsinger & Putbrezse. Format: Christian music. News progmg 2 hrs wkly. Target aud: 18-49. ■ David McAnally, chmn; Jeff D. Lyle, pres & gen mgr; Steve Swanson, opns mgr & mus dir; Mike Davis, gen sls mgr; Lary Ellis, adv dir; Matt Williams, asst mus dir; Earl Hill, chief engr. ■ Rates: $30; 24; 28; 18.

Bloomfield

KXOF(FM)—June 26, 1982: 106.3 mhz; 3 kw. Ant 300 ft. TL: N40 46 42 W92 23 48. Stereo. Box 186 (52537). (515) 664-3721. FAX: (515) 664-3721. Licensee: Horizon Broadcasting Inc. (acq 7-24-89; $130,000; FTR 7-24-89). Net: ABC/D; Brownfield. Rep: Farmakis, Agri Spot Sls. Format: Country, gospel. ■ Doug Smiley, pres & chief engr; Linda Hamilton, gen mgr & gen sls mgr; John Jannenga, prom mgr, progmg dir & mus dir.

Boone

***KFGQ(AM)**—1927: 1260 khz; 5 kw-D, 33 w-N, DA-2. TL: N42 02 55 W93 53 54. 924 W. 2nd St. (50036). (515) 432-2092. Licensee: Boone Biblical Ministries Inc. Format: Relg. ■ J.L. Black, pres; D.R. James, gen mgr; Steven Huffman, chief engr.

***KFGQ-FM**—1950: 99.3 mhz; 2.55 kw. Ant 351 ft. TL: N42 02 55 W93 53 54. Dups AM 100%.

KRUU(FM)—May 15, 1975: 98.3 mhz; 3 kw. Ant 210 ft. TL: N42 01 22 W93 52 36 (CP: 25 kw, ant 500 ft.). Stereo. 5161 Maple Dr., Ames (50317). (515) 265-5788. FAX: (515) 262-2032. Licensee: Radio Ingstad Iowa Inc. Group owner: James Ingstad Broadcasting Inc. (acq 6-86). Net: ABC/I. ■ J. Michael McKoy, gen mgr.

KWBG(AM)—Jan 15, 1950: 1590 khz; 1 kw-D, 500 w-N, DA-N. TL: N42 01 22 W93 52 36. Box 366 (50036). (515) 432-2046. FAX: (515) 432-1448. Licensee: G.O. Radio, Boone Inc. Group owner: GO Radio Inc. (acq 7-19-93; $435,000; FTR 8-9-93). Net: ABC/I. Format: MOR. News staff one; news progmg 18 hrs wkly. Target aud: 35 plus. Spec prog: Farm 15 hrs wkly. ■ Bradley Olson, stn mgr; Edgar Johnson, progmg dir; Jim Turbes, news dir. ■ Rates: $16; 12; 14; 10.

Britt

NEW FM—Not on air, target date unknown: 99.5 mhz; 6 kw. Ant 124 ft. 3708 240th Tanglefoot, Clear Lake (50428). Licensee: Robert W. Hawley.

Brooklyn

KSKB(FM)—March 1, 1988: 99.1 mhz; 50 kw. Ant 175 ft. TL: N41 42 36 W92 27 54. Stereo. Box 440, (52211). 505 Josephine St., Titusville, FL (32796). (515) 522-7202; (407) 267-3000. FAX: (407) 264-9370. Licensee: Florida Public Radio Inc. (acq 1-8-90). Format: Adult contemp Christian music. Target aud: General. Spec prog: Ger one hr, Pol one hr wkly. ■ Edie Kuntz, gen mgr.

Burlington

KBUR(AM)—July 1941: 1490 khz; 1 kw-U. TL: N40 49 26 W91 08 33. Stereo. Hrs opn: 24. Box 70, 1411 N. Roosevelt Ave. (52601). (319) 752-2701. FAX: (319) 752-5287. Licensee: LWM Inc. (acq 10-1-88). Net: ABC/I. Rep: McGavren Guild. Wash atty: Dow, Lohnes & Albertson. Format: Adult contemp, MOR, news/talk. News staff 3; news progmg 28 hrs wkly. Target aud: General; adults 25 plus. Spec prog: Farm 14 hrs wkly. ■ James M. Livengood, pres & gen mgr; John Weir, gen sls mgr; Steve Hexom, progmg dir; J.K. Martin, news dir; Vernave V. Garcia, chief engr.

KGRS(FM)—Co-owned with KBUR(AM). Nov 27, 1968: 107.3 mhz; 100 kw. Ant 429 ft. TL: N40 49 26 W91 08 33. Stereo. Prog sep from AM. Net: ABC/FM. Format: Adult contemp. News staff 3; news progmg 15 hrs wkly. Target aud: 25-45. ■ John Weir, stn mgr; Cosmo Leone, progmg dir & mus dir.

KCPS(AM)—July 30, 1965: 1150 khz; 500 w-D, 100 w-N, DA-1. TL: N40 51 11 W91 08 10. Box 946, 408 N. Main St. (52601). (319) 754-6698. FAX: (319) 754-8899. Licensee: John Giannettino (acq 1-88). Net: CBS, MBS, NBC Talknet, Tribune. Rep: Katz & Powell. Format: Talk radio. News staff 3; news progmg 20 plus hrs wkly. Target aud: 25-54; middle-aged, upscale and well informed adults. Spec prog: Agri-business 10 hrs, pro sports 10 hrs wkly. ■ Chip Giannettino, gen mgr, opns mgr, gen sls mgr & progmg dir; Joe Loffler, vp sls; Roger Williams, sls dir; Kevin Francis, mus dir; Gary Saunders, news dir; John O'Lenahan, chief engr. ■ Rates: $15; 15; 15; 7.

KDMG(FM)—July 19, 1993: 103.1 mhz; 12 kw. Ant 445 ft. TL: N40 44 03 W91 15 14. Hrs opn: 24. Box 832, 2850 Mt. Pleasant St. (52601). (319) 752-5402; (319) 754-1103. FAX: (319) 752-4715. Licensee: Pritchard Broadcasting Co. Rep: Katz & Powell. Wash atty: Donald E. Ward P.C. Format: Pure digital country. News staff one. Target aud: 25-54. ■ John Pritchard, pres; David Brown, gen mgr; Gail L. Holford, opns mgr, prom dir & progmg dir; Chet Young, gen sls mgr; Dave Lavender, asst mus dir; Mike Wilson, news dir & pub affrs dir; Roger Lundeen, chief engr. ■ Rates: $10.94; 10.94; 10.94; 10.94.

KGRS(FM)—Listing follows KBUR(AM).

KKMI(FM)—Oct 22, 1981: 93.5 mhz; 3.0 kw. Ant 300 ft. TL: N40 49 14 W91 07 00. Stereo. Hrs opn: 24. Box 832, 2850 Mt. Pleasant St. (52601). (319) 752-5402. FAX: (319) 752-4715. Licensee: Pritchard Broadcasting Co. (acq 8-5-91). Rep: Katz & Powell. Wash atty: Donald Ward. Format: Adult contemp/oldies. News staff one; news progmg 8 hrs wkly. Target aud: 25-55; upscale. Spec prog: Pub affrs. ■ John T. Pritchard, pres; David W. Brown, gen mgr & stn mgr; Gail L. Holford, opns mgr & progmg dir; Chet Young, rgnl sls mgr; Gail Holford, prom dir; Dave Lavendar, mus dir; Mike Wilson, news dir & pub affrs dir; Roger Lundeen, chief engr. ■ Rates: $10.80; 10.80; 10.80; 9.

Carroll

KCIM(AM)—June 8, 1950: 1380 khz; 1 kw-U, DA-2. TL: N42 02 29 W94 53 06. 1119 E. Plaza Dr. (51401). (712) 792-4321. FAX: (712) 792-6667. Licensee: Carroll Broadcasting Co. (acq 8-1-85; $1.5 million; with co-located FM; FTR 5-20-85). Net: CBS. Rep: Katz. Format: Adult contemp, farm. ■ Neil Trobak, gen mgr; Karolee Lehman, gen sls mgr.

KKRL(FM)—Co-owned with KCIM(AM). Jan 18, 1967: 93.7 mhz; 100 kw. Ant 300 ft. TL: N42 03 14 W94 53 06. Stereo. Prog sep from AM. Format: CHR.

Cedar Falls

KCFI(AM)—Feb 2, 1958: 1250 khz; 500 w-U, DA-2. TL: N42 32 41 W92 29 16. 721 Shirley St. (50613). (319) 277-1918. FAX: (319) 277-5202. Licensee: Cedar Valley Broadcasting Inc. (acq 3-11-92; $275,000; FTR 4-6-92). Net: ABC/D. Format: News, sports, talk. ■ David Rabbitt, gen mgr & gen sls mgr; Kelly Neff, mus dir; Pat Blank, news dir.

***KHKE(FM)**—April 1, 1974: 89.5 mhz; 10 kw. Ant 410 ft. TL: N42 23 58 W92 19 15. Stereo. Hrs opn: 6 AM-midnight. Univ. of Northern Iowa (50614-0359). (319) 273-6400. FAX: (319) 273-2682. Licensee: Univ. of Northern Iowa. Net: APR. Format: Classical, jazz. News staff 3; news progmg 17 hrs wkly. Target aud: General. Spec prog: New age 7 hrs, news 17 hrs wkly. ■ Constantine Curris, pres; Doug Vernier, gen mgr; Jons Olsson, dev dir; Dave Hays, prom dir; Carl Jenkins, progmg dir; Al Schares, mus dir; Greg Shanley, news dir; Walt Alliss, chief engr.

***KUNI(FM)**—Sep 15, 1960: 90.9 mhz; 100 kw. Ant 1,782 ft. TL: N42 18 59 W91 51 31. Stereo. Hrs opn: 24. Univ. of Northern Iowa (50614-0359). (319) 273-2682. Licensee: Univ. of Northern Iowa. Net: NPR, APR. Format: Div. class. News staff 3; news progmg 35 hrs wkly. Target aud: General. Spec prog: Black 15 hrs, folk 12 hrs, new age 12 hrs blues & R&B 10 hrs wkly. ■ Constantine Curris, pres; Doug Vernier, gen mgr; Jons Olsson, dev dir; Dave Hays, prom dir; Carl Jenkins, progmg dir; Al Schares, mus dir; Greg Shanley, news dir; Walt Alliss, chief engr.

Cedar Rapids

***KCCK-FM**—Sept 5, 1972: 88.3 mhz; 10 kw. Ant 420 ft. TL: N41 54 33 W91 39 17. Stereo. Hrs opn: 5 AM-midnight, 24 hrs wknds. 6301 Kirkwood Blvd. S.W. (52406). (319) 398-5446. FAX: (319) 398-5492. Licensee: Kirkwood Community College. Net: APR, AP. Wash atty: Wilkinson, Barker, Knauer & Quinn. Format: Jazz, information. News staff 2; news progmg 18 hrs wkly. Target aud: 25-54; educated, affluent, active in community. Spec prog: New age 7 hrs wkly. ■ Norm Nielson, pres; Steve Carpenter, gen mgr & opns dir; Sue Hawn, dev dir; Liz Hoskins, vp mktg; Ken Rinehart, progmg dir & mus dir; Dianne Allender, asst mus dir; George Dorman, news dir; Orv Thein, vp engrg; Don Lohse, engrg dir; Dave Maley, chief engr.

KCRG(AM)—1947: 1600 khz; 5 kw-U, DA-N. TL: N41 58 21 W91 32 04. Stereo. Hrs opn: 24. 2nd Ave. at 5th St. S.E. (52401); Box 816 (52406-0816). (319) 398-8422. FAX: (319) 368-8505. Licensee: Cedar Rapids TV Co. Net: ABC/I. Rep: Katz & Powell. Wash atty: Wiley, Rein & Fielding. Format: Country, news/talk. News progmg 15 hrs wkly. Target aud: 25-54. Spec prog: Czech polka 4 hrs wkly. ■ Joseph F. Hladky, pres; Bob Allen, gen mgr; Craig Hesser, gen sls mgr; Bob Lorenzen, prom mgr; Wally Pasbrig, progmg dir & mus dir; Dean Bunting, news dir; Bruce Kruse, chief engr. ■ KCRG-TV affil.

KFMW(FM)—See Waterloo.

KHAK(AM)—July 1, 1961: 1360 khz; 1 kw-D, 124 w-N, DA-1. TL: N41 55 28 W91 36 55. Hrs opn: 24. Suite 450, 425 Second St. S.E. (52401). (319) 365-9431; (319) 365-3698. FAX: (319) 363-8062. Licensee: Quass Broadcasting Co. (acq 9-26-88). Net: ABC/E. Rep: Christal. Wash atty: Latham & Watkins. Format: Modern country.

Newsstaff 2; news progmg 7 hrs wkly. Target aud: 25-54; general. ■ Mary Quass, CEO, pres, gen mgr & natl sls mgr; Kerry Murray, gen sls mgr; Susan Glaza, prom dir; Jeff Winfield, progmg dir; Dawn Johnson, mus dir; Britta Lee, news dir; Matt Paul, pub affrs dir; George Nicholas, chief engr. ■ Rates: $85; 75; 80; 20.

KHAK-FM—July 1, 1961: 98.1 mhz; 100 kw. Ant 485 ft. TL: N41 55 28 W91 36 55. Stereo. Dups AM 100%. ■ Rates: Same as AM.

KMRY(AM)—August 1949: 1450 khz; 1 kw-U. TL: N42 00 25 W91 42 29. 1957 Blairsferry Rd. N.E. (52402). (319) 393-1450. Licensee: Dulaney Broadcasting. Inc. (acq 4-1-84; $300,000; FTR 3-19-84). Net: SMN. Format: Nostalgia. News staff one. Target aud: 40 plus; affluent, upscale adults with large disposable income. ■ Mike Dulaney, pres & gen mgr; Rick Sampson, opns mgr & news dir; Dallas Hemmen, gen sls mgr; Tim Busch, chief engr.

KQCR(FM)—Apr 29, 1975: 102.9 mhz; 100 kw. Ant 390 ft. TL: N42 04 51 W91 41 45. Stereo. Box 876, 1110 26th Ave. S.W. (52406). (319) 363-2061. Licensee: Cedar Rapids-KQCR L.P. (acq 5-1-85; $1.9 million; FTR 2-25-85). Wash atty: Fisher, Wayland, Cooper & Leader. Format: CHR. Target aud: 25-34; working women. ■ Bill Clymer, gen mgr; Jeff Glover, rgnl sls mgr; Scotty Snipes, progmg dir; Gail Lewis, mus dir; Clynde Clymer, pub affrs dir; Joe Spinks, chief engr. ■ Rates: $38; 34; 38; 28.

KTOF(FM)—May 1971: 104.5 mhz; 100 kw. Ant 500 ft. TL: N42 04 51 W91 41 45. Stereo. Hrs opn: 24. 1957 Blairsferry Rd. N.E. (52402). (319) 393-1045. FAX: (319) 393-5060. Licensee: Young Broadcasting Co. (acq 1-26-77). Net: Moody. Wash atty: Miller & Fields. Format: Relg, inspirational. Target aud: 25-54. ■ James Young, pres; Eugene Dowie, exec vp; Tim Calcara, gen mgr, gen sls mgr, prom mgr & adv mgr; Tom Murphy, progmg dir & mus dir; Wendi Fish, pub affrs dir; Mike Rieff, chief engr. ■ Rates: $12.50; 12.50; 12.50; 12.50.

WMT(AM)—1922: 600 khz; 5 kw-U, DA-N. TL: N42 03 40 W91 32 44. Box 2147 (52406). (319) 395-0530. FAX: (319) 393-0918. Licensee: Wonderful Music and Talk Inc. (acq 9-25-86; $8 million; FTR 8-11-86). Net: CBS. Rep: Katz. Format: Personality, MOR. Target aud: 35 plus. Spec prog: Farm 19 hrs wkly. ■ Forrest Mitchell, chmn & gen mgr; Rick Sellers, vp opns & vp progmg; Jim Doyne, vp sls; Vic McGill, natl sls mgr; Wayne Johnson, mus dir; Jim Boyd, news dir; James Davies, chief engr.

WMT-FM—Feb 16, 1963: 96.5 mhz; 100 kw. Ant 540 ft. TL: N42 01 43 W91 38 27. Stereo. Prog sep from AM. Net: CBS Spectrum. Format: Adult contemp. Target aud: 25-49. ■ Randy Lee, progmg dir & mus dir.

Centerville

KCOG(AM)—Mar 1, 1949: 1400 khz; 500 w-D, 1 kw-N. TL: N40 44 40 W92 54 32. Hrs opn: 5 AM-midnight. 402 N. 12th St. (52544). (515) 437-4242. Licensee: KCOG Inc. (acq 6-1-84; $406,000; FTR 4-16-84). Net: USA; Brownfield. Format: MOR. ■ Richard Calzascia, pres; Fred Jenkins, gen mgr & chief engr; Carolyn Jenkins, gen sls mgr.

KMGO(FM)—Co-owned with KCOG(AM). Oct 1, 1974: 98.7 mhz; 100 kw. Ant 500 ft. TL: N40 47 34 W92 52 47. Stereo. Hrs opn: 24. (515) 856-3996. Licensee: KMGO Inc. (acq 6-5-85). Format: Country. ■ Larry Stout, progmg dir.

Chariton

KELR-FM—Nov 15, 1979: 105.5 mhz; 1.7 kw. Ant 390 ft. TL: N41 00 50 W93 17 23. Stereo. Hrs opn: 17. 927 1/2 Braden Ave. (50049); Box 693 (50049). (515) 774-8494. FAX: (515) 774-8495. Licensee: Dwaine F. Meyer (acq 8-85). Net: ABC/E, Westwood One. Format: MOR, relg. News staff 2; news progmg 30 hrs wkly. Target aud: 28 plus. ■ Dwaine Meyer, pres; Kandy Mikesell, gen mgr; Jason L. Mikesell, opns dir, progmg dir & mus dir; Steven Mikesell, sls dir; Kriston Johnston, gen sls mgr; Doris K. Mikesell, news dir; Randy Parker, vp engrg. ■ Rates: $8; 8; 8; 6.

Charles City

KCHA(AM)—November 1949: 1580 khz; 500 w-D, 10 w-N. TL: N43 03 05 W92 40 00. 207 N. Main St. (50616). (515) 228-1000; (515) 228-1321. FAX: (515) 228-1200. Licensee: Mega Media Ltd. (group owner). Net: NBC. Format: Adult contemp. News progmg 12 hrs wkly. Target aud: General. Spec prog: Farm 12 hrs wkly. ■ James B. Hebel, CEO; James Hebel, chmn & gen mgr; Debra Lowe, opns mgr; Jim Bernard, gen sls mgr; Stan McHenry, prom mgr; John Waters, progmg dir & mus dir; Mike Lyman, news dir & pub affrs dir; Tim Cook, chief engr.

KCHA-FM—October 1971: 95.9 mhz; 3 kw. Ant 300 ft. TL: N43 03 05 W92 40 00. Stereo. Dups AM 95%. Rep: Farmakis. ■ James Hebel, pres.

Cherokee

KCHE(AM)—January 1953: 1440 khz; 500 w-D. TL: N42 47 21 W95 33 06. Box 1440, 201 S. 5th (51012). (712) 225-2511. FAX: (712) 225-3782. Licensee: Sioux Valley Broadcasting Inc. (acq 9-1-76). Format: MOR. Spec prog: Farm 12 hrs wkly. ■ John M. O'Connor, pres, gen mgr & gen sls mgr; Scott Hagerty, progmg dir; Dave Lund, news dir; Kirby Moral, chief engr.

KCHE-FM—Dec 9, 1976: 92.1 mhz; 3 kw. Ant 302 ft. TL: N42 47 21 W95 33 06. Stereo. Hrs opn: 5:30 AM-11 PM. Dups AM 90%. Net: ABC, Radio Iowa. Rep: Farnakis. Wash atty: Chris Smallwood. News staff 2; news progmg 28 hrs wkly. Spec prog: Relg 4 hrs wkly. ■ Kay O'Connor, gen sls mgr; Scott Hagerty, mus dir. ■ Rates: $11.50; 9.50; 5.50; 5.

Clarinda

KKBZ(FM)—Sept 25, 1990: 106.1 mhz; 50 kw. Ant 492 ft. TL: N40 33 12 W95 07 18. Stereo. Hrs opn: 5 AM-midnight. Box 960, 209 N. Elm, Shenandoah (51601). (712) 246-5270. FAX: (712) 246-5275. Licensee: May Broadcasting Co. Group owner: May Broadcasting. Net: SMN, Radio Iowa, Missourinet. Rep: Katz. Format: Oldies News staff 2; news progmg 5 hrs wkly. Target aud: 25-44. ■ Edward W. May, pres; Susan Friehe Christensen, gen mgr; Randy Rasmussen, prom mgr; Don Hansen, progmg dir; Bill Bone, news dir; Steve Tunwall, chief engr.

Clarion

KIAQ(FM)—May 18, 1964: 96.9 mhz; 100 kw. Ant 578 ft. TL: N42 40 18 W94 09 11. Stereo. 1014 Central Ave., Fort Dodge (50501). (515) 573-5748. FAX: (515) 573-3376. Licensee: Radio Iowa Broadcasting Inc. Group owner: James Ingstad Broadcasting Inc. (acq 7-2-92; $785,000; FTR 7-27-92). Rep: Katz. Format: CHR. News staff 2; news progmg 5 hrs wkly. Target aud: 25-54. ■ Jim Ingstad, pres; Michael J. Parry, gen mgr; Pamela Ladlie, gen sls mgr; Phil Jaye, prom mgr & mus dir; Jessica Jamieson, news dir; Paul Tichenal, engrg dir.

Clear Lake

KLKK(FM)—Feb 16, 1978: 103.1 mhz; 6 kw. Ant 300 ft. TL: N43 03 58 W93 22 53. Stereo. Hrs opn: 24. Box 1300 (50401); 341 Yorktown Pike, Mason City (50401). (515) 423-1300. FAX: (515) 423-2906. Licensee: James Ingstad Broadcasting of Iowa Inc. Group owner: James Ingstad Broadcasting Inc. (acq 1-28-93; $294,000; FTR 2-22-93). Net: AP. Format: Adult contemp, oldies. News progmg 42 hrs wkly. Target aud: 25-54; older adults. Spec prog: Relg 2 hrs wkly. ■ John Linder, pres & gen sls mgr; Kevin Lein, gen mgr; Scott Jeffreys, chief engr. ■ Rates: $16; 10; 16; 10.

Clinton

KCLN-FM—Listing follows KLNT(AM).

KLNT(AM)—Dec 21, 1956: 1390 khz; 1 kw-D, 91 w-N, DA-2. TL: N41 54 32 W90 13 16. Hrs opn: 6 AM-midnight. 1853 442nd Ave. (52732). (319) 243-1390. Licensee: K to Z Ltd. (group owner; acq 3-15-90). Net: ABC/E; Tribune. Rep: Katz. Wash atty: Miller & Fields. Format: 40s, 50s, 60s music, big band. News staff 2. Target aud: 40 plus. Spec prog: Farm 10 hrs wkly. ■ Gene Kauffman, vp & gen mgr; Jim Bartlett, opns mgr; Jeff Schultz, gen sls mgr; Wayne Larkey, progmg dir; Mike Winkel, news dir; Bill Dieckman, chief engr.

KCLN-FM—Co-owned with KLNT(AM). Dec 7, 1970: 97.7 mhz; 3 kw. Ant 300 ft. TL: N41 54 32 W90 13 20. Stereo. Hrs opn: 5 AM-1 AM. Prog sep from AM. Format: Adult contemp. Target aud: 25-49.

KMXG(FM)—July 1974: 96.1 mhz; 100 kw. Ant 980 ft. TL: N41 37 58 W90 24 38. Stereo. Hrs opn: 24. Suite 303, 3535 E. Kimberly Rd., Davenport (52807). (319) 344-7060. Licensee: Signal Hil Communications Inc. (acq 2-25-93; $1.256 million; FTR 3-15-93). Net: Unistar. Rep: Eastman. Format: Adult contemp. News staff one; news progmg 3 hrs wkly. Target aud: 25-49; yuppies, baby boomers, upscale professionals. Spec prog: Jazz 2 hrs wkly. ■ Vicki Palmer, gen mgr; Dave Seran, gen sls mgr; Chuck O'Brien, progmg dir; Zach Taylor, mus dir; Audrey Honig, news dir; Tom Messerli, chief engr. ■ Rates: $25; 22; 25; 20.

KROS(AM)—Sept 28, 1941: 1340 khz; 1 kw-U. TL: N41 51 36 W90 12 18. Stereo. Hrs opn: 5:30 AM-midnight. Box 0518, 870 13th Ave. N. (52732). (319) 242-1252. FAX: (319) 242-4825. Licensee: KROS Broadcasting Inc. (acq 12-31-86; $232,500; FTR 11-24-86). Net: MBS; Iowa Net., Radio Iowa. Format: MOR, adult contemp, news/talk. News staff 2; news progmg 38 hrs wkly. Target aud: General; loc audience. Spec prog: Farm 5 hrs, relg 4 hrs, folk 2 hrs, jazz 2 hrs, blues one hr, women 5 hrs, country 6 hrs, big band 3 hrs wkly. ■ Gerald Parker, pres; Don Schneider, gen mgr; Lauren Hyde, gen sls mgr; Paul Clark, progmg dir; Val Hayes, mus dir; Dave Vickers, news dir; William Scott, chief engr. ■ Rates: $13; 13; 13; 6.

Council Bluffs

KESY(AM)—See Omaha, Neb.

KESY-FM—See Omaha, Neb.

***KIWR(FM)**—Nov 23, 1981: 89.7 mhz; 100 kw. Ant 1,100 ft. TL: N41 18 40 W96 01 37. Stereo. Hrs opn: 5 AM-midnight (M-F)/6 AM- midnight (Sat & Sun). 1700 College Rd. (51503). (712) 325-3254. Licensee: Iowa Western Community College. Net: NPR. Format: News, jazz, classical. News staff one; news progmg 36 hrs wkly. Target aud: 25-54; well educated, upper & middle-upper income. ■ Scott Hanley, gen mgr, dev mgr, gen sls mgr & progmg dir; Mimi Schneider, Roger Vaad, mus dirs; Bill Rodgers, pub affrs dir; Dave Ludwig, chief engr. ■ Rates: $15; 10; 15; na.

KLNG(AM)—1947: 1560 khz; 1 kw-D. TL: N41 12 28 W95 54 4. Hrs opn: 6 AM-sunset. 3851 S. Omaha Bridge Rd. (51501). (712) 366-5564. FAX: (712) 366-3342. Licensee: Wilkins Communications Network Inc. (group owner; acq 4-89; $250,000). Net: CBN, USA. Format: Christian talk & mus, ethnic. Spec prog: Sp 17 hrs wkly. ■ Robert L. Wilkins, pres; Johnny Dale, progmg dir. ■ Rates: $12; 12; 12; na.

KQKQ-FM—1969: 98.5 mhz; 100 kw. Ant 1,074 ft. TL: N41 18 25 W96 01 37. Stereo. 1001 Farnam-on-the-Mall, Omaha, NE (68102). (402) 342-2000. FAX: (402) 342-5874; (402) 346-5748. Licensee: Mitchell Broadcasting Co. Rep: Katz. Format: Contemporary Hit. Spec prog: Alternative 3 hrs wkly. ■ John C. Mitchell, pres; Marty Riemenschneider, sr vp; Daniel Charleston, gen sls mgr; Karen Menke, prom mgr; Dan Kieley, progmg dir; Adam Thunder, mus dir; Terrianne Hannibal, news dir; Allen Sherrill, chief engr.

Cresco

KCZQ(FM)—Apr 1, 1991: 102.3 mhz; 3 kw. Ant 328 ft. TL: N43 25 47 W92 09 49. Stereo. 207 N. Main St., Charles City (50616); 116 First Ave. W. (52136). (515) 228-1000; (319) 547-1000. FAX: (515) 228-1200. Licensee: Mega Media Ltd. (group owner). Net: NBC. Rep: J.L. Farmakis. Format: Adult contemp. News progmg 12 hrs wkly. Target aud: General. Spec prog: Farm 12 hrs wkly. ■ James B. Hebel, pres, gen mgr & gen sls mgr; Steve Danielson, stn mgr; Debra Lowe, opns mgr; Jim Bernard, progmg dir; John Waters, mus dir; Stan McHenry, asst mus dir; Mike Lyman, news dir & pub affrs dir; Tim Cook, chief engr.

Creston

KSIB(AM)—Dec 7, 1946: 1520 khz; 1 kw-D. TL: N41 02 16 W94 23 38. Box 426 (50801). (515) 782-2155. FAX: (515) 782-6963. Licensee: G.O. Radio Inc. (group owner; acq 2-82; grpsl; FTR 2-22-82). Net: AP; Iowa Net. Rep: Frederick Smith, Midwest. Format: C&W. News staff one; news progmg 20 hrs wkly. Target aud: General. ■ Glenn Olson, pres; Dave Rieck, gen mgr; David Passehl, progmg dir & mus dir; Mike Peterson, news dir; Charlie Maley, chief engr. ■ Rates: $18; 14; 18; 12.

KITR(FM)—Co-owned with KSIB(AM). March 1966: 101.3 mhz; 3 kw. Ant 255 ft. TL: N41 03 41 W94 22 30 (CP: 18.75 kw, ant 364 ft.). Stereo. Dups AM 95%. Net: ABC/D; Brownfield. News staff one; news progmg 10 hrs wkly. Target aud: General. ■ Rates: Same as AM.

Davenport

***KALA(FM)**—Nov 4, 1967: 88.5 mhz; 100 w. Ant 110 ft. TL: N41 32 28 W90 34 57. Stereo. 518 West Locust St. (52803). (319) 383-8911. FAX: (319) 383-8909. Licensee: St. Ambrose University (acq 11-4-67). Format: Jazz, progressive, urban contemp. Spec prog: Sp 15 hrs, gospel 11 hrs wkly. ■ David Baker, gen mgr & mus dir; Steve Tappa, asst mus dir; Alan Sivell, news dir; Kenneth E. Colwell, chief engr.

KFMH(FM)—(Muscatine). February 1949: 99.7 mhz; 100 kw. Ant 895 ft. TL: N41 26 43 W91 04 36 Stereo. Hrs

Broadcasting & Cable Yearbook 1994
B-133

opn: 24. Valley Fair, 2720 W. Locust St., Davenport (52804); 529 S. Gilbert St., Iowa City (52240). (319) 391-9900; (319) 354-5958. FAX: (319) 391-8375. Licensee: Flambo Broadcasting Inc. (acq 11-1-81; $1.2 million; sold co-located AM stn / 1992; FTR 11-9-81). Rep: Katz & Powell. Wash atty: Fisher, Wayland, Cooper & Leader. Format: AOR. News staff one. Target aud: 18-49 adults. Spec prog: Jazz 4 hrs wkly. ■ John Flambo, pres & gen mgr; Steve Bridges, exec vp & stn mgr; Judy Thoma, sls dir; Sean Tracy, progmg dir & mus dir; Andy Andresen, chief engr. ■ Rates: $35; 28; 28; 15.

KFQC(AM)—September 1952: 1580 khz; 500 w-D, 7 w-N. TL: N41 34 15 W90 34 53. 5315 Tremont Ave. (52807-2640). Box 1533 (52809). (319) 386-9229. Licensee: Christian Family Media Inc. (acq 5-22-90; $200,000; FTR 6-11-90). Rep: Lotus. Format: Pop stardards, nostalgia. ■ Richard Andresen, gen mgr; Mark Lucas, gen sls mgr.

KJOC(AM)—1947: 1170 khz; 1 kw-U, DA-2. TL: N41 23 22 W90 31 08. 1229 Brady St. (52803). (319) 326-2541. Licensee: Goodrich Broadcasting Inc. (group owner; acq 4-9-87). Net: CBS, ESPN. Rep: Katz. Format: Sports Target aud: 18-49. ■ Bob Goodrich, pres; David Bevins, gen mgr; Steve Watt, gen sls mgr; Dan Burich, prom dir; Ray Sherman, progmg dir; Steve Gunner, mus dir; Larry Timmons, chief engr.

KRVR(FM)—Sept 1, 1966: 106.5 mhz; 60 kw. Ant 210 ft. TL: N41 32 14 W90 34 30. Stereo. Corporate East, 1910 E. Kimberly Rd. (52807). (319) 359-1065. FAX: (319) 359-8524. Licensee: K-River Broadcasting Inc. (acq 6-9-93; $1 million; FTR 6-28-93). Format: Adult contemp. Target aud: 25-54. ■ Larry R. Rosmilso, gen mgr; Terri Van Dyke, stn mgr; Arla Taylor, opns dir; Lisa Lauman, opns mgr; Sandy McKay, progmg dir; Mark Minnick, news dir; Don Bargmann, chief engr. ■ Rates: $39; 39; 39; 25.

KUUL(FM)—Listing follows WOC(AM).

WLLR(AM)—See Moline, Ill.

WOC(AM)—February 1922: 1420 khz; 5 kw-U, DA-2. TL: N41 33 00 W90 28 37. Hrs opn: 24. 3535 E. Kimberly Rd. (52807). (319) 344-7000. FAX: (319) 344-7065; TWX: 910-525-1189. Licensee: Signal Hill Communications Inc. (acq 8-24-89). Net: ABC/I, CNN, NBC, NBC Talknet, AP; Ill. Net, Radio Iowa. Rep: Christal. Wash atty: Baker & Hostetler. Format: News, talk, info. News staff 5. Target aud: 35-64; information-oriented adults. Spec prog: Farm 10 hrs wkly. ■ Vickie Palmer, pres; Dave Seran, gen sls mgr; Bob Shomper, progmg dir; John Bauman, news dir; Jon Book, chief engr. ■ Rates: $45; 35; 30; 18.

KUUL(FM)—Co-owned with WOC(AM). October 1948: 103.7 mhz; 100 kw. Ant 1,191 ft. TL: N41 32 49 W90 28 35. Stereo. Hrs opn: 24. Prog sep from AM. Net: CBS Spectrum, Unistar. Format: Oldies. News progmg 2 hrs wkly. Target aud: 25-54. ■ Dave Seran, rgnl sls mgr; David Sands, mus dir. ■ Rates: $72; 51; 55; 18.

Decorah

KDEC(AM)—May 1947: 1240 khz; 1 kw-U. TL: N43 19 26 W91 47 04. Hrs opn: 5 AM-10 PM (Mon-Fri). Box 27, 110 Highland Dr. (52101). (319) 382-4251. FAX: (319) 382-9540. Licensee: Decorah Radio Inc. (acq 10-85; $380,000; FTR 8-19-85). Net: ABC/D; Tribune. Rep: Farmakis. Wash atty: Reddy, Begley & Martin. Format: MOR. News staff one; news progmg 12 hrs wkly. Target aud: 35 plus. ■ Paul Scott, gen mgr; Dennis Green, stn mgr; Gary Rustad, gen sls mgr; Mitch Teich, news dir; Brett Mashek, chief engr. ■ Rates: $11; 8; 8; 8.

KRDI-FM—Co-owned with KDEC(AM). Sept 2, 1986: 100.5 mhz; 30 kw. Ant 420 ft. TL: N43 19 26 W91 47 04. Stereo. Hrs opn: 19. Prog sep from AM. Format: Adult contemp. News staff one; news progmg 10 hrs wkly. Target aud: 18-45. ■ Pat Linton, progmg dir & mus dir. ■ Rates: $21; 16; 16; 16.

***KLCD(FM)**—July 15, 1977: 89.5 mhz; 100 w. Ant 140 ft. TL: N43 18 56 W91 47 18. Stereo. 735 Marquette Bank Bldg., Rochester, MN (55904). (507) 282-0910. FAX: (507) 282-2107. Licensee: Minnesota Public Radio Inc. Net: NPR, APR. Format: Class, news. News staff 4; news progmg 30 hrs wkly. Spec prog: Jazz 14 hrs wkly. ■ William Kling, pres; Rich Dietman, gen mgr; Gina Wegwerth, dev dir; Paula Kabe, mktg dir; Carol Gunderson, news dir; Don Kolbert, chief engr.

***KLNI(FM)**—1993: 88.7 mhz; 100 w. Ant -36 ft. TL: N43 18 35 W91 48 30. Hrs opn: 24. c/o 45 E. 7th St., St. Paul, MN (55101). Licensee: Minnesota Public Radio. (group owner; acq 6-10-92). Net: NPR, APR. Format: News/information. News staff 3. ■ Dennis Hamilton, exec vp; Rich Dietman, gen mgr; Gina Wegwerth, dev dir.

KRDI-FM—Listing follows KDEC(AM).

***KWLC(AM)**—December 1926: 1240 khz; 1 kw-U. TL: N43 18 38 W91 48 41. 700 College Dr. (52101). (319) 387-1240. Licensee: Luther College. Net: CNN. Format: Div, progsv. News progmg 4 hrs wkly. Spec prog: Classic rock, class, educ, jazz, relg, folk, rap & house music, sports 6 hrs wkly. ■ Beth Seibert, stn mgr, news dir & pub affrs dir; Brent Veninga, mktg dir, prom dir & progmg dir; Nick Camilieri-Preziosi, mus dir; James Veeder, chief engr.

Denison

KDSN(AM)—Apr 11, 1956: 1530 khz; 500 w-D. TL: N42 02 11 W95 19 50. Box 670, 1530 Ridge Rd. (51442). (712) 263-3141. FAX: (712) 263-2088. Licensee: M & J Radio Corp. (acq 8-3-93; $450,000 with co-located FM; FTR 8-23-93). Net: ABC/D; Brownfield, Iowa Radio Net. Format: Country, adult contemp. News staff one; news progmg 14 hrs wkly. Target aud: General. Spec prog: Farm 7 hrs, polka 4 hrs wkly. ■ Jeff Fuller, pres & gen mgr; Michael Dudding, exec vp & gen sls mgr; Tom Hamilton, progmg dir & mus dir; Brian Schmid, news dir; Dick Keane, chief engr. ■ Rates: $12.50; 10.50; 10.50; 10.50.

KDSN-FM—Aug 1, 1968: 107.1 mhz; 3.3 kw. Ant 300 ft. TL: N42 02 11 W95 19 50. Stereo. Prog sep from AM. Format: Adult contemp. News progmg 15 hrs wkly. Target aud: 25-54. Spec prog: Farm 7 hrs wkly. ■ Rates: Same as AM.

Des Moines

***KDFR(FM)**—1989: 91.3 mhz; 4 kw. Ant 446 ft. TL: N41 36 59 W93 31 36. 2350 N.E. 44th Court (50317). (515) 262-0449. Licensee: Family Stations Inc. (group owner). Format: Relg. ■ Harold Camping, pres; Larry Vavroch, gen mgr & opns mgr.

KDMI(AM)—July 21, 1921: 1460 khz; 5 kw-U, DA-N. TL: N41 38 45 W93 32 12. Stereo. Hrs opn: 24. 3900 N.E. Broadway (50317-8942). (515) 265-6181. Licensee: American Radio Systems License Corp. Group owner: American Radio Systems (acq 9-15-93; with co-located FM; FTR 10-4-93). Net: NBC the Source. Rep: Eastman. Format: Rock. Target aud: 18-49. ■ Peter McLane, vp & gen mgr; Dan Abbuehl, gen sls mgr; Phil Wilson, progmg dir; Jack Emerson, mus dir; Larry Morgan, news dir; Rick Chalfant, chief engr.

KGGO-FM—Co-owned with KDMI(AM). May 31, 1964: 94.9 mhz; 100 kw. Ant 1,059 ft. TL: N41 37 54 W93 27 24. Stereo. Dups AM 100%. ■ Jeff Lynn, prom mgr.

***KDPS(FM)**—Apr 16, 1952: 88.1 mhz; 5.2 kw. Ant 285 ft. TL: N41 35 01 W93 38 28. 1800 Grand Ave. (50309-3399). (515) 242-7723. FAX: (515) 242-7598. Licensee: Des Moines Independent School Dist. Format: Div, educ. ■ Judith Richardson, gen mgr; Bill Springer, progmg dir, mus dir & news dir; Glendon McLean, chief engr.

KGGO-FM—Listing follows KDMI(AM).

KHKI(FM)—1961: 97.3 mhz; 115 kw. Ant 500 ft. TL: N41 39 47 W93 45 21. Stereo. 2907 Merle Hay Rd. (50310). (515) 274-4968. Licensee: American Radio Systems License Corp. Group owner: American Radio Systems (acq 9-15-93; FTR 10-4-93). Net: MBS. Format: Relg. ■ Ralph Duckworth Jr., pres; Maxine Bruinekool, gen mgr; Jerry Slegh, stn mgr & progmg dir.

KIOA(AM)—April 1947: 940 khz; 10 kw-D, 5 kw-N, DA-2. TL: N41 28 35 W93 22 26. 1416 Locust St. (50309). (515) 280-1350. Licensee: Saga Communications of Iowa Inc. Group owner: Saga Communications Inc. (acq 4-19-93; $2.7 million with co-located FM; FTR 5-3-93). Net: ABC/E. Rep: Banner. Format: Oldies. ■ Phil Hoover, pres & gen mgr; Bill Shannon, opns dir; Pete Paquette, prom mgr; Kipper McGee, progmg dir; Polly Carver-Kimm, news dir; John Kosobucki, chief engr.

KIOA-FM—Sept 18, 1964: 93.3 mhz; 100 kw. Ant 1,063 ft. TL: N41 37 54 W93 27 24. Stereo. Dups AM 100%.

KJJY-FM—Listing follows KKSO(AM).

KKDM(FM)—Not on air, target date unknown: 107.5 mhz; 50 kw. Ant 492 ft. Box 1797, 1001 Grand Ave. (50306). Licensee: Midwest Radio Inc.

KKSO(AM)—Mar 13, 1947: 1390 khz; 1 kw-U, DA-1. TL: N41 35 18 W93 31 38. 5161 Maple Dr. (50317). (515) 262-9200. Licensee: Fuller-Jeffrey Broadcasting of Greater Des Moines. Group owner: Fuller-Jeffrey Broadcasting Companies Inc. (acq 7-1-86; $400,000; FTR 5-12-86). Net: UPI. Rep: McGavren Guild. Format: Country. News staff 2; news progmg 10 hrs wkly. Target aud: 25 plus. ■ Robert F. Fuller, pres; J. Michael McKoy, vp & gen mgr; Beverlee Brannigan, chief opns; Jim Lobaito, rgnl sls mgr; Tina Norris, prom mgr; Eddie Hatfield, mus dir; Susan Hudson, news dir; Eldon L. Schlenker, chief engr. ■ Rates: $125; 85; 98; 45.

KJJY-FM—(Ankeny). Co-owned with KKSO(AM). Feb 4, 1978: 92.5 mhz; 41 kw. Ant 541 ft. TL: N41 39 53 W93 45 24. Stereo. Net: McGavren Guild. Format: Pop country. ■ Rates: Same as AM.

KLYF(FM)—Listing follows WHO(AM).

KRNT(AM)—Mar 17, 1935: 1350 khz; 5 kw-U, DA-N. TL: N41 33 34 W93 34 40. 1416 Locust (50309). (515) 280-1350. Licensee: Saga Communications Inc. (group owner; acq 8-88; $3.25 million with co-located FM; FTR 8-1-88). Net: CBS, MBS, Unistar. Rep: Katz. Format: MOR. ■ Phil Hoover, gen mgr; Mark Pierce, gen sls mgr; Kipper McGee, progmg dir; Dale Woolery, news dir; Joe Farrington, chief engr.

KSTZ(FM)—1970: 102.5 mhz; 100 kw. Ant 1,248 ft. TL: N41 48 01 W93 36 27. Stereo. 1416 Locust (50309). (515) 280-1350. Licensee: James Ingstad Broadcasting Inc. (group owner; acq 10-5-93; $5,000; FTR 10-25-93). Net: ABC/FM. Format: CHR. ■ Chuck Knight, progmg dir; Bob Lewis, mus dir.

***KUCB-FM**—Aug 7, 1981: 89.3 mhz; 10 kw. Ant 100 ft. TL: N41 36 15 W93 37 43. Stereo. Box 1316, Radio Station KUCB-FM (50309). (515) 246-1588. Licensee: Center for the Study & Applications of Black Economic Development. Format: Eclectic, pub info & educ. Spec prog: African history 20 hrs, reggae 12 hrs, talk 13 hrs, jazz & blues 10 hrs, gospel 12 hrs, contemp 20 hrs wkly. ■ Wayne Ford, pres; Eugene Fowler, gen mgr; Kalonji Saadia, Sekou Mtyari (asst), stn mgrs; Ako Abdul-Sumad, progmg dir; Pat Fowler, news dir; Mr. Farrington, chief engr.

KWKY(AM)—Feb 2, 1948: 1150 khz; 1 kw-U, DA-2. TL: N41 27 07 W93 40 44. Box 662 (50303); 501 Hwy. 28, Norwalk (50211). (515) 981-0981. FAX: (515) 981-0840. Licensee: Norseman Broadcasting (acq 3-11-61). Net: USA. Wash atty: Putbrese, Hunsaker & Ruddy. Format: Relg, sports. Target aud: General. ■ Charles E. Putbrese, gen mgr; Thelma Shelton, opns mgr; Robert Simms, rgnl sls mgr; Tom Vandeberg, progmg dir & mus dir; Bobby Dick, news dir; Howard Kling, chief engr.

WHO(AM)—Apr 10, 1924: 1040 khz; 50 kw-U. TL: N41 39 12 W93 20 56. 1801 Grand Ave. (50309). (515) 242-3500. FAX: (515) 242-3798; (515) 242-3553. Licensee: Palmer Broadcast Limited Partnership. Net: NBC, NBC Talknet, Wall Street, ABC. Rep: Christal. Format: News\talk. News staff 9. Target aud: General. Spec prog: Farm 15 hrs wkly. ■ Bill Ryan, pres; Joe Lentz, gen mgr; Mark Haverson, stn mgr; Mark Haherson, natl sls mgr; Matt Gillon, rgnl sls mgr; Van Harden, progmg dir; Bob Quinn, news dir; Raleigh Rubenking, chief engr.

KLYF(FM)—Co-owned with WHO(AM). Feb 1, 1948: 100.3 mhz; 100 kw. Ant 1,700 ft. TL: N41 48 33 W93 36 53. Stereo. Prog sep from AM. Format: Adult contemp. Target aud: 25-54. ■ Tim Gardner, progmg dir; Pam Dixon, news dir. ■ WHO-TV affil.

Dubuque

KATF(FM)—Listing follows KDTH(AM).

KDTH(AM)—May 4, 1941: 1370 khz; 5 kw-U, DA-N. TL: N42 29 06 W90 38 39. Hrs opn: 24. Box 659, 8th & Bluff Sts. (52004). (319) 588-5700. Licensee: Woodward Communications Inc. (group owner). Net: CBS, AP. Rep: Eastman. Wash atty: Bryan & Cave. Format: Full service MOR. News staff 4; news progmg 25 hrs wkly. Target aud: 35 plus; responsible adults with established careers and households. Spec prog: Farm 8 hrs wkly. ■ John Hafkemeyer, gen mgr; Kathy Schmitt, gen sls mgr; Larry Blatz, natl sls mgr; Bob Gelms, progmg dir; Michael Kaye, mus dir; Jim Wise, news dir; Marc Karrmann, chief engr. ■ Rates: $30; 20; 15; 8.

KATF(FM)—Co-owned with KDTH(AM). June 25, 1967: 92.9 mhz; 100 kw. Ant 999 ft. TL: N42 31 43 W90 36 56. Stereo. Hrs opn: 24. Prog sep from AM. (319) 588-5678. Net: ABC. Format: Adult contemp. News progmg 3 hrs wkly. Target aud: 25-54; adults establishing families, careers & households. ■ Tommy Allen, progmg dir; Tommy Edwards, mus dir. ■ Rates: $25; 25; 30; 10.

KGGY(FM)—Mar 8, 1980: 102.3 mhz; 2.4 kw. Ant 410 ft. TL: N42 32 28 W90 36 46. Stereo. Hrs opn: 24. Suite 800, 909 Main St. (52001). (319) 557-8888. Licensee: Eagle Communications of Iowa Inc. Group owner: Eagle Communications (acq 6-7-87). Net: Unistar. Format: Classic rock, oldies. News staff one; news progmg 2 hrs wkly. Target aud: 18-49; in high school or college in the 60's and 70's. ■ Kirby Confer, pres; Don Neer, gen mgr; Mike Callaghan, progmg dir; Mary Ernst, news dir. ■ Rates: $20; 18; 20; 14.

KLYV(FM)—Listing follows WDBQ(AM).

WDBQ(AM)—Oct 30, 1933: 1490 khz; 1 kw-U. TL: N42 30 10 W90 42 24. Stereo. Box 1280, 5490 Saratoga Rd. (52001). (319) 583-6471. FAX: (319) 583-4535. Licensee: Communications Properties Inc. (group owner; acq 9-15-78). Net: ABC/D. Rep: Banner, Radio Iowa. Wash atty: Peper & Martin. Format: Adult contemp, oldies. News staff 3. ■ Philip T. Kelly, pres; Kevin T. Kelly, gen mgr; Paul Hemmer, progmg dir; Jack Kilcoyne, news dir; Tom White, chief engr. ■ Rates: $25; 20; 22; 18.

KLYV(FM)—Co-owned with WDBQ(AM). Sept 1, 1965: 105.3 mhz; 50 kw. Ant 330 ft. TL: N42 30 10 W90 42 11. Stereo. (319) 557-1040. Net: NBC the Source. Rep: Banner. Format: CHR. News staff 2. Target aud: 18-49. ■ Kevin T. Kelly, vp; Joe Dawson, progmg dir; Scott Thomas, mus dir; Tom White, engrg dir.

Dyersville

KDST(FM)—Aug 25, 1985: 99.3 mhz; 3 kw. Ant 298 ft. TL: N42 25 43 W91 12 50. Stereo. 239 1/2 First Ave. E. (52040). (319) 875-8193. FAX: (319) 875-8193. Licensee: Design Homes Inc. (acq 12-88); $22,079; FTR 12-26-88). Net: SMN; Brownfield. Format: Country. News staff 5. Target aud: 25-45. Spec prog: Farm. ■ Franklin Weeks, pres; John Lightfoot, vp, gen mgr, gen sls mgr & chief engr; Roger Lambert, opns mgr, progmg dir & news dir. ■ Rates: $12.50; 11.50; 9.50; 9.50.

Eagle Grove

KJYL(FM)—Not on air, target date unknown: 100.7 mhz; 25 kw. Ant 328 ft. Box 72, Blue Earth, MN (56013). Licensee: Minn-Iowa Christian Broadcasting Inc.

Eddyville

KKSI(FM)—July 30, 1990: 101.5 mhz; 49 kw. Ant 498 ft. TL: N41 07 57 W92 42 12. Stereo. Hrs opn: 24. Box 1110, Penn Central Mall, 200 High Ave, Oskaloosa (52577); 416 E. Main, Ottumwa (52501). (515) 673-6402; (515) 682-0498. FAX: (515) 684-5832. Licensee: "O"-Town Communications, Inc. Group owner: Linder Broadcasting Group (acq 2-15-91); $1,240; FTR 3-11-91). Net: ABC. Wash atty: Miller & Fields. Format: Adult contemp, classic rock, oldies. News staff one; news progmg 4 hrs wkly. Target aud: 25-54; females, young adults. Spec prog: Farm one hr, gospel one hr wkly. ■ Don Linder, pres; Greg List, stn mgr; Pat Snyder, progmg dir; Rich Brown, asst mus dir; Carmela Sample, news dir; Mark McVey, chief engr.

Eldora

KDAO-FM—June 1, 1992: 99.5 mhz; 3 kw. Ant 328 ft. TL: N42 15 49 W93 03 57. Stereo. Hrs opn: 24. Box 538, Marshalltown (50158). (515) 752-4102. Licensee: Eldora Broadcasting Co. (acq 12-18-91; $15,000 for CP; FTR 1-13-92). Net: ABC/C. Format: Adult contmep. Target aud: 25-54. ■ Mark Osmundson, gen mgr; Rich Davis, opns mgr.

Elkader

KADR(AM)—May 15, 1983: 1400 khz; 1 kw-U. TL: N42 50 57 W91 24 43. Rt. 1, Box 86 (52043). (319) 245-1400. FAX: (319) 245-1402. Licensee: KADR-AM 14, div of Design Homes Inc. (acq 3-20-85). Net: SMN. Rep: Farmakis. Format: Adult contemp. News staff one. ■ Franklin Weeks, CEO & pres; John Lightfoot, vp, gen mgr, gen sls mgr & chief engr; Troy Thein, chief opns, progmg mgr & mus dir; Dan Berns, news dir. ■ Rates: $15; 13; 13; 11.

KCTN(FM)—See Garnavillo.

Emmetsburg

KEMB(FM)—Jan 10, 1977: 100.1 mhz; 3 kw. Ant 300 ft. TL: N43 01 20 W94 41 59. Stereo. Box 390, 2215 Main St. (50536). (712) 852-4551. FAX: (712) 852-2088. Licensee: Jacobson Broadcasting Corp. (acq 10-28-89; FTR 9-18-89). Net: ABC/D, Iowa Net. Rep: Farmakis. Wash atty: Lauren A. Colby. Format: Oldies. Spec prog: Farm 10 hrs wkly. ■ Roger J. Jacobson, pres; Mike Joseph, progmg dir; Brent Wiethorn, news dir; Doug Burton, chief engr.

Epworth

NEW FM—Not on air, target date unknown: 97.3 mhz; 20 kw. Ant 367 ft. 1030 Boyer, Dubuque (52001). Licensee: Hemmer Broadcasting.

Estherville

KILR(AM)—Dec 23, 1967: 1070 khz; 250 w-D, DA. TL: N43 25 28 W94 49 30. Box 453, Hwy. 4 N. (51334-0453). (712) 362-2644. Licensee: Jacobson Broadcasting Co. Inc. (acq 7-1-82; $610,000 with co-located FM; FTR 7-5-82). Net: ABC/I. Rep: Farmakis. Wash atty: Lauren Colby. Format: Adult contemp, oldies, news/talk. News staff one; news progmg 24 hrs wkly. Target aud: 29-65; local baby boomers. Spec prog: Farm 4 hrs, relg 11 hrs wkly. ■ Roger J. Jacobson, pres, gen mgr & gen sls mgr; Barbara J. Jacobson, CFO; Peggy Zahrt, opns mgr; Debbi Hecht, prom dir; Greg Alan, progmg dir & news dir; Doug Burton, chief engr.

KILR-FM—Oct 17, 1969: 95.9 mhz; 6 kw. Ant 300 ft. TL: N43 25 49 W94 49 30. Stereo. Dups AM 100%. ■ Debbi Hecht, adv dir.

Fairfield

***KHOE(FM)**—Not on air, target date unknown: 90.5 mhz; 100 w. Ant 98 ft. TL: N41 00 59 W91 58 09. Box 209 (52556); 402, 1000 N. 4th St. (52556). (515) 469-5463. FAX: (515) 472-1141. Licensee: Fairfield Educational Radio Station.

KIIK-FM—Listing follows KMCD(AM).

KMCD(AM)—March 3, 1958: 1570 khz; 250 w-D, 108 w-N. TL: N41 00 25 W92 00 50. 57 1/2 S. Court (52556). (515) 472-4191. FAX: (515) 472-2071. Licensee: Galesburg Broadcasting Co. (group owner; acq 9-1-79). Net: ABC/I, CNN. Format: Country. News staff one; news progmg 22 hrs wkly. Target aud: 40 plus. Spec prog: Farm 10 hrs wkly. ■ Kent Osborne, gen mgr, progmg dir & mus dir; Bob Hudgins, news dir.

KIIK-FM—Co-owned with KMCD(AM). 1977: 95.9 mhz; 2.05 kw. Ant 400 ft. TL: N40 58 47 W92 05 45 (CP: 4.1 kw). Stereo. Prog sep from AM. Net: ABC/R. Format: Top-40. News staff one; news progmg 12 hrs wkly. Target aud: 18-39. Spec prog: Farm 7 hrs wkly.

Forest City

KIOW(FM)—Nov 8, 1978: 107.3 mhz. 25 kw. Ant 328 ft. TL: N43 17 02 W93 37 50. Stereo. Hrs opn: 24. Box 308, 18643 360th St. (50436). (515) 582-3121. FAX: (515) 582-2990. Licensee: Pilot Knob Broadcasting Inc. Net: NBC, Westwood One. Radio Iowa. Rep: Farmakis. Home Town Radio Net. Format: Country, adult contemp, news. News staff one; news progmg 15 hrs wkly. Target aud: 12-64. Spec prog: Farm 15 hrs, contemp hits 19 hrs wkly. ■ Tony Coloff, pres, gen mgr & chief engr; Susan I. Coloff, exec vp; Melody Schlake, gen sls mgr; Gary Rayhons, adv mgr; Dale Aman, progmg dir; Mark Skaar, news dir. ■ Rates: $10.30; 10.30; 10.30; 10.30.

Fort Dodge

***KICB(FM)**—September 1971: 88.1 mhz; 200 w. Ant 130 ft. TL: N42 29 27 W94 12 01. Stereo. 330 Ave. M (50501). (515) 576-6049. Licensee: Iowa Central Community College. Format: Oldies, progressive, AOR. News progmg 12 hrs wkly. Target aud: 13-34; young men and women with progressive tastes. Spec prog: Rap 2 hrs wkly. ■ Robert W. Wood, gen mgr & chief engr.

KKEZ(FM)—Listing follows KWMT(AM).

***KTPR(FM)**—Sept 15, 1980: 91.1 mhz; 100 kw. Ant 1,052 ft. TL: N42 49 03 W94 24 41. Stereo. Hrs opn: 5 AM-12 midnight. 330 Ave. M (50501). (515) 955-5877. FAX: (515) 576-7206. Licensee: Iowa Central Community College. Net: NPR. Format: Class, jazz, news. News staff 2; news progmg 34 hrs wkly. Target aud: General; educated, affluent. Spec prog: Black 2 hrs, nostalgia 4 hrs, new age 7 hrs wkly. ■ Scott Lewison, gen mgr; Bob Kern, progmg dir; John Pemble, mus dir; Ted Green, asst mus dir; Lisa Phillips, news dir; Kay Miska, pub affrs dir; Ed Miltner, chief engr.

KUEL(FM)—Listing follows KVFD(AM).

KVFD(AM)—Dec 24, 1939: 1400 khz; 1 kw-U. TL: N42 28 44 W94 12 10. Box Y, 3566 5th Ave. S. (50501). (515) 955-1400. FAX: (515) 955-5844. Licensee: Sorenson Broadcasting Co. (group owner; acq 6-20-88; $875,000 with co-located FM; FTR 6-20-88). Rep: Katz & Powell, O'Malley. Format: Memory music. ■ Dean Sorenson, pres; Bill Grady, gen mgr; Ed Miska, opns mgr; Bill Higgins, mus dir; Amy Reasner-Crossley, news dir; Ed Miltner, chief engr.

KUEL(FM)—Co-owned with KVFD(AM). July 28, 1975: 92.1 mhz; 3 kw. Ant 300 ft. TL: N42 28 44 W94 12 10 (CP: Ant 321 ft.). Stereo. (515) 955-5656. Format: Unistar-oldies. ■ Bill Grady, gen sls mgr.

KWMT(AM)—April 1956: 540 khz; 5 kw-D, 200 w-N, DA-2. TL: N42 22 94 W94 12 27. Box 578, 540 A St. (50501). (515) 576-7333. FAX: (515) 955-4250. Licensee: KWMT Radio Inc. Net: ABC/C. Rep: McGavren Guild. Wash atty: Reddy, Begley & Martin. Format: Country. News staff 3; news progmg 10 hrs wkly. Target aud: General. Spec prog: Farm. ■ John P. Jenkins, CEO; Jon W. Jenkins, pres & gen mgr; Beck O'Brien, gen sls mgr; Dale Eichor, progmg dir & mus dir; Jerry Sheeder, news dir; Barry Walsh, chief engr.

KKEZ(FM)—Co-owned with KWMT(AM). 1966: 94.5 mhz; 100 kw. Ant 640 ft. TL: N42 29 43 W94 12 33. Stereo. Hrs opn: 24. Prog sep from AM. Format: Adult contemp. News staff 3; news progmg 5 hrs wkly. Target aud: 18-49. ■ Amy Alberts, mus dir.

Fort Madison

KBKB(AM)—Feb 6, 1948: 1360 khz; 1 kw-D, 35 w-N. TL: N40 39 30 W91 16 20. Box 369, US 61 N. (52627). (319) 372-1241. FAX: (319) 372-5254. Licensee: Talley Broadcasting Co. Group owner: Talley Radio Stations (acq 5-1-60). Net: NBC. Rep: Farmakis, Heartland Broadcasting Net. Wash atty: Fisher, Wayland, Cooper & Leader. Format: Adult contemp. News staff 2; news progmg 30 hrs wkly. Target aud: 24-50. Spec prog: News/talk 15 hrs wkly. ■ Hayward L. Talley, pres; John R. Peters, vp, gen mgr & chief engr; David Clark, opns mgr & progmg dir; Mardie Smith, gen sls mgr; Todd Wise, mus dir; Mike Steenberg, news dir; Dick Specht, pub affrs dir. ■ Rates: $13.50; 9; 13.50; 9.

KBKB-FM—June 1, 1973: 101.7 mhz; 50 kw. Ant 466 ft. TL: N40 43 25 W91 13 49. Stereo. Hrs opn: 24. Dups AM 67%. Format: Adult contemp. News staff 2; news progmg 7 hrs wkly. Target aud: 25-50. ■ Rates: Same as AM.

Garnavillo

KCTN(FM)—Dec 6, 1982: 100.1 mhz; 3 kw. Ant 300 ft. TL: N42 53 06 W91 19 11. Stereo. Hrs opn: 24. Route 1, Box 86, Elkader (52043). (319) 245-1400. FAX: (319) 245-1402. Licensee: KCTN-FM 100, div of Design Homes Inc. Net: Brownfield. Rep: J.L. Farmakis. Format: Country. News staff one. Target aud: 24-55; farmers and rural communities. Spec prog: Farm. ■ Franklin Weeks, pres; John Lightfoot, vp, gen mgr, gen sls mgr, vp mktg & vp prom; Troy Thein, chief opns & progmg mgr; Michael Johnson, mus dir; Dan Berns, news dir. ■ Rates: $13.50; 12; 12; 11.

Grinnell

***KDIC(FM)**—May 1968: 88.5 mhz; 100 w. Ant 124 ft. TL: N41 44 53 W92 43 10. Stereo. Hrs opn: 24. Grinnell College (50112). (515) 269-3335. Licensee: Trustees of Iowa College. Format: Class rock, progsv, urban contemp. News progmg 4 hrs wkly. College students, professors, town. Spec prog: Class 12 hrs, Black 12 hrs wkly. ■ Jason Eckert, stn mgr; Matt Miller, prom mgr; Jason Eckert, progmg mgr; Ken Viste, mus dir; Ken Viste, Monica Ware, asst mus dirs; Mike Bilden, news dir; Jason Reynolds, pub affrs dir.

KGRN(AM)—Nov 15, 1957: 1410 khz; 500 w-D, 47 w-N. TL: N41 44 44 W92 42 36 (CP: 300 w-D, 33 w-N, TL: N41 46 35 W92 38 56). Box 660 (50112). (515) 236-6106. Licensee: Mitchell Broadcasting Co. (acq 8-25-92; FTR 9-14-92). Net: Iowa Net. Rep: Farmakis. Format: MOR. Spec prog: Farm 12 hrs, C&W 12 hrs wkly. ■ Frosty Mitchell, pres; Russ Crawford, gen mgr; Mark McDowell, progmg dir & mus dir; Don Bradley, news dir; Jim Davies, chief engr.

KRTI(FM)—Not on air, target date unknown: 106.7 mhz; 50 kw. Ant 492 ft. 310 6th Ave. (50112). (515) 236-5784. Licensee: Janet A. Carl. ■ Tom Grady, gen mgr.

Grundy Center

KGCI(FM)—Oct 8, 1983: 97.7 mhz; 16 kw. Ant 407 ft. TL: N42 23 28 W92 13 57 Stereo. Black's Bldg., 501 Sycamore, Waterloo (50703). (319) 232-9898. FAX: (319) 824-5856. Licensee: Grundy Broadcasting. Format: Country. News staff 2: news progmg 3 hrs wkly. Target aud: General; 18 plus. Spec prog: Farm one hr wkly. ■ Audrey Osmundson, pres; Dean L. Osmundson, gen mgr & sls dir; Mike Baumgartner, progmg dir & mus dir; Rob Stephens, asst mus dir; Elwin Huffman, news dir; Stan Siems, chief engr.

Hampton

KLMJ(FM)—May 16, 1983: 104.9 mhz; 4.5 kw. Ant 255 ft. TL: N42 49 45 W93 11 10. Stereo. Hrs opn: 17. Box 495, 1509 Fourth St. N.E. (50441). (515) 456-5656. FAX: (515) 456-5655. Licensee: C.D. Broadcasting (acq 10-

93; $60,000; FTR 10-11-93). Net: ABC/D. Radio Iowa. Rep: Farmakis. Format: Adult contemp, C&W, oldies. News staff one; news progmg 14 hrs wkly. Target aud: General; 25 plus. Spec prog: Farm 16 hrs wkly. ■ Craig Donnelly, gen mgr, gen sls mgr & adv mgr; Pat Palmer, opns mgr & progmg dir; Mike Betton, mus dir; Mark Saylor, news dir & pub affrs dir; Stan Siems, chief engr. ■ Rates: $11; 11; 11; 11.

KRNQ(FM)—Not on air, target date unknown: 98.9 mhz; 6 kw. Ant 325 ft. TL: N42 39 15 W93 14 37. Hrs opn: 24. Box 366, 553 3rd Ave. N.W. (55350); 2110 E. 10th St. (55336). (612) 587-5696; (612) 864-6700. FAX: (612) 587-1113; (612) 864-6750. Licensee: James Ingstad Broadcasting Inc. (group owner; acq 10-5-93; $5,000; FTR 10-25-93). Net: ABC. Format: Variety hit radio. News staff one; Target aud: 18-49; an appeal to all age groups. ■ John Linder, pres & gen mgr; John Mons, stn mgr, opns mgr & prom dir; Bruce Kottke, Dale Koktan, sls dirs; John Beck, mus dir & pub affrs dir; Janis Rannow, news dir; Scott Jeeffrey, vp engrg.

Harlan

KNOD(FM)—Nov 12, 1979: 105.3 mhz; 25 kw. Ant 300 ft. TL: N41 37 00 W95 16 10. Stereo. Box 723 (51537). (712) 755-3883. Licensee: KNOD Radio. Net: ABC/D; Brownfield. Format: Adult contemp, C&W, news. News staff one. Target aud: 25-50. Spec prog: Farm 3 hrs, relg 2 hrs wkly. ■ John Talbott, pres; Ron Novotny, opns mgr, dev dir, gen sls mgr, prom mgr & progmg dir; John Knoell, mus dir; Nancy Olson, news dir; John Talbott, Larry Miller, chiefs engr. ■ Rates: $9; 9; 9; 9.

Hudson

NEW FM—Not on air, target date unknown: 96.1 mhz; 3 kw. Ant 312 ft. 73 Kercheval Ave., Grosse Point Farms, MI (48236). Licensee: Donald L. Rabbitt (acq 6-3-93; $10,658; FTR 6-21-93).

Humboldt

KHBT(FM)—Aug 5, 1970: 97.7 mhz; 3 kw. Ant 275 ft. TL: N42 43 57 W94 12 23. Stereo. Box 217, 2196 Montana Ave. (50548). (515) 332-4100. Licensee: Signature Communications Inc. (acq 7-1-93; $148,000; FTR 6-14-93). Net: AP,CNN. Format: Btfl mus, easy lstng. News progmg 30 hrs wkly. Target aud: General. Spec prog: Farm 10 hrs wkly. ■ Frank Hayer, gen mgr; Paulette Lyndberg, gen sls mgr.

Ida Grove

KIDA-FM—September 1981: 92.9 mhz; 16 kw. Ant 295 ft. TL: N42 15 16 W95 23 29. Stereo. 513 W. Second St. (51445). (712) 364-9200. FAX: (712) 364-2559. Licensee: Golden Midwest Radio Corp. (acq 2-1-93; FTR 2-22-93). Net: ABC/D; Brownfield, Radio Iowa. Rep: Farmakis. Format: Country. Spec prog: Farm 10 hrs, big band 3 hrs wkly. ■ Dan Dobson, gen mgr; Johnny Lynn Nordecker, news dir; Jeff Briesen, chief engr.

Independence

KQMG(AM)—Dec 10, 1959: 1220 khz; 250 w-D, 166 w-N. TL: N42 28 34 W91 52 31. 231 1/2 First St. E. (50644). (319) 334-2549. FAX: (319) 334-6153. Licensee: Midwest Broadcasting Inc. (acq 12-2-91; $192,500 with co-located FM; FTR 12-16-91). Net: AP. Format: Adult contemp, oldies. News staff 13; news progmg 17 hrs wkly. Spec prog: Farm 6 hrs wkly. ■ Dean Schlitter, pres; Tim Lary, news dir. ■ Rates: $12; 12; 12; 6.

KQMG-FM—Jan 1, 1972: 95.3 mhz; 3 kw. Ant 200 ft. TL: N42 28 34 W91 52 31. Stereo. Dups AM 100%. ■ Dean Schlitter, gen mgr.

Iowa City

KCJJ(AM)—Jan 15, 1977: 1560 khz; 840 w-U, DA-1. TL: N41 36 03 W91 30 02. Stereo. Hrs opn: 24. Box 2118, 4404 SE Napoleon St. (52244); RR 4, Sand Rd. (52240). (319) 354-1244. FAX: (319) 354-1286. Licensee: River City Radio, Inc. (acq 6-24-91; $100,000 for half-interest, family deal; FTR 7-15-91). Net: Unistar. Format: Adult contemp, oldies. News staff one; news progmg 18 hrs wkly. Target aud: 35 plus; general. Spec prog: Farm 3 hrs, big band 4 hrs, sports talk one hr, 60 plus 7 hrs wkly. ■ Cordell Braverman, pres & gen mgr; Rosemary Roelf, vp opns & vp mktg; Rod Haag, progmg dir; Paul Morsch, news dir; Terrence Noezil, pub affrs dir; Mike Roelf, vp engrg. ■ Rates: $18; 13; 13; 8.

KKRQ(FM)—Listing follows KXIC(AM).

KRNA(FM)—Oct 4, 1974: 94.1 mhz; 100 kw. Ant 981 ft. TL: N41 45 00 W91 50 16. Stereo. Hrs opn: 24. 2105 A.C.T. Cir. (52245-9636). (319) 351-9300; (319) 362-0393. FAX: (319) 351-4943. Licensee: KRNA Inc. Rep: Roslin. Wash atty: Dow, Lohnes & Albertson. Format: Rock (AOR). News staff 2; news progmg 2 hrs wkly. Target aud: 18-49. ■ Eliot A. Keller, pres, gen mgr & news dir; Robert K. Norton Jr., exec vp, opns mgr, progmg dir, mus dir & chief engr; David M. Kelch, vp sls; Joe Nugent, pub affrs dir. ■ Rates: $65; 57; 65; 57.

***KRUI-FM**—March 28, 1984: 89.7 mhz; 100 w. Ant 90 ft. TL: N41 39 29 W91 32 40. Stereo. Hrs opn: 24. 897 South Quad (52242). (319) 335-9525. FAX: (319) 335-9526. Licensee: Student Broadcasters Inc. Net: AP. Format: Div, educ, progsv. News progmg 7 hrs wkly. Target aud: 18-34; Univ. of Iowa students & surrounding community. Spec prog: Black 12 hrs, jazz 3 hrs, blues 3 hrs, reggae 2 hrs, heavy metal 3 hrs, dance 3 hrs, Sp 3 hrs wkly. ■ Tom Langenberg, gen mgr; Mike Moyle, chief opns; Pat Madigan, mktg dir, prom dir & adv dir; A. J. Bautista, progmg dir & chief engr; Anthony Calandra, mus dir; Nicole Stavish, news dir.

***KSUI(FM)**—Listing follows WSUI(AM).

KXIC(AM)—June 7, 1948: 800 khz; 1 kw-D, 199 w-N, DA-2. TL: N41 41 15 W91 32 39. Box 2388 (52244). (319) 354-9500. FAX: (319) 354-9504. Licensee: Iowa City Broadcasting. Net: ABC/E. Format: News & info. ■ Steve Winkey, gen mgr; Roy Justis, news dir.

KKRQ(FM)—Co-owned with KXIC(AM). May 1, 1966: 100.7 mhz; 100 kw. Ant 1,350 ft. TL: N41 45 26 W91 31 31. Stereo. Prog sep from AM. Net: ABC/C. Format: Music of the 50s, 60s & 70s. ■ Phil Maicke, progmg dir; Greg Runyon, mus dir.

***WSUI(AM)**—1919: 910 khz; 5 kw-U, DA-N. TL: N41 39 45 W91 34 30. 3300 Engr Bldg, Univ. of Iowa (52242). (319) 335-5730. Licensee: The Univ. of Iowa. Net: NPR. Format: Information. ■ John Monick, gen mgr; Dennis Reese, progmg dir; Terry Edmonds, chief engr.

***KSUI(FM)**—Co-owned with WSUI(AM). 1948: 91.7 mhz; 100 kw. Ant 1,310 ft. TL: N41 43 15 W91 20 30. Format: Fine Arts, class. ■ John Fisher, progmg dir.

Iowa Falls

KIFG(AM)—July 22, 1962: 1510 khz; 1 kw-D, 500 w CH. TL: N42 30 49 W93 12 57. Box 307, 308 1/2 Stevens (50126). (515) 648-4281; (515) 648-4282. FAX: (515) 648-3283. Licensee: John P. Whitesell (acq 7-90; $129,000 with co-located FM; FTR 7-23-90). Net: AP. Rep: Keystone (unwired net). Format: Adult contemp. News staff one; news progmg 14 hrs wkly. Target aud: 25 plus. Spec prog: Farm 5 hrs, country 10 hrs wkly. ■ John P. Whitesell, pres; James W. Starr, gen mgr & gen sls mgr; Al Reiter, progmg dir; Gene Newgoard, mus dir; Stan Siems, chief engr. ■ Rates: $8.75; 8.75; 8.75; 8.75.

KIFG-FM—Oct 1, 1965: 95.3 mhz; 4.7 kw. Ant 237 ft. TL: N42 30 49 W93 12 57. Stereo. Hrs opn: 17. Dups AM 100%.

Jefferson

KLSN(FM)—Oct 1, 1981: 98.9 mhz; 3 kw. Ant 101 ft. TL: N42 00 59 W94 22 26. Stereo. 116 E. State (50129). (515) 386-2215. Licensee: Breakthrough Broadcasting Ltd. (acq 11-4-91; $90,000; FTR 11-25-91). Net: ABC; Iowa Radio Net., Brownfield. Format: Adult contemp, oldies. News staff one; news progmg 9 hrs wkly. Target aud: 35 plus; rural farm community, middle class adults. Spec prog: Farm 15 hrs wkly. ■ Lauri Struve, gen mgr; Elaine Phelp-Capek, opns mgr; James Casey, sls dir & adv dir. ■ Rates: $15; 11.25; 11.25; 7.50.

Keokuk

KOKX(AM)—Oct 19, 1947: 1310 khz; 1 kw-D, 500 w-N, DA-N. TL: N40 22 50 W91 21 09. Box 427, 108 Washington (52632). (319) 524-5410. FAX: (319) 524-7275. Licensee: Withers Broadcasting of Iowa. Group owner: Withers Broadcasting Co. (acq 7-15-81; $900,000 with co-located FM; FTR 7-13-81). Net: MBS. Rep: D & R Radio. Format: Adult contemp. News staff one; news progmg 18 hrs wkly. Target aud: 25-54; active adults of the 90s. Spec prog: Farm 6 hrs wkly. ■ W. Russell Withers Jr., pres; Celley Coffield, gen mgr & gen sls mgr; Tim Hawkins, opns dir & progmg dir; Andy Jeffries, mus dir; Jeff Killoren, news dir; Kevin Potter, chief engr. ■ Rates: $17; 16; 17; 15.

KOKX-FM—Jan 30, 1973: 95.3 mhz; 3 kw. Ant 175 ft. TL: N40 24 38 W91 25 57 (CP: 96.3 mhz; 50 kw, ant 492 ft.). Stereo. Hrs opn: 24. Format: Modern country. News staff one; news progmg 4 hrs wkly. Target aud: 25-54. Spec prog: Farm 5 hrs wkly. ■ Andy Jefferies, news dir. ■ Rates: Same as AM.

KYAT(FM)—Not on air, target date unknown: 105.9 mhz; 50 kw. Ant 492 ft. TL: N40 14 42 W91 34 22. c/o 847 Todd Preis Dr., Nashville, TN (37221). Licensee: David M. Lister.

Knoxville

KNIA(AM)—Aug 30, 1960: 1320 khz; 500 w-D, 222 w-N. TL: N41 19 40 W93 06 34. Hrs opn: 5 AM-11 PM. Box 31 (50138). (515) 842-3161. Licensee: M and H Broadcasting Inc. (acq 2-23-93; $768,000 with co-located FM; FTR 3-15-93). Net: AP. Format: Adult contemp. Spec prog: Relg 18 hrs wkly. ■ Mel Suhr, pres & sr vp; Jim Butler, gen mgr; Greg McComish, progmg dir & mus dir; Greg May, news dir.

KRLS(FM)—Co-owned with KNIA(AM). July 16, 1973: 92.1 mhz; 3 kw. Ant 300 ft. TL: N41 21 40 W93 00 15 (CP: 15.5 kw, ant 308 ft.). Stereo. Dups AM 100%. ■ Mike McGuire, news dir.

Le Mars

KLEM(AM)—Oct 12, 1954: 1410 khz; 1 kw-D, 63 w-N. TL: N42 49 05 W96 10 00. 37 2nd Ave. N.W. (51031). (712) 546-4121. Licensee: KLEM Inc. (acq 7-6-61). Net: AP. Format: Adult contemp. Spec prog: Farm 18 hrs wkly. ■ Paul W. Olson, pres & gen mgr; Roger Miller, gen sls mgr; Dave Ruden, progmg dir & mus dir; Larry Schmitz, news dir; Stan Culley, chief engr.

KKMA(FM)—Co-owned with KLEM(AM). Jan 1, 1967: 99.5 mhz; 100 kw. Ant 790 ft. TL: N42 28 56 W96 15 30. Stereo. Prog sep from AM. Wash atty: Gardner, Carton & Douglas.

Manchester

KMCH(FM)—Dec. 5, 1991: 94.7 mhz; 6 kw. Ant 328 ft. TL: N42 31 42 W91 22 53. Hrs opn: 24. Box 497, Professional Services Bldg., 223 W. Main (52057). Licensee: Susan I. Coloff. Rep: Farmakis Inc. Format: Adult contemporary, C&W. News staff one; news progmg 20 hrs wkly. Target aud: 25-64; northeast Iowa adults and farm population. Spec prog: Farm 7 hrs, sports 7 hrs, relg 4 hrs wkly. ■ Anthony G. Coloff, pres; James A. Coloff, gen mgr & gen sls mgr; Jackie Coates, mktg dir; James R. Dalton, progmg dir; Anthony James, mus dir; Laura Blobaum, news dir; Lori Scovel, pub affrs dir; George Nicholas, chief engr. ■ Rates: $14.70; $14.70; 14.70; 14.70.

Maquoketa

KMAQ(AM)—Aug 26, 1958: 1320 khz; 500 w-U. TL: N42 05 26 W90 37 43. Box 940, 129 N. Main St. (52060). (319) 652-2426. Licensee: Maquoketa Broadcasting Co. (acq 1965). Net: ABC/D; Brownfield, Radio Iowa. Rep: Farmakis. Wash atty: Miller & Fields. Format: C&W. News staff one; news progmg 20 hrs wkly. Target aud: General; adults, high percentage of farmers. Spec prog: Farm 10 hrs, polka 3 hrs wkly. ■ Dennis W. Voy, pres, gen mgr & progmg dir; Leighton Hepker, gen sls mgr & prom mgr; Chris Clasen, mus dir; Lyle Schepers, news dir; Tom Messerli, chief engr.

KMAQ-FM—Sept 1, 1967: 95.3 mhz; 3 kw. Ant 328 ft. TL: N42 05 26 W90 37 43. Stereo. Prog sep from AM. Net: ABC/D; Radio Iowa. Format: MOR.

Marshalltown

KDAO(AM)—Dec 16, 1978: 1190 khz; 250 w-D. TL: N42 04 17 W92 55 19. Box 538, 1930 N. Center St. (50158). (515) 752-4122. Licensee: MTN Broadcasting Inc. Net: ABC/C. Format: Adult contemp. Target aud: 25-54. ■ Mark K. Osmundson, pres & gen mgr; Rich Davis, sls dir.

KFJB(AM)—September 1923: 1230 khz; 1 kw-U. TL: N42 04 01 W92 58 10. Hrs opn: 5 AM-midnight. Box 698, 123 W. Main St. (50158). (515) 753-3361. FAX: (515) 752-7201. Licensee: Marshalltown Broadcasting Inc. (acq 12-29-86). Net: ABC/D; Brownfield. Rep: Torbet; Hyett/Ramsland. Format: Oldies. News staff 2; news progmg 12 hrs wkly. Target aud: 25-54. ■ David L. Nelson, pres; John Reardon, exec vp, gen mgr & gen sls mgr; Bob Moore, progmg dir & mus dir; Kevin Pink, Loren Lembke (asst), news dirs; Phil Benjamin, chief engr.

KXIA(FM)—Co-owned with KFJB(AM). January 1968: 101.1 mhz; 75 kw. Ant 300 ft. TL: N42 01 19 W92 59 51. Stereo. Hrs opn: 24. Prog sep from AM. Format: C&W. News staff 2; news progmg 6 hrs wkly. ■ Mike Watson, progmg dir; John Simmons, mus dir.

Mason City

***KCMR(FM)**—May 3, 1979: 97.9 mhz; 6 kw. Ant 300 ft. TL: N43 07 18 W93 11 32 (CP: Ant 315 ft.). Stereo. Box 979, 600 First St. N.W. (50402-0979). (515) 424-9300.

Licensee: TLC Broadcasting Corp. Format: Easy lstng, inspirational. Spec prog: Class 5 hrs, nostalgia 10 hrs wkly. ■ Larry Salge, gen mgr & chief engr; Karen Vaage, progmg dir & mus dir.

KGLO(AM)—Jan 17, 1937: 1300 khz; 5 kw-U, DA-N. TL: N43 08 50 W93 14 19. 341 Yorktown Pike (50401). (515) 423-1300. FAX: (515) 423-2906. Licensee: James Ingstad Broadcasting of Iowa Inc. Group owner: James Ingstad Broadcasting Inc. (acq 3-31-90; with co-located FM; FTR 1-29-90). Net: CBS. Rep: Katz. Format: MOR. News staff 2; news progmg 20 hrs wkly. Target aud: 25-35; adults. Spec prog: Farm 15 hrs wkly. ■ Kevin Lein, gen mgr; Tim Fleming, opns mgr & progmg mgr; Barbara J. Salz, gen sls mgr & mktg mgr; John Swinton, mus dir.

KIAI(FM)—Co-owned with KGLO(AM). November 1985: 93.9 mhz; 100 kw. Ant 790 ft. TL: N43 08 50 W93 14 39. Stereo. Box 1300 (50401). Format: Country.

KLSS-FM—Listing follows KRIB(AM).

KRIB(AM)—April 1948: 1490 khz; 1 kw-U. TL: N43 08 05 W93 12 30. Stereo. Box 1837, 19 First St. NE (50401). (515) 423-8634. FAX: (515) 423-8206. Licensee: Music Man Broadcasting Inc. Net: ABC/E; Iowa Net. Rep: McGavren Guild. Format: Oldies. News staff 2; news progmg 25 hrs wkly. Target aud: 25-54. Spec prog: Relg 5 hrs wkly. ■ Paul C. Hedberg, pres; Mark Hedberg, vp & gen mgr; Stu Tell, progmg dir; Rich Sprouse, news dir; Mike Hendrickson, chief engr.

KLSS-FM—Co-owned with KRIB(AM). Nov 1, 1967: 106.1 mhz; 100 kw. Ant 315 ft. TL: N43 08 31 W93 06 40. Stereo. Prog sep from AM. Format: Adult contemp. News staff 2. Target aud: 18-54. ■ Harry Oneil, mus dir. ■ Rates: $40; 34; 40; 24.

***KRNI(AM)**—Mar 1, 1948: 1010 khz; 1 kw-D, 15.8 w-N. TL: N43 08 31 W93 06 40. Hrs opn: 6 AM-midnight. Rebroadcasts KHKE(FM) Cedar Falls, 100%. c/o KHKE-FM, Univ. of Northern Iowa, Cedar Falls (50614-0359). (319) 273-6400. FAX: (319) 273-2862. Licensee: University of Northern Iowa (acq 8-31-90; FTR 8-27-90). Net: APR. Format: Class, jazz. News staff 3; news progmg 14 hrs wkly. Target aud: General. ■ Constantine Curris, pres; Doug Vernier, gen mgr; Jons Olsson, dev dir; David Hays, mktg dir; Carl Jenkins, progmg dir; Al Schares, mus dir; Greg Shanley, news dir; Walt Alliss, chief engr.

***KUNY(FM)**—Co-owned with KRNI(AM). Dec 15, 1987: 91.5 mhz; 8 kw-V. Ant 371 ft. TL: N43 09 27 W93 08 11. Stereo. Hrs opn: 24. c/o KUNI, Univ. of Northern Iowa, Cedar Falls (50614-0359). Net: APR, NPR. Format: Div. News staff 2; news progmg 35 hrs wkly. Spec prog: Black 12 hrs wkly.

Mount Pleasant

KILJ(AM)—December 1974: 1130 khz; 250 w-D. TL: N40 57 32 W91 35 01. 281 Radio Rd. (52641). (319) 385-8728. Licensee: KILJ AM Ltd. (acq 5-15-84; $210,000; FTR 3-26-84). Net: ABC/D. Format: Oldies. ■ Mike Stoffregen, pres & gen sls mgr; John R. Kuhens, gen mgr, progmg dir & mus dir; Tammara Bennett, news dir; Fred Jenkins, chief engr.

KILJ-FM—October 1970: 105.5 mhz; 24 kw. Ant 338 ft. TL: N40 56 32 W91 34 08 (CP: 3.3 kw). Stereo. Dups AM 25%. Net: ABC/D; Brownfield, Radio Iowa. Format: Country. News staff one. Target aud: 25-54.

Mount Vernon

***KRNL-FM**—Apr 1, 1948: 89.7 mhz; 10 w. Ant 984 ft. TL: N41 55 24 W91 25 18. Stereo. Cornell College (52314). (319) 895-4431. Licensee: Cornell College. Format: Free form. Target aud: 18-25; college students. ■ Zayda Hernandez, gen mgr; Don Brodale, stn mgr & news dir; Joseph Pavelich, prom dir; Ken Adrian, progmg dir; Corey Kaul, mus dir; Joesph Pavelich, pub affrs dir.

Muscatine

KFMH(FM)—Licensed to Muscatine. See Davenport.

KWPC(AM)—Jan 5, 1947: 860 khz; 250 w-D, 8w-N. TL: N41 26 43 W91 04 36. Stereo. Hrs opn: 5:30 AM-midnight. 3218 Mulberry Ave. (52761). (319) 263-2442. FAX: (319) 263-9206. Licensee: Muscatine Communications Inc. (acq 12-23-92; $300,000; FTR 1-25-93). Net: AP, USA; Brownfield. Format: Adult contemp, new age. News staff 3; news progmg 18 hrs wkly. Target aud: 25-54. Spec prog: Sp 6 hrs wkly. ■ John A. Schwandke, pres & gen mgr; Tim Scott, opns dir, progmg dir & mus dir; Warren J. Schwandke, rgnl sls mgr; Peggy Senzarino, news dir; Larry Kemper, chief engr. ■ Rates: $19.50; 19.50; 19.50; 19.50.

New Hampton

KCZE(FM)—Dec 1, 1992: 95.1 mhz; 5.5 kw. Ant 328 ft. TL: N43 02 46 W92 18 09. Stereo. 207 N. Main St., Charles City (50616); 108 W. Main St. (50659). (515) 228-1000; (515) 394-1000. FAX: (515) 228-1200. Licensee: Mega Media Ltd. (group owner). Net: NBC. Rep: J.L. Farmakis. Format: Adult contemp. News progmg 12 hrs wkly. Target aud: General. Spec prog: Farm 12 hrs wkly. ■ James B. Hebel, pres, gen mgr & gen sls mgr; Al Halder, stn mgr; Debra Lowe, opns mgr; Jim Bernard, progmg dir; John Waters, mus dir; Stan McHenry, asst mus dir; Mike Lyman, news dir; Gary Wenger, pub affrs dir; Tim Cook, chief engr.

New Sharon

KCWN(FM)—Not on air, target date unknown: 99.9. mhz; 25 kw. Ant 297 ft. 612 Franklin St., Pella (50219). Licensee: Crown Broadcasting Co.

Newton

KCOB(AM)—Sept 15, 1955: 1280 khz; 1 kw-D, 500 w-N. TL: N40 44 11 W93 01 12. 611 First Ave. E. (50208). (515) 792-5262. FAX: (515) 792-8403. Licensee: Central Iowa Broadcasting Inc. Net: CNN. Format: Country. News staff one; news progmg 15 hrs wkly. Target aud: 25-50. Spec prog: Farm 4 hrs wkly. ■ John E. Carl, pres; Frank Liebl, gen mgr & gen sls mgr; Terry Walters, progmg dir; Colleen Blazek, news dir; Walt Keith, chief engr. ■ Rates: $18; 16; 16; 10.

KCOB-FM—Jan 3, 1969: 95.9 mhz; 2.5 kw. Ant 354 ft. TL: N41 44 11 W93 01 12 (CP: 5.1 kw). Stereo. Hrs opn: 18. Dups AM 100%.

Northwood

KYTC(FM)—Oct 15, 1990: 102.7 mhz; 6 kw. Ant 318 ft. TL: N43 29 18 W93 14 12. Stereo. Hrs opn: 24. 839 Central Ave. (50459). (515) 324-1116. Licensee: Tri-Cities Broadcasting Ltd. (acq 11-15-90). Net: Tribune. Format: Oldies. News staff one; news progmg 6 hrs wkly. Target aud: 25-54. Spec prog: Gospel one hr, relg 2 hrs wkly. ■ Andrew P. Mark, pres; Marlin Hanson, chief engr. ■ Rates: $12; 12; 12; 9.

Oelwein

KOEL(AM)—July 23, 1950: 950 khz; 5 kw-D, 500 w-N, DA-2. TL: N42 39 26 W91 54 02. Hrs opn: 24. Box 391, 1259 Park Rd. (50662). (319) 283-1234. FAX: (319) 283-3615. Licensee: Independence Broadcasting Oelwein Corp. Group owner: Independence Broadcasting Corp. (acq 12-24-86; 6.75 million with co-located FM; FTR 12-1-86). Net: ABC/I. Rep: Banner. Format: Full svc adult contemp. News staff 3; news progmg 30 hrs wkly. Target aud: 35 plus. Spec prog: Farm 16 hrs wkly. ■ John Goodwill, CEO; Tom Parsley, gen mgr; Dave Horton, opns mgr; Mark Schmitz, gen sls mgr; Ryan Peterson, mus dir; Pam Ohrt, news dir; Arnold Zaruba, chief engr.

KOEL-FM—Dec 29, 1971: 92.3 mhz; 100 kw. Ant 1,000 ft. TL: N42 40 53 W91 52 52 (CP: 95.3 mhz, ant 991 ft.). Stereo. Hrs opn: 24. Prog sep from AM. 4708 University Ave., Cedar Falls (50613). (319) 277-0350. Net: ABC/E. Format: Country. ■ Tom Thomas, opns mgr; Ric Anthony, mus dir.

Osage

KCZY(FM)—July 9, 1980: 103.7 mhz; 6 kw. Ant 154 ft. TL: N43 19 20 W92 51 22 (CP: 6 kw, ant 154 ft.). Stereo. 207 N. Main St., Charles City (50616); 200 N. 7th St., (50461). (515) 228-1000; (515) 732-1000. FAX: (515) 228-1200. Licensee: Mega Media Ltd. (group owner). Net: NBC. Rep: Farmakis. Format: Adult contemp. News progmg 12 hrs wkly. Target aud: General. Spec prog: Farm 12 hrs wkly. ■ James B. Hebel, CEO, pres & gen mgr; Debra Lowe, opns mgr; Jim Hebel, gen sls mgr; Jim Bernard, progmg dir; John Waters, mus dir; Stan McHenry, asst mus dir; Mike Lyman, news dir & pub affrs dir; Tim Cook, chief engr.

Osceola

KJJC(FM)—Oct 4, 1982: 106.9 mhz; 50 kw. Ant 650 ft. TL: N41 01 05 W93 48 55. Stereo. Hrs opn: 24. Box 556 (50125). (515) 961-9804. FAX: (515) 961-3354. Licensee: Lifestyle Communications Inc. (acq 6-12-87; $500,000; FTR 4-20-87). Format: C&W. News staff 2; news progmg 4 hrs wkly. Target aud: 18-44; women. Spec prog: Farm 8 hrs wkly. ■ James S. McBride, pres; Steve Russell, vp & gen mgr; Kim Carrison-Hartley, vp prom; Ron Stevens, progmg dir; Jonnie Lynn Nordacker, news dir. ■ Rates: $21.50; 17.50; 17.50; 10.

Oskaloosa

KBOE(AM)—Nov 15, 1950: 740 khz; 250 w-D, 12 w-N. TL: N41 19 15 W92 38 44 (CP: 10 w-N). Hrs opn: 5 AM-midnight. Box 380, Hwy. 63 N. (52577). (515) 673-3493; (515) 673-3481. FAX: (515) 673-3495. Licensee: Jomast Corp. (acq 6-85; $850,000 with co-located FM; FTR 6-3-85). Net: ABC/D; Brownfield, Radio Iowa. Rep: Midwest. Format: Country. News staff one; news progmg 15 hrs wkly. Target aud: 25-50. Spec prog: Farm 5 hrs, gospel 11 hrs wkly. ■ Brad Muhl, pres; Scott Ewing, gen mgr & gen sls mgr; Bob Palameter, prom mgr; Ralph Bright, progmg dir & mus dir; Gary Engel, news dir; Gary Wilson, chief engr.

KBOE-FM—Feb 7, 1964: 104.9 mhz; 50 kw. Ant 492 ft. TL: N41 19 15 W92 38 44. Stereo. Hrs opn: 5 AM-midnight. Dups AM 100%.

***KIGC(FM)**—1975: 88.7 mhz; 230 w. Ant 93 ft. TL: N41 18 37 W92 38 49 (CP: ant 123 ft.). Stereo. Hrs opn: 8 AM-midnight. Student Union, William Penn College (52577). (515) 673-1095; (515) 673-1092. Licensee: William Penn College. Format: Adult contemp, div. News progmg one hr wkly. Target aud: 13-25. Spec prog: Jazz 2 hrs, Black 8 hrs wkly. ■ Don DeBoef, gen mgr & chief engr.

Ottumwa

KBIZ(AM)—1941: 1240 khz; 1 kw-U. TL: N41 00 00 W92 23 23. Box 190, Broadcast Ctr., 209 S. Market (52501). (515) 682-4535. FAX: (515) 684-5892. Licensee: Gillbro Communications Ltd. Net: CBS. Rep: Katz & Powell. Format: Classic oldies. News staff 2. Target aud: 25-54. Spec prog: Farm 12 hrs wkly. ■ Mel Moyer, gen mgr; Jaunita Hootman, rgnl sls mgr; Tom Rodgers, mus dir; Bill Willis, chief engr.

KTWA(FM)—Co-owned with KBIZ(AM). Dec 1984: 92.7 mhz; 3 kw. Ant 328 ft. TL: N41 01 29 W92 28 09. Prog sep from AM. Net: SMN. Format: Adult contemp.

KLEE(AM)—Aug 1, 1954: 1480 khz; 500 w-D, 33 w-N. TL: N41 01 27 W92 28 56. Stereo. Hrs opn: 24. 212 1/2 E. Main St. (52501). (515) 682-8711; (515) 682-8712. Licensee: FMC Broadcasting Inc. (acq 1-16-92; $400,000 with co-located FM; FTR 2-10-92). Net: NBC, NBC Talknet, MBS; Iowa Radio Net., Brownfield. Format: Country, news/talk. News staff one; news progmg 28 hrs wkly. Target aud: General; people on the move. Spec prog: Gospel 6 hrs, polka one hr wkly. ■ Thomas A. Palen, pres & gen mgr; Bill Bishop, chief opns & pub affrs dir; Newell Palen, gen sls mgr; Tom Palen, prom dir; Jill Green, mus dir; Fred Jenkins, chief engr. ■ Rates: $11; 10; 11; 10.

KOTM-FM—Co-owned with KLEE(AM). March 22, 1976: 97.7 mhz; 6 kw. Ant 200 ft. TL: N41 01 27 W92 28 56. Stereo. Prog sep from AM. Net: NBC the Source, Westwood One. Format: Contemp hit. News staff one; news progmg 14 hrs wkly. Target aud: Teens-50. ■ Rates: Same as AM.

KTWA(FM)—Listing follows KBIZ(AM).

Pella

***KCUI(FM)**—June 2, 1961: 89.1 mhz; 10 w. Ant 20 ft. TL: N41 24 00 W92 55 00. Hrs opn: 6 AM-2 AM. Central College (50219). (515) 628-5263; (515) 628-5262. Licensee: Central University of Iowa. Format: Classic rock, CHR, prog. News staff 2; news progmg 10 hrs wkly. Target aud: 15-30 plus; college campus and surrounding communities. Spec prog: Farm, folk, Ger, Fr, Pol, Sp, country, pub svc 5 hrs, new age 2 hrs, jazz 3 hrs wkly. ■ Cory Springhorn, gen mgr.

KFMG(FM)—Aug 1, 1976: 103.3 mhz; 100 kw. Ant 745 ft. TL: N41 32 18 W93 17 58 (CP: 98 kw, ant 1,043 ft.). Stereo. Hrs opn: 24. Suite 103, 108 3rd St., Des Moines (50309). (515) 282-1033. FAX: (515) 282-1062. Licensee: Intergalactic Communications Inc. (acq 4-20-92; $1.43 million; FTR 3-23-92). Net: Unistar. Rep: Katz & Powell. Format: Adult AOR. News staff one; news progmg 4 hrs wkly. Target aud: 25-44. Spec prog: Jazz 6 hrs wkly. ■ Ron Sorenson, pres, gen mgr & mus dir; Mark Vos, stn mgr & progmg dir; Dennis Brdicko, gen sls mgr; Vicki Sharp, prom dir; Douglass Cooper, news dir & pub affrs dir; Rich Sweetman, chief engr.

KNIA(AM)—See Knoxville.

Perry

KDLS(AM)—May 10, 1961: 1310 khz; 500 w-D, 300 w-N, DA-2. TL: N41 49 58 W94 02 15. Box 548, 2260 141st Dr. (50220). (515) 465-5357. Licensee: Perry Broadcasting Co. Net: MBS. Rep: Farmakis. Format:

Broadcasting & Cable Yearbook 1994
B-137

Iowa

Farm, C&W. Target aud: General. ■ Shirley Whitehead, pres; Marcia Murphy, gen mgr; John Patrick, opns dir; progmg dir, mus dir & news dir; Patrick Graney, gen sls mgr; Bill Zollman, chief engr.

KDLS-FM—Feb 26, 1971: 101.7 mhz; 3 kw. Ant 300 ft. TL: N41 49 58 W94 02 15. Stereo. Hrs opn: 6 AM-midnight. Dups AM 5%. Format: Country.

Red Oak

KOAK(AM)—Aug 16, 1968: 1080 khz; 250 w-D. TL: N41 01 00 W95 12 46. Box 465 (51566). (712) 623-2584. FAX: (712) 623-2583. Licensee: Montgomery County Broadcasting Co. Inc. (acq 3-1-84; $260,000 with co-located FM; FTR 2-20-84). Net: CBS. Format: MOR. ■ September Turner, gen mgr; Rod Bolton, gen sls mgr; Charles Maley, chief engr.

KOAK-FM—September 1979: 95.3 mhz; 20.4 kw. Ant 364 ft. TL: N41 01 00 W95 12 46. Stereo. Dups AM 100%.

Rock Valley

KQEP(FM)—Not on air, target date unknown: 106.9 mhz; 3 kw. Ant 328 ft. TL: N43 11 17 W96 17 44. 1943 Greenview, Northbrook, IL (60062). Licensee: Robert M. Mason.

Sheldon

KIWA(AM)—Oct 27, 1961: 1550 khz; 500 w-D, 11 w-N. TL: N43 11 00 W95 52 05. Hrs opn: 6 AM-midnight. 411 9th St. (51201). (712) 324-2597. FAX: (712) 324-2340. Licensee: Sheldon Broadcasting Co. Inc. (acq 10-27-61). Net: ABC/E. Rep: Farmakis. Format: MOR, country. News staff 2; news progmg 15 hrs wkly. Target aud: General; adult, farm, urban. ■ E.C. Stangland, pres; Frank Luepke, gen mgr & gen sls mgr; Walt Pruiksma, prom mgr; Bob Grote, progmg dir, mus dir & chief engr; Karen Mitchell, news dir. ■ Rates: $17; 17; 15; 15

KIWA-FM—Oct 1, 1971: 105.3 mhz; 50 kw. Ant 292 ft. TL: N43 11 00 W95 52 05. Stereo. Hrs opn: 6 AM-midnight. Format: C&W music/talk. News progmg 15 hrs wkly. Target aud: General. ■ Rates: $17; 17; 17; 14.

Shenandoah

KMA(AM)—Aug 12, 1925: 960 khz; 5 kw-U, DA-N. TL: N40 46 48 W95 21 23. Hrs opn: 5 AM-midnight. Box 960, 209 N. Elm, (51601). (712) 246-5270. FAX: (712) 246-5275. Licensee: May Broadcasting Co. (group owner). Net: ABC/I, Radio Iowa. Rep: Katz. Format: Country, news/talk. News staff 2; news progmg 15 hrs wkly. Target aud: 35-54. Spec prog: Farm. ■ Edward W. May, pres; Susan Friehe Christensen, gen mgr; Don Hansen, opns dir; Mark End, natl sls mgr; Tim Wayne, mus dir; Bill Bone, news dir; Steve Tunwall, chief engr.

*****KYFR(AM)**—1924: 920 khz; 5 kw-D, 2.5 w-N, DA-2. TL: N40 37 22 W95 14 42. Hrs opn: 24. 618 1/2 W. Sheridan Ave. (51601). (712) 246-5151. Licensee: Family Stations Inc. (group owner; acq 1976). Format: Relg. ■ Harold Camping, pres; Mike DeStefano, stn mgr; Darlene Farmer, chief engr.

Sioux Center

*****KDCR(FM)**—Aug 16, 1968: 88.5 mhz; 100 kw. Ant 320 ft. TL: N43 05 00 W96 09 50. Stereo. Dordt College Campus 498 4th Ave. N.E. (51250). (712) 722-0885. FAX: (712) 722-6244. Licensee: Dordt College Inc. (acq 1-19-90). Net: USA. Format: Class, relg. Spec prog: Farm 2 hrs, Dutch one hr wkly. ■ Dennis DeWaard, gen mgr & progmg dir; Jim Bolkema, mus dir; Tim Vos, news dir.

KTSB(FM)—Listing follows KVDB(AM).

KVDB(AM)—Nov 17, 1969: 1090 khz; 500 w-D, DA. TL: N43 03 22 W96 10 17. Hrs opn: Sunrise-sunset. 128 20th St. S.E. (51250). (712) 722-1090; (712) 722-1091. FAX: (712) 722-1102. Licensee: Tri-State Broadcasters. Rep: Farmakis. Wash atty: Lauren Colby. Format: Country, gospel. News staff one; news progmg 17 hrs wkly. Target aud: General. ■ Don Broek, pres; Shirley Wierda, gen sls mgr; Tom Aldrich, progmg dir; John Sliegers, news dir; Rich Haan, chief engr. ■ Rates: $14; 13; 11; 9.

KTSB(FM)—Co-owned with KVDB(AM). Oct 17, 1974: 94.3 mhz; 3 kw. Ant 300 ft. TL: N43 03 22 W96 10 17 (CP: 93.9 mhz, 50 kw, ant 492 ft.). Stereo. Dups AM 20%. Format: Adult contemp. ■ Don Broek, vp opns, vp sls & vp adv; Tom Juhl, vp mktg; Tom Aldrich, vp prom, vp progmg & mus dir; Rich Haan, vp engrg.

Sioux City

KGLI(FM)—Listing follows KWSL(AM).

KMNS(AM)—May 1, 1949: 620 khz; 1 kw-U, DA-2. TL: N42 22 15 W96 27 00. Box 177, 901 Steuben St. (51102). (712) 258-0628. FAX: (712) 277-3299. Licensee: Chesterman Communications Sioux City Inc. (acq 5-29-92; with co-located FM). Net: MBS. Rep: Christal. Format: C&W. Spec prog: Farm 20 hrs wkly. ■ George Pelletier, vp & gen mgr; Woody Gottburg, news dir; Jerry Gibbs, chief engr.

KSEZ(FM)—Co-owned with KMNS(AM). Feb 6, 1960: 97.9 mhz; 100 kw. Ant 643 ft. TL: N42 29 48 W96 18 55. Stereo. (712) 258-6740. Net: NBC the Source. Format: AOR. ■ Tim Harrison, progmg dir; Randy Michaels, mus dir.

*****KMSC(FM)**—April 1978: 88.3 mhz; 10 w. Ant 105 ft. TL: N42 28 28 W96 21 34. 1501 Morningside Ave. (51106). (712) 274-5299; (712) 274-5684. FAX: (712) 274-5420. Licensee: Morningside College Board of Directors. Format: Top-40, alternative. News staff 3; news progmg 4 hrs wkly. Target aud: 12-24; high school-college students. ■ David Diamond, chmn; Darrin Fullerton, gen mgr, stn mgr, opns mgr & mus dir; Staci D. Isaacson, dev dir; Jennifer Buys, dev mgr; Chris Bogenrief, prom dir & pub affrs dir; Richard Mackey, progmg dir; Tracy Schumacher, asst mus dir; Denise Gard, news dir; John Bennett, chief engr.

KSCJ(AM)—1927: 1360 khz; 5 kw-D, 1 kw-N, DA-N. TL: N42 33 24 W96 20 12. 2000 Indian Hills Dr. (51104). (712) 239-2100. FAX: (712) 239-3346. Licensee: Flagship Communications LP (acq 8-16-89; $962,611; FTR 9-5-89). Net: ABC/I, NBC Talknet, AP; Iowa Net. Rep: Katz-Powell. Format: News/talk, adult contemp. News staff 3; news progmg 24 hrs wkly. Target aud: 25-54. Spec prog: Farm 16 hrs wkly. ■ Tom Spies, gen mgr; Denny Bullock, gen sls mgr; Randy Renshaw, progmg dir; Dick Michaels, news dir; Samuel Seldon, chief engr.

KSEZ(FM)—Listing follows KMNS(AM).

KTFC(FM)—July 1, 1965: 103.3 mhz; 100 kw. Ant 271 ft. TL: N42 29 05 W96 18 10. Stereo. Hrs opn: 24. 1534 Buchanan Ave. (51106). (712) 252-4621; (712) 252-0327. Licensee: Donald A. Swanson. Format: Gospel. Spec prog: Farm one hr, news 10 hrs wkly. ■ Don Swanson, pres, gen mgr & chief engr; Charles Solomon, gen sls mgr.

*****KWIT(FM)**—Jan 31, 1978: 90.3 mhz; 100 kw. Ant 910 ft. TL: N42 28 56 W96 15 30. Stereo. Hrs opn: 24. 4647 Stone Ave. (51106-1997). Box 265 (51102-0265). (712) 274-6406. FAX: (712) 274-6411. Licensee: Western Iowa Tech Community College. Net: APR, NPR. Format: Classical, jazz, news/talk. News staff 2; news progmg 36 hrs wkly. Target aud: 25-54. Spec prog: New age 2 hrs, blues one hr, Sp 2 hrs wkly. ■ Dan R. Brooks, gen mgr; Douglas Kizzier, opns dir & mus dir; Gerald Iverson, dev dir, mktg dir & prom mgr; Sandra Ellis, sls dir; Gretchen Gondek, asst mus dir & pub affrs dir; Judeka Drogt, news dir; Dennis Semple, chief engr.

KWSL(AM)—April 1938: 1470 khz; 5 kw-U, DA-2. TL: N42 24 42 W96 25 30. Stereo. Box 1737 (51102). (712) 255-1470. Licensee: Cardinal Communications Inc. (group owner; acq 6-84; $725,000; FTR 4-2-84). Net: CNN, Unistar. Rep: Torbet. Wash atty: Dow, Lohnes & Albertson. Format: MOR, news, big band. News staff one; news progmg 24 hrs wkly. Target aud: 35 plus. Spec prog: Farm 2 hrs wkly. ■ John D. Daniels, pres; Ted Mann, vp & gen mgr; Rick Schorg, gen sls mgr; Candice Nash, prom mgr; Kevin Collins, progmg dir; Mike Newhouse, news dir; Ted Mahn, chief engr.

KGLI(FM)—Co-owned with KWSL(AM). Mar 11, 1974: 95.5 mhz; 100 kw. Ant 900 ft. TL: N42 30 53 W96 18 13 (CP: Ant 984 ft.). Stereo. Prog sep from AM. (712) 258-5595. FAX: (712) 252-2430. Net: ABC/C. Format: Hot adult contemp. Target aud: 25-54.

Sioux Rapids

KTFG(FM)—1991: 102.9 mhz; 50 kw. Ant 479 ft. TL: N42 54 34 W95 09 35. 1534 Buchanan Ave. Sioux City (51106). (712) 283-2335. Licensee: Donald A. Swanson. Format: Gospel. ■ Donald A. Swanson, gen mgr.

Spencer

KICD(AM)—December 1942: 1240 khz; 1 kw-U. TL: N43 10 00 W95 08 45. Box 7248 (51301). (712) 262-1240. FAX: (712) 262-2076. Licensee: Iowa Great Lakes Broadcasting Co. (acq 4-45). Net: CBS. Rep: Katz. Format: Farm, MOR. ■ William R. Sanders, pres, gen mgr & gen sls mgr; Bill Campbell, progmg dir; Curtis Dean, news dir; Joseph Schloss, chief engr.

KICD-FM—Sept 17, 1965: 107.7 mhz; 100 kw. Ant 310 ft. TL: N43 10 00 W95 08 45. Stereo. Prog dups AM 30%. Format: Country, farm. ■ Rhonda Wedeking, progmg dir.

KIGL(FM)—February 1979: 104.9 mhz; 3 kw. Ant 298 ft. TL: N43 09 24 W95 04 53. Stereo. Hrs opn: 24. Box 7248, 2600 N. Hwy. Blvd. (51301). (712) 262-3300; (712) 262-1240. FAX: (712) 262-2076. Licensee: Iowa Great Lakes Broadcasting Co. Inc. (acq 9-3-93; $250,000; FTR 9-27-93). Net: CNN. Wash atty: Leventhal, Senter & Lerman. Format: Hot adult contemp. News staff 2; news progmg 14 hrs wkly. Target aud: 25-54. ■ William R. Sanders, gen mgr. ■ Rates: $16; 16; 16; 16.

Spirit Lake

KUOO(FM)—April 1, 1985: 103.9 mhz; 50 kw. Ant 492 ft. TL: N43 20 34 W93 12 24. Stereo. Box 528, Hwy. 9 W. (51360). (712) 336-5800. FAX: (712) 336-1634. Licensee: Campus Radio Co. Inc. Group owner: Hedberg Broadcasting Group. Net: NBC. Format: Adult contemp. News staff 2; news progmg 16 hrs wkly. Target aud: 25-54. Spec prog: Farm 5 hrs wkly. ■ Paul C. Hedberg, pres; Ronald Kruse, gen mgr; Jeff Thee, prom dir; Joey Elbert, progmg dir; Mike Dye, mus dir; Paul Koch, news dir; Mike Hendrickson, chief engr. ■ Rates: $24; 21; 24; 21.

Storm Lake

KAYL(AM)—November 1948: 990 khz; 250 w-D. TL: N42 37 56 W95 09 54 (CP: TL: N42 38 05 W95 10 10). Box 1037, 604 Lake Ave. (50588). (712) 732-3520. FAX: (712) 732-1746. Licensee: Northwest Iowa Broadcasting Co. Group owner: Hedberg Broadcasting Group (acq 7-90; $921,400 with co-located FM; FTR 8-6-90). Net: ABC/I. Format: MOR, div. Spec prog: Farm 20 hrs wkly. ■ Paul Hedberg, pres; Mike Puetz, gen mgr; Joel Hermann, news dir; Mike Hendrickson, chief engr.

KAYL-FM—February 1949: 101.5 mhz; 100 kw. Ant 331 ft. TL: N42 37 56 W95 09 54 (CP: Ant 400 ft., TL: N42 38 05 W95 10 10). Stereo. Format: Adult contemp, loc news & sports.

Stuart

KKRF(FM)—Aug 12, 1993: 107.9 mhz; 2.75 kw. Ant 472 ft. TL: N41 30 25 W94 18 06. Stereo. Hrs opn: 24. 212 S. Division (50250); R.R. #2, Box 106A, La Crescent, MN (55947). (515) 523-1107. FAX: (515) 523-1817. Licensee: Coon Valley Communications. Format: Traditional country. News staff 2; news progmg 10 hrs wkly. Target aud: 25-64. Spec prog: Farm 5 hrs wkly. ■ Lee Norman, pres & stn mgr; Pat Delaney, CFO, mus dir & engrg dir; Steve Fuerst, opns mgr & news dir; Dawn Jensen, sls dir.

Twin Lakes

KTLB(FM)—Oct 5, 1975: 105.9 mhz; 25 kw. Ant 328 ft. TL: N42 32 09 W94 40 48. Stereo. Hrs opn: 18. Box 105, 2269 N. Twin Lakes Rd., Rockwell City (50579). (712) 297-7586. FAX: (712) 297-7588. Licensee: Twin Lakes Broadcasting Inc. Net: ABC/D; Brownfield, Radio Iowa. Format: Adult contemp, country. News staff one; news progmg 15 hrs wkly. Target aud: 20 plus; farmers. Spec prog: Big band 4 hrs, farm 15 hrs, gospel 2 hrs, relg 2 hrs wkly. ■ Frank Donnelly, pres, gen mgr, gen sls mgr & prom mgr; Sheila R. Phipps, mus dir & pub affrs dir; Bill Hiler, chief engr. ■ Rates: $12; 8.25; 8.25; 6.

Vinton

KVYV(FM)—Not on air, target date unknown: 107.1 mhz; 6 kw. Ant 328 ft. TL: N42 03 57 W91 54 06. c/o Box 2126, McCabe & Allen, Manassas Park, VA (22111). Licensee: Kenneth C. Rosato.

Washington

KCII(AM)—Nov 12, 1961: 1380 khz; 500 w-D. TL: N41 18 18 W91 42 36. Hrs opn: 5:30 AM-11 PM. Box 524, 110 E. Main St. (52353). (319) 653-2113. FAX: (319) 653-3500. Licensee: Washington Radio Inc. (acq 10-1-70). Net: AP. Rep: Rgnl Reps. Format: Adult contemp, oldies. News staff one; news progmg 4 hrs wkly. Target aud: 25-54. Spec prog: Farm, Local & University of Iowa sports. ■ Brian Sines, gen mgr; Joe Williams, progmg dir; Mary Ann Haas, mus dir; Jim Buitendorp, news dir; Mike Worley, chief engr. ■ Rates: $18.25; 17.25; 18.25; 16.25.

KCII-FM—1975: 95.3 mhz; 3 kw. Ant 300 ft. TL: N41 18 18 W91 42 36. Stereo. Dups AM 100%. ■ Rates: Same as AM.

Waterloo

KBBG(FM)—July 26, 1978: 88.1 mhz; 9.5 kw. Ant 150 ft. TL: N42 30 35 W92 19 35. Stereo. Hrs opn: 19. 527 1/2 Cottage St. (50703). (319) 234-1441; (319) 235-1515. Licensee: Afro-American Community Broadcasting Inc. Net: American Urban. Format: Black, btfl mus, jazz. Target aud: General. Spec prog: Gospel. ■ Louise Porter, pres; Bennie Walker Jr., gen mgr, progmg dir & news dir; Tracy Wilson, mus dir.

KFMW(FM)—Listing follows KWLO(AM).

KNWS(AM)—1953: 1090 khz; 1 kw-D. TL: N42 26 38 W92 17 58. 4880 Texas (50702). (319) 296-1975. FAX: (319) 296-1977. Licensee: Northwestern College. Group owner: Northwestern College Radio Network (acq 4-2-53). Net: UPI. Format: Relg, news. News staff one. Target aud: 25-54. ■ Jeff Seeley, gen mgr; Betty Brandhorst, mus dir; Pat Beiner, news dir; David Dobes, chief engr.

KNWS-FM—1965: 101.9 mhz; 100 kw. Ant 1,010 ft. TL: N42 24 48 W92 00 25. Stereo. Dups AM 20%. Format: Good mus & relg.

KOKZ(FM)—Listing follows KXEL(AM).

KWLO(AM)—November 1947: 1330 khz; 5 kw-U, DA-2. TL: N42 28 56 W92 16 16. Stereo. Hrs opn: 24. Box 1330 (50704); 514 Jefferson St. (50701). (319) 234-2200. Licensee: Park Radio of Iowa Inc. Group owner: Park Communications Inc. (acq 10-6-86). Net: NBC, MBS. Rep: Katz. Wash atty: Wiley, Rein & Fielding. Format: Full service w/classic oldies News staff 6; news progmg 65 hrs wkly. Spec prog: Sports, farm. ■ Roy H. Park, chmn; Wright M. Thomas, pres; Rick Prusator, vp; Don Morehead, gen mgr; Fred Hendrickson, gen sls mgr; Brad Williams, prom mgr; Dave McCormick, progmg dir; Kathy Flynn, news dir; Roger Lundeen, chief engr.

KFMW(FM)—Co-owned with KWLO(AM). November 1968: 107.9 mhz; 100 kw. Ant 1,850 ft. TL: N42 24 04 W91 50 43 (CP: 76.54 kw). Stereo. Hrs opn: 24. Prog sep from AM. Net: Unistar. Format: Classic rock, AOR, CHR. ■ Mark Hansen, progmg dir & mus dir.

KXEL(AM)—July 14, 1942: 1540 khz; 50 kw-U, DA-N. TL: N42 10 46 W92 18 15. Box 1540, 3721 Independence Ave. (50703). (319) 233-3371. Licensee: Bahakel Communications (acq 1-11-58). Net: ABC/l. Rep: Katz. Format: C&W. Spec prog: Farm 18 hrs wkly. ■ Cy N. Bahakel, pres; Tim Mathews, gen sls mgr; Dan Olson, progmg dir; Harlan Hanna, news dir; Leonard Tompkins, chief engr. ■ Rates: $38; 31; 38; na.

KOKZ(FM)—Co-owned with KXEL(AM). Nov 21, 1962: 105.7 mhz; 100 kw. Ant 1,403 ft. TL: N42 24 35 W92 05 10. Stereo. Net: ABC/C. Format: Contemp hit. Target aud: 18-49; upscale, college educated. ■ Tim Mathew, gen mgr. ■ Rates: $47; 40; 47; 36.

Waukon

KNEI(AM)—July 1, 1967: 1140 khz; 1 kw-D. TL: N43 17 13 W91 28 06. Box 151, Hwy. 9 N. (52172). (319) 568-3476. FAX: (319) 568-3391. Licensee: David H. Hogendorn (acq 1972). Net: CBS; Radio Iowa, Brownfield. Wash atty: Sam Miller. Format: Country. News staff one; news progmg 21 hrs wkly. Target aud: 25-65. ■ David H. Hogendorn, pres & gen mgr; Chuck Bloxham, opns dir & gen sls mgr; Chuck Allen, vp prom & progmg dir; Chelsey Wagner, mus dir; Tom Brehmer, news dir; Rod Perry, chief engr. ■ Rates: $8.50; 8.50; 8.50; 8.50.

KNEI-FM—Sept 1, 1968: 103.9 mhz; 3 kw. Ant 200 ft. TL: N43 17 32 W91 27 35 (CP: 103.5 mhz, 30 kw, ant 492 ft., TL: N43 17 38 W91 29 57). Stereo. Dups AM 100%. Box 492, Hwy. 9 N. (52172).

Waverly

KWAR(FM)—Sept 15, 1951: 89.1 mhz; 40 w. Ant 125 ft. TL: N42 43 24 W92 28 05. Box 1003, Wartburg College (50677-0903). (319) 352-8222. FAX: (319) 352-8501. Licensee: Wartburg College. Format: Educ, div. Spec prog: Class 10 hrs, jazz 10 hrs wkly.

KWAY(AM)—May 6, 1958: 1470 khz; 1 kw-D, 61 w-N, DA-2. TL: N42 42 13 W92 28 21. Box 307 (50677). (319) 352-3550. FAX: (319) 352-3601. Licensee: Al Suhr Enterprises. Net: AP. Format: 50s and 60s. ■ Al Suhr, pres & gen mgr; Bob Foster, progmg dir.

KWAY-FM—Dec 21, 1971: 99.3 mhz; 3 kw. Ant 180 ft. TL: N42 42 13 W92 28 21. Format: Light adult contemp. ■ Bob Foster, opns mgr.

Webster City

KQWC(AM)—Feb 5, 1950: 1570 khz; 250 w-D, 132 w-N. TL: N42 27 45 W93 48 05 (CP: 147 w). Box 550 (50595). (515) 832-1570. FAX: (515) 832-2079. Licensee: Gorich Radio Corp. Group owner: GO Radio Inc. (acq 10-24-91; $650,000 with co-located FM; FTR 11-11-91). Net: NBC/D, NBC Talknet. Rep: Farmakis. Format: Adult contemp, news, talk. News staff one; news progmg 28 hrs wkly. Target aud: 25-70; affluent with max spendable income. Spec prog: Farm 8 hrs wkly. ■ Glenn R. Olson, pres; Larry M. Schultz, gen mgr & gen sls mgr; Tony Thomas, progmg dir; Patrick Powers, news dir; Charlie Mailey, chief engr. ■ Rates: $17; 13.5; 17; 12.

KQWC-FM—1969: 95.7 mhz; 25 kw. Ant 328 ft. TL: N42 28 04 W93 47 48. Stereo. 1020 E. Second St. (50595). (Acq 1972). Net: ABC/D. News progmg 30 hrs wkly. ■ Frank Vance, opns dir; Kent Bailey, sls dir & mktg dir; Scott Schumaker, prom dir; Tony Thomas, mus dir. ■ Rates: Same as AM.

West Des Moines

KWDM(FM)—March 1976: 88.7 mhz; 100 w. Ant 170 ft. TL: N41 35 25 W93 45 10. Stereo. Hrs opn: 12. Valley High School, 1140 Valley West Dr. (50266). (515) 226-2600. Licensee: West Des Moines Community School District. Wash atty: Reddy, Begley & Martin. Format: Class rock, talk. News staff one; news progmg 3 hrs wkly. Target aud: General; educ facility-var progmg. Spec prog: Sports 3 hrs wkly.

Winterset

KBBM(FM)—Not on air, target date unknown: 95.7 mhz; 6 kw. Ant 328 ft. TL: N41 24 02 W93 54 58. Box 736, Myrtle Beach, SC (29577). Licensee: Pro Radio Inc. (acq 8-18-92; $51,000; FTR 9-7-92).

Kansas

LAUREN A. COLBY
301-663-1086
COMMUNICATIONS ATTORNEY
Special Attention to
Difficult Cases

Abilene

KABI(AM)—April 8, 1963: 1560 khz; 250 w-D. TL: N38 55 46 W97 14 48. Box 69, 200 N. Broadway (67410). (913) 263-1560. FAX: (913) 263-0166. Licensee: Eagle Broadcasting Co. (acq 10-24-91; $650,000 with co-located FM; FTR 11-11-91). Net: CBS. Format: Country. News staff one. Target aud: 35 plus; local residents Dickinson County. ■ John Vanier II, pres; Jerry Hinrikus, vp; Joe Eck, opns mgr & chief engr; Larry Avery, vp sls; Bruce Crandall, progmg mgr; John Anderson, news dir.

KSAJ-FM—Co-owned with KABI(AM). Dec 10, 1968: 98.5 mhz; 100 kw. Ant 443 ft. TL: N38 47 50 W97 13 01. Stereo. Prog sep from AM. Format: Oldies. News staff one. Target aud: 25-54; baby boomers. ■ Jerry Hinrikus, gen mgr; Bruce Crandall, progmg dir.

Andover

KDLE(FM)—Not on air, target date unknown: 93.9 mhz; 25 kw. Ant 328 ft. 331 Lookout Point, Hot Springs, AR (71913). Licensee: Viola Ann Violet and Gary Violet.

Arkansas City

KSOK(AM)—Jan 1, 1947: 1280 khz; 1 kw-D, 100 w-N. TL: N37 05 19 W97 01 56. Hrs opn: 24. Box 917 (67005); Box 843. Winfield (67156). (316) 442-5400; (316) 221-1440. FAX: (316) 442-5401. Licensee: Cowley County Communications. Net: NBC, Unistar, Talknet; Kan. Info. Format: Country, news/talk. News staff one; news progmg 10 hrs wkly. Target aud: 34 plus; agriculturally oriented listeners seeking info. Spec prog: Farm 10 hrs, relg 5 hrs wkly. ■ Kelly Porter, gen sls mgr; Marty Mutti, progmg dir; Cheryl Higgins, news dir; Dave Foster, chief engr. ■ Rates: $14.35; 10.35; 12.35; 6.

KYQQ(FM)—Nov 1, 1979: 106.5 mhz; 100 kw. Ant 1,278 ft. TL: N37 21 24 W96 57 55. Stereo. Hrs opn: 24. Box 650, Wichita (67201); Suite 480, 100 E. English, Wichita (67202). (316) 265-1065. FAX: (316) 265-0246. Licensee: Harris Broadcasting Systems Inc. (acq 3-3-90).

Wash atty: Fisher Wayland. Format: Hot country. News progmg one hr wkly. Target aud: 18-49; upper income, well educated. Spec prog: Relg 2 hrs wkly. ■ Will R. Harris, chmn; Des Taylor, gen mgr; Gerre Miller, opns dir; Doug Downs, progmg dir; Cliff Roberts, mus dir; Larry Waggoner, chief engr. ■ Rates: $35; 30; 32; 25.

Atchison

KERE(AM)—July 28, 1939: 1470 khz; 1 kw-U, DA-1. TL: N39 37 09 W94 59 27. Box G (66002). (913) 367-1470. FAX: (913) 367-7021. Licensee: KARE Radio Inc. (acq 1-2-81). Net: NBC. Rep: Savalli, Gray. Format: Adult contemp. Spec prog: Farm 7 hrs wkly. ■ William D. Purkis, pres & gen mgr; James Ervin, gen sls mgr; Harold Scheopner, progmg dir & news dir; Sam Van Horn, chief engr.

Augusta

KLLS(FM)—Apr 1, 1992: 104.5 mhz; 46 kw. Ant 512 ft. TL: N37 48 13 W96 57 04. Hrs opn: 24. 1632 S. Maize Rd., Wichita (67202). Licensee: Lesso Inc. (acq 3-18-92). Format: Hot Adult contemp. News staff 2; news progmg 8 hrs wkly. Target aud: 25-54. ■ Larry Steckline, pres; Greg Steckline, vp & gen mgr; Dane Daniel, prom dir; Doug Burton, progmg dir; Bill Nolan, engrg dir. ■ Rates: $20; 15; 20; 10.

Baldwin City

KNBU(FM)—Nov 29, 1965: 89.7 mhz; 100 w. Ant 118 ft. TL: N38 46 45 W95 11 15. 7th and Dearborn Sts. (66006). (913) 594-6451 EXT. 329. FAX: (913) 594-3570. Licensee: Baker University. Net: Unistar. Format: C&W, classic rock. Spec prog: Jazz 15 hrs wkly. ■ Richard Bayha, gen mgr; Pat Tubach, progmg dir. ■ KNBU-TV affil.

Baxter Springs

KMOQ(FM)—Feb 1, 1980: 107.1 mhz; 3 kw. Ant 300 ft. TL: N37 07 34 W94 42 12. Stereo. 2905 E. 4th St., Joplin, MO (64801). (417) 623-2107. FAX: (417) 782-5111. Licensee: T.G.S. Communications Inc. (acq 2-17-87; $350,000; FTR 12-15-86). Net: SMN. Format: Oldies. Target aud: 25-54. ■ Thomas Schulte, pres & gen mgr; Patty Schulte, stn mgr; Lon Larkin, progmg dir; Jack Leutzinger, chief engr.

Belle Plaine

KOUY(FM)—Not on air, target date unknown: 92.7 mhz; 4.6 kw. Ant 754 ft. 331 Point Lookout, Hot Springs, AR (71913). Licensee: Daniel D. Smith (acq 2-16-93; $10,700; FTR 3-8-93).

Belleville

KREP(FM)—June 26, 1984: 92.1 mhz; 6 kw. Ant 300 ft. TL: N39 45 00 W97 36 48. Stereo. Hrs opn: 17. 2307 W. Frontage Rd. (66935). (913) 527-2266; (913) 527-2267. FAX: (913) 527-5919. Licensee: First Republic Broadcasting Corp. Net: ABC/D. Format: Country. News staff one; news progmg 20 hrs wkly. Target aud: 25-55. Spec prog: Farm markets. ■ Deborah M. Ball, pres; John K. Montgomery, gen sls mgr & prom mgr; Steve St. James, news dir; Herbert R. Hoeflicker, chief engr. ■ Rates: $10; 10; 10; 10.

Beloit

KVSV(AM)—Nov 21, 1979: 1190 khz; 2.5 kw-D, DA. TL: N39 26 53 W98 04 45. Box 7 (67420). (913) 738-2206. Licensee: Solomon Valley Broadcasting Inc. (acq 10-15-82; FTR 10-18-82). Net: ABC/D; Kan. Agri. Format: Full svc adult contemp. News staff one; news progmg 11 hrs wkly. Target aud: General; adults. Spec prog: Farm 7 hrs wkly. ■ Charles K. Frodsham, pres, gen mgr; Kent Heier, news dir.

KVSV-FM—Nov 11, 1980: 105.5 mhz; 50 kw. Ant 443 ft. TL: N39 28 09 W98 05 37. Stereo. Hrs opn: 6 AM-midnight. Prog sep from AM. Format: Btfl mus.

Burlington

KSNP(FM)—June 14, 1990: 95.3 mhz; 6 kw. Ant 349 ft. TL: N38 10 08 W95 39 07. Box 233 (66839). (316) 364-8807. FAX: (316) 364-2573. Licensee: Coffey County Broadcasting Co. Net: ABC; Kansas Info, Kansas Agri. Format: Adult contemp. ■ Bob Lawrence, gen mgr.

Caney

KEOJ(FM)—Oct 15, 1992: 101.1 mhz; 3 kw. Ant 328 ft. TL: N36 58 19 W95 53 47. Stereo. Hrs opn: 24. Box 1250,

Kansas

Old Frankoma Rd., Sapulpa, OK (74067). (918) 224-2620. FAX: (918) 224-4984. Licensee: KXOJ Inc. (group owner; acq 4-29-92; grpsl). Net: UPI. Format: Contemp Christian music. Target aud: 18-35; young married Christians. ■ Mike Stephens, pres & gen mgr; Joy Stephens, vp; Dale Stephens, stn mgr; Jim Malone, mktg dir & adv dir; Seth Andrews, prom dir; Randall Nance, progmg dir; Bill Davis, chief engr. ■ Rates: $13.75; 13.75; 13.75; 13.75.

Chanute

KKOY(AM)—Nov 17, 1952: 1460 khz; 1 kw-D, 57 w-N. TL: N37 41 25 W95 28 08. Hrs opn: 6 AM-midnight. Box 788 (66720). (316) 431-3700; (316) 431-1460. FAX: (316) 431-4643. Licensee: Neosho County Broadcasting Inc. (acq 5-1-68). Net: ABC/I, ABC TalkRadio; Kansas Info, Kansas Agri. Format: Adult contemp, news/talk. News staff 3. ■ Dale W. McCoy Jr., pres & gen mgr; Wayne Sparks, gen sls mgr; Mike Sutcliffe, progmg dir; Brian Edwards, news dir; Taylor Fast, chief engr. ■ Rates: $14; 10; 14; 10.

KKOY-FM—Jan 1, 1971: 105.5 mhz; 3 kw. Ant 170 ft. TL: N37 41 25 W95 28 08. Stereo. Hrs opn: 6 AM-midnight. Prog sep from AM. Net: ABC. Format: Oldies. ■ Rates: Same as AM.

Clay Center

KCLY(FM)—Jan 6, 1978: 100.9 mhz; 2.8 kw. Ant 255 ft. TL: N39 21 53 W97 05 32 (CP: 6 kw). Stereo. Box 16, 5th and Lincoln (67432). (913) 632-5661. Licensee: Taylor Communications. Net: ABC/D; Kan. Info. Rep: Keystone (unwired net). Format: C&W. ■ Phil Taylor, pres; Vernadell Yarrow, gen mgr.

Clearwater

KSPG(FM)—Not on air, target date Spring 1994: 98.7 mhz; 50 kw. Ant 492 ft. TL: N37 24 11 W97 35 22. Stereo. Hrs opn: 24. 331 Lookout Pt. Hot Springs, AR (71913). (501) 525-1736. FAX: (501) 525-1100. Licensee: Gary L. Violet (group owner). Wash atty: Blair, Joyce & Silva. Format: Hot country. ■ Gary Violet, gen mgr & chief engr; Ann Violet, opns mgr; Dan Smith, sls dir; Lymon James, vp progmg; Jack Wellman, mus dir; Bruce Adamek, pub affrs dir. ■ Rates: $10; 10; 10; 10.

Coffeyville

KGGF(AM)—1930: 690 khz; 10 kw-D, 5 kw-N, DA-2. TL: N37 08 58 W95 28 27. Box 1087, 306 W. 8th St. (67337). (316) 251-3800. FAX: (316) 252-9210. Licensee: KGGF-KUSN Inc. Group owner: Mahaffey Enterprises Inc. (acq 12-26-90; $750,000 with co-located FM; FTR 1-14-91). Net: ABC/E. Rep: Banner. Format: News/talk. News staff 3; news progmg 32 hrs wkly. Target aud: 35 plus. ■ Bob Tesh, prom mgr & progmg dir; Lance Allred, news dir; Bob Cauthon, chief engr.

KUSN(FM)—Co-owned with KGGF(AM). Sept 1, 1983: 98.9 mhz; 6 kw. Ant 300 ft. TL: N37 06 28 W95 43 22 (CP: 6 kw, ant 305 ft.). Stereo. Format: Adult contemp.

Colby

KQLS(FM)—Listing follows KXXX(AM).

*****KTCC(FM)**—May 1974: 91.9 mhz; 3 kw. Ant 199 ft. TL: N39 22 34 W101 03 08. Stereo. Hrs opn: 24. 1255 S. Range (67701). (913) 462-3984, ext. 282; (913) 462-6762. FAX: (913) 462-8315. Licensee: Colby Community College. Net: AP, CNN. Format: CHR. News staff 2; news progmg 14 hrs wkly. Target aud: 18-25. ■ Jon Burlew, gen mgr, mktg dir, adv dir & mus dir; Carrie Jones, stn mgr, prom mgr, progmg dir & asst mus dir; Bernie Schmid, chief engr.

KXXX(AM)—August 1947: 790 khz; 5 kw-D. TL: N39 23 35 W101 00 06. Hrs opn: 16. 1065 S. Range (67701). (913) 462-3984. FAX: (913) 462-3307. Licensee: Lesso Inc. (group owner). Net: MBS. Rep: McGavren Guild. Format: Contemp country. News staff one; news progmg 5 hrs wkly. Target aud: 35-55; rural audience. ■ Bob Isaacson, gen mgr; Dave Lamb, progmg dir & mus dir; Bill Nolan, chief engr.

KQLS(FM)—Co-owned with KXXX(AM). September 1971: 100.3 mhz; 100 kw. Ant 610 ft. TL: N39 28 50 W100 54 34. Stereo. (913) 462-3306. Format: Adult contemp. Target aud: 18-34; general.

Columbus

KOCD(FM)—Dec 25, 1982: 105.3 mhz; 6.1 kw. Ant 308 ft. TL: N37 14 47 W94 44 52 (CP: 25 kw, ant 210 ft., TL: N37 01 57 W94 49 44). Stereo. Hrs opn: 24. 3001 W. 13th St., Joplin, MO (64801). (417) 624-1230. FAX: (417) 624-7101. Licensee: Saturn Communications Inc. (acq 1-11-

90; $200,000; FTR 1-15-90). Rep: Katz. Format: AOR. News staff one; news progmg 2 hrs wkly. Target aud: 18-49. Spec prog: Blues 5 hrs wkly. ■ Andrew S. Wolfson, pres; Kevin McKelvy, gen mgr; Vance Lewis, opns mgr & progmg dir; Dennis Burns, gen sls mgr; Darren Hansen, prom mgr & pub affrs dir; Ann Harlo, mus dir; Jack Leutzinger, chief engr. ■ Rates: $25; 28; 22; 18.

Concordia

KCKS(FM)—Listing follows KNCK(AM).

KNCK(AM)—Feb 6, 1954: 1390 khz; 500 w-D, 54 w-N. TL: N39 33 58 W97 41 04. Box 629, Rte one W. 11th St. (66901). (913) 243-1414. Licensee: KNCK Inc. (acq 10-18-89; $190,000 with co-located FM; FTR 11-6-89). Net: SMN; Kan. Agri., Kan. Info. Format: Country. Target aud: 45 plus. ■ Joe Jimdra, pres, gen mgr & progmg dir; Marvin Hoffman, chief engr.

KCKS(FM)—Co-owned with KNCK(AM). Sept 1, 1978: 95.3 mhz; 2.5 kw. Ant 329 ft. TL: N39 33 58 W97 41 04. Stereo. Format: Oldies.

*****KVCO(FM)**—May 1, 1977: 88.3 mhz; 126.5 w. Ant 77 ft. TL: N39 33 17 W97 39 48. Stereo. Box 1002, 2221 Campus Dr. (66901). (913) 243-1435. Licensee: Cloud County Community College. Net: CNN. Format: Div. News progmg 3 hrs wkly. Target aud: 16-30 plus; students and young adults. ■ David Norlin, gen mgr.

Copeland

*****KJIL(FM)**—Sept 5 1992: 99.1 mhz; 100 kw. Ant 935 ft. TL: N37 29 01 W100 34 53. Hrs opn: 24. Box 991, 909 W. Carthage, Meade (67864-0991). (316) 873-2991. FAX: (316) 873-2755. Licensee: Great Plains Christian Radio Inc. Net: Moody, Skylight, USA. Format: Contemp Christian. Target aud: Evangelical Christians ages 25-60. ■ Don Hughes, gen mgr; Michael Luskey, opns dir; Rebecca Ottun, pub affrs dir; Jerry Miller, chief engr.

KYBD(FM)—Not on air, target date unknown: 98.1 mhz; 100 kw. Ant 666 ft. TL: N37 30 00 W100 40 00. c/o Sound Broadcasting Inc., 37 Martin St., Rehoboth, MA (02769). Licensee: Sound Broadcasting Inc.

Derby

KRZZ-FM—1978: 96.3 mhz; 50 kw. Ant 492 ft. TL: N37 37 03 W97 20 11. Stereo. 2402 E. 37th St., Witchita (67219). (316) 832-9600. FAX: (316) 838-2800. Licensee: Prism Radio Partners (acq 1993; FTR 9-20-93). Net: CBS. Rep: D&R Radio. Format: AOR. Target aud: 25-54; baby boomers. ■ Tim Link, gen mgr; Jack Oliver, opns dir; Greg Berger, progmg dir; Justin Bernrose, chief engr.

Dodge City

KDCC(AM)—1992: 1550 khz; 1 kw-D, 90 w-N, DA-2. TL: N37 47 09 W100 01 55 (CP: TL: N37 47 14 W100 01 55). Hrs opn: 7 AM-6 PM. 3004 N. 14th (67801). (316) 225-6783. FAX: (316) 225-0918. Licensee: Dodge City Community College (acq 6-7-92; $11,400; FTR 7-27-92). Format: Oldies, div. Spec prog: Christian, Spanish. ■ John Ewy, gen mgr; Chris Bowen, opns mgr.

*****KONQ(FM)**—Co-owned with KDCC(AM). April 26, 1978: 91.9 mhz; 2.6 kw. Ant 123 ft. TL: N37 46 33 W100 02 12. (316) 225-6720. Format: Var. Spec prog: Class 10 hrs, jazz 10 hrs, Black 10 hrs, Sp 5 hrs wkly.

KDGB(FM)—Not on air, target date unknown: 93.9 mhz; 100 kw. Ant 511 ft. TL: N38 00 07 W101 14 45. c/o Lesso Inc., 1632 Maize Rd., Wichita (67209). Licensee: Lesso Inc. ■ Larry Steckline, pres.

KGNO(AM)—June 30, 1930: 1370 khz; 5 kw-D, 1 kw-N, DA-N. TL: N37 47 33 W100 00 35. Box 1398, 908 W. Frontview (67801-1398). (316) 227-4444. FAX: (316) 227-4432. Licensee: Lesso Inc. (group owner; acq 9-1-93; grpsl; FTR 9-13-93). Net: MBS, Mid-American Ag. Rep: Katz. Format: Full svc country. News staff one; news progmg 25 hrs wkly. Target aud: 25-54. Spec prog: Farm 15 hrs wkly. ■ Larry Steckline, pres; Mike Kinnan, gen mgr & natl sls mgr; Dave Murdock, opns dir & progmg dir; Bonita McClure, gen sls mgr; Dave Sparks, news dir; Darla Hall, pub affrs dir; Jerry Miller, chief engr.

KOLS(FM)—Co-owned with KGNO(AM). May 1966: 95.5 mhz; 100 kw. Ant 570 ft. TL: N37 38 28 W100 20 40. Stereo. Hrs opn: 24. Prog sep from AM. Format: Adult contemp. News progmg 5 hrs wkly. Target aud: 25-49. ■ Dave Murdock, opns mgr; Mike Kinnan, gen sls mgr; Dave Jackson, progmg dir.

*****KONQ(FM)**—Listing follows KDCC(AM).

El Dorado

KSRX(AM)—Nov 16, 1953: 1360 khz; 500 w-D. TL: N37 48 47 W96 48 44. Box 550 (67042). (316) 321-1360. Licensee: New Life Fellowship Inc. (acq 9-6-91; $1.05 million with co-located FM; FTR 9-23-91). Format: Country, news/talk. Spec prog: Farm. ■ Rates: $6; 6; 6; na.

KTLI(FM)—Co-owned with KSRX(AM). Feb 15, 1972: 99.1 mhz; 45 kw. Ant 492 ft. TL: N37 48 47 W96 48 44 (CP: 100 kw, ant 981 ft., TL: N37 56 22 W96 59 20). Stereo. Prog sep from AM. Suite 201, 400 N. Woodlawn, Wichita (67208). (316) 684-3699. FAX: (316) 436-1329. Format: Contemp Christian. ■ Rates: $12; 12; 12; 12.

Ellsworth

KSKU(FM)—See Hutchinson.

Emporia

KEGS(FM)—Jan 16, 1985: 101.7 mhz; 3.3 kw. Ant 300 ft. TL: N38 21 45 W96 07 02. Stereo. Hrs opn: 24. 322 Commercial, Emporia (66801). (316) 343-8525. Licensee: Lesso Inc. (group owner; acq 8-10-92; $230,844; FTR 8-31-92). Net: MBS, Mid-America Ag. Format: Country. Target aud: 25-54. ■ Gregory R. Steckline, pres; Greg Steckline, vp; Becky Bloomquist, stn mgr; Bill Nolan, chief engr. ■ Rates: $15; 12; 12; 8.

KFFX(FM)—Listing follows KVOE(AM).

KGZF(FM)—Not on air, target date unknown: 99.5 mhz; 3 kw. Ant 328 ft. TL: N38 20 57 W96 16 06. Box 985 (66801-0985). Licensee: Michael D. Law (acq 8-17-92; $,2,700; FTR 9-7-92).

*****KNGM(FM)**—Jan 11, 1987: 91.9 mhz; 3 kw. Ant 263 ft. TL: N38 24 35 W96 13 30. Stereo. Hrs opn: 24. Box 506, 815 Graham (66801). (316) 343-9292. Licensee: Christian Action Team Inc. Net: Moody. Format: Contemporary Christian. News staff one. Target aud: Young families & young adults. ■ Jeff Shirley, pres & sr vp; Jeanne Hines, vp; Steve Pearson, gen mgr & news dir; Scott Pearson, progmg dir.

KVOE(AM)—Jan 21, 1939: 1400 khz; 1 kw-U. TL: N38 23 10 W96 10 36. Box 968, 1420 C of E Dr. (66801). (316) 342-1400. FAX: (316) 342-0804. Licensee: Valu-Broadcasting Inc. (group owner; acq 1-7-87). Net: ABC/I. Wash atty: Eugene Smith. Format: Adult contemp, oldies, news. News staff 2; news progmg 20 hrs wkly. Target aud: 35-54. ■ Steve Sauder, CEO; Lea Firestone, pres & gen mgr; Ron Thomas, opns mgr; Lee Schroeder, gen sls mgr; Steven Yewell, Jeff O'Dell, news dirs; Ed Lipson, chief engr. ■ Rates: $16.50; 14.50; 15.50; 13.50.

KFFX(FM)—Co-owned with KVOE(AM). June 15, 1966: 104.9 mhz; 3 kw. Ant 279 ft. TL: N38 23 10 W96 10 36. Stereo. Hrs opn: 24. Prog sep from AM. Format: Classic rock, rock (AOR). News staff 2; news progmg 4 hrs wkly. Target aud: 18-34. ■ Mike Menter, progmg dir. ■ Rates: Same as AM.

Eureka

KOTE(FM)—October 1988: 93.5 mhz; 3 kw. Ant 321 ft. TL: N37 47 29 W96 17 25. Stereo. Hrs opn: 18. Box 331, R.R. 3 (67045). (316) 583-7414. FAX: (316) 583-7233. Licensee: Newwood Productions L.P. Net: Jones Satellite Audio; Kan. Info., Kan. Agri. Format: C&W. Target aud: General. Spec prog: Blues 2 hrs wkly. ■ Jay Brown, CEO, gen mgr, news dir & chief engr. ■ Rates: $10; 10; 10; na.

Fairway

KCNW(AM)—Apr 16, 1953: 1380 khz; 2.5 kw-D, 29 w-N. TL: N39 04 19 W94 40 58. 4535 Metropolitan Ave., Kansas City, (66106). (913) 236-5269. FAX: (913) 236-9583. Licensee: Jim Runsdorf, liquidating agent. Group owner: Children's Broadcasting Corp. Net: CBN. Format: Contemp Christian music. News staff one. Target aud: 18-49; Christians. ■ Richard V. Marsh, exec vp; Nicholas Marchi, vp; Ken Hinson, opns mgr & progmg dir; Nick Marchi, mus dir; Beth Gatton, pub affrs dir. ■ Rates: $15; 10; 15; 10.

Fort Scott

KMDO(AM)—Oct 8, 1954: 1600 khz; 1 kw-D, 50 w-N. TL: N37 48 35 W94 42 22 (CP: TL: N37 48 27 W94 42 33). Box 72, 2 N. National (66701). (316) 223-4500; (316) 223-4501. FAX: (316) 223-5662. Licensee: Fort Scott Broadcasting Co. (acq 2-1-60). Net: Keystone (unwired net). Format: Country. News staff one; news progmg 20 hrs wkly. Target aud: General; 30 plus. ■ Tim McKenny, pres, gen mgr & progmg dir; Nicki Hall, mus dir; Dave Masick, chief engr.

KOMB(FM)—Co-owned with KMDO(AM). Jan 23, 1981: 103.9 mhz; 2 kw. Ant 400 ft. TL: N37 48 27 W98 42 33. Stereo. Format: CHR. ■ Lori Hall, mus dir.

***KVCY(FM)**—November 1983: 101.7 mhz; 3 kw. Ant 250 ft. TL: N37 47 47 W94 42 20 (CP: Ant 328 ft.). Stereo. 2 N. Judson (66701); 3434 W. Kilbourn Ave., Milwaukee, WI (53208). (414) 935-3000. FAX: (414) 935-3015. Licensee: Wisconsin Voice of Christian Youth Inc. (group owner). Format: Relg. ■ Vic Eliason, vp & gen mgr; Jim Schneider, progmg dir, progmg mgr & pub affrs dir; Gordon Morris, news dir; Andy Eliason, chief engr.

Garden City

***KANZ(FM)**—June 29, 1980: 91.1 mhz; 100 kw. Ant 650 ft. TL: N37 46 40 W100 52 08. Stereo. 210 N. 7th St. (67846-5519). (316) 275-7444. FAX: (316) 275-7496. Licensee: KANZA Society Inc. Net: APR, NPR. Format: Div, educ, class. News staff one; news progmg 24 hrs wkly. Spec prog: Jazz 15 hrs, Sp 6 hrs wkly. ■ Dave Parman, pres; Dale Bolton, gen mgr; Deborah Wepelman, opns dir; Janet Barlow, dev dir; Byron Caloz, progmg dir; Kevin O'Connor, mus dir; Eric Angevine, news dir; Sheldon Marcus, chief engr.

KBUF(AM)—(Holcomb). 1948: 1030 khz; 25 kw-D, 1 kw-N, DA-2. TL: N38 00 01 W100 53 54. 1309 E. Fulton, Garden City (67846). (316) 276-2366. FAX: (316) 276-3568. Licensee: KBUF Partnership. Group owner: Robert Ingstad Broadcast Properties (acq 11-1-79). Net: ABC/I; Mid-America Ag. Rep: Banner. Format: C&W. News staff one. Target aud: 25-54. Spec prog: Farm 15 hrs wkly. ■ Scott W. Smith, gen mgr; Rick Thomeczek, gen sls mgr; Corey Hayze, progmg dir; Storm Denison, mus dir; Don Britnall, chief engr.

KKJQ(FM)—Co-owned with KBUF(AM). Nov 20, 1962: 97.3 mhz; 100 kw. Ant 850 ft. TL: N37 46 48 W100 27 36. Stereo. Prog sep from AM. Format: Country, adult contemp. Target aud: 18-49. Spec prog: Oldies 10 hrs wkly.

KIUL(AM)—May 20, 1935: 1240 khz; 1 kw-U. TL: N37 59 52 W100 54 25. 308 N. Seventh St., (67846). (316) 276-3251. FAX: (316) 276-3649. Licensee: Threjay Inc. (acq 10-1-91). Net: CBS; Kan. Info., Kan. Agri. Wash atty: Dow, Lohnes & Albertson. Format: MOR. News staff one; news progmg 10 hrs wkly. Target aud: 45 plus; upscale adults. Spec prog: Farm 5 hrs wkly. ■ Ronald C. Isham, pres & gen mgr; Scott Roberts, opns mgr & progmg dir; Doug Wagner, gen sls mgr; Rob Houston, news dir; Don Brintall, chief engr. ■ Rates: $30; 26; 30; 11.

KKJQ(FM)—Listing follows KBUF(AM).

KWKR(FM)—See Leoti.

Girard

KSEK-FM—Sept 1, 1988: 99.1 mhz; 3 kw. Ant 325 ft. TL: N37 29 02 W94 50 08. 1604 E. Quincy, Pittsburg (66762). (316) 724-8164. FAX: (316) 232-6341. Licensee: Freeman Broadcasting Inc. (acq 2-19-92; $160,166 with KPHN[AM] Pittsburg; FTR 3-16-92). Net: SMN. Format: Classic rock. ■ Rob Freeman, pres & gen mgr; Lisa Freeman, stn mgr; Taylor Fast, chief engr.

Goodland

KGCR(FM)—March 1, 1988: 107.7 mhz; 100 kw. Ant 446 ft. TL: N39 22 03 W101 26 44. Stereo. Hrs opn: 24. Box 948 (4 mi. W. of Brewster) (67735). (913) 694-2877. Licensee: Grace Communications. Net: Moody, USA. Format: Relg. News staff one; news progmg 30 hrs wkly. Target aud: 25-54; Christian families. Spec prog: Farm 2 hrs wkly. ■ Allen Quenzer, pres & gen mgr; Roger Resler, stn mgr, gen sls mgr, adv mgr & asst mus dir; Roger Resler, Allen Quenzer, progmg dirs; Herb Roszhart, mus dir; James Claassen, news dir. ■ Rates: $5.25; 5.25; 5.25; 5.25.

KKCI(FM)—Listing follows KLOE(AM).

KLOE(AM)—1947: 730 khz; 1 kw-D, 20 w-N. TL: N39 20 04 W101 45 28. Box 569 (67735-0569). (913) 899-2309. FAX: (913) 899-3062. Licensee: Robert E. Schmidt. Group owner: Beach-Schmidt Group (acq 3-20-91; grpsl; FTR 4-8-91). Net: CBS; Kan. Agri. Format: Adult contemp, farm. ■ Kay Melia, gen mgr; Marty Melia, opns mgr; Jan Elliot, gen sls mgr; Ron Rempe, mus dir; Kelly Hullet, news dir; George Price, chief engr.

KKCI(FM)—Co-owned with KLOE(AM). Sept 15, 1990: 102.5 mhz; 100 kw. Ant 712 ft. TL: N39 23 19 W101 33 34. Licensee: Eagle Communications Group owner: Beach-Schmidt Group (acq 4-90; $40,000; FTR 5-21-90). ■ Marty Mella, gen mgr. ■ KLOE-TV affil.

Great Bend

***KHCT(FM)**—Aug 3, 1992: 90.9 mhz; 50 kw. Ant 781 ft. TL: N38 37 04 W98 56 32. Suite 300, 815 N. Walnut St., Hutchinson (67501). (316) 665-3500; (316) 665-3555. Licensee: Hutchinson Community College. Net: NPR. Format: Classical, new age, news. News progmg 27 hrs wkly. Spec prog: Jazz one hr wkly. ■ David Horning, gen mgr; Anthony Hunt, dev dir; Patsy Terrell, prom mgr; Sharon Dudgeon, progmg dir; Carolyn Gardner, asst mus dir; Ric Jung, chief engr.

KHOK(FM)—(Hoisington). 1978: 100.7 mhz; 100 kw. Ant 430 ft. TL: N38 32 49 W98 45 59. Stereo. Hrs opn: 6 AM-1 AM. Box 48, 5501 10th, Great Bend (67530). (316) 792-3647; (316) 792-3101. Licensee: Robert E. Schmidt. Group owner: Eagle Communications Group (acq 3-20-91; $290,000 grpsl; FTR 4-8-91). Net: NBC the Source. Format: CHR. News staff one; news progmg one hr wkly. Target aud: 18-44. Spec prog: Relg 2 hrs wkly. ■ Robert E. Schmidt, vp; Rick Nulton, gen mgr & gen sls mgr; Rick Elder, sls dir; Scott Donovan, prom mgr, progmg dir & mus dir; Dave Alexander, asst mus dir; Gale Scheurman, chief engr. ■ Rates: $12; 10; 10; 8.

KVGB(AM)—March 10, 1937: 1590 khz; 5 kw-U, DA-N. TL: N38 18 50 W98 47 35. 1200 Baker St. (67530). (316) 792-4317. Licensee: Forward of Kansas Inc., debtor in possession. Net: ABC. Format: Country, farm. ■ Sam Jones, stn mgr; George Dietz, gen sls mgr; John T. O'Conner, mus dir; Tim McQuade, news dir; Lloyd Messner, chief engr.

KVGB-FM—Jan 17, 1977: 104.3 mhz; 96 kw. Ant 810 ft. TL: N38 25 54 W98 46 18. Stereo. Dups AM 50%.

KZLS(FM)—Feb 3, 1986: 107.9 mhz; 100 kw. Ant 886 ft. TL: N38 46 16 W98 44 17. Stereo. Hrs opn: 24. Box 11 (67530). (316) 792-7108. FAX: (316) 792-7051. Licensee: Lesso Inc. (group owner; acq 1993; grpsl; FTR 9-13-93). Net: Mid-American Ag. Wash atty: Blooston, Mordkofsky, Jackson & Dickens. Format: Adult contemp. News staff one; news progmg 5 hrs wkly. Target aud: 25-54. ■ Larry Steckline, CEO; Stan Unruh, gen mgr; Tommy Steel, progmg dir & mus dir; Julie Smith, asst mus dir & news dir; Jerry Miller, chief engr.

Hays

KAYS(AM)—Oct 15, 1948: 1400 khz; 1 kw-U. TL: N38 53 29 W99 22 03. Stereo. Hrs opn: 18. Box 817, 2300 Hall St. (67601). (913) 625-2578. Licensee: Robert E. Schmidt. Group owner: Eagle Communications (acq 3-20-91; grpsl; FTR 4-8-91). Net: NBC. Format: Oldies. News staff one; news progmg 6 hrs wkly. Target aud: General; adults. Spec prog: Local sports. ■ Robert E. Schmidt, pres; Gary D. Shorman, vp; Joe Engel, gen mgr; Greg Schmidt, gen sls mgr; Mike Cooper, progmg dir; Todd Nelson, news dir; Ken Giebler, chief engr. ■ Rates: $11; 11; 11; 11.

KHAZ(FM)—Co-owned with KAYS(AM). May 1, 1985: 99.5 mhz; 100 kw. Ant 515 ft. TL: N38 56 29 W99 21 22. Stereo. Hrs opn: 18. Prog sep from AM. Box 6 (67601). Net: Mid-American Ag. Format: Country. News progmg 4 hrs wkly. Target aud: 25-54. Spec prog: Farm 10 hr wkly. ■ Mark Hinga, opns mgr; Frank Muselek, gen sls mgr; Mike Korner, progmg dir. ■ Rates: $12; 12; 12; 12.

KJLS(FM)—June 27, 1974: 103.3 mhz; 100 kw. Ant 463 ft. TL: N38 55 20 W99 21 11. Stereo. Hrs opn: 24. Box 364, 107 W. 13th, (67601). (913) 628-1064. FAX: (913) 628-1822. Licensee: Radio Inc. dba KJLS (acq 11-83). Net: ABC/E. Format: Adult contemp. Target aud: 25-49. Spec prog: Solid gold 5 hrs, CHR 3 hrs wkly. ■ Rick Kuehl, pres; Kyle Ermoian, gen mgr; Ken Billinger, opns dir & mus dir; Steve Klitzke, rgnl sls mgr; Chris Sook, mktg dir; Leon Frank, chief engr. ■ Rates: $10; 9; 8; 7.

Haysville

KXLK(FM)—Aug 25, 1985: 105.3 mhz; 100 kw. Ant 1,000 ft. TL: N37 46 40 W97 30 37. Stereo. 626 N. Broadway, Wichita (67214). (316) 267-0800. FAX: (316) 267-0512. Licensee: Midcontinent Broadcasting Co. of Kansas. Group owner: Midcontinent Media Inc. Net: AP. Rep: Banner. Format: Adult contemp. News staff 2; news progmg 3 hrs wkly. Target aud: 25-49. Spec prog: Relg 2 hrs wkly. ■ Larry Bentson, pres; Jeff Clark, gen mgr; Jackie Wise, gen sls mgr; Robin Ragland-Smith, prom mgr; Jeff Couch, progmg dir; Greg Gann, mus dir; Steve McIntosh, news dir; Larry Waggoner, chief engr.

Herington

KDMM(FM)—Not on air, target date August 1994: 105.7 mhz; 12.5 kw. Ant 500 ft. TL: N38 37 01 W96 59 09. Stereo. Hrs opn: 24. Box 175 (67449). (913) 258-2388. Licensee: Marie and Donald D. Willis. Format: Traditional country. ■ Donald D. Willis, pres, gen mgr & chief engr; Evelyn M. Willis, adv mgr.

Hiawatha

KNZA(FM)—Aug 18, 1977: 103.9 mhz; 3 kw. Ant 300 ft. TL: N39 46 23 W95 31 34 (CP: 50 kw. Ant 492 ft.). Stereo. Hrs opn: 5 AM-midnight. Box 104, Hwy. 73 S. (66434-0104). (913) 547-3461. FAX: (913) 547-9900. Licensee: KNZA Inc. (acq 6-83; $587,500; FTR 6-20-83). Net: ABC/D. Format: C&W. News staff one; news progmg 10 hrs wkly. Target aud: General. Spec prog: Farm 14 hrs wkly. ■ Greg Buser, gen mgr; Robert Hilton, opns mgr; L. J. Trant, progmg dir; Murray McGee, news dir; Mike Douthat, chief engr. ■ Rates: $24; 21; 21; 10.

Hill City

***KZNA(FM)**—1986: 90.5 mhz; 100 kw. Ant 600 ft. TL: N39 15 56 W99 49 48. Stereo. Hrs opn: 19. 210 N. 7th., Garden City (67846-5519). (316) 275-7444. FAX: (316) 275-7496. Licensee: Kanza Society Inc. Net: APR, NPR. Format: Div, ed. Spec prog: Jazz 15 hrs, Sp 6 hrs wkly. ■ Dave Parman, pres; Deborah Wepelman, opns mgr; Janet Barlow, dev dir; Byron Caloz, progmg dir; Kevin O'Connor, mus dir; Eric Angevine, pub affrs dir; Sheldon Marcus, chief engr.

Hoisington

KHOK(FM)—Licensed to Hoisington. See Great Bend.

Holcomb

KBUF(AM)—Licensed to Holcomb. See Garden City.

Horton

KADF(FM)—Not on air, target date unknown: 93.7 mhz; 25 kw. Ant 328 ft. 1106 Santa Fe, Atchison (66002). Licensee: William D. Purkis.

Hugoton

KFXX-FM—Sept 16, 1983: 106.7 mhz; 35 kw. Ant 259 ft. TL: N37 19 03 W101 20 16. Stereo. Hrs opn: 24. Dups KULY(AM) Ulysses 90%. Box 1067, 2917 S. Colorado, Ulysses (67880). (316) 353-1067. FAX: (316) 356-3635. Licensee: A & B Broadcasting Inc. (group owner; acq 4-14-92; $220,000 with KULY(AM) Ulysses; FTR 5-4-92). Net: ABC/D, Jones Satellite Audio; Kan. Info. Wash atty: B. Jay Baraff. Format: Country, news/talk. News staff 2; news progmg 15 hrs wkly. Target aud: 25-44. Spec prog: Farm 12 hrs, gospel 7 hrs wkly. ■ Monte Spearman, gen mgr; Kristi Spearman, opns mgr; Kay Anderson, dev dir & adv dir; Jerry Sullivan, sls dir; Jolene Eisenhour, mktg dir & pub affrs dir; Ty Harmon, prom dir & progmg dir; Eddie Ochoa, mus dir; John O'Sullivan, news dir; Chuck Springer, chief engr. ■ Rates: $11; 11; 11; 7.

Hutchinson

***KHCC-FM**—Sept 11, 1972: 90.1 mhz; 100 kw. Ant 1,080 ft. TL: N38 03 40 W97 45 49. Hrs opn: 19. Suite 300, 815 N. Walnut, (67501-6217). (316) 665-3555. FAX: (316) 662-6740. Licensee: Hutchinson Community College. Net: NPR. Format: Class, new age, news. News progmg 27 hrs wkly. Spec prog: Jazz one hr wkly. ■ David M. Horning, gen mgr; Anthony Hunt, dev dir; Patsy Terrell, prom mgr; Sharon Dudgeon, progmg dir; Carolyn Gardner, mus dir; Ric Jung, engrg dir.

KHUT(FM)—Listing follows KWBW(AM).

KIUS(FM)—Listing follows KWHK(AM).

KSKU(FM)—April 10, 1970: 106.1 mhz; 100 kw. Ant 659 ft. TL: N38 16 33 W98 12 11. Stereo. Hrs opn: 24. 106 N. Main St. (67501). (316) 665-5758. FAX: (316) 665-6655. Licensee: Ad Astra Per Aspera Broadcasting Inc. (acq 9-17-86; $366,816; FTR 6-9-86). Wash atty: Hopper & Kanouf. Format: Adult contemp, CHR. News staff one; news progmg 2 hrs wkly. Target aud: 12-49; listeners throughout central Kansas. ■ Cliff C. Shank, pres; Mike Hill, vp, vp sls & vp adv; Vicki Shank, stn mgr & vp mktg; Tom Simon, opns mgr, progmg dir & mus dir; Monica Norris, prom dir; Thomas Norris, news dir; Michael Paul, pub affrs dir; Rod Rogers, chief engr. ■ Rates: $36; 34; 35; 33.

KWBW(AM)—May 28, 1935: 1450 khz; 1 kw-U. TL: N38 04 02 W97 57 53. Box 1036 (67504-1036). (316) 662-4486. FAX: (316) 662-5357. Licensee: KAYS Inc. (acq 11-4-91; with co-located FM). Net: NBC. Format: Talk, MOR. Spec prog: Black 2 hrs, gospel 11 hrs wkly. ■ Dan Deming, gen mgr & progmg dir; Ed Rudloff, chief engr.

Kansas

KHUT(FM)—Co-owned with KWBW(AM). March 15, 1972: 102.9 mhz; 28.5 kw. Ant 496 ft. TL: N38 02 36 W98 00 53 (CP: TL: N38 02 39 W98 00 56). Format: C&W. Spec prog: Gospel 5 hrs wkly. ■ Mark Trotman, stn mgr; Terry Drouhard, progmg dir.

KWHK(AM)—Nov 1, 1946: 1260 khz; 1 kw-D, 500 w-N, DA-2. TL: N38 06 07 W97 56 08. 106 W. 43rd (67602). (316) 663-9174. FAX: (316) 663-3736. Licensee: Kansas/Nebraska Christian Broadcasting Inc. (acq 3-28-93; $600,000 with co-located FM; FTR 7-3-90). ■ Thomas Russell, gen mgr.

KIUS(FM)—Co-owned with KWHK(AM). January 1990: 97.1 mhz; 25 kw. Ant 500 ft. TL: N37 57 54 W97 49 26. Stereo.

KZSN-FM—Oct 7, 1968: 102.1 mhz; 100 kw. Ant 1,032 ft. TL: N37 47 47 W97 31 59. Stereo. 5610 E. 29th St. N., Wichita (67220). (316) 683-4566. FAX: (316) 683-4609. Licensee: H & D Entertainment Inc. Group owner: H & D Broadcast Group (acq 6-29-93; with KZSN[AM] Wichita; FTR 8-2-93). Net: AP. Rep: Katz, Midwest. Format: Country. News staff one. Target aud: General. ■ Jerry Atchley, pres; Jim Worthington, vp & gen mgr; Lisa Allan, gen sls mgr; Amy Novotny, prom mgr; Pat Moyer, progmg dir & news dir; Dan Holiday, mus dir; Ralph Cramm, chief engr.

Independence

KIND(AM)—Dec 8, 1947: 1010 khz; 250 w-D, 32 w-N. TL: N37 13 07 W95 43 30. Box A, 113 S. 8th St. (67301). (316) 331-3000. Licensee: Central Broadcasting Inc. Net: Moody; Kan. Info, Kan. Agri. Format: Div, full svc. Target aud: General. Spec prog: Jazz. ■ Nelson Rupard, gen mgr. ■ Rates: $6.75; 6.75; 6.75; 6.75.

KIND-FM—May 10, 1969: 101.7 mhz; 1.6 kw. Ant 155 ft. TL: N37 13 07 W95 43 30 (CP: 3 kw., ant 226 ft.). Dups AM 100%.

Iola

KALN(AM)—July 25, 1961: 1370 khz; 500 w, 62 w-N DA. TL: N37 54 07 W95 24 26. Box 710 (66749). (316) 365-3151. Licensee: Iola Broadcasting Inc. (acq 9-1-73). Format: Country. ■ Michael P. Russell, pres & gen mgr; Lovetta R. Russell, CFO; Kennie Graves, chief engr.

KIKS-FM—Co-owned with KALN(AM). June 9, 1977: 99.3 mhz; 3 kw. Ant 300 ft. TL: N37 54 04 W95 24 04. Stereo. Dups AM 60%. Format: Adult contemp.

Junction City

KJCK(AM)—May 15, 1949: 1420 khz; 1 kw-D, 500 w-N, DA-N. TL: N39 01 33 W96 48 36. Box 789 (66441). (913) 762-5525. FAX: (913) 762-5387. Licensee: Platinum Broadcasting Inc. (acq 9-4-86). Net: ABC/E. Format: C&W. ■ Daryl W. Gatza, pres & gen mgr; Mark Ediger, opns dir & progmg dir; Jerry Brechieson, news dir; Randy Stewart, chief engr.

KJCK-FM—July 22, 1965: 94.5 mhz; 100 kw. Ant 630 ft. TL: N39 00 53 W96 52 15. Stereo. Prog sep from AM. Net: ABC/FM. Format: CHR.

Kansas City

KFKF-FM—May 28, 1963: 94.1 mhz; 100 kw. Ant 994 ft. TL: N39 00 57 W94 30 24. Stereo. Box 236394 (64126). (816) 753-4000. Licensee: KFKF Broadcasting Co. Format: Contemp country. ■ Dan Wastler, vp & gen mgr; Don Crawley, progmg dir; Tony Stevens, mus dir; Randy Birch, news dir; Dan Mitchell, chief engr.

KNHN(AM)—1925: 1340 khz; 1 kw-U. TL: N39 06 50 W94 40 05. Hrs opn: 24. 4121 Minnesota Ave. (66102). (913) 342-1600; (913) 342-1340. FAX: (913) 342-1351. Licensee: KCBR-AM L.P. Net: CNN. Format: Headline News. ■ William R. Johnson, gen mgr; LeAnn Petty, progmg dir; Bob Mead, news dir; Ed Treese, chief engr.

KUDL(FM)—Oct 9, 1959: 98.1 mhz; 100 kw. Ant 994 ft. TL: N39 04 23 W94 29 06. Stereo. Suite 410, 3 Broadway, Shawnee Mission (64111). (816) 753-0933. FAX: (816) 753-6654. Licensee: Apollo Radio Ltd. (group owner; acq 8-3-93). Net: AP. Rep: Christal. Format: Adult contemp. ■ Fred Muir, gen mgr; Mike Payne, gen sls mgr; Linda Stultz, prom dir; Tom Land, progmg dir; Darcie Blake, news dir; Ben Weiss, chief engr.

Kingman

KTCM(FM)—Sept 15, 1989: 100.3 mhz; 48 kw. Ant 505 ft. TL: N37 29 59 W98 10 24. Stereo. 315 W. D Ave. (67068). (316) 532-5811. FAX: (316) 532-5959. Licensee: New Life Fellowship Inc. (acq 10-26-93; $355,000; FTR 11-8-93). Net: SMN. Format: CHR. News staff one. Target aud: 17-40; Kingman area residents. ■ John Pohlman, gen mgr; Lesley Miller, opns mgr; Lyman James, progmg dir; Dan Gentry, chief engr.

Larned

KANS(AM)—Nov 4, 1963: 1510 khz; 1 kw-D (500 w-CH). TL: N38 09 54 W99 06 05. 200 E. 8th (67550). (316) 285-2127. FAX: (316) 285-2102. Licensee: C&C Consulting Inc. (acq 11-6-90; $325,000 with co-located FM; FTR 11-19-90). Net: SMN; Kan. Info, Kan. Agri. Rep: Gray. Format: Adult contemp. News staff one; news progmg 10 hrs wkly. Target aud: General; people looking for local information. Spec prog: Farm 10 hrs, gospel 6 hrs, relg 5 hrs wkly. ■ Ed Lipson, pres & chief engr; R.D. Carter, gen mgr, gen sls mgr & progmg dir; Dan Cormack, mus dir.

KQDF-FM—Co-owned with KANS(AM). Nov 1, 1965: 96.7 mhz; 3 kw. Ant 290 ft. TL: N38 09 54 W99 06 05 (CP: Ant 265 ft.). Stereo. Prog sep from AM. Format: Oldies.

Lawrence

*****KANU(FM)**—Sept 15, 1952: 91.5 mhz; 100 kw. Ant 698 ft. TL: N38 57 18 W95 15 57. Stereo. Hrs opn: 24. Broadcasting Hall, Univ. of Kansas (66045-2672). (913) 864-4530. Licensee: University of Kansas. Net: APR, NPR; Kan. Pub. Wash atty: Arter & Hadden. Format: News, class, jazz. News staff 3; news progmg 35 hrs wkly. Target aud: 25-49; upscale. Spec prog: Bluegrass 4 hrs, Celtic 2 hrs, blues 4 hrs. ■ Howard Hill, gen mgr; Sam Chapman, opns dir; Judy Keller, dev dir; Cheryl Patterson, prom dir; Darrell Brogdon, progmg dir; Rachel Hunter, mus dir; Vance Hiner, news dir; Bob Pearson, chief engr.

*****KFKU(AM)**—Co-owned with KANU(FM). Sept 15, 1924: 1250 khz; 5 kw-U, DA-N. TL: N39 04 55 W95 32 45. Stn currently dark.

*****KJHK(FM)**—1975: 90.7 mhz; 100 w. Ant 163 ft. TL: N38 57 30 W95 15 00. Stereo. Hrs opn: 24. Rm. 2051-A, Dole Ctr., Univ. of Kansas (66045). (913) 864-3993; (913) 864-4745. FAX: (913) 864-0614. Licensee: Univ. of Kansas. Net: ABC/E. Format: Rock, jazz. News progmg 15 hrs wkly. Target aud: 18-24. Spec prog: Reggae 3 hrs, blues 2 hrs wkly. ■ Tim Mensendiek, gen mgr; Adrienne Rivers, prom dir; John Broholm, news dir; Mitch Gabe, chief engr.

KLWN(AM)—Feb 22, 1951: 1320 khz; 500 w-D, 250 w-N. TL: N38 55 52 W95 15 56. Hrs opn: 5 AM-11 PM. Box 3007, 3035 Iowa St. (66046). (913) 843-1320; (913) 843-1321. FAX: (913) 841-1320. Licensee: Lawrence Broadcasters Inc. Net: AP. Format: Adult contemp, news/talk. News staff 3; news progmg 13 hrs wkly. Target aud: 25-59; educated adults, family units. Spec prog: Farm one hr, relig 6 hrs wkly. ■ Arden Booth, pres; Hank Booth, gen mgr; Bob Newton, stn mgr; Warner Lewis, gen sls mgr; Larry Wilson, prom dir; progmg dir & mus dir; Barb Quinn, news dir; Brian Short, chief engr. ■ Rates: $28.50; 22; 28.50; 12.50.

KLZR(FM)—Co-owned with KLWN(AM). Aug 20, 1963: 105.9 mhz; 100 kw. Ant 771 ft. TL: N39 02 21 W95 26 59. Stereo. Hrs opn: 24. Prog sep from AM. (913) 842-1059. Net: AP, SMN. Format: Alternative. News staff 3; news progmg one hr wkly. Target aud: 18-35; college students, young adults. ■ Tim Barrett, prom dir & progmg dir; John Flood, pub affrs dir. ■ Rates: Same as AM.

Leavenworth

KKLO(AM)—1946: 1410 khz; 5 kw-D, 500 w-N, DA-2. TL: N39 16 30 W94 54 30 (CP: 5 kw-N). 481 Muncie Rd. (66048). (913) 727-1410. Licensee: Chara Communications Inc. (acq 6-1-92; $450,000; FTR 6-22-92). Format: Christian top-40. News staff one; news progmg 15 hrs wkly. Target aud: 25-49; upscale, educated, loyal Christian listeners. ■ Todd Chase, gen mgr & progmg dir; Wayne Combs, news dir; Dave Barnett, chief engr.

KQRC-FM—Licensed to Leavenworth. See Kansas City, Mo.

Leoti

KWKR(FM)—Nov 1, 1983: 99.9 mhz; 100 kw. Ant 395 ft. TL: N38 16 39 W101 17 50. Stereo. 308 N. 7th St., Garden City, (67846). (316) 276-3251. FAX: (316) 276-3649. Licensee: Threjay Inc. (acq 10-1-91). Net: Unistar. Wash atty: Dow, Lohnes & Albertson. Format: Classic rock. News staff one; news progmg 2 hrs wkly. Target aud: 25-44; primarily young adults. Spec prog: Sp 3 hrs wkly. ■ Ronald C. Isham, pres; Judith Isham, vp; Doug Wagner, gen sls mgr; Don Jantzen, progmg dir; Rob Houston, news dir; Don Brintall, chief engr. ■ Rates: $30; 25.50; 30; 10.50.

Liberal

KSCB(AM)—July 25, 1948: 1270 khz; 1 kw-D, 500 w-N, DA-N. TL: N37 03 15 W100 53 39. Hrs opn: 24. Box 3125 (67905-3125); 1600 E. Eighth St. (67901). (316) 624-3891; (800) 373-3891. FAX: (316) 624-9472. Licensee: Seward County Broadcasting Co. Net: ABC; Kan. Info, EIB. Rep: Roslin. Wash atty: Fisher, Wayland, Cooper & Leader. Format: Country. News staff one; news progmg 21 hrs wkly. Target aud: 25-54. ■ Jack Landon, pres; Stuart Melchert, vp & gen mgr; Jami Snell, gen sls mgr; Mark David, progmg dir & mus dir. ■ Rates: $15.20; 13.20; 15.20; 13.20.

KSCB-FM—July 10, 1978: 107.5 mhz; 100 kw. Ant 511 ft. TL: N37 02 45 W101 06 11. Stereo. Hrs opn: 24. Prog separate from AM. Net: ABC/C. Format: Adult contemp. News progmg 7 hrs wkly. Target aud: 25-49; mobile adults. ■ Rates: Same as AM.

KSLS(FM)—Listing follows KYUU(AM).

KYUU(AM)—Sept 15, 1960: 1470 khz; 1 kw-D, 125 w-N. TL: N37 03 17 W100 53 06. RR 2, Box 431 (67901). (316) 624-8156. FAX: (316) 624-8157. Licensee: Lawrence E. Steckline. Group owner: Lesso Inc. Net: MBS; Mid-America Ag. Rep: McGavren Guild. Format: Pure gold, class rock 50s, 60s, 70s. News staff one; news progmg 15 hrs wkly. Target aud: 25-54. Spec prog: Farm 12 hrs, Sp 5 hrs wkly. ■ Lawrence Steckline, pres; Steve Williams, gen mgr; Larry Howell, stn mgr; Shelby Marchel, gen sls mgr; Woody Harrelson, progmg dir; Orlando Aguilar, mus dir & news dir; Bill Nolan, chief engr.

KSLS(FM)—Co-owned with KYUU(AM). July 1978: 101.5 mhz; 100 kw. Ant 550 ft. TL: N37 03 20 W100 48 40. Stereo. Format: Country.

KZQD(FM)—Not on air, target date unknown: 105.1 mhz; 50 kw. Ant 492 ft. TL: N37 17 39 W100 51 38. Alpha Broadcasting Inc., 2250 N. Rock Rd. #121, Wichita (67226). Licensee: Alpha Broadcasting Inc.

Lindsborg

KQNS-FM—Oct 8, 1985: 95.9 mhz; 1.3 kw. Ant 455 ft. TL: N38 40 00 W97 41 30. Stereo. Box 2508, Salina (67402-2060). (913) 826-9636. FAX: (913) 827-3506. Licensee: Davies Communications Inc. (acq 10-5-92; $125,000; FTR 11-2-92). Format: AOR/Rock. Target aud: 20-45. ■ Bruce Chalmers, gen mgr, progmg dir & news dir; Debra Rogan, gen sls mgr.

Lyons

KSKU(FM)—See Hutchinson.

Manhattan

KJCK-FM—See Junction City.

*****KKSU(AM)**—Dec 1, 1924: 580 khz; 5 kw-D. (ST-WIBW). TL: N39 13 00 W96 35 10. Rm. 20, McCain Auditorium, Kansas State Univ. (66506). (913) 532-5851. FAX: (913) 532-5709. Licensee: Kansas State Univ. Net: NPR; Kan. Pub. Licensee: Educ, news/talk. News staff one; news progmg 15 hrs wkly. Target aud: General. ■ Jon Wefald, pres; Ralph S. Titus, gen mgr, progmg dir & mus dir; Richard Baker, news dir; Delbert Staab, chief engr.

*****KSDB-FM**—Co-owned with KKSU(AM). 1950: 91.9 mhz; 1.4 kw. Ant 290 ft. TL: N39 09 49 W96 31 54. Stereo. Hrs opn: 19 A.Q. Miller School of Journalism, Room 104, Kedzie Hall (66506). (913) 532-3292. FAX: (913) 532-7309. Net: CNN. Format: Progsv, rock. News progmg 12 hrs wkly. Target aud: 18-34; young adults. ■ Carol Oukrop, pres; Joe Montgomery, gen mgr; Eric Melin, mus dir; Gary Pettet, chief engr.

KMAN(AM)—June 1950: 1350 khz; 500 w-D, 40 w-N. TL: N39 13 00 W96 33 30. Stereo. Hrs opn: 24. Box 1350 (66502); 2414 Casement Rd. (66502). (913) 776-1350; (913) 776-4851. FAX: (913) 539-1000. Licensee: Manhattan Broadcasting Co. Group owner: Seaton Stns. Net: MBS, NBC Talknet; Kan. Info. Wash atty: Fisher, Wayland, Cooper & Leader. Format: Adult contemp, news/talk, sports. News staff 2; news progmg 60 hrs wkly. Target aud: 30 plus. ■ Edward Seaton, pres; Richard T. Wartell, gen mgr; Dave Lewis, progmg dir; Jason Wright, mus dir; Ken Scott, news dir; Kevin Block, chief engr. ■ Rates: $20; 16; 20; 16.

KMKF(FM)—Co-owned with KMAN(AM). Sept 1, 1972: 101.5 mhz; 39 kw. Ant 577 ft. TL: N39 15 55 W96 27 56. Stereo. Hrs opn: 24. Prog sep from AM. Format: Rock (AOR). News staff 2; news progmg 2 hrs wkly. Target aud: 18-35. ■ Jason Whisnand, prom mgr & progmg dir. ■ Rates: Same as AM.

KQLA(FM)—(Ogden). Feb 14, 1986: 103.9 mhz; 3 kw. Ant 315 ft. TL: N39 09 21 W96 36 44 (CP: 103.5 mhz, 50 kw). Stereo. Hrs opn: 24. Box 104, 5008 Skyway Dr., Manhattan (66502); Box 1104, Junction City (66441). (913) 776-0104; (913) 238-0104. FAX: (913) 776-0110. Licensee: Kaw Valley Broadcasting Co. Net: ABC/C. Rep: Katz & Powell. Wash atty: Mullin, Rhyne, Emmons & Topel. Format: CHR, hot AC. News staff one; news progmg 2 hrs wkly. Target aud: 18-44; mobile, educated persons with quality income. Spec prog: Gospel 2 hrs, urban contemp 4 hrs wkly. ■ Jody McCoy, pres; Jim Bond, CFO & vp; Ed Klimek, gen mgr & prom mgr; Jerry Teol, gen sls mgr; Mike Temaat, progmg dir & mus dir; J.P. Phelps, asst mus dir; Jeff Wichman, news dir & pub affrs dir; Tom Toenjes, chief engr. ■ Rates: $14; 12; 17; 12.

*****KSDB-FM**—Listing follows KKSU(AM).

Marysville

KNDY(AM)—July 10, 1956: 1570 khz; 250 w-D. TL: N39 51 02 W96 38 52. Hrs opn: 24. R.R. 3 (66508). (913) 562-2361. Licensee: Dierking Communications Inc. (acq 9-6-88). Net: ABC/D; Mid-America Ag. Format: Farm, C&W. News progmg 24 hrs wkly. Target aud: General. ■ Bruce Dierking, pres, gen mgr & gen sls mgr; Jeff Jacques, mus dir; Paul Gaston, chief engr.

KNDY-FM—July 23, 1974: 103.1 mhz; 9 kw. Ant 389 ft. TL: N39 52 12 W96 44 45. Stereo. Hrs opn: 24. Dups AM 10%. Net: ABC/D. Format: C&W. ■ Paul Lovell, gen sls mgr; Jeff Jacques, progmg dir; Myron Nolind, chief engr.

McPherson

KNGL(AM)—Jan 4, 1949: 1540 khz; 250 w-D. TL: N38 20 30 W97 40 12. Box 1069 (67460). (316) 241-1504. FAX: (316) 241-3078. Licensee: Davies Communications Inc. (acq 10-1-85; $589,000 with co-located FM; FTR 8-19-85). Net: AP. Format: Adult contemp, oldies. News staff 3; news progmg 21 hrs wkly. Target aud: 25-54. Spec prog: Relg 5 hrs wkly. ■ Jerry Davies, pres, gen mgr & gen sls mgr; Diane Davies, exec vp, prom dir, progmg dir & mus dir; Bud DeArvil, news dir; Shawn White, chief engr.

KBBE(FM)—Co-owned with KNGL(AM). Jan 12, 1974: 96.7 mhz; 6 kw. Ant 245 ft. TL: N38 20 30 W97 40 12. Stereo. Format: Adult contemp, cross-country mix.

Medicine Lodge

KREJ(FM)—January 1990: 101.7 mhz; 50 kw. Ant 492 ft. TL: N37 13 58 W98 39 43. Hrs opn: 24. 301 S. Main (67104). (316) 886-3537. FAX: (316) 886-3537. Licensee: Florida Public Radio Inc. (acq 5-90; FTR 6-11-90). Net: Moody. Format: Relg. Target aud: General. ■ Mike Henry, gen mgr; Randy Henry, chief engr.

Minneapolis

KILS(FM)—Not on air, target date unknown: 92.7 mhz; 50 kw. Ant 492 ft. TL: N39 00 52 W97 37 42. Licensee: Lesso Inc. (group owner; acq 4-23-93; $72,162; FTR 5-17-93).

Mission

KBEA(AM)—October 1957: 1480 khz; 1 kw-D, 500 w-N, DA-2. TL: N39 04 05 W94 42 09. Hrs opn: 24. 1701 S. 55th L St., Kansas City (66106). (913) 432-1480. FAX: (913) 287-5209. Licensee: Ingram Enterprises. Net: ABC/C, MBS, USA. Format: Music of your life. Target aud: 25 plus. ■ Robert P. Ingram, pres; James E. Cunningham, vp; Lawyer Ward, gen sls mgr; Dave Wilson, progmg dir; Lee Wheeler, chief engr.

KCNW(AM)—See Fairway.

KXTR(FM)—See Kansas City, Mo.

Newton

KJRG(AM)—May 24, 1953: 950 khz; 500 w-D, 147 w-N. TL: N38 02 45 W97 22 24. Box 567 (67114). (316) 283-5150. Licensee: KJRG Inc. (acq 7-59). Format: Relg. ■ George Anderson, pres; Gordon Anderson, gen mgr; Daisyann Anderson, gen sls mgr; Larry Sperling, news dir; Robin McDaniel, chief engr.

KOEZ(FM)—Co-owned with KJRG(AM). 1959: 92.3 mhz; 100 kw. Ant 650 ft. TL: N38 01 09 W97 23 01. Stereo. Prog sep from AM. Net: Wall Street. Format: Btfl mus.

North Fort Riley

KBLS(FM)—Jan 1, 1993: 102.5 mhz; 100 kw. Ant 492 ft. TL: N38 57 05 W96 47 45. Stereo. Hrs opn: 24. Box 69, 200 N. Broadway, Abilene (67410). (913) 263-1560. Licensee: The Eagle Broadcasting Company Inc. (acq 4-5-93; $585,000; FTR 4-26-93). Format: Light adult contemp. News staff one. Target aud: 25-54; women. ■ John Vanier, pres; Jerry Hinrikus, vp & gen mgr; Larry Avery, sls dir; Bruce Crandall, progmg dir; Joe Eck, chief engr.

North Newton

*****KBCU(FM)**—Apr 6, 1989: 88.1 mhz; 149 w. Ant 56 ft. TL: N38 04 26 W97 20 35. Hrs opn: 7 AM-midnight (Mon-Fri), noon-midnight (Sat-Sun). 300 E. 27th St. (67117). (316) 284-5228; (316) 284-5368. FAX: (316) 284-5286. Licensee: Bethel College. Net: Kan. Info. Wash atty: Duncan, Weinberg, Miller & Pembroke. Format: Div. News progmg 5 hrs wkly. Target aud: General; college students & local listeners. ■ Thane Chastain, gen mgr; Aaron Hull, vp mktg; Chad Frey, vp progmg; Don Duncan, mus dir; Matt Pankratz, news dir; Brian Mast, pub affrs dir; Ron Glanzer, engrg dir.

Norton

KQNK(AM)—Oct 30, 1963: 1530 khz; 1 kw-D. TL: N38 35 04 W95 15 57. Box 220 (67654). (913) 877-3378. Licensee: Pioneer Country Broadcasting Inc. (acq 6-1-83; $260,000; FTR 6-20-83). Net: ABC/I. Rep: Keystone (unwired net). Format: MOR. ■ Larry Black, pres & gen mgr; Tom Schmeio, chief engr.

KVNV(FM)—Co-owned with KQNK(AM). Mar 1, 1993: 106.7 mhz; 51 kw. Ant 92 ft. TL: N39 49 37 W99 52 08.

Oberlin

KFNF(FM)—July 1977: 101.1 mhz; 100 kw. Ant 420 ft. TL: N39 49 33 W100 39 09. Stereo. Box 108, 6 Miles W. of Oberlin (67749). (913) 475-2225; (913) 475-2226. FAX: (913) 475-2510. Licensee: Valu-West Inc. Group owner: Valu-Line Inc. (acq 12-26-88; $155,000; FTR 12-26-88). Net: MBS; Kan. Agri. Format: C&W. Target aud: General. Spec prog: Gospel 6 hrs, oldies 3 hrs wkly. ■ Steve Sauder, pres; Lea Firestone, vp & gen mgr; Marty Hill, stn mgr, opns mgr, prom dir, progmg dir & pub affrs dir; Carolyn Roberson, gen sls mgr & adv mgr; Ed Lipson, chief engr.

Ogden

KQLA(FM)—Licensed to Ogden. See Manhattan.

Olathe

KCCV-FM—Not on air, target date unknown: 92.3 mhz; 3 kw. Ant 328 ft. TL: N38 49 34 W94 49 32. 10550 Barkley, Overland Park (66212). (913) 642-7600. Licensee: Bott Broadcasting Co. (group owner; acq 7-1-92; $537,500; FTR 8-3-92). ■ Richard Bott II, gen mgr.

Osage City

KZOC(FM)—July 26, 1982: 92.9 mhz; 50 kw. Ant 480 ft. TL: N38 31 47 W96 05 09. Stereo. Hrs opn: 24. Box 83, 520 Market St. (66523); Box 893, 706 Commercial, Emporia (66801). (913) 528-4128; (316) 342-7655. FAX: (913) 528-4270. Licensee: Osage Radio Inc. Net: USA Kan. Info. Rep: Schneider. Wash atty: Blair & Silva. Format: Country. News staff one. Target aud: 25-54. Spec prog: Farm 18 hrs, relg 5 hrs wkly. ■ E.E. McCoy, pres, gen mgr & gen sls mgr; ED Funston, progmg dir; Ed Funston, mus dir & news dir; Jim Droegge, chief engr. ■ Rates: $21; 17; 17; 8.

Ottawa

KOFO(AM)—Sept 24, 1949: 1220 khz; 250 w-D, 40 w-N. TL: N38 35 04 W95 15 57. Hrs opn: 6 AM-10 PM (Mon-Sat), 6 AM-6 PM (Sun). Box 16, 320 E. Radio Rd. (66067). (913) 242-1220. FAX: (913) 242-1442. Licensee: Brandy Communications Inc. Net: ABC/E; Kan. Info., Kan. Agri. Format: C&W. News staff one; news progmg 5 hrs wkly. Target aud: 25-54. Spec prog: Farm 2 hrs wkly. ■ Brad Howard, pres, gen mgr, progmg dir & chief engr; Kathy Niehoff, gen sls mgr; Jay Bacon, mus dir; Brian Ketterer, news dir. ■ Rates: $9; 9; 9; 9.

*****KTJO-FM**—May 1951: 88.9 mhz; 150 w. Ant 98 ft. TL: N38 36 16 W95 15 49. Stereo. Box 110, Ottawa University, 1001 S. Cedar (66067). (913) 242-5200, ext. 5440. FAX: (913) 242-7429. Licensee: Ottawa University. Format: Div, contemp hit, contemp Christian. News progmg 5 hrs wkly. Target aud: General; the Ottawa Univ. community and the City of Ottawa, KS. ■ Barry King, gen mgr.

KZTO(FM)—March 1, 1962: 95.7 mhz; 100 kw. Ant 987 ft. TL: N38 50 15 W95 29 51 (CP: 98.6 kw). Hrs opn: 24.

2200 W. 25th St., Lawrence (66047). (913) 841-9696. FAX: (913) 841-9726. Licensee: American Broadcasting Systems Inc. (group owner; acq 12-4-91; $2.3 million; FTR 1-6-92). Net: CNN. Format: Adult contemp. News progmg 14 hrs wkly. Target aud: 25-54. Spec prog: Relg one hr wkly. ■ Ron Shaffer, pres; Helen Castleberry, gen mgr; Ron Miller, adv mgr; Scott Parks, progmg dir; John Collinson, chief engr.

Overland Park

KCCV(AM)—December 1989: 760 khz; 6 kw-D, DA. TL: N39 02 26 W94 30 32. 10550 Barkley (66212). (913) 642-7600. FAX: (913) 642-2424. Licensee: Bott Broadcasting (group owner). Net: USA. Format: Relg, news/talk. Target aud: 35-64; family oriented, mature. ■ Richard P. Bott, pres; Richard Bott II, exec vp & gen mgr; Ken Monroe, progmg dir.

Parsons

KLKC(AM)—1948: 1540 khz; 250 w-D. TL: N37 20 35 W95 13 55. Box 853 (67357). (316) 421-6400. FAX: (316) 421-5571. Licensee: Community Broadcasting Co. Inc. (acq 2-54). Format: Adult contemp. News staff one; news progmg 12 hrs wkly. Target aud: Young adults-60. Spec prog: Farm 2 hrs, big band 3 hrs wkly. ■ Richard R. Combs, pres & chief engr; Gary Cantrell, gen mgr, stn mgr & gen sls mgr; Steve Lardy, progmg dir; Ken Dickenson, mus dir; Annette Tucker, news dir.

KLKC-FM—October 1978: 93.5 mhz; 3 kw. Ant 267 ft. TL: N37 20 35 W95 13 55. Dups AM 80%.

Phillipsburg

KKAN(AM)—Dec 31, 1959: 1490 khz; 1 kw-U. TL: N39 47 32 W99 19 55. Box 548 (67661). (913) 543-2151; (913) 543-6593. Licensee: Walter C. Seidel (acq 3-29-88). Net: NBC, AP; Kan. Info. Format: Div, news. News staff one. Target aud: General; rural population & small towns. Spec prog: Farm 10 hrs, gospel 12 hrs wkly. ■ Walter C. Seidel, pres & gen mgr; Kirby Mullen, gen sls mgr; Bob Yates, progmg dir & mus dir; Tad Felts, news dir; Fred Zillinger, chief engr.

KQMA-FM—Co-owned with KKAN(AM). July 14, 1984: 92.5 mhz; 100 kw. Ant 510 ft. TL: N39 37 02 W99 17 55. Stereo. Dups AM 60%. 693 Third St. (67661). Net: AP.

Pittsburg

KKOW(AM)—Oct 11, 1937: 860 khz; 10 kw-D, 5 kw-N, DA-N. TL: N37 24 46 W94 38 16. Hrs opn: 24. Rte. 5, Box 45 (66762). (316) 231-7200. FAX: (316) 231-3321. Licensee: American Media Investment Inc. (acq 6-89; $400,000 with co-located FM; FTR 6-26-89). Net: CBS. Rep: McGavren Guild. Format: C&W, farm. News staff 2; news progmg 5 hrs wkly. Target aud: General. ■ O. Gene Bicknell, pres; Lance Sayler, gen mgr; Mike Gilmore, gen sls mgr; Lisa Miller-Ewing, prom dir; Bob Capps, progmg dir & mus dir; Mike Smith, Bob Capps, news dirs; Taylor Fast, chief engr.

KKOW-FM—April 20, 1975: 96.9 mhz; 100 kw. Ant 278 ft. TL: N37 23 44 W94 40 42. Stereo. Net: McGavren Guild. Format: Contemp country. ■ Gayle Poteet, progmg dir & mus dir.

KPHN(AM)—1948: 1340 khz; 1 kw-U. TL: N37 23 44 W94 40 42. 1604 E. Quincy (66762). (316) 232-1340; (316) 235 1340. FAX: (316) 232-6341. Licensee: Freeman Broadcasting Inc. (acq 5-20-93; $140,000 FTR 6-7-93). Net: SMN. Format: News/talk. News staff 2. Target aud: 25 plus. Spec prog: High School basketball & football. ■ Bill Johnson, pres; Cheryl Mcloyd, gen mgr & stn mgr.

*****KRPS(FM)**—Apr 29, 1988: 89.9 mhz; 100 kw. Ant 1,000 ft. TL: N37 18 44 W94 48 58. Stereo. Hrs opn: 24. Box 899 (66762). (316) 231-7000. FAX: (316) 232-2430. Licensee: Pittsburg State Univ. Net: NPR, APR. Format: Fine arts. News progmg 30 hrs wkly. Target aud: 35 plus; older, better educated, higher income. Spec prog: Folk 3 hrs, jazz 21 hrs, blues 4 hrs, new age 4 hrs wkly. ■ Jon R. Howard, gen mgr; Terri Falis, opns mgr; Missi Lindsay, mktg mgr; Kristine Allen, progmg dir; Keith Retzer, chief engr.

Pratt

KWLS(AM)—Sept 19, 1963: 1290 khz; 5 kw-D, 500 w-N, DA-2. TL: N37 38 34 W98 40 39. Box 486 (67124). (316) 672-5581. FAX: (316) 672-5583. Licensee: Lesso Inc. (group owner; acq 1-1-78). Net: ABC/E, MBS; Mid America Ag. Format: C&W, farm. News staff one; news progmg 3 hrs wkly. Target aud: 25 plus; rural. ■ Larry Steckline, pres; Ron Metzinger, gen mgr & gen sls mgr;

Carl Raida, prom mgr, progmg dir & mus dir; Edward L. Kidd, news dir; Bill Nolan, chief engr.

KGLS(FM)—Co-owned with KWLS(AM). July 1, 1965: 93.1 mhz; 100 kw. Ant 1,007 ft. TL: N37 55 50 W98 19 04. Stereo. Dups AM 20%. 1120 N. Halstgad, Hutchinson (67501). Format: Country, farm.

Russell

KRSL(AM)—Jan 11, 1956: 990 khz; 250 w-D, 30 w-N. TL: N38 54 22 W98 51 39. Box 666 (67665). (913) 483-3121. FAX: (913) 483-6511. Licensee: West Central Radio Inc. (acq 10-24-89; $404,000 with co-located FM; FTR 11-13-89). Format: Adult contemp. News staff one; news progmg 10 hrs wkly. Target aud: General; 24 plus. Spec prog: Polka 4 hrs, farm 2 hrs wkly. ■ Wayne Grabbe, pres, gen mgr & mktg mgr; Robert Musgrave, exec vp; Fred L. Thompson, sr vp; Naomi Miller, opns dir; Gordon Gorton, dev dir, sls dir & adv dir; Ken Geibler, news dir & engrg dir. ■ Rates: $13; 10; 13; 10.

KCAY(FM)—Co-owned with KRSL(AM). July 1, 1965: 95.9 mhz; 1.35 kw. Ant 487 ft. TL: N38 54 22 W98 51 39. Stereo. Dups AM 96%. Spec prog: Wilson Czeck polka party and Waxworks (oldies format geared to the 30s & 40s). ■ Robert Musgrave, vp; Naomi Miller, dev dir. ■ Rates: Same as AM.

Salina

KCVS(FM)—October 1988: 104.9 mhz; 3 kw. Ant 269 ft. TL: N38 53 23 W97 38 46. 110 E. Walnut (67401). (913) 823-5200. FAX: (913) 823-8596. Licensee: United American Broadcasting. Format: Inspir. ■ Gayland Gaut, gen mgr; Shaun Fitzpatrick, progmg dir; Dwight Downing, chief engr.

KFRM(AM)—1947: 550 khz; 5 kw-D, 110 w-N, DA-2. TL: N39 2610 W97 3940. Rte 1, Concordia (66901). (316) 243-1114. FAX: (913) 243-2012. Licensee: H.R.H. Broadcasting Corp. (acq 7-30-93; $25,000; FTR 8-23-93). Net: ABC/D; Brownfield. Wash atty: Sidley & Austin. Format: Country. News progmg 8 hrs wkly. Target aud: 25-55. Spec prog: Farm 5 hrs, gospel 5 hrs wkly. ■ Curt Shoemaker, gen mgr.

***KHCD(FM)**—Jan 28, 1988: 89.5 mhz; 100 kw. Ant 925 ft. TL: N39 06 16 W97 23 15. Stereo. Satellite of KHCC-FM Hutchinson. Suite 300, 815 N. Walnut, Hutchinson (67501). (316) 665-3555. Licensee: Hutchinson Community College. Net: NPR. Format: Class, new age, news. News progmg 27 hrs wkly. Spec prog: Jazz one hr wkly. ■ David M. Horning, gen mgr; Patsy Terrell, prom mgr; Sharon Dudgeon, progmg dir; Carolyn Gardner, mus dir; Ric Jung, engrg dir.

KINA(AM)—April 20, 1964: 910 khz; 500 w-D, 29 w-N, DA-2. TL: N38 45 52 W97 32 30. Box 2060, 203 S. Santa Fe, (67402-2060). (913) 825-0266. FAX: (913) 825-0269. Licensee: Smoky Hill Broadcasting Inc. Net: CNN; Kan. Info., Kan. Ag. Format: Original hits. Target aud: 45 plus. Spec prog: Farm 4 hrs wkly. ■ L.P. Justus, pres & gen mgr; Ken Jennison, gen sls mgr; Dan Helm, progmg dir; Gary Houser, mus dir; Bryan Thompson, news dir.

***KKRC(FM)**—Not on air, target date unknown: 90.7 mhz; 1 kw. Ant 253 ft. TL: N38 53 23 W97 38 46. 400 W. Lake Brantley, Altamonte Springs, FL (32714). Licensee: North Central Kansas Broadcasting Inc. (acq 1993; FTR 9-13-93).

KSAL(AM)—May 18, 1937: 1150 khz; 5 kw-U, DA-N. TL: N38 53 08 W97 30 58. Box 80 (67402). (913) 823-1111. Licensee: Independence Broadcasting Salina Corp. Group owner: Independence Broadcasting Corp. (acq 12-24-86; grpsl; FTR 12-1-86). Net: ABC/I. Rep: Banner. Format: Full svc adult contemp. News staff 3; news progmg 20 hrs wkly. Target aud: General. Spec prog: Farm 6 hrs wkly. ■ John Goodwill, pres; Larry Riggins, gen mgr, natl sls mgr & rgnl sls mgr; Bob Protzman, gen sls mgr; Jay Michaels, progmg dir; Mark Beaver, mus dir; Dave Foor, news dir; Don Englehardt, chief engr. ■ Rates: $30; 26; 27; 20.

KYEZ(FM)—Co-owned with KSAL(AM). May 1, 1975: 93.7 mhz; 100 kw. Ant 510 ft. TL: N38 57 14 W97 36 29. Stereo. 1510 E. Iron (67401). Net: MBS. Format: C&W. Target aud: 25-54. ■ Carolyn Carpenter, gen sls mgr. ■ Rates: Same as AM.

KSKG(FM)—1961: 99.9 mhz; 100 kw. Ant 570 ft. TL: N38 47 36 W97 31 33. Box 6198 Salina (67401-0198). (913) 825-4631. FAX: (913) 825-6100. Licensee: Eagle Communications Inc. Net: ABC/FM. Format: CHR. Spec prog: Farm 2 hrs, church 3 hrs wkly. ■ Gary Shorman, vp; Rod Rogers, chief engr.

KYEZ(FM)—Listing follows KSAL(AM).

Scott City

KFLA(AM)—Oct 13, 1962: 1310 khz; 500 w-D, 147 w-N. TL: N38 31 35 W100 54 42. Route 1, Box 14 (67871). (316) 872-5345. FAX: (316) 872-5346. Licensee: Western Kansas Wireless Inc. (acq 3-26-93; $175,000 with co-located FM; FTR 4-12-93). Net: Kan. Agri, Kan. Info. Format: Relg. Spec prog: Farm 5 hrs wkly. ■ Scott Smith, gen mgr.

KSKL(FM)—Co-owned with KFLA(AM). Nov 9, 1964: 94.5 mhz; 100 kw. Ant 345 ft. TL: N38 31 35 W100 34 42. Stereo. Net: Kan. Info. Format: Oldies.

Seneca

KMZA(FM)—Oct 15, 1992: 92.1 mhz; 4.5 kw. Ant 377 ft. TL: N39 49 50 W96 02 39. Stereo. Hrs opn: 5 AM-midnight. Rebroadcasts KNZA(FM) Hiawatha 90%. Box 92 (66538); 427 Main St. (66538). (913) 336-6166. FAX: (913) 336-3600. Licensee: KNZA Inc. Net: ABC/D. Format: Country, local. News staff one; news progmg 10 hrs wkly. Target aud: General. Spec prog: Farm 7 hrs wkly. ■ Greg Buser, pres & gen mgr; Robert Hilton, opns mgr; Mike Douthut, chief engr. ■ Rates: $13.50; 13.50; 13.50; 6.

Topeka

KDVV(FM)—Listing follows KTOP(AM).

***KJTY(FM)**—Aug 31, 1985: 88.1 mhz; 50 kw. Ant 350 ft. TL: N39 11 25 W95 39 29 (CP: 100 kw). Stereo. Hrs opn: 24. 1005 S.W. 10th St. (66604). (913) 357-8888. Licensee: Joy Public Broadcasting Corp. Net: MBN, USA. Format: Relg. News progmg 15 hrs wkly. Target aud: 25-49. Spec prog: Black, Children 5 hrs wkly. ■ Lowell M. Bush, pres; Ed Smith, gen mgr & chief engr.

KMAJ(AM)—July 1947: 1440 khz; 5 kw-D, 1 kw-N, DA-1. TL: N39 01 17 W95 34 15. Box 4407 (66604). (913) 272-2122. FAX: (913) 272-6219. Licensee: Midland Broadcasters Inc. (acq 2-62). Net: ABC/I. Rep: Torbet. Format: Talk. News staff one. Target aud: General. ■ Fred P. Reynolds, pres; Fritz Reynolds, gen mgr; Bill Reed, gen sls mgr; Mary Franco, progmg dir; Jan Lunsford, news dir.

KMAJ-FM—July 1, 1971: 107.7 mhz; 100 kw. Ant 1,214 ft. TL: N39 01 34 W95 54 58. Stereo. Prog sep from AM. Format: Adult contemp.

KTOP(AM)—July 1947: 1490 khz; 1 kw-U. TL: N39 04 39 W95 40 46. Box 1478 (66601); 715 Harrison St. (66603). (913) 234-3444. FAX: (913) 234-6654. Licensee: UNO Broadcasting Corp. (group owner; acq 10-87). Net: MBS. Rep: Banner. Format: Big band. News staff one; news progmg 18 hrs wkly. Target aud: 45 plus. ■ Robert Tezak, pres; Greg Phillips, opns mgr; Steve Lewis, gen sls mgr. ■ Rates: $24; 22; 24; 20.

KDVV(FM)—Co-owned with KTOP(AM). May 29, 1960: 100.3 mhz; 100 kw. Ant 984 ft. TL: N38 57 15 W95 54 43. Stereo. Prog sep from AM. Format: Adult rock & roll. Target aud: 18-54.

KTPK(FM)—Nov 25, 1974: 106.9 mhz; 100 kw. Ant 1,210 ft. TL: N39 01 34 W95 54 58. Stereo. Hrs opn: 24. 3003 S. Van Buren at 30th. (66611). (913) 267-2300; (913) 297-1069. FAX: (913) 267-5875. Licensee: Topeka Broad Comm Inc. (acq 12-29-88). Net: ABC/D. Rep: D & R Radio. Wash atty: James Gammon. Format: Modern country. News staff 2; news progmg 6 hrs wkly. Target aud: 25-64; mobile, family-oriented adults. ■ H. Pat Powers, CEO, exec vp & gen mgr; Pierce McNally, pres; Phil Tysinger, vp, vp sls, gen sls mgr, vp adv & adv mgr; Lynn Higbee, stn mgr & news dir; Marlene Adkison, opns dir, progmg dir & mus dir; Lee O'Day, prom dir; Robin Valentine, prom mgr; Rick Douglas, asst mus dir & pub affrs dir; Mike Slocum, chief engr.

KWIC(FM)—Not on air, target date unknown: 92.5 mhz; 6 kw. Ant 292 ft. c/o Margaret Escriva, 17006 Silver Sky Lane, Houston, TX (77095). Licensee: Margaret Escriva.

WIBW(AM)—May 8, 1927: 580 khz; 5 kw-U, DA-N (S-KKSU). TL: N39 05 05 W95 46 58. Hrs opn: 19. Box 119 (66601); 5600 W. 6th St. (66606). (913) 272-3456. FAX: (913) 272-0117. Licensee: Stauffer Communications Inc. (group owner; acq 2-1-57). Net: CBS Spectrum, ABC, Sun. Rep: Katz. Wash atty: Dow, Lohnes & Albertson. Format: Full svc country, farm & sports. News staff 4. Target aud: 25 plus. Spec prog: Relg 6 hrs wkly. ■ Al Lobeck, gen mgr; Craig Colboch, gen sls mgr; Mike Matson, news dir; Ed O'Donnell, chief engr.

WIBW-FM—Sept 1, 1961: 97.3 mhz; 100 kw. Ant 1,220 ft. TL: N39 00 19 W96 02 58. Stereo. Hrs opn: 24. Net: SMN. Format: Country. News progmg 7 hrs wkly. Target aud: 25-54. ■ Kevin Wagner, progmg dir. ■ WIBW-TV affil.

Ulysses

KULY(AM)—Mar 1, 1965: 1420 khz; 1 kw-D, 500 w-N, DA-N. TL: N37 14 28 W101 21 49. Box 1420 (67880). (316) 356-1420. FAX: (316) 356-3635. Licensee: A & B Broadcasting Inc. (group owner; acq 4-14-92; $220,000 with KFXX-FM Hugoton; FTR 5-4-92). Net: ABC/D; Kan. Info., Kan. Agri. Wash atty: B. Jay Baraff. Format: C&W. News staff one; news progmg 24 hrs wkly. Target aud: 25-44; middle to upper class workers, farmers & housewives. Spec prog: Met Opera 4 hrs, farm 12 hrs, gospel 7 hrs wkly. ■ Monte Speavman, gen mgr; John O'Sullivan, opns dir, dev dir & news dir; Jerry Sullivan, sls dir; Monte Spearman, gen sls mgr, natl sls mgr & rgnl sls mgr; Ty Harmon, progmg dir & mus dir; Chuck Springer, chief engr. ■ Rates: $11; 11; 11; 3.

Wamego

KHCA(FM)—Mar 6, 1986: 95.3 mhz; 6 kw. Ant 328 ft. TL: N39 12 35 W96 21 05. Stereo. 103 N. 3rd, Manhattan (66502). (913) 456-9530; (913) 537-9595. FAX: (913) 537-2955. Licensee: KHCA Inc. (acq 9-18-91; $126,000; FTR 10-7-91). Net: CBN. Format: Christian adult contemp/rock. News staff one; news progmg 15 hrs wkly. ■ Jerry Hutchinson, pres & news dir; Jerry Hutchinson, Tim Dykes (asst), gen mgrs; Phil Padilla, progmg dir & mus dir; Kevin Block, chief engr. ■ Rates: $8.50; 7.50; 8.50; 7.50.

Wellington

KLEY(AM)—Nov 19, 1966: 1130 khz; 250 w-D, DA. TL: N37 14 28 W97 24 04. Hrs opn: 6 AM-6 PM. R.R. 3, Box 1AA (67152). (316) 326-3341. FAX: (316) 326-8512. Licensee: Johnson Enterprises Inc. (acq 5-1-89; $575,000 with co-located FM; FTR 3-27-89). Net: AP, Unistar; Kan. Info, Kan. Agri. Format: Country. News staff one; news progmg 20 hrs wkly. Target aud: General. Spec prog: Farm 10 hrs, relg 4 hrs wkly. ■ E. Gordon Johnson, pres, gen mgr, gen sls mgr & prom mgr; Vernon Napier, opns mgr, progmg dir & engrg dir; Tom Dobbins, news dir. ■ Rates: $9; 7.40; 7.40; 6.30.

KWME(FM)—Co-owned with KLEY(AM). Aug 27, 1979: 93.5 mhz; 3 kw. Ant 200 ft. TL: N37 14 28 W97 24 04. Stereo. Dups AM 10%. Format: EZ lstng. Target aud: 35-64.

Wichita

***KCFN(FM)**—Apr 23, 1978: 91.1 mhz; 100 kw. Ant 345 ft. TL: N37 48 01 W97 17 50. Stereo. Hrs opn: 24. Suite 201, 400 N. Woodlawn (67208). (316) 688-5236. FAX: (316) 436-1329. Licensee: New Life Fellowship Inc. (group owner; acq 4-1-92; $205,000; FTR 4-20-92). Format: Christian. News progmg 2 hrs wkly. Target aud: 35-65; general. Spec prog: Big band 4 hrs, Broadway 2 hrs, jazz 4 hrs wkly. ■ John Pohlman, gen mgr; Bob Thornton, prom dir; Dan Gentry, chief engr.

KEYN-FM—Listing follows KQAM(AM).

KFDI(AM)—September 1923: 1070 khz; 10 kw-D, 1 kw-N, DA-N. TL: N37 42 47 W97 19 59. Hrs opn: 24. Box 1402, 4200 N. Old Lawrence Rd. (67201). (316) 838-9141. Licensee: Wichita Great Empire Broadcasting. Group owner: Great Empire Broadcasting Inc. (acq 1-17-66). Net: ABC. Rep: Torbet, R&R. Wash atty: Dow, Lohnes & Albertson. Format: C&W. News staff 7. Target aud: 25-54. ■ F.F. Mike Lynch, pres; Mike Oatman, vp; John Speer, opns mgr; Spike Santee, gen sls mgr; Bryce LeGrand, prom dir; Scott Piper, progmg dir; Gary Hightower, mus dir; Dan Dillon, news dir; Julie Pritchard, pub affrs dir; Cliff Koch, chief engr.

KFDI-FM—June 6, 1963: 101.3 mhz; 100 kw. Ant 1,139 ft. TL: N37 47 47 W97 31 59. Stereo. Dups AM 45%. Format: C&W. ■ John Speer, progmg dir.

KFH(AM)—May 26, 1922: 1330 khz; 5 kw-U, DA-N. TL: N37 42 47 W97 14 51. Stereo. Hrs opn: 24. 626 N. Broadway (67214). (316) 267-0800. FAX: (316) 267-0512. Licensee: Midcontinent Broadcasting Co. of Kansas. Group owner: Midcontinent Media Inc. (acq 1988; $800,000 FTR 12-5-88). Net: CBS, AP, MBS. Rep: Banner. Format: News/talk. News staff 2; news progmg 14 hrs wkly. Target aud: 25-54. ■ Larry Bentson, pres; Jeff Clark, gen mgr; Jackie Wise, gen sls mgr; Barry Casey, prom dir, progmg dir & mus dir; Janet Neel, news dir; Tony Duesing, pub affrs dir; Larry Waggoner, chief engr.

KFRM(AM)—See Salina.

***KIBN(FM)**—Mar 25, 1990: 90.7 mhz; 25 kw-H, 23 kw-V. Ant 335 ft. TL: N37 21 53 W97 20 30. Hrs opn: 24. Suite

Stations in the U.S.

Kentucky

201, 400 N. Woodlawn (67208). (316) 686-7744; (316) 436-5426. FAX: (316) 436-1329. Licensee: New Life Fellowship Inc. Net: American Urban. Format: Div, relg, urban contemp. News progmg 10 hrs wkly. Target aud: 25-54; upscale females. ■ David G. Brace, pres; Sherdeill H. Breatheh Sr., adv dir; Carla M. Williams, progmg dir; Larry Wagner, chief engr.

KICT-FM—April 28, 1972: 95.1 mhz; 100 kw. Ant 1,026 ft. TL: N37 47 58 W97 31 58. Stereo. 734 N. Maize Rd. (67212). (316) 722-5600. FAX: (316) 722-0722. Licensee: Granite Broadcasting Corp. (acq 11-30-92; $1 million; FTR 12-21-92). Net: ABC/R. Rep: McGavren Guild. Format: Rock. News staff 2. Target aud: 18-49. Spec prog: Heavy rock 8 hrs wkly. ■ Barry Gaston, pres; gen mgr & stn mgr; Brian McDonough, gen sls mgr; Rick Regan, prom mgr; Ron Eric Taylor, progmg dir; Sherry McKinnon, mus dir; Jan Harrison, news dir.

KKRD(FM)—Listing follows KNSS(AM).

*KMUW(FM)—April 26, 1949: 89.1 mhz; 100 kw. Ant 450 ft. TL: N37 45 01 W97 18 12. Stereo. Hrs opn: 19. 3317 E. 17th St. (67208). (316) 682-5737. FAX: (316) 689-3946. Licensee: Wichita State Univ. Net: NPR/Kan. Info. Wash atty: Schwartz, Woods & Miller. Format: Class, jazz, news. News staff 2; news progmg 8 hrs wkly. Target aud: General. Spec prog: Gospel 6 hrs, Sp 2 hrs wkly. ■ Gary Shivers, gen mgr; Pat Hayes, dev dir; Mark McCain, progmg dir; Gordon Bassham, news dir; Ross Pierce, chief engr.

KNSS(AM)—Oct 28, 1947: 1240 khz; 630 kw-U. TL: N37 43 06 W97 19 05. 2402 E. 37th N. (67219). (316) 832-9600. FAX: (316) 838-2800. Licensee: Prism Radio Partners (acq 1993; with co-located FM; FTR 9-20-93). Net: ABC TalkRadio, CBS, MBS, NBC. Rep: D & R Radio. Format: All news, talk. News staff 6; news progmg 40 hrs wkly. Target aud: 35 plus; professionals. ■ Tim Link, gen mgr; Ken Clifford, sls dir; Mary Beal, progmg dir; Denis Martyn, news dir; Jeff Bemrose, chief engr.

KKRD(FM)—Co-owned with KNSS(AM). Apr 17, 1967: 107.3 mhz; 100 kw. Ant 884 ft. TL: N37 46 37 W97 31 01. Stereo. Rep: D & R Radio. Format: CHR. ■ Jack Oliver, progmg dir; Scott Smith, news dir.

KQAM(AM)—1950: 1410 khz; 5 kw-D, 1 kw-N, DA-2. TL: N37 44 05 W97 21 06. Hrs opn: 24. 2829 Salina Ave. (67204). (316) 838-7744. FAX: (316) 832-0061. Licensee: Clear Channel Radio Licenses Inc. (group owner; acq 8-5-92; with co-located FM). Net: MBS. Rep: Eastman. Format: Nostalgia, big band, news/talk. News staff one. Target aud: 35-64. ■ Richard Parrish, vp & gen mgr; Dan Hogan, gen sls mgr; Elise Schowalter, prom dir; Jerry Vaughn, progmg dir; Dan O'Neal, news dir; Hank Langlinias, chief engr.

KEYN-FM—Co-owned with KQAM(AM). October 1968: 103.7 mhz; 95 kw. Ant 859 ft. TL: N37 46 37 W97 31 01. Stereo. Hrs opn: 24. Prog sep from AM. Net: ABC. Format: Adult contemp, oldies. Target aud: 25-49; baby boomers. ■ April McQuilken, opns dir; Dennis Kinkaid, progmg dir.

KRBB(FM)—Sept 19, 1948: 97.9 mhz; 100 kw. Ant 993 ft. TL: N37 42 47 W97 14 51. Stereo. Hrs opn: 24. Suite 300, 200 N. Broadway (67202). (316) 265-9800. FAX: (316) 265-1162. Licensee: Marathon Broadcasting (acq 9-27-89). Rep: Christal. Format: Adult contemp. News staff one. Target aud: 28-48. Spec prog: Jazz 6 hrs, relg one hr wkly. ■ Sid Sayovitz, pres; Chet Tart, exec vp & gen mgr; Bob Morrison, sls dir; Brett Harris, prom mgr & progmg dir; Ken Payne, mus dir; Tracy Cassidy, news dir; Larry Waggoner, chief engr. ■ Rates: $45; 55; 50; 38.

KRZZ-FM—See Derby.

KSGL(AM)—August 1957: 900 khz; 250 w-D, 28 w-N, DA-2. TL: N37 41 33 W97 22 54. 3337 W. Central (67203). (316) 942-3231. Licensee: Agape Communications Inc. Net: USA. Format: Relg. News staff 5. ■ Don Clifford, pres; Norbert Atherton, sr vp & chief engr; Terry Atherton, gen mgr & progmg dir; Gary Dark, gen sls mgr; John Mills, mus dir; Martin Shay, pub affrs dir.

*KYFW(FM)—Oct 1, 1986: 88.3 mhz; 17 kw. Ant 141 ft. TL: N37 40 22 W97 20 08. Stereo. Hrs opn: 24. 239 Harral, Derby (67037). (316) 788-7883. Licensee: Bible Broadcasting Network (group owner; acq 6-26-89). Format: Christian music. ■ Lowell Davey, pres; Matt Johnson, gen mgr & prom mgr; Harold Richards Jr., progmg dir.

KYQQ(FM)—See Arkansas City.

KZSN(AM)—1936: 1480 khz; 5 kw-D, 1 kw-N, DA-2. TL: N37 44 21 W97 16 14. Rebroadcasts KZSN-FM Hutchinson. 5610 E. 29th St. N. (67220). (316) 683-4566. FAX: (316) 683-4609. Licensee: Southern Skies Corp. (group owner; acq 2-1-86). Net: AP. Rep: Katz. Format: Country.

Target aud: 45 plus. ■ Jerry Atchley, pres; Jim Worthington, vp & gen mgr; Pat Moyer, opns mgr, progmg dir & news dir; Lisa Allan, gen sls mgr; Juvetta Stump, prom mgr; Ralph Craig Jr., chief engr.

Winfield

KKLE(AM)—Aug 19, 1963: 1550 khz; 250 w-D, 52 w-N. TL: N37 14 21 W97 00 43. Suite 300, First Natl. Bank Bldg. (67156). (316) 221-3341. FAX: (316) 221-3342. Licensee: Johnson Enterprises Inc. (group owner; acq 1988). Net: MBS. Format: Adult contemp, MOR. News staff one; news progmg 7 hrs wkly. Target aud: 25 plus. ■ Gordon Johnson, pres & gen mgr; G.A. Wiles, gen sls mgr; Vernon Napier, progmg dir; Tony Purcell, news dir.

KKWM(FM)—Co-owned with KKLE(AM). Not on air, target date August 1994: 95.9 mhz; 50 kw. Ant 492 ft. TL: N37 06 42 W96 40 50.

*KSWC(FM)—November 1967: 100.3 mhz; 10 w. Ant 70 ft. TL: N37 14 42 W96 54 19. 100 College St. (67156). (316) 221-4150. FAX: (316) 221-8382. Licensee: Southwestern College. Format: Progsv, AOR, urban contemp. News progmg one hr wkly. Target aud: 21 & younger. ■ William DeArmond, gen mgr.

KWKS(FM)—1980: 107.9 mhz; 50 kw. Ant 397 ft. TL: N37 14 42 W96 54 19. Stereo. Hrs opn: 24. Prog sep from AM. Box 843, Strother Field Terminal Bldg. (67156-0843). Box 917, Arkansas City (67005). (316) 221-1440; (316) 442-5400. FAX: (316) 221-7782. Licensee: Cowley County Communications. Net: SMN; Kan. Info. Format: Oldies. News staff one; news progmg 10 hrs wkly. Target aud: 29-54; upscale yuppies & blue collar workers, baby boomers. Spec prog: Nostalgia 3 hrs, relg 2 hrs wkly. ■ Kelly Porter, gen sls mgr; Marty Mutti, progmg dir; Cheryl Higgins, news dir; Dave Foster, chief engr. ■ Rates: $15; 12.50; 15; 12.50.

Kentucky

LAUREN A. COLBY
301-663-1086
COMMUNICATIONS ATTORNEY
Special Attention to Difficult Cases

Albany

WANY(AM)—Oct 25, 1958: 1390 khz; 1 kw-D. TL: N36 41 54 W85 09 00. Box 400 (42602). (606) 387-5186. Licensee: Albany Broadcasting Co. Net: UPI; Ky. Agri. Rep: Keystone (unwired net). Format: Top-40, C&W. Spec prog: Farm 2 hrs, Gospel 6 hrs wkly. ■ Sidney Scott, gen mgr & gen sls mgr; Randy Speck, prom mgr, progmg dir, mus dir & news dir; Robert Huddleston, chief engr.

WANY-FM—April 18, 1966: 106.3 mhz; 2.7 kw. Ant 155 ft. TL: N36 41 54 W85 09 00. Dups AM 75%.

Allen

WMDJ-FM—Sept 1, 1984: 100.1 mhz; 1.3 kw. Ant 492 ft. TL: N37 35 12 W82 42 57 (CP: 2.6 kw). Stereo. Box 530, Martin (41649). (606) 874-8005. FAX: (606) 874-0057. Licensee: Floyd County Broadcasting (acq 12-84; grpsl; FTR 12-31-84). Net: NBC. Format: C&W, oldies. ■ Dale McKinney, pres, gen sls mgr, prom mgr & news dir; Rich Caudill, gen mgr, progmg dir & mus dir; Jim Daniels, chief engr.

Ashland

WCMI(AM)—1935: 1340 khz; 1 kw-U. TL: N38 26 45 W82 36 36. Box 949 (41105). (606) 329-1777. FAX: (606) 324-3377. Licensee: First Comm Inc. (acq 11-79). Net: ABC/E, ABC TalkRadio, MBS; Ky. Net. Format: News, talk, gospel. ■ Dick Martin Jr., pres & gen mgr; Charles Dunlap, gen sls mgr; Scott Martin, progmg dir; Ted Robinson, news dir; Don Rees, chief engr.

WCMI-FM—See Catlettsburg.

WRVC-FM—1948: 93.7 mhz; 100 kw. Ant 741 ft. TL: N38 23 14 W82 39 45. Stereo. Box 1150, Huntington, WV (25713). (304) 523-8401. FAX: (304) 523-4848. Licensee: Fifth Avenue Broadcasting (acq 1988). Net: NBC. Rep: Banner. Wash atty: Arent, Fox, Kitner, Plotkin & Kahn. Format: Oldies. News staff one. Target aud: 25-49; well educated. ■ Mike Kirtner, pres & gen mgr; Mark

Jesse, gen sls mgr; Jeff Crawford, prom dir, progmg dir & mus dir; Teresa Nichols, news dir & pub affrs dir; Bill Geyer, chief engr.

WTCR-FM—See Huntington, W.Va.

Barbourville

WYWY(AM)—Dec 13, 1955: 950 khz; 1 kw-D. TL: N36 50 26 W83 52 16. Box 778, 222 Daniel Boone Dr. (40906). (606) 546-4128. FAX: (606) 546-4138. Licensee: Barbourville Community Broadcasting Co. (acq 11-66). Format: Relg. News staff one; news progmg 2 hrs wkly. ■ Elmer Engle, pres; Chad Engle, gen mgr; Doug Hammons, chief engr.

WYWY-FM—Oct 2, 1974: 96.1 mhz; 25 kw. Ant 300 ft. TL: N36 51 55 W83 53 55. Stereo. Prog sep from AM. Format: Country. News progmg 4 hrs wkly. Target aud: 25-34. ■ James Engle, pres; Ed Thomas, gen sls mgr; Danny Miracle, prom dir. ■ Rates: $7.50; 6.50; 7.50; 6.50.

Bardstown

WBRT(AM)—December 1954: 1320 khz; 1 kw-D. TL: N37 49 09 W85 29 10. 106 S. 3rd (40004). (502) 348-3943. FAX: (502) 348-4043. Licensee: Nelson County Broadcasting (acq 9-66). Net: ABC/E; Ky. Net. Rep: Rgnl Reps. Format: C&W. News staff one. Target aud: 20 plus. Spec prog: Farm 10 hrs wkly. ■ Tom Isaac, pres & gen mgr; Peter Boyce, chief engr.

WOKH(FM)—Co-owned with WBRT(AM). October 1979: 96.7 mhz; 3 kw. Ant 160 ft. TL: N37 49 09 W85 29 10. Stereo. Prog sep from AM. Format: Adult contemp, classic rock.

Beattyville

WLJC(FM)—May 12, 1965: 102.1 mhz; 1.2 kw. Ant 520 ft. TL: N37 36 23 W83 41 16. 219 Radio Station Loop (41311). (606) 464-3600. FAX: (606) 464-0044. Licensee: Hour of Harvest Inc. Rep: Rgnl Reps. Format: Relg. ■ Forest Drake, pres & gen mgr; John Drake, gen sls mgr; Rachel Drake, progmg dir; Ida Hogan, mus dir; Jonathan Drake, chief engr.

Beaver Dam

WLLS(AM)—See Hartford.

WLLS-FM—See Hartford.

Benton

WCBL(AM)—Dec 13, 1954: 1290 khz; 5 kw-D. TL: N36 51 30 W88 20 13. Hrs opn: 5 AM-12 AM. Box 387, Hwy. 408 E. (42025). (502) 527-3102. FAX: (502) 527-5606. Licensee: Purchase Broadcasting Co. Net: NBC. Ky. Network. Format: Country. News staff one; news progmg 7 hrs wkly. Target aud: General. ■ Julie Sweet, pres; Mark Sweet, vp; Jim Freeland, gen mgr & gen sls mgr; Sherry Rickman, opns mgr; Paul Lamb, rgnl sls mgr; Dan Davis, progmg dir; Cathy Greer, mus dir & news dir; Faye Phillips, pub affrs dir; Earl Abanathy, chief engr. ■ Rates: $8; 8; 8; 8.

WCBL-FM—Mar 3, 1966: 102.3 mhz; 3 kw. Ant 298 ft. TL: N36 51 30 W88 20 13 (CP: 3.3 kw). Prog sep from AM. Rep: NBC. Format: Oldies.

*WVHM(FM)—Not on air, target date unknown: 90.5 mhz; 8 kw-V. Ant 351 ft. TL: N36 48 31 W88 13 26. Box 281, Hardin (42048). (502) 437-4905. Licensee: Heartland Ministries. Net: Moody, USA. Format: Gospel. ■ Darell Gibson, pres; Cycel Glass, stn mgr; Mike Wood, progmg dir.

Berea

WKXO(AM)—July 18, 1971: 1500 khz; 250 w-D. TL: N37 35 12 W84 18 04. Hrs opn: 6 AM-7 PM. Box 307, 406 Chestnut St. (40403). (606) 986-9321. FAX: (606) 986-8675. Licensee: Berea Broadcasting Inc. Group owner: Pioneer Communications (acq 7-2-82; $155,000; FTR 7-26-82). Net: ABC/E; Ky. Net. Format: C&W, news. News staff one; news progmg 3 hrs wkly. Target aud: 21 plus. Spec prog: Gospel 6 hrs wkly. ■ Robert J. Spradlin, pres; Rich Middleton, progmg dir. ■ Rates: $8; 8; 8; na.

WKXO-FM—Sept 27, 1990: 106.7 mhz; 1.95 kw. Ant 584 ft. TL: N37 30 15 W84 12 58. Stereo. Hrs opn: 24. Dups AM 50%.

Bowling Green

WBGN(AM)—Nov 24, 1959: 1340 khz; 1 kw-U. TL: N37 00 34 W86 27 09. Hrs opn: 24. Box 900, 948 Fairview

Ave. (42101). (502) 842-1638. Licensee: Hilltopper Broadcasting Inc. (acq 4-88). Net: NBC, CBS; Ky. Net. Rep: Rgnl Reps. Wash atty: Pepper & Corazzini. Format: News/talk. News staff one; news progmg 20 hrs wkly. Target aud: 25-49. ■ Wes Strader, pres; Barry Williams, gen mgr; Hank Brosche, gen sls mgr; Rob Beasley, chief engr. ■ Rates: $8.50; 7.50; 8.50; 7.50.

*WCVK(FM)—April 22, 1986: 90.7 mhz; 14 kw. Ant 448 ft. TL: N37 00 18 W86 31 19. Stereo. Box 539 (42102); 1403 Scottsdale Rd. (42102). (502) 781-7326. FAX: (502) 781-8005. Licensee: Bowling Green Community Broadcasting Inc. Net: USA. Format: Relg, MOR. News staff 2; news progmg 6 hrs wkly. Target aud: 25-54; Christian men & women. Spec prog: Black 2 hrs wkly.■James G. Chapman, pres; David Queen, gen mgr; Ken Burns, progmg dir; Chris Scott, chief engr.

WDNS(FM)—Listing follows WKCT(AM).

WKCT(AM)—Nov 1, 1947: 930 khz; 5 kw-D, 500 w-N, DA-N. TL: N37 01 53 W86 26 18. Hrs opn: 24. Box 930, 804 College St. (42102-0930). (502) 781-2121. FAX: (502) 842-0232. Licensee: Daily News Broadcasting Co. Net: CBS. Rep: Katz & Powell. Wash atty: Pepper & Corazzini. Format: MOR. News staff one; news progmg 25 hrs wkly. Target aud: 30 plus. Spec prog: Farm 2 hrs wkly. ■ John B. Gaines, pres; David O. White, gen mgr & gen sls mgr; Cynthia Shaluta, adv mgr; Al Arbogast, progmg dir & news dir; Robert J. Hendrick, chief engr. ■ Rates: $18; 14; 16; 9.

WDNS(FM)—Co-owned with WKCT(AM). March 12, 1973: 98.3 mhz; 6 kw. Ant 300 ft. TL: N37 02 45 W86 21 53. Stereo. Hrs opn: 24. Format: Classic rock, AOR. News staff one; news progmg 7 hrs wkly. Target aud: 18-44. ■ David White, progmg dir.

*WKYU-FM—November 1980: 88.9 mhz; 100 kw. Ant 721 ft. TL: N37 05 22 W86 38 05. Stereo. Hrs opn: 24. 248 Academic Complex, Western Kentucky Univ. (42101). (502) 745-5489. FAX: (502) 745-2084. Licensee: Western Kentucky Univ. Net: NPR, APR, Ky. Net. Wash atty: Cohn & Marks. Format: Class. News staff 3; news progmg 37 hrs wkly. Target aud: General. Spec prog: Jazz 15 hrs, folk 5 hrs wkly. ■ Thomas Meredith, pres; David T. Wilkinson, gen mgr; Jane Moore, opns mgr; Melinda Craft, dev mgr; Lee Stott, mus dir; Dan Modlin, news dir; Chris Scott, chief engr. ■ WKYU-TV affil.

WLBJ(AM)—June 1940: 1410 khz; 5 kw-D, 1 kw-N, DA-N. TL: N36 59 46 W86 24 13. Box 689, 200 Scott Lane (42102). (502) 843-3212. Licensee: Bowling Green Broadcasters Inc. Group owner: Bahakel Communications (acq 1-56). ■ Cy N. Bahakel, pres.

WMJM(FM)—May 1965: 96.7 mhz; 13.5 kw. Ant 521 ft. TL: N36 57 25 W86 40 14. Stereo. Hrs opn: 24. Suite 2, 2465 Russellville Rd. (42101). (502) 843-3333. FAX: (502) 843-0454. Licensee: WBZD Inc. Group owner: Donald Alt (acq 10-3-91; $250,000 FTR 10-28-91). Net: SMN. Format: Adult contemp. Target aud: 18-54. ■ Shannon Allen, stn mgr; Michael Golchert, chief engr.

*WWHR(FM)—Aug 18, 1988: 91.7 mhz; 100 w. Ant 10 ft. TL: N36 59 00 W86 27 24. Stereo. Western Kentucky Univ., Academic Complex 153 (42101). (502) 745-5350. FAX: (502) 745-2084. Licensee: Western Kentucky University. Net: AP. Format: Alternative. Target aud: College students. ■ Charles M. Anderson, gen sls mgr; Jeff Roper, progmg dir.

Brandenburg

WMMG(AM)—July 1984: 1140 khz; 250 w-D. TL: N37 59 05 W86 09 24. 1715 Bypass Rd. (40108). (502) 422-3961; (502) 422-4440. FAX: (502) 422-3464. Licensee: Meade County Broadcasting Inc. Net: Ky. Net. Rep: Rgnl Reps. Format: Country. News staff one; news progmg 16 hrs wkly. Spec prog: Relg 8 hrs wkly. ■ Shawn Lynch, gen mgr & prom mgr; Diane Wood, gen sls mgr; Lee Bramlett, progmg dir & news dir; Jody Benham, mus dir; Scott Benham, asst mus dir; Greg Happel, chief engr. ■ Rates: $6.75; 6.75; 6.75; 6.75.

WMMG-FM—Aug 23, 1972: 93.5 mhz; 3.4 kw. Ant 290 ft. TL: N37 59 05 W86 09 24 Stereo. Dups AM 100%.

Buffalo

WXAM(AM)—Nov 26, 1974: 1430 khz; 1 kw-D. TL: N37 31 49 W85 42 49. Box 177, Hodgenville (42748). (502) 358-4707. FAX: (502) 358-4755. Licensee: Mark Goodman Productions Inc. (acq 2-1-89; $99,292; FTR 2-13-89). Net: ABC/I. Format: Country. ■ Mark Goodman, pres & gen mgr; Carolyn Goodman, vp & news dir; Ron Dowdell, chief engr.

Burkesville

WKYR(AM)—Dec 15, 1975: 1570 khz; 1 kw-D. TL: N36 4647 W85 2200. Box 340 (42717). (502) 433-7191. FAX: (502) 433-7195. Licensee: WKYR Inc. (acq 3-3-76). Net: ABC/E. Rep: Rgnl Reps, Keystone (unwired net). Format: General. Spec prog: Farm 5 hrs wkly. ■ Ray Mullinix, CEO, pres, gen mgr & progmg dir; Silas A. Norris, sr vp; Carol Mirill, sls dir; Don Johnson, mus dir; Randy Speck, news dir; Larry Nelson, chief engr.

WKYR-FM—October 1988: 107.9 mhz; 6 kw. Ant 312 ft. TL: N36 47 26 W85 22 47. Stereo. Dups AM 100%.

Burnside

WKEQ(AM)—Feb 28, 1984: 910 khz; 500 w-D. TL: N37 01 46 W84 36 28. Box 1464, 1464 Boat Dock Rd., Somerset (42501). (606) 679-8594. FAX: (606) 678-2020. Licensee: Lenn R. Pruitt. Net: CBS Spectrum. Format: Classic rock. News staff one; news progmg 5 hrs wkly. Target aud: 18-50. ■ Lenn R. Pruitt, pres; Eddy Pruitt, gen mgr; Nolan Canner, opns mgr; Gib Gossler, news dir; Bruce Correll, chief engr.

WJDJ(FM)—Co-owned with WKEQ(AM). Aug 17, 1985: 93.9 mhz; 50 kw. Ant 492 ft. TL: N37 09 15 W84 27 35. Stereo. Prog sep from AM. Net: SMN. Format: CHR.

Cadiz

WKDZ(AM)—Apr 8, 1966: 1110 khz; 1 kw-D. TL: N36 52 57 W87 50 44. Drawer D, 1487 Will Jackson Rd. (42211-0316). (502) 522-3232. FAX: (502) 522-1110. Licensee: Ham Broadcasting Co. (acq 1-22-91; $200,000 with co-located FM; FTR 2-11-91). Net: MBS. Format: Country. News staff one. Target aud: 25-54. Spec prog: Farm 2 hrs wkly, relg 6 hrs wkly. ■ D.J. Evert, pres; Cinthia Allan, gen mgr; Tom Rogers, progmg dir & mus dir; David Fowler, news dir; Larry Mcdow, chief engr.

WKDZ-FM—May 18, 1972: 106.3 mhz; 3 kw. Ant 317 ft. TL: N36 52 57 W87 50 44. Stereo. Prog sep from AM. Format: Lite rock, MOR. ■ Gary Kidd, gen sls mgr.

Calvert City

WCCK(FM)—Not on air, target date unknown: 95.7 mhz; 3 kw. Ant 328 ft. 647 Main St. (42029). Licensee: Stice Communications Inc.

Campbellsville

WCKQ(FM)—Dec 1, 1964: 104.1 mhz; 2.25 kw. Ant 374 ft. TL: N37 19 29 W85 18 36. Stereo. 50 Friendship Pike (42718); Box 1053 (42719). (502) 789-2401. Licensee: Heartland Communications (acq 9-85; $725,000 with co-located AM; FTR 9-23-85). Net: CBS, CBS Spectrum, Westwood One. Rep: Rgnl Reps. Format: Adult contemp. News staff 2. Target aud: 18-54. ■ George E. Owen Jr., pres & gen mgr; Steve George, sls dir; Kim Cary, progmg dir; Tom McClendon, mus dir; Tom Redmon, news dir; Mike Graham, chief engr. ■ Rates: $18; 11; 18; 7.

WTCO(AM)—Co-owned with WCKQ(FM). Mar 1948: 1450 khz; 1 kw-U. TL: N37 20 07 W85 22 33. Prog sep from FM. (502) 789-1450. Net: Jones Satellite Audio. Format: Country. Target aud: 25-64. ■ Rates: $7; 6; 7; 5.

WGRK-FM—See Greensburg.

WTCO(AM)—Listing follows WCKQ(FM).

WVLC(FM)—Not on air, target date unknown: 99.9 mhz; 3 kw. Ant 328 ft. 173 W. Owl Creek Rd. (42718). Licensee: Patricia Rodgers.

Cannonsburg

WOKT(AM)—December 1987: 1040 khz; 2.5 kw-D, DA-D. TL: N38 23 39 W82 41 53. Hrs opn: Sunrise-sunset. Box 5730, Ashland (41105); 3027 Lester Ln., Ashland (41102). (606) 928-3778. Licensee: WOKT Inc. Group owner: Baker Family Stations. Net: USA. Format: Relg, talk. Target aud: General. ■ Edward A. Baker, pres; Brian Corea, gen mgr; Elliot Gehringer, chief engr. ■ Rates: $7.50; 7.50; 7.50; na.

Carlisle

WWLW(FM)—Not on air, target date unknown: 100.7 mhz; 6 kw. Ant 269 ft. Stereo. Hrs opn: 24. 10 Trinity Place, Fort Thomas (41075). Licensee: TAMI Inc. Wash atty: Miller & Miller. Format: Diversified. News staff one; news progmg 14 hrs wkly. Target aud: General. Spec prog: Sports, farm 5 hrs, the Dead hour one hr, your day's court 5 hrs wkly.

Carrollton

WIKI(FM)—April 12, 1968: 95.3 mhz; 3 kw. Ant 423 ft. TL: N38 39 58 W85 16 51. Stereo. Hrs opn: 24. Wiki Building, 102 E. Main St., Madison, IN (47250). (502) 732-6686; (812) 265-6878. Licensee: WIKI Inc. (acq 11-1-84; $170,000; FTR 6-4-84). Net: Jones Satellite Audio. Rep: Rgnl Reps. Wash atty: Erwin Krasnow. Format: Country. News progmg 6 hrs wkly. Target aud: General; ages 10-90. ■ George Freeman, pres & gen mgr.

Catlettsburg

WCMI-FM—Jan 19, 1972: 92.7 mhz; 3 kw. Ant 298 ft. TL: N38 27 58 W82 35 27. Stereo. Hrs opn: 20. Box 949, Ashland (41105). (606) 329-1777. Licensee: First Comm Inc. Net: ABC/A, MBS. Format: Adult contemp. ■ Dick Martin Jr., pres & gen mgr; Charlie Dunlap, gen sls mgr; Scott Martin, progmg dir & mus dir; Ted Robinson, news dir; Don Rees, chief engr.

Cave City

WHHT(FM)—Sept 2, 1988: 103.7 mhz; 13.5 kw. Ant 449 ft. TL: N37 06 39 W85 58 41 Stereo. Hrs opn: 24. Box 457, 605C Happy Valley Rd., Glasgow (42142). (502) 651-6050; (502) 651-6060. FAX: (502) 651-7666. Licensee: Newberry Broadcasting Inc. Net: Unistar. Wash atty: Pepper & Corazzini. Format: Adult contemp, CHR. News staff one; news progmg 7 hrs wkly. Target aud: 25-44. ■ Steven W. Newberry, pres; Vickie K. Hatchett, vp; Dale Thornhill, gen mgr; Craig Davis, opns mgr; Timothy Hurst, gen sls mgr; Rex Holiday, progmg dir; Greg Happle, chief engr. ■ Rates: $10; 9; 10; 8.

Central City

WNES(AM)—Jan 1, 1955: 1050 khz; 1 kw-D, 172 w-N. TL: N37 16 09 W87 08 32. Box 471 (42330). (502) 754-3000. FAX: (502) 754-3003. Licensee: Victoria B. Anderson (acq 9-28-89). Net: CBS; Ky. Net. Format: Btfl mus. News staff one. Spec prog: Farm 7 hrs wkly. ■ Andy Anderson, pres & gen mgr; Stan Barnett, progmg mgr; Frank Hertel, chief engr.

WQXQ(FM)—Co-owned with WNES(AM). Dec 18, 1956: 101.9 mhz; 100 kw. Ant 215 ft. TL: N37 16 09 W87 08 32 (CP: Ant 676 ft.). Format: Country.

Columbia

WAIN(AM)—Aug 1, 1951: 1270 khz; 1 kw-D, 68 w-N. TL: N37 06 36 W85 16 42. Box 77 (42728). (502) 384-2134. FAX: (502) 384-6722. Licensee: Key Broadcasting. Group owner: Key Broadcasting Inc. Net: ABC/I. Rep: Rgnl Reps. Format: Contemp country, AOR. News staff one; news progmg 8 hrs wkly. Target aud: 25-65. Spec prog: Farm 2 hrs, gospel 18 hrs wkly. ■ Terry Forcht, pres; Louise Wooten, gen mgr, gen sls mgr, prom mgr & vp adv; Don Salmon, progmg dir; Ron Cowell, mus dir; Lisa Fisher, news dir; Greg Happel, chief engr. ■ Rates: $10; 9; 10; 7.

WAIN-FM—March 1, 1968: 93.5 mhz; 4.7 kw. Ant 220 ft. TL: N37 06 36 W85 16 42. Stereo. Dups AM 100%. ■ Don Salmon, chief opns & progmg mgr; Loiuse Wooten, adv mgr; Ron Cowell, news dir; Greg Happel, vp engrg. ■ Rates: Same as AM.

Corbin

WCTT(AM)—May 9, 1947: 680 khz; 1 kw-U, DA-N. TL: N36 54 09 W84 04 50. Box 372, 105 N. Kentucky St. (40701). (606) 528-4717. FAX: (606) 523-2068. Licensee: Crawford Broadcasting (acq 6-81; $356,250 with co-located FM; FTR 6-22-81). Net: NBC; Ky. Net. Rep: Rgnl Reps. Format: C&W. ■ John L. Crawford, pres; James L. Crawford, vp; John L. Crawford II, gen mgr; Johnny Reeves, gen sls mgr; Donald Sutton, progmg dir; Glenn Parks, mus dir; Loren Hooker, news dir; Gary Durham, chief engr.

WCTT-FM—June 1, 1967: 107.3 mhz; 50 kw. Ant 492 ft. TL: N36 54 09 W84 04 55. Stereo. Prog sep from AM. Net: SMN. Format: Adult contemp.

WKDP(AM)—Nov 23, 1961: 1330 khz; 5 kw-D, DA. TL: N36 56 20 W84 04 44. Box 742 (40702); 400 E. Center St. (40701). (606) 528-6617. FAX: (606) 528-4487. Licensee: Eubanks Broadcasting Inc. (acq 12-28-89). Net: ABC/C. Format: Relg, talk. News staff 2; news progmg 25 hrs wkly. Target aud: 30-64. ■ Dallas R. Eubanks, pres; John Holbrook, gen mgr; Don Hodge, prom mgr & progmg dir; Mark Daniels, mus dir; Cathy Hall, news dir; Derek Eubanks, chief engr. ■ Rates: $13.75; 11.10; 11.70; 10.25.

Stations in the U.S.

WKDP-FM—1967: 99.5 mhz; 25 kw. Ant 709 ft. TL: N36 57 14 W84 58 41. Stereo. Prog sep from AM. Net: ABC. Wash atty: Fisher, Wayland, Cooper & Leader. Format: Country. Spec prog: Relg 5 hrs wkly. ■ John Holbrook, prom mgr & progmg dir.

Covington

WCVG(AM)—Oct 29, 1965: 1320 khz; 500 w-D, 430 w-N, DA-2. TL: N39 02 44 W84 30 30. 1591 Boyle Rd., Hamilton, OH (45013). (513) 248-1072. Licensee: Richard L. Plessinger Sr. Group owner: Plessinger Radio Group (R.L. Plessinger Holding Co.) (acq 1987). Net: ABC/R. Format: Rock, CHR. Target aud: General. ■ Rick Plessinger, gen mgr.

Cumberland

WCPM(AM)—October 1951: 1280 khz; 1 kw-D. TL: N36 58 25 W82 59 15. Hrs opn: Sunrise-sunset. 101 Keller St. (40823). (606) 589-4623. Licensee: Cumberland City Broadcasting (acq 11-1-57). Net: USA. Wash atty: John B. Kenkel. Format: C&W til 4 PM, then AOR. News progmg 9 hrs wkly. Target aud: 18-65; adults til 4 PM & teens and adults after. Spec prog: Black 3 hrs, relg 9 hrs, farm one hr wkly. ■ George Bibb, pres, gen mgr, gen sls mgr, news dir & chief engr; Laura Hollitt, opns mgr; Tammy Tuttle, mus dir. ■ Rates: $3.30; 3.30; 3.30; na.

WSEH(FM)—Not on air, target date unknown: 102.7 mhz; 165 w. Ant 1,847 ft. TL: N36 54 50 W82 53 40. 111 Third St., Harlan (40831). Licensee: Cumberland City Broadcasting Inc. (acq 2-23-93; $20,790; FTR 3-22-93).

Cynthiana

WCYN(AM)—Sept 1, 1956: 1400 khz; 500 w-D, 1 kw-N. TL: N38 24 20 W84 17 32. 10 Court St. (41031). (606) 234-5108. FAX: (606) 234-1425. Licensee: WCYN Radio. Net: Ky. Agri, Ky. Net. Rep: Keystone (unwired net), Rgnl Reps. Format: Country. News staff one; news progmg 10 hrs wkly. Target aud: General. Spec prog: Farm 15 hrs, relg 11 hrs wkly. ■ Anne Anderson, pres & gen mgr; Ann Anderson, gen sls mgr; Charlie Garnett, news dir; Jim Plumber, chief engr.

WCYN-FM—June 1, 1970: 102.3 mhz; 1.9 kw. Ant 400 ft. TL: N38 24 39 W84 19 07. Dups AM 100%.

Danville

*WDFB-FM—Not on air, target date unknown: 88.1 mhz; 170 w. Ant 328 ft. TL: N37 35 46 W84 50 19. Box 106 (40423). Licensee: Alum Springs Educational Corp. (acq 6-8-92).

WHIR(AM)—Oct 27, 1947: 1230 khz; 1 kw-U. TL: N37 40 28 W84 46 06. Stereo. Hrs opn: 24. Box 1230, Burgin Rd. (40422). (606) 236-2711. Licensee: Perkey Inc. (acq 5-87). Net: CNN, Ky. Net. Ky. Net. Rep: Rgnl Reps. Format: Adult contemp. News staff 2; news progmg 2 hrs wkly. Target aud: 25-54. ■ Wayne Perkey, pres; John Randolph, vp & stn mgr; Brian Conn, opns dir & progmg dir; Norm King, gen sls mgr; Fran Randolph, mus dir; Hershel McKinley, news dir; Larry Baysinger, chief engr. ■ Rates: $16; 14; 16; 7.

WMGE(FM)—Co-owned with WHIR(AM). Oct 27, 1969: 107.1 mhz; 3 kw. Ant 185 ft. TL: N37 40 28 W84 46 06. Stereo. Hrs opn: 24. Prog sep from AM. Net: CNN. Format: Country. ■ Rates: Same as AM.

Eddyville

WWLK(AM)—May 2, 1981: 900 khz; 1 kw-D, 250 w-N, DA-2. TL: N37 04 26 W88 04 48. Box 90, Gregory Rd. (42038). (502) 388-9726. Licensee: Tilent Inc. Group Owner: Bible Time Ministries Inc. Non Profit (acq 7-20-89; $65,000; FTR 8-14-89). Net: CBN. Format: Relg. News progmg 7 hrs wkly. Target aud: General. Spec prog: Southern gospel music & church programs. ■ Jim Baggett, pres, gen mgr, gen sls mgr & progmg dir; Earl Adanathy, chief engr. ■ Rates: $3; 3; 3; 3.

Edmonton

WKNK(FM)—April 5, 1990: 99.1 mhz; 3 kw. Ant 328 ft. TL: N37 01 33 W85 33 14. Stereo. Hrs opn: 24. Box 457, 605 C Happy Valley Rd., Glasgow (42141). (502) 432-7600. Licensee: Newberry Broadcasting Inc. (acq 4-2-93; 10% of stock of Newberry Broadcasting; FTR 4-26-93). Net: Ky. Net. Format: Country. News staff one; news progmg 10 hrs wkly. Target aud: 25-54. Spec prog: Farm 15 hrs wkly. ■ Dale Thomhill, vp & gen mgr; Brian Smith, opns mgr; Vickie Hatchett, vp sls; Todd Belcher, progmg dir; Greg Happle, chief engr.

Elizabethtown

WIEL(AM)—Oct 1, 1950: 1400 khz; 1 kw-U. TL: N37 41 11 W85 52 19. Box L, 406 S. Mulberry (42701). (502) 769-1400. (502) 769-1401. FAX: (502) 769-6349. Licensee: Elizabethtown Broadcasting Co. (acq 5-6-85; grpsl; FTR 5-6-85). Net: ABC/E, SMN. Rep: Rgnl Reps. Wash atty: Fisher, Wayland & Cooper. Format: Oldies. News staff one; news progmg 4 hrs wkly. Target aud: 24-54. ■ D. Michael Coyle, chmn; Charles P. Harper, pres, gen mgr, gen sls mgr & mktg dir; Barry Black, opns dir; progmg mgr, mus dir, news dir & pub affrs dir; Robert Horsley, chief engr.

WKMO(FM)—See Hodgenville.

*WKUE(FM)—Oct 15, 1990: 90.9 mhz; 5.2 kw. Ant 633 ft. TL: N37 44 46 W85 53 18. Stereo. Hrs opn: 24. Academic Complex 248, Western Kentucky Univ., Bowling Green (42101). (502) 745-5489. FAX: (502) 745-2084. Licensee: Western Kentucky Univ. Net: NPR, APR, AP, Ky. Net. Wash atty: Cohn & Marks. Format: Class, news/talk. News staff 2; news progmg 30 hrs wkly. Target aud: General. Spec prog: Jazz 20 hrs, folk 5 hrs wkly. ■ Thomas Meredith, pres; David T. Wilkinson, gen mgr; Jane Moore, opns mgr; Melinda Craft, dev mgr; Lee Stott, mus dir; Dan Modlin, news dir; Chris Scott, chief engr. ■ WKYU-TV affil.

WQXE(FM)—Nov 24, 1969: 98.5 mhz; 1.9 kw. Ant 385 ft. TL: N37 44 46 W85 53 18. Stereo. Box 517, 245 W. Dixie (42701). (502) 737-8000. FAX: (502) 737-7229. Licensee: Hardin County Broadcasting Co. Net: ABC/I. Format: Adult contemp. News staff 2; news progmg 4 hrs wkly. Target aud: 25-54; upscale, dual income families. ■ Billy R. Evans, pres & gen mgr; Larry Tarter, gen sls mgr; Marilyn Evans, prom mgr; David Siders, progmg dir; Mark Stevens, mus dir; Ed Huckleberry, news dir; Greg Happel, chief engr.

Elkhorn City

WBPA(AM)—Nov 24, 1979: 1460 khz; 5 kw-D. TL: N37 18 25 W82 19 53. Box 2200, 205 N. Mayo Trail, Pikeville (41501). (606) 437-7323. FAX: (606) 432-2809. Licensee: Gary K. Justice (acq 3-7-90; $268,303 with co-located FM; FTR 3-26-90). Net: ABC; Ky. Net. Format: Country. News staff one; news progmg 12 hrs wkly. Target aud: 25-49. ■ Gary K. Justice, pres; Pat Hall, gen sls mgr & prom mgr; Rondel Smith, progmg dir; Sam Runyon, chief engr. ■ Rates: $7.25; 7.25; 7.25; na.

WPKE-FM—Co-owned with WBPA(AM). Sept 21, 1974: 103.1 mhz; 120 w. Ant 1,371 ft. TL: N37 16 05 W82 21 37. Stereo. Prog sep from AM. Format: Adult contemp, oldies. News progmg 21 hrs wkly. Target aud: General. ■ Pat Hall, gen mgr. ■ Rates: Same as AM.

Elkton

WEKT(AM)—July 21, 1977: 1070 khz; 500 w-D. TL: N36 48 33 W87 09 38. Box 577, Marion St. (42220). (502) 265-5636. Licensee: M&R Broadcasting Inc. (acq 12-19-89; $57,000; FTR 1-16-89). Net: Unistar. Format: Country, oldies, relg. ■ Marshall Sidebottom, pres; Raymond Shoemate, vp progmg; Brian Sidebottom, mus dir; Karl C. Rankin, news dir & chief engr.

Eminence

WKXF(AM)—June 1, 1956: 1600 khz; 500 w-D, 48 w-N. TL: N38 21 02 W85 11 11. Box 194 (40019). (502) 845-4200. FAX: (502) 845-2716. Licensee: Superior Market-Eminence Inc. (acq 4-1-93; $40,000; FTR 4-19-93). Format: Country. News staff one; news progmg 6 hrs wkly. Target aud: 25 plus. ■ Keith Miller, gen mgr; Estill Roberts, progmg dir; Bryan Heilman, mus dir.

WXLN-FM—July 4, 1988: 105.7 mhz; 3 kw. Ant 325 ft. TL: N38 21 09 W85 11 09. Prog sep from AM. Box 655, New Albany IN (47151). (812) 581-1570. FAX: (812) 944-7782. Licensee: Cross Country Communications Inc. (acq 12-2-92; $210,000; FTR 12-21-92). Format: Christian. ■ Debra Kaiser, gen mgr & progmg dir; George Zarris, stn mgr; Wayne Wilson, news dir & chief engr.

Erlanger

WIZF(FM)—Sept 22, 1965: 100.9 mhz; 1.25 kw. Ant 508 ft. TL: N39 06 18 W84 33 24 (CP: 2.25 kw, ant 518 ft.). Stereo. Suite 316, 7030 Reading Rd., Cincinnati, OH (45237). (513) 351-5900. FAX: (513) 351-0020. Licensee: Inter-Urban Broadcasting of Cincinnati Inc. (acq 11-86; $2 million; FTR 8-4-86). Net: AP, Unistar. Format: Urban contemp. News progmg 4 hrs wkly. Target aud: General. Spec prog: Jazz. ■ Fritz Valentine, pres; Tom Owens, prom mgr; Tori Turner, progmg dir; Edna Howell, news dir; Joe Stenger, chief engr.

Falmouth

WIOK(FM)—June 1981: 107.5 mhz; 610 w. Ant 695 ft. TL: N38 43 15 W84 22 27. Stereo. Hrs opn: 24. Box 50 (41040). (606) 491-3480; (606) 472-5511. FAX: (606) 472-2875. Licensee: Hammond Broadcasting Inc. Net: Ky. Net. Rep: Rgnl Reps. Format: Gospel, religious country. News progmg 8 hrs wkly. Target aud: 35-64; women. ■ Gil Hammond, Jan Hammond, gen mgrs; Ken Jasper, gen sls mgr; Bruce Edwards, progmg dir, mus dir, pub affrs dir & chief engr; Mike Schmidt, news dir. ■ Rates: $10; 7; 10; 7.

Flemingsburg

WBPK(FM)—Not on air, target date unknown: 106.3 mhz; 1.8 kw. Ant 400 ft. TL: N38 24 43 W83 34 49. Stereo. one Radio Dr. Rt. 3 (41041). (606) 849-4433. Licensee: Fleming County Broadcasters Inc. Format: AOR. ■ Garey A. Beckett, pres, gen mgr & progmg dir; Chris O'Neill, news dir; J.E. Kieffer, chief engr.

WFLE(AM)—November 1981: 1060 khz; 1 kw-D, DA. TL: N38 27 01 W83 44 06. Route 3, One Radio Dr. (41041). (606) 849-4433. FAX: (606) 845-9353. Licensee: Flemingsburg FM Broadcasters Inc. Net: CNN. Format: C&W. News staff 2; news progmg 9 hrs wkly. Target aud: 25-54. ■ Ernest Sparkman, pres; Carl Haight, gen mgr, gen sls mgr & news dir; Cathy Campbell, prom mgr; Kim Hester, progmg dir; Brent Mulliken, mus dir; Jim Hay, chief engr.

WFLE-FM—February 1993: 106.3 mhz; 1.61 kw. Ant 449 ft. TL: N38 24 42 W83 34 41.

Florence

WBND(AM)—September 1984: 1160 khz; 1 kw-D, DA. TL: N38 59 23 W84 41 21 (CP: 1160 khz; 5 kw-D, 1 kw-N, DA-2, TL: N38 59 00 W84 41 44). Stereo. Suite 312E, 250 W. Court St., Cincinnati, OH (45202). (513) 241-1180. FAX: (513) 381-1160. Licensee: WMLX Inc. (acq 2-23-93; $175,000; FTR 3-15-93). Net: SMN. Rep: Major Mkt. Format: Nostalgia. Target aud: 35 plus. ■ Ken McDowell, pres & gen mgr; Deane D. Osborne, vp; Jim Stitt, stn mgr & chief engr; Deane Osborne III, gen sls mgr; Jackie Norton, prom mgr; Ted Martin, progmg dir; Brian Wright, news dir. ■ Rates: $25; 25; 25; na.

Fort Campbell

WABD(AM)—July 27, 1963: 1370 khz; 1 kw-D, 53 w-N. TL: N36 38 28 W87 26 04. Box 2249, 150 Stateline Rd., Clarksville, TN (37042); Box 521, Ft. Campbell, KY (42223). (615) 431-4984. FAX: (615) 431-4986. Licensee: Southern Broadcasting Corp. (acq 12-1-86; $1,425,000 with co-located FM; FTR 10-13-86). Net: AP. Rep: MidSouth. Format: Black. News staff one; news progmg 2 hrs wkly. Target aud: 18-34. Spec prog: Gospel 10 hrs, relg 4 hrs wkly. ■ Tom Cassetty, pres & gen mgr; Steve King, gen sls mgr; Brent Barbour, progmg dir; Karen Griffin, mus dir; Chris Baker, news dir; J.C. Morrow, chief engr.

WCVQ(FM)—Co-owned with WABD(AM). August 1969: 107.9 mhz; 100 kw. Ant 950 ft. TL: N36 32 23 W87 39 45. Stereo. Hrs opn: 24. Prog sep from AM. Net: ABC/C. Format: Adult contemp. Target aud: 25-54. ■ Lee Erwin, prom mgr; Michael Johnson, progmg dir & mus dir; Bette Morris, pub affrs dir.

Fort Knox

WASE-FM—Oct 1, 1967: 105.5 mhz; 3 kw. Ant 299 ft. TL: N37 51 06 W85 56 45 (CP: 3.6 kw, ant 417 ft., TL: N37 45 57 W85 54 38). Stereo. Hrs opn: 24. Box 2087, Elizabethtown (42702); 4296 S. Wilson Rd., Elizabethtown (42701). (502) 769-1055. FAX: (502) 769-1052. Licensee: W&B Broadcasting Co. (acq 5-1-84); grpsl; FTR 2-17-84). Net: Unistar. Wash atty: Miller & Miller. Format: Oldies. News staff one; news progmg 2 hrs wkly. Target aud: 25-54. ■ Bill Walters, pres; Mike Baldwin, gen mgr; Bob Craft, progmg dir & mus dir; Kendra Stewart, news dir; Rick Caldwell, chief engr. ■ Rates: $15.50; 15.50; 15.50; 5.

Frankfort

WFKY(AM)—February 1946: 1490 khz; 1 kw-U. TL: N38 12 46 W84 52 31. Box 757, 120 Mero (40602). (502) 223-8281. FAX: (502) 223-0723. Licensee: Radio Enterprises of Kentucky Inc. Net: CBS. Rep: Regional. Format: Adult contemp, news/talk. News staff one. Target aud: 25-55. Spec prog: Relg 6 hrs wkly. ■ Richard D. Rowley, pres; Gary White, gen mgr; John Roberts, opns mgr; Amy Norville, gen sls mgr. ■ Rates: $9; 9; 9; 9.

Broadcasting & Cable Yearbook 1994

Kentucky

WKYW(FM)—Co-owned with WFKY(AM). Jan 1, 1967: 104.9 mhz; 3 kw. Ant 300 ft. TL: N38 13 19 W84 54 55. Stereo. Dups AM 5%. Format: Adult contemp, oldies. ■ Rates: Same as AM.

WKED(AM)—Nov 17, 1977: 1130 khz; 500 w-D, DA. TL: N38 12 13 W84 54 51. Hrs opn: 6 AM-7 PM. Suite 509, 306 W. Main St. (40601). (502) 875-1130. Licensee: Allan Communications Inc. (acq 10-8-81; $350,000; FTR 9-7-81). Net: CNN, Unistar. Wash atty: Dow, Lohnes & Albertson. Format: C&W. News staff 2; news progmg 15 hrs wkly. Target aud: 25-54; info & personality oriented adults. Spec prog: Relg 2 hrs wkly. ■ Leigh W. Allan, pres, gen mgr, progmg dir, mus dir & chief engr; Kenneth O. Mitchell, vp, gen sls mgr & prom mgr; Kathleen A. Allan, opns dir; Sharon Roark, news dir; Josephine Jacovino, pub affrs dir. ■ Rates: $11; 9.25; 11; na.

WKED-FM—April 15, 1991: 103.7 mhz; 2.5 kw. Ant 350 ft. TL: N38 13 17 W84 54 52. Stereo. Hrs opn: 24. Prog sep from AM. Format: Adult contemp. News staff 2; news progmg 4 hrs wkly. Target aud: 25-54. ■ Rates: Same as AM.

WKYW(FM)—Listing follows WFKY(AM).

Franklin

WFKN(AM)—Apr 25, 1954: 1220 khz; 250 w-D, 90 w-N. TL: N36 44 20 W86 34 42. Hrs opn: 6 AM-11 PM. Box 309, 103 N. High St. (42135). (502) 586-4481. FAX: (502) 586-6031. Licensee: The Franklin Favorite-WFKN Inc. (acq 6-74). Net: ABC/E; Ky. Net. Rep: Rgnl Reps. Wash atty: Dennis Kelly. Format: Country. News staff 2; news progmg 16 hrs wkly. Target aud: General. Spec prog: Relg, farm 6 hrs wkly. ■ Henry D. Stone, pres, gen mgr & prom mgr; Tami Carey, gen sls mgr & adv mgr; Richard Upton, progmg dir; Ken Cline, mus dir; Keith Pyles, news dir. ■ Rates: $4.30; 4.30; 4.30; 4.30.

Fulton

WKZT(AM)—July 8, 1951: 1270 khz; 1 kw-D, 54 w-N. TL: N36 30 54 W88 54 16. Stereo. Box 1380, Middle Rd. Hwy. 166 (42041). (502) 472-1270; (502) 472-1189. TWX: 502-472-0460. Licensee: River Country Broadcasting Inc. (acq 5-90; $80,000; FTR 6-11-90). Net: ABC/E. Format: Country, gospel. News progmg 2 hrs wkly. Target aud: 40 plus. ■ Charles Whitlow, pres & gen mgr; Scotty Bell, gen sls mgr & news dir; Lowell Cole, chief engr. ■ Rates: $9; 6; 6; 5.

WWKF(FM)—September 1954: 99.3 mhz; 3.3 kw. Ant 337 ft. TL: N36 27 59 W88 56 47. Stereo. Hrs opn: 24. 1729 Nailling Dr., Union City, TN (38261). (901) 885-1240. FAX: (901) 885-3405. Licensee: WENK of Union City Inc. Group owner: WENK Broadcast Group Inc. (acq 10-1-82; $473,131; FTR 10-18-82). Net: ABC/R, Unistar. Rep: Keystone (unwired net), MidSouth. Wash atty: Philip R. Hochberg. Format: CHR. News staff 2. Target aud: 18-34. ■ Terry L. Hailey, pres, gen mgr & progmg dir; Wilma Johnson, opns mgr; Mary Bondurant, gen sls mgr; James J. Cawley, news dir; Charles R. Holland, chief engr. ■ Rates: $9.85; 9.85; 9.85; 9.85.

Garrison

WNUU(FM)—Not on air, target date unknown: 98.3 mhz; 2.6 kw. Ant 492 ft. TL: N38 36 19 W83 03 37. c/o 2335 Bonnycastle Ave. Louisville (40205). Licensee: Henson Media Inc.

Georgetown

WBBE(AM)—Sept 6, 1957: 1580 khz; 10 kw-D, 45 w-N, DA-2. TL: N38 10 05 W84 35 37. Box 12890, Lexington (40583). (606) 299-1103. FAX: (606) 280-9642. Licensee: Kentucky Radio Ltd. Partners (acq 10-6-89; $1.75 million with co-located FM; FTR 6-12-89). Rep: Eastman Radio, Rgnl Reps. Format: Traditional country. ■ Chuck Dunaway, gen mgr & gen sls mgr; Wayne Long, chief engr.

WTKT-FM—Co-owned with WBBE(AM). Sept 10, 1973: 103.3 mhz; 6 kw. Ant 300 ft. TL: N38 11 24 W84 28 57. Stereo. Prog sep from AM. Format: Oldies. Target aud: 25-49; upwardly mobile professionals. Spec prog: Jazz 6 hrs wkly. ■ Gil Dunn, prom mgr; Don Edwards, progmg dir; Dan Cassidy, news dir.

*****WRVG(FM)**—Oct 1, 1963: 89.9 mhz; 140 w. Ant 33 ft. TL: N38 12 27 W84 33 24. Hrs opn: 24. Box 301, Arts Bldg., Georgetown College (40324). (502) 863-8110. Licensee: Georgetown College. Format: Top-40. Spec prog: Class 6 hrs, relg 12 hrs, black 3 hrs, jazz 3 hrs wkly. ■ Paula Curry, gen mgr.

WTKT-FM—Listing follows WBBE(AM).

Glasgow

WCDS(AM)—Oct 1, 1962: 1440 khz; 5 kw-D. TL: N36 58 10 W85 56 24. Box 158 (42142-0158). (502) 651-3132. FAX: (502) 651-8472. Licensee: Ward Communications Corp. (acq 12-26-91; $575,000 with co-located FM; FTR 1-14-91). ■ Sarah Barrick, gen mgr; Ann Morgan, gen sls mgr; Johnny Barrick, news dir; Orville Cox, chief engr.

WWWQ(FM)—Co-owned with WCDS(AM). July 14, 1972: 105.3 mhz; 25 kw. Ant 318 ft. TL: N36 54 50 W85 43 20. Stereo. Format: Top-40, adult contemp.

WCLU(AM)—Sept 25, 1946: 1490 khz; 1 kw-U, DA-1. TL: N37 00 19 W85 54 42. Box 1628, 229 W. Main St. (42142). (502) 651-9149. FAX: (502) 651-9222. Licensee: Royse Radio Inc. Net: CBS. Format: Full svc. News staff 6. Target aud: 30 plus; listeners with disposable income. ■ Henry Royse, pres; Jim Moody, news dir. ■ Rates: $6.50; 6.50; 6.50; 6.50.

WGGC(FM)—June 23, 1961: 95.1 mhz; 100 kw. Ant 988 ft. TL: N37 00 19 W85 55 42. Box 219 (42142-0129). 510 Happy Valley Rd. (42141). (502) 651-2142. FAX: (502) 651-2141. Licensee: Heritage Communications Inc. Format: C&W, farm. ■ Moena E. Sadler, pres; William Evans, gen mgr.

WWWQ(FM)—Listing follows WCDS(AM).

Gray

WKYZ(AM)—Nov 8, 1984: 1590 khz; 500 w-D, 26 w-N. TL: N36 56 44 W84 01 09. Stereo. Box 813 (40701). (606) 523-1590. Licensee: Crown Communications Inc. (acq 9-10-86; $470,000; FTR 8-18-86). Net: USA. Format: MOR, oldies. Target aud: 35-55. Spec prog: Relg 12 hrs wkly. ■ David L. Carrier, pres & gen sls mgr; Joey Kesler, gen mgr & news dir; Kathy Hubbs, prom mgr; Andrea Kesler, progmg dir; James H. Evans, chief engr.

Grayson

WGOH(AM)—June 1, 1959: 1370 khz; 5 kw-D, 21 w-N. TL: N38 19 44 W82 58 33. Hrs opn: 6 AM-2 hrs past sunset. Box 487, US 60 W. (41143). (606) 474-5144; (606) 474-5145. FAX: (606) 474-7777. Licensee: Carter County Broadcasting Co. Net: CBS. Rep: Rgnl Reps. Format: Country. News staff one; news progmg 20 hrs wkly. Target aud: 35-65. Spec prog: Bluegrass 15 hrs, gospel 8 hrs wkly. ■ Francis M. Nash, gen mgr, gen sls mgr & progmg dir; Jim Phillips, news dir; William H. Craig, chief engr. ■ Rates: $5; 4.60; 4.60; 4.60.

WUGO(FM)—Co-owned with WGOH(AM). February 1967: 102.3 mhz; 4.8 kw. Ant 360 ft. TL: N38 19 44 W82 58 33. Stereo. Hrs opn: 6 AM-midnight. Prog sep from AM. Format: Adult contemp, classic rock, oldies. News progmg 18 hrs wkly. Target aud: 25-54. ■ Rates: Same as AM.

*****WKCC(FM)**—Oct. 1973: 96.7 mhz; 10 w. Ant 55 ft. TL: N38 20 18 W82 56 38. Kentucky Christian College, 617 N. Carol Malone Blvd. (41143-1199). (606) 474-3257; (606) 474-3749. Licensee: Kentucky Christian College. Net: USA. Format: Relg, new/talk. News progmg one hr wkly. Target aud: General. Spec prog: Children 3 hrs wkly. ■ Mic Marshall, gen mgr; Joel Seymour, progmg dir; Tom Harrigan, mus dir; Scott Tucker, news dir.

WUGO(FM)—Listing follows WGOH(AM).

Greensburg

WAKY(AM)—March 15, 1972: 1540 khz; 1 kw-D. TL: N37 15 34 W85 30 57. Box 246, Buckner Hill Rd. (42743); Box 1081, Campbellsville (42719). (502) 932-7401; (502) 789-1464. FAX: (502) 932-7402. Licensee: Veer Broadcasting. Rep: Rgnl Reps. Format: Oldies. Target aud: 25-54. Spec prog: Farm 15 hrs wkly. ■ James M. Hay, pres; Michael R. Wilson, vp, gen mgr & chief engr; Joy L. Wilson, gen sls mgr; Torry Petrick, news dir.

WGRK-FM—Co-owned with WAKY(AM). Dec 15, 1977: 103.1 mhz; 2.2 kw. Ant 375 ft. TL: N37 15 34 W85 30 57 (CP: 4.6kw). Stereo. Hrs opn: 24. Dups AM 50%. Format: Big country hits.

Greenup

WLGC(AM)—April 1, 1985: 1520 khz; 5 kw-D. TL: N38 35 44 W82 51 20. Stereo. Box 685, Suite B, Main St. and Harrison (41144). (606) 473-7377; (800) 551-1057. FAX: (606) 473-5086. Licensee: Greenup County Broadcasting Inc. Net: ABC/D. Format: Southern Gospel. News progmg 7 hrs wkly. Target aud: 30-70. ■ Phillip Bruce Leslie, pres; Robert Scheibly, vp; Mark Justice, prom mgr; Bill Geyer, news dir.

WLGC-FM—Sept 1, 1982: 105.7 mhz; 25 kw. Ant 479 ft. TL: N38 35 34 W82 51 20. Stereo. Prog sep from AM. (606) 473-7377. Net: Ky. Net. Format: Country. Target aud: 25-54; middle income listeners. ■ Otto Collins, gen sls mgr; Mark Justice, prom mgr, progmg dir & mus dir; Bill Geyer, news dir.

Greenville

WWHK(FM)—Dec 11, 1981: 105.5 mhz; 3 kw. Ant 300 ft. TL: N37 11 45 W87 12 38. Stereo. Box 254 (42345); Hwy. 189 (42345). (502) 298-3268. Licensee: Greenville Broadcasting Co. Group owner: Spinks Group (acq 8-31-83). Net: ABC/E; Ky. Net. Format: Contemp hit. News staff one; news progmg 10 hrs wkly. Target aud: 18-40. ■ Hayward F. Spinks, pres; Lloyd Spivey, gen mgr & chief engr; Wanda Winstead, gen sls mgr; Debbie Harris, prom mgr; Lanie Murser, progmg dir; Sheila Pierson, news dir. ■ Rates: $5; 5; 5; 4.

Hardinsburg

WHIC(AM)—July 6, 1968: 1520 khz; 1 kw-D. TL: N37 45 45 W86 26 22. Box 203 (40143). (502) 756-2105. FAX: (502) 756-6367. Licensee: H.I.C. Broadcasting Inc. Group owner: Key Broadcasting Inc. (acq 5-12-82; $500,000 with co-located FM; FTR 5-31-82). Net: CNN. Rep: Rgnl Reps. Format: C&W. News staff 2; news progmg 4 hrs wkly. ■ Terry E. Forcht, pres; Brent Black, opns mgr, progmg dir & mus dir; Karen Embry, gen sls mgr; Miguel Zergara, news dir; Greg Happel, chief engr. ■ Rates: $8; 6; 8; 6.

WHIC-FM—July 9, 1970: 94.3 mhz; 3.4 kw. Ant 290 ft. TL: N37 45 40 W86 26 22 (CP: 30 kw, ant 525 ft.). Stereo. Dups AM 80%. ■ Rates: Same as AM.

WXBC(FM)—Aug 15, 1992: 104.3 mhz; 3 kw. Ant 328 ft. TL: N37 43 13 W86 26 08. Stereo. Hrs opn: 24. Box 143, 220 "B" S. Main St. (40143). (502) 756-1043. FAX: (502) 756-1086. Licensee: Breckinridge Broadcasting Co. Inc. Net: ABC/D; Ky Net. Wash atty: Booth, Freret & Imlay. Format: Vaiety, adult contemp, country. News progmg 15 hrs wkly. Target aud: General. Spec prog: Farm 5 hrs, relg 7 hrs, news 15 hrs wkly. ■ Jo Ann Keenan, CEO, CFO, sls dir & adv dir; Jim Wooley, pres, stn mgr, news dir & pub affrs dir; Jo Ann Kennan, gen mgr; Dennis Day, chief opns & progmg dir; Jeff Morgan, prom dir & mus dir; Greg Happel, chief engr.

Harlan

WFSR(AM)—April 1976: 970 khz; 5 kw-D, 94 w-N. TL: N36 50 59 W83 23 41. Box 818, 210 N. Main (40831). (606) 573-1470. FAX: (606) 573-1473. Licensee: Eastern Broadcasting. Net: CNN, AP. Format: Country. News staff one. Target aud: 25-54; adult purchasers. ■ Don Parsons, pres; Barbara Sloan, gen sls mgr; Scott Caldwell, prom mgr, progmg dir & mus dir; Bernard Leonard, chief engr.

WTUK(FM)—Co-owned with WFSR(AM). Not on air, target date unknown: 105.1 mhz; 270 w. Ant 1,037 ft. TL: N36 54 09 W83 18 01. ■ WYMT(TV) affil.

WHLN(AM)—May 30, 1941: 1410 khz; 5 kw-D, 94 w-N. TL: N36 52 02 W83 19 36. Box 898 (40831). (606) 573-2540. FAX: (606) 573-7557. Licensee: Radio Harlan Inc. (acq 6-1-56). Net: SMN. Rep: Rgnl Reps. Format: Adult contemp. ■ James T. Morgan, pres & gen mgr; James O. Morgan, vp, gen sls mgr, prom mgr & progmg dir; Tracy M. Turner, news dir; Frank Folsom, chief engr.

WTUK(FM)—Listing follows WFSR(AM).

Harrodsburg

WHBN(AM)—June 25, 1955: 1420 khz; 1 kw-D, 46 w-N. TL: N37 44 03 W84 48 50. Box 247, Ole Opera House, 400 Beaumont Avenue (40330). (606) 734-4321. FAX: (606) 734-5786. Licensee: Fort Harrod Broadcasting Corp. (acq 3-60). Net: Ky. Net. Rep: Rgnl Reps. Format: C&W, variety. News staff one; news progmg 9 hrs wkly. Target aud: General. Spec prog: Black one hr, relg 15 hrs wkly. ■ Robert L. Martin, pres, gen mgr, gen sls mgr, prom mgr & progmg dir; Nadine Cole, news dir; Tom Devine, chief engr. ■ Rates: $7.35; 7.35; 7.35; 7.35.

WHBN-FM—Dec 9, 1969: 99.3 mhz; 3 kw. Ant 265 ft. TL: N37 44 03 W84 48 50. Stereo. Hrs opn: 6 AM-midnight. Dups AM 100%. FAX: (606) 734-7524. ■ Rates: Same as AM.

Hartford

WLLS(AM)—June 21, 1969: 1600 khz; 1 kw-D, DA. TL: N37 26 36 W86 53 57. Hrs opn: 6 AM-sunset. Spink's Shopping Center, 1121 S. Main (42347). (502) 298-3268; (502) 298-3269. FAX: (502) 298-9326. Licensee: Hayward F. Spinks. Group owner: Spinks Group. Net: ABC/E, Ky. Net. Rep: Rgnl Reps. Format: Country, rock. Target aud: General. ■ Hayward F. Spinks, pres; Lloyd Spivey, gen mgr, gen sls mgr & chief engr; Carol Haynes, opns mgr & progmg dir; Leonard Renfrow, mus dir & news dir. ■ Rates: $5; 5; 5; 5.

WLLS-FM—May 18, 1972: 106.3 mhz; 3 kw. Ant 280 ft. TL: N37 26 36 W86 53 57. Stereo. Hrs opn: 16. Dups AM 100%. ■ Rates: Same as AM.

Hawesville

WKCM(AM)—Nov 7, 1972: 1160 khz; 2.5 kw-D, 1 kw-N, DA-N. TL: N37 54 20 W86 45 30. Stereo. Hrs opn: 24. Box 335, Old U.S. Hwy. #60 W. (42348). (812) 927-8121. FAX: (812) 547-8121. Licensee: Hancock Communications Inc. Group owner: The Cromwell Group Inc. Net: Ky. Agri. Format: Oldies. News staff one; news progmg 10 hrs. Target aud: 25-54; general. Spec prog: Farm 3 hrs, sports 6 hrs wkly. ■ Bayard H. Walters, pres; Robert Munson, gen mgr & progmg dir; Mark Rogers, news dir; Watt Hairston, Bob Horsley (local), chiefs engr. ■ Rates: $10; 10; 10; 6.

WKCM-FM—May 1993: 102.9 mhz; 2.6 kw. Ant 505 ft. TL: N37 53 47 W86 45 59. Licensee: The Cromwell Group Inc. of Kentucky. Group owner: The Cromwell Group Inc. (acq 1993; $170,000; FTR 9-6-93).

Hazard

*WEKH(FM)—February 1985: 90.9 mhz; 33 kw. Ant 1,005 ft. TL: N37 11 34 W83 11 16. Stereo. Hrs opn: 24. Rebroadcasts WEKU-FM Richmond 100%. Eastern Kentucky Univ., Perkins 102, Richmond (40475-3127). (606) 622-1655. Licensee: Board of Regents, Eastern Kentucky Univ. Net: APR, NPR. Format: Class, news mag, info. News staff 4; news progmg 35 hrs wkly. Target aud: General. Spec prog: Women's programs 2 hrs wkly. ■ Tim Singleton, stn mgr; John Francis, opns mgr; Judy Flavell, dev dir & prom mgr; Loy Lee, mus dir; Marie Mitchell, news dir; Bill Browning, chief engr.

WJMD(FM)—July 26, 1989: 104.7 mhz; 2.5 kw. Ant 1,135 ft. TL: N37 11 36 W83 11 04. Stereo. Hrs opn: 24. Box 7001 (41702); 125 Morgan St. (41701). (606) 439-3358. Licensee: Hazard Broadcasting Services. Net: USA. Format: Relg. News staff 2; news progmg 7 hrs wkly. Target aud: General. ■ Michael R. Barnett, pres & gen mgr; Lema Barnett, progmg dir; Rae Ann Barnett, mus dir; Robert Hale, chief engr. ■ Rates: $7; 7; 7; 7.

WKIC(AM)—Nov 23, 1947: 1390 khz; 5 kw-D. TL: N37 14 19 W83 12 41. Stereo. Box 7898 (41701). (606) 436-2121. FAX: (606) 436-4172. Licensee: Mountain Broadcasting Service Inc. (acq 12-67). Net: ABC/E, Westwood One; Ky. Net. Rep: Rgnl Reps. Format: Contemp hit. ■ Faron Sparkman, gen sls mgr; Paula Campbell, progmg dir; Shane Sparkman, news dir; Bob Hale, chief engr.

WSGS(FM)—Co-owned with WKIC(AM). Feb 3, 1959: 101.1 mhz; 100 kw. Ant 1,463 ft. TL: N37 11 38 W83 10 52. Stereo. Prog sep from AM. Radio Bldg. Main & Morgan Sts. (41702). Net: ABC. Ky. News Net. Rep: Regional Reps. Format: Country. ■ Faron Sparkman, pres

WQXY(AM)—Mar 1, 1988: 1560 khz; 1 kw-D, 500 w-CH, DA. TL: N37 16 27 W83 11 29. Stereo. Box 1981 (41702-1981); First Federal, 477 Main (41701). (606) 436-0156. FAX: (606) 436-0156. Licensee: Black Gold Broadcasting (acq 8-90; $97,500; FTR 9-24-90). Net: SMN, AP. Format: Oldies, news. News staff 3; news progmg 10 hrs wkly. Target aud: 25-54; educated, mobile, child-rearing couples in suburbs, blue collar workers. ■ John Edwards, pres; Colin Cox, execvp; R. Brian Baker, gen mgr & sls mgr; Ruby Nickles, opns mgr; William Gorman Jr., progmg dir; Pat Clarke, mus dir; Philip Hayes, chief engr. ■ Rates: $5; 5; 5; 5.

WSGS(FM)—Listing follows WKIC(AM).

Henderson

WGBF-FM—Dec 1, 1971: 103.1 mhz; 3 kw. Ant 460 ft. TL: N37 46 54 W87 37 24 (CP: 3.16 kw, ant 453 ft.). Stereo. Hrs opn: 24. Box 297, Evansville, IN (47702). (812) 477-8811. Licensee: Aiken Communications Corp. (acq 5-9-87). Net: Unistar, NBC the Source. Rep: Banner. Wash atty: Fisher, Wayland, Cooper & Leader. Format: Rock. News staff 2; news progmg 3 hrs wkly. Target aud: 18-49. ■ Larry Aiken, pres, gen mgr & stn mgr; Mike Bevers, vp & gen sls mgr; Tony Couch, progmg dir & mus dir; Dan Egierski, news dir; Steve Chandler, chief engr.

WKDQ(FM)—1947: 99.5 mhz; 100 kw. Ant 944 ft. TL: N37 49 36 W87 33 00. Stereo. Hrs opn: 24. Box 435, 3020 Hwy. (42420). (502) 827-8995. FAX: (502) 827-5756. Licensee: Bristol Broadcasting Co. Inc. Group owner: Nininger Stns. (acq 12-16-86). Net: ABC/I. Rep: Christal. Format: Country. Target aud: 25-54. ■ Mike Robinson, gen mgr; Dave Evans, prom dir; Bruce Clark, progmg dir; Gene Stewart, news dir; Shelby Wilkinson, chief engr.

*WKPB(FM)—April 1, 1990: 89.5 mhz; 23 kw. Ant 1,502 ft. TL: N37 51 06 W87 19 43 (CP: 43 kw, ant 377 ft.). Stereo. Hrs opn: 24. Western Kentucky Univ., 248 Academic Complex, Bowling Green (42101). (502) 745-5489. FAX: (502) 745-2084. Licensee: Western Kentucky Univ. Net: NPR, APR, AP, Ky. Net. Wash atty: Cohn & Marks. Format: Class, news/talk. News staff 3; news progmg 30 hrs wkly. Target aud: General. Spec prog: Jazz 14 hrs, folk 5 hrs wkly. ■ Dr. Thomas Meredith, pres; David T. Wilkinson, gen mgr; Jane Moore, opns mgr; Melinda Craft, dev mgr; Lee Scott, mus dir; Dan Modlin, news dir; Chris Scott, chief engr. ■ WKYU-TV affil.

WSON(AM)—Dec 17, 1941: 860 khz; 500 w-U, DA-N. TL: N37 51 11 W87 32 12. Box 418, 230 Second St. (42420). (502) 826-3923. FAX: (502) 826-7572. Licensee: Henry G. Lackey. Group owner: Lackey Group (acq 7-31-79). Net: Ky. Net. Rep: Rgnl Reps. Format: Big band, stardust. Spec prog: Farm 2 hrs wkly. ■ Henry G. Lackey, pres, gen mgr & gen sls mgr; Bill Stephens, news dir.

Highland Heights

*WNKU(FM)—Apr 29, 1985: 89.7 mhz; 12 kw. Ant 318 ft. TL: N39 02 21 W84 27 57. Stereo. Hrs opn: 19. Box 337 (41076); 301 Landrum Academic Center, Nunn Dr. (41099-5999). (606) 572-6500. FAX: (606) 572-6604. Licensee: Northern Kentucky Univ. Net: APR, NPR. Wash atty: Arter & Hadden. Format: Folk & acoustic alternative music, news. News staff 2; news progmg 36 hrs wkly. Target aud: 35-49. Spec prog: Ger 2 hrs wkly. ■ David Arnold, gen mgr & progmg dir; Colin Cordy, opns mgr; Vickie Ellis, dev dir, mktg dir & prom mgr; Maryanne Zeleznik, news dir; Don Smith, chief engr.

Hindman

WKCB(AM)—Jan 26, 1971: 1340 khz; 6 kw-U. TL: N37 19 45 W83 00 17. Box 864 (41822). (606) 785-3129. Licensee: Hindman Broadcasting Corp. (acq 9-15-89; $100,000 with co-located FM; FTR 10-23-89). Net: ABC/E; Ky. Net. Rep: Rgnl Reps. Format: Adult contemp, C&W. ■ Randy Thompson, pres & gen mgr; Sandy Short, progmg dir; Tom Cody, news dir; Noll Davis, chief engr.

WKCB-FM—Dec 13, 1974: 107.1 mhz; 770 w. Ant 650 ft. TL: N37 19 56 W82 56 52. Stereo. Dups AM 100%.

Hodgenville

WKMO(FM)—March 1974: 106.3 mhz; 3 kw. Ant 400 ft. TL: N37 40 21 W85 44 34. Stereo. Box L, 406 S. Mulberry, Elizabethtown (42701). (502) 769-0106, (502) 769-0107. FAX: (502) 769-6349. Licensee: Elizabethtown Broadcasting Co. (acq 5-85; grpsl; FTR 5-6-85). Net: ABC/E. Rep: Keystone (unwired net), Rgnl Reps. Wash atty: Fisher, Wayland, Cooper & Leader. Format: Country. News staff one; news progmg 4 hrs wkly. Target aud: 24-54. Spec prog: Farm 2 hrs wkly. ■ D. Michael Coyle, chmn; Charles P. Harper, pres, gen mgr, gen sls mgr & mktg dir; Barry Black, opns mgr, prom dir, progmg dir, mus dir & news dir; Robert Horsley, chief engr.

WXAM(AM)—See Buffalo.

Hopkinsville

WHOP(AM)—Jan 8, 1940: 1230 khz; 830 w-U. TL: N36 52 54 W87 30 44. Hrs opn: 24. Box 709, 220 Dink Embry's Buttermilk Rd. (42241-0709). (502) 885-5331. FAX: (502) 885-2688. Licensee: Hopkinsville Broadcasting Co. Group owner: Lackey Group. Net: CBS, Ky. Net. Rep: Rgnl Reps. Wash atty: Pepper & Corazzini. Format: News/talk, MOR. News staff 2. Target aud: 25-65. ■ Roger H. Jeffers, pres & gen mgr; Jerry Stegall, gen sls mgr; Tony Winfield, progmg dir & mus dir; Jim Love, news dir; Marvin Mahoney, chief engr. ■ Rates: $24.50; 22.50; 24.50; 22.50.

WHOP-FM—May 1948: 98.7 mhz; 100 kw. Ant 304 ft. TL: N36 52 54 W87 30 44. Stereo. Hrs opn: 24. Prog sep from AM. Format: C&W. Target aud: 18-54. Spec prog: Farm 17 hrs wkly. ■ Rates: $23; 23; 23; 23.

*WNKJ(FM)—Aug 3, 1981: 89.3 mhz; 12 kw. Ant 330 ft. TL: N36 48 34 W87 24 20. Stereo. Box 1029 (42241-1029); 1100 E. 18th St. (42240). (502) 886-9655. Licensee: Pennyrile Christian Community Inc. Net: Moody. Format: Christian. News progmg 12 hrs wkly. Target aud: General. Spec prog: Black 5 hrs, Korean one hr wkly. ■ Joan S. Amis, pres; Jim D. Adams Jr., gen mgr; Joseph P. Barner, mus dir; Donald E. Griffey, chief engr.

WQKS(AM)—Sept 19, 1954: 1480 khz; 1 kw-D, 24 w-N. TL: N36 52 15 W87 30 43. 905 S. Main St. (42240-2098). (502) 886-1480. FAX: (502) 886-6286. Licensee: Regional Broadcasting Inc. (acq 7-90; $756,000 with co-located FM; FTR 8-6-90). Net: Natl Black. Rep: Rgnl Reps. Format: Urban contemp. Spec prog: Farm one hr, relg 6 hrs wkly. ■ Rick Shaw, gen mgr; Reggie Rouse, progmg dir; Don Stewart, news dir; Larry McDowell, chief engr.

WZZF-FM—Co-owned with WQKS(AM). July 1, 1960: 100.3 mhz; 100 kw. Ant 602 ft. TL: N36 56 58 W87 40 18. Stereo. Prog sep from AM. (502) 886-1100. Net: ABC/FM, AP. Format: CHR.

Horse Cave

WXPC(FM)—Not on air, target date unknown: 100.7 mhz; 3 kw. Ant 328 ft. TL: N37 08 43 W85 56 11. Box 312, Cave City (42127). Licensee: Newberry Broadcasting Inc. (acq 3-8-93; $30,000; FTR 3-29-93).

Hyden

WZQQ(FM)—Nov 7, 1988: 97.9 mhz; 5.7 kw. Ant 335 ft. TL: N37 10 14 W83 22 49. Box 7280, Main St., Hazard (41702). (606) 436-9898. Licensee: Leslie County Broadcasting Inc. (acq 10-16-92; $178,000; FTR 11-23-92). Net: SMN. Format: CHR. News progmg 50 hrs wkly. General. ■ Stuart Shane Sparkman, CEO; Mike Reeves, gen mgr & gen sls mgr; Jimmy Napier, chief engr.

Inez

WBTH(AM)—See Williamson, W.Va.

WXCC(FM)—See Williamson, W.Va.

Irvine

WIRV(AM)—July 2, 1960: 1550 khz; 1 kw-D. TL: N37 42 26 W83 58 15 (CP: TL: N37 42 57 W83 58 29). Box 281, 1030 Winchester Rd. (40336). (606) 723-5138; (606) 723-5139. FAX: (606) 723-5180. Licensee: Kentucky River Broadcasting Co Inc. Net: Ky. Net. Rep: Rgnl Reps. Format: Country. News staff one; news progmg 7 hrs wkly. ■ Kelly T. Wallingford, pres, gen mgr & gen sls mgr; Vicki Hoppe, progmg dir, mus dir & news dir.

WCYO(FM)—Co-owned with WIRV(AM). Aug 1991: 106.1 mhz; 1.2 kw. Ant 653 ft. TL: N37 43 12 W83 56 54 (CP: 600 w, ant 725 ft.; TL: N37 43 38 W83 56 34). Hrs opn: 24. Prog sep from AM. Net: ABC/D. ■ Dan Frederick, asst mus dir & news dir; Jane Harris, pub affrs dir. ■ Rates: $7; 7; 7; 5.

Jackson

WEKG(AM)—March 7, 1969: 810 khz; 5 kw-D. TL: N37 34 41 W83 24 19. 1024 College Ave. (41339). (606) 666-7531. Licensee: Intermountain Broadcasting Co. Net: Ky. Net. Format: Country. ■ James M. Hay, pres, gen mgr & stn mgr; Doug Neace, gen sls mgr.

WJSN-FM—Co-owned with WEKG(AM). Jan 1, 1979: 97.1 mhz; 638 w. Ant 610 ft. TL: N37 32 46 W83 23 42 (CP: 895 w, ant 827 ft.). Stereo. Format: Adult contemp/CHR.

Jamestown

WJKY(AM)—Sept 3, 1967: 1060 khz; 1 kw-D. TL: N37 01 31 W85 04 23. Box 1326, Russell Springs (42642). (502) 866-3487. FAX: (502) 866-2060. Licensee: Lake Cumberland Broadcasters (acq 7-1-70). Net: SMN. Format: Country. ■ May Hoover, gen mgr; Paul Goodman, gen sls mgr; Darren George, mus dir & news dir; Larry Nelson, chief engr.

WJRS(FM)—Co-owned with WJKY(AM). Sept 3, 1966: 104.9 mhz; 2 kw. Ant 360 ft. TL: N37 01 31 W85 04 23. Box 336, Jamestown (42629). (502) 343-4444. Net: SMN; Ky. Agri.

Jeffersontown

WLSY-FM—Dec 1, 1978: 101.7 mhz; 1.4 kw. Ant 413 ft. TL: N38 11 04 W85 29 57 (CP: 1.89 kw). Stereo. c/o Media Capital Inc., 4224 E. West Hwy., Chevy Chase, MD (20815). (502) 581-9798. Licensee: Channel Chek Inc. (acq 8-14-92; $350,000; FTR 9-7-92). Format: Urban contemp. ■ Rod Burbridge, gen mgr.

Kentucky

Directory of Radio

Jenkins

WIFX-FM—May 10, 1975: 94.3 mhz; 2.8 kw. Ant 1,492 ft. TL: N37 06 38 W82 44 18. Box 729, Whitesburg (41858). (606) 633-9430. FAX: (606) 633-3314. Licensee: Letcher County Broadcasting Inc. (acq 7-1-93; $37,000; FTR 7-26-93). Net: Unistar. Format: Top-40. ■ G.C. Kincer, gen mgr; Diane Watts, gen sls mgr; Ted Meadows, mus dir.

WKVG(AM)—Feb 1, 1970: 1000 khz; 1 kw-D. TL: N37 09 59 W82 37 13. Hrs opn: Sunrise-sunset. Box 613, Pound, VA (24279-0613). 20 Main St. (41537). (703) 796-5636; (703) 796-6011. FAX: (606) 832-4656. Licensee: Martins and Assoc. Inc. (acq 6-15-92; $40,000; FTR 6-7-92). Net: USA. Format: Gosp, Relg. News progmg 7-10 hrs wkly. Target aud: General. ■ Jerry Martin, gen mgr & progmg dir; Orbin Engle, stn mgr & mus dir; Jean Martin, gen sls mgr & adv dir; David Vanover, news dir; Carl Henderson, Jerry Martin, chiefs engr.

Junction City

WDFB(AM)—May 20, 1985: 1170 khz; 1 kw-D, DA. TL: N37 35 46 W84 50 19. Hrs opn: Sunrise-sunset. Box 106, Danville (40423-0106); 3596 Alum Springs Rd., Danville (40422). (606) 236-9333. FAX: (606) 236-9333. Licensee: Alum Springs Vision & Outreach. Net: USA. Format: Relg. Target aud: General. ■ Donald A. Drake, pres; Mildred Drake, exec vp, gen mgr, progmg dir & mus dir; Jim Gaskin, sls dir, adv mgr & chief engr.

Keavy

*****WVCT(FM)**—January 1984: 91.5 mhz; 113 w. Ant 88 ft. TL: N36 58 21 W84 07 28. Stereo. 968 W. City Dam Rd. (40737). (606) 528-4671. FAX: (606) 528-8604. Licensee: Victory Training School Corp. Format: Educ, relg. ■ Charles Sivley, pres & gen mgr; Rhonda Kidd, progmg dir; Wayne Kidd, chief engr.

Lancaster

WKYY(AM)—Nov 5, 1966: 1280 khz; 1 kw-D. TL: N37 37 56 W84 34 02. 551 Buckeye Rd. (40444-9302). (606) 792-2152. Licensee: Lancaster Broadcasters Inc. Net: Ky. Net. Rep: Rgnl Reps. Format: Country. ■ LaJeune Cantwell, pres, gen mgr & gen sls mgr; Kim Cantwell, prom mgr, progmg dir, mus dir & news dir; Gary Durham, chief engr.

WRNZ(FM)—Oct 1, 1988: 105.1 mhz; 3 kw. Ant 325 ft. TL: N37 36 06 W84 34 27. Stereo. 324 Main St., Danville (40422). (606) 236-7106; (606) 236-1461. FAX: (606) 236-1461. Licensee: Hometown Broadcasting of Lancaster Inc. Net: Jones Satellite Audio; Ky. Net. Format: Oldies. News staff one; news progmg 2 hrs wkly. Target aud: 25-54; upscale, white collar. ■ Robert Lee Scheibly, pres; Steve Hayes, gen mgr & progmg dir; Jim Parman, opns dir; Charlie Perry, prom mgr & mus dir; Jim Parmon, news dir; Bill Geyer, chief engr. ■ Rates: $10; 8; 8; 6.

Lawrenceburg

WKYL(FM)—May 11, 1993: 102.1 mhz; 3 kw. Ant 328 ft. TL: N38 01 37 W84 52 59. Stereo. Hrs opn: 24. 1010 Industry Rd.; 1324 Drydock Rd. (40342). (502) 839-1021; (502) 839-6796. FAX: (502) 839-7559. Licensee: FWJR Communications, Inc. Net: Jones Satellite Audio. Wash atty: Pepper & Corazzini. Format: Soft adult contemp. News progmg 4 hrs wkly. Target aud: 30-50; higher income; especially at work listeners. Spec prog: Relg 5 hrs, rgnl high school sports 4 hrs wkly. ■ Finley Willis Jr., CEO, gen mgr & gen sls mgr; Brian Teater, opns dir; progmg dir & mus dir; Robin Powers, rgnl sls mgr. ■ Rates: $6.25; 5; 6.25; 3.

Lebanon

WLBN(AM)—October 1954: 1590 khz; 1 kw-D, 74 w-N, DA-1. TL: N37 33 55 W85 14 47. Box 680, Radio Station Rd. (40033); Remote Studios, Masonic Bldg., Main St., Springfield (40069). (502) 692-3126; (606) 336-7486. FAX: (502) 692-6003. Licensee: Lebanon-Springfield Broadcasting Co. Inc. (acq 7-1-85; $300,000 with co-located FM; FTR 6-10-85). Net: Moody, MBS. Rep: Rgnl Reps. Wash atty: Leonard Joyce. Format: Adult contemp, talk. News staff 3; news progmg 13 hrs wkly. Target aud: 18-65; rural, students & business people. Spec prog: Gospel 5 hrs, open mike 5 hrs wkly. ■ J.T. Whitlock, pres & gen mgr; Cherry Gibson, stn mgr & gen sls mgr; Tommy Burris, prom mgr; Carl Briggs, adv mgr; Jamie Whitlock, progmg dir; Frank Kemp, mus dir; Alvin Wren,

news dir; J.B. Crawley, chief engr. ■ Rates: $5.95; 5.95; 5.95; 5.95.

WLSK(FM)—Co-owned with WLBN(AM). Oct 1, 1979: 100.9 mhz; 3 kw. Ant 200 ft. TL: N37 35 12 W85 12 15. Stereo. Hrs opn: 5:30 AM-midnight. Prog sep from AM. Net: MBS. Format: Modern country. News staff 3; news progmg 19 hrs wkly. Spec prog: Seasonal Univ. of Ky & local sports wkly. ■ J.T. Whitlock, CEO; Carl Briggs, sls dir & adv mgr; Linda Nally, mktg dir; Cherry Gibson, adv dir; Tommy Burris, progmg dir & mus dir; Frank Kemp, asst mus dir. ■ Rates: $7.70; 7.70; 7.70; 7.70.

Leitchfield

WMTL(AM)—Jan 17, 1959: 870 khz; 500 w-D. TL: N37 30 40 W86 17 15. 2160 Brandenburg Rd. (42754). (502) 259-3165. FAX: (502) 259-5693. Licensee: Rough River Broadcasting Co. Inc. (acq 5-76). Net: SMN. Format: C&W. ■ Kenneth H. Goff, pres; Greg Gribbins, gen mgr & gen sls mgr; Leslie Goff, news dir; Ed Thomas, chief engr.

WKHG(FM)—Co-owned with WMTL(AM). Oct 29, 1967: 104.9 mhz; 3.5 kw. Ant 250 ft. TL: N37 30 40 W86 17 15. Stereo. Prog sep from AM. (502) 259-5692. Net: ABC/I, SMN. Format: Adult contemp.

Lewisport

WKCM(AM)—See Hawesville.

Lexington

WGKS(FM)—Listing follows WLXG(AM).

WKQQ(FM)—July 15, 1969: 98.1 mhz; 100 kw. Ant 561 ft. TL: N38 02 07 W84 27 04. Stereo. Box 100 (40590); 1087 New Circle Rd. (40505). (606) 252-6694. FAX: (606) 252-8505. Licensee: Village Companies (group owner; acq 12-1-74). Net: AP. Format: AOR, classic rock. Target aud: 25-49. ■ James Heavner, pres; Keith Yarber, gen mgr; Tim Wagner, gen sls mgr; Linda Huston, prom mgr; Peter Delloro, progmg dir; Tony Tilford, mus dir; Katie Cline, news dir; Fred Pace, chief engr. ■ Rates: $81; 69; 76; 40.

WLAP(AM)—September 1922: 630 khz; 5 kw-D, 1 kw-N, DA-2. TL: N38 07 25 W84 26 45. Box 11670, 3549 Russell Cave Rd. (40577-1670). (606) 293-0563. Licensee: Trumper Communications of Kentucky. Group owner: Trumper Communications Inc. (acq 12-31-86). Rep: D & R Radio. Format: Oldies. ■ Daniel C. Dorsett, vp & gen mgr; Karen Wesley, gen sls mgr; Brian Wright, news dir; Phillip J. Fraley, chief engr.

WMXL(FM)—Co-owned with WLAP(AM). 1940: 94.5 mhz; 100 kw. Ant 640 ft. TL: N38 07 25 W84 26 45. Stereo. Prog sep from AM. Format: Adult contemp.

WLXG(AM)—1946: 1300 khz; 2.5 kw-D, 1 kw-N, DA-N. TL: N38 05 50 W84 31 45. 1300 Greendale Rd. (40511); Box 11788 (40578). (606) 233-1515. Licensee: L. M. Communications Inc. (group owner; acq 7-1-84). Net: CNN, ABC, NBC, ESPN, MBS. Format: News/talk. Target aud: 25-54; adults. Spec prog: Cincinnati Reds Baseball, Cincinnati Bengals football, SCC Game of the Week. ■ Lynn Martin, pres; Dave Curtis, gen mgr.

WGKS(FM)—(Paris). Co-owned with WLXG(AM). June 5, 1968: 96.9 mhz; 50 kw. Ant 492 ft. TL: N38 07 32 W84 21 12. Stereo. Prog sep from AM. Net: ABC. Rep: D & R Radio. Format: KISS FM/Adult Contemp.

WMXL(FM)—Listing follows WLAP(AM).

*****WRFL(FM)**—Mar 3, 1988: 88.1 mhz; 250 w. Ant 288.6 ft. TL: N38 02 19 W84 30 16. Box 777, University Stn. (40506-0025). (606) 257-4636. FAX: (606) 258-1039. Licensee: Radio Free Lexington Inc. Format: Alt/free form. Spec prog: Christian 3 hrs, heavy metal 6 hrs, reggae 3 hrs, rap-hip-hop 3 hrs, underground 3 hrs, psychedelic 3 hrs, folk 3 hrs, blues 3 hrs, dance 3 hrs, jazz 6 hrs wkly. ■ Wayne Karczewski, gen mgr; Rick Jamie, progmg dir.

*****WUKY(FM)**—March 13, 1941: 91.3 mhz; 95 kw. Ant 1,004 ft. TL: N37 47 18 W84 40 49. Stereo. Hrs opn: 24. Univ. of Kentucky, 340 McVey (40506-0045). (606) 257-3221; (606) 257-4248. FAX: (606) 257-6291. Licensee: Univ. of Kentucky. Net: APR, AP, NPR. Format: News, jazz/blues, class. News staff one; news progmg 63 hrs wkly. Target aud: General. ■ Roger Chesser, gen mgr & mus dir; Helen Wigger, opns mgr; Gail Koon Bennett, dev mgr; David Farmer, pub affrs dir; Joe Woody, chief engr.

WVLK(AM)—October 1947: 590 khz; 5 kw-D, 1 kw-N, DA-2. TL: N38 06 42 W84 34 36 (CP: 1.6 kw-N). Stereo. Hrs opn: 24. Box 1559 (40592). (606) 253-5900. FAX: (606) 253-5903. Licensee: WVLK Radio Inc. Group owner: Bluegrass Broadcasting Co. Inc. (acq 1-79). Net: NBC Talknet, ABC/I; Ky. Net. Rep: Katz. Format: Adult contemp, talk. Spec prog: Farm 5 hrs wkly. ■ Ralph E. Hacker, pres; Robert Lindsey, opns mgr & progmg dir; Connie Joiner, vp sls; Terry Barton, gen sls mgr; Tom Leach, news dir; Tom Devine, chief engr.

WVLK-FM—February 1962: 92.9 mhz; 100 kw. Ant 854 ft. TL: N38 02 22 W84 24 11. Stereo. Prog sep from AM. Format: Country.

Lexington-Fayette

WJGG(FM)—July 30, 1992: 104.5 mhz. 1139 Dunbarton Lane, Lexington (40502). Licensee: J.L. Givens Associates Ltd.

Liberty

WKDO(AM)—November 1963: 1560 khz; 1 kw-D. TL: N37 18 22 W84 55 02. Box B, Hwy. 1649 (42539). (606) 787-7331; (606) 787-7838. FAX: (606) 787-2166. Licensee: Radio Station WKDO (acq 11-27-75). Net: USA. Format: Country, relg. News progmg 10 hrs wkly. Target aud: 18-49. ■ Carlos Wesley, pres, gen mgr & gen sls mgr; Rick Wesley, prom mgr, progmg dir & mus dir; Ricky Melson, chief engr. ■ Rates: $7; 7; 7; 7.

WKDO-FM—January 1977: 98.7 mhz; 25 kw. Ant 239 ft. TL: N37 18 22 W84 55 02. Stereo. Hrs opn: 16. Format: Modern country, classic rock. News staff 3; news progmg 21 hrs wkly. Target aud: 15-35.

London

WFTG(AM)—Sept 1, 1955: 1400 khz; 1 kw-U. TL: N37 08 28 W84 04 45 (CP: 980 khz; 1 kw-D). Box 1988 (40743-0647). (606) 864-2148. FAX: (606) 864-0645. Licensee: F.T.G. Broadcasting Inc. (acq 8-5-92; $410,000; FTR 8-24-92). Net: AP. Format: Adult contemp. ■ Francis Wilhort, gen mgr; Drew Taylor, progmg mgr.

WWEL(FM)—Co-owned with WFTG(AM). Sept 15, 1970: 103.9 mhz; 3 kw. Ant 190 ft. TL: N37 08 28 W84 04 45. Stereo. (606) 864-2048. Net: SMN. Format: Country. ■ Betty Miles, news dir.

WMAK(AM)—Aug 8, 1981: 980 khz; 900 w-D, U. TL: N37 10 16 W84 06 39. Hrs opn: 24. 568 Old Richmond Rd. (40741). (606) 878-0980. FAX: (606) 878-0980. Licensee: Gizmo Communications Inc. (acq 12-11-90; $125,000; FTR 1-7-91). Net: ABC/E, SMN. Format: Gospel. News progmg 5 hrs wkly. Target aud: 25-54; male/female. Spec prog: Relg 6 hrs wkly. ■ James S. Parks, CEO & chmn; Rich Hunter, gen mgr & mus dir; Rich Hunter, James Parks, gen sls mgrs; Doug Stallard, chief engr. ■ Rates: $3.50; 3; 3.25; 2.50.

WWEL(FM)—Listing follows WFTG(AM).

Louisa

WBTH(AM)—See Williamson, W.Va.

WSAC(FM)—May 17, 1991: 92.3 mhz; 4.48 kw. Ant 377 ft. TL: N38 10 33 W82 37 39. Box 176, 112 Madison St. (41230). (606) 638-9203. FAX: (606) 638-9559. Licensee: Louisa Communications Inc. Net: CNN. Format: Adult contemp. ■ Harold Britton, pres; Lisa Strobel, gen mgr; Sheila McCarty, gen sls mgr; Mike Copley, prom mgr; Diana Ambler, progmg dir; Chris Miller, news dir; Bill Geyer, chief engr.

WVKY(AM)—Dec 15, 1970: 1270 khz; 1 kw-D, 100 w-PSSA. TL: N38 05 18 W82 36 44. Box 176 (41230). (606) 638-9203; (606) 638-9210. Licensee: Louisa Communications Inc. (acq 6-30-93; FTR 7-26-93). Net: ABC/D; Ky. Net. Rep: Rgnl Reps. Format: C&W. News staff one; news progmg 8 hrs wkly. Target aud: General. Spec prog: Gospel. ■ Harold Britton, pres; Lisa Strobel, gen mgr; Sheila McCarty, gen sls mgr; Gary Strobel, prom mgr, progmg dir & mus dir; Chris Bevins, news dir; Emmitt Ratliss, chief engr.

WXCC(FM)—See Williamson, W.Va.

Louisville

WAMZ(FM)—Listing follows WHAS(AM).

WAVG(AM)—Dec 30, 1933: 970 khz; 5 kw-U, DA-2. TL: N38 19 05 W85 44 39. Stereo. Hrs opn: 24. Box 1897 (40201-1897). Box 726, 213 Magnolia, Jeffersonville, IN (47130). (502) 587-0970; (812) 283-3577. FAX: (812) 285-5060. Licensee: Sunnyside Communications Inc. (acq 10-16-91; $425,000 with WXVW-AM, Jeffersonville, Ind.; FTR 11-4-91). Net: SMN, CBS. Rep: Savalli. Rgnl Reps.Wash atty: Jones, Waldo, Holbrook & McDonough. Format: Adult standards. News staff one; news progmg 21 hrs wkly. Target aud: 35-65 plus; people with most discretionary incomes. ■ Charles J. Jenkins, pres & gen sls mgr; Betty Kelley, prom dir; Ron Chilton, progmg dir; Bob MacIntosh, pub affrs dir; Steve Petty, chief engr. ■ Rates: $27; 27; 27; 27.

WDJX(AM)—November 1948: 1080 khz; 10 kw-D, 1 kw-N, DA-2. TL: N38 18 29 W85 49 45. Suite 100, 612 4th Ave. (40202). (502) 589-4800. FAX: (502) 587-0212. Licensee: American Radio Systems License Corp. Group owner: American Radio Systems (acq 9-15-93; with co-located FM; FTR 10-4-93). Rep: Eastman. Format: Adult CHR. News staff one. Target aud: 18-34; women. ■ David Pearlman, pres; William V. Wells, gen mgr; Mike Horlander, sls dir; Don Snelling, prom mgr; Chris Shebel, progmg dir; Jill Meyer, mus dir; James Banzer, news dir; Jerry Snapp, chief engr.

WDJX-FM—Aug 1, 1963: 99.7 mhz; 24 kw. Ant 720 ft. TL: N38 21 53 W85 50 18. Stereo. Dups AM 100%. ■ Karen Strong, prom mgr.

WFIA(AM)—March 1947: 900 khz; 1 kw-U. TL: N38 16 12 W85 42 25. 300 W. Liberty St. (40202). (502) 583-4811. FAX: (502) 583-4820. Licensee: Radio 900 Inc. (acq 2-22-90; $2.1 million with co-located FM; FTR 3-12-90). Format: Christian teaching. ■ Jim Kincer, pres; Joyce Kincer, opns mgr.

WHKW(FM)—Co-owned with WFIA(AM). 1974: 103.9 mhz; 1.35 kw. Ant 490 ft. TL: N38 15 20 W85 45 28. Stereo. Prog sep from AM. Format: Adult contemp Christian.

***WFPK(FM)**—Oct 4, 1954: 91.9 mhz; 100 kw. Ant 350 ft. TL: N38 14 40 W85 45 27. Stereo. 301 York St. (40203-2257). (502) 561-8640. Licensee: Louisville Free Public Library. Net: APR. Format: Class. Target aud: 25 plus. ■ Gerry Weston, gen mgr; Lori Boyd, opns mgr; Amy Wagner, dev dir; Jim Beckham, sls dir; Phil Bailey, mus dir; Donald Backherms, chief engr.

***WFPL(FM)**—Feb 20, 1950: 89.3 mhz; 100 kw. Ant 310 ft. TL: N38 14 40 W85 45 27. Stereo. 301 York St. (40203-2257). (502) 561-8640. Licensee: Louisville Free Public Library. Format: News/talk, jazz. ■ Gerry Weston, gen mgr; Lori Boyd, opns mgr; Amy Wagner, dev dir; Jim Beckham, sls dir; Phil Bailey, mus dir; Diane Bryant, news dir; Donald Backherms, chief engr.

WHAS(AM)—July 18, 1922: 840 khz; 50 kw-U. TL: N38 15 40 W85 25 43. Stereo. Hrs opn: 24. Box 1084 (40201); 520 W. Chestnut St. (40202). (502) 582-7840. FAX: (502) 582-7837. Licensee: Clear Channel Radio Licenses Inc. (acq 7-24-92; with co-located FM). Net: ABC/I. Rep: Christal. Wash atty: Cohn & Marks. Format: Adult contemp, MOR, news/talk. News staff 8; news progmg 14 hrs wkly. Target aud: 25-54. Spec prog: Farm 15 hrs, relg 3 hrs wkly. ■ Robert Scherer, vp & gen mgr; Skip Essick, opns dir, progmg dir & mus dir; Mark Thomas, gen sls mgr; Jane Vance, natl sls mgr; Jerry Solomon, rgnl sls mgr; Keli Bennett, prom dir; Brian Rublein, news dir; Charles Strickland, chief engr.

WAMZ(FM)—Co-owned with WHAS(AM). September 1966: 97.5 mhz; 100 kw. Ant 500 ft. TL: N38 03 49 W85 43 52 (CP: Ant 649 ft.). Stereo. Hrs opn: 24. Prog sep from AM. Format: Country. News staff 2. Target aud: 25-54. ■ Coyote Calhoun, opns mgr & progmg dir; George Demaree, gen sls mgr; Marji Pilato, prom mgr; Bobby Jack Murphy, mus dir; Vaness Anderson, pub affrs dir.

WHKW(FM)—Listing follows WFIA(AM).

WLLV(AM)—June 1940: 1240 khz; 1 kw-U. TL: N38 14 49 W85 42 19. 515 S. 3rd St. (40202). (502) 581-1240. FAX: (502) 583-4301. Licensee: Almighty Broadcasting Co. (acq 12-8-93; $375,000; FTR 1-3-94). Net: Natl Black. Rep: Katz. Format: Black Gospel. ■ Archie Dale, pres, gen mgr & gen sls mgr; James Ford, progmg dir & mus dir; Kenny Miles, news dir; Bill Brown, chief engr.

WLOU(AM)—1948: 1350 khz; 5 kw-U, DA-N. TL: N38 13 45 W85 46 47. 2549 S. Third St. (40208). (502) 636-3535. FAX: (502) 637-7943. Licensee: Johnson Communications (acq 1982; $1.6 million; FTR 11-15-82). Net: American Urban, Natl Black. Format: Black, urban contemp. Target aud: 25-54; mature adults. ■ Linda Johnson Rice, pres; Venissa Jentry, opns mgr; Ange Canessa, progmg dir.

WLRS(FM)—October 1964: 102.3 mhz; 3 kw. Ant 300 ft. TL: N38 14 37 W85 45 34. Hrs opn: 24. 320 B Distillery Commons (40206). (502) 585-5178. FAX: (502) 587-6274. Licensee: Blue River Communications L.P. (group owner: acq 7-1-92; $10 & assumption of debt; FTR 7-20-92). Net: ABC/FM. Rep: Target. Format: Adult comtemp. Target aud: Women 25-49; working women with emphasis on workday listening. ■ James Champlin, chmn; Christopher Baker, gen mgr & natl sls mgr; George Linsey, opns mgr; Barry Epstein, gen sls mgr & adv mgr; Susan Wells, prom dir; Joe Kelly, progmg dir & mus dir; Gil Daugherty, news dir; Don Backherms, chief engr. ■ Rates: $75; 85; 75; 40.

WLSY-FM—See Jeffersontown.

WQMF(FM)—See Jeffersonville, Ind.

WTFX(FM)—Not on air, target date unknown: 100.5 mhz; 37.6 kw. Ant 567 ft. TL: N38 03 49 W85 43 52. 558 Fourth Ave. (40202). (502) 585-1005. Licensee: Louisville Broadcasters Ltd. ■ Jim Cooley, gen mgr.

WTMT(AM)—Aug 20, 1958: 620 khz; 500 w-U, DA-2. TL: N38 18 59 W85 42 08. 162 W. Broadway (40202). (502) 583-6200. FAX: (502) 589-2979. Licensee: Jefferson Broadcasting Co. Rep: Masla. Format: C&W. ■ Lee Stinson, pres & gen mgr; Lee Stinson Jr., vp & gen sls mgr; E.J. Clark, progmg dir, mus dir & news dir.

***WUOL(FM)**—Dec 20, 1976: 90.5 mhz; 35 kw. Ant 580 ft. TL: N38 21 23 W85 50 52. Stereo. Hrs opn: 24. Strickler Hall, Univ. of Louisville (40292). (502) 852-6467. FAX: (502) 852-7042. Licensee: Univ. of Louisville. Net: Beethoven; Ky. Pub. Format: Class, talk. News progmg 7 hrs wkly. Target aud: General; those interested in quality mus & info. Spec prog: Jazz one hr, Broadway musicals 7 hrs wkly. ■ Jay Landers, stn mgr; Michael Toulouse, opns dir; Vicky Costello, Cindy Robinson (asst), mktg dirs; Bill Underwood, progmg dir; David Brownstein, mus dir; Randi Hansen (asst), pub affrs dir; Herb Barbee, chief engr.

WVEZ-FM—Listing follows WWKY(AM).

WWKY(AM)—1936: 790 khz; 5 kw-D, 1 kw-N, DA-2. TL: N38 11 34 W85 31 14. Stereo. 558 Fourth Ave. (40202). (502) 587-1069. FAX: (502) 589-1722. Licensee: Prism Radio Partners Ltd. (acq 4-30-93; $6.375 million with co-located FM; FTR 5-24-93). Net: Daynet, NBC News, NBC Talknet. Rep: McGavren Guild. Format: Talk. News staff one; news progmg 10 hrs wkly. Target aud: 25-54. Spec prog: Relg 4 hrs, pub affrs, sports 4 hrs wkly. ■ Bill Phalen, CEO; James Cooley, gen mgr; Steve Fehder, gen sls mgr; Andra Kotcho, prom dir; Chuck Tyler, progmg dir & mus dir; Stan Cook, news dir; Jerry Shea, chief engr.

WVEZ-FM—Co-owned with WWKY(AM). Apr 1, 1967: 106.9 mhz; 24.5 kw. Ant 670 ft. TL: N38 22 20 W85 49 32. Stereo. Format: Adult contemp. News staff one; news progmg 5 hrs wkly. Target aud: 24-54; upper-scale, working women.

WXVW(AM)—See Jeffersonville, Ind.

WZCC(AM)—See New Albany, Ind.

Madisonville

WFMW(AM)—January 1947: 730 khz; 500 w-D, 215 w-N. TL: N37 21 03 W87 29 25. Stereo. Hrs opn: 24. Box 338, 2380 N. Main St. (42431). (502) 821-4096. FAX: (502) 821-5954. Licensee: Sound Broadcasters (acq 4-30-73). Net: CNN. Rep: Rgnl Reps, Keystone (unwired net). Format: C&W. News staff one; news progmg 13 hrs wkly. Target aud: 18 plus. ■ Robert T. Kelley, pres & gen mgr; Dan Koeber, progmg dir; Chris Gardener, news dir; Charles Wilson, chief engr.

WKTG(FM)—Co-owned with WFMW(AM). April 19, 1949: 93.9 mhz; 27.1 kw. Ant 295 ft. TL: N37 21 05 W87 29 25. Stereo. Hrs opn: 24. Prog sep from AM. (502) 821-1156. Net: USA, Unistar. Format: AOR, classic rock. News staff one; news progmg 3 hrs wkly. Target aud: 20-45. ■ Bob Mays, progmg dir.

***WSOF-FM**—February 1977: 89.9 mhz; 39.4 kw. Ant 282 ft. TL: N37 19 11 W87 30 57. Stereo. Box 1246, 1415 Island Ford Rd. (42431). (502) 825-3004. Licensee: Madisonville Christian School, a div of Madisonville Baptist Temple Inc. Net: USA. Format: Christian educ. News progmg 7 hrs wkly. Target aud: General; Christian. ■ Gary Hall, pres & chief engr; Ben Hall, progmg dir & mus dir.

WTTL(AM)—Sept 16, 1956: 1310 khz; 1.5 kw-D, 500 w-N, DA-N. TL: N37 20 12 W87 32 41. 265 S. Main St. (42431). (502) 821-1310. FAX: (502) 825-3260. Licensee: Hopkins County Broadcasters (acq 6-8-92; $100,000; FTR 6-29-92). Net: ABC/C. Format: Contemp, MOR. Spec prog: Black 20 hrs wkly. ■ Marshall Smith, pres; Val Smith, gen mgr; Stan Harvey, prom mgr; Jerry McKonly, progmg dir & mus dir; Ed Thomas, chief engr.

WTTL-FM—Sept 7 1992: 106.9 mhz; 2 kw. Ant 528 ft. TL: N37 22 51 W87 28 04. Hrs opn: 6 AM-midnight. Format: Adult contemp.

Manchester

WKLB(AM)—Sept 26, 1981: 1290 khz; 50 kw-U. TL: N37 09 29 W83 47 06 (CP: 50 kw). Stereo. Hrs opn: 24. Box 448, 106 Richmond Rd. (40962). (606) 598-2445; (606) 598-2653. FAX: (606) 598-6638. Licensee: Barker Broadcasting Co. Larry Barker (acq 1981). Net: ABC/E, Ky. Net. Rep: Rgnl Reps. Wash atty: Robert Olender. Format: Country. News staff one; news progmg 8 hrs wkly. Target aud: 24-65; working people. Spec prog: Farm one hr, gospel 4 hrs wkly. ■ Larry Barker, pres, gen mgr, gen sls mgr, mktg mgr & prom mgr; Lynda Barker, news dir; Bob Hale, chief engr.

WTBK(FM)—Oct 1989: 105.7 mhz; 7.5 kw. Ant 462 ft. TL: N37 08 57 W83 45 09. Stereo. Hrs opn: 19. Old Royal Hotel, 305 Bridge St. (40962). (606) 598-7588; (606) 598-7559. FAX: (606) 598-6016. Licensee: Manchester Communications Inc. (acq 3-24-89). Net: AP, Westwood One. Format: Classic rock. News staff one; news progmg 10 hrs wkly. Target aud: General; 30 plus in the morning; 16-40 at night. Spec prog: Talk 8 hrs wkly. ■ Joe W. Burchell, pres; Krista E. Robles, gen mgr; Earl Owens, dev mgr, news dir & pub affrs dir; David Miller, gen sls mgr & prom mgr; David Begley, progmg dir & mus dir; Pete Boyce, chief engr. ■ Rates: $8; 8; 8; 5.

WWLT(AM)—1956: 1450 khz; 1 kw-U. TL: N37 09 04 W83 45 45. Hrs opn: 19. Rt 5, Box 50, Radio Hill (40962). (606) 598-5102. FAX: (606) 598-8343. Licensee: Wilderness Hills Broadcasting Co. Group owner: Vernon R. Baldwin Inc. (acq 1956). Net: USA. Rep: Rgnl Reps. Wash atty: Lauren A. Colby. Format: Gospel. News progmg 11 hrs wkly. Target aud: General. Spec prog: Farm one hr wkly. ■ Vernon R. Baldwin, pres; Lonnie Marcum, gen mgr, progmg dir & mus dir; Roy Steck, chief engr.

WWXL-FM—Co-owned with WWLT(AM). Aug 9, 1967: 103.1 mhz; 3 kw. Ant 328 ft. TL: N37 09 13 W83 46 26. Stereo. Dups AM 100%.

Marion

WMJL(AM)—July 10, 1968: 1500 khz; 250 w-D. TL: N37 20 11 W88 04 12 (CP: 1.75 kw. TL: N37 20 16 W88 04 03). Hrs opn: Sunrise-Sunset. Box 68, 251 Club Dr. (42064). (502) 965-2271. Licensee: Crittenden County Broadcasting Co. Net: ABC/E; Ky. Net. Rep: Rgnl Reps. Format: Country. News staff one; news progmg 12 hrs wkly. Target aud: General. Spec prog: Local news, farm 3 hrs, community announcements one hr wkly. ■ Sam Crawley, pres; Henry Hina, gen mgr, gen sls mgr, adv mgr & news dir; Brad Dossett, mus dir; Joseph Greenwell, chief engr. ■ Rates: $3.75; 3.75; 3.75; 3.75.

WMJL-FM—June 1993: 102.7 mhz; 3 kw. Ant 328 ft. TL: N37 20 16 W88 04 03. Stereo. Hrs opn: 6 AM-10 PM. Dups AM 100%. (acq 3-12-91; FTR 4-1-91). ■ Rates: Same as AM.

Martin

WMDJ(AM)—Nov 1, 1982: 1440 khz; 2.5 kw-D. TL: N37 35 33 W82 43 43. Box 530, Old Hwy. 80 (41649). (606) 874-8005. FAX: (606) 874-0057. Licensee: Floyd County Broadcasting Co. Inc. (acq 1-19-81). Net: NBC. Rep: Rgnl Reps. Wash atty: Russ Powell. Format: C&W, oldies. News staff 3; news progmg 35 hrs wkly. Target aud: 25-65; young adults to middle-aged teenie boppers. Spec prog: Sports with Cincinnati Reds. ■ Dale McKinney, gen mgr & progmg dir; Rick Caudill, stn mgr; Mona

Kentucky

Allen, gen sls mgr; Bill Marshall, mus dir; Rick Caudille, news dir; Jim Daniels, chief engr.

Mayfield

WNGO(AM)—Jan 7, 1947: 1320 khz; 1 kw-D, 97 w-N. TL: N36 45 37 W88 38 20. Hrs opn: 5 AM-10 PM. Box 679, Paducah Rd. (42066). (502) 247-5122. FAX: (502) 247-4207. Licensee: West Kentucky Broadcasting Inc. (acq 11-3-57). Net: ABC/E; Ky. Agri. Wash atty: Mullin, Rhyne, Emmons & Topel. Format: Country. News staff one. Target aud: 24-54. Spec prog: Farm 4 hrs wkly. ■ Charles W. Stratton, pres; Roth Stratton, gen mgr, gen sls mgr & vp prom; Jerry Snowden, prom dir, progmg dir & mus dir; Jean Richardson, adv dir; Joe Crotty, (asst) mus dir & pub affrs dir; Mark McClain, news dir; Joe Bellis, chief engr.

WXID(FM)—Co-owned with WNGO(AM). Nov 2, 1955: 94.7 mhz; 32 kw. Ant 442 ft. TL: N36 45 59 W88 38 55 (CP: 31.5 kw, ant 443 ft.). Stereo. Hrs opn: 24. Dups AM 100%.

WYMC(AM)—Oct 18, 1976: 1430 khz; 1 kw-U, DA-N. TL: N36 47 12 W88 39 16. Stereo. Box V, Keybottom Rd. (42066). (502) 247-1430. FAX: (502) 247-1825. Licensee: JDM Communications Inc. (acq 12-31-90; $277,649; FTR 1-21-91). Net: NBC, NBC Talknet, SMN. Wash atty: Wiley, Rein & Fielding. Format: MOR. News staff one; news progmg 12 hrs wkly. Target aud: 35-64; affluent, business oriented. Spec prog: Farm 8 hrs wkly. ■ Jim Moore, gen sls mgr; Vince Dawson, prom mgr; Randy Reeves, news dir; Allen Fowler, chief engr.

Maysville

WFTM(AM)—Jan 1, 1948: 1240 khz; 1 kw-U. TL: N38 38 10 W83 45 38. Hrs opn: 6 AM-11 PM. 626 Forest Ave. (41056). (606) 564-3361. FAX: (606) 564-4291. Licensee: Standard Tobacco Co. Net: MBS, Westwood One, CBS. Rep: Keystone (unwired net), Rgnl Reps. Format: Oldies, country. News staff 2; news progmg 10 hrs wkly. Target aud: General. Spec prog: Farm 6 hrs, gospel 5 hrs, relg 5 hrs wkly. ■ J.M. Finch, pres; J. A. Finch, vp; Doug McGill, gen mgr, gen sls mgr & chief engr; Danny Weddle, news dir. ■ Rates: $5.10; 5.10; 5.10; 5.10.

WFTM-FM—Oct 26, 1965: 95.9 mhz; 3 kw. Ant 207 ft. TL: N38 38 04 W83 46 48. Hrs opn: 6 AM-11 PM. Dups AM 30%. Format: Country, oldies, relg. ■ Robert Roe, mus dir. ■ Rates: Same as AM.

McDaniels

*****WBFI(FM)**—Sept 7, 1987: 91.5 mhz; 5 kw. Ant 190 ft. TL: N37 36 06 W86 22 13. Box 2, Hwy. 259 S. (40152). (502) 257-2689. FAX: (502) 257-8344. Licensee: Bethel Fellowship Inc. Format: Relg, educ. ■ Ronald W. Miller, pres; James Coates, gen mgr.

McKee

WWAG(FM)—Nov 1, 1990: 107.9 mhz; 2 kw. Ant 400 ft. TL: N37 23 39 W83 54 32. Hrs opn: 18. 1680 State Rd., Hwy. 1071, Tyner (40486-9543). (606) 287-9924; (606) 598-5102. Licensee: Wilderness Hills Inc. Group owner: Vernon R. Baldwin Inc. (acq 7-90; $65,000; FTR 8-13-90). Net: USA. Rep: Rgnl Reps. Wash atty: Lauren A. Colby. Format: Gospel. Target aud: General. ■ Vernon R. Baldwin, pres; Paul Merryman, gen mgr, progmg dir & mus dir; Roy Stack, chief engr.

Middlesboro

WFXY(AM)—Mar 1, 1969: 1490 khz; 1 kw-U. TL: N36 36 47 W83 42 34. Stereo. Hrs opn: 24. Box 999, 2118 Cumberland Ave., (40965). (606) 248-1560; (606) 248-1574. FAX: (606) 248-6397. Licensee: Country-Wide Broadcasters Inc. (acq 6-1-76). Net: ABC/D, MBS; Ky. Net., Tenn. Radio Net. Rep: Rgnl Reps. Wash atty: Bechtel & Cole. Format: Adult contemp. News staff 2; news progmg 20 hrs wkly. Target aud: 25-54; community-oriented. Spec prog: Black 2 hrs, gospel 3 hrs, relg 3 hrs wkly. ■ Warren Pursifull, pres & gen mgr; Ben Harold, opns mgr; James R. Pursifull Jr., prom mgr; Dominica Reynolds, progmg mgr; Clarence Yeary, mus dir; Terry Michael, news dir; Beulah Pursifull, pub affrs dir; David Laws, chief engr. ■ Rates: $6; 6; 6; 4.

WMIK(AM)—Nov 15, 1948: 560 khz; 500 w-D, 88 w-N. TL: N36 37 38 W83 42 52. Box 608 (40965). (606) 248-5842. FAX: (606) 248-7660. Licensee: Cumberland Gap Broadcasting Co. Net: UPI. Format: C&W. Spec prog: Farm one hr, Gospel 2 hrs wkly. ■ Judy Lusk, gen mgr.

WMIK-FM—June 4, 1971: 92.7 mhz; 130 w. Ant 1,438 ft. TL: N36 35 50 W83 47 49. Stereo. Prog sep from AM. Net: UPI; Tenn. Net., Ky. Net. Format: Top-40.

Millerstown

*****WJCR-FM**—Not on air, target date unknown: 90.1 mhz; 100 kw. Ant 383 ft. TL: N37 25 57 W86 01 50. Stereo. Hrs opn: 24. Box 91, 13101 Raider Hollow Rd., Upton (42784). (502) 369-8614. FAX: (502) 737-5252. Licensee: FM 90.1 Inc. Wash atty: Thomas Hutton. Format: Southern gospel music. Target aud: General. ■ Don Powell, pres, gen mgr & progmg dir; Gerri Powell, exec vp & adv mgr; Dexter Pepper, sls dir; Gerrie Powell, gen sls mgr; Gary Richardson, mus dir; Wanda Richardson, pub affrs dir; Alvin Despain, engrg dir.

Monticello

WFLW(AM)—May 19, 1955: 1360 khz; 1 kw-D. TL: N36 49 30 W84 51 20. Hrs opn: 6 AM-6 PM. 150 Worsham Ln. (42633). (606) 348-8427; (606) 348-7083. FAX: (606) 348-3867. Licensee: Regional Broadcasting Co. (acq 1-1-67). Net: Ky. Net. Rep: Keystone (unwirwed net), Rgnl Reps. Wash atty: Richard Hayes Jr. Format: Country. News staff 2. Target aud: General. Spec prog: Farm 5 hrs, gospel 10 hrs, bluegrass 3 hrs wkly. ■ Steve Staples Sr., pres & gen mgr; Debbie S. Brown, opns mgr & mus dir; Edwin Neal, news dir; Bruce Correll, chief engr. ■ Rates: $10; 8; 8; na.

WKYM(FM)—Co-owned with WFLW(AM). Dec 19, 1965: 101.7 mhz; 1.75 kw. Ant 617 ft. TL: N36 48 08 W84 50 51 (CP: 1.75 kw, ant 617 ft.). Stereo. Hrs opn: 5 AM-midnight. Prog sep from AM. Licensee: Stephen W. Staples Sr. dba Regional Broadcasting Co. Net: Westwood One. Rep: Rgnl Reps. Format: Adult contemp. Target aud: 18-44; young adults. ■ Rory Cundiff, prom mgr; Stephen Staples Jr., adv mgr. ■ Rates: $10; 8; 8; 8.

WMKZ(FM)—June 1, 1990. 93.1 mhz; 2.15 kw. Ant 558 ft. TL: N36 48 29 W84 50 46. Stereo. Box 89, Old Hwy. 90 (42633). (606) 348-3393; (606) 348-3330. FAX: (606) 348-3330. Licensee: Monticello-Wayne County Media Inc. Net: USA, Drake-Chenault. Wash atty: Jim Freeman. Format: Country. 9 hrs wkly. Target aud: 24-55; general.■Glen Massengale, pres; Joel Catron, gen mgr, gen sls mgr & mus dir; Annie Burton, prom mgr; Mary Ellis, progmg dir & news dir; Ernie Sutton, chief engr. ■ Rates: $7.50; 7.50; 7.50; 6.

Morehead

WKCA(FM)—See Owingsville.

*****WMKY(FM)**—June 1965: 90.3 mhz; 37 kw. Ant 895 ft. TL: N38 10 38 W83 24 18 (CP: 100 kw, ant 909 ft.). Stereo. Box 903, Morehead State Univ. (40351). (606) 783-2001. FAX: (606) 783-2335. Licensee: Morehead State Univ. Net: APR, NPR, UPI; Ky. Net. Format: Div. Spec prog: Black 5 hrs, bluegrass 2 hrs wkly. ■ Larry Netherton, gen mgr; James B. Hall, opns mgr & engrg dir; Ron Mace, prom mgr; Paul Hitchcock, mus dir; Tom Lewis, news dir; Ray Roberts, chief engr.

WMOR(AM)—Feb 18, 1955: 1330 khz; 1 kw-D. TL: N38 10 12 W83 26 02. Box 940, 113 E. First St. (40351). (606) 784-4141. Licensee: Dream Enterprises Inc. Net: ABC/I, Moody. Format: Christian. ■ Jim Forrest, pres & gen mgr; Merv Lawson, chief engr.

WMOR-FM—June 15, 1965: 92.1 mhz; 3 kw. Ant 288 ft. TL: N38 10 53 W83 26 55. Prog sep from AM. Format: Top-40.

WWDQ(FM)—Not on air, target date 1994: 96.3 mhz; 6 kw. Ant 328 ft. TL: N38 10 56 W83 26 56. Stereo. Box 1010, Owingsville (40360). Licensee: Gateway Radio Works Inc.

Morganfield

WMSK(AM)—Nov 21, 1960: 1550 khz; 250 w-D. TL: N37 40 00 W87 55 40. Box 369 (42437). (502) 389-1550. FAX: (502) 389-1550. Licensee: Union County Broadcasting Inc. Net: ABC/E. Rep: Hopewell, Rgnl Reps. Format: C&W. ■ J.B. Crawley, pres; Don Sheridan, gen sls mgr; Joseph Greenwell, chief engr.

WMSK-FM—Aug 8, 1967: 95.3 mhz; 3 kw. Ant 300 ft. TL: N37 40 00 W87 55 40. Dups AM 100%.

Morgantown

WLBQ(AM)—1976: 1570 khz; 1 kw-D, 150 w-N. TL: N37 14 10 W86 42 29. Hrs opn: 6 AM-10 PM. Box 130, 210 S. Main St. (42261). (502) 526-3321. FAX: (502) 526-3996. Licensee: Butler County Broadcasting Co. Format: Country, adult contemp. ■ Charles Black, pres; Mary Alice Black, gen sls mgr; Lynne Hutcheson, progmg dir & news dir; Mike Bova, mus dir; Dennis Daugherty, chief engr. ■ Rates: $5; 5; 5; na.

Mt. Sterling

WKCA(FM)—See Owingsville.

WMST(AM)—Oct 17, 1957: 1150 khz; 500 w-D, 54 w-N. TL: N38 02 41 W83 54 05. 34 Broadway (40353). (606) 498-1150. Licensee: Mount Sterling Broadcasting Co. Net: ABC/E; Ky. Net. Rep: Rgnl Reps. Format: Adult contemp.■Janet Lucas, pres; Vernice Taylor, gen mgr; John Wolfe, progmg dir.

WMST-FM—May 28, 1968: 105.5 mhz; 3 kw. Ant 300 ft. TL: N38 05 36 W83 56 39. Stereo. Prog sep from AM. Format: Country.

Mt. Vernon

WRVK(AM)—April 30, 1957: 1460 khz; 500 w-D. TL: N37 23 49 W84 19 45. Box 1288, Red Foley Rd. (40456). (606) 256-2146. FAX: (606) 256-9146. Licensee: Cumberland Media Inc. (acq 6-10-88). Net: ABC/D; Ky. Net. Format: Country, southern gospel. Target aud: General. ■ Larry A. Burdette, pres & gen mgr; Gail F. Burdette, progmg dir.

WXJJ(FM)—Not on air, target date unknown: 102.9 mhz; 2.5 kw. Ant 328 ft. TL: N37 21 32 W84 27 40. c/o William S. Daugherty III, 123 Whispering Hill Dr., Berea (40403). Licensee: William S. Daugherty III.

Munfordville

WLOC(AM)—Feb. 1993: 1150 khz; 1 kw-D, 61 w-N. TL: N37 16 30 W85 55 00. Box 307 (42765). (502) 524-4121. Licensee: South Central Kentucky Broadcasting Co. (acq 6-60). Net: ABC. Rep: Rgnl Reps. Wash atty: Pepper & Corazzini. Format: Country. News staff one; news progmg 20 hrs wkly. Target aud: General. Spec prog: Gospel 19 hrs wkly. ■ Carl Piccuito, gen mgr, progmg dir & news dir; Terry Burnett, stn mgr; David Spence, gen sls mgr; Joy Berry, mus dir; Wayne Sims, chief engr. ■ Rates: $10; 9; 9; 7.

WLOC-FM—Aug 1, 1964: 102.3 mhz; 3 kw. Ant 99 ft. TL: N37 16 30 W85 55 00. Prog sep from AM. Format: Div, C&W, btfl mus. Spec prog: Farm 2 hrs wkly.

Murray

WBLN-FM—Listing follows WSJP(AM).

*****WKMS-FM**—May 11, 1970: 91.3 mhz; 100 kw. Ant 602 ft. TL: N36 55 18 W88 05 50. Stereo. Hrs opn: 5 AM-Midnight M-Th; 5AM-3AM Fri; 6 AM-1 AM Sat; 6 AM-Midnight Sun. Box 2018, University Station, (42071). (502) 762-4745. FAX: (502) 762-4359. Licensee: Board of Regents, Murray State Univ. Net: NPR. Format: Class, jazz, news. News staff 2. ■ Kate Lochte, gen mgr & prom mgr; Grady Kirkpatrick, opns dir & progmg mgr; Anita Bugg, news dir; Allen Fowler, chief engr.

WNBS(AM)—July 1948: 1340 khz; 1 kw-U. TL: N36 37 42 W88 18 04. Hrs opn: 24. Box 1340, 1500 Diuguid Rd. (42071). (502) 753-2400. FAX: (502) 753-9434. Licensee: Jackson Purchase Broadcasting Co. (acq 4-9-93; $170,000; FTR 4-26-93). Net: USA. Rep: Rgnl Reps. Format: Southern gospel. News staff one; news progmg 10 hrs wkly. Target aud: 25-55. Spec prog: Farm 6 hrs wkly. ■ Dr. Sam Parker, pres & gen mgr & news dir; Dal Barrett, gen sls mgr; Bill Bell, progmg dir; Allen Fowler, chief engr. ■ Rates: $6.50; na; na; na.

WSJP(AM)—Sept 12, 1978: 1130 khz; 2.5 kw-D, 250 w-N, DA-2. TL: N36 38 09 W88 19 12. Hrs opn: 24. 1500 Diuguid Dr. (42071). (502) 753-2400. FAX: (502) 753-9434. Licensee: WML Communications Inc. (acq 5-14-92; $1,225,000 with co-located FM; FTR 6-1-92). Net: Unistar Country, CNN Radio News; Ky. Net., Ky. Agri. Format: News/talk. News staff one; news progmg 20 hrs wkly. Target aud: 35 plus. Spec prog: Relg 6 hrs wkly. ■ Dr. Sam Parker, pres & gen mgr; Greg Delaney, gen sls mgr; Wendy Parker, progmg dir; Allen Fowler, chief engr. ■ Rates: $10.95; 9.95; 10.95; 8.95.

WBLN-FM—Co-owned with WSJP(AM). June 23, 1967: 103.7 mhz; 100 kw. Ant 661 ft. TL: N36 32 58 W88 19 52. Stereo. Hrs opn: 24. Prog sep from AM. Rep: Rgnl Reps. Format: Adult contemp. News progmg 4 hrs wkly. Target aud: 18-45. ■ Rates: $19.95; 17.95; 19.95; 13.95.

Neon

WNKY(AM)—Aug 31, 1956: 1480 khz; 5 kw-D. TL: N37 11 54 W82 42 42. Box 248 (41840). Licensee: Letcher County Broadcasting Inc. (acq 6-25-93; $60,000; FTR 7-19-93). ■ Charles Whitaker, pres; Gary Ganter, gen mgr. ■ Rates: $4; 4; 4; na.

Newburg

WXKN(AM)—Not on air, target date unknown: 680 khz; 1.3 kw-D, 450 w-N, DA-2. TL: N38 05 31 W85 40 56. Licensee: River City Communications Inc. (acq 7-31-92; $1,000; FTR 8-17-92).

Newport

WNOP(AM)—Aug 21, 1948: 740 khz; 1 kw-D, DA. TL: N39 05 41 W84 34 59. 1518 Dalton St. Cincinnati, OH (45214). (513) 241-9667. FAX: (513) 421-5194. Licensee: Dayton Heidelberg Distributing Co. Group owner: A-V Communications Inc. (acq 6-2-87). Format: News. ■ Albert W. Vontz, pres & gen mgr; William Faulkner, stn mgr & progmg dir; Fredric Williams, chief engr.

Nicholasville

WCGW(AM)—Sept 15, 1986: 770 khz; 1 kw-D. TL: N37 53 07 W84 31 46. Stereo. Lexington Green, Suite 600, 3191 Nicholasville Rd., Lexington (40503). (606) 245-1900. FAX: (606) 245-1806. Licensee: Mortenson Broadcasting Co. (group owner). Net: USA. Format: Southern gospel. News progmg 6 hrs wkly. Target aud: 25-54; above average in education, family size, income. ■ Jack Mortenson, pres; Dennis J. Smith, gen mgr & gen sls mgr; Tim Hall, progmg dir & mus dir; Dave Johnson, chief engr. ■ Rates: $20; 15; 20; na.

WCKU(FM)—Aug 29, 1988: 102.5 mhz; 3 kw. Ant 300 ft. TL: N37 49 52 W84 30 18. Stereo. Hrs opn: 24. Suite 102, 651 Perimeter Dr., Lexington (40517). (606) 269-9540. FAX: (606) 269-9241. Licensee: High Communications Partnership. Group owner: High Media Group. (acq 1989). Net: ABC, Unistar, SMN. Rep: Torbet, Rgnl Reps. Wash atty: Pellegrin & Levine. Format: Urban contemp. News staff one; news progmg one hr wkly. Target aud: 18-44. Spec prog: Gospel 6 hrs, jazz 4 hrs, oldies 5 hrs wkly. ■ Terry Kile, pres; Tony Gray, gen mgr & gen sls mgr; Bill Clary, opns mgr & progmg dir; John Sandy, mktg dir; Jodi Berry, prom dir; Don Saunders, mus dir; Heather Braun, news dir; William Smith, chief engr. ■ Rates: $50; 50; 50; 50.

WNVL(AM)—December 1962: 1250 khz; 500 w-D. TL: N37 54 18 W84 33 25. Box 247, 108 N. Main St. (40356). (606) 885-6031. FAX: (606) 887-4650. Licensee: Laney Communications Inc. (acq 2-4-92; $125,000; FTR 2-24-92). Net: AP; Ky. Agri. Format: Modern country. ■ Bill Laney, pres; Keith Chafin, opns mgr.

Okolona

***WJIE(FM)**—Jan 1, 1988: 88.5 mhz; 24.5 kw. Ant 623 ft. TL: N38 01 59 W85 45 16. Stereo. Hrs opn: 24. 5400 Minors Ln., Louisville (40219). (502) 968-1220. FAX: (502) 962-3143. Licensee: Evangel Schools Inc. Net: USA, Moody. Wash atty: Pepper & Corazzini. Format: Relg. News progmg 7 hrs wkly. Target aud: 25-49; Christian adults. ■ Steve Butler, gen mgr; Andy Haynes, progmg dir; Jim Galipeau, mus dir; John Bradshaw, chief engr.

Owensboro

WBKR(FM)—Listing follows WOMI(AM).

***WKWC(FM)**—Jan 21, 1983: 90.3 mhz; 5 kw. Ant 100 ft. TL: N37 44 37 W87 07 12. Stereo. Hrs opn: 8 AM-midnight. Massie Hall, 3000 Frederica St. (42301). (502) 685-5937; (502) 926-3111, ext. 237. Licensee: Kentucky Wesleyan College. Format: Class, jazz. News progmg 2 hrs wkly. Target aud: 12 plus. Spec prog: Black 15 hrs, relg 15 hrs wkly. ■ Pam Gray, gen mgr, gen sls mgr, progmg dir & mus dir; Rebecca Jackson, news dir; Rick Graves, chief engr. ■ WKWC-TV affil.

WOMI(AM)—March 7, 1938: 1490 khz; 830 w-U. TL: N37 44 29 W87 06 58. Hrs opn: 24. Box 1330 (42302). (502) 683-1558. Licensee: Tri-State Broadcasting Inc. Group owner: Brill Media Company Inc. (acq 7-7-93; $2.46 million with co-located FM; FTR 7-26-93). Net: NBC, BRN; Ky Net. Rep: Banner. Format: News/talk. News staff 3. Target aud: 35-64. ■ Alan Brill, CEO; Gary Exline, pres, gen mgr & gen sls mgr; Dave Lovell, prom mgr; Tom Massie, progmg dir; Lee Denney, news dir; Rick Crago, engrg dir. ■ Rates: $50; 45; 50; 25.

WBKR(FM)—Co-owned with WOMI(AM). 1948: 92.5 mhz; 91 kw. Ant 1,049 ft. TL: N37 36 29 W87 03 15. Stereo. Prog sep from AM. FAX: (502) 685-2500. Rep: Banner. Format: Country. Target aud: 25-54. Spec prog: Farm 2 hrs wkly. ■ Chuck Urban, opns dir & progmg dir; Dave Spenser, mus dir. ■ Rates: $50; 45; 50; 35.

WSTO(FM)—Listing follows WVJS(AM).

WVJS(AM)—Nov 26, 1947: 1420 khz; 5 kw-D, 1 kw-N, DA-2. TL: N37 46 32 W87 09 31. Box 1828 (42302). (502) 685-2991. FAX: (502) 685-0854. Licensee: Owensboro on the Air Inc. (acq 12-26-91; with co-located FM). Net: ABC/C. Format: Oldies. Spec prog: Farm one hr wkly. ■ Leornard J. Norcia, gen mgr; Joseph Lowe, prom mgr & progmg dir; Jerry Birge, news dir; Mike Flemming, chief engr.

WSTO(FM)—Co-owned with WVJS(AM). June 7, 1948: 96.1 mhz; 100 kw. Ant 1,000 ft. TL: N37 46 20 W87 21 27. Stereo. Prog sep from AM. Format: CHR. Target aud: 18-34. ■ Barry Witherspoon, progmg dir.

Owingsville

WKCA(FM)—Dec 1, 1983: 107.1 mhz; 3 kw. Ant 370 ft. TL: N38 11 16 W83 46 34. Stereo. Hrs opn: 24. Box 1010, 113 S. Court St. (40360). (606) 674-2266. FAX: (606) 674-6700. Licensee: Gateway Radio Works Inc. Net: SMN; Ky. Agri. Wash atty: Blair, Joyce & Silva. Format: C&W. News staff one; news progmg 10 hrs wkly. Target aud: 25-54. Spec prog: Farm 2 hrs wkly. ■ Hays McMakin, pres; Ann Thomas, stn mgr; Jeff Ray, gen sls mgr; Robert Haydon, mktg mgr; Becky Young, progmg dir; Bill Chadwell, news dir; Ernest Sutton, chief engr.

Paducah

WDDJ(FM)—Listing follows WPAD(AM).

WDXR(AM)—Dec 24, 1957: 1450 khz; 1 kw-U. TL: N37 05 55 W88 37 19. Stereo. Hrs opn: 24. Box 2250, One Executive Blvd. (42002-2250). (502) 443-1000. FAX: (502) 442-1000. Licensee: Mason-Dixon Broadcasting Co. (acq 9-3-91; $20,300 with WDXR-FM Golconda, IL; FTR 8-5-91). Net: CNN. Wash atty: Rosenman & Colin. Format: News, Sports. News staff one; news progmg 5 hrs wkly. Target aud: 30-65. Spec prog: Local, regional, & national sports. ■ David Emerson, pres; Karen Cox, opns mgr, mktg mgr & prom mgr; Randy Scheiding, gen sls mgr & adv mgr; Emily Brown, news dir & pub affrs dir; Joe Bellis, chief engr. ■ Rates: $15; 10; 12; 7.

WKYQ(FM)—Listing follows WKYX(AM).

WKYX(AM)—1946: 570 khz; 1 kw-D, 500 w-N, DA-2. TL: N37 00 53 W88 36 46. Stereo. Hrs opn: 24. Box 2397 (42002); 6000 WKYX/WKYQ Rd. (42003). (502) 554-8255. FAX: (502) 554-5468. Licensee: Bristol Broadcasting Co. Inc. Group owner: Nininger Stns. (acq 11-23-71). Net: ABC/C. Rep: McGavren Guild. Format: Adult contemp, talk, sports. News staff 2. Target aud: 25-54; middle to upper income loyal Paducahan due to long time community service. Spec prog: Relg 6 hrs wkly. ■ Gary Morse, gen mgr & gen sls mgr; John Jones, progmg dir; Kevin Anderson, news dir; Greg Walker, chief engr. ■ Rates: $20; 20; 20; 10.

WKYQ(FM)—Co-owned with WKYX(AM). 1947: 93.3 mhz; 89 kw. Ant 440 ft. TL: N37 00 53 W88 36 46 (CP: 100 kw, ant 981 ft.). Stereo. Hrs opn: 24. Prog sep from AM. (502) 554-0093. Net: ABC/I. Format: C&W. Target aud: Wide variety lifestyle due to long time share of adult audience. Spec prog: Gospel 2 hrs wkly. ■ Kent King, progmg dir; Jeff Lawrence, mus dir. ■ Rates: $65; 65; 65; 30.

WPAD(AM)—Aug 23, 1930: 1560 khz; 10 kw-D, 5 kw-N, DA-3. TL: N37 03 08 W88 36 03. Box 450, 1700 N. 8th St. (42001). (502) 442-8231. Licensee: Purchase Broadcasting Inc. (acq 1-24-91; $1.8 million with co-located FM; FTR 2-11-91). Net: MBS, Unistar. Rep: Eastman, Katz; Rgnl Reps.Wash atty: David Hunsaker. Format: Music of your life (40s, 50s, 60s), U.K sports. News staff one; news progmg 22 hrs wkly. Target aud: 35-64; upscale. Spec prog: Relg 7 hrs wkly. ■ R. Lee Hagan, pres; Keith Kraus, gen mgr, stn mgr & gen sls mgr; Rod Phillips, opns mgr; Dee Gillihan, sls dir; Jennifer Taylor, progmg dir; Lori Barrett, news dir & pub affrs dir; Charlie Wilson, chief engr. ■ Rates: $18; 15; 17; 10.

WDDJ(FM)—Co-owned with WPAD(AM). Nov 26, 1946: 96.9 mhz; 100 kw. Ant 340 ft. TL: N37 05 55 W88 37 19. Stereo. Hrs opn: 24. Prog sep from AM. Net: ABC/FM. Format: Adult contemporary hit radio, classic rock. News progmg 2 hrs wkly. Target aud: 18-49; active, white-collar, plus impulsive teens. ■ Dee Gillihan, gen sls mgr; Keith Kraus, natl sls mgr & rgnl sls mgr; Rod Phillips, progmg dir; Jamie Roberts, mus dir. ■ Rates: $26; 22; 25; 20.

WREZ(FM)—See Metropolis, Ill.

WRIK-FM—See Metropolis, Ill.

Paintsville

WKLW(AM)—Mar 18, 1985: 600 khz; 5 kw-D, 500 w-N. TL: N37 47 19 W82 47 07. Stereo. Drawer 1407, Suite 6, Woodland Place (41240). (606) 789-6664. FAX: (606) 789-6669. Licensee: B&G Broadcasting Inc. Net: NBC, Unistar, Westwood One. Wash atty: Midlen & Guillot. Format: Adult contemp, classic rock. News staff 2; news progmg 6 hrs wkly. Target aud: 25-49; middle to upper class adults. ■ Alan Burton, pres, gen mgr, opns mgr & chief engr; William D. Gibson, vp; Robert Castle, gen sls mgr & adv dir; Tim Michales, prom mgr; Craig Reynolds, progmg dir & news dir. ■ Rates: $18; 14; 18; 12.

WKLW-FM—June 18, 1993: 94.7 mhz; 4.9 kw. TL: N37 42 42 W82 48 03. Hrs opn: 24. Dups AM 100%.

WSIP(AM)—April 24, 1949: 1490 khz; 1 kw-U. TL: N37 48 21 W82 46 01. Box 591, 124 Main St. (41240). (606) 789-5311. FAX: (606) 789-7200. Licensee: S.I.P. Broadcasting Inc. Group owner: Key Broadcasting Inc. (acq 2-84). Net: CBS; Ky. Net. Rep: Rgnl Reps. Format: Country. News staff one. Target aud: General. ■ Terry Forcht, pres; Glenna Adkins, gen mgr & gen sls mgr; Mike Fyffe, opns mgr; Jason Blanton, mus dir & news dir; Paul Manuel, chief engr.

WSIP-FM—Jan 12, 1965: 98.9 mhz; 94 kw. Ant 600 ft. TL: N37 47 45 W82 48 04. Stereo. Dups AM 100%. ■ Jason Blanton, progmg dir.

Paris

WGKS(FM)—Licensed to Paris. See Lexington.

WYGH(AM)—January 1993: 1440 khz; 1 kw-D. TL: N38 13 30 W84 14 59. 129 High St. (40361); 2034 N. Hwy. 39, Somerset (42501). (606) 987-1440. FAX: (606) 679-1342. Licensee: Somerset Educational Broadcasting Foundation Format: Relg. ■ David Carr, gen mgr.

Philpot

WBIO(FM)—Not on air, target date unknown: 94.7 mhz; 3 kw. Ant 328 ft. TL: N37 41 51 W86 59 26. c/o WKCM(AM), Box 335, Old U.S. Hwy. #60W., Hawesville (42348). (502) 927-8121. FAX: (502) 927-8122. Licensee: Hancock Communications Inc. Group owner: The Cromwell Group Inc. (acq 6-17-93; $90,565; FTR 7-5-93). ■ Teresa Grimes, gen mgr.

Pikeville

WBTH(AM)—See Williamson, W.Va.

WDHR(FM)—Listing follows WPKE(AM).

***WJSO(FM)**—Oct 28, 1987: 90.1 mhz; 3.8 kw. Ant 455 ft, TL: N37 27 52 W82 32 45. Hrs opn: 24. Box 3457 (41502). (606) 432-0351. FAX: (312) 329-4468. Licensee: Moody Bible Institute of Chicago (group owner; acq 12-18-91; donation; FTR 1-13-92). Format: Relg. News progmg 15 hrs wkly. Target aud: 35-55. ■ Dr. Joseph Stowell, pres; Bob Neff, vp; Phil Shappard, gen mgr; Ken Robinson, chief engr.

WLSI(AM)—Jan 20, 1949: 900 khz; 5 kw-D. TL: N37 29 06 W82 32 44. Hrs opn: 6 AM-midnight. Box 352, 200 N. Mayo Trail. (41502). (606) 437-7323. FAX: (606) 437-9133. Licensee: Cumberland Publishing Co. Inc. Net: AP, MBS. Rep: Rgnl Reps. Format: Country. News staff one; news progmg 21 hrs wkly. Target aud: 25-49. ■ Gary Justice, gen mgr; Gary Slone, opns mgr; Geraldine Fields, gen sls mgr & prom mgr; Sam Runyon, chief engr. ■ Rates: $7.25; 7.25; 7.25; na.

WPKE(AM)—July 31, 1949: 1240 khz; 1 kw-U. TL: N37 28 53 W82 31 27. Stereo. Hrs opn: 24. Box 2200, 1240 Radio Dr. (41501). (606) 437-4051. FAX: (606) 432-2809. Licensee: East Kentucky Broadcasting Corp. (group owner; acq 1962). Net: ABC/E, Ky. Net. Rep: Rgnl Reps. Wash atty: Erwin Krasnow. Format: Adult contemp, classic rock. News staff one; news progmg 5 hrs wkly. ■ Walter E. May, pres, gen mgr & opns mgr; Daniel K. P'Lool, vp sls, gen sls mgr, natl sls mgr, rgnl sls mgr & adv mgr; Lindy Sargent, prom mgr; Brian Prater, progmg dir; Cindy Sargent, progmg mgr & mus dir; Myra Chico, news dir; Tim Daniels, chief engr.

WDHR(FM)—Co-owned with WPKE(AM). Mar 25, 1966: 92.1 mhz; 3 kw. Ant 500 ft. TL: N37 27 58 W82 33 02 (CP: 93.1 mhz, 16.5 kw, ant 856 ft., TL: N37 27 57 W82 33 04). Stereo. Hrs opn: 24. Prog sep from AM. Box 2228 (41501). (606) 432-8103. Net: ABC, Ky. Net. Format: C&W. News staff 2. ■ Walter E. May, vp, gen mgr & stn mgr; Cindy Sargent, vp opns; Dan P'Pool, gen sls mgr; Brian Prater, mus dir; Myra Chico, news dir. ■ Rates: $16.90; 16.90; 16.90; na.

WXCC(FM)—See Williamson, W.Va.

Kentucky

Pineville

WANO(AM)—March 16, 1957: 1230 khz; 1 kw-U. TL: N36 46 07 W83 42 59. HC 84, Box one (40977). (606) 337-2100. FAX: (606) 337-5900. Licensee: Jimmie R. Branham (acq 2-1-86; $210,000; FTR 1-6-86). Net: ABC. Format: C&W, gospel. News staff one; news progmg 21 hrs wkly. Target aud: General. ■ Mary Branham, gen mgr; Jimmie R. Branham, gen sls mgr; Jim Jones, adv mgr; Clayton Hart, progmg dir & mus dir; Jim Branham, chief engr.

WRIL(FM)—Feb 24, 1973: 106.3 mhz; 350 w. Ant 750 ft. TL: N36 45 15 W83 42 23 (CP: 1.045 kw, ant 768 ft.). HC 84, Box one (40977). (606) 337-2100. FAX: (606) 337-5900. Licensee: Pine Hills Broadcasting Inc. (acq 2-22-84; $300,000; FTR 3-5-84). Net: ABC/E. Format: C&W, gospel. ■ Mary Branham, gen mgr; Clayton Hart, progmg dir; Jim Branham, chief engr.

Pippa Passes

*****WOAL-FM**—Nov 1, 1986: 91.7 mhz; 3 kw. Ant 100 ft. TL: N37 19 45 W82 52 30. Stereo. Alice Lloyd College, Purpose Rd. (41844). (606) 368-2101. EXT. 4603. FAX: (606) 368-2125. Licensee: Alice Lloyd College. Net: AP. Format: Easy lstng, adult contemp. Teenagers and young adults. ■ Fred Mullinax, pres; John Jukes, gen mgr.

Prestonsburg

WDOC(AM)—November 1957: 1310 khz; 5 kw-D. TL: N37 41 10 W82 46 42. Box 309 (41653). (606) 886-2338. FAX: (606) 886-1206. Licensee: WDOC Inc. Net: ABC/I. Rep: Rgnl Reps. Format: Oldies. ■ Gormon Collins Sr., pres; Gormon Collins Jr., gen mgr & gen sls mgr; Jerry Grass, progmg dir; James Allen, mus dir; Norm Mircum, news dir; Russel Lifferty, chief engr.

WQHY(FM)—Co-owned with WDOC(AM). Feb 11, 1968: 95.5 mhz; 100 kw. Ant 1,000 ft. TL: N37 41 45 W82 45 24. Stereo. Prog sep from AM. (606) 886-8409. Format: Adult contemp.

WPRT(AM)—Dec 5, 1952: 960 khz; 5 kw-D. TL: N37 40 14 W82 45 14. Box 2200, Pikesville (41501). (606) 886-4375. Licensee: Jeffrey L. and Arnold E. Meek (acq 9-17-90; $300,000 with co-located FM; FTR 10-8-90). Net: Westwood One; Ky. Net. Format: C&W. ■ Jeffrey L. Meek, pres & gen mgr; Debbi Manuel, opns mgr; Dan P. Poop, gen sls mgr; Cindy Sargent, progmg dir; Jim Januls, chief engr.

WXKZ-FM—Co-owned with WPRT(AM). Feb 10, 1967: 105.5 mhz; 3.5 kw. Ant 390 ft. TL: N37 39 24 W82 45 58. Stereo. 31 Francis Ct. (41053). (606) 886-2053. Format: CHR/AOR. ■ Don Lewis, gen sls mgr; Debra Scutchfield, mus dir.

WQHY(FM)—Listing follows WDOC(AM).

WXKZ-FM—Listing follows WPRT(AM).

Princeton

WPKY(AM)—March 15, 1950: 1580 khz; 250 w-D. TL: N37 07 14 W87 51 31. Hrs opn: 6 AM-10 PM. Box 148 (42445). (502) 365-2072. FAX: (502) 365-2073. Licensee: Dart Inc. (acq 11-19-93). Format: Adult contemp. Target aud: General. Spec prog: Farm 5 hrs wkly. ■ Randy Gardner, gen mgr; Twyman Boren, gen sls mgr; Betty Boren, progmg dir & mus mgr; Shirley Gray, news dir; Leslie Goodaker, chief engr.

WAVJ(FM)—Co-owned with WPKY(AM). April 1, 1969: 104.9 mhz; 3 kw. Ant 187 ft. TL: N37 07 14 W83 51 31. Stereo. Dups AM 99%.

Providence

WHRZ(FM)—April 9, 1976: 97.7 mhz; 6 kw. Ant 328 ft. TL: N37 24 52 W87 34 23. Stereo. Hrs opn: 17. Box 475, 552 E. Center St., Madisonville (42431); Box 127, 405 E. Main (42450). (502) 825-1081; (502) 667-2044. FAX: (502) 825-1082. Licensee: Tradewater Broadcasting Co. Inc. Net: ABC/D; Ky. Net. Format: Country. News staff 2; news progmg 21 hrs wkly. Target aud: 18-65. Spec prog: Farm 2 hrs wkly. ■ B. Douglas Hamby, pres, gen mgr & gen sls mgr; Ron Walker, progmg dir & mus dir; Keith Farrell, news dir; Marvin Mahoney, chief engr. ■ Rates: $7.50; 7.50; 7.50; 7.50.

Radcliff

WLVK(FM)—1994: 103.5 mhz; 6 kw. Ant 321 ft. TL: N37 46 57 W85 54 38. Stereo. Hrs opn: 24. Box 2087, Elizabethtown (42702); 4296 S. Wilson Rd. Elizabethtown (42701). (502) 769-1055. FAX: (502) 769-1052. Licensee: WLVK Inc. Net: Unistar. Wash atty: Miller & Miller. Format: Oldies. News staff one; news progmg 4 hrs wkly. Target aud: 25-54. ■ Bill Walters, pres & gen mgr; Rene Hart, opns mgr; Kendra Stewart, news dir. ■ Rates: $15.50; 15.50; 15.50; 5.

Reidland

WZZL(FM)—Not on air, target date unknown: 106.7 mhz; 1.35 kw. Ant 492 ft. TL: N37 03 23 W88 27 22. 505 S. 7th St., Paducah (42001). Licensee: WMOK Inc. (group owner: acq 7-28-92; $100,000; FTR 8-24-92).

Richmond

WCBR(AM)—March 1969: 1110 khz; 250 w-D. TL: N37 44 09 W84 16 05. Box 570, College Park Center, EKU By-Pass (40476-0570). (606) 623-1235. FAX: (606) 623-7094. Licensee: WCBR Radio Inc. (acq 10-79). Net: SMN; Hometown Radio. Format: MOR, big band, btfl mus. News staff 6; news progmg 5 hrs wkly. Target aud: 35plus; older adult listener. Spec prog: Local talk shows, news, sports. ■ George W. Robbins, pres & gen sls mgr; David L. Humes, exec vp; Danny Davis, vp prom & vp progmg; Rob Burton, news dir; William Browning, chief engr. ■ Rates: $16; 8; 14; 6.

WMCQ-FM—Co-owned with WCBR(AM). May 12, 1972: 101.7 mhz; 6 kw. Ant 300 ft. TL: N37 44 09 W84 16 05. Stereo. Hrs opn: 24. Prog sep from AM. Format: 50s & 60s oldies. News staff one; news progmg 6 hrs wkly. Target aud: 25-54; mid to upper scale adults. ■ William Robbins, pres. ■ Rates: $10; 6; 9; 5.

*****WEKU-FM**—September 1968: 88.9 mhz; 50 kw. Ant 720 ft. TL: N37 52 45 W84 19 33. Stereo. Hrs opn: 24. Eastern Kentucky Univ., 102 Perkins Bldg. (40475-3127). (606) 622-1655. Licensee: Board of Regents, Eastern Kentucky University. Net: APR, NPR. Format: Class, news magazine, info. News staff 4; news progmg 35 hrs wkly. Target aud: General. Spec prog: Women's programs 2 hrs wkly. ■ Tim Singleton, stn mgr; John Francis, opns mgr; Judy Flavell, dev dir & prom mgr; Loy Lee, mus dir; Marie Mitchell, news dir; Bill Browning, chief engr.

WEKY(AM)—Oct 17, 1953: 1340 khz; 1 kw-U. TL: N37 43 00 W84 18 25. Stereo. 128 Big Hill Ave. (40475). (606) 623-1340. FAX: (606) 623-1439. Licensee: Berea Broadcasting Company Inc. Group owner: Pioneer Communications (acq 6-23-93; $130,000; FTR 7-19-93). Net: ABC/C. Rep: Rgnl Reps. Format: Adult contemp. News staff one. Target aud: 25-54. Spec prog: Black 12 hrs wkly. ■ Bob Spradlin, pres; Rich Middleton, opns mgr & progmg dir; Mike Bryant, news dir; Bill Browning, chief engr.

WMCQ-FM—Listing follows WCBR(AM).

Russell Springs

WJKY(AM)—See Jamestown.

WJRS(FM)—See Jamestown.

WTCO-FM—Not on air, target date unknown: 92.7 mhz; 6 kw. Ant 328 ft. TL: N37 00 31 W85 12 14. Box 471, Columbia (42728). Licensee: Heartland Communications Inc. (group owner; acq 9-4-92; $28,500; FTR 9-28-92).

Russellville

WRUS(AM)—Aug 28, 1953: 610 khz; 2.5 kw-D, 73 w-N. TL: N36 48 51 W86 52 50 (CP: 500 w-N, TL: N36 52 29 W86 52 56 (night)). Box 298 (42276). (502) 726-2471. FAX: (502) 726-3095. Licensee: The Tremont Group Ltd. Group owner: Amaturo Group Ltd. (acq 6-13-91; $10; FTR 7-1-91). Net: ABC/D. Rep: Eastman, Intermountain. Format: Adult contemp, farm, div. ■ Bill McGinnis, gen mgr; H.R. Ashby, gen sls mgr; Don Neagle, news dir; Michael Golchert, chief engr.

WBVR(FM)—Co-owned with WRUS(AM). March 28, 1965: 101.1 mhz; 100 kw. Ant 1,047 ft. TL: N36 50 40 W86 55 11 (CP: Ant 1,298 ft. TL: N36 52 29 W86 52 56). Stereo. (502) 726-3555. (acq 7-90; $6 million; FTR 8-6-90). Format: C&W.

St. Matthews

WRKA(FM)—Oct 19, 1964: 103.1 mhz; 6 kw. Ant 312 ft. TL: N38 16 03 W85 41 53. Stereo. 10001 Linn Stn Rd., Louisville (40223). (502) 423-9752. FAX: (502) 423-0231. Licensee: Franklin Communications Partners L.P. Group owner: WESHAM Broadcasting Co. (acq 7-16-92; grpsl; FTR 8-3-92). Rep: Banner. Format: Oldies. ■ Kenneth S. Johnson, pres; Bill Hazen, gen mgr; Chuck Cunningham, gen sls mgr; Fred North, progmg dir; Stevie Jenson, mus dir; Dawne Gee, news dir; Greg Hahn, chief engr.

Salyersville

WRLV(AM)—September 1979: 1140 khz; 1 kw-D. TL: N37 44 58 W83 05 19. Box 550, 225 Church St., Rt. 40 W. (41465). (606) 349-6125. FAX: (606) 297-1510. Licensee: Licking Valley Radio Corp. Net: ABC/E. Rep: Rgnl Reps. Format: Relg. News staff 2; news progmg 8 hrs wkly. Target aud: 35-65. ■ C.K. Belhassen, pres & gen mgr; Dan Lions, gen sls mgr; Pam Pack, prom mgr; Nolan Hall, progmg dir & mus dir; Chris Bailey, news dir; Jim Daniels, chief engr.

WRLV-FM—Aug 25, 1989: 97.3 mhz; 5.2 kw. Ant 350 ft. TL: N37 45 30 W83 03 52. Stereo. Prog sep from AM. Format: Country. Target aud: 18-55. ■ C.K Belhassen, prom mgr; Charlene Belhassen, progmg dir; Bryan Dyer, mus dir.

Scottsville

WLCK(AM)—Feb 27, 1958: 1250 khz; 1 kw-D. TL: N36 44 24 W86 10 20 (CP: 860 w. TL: N36 44 25 W86 10 31). Hrs opn: 6 AM-9 PM. Box 158, 104.5 Public Square (42164). (502) 237-3149. FAX: (502) 237-3533. Licensee: Sherandan Broadcasting Co. (acq 7-3-85). Net: USA. Rep: Rgnl Reps. Format: Relg. News staff one. Target aud: General. Spec prog: Farm 3 hrs wkly. ■ Danny Tabor, pres & gen mgr; David Holder, mus dir; Chris Nelson, news dir.

WVLE(FM)—Co-owned with WLCK(AM). Feb 26, 1967: 99.3 mhz; 3 kw. Ant 328 ft. TL: N36 44 24 W86 10 20 Stereo. Prog sep from AM. (502) 237-3148. Net: ABC/I. Format: C&W. News progmg 20 hrs wkly.

Shelbyville

WCND(AM)—June 3, 1964: 940 khz; 250 w-D. TL: N38 13 00 W85 09 45. Box 248, 416 Main St. (40066). (502) 633-3814; (502) 647-2101. FAX: (502) 633-9923. Licensee: Shelby County Broadcasting Inc. (acq 6-9-92; $250,000; with co-located FM; FTR 6-29-92). Net: Ky. Net. Format: Country. News staff one; news progmg 16 hrs wkly. Target aud: 18-54. Spec prog: Farm 6 hrs wkly. ■ R. Lee Hagen, pres; Sheila H. Hawkins, vp & gen mgr; Ron Wainscott, opns mgr; Vicki Elliott, gen sls mgr; Drew Lambert, asst mus dir; Scott Allen, pub affrs dir.

WTHQ(FM)—Co-owned with WCND(AM). Sept 30, 1989: 101.3 mhz; 3 kw. Ant 328 ft. TL: N38 00 08 W85 41 56. Stereo. Hrs opn: 24. Dups AM 100%.

Shepherdsville

WBUL(AM)—Oct 29, 1955: 1470 khz; 1 kw-D, 54 w-N. TL: N37 51 06 W85 56 45. Stn currently dark. 220 Potters Ln., Clarksville, IN (47129). (812) 941-1570. Licensee: Altes Broadcasting Corp. ■ George Zarris, gen mgr.

WEHR(FM)—Not on air, target date unknown: 105.1 mhz; 1.55 kw. Ant 446 ft. TL: N38 02 54 W85 46 04. Suite 106, 3103 Fern Valley Rd., Louisville (40213). (502) 962-8760. Licensee: Owensboro On the Air Inc. (acq 8-26-93; FTR 9-27-93). ■ Steve Cooke, gen mgr.

Smiths Grove

WBLG(FM)—Dec 1, 1986: 107.1 mhz; 50 kw. Ant 393 ft. TL: N36 50 35 W86 15 30. Stereo. Hrs opn: 24. Box 900, 948 Fairview Ave., Bowling Green (42101). (502) 843-0107. FAX: (502) 782-0767. Licensee: Hilltopper Broadcasting Inc. (acq 5-4-87). Net: NBC. Rep: Rgnl Reps. Wash atty: Pepper & Corazzini Format: Adult contemp. News staff one; news progmg 5 hrs wkly. Target aud: 25-49. ■ Wes Strader, pres; Barry Williams, gen mgr; Bryan Locke, opns mgr; Hank Brosche, gen sls mgr; Roy Brassfield, news dir; Rob Beasley, chief engr. ■ Rates: $15.75; 14.50; 15.75; 14.50.

Somerset

*****WDCL-FM**—July 1985: 89.7 mhz; 100 kw. Ant 570 ft. TL: N37 09 29 W85 09 50. Stereo. Hrs opn: 24. 248 Academic Complex, Western Kentucky Univ., Bowling Green (42101). (502) 745-5489. FAX: (502) 745-2084. Licensee: Western Kentucky Univ. Net: APR, AP, NPR, Ky. Net. Wash atty: Cohn & Marks. Format: Class, news. News staff 3; news progmg 30 hrs wkly. Target aud: General. Spec prog: Jazz 15 hrs, folk 5 hrs wkly. ■ Thomas Meredith, pres; David T. Wilkinson, gen mgr; Jane Moore, opns mgr; Melinda Craft, dev mgr; Lee Stott, mus dir; Dan Modlin, news dir; Chris Scott, chief engr. ■ WKYU-TV affil.

WLLK(FM)—Aug 14, 1989: 102.3 mhz; 3 kw. Ant 328 ft. TL: N37 04 41 W84 40 39. Hrs opn: 5 AM-midnight. Box

3404 (42564). (606) 679-2394. Licensee: Williams Communications Inc. (acq 6-24-92; $317,735; FTR 6-29-92). Format: Adult contemp. News progmg 6 hrs wkly. Target aud: 25-54. ■ Walt Williams, pres, gen mgr, gen sls mgr, progmg dir & mus dir; Melinda Williams, exec vp, mktg dir & prom dir; Bruce Correll, chief engr. ■ Rates: $8.80; 7.50; 8; 6.50.

WSEK(FM)—Listing follows WSFC(AM).

WSFC(AM)—Dec 14, 1947: 1240 khz; 790 w-U. TL: N37 07 06 W84 36 44. Stereo. Hrs opn: 5 AM-2 AM. Box 740 (42502-0740); First Radio Lane, 1910 N. Hwy. 1247 (42501). (606) 678-5151. FAX: (606) 678-2026. Licensee: First Radio Inc. (acq 12-15-80). Net: ABC/E. Rep: Rgnl Reps. Wash atty: Latham & Watkins. Format: Talk. News staff 2; news progmg 15 hrs wkly. Target aud: General. Spec prog: Farm 2 hrs wkly. ■ Nolan Kenner, pres, gen mgr & gen sls mgr; Gib Gosser, news dir; James Mercer, chief engr.

WSEK(FM)—Co-owned with WSFC(AM). Sept 1, 1964: 97.1 mhz; 6 kw. Ant 659 ft. TL: N36 57 40 W84 57 01. Stereo. Prog sep from AM. Net: MBS. Format: C&W. News progmg 10 hrs wkly. Spec prog: Farm one hr wkly.

***WTHL(FM)**—July 16, 1987: 90.5 mhz; 20 kw. Ant 590 ft. TL: N37 07 52 W84 33 15. Stereo. 2034 N. Hwy. 39 (42501). (606) 679-6300. FAX: (606) 679-1342. Licensee: Somerset Educational Broadcasting Foundation. Net: Moody. Format: Btfl, educ, relg, Christian. News progmg 24 hrs wkly. Target aud: 40 plus; people with conservative, traditional & relg values & interests. ■ S. David Carr, gen mgr; Homer Akers, chief engr.

WTLO(AM)—Nov 1, 1958: 1480 khz; 1 kw-D. TL: N37 05 15 W84 38 14. Stereo. Drawer B, 290 WTLO Rd. (42501). (606) 678-8151. FAX: (606) 678-8152. Licensee: Cumberland Communications Inc. (acq 11-6-74). Net: SMN. Rep: Keystone (unwired net). Format: Unforgetable Oldies. News staff one; news progmg 14 hrs wkly. Target aud: 45 plus; upscale & highly mobile. Spec prog: Farm one hr, relg 4 hrs wkly. ■ J. Allen Brown, pres, gen mgr & news dir; Brook Cary, opns mgr; Nancy Combs, gen sls mgr; Randy Warren, mus dir; James Freeman, chief engr. ■ Rates: $8.50; 8.50; 8.50; 8.50.

Springfield

WMQQ(FM)—Feb 17, 1989: 102.7 mhz; 1.9 kw. Ant 417 ft. TL: N37 41 43 W85 19 06. Hrs opn: 24. Box 248, Hwy. 150, Bardstown Rd. (40069). (606) 336-7762. FAX: (606) 336-7763. Licensee: Washington-Marion Sound Corp. Net: SMN; Ky. Net. Format: Oldies, news. News staff 4; news progmg 20 hrs wkly. Target aud: 25-55. Spec prog: Sports 12 hrs, farm 10 hrs wkly. ■ Ed O'Daniel, pres; Margaret O'Daniel, vp, gen mgr, stn mgr, gen sls mgr & prom mgr; Sheila Spaulding, adv dir; Roger Gribbins, news dir; Frank Hertel, chief engr. ■ Rates: $7; 7; 7; 6.

Stamping Ground

WKYI(FM)—Not on air, target date unknown: 99.1 mhz; 1.5 kw. Ant 200 ft. TL: N38 16 24 W84 33 51. 110 E. Main St., Georgetown (40324). Licensee: Scott County Communications Inc.

Stanford

WRSL(AM)—Nov 1, 1961: 1520 khz; 1 kw-D. TL: N37 33 03 W84 38 45. Stereo. Box 300 (40484). (606) 365-2126. Licensee: Lincoln-Garrard Broadcasting Inc. (acq 12-23-70). Format: Relg. Spec prog: Farm & community affrs 4 hrs wkly. ■ Ruth Smith, pres, gen mgr & gen sls mgr; Joesph Smith, progmg dir; David Lee, chief engr.

WRSL-FM—May 22, 1967: 95.9 mhz; 3 kw. Ant 85 ft. TL: N37 33 03 W84 38 45. Prog sep from AM. Format: Country.

Stanton

WBFC(AM)—June 21, 1975: 1470 khz; 1 kw-D. TL: N37 53 21 W83 51 57. 41 Faulkner Rd. (40380). (606) 663-2888. Licensee: Jerry Wilson. Format: Relg. Target aud: 25 plus. Spec prog: Farm 2 hrs wkly. ■ Jerry Wilson, pres & gen mgr. ■ Rates: $3; 3; 3; na.

WSKV(FM)—Aug 10, 1974: 104.9 mhz; 440 w. Ant 680 ft. TL: N37 45 43 W83 50 36. Stereo. Hrs opn: 24. Box 610 28 W Hall's Rd. (40380). (606) 663-2811. FAX: (606) 663-2895. Licensee: Parks Broadcasting Inc. (acq 1984). Net: Ky. Net. Format: Country, bluegrass. Target aud: General. ■ Walter Parks, pres, progmg dir & chief engr; John Meins, gen sls mgr; Jim Chadwick, mus dir & news dir.

Tompkinsville

WTKY(AM)—May 28, 1960: 1370 khz; 2.1 kw-D. TL: N36 43 27 W85 40 53. Box 352, Hwy. 1049, Radio Station Rd. (42167). (502) 487-6119. FAX: (502) 487-8462. Licensee: Whittimore Enterprises Inc. (acq 12-3-84). Net: CBS Spectrum, CBS. Format: C&W. ■ J.K. Whittimore, pres & chief engr; Bernice Whittimore, gen mgr.

WTKY-FM—Jan 20, 1972: 92.1 mhz; 6 kw. Ant 328 ft. TL: N36 43 27 W85 40 53. Dups AM 80%.

Valley Station

WQNF(FM)—Not on air, target date unknown: 105.9 mhz; 3 kw. Ant 328 ft. TL: N38 08 14 W85 56 10. 5122 Dawn Dr., Shively (40216). Licensee: Valley Radio.

Vanceburg

WKKS(AM)—June 1, 1958: 1570 khz; 1 kw-D. TL: N38 35 50 W83 20 50. 1106 Fairlane Dr. (41179). (606) 796-3031. Licensee: Brown Communications Inc. (acq 1984). Net: SMN Format: Country. Spec prog: Gospel 16 hrs, oldies 7 hrs, classic country 4 hrs wkly. ■ Dennis Brown, pres, gen mgr & progmg dir; Howard Potts, chief engr.

WKKS-FM—1983: 104.9 mhz; 3 kw. Ant 298 ft. TL: N38 36 19 W83 19 57. Dups AM 95%.

Vancleve

WMTC(AM)—June 1948: 730 khz; 5 kw-D, DA. TL: N37 36 12 W83 26 39. Box 8, Fisher Radio Bldg., 1003 Kentucky Hwy. 541 (41385). (606) 666-5006; (606) 666-7534. FAX: (606) 666-7534. Licensee: Kentucky Mountain Holiness Assn. Wash atty: Pepper & Corazzini. Format: Relg. News progmg 14 hrs wkly. Spec prog: Farm 2 hrs, class 15 hrs wkly. ■ John Eldon Neihof, pres; Seldon Short, vp, gen mgr & sls dir; Stephen Richmond, prom mgr; Janet Short, progmg dir; Carlene Light, asst mus dir; Kenneth Amspaugh, chief engr.

WMTC-FM—Jan 1, 1991: 99.9 mhz; 3 kw. Ant 328 ft. TL: N37 36 23 W83 26 48. Hrs opn: 6 AM-10 PM. Dups AM 100%.

Versailles

WJMM-FM—July 16, 1973: 106.3 mhz; 3 kw. Ant 316 ft. TL: N38 02 44 W84 39 29. Stereo. Hrs opn: 24. Lexington Green Suite 600, 3191 Nicholasville Rd., Lexington (40503); 3950 Lexington Rd. (40383). (606) 245-1900; (606) 873-8096. FAX: (606) 245-1806; (606) 873-1318. Licensee: Mortenson Broadcasting Co. (group owner). Net: USA. Format: Relg. Target aud: 25-49; female. ■ Jack M. Mortenson, pres; Ed Wright, gen mgr & progmg dir; Al Dodak, opns dir & mus dir; Dennis Blais, pub affrs dir & chief engr. ■ Rates: $21; 19; 19; 10.

Vine Grove

WRZI(FM)—Sept 1, 1993: 101.5 mhz; 6 kw. Ant 328 ft. TL: N37 35 07 W85 50 20. Stereo. Hrs opn: 24. 120 Dixie Hwy N., Elizabethtown (42701). (502) 769-5556. Licensee: Radio Partners Inc. Wash atty: Roy Perkins. Format: Light adult contemp. ■ Robin Heffer, gen mgr.

Virgie

WZLK(FM)—Not on air, target date unknown: 107.5 mhz; 580 w. TL: N37 22 47 W82 34 11. Rt. 122, Box 1800, Robinson Creek (41560). Licensee: Kenneth Osborne.

Warsaw

WKID(FM)—See Vevay, Ind.

West Liberty

WLKS(AM)—July 25, 1965: 1450 khz; 1 kw-U. TL: N37 55 36 W83 16 41. Stereo. Hrs opn: 24. Box 338, 129 College St. (41472). (606) 743-3145. FAX: (606) 743-7792. Licensee: Morgan County Industries Inc. Net: Unistar, Westwood One. Rep: Keystone (unwired net), Rgnl Reps. Format: Country. News staff one; news progmg 35 hrs wkly. Target aud: General. Spec prog: Oldies 19 hrs, farm 5 hrs wkly. ■ C.C. Smith, pres; Glenn Woodward, gen mgr & news dir; Darla Rudd, stn mgr & vp opns; Paul Lyons, progmg dir, mus dir & chief engr. ■ Rates: $5.06; 5.06; 5.06; 5.06.

WLKS-FM—Not on air, target date unknown: 102.9 mhz; 6 kw. Ant 328 ft. TL: N37 55 36 W83 16 41.

Westwood

WLUA(FM)—Not on air, target date unknown: 99.7 mhz; 3 kw. Ant 328 ft. TL: N38 26 20 W82 47 51. 2809 Lexington St., Ashland (41101). Licensee: Cope Communications Inc.

Whitesburg

***WMMT(FM)**—Nov 1, 1985: 88.7 mhz; 1 kw. Ant 1,411 ft. TL: N37 06 38 W82 44 15. Stereo. Hrs opn: 24. 306 Madison St. (41858). (606) 633-0108. Licensee: Appalshop Inc. Net: Ky. Pub. Format: Div. News staff 2; news progmg 2 hrs wkly. Target aud: General. Spec prog: Class 2 hrs, jazz 5 hrs, Sp one hr, bluegrass 10 hrs, blues 2 hrs, African one hr, women's 2 hrs, local pub affrs 3 hrs wkly. ■ Rich Kirby, stn mgr; Jim Webb, progmg dir; Buck Maggard, mus dir; Tom Hansell, asst mus dir; Maxine Kenny, news dir & pub affrs dir; Don Mussell, chief engr.

WTCW(AM)—Feb 19, 1953: 920 khz; 5 kw-D, 47 w-N. TL: N37 08 04 W82 46 08 (CP: TL: N37 08 46 W82 46 01). HC 87, Box 1140 (41858). (606) 633-4434; (606) 633-2711. FAX: (606) 633-4445. Licensee: T.C.W. Broadcasting Co. Inc. Group owner: Key Broadcasting Inc. (acq 1-1-86); $765,000 with co-located FTR 10-7-85). Net: CBS; Ky. Net. Rep: Rgnl Reps. Format: C&W, relg. News staff one. Target aud: 30 plus. Spec prog: Bluegrass 10 hrs wkly. ■ Terry Forcht, pres; Gregory Yaden, gen mgr; Bob Hale, chief engr.

WXKQ(FM)—Co-owned with WTCW(AM). Nov 25, 1964: 103.9 mhz; 210 w. Ant 940 ft. TL: N37 04 27 W82 48 44. Stereo. Dups AM 40%. Format: Modern Country.

Whitley City

WHAY(FM)—Dec 1, 1990: 105.9 mhz; 3 kw. Ant 328 ft. TL: N36 44 39 W84 28 37. Hrs opn: 24. Box 69 (42653). (606) 376-2218. Licensee: Tim Lavender. Format: Country. ■ Don Lewis, gen mgr, gen sls mgr, mktg dir, progmg dir & adv dir; Dave Howe, opns mgr, prom mgr, progmg dir & mus dir; Jim Freeman, chief engr. ■ Rates: $6.25; 6.25; 6.25; 6.25.

Wickliffe

WBCE(AM)—Jan 4, 1981: 1200 khz; 1 kw-D. TL: N36 58 54 W89 04 39. Box 128 (42087). (502) 335-5171. Licensee: Bible Time Ministries Inc. Net: CBN. Format: Relg. Target aud: General. Spec prog: Southern gospel music. ■ Jim Baggett, pres & gen mgr; Charlotte Seratt, progmg dir & mus dir; Earl Abernathy, chief engr.

WGKY(FM)—January 1987: 95.9 mhz; 3 kw. Ant 759 ft. TL: N36 56 24 W88 57 59. Stereo. Box 500, Hwy. 286 (42087). (502) 335-3696. FAX: (502) 335-3698. Licensee: Purchase Sound Inc. (acq 10-86; $65,000; FTR 6-30-86). Net: SMN. Format: Classical rock. News staff one; news progmg 10 hrs wkly. Target aud: 24-54. ■ Brian Jennings, pres & progmg dir; Tim Taylor, opns mgr; Christy Peters, gen sls mgr; Randy Reeves, news dir; Allen Fowler, chief engr.

Williamsburg

WEKC(AM)—Sept 21, 1981: 710 khz; 4.2 kw-D. TL: N36 46 28 W84 10 05. Box 1298 (40769). (606) 549-3000. FAX: (606) 549-5463. Licensee: Williamsburg Broadcasting Co. Inc. Net: CBS. Format: Country. ■ F. Lamont McAnally, pres, gen mgr & chief engr; Shelby Prewitt, opns mgr; Jim Castro, gen sls mgr; Monty McAnally, progmg dir.

WEZJ(AM)—March 7, 1959: 1440 khz; 2.5 kw-D, 500 w-N, DA-1. TL: N36 43 48 W84 09 04. 522 Main St. (40769). (606) 549-2285. FAX: (606) 549-5565. Licensee: Whitley County Broadcasting Inc. (acq 6-75). Net: ABC/I; Ky. Net. Rep: Rgnl Reps. Format: C&W. ■ Paul Estes, pres, gen mgr & gen sls mgr; Theresa Estes, prom mgr & progmg dir; David Estes, mus dir; David Paul, news dir; Dave Smith, chief engr.

WEZJ-FM—Nov, 1990: 104.3 mhz; 1.4 kw. Ant 656 ft. TL: N36 44 43 W84 11 24.

Williamstown

WNKR(FM)—April 1, 1992: 106.5 mhz; 1.41 kw. Ant 476 ft. TL: N38 40 54 W84 39 33. Stereo. Hrs opn: 24. 11 N. Main St., Dry Ridge (41035). (606) 824-9106; (800) 925-1220. FAX: (606) 824-9835. Licensee: 21st Century Media. Net: Ky. Net. Rep: Rgnl Reps. Format: Country. News staff one; news progmg 7 hrs wkly. Target aud: 25-54. Spec prog: Bluegrass 8 hrs, regional one hr wkly. ■ Joseph Schildmeyer, CEO & pres; Ron Lawson, gen mgr, progmg mgr & mus dir; Brad Mundstock, stn mgr &

pub affrs dir; Nicole Studer, sls dir; Lauren Abel, news dir; Ron Bricker, chief engr. ■ Rates: $ 27; 27; 27; 27.

Winchester

WHRS(AM)—Oct 19, 1954: 1380 khz; 2.5 kw-D, 40 w-N. TL: N38 00 46 W84 09 38. 53 S. Main St. (40391). (606) 744-2864. FAX: (606) 744-9100. Licensee: WHRS Inc. (acq 11-13-92); $60,000; FTR 11-23-92). Net: Ky. Net. Rep: Rgnl Reps. Wash atty: Pepper & Corazzini. Format: Country. News progmg 5 hrs wkly. Target aud: 25-54; adults. ■ J. Tim Smith, pres & gen mgr; John Stotts, gen sls mgr; Janel Snow, progmg dir; Jim Plummer, chief engr. ■ Rates: $7; 5; 6; 4.

WWYC(FM)—1974: 100.1 mhz; 32 kw. Ant 490 ft. TL: N38 01 47 W84 16 46. Stereo. Box 11670, Lexington (40577); 3549 Russell Cave Rd., Lexington (40511). (606) 293-0563. FAX: (606) 299-3898. Licensee: Trumper Communications of Kentucky L.P. (acq 12-14-92); $1.513 million; FTR 1-11-93). Format: Country. ■ Daniel C. Dorsett, vp & gen mgr; Karen Wesley, gen sls mgr; Kevin Ray, progmg dir.

Louisiana

LAUREN A. COLBY
301-663-1086
COMMUNICATIONS ATTORNEY
Special Attention to Difficult Cases

Abbeville

KROF(AM)—July 9, 1948: 960 khz; 1 kw-D, 95 w-N. TL: N30 00 40 W92 07 21. Box 610, Hwy. 167 N. (70511-0610). (318) 893-2531. FAX: (318) 893-2569. Licensee: Abbeville Broadcast Service Inc. Format: Oldies. Spec prog: French-Cajun 10 hrs wkly. ■ Garland Bernard, gen mgr; Anthony Keith, progmg dir; Dave Milner, news dir. ■ Rates: $15; 15; 15; 15.

KROF-FM—June 1, 1974: 105.1 mhz; 25 kw. Ant 300 ft. TL: N30 00 40 W92 07 21 (CP: Ant 292 ft.). Stereo. Hrs opn: 24. Dups AM 100%.

Alexandria

KALB(AM)—Sept 21, 1935: 580 khz; 5 kw-D, 1 kw-N, DA-N. TL: N31 18 25 W92 25 00. Box 471 (71301). (318) 443-2543; (318) 443-2592. FAX: (318) 443-7306. Licensee: Alexandria Broadcasting Co. (acq 1946). Net: SMN. Rep: Katz. Format: Oldies. Spec prog: Sports 15 hrs wkly. ■ Robert May, gen mgr.

KZMZ(FM)—Co-owned with KALB(AM). 1947: 96.9 mhz; 95 kw. Ant 1,450 ft. TL: N31 02 15 W92 29 45. Stereo. Prog sep from AM. 400 Washington Ave. (71301). Wash atty: Wiley, Rein & Fielding. Format: Adult hit radio. ■ Joseph Villamarette, chief engr.

KFAD(FM)—Not on air, target date unknown: 93.9 mhz; 6 kw. Ant 328 ft. TL: N31 16 04 W92 26 24. Box 8798, Alexandria (71306). (318) 473-0098. Licensee: FM Broadcasting Corp. ■ Pat Strother, gen mgr.

*KLSA(FM)—1987: 90.7 mhz; 100 kw. Ant 1,243 ft. TL: N31 33 56 W92 32 50. 8100 Hwy. 71 S. (71302). (318) 473-6454. FAX: (318) 797-5154. Licensee: Board of Supervisors, Louisiana State Univ. and Agricultural Mechanical College. Format: Class, news & jazz. ■ Catherine Fraser, gen mgr; Jean Hardman, mktg mgr; Mary Masters, progmg dir; Greg Carter, news dir; Rod Matthews, chief engr.

KQID(FM)—Listing follows KSYL(AM).

KRRV(AM)—December 1953: 1410 khz; 1 kw-D, 49.5 w-N, ND-1. TL: N31 16 58 W92 26 25. Hrs opn: 24. Box 591, (71309); 1515 Jackson St. (71301). (318) 443-7454; (318) 442-1410. FAX: (318) 442-2747. Licensee: KDBS Inc. (acq 1954; $10,000). Net: ABC/E. Rep: Banner. Format: Modern country. News staff 2; news progmg 4 hrs wkly. Target aud: 25-54. ■ Dr. Judy Karst, pres & gen mgr; Wayne Bettoney, gen sls mgr; Dwight Moore, progmg dir; Michael Bailey, mus dir; Wendy Williams, news dir; Charles Flowers, chief engr.

KRRV-FM—May 11, 1969: 100.3 mhz; 100 kw. Ant 1,055 ft. TL: N31 01 59 W92 30 08. Stereo. Hrs opn: 24. Dups AM 100%.

KSYL(AM)—April 1, 1947: 970 khz; 1 kw-U, DA-N. TL: N31 19 33 W92 29 17. Stereo. Box 7057 (71306). (318) 445-1234. FAX: (318) 445-7231. Licensee: Cenla Broadcasting Inc. (acq 8-1-80). Rep: Torbet. Format: Adult contemp. ■ Taylor C. Thompson, pres & gen mgr; Charles J. Soprano, vp; Randy Reynolds, gen sls mgr; Pat Cloud, mus dir; Lenny Dupree, chief engr.

KQID(FM)—Co-owned with KSYL(AM). Sept 17, 1978: 93.1 mhz; 100 kw. Ant 1,700 ft. TL: N31 38 20 W92 12 18. Stereo. 1115 Texas Ave. (71301). Net: ABC/C. Format: Top-40.

*KYFE(FM)—Not on air, target date unknown: 91.7 mhz; 1 kw. Ant 249 ft. TL: N31 16 04 W92 26 04. Box 1818, 1300 N. Battlefield Blvd., Chesapeake, VA (23320). Licensee: Bible Broadcasting Network (group owner).

KZMZ(FM)—Listing follows KALB(AM).

Amite

WABL(AM)—January 1956: 1570 khz; 500 w-D. TL: N30 42 31 W90 31 31. Box 787 (70422). (504) 748-8385. FAX: (504) 748-3918. Licensee: Amite Broadcasting Co. (acq 9-85). Format: News/talk, C&W. News progmg 40 hrs wkly. Target aud: 20-55. ■ Charles Hart, gen mgr; Greg Dreher, gen sls mgr; Fran Durio, progmg dir; Terry Mixon, chief engr.

Angola

*KLSP(FM)—Aug 12, 1986: 91.7 mhz; 100 w. Ant 90 ft. TL: N30 57 17 W91 35 45. Louisiana State Penitentiary (70712). (504) 655-4411. Licensee: Angola Educational Foundation Inc. Format: Div. News progmg 3 hrs wkly. Target aud: General; predominately all-male inmate & mixed. Spec prog: Black 10 hrs, C&W 6 hrs, jazz 7 hrs, poets corner one hr, legal wave 3 hrs wkly. ■ John P. Whitley, gen mgr; R. Dwayne McFatter, stn mgr; Prentice Robinson, progmg dir.

Ball

KWDF(AM)—1986: 840 khz; 10 kw-D. TL: N31 22 41 W92 28 27. 3735 Rigolette Rd., Pineville (71360). (318) 640-4373; (318) 640-9001. FAX: (318) 640-1321. Licensee: William D. Franks & A.T. Moore dba Ball Broadcasting Co. Net: USA. Format: Southern gospel, relg. ■ Tommy Moore, gen mgr & chief engr; Rich Dupree, gen sls mgr, progmg dir & prom mgr; Sharon Thorne, mus dir & news dir.

Basile

KBAZ(FM)—May 4, 1990: 102.1 mhz; 3 kw. Ant 328 ft. TL: N30 28 52 W92 35 50. Hrs opn: 24. 109 S. Second St., Eunice (70535). (318) 457-3543. FAX: (318) 457-2917. Licensee: Nezpique Communications Inc. Net: SMN. Format: Country. News progmg 2.5 hrs wkly. Target aud: General; middle-income age 25-55. Spec prog: Fr 5 hrs, relg one hr wkly. ■ Robert Fontenot, gen mgr & gen sls mgr; Jocelyn Bradley, progmg dir, mus dir & news dir; Tony Evans, chief engr.

Bastrop

KRVV(FM)—1977: 100.1 mhz; 50 kw. Ant 490 ft. TL: N32 40 20 W91 55 06. Stereo. Hrs opn: 24. Box 4808, 1109 Hudson Lane, Monroe (71211). (318) 322-1914. FAX: (318) 388-0569. Licensee: Holladay Broadcasting of Louisiana Inc. (acq 10-15-91; $1,035,891; FTR 11-4-91). Rep: McGavern Guild. Wash atty: Kaye, Scholer, Fierman, Hays & Handler. Format: Urban. Target aud: General; 18-54. ■ Clay Holladay, pres; Larry Green, gen sls mgr; Victor Mathis, progmg dir; Roger Bennet, chief engr. ■ Rates: $18; 18; 18; 12.

KTRY(AM)—February 1948: 730 khz; 250 w-D. TL: N32 49 10 W91 54 29. Box 1075 (71220). (318) 281-1850. Licensee: North Delta Broadcasting Inc. (acq 11-14-77). Net: Natl Black. Format: Black. ■ Henry Cotton, pres, gen mgr & progmg dir; Lewis McDuff, mus dir; Raife Smith, chief engr.

KTRY-FM—Mar 1, 1974: 94.3 mhz; 3 kw-H. Ant 289 ft. TL: N32 49 10 W91 54 29. Stereo. (318) 281-1850. Rep: Lazar. Spec prog: Jazz 8 hrs wkly. ■ Mike Cain, mus dir.

NEW FM—Not on air, target date unknown: 103.3 mhz; 3 kw. Ant 100 ft. 3712 Cornell Dr., Shreveport (71107). Licensee: Max BCG Co.

Baton Rouge

KBRH(AM)—Listing follows WBRH(FM).

*KLSU(FM)—October 1981: 91.1 mhz; 5 kw. Ant 159 ft. TL: N30 24 37 W91 10 37. Stereo. Hrs opn: 6 AM-2 AM. LSU B-46 Hodges Hall (70803). (504) 388-1698. Licensee: Louisiana State Univ. Rep: Rgnl Reps. Format: Jazz, div, progsv. News progmg 3 hrs wkly. Target aud: 18-25; university students & college age listeners. Spec prog: Class 3 hrs, blues 3 hrs, international 3 hrs, reggae 3 hrs wkly. ■ Ken Nagelberg, gen mgr; Katty Biscone, stn mgr; Monique Wheeler, opns dir; Sharon Schoenfeld, adv dir; Darren Gauthier, progmg dir; Kathleen Gregory, mus dir; Darin Mann, news dir; Keith Stokes, chief engr.

*WBRH(FM)—September 1977: 90.3 mhz; 7 kw. Ant 154 ft. TL: N30 26 45 W91 09 31. Stereo. 2825 Government St. (70806). (504) 383-3243. FAX: (504) 343-9226. Licensee: East Baton Rouge Parish School Board. Format: Jazz. News progmg 3 hrs wkly. Target aud: 25-54; men. ■ Danny Dean, gen mgr & progmg dir; Martin Johnson, gen sls mgr; Keith Stokes, chief engr.

KBRH(AM)—Co-owned with WBRH(FM). 1953: 1260 khz; 1 kw-D, 127 w-N. TL: N30 27 40 W91 14 39. Hrs opn: 24. (Acq 7-7-93; FTR 8-2-93). Format: News/Talk.

WCKW-FM—See La Place.

WFMF(FM)—Listing follows WJBO(AM).

WGGZ(FM)—Oct 1, 1968: 98.1 mhz; 100 kw. Ant 1,550 ft. TL: N30 21 58 W91 12 47. Stereo. Hrs opn: 24. Box 2231 (70821); 929-B Government (70802). (504) 388-9898. Licensee: Guaranty Broadcasting Corp. Net: Unistar. Rep: Katz. Wash atty: Wiley, Rein & Fielding. Format: Oldies. News staff one; news progmg 7 hrs wkly. Target aud: 25-54. ■ George A. Foster Jr., chmn & pres; Michael Adams, vp & gen mgr; Mike Norwood, gen sls mgr; J. J. Stone, prom mgr & progmg dir; Jack Flash, mus dir; Kevin Meeks, news dir; Arthur Hoover, chief engr. ■ Rates: $80; 60; 80; 50.

WIBR(AM)—July 18, 1948: 1300 khz; 5 kw-D, 1 kw-N, DA-2. TL: N30 28 25 W91 13 34. 9737 N. Winston Ave. (70809-2531). (504) 292-9556. FAX: (504) 344-2666. Licensee: Southern Communications Inc. (acq 2-7-86; $450,000; FTR 12-9-85). Net: La. Net. Rep: Christal. Format: Sports. News progmg 3 hrs wkly. Target aud: 25-54. ■ Lew Campbell, pres & gen mgr; Don Nelson, gen sls mgr; Gary Hail, prom mgr; Joe Redmond, progmg dir & mus dir; Margaret Taylor, news dir; Dane Robinson, chief engr. ■ Rates: $25; 20; 25; 10.

WJBO(AM)—Dec 11, 1934: 1150 khz; 5 kw-U, DA-1. TL: N30 27 47 W91 16 10. Box 496 (70821); Suite One, 3955 Government St. (70806). (504) 383-5271. FAX: (504) 343-4785. Licensee: George Jenne. Group owners: Baton Rouge Broadcasting Co., Transcontinental Broadcasting Co. and WLIN Inc. (acq 10-1-89; $9,091,194 with co-located FM; FTR 7-24-89). Net: ABC/R, ABC TalkRadio, AP, CBS Spectrum, NBC Talknet, Unistar, Westwood One. Rep: D & R Radio. Format: Talk, news & sports. News staff 4; news progmg 14 hrs wkly. Target aud: 20 plus. ■ George Jenne, pres & gen mgr; Eddie Martiny, gen sls mgr; Mark Summers, progmg dir; Sylvia Weatherspoon, news dir; Keith Stokes, chief engr.

WFMF(FM)—Co-owned with WJBO(AM). 1941: 102.5 mhz; 85 kw. Ant 1,260 ft. TL: N30 17 49 W91 11 40. Stereo. Prog sep from AM. Format: CHR. News staff 4; news progmg 5 hrs wkly. Target aud: 12 plus. ■ Johnny Ahysen, progmg dir & mus dir.

WKJN-FM—See Hammond.

WLUX(AM)—(Port Allen). 1963: 1550 khz; 5 kw-D. TL: N30 30 07 W91 12 39. Box 262550, Baton Rouge (70826); 8919 World Ministry Ave., Baton Rouge (70810). (504) 768-3867. FAX: (504) 768-3729. Licensee: Jimmy Swaggart Ministries (acq 1973). Net: USA. Wash atty: Latham & Watkins. Format: Relg. Target aud: 35-59; middle-class female. ■ Jimmy Swaggart, pres; Sean Daigre, gen mgr & progmg dir; Mike Patton, chief engr. ■ Rates: $11.80; 9.60; 11.80; na.

WNDC(AM)—Nov 1, 1946: 910 khz; 1 kw-U, DA-1. TL: N30 34 48 W91 07 50. 3000 Tecumseh St. (70805). (504)

Stations in the U.S.   Louisiana

357-4571. FAX: (504) 356-7784. Licensee: Church Point Ministries Inc. (acq 3-1-89). Format: Black gospel. Target aud: 18-59. ■ Dwight Pate, pres; Shirley Jones, gen mgr.

*WRKF(FM)—Jan 18, 1980: 89.3 mhz; 28 kw. Ant 935 ft. TL: N30 22 22 W91 12 16. Stereo. Hrs opn: 24. 3050 Valley Creek (70808). (504) 926-3050. Licensee: Public Radio Inc. Net: NPR, APR. Format: Class. News staff one; news progmg 35 hrs wkly. Target aud: General. ■ Eric DeWeese, pres & gen mgr; Susan Hidalo-Smith, vp dev; Constance Nauratil, mus dir; Debra Holden, news dir; Lew Carter, pub affrs dir; Paul Burt, chief engr.

WTGE-FM—Sept 10, 1966: 100.7 mhz; 97 kw. Ant 1,499 ft. TL: N30 19 35 W91 16 36. Stereo. Hrs opn: 24. 5220 Essen Lane (70809). (504) 766-3233. FAX: (504) 766-4112. Licensee: Vetter Communications Co. Inc. (acq 7-1-89; $5,000,000; FTR 1-20-89). Rep: Eastman. Wash atty: Dow, Lohnes & Albertson. Format: Rock. News staff one; news progmg 3 hrs wkly. Target aud: 18-49. ■ Cyril Vetter, pres; Jim Thompson, gen mgr; Larry Dietz, stn mgr; Brad Leggett, gen sls mgr; Andy Holt, progmg dir; Kathy Jones, mus dir; Larry Davis, news dir; Dane Robinson, chief engr. WVLA-TV affil. ■ Rates: $60; 60; 60; 30.

WXOK(AM)—February 1953: 1460 khz; 5 kw-D, 1 kw-N, DA-3. TL: N30 28 08 W91 12 24. 7707 Waco Dr. (70806). (504) 926-1106. FAX: (504) 928-1606. Licensee: Citywide Broadcasting Corp. (acq 9-20-90; $1,000,000; FTR 10-8-90). Net: ABC/C. Rep: Torbet. Format: Black, news. News staff 2; news progmg 30 hrs wkly. Target aud: 18 plus. ■ Peter Moncrieffe, pres & gen mgr; Kay Taylor, gen sls mgr; Chris Clay, progmg dir & mus dir; Mike Patton, chief engr.

WYNK(AM)—1956: 1380 khz; 5 kw-D, DA. TL: N30 27 39 W91 13 23. Box 14061 (70898-4061). (504) 231-1860. FAX: (504) 231-1879. Licensee: Narrangasett Radio L.P. Group owner: Narrangasett Radio Inc. (acq 11-12-86; grpsl; FTR 11-24-86). Net: ABC. Rep: Torbet. Wash atty: Reed, Smith, McClay, Pierson, Ball & Dowd. Format: Modern country. Target aud: 25-54. Spec prog: Fr 2 hrs wkly. ■ Manual Broussard, pres; John L. Peroyea, gen mgr; Donna Andre, gen sls mgr; Stephanie Williamson, prom mgr; Brian King, progmg dir & mus dir; Viki Varstel, news dir; Richard Petty, chief engr. ■ Rates: $130; 120; 115; 35.

WYNK-FM—Dec 7, 1968: 101.5 mhz; 100 kw. Ant 1,500 ft. TL: N30 19 35 W91 16 36 (CP: Ant 1,283 ft.). Stereo. Hrs opn: 24. Dups AM 100%. 5th Floor, 5555 Hilton Ave. (70808). Net: ABC/E. News staff one. Target aud: 18-54. Spec prog: Cajun French 3 hrs wkly. ■ Stephanie Williamson, mktg dir; Amy Johns, pub affrs dir. ■ Rates: Same as AM.

Bayou Vista

KDLP(AM)—February 1977: 1170 khz; 500 w-D. TL: N29 27 28 W91 17 41. 128 Pluto St. (70381). (504) 395-2853. Licensee: Teche Broadcasting Corp. Net: Unistar; La. Net. Format: C&W. ■ Paul J. Cook, pres & gen mgr; Ernest Dean Polk, opns mgr, news dir & chief engr; Jimmy McDowell, gen sls mgr; Bobby Richard, progmg dir & mus dir.

KQKI(FM)—Co-owned with KDLP(AM). Dec 31, 1976: 95.3 mhz; 3 kw. Ant 299 ft. TL: N29 29 38 W91 17 41 (CP: 25 kw). Dups AM 100%.

Belle Chasse

KMEZ(FM)—March 1990: 102.9 mhz; 5.2 kw. Ant 604 ft. TL: N29 57 14 W89 56 58. Suite 440, 1450 Poydras New Orleans (70112). (504) 593-2171. FAX: (504) 367-8024. Licensee: Coastal Broadcasting Inc. (acq 8-20; FTR 9-10-90). Format: New adult contemp. ■ Tac Carrere, pres; Nick Ferrera, progmg dir.

Benton

KLKL(FM)—1981: 92.1 mhz; 3 kw. Ant 299 ft. TL: N32 39 19 W93 41 38. Stereo. Hrs opn: 24. 1000 Grimmet, Shreveport (71107). (318) 221-5357; (318) 221-9696. FAX: (318) 332-0758. Licensee: Progressive United Corporation (acq 1993; $325,000; FTR 9-6-93). Net: ABC, Unistar. Rep: Katz & Powell. Format: Oldies. Target aud: 35 plus; upper income, upwardly mobile. ■ William R. Fry, pres & stn mgr; John Hill, opns mgr & vp prom; Don Zimmerman, gen sls mgr; Howard Clark, progmg dir; Rick Benson, vp engrg.

Berwick

KBZE(FM)—July 4, 1990: 105.9 mhz; 1.8 kw. Ant 403 ft. TL: N29 45 27 W91 10 25. Stereo. Hrs opn: 24. Drawer N, Morgan City (70381); Offshore Oil Center, 6502 Hwy. 90 East, Morgan City (70380). (504) 385-6266. FAX:

(504) 385-6268. Licensee: HubCast Broadcasting Inc. (acq 3-5-93; $105,500; FTR 8-9-93). Format: Urban adult contemp. News staff one; news progmg 4 hrs wkly. Target aud: 24-54; middle to upper income. Spec prog: Gospel 10 hrs wkly. ■ Howard Castay Jr., pres & gen mgr; Walter Stevens, exec vp; Darlene Arceneaux, gen sls mgr; Ray Robicheaux, progmg dir & mus dir; Sonja Jones, news dir & pub affrs dir. ■ Rates: $7.75; 7.75; 6.75; 4.25.

Bogalusa

WBOX(AM)—March 1, 1954: 920 khz; 1 kw, DA-N. TL: N30 50 29 W89 50 06. Box 280 (70427). (504) 732-4288; (504) 839-2990. FAX: (601) 736-2617. Licensee: Bogue Chitto Communications Co. (group owner). Format: Contemp country. ■ Thomas McDaniel, pres; Ben R. Strickland, gen mgr; Chris Blackburn, opns mgr.

WBOX-FM—See Varnado.

WIKC(AM)—May 15, 1947: 1490 khz; 1 kw-U. TL: N30 47 30 W89 52 47. Box 638, 607 Rio Grande St. (70427). (504) 732-4190. FAX: (504) 735-8186, ext. 2. Licensee: Timberlands Broadcasting Corp. (acq 6-29-82). Net: USA. Format: Variety. News progmg 12 hrs wkly. Target aud: General. ■ G.S. Adams Jr.. pres, gen mgr & gen sls mgr.

Bossier

KRMD(AM)—See Shreveport.

KRMD-FM—See Shreveport.

Boyce

KBCE(FM)—Mar 29, 1982: 102.3 mhz; 6 kw. Ant 289 ft. TL: N31 22 21 W92 38 09. Box 69 (71409); Suite 6, 2826 Lee St., Alexandria (71301). (318) 793-4003; (318) 445-1360. FAX: (318) 793-8888. Licensee: Trinity Broadcasting Corp. Net: American Urban. Rep: D & R Radio. Format: Urban contemp. News progmg one hr wkly. Target aud: General. Spec prog: Gospel 19 hrs, jazz 3 hrs, blues one hr, talk one hr wkly. ■ Gus E. Lewis, pres & gen mgr; Gus Lewis, gen sls mgr; Donnie Taylor, progmg dir; Woody Fryar, chief engr. ■ Rates: $20; 18; 20; 15.

Breaux Bridge

KFTE(FM)—Nov. 15, 1992. 96.5 mhz; 22.5 kw. Ant 328 ft. TL: N30 06 09 W91 59 30. Stereo. Hrs opn: 24. 202 A Galbert Rd., Lafayette (70506). (318) 232-2242. FAX: (318) 235-4181. Licensee: Mid-Acadiana Broadcasting Corp. (acq 9-17-93; $517,750; FTR 10-18-93). Wash atty: Arent, Fox, Kintner, Plotkin & Kahn. Format: Easy lstng. ■ Ernie Alexander, pres; Charles Sonnier, exec vp.

Brusly

KRVE(FM)—Sept 9, 1989: 96.1 mhz; 43 kw. Ant 449 ft. TL: N30 29 34 W91 00 15. Stereo. Box 68, 601 Hatchell Ln., Denham Springs (70727). (504) 665-5154. FAX: (504) 499-9696. Licensee: MCFORHUN Inc. Format: Adult contemp. Target aud: 25-54. ■ Rip Miller, gen mgr & gen sls mgr; Bob Murphy, progmg dir.

Bunkie

KRBG(FM)—Not on air, target date unknown: 104.3 mhz; 18 kw. Ant 384 ft. TL: N31 05 14 W92 21 34. Drawer B, Flat River, MO (63601). Licensee: Carolina Communications (acq 8-31-92; $2,000; FTR 9-21-92).

Clinton

WQCK(FM)—Sept 23, 1981: 92.7 mhz; 32 kw. Ant 604 ft. TL: N30 51 03 W91 04 31. Stereo. Hrs opn: 24. Box 7934 (70722); 5280 Groom Rd., Baker (70714). (504) 777-7780. FAX: (504) 774-7785. Licensee: Hoffman Media of Louisiana Inc. Group Owner: Hoffman Communications/Hoffman Media Inc. (acq 11-4-86; $300,000; FTR 9-29-86). Net: CBN. Format: Contemp Christian. Target aud: 25-49. ■ Hubert Hoffman, pres; Michael Allen, gen mgr; Dave Cruse, opns mgr, progmg dir & mus dir; Sheryl Hamilton, gen sls mgr; Harvey LeBlanc, chief engr. ■ Rates: $25; 20; 25; 20.

Columbia

KCTO(AM)—November 1968: 1540 khz; 1 kw-D. TL: N32 05 35 W92 05 22. Box 1319, The Radio Group Bldg., #1 Radio Rd. (71418). (318) 649-2756; (318) 649-7959. Licensee: KCTO Broadcasting Co. Group owner: The Radio Group (acq 1-26-77). Net: Unistar. Format: Gospel. Target aud: 25-54. Spec prog: Farm 3 hrs wkly. ■ Tom D. Gay, pres & gen mgr; William Mann, opns mgr &

progmg dir; Pat Hurley, chief engr. ■ Rates: $4.50; 4.50; 4.50; na.

KCTO-FM—Jan 21, 1980: 103.1 mhz; 25 kw. Ant 348 ft. TL: N32 09 25 W92 10 58 Stereo. Hrs opn: 24. Prog sep from AM. Format: Oldies. News progmg 7 hrs wkly. Target aud: 25-54. ■ Rates: $6.50; 6.50; 6.50; 4.50.

Coushatta

KRRP(AM)—May 1981: 950 khz; 500 w-D, 209 w-N, DA-2. TL: N31 56 49 W93 20 13. Hrs opn: 6 AM-6 PM. Rt. 4, Box 197, Jordan Ferry Rd. (71019). (800) 259-9490. Licensee: James G. Bethard. Net: USA; La. Net. Format: Gospel. News staff one; news progmg 11 hrs wkly. Target aud: General. ■ John Brewer, gen mgr; Tammie Blanchard, prom mgr, progmg dir & pub affrs dir; George Moore, news dir; A.T. Moore, chief engr. ■ Rates: $3; 3; 3; na.

KSBH(FM)—Co-owned with KRRP(AM). Nov 15, 1992: 94.9 mhz; 25 kw. Ant 328 ft. TL: N31 51 34 W93 13 00. Stereo. Hrs opn: 24. Net: Jones Satellite Audio; La. Net. Format: Country. Target aud: 18-54. ■ Rates: $8; 8; 8; 3.

Covington

WASO(AM)—November 1953: 730 khz; 250 w-D, 25 w-N. TL: N30 29 37 W90 08 37. Box 568 (70434). (504) 892-1600. FAX: (504) 892-1697. Licensee: America First Communications Inc. (acq 7-7-92; $200,000; FTR 7-27-92). Net: NBC, NBC Talknet, MBS, CNN. Format: News, talk & sports. News staff 4. Target aud: 25 plus. ■ Herman Lombas, pres; Robert Namer, gen mgr & gen sls mgr; Curtis Sharp, opns mgr & progmg dir; Layton Martens, news dir; Matthew Quave, pub affrs dir; Ernie Harvey, chief engr. ■ Rates: $36; 36; 36; na.

Crowley

KAJN-FM—Oct 1, 1977: 102.9 mhz; 95 kw. Ant 1,499 ft. TL: N30 02 19 W92 22 15. Stereo. Hrs opn: 24. Box 1469, 110 W. 3rd St. (70527-1469). (318) 783-1560. FAX: (318) 783-1674. Licensee: Rice Capital Broadcasting. Net: CNN, USA. Wash atty: Fletcher, Heald & Hildreth. Format: Relg. News staff one; news progmg 3 hrs wkly. Target aud: 25-44. Spec prog: Black 2 hrs wkly. ■ Barry D. Thompson, CEO, chmn, pres, gen mgr & progmg dir; Annette G. Thompson, CFO, exec vp & vp; Chip Bailey, gen sls mgr; Craig Thompson, mus dir; Joe Gall, news dir; Brandon Johnson, pub affrs dir; Tony Evans, chief engr. ■ Rates: $32; 27; 32; 27.

KPWS(AM)—Co-owned with KAJN-FM. 1972: 1560 khz; 1 kw-D, DA. TL: N30 11 36 W92 23 29. Prog sep from FM. Format: Country gospel. Target aud: 25-64. Spec prog: Fr 2 hrs, farm 4 hrs, Black 3 hrs wkly.

KSIG(AM)—May 1947: 1450 khz; 1 kw-U. TL: N30 13 50 W92 21 45. Box 228 (70527); 320 N. Parkerson Ave. (70526). (318) 783-2520. FAX: (318) 783-2521. Licensee: Acadia Broadcast Partners Inc. (acq 12-7-92; $350,000; FTR 1-4-93). Net: ABC/C. Rep: MidSouth. Format: Country, Louisiana music. Spec prog: Fr 18 hrs, farm 5 hrs wkly. ■ Phil Lizotte, pres & stn mgr; Charles Ellis, chief engr.

De Ridder

KDLA(AM)—Nov 11, 1950: 1010 khz; 1 kw-D, 40 w-N. TL: N30 52 43 W93 17 25. Hrs opn: Sunrise-sunset. Box 1088, One Hooks Rd. (70634). (318) 462-1017; (800) 858-4424. FAX: (318) 463-6728. Licensee: Carol E. Simmons. Net: Jones Satellite Audio; La. Net. Format: Adult contemp. 18-54. ■ Carol E. Simmons, pres, stn mgr & progmg dir; Steve Donalson, engrg dir & chief engr. ■ Rates: $11.50; 10; 10; 10.

KEAZ(FM)—Co-owned with KDLA(AM). Sept 6, 1991: 101.7 mhz; 3 kw. Ant 299 ft. TL: N30 52 43 W93 17 25. Stereo. Hrs opn: 24. Net: SMN. Format: Pure Gold. ■ Rates: $11.50; 11.50; 11.50; 10.

KROK(FM)—Nov 1, 1985: 92.1 mhz; 3 kw. Ant 470 ft. TL: N30 53 41 W93 16 02. Stereo. Hrs opn: 24. Box 1180, Rt. 4, Yankee Ridge Rd. (70634). (318) 463-9298; (318) 463-9292. FAX: (318) 463-9291. Licensee: West Central Broadcasting Co. Inc. Wash atty: James Popham. Format: AOR. Target aud: 18-54. Spec prog: Blues. ■ Doug Stannard, pres, gen mgr & progmg dir; Dennis McClintock, opns mgr; Lou Orleans, mus dir. ■ Rates: $17.65; 17.65; 17.65; 17.65

Delhi

KKRP(FM)—September 1991: 93.5 mhz; 3 kw. Ant 328 ft. TL: N32 37 45 W91 33 13. Rt. 3, Box 55M (71232). (318) 878-9469. Licensee: KT Enterprises Inc. (acq 8-19-92; $125,000; FTR 9-14-92). Format: News/talk.

Broadcasting & Cable Yearbook 1994
B-157

Louisiana | Directory of Radio

News staff one; news progmg 12 hrs wkly. Target aud: General. ■ Kerney Thomas, pres; Darrell Jones, opns mgr.

Denham Springs

WBIU(AM)—April 15, 1959: 1210 khz; 10 kw-D, 1 kw-N, DA-N. TL: N30 31 20 W90 58 15. Stereo. Hrs opn: 18. 601 Hatchell (70726). (504) 665-5154. FAX: (504) 499-9696. Licensee: Livingston Communications Inc. (acq 2-10-84; $235,000; FTR 2-6-84). Net: USA. Format: Christian talk/Christian country, Southern Gospel mus. News staff one. Target aud: 25-54. ■ Nancy David, pres; Rip Miller, gen mgr & gen sls mgr; Danny Church, progmg dir; Sam North, news dir; Richard Petty, chief engr. ■ Rates: $20; 18; 18; 12.

Donaldsonville

KKAY-FM—1972: 104.9 mhz; 3 kw. Ant 299 ft. TL: N30 05 57 W91 00 13. Hrs opn: 6 AM-10 PM. Rebroadcasts KKAY(AM) White Castle. 3365 Hwy. One S. (70346). (504) 473-5764. FAX: (504) 473-6397. Licensee: La Fourche Valley Enterprises. Format: Country. Target aud: General. ■ Michael P. Leblanc, pres & chief engr; Rick Rousseau, stn mgr & news dir. ■ Rates: $13; 13; 13; 13.

Dry Prong

*****KVDP(FM)**—Aug 13, 1985: 89.1 mhz; 3 kw. Ant 207 ft. TL: N31 35 20 W92 30 59 (CP: Ant 295 ft.). Stereo. Box 214 (71423). (318) 899-5837. FAX: (318) 899-7624. Licensee: Dry Prong Educational Broadcasting Foundation Inc. (acq 11-24-92; FTR 12-21-92). Net: USA. Format: Relg, educ. ■ Coy Edwards, pres; Leta Edwards, gen mgr; Donna Cline, mus dir; Lonnie Hutto, chief engr.

Dubach

KPCH(FM)—June 4, 1984: 97.7 mhz; 3 kw. Ant 299 ft. TL: N32 39 11 W92 40 38. Stereo. Box 977, 2608 N. Trenton, Ruston (71270); (318) 251-3697; (318) 251-0699. FAX: (318) 251-9230. Licensee: William W. Brown (acq 12-86; $355,000). Net: Unistar; La. Net. Format: Oldies, sports. News staff one; news progmg 8 hrs wkly. Target aud: 25-54; upper income, educ level. Spec prog: Gospel 5 hrs, Down Memory Lane 7 hrs wkly. ■ William W. Brown, vp, gen mgr, stn mgr & gen sls mgr; Cary Brown, prom mgr; William W. Brown Jr., progmg dir & mus dir; Tommy Moore, chief engr. ■ Rates: $21.76; 21.76; 21.76; 21.76.

Erath

KPEL-FM—April 1992: 107.7 mhz; 25 kw. Ant 328 ft. TL: N30 02 54 W91 59 49 (CP: 10 kw, ant 469 ft.). Stereo. Hrs opn: 24. Box 52046, 1749 Bertrand Dr., Lafayette (70506). (318) 233-7003. FAX: (318) 234-7360. Licensee: KPEL-FM Inc. (acq 11-1-93). Net: CBS, MBS, NBC Talknet; La. Net. Rep: Christal. Format: News/talk. News staff 2; news progmg 25 hrs wkly. Target aud: 35-54; male. ■ Mike Mitchell, gen mgr; Bill Branton, news dir; Marty Melancon, pub affrs dir; Tony L. Evans, chief engr.

Erwinville

*****KPAE(FM)**—Sept 30, 1985: 91.5 mhz; 5 kw. Ant 167 ft. TL: N30 32 09 W91 24 52. Stereo. 13028 U.S. Hwy. 190 W., Port Allen (70767). (504) 627-4578. Licensee: Port Allen Educational Broadcasting Foundation. Net: Moody. Format: Relg, educ. Target aud: General. ■ Willie F. Kennedy, pres; Lonnie Hutto, chief engr.

Eunice

KEUN(AM)—October 1952: 1490 khz; 1 kw-U. TL: N30 28 17 W92 24 51. 330 W. Laurel (70535). (318) 457-3041. FAX: (318) 457-3081. Licensee: Tri-Parish Broadcasting Co. Inc. (acq 9-19-80). Format: C&W, Sports/News, French/Cajun. News staff one; news progmg 5 hrs wkly. Target aud: 25 plus. Spec prog: Zydico 6 hrs wkly. ■ Karl Rene De Rouen, pres & gen mgr; Steve Gauthier, opns mgr, progmg dir, mus dir & news dir; Linda Bellow, gen sls mgr; Karl Rene DeRauen, prom mgr; Paul Seibert, chief engr. ■ Rates: $12; 7.50; 11; 6.

KJJB(FM)—Co-owned with KEUN(AM). Oct 22, 1981: 105.5 mhz; 3 kw. Ant 300 ft. TL: N30 26 16 W92 26 04. Stereo. Hrs opn: 24. (acq 10-7-93; $220,750; FTR 10-25-93). Net: SMN; La. Net. Format: Pure gold. News staff one; news progmg 10 hrs wkly. Target aud: 25-54. Spec prog: Fr 5 hrs wkly. ■ Tony Evans, chief engr.

Farmerville

KWJM(FM)—Apr 19, 1979: 92.7 mhz; 6 kw. Ant 328 ft. TL: N32 48 21 W92 22 24. Stereo. Hrs opn: 24. 113 N. Main St. (71241). (318) 368-3094. FAX: (318) 368-2203. Licensee: Union Broadcasting Co., Inc. Net: CBS; La. Net. Format: Adult contemp. News progmg 18 hrs wkly. Target aud: 24-65; adult audience with incomes to buy. ■ Don Barron, pres; Doyle Barron, gen mgr & stn mgr; Glynn Hayes, progmg mgr & mus dir; Larry Young, chief engr. ■ Rates: $10; 10; 10; 10.

Ferriday

KFNV(AM)—1956: 1600 khz; 1 kw-D. TL: N31 35 04 W91 32 15. Box 512, Ferriday, MS (71334); 917 S. Wallace Blvd. (71334). (318) 757-4200. Licensee: Big River Broadcasting. Group owner: The Radio Group. Net: Unistar; La. Net. Format: Relg. News staff one; news progmg 3 hrs wkly. Target aud: General. Spec prog: Black 12 hrs wkly. ■ Tom Gay, pres; Hugh Matthews, gen mgr, gen sls mgr, progmg dir, mus dir & news dir; Pat Hurley, chief engr. ■ Rates: $10; 9; 10; 9.

KFNV-FM—October 1971: 107.1 mhz; 18.5 kw. Ant 233 ft. TL: N31 36 08 W91 32 27. Stereo. Format: Adult contemp. Spec prog: Farm 2 hr wkly. ■ Rates: $6.50; 6.50; 6.50; na.

Folsom

KGZC(FM)—Not on air, target date unknown: 104.9 mhz; 3 kw. Ant 328 ft. TL: N30 38 28 W90 04 28. 71207 Shady Lake Dr., Covington (70433). (504) 893-3944. Licensee: Enon Broadcasting Inc.

Franklin

KFRA(AM)—June 4, 1961: 1390 khz; 500 w-D. TL: N29 50 14 W91 32 22. Box 1111, 103 Wilson St. (70538). (318) 828-5372. FAX: (318) 828-5373. Licensee: Franklin Broadcasting Co. Inc. (acq 1-1-85; $475,000 with co-located FM; FTR 1-21-85). Format: Adult contemp. News staff one; news progmg 8 hrs wkly. Target aud: 24-49. Spec prog: Relg 3 hrs wkly. ■ S.A. Lopez, pres; Roger Robinson, gen mgr & news dir; Tiffany Dennis, progmg dir & mus dir; Nolton Guillory, chief engr.

KFMV(FM)—Co-owned with KFRA(AM). May 9, 1975: 105.5 mhz; 3 kw. Ant 300 ft. TL: N29 50 14 W91 32 22. Stereo. Dups AM 100%. Net: La. Net. Wash atty: James Cook. ■ Rates: $8.20; 8.20; 8.20; 7.

Franklinton

WFCG(AM)—Dec 5, 1966: 1110 khz; 1 kw-D. TL: N30 51 34 W90 09 57. Box 604 (70438). (504) 839-4110. Licensee: GACO Broadcasting Corp. Net: AP. Format: C&W. Spec prog: Black 12 hrs wkly. ■ J.A. Gatewood, pres, gen sls mgr & chief engr; M.K. Gatewood, gen mgr & news dir; Vickie DeCarlo, mus dir.

Galliano

KLEB-FM—Licensed to Galliano. See Golden Meadow.

Garyville

WCKW(AM)—Dec 22, 1970: 1010 khz; 500 w-D, 42 w-N. TL: N30 04 35 W90 37 17. Stereo. Hrs opn: 24. Rebroadcasts WCKW-FM La Place 100%. Box 5905, Metairie (70009); 3501 N. Causeway Blvd., #700, Metairie (70002). (504) 831-8811. Licensee: 222 Corp. Rep: Banner. Format: Classic rock. Target aud: 18-54. Spec prog: Black 6 hrs, gospel 12 hrs wkly. ■ Sidney J. Levet III, pres & chief engr; Sidney J. Levet IV, stn mgr; Bryce Taylor, gen sls mgr; Steve Levet, natl sls mgr; Wayne Watkins, progmg dir.

Golden Meadow

KLEB(AM)—May 13, 1963: 1600 khz; 5 kw-D, 250 w-N. TL: N29 22 41 W90 15 50. Box 726, 315 Callais Ln. (70357). (504) 475-5141. FAX: (504) 475-6390. Licensee: Callais Broadcasting Inc. (acq 8-20-85; $852,500 with co-located FM; FTR 6-17-85). Format: C&W. Spec prog: Fr 12 hrs wkly. ■ Harold Callais, pres; Tina Callais, gen mgr; Angel Martinez, gen sls mgr; Tom Gregory, progmg dir.

KLEB-FM—(Galliano). Nov 16, 1975: 94.3 mhz; 25 kw. Ant 308 ft. TL: N29 33 01 W90 21 04. Prog sep from AM. Net: SMN. Format: Adult contemp.

Grambling

*****KGRM(FM)**—January 1974: 91.5 mhz; 50 kw. Ant 492 ft. TL: N32 30 56 W92 43 27. Stereo. Hrs opn: 6 AM-midnight. Drawer K (71245); Dunbar Hall Rm. 220, Grambling State Univ. (71245). (318) 274-3244; (318) 274-2734. FAX: (318) 274-3245. Licensee: Grambling State Univ. Format: Urban contemp. Target aud: Black community. Spec prog: Gospel 17 hrs, jazz 15 hrs wkly. ■ Dr. Harold Lundy, CEO; Calvin Miles, gen mgr; David Dickinson, opns mgr; Tommy Moore, chief engr.

Gretna

KGLA(AM)—Jan 6, 1969: 1540 khz; 1 kw-D. TL: N29 53 27 W90 05 05. Box 428, Marrero (70072). (504) 347-8491. FAX: (504) 340-3747. Licensee: Crocodile Broadcasting Corp. Inc. dba CBC Inc. (acq 2-11-92; $300,000; FTR 3-2-92). Net: UPI. Rep: Caballero. Format: Sp. ■ Ernesto Schwiekent, pres & gen mgr; Maria Dip, news dir; Ernest Harvey, chief engr.

KKNO(AM)—Sept 10, 1989: 750 khz; 250 w-D, DA. TL: N29 53 15 W90 05 03. Suite 204, 16 Westbank Expressway (70053). (504) 366-5505. FAX: (504) 363-2230. Licensee: Robert C. Blakes Sr. (acq 6-24-93; $275,000; FTR 7-12-93). Format: Christian gospel. Target aud: General. ■ Robert C. Blakes Sr., CEO; Kyle Jones, gen mgr & progmg dir; Steve O. Allen, vp opns; Patricia Buckhalton, gen sls mgr; Richard Hartwell, chief engr. ■ Rates: $15; 15; 15; na.

Hammond

*****KSLU(FM)**—Nov 11, 1974: 90.9 mhz; 3 kw. Ant 143 ft. TL: N30 30 53 W90 27 59. Stereo. Hrs opn: 24. SLU Box 783, D. Vickers Hall, Tennessee & Sycamore Sts. (70402). SLU Box 803, University Station (70402). (504) 549-2330; (504) 549-5758. FAX: (504) 549-3960. Licensee: Southeastern Louisiana Univ. Net: APR. Format: Jazz, class, news/talk. News staff one; news progmg 30 hrs wkly. Target aud: General. Spec prog: Folk, black. ■ Ron Nethercutt, gen mgr; Joyce Savoie, dev mgr; Paul Varnado, gen sls mgr & prom mgr; Craig Williams, progmg dir; John Pisicotta, mus dir; Ken Benitez, news dir; Larry Ward, chief engr.

WCKW-FM—See La Place.

WFPR(AM)—Nov 15, 1947: 1400 khz; 1 kw-U. TL: N30 30 31 W90 30 18. Hrs opn: 24. Box 1829, 200 E. Thomas (70404). (504) 542-1400. FAX: (504) 542-9377. Licensee: Radio Works Inc. (acq 9-7-93; $625,000 with co-located FM; FTR 9-27-93). Net: SMN; La. Net. Format: Modern country. ■ John A. Chauvin, pres; Steve Chauvin, gen mgr & gen sls mgr; John A. Chauvin Jr., progmg dir; John Scott, mus dir; Mary Pirosko, news dir. ■ Rates: $27; 14; 16; na.

WHMD(FM)—Co-owned with WFPR(AM). Aug 26, 1974: 107.1 mhz; 3 kw. Ant 328 ft. TL: N30 30 31 W90 30 18. Stereo. Prog sep from AM. (504) 345-1070. ■ Nanette C. Guerin, gen sls mgr. ■ Rates: Same as AM.

WKJN-FM—Apr 3, 1965: 103.3 mhz; 100 kw. Ant 1,004 ft. TL: N30 24 06 W90 50 43. Stereo. Hrs opn: 24. 9737 N. Winston Ave., Baton Rouge (70809-2531). (504) 292-9556. FAX: (504) 291-6420. Licensee: Southern Communications Corp. (group owner; acq 6-88; $6 million; FTR 6-20-88). Net: MBS; La. Net. Rep: Eastman. Format: Country. News staff one; news progmg 3 hrs wkly. Target aud: 25-54. Spec prog: Cajun 3 hrs wkly. ■ Lew Campbell, pres & natl sls mgr; Don Nelson, gen mgr & gen sls mgr; Randy Rice, stn mgr & mus dir; Darrell Picou, rgnl sls mgr; Gary Hail, prom mgr & progmg dir; Joe Redmond, asst mus dir; Margaret Taylor, news dir & pub affrs dir; Dane Robinson, chief engr.

Haughton

KDKS-FM—Not on air, target date unknown: 103.7 mhz; 6 kw. Ant 328 ft. TL: N32 31 20 W93 30 05. 949 Poleman Rd., Shreveport (71107). Licensee: Cary D. Camp. ■ A.E. Fryar Jr., pres.

Haynesville

KLVU(AM)—September 1956: 1580 khz; 1 kw-D, 86 w-N. TL: N32 58 47 W93 08 38. Stn currently dark. c/o Hawkins Broadcasting Co., 506 Dante Ave., Glenwood, IL (60425); 7830 Hwy 79 S., Emerson, AR (71740). (501) 547-3670. Licensee: Hawkins Broadcasting Co. (acq 4-4-90; $200,000 with co-located FM; FTR 4-16-90). Paul Thomas, gen mgr; Ray Lory, chief engr.

KWHN-FM—Co-owned with KLVU(AM). September 1984: 105.9 mhz; 3 kw. Ant 203 ft. TL: N33 03 13 W93 10 27. Stereo. Hrs opn: 6:30 AM-10 PM. Dups AM 100%.

Stations in the U.S.   Louisiana

Homer

KZXB(FM)—Not on air, target date unknown: 106.7 mhz; 50 kw. Ant 492 ft. TL: N32 37 03 W93 14 36. 3712 Cornell Ave., Shreveport (71107). Licensee: NWLA Broadcasting Co.

Houma

KCIL(FM)—Listing follows KJIN(AM).

KHOM(FM)—Nov 15, 1968: 104.1 mhz; 100 kw. Ant 1,945 ft. TL: N29 57 13 W90 43 25. Stereo. Hrs opn: 24. Box 728, Stn. 2, 2306 W. Main St. (70360). (504) 876-5466. Licensee: KHOM Associates. Net: NBC. Rep: Torbet. Format: Oldies. News staff one; news progmg 2 hrs wkly. Target aud: 25-54. ■ Raymond A. Saadi, CEO & gen mgr; James J. Boquex Jr., pres; Darrin Guidry, stn mgr; Chuck White, progmg dir; Jeff Zerinque, news dir; Roy Vicknair, pub affrs dir.

KJIN(AM)—April 1, 1946: 1490 khz; 1 kw-U. TL: N29 34 14 W90 43 42. Box 2068, 906 Belanger (70361). (504) 851-1020; (504) 851-1025. FAX: (504) 872-4403. Licensee: Guaranty Broadcasting Corp. Rep: Roslin. Format: Country. News staff one; news progmg 3 hrs wkly. Target aud: 25-54. Spec prog: Fr 2 hrs wkly. ■ George Foster, CEO; Michael Adams, vp; Michael Stone, gen mgr & progmg dir; Jan Jackson, gen sls mgr; Don Thomas, prom mgr; Mark Murphy, asst mus dir; Jennie Childs, news dir; Bo Hoover, chief engr.

KCIL(FM)—Co-owned with KJIN(AM). Dec 31, 1965: 107.5 mhz; 100 kw. Ant 649 ft. TL: N29 26 48 W90 44 34 (CP: Ant 981 ft., TL: N29 26 48 W90 44 34). Stereo. Dups AM 91%. Format: Country, French.

Jena

KJNA(AM)—Oct 4, 1962: 1480 khz; 500 w-D, 155 w-N. TL: N31 40 37 W92 07 02. Box 1340, 2nd & Elm Sts. (71342). (318) 992-4155. Licensee: Riverside Radio Group of LA. Inc. (acq 1993). Net: Unistar. Format: C&W. News staff one; news progmg 20 hrs wkly. Target aud: 25-54. Spec prog: Farm 3 hrs wkly. ■ Tom D. Gay, pres; Larry Evans, gen mgr & gen sls mgr; B. Mitchell, progmg dir & mus dir; Pat Hurley, chief engr.

KJNA-FM—November 1976: 99.3 mhz; 3 kw. Ant 299 ft. TL: N31 41 51 W92 05 43. Stereo. Hrs opn: 24. Dups AM 100%.

Jennings

KJEF(AM)—November 1950: 1290 khz; 1 kw-U. TL: N30 12 38 W92 39 55. Stereo. Hrs opn: 24. Drawer 1248, 1215 S. Lake Arthur Ave. (70546). (318) 824-2934. FAX: (318) 824-1384. Licensee: Jennings Broadcasting Co. Net: NBC; La. Net. Format: C&W. Target aud: General. Spec prog: Fr 12 hrs, gospel 6 hrs wkly. ■ Clovis L. Bailey, pres & chief engr; Bill Bailey, gen mgr, gen sls mgr & progmg dir.

KJEF-FM—January 1963: 92.9 mhz; 33 kw. Ant 600 ft. TL: N30 00 31 W92 46 47. Stereo. Hrs opn: 24. Dups AM 100%. ■ Rates: $14; 10; 14; 8.

Jonesboro

KTOC(AM)—Dec 4, 1958: 920 khz; 1 kw-D. TL: N32 13 28 W92 43 27. Stereo. Hrs opn: 5:30 AM-10 PM. Box 690, 1300 1/2 Gansville Rd. (71251). (318) 259-4600. FAX: (318) 259-3914. Licensee: Jackson Parish Broadcasters. Net: La. Net. Format: Country, relg, classic rock. News staff one; news progmg 6 hrs wkly.

KTOC-FM—Oct 1, 1967: 104.9 mhz; 3 kw. Ant 246 ft. TL: N32 13 28 W92 43 27 (CP: 8 kw). Stereo. Format: Southern gospel, classic country, solid gold.

Kaplan

KMDL(FM)—Aug 1, 1981: 97.3 mhz; 42 kw. Ant 535 ft. TL: N30 02 54 W91 59 49. Stereo. Hrs opn: 24. 202A Galbert Rd., Lafayette (70506). (318) 232-2242; (318) 235-0973. FAX: (318) 235-4181. Licensee: Mid-Acadiana Broadcasting Corp. Net: AP. Rep: Banner. Wash atty: Ashton Hardy. Format: Country. News staff one; news progmg 7 hrs wkly. Target aud: 25-54. Spec prog: Cajun-French 3 hrs wkly. ■ Ernest J. Alexander, pres; Debbie Blackwell, opns dir; Sharon Scheuermann, gen sls mgr; Stephanie Crist, prom dir; David Michael, progmg dir & mus dir; Tony Evans, chief engr. ■ Rates: $46; 39; 46; 21.50.

Kentwood

WYCT(FM)—Dec 14, 1967: 94.1 mhz; 100 kw. Ant 981 ft. TL: N30 51 18 W90 39 59. Stereo. 7707 Waco Ave. Baton Rouge (70806). (504) 927-7060. FAX: (504) 928-1606. Licensee: Citywide Broadcasting Corp. (acq 7-30-93; $2.3 million; FTR 8-30-93). Format: C&W. ■ Jim Thompson, gen mgr; Susan Dowdy, gen sls mgr; Dick Daniels, progmg dir.

La Place

WCKW-FM—Jan 10, 1966: 92.3 mhz; 100 kw. Ant 2,000 ft. TL: N29 57 13 W90 43 25. Stereo. Hrs opn: 24. Box 5905, Suite 700, 3501 N. Causeway Blvd., Metairie (70009). (504) 831-8811. Licensee: 222 Corp. Rep: Banner. Format: AOR, classic rock. Target aud: 18-49; men. ■ Sidney J. Levet III, pres & gen mgr; Sidney J. Levet IV, stn mgr; Bryce Taylor, gen sls mgr; Stephen Levet, natl sls mgr; Wayne Watkins, progmg dir; Karol Brandt, pub affrs dir.

Lacombe

KPXF(FM)—Not on air, target date unknown: 94.7 mhz; 3 kw. TL: N30 18 31 W89 53 09. 775 I Bayou Liberty Rd., Slidell (70460). Licensee: North Lake Radio Inc.

Lafayette

KACY(AM)—Nov 15, 1960: 1520 khz; 10 kw-D, 500 w-N, DA-N. TL: N30 16 51 W92 00 53. Stereo. Hrs opn: 24. 202 Galbert Rd. (70506); Box J (70502). (318) 232-2632. FAX: (318) 233-3779. Licensee: Media Properties, An Alabama General Partnership (acq 6-29-87). Net: ABC. Rep: Banner. Format: Sports, talk. News staff one. Target aud: 35-64. ■ Rish Wood, pres; Chuck Wood, exec vp, gen mgr & gen sls mgr; Jimmy Cole, opns mgr; Diane Ducey, prom dir & news dir; Jimmie Cole, progmg dir; Tony Evans, chief engr.

KSMB(FM)—Co-owned with KACY(AM). 1964: 94.5 mhz; 100 kw. Ant 1,079 ft. TL: N30 21 44 W92 12 53. Stereo. (318) 232-1311. Net: ABC/A. Format: Top-40. Target aud: 18-49; active on-the-go adults. ■ Mary Galyean, prom dir; Bobby Novosad, progmg dir; Kurt Kruzer, mus dir.

KJCB(AM)—April 9, 1982: 770 khz; 1 kw-D, 500 w-N, DA-N. TL: N30 17 55 W91 59 30. Stereo. 413 Jefferson St. (70501). (318) 233-4262. FAX: (318) 235-9681. Licensee: R & M Broadcasting Inc. (acq 11-16-92; $100,000; FTR 12-14-92). Net: ABC/I. Rep: Katz. Format: Urban contemp. News staff one; news progmg 2 hrs wkly. Target aud: 25-54. Spec prog: Gospel, jazz. ■ JeNelle Chargois, gen mgr & sls dir; Marcus Quinn, prom dir & progmg dir; Joshua Jackson, asst mus dir; Mac Dule, chief engr. ■ Rates: $19; 19; 19; 15.

KPEL(AM)—Jan 2, 1950: 1420 khz; 1 kw-D, 750 w-N, DA-N. TL: N30 16 38 W92 03 51. Rebroadcasts KPEL-FM Erath, 100%. Box 52046 (70505). (318) 233-7003. FAX: (318) 234-7360. Licensee: Radio KPEL Inc. Group owner: Communications Corp. (acq 5-28-76). Net: ABC/E, ABC/I, ABC TalkRadio, CBS, NBC Talknet, MBS, La. Net. Rep: Christal. Format: News/talk. News progmg 25 hrs wkly. Target aud: 35-54; male. ■ Tom Galloway, CEO; Jeff Scarpelli, pres; Sheldon Galloway, gen mgr; Conrad Maxwell, stn mgr & gen sls mgr; Darryl Parks, opns mgr & mktg mgr; John Reed, sls dir; Kathie Lane, prom dir; Ray Sutley, progmg mgr; Tony L. Evans, chief engr.

KTDY(FM)—Co-owned with KPEL(AM). Sept 15, 1966: 99.9 mhz; 100 kw. Ant 984 ft. TL: N30 12 04 W91 46 33. Stereo. 1749 Bertrand (70505). (318) 233-6000. Net: Christal. Format: Adult contemp. News staff one. Target aud: 25-54; female. ■ Jim Akers, sls dir; Darryl Parks, mktg dir & progmg dir; Kathie Lane, mus dir.

KRRQ(FM)—Not on air, target date unknown: 95.5 mhz; 6 kw. Ant 328 ft. TL: N30 10 26 W92 07 59. c/o Lafayette FM Joint Venture, 3530 N.E. 25 Terrace, Fort Lauderdale, FL (33308). (318) 856-4666. Licensee: Lafayette FM Joint Venture (acq 3-5-93; FTR 3-29-93).

*****KRVS(FM)**—1962: 88.7 mhz; 100 kw. Ant 449 ft. TL: N30 15 25 W92 09 38. Stereo. USL Box 42171, Hebrard Blvd. (70504). (318) 231-5668. FAX: (318) 231-6101. Licensee: Univ. of Southwestern Louisiana. Net: NPR. Format: Class, jazz, Cajun. Target aud: General. ■ Dave Spizale, gen mgr; Bill Says, opns mgr; Judith Meriwether, prom mgr; Pete Bergeron, progmg dir; Mac Dule, chief engr.

*****KSJY(FM)**—Feb 7, 1988: 90.9 mhz; 510 w. Ant 207 ft. TL: N30 17 08 W92 04 03 (CP: 6 kw, ant 476 ft.). Hrs opn: 24. Suite C-1, 221 S. Park Rd. (70508). (318) 837-6229. Licensee: Lafayette Educational Broadcasting Foundation Inc. Net: SMN. Format: Relg. Target aud: General. ■ Francis Martin, pres; Gary W. Reynolds, gen mgr; Elena Viator, progmg dir; Mac Dulla, chief engr.

KSMB(FM)—Listing follows KACY(AM).

KTDY(FM)—Listing follows KPEL(AM).

KVOL(AM)—May 18, 1935: 1330 khz; 5 kw-D, 1 kw-N, DA-2. TL: N30 14 29 W92 03 31. 123 E. Main St. (70501). (318) 233-1330. FAX: (318) 237-7733. Licensee: Cavaness Broadcasting Corp. (acq 11-88). Net: MBS, Unistar, Westwood One. Rep: McGavren Guild. Format: Rhythm & Blues. News staff one; news progmg 4 hrs wkly. Target aud: 25-54; middle and upper income. ■ Roger Cavaness, pres.

KXKC(FM)—See New Iberia.

*****KYFI(FM)**—Not on air, target date unknown: 91.9 mhz; 1.5 kw. Ant 536 ft. TL: N30 10 26 W92 07 59. Box 1818, Chesapeake, VA (23320). Licensee: Bible Broadcasting Network Inc. (group owner).

Lake Charles

KAOK(AM)—May 10, 1947: 1400 khz; 1 kw-U. TL: N30 12 35 W93 12 43. Hrs opn: 24. Drawer S (70602). (318) 882-0514. FAX: (318) 882-6731. Licensee: Toot Toot Communications (acq 9-1-92; $94,700; FTR 9-21-92). Net: ABC/E, NBC Talknet, Moody, CBS. La. Net. Format: News/talk, info & sports, big band. News staff 3; news progmg 168 hrs wkly. Target aud: 25 plus; Baby Boomers. Spec prog: Cajun 20 hrs, black 16, relg 7 hrs, gospel 5 hrs wkly. ■ Sidney Simien, pres & mus dir; Carol Simien, , vps; Ed Prendergrast, gen mgr, opns mgr & gen sls mgr, progmg mgr & news dir; Carol Simien, vp opns, mktg dir & pub affrs dir; Paul Douglass, engrg dir. ■ Rates: $18; 16; 18; 14.

KBIU(FM)—Listing follows KXZZ(AM).

KEZM(AM)—See Sulphur.

KHLA(FM)—Listing follows KLCL(AM).

KLCL(AM)—May 12, 1935: 1470 khz; 5 kw-U, 500 w-N. TL: N30 15 31 W93 16 07. Box 3067 (70602). (318) 433-1641. FAX: (318) 433-2999. Licensee: Broadcasters & Publishers Inc. (group owner; acq 9-15-92; grpsl; FTR 10-19-92). Net: SMN. La. Net. Rep: Eastman. Wash atty: Roberts & Eckard, PC. Format: MOR. News staff 2. Target aud: 35-64. Spec prog: Farm 2 hrs, big band 4 hrs, Cajun 14 hrs wkly. ■ George Swift, pres & gen mgr; Tom Hoefer, opns mgr & progmg mgr; Jeff Ransdell, mus dir; Scott Alston, news dir; Bruce Merchant, chief engr. ■ Rates: $16; 16; 16; 13.

KHLA(FM)—Co-owned with KLCL(AM). Nov 8, 1965: 99.5 mhz; 100 kw. Ant 371 ft. TL: N30 14 41 W93 20 52 (CP: Ant 1,466 ft., TL: N30 26 10 W93 04 05). Stereo. Prog sep from AM. Net: Unistar. Format: Adult contemp. Target aud: 25-54. ■ Thom Hager, sls dir. ■ Rates: $28; 28; 28; 25.

*****KOJO(FM)**—Not on air, target date unknown: 91.7 mhz; 3 kw. Ant 328 ft. TL: N30 16 10 W93 03 51. 2921 Brown Trail, No. 140, Bedford, TX (76021). (817) 498-7001. Licensee: Southwest Educational Media Foundation Inc.

KTQQ(FM)—See Sulphur.

KXZZ(AM)—1947: 1580 khz; 1 kw-U, DA-N. TL: N30 15 28 W93 11 55. Stereo. Box 1725 (70602); 311 Alamo St. (70601). (318) 436-7277. FAX: (318) 436-7278. Licensee: Dixie Broadcasters Inc. (acq 5-2-60). Net: American Urban. Rep: Katz, ABC. Wash atty: Bryan, Cave, McPheeters & McRoberts. Format: Urban contemp. Target aud: 18-49. Spec prog: Zydeco 4 hrs wkly. ■ Dixie Johnson, CEO; Albert D. Johnson, pres; Danny Johnson, vp; John Davis, gen mgr & gen sls mgr; James Williams, progmg dir & mus dir.

KBIU(FM)—Co-owned with KXZZ(AM). Dec 1, 1976: 103.7 mhz; 100 kw. Ant 425 ft. TL: N30 14 41 W93 20 52. Stereo. Prog sep from AM. (acq 2-22-83). Format: CHR. Target aud: 18-35. ■ Hollywood Harrison, progmg dir & mus dir.

KYKZ(FM)—January 1976: 96.1 mhz; 97 kw. Ant 1,204 ft. TL: N30 17 26 W93 34 35. Stereo. Box 999, (70602); 716 Hodges St., (70601). (318) 439-3300. FAX: (318) 433-7701. Licensee: Southwest TV and Radio Inc. (acq 3-87). Net: ABC/I. Rep: Banner. Format: Modern country. News staff 3; news progmg 8 hrs wkly. Target aud: General. ■ G. Russell Chambers, pres; Jerry Goos, gen mgr; Johnette LaBorde, gen sls mgr; Eric Nielson, progmg dir & mus dir; Carroll Collins, news dir; Al Smith, chief engr.

KZWA(FM)—Not on air, target date unknown: 105.3 mhz; 50 kw. Ant 492 ft. TL: N30 05 48 W93 28 41. Box 699 (70602). (318) 477-4000. Licensee: B & C Corp. (acq 11-23-92; FTR 12-21-92).

Louisiana Directory of Radio

Lake Providence

KLPL(AM)—June 27, 1957: 1050 khz; 250 w-D. TL: N32 49 02 W91 12 35. Box 469 (71254). (318) 559-2340. Licensee: Arthur L. Thomas (acq 11-13-92; $30,000 with co-located FM; FTR 11-30-92). Net: Prog Farm. Format: C&W, Black. News staff one. Target aud: General. Spec prog: Cajun 2 hrs, farm 8 hrs wkly. ■ Calvin Thomas, gen mgr; Isaiah Robinson, mus dir & news dir.

KLPL-FM—Jan 28, 1975: 92.7 mhz; 2 kw. Ant 144 ft. TL: N32 49 02 W91 12 35. Stereo. Format: C&W. Spec prog: Farm 10 hrs, Cajun 2 hrs wkly.

Larose

KLRZ(FM)—July 29, 1993: 100.3 mhz; 50 kw. Ant 328 ft. TL: N29 32 46 W90 24 35. Hrs opn: 24. Drawer 1350 11603 Hwy. 308 (70373). (504) 798-7792. FAX: (504) 798-7793. Licensee: Electronics Unlimited Inc. Net: Westwood One. Format: CHR. News staff one. Target aud: 18-34; males & females. ■ Jerry Gisclair, pres, gen mgr & opns mgr; Terry Harris, gen sls mgr; Freddy Zeringue, prom dir; Shana Rose, news dir; James Bellanger, pub affrs dir; Scott Pierce, chief engr. ■ Rates: $30; 30; 30; 30.

Leesville

KJAE(FM)—Listing follows KLLA(AM).

KLLA(AM)—September 1956: 1570 khz; 1 kw-D. TL: N31 06 24 W93 17 38. Box 1323 (71446). (318) 239-3403. FAX: (318) 238-9283. Licensee: Pene Broadcasting Co. (acq 12-1-76). Net: AP. Format: MOR. ■ Nick Pollacia, pres, gen mgr & chief engr; Nita Clarke, gen sls mgr; Lenny Roach, progmg dir.

KJAE(FM)—Co-owned with KLLA(AM). October 1979: 92.7 mhz; 3 kw. Ant 164 ft. TL: N31 08 28 W93 17 44 (CP: Ant 328 ft.). Stereo. Prog sep from AM. Format: C&W.

KVVP(FM)—Jan 20, 1977: 105.5 mhz; 9 kw. Ant 328 ft. TL: N31 03 01 W93 16 35 (CP: 25 kw, TL: N30 57 40 W93 13 12). Stereo. Hrs opn: 24. Drawer K, Hwy. 171 (71446). (318) 537-5887. Licensee: Stannard Broadcasting Co. Inc. Net: MBS; La. Net. Rep: Dora-Clayton. Wash atty: Jim Popham. Format: C&W. News staff one; news progmg 15 hrs wkly. Target aud: General; adults with spending power. Spec prog: Relg 9 hrs wkly. ■ John S. Stannard, pres & gen mgr; Alan Taylor, stn mgr, gen sls mgr, progmg dir & news dir; Peggy Ford, prom mgr; Bob Coriell, mus dir; Randy Schell, chief engr.

Mansfield

KDXI-FM—September 1976: 92.7 mhz; 3 kw. Ant 299 ft. TL: N32 01 18 W93 44 18. Stereo. Drawer 1306 (71052).

Many

KWLA(AM)—August 1962: 1400 khz; 1 kw-U. TL: N31 34 31 W93 29 46. Stereo. 605 San Antonio (71449). (318) 256-5177. Licensee: WLV-TV Inc. (acq 1983; $170,000; FTR 6-6-83). Net: SMN; La. Net. Format: Oldies but goodies. News staff one; news progmg 6 hrs wkly. Target aud: General. ■ Rhonda Singletary, gen mgr; Cindy Izemack, gen sls mgr; Tommy O'Con, news dir; Kenny Carter, chief engr. ■ Rates: $8; 8; 8; 8.

KWLV(FM)—Co-owned with KWLA(AM). Nov 12, 1977: 107.1 mhz; 25 kw. Ant 253 ft. TL: N31 36 27 W93 24 05. (318) 256-5924. Net: MBS. Format: Country. News staff one; news progmg 8 hrs wkly. ■ Rates: Same as AM.

Marksville

KAPB(AM)—Oct 28, 1954: 1370 khz; 1 kw-D, 40 w-N. TL: N31 07 27 W92 04 40. Hrs opn: 6 AM-6 PM. Box 7, 100 Chester (71351). (318) 253-5272. Licensee: Three Rivers Radio Co. Group owner: The Radio Group (acq 11-1-88). Net: CNN; Prog Farm. Format: Country. News progmg 8 hrs wkly. Target aud: 18-49. Spec prog: Farm 6 hrs, Fr 3 hrs, Cajun 3 hrs, Relg 4 hrs wkly. ■ Tom Gay, pres; Johnny Bordelon, gen mgr & adv mgr; Janice Armand, gen sls mgr & prom mgr; Pat Tassin, progmg dir; Pat Hurely, chief engr. ■ Rates: $12.50; 8; 9.50; 8.

KAPB-FM—Aug 14, 1971: 97.7 mhz; 3 kw. Ant 328 ft. TL: N31 07 27 W92 04 40. Stereo. Dups AM 100%. ■ Rates: Same as AM.

Maurice

KFXZ(FM)—June 13, 1985: 106.3 mhz; 1.3 kw. Ant 495 ft. TL: N30 04 16 W92 11 53. Stereo. 3225 Ambassador Caffery Pkwy., Lafayette (70506). (318) 898-1112. FAX: (318) 988-0443. Licensee: Citywide Broadcasting of Lafayette Inc. (acq 2-20-90; $1.3 million; FTR 3-12-90). Rep: D & R Radio. Format: Urban contemp. News progmg 2 hrs wkly. Target aud: 12-34. Spec prog: Gospel 4 hrs; Zydeco 4 hrs wkly. ■ Al J. Wallace, gen mgr; John Marver, gen sls mgr; Corey Martin, progmg dir & mus dir.

Minden

KASO(AM)—April 1, 1952: 1240 khz; 1 kw-U. TL: N32 37 50 W93 16 56. Box 1240 (71055). (318) 377-1240. Licensee: Cook Enterprises Inc. (acq 11-15-63). Net: MBS. Format: Country. ■ Harold Ray Boe Cook, pres & gen mgr; Jesse Lowe, progmg dir; Tommy Moore, chief engr.

KASO-FM—July 1, 1978: 95.3 mhz; 3 kw. Ant 144 ft. TL: N32 37 50 W93 16 56. Format: 60s, 70s, 80s.

Monroe

***KEDM(FM)**—April 23, 1991: 90.3 mhz; 87.1 kw. Ant 863 ft. TL: N91 59 28 W32 39 38. Stereo. Hrs opn: 24. 225 Stubbs Hall (71209-6805). (318) 342-5556. FAX: (318) 342-5570. Licensee: Northeast Louisiana Univ. Net: NPR, APR; La. Net. Wash atty: Dow, Lohnes & Albertson. Format: News, class, jazz. News staff one; news progmg 44 hrs wkly. Target aud: 35 plus; involved, upscale, educated, movers & shakers. Spec prog: New age 7 hrs, blues 4 hrs wkly. ■ Kerry Cordray, gen mgr & progmg dir; Beverly Banks, dev dir & prom dir; Sunny Meriwether, news dir; Mark Wilson, chief engr.

KJLO-FM—Listing follows KMLB(AM).

KLIC(AM)—1230 khz; 1 kw-U. TL: N32 29 16 W92 05 25. Hrs opn: 24. 1700 Parkview Dr. (71202); Box 4370 (71211). (318) 387-1230. Licensee: Fountain of Love Ministries (acq 10-28-92; $165,000; FTR 11-23-92). Format: MOR, Christian. ■ Jim Stewart, pres & gen mgr; Lonnie Hutto, vp & chief engr.

KMLB(AM)—July 1, 1930: 1440 khz; 5 kw-D, 1 kw-N, DA-N. TL: N32 33 10 W92 04 24. Hrs opn: 24. Box 4808 (71211). (318) 361-0786. FAX: (318) 388-0569. Licensee: New South Communications Inc. (group owner; acq 12-15-86). Net: NBC Talknet, MBS, Unistar. Rep: McGavren Guild. Wash atty: Kaye Scholar. Format: Talk/news. Target aud: 25-54. ■ Ed Holladay, pres; Bob Holladay, gen mgr; Mike Downhour, gen sls mgr; Grey Guylas, progmg dir; Roger Bennet, chief engr. ■ Rates: $15; 15; 15; 9.

KJLO-FM—Co-owned with KMLB(AM). July 1946: 104.1 mhz; 100 kw. Ant 1,017 ft. TL: N32 39 36 W92 05 15. Stereo. Hrs opn: 24. (318) 388-2323. Format: Country. News staff one. Spec prog: Gospel 4 hrs wkly. ■ Bill Galloway, gen sls mgr; Mike Blakeney, progmg dir. ■ Rates: $39; 39; 39; 24.

KMYY(FM)—Nov 15, 1965: 106.1 mhz; 97 kw. Ant 1,017 ft. TL: N32 39 36 W92 05 15. Stereo. 1200 N. 18th St. (71201). (318) 387-3922. FAX: (318) 322-4585. Licensee: Opus Media Group Inc. (acq 2-12-90; grpsl; FTR 3-12-90). Net: ABC/FM. Rep: Banner. Format: CHR, adult contemp. News staff one; news progmg 35 hrs wkly. Target aud: 25-49. ■ Bob Barnett, gen mgr; Dave Roberts, progmg dir; Michelle Hunt, news dir; Randi Guess, pub affrs dir; Joey Guy, chief engr. ■ Rates: $27; 21; 25; 13.

***KNLU(FM)**—Apr 23, 1973: 91.1 mhz; 8.5 kw. Ant 716 ft. TL: W32 39 38 N91 59 28 Stereo. Hrs opn: 18. 128 Stubbs Hall, (71209-8821). (318) 342-5658; (318) 342-5659. Licensee: Northeast Lousiana Univ. Wash atty: Dow, Lohnes & Albertson. Format: Rock, jazz. News progmg 2 hrs wkly. Target aud: 12-34. Spec prog: Blues 3 hrs wkly. ■ Joel Willer, gen mgr; Mark Wilson, chief engr.

KNOE(AM)—Oct 4, 1944: 540 khz; 5 kw-D, 1 kw-N, DA-2. TL: N32 32 36 W92 10 45. Box 4067 (71211). (318) 388-8888. FAX: (318) 322-8774. Licensee: James A. Noe Jr. Net: SMN. Rep: McGavren Guild. Format: Gold hits of the 50s, 60s & 70s. ■ James A. Noe Jr., pres; George Noe, gen mgr; Russell Mitchell, opns mgr; Roy Frostenson, news dir; Jerry Harkins, chief engr.

KNOE-FM—Jan 29, 1967: 101.9 mhz; 97 kw-H, 96 kw-V. Ant 1,670 ft. TL: N32 11 45 W92 04 10. Stereo. Prog sep from AM. Format: CHR. ■ Russell Mitchell, mus dir. ■ KNOE-TV affil.

KRVV(FM)—See Bastrop.

***KYFL(FM)**—Oct 8, 1992: 89.5 mhz; 1 kw. Ant 397 ft. TL: N32 28 38 W92 11 08. Stereo. Hrs opn: 24. Suite one, 4007 Whites Ferry Rd., West Monroe (71291). (318) 396-6284 Licensee: Bible Broadcasting Network. (group owner). Format: Conservative Christian. News progmg 3 hrs wkly. Target aud: General. ■ John Fetterhoft, gen mgr.

Moreauville

KLIL(FM)—July 25, 1980: 92.1 mhz; 3 kw. Ant 300 ft. TL: N31 02 53 W91 59 47. Stereo. Box 365 (71355). (318) 985-2929. FAX: (318) 985-2995. Licensee: Cajun Broadcasting Inc. Net: La. Net. Rep: Miller. Format: Top-40, oldies, farm. News progmg 10 hrs wkly. Spec prog: Cajun Fr 2 hrs wkly. ■ Louis B. Coco Jr., pres, gen mgr, mktg dir, news dir & chief engr; Michael Ricaud, gen sls mgr; Louis Coco III, prom dir; Helen Roy, adv dir; John Coco, progmg dir; Amy Coco, mus dir.

Morgan City

KMRC(AM)—April 1954: 1430 khz; 500 w-D, 100 w-N. TL: N29 45 03 W91 10 24. Hrs opn: 24. Box 1430 (70381); 409 Duke St. (70380). (504) 384-1430. FAX: (504) 384-2351. Licensee: Tri-City Broadcasting Inc. Format: Adult contemp. News staff one; news progmg 5 hrs wkly. Target aud: 25-54; middle to upper income. Spec prog: Gospel 10 hrs wkly. ■ Warren J. Fortier, pres; Tim Benoit, gen mgr & chief engr; Dennis Miller, gen sls mgr; Brett Ross, prom dir, progmg dir & mus dir; Warren Souldier, news dir. ■ Rates: $9; 6; 9; 4.

KFXY(FM)—Co-owned with KMRC(AM). Aug 1, 1967: 96.7 mhz; 6 kw. Ant 390 ft. TL: N29 45 63 W91 10 24. Stereo. Hrs opn: 24 Prog sep from AM. Format: Contemp hit. News progmg 2 hrs wkly. Target aud: 18-34; majority women. Spec prog: Gospel 6 hrs wkly. ■ Tim Benoit, vp sls. ■ Rates: $15; 12; 15; 8.

Natchitoches

KDBH(FM)—July 1, 1965: 97.7 mhz; 3 kw. Ant 328 ft. TL: N31 45 47 W93 03 47 (CP: 97.3 mhz, 11 kw). Stereo. Box 1420 (71458-1420). (318) 352-9596. Licensee: Cane River Communications Inc. (acq 10-25-90; $267,000 with co-located AM; FTR 11-19-90). Net: ABC/I; La. Net. Wash atty: Kaye Scholer. Format: C&W. ■ Joe Cunningham Jr., pres & gen mgr; Melody Busby, gen sls mgr; Ed Gobel, mus dir; Bill Perdue, news dir; Belden Williams, chief engr. ■ Rates: $6; 6; 6; 6.

KNOC(AM)—Co-owned with KDBH(FM). May 1, 1947: 1450 khz; 1 kw-U. TL: N31 45 47 W93 03 47. Hrs opn: 5:30 AM-midnight. Prog sep from FM. Box 607, 720 Front St. (71458-0607). Net: ABC/C. Format: Oldies, talk. News staff 2; news progmg 20 hrs wkly. Target aud: 25-59; upper-middle class. Spec prog: Farm one hr, gospel 6 hrs wkly. ■ Rates: Same as FM.

***KNWD(FM)**—September 1975: 91.7 mhz; 255 w-H. Ant 164 ft. TL: N31 44 51 W93 05 47. Stereo. Hrs opn: 24. Box 3038, NSU (71497); South Hall, Northwestern State Univ. (71497). (318) 357-5693; (318) 357-4180. FAX: (318) 357-6564. Licensee: Northwestern State Univ. of Louisiana. Format: Black, progsv, rock. News staff one; news progmg 3 hrs wkly. Target aud: 18-25; male, female, all races . Spec prog: Gospel 6 hrs, heavy metal 2 hrs, blues 2 hrs wkly. ■ Paul Parker, gen mgr; Jeff Burkett, prom dir; Ron Bolton, progmg dir; Tim Barr, mus dir; Ricky Darbonne, Vernassa Fields, asst mus dirs; Bridgette Morvant, news dir; Sean Schneyer, pub affrs dir; Clark Hyams, engrg mgr; Gene Chance, chief engr.

KZBL(FM)—Oct 8, 1985: 95.9 mhz; 3 kw. Ant 299 ft. TL: N31 48 18 W93 01 29. Stereo. Hrs opn: 24. Box 18 (71458-0018); 1115 Washington St. (71457). (318) 352-9696. FAX: (318) 352-4364. Licensee: Bundrick Communications Inc. (acq 12-26-88). Net: CNN. Format: Adult contemp. Target aud: 18-49. ■ Hal M. Bundrick, pres & gen mgr; Woody Fryar, chief engr.

New Iberia

KANE(AM)—August 1946: 1240 khz; 1 kw-U. TL: N30 01 03 W91 50 10. Stereo. Hrs opn: 24. 2316 E. Main (70560). (318) 365-3434. FAX: (318) 367-5385. Licensee: New Iberia Broadcasting Co. Inc. Net: ABC/E. Format: Adult contemp. News staff one; news progmg 30 hrs wkly. Target aud: 25-54. Spec prog: Farm 2 hrs wkly. ■ Art Suberbielle, pres & gen mgr; Ken Romero, opns dir, prom mgr, progmg dir, mus dir & chief engr; Wayne LeJeune, news dir. ■ Rates: $18; 16; 18; 14.

KDEA(FM)—1991: 93.7 mhz; 34 kw. Ant 590 ft. TL: N29 49 31 W91 39 50. 123 E. Main St., Lafayette (70501). (318) 233-1330. FAX: (318) 237-7733. Licensee: Cajun Consulting Inc. (acq 10-3-91; $101,000 for CP; FTR 10-28-91). ■ Roger W. Cavaness, gen mgr; Jimmy Akers, stn mgr; Randy Abadie, progmg mgr; Jim Cope, chief engr.

KNIR(AM)—June 1, 1951: 1360 khz; 1 kw-D, 209 w-N. TL: N30 01 32 W91 49 20. Hrs opn: 24. Box 12948 (70562-2948); 145 W. Main St. (70560). (318) 365-6651. FAX: (318) 365-6314. Licensee: Donald Bonin dba

KXKC/KNIR. Net: Unistar. Rep: Katz; Midsouth.Format: Nostalgia. News staff 2; news progmg 10 hrs wkly. Target aud: 35 plus. ■ Donald Bonin, gen mgr; Eddie Provost, stn mgr; Jerry Methvin, opns mgr; Louis Cowen, gen sls mgr; Patrick Bonin, prom mgr; Renee Revett, progmg dir; Kelly Thompson, mus dir; Mary Brown, news dir; Rick Morel, chief engr. ■ Rates: $12; 12; 12; 10.

KXKC(FM)—Co-owned with KNIR(AM). January 1969: 99.1 mhz; 100 kw. Ant 1,039 ft. TL: N30 12 4 W91 46 33. Stereo. Hrs opn: 24 Prog sep from AM. Licensee: Donald Bonin. Rep: Katz. Format: Country. News staff 2; news progmg 10 hrs wkly. Target aud: 18-44. ■ Jerry Methvin, chief opns.

New Orleans

KGLA(AM)—See Gretna.

WBOK(AM)—February 1951: 1230 khz; 1 kw-U. TL: N29 59 18 W90 02 45. 1639 Gentilly Blvd. (70119). (504) 943-4600. FAX: (504) 944-4662. Licensee: Christian Broadcasting Corp. Group owner: Willis Broadcasting Corp. (acq 1983; $700,000; FTR 7-4-83). Rep: Roslin. Format: Gospel. Target aud: 25 plus. ■ Bishop L.E. Willis, pres; Annette G. Pete, gen mgr; Bob Frost, progmg dir; Danny Miller, chief engr.

***WBSN-FM**—Feb 5, 1979: 89.1 mhz; 10 kw. Ant 525 ft. TL: N29 57 01 W89 57 29 (CP: 8 kw, ant 643 ft.). Stereo. Hrs opn: 24. 3939 Gentilly Blvd. (70126). (504) 286-3600. FAX: (504) 286-3580. Licensee: New Orleans Baptist Theological Seminary (acq 1-79). Format: Contemp Christian. Target aud: 25-49; active, Christian oriented families. ■ Stan Watts, gen mgr; Brian Sanders, gen sls mgr & adv dir; Wayne Michaels, progmg dir; Doug Booth, chief engr.

WBYU(AM)—1950: 1450 khz; 1 kw-U. TL: N29 57 49 W90 06 34. 1515 St. Charles Ave. (70130). (504) 522-1450. FAX: (504) 528-9244. Licensee: Radio Vanderbilt Inc. (acq 4-20-79). Net: SMN. Rep: Roslin. Format: Nostalgia, easy lstng. Target aud: 35 plus. ■ Seymour Smith, pres; David Smith, vp, gen mgr & gen sls mgr; Bob Middleton, progmg dir & mus dir; Jay Gardener, news dir; Ken Devine, chief engr. ■ Rates: $60; 60; 60; 50.

WCKW-FM—See La Place.

WEZB(FM)—Sept 1, 1945: 97.1 mhz; 100 kw. Ant 984 ft. TL: N29 55 11 W90 01 29. Stereo. Box 53447 (70153); 601 Loyola-Poydras Plaza (70113). (504) 581-7002. FAX: (504) 523-2857. Licensee: EZ Communications Inc. (group owner; acq 1-2-72). Rep: Major Mkt. Format: CHR. News staff one; news progmg 3 hrs wkly. Target aud: 18-34; females. ■ Alan Box, pres; Mark Leunissen, vp & gen mgr; Chester Schofield, gen sls mgr; Ann Rogers, prom dir; Scott Wright, progmg dir; Joey Giovingo, mus dir; Janet Gross, news dir; Tim Boots, chief engr.

WGSO(AM)—Jan 27, 1946: 990 khz; 1 kw-D, 400 w-N. TL: N29 57 24 W90 04 34. 3525 N. Causeway Blvd., Metarie (70002). (504) 834-9587. FAX: (504) 833-8560. Licensee: Phase II Broadcasting Inc. Net: CBS Spectrum, Unistar. Rep: D & R Radio. Format: Oldies. ■ Edmond J. Muniz, pres & gen mgr; Denise Hamilton, gen sls mgr; Bob Mitcell, progmg dir; Ben Suddeth, news dir; Ernest L. Harvey Jr., chief engr.

WLMG(FM)—Listing follows WWL(AM).

WNOE(AM)—1925: 1060 khz; 50 kw-D, 5 kw-N, DA-2. TL: N29 52 46 W89 59 51. Stereo. 529 Bienville (70130). (504) 529-1212. FAX: (504) 525-1011. Licensee: New-Market Media Corp. (group owner; acq 11-28-89; $7,240,000 with co-located FM; FTR 10-2-89). Net: MBS. Rep: McGavern Guild. Wash atty: Kaye, Scholer, Fierman, Hays & Hanoler. Format: C&W. ■ Tom Kennedy, vp; Ted Stacker, opns mgr; Richard Hinshaw, gen sls mgr; Earl Boaz, prom mgr; Richard Blake, mus dir; Ray Romero, news dir; Doug Booth, chief engr.

WNOE-FM—Sept 15, 1968: 101.1 mhz; 100 kw. Ant 1,004 ft. TL: N29 58 57 W89 57 09. Stereo. Prog sep from AM.

WQUE(AM)—July 23, 1923: 1280 khz; 5 kw-U, DA-1. TL: N29 53 43 W90 00 16. Stereo. 2228 Gravier (70119). (504) 827-6000. FAX: (504) 827-6045. Licensee: Clear Channel Radio Licenses Inc. (acq 7-24-92). Rep: Christal. Wash atty: Cohn & Marks. Format: Contemp hit, urban contemp. News staff one; news progmg one hr wkly. ■ Lowry Mays, pres; Ken Went, gen mgr; Jerod Stevens, mus dir; Monica Pierre, news dir; J.P. Robillard, chief engr. ■ Rates: $165; 135; 150; 125.

WQUE-FM—Jan 1, 1949: 93.3 mhz; 93 kw. Ant 459 ft. TL: N29 57 24 W90 04 31 (CP: 100 kw, ant 984 ft., TL: N29 55 11 W90 01 29). Stereo. Dups AM 100%. ■ Ron Burgess, gen sls mgr; Jerod Stevens, progmg dir. ■ Rates: Same as AM.

***WRBH(FM)**—1980: 88.3 mhz; 54 kw. Ant 600 ft. TL: N29 57 01 W89 57 29. 3606 Magazine St. (70115). (504) 899-1144. FAX: (504) 899-1165. Licensee: Radio for the Blind and Print Handicapped Inc. Format: Radio Reading Svc. ■ Tim Green, gen mgr; Randy Savoie, progmg dir.

WRNO-FM—Oct 17, 1967: 99.5 mhz; 100 kw. Ant 1,004 ft. TL: N29 58 57 W89 57 09. Stereo. 4539 I-10 N. Service Rd. W., Metairie (70006). (504) 889-2424. FAX: (504) 454-2472. Licensee: Radio WRNO-FM Inc. (acq 11-3-92; $500,000; FTR 11-23-92). Net: ABC/FM. Rep: Major Mkt. Format: Rock. Target aud: 18-49. ■ J. Mark Costello III, pres; Bill May, progmg dir & mus dir.

WSHO(AM)—1926: 800 khz; 1 kw-D, 233 w-N, DA-1. TL: N29 50 42 W90 06 39. 1001 Howard Ave. (70113). (504) 527-0800. FAX: (504) 527-0881. Licensee: Cascade Broadcasting of Louisiana Inc. (acq 12-2-82; $920,000; FTR 11-18-82). Net: CBN, USA. Format: Christian music and talk. News progmg 10 hrs wkly. Target aud: 25-54. ■ David Jack, pres; William Ainsworth, gen mgr, opns mgr & prom mgr; Dennis Boutillier, gen sls mgr; David Gerdes, progmg dir & news dir; John Johnston, chief engr.

WSLA(AM)—See Slidell.

WSMB(AM)—April 21, 1925: 1350 khz; 5 kw-U, DA-2. TL: N29 55 27 W90 02 04. Hrs opn: 24. Suite 440, 1450 Poydras (70112). (504) 593-2100. FAX: (504) 593-1850. Licensee: Winston Communications (acq 7-1-88). Format: News/talk. ■ Johnny Andrews, stn mgr.

WTIX(AM)—1948: 690 khz; 10 kw-D, 5 kw-N, DA-2. TL: N29 57 53 W89 57 31. Hrs opn: 24. 3313 Kingman St., Metarie (70006). (504) 888-9849. FAX: (504) 888-8329. Licensee: WTIX Inc. Group owner: GHB Radio Group (acq 2-12-92; $800,000; FTR 3-16-92). Net: NBC, BRN, Talknet, Dow Jones. Wash atty: Cohn & Marks. Format: Big band, jazz. News staff 2; news progmg 30 hrs wkly. Target aud: 25 plus; affluent, educated, professional. ■ George H. Buck Jr., pres & stn mgr; Robert Namer, gen mgr & gen sls mgr; Mal Banks, opns dir; Jay Richards, Ron Hunter, progmg dirs. ■ Rates: $60; 25; 40; 25.

WTKL(FM)—February 1953: 95.7 mhz; 100 kw. Ant 984 ft. TL: N29 55 11 W90 01 29. Stereo. Suite 1053, 3525 N. Causeway Blvd., Metairie (70002). (504) 834-9587. FAX: (504) 833-8560. Licensee: Phase II Broadcasting Inc. (acq 2-3-93; $3.25 million; FTR 3-1-93). Rep: Eastman. Wash atty: Latham & Watkins. Format: Oldies. News staff one. Target aud: 25-54. ■ Ed Nuniz, pres & gen mgr; Dennis Hamilton, gen sls mgr; Don Amez, prom dir; Steve Sutter, progmg dir & mus dir; Ben Sudduth, news dir; Wayne Andrews, chief engr. ■ Rates: $75; 60; 60; 40.

***WTUL(FM)**—Nov 14, 1974: 91.5 mhz; 1.5 kw. Ant 161 ft. TL: N29 56 18 W90 07 07. Stereo. Hrs opn: 24. Tulane Univ. Ctr. (70118). (504) 865-5887. Licensee: Tulane Educational Fund. Format: Progsv rock, classical, jazz. News progmg 3 hrs wkly. Target aud: General. Spec prog: Class 15 hrs, country 3 hrs, reggae 2 hrs, blues 2 hrs, New Orleans music 2 hrs, folk 2 hrs, rap 2 hrs, world music 2 hrs, techno 2 hrs wkly. ■ Ardis Eschenberg, gen mgr; Jia Gilani, progmg dir; Colin Borstel, news dir; Mark Musgrove, chief engr.

WVOG(AM)—April 23, 1964: 600 khz; 1 kw-D. TL: N29 57 25 W90 09 33. Hrs opn: 5:30 AM-8:30 PM. 2730 Loumour Ave., Metairie (70001). (504) 831-6941. Licensee: F.W. Robbert Broadcasting Co. (group owner; acq 6-28-74). Net: USA. Format: Relg, talk. News progmg 2 hrs wkly. Target aud: 30 plus. ■ Fred Westenberger, pres & gen mgr; Eric Westenberger, gen sls mgr; Ken Devine, chief engr. ■ Rates: $10; 10; 10; 10.

WWL(AM)—Mar 31, 1922: 870 khz; 50 kw-U, DA-1. TL: N29 50 14 W90 07 55. Hrs opn: 24. Suite 440, 1450 Poydras (70112). (504) 593-6376. FAX: (504) 593-2102. Licensee: Keymarket Communications (group owner; acq 8-14-89; $12.85 million with co-located FM; FTR 7-10-89). Net: CBS, ABC/I. Rep: Katz. Format: News/talk. ■ Kerby Confer, chmn; Barry Drake, pres; Donald Alt, vp; Johnny Andrews, gen mgr; Bob Christopher, opns mgr; Eve Minitillo Versteeg, gen sls mgr; Jay Ory, prom dir; Diane Newman, progmg mgr; Walt Pierce, news dir; Ernie Kain, chief engr.

WLMG(FM)—Co-owned with WWL(AM). March 15, 1970: 101.9 mhz; 100 kw. Ant 984 ft. TL: N29 55 11 W90 01 29. Stereo. Hrs opn: 24. Prog sep from AM. Format: Adult contemp. ■ Ken Hoag, gen sls mgr; Pam Montz, prom mgr; Nick Ferrara, progmg dir; Johnny Scott, mus dir; David Blake, news dir. ■ WWL-TV affil.

***WWNO(FM)**—Feb 20, 1972: 89.9 mhz; 50 kw. Ant 640 ft. TL: N29 57 01 W89 57 29. Stereo. Hrs opn: 24. Univ. of New Orleans, 2000 Lakeshore Dr. (70148). (504) 286-7000. FAX: (504) 286-7317. Licensee: Louisiana State Univ. Net: APR, NPR. Format: Class, news. News progmg 32 hrs wkly. Target aud: 35 and older; well-educated professionals, mgrs, artists and art patrons. Spec prog: Jazz 18 hrs, new age one hr wkly. ■ John S. Batson, gen mgr; Ron C. Curtis, opns dir; Patricia Miscenich, dev mgr; Ric Frances, sls dir; Fred Kasten, prom mgr; Suzanne Dobkin, progmg dir; Larry Guillot, mus dir; Robert Carroll, chief engr.

***WWOZ(FM)**—Dec 6, 1980: 90.7 mhz; 19 w. Ant 279 ft. TL: N29 57 01 W90 09 16 (CP: 4 kw, ant 508 ft., TL: N29 57 24 W90 04 31). Stereo. Hrs opn: 20. Box 51840 (70151); 1201 St. Phillip St. (70116). (504) 568-1238; (504) 568-1239. FAX: (504) 558-9332. Licensee: Friends of WWOZ Inc. (acq 10-14-86). Wash atty: Haley, Bader & Potts. Format: Jazz, R&B. Target aud: General. ■ David Freedman, gen mgr; Virginia Prescott, progmg dir & mus dir; Damond Jacob, chief engr.

WYLD(AM)—1949: 940 khz; 10 kw-D, 500 w-N, DA-2. TL: N29 54 00 W90 00 17. 2228 Gravier St. (70119). (504) 827-6000; (504) 827-6045. FAX: (504) 826-7723. Licensee: Snowden Broadcasting of New Orleans Inc. Net: ABC. Rep: D & R Radio. Wash atty: Crowell & Moring. Format: Gospel. Target aud: 25-54. ■ Jim Snowden, gen mgr; Skill Dillard, progmg dir; Denise Verrey, news dir; J.P. Robillar, chief engr.

WYLD-FM—1971: 98.5 mhz; 100 kw. Ant 984 ft. TL: N29 55 11 W90 01 29. Stereo. Format: Urban contemp, news. News staff 2; news progmg 5 hrs wkly. Spec prog: Jazz 5 hrs wkly.

New Roads

KQXL-FM—Oct 1, 1979: 106.5 mhz; 50 kw. Ant 485 ft. TL: N30 37 24 W91 09 50. Stereo. Hrs opn: 24. 7707 Waco Ave., Baton Rouge (70806). (504) 926-1106. FAX: (504) 928-1606. Licensee: Citywide Broadcasting Corporation. Net: ABC/FM, CBS. Rep: Banner. Format: Black, urban contemp. News staff one. Target aud: 18-54; Black adults. ■ Peter Moncrieffe, pres & gen mgr; Jim Thompson, stn mgr; Bobbie Coates, natl sls mgr; Kay Taylor (local), rgnl sls mgr; Chris Clay, progmg dir; Lou Bennett, mus dir; Isiah Carey, news dir; Mya Vernon, pub affrs dir; Paul Burt, chief engr.

Norco

WADU(AM)—1987: 830 khz; 5 kw-D, 750 w-N, DA-2. TL: N30 03 00 W90 22 41. 1500 E. Airline Hwy., La Place (70068). (504) 651-9238. FAX: (504) 468-3354. Licensee: River Road Radio Inc. Format: Hispanic. ■ Virgie H. duTreil, pres, gen mgr & progmg dir.

North Fort Polk

KCIJ(FM)—Not on air, target date Spring 1994: 106.7 mhz; 6 kw. Ant 328 ft. TL: N31 03 46 W93 16 11. 714 Tilly Rd., Leesville (71446). (318) 535-9102. Licensee: Burwell Broadcasting. Format: Christian.

Oak Grove

KWCL-FM—Jan 30, 1973: 96.7 mhz; 3 kw. Ant 289 ft. TL: N32 51 33 W91 21 26 (CP: 25 kw, ant 286 ft.). Stereo. Box 260 (71263). (318) 428-9670. FAX: (318) 428-2476. Licensee: KWCL-FM Broadcasting Co. Inc. (acq 7-24-92). Wash atty: Miller & Miller. Format: Country classic. News staff 6; news progmg 17 hrs wkly. Target aud: General. ■ Irene Robinson, gen mgr, gen sls mgr & sls dir; Don Copes Jr., mus dir & news dir; Randy Meadows, pub affrs dir; Ivy Robinson, engrg dir & chief engr. ■ Rates: $6; 6; 6; 5.

Oakdale

KICR-FM—1972: 98.7 mhz; 10 kw. Ant 1,053 ft. TL: N30 48 30 W92 38 30. Stereo. Hrs opn: 24. Box 8798, Alexandria (71306); 3620 Bayou Rapides Rd., Alexandria (71303). (318) 473-0098; (318) 473-9898. Licensee: B&D Communications (acq 2-19-90; $492,300; with co-located FM; FTR 2-19-90). Net: AP, Unistar. Format: C&W. News staff one; news progmg 20 hrs wkly. ■ Bob Holladay, pres; Patricia Strother, gen mgr & gen sls mgr; Jack Sharp, natl sls mgr; Steve Casey, progmg dir; Rick Stevens, pub affrs dir; Roger Bennett, chief engr.

KICR(AM)—1952: 900 khz; 250 w-D.

Opelousas

KOGM(FM)—Listing follows KSLO(AM).

KSLO(AM)—September 1947: 1230 khz; 1 kw-U. TL: N30 31 31 W92 06 17. Box 1150, 232 N. Court (70571-1150). (318) 942-2633. FAX: (318) 942-2633. Licensee: KSLO Broadcasting Co. Inc. Net: ABC/I. Format: C&W,

Black, news/talk. Spec prog: Fr 20 hrs wkly. ■ Wandell Allegood, pres & gen mgr; Johnny Wright, gen sls mgr. ■ Rates: $17.90; 17.90; 17.90; 17.90.

KOGM(FM)—Co-owned with KSLO(AM). June 18, 1965: 107.1 mhz; 3 kw-H. Ant 203 ft. TL: N30 31 31 W92 06 17. Stereo. Prog sep from AM. Net: SMN. Format: Adult contemp. ■ Johnny Wright, sls dir.

KVOL-FM—Aug 3, 1989: 105.9 mhz; 3.4 kw. Ant 433 ft. TL: N30 27 53 W92 04 31. 123 E. Main St., Lafayette (70501). (318) 233-1330. FAX: (318) 237-7733. Licensee: Cavaness Broadcasting Inc. (acq 4-18-90; $43,333; FTR 5-14-90). Rep: D & R Radio. Format: R&B. Target aud: 20-54. Spec prog: Creole. ■ Roger Cavaness, gen mgr; Horatio Handy, gen sls mgr; Randy Abadie, progmg dir; Lynette Broussard, mus dir.

Pineville

KTLD(AM)—Sept 13, 1974: 1110 khz; 500 w-D. TL: N31 21 52 W92 27 15. Stereo. 34D MacArthur Dr., Alexander (71303). (318) 473-4388. Licensee: Hill Country Broadcasting Inc. ■ Troy DeRamus, pres; Steve Cathie, gen mgr.

Port Allen

WLUX(AM)—Licensed to Port Allen. See Baton Rouge.

Port Sulphur

KAGY(AM)—Aug 17, 1966: 1510 khz; 1 kw-D. TL: N29 29 03 W89 42 15. Box 1307, Hwy. 23 S., Buras (70041). (504) 657-5249. Licensee: Miracle Assembly of God Inc. (acq 8-11-92; $0, donated; FTR 8-31-92). Net: USA. Format: Gospel. Target aud: 24-54. Spec prog: Fr 3 hrs, relg 3 hrs wkly. ■ Max Latham, pres & gen mgr.

KGTR(FM)—July 4, 1989: 106.7 mhz; 100 kw. Ant 981 ft. TL: N29 48 30 W89 45 42. Hrs opn: 24. Suite 4200, 1001 Howard Ave., New Orleans (70113). (504) 528-1067. FAX: (504) 522-6544. Licensee: NewMarket Media Corp. (group owner; acq 9-15-93; $3.35 million; FTR 10-11-93). Rep: McGavren Guild. Format: Oldies. News staff one. Target aud: 25-54. ■ Tom Kennedy, vp & gen mgr; Ted Stecker, chief opns & progmg dir; Drew Bienvenu, gen sls mgr; Susie Prats, natl sls mgr; Earl Boaz, prom mgr; Richard Blake, mus dir; Josh Halstead, pub affrs dir; Marc Musgrove, chief engr. ■ Rates: $60; 60; 60; 35.

Rayne

KCRL(FM)—Not on air, target date unknown: 106.7 mhz; 3 kw. Ant 328 ft. TL: N30 18 17 W92 20 47. 205 E. Edwards St. (70578). Licensee: Broadcast Partners Inc. (acq 12-18-92; $60,000; FTR 1-11-93).

Rayville

KTJC(FM)—September 1984: 92.3 mhz; 26 kw. Ant 492 ft. TL: N32 27 51 W91 39 10. Stereo. Hrs opn: 16. 1207 Louisa St. (71269). (318) 728-5852. Licensee: Kenneth W. Diebel. Format: Southern gospel. ■ Kenneth W. Diebel, gen mgr & chief engr.

KXLA(AM)—1957: 990 khz; 1 kw-D, 250 w-N, DA-2. TL: N32 28 55 W91 47 46. Stereo. Box 990 (71269). (318) 728-6990. FAX: (318) 396-5348. Licensee: Ouachita Broadcasters Inc. (acq 5-26-92; $160,000; FTR 6-15-92). Format: Black, gospel. ■ Matthew Pearce, gen mgr; Rev. Charles Thomas, progmg dir & mus dir; Tim Waterhouse, chief engr.

Reserve

WADU-FM—August 1991: 94.9 mhz; 1.9 kw. Ant 407 ft. TL: N30 04 37 W90 37 19. Stn currently dark. 1500 E. Airline Hwy., LaPlace (70068). (504) 651-9238. FAX: (504) 468-3354. Licensee: Virgie Hare du Treil. Format: Btfl music. ■ Virgie H. duTreil, pres & gen mgr.

Richwood

NEW FM—Not on air, target date unknown: 100.9 mhz; 6 kw. Ant 328 ft. 106 Garway Cove, Clinton, MS (39058). Licensee: Russ Robinson.

Ruston

***KLPI-FM**—1973: 89.1 mhz; 4 kw. Ant 285 ft. TL: N32 31 09 W92 39 02. Stereo. 900 Gilman (71270); Box 8638 T.S. (71272). (318) 257-4851; (318) 257-3689. Licensee: Louisiana Tech Univ. Net: La. Net. Wash atty: Arent, Fox, Kintner, Plotkin & Kahn. Format: Div. News staff one; news progmg 3 hrs wkly. Target aud: 18-24; college students. Spec prog: Black 3 hrs, classical 3 hrs, oldies 12 hrs, punk rock 3, reggae 6 hrs wkly. ■ Dr. Dan Reneau, pres; Michel Boulware, gen mgr; Darren Standish, progmg dir; John Fernandes, mus dir; Emery Geyer, news dir; Jerry Harkins, chief engr.

KRUS(AM)—Nov 7, 1947: 1490 khz; 1 kw-U. TL: N32 30 48 W92 39 56. Box 430, 500 N. Monroe St. (71273-0430). (318) 255-2530. FAX: (318) 255-2100. Licensee: Ruston Broadcasting Co. Inc. (acq 4-1-69). Net: APR. Format: Urban contemp, blues. News staff one; news progmg 10 hrs wkly. Target aud: 25-55; Black. Spec prog: Black gospel 12 hrs wkly. ■ Dan Hollingsworth, pres, gen mgr, vp sls & chief engr; James Cooper, opns dir & mus dir; Mary Poe, prom mgr; Gene Haynes, news dir. ■ Rates: $11.77; 11.77; 11.77; 11.77.

KXKZ(FM)—Co-owned with KRUS(AM). June 29, 1966: 107.5 mhz; 98 kw. Ant 1,066 ft. TL: N32 26 38 W92 42 42. Stereo. Hrs opn: 24. Prog sep from AM. Box 2264, Monroe (71207). (318) 255-5000; (318) 388-6111. Net: AP. Format: C&W. News staff one; news progmg 7 hrs wkly. Target aud: 25-54. ■ Dan Hollingsworth, CEO, sls dir & progmg dir; Bob Day, mus dir; Shantele Smith, Karen Jones, news dirs. ■ Rates: $32; 32; 32; 32.

Shreveport

KBCL(AM)—September 1957: 1070 khz; 250 w-D. TL: N32 32 14 W93 43 28. 316 B Gregg St. (71104). (318) 861-1070. Licensee: Results Unlimited Inc. (acq 6-1-83; $220,000; FTR 7-11-83). Format: Contemp & traditional Christian music. ■ Randy Alewyne, pres & progmg mgr; Don Hanley, gen mgr, gen sls mgr & progmg dir; Tommy Moore, chief engr. ■ Rates: $5; 3; 5; na.

***KDAQ(FM)**—Dec 21, 1984: 89.9 mhz; 100 kw. Ant 932 ft. TL: N32 40 41 W93 55 35. Stereo. One University Place (71115). (318) 797-5150. FAX: (318) 797-5154. Licensee: Louisiana State Univ. Board of Supervisors. Net: NPR. Format: Class, news, jazz, blues. News staff 2; news progmg 34 hrs wkly. Target aud: General. ■ John Darling, pres; Catherine Fraser, gen mgr; Jene Hardman, gen sls mgr; Jean Hardman, mktg dir; Mary Masters, progmg dir; Kermit Poling, mus dir; Rod Matthews, chief engr.

KEEL(AM)—1922: 710 khz; 50 kw-D, 5 kw-N, DA-2. TL: N32 40 35 W93 51 35. Box 20007 (71120); 710 Spring St. (71101). (318) 425-8692. FAX: (318) 425-1490. Licensee: Multimedia Broadcasting Co. (group owner; acq 1975). Net: ABC/I, AP, NBC, Unistar; La. Net. Rep: Katz. Format: News, MOR, sports, talk. News staff 5. Target aud: 25-54. ■ Leeann Lewis, gen mgr; Deloras Davenport, prom mgr, progmg dir & mus dir; Jeff Stierman, news dir; Rick Benson, chief engr.

KITT(FM)—Co-owned with KEEL(AM). May 17, 1968: 93.7 mhz; 95 kw. Ant 1,010 ft. TL: N32 40 39 W93 55 41. Stereo. Prog sep from AM. Format: Adult contemp. News staff 2. ■ Nelda Coleman, gen mgr.

KFLO(AM)—July 10, 1975: 1300 khz; 5 kw-D. TL: N32 31 48 W93 48 16. Box 7277 (71137); 2097 N. Hearne Ave. (71107). (318) 222-2744. FAX: (318) 425-3057. Licensee: Nor-Max Broadcasting Co. (acq 6-1-77). Format: Relg, sports. ■ Tommy Moore, pres; Danny Perkins, gen sls mgr; Kathy Mellinger, progmg dir; A.T. Moore, chief engr. ■ Rates: $12; 12; 12; 12.

KIOU(AM)—1950: 1480 khz; 1 kw-D. TL: N32 31 30 W93 48 30. Hrs opn: 6 AM-6 PM. Box 197 (71161). (318) 222-0272. FAX: (318) 222-0482. Licensee: KCIJ Communications, Inc. Format: Religious. Target aud: General. ■ Peter Stinson, gen sls mgr.

KITT(FM)—Listing follows KEEL(AM).

KMJJ-FM—Dec 5, 1976: 100.1 mhz; 50 kw. Ant 462 ft. TL: N32 30 24 W93 45 13. 725 Austin Pl. (71101). (318) 227-8020. FAX: (318) 227-9826. Licensee: SunGroup Inc. (group owner; acq 10-5-89; grpsl; FTR 10-23-89). Format: Urban contemp. ■ John Wilson, gen mgr; Mike Anthony, progmg dir & mus dir.

KOKA(AM)—Aug 1, 1954: 980 khz; 5 kw-D. TL: N32 34 18 W93 44 39. 1315 Milam St. (71101); Box 103 (71161). (318) 221-9802; (318) 222-3122. FAX: (318) 459-1493. Licensee: Cary D. Camp (acq 6-30-89; $230,000; FTR 7-3-89). Net: NBC. Rep: D & R Radio. Format: Relg, Black. Target aud: 25-64; middle-aged, middle class, Black adults. ■ Cary D. Camp, pres; Diane M. Camp, gen mgr; Eddie Giles, progmg dir; A.T. Moore, chief engr. ■ Rates: $18; 12; 15; 12.

KRMD-FM—August 1948: 101.1 mhz; 98 kw. Ant 1,119 ft. TL: N32 41 08 W93 56 00. Stereo. Box 41011, 3109 Alexander St. (71134-1101). (318) 865-5173. FAX: (318) 865-3657. Licensee: AmCom of Louisiana Inc. (acq 10-17-85; $5 million with co-located AM; FTR 7-15-85). Net: CBS; La. Net. Rep: Eastman. Format: Contemp country. News staff one; news progmg 3 hrs wkly. Target aud: 25-54. ■ George R. Francis, pres; Gene Dickerson, vp & gen mgr; Jerry Frentress, opns mgr & gen sls mgr; Brandi Myers, prom mgr; Rick Stephenson, progmg dir; David Franklin, mus dir; Tony King, news dir; Rudy Johnson, chief engr.

KRMD(AM)—June 1928: 1340 khz; 1 kw-U. TL: N32 29 36 W93 45 55. Dups FM 100%.

***KSCL(FM)**—Mar 11, 1976: 91.3 mhz; 150 w. Ant 79 ft. TL: N32 29 01 W93 43 53. Stereo. Hrs opn: 12. 2911 Centenary Blvd. (71104). (318) 869-5297; (318) 869-5269. FAX: (318) 869-5026. Licensee: Centenary College of Louisiana. Format: College alternative, div. Target aud: General. Spec prog: Black 3 hrs, folk 6 hrs, jazz 3 hrs, reggae 4 hrs, new age one hr, blues one hr, world beat 3 hrs wkly. ■ Christopher S. Case, stn mgr; Sandy Barnett, progmg dir & mus dir; Mary Katherine Penuel, asst mus dir; Bobby Hamm, news dir & pub affrs dir; Daryl Bordelon, chief engr.

KTUX(FM)—(Carthage, Tex). April 1, 1985: 98.9 mhz; 100 kw. Ant 1,049 ft. TL: N32 23 19 W94 01 10. Stereo. Hrs opn: 24. 5005 W. Monkhouse, Shreveport, LA (71109). (318) 635-9999. FAX: (318) 636-7441. Licensee: KTUX Inc. (acq 2-3-83). Rep: Banner, Katz. Wash atty: John Fiorinni. Format: Hit Rock. Target aud: 18-49; super-active adults. ■ Ken Stephens, pres; Elinor Lewis Stephens, gen mgr; Ken Shepherd, opns dir; Tom Laengle, gen sls mgr; John Trapane, progmg dir; Rudy Johnson, chief engr.

KVKI-FM—May 1959: 96.5 mhz; 95 kw. Ant 797 ft. TL: N32 35 38 W93 51 39. Stereo. Hrs opn: 24. 1300 Grimmett Dr. (71107). (318) 221-9696. FAX: (318) 222-0758. Licensee: Progressive United Corp. (acq 8-10-90; $1.5 million with co-located FM; FTR 8-27-90). Rep: Katz & Powell. Format: Adult contemp. News staff one. Target aud: 25-54; female. ■ William R. Fry, pres & gen mgr; John Hill, opns mgr & prom dir; Don Zimmerman, gen sls mgr; Howard Clark, progmg mgr; Katherine Usher, news dir & pub affrs dir; Tommy Moore, vp engrg. ■ Rates: $35; 30; 35; 18.

KWKH(AM)—September 1925: 1130 khz; 50 kw-U, DA-N. TL: N32 42 15 W93 52 52. Hrs opn: 24. Box 31130 (71130-1130); 6341 Westport Ave. (71129-2498). (318) 688-1130. FAX: (318) 687-8574. Licensee: Shreveport Great Empire Broadcasting. Group Owner: Great Empire Broadcasting Inc. (acq 6-16-77). Net: MBS. Rep: Christal. Format: Country. News staff 4; news progmg 18 plus hrs wkly. Target aud: 25-54. Spec prog: Bluegrass one hr wkly. ■ F. F. Lynch, pres; Frank Gunn, vp & gen mgr; Steve McDonald, opns mgr & progmg dir; Jim Vidler, gen sls mgr; Tim Carr, prom dir; Danny Fox, mus dir; John Lee, news dir; Johnny Lafitte, engrg mgr; Peter Palagonia, chief engr.

KWKH-FM—Nov 5, 1948: 94.5 mhz; 99 kw. Ant 1,096 ft. TL: N32 40 13 W93 55 59. Stereo. Hrs opn: 24. Dups AM 40%. news progmg 15 hrs wkly.

Slidell

WLTS-FM—Sept 8, 1970: 105.3 mhz; 100 kw. Ant 902 ft. TL: N29 58 57 W89 57 09. Stereo. 3525 N. Causeway Blvd., Metarie (70002). (504) 834-9587. Licensee: Phase II Broadcasting Inc. (acq 1-1-74). Net: CBS Spectrum, Unistar. Format: Adult contemp, lite rock. ■ Edmund J. Muniz, pres, gen mgr & gen sls mgr; Bob Mitchell, progmg dir; Johnny Scott, mus dir; Ben Sudduth, news dir; Ernest L. Harvey Jr., chief engr.

WSLA(AM)—Dec 5, 1963: 1560 khz; 1 kw-U, DA-N. TL: N30 15 08 W89 45 46. Stereo. Hrs opn: 24. Box 1175, 38230 Coast Blvd. (70459). (504) 643-1560. Licensee: MAPA Broadcasting L.L.C. (acq 7-2-93; $100; FTR 8-2-93). Net: MBS, CNN. Format: News/talk. News staff 7; news progmg 12 hrs wkly. Target aud: 25 plus; news intensive audience. ■ Paul Mayoral, pres & gen mgr; Jim Summers, opns mgr & progmg dir; Danny Miller, chief engr. ■ Rates: $25; 15; 20; 10.

Springhill

KTKC(FM)—Sept 5, 1975: 92.7 mhz; 3 kw. Ant 174 ft. TL: N33 00 28 W93 28 43. Stereo. Hrs opn: 18. Box 127 (71075). (318) 539-4616. Licensee: Springhill Broadcasting Co. (acq 2-3-59). Net: ABC, SMN; L.A. Net. Format: Oldies. News progmg 10 hrs wkly. Target aud: 35-54. ■ Johnnie K. Hill, pres; David Graham, gen mgr; Keith Hill, progmg dir; Rick Benson, chief engr. ■ Rates: $7; 7; 7; 6.

KBSF(AM)—Co-owned with KTKC(FM). June 30, 1954: 1460 khz; 1 kw-D, 220 w-N. TL: N33 00 02 W93 28 43. Hrs opn: Sunrise-sunset. Prog sep from FM. Format:

Oldies, Black. Spec prog: Gospel 3 hrs wkly. ■ Johnie Hill, pres. ■ Rates: $5; 5; 5; na.

Sulphur

KEZM(AM)—1955: 1310 khz; 500 w-D, 50 w-N, DA-2. TL: N30 13 27 W93 22 44. Stereo. Hrs opn: 24. 101 W. Napoleon (70663); 320 Parish Rd. (70663). (318) 527-3611; (318) 527-9644. FAX: (318) 527-0213. Licensee: Ladas Broadcasting Corp. (acq 1-87; $163,280; FTR 12-8-86). Net: SMN. Rep: Katz & Powell. Wash atty: Smithwick & Belendiuk. Format: Oldies. News staff 2; news progmg 7 hrs wkly. Target aud: 25-45; up scale baby-boomers. Spec prog: Loc sports. ■ Harry Ladas, pres & gen mgr; Margaret Corbin, sls dir; Hal Comeaux, progmg dir & news dir. ■ Rates: $15.50; 14.50; 15.50; 11.50.

KTQQ(FM)—Dec 17, 1977: 100.9 mhz; 3 kw. Ant 328 ft. TL: N30 14 15 W93 17 56. Stereo. Hrs opn: 24. Box 2418 (70664-2418); 101 Advent Ave. (70663). (318) 625-7777. FAX: (318) 625-7787. Licensee: 21st Century Communications Inc. (acq 3-91; $650,000). Net: La. Net. Rep: Christal. Wash atty: Kaye, Scholer. Format: Country. News staff one. Target aud: General; Adult country music fans. ■ Keith Baine Martin, CEO, pres, gen mgr, gen sls mgr & natl sls mgr; Christopher J. Dunn, CFO & vp; John Breland, prom mgr; Mike Ruiz, progmg dir; Gary Shannon, mus dir; Alan Dickerson, chief engr.

KYKZ(FM)—See Lake Charles.

Tallulah

KBYO(AM)—Sept 4, 1954: 1360 khz; 500 w-D. TL: N32 25 37 W91 13 15. Box 1112 (71282); Hwy. 80 W. (71282). (318) 574-1500. Licensee: Sharing Inc. (acq 5-89; $103,000; FTR 1-16-89). Format: Urban contemp. News progmg 10 hrs wkly. Target aud: 18-54. ■ Tommy Johnson, pres; Everet J. Stroop, gen mgr & gen sls mgr.

KBYO-FM—Apr 29, 1983: 104.9 mhz; 3 kw. Ant 320 ft. TL: N29 45 35 W90 49 30 (CP: 104.5 mhz, 25kw). Stereo. Prog sep from AM. Net: ABC/I. Format: Country. News staff 2; news progmg 80 hrs wkly. ■ Everet J. Stroop, vp, gen mgr & gen sls mgr; Cherri Jones, progmg dir; Laura Cowley, mus dir.

Thibodaux

***KNSU(FM)**—Feb 15, 1972: 91.5 mhz; 10 w-horiz. Ant 292 ft. TL: N29 47 35 W90 48 09 (CP: 91.3 mhz, 3 kw, ant 285 ft., TL: N29 45 35 W90 49 30). Hrs opn: 10 AM-2 AM (Mon-Fri), noon-2 AM (Sat-Sun). Box 2664, Nicholls State Univ. (70310). (504) 448-4448. Licensee: Board of Trustees, Nicholls State Univ. Format: Classic rock, progsv. News progmg 10 hrs wkly. Target aud: 18 plus. ■ Simeon Wildman, stn mgr; Holly Naquin, progmg dir; Richie Parker, mus dir; Hoyt Ledet, news dir; Robert Blazier, chief engr.

KTIB(AM)—Dec 24, 1953: 640 khz; 5 kw-D, 1 kw-N, DA-2. TL: N29 50 05 W90 54 48. Stereo. Hrs opn: 5:30 AM-midnight. Box 682, 108 Green St. (70301). (504) 447-9006. FAX: (504) 446-2338. Licensee: LaTerr Broadcasting Corp. (acq 11-16-73). Net: NBC. Format: MOR. News staff 2; news progmg 13 hrs wkly. Target aud: 35 plus. Spec prog: Fr 3 hrs wkly. ■ James J. Buquet, pres; Raymond Saadi, gen mgr; Marie S. Bergeron, stn mgr; Lynn Pitts, news dir; Roy Pugh, chief engr.

KXOR(FM)—May 1, 1966: 106.3 mhz; 6 kw. Ant 302 ft. TL: N29 43 18 W90 46 33. Stereo. Hrs opn: 24. 106 Ridgefield Rd. (70301). (504) 446-5604; (504) 876-7625. FAX: (504) 446-5605. Licensee: KXOR Inc. Group owner: Gulf South Broadcasters Ltd. Net: ABC/FM, Unistar, La. Net. Format: Contemp hit. News progmg 20 hrs wkly. Target aud: 18-54. Spec prog: LSU Sports, local high school football. ■ Bobby Martinez, gen mgr & gen sls mgr; Max Johnson, progmg dir & mus dir; Kevin Duplantis, chief engr. ■ Rates: $20; 20; 20; 20.

Tioga

KLAA(FM)—May 25, 1984: 103.5 mhz; 50 kw. Ant 476 ft. TL: N31 25 39 W92 24 18. Stereo. Hrs opn: 24. 1115 Texas Ave., Alexandria (71301). (318) 445-1234. FAX: (318) 445-7231. Licensee: Cajun Communications Inc. (acq 11-5-92; $6,928; FTR 11-30-92). Net: MBS. Rep: D & R Radio. Wash atty: Dow, Lohnes & Albertson. Format: Country. News staff one; news progmg 4 hrs wkly. Target aud: 25-54; working people, upscale professionals. ■ Roger Cabanis, pres; Taylor Thompson, gen mgr. ■ Rates: $24; 14; 24; 11.

KXKW(AM)—Not on air, target date unknown: 680 khz; 380 w-D, 740 w-N, DA-N. TL: N31 25 39 W92 24 18. 123 E. Main St., Lafayette (70501). Licensee: Cavaness Broadcasting Inc.

Varnado

WBOX-FM—November 1985: 92.9 mhz; 3 kw. Ant 321 ft. TL: N30 54 10 W89 57 36. Stereo. Box 280, Bogalusa (70427). (504) 732-4288; (504) 839-2990. FAX: (601) 736-2617. Licensee: Bogue Chitto Communications Co. (group owner). Format: Contemp country. ■ Thomas McDaniel, pres; Ben R.R. Strickland, gen mgr; Chris Blackburn, opns mgr.

Vidalia

KAIN(AM)—Licensed to Vidalia. See Natchez, Miss.

KVLA(AM)—December 1984: 1400 khz; 1 kw-U. TL: N31 34 01 W91 25 16. Box 1129, No. 12 Dotson (71373). (318) 336-7466. Licensee: Robert Cupit (acq 9-12-89; $72,000; $1,000 monthly; FTR 10-2-89). Net: CBS Spectrum; La. Net. Wash atty: Lee Peltzman. Format: Btfl mus, big band. Target aud: 21 plus. Spec prog: Talk 15 hrs (Rush Limbaugh Show), class 7 hrs wkly; high school and college football. ■ Bob Cupit, pres, gen mgr, news dir & chief engr; Lou Cupit, gen sls mgr; David Cupit, progmg dir. ■ Rates: $7; 7; 7; 6.

WQNZ(AM)—See Natchez, Miss.

Ville Platte

KVPI(AM)—November 1953: 1050 khz; 250 w-D, 10 w-N. TL: N30 41 39 W92 18 46. Drawer J, 809 W. LaSalle St. (70586). (318) 363-2124. FAX: (318) 363-3574. Licensee: Ville Platte Broadcasting Co. Format: C&W. Spec prog: Fr 15 hrs, farm 12 hrs wkly. ■ Lionel B. Deville, pres; Jim Soileau, gen mgr & gen sls mgr; Bonnie Fontenot, opns mgr; Butch DeVille, prom mgr; Mark Lane, progmg dir & news dir; Cheryl DeBaillon, mus dir; J.L. Sylvester, chief engr. ■ Rates: $8.75; 7.50; 8.75; 7.50.

KVPI-FM—Feb 26, 1967: 92.5 mhz; 3 kw-H. Ant 220 ft. TL: N30 41 39 W92 18 46. Stereo. Dups AM 20%. Format: Adult contemp, oldies. Spec prog: Black 10 hrs wkly. ■ Rates: Same as AM.

Vivian

KNCB(AM)—Apr 9, 1966: 1320 khz; 5 kw-D. TL: N32 54 08 W93 58 59. Box 1072, 17525 Hwy. One N. (71082). (318) 375-3278; (318) 375-5483. FAX: (318) 375-3329. Licensee: North Caddo Broadcasting Co. (acq 4-9-66). Net: AP. Format: C&W, oldies, relg. News staff one. Target aud: General. ■ Ruby J. Collins, gen mgr & gen sls mgr; Cherry Garner, progmg dir, mus dir & pub affrs dir; Gary Spikes, news dir; Lloyd Cox, chief engr. ■ Rates: $10; 8.15; 10; na.

KNCB-FM—Not on air, target date unknown: 95.7 mhz; 3 kw. Ant 285 ft. TL: N32 54 07 W93 58 58. ■ Ruby Collins, gen mgr.

Washington

KNEK(AM)—Aug 18, 1980: 1190 khz; 250 w-D. TL: N30 35 09 W92 04 00. Box 598 (70589). (318) 826-3921. FAX: (318) 826-3206. Licensee: David R. Price (acq 1-16-89; $3,900; FTR 6-12-89). Net: La. Net. Format: C&W. Spec prog: Farm 4 hrs wkly. ■ David Price, gen mgr; Tyrone Davis, progmg dir.

KNEK-FM—1989: 104.7 mhz; 3 kw. Ant 223 ft. TL: N30 26 45 W92 09 24. Prog sep from AM.

West Monroe

KMBS(AM)—August 1956: 1310 khz; 5 kw-D, 49 w-N. TL: N32 29 02 W92 09 10. 613 N. 5th St. (71294). (318) 387-1333. FAX: (318) 325-0081. Licensee: Red Bear Broadcasting (acq 6-10-93; $200,000; FTR 6-28-93). Format: News/talk. ■ Chuck Redden, gen mgr; Doug Seegers, sls mgr, mus dir & news dir; Ernest Sandidge, chief engr.

KYEA(FM)—Aug 1, 1967: 98.3 mhz; 50 kw. Ant 492 ft. TL: N32 39 38 W91 59 28. Stereo. Hrs opn: 24. 516 Martin St. (71292). (318) 322-1491. FAX: (318) 325-7203. Licensee: Phoenix Broadcasting Corp. Net: ABC/C. Rep: D & R Radio. Format: Urban contemp. Target aud: 18-54; mid to upper income. Spec prog: Gospel 20 hrs wkly. ■ Frank Stemley, pres; Bradley Wilkinson, gen mgr, stn mgr & vp sls; Barbara Dawson-Monk, gen sls mgr; Kelly Karson, prom dir; Rocky Love, progmg dir & mus dir; Rodney Evans, chief engr. ■ Rates: $38; 32; 38; 22.

White Castle

KKAY(AM)—November 1976: 1590 khz; 1 kw-D. TL: N30 11 01 W91 06 27. Hrs opn: 6 AM-sunset. 3365 Hwy. One S., Donaldsonville (70346). (504) 473-5764. FAX: (504) 473-6397. Licensee: La Fourche Valley Enterprises. Format: Relg. News progmg 6 hrs wkly. Target aud: 25 plus; relg with a love of Southern and Black gospel. ■ Michael P. Leblanc, pres, gen mgr & chief engr; Patricia Guillot, gen sls mgr; Ric Rousseau, news dir.

Winnfield

KVCL(AM)—Dec 17, 1955: 1270 khz; 1 kw-D, 500 w-CH. TL: N31 56 58 W92 37 37 (CP: 820 w-D). Stereo. Box 548, Harrison Bdcstg. Org. Bldg., No. One, KVCL Rd. (71483). (318) 628-7355; (318) 628-5822. FAX: (318) 628-7355. Licensee: Harrison Broadcast Organization Inc. (acq 3-7-90; $475,000 with co-located FM; FTR 3-26-90). Net: Unistar; La. Net. Wash atty: Brinig & Bernstein. Format: Country, div. News staff 2; news progmg 21 hrs wkly. Target aud: General. Spec prog: Black 3 hrs, relg 15 hrs, gospel 5 hrs, big band 3 hrs wkly. ■ George B. Harrison, CEO, pres, gen mgr & mktg mgr; Patricia J. Harrison, exec vp, prom mgr & pub affrs dir; George Feger, gen sls mgr; Meloney Brooks, natl sls mgr & adv mgr; Mike Parker, progmg dir & asst mus dir; Don Garrett, news dir; Woody Fryar, George B. Harrison, chiefs engr. ■ Rates: $10; 10; 10; 10.

KVCL-FM—Nov 3, 1966: 92.1 mhz; 6 kw. Ant 284 ft. TL: N31 56 58 W92 37 37. Stereo. Hrs opn: 24. Format: Country. ■ WINN Cable TV affil.

Winnsboro

KMAR(AM)—March 1, 1957: 1570 khz; 1 kw-D. TL: N32 11 40 W91 45 30. Box 312 (71295). (318) 435-5141. Licensee: Boeuf River Broadcasting Co. Group owner: The Radio Group (acq 11-89; $200,000 with co-located FM; FTR 11-6-89). Format: Country. ■ Tom Gay, gen mgr; Pete Peebles, stn mgr & opns mgr; Terry Hibbard, natl sls mgr; Pat Hurley, chief engr.

KMAR-FM—August 1969: 95.9 mhz; 3 kw. Ant 171 ft. TL: N32 11 40 W91 45 30. Stereo. Dups AM 100%.

Maine

Auburn

WKZS(FM)—February 1977: 99.9 mhz; 50 kw. Ant 492 ft. TL: N43 57 07 W70 17 46. Stereo. Hrs opn: 24. Box 929, Lewiston (04240). (207) 786-2496; (207) 784-5581. FAX: (207) 784-5581. Licensee: The Great Down East Wireless Talking Machine Co. (acq 1977). Rep: D & R Radio; Ginsberg, Feldman & Brest. Format: Adult contemp. News staff 2; news progmg 5 hrs wkly. Target aud: 25-54. ■ Ronald R. Frizzell, pres, gen mgr & gen sls mgr; Mark Ericson, opns mgr; Dave Bailey, prom mgr; Ann Matthews, progmg dir; Matt Ledin, news dir; Tom Whiting, chief engr.

WTHT(FM)—See Portland.

WZOU(AM)—See Lewiston.

Augusta

WABK(AM)—See Gardiner.

WABK-FM—See Gardiner.

WFAU(AM)—Oct 2, 1946: 1340 khz; 1 kw-U. TL: N44 19 43 W69 45 53. 160 Bangor St. (04330). (207) 622-4944. FAX: (207) 622-1340. Licensee: Seacoast Broadcasting Inc. (acq 5-7-88). Net: Unistar, CBS. Rep: Kettell-Carter. Format: MOR. News staff 2; news progmg 3 hrs wkly. Target aud: 35 plus. Spec prog: Fr 2 hrs wkly. ■ William Devine, pres & gen mgr; G.W. Mitchell Dugan, gen sls mgr; Don Brown, progmg dir; Suzanne Goucher, news dir; Richard Hyatt, chief engr.

WKCG(FM)—Co-owned with WFAU(AM). July 1961: 101.3 mhz; 50 kw. Ant 321 ft. TL: N44 18 51 W69 50 03. Stereo. Prog sep from AM. Format: Contemp country. Target aud: 25-54. ■ Bob Dow, prom mgr; Jim Walker, mus dir.

WMME(AM)—Feb 23, 1932: 1400 khz; 1 kw-U. TL: N44 17 30 W69 46 27. Hrs opn: 24. 52 Western Ave., Augusta (04330).] (207) 623-4735. FAX: (207) 626-5948. Licensee: Pilot Communications of Augusta Inc. (acq 2-18-93; $1.1 million with co-located FM; FTR 3-8-93). Rep: D & R Radio. Format: Contemp hit. News staff one. Target aud: 20-40; young adults. ■ Jim Mann, gen mgr; Tom Mitchel, progmg dir; Jeff Andrews, mus dir; Renee Nelson, news dir; Dick Hyatt, chief engr.

WMME-FM—Jan 14, 1981: 92.3 mhz; 50 kw. Ant 500 ft. TL: N44 20 07 W69 41 01. Stereo. Dups AM 100%.

Bangor

WABI(AM)—1924: 910 khz; 5 kw-U, DA-N. TL: N44 46 44 W68 44 22. Hrs opn: 18 27 State St. (04401). (207) 947-9100. FAX: (207) 94-RADIO; TWX: 910-240-1221. Licensee: Rockland Radio Corp. Net: Unistar, CNN. Rep: Torbet, Kettell-Carter. Wash atty: Dow, Lohnes & Albertson. Format: "Memories." News staff one; news progmg 4 hrs wkly. Target aud: 35 plus. ■ Peter K. Orne Sr., pres & gen mgr; Micah Malloy, gen sls mgr; George Hale, progmg dir; Jon Small, news dir; Stacey Brann, chief engr. ■ WABI-TV affil.

WYOU-FM—Co-owned with WABI(AM). Mar 15, 1961: 97.1 mhz; 5 kw. Ant 1,230 ft. TL: N44 42 13 W69 04 07. Stereo. Hrs opn: 24. Net: ABC/E. Format: C&W. News staff one; news progmg 2 hrs wkly. Target aud: General. ■ Neil Orne, opns mgr.

WEZQ(FM)—June 9, 1976: 92.9 mhz; 20 kw. Ant 787 ft. TL: N44 45 35 W68 33 55. Stereo. Hrs opn: 24. Box 1129, 68 State St., Ellsworth (04401). (207) 667-9555. FAX: (207) 667-2436. Licensee: Dudman Communications Corp. (acq 1993; $300,000; FTR 9-6-93). Net: Unistar. Rep: D & R Radio. Wash atty: Fisher, Wayland, Cooper & Leader. Format: Soft adult contemp., love songs. News staff one. Target aud: 25-54. ■ Martha Dudman, pres & gen mgr; Fred Miller, vp opns & vp progmg; Gail Ruwe, gen sls mgr; Jason Dumont, prom dir; Laura Neal, news dir & pub affrs dir; Dick Hyatt, chief engr.

***WHCF(FM)**—Aug 10, 1981: 88.5 mhz; 100 kw. Ant 1,604 ft. TL: N45 07 46 W68 21 28. Stereo. Hrs opn: 24. Box 5000, WHCF, 1476 Broadway (04402-5000). (207) 947-2751. (207) 947-6576. FAX: (207) 947-0010. Licensee: Bangor Baptist Church. Net: USA, MBN, Skylight. Wash atty: Harry Martin. Format: Inspirational Christian. News staff one; news progmg 7 hrs wkly. Target aud: 30-55. ■ Richard Rockwell, pres; Thomas Obey, gen mgr & adv mgr; James McLeod, opns mgr & progmg dir; Charlie Hartman, prom dir; Mike Dalton, mus dir; Virgil Phinney, news dir; Hal Welch, chief engr.

***WHSN(FM)**—September 1974: 89.3 mhz; 140 w. Ant 69 ft. TL: N44 49 30 W68 47 48. Stereo. One College Cir. (04401). (207) 947-3987. FAX: (207) 947-3987. Licensee: Husson College Board of Trustees. Format: Top-40, AOR. News progmg 7 hrs wkly. Target aud: 12-25; high school and college students. Spec prog: Alternative/new rock 8 hrs wkly. ■ Ben Haskell, gen mgr; Dave MacLaughlin, chief engr.

WKIT-FM—See Brewer.

***WMEH(FM)**—Sept 14, 1970: 90.9 mhz; 13.5 kw. Ant 850 ft. TL: N44 45 36 W68 33 59. Stereo. Hrs opn: 24. 1450 Lisbon St., Lewiston (04240); 65 Texas Ave. (04401). (207) 783-9101; (207) 941-1010. FAX: (207) 942-2857. Licensee: Maine Public Broadcasting Corp. (acq 6-23-92; FTR 7-13-92). Net: NPR, APR. Wash atty: Dow, Lohnes & Albertson. Format: Classical, pub affrs. ■ Robert H. Gardiner, pres; Russell Peotter, dev dir & mktg dir; Deb Turner, dev mgr; Bernard Roscetti, progmg dir; Charles Beck, progmg mgr & mus dir; Vic Hathaway, asst mus dir; Andrea DeLeon, news dir; Alexander G. Maxwell Jr., engrg dir; David Roy, chief engr.

WWFX(FM)—See Belfast.

WWMJ(FM)—See Ellsworth.

WYOU-FM—Listing follows WABI(AM).

WZON(AM)—December 1926: 620 khz; 5 kw-U, DA-N. TL: N44 49 44 W68 47 08. Hrs opn: 24. Box 1929 (04402); 861 Broadway (04401). (207) 942-4656. FAX: (207) 942-4657. Licensee: The Zone Corp. (acq 9-1-93; $236,200 FTR 9-27-93). Net: ARN, CBS, NBC Talknet. Format: Talk, news/talk. News staff 2; news progmg 40 hrs wkly. Target aud: General; information & entertainment seekers. ■ Brent Slowikowski, gen mgr; Linda Cummings, gen sls mgr & natl sls mgr; Brent Cummings, prom dir; Kathy Philbrick, news dir; Howard Soule, chief engr. ■ Rates: $20; 15; 12; 10.

Bar Harbor

WEJS(FM)—Not on air, target date unknown: 107.7 mhz; 6.3 kw. Ant 39 ft. Licensee: Richard D. Bush.

WLKE(FM)—Not on air, target date unknown: 99.1 mhz; 16.7 kw. Ant 403 ft. TL: N44 32 53 W68 18 53. Box 580, Yarmouth (04096). Licensee: Star Broadcasting of Maine Inc. (acq 1-3-92; $45,000; FTR 2-24-92).

Bath

WCME(FM)—See Boothbay Harbor.

WJTO(AM)—Sept 30, 1957: 730 khz; 1 kw-D, 29 w-N. TL: N43 52 39 W69 50 49 (CP: 10 kw-D, 500 w-N). Hrs opn: 24. Rebroadcasts WLAM(AM) Gorham 96%. Box 308, Austin Rd. (04530-0708). (207) 443-6671. FAX: (207) 443-8610. Licensee: Kaleidescope Inc. (acq 1-91; $701,750 with co-located FM). Net: ABC/E. Wash atty: Wilmer, Cutler & Pickering. Format: Music of your life. News staff one; news progmg 3 hrs wkly. Target aud: General, 40 plus; adults in Bath/Brunswick region. ■ J. Frank Burke, pres & gen mgr; Susan M. Burke, sr vp; Rick Reilly, gen sls mgr; Liz Hamlin, progmg dir, mus dir & pub affrs dir; Richard Hyatt, chief engr. ■ Rates: $6; 6; 6; 4.

WKRH(FM)—Co-owned with WJTO(AM). June 1971: 105.9 mhz; 50 kw. Ant 499 ft. TL: N44 04 09 W69 55 28. Stereo. Hrs opn: 24. Prog sep from AM. Net: ABC/SMN. Format: Classic rock. News staff one; news progmg one hr wkly. Target aud: 25-44. ■ J. Frank Burke, CEO; Susan Burke, exec vp; Mac Dickson, progmg dir; Liz Hamlin, news dir. ■ Rates: $18; 18; 18; 14.

Belfast

WWFX(FM)—March 7, 1986: 104.7 mhz; 10 kw. Ant 1,099 ft. TL: N44 34 51 W68 53 51. Stereo. Suite 207, 12 Acme Rd., Brewer (04412). (207) 989-7363. FAX: (207) 989-7366. Licensee: Group H Radio Inc. (acq 12-18-92; $525,000; FTR 1-11-93). Rep: Banner. Format: Contemp hit. News staff one. Target aud: 18-49. ■ George Baines, gen mgr; Sky Taylor, opns mgr, prom mgr & news dir; Rod Towne, gen sls mgr & adv dir; Kid Kelly, mus dir; Neil Wetmore, chief engr.

Biddeford

WIDE(AM)—1948: 1400 khz; 1 kw-U. TL: N43 28 52 W70 29 08. Hrs opn: 19. Box 667, Business Park, Alfred Rd. (04005). (207) 282-5121. FAX: (207) 282-3228. Licensee: Fuller-Jeffrey Broadcasting Corp. (acq 12-18-92; $600,000 with co-located FM; FTR 1-18-93). Net: ABC/I, CBS, Mutual. Rep: Keystone (unwired net). Wash atty: Bryan Cave. Format: News/talk, sports. News staff 2; news progmg 10 hrs wkly. Target aud: 25-54; upscale progressional. ■ R.F. "Doc" Fuller, pres; Eve Rubins, gen mgr; J.J. Jeffrey, opns dir; John Carter, sls dir; Carl Dana, progmg dir; John Olore, news dir; Eugene Terwilliger, engrg dir. ■ Rates: $35; 30; 28; 16.

WSTG(FM)—Co-owned with WIDE(AM). Aug 1972: 94.3 mhz; 13 kw. Ant 449 ft. TL: N43 32 34 W70 24 12 (CP: 12 kw, ant 472 ft.). Stereo. Hrs opn: 24. Prog sep from AM. One City Ctr., Portland (04101). Format: Rock. News staff one. Target aud: General; today's adult. ■ Tom Clark, mus dir. ■ Rates: $40; 30; 25; 20.

Blue Hill

***WERU-FM**—June 1, 1988: 89.9 mhz; 15 kw. Ant 899 ft. TL: N44 26 04 W68 35 25. Stereo. Hrs opn: 6 AM-1 AM. The Henhouse, Blue Hill Falls (04615). (207) 374-2313. Licensee: Salt Pond Community Broadcasting Co. Format: Div, educ. Target aud: General. Spec prog: Class 5 hrs, jazz 18 hrs, folk 15 hrs, blues 5 hrs, reggae 4 hrs, Afro-beat 4 hrs, pub affrs 9 hrs wkly. ■ Paul Brayton, pres; Jeffrey Kobrock, gen mgr; Becky McCall, opns mgr; Laura Grunfeld, dev dir; Hank Whitsett, gen sls mgr; Jeffrey Hansen, progmg dir; Cathy Melio, news dir; Don McKillop, chief engr.

Boothbay Harbor

WCME(FM)—April 1, 1984: 96.7 mhz; 25 kw. Ant 449 ft. TL: N44 01 31 W69 34 17. Stereo. Hrs opn: 24. Box 580, Yarmouth (04096); (207) 865-1199. FAX: (207) 865-3299. Licensee: Bay Communications Inc. Net: SMN, CNN. Wash atty: Brown, Finn & Nietert. Format: Country. News staff one; news progmg 12 hrs wkly. Target aud: 25-49; younger than traditional country. ■ Robert J. Cole, pres; Roger Fenn, gen mgr; Ken Minott, progmg dir & mus dir; Thomas Cole, engrg dir; Thomas R. Cole, chief engr.

Brewer

WKIT-FM—Feb 14, 1979: 100.3 mhz; 50 kw. Ant 850 ft. TL: N44 40 39 W68 45 15. Stereo. Hrs opn: 24. Box 2637, Bangor (04402-2637). Pearl Building, 8 Harlow St., Bangor (04401). (207) 990-2800. FAX: (207) 990-2444. Licensee: H&L Broadcasting Inc. (acq 5-1-91; $293,000 with co-located AM; FTR 5-20-91). Rep: Eastman. Wash atty: Fisher, Wayland, Cooper & Leader. Format: AOR. News staff one. Target aud: 18-49. ■ Raymond Lynch Jr., CEO; Eric Hake, exec vp; Michael O'Hara, gen mgr, vp mktg & mus dir; Dan Comeau, rgnl sls mgr; Bobby Russell, progmg dir; Glen Simpson, news dir; Howie Soles, chief engr. ■ Rates: $48; 34; 40; 25.

WNSW(AM)—Co-owned with WKIT-FM. 1974: 1200 khz; 10 kw-U, DA-1. TL: N44 46 23 W68 49 45. Hrs opn: 5 AM-midnight. Format: News, sports, weather. News progmg 133 hrs wkly. Target aud: 25-54; post grad. ■ Rates: $16; 14; 16; 13.

WQCB(FM)—Jan 20, 1986: 106.5 mhz; 98 kw. Ant 1,079 ft. TL: N45 03 26 W69 11 27. Stereo. Hrs opn: 24. Box 100, 49 Acme Rd. (04412). (207) 989-5631. FAX: (207) 989-5685. Licensee: Castle Broadcasting. Net: AP. Rep: McGavren Guild. Wash atty: Koteen & Naftalin. Format: Contemp country. News staff 2; news progmg 4 hrs wkly. Target aud: 25-54. ■ Katherine K. Dolley, gen mgr; Mark Parent, opns mgr & prom mgr; Candace Doucette, natl sls mgr; Robert S. Duchesne, progmg dir; Dave Glidden, mus dir; Suzanne Thomas, news dir; Neal Wetmore, chief engr.

Brunswick

***WBOR(FM)**—April 1957: 91.1 mhz; 300 w-H. Ant 154 ft. TL: N43 54 34 W69 57 43. Stereo. Hrs opn: 7 AM-2 AM. Moulton Union, Bowdoin College (04011). (207) 725-3250; (207) 725-3210. FAX: (207) 725-3510. Licensee: President & Trustees of Bowdoin College. Format: Div. Target aud: General. Spec prog: Class 10 hrs, jazz 20 hrs, folk 12 hrs, urban contemp 10 hrs, reggae 10 hrs, sports talk 5 hrs wkly. ■ Bill Fruth, gen mgr; Bart D'Alauro, stn mgr; Brian Curtis, opns mgr & news dir; Zach Hooper, dev dir; Erin Hunter, dev mgr; Marisa Langston, mktg dir & adv mgr; Rachel Rudman, mktg mgr, prom dir & adv dir; John Lawler, progmg dir; Christopher Hever, mus dir; Timothy Rotramel, asst mus dir; Sanjay Hegde, pub affrs dir.

WCLZ(AM)—December 1955: 900 khz; 1 kw-D, 66 w-N. TL: N43 55 40 W69 59 43. Box 2007 (04104). (207) 725-5505. FAX: (207) 725-5121. Licensee: Riverside Broadcasting L.P. (acq 5-18-92; $525,000 with co-located FM; FTR 6-8-92). Net: BRN. Format: Business. Target aud: 25-54. ■ Michael Waggoner, gen mgr; Andy Armstrong, chief engr.

WCLZ-FM—Apr 11, 1965: 98.9 mhz; 48 kw. Ant 400 ft. TL: N43 55 40 W69 59 43. Stereo. Prog sep from AM. Format: New adult contemp. News staff one; news progmg 2 hrs wkly. ■ Kim Anderson, gen mgr.

WKRH(FM)—See Bath.

Calais

***WMED(FM)**—Nov 1983: 89.7 mhz; 30 kw. Ant 525 ft. TL: N45 01 44 W67 19 25. Stereo. Rebroadcasts WMEH(FM) Bangor 100%. 1450 Lisbon St., Lewiston (04240); 65 Texas Ave., Bangor (04401). (207) 783-9101; (207) 941-1010. FAX: (207) 783-5193; (207) 942-2857. Licensee: Maine Public Broadcasting Corp. (acq 6-23-92). Net: NPR, APR. Format: Classical, pub affrs. ■ Robert H. Gardiner, pres; Russell Peotter, dev dir & mktg dir; Deb Turner, dev mgr; Bernard Roscetti, progmg dir; Charles Beck, progmg mgr & mus dir; Vic Hathoway, asst mus dir; Andrea DeLeon, news dir; Alexander G. Maxwell Jr., engrg dir; David Roy, chief engr.

WQDY(AM)—July 1, 1959: 1230 khz; 1 kw-U. TL: N45 10 55 W67 15 59. Hrs opn: 5 AM-midnight. Box 403, 281 Main St. (04619). (207) 454-7545. FAX: (207) 454-3062. Licensee: IBC Inc. (acq 10-78). Net: ABC/I. Wash atty: Fletcher, Heald & Hildreth. Format: Adult contemp, classic rock, country. Target aud: General. Spec prog: Ballroom 2 hrs, relg 2 hrs wkly. ■ Dan Hollingdale, pres; Mike Goodine, gen mgr & gen sls mgr; Armina Hansen, rgnl sls mgr; Rob Hunter, prom dir; Bill Conley, progmg dir & mus dir; Tom McLaughlin (US), Mac Nevers (Canada), news dirs; Roger Holst, chief engr.

WQDY-FM—Jan 14, 1976: 92.7 mhz; 3 kw. Ant 299 ft. TL: N45 10 02 W67 16 38. Stereo. Hrs opn: 5 AM-midnight. Dups AM 100%.

Camden

WQSS(FM)—May 1988: 102.5 mhz; 7.9 kw. Ant 1,201 ft. TL: N44 12 40 W69 09 06. Stereo. Hrs opn: 24. Box 1228, 21 Elm St. (04843). (207) 236-2452. FAX: (207) 236-4227. Licensee: Meguntícook Gramaphone and Radio Inc. (acq 7-86; $50,000; FTR 7-7-86). Net: ABC. Rep: D & R Radio. Wash atty: Ginsberg Feldman. Format: Adult contemp. News staff one; news progmg 10 hrs wkly. Target aud: 25-54. ■ Kevin Keogh, pres & gen mgr; Sandy Ellsworth, gen sls mgr; Carolyn Roney, progmg dir; Tim McLeod, news dir; Bob Perry, chief engr. ■ Rates: $30; 25; 30; 22.

Stations in the U.S.

Maine

Caribou

WBPW(FM)—See Presque Isle.

WCXU(FM)—Nov 15, 1986: 97.7 mhz; 6 kw. Ant 328 ft. TL: N46 47 26 W67 55 07. Stereo. Hrs opn: 24. R.R. 2, 2100 E. Greenridge Rd. (04736-9609). (207) 473-7513. FAX: (207) 472-3221. Licensee: The Canxus Broadcasting Corp. (group owner). Net: NBC, Unistar. Rep: Kettell-Carter. Wash atty: Koteen & Naftalin. Format: Adult contemp, news. News staff one; news progmg 21 hrs wkly. Target aud: 25-54. ■ Dennis H. Curley, pres; Richard Chandler, gen mgr & opns mgr; Don Wilson, stn mgr; Mark Stewert, prom mgr & progmg dir; Douglas Christensen, news dir; Dennis Curley, chief engr. ■ Rates: $15.35; 11.40; 13.90; 6.80.

WFST(AM)—July 15, 1956: 600 khz; 5 kw-D, 127 w-N. TL: N46 53 12 W68 02 44 (CP: TL: N46 45 52 W67 59 23). Box 312, US Rt. 1, Presque Isle (04769). (207) 769-6600. Licensee: Northern Broadcast Ministries Inc. (acq 6-8-93; $54,000; FTR 6-28-93).

Dennysville

WVZD(FM)—Not on air, target date unknown: 102.9 mhz; 3 kw. Ant 328 ft. TL: N44 55 31 W67 19 47. Licensee: Brian E. Lamont.

Dexter

WGUY(FM)—1993: 102.1 mhz; 26.5 kw. Ant 672 ft. TL: N45 02 40 W69 15 01. Hrs opn: 24. Box 32, 378 Main St. (04930). (207) 924-1021. FAX: (207) 924-3299. Licensee: Innovative Advertising Consultants Inc. Wash atty: Fletcher, Heald & Hildreth. Format: Oldies (60s & 70s). News progmg 2 hrs wkly. Target aud: 25-54. ■ Daniel F. Priestley, pres & gen mgr; Jocelynn Priestley, exec vp & stn mgr; Tammy Dowling, vp sls; Dean Taylor, mus dir; Chuck Foster, news dir; Adam White, pub affrs dir; Neal Wetmore, chief engr. ■ Rates: $11; 10; 11; 8.

Dover-Foxcroft

WDME-FM—November 1980: 103.1 mhz; 3 kw. Ant 285 ft. TL: N45 12 58 W69 14 40 (CP: 4.8 kw, ant 358 ft., TL: N45 12 58 W69 14 34). Box 357, Guilford Rd. (04426). (207) 564-2642. FAX: (207) 564-8905. Licensee: Community Communications Inc. (acq 2-82; $3,135; FTR 2-16-82). Net: ABC/I. Rep: New England. Format: Adult contemp. ■ Frederic Hirsch, pres, gen mgr, progmg dir & news dir; Judy Craig, gen sls mgr; Sydney Marshall, chief engr.

Eastport

***WSHD(FM)**—April 1984: 91.7 mhz; 10 w. Ant 98 ft. TL: N44 54 30 W66 59 24. Shead High School, 89 High Street (04631). (207) 853-6254. FAX: (207) 853-2919. Licensee: Shead High School. Format: Div. Target aud: General. ■ Tom McLaughlin, gen mgr, prom mgr & progmg dir; Steve Cannon, mus dir; Roger Holst, chief engr.

Ellsworth

WDEA(AM)—Dec 13, 1958: 1370 khz; 5 kw-U, DA-2. TL: N44 28 00 W68 28 11. Box 1129, 68 State St. (04605). (207) 667-9555. FAX: (207) 667-2436. Licensee: Dudman Communications Corp. (acq 5-14-80; $600,000 with co-located FM; FTR 5-26-80). Net: CBS, SMN. Rep: D & R Radio. Wash atty: Fisher, Wayland, Cooper & Leader. Format: MOR, big band. News staff one. Target aud: 35 plus. Spec prog: loc high school sports. ■ Helen Sloane Dudman, chmn; Martha T. Dudman, pres & gen mgr; Fred Miller, vp opns; Gail Ruwe, gen sls mgr; Jason Dumont, prom dir; Dan White, progmg dir; Laura Neal, news & pub affrs dir; Richard Hyatt, chief engr.

WWMJ(FM)—Co-owned with WDEA(AM). Dec 27, 1965: 95.7 mhz; 11.5 kw. Ant 1,029 ft. TL: N44 39 31 W68 36 20. Stereo. Prog sep from AM. Net: ABC/I. Rep: D & R Radio. Format: Oldies. News staff one. Target aud: 25-54. ■ Linda Cummings, vp sls; Fred Miller, vp progmg; Dan White (asst), progmg dir.

WKSQ(FM)—May 27, 1982: 94.5 mhz; 11.5 kw. Ant 1,027 ft. TL: N44 39 31 W68 36 17. Stereo. Hrs opn: 24. Box 9494, Buttermilk Rd. (04605); Suite 212, One Cumberland Pl., Bangor (04401). (207) 667-7573. FAX: (207) 667-9494. Licensee: Acadia Broadcasting Co. Rep: Christal. Wash atty: Koteen & Naftalin. Format: Adult contemp. News staff 2; news progmg 7 hrs wkly. Target aud: 25-54. ■ Mark Osborne, pres; Natalie Knox, exec vp; Keryn W. Smith, gen sls mgr; Ric Tyler, prom mgr; Thom Shepard, progmg dir; Chris Mackowski, news dir.

WWMJ(FM)—Listing follows WDEA(AM).

Fairfield

WCTB(FM)—Not on air, target date unknown: 93.5 mhz; 13.5 kw. Ant 440 ft. TL: N44 44 07 W69 41 18. Stereo. R.R. 1, Box 157, Harrison (04040-9711). Licensee: Somerset County Broadcasting Inc.

Farmington

WKTJ-FM—Aug 21, 1973: 99.3 mhz; 1.5 kw. Ant 400 ft. TL: N44 39 22 W70 11 48. Hrs opn: 18. Box 590, Voter Hill Rd. (04938). (207) 778-3000; (207) 778-3400. FAX: (207) 778-3000. Licensee: Franklin Broadcasting Corp. Rep: Kettell-Carter. Format: Adult contemp, country. Target aud: 25 plus. ■ Alfredo Ibarguen, pres & chief engr; Claire Taylor, gen mgr; Muriel Powers, stn mgr; Steve Bull, gen sls mgr; prom dir & progmg dir; Russell Nutt, mus dir, news dir & pub affrs dir. ■ Rates: $10.50; 10.50; 10.50; 10.50.

***WUMF-FM**—February 1972: 100.5 mhz; 13 w-H. Ant -190 ft. TL: N44 40 09 W70 09 00. Stereo. 86 Main St. (04938). (207) 778-7352. Licensee: Univ. of Maine at Farmington. Format: AOR, progsv. ■ Becka Meir, stn mgr; Rick Hersom, progmg dir; Mike Gaito, mus dir.

Fort Kent

WLVC(AM)—July 30, 1975: 1340 khz; 250 w-D, 1 kw-N. TL: N47 14 33 W68 36 47. Hrs opn: 18. 6 10th Ave., Madawaska (04756). (207) 728-4000; (207) 728-4001. FAX: (207) 728-4001. Licensee: Lamoille Broadcasting and Communications (acq 2-6-90; grpsl; FTR 2-26-90). Net: SMN. Format: Full svc adult contemp. Target aud: 25-54. ■ Kristin McQuarrie, gen mgr, gen sls mgr & adv dir; Monique Miller, stn mgr, opns mgr, progmg dir & mus dir; Ira Miller, prom mgr, news dir & pub affrs dir.

WMEF(FM)—Not on air, target date unknown: 106.5 mhz; 25 kw. Ant 302 ft. 65 Texas Ave., Bangor (04401). Licensee: Maine Public Broadcasting Corp.

WUFK(FM)—July 1974: 92.1 mhz; 13.85 w. Ant - 321 ft. TL: N47 15 02 W68 35 25. Annex Bldg., Pleasant St., Fort Kent (04743); Box 108, Univ. of Maine, 25 Pleasant St., Fort Kent (04743). (207) 834-3162; (207) 834-3712. Licensee: Univ. of Maine. Format: Div, progsv, rock. Target aud: 12-35. Spec prog: Irish/Gaelic folk show 3 hrs wkly. ■ A. Alan Daigle, gen mgr & prom mgr; Charles Zafonte, chief engr.

Gardiner

WABK(AM)—Sept 23, 1968: 1280 khz; 5 kw-U, DA-N. TL: N44 14 53 W69 48 51. Stereo. Hrs opn: 24. Box 1280, Northern Ave. (04345). (207) 582-3303. FAX: (207) 582-8144. Licensee: Kennebec-Tryon Broadcasting Corp. Group owner: Northeast Communications Corp. Net: ABC/I. Rep: Eastman, Kadetsky. Wash atty: Reddy, Begley & Martin. Format: Adult contemp, news, talk. News staff one; news progmg 34 hrs wkly. Target aud: 25-54. ■ Jeff Fisher, pres; Richard Walsh, gen mgr; Ryan Cote, opns dir; Bill Craig, gen sls mgr; Brant Curtiss, prom mgr & progmg dir; Steven Colella, mus dir; Don Bumpus, news dir; Richard Hyatt, chief engr.

WABK-FM—Apr 1, 1974: 104.3 mhz; 50 kw. Ant 492 ft. TL: N44 18 36 W69 49 51. Stereo. Dups AM 85%. Format: Adult contemp.

Gorham

WLAM(AM)—March 3, 1980: 870 khz; 10 kw-D, 1 kw-N. TL: N43 41 19 W70 30 34. Box 929, Lewiston (04243). (207) 784-5401. FAX: (207) 784-5581. Licensee: Great Portland Wireless Talking Machine Co. (acq 8-91). Net: SMN. Format: Music for your life. ■ Ron Frizzell, gen mgr; Armand Girard, chief engr.

***WMPG(FM)**—Sept 1, 1973: 90.9 mhz; 110 w-H, 1 kw-V. Ant 233 ft. TL: N43 40 50 W70 26 59. Stereo. Hrs opn: 24. 96 Falmouth St., Portland (04103); 92 Bedford St. (04103). (207) 780-4974. Licensee: Trustees Univ. of Maine. Format: Div, community-oriented. News progmg 5 hrs wkly. Target aud: General; any group currently underserved by other loc stns. Spec prog: Jazz 10 hrs, Black 10 hrs, folk 10 hrs, Sp 2 hrs, Indian 2 hrs, gospel 3 hrs, Cambodian 2 hrs, Swedish one hr, African one hr, Irish 2 hrs wkly. ■ Rob Rosenthal, stn mgr; Joanne Laugherty, dev dir; Jim Rand, progmg dir; Fred Kennedy, mus dir; Arnold Orlean, chief engr.

Harpswell

***WMSJ(FM)**—Not on air, target date unknown: 91.9 mhz; 6 kw. Ant 148 ft. TL: N43 44 16 W69 59 43. Box 432, Freeport (04132). Licensee: Downeast Christian Communications.

Houlton

WHGS(AM)—July 10, 1950: 1340 khz; 1 kw-U. TL: N46 08 45 W67 50 35. Box 40 (04730). (207) 532-6587. FAX: (207) 532-4251. Licensee: Peak Communications Inc. (acq 3-31-86; $280,000 with co-located FM; FTR 1-20-86). Net: NBC the Source. Rep: Torbet. Format: Adult contemp. News staff one; news progmg 8 hrs wkly. Target aud: 25-54. ■ Dale Tudor, pres; Larry Palmer, gen mgr; Kevin Given, prom dir & progmg dir; Paul Martin, news dir; Sandy Haynes, chief engr.

WHOU-FM—Co-owned with WHGS(AM). Jan 13, 1976: 100.1 mhz; 3 kw. Ant 298 ft. TL: N46 08 45 W67 50 35. Dups AM 90%. ■ Paul Martin, progmg dir.

Howland

WSNV(FM)—Not on air, target date unknown: 103.9 mhz; 54 kw. Ant 1,535 ft. TL: N45 07 46 W68 21 28. Box 580, Lighthouse Park, Yarmouth (04096-0580). (207) 865-1196. Licensee: Bay Communications Inc. Wash atty: Brown, Finn & Nietert. ■ Robert J. Cole, pres; Thomas Cole, chief engr.

Kennebunk

WBQQ(FM)—Nov 1991: 99.3 mhz; 3 kw. Ant 324 ft. TL: N43 24 16 W70 26 15. Hrs opn: 24. Unit 99.3, 169 Port Rd. (04043). (207) 967-0993. Licensee: Vega Corp. Rep: CMBS. Format: Class. Target aud: 35-64; upscale. ■ Alexander M. Tanger, chmn; Brenda Tanger, pres; Louis Vitali, sr vp; Alan Armstage, opns mgr; Roger Brace, chief engr. ■ Rates: $25; 25; 25; 15.

Kennebunkport

WXPT(FM)—Not on air, target date unknown: 104.7 mhz; 3 kw. Ant 292 ft. TL: N43 26 36 W70 26 38. Box 266, Kennebunk (04043). Licensee: Vega Corp. (acq 2-5-93; $135,000; FTR 3-1-93).

Kittery

WXBB(FM)—December 1992: 105.3 mhz; 2.2 kw. Ant 371 ft. TL: N43 10 28 W70 46 50. Stereo. Box 370, Dover, NH (03820). (603) 749-9750. FAX: (603) 749-1459. Licensee: Bear Broadcasting Co. (group owner; acq 10-11-91; $750,000; FTR 11-4-91). Format: Hot country. ■ Philip Urso, pres; Marty Lessard, gen mgr.

Lewiston

***WRBC(FM)**—Oct 6, 1958: 91.5 mhz; 150 w. Ant 16 ft. TL: N44 06 18 W70 12 32. Stereo. Hrs opn: 24. Box 495, Bates College, 31 Frye St. (04240). (207) 777-7532; (207) 777-7915. FAX: (207) 786-6123; (207) 786-6035. Licensee: President and Trustees of Bates College. Format: Div. Target aud: General; anyone searching for something different. Spec prog: Fr 2 hrs, jazz 4 hrs, metal 4 hrs, talk specialty shows 2 hrs, classic rock 11 hrs, new music 16 hrs, Maine artists 3 hrs, blues 2 hrs, 60s punk 2 hrs, Chicago music 2 hrs, folk 6 hrs wkly. ■ Denis Howard, gen mgr & mus dir; Lisa Adams, prom dir; Tania Davenport, progmg dir; Jenni Matz, pub affrs dir; Arnold Olean, chief engr.

WTHT(FM)—Licensed to Lewiston. See Portland.

WTME(AM)—Aug 21, 1938: 1240 khz; 1 kw-U. TL: N44 06 55 W70 14 56. Rebroadcasts WKTQ(AM) South Paris 80%. Box 72, Norway (04268). (207) 743-5911. FAX: (207) 743-5913. Licensee: Christian Family Radio Inc. Group owner: Gleason Marketing Services (acq 11-28-90). Net: USA. Rep: Cyr Associates Inc. Wash atty: Miller & Fields. Format: Christian, news/talk. News progmg 12 hrs wkly. Target aud: General. ■ Richard D. Gleason, pres & gen mgr; Don Mayberry, stn mgr; Tim Henry, progmg dir & news dir; Bob Perry, chief engr. ■ Rates: $12; 12; 12; 12.

WXGL-FM—Feb 29, 1948: 93.9 mhz; 27.5 kw. Ant 633 ft. TL: N44 08 40 W70 01 22. 25 Westminster St. (04243); (207) 784-6921. FAX: (207) 782-1827. Licensee: Stephen E. Powell (acq 1993; $700,000; FTR 9-13-93). Format: Oldies. ■ David O. Dulac, pres & gen mgr; Pat McKay, progmg dir; Larry Donovan, news dir.

WZOU(AM)—Sept 4, 1947: 1470 khz; 5 kw-U, DA-1. TL: N44 03 47 W70 15 00. Box 929 (04240). (207) 784-5401. FAX: (207) 784-5581. Licensee: Great Down East Wireless Talking Machine Co. (acq 7-29-75). Net: ABC/I, NBC Talknet. Rep: D & R Radio. Format: Music of your life. Spec prog: Fr 2 hrs wkly. ■ Don Steele, opns mgr; Donna Steele, progmg dir; Chris Chapman, mus dir; Matt Ledis, news dir.

Maine Directory of Radio

Lincoln

WSYY(AM)—See Millinocket.

WTOX(AM)—Nov 9, 1964: 1450 khz; 1 kw-U. TL: N45 21 52 W63 31 36. Box 9, Park Ave. (04457). (207) 794-6499. FAX: (207) 794-3583. Licensee: Northland Communications Corp. (acq 6-1-89; $240,000 with co-located FM; FTR 6-12-89). Net: Sun. Format: Talk. Target aud: General. ■ Roger Parent Jr., pres; Margaret Hayes, gen mgr & gen sls mgr; Steve Campbell, stn mgr; Michael Dow, progmg dir & mus dir; Sandy Haynes, chief engr.

WHMX(FM)—Co-owned with WTOX(AM). Apr 1, 1975: 105.7 mhz; 50 kw. Ant 413 ft. TL: N45 20 34 W68 30 25. Stereo. Hrs opn: 24. Prog sep from AM. Format: Country, rock, oldies, mix of hits.

Machias

WALZ(AM)—Dec 5, 1965: 1400 khz; 1 kw-U. TL: N44 43 49 W67 28 21. Stn currently dark. 12 Cooper St. (04654). Licensee: Henry Chausse (acq 2-27-90). ■ Robert Newsham, pres.

WALZ-FM—Nov 25, 1978: 95.3 mhz; 3 kw. Ant 220 ft. TL: N44 44 08 W67 30 11. Stereo. Stn currently dark.

Madawaska

WCXX(FM)—Jan 30, 1988: 102.3 mhz; 1.75 kw. Ant 384 ft. TL: N47 19 54 W68 20 31. Stereo. Box X (04756). (207) 473-7513. FAX: (207) 472-3221. Licensee: CanXus Broadcasting Corp. Net: NBC. Rep: Major Mkt, Kettel-Carter, Savalli. Wash atty: Koteen & Naftalin. Format: Adult contemp, news. News staff one; news progmg 16 hrs wkly. Target aud: 18-54. ■ Dennis H. Curley, pres; Richard Chandler, gen mgr; Don Wilson, stn mgr; Mark Stewart, opns mgr; Don Nadeau, mus dir; Douglas Christensen, news dir.

WSJR(AM)—Dec 1, 1962: 1230 khz; 1 kw-U. TL: N47 21 07 W68 18 21. Hrs opn: 24. 6 10th Ave. (04756). (207) 728-4000; (207) 728-4001. FAX: (207) 728-4001. Licensee: Lamoille Broadcasting and Communications (acq 2-6-90; grpsl; FTR 2-26-90). Net: SMN. Format: Full svc adult contemp. Target aud: 25-54. ■ Kristin McQuarrie, gen mgr, gen sls mgr & adv mgr; Monique Miller, stn mgr, opns mgr, progmg dir & mus dir; Ira Miller, prom mgr, news dir & pub affrs dir.

Madison

WHAA(FM)—Not on air, target date Spring 1994: 97.5 mhz; 6 kw. Ant 328 ft. TL: N44 47 32 W69 58 10. Hrs opn: 24. 378 Main St., Dexter (04930). (207) 924-1021. FAX: (207) 924-3299. Licensee: Innovative Advertising Consultants Inc. (acq 9-30-91; $6,000 for CP; FTR 10-28-91). Wash atty: Fletcher, Heald & Hildreth.

Mexico

WTBM(FM)—Sept 15, 1988: 100.7 mhz; 180 w. Ant 1,289 ft. TL: N44 34 56 W70 37 59. Box 72, Norway (04268). (207) 743-5911. FAX: (207) 743-5913. Licensee: Mountain Valley Broadcasting Inc. Gleason Marketing Broadcasting Inc. (acq 12-90; $300,000; FTR 10-22-90). Net: USA. Rep: CYR Associates Inc. Format: Country. ■ Richard Gleason, CEO, chmn & CFO; Don Mayberry, gen mgr; Tim Henry, progmg dir & news dir; Dick Cushman, chief engr. ■ Rates: $12; 12; 12; 12.

Millinocket

WSYY(AM)—Dec 7, 1963: 1240 khz; 1 kw-U. TL: N45 40 24 W68 43 07. Box 1240 (04462). (207) 723-9657. FAX: (207) 723-5900. Licensee: Katahdin Communications Inc. (acq 12-29-86; $295,000 with co-located FM; FTR 11-10-86). Net: AP, Jones. Format: Adult contemp. News staff one. Target aud: General. Spec prog: Relg 2 hrs wkly. ■ James N. Talbot, pres & chief engr; Steve Campbell, stn mgr; David Keyes, vp opns. ■ Rates: $11.75; 11.75; 11.75; 11.75.

WSYY-FM—Apr 12, 1978: 94.9 mhz; 23.5 kw. Ant 692 ft. TL: N45 52 58 W68 47 54. Stereo. Dups AM 95%. ■ Rates: Same as AM.

Norway

WOXO-FM—Dec 12, 1970: 92.7 mhz; 2 kw. Ant 360 ft. TL: N44 12 24 W70 33 18. Stereo. Box 72, 114 Main St. (04268). (207) 743-5911. FAX: (207) 743-5913. Licensee: Tri County Broadcasting Inc. Group owner: Gleason Marketing Services (acq 12-12-75). Net: USA. Rep: CYR Assoc. Wash atty: Miller & Fields. Format: Country, Sports. News progmg 12 hrs wkly. Target aud: General. ■ Richard D. Gleason, pres & gen mgr; Don Mayberry, stn mgr & gen sls mgr; Tim Henry, progmg dir & news dir; Bob Perry, chief engr. ■ Rates: $17; 17; 17; 17.

Old Town

WBZN(FM)—Not on air, target date unknown: 107.3 mhz; 50 kw. Ant 308 ft. TL: N45 02 06 W68 40 57. 727 Hammond St., Bangor (04401). (207) 947-4487. Licensee: Eclipse Broadcasting Inc. (acq 7-12-93; $55,000; FTR 8-9-93). Format: CHR. ■ David Turek, gen mgr.

Orono

***WMEB-FM**—Sept 6, 1988: 91.9 mhz; 380 w-H. Ant 66 ft. TL: N44 54 04 W68 40 07. Stereo. Univ of Maine, Room 106, 5725 E. Annex (04469-5725). (207) 581-2332; (207) 581-2335. FAX: (207) 581-4343. Licensee: Board of Trustees, Univ. of Maine. Format: Progsv, rock. News staff 2; news progmg 5 hrs wkly. Target aud: General. Spec prog: Jazz 13 hrs, reggae 7 hrs, new age 3 hrs, heavy metal 10 hrs, blues 7 hrs, rap 5 hrs, folk 4 hrs, Fr 4 hrs, international 3 hrs wkly. ■ Ryan McKinney, stn mgr; Jeffrey Tardiff, prom dir; David Nicholson, progmg mgr; Ryan Toppan, mus dir; Robert Turkington, news dir; Dave Bartlett, chief engr.

Pittsfield

WPBC(FM)—Dec 1993: 99.5 mhz; 3 kw. Ant 243 ft. TL: N44 51 12 W69 19 17. Radio Station WPBC(FM), 727 Hammond St., Bangor (04401). (207) 947-3600. FAX: (207) 947-3600. Licensee: Action Communications Partnership (acq 1-3-92; $6,000 for CP; FTR 1-27-92). Format: Adult contemp/CHR. ■ David Turek, gen mgr.

Portland

WBLM(FM)—February 1966: 102.9 mhz; 100 kw. Ant 1,460 ft. TL: N43 55 28 W70 29 28. Stereo. One City Ctr. (04101). (207) 774-6364. FAX: (207) 774-8707. Licensee: Fuller-Jeffrey Broadcasting of the Great State of Maine. Group owner: Fuller-Jeffrey Broadcasting Companies Inc. (acq 12-89; $4.5 million; FTR 12-11-89). Rep: McGavren Guild. Format: AOR. News staff one. Target aud: 18-49; active, involved, fun-loving. ■ Robert F. Fuller, pres; J. J. Jeffrey, vp; Eve Rubins, gen mgr; Michael Sambrook, stn mgr; Herbert Ivy, opns mgr & progmg dir; Brian James, mus dir; Celeste Nadeau, news dir; Eugene Terwilliger, chief engr.

WCSO(FM)—June 1, 1960: 97.9 mhz; 16 kw. Ant 889 ft. TL: N43 51 06 W70 19 40 (CP: 37.5 kw, ant 567 ft., TL: N43 45 32 W70 19 14). Stereo. Box 6713, 583 Warren Ave. (04103). (207) 775-6321. FAX: (207) 772-8087. Licensee: Atlantic Morris Broadcasting Corp. Group owner: Atlantic Morris Broadcasting Inc. (acq 7-25-91; $985,000; with WLPZ[AM] Westbrook, ME; FTR 8-12-91). Rep: Christal, Kettell-Carter. Format: Adult contemp. ■ Rob Breiner, gen mgr; T.J. Holland, progmg dir; Dick Gosselin, news dir; Andy Armstrong, chief engr.

WGAN(AM)—Aug 3, 1938: 560 khz; 5 kw-U, DA-2. TL: N43 41 22 W70 19 00 (CP: 4.8 kw-U, DA-1). 420 Western Ave., South Portland (04106). (207) 774-4561. FAX: (207) 774-3788. Licensee: Saga Communications of New England Inc. (group owner; acq 6-2-92; grpsl, including co-located FM). Net: NBC, NBC Talknet. Rep: Katz. Format: Adult contemp, news/talk. ■ Bruce Biette, gen mgr; Ken Christian, progmg dir; William Muldoon, news dir.

WMGX(FM)—Co-owned with WGAN(AM). June 10, 1977: 93.1 mhz; 50 kw. Ant 443 ft. TL: N43 41 27 W70 15 25. Stereo. Prog sep from AM. Format: Adult contemp. ■ Randi Kirshbaum, progmg dir.

WHOM(FM)—See Mt. Washington, N.H.

WKZS(FM)—See Auburn.

WLOB(AM)—Feb 2, 1957: 1310 khz; 5 kw-U, DA-2. TL: N43 41 22 W70 20 06. Hrs opn: 6 AM-10 PM. 779 Warren Ave. (04103). (207) 775-1310. Licensee: Carter Broadcasting Corp. (group owner). Net: USA. Format: Relg, talk. News progmg 6 hrs wkly. Target aud: General. ■ Ken Carter, pres & gen mgr; Michael Whitney, progmg dir; Richard Ringenback, pub affrs dir; Tina Smith, chief engr.

***WMEA(FM)**—April 1974: 90.1 mhz; 49 kw. Ant 1,919 ft. TL: N43 51 33 W70 42 43. Stereo. Hrs opn: 24. 65 Texas Ave., Bangor (04401); 1450 Libson St., Lewiston (04240). (207) 941-1010; (207) 783-9101. FAX: (207) 942-2857. Licensee: Maine Public Broadcasting Corp. (acq 6-23-92). Net: NPR, APR, Eastern Pub. Format: Class, pub affairs. ■ Robert Gardiner, gen mgr; Bernard Roscetti, stn mgr; Russ Peotter, mktg dir; Charles Beck, progmg dir; Andrea DeLeon, news dir; Alexander G. Maxwell Jr., engrg dir; David Roy, chief engr. ■ WMEA-TV. affil.

WMGX(FM)—Listing follows WGAN(AM).

WPOR(AM)—March 1946: 1490 khz; 1 kw-U. TL: N43 39 48 W70 16 16. Hrs opn: 24. 15 Baxter Blvd. (04101). (207) 773-8111. FAX: (207) 772-0870. Licensee: Ocean Coast Properties (acq 3-2-71). Net: ABC/E. Rep: McGavren Guild. Format: Country. News staff 2. Target aud: 25-54; general. ■ Phil Corper, pres; Robert Gold, gen mgr; Bonnie Grant, gen sls mgr; Mike Nelson, prom mgr; Tom Hennessey, progmg dir; Hal Knight, mus dir; Mike Audet, news dir; Gene Terwilliger, chief engr.

WPOR-FM—Oct 31, 1967: 101.9 mhz; 32.5 kw. Ant 606 ft. TL: N43 45 45 W70 19 30. Stereo. Dups AM 100%. News progmg 5 hrs wkly.

WTHT(FM)—(Lewiston). Mar 1, 1973: 107.5 mhz; 35 kw. Ant 610 ft. TL: N43 57 07 W70 17 46. Stereo. 1335 Washington Ave., Portland (04103). (207) 797-0780. FAX: (207) 797-0368. Licensee: Beacon Broadcasting Corp. (group owner; acq 12-89). Net: Unistar. Rep: D & R Radio. Format: Hot country. News staff one. ■ Alford H. Lessner, pres; Jon Van Hoogenstyn, gen mgr; Dan Fennell, rgnl sls mgr; Jim Schaeffer, news dir; John Hussey, chief engr.

WYNZ(FM)—See Westbrook.

WZAN(AM)—July 13, 1925: 970 khz; 5 kw-U, DA-N. TL: N43 36 19 W70 19 18. 420 Western Ave, South Portland (04106). (207) 774-4561. FAX: (207) 774-3788. Licensee: Saga Communications of New England Inc. Group owner: Saga Communications Inc. (acq 6-23-93; $350,000 with WYNZ-FM Westbrook; FTR 7-12-93). Net: CBS. Rep: Eastman. Format: Nostalgia. Target aud: 25-54. ■ Ed Christian, pres; Bruce Biette, gen mgr; Brian Meany, gen sls mgr; Don Matsen, progmg dir & news dir.

WZPK(FM)—See Berlin, N.H.

Presque Isle

WBPW(FM)—September 1973: 96.9 mhz; 100 kw. Ant 440 ft. TL: N46 45 52 W67 59 23 (CP: Ant 1,479 ft., TL: 46 31 16 W67 48 51). Stereo. Box 312, Rt. 1 (04769). (207) 769-6600. FAX: (207) 764-5274. Licensee: Four Seasons Communications Inc. Group owner: Martz Communications Group (acq 10-24-85; $350,000; FTR 9-2-85). Net: Westwood One. Rep: Banner, All-Canada. Format: Hot country. News staff one. Target aud: 18-49. ■ Timothy D. Martz, pres; Keith Neve, gen mgr; J.R. Mitchell, progmg dir; Barbara Whitzman, news dir; Andy Rebscher, chief engr.

***WMEM(FM)**—1975: 106.1 mhz; 99 kw. Ant 1,079 ft. TL: N46 33 06 W67 48 38. Rebroadcasts WMEH(FM) Bangor 100%. 1450 Lisbon St., Lewiston (04240); 65 Texas Ave., Bangor (04401). (207) 783-9101; (207) 941-1010. FAX: (207) 783-5193; (207) 942-2857. Licensee: Maine Public Broadcasting Corp. (acq 6-23-92). Net: NPR, APR; Eastern Pub. Wash atty: Dow, Lohnes & Albertson. Format: Classical, pub affrs. ■ Robert H. Gardiner, pres; Russell Peotter, dev dir & mktg dir; Deb Turner, dev mgr; Bernard Roscetti, progmg dir; Charles Beck, progmg mgr & mus dir; Vic Hathaway, asst mus dir; Andrea DeLeon, news dir; Alexander G. Maxwell Jr., engrg dir; David Roy, chief engr.

WOZI(FM)—Feb 2, 1981: 101.7 mhz; 1.35 kw-H. Ant 420 ft. TL: N46 44 28 W67 56 10. Stereo. Box 1117 (04769). (207) 762-5211. FAX: (207) 764-3927. Licensee: Carlos-Franklin Comm. Inc. (acq 11-85; $178,944; FTR 11-25-85). Net: CBS. Format: C&W. ■ Mike Carlos, gen mgr & gen sls mgr; George Kelley, progmg dir; Bill Ducharme, chief engr.

WTMS-FM—1981: 96.1 mhz; 95 kw. Ant 1,309 ft. TL: N46 32 55 W67 48 35. Stereo. 160 Airport Dr. (04769). (207) 768-5141. FAX: (207) 768-9347. Licensee: Cavan Communications Inc. (acq 11-1-87). Format: Rock, Top-40. ■ Dominic Monahan, pres; Mary Meo, gen mgr; Andrew Rebscher, chief engr.

WTMS(AM)—June 24, 1960: 1390 khz; 5 kw-U, DA-N. TL: N46 39 17 W68 03 01. Stn currently dark.

***WUPI(FM)**—July 26, 1973: 92.1 mhz; 17 w-H. Ant -39 ft. TL: N46 40 15 W68 01 00. Hrs opn: 15. Box 64, Normal Hall, 181 Main St. (04769). (207) 764-0311, ext. 309. Licensee: Univ. of Maine. Net: Westwood One. Format: AOR. News staff 2; news progmg 3 hrs wkly. Target aud: 16-35. Spec prog: Class 4 hrs, Black 2 hrs, country 2 hrs, jazz 2 hrs, heavy metal 4 hrs, punk 2 hrs, Russian 2 hrs, Kenyan 2 hrs, Indian 2 hrs wkly. ■ Brian Massey, pres, gen mgr, stn mgr & dev mgr; Jeff Heneghan, vp; Scott Gordon, opns dir & mus dir; Steve Trafford, sls dir & pub affrs dir; Vickie Harris, prom mgr & adv mgr; Rick Velin, chief engr.

Rockland

WRKD(AM)—Oct 1, 1952: 1450 khz; 1 kw-U. TL: N44 06 22 W69 06 31. Stereo. Hrs opn: 24. Box 130, 415 Main St. (04841). (207) 594-1450; (207) 596-1033. FAX: (207) 594-2234. Licensee: Rockland Radio Corp. (acq 12-5-90; with co-located FM). Net: SMN. Format: MOR, beautiful mus, oldies. News staff one; news progmg 11 hrs wkly. Target aud: 35 plus. ■ Peter K. Orne, pres & gen mgr; Elaine Knowlton, vp; Neil Orne, vp opns, vp progmg & progmg dir; Gordon Page, vp sls & gen sls mgr; Don Shields, news dir; Michelle Anderson, pub affrs dir; Stacey Brann, chief engr. ■ Rates: $15; 10; 14; 9.

WMCM(FM)—Co-owned with WRKD(AM). April 16, 1968: 103.3 mhz; 31.2 kw. Ant 587 ft. TL: N44 07 34 W69 08 19. Stereo. Hrs opn: 24. Prog sep from AM. Net: SMN. Format: C&W. News staff one. Target aud: General. ■ Rates: $30; 22; 25; 15.

Rumford

WRUM(AM)—Aug 21, 1953: 790 khz; 1 kw-D, 50 w-N. TL: N44 30 53 W70 31 01. 89 Congress St. (04276). (207) 364-7969; (207) 364-7960. Licensee: Carter Broadcasting Corp. (acq 5-7-87; $587,000 with co-located FM; FTR 5-25-87). Net: SMN. Format: Big band. Target aud: 35 plus. ■ Ken Carter, pres; Michael Breton, gen mgr; Richard Cushman, chief engr.

WWMR(FM)—Co-owned with WRUM(AM). Nov 15, 1975: 96.3 mhz; 100 kw. Ant 1,433 ft. TL: N44 34 56 W70 37 59. Stereo. Format: Div.

Saco

WHYR(FM)—July 18, 1982: 95.9 mhz; 3.3 kw. Ant 300 ft. TL: N43 33 24 W70 30 31 (CP: 6 kw, ant 328 ft.). Stereo. Box 567, 200 Main St. (04072). (207) 283-1116; (207) 284-9600. FAX: (207) 283-1234. Licensee: Vacationland Broadcasting Service Inc. Rep: Roslin. Format: Top-40. ■ Bart Bailey, gen mgr & chief engr; Astraid Bailey, stn mgr; Fred Miller, gen sls mgr; Rob Snyder, progmg dir; Jason Guy, mus dir; Peter Hathaway, news dir.

WIDE(AM)—See Biddeford.

WSTG(FM)—See Biddeford.

Sanford

WCDQ(FM)—Listing follows WSME(AM).

*WSEW(FM)—Not on air, target date unknown: 88.5 mhz; 100 w. Ant 387 ft. TL: N43 25 11 W70 48 09. Licensee: Word-Radio Educational Foundation.

WSME(AM)—Nov 9, 1957: 1220 khz; 1 kw-D, 234 w-N. TL: N43 25 53 W70 45 44. Hrs opn: 24. Box 631 (04073). (207) 324-7271. FAX: (207) 324-2464. Licensee: WSME Inc. (acq 7-86). Net: MBS. Format: News/talk. ■ Donald Crown, gen mgr; Tim Maxfield, gen sls mgr; Russ Dumont, progmg dir; Bob Perry, chief engr.

WCDQ(FM)—Co-owned with WSME(AM). Oct 10, 1975: 92.1 mhz; 1.2 kw. Ant 525 ft. TL: N43 35 24 W70 22 20. Stereo. Hrs opn: 24. Prog sep from AM. Format: Classic rock. News staff one. Target aud: General. Spec prog: Blues 3 hrs, reggae 2 hrs wkly. ■ Donald Crown, pres; Russ Dumont, gen mgr.

Scarborough

WPKM(FM)—1960: 106.3 mhz; 3 kw. Ant 299 ft. TL: N43 35 24 W70 22 20. Stereo. Box 610, 17 Elmwood Ave. (04074). (207) 883-9596. FAX: (207) 883-9530. Licensee: WPKM FM Inc. (acq 4-18-88). Rep: CMBS. Format: Classical. News staff 2; news progmg 3 hrs wkly. Target aud: 25-54; upscale, affluent, management, professionals. Spec prog: Jazz 5 hrs wkly. ■ Charles C. McCreery, pres; JoAnn Fisher, gen mgr & gen sls mgr; Katherine A. Blake, stn mgr; John Spritz, progmg dir & mus dir; Gene Terwilliger, chief engr. ■ Rates: $25; 22; 25; 16.

Searsport

WBYA(FM)—Not on air, target date unknown: 101.7 mhz; 6 kw. Ant 236 ft. TL: N44 25 50 W68 52 59. Box 564, Union (04862). Licensee: Searsport Broadcasting Partnership.

Skowhegan

WHQO(FM)—September 1989: 107.9 mhz; 6.50 kw. Ant 676 ft. TL: N44 42 46 W69 43 36 (CP: 5.98 kw, ant 666 ft.). Stereo. Box 698 (04976-0698). (207) 474-0108. FAX: (305) 474-0341. Licensee: Robert R. Harvey (acq 2-15-91; $185,000; FTR 3-11-91). Format: Oldies, top-40. Target aud: 25-54; baby boomers who grew up with Top-40 radio. ■ Robert R. Harvey, pres, gen mgr & progmg dir; Tim Smith, chief engr.

WSKW(AM)—1956: 1160 khz; 10 kw-D, 1 kw-N. TL: N44 44 43 W69 41 36. Box 159, Middle Rd. (04976). (207) 474-5171. Licensee: Mountain Wireless Inc. (acq 8-19-87). Net: CNN, Unistar. Rep: Katz & Powell. Format: AM only, local news. News staff one; news progmg 5 hrs wkly. Target aud: 40 plus; older, local audience. Spec prog: High school sports, Univ. of Maine sports, Sunday religion. ■ Alan W. Anderson, pres & gen mgr; Mike Estrada, vp opns & news dir; Tim Gatz, gen sls mgr; Gene Terwilliger, chief engr.

WTOS-FM—Co-owned with WSKW(AM). Nov 13, 1969: 105.1 mhz; 50 kw. Ant 2,431 ft. TL: N45 01 54 W70 18 50. Stereo. Hrs opn: 24. Prog sep from AM. Format: Rock (AOR). News progmg 3 hrs wkly. Target aud: Adults; 18-49. ■ Tim Gatz, sls dir; Bill Schissler, progmg dir.

South Paris

WKTQ(AM)—Oct 28, 1955: 1450 khz; 1 kw-U, DA-1. TL: N44 13 16 W70 31 43. Prog dups WTME(AM) Lewiston. PO Box 72, 114 Main St., Norway (04268). (207) 743-5911. FAX: (207) 743-5913. Licensee: Penneseewassee Broadcasting Co. Group owner: Gleason Marketing Services (acq 7-27-76). Net: USA. Wash atty: Miller & Fields. Format: Christian, news/talk. News progmg 12 hrs wkly. Target aud: General. ■ Richard D. Gleason, pres & gen mgr; Don Mayberry, stn mgr & gen sls mgr; Tim Henry, progmg dir & news dir; Bob Perry, chief engr. ■ Rates: $12; 12; 12; 12.

WOXO-FM—See Norway.

Standish

*WSJB-FM—Apr 1, 1984: 91.5 mhz; 360 w. Ant 85 ft. TL: N43 49 32 W70 29 03. Stereo. St. Joseph's College, Windham (04062). (207) 892-6766. Licensee: Trustees of St. Joseph's College. Net: AP. Format: Div. News progmg 3 hrs wkly. Target aud: College students. Spec prog: Class 2 hrs, C&W 3 hrs, jazz 3 hrs wkly. ■ Bill Yates, gen mgr; Jim Carter, chief engr.

Thomaston

WAVX(FM)—May 29, 1992: 106.9 mhz; 29.5 kw. Ant 633 ft. TL: N44 06 30 W69 09 28. Stereo. Hrs opn: 24. Suite 101A, 119 Tillson Ave., Rockland (04841). (207) 594-9283. FAX: (207) 594-1620. Licensee: Northern Lights Broadcasting Co. Wash atty: Smithwick & Belendiuk. Format: Class. News progmg 2 hrs wkly. Target aud: 35 plus; affluent, upscale adults. Spec prog: Children one hr, drama one hr wkly. ■ Jonathan L. Le Veen, pres; Julie Allen, opns dir; Mary McPherson, gen sls mgr; Laurena Gilbert, prom dir; Geri Coughlin, progmg dir; Eugene Terwilliger, chief engr. ■ Rates: $25; 16; 25; 14.

Topsham

WPME(FM)—1993: 95.5 mhz; 3 kw. Ant 456 ft. TL: N43 54 12 W70 02 13. Box 580, Yarmouth (04096). (207) 865-1199. Licensee: Coastal Broadcasting Inc. (acq 12-6-93; $263,585; FTR 1-3-94). Format: Country. ■ Marilyn Quinn, gen mgr.

Waterville

WEBB(FM)—Listing follows WTVL(AM).

WJBI-FM—See Winslow.

*WMEW(FM)—Nov 1983: 91.3 mhz; 3 kw. Ant 299 ft. TL: N44 29 23 W69 39 05. Stereo. Hrs opn: 24. Rebroadcasts WMEH(FM) Bangor 100%. 1450 Lisbon St., Lewiston (04240); 65 Texas Ave., Bangor (04401). (207) 783-9101; (207) 942-2857. FAX: (207) 783-5193; (207) 942-2857. Licensee: Maine Public Broadcasting Corp. (acq 6-23-92; FTR 7-13-92). Net: NPR, APR; Eastern Pub. Wash atty: Dow, Lohnes & Albertson. Format: Classical, pub affrs. ■ Robert H. Gardiner, pres; Russell Peotter, dev dir & mktg dir; Deb Turner, dev mgr; Bernard Roscetti, progmg dir; Charles Beck, progmg mgr; Chareles Beck, mus dir; Vic Hathoway, asst mus dir; Andrea DeLeon, news dir; Alexander G. Maxwell Jr., engrg dir; David Roy, chief engr.

*WMHB(FM)—Oct 1, 1974: 90.5 mhz; 110 w. Ant 98 ft. TL: N44 33 57 W69 39 49. Stereo. Hrs opn: 24. Colby College (04901-4977). (207) 872-3686; (207) 872-3348. FAX: (207) 872-3555. Licensee: Mayflower Hill Broadcasting Corp. Format: Div. News progmg one hr wkly. Target aud: General; 5 to 100 yrs, we cater to everyone. Spec prog: Black 12 hrs, folk 12 hrs, jazz 8 hrs, blues 6 hrs, country 10 hrs, new age 2 hrs, Broadway 2 hrs, disco 2 hrs, metal 6 hrs wkly. broad hrs, R&B 16 hrs, new age 6 hrs, folk 16 hrs, heavy metal 4 hrs wkly. ■ Jessica Hill, pres & gen mgr; Niki Shinneman, dev dir & sls dir; Ray Beaudoin, prom dir; Dina Pfister-Mandes, progmg mgr; Michael Smoot, mus dir; Jens Kueter, Faisel Zaman, Stephen Motion, (asst) mus dirs.

WTVL(AM)—June 19, 1946: 1490 khz; 1 kw-U. TL: N44 33 52 W69 36 39. 36 Silver St. (04901). (207) 873-3311. FAX: (207) 873-3313. Licensee: WTVL Corp. Group owner: Close Communications. Format: Soft rock. ■ Douglas Warner, stn mgr & gen sls mgr; John Paradise, progmg dir & mus dir; Eric Leimbach, news dir; Joe Roy, chief engr.

WEBB(FM)—Co-owned with WTVL(AM). Mar 26, 1968: 98.5 mhz; 50 kw. Ant 305 ft. TL: N44 33 52 W69 36 39. Stereo. Dups AM 100%.

Westbrook

WLPZ(AM)—Nov 8, 1959: 1440 khz; 5 kw-D, 1 kw-N, DA-1. TL: N43 40 50 W70 22 47. Box 6713, Portland (04101). (207) 775-6321. FAX: (207) 772-8087. Licensee: Porter Communications Systems Inc (group owner; acq 7-25-91; $985,000 with WCSO[FM] Portland; FTR 8-12-91). Format: Sports, talk. Target aud: 18-65; male. ■ Rob Breiner, gen mgr & natl sls mgr; Tom Sayler, opns mgr & progmg dir; Peter Mutino, gen sls mgr; Lisa Daniels, prom mgr; Dick Gosselin, news dir; Andy Armstrong, chief engr.

WPKM(FM)—See Scarborough.

WYNZ(FM)—February 1976: 100.9 mhz; 3 kw. Ant 225 ft. TL: N43 39 02 W70 15 54. Stereo. 42 Western Ave., South Portland (04106). (207) 774-4561. FAX: (207) 774-3788. Licensee: Saga Communications of New England Inc. Group owner: Saga Communications Inc. (acq 6-23-93; $350,000 with WYNZ[AM] Portland; FTR 7-12-93). Rep: Eastman. Format: Oldies. Target aud: 25-54. ■ Edward K. Christian, pres; Bruce A. Biette, vp & gen mgr; Brian B. Meany, gen sls mgr; Don Matsen, progmg dir; Bill Muldoon, news dir.

Winslow

WJBI-FM—Not on air, target date unknown: 95.3 mhz; 5.3 kw. Ant 348 ft. TL: N44 29 18 W69 39 08. 1943 Thistlewood Ct., Ashtabula, OH (44004). (216) 997-1025. Licensee: Bulmer Communications Group (group owner).

York Center

WCQL-FM—June 1987: 95.3 mhz; 1.40 kw H., 1.35 kw V. Ant 682 ft. TL: N43 13 24 W70 41 35 (CP: 1.42 kw, ant 682 ft.). Stereo. Hrs opn: 24. 1555 Islington St., Portsmouth, NH (03801). (603) 430-9500. FAX: (603) 430-9501. Licensee: Sunshine Group Broadcasting Inc. (acq 3-13-89; $1 million; FTR 2-13-89). Rep: Katz. Format: Oldies. News staff one; news progmg 7 hrs wkly. Target aud: 25-54. ■ George Silverman, pres & gen mgr; Mark White, gen sls mgr; Scott Mason, progmg dir; Kim Engle, news dir.

Maryland

Aberdeen

WAMD(AM)—May 1, 1957: 970 khz; 500 w-U, DA-2. TL: N39 30 35 W76 11 38. Box 970 (21001). (410) 272-4400. Licensee: Mackk Broadcasting Co. (acq 5-1-78). Format: Adult contemp. ■ John Contino, pres; Jim McMahan, vp & gen sls mgr.

Annapolis

WANN(AM)—Jan 10, 1947: 1190 khz; 10 kw-D, DA. TL: N38 56 32 W76 28 54. Stereo. Box 631 (21404); WANN Studios and Offices, 1081 Bay Ridge Rd. (21403). (410) 269-0700. Licensee: Annapolis Broadcasting Corp. Wash atty: Christopher J. Reynolds. Format: Country. News staff one; news progmg 2 hrs wkly. Target aud: 25-54; Adults 25 plus. Spec prog: Relg 8 hrs wkly. ■ Morris H. Blum, pres, gen mgr & pub affrs dir; Robert Z. Goldberg, vp sls, mktg dir & adv dir; Bob White, prom dir, progmg dir & mus dir; Jeffrey S. Blum, news dir; M.W. Pittman, vp engrg.

*WFSI(FM)—May 16, 1960: 107.9 mhz; 50 kw. Ant 500 ft. TL: N38 59 45 W76 39 27. Stereo. Hrs opn: 24. 918 Chesapeake Ave. (21403). (410) 268-6200. FAX: (410) 268-0931. Licensee: Family Stations Inc. (group owner; acq 1-7-72). Wash atty: Irwin, Campbell & Crowe. Format: Relg. ■ Harold Camping, pres; Scott Smith, vp; W. Sadlier, stn mgr.

LAUREN A. COLBY
301-663-1086
COMMUNICATIONS ATTORNEY
Special Attention to Difficult Cases

WHFS(FM)—1947: 99.1 mhz; 50 kw. Ant 459 ft. TL: N38 59 46 W76 39 26. Stereo. Hrs opn: 24. 8201 Corporate Dr., Suite 550, Landover (20785). (301) 306-0991; (301) 880-4338. FAX: (301) 731-0431. Licensee: Duchossois Communications Co. of Maryland. Group owner: Duchossois Communications Co. (acq 1-15-88; $8.25 million). Net: AP. Rep: Banner. Wash atty: Tierney & Swift. Format: AOR, modern rock. News staff one. Target aud: 18-49; upscale professionals. Spec prog: Blues 2 hrs, reggae 2 hrs wkly. ■ Rolland Johnson, CEO & pres; T. Alan Hay, vp & gen mgr; Jeanell Hines, gen sls mgr; Joanne Connolly, mktg mgr; Bill Glasser, prom mgr; Robert Benjamin, progmg dir; Bob Waugh, mus dir; Rob Timm, news dir; Randy Scott, engrg dir.

WNAV(AM)—1949: 1430 khz; 5 kw-D, 1 kw-N, DA-N. TL: N38 59 00 W76 31 21. Box 829 (21404); 236 Admiral Dr. (21401). (410) 263-1430. FAX: (410) 268-5360. Licensee: Encore Broadcasting of Maryland Inc. (acq 9-89). Net: NBC. Sports Format: Oldies/Full Service. News staff 2. Target aud: 25-54. Spec Prog: Baltimore Orioles Baseball, Naval Acad. ■ Jacob Einstein, CEO; David C. Holmes, pres; Stephen Hopp, gen mgr; Patricia Fiedler, rgnl sls mgr; John Moran, news dir; George Rond, chief engr.

WXZL(FM)—Listing follows WYRE(AM).

WYRE(AM)—1946: 810 khz; 250 w-D. TL: N38 58 13 W76 30 28. 112 Main St. (21401). (410) 626-0103. FAX: (410) 267-7634. Licensee: Vision Broadcasting Co. Ltd. (acq 3-1-91). Wash atty: Baraff, Koerner, Olender & Hochberg. Format: Adult contemporary. Target aud: 35-54; upscale, mature audience. ■ Neal Heaton, gen mgr & sls dir; Reda Kessler, prom dir; Ray Hoffman, progmg dir; Gary Michaels, news dir & pub affrs dir. ■ Rates: $35; 35; 35; 25.

WXZL(FM)—(Grasonville). Co-owned with WYRE(AM). Apr 1, 1990: 103.1 mhz; 3 kw. Ant 328 ft. TL: N38 58 04 W76 14 36 (CP: 6 kw, TL: N38 56 37 W76 10 43). Stereo. Net: Unistar. Format: Pure rock/AOR. Target aud: 18-34. ■ Richard Winn, gen mgr; Michael Lee, progmg dir.

Baltimore

WANN(AM)—See Annapolis.

WBAL(AM)—Nov 2, 1925: 1090 khz; 50 kw-U, DA-N. TL: N39 22 33 W76 46 21. Hrs opn: 24. 3800 Hooper Ave. (21211). (301) 467-3000. Licensee: WBAL Div., The Hearst Corp. Group owner: Hearst Broadcasting Group (acq 1-14-35). Net: CBS. Rep: D & R Radio. Wash atty: Tharrington, Smith & Hargrove. Format: News/talk. Target aud: 25-54. Spec prog: Sports. ■ Edward C. Kiernan, vp & gen mgr; Jeffrey Beauchamp, stn mgr; John Grimes, opns mgr; Larry Doyle, gen sls mgr; Irv Zelt, natl sls mgr; Bob Cecil (local), rgnl sls mgr; Laurie Fleishman, prom mgr; Mark Miller, news dir; Hank Volpe, chief engr.

WIYY(FM)—Co-owned with WBAL(AM). Dec 7, 1958: 97.9 mhz; 13.5 kw. Ant 945 ft. TL: N39 20 05 W76 39 03. Stereo. Prog sep from AM. Net: ABC/R. Format: AOR. Target aud: 18-34. ■ Irvin R. Zelt, gen sls mgr; Wendy LaGrant (local), rgnl sls mgr; Mary France, prom mgr; Russ Mottla, progmg dir; Jonathan Shapiro, mus dir; Bob Lopez, news dir. ■ WBAL-TV affil.

WBGR(AM)—July 27, 1955: 860 khz; 2.5 kw-D, 66 w-N, DA-2. TL: N39 18 43 W76 29 26. 3000 Druid Park Dr. (21215). (410) 367-7773. Licensee: Mortenson Broadcasting Co. (group owner; acq 11-7-80; $700,000; FTR 11-24-80). Format: Relg/gospel. News staff one. Target aud: 18-49. ■ Su Wood, gen mgr, gen sls mgr & pub affrs dir; Naomi Durant, prom dir; Nor Ven Goldberry, progmg dir & mus dir; David Brown, news dir; Charles Fant, chief engr.

***WBJC(FM)**—April 6, 1951: 91.5 mhz; 50 kw. Ant 500 ft. TL: N39 23 11 W76 43 52. Stereo. 2901 Liberty Heights Ave. (21215). (410) 333-5100. Licensee: Baltimore City Community College (acq 4-22-91). Net: AP, APR, NPR. Format: Classical. ■ Cary Smith, gen mgr; Tom Hill, opns mgr; Jonathan Palevsky, progmg dir & mus dir; Frank Zeiler, chief engr.

WBMD(AM)—Dec 7, 1947: 750 khz; 1 kw-D. TL: N39 19 26 W76 32 56. Hrs opn: Sunrise-sunset. 4th Floor, 305 Washington Ave., Towson (21204). (410) 481-9000. FAX: (410) 825-2442. Licensee: Inner Harbor Broadcasting. Group owner: Sconnix Broadcasting Co. (acq 3-1-89; grpsl; FTR 1-23-89). Format: Relg. Spec prog: Gr one hr, Pol 2 hrs, Greek 2 hrs, Lithuanian one hr wkly. ■ Randall T. Odeneal, pres; James Bradford Murray, vp & gen mgr; Clark West, stn mgr; Mike McGraw, mus dir; Kevin Allensworth, chief engr.

***WBYQ(FM)**—Sept 17, 1974: 96.7 mhz; 19 w. Ant 75 ft. TL: N39 16 04 W76 30 57. Stereo. Office of Student Life, Essex Community College, 7201 Rossville Blvd. (21237). (410) 780-6572. FAX: (410) 686-9503. Licensee: Essex Community College (acq 8-1-86). Format: Educ. Target aud: 25-66. Spec prog: Classical 3 hrs, big band 6 hrs, nostalgia 6 hrs wkly. ■ Dr. Donald Slowinski, pres; Mitchell Perkins, gen mgr; Alex Soroka, chief engr.

WCAO(AM)—May 8, 1922: 600 khz; 5 kw-U, DA-1. TL: N39 25 47 W76 45 42. 1829 Reisterstown Rd. (21208). (410) 653-2200. Licensee: Summit-Baltimore Broadcasting Inc. Group owner: Summit Communications Group Inc. Net: NBC. Rep: McGavren Guild. Format: Black gospel. ■ Roy Deutschman, vp & gen mgr; Roy Sampson, opns mgr; Bill Ahlfield, dev dir; Bill Hopkinson, gen sls mgr; Dean Smith, natl sls mgr; Larry Jennings, rgnl sls mgr; MarLear Alston, prom mgr; Lee Michaels, mus dir; April Ryan, news dir; Mary Clayburn, pub affrs dir; Erich Steinnagel, chief engr.

WXYV(FM)—Co-owned with WCAO(AM). Dec 15, 1947: 102.7 mhz; 50 kw. Ant 436 ft. TL: N39 23 11 W76 43 52. Stereo. Prog sep from AM. Format: Urban contemp. ■ Roy Sampson, progmg dir; Stan Jacobs, mus dir; Jean Ross, pub affrs dir.

WCBM(AM)—1924: 680 khz; 10 kw-D, 5 kw-N, DA-2. TL: N39 24 30 W76 46 34. 68 Radio Plaza, Owings Mills (21117-3602). (410) 356-3003; (410) 581-0450. FAX: (410) 581-0150. Licensee: Bennett Gilbert Gaines, interlocutory receiver. Net: ABC/I, ABC TalkRadio, ARN. Rep: Katz. Format: Contemp talk. News staff 3. Target aud: 25-54; informed adults with major purchasing power. Spec prog: Jewish one hr, relg one hr wkly. ■ Nick Mangione Jr., gen mgr; Sean Casey, opns mgr & progmg dir; Ken Maylath, news dir; Vernon Anderson, pub affrs dir; Mike Fast, engrg dir. ■ Rates: $100, 80, 90, 60.

***WEAA(FM)**—Jan 10, 1977: 88.9 mhz; 12.5 kw. Ant 220 ft. TL: N39 20 31 W76 35 13. Stereo. Hrs opn: 18 Mon.-Fri.; 24 Sat.-Sun. Banneker Rm 202, Hillen Rd. & Coldspring Ln., (21239). (410) 319-3564. FAX: (410) 319-3698. Licensee: Morgan State University. Net: NPR, AP. Format: Jazz, news, info. News staff one; new progmg 13 hrs wkly. Target aud: 25-49. Spec prog: Caribbean, gospel; oldies 4 hrs, talk 14 hrs wkly. ■ Earl Richardson, pres; Wendy Williams (acting) gen mgr; Lori Brunson, dev dir; Curtis Brown, mktg dir; Paula C. Smith, prom dir; Lawrence Shorter, progmg dir & mus dir; Gary Ellerbe, asst mus dir; Gale Reed, news dir; Roslyn Nelson, pub affrs dir; Charles M. Fant, chief engr.

WERQ-FM—1960: 92.3 mhz; 37 kw. Ant 571 ft. TL: N39 20 20 W76 40 02. Stereo. 1111 Park Ave. (21201). (410) 523-6900. FAX: (410) 669-2127. Licensee: Radio One of Maryland (group owner; acq 6-21-93; $9 million with co-located AM; FTR 7-19-93). Net: AP. Rep: Major Mkt. Wash atty: Arent, Fox, Kintner, Plotkin & Kahn. Format: CHR, news/talk. News progmg 2 hrs wkly. Target aud: 18-34; young adults. ■ Cathy Hughes, CEO & chmn; Alfred Liggins, pres; Mike Covington, CFO; Lee Michaels, vp; Bill Hopper, gen mgr; Pam Somers, stn mgr & gen sls mgr; Bob Phillips, natl sls mgr; Hal Martin, mktg dir & prom mgr; Russ Allen, progmg dir; Kristie Wiemer, mus dir; Karl Goreing, chief engr.

WOLB(AM)—Co-owned with WERQ-FM. Nov 25, 1947: 1010 khz; 1 kw-D, 27 w-N. TL: N39 16 38 W76 37 59. Hrs opn: 24. Prog dups FM 100%. Rep: Major Mkt. News progmg 5 hrs wkly. Target aud: 35 plus; African American adults. Spec prog: Relg 2 hrs, Sp 2 hrs wkly.

WITH(AM)—Mar 1, 1941: 1230 khz; 1 kw-U. TL: N39 18 58 W76 36 03. Suite 650, 5 Light St. (21202). (410) 528-1230. FAX: (410) 528-1256. Licensee: Capital Kids' Radio Co. (acq 3-25-93; $762,500; FTR 4-12-93). Net: MBS. Rep: Roslin. Format: Big band, swing era & top hits of the 40s-80s. News progmg 2 hrs wkly. Target aud: 35 plus; nostalgia audience. Spec prog: It 2 hrs wkly. ■ James McCotter, pres; Cathleen Brunty, stn mgr; Niles Seaberg, vp progmg.

WIYY(FM)—Listing follows WBAL(AM).

WJFK(AM)—June 8, 1922: 1300 khz; 5 kw-U, DA-2. TL: N39 20 00 W76 46 13. Hrs opn: 24. 10800 Main St., Fairfax, VA (22030). (703) 691-1900. FAX: (703) 385-0189. Licensee: Infinity Broadcasting Corp. (group owner; acq 5-29-89; $32 million with co-located FM; FTR 4-24-89). Rep: Christal. Wash atty: Leventhal, Senter & Lerman. Format: Adult contemp. News staff 2. Target aud: 25-54. ■ Mel Karmazin, pres; Ken Stevens, gen mgr; Alan Leinwand, gen sls mgr; Tami Sacks, prom mgr; Jeremy Coleman, progmg dir; Mike Elston, news dir; Dan Ryson, chief engr.

WLIF-FM—Co-owned with WJFK(AM). Dec 24, 1970: 101.9 mhz; 13.5 kw. Ant 960 ft. TL: N39 25 02 W76 33 23. Stereo. Dups AM 100%. Suite 850, One W. Pennsylvania Ave., Towson (21204). (410) 823-1570. FAX: (410) 821-5482. ■ Kelly Swift, prom dir; Gary Balaban, progmg dir; Sloane Brown, news dir.

***WJHU-FM**—May 23, 1979: 88.1 mhz; 10 kw. Ant 360 ft. TL: N39 19 53 W76 39 28. Stereo. 2216 N. Charles St. (21218). (410) 516-9548. FAX: (410) 516-1976. Licensee: The Johns Hopkins Univ. Net: APR, NPR. Format: Class, jazz, news/talk. News staff one; news progmg 21 hrs wkly. ■ Dennis Kita, gen mgr; Lesley Gillman, dev dir & sls dir; Peter Moskowitz, progmg dir; Christopher Czeh, chief engr.

WKDB(AM)—See Towson.

WLIF-FM—Listing follows WJFK(AM).

WOLB(AM)—Listing follows WERQ-FM.

WPOC(FM)—Feb 4, 1960: 93.1 mhz; 16 kw. Ant 860 ft. TL: N39 17 13 W76 45 16. Stereo. 711 W. 40th St. (21211). (410) 366-3693. Licensee: Nationwide Communications Inc. Group owner: Nationwide Mutual Insurance Co. (acq 8-15-74). Net: ABC/E. Rep: McGavren Guild. Format: country. ■ Jennifer Grimm, gen mgr; Jim Dolan, gen sls mgr; Sheila Silverstein, prom mgr; Robert Moody, progmg dir; Greg Cole, mus dir; Merrie Street, news dir.

WQSR(FM)—See Catonsville.

WRBS(FM)—Aug 1, 1964: 95.1 mhz; 50 kw. Ant 499 ft. TL: N39 15 21 W76 40 29. Stereo. 3600 Georgetown Rd. (21227). (410) 247-4100. FAX: (410) 247-4533. Licensee: Peter and John Radio Fellowship Inc. (acq 9-64). Net: AP, Moody. Format: Inspirational. ■ Rev. John O. Bisset, pres; J. Thomas Bisset, gen mgr; Gary Carr, gen sls mgr; Steve Lawhon, progmg dir & mus dir; Henry Barnes, asst mus dir; David Paul, news dir; Peter Allen, chief engr. ■ Rates: $45; 45; 45; 45.

WVRT(FM)—1949: 104.3 mhz; 50 kw. Ant 420 ft. TL: N39 25 46 W76 27 01. Stereo. 3701 Malden Ave. (21211). (410) 466-9272. Licensee: Capitol Broadcasting Co. Inc. (acq 10-15-93; $9.7 million; FTR 11-8-93). Format: Mass appeal contemp.

WWIN(AM)—1951: 1400 khz; 1 kw-U. TL: N39 19 21 W76 36 33. Stereo. Hrs opn: 24. 6th Flr., 200 S. President St. (21202). (410) 332-8200. FAX: (410) 752-2252. Licensee: Radio One of Maryland Inc. (acq 1-23-92; 7.5 million; with WWIN-FM Glen Burnie). Net: ABC/C. Rep: D & R Radio. Wash atty: Verner, Liipert, Bernhard, McPherson & Hand. Format: Gospel inspirational. News staff one. news progmg one hr wkly. Target aud: 25-54; Black religious. ■ Catherine L. Hughes, CEO; Alfred C. Liggins, pres; Michael A. Covington, CFO; William B. Hooper, gen mgr; Pam Somers, stn mgr; Marvin Betts, prom dir; Lee Michaels, vp progmg; Terri Avery, progmg dir & mus dir; Glenda McCartney, news dir; Karl Goehring, chief engr.

WWIN-FM—See Glen Burnie.

WWLG(AM)—April 5, 1955: 1360 khz; 5 kw-D, 1.7 kw-N, DA-2. TL: N39 19 39 W76 39 48. Box 1591 (21203); Radisson Plaza Lord Baltimore Hotel (21201). (410) 576-8860. FAX: (410) 576-8863. Licensee: Houlpeka Limited Liability Co. (acq 1993; $675,000; FTR 9-13-93). Net: American Urban. Format: Big band, nostalgia. ■ Paul Kopelke, Jim Ward, gen mgrs.

WWMX(FM)—1960: 106.5 mhz; 7.4 kw. Ant 1,217 ft. TL: N39 20 10 W76 38 59. Stereo. Suite 201, 600 Washington Ave. (21204-3913). (410) 825-5400. FAX: (410) 583-1065. Licensee: Capitol Broadcasting Co. Inc. (group owner; acq 11-86; grpsl; FTR 9-22-86). Rep: Katz. Format: Adult contemp. ■ James Goodmon, pres; Arduth Gregory, vp & gen mgr; Robert Kiersznowski, gen sls mgr; Dawn Tritiak, prom mgr; Steve Cross, mus dir; Fred Klimes, chief engr.

WXYV(FM)—Listing follows WCAO(AM).

Bel Air

***WHFC(FM)**—1972: 91.1 mhz; 1.1 kw. Ant 226 ft. TL: N39 33 22 W76 16 48. Stereo. 401 Thomas Run Rd. (21015-1698). (410) 836-4358. FAX: (410) 836-4358. Licensee: Harford Community College. Format: Class, jazz, adult alt. News progmg 10 hrs wkly. Target aud: 24-42; upwardly mobile professionals. ■ John Davlin, gen mgr; Jeff Dean, mus dir; Ralph Hilsher, chief engr.

WHRF(AM)—June 11, 1963: 1520 khz; 250 w-D, DA. TL: N39 31 17 W76 21 45 (CP: 830 khz, 1 kw-N, DA-2, TL: N39 34 18 W76 26 57). 307 S. Tollgate Rd, 2nd Flr. (21014). (410) 638-0500. FAX: (410) 893-3951. Licensee: New Harford Group Inc. (acq 11-4-91). Net: ABC/E. Format: News/talk. ■ Pat McDonnough, pres; Gwen Corkran, gen sls mgr.

Berlin

WOCQ(FM)—June 25, 1981: 103.9 mhz; 3 kw. Ant 328 ft. TL: N38 22 58 W75 18 58. Stereo. Hrs opn: 24. Box 1850, Ocean City (21842); 11210 Bell Rd., Whaleysville (21872). (410) 641-0001. FAX: (410) 641-0930. Licensee: Musicradio of Maryland Inc. Net: ABC/E. Rep: Katz & Powell. Wash atty: James Koerner. Format: Contemp hit. News staff one; news progmg 4 hrs wkly. Target aud: 18-49. Rep: Roslin. Spec prog: "Casey's Top-40" 4 hrs, "The Countdown" with Walt Love 2 hrs wkly. ■ Darryl Nixon, chmn, pres & gen mgr; Skip McCloskey, opns mgr & chief engr; Ed Fennessey, gen sls mgr; Gary Smith, rgnl sls mgr; Don Duckman, progmg dir; Mari Lou Shuster, mus dir; George Kreiner, asst mus dir. ■ Rates: $45; 40; 45; 30.

Bethesda

WARW(FM)—October 1959: 94.7 mhz; 22.5 kw. Ant 780 ft. TL: N38 57 49 W77 06 12 (CP: 20.5 kw, ant 771 ft.). Hrs opn: 24. 5912 Hubbard Dr., Rockville (20852). (301) 984-6000. FAX: (301) 468-2490. Licensee: CBS Inc. Group owner: CBS Broadcast Group (acq 8-1-85; grpsl; FTR 6-10-85). Rep: CBS Radio Reps. Format: Rock and roll oldies. News staff 1. Target aud: General; adults 25-54. ■ Nancy Widmann, pres; Sarah Taylor, vp & gen mgr; Donna Ragland, gen sls mgr; Jim Zagami, natl sls mgr; Jimmy Lynn, prom mgr; Craig Ashwood, progmg dir; Beverly Fox, news dir & pub affrs dir; Jon Banks, chief engr.

WGMS-FM—See Washington, D.C.

WMMJ(FM)—Nov 12, 1961: 102.3 mhz; 2.9 kw. Ant 480 ft. TL: N38 56 09 W77 05 33. Stereo. 400 H St. N.E., Washington, DC (20002). (202) 675-4800. FAX: (202) 675-4842. Licensee: Almic Broadcasting Co. (acq 10-26-87; $7.5 million; FTR 10-26-87). Format: AC/Motown. News staff one. ■ Alfred Liggins, pres; Ed Turner, gen mgr; Tony Washington, gen sls mgr; Emma O'Neil, prom dir; Lee Michaels, progmg dir; Jim Allen, news dir; Karl Goehering, chief engr.

WTEM(AM)—Jan 2, 1946: 570 khz; 5 kw-D, 1 kw-N, DA-2. TL: N39 02 07 W77 10 11. Hrs opn: 24. One Central Plaza, 11300 Rockville Pike, Rockville (20852). (301) 468-1800. FAX: (301) 468-0491. Licensee: Classical Acquisition L.P. Group owner: Colfax Communications Inc. Rep: Eastman. Format: Sports. ■ Bennets Zier, gen mgr; Bob Snyder, gen sls mgr; Michelle Snyder, mktg dir; Brendan Hurley, prom mgr; Doug Gonden, progmg dir; Ron Sofologis, chief engr. ■ Rates: $200; 185; 170; na.

WUST(AM)—See Washington, D.C.

Braddock Heights

WZYQ(FM)—Apr 8, 1972: 103.9 mhz; 380 w. Ant 910 ft. TL: N39 27 50 W77 29 44. Stereo. Hrs opn: 24. Box 1129, 6633 Mt. Phillip Rd. (21702). (301) 663-5400. FAX: (301) 663-0636. Licensee: Musical Heights Inc. Rep: Roslin. Format: CHR. News staff one; news progmg 5 hrs wkly. Target aud: 25-49. ■ Leo Shank, pres; Jim Riley, gen mgr; Nancy Fowler, opns mgr; Nancy Burns, gen sls mgr; Anne Marie DeBremond, rgnl sls mgr; Diana Gibson, prom mgr; Bob Maxwell, progmg dir & mus dir; Dallas Kincaid, asst mus dir; Ted Ritter, news dir; Howard Fisher, chief engr.

Brunswick

WTRI(AM)—Oct 2, 1966: 1520 khz; 500 w-D, 250 w-CH. TL: N39 18 45 W77 36 31 (CP: 9.3 kw-D, 5.8 kw-CH, DA). Stereo. 214 13th Ave. (21716). (301) 834-6998. FAX: (703) 822-9092. Licensee: Tri-State Broadcasting Inc. (acq 11-8-91); $115,000; FTR 12-2-91). Format: All local music. News progmg 15 hrs wkly. Target aud: 20-45. Spec prog: Talk 2 hrs, farm 2 hrs, relg 7 hrs, sports 5 hrs wkly. ■ Elizabeth Roberts, pres, gen mgr & progmg dir; Andrea Kershaw, mus dir; Tom Whalen, news dir; Fran Little, chief engr.

California

WRFK(FM)—Mar 1, 1993: 102.9 mhz; 3.7 kw. Ant 407 ft. TL: N38 20 53 W76 37 40. Stereo. Stn currently dark. Box 2470, La Plata (20646). (301) 870-5550. Licensee: Somar Communications Inc. (acq 1993; $130,000; FTR 5-24-93). Wash atty: Fisher, Wayland, Cooper & Leader. ■ Roy Robertson, pres.

Cambridge

WCEM(AM)—1947: 1240 khz; 1 kw-U. TL: N38 35 02 W76 04 56. Box 237 (21613); 2 Bay St. (21613). (410) 228-4800. FAX: (410) 228-0130. Licensee: MTS Broadcasting (acq 6-20-93; $1,800,001 with co-located FM; FTR 8-9-93). Net: ABC/I. Rep: Republic. Format: C&W. News staff 2. Target aud: 25-54. ■ Sharon Palamaras, gen mgr; Joel Scott, opns mgr; Blake Wise, gen sls mgr; Al Miller, progmg dir & mus dir; Norm Elliott, news dir; Bruce Patrick, pub affrs dir; Gary Crouch, chief engr.

WCEM-FM—Jan 29, 1968: 106.3 mhz; 3 kw. Ant 298 ft. TL: N38 35 02 W76 04 56. Stereo. FTR 8-23-93. Net: ABC/I. Format: Adult contemp. Target aud: 18-49. ■ John Harris, progmg dir; Joel Scott, mus dir; Bruce Patrick, asst mus dir.

WFBR(FM)—Not on air, target date unknown: 94.3 mhz; 6 kw. Ant 328 ft. TL: N38 37 53 W76 01 33. 35 Solomons Island Rd., Annapolis (21401). Licensee: CWA Broadcasting Inc.

Catonsville

WQSR(FM)—Nov 22, 1963: 105.7 mhz; 50 kw. Ant 492 ft. TL: N39 19 26 W76 32 56. Stereo. 305 Washington Ave., Towson (21204). (410) 825-1000. FAX: (410) 337-2772. Licensee: Inner Harbor Broadcasting. Group owner: Sconnix Broadcasting Co. (acq 3-1-89; grpsl; FTR 1-23-89). Rep: Christal. Format: Oldies. News staff one. Target aud: 25-54. ■ Randall T. Odeneal, pres; James Bradford Murray, vp & gen mgr; Buz Hiken, gen sls mgr; Rosemary Kay Weiner, prom mgr; J. D. Adams, progmg dir; Linda Sherman, news dir; Kevin Allensworth, chief engr.

Chestertown

WCTR(AM)—June 16, 1963: 1530 khz; 250 w-D. TL: N39 13 35 W76 05 20. Box 700, 231 Flatland Rd. (21620). (410) 778-1530. FAX: (410) 778-4800. Licensee: Kent Broadcasting Corp. (acq 12-29-86; FTR 11-10-86). Format: Moody. Format: MOR, news/talk. News progmg 9 hrs wkly. Target aud: General. Spec prog: Farm 5 hrs wkly. ■ David Taylor, pres; Jody Taylor, vp, gen mgr & gen sls mgr; John Link, progmg dir; Dave Schmidt, chief engr.

College Park

***WMUC-FM**—Sept 10, 1979: 88.1 mhz; 8.5 w. Ant 3 ft. TL: N38 58 59 W76 56 37. Stereo. Box 99, University of Maryland, (20742). (301) 314-7865. FAX: (301) 314-7879. Licensee: University of Maryland. Format: Alternative ■ Steve Stofberg, gen mgr; David Barnes, progmg dir; Hal Miller, mus dir; Gil Yaker, chief engr.

Crisfield

WLSL(FM)—Not on air, target date unknown: 96.9 mhz; 3 kw. Ant 328 ft. TL: N37 59 57 W75 49 43. 2461 Eisenhower Ave., Alexandria, VA (22331-0100). (703) 960-4700. Licensee: Hoffman Broadcasting Inc. (acq 5-89; $25,000; FTR 5-29-89).

Cumberland

WALI(AM)—1948: 1230 khz; 1 kw-U. TL: N39 38 36 W78 44 35. 516 White Ave. (21502). (301) 777-5400. FAX: (301) 777-5404. Licensee: Northeast Broadcasting of Cumberland Inc. (acq 4-25-91; $1.8 million with co-located FM; FTR 5-13-91). Net: Unistar. Wash atty: Wilkinson, Barker, Knaver & Quinn. Format: Oldies. News staff 2; news progmg 5 hrs wkly. Target aud: 25-54. Spec prog: Sports talk. ■ James P. O'Leary, pres & gen mgr; Cathy Butts, vp sls; Pat Sullivan, progmg dir; Bill Weber, mus dir; Grant Garland, news dir; Rick Williams, chief engr. ■ Rates: $12; 10; 12; 5.

WROG(FM)—Co-owned with WALI(AM). 1948: 102.9 mhz; 32 kw. Ant 1,440 ft. TL: N39 34 56 W78 53 53. Stereo. Prog sep from AM. Format: Contemp country. News staff one. Target aud: 25-49. ■ Cathy Butts, sls dir. ■ Rates: $12; 10; 12; 11.

WCBC(AM)—June 24, 1953: 1270 khz; 5 kw-D, 1 kw-N, DA-2. TL: N39 40 28 W78 46 48. Box 1290, 35 Baltimore St. (21502). (301) 724-5000. FAX: (301) 722-8336. Licensee: Cumberland Broadcasting Co. Inc. (acq 4-8-76). Net: ABC, MBS, NBC Talknet, Westwood One. Format: Adult contemp. Target aud: 25 plus. ■ David B. Aydelotte Sr., pres; David N. Aydelotte, gen mgr; Mary Clites, gen sls mgr; Jim Robey, progmg dir; Bryan Gowans, news dir; Martin White, chief engr.

WKGO(FM)—Listing follows WTBO(AM).

WROG(FM)—Listing follows WALI(AM).

WTBO(AM)—Dec 13, 1928: 1450 khz; 1 kw-U. TL: N39 38 43 W78 45 05. Box 1644, 350 Byrd Ave. (21502). (301) 722-6666. Licensee: WTBO-WKGO Corp. Group owner: Dix Communications (acq 11-1-77). Net: Unistar. Rep: Dome & Associates. Format: Nostalgia. News staff one; news progmg 20 hrs wkly. Target aud: 40 plus. ■ Albert E. Dix, pres; Beda M. Riley, gen mgr; Richard Cornwell, gen sls mgr; Tim Martin, progmg dir; Jim Van, news dir; Craig Leasure, chief engr.

WKGO(FM)—Co-owned with WTBO(AM). April 1962: 106.1 mhz; 4 kw. Ant 1,400 ft. TL: N39 34 54 W78 53 58. Stereo. Hrs opn: 24. Prog sep from AM. Format: Top-40, CHR. News staff one; News progmg 3 hrs wkly. Target aud: 18-34.

Denton

WKDI(AM)—Dec 27, 1988: 840 khz; 1 kw-D, DA. TL: N38 53 53 W75 51 10. Stereo. Hrs opn: Sunrise-sunset. Box 309, 24580 Station Rd. (21629). (410) 479-2288. Licensee: Bayshore Communications Inc. Net: USA. Format: Christian. News progmg 12 hrs wkly. Target aud: 25-49; middle income Christians. ■ Edward A. Baker, pres; Michael A. McCoy, gen mgr & gen sls mgr; Michael McCoy, progmg dir & mus dir; David Schmidt, chief engr. ■ Rates: $12; 10; 12; 10.

Easton

WCEI(AM)—Sept 29, 1960: 1460 khz; 1 kw-D, 500 w-N, DA-2. TL: N38 46 13 W76 04 55. Stereo. 306 Port St. (21601). (410) 822-3301. Licensee: Clark Broadcasting Co. (acq 8-14-81; $512,500 with co-located FM; FTR 9-7-81). Net: AP, FNN, Motor Racing Net. Wash atty: Dow, Lohnes & Albertson. Format: Big band. News staff 2; news progmg 6 hrs wkly. Target aud: 45 plus; mature adults. ■ James A. Hammond, vp & gen mgr; Bill Crisp, progmg dir; Steve Hunter, mus dir; Anita Stewart, news dir; Dave Schmidt, chief engr.

WCEI-FM—May 14, 1975: 96.7 mhz; 25 kw. Ant 245 ft. TL: N38 46 13 W76 04 55. Stereo. Hrs opn: 24. Prog sep from AM. Net: AP, Unistar. Format: Adult contemp, oldies. Target aud: 25-54.

Elkton

***WOEL-FM**—September 1978: 89.9 mhz; 3 kw. Ant 259 ft. TL: N39 35 35 W75 51 49. Box 246 (21922). (410) 392-3225. Licensee: Maryland Baptist Bible College. Net: USA. Format: Relg. ■ Pastor Allen Dickerson, gen mgr.

WSER(AM)—Aug 22, 1963: 1550 khz; 1 kw-D, 10 w-N, DA-2. TL: N39 35 45 W75 47 50. 192 Maloney Rd. (21921). (410) 398-3883. FAX: (410) 392-9882. Licensee: First Philadelphia Properties Inc. (acq 7-7-87; $310,000; FTR 6-15-87). Net: ABC/E. Format: Adult contemp. Target aud: 25-54; primarily females. Spec prog: Relg 3 hrs, farm one hr wkly. ■ Brian Barrabee, pres; Mark Crouch, gen mgr; Charles Doll, gen sls mgr; Polly Barrabee, prom mgr & progmg dir; Joe Vietri, mus dir; Dave Langley, news dir; Mike S. Phinney, chief engr. ■ Rates: $15; 15; 15; na.

Emmittsburg

***WMTB-FM**—Oct 1, 1977: 89.9 mhz; 100 w. Ant 144 ft. TL: N39 41 02 W77 21 25. Hrs opn: Noon-3 PM. WMTB-FM, Mount Saint Mary's College, Emmittsburg (21727-7799). (301) 447-6122. Licensee: Mount Saint Mary's College. Format: Classic rock, new age. News progmg 2 hrs wkly. Target aud: General; college and community. Spec prog: Folk nine hr, gospel one hr, relg 4 hrs wkly. ■ John Fitzpatrick, gen mgr; T.J. Rainsford, progmg dir; David Cooper, mus dir; David McKay, news dir; Joseph Goetz, engrg dir & chief engr.

Federalsburg

WWPL(FM)—Dec 2, 1978: 107.1 mhz; 3.9 kw. Ant 408 ft. TL: N38 46 02 W75 44 46 Hrs opn: 5 AM-midnight. Box P, 6301 Meadow Dr., Hurlock (21643). (410) 754-9580. FAX: (410) 754-9580. Licensee: P.M. Broadcast Engineering Inc. (acq 9-26-91; $170,000; FTR 10-28-91). Net: ABC. Format: Easy lstng. News progmg 4 hrs wkly. Target aud: 35 plus; adults, affluent. ■ Mike Powell, pres & gen mgr. ■ Rates: $10; 9; 10; 5.

Frederick

WARX(FM)—See Hagerstown.

WFMD(AM)—Jan 1, 1936: 930 khz; 5 kw-D, 2.5 kw-N, DA-2. TL: N39 24 55 W77 27 41. Stereo. Box 151 (21705); 5966 Grove Hill Rd. (21702). (301) 663-4181. FAX: (301) 663-5494. Licensee: James L. Gibbons Radio Inc. (acq 11-1-67). Net: CBS, Daynet, NBC Talknet. Format: News/talk. News staff 4; news progmg 30 hrs wkly. Target aud: 25-54; Frederick County adults. ■ Jim Gibbons, pres; Jim Gibsons, gen mgr; John Fieseler, progmg dir; Randy Gray, news dir; Roger Lide, chief engr.

WFRE(FM)—Co-owned with WFMD(AM). Feb 19, 1961: 99.9 mhz; 9 kw. Ant 1,100 ft. TL: N39 29 59 W77 29 58. Stereo. Prog sep from AM. (301) 663-4337. Net: Wall Street. Format: Easy lstng. ■ Tom Gibbons, stn mgr.

WQSI(AM)—Dec 15, 1960: 820 khz; 4.3 kw-D, 430 w-N, DA-N. TL: N39 24 42 W77 28 20. Hrs opn: 24. Box 1129, 6633 Mt. Phillip Rd., (21702). (301) 663-5400. FAX: (301) 663-0636. Licensee: Musical Heights Inc. Net: ABC/I. Rep: Roslin. Format: Country. News staff one; news progmg 15 hrs wkly. Target aud: 25-54. ■ Leo L. Shank, pres; Jim Riley, gen mgr; Nancy Fowler, opns mgr; Nancy Burns, gen sls mgr; Anne-Marie DeBremond, rgnl sls mgr; Ray Romano, prom mgr, progmg dir & mus dir; Ted Ritter, news dir; Howard Fisher, chief engr.

Frostburg

WFRB(AM)—Dec 20, 1958: 560 khz; 5 kw-D. TL: N39 41 02 W78 57 57. Hrs opn: 6 AM-2 hrs post-sunset. Box 373, Rt. 2 (21532). (301) 689-8871. FAX: (301) 689-8880. Licensee: Western Maryland Broadcasting Co. Inc. Net: ABC/E, AP. Format: C&W, relg, news/talk. News staff 2; news progmg 10 hrs wkly. Target aud: 25-55; those gainfully employed, in the market for goods and svcs. ■ D.C. Loughry, pres & gen mgr; Chris Bagley, opns mgr & prom mgr; R. Dean Hillegas, gen sls mgr; Greg Barrett, mus dir; Jim Welsh, news dir; Allen Brown, pub affrs dir; Robert May, chief engr. ■ Rates: $14; 12.90; 14; 11.80.

WFRB-FM—Oct 1, 1965: 105.3 mhz; 16.5 kw. Ant 960 ft. TL: N39 41 02 W78 57 57. Stereo. Hrs opn: 24. Dups AM 50%. Format: Country. News staff 2; news progmg 5 hrs wkly. ■ Rates: Same as AM.

*WFWM(FM)—April 1986: 91.7 mhz; 150 w. Ant 1,242 ft. TL: N39 34 54 W78 53 53. Stereo. Hrs opn: 24. Compton Hall, CG 4A, Frostburg State Univ. (21532). (301) 689-4143. FAX: (301) 689-7040. Licensee: Frostburg State Univ. Format: Class, jazz, alternative. News progmg 2 hrs wkly. Target aud: General. Spec prog: Educ 11 hrs wkly. ■ Rene G. Atkinson, gen mgr, prom mgr & progmg mgr; Lisa Browning, opns mgr; Coleen Peterson, vp dev; Jos Groen, mus dir; Martin White, engrg dir & chief engr; Jim Kerr, engrg mgr.

*WLIC(FM)—Oct 1989: 97.1 mhz; 145 w. Ant 1,401 ft. TL: N39 34 56 W78 53 53 (CP: 150 w, ant 1,355 ft.). Stereo. Hrs opn: 24. Rebroadcasts WAIJ(FM) Grantsville 100%. Box 540, He's Alive Corp. Offices, 34 Springs Rd., Grantsville (21536). (301) 895-3292; (301) 729-0778. FAX: (301) 895-3293. Licensee: He's Alive Inc. (group owner). Net: USA. Wash atty: Lee Peltzman. Format: Gospel, Christian adult contemp. Target aud: General. ■ Dewayne Johnson, pres; Wally Weeks, gen mgr, progmg dir & mus dir; Martin White, chief engr.

Funkstown

WPVG(AM)—Sept 26, 1991: 1160 khz; 1 kw-D, 500 w-N. TL: N39 11 16 W77 12 56. Box 728 (21734). (301) 733-8900. FAX: (301) 733-8900. Licensee: Peter V. Gureckis dba WPVG Inc. Format: Hot country. Target aud: 40 plus. ■ Peter V. Gureckis, pres; Michael Gureckis, gen mgr & gen sls mgr; Dave Reichard, prom mgr; Sam Wolfe, mus dir; Mike Powell, chief engr.

Gaithersburg

WMET(AM)—Jan 31, 1983: 1150 khz; 1 kw-D, 500 w-N, DA-2. TL: N39 11 16 W77 12 56. Suite 203, 2401 Research Blvd., Rockville (20850). (301) 921-0093. FAX: (301) 926-8227. Licensee: Beltway Communications Corp. (acq 11-3-86; $525,000; FTR 8-4-86). Format: News/talk. News staff 2; Target aud: 25-54; upscale, educated. ■ Ernest Davis, pres & gen mgr; Richard J. Mangus, vp opns & progmg dir; Tom McGinley, chief engr.

Glen Burnie

WJRO(AM)—May 15, 1963: 1590 khz; 1 kw-U, DA-2. TL: N39 10 36 W76 37 20. Box 159 (21061). (410) 761-1590. Licensee: Erald Broadcasting Inc. (acq 3-13-81; $350,000; FTR 3-30-81). Net: AP. Format: Relg, gospel. ■ George Dietrich, pres & gen mgr; Larnell Phillips, gen sls mgr, progmg dir & mus dir; Alex Soroka, chief engr.

WWIN-FM—Sept 15, 1964: 95.9 mhz; 3 kw-H, 2.55 kw-V. Ant 299 ft. TL: N39 12 16 W76 34 07. Hrs opn: 24. 6th Flr., 200 S. President St., Baltimore (21202). (410) 332-8200. FAX: (410) 752-2252. Licensee: Radio One of Maryland Inc. (acq 1-2-92; $7.5 million with WWIN(AM) Baltimore). Rep: D & R Radio. Wash atty: Verner, Liipfert, Bernhard, McPherson & Hand. Format: Black adult contemp. News staff one; news progmg one hr wkly. Target aud: 35-54. ■ Catherine L. Hughes, CEO; Alfred C. Liggins, pres; Michael A. Covington, CFO; William B. Hooper, gen mgr; Pam Somers, vp progmg; Terri Avery, progmg dir & mus dir; Glenda McCartney, news dir; Carl Goehring, chief engr.

Grantsville

*WAIJ(FM)—Oct 1984: 90.3 mhz; 1 kw-H, 880 w-V. Ant 561 ft. TL: N39 42 14 W79 05 31. Stereo. Hrs opn: 24. Box 540, He's Alive Corp. Offices, 34 Springs Rd. (21536). (301) 895-3292. FAX: (301) 895-3293. Licensee: He's Alive Inc. (group owner). Net: USA. Wash atty: Lee Peltzman. Format: Gospel, Christian adult contemp. Target aud: 23-40. ■ Dewayne Johnson, pres & gen mgr; Wally Weeks, stn mgr & progmg dir; Mark VanOuse, prom mgr; Rick Williams, chief engr.

Grasonville

WXZL(FM)—Licensed to Grasonville. See Annapolis.

Hagerstown

WARK(AM)—July 20, 1947: 1490 khz; 1 kw-U. TL: N39 37 35 W77 42 40. 880 Commonwealth Ave. (21740). (301) 733-4500; (800) 222-9279. Licensee: Manning Broadcasting Inc. (acq 10-1-82; $730,000 with co-located FM; FTR 10-11-82). Net: SMN. Rep: Katz & Powell. Wash atty: Dow, Lohnes & Albertson. Format: Oldies. News staff one; news progmg 8 hrs wkly. Target aud: 25-54. ■ Eugene J. Manning, pres & gen mgr; J. Frederick Manning, vp opns; Thomas McCanner, sls dir; Susan Burns, progmg dir; Fran Little, chief engr.

WARX(FM)—Co-owned with WARK(AM). March 1957: 106.9 mhz; 15.5 kw. Ant 855 ft. TL: N39 29 43 W77 36 42. Stereo. Hrs opn: 24. Net: Westwood One, MBS. Format: Oldies. Spec prog: Jazz 3 hrs wkly.

*WETH(FM)—June 1993: 89.1 mhz; 900 w. Ant 1,338 ft. TL: N39 41 39 W77 30 50. Box 2626, Washington, DC (20013). Licensee: Greater Washington Education Telecommunication Assoc. Net: NPR, APR. Format: Folk. ■ Neil Mahrer, exec vp; Tom Livingston, sr vp; Cynthia Cotton, opns mgr; Mike Soper, vp dev; Elise Addy, vp prom; Mary Stewart, prom mgr; Marilyn Cooley, mus dir; Joe Davis, chief engr.

WHAG(AM)—(Halfway). June 9, 1962: 1410 khz; 1 kw-D, 99 w-N, DA-2. TL: N39 37 03 W77 44 17. Hrs opn: 6 AM-7 PM. 1250 Maryland Ave., Hagerstown (21740). (301) 797-7300. FAX: (301) 797-5659. Licensee: Gemini Broadcast Group (acq 7-1-85; $890,000 with co-located FM; FTR 4-22-85). Net: ABC TalkRadio, CNN. Format: News/talk. News staff 2; news progmg 7 hrs wkly. Target aud: 25-64; news-talk information profile; older, upscale. ■ Kibby Albright, gen mgr & gen sls mgr; Will Kauffman, news dir; Peter Loewenheim, chief engr. ■ Rates: $18; 19; 18; na.

WQCM(FM)—(Halfway). Co-owned with WHAG(AM). January 1965: 96.7 mhz; 4.8 kw. Ant 164 ft. TL: N39 37 03 W77 44 17. Prog sep from AM. Net: ABC. Format: Classic rock, AOR. News staff 2. Target aud: 18-54; adults, young families. ■ David W. Miller, progmg dir; Will Kauffman, mus dir; Sean O'Mealy, (asst) mus dir; Randy Mitchell, pub affrs dir. ■ Rates: $26; 24; 26; 18.

WJEJ(AM)—October 1932: 1240 khz; 1 kw-U. TL: N39 40 00 W77 43 30. Hrs opn: 5 AM-2 AM. 1135 Haven Rd. (21742). (301) 739-2323. FAX: (301) 797-7408. Licensee: Hagerstown Broadcasting Co Inc (acq 12-21-72). Net: CBS, AP. Wash atty: Baraff, Koerner, Olender & Hochberg. Format: Adult contemp. News staff one; news progmg 21 hrs wkly. Target aud: 35 plus. Spec prog: Farm one hr, talk 8 hrs wkly. ■ John T. Staub, pres & gen mgr; Louis J. Scally, progmg dir & chief engr; Travis Medcalf, mus dir; Tom Bradley, news dir.

WWMD(FM)—Co-owned with WJEJ(AM). 1946: 104.7 mhz; 8.3 kw. Ant 1,379 ft. TL: N39 41 47 W77 30 47. Stereo. Hrs opn: 5 AM-2 AM. Prog sep from AM. (301) 739-2326. Format: Easy lstng. News progmg 11 hrs wkly. Target aud: Mature, upscale, educated professionals. ■ Travis Medcalf, pub affrs dir; David Butler, chief engr.

WQCM(FM)—Listing follows WHAG(AM).

WWMD(FM)—Listing follows WJEJ(AM).

WYII(FM)—See Williamsport.

Halfway

WHAG(AM)—Licensed to Halfway. See Hagerstown.

WQCM(FM)—Licensed to Halfway. See Hagerstown.

Havre de Grace

WASA(AM)—May 15, 1948: 1330 khz; 5 kw-D, 500 w-N, DA-N. TL: N39 33 55 W76 07 08. Box 97, 1605 Level Rd. (21078). (410) 939-0800; (410) 575 6511. FAX: (410) 939-1861. Licensee: KME Broadcasting Corp. (acq 8-14-92; $150,000; FTR 8-31-92). Net: CBS, CBS Spectrum, USA. Format: Classic country. News staff one. Target aud: General. Spec prog: Black. ■ Kurt M.] Elasauage, pres; Donald Kampes, gen mgr; Paul Sheldon, progmg dir & chief engr.

WXCY(FM)—June 19, 1960: 103.7 mhz; 50 kw. Ant 341 ft. TL: N39 33 55 W76 07 08. Stereo. Hrs opn: 24. Box 269, 707 Revolution St. (21078). (410) 939-1100; (410) 939-1101. FAX: (410) 939-1104. Licensee: Prettyman Broadcasting Co. (group owner; acq 3-6-89). Net: Unistar. Rep: Katz & Powell. Format: Modern country. News staff 2. Target aud: 25-54. Spec prog: Relg 2 hrs, NASCAR races 6 hrs wkly. ■ Bill Prettyman, pres; Bob Bloom, gen mgr; Jeanne Fotiadis, rgnl sls mgr; Rico Richards, prom dir; Dave Hovel, progmg dir; Dave Roberts, mus dir; Jane Bellmeir, news dir; Libby Cole, pub affrs dir; Tom Ringer, engrg dir; Ken Carey, chief engr. ■ Rates: $50; 40; 50; 35.

Hurlock

WAAI(FM)—June 1, 1989: 100.9 mhz; 1.3 kw. Ant 502 ft. TL: N38 37 28 W75 53 20. Stereo. Hrs opn: 24. Box 1300, 6301 Meadow Dr. (21643). (410) 754-3032; (410) 376-3032. Licensee: Apex Associates Inc. Net: Unistar, CNN. Wash atty: Roberts & Eckard. Format: Country. News staff one; news progmg 6 hrs wkly. Target aud: 25-54; general. Spec prog: Gospel 3 hrs wkly. ■ Keith Mayo, pres, gen mgr & chief engr; Troy Hill, opns mgr; William Bukowski, progmg dir; Ed Lewis, news dir. ■ Rates: $18; 9; 12; 8.

Indian Head

WNTL(AM)—June 1986: 1030 khz; 50 kw-D, DA. TL: N38 33 53 W76 49 01. Stereo. Box 1650, Waldorf (20604). (301) 870-8700. FAX: (301) 870-6714. Licensee: WBZE Inc. Wash atty: Roy F. Perkins Jr. Format: Country. Spec prog: Arabic. ■ Peter V. Gureckis, pres; Steve P. Gureckis, vp sls; Elizabeth A. Gureckis, vp progmg; Douglas Dillman, news dir; Michael Powell, chief engr.

La Plata

WMOM(AM)—October 1965: 1560 khz; 1 kw-D. TL: N39 32 36 W76 59 37. Box 2470 (20646). (301) 934-9666. FAX: (301) 884-0280. Licensee: Somar Communications Inc. (acq 4-12-91; $65,000; FTR 5-6-91). Format: Adult contemp. News progmg 5 hrs wkly. Target aud: 25 plus. Spec prog: Farm 2 hrs, sports 8 hrs, loc pub affrs one hr wkly. ■ Roy Robertson, gen mgr.

Laurel

WILC(AM)—Dec 23, 1965: 900 khz; 1.9 kw-D, 500 w-N. TL: N39 04 57 W76 50 19. Box 42 (20707). (301) 953-2332. FAX: (301) 206-2841. Licensee: ILC Corp. (acq 11-5-85). Rep: Caballero. Format: Sp, latin mus, news. News staff 2. Target aud: General. ■ Dr. Israel Lopez, pres; Alejandro Carrasco, gen mgr, gen sls mgr, progmg dir & mus dir; Ione Molinares, news dir; Roger Oufalt, chief engr.

Lexington Park

WPTX(AM)—Apr 20, 1953: 920 khz; 5 kw-D, 1 kw-N, DA-2. TL: N38 16 57 W76 33 35. St. AndrewsChurch Rd. (20653). (301) 475-8383. FAX: (301) 475-7832. Licensee: Southern Maryland Broadcasting. Group owner: Emmet Broadcasting Co. (acq 6-1-89; $900,000 with co-located FM; FTR 6-12-89). Net: ABC/I. Format: Country. News staff one; news progmg 15 hrs wkly. Target aud: 24-59; upscale, information oriented adults. ■ Grenville T. Emmet, pres; Ray Holbrook, gen mgr; Mike Lucas, opns mgr; Christine Macinnon, news dir; Mike Powell, chief engr.

WMDM-FM—Co-owned with WPTX(AM). Dec 16, 1976: 97.7 mhz; 3 kw. Ant 273 ft. TL: N38 16 57 W76 33 35. Stereo. Prog sep from AM. Net: ABC/FM. Format: Top-40. News progmg 3 hrs wkly. Target aud: 18-45; upwardly mobile young adults. ■ Beverly Farmer, progmg dir & mus dir.

Mechanicsville

WSMD(FM)—Sept 1, 1988: 98.3 mhz; 3 kw. Ant 328 ft. TL: N38 24 49 W76 46 31. Stereo. Hrs opn: 24. Box 2470, La Plata (20646); The Morgan Bldg., Rt. 5 (20659). (301) 870-5550; (301) 884-5550. FAX: (301) 884-0280. Licensee: Somar Communications Inc. Net: ABC/E. Wash atty: Fisher, Wayland, Cooper & Leader. Format: Adult contemp. News staff one; news progmg 6 hrs wkly. Target aud: 18-49; middle to upper income adults. Spec prog: Pub svc 3 hrs, Crime Solvers one hr, news 14 hrs wkly. ■ Roy Robertson, pres & gen mgr; Sharon McGuire, gen sls mgr; Kevin Strom, chief engr. ■ Rates: $45; 35; 40; 30.

Middletown

WAFY(FM)—May 7, 1990: 103.1 mhz; 3 kw. Ant 328 ft. TL: N39 24 35 W77 31 19. Stereo. Hrs opn: 24. Box 600, 4707 Schley Ave., Braddock Heights (21714). (301) 371-7900; (301) 473-4700. FAX: (301) 371-7901. Licensee: Barbara D. Marmet. Wash atty: Harold K. McCombs Jr. Format: Adult contemp. Target aud: 25-54; upscale, well-educated, great radio commitment. ■ Barbara Marmet, gen mgr; Josh Brooks, gen sls mgr; Bill Madden, prom mgr; Norm Schmidt, mus dir; Anne Kramer, news dir; David Keefer, chief engr.

Morningside

WPGC(AM)—October 1954: 1580 khz; 50 kw-D, 250 w-N, DA. TL: N38 52 07 W76 53 48. Hrs opn: 24. Box 10239, Washington, DC (20018); Suite 800, 6301 Ivy Lane, Greenbelt, MD (20770). (301) 441-3500. FAX: (301) 345-9505; (301) 441-9555. Licensee: Cook Inlet Radio License Partnership L.P. (acq 6-8-92; with co-located FM). Net: BRN, AP, Unistar. Rep: Banner. Wash atty: Covington & Burling. Format: News/talk (financial). News staff 10. Target aud: 25-54; Washington business/decision makers. Spec prog: Business/financial news. ■ Benjamin Hill, pres & gen mgr; Dale Williamson, vp; Gene Harley, stn mgr; Steve Chaconas, opns mgr, progmg dir & news dir; Michelle Royal, gen sls mgr; Tom McGinley, chief engr.

WPGC-FM—February 1959: 95.5 mhz; 50 kw. Ant 500 ft. TL: N38 51 48 W76 54 38. Stereo. Hrs opn: 24. Prog sep from AM. Net: AP, NBC. Wash atty: Covington & Burling. Format: CHR. News staff one. Target aud: 18-54; general. ■ Sam Rogers, stn mgr & gen sls mgr; Jay Stevens, opns dir & progmg dir; Cindy Friedman, rgnl sls mgr; Dawn Scott, prom mgr; Al DeAngelo, mus dir; Lejaun McCain, asst mus dir; David Haines, news dir; Josh Spiegel, pub affrs dir; Tom McGinley, engrg dir.

Mountain Lake Park

WKHJ(FM)—July 9, 1990: 98.9 mhz; 490 w. Ant 662 ft. TL: N39 24 37 W79 17 51. Stereo. Hrs opn: 24. Box 2337, 407 Lothian St. (21550). (301) 334-4272; (301) 334-2086. FAX: (301) 334-2152. Licensee: Southern Highlands Inc. Net: CNN. Format: Adult contemp. News staff one; news progmg 12 hrs wkly. Target aud: 18-49. ■ Roger L. Ruff, pres & chief engr; Terry King, gen mgr, opns mgr & gen sls mgr; Cathy G. Clocker, prom dir & mus dir; Greta E. Edgar, progmg dir; James Shaffer, news dir; Alice Winston, pub affrs dir. ■ Rates: $14.20; 11.40; 14.20; 11.40.

Oakland

WKHJ(FM)—See Mountain Lake Park.

WMSG(AM)—May 19, 1963: 1050 khz; 1 kw-D, 75 w-N. TL: N39 25 15 W79 25 00. Box 271 (21550). (301) 334-3800; (301) 334-3700. FAX: (301) 334-5800. Licensee: Oakland Radio Station Corp. Net: CBS. Format: Country. News staff one. Target aud: General. ■ Brenda Butscher, pres & gen mgr; Todd Derham, progmg dir & mus dir; Brian Edwards, engrg dir. ■ Rates: $9.15; 7.25; 9.15; 5.80.

WXIE(FM)—Co-owned with WMSG(AM). 1966: 92.3 mhz; 1.4 w. Ant 689 ft. TL: N39 26 41 W79 31 42. Stereo. Prog sep from AM. (301) 334-1100. Net: ABC. Format: Classic rock.

Ocean City

WETT(AM)—July 1, 1960: 1590 khz; 1 kw-D, 500 w-N, DA-2. TL: N38 24 16 W75 07 37. Hrs opn: 24. Box 785 (21842). (410) 723-6505. FAX: (410) 723-6508. Licensee: R. Akin Esq. & Banking Services Corp. Group owner: Benchmark Communications Radio. Rep: Banner. Format: News, sports. News staff 2; news progmg 25 hrs wkly. Target aud: 25-54. ■ Chris Wallace, gen mgr; Doug Welldon, gen sls mgr; Bonnie Jones, gen sls mgr; Duke Brooks, progmg dir & news dir; Jeff Twilley, chief engr.

WKHI(FM)—See Bethany Beach, Del.

WOCQ(FM)—See Berlin.

WRXS(FM)—Not on air, target date unknown: 106.9 mhz; 3 kw. Ant 328 ft. 517 Croaton Rd., Virginia Beach, VA (23451). Licensee: J.H. Communications.

WWFG(FM)—June 30, 1978: 99.9 mhz; 50 kw. Ant 319 ft. TL: N38 20 07 W75 09 04. Stereo. 2301 Coastal Hwy. (21842). (410) 289-3456. FAX: (410) 289-3299. Licensee: Benchmark Radio Aquisition Fund IV Ltd. Group owner: Benchmark Communications Radio (acq 1993; $2 million; FTR 9-13-93). Format: Country. News staff one; news progmg 3 hrs wkly. Target aud: 25 plus; affluent, upwardly mobile, male & female. ■ Chris Walus, gen mgr; Doug Welldon, stn mgr; J. J. McKay, opns mgr & progmg dir; Stevie Prettyman, gen sls mgr; Brian K. Hall, news dir; Norman Schultz, chief engr.

Ocean City-Salisbury

WQHQ(FM)—Licensed to Ocean City-Salisbury. See Salisbury.

Ocean Pines

WZJO(FM)—Not on air, target date unknown: 97.1 mhz; 2.10 kw. Ant 394 ft. TL: N38 23 50 W75 10 50. Box 909, c/o Prettyman Broadcasting, Salisbury (21803). (410) 742-3212. Licensee: Prettyman Broadcasting (group owner; acq 12-3-93; $60,000; FTR 12-20-93). ■ William E. Prettyman Jr., pres.

Owings Mills

WCBM(AM)—See Baltimore.

Pocomoke City

WDMV(AM)—Aug 1, 1955: 540 khz; 500 w-D, 243 w-N. TL: N38 03 11 W75 34 11 (CP: COL: Brinklow, 1 kw, TL: N39 15 42 W77 03 19). Box 210, 1637 Dunn Swamp Rd. (21851). FAX: (410) 957-4940. Licensee: Birach Broadcasting Corp. (acq 11-25-92; $127,500; FTR 12-14-92). Wash atty: Pepper & Corazzini. ■ Sid Friedman, pres.

WMYJ(FM)—May 1, 1992: 106.5 mhz; 1.8 kw. Ant 341 ft. TL: N37 58 38 W75 32 36. Box 810 (21851). (410) 957-4300. FAX: (410) 957-4930. Licensee: Transmedia, Inc. Net: NBC. Wash atty: Cohn & Marks. Format: A/C, Oldies. News progmg 8 hrs wkly. Target aud: 25-54. ■ "Choppy" Layton, pres & gen mgr; Bill LeCato, prom dir, progmg dir & mus dir; Norman Schultz, chief engr.

Potomac-Cabin John

WCTN(AM)—1965: 950 khz; 2.5 kw-D, 47 w-N, DA-2. TL: N39 02 12 W77 12 09. No. 211, 7825 Tuckerman Ln., Potomac (20854). (301) 299-7026. FAX: (301) 299-5301. Licensee: Seven Locks Broadcasting Co. Inc. (acq 10-15-85). Net: USA. Rep: John Vogt. Wash atty: Fisher, Wayland, Cooper & Leader. Format: Adult contemp, relg. News progmg 8 hrs wkly. Target aud: 22-45. Spec prog: Adult contemp Christian. ■ Jim McIlvaine, CEO & chmn; John Vogt, pres & gen mgr; Steve Sparks, vp; Rebecca Wong, opns mgr; Nancy Burke, prom dir; Sally Vogt, mus dir; John Vogt, Nancy Burke, pub affrs dirs; Robert Allen, chief engr. ■ Rates: $35; 25; 30; na.

Prince Frederick

WMJS(FM)—August 1971: 92.7 mhz; 2.1 kw. Ant 565 ft. TL: N38 30 52 W76 37 03. Stereo. Hrs opn: 24. Box 547 (20678). (410) 535-2201. Licensee: MJS Communications Inc. (acq 6-19-73). Net: AP. Wash atty: Miller & Miller. Format: Oldies. News progmg 7 hrs wkly. Target aud: General. ■ Melvin Gollub, pres & gen mgr; Ada Gollub, gen sls mgr; Martin Madden, progmg dir. ■ Rates: $25.50; 17.50; 25.50; 17.50.

Princess Anne

***WESM(FM)**—March 29, 1987: 91.3 mhz; 50 kw. Ant 347 ft. TL: N38 12 37 W75 40 56. Stereo. Hrs opn: 24. Univ. of Maryland Eastern Shore, Backbone Rd. (21853). (410) 651-2816; (410) 651-2817. FAX: (410) 651-2819. Licensee: Univ. of Maryland Eastern Shore. Net: NPR, APR, American Urban. Format: Jazz, Black, relg. News staff one; news progmg 15 hrs wkly. Target aud: General. Spec prog: Blues 4 hrs, reggae 6 hrs, big band 8 hrs, gospel 20 hrs wkly. ■ William P. Hythe, pres; Robert A. Franklin, gen mgr; Michael Jenkins, progmg mgr & mus dir; Robin Peace, news dir & pub affrs dir; David Schmidt, chief engr.

WOLC(FM)—Dec 24, 1976: 102.5 mhz; 50 kw. Ant 500 ft. TL: N38 06 43 W75 39 14. Stereo. Box 130, Crisfield Ln. (21853). (410) 543-9652. FAX: (410) 651-9652. Licensee: Maranatha Inc. Net: AP, USA. Wash atty: Grover Cooper. Format: Relg. Target aud: 35-50; older baby boomers. ■ Don Andrews, pres; Jim East, gen mgr; Kelly Taylor, sls dir; Greg Fentress, progmg dir; Mark Bownet, chief engr. ■ Rates: $14.20; 14.20; 14.20; 14.20.

Rockville

WINX(AM)—November 1951: 1600 khz; 1 kw-D, 500 w-N, DA-N. TL: N39 05 51 W77 09 07. Hrs opn: 6 AM-midnight. Box 1726, Radio Center, 8 Baltimore Rd. (20850). (301) 424-9292. FAX: (301) 424-8266. Licensee: Radio Broadcast Communications Inc. (acq 1-15-93; $150,000; FTR 2-8-93). Rep: Roslin. Format: Oldies. News staff one; news progmg 11 hrs wkly. Target aud: 25-54; upscale, suburban adults. Spec prog: Black one hr, Jewish 3 hrs, Greek 2 hrs wkly. ■ Bill Parris, pres; Gene Alim, vp, gen mgr & vp adv; Gary Gross, opns dir, progmg dir & news dir; Martin Miller, gen sls mgr; Bill Vickers, chief engr. ■ Rates: $30; 25; 30; 20.

Salisbury

***WDIH(FM)**—June 1990: 90.3 mhz; 378 w. Ant 180 ft. TL: N38 24 28 W75 36 16. Box 186, Salisbury (21801). (410) 546-7772. Licensee: Salisbury Educational Broadcasting Foundation. Format: Christian preaching & music. ■ Rev. George Copeland, gen mgr; Craig Baker, chief engr.

WDMV(AM)—See Pocomoke City.

WICO(AM)—September 1957: 1320 khz; 1 kw-D, 36 w-N. TL: N38 21 39 W75 37 00. Box 909 (21803). (410) 742-3212. FAX: (410) 548-1543. Licensee: Prettyman Broadcasting Co. (group owner; acq 9-10-81; $1.06 million with co-located FM; FTR 10-5-81). Net: ABC. Rep: Torbet. Format: Talk, info. ■ Bill Prettyman, pres, gen mgr & gen sls mgr; Joe Edwards, progmg dir; C. R. Hook, mus dir; Thomas Ringer, chief engr.

WICO-FM—Sept 3, 1969: 94.3 mhz; 3 kw. Ant 299 ft. TL: N38 21 39 W75 37 00 (CP: Ant 328 ft.). Stereo. Format: Country. ■ Pat Ford, news dir.

WJDY(AM)—March 14, 1958: 1470 khz; 5 kw-D, DA. TL: N38 23 30 W75 38 48. 1633 N. Division St. (21801). (410) 742-5191. FAX: (410) 749-9079. Licensee: Connor FM Broadcasting Corp. (acq 11-1-77). Rep: Roslin. Wash atty: Eugene F. Mullin. Format: Black adult contemp, urban contemp, gospel. Target aud: 25-54; Black adults. ■ J. Parker Connor, pres; J. P. Connor Jr., vp & gen mgr; John Rupprecht, chief engr.

WSBY-FM—Co-owned with WJDY(AM). Dec 13, 1989: 98.9 mhz; 6 kw. Ant 328 ft. TL: N38 18 00 W75 37 41. Stereo. Prog sep from AM. Net: CBS. Format: Oldies. Spec prog: Farm 2 hrs wkly.

WLVW-FM—July 25, 1982: 105.5 mhz; 2.1 kw. Ant 384 ft. TL: N38 24 26 W75 35 57. Stereo. Box U (21801). (410) 860-2260. FAX: (410) 742-2329. Licensee: HVS Partners (acq 1-14-93; $2.7 million with WHBX(FM) Tallahassee, FL; FTR 2-15-93). Format: Oldies. ■ Tom Lattimer, gen mgr; Bonnie Jones, gen sls mgr; Tom Walsh, progmg dir & mus dir; Karen Thomas, news dir; Don Williamson, chief engr.

WQHQ(FM)—Listing follows WTGM(AM).

WSBY-FM—Listing follows WJDY(AM).

***WSCL(FM)**—May 29, 1987: 89.5 mhz; 27 kw. Ant 600 ft. TL: N38 39 15 W75 36 42. Stereo. Hrs opn: 24. Box 2596, S. Salisbury Blvd. (21801). (410) 543-6895. Licensee: Salisbury State University Foundation Inc. Net: AP, NPR, APR. Format: Classical, news. News staff one; news progmg 29 hrs wkly. Target aud: General. Spec prog: Opera 3 hrs wkly. ■ Fred Marino, gen mgr; Ken Basile, sls dir; Pam Andrews, progmg dir; Julianne Welby, news dir; Bruce Blanchard, chief engr.

WTGM(AM)—Sept 13, 1940: 960 khz; 5 kw-U, DA-2. TL: N38 25 44 W75 37 26. Hrs opn: 24. Box U (21802). (410) 546-1055; (410) 742-1923. FAX: (410) 742-2329. Licensee: HVS Partners (group owner; acq 6-26-89; with co-located FM; FTR 6-26-89). Net: AP. Rep: Banner. Format: Sports. News staff one. Target aud: 25-54. ■ Ron Jay Gillenardo, gen mgr; Sandi Alexander, opns mgr & prom mgr; Don Bailey, gen sls mgr; Mike Boggs, progmg dir; Mike James, news dir; Jeff Twilley, chief engr. ■ Rates: $40; 40; 40; 20.

WQHQ(FM)—(Ocean City-Salisbury). Co-owned with WTGM(AM). July 1, 1985: 104.7 mhz; 33 kw. Ant 610 ft. TL: N38 23 15 W75 17 30. Stereo. Prog sep from AM. Wash atty: Arent, Fox, Kintner, Plotkin & Kahn. Format:

Massachusetts

Adult contemp. Target aud: 25-54. ■ Rates: $70; 70; 60; 40.

WWFG(FM)—See Ocean City.

Silver Spring

WGAY(FM)—See Washington, D.C.

WKDL(AM)—Licensed to Silver Spring. See Washington, D.C.

WWDC(AM)—See Washington, D.C.

Takoma Park

*****WGTS-FM**—May 8, 1957: 91.9 mhz; 29.5 kw. Ant 165 ft. TL: N38 59 12 W77 00 04 Stereo. Hrs opn: 24. 7600 Flower Ave. (20912). (301) 891-4200. FAX: (301) 270-9191. Licensee: Columbia Union College Broadcasting Inc. Format: Classical, relg. Target aud: General. ■ Don Wheeler, gen mgr & chief engr; John Konrad, opns mgr & progmg dir; Sharon Kay Kendall, mus dir.

Thurmont

WTHU(AM)—June 12, 1967: 1450 khz; 500 w-D, 400 w-N. TL: N39 37 37 W77 24 11. Hrs opn: 24. 10 Radio Ln. (21788). (301) 271-2188. Licensee: Charles R. Walmer (acq 4-20-92; $125,000; FTR 5-11-92). Net: CNN; Agri-net. Format: Classic hits, talk. News staff 5; news progmg 15 hrs wkly. Target aud: 25-49; two paycheck households with discretionary income. Spec prog: Jazz 4 hrs, sports 3 hrs, relg 5 hrs wkly. ■ Charles R. Walmer, exec vp & gen mgr; Bill McCarey, chief engr.

Towson

WKDB(AM)—Oct 27, 1955: 1570 khz; 5 kw-D, 236 w-N. TL: N39 25 04 W76 33 23. Radio Zone, 8555 16th St., Silver (20910). (410) 339-5252. Licensee: Capital Kids' Radio Co. (acq 12-3-93; $483,250; FTR 12-20-93). Format: Children. ■ Joan Schultz, gen mgr.

WLIF-FM—See Baltimore.

*****WTMD(FM)**—Feb 12, 1976: 89.7 mhz; 10.16 kw. Ant 236 ft. TL: N39 23 45 W76 36 29. Stereo. Hrs opn: 19. Media Center, Towson State Univ. (21204). (410) 830-8938; (410) 830-8936. FAX: (410) 830-2686. Licensee: Towson State Univ. Format: New adult contemp. News progmg 6 hrs wkly. Target aud: 18-65. Spec prog: Black one hr, folk 3 hrs, Pol 2 hrs, oldies 3 hrs, blues 3 hrs, reggae 2 hrs wkly. ■ S. James English III, gen mgr; James Armstrong, progmg dir; Dick Rader, chief engr.

Waldorf

WXTR-FM—February 1965: 104.1 mhz; 22 kw. Ant 764 ft. TL: N38 37 07 W76 50 42 (CP: 22 kw, ant 764 ft.). Stereo. Hrs opn: 24. 5210 Auth Rd., Marlow Heights (20746). (301) 899-3014. FAX: (301) 899-6011. Licensee: Radio Ventures I (group owner; acq 4-1-90; $33 million; FTR 2-26-90). Net: AP. Rep: McGavren Guild. Format: Oldies. ■ Robert J. Longwell, pres & gen mgr; Warren Wright, gen sls mgr; Paul Campbell, prom mgr; Bob Duckman, progmg dir & mus dir; Jim Hawk, news dir; Dennis Crowley, pub affrs dir; Ward Fetrow, chief engr.

Westernport

WWPN(FM)—Oct 1, 1993: 101.1 mhz; 6 kw. Ant -541 ft. TL: N39 29 14 W79 03 13. 12 N. Lavale St., Lavale (21502). (303) 463-5100. Licensee: Ernest F. Santmyire. Format: Relg.

Westminster

WGRX(FM)—Nov 1, 1959: 100.7 mhz; 16 kw. Ant 858 ft. TL: N39 36 59 W76 51 37. Stereo. Hrs opn: 24. Suite 204, 540 E. Belvedere Ave., Baltimore (21212). (410) 435-9487. FAX: (410) 435-0633. Licensee: Shamrock Communications Inc. (group owner; acq 4-7-81; $1.74 million with co-located FM; FTR 5-4-81). Net: ABC/FM. Rep: D & R Radio. Format: Classic rock and roll. News staff one; news progmg 2 hrs wkly. Target aud: 25-49. ■ George Duffy, gen mgr; Chris Ganoudis, gen sls mgr; Bob McLaughlin, prom dir; Steve McNee, progmg dir; Lee Gary, mus dir; Teresa Blythe, news dir & pub affrs dir; Fred Klimes, chief engr.

WTTR(AM)—Co-owned with WGRX(FM). July 1953: 1470 khz; 1 kw-U, DA-N. TL: N39 34 37 W77 01 21. Hrs opn: 5 AM-midnight. Prog sep from AM. 101 WTTR Ln. (21158). (410) 848-5511; (410) 876-1515. FAX: (410) 876-5095. Net: ABC/D. Format: Full svc adult contemp. News staff 2; news progmg 12 hrs wkly. Target aud: 25-54. Spec prog: Farm 4 hrs wkly. ■ Dwight Dingle, gen mgr; Brian Beddow, prom mgr, progmg dir & mus dir; Lisa Becker, news dir & pub affrs dir. ■ Rates: $26; 21; 21; 17.

Wheaton

WASH(FM)—See Washington, D.C.

WMDO(AM)—1954: 1540 khz; 5 kw-D. TL: N39 00 50 W77 01 46. 9th Fl., 962 Wayne Ave., Silver Spring (20910). (301) 589-4800. FAX: (301) 495-9556. Licensee: Los Cerezos Television Co. (acq 3-31-89; $750,000). Net: CRC, UPI. Rep: Katz Hispanic. Wash atty: Leventhal, Senter & Lerman. Format: Spanish. News staff 5; news progmg 21 hrs wkly. Target aud: General; Hispanic, Central & Latin American, Caribbean listeners. ■ Antonio Guernica, pres & gen mgr; Rudy Guernica, opns mgr; Elio Aguilar, gen sls mgr; Mario Sol, progmg dir; Ernesto Clavijo, news dir & pub affrs dir; David Hubley, chief engr. ■ Rates: $75; 60; 70; 50.

Williamsport

*****WCRH(FM)**—July 24, 1976: 90.5 mhz; 10 kw. Ant 884 ft. TL: N39 39 34 W77 57 56. Stereo. Hrs opn: 24. Box 439 (21795). FAX: (301) 582-2707. Licensee: Cedar Ridge Children's Home and School Inc. Net: Moody. Wash atty: Ross & Hardies. Format: Relg. News staff one; news progmg 9 hrs wkly. Target aud: 25-45. ■ Ward Childerston, gen mgr; Suzanna Snyder, mus dir; Robert Dunkle, news dir; Jeff Bean, pub affrs dir; Harry Scott, chief engr.

WYII(FM)—Nov 15, 1972: 95.9 mhz; 3 kw. Ant 300 ft. TL: N39 36 17 W77 46 49. Stereo. Hrs opn: 24. 6 E. Potomac St. (21795). (301) 223-8800. FAX: (301) 223-8830. Licensee: OEA Inc. Net: NBC. Wash atty: Southmayd, Simpson & Miller. Format: Modern country. News progmg 15 hrs wkly. Target aud: 25-54. ■ Kenneth F. Smith, pres, gen mgr & chief engr; Bob Merritt, gen sls mgr; Lois LaPorte, prom mgr; Casey Brooks, progmg dir, mus dir & news dir. ■ Rates: $20; 18.50; 20; 16.

Worton

*****WKHS(FM)**—March 28, 1974: 90.5 mhz; 17.5 kw. Ant 215 ft. TL: N39 16 55 W76 05 26. Stereo. Box 905, Rts. 297 & 298 (21678). (410) 778-4249. Licensee: Board of Education of Kent County. Net: AP. Format: Adult contemp, progressive. News progmg 10 hrs wkly. Target aud: 12 plus. Spec prog: Oldies 6 hrs, children 5 hrs, country 2 hrs, big band 2 hrs, R&B 2 hrs, jazz 2 hrs wkly. ■ Robert G. Futterman, gen mgr; Rob Dey, mus dir; Chris Singleton, chief engr.

Massachusetts

Allston

*****WGBH(FM)**—See Boston.

Amherst

*****WAMH(FM)**—1955: 89.3 mhz; 1.5 kw. Ant 720 ft. TL: N42 21 51 W72 25 24 (CP: 5 kw). Stereo. Box 1815, Amherst College, Box 5000 (01002-5000). (413) 542-2224. FAX: (413) 542-2305. Licensee: Trustees of Amherst College. Format: Progsv. News progmg 6 hrs wkly. Target aud: 18-24; college students. Spec prog: Black 12 hrs, classical 3 hrs, jazz 8 hrs, Sp 2 hrs, Japanese 2 hrs, comedy 3 hrs, talk 2 hrs wkly. ■ Megan Brown, stn mgr; Chandra Tobey, mus dir; Petra Mayer, chief engr.

*****WFCR(FM)**—May 6, 1961: 88.5 mhz; 35 kw. Ant 718 ft. TL: N42 21 49 W72 25 24. Stereo. Hrs opn: 21. Box 33630, Hampshire House, Univ. of Mass. (01003-3630). (413) 545-0100. Licensee: Univ. of Massachusetts. Net: NPR. Format: Class, news/talk. Target aud: General. Spec prog: Sp 4 hrs, jazz 9 hrs, folk 4 hrs, world mus 4 hrs wkly. ■ Joan G. Rubel, gen mgr; Rena Fischer, dev dir; Mark Auerbach, prom dir; Richard Malawista, progmg dir; John A. Montanari, mus dir; Pippin Ross, news dir; Richard Rzeszutek, chief engr.

*****WMUA(FM)**—1958: 91.1 mhz; 1 kw. Ant 26 ft. TL: N42 23 31 W72 31 13. Stereo. Hrs opn: 24. Univ. of Massachusetts, 102 Campus Ctr. (01003). (413) 545-2876. FAX: (413) 545-4751. Licensee: Board of Trustees of Univ. of Mass. Net: AP. Format: Div/variety, Black, jazz. Target aud: General; U-Mass. students & Connecticut Valley residents. Spec prog: Pol 6 hrs, Sp 9 hrs, folk 15 hrs, gospel 9 hrs, blues 15 hrs, womens 12 hrs, international 12 hrs wkly. ■ Kenley Obas, chmn; Alan Wilcox, gen mgr; Glenn Siegel, opns dir; Michael Tow, sls dir; Meredith Makowski, prom dir; Ruth Nalkin, mus dir; Helen Hong, news dir; Dacia Campbell, pub affrs dir; Daniel Ferreira, chief engr.

WRNX(FM)—Listing follows WTTT(AM).

WTTT(AM)—Apr 2, 1963: 1430 khz; 5 kw-D, DA. TL: N42 21 25 W72 29 13. Hrs opn: 6 AM-midnight. Box 67 (01004). (413) 256-6794. FAX: (413) 256-3171. Licensee: Hampshire County Broadcasting Ltd. (acq 4-12-91; with co-located FM; FTR 5-6-91). Net: CNN. Wash atty: Ginsberg, Feldman. Format: CNN News. News staff 2; news progmg 126 hrs wkly. Spec prog: Class 2 hrs wkly. ■ Thomas G. Davis, gen mgr & gen sls mgr; Amy Hamel, prom mgr; James Asker, progmg dir; Bruce Stebbins, mus dir; James Gemmell, news dir; Bob Shotwell, chief engr.

WRNX(FM)—Co-owned with WTTT(AM). Nov 12, 1990: 100.9 mhz; 1.35 kw. Ant 692 ft. TL: N42 18 24 W72 31 59. Format: Renaissance rock.

Andover

*****WPAA(FM)**—May 1, 1965: 91.7 mhz; 25 w. Ant 209 ft. TL: N42 38 54 W71 07 51. Phillips Academy (01810). (508) 749-4384. Licensee: Trustees of Phillips Academy. Format: AOR. ■ Eric Gottesman, gen mgr.

Athol

WCAT(AM)—See Orange-Athol.

WCAT-FM—Dec 4, 1989: 99.9 mhz; 1.85 kw. Ant 407 ft. TL: N42 35 39 W72 12 02. Stereo. Hrs opn: 24. Box 90, 660 E. Main, Orange (01364). (508) 544-2321; (508) 544-2322. Licensee: P&S Broadcasting Inc. Net: SMN. Rep: Katz & Powell. Format: Hot adult comtemp. ■ Jean S. Partridge, pres, gen mgr, stn mgr, opns mgr & gen sls mgr; Steve Elliott, prom mgr, progmg dir, mus dir & news dir. ■ Rates: $12; 12; 12; 12.

Attleboro

WARA(AM)—Oct 8, 1950: 1320 khz; 5 kw-U, DA-2. TL: N41 57 33 W71 19 37. 8 N. Main St., (02703). (508) 222-1320; (508) 222-1321. FAX: (508) 761-9239. Licensee: Ten Mile Communications Inc. (acq 7-90). Net: AP. Rep: Christal. Format: News/talk, info, sports. News staff 2; news progmg 24 hrs wkly. Target aud: 25 plus; middle-upper middle class. Spec prog: Relg one hr wkly. ■ Peter H. Ottmar, pres; Gene Lombardi, vp; Jeff Lowe, gen sls mgr; Larry Tocci, progmg dir; Fran Liro, news dir; Grady Moates, chief engr.

Barnstable

WQRC(FM)—July 20, 1970: 99.9 mhz; 50 kw. Ant 378 ft. TL: N41 41 19 W70 20 49. Stereo. Hrs opn: 24. 737 W. Main St., Hyannis (02601). (508) 771-1224. FAX: (508) 775-2605. Licensee: Sandab Communications Inc. (group owner; acq 4-16-92; grpsl; FTR 1-13-92). Net: AP. Rep: Christal. Wash atty: Covington-Bunley. Format: Light AC, news/info, jazz. News staff 3; news progmg 32 hrs wkly. Target aud: 25 plus; Cape Cod's affluent adult population. ■ Stephen D. Seymour, pres; Gregory D. Bone, vp & gen mgr; Zoe Zuest, opns mgr; Stephen M. Colella, gen sls mgr; Lisa Sheehy, prom mgr; Robert Seay, news dir.

Beverly

WNSH(AM)—Dec 23, 1963: 1570 khz; 1 kw-U, DA-2. TL: N42 33 08 W70 55 43. Box 344 (01915). (508) 468-5233; (508) 468-6011. Licensee: FSAM Corp. (acq 10-24-91). Format: Adult contemp. News staff 2; news progmg 15 hrs wkly. Target aud: 25-45. Spec prog: Pub affrs 2 hrs wkly. ■ Neil Whitehouse, pres & gen mgr; Gary Tolley, gen sls mgr; Brendan Lynch, prom mgr; James Gardener, chief engr.

Boston

WBCN(FM)—May 1958: 104.1 mhz; 20.9 kw. Ant 771 ft. TL: N42 20 50 W71 04 59. Stereo. 1265 Boylston St. (02215). (617) 266-1111. FAX: (617) 437-6690; (617) 247-2266. Licensee: Infinity Broadcasting Corp. (group owner; acq 2-16-79). Format: Rock/AOR. ■ Mel Karmazin, pres; Tony Berardini, gen mgr; Nancy Dietrich, gen sls mgr; Larry Loprete, prom mgr; Carter Alan, mus dir; Jim Rakiey, chief engr.

WBCS(FM)—1945: 96.9 mhz; 12.5 kw. Ant 1,010 ft. TL: N42 18 12 W71 13 08 (CP: 8.8 kw, ant 1151 ft., TL: N42 18 27 W71 13 27). Stereo. 330 Stuart St. (02116). (617) 542-0241. FAX: (617) 542-0620. Licensee: Greater Boston Radio, Inc. (group owner; acq 3-31-93; $11.655 million; FTR 4-19-93). Rep: D & R Radio. Format: Country. News progmg 5 hrs wkly. Target aud: 25-54. ■ Michael McDermott, prom mgr; Jim Murphy, progmg dir; Jimmy Rogers, mus dir; Paul Shullins, chief engr.

WBMX(FM)—Listing follows WRKO(AM).

WBOS(FM)—See Brookline.

***WBUR(FM)**—March 1950: 90.9 mhz; 7.2 kw. Ant 1,046 ft. TL: N42 18 27 W71 13 27. Stereo. 630 Commonwealth Ave. (02215). (617) 353-2790. FAX: (617) 353-4747. Licensee: Executive Committee of the Trustees of Boston Univ. Net: NPR, APR. Format: News, class, jazz. News staff 28; news progmg 70 hrs wkly. Target aud: 25-65. intellectual adults interested in news and politics. Spec prog: Sp 5 hrs wkly. ■ Jane Christo, gen mgr; Peter Lydotes, opns mgr; Nancy Boach, sls dir; Jay Clayton, mktg dir; Leticia Nieves, prom mgr; George Boosey, progmg mgr; George Preston, mus dir; Sam Fleming, news dir; Jeffrey Hutton, engrg dir; Michael Le Clair, chief engr.

WBZ(AM)—Sept 19, 1921: 1030 khz; 50 kw-U, DA-1. TL: N42 16 44 W70 52 34. Stereo. 1170 Soldiers Field Rd. (02134). (617) 787-7000. Licensee: Westinghouse Broadcasting Inc. (group owner). Net: ABC/I. Rep: Group W. Format: News all day, talk all night. News staff 20; news progmg 75 hrs wkly. Target aud: 25-54. Spec prog: Relg 2 hrs, countryside-agri one hr wkly. ■ Dan Mason, pres; Chris Hill Staffier, gen sls mgr; Camela Masi, mktg dir; Carmela Masi, prom mgr; Brian Whittemore, progmg mgr & news dir; Nancy Whittemore, pub affrs dir; Mark Manuelian, chief engr.

WCLB-FM—See Framingham.

WCRB(FM)—See Waltham.

WEEI(AM)—Sept 29, 1924: 590 khz; 5 kw-U, DA-1. TL: N42 24 24 W71 05 14. Hrs opn: 24. Suite 220, 529 Main St., Charlestown (02129). (617) 242-5900. FAX: (617) 241-9925. Licensee: Boston Celtics Communications Ltd. (acq 4-18-90). Net: ABC, CNN, AP. Rep: CBS. Format: Sports, sports talk. Target aud: General. ■ Aaron Daniels, gen mgr; John Mitchell, gen sls mgr; Pat Donley, prom mgr; Phil Sirkin, progmg dir; Don Albanese, chief engr. ■ WFXT-TV affil.

***WERS(FM)**—Nov 14, 1949: 88.9 mhz; 4 kw. Ant 614 ft. TL: N42 21 08 W71 03 25. Stereo. 126 Beacon St. (02116). (617) 578-8892. FAX: (617) 578-8804. Licensee: Emerson College. Net: MBS. Format: Div. News progmg 2 hrs wkly. ■ Fran Ellis Berger, gen mgr; Rick Levy, chief engr.

WEZE(AM)—1922: 1260 khz; 5 kw-U, DA-N. TL: N42 16 30 W71 02 31. Box 9121 (02171-9121). (617) 328-0880. FAX: (617) 328-0375. Licensee: New England Continental Media Inc. Group owner: Salem Communications Corp. (acq 9-21-77). Net: USA. Format: Relg, talk. Target aud: General. Spec prog: Sp one hr, Black 2 hrs, Portuguese one hr, Haitian 2 hrs wkly. ■ Edward G. Atsinger III, pres; Gordon Marcey, gen mgr; Alex Canavan, gen sls mgr; Bob Patterson, progmg dir; Ireta Maxwell, pub affrs dir; Richard Jolls, chief engr.

***WGBH(FM)**—Oct 6, 1951: 89.7 mhz; 98 kw. Ant 650 ft. TL: N42 12 42 W71 06 51. Stereo. Hrs opn: 24. 125 Western Ave. (02134). (617) 492-2777. FAX: (617) 787-0714; TWX: 710-330-6887. Licensee: WGBH Educational Foundation. Net: APR, NPR; Eastern Pub. Format: Class, jazz, news. News progmg 22 hrs wkly. Target aud: General. Spec prog: Folk 10 hrs, blues 8 hrs, Irish 2 hrs, cultural 3 hrs wkly. ■ Henry Becton, pres; Marita Rivero, gen mgr; John Voci, opns mgr; Roberta MacCarthy, dev dir; Jill Medvedow, progmg dir; Jon Solins, mus dir. ■ *WGBH-TV, WGBX-TV, WGBY-TV affils.

WHDH(AM)—Dec 1, 1926: 850 khz; 50 kw-U, DA-2. TL: N42 16 41 W71 16 02. Hrs opn: 24. 7 Bulfinch Pl. (02114). (617) 725-0777. FAX: (617) 742-4604. Licensee: Atlantic Radio Corp. Group owner: American Radio Systems (acq 10-29-92; $3 million; FTR 11-23-92). Net: NBC, NBC Talknet. Rep: Banner. Wash atty: Hogan & Hartson. Format: Talk. News staff 6. Target aud: 25-54. ■ Lynn O'Connell, gen sls mgr; Frank Murgagh, mktg dir; Al Mayers, progmg dir; Deb Robi, news dir; Dana Puopolo, chief engr.

WHRB(FM)—See Cambridge.

WILD(AM)—1946: 1090 khz; 5 kw-D. TL: N42 24 40 W71 04 28. 90 Warren St. (02119). (617) 427-2222. FAX: (617) 427-2677. Licensee: Nash Communications Corp. (acq 8-26-80; $1 million; FTR 7-21-80). Net: ABC. Rep: Roslin. Format: Urban contemp. News staff one. Target aud: General. ■ Bernadine Nash, CEO & pres; Monte Bowens, gen mgr; Neal Perlstein, gen sls mgr; Ken Johnston, progmg dir; Dana Hall, mus dir; Brian Higgins, news dir; Grady Moates, chief engr.

WJIB(AM)—(Cambridge). 1948: 740 khz; 250 w-D, 5 w-N. TL: N42 23 13 W71 08 21. Stereo. Hrs opn: 24. Box 848, Boston (02194). (617) 868-7400. Licensee: Bob Bittner Broadcasting Inc. (acq 9-12-91). Net: USA. Wash atty: Wilkes, Artis, Hedrick & Lane. Format: Btfl music. News progmg 4 hrs. wkly. Target aud: 30-70; the affluent type that listens to btfl music. Spec prog: Gospel 6 hrs wkly. ■ Bob Bittner, pres, gen mgr & mus dir; Peter George, chief engr. ■ Rates: $29; 29; 29; na.

WJMN(FM)—Mar 31, 1948: 94.5 mhz; 11.5 kw. Ant 1,053 ft. TL: N42 18 27 W71 13 27. Stereo. 235 Bear Hill Rd., Waltham (02154-1014). (617) 290-0009. FAX: (617) 290-0722. Licensee: Ardman Broadcasting Corp. (group owner; acq 6-16-87). Rep: Eastman. Format: CHR. Target aud: 12-44. ■ Alan Chartrand, vp & gen mgr; Christopher McWade, gen sls mgr; Cathy Ritter, natl sls mgr; Jim Berry, mktg mgr; Leslie Cipolla, prom dir; Michael Colby, progmg dir; Eric Anderson, mus dir; Lori Duchesne, news dir; Christopher Hall, chief engr.

WMEX(AM)—Jan 1, 1979: 1150 khz; 5 kw-U, DA-2. TL: N42 24 49 W71 12 40. Stereo. 330 Stuart St. (02116). (617) 542-0241. FAX: (617) 542-5809. Licensee: Greater Boston Radio. Group owner: Greater Media Inc. (acq 2-85). Rep: McGavren Guild. Format: Adult contemp. Target aud: 25-54. ■ Peter H. Smyth, vp & gen mgr; Don Kelley, opns mgr & news dir; Frank Kelley, gen sls mgr; Margaret Murphy, natl sls mgr; Michael McDermott, prom dir; Nancy Quill, mus dir; Paul Shulins, chief engr.

WMJX(FM)—Co-owned with WMEX(AM). Jan 6, 1982: 106.7 mhz; 21.5 kw. Ant 750 ft. TL: N42 20 50 W71 04 59. Stereo. Dups AM 100%. Net: AP.

WNTN(AM)—See Newton.

WODS(FM)—1948: 103.3 mhz; 16.5 kw. Ant 938 ft. TL: N42 18 27 W71 13 27. Stereo. Hrs opn: 24. 30 Winter St. (02108). (617) 426-2200. FAX: (617) 728-1958. Licensee: CBS Inc. Group owner: CBS Broadcast Group. Net: CBS Spectrum. Rep: CBS Radio. Format: Oldies. ■ Bob Pates, vp & gen mgr; JoAnne Adduci, gen sls mgr; Barbara Crouse, prom dir; Rick Shockley, progmg dir; Sandy Benson, mus dir; Gordon Hill, news dir; Charles "Buddy" Giordano, chief engr.

***WRBB(FM)**—October 1970: 104.9 mhz; 10.9 w. Ant 89 ft. TL: N42 20 19 W71 05 28. Hrs opn: 24. 360 Huntington Ave. (02115). (617) 373-4338; (617) 373-2790. Licensee: Northeastern Univ. Net: MBS. Format: Alternative rock, urban contemp. News staff one; news progmg 2 hrs wkly. Target aud: 12-35; college, urban. Spec prog: Sp 4 hrs, relg 4 hrs, West Indian 5 hrs wkly. ■ Chris Adams, gen mgr; Lou Conrad, stn mgr; Scott Souza, adv mgr; Christian Del Prete, progmg mgr; R.J. Bartsch, mus dir; Kristi Bartlett, asst mus dir; Chris Perkins, news dir; Nicole Ulrick, pub affrs dir; Todd Lariviere, engrg dir; Ray Fallon, chief engr.

WRKO(AM)—1922: 680 khz; 50 kw-U, DA-2. TL: N42 2925 W71 1305. 3 Fenway Plaza (02215). (617) 236-6800. FAX: (617) 236-6834. Licensee: American Radio Systems (group owner; (acq 12-20-88). Net: MBS, Unistar, CBS. Rep: Eastman. Format: Talk. Spec prog: Black 2 hrs, relg one hr wkly. ■ Steve Dodge, chmn; Joe Winn, pres & gen mgr; Lynn O'Connell, gen sls mgr; Dereen Wong, natl sls mgr; Frank Murtagh, mktg dir; Jeff Demers, prom dir; Paula O'Connor, progmg mgr; Deb Robi, news dir; Paul Donovan, engrg dir; Larry Bruce, chief engr.

WBMX(FM)—Co-owned with WRKO(AM). 1948: 98.5 mhz; 9 kw. Ant 1,145 ft. TL: N42 18 27 W71 13 27. Stereo. Prog sep from AM. Format: Adult contemp. ■ Jenny McCann, gen mgr; Gary Rozynek, gen sls mgr; Lee Ann Callahan, mktg dir; Greg Strassell, progmg dir.

WROL(AM)—Oct 8, 1950: 950 khz; 5 kw-D. TL: N42 26 15 W70 59 40. Hrs opn: 6 AM-midnight. Suite 315, 20 Park Plaza (02116). (617) 423-0210. FAX: (617) 482-9305. Licensee: Pilgrim Broadcasting Co. Group owner: Carter Broadcasting. Format: Talk, relg. Target aud: Adults. Spec prog: Fr 15 hrs, Sp 10 hrs wkly. ■ Ken Carter, pres & gen mgr; Kurt Carberry, gen sls mgr; Bill Porter, progmg dir; Phillip Shea, chief engr.

WSSH(AM)—1934: 1510 khz; 50 kw-U, DA-2. TL: N42 23 10 W71 12 01. Stereo. Suite 2500 500 W. Cummings Park, Woburn (01801). (617) 938-0660; (617) 935-9774. Licensee: Noble Broadcast of Ballybunion Inc. Group owner: Noble Broadcast Group (acq 6-11-87; $3.7 million; FTR 6-15-87). Wash atty: Haley, Bader & Potts. Format: Talk. Target aud: 25-54. ■ Michael J. Klein, gen mgr & chief engr; Lynn O'Connell, gen sls mgr.

WSSH-FM—See Lowell.

***WUMB-FM**—Sept 19, 1982: 91.9 mhz; 660 w. Ant 207 ft. TL: N42 15 27 W71 01 44. Stereo. Hrs opn: Mon-Fri 5 AM-1 AM, Sat-Sun 6 AM-1 AM. Univ. of Mass.-Boston, 100 Morrissey Blvd. (02125-3393). (617) 287-6900. FAX: (617) 287-6916. Licensee: The Univ. of Massachusetts. Format: Acoustic/folk, R&B, ballets. News progmg 5 hrs wkly. Target aud: 25-40. Spec prog: Chinese one hr, children one hr, Sp 5 hrs, talk/news 17 hrs, elderly 5 hrs wkly. ■ Patricia A. Monteith, gen mgr; Brian Quinn, progmg dir; Isabel Freeman, mus dir; Grady Moates, chief engr.

WUNR(AM)—(Brookline). 1947: 1600 khz; 5 kw-U, DA-1. TL: N42 17 20 W71 11 22. 160 N. Washington St., Boston (02114). (617) 367-9003. FAX: (617) 367-2265. Licensee: Champion Broadcasting System Inc. Rep: Caballero. Format: Ethnic, Sp. Spec prog: It 12 hrs, Pol 2 hrs, Portuguese 2 hrs, Asia 2 hrs, Irish 2 hrs, Greek 17 hrs, Black 20 hrs wkly. ■ Herbert S. Hoffman, pres; Patricia Domeniconi, gen mgr; Eric Hayes, opns mgr; Velma May, progmg dir, mus dir, news dir & pub affrs dir; Blair Harden, chief engr.

WXKS-FM—See Medford.

WZLX(FM)—Jan 1, 1979: 100.7 mhz; 21.5 kw. Ant 777 ft. TL: N42 20 50 W71 04 59. Stereo. 200 Clarendon St. (02116). (617) 267-0123. FAX: (617) 421-9305. Licensee: Infinity Broadcasting Corp. (group owner; acq 12-18-92; grpsl; FTR 1-25-93). Rep: Christal. Format: Classic rock. News staff one. Target aud: 25-54; males. ■ Jerry Charm, gen mgr; Chris Paquin, gen sls mgr; Samantha Ryan, prom mgr; Buzz Knight, progmg mgr; Paul Lemieux, mus dir; Lori Kelman, news dir; Bruce Parsons, chief engr. ■ Rates: $275; 300; 300; 150.

Boxford

***WBMT(FM)**—Jan 30, 1978: 88.3 mhz; 710 w. Ant 17 ft. TL: N42 37 39 W70 58 21. RFD Topsfield (01983). (508) 887-8830. Licensee: Masconomet Regional High School System. Format: AOR. ■ Glenn Walker, gen mgr; Matthew Baldassarri, stn mgr.

Bridgewater

***WBIM-FM**—November 1972: 91.5 mhz; 180 w. Ant 71 ft. TL: N41 59 15 W70 58 21. Stereo. Campus Center, Bridgewater State College (02325). (508) 697-1303. FAX: (508) 697-1705. Licensee: Bridgewater State College. Net: ABC/FM. Format: Div, progsv. Spec prog: Black 3 hrs, country 2 hrs, reggae 2 hrs wkly. ■ John Curtin, stn mgr; Laurie Andrews, mus dir; Richard F. Cubi, chief engr.

Brockton

WBET(AM)—Nov 27, 1946: 1460 khz; 5 kw-D, 1 kw-N, DA-N. TL: N42 04 23 W71 02 39. Box 787, 60 Main St. (02403). (508) 587-2400. FAX: (508) 586-7903. Licensee: Enterprise Publishing Co. Net: CNN. Rep: Kettell-Carter. Format: Adult contemp. Spec prog: Gospel one hr, It 2 hrs, Pol 2 hrs, Irish 2 hrs wkly. ■ Charles K. Bergeron, gen mgr; Paul Cunningham, gen sls mgr; Matthew McLaughlin, prom mgr; Peter Rivoira, progmg dir & mus dir.

WCAV(FM)—Co-owned with WBET(AM). July 21, 1948: 97.7 mhz; 3 kw. Ant 300 ft. TL: N42 04 23 W71 02 39. Format: C&W. Spec prog: Greek one hr, gospel 2 hrs wkly. ■ Mike Casey, progmg dir & mus dir.

WMSX(AM)—July 17, 1961: 1410 khz; 1 kw-D, DA. TL: N42 03 30 W71 02 40. 288 Linwood St. (02401). (508) 587-1410. FAX: (508) 586-4996. Licensee: Metro South Broadcasting Inc. (acq 6-16-89; $175,000; FTR 7-3-89). Format: Talk. ■ Donald Sandler, pres, gen mgr, progmg dir. ■ Rates: $21; 19; 21; na.

Brookline

WBOS(FM)—1955: 92.9 mhz; 8.8 kw. Ant 1,100 ft. TL: N42 18 27 W71 13 27. Stereo. Hrs opn: 24. 1200 Soldier's Field Rd., Boston (02134). (617) 254-9267. FAX: (617) 782-8757. Licensee: GCI Boston Inc. Group owner: Granum Communications (acq 2-5-92; $9 million (est); FTR 3-2-92). Rep: Katz. Wash atty: Rubin, Winston & Diercks. Format: Soft album rock. News staff 2; news progmg 3 hrs wkly. Target aud: 25-49; baby-boomers seeking diverse selection of quality album music. ■ John

Massachusetts

Layton, vp & gen mgr; Tricia Baker, gen sls mgr; Jim Herron, progmg dir; Merilee Kelly, mus dir; John Kennedy, chief engr. ■ Rates: $225; 200; 225; 125.

WUNR(AM)—Licensed to Brookline. See Boston.

Cambridge

WBCS(FM)—See Boston.

WHRB(FM)—May 1957: 95.3 mhz; 3 kw. Ant 110 ft. TL: N42 22 20 W71 07 09. Stereo. Hrs opn: 24. 45 Quincy St. (02138). (617) 495-4818. FAX: (617) 496-3990. Licensee: Harvard Radio Broadcasting Co. Inc. Format: Class, jazz, AOR. News progmg 4 hrs wkly. Spec prog: Black 18 hrs, country 5 hrs, Sp 3 hrs, reggae 3 hrs, folk 15 hrs wkly. ■ Doug DeMay, pres; Jeremy Rassen, gen mgr & chief engr; Manny Biderman, sls dir; Andrea Perini, mus dir; Dave Mazieres, news dir. ■ Rates: $40; 40; 40; 40.

WJIB(AM)—Licensed to Cambridge. See Boston.

*WMBR(FM)—Apr 10, 1961: 88.1 mhz; 360 w. Ant 285 ft. TL: N42 21 42 W71 05 03. Stereo. 3 Ames St. (02142). (617) 253-4000; (617) 253-2810. Licensee: Technology Broadcasting Corp. Format: Div, underground progressive, rock. News prgmg 4 hrs wkly. Target aud: General. Spec prog: Black 15 hrs, class 2 hrs, relg 4 hrs, jazz 14 hrs, folk 6 hrs, French 2 hrs, gospel 2 hrs wkly. ■ Todd Glickman, pres; Dayo Ogunyemi, gen mgr; Joan Hathaway, stn mgr; Ert Dredge, prom dir; Bill Stockton, progmg dir; Rodney Marable, mus dir; Bob Dubrow, asst mus dir; Dave Goodman, news dir; Trish Anderton, chief engr.

Charlton

*WBPV(FM)—1976: 90.1 mhz; 100 w. Ant 390 ft. TL: N42 08 01 W71 57 26. 57 Old Muggett Hill Rd. (01507). (508) 248-5971. Licensee: Bay Path Vocational High School. Format: Educ, rock. Target aud: General. ■ Clifford Cloutier, gen mgr.

Chatham

WFCC-FM—March 24, 1987: 107.5 mhz; 50 kw. Ant 341 ft. TL: N41 44 14 W70 00 40. Stereo. Hrs opn: 18. One Villages Dr., Brewster (02631). (508) 896-9322. Licensee: Dolphin Productions Inc. (acq 9-19-92; $579,000; FTR 11-2-92). Rep: CMN; Kettell-Carter. Format: Classic. News progmg 2 hrs wkly. Target aud: 25 plus; upscale, affluent, educated adults. ■ Alan Stanley, chmn & pres; Allan Stanley, gen mgr, adv dir & progmg dir; Edward J. Cochran, sls dir; Barbara Stanley, prom dir & pub affrs dir; Janice Gray, progmg dir; Don Moore, chief engr. ■ Rates: $20; 20; 20; 20.

Cherry Valley

WCRN(AM)—Not on air, target date unknown: 830 khz; 3 kw-D, 1 kw-N, DA-2. TL: N42 14 47 W71 55 51. 20 Park Plaza, Suite 315, Boston (02116). Licensee: Carter Broadcasting Corp. (acq 1-16-90).

Chicopee

WACE(AM)—Dec 1, 1946: 730 khz; 5 kw-U. TL: N42 10 01 W72 37 31. Hrs opn: 24. 326 Chicopee St. (01013). (413) 594-6654. Licensee: Carter Broadcasting Corp. (acq 12-24-86). Format: Relg, Sp. Spec prog: Pol 2 hrs, Irish 2 hrs wkly. ■ Ken Carter, pres, gen mgr & gen sls mgr; Cal McClain, progmg dir & news dir; Alan McAlary, mus dir; Bob Shotwell, chief engr.

Concord

WADN(AM)—Aug 28, 1989: 1120 khz; 5 kw-D, 1 kw-N, DA-2. TL: N42 26 54 W71 25 39. Hrs opn: 5 AM-10 PM. Radio Station WADN(AM), Damonmill Sq. (01742). (508) 371-3200. FAX: (508) 369-6368. Licensee: Assabet Communications Corp. (acq 1-23-93; $280,000; FTR 3-15-93). Rep: New England Spot Sls. Format: Contemp folk/acoustic. News progmg 17 hrs wkly. Target aud: 35 plus; upscale, suburban families. Spec prog: Children's one hr, math audubon one hr, BBC 7 hrs wkly. ■ Ned Crecelius, pres & gen mgr; Jim Parry, progmg dir; Kate Borger, mus dir.

*WIQH(FM)—December 1971: 88.3 mhz; 10 w. Ant 30 ft. TL: N42 26 48 W71 20 49. 500 Walden St. (01742). (508) 371-4680. Licensee: Concord-Carlisle Regional School District. Format: AOR, progsv. News progmg one hr wkly. Target aud: 12-21; teenagers. ■ Laurel Millette, gen mgr; Ned Roos, chief engr.

Danvers

WNSH(AM)—See Beverly.

Dedham

WBMA(AM)—Not on air, target date unknown: 890 khz; 10 kw-D, 1 kw-N, DA-2. TL: N42 16 54 W71 11 15. 3108 Fulton Ave., Sacramento, CA (95821). (916) 481-8191. Licensee: Family Stations Inc. (group owner). Format: Div, relg. Spec prog: Class 10 hrs, Black 4 hrs wkly. ■ Harold Camping, pres; John Lewis, chief engr.

Deerfield

*WGAJ(FM)—May 1982: 91.7 mhz; 100 w. Ant 314 ft. TL: N42 32 05 W72 35 32. Stereo. Deerfield Academy (01342). (413) 773-8412. Licensee: Trustees of Deerfield Academy. Format: AOR. Spec prog: Black 5 hrs, jazz 2 hrs. ■ Nora Zuckerman, gen mgr; Dan Garrison, stn mgr.

Dudley

*WNRC(FM)—1975: 95.1 mhz; 14.7 w. Ant 125 ft. TL: N42 02 40 W71 55 52. Box 9, Nichols College, Center Rd. (01571). (508) 943-8320. Licensee: Nichols College. ■ Scott Duszalk, stn mgr.

East Longmeadow

WAQY(AM)—1947: 1600 khz; 5 kw-D, 2.5 kw-N, DA-2. TL: N42 04 30 W72 31 40. Hrs opn: 24. Simulcast with WAQY-FM, Springfield. 45 Fisher Ave. (01028). (413) 525-4141. Licensee: Saga Communications of New England Inc. (group owner; acq 6-2-92; grpsl). Rep: Katz. Format: AOR. Target aud: 18-49; upscale young adults. ■ Edward Christian, chmn; Warren Lada, pres, vp & gen mgr; Norm McKee, CFO; Larry Goldberg, gen sls mgr; Pam Tardiff, prom dir; Keith Masters, progmg dir; Becca Reed, mus dir; Howard Frost, engrg mgr. ■ Rates: $180; 180; 180; 180.

Easton

*WSHL-FM—Jan 1, 1973: 91.3 mhz; 100 w. Ant 66 ft. TL: N42 03 27 W71 04 47. Stereo. Hrs opn: 24. Stonehill College, College Center, 320 Washington St., North Easton (02357). (508) 238-2612; (508) 238-8414. Licensee: Stonehill College. Format: Div. Target aud: 19-30. ■ Justin Dulude, gen mgr & opns dir; Katie Couzens, prom dir; Christopher Rogers, adv dir; Rick Laidlaw, progmg dir; Nick Banks, mus dir; Catherine Childs, news dir; Peter Quentin George, chief engr.

Fairhaven

WFHN(FM)—March 1, 1989: 107.1 mhz; 3 kw. Ant 370 ft. TL: N41 38 26 W70 55 03. Stereo. 220 Union St., New Bedford (02740). (508) 999-6690. FAX: (508) 999-1420. Licensee: Fairhaven to Dover Broadcasting Inc. Group owner: H & D Broadcast Group (acq 3-14-90; $4 million; FTR 4-2-90). Rep: Christal. Format: Adult contemp. Target aud: 18-49. ■ Gerald A. Poch, pres; Steven Bogue, gen mgr; Anita Robinson, stn mgr; Jean Marie Manning, gen sls mgr; Joe Limardi, progmg dir; Frank Goremus, chief engr.

WLAW(AM)—Not on air, target date unknown: 1270 khz; 5 kw-U, DA-2. TL: N41 39 06 W70 54 59. 35 Orchard St., New Bedford (02740). (508) 997-2929. Licensee: Edmund Dinis.

Fall River

WCTK(FM)—See Providence.

WHTB(AM)—May 13, 1948: 1400 khz; 1 kw-U. TL: N41 41 23 W71 08 43. Hrs opn: 5 AM-11 PM. Box 927 (02722). (508) 678-9727. FAX: (508) 673-0310. Licensee: S N E Broadcasting Ltd. (acq 5-8-89; $650,000; FTR 5-29-89). Net: CNN. Rep: McGavren Guild, Interep. Format: News/talk, sports, oldies. News staff 2; news progmg 20 hrs wkly. Target aud: 25-64; 66% Portuguese (ethnic). Spec prog: Portuguese 6 hrs, Pol 2 hrs, Irish one hr, Fr one hr wkly. ■ Robert S. Karam, pres; James J. Karam, CFO; Pete Vincelette, gen mgr & gen sls mgr; Steve Sorel, chief engr. ■ Rates: $25; 20; 22; 15.

WSAR(AM)—1921: 1480 khz; 5 kw-U, DA-1. TL: N41 43 26 W71 11 21. Box 927 (02722); One Home St., Somerset (02725). (508) 678-9727. FAX: (508) 678-9727. Licensee: Bristol County Broadcasting Inc. (acq 10-26-92; $440,000; FTR 11-23-92). Net: ABC/D. Rep: Banner. Format: Div, talk. News staff 3. Target aud: 25 plus. Spec prog: Portuguese 3 hrs wkly. ■ Robert S. Karam, pres; Hector Gauthier, vp; Pete Vincelette, gen mgr & gen sls mgr.

Falmouth

WCIB(FM)—1970: 101.9 mhz; 50 kw. Ant 479 ft. TL: N41 33 31 W70 35 46. Stereo. Box C, 60 Spring Bars Rd. (02540). (508) 548-3102. FAX: (508) 540-9430. Licensee: Ardman Broadcasting Corp. of Cape Cod. Group owner: Ardman Broadcasting Corp. (acq 6-4-90; $2.5 million; FTR 7-2-90). Net: ABC/D. Rep: Katz. Format: Hot new country ■ Paul Seccareccio, gen mgr; Dana Panepinto, gen sls mgr; Mark Erickson, progmg dir; Joe Jorjoura, chief engr.

WFAL(FM)—Feb 12, 1987: 101.1 mhz; 3.7 kw. Ant 253 ft. TL: N41 36 50 W70 35 56. Stereo. Hrs opn: 24. Dups WFXR(FM) Harwichport 100%. 105 Stevens St. (02601). (508) 457-4122. FAX: (508) 775-6088. Licensee: J.J. Taylor Companies Inc. Net: Unistar. Rep: Eastman. Wash atty: Pepper & Corazzini. Format: Country. News staff 2; news progmg 3 hrs wkly. Target aud: 18-49. ■ Bonnie McCarty, gen mgr; Ted Morgan, opns mgr; Frank Feeley, gen sls mgr; Keith Lemire, progmg dir; Skip Comeau, chief engr.

Fitchburg

WEIM(AM)—Oct 6, 1941: 1280 khz; 5 kw-D, 1 kw-N, DA-2. TL: N42 35 40 W71 50 12. Hrs opn: 20. Box 727, 762 Water St. (01420). (508) 343-3766. FAX: (508) 345-6397. Licensee: WEIM Corp. (acq 8-1-87). Net: ABC/C. Rep: Banner, Knight Radio Sales. Wash atty: Pepper & Corazzini. Format: Adult contemp, news/talk, sports. News staff 2; news progmg 28 hrs wkly. Target aud: 25-54; loc listeners. ■ Frank Filippone, CEO, pres & gen mgr; Martha Filippone, chmn; Anne Filippone-Bisbee, opns mgr; Woodie Cross, sls mgr; Jack Raymond, progmg dir & mus dir; Ray Chalifoux, pub affrs dir; Mark Bisbee, chief engr. ■ Rates: $31; 25; 28; 23.

WFGL(AM)—February 1950: 960 khz; 2.5 kw-D, 1 kw-N, DA-2. TL: N42 35 24 W71 49 41. Stn currently dark. 5th Fl., 250 Commercial St., Worcester (01608). (508) 752-1045. Licensee: Montachusett Broadcasting. Group owner: Deer River Broadcasting Group (acq 1979).

WXLO-FM—Licensed to Fitchburg. See Worcester.

*WXPL(FM)—August 1985: 91.3 mhz; 100 w. Ant 134 ft. TL: N42 35 18 W71 47 26. Stereo. 160 Pearl St. (01420). (508) 345-0276. FAX: (508) 345-7922. Licensee: Fitchburg State College. Format: Progsv. News progmg 4 hrs wkly. Target aud: 16-25. Spec prog: Class 2 hrs, jazz 4 hrs, sports 2 hrs wkly. ■ Vincent J. Mara, pres; Margaret Ricardo, gen mgr; Tara Kerrigan, chief engr.

Framingham

WBIV(AM)—See Natick.

WCLB-FM—Listing follows WKOX(AM).

*WDJM-FM—1973: 91.3 mhz; 100 w. Ant 89 ft. TL: N42 17 44 W71 26 18. Stereo. Suite 512, 100 State St. (01701). (508) 620-1220. FAX: (508) 626-4939. Licensee: Framingham State College. Format: Alternative. Target aud: 15-35; college, surrounding community & commuters. Spec prog: Jazz 3 hrs, Sp 8 hrs, rap 3 hrs, metal 2 hrs, hard core 2 hrs, industrial 4 hrs, local 2 hrs, urban contemp 2 hrs wkly. ■ Andrew Aldous, gen mgr; Sandy Porter, stn mgr; Ben Cunningham, progmg dir.

WKOX(AM)—April 1947: 1200 khz; 10 kw-D, 1 kw-N, DA-N. TL: N42 17 17 W71 25 53 (CP: 50 kw). Hrs opn: 24 100 Mt. Wayte Ave. (01701). (508) 820-2400. FAX: (508) 820-2458. Licensee: Fairbanks Communications Inc. (group owner; acq 1-71). Net: ABC/E, AP. Rep: Banner. Wash atty: Haley, Bader & Potts. Format: Metrowest news, traditional country. News staff 2; news progmg 20 hrs wkly. Target aud: 25-54; upscale suburban/metropolitan Boston residents. Spec prog: Sp 2 hrs, It one hr, sports 15 hrs, Jewish one hr wkly. ■ Richard M. Fairbanks, pres; James C. Hilliard, exec vp; Charles N. Shapiro, gen mgr & gen sls mgr; Bob Christy, opns mgr; Scott Gibbons, prom dir & progmg dir; Gene Molter, news dir; Al Carp, chief engr. ■ Rates: $50; 25; 35; 15;.

WCLB-FM—Co-owned with WKOX(AM). 1959: 105.7 mhz; 8.5 kw. Ant 1,144 ft. TL: N42 18 27 W71 13 27. Stereo. Prog sep from AM. Prudential Tower, Boston (02199). (617) 375-2100. FAX: (617) 375-2158. Format: Hot new country. Target aud: 25-54. ■ James C. Hilliary, gen mgr; Tim Reeves, gen sls mgr; Leigh Burdett, natl sls mgr; Jim Harris, rgnl sls mgr; Cara Storm, prom dir; George Johns, progmg dir; Len Mailloux, news dir.

Franklin

*WGAO(FM)—1975: 88.3 mhz; 125 w. Ant 174 ft. TL: N42 05 08 W71 23 54. Stereo. 99 Main St. (02038). (508) 528-4210. Licensee: Dean Junior College. Net: UPI. Format: Classic rock, contemp hit, AOR. News progmg 5 hrs wkly. Target aud: 15-25. ■ Nancy Kerr, gen mgr; Vic Michaels, opns dir; Rich Pezzoulo, news dir; Roger Turner, chief engr.

Gardner

WGAW(AM)—1946: 1340 khz; 1 kw-U. TL: N42 35 33 W71 59 20. Box 87, Green St. (01440). (508) 632-1340. FAX: (508) 632-1332. Licensee: WGAW Inc. (acq 11-59). Net: AP. Format: Adult contemp, talk. ■ Douglas Rowe, gen mgr; Mark Nardini, opns dir; Mark Rossi, progmg dir & mus dir; Rick Kenadack, chief engr.

Gloucester

WBOQ(FM)—Sept 14, 1964: 104.9 mhz; 1.5 kw. Ant 446 ft. TL: N42 35 36 W70 43 28. Stereo. Hrs opn: 24. 8 Enon St., North Beverly (01915). (508) 927-1049. FAX: (508) 921-2635. Licensee: Southfield Communications L.P. (acq 7-14-88). Rep: CMBS. Format: Class. News progmg 3 hrs wkly. Target aud: 25-54; mass appeal classical favorites. ■ Douglas H. Tanger, pres & gen mgr; Scott J. Hooper, opns mgr; Alan Tolz, gen sls mgr; Heather Kent, mus dir. ■ Rates: $40; 40; 40; 40.

LAUREN A. COLBY
301-663-1086
COMMUNICATIONS ATTORNEY
Special Attention to Difficult Cases

Great Barrington

WAMQ(FM)—November 1988: 105.1 mhz; 1.1 kw. Ant 1,708 ft. TL: N42 09 46 W73 28 26. Stereo. Hrs opn: 24. Rebroadcasts WAMC (FM) Albany 100%. 318 Central Ave., Albany, NY (12206). (800) 323-9262; (518) 465-5233. Licensee: WAMC. Group owner: WAMC/Northeast Public Radio (acq 3-5-93; $325,000; FTR 3-29-93). Net: NPR, APR. Format: Lite adult contemp. Target aud: 18-54. ■ Alan Chartock, CEO; David Galletly, gen mgr.

WSBS(AM)—December 1957: 860 khz; 2.7 kw-D. TL: N42 12 52 W73 20 45. Hrs opn: 5:30 AM-7 PM. Box 297, Stockbridge Rd., Rt. 7 (01230). (413) 528-0860. FAX: (413) 528-2162. Licensee: Berkshire Broadcasting Co. Group owner: Berkshire Group (acq 9-12-68). Net: CNN. Rep: Kettell-Carter. Wash atty: Wilkinson, Barker, Knauer & Quinn. Format: Adult contemp. News staff 2; news progmg 10 hrs wkly. Target aud: General. ■ Donald A. Thurston, pres; Corydon L. Thurston, gen mgr; Joan Roger, gen sls mgr; Gerard Reardon, progmg dir; Dick Lindsay, news dir; Paul Willey, chief engr. ■ Rates: $25; 20; 25; na.

Greenfield

WGAM(AM)—Aug 26, 1980: 1520 khz; 10 kw-D, DA. TL: N42 36 12 W72 36 21. Box 910 (01302); 158 Main St. (01301). (413) 774-2321. FAX: (413) 774-2683. Licensee: Radio Skutnik Inc. (acq 10-16-92; $500,000; with co-located FM; FTR 11-23-92). Net: ABC/I, Unistar. Rep: Torbet. Format: Adult contemp. News progmg 7 hrs wkly. Target aud: 35 plus. Spec prog: Big band 2 hrs wkly. ■ Edward Skutnik, pres, gen mgr, gen sls mgr & prom mgr; Jim Hemingway, chief engr.

WRSI(FM)—Co-owned with WGAM. July 26, 1981: 95.3 mhz; 320 w. Ant 780 ft. TL: N42 41 50 W72 36 20. Stereo. Prog sep from AM. Format: Div, classic rock/AOR. Target aud: 18-45. Spec prog: Class 6 hrs, jazz 6 hrs, C&W 6 hrs, oldies 5 hrs. ■ Edward W. Skutnik, chief engr.

WHAI(AM)—May 15, 1938: 1240 khz; 1 kw-U. TL: N42 35 21 W72 37 08. Hrs opn: 24. Box 32 (01302); 81 Woodard Rd. (01301). (413) 774-4301. FAX: (413) 773-5637. Licensee: Haigis Broadcasting Corp. Net: CBS. Wash atty: Wiley, Rein & Fielding. Format: Adult contemp, country. News staff 2; news progmg 20 hrs wkly. Target aud: 25-49. Spec prog: Oldies 13 hrs wkly. ■ Ann H. Banash, pres & gen mgr; Robert Diamond, gen sls mgr; Jay E. Deane, progmg dir; Rick Archer, mus dir; Dyson Shultz, news dir; William J. Wiles, chief engr. ■ Rates: $36.75; 25.10; 31; 20.70.

WHAI-FM—May 15, 1948: 98.3 mhz; 2 kw. Ant 403 ft. 100%. ■ Rates: Same as AM.

WRSI(FM)—Listing follows WGAM.

WXOD(FM)—See Winchester, N.H.

Harwich

*WCCT-FM—May 1988: 90.3 mhz; 160 w-H, 640 w-V. Ant 125 ft. TL: N41 42 40 W70 04 34. Hrs opn: 24. Rebroadcasts WBUR(FM) Boston 90%. Cape Cod Tech., Pleasant Lake Ave., (02645). (508) 432-4500, ext. 226. FAX: (508) 432-7916. Licensee: Cape Cod Regional Technical High School (acq 11-11-87). Net: NPR. Format: Div. News progmg 30 hrs wkly. Target aud: 20-65; educated adults. ■ Tim Carrole, CEO; Oscar Doame, chmn; Burt Fisher, gen mgr & chief engr.

Harwichport

WFXR(FM)—May 11, 1989: 93.5 mhz; 3 kw. Ant 328 ft. TL: N41 44 19 W70 00 40. Stereo. Hrs opn: 24. 105 Stevens St., MA (02601). (508) 457-4122. FAX: (508) 775-6088. Licensee: J.J. Taylor Companies Inc. Net: Unistar. Rep: Eastman. Wash atty: Pepper & Corazzini. Format: Country. ■ Bonnie McCarthy, gen mgr; Ted Morgan, opns mgr; Frank Feeley, gen mgr; Keith Lemire, progmg dir; Skip Comeau, chief engr.

Haverhill

WHAV(AM)—1947: 1490 khz; 1 kw-U. TL: N42 46 22 W71 06 01. Hrs opn: 24. Box 1490, 30 How St. (01831). (508) 374-4733. FAX: (508) 373-8023. Licensee: Northeast Broadcasting Co. (group owner; acq 1981). Net: Unistar. Format: Full svc, adult contemp, news/talk. News staff one. Target aud: General. Spec prog: Pol one hr, Sp 3 hrs wkly. ■ Suzan Robinson, gen mgr & stn mgr; Mark LeMay, news dir.

WLYT(FM)—Co-owned with WHAV(AM). June 1959: 92.5 mhz; 25 kw. Ant 710 ft. TL: N42 46 23 W71 06 01. Stereo. Hrs opn: 24. Prog sep from AM. Format: Adult contemp. Target aud: 25-49.

Holliston

*WHHB(FM)—Apr 17, 1979: 91.5 mhz; 10 w. Ant 52 ft. TL: N42 12 29 W71 26 19 (CP: 99.9 mhz, 18 w, ant 187 ft., TL: N42 12 16 W71 25 53). Holliston High School, 370 Hollis St. (01746). (508) 429-0679. Licensee: Holliston High School. Format: Div. ■ William Curboy, stn mgr.

Holyoke

*WCCH(FM)—1977: 103.5 mhz; 10 w. Ant 258 ft. TL: N42 11 55 W72 38 27. Hrs opn: 6 AM-11 PM. 303 Homestead Ave. (01040). (413) 538-7000, ext. 488. Licensee: Holyoke Community College. Format: Progsv. Spec prog: Black 2 hrs, class 2 hrs, country 2 hrs, jazz 2 hrs, Sp 2 hrs, R&B 6 hrs wkly. ■ Edward Brown, chmn & pres; Kevin Morartg, gen mgr & progmg mgr; Adam Wheeler, prom mgr; Dana Morse, mus dir; Karen Sumwalt, news dir; Gary Mollett, chief engr.

Hyannis

WCOD-FM—June 2, 1967: 106.1 mhz; 50 kw. Ant 450 ft. TL: N41 43 46 W70 10 01. Stereo. Hrs opn: 24. 105 Stevens St., (02601). (508) 775-6800. FAX: (508) 775-6088. Licensee: J.J. Taylor Companies Inc. Group owner: Taylor Communications Inc. (acq 12-19-86). Net: AP. Rep: Banner. Format: Adult contemp. News staff 2. Target aud: 25-54. Spec prog: Acoustic/folk 4 hrs wkly. ■ John J. Taylor III, pres; Paul Levesque, exec vp; Bonnie McCarthy, gen mgr; Autumn Quinn, opns mgr; Frank Feeley, gen sls mgr; Chris Boles, progmg dir; Bill Lowell, news dir; Skipi Comeau, chief engr.

WPXC(FM)—Jan 9, 1987: 102.9 mhz; 6 kw. Ant 325 ft. TL: N41 41 19 W70 20 49. Stereo. Hrs opn: 24 154 Barnstable Rd. (02601). (508) 778-2888. FAX: (508) 362-5557. Licensee: Radio Hyannis Inc. Rep: McGavren Guild. Wash atty: Adrian Cronauer, Maloney & Burch. Format: Classic hits/AOR. News staff 3; news progmg 4 hrs wkly. Target aud: General. ■ Albert Makkay Sr., pres; Maureen Makkay, vp; Albert Makkay Jr., gen mgr; Brad Goodwin, gen sls mgr; Allison Makkay, natl sls mgr; Dennis W. Harwich, vp adv; Colleen Makkay, vp adv; Phil Manicki, vp progmg; Brian Kelly, mus dir; Chris Barnes, news dir & pub affrs dir; Grady Moates, chief engr.

WQRC(FM)—See Barnstable.

Lawrence

WCCM(AM)—August 1947: 800 khz; 1 kw-D. TL: N42 40 26 W71 11 26. 33 Franklin St. (01840). (508) 683-7171. FAX: (508) 681-0786. Licensee: Gowdy Family L.P. (group owner; acq 5-31-63). Net: MBS. Rep: Katz & Powell. Format: Talk/news. ■ Curt Gowdy, pres; Jerre Gowdy, vp; Trever Gowdy, gen mgr & gen sls mgr; Bruce Arnold, progmg dir; Bob Schufrieder, news dir.

WCGY(FM)—Co-owned with WCCM(AM). April 1960: 93.7 mhz; 50 kw. Ant 430 ft. TL: N42 40 26 W71 11 26 (CP: 29.5 kw, ant 640 ft., TL: N42 35 42 W71 02 18). Stereo. Prog sep from AM. Format: Classic rock. ■ Dave Cooper, progmg dir.

WLLH(AM)—See Lowell.

Leicester

WVNE(AM)—June 19, 1991: 760 khz; 25 kw-D. TL: N42 14 57 W72 04 41. Suite 201, 70 James St., Worcester (01603). (508) 831-9863. Licensee: Blount Masscom Inc. (acq 5-15-90; FTR 6-4-90). Net: USA, Moody. Format: Religious. Target aud: 25-54. ■ William A. Blount, pres, gen mgr & progmg dir; Deborah C. Blount, exec vp; David O. Young, vp; Steve Tuzeneu, opns mgr & mus dir; Gary Todd, gen sls mgr; Eleanor Hubbard, pub affrs dir; Lincoln Hubbard, chief engr. ■ Rates: $18; 18; 18; 18.

Leominster

WEIM(AM)—See Fitchburg.

Lowell

WCAP(AM)—June 10, 1951: 980 khz; 5 kw-U, DA-2. TL: N42 39 16 W1 21 43. Hrs opn: 24. 243 Central St. (01852). (508) 454-0404; (617) 729-4270. FAX: (508) 458-9124. Licensee: Northeast Radio Inc. Net: ABC/D, Daynet. Rep: Kettell-Carter. Format: Talk, news. News staff 3; news progmg 17 hrs wkly. Target aud: 25 plus. ■ Israel Cohen, pres; Maurice Cohen, gen mgr; Pauline Yates, stn mgr; Joe Corcoran, opns mgr; John Stuart, news dir; Kevin Bowland, chief engr.

*WJUL(FM)—Nov 6, 1967: 91.5 mhz; 1.7 kw. Ant 39 ft. TL: N42 39 10 W71 19 38. Stereo. Hrs opn: 18. One University Ave. (01854). (508) 452-9073. Licensee: Univ. Mass.-Lowell Bd of Trustees. Format: Div, progsv rock. Target aud: 16-25. Spec prog: Sp 15 hrs, Portuguese 2 hrs, Armenian 2 hrs, Indian 2 hrs, jazz 8 hrs, Black 2 hrs, reggae 4 hrs, heavy metal 4 hrs, soul 4 hrs, avante garde 4 hrs, class 4 hrs wkly. ■ Paul R. Gerry III, pres; Tom Pepres, sr vp; Tim Waltner, vp & gen mgr; Josh Etner, stn mgr; Paul R. Gerry, chief engr.

WLLH(AM)—1934: 1400 khz; 1 kw-U. TL: N42 39 29 W71 19 04. Box 1818, 40-44 Church St. (01853). (508) 458-8486; (508) 682-2148. FAX: (508) 452-0980. Licensee: The Great Merrimack Valley Wireless Talking Machine Co. (acq 12-1-86). Net: ABC/C. Rep: Kadetsky. Format: Sp, news/talk. News staff 2 Target aud: 25-54. Spec prog: Black one hr, Greek 2 hrs, Portuguese 2 hrs, Indian one hr, Brazilian one hr, Cambodian 6 hrs wkly. ■ Donald T. Fitzgibbons, pres; Perry Kapiloff, gen mgr; Frank Messina, gen sls mgr; Bob Ellis, progmg dir & news dir; Joyce Apostolos, mus dir; Joe Soucie, chief engr. ■ Rates: $30; 25; 30; 25.

WSSH-FM—1947: 99.5 mhz; 32 kw. Ant 600 ft. TL: N42 39 16 W71 13 09. Stereo. 1200 Soldiers Field Rd., Boston (02134). (617) 254-9267. FAX: (617) 782-8757. Licensee: Granum Communications (acq 4-23-93; $18.5 million; FTR 3-29-93). Net: Unistar. Rep: Major Mkt. Format: Adult contemp. Target aud: 25-54. ■ John R. Laton, gen mgr; Greg Janoff, gen sls mgr; Susan Rosenbenk, prom dir; Chuck Morgan, progmg dir; John Kennedy, chief engr.

Lynn

WFNX(FM)—Aug 5, 1963: 101.7 mhz; 1.65 kw. Ant 440 ft. TL: N42 25 52 W71 05 20. Stereo. 25 Exchange St. (01901). (617) 595-6200; (617) 595-1017. FAX: (617) 595-3810. Licensee: MCC Broadcasting Inc. (acq 11-10-82; FTR 11-29-82). Format: Adult new rock. News staff one. Target aud: 18-49; well educated, affluent & socially active trend setters. Spec prog: Jazz 8 hrs, gay talk show 4 hrs, loc mus 3 hrs wkly. ■ Stephen Mindich, CEO & chmn; H. Barry Morris, pres; Charlie Walter, CFO; Andy Kingston, gen sls mgr; Greg Orcutt, natl sls mgr; Carola Cadley, mktg mgr; Ginny Markowitz, prom mgr; Kurt St.Thomas, progmg dir; Troy Smith, mus dir; Henry Santoro, news dir; Marc Gordon, chief engr. ■ Rates: $225; 190; 200; 175.

Massachusetts

WLYN(AM)—November 1947: 1360 khz; 700 w-D, 76 w-N. TL: N42 27 17 W70 58 44. 25 Exchange St. (01903). (617) 581-5722. Licensee: Puritan Broadcast Service Inc. Net: ABC/E. Rep: Frederick. Format: Ethnic. Spec prog: It 4 hrs, Pol 2 hrs, Greek 4 hrs wkly. ■ Paul Allen, gen mgr; Ed White, progmg dir; Mike Klein, chief engr.

Marion

*WWTA(FM)—Not on air, target date unknown: 88.5 mhz; 19 w-H, 100 w-V. Ant 53 ft. TL: N41 42 32 W70 45 57. Front St. (02738). Licensee: Tabor Academy.

Marlboro

WSRO(AM)—January 1958: 1470 khz; 5 kw-U, DA-N. TL: N42 21 59 W71 34 22. Stereo. Hrs opn: 24. 48 Fitchburg St. (01752). (508) 485-9291. FAX: (508) 624-6496. Licensee: WSRO Inc. (acq 1-12-61). Net: AP, CNN. Format: Full service. News staff 3. Target aud: 35 plus; people living between Worcester & Boston. ■ Douglas J. Rowe, pres; John Crohan, gen mgr; Bernie Toole, gen sls mgr; Kris Shore, progmg dir & mus dir; Rick Kenadack, chief engr.

Marshfield

WATD-FM—Dec 5, 1977: 95.9 mhz; 2.8 kw. Ant 350 ft. TL: N42 06 40 W70 42 14. Stereo. Hrs opn: 24. 130 Enterprise Dr. (02050). (617) 837-1166. FAX: (617) 837-1978. Licensee: Marshfield Broadcasting Co. Format: Adult contemp, blues, oldies. News staff 2; news progmg 10 hrs wkly. Target aud: 25-64; South Shore residents. Spec prog: Irish 6 hrs wkly. ■ Edward Perry, pres & gen mgr; Taylor Morgan, prom dir; Cathy Doran, progmg dir; Robert Stone, news dir; Ed Perry, engrg dir. ■ Rates: $22; 18; 20; 15.

Maynard

*WAVM(FM)—April 1974: 91.7 mhz; 16 w. Ant -7 ft. TL: N42 25 18 W71 27 02. Stereo. Hrs opn: 24. Maynard High School, Great Rd. (01754). (508) 897-5213; (508) 897-5179. Licensee: Maynard Public Schools. Format: Noncoml div. Target aud: General. Spec prog: Oldies one hr wkly. ■ Joseph Magno, stn mgr.

Medford

*WMFO(FM)—March 1971: 91.5 mhz; 125 w. Ant 135 ft. TL: N42 24 27 W71 07 15. Stereo. 490 Boston Ave. (02153); Box 65 (02155). (617) 625-0800; (617) 381-3800. FAX: (617) 625-6072. Licensee: Trustees of Tufts College. Format: Freeform. Spec prog: Black 12 hrs, class 3 hrs, Portuguese 3 hrs, Native American 6 hrs, Sp 3 hrs, Haitian 4 hrs wkly. ■ Dustin Tracey, gen mgr; Carlos Aramoya, progmg dir; Derrick Smith, mus dir; Michael LeClair, chief engr.

WXKS(AM)—Jan 20, 1952: 1430 khz; 5 kw-D, 1 kw-N, DA-N. TL: N42 24 11 W71 04 29. Hrs opn: 24. Box 128, 99 Revere Beach Pkwy. (02155). (617) 396-1430. FAX: (617) 391-3064. Licensee: Kiss L.P. Group owner: Pyramid Broadcasting (acq 7-15-86). Net: Unistar. Wash atty: David Tillotson, esq. Format: Nostalgia, big band. Target aud: 35 plus. ■ Richard Balsbaugh, CEO; John Madison, sr vp, gen mgr & vp sls; Arnie Ginsburg, progmg mgr; Bill Costa, news dir; Bob Wotiz, chief engr.

WXKS-FM—Sept 1, 1960: 107.9 mhz; 20.5 kw. Ant 771 ft. TL: N42 20 50 W71 04 59. Stereo. Hrs opn: 24. Net: Format: CHR. Target aud: 18-34. ■ Kenneth J. O'Keefe, CFO; Beverly Tilden, prom mgr; Steve Rivers, progmg dir; Cadillac Jack McCartney, mus dir.

Middleborough Center

WCEG(AM)—Not on air, target date unknown: 1530 khz; 1 kw-D. TL: N41 55 28 W70 56 10. 66 Cambridge St., Middleboro (02346-2004). Licensee: Metro South Broadcasting Network Inc. (acq 12-8-92; $150,000; FTR 1-4-93).

Milford

WMRC(AM)—Oct 6, 1956: 1490 khz; 1 kw-U. TL: N42 08 12 W71 30 50. 11 Congress St. (01757). (508) 473-1490. FAX: (508) 478-2200. Licensee: Thomas M. McAuliffe (acq 7-23-90; $250,000; FTR 8-13-90). Net: AP. Rep: New England Spot Sls. Format: Adult contemp, news/talk. News staff 3. Target aud: 25-54. Spec prog: Portuguese 2 hrs wkly. ■ Thomas M. McAuliffe, pres; Bill Robert, progmg dir & mus dir; Edward Thompson, news dir; Doug Kehrig, chief engr. ■ Rates: $22; 22; 22; 22.

Milton

*WMLN-FM—Apr 1, 1975: 91.5 mhz; 170 w. Ant 98 ft. TL: N42 14 27 W71 06 52. Hrs opn: 24. 1071 Blue Hill Ave. (02186). (617) 333-0311; (617) 333-0500. FAX: (617) 333-0309. Licensee: Curry College. Net: NBC. Format: Jazz, rock, div, AOR. News progmg 15 hrs wkly. Target aud: General. Spec prog: Oldies 4 hrs, blues 3 hrs, pub affrs 2 hrs wkly. ■ Alan H. Frank, gen mgr.

Nantucket

WRZE(FM)—June 15, 1981: 96.3 mhz; 50 kw. Ant 405 ft. TL: N41 16 07 W70 10 49. Stereo. Hrs opn: 24. 154 Barnstable Rd., Hyannis (02601). (508) 778-2888. Licensee: Radio Nantucket Inc. (acq 11-25-92; $500,000; FTR 12-14-92). Wash atty: Maloney & Burch. Format: CHR, adult contemp. News staff 2; news progmg 8 hrs wkly. Target aud: 18-49. ■ Albert Makkay Sr., pres; Albert Makkay, gen mgr; Allison Makkay, natl sls mgr; Dennis W. Harwich, prom dir; Steve McVie, progmg dir; Corey Chase, mus dir; Chris Barnes, news dir & pub affrs dir; Skip Comeau, vp engrg.

Natick

WBIV(AM)—November 1972: 1060 khz; 25 kw-D, 2.5 kw-N, DA-2. TL: N42 14 49 W71 25 30. Suite 204, 1105 Commonwealth Ave., Boston (02215). (617) 782-4848. Licensee: Boston SRN Inc. Group owner: Satellite Radio Network (acq 11-30-90; $1.3 million; FTR 12-31-90). Format: Contemp Christian/Time Brokered. Target aud: General. Spec prog: Cape Verdean 4 hrs, Indian 3 hrs, folk 2 hrs, public affrs one hr wkly. ■ Robert Tarpin, gen mgr; Walter Dixon, pub affrs dir; Grady Moates, chief engr. ■ Rates: $30; 30; 30; 20.

New Bedford

WBSM(AM)—July 17, 1949: 1420 khz; 5 kw-D, 1 kw-N, DA-2. TL: N41 39 02 W70 54 58. 22 Sconticut Neck Rd., Fairhaven (02719). (508) 993-1767. FAX: (508) 999-1420. Licensee: Dover Broadcasting Inc. Group owner: H & D Broadcast Group (acq 3-14-90; grpsl; FTR 3-9-90). Net: NBC, NBC Talknet. Rep: Christal. Format: News, talk. ■ Gerald Poch, pres; Stephen Bogue, gen mgr; Jean Marie Manning, gen sls mgr; Joe Lemardy, progmg dir; Jim Marshall, news dir; Frank Deramos, chief engr.

WCTK(FM)—Licensed to New Bedford. See Providence, R.I.

WJFD-FM—Feb 22, 1949: 97.3 mhz; 50 kw. Ant 500 ft. TL: N41 38 20 W70 52 27. Stereo. Hrs opn: 24. 270 Union St. (02740). (508) 997-2929; (508) 997-2920. FAX: (508) 990-3893. Licensee: Edmund Dinis (acq 6-23-86). Format: Ethnic. Target aud: General; Portuguese-speaking community. ■ Edmund Dinis, pres; Maria DaSilva, opns dir; Josef Faustino, news dir; Gregory Lynam, chief engr.

WNBH(AM)—Licensed to New Bedford. See Providence, R.I.

Newburyport

WNBP(AM)—March 10, 1957: 1450 khz; 1 kw-U. TL: N42 49 23 W70 51 42. Hrs opn: 18. Box 1450, 6 Federal St. (01950). (508) 462-1450. (508) 465-6666. FAX: (508) 462-0333. Licensee: Damon Radio Inc. (acq 6-22-89; $420,000; FTR 5-29-89). Net: AP. Rep: New England. Wash atty: McCabe & Allen. Format: Adult contemp. Target aud: 25-54. Spec prog: Irish 4 hrs wkly. ■ Win Damon, pres, gen mgr & sls dir; Matt Stevens, progmg dir; John Evans, news dir; Dan Guy, engrg dir.

Newton

WNTN(AM)—Apr 1, 1968: 1550 khz; 10 kw-D. TL: N42 21 27 W71 14 30. 143 Rumford Ave. (02166). (508) 969-1550. Licensee: Newton Broadcasting Corp. (acq 11-15-75). Rep: Herbert Groskin. Format: Talk/ethnic. Target aud: 40 plus. Spec prog: Greek 17 hrs, It 2 hrs, Irish 8 hrs, Fr/Haitian 3 hrs, Indian one hr wkly. ■ Orestes Demetriades, pres; Rob Rudnick, stn mgr; John Frassica, news dir; Leo Sullivan, chief engr.

*WZBC(FM)—April 1974: 90.3 mhz; 1 kw. Ant 220 ft. TL: N42 20 05 W71 10 31. Stereo. McElroy 107, Boston College (02167). (617) 552-8000. FAX: (617) 552-2158. Licensee: Trustees of Boston College. Format: Progsv. Spec prog: Class 3 hrs, jazz 6 hrs, Black 2 hrs, C&W 5 hrs, Haitian 4 hrs wkly. ■ P.J. Proscia, gen mgr; Steve Riggs, chief engr.

Norfolk

WDIS(AM)—March 20, 1978: 1170 khz; 1 kw-D, DA. TL: N42 05 32 W71 18 13. Box 207, 100 Pond St. (02056).

(508) 384-8255. FAX: (508) 384-1530. Licensee: Discussion Radio Inc. (acq 8-12-92; $65,000; FTR 9-7-92). Net: MBS. Format: News/talk. Spec prog: Pol 2 hrs wkly. ■ John Pacitto, gen mgr; Kevin Moriarty, progmg dir. ■ Rates: $25; 25; 25; na.

North Adams

*WJJW(FM)—Sept 5, 1973: 91.1 mhz; 423 w. Ant -830 ft. TL: N42 41 27 W73 06 16. Stereo. N. Adams State College, Campus Center (01247). (413) 663-9136. Licensee: North Adams State College. Format: Progsv. Spec prog: Jazz 4 hrs, Pol 3 hrs, class 3 hrs wkly. ■ Harry Hawkins, gen mgr; Glen Harrison, progmg dir; Ed Baker, mus dir; Paul Wiley, chief engr.

WMNB(FM)—Listing follows WNAW(AM).

WNAW(AM)—Nov 23, 1947: 1230 khz; 1 kw-U. TL: N42 41 03 W73 06 23. Box 707, 466 Curran Hwy. (01247-0707). (413) 663-6567. FAX: (413) 662-2143. Licensee: Berkshire Broadcasting Co. Inc. Group owner: Berkshire Group (acq 7-22-66). Net: CNN. Rep: Kettell-Carter. Wash atty: Wilkinson, Barker, Knauer & Quinn. Format: Full svc adult contemp. News staff 3; news progmg 14 hrs wkly. Target aud: Adults. ■ Donald A. Thurston, pres; Corydon L. Thurston, vp & gen mgr; Rod Bunt, progmg mgr; Ronald Plock, news dir; A. Paul Willey, chief engr.

WMNB(FM)—Co-owned with WNAW(AM). July 12, 1964: 100.1 mhz; 3 kw. Ant 501 ft. TL: N42 41 51 W73 03 52. Stereo. Prog sep from AM. Format: Btfl mus. Target aud: 35 plus. ■ Dave Fierro, progmg mgr. ■ Rates: $22; 22; 22; 15.

North Dartmouth

*WSMU-FM—September 1973: 91.1 mhz; 1.2 kw. Ant 300 ft. TL: N41 37 43 W71 00 24. Stereo. Old Westport Rd. (02747). (508) 999-8149. FAX: (508) 999-8173. Licensee: Univ. of Mass.-Dartmouth. Net: ABC/FM. Format: Progsv, alt rock. ■ Tom Bednarz, gen mgr; Ed Woytaskek, chief engr.

Northampton

WEIB(FM)—Not on air, target date unknown: 106.3 mhz; 3 kw. Ant 289 ft. TL: N42 22 29 W72 40 24. Stereo. Hrs opn: 24. 8 N. King St., Northhampton (01060). Licensee: Cutting Edge Broadcasting Inc. Wash atty: Hutton, Feore & Cooke. ■ Carol Moore Cutting, pres & gen mgr.

WHMP(AM)—December 1950: 1400 khz; 1 kw-U. TL: N42 19 36 W72 39 28. Box 268, 15 Hampton Ave. (01061). (413) 586-7400. Licensee: Multi-Market Radio of Northampton Inc. (acq 1993). Net: NBC, NBC Talknet. Rep: Katz & Powell; Kettell-Carter. Format: MOR, nostalgia, adult contemp. News staff 3; news progmg 10 hrs wkly. Target aud: 35 plus. Spec prog: Pol 3 hrs wkly. ■ Rick Heideman, gen mgr & stn mgr; Mike Dion, opns mgr & mus dir; Ted Baker, prom mgr & progmg dir; Ron Hall, news dir; Tom Ray, chief engr. ■ Rates: $27; 15; 20; 8.

WHMP-FM—Nov 1, 1956: 99.3 mhz; 3 kw. Ant 321 ft. TL: N42 22 29 W72 40 24. Stereo. Prog sep from AM. Format: CHR. ■ Mike Dion, progmg dir.

*WOZQ(FM)—1981: 91.9 mhz; 200 w. Ant 115 ft. TL: N42 19 13 W72 38 14. Stereo. Davis Center, Smith College (01063). (413) 585-4977. Licensee: Trustees of Smith College. Net: AP. Format: Educ, div. News progmg 3 hrs wkly. Target aud: 15-30; college students & area businesses. Spec prog: Black 10 hrs, class 3 hrs, Ger one hr, Pol 3 hrs, Portuguese 2 hrs, Sp 3 hrs, Indian 2 hrs wkly. ■ Nicki Shute, stn mgr.

Northfield

*WNMH(FM)—Sept 10, 1984: 91.5 mhz; 235 w. Ant 308 ft. TL: N42 42 52 W72 26 38. Stereo. Box 2697, Northfield Mt. Hermon School, (01360); Revell Hall, 206 Main St. (01360). (413) 498-3603. FAX: (413) 498-3329. Licensee: Northfield Mount Hermon School. Net: ABC/I. Format: Div. News progmg 3 hrs wkly. Target aud: Student body & surrounding communities. Spec prog: Class 2 hrs, jazz 10 hrs, Sp 4 hrs, black 8 hrs, Fr 2 hrs wkly. ■ W.S. Hattendorf Jr., pres; Todd Darten, stn mgr; Nick Heikkila, vp opns; Graham Schera, vp dev; Trevett McCandlis, Harry Hernandez, vps prom; Kathrine Flynn, news dir.

Orange

WFUB(FM)—Not on air, target date unknown: 97.3 mhz; 3 kw. Ant 328 ft. TL: N42 37 19 W72 21 58. Box 973 (01364). Licensee: Deane Brothers Broadcasting Corp.

Orange-Athol

WCAT(AM)—May 13, 1956: 700 khz; 2.5 kw-D. TL: N42 35 06 W72 16 56. Box 90, 660 E. Main St., Orange (01364). (508) 544-2321. Licensee: P&S Broadcasting Inc. (acq 12-1-75). Rep: Katz. Format: News/talk. News staff 2. Target aud: Adults 35 plus. ■ Jean S. Partridge, pres, gen mgr, opns mgr, gen sls mgr & adv dir; Steve Elliott, prom mgr, progmg dir, mus dir & news dir. ■ Rates: $12; 12; 12; 12.

Orleans

WKPE(AM)—April 10, 1970: 1170 khz; 1 kw-D, DA. TL: N41 46 48 W70 00 36. Radio Center (02653). (508) 255-3220. FAX: (508) 255-9787. Licensee: Cape Media Inc. Group owner: Roth Communications (acq 8-15-83; $2.05 million with co-located FM; FTR 9-5-83). Rep: Katz. Format: Oldies. ■ Peter Crawford, CEO; David Roth, pres; Dave Parsons, stn mgr; Shari Brown, rgnl sls mgr; Steve Binder, progmg mgr & chief engr; Joe Rossetti, news dir.

WKPE-FM—July 25, 1974: 104.7 mhz; 50 kw. Ant 504 ft. TL: N41 46 48 W70 00 36. Stereo. Dups AM 100%.

Pittsfield

WBEC(AM)—March 1947: 1420 khz; 1 kw-U, DA-N. TL: N42 26 40 W73 16 43. Hrs opn: 24. Box 958, 211 Jason St. (01202). (413) 499-3333. FAX: (413) 442-1590. Licensee: Aritaur Communications (Mass) Inc. (acq 6-1-93; $500,000 with co-located FM; FTR 5-17-93). Net: ABC/I. Rep: Torbet. Wash atty: Smithwick & Belendiuk Format: News/talk. News staff 4; news progmg 15 hrs wkly. Target aud: 25-55. Spec prog: Relg 3 hrs wkly. ■ Joseph V. Gallagher, pres; Dave Winchester, opns mgr; Todd Mallinson, gen sls mgr; Jack Styczynski, news dir.

WBEC-FM—October 1967: 105.5 mhz; 975 w. Ant 590 ft. TL: N42 24 44 W73 17 05. Stereo. Hrs opn: 24. Prog sep from AM. Format: Expanded contemp hit. News progmg 3 hrs wkly. Target aud: 18-54. ■ Terrie Michaels, prom mgr; Joanne Billow, progmg dir; Terry Michaels, mus dir.

WBRK(AM)—Feb 20, 1938: 1340 khz; 1 kw-U. TL: N42 27 00 W73 12 55. 100 North St. (01201). (413) 442-1553. FAX: (413) 445-5294. Licensee: WBRK Inc. (acq 6-30-84). Net: MBS, CBS. Rep: Savalli, Kettell-Carter. Format: Adult contemp, talk. Spec prog: Pol 2 hrs, Irish one hr, relg 2 hrs wkly. ■ Willard H. Hodgkins, pres; John Campoli, exec vp; Michael J. Bunn, vp opns; Robert Shade, vp sls; Richard Weinberg, vp progmg; Michael Leary, news dir; Donald Coleman, chief engr.

WRCZ(FM)—Co-owned with WBRK(AM). Oct 10, 1970: 101.7 mhz; 3 kw. Ant 145 ft. TL: N42 28 31 W73 16 07. Stereo. Dups AM 20%. Format: Classic rock.

WUHN(AM)—Sept 9, 1971: 1110 khz; 5 kw-D, DA. TL: N42 26 22 W73 17 30. Hrs opn: Sunrise-sunset. Box 1265, 501 East St. (01202-1265). (413) 499-1100. FAX: (413) 499-1800. Licensee: Weiner Broadcasting Inc. (acq 1-15-88). Net: SMN. Rep: Eastman. Wash atty: Cohn & Marks. Format: Pure gold. News staff one; news progmg 14 hrs wkly. Target aud: 25-54; baby boomers. ■ Phillip A. Weiner, CEO; Philip A. Weiner, pres; Denise A. Shoblom, vp & gen mgr; David Isby, stn mgr, prom dir & progmg dir; Dick Savage, gen sls mgr; Steve Elliott, news dir; Mike Alderman, chief engr.

WUPE(FM)—Co-owned with WUHN(AM). 1975: 95.9 mhz; 1 kw. Ant 560 ft. TL: N42 24 44 W73 17 05. Stereo. Hrs opn: 24. Prog sep from AM. Net: Unistar. Format: Lite adult contemp. News progmg 28 hrs wkly. Target aud: 25-54; young adults with families.

Plymouth

WPLM(AM)—Aug 8, 1955: 1390 khz; 5 kw-U, DA-2. TL: N41 58 05 W70 42 06. Pilgrim Hwy., Rt. 3 (02360); Box 1390 (02362). (508) 746-1390. FAX: (508) 830-1128. Licensee: Plymouth Rock Broadcasting Co. Inc. Net: UPI. Rep: Kirby. Format: Big band. ■ Dr. Laurie Campbell, pres; Rob Monahan, gen mgr; Steve Williams, progmg dir; Don Latulip, news dir.

WPLM-FM—June 25, 1961: 99.1 mhz; 50 kw. Ant 430 ft. TL: N41 58 02 W70 42 04. Dups AM 100%.

Provincetown

*WOMR(FM)—Mar 21, 1982: 91.9 mhz; 810 w. Ant 155 ft. TL: N42 03 54 W70 09 34. Stereo. Hrs opn: 6 AM-midnight. Box 975, 14 Center St. (02657). (508) 487-2106; (508) 487-2619. Licensee: Lower Cape Communications Inc. Format: Class, jazz, folk. News progmg 3 hrs wkly. Target aud: General. Spec prog: March 2 hrs, blues 3 hrs, rock 12 hrs, pub affrs 15 hrs, bluegrass 3 hrs, children's 6 hrs wkly. ■ Thomas Conklin, pres; Jeanne Brossart, gen mgr; Len Bowen, mus dir; Erraeon Perry, engrg mgr.

Quincy

WJDA(AM)—Sept 13, 1947: 1300 khz; 1 kw-D. TL: N42 15 35 W70 58 36. Hrs opn: 5 AM-9 PM Mon.-Sat.; 6 AM-6 PM Sun. Box 130, (02269). (617) 479-1300. FAX: (617) 479-0622. Licensee: South Shore Broadcasting Co. Net: AP, SMN. Format: MOR, SMN's "Stardust" format. News staff 2; news progmg 10 hrs wkly. Target aud: 35 plus. ■ James D. Asher, pres; John Nicholson, gen mgr; Michael Benjamin, gen sls mgr; Roy Lind, progmg dir; Joe Catalano, news dir; Douglas Lane, chief engr. ■ Rates: $35; 23; 35; na.

Rockland

*WRPS(FM)—Feb 8, 1974: 88.3 mhz; 100 w. Ant 120 ft. TL: N42 07 43 W70 55 01. 34 Goddard Ave. (02370). (617) 871-0724. Licensee: Rockland Public Schools. Format: Pub svc. ■ Stephen J. Budkiewicz, gen mgr; Newton Stephen, chief engr.

Salem

WESX(AM)—Jan 1, 1939: 1230 khz; 1 kw-U. TL: N42 31 06 W70 51 41. Box 710 (01970); Nagus Ave., Marblehead (01945). (508) 744-1230. FAX: (508) 744-1853. Licensee: North Shore Broadcasting Co. (acq 4-1-50). Net: AP. Format: Adult contemp, big band, news. News staff 2; news progmg 20 hrs wkly. Target aud: General. Spec prog: Pol 2 hrs, relg 2 hrs, Irish 2 hrs wkly. ■ James D. Asher, pres; Stuart Egenberg, gen sls mgr; Al Needham, news dir; Doug Lane, chief engr.

*WMWM(FM)—1976: 91.7 mhz; 130 w. Ant 132 ft. TL: N42 30 14 W70 53 26. Stereo. Hrs opn: 15 Campus Center, 352 Lafayette St. (01970). (508) 745-9170; (508) 745-9401. FAX: (508) 740-7204. Licensee: Salem State College. Format: Progsv, educ. News progmg one hr wkly. Target aud: General. Spec prog: Black 16 hrs, jazz 3 hrs, relg 3 hrs wkly. ■ Chris Moradi, gen mgr; Clark Sullivan, opns mgr; Gary Sciola, progmg dir; Julie Chadwick, mus dir; Bob Nelson, pub affrs dir; Marc Gordon, chief engr.

Sandwich

*WSDH(FM)—1976: 91.5 mhz; 310 w. Ant 150 ft. TL: N41 44 06 W70 27 35. Hrs opn: 10 AM-4 PM Mon.-Fri. Sandwich High School, 365 Quaker Meetinghouse Rd., East Sandwich (02537). (508) 888-0420. FAX: (508) 833-8392. Licensee: Sandwich Public Schools. Format: CHR, classic rock, educ. News staff one. Target aud: 12-20; high school students. ■ Richard Rose, gen mgr; Tom O'Connell, chief engr.

Sheffield

*WBSL-FM—September 1973: 91.7 mhz; 250 w. Ant 50 ft. TL: N42 06 57 W73 25 00. Hrs opn: 8. Berkshire School, 245 N. Undermountain Rd. (01257). (413) 229-6683; (413) 229-8511, ext. 235. Licensee: Berkshire School Inc. Net: AP. Format: Adult contemp, jazz, progsv. Target aud: General. Spec prog: Jazz 15 hrs, Black 2 hrs, folk 2 hrs, Sp 2 hrs, Pol one hr wkly. ■ Joanne A. Dinsmore, gen mgr & progmg dir; Thomas P. Jaworski, opns dir & chief engr.

South Hadley

*WMHC(FM)—May 14, 1957: 91.5 mhz; 100 w. Ant -18 ft. TL: N42 15 12 W72 34 40. Stereo. Mt. Holyoke College (01075). (413) 538-2044; (413) 538-2019. Licensee: President & Trustees of Mount Holyoke College. Net: AP. Format: Rock, rap, variety/div. News progmg 7 hrs wkly. Target aud: General. Spec prog: Black 15 hrs, class 15 hrs, jazz 15 hrs wkly. ■ Lisa Kovalivich, gen mgr; Jennifer Rochlis, chief engr.

South Yarmouth

WATB(FM)—Not on air, target date unknown: 103.9 mhz; 3 kw. Ant 315 ft. TL: N41 41 30 W70 08 43. One Park Ctr., Hyannis (02601). Licensee: Cape Cod Radio Inc. ■ John W. Miller, pres.

Southbridge

WESO(AM)—March 20, 1955: 970 khz; 1 kw-D, 21 w-N. TL: N42 03 59 W71 59 28. Hrs opn: 6 AM-midnight. 26 Hamilton St. (01550). (508) 764-4381. FAX: (508) 764-2682. Licensee: John R. Neuhoff Jr. (acq 12-20-88; $1.1 million with co-located FM; FTR 1-16-89). Net: AP. Rep: Torbet. Format: Adult contemp. Spec prog: Pol 2 hrs, Sp 2 hrs wkly. ■ John R. Neuhoff, pres; Don Fitzgibbons, gen mgr & gen sls mgr; Russ Dowd, opns mgr; Steve Geer, prom dir, mus dir & progmg dir; Dave Goblaskas, news dir; Richard Lavalle, chief engr. ■ Rates: $30; 27; 30; 18.

WQVR(FM)—Co-owned with WESO(AM). Nov 1, 1968: 100.1 mhz; 3 kw. Ant 295 ft. TL: N42 02 16 W71 59 20 (CP: 1.74 kw, ant 590 ft.). Stereo. Prog sep from AM. Net: AP, Jones Satellite Audio. Format: Country. Spec prog: Pol 2 hrs, Greek one hr wkly. ■ Joe Grivalski, mus dir.

Springfield

WACE(AM)—See Chicopee.

WACM(AM)—See West Springfield.

*WAIC(FM)—February 1967: 91.9 mhz; 230 w. Ant 66 ft. TL: N42 06 44 W72 33 29. Stereo. 1000 State St. (01109). (413) 736-7662. Licensee: American International College. Format: Div. Target aud: 16-40. Spec prog: Gospel. ■ Damon Johnson, gen mgr; Jason Larrier, progmg dir.

WAQY-FM—Dec 17, 1966: 102.1 mhz; 50 kw. Ant 780 ft. TL: N42 05 00 W72 42 16. Stereo. Hrs opn: 24. 45 Fisher Ave., East Longmeadow (01028). (413) 525-4141. FAX: (413) 525-4334. Licensee: Saga Communications of New England Inc. (group owner; acq 6-2-92; grpsl). Rep: Katz. Wash atty: Smithwick & Belendiuk. Format: Class rock. Target aud: General; upscale young adults with high income. ■ Edward Christian, CEO & chmn; Warren Lada, pres, vp & gen mgr; Norm Rawls, CFO; Larry Goldberg, gen sls mgr; Pam Tardiff, prom dir; Keith Masters, progmg dir; Becca Reed, mus dir; John O'Brien, news dir; Tom Ray, chief engr.

WHYN(AM)—1941: 560 khz; 5 kw-D, 1 kw-N, DA-2. TL: N42 11 58 W72 41 03 (CP: N42 11 37 W72 41 02). Stereo. Hrs opn: 24. Box 9013, 1331 Main St. (01102-9013). (413) 781-1011. FAX: (413) 734-4434. Licensee: Radio Station Management Inc. (acq 1993; grpsl); FTR 9-20-93). Net: ABC/I. Rep: McGavren Guild. Wash atty: Haley, Bader & Potts. Format: Full svc adult contemp. News staff 6. Target aud: General. ■ Donald Wilks, pres; Marc Berman, gen mgr & gen sls mgr; Anne Strong, prom mgr; Bill Hess, progmg dir; Paul Healy, news dir; Ken Jones, chief engr.

WHYN-FM—1946: 93.1 mhz; 8.9 kw. Ant 1,000 ft. TL: N42 14 28 W72 38 56. Stereo. Prog sep from AM. Format: Adult contemp. Target aud: 25-54.

WMAS(AM)—Sept 1, 1932: 1450 khz; 1 kw-U. TL: N42 06 32 W72 36 44. Stereo. Box 1139 (01101). (413) 737-1414. FAX: (413) 737-1488. Licensee: Lappin Communications Inc. (acq 5-8-78). Net: MBS, ABC. Rep: Banner. Format: MOR, talk. Spec prog: Black one hr, relg 2 hrs wkly. ■ Bruce Peckover, vp & gen mgr; Karen McCarthy, prom dir; Chris Carr, progmg dir; Jon Evans, news dir; Chuck Herlihy, chief engr.

WMAS-FM—Dec 1, 1947: 94.7 mhz; 50 kw. Ant 194 ft. TL: N42 06 32 W72 36 44. Stereo. Prog sep from AM. Rep: Banner. Format: Adult contemp. ■ Tom Holt, progmg dir; Keith Stephens, mus dir.

*WNEK-FM—Feb 17, 1976: 105.1 mhz; 13 w. Ant -23 ft. TL: N42 06 55 W72 31 05. Stereo. Western New England College, 1215 Wilbraham Rd, (01119-2684). (413) 782-1582. Net: AP, ABC/C. Format: Div. News staff 8; news progmg 5 hrs wkly. Target aud: 15-35; college community, greater Springfield area. Spec prog: Black 8 hrs wkly. ■ Jeff Bruce, gen mgr & chief engr; Darryl Brown, prom dir; Jon Constant, progmg dir; Melissa Wojcik, mus dir; Kirk Shute, news dir; Troy Dube, pub affrs dir.

WNNZ(AM)—(Westfield). July 8, 1987: 640 khz; 50 kw-D, 1 kw-N, DA-2. TL: N42 10 46 W72 45 05 (CP: 15 kw-N). Stereo. Hrs opn: 24. Box 640, 249 Union St. (01086); Box 30064, Springfield (01103). (413) 562-7666. FAX: (413) 562-1959. Licensee: Celia Communications Inc. Net: CBS, ABC. Rep: Eastman, Kadetsky. Wash atty: Akin, Gump, Strauss, Hauer & Feld. Format: Talk. News staff one; news progmg 10 hrs wkly. Target aud: 25-54; upscale adults. ■ Curtis H. Hahn, pres; Celia F. Hahn, gen mgr & stn mgr; John Baibak, news dir; Karen Scully, pub affrs dir; Bill Weeks, chief engr. ■ Rates: $35; 30; 35; 25.

*WSCB(FM)—Mar 1, 1958: 89.9 mhz; 100 w. Ant 35 ft. TL: N42 05 59 W72 33 30. 263 Alden St. (01109). (413) 748-3722. Licensee: Pres & Trustees of Springfield College. Format: Div. ■ Jason Arnold, gen mgr; Gary Mullett, chief engr.

WSPR(AM)—June 1936: 1270 khz; 5 kw-D, 1 kw-N, DA-2. TL: N42 05 24 W72 36 11. 195 High St., Holyoke (01040). (413) 536-7229. Licensee: Edmund Dinis (acq 2-2-93; $70,000; FTR 2-22-93). Format: Portugese. ■ Edmund Dinis, pres; Carlos Gonzalez, gen mgr.

***WTCC(FM)**—Aug 19, 1971: 90.7 mhz; 4 kw. Ant 92 ft. TL: N42 06 32 W72 34 45. Stereo. One Armory Sq. (01105). (413) 781-6628. FAX: (413) 781-5805. Licensee: Springfield Technical Community College. Format: Div, Black. News progmg 2 hrs wkly. Target aud: General. Spec prog: Class 3 hrs, country 4 hrs, Greek 2 hrs, It 2 hrs, Pol 2 hrs, Sp 14 hrs wkly. ■ James Dowd, pres; Rick Eckstein, gen mgr; Fred Krampits, chief engr.

Stockbridge

***WCWL(FM)**—April 1, 1975: 91.3 mhz; 250 w. Ant 40 ft. TL: N42 20 38 W73 17 20. 200 Stockbridge Rd., Lenox (01240). Licensee: Christian Theatre of the Air (acq 10-7-93; FTR 10-25-93). ■ Tammy Chamberlin, gen mgr; Geoff Hartman, progmg dir.

Sudbury

***WYAJ(FM)**—September 1980: 88.1 mhz; 4 w. Ant 220 ft. TL: N42 22 30 W71 24 28. 390 Lincoln Rd. (01776). (508) 443-9961. Licensee: Lincoln-Sudbury Broadcasting Foundation Inc. Format: Educ. Spec prog: Black 6 hrs, class 3 hrs, jazz 5 hrs, local rock artists 3 hrs wkly. ■ Fredrick Walker, pres; Christopher Trimper, chief engr.

Taunton

WPEP(AM)—Dec 22, 1949: 1570 khz; 1 kw-D, 227 w-N. TL: N41 53 00 W71 03 50. Hrs opn: 24. 41 Taunton Green (02780). (508) 822-1570. Licensee: Space Communication Systems Inc. (acq 9-30-93; $200,000; FTR 10-18-93). Rep: New England. Wash atty: Leventhal, Senter & Lerman. Format: News/talk. News staff 3; news progmg 20 hrs wkly. Target aud: 30 plus. Spec prog: Sp 3 hrs, Portuguese 5 hrs wkly. ■ David T. Gay, pres; Edward F. Fowler Jr., vp; George Colajezzi, gen mgr & progmg dir; Anthony W. Lopes, sls dir; Caroline Nyquist, news dir; Donna L. Colajezzi, pub affrs dir; Ransom Y. Place III, chief engr. ■ Rates: $18; 16; 17; 13.

WSNE(FM)—Jan 26, 1966: 93.3 mhz; 50 kw. Ant 620 ft. TL: N41 51 56 W71 17 22. Stereo. 100 Boyd Ave., East Providence, RI (02914). (401) 438-9300. Licensee: WSNE Inc. Group owner: Beck-Ross Communications Inc. (acq 3-20-86; $7,500,000; FTR 1-13-86). Net: AP. Rep: Eastman. Format: Adult contemp. News staff one. Target aud: 25-54; mostly women. Spec prog: Pub affrs 4 hrs wkly. ■ James Champlin, pres; William Campbell, vp & gen mgr; Robert Melfi, vp opns & gen sls mgr; Kathy Scully, rgnl sls mgr; Leslie Seiler, prom mgr & mus dir; David Jones, vp progmg; Steve Peck, progmg dir; Charles Hinman, news dir; Steve Lariviere, William Parks, chiefs engr. ■ Rates: $150; 150; 125; 35.

Tisbury

WMVY(FM)—June 1, 1981: 92.7 mhz; 3 kw. Ant 300 ft. TL: N41 26 17 W70 36 47 (CP: Ant 328 ft., TL: N41 26 17 W70 36 47). Stereo. Hrs opn: 21. Box 1148, 57 Carrols Way, Vineyard Haven (02568). (508) 693-5000. FAX: (508) 693-8211. Licensee: Broadcast Properties Inc. (acq 1-26-90). Net: AP, Moody. Rep: Banner. Format: AOR. News staff one. Target aud: 25-49; upper income, active consumer group. Spec prog: Class 4 hrs, jazz 4 hrs wkly. ■ Susan Pickering, gen mgr; Laurel Redington, prom dir; Barbara Dacey, progmg dir & mus dir; Mitch Wertlieb, news dir; Tom Bardwell, chief engr.

Truro

WCDJ(FM)—Not on air, target date unknown: 102.3 mhz; 3 kw. Ant 190 ft. TL: N42 01 03 W70 04 23. 25 Brookledge St., Boston (02121). Licensee: Truro Wireless Inc. (acq 11-8-91).

Walpole

***WSRB(FM)**—February 1975: 91.5 mhz; 14 w. Ant 83 ft. TL: N42 08 12 W71 14 56. 275 Common St. (02081). (508) 660-7257. FAX: (508) 668-1167. Licensee: Walpole Public Schools. Format: Educ, div. ■ Lester Burch, pres; Charles H. Ross Jr., chief engr.

Waltham

***WBRS(FM)**—Feb 5, 1968: 100.1 mhz; 25 w. Ant 151 ft. TL: N42 22 09 W71 15 28. Stereo. Hrs opn: 24. Brandeis Univ., 415 South St. (02254). (617) 736-5277. Licensee: Brandeis Univ. Format: Div. News progmg 5 hrs wkly. Target aud: General. Spec prog: Black 14 hrs; class 3 hrs; country 2 hrs; Fr, Ger, Italian 15 hrs; Portuguese & Sp 2 hrs; Yiddish one hr; reggae 7 hrs; blues 14 hrs; live music 12 hrs; gospel 4 hrs; Hatian 8 hrs; new age 14 hrs; American Indian 2 hrs; children's 2 hrs; Vietnamese 2 hrs; Greek 4 hrs; folk 6 hrs wkly. ■ Chuck Tanowitz, pres; Marshall Stevenson, gen mgr; Brandon Magee, progmg dir; Barry Rothman, mus dir; J.J. Bernay, news dir; Dana Puopolo, chief engr.

WCRB(FM)—1954: 102.5 mhz; 15 kw. Ant 918 ft. TL: N42 18 37 W71 14 14. Stereo. 750 South St. (02154). (617) 893-7080. Licensee: Charles River Broadcasting Co. Net: UPI. Format: Class. News staff one. Target aud: General. Spec prog: Jazz 2 hrs, comedy one hr wkly. ■ Cynthia D. Scullin, pres; Diane Hagmann, gen sls mgr; Marian Alper, prom mgr; John Dodge, progmg dir; Rodney Flora, mus dir; Laura Carlo, news dir; David Maxson, chief engr.

WRCA(AM)—1948: 1330 khz; 5 kw-U, DA-2. TL: N42 21 16 W71 15 44. Stereo. Hrs opn: 24. Bldg. 1400, 552 Massachusetts Ave., Cambridge (02139). (617) 492-3300. Licensee: The Boston Radio Group Inc. (acq 4-10-89; $1.15 million; FTR 4-24-89). Net: ABC/D. Format: Ethnic. News progmg 10 hrs wkly. Target aud: General. Spec prog: Sp, Fr, Indian 5 hrs, Portuguese one hr, Arabic 2 hrs wkly. ■ Harold Bausemer, gen mgr; Grady Moates, chief engr.

Ware

WARE(AM)—July 11, 1948: 1250 khz; 5 kw-D, 2.5 kw-N, DA-2. TL: N42 14 41 W72 12 30. Box 210, 90 South St. (01082). (413) 967-6231. FAX: (413) 967-4456. Licensee: Quadra Communications Inc. (acq 9-22-92; $400,000; FTR 11-2-92). Net: CBS Spectrum. Wash atty: Cohen & Marks. Format: Oldies. News staff 2. Target aud: 30 plus. Spec prog: Pol 3 hrs, country 5 hrs wkly. ■ Wayne Higney, pres & gen mgr; Norm Phillips, gen sls mgr; Kevin Lynn, news dir; Burton Landry, chief engr. ■ Rates: $21; 20; 21; 20.

Webster

WGFP(AM)—Apr 1, 1980: 940 khz; 1 kw-D. TL: N42 03 17 W71 50 00. Hrs opn: 6 AM-6 PM. Douglas Rd. (01570). (508) 943-9400. FAX: (508) 943-0405. Licensee: Okun Broadcasting Corp. (acq 3-23-84; FTR 3-19-84). Net: ABC/E, ABC/I. Format: News/talk. News staff 2. Target aud: General. Spec prog: Pol one hr wkly, children one hr. ■ Alan S. Okun, pres & gen mgr; Kevin Casey, opns mgr; Chip Jarry, gen sls mgr & prom mgr; Larry Milesky, rgnl sls mgr; Gillean Smith, news dir & pub affrs dir.

WXXW(FM)—Not on air, target date unknown: 98.9 mhz; 3 kw. Ant 328 ft. TL: N42 02 30 W71 59 18. Douglas Rd. (01570). Licensee: Okun Broadcasting Corp.

Wellesley

***WZLY(FM)**—Sept 20, 1976: 91.5 mhz; 10 w. Ant 164 ft. TL: N42 17 35 W71 18 21. Stereo. Hrs opn: 7 AM-1 AM. Schneider Center, Wellesley College (02181). (617) 235-9150; (617) 237-4433. Licensee: Wellesley College. Net: AP. Format: Div, progsv, AOR. News progmg 5 hrs wkly. Target aud: General; Wellesley Town and college community. Spec prog: Class 4 hrs, folk 2 hrs, It one hr, jazz 2 hrs, relg 2 hrs, Sp one hr, Japanese one hr, Chinese one hr, Russian one hr, reggae 2 hrs, women's 2 hrs, blues 2 hrs, bluegrass 2 hrs wkly. ■ Jacquelys Fletcher, gen mgr; Neerja Khaneja, sls dir; Sara Commisso, prom mgr; Jennifer Spillane, progmg dir; Jen Tilson, Lori Romero, Sonali Banerjee, mus dirs; Sangita Chandra, news dir; Ann Mrkic, pub affrs dir; Dave Powers, chief engr.

West Barnstable

***WKKL(FM)**—Sept 19, 1977: 90.7 mhz; 205 w. Ant 71 ft. TL: N41 41 31 W70 20 16. Rt. 132, Cape Cod Community College (02668). (508) 362-7766. Licensee: Board of Trustees, Cape Cod Community Colleges. Format: Progsv rock, educ. ■ Steven M. Leclair, gen mgr; Skip Comeau, chief engr.

West Springfield

WACM(AM)—Aug 28, 1949: 1490 khz; 1 kw-U. TL: N42 06 06 W72 37 22. 34 Sylvan St. (01089). (413) 781-5200. FAX: (413) 734-2240. Licensee: Carmelina G. Silva (acq 12-30-86). Rep: New England. Format: 24 hr Sp. Spec prog: News, relg, talk. ■ Carmelina G. Silva, pres; Jack Silva, gen mgr, gen sls mgr & progmg dir; Anita Rivera, mus dir & news dir.

West Yarmouth

WUOK(AM)—Dec 30, 1991: 1240 khz; 1 kw-U. TL: N41 38 07 W70 14 06. Stereo. Hrs opn: 24. Box 668 (02673). (508) 775-7400. Licensee: Boch Broadcasting Ltd. (acq 5-31-91; $825,000 with co-located FM; FTR 6-24-91). Net: CBS, Unistar, CNN. Rep: Christal. Format: News, loc sports, talk. ■ Ernie Boch, CEO; Cary Pahigian, gen mgr; Keith Corey, progmg dir.

WXTK(FM)—Co-owned with WUOK(AM). Dec 30, 1991: 94.9 mhz; 50 kw. Ant 246 ft. TL: N41 38 07 W70 14 06 (CP: Ant 394 ft., TL: N41 41 11 W70 08 09). Stereo. Dups AM 15%. Net: Sun, Daynet, NBC Talknet. Format: News/talk.

Westfield

WNNZ(AM)—Licensed to Westfield. See Springfield.

***WSKB(FM)**—October 1974: 89.5 mhz; 100 w. Ant 130 ft. TL: N42 07 55 W72 47 51. Stereo. Western Ave. (01086). (413) 572-5427. Licensee: Pres and Trustees of Westfield State College. Format: Progsv. News progmg 5 hrs wkly. Target aud: General. Spec prog: Class 3 hrs, folk 3 hrs, French one hr, jazz 6 hrs wkly. ■ Steve Joels, gen mgr.

Winchendon

WINQ(FM)—Jan 1983: 97.7 mhz; 1.85 kw. Ant 417 ft. TL: N42 42 10 W72 02 18. Stereo. Hrs opn: 24. 3 Central St. (01475). (508) 297-3698. FAX: (508) 297-9970. Licensee: Central Broadcasting Corp. (acq 5-92; $150,000; FTR 4-13-92). Format: Hot adult contemp. News staff 2; news progmg 9 hrs wkly. Target aud: 25-54. ■ Bill Maxwell, pres & gen mgr; Scott Bingham, stn mgr & natl sls mgr; Rod Hill, gen sls mgr; Ben Parker, progmg dir; Marc S. Cole, asst mus dir; Doug Ely, news dir & pub affrs dir. ■ Rates: $24; 20; 24; 16.

Worcester

WAAF(FM)—Listing follows WVEI(AM).

***WCHC(FM)**—Sept 19, 1977: 88.1 mhz; 100 w. Ant 6.56 ft. TL: N42 14 15 W71 48 31. Box G, Holy Cross College (01610). (508) 793-2475. FAX: (508) 793-2471. Licensee: Trustees of the College of the Holy Cross. Net: UPI. Format: Progsv. ■ Ed Kenney, gen mgr; Carl Dagostino, chief engr.

***WCUW(FM)**—Dec 4, 1973: 91.3 mhz; 630 w. Ant 145 ft. TL: N42 15 46 W71 47 59. Stereo. 910 Main St. (01610). (508) 753-1012; (508) 753-2284. Licensee: WCUW Inc. Format: Div, Black, Sp. News progmg one hr wkly. Target aud: General. Spec prog: Class 5 hrs, C&W 2 hrs, Fr 2 hrs, jazz 6 hrs, Sp 19 hrs, Asian one hr, Pol 5 hrs, Irish 2 hrs, Scotish 2 hrs, Jewish one hr, women 3 hrs, blues 6 hrs, Albanian one hr, India 2 hrs, Haitian one hr, Gr 2 hrs, bluegrass 3 hrs, Folk 15 hrs wkly. ■ Bernard Baldyga, pres; Joe Cutroni, gen mgr; Michael Sullivan, vp dev; John Walsh, pub affrs dir; Steve Tuzuenu, chief engr.

***WICN(FM)**—Nov 21, 1969: 90.5 mhz; 8.1 kw. Ant 368 ft. TL: N42 20 07 W71 42 54. Stereo. Hrs opn: 6 AM-3 AM. 6 Chatham St. (01609). (508) 752-0700. Licensee: WICN Public Radio Inc. Net: NPR. Format: Div, jazz, class. News progmg 16 hrs wkly. Target aud: 35 plus. Spec prog: Armenian 2 hrs, Irish 2 hrs, Lithuanian one hr, folk 12 hrs, bluegrass 4 hrs, world 2 hrs, new age 3 hrs, Celtic one hr wkly. ■ Peter Christianson, CEO, gen mgr & stn mgr; James H. Harrington, pres; Thomas Devlin, opns dir; Allison Savicz, dev dir & mktg dir; Eugene R. Petit, progmg dir; Glenda C. Reiss, mus dir; Don De Marsh, chief engr.

WNEB(AM)—Dec 18, 1946: 1230 khz; 1 kw-U. TL: N42 16 23 W71 49 23. Box 848, Boston (02194). (617) 868-7400. Licensee: AAMAR Communications Inc. (acq 12-1-86; $850,000; FTR 9-22-86). ■ Bob Bittner, gen mgr.

WORC(AM)—February 1925: 1310 khz; 5 kw-D, 1 kw-N, DA-2. TL: N42 13 19 W71 49 02. Stereo. Hrs opn: 24. 108 Grove St. (01605). (508) 799-0581. Licensee: Davis Radio Corp. (acq 11-13-89; $600,000; FTR 11-27-89). Net: Unistar, CNN. Rep: Kettell-Carter. Wash atty: Ginsburg, Feldman & Bress. Format: Oldies. News staff one. Target aud: 29-54; upscale adults. Spec prog: Sports 8 hrs, Pol one hr, Greek one hr, Sp one hr, Irish one hr wkly. ■ Andrew Davis, pres; Alan Berman, gen sls mgr; Jeffrey Davis, prom mgr; Dave Ogara, progmg dir; Frank Foley, news dir. ■ Rates: $40; 30; 30; 20.

WSRS(FM)—Listing follows WTAG(AM).

WTAG(AM)—May 1, 1924: 580 khz; 5 kw-U, DA-2. TL: N42 20 13 W71 49 15. Box 58, W. Side Stn. (01602). (508) 795-0580. FAX: (508) 757-1779. Licensee: Knight

Communications Corp. Group owner: Knight Quality Group Stns (acq 8-14-87). Net: NBC, NBC Talknet. Rep: Banner, Knight Quality Stations. Format: Adult contemp, talk. News staff 6; news progmg 40 hrs wkly. Target aud: General. ■ Scott Knight, pres; Bud Paras, gen mgr & gen sls mgr; Heather Copelas, prom mgr; Scott Pare, progmg dir; George Brown, mus dir; Paul Tuthill, news dir; John Andrews, chief engr.

WSRS(FM)—Co-owned with WTAG(AM). June 17, 1940: 96.1 mhz; 14 kw. Ant 863 ft. TL: N42 18 34 W71 54 10. Stereo. Prog sep from AM. Box 961, W. Side Stn. (01602). (508) 757-9696. (acq 3-63). Format: Soft adult contemp. Target aud: 25-54. ■ Vicky Greene, news dir.

WVEI(AM)—1926: 1440 khz; 5 kw-U. TL: N42 20 13 W71 49 15. Suite 4000, 200 Friberg Pkwy., Westborough (01581-3911). (508) 752-5611. Licensee: Zapis Communications Corp. (acq 6-21-89). Net: ABC/D. Rep: CBS. Format: Sports. ■ Bruce Mattman, gen mgr; Glenn Lucas, natl sls mgr; Ron Valeri, progmg dir; Eric Fitch, chief engr.

WAAF(FM)—Co-owned with WVEI(AM). June 15, 1961: 107.3 mhz; 18.6 kw. Ant 820 ft. TL: N42 18 13 W71 53 51. Stereo. (508) 836-9223. FAX: (508) 366-0745. Net: Unistar. Format: AOR. News staff one. Target aud: 25-54. ■ Xen Zapis, pres; Stuart Siden, gen sls mgr; Sarah Duhaime, prom mgr; Chris Engel, news dir.

WVNE(AM)—See Leicester.

WXLO-FM—(Fitchburg). August 1960: 104.5 mhz; 37 kw. Ant 563 ft. TL: N42 30 27 W71 49 37. Stereo. Hrs opn: 24. Suite 530, 250 Commercial St., Worcester (01608). (508) 752-1045. FAX: (508) 793-0324. Licensee: Montachussett Broadcasting. Group owner: Deer River Broadcasting Group. Net: AP Radio. Rep: McGavren Guild. Wash atty: Kaye, Scholer, Fierman, Hays & Handler. Format: Adult contemp. News progmg 5 hrs wkly. Target aud: 25-54. Spec prog: Oldies (Super-Gold) 5 hrs wkly. ■ Robin B. Martin, CEO; James P. Williams Jr., pres; Richard A. Krezwick, gen mgr; Steve Gallagher, progmg dir; Lynne MacNamee, news dir; Sid Schweiger, chief engr.

Michigan

LAUREN A. COLBY
301-663-1086
COMMUNICATIONS ATTORNEY
Special Attention to
Difficult Cases

Adrian

WABJ(AM)—Nov 13, 1946: 1490 khz; 1 kw-U. TL: N41 54 02 W84 00 51. Hrs opn: 24. 121 W. Maumee St. (49221). (517) 265-1500. FAX: (517) 263-4525. Licensee: Friends Communication of Michigan Inc. (acq 10-1-90; grpsl; FTR 10-29-90). Net: ABC/I, NBC Talknet, Mich. Net, Mich. Farm. Rep: Patt. Format: News/talk. News staff 2; news progmg 9 hrs wkly. Target aud: General. Spec prog: Farm 7 hrs, relg 3 hrs wkly. ■ Bob Elliot, chmn & pres; Bruce Goldsen, Sue Goldsen, vps; Bruce Goldsen, gen mgr; Sue Goldsen, gen sls mgr; Jeff Hager, progmg dir & news dir; Maureen Bristoll, pub affrs dir. ■ Rates: $14; 12; 12; 5.

WQTE(FM)—Co-owned with WABJ(AM). Sept 1, 1976: 95.3 mhz; 3 kw. Ant 299 ft. TL: N41 48 15 W84 05 25. Stereo. Hrs opn: 24. Prog sep from AM. (517) 263-6425. Net: ABC/I, SMN. Format: Country. News progmg 2 hrs wkly. Target aud: 25-54. Spec prog: Gospel 2 hrs wkly. ■ Greg Green, progmg dir; Mike McIntyre, mus dir; Jeff Hager, news dir; Maureen Bristoll, pub affrs dir. ■ Rates: $18; 14; 16; 8.

WLEN(FM)—June 9, 1965: 103.9 mhz; 3 kw. Ant 299 ft. TL: N41 54 11 W83 59 13. Stereo. Hrs opn: 24. Box 687, 242 W. Maumee St. (49221). (517) 263-1039. FAX: (517) 265-5362. Licensee: Lenawee Broadcasting Co. Net: MBS. Format: Adult contemp, C&W. Target aud: 25-54. Spec prog: Farm 6 hrs, Sp 4 hrs wkly. ■ Julie M. Koehn, pres & gen mgr; Doug Spade, opns mgr; Pati Hayes, gen sls mgr; Dale Gaertner, progmg dir & mus dir; Mike Clement, news dir; Larry Cox, chief engr. ■ Rates: $17.93; 17.93; 15.76.

WQTE(FM)—Listing follows WABJ(AM).

*****WVAC-FM**—Feb 13, 1967: 107.9 mhz; 13 w-H. Ant 79 ft. TL: N41 53 55 W84 03 33. Adrian College, 110 S. Madison St. (49221). (517) 265-5161, ext. 4540. FAX: (517) 264-3331. Licensee: Adrian College Board of Trustees. Format: Div. ■ Steven Shehan, gen mgr.

Albion

WALM(AM)—Nov 2, 1952: 1260 khz; 1 kw-D, 500 w-N, DA-N. TL: N42 13 48 W84 47 19. 10980 25 1/2 Mile Rd., Marshall (49224). (517) 629-5516. Licensee: Katherine L. Voigt (acq 2-8-93; $25,000; FTR 3-1-93). Net: AP. Format: Light adult contemp. News staff 4. Target aud: 25-50. Spec prog: Big band 12 hrs, relg 3 hrs wkly. ■ Katherine L. Voigt, CEO; David Moore-Ashbolt, gen mgr & stn mgr; Terry Oosterbaan, opns mgr & progmg dir; Larry D. Keiser, gen sls mgr; Dana Drummond, news dir; Harry Langman, chief engr.

WELL-FM—(Marshall). Oct 1, 1968: 104.9 mhz; 3 kw. Ant 300 ft. TL: N42 18 47 W84 55 46. 390 Golden Ave., Battle Creek (49015). (616) 963-5555. FAX: (616) 963-5185. Licensee: Liggett Broadcast Inc. (group owner; acq 2-4-93; $127,500 with WELL[AM] Battle Creek; FTR 3-22-93). Format: Hot country. ■ Mark Andrews, gen mgr.

*****WUFN(FM)**—April 1971: 96.7 mhz; 1.5 kw. Ant 469 ft. TL: N42 15 58 W84 38 49. Stereo. 13799 Donovan Rd. (49224). (517) 531-4478. Licensee: Family Life Broadcasting System. (group owner). Net: USA, AP, MBS. Format: Relg. News staff one; news progmg 22 hrs wkly. Target aud: General. ■ Warren Bolthouse, pres; John Harrison, gen mgr; Rod Robison, dev dir; Dave Kersey, progmg dir; Jon Couch, mus dir; Ruth Yuen, news dir; Richard Lindley, chief engr.

Allegan

WKGH(FM)—Apr 1991: 92.3 mhz; 860 w. Ant 600 ft. TL: N42 34 52 W85 45 17. Stereo. Hrs opn: 24. Box 50-789, Kalamazoo (49005). (616) 673-8094; (800) 964-9544. FAX: (616) 673-8717. Licensee: Midpoint Broadcasting. Net: SMN; Patt Media. Format: Oldies. News staff one; news progmg 6 hrs wkly. Target aud: 35-54. ■ Michael Maciejewski, CEO, gen mgr & chief engr; Mitch Ambler, vp sls & vp mktg; John Thierwechter, prom dir; Jim Zippo, progmg dir; Coletta Dunn, pub affrs dir. ■ Rates: $19; 17; 18; 15.50.

Allendale

*****WGVU-FM**—July 15, 1983: 88.5 mhz; 3 kw. Ant 311 ft. TL: N43 03 24 W85 57 31. Stereo. Hrs opn: 24. Grand Valley State Univ., 301 W. Fulton, Grand Rapids (49504-6492). (616) 771-6666; (800) 442-2771. FAX: (616) 771-6625. Licensee: Board of Control of Grand Valley State Univ. Net: AP, NPR; Mich. Pub. Wash atty: Cohn & Marks. Format: Jazz, news. News staff 2; news progmg 26 hrs wkly. Target aud: 25 plus; mid to upper educ & income levels. ■ Michael T. Walenta, gen mgr; Gary DeSantis, dev mgr; Jan McKinnon, sls dir; Kevin Frazier, prom mgr; Robert Willey, progmg dir; David Moore, news dir; Bob Lumbert, chief engr.

Alma

WFYC(AM)—Aug 17, 1948: 1280 khz; 1 kw-D, 45 w-N. TL: N43 22 08 W84 36 19. Box 669, 5310 N. State Rd. (48801). (517) 463-3175. Licensee: Sommerville Broadcasting. Inc. (acq 4-19-85). Net: ABC/D, Unistar. Wash atty: Earl Stanley. Format: Country. Target aud: 25-50. Spec prog: Farm 4 hrs wkly. ■ David W. Sommerville, pres & gen mgr; James P. Sommerville, stn mgr & progmg dir; Richard D. Sommerville, prom mgr; John Roslund, mus dir; Peter Fronczak, chief engr.

WFYC-FM—November 1964: 104.9 mhz; 3 kw-H, 430 w-V. Ant 299 ft. TL: N43 22 08 W84 36 19. Stereo. Hrs opn: 6 AM-11 PM. Dups AM 100%.

WMLM(AM)—See St. Louis.

*****WQAC-FM**—March 27, 1993: 90.9 mhz; 100 w. Ant 66 ft. TL: N43 22 50 W84 40 14. Hrs opn: 7 AM-2 AM Mon-Fri, noon-2 AM Sat-Sun. 614 W. Superior St. (48801). (517) 463-7301. FAX: (517) 463-7277. Licensee: Alma College. Format: Rock (AOR). Target aud: 13-24; high school and college students. Spec prog: Classic rock 4 hrs, all 80s 2 hrs, hip hop 3 hrs, techno 5 hrs, dance 4 hrs, jazz 2 hrs, relg 2 hrs wkly. ■ Karen Haviland, stn mgr; Mark Gorczyca, prom dir; Brad Engel, progmg dir; Jeff Kren, mus dir; Lisa Edwards, news dir; Jen Petrocelli, pub affrs dir; Brett McDowell, engrg dir.

Alpena

WATZ(AM)—1946: 1450 khz; 1 kw-U. TL: N45 03 58 W83 29 06. Hrs opn: 19.5. Box 536, 123 Prentiss (49707). (517) 354-8400. FAX: (517) 354-3436. Licensee: WATZ Radio Inc. Group owner: Midwestern Broadcasting Co. Net: ABC/E; Mich. Farm. Rep: Katz. Format: Country, talk. News staff 2; news progmg 31 hrs wkly. Target aud: 35-64. Spec prog: Rush Limbaugh 15 hrs, farm 4 hrs, Ger 2 hrs, Pol 2 hrs, relg 2 hrs wkly. ■ Ross Biederman, pres; Don Rhea, gen mgr; Steve Wright, progmg dir; Bruce Johnson, news dir; Jim Sofonia, chief engr. ■ Rates: $17; 17; 17; 17.

WATZ-FM—1967: 99.3 mhz; 17 kw. Ant 843 ft. TL: N44 51 25 W83 32 04. Stereo. Hrs opn: 19.5. Format: Country. Target aud: 25-54. ■ Rates: Same as AM.

*****WCML-FM**—April 24, 1978: 91.7 mhz; 100 kw. Ant 1,171 ft. TL: N45 08 17 W84 09 44. Stereo. Hrs opn: 24. Public Broadcasting Cntr., Central Mich. Univ., Mt. Pleasant (48859). (517) 774-3105. FAX: (517) 774-4427. Licensee: Central Michigan Univ. Net: NPR, APR; Mich. Pub. Format: Jazz, class, news & info. News staff 2; news progmg 30 hrs wkly. Target aud: General. ■ Thomas Hunt, gen mgr; Linda Hyde, prom dir; Ray Ford, progmg dir; Randy Kapenga, chief engr. ■ *WCML-TV affil.

WHSB-FM—May 1965: 107.7 mhz; 99 kw. Ant 760 ft. TL: N45 03 40 W83 43 05. Stereo. 1491 M-32 W. (49707). (517) 354-4611. FAX: (517) 354-4014. Licensee: Daraka Broadcasting Inc. (acq 4-1-89). Net: ABC/C. Rep: Michigan. Format: Adult contemp, CHR. News staff 3. Target aud: 25-54. ■ David R. Karschnick, pres & gen mgr; David R. Karschnick Jr., gen sls mgr; Darrel Kelly, progmg dir; Kerwin Kitzman, mus dir; John Pines, news dir; Harvey Klann, chief engr.

Ann Arbor

WAAM(AM)—October 1947: 1600 khz; 5 kw-U, DA-2. TL: N42 11 32 W83 41 09. Stereo. Hrs opn: 24. 4230 Packard Rd. (48108). (313) 971-1600. FAX: (313) 973-2916. Licensee: Whitehall Convalescent Homes Inc. (acq 9-15-83; $500,000; FTR 10-3-83). Net: NBC Talknet, MBS. Rep: Patt. Wash atty: Bryan, Cave, McPheeters & McRoberts. Format: MOR, news/talk. News staff 4; news progmg 20 hrs wkly. Target aud: 35 plus; adult home owners & professionals. Spec prog: Relg 5 hrs, sports 4 hrs, old time radio 8 hrs wkly. ■ Lloyd Johnson, pres; Catherine Kalman, gen mgr; Keith Peters, gen sls mgr; Kenneth Kelly, progmg dir & mus dir; Ted Heusel, news dir; John Grevers, chief engr. ■ Rates: $36; 28; 32; 19.

*****WCBN-FM**—Jan 1972: 88.3 mhz; 200 w-V. Ant 177 ft. TL: N42 16 37 W83 44 07. Stereo. Hrs opn: 24. 530 Student Activities Bldg. (48109). (313) 763-3501. Licensee: Regents of the Univ. of Michigan. Format: Div. Target aud: 18-49. Spec prog: Jazz 18 hrs, Sp 3 hrs, folk 3 hrs, pub affrs 5 hrs, gospel one hr, Fr one hr wkly. ■ Ted Oberg, gen mgr; Dirk Schulze, progmg dir; Brendan Gillen, mus dir; Alex Grossberg, news dir; Patrick Halladay, pub affrs dir; Paul Townsend, chief engr.

WIQB-FM—March 1962: 102.9 mhz; 49 kw-H, 42 kw-V. Ant 499 ft. TL: N42 15 04 W83 48 28. Stereo. Box 8605 (48107); 3001 Brassow Rd., Saline (48176). (313) 944-2881. FAX: (313) 429-7837. Licensee: Trans-America Comm Corp. (acq 11-10-86; $4,348,000; FTR 10-20-86). Rep: McGavren Guild. Format: Rock. ■ Mike Solan, gen mgr; Joe Urbiel, stn mgr; Nick Guerra, gen sls mgr; Reid Paxton, mus dir; Kelly Wright, news dir; John Grevers, chief engr.

WQKL(FM)—Listing follows WTKA(AM).

WTKA(AM)—Apr 26, 1945: 1050 khz; 5 kw-D, 500 w-N, DA-2. TL: N42 14 32 W83 45 55 (CP: 10 kw-D, TL: N42 08 46 W83 39 36). Box 300, 24 Frank Lloyd Wright Dr. (48106). (313) 930-5000. FAX: (313) 741-1071. Licensee: MW Blue Partnership (acq 9-30-92; $750,000 with co-located FM; FTR 11-2-92). Net: ABC/I. Rep: Michigan. Format: Adult contemp. Spec prog: Farm 9 hrs wkly. ■ Robert Murthum, pres & gen mgr; Dean Erskine, progmg dir; Rachel Wolski, chief engr.

WQKL(FM)—Co-owned with WTKA(AM). Feb 14, 1967: 107.1 mhz; 3 kw. Ant 289 ft. TL: N42 16 41 W83 44 32. Prog sep from AM. Format: Jazz. ■ James Baugh, vp & stn mgr; Dave Anthony, progmg dir.

*****WUOM(FM)**—1948: 91.7 mhz; 93 kw. Ant 780 ft. TL: N42 24 24 W83 54 34. Stereo. Hrs opn: 24. Univ. of Michigan, 5501 L.S.A. Bldg. (48109-1382). (313) 764-9210. FAX: (313) 747-3488. Licensee: The Regents of Univ. of Michigan. Net: NPR, APR. Mich. Pub. Format: Class, News. News staff 3; news progmg 30 hrs wkly.

Michigan

Target aud: 35-64. Spec prog: Jazz 6 hrs wkly. ■ Joel Seguine, stn mgr; Shelley MacMillan, dev dir; Harriet Teller, prom mgr; Lisa McCormack, progmg dir; Bob Whitman, news dir; Jim Paffenbarger, chief engr.

Ashley

WJSZ(FM)—Not on air, target date unknown: 92.5 mhz; 3 kw. Ant 328 ft. TL: N43 10 55 W84 26 58. 204 Stratford Dr., Owosso (48867). Licensee: William V. Constine.

Atlanta

WAIR(FM)—Licensed to Atlanta. See Petoskey.

Auburn Hills

***WAHS(FM)**—1975: 89.5 mhz; 100 w. Ant 141 ft. TL: N42 37 42 W83 13 56. Attn: Toni Shoemaker, 2800 Waukegan St. (48326). (313) 852-3961. Licensee: Avondale School District. ■ Toni Shoemaker, gen mgr.

Bad Axe

WLEW(AM)—1950: 1340 khz; 1 kw-U, DA-D. TL: N43 47 56 W83 01 21. Hrs opn: 24. 935 S. Van Dyke Rd. (48413). (517) 269-9931. FAX: (517) 269-7702. Licensee: Thumb Broadcasting Inc. (acq 9-15-93; with co-located FM; FTR 10-11-93). Format: Country. News staff 2; news progmg 19 hrs wkly. Target aud: 18-50. Spec prog: Farm 4 hrs, Pol 2 hrs wkly. ■ Richard A. Ayman, CEO, pres, gen mgr & progmg dir; Thomas Meyer, opns mgr; Jack Thomas, mus dir; Craig Routzen, news dir; John T. Vobbe, chief engr. ■ Rates: $14.20; 13.20; 14.20; 12.20.

WLEW-FM—1956: 102.1 mhz; 50 kw. Ant 492 ft. TL: N43 53 28 W83 07 26. Stereo. Hrs opn: 24. Prog sep from AM. Format: Adult contemp. News progmg 18 hrs. Target aud: 25-50. ■ Matthew A. Aymen, vp & adv mgr; Thomas L. Meyer, stn mgr. ■ Rates: $16.45; 16.45; 16.45; 16.45.

Baraga

WODQ(FM)—Not on air, target date unknown: 104.3 mhz; 100 kw. Ant 997 ft. TL: N46 39 47 W88 20 45. Stereo. 5595 Liberty Rd., Chagrin Falls, OH (44022). (216) 498-1221. Licensee: Zephyr Broadcasting Inc. Group owner: Martz Communications Group (acq 3-5-90; $10,000; FTR 3-19-90). Wash atty: Cohn & Marks. ■ Timothy D. Martz, pres.

Battle Creek

WBCK(AM)—July 9, 1948: 930 khz; 5 kw-D, 1 kw-N, DA-2. TL: N42 17 40 W85 11 00. 390 Golden Ave. (49015). (616) 963-5555. FAX: (616) 963-5185. Licensee: Liggett Broadcast Inc. (group owner; acq 7-87; $430,000; FTR 8-3-87). Net: NBC, NBC Talknet. Rep: Eastman. Format: Full svc. News staff 2. Target aud: 25-54. ■ Jim Jensen, pres; Jack McDezitt, gen mgr; Mark E. Andrews, gen sls mgr; Sean Stevens, prom mgr; Tom McHale, news dir; Craig Bowman, chief engr.

WBXX(FM)—Co-owned with WBCK(AM). Feb 28, 1975: 95.3 mhz; 3 kw. Ant 269 ft. TL: N42 17 17 W85 09 54 (CP: Ant 285 ft, TL: N42 17 31 W85 10 59). Stereo. Prog sep from AM. Box 3495 (49016). Group owner: Liggett Broadcast Group (acq 2-1-86). Net: UPI. Format: Top-40. News staff one; news progmg 2 hrs wkly. Target aud: 18-49. ■ Robert G. Liggett Jr., pres; Joe Friday, mus dir.

WELL(AM)—July 1, 1993: 1600 khz; 1 kw-U. TL: N42 18 15 W85 11 31. 390 Golden Ave. (49015). (616) 963-5555. Licensee: Liggett Broadcast Inc. (group owner; acq 2-4-93; $127,500 with WELL-FM Marshall; FTR 3-22-93). Net: MBS. Rep: Eastman. Format: Hot country. ■ Mark Andrews, gen mgr & gen sls mgr; Bridgette Donahue, news dir; Craig Bowman, chief engr.

WKFR-FM—June 11, 1963: 103.3 mhz; 50 kw. Ant 500 ft. TL: N42 21 19 W85 20 28. Stereo. Hrs opn: 24. P.O. Box 50911, 4154 Jennings Dr., Kalamazoo (49005-0911). (616) 344-0111. FAX: (616) 344-4223. Licensee: Crystal Radio Group (acq 8-31-93). Rep: Katz. Wash atty: Reed, Smith, Shaw & McClay. Format: CHR. News staff 3. Target aud: 18-49. ■ David L. Hicks, CEO; Ed Sackely, pres; Phil Britiain, chief opns; Bob Miller, Steve Steineoff, gen sls mgrs; Glen Dillion, progmg dir & mus dir; John Kulba, news dir; David Benson, pub affrs dir; Dale Schiesser, chief engr. ■ Rates: $54; 50; 54; 45.

WOLY(AM)—Nov 22, 1963: 1500 khz; 1 kw, DA. TL: N42 17 30 W85 10 08. 15074 6+ Mile Rd. (49016). (616) 965-1515. FAX: (616) 965-1315. Licensee: Christian Family Network (acq 1-89; $100,000; FTR 1-23-89). Net: CBN; USA. Format: Contemp Christian mus & progmg. News progmg 5 hrs wkly. Target aud: General. Spec prog: Black 6 hrs wkly. ■ James Elsman, pres; Dail Jenks, vp & gen mgr; Harry Langman, chief engr. ■ Rates: $15; 10; 12; na.

Bay City

***WCHW-FM**—Sept 1, 1973: 91.3 mhz; 110 w-H. Ant 125 ft. TL: N43 35 19 W83 52 28. 1624 Columbus Ave. (48708). (517) 892-1741. FAX: (517) 892-7946. Licensee: Bay City Public School District. Format: AOR. ■ Lawrence E. Sundberg, gen mgr; Kevin Grudzinski, progmg dir; Cliff Saladine, chief engr.

WHNN(FM)—1947: 96.1 mhz; 100 kw-H, 90 kw-V. Ant 1,020 ft. TL: N43 33 10 W83 41 24. Stereo. Hrs opn: 24. 5196 State Rd., Saginaw (48603). (517) 799-1000. FAX: (517) 790-1943. Licensee: Robert G. Liggett Jr. Group owner: Liggett Broadcast Inc. (acq 1973). Net: Unistar. Rep: Republic. Format: Oldies. News staff one; news progmg 6 hrs wkly. Target aud: 25-54. ■ James A. Jensen, pres; Daniel E. Stewart, vp; Jim Spangenberg, gen sls mgr; Scott Stine, progmg dir; Jim Owen, mus dir; Kathy Burns, news dir; Kevin Hawley, chief engr.

WIOG(FM)—September 1969: 102.5 mhz; 86 kw. Ant 860 ft. TL: N43 28 24 W83 50 40. Stereo. Box 1945, 1795 Tittabawassee, Saginaw (48603). (517) 752-3456. FAX: (517) 754-5046. Licensee: Booth American Co. (group owner; acq 9-21-86; $4.6 million; FTR 5-26-86). Net: ABC/C, NBC the Source. Format: CHR. News staff one; news progmg 6 hrs wkly. Target aud: 18-34. ■ John L. Booth, pres; John F. Casey, vp & gen mgr; Jerry Noble, opns dir, progmg dir & mus dir; Sue Smith, prom mgr; Dave Maurer, news dir; Cliff Graff, chief engr. ■ Rates: $66; 66; 69; 49.

WMAX(AM)—June 5, 1925: 1440 khz; 5 kw-D, 2.5 kw-N, DA-2. TL: N43 31 27 W83 57 58. Hrs opn: 24. Suite 100, 3071 Bay Rd., Saginaw (48603). (517) 799-0060. FAX: (517) 799-4680. Licensee: Saginaw Bay Broadcasting Corp. (acq 4-17-92). Net: CNN. Format: Sports. News staff 12; news progmg 168 hrs wkly. Target aud: 25-54; mature upscale adults. ■ Joseph Mengden, CEO.

WSGW(AM)—See Saginaw.

***WTRK(FM)**—Not on air, target date unknown: 89.1 mhz; 2 kw. Ant 328 ft. 919 29th St. (48708). Licensee: Beyond The Bay Media Group.

***WUCX-FM**—September 1989: 90.1 mhz; 30 kw. Ant 479 ft. TL: N43 33 10 W83 41 24. Stereo. Public Broadcasting Ctr., Mt. Pleasant (48859). (517) 774-3105. FAX: (517) 774-4427. Licensee: Central Michigan Univ. Net: AP, NPR; Mich. Pub. Format: Class, jazz, news. News staff 2; news progmg 35 hrs wkly. Target aud: General. ■ Tom Hunt, gen mgr; Linda Hyde, prom mgr; Ray Ford, progmg dir; Neal Johnson, news dir; Randy Kapenga, chief engr.

Bear Lake

WRQT(FM)—Nov 2, 1987: 100.1 mhz; 3 kw. Ant 328 ft. TL: N44 25 18 W86 07 17. Stereo. Hrs opn: 24. Box 65, 12013 West St. (49614). (616) 864-2400. FAX: (616) 864-2401. Licensee: Andrew L. Banas (acq 8-19-93; $5,000). Format: Rock. News staff 2. Target aud: 18-49; middle income males. Spec prog: Pol 2 hrs wkly. ■ Rojer L. Hoppe Sr., srvp; Roger L. Hoppe II, progmg dir; Donald R. McComb, chief engr.

Beaverton

WMRX-FM—Sept 15, 1980: 97.7 mhz; 2.03 kw. Ant 400 ft. TL: N43 53 16 W84 31 45. Stereo. 1510 Bayliss St., Midland (48640). (517) 631-1490; (517) 631-2220. FAX: (517) 631-9679. Licensee: Maines Broadcasting Inc. (acq 10-1-83; $70,000; FTR 10-17-83). Net: UPI. Rep: Masla. Format: Adult contemp. ■ Thomas Steel, pres & gen mgr; Joe Goddeyne, chief engr.

Benton Harbor

WHFB-FM—Licensed to Benton Harbor. See Benton Harbor-St. Joseph.

Benton Harbor-St. Joseph

WHFB(AM)—Sept 22, 1947: 1060 khz; 5 kw-D, 2.5 kw-CH. TL: N42 04 44 W86 28 00. Stereo. 2100 Fairplain Ave., Benton Harbor (49022). (616) 925-9300. FAX: (616) 925-0065. Licensee: WHFB Broadcast Associates L.P. Group owner: WinCom Communications Group Inc. (acq 8-85). Net: ABC/I; Mich. Farm. Rep: Katz. Format: Nostalgia. News staff 3. Target aud: General. Spec prog: Farm 4 hrs wkly. ■ Donn Winther, pres; Bob Ganzak, gen mgr; Tony Vivacqua, vp & gen sls mgr; Gregg Rizzo, mktg dir; Jim Miller, prom mgr; Doug Hawkes, progmg dir; Bill Stanley, news dir; Robert Henning, chief engr. ■ Rates: $30; 25; 28; na.

WHFB-FM—(Benton Harbor). Oct 10, 1947: 99.9 mhz; 50 kw. Ant 497 ft. TL: N42 03 17 W86 27 31. Stereo. Format: Adult contemp. News staff 3; news progmg 10 hrs wkly. Target aud: 25-54. ■ Rates: $40; 30; 35; 20.

WIRX(FM)—Listing follows WSJM(AM).

WSJM(AM)—(St. Joseph). Nov 18, 1956: 1400 khz; 880 w-U. TL: N42 05 12 W86 26 40. Box 107 (49085); 580 E. Napier, Benton Harbor (49022). (616) 925-1111; (616) 925-9756. FAX: (616) 925-1011. Licensee: WSJM Inc. Group owner: Mid-West Family Stns. (acq 1-1-59). Net: NBC, NBC Talknet, CNN, FNN. Rep: Christal. Wash atty: Fisher, Wayland, Cooper & Leader. Format: Full svc news/talk. News staff 4. Target aud: 25-54. Spec prog: Black 3 hrs wkly. ■ Gayle Olson, pres & gen mgr; David Wisniewski, Jeff Schmidt, gen sls mgrs; Brenda Layne, prom mgr; Bob DeWitt, progmg dir & news dir; Spencer Sheldon, chief engr.

WIRX(FM)—(St. Joseph). Co-owned with WSJM(AM). June 20, 1966: 107.1 mhz; 1.2 kw. Ant 498 ft. TL: N42 04 19 W86 22 14. Stereo. Prog sep from AM. (616) 925-9479. Net: NBC the Source. Format: CHR. Target aud: 18-49. ■ Brian Maloney, progmg dir; Mark Adams, mus dir.

Berrien Springs

***WAUS(FM)**—Licensed to Berrien Springs. See South Bend, Ind.

Beulah

WMNW(FM)—Not on air, target date unknown: 92.1 mhz; 1.65 kw. Ant 443 ft. TL: N44 38 34 W86 01 42. Suite 51G, 8420 Deadstream Rd., Honor (49640). Licensee: Roger L. Hoppe II.

Big Rapids

WBRN(AM)—Jan 6, 1953: 1460 khz; 5 kw-D, 2.5 kw-N, DA-N. TL: N43 39 57 W85 28 59. Stereo. Hrs opn: 24. Box 1460, 13574 Northland Dr. (49307). (616) 796-7684. FAX: (616) 796-6227. Licensee: WBRN Inc. (acq 10-1-55). Rep: Michigan. Format: C&W. Target aud: General. Spec prog: Farm 6 hrs wkly. ■ John A. White II, CEO & pres; James C. Nostrant, gen mgr; John C. Smith, news dir; Garnet Zimmerman, chief engr.

WBRN-FM—September 1964: 100.9 mhz; 6 kw. Ant 318 ft. TL: N43 39 49 W85 28 54. Stereo. Hrs opn: 24. Prog sep from AM. Format: Adult contemp.

WPZX(FM)—June 30, 1982: 102.3 mhz; 10.5 kw. Ant 436 ft. TL: N43 41 01 W85 34 56. Stereo. Hrs opn: 24. 220 S. Michigan (49307). (616) 796-7000. FAX: (616) 796-7004. Licensee: West Michigan Radio Inc. Group owner: Michigan Communications Group (acq 8-22-89; $425,000; FTR 9-11-89). Net: ABC, Westwood One, Unistar, USA. Rep: Patt. Format: Contemp hit/top-40. News progmg 8 hrs wkly. Target aud: 18-34. Spec prog: Relg one hr wkly. ■ Russell Balch, pres; Bill Kelso, gen mgr; Brian Goodenow, opns mgr, progmg dir & mus dir; Judy Johnston, gen sls mgr & vp prom; Art Kinsey, chief engr. ■ Rates: $16; 14; 16; 12.

Birmingham

WCSX(FM)—Sept 1, 1958: 94.7 mhz; 13.5 kw. Ant 945 ft. TL: N42 27 13 W83 09 50. Stereo. Hrs opn: 24. One Radio Plaza, Detroit (48220). (313) 398-7600. FAX: (313) 542-0313. Licensee: Greater Michigan Radio Inc. Group owner: Greater Media Inc. (acq 7-3-73). Net: Unistar. Rep: McGavren Guild. Format: Classic rock. Target aud: 25-54; males. ■ Tom Bender, gen mgr; Bruce Stoller, gen sls mgr; Tom Daldin, prom mgr; Ralph Cipolla, progmg dir; Bob Dietsch, chief engr.

Bloomfield Hills

***WBFH(FM)**—Oct 1, 1976: 88.1 mhz; 360 w. Ant 180 ft. TL: N42 34 42 W83 17 10 Stereo. 4200 Andover Rd. (48302). (313) 645-4740. FAX: (313) 645-4744. Licensee: Board of Educ of Bloomfield Hills School District. Net: AP. Format: Div, contemp hit, rock/AOR. Target aud: 12-34. Spec prog: Prep sports 6 hrs, big band 5 hrs wkly. ■ Pete Bowers, gen mgr; Ronald C. Wittebols (night), stn mgr; John Grevers, chief engr.

Boyne City

WBCM(FM)—April 10, 1978: 93.5 mhz; 14.1 kw. Ant 928 ft. TL: N45 10 44 W85 05 42. Stereo. Hrs opn: 24. Box 472, Traverse City (49685). (616) 582-6791; (616) 947-7675. FAX: (616) 929-3988. Licensee: Biederman In-

Stations in the U.S.   Michigan

vestments Inc. (acq 9-6-90; $250,000; FTR 10-1-90). Net: ABC/I. Rep: Katz. Wash atty: Cordon & Kelly. Format: Modern country. News staff 4; news progmg 25 hrs wkly. Target aud: 25-54. Spec prog: Farm one hr wkly. ■ Ross Biederman, pres; Jon Patrick, gen sls mgr; Jack O'Malley, progmg dir; Ryan Dobry, mus dir; Kim Chiodo, news dir; Jim Sofonia, chief engr.

Bridgman

WCSE(FM)—Not on air, target date unknown: 97.5 mhz; 1.9 w. Ant 413 ft. TL: N41 59 19 W86 31 46. 728 Superior St., South Haven (49090). Licensee: Dunes Broadcasting Inc.

Bronson

*WCVM(FM)—Not on air, target date unknown: 94.7 mhz; 4.8 kw. Ant 364 ft. 1573 W. Chicago Rd., Coldwater (49036). Licensee: Michiana Christian Broadcasters Inc.

Buchanan

WSMK(FM)—1991: 99.1 mhz; 3 kw. Ant 328 ft. TL: N41 52 51 W86 18 13. 925 N. 5th St., Niles (49120). (616) 683-4343. FAX: (616) 683-9429. Licensee: Marion R. Williams. ■ Cathy Norris, gen mgr.

Cadillac

WATT(AM)—September 1945: 1240 khz; 1 kw-U. TL: N44 13 27 W85 24 06. Box 520 (49601). (616) 775-1263. FAX: (616) 779-2844. Licensee: MacDonald Broadcasting Co. (group owner; acq 6-80; grpsl; FTR 6-16-80). Net: Unistar. Rep: Christal, Michigan. Format: Oldies of the 40s, 50s & 60s. ■ Ken MacDonald, pres; Cori Lindell, gen mgr; Chuck DiStefano, progmg dir; Jeremy Sandlin, mus dir; Dan Emery, news dir; Garry Harding, chief engr.

WWLZ(FM)—Co-owned with WATT(AM). July 7, 1974: 96.7 mhz; 1.7 kw. Ant 443 ft. TL: N44 14 56 W85 18 48. (Acq 5-83; $270,000; FTR 5-9-83). Format: Adult contemp. ■ Andrew MacDonald, vp; Dan Parker, gen mgr; Bob Bier, progmg dir.

WKJF(AM)—May 26, 1968: 1370 khz; 5 kw-D, 1 kw-N, DA-N. TL: N44 13 54 W85 24 45. Stereo. 1111 S. Mitchell (49601). (616) 775-0143. FAX: (616) 775-5217. Licensee: Hagar Broadcasting & Investments (group owner; acq 10-5-91; $350,000 with co-located FM; FTR 10-7-91). Net: ABC. Rep: Patt. Format: Adult contemp. ■ Julia M. Hagar, pres & stn mgr; Steve Masters, opns mgr.

WKJF-FM—Oct 15, 1961: 92.9 mhz; 100 kw-H. Ant 895 ft. TL: N44 08 12 W85 20 33. Stereo. Prog sep from AM.

*WOLW(FM)—May 26, 1988: 91.1 mhz; 50 kw-H, 28 kw-V. Ant 700 ft. TL: N44 16 33 W85 42 49. Stereo. Hrs opn: 24. Box 695, 1511 M-32 E. Gaylord, Gaylord (49735). (517) 732-6274. FAX: (517) 732-8171. Licensee: Northern Christian Radio Inc. Net: Moody, USA, Skylight. Wash atty: Jeffery Southmayd. Format: Educ, relg. News progmg 10 hrs wkly. Target aud: 25-55. Spec prog: Classical one hr wkly. ■ David A. Malin, CEO; Peter J. Vellenga, chmn; Dan Maguine, mus dir; George Lake Jr., chief engr.

WWLZ(FM)—Listing follows WATT(AM).

WYTW(FM)—Sept 15, 1985: 107.1 mhz; 1.25 kw. Ant 499 ft. TL: N44 10 18 W85 20 17 (CP: 2.75 kw, ant 482 ft., TL: N44 10 16 W85 20 13). Stereo. Rebroadcasts WMCK(FM) St. Ignace 100%. Box 669, 101 E. Harris St. (49601). (616) 775-1071. FAX: (616) 775-3707. Licensee: Four Seasons Broadcasting Co. Inc. (acq 6-3-83). Net: SMN. Format: Country. News staff one. Target aud: 25-54. Spec prog: Farm, relg, dining guide. ■ Donald Benson, pres; Don Mayle, gen mgr.

Caro

WKYO(AM)—May 19, 1962: 1360 khz; 1 kw-U, DA-2. TL: N43 27 32 W83 23 39. Box 151 (48723). (517) 673-2136. Licensee: Jackson Communications Ltd. (acq 6-13-90; $425,000 with co-located FM; FTR 7-9-90). Net: ABC/E; Mich. Farm. Format: MOR, news, talk. Spec prog: Farm 18 hrs wkly. ■ William G. Jackson, pres, gen mgr & gen sls mgr; Mike Nelson, progmg dir & mus dir; Ed Czelad, chief engr.

WIDL(FM)—Co-owned with WKYO(AM). Oct 16, 1974: 92.1 mhz; 6 kw. Ant 318 ft. TL: N43 28 51 W83 20 31. Stereo. Prog sep from AM. (517) 673-9435. Format: AC gold.

Carrollton

WTCF(FM)—Licensed to Carrollton. See Saginaw.

Cassopolis

WLLJ(AM)—Aug 1988: 910 khz; 1 kw-D, 35 w-N, DA-1. TL: N41 57 14 W86 00 59. Stereo. Hrs opn: 24. Suite 310, 3371 Cleveland Rd. Ext., South Bend, IN (46628); 6036 S. Bishop, Chicago, IL (60636). (616) 445-3526. Licensee: Larry Langford. Net: SMN. Wash atty: Lauren A. Colby. Format: Urban contemp, urban oldies. Target aud: 25-49; middle class Black adults. Spec prog: Blues 4 hrs, gospel 10 hrs wkly. ■ Larry Langford, pres; Abe Thompson, gen mgr & sls dir; Roger Lindo, progmg dir; William Langford Jr., chief engr. ■ Rates: $9; 9; 9; na.

Charlevoix

WKHQ-FM—May 16, 1980: 105.9 mhz; 100 kw. Ant 899 ft. TL: N45 10 44 W85 05 40 (CP: Ant 1,003 ft., TL: N45 10 43 W85 05 42). Stereo. Hrs opn: 24. Box 237, 413 Bridge St. (49720). (616) 547-4454. FAX: (616) 547-5378. Licensee: Jay Meyers - receiver. Rep: McGavren Guild. Wash atty: Koteen & Naftalin. Format: CHR. News staff one. Target aud: 18-34. ■ Robert G. Mallery, gen mgr; Patricia Scott, gen sls mgr; Marvin Veurink, chief engr. ■ Rates: $35; 35; 35; 20.

WMKT(AM)—Co-owned with WKHQ-FM. July 20, 1974: 1270 khz; 5 kw-U, DA-N. TL: N45 16 22 W85 15 08. Hrs opn: 24. Prog sep from FM. Net: BRN. Format: All business news and talk. News staff one. Target aud: 35 plus; listeners with spendable income. ■ Rates: $10; 10; 10; 7.

Charlotte

WLCM(AM)—Aug 25, 1956: 1390 khz; 5 kw-U, DA-1. TL: N42 34 02 W84 51 58. Hrs opn: 6:30 AM-local sunset M-F; 7 AM-local sunset Sat. & Sun. Box 338, 1613 W. Lawrence (48813). (517) 543-8200. FAX: (517) 543-7779. Licensee: Midwest Broadcasting Corp. (acq 1-5-93; assumption of land contract; FTR 1-25-93). Net: USA. Format: Relg. News progmg 2 hrs wkly. Target aud: 25-55; general. ■ John Yinger, gen mgr; David Huva, stn mgr, opns dir & chief engr; Jeff Cohen, gen sls mgr. ■ Rates: $10; 10; 10; 10.

WMMQ(FM)—Dec 29, 1965: 92.7 mhz; 1.5 kw. Ant 466 ft. TL: N42 38 31 W84 47 55. Stereo. Hrs opn: 24. 2517 E. Mt. Hope, Lansing (48910). (517) 482-9292; (517) 487-5986. FAX: (517) 487-0208. Licensee: Goodrich Broadcasting Inc. (group owner; acq 4-8-93; $900,000; FTR 5-3-93). Net: CBS Spectrum, Unistar. Great Lake Media Group. Rep: D & R Radio. Wash atty: Reddy, Begley & Martin. Format: Classic rock & roll. News progmg 3 hrs wkly. Target aud: 18-44; baby boomers who grew up listening to the Beatles, Who & Stones. ■ Bob Ottaway, pres; Mike St. Cyr, gen mgr & chief engr; Bob Bolac, gen sls mgr; Bill Daniels, prom mgr; Bill Elliott, progmg dir & mus dir; Mark Maloney, news dir; Ken Pesonen, engrg mgr. ■ Rates: $60; 60; 60; 30.

Cheboygan

WCBY(AM)—Oct 28, 1954: 1240 khz; 1 kw-U. TL: N45 39 38 W84 29 26. 1356 MacKinaw Ave. (49721). (616) 627-2341. FAX: (616) 627-7000. Licensee: Reynolds Communications Inc. (acq 2-89; $742,181 with co-located FM; FTR 2-20-89). Net: ABC/I. Rep: Michigan. Format: MOR. ■ Del Reynolds, pres & gen mgr; Mary Reynolds, natl sls mgr; Greg Schmaltz, progmg dir; Greg Fletcher, mus dir; Mike Grisdale, news dir.

WGFM(FM)—Co-owned with WCBY(AM). Aug 15, 1968: 105.1 mhz; 100 kw. Ant 610 ft. TL: N45 26 50 W84 28 30. Stereo. Prog sep from AM. Net: Unistar. Format: Classic hits.

Clare

WCFX(FM)—June 28, 1967: 95.3 mhz; 6 kw. Ant 328 ft. TL: N43 44 41 W84 48 09. Stereo. 5847 Venture Way, Mt. Pleasant (48858). (517) 772-4173. FAX: (517) 773-1236. Licensee: Mackin Broadcasting Inc. (acq 1-22-90; $325,000; FTR 3-5-90). Net: Mich. Net. Rep: Roslin. Format: CHR, adult contemp. News progmg 4 hrs wkly. Target aud: 18-49. Spec prog: Relg one hr, oldies 3 hrs wkly. ■ J. D. Mackin, gen mgr; Kent Bergstrom, progmg dir & news dir; Robert Wang, mus dir.

Coldwater

WNWN(FM)—Licensed to Coldwater. See Kalamazoo.

WTVB(AM)—Aug 7, 1949: 1590 khz; 5 kw-D, 1 kw-N, DA-N. TL: N41 54 34 W85 00 21. Box 1590, 174 N. Angola Rd. (49036). (517) 279-9767. FAX: (517) 279-9767. Licensee: Tri-State Broadcasting (acq 4-1-72). Net: ABC/I. Rep: Christal. Wash atty: Tierney & Swift. Format: Adult contemp. News progmg 10 hrs wkly. Spec prog: Farm 6 hrs wkly. ■ Gary Mallernee, pres & gen mgr; Ken Delaney, opns dir & progmg dir; Jim Suski, rgnl sls mgr; Jim Whelan, news dir; Chris Arnaut, chief engr.

Coleman

WPRJ(FM)—Dec 7, 1992: 101.5 mhz; 2.2 kw. Ant 400 ft. TL: N43 48 41 W84 27 57. Stereo. Hrs opn: 6 AM-midnight. Box 236, 5444 N. Coleman Rd. (48618). (517) 465-WPRJ. Licensee: Come Together Ministries Inc. (acq 11-9-89; $8,000; FTR 11-27-89). Wash atty: Reddy, Begley & Martin. Format: Full time Christian adult contemp, praise. Target aud: 18 plus; youth, young singles and married. ■ Gary H. Bugh, pres & progmg dir; Patty Jo Bugh, vp; Connie Wieber, opns mgr; Jeff Schultz, sls dir; Brian Erwin, mus dir; Ed Czelada, chief engr.

Dearborn

*WHFR(FM)—Dec 20, 1985: 89.3 mhz; 270 w. Ant 98 ft. TL: N42 19 26 W83 14 09 (CP: ant 98 ft.). Stereo. Hrs opn: 9 AM-10 PM Sat.-Thurs., 9 AM-midnight Fri. Henry Ford Community College, 5101 Evergreen Rd. (48128). (313) 845-9676; (313) 845-6477. FAX: (313) 845-6321. Licensee: Henry Ford Community College. Format: Div. News progmg one hr wkly. Target aud: 12-60; people searching for alternatives to coml monotony. Spec prog: Jazz 15 hrs, class 4 hrs, world mus 3 hrs, big band 3 hrs, blues 3 hrs wkly. ■ Jay B. Korinek, gen mgr.

WMTG(AM)—Dec 29, 1946: 1310 khz; 5 kw-U, DA-2. TL: N42 15 50 W83 15 14. 15001 Michigan Ave. (48126). (313) 846-8500. FAX: (313) 846-1068. Licensee: Renaissance Communications Inc. Group owner: Fairmont Communications Corp. Net: SMN. Rep: McGavren Guild. Format: Classic soul. ■ Gary Fisher, pres & gen mgr; John Long, gen sls mgr; Jim Harper, progmg dir; Fred Miller, chief engr.

WNIC(FM)—Licensed to Dearborn. See Detroit.

Detroit

WCAR(AM)—See Livonia.

*WDET-FM—Dec 18, 1948: 101.9 mhz; 79 kw. Ant 450 ft. TL: N42 21 28 W83 03 55. Stereo. Hrs opn: 24. First Fl., 6001 Cass Ave. (48202). (313) 577-4146. FAX: (313) 577-1300. Licensee: Wayne State Univ. (acq 5-52). Net: NPR; Mich. Pub. Wash atty: Jeff Olsen. Format: News, adult alternative acoustic. News staff 4; news progmg 43 hrs wkly. Target aud: 35-54; sophisticated, varied music tastes & news consumers. Spec prog: Class 4 hrs, folk 4 hrs, gospel 2 hrs, Sp 2 hrs, bluegrass 3 hrs, blues 8 hrs, reggae 2 hrs wkly. ■ Caryn G. Mathes, gen mgr; John Patouhas, opns dir; Robert Jones, sls dir; Diane Taylor, mktg dir; Judy C. Adams, progmg dir; Ann Delisi, mus dir; Roger Adams, news dir; Malloy Farley, chief engr.

*WDTR(FM)—Feb 5, 1948: 90.9 mhz; 42 kw-H, 38 kw-V. Ant 437 ft. TL: N42 22 25 W83 06 50. Stereo. Hrs opn: 8:30 AM-8:30 PM. 9345 Lawton Ave. (48206). (313) 596-3507. FAX: (313) 596-3588. Licensee: Board of Education, City of Detroit. Wash atty: Derrick Humphries. Format: Educ. Target aud: General; intergenerational-urban/suburban. Spec prog: Black 8 hrs, jazz one hr, Sp one hr, alternative mus one hr, gospel 2 hrs, blues 4 hrs wkly. ■ Lynne W. Boyle, gen mgr, prom dir & pub affrs dir.

WGPR(FM)—1961: 107.5 mhz; 50 kw. Ant 360 ft. TL: N42 21 28 W83 03 56. Stereo. 3146 Jefferson E. (48207). (313) 259-8862. FAX: (313) 259-6662. Licensee: WGPR Inc. (acq 7-64). Net: American Urban. Wash atty: Hogan & Hartson. Format: Urban contemp. Target aud: 18-49. ■ George Mathews, CEO & pres; James O. Dogan, vp & stn mgr; Celestine Harris, prom mgr; Joe Spencer, progmg dir; Lucia Harvin, news dir; Al Ruedemann, chief engr. ■ WGPR-TV affil.

WHYT(FM)—Listing follows WJR(AM).

WJLB(FM)—1926: 97.9 mhz; 50 kw. Ant 489 ft. TL: N42 24 22 W83 06 44. Stereo. Suite 633, 645 Griswold (48226). (313) 965-2000. Licensee: Booth Broadcasting. Group owner: Booth American Co. Rep: Major Mkt. Format: Black contemp. News staff 2; news progmg 3 hrs wkly. Target aud: 18-49; Black adults. ■ Verna S. Green, vp & gen mgr; Sheldon Leshner, gen sls mgr; Maureen Barkume, prom mgr; Steve Hegwood, progmg dir; Mildred Gaddis, news dir; Thomas Christie, chief engr.

WJOI(FM)—Listing follows WWJ(AM).

Broadcasting & Cable Yearbook 1994
B-181

WJR(AM)—May 4, 1922: 760 khz; 50 kw-U. TL: N42 10 07 W83 13 00. 2100 Fisher Bldg. (48202). (313) 875-4440. FAX: (313) 875-9636. Licensee: Capital Cities/ABC Inc. Group owner: Capital Cities/ABC Broadcast Group (acq 1986). Net: ABC/I. Rep: Katz. Format: Full svc, news/talk. News staff 11; news progmg 25 hrs wkly. Target aud: 12 plus. ■ Jim Long, vp & gen mgr; Mike Fezzey, gen sls mgr; Phil Boyce, progmg dir; Dick Haefner, news dir; Ed Buterbaugh, chief engr.

WHYT(FM)—Co-owned with WJR(AM). June 1, 1948: 96.3 mhz; 20 kw. Ant 787 ft. TL: N42 27 13 W83 09 50. Stereo. Prog sep from AM. (313) 871-3030. Net: ABC/C. Format: Contemp hit. ■ John E. Cravens, pres & gen mgr; Jack Johnson, gen sls mgr; Rick Gillette, progmg dir; Mark Jackson, mus dir; Rik Jagger, news dir; Hal Buttermore, chief engr.

WJZZ(FM)—May 26, 1960: 105.9 mhz; 20 kw. Ant 725 ft. TL: N42 28 16 W83 12 03. Stereo. 2994 E. Grand Blvd. (48202). (313) 871-0590. FAX: (313) 871-8770. Licensee: Bell Broadcasting Co. Rep: Torbet. Format: Jazz. Target aud: 25-49. Spec prog: Sports 2 hrs, entertainment guide 2 hrs wkly. ■ Terry Arnold, pres; Robert Bass, gen mgr; O'Neal Stevens, progmg dir; Rosetta Hines, mus dir; Treva Bell Bass, chief engr.

WKQI(FM)—Feb 12, 1949: 95.5 mhz; 100 kw. Ant 437 ft. TL: N42 28 22 W83 11 59. Stereo. Hrs opn: 24. 15401 W. 10 Mile Rd., Oak Park (48237). (313) 967-3750. Licensee: Broadcasting Partners of Detroit Inc. Rep: Banner. Format: Adult CHR. ■ Perry L. Lewis, chmn; Barry Mayo, pres; Nathan W. Pearson Jr., CFO; John Fullam, gen mgr; Peter Connolly, gen sls mgr; Susan Griffith, natl sls mgr; Suzanne Belanger, prom dir; Steve Weed, progmg dir. ■ Rates: $450; 275; 250; 50.

WLLZ(FM)—1961: 98.7 mhz; 50 kw. Ant 462 ft. TL: N42 23 42 W83 08 58. Stereo. 31555 Fourteen Mile Rd., Farmington Hills (48334). (313) 855-5100. Licensee: Group W Radio. Group owner: Westinghouse Broadcasting Co. (acq 12-89; grpsl; FTR 12-11-89). Net: Unistar. Rep: Group W Sls. Format: AOR. ■ Buzz Van Houten, vp & gen mgr; John Moran, gen sls mgr; Jon Robbins, mktg dir, prom mgr & progmg dir; Todd Thomas, mus dir; Sandy Kovach, news dir; Ross Lusk, chief engr.

WLQV(AM)—1925: 1500 khz; 50 kw-D, 5 kw-N, DA-2. TL: N42 13 51 W83 11 55. Hrs opn: 24. Suite 650, 29200 Vassar Dr., Livonia (48152). (313) 477-4600. FAX: (313) 477-6911. Licensee: Midwest Broadcasting Corp. Too (acq 9-1-93; $2.1 million; FTR 9-27-93). Net: USA. Format: Relg. Target aud: 30-55; adult middle class. Spec prog: Black 10 hrs wkly. ■ Micheal Glinter, pres; Jon R. Yinger, gen mgr; Mark Ennis, opns mgr; Bob Covington, chief engr.

WLTI(FM)—July 9, 1947: 93.1 mhz; 26.5 kw. Ant 669 ft. TL: N42 28 16 W83 12 03. Stereo. Hrs opn: 24. Suite 1000, 28411 Northwestern Hwy., Southfield (48034-5540). (313) 354-9300. FAX: (313) 354-1474. Licensee: Viacom Broadcasting Inc. (group owner; acq 12-2-88). Format: Adult contemp. Spec prog: Talk one hr wkly. ■ George Kenyon, vp; Marcy Cybert, gen sls mgr; Jeff Silvers, progmg dir; Lecia Macryn, mus dir; Gail McNight, news dir; Mark Phelps, chief engr.

WMTG(AM)—See Dearborn.

WMUZ(FM)—Nov 11, 1958: 103.5 mhz; 50 kw. Ant 500 ft. TL: N42 22 40 W83 14 32. 12300 Radio Place (48228). (313) 272-3434. FAX: (313) 272-5045. Licensee: WMUZ Radio Inc. Group owner: Crawford Broadcasting Co. Format: Adult Christian contemp. ■ Donald B. Crawford, pres; Frank Franciosi, gen mgr; Douglas Burns, progmg dir; Dave Whitaker, mus dir; Bill Johnson, chief engr.

WMXD(FM)—Listing follows WXYT(AM).

WNIC(FM)—(Dearborn). December 1946: 100.3 mhz; 32 kw. Ant 600 ft. TL: N42 23 22 W83 08 53. Stereo. 15001 Michigan Ave., Dearborn (48126). (313) 846-8500. FAX: (313) 846-1068. Licensee: Renaissance Communications Inc. Group owner: Fairmont Communications Corp. Rep: McGavren Guild. Format: Adult contemp. ■ Gary Fisher, pres & gen mgr; Jim Harper, progmg dir; Fred Miller, chief engr.

WNZK(AM)—(Westland). Oct 12, 1985: 690 khz-D, 680 khz-N; 2.5 kw. TL: N42 05 55 W83 19 48. Suite 1190, 21700 Northwestern Hwy., Southfield (48075). (313) 557-3500. FAX: (313) 557-3241. Licensee: Birach Broadcasting Corp. (acq 1984). Format: All foreign language. News progmg 32 hrs wkly. Target aud: General. ■ Sima Birach, gen mgr.

WOMC(FM)—Mar 5, 1948: 104.3 mhz; 190 kw. Ant 361 ft. TL: N42 28 25 W83 06 56. Stereo. 2201 Woodward Heights Blvd. (48220). (313) 546-9600. FAX: (313) 546-5446. Licensee: Infinity Broadcasting of Michigan. Group owner: Infinity Broadcasting Corp. (acq 4-28-88). Net: Unistar. Rep: Torbet. Format: Oldies. News staff one; news progmg 4 hrs wkly. Target aud: 25-54; upscale. ■ Elaine R. Baker, vp & gen mgr; Suzie Player, gen sls mgr; Thom McGinty, prom dir; Phil West, progmg dir; Barry Argenbright, mus dir; Marie Osborne, news dir; Bill Bommarito, chief engr.

WQBH(AM)—1926: 1400 khz; 1 kw-U. TL: N42 24 22 W83 06 44. Penobscot Bldg. Suite 2050 (48226). (313) 965-4500. Licensee: TXZ Corp. (acq 4-23-82; $2 million; FTR 5-10-82). Rep: Patt. Format: Black adult. News staff 2. Target aud: 34-49; Black adult. ■ Tom Bruetsch, gen mgr & news dir; Jay Butler, progmg dir; Don Mosack, chief engr.

WQRS(FM)—March 6, 1960: 105.1 mhz; 21.7 kw. Ant 726 ft. TL: N42 28 16 W83 12 03. Stereo. Suite 200, 28588 Northwestern Hwy., Southfield (48034). (313) 355-1051. Licensee: Marlin Broadcasting Inc. (group owner; acq 12-85; $4.07 million; FTR 9-2-85). Net: Concert Music Net. Rep: CMBS. Format: Class. Target aud: General; professional, upscale, educated. ■ Howard P. Tanger, pres; Steven Krakow, sr vp; Jenny Northern, gen mgr; Bill DeYoe, gen sls mgr; David Wagner, progmg dir; Charles Greenwell, mus dir; Nick Mast, chief engr.

WRIF(FM)—Jan 1, 1948: 101.1 mhz; 27.2 kw. Ant 879 ft. TL: N42 28 15 W83 15 00. Stereo. 26500 Northwestern Hwy 203, Southfield (48076). (313) 827-1111. FAX: (313) 827-9538. Licensee: Great American Television & Radio Co. Inc. Group owner: Great American Broadcasting (acq 12-15-87). Net: ABC/R. Rep: Banner. Format: AOR. News staff one. Target aud: 18-34; men. ■ Tom Bender, gen mgr; Jim Bernardin, gen sls mgr; Greg Husham, progmg dir; Trudi Daniels, news dir; Mike Kernen, chief engr.

WWJ(AM)—Aug 20, 1920: 950 khz; 5 kw-U, DA-N. TL: N42 26 47 W83 10 23. Box 5005, 16550 W. Nine Mile Rd. Southfield (48086-5005). (810) 423-3300. FAX: (810) 423-3326; (810) 224-4504. Licensee: CBS Inc. Group owner: CBS Broadcast Group (acq 3-9-89; FTR 2-27-89). Net: CBS, AP, CNBC. Rep: CBS. Format: All news. News staff 32. Target aud: General. Spec prog: Detroit Lions, Detroit Pistons, Univ. of Michigan Wolverines. ■ Roger Nadel, vp & gen mgr; Tom O'Brien, gen sls mgr; Cathy Goltz, prom mgr; Deidra White, progmg dir & news dir; Bob Ostazewski, chief engr.

WJOI(FM)—Co-owned with WWJ(AM). May 9, 1941: 97.1 mhz; 12 kw. Ant 890 ft. TL: N42 28 59 W83 12 20. Stereo. Prog sep from AM. (313) 423-3398. Format: Easy lstng. ■ Mike Oakes, progmg dir.

WWWW(AM)—Dec 17, 1939: 1130 khz; 50 kw-D, 10 kw-N, DA-2. TL: N42 06 39 W83 11 52. 2930 E. Jefferson (48207). (313) 259-4323. FAX: (313) 259-9079. Licensee: Shamrock Broadcasting Inc. (group owner; acq 5-15-86). Net: AP, UPI, Unistar. Rep: Eastman. Format: Country. Target aud: 25-54. ■ Phil Lamka, gen mgr; Barry Mardit, progmg dir; Sharon Foster, mus dir; Tony Miller, news dir; Ralph Hunt, chief engr.

WWWW-FM—Oct 16, 1960: 106.7 mhz; 61 kw. Ant 510 ft. TL: N42 19 55 W83 02 42 (CP: 28.5 kw, ant 728 ft., TL: N42 19 45 W83 02 25). Stereo. (acq 7-79). ■ Barry Mardit, progmg dir; Sharon Foster, mus dir.

WXYT(AM)—Oct 10, 1925: 1270 khz; 5 kw-U, DA-N. TL: N42 27 58 W83 15 00. Box 905, 15600 W. 12 Mile Rd., Southfield (48037). (313) 569-8000. FAX: (313) 569-9866. Licensee: Fritz Broadcasting Inc. (acq 10-8-84). Net: CNN, Unistar, NBC Talknet, MBS. Rep: D & R Radio. Wash atty: Covington & Burling. Format: News/talk. ■ Charles Fritz Sr., chmn; Jock Fritz, pres, gen mgr & gen sls mgr; Michael Packer, vp opns, opns dir & progmg dir; Stacy Heike, prom mgr; Lisa Barry, news dir; Neil Schwanitz, chief engr.

WMXD(FM)—Co-owned with WXYT(AM). Dec 8, 1964: 92.3 mhz; 21.5 kw-H, 16.5 kw-V. Ant 699 ft. TL: N42 19 45 W83 02 25 (CP: 50 kw, ant 459 ft.). Stereo. Prog sep from AM. Format: Urban contemp. ■ Kris McClendon, opns dir & progmg dir.

WYCD(FM)—May 4, 1960: 99.5 mhz; 21 kw-H, 19-V. Ant 755 ft. TL: N42 28 16 W83 12 03. Stereo. Suite 500, 306 S. Washington, Royal Oak (48067). (313) 398-1100. FAX: (313) 543-3699. Licensee: Alliance Broadcasting Motown Ltd. Group owner: Alliance Broadcasting (acq 8-19-92; $4.55 million; FTR 9-7-92). Net: NBC the Source. Rep: Major Mkt. Wash atty: Fisher, Wayland, Cooper & Leader. Format: Young country. News progmg one hr wkly. Target aud: 12-34. ■ Scott Meier, gen mgr; Ann Boss, prom mgr; Al Casey, progmg dir; Jeff Breitner, chief engr.

Dewitt

WQHH(FM)—1991: 96.5 mhz; 3 kw. Ant 328 ft. TL: N42 51 06 W84 40 06. 1011 Northcrest Rd., Suite 4, Lansing (48906). (517) 484-9600. FAX: (517) 484-9699. Licensee: Mid Michigan FM Inc. Format: Urban contemp.

Dimondale

WXLA(AM)—Sept 20, 1982: 1180 khz; 1 kw-D, DA. TL: N42 39 01 W84 34 49. Hrs opn: 12. Suite 4, 1011 Northcrest, Lansing (48906). (517) 484-9600. FAX: (517) 484-9699. Licensee: Diamond Broadcasters Inc. (acq 9-20-82). Format: Adult contemp, urban contemp. Target aud: 25-54; mature audience. Spec prog: Gospel 5 hrs, jazz 3 hrs, relg 5 hrs wkly. ■ Helena Dubose, pres, gen mgr & gen sls mgr; Helana Dubose, prom mgr; Joe Goldbach, progmg dir & mus dir; Larry Estlack, chief engr.

Dowagiac

***WAUS(FM)**—See South Bend.

WDOW(AM)—September 1960: 1440 khz; 1 kw-D, 89 w-N. TL: N41 59 35 W86 05 10. Box 150 (49047). (616) 782-5106. FAX: (616) 782-5107. Licensee: Dowagiac Broadcasting Co. Inc. Group owner: Kuiper Stns. (acq 11-89; $200,000 with co-located FM; FTR 11-27-89). Net: UPI. Rep: Keystone (unwired net). Format: MOR, btfl mus. Spec prog: Farm 7 hrs wkly. ■ William E. Kuiper Sr., pres; Dean Bussler, gen mgr, prom mgr & progmg dir; Kent Fulmer, news dir.

WDOW-FM—January 1971: 92.1 mhz; 3.3 kw. Ant 299 ft. TL: N41 59 52 W86 03 14. Dups AM 95%.

East Jordan

***WIZY(FM)**—June 25, 1989: 100.9 mhz; 2.8 kw. Ant 489 ft. TL: N45 10 40 W85 05 57. Stereo. Hrs opn: 24. Rebroadcasts WIAA(FM) Interlochen 100%. Box 199, One Lyon St., Interlochen (49643). (616) 276-6171. FAX: (616) 276-6279. Licensee: Interlochen Center for the Arts (acq 5-23-90). Net: NPR, APR, AP; Mich. Pub. Wash atty: Arter & Hadden. Format: Class mus, news. News staff 2; news progmg 20 hrs wkly. Target aud: 35 plus; upper income, arts-oriented, civic-minded professionals. ■ Thom Paulson, gen mgr & dev mgr; Eileen McCann, prom mgr; Frank Slaughter, adv mgr; Edward Catton, progmg dir & mus dir; Robert Allen, news dir & pub affrs dir; L.D. Greilick, engrg dir.

East Lansing

***WDBM(FM)**—Feb 24, 1989: 88.9 mhz; 2 kw. Ant 279 ft. TL: N42 42 20 W84 28 30. Stereo. Hrs opn: 24. 310 Auditorium Bldg., Mich. State Univ. Campus (48824). (517) 353-4414. FAX: (517) 355-4237. Licensee: Board of Trustees of Michigan State Univ. Format: Alternative rock. News progmg 10 hrs wkly. Target aud: 18-34; students of MSU. Spec prog: Blues 4 hrs, jazz 5 hrs, rap/house 5 hrs, heavy metal 4 hrs, progsv country 4 hrs, industrial 2 hrs, punk 2 hrs, Christian rock 4 hrs, TDK new music report one hr, women's prog 2 hrs, reggae 4 hrs wkly. ■ Pat Norager, gen mgr; Rod St. Amand, stn mgr; Dana Hughes, opns dir; Kim Treat, mktg dir; Mike Mann, progmg dir; Brian Halahan, mus dir; Cybil Wallace, news dir; Harold Beer, chief engr.

WFMK(FM)—July 16, 1959: 99.1 mhz; 28 kw. Ant 600 ft. TL: N42 40 33 W84 30 00. Stereo. Hrs opn: 24. Box 991 (48826); 146-R E. Grand River, Williamston (48895). (517) 349-4000. FAX: (517) 379-2020. Licensee: Liggett Broadcast Inc. (group owner; acq 1970). Rep: Eastman. Wash atty: Fisher, Wayland, Cooper & Leader. Format: Adult contemp. News staff one; news progmg 2 hrs wkly. Target aud: 25-54. ■ Robert Liggett, chmn; Jim Jensen, pres; Rod Krol, vp & gen mgr; Ray Marshall, progmg dir; Gary Austin, news dir & pub affrs dir; Craig Bowman, chief engr. ■ Rates: $75; 75; 75; 40.

***WKAR(AM)**—Aug 18, 1922: 870 khz; 10 kw-D, DA. TL: N42 42 19 W84 28 30. 283 Communication Arts Bldg., Michigan State Univ. (48824-1212). (517) 355-6540; (517) 355-2300. FAX: (517) 353-7124. Licensee: Board of Trustees of Michigan State Univ. Net: NPR, AP, APR; Mich. Pub. Wash atty: Schwartz, Woods & Miller. Format: News & talk. News staff 8; news progmg 60 hrs wkly. Spec prog: Sp 3 hrs wkly. ■ Steven Meuche, gen mgr; Harold Prentice, opns mgr & mus dir; Jayne Marsh, dev dir & gen sls mgr; Diane Hutchens, prom dir; Jane Linn, adv dir; Curt Gilleo, progmg dir & news dir; Gary Blievernicht, vp engrg.

***WKAR-FM**—Oct 10, 1948: 90.5 mhz; 86 kw-V, 57 hw-V. Ant 895 ft. TL: N42 42 08 W84 24 51. Prog sep from AM. Format: Class. News progmg 24 hrs wkly. Spec prog:

Stations in the U.S. — Michigan

Jazz 7 hrs wkly. ■ Harold Prentice, progmg dir. ■ *WKAR-TV affil.

WMMQ(FM)—See Charlotte.

WVFN(AM)—September 1964: 730 khz; 500 w-D, 17.5 w-N, DA-2. TL: N42 38 45 W84 33 39. 2517 E. Mt. Hope Ave., Lansing (48910). (517) 487-5986. FAX: (517) 487-0208. Licensee: Goodrich Broadcasting Inc. (group owner; acq 7-81; $2.35 million with co-located FM; FTR 7-20-81). Rep: Katz. Format: CHR. News staff one; news progmg 2 hrs wkly. Target aud: 18-49. ■ Dan Gutowsky, progmg dir.

WVIC-FM—Co-owned with WVFN(AM). Nov 16, 1963: 94.9 mhz; 49 kw. Ant 499 ft. TL: N42 38 44 W84 33 38. Stereo. Dups AM 100%. ■ Jim Lawson, progmg dir; Tim Richards, mus dir; Mark Maloney, news dir.

Elmwood Township

WLJN(AM)—Dec 23, 1982: 1400 khz; 1 kw-U. TL: N44 46 34 W85 39 40 (CP: 640 w). Box 1400, 33930 S. Morgan Hill Rd., Traverse City (49685). (616) 946-1400. FAX: (616) 946-3959. Licensee: Good News Media Inc. Format: Relg, contemp. Target aud: General. ■ John Van Tholen, pres; Raymond Hashley, gen mgr; Brian Harcey, progmg dir; Donald Parker, chief engr.

Elsie

*WOES(FM)—See Ovid-Elsie.

Escanaba

WCHT(AM)—Dec 1, 1958: 600 khz; 1 kw-D, 191 w-N, DA-2. TL: N42 40 28 W87 08 41. Suite 300, 524 Ludington St. (49829). (906) 789-0600. FAX: (906) 789-0600. Licensee: MW Multicom. Group owner: Mid-West Family Stns. Net: ABC/E. Rep: Christal. Format: Oldies, news/talk. News staff one; news progmg 18 hrs wkly. Target aud: 25-54. Spec prog: Farm one hr wkly. ■ Richard Duerson, pres; Rick Duerson, gen mgr; Ann Plummer, gen sls mgr; Mike Daniels, progmg dir & mus dir; Nick Sawyer, news dir; Jeff Gerber, chief engr.

WGLQ(FM)—Co-owned with WCHT(AM). Sept 11, 1976: 97.1 mhz; 100 kw. Ant 1,070 ft. TL: N46 08 04 W85 56 02. Stereo. (906) 789-9700. Net: ABC/C. Format: Adult contemp.

WDBC(AM)—Sept 4, 1941: 680 khz; 10 kw-D, 1 kw-N, DA-2. TL: N45 45 53 W87 05 48. 604 Ludington St. (49829). (906) 786-6144. FAX: (906) 789-9959. Licensee: KMB Broadcasting Co. Inc. (acq 12-31-88). Net: CBS. Rep: Banner. Format: Full svc adult contemp. News staff one; news progmg 35 hrs wkly. Target aud: 25-54. Spec prog: Relg 4 hrs wkly. ■ Betsy Cooke, pres; Alice Sabuco, gen mgr & gen sls mgr; Kevin Scannell, progmg dir; Kevin Morter, news dir; Fred Miller, chief engr. ■ Rates: $19.50; 19.50; 19.50; 15.

WYKX(FM)—Co-owned with WDBC(AM). Dec 22, 1977: 104.7 mhz; 100 kw. Ant 351 ft. TL: N45 55 41 W87 16 00 (CP: 1 kw-N, TL: N45 52 43 W87 28 00). Stereo. Prog sep from AM. (906) 786-3800. Net: SMN. Format: Country. ■ Lee Jeffries, progmg dir. ■ Rates: Same as AM.

WGLQ(FM)—Listing follows WCHT(AM).

WYKX(FM)—Listing follows WDBC(AM).

Essexville

WIXC(FM)—Jan 1, 1992: 97.3 mhz; 3 kw. Ant 328 ft. TL: N43 36 48 W83 45 51. Hrs opn: 24. Box 973, Bay City (48707); 81 S. Tuscola Rd., Bay City (48708). (517) 892-9700. FAX: (517) 892-0973. Licensee: WIXC L.P. Rep: D & R Radio. Wash atty: Fisher, Wayland, Cooper & Leader. Format: Hot country. News progmg 3 hrs wkly. Target aud: 18-49 primary, 25-54 secondary; adults with an affinity for the country lifestyle. ■ Geary S. Morrill, pres & gen mgr; Kevan Kavanaugh, vp & natl sls mgr; Steve Williams, prom dir & pub affrs dir; John H. Dakins, progmg dir & mus dir; Pat Garrison, asst mus dir; Jackie Mack, news dir. ■ Rates: $43; 38; 41; 21.

Farmington Hills

*WORB(FM)—May 1976: 90.3 mhz; 12 w. Ant 138 ft. TL: N42 29 35 W83 25 04. J Building, 27055 Orchard Lake Rd. (48334). (313) 471-7718. FAX: (313) 471-7544. Licensee: Oakland Community College. Format: Free form. Target aud: 14-21 primary; 25-33 secondary; teenagers & young professionals. Spec prog: Black 4 hrs wkly. ■ Ron Burda, gen mgr; Frank Rotondo, stn mgr & progmg dir; Scott Zacharias, mus dir; Michael La Bond, chief engr.

Fenton

WWON(AM)—Nov 15, 1985: 1160 khz; 1 kw-U, DA-1. TL: N42 38 30 W83 43 50. 15130 North Rd. (48430). (810) 629-1300. FAX: (810) 629-7044. Licensee: GWC Inc. (acq 4-20-93; $220,000; FTR 5-3-93). Net: American Urban. Format: Relg. ■ Larry Robinson, pres; Joyce Cooper, gen mgr; Rev. James A. Williams Jr., progmg dir; Michael Bradford, chief engr.

Flint

WCRZ(FM)—Listing follows WFNT(AM).

WDZZ-FM—Listing follows WFDF(AM).

*WFBE(FM)—Oct 5, 1953: 95.1 mhz; 50 kw. Ant 243 ft. TL: N43 01 13 W83 40 40. Stereo. Hrs opn: 5 AM-1 AM. 605 Crapo St. (48503). (313) 760-1148. FAX: (313) 760-6790. Licensee: Flint Board of Educ. Net: APR. Wash atty: Schwartz, Woods & Miller. Format: Classical, jazz, new age. News progmg 26 hrs wkly. Target aud: General; public radio listeners. Spec prog: Folk 3 hrs, lt one hr, ethnic one hr, alternative 4 hrs, community affrs 10 hrs wkly. ■ John R. Szucs, gen mgr; Pam Bakken, opns dir; Jody Arvoy, dev dir; Tom Butts, chief engr.

WFDF(AM)—May 25, 1922: 910 khz; 5 kw-D, 1 kw-N, DA-2. TL: N42 58 22 W83 37 30. Suite 1830, One E. 1st St. (48502). (313) 238-7300. FAX: (313) 238-7310. Licensee: Erie Coast Communications Net: CBS, MBS. Rep: D & R Radio. Format: Big band, oldies. ■ Michael Dach, gen mgr; Debbie Collins, gen sls mgr; Peggy Raleigh, progmg dir; Les Root, news dir; Dan Greer, chief engr.

WDZZ-FM—Co-owned with WFDF(AM). Sept 29, 1979: 92.7 mhz; 3 kw. Ant 260 ft. TL: N43 00 57 W83 41 24. Stereo. Format: Urban contemp. Spec prog: Jazz 11 hrs, gospel 8 hrs wkly. ■ Terry Chisolm, progmg dir; Theresa Turner, news dir.

WFLT(AM)—Dec 5, 1955: 1420 khz; 500 w-D, 142 w-N, DA-2. TL: N43 01 15 W83 38 36. 317 S. Averill (48506). (313) 239-5733. Licensee: Metropolitan Missionary Baptist Church (acq 7-2-90; $225,000; FTR 7-23-90). Net: MBS. Rep: Michigan. Format: Black gospel. ■ Jesse Scott, gen mgr; Rory Cavette, gen sls mgr & progmg dir; Mike Moffitt, chief engr.

WFNT(AM)—Apr 10, 1953: 1470 khz; 5 kw-D, 1 kw-N, DA-2. TL: N42 58 22 W83 38 24. Hrs opn: 24. G 3338 E. Bristol Rd. (48501). (313) 742-1470. FAX: (313) 742-5170. Licensee: Faircom Flint Inc. Group owner: Faircom Inc. (acq 10-22-86; $7.5 million with co-located FM; FTR 8-11-86). Rep: Katz. Wash atty: Haley, Bader & Potts. Format: News/talk. News staff 3. ■ Joel Fairman, pres; John Risher, vp & gen mgr; Lynette Mackenzie, gen sls mgr; Andy Isola, prom dir; Anne Downley, progmg dir & mus dir; Chris Pavelich, news dir; Bill Sanderson, chief engr. ■ Rates: $94; 94; 94; 94.

WCRZ(FM)—Co-owned with WFNT(AM). Nov 4, 1961: 107.9 mhz; 50 kw. Ant 331 ft. TL: N42 58 49 W83 34 40. Stereo. Prog sep from AM. Box 1080 (48501). (313) 743-1080. Net: CBS Spectrum. Format: Adult contemp. ■ Jay Patrick, opns mgr & progmg dir. ■ Rates: Same as AM.

*WFUM-FM—Aug 23, 1985: 91.1 mhz; 18 kw. Ant 489 ft. TL: N42 53 57 W83 27 42. Stereo. 1321 E. Court St. (48503). (313) 762-3028. Licensee: Regents of the Univ. of Michigan. Net: NPR. Format: Classical. Spec prog: Jazz 10 hrs wkly. ■ Gordon Lawrence, gen mgr.

WTAC(AM)—Apr 26, 1946: 600 khz; 1 kw-D, 500 w-N, DA-2. TL: N42 56 23 W83 37 41. Hrs opn: 6 AM-midnight. G-6171 S. Center Rd., Grand Blanc (48439). (313) 694-4146. FAX: (313) 239-6401. Licensee: Midwest Broadcasting Corp. (acq 1-22-93; $400,000; FTR 2-8-93). Format: Christian adult contemp. ■ Evelyn Shaw, stn mgr; Jimi Reid, progmg dir; Paul Porter, mus dir; Don McComb, chief engr.

WWCK(AM)—Nov 11, 1946: 1570 khz; 1 kw-D, 238 w-N. TL: N43 00 38 W83 39 09. 3217 Lapeer Rd. (48503). (313) 744-1570. FAX: (313) 743-2500. Licensee: Majac of Michigan Inc. (acq 12-20-88; $2.4 million with co-located FM; FTR 1-9-89). Rep: Christal. Format: CHR Top-40. ■ Marc Steenbarger, pres, gen mgr, gen sls mgr & mus dir; Lee St. Michaels, progmg dir; Marlin Kibbee, Debbi Gilbert, news dirs; Mark Meyer, chief engr.

WWCK-FM—September 1964: 105.5 mhz; 25 kw. Ant 328 ft. TL: N43 00 38 W83 39 09. Stereo. Dups AM 90%. Net: NBC the Source.

Frankenmuth

WKNX(AM)—Licensed to Frankenmuth. See Saginaw.

Frankfort

WBNZ(FM)—Oct 2, 1978: 99.3 mhz; 50 kw. Ant 410 ft. TL: N44 36 38 W86 09 38. Stereo. Hrs opn: 5 AM-2 AM. 1532 Forrester Rd. (49635). (616) 352-9603. FAX: (616) 352-7877. Licensee: Crystal Clear Communications Inc. (acq 6-25-91; $84,000; FTR 7-15-91). Rep: Patt. Format: Adult contemp. News staff one; news progmg 3 hrs wkly. Target aud: 25-54. Spec prog: Folk 2 hrs, big band 2 hrs wkly. ■ Marc McGuire, CEO, chmn, gen mgr & gen sls mgr; Vicki McGuire, vp; Tim Burke, progmg dir & mus dir; John Rutherford, news dir; Walker Sisson, chief engr. ■ Rates: $13.50; 12; 13.50; 10.

Fremont

WSHN(AM)—May 23, 1961: 1550 khz; 1 kw-D. TL: N43 28 15 W85 56 25. Box 190, 517 Beebe St. (49412). (616) 924-4700; (800) 968-9746 (in MI). FAX: (616) 924-9746. Licensee: Stuart P. Noordyk. Group owner: WSHN Inc. (acq 5-23-61). Net: Mich. Net. Rep: Patt. Format: Country. ■ Stu Noordyk, pres; Don Noordyk, gen mgr; John Russell, news dir; David Grant, chief engr.

WSHN-FM—1971: 100.1 mhz; 2.75 kw. Ant 295 ft. TL: N43 28 15 W85 56 25. Stereo. Dups AM 100%. (409) 336-5793. FAX: (409) 336-5250. Licensee: Trinity River Valley Broadcasting Co. Format: Adult contemp, oldies, recurrent country. Target aud: Adult. Spec prog: Black ■ William Buchanan, pres & gen mgr; Jay Scott, progmg dir; J.R. Austin, mus dir; Allen Wayne, asst mus dir; Sam Sailar, news dir; Barbara Moss, pub affrs dir.

Gaylord

WKPK(FM)—Nov 18, 1972: 106.7 mhz; 100 kw. Ant 580 ft. TL: N45 02 42 W84 50 44. Stereo. Hrs opn: 24. Box 190, 308 W. Main (49735). (517) 732-2474. Licensee: Alpine Broadcasting Co. Net: Unistar. Rep: Patt. Format: Adult Top-40. Target aud: 18-49; rgnl orientation including Traverse City, Petoskey, Cheboygan-active life style. ■ John D. DeGroot, pres & gen mgr; Lisa Landers, gen sls mgr; Jake Edwards, progmg dir; Craig Russeu, mus dir; Robert Sheen, news dir; Robert Stutesman, chief engr. ■ Rates: $17; 17; 17; 17.

WMJZ-FM—Listing follows WSNQ(AM).

*WPHN(FM)—Apr 7, 1985: 90.5 mhz; 100 kw. Ant 1,000 ft. TL: N45 08 17 84 09 44. Stereo. Hrs opn: 24. Box 695 (49735-0695); 1511 M-32 E. (49735). (517) 732-6274. Licensee: Northern Christian Radio Inc. Net: Moody, USA, Skylight. Wash atty: Jeffrey D. Southmayd. Format: Relg, educ. News progmg 10 hrs wkly. Target aud: 25-55. Spec prog: Class 5 hrs wkly. ■ David A. Malin, CEO; Peter J. Vellenga, chmn; George Lake Jr., chief engr.

WSNQ(AM)—July 29, 1950: 900 khz; 1 kw-D, 101 w-N. TL: N45 01 25 W84 39 15. Hrs opn: 24. Box 25, 650 E. Main (49735). (517) 732-2341; (517) 732-3446. FAX: (517) 732-6202. Licensee: Classic Radio Inc. (acq 6-29-86). Net: Sun.; Mich. Net. Rep: Patt. Format: News/talk. News staff one; news progmg 15 hrs wkly. Target aud: 35-54. Spec prog: Pol 2 hrs, relg 2 hrs wkly. ■ William F. Rolinski, CEO; Barbara Thiel, pres; Diane Williams, vp; Tom Bill, sls dir; Brent Cogswell, progmg dir; Dan Heaton, news dir; George Lake, chief engr.

WMJZ-FM—Co-owned with WSNQ(AM). 1984: 95.3 mhz; 3 kw. Ant 325 ft. TL: N45 01 25 W84 39 15. Stereo. Hrs opn: 24. Prog sep from AM. Net: Unistar. Format: Adult contemp, full svc. Target aud: 25-54. Spec prog: Loc sports 26 hrs wkly. ■ Tom Gill, gen mgr.

Gladstone

WENL(FM)—Not on air, target date unknown: 105.5 mhz; 6 kw. Ant 256 ft. TL: N45 46 56 W87 04 40. Stereo. Martz Communications Group, 5595 Liberty Rd., Chagrin Falls, OH (44022). (216) 498-1221. Licensee: Zephyr Broadcasting Inc. Group owner: Martz Communications Group (acq 3-5-90; $5,000; FTR 3-19-90). Wash atty: Cohn & Marks. ■ Timothy D. Martz, pres.

Gladwin

WGDN(AM)—Dec 7, 1974: 1350 khz; 1 kw-D, DA. TL: N43 57 03 W84 30 34. 3601 W. Woods Rd. (48624). (517) 426-1350. Licensee: Apple Broadcasting Co. Inc. (acq 3-87; $75,000 with co-located FM; FTR 12-22-86). Format: Adult contemp. Target aud: 35 plus. ■ Timothy L. Coston, pres; Steve Coston, gen mgr; Chuck Cobb, progmg dir; Charlie Cobb, mus dir; Ralph Haines, chief engr.

WGDN-FM—Feb 7, 1978: 103.1 mhz; 11.5 kw. Ant 453 ft. TL: N43 57 03 W84 30 34. Stereo. Prog sep from AM. Net: USA. Format: Btfl mus. ■ Rates: $9; 9; 9; na.

Glen Arbor

WGFN(FM)—February 1991: 98.1 mhz; 7.9 kw. Ant 590 ft. TL: N44 49 15 W85 59 42. Stereo. Hrs opn: 24. 1356 Macanaw, Sheboygan (49721). (616) 627-6105. FAX: (616) 627-7000. Licensee: Cherry Capital Media Inc. (acq 7-24-92; FTR 8-17-92). Net: Unistar. Format: Classic rock. News staff one. Spec prog: Jazz 4 hrs wkly. ■ Del Reynolds, pres & gen mgr; Michael Bradford, chief engr. ■ Rates: $15; 11; 15; 9.50.

Grand Haven

WGHN(AM)—July 16, 1956: 1370 khz; 500 w-D. TL: N43 02 17 W86 13 46. Box 330, One S. Harbor (49417). (616) 842-8110. Licensee: WGHN Inc. (acq 2-14-83; $260,500 with co-located FM; FTR 3-7-83). Net: CBS; Mich. News Net., Mich. Farm. Rep: Patt. Format: Adult contemp. News staff one; news progmg over 30 hrs wkly. Target aud: 25-54. Spec prog: Agriculture & farm 5 hrs wkly. ■ William Struyk, pres, gen mgr & gen sls mgr; Doug Peets, mus dir; Ron Stevens, news dir. ■ Rates: $16; 14; 16; 12.

WGHN-FM—Jan 28, 1969: 92.1 mhz; 3 kw. Ant 246 ft. TL: N43 03 23 W86 14 27. Stereo. Hrs opn: 5 AM-midnight. Dups AM 95%. Net: CBS. Mich. News Net., Mich. Farm.

Grand Rapids

WBCT(FM)—October 1951: 93.7 mhz; 320 kw. Ant 781 ft. TL: N42 37 56 W85 32 16. Stereo. Hrs opn: 24. 280 Ann St., N.W. (49504). (616) 363-7701. FAX: (616) 361-7156. Licensee: Radio Associates of Michigan Inc. Group owner: Radio Associates (acq 4-15-92; $4.62 million with WKZO[AM] Kalamazoo; FTR 5-11-92). Net: ABC/R. Rep: D & R Radio. Format: Country. News staff one; news progmg 3 hrs wkly. Target aud: 25-49. ■ Ken Miller, CEO; Bob Salmon, pres; Tim Feagan, gen mgr; Lee Cory, opns mgr & progmg dir; Dave Paulis, gen sls mgr; Kelly Iras, mus dir; John Semore, chief engr. ■ Rates: $90; 90; 90; 50.

***WBLU-FM**—Aug 18, 1979: 88.9 mhz; 650 w. Ant 400 ft. TL: N42 59 15 W85 37 26. Stereo. Rebroadcasts WBLV(FM) Twin Lake. Blue Lake Fine Arts Camp, Twin Lake (49457); Suite 200B, Waters Bldg., 161 Ottawa N.W. (49503). (616) 894-2616; (616) 458-9258. FAX: (616) 893-2457. Licensee: Blue Lake Fine Arts Camp (acq 3-1-93; $200,000; FTR 3-15-93). Net: APR, NPR; Mich. Pub. Format: Class, jazz, news. News progmg 20 hrs wkly. Target aud: Adult. Spec prog: Folk 5 hrs wkly. ■ Buck Matthews, gen mgr & gen sls mgr; Gordon Christianson, opns dir; Dave Myers, progmg dir; Bonnie Bierma, mus dir; Brad Aspey, pub affrs dir; Don Hoogeboom, chief engr.

***WBYW(FM)**—May 18, 1978: 89.9 mhz; 390 w. Ant 144 ft. TL: N43 01 25 W85 35 30. Stereo. Hrs opn: 20. Box 2892 (49501-2892); 3066 3 Mile Rd. (49504). (616) 453-3711. Licensee: Grand Rapids Public Broadcasting Corp. (acq 4-23-76). Format: International. Target aud: General; ethnic progmg. Spec prog: Ger 2 hrs, Sp 12 hrs, class 2 hrs, Indian 2 hrs, black 8 hrs, big band 10 hrs, American Indian 2 hrs, Israeli 2 hrs wkly. ■ John Labinskas, gen mgr. ■ Rates: $15; 20; 30; 35.

WBYY(AM)—See Rockford.

***WCSG(FM)**—June 9, 1973: 91.3 mhz; 37 kw. Ant 570 ft. TL: N42 47 46 W85 38 58. Stereo. 1159 E. Beltline Ave. N.E. (49505). (616) 942-1500. Licensee: Grand Rapids Baptist College and Seminary. Net: ABC/I, Skylight. Format: Relg. News staff 2. Target aud: 35-55. ■ Dr. Rex Rogers, pres; Lee Geysbeek, vp; Jack Havemen, dev dir; Tammie George, prom dir; Cal Olson, mus dir; Becky Carlson, news dir; Dave Gale, chief engr.

WCUZ(AM)—February 1945: 1230 khz; 1 kw-U. TL: N42 59 42 W85 40 36. Stereo. Hrs opn: 24. 140 Monroe Ctr. (49503). (616) 451-2551. FAX: (616) 451-0931. Licensee: Pathfinder Communications Corp. Group owner: Federated Media (acq 6-10-73). Net: ABC/I. Rep: Christal. Wash atty: Dow, Lohnes & Albertson. Format: Country. News staff 2; new progmg 7 hrs wkly. Target aud: 25-54; conservative. ■ John F. Dille III, pres; Ronald Dykstra, gen mgr; Brian Wright, opns mgr; Randy Prichard, gen sls mgr; Sheila Gunneson, mktg dir, prom mgr & adv dir; Ed Buchanan, mus dir; John Bry, news dir; David Gale, chief engr.

WCUZ-FM—1965: 101.3 mhz; 50 kw. Ant 420 ft. TL: N43 02 28 W85 21 28 (CP: Ant 702 ft., TL: N43 02 28 W85 31 04). Stereo. Hrs opn: 24. Dups AM 50%. Target aud: 25-54.

WFGR(FM)—Not on air, target date unknown: 98.7 mhz; 2.75 kw. Ant 492 ft. TL: N43 01 57 W85 41 47. Suite 425, 220 Lyon St. N.W. (49503). (616) 458-2600. Licensee: Haith Broadcasting Corp. ■ Tom Beauvais, gen mgr; Dave Ayrault, stn mgr.

WFUR(AM)—Nov 1947: 1570 khz; 1 kw-D, 306 w-N. TL: N42 57 14 W85 41 52. 399 Garfield Ave. S.W. (49504). (616) 451-9387. FAX: (616) 451-8460. Licensee: Furniture City Broadcasting Corp. Group owner: Kuiper Stns. (acq 3-10-50). Net: USA. Format: Relg. ■ William E. Kuiper Sr., pres & gen mgr.

WFUR-FM—Sept 1960: 102.9 mhz; 50 kw. Ant 492 ft. TL: N42 57 13 W85 41 55. Stereo. Hrs opn: 24. Prog sep from AM. Format: Btfl mus, relg mus.

WGRD(AM)—Nov 1, 1947: 1410 khz; 1 kw-D. TL: N42 59 14 W85 37 76. Suite 200, 38 W. Fulton (49503). (616) 459-4111. FAX: (616) 459-6887. Licensee: All Channel TV Service (acq 10-9-92; no financial consideration with co-located FM; FTR 11-23-92). Net: SMN, BRN. Rep: D & R Radio. Format: News/talk, bus. Target aud: 35 plus; professionals. ■ David Gates, gen mgr; Jill Schmiecher, gen sls mgr; Kevin Gossett, progmg dir & mus dir; Rick Hood, chief engr.

WGRD-FM—Aug 1, 1962: 97.9 mhz; 13 kw. Ant 590 ft. TL: N42 47 46 W85 38 58. Stereo. Prog sep from AM. Format: Contemp hit. ■ Rates: $120; 100; 110; 95.

***WGVU(AM)**—(Kentwood). Dec 25, 1954: 1480 khz; 5 kw-U, DA-N. TL: N42 57 13 W85 41 36 (CP: 2 kw-D, 5 kw-N). Hrs opn: 24. 301 W. Fulton, Grand Rapids (49504). (616) 771-6666. FAX: (616) 771-6625. Licensee: Grand Valley State Univ. (acq 4-7-92; $240,000 part sale & part gift; FTR 4-27-92). Net: NRP, APR. Format: News and information. News staff 2; news progmg 89 hrs wkly. Target aud: 35-44; college-educated men with average income. ■ Gary DeSantis, dev mgr; Jan McKinnon, sls dir; Michael Walenta, gen sls mgr; Rob Willey, progmg mgr; David Moore, news dir; Bob Lambert, chief engr. ■ Rates: $21; 21; 21; na.

***WGVU-FM**—See Allendale.

WKLQ(FM)—See Holland.

WKWM(AM)—See Kentwood.

WLAV(AM)—Sept 18, 1940: 1340 khz; 1 kw-U. TL: N42 57 02 W85 41 55. Hrs opn: 24. Trade Ctr., 3rd Fl., 50 Louis N.W. (49503). (616) 456-5461. FAX: (616) 451-3299. Licensee: Radio Group Corp. (acq 8-26-86). Rep: Major Mkt. Format: Modern rock. Target aud: 18-34; modern rockers. Spec prog: Sp one hr wkly. ■ Joel T. Schaaf, vp, gen mgr & natl sls mgr; David Burns, gen sls mgr; Marianne Dupree, prom dir; Mark Steven, progmg dir; Brian Tinnes, news dir; June Egan, pub affrs dir; Dave Grant, chief engr. ■ Rates: $25; 25; 30; 20.

WLAV-FM—January 1947: 96.9 mhz; 50 kw. Ant 499 ft. TL: N43 02 01 W85 31 15. Stereo. Prog sep from AM. Format: AOR. News staff one. Target aud: 18-44. ■ Marianne Dupree, prom mgr & mus dir.

WLHT(FM)—Feb 28, 1962: 95.7 mhz; 40 kw. Ant 551 ft. TL: N43 01 57 W85 41 47. Stereo. Box 96 (49501). (616) 451-4800. FAX: (616) 451-0113. Licensee: Liggett Broadcast Inc. (group owner; acq 12-80; $1.38 million; FTR 12-15-80). Rep: Eastman. Wash atty: Fisher, Wayland, Cooper & Leader. Format: Adult contemp. News staff one; news progmg 3 hrs wkly. Target aud: 25-49. ■ James A. Jensen, pres; Philip Catlett, gen mgr; Fred Barr, gen sls mgr; Steve Dirksen, progmg dir; Michael Sirianni, mus dir; Charles LaTour, news dir; Craig Bowman, chief engr. ■ Rates: $135; 125; 110; 50.

WODJ(FM)—(Greenville). May 22, 1962: 107.3 mhz; 50 kw. Ant 492 ft. TL: N43 01 10 W85 20 58. Stereo. Suite F, 2610 Horizon Dr. S.W., Grand Rapids (49546). Licensee: Goodrich Broadcasting Inc. Format: Oldies. Target aud: 25-54. ■ Tom Duda, gen mgr; Michael W. Kay, progmg dir; Mike St. Cyr, chief engr.

WOOD(AM)—1924: 1300 khz; 5 kw-U, DA-N. TL: N42 51 24 W85 39 03. Stereo. Hrs opn: 24. College Park Plaza, 180 N. Division (49503-3186). (616) 459-1919. FAX: (616) 732-3330. Licensee: Wood Radio Ltd Partnership (acq 11-91; $10.5 million with co-located FM; FTR 9-2-91). Net: NBC Talknet. Rep: Katz. Wash atty: Cole Raywid Braverman. Format: Full svc adult contemp. News progmg 24 hrs wkly. Target aud: 35-54. Spec prog: Farm 6 hrs wkly. ■ Bruce H. Holberg, pres & vp; Paul Boscarino, stn mgr; Dick Stoimenoff, natl sls mgr; Stan Atkinson, progmg dir; David Isaacs, news dir; Don Missad, chief engr.

WOOD-FM—1962: 105.7 mhz; 265 kw. Ant 810 ft. TL: N42 41 13 W85 30 35. Stereo. Hrs opn: 24. Dups AM 15%. Format: Easy lstng. News progmg 10 hrs wkly.

***WVGR(FM)**—Dec 7, 1961: 104.1 mhz; 108 kw. Ant 600 ft. TL: N42 41 13 W85 30 35. Stereo. Hrs opn: 24. Satellite of *WUOM(FM) Ann Arbor. 5501 LSA Bldg., University of Michigan, Ann Arbor, (48109-1382). (616) 956-7711; (313) 764-9210. FAX: (313) 747-3488. Licensee: Regents of the U. of Michigan. Net: NPR, APR. Mich. Pub. Format: Class, news. News staff 3; news progmg 30 hrs wkly. Target aud: 35-64. Spec prog: Jazz 6 hrs wkly. ■ Joel Seguine, stn mgr; Shelley MacMillan, dev dir; Harriet Teller, prom mgr; Lisa McCormack, progmg dir; Bob Whitman, news dir; Jim Paffenbarger, chief engr.

Grayling

WGRY(AM)—Aug 1, 1970: 1230 khz; 750 w-U. TL: N44 39 05 W84 44 18. Hrs opn: 5:30 AM-midnight. 6514 Old Lake Rd. (49738). (517) 348-6171; (517) 348-4132. FAX: (517) 348-6181. Licensee: Dewitt Radio Inc. (acq 9-88). Net: MBS; Mich. Net. Rep: Michigan, Patt. Format: Country. News staff one; news progmg 16 hrs wkly. Target aud: 25 plus. ■ William S. Gannon, pres & gen mgr; Scott Marshall, stn mgr; Dave Sherbert, opns mgr, progmg dir, mus dir & news dir; Delton Winkel, gen sls mgr; Robert Stutsman, chief engr. ■ Rates: $12; 12; 12; 10.

WQON(FM)—June 16, 1977: 100.3 mhz; 50 kw. Ant 436 ft. TL: N44 36 50 W84 41 05. Stereo. 6514 Old Lake Rd. (49738). (517) 348-6171. FAX: (517) 348-6181. Licensee: Dewitt Radio Inc. (acq 10-6-93; FTR 10-25-93). Net: SMN. Rep: Patt. Format: Adult contemp. News staff 2; news progmg 3 hrs wkly. Target aud: 25-54. ■ Scott Marshall, stn mgr, dev mgr, gen sls mgr, mktg mgr & prom mgr; Dave Sherbert, opns mgr, progmg mgr & news dir. ■ Rates: $9; 9; 9; 9.

Greenville

WODJ(FM)—Licensed to Greenville. See Grand Rapids.

WPLB(AM)—May 19, 1960: 1380 khz; 1 kw-D, 500 w-N, DA-N. TL: N43 09 18 W85 15 25. Box 578 (48838). (616) 754-3656. FAX: (616) 754-2390. Licensee: Kortes Communications Inc. (acq 9-8-92; $185,000; FTR 10-5-92). Format: MOR, talk, sports. ■ Jeff Kortes, pres, gen mgr & gen sls mgr; Jim St. Clair, progmg dir; Chuck Hill, mus dir. ■ Rates: $18; 16; 18; 10.

Gulliver

WCMM(FM)—1982: 94.7 mhz; 100 kw. Ant 659 ft. TL: N 45 58 01 W86 29 18. Stereo. Box 220, Manistique (49854); 1501 Deer St., Manistique (49854). (906) 341-8444. FAX: (906) 341-6222. Licensee: WSHN Inc. (group owner; acq 12-26-91; grpsl; FTR 1-14-91). Net: ABC. Format: Country. News staff 2; news progmg 15 hrs wkly. Target aud: 18-54; younger, contemp. Target aud: mobile adult workers. ■ Stu Noordyk, CEO; Todd Noordyk, gen mgr & progmg dir; L. David Vaughan, vp opns; Rick Duerson, vp dev; Ann Plummer, vp sls; Cindy Beshaw, vp mktg; Art Voight, mktg dir; Ron Rizdon, mus dir; Beth Ann Gyorke, news dir; William Becks, vp engrg. ■ Rates: $13; 11; 13; 11.

Hancock

WMPL(AM)—March 2, 1957: 920 khz; 1 kw-D, 206 w-N. TL: N47 06 05 W88 35 26. Box 547 (49930). (906) 482-3700. FAX: (906) 482-1540. Licensee: Copper Country Enterprises Inc. (acq 9-1-69). Net: USA. Rep: Michigan. Format: Talk/news, info. News progmg 20 hrs wkly. Target aud: General; young adults including college students. ■ W.G. Blake, pres; Robert Olson, gen mgr; Bob Olson, gen sls mgr; Mitchell Lake, news dir; George Kinnenen, chief engr.

WZRK(FM)—Co-owned with WMPL(AM). 1968: 93.5 mhz; 3 kw-H. Ant 249 ft. TL: N47 06 05 W88 35 26 (CP: 13.5 kw, ant 456 ft.). Prog sep from AM. (906) 482-1540. Net: SMN. Wash atty: Booth & Freret. Format: Pure gold. ■ Marianne Schulze, gen sls mgr; Marc Carver, progmg dir.

Harbor Springs

***WCMW-FM**—Aug 15, 1988: 103.9 mhz; 28 kw. Ant 663 ft. TL: N45 29 02 W84 58 00. Stereo. Hrs opn: 24. Public Broadcasting Ctr., Central Michigan Univ., Mt. Pleasant (48859). (517) 774-3105. FAX: (517) 774-4427. Licensee: Central Michigan University (acq 7-21-93; $325,000; FTR 8-23-93). Net: NBC the Source. Rep: Patt. Format: Classical jazz, news/info. News staff one; news progmg 7 hrs wkly. Target aud: 25-54. Spec prog:

Folk 3 hrs wkly. ■ Thomas Hunt, gen mgr; Linda Hyde, prom dir; Ray Ford, progmg dir; Susan MacTaggart-Dennis, mus dir; Randy Kapenga, chief engr. ■ Rates: $25; 17; 20; 10.

Harrison

WKKM(FM)—Mar 26, 1975: 92.1 mhz; 6 kw. Ant 300 ft. TL: N43 59 38 W84 50 13. Hrs opn: 24. Box 549, 209 E. Spruce St. (48625-0549). (517) 539-7105. Licensee: David A. Carmine. Net: ABC/E. Format: Country. News progmg 10 hrs wkly. Target aud: General; mature adults. ■ David A. Carmine, CEO, gen mgr & chief engr. ■ Rates: $4.75; 4.75; 4.75; 4.75.

Hart

WCXT(FM)—Sept 14, 1983; 105.3 mhz; 100 kw. Ant 649 ft. TL: N43 40 34 W86 14 21 (CP: Ant 1,076 ft.). Stereo. 220 Polk Rd. (49420). (616) 873-7129. FAX: (616) 873-7120. Licensee: Waters Broadcasting Corp. Format: Light mix adult contemp. Target aud: 25-54; adult women. ■ Nancy Waters, pres; Mark Waters, progmg dir.

Hastings

WBCH(AM)—November 1957: 1220 khz; 250 w-D, 48 w-N. TL: N42 37 36 W85 16 39. Box 88 (49058). (616) 945-3414. FAX: (616) 945-3470. Licensee: Barry Broadcasting Co. (acq 8-17-58). Net: ABC/E, Unistar; Mich. Farm, MNN. Rep: Michigan. Format: Hit Country. News staff one; news progmg 16 hrs wkly. Target aud: 25-60. ■ Kenneth R. Radant, pres, gen mgr & gen sls mgr; Steve Radant, vp, stn mgr, prom mgr, progmg dir & mus dir; Buzz Youngs, news dir; Dean Bass, chief engr. ■ Rates: $10.50; 9.50; 10.50; 9.50.

WBCH-FM—December 1967: 100.1 mhz; 3 kw. Ant 295 ft. TL: N42 37 36 W85 16 39. Stereo. Dups AM 100%. ■ Rates: Same as AM.

Highland Park

*WHPR(FM)—May 21, 1954: 88.1 mhz; 11 w-H. Ant 105 ft. TL: N42 24 50 W83 05 48. Stn currently dark. 20 Bartlett (48203). (313) 250-0440, ext. 066. FAX: (313) 868-4950. Licensee: School District of Highland Park.

Hillman

WKJZ(FM)—Not on air, target date unknown: 94.9 mhz; 50 kw. Ant 492 ft. TL: N45 01 33 W83 54 52. 3964 E. Lawrence Dr., Oscoda (48750). Licensee: Carroll Enterprises Inc. (acq 6-29-92; FTR 7-27-92).

Hillsdale

WCSR(AM)—May 21, 1959: 1340 khz; 500 w-D, 1 kw-N. TL: N41 55 41 W84 38 10. 170 N. West St. (49242). (517) 437-4444. Licensee: WCSR Inc. (acq 11-15-61). Net: Mich. Farm. Format: Adult contemp, MOR. News staff one; news progmg 14 hrs wkly. Target aud: General; county-wide 25 plus. Spec prog: Farm 3 hrs, relg 10 hrs wkly. ■ Tony Flynn, pres; Dick Mumey, gen mgr; Bob Flynn, mus dir; Park Hayes, news dir; Ed Trombley, chief engr.

WCSR-FM—May 19, 1973: 92.1 mhz; 6 kw. Ant 243 ft. TL: N41 55 41 W84 38 10. Stereo.

Holland

WHTC(AM)—July 1948: 1450 khz; 1 kw-U. TL: N42 47 41 W86 06 22. Hrs opn: 5 AM-midnight. Box 1467 (49422); 87 Central Ave. (49423). (616) 392-3121; (616) 459-9888. FAX: (616) 392-8066. Licensee: Holland Communications Inc. Group owner: Walton Co. (acq 1981). Net: MBS, CBS; Mich. Farm. Rep: Patt. Format: MOR, news/talk. News staff one; news progmg 15 hrs wkly. Target aud: 25 plus. Spec prog: Sp 3 hrs wkly. ■ Michael Walton, pres; Kendal Showers, opns dir & progmg dir; Michael Hatton, gen sls mgr; Dennis Kortman, news dir; Patty Vandenberg, pub affrs dir; Ron Steenwyck, chief engr.

WKEZ(FM)—Co-owned with WHTC(AM). September 1962: 96.1 mhz; 50 kw-H, 45 kw-V. Ant 492 ft. TL: N42 49 10 W85 52 09. Stereo. Hrs opn: 24. Prog sep from AM. Box 1467, 87 Central St. (49422); Suite E2, 2600 Horizon S.E., Grand Rapids (49546). Net: CBS Spectrum. Format: Easy lstng. Target aud: 35 plus; upscale adults. ■ Margie Boerman, pub affrs dir.

WJQK(FM)—Listing follows WWJQ(AM).

WKEZ(FM)—Listing follows WHTC(AM).

WKLQ(FM)—March 21, 1961: 94.5 mhz; 50 kw. Ant 499 ft. TL: N42 51 20 W85 57 45. Stereo. Hrs opn: 24. Peoples Bldg., 60 Monroe Ctr. N.W., Grand Rapids (49503). (616) 774-8461. FAX: (616) 774-0351. Licensee: Michigan Media Inc. Group owner: Bloomington Broadcasting Corp. (acq 10-31-83). Rep: Banner Wash atty: Reddy, Begley & Martin. Format: AOR. Target aud: 18-49. ■ Bart Brandmiller, pres & gen mgr; Jennifer Stoll, gen sls mgr; Mike Tinnes, progmg dir; Dave Wellington, mus dir; Ron Steenwyk, chief engr.

*WTHS(FM)—Oct 15, 1984: 89.9 mhz; 1 kw. Ant 154 ft. TL: N42 47 16 W86 06 02. Stereo. Hrs opn: 24. DeWitt Centre, Hope College (49423). (616) 394-7878; (616) 394-7880. Licensee: Hope College Board of Trustees. Wash atty: Lauren Colby. Format: Alternative. News progmg 7 hrs wkly. Target aud: 15-30; students & adults. Spec prog: Jazz 6 hrs, relg 14 hrs, Sp 8 hrs wkly. ■ Trent Wakenight, gen mgr; Ward Holloway, mus dir; Ed Walters, chief engr.

WWJQ(AM)—Nov 2, 1956: 1260 khz; 5 kw-D, 1 kw-N, DA-1. TL: N42 43 56 W86 06 06. Hrs opn: 24. 5658-143rd Ave. (49423). (616) 394-1260. FAX: (616) 394-9008. Licensee: Lanser Broadcasting Corp. (acq 11-1-83; $950,000; FTR 10-3-83). Net: ABC/I, AP. Rep: Michigan. Wash atty: Reddy, Begley & Martin. Format: Relg. News staff one; news progmg 9 hrs wkly. Target aud: 35 plus; mature adults. Spec prog: Sp 2 hrs, farm one hr wkly. ■ Leslie J. Lanser, pres & gen mgr; Ramona Gainey, gen sls mgr; Jack Moelker, news dir; Verne Bawinkle, chief engr.

WJQK(FM)—(Zeeland). Co-owned with WWJQ(AM). Aug 23, 1971: 99.3 mhz; 5.1 kw. Ant 354 ft. TL: N42 47 31 W86 01 12 (CP: 4.7 kw, ant 371 ft., TL: N42 48 59 W85 57 24). Stereo. Hrs opn: 24. Licensee: Beacon Broadcasting Co. (acq 1-1-87). Net: ABC/D, AP. Format: Contemp Christian. News progmg 7 hrs wkly. Target aud: 25-49. ■ Dale Kompik, progmg mgr; Donn Rae, mus dir.

Houghton

WAAH(FM)—Sept 1, 1989: 102.3 mhz; 1.05 kw. Ant 554 ft. TL: N47 06 13 W88 34 04. 610 Sheldon Ave. (49931). (906) 482-7080; (906) 482-7081. FAX: (906) 482-9489. Licensee: Houghton Radio Group of N.C. Inc., creditor in possession (acq 5-26-92; no financial consideration; FTR 6-15-92). Net: SMN. Format: Adult contemp. ■ Gary Linna, gen mgr; Craig Sporalski, gen sls mgr; John Samuli, chief engr.

WCCY(AM)—1929: 1400 khz; 1 kw-U. TL: N47 08 06 W88 33 53. Hrs opn: 24. 313 Montezuma Ave. (49931). (906) 482-7700. Licensee: Al Greenfield, dba The Greenfield Group, receiver (group owner; acq 12-6-91; grpsl). Net: ABC/E. Rep: Patt. Format: Country. News staff one; news progmg 18 hrs wkly. Target aud: 25-65. Spec prog: Relg one hr, pub affrs one hr wkly. ■ Al Greenfield, pres; Justin M. Marzke, gen mgr; Edmund Janisse, gen sls mgr; Norm Koski, progmg dir; Dick Storm, news dir; Arthur Siewart, chief engr. ■ Rates: $10; 8; 10; 7.50.

WOLF-FM—Co-owned with WCCY(AM). March 7, 1980: 97.7 mhz; 875 w. Ant 508 ft. TL: N47 08 27 W88 32 26. Stereo. Prog sep from AM. Net: ABC/D. Format: Adult contemp, rock. News staff one; news progmg 15 hrs wkly. Target aud: 18-45. ■ Edward Janisse, sls dir; Kevin Erickson, progmg dir & mus dir. ■ Rates: $12; 12; 12; 12.

*WGGL-FM—February 1982: 91.1 mhz; 100 kw. Ant 809 ft. TL: N47 02 08 W88 41 43. Stereo. Hrs opn: 24. Box 45 (49931). (906) 482-8912. FAX: (906) 482-1207. Licensee: Minnesota Public Radio Inc. Net: APR, NPR; Minn. Pub. Format: Class, news. News staff one. Target aud: General. ■ William H. Kling, pres; Jill Burkland, stn mgr; Ron Gnadinger, opns mgr; Karen Bell-Hanson, dev dir; John Samuli, chief engr.

WOLF-FM—Listing follows WCCY(AM).

Houghton Lake

WHGR(AM)—July 1954: 1290 khz; 4.9 kw-D. TL: N44 17 51 W84 42 26. Hrs opn: 18. Box 468, 830 W. Houghton Lake Dr., Prudenville (48651). (517) 366-5364. FAX: (517) 366-6200. Licensee: Northlands Communications Inc. (acq 1988; $900,000). Net: ABC/I. Rep: Patt. Wash atty: Lauren Colby. Format: Nostalgia, easy lstng. News staff one; news progmg 2 hrs wkly. Target aud: 35 plus; general. ■ John M. Salov, pres & gen mgr; Barb Rigling, stn mgr; Corinne Williamson, prom mgr; Chris Allen, mus dir; Michael Bradford, chief engr. ■ Rates: $25; 18; 25; 15.

WUPS(FM)—Co-owned with WHGR(AM). July 1, 1961: 98.5 mhz; 100 kw. Ant 981 ft. TL: N44 17 18 W84 44 30. Stereo. Hrs opn: 24. Prog sep from AM. Net: ABC/C. Format: Adult contemp. News staff 2; news progmg 6 hrs wkly. Target aud: 25-54; general. ■ Rates: $38; 25; 38; 20.

Howell

WHMI(AM)—Feb 17, 1957: 1350 khz; 500 w-D, 29 w-N. TL: N42 36 09 W83 59 18. Hrs opn: 5 AM-1 AM. Box 935 (48844); 1372 W. Grand River (48843). (517) 546-0860. FAX: (517) 546-1758. Licensee: The Livingston Radio Co. (acq 3-3-89). Net: ABC/C, Westwood One. Rep: Michigan. Wash atty: Arent, Fox, Kintner, Plotkin & Kahn. Format: Adult contemp. News staff one; news progmg 10 hrs wkly. Target aud: 18-54. ■ Greg Jablonski, pres & chief engr; Marcia Jablonski, gen mgr; Al Pervin, gen sls mgr; Bonnie Mobley, prom mgr; Reed Kittredge, progmg dir; Jeff Welling, mus dir; Tim LaMotte, news dir.

WHMI-FM—Sept 1, 1977: 93.5 mhz; 3 kw. Ant 300 ft. TL: N42 39 47 W83 56 24. Stereo. Hrs opn: 5 AM-1 AM. Dups AM 97%.

Inkster

WJZZ(FM)—See Detroit.

WMKM(AM)—November 1956: 1440 khz; 1 kw-U. TL: N42 15 22 W83 21 48. Hrs opn: 24. 1514 E. Jefferson Ave., Detroit (48207). (313) 393-1044. Licensee: Great Lakes Radio Inc. (acq 11-27-89; $550,000; FTR 12-18-89). Net: Natl Black, Westwood One. Wash atty: Hogan & Hartson. Format: Black gospel. News progmg 4 hrs wkly. Target aud: 35 plus; adult black church audience. ■ Michael J. Gallagher, pres, gen mgr & sls mgr; Crystal D. Sampson, stn mgr & progmg dir; Roger Carter, mus dir; Michael Bradford, engrg dir. ■ Rates: $32; 32; 32; 32.

Interlochen

*WIAA(FM)—July 22, 1963: 88.7 mhz; 100 kw. Ant 1,225 ft. TL: N44 16 33 W85 42 49. Stereo. Hrs opn: 24. Box 199, Interlochen Ctr. for the Arts (49643). (616) 276-6171. FAX: (616) 276-6279. Licensee: Interlochen Center for the Arts. Net: NPR, APR, Mich. Pub. Wash atty: Arter & Hadden. Format: Class. News staff one; news progmg one hr wkly. Target aud: 35-65 plus; professional, arts-oriented, upper-income. Spec prog: Jazz 2 hrs, folk one hr wkly. ■ Thom Paulson, vp & dev dir; Eileen McCann, prom mgr; Edward Catton, progmg dir; Robert Allen, news dir & pub affrs dir; L. D. Greilick, chief engr.

Ionia

WION(AM)—Feb 1, 1953: 1430 khz; 5 kw-D, 330 w-N, DA-2. TL: N43 00 16 W85 05 09. Box 143, 1150 Haynor Rd. (48846). (616) 527-4400. Licensee: MacPherson Broadcasting Co. (acq 1993; FTR 9-6-93). Net: ABC/E; Mich. Farm. Rep: Michigan. Format: Country. Spec prog: Farm 8 hrs wkly. ■ Phyllis MacPherson, pres; Phil Cloud, progmg dir; Don Grunow, mus dir; Steve Howard, news dir; Don Missad, chief engr.

Iron Mountain

WIMK(FM)—Listing follows WMIQ(AM).

WJNR-FM—Aug 17, 1972: 101.5 mhz; 47 kw. Ant 620 ft. TL: N45 49 15 W88 02 38 (CP: 100 kw, ant 613 ft.). Stereo. Box 1062, 219 E. A St. (49801). (906) 774-5731. FAX: (906) 774-4542. Licensee: Wheeler Broadcasting of Michigan Inc. Group owner: Wheeler Broadcasting Inc. (acq 4-30-87). Format: Adult contemp. ■ Ray Wheeler, pres; Carrie Toretta, gen mgr; Dick Nimmer, chief engr.

WMIQ(AM)—January 1947: 1450 khz; 1 kw-U. TL: N45 49 16 16 W88 03 16. Box 10, 101 Kent St. (49801). (906) 774-4321. FAX: (906) 774-7799. Licensee: Iron Mountain-Kingsford Broadcasting Co. (acq 9-68). Net: ABC/E. Format: Classic hits. ■ Charles R. Henry, pres; Greg Jeffen, gen mgr; Kevin Rosenbloom, chief engr.

WIMK(FM)—Co-owned with WMIQ(AM). Dec 27, 1981: 93.1 mhz; 100 kw. Ant 590 ft. TL: N45 49 16 W88 02 28. Stereo. Prog sep from AM. Format: Hit rock. ■ Greg Jeffen, gen mgr.

Iron River

WIKB(AM)—Nov 18, 1949: 1230 khz; 1 kw-U. TL: N46 03 55 W88 38 17. Hrs opn: 5 AM-11 PM Mon.-Sat., 7 AM-10 PM Sun. Box AC (49935). (906) 265-5104. FAX: (906) 265-3486. Licensee: Northland Adv. Inc. (acq 1-1-65). Net: NBC. Rep: Roslin. Format: Oldies. News staff one; news progmg 15 hrs wkly. Target aud: General. ■ Gene Halker, pres; Jay Barry, gen mgr, gen sls mgr &

chief engr; Bill Leonoff, opns mgr & news dir. ■ Rates: $24; 24; 24; na.

WIKB-FM—Sept 25, 1981: 99.1 mhz; 50 kw. Ant 492 ft. TL: N46 06 03 W88 32 23. Stereo. Hrs opn: 5 AM-11 PM M-S, 7 AM-10 PM Sun. Dups AM 99%. Rep: Roslin. ■ Rates: Same as AM.

Ironwood

WIMI(FM)—Listing follows WJMS(AM).

WJMS(AM)—Nov 3, 1931: 590 khz; 5 kw-D, 1 kw-N, DA-N. TL: N46 25 25 W90 12 30. Hrs opn: 24. 222 S. Lawrence St. (49938). (906) 932-2411. Licensee: Roberts Broadcasting Inc. (group owner; acq 10-74). Net: CBS. Rep: D & R Radio. Format: Country. News staff one. Target aud: 25 plus. ■ W. Donald Roberts, pres; Edward Rickard, gen mgr; Scott Jaegar, gen sls mgr; Steve Resnick, progmg dir; Charles Gennero, chief engr.

WIMI(FM)—Co-owned with WJMS(AM). March 1976: 99.7 mhz; 100 kw. Ant 561 ft. TL: N46 25 25 W90 14 53. Stereo. Prog sep from AM. FAX: (906) 932-2485. Net: CBS Spectrum. Format: Adult contemp.

WUPM(FM)—Oct 17, 1977: 106.9 mhz; 53 kw. Ant 495 ft. TL: N46 28 18 W90 00 43. Box 107, 813 E. Cloverland Dr. (49938). (906) 932-5234. FAX: (906) 932-1548. Licensee: Big G Little O Inc. Net: ABC/C. Format: Adult contemp, top-40. ■ Charles H. Gervasio, pres & gen mgr; Ed McCullough, gen sls mgr; Greg Daniels, progmg dir.

Ishpeming

WIAN(AM)—1947: 1240 khz; 1 kw-U. TL: N46 30 16 W87 40 46. 110 W. Canada St. (49849). (906) 486-9937. FAX: (906) 225-1324. Licensee: Goetz Communications (acq 5-16-89). Net: NBC. Format: C&W. ■ Nathan Goetz, pres; Ron Wales, gen mgr; Janet Krause, gen sls mgr; Vicky Chystal, progmg dir; Victoria Prewitt, mus dir; Tom Feldhusen, news dir; Coral Howell, chief engr.

WJPD(FM)—Co-owned with WIAN(AM). May 15, 1975: 92.3 mhz; 100 kw. Ant 469 ft. TL: N46 30 51 W87 28 54. Stereo. Dups AM 100%. ■ Chuck Wilson, gen sls mgr; Norman Koski, progmg dir.

WMQT(FM)—Listing follows WMVN(AM).

WMVN(AM)—June 26, 1959: 970 khz; 5 kw-D. TL: N46 30 20 W87 32 24. Hrs opn: Sunrise-sunset. Box 467, N. 2nd & Ash St. (49849). (906) 485-5566. FAX: (906) 485-4585. Licensee: Taconite Broadcasting Inc. (acq 8-8-71). Net: USA. Format: Contemp Christian. Target aud: 12 plus; Christian youth. ■ William J. Blake, pres & gen mgr; Joe Austin, progmg dir.

WMQT(FM)—Co-owned with WMVN(AM). Jan 26, 1974: 107.5 mhz; 98 kw. Ant 528 ft. TL: N46 28 42 W87 37 21. Stereo. Hrs opn: 24. Prog sep from AM. (906) 485-5523. Net: NBC the Source. Rep: D & R Radio. Format: Adult contemp. News staff 2. Target aud: 18-49. ■ William J. Blake, pres & gen mgr; Tom Mogush, gen sls mgr; Jim Koski, progmg dir. ■ Rates: $28; 24; 22; 22.

Jackson

WIBM(AM)—1925: 1450 khz; 1 kw-U. TL: N42 13 16 W84 26 03. 2511 Kibby Rd. (49203). (517) 787-1450. FAX: (517) 784-9426. Licensee: Regional Hit Radio Inc. (acq 2-3-93; $2.5 million with co-located FM; FTR 3-1-93). Net: Unistar. Rep: Major Mkt. Format: Oldies. Spec prog: Pol 2 hrs, Sp one hr wkly. ■ Larry W. Patton, gen mgr; Debbie Whitaker, gen sls mgr; Dwayne Carver, progmg dir; Monica Harris, news dir.

WIBM-FM—1955: 94.1 mhz; 40 kw. Ant 551 ft. TL: N42 23 32 W84 40 00. Stereo. Dups AM 70%. ■ Tim Dalrymple, gen sls mgr; Allan Gibbs, progmg dir.

WJCO(AM)—January 1962: 1510 khz; 5.4 kw-D, DA. TL: N42 11 10 W84 22 39. Stereo. 1293 Floyd Ave. (49201). (517) 784-1510. FAX: (517) 782-9607. Licensee: Powerhouse Broadcast System Inc. Net: CBS, Westwood One. Rep: Patt. Format: C&W, news. News staff 2. Target aud: 25-54 plus; professional. Spec prog: Bluegrass 2 hrs, children's one hr wkly. ■ Zail Greenbain, pres & gen mgr; Cash McCall, opns mgr; Michael Bruening, prom mgr; Virginia Burroughs, mus dir; Robert Burnham, chief engr.

WJXQ(FM)—May 30, 1976: 106.1 mhz; 50 kw. Ant 489 ft. TL: N42 23 28 W84 37 22. Stereo. Hrs opn: 24. Box 26007, Lansing (48909); Suite 106, 2495 N. Cedar, Holt (48842). (517) 699-0111; (517) 788-6360. FAX: (517) 699-1880. Licensee: Regional Radio Corp. (acq 1969). Net: ABC/R. Rep: D & R Radio. Wash atty: Smithwick & Belendiuk. Format: AOR. News staff one; news progmg one hr wkly. Target aud: 18-44; baby boomers with an inclination for rock'n roll. ■ Myron P. Patten, pres; Dennis Mockler, vp & gen mgr; Debbie Whitaker-Platt, gen sls mgr; John Robinson, prom dir; Mark Stevens, progmg dir; Deb Hart, news dir; Michael Bradford, chief engr. ■ Rates: $75; 65; 70; 35.

WKHM(AM)—Dec 7, 1951: 970 khz; 1 kw-U, DA-2. TL: N42 11 39 W84 25 50. 1700 Glenshire Dr. (49201). (517) 787-9546. FAX: (517) 787-7517. Licensee: Cascades Broadcasting Inc. (acq 10-28-85; $567,000; FTR 9-9-85). Net: ABC/I. Rep: Christal. Format: Adult contemp, sports, talk. ■ Richard Ambs, pres; Greg O'Connor, progmg dir; Tom Krawczak, mus dir; Rob Pascoe, news dir; Michael Bradford, chief engr.

Kalamazoo

***NEW FM**—Not on air, target date unknown: 88.3 mhz; 10 kw. Ant 121 ft. 18 Zumberge Hall, Allendale (49401). Licensee: Grand Valley State University Board of Control.

WHEZ(AM)—See Portage.

***WIDR(FM)**—July 7, 1975: 89.1 mhz; 100 w. Ant 158 ft. TL: N42 16 55 W85 37 05. Stereo. Hrs opn: 24. Box 1511, Faunce Student Services, Western Mich Univ. (49007). (616) 387-6301; (616) 387-6305. Licensee: Western Michigan Univ. Board of Trustees. Net: AP. Format: Progsv rock. Target aud: 18-25; college students. Spec prog: Black 8 hrs, gospel 2 hrs, jazz 4 hrs, blues 3 hrs, folk 2 hrs, world 2 hrs, reggae one hr wkly. ■ Mark Hammady, gen mgr; Tammara Ball, prom dir; Walker Sisson, chief engr.

***WKDS(FM)**—October 1982: 89.9 mhz; 100 w. Ant 150 ft. TL: N42 14 36 W85 34 19. Stereo. Hrs opn: 8 AM-9 PM (Mon-Fri). 606 E. Kilgore Rd. (49001). (616) 337-0899; (616) 337-0271. FAX: (616) 337-0251. Licensee: Kalamazoo Board of Educ. Wash atty: Arent, Fox, Kinter, Plotkin & Kahn. Format: Div, educ. News progmg 3 hrs wkly. Target aud: High school & college students. ■ Robert Kucera, gen mgr; Del Farnsworth, prom mgr; Kristin Kirkpatrick, progmg dir; John Badham, chief engr.

WKFR-FM—See Battle Creek.

WKMI(AM)—August 1947: 1360 khz; 5 kw-D, 1 kw-N, DA-2. TL: N42 19 36 W85 31 39. Hrs opn: 24. Box 50911, 4154 Jennings Dr. (49005-0911). (616) 344-0111. FAX: (616) 344-4223. Licensee: Hicks Broadcasting Corp. (acq 7-86; grpsl; FTR 2-19-90). Net: ABC/I, Daynet. Rep: Katz. Wash atty: Reed, Smith, Shaw & McClay. Format: News/talk. News staff 3. Target aud: 25-54. ■ Ed Sackley, pres; Robert Miller, stn mgr; Phil Britain, chief opns; Steve Steimenoff, gen sls mgr; Glen Dillon, progmg dir; Dale Schiesser, chief engr. ■ Rates: $24; 20; 24; 14.

WKPR(AM)—Oct 20, 1960: 1420 khz; 1 kw-D, DA. TL: N42 18 46 W85 37 06. Box 50867, (49005); 2244 Ravine Rd. (49004). (616) 381-1420. Licensee: Kalamazoo Broadcasting Co. Group owner: Kuiper Stns. Net: USA. Format: Relg. Target aud: 25 plus. ■ William E. Kuiper Sr., pres; Doug Telfer, stn mgr, news dir & pub affrs dir; William E. Kuiper Jr., chief engr. ■ Rates: $8; 8; 8; na.

WKZO(AM)—Sept 10, 1931: 590 khz; 5 kw-U, DA-N. TL: N42 21 00 W85 33 43. Hrs opn: 24. 590 W. Maple St. (49008). (616) 345-2101. FAX: (616) 382-1041. Licensee: Radio Associates of Michigan Inc. Group owner: Radio Associates (acq 4-15-92; $4.62 million with WBCT[FM] Grand Rapids; FTR 5-11-92). Net: CBS, MBS; Mich. Net; Mich. Farm. Rep: McGavren Guild. Format: News/talk. News staff 15. Target aud: 35-64; upscale; 60% male, 40% female. Spec prog: Farm 10 hrs, relg 5 hrs wkly. ■ Robert Salmon, pres; David Steere, exec vp, gen mgr & stn mgr; Jerry Raffel, gen sls mgr; Mike Keyworth, prom mgr & progmg dir; Mark Fricke, news dir; Todd Van Dyke, pub affrs dir; Charles Gustafson, chief engr.

***WMUK(FM)**—Jan 8, 1951: 102.1 mhz; 50 kw. Ant 490 ft. TL: N42 25 03 W85 31 55. Stereo. Hrs opn: 5:30 AM-12:30 AM. Friedmann Hall, W. Michigan Univ. (49008-5003). (616) 387-5715. FAX: (616) 387-4630. Licensee: Western Michigan Univ. Net: NPR; Mich. Pub. Format: Classical, pub affrs, news/talk. News staff 2; news progmg 38 hrs wkly. Target aud: General. Spec prog: Sp one hr, jazz 6 hrs, bluegrass 8 hrs wkly. ■ Garrard D. Macleod, gen mgr & progmg dir; Klay Woodworth, opns dir; Elizabeth King, dev mgr; Floyd Pientka, mus dir; Anthony E. Griffin, news dir; Mark Tomlonson, chief engr.

WNWN(FM)—(Coldwater). Nov 11, 1950: 98.5 mhz; 50 kw. Ant 500 ft. TL: N42 03 28 W84 59 51. Stereo. Hrs opn: 24. 6021 S. Westnedge Ave., Kalamazoo (49002). (616) 342-0070. FAX: (616) 342-8948. Licensee: Tri-State Broadcasting (acq 4-1-72). Net: ABC/E. Wash atty: Tierney & Swift. Format: Contemp country. News staff 3; news progmg 5 hrs wkly. Target aud: 25-54. ■ Gary B. Mallernee, pres & gen mgr; Jim Suski, gen sls mgr; Denny Bice, progmg dir & mus dir; Jim Whelan, news dir; Mike Peters, chief engr.

WQLR(FM)—Listing follows WQSN(AM).

WQSN(AM)—Feb 4, 1956: 1470 khz; 800 w-D, 1 kw-N. TL: N42 21 41 W85 34 37. Stereo. 4200 W. Main St. (49006). (616) 345-7121. Licensee: Fairfield Broadcasting Co. (group owner; acq 7-1-85; $175,000; FTR 4-1-85). Rep: Banner. Wash atty: David Tillorson. Format: Sports. Target aud: 25-64; sports fans, primarily men. ■ Stephen C. Trivers, pres & gen mgr; William J. Wertz, sr vp; Ken Lanphear, opns mgr & progmg dir; Dennis Martin, gen sls mgr; Dan Chamberlin, prom mgr; Jodi Victor, news dir; Bob Torstenson, chief engr.

WQLR(FM)—Co-owned with WQSN(AM). June 19, 1964: 106.5 mhz; 33 kw. Ant 600 ft. TL: N42 28 32 W85 29 22. Stereo. Prog sep from AM. Rep: Banner. Format: Adult contemp. News staff one. Target aud: 25-54; two-income home owners; families. ■ William J. Wertz, mus dir.

WRKR(FM)—(Portage). Oct 13, 1988: 107.7 mhz; 50 kw. Ant 500 ft. TL: N42 07 43 W85 20 16. Stereo. Hrs opn: 24. Box 50911, 4154 Jennings Dr., Kalamazoo (49005-0911). (616) 344-0111; (616) 964-7173. FAX: (616) 344-4223. Licensee: Crystal Radio Group Inc. (group owner; acq 6-18-93; FTR 7-5-93). Net: ABC/R. Rep: Katz. Wash atty: Fisher, Wayland, Cooper & Leader. Format: Classic rock, AOR. News staff 2; news progmg 4 hrs wkly. Target aud: 18-44 adults. Spec prog: Blues 3 hrs wkly. ■ Ed Sackley, CEO, pres & gen mgr; David L. Hicks, chmn & exec vp; John Strandin, vp; Phil Britain, opns mgr; David L. Hines, sls dir; Steve Stoimenoff, gen sls mgr; Mike Childs, progmg dir & mus dir; Tom Hill, asst mus dir; Leanne Agne, news dir & pub affrs dir; Walker Sisson, chief engr.

Kalkaska

***WKAL(AM)**—Sept 15, 1982: 1420 khz; 500 w-D, DA. TL: N44 43 12 W85 10 23. Box 580 (49646). (616) 258-8803; (616) 258-9167. FAX: (616) 258-4474. Licensee: Kalkaska Area Educational Foundation Inc. (acq 1-18-91; FTR 2-4-91). Format: Classical, educ, div. News progmg 5 hrs wkly. Target aud: General; county residents. ■ Doyle Disbrow, pres; Scott Yost, engrg mgr.

WKLT(FM)—April 8, 1979: 97.5 mhz; 32 kw. Ant 670 ft. TL: N44 47 29 W85 14 20. Stereo. Hrs opn: 24. 745 S. Garfield, Traverse City (49684). (616) 947-0003. FAX: (616) 947-7002. Licensee: Northern Radio of Michigan (acq 1-82; $320,000; FTR 1-18-82). Net: ABC/R. Rep: Banner. Wash atty: Reddy, Begley & Martin. Format: Rock. News progmg 2 hrs wkly. Target aud: 25-54; baby boomers & young adults. Spec prog: Comedy 2 hrs wkly. ■ Richard Dills, pres; Reggie Box, gen mgr & natl sls mgr; DeeAnn Davis, gen sls mgr; Tom Pluister, prom mgr; David Fortney, progmg dir; Brian Sullivan, mus dir; Pete Misiak, news dir; Susan Melton, pub affrs dir; Dennis Murray, chief engr.

Kentwood

***WGVU(AM)**—Licensed to Kentwood. See Grand Rapids.

WKWM(AM)—Sept 18, 1978: 1140 khz; 5 kw-D, DA. TL: N42 56 13 W85 27 20. Box 828 (49518). (616) 676-1237. FAX: (616) 676-2329. Licensee: Richard Culpepper. Net: American Urban. Rep: Patt. Wash atty: Lauren Colby. Format: Urban contemp. Target aud: 18-49. Spec prog: Jazz 6 hrs, relg 12 hrs wkly. ■ Richard Culpepper, gen mgr & chief engr; Tracy Darby, opns mgr; Coy Davis, gen sls mgr; Lee Cadena, prom dir & mus dir.

Kingsford

***WEUL(FM)**—Feb 11, 1990: 98.1 mhz; 240 w. Ant 482 ft. TL: N45 49 58 W88 04 57. 130 Carmen Dr., Marquette (49855). (906) 249-1423. Licensee: Gospel Opportunities Inc. Format: Christian. ■ W. Curtis Marker, gen mgr & progmg dir; Terry Dalby, chief engr.

Lakeview

WPLB-FM—November 1989: 106.3 mhz; 3 kw. Ant 328 ft. TL: N43 24 33 W85 15 53. Stereo. Box 578, 9181 S. Greenville Rd., Greenville (48838). (616) 754-3656. Licensee: Kortes Communications Inc. (acq 3-19-93; $72,500; FTR 4-12-93). Format: Country. ■ Jeff Kortes, gen mgr.

Lansing

WILS(AM)—July 17, 1947: 1320 khz; 5 kw-D, 1 kw-N, DA-2. TL: N42 41 30 W84 33 38. 600 W. Cavanaugh Rd. (48910). (517) 393-1320. FAX: (517) 393-0882. Licensee: MacDonald Broadcasting Co. (group owner; acq 3-9-89); $2,150,000 with co-located FM; FTR 3-27-89). Rep: Christal. Format: Classic country. News staff one. Target aud: 25-54; Spec prog: Smart shopper 6 hrs wkly. ■ John Dew, vp & gen mgr; Rick Walker, opns mgr & progmg mgr; Julie Lindell (local); Jeff Mason, prom mgr & pub affrs dir; Larry Estlack, chief engr.

WILS-FM—January 1967: 101.7 mhz; 2.1 kw. Ant 377 ft. TL: N42 41 30 W84 33 38. Stereo. Box 25008 (48909). Target aud: 18-49; upscale adults. ■ Rates: $35; 35; 35; 35.

WITL(AM)—June 26, 1961: 1010 khz; 500 w-D, 13 w-N, DA-2. TL: N42 40 32 W84 30 06. Stereo. 3200 Pine Tree Rd. (48911). (517) 393-1010. FAX: (517) 393-3650. Licensee: MSP Communications Inc. (acq 11-16-88; $10.22 million with co-located FM; FTR 12-19-88). Net: ABC/I. Rep: Banner. Format: Country. News staff 2; news progmg 11 hrs wkly. Target aud: 25-54. ■ Gregory K. Capogna, gen mgr; Bill Pacelli, gen sls mgr; Mike Bellemy, prom mgr; Jay J. McCrae, progmg dir; Meyno Lyons, news dir; Kevin Larke, chief engr.

WITL-FM—April 15, 1964: 100.7 mhz; 26.5 kw. Ant 640 ft. TL: N42 40 33 W84 30 00. Stereo. Dups AM 98%.

WJIM(AM)—1934: 1240 khz; 1 kw-U. TL: N42 44 22 W84 30 39. Hrs opn: 24. Suite 16A, 300 N. Clippert (48912). (517) 332-0975. FAX: (517) 332-2418. Licensee: Liggett Broadcast Inc. (group owner; acq 5-93); $3.5 million with co-located FM; FTR 5-10-93). Net: NBC, NBC Talknet. Rep: Eastman. Format: News, info, talk. Target aud: 25-54. ■ Jim Jensen, pres; Rod Krol, exec vp; Tim Spires, gen mgr & vp prom; Jack Robbins, prom mgr & progmg mgr; Don Riggs, news dir; Ted Frantz, chief engr.

WJIM-FM—June 1960: 97.5 mhz; 28 kw-H. Ant 440 ft. TL: N42 44 23 W84 30 43 (CP: 50 kw, ant 492 ft., TL: N42 38 45 W84 33 38). Stereo. Hrs opn: 24. Prog sep from AM. Net: Westwood One, MBS; Mich. Net. Format: Adult contemp.

WJXQ(FM)—See Jackson.

*WLNZ(FM)—Not on air, target date unknown: 89.7 mhz; 100 w. Ant 98 ft. Box 40010 (48901). Licensee: Lansing Community College.

WMMQ(FM)—See Charlotte.

WVFN(AM)—See East Lansing.

WVIC-FM—See East Lansing.

WWDX(FM)—See St. Johns.

WWSJ(AM)—See St. Johns.

Lapeer

*WMPC(AM)—Dec 6, 1926: 1230 khz; 1 kw-U. TL: N43 04 46 W83 18 35. Hrs opn: 24 Box 104, 1800 N. Lapeer Rd. (48446). (313) 664-6211. FAX: (313) 664-5361. Licensee: The Calvary Bible Church of Lapeer Inc. Net: AP, Skylight. Format: Relg. News staff one; news progmg 24 hrs wkly. Target aud: General. ■ Arnold L. Bracy, gen mgr; Greg Yoder, news dir; Robert Wolfe, chief engr.

WWGZ(AM)—Nov 16, 1962: 1530 khz; 5 kw-D, DA-D. TL: N43 01 35 W83 17 12. 286 W. Nepessing St. (48446). (313) 664-8555; (313) 238-1038. FAX: (313) 664-8990. Licensee: Covenant Communications Corp. (acq 76-14-90); with co-located FM; FTR 7-15-91). Net: USA. Rep: Patt. Wash atty: Earl Stanley. Format: Classic country. News staff one; news progmg 9 hrs wkly. Target aud: 35 plus. Spec prog: Farm 5 hrs, rgn'l 3 hrs, sports 4 hrs wkly. ■ Donald E. Weber, CEO, pres & gen mgr; Jay Alexander, vp & opns mgr; Joe Bellanca, gen sls mgr; Cindy Miller, prom mgr; Jerry Tarrants, progmg dir; Jeff Holbrook, mus dir; Juli Jay, news dir & pub affrs dir; Ed Czelada, chief engr. ■ Rates: $12; 8; 12; 12.

WWGZ-FM—Feb 6, 1968: 103.1 mhz; 3 kw. Ant 299 ft. TL: N43 04 49 W83 11 30. Stereo. Net: Westwood One. Wash atty: Wilkinson, Barker, Knauer & Quinn. Format: Adult rock. Target aud: 25-40; college educated men & women. Spec prog: In concert: Sunday blues, "On the Edge"(AOR), Spiriting (gospel). ■ Cindy Miller, prom dir; Juli Jay, mus dir. ■ Rates: $20; 18; 20; 8.

Leland

WTRV(FM)—Aug 9, 1991: 94.3 mhz; 3.6 kw. Ant 426 ft. TL: N46 54 48 W85 49 18 (CP: 14.88 kw). Stereo. Hrs opn: 24. Prog dups WAIR(FM), Atlanta. 322 Bay St., Petoskey (49770); 207 Grandview Pkwy., Traverse City (49684). (616) 348-2000. FAX: (616) 348-2092. Licensee: Grand Traverse Broadcasting Co. Net: CBS, Unistar. Rep: Patt. Wash atty: Reddy, Begley & Martin.

Format: Oldies. News staff one; news progmg 7 hrs wkly. Target aud: 25-54. ■ Richard D. Stone, pres & gen mgr; Cliff Carey, stn mgr & opns mgr; Carlin Smith, news dir.

Lexington

WBTI(FM)—July 13, 1991: 96.9 mhz; 3 kw. Ant 328 ft. TL: N43 12 34 W82 32 10. Stereo. Hrs opn: 24. Broadcast House, 2379 Military St., Port Huron (48060); 251 Campbell St., Sarnia, ON (N7T 2H2). (313) 987-4100; (519) 337-5853. Licensee: Hanson Communications Inc. (acq 6-29-92; $350,000; FTR 7-20-92). Rep: Patt. Format: CHR. Target aud: 18-34. ■ Lee C. Hanson, pres & gen mgr; Al Tyrrell, gen sls mgr; Kevin Miller, progmg dir & news dir; Eric C. Hanson, chief engr.

Livonia

WCAR(AM)—Oct 23, 1963: 1090 khz; 250 w-D, 500 w-N, DA-2. TL: N42 19 46 W83 21 43. 32500 Park Ln., Garden City (48135). (313) 525-1111. FAX: (313) 525-3608. Licensee: Wolpin Broadcasting Co. Group owner: Twin W Communications Inc. (acq 5-1-69). Format: Talk, ethnic. Spec prog: Japanese one hr, Arabic 3 hrs, Hispanic 5 hrs wkly. ■ Walter Wolpin, pres; Jack Bailey, gen mgr; Michael Borkowski, gen sls mgr; David Wallace Johnson, progmg dir & news dir; Bob Burnham, chief engr.

Ludington

WKLA(AM)—Oct 9, 1944: 1450 khz; 1 kw-U. TL: N43 57 05 W86 25 28. 5941 W., U.S. 10 (49431). (616) 843-3438. Licensee: Chickering Associates Inc. (acq 9-4-90; $450,000 with co-located FM; FTR 9-24-90). Format: Easy lstng. ■ John E. Chickering, pres; Kathy Gale, gen mgr; Jim Frost, gen sls mgr; Ray Cummins, news dir; Bob Engblade, chief engr.

WKLA-FM—May 1971: 106.3 mhz; 4.1 kw. Ant 400 ft. TL: N43 03 30 W86 24 59. Stereo. Dups AM 19%. Format: Adult contemp.

WKZC(FM)—See Scottville.

Mackinaw City

WFGE(FM)—Sept 6, 1989: 94.3 mhz; 3 kw. Ant 300 ft. TL: N45 46 49 W84 44 06. Stereo. Stn currently dark. Box 422, Ashley, IN (46705). (616) 436-7022. Licensee: Robert A. Naismith (acq 2-20-92). ■ Sonora S. Wray, pres; Otto Mashun, progmg dir; James A. Chase, chief engr.

Manistee

WMTE(AM)—June 7, 1951: 1340 khz; 1 kw-U. TL: N44 14 07 W86 19 05. Box 190, 359 River St. (49660). (616) 723-9906. Licensee: Manistee Broadcasting Corp. (acq 11-86). Net: NBC, NBC Talknet. Rep: Michigan. Format: Classic rock. Target aud: 35 plus. ■ Paul Bosschem, pres; Laurie Foster, progmg dir & mus dir; Bernie Schroeder, news dir; Thomas Peterson, chief engr.

WMTE-FM—Aug 1, 1970: 97.7 mhz; 3 kw. Ant 200 ft. TL: N48 14 07 W86 19 05. Prog dups from AM. Net: Mich. Net. Format: Jazz. Target aud: 21-50.

WXYQ(FM)—Not on air, target date May 1, 1994: 101.5 mhz. 3 kw. Ant 105 ft. TL: N44 12 18 W86 17 22. Stereo. Hrs opn: 24. Suite 106, 4359 S. Howell Ave., Milwaukee WI (53207). (414) 482-2638; (414) 482-1980. FAX: (414) 483-1980. Licensee: Bay View Broadcasting Inc. Format: Adult contemp. Spec prog: Pol 6 hrs wkly. ■ Rates: $12; 10; 10; 5.

Manistique

WTIQ(AM)—Feb 11, 1968: 1490 khz; 1 kw-U. TL: N45 57 51 W86 16 37. Stereo. Box 220, 1501 Deer St. Manistique (49854). (906) 341-6601. FAX: (906) 341-2024. FAX: (906) 341-6222. Licensee: WSHN Inc. (group owner; acq 12-24-90; grpsl; FTR 1-14-91). Net: MBS; MNN. Wash atty: Meyer, Faller, Weisman & Rosenberg. Format: Soft hits. News staff 2; news progmg 40 hrs wkly. Target aud: 25-54; blue & white collar. ■ Todd Noordyk, gen mgr & vp sls; L. David Vaugn, stn mgr; Art Udight, vp prom; L. David Vaughn, vp progmg; Beth Ann Gyorke, news dir; Bill Becks, vp engrg. ■ Rates: $9; 9; 9; 9.

Marine City

WIFN(AM)—Dec 10, 1951: 1590 khz; 1 kw-D, 102 w-N, DA-1. TL: N42 43 42 W82 31 15. Box 310, 5300 Marine City Hwy. (48039). (313) 765-8893; (313) 329-9666. FAX: (313) 765-8894. Licensee: Richard S. Somerville, trustee (acq 5-29-92; $110,000; FTR 6-22-92). Net: Mutual. Wash atty: Wilkinson, Barker & Quinn. Format:

Country, talk. News staff one; news progmg 14 hrs wkly. Target aud: General; 25-54. Spec prog: Pol 3 hrs wkly. ■ David Ball, pres; Rick Schremp, opns mgr & progmg dir; Dave Haze, mus dir; Denis Napolitan, news dir. ■ Rates: $17; 17; 17; 17.

Marlette

WBGV(FM)—Not on air, target date unknown: 92.5 mhz; 3 kw. Ant. 328 ft. TL: N43 17 10 W82 58 17. Box 224 (48453). Licensee: GB Broadcasting Co. (acq 6-5-92).

Marquette

WDMJ(AM)—July 1, 1931: 1320 khz; 5 kw-D, 1 kw-N, DA-N. TL: N46 32 40 W87 26 42. 845 W. Washington St. (49855). (906) 225-1313. FAX: (906) 225-1324. Licensee: John H. Hackman Group owner: Goetz Broadcasting Corp. (acq 8-29-89; $90,000; FTR 9-11-89). Net: ABC/E. Rep: Michigan. Format: Classic rock. News staff one; news progmg 12 hrs wkly. Target aud: 25-54. ■ Ron Wales, gen mgr; Victoria Pruett, progmg mgr.

WFXD(FM)—Apr 6, 1974: 103.3 mhz; 100 kw. Ant 544 ft. TL: N46 30 52 W87 28 37. Stereo. Hrs opn: 24. 832 W. Washington St. (49855). (906) 228-6800. FAX: (906) 228-5766. Licensee: Vista Pointe Communications, Inc. (acq 4-25-90; $445,000; FTR 5-21-90). Net: MBS, SMN. Rep: Christal. Wash atty: Lukas, McGowan, Nace & Gutierrez. Format: Oldies. News staff one; news progmg 12 hrs wkly. Target aud: 25-54. ■ William J. Young, chmn; Kris Erik Stevens, pres; David Peterson, gen mgr, prom mgr & progmg dir; Barry Ray, news dir & pub affrs dir; Al Meeves, chief engr. ■ Rates: $15; 13; 15; 13.

*WHWL(FM)—Dec 16, 1965: 95.7 mhz; 100 kw. Ant 531 ft. TL: N46 29 52 W87 24 59. Stereo. 130 Carmen Dr. (49855). (906) 249-1423. Licensee: Gospel Opportunities Inc. (acq 4-19-76). Format: Relg. ■ Curt Marker, gen mgr; Terry Dalby, chief engr.

WIAN(AM)—See Ishpeming.

*WNMU-FM—August 1963: 90.1 mhz; 100 kw. Ant 930 ft. TL: N46 21 09 W87 51 32. Stereo. Learning Resources Ctr., Northern Michigan U., Elizabeth Harden Circle Dr. (49855). (906) 227-2600. FAX: (906) 227-2905. Licensee: Board of Control of Northern Michigan University. Net: NPR, APR, AP; Mich. Pub. Wash atty: Cohn & Marks. Format: Classical, jazz, news. News staff one; new progmg 31 hrs wkly. Spec prog: Educ. ■ Scott Seaman, gen mgr; Susan Sherman, stn mgr; Bill Hart, opns mgr; Gregg Beukema, prom mgr; Stan Wright, mus dir; Jim Russell-Parks, news dir; Earl Littich, chief engr.

WUPK(FM)—Not on air, target date unknown: 94.1 mhz; 4.5 kw. Ant 377 ft. TL: N46 30 52 W87 28 37. Box 190, 105 E. Kent St., Iron Mountain (49801). Licensee: Iron Range Broadcasting Co. Inc.

*WUPX(FM)—Not on air, target date unknown: 91.5 mhz; 200 w. Ant 138 ft. TL: N46 34 44 W87 23 42. Cohodas Administration Ctr. (49855). (906) 227-2348. Licensee: Board of Control of Northern Michigan University. ■ WNMU-TV affil.

Marshall

WALM(AM)—See Albion.

WELL-FM—Licensed to Marshall. See Albion.

Mason

*WUNN(AM)—May 11, 1967: 1110 khz; 1 kw-D, DA. TL: N42 33 04 W84 24 15. Box 288, 1571 Tomlinson Rd. (48854). (517) 676-2488. FAX: (517) 676-3705. Licensee: Family Life Broadcasting System (group owner; acq 1-1-69). Net: AP. Format: Relg. News progmg 5 hrs wkly. Target aud: General; Christian families. ■ Warren Bolthouse, pres; Randy Carlson, exec vp; Dave Phelps, gen mgr; Rod Robison, dev dir; Jon Couch, mus dir; Dick Lindley, engrg mgr.

Menominee

WAGN(AM)—Nov 14, 1952: 1340 khz; 1 kw-U. TL: N45 06 27 W87 36 25. Hrs opn: 20. Box 365, 413 Tenth Ave. (49858). (906) 863-5551. Licensee: Good Neighbor Broadcasting Inc. (acq 10-90). Net: ABC/I, Moody. Wash atty: McCabe & Allen. Format: MOR, oldies. News staff 2; news progmg 15 hrs wkly. Target aud: 30 plus; older, affluent adults. Spec prog: CBS radio sports, local sports. ■ William Sauve, pres, gen mgr & gen sls mgr; Chuck Patrick, progmg dir; Jim Callow, news dir & chief engr. ■ Rates: $8; 8; 8; 8.

WHYB(FM)—Co-owned with WAGN(AM). Oct 24, 1984: 103.9 mhz; 3 kw. Ant 300 ft. TL: N45 04 00 W87 39 55. Stereo. Hrs opn: 24. FAX: (906) 863-5679. (acq

Country. News staff 2; news progmg 5 hrs wkly. Target aud: 35-64. ■ Jim Callow, opns mgr. ■ Rates: $11; 11; 11; 11.

WMAM(AM)—See Marinette, Wis.

Midland

WKQZ(FM)—Dec 14, 1976: 93.3 mhz; 39.2 kw. Ant 554 ft. TL: N43 50 46 W84 05 32. Stereo. Box 6393, Saginaw (48608); 2080 Gordonville Rd. (48640). (517) 695-5115. FAX: (517) 695-5376. Licensee: Windward Communications Inc. (acq 9-15-90; $2.01 million; FTR 7-9-90). Net: ABC/R. Rep: Banner. Wash atty: Reddy, Begley & Martin. Format: AOR. Target aud: 25-44; males. ■ R. Charles McLravy, pres; Michael C. Thomas, gen mgr; Rick Church, opns mgr, progmg dir & mus dir; Ray Nelson, gen sls mgr; Joe Volk, news dir; Doug Brinks, chief engr.

WMPX(AM)—Sept 11, 1948: 1490 khz; 1 kw-U, DA-2. TL: N43 36 48 W84 13 17. Hrs opn: 24. 1510 Bayliss St. (48640); Box 1513 (48642). (517) 631-1490; (517) 631-2220. FAX: (517) 695-9679. Licensee: Steel Broadcasting Inc. (acq 8-19-81; $900,000; FTR 8-24-81). Net: SMN. Rep: Patt. Format: Adult contemp. News staff one; news progmg 9 hrs wkly. Target aud: General. Spec prog: Sounds of Sinatra; relg 3 hrs wkly. ■ Thomas Steel, pres & gen mgr; Thomas Schelich, gen sls mgr; Lee Monday, pub affrs dir; Joe Goddeyne, chief engr. ■ Rates: $25; 25; 25; 12.50.

***WUGN(FM)**—Dec 2, 1973: 99.7 mhz; 100 kw. Ant 712 ft. TL: N43 30 56 W84 32 49. Stereo. Box 366, 510 E. Isabella Rd. (48640). (517) 631-7060. Licensee: Family Life Broadcasting System (group owner; acq 9-26-73). Net: MBN. Format: Relg. ■ Warren Bolthouse, pres; Peter Brooks, gen mgr; Lee Welch, news dir; Tim Coston, chief engr.

Mio

WCLX(FM)—Not on air, target date 1994: 93.9 mhz; 50 kw. 433 ft. TL: N44 43 40 W84 21 35. Stereo. Hrs opn: 24. Rebroadcasts WCLS(FM) Oscoda 90%. Box 296, Suite 8, 5737 North U.S. 23, Oscoda (48750). (517) 739-8180. FAX: (517) 739-7788. Licensee: Todd A. Mohr. Group owner: Spectrum Communications. Rep: Patt. Format: Soft adult contemp.

Monroe

WCSX(FM)—See Birmingham.

***WEJY(FM)**—November 1978: 97.5 mhz; 8 w. Ant 135 ft. TL: N41 55 07 W83 26 12. 1275 N. Macomb St. (48161); Monroe High School, 901 Herr Rd., (48161). (313) 241-1491, EXT. 252. Licensee: Monroe Public Schools (acq 8-77). Format: AOR, var/div. News progmg 5 hrs wkly. Target aud: 15-24. ■ Eric Diroff, gen mgr; Leisa Castellese, progmg dir; Ethan Klump, mus dir; Tennille Teague, news dir; Christine Edwards, pub affrs dir; Milward Beaudry, chief engr.

WHND(AM)—July 12, 1956: 560 khz; 500 w-D, 27 w-N. TL: N41 53 28 W83 25 39. One Radio Plaza (48220). (313) 398-7600. FAX: (313) 542-0313. Licensee: Greater Michigan Radio Inc. Group owner: Greater Media Inc. Rep: McGavren Guild. Format: Oldies. ■ Tom Bender, gen mgr; Bruce Stoller, gen sls mgr; Richard D. Haase, progmg dir; Bob Dietsch, chief engr.

WTWR-FM—July 16, 1967: 98.3 mhz; 1.4 kw. Ant 465 ft. TL: N41 50 43 W83 27 59. Stereo. 7 S. Monroe St. (48161). (313) 242-6600. FAX: (313) 242-6599. Licensee: Lesnick Communications Inc. (acq 8-2-82; $570,000; FTR 9-20-82). Rep: Patt. Format: Adult contemp. News staff one. Target aud: 25-54. ■ Bruce Randolph Lesnick, pres; Tom Treece, stn mgr; Terri McCormick, progmg dir & mus dir; John Zadikian, news dir; Bill Mullen, chief engr. ■ Rates: $28; 24; 26; 20.

Mount Clemens

WBRB(AM)—May 18, 1957: 1430 khz; 500 w-U, DA-2. TL: N42 32 43 W82 54 03. 32500 Parklane, Garden City (48135). (313) 525-1111. Licensee: Wolpin Broadcasting Co. (acq 10-26-92; $1,005; FTR 11-23-92). ■ Jack Bailey, gen mgr.

WDZR(FM)—Nov 6, 1960: 102.7 mhz; 50 kw. Ant 499 ft. TL: N42 32 39 W82 54 09. Stereo. Hrs opn: 24. 850 Stephenson Hwy. 405, Troy (48083). (313) 589-7900. Licensee: Ragan A. Henry National Radio, L.P. Group owner: Ragan Henry Broadcast Group Inc. Net: ABC, SMN, NBC the Source. Rep: D & R. Format: Hard rock. News staff one; news progmg 10 hrs wkly. Target aud: 18-39; rock & rollers of all ages that like today's rock & roll. ■ Ragan A. Henry, pres; Robert Schutt, vp; Joe Bevilacqua, prom dir; Bill Mullin, chief engr. ■ Rates: $90; 110; 120; 80.

Mount Pleasant

WCEN(AM)—Aug 8, 1949: 1150 khz; 1 kw-D, 500 w-N, DA-2. TL: N43 34 36 W84 45 57. Stereo. Hrs opn: 24. Box 407, 4151 Bluegrass Rd. (48804-0407). (517) 773-5961. FAX: (517) 772-9420. Licensee: Sommerville Broadcasting (acq 5-1-86; $1.35 million with co-located FM; FTR 3-31-86). Net: Moody. Rep: Patt. Wash atty: Wilkinson, Barker, Knauer & Quinn. Format: Oldies. News staff 2; news progmg 20 hrs wkly. Target aud: 35 plus; middle class, above-average income. Spec prog: Farm 5 hrs wkly. ■ Richard Sommerville, pres & gen mgr; James Sommerville, opns mgr & mus dir; Sharon McVicker, gen sls mgr; Duane Taft, news dir; Richard Leonard, chief engr. ■ Rates: $27; 27; 27; 18.

WCEN-FM—Aug 8, 1963: 94.5 mhz; 100 kw. Ant 994 ft. TL: N43 43 36 W84 36 16. Stereo. Hrs opn: 24. Prog sep from AM. Net: MBS. Format: Modern country. Target aud: 25-54. medium income, both rural & urban. ■ Rates: Same as AM.

WCFX(FM)—See Clare.

***WCMU-FM**—April 6, 1964: 89.5 mhz; 100 kw. Ant 423 ft. TL: N43 34 24 W84 46 21. Stereo. Hrs opn: 24. Public Broadcasting Ctr., Central Michigan Univ. (48859). (517) 774-3105. FAX: (517) 774-4427. Licensee: Central Michigan U. Net: NPR, APR; Mich. Pub. Wash atty: Dow, Lohnes & Albertson. Format: Class, jazz, news & info. News staff 2; news progmg 30 hrs wkly. Target aud: General. ■ Thomas Hunt, gen mgr; Linda Hyde, prom mgr; Ray Ford, progmg dir; Randy Kapenga, chief engr. ■ *WCMU-TV affil.

WCZY-FM—Aug 20, 1991: 104.3 mhz; 3 kw. Ant 328 ft. TL: N43 35 39 W84 49 26. Stereo. 4065 E. Wing Rd. (48858). (517) 772-9664; (517) 773-5000. Licensee: Central Michigan Communications Inc. Net: Jones Satellite Audio. Rep: Michigan. Wash atty: Reddy, Begley & Martin. Format: Easy lstng. News staff one. Target aud: Adults; 30 plus. ■ Mike Carey, pres, gen mgr & gen sls mgr; Steve Conley, progmg dir & mus dir; Jim Hughes, news dir; Darel Vanderhoof, chief engr. ■ Rates: $9.75; 9.75; 9.75; 9.75.

***WMHW-FM**—Nov 20, 1972: 91.5 mhz; 307 w. Ant 112 ft. TL: N43 35 12 W84 46 24. Stereo. 180 Moore Hall, Central Mich U. (48859). (517) 774-7287; (517) 774-3851. Licensee: Bd of Trustees, Central Michigan U. Format: New age, progressive. ■ J. Robert Craig, gen mgr; Jerry Henderson, opns mgr; Randy Kapenga, chief engr.

Munising

WQXO(AM)—Sept 20, 1955: 1400 khz; 1 kw-U. TL: N46 24 30 W86 38 22. Hrs opn: 24. Box 100, 110 W. Onota St. (49862). (906) 387-4000; (800) 236-4007. FAX: (906) 387-5161. Licensee: Mid Pen Broadcasting Inc. (acq 1-15-91; with co-located FM). Net: SMN; Mich. Net. Rep: Patt. Wash atty: Haley, Bader & Potts. Format: Big band, oldies. Target aud: 25-54. ■ Wallace D. Steinhoff, pres; Thomas E. Brazil, gen mgr; Wendy Doucette, progmg dir; Dan Beiley, news dir; Al Meeves, chief engr. ■ Rates: $6.50; 6.50; 6.50; 6.50.

WHCH(FM)—Co-owned with WQXO(AM). June 21, 1974: 98.3 mhz; 32 kw. Ant 357 ft. TL: N46 24 53 W86 40 27. Stereo. Hrs opn: 24. Prog sep from AM. 309 S. Front Marquette (49855). (906) 225-0660. FAX: (906) 228-3766. Net: Unistar, Westwood One. Rep: Patt. Format: Hot country hits. Target aud: 18-54. ■ Rates: $8.50; 8.50; 8.50; 8.50.

Muskegon

WKBZ(AM)—1926: 850 khz; 1 kw-U, DA-1. TL: N43 08 05 W86 15 14. Hrs opn: 24. Box 238, 592 Pontaluna Rd. (49443). (616) 798-2141. FAX: (616) 798-3677. Licensee: KBZ Broadcasting Inc. (acq 1986; grpsl; FTR 10-27-86). Net: ABC/C, Moody, Westwood One. Rep: Roslin. Wash atty: Fletcher, Heald & Hildreth. Format: Adult contemp, full svc. News staff 2; news progmg 76 hrs wkly. Target aud: 25-54. ■ David Lorenz, gen mgr; William Hintzelman, news dir; Lynn Kolk, chief engr.

WKBZ-FM—Not on air, target date unknown: 107.9 mhz; 2.6 kw. Ant 348 ft. TL: N43 17 41 W86 13 12 (CP: 25 kw, ant 328 ft.). Box 4217, Muskegon Heights (49444). Licensee: Richard L. Culpepper. Rep: Patt. Format: Urban contemp. Target aud: 18-49. ■ Richard L. Culpepper, pres, gen mgr & gen sls mgr; Sammie L. Jordan, prom mgr, progmg dir, mus dir & news dir; John Seymour, chief engr.

WMHG(FM)—See Whitehall.

WMUS(AM)—June 15, 1947: 1090 khz; 1 kw-D. TL: N43 16 35 W86 15 10. Hrs opn: 6 AM-sunset plus 2 hrs. Dups FM 100%. Lakeview Center, 3565 Green St., Norton Shores (49444); Box 2871, Riverview Center, Suite 213, 678 Front St., Grand Rapids (49501). (616) 744-1671; (616) 451-8766. FAX: (616) 733-1107. Licensee: Greater Muskegon Broadcasters Inc. Net: ABC/D. Rep: D & R Radio. Wash atty: John Garziglia. Format: Contemp country. News staff one. Target aud: 25-54 primary; 35-64 secondary. ■ Tim Achterhoff, pres & gen mgr; Dave Wiehe, gen sls mgr; Peg Daniels, prom mgr; Kevin King, progmg dir; Mark Dixon, mus dir; Rod Kackley, news dir; Mike Maciejewski, chief engr. ■ Rates: $60; 50; 60; 30.

WMUS-FM—1962: 106.9 mhz; 50 kw. Ant 480 ft. TL: N43 13 47 W86 05 05. Stereo. Hrs opn: 24. Dups AM 100%. ■ Rates: Same as AM.

WSFN(AM)—1949: 1600 khz; 5 kw-U, DA-N. TL: N43 11 50 W86 13 22. 875 E. Summit Ave. (49444). (616) 733-2126. FAX: (616)-739-9037. Licensee: Goodrich Theatres Inc. Group owners: Goodrich Broadcasting Inc. (acq 2-7-86; $325,000; FTR 2-24-86). Rep: Katz. Format: Sports talk. News staff one; news progmg 2 hrs wkly. Target aud: 25-54; sports-minded males. ■ Robert Goodrich, pres; Tim Huelsing, gen mgr; Mike Marshal, rgnl sls mgr; Chris Thompson, prom dir; Jim Richards, progmg dir.

WSNX-FM—Co-owned with WSFN(AM). Nov 18, 1971: 104.5 mhz; 50 kw. Ant 361 ft. TL: N43 12 13 W86 01 49 (CP: 32 kw, ant 620 ft., TL: N43 12 16 W86 01 35). Stereo. Prog sep from AM. (acq 12-85; $1.1 million; FTR 12-23-85). Format: Contemporary hit.

Muskegon Heights

WMRR(FM)—March 29, 1974: 101.7 mhz; 15 kw. Ant 305 ft. TL: N43 16 38 W86 20 05. Stereo. Hrs opn: 24. Licensee: Goodrich Broadcasting Inc. (group owner; acq 3-10-93; $625,000; FTR 3-29-93).

WQWQ(AM)—February 1963: 1520 khz; 10 kw-D, 1 kw, DA-2. TL: N43 08 28 W86 14 50. Hrs opn: 24. 6083 Martin Rd. (49444). (616) 798-2245. FAX: (616) 798-3819. Licensee: Pathfinder Communications Corp. Group owner: Federated Media (acq 2-13-90; $1.2 million with co-located FM; FTR 3-5-90). Rep: Michigan. Format: Nostalgia, big band, oldies. Spec prog: Relg 5 hrs wkly. ■ Ron Dykstra, vp; William R. Shoup Jr., opns mgr; Bill Shoup Jr., progmg dir; Dave Gale, chief engr.

Newberry

WNBY(AM)—May 16, 1966: 1450 khz; 1 kw-U. TL: N46 18 41 W85 30 44. Box 501, Newberry Ave., Hwy. M-123 (49868). (906) 293-3221; (906) 293-5200. FAX: (906) 293-8275. Licensee: Peggy L. St. Andre (acq 1-7-93; estate transfer with co-located FM; FTR 2-1-93). Net: ABC/I; Mich. Farm. Rep: Patt. Format: MOR. News staff one; news progmg 10 hrs wkly. Target aud: 35 plus. Spec prog: Polka 2 hrs wkly. ■ Peggy St. Andre, gen sls mgr; Tom Bierch, prom mgr; Ray Rylett, chief engr. ■ Rates: $10; 10; 10; 10.

WNBY-FM—1977: 93.7 mhz; 3.5 kw. Ant 262 ft. TL: N46 18 48 W85 30 38 (CP: 6 kw, ant 279 ft.). Stereo. Dups AM 80%. Net: Mich. Net. Format: Oldies. Target aud: 25-45. Spec prog: Professional football & hockey, major league baseball. ■ Rates: Same as AM.

WUPQ(FM)—April 24, 1989: 97.9 mhz; 50 kw. Ant 352 ft. TL: N46 18 53 W85 33 45. Stereo. Hrs opn: 24. Box 152, S. Newberry Ave. (49868). (906) 293-8522. Licensee: Leon B. Van Dam. Net: NBC. Format: Easy adult contemp. News progmg 32 hrs wkly. Target aud: 25-54. ■ Lee Van Dam, pres & gen mgr; Karen Eastman, gen sls mgr. ■ Rates: $7.50; 7.50; 7.50; 5.

Niles

***WAUS(FM)**—See South Bend.

WNIL(AM)—Dec 6, 1956: 1290 khz; 500 w-D. TL: N41 49 22 W86 17 03. Box 370, 210 S. Phillip Rd. (49120). (616) 683-5432. FAX: (616) 683-2758. Licensee: Niles Broadcasting Co. (acq 1-1-59). Net: MBS. Rep: Roslin, Michigan. Wash atty: Wilkinson, Barker, Knauer & Quinn. Format: Contemp, MOR. News staff 2. Target aud: 35 plus. Spec prog: Country 10 hrs wkly. ■ J. Eric Plym, pres; Charles E. Frey, gen mgr; Micki Johnson, gen sls mgr; Sue Frey, mus dir; Shannon Carter, news dir; Roland Earnst, chief engr. ■ Rates: $49; 46; 49; na.

WAOR(FM)—Co-owned with WNIL(AM). Sept 13, 1968: 95.3 mhz; 3.3 kw. Ant 298 ft. TL: N41 49 22 W86 17 03. Stereo. Format: AOR.

Broadcasting & Cable Yearbook 1994
B-188

North Muskegon

WLCS(FM)—November 1983: 98.3 mhz; 2.6 kw. Ant 321 ft. TL: N43 16 34 W86 14 45. Stereo. 6083 Martin Rd. Muskegon (49444). (616) 733-9819. FAX: (616) 733-1959. Licensee: The New Black and Gold Co. Inc. (acq 11-22-85). Net: Unistar. Rep: Roslin. Format: Oldies. News staff one; news progmg 4 hrs wkly. Target aud: 25-54; general. ■ Mike Murphy, Dan Vandermyde, vps; Mike Murphy, vp opns; Dan Vandermyde, vp sls & news dir; Bill Marshall, pub affrs dir; Mike Maciewjewski, chief engr.

Norway

WZNL(FM)—Mar 15, 1990: 94.3 mhz; 1.3 kw. Ant 502 ft. TL: N45 47 15 W87 51 52. 333 S. Stephenson Ave., Iron Mountain (49801). (906) 779-2971. Licensee: Zephyr Broadcasting Inc. Group owner: Martz Communications Group (acq 1-24-90; grpsl; FTR 2-19-90). Format: Easy contemp. ■ Timothy D. Martz, pres; Veronica Roberts, gen mgr & gen sls mgr; Tim James, opns mgr.

Novi

*****WOVI(FM)**—Sept 4, 1978: 89.5 mhz; 100 w. Ant 67 ft. TL: N42 27 49 W83 29 28. Stereo. Hrs opn: 40. Novi High School, 24062 Taft Rd., (48375). (313) 349-5574; (313) 344-8300. Licensee: Board of Education Novi School District (acq 3-8-76). Format: Alternative. Target aud: General. ■ David Legg, stn mgr.

Oakland

*****WAEK(FM)**—Not on air, target date unknown: 88.3 mhz; 126 w-V. Ant 316 ft. 49 Oakland Center, Rochester (48309). Licensee: Oakland University.

Olivet

*****WOCR(FM)**—Apr 22, 1975: 89.7 mhz; 10 w. Ant 70 ft. TL: N42 26 31 W84 55 30. Stereo. Kirk Center, Olivet College (49076). (616) 749-7598. FAX: (616) 749-7121. Licensee: Olivet College. Format: CHR. News progmg one hr wkly. ■ Stuart Blacklaw, pres; Jason Houchins, gen mgr; Mike Adams, stn mgr; Josh Hosler, progmg dir.

Ontonagon

*****WOAS(FM)**—Nov 15, 1978: 88.5 mhz; 10 w. Ant 124 ft. TL: N46 52 30 W89 18 00. 701 Parker (49953). (906) 884-4422. FAX: (906) 884-2942. Licensee: Ontonagon Area School District. Format: Div, educ. News staff one; news progmg 5 hrs wkly. Target aud: General; local residents of the area. Spec prog: Finnish one hr, jazz 8 hrs, Walk of Life 3 hrs wkly. ■ Mike Bennett, gen mgr; Jim Bradley, chief engr.

WUPY(FM)—1987: 101.1 mhz; 30 kw. Ant 620 ft. TL: N46 44 49 W89 11 27. Stereo. Hrs opn: 24. 610 Greenland Rd. (49953). (906) 884-9668. FAX: (906) 884-4985. Licensee: S&S Broadcasting Inc. (acq 7-90). Net: NBC, CBS. Format: Country. News staff one; news progmg 10 hrs wkly. Target aud: 25 plus. Spec prog: Finnish 2 hrs, oldies 4 hrs, polkas one hr wkly. ■ Robert Schulz, pres; Skip Schulz, gen mgr & prom mgr; Bruce Nelson-Stratton, opns mgr; Sandy Schulz, gen sls mgr; Bruce Nelson, progmg dir; Paul Locatelli, news dir; Dave Danks, chief engr. ■ Rates: $7.25; 7.25; 7.25; 6.25.

Orchard Lake

*****WBLD(FM)**—May 28, 1974: 89.3 mhz; 10 w. Ant 110 ft. TL: N42 33 56 W83 21 32. Stereo. 4925 Orchard Lake Rd., West Bloomfield (48322). (313) 539-2595. Licensee: West Bloomfield Board of Education. Format: Div, rock. ■ Paul S. Townley, stn mgr; Randy G. Long, chief engr.

Oscoda

WCLS(FM)—Aug. 29, 1992: 100.7 mhz; 20.5 kw. Ant 360 ft. TL: N44 34 42 W83 22 40. Stereo. Hrs opn: 24. Box 296, Suite 8, 5737 N. US 23 (48750). (517) 739-8180. FAX: (517) 739-7788. Licensee: Todd A. Mohr. Group owner: Spectrum Communications, Inc. (acq 1-31-91). Rep: Patt. Wash atty: Carter, Ledyard & Milburn. Format: Soft adult contemp. News staff one; news progmg 4 hrs wkly. Target aud: 25-54; music intensive soft AC format targeted to adults. ■ Todd Mohr, pres & gen mgr; Keith Michaels, gen mgr & prom mgr; Dennis Hutchinson, progmg mgr & mus dir; Doug Waggoner, news dir; Mike Maciejewski, chief engr. ■ Rates: $12; 12; 12; 12.

Otsego

WQXC(AM)—1958: 980 khz; 1 kw-D. TL: N42 27 33 W85 43 58. Box 980 (49078). (616) 692-6851. FAX: (616) 692-6861. Licensee: Forum Communications Inc. (group owner; acq 3-83). Net: UPI. Format: Adult contemp. ■ Robert Brink, pres & gen mgr; Denny Cooley, progmg dir & mus dir; Ken Jacoby, news dir; Walker Sisson, chief engr.

WQXC-FM—Apr 17, 1981: 100.9 mhz; 3 kw. Ant 299 ft. TL: N42 30 31 W85 46 08. Stereo. Dups AM 100%.

Ovid-Elsie

*****WOES(FM)**—March 21, 1978: 91.3 mhz; 535 w. Ant 140 ft. TL: N43 02 44 W84 23 14. Stereo. Hrs opn: 8 AM-4 PM. 8989 Colony Rd., Elsie (48831). (517) 834-2271, ext. 35. FAX: (517) 862-4463. Licensee: Ovid-Elsie Area Schools (acq 1978). Format: Adult contemp, top-40. Spec prog: Class one hr, Pol one hr, Czech one hr, stage & screen one hr wkly. ■ George Bishop, gen mgr; Kevin Somers, opns mgr; Jim Dorman, chief engr.

Owosso

WOAP(AM)—Jan 1, 1948: 1080 khz; 1 kw-D. TL: N43 01 48 W84 10 39. Box 128, 2301 N., M-52 (48867). (517) 725-8196. FAX: (517) 725-6626. Licensee: Michigan Radio Group Inc. Group owner: Michigan Communications Group (acq 5-15-87; $750,000 with co-located FM; FTR 5-25-87). Net: AP; Mich. Net, Mich. Farm. Rep: Patt. Wash atty: Pepper & Corazzini. Format: News/talk. News staff one; news progmg 20 hrs wkly. Target aud: General. Spec prog: Farm 2 hrs, polka 3 hrs, relg 4 hrs, loc pub affairs 2 hrs wkly. ■ Russell C. Balch, pres; Art Kinsey, gen mgr & stn mgr; Ann Bakita, opns mgr; Joe Williams, news dir. ■ Rates: $13; 10; 13; 8.

WMZX(FM)—Co-owned with WOAP(AM). Dec 2, 1965: 103.9 mhz; 6 kw. Ant 255 ft. TL: N43 01 48 W84 10 39. Stereo. Prog sep from AM. Net: AP. Format: Soft adult contemp. News progmg 18 hrs wkly. Target aud: 25-54. Spec prog: Class one hr, relg one hr, sports 4 hrs wkly. ■ Rates: Same as AM.

Petoskey

WAIR(FM)—Listing follows WJML(AM).

WJML(AM)—Dec 6, 1966: 1110 khz; 10 kw-D, DA. TL: N45 20 05 W84 55 34. 2175 Click Rd. (49770). (616) 348-5000. Licensee: Stone Communications, Inc. (acq 10-8-91; $24,000; FTR 1-6-92). Net: CBS, CNN. Rep: Patt. Wash atty: Reddy, Begley & Martin. Format: News/talk. News progmg 72 hrs wkly. Target aud: 25 plus. Spec prog: Relg 8 hrs wkly. ■ Richard D. Stone, pres & gen mgr; Richard Blackmore, opns mgr & news dir.

WAIR(FM)—(Atlanta). Co-owned with WJML(AM). Oct 20, 1988: 92.5 mhz; 100 w. Ant 868 ft. TL: N45 01 00 W84 21 10. Stereo. Hrs opn: 24. Prog dups WTRV-FM. FAX: (616) 348-2092. Licensee: W-AIR Inc. Net: CBS, Unistar. Format: Oldies. News staff one; ■ Cliff Carey, stn mgr; Paula Adams, rgnl sls mgr.

WKHQ-FM—See Charlevoix.

WKLZ(FM)—Dec 7, 1965: 98.9 mhz; 50 kw. Ant 800 ft. TL: N45 28 40 W84 57 04. Stereo. Hrs opn: 24. Simulcast WKLT-FM. 2175 Click Rd. (49770); 745 S. Garfield Ave., Traverse City (49684). (616) 347-8191; (616) 947-0003. FAX: (616) 947-7002. Licensee: Northern Radio of Petoskey Inc. (acq 8-15-91; $800,000). Net: ABC. Rep: Banner. Wash atty: Reddy, Begley & Martin. Format: Rock/AOR. News progmg 2 hrs wkly. Target aud: 18-49; baby boomers, young adults. ■ Richard Dills, pres; Reggie Box, gen mgr; gen sls mgr & rgnl sls mgr; Marion Kalbfleisch, stn mgr; DeeAnn Davis, natl sls mgr; Susan Melton, prom dir & pub affrs dir; David Fortney, progmg dir; Brian Sullivan, mus dir; Pete Misiak, news dir; Dennis Murray, chief engr.

WMBN(AM)—May 1946: 1340 khz; 1 kw-U. TL: N45 20 50 W84 58 01. Box 286 (49770). (616) 347-8713. FAX: (616) 347-9920. Licensee: MacDonald Broadcasting Co. (group owner; acq 6-80; $250,000; FTR 6-16-80). Net: NBC, MBS. Rep: Christal, Michigan. Format: Classic rock. News staff one; news progmg 6 hrs wkly. Target aud: 25 plus. ■ Ken MacDonald Jr., pres; Patricia MacDonald-Garber, sr vp & gen mgr; Phill Orth, gen sls mgr; Dave Scott, progmg dir; Robert Carey, mus dir; Bob Wagar, news dir; Gary Harding, chief engr.

WMBN-FM—Jan 1, 1967: 96.3 mhz; 100 kw. Ant 981 ft. TL: N45 19 17 W84 52 33. Stereo. Prog sep from AM. Format: Easy lstng. Target aud: young, upwardly mobile adults. ■ Patricia MacDonald Garber, gen mgr; Tom Michaels, progmg dir; Christopher Hart, news dir; Chuck Scott, chief engr.

Pickford

WADW(FM)—Not on air, target date unknown: 105.5 mhz; 6 kw. Ant 328 ft. 30 S. Mercer St., Princeton, IL (61356). Licensee: Seaway Broadcasting Inc.

Pinconning

WBTZ(FM)—Nov 15, 1983: 100.9 mhz; 1.3 kw. Ant 495 ft. TL: N43 50 46 W84 05 32 (CP: 2.6 kw). Stereo. Hrs opn: 24. 2080 E. Gordonville Rd., Midland (48640). (517) 695-5115. FAX: (517) 695-5376. Licensee: P & G Media Corporation (acq 3-11-91; $55,000; FTR 3-11-91). Rep: Banner. Format: Adult contemp. Target aud: 25-54; primarily upscale women, men secondary. ■ Mike Thomas, gen mgr. ■ Rates: $15; 13; 15; 8.

Pittsford

*****WPCJ(FM)**—Oct 23, 1985: 91.1 mhz; 100 w. Ant 125 ft. TL: N41 53 04 W84 28 15 (CP: 270 w, ant 184 ft.). Hrs opn: 13. 940 Beecher Rd. (49271). (517) 523-3427. Licensee: Pittsford Educational Broadcasting Foundation. Net: Moody. Format: Educ, relg. News progmg 10 hrs wkly. Target aud: General; rural. ■ Richard Krage, stn mgr; Ed Trombley, chief engr.

Plymouth

*****WSDP(FM)**—Feb 14, 1972: 88.1 mhz; 200 w. Ant 73 ft. TL: N42 20 50 W83 29 51. Stereo. Hrs opn: 7:30 AM-11 PM. 46181 Joy Rd., Canton (48187). (313) 451-6266; (313) 453-0035. Licensee: Plymouth Canton Community Schools. Format: AOR, new mus. News progmg 3 hrs wkly. Target aud: General. Spec prog: Heavy metal 3 hrs, hardcore/thrash 2 hrs wkly. ■ J.M. Hoben, pres; Bill Keith, gen mgr & stn mgr; Reshma Shah, prom dir; Sweena Aulakh, progmg dir & mus dir; Kara Fiegenschuh, asst mus dir; Beth Eckerty, news dir; Steve Martin, chief engr.

Port Huron

WHLS(AM)—Aug 8, 1938: 1450 khz; 1 kw-U. TL: N42 58 37 W82 27 52. Box 807, 808 Huron Ave. (48061-0807). (313) 987-1450. FAX: (313) 987-9380. Licensee: Wismer Broadcasting Inc. (acq 1-1-56). Net: AP. Rep: Michigan. Format: Oldies, news/talk. News staff 2; news progmg 18 hrs wkly. Target aud: 18-50; middle class. ■ John F. Wismer, pres & gen mgr; Lawrence Smith, gen sls mgr; Matt Brown, progmg dir; Gary Girard, news dir; Carl White, chief engr.

WSAQ(FM)—Co-owned with WHLS(AM). Aug 7, 1964: 107.1 mhz; 6 kw. Ant 298 ft. TL: N42 58 37 W82 27 52. Stereo. Format: Country. Target aud: 25-55. ■ Brian Harper, prom dir; Bob Pouget, progmg dir.

*****WNFA(FM)**—May 15, 1986: 88.3 mhz; 1.3 kw. Ant 227 ft. TL: N42 59 36 W82 28 06. Stereo. Hrs opn: 24. 2865 Maywood Dr. (48060). (313) 985-3260. FAX: (313) 985-7712. Licensee: Ross Bible Church. Net: Moody, Skylight, USA. Wash atty: Jeff Southmayd. Format: Relg, inspirational. News progmg 14 hrs wkly. Target aud: 25-44; females. ■ Jeff Jacobsen, stn mgr; Lori McNaughton, opns dir; Ellyn Davey, mus dir; Ed Czelada, chief engr.

*****WORW(FM)**—May 31, 1973: 91.9 mhz; 188 w. Ant 78 ft. TL: N43 01 30 W82 26 10 (CP: 180 w). 1799 Krafft Rd., Fort Gratiot (48059). (313) 984-2675. Licensee: Port Huron Area School District. Format: Top-40. ■ Susan M. Doherty, pres & gen mgr; Mike Apple, progmg dir; David Huston, chief engr.

WPHM(AM)—Dec 6, 1947: 1380 khz; 5 kw-U, DA-2. TL: N42 51 50 W82 29 40. Hrs opn: 24. Broadcast House, 2379 Military St. (48060). (313) 987-4100; (313) 987-9746. Licensee: Hanson Communications Inc. (acq 12-1-86). Net: ABC/I, NBC Talknet, MBS. Rep: Patt. Format: Adult contemp, talk, news/info, sports. News progmg 28 hrs wkly. Target aud: 25-54. Spec prog: Farm one hr wkly. ■ Lee C. Hanson, pres & gen mgr; Al Tyrrell, gen sls mgr; Kevin Miller, progmg dir & news dir; Eric C. Hanson, chief engr.

WSAQ(FM)—Listing follows WHLS(AM).

*****WSGR-FM**—October 1971: 91.3 mhz; 100 w. Ant 87 ft. TL: N42 58 43 W82 25 45. Stereo. Box 5015, 323 Erie St. (48061-5015). (313) 989-5564. FAX: (313) 984-2852. Licensee: St. Clair County Community College. Format: Rock, eclectic. Target aud: General; all age groups. Spec prog: Metal/hard rock 20 hrs, dance/rap/techno 14 hrs, jazz/new age 8 hrs, film soundtks 6 hrs, reggae 4 hrs wkly. ■ John Hill, gen mgr; Jason Smith, progmg dir;

Michigan

Lance Billow, mus dir; James Stevenson, Mark Morden, asst mus dirs.

Portage

WFAT(FM)—Listing follows WHEZ(AM).

WHEZ(AM)—July 25, 1986: 1560 khz; 4.1 kw-D, DA. TL: N42 10 59 W85 35 30 (CP: 5 kw). Hrs opn: Sunrise-sunset. 6021 S. Westnedge Ave., Kalamazoo (49002). (616) 342-0070. Licensee: Tri-State Broadcasting Inc. (acq 8-85; FTR 7-15-85). Rep: Christal. News staff 3; news progmg 5 hrs wkly. Target aud: 25-54; emphasis on 35-50 age group. ■ Gary B. Mallernee, pres & gen mgr; Jim Suski, gen sls mgr; Eric Anderson, progmg dir; Denny Bice, mus dir; Jim Whelan, news dir; Mike Peters, chief engr.

WFAT(FM)—Co-owned with WHEZ(AM). June 1992: 96.5 mhz; 3 kw. Ant 321 ft. TL: N42 12 55 W85 36 37. (616) 342-8948. Format: Oldies.

WRKR(FM)—Licensed to Portage. See Kalamazoo.

Rockford

WBYY(AM)—1965: 810 khz; 500 w-D. TL: N43 07 03 W85 34 06. Stereo. 3090 28th St. S.E. (49507). (616) 949-8585. FAX: (616) 949-6262. Licensee: RDL Productions Inc. (acq 10-22-91; $327,000; FTR 11-11-91). Net: ABC/E, Jones Satellite Audio. Format: Adult contemp, oldies. Target aud: 30 plus. ■ Randall Disselkoen, pres & gen mgr; Mark Roberts, opns mgr & progmg mgr.

Rogers City

WHAK(AM)—May 1949: 960 khz; 5 kw-D. TL: N45 23 53 W83 55 19. 5667 M-68 Hwy. (49779). (517) 734-9960. Licensee: Ives Broadcasting Inc. (acq 8-4-92; $100,000; FTR 8-24-92). Net: NBC. Rep: Michigan. Format: Contemp country. ■ Dave Carsnik, gen mgr; Bob Edwards, progmg dir & mus dir; Mike Rogers, Peter Jakey (sports), news dirs; Harvey Klann, chief engr. ■ Rates: $10.60; 10.60; 10.60; na.

WMLQ(FM)—June 16, 1984: 96.7 mhz; 26 kw. Ant 383 ft. TL: N45 21 01 W83 47 00. Stereo. Box 297 (49779). (517) 734-4797. Licensee: North South Radio Group Inc. Net: SMN. Rep: Patt. Format: Adult contemp. Target aud: 45 plus. ■ John D. DeGroot, pres; Karl Grambau, stn mgr & news dir; Mike Butler, progmg dir; Robert Stutesman, chief engr. ■ Rates: $9; 8; 9; 8.

Roscommon

WGRY-FM—March 1990: 101.1 mhz; 3.4 kw. Ant 444 ft. TL: N44 34 31 W84 42 19. Stereo. Hrs opn: 5:30 AM-midnight. 6514 Old Lake Rd., Grayling (49738). (517) 348-6171; (517) 348-4132. FAX: (517) 348-6181. Licensee: Gannon Broadcasting Systems Inc. (acq 9-88). Net: MBS. Rep: Patt. Format: Country. News staff one; news progmg 16 hrs wkly. Target aud: 25 plus. ■ William S. Gannon, pres & gen mgr; Scott Marshall, stn mgr; Dave Sherbert, opns mgr, progmg dir, mus dir & news dir; Delton Winkel, gen sls mgr; Robert Stutsman, chief engr. ■ Rates: $12; 12; 12; 10.

Royal Oak

WEXL(AM)—October 1923: 1340 khz; 1 kw-U, DA-D. TL: N42 28 25 W83 06 56. 317 E. Eleven Mile Rd. (48067). (313) 544-2200. Licensee: Sparks Broadcasting Co. Inc. Net: UPI. Format: Relg. ■ G. Sparks, pres, gen mgr & chief engr; Ida Vettraino, gen sls mgr.

Saginaw

WGER-FM—Feb 19, 1969: 106.3 mhz; 3 kw. Ant 300 ft. TL: N43 28 38 W83 57 00. Stereo. 6165 Bay Rd. (48604). (517) 792-1063. FAX: (517) 792-1977. Licensee: F-B Communications Inc. (acq 9-23-86). Net: MBS. Rep: McGavren Guild. Format: Adult contemp. Target aud: 25-54; upscale, mid/high level income. ■ Jack Fitzgerald, chmn; Bill Harnsberger, vp; Jerry O'Donnell, gen mgr; Chris Reynolds, prom mgr, progmg mgr & mus dir; Bill Sanderson, chief engr. ■ Rates: $55; 45; 50; 30.

WHNN(FM)—See Bay City.

WIOG(FM)—See Bay City.

WKCQ(FM)—Listing follows WSAM.

WKNX(AM)—(Frankenmuth). April 17, 1947: 1210 khz; 10 kw-D, DA-D. TL: N43 20 30 W83 53 52. 306 W. Genesee, Frankenmuth (48734). (517) 652-3265. FAX: (517) 652-3291. Licensee: Bell Broadcasting Co. (acq 12-2-93; $270,000; FTR 12-20-93). Net: AP. Rep: Patt. Format: Big band. Spec prog: Black 2 hrs, Sp 9 hrs, Ger 3 hrs, Pol 5 hrs, It one wkly. ■ Robert Dana MacVay, pres;

Robert G. Dyer, gen mgr & gen sls mgr; Linda Trestrail, prom mgr; Joseph Pratt, news dir.

WSAM(AM)—1940: 1400 khz; 1 kw-U. TL: N43 25 00 W83 55 05. Box 1776, 2000 Whittier (48605). (517) 752-8161. FAX: (517) 752-8102. Licensee: MacDonald Broadcasting Co. (group owner; acq 11-1-62). Net: ABC/D. Rep: D & R Radio. Wash atty: Fletcher, Heald & Hildreth. Format: MOR/full service. News staff 2; news progmg 5 hrs wkly. Target aud: 25 plus. ■ Carolyn Ann MacDonald, CEO; Kenneth MacDonald Jr., pres & gen mgr; Patricia Webb, MacDonald Garber, sr vps; Andrew Reale MacDonald, vp; Duane Alverson, gen sls mgr; Barb Sheltraw, prom mgr; Bill Anders, progmg dir; Mike McClain, mus dir; Lyle Kleman, news dir; Gary Harding, chief engr. ■ Rates: $30; 25; 20; 5.

WKCQ(FM)—Co-owned with WSAM. 1947: 98.1 mhz; 50 kw. Ant 500 ft. TL: N43 25 04 W83 58 06. Stereo. Prog sep from AM. Format: Country. Spec prog: Sp 3 hrs, Ger 3 hrs wkly. ■ Jim Kramer, opns mgr; Fritz Kuhlman, progmg dir & mus dir.

WSGW(AM)—Aug 11, 1950: 790 khz; 5 kw-D, 1 kw-N, DA-2. TL: N43 27 40 W83 48 48. Hrs opn: 24. Box 1945, 1795 Tittabawassee (48605). (517) 752-3456. FAX: (517) 754-5046. Licensee: Booth American Co. (group owner). Net: NBC; NBC Talknet; AP; CBS; MBS; Mich. Net., Mich. Farm. Rep: Katz. Format: News/talk. News staff 5; news progmg 40 hrs wkly. Target aud: General; emphasis on adults 35-64. Spec prog: Farm 10 hrs wkly. ■ John L. Booth, pres; John Casey, vp, gen mgr & progmg dir; Sue Smith, prom mgr; Dave Maurer, news dir; Cliff Graff, chief engr. ■ Rates: $45; 35; 39; 25.

WTCF(FM)—(Carrollton). Mar 11, 1991: 100.5 mhz; 3 kw. Ant 500 ft. TL: N43 33 43 W85 58 54. Stereo. Box 24. Box 5649, 902 S. Euclid Ave., Saginaw (48603). Licensee: Mid-America Broadcasting Inc. (group owner). Net: CNN. Rep: Katz & Powell. Wash atty: Booth, Freret & Imlay. Format: CHR. News staff one. Target aud: 18-49 plus teenagers. ■ Bob Friedle, pres, opns mgr & engrg dir; Richard J. Doud, vp & stn mgr; Kim Jewell, gen sls mgr, natl sls mgr & rgnl sls mgr; Lee Ann Curtis, prom dir; Steve Williams, progmg dir; Amy Wilda, mus dir; Mary Doud, pub affrs dir. ■ Rates: $50; 45; 50; 35.

WTLZ(FM)—Nov 15, 1968: 107.1 mhz; 4.9 kw. Ant 400 ft. TL: N43 21 14 W83 55 06. Stereo. Hrs opn: 24. Box 107 (48606); Suite 514, 126 N. Franklin (48607). (517) 754-1071. FAX: (517) 754-4292. Licensee: WTL Inc. Group owner: WTL Inc. (acq 7-22-88). Net: American Urban. Wash atty: Pepper & Corazzini. Format: Contemp urban (Churban). Target aud: 18-35; upscale, Blacks, women. Spec prog: Gospel 6 hrs wkly. ■ Jack Lich, pres; Lynell Gordon-Young, gen mgr; Julia Ruffin, mktg dir; Dante Toussaint, prom mgr; Kermit Crockett, progmg dir; Tony Lamptey, mus dir; Kevin Halley, chief engr.

WUVE(FM)—Not on air, target date unknown: 104.5 mhz; 2.45 kw. Ant 469 ft. TL: N43 23 34 W83 55 37. 10750 Cushdon Ave., Los Angeles, CA (90064). Licensee: Thomas M. Eells.

St. Ignace

WIDG(AM)—June 7, 1966: 940 khz; 5 kw-D. TL: N45 52 04 W84 47 09. Hrs opn: Sunrise - sunset. 334 N. State St. (49781). (906) 643-9494. Licensee: Mighty-Mac Broadcasting Co. Net: NBC. Rep: Unirep, Patt. Format: C&W. ■ Donald E. Benson, pres; Tim Fenlon, gen mgr; George Crapser, gen sls mgr; Rob Ryan, progmg dir; Scott Hooker, news dir; Marvin Veurink, chief engr.

WMKC(FM)—Co-owned with WIDG(AM). Feb 8, 1982: 102.9 mhz; 100 kw. Ant 374 ft. TL: N45 52 07 W84 47 09. Stereo. Prog sep from AM.

St. Johns

WWDX(FM)—July 15, 1972: 92.1 mhz; 6 kw. Ant 400 ft. TL: N42 53 29 W84 34 27. Stereo. Suite 101, 220 M.A.C., East Lansing (48823). (517) 332-8700. FAX: (517) 332-6418. Licensee: Landsmen Communications Ltd. (acq 5-4-93; $550,000; FTR 5-24-93). Net: ABC. Rep: D & R Radio. Wash atty: Harry Martin. Format: Modern rock. Target aud: 25-54; upscale, educated professionals. ■ Curtis E. Spain, Allan Wilson, gen mgrs; Michael Greenwalt, gen sls mgr; Greg St. James, progmg dir; Sandy Horiwitz, mus dir; Larry Eastlack, engrg mgr. ■ Rates: $25; 23; 24; 20.

WWSJ(AM)—Sept 23, 1959: 1580 khz; 1 kw-D, DA. TL: N42 58 14 W84 32 59. Hrs opn: 6 AM-8 PM. Box 276, 1363 W. Parks Rd. (48879). (517) 224-7911. Licensee: WSJ/WQON Inc. Net: Mich. Farm. Format: Country. ■ Robert D. Ditmer, pres, gen sls mgr & news

dir; Mark Hull, gen mgr & progmg dir; Ed Czendla, chief engr.

St. Joseph

*WAUS(FM)—See South Bend.

WHFB(AM)—See Benton Harbor-St. Joseph.

WHFB-FM—See Benton Harbor-St. Joseph.

WIRX(FM)—Licensed to St. Joseph. See Benton Harbor-St. Joseph.

WSJM(AM)—Licensed to St. Joseph. See Benton Harbor-St. Joseph.

St. Louis

WFYC(AM)—See Alma.

WFYC-FM—See Alma.

WMLM(AM)—Dec 15, 1977: 1520 khz; 1 kw-U, DA-2. TL: N43 21 08 W84 36 15. 4170 N. State Rd., Alma (48801). (517) 463-4013; (517) 463-4014. Licensee: Siefker Broadcasting Co. Net: ABC/E. Format: C&W. Target aud: General. Spec prog: Farm 5 hrs, big band 4 hrs, gospel 2 hrs wkly. ■ Gregory Siefker, pres & gen mgr; Jerry Ross, mus dir. ■ Rates: $8.50; 7; 8.50; 4.

Salem Township

WSDS(AM)—1962: 1480 khz; 750 w-D, DA-2, 5 kw-N. TL: N42 15 42 W83 37 10. Hrs opn: 19. 580 W. Clark Rd., Ypsilanti (48198). (313) 484-1480. FAX: (313) 484-1481. Licensee: Koch Broadcasting (acq 6-1-68). Net: MBS. Format: Country, news. Target aud: 25 plus. Spec prog: Bluegrass 6 hrs wkly. ■ Bob Weber Koch, pres; Michael Calanan, gen mgr & gen sls mgr; Jeffrey Van Riper, opns mgr, prom dir & progmg dir; Christine Sharp, mus dir; Kirsten Hayes, pub affrs dir; Tom Gardull, chief engr. ■ Rates: $19; 15; 19; 15.

Saline

WAMX(AM)—1958: 1290 khz; 500 w-D, DA. TL: N42 12 17 W83 47 19. Box 8605, Ann Arbor (48107); 3001 Brassow Rd. (48176). (313) 429-3333. FAX: (313) 429-7837. Licensee: Mediabase Research Corp. (acq 11-10-86; grpsl; FTR 10-20-86). Net: MBS. Rep: McGavren Guild. Format: Oldies. ■ Mike Solan, gen mgr; Joe Urbiel, stn mgr; Nick Guerra, gen sls mgr; Dave Michaels, mus dir; Kelly Wright, news dir; John Grevers, chief engr.

Sandusky

WMIC(AM)—June 27, 1968: 660 khz; 1 kw-D, DA. TL: N43 23 34 W82 49 57. 19 S. Elk (48471). (313) 648-2700. FAX: (313) 648-3242. Licensee: Sanilac Broadcasting Co. Net: ABC/I; Mich. Farm. Format: Country. News staff 2; news progmg 25 hrs wkly. Target aud: General; 25 plus. Spec prog: Farm 12 hrs, Pol 4 hrs wkly. ■ Bob Armstrong, gen mgr, stn mgr & gen sls mgr; Ken Cenci, mus dir; Jim Daniels, news dir; Kevin Larke, chief engr. ■ Rates: $9.40; 9.40; 9.40; 9.40.

WTGV-FM—Co-owned with WMIC(AM). Aug 16, 1971: 97.7 mhz; 3 kw. Ant 325 ft. TL: N43 23 33 W82 49 56. Stereo. Hrs opn: 24. Prog sep from AM. Format: MOR. ■ Rates: $7.50; 7.50; 7.50; 7.50.

*WNFR(FM)—Not on air, target date unknown: 90.7 mhz. Ant 328 ft. 2865 Maywood Dr., Port Huron (48060). Licensee: Ross Bible Church.

WTGV-FM—Listing follows WMIC(AM).

Saugatuck

WEVS(FM)—July 4, 1987: 92.7 mhz; 2.15 kw. Ant 387 ft. TL: N42 41 10 W86 10 05. Stereo. Box 927, 3676 63rd St., (49453). (616) 857-1721. Licensee: Conrad Communications Corp. Net: CBS. Format: Adult contemp, oldies, classic rock. Target aud: 25-54. ■ Christopher C. Conrad, pres & gen mgr; Bill Riechts, sls dir; Shannon Lowe, prom mgr & news dir; David Roper, adv dir; Harry Ford, progmg dir; Joe Stokes, mus dir & pub affrs dir; Walker Sisson, chief engr. ■ Rates: $8.50; 7; 8.50; 5.50.

Sault Ste. Marie

*WCMZ-FM—July 13, 1990: 98.3 mhz; 25 kw. Ant 328 ft. TL: N46 29 10 W84 13 49. Stereo. Hrs opn: 24. Public Broadcasting Center, Mount Pleasant (48859). (517) 774-3105. FAX: (517) 774-4427. Licensee: Central Michigan Univ. Net: APR, NPR; Mich. Pub. Wash atty: Dow, Lohnes & Albertson. Format: Class, jazz, news. News staff 2; news progmg 35 hrs wkly. Target aud: General. ■ Thomas Hunt, gen mgr; Linda Hyde, prom mgr; Ray Ford, progmg dir; Randy Kapenga, chief engr.

WKNW(AM)—Listing follows WYSS(FM).

***WLSO(FM)**—Not on air, target date unknown: 90.1 mhz; 100 w. Ant 98 ft. 1000 College Dr. (49783). Licensee: Lake Superior State Univ.

WSOO(AM)—June 1, 1940: 1230 khz; 1 kw-U. TL: N46 26 16 W84 22 42. Box 1230 (49783). (906) 632-2231. (906) 632-4411. Licensee: Fabiano-Strickler Communications (acq 9-22-81; $270,000 with co-located FM; FTR 10-12-81). Net: ABC/I. Rep: Michigan. Format: Adult contemp. ■ James C. Fabiano, pres; Tom Ewing, gen mgr; Paul Stabile, progmg dir; Larry McNeal, news dir; Larry Norman, chief engr.

WSUE(FM)—Co-owned with WSOO(AM). 1978: 101.3 mhz; 100 kw. Ant 978 ft. TL: N46 26 16 W84 22 42. Prog sep from AM. Format: Classic rock.

WYSS(FM)—July 12, 1972: 99.5 mhz; 26.5 kw. Ant 275 ft. TL: N46 23 48 W84 23 52 (CP: 100 kw). Stereo. 1402 Ashmun St. (49783). (906) 635-0995. FAX: (906) 635-1216. Licensee: Algoma Broadcasting Co. Group owner: Martz Communications Group (acq 5-21-86; $540,000). Net: ABC/C, Westwood One. Rep: Patt. Wash atty: Cohn & Marks. Format: Contemp hit. News staff 2. Target aud: 18-49. ■ Timothy D. Martz, pres; Mike Boldt, gen mgr & gen sls mgr; Terry Carr, progmg dir & mus dir; Ronald Dewey, news dir; Paul Buck, chief engr.

WKNW(AM)—Co-owned with WYSS(FM). Aug 25, 1990: 1400 khz; 250 w-U. TL: N46 29 18 W84 19 45. Stereo. Hrs opn: 24. Prog sep from FM. Net: MBS. Format: Full svc, news/talk. ■ John Bell, progmg dir.

Scottville

WKZC(FM)—Feb 16, 1983: 94.9 mhz; 17 kw. Ant 400 ft. TL: N44 03 27 W86 24 58. Stereo. Hrs opn: 5 AM-2 AM. 5941 W. U.S. 10, Ludington (49431). (616) 843-3438. Licensee: Chickering Associates Inc. (acq 5-20-93; $190,000; FTR 6-14-93). Net: SMN. Rep: Patt. Wash atty: Bechtel & Cole. Format: Contemp country. News staff one; news progmg 5 hrs wkly. Target aud: 25-54. ■ John Chickering, pres, gen mgr & progmg dir; Bob Engblade, opns mgr & chief engr; Kathy Gale, rgnl sls mgr; Ray Cummins, news dir. ■ Rates: $14; 10; 10; 7.

Shepherd

WMMI(AM)—Feb 2, 1987: 830 khz; 1 kw-D. TL: N43 33 42 W84 45 00. Stereo. 4065 E. Wing Rd., Mt. Pleasant, (48858). (517) 772-9664; (517) 773-5000. Licensee: Central Michigan Communications Inc. (acq 8-15-88). Net: SMN; Great Lakes Media Group. Rep: Michigan (spot sales). Wash atty: Reddy, Begley & Martin. Format: Oldies. News staff one; news progmg 5 hrs wkly. Target aud: 25-54; general. ■ Mike Carey, pres; Steve Conley, progmg dir & mus dir; Jim Hughes, news dir; Darel Vanderhoof, chief engr. ■ Rates: $9.75; 9.75; 9.75; 9.75.

South Haven

WCSY(AM)—1961: 940 khz; 1 kw-D, 6 w-N, DA-D. TL: N42 24 34 34 W86 16 01. 510 Williams St. (49090). (616) 637-6397. FAX: (616) 637-2675. Licensee: Cosy Broadcasting Inc. (acq 10-1-81; $187,000; FTR 9-21-81). Net: ABC/E; Mich. Farm. Format: Adult contemp. Spec prog: Farm 3 hrs wkly. ■ Don Anderson, pres & gen mgr; Joe Jason, opns mgr; Dick Shier, news dir; Walker Sisson, chief engr.

WCSY-FM—Oct 31, 1981: 98.3 mhz; 2 kw. Ant 400 ft. TL: N42 18 02 W86 15 03. Stereo. Dups AM 100%.

Southfield

***WSHJ(FM)**—Feb 28, 1967: 88.3 mhz; 125 w. Ant 43 ft. TL: N42 28 12 W83 15 50. Stereo. Hrs opn: 7:30 AM-10 PM. 24675 Lahser Rd. (48034). (313) 746-8630; (303) 746-8631. Licensee: Board of Education Southfield Public Schools. Net: ABC/C. Format: Contemp hits, oldies, educ. Target aud: General; student & families. Spec prog: Foreign 3 hrs wkly. ■ Jon L. Fruytier, gen mgr; Max Peelman, opns dir; Babette Chapman, prom dir; Levi Bayne, progmg dir; Kevin Fowler, mus dir; Kennyle Jones, pub affrs dir; Robert Younker, chief engr.

Spring Arbor

***KTGG(AM)**—Aug 15, 1985: 1540 khz; 450 w-D, 200 w-CH. TL: N42 09 13 W84 32 58. Spring Arbor College, 106 Main St., Sayre Hall (49283). (517) 750-1200; (517) 750-2709. FAX: (517) 750-2108; (517) 750-1604. Licensee: Spring Arbor College Communications. Format: Gospel. News progmg 11 hrs wkly. Target aud: 18-49; rural to urban. Spec prog: Children's 18 hrs wkly. ■ Carl V. Jacobson, gen mgr; Michelle Stone, opns dir & progmg dir; Ed Trombley, chief engr.

***WSAE(FM)**—Co-owned with KTGG(AM). Oct 2, 1963: 106.9 mhz; 2.88 kw. Ant 349 ft. TL: N42 09 13 W84 32 58 (CP: 3.9 kw). Stereo. Hrs opn: 6 AM-midnight. Wash atty: Lauren Colby. Format: Christian contemp. Spec prog: Children 10 hrs wkly.

Standish

WSTD(FM)—January 1990: 96.9 mhz; 3 kw. Ant 328 ft. TL: N44 02 08 W84 00 31. Stereo. Hrs opn: 24. Box 969, 1670 Able Rd., Sterling (48659). (517) 654-2400. FAX: (517) 654-2440. Licensee: Agri-Valley Communications Inc. Net: MBS. Format: Adult contemp. News staff one. Target aud: General. ■ Edwin H. Eichler, pres & gen mgr; Tim LaVere, news dir; Kyle Arnett, pub affrs dir; Larry Hilton, chief engr. ■ Rates: $13; 13; 13; 10.

Sterling Heights

***WUFL(AM)**—Oct 26, 1988: 1030 khz; 5 kw-D, DA. TL: N42 36 19 W82 54 37. Suite 328, 42669 Garfield Rd., Clinton Township (48038); Box 1030 (48311). (313) 263-1030. FAX: (313) 228-1030. Licensee: Family Life Broadcasting System (group owner; acq 10-25-88). Net: Moody, Skylight, USA. Format: Relg. News staff one. Target aud: 25-49; evangelical Christians. ■ Rev. Warren Bolthouse, pres; Steven K. Wright, gen mgr; Greg Kinzy, opns mgr; Jon Couch, mus dir; Shelly Trayer, news dir; Bill Mullen, chief engr.

Sturgis

WMSH(AM)—1951: 1230 khz; 1 kw-U, DA-1. TL: N41 46 11 W85 25 09 (CP: 2.16 kw). Box 7080, 70808 S. Nottawa Rd. (49091). (616) 651-2383; (616) 651-2384. FAX: (616) 659-1111. Licensee: Forum Communications Inc. (group owner; acq 1-1-89; $370,000 with co-located FM; FTR 1-16-89). Net: ABC. Format: Adult contemp, oldies. News staff 2; news progmg 7 hrs wkly. Target aud: 18-49. ■ Robert Brink, pres; Thomas Flynn, gen mgr & gen sls mgr; Randy Rowley, prom mgr, progmg dir & mus dir; John Chandler, news dir; Walker Sisson, chief engr.

WMSH-FM—1951: 99.3 mhz; 1.4 kw. Ant 390 ft. TL: N41 46 11 W85 25 09. Stereo. Dups AM 100%.

Tawas City

WHST(FM)—Nov 1, 1972: 107.3 mhz; 6 kw. Ant 280 ft. TL: N44 16 27 W83 39 42. Stereo. Hrs opn: 24 130 Newman St., E. Tawas (48730). (517) 362-6149. FAX: (517) 362-6351. Licensee: Ives Broadcasting Inc. (acq 1-27-93; $190,000; FTR 2-15-93). Net: CBS, Westwood One. Rep: Patt. Wash atty: David Tillotson. Format: Adult contemp. News staff one; news progmg 12 hrs wkly. Target aud: 25-54. ■ David Karschnick, pres & gen mgr; Jack Dragmiller, sls dir; Darrell Kelly, prom dir & progmg dir; John Pines, news dir & pub affrs dir; Harvey Klann, chief engr. ■ Rates: $17.65; 14.10; 15.30; 9.40.

WIOS(AM)—Sept 27, 1958: 1480 khz; 1 kw-D, DA. TL: N44 15 48 W83 32 42. Box 549, 523 Meadow (48764); Box 104 (48764). (517) 362-3417; (517) 362-3627. FAX: (517) 362-4544. Licensee: Carroll Enterprises Inc. (acq 5-1-69). Net: ABC/I; Mich. Farm, Mich. Net. Rep: Michigan. Wash atty: Booth, Freret & Imlay. Format: Easy lstng, talk. Target aud: 25 plus; general. Spec prog: Big band 6 hrs wkly. ■ John Carroll Jr., CEO, pres & gen mgr; John Carroll Sr., chmn; Kevin Allen, opns dir, progmg dir & mus dir; Tim Carroll, gen sls mgr.

WKJC(FM)—Co-owned with WIOS(AM). October 1979: 104.7 mhz; 50 kw. Ant 492 ft. TL: N44 24 43 W83 37 17. Stereo. Prog sep from AM. Format: Modern C&W.

Taylor

WCHB(AM)—1990: 1200 khz; 25 kw-D, 700 w-N, DA-2. TL: N42 09 24 W83 19 56. 32790 Henry Ruff Rd., Inkster (48141). (313) 278-1440. FAX: (313) 722-8495. Licensee: Bell Broadcasting Co. Format: Blues & gospel. ■ Terry Arnold, CEO; Dr. Wendell Cox, vp & gen mgr; Sidney Johnson, opns mgr & progmg dir; Treva Bass, chief engr.

Three Rivers

WLKM(AM)—May 3, 1962: 1510 khz; 500 w-D. TL: N41 55 41 W85 38 18. Hrs opn: Sunrise-sunset. 59750 Constantine Rd. (49093-9394). (616) 278-1815. Licensee: Voice of Three Rivers Inc. (acq 1970). Net: MBS; Mich. Farm. Rep: Patt. Format: Soft adult contemp, news. News staff one; news progmg 17 hrs wkly. Target aud: 21-54. Spec prog: Farm 3 hrs wkly. ■ Carl L. Shipley, pres; Dennis Rumsey, vp & gen mgr; Kathy Loker, gen sls mgr; J. Patrick Lafferty, news dir; Walker Sisson, chief engr. ■ Rates: $15; 13.50; 15; 8.50.

WLKM-FM—Mar 1975: 95.9 mhz; 3 kw. Ant 289 ft. TL: N41 55 41 W85 38 18. Stereo. Hrs opn: 24. Dups AM 95%. ■ Rates: Same as AM.

Traverse City

WCCW(AM)—July 15, 1960: 1310 khz; 5 kw-D. TL: N44 46 11 W85 41 22. Box 666 (49685). (616) 946-6211. FAX: (616) 946-1914. Licensee: Fabiano-Strickler Communications Inc. (acq 4-6-84; $755,000 with co-located FM; FTR 3-5-84). Net: ABC/I. Rep: Katz, Michigan. Format: MOR. ■ Hal Paine, gen mgr; George Bliss, gen sls mgr; Brian Hale, progmg dir; Dave Gauthier, news dir; Dennis Murray, chief engr.

WCCW-FM—Nov 8, 1967: 107.5 mhz; 840 w. Ant 518 ft. TL: N44 46 11 W85 41 22 (CP: 107.5 mhz, 660 w, ant 702 ft., TL: N44 46 02 W85 41 26). Stereo. Prog sep from AM. Net: ABC/E. Format: Classic hits/gold. ■ Brian Hale, progmg dir.

WLDR(FM)—July 17, 1966: 101.9 mhz; 100 kw. Ant 538 ft. TL: N44 46 13 W85 41 43 (CP: Ant 630 ft.). Stereo. 118 S. Union St. (49684). (616) 947-3220. FAX: (616) 947-7201. Licensee: Great Northern Broadcasting System Inc. Net: Unistar. Format: Adult contemp. News staff one. Target aud: 25-54. ■ Donald Wiitala, pres & gen mgr; Dave Maxson, opns dir, progmg dir & news dir; Steve Fordyce, gen sls mgr; Angie Handa, mus dir; Dennis Murray, chief engr. ■ Rates: $30; 28; 29; 24.

***WLJN-FM**—Oct 1, 1989: 89.9 mhz; 10 kw. Ant 443 ft. TL: N44 46 34 W85 39 40. Stereo. Box 1400, 33930 Morgan Hill Rd. (49684). (616) 946-1400. FAX: (616) 946-3959. Licensee: Good News Media Inc. Format: Relg. Target aud: General. ■ John Van Tholen, pres; Raymond Hashley, gen mgr; Brian Harcey, progmg dir & news dir; Donald Parker, chief engr.

WMBN-FM—See Petoskey.

***WNMC-FM**—October 1967: 90.9 mhz; 150 w. Ant -88 ft. TL: N44 45 57 W85 34 49. Stereo. 1701 E. Front St. (49684). (616) 922-1091. Licensee: Northwestern Michigan College. Format: Div, jazz, rock. Spec prog: Black 20 hrs, Sp 3 hrs wkly. ■ Teresa O'Hara, gen mgr; Keith Schwartz, progmg dir; Michael Lloyd, mus dir; Dennis Murray, chief engr. ■ Rates: $2; 2; 2; 2.

WTCM(AM)—1941: 580 khz; 5 kw-D, 500 w-N, DA-2. TL: N44 43 18 W85 42 18. Stereo. Hrs opn: 24. 314 E. Front St. (49684). (616) 947-7675. FAX: (616) 929-3988. Licensee: WTCM Radio Inc. (group owner: Paul Bunyan Network). Net: ABC/I, MBS; Mich. Net. Rep: Katz. Wash atty: Cordon & Kelly. Format: News/talk. News staff 4; news progmg 12 hrs wkly. Target aud: 25-54. Spec prog: Farm 5 hrs wkly. ■ Ross Biederman, pres; Jon Patrick, sls dir; Norm Jones, prom dir; Jack O'Malley, progmg dir; Kim Chido, news dir; Jim Sofonia, chief engr. ■ Rates: $10; 10; 10; 10.

WTCM-FM—Dec 13, 1965: 103.5 mhz; 100 kw. Ant 989 ft. TL: N44 27 31 W85 42 02. Stereo. Hrs opn: 24. Prog sep from AM. Format: C&W. News staff 4; news progmg 15 hrs wkly. Target aud: 25-54. ■ Ross Biederman, gen mgr; Jon Patrick, natl sls mgr; Ryan Dobry, mus dir; Merlin Dumbrille, pub affrs dir. ■ Rates: $55; 27; 36; 27.

Tuscola

WKMF-FM—Sept 14, 1987: 101.7 mhz; 3 kw. Ant 328 ft. TL: N43 16 12 W83 30 14. 306 W. Genesee St., Frankenmuth (48734); 3338 Bristol Rd., Burton (48529). (313) 742-1470. FAX: (313) 742-5170. Licensee: Radiocom Ltd. Net: AP. Rep: Patt. Format: Country. ■ John Risher, gen mgr.

Twin Lake

***WBLV(FM)**—July 3, 1982: 90.3 mhz; 100 kw. Ant 649 ft. TL: N43 33 00 W86 02 34. Stereo. Hrs opn: 24. Blue Lake Fine Arts Camp (49457); Suite 200B, Waters Building, 161 Ottawa N.W., Grand Rapids (49503). (616) 894-2616; (616) 458-9258. FAX: (616) 893-2457. Licensee: Blue Lake Fine Arts Camp. Net: APR, NPR; Mich. Pub. Wash atty: Meyer, Faller, Weisman & Rosenberg. Format: Class, jazz, news. News progmg 20 hrs wkly. Target aud: Adult. Spec prog: Folk 5 hrs wkly. ■ William F. Stansell, pres; Buck Matthews, gen mgr & gen sls mgr; Gordon Christianson, opns dir; Dave Myers, progmg dir; Bonnie Bierma, mus dir; Brad Aspey, pub affrs dir; Don Hoogeboom, chief engr.

Vassar

WOWE(FM)—July 1, 1990: 98.9 mhz; 3 kw. Ant 328 ft. TL: N43 17 56 W83 30 34. 107 S. Main St. (48768). (517) 823-3399. FAX: (517) 823-3381. Licensee: Michael Joseph Shumpert. Format: CHR, urban contemp. ■ Mi-

Minnesota

chael Shumpert, pres & gen mgr; Kevin Askew, mus dir; Marsha Westbrook, news dir; Ed Czelada, chief engr.

Walker

WQFN(FM)—Not on air, target date unknown: 100.5 mhz; 3 kw. Ant 328 ft. TL: N43 01 01 W85 44 25. 1051 Fremont N.W., Grand Rapids (49504). Licensee: William E. Kuiper Jr.

Walled Lake

WPON(AM)—December 1954: 1460 khz; 1 kw-D, 760 w-N, DA-2. TL: N42 32 38 W83 29 58. 2222 Franklin Rd., Bloomfield Hills (48302). (313) 332-8883. FAX: (313) 332-8899. Licensee: Foreign Radio Programs Inc. (acq 12-4-82; $1,065,000; FTR 12-6-82). Format: Ethnic, adult contemp, talk. Target aud: General; diverse metropolitan ethnic groups. ■ Yolanda Zaparackas, gen mgr; Paul Harding, progmg dir, mus dir & chief engr. ■ Rates: $40; 40; 40; 25.

Warren

***WPHS(FM)**—March 20, 1964: 89.1 mhz; 110 w. Ant 150 ft. TL: N42 31 00 W83 00 36. Stereo. Hrs opn: 9:30 AM-8 PM. P.K. Cousino High School, 30333 Hoover Rd. (48093); Warren Consolidated Schools, 31300 Anita (48093). (313) 751-3689; (313) 574-3137. FAX: (313) 751-3755. Licensee: Warren Consolidated Schools (acq 1963). Wash atty: James Cooke. Format: Country, rock (AOR), CHR. News progmg 10 hrs wkly. Target aud: 12-27; males, 17-25. Spec prog: Auto news one hr, jazz one hr, blues one hr, Pol 2 hrs, Black 4 hrs, news 5 hrs, sports 3 hrs wkly. ■ Dr. Mary Barry Cybulski, pres; Jennifer Schermerhorn, gen mgr; Mathew Fieler, opns mgr; David Nowakowski, gen sls mgr; Cinzia Mancini, Paul Lefebvre, Scott Schwabe, vps prom; Diane Semoar, vp progmg; Sarah Donovan, mus dir; Christopher Sherwood, asst mus dir; Richard Slusher, chief engr. WCS-TV affil. ■ Rates: $15; 15; 15; 15.

West Branch

WBMB(AM)—June 7, 1972: 1060 khz; 1 kw-D. TL: N44 17 57 W84 15 59. c/o WHSB(FM), 1491 M-32 W., Alpena (49707). (517) 354-4611. FAX: (517) 354-4014. Licensee: Ives Broadcasting Inc. (acq 6-21-93; $75,000 with co-located FM; FTR 7-19-93). Net: Westwood One. Format: Adult contemp, oldies. Spec prog: Pol 6 hrs wkly. ■ David R. Karschnick, pres & gen mgr.

WBMI(FM)—Co-owned with WBMB(AM). Nov 7, 1977: 105.5 mhz; 3 kw. Ant 312 ft. TL: N44 17 57 W84 15 59. Stereo. Dups AM 100%. ■ Rates: Same as AM.

Westland

WNZK(AM)—Licensed to Westland. See Detroit.

Whitehall

WEFG(AM)—Oct 21, 1959: 1490 khz; 1 kw-U. TL: N43 23 04 W86 19 30. Stereo. Hrs opn: 24. Box 1204, Muskegon (49443). (616) 893-2247; (800) 968-7529. FAX: (616) 893-2147. Licensee: Pyramid Broadcasting Co. (acq 3-15-81). Net: MBS, NBC. Format: C&W. News staff 2; news progmg 2 hrs wkly. Target aud: 25-54. Spec prog: Relg, farm one hr wkly. ■ Van Carsa, gen mgr; Mike St. James, progmg dir; Ingrid Van Damme, news dir. ■ Rates: $13; 13; 13; 13.

WEFG-FM—April 1, 1991: 97.5 mhz; 3 kw. Ant 430 ft. TL: N43 23 04 W86 19 30. Stereo. Hrs opn: 24. Dups AM 100%. Net: Unistar. Format: Country. News staff one; news progmg one hr wkly. Target aud: 25-49. ■ Peter Rothfuss, vp opns; Jim McNeely, dev dir.

WMHG(FM)—1975: 95.3 mhz; 2 kw. Ant 360 ft. TL: N43 21 14 W86 19 38. Stereo. Box 238, 592 Pontaluna Rd., Muskegon (49443). (616) 798-2141. FAX: (616) 798-3677. Licensee: KBZ Broadcasting Inc. (acq 1986; $475,000; FTR 10-27-86). Net: ABC/C, Moody, Westwood One. Rep: Roslin. Wash atty: Fletcher, Heald & Hildreth. Format: Adult contemp. News progmg 3 hrs wkly. Target aud: 25-54. ■ Scott Taylor, progmg dir; Mark Frost, mus dir; William Heintzelman, news dir; Lynn Kolk, chief engr.

Wyoming

***WYCE(FM)**—Nov 1, 1983: 88.1 mhz; 1 kw. Ant 62 ft. TL: N42 54 45 W85 41 06. 2820 Clyde Park Ave. S.W. (49509-2995). (616) 530-7509. FAX: (616) 531-8350. Licensee: Grand Rapids Cable Access Center Inc. (acq 5-31-89; $30,616; FTR 6-19-89). Format: Alternative, adult contemp. ■ Lee Ferraro, stn mgr; Thom Bland, progmg dir.

WYGR(AM)—Nov 14, 1964: 1530 khz; 500 w-D. TL: N42 55 38 W85 44 50. Box 9591 (49509). (616) 532-1168; (616) 249-1530. Licensee: WYGR Broadcasting (acq 3-18-89). Net: USA. Rep: Patt. Wash atty: Meyer, Faller, Weisman & Rosenberg, P.C. Format: Talk, big band. Target aud: 45 plus; upscale. Spec prog: Black 2 hrs, relg 4 hrs, Polka 6 hrs, sports 3 hrs, Indian one hr wkly. ■ Roland Rusticus, gen mgr; Richard Pastoor, gen sls mgr; Scott Pastoor, prom mgr.

Ypsilanti

***WEMU(FM)**—Dec 8, 1965: 89.1 mhz; 15.5 kw. Ant 289 ft. TL: N42 15 48 W83 37 34. Stereo. Hrs opn: 24. Box 350, Eastern Michigan Univ., 426 King Hall (48197-0350). (313) 487-2229; (313) 487-8936. FAX: (313) 487-1015. Licensee: Eastern Michigan Univ. Net: AP, NPR; Mich. Pub. Wash atty: Cohn & Marks. Format: News, jazz. News staff 2; news progmg 39 hrs wkly. Target aud: General. ■ Arthur Timko, gen mgr; Mary Motherwell, dev dir; Linda Yohn, mus dir; Clark Smith, news dir; Ray Cryderman, chief engr.

WWCM(AM)—Nov 16, 1962: 990 khz; 500 w-D, 250 w-N, DA-2. TL: N42 15 55 W83 36 42. Stereo. 17 N. Huron St. (48197). (313) 482-4000. FAX: (313) 482-4995. Licensee: Word Broadcasting Inc. Net: MBS. Rep: Radio Spot Sls. Format: Adult contemp Christian. ■ Lou Velker, pres & gen mgr; Daniel Poole, gen sls mgr; Jack Hickey, prom mgr, progmg dir & mus dir; Jim Wade, chief engr.

Zeeland

***WGNB(FM)**—Jan 21, 1989: 89.3 mhz; 30 kw. Ant 500 ft. TL: N42 50 14 W85 59 17. Stereo. Hrs opn: 24. Box 40, 3764 84th Ave. (49464). (616) 772-7300. Licensee: The Moody Bible Institute of Chicago Inc. (group owner; acq 2-5-91; FTR 2-25-91). Net: AP, Moody. Format: Relg. News progmg 15 hrs wkly. Target aud: 35-64; Evangelical Christians. ■ Dr. Joseph Stowell, pres; Dennis Shere, sr vp; Robert Neff, vp; J. Scott Keegan, gen mgr & progmg dir; Scott Curtis, mus dir; James Klopfenstein, chief engr.

WISZ(AM)—February 1990: 640 khz; 1 kw-D, 250 w-N. TL: N42 47 31 W86 01 11. Hrs opn: 24. c/o Radio Station WBYY, 3090 28th St. S.E., Grand Rapids (49512). (616) 949-8585. FAX: (616) 949-9262. Licensee: Randall C. Disselkoen (acq 7-8-93; $37,000; FTR 8-2-93). Format: Kids music. ■ Randy Disselkoen, pres & gen sls mgr; Randall C. Disselkoen, gen mgr; Mark Roberts, prom mgr, progmg dir & mus dir.

WJQK(FM)—Licensed to Zeeland. See Holland.

WWJQ(AM)—See Holland.

Minnesota

LAUREN A. COLBY
301-663-1086
COMMUNICATIONS ATTORNEY
Special Attention to Difficult Cases

Ada

KRJB(FM)—Sept 1, 1985: 106.3 mhz; 3 kw. Ant 276 ft. TL: N47 18 41 W96 31 13. Stereo. 312 W. Main St. (56510). (218) 784-2844. FAX: (218) 784-3749. Licensee: R & J Broadcasting (acq 10-1-87). Net: CNN; MNN. Format: Country. ■ Jim Birkemeyer, vp mktg, vp prom, vp adv & vp progmg; K-Lyne Hegreberg, mus dir; Jim Peterick, asst mus dir & news dir; Woody Roux, pub affrs dir; Dean Johnson, vp engrg. ■ Rates: $13; 13; 13; 11.

Aitkin

KKIN(AM)—June 1, 1961: 930 khz; 2.5 kw-D, 400 w-N. TL: N46 32 26 W93 39 22. Stereo. Hrs opn: 24. Box 930, Hwy. 169 N. (56431). (218) 927-2344. FAX: (218) 927-2100. Licensee: Upper Minnesota Broadcasting Corp. (acq 3-10-69). Net: Unistar, UPI, ABC; MNN. Wash atty: Tim Brady. Format: C&W. Target aud: General. ■ Michael P. Patterson, pres; Boyd Bremner, gen mgr; Mace Twigg, progmg dir; John Thoten, news dir; Mark Persons, chief engr.

KEZZ(FM)—Co-owned with KKIN(AM). Jan 3, 1972: 94.3 mhz; 3 kw. Ant 328 ft. TL: N46 32 07 W93 50 26. Stereo. Hrs opn: 24. Prog sep from AM. Format: Adult contemp. ■ Boyd Bremner, gen sls mgr; John Heltemes, mus dir; Bunny Vall, news dir.

Albany

KASM(AM)—Nov 20, 1950: 1150 khz; 2.5 kw-D, 23 w-N. TL: N45 37 59 W94 36 00 (CP: 2.1 kw, TL: N45 37 53 W94 36 00). Box 390, Albany, ND (56307). (612) 845-2184. FAX: (612) 845-2187. Licensee: KASM of Minnesota Inc. (acq 4-24-92; $750,000 with co-located FM; FTR 5-11-92). Net: MAGNET. Rep: Torbet; Hyett/Ramsland.Wash atty: Baker & Hostetler. Format: Country, news, polka. Target aud: 36 plus. Spec prog: Oldies, Ger mus 2 hrs wkly. ■ Steve Gretsch, gen mgr.

KASM-FM—Not on air, target date May 1993: 105.5 mhz; 3 kw. Ant 328 ft. TL: N45 37 53 W94 36 00.

Albert Lea

KATE(AM)—October 1937: 1450 khz; 1 kw-U. TL: N43 38 00 W93 22 15. Stereo. Hrs opn: 24. Box 971, 305 S. First Ave. (56007). (507) 373-2338. FAX: (507) 373-4730. Licensee: Communications Properties Inc. (group owner; FTR; 4-16-90). Net: ABC/I. Rep: Banner. Format: MOR, C&W, div. News staff 3; news progmg 30 hrs wkly. Target aud: 12 plus; general. Spec prog: Farm 18 hrs, Sp 2 hrs wkly. ■ Phil Kelly, pres; Dave Nolander, gen mgr; Vern Rasmussen, gen sls mgr; Bill Elliot, prom mgr, progmg dir & news dir; Darrel Amundson, mus dir; Dercey Christianson, chief engr.

KCPI(FM)—Co-owned with KATE(AM). July 1974: 95.3 mhz; 3 kw. Ant 299 ft. TL: N43 38 00 W93 22 15 (CP: 94.9 mhz, 50 kw, ant 466 ft., TL: N43 52 04 W93 16 16). Stereo. Hrs opn: 24. Prog sep from AM. Format: Oldies based adult contemp. News progmg 12 hrs wkly. Target aud: 25-45. ■ Bill Elliott, opns mgr.

KQPR-FM—Aug 14, 1990: 96.1 mhz; 6 kw. Ant 328 ft. TL: N43 34 54 W93 23 42. Stereo. Hrs opn: 24. Box 1106, D-D Bldg., Suite L, 326 S. Broadway (56006). (507) 373-9600. FAX: (507) 373-9045. Licensee: Radio Albert Lea Inc. Group owner: Robert E. Ingstad Broadcast Properties. Net: ABC/R. Rep: Torbet. Format: Adult contemp. News staff one. Target aud: General. ■ Robert Ingstad, pres; Tammi Jensen, stn mgr; Bob Berrell, progmg dir; Cathy Kalis, pub affrs dir; Paul Trichenal, chief engr. ■ Rates: $19; 19; 19; 13.50.

Alexandria

KIKV-FM—Dec 25, 1970: 100.7 mhz; 100 kw. Ant 1,023 ft. TL: N45 41 03 W95 08 14. Stereo. Box 1024, 604 3rd Ave. W. (56308). (612) 762-2154. Licensee: BDI Broadcasting Inc. Group owner: Omni Broadcasting Co. (acq 9-25-89; $855,000; FTR 10-16-89). Net: ABC/C; Linder Farm. Rep: Katz. Format: Country. News staff one. Target aud: 25-54. Spec prog: Farm 20 hrs wkly. ■ Lou Buron, pres; Dave Vagle, gen mgr; Trudy Blanshan, gen sls mgr; Rick Blanshan, progmg dir; Jim Rohn, news dir; Wendel Sowers, chief engr.

KSTQ(FM)—April 2, 1984: 99.3 mhz; 6 kw. Ant 285 ft. TL: N45 52 48 W95 18 40. Stereo. Hrs opn: 24. Box 1114, 601 Broadway (56308); Box 241, Glenwood (56334). (612) 763-6515; (612) 763-5999. FAX: (612) 763-7779. Licensee: Branstock Communications Inc. (acq 6-18-93; $550,000; FTR 7-19-93). Net: Jones Satellite Audio. Format: Adult contemp/soft hits, news/talk. Target aud: 25-54. Spec prog: Jazz one hr, relg 3 hrs wkly. ■ Steve R. Nester, pres; John Messenger, gen mgr & progmg dir; Chuck Schott, gen sls mgr; Steven R. Nestor, mktg dir; Paul Rykhus, prom dir; Patty Wicken, news dir; Steven Youngberg, chief engr.

KXRA(AM)—July 27, 1949: 1490 khz; 1 kw-U. TL: N45 52 30 W95 21 30. Hrs opn: 5 AM-midnight. Box 69, 1312 Broadway (56308). (612) 763-3131. FAX: (612) 763-5641. Licensee: Paradis Broadcasting of Alexandria Inc. (acq 10-1-88). Net: NBC; MNN. Format: News/talk. News staff one. Target aud: 45 plus. Spec prog: Farm 5 hrs, relg 2 hrs wkly. ■ Mel Paradis, pres; Brett Paradis, gen mgr & gen sls mgr; Steve Sherwin, prom mgr & progmg dir; Dennis Anhalt, news dir; Wendell Sowers, chief engr. ■ Rates: $12; 10; 12; 6.

KXRA-FM—May 1, 1968: 92.3 mhz; 13.5 kw. Ant 446 ft. TL: N45 52 30 W95 21 30. Stereo. Prog sep from AM. Net: NBC the Source. Format: CHR. Target aud: 20-40. ■ Ron Revere, progmg dir; Mike Loman, mus dir.

Anoka

KBCW(AM)—(Brooklyn Park). April 15, 1956: 1470 khz; 5 kw-U, DA-2. TL: N45 05 17 W93 22 59. Stn currently dark. 5820 74th Ave. N., No. 101, Brooklyn Park (55443-3140). Licensee: North Suburban Radio Co. (acq 12-1-77). ■ Bruce B. James, pres; Jeff Boone, gen mgr.

KQQL(FM)—Aug 1, 1968: 107.9 mhz; 100 kw. Ant 1,080 ft. TL: N45 20 12 W93 23 28. Stereo. Suite 1319, 100 Washington Sq., Minneapolis (55401). (612) 338-8118. FAX: (612) 333-1616. Licensee: Radio 100 L.P. Group owner: Colfax Communications Inc. (acq 12-16-92; $14 million; FTR 1-11-93). Format: Oldies. News staff one. Target aud: 35-54. ■ Kevin McCarthy, vp & gen mgr; Shelly Malecha, gen sls mgr; Ann Licater, prom mgr; Kevin Methenez, progmg dir; Mike Troge, chief engr.

Appleton

***KRSU(FM)**—Oct 25, 1989: 91.3 mhz; 75 kw. Ant 1,158 ft. TL: N45 10 03 W96 00 02. Stereo. Hrs opn: 24. 45 E. 7th St., St. Paul (55101). (612) 290-1500. FAX: (612) 290-1260. Licensee: Minnesota Public Radio Inc. Net: NPR, APR; Minn. Pub. Format: Classical, news. ■ William H. Kling, pres; Valerie Arganbright, gen mgr; Ralph Homberger, engrg dir.

Atwater

KYRS(FM)—Licensed to Atwater. See Litchfield.

Austin

KAUS(AM)—May 30, 1948: 1480 khz; 1 kw-U, DA-2. TL: N43 37 20 W92 59 26. Hrs opn: 24. Box 159, Hwy. 105 S. (55912). (507) 437-7666; (507) 437-1480. FAX: (507) 437-7669. Licensee: Orion Broadcasting Co. Group owner: Nolan Broadcast Group (acq 12-12-78). Net: NBC, MBS. MNN. Rep: Eastman. Wash atty: Wiley, Rein & Fielding. Format: Oldies, adult contemp, news/talk. News staff 3; news progmg 20 hrs wkly. Target aud: 25-54. ■ Phil Nolan, pres; Ken S. Soderberg, gen sls mgr; Duane Germaine, progmg dir; Dan Conradt, news dir; Marv Olson, chief engr.

KAUS-FM—1963: 99.9 mhz; 100 kw. Ant 900 ft. TL: N43 37 42 W93 09 12. Stereo. Hrs opn: 24. Prog sep from AM. Net: MBS; Rep: Eastman. Format: Country. News staff 2; news progmg 12 hrs wkly. Target aud: 25-54. ■ Phil Nolan, CEO & gen mgr; Marv Olson, progmg dir & engrg dir; Scott Soderberg, mus dir.

***KMSK(FM)**—Jan 12, 1981: 91.3 mhz; 135 w. Ant 221 ft. TL: N43 40 39 W93 00 04. Stereo. Hrs opn: 6 AM-1 AM. Rebroadcasts KMSU(FM) Mankato. Box 153, Box 8400 Mankato State Univ. (56002-8400). (507) 389-5679. FAX: (507) 389-1899. Licensee: Mankato State University (acq 12-23-91). Net: NPR. Wash atty: Cohn & Marks. Format: Public affrs, educ, mus. News staff one; news progmg 50 hrs wkly. Target aud: General; upscale, educated. Spec prog: Drama 3 hrs, folk/ethnic 5 hrs, new age 5 hrs wkly. ■ Margaret Preska, CEO; William McGinley, gen mgr; Susan Wood, dev dir & prom mgr; Henrey Busse Jr., mus dir; Fred Vette, news dir; Ron Dick, chief engr.

KQAQ(AM)—Apr 16, 1960: 970 khz; 5 kw-D, 500 w-N, DA-2. TL: N43 42 27 W92 56 45. Hrs opn: 5 AM-midnight. Rt. 1, Box 50, Rochester (55912). (507) 437-9213. Licensee: Robert E. Ingstad and Janice M. Ingstad (group owner; acq 6-10-92; $160,000; FTR 7-6-92). Net: NBC, NBC Talknet, Linder Farm, Tribune. Rep: Katz. Format: Talk. News staff one; news progmg 10 hrs wkly. Target aud: 25-54. ■ Larry Edwards, pres; Bob Junge, gen mgr; James C. Ruud, gen sls mgr & prom mgr; Robin Thorpe, progmg dir & mus dir; Ted Anthony, news dir; Donald Franz, chief engr. ■ Rates: $12.50; 40; 12.50; 10.

Baxter

WJJY(AM)—Aug 29, 1987: 1270 khz; 5 kw-U, DA-N. TL: N46 17 55 W94 16 42. 410 Front St., Brainerd (56401). (218) 828-1244. FAX: (218) 828-1119. Licensee: Tower Broadcasting Corp. Net: ABC, CBS. Format: Oldies. News staff one; news progmg 20 hrs wkly. Target aud: 25 plus. ■ James R. Pryor, pres, gen mgr & chief engr; Steve Foy, gen sls mgr; Hugh K. Phillips, progmg dir & news dir. ■ Rates: $8; 8; 8; 8.

Bemidji

KBHP(FM)—Listing follows KBUN(AM).

***KBSB(FM)**—Jan 19, 1970: 89.7 mhz; 115 w. Ant 126 ft. TL: N47 29 00 W94 52 27. Hrs opn: 17. 215 Deputy Hall, Bemidji State Univ. (56601). (218) 755-2059. FAX: (218) 755-4119. Licensee: Bemidji State Univ. Format: Diversified, contemp hit. Target aud: 16-35; college & high school students. Spec prog: Big band 2 hrs, country 3 hrs wkly. ■ Roger Paskvan, gen mgr; Nicole Pheroux, stn mgr; Tony Poetz, progmg dir.

KBUN(AM)—1946: 1450 khz; 1 kw-U, DA-1. TL: N47 27 56 W94 54 37. Hrs opn: 24. Box 1656, 502 Beltrami Ave. (56601). (218) 751-4120. Licensee: Paul Bunyan Broadcasting Co. Group owner: Omni Broadcasting Co. (acq 6-22-89; FTR 6-26-89). Net: MBS. Format: Sports talk. News staff one. Target aud: 18-54. ■ Louis H. Buron Jr., CEO, pres & gen mgr; Mary A. Campbell, CFO & exec vp; Peggy Hanson, gen sls mgr; Todd Haugen, progmg dir; Kevin Jackson, progmg mgr; Mardy Karger, news dir & pub affrs dir.

KBHP(FM)—Co-owned with KBUN(AM). Aug 3, 1972: 101.1 mhz; 100 kw. Ant 331 ft. TL: N47 22 18 W94 52 56. Stereo. Hrs opn: 24. Prog sep from AM. Format: Country.

***KCRB-FM**—Dec 22, 1982: 88.5 mhz; 95 kw. Ant 994 ft. TL: N47 42 03 W94 29 15. Hrs opn: 24. Box 578 (56601). (218) 751-8864. FAX: (218) 751-8640. Licensee: Minnesota Public Radio Inc. Net: APR, NPR; Minn. Pub. Format: Class, news, info. News staff one; news progmg 25 hrs wkly. ■ William H. Kling, pres; Dennis Hamilton, gen mgr; Marilyn Heltzer, stn mgr; Dave Cox, news dir.

KKBJ(AM)—Oct 31, 1977: 1360 khz; 5 kw-D, 2.5 kw-N, DA-N. TL: N47 26 32 W94 55 07. Box 1360, 2115 Washington Ave. S. (56601). (218) 751-5950. FAX: (218) 751-5953. Licensee: CD Broadcasting Corp of Bemidji. Group owner: CD Broadcasting Corp. (acq 12-31-87). Net: ABC/D. Format: Country, talk. News progmg 15 hrs wkly. Target aud: 25-54. ■ Chris Dahl, pres; Mike Anderson, gen mgr; Brian Edward, opns mgr; Barbara Baer, gen sls mgr; Mike Murphy, progmg dir & mus dir; Ken Bartz, chief engr. ■ Rates: $15; 11; 13; 9.

KKBJ-FM—Aug 8, 1983: 103.7 mhz; 100 kw. Ant 460 ft. TL: N47 33 19 W94 47 59. Stereo. Hrs opn: 24. Prog sep from AM. Net: ABC/E. Format: Contemp hit. ■ Brian Edwards, progmg dir & mus dir. ■ Rates: Same as AM.

***KNBJ(FM)**—Not on air, target date June 1, 1994: 91.3 mhz; 60 kw. Ant 974 ft. Hrs opn: 24. Rebroadcasts KNOW-FM St. Paul 90%. 45 E. Seventh St., Saint Paul (55101); Box 578 (56601). (218) 751-8864. FAX: (218) 751-8640. Licensee: Minnesota Public Radio. Net: APR, NPR; Minn. Pub. Format: News. ■ William H. King, pres; Dennis Hamilton, vp; Ellen Blanchard, dev dir; Joelle Andette, asst mus dir.

Benson

KSCR(AM)—December 1956: 1290 khz; 500 w-D. TL: N45 19 06 W95 33 48. 105 13th St. N. (56215). (612) 843-3290. FAX: (612) 843-3955. Licensee: Davies Broadcasting Co. (acq 11-8-91; $200,000; with co-located FM; FTR 12-2-91). Net: SMN; MNN. Wash atty: Leventhal, Senter & Lerman. Format: Pop standards. News staff one; news progmg 25 hrs wkly. Target aud: 35-65; 24 plus in the morning. Spec prog: Farm 10 hrs wkly. ■ Dan Davies, pres & gen mgr; Barb Erickson, gen sls mgr; Pat Thorson, progmg dir & mus dir; Jason Brandt, news dir; Steve Youngberg, chief engr.

KSCR-FM—April 26, 1968: 93.5 mhz; 3 kw. Ant 200 ft. TL: N45 19 06 W95 33 48. Stereo. Dups AM 100%.

Blackduck

WBJI(FM)—1991: 98.3 mhz; 50 kw. Ant 456 ft. TL: N47 33 19 W94 47 59. 102 1/2 Lincoln Ave., Bemidji (56601). Licensee: R.P. Broadcasting Inc. ■ Randy Cable, gen mgr.

Blue Earth

KBEW(AM)—Aug 29, 1963: 1560 khz; 1 kw-D. TL: N43 38 48 W95 33 48. Box 278 (56013). (507) 526-2181. FAX: (507) 526-7468. Licensee: KBEW Radio Inc. Group owner: Result Radio Group (acq 2-1-81). Net: ABC/E. Rep: Katz. Format: Country. News staff one. Target aud: General. ■ Jerry Papenfuss, pres & gen mgr; Roy Haven, stn mgr & progmg dir; Wanda Nichols, adv mgr; Norm Hall, news dir; Mike Hendrickson, chief engr.

KBEW-FM—Not on air, target date unknown: 98.1 mhz; 25 kw. Ant 328 ft. TL: N43 38 44 W94 05 33.

KJLY(FM)—Nov 1, 1983: 104.5 mhz; 50 kw. Ant 495 ft. TL: N43 39 41 W94 06 29. Stereo. Box 72, County Rd. 6. (56013). (507) 526-3233. FAX: (507) 526-3235. Licensee: Minn-Iowa Christian Broadcasting. Net: Moody, USA. Format: Inspirational relg. News staff one; news progmg 21 hrs wkly. Target aud: 25-55. Spec prog: Farm 5 hrs, childrens 4 hrs wkly. ■ Maurice Schwen, pres; Paul Schneider, gen mgr & progmg dir; Matthew Dorfner, opns dir; Rob Stauter, mus dir; Paul Egeness, news dir; Steve Larson, chief engr.

Brainerd

KABD(FM)—Not on air, target date unknown: 103.5 mhz; 6 kw. Ant 328 ft. 2437 Sylvan Birch Ln. W (56401). Licensee: June A. Persons.

***KBPR(FM)**—Licensed to Brainerd. See Collegeville.

KLIZ(AM)—Aug 6, 1946: 1380 khz; 5 kw-U, DA-N. TL: N46 19 56 W94 10 26. Hrs opn: 24. 2700 E. Oak St. (56401). Box 980 (56401). (218) 829-2853. FAX: (218) 829-6983. Licensee: Sioux Valley Broadcasting (acq 10-1-89). Net: AP, NBC Talknet, NBC; MNN, Midwest Radio. Rep: Hyett/Ramsland. Format: Contemp country, sports, news/talk. News staff one; news progmg 30 hrs wkly. Target aud: 25-54. ■ Jeff Hilborn, gen mgr; Don Jahnke, gen sls mgr; Tim Norton, progmg dir; Jerry Freed, news dir; Doug Stromberg, chief engr.

KLIZ-FM—May 23, 1960: 107.5 mhz; 100 kw. Ant 350 ft. TL: N46 19 56 W94 10 26. Stereo. Prog sep from AM. Format: Classic rock. News progmg 3 hrs wkly. Target aud: 18-49.

KVBR(AM)—May 16, 1964: 1340 khz; 1 kw-U. TL: N46 20 51 W94 10 52. Hrs opn: 24. KVBR Bldg., 411 Laurel St. (56401). (218) 829-8747. FAX: (218) 829-8748. Licensee: Greater Minnesota Broadcasting Corp. (acq 3-3-86; $450,000; FTR 2-3-86). Net: ABC/I, AP. Format: Country. News staff one; news progmg 20 hrs wkly. Target aud: 35-65. ■ Charles B. Persons, pres, gen mgr, gen sls mgr & prom mgr; Dave Torkelson, vp progmg; Don Kelley, news dir; Mark W. Persons, chief engr. ■ Rates: $12; 12; 12; 9.

WJJY-FM—July 21, 1978: 106.7 mhz; 100 kw. Ant 448 ft. TL: N46 26 36 W94 22 58. Stereo. 410 Front St. (56401). (218) 828-1244. FAX: (218) 828-1119. Licensee: Tower Broadcasting Corp. Net: MBS. Format: Full svc adult contemp. News staff one; news progmg 20 hrs wkly. Target aud: 25 plus. ■ James R. Pryor, pres & gen mgr; Tom Albrecht, gen sls mgr; Mark Hegstrom, prom mgr; Hugh K. Phillips, progmg dir & news dir; Barry Brueland, mus dir; M.W. Persons, chief engr. ■ Rates: $15; 13; 15; 13.

Breckenridge

KBMW(AM)—Licensed to Breckenridge. See Wahepton, N.D.

KLTA(FM)—Feb 17, 1970: 107.9 mhz; 100 kw. Ant 713 ft. TL: N46 32 41 W96 37 33. Stereo. Suite 201, 2501 13th Ave. SW, Fargo, ND (58103). (701) 237-4500. FAX: (701) 235-9082. Licensee: T & J Broadcasting Inc. Tom Ingstad Broadcasting Group. Rep: Christal. Format: Adult contemp. Target aud: 25-54; adults; skews female. ■ Randy Holland, CEO; Tom Ingstad, pres; Nancy Odney, gen mgr; Michael Brooks, rgnl sls mgr; Dan Michaels, progmg mgr; Bill Csongradi, mus dir; Ken Bartz, chief engr.

Breezy Point

KLKS(FM)—June 14, 1984: 104.3 mhz; 50 kw. Ant 492 ft. TL: N46 36 13 W94 15 04. Stereo. Hrs opn: 5 AM-1 AM Box 300 (56472); Ski Chalet Dr. (56472). (218) 562-4884; (218) 829-2997 (SALES OFFICE BRAINIERD). FAX: (218) 562-4058; (218) 829-9341 (SALES OFFICE BRAINIERD). Licensee: Lakes Broadcasting Group Inc. Net: CNN. Wash atty: Hogan & Artson. Format: MOR, div, oldies. News staff 2; news progmg 25 hrs wkly. Target aud: 40 plus. ■ Allen Gray, CEO, chmn & pres; Diane Anderson, CFO & vp opns; Robert L. "Bob" Bundgaard, sr vp & gen mgr, progmg dir; Thomas Kenow, vp sls.

Brooklyn Park

KBCW(AM)—Licensed to Brooklyn Park. See Anoka.

Browerville

KXDL(FM)—Licensed to Browerville. See Long Prairie.

Buffalo

KRWC(AM)—Nov 16, 1971: 1360 khz; 500 w-D. TL: N45 10 00 W93 55 11. Hrs opn: 6 AM-6:30 PM. Box 267 (55313). (612) 682-4444. FAX: (612) 682-3542. Licensee: Donnell Inc. (acq 10-15-75). Net: MBS; MNN. Format: Country. News staff one; news progmg 16 hrs wkly. Target aud: 25 plus. ■ Kurt Weiche, pres, gen mgr & gen sls mgr; Tim Matthews, progmg dir & mus dir; Mike Henry, news dir; John George, chief engr. ■ Rates: $11; 11; 11; na.

Caledonia

KKOO(FM)—Not on air, target date unknown: 94.7 mhz; 3 kw. Ant 328 ft. TL: N43 42 34 W91 27 52. 15251 N.E. 18th Ave., North Miami Beach, FL (33162). (305) 949-8326. Licensee: Oasis Broadcasting Partners Inc.

Cambridge

WLOL(FM)—May 5, 1973: 105.3 mhz; 25 kw. Ant 298 ft. TL: N45 31 17 W93 10 27. Stereo. Hrs opn: 24. Box 191, 540 Emerson Ave. N. (55008). (612) 339-2215; (612) 689-1055. FAX: (619) 339-3163. Licensee: Intrepid Broadcasting Inc. (acq 7-91; $800,000). Net: ABC/D, SMN. Wash atty: Leventhal, Senter & Lerman. Format: Adult contemp. News staff one; news progmg 24 hrs wkly. Target aud: 25-54. Spec prog: Farm 8 hrs wkly. ■ Todd J. Garamella, pres & gen mgr; Ray Foslid, gen sls mgr; Berni Orbeck, prom mgr; Brian Zepp, progmg dir & mus dir; Donn Fredlund, news dir; Steve Youngberg, chief engr. ■ Rates: $18; 18; 18; 18.

Cloquet

WKLK(AM)—Jan 31, 1950: 1230 khz; 1 kw-U, DA-1. TL: N46 44 58 W92 25 17. 807 Cloquet Ave. (55720-1613). (218) 879-4534. FAX: (218) 879-1962. Licensee: QB Broadcasting Ltd. (acq 5-12-92; $200,000 with co-located FM; FTR 6-1-92). Net: AP, SMN. Format: Oldies. News staff one; news progmg 16 hrs wkly. Target aud: Community oriented. Spec prog: Farm one hr, polka 2 hrs, relg 5 hrs, talk one hr, health issues one hr, political one hr wkly. ■ Al Quarnstrom, CEO & gen mgr; Linda Quarnstrom, vp; Jim Ruzic, gen sls mgr; Scott Conrad, progmg dir; Mark Larson, news dir; Bill Meyes, chief engr.

WKLK-FM—April 30, 1992: 96.5 mhz; 6 kw. Ant 315 ft. TL: N46 44 58 W92 25 17.

***WSCN(FM)**—Nov 17, 1975: 100.5 mhz; 100 kw. Ant 875 ft. TL: N46 47 21 W92 06 51. Stereo. Hrs opn: 24. 224 Holiday Ctr., Duluth (55802). (218) 722-9411. FAX: (218) 720-4900. Licensee: Minnesota Public Radio (acq 12-88; $200,000; FTR 12-19-88). Net: APR, NPR; Minn. Pub. Format: All news. ■ William H. Kling, pres; John R. Snee, gen mgr; Carol Howe, dev dir; Bob Kelleher, news dir; Jon Blomstrand, chief engr.

Cold Spring

KMXK(FM)—Aug 30, 1968: 94.9 mhz; 50 kw. Ant 492 ft. TL: N45 23 53 W94 25 15. Stereo. Box 220, St. Cloud (56302). (612) 251-4422. FAX: (612) 255-1806. Licensee: Andrew Higler. Format: Oldies. ■ Steve Stewart, gen mgr; Kathy Merchant, natl sls mgr.

Coleraine

KGPZ(FM)—Not on air, target date unknown: 96.1 mhz; 100 kw. Ant 577 ft. TL: N47 19 31 W93 16 18. 419 W. Michigan St., Duluth (55802). Licensee: Latto Northland Broadcasting Inc. Group owner: Lew Latto Group of Northland Radio Stations.

Collegeville

***KBPR(FM)**—(Brainerd). February 1988: 90.7 mhz; 34.2 kw. Ant 679 ft. TL: N46 25 21 W94 27 41. Stereo. Hrs opn: 24. Box 7011, Collegeville (56321). (218) 829-1072. FAX: (612) 363-4948. Licensee: Minnesota Public Radio. Net: APR, NPR; Minn. Pub. Format: Class, news, info. News staff 2. Target aud: General. ■ William H. Kling, pres; Anne Hovland, vp dev; Ginger Sisco, vp mktg; Vic Bremer, vp progmg; Loren Omoto, news dir; Ralph Hornberger, engrg dir; Rob Daly, chief engr.

***KNSR(FM)**—Aug 29, 1988: 88.9 mhz; 100 kw. Ant 728 ft. TL: N45 29 52 W94 32 14. Stereo. Hrs opn: 24. Box 7011, St. John's University (56321). (612) 363-7702. FAX: (612) 363-4948. Licensee: Minnesota Public Radio. Net: APR, NPR; Minn. Pub. Format: All news. News staff 2. Target aud: General. ■ William H. Kling, pres; Anne Hovland, vp dev; Ginger Sisco, vp mktg; Vic Bremer, vp progmg; Dick Forney, progmg mgr; Loren Omoto, news dir; Ralph Hornberger, engrg dir; Rob Daly, chief engr.

***KSJR-FM**—Jan 21, 1967: 90.1 mhz; 100 kw. Ant 700 ft. TL: N45 29 52 W94 32 14. Stereo. Hrs opn: 24. Box 7011, St. John's University (56321). (612) 363-7702. FAX: (612) 363-4948. Licensee: Minnesota Public Radio. Net: APR; Minn. Pub. Format: Class. News staff 2. Target aud: General. ■ William H. Kling, pres; Anne Hovland, vp dev; Ginger Sisco, vp mktg; Vic Bremer, vp progmg; Arthur Cohen, progmg mgr; Loren Omoto, news dir; Ralph Hornberger, engrg dir; Rob Daly, chief engr.

Crookston

KQHT(FM)—Licensed to Crookston. See Grand Forks, N.D.

KROX(AM)—April 1948: 1260 khz; 1 kw-D, 500 w-N, DA-N. TL: N47 47 20 W96 35 40. Box 620, 208 S. Main St. (56716-1969). (218) 281-1140. FAX: (218) 281-5036. Licensee: Gopher Communications Co. (acq 5-11-87). Net: MBS; MNN, Midwest Radio Net. Rep: Hooper Jones. Format: Adult contemp. News staff 2; news progmg 40 hrs wkly. Spec prog: Farm 10 hrs wkly. ■ Frank Fee, gen mgr & progmg dir; Mark Anderson, mus dir; Jerry Dahlberg, news dir; Stan Mueller, chief engr.

KYCK(FM)—March 4, 1980: 97.1 mhz; 100 kw. Ant 360 ft. TL: N47 49 17 W96 49 03. Stereo. Box 5210, Suite 2B, 301 N. 3rd St., Grand Forks, ND (58206). (701) 746-4516. FAX: (701) 746-6375. Licensee: SS Broadcasting. Group owner: Leighton Enterprises Inc. Net: ABC/D. Rep: D & R Radio. Format: C&W, farm. ■ Al Leighton, pres; Jerry Gutensohn, gen mgr; Jaci Anderson, progmg dir; Ron Kennedy, mus dir & news dir; Dan Mueller, chief engr.

Crosby

KTCF(FM)—Oct 10, 1990: 101.5 mhz; 25 kw. Ant 328 ft. TL: N46 33 39 W94 00 15 (CP: 25 kw, TL: N46 32 05 W93 52 41). 27 First St., S.W. (56441). (218) 546-8155. FAX: (218) 546-8056. Licensee: First Radio Station of Crosby Inc. Net: Unistar, CNN. Format: Country. ■ Steve Hasskamp, pres & chief engr; Margaret Hasskamp, gen mgr & mus dir; Tom Lang, progmg dir.

Detroit Lakes

KDLM(AM)—October 1951: 1340 khz; 1 kw-U. TL: N46 50 14 W95 50 17. Hrs opn: 5:30 AM-midnight. Box 746, 1340 Richwood Rd. (56502). (218) 847-5624. FAX: (218) 847-7657. Licensee: Lakes to Plains Broadcasting Inc. Group owner: Leighton Enterprises Inc. (acq 8-22-90; $1.41 million with co-located FM; FTR 9-10-90). Net: CBS; MNN. Format: Adult contemp. Target aud: 21 plus. ■ Alver Leighton, chmn; Robert D. Spilman, pres & gen sls mgr; Scott Abbey, gen mgr; Andy Lia, progmg dir; Maureen Brown, news dir; Craig Bomgaars, chief engr.

KKDL(FM)—Co-owned with KDLM(AM). Jan 2, 1976: 95.1 mhz; 100 kw. Ant 970 ft. TL: N46 40 27 W96 13 39. Stereo. Hrs opn: 24. Prog sep from AM. Format: Golden oldies. News staff one; news progmg 8 hrs wkly. Target aud: 25-54; Fargo-Moorhead, metro and TSA listeners. ■ Alver Leighton, CEO; Scott Abbey, stn mgr; David Howey, prom dir; Bob Wayne, progmg dir & mus dir.

Duluth

KDAL(AM)—Nov 26, 1936: 610 khz; 5 kw-U, DA-N. TL: N46 43 13 W92 10 34. 425 W. Superior St. (55802). (218) 722-4321. FAX: (218) 722-5423. Licensee: Shockley Communications Co. (group owner; acq 4-88). Net: CBS; MNN, Midwest Radio. Rep: Hyett-Ramsland, Katz. Format: Div. News staff 3; news progmg 34 hrs wkly. Target aud: 35-64. ■ Terry K. Shockley, pres; Debra Messer, gen mgr & gen sls mgr; Mike Langevin, opns dir; John Schadl, news dir; John Talcot, engrg mgr.

KDAL-FM—July 1985: 95.7 mhz; 100 kw. Ant 830 ft. TL: N46 47 07 W92 07 15. Stereo. Prog sep from AM. Format: Adult contemp, gold. Target aud: 25-49. ■ Mike Langevin, progmg dir; Lauri Lynn, mus dir; John Schadl, asst mus dir.

***KDNI(FM)**—Licensed to Duluth. See Roseville.

***KDNW(FM)**—Not on air, target date unknown: 97.3 mhz; 40 kw. Ant 548 ft. TL: N46 47 20 W92 07 04. Stereo. Hrs opn: 24. 3003 N. Snelling Ave., St. Paul (55113). Licensee: Northwestern College Radio Foundation (acq 12-4-91; $20,000; FTR 1-6-92). Format: Relg. ■ Mel Johnson, chmn; Donald Ericksen, pres; Paul Ramseyer, exec vp; Paul Harkness, gen mgr, stn mgr, prom mgr, progmg dir & chief engr; Gordy Mesedahl, opns dir; Bob Nus, mus dir; Gordon Mesedahl, news dir.

KLXK(FM)—Jan 1, 1994: 101.7 mhz; 1.5 kw. Ant 466 ft. TL: N46 47 07 W92 07 15. Box 106, c/o Segue Communications Corp., Princeton (55371). (612) 389-1300. Licensee: Segue Communications Corp. (acq 10-21-92; $40,000; FTR 11-23-92). ■ Paul B. Steigerwald, CEO.

KQDS-FM—Apr 1, 1976: 94.9 mhz; 100 kw. Ant 730 ft. TL: N46 47 41 W92 07 05. Stereo. 2001 London Rd. (55812). (218) 728-6421. FAX: (218) 728-5809. Licensee: Great Duluth Broadcasting Co. Inc. Net: ABC/R. Format: AOR. News progmg 2 hrs wkly. Target aud: 18-49. ■ Tim Achterhoff, pres; Steve James, gen mgr & gen sls mgr; Jim Lien, mktg dir; Mike Keller, progmg dir; Paul St. Andrew, mus dir.

KQDS(AM)—Mar 11, 1963: 1490 khz; 1 kw-U. TL: N46 47 42 W92 07 08. Dups FM 100%.

***KUMD-FM**—May 26, 1971: 103.3 mhz; 95 kw. Ant 820 ft. TL: N46 47 31 W92 07 21. Stereo. Hrs opn: 5 AM-1 AM (Mon-Thu), 5 AM-3 AM (Fri), 6 AM-3 AM (Sat), 6 AM-midnight (Sun). 130 Humanities Bldg. (55812). (218) 726-7181. FAX: (218) 726-6571. Licensee: Board of Regents of U. of Minn. (acq 8-75). Net: APR. Format: News/info, new adult contemp. News staff 2; news progmg 39 hrs wkly. Target aud: 25-45. ■ Paul Schmitz, gen mgr; Paul Damberg, dev dir; John Ziegler, progmg dir & mus dir; Stephanie Hemphill, news dir; Kirk Kersten, chief engr.

KXTP(AM)—See Superior, Wis.

WAKX(FM)—June 14, 1972: 98.9 mhz; 100 kw. Ant 600 ft. TL: N46 47 30 W92 06 59. Stereo. Hrs opn: 24. Northland Bldg, 419 W. Michigan St (55802). (218) 727-7271. FAX: (218) 727-7108. Licensee: Stereo Broadcasting. Group owner: Lew Latto Group of Northland Radio Stns. (acq 11-1-74). Rep: Katz & Powell; O'Malley Communications. Wash atty: John McVeigh; Fisher, Wayland, Cooper & Leader. Format: Classic rock. Target aud: 25-49. ■ Lew Latto, pres & gen mgr; Eric Allen, opns mgr; Wilfred A. Meys, chief engr. ■ Rates: $90; 55; 80; 20.

WAVC(FM)—Listing follows WEBC(AM).

WDSM(AM)—See Superior, Wis.

WEBC(AM)—June 1924: 560 khz; 5 kw-U, DA-2. TL: N46 38 37 W91 59 09. 1001 E. 9th St. (55805). (218) 728-4484. FAX: (218) 728-1779. Licensee: North Land Broadcasting Inc. Group owner: Brill Media Co. Inc. (acq 5-21-84; $2 million with co-located FM; FTR 4-23-84). Net: ABC/I. Rep: Christal. Format: News/talk. ■ Charles Norman, pres & gen mgr; Roger Johnson, opns mgr; Chuck Gehlen, gen sls mgr; Julie Anderson, mktg dir & prom dir; Dave Walter, progmg dir & news dir; Paul Kero, chief engr.

WAVC(FM)—Co-owned with WEBC(AM). 1966: 105.1 mhz; 100 kw. Ant 789 ft. TL: N46 47 21 W92 06 51. Stereo. Dups AM 2%. (acq 1-83). Net: Unistar. Format: Country News staff one; news progmg 3 hrs wkly. Target aud: General. ■ Pat Puchalla, progmg dir; Tim Michaels, mus dir.

***WIRR(FM)**—(Virginia-Hibbing). December 1985: 90.9 mhz; 21 kw. Ant 552 ft. TL: N47 29 46 W92 47 05. Stereo. Hrs opn: 24. 224 Holiday Ctr., Duluth (55802). (218) 722-9411. FAX: (218) 720-4900. Licensee: Minnesota Public Radio Inc. Net: APR, NPR; Minn. Pub. Format: Class, news & info. News staff 3. Target aud: General. ■ William H. Kling, pres; John Snee, gen mgr; Janet Carter, opns dir; Carol Howe, dev dir; Cynthia Johnson, prom mgr; Bob Kelleher, news dir; Jon Blomstrand, chief engr.

***WSCD-FM**—Co-owned with WIRR(FM). 1975: 92.9 mhz; 70 kw. Ant 614 ft. TL: N46 47 20 W92 07 04. Stereo. Prog sep from WIRR(FM) Virginia-Hibbing. (218) 722-9411. ■ Carol Howe, prom mgr.

***WNCB(FM)**—Nov 1, 1982: 89.3 mhz; 2.4 kw. Ant 430 ft. TL: N46 47 14 W92 06 53 (CP: 2.4 kw). Stereo. 2828 Piedmont Ave. (55811-2938). (218) 722-3017. Licensee: North-Central Christian Broadcasting. Net: USA. Format: Adult contemp, contemp hits, relg. News progmg 5 hrs wkly. Target aud: 20-30. ■ Robert Baker, pres; Jeffrey Stromquist, gen mgr; Brett M. Gibson, progmg dir; Elizabeth Stromquist, mus dir; Douglas Krantz, chief engr.

***WSCD-FM**—Listing follows WIRR(FM).

WWJC(AM)—April 26, 1963: 850 khz; 10 kw-D. TL: N46 39 19 W92 12 40. 1120 E. McCuen St. (55808). (218) 626-2738. Licensee: WWJC Inc. Net: USA, CBN. Format: Relg. Spec prog: Talk 8 hrs wkly. ■ Robert Krejcie, pres; Ted Elm, gen mgr & progmg dir; John Talcott, chief engr.

Eagan

KMZZ(AM)—See Minneapolis-St. Paul.

East Grand Forks

KCNN(AM)—Aug 14, 1959: 1590 khz; 5 kw-D, 1 kw-N, DA-2. TL: N47 52 41 W97 00 24. Box 560 (56721). (701) 772-2204. Licensee: KRAD Inc. (acq 4-85). Net: CBS, MBS. Format: News, talk. Spec prog: Farm 6 hrs wkly. ■ David L. Norman, pres & gen mgr; Scott J. Hennen, stn mgr; D.L. Harvey, news dir; John Aasen, chief engr.

KZLT-FM—Co-owned with KCNN(AM). April 1, 1975: 104.3 mhz; 100 kw. Ant 550 ft. TL: N47 48 37 W96 55 46. Prog sep from AM. Format: Adult contemp. Spec prog:

Solid gold 8 hrs wkly. ■ Scott Hennen, progmg dir; Josh Jones, mus dir.

KSNR(FM)—(Thief River Falls). May 1976: 100.3 mhz; 100 kw. Ant 620 ft. TL: N47 58 38 W96 36 42. Stereo. Hrs opn: 24. Box 40 (56701); 323 4th St. N.W., East Grand Forks (56721). (218) 681-1230; (218) 773-6245. FAX: (218) 773-6140. Licensee: Border States Broadcasting Corp. (acq 5-28-92; with KTRF(AM) Thief River Falls). Net: SMN. Wash atty: Haley, Bader & Potts. Format: Oldies. News staff one; news progmg 10 hrs wkly. Target aud: 25-54; boomers & kids. Spec prog: Farm one hr wkly. ■ Steve Glasmann, pres; Joel Swanson, gen mgr & gen sls mgr; Scott Swygman, rgnl sls mgr; Nancie Stroeh, prom mgr; Bob Hultgren, Mark Stromsadt, progmg dirs; Bob Hultgren, mus dir & engrg mgr; Todd McDonald, Lee Richards, news dirs; Bob Hultgren, Todd McDonald, pub affrs dirs; Stan Mueller, chief engr. ■ Rates: $15; 14; 13; 12.

KZLT-FM—Listing follows KCNN(AM).

Eden Prairie

KCFE(FM)—Not on air, target date unknown: 105.7 mhz; 3 kw. Ant 328 ft. TL: N44 51 40 W93 31 18 (CP: 6 kw, ant 239 ft.). c/o 1748 20th Ave. N.W., New Brighton (55112). Licensee: Southwest Suburban Broadcasting Inc. (acq 10-25-93; $50,000; FTR 11-8-93).

Ely

WELY(AM)—Oct 2, 1954: 1450 khz; 1 kw-U, DA-N. TL: N47 53 37 W91 51 59 (CP: TL: N47 53 40 W91 51 50). Box 630, Central & Allaire (55731). (218) 365-3285. FAX: (218) 365-2636. Licensee: BJL Broadcasting Corp. (acq 12-16-76; $175,000). Net: Mutual, ABC/E; Minn. News. Wash atty: Brown, Finn & Nietert. Format: MOR. Target aud: General; senior citizens. Spec prog: C&W 6 hrs, relg 6 hrs, class 6 hrs wkly. ■ Jeanne A. Larson, pres, gen mgr, opns mgr, gen sls mgr & mktg mgr; Bradley S. Jones, CFO & chief engr; Harry Reed II, vp. ■ Rates: $7.50; 7.50; 7.50; na.

WELY-FM—July 25, 1992: 92.1 mhz; 6 kw. Ant 328 ft. TL: N47 53 40 W91 51 50. Stereo. Net: SMN. Format: Adult contemp.

Eveleth

WEVE(AM)—December 1948: 1340 khz; 1 kw-U. TL: N47 28 40 W92 32 00. Hrs opn: 24. Box 650, Old Hwy. 53 & Cemetery Rd. (55734). (218) 741-5922; (800) 247-0089. FAX: (218) 741-7302. Licensee: Stereo Broadcasting Inc. Group owner: Lew Latto Group of Northland Radio Stns. (acq 5-1-78). Net: ABC/E, ABC/I. Rep: Katz & Powell. Format: Adult contemp. News staff one. Target aud: 25-54. Spec prog: Finnish one hr wkly. ■ Lew Latto, pres; Jerry Sylvester, vp, gen mgr & adv mgr; Dennis Jerald, progmg dir & mus dir; Peter Mackowski, news dir; Wilfred Meys, chief engr.

WEVE-FM—June 26, 1978: 97.9 mhz; 71 kw. Ant 555 ft. TL: N47 33 53 W92 13 26. Stereo. Hrs opn: 24. Dups AM 90%. News staff one; news progmg one hr wkly. Spec prog: Relg 5 hrs wkly. ■ Rates: $15; 15; 12.50; 12.50.

Fairmont

KSUM(AM)—Jan 1, 1949: 1370 khz; 1 kw-U, DA-2. TL: N43 37 45 W94 29 00. Stereo. Box 491, 1371 W. Lair Rd. (56031). (507) 235-5595. Licensee: Woodward Broadcasting Inc. (acq 11-1-62). Net: CNN. Rep: Torbet, Hyett-Ramsland. Format: Country. News staff one; news progmg 10 hrs wkly. Target aud: General. Spec prog: Farm 18 hrs wkly. ■ Woody Woodward, pres & gen mgr; Donald Kliewer, gen sls mgr; Pat Murphy, progmg dir; Jeff Hagen, news dir; Lee Bramer, chief engr. ■ Rates: $35; 29; 29; 29.

KFMC(FM)—Co-owned with KSUM(AM). July 31, 1978: 106.5 mhz; 100 kw. Ant 400 ft. TL: N43 37 45 W94 29 00. Stereo. Hrs opn: 24. Prog sep from AM. Format: Adult contemp, oldies. Target aud: 25-54. Spec prog: Farm 4 hrs wkly. ■ Donald Kliewer, vp sls. ■ Rates: Same as AM.

Faribault

KDHL(AM)—Jan 10, 1948: 920 khz; 5 kw-U, DA-2. TL: N44 15 47 W93 16 29. Hrs opn: 24. Box 30, 601 Central Ave. (55021-0030). (507) 334-0061. FAX: (507) 334-7057. Licensee: Radio Ingstad Minn. Inc. Net: ABC/I. Format: Country, old-time. ■ Robert E. Ingstad, pres; Jeff Kutznik, gen mgr; Kymn Anderson, gen sls mgr; John Taylor, progmg dir; Gordy Kosfeld, news dir.

KQCL(FM)—Co-owned with KDHL(AM). Jan 10, 1968: 95.9 mhz; 3 kw. Ant 328 ft. TL: N44 21 25 W93 11 31. Stereo. Format: Adult contemp. News staff one; news progmg 14 hrs wkly. Target aud: 18-49. ■ Jeff Kutzink, progmg dir.

Fergus Falls

KBRF(AM)—Oct 20, 1926: 1250 khz; 5 kw-D, 1 kw-N, DA-N. TL: N46 17 19 W96 06 17 (CP: 2.2 kw-N, Non-DA-D. TL: N46 17 53 W95 58 42). Hrs opn: 24. Box 494, 728 Western Ave. N. (56537). (218) 736-7596. FAX: (218) 736-2836. Licensee: Fergus Falls Radio Inc. Group owner: Result Radio Inc. (acq 1-30-78). Net: Westwood One, MBS; MNN. Rep: Roslin. Format: Country. News staff one; news progmg 15-20 hrs wkly. Target aud: 25 plus. Spec prog: Farm 15 hrs, relg 7 hrs wkly. ■ Jerry Papenfuss, pres; Randy Vangrud, gen mgr; Barbara Vangrud, opns mgr; John Burns, gen sls mgr; Sue Tate, prom mgr; Charlie Kampa, progmg dir; Chuck Aamot, mus dir; James Sturgeon, news dir; Ken Howe, chief engr. ■ Rates: $18.65; 17.65; 18.65; 13.25.

KZCR(FM)—Co-owned with KBRF(AM). Jan 19, 1968: 103.3 mhz; 100 kw. Ant 620 ft. TL: N46 28 06 W96 11 54. Stereo. Prog sep from AM. Net: MBS. Format: Classic hit rock. News staff 2; news progmg 10 hrs wkly. Target aud: 18-49. ■ Barbara Vangrud, progmg dir. ■ Rates: Same as AM.

KJJK(AM)—Dec 1, 1986: 1090 khz; 1 kw-D, DA. TL: N46 14 43 W95 58 46. Box 724, 2450 College Way (56537). (218) 736-5408. FAX: (218) 736-5400. Licensee: Otter Tail Media Group Inc. (acq 1-23-90; $502,484 with co-located FM; FTR 2-19-90). Net: ABC/D. Rep: Katz & Powell, O'Malley Communications. Wash atty: Lukas, McGowan, Nace & Gutierrez. Format: Hits of 40's, 50's, 60's. News staff one; news progmg one hr wkly. Target aud: 45 plus. Spec prog: Paul Harvey News. ■ Larry Dorn, pres; Larry Nornes, vp & gen mgr; Mark Bjoralt, gen sls mgr; Ernie Roers, prom mgr; John Brisson, progmg dir; Katie Scott, news dir; Ken Bartz, chief engr. ■ Rates: $12; 10; 12; 6.70.

KJJK-FM—Oct 14, 1981: 96.5 mhz; 100 kw. Ant 480 ft. TL: N46 14 43 W95 58 46. Stereo. Hrs opn: 24. Prog sep from AM. Net: ABC/D Minn News Net. Format: Country. News staff one; news progmg 3 hrs wkly. Target aud: 21-54; today's country music fans. ■ Larry Nornes, stn mgr; Ernie Roers, opns mgr; Mark Anderson, mus dir. ■ Rates: Same as AM.

KZCR(FM)—Listing follows KBRF(AM).

Forest Lake

WLKX-FM—Oct 28, 1978: 95.9 mhz; 3 kw. Ant 300 ft. TL: N45 17 40 W93 04 22. Stereo. Hrs opn: 24. 15226 W. Freeway Dr. (55025). (612) 464-6796. FAX: (612) 464-3638. Licensee: Lakes Broadcasting Co. Inc. Format: Country. News staff one; news progmg 20 hrs wkly. Target aud: General. Spec prog: Auction show 9 hrs, relg 6 hrs wkly. ■ Ed Cary, Joanne Cary, Cathleen Cary, CEOs; Elgie S. Cary, pres; Joanne M. Cary, vp; Mark Lowe, gen sls mgr; Douglas Hammer, prom mgr; Cathleen Cary, progmg dir & mus dir; Jeff Stevens, news dir. ■ Rates: $18.90; 18.90; 18.90; 18.90.

Fosston

KKCQ(AM)—Dec 12, 1966: 1480 khz; 5 kw-D, 2.5 kw-N, DA-N. TL: N47 33 44 W95 43 50. Hrs opn: 6 AM-10 PM. Box 606, Hwy. 2 E. (56542). (218) 435-1919. FAX: (218) 435-1480. Licensee: Pine to Prairie Broadcasting Inc. (acq 1-22-92; $335,000 with co-located FM; FTR 2-10-92). Net: ABC/I, Unistar; MNN. Wash atty: Eugene T. Smith. Format: Big band. News staff one; news progmg 4 hrs wkly. Target aud: 25-54; family-oriented adults. Spec prog: Farm 5 hrs, relg 4 hrs wkly. ■ Larry Roed, pres & pub affrs dir; Phil Ehlke, gen mgr & gen sls mgr; Jacque Johnson, progmg dir & mus dir; Dave Suedin, news dir; Mark Persons, chief engr. ■ Rates: $10.95; 9.95; 9.95; 6.95.

KKCQ(FM)—June 13, 1969: 107.1 mhz; 50 kw. Ant 482 ft. TL: N47 33 44 W95 43 30 Stereo. Hrs opn: 6 AM-10 PM. Prog sep from AM. Format: Relg. ■ Larry Roed, CEO & gen mgr; Phil Ehlke, stn mgr; Kevin Arvidson, progmg dir. ■ Rates: Same as AM.

Glencoe

KARP(FM)—Sept 23, 1993: 96.1 mhz; 13.5 kw. Ant 449 ft. TL: N44 55 10 W94 10 28. Hrs opn: 24. Box 366, 553 3rd Ave. N.W., Hutchinson (55350); 2110 E. 10th St. (55336). (612) 587-5696; (612) 864-6700. FAX: (612) 587-1113; (612) 864-6750. Licensee: Minnesota Valley Broadcasting (acq 10-18-93; 25,000). Net: ABC. Format: Variety hit radio. News staff one. Target aud: 18-49; an appeal to all age groups. ■ John Linder, gen mgr; John Mons, stn mgr, opns mgr & prom mgr; Bruce Kottke, Dale Kotkan, sls dirs; John Beck, mus dir & pub affrs dir; Janis Rannow, news dir; Scott Jeffrey, vp engrg. ■ Rates: $13.50; 12.50; 13.50; 10.50.

Glenwood

KMGK(FM)—March 11, 1983: 107.1 mhz; 3 kw. Ant 300 ft. TL: N45 36 53 W95 23 28. Stereo. Hrs opn: 24. Box 215, 605 S. Lakeshore Dr. (56334). (612) 634-5358. FAX: (612) 763-5999. Licensee: KMGK Inc. (acq 6-18-93). Format: Adult contemp. News staff one. Target aud: 25-54. ■ Steven R. Nestor, CEO, progmg dir & news dir; John Messenger, gen mgr, opns dir & mus dir; Paul Rykhus, gen sls mgr & vp mktg; Chuck Schott, prom dir; Pat] Cochran, pub affrs dir; Steve Youngberg, chief engr. ■ Rates: $10; 9; 10; 8.

Golden Valley

KQRS(AM)—May 13, 1948: 1440 khz; 5 kw-D, 500 w-N, DA-N. TL: N44 59 20 W93 21 06. Hrs opn: 24. 917 N. Lilac Dr., Minneapolis (55422). (612) 545-5601. Licensee: Capital Cities/ABC Inc. Group owner: Capital Cities/ABC Broadcast Group (acq 6-30-86). Net: ABC/R. Rep: Katz. Format: AOR. News staff one; news progmg 5 hrs wkly. Target aud: 18-49; Baby boomers/Generation X audience ■ Mark S. Steinmetz, pres & gen mgr; Amy Waggoner, gen sls mgr; John Lassman, prom mgr & mus dir; Dave Hamilton, progmg dir; Wade Linder, asst mus dir; Terri Traen, news dir; Ranee Johnson, pub affrs dir; David Szaflarski, chief engr.

KQRS-FM—Sept 1, 1963 92.5 mhz 100 kw Ant 900 ft. TL: N44 59 20 W93 21 06 (CP: Ant 1,033 ft.). Stereo. Hrs opn: 24. Dups AM 100% Format: Rock.

KYCR(AM)—Licensed to Golden Valley. See Minneapolis-St. Paul.

Grand Rapids

***KAXE(FM)**—Apr 23, 1976: 91.7 mhz; 100 kw. Ant 460 ft. TL: N47 15 17 W93 26 03. Stereo. 1841 E. Hwy. 169 (55744). (218) 326-1234. FAX: (218) 326-1235. Licensee: Northern Community Radio Network. Net: NPR, APR. Format: Div. News staff one; news progmg 45 hrs wkly. Target aud: General. Spec prog: Folk 6 hrs, Black 2 hrs, classic 2 hrs, C&W 3 hrs, jazz 6 hrs, Finnish 2 hrs, polka 2 hrs, American Indian 3 hrs, farm one hr wkly. ■ Maggie Montgomery, pres; Pam Leschak, gen mgr; Michael Olson, dev dir; Chris Julin, progmg dir; Terry O'Brien, mus dir; Michelle Johnson, news dir & pub affrs dir.

KMFY(FM)—Listing follows KOZY(AM).

KOZY(AM)—Jan 29, 1948: 1320 khz; 5 kw-U, DA-2. TL: N47 10 22 W93 27 10. Hrs opn: 24. Box 597, 507 11th St., S.E. (55744). (218) 326-3446. FAX: (218) 326-3448. Licensee: Kirwin Broadcasting Inc. (acq 10-27-86; $375,000; FTR 9-22-86). Net: ABC/MNN. Format: Adult contemp. News staff 7. ■ Bill Kirwin, pres & gen mgr; Mike Iaizzo, gen sls mgr; Dale Randall, progmg dir & news dir.

KMFY(FM)—Co-owned with KOZY(AM). Dec 5, 1975: 96.9 mhz; 100 kw. Ant 450 ft. TL: N47 15 17 W93 26 03. Stereo. Hrs opn: 24. Prog sep from AM. News staff 5. Target aud: 35-54.

Granite Falls

KKRC(FM)—Oct 5, 1993: 93.9 mhz; 6 kw. Ant 262 ft. TL: N44 54 06 W95 32 53. Box 1420, 126 Ridge Ln., Mankato (56001). (507) 345-4537. Licensee: John Linder. Group owner: Linder Broadcasting Group. Format: Adult contemp. ■ John Linder, gen mgr.

KMGM(FM)—See Montevideo.

Hastings

KDWA(AM)—Oct 24, 1963: 1460 khz; 1 kw-D, 45 w-N. TL: N44 42 49 W92 50 30. Box 215, 1718 Vermillion St. (55033). (612) 437-1460. FAX: (612) 438-3042. Licensee: K & M Broadcasting Inc. (acq 6-30-92; $161,000; FTR 7-20-92). Net: Mutual; MNN. Format: Country. News staff one; news progmg 18 hrs wkly. Target aud: 25-50. Spec prog: Local news & sports. ■ Dan Massman, CEO, gen mgr & vp sls; Roy Kline, pres, vp opns, progmg dir & mus dir; Dave Douglas, chief engr. ■Rates: $10; 8; 10; 5.

Hibbing

KMFY(FM)—See Grand Rapids.

***WIRR(FM)**—See Duluth.

Minnesota Directory of Radio

WKKQ(AM)—(Nashwauk). June 2, 1975: 650 khz; 10 kw-D, 500 w-N, DA-N. TL: N47 22 31 W93 00 56 (CP: 10 kw-D, 1 kw-N). Box 1060, Hibbing (55746). (218) 262-4545; (218) 262-3535. FAX: (218) 262-2407. Licensee: Midwest Communications. Group owner: Midwest Communications Inc. (acq 12-85; $1,100,000 with co-located FM; FTR 12-9-85). Net: ABC/E. Rep: Banner. Format: Country. News staff 2; news progmg 2 hrs wkly. Target aud: 35 plus. Spec prog: Pol 2 hrs wkly. ■ Duke Wright, pres; Sharon Flaherty, gen mgr & gen sls mgr; Pam Quinn, progmg dir; Mark Anthony, mus dir; Craig Holgate, news dir; Danny Klaysmat, chief engr. ■ Rates: $20; 15; 18; 13.

WTBX(FM)—Co-owned with WKKQ(AM). Dec 31, 1980: 93.9 mhz; 100 kw. Ant 548 ft. TL: N47 22 31 W93 00 56. Stereo. Prog sep from AM. Net: ABC/FM. Format: CHR. Target aud: 18-40. ■ Bill Kaye, progmg dir; Deanne Davis, mus dir. ■ Rates: Same as AM.

WMFG(AM)—1935: 1240 khz; 1 kw-U. TL: N47 24 30 W92 57 04. Box 99, 807 W. 37th St. (55746). (218) 263-7531. FAX: (218) 263-6112. Licensee: Sounds Unlimited of Red Wing Inc. (acq 3-1-93; $255,000 with co-located FM; FTR 3-22-93). Net: SMN; MNN. Format: Oldies. News staff 2; news progmg 13 hrs wkly. Target aud: 25-55. Spec prog: Relg 4 hrs, polka 4 hrs wkly. ■ Al Quamstrom, pres; Dennis Martin, sr vp, gen mgr & natl sls mgr; Jim Ramsland, rgnl sls mgr; Keith Knox, progmg dir & mus dir; John Hendrickson, news dir.

WMFG-FM—1971: 106.3 mhz; 600 w-H. Ant 269 ft. TL: N47 24 30 W92 57 04 (CP: 25 kw, ant 259 ft.). Stereo. Dups AM 100%. News staff one; news progmg 12 hrs wkly. Target aud: 25-54. ■ Dennis Martin, gen sls mgr; Craig Coomb, adv mgr; John Hendrickson, vp progmg; Bill Meyes, engrg dir.

WTBX(FM)—Listing follows WKKQ(AM).

Hutchinson

KDUZ(AM)—Sept 16, 1953: 1260 khz; 1 kw-D, 64 w-N. TL: N44 54 24 W94 21 59. Hrs opn: 19. 20132 Hwy. 15 N. (55350-5643). (612) 587-2140. FAX: (612) 587-5158. Licensee: North American Broadcasting Co. Net: ABC/I; Linder Farm. Rep: Katz. Format: Country. News staff 3; news progmg 21 hrs wkly. Target aud: 30 plus; general. Spec prog: Farm 18 hrs, gospel 3 hrs, polka 8 hrs wkly. ■ Larry Graf, pres, gen mgr & gen sls mgr; Joyce Wieweck, vp; Jim Ohnstad, progmg dir; Terry Rosati, news dir; Lon Roach, pub affrs dir; Steve Youngberg, chief engr. ■ Rates: $18.20; 16.60; 18.20; 16.60.

KKJR(FM)—Co-owned with KDUZ(AM). June 6, 1968: 107.1 mhz; 4.4 kw. Ant 195 ft. TL: N44 54 24 W94 21 59. Stereo. Hrs opn: 24. Net: SMN. News staff 3; news progmg 3 hrs wkly. Target aud: 18 plus. ■ Jon Carrigan, opns mgr & progmg dir; Vicky Sexton, gen sls mgr. ■ Rates: $16.20; 14.60; 16.20; 14.60.

International Falls

KBHW(FM)—Jan 4, 1983: 99.5 mhz; 100 kw. Ant 580 ft. TL: N48 33 45 W93 49 22. Stereo. Box 433 (56649). (218) 285-7398; (218) 283-2420. Licensee: Minnesota Christian Broadcasting Inc. Net: AP, USA, Moody. Format: Relg. News progmg 15 hrs wkly. Target aud: General. ■ John W. Blankman, gen mgr & stn mgr; Bruce Christopherson, progmg dir & chief engr; Jon Hall Blankman, mus dir & pub affrs dir; Bruce A. Christopherson, news dir.

KGHS(AM)—Sept 1, 1959: 1230 khz; 500 w-D, 250 w-N. TL: N48 35 29 W93 22 54. 201 3rd St. (56649). (218) 283-3481. FAX: (218) 283-3087. Licensee: Communications International Assoc. Inc. (acq 12-26-83). Net: MBS; MNN. Format: Adult contemp, oldies. News staff one; news progmg 10 hrs wkly. ■ F.H. Walter, pres; Charles Radford, gen mgr & prom mgr; Brad King, gen sls mgr; Dave Stelton, progmg dir; Gerald Franzen, mus dir; Lon Francis, news dir; Scott Crowe, chief engr.

KSDM(FM)—Co-owned with KGHS(AM). March 17, 1979: 104.1 mhz; 8.5 kw. Ant 200 ft. TL: N48 35 39 W93 22 56. Stereo. Prog sep from AM. Box 591 (56649). (218) 283-2622. Format: Country. ■ Brad King & Margo Walter, prom mgr; Dave Stelton, mus dir.

Jackson

KKOJ(AM)—July 10, 1980: 1190 khz; 5 kw-D, DA. TL: N43 31 45 W95 00 02. Box 29, R.R. 2 (56143). (507) 847-5400. FAX: (507) 847-5745. Licensee: Kleven Broadcasting Co. of Minn. Net: Linder Farm. Rep: Katz. Format: Modern country. News staff one; news progmg 20 hrs wkly. Target aud: General. Spec prog: Farm 15 hrs wkly. ■ Les Kleven, pres & chief engr; Doug Johnson, gen mgr; Terry Wheeler, gen sls mgr & mus dir; Larry Anderson, progmg dir; Steve Schwaller, news dir. ■ Rates: $13.50; 13.50; 13.50; 13.50.

KRAQ(FM)—Spring 1993: 105.7 mhz; 25 kw. Ant 328 ft. TL: N43 36 54 W94 57 48. Box 29 (56143). Box 687, Sturgis, SD (57785). (507) 847-5400. FAX: (507) 847-5745. Licensee: Jackson Broadcasting Co. ■ Doug Johnson, gen mgr; Larry Anderson, progmg dir.

La Crescent

KQEG(FM)—Licensed to La Crescent. See La Crosse, Wis.

***KXLC(FM)**—Nov 24, 1991: 91.1 mhz; 230 w. Ant 843 ft. TL: N43 48 16 W91 22 18. Stereo. Hrs opn: 24. 735 Marquette Bank Bldg., Rochester (55904). (507) 282-0910. FAX: (507) 282-2107. Licensee: Minnesota Public Radio (acq 4-9-90). Net: NPR, APR; Minn. Pub. Format: News. News staff 3. Target aud: General. ■ William H. Kling, pres; Richard Dietman, gen mgr; Carol Schotzko, opns dir; Becky Gonzalez, dev dir; Bridget Parks, mktg dir; Carol Gunderson, news dir; Don Kolbert, chief engr.

Lake City

KMFX(FM)—Feb 14, 1991: 102.5 mhz; 9.4 kw. Ant 528 ft. TL: N44 16 45 W92 23 38. Radio Station KMFX(FM), 29 7th St. N.E., Rochester (55906). (507) 288-3888. FAX: (507) 288-7815. Licensee: Radio Ingstad Minnesota Inc. Format: Country. ■ Bob Jung, gen mgr; Mary Anne Nonn, gen sls mgr.

Lakeville

WTCX(FM)—February 1993: 105.1 mhz; 2.6 kw. Ant 499 ft. TL: N44 42 05 W93 09 02. Box 581367, Minneapolis (55458). (612) 322-2222; (612) 322-4343. FAX: (612) 322-4646. Licensee: Southern Twin Cities Area Radio Inc. ■ Tom Lijewski, pres.

Litchfield

KLFD(AM)—Jan 2, 1959: 1410 khz; 500 w-D, 47 w-N. TL: N45 07 02 W94 33 13. Stereo. Hrs opn: 5:30 AM-midnight. 234 N. Sibley Ave. (55355). (612) 693-3281. FAX: (612) 693-3283. Licensee: Mid-Minnesota Broadcasting Co. (acq 11-26-91; $42,500; FTR 12-16-91). Net: AP. Wash atty: Leventhal, Senter & Lerman. Format: Oldies, country. News staff one; news progmg 10 hrs wkly. Target aud: 25-54. Spec prog: Local sports progmg, farm 20 hrs, relg 3 hrs wkly. ■ Bob Greenhow, pres; Steve Neighbors, vp opns; Sue Rose, gen sls mgr; Randy Domstrad, prom dir; Randy Quinty, progmg dir; Dean Tongen, news dir; Craig Bomgarrs, chief engr. ■ Rates: $9; 9; 9; 4.

KYRS(FM)—(Atwater). Nov 26, 1988: 94.1 mhz; 3 kw. Ant 328 ft. TL: N45 04 24 W94 45 20. Stereo. Hrs opn: 24. Box 881, 718 N. Sibley Ave., Litchfield (55355). (612) 693-2817. FAX: (612) 693-2819. Licensee: KYRS Inc. Group owner: StarCom Inc. (acq 10-5-89; $282,000 FTR 10-23-89). Format: Country. Target aud: General. ■ Steven Potter, gen mgr & gen sls mgr; Greg Johnson, progmg mgr; Jared Mashburn, mus dir; Steve Youngberg, chief engr.

Little Falls

KFML(FM)—Listing follows KLTF(AM).

KLTF(AM)—October 1950: 960 khz; 5 kw-D, 35 w-N. TL: N46 00 16 W94 19 42. Hrs opn: Sunset-11 PM. 70 N.E. First Ave. (56345). (612) 632-5414. FAX: (612) 632-5415. Licensee: Little Falls Broadcasting Co. (acq 12-1-52). Net: AP, CNN. Format: Adult contemp, country, news/talk. News staff one; news progmg 24 hrs wkly. Target aud: 19-65; loc audience who listen for news & info. Spec prog: Farm 8 hrs, relg one hour, big band 5 hrs wkly. ■ Mark Lemme, pres, gen mgr & gen sls mgr; Harriet Turner, stn mgr; Gary Block, progmg dir & mus dir; Lee Ann Doucette, news dir; Alan Arquette, chief engr. ■ Rates: $15.60; 15.60; 15.60; 15.60.

KFML(FM)—Co-owned with KLTF(AM). November 1988: 94.1 mhz; 3 kw. Ant 275 ft. TL: N46 00 16 W94 19 42. Stereo. Prog sep from AM. Format: The best of yesterday & today. ■ Alan Arquette, progmg dir & mus dir. ■ Rates: $14.20; 14.20; 14.20; 14.20.

WYRQ(FM)—May 19, 1980: 92.1 mhz; 3 kw. Ant 299 ft. TL: N45 56 57 W94 17 48. Stereo. 70 S.E. First Ave. (56345). (612) 632-2992. FAX: (612) 632-2571. Licensee: WYRQ Inc. (acq 3-1-92). Net: NBC; MNN. Format: Country, farm. News staff one; news progmg 20 hrs wkly. Target aud: 25-54; farmers and working people. Spec prog: Polka 2 hrs wkly. ■ Jack Hansen, pres, gen mgr & chief engr; Steve Van Slooten, stn mgr, gen sls mgr & news dir; Damian Dupre, prom mgr & progmg dir.

Long Prairie

KEYL(AM)—Sept 15, 1959: 1400 khz; 1 kw-U. TL: N45 57 45 W94 52 09. Hrs opn: 5:30 AM-midnight. Box 187, 221 Lake St. (56347). (612) 732-2164. FAX: (612) 732-2284. Licensee: Prairie Broadcasting Co. (acq 7-1-88). Net: MBS; MNN. Rep: O'Malley Communications. Wash atty: Miller & Miller. Format: Country. News progmg 15 hrs wkly. Target aud: 25 plus. Spec prog: Farm 5 hrs, sports 10 hrs, radio drama one hr, relg 4 hrs wkly. ■ Donald D. Schermerhorn, pres; Darrell R. Anderson, gen mgr; Jim Borrett, opns mgr & news dir; Allen Bailey, gen sls mgr; Mary Stencel, prom mgr; Clif Cline, progmg dir & mus dir; Darrell Anderson, pub affrs dir; Dave Emewein, chief engr. ■ Rates: $9.50; 9.50; 9.50; na.

KXDL(FM)—(Browerville). May 15, 1992: 99.7 mhz; 6 kw. Ant 328 ft. TL: N46 03 15 W94 50 50. Hrs opn: 24. Box 187, 221 Lake St. S., Long Prairie, (56347). Licensee: Prairie Broadcasting Co. Net: SMN. Rep: O'Malley. Format: Oldies. News progmg 4 hrs wkly. Target aud: 25-54. Spec prog: Sports 2 hrs wkly. ■ Donald Schermerhorn, pres; Darrell Anderson, gen mgr; Jim Borrett, opns mgr & news dir; Alan Bailey, gen sls mgr; Dave Emwein, chief engr. ■ Rates: $9; 9; 9; 9.

Luverne

KQAD(AM)—Mar 1, 1971: 800 khz; 500 w-D, 80 w-N, DA-2. TL: N43 39 01 W96 10 19. Stereo. Hrs opn: 24. Box H (56156). (507) 283-4444. FAX: (507) 283-4445. Licensee: Raymond Lamb. Group owner: Broadcast Management Services Inc. (acq 9-88). Net: ABC/C. Rep: Katz & Powell, Repcom. Format: Adult contemp, farm. News staff one; news progmg 5 hrs wkly. Target aud: 35 plus. Spec prog: Relg 5 hrs wkly. ■ Ray Lamb, pres; Steve Graphenteen, gen mgr; Charlie Hamman, gen sls mgr; Keith Maine, progmg dir, mus dir & news dir; Bob Cook, chief engr.

KLQL(FM)—Co-owned with KQAD(AM). Nov 24, 1971: 101.1 mhz; 100 kw. Ant 530 ft. TL: N43 48 24 W96 12 23. Stereo. Hrs opn: 24. Prog sep from AM. Net: ABC/E. Format: C&W. News progmg 4 hrs wkly. Target aud: 25-54. Spec prog: Farm 10 hrs, gospel 5 hrs wkly. ■ Steve Graphantien, gen sls mgr; Bruce Thalhuber, progmg dir.

Madison

KLQP(FM)—Jan 31, 1983: 92.1 mhz; 3 kw. Ant 300 ft. TL: N45 01 37 W96 11 15. Stereo. Hrs opn: 5 AM-10 PM. Box 70, 623 W. 3rd St. (56256). (612) 598-7301. FAX: (612) 598-7955. Licensee: Lac Qui Parle Broadcasting Co. Inc. Net: CNN. Format: Country. Target aud: General. Spec prog: Farm 5 hrs wkly. ■ Maynard R. Meyer, CEO, gen mgr, news dir & chief engr; Julien J. Meyer, pres; Kris Kuechenmeister, opns mgr; Terry Overlander, gen sls mgr. ■ Rates: $7.25; 7.25; 7.25; 3.75.

Mankato

KDOG(FM)—Listing follows KTOE(AM).

KEEZ-FM—Apr 1, 1968: 99.1 mhz; 100 kw. Ant 864 ft. TL: N43 56 14 W94 24 41. Stereo. Hrs opn: 24. Box 3345, 102 Capital Rd. (56001). (507) 345-4646. Licensee: Gemini Broadcasting Co. Group owner: Nolan Broadcast Group (acq 1-1-93; $1.85 million; FTR 11-2-92). Net: MBS, Westwood One. Rep: Eastman. Format: Adult contemp. News staff one. Target aud: 25-54. ■ Phil Nolan, pres; Mike Nolan, vp & gen mgr; Dave Doetsuh, rgnl sls mgr; Mark Spangler, prom dir; Dan Hatter, progmg dir; Tim Allen, news dir & pub affrs dir; Maru Olson, vp engrg. ■ Rates: $25; 21.50; 25; 21.50.

***KGAC(FM)**—See St. Peter.

***KMSU(FM)**—Jan 7, 1963: 89.7 mhz; 20 kw. Ant 400 ft. TL: N44 08 34 W94 00 08. Stereo. Hrs opn: 24. Box 153, Warren St. Ctr., 1536 Warren St. (56001). (507) 389-5678. FAX: (507) 389-1899. Licensee: Mankato State Univ. Net: APR, NPR. Wash atty: Cohn & Marks. Format: News, class, jazz. News staff one; news progmg 50 hrs wkly. Target aud: General; upscale, educated. Spec prog: Drama 3 hrs, folk/ethnic 5 hrs, new age 5 hrs wkly. ■ Richard R. Rush, pres; Susan Ward, dev dir & prom mgr; Marilee Rickard, progmg dir; Henrey Busse Jr., mus dir; Fred Velte, news dir; Ron Dick, chief engr.

***KNGA(FM)**—See St. Peter.

KXLP(FM)—(New Ulm). Co-owned with KNUJ(AM). Nov 21, 1966: 93.1 mhz; 100 kw. Ant 489 ft. TL: N44 07 44 W94 11 15. Stereo. Prog sep from AM. Box 2268, North Mankato (56002). (507) 388-2900. FAX: (507) 345-4675. Net: NBC the Source. Rep: Katz & Powell. Format: Classic hits, adult contemp. News progmg 2 hrs wkly. Target aud: 25-54. Spec prog: Oldies 15 hrs wkly. ■ Chris Painter, stn mgr; Mary Degrood, gen sls mgr; Jo

Broadcasting & Cable Yearbook 1994
B-196

Baily, natl sls mgr; Terry Cooley, progmg dir; Dave Christianson, mus dir. ■ Rates: $28; 24; 28; 24.

KTOE(AM)—1950: 1420 khz; 5 kw-U, DA-N. TL: N44 10 06 W93 54 37. Box 1420 (56002). (507) 345-4537. FAX: (507) 345-5364. Licensee: Minnesota Valley Broadcasting Co. Group owner: Linder Broadcasting Group. Rep: Katz. Format: Adult contemp. Target aud: 25-54. ■ Don Linder, pres; John Linder, gen mgr; Denny Wassinger, gen sls mgr; Pete Steiner, prom mgr & progmg dir; Don Rivet, mus dir; Greg Husak, news dir; Scott Jeffries, chief engr.

KDOG(FM)—(North Mankato). Co-owned with KTOE(AM). April 1, 1985: 96.7 mhz; 18 kw. Ant 390 ft. TL: N44 13 20 W94 07 03. Stereo. Prog sep from AM. (507) 625-9197. Format: CHR. ■ Jay Paul, prom mgr; Dick Dietc, progmg dir; Greg Husak, mus dir.

KXLP(FM)—Listing follows KNUJ(AM).

KYSM(AM)—Licensed to Mankato. See North Mankato.

KYSM-FM—Licensed to Mankato. See North Mankato.

Maplewood

WCTS(AM)—Licensed to Maplewood. See Minneapolis-St. Paul.

Marshall

KBJJ(FM)—July 7, 1985: 107.5 mhz; 25 kw. Ant 213 ft. TL: N44 24 37 W95 51 43. Stereo. Box 520, 109 S. Fifth St. (56258). (507) 537-0566. FAX: (507) 537-0685. Licensee: Paradis Broadcasting of Marshall Inc. (acq 12-3-90; $250,000; FTR 12-31-90). Net: SMN. Format: Adult contemp. News staff one; news progmg 25 hrs wkly. Target aud: 25-54. ■ Tim Paradis, gen mgr; Ron Revere, opns mgr & progmg dir; Dennis Allen Jensen, news dir; Wendell Sowers, chief engr.

KKCK(FM)—Listing follows KMHL(AM).

KMHL(AM)—Nov 30, 1946: 1400 khz; 1 kw-U. TL: N44 26 55 W95 45 27 (CP: TL: N44 26 59 W95 45 43). Hrs opn: 24. Box 61, 1414 E. College Dr. (56258). (507) 532-2282. Licensee: KMHL Broadcasting Co. Group owner: Linder Broadcasting Group. Net: ABC/D; Linder Farm. Rep: Katz. Format: Farm, country, news/talk. News staff one; news progmg 20 hrs wkly. Target aud: 27 plus. Spec prog: Relg 7 hrs wkly. ■ Donald Linder, pres; Bruce Linder, vp; Brad Strootman, gen mgr & sls dir; Greg Schultz, progmg dir & pub affrs dir; Brian Johnson, mus dir; Fred Spencer, news dir; Craig Allen, engrg mgr; Scott Jeffries, chief engr. ■ Rates: $14; 12; 8.25; 8.25.

KKCK(FM)—Co-owned with KMHL(AM). Dec 13, 1967: 99.7 mhz; 100 kw. Ant 925 ft. TL: N44 26 55 W95 45 27. Stereo. Hrs opn: 24. Prog sep from AM. Net: ABC/FM. Rep: Katz. Format: Hot adult contemp/rock 40. News staff one; news progmg 8 hrs wkly. Target aud: 21-39. ■ Donald Linder, pres; Bruce Linder, exec vp; John Linder, sr vp; Tom Hager, opns mgr, prom mgr & progmg mgr; Greg Schultz, news dir; Craig Erpestad, chief engr. ■ Rates: $13.50; 13.50; 13.50; 13.50.

Minneapolis

***KBEM-FM**—Licensed to Minneapolis. See Minneapolis-St. Paul.

***KFAI(FM)**—Licensed to Minneapolis. See Minneapolis-St. Paul.

KFAN(AM)—Licensed to Minneapolis. See Minneapolis-St. Paul.

***KMOJ(FM)**—Licensed to Minneapolis. See Minneapolis-St. Paul.

***KNOW(AM)**—Licensed to Minneapolis. See Minneapolis-St. Paul.

KRXX-FM—Licensed to Minneapolis. See Minneapolis-St. Paul.

***KSJN(FM)**—Licensed to Minneapolis. See Minneapolis-St. Paul.

KTCJ(AM)—Licensed to Minneapolis. See Minneapolis-St. Paul.

KTCZ-FM—Licensed to Minneapolis. See Minneapolis-St. Paul.

***KTIS(AM)**—Licensed to Minneapolis. See Roseville.

***KTIS-FM**—Licensed to Minneapolis. See Minneapolis-St. Paul.

***KUOM(AM)**—Licensed to Minneapolis. See Minneapolis-St. Paul.

***WBOB-FM**—Licensed to Minneapolis. See Minneapolis-St. Paul.

WCCO(AM)—Licensed to Minneapolis. See Minneapolis-St. Paul.

WLTE(FM)—Licensed to Minneapolis. See Minneapolis-St. Paul.

WWTC(AM)—Licensed to Minneapolis. See Minneapolis-St. Paul.

Minneapolis-St. Paul

***KBEM-FM**—(Minneapolis). Oct 4, 1970: 88.5 mhz; 2.15 kw. Ant 370 ft. TL: N44 58 38 W93 15 55. Stereo. Hrs opn: 24. 1555 James Ave. N. (55411); 807 N.E. Broadway (55413). (612) 627-2833; (612) 529-5236. FAX: (612) 627-3106. Licensee: Special School District No. 1, Board of Education. Net: ABC/I, APR. Format: Jazz. News staff one; news progmg 14 hrs wkly. Target aud: 35 plus; jazz/progsv adults, new age concert/club/audiophiles. Spec prog: Bluegrass 5 hrs, Sp 3 hrs wkly. ■ Kay Sack, gen mgr; Robert Montesano, stn mgr; Craig Eichhorn, dev dir; Ted Allison, prom mgr; J.D. Ball, progmg dir; Terry Walker, mus dir; Ed Jones, news dir; Wayne Selly, chief engr.

KDWB-FM—Listing follows WDGY(AM).

KEEY-FM—Listing follows KFAN(AM).

***KFAI(FM)**—(Minneapolis). May 1, 1978: 90.3 mhz; 125 w. Ant 440 ft. TL: N44 58 29 W93 16 17. Stereo. 1808 Riverside Ave., Minneapolis (55454-1035). (612) 341-3144. FAX: (612) 341-4281. Licensee: Fresh Air Inc. Format: Div. News staff one; news progmg 7 hrs wkly. Target aud: General; underserved, under-represented communities. Spec prog: American Indian one hr, Black 10 hrs, class 4 hrs, folk 6 hrs, Fr 2 hrs, gospel 3 hrs, jazz 12 hrs, Sp 8 hrs wkly. ■ Denise Moyotte, gen mgr; Tamara Blaschko, prom mgr; John Kass, mus dir; Nolan Cramer, chief engr.

KFAN(AM)—(Minneapolis). 1923: 1130 khz; 50 kw-D, 25 kw-N, DA-2. TL: N44 38 48 W93 23 31. Hrs opn: 24. 611 Frontenac Pl., St. Paul (55104). (612) 645-7757. FAX: (612) 642-5223. Licensee: Shamrock Holdings Inc. Group owner: Shamrock Broadcasting Inc. (acq 6-4-93; grpsl; FTR 6-21-93). Net: MBS. Rep: Christal. Format: News/talk, sports. News progmg 20 hrs wkly. Target aud: 25-54; males. ■ Bill Clark, CEO; Marte Loughman, pres; Mick Anselmo, gen mgr & stn mgr; Lorna Gladstone, opns dir; David Haeg, gen sls mgr; Steve Labau, news dir; John Wailin, pub affrs dir; Harry Wilkins, engrg dir.

KEEY-FM—(St. Paul). Co-owned with KFAN(AM). June 1, 1969: 102.1 mhz; 100 kw. Ant 1,033 ft. TL: N45 03 30 W93 07 27. Stereo. Hrs opn: 24. Format: Adult contemp country. News staff one; news progmg 2 hrs wkly. Target aud: General. ■ Judy Dibble, prom mgr; Mark Bauer, mus dir; Pam Lewis, news dir; John Waylon, pub affrs dir.

KJJO(AM)—See St. Louis Park.

KLBB(AM)—(St. Paul). 1936: 1400 khz; 1 kw-U. TL: N44 57 28 W93 12 23. 1996 University Ave., St. Paul (55104). (612) 645-4403. FAX: (612) 645-8308. Licensee: LCC Inc. (acq 10-10-84). Net: Unistar. Wash atty: Haley, Badger & Potts. Format: Big band, MOR, nostalgia. News progmg 10 hrs wkly. Target aud: 35 plus. ■ Walter Richey, pres; John R. Kuehne, exec vp; Jonathon Giberson, gen mgr; Tim Momhan, gen sls mgr; Reed Hagen, progmg dir & mus dir; Marianne Berreth, news dir; Doug Thompson, chief engr.

***KMOJ(FM)**—(Minneapolis). Sept 15, 1978: 89.9 mhz; 1 kw. Ant 600 ft. TL: N44 59 00 W93 17 22. Stereo. Hrs opn: 24. 501 N. Bryant Ave., Minneapolis (55405). (612) 377-0595; (612) 377-5615. FAX: (612) 377-6919. Licensee: Center for Communication & Development (acq 1975). Format: Urban contemp. News staff 2; news progmg 4 hrs wkly. Target aud: General. ■ Ron Edwards, pres; Dorian Flowers, stn mgr, opns mgr, prom mgr & progmg dir; Walter Banks Jr., mus dir; Dan Zimmerman, chief engr.

KNOF(FM)—(St. Paul). Apr 10, 1960: 95.3 mhz; 3 kw. Ant 200 ft. TL: N44 56 48 W93 09 26. 1347 Selby Ave., St. Paul (55104). (612) 645-8271. Licensee: Selby Gospel Broadcasting Co. Format: Relg. Spec prog: Black 2 hrs wkly. ■ Grace Adam, pres & gen mgr; Larry Johnson, opns mgr, vp progmg & mus dir; James A. Peterson, chief engr.

***KNOW(AM)**—(Minneapolis). 1939: 1330 khz; 5 kw-U, DA-2. TL: N44 53 59 W93 10 15 (CP: 5 kw, DA-1, TL: N44 49 18 W93 13 06). 45 E. 7th St., St. Paul (55101). (612) 290-1500. FAX: (612) 290-1260. Licensee: Minnesota Public Radio Inc. FTR (7-29-91). Net: NPR, AP, APR; Minn. Pub. Format: News/talk. ■ William H. Kling, pres; Victor J. Bremer, vp; Anne Hovland, vp dev; Ginger Sisco, vp mktg; Victor J. Brener, progmg dir; Doug Thompson, chief engr.

***KNOW-FM**—Listing follows KSJN(FM).

KQRS(AM)—See Golden Valley.

KQRS-FM—See Golden Valley, Minn.

KRXX(AM)—(Richfield). Oct 18, 1949: 980 khz; 5 kw-U, DA-1. TL: N44 47 18 W93 12 54. Stereo. 2110 Cliff Rd., Eagan (55122). (612) 452-6200. FAX: (612) 452-9189. Licensee: Entertainment Communications Inc. Group owner: Entercom (acq 12-15-86). Rep: D & R Radio. Format: AOR. Target aud: 18-34. ■ Greg Steele, opns mgr; Terry Volbert, gen sls mgr; Annie Miners, prom mgr; Ron Kazda, chief engr.

KRXX-FM—(Minneapolis). Jan 6, 1961: 93.7 mhz; 100 kw. Ant 1,033 ft. TL: N45 03 30 W93 07 27. Stereo. Prog sep from AM. Format: CHR. Target aud: 25-54.

***KSJN(FM)**—(Minneapolis). 1956: 99.5 mhz; 100 kw. Ant 1,033 ft. TL: N44 03 30 W93 07 27. Stereo. 45 E. 7th St., St. Paul (55101). (612) 290-1500. FAX: (612) 290-1260. Licensee: Minnesota Public Radio Inc. Net: APR. Format: Class. ■ William H. Kling, pres; Victor J. Bremer, vp; Anne Hovland, dev dir; Ginger Sisco, prom mgr; Arthur Cohen, progmg dir; John Michel, mus dir; Loren Omoto, news dir; Doug Thompson, chief engr.

***KNOW-FM**—Co-owned with KSJN(FM). July 1, 1967: 91.1 mhz; 100 kw. Ant 1,310 ft. TL: N45 03 44 W93 08 21. Stereo. Prog sep from KSJN(FM) Minneapolis. Format: News/info. ■ Ginger Sisco, vp mktg; Victor Brimmer, progmg dir.

KSTP(AM)—(St. Paul). April 1924: 1500 khz; 50 kw-U, DA-N. TL: N45 01 32 W93 03 06. 2792 Maplewood Dr. (55109). (612) 481-9333. FAX: (612) 481-9324. Licensee: KSTP-AM Inc. Group owner: Hubbard Broadcasting Inc. Net: ABC/I. Rep: McGavren Guild. Format: Talk. Target aud: 25-54; male. Spec prog: Minnesota pro hockey. ■ Stanyley S. Hubbard, CEO; John Mayasich, pres; Virginia H. Morris, vp & gen mgr; Mike Boen, stn mgr & gen sls mgr; Craige Iwaszko, natl sls mgr; Steve Dubbels, rgnl sls mgr; Steve Konrad, progmg mgr; John MacDougall, pub affrs dir; Norm Paetznick, chief engr.

KSTP-FM—(St. Paul). Nov 1, 1965: 94.5 mhz; 100 kw. Ant 1,225 ft. TL: N45 03 45 W93 08 22. Stereo. Prog sep from AM. 3415 University Ave., Minneapolis (55414). (612) 642-4141. FAX: (612) 642-4142. Net: UPI. Format: Adult contemp. Target aud: 25-54; female. Spec prog: Oldies 4 hrs wkly. ■ John Rohm, gen mgr; Bob Davis, opns dir & progmg dir; Lisa Bittman, gen sls mgr; Kelly Wallis, prom dir; Pat McKeever, mus dir; Linda Evans, news dir; Ken Cummings, chief engr. ■ KSTP-TV affil.

KTCJ(AM)—(Minneapolis). Apr 5, 1962: 690 khz; 500 w-D, DA. TL: N45 01 25 W93 22 58 (CP: 1.5 kw-D, 500 w-N, TL: N44 44 58 W92 59 35). Stereo. Butler Sq., Suite 210C, 100 N. Sixth St., Minneapolis (55403). (612) 339-0000. FAX: (615) 333-2997. Licensee: National Radio Partners L.P. Group owner: American Media Inc. (acq 7-7-92; $12.75 million with co-located FM; FTR 7-27-92). Rep: Major Mkt. Format: Progsv, rock. Target aud: 25-44. Spec prog: New age 2 hrs, blues one hr, local music one hr, jazz 3 hrs wkly. ■ Doug Brown, gen mgr; Jim Gross, gen sls mgr; Jonathan Stymes, natl sls mgr; Melissa Siegel, rgnl sls mgr; Mike Noble, prom mgr; Jim Robinson, progmg dir; Jane Fredrickson, mus dir; Kyrie Sandum, news dir; Jonell Pernula, pub affrs dir; Bob Gagne, chief engr.

KTCZ-FM—(Minneapolis). Co-owned with KTCJ(AM). 1956: 97.1 mhz; 100 kw. Ant 1,033 ft. TL: N45 03 30 W93 07 27. Stereo. Hrs opn: 24. Prog sep from AM. ■ Ronald J. Kazda, gen mgr; Jeff Litt, gen sls mgr; Mike Traub, prom mgr; Lin Brehmer, progmg dir; Jane Fredricksen, news dir; Bob Gagne, chief engr. ■ Rates: $200; 200; 200; 125.

***KTIS-FM**—(Minneapolis). May 1949: 98.5 mhz; 100 kw. Ant 1,033 ft. TL: N45 03 30 W93 07 27. Stereo. Hrs opn: 24. 3003 N. Snelling Ave., St. Paul (55113). (612) 631-5000. FAX: (612) 631-5010. Licensee: Northwestern College. Net: Skylight. Wash atty: John Wilner. Format: Relg. News staff 2; news progmg 20 hrs wkly. Target aud: 25-45. ■ Mel Johnson, chmn; Dr. Donald Erickson, pres; Dan Stolz, CFO; Paul Ramseyer, vp; Don Rupp, stn mgr; Dale Thiessen, prom dir; Neil Stavem, pub affrs dir; Rod Thannum, chief engr.

***KUOM(AM)**—(Minneapolis). Jan 13, 1922: 770 khz; 5 kw-D. TL: N44 59 54 W93 11 18. Stereo. Hrs opn: Sunrise-sunset. Univ. of Minn., 550 Rarig Ctr., 330 21st Ave. (55455-0415). (612) 625-3500. FAX: (612) 624-6079. Licensee: University of Minnesota. Net: AP. Wash atty:

Dow, Lohnes & Albertson. Format: Progressive. News staff one; news progmg 5 hrs wkly. Target aud: 18-25. ■ Nils Hasselmo, pres; Andrew Marlow, stn mgr; Stuart Sanders, dev dir; Kindra Voss, sls dir; Marybeth Foss, prom dir; Jim Musil, progmg dir; Joel Stitzel, mus dir; David Olson, news dir.

KYCR(AM)—(Golden Valley). Oct 27, 1961: 1570 khz; 2.5 kw-U, 300 w-N, 500 w-CH. TL: N44 59 51 W93 21 10. Hrs opn: 24. 5730 Duluth St., Minneapolis (55422). (612) 544-3196; (612) 544-5478. FAX: (612) 544-0519. Licensee: Jim Runsdorf, liquidating agent. Group owner: Children's Broadcasting Corp. Net: USA, Moody. Wash atty: Putbrese, Hunsaker & Ruddy. Format: Contemp Christian. News progmg 6 hrs wkly. Target aud: 25-49; 60% female, 40% male. Spec prog: Black gospel 3 hrs wkly. ■ Christopher T. Dahl, CEO, chmn & pres; James G. Gilbertson, CFO; Richard V. Marsh, exec vp; David F. Reeder, gen mgr & gen sls mgr; Rick Selin, opns dir & progmg dir; Jennifer Johnson, dev dir; Bruce Slinden, rgnl sls mgr & adv mgr; Jonas Nelson, prom mgr & mus dir; Sylvia Harder, pub affrs dir; David Ernewein, chief engr. ■ Rates: $35; 25; 30; 23.

***WBOB-FM**—(Minneapolis). June 26, 1965: 100.3 mhz; 97 kw. Ant 905 ft. TL: N45 20 12 W93 23 28 (CP: Ant 922 ft.). Stereo. Suite 1319, 100 Washington Sq. (55401). (612) 333-8118. Licensee: Radio 100 L.P. Group owner: Colfax Communications Inc. (acq 10-27-92; $10 million; FTR 11-23-92). Format: Continuous country. ■ Kevin McCarthy, gen mgr.

WCCO(AM)—(Minneapolis). Oct 2, 1924: 830 khz; 50 kw-U. TL: N45 10 40 W93 20 55 (CP: 46 kw-N, TL: N45 05 06 W93 31 06). 625 Second Ave. S., Minneapolis (55402). (612) 370-0611. FAX: (612) 370-0683. Licensee: WCCO Radio Inc. Group owner: Midwest Communications Inc. (acq 8-52). Net: CBS, AP. Rep: CBS Spot. Format: Var, personality. ■ Rand Gottlieb, gen mgr; Andy Stavast, gen sls mgr; Ginger Sisco, prom mgr; Jim Ashbery, progmg dir; Curt Lundgren, mus dir; Kit Borgman, news dir; Jerome L. Miller, chief engr.

WLTE(FM)—(Minneapolis). Co-owned with WCCO(AM). Aug 27, 1973: 102.9 mhz; 100 kw. Ant 1,033 ft. TL: N45 03 30 W93 07 27. Stereo. Hrs opn: 24. No. 470, 1111 3rd Ave. S., Minneapolis (55404). (612) 339-1029. FAX: (612) 339-5653. Licensee: CBS, Inc. Format: Soft adult contemp. News staff one; news progmg 5 hrs wkly. Target aud: 25-54. ■ Rand Gottlieb, gen mgr; Kathy Golbluff, gen sls mgr; Susan Pickarski, prom mgr; Gary Nolan, progmg dir & mus dir; Robin Anderson, news dir; Steve Brown, chief engr.

WCTS(AM)—(Maplewood). August 1964: 1030 khz; 50 kw-D, 1 kw-N, DA-2. TL: N44 52 01 W92 54 02. 1250 W. Broadway, Minneapolis (55411). (612) 522-7339. FAX: (612) 522-9663. Licensee: Central Baptist Theological Seminary of Minneapolis (acq 10-27-92; $1.5 million; FTR 11-23-92). Net: Unistar. Format: Christian mus. ■ Dennis Whitehead, gen mgr.

WDGY(AM)—(St. Paul). Sept 19, 1959: 630 khz; 5 kw-D, 500 w-N, DA-2. TL: N44 56 40 W92 55 52. Box 25130, St. Paul (55125); Suite 200, 708 S. third St., Minneapolis (55415). (612) 739-4433. FAX: (612) 739-4784. Licensee: Midcontinent Radio of Minnesota Inc. Group owner: Midcontinent Media Inc. (acq 10-30-89; $17,950,000 with co-located FM; FTR 11-13-89). Net: NBC, Mutual. Rep: Banner. Wash atty: Dow, Lohnes & Albertson. Format: Country. Target aud: 25-54. ■ Larry Bentson, CEO, chmn & pres; Greg Anderson, CFO; Mark Niblick, vp & vp dev; Marc Kalman, gen mgr; Thomas Garry, stn mgr & natl sls mgr; David Malmberg, progmg dir & mus dir; Michael Gorniak, engrg dir; Tom Dillon, chief engr.

KDWB-FM—(Richfield). Co-owned with WDGY(AM). August 1959: 101.3 mhz; 100 kw. Ant 1,033 ft. TL: N45 03 30 W93 07 27. Stereo. Hrs opn: 24. Prog sep from AM. Format: Contemp hit radio. News staff one. Target aud: 12-34. ■ Tom Gerry, sls dir; Paul Miraldi, prom dir; Kevin Peterson, progmg dir; Ed Lambert, mus dir; Lee Valsvik, news dir.

WLTE(FM)—Listing follows WCCO(AM).

***WMCN(FM)**—(St. Paul). Sept 15, 1979: 91.7 mhz; 10 w. Ant 1,004 ft. TL: N44 36 22 W93 10 04. Stereo. 1600 Grand Ave., St. Paul (55105). (612) 696-6082. Licensee: Macalester College. Format: Progsv, Black. Target aud: All ages. Spec prog: Country 4 hrs, Latin 4 hrs, multicultural 10 hrs, industrial 10 hrs, drama 5 hrs wkly. ■ Jordan Barnett, Skye Merriwether, gen mgrs; Roger Skalback, chief engr.

WWTC(AM)—(Minneapolis). Aug 10, 1925: 1280 khz; 5 kw-U, DA-N. TL: N44 57 41 W93 21 24. 5501 Excelsior Blvd., Minneapolis (55416). (612) 926-1280. FAX: (612) 926-8014. Licensee: CD Broadcasting Corp. of Minneapolis. Group owner: CD Broadcasting Corp. (acq 4-16-90; $950,000; FTR 5-7-90). Format: Children. Target aud: 12 and under; children. ■ Christopher T. Dahl, pres; Chris Botto, stn mgr; Michael Ostlund, progmg dir; Robin Blair, pub affrs dir; Gary Liasick, chief engr. ■ Rates: $82; 82; 82; 82.

Montevideo

KDMA(AM)—Dec 21, 1951: 1460 khz; 1 kw-U, DA-N. TL: N44 56 05 W95 44 50. Hrs opn: 19. Box 738, W. Hwy. 212 (56265). (612) 269-8815; (612) 269-5131. FAX: (612) 269-8449. Licensee: Eagle Broadcasting Corp. (acq 6-1-86; $450,000; FTR 7-21-86). Net: ABC/I; Linder Farm. Rep: Katz, O'Malley. Format: Country. News staff one. Spec prog: Farm 7 hrs wkly. ■ David A. Ramage, pres; Troy Ramage, vp; Deanna Hodge, gen mgr; Dwight Mulder, opns dir, progmg dir & mus dir; Linda Christianson, gen sls mgr; Tim Burns, prom dir; Andrew Hoppe, news dir; Steve Youngberg, chief engr. ■ Rates: $12.90; 12.90; 12.90; 12.90.

KMGM(FM)—Co-owned with KDMA(AM). Oct 1, 1982: 105.5 mhz; 3 kw. Ant 300 ft. TL: N44 51 24 W95 37 46. Stereo. Hrs opn: 24. Prog sep from AM. (Acq 6-1-87). Net: SMN. Format: Oldies. Target aud: 25-54. Spec prog: Farm one hr wkly. ■ Rates: Same as AM.

Monticello

KMOM(AM)—November 1981: 1070 khz; 10 kw-U, 2.5 kw-N, DA-2. TL: N45 16 30 W93 47 32. Box 900, 8610 Edomonson St. N.W. (55362). (612) 295-1070. FAX: (612) 295-1070. Licensee: Greg Davis (acq 9-9-88; $426,000; FTR 10-31-88). Net: USA. Format: Full service. News staff 2; news progmg 30 hrs wkly. Target aud: 25-55; rgnl communities. Spec prog: Relg 4 hrs wkly. ■ Greg Davis, pres, gen mgr & gen sls mgr; Dick Chaalek, opns mgr; Maggie Garin, prom dir; Dori Adams, news dir.

Moorhead

***KCCD(FM)**—June 1, 1992: 90.3 mhz; 100 kw. Ant 495 ft. TL: N 46 45 35 W96 36 26. Hrs opn: 24. 901 S. 8th St. (56562). (218) 299-3666. FAX: (218) 299-3418. Licensee: Minnesota Public Radio. Format: News/info. News staff 2; news progmg 168 hrs wkly. Target aud: General. ■ William H. King, pres; Lois Hanson, gen mgr; Vern Goodin, dev dir; Karen Nitzorski, prom dir; Dan Gunderson, news dir.

***KCCM-FM**—Oct 23, 1971: 91.1 mhz; 67 kw. Ant 656 ft. TL: N46 45 35 W96 36 26. Stereo. Hrs opn: 24. Concordia College, 901 8th St. S. (56562). (218) 299-3666. FAX: (218) 299-3418. Licensee: Minnesota Public Radio Inc. Net: APR, NPR; Minn. Pub. Format: Class music & cult progrmg. News staff 2. Target aud: General. ■ William H. Kling, pres; Lois Hanson, gen mgr; Vern Goodin, dev dir; Karen Nitzkorski, prom dir; Dan Gunderson, news dir; Ken Bartz, chief engr.

KFGO-FM—See Fargo, N.D.

KLTA(FM)—See Breckenridge.

KQWB(AM)—See Fargo, N.D.

KQWB-FM—Licensed to Moorhead. See Fargo, N.D.

KVOX(AM)—Nov 30, 1937: 1280 khz; 5 kw-D, 1 kw-N, DA-2. TL: N46 49 10 W96 45 56. Hrs opn: 24. Box 97, S. Hwy. 75 (56560). (218) 233-1522. FAX: (218) 233-8742. Licensee: KVOX Inc. (acq 7-1-89; $1.6 million with co-located FM; FTR 6-12-89). Net: ABC/D, SMN. Rep: Torbet, Hyett-Ramsland. Format: MOR. News progmg 12 hrs wkly. Target aud: 35-64. ■ David Nelson, pres; Clark Wideman, gen mgr & gen sls mgr; Melony McKaye, prom dir; Scott Winston, mus dir; Ken Bartz, chief engr. ■ Rates: $44; 36; 30; 27.

KVOX-FM—Nov 30, 1966: 99.9 mhz; 100 kw. Ant 444 ft. TL: N46 49 09 W96 45 56. Stereo. Hrs opn: 24. Prog sep from AM. Format: Country. News progmg 7 hrs wkly. Target aud: 25-54. ■ Rates: $18; 15; 12; 10.

Morris

KKOK-FM—Listing follows KMRS(AM).

KMRS(AM)—Sept 16, 1956: 1230 khz; 1 kw-U. TL: N45 36 11 W95 53 14. Box 570 (56267). (612) 589-3131. Licensee: Western Minnesota Broadcasting. Group owner: Hedberg Broadcasting Group. Net: NBC. Rep: McGavren Guild. Format: Farm, C&W. News staff one; news progmg 80 hrs wkly. Target aud: 35-64; farmers and agribusiness people. ■ Paul C. Hedberg, pres; Mark Ring, gen mgr; Bill Eckersen, progmg dir; Sue Dieter, news dir; Mike Hendrickson, chief engr.

KKOK-FM—Co-owned with KMRS(AM). Sept 16, 1976: 95.7 mhz; 100 kw. Ant 474 ft. TL: N45 36 11 W95 53 14. Stereo. Dups AM 15%. Format: Country.

***KUMM(FM)**—Sept 17, 1970: 89.7 mhz; 223 w. Ant 120 ft. TL: N45 35 20 W95 54 22. Stereo. Hrs opn: 24. Univ. of Minnesota-Morris (56267). (612) 589-6076. FAX: (612) 589-6075. Licensee: Univ. of Minnesota. Format: Progsv, alternative. Target aud: 18-30; primarily college students. Spec prog: Hip-Hop 2 hrs, class 3 hrs, jazz 3 hrs, reggae 2 hrs, blues 2 hrs, hardcore 2 hrs, Minnesota one hr, industrial 2 hrs, classic rock 2 hrs, dance 2 hrs wkly. ■ Greg Goranson, gen mgr; Kate Pomerenke, sls dir, mktg dir, prom dir & adv dir; Les Opatz, progmg dir; Chad Snow, mus dir; Steve Brand, news dir; Roger Boleman, engrg dir.

Nashwauk

WKKQ(AM)—Licensed to Nashwauk. See Hibbing.

WMFG(AM)—See Hibbing.

New Prague

KCHK(AM)—Sept 22, 1969: 1350 khz; 500 w-D, 70 w-N, DA-2. TL: N44 34 39 W93 30 16. Hrs opn: 5 AM-midnight. Box 251, 25821 Langford Ave. (56071). (612) 758-2571; (612) 758-2572. FAX: (612) 758-3170. Licensee: Kingsley H. Murphy Jr. (acq 1976). Net: USA; MNN. Wash atty: Rosenman & Colin. Format: Oldies. News progmg 7 hrs wkly. Target aud: 35-59. Spec prog: Old-time music 18 hrs, Pol 18 hrs wkly. ■ Kingsley Murphy Jr., pres; Jack B. Ludescher, gen mgr & gen sls mgr; Tom Goetzinger, progmg dir, news dir & chief engr; Matt Page, mus dir. ■ Rates: $8.85; 8.85; 8.85; 8.85.

KCHK-FM—Dec 1, 1990: 95.5 mhz; 3 kw. Ant 328 ft. TL: N44 27 41 W93 35 21. Stereo. Hrs opn: 5 AM-midnight. Dups AM 100%. Target aud: General; 25-64. ■ Tom Goetzinger, prom dir. ■ Rates: Same as AM.

New Ulm

KNUJ(AM)—May 1949: 860 khz; 1 kw-U. TL: N44 17 10 W94 25 50. Box 368, Grand Hotel Bldg. (56073). (507) 359-2921. FAX: (507) 359-4520. Licensee: James Ingstad Broadcasting Inc. (acq 3-8-86; $1,325,000 with co-located FM; FTR 12-23-85). Net: NBC. Rep: Hyett/Ramsland. Wash atty: Fisher, Wayland, Cooper & Leader. Format: News, farm, C&W. News staff 2; news progmg 30 hrs wkly. Target aud: 30 plus. Spec prog: Old-time 8 hrs wkly. ■ Jim Ingstad, pres; Jim Bartels, gen mgr; Marj Frederickson, gen sls mgr; Brian Filzen, progmg dir; Tim Babel, mus dir; Randy Harder, news dir; Paul Titchenal, chief engr. ■ Rates: $46; 28; 46; 28.

KXLP(FM)—Licensed to New Ulm. See Mankato.

Nisswa

KZPX(FM)—Not on air, target date unknown: 93.3 mhz; 100 kw. Ant 768 ft. TL: N44 41 19 W93 04 22. Suite 925, 88 S. 6th St., Minneapolis (55402). (612) 338-3888. Licensee: The Bellfonte Co.

North Mankato

KDOG(FM)—Licensed to North Mankato. See Mankato.

KYSM(AM)—(Mankato). July 25, 1938: 1230 khz; 1 kw-U. TL: N44 10 20 W94 02 23. Stereo. Hrs opn: 24. Box 2268, North Mankato (56002); 1807 Lee Blvd., North Mankato MN (56003). (507) 345-4673. FAX: (507) 345-4675. Licensee: F.B. Clements & Co. Net: SMN; MNN. Rep: Katz & Powell. Wash atty: Dow, Lohnes & Albertson. Format: Oldies. News staff 2; news progmg 20 hrs wkly. Target aud: 18 plus; baby boomers. Spec prog: Farm 4 hrs wkly. ■ Jim Ingstad, pres; Jo Guck Bailey, opns mgr; Chris Painter, Mary DeGrood, gen sls mgrs; Terry Cooley, progmg dir.

KYSM-FM—(Mankato). April 1948: 103.5 mhz; 81 kw. Ant 530 ft. TL: N44 10 20 W94 02 23 (CP: 100 kw, ant 541 ft.). Stereo. Hrs opn: 24. Prog sep from AM. Format: Country. News staff 2; news progmg 6 hrs wkly. Spec prog: Sp one hr wkly. ■ Rates: $15; 15; 15; 12.

Northfield

***KRLX(FM)**—Jan 25, 1975: 88.1 mhz; 100 w. Ant 16 ft. TL: N44 27 39 W93 09 21. Stereo. Carleton College, One N. College St. (55057). (507) 663-4102. Licensee: Carleton College. Net: UPI. Format: Diverse. News progmg 4 hrs wkly. Target aud: General; college-associated people and rural. ■ Shanan Becker, stn mgr; Alex Zinnes, mktg mgr; Alison Clark, Dave Cloutier, progmg mgrs; Dan Bass, mus dir; Steve Lennon, Simon Overbey, chiefs engr.

KYMN(AM)—Sept 27, 1968: 1080 khz; 1 kw-D. TL: N44 29 12 W93 06 20. Stereo. Box 201, 1985 320 St. W. (55057). (507) 645-5695. FAX: (507) 645-9768. Licensee: KYMN Inc. (acq 2-1-73). Format: Now & then adult contemp. News staff 3; news progmg 20 hrs wkly. Target aud: 25-55; parents with school-age children, employed adults. Spec prog: Class 2 hrs, farm 2 hrs wkly. ■ Wayne Eddy, pres & gen mgr; Robert Matheson, gen sls mgr; Rich Harris, progmg dir, mus dir & chief engr; Don McRae, news dir.

*****WCAL(FM)**—Dec 1, 1991: 89.3 mhz; 98 kw. Ant 768 ft. TL: N44 41 19 W93 04 22. Stereo. St. Olaf College, 1520 St. Olaf Ave. (55057). (507) 646-3071. Licensee: St. Olaf College. Net: NPR. Wash atty: Dow, Lohnes & Albertson. Format: Classical, educ. Target aud: General. Spec prog: Black 2 hrs, jazz 3 hrs, drama 2 hrs wkly. ■ Paul E. Peterson, gen mgr; Heather Ferguson, opns mgr; Tom Norgel, dev dir; Paul Krause, mktg mgr; Sarah Entenmann, prom mgr; Marty Pelikan, progmg dir; Gordon Wildman, mus dir; Tom Nelson, chief engr.

Olivia

KOLV(FM)—June 27, 1983: 101.7 mhz; 6 kw. Ant 285 ft. TL: N44 45 51 W94 55 45. Stereo. Box 6 (56277). (612) 523-1017. FAX: (612) 523-1018. Licensee: Olivia Broadcasting Co. Net: MBS; Linder Farm, American Ag. Rep: Keystone (unwired net). Format: Country, farm, div. Spec prog: Big band, adult contemp, oldies, top-40 wkly. ■ George S. Blum, pres, gen mgr & chief engr; Charles Blum, stn mgr, progmg dir & mus dir; Ruby Blum, gen sls mgr.

Ortonville

KCGN-FM—Licensed to Ortonville. See Milbank, S.D.

KDIO(AM)—July 23, 1956: 1350 khz; 1 kw-D. TL: N45 20 58 W96 27 10. Box 115, R.R. 264 (56278). (612) 839-2581. FAX: (612) 839-2581, Ext 13. Licensee: Tri-State Broadcasting Co. Net: MBS; Minn. News. Format: Adult contemp (weekdays), oldies (weekends). News staff one; news progmg 19 hrs wkly. Spec prog: Farm 10 hrs wkly. ■ Donald P. Egert, pres & gen sls mgr; James Egert, gen mgr & prom mgr. ■ Rates: $9.40; 8.60; 9.40; 8.60.

Osakis

KBHL(FM)—Mar 11, 1985: 103.9 mhz; 3 kw. Ant 341 ft. TL: N45 50 24 W95 05 56 (CP: 6 kw, ant 328 ft.). Stereo. Box 247, 515 Pike St. E. (56360). (612) 859-3000. Licensee: Christian Heritage Broadcasting (acq 3-85; $14,127.21; FTR 3-4-85). Net: Moody. Format: Christian. ■ David McIver, gen mgr; Todd Atwater, mus dir.

Owatonna

KRFO(AM)—1950: 1390 khz; 500 w-D, 100 w-N. TL: N44 04 29 W93 10 46. Hrs opn: 5 AM-midnight. Box K, 204 1/2 E. Pearl St. (55060). (507) 451-2250. FAX: (507) 451-8837. Licensee: James Ingstad Broadcasting Inc. (acq 8-8-89; $1,054,551 with co-located FM; FTR 8-28-89). Net: UPI, CNN; Minn Net. Format: Adult contemp. News staff one; news progmg 18 hrs wkly. Target aud: 35 plus. Spec prog: Sp 2 hrs wkly. ■ Jim Ingstad, pres; Jim Lowe, gen mgr & stn mgr; John Connor, gen sls mgr; Greg Owens, progmg dir; Dave Gerard, mus dir; Larry Allan, news dir; Jeff Urban, chief engr. ■ Rates: $14; 12; 14; 10.

KRFO-FM—Dec 29, 1966: 104.9 mhz; 4.7 kw. Ant 200 ft. TL: N44 04 29 W93 10 46. Stereo. Hrs opn: 18. Prog sep from AM. Format: Country. News staff one; news progmg 12 hrs wkly. Target aud: 25-54. ■ Rates: $12; 10; 12; 8.

Park Rapids

KPRM(AM)—Dec 1, 1962: 870 khz; 25 kw-D, 1 kw-N, DA-N. TL: N46 55 42 W95 00 22. Stereo. Box 49, Hwy. 34 E. (56470). (218) 732-3306. Licensee: De La Hunt Jr. Broadcasting. Net: NBC, NBC Talknet. Format: Country. News staff 2; news progmg 20 hrs wkly. Target aud: 25 plus. ■ E.P. De La Hunt Jr., pres & gen mgr; Carol J. De La Hunt, stn mgr; David De La Hunt Jr., chief engr.

KDKK-FM—Co-owned with KPRM(AM). December 1967: 97.5 mhz; 100 kw. Ant 440 ft. TL: N46 55 42 W95 00 22. Stereo. Prog sep from AM. Net: SMN. Format: Stardust Memory Music. Target aud: 40 plus. ■ E.P. De La Hunt Jr., progmg dir.

Paynesville

KZPK(FM)—Not on air, target date unknown: 98.9 mhz; 50 kw. Ant 492 ft. TL: N45 23 15 W94 24 47. Box 5119, St. Cloud (56302). (612) 251-7169. Licensee: Ronald J. Linder.

Pelican Rapids

KBOT(FM)—Not on air, target date unknown: 104.1 mhz; Box 30, Rt. 4 (56572). Licensee: Heart of the Lakes Broadcasting.

Pequot Lakes

KTIG(FM)—Apr 30, 1978: 100.1 mhz; 6 kw. Ant 300 ft. TL: N46 36 06 W94 18 55 (CP: 102.7 mhz, 40 kw, ant 541 ft.). Stereo. Hrs opn: 24. Box 409, 100 Brunes St. (56472). (218) 568-4422. Licensee: Minnesota Christian Broadcasters Inc. Net: Moody, USA, Skylight. Wash atty: Reddy, Begley & Martin. Format: Relg. News staff one. Target aud: General. ■ Dale Shelley, pres; Mike Heuberger, gen mgr & progmg dir; Tom Bonar, opns dir & news dir; Marietta Heuberger, mus dir; Dwayne Walker, chief engr.

Pine City

WCMP(AM)—June 13, 1957: 1350 khz; 1 kw-D. TL: N45 49 10 W92 59 45. Box 357 F, R.R. 2 (55063). (612) 629-7575. FAX: (612) 629-3933. Licensee: Pine City Broadcasting Co. Inc. (acq 2-12-92; $650,000 with co-located FM; FTR 3-16-92). Net: ABC/I; MNN. Wash atty: Blair-Joyce & Silva. Format: News, oldies, div. News staff one; news progmg 14 hrs wkly. Target aud: 30 plus; farmers, commuters, homemakers. Spec prog: Farm 6 hrs wkly. ■ Ken Buehler (owner), pres; Mike Hughes, opns mgr, progmg dir & mus dir; Dave Chmeil, gen sls mgr; Phil Maki, chief engr. ■ Rates: $18.60; 18.60; 18.60; 18.60.

WCMP-FM—Oct 15, 1977: 92.1 mhz; 3 kw. Ant 300 ft. TL: N45 54 07 W92 57 25. Stereo. Hrs opn: 5 AM-midnight. Prog sep from AM. Net: ABC/E; MNN. Format: Contemp country, sports, news. Target aud: 18 plus; commuters, working adults with families. ■ Rates: Same as AM.

Pipestone

KLOH(AM)—June 1955: 1050 khz; 1 kw-D, 238 w-N, DA-2. TL: N43 59 32 W96 20 37 (CP: 9 kw-D, 400 w-N). Stereo. Box 456 (56164). (507) 825-4282. Licensee: Wallace Christensen (acq 8-1-76). Net: ABC/D, SMN. Format: C&W, farm. ■ Wally Christensen, pres, gen mgr & gen sls mgr; Bernie Weimie, mus dir; Diane Marie, news dir; Paul Derby, chief engr.

KISD(FM)—Co-owned with KLOH(AM). Nov 20, 1968: 98.7 mhz; 100 kw. Ant 700 ft. TL: N43 53 01 W95 55 44 (CP: Ant 1,017 ft.). Stereo. Hrs opn: 24. Prog sep from AM. Net: SMN. Format: CHR, adult contemp, oldies. Target aud: 18-65. ■ Mylan Ray, mus dir.

Preston

KFIL(AM)—May 21, 1966: 1060 khz; 1 kw-D. TL: N43 40 48 W92 08 27. Box 377 (55965). (507) 765-3856. FAX: (507) 765-2738. Licensee: KFIL Inc. Group owner: Borgen Broadcasting Co. Net: MBS. MNN. Format: C&W. ■ Michael Borgen, pres & gen mgr; Jeff Borgen, vp & gen sls mgr; Bruce Fishbaugher, stn mgr; Janna Vaalemoen, progmg dir; Michael Sveen, mus dir.

KFIL-FM—Sept 1, 1970: 103.1 mhz; 6 kw. Ant 270 ft. TL: N43 40 48 W92 08 27. Stereo. Dups AM 80%. Box 377, St. Paul & River Sts. (55965). Format: Country.

Princeton

WQPM(AM)—Feb 1, 1967: 1300 khz; 1 kw-D, 83 w-N. TL: N45 32 58 W93 34 52. Hrs opn: 5 AM-1 AM. Box 106, 32215 124th St. (55371). (612) 389-1300; (612) 444-6741. FAX: (612) 389-1359. Licensee: Segue Communications Corp. (acq 6-16-92; $1.2 million with co-located FM; FTR 5-4-92). Net: USA; Minn. News Net. Wash atty: Mullin, Ryne, Emmons & Topel. Format: Contemp country. News staff one; news progmg 10 hrs wkly. Target aud: 25-54. Spec prog: Farm 9 hrs wkly. ■ Paul Stagg, pres & gen mgr; Don Peters, opns dir; Susan Schmidgall, vp sls; Todd Rust, progmg dir, news dir & chief engr; Chris London, mus dir.

WQPM-FM—Dec 1, 1974: 106.1 mhz; 35 kw. Ant 620 ft. TL: N45 23 00 W93 42 30. Stereo. Hrs opn: 5 AM-1 AM. Format: Contemp country. News progmg 7 hrs wkly. Spec prog: Gospel greats 3 hrs wkly. ■ Neil Freeman, progmg dir; Chris London, mus dir; Todd Rust, engrg dir.

Red Wing

KCUE(AM)—Jan 29, 1949: 1250 khz; 1 kw-D, 110 w-N. TL: N44 32 20 W92 31 25. Hrs opn: 24. Box 102, 113 Guernsey Ln. (55066). (612) 388-7151. FAX: (612) 388-7153. Licensee: Sorenson Broadcasting Corp. (group owner; acq 6-81; $1.1 million with co-located FM; FTR 6-22-81). Net: ABC/I; MNN. Format: News/talk, farm, relg. News staff 2; news progmg 7 hrs wkly. Target aud: 35 plus; information consumer. ■ Dean Sorenson, pres; Lester Tuttle, gen mgr; Tom Hughes, opns mgr; Paul Reding, gen sls mgr; Max Wells, progmg dir; Linda Andrews, news dir; Dave Emowein, chief engr. ■ Rates: $20; 10; 10; 5.

KWNG(FM)—Co-owned with KCUE(AM). Aug 26, 1965: 105.9 mhz; 20 kw. Ant 300 ft. TL: N45 15 W92 13 56. Stereo. Hrs opn: 24. Prog sep from AM. Net: ABC-FM. Rep: Katz & Powell. Format: Classics-60s, 70s & 80s. News staff 2; news progmg one hr wkly. Target aud: 25-44; family & yuppie. ■ Mitzi Warrington, gen sls mgr; Jennifer Luebke, mus dir. ■ Rates: $20; 15; 15; 7.

Redwood Falls

KLGR(AM)—Nov 1954: 1490 khz; 1 kw-U. TL: N44 32 33 W95 07 57 (CP: 470 w, TL: N44 32 35 W95 07 57). Box 65, Hwy. 19 W. (56283). (507) 637-2989. Licensee: CD Broadcasting Corp of Redwood Falls. Group owner: CD Broadcasting Co. (acq 10-86; $701,000 with co-located FM; FTR 10-27-86). Net: ABC/I; MNN. Format: C&W, farm. News staff 2; news progmg 20 hrs wkly. Target aud: General. ■ Mel Paradis, pres; Mike Neudecker, gen mgr; Marty Hembre, progmg dir; Tim Johnson, mus dir; Bruce Tolzmann, news dir & chief engr.

KLGR-FM—June 3, 1974: 97.7 mhz; 3 kw. Ant 305 ft. TL: N44 32 33 W95 07 57 (CP: 60 kw, ant 289 ft.). Stereo. Dups AM 20%. Format: Hot country.

Richfield

KDWB-FM—Licensed to Richfield. See Minneapolis-St. Paul.

KRXX(AM)—Licensed to Richfield. See Minneapolis-St. Paul.

Rochester

*****KFSI(FM)**—Apr 28, 1981: 88.5 mhz; 7 kw. Ant 320 ft. TL: N44 01 27 W92 32 36. Stereo. 4016 28th St. S.E. (55904). (507) 289-8585. Licensee: Faith Sound Inc. Net: Moody. Format: Contemp Christian. ■ Ray Logan, pres; Paul Logan, progmg dir.

*****KLSE-FM**—Dec 17, 1974: 91.7 mhz; 100 kw. Ant 953 ft. TL: N44 02 26 W92 20 28. Stereo. Hrs opn: 24. 735 Marquette Bank Bldg. (55904). (507) 282-0910; (507) 282-8000. FAX: (507) 282-2107. Licensee: Minnesota Public Radio Inc. Net: NPR, APR; Minn. Pub. Radio. Format: Class, news. News staff 4; news progmg 30 hrs wkly. ■ William H. Kling, pres; Rich Dietman, gen mgr; Becky Gonzalez, dev dir; Bridget Parks, mktg dir; Carol Gunderson, news dir; Don Kolbert, chief engr.

KNXR(FM)—Dec 24, 1965: 97.5 mhz; 100 kw. Ant 1,055 ft. TL: N44 02 32 W92 20 26. Stereo. Hrs opn: 6 AM-1 AM. 1620 Greenview Dr. S.W. (55902). (507) 288-7700. FAX: (507) 288-4531. Licensee: United Audio Corp. Net: ABC/E. Rep: Katz. Wash atty: Miller & Fields. Format: Adult traditional. Target aud: 35 plus. Spec prog: Class 4 hrs wkly. ■ Thomas H. Jones, pres & gen mgr; Donald H. Anderson, gen sls mgr.

KOLM(AM)—November 1963: 1520 khz; 10 kw-D. TL: N43 59 13 W92 25 05. 1220 4th Ave. S.W. (55902). (507) 288-1971. FAX: (507) 288-1520. Licensee: Olmsted County Broadcasting Co. Net: MBS. Rep: McGavren Guild. Wash atty: Gardner, Canton & Douglas. Format: Oldies. News staff 2. Target aud: 25-54. Spec prog: Farm 3 hrs wkly. ■ Howard G. Bill, pres; Dick Kadke, gen mgr; Denny Foster, opns mgr & progmg mgr; Jim Dahl, gen sls mgr; Bob David, mus dir; Katy Colbenson, news dir. ■ Rates: $38; 38; 38; 10.

KWWK(FM)—Co-owned with KOLM(AM). July 4, 1967: 96.5 mhz; 43 kw. Ant 528 ft. TL: N44 01 59 W92 36 10. Stereo. Prog sep from AM. Net: MBS. Rep: McGavren Guild. Format: Country. ■ Rates: $32; 28; 28; 22.

KRCH(FM)—Listing follows KWEB(AM).

KROC(AM)—October 1935: 1340 khz; 1 kw-U. TL: N44 01 47 W92 29 31. Hrs opn: 24. 122 4th St. S.W. (55902). (507) 286-1010. Licensee: Southern Minnesota Broadcasting Co. (group owner). Net: ABC/E, MBS. Rep: Torbet, Hyett/Ramsland. Format: MOR, oldies. News staff 3. Target aud: 30-64. Spec prog: Farm 12 hrs wkly. ■ Greg Gentling, pres & gen mgr; Rosanne Rybak, gen sls

Minnesota

mgr; Joe O'Brien, progmg dir; Tony Gentling, mus dir; Kim David, news dir; Dave Seavy, chief engr.

KROC-FM—July 1, 1965: 106.9 mhz; 100 kw. Ant 1,110 ft. TL: N43 34 15 W92 25 37. Prog sep from AM. Net: ABC/C. Format: CHR. News staff one. Target aud: 18-54. ■ Brent Ackerman, progmg dir; Bill Davis, mus dir.

*KRPR(FM)—1976: 89.9 mhz; 1.2 kw. Ant 500 ft. TL: N44 02 32 W92 20 26. Rochester Community College, 851 30th Ave. S.E. (55904). (507) 285-7231. FAX: (507) 285-7496. Licensee: Rochester Community College. Format: Educational, AOR. ■ Jim Kehoe, stn mgr; Chad Trom, mus dir; Dale Pederson, chief engr.

KWEB(AM)—Nov 27, 1957: 1270 khz; 5 kw-D, 1 kw-N, DA-2. TL: N43 58 47 W92 26 51. 29 7th St. N.E. (55906). (507) 288-3888. FAX: (507) 288-7815. Licensee: KRCH of Minnesota Inc. (acq 12-27-92; $2 million with co-located FM; FTR 1-18-93). Net: CNN, MNN. Rep: Katz & Powell. Format: Talk. News staff one; news progmg 28 hrs wkly. Target aud: Men. Spec prog: Sports. ■ Robert Ingstad, pres; Bob Jung, gen mgr & opns mgr; Mary Anne Nonn, gen sls mgr; Greg Henn, progmg dir; Brad Oistad, news dir; Jim Casey, chief engr. ■ Rates: $25; 20; 20; 15.

KRCH(FM)—Co-owned with KWEB(AM). Nov 1, 1968: 101.7 mhz; 39.1 kw. Ant 554 ft. TL: N44 06 59 W92 41 22. Stereo. Hrs opn: 24. Net: NBC the Source. Format: Classic rock. Target aud: 25-54. ■ Mike Hines, prom dir; Jack Hicks, progmg dir; Matt Montgomery, mus dir.

KWWK(FM)—Listing follows KOLM(AM).

*KZSE(FM)—February 1989: 90.7 mhz; 1.38 kw. Ant 259 ft. TL: N44 02 26 W92 20 28. Hrs opn: 24. 735 Marquette Bank Bldg. (55904). (507) 282-0910; (507) 282-8000. FAX: (507) 282-2107. Licensee: Minnesota Public Radio Inc. Net: NPR, APR; Minn. Pub. Format: News & info. News staff 3. ■ William H. Kling, pres; Rich Dietman, gen mgr; Becky Gonzalez, dev dir; Bridget Parks, mktg dir; Carol Gunderson, news dir; Don Kolbert, chief engr.

Roseau

KRWB(AM)—Apr 5, 1963: 1410 khz; 1 kw-U, DA-N. TL: N48 50 40 W95 43 41. Box 130 (56751). (218) 463-1410. Licensee: Marlin T. Obie (acq 7-1-85; $315,000; FTR 5-13-85). Net: ABC/I; MNN. Format: C&W. News staff one. Target aud: 25-54; general. ■ Marlin T. Obie, pres; Rob Obie, gen mgr; Jack L. McDonald, gen sls mgr; Natalie Gustasson, prom dir & progmg mgr; Brad Zoeller, mus dir; Pam Iverson, news dir; Ken Bartz, chief engr.

Roseville

*KDNI(FM)—(Duluth). Apr 16, 1983: 90.5 mhz; 1.3 kw. Ant 804 ft. TL: N46 47 21 W92 06 51 (CP: 97.3 mhz, 40 kw, ant 548 ft.). Stereo. Hrs opn: 24. 1101 E. Central Entrance, Duluth (55811); NWCR Foundation, 3003 N. Snelling Ave., Roseville (55113). (218) 722-6700; (612) 631-5000. FAX: (218) 722-1092. Licensee: Northwestern College Radio Foundation. Group owner: Northwestern College Radio Network (acq 12-18-92). Net: AP, Skylight. Wash atty: Bryan, Cave & McPheeters. Format: Relg, educ. News progmg 5 hrs wkly. Target aud: 25-54; baby boomers. ■ Paul Ramseyer, exec vp; Harv Hendrickson, vp; Paul Harkness, stn mgr & chief engr; Bob Nus, mus dir.

*KTIS(AM)—(Minneapolis). Feb 7, 1949: 900 khz; 25 kw-D, 300 w-N, DA-2. TL: N44 59 51 W93 21 10. Hrs opn: 24. 3003 N. Snelling, Roseville (55113). (612) 631-5000. FAX: (612) 631-5010. Licensee: Northwestern College. Group owner: Northwestern College Radio Network. Net: Skylight. Format: Relg. News staff 2; news progmg 20 hrs wkly. Target aud: 35-45. ■ Mel Johnson, chmn; Donald Ericksen, pres; Paul Ramseyer, vp; Don Rupp, gen mgr; Dale Thiessen, prom mgr; Neil Staven, pub affrs mgr; Rod Thannum, chief engr.

Rushford

KWNO-FM—Dec 18, 1991: 99.3 mhz; 2.56 kw. Ant 499 ft. TL: N43 56 32 W91 45 30. Box 466, Winona (55987). (507) 452-4722. FAX: (507) 487-4871. Licensee: Wheeler Broadcasting of Minnesota Inc. (acq 5-14-92; FTR 6-8-92). ■ Patrick Marek, gen mgr.

St. Cloud

*KCFB(FM)—Nov 17, 1986: 91.5 mhz; 800 w. Ant 119 ft. TL: N45 33 13 W94 11 27. Stereo. Hrs opn: 24. Box 1683 (56302). (612) 252-4214. Licensee: Fellowship Broadcasting Corp. of St. Cloud, Minn. Net: Moody. Format: Relg. Target aud: General. ■ Lawrence E. Simmons, pres & chief engr; Mary Ann Simmons, gen sls mgr.

KCLD-FM—Listing follows KNSI(AM).

KKSR(FM)—(Sartell). Aug 26, 1988: 96.7 mhz; 50 kw. Ant 453 ft. TL: N45 46 03 W94 08 04. Stereo. Hrs opn: 24. Box 699, St. Cloud (56302); 24 W. Division St., Waite Park (56387). (612) 253-9600. FAX: (612) 255-5276. Licensee: Sartell FM Inc. Group owner: Starcom Inc. Net: Unistar. Rep: O'Malley. Wash atty: Wiley, Rein & Fielding. Format: Adult contemp. News staff one. Target aud: 25-54. ■ Dennis Carpenter, pres; Sheldon Johnson, vp; Diana Fuhrman, opns mgr; Rick Anderson, rgnl sls mgr; Dennis Comfort, prom mgr; Carrie Preston, mus dir; Russ Bohaty, news dir; Ken Cummings, chief engr.

KNSI(AM)—June 1938: 1450 khz; 1 kw-U. TL: N45 32 21 W94 10 05. Stereo. Box 1458 (56302); 619 Mall Germain (56301). (612) 251-1450. Licensee: Leighton Enterprises Inc. (group owner; acq 9-15-75). Net: NBC Talknet, CNN. Rep: Roslin; CMR. Format: News/talk. News staff 2; news progmg one hr wkly. Target aud: general. ■ Al Leighton, pres; John J. Sowada, CFO, vp & stn mgr; Dennis Niess, vp sls & gen sls mgr; Nancy Zenner, prom mgr; Rock Lundorff, progmg dir; Craig Bomgaars, chief engr.

KCLD-FM—Co-owned with KNSI(AM). May 1, 1948: 104.7 mhz; 100 kw. Ant 984 ft. TL: N45 34 03 W94 30 43. Stereo. Prog sep from AM. Format: CHR. ■ John Ramsey, prom dir, progmg dir & mus dir; John Uran, prom mgr.

*KVSC(FM)—May 10, 1967: 88.1 mhz; 16.5 kw. Ant 446 ft. TL: N45 31 00 W94 13 52. Stereo. Hrs opn: 20. St. Cloud State Univ., 27 Stewart Hall (56301). (612) 255-3066. FAX: (612) 255-3126. Licensee: St. Cloud State Univ. Net: AP. Format: Div/variety, progsv, AOR. News staff one; news progmg 15 hrs wkly. Target aud: 17-60; educated, progsv. Spec prog: reggae, blues, class 3 hrs, jazz 12 hrs, Black 5 hrs wkly. ■ Dorothy Simpson, pres; Richard Hill, gen mgr; Jo McMullen, stn mgr & mktg dir; Kyle Smith, progmg dir; Kevin Young, news dir; Bill Nelson, chief engr.

KXSS(AM)—See Waite Park.

WJON(AM)—September 1950: 1240 khz; 1 kw-U. TL: N45 33 36 W94 08 20. Stereo. Box 220 (56302); 640 S.E. Lincoln Ave. (56303). (612) 251-4422. FAX: (612) 251-1855. Licensee: WJON Broadcasting Co. (acq 5-31-62). Net: ABC/I; MNN. Format: MOR, news/talk. News staff 2; news progmg 30 hrs wkly. Target aud: 25-plus. ■ Andy Hilger, CEO & pres; Carol Hilger, vp; Steve Stewart, stn mgr & gen sls mgr; Kathy Merchant, natl sls mgr; Mike Diem, progmg dir & mus dir; Bruce Gordon, news dir; Mark Young, chief engr. ■ Rates: $35.25; 22.90; 22.90; 17.65.

WWJO(FM)—Co-owned with WJON(AM). 1975: 98.1 mhz; 97 kw. Ant 1,000 ft. TL: N45 48 52 W94 01 38. Stereo. Hrs opn: 24. Prog sep from AM. Net: ABC/E; MNN. Format: Country. News progmg 14 hrs wkly. Target aud: 25 plus. ■ Mark Sprint, progmg dir & mus dir. ■ Rates: $52.90; 40.60; 40.60; 21.15.

St. James

KXAC(FM)—Nov. 1, 1992: 100.5 mhz; 50 kw. Ant 433 ft. TL: N43 52 29 W94 36 04. Hrs opn: 24. Box 465, Hwy. 4-30 N.W. (56081). (507) 375-3386. FAX: (507) 375-5050. Licensee: Rogers Broadcasting Inc. Net: MNN, Mutual. Wash atty: Miller & Miller. Format: Lite hits. News staff one; news progmg 17 hrs wkly. Target aud: 25-58. ■ Dick Rogers, exec vp, gen mgr, adv mgr & news dir; Phil Rogers, sr vp; Curt Rogers, stn mgr, chief opns & pub affrs dir; Gwen Finstad, gen sls mgr; Jeremy James, vp progmg; John McKenzie, mus mgr; Scott Schmeling, chief engr.

KXAX(FM)—July 24, 1983: 104.9 mhz; 3 kw. Ant 289 ft. TL: N44 03 15 W94 39 40. Stereo. Hrs opn: 24. Box 465, Highway 4-30 N.W. (56081). (507) 375-3386. FAX: (507) 375-5050. Licensee: Rogers Broadcasting Inc. Net: MNN. Wash atty: Miller & Miller. Format: Modern country. News staff one; news progmg 16 hrs wkly. Target aud: 25-54. Spec prog: Sp one hr wkly. ■ Dick Rogers, pres, gen mgr & progmg dir; Phil Rogers, exec vp; Curt Rogers, chief opns & mus dir.

St. Joseph

KKJM(FM)—Not on air, target date unknown: 92.9 mhz; 25 kw. Ant 328 ft. Box 68 (56374). Licensee: St. Joseph Broadcasters.

St. Louis Park

*KDXL(FM)—March 17, 1977: 106.7 mhz; 10 w. Ant 974 ft. TL: N44 56 36 W93 21 39. Stereo. Hrs opn: 7:30 AM-10 PM, M-F; 8 AM-6 PM, Sat. Sr. H.S., 6425 W. 33rd St. (55426). (612) 928-6272; (612) 928-6150. Licensee: Independent School District 283. Format: AOR, classic rock, progressive. Target aud: 15-30. ■ Tom Marble, stn mgr; Dick Johnson, chief engr.

KJJO(AM)—May 13, 1958: 950 khz; 1 kw-U, DA-2. TL: N44 52 08 W93 25 11. Hrs opn: 24. 11320 Valley View Rd., Eden Prairie (55344). (612) 941-5774. FAX: (612) 941-8750. Licensee: Park Broadcasting. Group owner: Park Communications Inc. (acq 12-68). Net: ABC/E. Rep: Major Mkt. Format: Contemp country. Target aud: 25-54. ■ Tom Tucker, gen mgr; Bill Fink, progmg dir; Scott James, mus dir; Dave Ernewein, chief engr.

KJJO-FM—July 1, 1962: 104.1 mhz; 100 kw. Ant 1,040 ft. TL: N45 06 21 W92 42 29. Stereo. Prog sep from AM. Net: ABC/I. ■ Lisa Toren, rgnl sls mgr; Suzanne Schultz, prom mgr.

St. Paul

KEEY-FM—Licensed to St. Paul. See Minneapolis-St. Paul.

KLBB(AM)—Licensed to St. Paul. See Minneapolis-St. Paul.

KNOF(FM)—Licensed to St. Paul. See Minneapolis-St. Paul.

KSTP(AM)—Licensed to St. Paul. See Minneapolis-St. Paul.

KSTP-FM—Licensed to St. Paul. See Minneapolis-St. Paul.

WDGY(AM)—Licensed to St. Paul. See Minneapolis-St. Paul.

*WMCN(FM)—Licensed to St. Paul. See Minneapolis-St. Paul.

St. Peter

*KGAC(FM)—Mar 29, 1985: 90.5 mhz; 75 kw. Ant 708 ft. TL: N44 13 20 W94 07 03. Stereo. Hrs opn: 24. Rebroadcasts KSJN(FM) Minneapolis 90%. Box 236 (56082); Gustavus Adolphus College, Bjorling Hall, 800 W. College Ave. (56082). (507) 933-7660. FAX: (507) 933-7662. Licensee: Minnesota Public Radio Inc. Net: APR; Minn. Pub. Format: Class, arts. News staff 2. Target aud: General. Spec prog: Folk/variety 17 hrs wkly. ■ William H. Kling, pres; Dennis Hamilton, vp; John Gaddo, gen mgr; Sally Brasher, dev mgr; Jennifer Kane, prom mgr; Lorna Benson, news dir; Scott Schmeling, chief engr.

*KNGA(FM)—March 1, 1992: 91.5 mhz; 8.5 kw. Ant 600 ft. TL: N44 13 20 W94 07 03. Stereo. Hrs opn: 24. Rebroadcasts KNOW(AM) Minneapolis 90%. Box 236 (56082); Adolphus College, Bjorling Hall, 800 W. College Ave. (56082). (507) 933-7660. FAX: (507) 933-7662. Licensee: Minnesota Public Radio. Net: NPR, APR; Minn. Pub. Format: News, information. News staff 2. Target aud: General. ■ William H. Kling, pres; Dennis Hamilton, vp; John Gaddo, gen mgr; Sally Brasher, dev mgr; Jennifer Kane, prom mgr; Lorna Benson, news dir; Scott Schmeling, chief engr.

KRBI(AM)—Aug 5, 1957: 1310 khz; 1 kw-D, 343 w-N, DA-1. TL: N44 19 51 W93 58 19. Hrs opn: 6 AM-midnight. 1031 W. Grace St. (56082). (507) 931-3220. FAX: (507) 931-4740. Licensee: Johnson Broadcasting Corp. (acq 4-1-60). Net: ABC/E. Rep: Walton. Format: Adult contemp, country, oldies. News staff 3. Target aud: General. ■ Robert Johnson, pres & gen mgr; Judy Conroy, gen sls mgr; Rick Johnson, progmg dir; Bruce Davis, mus dir; Joel Koetke, news dir; Gary Wilson, chief engr. ■ Rates: $10.60; 10.60; 10.60; 10.60.

KRBI-FM—Sept 1, 1966: 105.5 mhz; 3 kw. Ant 130 ft. TL: N44 19 41 W93 58 17. Stereo. Hrs opn: 6 AM-midnight. Dups AM 100%. ■ Rates: Same as AM.

Sartell

KKSR(FM)—Licensed to Sartell. See St. Cloud.

Sauk Centre

KMSR(FM)—1976: 94.3 mhz; 3 kw. Ant 286 ft. TL: N45 42 30 W95 08 18. Stereo. 508 Original Main St. (56378). (612) 352-6594. FAX: (612) 352-6594. Licensee: Friday Communications Inc. (acq 2-12-90; FTR 3-12-90). Net: MBS, SMN; MNN, MAGNET. Format: Oldies, MN pro sports. News staff one. Target aud: 25-49. Spec prog: Area sports 6 hrs wkly. ■ Rick Freitag, pres, gen mgr, gen sls mgr & vp progmg; Gail Freitag, vp; Renee Willhite, news dir; Wendall Sowers, chief engr.

Stations in the U.S.

Sauk Rapids

WVAL(AM)—Aug 3, 1963: 660 khz; 10 kw-D, 250 w-N, DA-2. TL: N45 36 18 W94 09 21. 10102nd St. N. (56379). (612) 252-6200. FAX: (612) 252-9367. Licensee: Tri-County Broadcasting Inc. Net: NBC, NBC Talknet, Unistar. Format: Oldies. Spec prog: Farm 3 hrs wkly. ■ Herb M. Hoppe, pres & gen mgr; Scott C. Klohn, opns mgr & news dir; Hal Hoover, progmg dir; Kim Daniels, mus dir; Garry Hoppe, chief engr.

WHMH-FM—Co-owned with WVAL(AM). Oct 31, 1975: 101.7 mhz; 3 kw. Ant 297 ft. TL: N45 35 48 W94 09 25 (CP: 6 kw, ant 308 ft.). Stereo. Prog sep from AM. Net: NBC the Source. Format: AOR. ■ Nigel Stewart, progmg dir; Randy Kaye, mus dir.

Shakopee

KKCM(AM)—Oct 6, 1963: 1530 khz; 8.6 kw-D, DA-D. TL: N44 48 26 W93 33 25. Box 357, 421 E. 1st Ave. (55379). (612) 496-1530. FAX: (612) 496-4292. Licensee: American Sunrise Communications (acq 4-1-89). Net: USA. Wash atty: Gammon & Grange. Format: Christian, news/talk. News progmg 20 hrs wkly. Target aud: 25-49; young adults. ■ John Boyd, pres; John Hull, gen mgr & chief engr; Brian Fisher, chief opns. ■ Rates: $15; 12; 15; na.

Slayton

KLOH-FM—1993: 103.1 mhz; 3 kw. TL: N43 59 43 W95 44 51. 2660 Broadway Ave. (56172). (507) 836-6125. Licensee: Wallace Christensen. Format: Country. ■ Wally Christensen, gen mgr.

Sleepy Eye

KNUJ-FM—Not on air, target date unknown: 107.3 mhz; 1.13 kw. Ant 528 ft. Rebroadcasts KNUJ(AM) New Ulm 70%. Box 368, New Ulm (56073). Licensee: Brown County Broadcasting Inc. Group owner: James Ingstad Broadcasting Inc. Format: Country, news/talk. News staff one; news progmg 20 hrs wkly. Target aud: 30 plus; general. ■ Jim Bartels, gen mgr; Marj Frederickson, sls dir; Brian Filaen, progmg dir. ■ Rates: $30; 30; 30; 15.

Spring Grove

KQYB(FM)—Aug 2, 1980: 98.3 mhz; 33 kw. Ant 607 ft. TL: N43 40 53 W91 45 28. Stereo. Hrs opn: 24. Box 308, Hwy. 44 W. (55974-0308). (507) 498-5720; (507) 498-5772. FAX: (507) 498-5766. Licensee: SUN Communications Inc. Net: SMN. Wash atty: Miller & Fields. Format: Hot country. News progmg one hr wkly. Target aud: General. Spec prog: Relg 3 hrs wkly. ■ Greg Wennes, pres; Phyllis Thorson, gen mgr & gen sls mgr; Phil Costigan, opns mgr; Joe Deschler, progmg dir; Lori Peterson, news dir; Pat Delaney, chief engr. ■ Rates: $15.75; 12.75; 15.75; 12.75.

Spring Valley

KNFX(FM)—Not on air, target date unknown: 104.3 mhz; 2.8 kw. Ant 472 ft. TL: N43 33 46 W92 25 29. 232 Third St., Valley City, ND (58072). Licensee: Radio Ingstad Minnesota Inc.

Springfield

KLPR(FM)—Not on air, target date unknown: 105.7 mhz; 3 kw. Ant 328 ft. TL: N44 14 13 W95 06 20. 232 3rd St. N.E., Valley City, ND (58072). Licensee: James Ingstad Broadcasting Inc.

Staples

KNSP(AM)—June 3, 1982: 1430 khz; 1 kw-D, 199 w-N. TL: N46 21 34 W94 46 55. Box 278, 213 N.E. 4th St. (56479). (218) 894-3441. FAX: (218) 894-3441. Licensee: Cardinal Broadcasting Inc. (acq 12-4-91; $86,188; FTR 1-6-92). Net: UPI. Format: 50s and 60s. Spec prog: Farm 6 hrs wkly. ■ Perry Kugler, pres; Larry Best, gen mgr; Barb Best, progmg dir & mus dir; Dennis Minks, news dir; Ralph Anderson, chief engr.

KNSP-FM—Not on air, target date unknown: 94.7 mhz; 3 kw. Ant 121 ft. TL: N46 21 34 W94 46 55. Licensee: Staples Broadcasting Inc.

KSKK(FM)—Not on air, target date unknown: 94.7 mhz; 6 kw. Ant 125 ft. Box 49, Park Rapids (56470). Licensee: NorMin Broadcasting Co.

Stewartville

KYBA(FM)—Feb 1, 1993: 105.3 khz; 50 kw. Ant 492 ft. TL: N43 40 23 W92 41 54. 104 Second St. N.W. (55976). (507) 533-4082. FAX: (507) 533-4083. Licensee: Southern Minnesota Broadcasting Co. (group owner; acq 6-30-93; $125,000; FTR 7-26-93). ■ Sue Daily, gen mgr; David Fezler, opns dir.

Stillwater

WIMN(AM)—March 13, 1949: 1220 khz; 5 kw-D, 254 w-N. TL: N45 03 15 W92 49 42. c/o Smith Broadcasting Co., 125 E. Third St., New Richmond, WI (54017); 104 N. Main St. (55082). (715) 246-2254; (612) 430-5006. FAX: (715) 246-7090; (612) 439-5015. Licensee: Smith Broadcasting Co. Group owner: Bob Smith Stns (acq 7-19-93; $75,000; FTR 8-9-93). Format: Nostalgia. ■ Daniel Smith, vp & gen mgr; Robert Van Cleve, news dir.

Thief River Falls

KKAQ(AM)—Nov 2, 1979: 1460 khz; 2.5 kw-U. TL: N48 07 21 W96 08 24. Hrs opn: 24. Box 218, 319 N. LaBree Ave. (56701). (218) 681-4900. FAX: (218) 681-6311. Licensee: Ault Marketing Inc. (acq 4-21-93; $375,000 with co-located FM; FTR 5-10-93). Net: ABC/I, Unistar. Wash atty: Eugene T. Smith. Format: Country. News staff one; news progmg 4 hrs wkly. Target aud: 25-54. Spec prog: Oldies 6 hrs wkly. ■ Curt Quesnell, gen mgr & gen sls mgr; Dave Halvorson, progmg dir.

KKDQ(FM)—Co-owned with KKAQ(AM). Nov 1, 1990: 99.3 mhz; 6 kw. Ant 170 ft. TL: N48 07 21 W96 08 24. Stereo. Hrs opn: 24. Prog sep from AM. Format: Country. News progmg 4 hrs wkly. Target aud: Young adults. ■ Rob Raymond, progmg dir.

*****KNTN(FM)**—Dec 13, 1991: 102.7 mhz; 100 kw. Ant 538 ft. TL: N47 58 38 W96 36 32. Stereo. Hrs opn: 24. c/o KCCM, Concordia College, 901 S. 8th St., Moorhead (56562). (218) 299-3666. FAX: (218) 299-3418. Licensee: Minnesota Public Radio Inc. (acq 11-26-90; $30,000; FTR 12-17-90). Net: NPR, APR; Minn. Pub. Format: News. News staff 2; news progmg 168 hrs wkly. Target aud: General. ■ William H. Kling, pres; Lois Hanson, gen mgr; Brooke Miller, dev dir; Karen Nitzkorski, prom mgr; Dan Gunderson, news dir; Jon Blomstrand, chief engr.

*****KQMN(FM)**—Nov 26, 1990: 91.5 mhz; 100 kw. Ant 449 ft. TL: N47 58 38 W96 36 32. Stereo. Hrs opn: 24. Prog sep from KNTN(FM). Concordia College, 901 S. 8th, Moorhead (56562). (218) 299-3666. FAX: (218) 299-3418. Licensee: Minnesota Public Radio Inc. Net: NPR, APR; Minn. Pub. Format: Classical music & cultural progmg. News staff 2. Target aud: General. ■ William H. Kling, pres; Lois Hanson, gen mgr; Vern Goodin, dev dir; Karen Nitzkorski, prom mgr; Dan Gunderson, news dir; Jon Blomstrand, chief engr.

KSNR(FM)—Licensed to Thief River Falls. See East Grand Forks.

*****KSRQ(FM)**—Nov 15, 1971: 90.1 mhz; 24 kw. Ant 338 ft. TL: N48 01 19 W96 22 12. Stereo. Hrs opn: 5 AM-11 PM. Thief River Falls Technical College, 1301 Hwy. 1 E. (56701). (218) 681-6364; (800) 222-2884. FAX: (218) 681-5519. Licensee: Joint Vocational Technical College District No. 22004 (acq 5-29-92). Net: CNN. Wash atty: Blair, Joyce & Silva. Format: Adult contemp, AOR, country. News progmg 10 hrs wkly. Target aud: 12-30. Spec prog: Christian rock 6 hrs wkly. ■ Orley Gunderson, pres; Howard Rokke, gen mgr; Donald Jorstad, stn mgr; Stan Mueller, chief engr.

KTRF(AM)—Jan 30, 1947: 1230 khz; 1 kw-U. TL: N48 07 47 W96 17 11. Hrs opn: 24. Box 40, Hwy 32 N. (56701). (218) 681-1230. FAX: (218) 681-3717. Licensee: Border States Broadcasting Corp. (acq 5-28-92; with KSNR(FM) Thief River Falls). Net: CBS; MNN. Wash atty: Haley, Bader & Potts. Format: MOR, news. News staff 2; news progmg 35 hrs wkly. Target aud: General; 25 plus. Spec prog: Farm 12 hrs wkly. ■ Steve Glasmann, pres; Joel Swanson, gen mgr & gen sls mgr; Jon Praska, rgnl sls mgr; Joel Swanson, Jon Praska, Sue Peterson, mktg mgrs; Colette Vetsch, Jon Praska, prom dirs; Joel Swanson, Sue Peterson, Mark Stromsodt, adv mgrs; Mark Stromsodt, Bob Hultgren, progmg dirs; Mark Stromsodt, Bob Hultgren, mus dirs; Todd McDonald, Lee Richards, news dirs; Sue Peterson, Todd McDonald, pub affrs dirs; Mark Stromsodt, engrg mgr; Stan Mueller, chief engr. ■ Rates: $15; 13; 11; 9.

Tracy

KARL(FM)—Not on air, target date unknown: 105.1 mhz; 3 kw. Ant 342 ft. TL: N44 13 58 W95 39 45 (CP: 4.3 kw, ant 387 ft.). Stereo. Box 218, 3rd St. (56175). (507) 629-3355. FAX: (507) 532-3739. Licensee: KMHL Broadcasting Co. (acq 12-17-92; $22,100; FTR 1-11-93). Format: Super hit country. News progmg 3 hrs wkly. Target aud: General. ■ Donald Linder, pres; Brad Strootman, gen mgr; Greg Schultz, opns mgr; Sharon Fenske, adv dir; Brian Johnson, progmg mgr & pub affrs dir. ■ Rates: $8.25; 8.25; 7.50; 6.25.

Two Harbors

WRSR(FM)—Not on air, target date unknown: 104.3 mhz; 3 kw. Ant 328 ft. TL: N46 59 51 W91 50 13. Stereo. 5001 W. 80th St., No. 901, Minneapolis (55437). (612) 835-1214. Licensee: Twin Ports Broadcasting Inc. Group owner: Starcom Inc.

Virginia

WHLB(AM)—Oct 12, 1936: 1400 khz; 1 kw-U. TL: N47 30 33 W92 32 31 (CP: N47 30 09 W92 33 44). Hrs opn: 24. Box 954, S. 17th St. & 6th Ave. (55792). (218) 741-2233; (218) 741-2234. FAX: (218) 741-1415. Licensee: Virginia Broadcasting Co. Inc. (acq 4-11-85). Net: MBS, SMN, ABC/E; MNN. Wash atty: Bob Rini. Format: Big band, MOR. News progmg 10 hrs wkly. Target aud: 35 plus; blue collar workers, retired men & women. Spec prog: Polka 8 hrs, relg 5 hrs wkly. ■ Frank C. Befera, pres & gen mgr; Steve Fleming, gen sls mgr; Neil Larson, progmg dir. ■ Rates: $9.50; 8.60; 9.50; 7.75.

WUSZ(FM)—Co-owned with WHLB(AM). June 2, 1971: 99.9 mhz; 100 kw. Ant 567 ft. TL: N47 22 52 W92 57 18. Stereo. Hrs opn: 24. Prog sep from AM. Net: MBS, ABC/E, DUSA; MNN. Wash atty: Rini & Coran. Format: Country. News progmg one hr wkly. Target aud: 25-49; blue & white collar workers & families. ■ Frank C. Befera, CEO & progmg dir; Steve Lah, mus dir. ■ Rates: $15.40; 14; 15.40; 12.60.

Virginia-Hibbing

*****WIRR(FM)**—Licensed to Virginia-Hibbing. See Duluth.

Wabasha

KWMB(AM)—April 1976: 1190 khz; 1 kw-D. TL: N44 20 44 W91 58 28. Box 46, 62 1/2 Pembroke Ave. (55981). (612) 565-4576. FAX: (612) 565-2616. Licensee: Radio Ingstad Minnesota Inc. (acq 6-6-90; $275,000 with KMFX-FM Lake City; FTR 6-25-90). Net: MBS; MNN. Format: C&W, farm. ■ Kelly Lafky, opns mgr & gen sls mgr; Carol Tentis, progmg dir & mus dir; Mike Yanckley, news dir; Jeff Urban, chief engr.

Wadena

KWAD(AM)—April 24, 1948: 920 khz; 1 kw-U, DA-N. TL: N46 22 15 W95 08 58. Hrs opn: 5 AM-1 AM. Box 551 (56482). (218) 631-1803. FAX: (218) 631-4557. Licensee: Ingstad Broadcasting Inc. Group owner: James Ingstad Broadcasting Inc. (acq 8-2-76). Net: ABC/I. Format: C&W. News staff one. Target aud: General. Spec prog: Farm 10 hrs wkly. ■ Jim Ingstad, pres; Rick Youngbauer, gen mgr; Randy Johnson, gen sls mgr; Dan Skogen, progmg dir; Kyle Gylsen, mus dir; Dan Skogan, news dir; Paul Titchenal, chief engr.

KKWS(FM)—Co-owned with KWAD(AM). Sept 23, 1968: 105.9 mhz; 100 kw. Ant 564 ft. TL: N46 36 00 W94 54 03. Stereo. ■ Mike Huber, progmg dir.

Waite Park

KXSS(AM)—Jan 1, 1981: 1390 khz; 2.5 kw-D, 1 kw-N, DA-2. TL: N45 32 35 W94 15 41. Stereo. Box 5009, 33rd Div., Cross Rds Mall, 1986 Julep Rd., St. Cloud (56302). (612) 253-1400. FAX: (612) 251-5129. Licensee: Sioux Valley Broadcasting Co. (acq 10-22-91; $800,000 with co-located FM; FTR 11-11-91). Format: CHR. News staff one; news progmg one hr wkly. Target aud: 18-49. ■ Bob Ramstorf, gen mgr; Tim Walstron, opns mgr; Adam North, prom mgr & mus dir.

KLZZ(FM)—Co-owned with KXSS(AM). July 1989: 103.7 mhz; 3 kw. Ant 328 ft. TL: N45 32 35 W94 15 41 (CP: 25 kw, TL: N45 29 02 W94 08 12). Dups AM 100%.

Walker

KLLZ(AM)—July 11, 1970: 1600 khz; 1 kw-D, 47 w-N. TL: N47 04 58 W94 35 21. Box 70, Hwy. 34 W. (56484). (218) 547-1200. FAX: (218) 547-2533. Licensee: Sioux Valley Broadcasting Co. (acq 4-9-91; $255,000 with co-

Mississippi

located FM; FTR 4-22-91). Net: MNN. Format: Adult contemp. Target aud: General. ■ Brad Walhof, gen mgr & gen sls mgr; James Schmelzer, news dir; Paul Tichanal, chief engr.

KLLZ-FM—May 6, 1984: 99.1 mhz; 50 kw. Ant 492 ft. TL: N47 12 42 W94 55 02. Stereo. Rebroadcasts KLIZ(FM) Brainerd 100%. Format: Classic rock. ■ Charlie Ferguson, gen mgr; Don Janke, gen sls mgr; Steve Gunner, progmg dir; Dan Wilde, mus dir; Tim Norton, news dir; Sam Morris, pub affrs dir; Jerry Weller, engrg dir. ■ Rates: $22.50; 17.25; 22.50; 17.25.

Warroad

KKWQ(FM)—August 1989: 92.5 mhz; 100 kw. Ant 472 ft. TL: N48 49 41 W92 23 16. Stereo. Box 53 (56763); 501 Lake St. N.E. (56763). (218) 386-3024. FAX: (218) 386-3090. Licensee: Demolee Communications Inc. Format: C&W. ■ Fredrick Demolee, pres & gen mgr; Vern Nash, gen sls mgr; Keith Leiran, progmg dir; Terry Olson, news dir; Stan Mueller, chief engr.

Waseca

KOWO(AM)—Dec 22, 1971: 1170 khz; 1 kw-D. TL: N44 02 45 W93 23 08. Box 505, 222 N. State St. (56093). (507) 835-5555. FAX: (507) 835-2030. Licensee: Waseca Communications Inc. (acq 6-11-84). Net: MBS; MNN, Midwest Radio. Wash atty: Miller & Miller. Format: Adult contemp. News staff 2; news progmg 12 hrs wkly. Target aud: 30-65; general, farm. ■ Richard W. Seehafer, pres & gen mgr; Carol B. Seehafer, vp; John Buck, opns mgr; Lori Stangler, gen sls mgr; John Seehafer, mus dir; Lee Rettig, news dir; Ron Olson, chief engr.

KRUE(FM)—Co-owned with KOWO(AM). June 1972: 92.1 mhz; 25 kw. Ant 286 ft. TL: N44 02 45 W93 23 08. Stereo. Hrs opn: 5:30 AM-midnight. Dups AM 100%. ■ Rates: $12; 11; 11; 10.

Willmar

KDJS(AM)—Mar 2, 1981: 1590 khz; 1 kw-D, 89 w-N, DA-2. TL: N45 05 07 W95 00 19. Hrs opn: 18. Box 380, 730 N.E. Hwy. 71 (56201). (612) 231-1600. FAX: (612) 235-7010. Licensee: Kandi Broadcasting (acq 6-7-83; $430,000; FTR 6-6-83). Net: CNN. Wash atty: Wilmer, Cutler & Pickering. Format: Oldies. News staff one. Target aud: 25-54. Spec prog: Farm 5 hrs wkly. ■ Perry Kugler, pres, gen mgr & gen sls mgr; Rob Ryan, progmg dir; Steve Hall, mus dir; Kathryn Sasse, news dir; Steve Youngberg, chief engr. ■ Rates: $13; 13; 13; 10.

KDJS-FM—May 17, 1993: 95.3 mhz; 50 kw. Ant 436 ft. TL: N45 01 23 W95 15 57. Stereo. Hrs opn: 24. Box 380, 730 N.E. Hwy. 71 (56201). (612) 231-1600. FAX: (612) 235-7010. Wash atty: Wilmer, Cutler & Pickering. Format: Country. News staff one. Target aud: 25-54. ■ Perry Kugler, pres, gen mgr & gen sls mgr; Rob Ryan, progmg dir; Steve Hall, mus dir; Katherine Sasse, news dir; Steve Youngberg, chief engr. ■ Rates: $16.50; 16.50; 16.50; 10.

KQIC(FM)—Listing follows KWLM(AM).

KWLM(AM)—1940: 1340 khz; 1 kw-U. TL: N45 08 00 W95 02 35. Hrs opn: 24. Box 838, 1340 N. 7th St. (56201). (612) 235-1340. FAX: (612) 235-9111. Licensee: Steven W. Linder (acq 4-5-91; $691,937 with co-located FM; FTR 4-22-91). Net: ABC/I; Linder Farm. Rep: Katz. Format: Full svc. News staff 3; news progmg 30 hrs wkly. Target aud: General. Spec prog: Farm 8 hrs wkly. ■ Steven W. Linder, vp; Doug Loy, gen mgr; Jeanne Kling, opns mgr & prom mgr; Kay Arne, news dir; Pete Hoagland, chief engr. ■ Rates: $21; 18.25; 16; 11.75.

KQIC(FM)—Co-owned with KWLM(AM). July 1, 1965: 102.5 mhz; 100 kw. Ant 830 ft. TL: N45 11 40 W95 05 01. Stereo. Prog sep from AM. (612) 235-3535. Net: ABC/D, NBC, MBS; Midwest Radio. Format: Adult contemp. Target aud: 18-49. Spec prog: Relg 2 hrs wkly. ■ Steve Linder, pres; Doug Loy, adv mgr; Steve Schug, progmg dir & mus dir. ■ Rates: $22.25; 20; 22.25; 17.

Windom

KDOM(AM)—Dec 28, 1958: 1580 khz; 1 kw-D, 2 w-N, DA-2. TL: N43 51 41 W95 05 50. Hrs opn: 6 AM-midnight. Box 218 (56101). (507) 831-3908. FAX: (507) 831-3913. Licensee: Windom Radio Inc. (acq 4-89; with co-located FM; FTR 4-14-80). Net: ABC/I; MNN. Rep: Katz. Format: Country, btfl mus, oldies. News staff one; news progmg 21 hrs wkly. Target aud: General; farm audience, housewives, business owners & laborers. ■ Rich Biever, pres, gen mgr & gen sls mgr; Sheri Biever, vp; Dave Cory, progmg dir; Todd Olson, news dir; Steve Larson, chief engr. ■ Rates: $19.50; 19.50; 17; 17.

KDOM-FM—Dec 8, 1976: 94.3 mhz; 5.7 kw. Ant 335 ft. TL: N43 53 06 W95 10 53. Stereo. Hrs opn: 6 AM-midnight. Dups AM 100%.

Winona

KAGE(AM)—Feb 17, 1957: 1380 khz; 4 kw-D. TL: N44 02 13 W91 37 09. Box 5767, 752 Bluffview Cir. (55987-5767). (507) 452-4000; (507) 452-2867. FAX: (507) 452-9494. Licensee: KAGE Inc. Group owner: The Result Radio Group (acq 1-73). Net: AP. Wash atty: Wiley, Rein & Fielding. Format: C&W. News staff 2; news progmg 19 hrs wkly. Target aud: General. Spec prog: Farm, relg. ■ Jerry Papenfuss, pres, gen mgr & gen sls mgr; Pat Papenfuss, opns mgr & progmg dir; Jim Trotter, mus dir; Darryl Smelser, news dir; Steve Schuh, chief engr. ■ Rates: $25; 25; 25; 25.

KAGE-FM—Aug 14, 1971: 95.3 mhz; 11 kw. Ant 495 ft. TL: N44 02 31 W91 40 47. Stereo. Hrs opn: 24. Prog sep from AM. Format: Adult contemp. News progmg 14 hrs wkly. Target aud: 25-54. ■ Rates: Same as AM.

KHME(FM)—June 4, 1992: 101.1 mhz; 6 kw. Ant 350 ft. TL: N44 01 18 W91 34 24. Hrs opn: 5 AM-12:30 AM. 360 Vila St. (55987). (507) 454-4663. FAX: (507) 454-1463. Licensee: Home Broadcast Company. Net: CNN. Wash atty: H.R. Martin. Format: Lite adult contemp. News staff one; news progmg 21 hrs wkly. Target aud: 35-54; women. ■ Bud Baechler, pres; Bill Withers, gen mgr; Patty Fitzpatrick, opns dir; Connie Hawkinson, gen sls mgr, mktg mgr & adv mgr; David Dicke, progmg dir & mus dir; David Welshhons, news dir; Karen Lideen, pub affrs dir; Steve Schuh, chief engr. ■ Rates: $11.85; 11.85; 11.85; 11.85.

***KQAL(FM)**—Dec 12, 1975: 89.5 mhz; 1.8 kw. Ant 628 ft. TL: N44 02 52 W91 38 40. Stereo. 234 P.A.C. Bldg., Winona State Univ. (55987). (507) 457-5226. Licensee: Winona State Univ. Net: AP, NPR. Format: Div. News staff 5; news progmg 5 hrs wkly. Target aud: General. Spec prog: Class 14 hrs, country one hr, jazz 20 hrs, public affairs/info 15 hrs, big band 4 hrs wkly. ■ Ajit Daniel, gen mgr; Ed Hurley, progmg dir; David Arney, mus dir; Kevin Spiegel, asst mus dir; Cindy Rusch, news dir; Michelle Derks, pub affrs dir; Mike Martin, chief engr.

***KSMR(FM)**—Nov 1, 1978: 92.5 mhz; 4 w. Ant -141 ft. TL: N42 02 47 W91 41 43. Stereo. St. Mary's College, #29, 700 Terrace Heights (55987). (507) 457-1613; (507) 457-1615. FAX: (507) 457-6930. Licensee: St. Mary's College. Format: AOR. Target aud: 18-24. ■ Tony Zielinski, gen mgr; Brian Cern, opns mgr; Jodi Benson, prom mgr; Pete Fehlen, progmg dir; Pete Fehlen, Brian Cern, mus dirs; Heather Coequyt, news dir; Steve Schuh, chief engr.

KWNO(AM)—January 1938: 1230 khz; 1 kw-U. TL: N44 01 52 W91 38 31. 216 Center St. (55987). (507) 452-4722. FAX: (507) 452-4871. Licensee: Wheeler Broadcasting of Minn Inc. Group owner: Wheeler Broadcasting Inc. (acq 10-1-85; $700,000; FTR 7-8-85). Net: ABC/I; MNN. Format: Oldies. News staff one; news progmg 21 hrs wkly. Target aud: 35 plus. Spec prog: Polka 5 hrs wkly. ■ Ray L. Wheeler, pres; Patrick Marek, gen mgr & gen sls mgr; Dave Williams, news dir; Mike Martin, chief engr.

Worthington

KWOA(AM)—Oct 11, 1947: 730 khz; 1 kw-U, 159 w-N. TL: N43 37 48 W95 40 32. Box 730, Hwy. 35 W. (56187). (507) 376-6165. FAX: (507) 376-5071. Licensee: Nobles Broadcasting Co. Ltd. (acq 7-1-88). Net: NBC, NBC Talknet; MAGNET. Rep: Torbet, Hyett/Ramsland. Wash atty: Baker & Hostetler. Format: News/talk. News staff one; news progmg 18 hrs wkly. Target aud: 35 plus. Spec prog: Farm. ■ Donald L. Rabbitt, pres; Mike Casper, gen mgr & gen sls mgr; Mark Seger, opns mgr, Darrell Stitt, progmg dir & mus dir; Greg VanWorner, news dir; Vince Fuhs, chief engr.

KWOA-FM—May 3, 1961: 95.1 mhz; 100 kw. Ant 660 ft. TL: N43 37 48 W95 40 32. Stereo. Hrs opn: 20. Prog sep from AM. Format: Adult contemp. News staff one; news progmg 10 hrs wkly. Target aud: 25-40. ■ Bruce Thalhuber, progmg dir & mus dir.

Worthington-Marshall

***KRSW-FM**—December 1973: 91.7 mhz; 99 kw. Ant 800 ft. TL: N43 53 01 W95 55 44. Stereo. 1450 College Way (56187). (507) 372-2904. Licensee: Minnesota Public Radio Inc. Net: APR, NPR. Format: Classical, jazz, news. ■ William H. Kling, pres; Valerie Arganbright, gen mgr; Mark Steil, news dir; Paul Derby, chief engr.

Mississippi

LAUREN A. COLBY
301-663-1086
COMMUNICATIONS ATTORNEY
Special Attention to Difficult Cases

Aberdeen

WWZQ(AM)—February 1952: 1240 khz; 1 kw-U. TL: N33 48 32 W88 32 33. Drawer 1240, 1031 S. Meridian St. (39730). (601) 369-9672. FAX: (601) 369-6136. Licensee: Tenn-Tom Broadcasting Corp. (acq 12-31-85; $400,000 with co-located FM; FTR 11-25-85). Net: CBS; Miss. Net., Prog Farm. Format: Light rock, soft adult contemp. ■ J.D. Buffington, pres & gen mgr; Vance Tucker, opns mgr; Olen Booth, chief engr.

WWZQ-FM—June 1, 1975: 105.3 mhz; 25 kw. Ant 299 ft. TL: N33 55 20 W88 33 25 (CP: 25 kw, ant 295 ft.). Stereo.

Ackerman

WFCA(FM)—1986: 107.9 mhz; 100 kw. Ant 614 ft. TL: N33 25 25 W89 24 13. Stereo. Box 12, School St., French Camp (39745). (601) 547-6414. FAX: (601) 547-9451. Licensee: French Camp Radio Inc. Net: MBS; Miss. Net. Format: Relg. ■ Stuart C. Irby Jr., pres; H. Richard Cannon, gen mgr; Charles S. Carroll, gen sls mgr; Margaret Maehlmann, mus dir; David E. Vincent, chief engr.

Amory

WAMY(AM)—Oct 23, 1955: 1580 khz; 1 kw-D. TL: N33 58 33 W88 29 29. Hrs opn: 5:30 AM-sunset. Box 458, Hwy. 278 W. (38821). (601) 256-9725. FAX: (601) 256-8512. Licensee: Stanford Communications Inc. (acq 9-21-92; $85,000 with co-located FM; FTR 11-9-92). Net: Unistar. Rep: Midsouth. Format: Country. Spec prog: Farm one hr wkly. ■ Ed Stanford, CEO, gen mgr & vp sls; Teresa Stanford, vp; Ken Wardlaw, opns mgr & mus dir; Olin Booth, chief engr.

WAFM(FM)—Co-owned with WAMY. 1974: 95.3 mhz; 3 kw. Ant 255 ft. TL: N33 58 33 W88 29 29. Stereo. Prog sep from AM. (601) 256-9726. Net: Unistar. Format: CHR.

WWZQ-FM—See Aberdeen.

Artesia

WQNN(FM)—Licensed to Artesia. See Columbus.

Baldwyn

WESE(FM)—Oct 1, 1980: 95.9 mhz; 5.4 kw. Ant 328 ft. TL: N34 26 32 W88 41 11. Stereo. Box 3300, 2812 Cliff, Tupelo (38803). (601) 842-1067. FAX: (601) 842-0725. License: Tupelo Broadcasting Corp. (acq 12-14-92; $250,000 with WTUP[AM] Tupelo; FTR 1-11-93). Net: SMN. Rep: Roslin. Format: Urban contemp. News staff one; news progmg 3 hrs wkly. Target aud: 25-54. ■ Terry L. Barber, pres & gen mgr; Dexter Witherspoon, opns mgr; Rick Joyner, progmg dir; Olen Booth, chief engr.

Batesville

WJBI(AM)—June 19, 1953: 1290 khz; 730 w-D, 91 w-N. TL: N31 18 13 W89 58 59. Box 73 (38606). (601) 563-4664. FAX: (601) 563-9002. Licensee: Batesville Broadcasting Co. Inc. (acq 4-1-78). Net: ABC/E. Format: Farm, MOR, relg. News staff 4. Target aud: 30 plus. Spec prog: Gospel. ■ J. Boyd Ingram, pres & chief engr; Tommy Darby, gen mgr & prom mgr; John P. Ingram, gen sls mgr; Kenny Goodwin, mus dir.

WBLE(FM)—Co-owned with WJBI(AM). Aug 1, 1978: 100.5 mhz; 50 kw. Ant 492 ft. TL: N34 18 13 W89 58 59. Stereo. Prog sep from AM. Format: Farm, C&W. News staff 2; news progmg 5 hrs wkly. Target aud: 25 plus. Spec prog: Black 3 hrs wkly.

Bay St. Louis

WBSL(AM)—March 1974: 1190 khz; 5 kw-D. TL: N30 19 25 W89 21 03. Hrs opn: 13. 1190 Casino Magic Dr. (39520). (601) 467-1190. Licensee: Hancock Broadcasting Corp. Format: Lite rock. ■ Bill Thrasher, gen mgr.

Broadcasting & Cable Yearbook 1994
B-202

Mississippi

Bay Springs

WIZK(AM)—June 26, 1971: 1570 khz; 5 kw-D. TL: N31 58 01 W89 18 05. Box 548, 150 Bay Ave. (39422). (601) 764-3151. Licensee: Cotton Valley Broadcasting Co. Net: SMN. Format: Real country. News staff one; news progmg 20 hrs wkly. Target aud: 25-54; baby boomers and older consumers. ■ Jerome Hughey, pres, gen mgr, gen sls mgr & prom mgr; Mitch Hughey, progmg dir & news dir; Tom Diaz, chief engr.

WIZK-FM—July 7, 1975: 93.5 mhz; 3 kw. Ant 328 ft. TL: N31 58 01 W89 18 05. Stereo. Dups AM 100%. Spec prog: Black gospel 21 hrs wkly.

Belzoni

WELZ(AM)—1959: 1460 khz; 1 kw-U. TL: N30 23 38 W88 59 58 (CP: TL: N33 10 24 W90 28 51). Box 299 (39038). (601) 247-1744. FAX: (601) 247-1744. Licensee: Humphreys County Broadcasting Co. Inc. (acq 12-19-91; $145,000; FTR 1-13-91). Net: Unistar; Miss. Net. Format: Country, gospel. ■ Herb Guthrie, pres, gen mgr & chief engr; Gene Luster, prom mgr & progmg dir; Dan Winsteav, news dir.

WVRD(FM)—Co-owned with WELZ(AM). 1986: 107.1 mhz; 3 kw. Ant 174 ft. TL: N33 10 24 W90 28 51. Stereo. Prog sep from AM. Format: Contemp hit.

WVRD(FM)—Listing follows WELZ(AM).

Biloxi

*WMAH-FM—December 1983: 90.3 mhz; 100 kw. Ant 1,410 ft. TL: N30 45 14 W88 56 44. Stereo. Hrs opn: 24. 3825 Ridgewood Rd., Jackson (39211). (601) 982-0500. FAX: (601) 982-6746. Licensee: Mississippi Authority for Educational Television. Net: APR, NPR. Format: Class, news. Spec prog: Jazz 10 hrs, new age 10 hrs, folk 3 hrs, bluegrass 3 hrs wkly. ■ Larry Miller, pres; William Fulton, gen mgr & progmg dir; Martin Mangold, chief engr.

WQID(FM)—Listing follows WVMI(AM).

WVMI(AM)—April 1, 1950: 570 khz; 5 kw-D, 1 kw-N, DA-2. TL: N30 28 29 W88 51 22. Stereo. Hrs opn: 24. Box 4606 (39535); 286 DeBuys Rd. (39531). (601) 388-2323. FAX: (601) 388-2362. Licensee: Telesouth Communications Inc. (acq 8-29-90; $2.1 million with co-located FM; FTR 9-24-90). Net: ABC/E. Rep: McGavren Guild. Format: News/talk. News staff 2; news progmg 21 hrs wkly. Target aud: 35-64. ■ Stephen C. Davenport, pres; Mike McCraw, opns dir; Melissa Miller, gen sls mgr. ■ Rates: $27; 32; 25; 20.

WQID(FM)—Co-owned with WVMI(AM). July 11, 1966: 93.7 mhz; 100 kw. Ant 1,012 ft. TL: N30 29 09 W88 42 53. Stereo. Hrs opn: 24. Prog sep from AM. Net: ABC/FM. Format: Contemp hit/top-40, classic rock. News staff one; news progmg 5 hrs wkly. Target aud: 25-54. ■ Shae Matthews, prom mgr; Todd Martin, progmg dir. ■ Rates: $40; 36; 40; 36.

WXBD(AM)—May 1948: 1490 khz; 1 kw-U. TL: N30 23 38 W88 59 58. Box 4779, 212 DeBuys Rd. (39531). (601) 388-1490. FAX: (601) 388-1966. Licensee: LES Radio Corp. (acq 10-21-92; $50,000 with WXLS-FM Gulfport; FTR 11-23-92). Net: SMN. Rep: Torbet. Format: Light rock, adult contemp. ■ Lawrence Steelman, gen mgr; Ken Clark, prom mgr & progmg dir.

Booneville

WBIP(AM)—Sept 1, 1950: 1400 khz; 1 kw-U. TL: N34 38 21 W88 34 33. Hrs opn: 5 AM-11 PM. Box 356, Hwy. 45 S. (38829-0356). (601) 728-5301. FAX: (601) 728-2572. Licensee: WBIP Broadcasting Corp. Net: Unistar; Miss. Net. Format: Country, southern gospel. News progmg 7 hrs wkly. Target aud: 24-54. Spec prog: Black 7 hrs wkly. ■ R. J. Bonds, pres & gen mgr; Don Murphy, vp; Harold Campbell, progmg dir & mus dir; Danny Ozbirn, chief engr. ■ Rates: $5; 5; 5; 5.

WBIP-FM—Jan 15, 1976: 99.3 mhz; 6 kw. Ant 300 ft. TL: N34 38 15 W88 34 45. Hrs opn: 5 AM-11 PM. Dups AM 80%. Format: Country. Spec prog: Black 6 hrs wkly. ■ Don D. Murphy, vp opns. ■ Rates: Same as AM.

*WMAE-FM—December 1983: 89.5 mhz; 85 kw. Ant 660 ft. TL: N34 40 00 W88 45 05. Stereo. Hrs opn: 24. Box 4343, 3825 Ridgewood Rd., Jackson (39211). (601) 982-6565. FAX: (601) 982-6746. Licensee: Mississippi Authority for Educational Television. Net: APR, NPR. Format: Class, news. News progmg 40 hrs wkly. Spec prog: Jazz 10 hrs, new age 10 hrs, folk 3 hrs, bluegrass 3 hrs. ■ Larry Miller, pres; William Fulton, gen mgr; Bill Pharr, dev dir; Alma Ellis, prom mgr; Kevin Farrell, pub affrs dir; Martin Mangold, chief engr.

Brandon

WRKN(AM)—June 1967: 970 khz; 1 kw-D, DA. TL: N32 17 20 W89 59 50. Box 145 (39043). (601) 825-5045. Licensee: WRKN Inc. (acq 2-71). Net: CBN. Format: Southern gospel. Spec prog: Relg, gospel, farm one hr wkly. ■ June Harris, pres & gen mgr; Jeff Steele, gen sls mgr; Vickie Ferrer, chief engr.

WRJH(FM)—Co-owned with WRKN(AM). Dec 1, 1974: 97.7 mhz; 3.4 kw. Ant 290 ft. TL: N32 12 10 19 W89 55 56. Stereo. Prog sep from AM. Licensee: WRJH Inc. Format: Relg. Spec prog: Farm one hr wkly. ■ Vickie Ferrer, mus dir.

Brookhaven

WCHJ(AM)—Aug 15, 1955: 1470 khz; 1 kw-D. TL: N31 33 39 W90 26 32. Hrs opn: 6 AM-6 PM. Box 711, 203 E. Monticello St. (39601). (601) 833-6221; (601) 833-9210. FAX: (601) 833-6221. Licensee: Bogue Chitto Communications Co. (group owner, acq 4-1-87). Net: ABC/E, Daynet. Format: News/talk. Target aud: General. Spec prog: Gospel 12 hrs wkly. ■ Thomas F. McDaniel, pres; William T. Reynolds, gen mgr & gen sls mgr; Ken Hollingsworth, opns mgr. ■ Rates: $4; 4; 4; na.

WBKN(FM)—Co-owned with WCHJ(AM). July 29, 1976: 92.1 mhz; 2.5 kw. Ant 351 ft. TL: N31 36 00 W90 27 09. Stereo. Hrs opn: 24. Prog sep from AM. Net: ABC/D. Format: Country. Target aud: 25-54. ■ Rates: $7; 6; 7; 4.

Bude

*WMAU-FM—December 1983: 88.9 mhz; 100 kw. Ant 960 ft. TL: N31 22 19 W90 45 05. Stereo. Hrs opn: 24. 3825 Ridgewood Rd., Jackson (39211). (601) 982-0500. Licensee: Mississippi Authority for Educational Television. Net: APR, NPR. Format: Class, news. Spec prog: Jazz 10 hrs, new age 5 hrs, folk 3 hrs, bluegrass 3 hrs wkly. ■ Larry Miller, pres; Bill Lovett, opns mgr; Norma Barnett, prom mgr; William Fulton, progmg dir; Martin Mangold, chief engr.

Byhalia

WHLE(FM)—Not on air, target date unknown: 94.9 mhz; 6 kw. Ant 328 ft. TL: N34 46 47 W89 26 42. Stereo. c/o Crain Broadcasting Co., 102 Brookhaven Dr., Columbia, TN (38401). (615) 381-4511. Licensee: Albert L. Crain. Group owner: Crain Broadcasting Co. (acq 3-30-93; FTR 4-19-93). ■ Albert L. Crain, gen mgr.

Canton

WMGO(AM)—Dec 9, 1954: 1370 khz; 1 kw-D, 28 w-N. TL: N32 37 36 W90 01 47. Hrs opn: 16. Box 182, 107 W. Peace St. (39046); 115 N. Union St. (39046). (601) 859-2373. Licensee: WMGO Broadcasting Corp. Inc. (acq 5-3-93; $100,000; FTR 5-24-93). Net: Unistar, Miss. Net. Rep: MidSouth. Format: Adult contemp, Black, urban contemp. News staff one; news progmg 10 hrs wkly. Target aud: 25-54; male & female. ■ Aubury Prince, gen mgr; Jerry Lousteau, stn mgr, vp opns, gen sls mgr, vp progmg & news dir; Aubrey Prince, vp sls; John Woods, Charlie Smith, Jerry Lousteau, mus dirs; Evelyn Jones, asst mus dir; Annie Lousteau, pub affrs dir; Phillip Scott, chief engr. ■ Rates: $8.20; 8.20; 8.20; 8.20.

WONG(AM)—April 1989: 1150 khz; 500 w-D. TL: N32 32 35 W90 03 36. Box 1151, Madison (39110). (601) 859-7978. FAX: (601) 859-8218. Licensee: John H. Pembroke. Format: Blues, soul classics & gospel. Target aud: 25 plus. ■ Bobbey Bobo, pres; Dolores Bobo, gen mgr; Kaple Hill, prom mgr, progmg dir & news dir; Richard Durr, chief engr. ■ Rates: $6.75; 5.50; 6.75; 5.50.

Carthage

WSSI(AM)—March 13, 1965: 1080 khz; 5 kw-D, DA. TL: N32 43 13 W89 32 48. Box 475, Hwy. 16 W. (39051). (601) 267-8361. Licensee: Michael D. and Linda D. Goodwin. Net: Unistar, Miss. Net. Format: Country, news/talk. News progmg 11 hrs wkly. Target aud: 12-85; general. Spec prog: Farm 2 hrs, American Indian one hr, Black 2 hrs, relg 2 hrs wkly. ■ Mike Goodwin, pres, gen mgr & gen sls mgr; Linda D. Goodwin, opns mgr; Bill Fulgham, chief engr. ■ Rates: $10; 9; 9; 8.

WSSI-FM—April 1979: 98.3 mhz; 3 kw. Ant 300 ft. TL: N32 43 13 W89 32 48. Prog sep from AM. Net: USA. Format: C&W. ■ Rates: Same as AM.

Centreville

WZFL(AM)—Jan 1, 1981: 1580 khz; 250 w-D. TL: N31 06 07 W91 02 27. 13028 U.S. Hwy. 190 W., Port Allen, LA (70767). (504) 627-4578. Licensee: Port Allen Educational Broadcasting Foundation (acq 7-15-93; $1,000; FTR 8-9-93). Format: Relg, educ. ■ Bob Cupit, pres; Willie F. Kennedy, gen mgr; Larry Feltus, progmg dir.

Charleston

WTGY(FM)—Apr 1, 1986: 95.7 mhz; 3.8 kw. Ant 300 ft. TL: N33 53 28 W90 03 09. Stereo. Hrs opn: 18. Box 9, Marshall Rd. (38921); Box 1106, Hwy. 8 West, Grenada (38901). (601) 647-5600; (601) 226-4644. Licensee: Charleston Broadcasting Co. Inc. (acq 9-85; $8,750; FTR 6-3-85). Net: ABC/C. Rep: Savalli, MidSouth. Format: C&W, farm. Spec prog: Black 12 hrs wkly. ■ Bobby B. Anderson, gen mgr & vp adv. ■ Rates: $11.50; 11.50; 11.50; 11.50.

Clarksdale

WAID(FM)—July 1, 1978: 106.3 mhz; 3 kw. Ant 299 ft. TL: N34 09 22 W90 37 52 (CP: 50 kw, ant 492 ft.). Stereo. Box 668, 20 E. 2nd St. (38614). (601) 627-2281. FAX: (601) 624-2900. Licensee: Radio Cleveland Inc. (group owner; acq 8-2-83; $185,000; FTR 1-8-83). Net: AP, SMN. Miss. Net. Format: Urban contemp. News staff one; news progmg 2 hrs wkly. Target aud: General. Spec prog: Farm 3 hrs wkly. ■ J.R. Denton Sr., pres; Greg Shurden, gen mgr, stn mgr, mktg mgr, prom mgr & adv mgr; John Kinberg, progmg dir & mus dir; Jimmy Powell, chief engr. ■ Rates: $6.50; 6.50; 6.50; 3.95.

WKDJ(FM)—Nov 1, 1988: 96.5 mhz; 6 kw. Ant 184 ft. TL: N34 11 33 W90 34 17 (CP: 25 kw, ant 263 ft., TL: N34 06 03 W90 24 53). Stereo. Box 1722, 112 LeFlore (38614). (601) 624-2997. Licensee: WKDJ Radio. Group owner: Superior Broadcast Group. Net: ABC/E. Format: Country. News staff one; news progmg 6 hrs wkly. Target aud: 25-55. Spec prog: Black 15 hrs wkly. ■ J. Boyd Ingram, pres; Shirl Peck, gen mgr; John P. Ingram, gen sls mgr.

WROX(AM)—1941: 1450 khz; 1 kw-U. TL: N34 12 40 W90 34 42. Hrs opn: 6 AM-10 PM. Suite 222, Central Bldg., 125 Third St. (38614-4209). (601) 627-7343. FAX: (601) 627-1000. Licensee: Weaver Communication Group Inc. (acq 8-12-92; $50,000; FTR 8-17-92). Net: CBS. Format: Adult Contemp, Black. Target aud: General. ■ Gerald E. Weaver, pres, gen mgr & prom mgr; Robert A. Weaver, vp.

WWUN-FM—1973: 101.7 mhz; 3 kw. Ant 198 ft. TL: N34 11 33 W90 34 17. Stereo. Box 1475 (38614). (601) 627-1113. Licensee: Delta Christian Radio Inc. (acq 1-28-92). Format: Black, gospel, farm. ■ U.J. Gilbert, pres, gen mgr & chief engr; Patricia Gilbert, gen sls mgr, prom mgr, progmg dir & mus dir.

Cleveland

WCLD(AM)—1949: 1490 khz; 1 kw-U. TL: N33 44 01 W90 42 50. Hrs opn: 24. Drawer 780 (38732). (601) 843-4091. Licensee: Radio Cleveland Inc. (group owner; acq 1957). Net: CNN. Format: Oldies. Target aud: 26-48. ■ Homer Sledge Jr., pres; Clint Webster, gen mgr; Ron Richards, opns mgr; Kevin Cox, gen sls mgr; George C. Shurden, chief engr.

WCLD-FM—1972: 103.9 mhz; 6 kw. Ant 300 ft. TL: N33 44 01 W90 42 50. Stereo. Prog sep from AM. Net: CNN. Format: Urban contemp. ■ Ron Richards, progmg dir.

WDFX(FM)—Not on air, target date unknown: 98.3 mhz; 25 kw. TL: N33 52 44 W90 43 04. Licensee: American Family Association Inc. (acq 5-3-93; $6,150; FTR 5-24-93).

WDTL-FM—May 22, 1970: 92.7 mhz; 3 kw. Ant 262 ft. TL: N33 45 12 W90 42 45. Stereo. Hrs opn: 24. Prog sep from AM. Box 1438, Suite 12, 201 E. Sunflower Rd. (38732). (601) 846-0927. FAX: (601) 843-0494. Licensee: Delta Radio Inc. Group owner: Contemporary Communications (acq 3-15-92; with co-located AM). Wash atty: Venable, Baetjer, Howard & Civiletti. Format: Country. News staff one. Target aud: 25-54. ■ Larry Fuss, pres & gen mgr; Brad Young, vp; Jim Gregory, vp opns; Belinda Mainka, sls dir; Donna Gregory, prom dir; Rob Sidney, mus dir; Kelly Rush, news dir; Kirk Harnack, engrg dir. ■ Rates: $8; 7; 8; 6.

Mississippi

WDTL(AM)—June 25, 1958: 1410 khz; 1 kw-D. TL: N33 40 25 W90 40 25 (CP: TL: N33 45 11 W90 42 50). Stn currently dark.

Clinton

WHJT(FM)—1974: 93.5 mhz; 3 kw. Ant 300 ft. TL: N32 20 15 W90 19 47. Stereo. Box 4247, Aren Hall, 100 S. Jefferson (39058). (601) 925-3458; (601) 925-3899. FAX: (601) 924-4506. Licensee: Mississippi College. Net: USA. Wash atty: Smithwick & Belendiuk. Format: Christian contemp. News progmg 7 hrs wkly. Target aud: 25-54. Spec prog: Relg 6 hrs wkly. ■ Russ Robinson, gen mgr & gen sls mgr; Jimmy Glenn Jr., opns mgr; Jan Millican, prom dir; Craig Lowrey, progmg dir; Clay Bartunek, mus dir; Kim Stevens, news dir; Bob Buie, engrg mgr; Jeff Cockern, chief engr. ■ Rates: $20; 18; 20; 18.

WTWZ(AM)—Oct 10, 1982: 1120 khz; 5 kw-D, 2.5 kw-CH. TL: N32 21 03 W90 20 22. 608C Hwy. 80 E. (39056); Box 31 (39060). (601) 924-8216. FAX: (601) 924-2768. Licensee: Terry E. Wood. Net: USA. Format: Contemp Christian. ■ Terry Wood, pres, gen mgr, gen sls mgr, prom mgr & progmg dir; Stan Carter, chief engr.

Coldwater

WVIM-FM—1976: 95.3 mhz; 1 kw. Ant 299 ft. TL: N34 46 42 W89 58 23. Stereo. Drawer 487, Hernando (38632). (601) 429-4465. Licensee: Tate & Desoto Broadcasting Co. Inc. Net: MBS. Format: C&W, Gospel. ■ Eddie Bond, pres; Ed Mounger, gen mgr; Karen Arnold, progmg dir; Barbara Vining, news dir; Robert Benjamin, chief engr.

Collins

WKNZ(FM)—Aug 15, 1978: 101.7 mhz; 1 kw. Ant 541 ft. TL: N31 31 49 W89 30 29 (CP: 2.25 kw). Stereo. Box 15935, Hattiesburg (39404). (601) 264-0443. FAX: (601) 264-5733. Licensee: Covington County Broadcasters Inc. (acq 6-28-93; $520,500; FTR 7-26-93). Net: Unistar. Format: Country. Target aud: 18-54; upwardly mobile. Spec prog: Gospel 2 hrs wkly. ■ Romeo Sullivan, gen mgr.

Columbia

WCJU(AM)—Dec 20, 1946: 1450 khz; 1 kw-U. TL: N31 14 14 W89 50 24. Stereo. Hrs opn: 17. Box 472 (39429). (601) 736-2616; (601) 736-2617. FAX: (601) 736-2617. Licensee: WCJU Inc. (acq 6-69). Net: ABC/C. Rep: Keystone (unwired net). Format: Talk. News staff 2; news progmg 30 hrs wkly. Target aud: 18-54. Spec prog: Gospel 4 hrs wkly. ■ T. McDaniel, pres. ■ Rates: $5.46; 2.70; 2.88; 2.70.

WFFF(AM)—Apr 14, 1961: 1360 khz; 1 kw-D, 159 w-N. TL: N31 15 44 W89 50 41. Box 550, 11 Gardner Shopping Center (39429). (601) 736-1360. FAX: (601) 736-1361. Licensee: Haddox Enterprises Inc. (acq 10-9-91; $250,000 with co-located FM; FTR 11-4-91). Net: MBS; Miss. Net. Format: C&W, relg. News staff 4; news progmg 8 hrs wkly. Target aud: General. Spec prog: Gospel 20 hrs wkly. ■ David Martin, pres & gen sls mgr; Ronnie Geiger, vp, progmg dir, mus dir, news dir & chief engr.

WFFF-FM—October 1966: 96.7 mhz; 3 kw. Ant 400 ft. TL: N31 15 44 W89 50 41. Stereo. Hrs opn: 17. Dups AM 10%. Net: MBS; Miss Net. Format: Adult contemp. Target aud: 25-54. ■ Ronnie Geiger, adv dir & vp engrg.

Columbus

WACR(AM)—1950: 1050 khz; 1 kw-D, 48 w-N, DA. TL: N33 30 36 W88 24 46. Box 1078 (39703); 1910 14th Ave. N. (39701). (601) 328-1050. FAX: (601) 328-1054. Licensee: T & W Communications Inc. (acq 1993; $110,000 with co-located FM; FTR 9-13-93). Rep: Roslin. Format: Relg. News progmg 4 hrs wkly. Target aud: General. ■ Bennie L. Turner, pres; Danny Byrd, opns mgr; Edna Turner, gen mgr; Jerold Jackson, progmg dir; Olen Booth, chief engr.

WACR-FM—Dec 15, 1978: 103.9 mhz; 3 kw. Ant 204 ft. TL: N33 30 36 W88 24 46 (CP: 50 kw, ant 492 ft.; TL: N33 24 20 W88 08 34). Stereo. Hrs opn: 24. Prog sep from AM. Format: Urban contemp. ■ Patricia Hill, mus dir. ■ Rates: $25; 21; 25; 17.

WJWF(AM)—Nov 1, 1969: 1400 khz; 1 kw-U. TL: N31 29 30 W88 24 14. Stn currently dark. Box 707 (39703). (601) 328-1400; (601) 328-1420. FAX: (601) 328-1421. Licensee: Radio Columbus Inc. Group owner: Gulf Central Radio Net. ■ J. W. Furr, pres; Carolin Lowry, gen mgr; Bob Green, gen sls mgr; Johnny Dees, progmg dir; Craig Carson, mus dir; Mike Comfort, Olin Booth, chiefs engr.

WMBC(FM)—Co-owned with WJWF(AM). Nov 1, 1969: 103.1 mhz; 22 kw. Ant 754 ft. TL: N33 29 30 W88 24 14. Stereo. Format: Modern country. ■ Bill Lemonds, progmg dir.

WKOR-FM—Dec 16, 1992: 94.9 mhz; 29.5 kw. Ant 492 ft. TL: N33 28 38 W88 16 25. Stereo. 206 8th St. N. (39701). (601) 327-1183. FAX: (601) 328-1122. Licensee: Donald R. DePriea Golden Triangle Radio. Group owner: Charisma Communications Group. Format: Hot country. ■ Terry L. Barber, pres; Dana Cobb, stn mgr; Bill Thurlow, progmg dir.

WMBC(FM)—Listing follows WJWF(AM).

*****WMUW(FM)**—Sept 28, 1981: 88.5 mhz; 980 w. Ant 87 ft. TL: N33 29 23 W88 25 18. Stereo. Box W-1619, Miss. Univ. for Women (39701). (601) 329-7255. Licensee: Mississippi Board of Trustees. Format: Alternative rock (AOR). Spec prog: C&W 10 hrs, jazz 10 hrs wkly. ■ Taylor Henry, gen mgr; Jennah Victor, progmg dir & mus dir; Christopher Jenkins, chief engr.

WQNN(FM)—(Artesia). 1985: 99.9 mhz; 6 kw. Ant 328 ft. TL: N33 39 14 W88 37 15. Hrs opn: 24. Box 8950, Columbus (39705). (601) 328-7124. FAX: (601) 329-1117. Licensee: Bravo Communications Inc. (acq 7-13-90; $460,000; FTR 8-6-90). Format: Adult CHR. ■ Bob Green, gen mgr.

Corinth

WADI(FM)—Listing follows WCMA(AM).

WCMA(AM)—March 1, 1946: 1230 khz; 1 kw-U. TL: N34 52 07 W88 31 17. 1608 S. John St. (38834). (601) 287-3101. FAX: (601) 287-9262. Licensee: Joe Taylor Jobe (acq 3-1-87). Rep: Midsouth. Format: C&W. ■ Joe Taylor Jobe, pres & gen mgr; Janet Baggett, gen sls mgr; Joan Jobe, progmg dir & mus dir; Phil Wammack, news dir; Joseph Jobe, chief engr.

WADI(FM)—Co-owned with WCMA(AM). Oct 26, 1968: 95.3 mhz; 4.2 kw. Ant 210 ft. TL: N34 55 45 W88 25 17. Stereo. Dups AM 100%.

WKCU(AM)—Oct 24, 1965: 1350 khz; 1 kw-D, 68 w-N. TL: N34 54 51 W88 30 42. 2112 Hwy. 72 E. (38834). (601) 286-8451. FAX: (601) 286-8452. Licensee: The Progressive Broadcasting Co. Net: MBS; Miss. Net. Rep: Midsouth. Format: Relg. ■ James D. Anderson, pres, gen mgr & chief engr; James H. Anderson, stn mgr; John Paul Anderson, gen sls mgr & prom mgr; Tina Gant, progmg dir & mus dir; Terry Anderson, news dir.

WXRZ(FM)—Co-owned with WKCU(AM). January 1967: 94.3 mhz; 3.3 kw. Ant 328 ft. TL: N34 54 51 W88 30 42. Stereo. Prog sep from AM. Format: Adult contemp. ■ Regina Pyle, prom mgr; Terry F. Anderson, mus dir; John P. Anderson, news dir.

Drew

WKZB(FM)—June 1, 1971: 95.3 mhz; 3 kw. Ant 344 ft. TL: N33 47 24 W90 34 28. Stereo. Hrs opn: 24. Box 1438, Cleveland (38732); 201 E. Sunflower Rd., Suite 12, Cleveland (38732). (601) 834-0927; (601) 745-9995. FAX: (601) 843-0494. Licensee: Delta Radio Inc. Group owner: Contemporary Communications (acq 8-6-93; $75,000). Format: Urban contemp. ■ Larry G. Fuss, pres & gen mgr; Brad S. Young, vp; Jim Gregory, vp opns; Doc Murphy, progmg dir & mus dir; Kirk Harnack, engrg dir. ■ Rates: $8; 7; 8; 6.

Ebenezer

WZBR(FM)—Not on air, target date unknown: 103.9 mhz; 6 kw. Ant 328 ft. TL: N32 53 14 W90 11 25. Box 87 (39064). Licensee: Jimbar Enterprises (acq 3-28-91; FTR 4-15-91).

Ellisville

WJKX(FM)—Oct 5, 1973: 102.5 mhz; 50 kw. Ant 492 ft. TL: N31 46 05 W89 10 12. Stereo. Box 17131, Hattiesburg (39402). (601) 582-2899. FAX: (601) 477-9043. Licensee: South Jones Broadcasters Inc. (acq 12-9-92; $50,000; FTR 1-4-93). Net: ABC/E; Miss. Net. Format: Relg. Target aud: 35 plus. Spec prog: Gospel 12 hrs wkly. ■ Gayril Gibson, pres & gen mgr; Jay Whitehurst, prom mgr; Buck Holston, chief engr.

Eupora

WEPA(AM)—May 3, 1974: 710 khz; 2.5 kw-D. TL: N33 32 41 W89 13 57. Box 710 (39744). (601) 258-7170; (601) 258-9696. FAX: (601) 258-9696. Licensee: Tri County Broadcasting Company Inc. Group owner: Air South Radio Inc. Wash atty: Frank Jazzo. Format: Modern country, relg. News progmg 6 hrs wkly. Target aud: General. ■ Olvie E. Sisk, pres; Harry E. Jackson, gen mgr; Carolyn Jackson, gen sls mgr; Bill Taylor, progmg dir & mus dir; B.J. Crabbs, chief engr. ■ Rates: $12; 10; 10; 10.

WLZA(FM)—Licensed to Eupora. See Starkville.

Fayette

WTYJ(FM)—Oct 17, 1983: 97.7 mhz; 3 kw. Ant 300 ft. TL: N31 40 32 W91 06 18. Stereo. Box 1248, Natchez (39121); 20 E. Franklin St. (39120). (601) 442-2522. FAX: (601) 446-9910. Licensee: Natchez Communications Inc. (acq 4-86; $200,000; FTR 4-14-86). Net: NBC. Format: Black. News staff one. Target aud: General. ■ James B. Nutter, pres; David Shaw, gen mgr.

Flowood

WPBQ(AM)—Feb 1, 1994: 1240 khz; 1 kw-U. TL: N32 18 22 W90 08 42. 141 McTyere, Jackson (39202). Licensee: PDB Corp. (acq 2-10-92; $4,00; FTR 3-2-92). Net: NBC Talknet, ABC/I, Daynet, BRN, CBS, Unistar. Wash atty: Haley, Bader & Potts. Format: News/talk. News staff one; news progmg 21 hrs wkly. Target aud: 25-54. ■ Donald B. Brady, pres. ■ Rates: $6; 6; 6; 6.

Forest

*****WMBU(FM)**—Not on air, target date unknown: 89.1 mhz; 100 kw. Ant 640 ft. Box 199, Dixon's Mills, AL (36736). Licensee: Central Mississippi Educational Radio Inc.

WQST(AM)—September 1955: 850 khz; 10 kw-D, DA. TL: N32 21 46 W89 25 09. Box 857, Hwy. 80 (39074). (601) 469-3701. FAX: (601) 469-1892. Licensee: American Family Association Inc. (acq 7-20-93; $700,000 with co-located FM; FTR 8-23-93). Net: AP. Rep: Midsouth. Format: Country. Target aud: 25-55. Spec prog: Gospel 15 hrs wkly. ■ Frank Edmondson, gen mgr; John Tatum, gen sls mgr; Ron Coulter, progmg dir.

WQST-FM—September 1962: 92.5 mhz; 100 kw. Ant 1,040 ft. TL: N32 21 48 W89 25 29. Stereo. Dups AM 100%. Format: Country. Spec prog: Farm 2 hrs, Gospel 6 hrs wkly. ■ John Riley, progmg dir; Tom Scott, chief engr.

Fulton

WFTA(FM)—Licensed to Fulton. See Tupelo.

WFTO(AM)—Aug 15, 1967: 1330 khz; 5 kw-D. TL: N34 14 50 W88 24 26. Hrs opn: 6 AM-sunset. Box 249, Radio Bldg., Hwy. 25 S. (38843). (601) 862-3191; (601) 842-7625. FAX: (601) 862-2233. Licensee: Air South Radio Inc. (group owner). Net: NBC. Format: Modern country. News progmg 5 hrs wkly. Target aud: General. ■ Olvie E. Sisk, pres & gen mgr; Ivous Sisk, gen sls mgr & prom mgr; James McPherson, progmg dir; Randy Love, mus dir; Fred Blalock, news dir; Gene Sisk, chief engr. ■ Rates: $10; 10; 10; 10.

Gluckstadt

WLIN(FM)—Jan 7, 1976: 101.7 mhz; 3 kw. Ant 300 ft. TL: N32 30 03 W90 02 28 (CP: 25 kw, ant 328 ft.). Stereo. Suite C, 102 Business Park Dr., Jackson (39213). (601) 956-0102. FAX: (601) 978-3980. Licensee: Aileron Communications Inc. (acq 11-85; grpsl; FTR 11-25-85). Net: Unistar. Rep: Rgnl Reps. Format: Soft adult contemp. ■ Marshall Magee, gen mgr; Joe Bennett, opns mgr.

Greenville

WBAD(FM)—See Leland.

WBAQ(FM)—May 1, 1970: 97.9 mhz; 24.5 kw-horiz. Ant 495 ft. TL: N33 23 50 W91 00 23. Stereo. Hrs opn: 5:30 AM-midnight. Box 656, 136 S. Broadway (38702). (601) 335-3383. FAX: (601) 335-3383. Licensee: Paul C. Artman (acq 5-70; FTR 2-17-86). Net: ABC/I; Prog Farm, Miss. Net. Format: EZ lstng. News progmg 14 hrs wkly. Target aud: 25-54; quality-conscious adults with spendable income. Spec prog: Class 2 hrs, farm 2 hrs, btfl sacred 4 hrs wkly. ■ Paul Artman Sr., pres; Paul Artman Jr., gen mgr; Chip Chipman, prom mgr; Randy L. Mays, progmg dir; Marion Stevens, mus dir; Kevin Warner, chief engr. ■ Rates: $9; 9; 9; 9.

WDDT(AM)—April 1956: 900 khz; 1 kw-D, 109 w-N. TL: N33 25 05 W90 59 42. c/o L.E. Willis, 645 Church St., Norfolk, VA (23541). (804) 624-6500. Licensee: WDDT Inc. (acq 8-22-90; $100,000; FTR 10-1-90). Net: MBS. Format: Contemp country. Spec prog: Farm 10 hrs wkly. ■ L.E. Willis, pres; Celestine Willis, stn mgr.

WDMS(FM)—Listing follows WGVM(AM).

WESY(AM)—See Leland.

WGVM(AM)—1948: 1260 khz; 5 kw-D. TL: N33 25 20 W91 01 41. Box 1438 (38701). (601) 334-4559. FAX: (601) 332-1315. Licensee: Mid-America Broadcasting Co. Rep: Midsouth. Format: C&W. Spec prog: Black 5 hrs, farm 12 hrs wkly. ■ David M. Segal, pres; Bob Ghetti, gen mgr & gen sls mgr; Ray Renfroe, progmg dir; Jerry Campbell, chief engr.

WDMS(FM)—Co-owned with WGVM(AM). December 1967: 100.7 mhz; 52 kw-H. Ant 449 ft. TL: N33 24 20 W91 01 41. Stereo. Prog sep from AM. Format: Adult contemp.

WIQQ(FM)—See Leland.

WNIX(AM)—August 1937: 1330 khz; 1 kw-D, 500 w-N, DA-N. TL: N33 24 36 W91 01 03. Hrs opn: 24. Box 1816, Delta Plaza Mall, Unit 39, 800 Hwy. One S. (38701). (601) 378-2617. FAX: (601) 378-8341. Licensee: The River Broadcasting Co. Inc. (acq 8-31-79). Rep: McGavren Guild. Wash atty: Baraff, Koerner, Olender & Hochberg, P.C. Format: Oldies, farm. News progmg 3 hrs wkly. Target aud: 24-55. Spec prog: Relg 6 hrs wkly. ■ George E. Pine, pres; James P. Karr Jr., vp, gen mgr & prom dir; Margret Kazan Karr, gen sls mgr; Arch Chapman, mktg dir; Chuck Early, progmg dir & pub affrs dir; Larry Thomas, mus dir; Percy Kuhn, chief engr.

Greenwood

WABG(AM)—February 1950: 960 khz; 1 kw-D, 500 w-N, DA-N. TL: N33 33 45 W90 12 38. 2001 Garrard Ave. (38930). (601) 453-7822. FAX: (601) 455-3311. Licensee: Greenwood Broadcasting Co. Inc. Group owner: Bahakel Communications. Net: AP, Prog Farm. Rep: Banner. Format: C&W. Spec prog: Farm 15 hrs, Black 10 hrs wkly. ■ Cy N. Bahakel, pres; John Rogers, gen mgr; Ed Wood, gen sls mgr; Tom Ainsworth, progmg dir; Brad LeBrun, chief engr. ■ WABG-TV affil.

WGNL(FM)—Dec 1, 1989: 104.3 mhz; 3 kw. Ant 312 ft. TL: N33 31 30 W90 09 52 (CP: 25 kw, ant 328 ft., TL: N33 21 56 W90 14 59). Stereo. Hrs opn: 24. Box 1801, 503 Ione St. (38930). (601) 453-1643. FAX: (601) 453-1646. Licensee: Team Broadcasting Co. Inc. Rep: Dora-Clayton. Wash atty: Emmons, Mullins & Rhyne. Format: Urban contemp. News staff one; news progmg 12 hrs wkly. Target aud: 18 plus. Spec prog: Jazz 6 hrs wkly. ■ Ruben C. Hughes, gen mgr & gen sls mgr; Maxine Hughes, opns mgr; Cyreio Hughes, progmg dir, mus dir & news dir. ■ Rates: $10.45; 9.85; 8.25; 7.65.

WGRM(AM)—1937: 1240 khz; 1 kw-U. TL: N33 31 55 W90 11 38 (CP: 730 w). Box 553 (39935-0553). 1110 Wright St. (38930). (601) 453-1240. Licensee: Twelve-forty Inc. Net: Unistar. Format: Adult contemp. Target aud: 25-45. Spec prog: Black 2 hrs wkly. ■ Clay Ewing, gen mgr & gen sls mgr; Rose Ewing, progmg dir.

WGRM-FM—July 17, 1989: 93.9 mhz; 3 kw. Ant 328 ft. TL: N33 32 02 W90 11 42.

WKXG(AM)—Jan 1, 1987: 1540 khz: 1 kw-D. TL: N33 31 12 W90 08 28. Hrs opn: 6 AM-10 PM. Box 1686, Browning Rd. (38930). (601) 453-2174. FAX: (601) 455-5733. Licensee: Mississippi Network Inc. (acq 8-1-88). Net: Miss. Net. Rep: Rgnl Reps. Format: Urban contemp. News progmg 3 hrs wkly. Target aud: 18-44. ■ Steve Davenport, pres; Wes Sterling, gen mgr & gen sls mgr; Herman Anderson, progmg dir; Keith Worell, chief engr.

WYMX(FM)—Co-owned with WKXG(AM). June 15, 1965: 99.1 mhz; 100 kw. Ant 1,029 ft. TL: N33 31 12 W90 08 28. Stereo. Prog sep from AM. Licensee: Telesouth Communications. Net: ABC/C. Format: Adult comtemp. News progmg 6 hrs wkly. ■ Hardin Browning, progmg dir.

***WMAO-FM**—December 1983: 90.9 mhz; 100 kw. Ant 880 ft. TL: N33 22 34 W90 32 32. Stereo. Hrs opn: 24. 3825 Ridgewood Rd., Jackson (39211). (601) 982-6565. FAX: (601) 982-6746. Licensee: Mississippi Authority for Educational Television. Net: APR, NPR. Format: Class, news. News progmg 40 hrs wkly. Spec prog: Jazz 10 hrs, new age 10 hrs, folk 3 hrs, bluegrass 3 hrs wkly. ■ Larry Miller, pres; William Fulton, gen mgr; Bill Pharr, dev dir; Alma Ellis, prom mgr; Kevin Farrell, pub affrs dir; Martin Mangold, chief engr.

WYMX(FM)—Listing follows WKXG(AM).

Grenada

WTGY(FM)—See Charleston.

WYKC(AM)—February 1949: 1400 khz; 1 kw-U. TL: N33 46 48 W89 48 09. Box 946 (38902). (601) 226-1400. FAX: (601) 226-4679. Licensee: Chatterbox Inc. (acq 1-16-81). Net: Prog Farm. Rep: Southern. Format: C&W, Black. ■ Bob Evans Jr., pres; Rett Evans, progmg dir; Ericka McCarty, news dir; Hollis Morrow, chief engr.

WQXB(FM)—Co-owned with WYKC(AM). Oct 16, 1970: 100.1 mhz; 3 kw. Ant 300 ft. TL: N33 46 36 W89 49 23. Stereo. (Acq 2-24-78). Net: ABC/C. Format: Adult contemp.

Gulfport

WGCM(AM)—1928: 1240 khz; 1 kw-U. TL: N30 22 38 W89 04 45. Hrs opn: 24. 11737 Klein Rd. (39503). (601) 863-3522. FAX: (601) 832-7699. Licensee: EJM Broadcasting (acq 11-26-89; grpsl; FTR 10-27-89). Net: SMN. Rep: Banner. Format: Big band, nostalgia. Target aud: 35 plus. ■ Ed Muniz, pres; Howard Yund, gen mgr; Leigh Moylan, gen sls mgr; Steve Spillman, progmg dir; Richard Marrell, news dir; Dominic Mitchel, chief engr.

WGCM-FM—Nov 14, 1969: 102.3 mhz; 25 kw. Ant 299 ft. TL: N30 22 28 W89 04 45. Stereo. Hrs opn: 24. Prog sep from AM. Format: Oldies. Target aud: 25-54.

WQFX(AM)—May 7, 1975: 1130 khz; 500 w-D. TL: N30 23 21 W89 06 23. Box 4566, Biloxi (39533). (601) 388-1490. Licensee: Southern Horizons Broadcasting Corp. (acq 3-26-93; $95,100 with co-located FM; FTR 4-12-93). Format: Power gospel. ■ Al Jenkins, stn mgr & mus dir; Frank Yates, chief engr.

WXRG(FM)—Co-owned with WQFX(AM). July 13, 1977: 96.7 mhz; 3 kw. Ant 245 ft. TL: N30 23 21 W89 06 23. Stereo. Box 4779, Biloxi (39535). (601) 435-7625. Format: Classic rock. ■ David Steere, pres & gen sls mgr; Lawrence E. Steelman, gen mgr; Al Jenkins, opns mgr & mus dir; Chantel Bradley, news dir; Frank Yates, chief engr.

WROA(AM)—Feb 27, 1955: 1390 khz; 5 kw-U, DA-2. TL: N30 27 30 W89 04 45. Box 2639 (39505). (601) 832-5111. FAX: (601) 832-7699. Licensee: Dowdy & Dowdy Partnership (acq 12-19-86). Net: NBC, Unistar. Rep: Masla. Format: Easy lstng. Spec prog: Farm one hr wkly. ■ Charles W. Dowdy, pres; Morgan Dowdy, gen mgr; Scott Gilreath, gen sls mgr; Steve Spillman, prom mgr; Bryan Rhodes, mus dir; Dominic Mitchum, chief engr.

WXLS-FM—1964: 107.1 mhz; 1.85 kw. Ant 394 ft. TL: N30 27 32 W89 04 45 (CP: 2.8 kw, ant 400 ft.). Stereo. Box 4779, 212 DeBuys Rd., Biloxi (39532). (601) 388-1490. FAX: (601) 388-1966. Licensee: LES Radio Corp. (acq 10-21-92; $50,000 with WXLS(AM) Biloxi; FTR 11-23-92). Net: NBC. Format: Light rock, adult contemp. ■ Jim Carlow (owner), pres; Lawrence E. Steelman, gen mgr.

WXRG(FM)—Listing follows WQFX(AM).

WZKX(FM)—See Poplarville.

Hattiesburg

WBKH(AM)—Sept 1, 1954: 950 khz; 5 kw-D. TL: N31 22 33 W89 19 49. 7501 Highway 49 N. (39402). (601) 582-9595. Licensee: Southern Air Communications Inc. (acq 11-22-89; grpsl; FTR 12-11-89). Format: Southern gospel. News progmg 3 hrs wkly. Target aud: 30 plus. ■ Kay Easterling, gen mgr; Freddie Kirkland, gen sls mgr; Merle Marie, mus dir; Dale Graham, chief engr.

WFOR(AM)—May 1924: 1400 khz; 1 kw-U. TL: N31 20 03 W89 19 08. Hrs opn: 24. 2414 W. Seventh (39401). (601) 544-1400. FAX: (601) 582-5481. Licensee: Radio Hattiesburg Inc. Group owner: Gulf Central Radio Net (acq 1965). Net: NBC, Unistar. Rep: Katz & Powell. Format: Oldies, MOR. Target aud: 35 plus. Spec prog: Relg 8 hrs wkly. ■ J. W. Furr, pres; David McPhail, gen mgr; Farley Shaw, opns mgr; Olon Booth, chief engr. ■ Rates: $24; 20; 24; 18.

WHER(FM)—Co-owned with WFOR(AM). July 1, 1966: 103.7 mhz; 100 kw. Ant 1,056 ft. TL: N31 31 37 W89 08 07. Stereo. Hrs opn: 24. Prog sep from AM. (601) 544-3232. Format: Country. Target aud: 25-54. Spec prog: Gospel 3 hrs, relg 2 hrs wkly. ■ Farley Shaw, progmg dir; Merle Kilzer, mus dir.

WHLV(AM)—September 1957: 1310 khz; 1 kw-D. TL: N31 21 00 W89 17 00 (CP: 5 kw). Box 17131 (39402). (601) 582-2899. FAX: (601) 477-3226. Licensee: Horizon Broadcast Communications Inc. (acq 12-24-86; $33,500; FTR 11-10-86). Net: USA, CBN, Skylight, Ambassador, Moody, UPI. Wash atty: William T. Abbott. Format: Relg. News staff one; news progmg 4 hrs wkly. Target aud: General. ■ D. Gayril Gibson, pres & gen mgr; Jimmie D. Gibson, gen sls mgr. ■ Rates: $12; 6; 12; 6.

WHSY(AM)—Sept 24, 1948: 1230 khz; 1 kw-U. TL: N31 20 55 W89 17 00. Hrs opn: 18. Drawer 1978 (39403); 833 Hwy. 11 N., Petal (39465). (601) 545-1230. FAX: (601) 545-1243. Licensee: Hub City Broadcasting Co. Group owner: Holt Broadcasting Service. Net: ABC/D, CBS; Miss. Net. Format: News/talk. News progmg 86 hrs wkly. Target aud: 35 plus; older audience with an interest in news. ■ Ted Tibbett, pres & gen sls mgr; Ted Tibbet, gen mgr; Glenn Smith, prom mgr; Will Martin, progmg dir; Dale Graham, chief engr. ■ Rates: $10; 7; 8; 5.

WHSY-FM—July 1, 1967: 104.5 mhz; 100 kw. Ant 984 ft. TL: N31 25 50 W89 08 51. Stereo. Hrs opn: 24. Dups AM 15%. Net: ABC/C. Format: Adult contemp. Target aud: General. ■ Will Martin, prom mgr; John Gatlin, mus dir. ■ Rates: $20; 12; 15; 10.

WJMG(FM)—Listing follows WORV(AM).

WMFM(FM)—See Petal.

WORV(AM)—June 7, 1969: 1580 khz; 1 kw-D, 88 w-N. TL: N31 20 33 W89 17 53. 1204 Graveline (39401). (601) 544-1941. Licensee: Vernon C. Floyd dba Circuit Broadcasting of Hattiesburg. Net: American Urban. Rep: Dora Clayton. Format: Urban contemp, gospel, relg. ■ Vernon C. Floyd, pres, gen mgr, gen sls mgr & chief engr. ■ Rates: $12; 12; 12; na.

WJMG(FM)—Co-owned with WORV(AM). May 10, 1982: 92.1 mhz; 3 kw. Ant 300 ft. TL: N31 20 33 W89 17 53. Stereo. Hrs opn: 24. Format: Adult contemp, urban contemp. ■ Rates: $14; 14; 14; 14.

***WUSM-FM**—May 10, 1973: 88.5 mhz; 3 kw. Ant 282 ft. TL: N31 21 02 W89 22 12. Stereo. Hrs opn: 6 AM-2 AM. Box 10045, Southern Hall, Rm. 107, Southern Stn. (39406-0045). (601) 266-4287; (601) 266-5615. FAX: (601) 266-4363. Licensee: Univ. of Southern Miss. Net: AP. Format: Class, jazz, educ. News staff 4; news progmg 22 hrs wkly. Target aud: General; college students & upper income univ. & community listeners. Spec prog: Blues 2 hrs, reggae 2 hrs, poetry one hr, new age 10 hrs, opera 3 hrs, pub affrs 10 hrs wkly. ■ Aubrey Lucas, pres; Dennis Webster, exec vp; Henry Lena, gen mgr; Jeff Rassier, prom mgr; Micheal Davis, mus dir; Clarence Vogel, chief engr.

Hazelhurst

WMDC(AM)—June 1, 1953: 1220 khz; 250 w-D, 46 w-N. TL: N31 53 34 W90 24 08. Box 680 (39083). (601) 894-1441. Licensee: Compiah County Broadcasting. Rep: Southern Spot Sls. Format: C&W. Spec prog: Farm 5 hrs, Black 18 hrs wkly. ■ A. M. Smith, stn mgr & chief engr; Jack Ellis, gen sls mgr.

WMDC-FM—Dec 24, 1970: 100.9 mhz; 3 kw. Ant 295 ft. TL: N31 53 34 W90 24 08. Dups AM 100%.

Heidelberg

WEEZ(FM)—May 1, 1980: 99.3 mhz; 3 kw. Ant 299 ft. TL: N31 52 31 W89 03 02 (CP: 50 kw, ant 492 ft., TL: N31 49 17 W89 18 37). Stereo. Hrs opn: 24. Box 367, 318 W. 5th St., Laurel (39441). (601) 425-4390. FAX: (601) 425-4486. Licensee: Gerald Williams (acq 10-91; $250,000 grpsl; FTR 11-4-91). Net: NBC, Miss. Net. Format: Relg. Target aud: General. ■ Gerald Williams, pres, gen sls mgr & news dir; Kathy McDonnieal, gen mgr & stn mgr; Bobby Brignac, opns mgr; Dora Patterson, progmg dir & mus dir; Dale Graham, chief engr. ■ Rates: $9; 9; 9; 7.

Holly Springs

WKRA(AM)—Sept 2, 1966: 1110 khz; 1 kw-D. TL: N34 47 11 W89 25 00. Hrs opn: Sunrise-sunset. Box 398 (38635); WKRA Bldg., 1400 B Salem Ave. (38635). (601) 252-1110. Licensee: Ralph H. Doxey (acq 12-19-88; $330,000 with co-located FM; FTR 1-16-89). Net: Unistar; Miss Net. Rep: Hopewell, Beaver. Format: C&W, talk. News staff one; news progmg 9 hrs wkly. Target aud: 25-55. Spec prog: Gospel 12 hrs wkly. ■ Ralph Doxey, gen mgr; Rick Williams, stn mgr, mus dir & news dir; Everitt Jones, gen sls mgr; Tom Scott, chief engr.

WKRA-FM—June 30, 1976: 92.7 mhz; 3 kw. Ant 299 ft. TL: N34 47 11 W89 25 00. Hrs opn: 24. Prog sep from AM. Format: Black, gospel. Target aud: General; Black community. Spec prog: Blues 12 hrs wkly. ■ Everitt Jones, progmg mgr & mus dir.

***WURC(FM)**—Oct 14, 1988: 88.1 mhz; 3 kw. Ant 328 ft. TL: N34 46 53 W89 26 49. 150 E. Rust Ave. (38635). (601) 252-8000, ext. 4560; (601) 252-5881. FAX: (601) 252-6107. Licensee: Rust College Inc. Format: Jazz, inspirational. News progmg 22 hrs wkly. Target aud: General; college students, alternative seekers, minority listeners. . ■ David L. Beckley, pres; Sylvester W. Oliver Jr., gen mgr; Edwin Smith, prom mgr; Wayne A. Fiddis, progmg dir; Sharron G. Hill, news dir; Gerald White, vp engrg.

Houston

WCPC(AM)—Oct 21, 1955: 940 khz; 50 kw-D, 250 w-N, DA-2. TL: N33 56 00 W89 00 33. Hrs opn: 4 AM-11 PM. Rt. 2, Box 10C, Hwy. 15 N. (38851). (601) 456-3071; (601) 456-3072. Licensee: WCPC Broadcasting Co. Inc. Net: Unistar; Miss Net. Rep: Midsouth. Wash atty: Leonard Joyce. Format: Country, gospel, Black, sports, farm. News staff one; news progmg 14 hrs wkly. Target aud: General; all ages. Spec prog: Farm, relg. ■ Robin H. Mathis, pres, gen mgr & gen sls mgr; Rick Huffman, prom mgr & adv mgr; Wayne Parks, progmg dir; Melanie Mathis Munlin, mus dir; Glenn Gann, news dir; John B. Skelton Jr., chief engr. ■ Rates: $21; 21; 21; 21.

WSYE(FM)—Sept 19, 1968: 93.3 mhz; 100 kw. Ant 1,804 ft. TL: N33 45 06 W88 52 40. Stereo. Box 1623, Suite H, 1705 S. Gloster, Tupelo (38802-1623). (601) 844-9793. FAX: (601) 844-7400. Licensee: New South Communications Inc. (group owner; acq 8-20-90; $1.5 million; FTR 9-10-90). Format: Adult contemp. News staff one; news progmg 2 hrs wkly. Target aud: 25-54. ■ Gwen Rakestraw, gen mgr; Lee Adams, progmg dir; Barry Walters, chief engr. ■ Rates: $26; 22; 24; 18.

Indianola

WDLJ(FM)—May 1990: 96.9 mhz; 6 kw. Ant 230 ft. TL: N33 27 32 W90 37 45. Hrs opn: 24. 517 E. Baker St. (38751). (601) 887-1091; (601) 887-1090. FAX: (601) 887-1092. Licensee: Son Rise Broadcasting Inc. (acq 7-13-90; $110,000; FTR 8-6-90). Net: USA. Format: Christian country. News staff one; news progmg 20 hrs wkly. Target aud: 35-64; strong family orientation, middle to upper incomes. ■ Andy Arant, CEO, pres, gen mgr, stn mgr & engrg mgr; Turner Arant, chmn; Denny Evans, vp opns, opns mgr, progmg dir & mus dir; Cal Hodges, vp sls & gen sls mgr; Charlotte Buchanan, news dir. ■ Rates: $5; 5; 5; 5.

WNLA(AM)—May 1953: 1380 khz; 500 w-D, 44 w-N. TL: N33 27 32 W90 37 45. Hrs opn: 12. Box 667, Hwy. 448 (38751). (601) 887-1380. Licensee: Shamrock Broadcasting Inc. (acq 10-1-84; $675,000 with co-located FM; FTR 8-25-84). Net: ABC/E; Miss. Net. Format: Black gospel. Target aud: 21-55; Black. ■ Gerry Brophy, pres, sls dir & engrg dir; Erin Ely, gen mgr & progmg dir; Bob Taylor, chief engr.

WNLA-FM—Sept 1, 1969: 105.5 mhz; 4.4 kw. Ant 200 ft. TL: N33 28 41 W90 38 28. Stereo. Hrs opn: 24. Prog sep from AM. Format: Adult contemp. News progmg 21 hrs wkly. Target aud: General; 21-55. ■ Erin Ely, opns dir.

Itta Bena

***WVSD(FM)**—June 23, 1991: 91.7 mhz; 3 kw. Ant 292 ft. TL: N33 31 05 W90 20 38. Hwy. 82 W. (38941). (601) 254-9041. FAX: (601) 254-6704. Licensee: Mississippi Valley State Univ. Format: Jazz, urban contemp, gospel. ■ Dr. William W. Sutton, pres; Samuel Brown, opns mgr; Brad Labrone, chief engr.

Iuka

WVOM(AM)—Sept 17, 1960: 1270 khz; 1 kw-D. TL: N34 47 34 W88 11 34. 311 W. Eastport (38852). (601) 423-6059. FAX: (601) 423-6059. Licensee: Billy R. McLain (acq 11-4-91; with co-located FM). Net: ABC/I. Format: Country. ■ Billy McClaine, gen mgr & gen sls mgr; Kent Mohundro, progmg dir; Jack Irvy, news dir; Jeff Vaughn, chief engr.

WFXO(FM)—Co-owned with WVOM(AM). Nov 5, 1970: 104.9 mhz; 50 kw. Ant 443 ft. TL: N34 46 35 W88 23 40. Prog sep from AM. Net: ABC/I. Format: Cotemp hit.

Jackson

WJDS(AM)—1929: 620 khz; 5 kw-D, 1 kw-N, DA-N. TL: N32 22 56 W90 11 26. Stereo. Hrs opn: 24. Box 31999, 1375 Beasley Rd. (39286). (601) 982-1062. FAX: (601) 362-1905. Licensee: R. Steven Hicks. Group owner: SFX Broadcasting Inc. (acq 7-19-89; grpsl; FTR 8-7-89). Net: ABC/D. Rep: McGavren Guild. Format: Adult contemp, oldies. News staff one; news progmg 10 hrs wkly. Target aud: 25-54; middle to upper income contemporary adults. Spec prog: Farm 2 hrs wkly. ■ R. Steven Hicks, pres; Kenneth E. Windham, gen mgr; David Perkins, opns mgr & progmg dir; Dianne Black, gen sls mgr; Randy Bell, news dir; George Thomas, chief engr.

WMSI(FM)—Co-owned with WJDS(AM). 1948: 103 mhz. 100 kw. Ant 1,800 ft. TL: N32 12 46 W90 22 54. Stereo. Hrs opn: 24. Prog sep from AM. Net: ABC/E. Format: C&W. News progmg 4 hrs wkly. Target aud: 25 plus. Spec prog: Farm one hr wkly. ■ David Perkins, progmg dir & mus dir.

WJDX(FM)—Listing follows WSLI(AM).

WJMI(FM)—Listing follows WOAD(AM).

***WJSU(FM)**—August 1975: 88.5 mhz; 3 kw-V. Ant 203 ft. TL: N32 17 47 W90 12 23. Stereo. Box 18450, Jackson State University, 1400 Lynch St. (39217). (601) 968-2140; (601) 968-2285. FAX: (601) 968-2007. Licensee: Jackson State Univ. Net: NPR, APR. Format: Jazz. News staff one; news progmg 7 hrs wkly. Target aud: 25-54; middle-class multiracial m/f who prefer jazz/alt mus. Spec prog: Gospel 18 hrs, reggae 2 hrs, blues 2 hrs wkly. ■ Dr. James E. Lyons, pres; Dr. Thomas J. Robinson, vp; Larry McAdoo, gen mgr; Trudy Shepherd, dev dir, prom dir, news dir & pub affrs dir; Bobbie Walker, progmg dir & mus dir; Ed Hobgood, chief engr. ■ Rates: $25; 25; 25; 25.

WJXN(AM)—March 1945: 1450 khz; 1 kw-U. TL: N32 18 42 W90 09 45. Hrs opn: 20. Box 24387 (39225); 916 Foley St. (39202). (601) 355-2518; (601) 944-1450. FAX: (601) 944-1450. Licensee: Willis Broadcasting (group owner; acq 1-30-89; $180,000; FTR 2-13-89). Net: CNN, USA. Format: News, talk, relg. News progmg one hr wkly. Target aud: 25-54; older adults. ■ Bishop L.E. Willis, pres; Celestine Willis, gen mgr & stn mgr; Tarra Haskin Gilbert, progmg dir.

WKTF(FM)—Nov 19, 1973: 95.5 mhz; 100 kw. Ant 1,060 ft. TL: N32 16 39 W90 17 41. Stereo. Box 31999 (39236). (601) 366-1989. FAX: (601) 366-2065. Licensee: Capstar Communications of Jackson Inc. Group owners: SFX Broadcasting Inc. (acq 10-12-93; $1,156,872; FTR 11-8-93). Net: CBS. Rep: D & R Radio. Wash atty: Cohn & Marks. Format: CHR. News staff one. Target aud: 18-34; female. ■ Ken Wyndham, gen mgr.

WKXI(AM)—1929: 1300 khz; 5 kw-D, 1 kw-N. TL: N32 23 12 W90 09 47. Box 9446 (39286); 222 Beasley Rd. (39206). (601) 957-1300. FAX: (601) 956-0516. Licensee: Opus Media Group (acq 2-12-90; grpsl; FTR 3-5-90). Net: American Urban, ABC. Rep: Banner. Format: Urban contemp. News staff one; news progmg 14 hrs wkly. Target aud: 25-54. ■ Kevin Webb, gen mgr; Becky Elkin, gen sls mgr; Stan Branson, progmg dir; Percy Davis, mus dir; Sean Stewart, news dir.

WTYX(FM)—Co-owned with WKXI(AM). Aug 10, 1971: 94.7 mhz; 100 kw. Ant 1,168 ft. TL: N32 16 53 W90 17 41. Stereo. Prog sep from AM. Format: Oldies. News staff one; news progmg 5 hrs wkly. ■ Ron Harrell, progmg dir; Jud Alford, mus dir; Donna Michaels, news dir.

WLIN(FM)—See Gluckstadt.

***WMPN-FM**—November 1984: 91.3 mhz; 100 kw. Ant 760 ft. TL: N32 16 53 W90 17 41. Stereo. Hrs opn: 24. 3825 Ridgewood Rd. (39211). (601) 982-6565. FAX: (601) 982-6746. Licensee: Mississippi Authority for Educational Television. Net: APR, NPR. Format: Class, news. News progmg 40 hrs wkly. Spec prog: Jazz 10 hrs, new age 10 hrs, folk 3, bluegrass 3 hrs wkly. ■ Larry Miller, pres; William Fulton, gen mgr & progmg dir; Bill Pharr, dev dir; Alma Ellis, prom dir; Bill Lovett, asst mus dir; Kevin Farrell, pub affrs dir; Martin Mangold, chief engr.

***WMPR(FM)**—1983: 90.1 mhz; 100 kw. Ant 500 ft. TL: N32 11 33 W90 05 28. Stereo. Box 9782 (39286); 416 W. County Line Rd. (39206). (601) 948-5853. FAX: (601) 948-6162. Licensee: J.C. Maxwell Broadcasting Group Inc. Format: Blues, gospel, urban contemp. ■ Charles Evers, pres; Sherry Duck, gen sls mgr; Shelton Gates, progmg dir & mus dir; Otha Caine, news dir; Bernard Smith, pub affrs dir; Sandy McKnight, chief engr.

WMSI(FM)—Listing follows WJDS(AM).

WOAD(AM)—1947: 1400 khz; 1 kw-U. TL: N32 19 12 W90 11 25. Hrs opn: 24. Box 10387 (39289); 1850 W. Lynch St. (39203). (601) 948-1515. FAX: (601) 354-1984. Licensee: Holt Communications Corp. Group owner. Net: NBC. Rep: D & R Radio. Format: Gospel. News staff one; news progmg 30 hrs wkly. Target aud: 25-54. ■ Arthur Holt, pres; Carl Haynes, vp & gen mgr; Gwen Cannon, stn mgr; Maria Epps, rgnl sls mgr; Jimmy Anthony, progmg dir & mus dir; Michelle Walker, news dir; Bruce Payne, pub affrs dir; Emmitt Rushing, chief engr. ■ Rates: $32; 26; 30; 24.

WJMI(FM)—Co-owned with WOAD(AM). 1967: 99.7 mhz; 100 kw. Ant 1,060 ft. TL: N32 16 39 W90 17 41. Stereo. Hrs opn: 24. Prog sep from AM. Net: ABC/FM. Format: Urban contemp. News staff one. Target aud: 18-49. ■ Paul Todd, progmg dir; Ernie Gaines, mus dir. ■ Rates: $56; 46; 53; 42.

WRKN(AM)—See Brandon.

WSLI(AM)—September 1938: 930 khz; 5 kw-U, DA-N. TL: N32 23 42 W90 09 14. Box 4214 (39205). (601) 925-3458. FAX: (601) 924-4506. Licensee: Spur Jackson Ltd. Group owner: Spur Capital Inc. (acq 5-9-90; $3,375,000; with co-located FM; FTR 6-4-90). Net: BRN, MBS. Rep: McGavern Guild. Format: Talk. News progmg 15 hrs wkly. ■ Rick Dawkins, gen mgr; Jimmy Glen Jr., stn mgr & progmg dir; Bob Buie, chief engr.

WJDX(FM)—Co-owned with WSLI(AM). Sept 16, 1966: 96.3 mhz; 100 kw. Ant 1,450 ft. TL: N32 14 26 W90 24 15. Stereo. Box 1999 (39286). (601) 982-1062. Net: ABC/D. Format: Adult contemp.

WSTZ-FM—(Vicksburg). June 1968: 106.7 mhz; 100 kw. Ant 1,365 ft., TL: N32 12 22 W90 24 50 (CP: Ant 1,059 ft. TL: N32 12 29 W90 24 50). Stereo. Suite 286, 4500 I 55 N., Jackson (39211). (601) 982-1067. FAX: (601) 981-5800. Licensee: Lewis Broadcasting Corp. (group owner). Rep: D & R Radio. Format: AOR. Target aud: 25-54. ■ Fred Pierce, pres; Kirk Sherwood, gen mgr; Pam Rivers, progmg dir & mus dir; Sara Kimmel, news dir; Randy Grammer, chief engr.

WTYX(FM)—Listing follows WKXI(AM).

WZRX(AM)—April 8, 1965: 1590 khz; 5 kw-D, 1 kw-N, DA-N. TL: N32 22 01 W90 13 26. Suite 286, 4500 I-55 N. (39211). (601) 982-1067. FAX: (601) 981-5800. Licensee: Capitol Radio. Group owner: Lewis Broadcasting Corp. (acq 3-86; $200,000; FTR 3-31-86). Net: Unistar. Rep: D & R Radio. Format: Blues & soul. Spec prog: Jazz 2 hrs wkly. ■ J. Curtis Lewis, pres; J. Fred Pierce, vp; Kirk Sherwood, gen mgr; Tiana Patterson, prom mgr; Pam Yates, progmg dir & mus dir; Sara Kimmel, news dir; Emmet Rushing, chief engr.

Kosciusko

WBKJ(FM)—Listing follows WKOZ(AM).

***WJTA(FM)**—1989: 91.7 mhz; 383 w. Ant 171 ft. TL: N33 05 54 W89 30 33. Hrs opn: 24. Box 742, 411 N. Jackson (39090). Licensee: Kosciusko Educational Broadcasting Foundation. Format: Relg, educ. News staff 2; news progmg 6 hrs wkly. Target aud: General. ■ Dr. William G. Suratt, pres & gen mgr; Arthur L. Suratt, gen sls mgr & progmg dir; H. J. Gunn, chief engr. ■ Rates: $3.50; 3.50; 3.50; 3.50.

WKOZ(AM)—Oct 31, 1947: 1340 khz; 1 kw-U. TL: N33 03 51 W89 36 12. Golf Course Rd. (39090). Box A (39090). (601) 289-1340. FAX: (601) 289-1340. Licensee: H. Mims Boswell Jr. (acq 6-1-62). Net: CNN. Format: Oldies, urban contemp. ■ H. Mims Boswell Jr., pres; Johnny Boswell, stn mgr & gen sls mgr; Bobby Leathers, chief engr.

WBKJ(FM)—Co-owned with WKOZ(AM). June 25, 1965: 105.1 mhz; 100 kw. Ant 355 ft. TL: N33 03 51 W89 36 12 (CP: Ant 981 ft., TL: N32 41 25 W89 52 06). Stereo. Prog sep from AM. (601) 289-1050. FAX: (601) 289-1050. Format: Country. ■ Rates: $10; 8; 10; 8.

WWFS(FM)—Not on air, target date unknown: 103.3 mhz; 25 kw. Ant 328 ft. TL: N32 58 27 W89 43 32. Rt. 2, Box 112, Sallis (39160). Licensee: Jesse Fleming.

Laurel

WAML(AM)—Oct 20, 1932: 1340 khz; 1 kw-U. TL: N31 40 01 W89 08 59. Hrs opn: 24. Box 367, 318 W. 5th St. (39441). (601) 425-4285. FAX: (601) 425-4486. Licensee: Gerald Williams (acq 10-91; $75,000 grpsl; FTR 11-4-91). Net: NBC. Rep: Midsouth. Format: Gospel, relg, news. Target aud: General. ■ Gerald Williams, pres, gen sls mgr & mus dir; Kathy McDonnieal, gen mgr & stn mgr; Bobby Brignac, opns dir; Dora Patterson, progmg dir; Dale Graham, chief engr. ■ Rates: $6; 6; 6.10; 5.10.

WIZK(AM)—See Bay Springs.

WIZK-FM—See Bay Springs.

WLAU(AM)—June 15, 1946: 1430 khz; 5 kw-D. TL: N31 42 51 W89 09 47. c/o Sarah Hodnett, 210 Locust St., Rolling Fork (01152). Licensee: Sarah Hodnett, trustee.

WNSL(FM)—Listing follows WQIS(AM).

WQIS(AM)—Feb 27, 1957: 890 khz; 10 kw-D. TL: N31 31 29 W89 14 31. Stereo. Box 151 (39440); 1260 Victory Rd. (39440). (601) 425-1491. FAX: (601) 426-8255. Licensee: Design Media Inc. (group owner; acq 1-30-89; $2,950,000; FTR 2-13-89). Net: ABC/FM. Rep: D & R Radio. Format: Urban contemp. News staff one. Spec prog: Gospel 11 hrs wkly. ■ John Thomas, pres; Glen Ulmer, progmg dir; Lyne Christian, mus dir; Olin Booth, chief engr.

WNSL(FM)—Co-owned with WQIS(AM). March 10, 1959: 100.3 mhz; 100 kw. Ant 1,050 ft. TL: N31 31 37 W89 08 07. Stereo. Prog sep from AM. Format: Adult contemp. ■ Rick James, stn mgr & progmg dir.

Leland

WBAD(FM)—Listing follows WESY(AM).

WESY(AM)—Apr 8, 1957: 1580 khz; 1 kw-D, 48 w-N. TL: N33 22 46 W90 55 47 (CP: 1 kw-N, DA-N). Box 5804, Greenville (38704); 7 Oaks Rd., Greenville (38701). (601) 378-9405; (601) 332-1580. FAX: (601) 335-5538. Licensee: East Delta Communications Inc. (acq 1980). Net: American Urban. Rep: Roslin, Southern. Format: Black, relg, gospel. ■ William D. Jackson, pres & gen mgr; Linda Elliott, gen sls mgr; Stanley S. Sherman, prom mgr; Nathan Williams, progmg dir; Dannu Jones, mus dir.

WBAD(FM)—Co-owned with WESY(AM). 1973: 94.3 mhz; 3 kw. Ant 300 ft. TL: N33 24 55 W90 59 18. Stereo. Hrs opn: 19. Prog sep from AM. (601) 335-9265. Licensee: Interchange Communications Inc. (acq 5-12-73). Wash atty: Arent, Fox, Kintner, Plotkin & Kahn. Format: Black, urban contemp. ■ Stanley S. Sherman, gen sls mgr.

WIQQ(FM)—Sept 1, 1985: 102.3 mhz; 3 kw. Ant 440 ft. TL: N33 23 59 W91 00 34. Stereo. Hrs opn: 24. Box 1816, Unit 39, Delta Plaza Mall, 800 Hwy. One S., Greenville (38702). (601) 378-2617. FAX: (601) 378-8341. Licensee: The River Broadcasting Co. Inc. Net: Prog Farm. Rep: McGavren Guild. Wash atty: Baraff, Koerner, Olender & Hochberg. Format: Top-40. News staff one; news progmg 2 hrs wkly. Target aud: 18-49; multi-paycheck & spendable income. Spec prog: Farm 6 hrs, jazz 2 hrs, relg 6 hrs wkly. ■ George E. Pine, pres; James P. Karr Jr., vp, gen mgr & vp prom; Floree Self, opns mgr; Margret Karr, gen sls mgr; Arch Chapman, mktg dir; Larry Thomas, progmg dir & mus dir; Chuck Early, pub affrs dir; Percy Kuhn, chief engr.

Lexington

WAGR-FM—June 1, 1990: 102.5 mhz; 6 kw. Ant 328 ft. TL: N33 09 06 W90 07 45 (CP: 12.5 kw, ant 459 ft.). Stereo. Drawer M (39095). (601) 834-1025. FAX: (601) 834-2612. Licensee: Fanny Tidwell Cothran. Net: Miss. Net. Format: Country, oldies. ■ Brad Cothran, gen mgr, progmg dir & news dir; Fanny Cothran, chief engr.

WLTD(FM)—July 20, 1980: 106.3 mhz; 3 kw. Ant 314 ft. TL: N33 06 14 W90 00 14 (CP: 25.5 kw, ant 689 ft.). Stereo. 224 Shiloh Dr., Jackson (39212-3048). Licensee: J. Scott Communications. ■ David Wilson, gen mgr; James Williams, progmg dir; Fiel Scott, chief engr.

WXTN(AM)—Oct 23, 1959: 1000 khz; 5 kw-D. TL: N33 06 39 W90 02 21. Drawer M (39095); 100 Radio Rd. (39095). (601) 834-1254. FAX: (601) 834-2612. Licensee: Fanny Cothran (acq 1985; $165,000; FTR 10-29-84). Format: Gospel, Black. ■ Fanny Cothran, pres; Brad M. Cothran, gen mgr.

Long Beach

WJZD(FM)—Not on air, target date unknown: 94.5 mhz; 3 kw. Ant 328 ft. TL: N30 22 25 W89 06 38. Box 6216, Gulfport (39506). Licensee: Beach Broadcasting L.P.

Lorman

***WPRL(FM)**—Oct 12, 1987: 91.7 mhz; 3 kw. Ant 300 ft. TL: N31 53 37 W91 08 54. Stereo. Hrs opn: 5 AM-1 AM, M-F; 6 AM-midnight, S-S. Box 269, Alcorn State Univ. (39096). (601) 877-6613; (601) 877-6290. FAX: (601) 877-6256. Licensee: Alcorn State Univ. Net: APR, NPR. Format: Jazz, urban contemp, rhythm & blues. News staff 2; news progmg 23 hrs wkly. Target aud: General; African-American, rural. Spec prog: Gospel 16 hrs wkly. ■ Dr. Shafiqur Rahman, gen mgr; Gregory Dace, opns mgr; Gregory Dace, Bruce Dungee, Darren Buckley, mus dirs; Patrick Strens, news dir; Charles Edmond, pub affrs dir.

Louisville

WLSM(AM)—Mar 11, 1953: 1270 khz; 5 kw-D. TL: N33 07 20 W89 01 05 (CP: 2.7 kw, TL: N33 70 20 W89 01 07). Box 279, Hwy. 14 E. (39339). (601) 773-3481. Licensee: Harrison Communications Inc. (acq 6-1-92; $425,000; with co-located FM; FTR 6-22-92). Net: ABC/D; Miss. Net. Format: Country, Black gospel. Target aud: 35-64. Spec prog: Relg 2 hrs wkly. ■ Phillip A. Harrison, pres, gen mgr, gen sls mgr, prom mgr & news dir; Stacy S. Harrison, stn mgr, progmg dir & mus dir; Lee Jackson, chief engr. ■ Rates: $8; 6; 8; 5.

WLSM-FM—Apr 22, 1966: 107.1 mhz; 3 kw. Ant 200 ft. TL: N33 07 20 W89 01 05. Stereo. Hrs opn: 5AM- 11 PM. Prog sep from AM. Net: ABC/D. Format: C&W. Target aud: 18-54. ■ Rates: Same as AM.

Lucedale

WRBE(AM)—Sept 3, 1960: 1440 khz; 5 kw-D. TL: N30 56 00 W88 36 20 (CP: TL: N30 55 58 W88 36 21). Box 827, Hwy. 98 W. (39452). (601) 947-8151. Licensee: Allen Broadcasting Co. Inc. (acq 1972). Net: AP. Rep: Dora-Clayton, Keystone (unwired net). Format: Country, gospel. News staff one; news progmg 10 hrs wkly. Target aud: General. ■ Douglas T. Luce, pres; Herman Kelly, vp, gen mgr, progmg dir & news dir; James Newman, chief engr.

WRBE-FM—Not on air, target date unknown: 106.9 mhz; 6 kw. Ant 258 ft. TL: N30 55 58 W88 36 21. Box 827 (39452). (601) 947-8151. Licensee: Allen Broadcasting Co. ■ Herman Kelly, vp & gen mgr.

Lumberton

WLUN(FM)—Dec 10, 1983: 95.3 mhz; 3 kw. Ant 289 ft. TL: N30 54 42 W89 24 59 (CP: 100 kw, ant 981 ft.). Box 723 (39577). (601) 928-7281; (800) 228-8779. FAX: (601) 928-7281. Licensee: Community Broadcasting Inc. Net: SMN. Format: Country. ■ A. R. Byrd, pres; Sheree Byrd, gen mgr.

Magee

WKXI-FM—Apr 11, 1970: 107.5 mhz; 98 kw. Ant 952 ft. TL: N32 15 28 W89 47 22. Stereo. 222 Beasley Rd., Jackson (39206); Box 9446, Jackson (39286). (601) 957-1300. FAX: (601) 956-0516. Licensee: CSB Communications Inc. Rep: Republic. Format: Adult contemp. News staff one; news progmg 2 hrs wkly. Target aud: 25-54. ■ Craig Scott, pres; Kevin Webb, gen mgr; Becky Elkin, gen sls mgr; Stan Branson, progmg dir & mus dir; Rob Jay, news dir.

Marion

WZMP(FM)—Mar 15, 1987: 95.1 mhz; 50 kw. Ant 606 ft. TL: N32 26 08 W88 36 24. Stereo. Box 5353, Meridian (39302); 2711 7th St., Meridian (39301). (601) 693-4851. FAX: (601) 693-0808. Licensee: Major Broadcasting Inc. (acq 12-19-89; grpsl; FTR 1-8-90). Net: SMN. Rep: Banner, MidSouth. Format: Country. Target aud: 25-54. ■ Ken Rainey, gen mgr; Earl Snowden, chief engr.

Marks

WQMA(AM)—Dec 1, 1969: 1520 khz; 250 w-D. TL: N34 15 42 W90 17 18. Box 1595, Clarksdale (38614); W. Marks Rd. (38646). (601) 326-8642. FAX: (601) 326-5164. Licensee: CK Broadcasting Inc. (acq 11-5-92; FTR 11-30-92). Wash atty: Leibowitz & Spencer. Format: Blues. Spec prog: Farm 4 hrs, relg 4 hrs wkly. ■ Charles R. Kendall, pres & gen mgr; Forrest Parker, sls dir & prom mgr; James Figgs, news dir; Billy Pinkston, chief engr. ■ Rates: $10; 6; 6; na.

McComb

WAKH(FM)—Co-owned with WAKK(AM). Oct 15, 1978: 105.7 mhz; 100 kw. Ant 489 ft. TL: N31 16 50 W90 27 05. Stereo. Prog sep from AM. FAX: (601) 684-4564. Net: SMN. Format: Country. ■ Bill Rush, progmg dir & mus dir.

WAKK(AM)—April 25, 1975: 1140 khz; 1 kw-D. TL: N31 14 51 W90 25 14. Box 1649, 206 N. Front (39648). (601) 684-4116. FAX: (601) 684-4654. Licensee: San-Dow Broadcasting Inc. (acq 8-5-93; $600,000: FTR 8-23-93). Net: Unistar; Miss. Net. Format: Urban gold. News staff one; news progmg 5 hrs wkly. Target aud: General. ■ Morgan Dowdy, pres; Wayne Dowdy, exec vp; Robbie Hamilton, gen mgr; Eugene Sharkey, gen sls mgr; Warren Ellis, progmg dir; Virgil Conerly, mus dir; Bill Rush, news dir; Hazel Denard, pub affrs dir; Richard Watts, chief engr.

WAPF(AM)—Apr 18, 1948: 980 khz; 5 kw-D, 152 w-N. TL: N31 12 51 W90 27 42. Drawer 1649, 317 Canal St. (39648). (601) 684-7470. FAX: (601) 684-4654. Licensee: Dowdy Broadcasting Co. Inc. (acq 9-86; $600,000 with co-located FM; FTR 7-28-86). Net: NBC. Rep: Southern. Format: Relg, talk. Target aud: General. ■ Morgan Dowdy, pres & exec vp; Robbie Hamilton, gen mgr; Eugene Sharky, gen sls mgr; Joanne Reynolds, progmg dir & mus dir; Susan Dowdy, news dir; Richard Watts, chief engr.

WHNY(AM)—1939: 1250 khz; 5 kw-D, 1 kw-N, DA-N. TL: N31 16 07 W90 26 03. Drawer 1905, Hwy. 570 S. Curve Rd. (39648). (601) 684-8140. Licensee: Broadcast Services Inc. Group owner: Holt Broadcasting Service. Net: ABC/C. Rep: Media Sls South. Format: News/talk, sports. News staff one; news progmg 3 hrs wkly. Target aud: 18 plus; two pay check households plus farm community. ■ Charles W. Holt, pres; Edna Crittenden, gen mgr, gen sls mgr & adv mgr; Brenda Lee, prom mgr; Randy Bullock, progmg dir, mus dir & news dir. ■ Rates: $6.75; 5.30; 6.75; 5.

McLain

WXAB(FM)—Not on air, target date unknown: 96.9 mhz; 6 kw. Ant 328 ft. TL: N31 04 55 W88 43 52. c/o Box 723, Wiggins (39577). Licensee: Community Broadcasting Co. Inc.

Meridian

WALT(AM)—1946: 910 khz; 5 kw-D, 1 kw-N. TL: N32 23 37 W88 40 08. Stereo. Box 5797 (39302). (601) 693-2661. FAX: (601) 483-0826. Licensee: New South Communications Inc. Group owner: New South Communications Inc. (acq 4-1-57). Net: ABC/E. Rep: McGavren Guild. Format: Urban contemp. News staff one. Target aud: 18-49. ■ F.E. Holladay, pres; Steve Poston, progmg dir & mus dir; Sheila McClain, news dir.

WOKK(FM)—Co-owned with WALT(AM). August 1967: 97.1 mhz; 100 kw. Ant 600 ft. TL: N32 19 45 W88 41 26. Stereo. Prog sep from AM. Format: Country. Target aud: 25-54. ■ Van Mac, progmg dir & mus dir.

WJDQ(FM)—February 1968: 101.3 mhz; 99 kw. Ant 581 ft. TL: N32 18 43 W88 41 33. Stereo. 4307 Hwy. 39 N. (39301). (601) 693-2381. Licensee: Broadcasters and Publishers Inc. (group owner; acq 1970). Net: ABC/C. Format: Contemp hit. ■ Dean Pearce, gen mgr; Jay Randall, mus dir; Mike Pierce, news dir.

***WMAW-FM**—December 1983: 88.1 mhz; 100 kw. Ant 1,050 ft. TL: N32 08 18 W89 05 36. Stereo. Hrs opn: 24. 3825 Ridgewood Rd., Jackson (39211). (601) 982-6565. FAX: (601) 982-6746. Licensee: Mississippi Authority for Educational Television. Net: APR, NPR. Format: Class, news. News progmg 40 hrs wkly. Spec prog: Jazz 10 hrs, new age 10 hrs, folk 3 hrs, bluegrass 3 hrs wkly. ■ Larry Miller, pres; William Fulton, gen mgr; Bill Pharr, dev dir; Kevin Farrell, pub affrs dir; Martin Mangold, chief engr.

WMER(AM)—Oct 16, 1973: 1390 khz; 5 kw-D, 250 w-N. TL: N32 20 41 W88 41 32. Box 1414 (39302); 2424 15th St. (39301). (601) 693-1414. FAX: (601) 485-8844. Licensee: New Life Outreach Ministries Inc. (acq 4-20-92; $42,500; FTR 5-11-92). Net: USA. Format: Relg. News staff one; news progmg 3 hrs wkly. Target aud: 25-54; upscale, young families, non-working mothers. ■ Michael Warren, gen mgr; Barry Walters, chief engr.

WMGP(AM)—December 1957: 1450 khz; 1 kw-U. TL: N32 23 09 W88 41 36. Box 5353 (39302). (601) 693-4851. FAX: (601) 693-0808. Licensee: Major Broadcasting Inc. (acq 12-19-90; grpsl; FTR 1-8-90). Net: SMN. Rep: Banner, Midsouth. Format: Urban contemp, gospel. ■ Ken Rainey, pres & gen mgr; Jeff Van, progmg dir; Earl Snowden, chief engr.

WMOX(AM)—Dec 1, 1945: 1010 khz; 10 kw-D, 1 kw-N, DA-2. TL: N32 23 42 W88 39 28. Box 5184 (39301). (601) 693-1891. FAX: (601) 483-1010. Licensee: Magnolia State Broadcasting Inc. (acq 12-21-92; $65,000; FTR 1-25-93). Net: Unistar. Rep: Savalli. Format: Country classics, news/talk. ■ Terry Burton, pres; Eddie Smith, gen mgr & gen sls mgr; Noel Adcock, progmg dir & mus dir; Mike Pearce, news dir; Jim Johnson, chief engr.

WNBN(AM)—Nov 1, 1987: 1290 khz; 1 kw-D, 90 w-N. TL: N32 21 42 W88 37 26. Hrs opn: 13. 1290 Hawkins Crossing Rd. (39301). (601) 483-3401. Licensee: Frank Rackley Jr. Format: Gospel, relg, urban contemp. Target aud: 18-54. Spec prog: Black, women's, business, inspirational. ■ Frank Rackley Jr., gen mgr; Beverly Nelson, progmg dir & mus dir; Jerry Clayton, chief engr.

WOKK(FM)—Listing follows WALT(AM).

WTUX(FM)—Not on air, target date unknown: 102.1 mhz; 800 w. Ant 610 ft. TL: N32 21 51 W88 38 34. Box 2425, Columbus (39704). Licensee: East Mississippi Broadcasters Inc. (acq 2-26-93; $243,500; FTR 3-22-93).

Mississippi State

***WMAB-FM**—December 1983: 89.9 mhz; 63 kw. Ant 1,080 ft. TL: N33 21 07 W89 08 56. Stereo. Hrs opn: 24. 3825 Ridgewood Rd., Jackson (39211). (601) 982-6565. FAX: (601) 982-6746. Licensee: Mississippi Authority for Educational Television. Net: APR, NPR. Format: Class, news. News progmg 40 hrs wkly. Spec prog: Jazz 10 hrs, new age 10 hrs, folk 3 hrs, bluegrass 3 hrs. ■ Larry Miller, pres; William Fulton, gen mgr; Bill Pharr, dev dir; Alma Ellis, prom mgr; Kevin Farrell, pub affrs dir; Martin Mangold, chief engr.

Mississippi

Monticello

WMLC(AM)—1969: 1270 khz; 1 kw-D. TL: N31 33 24 W90 08 06. Hrs opn: 6 AM-6 PM. Box 949, Hwy. 84 W. (39654). (601) 587-7997. FAX: (601) 587-7743. Licensee: Clinco Inc. Net: USA. Format: Country, gospel. News staff one; news progmg 4 hrs wkly. Target aud: 18 plus; middle to upper income. Spec prog: Relg 20 hrs, sports talk 5 hrs wkly. ■ Dave Nichols II, pres & gen mgr; Donna Lynn, progmg dir; Romona Dickson, mus dir; Travis Thomas, news dir; Fritz Muffler, chief engr. ■ Rates: $7; 5; 7; na.

WRQO(FM)—Nov 19, 1990: 102.1 mhz; 50 kw. Ant 500 ft. TL: N31 36 13 W90 12 26. Stereo. Hrs opn: 5 AM-midnight. Box Q, Nola Rd. (39654); Box 1084 (39654). (601) 587-9363; (601) 587-7625. FAX: (601) 587-7625. Licensee: The O'Neal Broadcasting Corp. Net: NBC; Miss. Net. Wash atty: Booth, Freret & Imlay. Format: Traditional country. News progmg 15 hrs wkly. Target aud: 25-54. Spec prog: Farm one hr, relg 10 hrs wkly. ■ Marcus Rusty O'Neal, pres, gen mgr & chief engr; Chuck Ivey, gen sls mgr; Rick Stevens, progmg dir.

Morton

WQST(AM)—See Forest.

Moss Point

WGUD(AM)—Licensed to Moss Point. See Pascagoula-Moss Point.

WZBA(FM)—Licensed to Moss Point. See Pascagoula-Moss Point.

Natchez

KAIN(AM)—(Vidalia, La). 1985: 1040 khz; 1 kw-D. TL: N31 30 48 W91 24 02. Box 17833, Beltline Hwy., Natchez, MS (39122). (601) 446-8803. Licensee: Peter J. Rinaldi. Net: USA. Miss Net. Format: News/talk. News staff 3; news progmg 15 hrs wkly. Target aud: 25 plus. Spec prog: Black 2 hrs, farm 3 hrs wkly. ■ Peter Rinaldi, pres; Vanessa Cupit, gen sls mgr; Brian Scuilli, progmg dir; Alan Goodwin, news dir; Kelly Martello, pub affrs dir; Larry Boland, chief engr. ■ Rates: $13.50; 12.35; 13.50; 11.75.

WMIS(AM)—May 18, 1941: 1240 khz; 1 kw-U. TL: N31 31 14 W91 23 09. Box 1248 (39121). (601) 442-2522. FAX: (601) 446-9918. Licensee: Natchez Broadcasting Co. Net: NBC. Format: Black. News staff one. Target aud: General; Black. Spec prog: Farm 6 hrs wkly. ■ Diana Ewing Nutter, pres; James B. Nutter, vp; David Shaw, gen mgr; James H. Dulaney, gen sls mgr; Johnnie Butler, progmg dir; Calvin Butler, mus dir; Larry Bolland, chief engr.

WNAT(AM)—Dec 4, 1949: 1450 khz; 1 kw-U. TL: N31 33 24 W91 23 00. Stereo. Hrs opn: 24. Box 768, No. 2, O'Ferral St. (39121). (601) 442-4895. FAX: (601) 446-8260. Licensee: First Natchez Corp. (acq 11-28-58). Net: ABC/E, SMN; Miss. Net. Rep: Katz & Powell, MidSouth. Format: Oldies. News staff 2. Target aud: 25-54. Spec prog: Gospel 18 hrs wkly. ■ Marie Z. Perkins, pres; William S. Perkins, vp; Larry Griffth, gen mgr; Jeff Holt, gen sls mgr; Betsy Arnold, prom mgr; Bill Crews, progmg dir. ■ WNTZ-TV affil.

WQNZ(FM)—Co-owned with WNAT(AM). March 1, 1968: 95.1 mhz; 98 kw. Ant 1,056 ft. TL: N31 30 33 W91 24 19. Stereo. Hrs opn: 24. Prog sep from AM. (601) 445-9500. Net: ABC/E; Prog Farm. Format: Country. News staff 2; news progmg 7 hrs wkly. Target aud: 25 plus. ■ Greg Knippers, mus dir. ■ Rates: $22; 20; 22; 18.

WTRC-FM—Not on air, target date unknown: 97.3 mhz; 3 kw. Ant 328 ft. TL: N31 31 05 W91 19 04. Box 2057 (39121). (601) 446-9730. Licensee: James C. Williams (acq 8-31-92; $36,000; FTR 9-21-92). ■ Bill Crews, gen mgr.

WTYJ(FM)—See Fayette.

New Albany

WNAU(AM)—March 27, 1955: 1470 khz; 500 w-U, DA-N. TL: N34 29 48 W89 00 52. Box 808 (38652). (601) 534-8133. Licensee: MPM Investment Group (acq 5-20-93; $60,000; FTR 6-7-93). Net: Miss. Net. Rep: Torbet, Midsouth. Format: Relg. Target aud: 25-54. Spec prog: Gospel. ■ Marty Cook, pres; Scott Spencer, gen mgr; Terry Cook, progmg dir; Olen Booth, chief engr.

WWKZ(FM)—Sept 28, 1966: 103.5 mhz; 100 kw. Ant 1,004 ft. TL: N34 23 52 W88 53 03. Stereo. Box 320, 3200 W. Main (38801). (601) 844-2134; (601) 844-4487. FAX: (601) 844-2887. Licensee: Broadcasters & Publishers Inc. (group owner; acq 9-15-92; grpsl; FTR 10-19-92). Net: Unistar, ABC. Rep: Torbet. Format: CHR. News staff one. Target aud: 18-49. ■ Jeffrey H. Shaw, gen mgr; Jim MacDonald, progmg dir; Olen Booth, engrg mgr. ■ Rates: $36; 34; 36; 28.

WWZD(FM)—Mar 3, 1986: 106.7 mhz; 50 kw. Ant 499 ft. TL: N34 26 08 W88 57 35. Stereo. Hrs opn: 24. Box 3300, 2812A Cliff Gookin Blvd., Tupelo (38803). (601) 842-1067. FAX: (601) 842-0725. Licensee: Tupelo Broadcasting Co. Group owner: Charisma Communications Group (acq 6-88). Net: NBC. Wash atty: William D. Freedman. Format: Country. Target aud: 25-54. ■ Terry L. Barber, gen mgr; T.J. McKay, progmg dir; Mark Summer, mus dir; Olen Booth, chief engr.

Ocean Springs

WOSM(FM)—Feb 12, 1971: 103.1 mhz; 50 kw. Ant 459 ft. TL: N30 24 34 W88 42 23. Stereo. 4720 Radio Rd. (39564). (601) 875-9031. FAX: (601) 875-6461. Licensee: Charles H. Cooper. Net: AP. Format: Relg. News progmg 14 hrs wkly. Target aud: General; 18-54, family. ■ C. H. Cooper, gen mgr & chief engr; Margaret Cooper, progmg dir; Gary McDowell, mus dir.

WWXX(FM)—Not on air, target date unknown: 92.5 mhz; Box 6554, Gulfport (39506). Licensee: Golden Gulf Coast Broadcasting Inc.

Olive Branch

WRXQ(FM)—Not on air, target date unknown: 95.7 mhz; 6 kw. Ant 328 ft. TL: N35 01 25 W89 53 57. c/o WREC(AM) and WEGR(FM), 203 Beale St., Memphis, TN (38103). (901) 578-1160; (901) 578-1103. Licensee: Olive Branch Broadcasting Corp. (acq 10-11-91). ■ Sherri Sawyer, gen mgr.

Oxford

*WMAV-FM—December 1983: 90.3 mhz; 100 kw. Ant 1,240 ft. TL: N34 17 26 W89 42 24. Stereo. Hrs opn: 24. 3825 Ridgewood Rd., Jackson (39211). (601) 982-0500. Licensee: Mississippi Authority for Educational Television. Net: APR, NPR. Format: Class, news. Spec prog: Jazz 10 hrs, new age 10 hrs, folk 3 hrs, bluegrass 3 hrs wkly. ■ Larry Miller, pres; Martin Mangold, chief engr.

WOXD(FM)—October 1988: 95.5 mhz; 3 kw. Ant 328 ft. TL: N34 18 10 W89 31 25. Stereo. Hrs opn: 5 AM-midnight. 2211 S. Lamar (38655). (601) 234-9634; (601) 234-9631. Licensee: Amber Communications Corp. (acq 10-29-93; $250,000 FTR 11-15-93). Rep: Mid-South. Format: Oldies, classic rock. Target aud: 25-54. ■ Vytas J. Paskus, pres & gen mgr.

WQLJ(FM)—Dec 31, 1984: 93.7 mhz; 25 kw. Ant 328 ft. TL: N34 18 58 W89 30 19. Stereo. Hrs opn: 24. Drawer 1077 (38655); 307 S. Lamar (38655). (601) 234-5107. FAX: (601) 234-6230. Licensee: Oxford Radio Inc. Net: Unistar; Miss. Net. Wash atty: Fletcher, Heald & Hildreth. Format: Adult contemp. News progmg 5 hrs wkly. Target aud: 18-45. Spec prog: Contemp Christian 9 hrs wkly. ■ David Kellum, pres, gen sls mgr, progmg dir & mus dir; Jack Gadd, prom mgr & adv mgr; Gary Darby, news dir; Dennis White, chief engr. ■ Rates: $15.30; 15.30; 15.30; 15.30.

WSUH(AM)—May 1, 1955: 1420 khz; 1 kw-D, 80 w-N. TL: N34 21 43 W89 30 04. Box 1056, 2015 University Ave. (38655). (601) 234-6881. Licensee: SAN-DOW Broadcasting Co. (acq 5-10-85). Format: News/talk. Target aud: 30-54; upscale adults. ■ Sam Cousley, gen mgr; John T. Walker, progmg dir.

WWMS(FM)—Co-owned with WSUH(AM). Jan 1, 1969: 97.5 mhz; 100 kw. Ant 1,000 ft. TL: N34 10 05 W89 09 23. Stereo. Prog sep from AM. Format: Country. Spec prog: Farm 2 hrs wkly.

Pascagoula

WGUD-FM—Licensed to Pascagoula. See Pascagoula-Moss Point.

WKNN-FM—December 1964: 99.1 mhz; 100 kw. Ant 1,012 ft. TL: N30 29 09 W88 42 53. Stereo. Hrs opn: 24. Box 6699, Biloxi (39532). (601) 392-7100. FAX: (601) 392-9500. Licensee: Southern Star of Mississippi, Inc. Net: ABC/I. Rep: McGavren-Guild. Format: Today's hot new country. News staff 2; news progmg 6 hrs wkly. Target aud: 25-54. ■ Bob Long, pres; Reggie Bates, gen mgr; Jay Austin, gen sls mgr; Rick Mize, progmg dir; Angie Thompson, asst mus dir; Hans Atwood, chief engr.

Pascagoula-Moss Point

WGUD(AM)—(Moss Point). May 1, 1964: 1460 khz; 1 kw-D, 370 w-N. TL: N30 26 54 W88 33 05. Hrs opn: 24. 4519 Jefferson Ave., Moss Point (39563). (601) 475-2111. Licensee: WGUD Stereo Inc. (acq 2-15-81). Net: CNN, Miss. Net. Rep: Katz & Powell. Format: News, sports. News staff one. Target aud: 25-54. ■ Glen Murphey, pres & gen mgr; Phil Moss, progmg dir & news dir; J.W. Newman, chief engr. ■ Rates: $15; 10; 15; 8.

WGUD-FM—(Pascagoula). June 1, 1976: 105.9 mhz; 25 kw. Ant 312 ft. TL: N30 22 05 W88 44 35. Stereo. Hrs opn: 24. Prog sep from AM. Box 307, Pascagoula (39568). Net: Miss. Net. Format: C&W. ■ Rates: $27; 19; 21; 13.

WZBA(FM)—(Moss Point). June 1, 1964: 104.9 mhz; 33 kw. Ant 600 ft. TL: N30 34 08 W88 22 48. Stereo. Hrs opn: 24. 1073 Dawes Rd., Mobile, AL (36695). (205) 639-1000. FAX: (205) 639-8959. Licensee: Jackson County Broadcasting Inc. (acq 2-15-81). Net: ABC/R. Format: Country. Target aud: 18-40. ■ C. Wayne Dowdy, pres; Paul Schultz, gen mgr, progmg dir & mus dir.

WZZJ(AM)—September 1951: 1580 khz; 5 kw-D, 50 w-N, DA-2. TL: N30 23 01 W88 32 07. 5115 Telephone Rd., Pascagoula (39567). (601) 762-5683. FAX: (601) 762-3118. Licensee: Barkley Evangelistic Association Inc. (acq 1-14-91; FTR 1-28-91). Net: ABC/I. Rep: McGavren Guild. Wash atty: Walker, Bordelon, Hamlin, Theriat & Hardy. Format: Contemp Christian. News staff 2; news progmg 6 hrs wkly. Target aud: 25-54. Spec prog: Black 4 hrs, farm one hr, relg 2 hrs wkly. ■ Kevin Grady, pres; Jean Sisk, gen sls mgr; Craig Jerome, chief engr. ■ Rates: $46; 38; 38; 25.

Pearl

WJNT(AM)—Oct 28, 1980: 1180 khz; 50 kw-D, 5 kw-N, DA-N. TL: N32 17 43 W90 06 54. Stereo. Suite 212, 1985 Lakeland Dr., Jackson (39216). (601) 353-2724; (601) 366-1150. FAX: (601) 366-1627. Licensee: Buchanan Broadcasting Co. Inc. Net: ABC, CBS. Format: News/talk. ■ Bob Buchanan, pres; Thena Gunn, gen mgr; James Thom, progmg dir; John Friskillo, news dir; Stan Carter, chief engr.

WLUE(FM)—Not on air, target date unknown: 93.9 mhz; 6 kw. Ant 328 ft. TL: N32 17 52 W89 59 56. 1006 Adkins Blvd., Jackson (39211). Licensee: Bobbye Imbragulio.

Petal

WMFM(FM)—January 1986: 106.3 mhz; 3 kw. Ant 400 ft. TL: N31 23 02 W89 10 44. Stereo. Hrs opn: 24. Box 16928, Hattiesburg (39404-6928); 2571 Old Richton Rd., Petal (39465). (601) 545-1063. Licensee: Hickman Broadcast Services Inc. Net: CNN. Wash atty: Lawrence Bernard Jr. Format: Lite adult contemp. News progmg 4 hrs wkly. Target aud: 25-54; upscale, educated and professional. Spec prog: Sports 3 hrs wkly. ■ Bill Hickman, CEO, pres & pub affrs dir; Yancey Sanford, opns dir, progmg dir & mus dir; Todd Adams, prom dir; Larry Morgan, chief engr. ■ Rates: $12; 12; 12; 12.

Philadelphia

WHOC(AM)—July 31, 1948: 1490 khz; 1 kw-U. TL: N32 45 52 W89 07 48. Box 26, 1016 W. Beacon St. (39350). (601) 656-1490. FAX: (601) 656-1458. Licensee: WHOC Inc. (acq 1-31-89; $300,000; FTR 2-20-89). Net: Unistar; Miss. Net. Format: Country. News progmg 12 hrs wkly. Target aud: General. Spec prog: Farm 2 hrs wkly. ■ Leah Jarrell, pres & gen mgr; Joe Vines, gen sls mgr & prom mgr; Benjie Coats, progmg dir; Benji Coats, mus dir; Rex Smith, chief engr.

WWSL(FM)—Co-owned with WHOC(AM). Jan 1, 1981: 102.3 mhz; 3 kw. Ant 200 ft. TL: N32 45 52 W89 07 48 (CP: 5.2 kw, ant 131 ft.). Stereo. (601) 656-7102. Licensee: H&GC Inc. Net: NBC, Westwood One; Miss. Net. Format: Oldies. ■ Laura Thrash, pres & gen mgr.

Picayune

WRJW(AM)—October 1949: 1320 khz; 5 kw-D, 75 kw-N. TL: N30 31 06 W89 38 41. Hrs opn: 16. Box 907, 2438 Hwy. 43 S. (39466). (601) 798-4835; (601) 799-1900. FAX: (601) 798-9755. Licensee: Pearl Rivers Communications Inc. (acq 8-2-91). Net: AP; Miss. Net. Format: Country. News staff 2; news progmg 10 hrs wkly. Target aud: 18-54; contemporary male & female country listeners. Spec prog: Black 8 hrs, farm 6 hrs, relg 16 hrs, sports 4 hrs wkly. ■ John Pigott, pres, dev dir & prom dir; Dot Pigott, vp, gen mgr & mktg dir; Delores Wood, stn mgr, opns dir, gen sls mgr, adv mgr & progmg dir; Sam Adkins, news dir; Denise Wood, pub affrs dir; Danny Miller, chief engr. ■ Rates: $12; 10; 12; 8.

WZRH(FM)—November 1973: 106.1 mhz; 50 kw. Ant 492 ft. TL: N30 31 06 W89 38 41. Stereo. Hrs opn: 24. 1601 Shortcut, Slidell, LA (70458). Licensee: Howes Broadcasting Inc. Rep: Katz & Powell. Format: Contemp hit, new age, modern rock. Target aud: 18-34; young professionals. ■ Dr. Randolph Howes, CEO; Art Roberts, gen mgr & sls dir; David Corso, rgnl sls mgr; Rebecca Young, prom dir; Kenny Vest, progmg dir; Christian Unruh, mus dir; Oscar Talbot, chief engr.

Pontotoc

WSEL(AM)—Nov 30, 1962: 1440 khz; 890 w-D, DA. TL: N34 15 10 W88 57 36. Stereo. Box 330 (38863). (601) 489-0297. Licensee: Ollie Collins Jr. (acq 5-5-92; $46,500 with co-located FM; FTR 6-1-92). ■ John Barnes, gen mgr.

WSEL-FM—Jan 1, 1966: 96.7 mhz; 3 kw. Ant 299 ft. TL: N34 15 10 W88 57 36. Stereo. Prog sep from AM. ■ Ollie Collins Jr., gen mgr.

Poplarville

WRPM(AM)—1963: 1530 khz; 10 kw-D, 1 kw-CH. TL: N30 48 55 W89 30 24. Hrs opn: 6 AM-6 PM. Box 352, Progress Rd. (39470). (601) 795-4900. FAX: (601) 795-4900. Licensee: Charles W. and J. Morgan Dowdy (acq 3-87; $2.25 million; with co-located FM; FTR 12-15-86). Net: ABC. Format: Country. Target aud: 22-54. ■ Bruce Dunn, gen mgr & gen sls mgr; Jean Dunn, stn mgr, prom dir, progmg dir & mus dir; Jason Kaufman, news dir & pub affrs dir; Dominic Mitchum, chief engr.

WZKX(FM)—Co-owned with WRPM(AM). Feb 14, 1966: 107.9 mhz; 92 kw. Ant 1,460 ft. TL: N30 44 48 W89 03 30. Box 2639, Gulfport (39503). (601) 832-5111. Format: CHR. ■ Morgan Dowdy, gen mgr; Steve Spillman, progmg dir.

Port Gibson

WKPG(AM)—November 1976: 1320 khz; 500 w-D. TL: N31 59 43 W91 00 52. Suite 14, 615 Market St. (39150). (601) 437-8413. Licensee: Evan Doss Jr. Corp. (acq 5-23-91; $25,000; FTR 6-10-91). Format: Gospel, oldies, blues. ■ Jerome Myles, gen mgr, gen sls mgr, progmg mgr & mus mgr; Emette Rushing, chief engr.

Prentiss

WJDR(FM)—June 1, 1982: 98.3 mhz; 6 kw. Ant 325 ft. TL: N31 29 43 W89 53 33. Stereo. Hrs opn: 4:30 AM-midnight. Box 351, Columbia (39429); 37 S. High School Ave. (39474). (601) 731-2298; (601) 792-2056. Licensee: Sunbelt Broadcasting Corp. (acq 12-1-85). Net: Unistar; Miss Net. Format: Country. News progmg 20 hrs wkly. Target aud: 25-54. Spec prog: Black 5 hrs wkly. ■ Thomas F. McDaniel, pres; Rob Schepers, stn mgr; Jack Boone, chief engr. ■ Rates: $6; 5; 5; 4.

Quitman

WBFN(AM)—Feb 2, 1968: 1500 khz; 1 kw-D. TL: N32 03 51 W88 43 29. Drawer 70 (39355). (601) 776-2931. Licensee: Quitman Broadcasting Co. (acq 5-2-83; $215,000 with co-located FM; FTR 5-23-83). Net: SMN. Rep: Keystone (unwired net). Format: C&W. Spec prog: Farm 2 hrs wkly. ■ Herman Kelly, pres; Terry Bonner, gen mgr, gen sls mgr & news mgr; Mike Fairchild, progmg dir; Jeff Corkran, chief engr.

WYKK(FM)—Co-owned with WBFN(AM). July 31, 1981: 98.9 mhz; 3 kw. Ant 295 ft. TL: N32 03 51 W88 43 29. Stereo. Dups AM 100%. ■ Rates: Same as AM.

Richland

WRBR(AM)—Not on air, target date unknown: 720 khz; 5 kw-D. TL: N32 18 48 W90 06 37. 949 Poleman Rd., Shreveport, LA (71107). (318) 424-4879. Licensee: Richland Broadcasting Co.

Richton

WESV(FM)—Not on air, target date unknown: 96.5 mhz; 6 kw. Ant 328 ft. TL: N31 21 01 W88 59 11. Box 9, Wiggins (39577). (601) 928-7281. Licensee: Vivian Inc. (acq 5-4-93; FTR 5-24-93). ■ A. R. Byrd, pres.

Ridgeland

WLRM(AM)—Dec 1, 1984: 780 khz; 5 kw-D. TL: N32 25 36 W90 12 19. Suite C, 102 Business Park Dr., Jackson (39213). (601) 956-0102. FAX: (601) 978-3980. Licen-

see: Exchequer Communications Inc. (acq 3-86; grpsl; FTR 11-25-85). Rep: Rgnl Reps. Format: Motivational. News staff 10 Target aud: Adult professionals. ■ Marshall Magee, gen mgr; Joe Bennett, opns mgr & progmg mgr.

Ripley

WCSA(AM)—Not on air, target date unknown: 1260 khz; 500 w-D. 10569 Collierville Rd., Collierville, TN (38017). (901) 853-8401. Licensee: Jesse R. Williams dba Tippah Broadcasting Co.

WKZU(FM)—June 1, 1979: 102.3 mhz; 3 kw. Ant 300 ft. TL: N34 42 05 W88 50 36. Stereo. Stn currently dark. 107 E. Spring St. (38663). (601) 837-1023. Licensee: Holliday Creations Inc. (acq 3-31-93; $131,010; FTR 4-19-93). Format: C&W. ■ Harry R. Holliday, gen mgr.

Rosedale

WMJW(FM)—Not on air, target date unknown: 107.5 mhz; 25 kw. Ant 328 ft. TL: N33 43 36 W90 43 53. Stereo. Box 73, Batesville (38606). (601) 563-4664. FAX: (601) 563-9002. Licensee: Carol B. Ingram. Net: ABC/E. Wash atty: Booth & Freret. Format: Contemporary hit. News progmg 8 hrs wkly. Target aud: 35 plus. ■ Carol B. Ingram, pres; J. Boyd Ingram, chief engr. ■ Rates: $8; 8; 8; 8.

Senatobia

***WKNA(FM)**—Jan 4, 1971: 88.9 mhz; 20 kw. Ant 405 ft. TL: N34 38 54 W90 01 21. Stereo. Hrs opn: 24. Rebroadcasts WKNO(FM) Memphis, 50%. Box 241880, Memphis, TN (38124); 900 Getwell Rd., Memphis, TN (38111). (901) 458-2521. FAX: (901) 458-2221. Licensee: Mid-South Public Communications Foundation. Net: APR, NPR. Wash atty: Schwartz, Woods & Miller. Format: Class, news. News staff one; news progmg 58 hrs wkly. Target aud: 35 plus. ■ Michael LaBonia, pres; Dan Campbell, gen mgr; Darel Snodgrass, opns mgr & progmg mgr; Charles McLarty, dev dir; Becky Kelly, dev mgr; Jim Eikner, gen sls mgr; Joel Hurd, prom mgr; Everette Rice, news dir; Russ Abernathy, engrg dir; Pat Lane, chief engr. ■ *WKNO-TV affil.

WSAO(AM)—Aug 8, 1962: 1140 khz; 5 kw-D. TL: N34 36 56 W89 56 09. Hrs opn: 5 AM-5 PM. Rt. 3, Box 29-X (38668). (601) 562-4445. Licensee: Christian Impact Inc. (acq 5-86; $135,000; FTR 4-21-86). Net: CBN; Miss. Net. Format: Christian, gospel, country, Black. News staff one. Target aud: General. ■ William Ray Ingram, pres & gen mgr; Jesse Ross, stn mgr; Kirk Harnack, chief engr.

Southaven

WAVN(AM)—June 4, 1990: 1240 khz; 580 w-U. TL: N34 58 57 W90 00 45. Hrs opn: 19. 1336 Brookhaven Dr. (38671); Rt. 6, Box 250, Byhalia (38611). (601) 393-8027; (601) 393-8056. FAX: (601) 393-8066. Licensee: Arlington Broadcasting Corp. Inc. (acq 8-31-92; $115,000; FTR 9-21-92). Net: Miss. Net. Format: Southern gospel. News progmg 7 hrs wkly. Target aud: General; 20-50. ■ Fred Flinn, pres & gen mgr; Rich Stewart, progmg dir; Rob Herring, chief engr. ■ Rates: $10; 10; 8; 5.

Starkville

WKOR(AM)—July 5, 1968: 980 khz; 1 kw-D. TL: N33 28 44 W88 44 40. Box 980 (39759). (601) 323-4980; (601) 327-1183. FAX: (601) 324-1170. Licensee: Charisma Broadcasting Co. Group owner: Charisma Communications Group (acq 6-7-77). Net: ABC/E. Rep: MidSouth, Southern. Format: CHR, news/talk. News staff one; news progmg 4 hrs wkly. Target aud: Adults; business professionals. Spec prog: Farm one hr, Black 20 hrs, gospel 6 hrs wkly. ■ Terry Barber, CEO; Joey C. McDonald, gen mgr; Jim Scott, prom mgr & vp progmg; Olen Booth, chief engr. ■ Rates: $16; 14; 16; 8.

WMSU(FM)—Co-owned with WKOR(AM). Sept 13, 1979: 92.1 mhz; 1.1 kw. Ant 500 ft. TL: N33 25 49 W88 45 17. Stereo. Dups AM 16%. 201 Lampkin St. (39759). Format: Country. Target aud: 25-54. ■ Terry Barber, pres. ■ Rates: $26; 24; 26; 18.

WLZA(FM)—(Eupora). Sept 1, 1978: 96.1 mhz; 50 kw. Ant 500 ft. TL: N33 28 18 W 89 13 36. Stereo. Hrs opn: 24. Box 844, Starkville (39759). (601) 324-9601. Licensee: Tri-county Broadcasting Company Inc. Group owner: Air South Radio Inc. Format: Adult contemp. ■ Olvie E. Sisk, pres; Harry E. Jackson, gen mgr; Karen Jackson, gen sls mgr; Joey Traywick, progmg mgr; John Brackston, mus dir. ■ Rates: $8; 8; 8; 8.

WMSU(FM)—Listing follows WKOR(AM).

***WMSV(FM)**—Not on air, target date unknown: 91.1 mhz; 14.1 kw. Ant 449 ft. Box 6101, WMSU-FM, Mississippi State (39762). Licensee: Mississippi State University.

WMXU(FM)—Listing follows WSSO(AM).

WSSO(AM)—Nov 8, 1948: 1230 khz; 1 kw-U. TL: N33 27 09 W88 49 15. 608 Yellowjacket Dr. (39759). (601) 323-1230. FAX: (601) 323-0573. Licensee: Starkville Broadcasting Co. Net: NBC; Miss. Net. Rep: Keystone (unwired net), Beaver. Format: Adult contemp. Spec prog: Black 12 hrs wkly. ■ Joe Phillips, pres; Rob Brown, progmg dir; Houston McDavitt, chief engr.

WMXU(FM)—Co-owned with WSSO(AM). July 15, 1968: 106.1 mhz; 3 kw. Ant 220 ft. TL: N33 17 38 W88 39 27. Stereo. Prog sep from AM. Format: Classic rock gold. ■ Terry O'Neil, progmg dir.

State College

WUMI(FM)—Not on air, target date unknown: 104.3 mhz; 3 kw. Ant 328 ft. TL: N33 27 07 W88 46 00. 3502 Spyglass Ct. Augusta, GA (30907). Licensee: PDB Corp., State College (acq 4-29-91; $4,000; FTR 5-20-91).

Taylorsville

WBBN(FM)—Mar 20, 1985: 95.9 mhz; 31 kw. Ant 625 ft. TL: N31 37 59 W89 28 40. Stereo. Rt. 2, Box 273B (39168). (601) 729-8100. FAX: (601) 729-8199. Licensee: Blakeney Communications Inc. Net: ABC/I. Format: Country. News staff one. Target aud: 25-54. ■ Larry Blakeney, pres, progmg dir & mus dir; Randall A. Blakeney, vp, gen mgr & chief engr; Debbie Blakeney, gen sls mgr; Malia Tucker, prom mgr; Craig Ford, news dir. ■ Rates: $36; 34; 36; 32.

Tupelo

***WAFR(FM)**—Aug 31, 1991: 88.3 mhz; 50 kw. Ant 492 ft. TL: N34 28 28 W88 43 41. Stereo. Hrs opn: 24. 107 Parkgate Dr. (38801); Box 3206 (38802). (601) 844-8888; (800) 844-4226. FAX: (601) 844-4176. Licensee: American Family Association. Net: USA. Format: Christian. News staff one; news progmg 3 hrs wkly. Target aud: 30-60; conservative Christian.

WELO(AM)—May 15, 1944: 580 khz; 1 kw-D, 500 w-N, DA-2. TL: N34 18 10 W88 42 17. Hrs opn: 24. Box 410 (38802); Hwy. 145 N. (38801). (601) 842-7658. FAX: (601) 842-0197. Licensee: Phoenix of Tupelo Inc. Group owner: Phoenix Communications Inc. (acq 8-15-89; $1,100,000 with co-located FM; FTR 6-26-89). Net: ABC/I; Miss. Net. Rep: Rgnl Reps. Format: Oldies, talk. News staff 2; news progmg 10 hrs wkly. Spec prog: Farm one hr wkly. ■ Sam Howard, pres; Jim Duke, opns mgr, progmg dir & news dir; Leslie Nabors, gen sls mgr; Tom Scott, chief engr.

WZLQ(FM)—Co-owned with WELO(AM). September 1968: 98.5 mhz; 100 kw-H. Ant 381 ft. TL: N34 18 09 W88 42 21 (CP: 100 kw, ant 991 ft., TL: N34 23 52 W88 53 03). Stereo. Prog sep from AM. Net: ABC/C. Format: Classic rock/AOR. Target aud: 18-49; baby boomers.

WFTA(FM)—(Fulton). Aug 19, 1976: 101.9 mhz; 100 kw. Ant 560 ft. TL: N34 15 46 W88 32 24. Stereo. Box 422, 855 Cliff Gookin Blvd., Tupelo (38801). (601) 842-7625; (601) 862-3191. FAX: (601) 862-2233. Licensee: Air South Radio Inc. (group owner). Format: Adult Contemp. News progmg 4 hrs wkly. Target aud 14-44. ■ Gene Sisk, pres & gen mgr; K.I. Sisk, gen sls mgr & prom mgr; Alan Potts, progmg dir; Fred Blalock, news dir; Billie J. Crabb, engrg dir; Olvie E. Sisk, chief engr.

WPMX(AM)—Aug 25, 1972: 1060 khz; 1 kw-D, 33 w-N, DA-1. TL: N34 14 18 W88 41 50. Hrs opn: 18. Box 980, Starkville (39759). (601) 842-1067. FAX: (601) 842-0725. Licensee: Tupelo Broadcasting Co. Group owner: Charisma Communications Group (acq 8-89; $72,000; FTR 8-21-89). Net: NBC. Wash atty: William D. Freedman. Format: Urban contemp. Target aud: General. Spec prog: Relg 12 hrs, blues 6 hrs wkly. ■ Terry L. Barber, gen mgr; Olen Booth, chief engr. ■ Rates: $9; 9; 9; 9.

WTUP(AM)—October 1953: 1490 khz; 1 kw-U. TL: N34 15 19 W88 41 46. Stereo. Hrs opn: 24. Box 3300, 2812 Cliff Gookin Blvd. (38803). (601) 842-1067. FAX: (601) 842-0725. Licensee: Tupelo Broadcasting Co. (acq 12-14-92; $250,000 with WESE(FM) Baldwyn; FTR 1-11-93). Net: SMN. Wash atty: Gurman, Kurtis, Blask & Freedman. Format: Big Band. News staff one; news progmg 12 hrs wkly. Target aud: 35 plus; older married couples. ■ Terry L. Barber, vp & gen mgr; Rusty Pugh, opns dir & progmg dir; Margaret Cooper, news dir; Olen Booth, chief engr.

Missouri   Directory of Radio

WZLQ(FM)—Listing follows WELO(AM).

Tylertown

WTYL(AM)—Feb 8, 1969: 1290 khz; 1 kw-D. TL: N31 07 50 W90 08 13. 930 Union Rd. (39667). (601) 876-2105. Licensee: Tylertown Broadcasting Co. Format: Country. Spec prog: Farm 6 hrs wkly. ■ Caroline Dylan, pres & gen mgr; Gail Ratcliff, progmg dir.

WTYL-FM—Apr 9, 1970: 97.7 mhz; 3 kw. Ant 145 ft. TL: N31 07 50 W90 08 13. Dups AM 90%.

University

WUMS(FM)—Apr 10, 1989: 92.1 mhz; 6 kw. Ant 328 ft. TL: N34 21 29 W89 32 30. Stereo. Farley Hall, Student Media Ctr. (38677). (601) 232-5395. FAX: (601) 232-5703. Licensee: Student Media Ctr. of the Univ. of Mississippi. Net: Westwood One. Format: AOR, college alternative. News staff 4; news progmg 2 hrs wkly. Target aud: 18-25; the college age students of the Oxford/Ole Miss area. Spec prog: Jazz 2 hrs, reggae one hr, classic oldies 2 hrs wkly. ■ S. Gale Denley, pres; Ashley Anderson, stn mgr; Melanie Wadkins, prom mgr; Corbin Daily, mus dir; Jerry Strickland, news dir; Jerry Campbell, chief engr.

Utica

WJXN-FM—Aug 28, 1990: 92.9 mhz; 6 kw. Ant 465 ft. TL: N32 06 09 W90 29 56. Stereo. Hrs opn: 5 AM-midnight. Box 24387, Jackson (39225,). 916 Foley St., Jackson (39202). (601) 355-2518. FAX: (601) 944-1450. Licensee: St. Pe Broadcasting Inc. (group owner; acq 1-11-90; $8,450; FTR 2-5-90). Net: USA, CBN. Format: Gospel. Target aud: 25 plus. ■ Bishop L.E. Willis, pres; Celestine Willis, stn mgr; Eric Sharpe, progmg dir; Tarra Haskin Gilbert, news dir. ■ Rates: $10; 10; 10; 10.

Vicksburg

WBBV(FM)—Aug 21, 1989: 101.1 mhz; 1.35 kw. Ant 259 ft. TL: N32 21 34 W90 50 80. Stereo. 899 Hwy. 61 N. (39180). (601) 638-0101. Licensee: Bishop Broadcasting Inc. Net: Unistar; Miss. Net. Format: Country. News progmg 16 hrs wkly. Target aud: 24-54. ■ Bob Bishop, pres, gen mgr & gen sls mgr; Ron Anderson, progmg dir, mus dir & news dir; Doug Wilson, chief engr. ■ Rates: $16; 16; 16; 16.

WIIN(FM)—Mar 19, 1966: 98.7 mhz; 100 kw. Ant 950 ft. TL: N32 12 29 W90 24 50. Stereo. Hrs opn: 24. Bldg. D, 1855 Lakeland Dr., Jackson (39216). (601) 362-9898. FAX: (601) 366-3698. Licensee: MS TV & Radio Inc. (acq 1-89; $1.1 million; FTR 1-23-89). Format: Country. Target aud: 25-54; upper-income and educ, even split male/female. ■ Russel Chambers, pres; Ken Paul, gen mgr; Len Hart, gen sls mgr; Mark Peeples, progmg dir; Lee Davis, mus dir; Emmette Rushing, chief engr.

WQBC(AM)—1931: 1420 khz; 5 kw-D, 500 w-N. TL: N32 19 56 W90 51 00. 3190 Porter's Chapel Rd. (39180). (601) 636-1108. FAX: (601) 636-7386. Licensee: Sharing Inc. (acq 10-87; $200,000; FTR 10-19-87). Format: News/talk. ■ Tommy Johnson, pres; Everett Stroop, vp & gen mgr; Gene Underwood, gen sls mgr; Bonnie Johnson, progmg dir & news dir; Emmette Rushing, chief engr.

WSTZ-FM—Licensed to Vicksburg. See Jackson.

WVIX(AM)—1948: 1490 khz; 1 kw-U. TL: N32 21 27 W90 51 29. 1501 Clay St. (39180). (601) 638-2049. FAX: (601) 638-2074. Licensee: John Henry Pembroke (acq 5-17-89; $100,000; FTR 6-12-89). Format: Hit kicking country.■ John Paul Douglas, gen mgr & chief engr; Kitty Carlson, stn mgr & gen sls mgr; "Cowboy" Otis Boozard, progmg dir.

Walnut

WLRC(AM)—June 21, 1982: 850 khz; 963 w-D. TL: N34 56 46 W88 52 44. Box 37 (38683). (601) 223-4071. Licensee: B.R. & Martha S. Clayton (acq 11-83; $100,000; FTR 11-28-83). Net: Unistar; Miss. Net. Rep: Midsouth. Format: Christian. ■ Scotti Clayton, gen mgr & progmg dir; Donnie Sipes, sls dir; Robin Clayton, mus dir; Carl Sampieri, chief engr. ■ Rates: $6; 6; 6; 6.

Water Valley

WYCG(FM)—Not on air, target date unknown: 105.5 mhz; 6 kw. Ant 247 ft. Box 9, Charleston (38921). Licensee: Bobby B. Anderson.

Waynesboro

WABO(AM)—Sept 11, 1954: 990 khz; 1 kw-D. TL: N31 40 48 W88 40 34. Box 507, 6746 Hwy. 84 W. (39367). (601) 735-4331. Licensee: Martin Broadcasting Inc. (acq 12-18-61). Net: ABC/I. Rep: Spot Sls. Format: Country, soul. ■ Nancy N. Martin, pres, gen mgr & news dir; Will Martin, prom mgr & mus dir; Marvin Longmire, progmg dir; Jeff Ketler, chief engr.

WABO-FM—June 13, 1973: 105.5 mhz; 3 kw. Ant 145 ft. TL: N31 40 48 W88 40 34. Stereo. Dups AM 50%. Format: Hot country.

Wesson

***WCLL-FM**—Oct 26, 1983: 90.7 mhz; 100 w. Ant 177 ft. TL: N31 41 28 W90 24 03. Hrs opn: Noon-midnight. Box 649, Sandifer Communications Bldg., Old Wesson Rd. (39191-0649). (601) 643-8384. FAX: (601) 643-2366. Licensee: Copiah-Lincoln Community College. Format: Adult contemp, educ. Target aud: 17-30; college students. ■ Burlian O. Walker, stn mgr; Lester Tarbutton, chief engr.

West Point

WROB(AM)—September 1947: 1450 khz; 1 kw-U. TL: N33 36 30 W88 39 15. Box 1336, 413 Forest (39773). (601) 494-1450. FAX: (601) 494-9762. Licensee: Bob McRaney Enterprises Inc. (group owner). Net: Miss. Net. Rep: Midsouth. Format: Top-40, Black. News progmg 10 hrs wkly. Target aud: General. Spec prog: Gospel 2 hrs wkly. ■ Bob McRaney Jr., pres, gen mgr, gen sls mgr, prom mgr & news dir; Ken Ramsey, progmg dir & mus dir; Jack King, chief engr.

WKBB(FM)—Co-owned with WROB(AM). April 14, 1974: 100.9 mhz; 3 kw. Ant 170 ft. TL: N33 36 30 W88 39 15. Stereo. Prog sep from AM. Net: Unistar. Format: Btfl mus. Target aud: 35-54. ■ Ken Ramsey, opns mgr; Samantha McRaney, sls dir. ■ Rates: $6.50; 6; 6; 6.

Wiggins

WIGG(AM)—February 1968: 1420 khz; 5 kw-D. TL: N30 52 18 W89 09 00. Box 723 (39577). (601) 928-7281. FAX: (601) 928-7281. Licensee: Community Broadcasting Co. Inc. Net: UPI; Miss. Net. Format: C&W. Spec prog: Farm 5 hrs wkly. ■ A.R. Byrd, pres & gen sls mgr; Tony Cospelich, gen mgr; Sheree Cospelich, opns dir; Paul Turner, chief engr.

WUSD(FM)—Not on air, target date unknown: 97.9 mhz; 3 kw. 210 Barronne St., New Orleans, LA (70112). Licensee: White Broadcasting Co.

Winona

WONA(AM)—Oct 25, 1958: 1570 khz; 1 kw-D. TL: N33 27 52 W89 44 11. Box 746 (38967). (601) 283-1570. FAX: (601) 283-1571. Licensee: Southern Electronics Co. Format: C&W, contemp. ■ Robert Evans Sr., pres; Johnny Pettit, vp, gen mgr & stn mgr; Sandra Pettit, gen sls mgr; J.P. Bowles, chief engr.

WONA-FM—Jan 4, 1976: 96.7 mhz; 3 kw. Ant 328 ft. TL: N33 29 34 W89 45 17. Stereo. Dups AM 100%.

Woodville

WLGG(FM)—Not on air, target date unknown: 95.9 mhz; 3 kw. Ant 328 ft. TL: N31 07 13 W91 20 32. 623 N. West Ave., McComb (39648). Licensee: PDB Broadcasting Co.

Yazoo City

WAZF(AM)—July 7, 1947: 1230 khz; 1 kw-U. TL: N32 51 58 W90 23 26 (CP: TL: N32 52 00 W90 23 28). Box 47 (39194). (601) 746-7735. Licensee: Sides, Robinson, Edwards Inc. (acq 4-29-93; $11,000; FTR 5-17-93). Net: Unistar, Miss. Net. Rep: Midsouth. Format: Black, oldies. News staff 2. Target aud: 35-55. ■ Dennis Littleton, gen mgr, prom mgr, progmg dir & news dir; Sue Dixon, gen sls mgr.

WJNS-FM—Dec 13, 1968: 92.1 mhz; 20 kw. Ant 300 ft. TL: N32 50 48 W90 23 18. Stereo. Box 24387, Jackson (39205). (601) 355-2518; (601) 746-5921. FAX: (601) 948-6052. Licensee: St. Pe Broadcasting Inc. (group owner; acq 6-3-88; $312,500; FTR 6-20-88). Net: CNN. Format: Relg. News staff one; news progmg 24 hrs wkly. Target aud: 25-54. Spec prog: Farm 16 hrs, weather 16 hrs wkly. ■ Edward St. Pe', pres; Celeste Willis, gen mgr; Phil Scott, chief engr. ■ Rates: $7; 7; 7; 7.

Missouri

LAUREN A. COLBY
301-663-1086
COMMUNICATIONS ATTORNEY
Special Attention to
Difficult Cases

Albany

KAAN-FM—See Bethany.

Arnold

***KCWA-FM**—Mar 26, 1987: 89.9 mhz; 150 w-H, 84 w-V. Ant 105 ft. TL: N38 26 35 W90 24 00. 1770 Missouri State Rd. (63010). (314) 296-0400. FAX: (314) 287-3181. Licensee: Arnold Educational Broadcasting Foundation. Format: Relg. ■ Kenneth Brown, pres; Darrell Deakins, gen mgr; Debbie Reed, stn mgr.

Asbury

KWXD(FM)—Not on air, target date unknown: 103.5 mhz; 3.8 kw. Ant 413 ft. TL: N37 14 24 W94 30 22. c/o 1612 Woodland Terrance, Pittsburg, KS (66762). Licensee: William Bruce Wachter.

Ash Grove

KZPD(FM)—Not on air, target date unknown: 104.1 mhz; 3 kw. Ant 194 ft. TL: N37 15 05 W93 41 12. 491 W. 3300 N., Vernal, UT (84078). Licensee: Ashgrove Inc.

Ashland

KBXR(FM)—Not on air, target date unknown: 106.1 mhz; 50 kw. Ant 492 ft. TL: N38 46 29 W92 33 22. 303 Elm Ave., Takoma Park, MD (20912). Licensee: Sobocomo Radio Inc.

Aurora

KGMY-FM—Feb 19, 1968: 100.5 mhz; 33 kw. Ant 600 ft. TL: N37 05 39 W93 31 05. Stereo. 840 S. Glenstone, Springfield (65802). (417) 869-1059. FAX: (417) 869-1000. Licensee: Aurora Broadcasting Inc. Format: Country.

KSWM(AM)—Oct 19, 1961: 940 khz; 1 kw-U. TL: N36 59 39 W93 42 58. 126 S. Jefferson (65605). (417) 678-0416. Licensee: Galen O. Gilbert. Group owner: Community Service Radio Group (acq 12-24-90; FTR 1-14-91). Net: Missourinet. Wash atty: Fletcher, Heald & Hildreth. Format: Country. News progmg 21 hrs wkly. Target aud: General; full service. ■ Galen O. Gilbert, pres; Jesse Gilbert, vp; Art Morris, stn mgr & opns mgr. ■ Rates: $12; 10; 8; 5.

Ava

KKOZ(AM)—1968: 1430 khz; 500 w-U. TL: N36 55 48 W92 39 19. Box 386 (65608). (417) 683-4193. Licensee: KKOZ Inc. (acq 12-83; $130,000; FTR 12-19-83). Net: ABC; Missourinet. Format: News/talk, farm, spec events. News progmg 15 hrs wkly. Target aud: 45 plus; farm orientated. ■ Joe Corum, pres, gen mgr & gen sls mgr; Art Corum, prom mgr, progmg dir, mus dir & news dir; Bob Woods, Joe Corum, chiefs engr. ■ Rates: $10.50; 10.50; 10.50; na.

KKOZ-FM—1990: 92.3 mhz; 6 kw. Ant 381 ft. TL: N36 55 48 W92 39 19. Licensee: Corum Industries Inc.

Ballwin

***KYMC(FM)**—February 1978: 89.7 mhz; 120 w-H. Ant 154 ft. TL: N38 37 15 W90 31 49 (CP: 120 w, ant 171 ft., TL: N38 37 23 W90 32 01). Stereo. Hrs opn: 24. Box 4038, 16464 Burkhardt Pl., Chesterfield (63006). (314) 530-0981. (314) 532-3100. Licensee: YMCA of Greater St. Louis-W. County Branch. Format: New music, progsv. Target aud: 12-35. Spec prog: Heavy metal 3 hrs. ■ Laura Jacobsen, stn mgr, progmg mgr & mus dir; Ross Levison, progmg dir; Adam Potts, asst mus dir; Loni Jonstone-Ross, news dir & pub affrs dir; Pat Ryan, chief engr.

Missouri

Bethany

KAAN(AM)—Dec 3, 1983: 870 khz; 1 kw-D. TL: N40 15 23 W94 09 23. Box 447, Hwy. 69 S. (64424). (816) 425-6380. FAX: (816) 425-6307. Licensee: Jerrell A. Shepherd. Group owner: Shepherd Group. Net: ABC/I; Missourinet. Format: Country. News staff 3; news progmg 10 hrs wkly. Target aud: 25 plus. Spec prog: Farm 10 hrs, relg one hr wkly. ■ Jerrell A. Shepherd, pres; Rodney D. Harris, gen mgr; Tom Lesnak, progmg dir & news dir; Gregg Richwine, chief engr.

KAAN-FM—Oct 27, 1978: 95.5 mhz; 50 kw. Ant 360 ft. TL: N40 15 23 W94 09 23. Hrs opn: 19. Dups AM 90%.

Birch Tree

KBMV(AM)—Sept 14, 1981: 1310 khz; 1 kw-D, 60 w-N. TL: N36 59 07 W91 32 54. Box 215, Birch St. (65438). (314) 292-3821. FAX: (314) 292-3636. Licensee: Jack G. Hunt. Net: ABC/E, SMN. Format: Country. News staff one. ■ Jessica Green, gen mgr, progmg dir, mus dir & news dir; Gaylord Harvey, gen sls mgr; Raymond Hijo, chief engr.

KBMV-FM—1983: 107.1 mhz; 3 kw. Ant 299 ft. TL: N36 59 07 W91 32 54 (CP: 16.2 kw, ant 407 ft.). Stereo. Dups AM 100%.

Blue Springs

KBEQ(AM)—Feb 2, 1984: 1030 khz; 1 kw-D, 500 w-N, DA-2. TL: N39 02 44 W94 14 06. Rebroadcasts KBEQ-FM Kansas City. 4710 Pennsylvania, Kansas City (64112). (816) 531-2535. FAX: (816) 968-4199. Licensee: Noble Broadcasting of Kansas City Inc. Group owner: Noble Broadcasting Group. Format: Young country. ■ Kathy Stinehour, gen mgr.

Bolivar

KYOO(AM)—November 1961: 1200 khz; 1 kw-D, ND. TL: N37 41 50 W93 25 45. 304 E. Jackson (65613). (417) 326-5259; (417) 326-5257. FAX: (417) 326-5250. Licensee: KYOO Broadcasting Co. (acq 6-89; $660,000; FTR 6-26-89). Format: Talk, country. News staff 2; news progmg 12 hrs wkly. ■ Mel Pulley, pres & gen mgr; Chris Keller, news dir; Shawn Gale, chief engr.

Bonne Terre

KDBB(FM)—September 1989: 104.3 mhz; 3 kw. Ant 328 ft. TL: N37 50 44 W90 34 31 (CP: 785 w, ant 630 ft., TL: N37 55 18 W90 33 24). Hrs opn: 24. Box B, 104 Juniper, Flat River (63601). (314) 431-1000. Licensee: Zindy Broadcasting Co. (acq 5-21-91; $350,000; FTR 6-10-91). Net: SMN. Format: Oldies, adult contemp. News progmg 20 hrs wkly. Target aud: 25-55. ■ Stephen B. Jones, pres; Glen Berry, progmg mgr.

Boonville

KCLR-FM—Oct 1, 1974: 99.3 mhz; 33.2 kw. Ant 590 ft. TL: N38 46 34 W92 32 45. Stereo. Box 1636, Columbia (65205). (314) 875-1099. FAX: (314) 875-2439. Licensee: Zimmer Broadcasting Co. Rep: Banner. Format: Country. News staff one. ■ Don Lynch, gen mgr.

KWRT(AM)—Aug 11, 1953: 1370 khz; 1 kw-D, 84 w-N. TL: N38 56 44 W92 46 14. 1600 Radio Hill Rd. (65233). (816) 882-6686. FAX: (816) 882-6688. Licensee: Big Country of Missouri Inc. Net: ABC/E; Missourinet. Format: C&W, big band. ■ Dick Billings, pres & gen mgr; Pat Billings, opns mgr; Matt Billings, progmg dir; Ted Bleil, progmg dir; Kevin Surgeon, chief engr.

KACJ(FM)—Co-owned with KWRT(AM). Not on air, target date unknown: 93.9 mhz; 6 kw. Ant 328 ft. Radio Hill Rd. (65233). Licensee: Big Country of Missouri Inc.

Bowling Green

KPCR(AM)—Dec 13, 1966: 1530 khz; 1 kw-D, 250 w-CH. TL: N39 21 57 W91 10 45. Hrs opn: Sunrise-sunset. Box 1, Hwy. 54 E. (63334). (314) 324-2283. FAX: (314) 324-2283. Licensee: Pike County Broadcasting Co. Net: Brownfield. Format: C&W. News progmg 12 hrs wkly. Target aud: General; adults who like to have fun with their radio. Spec prog: Farm 9 hrs wkly. ■ J. Paul Salois, pres, gen mgr & chief engr; Betty A. Salois, stn mgr & gen sls mgr; Mike Allen, progmg dir & mus dir. ■ Rates: $18; 18; 18; 8.

KPCR-FM—Aug 1, 1975: 94.1 mhz; 25 kw. Ant 270 ft. TL: N39 21 57 W91 10 45. Stereo. Hrs opn: 6 AM-10 PM. Dups AM 100%. ■ Rates: Same as AM.

Branson

***KLFC(FM)**—July 1988: 88.1 mhz; 100 w. Ant 328 ft. TL: N36 37 53 W93 18 15. Box 574 (65616). (417) 334-5532. Licensee: Vision Ministries Inc. Rep: Moody Broadcasting. Format: Relg. News progmg 8 hrs wkly. Target aud: General; resort and tourist community. ■ Jay Scribner, pres.

KOMC(AM)—Dec 21, 1956: 1220 khz; 1 kw-D, 53 w-N. TL: N36 37 12 W93 12 40. Hrs opn: 24. 202 Courtney St. (65616). (417) 334-6003; (417) 334-6012. FAX: (417) 334-7141. Licensee: Turtle Broadcasting Co. of Branson. Group owner: Orr & Earls Broadcasting Inc. (acq 11-21-86; $335,000). Net: CBS, ABC; Missourinet. Format: News/talk, nostalgia. News staff 2; news progmg 24 hrs wkly. Target aud: 40 plus. ■ Rod Orr, pres & gen mgr; Carol Orr, stn mgr; Greg Pyron, opns mgr; Steve Willoughby, mktg mgr; Bob Carignan, prom mgr; Scott McCaulley, progmg dir; Mike Summers, news dir. ■ Rates: $22; 15; 22; 15.

KRZK(FM)—Co-owned with KOMC(AM). March 1, 1971: 106.3 mhz; 5.7 kw. Ant 672 ft. TL: N36 43 52 W93 10 3. Stereo. Hrs opn: 24. Prog sep from AM. Net: ABC/D. Format: Country. News staff 2; news progmg 7 hrs wkly. Target aud: 25-49. Spec prog: Branson Backstage-talk one hr wkly. ■ Jessica James, progmg dir & mus dir.

Brookfield

KZBK(AM)—Feb 14, 1956: 1470 khz; 500 w-D, DA. TL: N39 50 26 W93 04 52. Hrs opn: 6 AM-sunset. 107 S. Main (64628). (816) 258-3383. Licensee: Best Broadcasting Inc. (acq 6-14-93; $70,000 with co-located FM; FTR 6-28-93). Format: Relg. News progmg 4 hrs wkly. Target aud: 30 plus. ■ Dwight Carver, gen mgr, gen sls mgr & chief engr. ■ Rates: $4.60; 4.60; 4.60; 4.60.

KZBK-FM—Sept 1981: 97.7 mhz; 3 kw. Ant 203 ft. TL: N39 50 26 W93 04 51 (CP: 96.9 mhz, 27.5 kw, ant 158 ft., TL: N39 50 26 W93 04 48). Hrs opn: 6 AM-10 PM. Prog sep from AM. (816) 258-7468. Net: Missourinet, Brownfield. Format: MOR, contemp hit. News progmg 9 hrs wkly. Target aud: 25 plus (D), under 30 (N). Spec prog: Class 4 hrs, farm 2 hrs, big band 11 hrs. ■ Rates: $5.35; 5.35; 5.35; 5.35.

Buffalo

KBFL(FM)—1965: 99.9 mhz; 4.1 kw. Ant 328 ft. TL: N37 38 17 W92 59 39. Stereo. Hrs opn: 6 AM-11 PM. Box 1385, Locust & Main Sts. (65622). (417) 345-2412. FAX: (417) 345-2410. Licensee: KBFL Broadcasting Co. (acq 7-6-93; $65,000; FTR 8-2-93). Net: CBS; Brownfield. Format: Country, top-100, adult contemp. News staff one; news progmg 15 hrs wkly. Target aud: General; grade school to senior adults. Spec prog: Gospel 2 hrs wkly. ■ Mel Pulley, Gretchen Pulley, exec vps; Chris Keller, gen mgr & progmg dir; Rebecca Menear, sls dir & adv dir; Lou Hagen, news dir. ■ Rates: $8; 6; 6; 6.

Butler

KMAM(AM)—May 11, 1962: 1530 khz; 500 w-D. TL: N38 14 56 W94 19 18. 800 E. Nursery St. (64730). (816) 679-4191. FAX: (816) 679-4193. Licensee: Bates County Broadcasting Co. Net: ABC/D; Brownfield. Format: C&W. News staff one; news progmg 10 hrs wkly. Target aud: General. Spec prog: Farm 15 hrs wkly. ■ B.D. Thornton, pres & gen mgr; Melody Greenwood, prom mgr; Lynda Lewis, progmg dir & mus dir; Bill Thornton, news dir; Don McClure, chief engr. ■ Rates: $10; 10; 10; 10.

KMOE(FM)—Co-owned with KMAM. Jan 15, 1975: 92.1 mhz; 4.7 kw. Ant 200 ft. TL: N38 14 56 W94 19 18 (CP: 4.725 kw, ant 148 ft.). Stereo. Hrs opn: 24. Dups AM 100%. ■ Jerry Thornton, sls mgr; B.D. Thornton, vp adv; Lynda Lewis, pub affrs dir. ■ Rates: Same as AM.

Cabool

KOZX(FM)—May 1978: 98.1 mhz; 3 kw. Ant 220 ft. TL: N37 07 58 W92 08 04. Stereo. 538 Main St. (65689). (417) 962-3303. FAX: (417) 962-4411. Licensee: Twin Cities Broadcasting Co. (acq 6-26-92; $115,000; FTR 7-20-92). Format: Country. Spec prog: Farm 2 hrs wkly. ■ Shelley Grosenbacher, pres & gen mgr; Mark Adams, progmg dir & mus dir.

California

KZMO(AM)—July 27, 1984: 1420 khz; 500 w-D, 225 w-N. TL: N38 38 12 W92 35 00. Hrs opn: 19. Box 307, Country Club Rd. (65018). (314) 796-3139. FAX: (314) 796-4131. Licensee: Town & Country Communications Inc. Net: ABC/D; Missourinet, Brownfield. Wash atty: Leibowitz & Spencer. Format: Country. News staff one; news progmg 19 hrs wkly. Target aud: 20 plus. Spec prog: Farm 5 hrs, gospel 3 hrs wkly. ■ Ray Rouse, pres, gen mgr & chief engr; Dennis Peter, gen sls mgr; Susan Rouse, prom mgr & progmg dir; Jeff Shackleford, mus dir; Walter Loeber, news dir.

KZMO-FM—July 27, 1984: 94.3 mhz; 1.75 kw. Ant 423 ft. TL: N38 38 12 W92 35 05. Stereo. Hrs opn: 19. Dups AM 100%. Net: ABC/D.

Camdenton

***KCVO-FM**—Sept 23, 1985: 91.7 mhz; 10 kw. Ant 435 ft. TL: N38 01 13 W92 45 27. Stereo. Hrs opn: 24. Box 800, Lake Road 5-92 (65020). (314) 346-3200. FAX: (314) 346-1010. Licensee: Lake Area Educational Broadcasting Foundation. Net: USA. Format: Educ, relg, news/talk. News progmg 7 hrs wkly. Target aud: 25-54. James J. McDermott, pres & gen mgr; Rick Steele, mus dir.

Cameron

KMRN(AM)—February 1971: 1360 khz; 500 w-D, 25 w-N. TL: N39 41 05 W94 14 22. 510 Northland Dr. (64429). (816) 632-6661. FAX: (816) 632-1334. Licensee: Cameron Radio Inc. (acq 1981). Net: ABC/D; Missourinet, Brownfield. Wash atty: Erwin Krasnow. Format: News/talk, country. News staff one; news progmg 40 hrs wkly. Target aud: General. Spec prog: Farm 12 hrs wkly. ■ Shellby L. Hendee, pres; J.F. Way, gen sls mgr; Mike Smith, news dir; John Meikle, chief engr.

Campbell

KKJJ(FM)—Not on air, target date unknown: 107.5 mhz; 20 kw. Ant 367 ft. TL: N36 29 55 W89 51 16. 204 Washington, Doniphan (63935). (314) 996-7215. Licensee: Jack G. Hunt.

Canton

KRRR(FM)—May 4, 1971: 100.9 mhz. 12.5 kw. Ant 308 ft. TL: N40 07 33 W91 31 42. Box 711, 119 N. Third, Hannibal (63401). (314) 221-3450. FAX: (314) 221-5331. Licensee: Bick Broadcasting. Rep: McGavren Guild. Format: Classic rock. ■ Teresa Pyle, gen sls mgr; Joel Sampson, progmg dir; Darren Martin, chief engr.

Cape Girardeau

KAPE(AM)—1951: 1550 khz; 5 kw-D, 50 w-N, DA-2. TL: N37 16 45 W89 33 28. Box 558 (63702); 901 S. Kings Hwy. (63701). (314) 335-5516. FAX: (314) 651-4100. Licensee: Withers Broadcasting Co. (group owner; acq 6-72). Net: MBS, Unistar, Westwood One. Rep: D & R Radio. Format: News/talk. News staff one; news progmg 3 hrs wkly. Target aud: 25-54; active, aware adults. ■ W. Russell Withers Jr., pres; Rick Lambert, gen mgr; Tom Marlow, news dir; Kevin Potter, chief engr.

KGMO(FM)—Co-owned with KAPE(AM). Mar 17, 1969: 100.7 mhz; 100 kw. Ant 699 ft. TL: N37 22 16 W89 31 52 (CP: Ant 987 ft.). Stereo. Prog sep from AM. Format: Oldies, 60s and 70s. News staff one; news progmg 2 hrs wkly. Target aud: 25-54. ■ Mike Ford, prom mgr; Jim Davis, mus dir.

KCGQ(AM)—June 10, 1966: 1220 khz; 250 w-D, 140 w-N. TL: N37 18 03 W89 29 27. Stereo. Hrs opn: 24. Box 2077, Suite 109, 106 Farrar Dr. (63701). (314) 335-9099. FAX: (314) 334-1220. Licensee: Target Media Inc. (acq 4-14-89; $225,000; FTR 5-1-89). Net: CNN, Unistar. Rep: Katz & Powell. Wash atty: Leventhal, Senter & Lerman. Format: Adult contemp. News staff one. Target aud: 35 plus. ■ Thomas P. Stine, pres & gen mgr; Craig Michaels, opns dir; Robert Scaneider, sls dir; Chris Razavi, prom dir; Jimmy Steele, progmg dir; J.J. Elliott, mus dir; Dean Field, news dir; Joe Bellis, chief engr.

KCGQ-FM—(Gordonville). 1978: 99.3 mhz; 4.2 kw. Ant 390 ft. TL: N37 22 07 W89 35 34. Stereo. Hrs opn: 24. Prog sep from AM. (Acq 4-22-86; grpsl; FTR 3-31-86). Target aud: 18-49.

KEZS-FM—Listing follows KZIM(AM).

KGMO(FM)—Listing follows KAPE(AM).

***KRCU(FM)**—Mar 3, 1976: 90.9 mhz; 6 kw. Ant 259 ft. TL: N37 18 37 W89 31 57. Stereo. One Univ. Plaza (63701). (314) 651-5070. Licensee: Board of Regents of S.E. Missouri State Univ. Net: NPR. Format: Classical, jazz, news. News progmg 32 hrs wkly. ■ Greg Petrowich, opns dir; Allen Lane, chief engr.

KYRX(FM)—(Chaffee). July 1, 1990: 104.7 mhz; 6 kw. Ant 328 ft. TL: N37 09 27 W89 36 20. Stereo. Box 558, Cape Girardeau (63702-0558). (314) 335-7600. Licensee: Chartres Media Inc. (acq 4-12-90; $33,587; FTR 5-7-90). Format: Hot adult contemp. News staff one. Target aud: 18-49. ■ Jim Davis, opns mgr & mus dir; Rick Lambert, gen sls mgr.

KZIM(AM)—1925: 960 khz; 5 kw-D, 500 w-N, DA-N. TL: N37 18 59 W89 29 06. Box 1610, 324 Broadway (63702). (314) 335-8291. FAX: (314) 335-4806. Licensee: Zimmer Enterprises Inc. Net: CBS, NBC Talknet. Rep: Banner. Wash atty: Fletcher, Heald & Hildreth. Format: News, talk. News staff 5 Target aud: 35-64. Spec prog: Farm 5 hrs, sports 10 hrs wkly. ■ Jerry Zimmer, pres; James Zimmer, gen mgr; Terry Hester, opns mgr & news dir; Gera Schemel, sls dir. ■ Rates: $30; 30; 30; 20.

KEZS-FM—Co-owned with KZIM(AM). Dec 10, 1970: 102.9 mhz; 100 kw. Ant 947 ft. TL: N37 24 23 W89 33 44. Stereo. Licensee: Zimmer Broadcasting Co. Inc. (acq 9-83; $70,000; FTR 9-5-83). Net: ABC/E. Format: Country. News staff one. Target aud: 25-54. ■ Kent Crider, opns dir. ■ Rates: $50; 50; 50; 30.

Carrollton

KAOL(AM)—Apr 18, 1959: 1430 khz; 500 w-U, 27 w-N. TL: N39 19 58 W93 32 15. Hrs opn: 24. KMZU Bldg., 102 N. Mason (64633). (816) 542-0404; (816) 542-0494. FAX: (816) 542-0404. Licensee: Kanza Inc. (acq 11-1-81; $665,000; with co-located FM; FTR 11-23-81). Rep: McGavren Guild. Format: C&W, farm. News staff 2; news progmg 10 hrs wkly. Target aud: 25-54; farm families and those with agricultural backrounds. ■ Mike L. Carter, pres & gen mgr; Miles Carter, opns mgr & progmg dir; Bob Tutt, gen sls mgr; Donn Emis, mus dir; Wayne Combs, news dir; Ken Wolf, chief engr. ■ Rates: $90; 90; 72; 32.

KMZU(FM)—Co-owned with KAOL(AM). July 13, 1962: 100.7 mhz; 98.6 kw. Ant 990 ft. TL: N39 22 05 W93 29 40. Stereo. Dups AM 100%. ■ Rates: Same as AM.

Carthage

KDMO(AM)—June 3, 1947: 1490 khz; 1 kw-U. TL: N37 10 58 W94 21 43. Hrs opn: 24. Box 426, 221 E. Fourth St. (64836). (417) 358-6054; (417) 358-2648. FAX: (417) 358-1278. Licensee: Ronald L. Petersen (acq 1-23-90). Net: ABC/I; Missourinet, Brownfield. Rep: Katz & Powell. Format: C&W. News staff one; news progmg 24 hrs wkly. Target aud: 35 plus. Spec prog: Farm 12 hrs wkly. ■ Ronald L. Petersen, pres & gen mgr; Mark Anthony, opns mgr; Mark Danielson, news dir. ■ Rates: $16.62; 11.06; 16.62; 11.06.

KMXL(FM)—Co-owned with KDMO(AM). Jan 10, 1972: 95.1 mhz; 50 kw. Ant 472 ft. TL: N37 10 58 W94 21 35. Stereo. Hrs opn: 24. Prog sep from AM. Net: ABC/D; Missourinet. Format: Adult contemp. News staff one; news progmg 5 hrs wkly. Target aud: 25-54; baby-boomers. ■ Rates: $16.95; 14.25; 16.95; 14.25.

Caruthersville

KCRV(AM)—Feb 22, 1950: 1370 khz; 1 kw-D, 63 w-N. TL: N36 12 50 W89 41 25. Box 909, Hwy. 84 W. (63830). (314) 333-1370; (314) 333-1371. FAX: (314) 333-1370. Licensee: Pemiscot Broadcasters Inc. Net: Moody; Prog Farm, Brownfield. Rep: MidSouth. Format: Country, gospel, farm. News staff one; news progmg 27 hrs wkly. Target aud: General; residents of Pemiscot County. Spec prog: Relg 23 hrs wkly. ■ J. Eric Taylor Jr., pres; Cleat Stanfill, gen mgr & news dir; Ed Delisle, gen sls mgr; Randy Tillman, progmg dir; Danny Nelson, mus dir; Emory P. Johnson, chief engr. ■ Rates: $9; 9; 9; 7.

KLOW(FM)—Co-owned with KCRV(AM). April 28, 1975: 103.1 mhz; 3 kw. Ant 200 ft. TL: N36 12 50 W89 41 25. Stereo. Prog sep from AM. Format: Adult contemp. News progmg 18 hrs wkly. ■ Rates: Same as AM.

Cassville

KRLK(FM)—Not on air, target date unknown: 100.1 mhz; 2.72 kw. Ant 489 ft. TL: N36 37 00 W93 48 31. Box 442 (65625). Licensee: Kevin M. and Patricia W. Wodlinger.

Centralia

KMFC(FM)—Feb 3, 1986: 92.1 mhz; 1.85 kw. Ant 418 ft. TL: N39 09 58 W92 09 52. Stereo. Box 26, 1249 E. Hwy. 22 (65240). (314) 682-5525. FAX: (314) 682-2744. Licensee: Clair Broadcasting Co. Format: Relg, Christian contemp. News progmg 8 hrs wkly. Target aud: 25-50. ■ Jerry D. Clair, pres; Thomas Winn, gen mgr; Tim Knight, gen sls mgr.

Chaffee

KYRX(FM)—Licensed to Chaffee. See Cape Girardeau.

Charleston

KCHR(AM)—1953: 1350 khz; 1 kw-D, 79 w-N. TL: N36 55 30 W89 17 45. Hrs opn: 6 AM-10 PM. First & Commercial St. (63834). (314) 683-6044. Licensee: South Missouri Broadcasting Co. Inc. Net: MBS, NBC Talknet. Format: C&W. News progmg one hr wkly. Target aud: General. Spec prog: Gospel 10 hrs, easy lstng 5 hrs wkly. ■ James L. Byrd III, pres; Danny Adams, gen mgr, gen sls mgr & news dir; Donna Adams, prom mgr, progmg dir & mus dir; Earl Abanathy, chief engr.

KWKZ(FM)—Not on air, target date unknown: 106.1 mhz; 3 kw. Ant 328 ft. TL: N36 57 29 W89 23 38. Licensee: Anderson Broadcasting Co. Inc. (acq 7-30-92).

Chillicothe

KCHI(AM)—Mar 3, 1950: 1010 khz; 250 w-D, 37 w-N. TL: N39 45 51 W93 33 21. Box 227, 421 Washington St. (64601). (816) 646-4173. FAX: (816) 646-2868. Licensee: Livingston Broadcasting Inc. (acq 7-1-84). Net: ABC/E; Missourinet. Format: Classic rock, oldies. News staff one; news progmg 25 hrs wkly. Target aud: 35-49. ■ Chris Beyer, gen mgr; Jerry Englert, progmg dir; Jim Hoffman, news dir. ■ Rates: $19.20; 19.20; 19.20; 19.20.

KCHI-FM—October 1976: 103.9 mhz; 1.55 kw. Ant 400 ft. TL: N39 48 52 W93 35 20. Stereo. Dups AM 95%.

***KRNW(FM)**—July 4, 1993: 88.9 mhz; 38 kw. Ant 525 ft. TL: N39 48 50 W93 35 20. Stereo. Hrs opn: 19. 800 University Dr., Admin. Bldg., Northwest Missouri State Univ., Maryville (64468). (816) 562-1163. FAX: (816) 562-1900. Licensee: Northwest Missouri State Univ. Format: News, class, jazz. News staff 2; news progmg 39 hrs wkly. Target aud: General. ■ Sharon C. Bonnett, stn mgr & progmg dir; Michael C. Johnson, opns mgr & progmg mgr; Gayle Hull, mktg mgr; Michael Johnson, prom mgr; John P. McGuire, news dir; Patty Andrews, pub affrs dir; Michael Douthat, engrg dir.

Clayton

***KFUO(AM)**—Dec 14, 1924: 850 khz; 5 kw-D. TL: N38 38 20 W90 18 57. Hrs opn: Sunrise-sunset. 85 Founders Ln. (63105). (314) 725-3030. FAX: (314) 725-3801. Licensee: Lutheran Church-Missouri Synod. Net: UPI. Wash atty: Arnold & Porter. Format: Relg. Target aud: General. ■ Paul Devantier, pres; Dennis Stortz, gen mgr; Chuck Rathert, progmg dir; Paul Clayton, mus dir; John Fischer, chief engr.

KFUO-FM—Jan 1, 1948: 99.1 mhz; 100 kw. Ant 1,026 ft. TL: N38 39 08 W90 17 03. Stereo. Prog sep from AM. (314) 725-0099. Net: NBC, Wall Street. Rep: CMBS. Format: Classical. ■ Ron Klemm, opns mgr; Glynelle Wells, sls dir; Jim Connett, progmg dir; John Roberts, mus dir. ■ Rates: $75; 75; 75; 50.

KSIV(AM)—1946: 1320 khz; 5 kw-D, 270 w-N, DA-N. TL: N38 36 26 W90 21 14. Hrs opn: 24. Suite 811, 1750 S. Brentwood Blvd., St. Louis (63144). (314) 961-1320. FAX: (314) 961-7562. Licensee: Bott Broadcasting (group owner; acq 2-25-82; FTR 3-15-82). Net: USA. Format: Christian info. radio. Target aud: 35-64; family-oriented, mature. ■ Richard P. Bott, pres; Michael McHardy, gen mgr.

***KWUR(FM)**—July 4, 1976: 90.3 mhz; 10 w. Ant 136 ft. TL: N38 38 45 W80 19 07. Stereo. Hrs opn: 24. Box 1182, Washington Univ., St. Louis (63130); Women's Building, Lindell & Skinker Blvds. (63130). (314) 935-5952; (314) 935-5987. FAX: (314) 935-8516. Licensee: Washington Univ. Format: Alternative. Target aud: 18 plus; those seeking alternative radio. Spec prog: Rap 24 hrs, metal 12 hrs, blues 6 hrs, jazz 6 hrs, folk 6 hrs, class 4 hrs, relg one hr, Sp 2 hrs, hardcore 2 hrs wkly. ■ Kelly Ireland, gen mgr; Brandon Bush, dev dir; Ben Walther, Ann Berman, prom dirs; Courtney LaFountain, progmg mgr; Kagin Lee, Mike Friedberg, mus dirs; Ian Murphy, Isaac Green, Pete Keusch, asst mus dirs; Patric Santo Petro, news dir; Anthony Friscia, Rachel DiMora, engrg mgrs.

Clinton

KDKD(AM)—1951: 1280 khz; 1 kw-D, 58 w-N. TL: N38 23 55 W93 46 19. Hrs opn: 19. Box 448, KDKD Bldg., 2201 N. Antioch Rd. (64735). (816) 885-6141. FAX: (816) 885-4801. Licensee: Clinton Radio Co. (acq 7-21-83; $825,000; with co-located FM; FTR 8-8-83). Net: ABC/I; Missourinet. Format: News/talk. News staff one; news progmg 10 hrs wkly. Target aud: 25-65. ■ Randel Boesen, pres & gen mgr; Bev Hansen, opns dir; Joan Boesen, sls dir & prom mgr; Jim Schmedding, gen sls mgr; Rhodes Carter, progmg mgr & asst mus dir; Tom Stanton, news dir; Charlie Branscombe, chief engr. ■ Rates: $20; 17; 17; 12.

KDKD-FM—1975: 95.3 mhz; 3 kw. Ant 174 ft. TL: N38 23 55 W93 46 19. Stereo. Hrs opn: 19. Prog sep from AM. (816) 885-7521. Net: ABC. Format: Contemp C&W.

KLRQ(FM)—Oct 5, 1990: 96.1 mhz; 100 kw. Ant 987 ft. TL: N38 28 27 W93 30 28. Hrs opn: 24. Box 446, Suite 9 & 10, 702 E. Ohio (64735). (816) 885-7517; (816) 885-7510. FAX: (816) 885-8318. Licensee: B & F Broadcasting Inc. Net: NBC the Source. Wash atty: Verner, Liipfert, Bernhard, McPherson and Hand. Format: Adult contemp, AOR. News staff one; news progmg 3 hrs wkly. Target aud: 18-50; young adults. ■ Nicole A. Blank, CEO; John M. Blank, chmn, gen mgr & engrg mgr; Dr. Bradley M. Townsend, pres; Niccole A. Blank, stn mgr; Darla K. Dillon, opns mgr; Kenneth L. Dillon, vp sls, progmg dir & mus dir; Mike Swafford, sls dir; John Blank, gen sls mgr; Barry Wilson, chief engr. ■ Rates: $12; 12; 12; 12.

Columbia

KARO(FM)—Feb 23, 1983: 101.5 mhz; 20 kw. Ant 604 ft. TL: N38 47 28 W92 17 43. Stereo. Hrs opn: 24. 503 Old 63 N. (65201); 221 1/2 Madison St., Jefferson City (65101). (314) 442-3116; FAX: (314) 449-7770; Licensee: Columbia FM Inc. Rep: Roslin. Format: Adult contemp. News staff 2; news progmg one hr wkly. Target aud: 25-54. ■ Al M. Germond, pres; David Baugher, gen mgr; John Ott, gen sls mgr; Dan Corkery, progmg dir; Mark Reardon, news dir; Mike McGowan, chief engr.

***KBIA(FM)**—1972: 91.3 mhz; 100 kw. Ant 610 ft. TL: N38 53 16 W92 15 48. Stereo. Univ. of Missouri, Columbia Campus, 409 Jesse Hall (65211). (314) 882-3431. FAX: (314) 882-2636. Licensee: Board of Curators, Univ. of Missouri. Group owner: The Curators of the Univ. of Missouri. Net: NPR, APR. Format: News, classical, jazz. News staff 5; news progmg 56 hrs wkly. Target aud: 35-64. ■ Michael Dunn, gen mgr; Roger Karwoski, stn mgr; Joy Ferguson, gen sls mgr & prom mgr; Peter Whorf, progmg dir; Cecil Hickman, news dir; Joe Fay, chief engr.

KCMQ(FM)—Dec 3, 1967: 96.7 mhz; 18 kw. Ant 344 ft. TL: N38 58 01 W92 18 39. Stereo. Hrs opn: 24. Box 1636, 810 E. Cherry (65201). (314) 875-1099. FAX: (314) 875-2439. Licensee: Zimmer Radio of Mid-Missouri Inc. (acq 7-15-93; $625,000; with co-located AM; FTR 8-9-93). Net: ABC/FM. Format: CHR. News staff 2; news progmg one hr wkly. Target aud: 18-49. ■ Don Lynch, gen mgr; Tim Meagher, gen sls mgr; Taylor Bryan, chief engr.

KTGR(AM)—Co-owned with KCMQ(FM). 1955: 1580 khz; 250 w-D, 19 w-N. TL: N38 58 01 W92 18 39. Stn currently dark.

***KCOU(FM)**—Oct 31, 1973: 88.1 mhz; 435 w. Ant 110 ft. TL: N38 56 23 W92 19 20. Stereo. 101-F Pershing Hall, Univ. of Missouri (65201). (314) 882-8262; (314) 882-7820. Licensee: Residence Halls Assoc. Inc. Net: ABC/I. Format: Progsv, rock. News progmg 5 hrs wkly. Target aud: 18-22; students & community members. Spec prog: Black 4 hrs, country 3 hrs, jazz 10 hrs, blues 2 hrs, reggae/African 2 hrs, punk/hardcore 2 hrs, industrial 2 hrs wkly. ■ Cliff Steele, progmg dir; Jess Deal, chief engr.

KFMZ(FM)—Oct 12, 1971: 98.3 mhz; 23.5 kw. Ant 711 ft. TL: N38 57 21 W92 16 24. Stereo. Hrs opn: 24. Box 1268, 1101 Walnut (65205). (314) 874-3000. FAX: (314) 443-1460. Licensee: Contemporary Broadcasting Inc. Group owner: Contemporary Media Broadcasting Group. Net: ABC/R. Rep: Christal. Wash atty: Rosenman & Colin Format: AOR. News staff one; news progmg 4 hrs wkly. Target aud: 18-49; ■ Mike Rice, pres; Janet Cox, exec vp; Richard Hauschild, gen mgr; Cindy Stratton, prom mgr; Chris Kellogg, progmg dir; Paul Malone, mus dir; J. Eric Hoehn, chief engr. ■ Rates: $35; 40; 35; 25.

KFRU(AM)—Oct 10, 1925: 1400 khz; 1 kw-U. TL: N38 57 52 W92 18 26. 503 Old Hwy., 63 N. (65201). (314) 449-4141. FAX: (314) 449-7770. Licensee: Columbia AM Inc. (acq 7-21-92; $448,841; FTR 8-10-92). Net: ABC/I, ABC TalkRadio, MBS; Missourinet. Format: News, talk. News staff 2; news progmg 15 hrs wkly. Target aud: General. ■ Al Germond, pres; David Baugher, gen mgr; John Ott, gen sls mgr; Steve Moore, progmg dir; Mark Reardon, news dir; Mike McGowan, chief engr.

KNCD(FM)—Not on air, target date unknown: 93.9 mhz; 3 kw. Ant 328 ft. TL: N38 52 10 W92 15 34. 2165 E. Raynell, Springfield (65804). Licensee: Thomas T. Cooke and Elmo L. Donze (acq 12-3-93; $46,500; FTR 12-20-93).

***KOPN(FM)**—Mar 1, 1973: 89.5 mhz; 36 kw-H. Ant 236 ft. TL: N38 59 47 W92 11 50 (CP: 36.4 kw, TL: N38 59 53 W92 11 48). Stereo. 915 E. Broadway (65201). (314)

Stations in the U.S.

Missouri

874-1139. Licensee: New Wave Corp. Format: Triple A music, AAA. News staff one; news progmg 28 hrs wkly. Target aud: Well educated, socially conscious. Spec prog: American Indian 3 hrs, Black 3 hrs, gospel 3 hrs, jazz 9 hrs, country 6 hrs, blues 12 hrs, bluegrass 6 hrs wkly. ■ P.T. Martin, gen mgr; Brian Mann, progmg dir & news dir; Steve Donofrio, engrg mgr; Sam Griffin, chief engr.

KTGR(AM)—Listing follows KCMQ(FM).

*__KWWC-FM__—Feb 2, 1965: 90.5 mhz; 1.25 kw. Ant 131 ft. TL: N38 57 12 W92 19 05. Stereo. Box 2114, Stephens College (65215). (314) 876-7297. FAX: (314) 876-7248. Licensee: Stephens College. Format: Div. News progmg 5 hrs wkly. Spec prog: Class 6 hrs, jazz 25 hrs, easy lstng 20 hrs, alternative 20 hrs, info 5 hrs, big band 3 hrs, Broadway 3 hrs wkly. ■ John Blakemore, CEO; Sarah Allen, gen mgr; Laura Beinecke, opns mgr; Max Orneles, chief engr.

Crestwood

KSHE(FM)—Feb 11, 1961: 94.7 mhz; 100 kw. Ant 1,019 ft. TL: N38 34 24 W90 19 30. Stereo. Hrs opn: 24. The Annex, Suite 101, 700 St. Louis Union Station, St. Louis (63103). (314) 621-0095. FAX: (314) 621-3428. Licensee: Emmis FM Broadcasting Corp. of St. Louis Group owner: Emmis Broadcasting Co. (acq 3-19-84; grpsl; FTR 1-30-84). Rep: D & R Radio. Format: Classic rock, AOR. News staff one; news progmg one hr wkly. Target aud: 18-40. ■ Steve Crane, CEO; Jeff Smulyan, chmn; Doyle Rose, pres; Howard Schrott, CFO; John R. Beck Jr., vp & gen mgr; Jim Owen, opns mgr & progmg dir; J. Marvin Sanders, gen sls mgr; Abigail Pollay, prom mgr; Al Hofer, mus dir; John Ulett, news dir; John Oelke, chief engr.

Cuba

KFXE(FM)—Not on air, target date unknown: 102.1 mhz; 3 kw. Ant 236 ft. TL: N38 03 49 W91 24 37. Rt. 3, Box 4331, Lake Rd. 54-24, Osage Beach (65065). Licensee: Lake Broadcasting Inc.

KGNN(AM)—June 28, 1978: 1410 khz; 5 kw-D, DA. TL: N38 05 06 W91 18 40. Hrs opn: 12. Box 617 (65453). (314) 885-3333; (314) 239-0400. Licensee: Missouri River Christian Broadcasting Inc. (acq 12-31-87). Net: Moody, USA. Format: Beautiful music, relg, news/talk. News progmg 4 hrs wkly. Target aud: General; inquisitive, conservative, liberal, philosophical, young & old. Spec prog: Gospel 10 hrs wkly. ■ J. C. Goggan, pres; gen mgr & gen sls mgr; Ken Bowles, vp opns mgr, news dir & chief engr. ■ Rates: $5; 5; 5; na.

De Soto

KHAD(AM)—Nov 1, 1968: 1190 khz; 5 kw-D, DA. TL: N38 08 22 W90 32 32. Box 696 (63020). (314) 586-4211. Licensee: Big River Broadcasting Inc. (acq 3-31-93; $67,500 with co-located FM; FTR 4-19-93). ■ Carla Hill-Smith, gen mgr; P.J. Johnson, chief engr.

KDJR(FM)—Co-owned with KHAD(AM). Jan 29, 1991: 100.1 mhz; 2 kw. Ant 400 ft. TL: N38 01 25 W90 34 02. Stereo.

Dexter

KDEX(AM)—Feb 1, 1956: 1590 khz; 1 kw-D, 78 w-N. TL: N36 47 20 W89 54 28. (CP: 620 w-D). Hrs opn: 5 AM-midnight. Box 249, Hwy. 114 E. (63841). (314) 624-3545; (314) 624-3591. FAX: (314) 624-3545. Licensee: Dexter Broadcasting Inc. (acq 7-15-88). Net: ABC/D, AP; Prog Farm. Wash atty: Fisher, Wayland, Cooper & Leader. Format: Country. News staff one; news progmg 6 hrs wkly. Target aud: 25-54. ■ Walter F. Turner, pres & gen mgr; Barbara B. Turner, gen sls mgr & prom mgr; Theresa Ryan Cox, progmg dir; Joeli Barbour, mus dir; Danny Walters, chief engr.

KDEX-FM—July 17, 1969: 102.3 mhz; 6 kw. Ant 53 ft. TL: N36 47 18 W89 54 22 Stereo. Dups AM 100%. ■ Barbara B. Turner, vp, stn mgr, opns mgr & natl sls mgr & mktg dir; Walter F. Turner, gen sls mgr & rgnl sls mgr; Gary Phillips, pub affrs dir; Daniel V. Walters, chief engr.

Doniphan

KDFN(AM)—Feb 4, 1963: 1500 khz; 2.5 kw-D, DA. TL: N36 36 53 W90 49 23. 116 S. Grand (63935). (314) 996-3124. FAX: (314) 996-7215. Licensee: Jack G. Hunt (acq 1963). Net: ABC/E; Missourinet. Format: Big band. News staff one. Target aud: General. Spec prog: Farm 5 hrs wkly. ■ Jack G. Hunt, pres; Gary Lee, gen mgr & gen sls mgr; Raymond Hodo, mus dir & chief engr; Dale Monroe, news dir.

KOEA(FM)—Co-owned with KDFN(AM). April 11, 1975: 97.5 mhz; 50 kw. Ant 577 ft. TL: N36 35 20 W90 49 10. Stereo. Prog sep from AM. Format: Country.

East Prairie

KYMO(AM)—Nov 15, 1965: 1080 khz; 500 w-D. TL: N36 47 42 W89 21 17 (CP: TL: N36 47 49 W89 21 19). Box 130 (63845). (314) 649-3597. Licensee: Usher Broadcasting (acq 6-1-69). Net: CNN. Format: Top-40. ■ H. Charles Beggs, pres; Barney L. Webster, gen mgr; Michael Bennett, progmg dir; Barney Webster, news dir; Earl Abanathy, chief engr.

KYMO-FM—Aug 5, 1991: 105.3 mhz; 3 kw. Ant 207 ft. TL: N36 47 49 W89 21 19.

El Dorado Springs

KESM(AM)—July 18, 1961: 1580 khz; 500 w-D. TL: N37 51 51 W94 00 54. Stereo. 200 Radio Ln. (64744). (417) 876-2741; (417) 876-2742. FAX: (417) 876-2743. Licensee: Wildwood Communications Inc. (acq 12-17-85). Net: NBC. Format: C&W, Gospel. Target aud: General. ■ Donald Kohn, pres, gen mgr & engrg mgr; Susan Kohn, stn mgr & gen sls mgr; Rhonda Carbin, news dir.

KESM-FM—June 1, 1965: 105.5 mhz; 6.0 kw. Ant 187 ft. TL: N37 51 51 W94 00 54. Stereo. Dups AM 50%. (Acq 12-17-85; $200,000 FTR 11-11-85). Format: Country, adult contemp.

Eldon

KBMX(FM)—Licensed to Eldon. See Osage Beach.

KLOZ(FM)—July 1, 1979: 92.7 mhz; 50 kw. Ant 590 ft. TL: N38 20 27 W92 35 33. Stereo. 209 E. Second St. (65026). (314) 392-3793. FAX: (314) 392-7617. Licensee: Capital Media Inc. (acq 9-4-92; FTR 9-28-92). Net: ABC/I. Format: Adult contemp. News staff one; news progmg 6 hrs wkly. Target aud: General. ■ Dennis Benne, gen mgr; J.C. Lake, progmg dir; Taylor Bryant, chief engr.

Excelsior Springs

KEXS(AM)—August 1968: 1090 khz; 1 kw-D. TL: N39 20 25 W94 14 26. 201 Industrial Park Rd. (64024). (816) 329-5880; (816) 637-6061. FAX: (816) 637-6063. Licensee: Crossway Communications Inc. (acq 7-1-89; $600,000; FTR 6-26-89). Net: USA. Format: Christian country. News progmg 2 hrs wkly. Target aud: 25-54. ■ Gary Babb, pres & gen mgr; Kevin Morgan, mus dir; Ben Weis, chief engr. ■ Rates: $18; 15; 17; na.

Farmington

KREI(AM)—Dec 7, 1947: 800 khz; 1 kw-D, 150 w-N. TL: N37 47 45 W90 24 30. Hrs opn: 24. Box 461, 1401 KREI Blvd. (63640). (314) 756-6476. FAX: (314) 756-1110. Licensee: KREI Inc. Group owner: Shepherd Group (acq 7-1-82; $160,000 with co-located FM; FTR 5-17-82). Net: ABC/I, NBC Talknet, MBS; Missourinet. Format: MOR, news/talk. News staff 8; news progmg 40 hrs wkly. Target aud: General. Spec prog: Farm 5 hrs wkly. ■ Jerrell Shepherd, pres; Richard Womack, gen mgr; Connie Pfeifer, gen sls mgr; Mark Toti, progmg dir & news dir; Kevin Brooks, chief engr. ■ Rates: $30; 18; 18; 12.

KTJJ(FM)—Co-owned with KREI(AM). June 5, 1977: 98.5 mhz; 100 kw. Ant 1,040 ft. TL: N37 43 07 W90 33 01. Stereo. Hrs opn: 24. Prog sep from AM. Net: ABC/E. Format: Country. News progmg 16 hrs wkly. Target aud: General. Spec prog: Farm 6 hrs, bluegrass 2 hrs wkly. ■ Rates: $44; 24; 24; 20.

Ferguson

*__KCFV(FM)__—Apr 17, 1972: 89.5 mhz; 100 w. Ant 159 ft. TL: N38 46 07 W90 17 16. Stereo. Hrs opn: 18. 3400 Pershall Rd., St. Louis (63135). (314) 595-4472; (314) 595-4478. FAX: (314) 595-4544. Licensee: St. Louis Community College District. Format: Progsv new music. News progmg 5 hrs wkly. Target aud: General. Spec prog: Rap 4 hrs, dance/industrial 4 hrs, loud music 4 hrs wkly. ■ Dianna L. Clark, gen mgr; Brad Hildebrand, chief engr.

Festus

KJCF(AM)—May 10, 1951: 1400 khz; 1 kw-U. TL: N38 13 56 W90 23 50. Hrs opn: 5:30 AM-10:30 PM. Box 368, 1400 Scenic Dr. (63028). (314) 937-7642; (314) 464-8680. FAX: (314) 937-3636. Licensee: KREI Inc. Group owner: Shepherd Group (acq 2-1-89; $230,000; FTR 2-1-89). Net: NBC; Missourinet. Format: Adult contemp, news/talk. News staff 4; news progmg 30 hrs wkly. Target aud: General. ■ Jerrell Shepherd, pres; Kirk Mooney, gen mgr; Hal Neisler, progmg dir; Kevin Brooks, chief engr.

Festus-St. Louis

KXEN(AM)—Licensed to Festus-St. Louis. See St. Louis.

Flat River

KFMO(AM)—July 1947: 1240 khz; 1 kw-U. TL: N37 51 10 W90 31 13. Box 36, St. Joe Dr., Park Hills (63601). (314) 431-2000. FAX: (314) 431-6350. Licensee: MKS Broadcasting Inc. (acq 3-16-92; FTR 4-6-92). Net: MBS, Westwood One. Format: Adult contemp, Christian. News staff 2; news progmg 36 hrs wkly. Target aud: 25-54; females. ■ M.L. Steinmetz III, pres; Larry D. Joseph, gen mgr & gen sls mgr; Greg Camp, progmg dir; John Carr, mus dir; Gilbert Collins, news dir. ■ Rates: $10, 9, 9, 9.

Florissant

KXOK-FM—Apr 15, 1977: 97.1 mhz; 100 kw. Ant 560 ft. TL: N38 46 45 W90 43 43. Stereo. Hrs opn: 24. 7777 Bonhomme Ave., No. 1600, St. Louis (63105-1998). (314) 727-0808. FAX: (314) 727-1220. Licensee: Legend Broadcasting of Missouri. Group owner: WPNT Inc. (acq 6-6-89; grpsl; FTR 6-26-89). Rep: Torbet. Format: CHR. News staff one. Target aud: 18-49. ■ Saul Frischling, pres; Michael Frischling, gen mgr; Alice Ross, gen sls mgr; Lee Williams, progmg dir; Scott Gordon, mus dir.

Fredricktown

KFTW(AM)—June 29, 1963: 1450 khz; 1 kw-U. TL: N37 35 00 W90 17 31. Box 71, Hwy. 00 (63645). (314) 783-6461. Licensee: Madison County Broadcasting Co. Inc. (acq 3-16-81). Net: ABC/D; Brownfield, Missourinet. Rep: Keystone (unwired net), Katz; Magic Circle. Format: C&W. Target aud: 35-65. Spec prog: Gospel 8 hrs wkly. ■ David E. Smith Sr., pres, gen mgr & gen sls mgr; David E. Smith, mus dir; Tom Hyatt, news dir; Earl Abernathy, chief engr.

Fulton

KFAL(AM)—Nov 14, 1950: 900 khz; 1 kw-D, 121 w-N. TL: N38 51 58 W91 57 15. Hrs opn: 19. 1805 Westminster Rd. (65251-0581). (314) 642-3341. FAX: (314) 642-3343. Licensee: KFAL Inc. Group owner: Meyer Communications Inc. Net: ABC/D. Rep: McGavren Guild. Format: C&W. News staff one; news progmg 9 hrs wkly. Spec prog: Relg 9 hrs wkly. ■ Kenneth E. Meyer, pres; Preston Semar, gen mgr; Dale Blankenship, chief engr. ■ Rates: $15; 12; 15; 7.

KKCA(FM)—Co-owned with KFAL(AM). 1970: 100.5 mhz; 6 kw. Ant 300 ft. TL: N38 51 58 W91 57 15. Stereo. Hrs opn: 19. Net: SMN. Format: Oldies. News progmg 2 hrs wkly.

Gainesville

KMAC(FM)—Jan 1, 1994: 99.7 mhz; 50 kw. Ant 492 ft. TL: N36 36 06 W92 25 48. Stereo. Hrs opn: 24. Box 653, Hwy. 160 W. & Hwy. 5 S. (65655); Box 2806, HC 2, Theodosia (65761). (417) 273-4308; (417) 679-3555. FAX: (417) 679-3008. Licensee: Dora J. Burnett. Wash atty: Aaron P. Shainis. Format: Oldies. Target aud: General. ■ Dora J. Burnett, pres; Kenneth Burnett, stn mgr.

Gallatin

KGOZ(FM)—Not on air, target date unknown: 101.7 mhz; 15 kw. Ant 423 ft. Box 128, Hwy. 65 N., Marshall (65340). Licensee: Missouri Valley Broadcasting Inc.

Gladstone

KGGN(AM)—Not on air, target date unknown: 890 khz; 1 kw-D, DA. TL: N39 20 03 W94 34 01. 18 N.W. Briarcliff Rd. (64116). Licensee: Michael Glinter.

Gordonville

KCGQ-FM—Licensed to Gordonville. See Cape Girardeau.

Halfway

KYOO-FM—Not on air, target date unknown: 93.1 mhz; 2.36 kw. Ant 367 ft. TL: N37 41 21 W93 20 11. 304 E. Jackson, Bolivar (65613). Licensee: KYOO Broadcasting Co.

Broadcasting & Cable Yearbook 1994

Missouri

Hannibal

KGRC(FM)—Nov 28, 1968: 92.9 mhz; 100 kw. Ant 490 ft. TL: N39 43 45 W91 24 15 (CP: 48.6 kw, ant 1,312 ft., TL: N39 54 00 W91 24 15). Stereo. Hrs opn: 24. Box 1205, 3702 Palmyra Rd. (63401); State & 8th Plaza, Quincy, IL (62301). (314) 221-2221; (217) 224-4102. FAX: (314) 221-3787; (314) 224-4133. Licensee: Staradio Corp. (group owner; acq 4-1-88). Net: ABC/FM. Rep: Katz & Powell. Wash atty: Pepper & Corazzini. Format: Adult contemp. News staff one; news progmg 4 hrs wkly. Target aud: 25-54; upscale adults. Spec prog: Jazz 4 hrs, oldies 3 hrs wkly. ■ Jack Whitley, pres; Pam Hunt, gen mgr & gen sls mgr; Karen Kelly, rgnl sls mgr; Reggie Coleman, progmg dir; Brian Myles, mus dir; Jeanne Robinson, news dir; Phil Reilly, chief engr. ■ Rates: $40; 35; 40; 35.

KHMO(AM)—April 1941: 1070 khz; 5 kw-D, 1 kw-N, DA-3. TL: N39 37 43 W91 22 34. Hrs opn: 24. Box 711, 119 N. Third St. (63401). (314) 221-3500. FAX: (314) 221-5331. Licensee: Bick Broadcasting (acq 8-1-85; $1,350,000; FTR 6-17-85). Net: CNN. Rep: McGavren Guild. Wash atty: Eugene T. Smith. Format: News/talk, sports, easy lstng. News staff 2; news progmg 22 hrs wkly. ■ Bud Janes, pres; Ed Foxall, gen mgr & gen sls mgr; Joel Sampson, progmg dir; Laurel Alridge, mus dir; John Hanvelt, news dir.

Harrisonville

KCFX(FM)—July 19, 1974: 101.1 mhz; 97.3 kw-H, 79.6 kw-V. Ant 994 ft. TL: N39 04 24 W94 29 06. Stereo. Suite 310, 10800 Farley, Overland Park KS (66210); Suite 1500, 13355 Noel Rd., Dallas, TX (75240). (913) 661-0101. FAX: (913) 345-2992. Licensee: Heritage Media Corp. (group owner; acq 4-13-92). Net: Unistar. Rep: Major Mkt. Format: Classic rock. News staff one; news progmg one hr wkly. Target aud: 25-54; baby boomers. ■ Bill Newman, pres & gen mgr; Donna Autry, opns dir; Pam Weinstein, sls dir; Howie Erenberg, prom dir; Beau Raines, progmg dir & mus dir; Rick Tamblyh, news dir; Janet Smith, pub affrs dir; Mark Lucas, chief engr.

Hayti

KCRV(AM)—See Caruthersville.

KLOW(FM)—See Caruthersville.

Houston

KBTC(AM)—June 28, 1962: 1250 khz; 1 kw-D, 51 w-N. TL: N37 19 45 W91 53 55. Hrs opn: 5 AM-midnight. Box 30 (65483). (417) 967-3353; (417) 967-4538. FAX: (417) 967-2281. Licensee: Texas County Radio Inc. (acq 9-87). Net: ABC/E; Missourinet. Wash atty: Fisher, Wayland, Cooper & Leader. Format: Country. News staff one; news progmg 7 hrs wkly. Target aud: 25-54; females. ■ Robert Berri, pres; Richard J. Berri, vp, gen mgr & prom mgr; John Yerby, gen sls mgr & adv dir; Keith Johnson, progmg dir; Scott Smith, mus dir & news dir.

KUNQ(FM)—Co-owned with KBTC(AM). May 1965: 99.3 mhz; 3 kw-H. Ant 300 ft. TL: N37 19 45 W91 53 55 (CP: 26 kw, ant 679 ft.). Stereo. News staff one; news progmg 12 hrs wkly. Spec prog: Farm 2 hrs wkly.

Huntsville

KTDI(FM)—Not on air, target date unknown: 92.5 mhz; 6 kw. Ant 328 ft. TL: N39 23 57 W92 26 04. Contemporary Media Broadcasting Group, 235 Jungerman Rd., St. Peters (63376). Licensee: Contemporary Broadcasting Inc. Group owner: Contemporary Media Broadcasting Group.

Independence

KJLA(AM)—1947: 1510 khz; 10 kw-D, DA. TL: N39 04 14 W94 26 58. 10841 E. 28th St. (64052). (816) 254-1073. Licensee: Tavastock Inc. (acq 9-29-89; $700,000; FTR 10-23-89). Format: Top 40. ■ Steve Dinkel, gen mgr; Bob Gould, gen sls mgr; Mark Feather, progmg dir; Craig Johnson, chief engr.

Jackson

KUGT(AM)—March 1972: 1170 khz; 250 w-D. TL: N37 22 54 W89 39 07. Box 546, 1301 Woodland (63755). (314) 243-0649. FAX: (314) 243-0640. Licensee: The Light & Power Co. (acq 5-1-89; $225,000; FTR 5-1-89). Net: CBN. Rep: Midsouth. Format: Relg. News progmg one hr wkly. Target aud: Young children to older adults. ■ Barbara England, gen mgr & sls dir; Dianne Stephens, mus dir. ■ Rates: $10; 10; 10; na.

Jefferson City

KFMZ(FM)—See Columbia.

***KJLU(FM)**—August 1973: 88.9 mhz; 40 kw. Ant 510 ft. TL: N38 27 29 W92 13 32. Stereo. Hrs opn: 6 AM-midnight. Box 29, 1004 E. Dunklin St. (65102). (314) 681-5301. Licensee: Board of Curators of Lincoln Univ. Net: ABC/FM. Format: Jazz, new age, urban contemp. News progmg 5 hrs wkly. Target aud: 18-54. Spec prog: Pub affrs, gospel, blues, reggae, oldies. ■ Jory A. Spears, gen mgr, stn mgr, progmg dir & mus dir; Dan Yeager, engrg mgr & chief engr.

KJMO(FM)—Listing follows KWOS(AM).

KLIK(AM)—February 1954: 950 khz; 5 kw-D, 500 w-N, DA-N. TL: N38 31 13 W92 10 42. Box 414 (65102). (314) 893-5696. FAX: (314) 635-FAXX. Licensee: Central Mo. Broadcasting Inc. Group owner: Brill Media Company Inc. (acq 6-1-81; $2,100,000; with co-located FM; FTR 5-4-81). Net: ABC/C. Format: Contemp country. Spec prog: Farm 12 hrs wkly. ■ Rich Nichols, pres, gen mgr & gen sls mgr.

KTXY(FM)—Co-owned with KLIK(AM). Dec 1, 1969: 106.9 mhz; 100 kw. Ant 1,250 ft. TL: N38 38 16 W92 29 34. Stereo. Prog sep from AM. Format: CHR.

KWOS(AM)—January 1937: 1240 khz; 1 kw-U. TL: N38 33 50 W92 11 21. Hrs opn: 24. Box 478 (65102). (314) 893-7857. Licensee: Triple-D Properties Inc. (acq 9-1-86; $700,000; FTR 6-16-86). Net: CBS, MBS; Missourinet. Format: News/talk. News staff 3; news progmg 39 hrs wkly. Target aud: 35 plus; mid to upper income-well informed. ■ Frank Newell, pres, gen mgr & progmg dir; Bob Kolb, gen sls mgr; John Marsh, news dir; Steve Morse, chief engr. ■ Rates: $17.75; 17.75; 12.75; 12.75.

KJMO(FM)—Co-owned with KWOS(AM). 1974: 100.1 mhz; 33 kw. Ant 600 ft. TL: N38 31 25 W92 24 25. Stereo. Hrs opn: 24. Prog sep from AM. 3109 S. Ten Mile Rd. (65109). (314) 893-5100. (Acq 7-15-81; $609,375; FTR 8-3-81). Net: NBC. Rep: Roslin. Format: Oldies. News staff 2. Target aud: 25-54; baby boomers. ■ Ted Ballenger, gen sls mgr; Warren Krech, progmg dir. ■ Rates: $22; 20; 21; 18.

Joplin

KFSB(AM)—Nov 21, 1948: 1310 khz; 5 kw-D, 1 kw-N, DA-2. TL: N37 07 03 W94 32 41. 2620 Dogwood Rd. (64801). (417) 624-1310. FAX: (417) 624-1817. Licensee: West Group Broadcasting (acq 11-30-88). Net: ABC/E. Rep: Banner. Format: Adult contemp. News staff one. Target aud: 25-54. ■ Paul Swint, pres & gen mgr; David Clemons, gen sls mgr; Rob Wells, progmg dir; Scott Curtis, news dir; Jack Leutzinger, chief engr. ■ Rates: $30; 20; 30; 15.

***KOBC(FM)**—Mar 17, 1969: 90.7 mhz; 30 kw. Ant 230 ft. TL: N37 06 16 W94 30 42. Stereo. Hrs opn: 18. 1111 N. Main St. (64801). (417) 781-6401. FAX: (417) 624-0090. Licensee: Ozark Christian College. Net: AP. Format: Contemp relg. News progmg 11 hrs wkly. Target aud: 25-49. ■ Ken Idleman, chmn; Rob Kime, gen mgr & progmg dir; Lisa Lunsford, mus dir; Mitch Piercy, chief engr.

KQYX(AM)—May 25, 1962: 1560 khz; 10 kw-D, DA. TL: N37 04 10 W94 32 49. Box 2625 (64803-2625); 2510 W. 20th St. (64804). (417) 781-1313. FAX: (417) 782-2134. Licensee: William B. Neal. Net: CNN, ABC TalkRadio. Rep: Katz & Powell. Wash atty: Leo Resnick. Format: News/talk. Target aud: 18-39. ■ William B. Neal, pres & gen mgr; Nancy Maxwell, gen sls mgr; Diane Smith, prom mgr & mus dir; Bob James, news dir; Jack Leutzinger, chief engr. ■ Rates: $28; 28; 28; 20.

KSYN(FM)—Co-owned with KQYX(AM). Dec 19, 1960: 92.5 mhz; 100 kw. Ant 430 ft. TL: N37 04 10 W94 32 49. Stereo. Prog sep from AM. Net: USA. Format: CHR. Target aud: 18-39. ■ Rates: $34; 34; 34; 26.

KWAS(AM)—June 1, 1946: 1230 khz; 1 kw-U. TL: N37 04 48 W94 33 10. Hrs opn: 24. 3001 W. 13th St. (64801). (417) 624-1230. FAX: (417) 624-7601. Licensee: Saturn Communications Inc. (acq 1-11-90; $200,000; FTR 1-29-90). Net: Unistar. Rep: Katz & Powell. Format: MOR. News staff one; news progmg 2 hrs wkly. Target aud: General. Spec prog: High school and college sports. ■ Andrew Wolfson, pres; Kevin McKelvy, gen mgr & stn mgr; Vance Lewis, opns dir & progmg mgr; Dennis Burns, gen sls mgr; Darron James, prom dir; Ann Harlow, mus dir; Darron Hanson, news dir; Jack Leutzinger, chief engr.

***KXMS(FM)**—Apr 5, 1986: 88.7 mhz; 10 kw. Ant 185 ft. TL: N37 05 57 W94 27 46. Stereo. Missouri Southern State College, Newman and Duquesne Rds. (64801). (417) 625-9356. Licensee: Board of Regents, Missouri Southern State College. Net: Beethoven. Format: Class. News progmg one hr wkly. Spec prog: Big band 2 hrs wkly. ■ Jeffrey D. Skibbe, stn mgr; Robert Harris, mus dir; Morris Sweet, chief engr.

WMBH(AM)—1927: 1450 khz; 1 kw-U. TL: N37 04 43 W94 32 26. 1309 Monroe, Joplin (64801). (417) 624-1025. FAX: (417) 781-6842. Licensee: Hendren-McChristian Communications (group owner; acq 6-11-92; $1.2 million; grpsl; FTR 6-29-92). Rep: Banner. Format: C&W, progsv, top-40. Spec prog: Farm one hr wkly. ■ Kim Hendren, pres; Linda Fair, gen mgr; Josh Duringer, progmg dir & mus dir.

WMBH-FM—November 1974: 102.5 mhz; 100 kw. Ant 410 ft. TL: N37 04 43 W94 32 26. Stereo. Format: Top-40, oldies. Spec prog: Class 3 hrs wkly.

Kansas City

KBEA(AM)—See Mission, Kan.

KBEQ-FM—Nov 1960: 104.3 mhz; 100 kw. Ant 987 ft. TL: N39 04 59 W94 28 49. Stereo. Hrs opn: 24. 4710 Pennsylvania (64112). (816) 531-2535. FAX: (816) 968-4199. Licensee: Noble Broadcast of Kansas City Inc. Group owner: Noble Broadcast Group (acq 10-87; $9.25 million; FTR 10-5-87). Rep: Torbet. Wash atty: Haley, Bader & Potts. Format: Young country. News staff one; news progmg one hr wkly. Target aud: 18-34. ■ Kathy Stinehour, vp; Brian Purdy, gen sls mgr; Sandy Wilkinson, prom dir; Mike Kennedy, progmg dir; Kimberly Ray, mus dir & news dir; Lee Wheeler, chief engr.

KCCV(AM)—See Overland Park, Kan.

KCFX(FM)—See Harrisonville.

KCMO(AM)—June 10, 1936: 810 khz; 50 kw-D, 5 kw-N, DA-N. TL: N39 18 21 W94 34 30. 508 Westport Rd. (64111). (816) 931-2681. FAX: (816) 932-7301. Licensee: Bonneville International (acq 10-27-93; with co-located FM; FTR 11-8-93). Net: CBS. Rep: McGavren Guild. Wash atty: Reed, Smith, Shaw & McClay. Format: News/talk. News staff 7; news progmg 30 hrs wkly. Target aud: 25-54. Spec prog: Sp one hr wkly. ■ Ron Carter, vp & gen mgr; Jane Graber, prom dir; Mike Elder, progmg dir; Katey McGuckin, pub affrs dir.

KCMO-FM—May 4, 1948: 94.9 mhz; 100 kw. Ant 1,057 ft. TL: N39 04 14 W94 34 59. Stereo. Prog sep from AM. Format: Oldies. News staff one; news progmg 3 hrs wkly. Spec prog: Pub affrs one hr wkly. ■ Brad Waldo, progmg dir.

KCNW(AM)—See Fairway, Kan.

***KCUR-FM**—October 1957: 89.3 mhz; 100 kw. Ant 820 ft. TL: N39 04 59 W94 28 49. Stereo. 5100 Rockhill Rd. (64110). (816) 235-1551. Licensee: Univ. of Missouri, Kansas City. Group owner: The Curators of the University of Missouri. Net: NPR, APR. Format: Pub affrs, news, jazz. News staff 3; news progmg 50 hrs wkly. Target aud: General; educated. Spec prog: Sp 2 hrs wkly. ■ Patricia Deal Cahill, gen mgr; Robert Barrientos, dev dir; Mary Jo Draper, news dir; Jim Jett, chief engr.

KEXS(AM)—See Excelsior Springs.

KFEZ(AM)—Sept 1, 1971: 1190 khz; 5 kw-D, 250 w-N, DA-N. TL: N39 03 49 W94 30 37. Stereo. Hrs opn: 24. Suite 300, 8826 Santa Fe, Overland Park, KS (66212). (913) 341-5552. FAX: (913) 341-0811. Licensee: Beal Broadcasting Co. Inc. (acq 8-29-91). Net: AP. Rep: Roslin. Wash atty: Booth, Freret & Imlay. Format: Adult standard, btfl mus, big band. Target aud: 35-64. Spec prog: Classical 17 hrs, jazz 5 hrs, relgious 5 hrs wkly. ■ Thomas E. Beal, CEO, pres, gen mgr & vp adv; Perry Beal, vp & gen sls mgr; Greg Funk, stn mgr; Steve Stalker, chief opns; Melissa Edris, prom dir; Melinda L. Beal, mus dir; Cinda Kirk, pub affrs dir; Fred Frank, chief engr. ■ Rates: $45; 30; 45; 26.

KJLA(AM)—See Independence.

***KKFI(FM)**—Feb 28, 1988: 90.1 mhz; 100 kw. Ant 503 ft. TL: N39 05 05 W94 28 47. Stereo. Hrs opn: 24. 900 1/2 Westport Rd. (64111). (816) 931-3122; (816) 931-5534. Licensee: Mid-Coast Radio Project Inc. Net: APR, NPR. Format: Jazz, prog, talk. News progmg 10 hrs wkly.

Target aud: General; women & minorities. Spec prog: Jazz/blues 19 hrs, Sp 16 hrs, international 7 hrs, women's 8 hrs, folk 4 hrs, American Indian 2 hrs wkly. ■ Trudie Hall, pres; Maria Banuelos, vp; Ed Haase, chief opns, progmg dir & news dir; Ed Treese, chief engr. ■ Rates: $30; 20; 30; 20.

*KLJC(FM)—Aug 9, 1970: 88.5 mhz; 100 kw. Ant 738 ft. TL: N39 04 24 W94 29 06. Stereo. c/o Calvary Bible College, 15800 Calvary Rd. (64147-1341). (816) 331-8700. FAX: (816) 331-4474. Licensee: Calvary Bible College. Net: Moody, USA. Format: Relg, educ, btfl music. ■ Dr. Donald Urey, pres; John Sims, gen mgr; John Hayden, mus dir; Darrell Nickolaus, chief engr.

KLTH(FM)—Listing follows KMBZ(AM).

KMBZ(AM)—1921: 980 khz; 5 kw-U, DA-N. TL: N39 02 17 W94 36 55. 4935 Belinder Rd., Westwood, KS (66205). (913) 677-8998. FAX: (913) 677-8935. Licensee: Bonneville International Corp. (group owner; acq 5-12-67). Net: NBC. Rep: D & R Radio. Format: News/talk. ■ Ron Carter, vp & gen mgr; Rob Hasson, gen sls mgr; Mike Elder, progmg dir; Noel Heckerson, news dir; Rich Myers, chief engr.

KLTH(FM)—Co-owned with KMBZ(AM). October 1962: 99.7 mhz; 100 kw. Ant 1,010 ft. TL: N39 05 01 W94 30 57. Stereo. Prog sep from AM. Format: Adult contemp.

KMXV(FM)—Mar 3, 1958: 93.3 mhz; 100 kw. Ant 1,066 ft. TL: N39 00 57 W94 30 57. Stereo. 3101 Broadway, No. 460 (64111). (816) 753-0933. FAX: (816) 753-6654. Licensee: Apollo Radio Ltd. (group owner; acq 1-19-90; $8.5 million; FTR 2-19-90). Rep: Banner. Format: Adult contemp. ■ William L. Stakelin, pres; Fred Murr, gen mgr; Mike Payne, gen sls mgr; Tom Land, progmg dir; Amanda Waters, news dir; Ben Weiss, chief engr.

KNHN(AM)—See Kansas City, Kan.

KPRS(FM)—Listing follows KPRT(AM).

KPRT(AM)—1950: 1590 khz; 1 kw-U. TL: N39 04 05 W94 32 10. Hrs opn: 24. 11131 Colorado Ave. (64137). (816) 763-2040. FAX: (816) 966-1055. Licensee: Mildred M. Carter. Rep: Eastman. Format: Gospel. ■ Michael Carter, pres; Audrey Thompson, opns mgr & natl sls mgr; Jay Cooper, gen sls mgr; Rich McCauley, prom mgr; Fred Bell, progmg dir; Eddie Blaze, mus dir; Robert Leedham, chief engr.

KPRS(FM)—Co-owned with KPRT(AM). 1963: 103.3 mhz; 100kw. Ant 994 ft. TL: N39 00 57 W94 30 24. Stereo. Prog sep from AM. Net: AP/FM. Rep: Katz, Eastman. Wash atty: Bryan Cave. Format: Urban contemp. News progmg one hr wkly. Target aud: 25-54; mid-upper income. ■ Mildred Carter, CEO; Rich McCauley, prom dir; Sam Weaver, progmg dir; Myron Feary, mus dir.

KQRC-FM—(Leavenworth, Kan) 1962: 98.9 mhz; 100 kw. Ant 990 ft. TL: N39 04 14 W94 54 39. Stereo. Suite #99, 4350 Shawnee Mission Pkwy., Shawnee Mission, KS (66205). (913) 384-9900. FAX: (913) 384-9911. Licensee: WTMJ Inc. (group owner; acq 8-22-89; $6 million; FTR 9-11-89). Net: NBC The Source. Rep: Banner. Wash atty: Crowell & Moring. Format: AOR. News staff one. Target aud: 25-54; above average education & income; upscale professionals. ■ Jon Schweitzer, gen mgr; Mike Wodlinger, stn mgr & gen sls mgr; Ina Erickson, dev dir; J. D. Allen, prom dir; Doug Sorensen, progmg dir; Valorie Knight, mus dir; Lee Wheeler, chief engr. ■ Rates: $75; 75; 75; 35.

KUDL(FM)—See Kansas City, Kan.

KXTR(FM)—Jan 1, 1959: 96.5 mhz; 99 kw. Ant 984 ft. TL: N39 00 57 W94 30 24. Stereo. Hrs opn: 24. 1701 S. 55th St. (66106). (913) 432-1480. FAX: (913)287-5209. Licensee: KXTR Broadcasting Co. (acq 1-1-76). Net: Unistar. Format: Class. Target aud: 25 plus; adults with above-average disposable income. ■ Robert P. Ingram, pres & gen mgr; James Cunningham, vp; Lawyer Ward, gen sls mgr & pub affrs dir; Patrick Neas, progmg dir; Lee Wheeler, chief engr. ■ Rates: $65; 62; 65; 52.

KYYS(FM)—Listing follows WDAF(AM).

WDAF(AM)—Feb 16, 1922: 610 khz; 5 kw-U. TL: N38 59 03 W94 37 40. 3020 Summit (64108). (816) 931-6100. FAX: (816) 932-8576. Licensee: Great American Broadcasting (group owner; acq 1987). Net: ABC/E. Rep: Katz. Format: Country. News staff 6. Target aud: 25-54; general. ■ Herndon Hasty, pres; Gary Lakey, gen sls mgr; Joe Nucci, natl sls mgr; Gregg Hibbeler, mktg dir; Deanna Posey, prom dir; Ted Cramer, progmg dir & asst mus dir; David Bryan, mus dir; Charles Gray, news dir; Ken Dillard, chief engr.

KYYS(FM)—Co-owned with WDAF(AM). March 5, 1961: 102.1 mhz; 100 kw. Ant 1,000 ft. TL: N39 04 20 W94 35 45. Prog sep from AM. (816) 561-9102. Format: AOR. News progmg one hr wkly. Target aud: 25-54. ■ Mike Campbell, gen mgr; Michelle England, prom dir; Scott Souhrada, progmg dir; Debbie Mitchell, mus dir. ■ WDAF-TV affil.

WHB(AM)—March 1922: 710 khz; 10 kw-D, 5 kw-N, DA-2. TL: N39 19 08 W94 29 48. Stereo. 102 N. Mason St., Carrollton (64633). (816) 224-6222. FAX: (816) 224-6222. Licensee: KANZA Inc. (acq 9-20-93; $600,000; FTR 10-18-93). Net: AP. Rep: Christal. Format: Country. ■ Mike Carter, gen mgr; Bob Tutt, gen sls mgr; Kathie Truitt, prom dir; Miles Carter, progmg dir; Wayne Combs, news dir; Ken Wolf, chief engr.

Kennett

KBOA(AM)—July 19, 1947: 830 khz; 10 kw-D. TL: N36 13 29 W90 04 31. Box 509 (63857). (314) 888-4616. FAX: (314) 888-4991. Licensee: KBOA Inc. Group owner: Meyer Communications Inc. (acq 10-1-83; $1.3 million with co-located FM; FTR 9-26-83). Net: AP; Missourinet. Rep: McGavren Guild. Format: Adult contemp, classic gold. News staff one. ■ Kenneth E. Meyer, pres; Jeff Wheeler, gen mgr & gen sls mgr; R.J. McAllister, news dir; Larry Anthony, chief engr.

KTMO(FM)—Co-owned with KBOA(AM). 1948: 98.9 mhz; 100kw. Ant 994 ft. TL: N36 07 53 W90 11 34. Stereo. Prog sep from AM. Format: C&W. Target aud: 24 plus.

KNNT(AM)—1963: 1540 khz; 1 kw-D. TL: N36 15 11 W90 02 56. Box 569 (63857). (314) 888-5333; (314) 888-1540. FAX: (314) 888-5333. Licensee: KBXM Inc. (acq 1982; $235,000; FTR 12-5-83). Net: ABC/I. Format: News/talk. Spec progmg: Farm 5 hrs, gospel 5 hrs wkly. ■ Gary Wilcoxson, pres; Mick Vandiver, gen & prom mgr; Larry Warbritton, gen sls mgr & adv mgr; Buck Harrison, progmg dir & mus dir; Tim Blair, news dir; Palmer Johnson, chief engr.

KTMO(FM)—Listing follows KBOA(AM).

Kirksville

KIRX(AM)—Oct 17, 1947: 1450 khz; 1 kw-U. TL: N40 12 24 W92 34 31. Hrs opn: 24. Box 130 (63501). (816) 665-9841; (816) 665-3781. FAX: (816) 665-0711. Licensee: KIRX Inc. (acq 10-1-85; $1.3 million; with co-located FM; FTR 8-12-85). Net: ABC/D, AP; Brownfield. Format: Country. News staff 2. Target aud: General. Spec prog: Talk 12 hrs, big band 3 hrs, farm 10 hrs wkly. ■ David L. Nelson, pres; Alvina M. Britz, exec vp & gen mgr; Steve Lloyd, gen sls mgr; Helen Adams, prom dir & progmg mgr; Chuck Knight, prom mgr; Troy Renner, mus dir; Carol Richardson, news dir; Phil Benjamin, chief engr.

KRXL(FM)—Co-owned with KIRX(AM). September 1967: 94.5 mhz; 100 kw. Ant 1,010 ft. TL: N40 13 32 W92 00 54 (CP: 90.4 kw). Stereo. Prog sep from AM. (816) 665-9828; Format: AOR, classic rock. Target aud: 25-54. ■ Trevor Stern, progmg mgr & mus dir; Richard Hutchinson, asst mus dir.

KLTE(FM)—May 20, 1991: 107.9 mhz; 100 kw. Ant 715 ft. TL: N39 57 23 W92 58 29. Suite 100, 3 Crown Dr. (63501). (816) 627-5583. FAX: (816) 665-8900. Licensee: The Word in Music Inc. Format: Contemp Christian. ■ Larry Alford, pres.

KRXL(FM)—Listing follows KIRX(AM).

KTUF(FM)—Feb 14, 1983: 93.7 mhz; 50 kw. Ant 492 ft. TL: N40 13 38 W92 36 35. Stereo. Hrs opn: 24. Box 218, 211 W. Washington St. (63501). (816) 627-1213. FAX: (816) 627-1213. Licensee: Admiral Broadcasting Corp. Net: AP. Format: Hot adult contemp. News staff one; news progmg 2 hrs wkly. Target aud: 14-55; teenage through yuppies to younger middle-age. ■ Irvin Davis, pres; Anne Blackwell, gen mgr, stn mgr & gen sls mgr; Debbie Blackwell, progmg dir; Mike Young, mus dir; Larry Byars, news dir; Clifton Brown, chief engr. ■ Rates: $16; 16; 16; 13.65.

Knob Noster

KXKX(FM)—June 24, 1983: 105.7 mhz; 3 kw. Ant 300 ft. TL: N38 46 28 W93 37 34 (CP: 30 kw). Stereo. Hrs opn: 24. Box 441, 610 E. Young, Warrensburg (64093). (816) 747-5122. FAX: (816) 747-7517. Licensee: Bick Broadcasting Co. (acq 7-19-89; $185,000; FTR 8-7-89). Net: ABC/I. Format: Country. News staff 2; news progmg 5 hrs wkly. Target aud: 25-54. ■ James E. Janes, pres; Dennis Polk, gen mgr & gen sls mgr; Byron Johnson, progmg dir; Robert Milner, progmg dir; Carl Zimmerscheid, chief engr. ■ Rates: $10.60; 8.25; 10.60; 8.25.

Lake Ozark

KABE(FM)—Not on air, target date unknown: 102.7 mhz; 6 kw. Ant 328 ft. 2279 Springs Landing Blvd., Longwood, FL (32779). Licensee: Herrin Broadcasting Inc.

Lamar

KHST(FM)—May 1, 1992. 99.9 mhz; 3 kw. Ant 328 ft. TL: N37 25 27 W94 16 12. Stereo. Hrs opn: 18. Box 100 (64759). (417) 682-6699. Licensee: Russell D. Weeks Jr. (acq 11-14-91; $12,000 for CP; FTR 12-2-91). Format: Country. ■ Russ Weeks, gen mgr.

Lebanon

KCLQ(FM)—Listing follows KLWT(AM).

KIRK(FM)—Listing follows KJEL(AM).

KJEL(AM)—Oct 20, 1973: 750 khz; 5 kw-D. TL: N37 41 10 W92 41 39. Hrs opn: 6 AM-6 PM. Box 1112, Dillworth Rd. (65536). (417) 532-9111. FAX: (417) 588-4191. Licensee: Ozark Broadcasting Inc. Group owner: Shepherd Group (acq 7-83; $450,000 with co-located FM; FTR 7-4-83). Net: ABC/I; Missourinet. Format: Country. News staff 2; news progmg 35 hrs wkly. Target aud: 35-64; middle America. Spec prog: Farm 8 hrs wkly. ■ Jerrell Shepherd, pres; Mike Edwards, gen mgr; John Fowler, opns mgr & progmg dir; Brenda Goodin, news dir; Bob Moore, chief engr. ■ Rates: $30; 28; 24; 14.

KIRK(FM)—Co-owned with KJEL(AM). Oct 20, 1973: 103.7 mhz; 100 kw. Ant 984 ft. TL: N37 49 10 W92 44 51. Stereo. Hrs opn: 24. News progmg 45 hrs wkly. Target aud: 25-54; affluent, business oriented. Spec progmg: New age 6 hrs, oldies 6 hrs wkly. ■ Rates: $36; 28; 22; 22.

KLWT(AM)—July 4, 1948: 1230 khz; 1 kw-U. TL: N37 40 40 W92 41 16. Hrs opn: 5 AM-midnight. Box 29, Rt. 2 (65536). (417) 532-2962. FAX: (417) 532-5184. Licensee: Lebanon Broadcasting Co. Net: MBS. Format: C&W, news/talk, sports. News staff 2; news progmg 5 hrs wkly. Target aud: 35 plus; higher income male. Spec prog: Farm 2 hrs wkly. ■ Deborah Moore, pres; Michael Hendee, gen mgr & vp prom; Larry Freeman, opns mgr, progmg dir & mus dir; Marian King, rgnl sls mgr; Mark Allen, news dir; Eugene Clay, chief engr. ■ Rates: $13; 10.50; 11.75; 2.50.

KCLQ(FM)—Co-owned with KLWT(AM). May 18, 1979: 107.9 mhz; 50 kw. Ant 365 ft. TL: N37 40 40 W92 41 16. Stereo. Hrs opn: 24. Prog sep from AM. Format: Pure gold of the 50s, 60s 70s & 80s. News staff 2; news progmg 3 hrs wkly. Target aud: 25-54; female. ■ Rates: $16.; 14; 15; 3.

Lexington

KISF(FM)—Sept 11, 1969: 107.3 mhz; 100 kw. Ant 1,184 ft. TL: N39 02 15 W93 55 48. Stereo. Hrs opn: 24. 10841 E. 28th St., Independence (64052). (816) 254-1073. FAX: (816) 254-6929. Licensee: KCFM Inc. Group owner: Meyer Communications Inc. Format: Top 40. News staff one. Target aud: 18-34; adults. ■ Regan Henry, CEO; Don Kidwell, pres; Stephen Dinkel, gen mgr; Mark Feather, progmg dir.

KLEX(AM)—Apr 19, 1956: 1570 khz; 250 w-D, 58 w-N. TL: N39 11 14 W98 35 00 03. Hrs opn: 5:30 AM-11 PM. 111 Main, Richmond (64085). (816) 776-3196. Licensee: Summit Operations Inc. (acq 7-24-90; $75,000; FTR 8-13-90). Wash atty: Erwin Krasnow. ■ Shelby L. Hendee, pres.

Liberty

KKCJ(FM)—Nov 9, 1979: 106.5 mhz; 100 kw. Ant 981 ft. TL: N39 04 23 W94 29 06. Stereo. Box 634, Kansas City (64126). (816) 531-1000. Licensee: Capital Broadcasting Inc. (acq 5-15-91; $2.6 million; FTR 6-10-91). Net: SMN. Rep: Republic. Format: Contemp country. News progmg one hr wkly. Target aud: 18-34. ■ Dan Wastler, vp & gen mgr; Don Crawley, opns mgr; Steve Douglas, progmg dir; Craig Johnson, chief engr. ■ Rates: $100; 100; 100; 100.

*KWJC(FM)—Apr 14, 1974: 91.9 mhz; 182 w. Ant 166 ft. TL: N39 14 52 W94 24 47. Stereo. William Jewell College (64068). (816) 781-8278. FAX: (816) 781-3164. Licensee: William Jewell College. Net: ABC/D. Format: Contemp Christian. News progmg 5 hrs wkly. Target aud: 12-34; young Christians in Kansas City. ■ Craig Larson, gen mgr; Fred Frank, chief engr.

Louisiana

KJFM(FM)—Sept 4, 1984: 102.1 mhz; 1.85 kw. Ant 387 ft. TL: N39 26 29 W91 02 19. Stereo. Box 438, 615 Georgia St. (63353). (314) 754-4583. Licensee: Foxfire Communications Inc. Net: ABC/C; Missourinet. Format: Country. News staff one; news progmg 16 hrs wkly. Target aud: 25-54. ■ Thom T. Sanders, pres & gen mgr; Gordon R. Sanders, progmg mgr.

Lutesville

KQUA(FM)—Not on air, target date unknown: 105.1 mhz; 1.75 kw. Ant 430 ft. TL: N37 23 01 W89 55 55. Box 855, Ironfield Dr., Mayfield, KY (42066). Licensee: Lutesville Broadcasting Inc. (acq 3-5-91; FTR 3-25-91).

Macon

KLTI(AM)—Jan 30, 1966: 1560 khz; 1 kw-D. TL: N39 42 34 W92 27 50. Box 189, Monroe City (63456). (314) 735-2754. Licensee: Monroe City Broadcasting Inc. (acq 3-17-93; $35,000; FTR 4-5-93). ■ John Jamison, pres; Faye Bleigh, gen mgr.

Madison

WGNU(AM)—See St. Louis, Mo.

Malden

KTCB(AM)—Sept 15, 1954: 1470 khz; 1 kw-D. TL: N36 33 08 W89 58 32. Hrs opn: 6 AM-sunset. Box 379, AB Hwy. S. (63863). (314) 276-5625. FAX: (314) 276-2282. Licensee: BBC Inc. (acq 4-88). Net: AP. Format: Southern gospel. News staff 3. Target aud: 35 plus. Spec prog: Country 6 hrs wkly. ■ Dave Green, pres, gen mgr & gen sls mgr; Denise Evans, prom mgr; Steve Connor, progmg dir & mus dir; Chuck Sutton, news dir; Jim McGowan, chief engr. ■ Rates: $8; 7; 7; 6.

KMAL(FM)—Co-owned with KTCB(AM). Nov 23, 1979: 92.7 mhz; 3 kw. Ant 193 ft. TL: N36 33 08 W89 58 42. Stereo. Hrs opn: 6 AM-midnight. Prog sep from AM. Box 1993, AB Hwy. S. (63863). Format: Adult contemp, urban contemp. News staff 2; news progmg 30 hrs wkly. Target aud: General. Spec prog: Black 6 hrs wkly. ■ Denise Evans, vp opns; Dave Green, vp sls; Steve Connor, vp progmg. ■ Rates: $10; 9; 8; 7.

Malta Bend

KRLI(FM)—Not on air, target date unknown: 97.5 mhz; 3.42 kw. Ant 879 ft. 802 E. 12th St., Carrollton (64633). Licensee: Miles J. Carter.

Mansfield

KTRI-FM—1978: 95.9 mhz; 3 kw. Ant 312 ft. TL: N37 02 18 W92 40 30. Stereo. Box 6610, Branson (65616). (417) 924-8696. FAX: (417) 924-8696. Licensee: Terry L. Claar. Net: AP. Rep: Keystone (unwired net), Magic Circle. Format: Classic country ■ Terry L. Claar, pres, gen mgr & gen sls mgr; Ken Luther, chief engr.

Marshall

KMMO(AM)—May 29, 1949: 1300 khz; 1 kw-D, 68 w-N. TL: N39 08 11 W93 13 24. Box 128 (65340). (816) 886-7422. FAX: (816) 886-6291. Licensee: Missouri Valley Broadcasting Inc. (acq 11-19-84; $690,000 with co-located FM; FTR 12-10-84). Net: CBS; Brownfield. Format: C&W. Spec prog: Farm 6 hrs wkly. ■ John Wilson, vp; Randall Wiseman, progmg dir; Brian Holsten, mus dir; Ken Lewellen, news dir.

KMMO-FM—December 1968: 102.9 mhz; 56 kw. Ant 380 ft. TL: N39 08 11 W93 13 24 (CP: 100 kw). Stereo. Dups AM 100%. Net: CBS. ■ Rates: Same as AM.

*****KMVC(FM)**—Nov 1, 1968: 91.7 mhz; 10 w. Ant 51 ft. TL: N39 06 24 W93 11 30 (CP: 93.1 mhz, 10 w. TL: N39 06 31 W93 11 29). Stereo. Hrs opn: 7 AM-11 PM Mon-Fri, 9 AM-11 PM Sat, noon-8 PM. Missouri Valley College, 500 E. College St. (65340). (816) 886-6924, ext. 193; (816) 886-6924, ext. 146. Licensee: Missouri Valley College. Format: Div. News progmg 3 hrs wkly. Target aud: 17-26; pre-, current & post-college age. Spec prog: Black 10 hrs, progsv 10 hrs, relg 16 hrs, classic rock 4 hrs, hip hop 10 hrs, urban 10 hrs wkly. ■ Karl E. Bean, gen mgr & vp progmg; Willailm D. Lehotz, stn mgr; Lee Peek, progmg dir; William Lehotz, progmg mgr; Ray Colaiacovo, mus dir; Julie Haefele, Rita Bates, asst mus dirs; Amy Kreitler, news dir.

Marshfield

KMRF(AM)—Nov 1, 1969: 1510 khz; 250 w-D. TL: N37 20 55 W92 54 28. Box K, 400 Hubble Dr. (65706). (417) 468-6188. Licensee: James R. and Mary Catherine Cooper (acq 11-30-92; $34,900; FTR 1-25-93). Net: USA; Missourinet, Brownfield. Format: Country. News staff one; news progmg 6 hrs wkly. Target aud: General. Spec prog: Gospel 7 hrs wkly. ■ Gene Muse, pres, stn mgr, gen sls mgr, progmg dir & pub affrs dir; Denny Goode, vp; Fred Fulbright, gen mgr; Dan Hale, prom dir. ■ Rates: $10; 8; 9; na.

KTOZ-FM—June 1982: 104.7 mhz; 3 kw. Ant 299 ft. TL: N37 17 57 W93 00 26 (CP: 35.3 kw, ant 581 ft., TL: N37 12 31 W92 54 21). Stereo. 2607 W. Bennet, Springfield (65807). (417) 831-7625. FAX: (417) 831-1231. Licensee: GMR, MO Inc. (acq 11-30-93; $280,000; FTR 12-20-93). Net: MBS. Format: Rock. ■ Frank Capsidas, pres; Dom Casual, opns mgr.

Maryville

KNIM(AM)—1953: 1580 khz; 250 w-D, 11 w-N. TL: N40 19 47 W94 52 31 (CP: 1 kw-D). Box 278 (64468). (816) 582-2151. FAX: (816) 582-3211. Licensee: Nodaway Broadcasting Corp. (acq 8-1-82). Net: ABC/D. Rep: Keystone (unwired net). Format: Adult contemp. Spec prog: Farm 5 hrs wkly. ■ Steve Mickelson, pres & gen mgr.

KNIM-FM—September 1972: 97.1 mhz; 25 kw. Ant 328 ft. TL: N40 19 41 W94 52 31 Stereo. Dups AM 80%.

*****KXCV(FM)**—1971: 90.5 mhz; 100 kw. Ant 500 ft. TL: N40 21 36 W94 53 00. Stereo. Wells Hall, 800 University Dr. (64468). (816) 562-1163; (816) 562-1164. FAX: (816) 562-1900. Licensee: Northwest Missouri State Univ. Net: AP, NPR, APR. Format: News, classical, jazz. News staff 2; news progmg 39 hrs wkly. Target aud: General. ■ Dean L. Hubbard, pres; Sharon Cross Bonnett, gen mgr & progmg dir; Michael Johnson, opns mgr, prom mgr & mus dir; Patty Holley, progmg dir; John McGuire, news dir; Michael Douthat, chief engr.

Memphis

KMEM-FM—Mar 29, 1982: 96.7 mhz; 25 kw. Ant 300 ft. TL: N40 29 59 W92 09 58. Stereo. Hrs opn: 5 AM-midnight. Box 121, 326 E. Jefferson (63555). (816) 465-7225; (816) 465-2715. FAX: (816) 465-2626. Licensee: Boyer Broadcasting Co. (acq 6-1-90; $72,500; FTR 3-12-90). Net: ABC/E, Missourinet, Iowa Net, Brownfield. Wash atty: Eugene Smith. Format: Country. News staff one; news progmg 15 hrs wkly. Target aud: General; agricultural audience and elderly. Spec prog: Farm 8 hrs, relg 4 hrs wkly. ■ Keith Boyer, pres; Ruthann Boyer, vp; Denise Boyer, gen mgr & mktg mgr; Jim Sears, opns mgr, progmg mgr & mus dir; Denise Boyer, Cindy Graber, Brenda Winn, gen sls mgrs; Rick Fischer, prom mgr; Denise Boyer, Cindy Graber, Brenda Winn, adv mgrs; Jim Sears, Melissa McCauley, Rick Fischer, news dirs; Don Pennick, chief engr. ■ Rates: $18; 18; 18; 16.50.

Mexico

*****KJAB-FM**—Oct 9, 1985: 90.1 mhz; 380 w. Ant 128 ft. TL: N34 10 28 W91 53 22. Hrs opn: 18. 310 N. Wade (65265). (314) 581-8606. Licensee: Mexico Educational Broadcasting Foundation. Net: USA. Format: Total Christian progmg, news/talk. Target aud: General. ■ Kevin Weber, gen mgr; Fran Keipp, stn mgr.

KWWR(FM)—Listing follows KXEO(AM).

KXEO(AM)—Dec 3, 1948: 1340 khz; 1 kw-U. TL: N39 10 01 W91 51 44. Hrs opn: 24. 1705 E. Liberty (65265). (314) 581-2340. Licensee: Ruth Anne Mongler (acq 2-4-91; with co-located FM; FTR 2-18-91). Net: MBS. Format: Gold. News progmg 4 hrs wkly. Target aud: 25-54. Spec prog: Farm 3 hrs wkly. ■ Ruth Anne Mongler, pres; Gary Leonard, gen mgr; Kent Morgan, gen sls mgr; Chuck Thomas, progmg dir; Mark Morgan, news dir. ■ Rates: $24.71; 21.18; 24.71; 21.18.

KWWR(FM)—Co-owned with KXEO(AM). Dec 14, 1966; 95.7 mhz; 100 kw. Ant 1,027 ft. TL: N39 11 42 W91 56 25. Stereo. Hrs opn: 24. Prog sep from AM. (314) 581-5500. Format: Country. Spec prog: Farm 4 hrs wkly. ■ Rates: $31.76; 25.88; 31.76; 25.88.

Moberly

KRES(FM)—Listing follows KWIX(AM).

KWIX(AM)—June 1950: 1230 khz; 1 kw-U. TL: N39 24 11 W92 25 57. Hrs opn: 24. Box 619, 300 W. Reed (65270). (816) 263-1500. Licensee: KWIX Inc. Group owner: Shepherd Group. Net: CBS, NBC Talknet. Rep: Katz. Format: Div. News staff 4; news progmg 30 hrs wkly. Target aud: General. ■ Jerrell A. Shepherd, pres; David Shepherd, opns mgr & gen sls mgr; Ken Kujawa, progmg dir; Brad Boyer, mus dir; Eric Chism, news dir. ■ Rates: $46; 36; 30; 20.

KRES(FM)—Co-owned with KWIX(AM). Oct 1966: 104.7 mhz; 100 kw. Ant 1025 ft. TL: N39 27 53 W92 42 07. Stereo. Prog sep from AM. Box 430 (65270). (816) 263-1600. Net: ABC/E. Format: Mod country, farm. News staff 5; news progmg 21 hrs wkly. ■ Rates: $50; 30; 20; 15.

KZZT(FM)—Apr 10, 1987: 105.5 mhz; 25 kw. Ant 328 ft. TL: N39 24 54 W92 24 36. Stereo. Hrs opn: 24. Box 128, Rt. 4, Jct. Hwy. 66/EE (65270). (816) 263-9390; (816) 263-1055. FAX: (816) 263-8800. Licensee: FM 105 Inc. Net: SMN, ABC. Wash atty: Bryan, Cave, McPheeters & McRoberts. Format: Hot adult contemporary. News progmg 5 hrs wkly. Target aud: 25-34; men & women with spendable income. Spec prog: Farm 3 hrs wkly. ■ Virginia S. Chirillo, pres; Dale A. Palmer, gen mgr, gen sls mgr, prom mgr & adv dir; Amy E. Aleshire, opns mgr; Mike Clayton, progmg mgr, news dir & pub affrs dir; Cory Curtis, mus dir; Alan West, chief engr. ■ Rates: $18.75; 18.75; 18.75; 12.

Monett

KRMO(AM)—August 1950: 990 khz; 2.5 kw-D, 47 w-N. TL: N36 56 15 W93 55 30. 1569 N. Central (65708). (417) 235-6041. FAX: (417) 235-6388. Licensee: Monett Communications Inc. (acq 4-80). Net: ABC/D; Brownfield, Missourinet. Format: Country, div, news. News staff one; news progmg 10 hrs wkly. Target aud: 35 plus. Spec prog: Farm 10 hrs, gospel 10 hrs wkly. ■ Kevin Wodlinger, pres & gen sls mgr; Patricia Wodlinger, stn mgr & progmg dir; Don Sullivan, news dir; James Helmkamp, chief engr. ■ Rates: $10; 10; 10; 10.

KKBL(FM)—Co-owned with KRMO(AM). December 1977: 95.9 mhz; 6 kw. Ant 269 ft. TL: N36 56 15 W93 55 30. Stereo. Prog sep from AM. Format: Adult contemp. ■ Rates: Same as AM.

Monroe City

KDAM(FM)—July 4, 1981: 106.3 mhz; 3 kw. Ant 302 ft. TL: N39 35 12 W91 47 57. Stereo. Hrs opn: 24. Box 189 (63456); 109 Winter (63456). (314) 735-2754. Licensee: John Jamison (acq 12-88). Net: ABC. Wash atty: Roger Begley. Format: Cool gold oldies. News staff 2; news progmg one hr wkly. Target aud: 18-35. ■ John Jamison, pres; Faye Bleigh, gen mgr.

Montgomery City

KMCR(FM)—Aug 15, 1977: 103.9 mhz; 3 kw. Ant 300 ft. TL: N38 59 12 W91 30 48. Stereo. Hrs opn: 24. Box 189, 405 E. Harrison (63361-0189). (314) 564-2275. Licensee: Montgomery Media. Net: ABC/E; Missourinet. Format: Adult contemp. News staff one; news progmg 3 hrs wkly. Target aud: General; 25-60, male/female. Spec prog: Farm 2 hrs, relg 2 hrs wkly. ■ Joel Greenberg, pres, gen mgr, gen sls mgr, progmg dir & news dir; Donna Nichols, sls dir; Ken Meacham, chief engr. ■ Rates: $12; 9; 10; 7.

Mount Vernon

KELE(FM)—Not on air, target date unknown: 106.7 mhz; 25 kw. Ant 328 ft. TL: N37 09 16 W93 36 58. Box 214044, Sacramento, CA (95821). Licensee: Edward J. Mahoney (acq 3-31-93; $24,000; FTR 4-26-93).

Mountain Grove

KCMG(AM)—Nov 16, 1954: 1360 khz; 1 kw-D. TL: N37 08 07 W92 14 59. Box 804 (65711). (417) 926-4650. FAX: (417) 926-7604. Licensee: Communication Works Inc. (acq 1984; $240,000). Net: ABC/D, Unistar; Brownfield, Missourinet. Rep: Keystone (unwired net). Format: All country. News staff one; news progmg 28 hrs wkly. Target aud: Farm oriented. ■ Lou Wehmer, gen mgr, opns mgr & chief engr; Fred Clift, gen sls mgr, prom mgr, adv mgr, progmg dir & mus dir. ■ Rates: $8; 8; 6.

KCMG-FM—Jan 1, 1977: 106.5 mhz; 3 kw. Ant 299 ft. TL: N37 08 07 W92 14 59. Stereo. Dups AM 100%. ■ David Hutton, gen mgr.

Mountain View

KXOZ(FM)—March 12, 1990: 96.9 mhz; 50 kw. Ant 420 ft. TL: N36 59 29 W91 47 41. Stereo. Hrs opn: 24. Box 358, Hwy. 60 W. (65548). (417) 934-6776; (417) 934-2244. FAX: (417) 934-6776. Licensee: James M. Hunt. Net: Unistar. Format: Adult contemp. News progmg 2 hrs wkly. Target aud: 25-54. ■ Jack Hunt, pres; Brian Keefe,

Stations in the U.S.

Missouri

gen mgr, gen sls mgr & progmg dir. ■ Rates: $7.75; 7; 7.75; 6.

Neosho

KBTN(AM)—Feb 1, 1954: 1420 khz; 1 kw-D, 500 w-N, DA-N. TL: N36 50 52 W94 19 12. Hrs opn: 5 AM-midnight. Box K, 216 W. Spring (64850). (417) 451-1420. Licensee: KBTN Inc. (acq 12-11-84). Net: SMN; Missourinet. Format: Country. News staff 2; news progmg 14 hrs wkly. Target aud: 18-54; adults. Spec prog: Farm 6 hrs wkly. ■ David L. Winegardner, pres & gen mgr; Carl Cobb, stn mgr; Ed Beach, news dir; Wilbur Blankenship, chief engr. ■ Rates: $17; 10; 10; 9.

***KNEO(FM)**—October 1986: 91.5 mhz; 348 w. Ant 80 ft. TL: N36 51 48 W94 23 18. Hrs opn: 17. Box 845, 700 Spencer Dr. (64850). (417) 451-5636. Licensee: Abundant Life Broadcasting Corp. Net: USA. Format: Gospel, MOR. News staff 3; news progmg 10 hrs wkly. Target aud: 21-50; rural people & older shut-ins. ■ Bill Nichols, pres; Mark Taylor, gen mgr & prom mgr; Larry Wise, progmg dir, mus dir & news dir; Ray Lark, chief engr.

Nevada

KNEM(AM)—1949: 1240 khz; 1 kw-U. TL: N37 49 50 W94 20 55. Hrs opn: 5:30 AM-midnight. Box 447, 414 E. Walnut (64772). (417) 667-3113. FAX: (417) 667-9797. Licensee: KNEM Communications Inc. (acq 6-13-83; $291,667; FTR 7-4-83). Net: ABC/D, Brownfield, Missourinet. Format: Country. News staff one; news progmg 30 hrs wkly. Target aud: General. Spec prog: Farm 7 hrs, Christian 5 hrs wkly. ■ F.D. Lightner, pres; Patrick A. Chambers, vp, gen mgr, gen sls mgr & progmg dir; Susan Thompson, opns mgr; Christina Hansell, mus dir; Dick Jones, news dir, engrg dir & chief engr. ■ Rates: $17.25; 14.67; 17.25; 12.94.

KNMO(FM)—Co-owned with KNEM(AM). Sept 10, 1984: 97.7 mhz; 3 kw. Ant 300 ft. TL: N37 51 37 W94 22 54. Stereo. Dups AM 100%. ■ Rates: Same as AM.

New Madrid

KMIS-FM—Licensed to New Madrid. See Portageville.

Nixa

KGBX-FM—Licensed to Nixa. See Springfield.

North Kansas City

KKCJ(FM)—See Liberty.

Osage Beach

KBMX(FM)—(Eldon). Oct 1, 1988: 101.9 mhz; 2.25 kw. Ant 545 ft. TL: N38 16 49 W92 35 07 (CP: 47.5 kw, 505 ft.). Stereo. Hrs opn: 24. Box 4881, Lake Rd. 54-24, Osage Beach (65065). (314) 348-0500. FAX: (314) 348-0625. Licensee: Lake Broadcasting Inc. Group owner: Contemporary Media Broadcasting Group (acq 2-22-88). Net: ABC/D. Wash atty: Rosenman & Colin. Format: Soft adult contemp. News staff one; news progmg 6 hrs wkly. Target aud: 25 plus; upscale adults. ■ Mike Rice, pres; Dan Leatherman, gen mgr; Jeff Karr, progmg dir; J. Eric Hoehn, chief engr.

KRMS(AM)—December 1952: 1150 khz; 1 kw-D, 55 w-N. TL: N38 07 29 W92 40 39. Hrs opn: 6 AM-midnight. Box 225, Hwy. 54 (65065). (314) 348-2772. FAX: (314) 348-2779. Licensee: KRMS/KYLC Inc. Group owner: Mahaffey Enterprises Inc. (acq 6-1-86). Net: CBS, NBC Talknet; Missourinet. Format: C&W. Spec prog: Farm 2 hrs wkly. ■ John Mahaffey, pres; David Schoolfield, vp & gen mgr; Kevin Roberts, progmg dir, mus dir & news dir; Pat Botts, chief engr.

KYLC(FM)—Co-owned with KRMS(AM). April 12, 1964: 93.5 mhz; 3 kw. Ant 300 ft. TL: N38 07 29 W92 40 39. Stereo. Prog sep from AM. Format: Contemporary, classic rock. Spec prog: The Jazz Show/David Sanborn; blues one hr wkly. ■ John Carroll, asst mus dir.

Osceola

KBUG(FM)—June 29, 1990: 92.3 mhz; 3.2 kw. Ant 259 ft. TL: N38 02 12 W93 33 44. Box 1420, Suite 6, Truman Hills Mall, Warsaw (65355). (816) 438-7343. FAX: (816) 438-7159. Licensee: Valkyrie Broadcasting Inc. (acq 3-26-90). Format: Country. ■ Jim McCollum, pres; Joey Anderson, gen mgr & gen sls mgr; Glenna Thrasher, prom mgr; Paula Spring, news dir.

Otterville

KOTT(FM)—Not on air, target date unknown: 107.7 mhz; 6 kw. Ant 328 ft. TL: N38 38 08 W92 57 28. 5345 Pin Oak Ln., Sedalia (65301). Licensee: Otterville Broadcasting L.P.

Overland

***KRHS(FM)**—Nov 7, 1977: 90.1 mhz; 10 w. Ant 60 ft. TL: N38 42 38 W90 21 22. 9100 St. Charles Rock Rd., St. Louis (63114). (314) 429-7111; (314) 429-3500. FAX: (314) 429-7114. Licensee: Ritenour Consolidated School District. Format: Educ, div. Target aud: General. ■ Alan Mitchell, gen mgr & stn mgr.

Owensville

KLZE(FM)—1986: 95.3 mhz; 50 kw. Ant 328 ft. TL: N38 15 22 W91 32 04. 309-B N. First St. (65066). Licensee: Davel Broadcasting. Format: Children. ■ Randy Wachter, gen mgr & chief engr.

Ozark

KZPF(FM)—Not on air, target date unknown: 92.9 mhz; 3 kw. Ant 328 ft. TL: N37 04 47 W93 10 58. 512 W. Edgewood, Springfield (65807). Licensee: Dorothy S. Lemmon.

Palmyra

KICK-FM—Sept 1, 1981: 97.9 mhz; 30 kw. Ant 341 ft. TL: N39 45 25 W91 29 57. Stereo. Hrs opn: 24. Box 711, Hannibal (63401-0711). (314) 221-3450. FAX: (314) 221-5331. Licensee: Bick Broadcasting Co. Rep: McGavren Guild. Format: Country. News staff 2. Target aud: 25-54; main stream adults. ■ Bud Janes, pres; Ed Foxall, gen mgr & gen sls mgr; Joel Sampson, progmg dir; Laurel Alridge, mus dir; Jon Hanvelt, news dir; Darren Martin, chief engr.

Parkville

***KGSP(FM)**—April 1972: 92.3 mhz; 10 w. Ant 100 ft. TL: N39 11 24 W94 40 49. Box 2, 8700 River Park Dr. (64152). (816) 741-2000, ext. 329. FAX: (816) 741-4911. Licensee: Bd. of Trustees of Park College. Format: Educ, contemp, AOR. Target aud: General; college students-any age. Spec prog: Folk 6 hrs, new age 6 hrs wkly. ■ Charles Welborn, gen mgr; Michael Dugas, progmg dir; Gregory McDonald, mus dir.

Perryville

KBDZ(FM)—Jan 30, 1990: 93.1 mhz; 1.6 kw. Ant 623 ft. TL: N37 38 56 W89 56 21. Stereo. Hrs opn: 24. Box 344, 10 Perry Plaza (63775); Box 428, Radio Hill, St. Genevieve (63670). (314) 883-2980; (314) 547-8005. Licensee: Donze Communications Inc. Net: Unistar Radio Net. Format: Adult contemp. News staff 3; news progmg 5 hrs wkly. Target aud: 25-54. Spec prog: Sports 5 hrs, relg 5 hrs, farm 2 hrs wkly. ■ Elmo L. Donze, pres, gen mgr & chief engr; Bob Scott, gen sls mgr, progmg dir & mus dir. ■ Rates: $16; 16; 16; 16.

Piedmont

KPWB(AM)—May 16, 1966: 1140 khz; 1 kw-D. TL: N37 08 29 W90 42 11. Rt. 3, Box 3202 (63957). (314) 223-4218. FAX: (314) 223-2351. Licensee: Hunt Broadcasting Group Inc. (acq 3-8-91; $200,000 with co-located FM; FTR 3-25-91). Net: ABC/D; Missourinet. Format: Gospel, C&W. ■ J.G. Hunt, pres; Gary Lee, gen mgr; Wil Wallace, news dir.

KPWB-FM—Sept 5, 1985: 104.9 mhz; 3 kw. Ant 300 ft. TL: N37 07 54 W90 41 28. Stereo. Prog sep from AM. Format: Country & adult contemp.

Point Lookout

***KCOZ(FM)**—Feb 12, 1962: 91.7 mhz; 200 w. Ant 151 ft. TL: N36 36 40 W93 14 29. Stereo. College of the Ozarks (65726). (417) 334-6411, ext. 4279. FAX: (417) 335-2618. Licensee: Southwest Missouri State University (acq 6-21-93; $10 and assumption of seller's obligation to National Telecommunications and Information Administration of approximately $39,712; FTR 7-19-93). Net: APR, NPR. Format: Class, news/talk, jazz. News staff 2. News progmg 40 hrs wkly. Target aud: Older, educated. Spec prog: Folk 10 hrs, new age 10 hrs wkly. ■ Jae Jones, gen mgr & chief engr; Eric Ewbank, opns mgr; Cynthia Swope, dev dir; Wendy Sebastian, mktg mgr; Matt Rupp, progmg dir & mus dir.

Poplar Bluff

KAHR(FM)—March 3, 1985: 96.7 mhz; 3 kw. Ant 328 ft. TL: N36 45 59 W90 28 52. Stereo. Box 1275 (63901). (314) 686-3700. FAX: (314) 686-1713. Licensee: Eagle Bluff Enterprises (acq 8-3-93; $350,000; FTR 8-30-93). Net: SMN. Format: Pure gold of the 50s, 60s & 70s. News staff 2. Target aud: 25-54; listeners living in the middle-class strata. ■ Gerald W. Hunt, pres & gen mgr; Jim Borders, gen sls mgr & prom mgr; Robbie Frish, progmg dir, mus dir & news dir. ■ Rates: $12.75; 12.75; 12.75; 12.75.

KJEZ(FM)—Aug 20, 1977: 95.5 mhz; 100 kw. Ant 860 ft. TL: N36 50 50 W90 19 52. Stereo. Hrs opn: 24. Box 130, 7 Hillsdale Plaza, Hwy. 67 N. (63901). (314) 686-2403. FAX: (314) 785-1119. Licensee: ACI Broadcasting of Poplar Bluff Inc. (acq 9-20-90; $900,000; FTR 10-8-90). Net: Unistar. Rep: Gary. Format: Adult contemp. News staff one; news progmg 10 hrs wkly. Target aud: 18-44. ■ Vince King, pres; Robbie Frish, stn mgr & opns dir; Yvonne Accuado, gen sls mgr & adv mgr; Tony James, progmg dir, news dir & pub affrs dir; Keith Taylor, mus dir; Charlie Lampe, chief engr. ■ Rates: $16; 12; 16; 10.

KKLR(FM)—Listing follows KWOC(AM).

KLID(AM)—May 22, 1961: 1340 khz; 1 kw-U. TL: N36 46 03 W90 22 11. Hrs opn: 6 AM-midnight. 102 N. 11th (63901). (314) 686-1600. Licensee: Browning Skidmore Broadcasting Inc. (acq 5-21-93; $60,000; FTR 6-14-93). Net: NBC. Rep: Midsouth. Format: Oldies. ■ Delores Skidmore, gen mgr & progmg dir; Neil Todd, mus dir; Earl Abernathy, chief engr.

***KLUH(FM)**—Oct 8, 1988: 90.5 mhz; 100 w. Ant 80 ft. TL: N36 44 44 W90 24 24 (CP: 700 w, ant 180 ft., TL: N36 42 07 W90 23 48). Box 1313 (63901-1313). (314) 686-1663. Licensee: Christian Educational Advancement Inc. Format: Relg. Target aud: General. ■ Donald Parsons, pres, gen mgr & chief engr.

***KOKS(FM)**—Oct 2, 1988: 89.5 mhz; 100 kw. Ant 423 ft. TL: N36 48 40 W90 27 50. Hrs opn: 24. Box 967 (63901). (314) 686-5080. Licensee: Calvary Educational Broadcasting Foundation. Format: All Christian/gospel. ■ Don Stewart, gen mgr; Mina Stewart, progmg dir; Charles Lampley, chief engr.

KWOC(AM)—May 10, 1938: 930 khz; 5 kw-D, 500 w-N, DA-N. TL: N36 43 15 W90 22 04. Hrs opn: 24. Box 399, 940 S. Westwood Blvd. (63901). (314) 785-0881. Licensee: Bluff City Broadcasting Co. Inc. (acq 12-87). Net: ABC/D, Brownfield. Rep: Banner. Format: Country. News staff one; news progmg 5 hrs wkly. Target aud: 25-54; adults with middle to upper income. ■ Jerry Zimmer, pres; Roger Hager, gen mgr & gen sls mgr; Scott Cox, progmg dir; Bill Steiger, news dir; Roy Phillips, chief engr.

KKLR(FM)—Co-owned with KWOC(AM). 1952: 94.5 mhz; 100 kw. Ant 807 ft. TL: N36 43 18 W90 22 10. Stereo. Prog sep from AM. Licensee: KKLR Broadcasting Co., Inc. (acq 2-88; $650,000; FTR 2-8-88). Format: Country. News staff one. Target aud: 18-49. ■ Toby Spenser, mus dir.

KZMA(FM)—Not on air, target date Jan 1, 1994: 103.5 mhz; 50 kw. Ant 492 ft. TL: N36 53 56 W90 18 27. Hrs opn: 24. R.R. 3, Box 558, Metropolis, IL (62960). Licensee: Twin Eagle Communications. Wash atty: Fisher, Wayland, Cooper & Leader. ■ Eugene F. Stratemeyer, Charlene S. Stratemeyer, CEOs; Eugene F. Stratemeyer, Charlene S. Stratemeyer, chrs; Eugene F. Stratemeyer, Charlene S. Stratemeyer, presdts; Eugene F. Stratemeyer, Charlene S. Stratemeyer, CFOs; Eugene F. Stratemeyer, Charlene S. Stratemeyer, gen mgrs; Eugene F. Stratemeyer, Charlene S. Stratemeyer, stn mgrs.

Portageville

KMIS(AM)—Sept 1, 1960: 1050 khz; 1 kw-D, 87 w-N. TL: N36 25 30 W89 41 39 (CP: 600 w). Hrs opn: 5 AM-10 PM. Box 250, Hwy. 162 E. (63873). (314) 379-5436; (314) 379-5647. FAX: (314) 379-2233. Licensee: Julie McCallum Sweet and Shelly McCallum Rudd (acq 2-8-90). Net: ABC/I. Format: Country. News staff one. Target aud: General. Spec prog: Relg/gospel 12 hrs wkly. ■ Julie M. Sweet, pres; Jim Freeland, gen mgr; Lisa Kelley, opns mgr; Ray Taylor, progmg dir, mus dir & news dir; Palmer Johnson II, chief engr. ■ Rates: $6; 6; 6; 6.

KMIS-FM—(New Madrid). Jan 31, 1976: 106.5 mhz; 50 kw. Ant 462 ft. TL: N36 25 30 W89 41 39. Stereo. Hrs opn: 5 AM-10 PM. Net: ABC. ■ Rates: Same as AM.

Potosi

KHCR(FM)—Not on air, target date unknown: 97.7 mhz; 9.4 kw. Ant 528 ft. TL: N37 52 51 W90 47 01. 511 W. 5th St., Washington (63090). Licensee: Prime Time Radio Inc. ■ Ken Kuenzie, pres & gen mgr.

KYRO(AM)—Feb 22, 1959: 1280 khz; 500 w-D. TL: N37 58 28 W90 45 44. Box 280, Hwy. 21 N. (63664). (314) 438-2136. FAX: (314) 438-3108. Licensee: James T. Porter & Debra S. Porter (acq 6-17-92; $100,000; FTR 7-6-92). Net: ABC/D; Missourinet. Wash atty: Cohn & Marks. Format: C&W. News staff one; new progmg 12 hrs wkly. Target aud: 25 plus; general. Spec prog: Gospel, bluegrass. ■ James T. Porter, pres & gen mgr; Debra S. Porter, vp; Louie Seiberlich, gen sls mgr, news dir & pub affrs dir; Jeremy Porter, prom mgr, progmg dir & mus dir; Tom Moon, chief engr.

Republic

KADI(FM)—June 18, 1990: 99.5 mhz; 6 kw. Ant 328 ft. TL: N37 09 54 W93 23 44. Stereo. Hrs opn: 24. Suite H, 1701 W. Sunshine, Springfield (65807). (417) 831-0995. FAX: (417) 831-0758. Licensee: Snowmen Broadcasting Inc. Net: CNN. Wash atty: Linda Eckard. Format: Adult contemp Christian mus. News progmg 8 hrs wkly. Target aud: General; mid 30s. ■ Don Hancock, pres; Linda Dorsey, gen mgr & gen sls mgr; Zach Anders, progmg dir; Shellie Scott, mus dir; Shawn Baker, chief engr.

Richmond

KAYX(FM)—Aug 1, 1990: 92.5 mhz; 6 kw. Ant 500 ft. TL: N39 14 52 W93 58 16. Stereo. Hrs opn: 5:30 AM-11 PM. 1111 Main (64085); Box 29, Rt. 1, Cameron (64429). (816) 776-3196; (816) 632-6661. Licensee: Summit Operations Inc. Wash atty: Erwin Krasnow. ■ Shellby Hendee, pres; Mike Hendee, gen mgr.

Rolla

***KMNR(FM)**—1974: 89.7 mhz; 450 w. Ant 230 ft. TL: N37 57 12 W91 46 29. Hrs opn: 24. Univ. of Missouri, 113 University Ctr. W. (65401). (314) 341-4272; (314) 341-4273. Licensee: Curators of the Univ. of Missouri (group owner). Net: AP. Format: Div, educ. Target aud: 18-25; college community. Spec prog: Jazz 3 hrs wkly. ■ Fred Goss, gen mgr; Jennifer Zung, stn mgr; Ben Harvey, adv dir; Woody Delp, progmg dir; Angela Haines, LeMar Dace, mus dirs; Thomas Erb, chief engr.

KMOZ(AM)—Aug 19, 1960: 1590 khz; 1 kw-D, 88 w-N. TL: N37 56 41 W91 48 40. Hrs opn: 6 AM-midnight. Box 728, 2100 A Hwy. 63 N. (65401). (314) 364-1590. Licensee: Progressive Broadcasting of Missouri (acq 6-1-76). Format: MOR. Target aud: 35 plus. Spec prog: Bluegrass 6 hrs wkly. ■ Edward W. Moynahan, pres, gen mgr, sls dir & natl sls mgr; Stan Hines, rgnl sls mgr & progmg dir; Paul Holmes, mus dir; Elizabeth Buehler, pub affrs dir; Chuck Knapp, chief engr. ■ Rates: $12; 11; 12; 11.

KQMX(FM)—Co-owned with KMOZ(AM). Nov 20, 1964: 94.3 mhz; 3 kw. Ant 114 ft. TL: N37 57 50 W91 45 54. Stereo. Hrs opn: 6 AM-midnight. Prog sep from AM. Net: Westwood One. Format: CHR, classic rock, oldies. Target aud: 18-44. ■ Rates: $12; 11; 11; 11.

KTTR(AM)—Sept 30, 1947: 1490 khz; 1 kw-U. TL: N37 56 42 W91 44 46. Box 727 (65401). (314) 364-2525. FAX: (314) 364-5161. Licensee: KTTR-KZNN Inc. Group owner: Mahaffey Enterprises Inc. (acq 6-1-84; $1.5 million; with co-located FM; FTR 4-16-84). Net: ABC/I; Missourinet. Format: News/talk, sports. News staff 2. Target aud: General. ■ John Mahaffey, pres; Hal Sell, gen mgr; Arlene Olander, gen sls mgr; Scott Johnson, progmg dir; Tom Colvin, news dir; Pat Botts, chief engr.

KZNN(FM)—Co-owned with KTTR(AM). Feb 12, 1973: 105.3 mhz; 100 kw. Ant 631 ft. TL: N37 52 39 W91 44 45. Stereo. Prog sep from AM. Net: ABC/D, Brownfield. Format: Modern country. News staff 2. Spec prog: Farm 3 hrs wkly. ■ Kevin Lewis, progmg dir.

***KUMR(FM)**—January 1964: 88.5 mhz; 100 kw. Ant 480 ft. TL: N37 47 56 W91 43 28. Stereo. Hrs opn: 19. G-6 Library, Univ. of Missouri-Rolla (65401). (314) 341-4386. FAX: (314) 341-4889. Licensee: The Curators of the Univ. of Missouri (group owner). Net: NPR, APR. Wash atty: Fisher, Wayland, Cooper & Leader. Format: Class, div, news. News staff one; news progm 35 hrs wkly. Target aud: General. Spec prog: Bluegrass 5 hrs, jazz 3 hrs, folk 5 hrs wkly. ■ Janet Turkovic, gen mgr; John Muesch, mktg mgr; Jim Sigler, progmg dir; Arleasha Mays, news dir; Charles Knapp, chief engr. ■ KOMU-TV affil.

KZNN(FM)—Listing follows KTTR(AM).

St. Charles

***KCLC(FM)**—October 1968: 89.1 mhz; 25.5 kw. Ant 257 ft. TL: N38 47 12 W90 29 49. Stereo. Hrs opn: 5:30 AM-2 AM. 209 S. Kings Hwy. (63301). (314) 949-4890; (314) 949-4891. Licensee: Lindenwood College. Net: ABC/D. Format: Jazz. News progmg 12 hrs wkly. Target aud: 24-54. Spec prog: Bluegrass 12 hrs, alternative rock 7 hrs, gospel 9 hrs, contemp Christian 7 hrs, blues 7 hrs wkly. ■ Dennis C. Spellmann, pres; Glen T. Cerny, gen mgr; Richard Reighard, opns mgr; Don Steinberg, mktg dir; Colin Killian, prom dir; Kammie Collins, mus dir; Greg Harmer, news dir; William Ott, chief engr.

KIRL(AM)—Apr 13, 1958: 1460 khz; 5 kw-D, 500 w-N, DA-2. TL: N38 47 56 W90 25 12. 3713 Hwy. 94 N. (63301). (314) 946-6600. Licensee: Bronco Broadcasting Co. Inc. (acq 1-2-80). Format: Jazz, relg. Spec prog: Farm 3 hrs wkly. ■ John Roland, pres; William White, gen mgr; Carl Johnson, gen sls mgr; Columbus Gregory, progmg dir; Howard Jamison III, news dir; Mike Rice, chief engr.

KXOK-FM—See Florissant.

St. James

KZYQ(FM)—Not on air, target date unknown: 99.7 mhz; 25 kw. Ant 328 ft. TL: N37 56 41 W91 42 23. Stereo. Box 727, Rolla (65401). (314) 364-2525. FAX: (314) 364-5161. Licensee: KTTR-KZNN Inc. Group owner: Mahaffey Enterprises Inc. ■ Hal Sell, gen mgr.

St. Joseph

KFEQ(AM)—Feb 16, 1926: 680 khz; 5 kw-U, DA-2. TL: N39 49 43 W94 48 20. Hrs opn: 24. Box 879, 4305 Frederick (64502). (816) 233-8881. FAX: (816) 364-6856. Licensee: KFEQ Inc. Group owner: Eagle Communications Group (acq 3-20-91; grpsl; FTR 4-8-91). Net: CBS; Rep: Katz. Format: Country, news/talk. News staff 4; news progmg 50 hrs wkly. Target aud: 18 plus; adults. Spec prog: Farm 20 hrs wkly. ■ Robert E. Schmidt, pres; Gene Millard, gen mgr; Kay Hutchinson, gen sls mgr; Dick Kline, rgnl sls mgr; Bob Orf, progmg dir; Brent Harmon, mus dir; Barry Birr, news dir.

KGNM(AM)—November 1955: 1270 khz; 1 kw-D, DA. TL: N39 44 39 W94 47 16. Hrs opn: 24. Box 7121, 2414 S. Leonard Rd. (64507). (816) 233-2577. FAX: (816) 233-2374. Licensee: Good News Ministries/Orama Inc. (acq 6-80; $400,000; FTR 6-30-80). Net: USA, Moody, CBN. Format: Relg, talk. Target aud: 30-55; conservative. Spec prog: Teen 6 hrs, preschoolers 2 hrs wkly. ■ Tim Doyle, gen mgr, progmg dir & mus dir; Vicki Lipira, pub affrs dir; Doug Dunlap, chief engr. ■ Rates: $186; 168; 186; 150.

KKJO(FM)—Listing follows KSFT(AM).

KSFT(AM)—June 1, 1946: 1550 khz; 5 kw-U, DA-N. TL: N39 42 23 W94 44 36. Hrs opn: 24. Box 8550 (64508); 1201 N. Woodbine (64506). (816) 279-6346. FAX: (816) 279-8280. Licensee: Cardinal Communications Inc. (group owner; acq 1-20-89). Net: ABC/I; Missourinet. Rep: Torbet. Format: Adult contemp, big band, btfl mus. News staff one. Target aud: 45-64. ■ John D. Daniels, pres; Ted Mahn, gen mgr & chief engr; Chris Meikel, opns dir; Reta Kneale, rgnl sls mgr; Bob Heater, news dir.

KKJO(FM)—Co-owned with KSFT(AM). Sept 1, 1962: 105.1 mhz; 100 kw. Ant 581 ft. TL: N39 40 51 W94 46 47 (CP: Ant 984 ft., TL: N39 33 08 W94 33 25). Stereo. Hrs opn: 24. Prog sep from AM. (Acq 7-28-80). Net: ABC/C. Format: Adult contemp, CHR. Target aud: 18-49. ■ Rick Austin, progmg dir; Chad Cruise, mus dir.

St. Louis

KASP(AM)—1927: 1380 khz; 5 kw-D, 1 kw-N, DA-3. TL: N38 31 27 W90 14 17. 2360 Hampton Ave. (63139). (314) 644-1380. FAX: (314) 644-6316. Licensee: Zimco Inc. (acq 11-29-93; $7 million with co-located FM; FTR 12-20-93). Rep: Katz. Format: Oldies. Target aud: 25-54; male. ■ Bill Viands, gen mgr; Joe Rush, gen sls mgr; Maureen Tenholder, prom dir; Kim Furlow, news dir; Bob Hoffman, chief engr.

WKBQ(FM)—(Granite City, Ill). Co-owned with KASP(AM). Nov 24, 1965: 106.5 mhz; 90 kw. Ant 1,027 ft. TL: N38 34 24 W90 19 30. Stereo. Format: CHR. ■ Kenny Knight, mus dir.

KATZ(AM)—Jan 3, 1955: 1600 khz; 5 kw-U, DA-N. TL: N38 39 19 W90 07 53. Box 4888, (63108). (314) 361-1108. FAX: (314) 361-2276. Licensee: Noble Broadcast of St. Louis Inc. Group owner: Noble Broadcast Group (acq 3-16-93; $2.75 million with KATZ-FM Alton; FTR 4-5-93). Format: R&B, Motown. ■ Linda O'Connor, gen mgr; Steve Mosier, gen sls mgr; Rod King, progmg dir; Daryl Mcquinn, chief engr.

***KDHX(FM)**—Oct 14, 1987: 88.1 mhz; 42.4 kw. Ant 1,314 ft. TL: N38 25 01 W90 25 59. Stereo. Box 63328 (63118); 3504 Magnolia (63118). (314) 664-3955. Licensee: Double Helix Corp. Net: APR. Format: Div. News staff one; news progmg 18 hrs wkly. Target aud: General. Spec prog: Black 12 hrs, class 4 hrs, country 10 hrs, jazz 12 hrs, Sp 4 hrs, folk 10 hrs, bluegrass 8 hrs, new age 6 hrs wkly. ■ Georgette Bronsman, gen mgr.

KEZK-FM—September 1968: 102.5 mhz; 100 kw. Ant 1,026 ft. TL: N38 34 24 W90 19 30. Stereo. 7711 Carondelet (63105). (314) 727-2160. FAX: (314) 727-7696. Licensee: Compass Radio of St. Louis Inc. Group owner: Compass Radio Group (acq 4-23-93; grpsl; FTR 5-10-93). Format: Soft adult contemp. News staff one. Target aud: 25-54; in office lstng. ■ Bob Hughes, CEO & pres; Jonathan Schwartz, CFO; Joe Cariffe, vp; Joe Cariife, gen mgr; Bob Burch, opns mgr & progmg mgr; Mike Jennewein, sls dir; Ruth Medina, prom mgr; Jim Cox, news dir; Sam Caputa, chief engr. ■ Rates: $200; 275; 200; 40.

KFNS(AM)—See Wood River, Ill.

***KFUO(AM)**—See Clayton.

KIRL(AM)—See St. Charles.

KJCF(AM)—See Festus.

KLOU(FM)—Listing follows KMOX(AM).

KMJM(FM)—Sept 28, 1972: 107.7 mhz; 100 kw. Ant 1,027 ft. TL: N38 34 24 W90 19 30. Stereo. Box 4888 (63108); 532 DeBaliviere Blvd. (63112). (314) 361-1108. FAX: (314) 361-2276. Licensee: Noble Broadcast of St. Louis. Group owner: Noble Broadcast Group (acq 6-86; grpsl; FTR 12-23-85). Rep: Christal. Format: Urban contemp. ■ Linda O'Connor, stn mgr; Steve Mosier, gen sls mgr; Chuck Atkins, progmg dir; Dave Wynter, mus dir; Doryl Mcquinn, chief engr.

KMOX(AM)—Dec 24, 1925: 1120 khz; 50 kw-U. TL: N38 43 20 W90 03 16. Stereo. Hrs opn: 24. One Memorial Dr. (63102). (314) 621-2345. FAX: (314) 444-3230. Licensee: CBS Inc. Group owner: CBS Broadcast Group (acq 1932). Net: CBS. Rep: CBS Radio. Format: News, info, talk, sports. News staff 12; news progmg 60 hrs wkly. Target aud: 25 plus. Spec prog: Jazz 4 hrs, relg one hr wkly. ■ Rod Zimmerman, vp & gen mgr; David Kelley, gen sls mgr; Ken Gioia, natl sls mgr; Kathy Muldoon, rgnl sls mgr; Renee LaFlam, prom dir & adv dir; Tom Langmyer, progmg dir; John Angelides, news dir; Marie Boykin, pub affrs dir; Paul Grundhauser, chief engr.

KLOU(FM)—Co-owned with KMOX(AM). Nov 1962: 103.3 mhz; 100 kw. Ant 920 ft. TL: N38 31 47 W90 17 58. Stereo. Hrs opn: 24. Prog sep from AM. FAX: (314) 621-3252. Format: Oldies. ■ Doug Wilson, opns mgr; Kathy Parks, rgnl sls mgr; Mary T. Kelly, prom mgr; Gary Kolarcik, mus dir.

KRJY(FM)—Dec 22, 1959: 96.3 mhz; 100 kw. Ant 650 ft. TL: N38 36 47 W90 20 09. Stereo. 8081 Manchester Rd. (63144). (314) 781-9600. FAX: (314) 781-0422. Licensee: Communications Fund Inc. (acq 1970). Format: Oldies. News staff one. Target aud: 25-54. ■ R.J. Miller, pres, gen mgr & mktg mgr; Ken Kraus, opns mgr & prom mgr; Gary Lewis, gen sls mgr; Jeff Allen, progmg dir; Bob Wayne, news dir; Sam Caputa, chief engr.

KSD(AM)—Feb 14, 1922: 550 khz; 5 kw-U, DA-N. TL: N38 39 12 W90 07 44. Stereo. 10155 Corporate Sq. (63132). (314) 997-5594. FAX: (314) 997-1283. Licensee: EZ Communications Inc. (group owner; acq 11-29-93; $15 million with co-located FM; FTR 12-13-93). Net: MBS. Rep: McGavren Guild. Format: Country. Target aud: 25-64. ■ Merrell Hansen, pres & gen mgr; John Kijowski, vp sls; Scott Strong, mktg dir; Bill Kratz, prom mgr; Lou Goad, mus dir; Robert Fox, news dir; Dave Obergoenner, vp engrg.

KSD-FM—November 1954: 93.7 mhz; 100 kw. Ant 859 ft. TL: N38 34 05 W90 19 55. Stereo. Prog sep from AM. Format: Classic rock. ■ John McRay, progmg dir; Mike Watermann, mus dir.

KSHE(FM)—See Crestwood.

KSIV(AM)—See Clayton.

KSTL(AM)—1948: 690 khz; 1 kw-D. TL: N38 37 01 W90 10 17. Hrs opn: Sunrise-sunset. 814 N. 3rd St. (63102). (314) 621-5785. Licensee: Radio St. Louis Inc. Wash atty: Bryan-Cave. Format: Relg, ethnic. Spec prog: Farm one hr, Greek one hr, Pol 2 hrs, German one hr, international 18 hrs, Russian one hr, Sp 10 hrs wkly. ■ C.F. Haverstick, pres; Doris Grebas, gen mgr; Mike Pyle, rgnl sls mgr; Dori Jones, prom dir; David Dale, progmg dir &

news dir; James Mitchell, chief engr. ■ Rates: $14; 14; 14.

*KWMU(FM)—June 2, 1972: 90.7 mhz; 97 kw. Ant 981 ft. TL: N38 34 50 W90 19 45 (CP: 100 kw, ant 1,000 ft.). Stereo. Hrs opn: 24. Univ. of Missouri-St. Louis, 8001 Natural Bridge Rd. (63121). (314) 553-5968. FAX: (314) 553-5993. Licensee: The Curators of the Univ. of Missouri (group owner). Net: NPR, AP. Wash atty: Fisher, Wayland, Cooper & Leader. Format: News, classical. News staff 4; news progmg 40 hrs wkly. Target aud: 27-45; upscale. ■ Patricia Wente, gen mgr; Mary Edwards, opns mgr; Shelley Kerley, dev dir; Jill Wagenblast, prom mgr; Tim Emmons, progmg dir; Joe Kupferer, chief engr.

KXEN(AM)—(Festus-St. Louis). May 10, 1951: 1010 khz; 50 kw-D, DA. TL: N38 45 43 W90 03 26 (CP: 500 w-N, DA-2). Box 8085, Granite City, IL (62040). (314) 436-6550. FAX: (618) 797-2293. Licensee: Mid-America Gospel. Group owner: Mid-America Gospel Radio. Net: USA. Format: Relg, gospel. ■ George Spicer, gen mgr & mus dir; Daniel A. Allen, stn mgr; Phillip W. French, gen sls mgr; Jay Madas, pub affrs dir; R.B. Niekamp, chief engr.

KXOK(AM)—Sept 19. 1938: 630 khz; 5 kw-U, DA-2. TL: N38 40 18 W90 06 52. Stereo. 24. #1600, 7777 Bonhomme Ave. (63105). (314) 727-0808. FAX: (314) 727-1220. Licensee: Legend Broadcasting of Missouri Inc. Group owner: WPNT Inc. (acq 6-6-89; grpsl; FTR 6-26-89). Rep: Torbet. Format: Black. Target aud: 25-54. Spec prog: Farm 5 hrs, jazz 2 hrs, business 4 hrs, travel one hr wkly. ■ Saul Frischling, pres; Michael Frischling, gen mgr; Alice Ross, gen sls mgr; Vicki Pimental, prom mgr; Marshall Rice, chief engr.

KYKY(FM)—1960: 98.1 mhz; 90 kw. Ant 1,027 ft. TL: N38 34 24 W90 19 30. Stereo. 3100 Market (63103). (314) 531-9898. FAX: (314) 531-9810. Licensee: E.Z. Communications Inc. (group owner; acq 1-27-85; $4,000,000; FTR 11-19-84). Format: Adult contemp. Target aud: 25-54. ■ Art Kellar, CEO; Alan Box, pres; Karen Carroll, gen mgr; Smokey Rivers, opns mgr; Susan Cervantes, gen sls mgr; Susan Wolin, natl sls mgr; Rachel Boxdorfer, mktg mgr; Kary Lockwood, prom mgr; Greg Hewitt, mus dir; Michelle Dibble, news dir; Joe Geerling, chief engr.

WEW(AM)—Apr 26, 1921: 770 khz; 1 kw-D. TL: N38 37 17 W90 04 36. 7720 Forsyth (63105). (314) 862-0815. FAX: (314) 862-1408. Licensee: Alliance Broadcasting Co. (acq 3-11-91; $300,000; FTR 3-11-91). Net: CNN. Format: Big band. ■ Doug Huber, pres; Brian Miller, opns mgr, progmg dir & mus dir.

WGNU(AM)—(Granite City, Ill.) Dec 1, 1961: 920 khz; 500 w-U, DA-2. TL: N38 45 33 W90 03 00. Hrs opn: 24. The Senate, Suite 1315, 275 N. Union Blvd., St. Louis, MO (63108-1236). (314) 454-6660; (618) 451-9950. FAX: (314) 454-6609. Licensee: Norman Broadcasting Co. Net: USA, Sun, IBN. Wash atty: Miller & Fields. Format: Talk. News staff 2; news progmg 2 hrs wkly. Target aud: 35 plus; active, educated adults. Spec prog: Black 18 hrs, Ger 3 hrs, relg 15 hrs, comedy one hr, Croatian one hr wkly. ■ Charles H. Norman, pres; Art Ford, gen mgr & gen sls mgr; John Minicky, mktg dir; Charles Geer, progmg dir & news dir; Joe Garcia, mus dir; Rich LaCroix, pub affrs dir; Harold McCarty, chief engr. ■ Rates: $25; 20; 20; 20.

WIL-FM—Listing follows WRTH(AM).

WKBQ(FM)—Listing follows KASP(AM).

WKKX(FM)—See Jerseyville, Ill.

WRTH(AM)—Feb 9, 1922: 1430 khz; 5 kw-U, DA-2. TL: N38 32 09 W90 11 26. 300 N. Tucker St. (63101). (314) 436-1600. FAX: (314) 436-6970. Licensee: Heritage Media Inc. Group owner: Heritage Media Corp. (acq 11-86; grpsl; FTR 11-17-86). Net: ABC/I. Rep: Banner. Format: MOR. Target aud: 35-64. ■ Dick Williams, pres & gen mgr; Bill Lenzen, gen sls mgr; Sydney Matta, prom mgr; F. Ray Massie, progmg dir; Mike Fuszner, mus dir; Gene Hirsch, news dir; Paul Sanford, chief engr.

WIL-FM—Co-owned with WRTH(AM). July 15, 1962: 92.3 mhz; 99 kw. Ant 984 ft. TL: N38 28 56 W90 23 53. Stereo. Prog sep from AM. Format: Contemp country. ■ Mark Langston, mus dir.

St. Robert

KFLD(FM)—Not on air, target date unknown: 96.5 mhz; 6 kw. Ant 328 ft. TL: N37 52 41 W92 01 05. 1268 Mautenne, St. Louis (63021). Licensee: Neil A. Rones and Luann C. Dalh.

Salem

KMMC(FM)—January 1971: 95.9 mhz; 4.8 kw. Ant 165 ft. TL: N37 38 01 W91 32 05. Stereo. Hrs opn: 6 AM-midnight. Box 650, Schafer Bldg., 1101 Hwy. 32 E. (65560). (314) 729-2404. FAX: (314) 729-5755. Licensee: Ultra-Sonic Broadcast Stations Inc. Net: USA, Ambassador, MBS. Format: Relg, gospel. News staff 4; news progmg 20 hrs wkly. Target aud: 18-52; full-time Christian station. ■ Dr. David Wheeler, pres; Ralph E. Gable, gen mgr, stn mgr, opns mgr, mktg mgr & prom dir; Edyie Gable, dev dir & progmg dir; Mark Seitz, gen sls mgr, mus dir & asst mus dir; Rick Henderson, chief engr. ■ Rates: $6; 6; 6; 4.50.

KSMO(AM)—November 1953: 1340 khz; 1 kw-U. TL: N37 37 36 W91 32 09. Hrs opn: 24. Box 229, 800 S. Main (65560). 729-6117. FAX: (314) 729-7337. Licensee: KSMO Enterprises (acq 11-84). Net: ABC/E; Missourinet, Brownfield. Wash atty: Julian Freret. Format: Country. News staff one; news progmg 18 hrs wkly. Target aud: General; middle class. Spec prog: Farm 4 hrs wkly. ■ Stanley M. Podorski, pres, gen mgr & progmg mgr; Melba Podorski, gen sls mgr; Stan Stevens, prom mgr & news dir; Cathy Farrar, mus dir; B.J. Rickerd, chief engr. ■ Rates: $9.10; 8.20; 8.75; 5.75.

Ste. Genevieve

KPNT(FM)—March 1967: 105.7 mhz; 100 kw. Ant 285 ft. TL: N37 59 37 W90 03 20. Stereo. Hrs opn: 24. 1215 Cole, St. Louis (63106). (314) 231-1057. FAX: (314) 231-1075. Licensee: River City Broadcasting (group owner). Net: ABC. Format: Mellow rock. Target aud: 18-34. ■ John Gutbrod, gen mgr; Ken Anthony, progmg dir & mus dir; Sherry Sissac, news dir; Marc Lehmuth, chief engr.

KSGM(AM)—See Chester, Ill.

Savannah

KSJQ(FM)—September 1991: 92.7 mhz; 50 kw. Ant 492 ft. TL: N39 58 34 W94 58 37. Box 879, St. Joseph (64502). (816) 233-8881. FAX: (816) 362-6856. Licensee: KFEQ Inc. Group owner: Eagle Communications Group (acq 1993; $450,000; FTR 9-13-93). Format: Country. ■ Gene Millard, gen mgr.

Sedalia

KDRO(AM)—Sept 13, 1939: 1490 khz; 1 kw-U. TL: N38 42 33 W93 15 53. Hrs opn: 24. 3106 W. Broadway (65301-2117). (816) 826-5005; (800) 440-1490. FAX: (816) 826-5255. Licensee: Mathewson Broadcasting Co. (acq 4-16-90; $300,000; FTR 5-7-90). Net: CBS; Brownfield, Missourinet. Format: Country. News staff 2; news progmg 11 hrs wkly. Target aud: General. Spec prog: Farm 6 hrs, Black one hr wkly. ■ James Mathewson, pres; Adam B. Fischer, vp; Bette Wise, gen mgr & gen sls mgr; Phil Sweamgin, prom mgr, progmg dir & mus dir; Bill Barrick, news dir; Stephen E. Bryant, pub affrs dir; Donald L. Harms, chief engr. ■ Rates: $13.10; 12.50; 13.10; 12.50.

KSDL(FM)—Listing follows KSIS(AM).

KSIS(AM)—Feb 18, 1954: 1050 khz; 1 kw-D, 86 w-N. TL: N38 43 52 W93 13 32. Stereo. Box 1056 (65302-1056). (816) 826-1056. FAX: (816) 827-5072. Licensee: Bick Broadcasting Co. (acq 1-1-87). Net: ABC/I. Format: Oldies. ■ Bud Janes, pres; Dennis Polk, gen mgr; Hal McKinney, gen sls mgr; Dick McQuitty, progmg dir; Bob Milner, news dir; Carl E. Zimmerschied, chief engr.

KSDL(FM)—Co-owned with KSIS(AM). May 11, 1964: 92.1 mhz; 3 kw. Ant 280 ft. TL: N38 43 52 W93 13 32. Stereo. Prog sep from AM. Format: Adult contemp.

Seligman

KESE(FM)—Aug 1, 1986: 93.3 mhz; 100 kw. Ant 492 ft. TL: N36 28 03 W94 10 25. Stereo. Hrs opn: 24. 216 N. Main, Bentonville, AR (72712). (501) 273-9039. Licensee: Elvis Moody (acq 12-85; $5,000; FTR 12-16-85). Net: USA. Format: Easy lstng. News staff one; news progmg 7 hrs wkly. Target aud: 35 plus; mature, upscale professionals. ■ Elvis Moody, gen mgr & stn mgr; Gary Borchard, opns dir & progmg dir.

Sikeston

KMPL(AM)—Mar 17, 1966: 1520 khz; 5 kw-D, 500 w-N, DA-3. TL: N36 49 25 W89 35 45. Box 970 (63801). (314) 471-1520. Licensee: Delta Radio Corp. (acq 4-1-73). Net: CBS, NBC Talknet. Rep: Walton. Format: MOR. Target aud: 35 plus. Spec prog: Farm 6 hrs wkly. ■ John C. David, pres; Amos Hargrave, chief engr. ■ Rates: $11.50; 11.50; 11.50; 11.50.

KSTG(FM)—Co-owned with KMPL(AM). Sept 12, 1968: 97.9 mhz; 12.5 kw. Ant 469 ft. TL: N36 59 52 W89 38 52. Stereo. Prog sep from AM. Format: Top-40. Target aud: 18-35. Spec prog: Black 4 hrs wkly. ■ Rates: Same as AM.

KSIM(AM)—July 17, 1948: 1400 khz; 1 kw-U. TL: N36 52 12 W89 36 32. 519 Greer Ave. (63801). (314) 471-1400. FAX: (314) 471-1402. Licensee: Prime Time Broadcasting Corp. (acq 10-1-84; $470,000; FTR 10-15-84). Net: ABC/C. Format: News/talk. News staff one; news progmg 10 hrs wkly. Target aud: 25-50. Spec prog: Loc sports, news, Paul Harvey. ■ James Zimmer, pres & gen mgr; Gera Schmoemel, gen sls mgr; Rick Sinclair, prom mgr & progmg dir; Bill Powers, news dir; Taylor Brian, chief engr. ■ Rates: $9; 9; 8; 7.

KSTG(FM)—Listing follows KMPL(AM).

Southwest City

KLTK(AM)—Mar 2, 1977: 1140 khz; 250 w-D. TL: N36 30 28 W94 36 34. 5409 W. Dogwood St., Roger, AR (72756). (417) 762-3835; (417) 762-3990. Licensee: Drake Communications Inc. (acq 9-22-93; $170,000 with co-located FM; FTR 10-11-93). Net: AP. Format: C&W. ■ Jeff Hutton, pres; David Ray, gen mgr; Linda Ladd, progmg dir.

KWMQ(FM)—Co-owned with KLTK(AM). October 1989: 100.3 mhz; 3 kw. Ant 328 ft. TL: N36 30 28 W94 36 35.

Sparta

KLTQ(FM)—March 1, 1989: 96.5 mhz; 3.2 kw. Ant 453 ft. TL: N37 05 17 W93 10 34 (CP: 50 kw, ant 492 ft., TL: N35 56 23 W93 17 15). Stereo. 3645 S. Ave., Springfield (65807). (417) 887-9650. FAX: (417) 887-2028. Licensee: KLTQ-96.5 FM Inc. (acq 6-28-93; FTR 7-26-93). Net: SMN. Format: Country. News staff 2. ■ James L. Gardner, pres & engrg dir; Stan Friend, progmg dir & mus dir.

Springfield

KGBX-FM—Listing follows KGMY(AM).

KGMY(AM)—Oct 31, 1926: 1400 khz; 1 kw-U. TL: N37 11 46 W93 19 21. Stereo. Broadcast Plaza, 840 S. Glenstone (65802). (417) 869-1059. FAX: (417) 869-1000. Licensee: Sunburst II Inc. (acq 1-17-89; $155,000; FTR 1-30-89). Net: Katz. Format: Today's country. News staff one. Target aud: 25-44; affluent, educated white-collar skewing 25-54 year olds. ■ John M. Borders, pres; Robert L. May, vp & gen mgr; Mark Thompson, progmg dir; Chris Cannon, mus dir.

KGBX-FM—(Nixa). Co-owned with KGMY(AM). December 1989: 105.9 mhz; 38 kw. Ant 558 ft. TL: N37 25 16 W93 24 06. Stereo. Hrs opn: 24. ■ Mitch Baker, progmg dir; Bryan Summers, mus dir; Mike Morgan, news dir; Sean Baker, chief engr.

KIDS(AM)—July 29, 1949: 1340 khz; 1 kw-U. TL: N37 12 30 W93 17 32. Box 1337 (65801); 610 College St. (65905). (417) 865-1340. Licensee: Kickapoo Prairie Broadcasting Inc. Format: Children. Target aud: 12-and-under; children and their parents. ■ Robert Kramer, pres; Jeanne Kramer, vp & gen mgr.

KLFJ(AM)—Nov 1, 1974: 1550 khz; 5 kw-D, 28 w-N. TL: N37 11 45 W93 19 07. 811 Boonville (65802). (417) 831-5535. FAX: (417) 831-5544. Licensee: Queen City Broadcasting Co. Net: USA. Format: Inspirational. ■ Don Burrell, pres; Lowell Hamilton, gen mgr & gen sls mgr; Alan Smith, prom mgr, progmg dir & mus dir; Robert Eastbum, pub affrs dir. ■ Rates: $8; 8; 8; 8.

KLPW(AM)—See Union.

*KSMU(FM)—May 7, 1974: 91.1 mhz; 40 kw. Ant 403 ft. TL: N37 10 16 W93 19 28 (CP: TL: N37 10 14 W93 19 25). Stereo. Hrs opn: 24. Southwest Missouri State Univ. (65804). (417) 836-5878. FAX: (417) 836-5889. Licensee: Southwest Missouri State Univ. Net: NPR. Wash atty: Baker & McKenzie. Format: News, class, educ. News staff one; news progmg 54 hrs wkly. Target aud: 35 plus. Spec prog: Jazz 10 hrs wkly. ■ Arlen Diamond, gen mgr; Mike Smith, opns mgr; Tammy Wiley, dev mgr & mktg mgr; Randy Stewart, mus dir; Dick Willingham, news dir; Doug Waugh, chief engr.

KTOZ(AM)—1972: 1060 khz; 500 w-D. TL: N37 11 29 W93 19 45. 2607 W. Bennett (65807). (417) 831-1060. FAX: (417) 831-1231. Licensee: Dixon Broadcasting Inc. (acq 4-6-89; $310,000; FTR 4-24-89). Net: MBS. Format: Big Band, nostalgia. ■ Larry D. Campbell, pres; Ron Johnson, gen sls mgr.

Missouri

KTTS(AM)—1926: 1260 khz; 5 kw-U, DA-N. TL: N37 15 51 W93 19 04. Stereo. Hrs opn: 24. Box 2180 (65801); 2330 W. Grand (65802). (417) 865-6614. FAX: (417) 865-9643. Licensee: Springfield Great Empire Broadcasting Inc. Group owner: Great Empire Broadcasting Inc. (acq 3-18-72). Net: Missourinet. Rep: Torbet. Format: C&W. News staff 6; news progmg 17 hrs wkly. Target aud: 35-54. Spec prog: Farm 5 hrs wkly. ■ Mike Lynch, pres; Curtis W. Brown, vp & gen mgr; George DeMarco, gen sls mgr; Don Paul, prom mgr & progmg dir; Warren McDonald, mus dir; Dan Shelley, news dir; John Nielsen, chief engr.

KTTS-FM—August 1948: 94.7 mhz; 100 kw. Ant 1,125 ft. TL: N37 13 26 W93 14 33. Stereo. Hrs opn: 24. Prog sep from AM. Wash atty: Dow, Lohnes & Albertson. Target aud: General. Spec prog: Farm 5 hrs wkly.

KTXR(FM)—June 12, 1962: 101.3 mhz; 100 kw. Ant 1,181 ft. TL: N37 11 40 W92 56 04. 3000 E. Chestnut Expwy. (65802). (417) 862-3751. FAX: (417) 869-7675. Licensee: Stereo Broadcasting Inc. Group owner: Meyer Communications Inc. Net: NBC. Format: Contemp easy lstng. ■ K. E. Meyer, pres; J. A. Meyer, vp & gen mgr; Dee Dugan, progmg dir & mus dir; Dale Blankenship, chief engr.

*KWFC(FM)—Apr 17, 1985: 89.1 mhz; 100 kw. Ant 250 ft. TL: N37 14 23 W93 17 05. Stereo. Box 8900 (65801); 2316 N. Benton (65803). (417) 869-0891. FAX: (417) 866-7525. Licensee: Baptist Bible College Inc. Format: Relg. News staff one; news progmg 6 hrs wkly. Target aud: General; conservative, church-oriented. ■ Bill Askew, gen mgr; Richard Morris, progmg dir; Tom Barnett, chief engr.

*KWND(FM)—July 12, 1993: 88.3 mhz; 12 kw. Ant 328 ft. TL: N37 10 30 W93 02 35. 2550 S. Campbell (65807). (417) 889-0883. Licensee: Lou Smith Ministries Inc. (group owner). Format: Christian contemp mus. ■ Mary L. Smith, pres; Darrell Ankarlo, gen mgr.

KWTO(AM)—Dec 25, 1933: 560 khz; 5 kw-U, DA-N. TL: N37 08 08 W93 16 36. Four Corporate Ctr., 1949 E. Sunshine, Suite 401 (65804). (417) 883-9000. FAX: (417) 883-4005. Licensee: Cole Media Inc. (acq 7-7-89; $4,250,000 with co-located FM; FTR 7-24-89). Net: ABC/E. Rep: Banner. Format: Talk. Spec prog: Farm 20 hrs wkly. ■ Dick Cole, pres; Kurt Boney, vp & gen mgr; Phil Gibson, progmg dir.

KWTO-FM—Nov 23, 1967: 98.7 mhz; 100 kw. Ant 600 ft. TL: N37 04 06 W93 18 31. Stereo. Prog sep from AM. Format: CHR. ■ Dave Alexander, progmg dir; Adam West, mus dir.

KXUS(FM)—Apr 17, 1969: 97.3 mhz; 100 kw. Ant 479 ft. TL: N37 14 23 W93 17 05 (CP: Ant 987 ft., TL: N37 11 10 W93 01 23). Stereo. Box 6048 (65801); 2920 E. Pythian (65802). (417) 831-9700. FAX: (417) 831-1142. Licensee: Demaree Media Inc., debtor in possession (group owner; acq 3-15-85). Net: ABC/R. Rep: Republic. Format: AOR. News staff one. Target aud: 18-49. ■ Pat Demaree, pres; Mike Crowder, stn mgr.

Sullivan

KTUI(AM)—Feb 14, 1966: 1560 khz; 1 kw-D. TL: N38 11 42 W91 11 12. Hrs opn: 6 AM-sunset. Box 99, 4045 N. Service Rd. W. #1 (63080-0099). (314) 468-5101. FAX: (314) 468-5884. Licensee: Meramec Valley Broadcasting Co. Net: UPI; Missourinet. Format: News/talk. News staff one. Target aud: General. ■ John C. Rice, gen mgr; Don DeBrecht, gen sls mgr; Sam Scott, prom dir & progmg dir; Bob Diestelkamp, news dir; Wilma Scott, pub affrs dir. ■ Rates: $10; 10; 10; na.

KTUI-FM—1981: 100.9 mhz; 3 kw. Ant 276 ft. TL: N38 11 42 W91 11 12. Licensee: Four Rivers Co. Net: ABC. Format: Top-40, country, sports. Target aud: General. ■ Sam Scott, gen sls mgr; Don DeBrecht, vp mktg; Angie Jackson, prom dir; Wilma Scott, adv dir; Bob Diestelkamp, progmg dir. ■ Rates: $11; 11; 11; 9.

Tarkio

KTRX(FM)—Aug 22, 1977: 93.5 mhz; 6 kw. Ant 235 ft. TL: N40 25 27 W95 24 40 (CP: 11 kw, ant 489 ft.). Rebroadcasts WHB(AM) Kansas City 80%. 102 N. Mason, Carrollton (64633). (816) 736-4127. FAX: (816) 736-4127. Licensee: Kanza Inc. Net: ABC/D. Format: Country, farm. Target aud: 25-54; farm & agricultural related. ■ Mike Carter, pres; Will Davis, gen mgr & sls mgr; Miles Carter, progmg dir. ■ Rates: $20; 20; 16; 16.

Thayer

KALM(AM)—Dec 11, 1953: 1290 khz; 1 kw-D, 56 w-N. TL: N36 32 58 W91 33 05. Hrs opn: 6 AM-sunset. Box 15, N. Hwy. 63 (65791). (417) 264-7211; (417) 264-7063. FAX: (417) 264-7212. Licensee: Ozark Radio Inc. Net: ABC/D; Brownfield, Missourinet. Rep: Keystone (unwired net). Wash atty: Richard J. Hays Jr. Format: C&W, relg. News staff one; news progmg 11 hrs wkly. Target aud: 18-65 plus; farmers, ranchers, rural families. ■ Shawn N. Marhefka, pres; Robert Eckman, gen mgr & gen sls mgr; Dave Watson, opns mgr & progmg dir; Mike Crase, prom mgr & news dir; Harold Robertson, Chris Skaggs, mus dirs; Dan Hickinbotham, pub affrs dir; Bill Martin, chief engr. ■ Rates: $9; 9; 9; na.

KAMS(FM)—See Mammoth Spring, Ark.

Trenton

KTTN(AM)—Apr 17, 1955: 1600 khz; 500 w-D. TL: N40 05 00 W93 33 30. Hrs opn: 6 AM-sunset. Box 307, 804 Main St. (64683). (816) 359-2261; (816) 748-4692. FAX: (816) 359-4126. Licensee: Luehrs Broadcasting Co. (acq 8-01-92). Net: ABC; Missourinet, Brownfield. Format: Country, news. News staff 2; news progmg 16 hrs wkly. Target aud: General; 16 plus. Spec prog: Farm 4 hrs, relg 7 hrs wkly. ■ John Anthony, pres & gen mgr; Tim Peery, vp & gen sls mgr; Mike Ranspell, opns dir; Drew Stickler, progmg dir & mus dir; Tom Mock, news dir; Randy Muselman, chief engr. ■ Rates: $13.30; 12; 9.15; 9.15.

KTTN-FM—Sept 15, 1978: 92.1 mhz; 2.1 kw. Ant 374 ft. TL: N40 05 00 W93 33 30. Stereo. Hrs opn: 19. Dups FM 95%. Net: ABC/D; Brownfield, Missouriet. Wash atty: Reddy, Begley Martin. Format: Classic rock, country, news. News staff 2. Target aud: General; 16 plus. ■ John Anthony, stn mgr. ■ Rates: Same as AM.

Troy

KZMM(FM)—Not on air, target date unknown: 100.7 mhz; 6 kw. TL: N39 03 13 W90 59 47. Hwy. 47, W. Tyme Sq. 102 A (63379). Licensee: James C. Magee.

Union

KLPW(AM)—Aug 18, 1954: 1220 khz; 1 kw-D, 151 w-N. TL: N38 28 57 W91 02 39. Hrs opn: 6 AM-8 PM. Box 623, Intersection of Hwys. A & BB, Washington (63090). (314) 583-5155; (314) 239-3355. FAX: (314) 583-1644. Licensee: Franklin Radio Corp. (acq 1-87; $410,000 with co-located FM; FTR 12-8-86). Net: ABC/I. Format: News/talk, adult contemp. News staff 2; news progmg 20 hrs wkly. Target aud: General. Spec prog: Relg 7 hrs wkly. ■ Richard Fister, pres; Kevin Anfield, gen mgr; Ray Heller, progmg dir & mus dir. ■ Rates: $16; 14; 14; 14.

KLPW-FM—Aug 1, 1966: 101.7 mhz; 2.1 kw-H. Ant 341 ft. TL: N38 28 57 W91 02 39. Stereo. Hrs opn: 24. Prog sep from AM. Format: Country. News staff 2; news progmg 7 hrs wkly. Target aud: General. Spec prog: Relg 6 hrs wkly. ■ Nona Lee Miller, mus dir. ■ Rates: Same as AM.

Vandalia

KLRK(FM)—June 13, 1983: 100.1 mhz; 3 kw. Ant 316 ft. TL: N39 19 00 W91 28 22. Stereo. c/o Webb Communications, 3800 Crystal Lane, Inverness, FL (32652). Licensee: Webb Communications (acq 5-24-88). ■ Robert Webb, pres & gen mgr; Karen Webb, stn mgr; Perry Moore, chief engr.

Versailles

KLGS(FM)—June 16, 1989: 95.1 mhz; 6 kw. Ant 328 ft. TL: N38 24 32 W92 45 42. Stereo. Hrs opn: 24. Box 409 (65084); Hwy. 52 E., Barnett (65011). (314) 378-5669; (800) 722-1195. FAX: (314) 378-6640. Licensee: Twin Lakes Communications Inc. (acq 11-89; $10,000; FTR 11-13-89). Net: CNN. Wash atty: Fletcher, Heald & Hildreth. Format: Country. News staff 2; news progmg 23 hrs wkly. Target aud: 25-54; loc rural audience and transient tourist population. Spec prog: Farm 2 hrs, relg 3 hrs wkly. ■ Douglas A. Fisher, chmn; James D. Fisher, pres, gen mgr & opns dir; Sheryl Lehman, sls dir; Richard Sterling, prom dir & asst mus dir; J.T. Gerlt, progmg dir & mus dir; Paul Ryan, news dir; Jay Fisher, chief engr.

Warrensburg

*KCMW-FM—Apr 1, 1962: 90.9 mhz; 100 kw. Ant 400 ft. TL: N38 55 54 W93 49 06. Stereo. Central Missouri State Univ., Corner of College and Clark (64093). (816) 543-4491. FAX: (816) 543-8863. Licensee: Central Missouri State Univ. Board of Regents. Net: NPR, APR. Format: Div. News staff one; news progmg 30 hrs wkly. Target aud: General. Spec prog: Black 3 hrs wkly. ■ Don Peterson, gen mgr; Bill Kim, progmg dir, mus dir & news dir; Dan Davis, chief engr.

KOKO(AM)—December 1953: 1450 khz; 1 kw-U. TL: N38 46 32 W93 43 12. Hrs opn: 5 AM-1 AM, M-S; 6 AM-1 AM, Sun. Box 398, 800 PCA Rd. (64093). (816) 747-9191. Licensee: Johnson Co. Broadcasters Inc. (acq 11-60). Net: MBS; Missourinet, Brownfield. Format: Adult contemp, news/talk. News staff one; news progmg 20 hrs wkly. Target aud: 25-54. Spec prog: Farm 4 hrs, relg 6 hrs wkly. ■ Avis G. Tucker, pres; Marion E. Woods, gen mgr, opns mgr, progmg dir, mus dir & chief engr; Linda Fischer, gen sls mgr; Bill Chase, prom dir; Kelly Hart, news dir; Lynn Eschliman, pub affrs dir. ■ Rates: $9.75; 9.75; 9.75; 7.90.

Warrenton

KWRE(AM)—Mar 9, 1949: 730 khz; 1 kw-D, 120 w-N. TL: N38 49 20 W91 08 15. Box 220 (63383). (314) 456-3311. Licensee: Kaspar Broadcasting Co. Net: SMN. Rep: Group W. Format: C&W. Spec prog: Farm 10 hrs wkly. ■ V.J. Kaspar, pres & chief engr; Mark Becker, gen sls mgr; Mike Thomas, mus dir & news dir.

KFAV(FM)—Co-owned with KWRE(AM). Not on air, target date unknown: 99.9 mhz; 2.5 kw. Ant 512 ft. TL: N38 50 20 W91 02 40. ■ V.J. Kasper, gen mgr.

Warsaw

KAYQ(FM)—Mar 10, 1980: 97.7 mhz; 3 kw. Ant 240 ft. TL: N38 17 12 W93 18 34. Stereo. Box 1420, Suite 6, Truman Hills Mall (65355). (816) 438-7343. FAX: (816) 438-7159. Licensee: Valkyrie Broadcasting Co. Inc. Format: Country. ■ Jim McCollum, pres; Joey Anderson, gen mgr & gen sls mgr; Glenna Thrasher, prom mgr; Kirk Lowery, progmg dir; Paula Spring, news dir.

Washington

*KGNV(FM)—Dec. 25, 1990: 89.9 mhz; one kw. Ant 213 ft. TL: N38 35 49 W91 06 17. Hrs opn: 24. Box 87 (63090). (314) 239-0400. Licensee: Missouri River Christian Broadcasting Inc. Net: Moody, USA. Format: Religious, news/talk, btfl music. News progmg 14 hrs wkly Target aud: General; inquisitive, conservative, liberal, philosophical, young & old. ■ James C. Goggan, pres & gen mgr; Ken Bowles, vp, opns mgr, progmg dir, news dir & chief engr. ■ Rates: $5; 5; 5; 5.

KLPW-FM—See Union.

KSLQ(AM)—Oct 19, 1985: 1350 khz; 500 w-D, 100 w-N, DA-1. TL: N38 34 44 W90 59 57. 511 W. 5th St. (63090). (314) 239-6800. FAX: (314) 239-0364. Licensee: Primetime Radio. Net: USA, Sun; Missourinet. Format: Adult contemp. News staff one. Target aud: 25-54. ■ Ken Kuenzie, pres, gen mgr & mus dir; Dennis Klautzer, progmg dir; Chris Dieckhause, news dir; Jeran Kuenzie, chief engr.

KSLQ-FM—Nov 21, 1989: 104.5 mhz; 3 kw. Ant 328 ft. TL: N38 36 03 W90 56 04. Stereo. Hrs opn: 24. Dups AM 25%. Format: Adult contemp, talk.

Waynesville

KFBD-FM—Listing follows KOZQ(AM).

KJPW(AM)—Apr 3, 1962: 1390 khz; 5 kw-D, 67 w-N. TL: N37 49 09 W92 09 06. Hrs opn: 19. Box D (65583); Business Loop 44 E., St. Robert (65583). (314) 336-4913; (314) 336-4450. FAX: (314) 336-2222. Licensee: Pulaski County Broadcasting Inc. (acq 6-1-74). Net: NBC; Missourinet. Wash atty: Cohn & Marks. Format: Country. News staff 2; news progmg 14 hrs wkly. Target aud: General. Spec prog: Relg 3 hrs wkly. ■ Millie Howlett-Brotherton, pres, gen mgr & gen sls mgr; Gary Knehans, prom mgr & progmg dir; Van Beydler, mus dir; Warren Goforth, news dir. ■ Rates: $9.50; 9.50; 9.50; 9.50.

KJPW-FM—May 2, 1968: 102.3 mhz; 1 kw. Ant 480 ft. TL: N37 49 09 W92 09 06. Stereo. Hrs opn: 19. Dups AM 95%. ■ Rates: Same as AM.

KOZQ(AM)—May 9, 1968: 1270 khz; 500 w-D. TL: N37 49 42 W92 10 27. Box 583 (65583). (314) 336-3133. Licensee: BD Inc. (acq 11-31-82; $500,000 with co-located FM; FTR 12-6-82). Net: Unistar. Rep: Magic Circle. Format: Top-40. Spec prog: Jazz 2 hrs wkly. ■ Dick Triggs, pres & gen mgr; Roland Wall, gen sls mgr; Brent Hayes, prom dir; Bob Lack, chief engr.

Stations in the U.S.

KFBD-FM—Co-owned with KOZQ(AM). Dec 9, 1964: 97.7 mhz; 3 kw. Ant 192 ft. TL: N37 49 42 W92 10 27. Stereo. Dups AM 100%. FAX: (314) 336-3133. ■ Rates: $16.50; 13; 13; 13.

Webb City

KIXQ(FM)—Sept 10, 1985: 93.9 mhz; 48 kw. Ant 505 ft. TL: N37 14 34 W94 30 21. Stereo. 2620 Dogwood Rd., Joplin (64801). (417) 624-1310. FAX: (417) 624-1817. Licensee: West Group Broadcasting. (acq 11-30-88). Net: ABC/E. Rep: Banner. Format: C&W. News staff one. Target aud: 25-54. ■ Paul Swint, gen mgr; Dave Clemens, gen sls mgr; Ralph Cherry, progmg dir; Scott Curtis, news dir; Jack Leutzinger, chief engr. ■ Rates: $130; 130; 110; 50.

KKLL(AM)—Mar 10, 1984: 1100 khz; 5 kw-D. TL: N37 06 23 W94 16 50. Box 211, 831 W. Daugherty (64870). (417) 673-1111; (417) 673-1100. FAX: (417) 781-1100. Licensee: Don & Gail Stubblefield. Format: Christian. ■ Don Stubblefield, pres, gen mgr & mus dir; Jim Young, gen sls mgr; Art Rogers, progmg dir; Jim Taylor, news dir; Jack Leutzinger, chief engr. ■ Rates: $7.25; 7.25; 7.25; 7.25.

KKLL-FM—Sept 1, 1988: 97.9 mhz; 6 kw. Ant 400 ft. TL: N37 06 11 W94 24 11. Stereo. Hrs opn: 6 AM-2 AM. Prog sep from AM. Net: USA. Target aud: General.

West Plains

KKDY(FM)—Mar 31, 1984: 102.5 mhz; 50 kw. Ant 485 ft. TL: N36 41 22 W91 53 45. Stereo. Hrs opn: 24. Box 10, 1562 Imperial Ctr. (65775). (417) 256-1025. FAX: (417) 256-2208. Licensee: Mackey Communications Corp. (acq 8-1-88). Net: Unistar. Wash atty: McCampbell & Young. Format: CHR. News progmg 10 hrs wkly. Target aud: 18-49. Spec prog: Contemp Christian 7 hrs wkly. ■ Joe F. Mackey, pres & gen mgr; Yancy Yates, gen sls mgr; Randal Gower, prom mgr; Bobby Helm, news dir. ■ Rates: $14.65; 14.65; 14.65; 14.65.

KSPQ(FM)—Listing follows KWPM(AM).

KWPM(AM)—1947: 1450 khz; 1 kw-U. TL: N36 44 28 W91 50 01. Hrs opn: 24. Rt. 2, Box 100 (65775). (417) 256-3131; (417) 256-5976. FAX: (417) 256-0948. Licensee: Neathery Communications Inc. (acq 8-25-76). Net: ABC/D, MBS; Talknet; Brownfield, Missourinet. Format: News/talk. News staff 4; news progmg 15 hrs wkly. Target aud: 25-54. Spec prog: Gospel 5 hrs, relg 10 hrs wkly. ■ Robert F. Neathery, pres; Bret R. Neathery, vp & gen mgr; Chuck Robson, opns mgr; John Thomason, gen sls mgr; John Deidiker, news dir; Gary Elam, pub affrs dir; Bill Martin, chief engr.

KSPQ(FM)—Co-owned with KWPM(AM). 1951: 93.9 mhz; 100 kw. Ant 650 ft. TL: N37 00 12 W91 54 24. Stereo. Prog sep from AM. Rt. 2, Box 100, E. Hwy. 160 (65775). (417) 256-2322. Format: AOR. News staff 2; news progmg 10 hrs wkly. Target aud: 45-65 plus. ■ John Deidiker, progmg dir.

Willard

KOSP(FM)—Aug 15, 1992: 105.1 mhz; 50 kw. Ant 492 ft. TL: N37 01 01 W93 30 31. 313-C E. Battlefield, Springfield (65807). (417) 886-5677. FAX: (417) 886-2155. Licensee: KOSP Partnership. Group owner: Mid-West Family Stations. Net: AP. Wash atty: Fisher, Wayland, Cooper & Leader. Format: Oldies. Target aud: 25-54. ■ Rex Hansen, vp & gen mgr.

Willow Springs

KUKU(AM)—Oct 1957: 1330 khz; 1 kw-D, 52 w-N. TL: N36 58 47 W91 59 29. Box 250 (65793). (417) 469-2500; (417) 469-3350. FAX: (417) 469-4812. Licensee: Neathery Broadcasting Inc. (acq 4-16-87). Format: Adult contemp, C&W. ■ Bret Neathery, pres; Larry D. Spence, gen mgr; Bill Martin, chief engr.

KUKU-FM—June 15, 1985: 100.3 mhz; 50 kw. Ant 492 ft. TL: N37 03 49 W92 01 39. Stereo. Hrs opn: 24. Prog sep from AM. Box 100, Rt. 2 West Plains (65775). (417) 256-3131. FAX: (417) 356-0948. Format: Country. News staff 2; news progmg 27 hrs wkly. Target aud: 29 plus. Spec prog: Farm 6 hrs wkly. ■ Bret Neathery, gen mgr.

Montana

LAUREN A. COLBY
301-663-1086
COMMUNICATIONS ATTORNEY
Special Attention to Difficult Cases

Anaconda

KGLM-FM—Jan 18, 1974: 97.7 mhz; 2.5 kw. Ant 940 ft. TL: N46 06 07 W112 56 59. Stereo. Hrs opn: 24. Box 772, Suite 210, 307 E. Park (59711); 105 Main (59711). (406) 563-8011. FAX: (406) 563-8259. Licensee: Aire/Ink Inc. (acq 7-89; $4,500; FTR 7-24-89). Net: SMN. Wash atty: Graybill, Ostrem, Warner & Crotty. Format: Country. News staff 2. Target aud: 18 plus. ■ David R. Fransen, pres; Edith I. Fransen, gen mgr; Mike McCoy, progmg dir; Tony Cuesta, vp engrg.

Baker

KATQ-FM—See Plentywood.

KFLN(AM)—July 14, 1964: 960 khz; 5 kw-D, 91 w-N. TL: N46 22 31 W104 16 25. Box 790 (59313); Hwy. 7, (59313). (406) 778-3371. FAX: (406) 778-3431. Licensee: Newell Broadcasting Corp. (acq 3-1-84; $870,000; FTR 3-5-84). Net: AP. Format: C&W. Spec prog: Farm 10 hrs wkly. ■ Russ Newell, pres & gen mgr; Nick Connors, gen sls mgr.

Belgrade

KGVW(AM)—Feb 1, 1959: 640 khz; 10 kw-D, 1 kw-N, DA-2. TL: N45 46 15 W111 13 26. Hrs opn: 6 AM-midnight. Box 167, 2050 Amsterdam Rd. (59714). (406) 388-4281. FAX: (406) 388-1700. Licensee: Christian Enterprise. Group owner: Enterprise Network (acq 5-31-62). Net: CBN. Format: Relg. News progmg 16 hrs wkly. Target aud: 35-64; professionals. Spec prog: Bobcat football and basketball. ■ Harold Erickson, pres; Bruce Erickson, exec vp & vp progmg; Mark Brashear, gen mgr & gen sls mgr; C. J. Swoboda, progmg dir; Dale Heidner, chief engr. ■ Rates: $9; 9; 9; 9.

KGVW-FM—Nov 1, 1963: 96.7 mhz; 6 kw. Ant 150 ft. TL: N45 41 36 W110 58 54. Stn currently dark. (Acq 5-86; $225,000; FTR 5-26-86).

Billings

KBLG(AM)—Sept 25, 1955: 910 khz; 1 kw-D, 63 w-N. TL: N45 45 10 W108 30 57. Hrs opn: 24. 2075 Central Ave. (59101). (406) 652-8400. FAX: (406) 652-4899. Licensee: Sunbrook Communications (group owner; acq 9-7-89; $175,000; FTR 1-23-89). Net: CBS, ABC Talk-Radio, MBS, NBC Talknet, ARN, Sun. Rep: McGavren Guild. Format: All news, talk. News staff one; news progmg 46 hrs wkly. Target aud: 35-64. Spec prog: Sports 10 hrs wkly. ■ Larry Roberts, pres; Patti Coffey, gen mgr; Chad Parrish, opns mgr; Steve Auga, gen sls mgr; Terry Keys, progmg dir; J.P. Donovan, news dir; Charlie Dozier, chief engr.

KRKX(FM)—Co-owned with KBLG(AM). July 1989: 94.1 mhz; 100 kw. Ant 1,023 ft. TL: N45 32 25 W108 38 31. Stereo. (406) 656-9410. (Acq 9-89; $101,777; FTR 9-25-89). Format: Classic rock. News progmg one hr wkly. Target aud: 25-54; the affluent. ■ Terry Keys, mus dir; Scott Monson, asst mus dir.

KCTR(AM)—Mar 20, 1951: 970 khz; 5 kw-U, DA-N. TL: N45 44 20 W108 32 38 (CP: N45 44 35 W108 32 37). Stereo. Hrs opn: 24. Box 1726 (59103); 27 N. 27th St., 23rd Fl., (59101). (406) 248-7827. FAX: (406) 252-9577. Licensee: Citadel Communications Corp. (group owner; acq 2-1-88). Net: ABC/I. Rep: Christal. Format: Modern country. News staff one; news progmg 2 hrs wkly. Target aud: 25-54. ■ Larry Wilson, pres; Paul V. Ehlis, gen mgr; Dennis Coffman, sls dir; Glenn Hebert, prom mgr; Jim Diamond, progmg dir; John Thomas, mus dir; Paul Mushaben, news dir; Randy Rocks, chief engr. ■ Rates: $50; 40; 32; 21.

KCTR-FM—Aug 14, 1979: 102.9 mhz; 100 kw. Ant 500 ft. TL: N45 45 59 W108 27 19. Stereo. Dups AM 100%. Format: Country.

***KEMC(FM)**—Apr 25, 1973: 91.7 mhz; 100 kw. Ant 520 ft. TL: N45 39 51 W108 34 14. Stereo. Hrs opn: 24. 1500 N. 30th St. (59101-0298). (406) 657-2978. FAX: (406) 657-2977. Licensee: Eastern Montana College. Net: NPR, APR. Format: Class, news. News staff one; news progmg 24 hrs wkly. Target aud: General. Spec prog: Jazz 16 hrs, folk 5 hrs wkly. ■ Marvin F. Granger, gen mgr; Lois Bent, opns mgr & progmg dir; Judy Larson, gen sls mgr; Alicia Lee, prom mgr; Brad Edwards, mus dir; Jackie Yamanaka, news dir; Randall Rocks, chief engr.

KGHL(AM)—June 8, 1928: 790 khz; 5 kw-U, DA-N. TL: N45 43 34 W108 36 35. Stereo. Hrs opn: 24. 2070 Overland Ave., Suite 103 (59102). (406) 656-1410. FAX: (406) 656-0110. Licensee: Pegasus Broadcasting of Billings Inc. (acq 5-31-91; $1 million with co-located FM; FTR 6-24-91). Net: CNN. Rep: Eastman, Intermountain Net, Art Moore. Wash atty: Fletcher, Heald & Hildreth. Format: C&W. News staff one; news progmg 4 hrs wkly. Target aud: 25-54. ■ Chris Brennan, CEO & gen mgr; John Burley, opns mgr & progmg dir; David Pederson, gen sls mgr; Scott Fredericks, prom mgr; Rick Lawrence, mus dir; Charles Dozier, chief engr.

KIDX(FM)—Co-owned with KGHL(AM). August 1978: 98.5 mhz; 85 kw. Ant 370 ft. TL: N45 45 51 W108 27 18. Stereo. Prog sep from AM. Rep: Eastman. Format: Adult contemp.

KKBR(FM)—Dec 17, 1963: 97.1 mhz; 28 kw. Ant 325 ft. TL: N45 45 51 W108 27 18. Stereo. Box 1276 (59103). (406) 248-7827. FAX: (406) 252-9577. Licensee: Citadel Communications Corp. (group owner; acq 5-26-93; $300,000; FTR 7-21-93). Format: Oldies. ■ Paul Ehlis, gen mgr; Curtis Thompson, progmg dir; Molly Grand, news dir.

KMAY(AM)—Sept 8, 1946: 1240 khz; 1 kw-U. TL: N45 45 26 W108 32 08. Box 1291, 1306 Central Ave. (59102). (406) 259-7900. FAX: (406) 252-8120. Licensee: Michael May Enterprises Inc. (acq 4-8-93; $14,000; FTR 4-26-93). Net: NBC. Rep: McGavren Guild. Format: Sports, talk. ■ Walter Christiansen, stn mgr.

KOHZ(FM)—Dec 6, 1987: 103.7 mhz; 100 kw. Ant 480 ft. TL: N45 46 00 W108 27 27. Stereo. Hrs opn: 24. Box 7088, 401 N. 31st St. (59103). (406) 248-2211. FAX: (406) 256-1037. Licensee: KOHZ Inc. Net: ABC/E. Rep: Banner, Target. Wash atty: Reddy, Begley & Martin. Format: Light adult contemp. Middle to upper income adults. ■ William R. Reier, pres; Michele Konzen, gen mgr & gen sls mgr; Ed Donohue, opns dir & progmg dir; Dick Jones, chief engr. ■ Rates: $22; 19; 21; 19.

KRKX(FM)—Listing follows KBLG(AM).

KURL(AM)—Oct 15, 1959: 730 khz; 5 kw-D, 236 w-N. TL: N45 45 29 W208 29 53. Hrs opn: 5:30 AM-midnight. Box 31038 (59107); 636 Haugen (59101). (406) 245-3121. FAX: (406) 248-6436. Licensee: Christian Enterprises Inc. Group owner: Enterprise Network (acq 1-20-62). Net: AP, USA. Format: Relg, syndicated talk. Target aud: 35-64. ■ Harold Erickson, pres; Bruce Erickson, exec vp; Herm Elenbaas, gen mgr; David Barrett, news dir; Kent Abendroth, chief engr. ■ Rates: $8.50; 9.50; 7.50; 6.50.

KYYA(FM)—April 5, 1969: 93.3 mhz; 100 kw. Ant 700 ft. TL: N45 45 37 W108 27 09. Stereo. Hrs opn: 24. 2075 Central Ave. (59102). (406) 652-8400. FAX: (406) 652-4899. Licensee: Sunbrook Communications Ltd. (acq 3-5-93; $415,000; FTR 3-22-93). Net: ABC/C. Rep: McGavren Guild. Format: Adult top-40. News staff one; news progmg 2 hrs wkly. Target aud: 18-49; mass audience, upscale adults. ■ Larry Roberts, chmn; Debbie Sundberg, gen mgr, gen sls mgr, natl sls mgr & rgnl sls mgr; Bruce Jensen, progmg dir & news dir; Charlie Fox, mus dir; Scott Simmons, asst mus dir; Tom Kelly, pub affrs dir; Louie Nunn, chief engr. ■ Rates: $21; 19; 21; 17.

Bozeman

KATH(FM)—Listing follows KBOZ(AM).

***KBMC(FM)**—Not on air, target date unknown: 102.1 mhz; 20.5 kw. Ant 768 ft. TL: N45 38 12 W111 16 20. 1500 N. 30th St., Billings (59101). (406) 657-2941. Licensee: Eastern Montana College (acq 3-29-91; FTR 4-15-91). Format: Class, jazz. ■ Marvin Granger, gen mgr.

KBOZ(AM)—Dec 19, 1975: 1090 khz; 5 kw-U, DA-N. TL: N45 36 58 W111 05 16. Box 20, 5445 Johnson Rd. (59715). (406) 586-5466. FAX: (406) 587-8201. Licensee: Citadel Communications Corp. (group owner; acq 9-86). Net: ABC/E, ABC/I, Unistar. Rep: Art Moore. Wash atty: Reed & Associates. Format: Country. News staff 2; news progmg 6 hrs wkly. Target aud: 25-64. Spec prog: Farm one hr wkly. ■ Larry Wilson, CEO; Vicki Mann, vp & gen mgr; Dean Alexander, vp sls & gen sls mgr; Terry Kegley, progmg dir; John Russell, news dir; Steve Campbell, vp engrg; Jim Bender, engrg mgr. ■ Rates: $27.75; 24.60; 27.75; 15.35.

KATH(FM)—Co-owned with KBOZ(AM). Nov 1, 1980: 93.7 mhz; 100 kw. Ant 245 ft. TL: N45 41 35 W110 58 50. Stereo. Prog sep from AM. Net: ABC/E. Format: Hot country. News staff 2; news progmg 4 hrs wkly. Target aud: 25-54. ■ Peter Masse, progmg dir; Roger Nelson, mus dir. ■ Rates: Same as AM.

***KGLT(FM)**—December 1963: 91.9 mhz; 2 kw. Ant 365 ft. TL: N45 41 35 W110 59 00. Stereo. Rm. 325, S.U.B., Montana State Univ. (59717). (406) 994-3001. Licensee: Montana State Univ. Net: AP. Format: Div, educ. Target aud: General. Spec prog: Black one hr, class 11 hrs, folk 12 hrs wkly. ■ Philip Charles, Landon Woodward (asst), gen mgrs; D.G. Poymter, vp mktg; Landon Woodword, vp progmg; Michael Weaver, Rob Work, mus dirs; John Campbell, chief engr.

KMMS(AM)—Oct 15, 1939: 1450 khz; 1 kw-U. TL: N45 39 33 W111 03 22. 125 W. Mendenhall (59715). (406) 586-2343. FAX: (406) 587-2202. Licensee: Gilbert Broadcasting Corp of Montana (acq 4-25-91; $829,000 with co-located FM; FTR 5-20-91). Net: AP, CNN. Rep: Target Radio. Wash atty: Pepper & Corazzini. Format: News/talk. News staff 2; news progmg 20 hrs wkly. Target aud: 35-64. ■ Kip Gilbert, pres; Joan Gilbert, gen sls mgr; Kay Ruh, prom mgr; George Carter, progmg dir.

KMMS-FM—Aug 14, 1986: 95.1 mhz; 94 kw. Ant 781 ft. TL: N45 40 24 W110 52 02. Format: Adult rock.

KZLO(AM)—May 22, 1950: 1230 khz; 1 kw-U, DA-2. TL: N45 42 02 W111 02 49. Hrs opn: 18. 219 E. Main St. (59715-4747). 1450 W. Kagy Blvd. (59715). (406) 585-1230. FAX: (406) 586-8659. Licensee: Reier Broadcasting Co. Inc. (acq 2-19-93; $125,000; FTR 5-17-93). Net: CBS; Agri-Net, Mont. Net. Rep: Eastman/Intermountain. Format: Best hits of last 40 yrs. News progmg 15 hrs wkly. Target aud: 30 plus; affluent adults. ■ Judy Cowdrey, pres; Katalin Pados, gen sls mgr. ■ Rates: $12; 11; 12; 10.

KZLO-FM—1983: 99.9 mhz; 100 kw. TL: N45 41 34 W110 58 57. Box 519 (59771). (406) 587-9999. Licensee: Reier Broadcasting Co. Inc. Format: Hot country. ■ Bill Reier, gen mgr; Craig Sullivan, progmg dir.

Butte

KAAR(FM)—Nov 1, 1988: 92.7 mhz; 3 kw. Ant 24 ft. TL: N46 01 34 W112 32 07. Hrs opn: 6 AM-midnight. 3219 Harrison Ave. (59701). (406) 494-1030. FAX: (406) 494-6020. Licensee: Sunbrook Communications Ltd. (group owner; acq 3-31-93; $90,000; FTR 4-19-93). Net: NBC, MBS. Rep: McGavren Guild. Format: Country, rock. News progmg 8 hrs wkly. Target aud: General. ■ Bob Toole, gen mgr. ■ Rates: $4.25; 4.25; 4.25; 4.25.

KBOW(AM)—Feb 14, 1947: 550 khz; 5 kw-D, 1 kw-N, DA-N. TL: N45 58 30 W112 34 18. Box 3389, 660 Dewey Blvd. (59702). (406) 494-7777. FAX: (406) 494-5534. Licensee: KBOW Inc. (acq 4-1-62). Net: CBS. Rep: Eastman/Intermountain, Art Moore. Wash atty: Haley, Bader & Potts. Format: C&W. News staff 2; news progmg 24 hrs wkly. Target aud: General; 25 plus. Spec prog: Farm 5 hrs wkly. ■ Shag Miller, pres; Ron Davis, gen mgr; Francie York, gen sls mgr; Tim Beggs, progmg dir; Karen Sullivan, news dir; Ed Bauer, chief engr.

KOPR(FM)—Co-owned with KBOW(AM). Oct 26, 1972: 94.1 mhz; 100 kw. Ant 1,840 ft. TL: N46 00 23 W112 26 28 (CP: 58.4 kw). Stereo. Hrs opn: 24. Net: ABC/C; Intermountain. Format: Adult contemp. News staff 2; news progmg 5 hrs wkly. Target aud: 25-45. ■ Phil Davenport, gen sls mgr.

***KMSM-FM**—1975: 91.5 mhz; 50 w. Ant 93 ft. TL: N46 00 43 W112 33 23. Stereo. Hrs opn: 24. Student Union Bldg, Montana Tech. (59701). (406) 496-4391; (406) 496-4389. FAX: (406) 496-4133. Licensee: Associated Students of Mont. Tech. Wash atty: Pepper & Corazzini. Format: Educ, div. News progmg 2 hrs wkly. Target aud: General; very diversified group. Spec prog: Jazz 5 hrs, relg 3 hrs, class 2 hrs wkly. ■ Ross Metcalfe, stn mgr; Greg Owen, progmg mgr & mus dir; John Haney, news dir; Pat Leathrum, chief engr.

KOPR(FM)—Listing follows KBOW(AM).

KQUY-FM—Listing follows KXTL(AM).

KXTL(AM)—1927: 1370 khz; 5 kw-U. TL: N46 09 37 W112 37 54. Stereo. Box 3788 (59702); 3219 Harrison Ave. (59701). (406) 494-4442. FAX: (406) 494-6020. Licensee: Sunbrook Communications (group owner; acq 9-86; $597,000 with co-located FM; FTR 7-21-86). Net: NBC, MBS. Rep: McGavren Guild. Format: MOR. News progmg 20 hrs wkly. Target aud: 25-54. ■ Larry Roberts, pres; Bob Toole, gen mgr; Charlotte Elich, gen sls mgr.

KQUY-FM—Co-owned with KXTL(AM). Feb 7, 1980: 95.5 mhz; 50 kw. Ant 1,820 ft. TL: N46 00 29 W112 26 30. Stereo. Prog sep from AM. (406) 494-5895. Net: MBS; Mont. Net. Rep: Torbet, McGavren Guild. Format: Adult contemp. News progmg 7 hrs wkly. Target aud: 25-54. ■ Dave Levin, opns mgr.

Chinook

KRYK(FM)—Licensed to Chinook. See Havre.

Columbia Falls

KCWX(FM)—January 1994: 95.9 mhz; 6 kw. Ant 285 ft. TL: N48 27 35 W114 20 25. Box 396, Whitefish (59937). Licensee: Frank Copsidas Jr.

Deer Lodge

KDRG(AM)—1963: 1400 khz; 1 kw-U. TL: N46 24 26 W112 43 08. Box 811, North of Deer Lodge, Sam Beck Rd. (59722). (406) 846-1221. FAX: (406) 563-8259. Licensee: Aire/Ink Inc. (acq 8-20-87). Format: Oldies. News staff 2. Target aud: 18 plus. Spec prog: Farm 2 hrs wkly. ■ David R. Fransen, pres & gen mgr; Edith I. Fransen, gen sls mgr; Mike McCoy, progmg dir & news dir.

Dillon

KDBM(AM)—Jan 1, 1957: 1490 khz; 1 kw-U. TL: N45 14 13 W112 38 32. Box 950 (59725). (406) 683-2800. Licensee: Beaverhead Madison Broadcasting (acq 4-1-88). Net: ABC/I. Rep: Eastman. Format: Country. ■ Larry Chaffin, pres, gen mgr & gen sls mgr; Wally Feldt, progmg dir; Greta Chaffin, news dir.

KDBM-FM—August 1972: 98.3 mhz; 10.5 kw. Ant 495 ft. TL: N45 14 22 W112 40 03. Stereo. Prog sep from AM. Format: AOR. News staff one. Target aud: General.

East Helena

KHKR(AM)—May 26, 1988: 680 khz; 5 kw-D. TL: N46 33 58 W111 54 12. Box 4111, Helena (59604). (406) 449-4251. FAX: (406) 449-3553. Licensee: Big Sky Communications Inc. Format: News/talk. ■ Roger Lonnquest, gen mgr; Kurt Kittelson, progmg dir.

KHKR-FM—Apr 13, 1989: 104.1 mhz; 100 kw. Ant 1,896 ft. TL: N46 44 50 W112 19 49. Stereo. (Acq 9-85; $60,000; FTR 9-2-85). Format: Country.

East Missoula

KLCY(AM)—Licensed to East Missoula. See Missoula.

Forsyth

KIKC(AM)—Oct 10, 1975: 1250 khz; 5 kw-D. TL: N46 15 30 W106 41 21. Box 1250, Hwy. 10 W. (59327). (406) 356-2711. FAX: (406) 356-2712. Licensee: Peter P. Kozloski (acq 3-8-91; grpsl; FTR 4-1-91). Net: USA. Rep: Art Moore Inc. Format: Country. News progmg 3 hrs wkly. Target aud: 25-54; farmers & ranchers. ■ Pete Koslowski, pres; Bill Harrington, gen mgr.

KIKC-FM—September 1980: 101.3 mhz; 100 kw. Ant 1,010 ft. TL: N46 10 32 W106 24 21. Stereo. Dups AM 100%. (406) 232-2002.

Fort Belknap Agency

***KAEP(FM)**—Not on air, target date unknown: 88.1 mhz; 90 kw. Ant 340 ft. Box 159, Harlem (59526). Licensee: Fort Belknap College.

Glasgow

KLAN(FM)—Mar 1, 1983: 93.5 mhz; 3 kw. Ant 300 ft. TL: N48 05 42 W106 37 08. Stereo. Box 671 (59230). (406) 228-9336. FAX: (406) 228-9338. Licensee: Glasgow Broadcasting Inc. Format: Adult contemp.

KLTZ(AM)—Aug 14, 1954: 1240 khz; 1 kw-U. TL: N48 13 09 W106 38 54. Box 671, 504 2nd Ave. S. (59230). (406) 228-9336. Licensee: Holter Broadcasting Inc. Net: ABC/I, Northern Agri-Net. Rep: Eastman. Format: C&W. News staff one. Target aud: 25 plus. ■ W.L. Bill Holter, pres; Shirley Kirkland, gen mgr & gen sls mgr; Annette Vegge, dev mgr; Tim Phillips, progmg dir; Larry Gilliland, asst mus dir; Rick Schultz, news dir; John Sisson, chief engr.

Glendive

KDZN(FM)—Dec 21, 1969: 96.5 mhz; 100 kw. Ant 400 ft. TL: N47 05 15 W104 48 04. Stereo. Hrs opn: 6 AM-midnight. Box 460, 116 S. Merrill (59330). (406) 365-6996. FAX: (406) 365-6996. Licensee: Magic-Air Communications Co. (acq 5-86; $100,000; FTR 4-21-86). Format: Adult contemp. News progmg 4 hrs wkly. Target aud: 25-54. ■ Burt H. Oliphant, pres & gen sls mgr; L. Brent Oliphant, gen mgr & chief engr; Jeff S. Oliphant, progmg dir & mus dir.

KGLE(AM)—Aug 22, 1962: 590 khz; 1 kw-D. TL: N47 05 50 W104 47 09. Box 931 (59330). (406) 365-3331. Licensee: Friends of Christian Radio Inc. (acq 1-12-93; $90,000; FTR 2-1-93). Net: CBN. Format: Relg, farm. Target aud: General, 35-64. ■ Merle Mullet, pres; Paul Malone, vp; Jim McBride, gen mgr & progmg dir; Bill Lindsay, mus dir & news dir; Art Gehnert, chief engr.

KXGN(AM)—Sept 23, 1948: 1400 khz; 1 kw-U. TL: N47 05 40 W104 42 50. 210 S. Douglas (59330). (406) 365-3377. FAX: (406) 365-2181. Licensee: Glendive Broadcasting Corp. Net: ABC/I. Rep: Intermountain, Eastman. Format: MOR. ■ Stephen Marks, pres; Dan Frenzel, gen mgr; Paul Sturlaugson, gen sls mgr. ■ KXGN-TV affil.

Great Falls

KAAK(FM)—Listing follows KXGF(AM).

KEIN(AM)—July 1922: 1310 khz; 5 kw-D, 1 kw-N. TL: N47 31 20 W111 23 18. Box 1239 (59403); 811 First Ave. N. (59401). (406) 761-1310. FAX: (406) 454-3775. Licensee: Roan Communications (acq 10-6-93; $325,000 with co-located FM; FTR 10-25-93). Net: SMN. Format: Country. ■ Ron Young, gen mgr; Conrad Young, progmg dir & mus dir.

KLFM(FM)—Co-owned with KEIN(AM). Feb 14, 1982: 92.9 mhz; 100 w. Ant 450 ft. TL: N47 31 57 W111 16 41. Stereo. Prog sep from AM. Format: Adult contemp. Target aud: 25-54. ■ Conrad Young, opns mgr.

***KGPR(FM)**—April 1984: 89.9 mhz; 9 kw. Ant 368 ft. TL: N47 31 57 W111 16 41. Stereo. Hrs opn: 24. Rebroadcasts KUFM(FM) Missoula 100%. Box 3343, 1400 First Ave. N. (59403). (406) 761-8292. FAX: (406) 761-0415. Licensee: Great Falls Public Radio Assn. Net: APR, NPR. Format: Classical, educ, news. News progmg 44 hrs wkly. Target aud: General. ■ Peter Briant, pres; Judy Wilsey, vp; Tim Christensen, stn mgr, progmg dir & mus dir; Kerry Callahan Bronson, news dir & pub affrs dir; Jim Van Cleave, chief engr.

KLFM(FM)—Listing follows KEIN(AM).

KMON(AM)—May 30, 1947: 560 khz; 5 kw-U, DA-N. TL: N47 25 29 W111 17 20. Stereo. Hrs opn: 24. Box 3309, Suite 210, 20 3rd St. N. (59401). (406) 761-7600. FAX: (406) 761-5511. Licensee: Staradio Corp. (group owner; acq 5-3-91; $450,000; with co-located FM; FTR 1-7-91). Net: ABC/I. Rep: IMN/Eastman, Art Moore. Wash atty: Greg Skall. Format: Country. News staff one; news progmg 20 hrs wkly. Target aud: 35-64. Spec prog: Farm 25 hrs, sports 5 hrs wkly. ■ Jack Whitley, pres; Howard Doss, exec vp; Jim Senst, vp & gen mgr; Terry Strickland, gen sls mgr; Dave Wilson, progmg dir; Skip Walters, mus dir; Brent Stanghelle, news dir; Mark Hoskins, chief engr. ■ Rates: $21.40; 21.40; 21.40; 18.80.

KMON-FM—Oct 1, 1972: 94.5 mhz; 36 kw. Ant 470 ft. TL: N47 32 09 W111 17 02. Stereo. Format: Hot Country. ■ Steve Keller, progmg dir. ■ Rates: Same as AM.

KMSL(AM)—1955: 1450 khz; 1 kw-U. TL: N47 31 26 W111 18 04. 525 Central Ave. (59405). (406) 761-2800. FAX: (406) 452-9467. Licensee: JS Marketing and Communications Inc. (group owner; acq 5-26-92; $267,000 with co-located FM; FTR 6-15-92). Net: Unistar. Rep: Christal. Format: Oldies, talk. Target aud: 25-54. Spec prog: Sports. ■ Pat Gittings, gen mgr; Dave France, opns mgr & progmg dir; Lance Palagi, mus dir; Skip Schudard, chief engr. ■ Rates: $15.60; 15.60; 15.60; 15.60.

KQDI-FM—Co-owned with KMSL(AM). Dec 31, 1963: 106.1 mhz; 100 kw. Ant 276 ft. TL: N47 31 57 W111 16 41. Stereo. Prog sep from AM. Format: Classic rock, AOR. News progmg 2 hrs wkly. Target aud: 18-49.

KOOZ(FM)—Not on air, target date unknown: 100.3 mhz; 100 kw. Ant 987 ft. TL: N47 36 26 W111 21 27. Stereo. Box 1787, Cleveland, MS (38732). (601) 846-1787. FAX: (601) 843-0494. Licensee: Contemporary Communications (group owner). Format: Country. News progmg 2 hrs wkly. Target aud: 35 plus. ■ Larry G. Fuss, chmn & pres.

KQDI-FM—Listing follows KMSL(AM).

KXGF(AM)—1947: 1400 khz; 1 kw-U. TL: N47 27 56 W111 20 22. Box 3129 (59403); 1300 Central Ave. W., (59404). (406) 727-7211. FAX: (406) 727-7218. Licensee: Sunbrook Communications (group owner; acq 11-87; $106,500; FTR 11-16-87). Net: SMN; Mont. Net. Rep: McGavren Guild. Format: MOR. News staff one; news progmg 8 hrs wkly. Target aud: 35-64. Spec prog: Farm

2 hrs wkly. ■ Larry Roberts, pres; Roger J. Gelder, gen mgr; Terry Jones, sls dir; J.J. Hemmingway, progmg dir; Skip Schuckard, chief engr.

KAAK(FM)—Co-owned with KXGF(AM). June 19, 1972: 98.9 mhz; 100 kw. Ant 500 ft. TL: N47 32 08 W111 17 02. Stereo. Prog sep from AM. Net: MBS; Mont. Net. Rep: McGavren Guild. Format: Adult contemp. News staff one; news progmg 10 hrs wkly. Target aud: 25-54.

***NEW FM**—Not on air, target date unknown: 90.9 mhz; 100 kw. Ant 476 ft. Hrs opn: 24. Rebroadcasts WJYL(FM) New Washington, IN. Box 1547, WCTV Building, 120 W. Court Ave., Jeffersonville, IN (47131). (812) 284-2600. FAX: (812) 282-4177. Licensee: Brightness Ministries Inc. Net: CBN. Format: Urban contemp (Christian). Target aud: 18-34. ■ John W. Smith Sr., CEO; Mary L. Smith, chmn; John W. Smith Jr., pres; Darlene Smith, CFO.

Hamilton

KLYQ(AM)—Feb 3, 1961: 1240 khz; 1 kw-U. TL: N46 15 22 W114 09 45. Box 668, Suite L, 217 N. 3rd St. (59840). (406) 363-3010. FAX: (406) 363-6436. Licensee: Benedict Communications L.P. (acq 12-16-86). Net: AP, ABC/I; Northern Ag. Net. Format: C&W, news. News staff one; news progmg 25 hrs wkly. Target aud: 25-49. ■ Steve Benedict, CEO & gen mgr; Donna Larson, sls dir; Don Davis, progmg dir & mus dir; Steve Fullerton, news dir; Mike Daniels, chief engr.

KBMG(FM)—Co-owned with KLYQ(AM). Feb 11, 1969: 95.9 mhz; 16 kw. Ant 393 ft. TL: N46 13 46 W114 14 01. Stereo. Prog sep from AM. Format: Adult contemp, oldies. News progmg 15 hrs wkly. Spec prog: 60s mus 3 hrs wkly. ■ Steve Fullerton, opns dir, progmg dir & mus dir.

Hardin

KDWG(FM)—1975: 95.5 mhz; 100 kw. Ant 984 ft. TL: N45 44 29 W108 08 19. Stereo. Suite 103, 2070 Overland Stn., Billings (59102). (406) 656-1410. FAX: (406) 656-0110. Licensee: Guarantee Broadcasting. Group owner: Pegasus Broadcasting Inc. Net: CBS. Rep: Intermountain Net. Format: Country. ■ Dan Snyder, gen mgr; David Peterson, adv mgr.

KKUL(AM)—Dec 28, 1962: 1230 khz; 1 kw-U. TL: N45 42 55 W107 35 59. Hrs opn: 24. Box 390 (59034). (406) 665-2131. FAX: (406) 656-0110. Licensee: First Security Bank of Livingston (acq 11-4-91; $21,000; FTR 12-2-91). Net: Drake-Chenault, Jones Satellite Audio; Intermountain. Rep: Art Moore. Format: Oldies. News progmg 2 hrs wkly. Target aud: 25-54; modern country fans. ■ Sterling Watan, CEO & pres; Bridgett Rice, gen mgr. ■ Rates: $18; 12; 14; 10.

Havre

***KNMC(FM)**—February 1979: 90.1 mhz; 10 w. Ant 56 ft. TL: N48 32 30 W109 41 06 (CP: 375 w, ant -112 ft., TL: N48 32 31 W109 41 17). Stereo. Cowen Hall, Cowen Dr. (59501). (406) 265-3709; (406) 265-3702. Licensee: Northern Montana College. Format: Educ. Spec prog: Class 10 hrs wkly. ■ Cliff Whittemore, gen mgr.

KOJM(AM)—Oct 31, 1947: 610 khz; 1 kw-U, DA-2. TL: N48 34 48 W109 38 54. Hrs opn: 19. Box 7000, Wildhorse Rd. (59501). (406) 265-7841. FAX: (406) 265-8855. Licensee: North Montana Broadcasters Inc. (acq 4-1-67). Net: ABC/I. Rep: Art Moore. Wash atty: Cohn & Marks. Format: Adult contemp. News progmg 6 hrs wkly. Target aud: 18-54. Spec prog: Farm 4 hrs wkly. ■ C. David Leeds, pres; John L. Mosher, gen mgr & gen sls mgr; Greg Ellendson, progmg dir; Dan Shepherd, news dir; Rob Yaw, chief engr.

KPQX(FM)—Co-owned with KOJM(AM). March 8, 1975: 92.5 mhz; 100 kw. Ant 1,485 ft. TL: N48 10 55 W109 41 01 (CP: 95.6 kw). Stereo. Hrs opn: 19. Prog sep from AM. Net: ABC/E. Format: Country. News staff 2. Spec prog: Farm 6 hrs wkly. ■ Kathee Jensen, mus dir.

KRYK(FM)—(Chinook). Nov 19, 1983: 101.3 mhz; 100 kw. Ant 688 ft. TL: N48 23 29 W109 17 50. Stereo. Hrs opn: 6 AM-11 PM. Box 1509, Hwy. 2 W., Chinook (59523). (406) 357-2296. Licensee: Rick D. Davies. Net: CBS. Wash atty: Lauren Colby. Format: Adult contemp, oldies. News progmg 18 hrs wkly. Target aud: 18-64; general. Spec prog: Farm 3 hrs, big band 2 hrs wkly. ■ Rick D. Davies, gen mgr, stn mgr & gen sls mgr; Carla Anderson, mktg dir; Sharmon Moxley, prom dir; Debra Davies, vp adv; K.D. Michaels, mus dir; Chuck Mulluck, asst mus dir; Jon Krinke, pub affrs dir; Sam Zuidema, chief engr. ■ Rates: $6.70; 6.70; 6.70; 6.70.

***KXEI(FM)**—July 28, 1983: 95.1 mhz; 98 kw. Ant 1,699 ft. TL: N48 10 42 W109 41 21. Stereo. Hrs opn: 24. Box 2426, 315 First St. (59501). (406) 265-5845. FAX: (406) 265-8860. Licensee: Hi-Line Radio Fellowship Inc. Net: Moody, Skylight. Wash atty: Cohn & Marks. Format: Relg. News progmg 13 hrs wkly. Target aud: General; those looking for alternative progmg. Spec prog: C&W one hr, farm one hr wkly. ■ Ed Matter, gen mgr; Paul Rangen, progmg dir & mus dir; Sam Zudemia, chief engr.

Helena

KBLL(AM)—September 1937: 1240 khz; 1 kw-U. TL: N46 35 24 W112 00 59. 1400 11th Ave. (59601). (406) 442-6620; (406) 443-1240. FAX: (406) 442-6161. Licensee: Holter Broadcasting Corp. (acq 7-16-73). Net: ABC/C, NBC Talknet. Rep: Intermountain, Art Moore. Wash atty: Dow, Lohnes & Albertson. Format: Oldies. News progmg 24 hrs wkly. Target aud: 29-54; high buying power. ■ W.L. Holter, pres; Jann Holter-Berntsen, vp; Jim Schaeffer, gen mgr & gen sls mgr; Mike Kandilas, progmg dir & mus dir; Al Johnson, news dir; Shawn Ketchum, chief engr. ■ Rates: $9.90; 8.25; 9.90; 8.25.

KBLL-FM—August 1979: 99.5 mhz; 30 kw. Ant 790 ft. TL: N46 46 12 W112 01 22. Stereo. Prog sep from AM. Net: NBC. Format: C&W. News progmg 19 hrs wkly. ■ Jim Schaeffer, adv dir. ■ Rates: Same as AM.

KCAP(AM)—Oct 1949: 1340 khz; 1 kw-U. TL: N46 36 43 W112 03 13. 110 Broadway (59601). (406) 442-4490. FAX: (406) 442-7356. Licensee: Pegasus Broadcasting of Montana Inc. (acq 10-8-86). Net: CBS, Moody. Rep: Art Moore. Format: News/talk. News staff 2; news progmg 21 hrs wkly. Target aud: 25-54. ■ Jim Willard, gen mgr; Duane Bruce, gen sls mgr; Steve Blair, progmg dir & mus dir; Cato Butler, news dir; Jackie Johnson, pub affrs dir; Jeff Block, chief engr. ■ Rates: $9; 9; 9; 7.50.

KZMT(FM)—Co-owned with KCAP(AM). 1975: 101.1 mhz; 95 kw. Ant 1,899 ft. TL: N46 44 52 W112 19 47. Stereo. Prog sep from AM. (406) 442-4468. Net: MBS. Format: Hot adult contemp. Target aud: 18-54; upscale, entrepeneurial, adults. ■ Rates: $12; 12; 12; 12.

KMTX(AM)—Nov 1, 1976: 950 khz; 5 kw-U, DA-N. TL: N46 40 28 W112 01 05. Box 1183 (59624). (406) 442-0400. FAX: (406) 449-7602. Licensee: Capital Investment. Net: AP. Format: Easy lstng. ■ James O'Connell, pres; Dean Williams, gen mgr; Ron Remington, chief engr.

KMTX-FM—Jan 19, 1985: 105.3 mhz; 86.9 kw. Ant 1,878 ft. TL: N46 44 52 W112 19 47 (CP: 100 kw, ant 1,954 ft.). Stereo. Prog sep from AM. Net: SMN. Format: Adult contemp.

***KUFM(FM)**—See Missoula.

***KVCM(FM)**—Not on air, target date unknown; 103.1 mhz; 100 kw. Ant 1,916 ft. TL: N46 44 50 W112 19 49. Box 4111 (59604). Licensee: Hi-Line Radio Fellowship Inc.

KZMT(FM)—Listing follows KCAP(AM).

Kalispell

KALS(FM)—November 1974: 97.1 mhz; 26 kw. Ant 2,488 ft. TL: N48 00 48 W114 21 55. Stereo. Box 9710 (59904-2710). (406) 752-5257. FAX: (406) 752-3416. Licensee: North Valley Broadcasting Enterprises Inc. Group owner: Enterprise Network. Format: Foreign, adult contemp. Spec prog: Class one hr wkly. ■ Harold Erickson, pres; Brad Rauch, gen mgr; Renee Morand, gen sls mgr; David Brown, progmg dir, progmg mgr & mus dir; Kent Abendroth, chief engr.

KBBZ(FM)—Sept 12, 1983: 98.5 mhz; 58 kw. Ant 2,378 ft. TL: N48 30 42 W114 22 14 (CP: 60 kw, ant 2,313 ft.). Stereo. Box 880, Whitefish (59937). (406) 862-5565. FAX: (406) 862-5566. Licensee: Bee Broadcasting Inc. (acq 6-12-83; $315,000; FTR 9-26-83). Net: ABC/C, ABC/FM. Format: Classic rock. ■ Benny Bee, pres; James Paulsen, gen mgr; Dennis Bee, gen sls mgr; John Michaels, progmg dir.

NEW FM—November 1993: 106.3 mhz; 3.9 kw. Ant 403 ft. Box 880, Whitefish (59937). (406) 862-8988. Licensee: Cloud Nine Broadcasting Inc. Format: Country. ■ Benny Bee Jr., gen mgr.

KGEZ(AM)—Mar 24, 1927: 600 khz; 5 kw-D, 1 kw-N, DA-2. TL: N48 09 40 W114 16 51. Box 169 (59903). (406) 752-2600. FAX: (406) 257-0459. Licensee: Skyline Broadcasters Inc. (acq 1958). Net: CBS, AP. Format: Oldies. News staff one; news progmg 25 hrs wkly. Target aud: 25-60. Spec prog: Farm 5 hrs wkly. ■ William E. Danford, gen mgr; Steve Breeze, gen sls mgr; Barry Morris, progmg dir & mus dir; Steve Sevener, news dir.

KOFI(AM)—Nov 11, 1955: 1180 khz; 50 kw-D, 10 kw-N, DA-N. TL: N48 11 52 W114 15 03. Stereo. Hrs opn: 24. Box 608, 317 First Ave. E. (59901). (406) 755-6690. Licensee: KOFI Inc. (acq 9-11-90; $750,000; with co-located FM; FTR 10-1-90). Net: MBS, AP, NBC Talknet, Westwood One. Rep: Tacher. Wash atty: Reddy, Begley & Martin. Format: Full svc/soft contemp. News staff 2; news progmg 35 hrs wkly. Target aud: 25-54. ■ Gerald W. Adams, pres, gen mgr, gen sls mgr & natl sls mgr; Jack Stevens, progmg dir; George Ostrom, news dir; Ron Hirsch, chief engr.

KOFI-FM—June 10, 1988: 103.9 mhz; 100 kw-H, 55 kw-V. Ant 571 ft. TL: N48 05 39 W114 16 11. Stereo. Hrs opn: 24. Net: SMN. Format: Country. News staff 2; news progmg 3 hrs wkly. Target aud: 18-49. ■ Scott Davis, mus dir.

KQRK(FM)—See Ronan.

Kinsey

KMTA(AM)—October 1986: 1050 khz; 10 kw-D, 136 w-N. TL: N46 24 04 W105 39 06. Hrs opn: 19. 1218 Pioneer Bldg., 336 N. Robert St., St. Paul, MN (55101). (612) 222-5555. FAX: (612) 222-5556. Licensee: Miles City Broadcasting Corp. Net: CBS. Format: Country, news/talk. News staff one; news progmg 6 hrs wkly. Target aud: 18-54; general. Spec prog: Farm 6 hrs, relg one hr, local sports 3 hrs wkly. ■ Paul Baillon, chmn.

Laurel

KBSR(AM)—September 1979: 1490 khz; 1 kw-U. TL: N45 39 11 W108 45 09. Hrs opn: 24. 117 E. Main St. (59044). (406) 628-8271. FAX: (406) 628-8271. Licensee: Big Sky Radio Inc. (acq 10-93). Net: Jones Satellite Audio. Format: Classic rock, talk. Target aud: 35 plus; professional, bus people. Spec prog: Sp, sports. ■ Richard Solberg, pres & gen mgr. ■ Rates: $10; 7; 7; 5.

KTWM(FM)—Not on air, target date unknown: 101.7 mhz; 100 kw. Ant 420 ft. TL: N47 04 13 W108 34 14. 5630 Billy Casper Dr., Billings (59106). Licensee: Jubilee Radio Network of Montana.

Lewistown

KXLO(AM)—1947: 1230 khz; 1 kw-U. TL: N47 01 13 W109 24 26. Box 620 (95457); 620 Northeast Main (95457). (406) 538-3441. FAX: (406) 538-3495. Licensee: KXLO Broadcast Inc. (acq 4-16-73). Net: ABC/I, CBS; Intermountain. Rep: Eastman/Intermountain. Format: Country. News staff one; news progmg 25 hrs wkly. Target aud: General. Spec prog: Farm. ■ Fred Lark, pres, gen mgr & gen sls mgr; Jerry Foster, prom dir, progmg dir & progmg mgr; Becky Passow, mus dir; Joe Zahler, news dir; Tony Cuesta, chief engr. ■ Rates: $9; 7.50; 9; 7.50.

KLCM(FM)—Co-owned with KXLO(AM). April 1975: 95.9 mhz; 3 kw. Ant 205 ft. TL: N47 04 13 W109 24 26. Stereo. Prog sep from AM. Licensee: Montana Broadcast Communications Inc. Rep: ABC. Format: Adult contemp. News progmg 6 hrs wkly. Target aud: 18-54. ■ Joe Zahler, pub affrs dir. ■ Rates: $7.50; 6; 7.50; 6.

Libby

KLCB(AM)—Dec 23, 1950: 1230 khz; 1 kw-U. TL: N48 22 14 W115 32 19. Hrs opn: 16. Box 730 (59923); 251 W. Cedar St. (59932). (406) 293-6234. Licensee: Lincoln County Broadcasters Inc. (acq 12-66). Net: ABC/I. Format: Country. News staff one; news progmg 13 hrs wkly. Target aud: 25-54. ■ Duane Williams, vp & gen mgr.

KTNY(FM)—Co-owned with KLCB(AM). Apr 5, 1986: 101.7 mhz; 3 kw. Ant -1,029 ft. TL: N48 22 14 W115 32 19. Stereo. Hrs opn: 16. Net: ABC/E. Format: MOR. News progmg 16. hrs wkly. Target aud: 35 plus.

Livingston

KBOZ-FM—December 1977: 97.5 mhz; 100 kw. Ant 265 ft. TL: N45 39 26 W110 48 22. Stereo. Box 20, Bozeman (59715). (406) 586-5466. Licensee: Citadel Communications Corp. (group owner; acq 7-1-93). Format: Country. ■ Vicki Mann, gen mgr.

KPRK(AM)—Jan 10, 1947: 1340 khz; 1 kw-U. TL: N45 40 21 W110 32 21. Hrs opn: 5:30 AM-midnight. Box 691, Hwy. 10 E. (59047). (406) 222-2841; (406) 222-1340. FAX: (406) 222-1341. Licensee: Livingston Broadcasting Inc. Net: ABC/I. Format: C&W. News staff one; news progmg 12 hrs wkly. Target aud: 25-64; general. Spec prog: Sports. ■ Jann Holter Berntsen, pres & gen mgr; Charles W. Shields, gen sls mgr & prom dir; Terry Michael, progmg dir & mus dir; Skip Shiver, news dir; Ed Bauer, chief engr. ■ Rates: $12; 12; 12; 12.

Nebraska

Malta

KLTZ(AM)—See Glasgow.

KMMR(FM)—Sept 9, 1980: 100.1 mhz; 2.25 kw. Ant 370 ft. TL: N48 15 17 W107 49 18 (CP: Ant 377 ft.). Stereo. Hrs opn: 6 AM-midnight. Box 1073, 155 1/2 S. 1st Ave E. (59538). (406) 654-2472. FAX: (406) 654-2506. Licensee: Malta Broadcasting Corp. (acq 4-4-86). Net: ABC/I. Rep: Art Moore. Format: MOR. News progmg 3 hrs wkly. Target aud: 18-65; general, rural. ■ W.L. Holter, pres; Greg Kielb, gen mgr, gen sls mgr & news dir; Sonia Young, progmg dir & mus dir; Raymond Johnson, chief engr. ■ Rates: $8.25; 8.25; 8.25; 8.25.

Miles City

KATL(AM)—Sept 4, 1941: 770 khz; 10 kw-D, 1 kw-N, DA-N. TL: N46 23 46 W105 46 44. Hrs opn: 24. Box 700, 810 S. Haynes Ave. (59301). (406) 232-2280; (406) 232-7700. FAX: (406) 232-2281. Licensee: Star Printing Co. Net: ABC/I, Unistar. Rep: Intermountain/Eastman, Art Moore. Format: Adult contemp. News staff one; news progmg 17 hrs wkly. Target aud: 25-54. ■ John Sullivan, pres; Donald L. Richard, gen mgr, prom mgr, mus dir & chief engr; Albert Homme, gen sls mgr; Donald L. Richard, Cindy Kay Lehman, news dirs. ■ Rates: $11.50; 11.50; 11.50; 11.50.

*KECC(FM)—Nov 17, 1988: 90.7 mhz; 500 w. Ant 502 ft. TL: N46 23 22 W105 45 22. Stereo. Hrs opn: 24. Rebroadcasts KEMC(FM) Billings 100%. 2715 Dickinson St. (59301). (406) 232-3031. FAX: (406) 232-5705. Licensee: Miles Community College. Net: NPR, APR. Format: Div. News progmg 39 hrs wkly. Target aud: General. ■ Sydney Sonneborn, stn mgr.

KIKC-FM—See Forsyth.

KMCM-FM—Nov 8, 1984: 92.5 mhz; 100 kw. Ant 628 ft. TL: N46 24 04 W105 39 06. Stereo. Hrs opn: 24. Box 1426, 508 Main St. (59301). (406) 232-5626. FAX: (406) 232-3692. Licensee: Miles City Broadcasting Corp. (acq 9-86). Net: CBS. Format: Adult contemp. News staff one; news progmg 3 hrs wkly. Target aud: 18-54; programmed for general audience appeal. Spec prog: Farm one hr wkly. ■ Paul Baillon, vp.

Missoula

KDXT(FM)—Listing follows KGRZ(AM).

KGRZ(AM)—1947: 1450 khz; 1 kw-U. TL: N46 52 36 W114 00 47. Box 4106 (59806); 1600 N. Ave W. (59801). (406) 728-1450. FAX: (406) 721-3020. Licensee: Sunbrook Communications (group owner; acq 5-86; $800,000; FTR 5-5-86). Net: NBC. Rep: McGavren Guild. Wash atty: Fisher, Wayland, Cooper & Leader. Format: MOR. News progmg 15 hrs wkly. Target aud: 55 plus. Spec prog: Farm 2 hrs wkly. ■ Larry Roberts, pres; Chad Parrish, gen mgr; Carla Hilleboe, gen sls mgr; Bill McPherson, rgnl sls mgr; Joe Bowers, chief engr.

KDXT(FM)—Co-owned with KGRZ(AM). April 29, 1977: 93.3 mhz; 43 kw. Ant 2,440 ft. TL: N47 02 24 W113 59 00. Stereo. Prog sep from AM. (406) 728-9399. Format: Adult contemp. News progmg 8 hrs wkly. Target aud: 18-49. ■ Scott Richards, progmg dir & mus dir.

KGVO(AM)—Jan 18, 1931: 1290 khz; 5 kw-U, DA-N. TL: N46 49 47 W114 04 45. Box 7279 (59806); 400 Ryman St. (59802). (406) 728-9300. FAX: (406) 542-2329. Licensee: Western Broadcasting Co. (acq 12-28-92; $200,000; FTR 1-25-93). Net: CBS, MBS. Rep: Republic. Format: News/talk. News staff one; news progmg 28 hrs wkly. Target aud: General. ■ Dale Moore Jr., CEO; Mark Ward, pres; Randy White, CFO; Ronald Ellingson, stn mgr; Denny Bedard, opns mgr; Dawn Correll, gen sls mgr; Kimberly Murray, prom dir; Pete Deneault, news dir; Tony Questa, chief engr.

KLCY(AM)—(East Missoula). June 27, 1959: 930 khz; 5 kw-D, 1 kw-N, DA-N. TL: N46 51 57 W114 04 57. 400 Ryman, Missoula (59802). (406) 728-9300. FAX: (406) 542-2329. Licensee: Western Broadcasting (acq 6-89). Net: ABC/C, AP. Rep: Eastman, Art Moore. Wash atty: Cohn & Marks. Format: Adult contemp. News staff one. Target aud: 35-54; adult spenders. ■ Mark Ward, gen mgr; Dawn Correll, gen sls mgr; Rick Sanders, progmg dir. ■ Rates: $15; 14; 13; 10.

KYSS-FM—Co-owned with KLCY(AM). May 11, 1969: 94.9 mhz; 15 kw. Ant 2,509 ft. TL: N47 02 24 W113 59 00. Stereo. Prog sep from AM. Net: ABC/I. Format: Modern C&W. ■ Mark E. Ward, pres; Paul Procter, progmg dir; Mike Doty, mus dir. ■ Rates: Same as AM.

KMSO(FM)—Feb 9, 1985: 102.5 mhz; 25 kw. Ant 874 ft. TL: N46 47 49 W114 00 59. Stereo. Hrs opn: 24. Box 2940, 725 Strand (59801). (406) 542-1025. FAX: (406) 721-1036. Licensee: Sheila Callahan & Friends Inc. Net: Mutual. Rep: Katz & Powell; Tacher. Format: Adult contemp. News staff one; News progmg 10 hrs wkly. Target aud: 25-54; upscale, professional, well-educated, management level. Spec prog: news magazine 3 hrs, relg one hr wkly. ■ Sheila Callahan, chmn & pres; Max Murphy, CFO & chief engr; Robert Borino, chief opns, progmg dir & mus dir; Jim Coulter, gen sls mgr & prom dir. ■ Rates: $12; 12; 12; 11.

*KUFM(FM)—Jan 31, 1965: 89.1 mhz; 17 kw. Ant 2,510 ft. TL: N47 02 24 W113 59 00 (CP: 32 kw, ant 2,473 ft., TL: N47 01 58 W113 59 29). Univ. of Montana. (59812). (406) 243-4931. FAX: (406) 243-3299. Licensee: Univ. of Montana. Net: NPR. Format: Div. ■ Terry Conrad, gen mgr & progmg dir; Charles Lubrecht, chief engr.

KYLT(AM)—July 15, 1955: 1340 khz; 1 kw-U. TL: N46 52 56 W113 59 08. Box 2277 (59806). (406) 728-5000. FAX: (406) 549-0503. Licensee: Smith Broadcasting (acq 5-90). Net: Unistar. Format: Oldies. News staff one. Target aud: 35-55. ■ Gregg Deorfler, pres; Dan Gittings, gen mgr; Craig Johnson, progmg dir; Bill Williams, mus dir; Vern Argo, chief engr.

KZOQ-FM—Co-owned with KYLT(AM). July 29, 1974: 100.1 mhz; 3 kw. Ant -300 ft. TL: N46 52 56 W113 59 08 (CP: 12.15kw). Stereo. Net: ABC/R. Format: AOR. News staff one. Target aud: 18-34.

KYSS-FM—Listing follows KLCY(AM).

KZOQ-FM—Listing follows KYLT(AM).

Plentywood

KATQ(AM)—Sept 14, 1979: 1070 khz; 5 kw-D. TL: N48 46 03 W104 32 45. 112 3rd Ave. (59254). (406) 765-1480. FAX: (406) 765-2357. Licensee: Radio International-KATQ Broadcast Association Inc. (acq 1-13-92; $5,000 with co-located FM; FTR 2-10-92). Net: ABC/E. Format: Country. Spec prog: Top-40, farm 5 hrs, relg 6 hrs wkly. ■ Mary Nielson, pres; Joy Fanning, gen mgr, prom mgr, progmg dir & mus dir.

KATQ-FM—June 1, 1962: 100.1 mhz; 3 kw. Ant 34 ft. TL: N48 47 06 W104 32 00. Dups AM 100%.

Polson

KERR(AM)—Mar 22, 1976: 750 khz; 50 kw-D, 1 kw-N, DA-N. TL: N47 38 34 W114 07 25. 581 N. Reservoir Rd. (59860). (406) 883-5255. FAX: (406) 883-4441. Licensee: Anderson Broadcasting Co. Net: ABC/E, Unistar. Format: Country. News progmg 14 hrs wkly. Target aud: General. ■ Mark Rowe, gen mgr & gen sls mgr; Mitch Miller, progmg dir; Tony Questa, chief engr.

Red Lodge

KMXE(FM)—Not on air, target date unknown: 99.3 mhz; 45 kw. Ant -359 ft. TL: N45 11 15 W109 14 46. Stereo. Box 460, Glendive (59330). (406) 365-6996. Licensee: Silver Rock Communications (acq 7-19-89; $30,000; FTR 8-7-89). Format: MOR. News staff 2. Target aud: 25-59; upwardly mobile. ■ Leslie Brent-Oliphant, pres, gen mgr & chief engr; Burt H. Oliphant, gen sls mgr; Jeffrey S. Oliphant, progmg dir & mus dir; Peggy S. Oliphant, news dir.

Ronan

KQRK(FM)—Oct 4, 1981: 92.3 mhz; 60 kw. Ant 3,500 ft. TL: N47 46 25 W114 16 04. Stereo. Hrs opn: 24. 581 N. Reservoir Rd. Polson (59860). (406) 883-9200. FAX: (406) 883-4441. Licensee: Anderson Broadcasting Co. Net: Unistar. Format: Adult contemp. Target aud: 25-49. ■ Lorraine V. Anderson, pres; Mark Rowe, gen mgr & gen sls mgr; Wayne Fox, progmg dir; Tony Questa, chief engr.

Scobey

KCGM(FM)—June 21, 1971: 95.7 mhz; 52 kw. Ant 660 ft. TL: N48 48 03 W105 21 00. Stereo. Box 220 (59263). (406) 487-2293. Licensee: Prairie Communications Inc. Net: AP. Format: Country. Spec prog: Farm 6 hrs wkly. ■ Clifford Hagfeldt, pres; Dixie Halverson, gen mgr & gen sls mgr; Wallace Fladager, progmg dir; Paul Richardson, chief engr.

Shelby

KSEN(AM)—Aug 11, 1947: 1150 khz; 5 kw-U, DA-2. TL: N48 28 54 W111 53 03. Hrs opn: 19. 830 Oilfield Ave. (59474). (406) 434-5241. FAX: (406) 434-2122. Licensee: Tri-County Radio Corp. Net: ABC/I. Rep: Eastman, Art Moore. Format: Div. News staff one; news progmg 15 hrs wkly. Target aud: 25-59. Spec prog: Farm 8 hrs wkly. ■ Jerry Black, pres, gen mgr & stn mgr; Bob Norris, vp & progmg dir; Annette Gollehan, opns mgr; Mark Daniels, news dir; Anne James, pub affrs dir; Tony Questa, chief engr. ■ Rates: $18.10; 13.90; 13.90; 12.50.

KZIN-FM—Co-owned with KSEN(AM). Dec 9, 1978: 96.3 mhz; 100 kw. Ant 570 ft. TL: N48 19 42 W112 02 03 (CP: Ant 550 ft.). Stereo. Hrs opn: 19. Dups AM 13%. Net: ABC/D. Format: Adult contemp. News staff one; news progmg 6 hrs wkly. Target aud: 18-49. Spec prog: Farm 4 hrs wkly. ■ Anne James, opns dir, progmg dir & mus dir. ■ Rates: $14.70; 11.30; 11.30; 10.20.

West Yellowstone

KWYS(AM)—Dec 20, 1967: 920 khz; 1 kw-D. TL: N44 38 56 W111 05 50. Box 9, 135 Gibbon (59758). (406) 646-7361. Licensee: GNP Inc. (acq 8-87). Net: CNN. Format: Country. Spec prog: Class one hr, big band 4 hrs wkly. ■ Gary Petersen, pres.

Whitefish

KJJR(AM)—Feb 14, 1979: 880 khz; 10 kw-D, 500 w-N. TL: N48 23 44 W114 19 11 (CP: 1 kw-N, DA-N). Box 880 (59937). (406) 862-5565. FAX: (406) 862-5566. Licensee: Bee Broadcasting Inc. Net: ABC/C. Format: Talk. ■ Benny Bee, pres; James Paulsen, gen mgr; Dennis Bee, gen sls mgr; Andy Shamely, progmg dir; Johnny Owen, news dir.

Wolf Point

KVCK(AM)—Sept 1, 1957: 1450 khz; 1 kw-U. TL: N48 05 18 W105 39 22. Hrs opn: 18. 324 Main St. (59201). (406) 653-1900. Licensee: Wolf Town Wireless Inc. (acq 8-31-92; $120,000 with co-located FM; FTR 11-16-92). Net: ABC/C. Rep: InterMountain. Format: C&W. Spec prog: Farm 6 hrs wkly. ■ Marvin Presser, pres; Randy Brooks, gen mgr; Marlene Johnson, mus dir & news dir; LeRoy Abel, chief engr.

KVCK-FM—Sept 1, 1981: 92.7 mhz; 860 w. Ant 508 ft. TL: N48 11 09 W105 40 08. Stereo. Prog sep from AM. 324 Main St. (59201). (406) 653-1902. Licensee: Wolf Town Wireless Inc. Format: Adult contemp. Spec prog: Farm one hr, American Indian one hr wkly.

Nebraska

LAUREN A. COLBY
301-663-1086
COMMUNICATIONS ATTORNEY
Special Attention to Difficult Cases

Ainsworth

KBRB(AM)—Feb 6, 1968: 1400 khz; 1 kw-U. TL: N42 33 16 W99 49 52. Hrs opn: 6 AM-10 PM. Box 285, 122 E. Second St. (69210). (402) 387-1400. Licensee: K. B. R. Broadcasting Co. Net: ABC/D; Brownfield. Format: C&W, MOR. News progmg 30 hrs wkly. Target aud: General. ■ Lorris C. Rice, pres, gen mgr & gen sls mgr; Kenneth W. Heuer, progmg dir; Randy Brudigan, chief engr. ■ Rates: $8; 8; 8; 8.

KBRB-FM—May 30, 1983: 92.7 mhz; 4.5 kw. Ant 331 ft. TL: N42 33 16 W99 49 52. Stereo. Hrs opn: 6 AM-10 PM. Dups AM 20%. Net: ABC; Brownfield. Format: Adult contemp. News progmg 10 hrs wkly.

Alliance

KAAQ(FM)—Listing follows KCOW(AM).

KCOW(AM)—Jan 1949: 1400 khz; 1 kw-U. TL: N42 06 26 W102 53 15. Hrs opn: 20. Box 600, 1210 W. 10th St. (69301). (308) 762-1400. FAX: (308) 762-7804. Licensee: KLOE Inc. Eagle Communications Inc. (acq 3-20-91; grpsl; FTR 4-8-91). Net: ABC/I. Rep: Eastman; Art Moore. Format: Adult contemp, news/talk. News staff one; news progmg 22 hrs wkly. Target aud: General; 25-54. Spec prog: Farm 8 hrs wkly. ■ Robert Schmidt, pres; Gary Shorman, vp; Michael M. Garwood, gen mgr; Mike Glesinger, opns mgr; John Jones, gen sls mgr & adv dir; Kevin Horn, prom dir, progmg dir & pub affrs dir; Jim Shull, news dir; Bill Bauer, chief engr. ■ Rates: $15.75; 13; 13; 11.50.

KAAQ(FM)—Co-owned with KCOW(AM). Sept 30, 1985: 105.9 mhz; 100 kw. Ant 700 ft. TL: N41 50 29 W103

05 07. Stereo. Hrs opn: 20. Net: ABC/E. Format: C&W. News staff 2; news progmg 15 hrs wkly. Target aud: 18-54. Spec prog: Farm 4 hrs wkly. ■ Rates: $30; 25; 25; 20.

KPNY(FM)—1978: 102.1 mhz; 100 kw. Ant 521 ft. TL: N42 07 01 W103 07 09. Stereo. Hrs opn: 6 AM-midnight. Box 245, 221 E. Third (69301). (308) 762-2000. FAX: (308) 635-1984. Licensee: Halstead Communications Inc. (acq 1988). Net: SMN. Format: Hot adult contemp. News staff one; news progmg 5 hrs wkly. Target aud: 18-35. ■ Leon Halstead, pres; Lee Hall, gen mgr; Mel Sauer, progmg dir; Bill Bauer, chief engr.

*KTNE-FM—May 1990: 91.1 mhz; 92.3 kw. Ant 1,325 ft. TL: N41 50 24 W103 03 18. Stereo. Hrs opn: 18. Box 83111, Lincoln (68501); 1800 N. 33rd St., Lincoln (68503). (402) 472-3611. FAX: (402) 472-1785. Licensee: Nebraska Educational Telecommunications Commission. Net: APR, NPR; Neb. Pub. Wash atty: Dow, Lohnes & Albertson. Format: Classical, news. News staff one; news progmg 20 hrs wkly. Target aud: 35 plus; general. Spec prog: Jazz 2 hrs, American Indian one hr, folk 2 hrs wkly. ■ Steve Robinson, gen mgr; Kathryn Stephens, prom mgr; Frank Hoffman, progmg dir; Bill Ramsay, chief engr.

Auburn

KCOE(FM)—Sept 18, 1981: 105.5 mhz; 3 kw. Ant 154 ft. TL: N40 22 54 W95 51 31. 1719 Courthouse Ave. (68305). (402) 274-1055. Licensee: Coe-Coe Broadcasters Inc. Net: ABC/D; Brownfield. Rep: Soderlund. Format: Country. ■ Judy Coe, pres & gen mgr.

Aurora

KLRB(FM)—Mar 1, 1980: 97.3 mhz; 50 kw. Ant 354 ft. TL: N40 52 44 W98 05 36. Stereo. Box 1465, Grand Island (68802); 3280 Woodridge Blvd. Grand Island (68803). (402) 694-4422; (308) 381-3697. Licensee: WrightWay Broadcasting Corp. Net: AP. Format: Classic Rock. News staff one; news progmg 2 hrs wkly. Target aud: 18-49. ■ J.D. Bleu, opns mgr & progmg dir; Scott Park, gen sls mgr; Rerry Carnos, news dir.

*KROA(FM)—See Grand Island.

Bassett

*KMNE-FM—June 1991: 90.3 mhz; 92.3 kw. Ant 1,292 ft. TL: N42 20 05 W99 29 01. Stereo. Box 83111, 1800 N. 33rd St., Lincoln (68501). (402) 472-3611. Licensee: Nebraska Educational Telecommunications Commission. Net: NPR, APR. Format: Educ, class, news/talk. News staff 3. Target aud: General. ■ Jack McBride, gen mgr; Steve Robinson, stn mgr; Jeff Smith, opns mgr; Dave Holmquist, dev mgr; Kathryn Stephens, prom dir; Frank Hoffman, progmg dir; Nancy Finken, news dir; Ralph Sanchez, chief engr.

Beatrice

KTGL(FM)—Licensed to Beatrice. See Lincoln.

KWBE(AM)—June 12, 1949: 1450 khz; 1 kw-U. TL: N40 15 49 W96 46 27. Hrs opn: 5:30 AM-11:15 PM M-Sat., 6 AM-11:15 PM Sun. Box 10, 200 Sherman St. (68310). (402) 228-5923. FAX: (402) 228-3704. Licensee: Community Media. Group owner: Warner Stations (acq 6-90; $325,000; FTR 6-11-90). Net: ABC/I. Rep: Katz & Powell. Format: Adult contemp, news/talk. News staff one; news progmg 25 hrs wkly. Target aud: 30-54; mature, affluent adults. Spec prog: Farm 14 hrs wkly. ■ Joan Wood, gen mgr & natl sls mgr; Rosemary Lamberson, gen sls mgr; Don Johnson, progmg dir & mus dir; Doug Kennedy, news dir; Bill Sayer, chief engr.

Bellevue

KOIL(AM)—Mar 19, 1987: 1180 khz; 5 kw-D, 1 kw-N. TL: N41 16 12 W95 47 10 (CP: TL: N36 15 58 W95 38 23). Stereo. Hrs opn: 24. 1001 Farnam-on-the-Mall, Omaha (68102). (402) 342-2000. FAX: (402) 342-5874; (402) 346-5748. Licensee: Mitchell Broadcasting Co. Net: CBS. Rep: Katz. Format: Adult standards. ■ John C. Mitchell, pres; Marty Riemenschneider, exec vp; Neil Nelkin, opns mgr; Daniel Charleston, gen sls mgr; Brian Barks, news dir; Allen Sherrill, chief engr.

Bennington

KRRK(FM)—June 10, 1991: 93.3 mhz; 6 kw. Ant 350 ft. TL: N41 22 57 W96 07 57. Stereo. 1600 S. 72nd St., Omaha (68124). (402) 393-8780; (402) 393-8455. FAX: (402) 398-1997. Licensee: 93.3 Inc. Rep: Katz. Format: 90s AOR. ■ Matt Markel, pres, gen mgr & progmg dir; Pam Lee, gen sls mgr; Jim Garrett, prom dir; Chuck Ramold, engrg mgr. ■ Rates: $45; 45; 45; 45.

Blair

*KDCV-FM—Oct 1, 1972: 91.1 mhz; 10 w. Ant 60 ft. TL: N41 33 07 W96 09 20. Dana College (68008). (402) 426-7205. FAX: (402) 426-7386. Licensee: Dana College. Format: Alternative. ■ Merv Christopherson, pres; Darrell W. Dibben, gen mgr; Brad Volcek, vp prom; Jon Rademacher, progmg dir; R. J. Redden, mus dir; Paula Cultice, news dir; Arvin Hernes, chief engr.

KISP(FM)—Dec 11, 1979: 106.3 mhz; 3 kw. Ant 469 ft. TL: N41 37 03 W96 04 23 (CP: 25 kw, ant 301 ft.). Stereo. Sunrise Broadcasting Corp., 131 E. 62nd St., New York, NY (10021). (212) 319-7210. Licensee: Sunrise Broadcasting Corp. (group owner; acq 1-12-90). ■ Joerg Klebe, pres; Kevin Van Grouw, vp & gen mgr; Don Morgan, gen sls mgr; Thom Morrow, news dir; Richard Dennis, chief engr.

Broken Bow

KCNI(AM)—Sept 28, 1949: 1280 khz; 1 kw-D. TL: N41 24 31 W99 40 28. Hrs opn: 6 AM-6 PM. Box 409, W. Hwy, #2 Calaway Rd. (68822). (308) 872-5881. Licensee: Custer County Broadcasting Co. Net: NBC. Rep: Soderlund. Format: C&W. News staff one; news progmg 24 hrs wkly. Target aud: General; rural audience of all ages with focus on 25-65. Spec prog: Farm and country mus specials. ■ David Birnie, vp, gen mgr, stn mgr, sls dir & progmg dir; Tom Hilkemeier, opns dir & news dir; Linda Henderson, pub affrs dir; Jim Drouegge, chief engr.

KBBN-FM—Co-owned with KCNI(AM). June 15, 1982: 98.3 mhz; 3.4 kw. Ant 332 ft. TL: N41 23 49 W99 37 02. Stereo. Hrs opn: 6 AM-11 PM. Net: NBC the Source. Format: Classic/adult rock. News staff one; news progmg 10 hrs wkly. Target aud: 24-45; baby boomers and on either edge of age breakdown.

Central City

KZEN(FM)—July 22, 1985: 100.3 mhz; 100 kw. Ant 1,854 ft. TL: N41 32 28 W97 40 45. Stereo. Box 100, 1608 16th St. (68826). (308) 946-3816. FAX: (308) 946-3612. Licensee: Osage Radio Inc. Rep: Banner; Howard Anderson Co. Format: Country, farm. Target aud: Rgnl, rural and small town audience. Spec prog: Religious 3 hrs wkly. ■ Gene McCoy, pres & gen mgr; Michael O'Connor, sls dir; Prince Mayne, progmg dir; Dave Andrews, mus dir; John Ellefson, news dir; Don Denver, chief engr. ■ Rates: $105; 85; 105; 35.

Chadron

*KCNE-FM—Aug 29, 1991: 91.9 mhz; 8.4 kw. Ant 338 ft. TL: N42 48 47 W103 00 22. Stereo. Box 83111, 1800 N. 33rd St., Lincoln (68501). (402) 472-3611. Licensee: Nebraska Educational Telecommunications Commission. Net: APR, NPR. Format: Educ, class, news/talk. News staff 3. Target aud: General. ■ Jack McBride, gen mgr; Steve Robinson, stn mgr; Jeff Smith, opns mgr; Dave Holmquist, dev dir; Kathryn Stephens, prom dir; Frank Hoffman, progmg dir; Nancy Finken, news dir; Ralph Sanchez, chief engr.

KCSR(AM)—May 9, 1954: 610 khz; 1 kw-D, 137 w-N. TL: N42 49 56 W103 01 00. Hrs opn: 24. 226 Bordeaux (69337). (308) 432-5545; (308) 432-2233. FAX: (308) 432-2960. Licensee: Chadred Communications Inc. (acq 8-30-91; $150,000). Net: ABC/I. Rep: Intermountain, Art Moore. Format: C&W, news. News staff one; news progmg 20 hrs wkly. Target aud: 25-54; people in the ranch, farm & agri industry. Spec prog: Farm 25 hrs wkly. ■ Dennis A. Brown, pres; Kathi Brown, vp, gen sls mgr, natl sls mgr & rgnl sls mgr; Doug Abbott, progmg dir; Steve Donker, mus dir; Mike Ricciardi, news dir; Ed Davenport, chief engr. ■ Rates: $14; 12; 12; 9.75.

KQSK(FM)—Sept 15, 1979: 97.5 mhz; 100 kw. Ant 840 ft. TL: N42 38 06 W103 06 12. Stereo. Box 1117, 331 Main (69337). (308) 432-2060. FAX: (308) 432-2059. Licensee: KLOE Inc. (acq 6-13-91; $125,000; FTR 7-1-91). Net: ABC/C. Format: Modern country. Target aud. 12-54; yuppies of the country-agri group. ■ Mike Garwood, gen mgr; John A. Howard, stn mgr; John Axtell, news dir.

Chester

*KVYM(FM)—Not on air, target date unknown: 89.9 mhz; 50 kw. Ant 492 ft. TL: N40 02 23 W97 23 25. Unit 3 c/o M. Jackson, Hutchinson, KS (67501). Licensee: Kansas Nebraska Christian Broadcasting Inc. (acq 6-5-92).

Columbus

KJSK(AM)—Apr 28, 1948: 900 khz; 1 kw-D, 66 w-N. TL: N41 26 12 W97 23 47. Box 99, RR3, Shady Lake Rd. (68602). (402) 564-2891. FAX: (402) 564-1999. Licensee: Heartland Broadcasting Inc. Group owner: Anderson Stations (acq 11-8-90; $101,500 with co-located FM; FTR 11-26-90). Net: USA, CBN; Brownfield. Wash atty: Blair, Joyce & Silva. Format: Relg. News staff one; news progmg 13 hrs wkly. ■ Timothy P. McMahan, pres; Stan Tafoya, gen mgr; James Nickel, opns dir; K.C. Hunter, news dir. ■ Rates: $10; 10; 6; 6.

KLIR(FM)—Co-owned with KJSK(AM). August 1964: 101.1 mhz; 100 kw. Ant 760 ft. TL: N41 16 55 W97 24 30. Stereo. Prog sep from AM. (402) 564-9101. Net: ABC/D. Format: Adult contemp. News staff one. Target aud: General. Spec prog: Relg 4 hrs wkly. ■ K.C. Hunter, opns mgr; Jon Michaels, mus dir; James Nickel, chief engr. ■ Rates: $12; 10.50; 12; 8.

KKOT(FM)—Listing follows KTTT(AM).

KLIR(FM)—Listing follows KJSK(AM).

*KTLX(FM)—July 1974: 91.9 mhz; 100 w. Ant 78 ft. TL: N41 26 26 W97 21 14. c/o Trinity Lutheran Church, 2200 25th St. (68601). (402) 564-8548. Licensee: TLC Educational Corp. Format: Educ, relg. ■ Gary Spuit, pres & gen mgr.

KTTT(AM)—Dec 2, 1962: 1510 khz; 500 w-D. TL: N41 27 14 W97 24 20. Box 518 (68602-0518); 1367 33rd Ave. (68601). (402) 564-2866. FAX: (402) 564-2867. Licensee: Husker Broadcasting Inc. Group owner: Radio One Broadcasting Inc. (acq 8-1-89; $850,000 with co-located FM; FTR 8-14-89). Net: ABC/E. Format: Soft adult contemp. Target aud: 25-65. ■ Wayne Walker, gen mgr; Scott Fisher, opns mgr; Bob Cook, chief engr.

KKOT(FM)—Co-owned with KTTT(AM). Nov 25, 1969: 93.5 mhz; 1 kw. Ant 981 ft. TL: N41 32 28 W97 40 45. Stereo. Prog sep from AM. Net: ABC/E. Format: AOR. Target aud: 30 plus; young families. ■ Ryan Knight, mus dir.

Cozad

KAMI(AM)—November 1965: 1580 khz; 1 kw-D. TL: N40 50 18 W99 56 20. Hrs opn: 8 AM-5 PM. 835 Meridian St. (69130). (308) 784-1580. Licensee: VectoRadio Inc. (acq 7-1-85). Format: Talk. News progmg 6 hrs wkly. Target aud: 25-54. ■ Chuck Larsen, pres & gen mgr; Larry Cotnoir, pub affrs dir; Jerry Johnson, chief engr.

KAMI-FM—Aug 4, 1983: 104.5 mhz; 100 kw. Ant 360 ft. TL: N40 46 35 W100 01 47. Stereo. Hrs opn: 24. Dups AM 100%. Target aud: 25-54.

Crete

*KDNE(FM)—Aug 30, 1993: 91.9 mhz; 200 w. Ant 66 ft. TL: N40 37 16 W96 57 04. Stereo. 1014 Boswell Ave. (68333). FAX: (402) 826-8199. Licensee: Doane College Board of Trustees. Format: Progressive Target aud: General. ■ Douglas A. Switzer, gen mgr; Mark Jorgensen, stn mgr; Geoff Hoffman, chief opns; Maura Dawson, prom dir; Regnad Kcin, progmg mgr; Lance Fisher, mus dir; Ben Emmett, news dir; Taunya Bunte, pub affrs dir; Herman Siegl, chief engr.

KKNB(FM)—Aug 20, 1976: 104.1 mhz; 50 kw. Ant 613 ft. TL: N40 31 06 W96 46 07. Stereo. Hrs opn: 24. Suite C, 5143 S. 48th St., Lincoln (68516). (402) 421-2223. Licensee: Rock Steady Inc. (acq 4-1-93; $185,300; FTR 4-19-93). Format: New rock. News staff one. Target aud: 18-34. ■ Doug Agnew, pres & stn mgr; Dave Douglass, progmg dir & mus dir; Julie Foxx, news dir.

Crookston

*KINI(FM)—Jan 1976: 96.1 mhz; 57 kw. Ant 500 ft. TL: N43 07 50 W100 54 02. Stereo. Hrs opn: 24. Box 419, 100 S. Main, St. Francis, SD (57572). (605) 747-2291. FAX: (605) 747-5057. Licensee: Rosebud Educational Society Inc. (acq 1-78). Net: AP. Wash atty: Haley, Bader & Potts. Format: Adult contemp, rock, country. News staff one; news progmg 12 hrs wkly. Target aud: General; Indian & white. Spec prog: Jazz 4 hrs, American Indian 4 hrs, gospel 6 hrs, relg 6 hrs wkly. ■ Robert Tillman, pres; Marlon Leneaugh, exec vp; Bernard Whiting Jr., gen mgr, stn mgr, asst mus dir & news dir; Lynelle Knox, progmg dir & pub affrs dir; Ryan Holy Eagle, mus dir; Gerald Calhoun, engrg mgr.

Dakota City

KTFJ(AM)—Not on air, target date unknown: 1250 khz; 500 w-D, 700 w-N, DA-2. TL: N42 26 33 W96 15 41. Hrs opn: 24. Box 102-A, Rte. 2, Sioux City, IA (51106). (712) 252-4621. Licensee: Donald A. Swanson. Net: USA. Format: Gospel ■ Don A. Swanson, pres, gen mgr, progmg dir & chief engr.

Fairbury

KGMT(AM)—June 13, 1960: 1310 khz; 500 w-D, 97 w-N. TL: N40 06 58 W97 09 05. 414 4th St. (68352). (402) 729-3382. FAX: (402) 729-3446. Licensee: Siebert Communications Inc. (acq 8-1-84; $375,000; FTR 6-18-84). Net: ABC/D. Rep: Farmakis. Wash atty: Fisher, Wayland, Cooper & Leader. Format: Adult contemp, oldies. News staff one; news progmg 30 hrs wkly. Target aud: 25-52. Spec prog: Farm 18 hrs wkly. ■ Rick Siebert, pres, gen mgr & gen sls mgr; Randy Bauer, progmg dir & mus dir; Nikki Colling, news dir; Don Denver, chief engr. ■ Rates: $10; 12; 10; 8.

KUTT(FM)—Co-owned with KGMT(AM). December 1983: 99.3 mhz; 3 kw. Ant 310 ft. TL: N40 11 04 W97 05 15 (CP: 100 kw, ant 640 ft.). Stereo. Format: C&W. Spec prog: Farm 12 hrs wkly.

Falls City

KTNC(AM)—Aug 3, 1957: 1230 khz; 500 w-D, 1 kw-N. TL: N40 03 57 W95 36 55. Hrs opn: 5:25 AM-10:30 PM Mon-Sat, 6:30 AM-10:30 PM Sun. Box 589, 1514 Stone St. (68355). (402) 245-2453. FAX: (402) 245-2774. Licensee: C.R. Communications Inc. (acq 8-1-81; $270,000; with co-located FM; FTR 7-13-81). Net: ABC/E; Brownfield. Rep: Gray, Farmakis; Soderlund Co.Format: MOR, Oldies. News staff one; news progmg 23 hrs wkly. Target aud: 25 plus; farmers, businessmen, employees, retirees. Spec prog: Christian mus one hr, polka one hr wkly. ■ Charles A. Radatz, pres & gen mgr; Darlene Tisdel, rgnl sls mgr; John Nixon, progmg dir & mus dir; Jennifer Sines, pub affrs dir. ■ Rates: $14.10; 13.80; 14.10; 13.50.

Fremont

KHUB(AM)—December 1939: 1340 khz; 500 w-D, 1 kw-N. TL: N41 25 58 W96 27 16. Hrs opn: 5 AM-midnight. Box 669, 118 E. Fifth (68025). (402) 721-5012. FAX: (402) 721-5023. Licensee: KHUB Inc. (acq 4-22-76). Net: ABC/I. Format: MOR. News staff one; news progmg 25 hrs wkly. Target aud: 35 plus; mature adults. Spec prog: Farm 6 hrs wkly. ■ Fred Pyle, pres, gen mgr & sls dir; Ted Venema, opns mgr & progmg dir; Susan Brandt, gen sls mgr; Mike Mascoe, news dir.

KFMT(FM)—Co-owned with KHUB(AM). July 1972: 105.5 mhz; 1.2 kw. Ant 450 ft. TL: N41 24 40 W96 31 53. Stereo. Hrs opn: 5 AM-midnight. Format: Country. Target aud: 25-54.

Gering

KMOR(FM)—See Scottsbluff.

Gordon

KSDZ(FM)—May 19, 1979: 95.5 mhz; 30 kw. Ant 310 ft. TL: N42 47 56 W102 15 40. Hrs opn: 24. Box 390, W. Hwy. 20 (69343). (308) 282-2500. Licensee: DJ Broadcasting Inc. (acq 12-26-91; $190,000; FTR 1-13-92). Net: MBS, ABC/D, Mid-American Ag, Brownfield, Jones Satellite Audio. Format: C&W, rockin' oldies. ■ Jim Lambley, pres, gen mgr & gen sls mgr; Randy Brudingan, chief engr. ■ Rates: $9.30; 9.30; 9.30; 7.75.

Grand Island

KMMJ(AM)—Nov 1925: 750 khz; 10 kw-U, DA-1. TL: N41 08 05 W97 59 38. Hrs opn: Sunrise-sunset. Box 1847, 3280 Woodridge Blvd. (68802). (308) 382-2800. Licensee: Cornhusker Radio Inc. Group owner: Forum Publishing Co. (acq 3-1-89). Net: MBS, SMN. Rep: McGavren Guild, Howard Anderson. Format: Country, news, farm. News staff 2; news progmg 2 hrs wkly. Target aud: 25 plus; agriculturally oriented. Spec prog: Polka 3 hrs wkly. ■ Scott Park, gen mgr, gen sls mgr, natl sls mgr & rgnl sls mgr; Dan Arrasmith, mus dir; Harry Albers, chief engr.

KRGI(AM)—Apr 1, 1953: 1430 khz; 5 kw-D, 1 kw-N, DA-N. TL: N40 62 26 W98 16 24. Box 4907 (68802-4907); 3205 W. N. Front St. (68803). (308) 381-1430. FAX: (308) 382-6701. Licensee: JRK Broadcasting Ltd. (acq 10-1-91; with co-located FM; FTR 10-14-91). Net: ABC/I. Rep: Christal. Wash atty: Reddy, Begley, & Martin. Format: Adult contemp. News staff 3. Target aud: 25-54. ■ John R. Kidd, pres; Lyle W. Nelson, gen mgr & gen sls mgr; Shaun Schleif, stn mgr, opns mgr & progmg dir; Chris Lowery, mus dir; Rich Dillman, news dir; Gene Homung, chief engr. ■ Rates: $34; 30; 32; 19.

KRGI-FM—Oct 30, 1975: 96.5 mhz; 100 kw. Ant 416 ft. TL: N40 51 53 W98 23 47 Stereo. Hrs opn: 24. Prog sep from AM. Format: C&W. ■ Rates: $37; 33; 35; na.

*KROA(FM)—Aug 11, 1967: 95.7 mhz; 100 kw. Ant 460 ft. TL: N40 47 11 W98 22 00. Stereo. Hrs opn: 24. Box K, Doniphan (68832). (402) 845-6595. Licensee: Grace College (acq 3-77). Net: Moody. Format: Relg. Target aud: General. Spec prog: Class one hr wkly. ■ Dr. Neal McBride, pres; Gordon Wheeler, stn mgr; Mark Krumwiede, chief engr.

KSYZ-FM—Nov 1982: 107.7 mhz; 100 kw. Ant 899 ft. TL: N40 51 53 W98 23 47 (CP: N40 42 07 W98 35 20). Stereo. Box 5108 (68802); 3532 W. Capital Ave. (68803). (308) 382-0108. Fax: (308) 384-8900. Licensee: Mid-Nebraska Broadcasting (acq 10-88). Net: Unistar. Rep: Roslin. Format: Adult contemp. News staff one. Target aud: 25-42. ■ Jay Vavricek, gen mgr; Brian Gallagher, progmg dir.

Hastings

*KCNT(FM)—Feb 22, 1971: 88.1 mhz; 2 kw. Ant 182 ft. TL: N40 34 52 W98 19 58. Box 1024 (68902). (402) 461-2458. Licensee: Central Community College. Format: CHR, educ. ■ John L. Brooks, gen mgr; Rick Horn, chief engr.

KEZH(FM)—Listing follows KICS(AM).

KHAS(AM)—Sept 30, 1940: 1230 khz; 1 kw-U. TL: N40 34 40 W98 24 17. Box 726, 906 W. 2nd (68901); 200 Tribune Bldg., (68902). (402) 462-5101. Fax: (402) 461-3866. Licensee: KHAS Broadcasting Inc. (acq 7-1-93; $200,000; FTR 6-28-93). Net: CBS. Rep: Katz. Format: Adult contemp. News staff one; news progmg 5 hrs wkly. Target aud: 35 plus. Spec prog: Farm 2 hrs, class 2 hrs wkly. ■ Wayne Specht, pres, gen mgr, gen sls mgr & mus dir; Mike Smithson, progmg dir & asst mus dir; Troy Gehlsen, news dir; Erv Siemoneit, chief engr. ■ Rates: $12.75; 11; 11; 10.

*KHNE-FM—June 1990: 89.1 mhz; 64.3 kw. Ant 328 ft. TL: N40 46 17 W98 05 22. Stereo. Hrs opn: 18. Box 83111, Lincoln (68501); 1800 N. 33rd St., Lincoln (68503). (402) 472-3611. FAX: (402) 472-1785. Licensee: Nebraska Educational Telecommunications Commission. Net: APR, NPR; Neb. Pub. Wash atty: Dow, Lohnes & Albertson. Format: Class, news. News staff one; news progmg 20 hrs wkly. Target aud: General. Spec prog: Jazz 2 hrs, American Indian one hr, folk 2 hrs wkly. ■ Steve Robinson, gen mgr; Kathryn Stephens, prom mgr; Frank Hoffman, progmg dir; Nancy Finken, news dir; Bill Ramsay, chief engr.

KICS(AM)—Apr 15, 1964: 1550 khz; 500 w-D. TL: N40 34 09 W98 21 57. Hrs opn: 6 AM-10 PM. Box 1005 (68902). (402) 463-1314. FAX: (402) 463-2526. Licensee: Heartland Radio Inc. (acq 6-90; $570,000 with co-located FM; FTR 9-10-90). Format: Div, oldies. News staff one; news progmg 12 hrs wkly. Target aud: 35 plus. ■ Michael O'Connor, gen mgr; Mike Will, progmg dir; Johnny James, mus dir; Jim Droge, chief engr.

KEZH(FM)—Co-owned with KICS(AM). February 1965: 101.5 mhz; 50 kw. Ant 265 ft. TL: N40 34 09 W98 21 57 (CP: 100 kw, ant 1,004 ft.). Stereo. Prog sep from AM. Format: Country. Target aud: 25-54.

Holdrege

KUVR(AM)—Oct 20, 1956: 1380 khz; 500 w-D. TL: N40 26 26 W99 23 58. Box 465, 613 4th Ave. (68949). (308) 995-4020. Licensee: High Plains Broadcasting Inc. (acq 9-88). Net: ABC/I, AP. Rep: Eastman, Intermountain Net, Soderlund. Wash atty: Anne Thomas Paxson. Format: Soft adult contemp. Spec prog: Swedish one hr, farm 5 hrs, big band 5 hrs, contemp gospel 5 hrs wkly. ■ Peggy Jean Goth, pres, gen mgr & gen sls mgr; Ruth Pearson, mktg dir; Keith Richards, progmg dir; Dixon Porters, mus dir; Randy Issler, news dir; Harold Erickson, chief engr.

KUVR-FM—Oct 1970: 97.7 mhz; 3 kw. Ant 240 ft. TL: N40 26 26 W99 23 58. Dups AM 100%. Net: Daynet.

Kearney

KGFW(AM)—1927: 1340 khz; 1 kw-U. TL: N40 40 40 W99 05 00. Box 669, 2223 Central Ave. (68848). (308) 237-2131. Licensee: Central Nebraska Broadcasting Inc. Net: MBS, CBS; Brownfield. Rep: Eastman. Format: Full svc adult contemp. News staff 2; news progmg 25 hrs wkly. Target aud: 25 plus. ■ John C. Mitchell, pres; Marty Reirenschreider, exec vp; John McDonald, gen mgr; Dirk Christensen, opns mgr & progmg dir; Paul Wice, news dir; Val Lane, chief engr. ■ Rates: $12; 12; 12; 12.

KQKY(FM)—Co-owned with KGFW(AM). October 1979: 105.9 mhz; 96.6 kw. Ant 1,010 ft. TL: N40 39 28 W98 52 04. (Acq 4-87). Net: ABC/FM. Format: CHR. News progmg 2 hrs wkly. Target aud: 18-34; young adult. ■ Mitch Cooley, progmg dir; Mark Reid, mus dir. ■ Rates: $18; 18; 18; 18.

KKPR(AM)—Dec 5, 1956: 1460 khz; 5 kw-D, 56 w-N. TL: N40 42 45 W99 10 15. Box 130 (68848); 403 E. 25th St. (68847). (308) 236-9900. FAX: (308) 234-6781. Licensee: Platte River Radio Inc. (acq 11-30-93; $750,000 with co-located FM; FTR 12-13-93). Rep: Torbet. Format: Oldies. ■ Craig Eckert, gen mgr; Dan Beck, progmg dir; Doug Koehn, chief engr.

KKPR-FM—Nov 1, 1962: 98.9 mhz; 100 kw. Ant 700 ft. TL: N40 48 53 W98 46 12. Stereo. Prog sep from AM. Format: CHR. Target aud: 18-34. ■ Rates: Same as AM.

KQKY(FM)—Listing follows KGFW(AM).

KRNY(FM)—1987: 102.3 mhz; 25 kw. Ant 328 ft. TL: N40 42 35 W99 05 55. Stereo. Hrs opn: 24. Suite 300, 2202 Central Ave. (68847). (308) 236-8600. Licensee: Nebraska Media Concepts. Wash atty: Haley, Bader, & Potts. Format: Contemp country. News progmg 5 hrs wkly. Target aud: 25 plus. ■ Oliver High, pres; Jean Esposito, gen mgr; Arttie Parker, chief opns & progmg dir; Beth Tollefsen, gen sls mgr; Jim Droege, chief engr. ■ Rates: $10; 10; 10; 10.

*KSCV(FM)—Mar 8, 1968: 91.3 mhz; 1 kw. Ant 100 ft. TL: N40 42 30 W99 05 45. Stereo. Hrs opn: 6 AM-midnight. Univ. of Neb. at Kearney (68849). (308) 234-8217. Licensee: Univ. of Nebraska at Kearney. Format: Jazz, new age, AOR. Spec prog: Class 18 hrs wkly. ■ Roy Hyatte, gen mgr.

Kimball

KIMB(AM)—1958: 1260 khz; 1 kw-D, 500 w-N. TL: N41 15 42 W103 40 06. 414 W. Second St., (69145). (308) 235-3634. Licensee: David S. Young (acq 8-25-92; $50,000; FTR 9-14-92). Net: CNN, SMN. Format: Country, news. News progmg 21 hrs wkly. Target aud: General. Spec prog: sports, farm 7 hrs wkly. ■ David Young, CEO; Jim McDonald, chief engr.

Lexington

*KLNE-FM—May 4, 1990: 88.7 mhz; 43.8 kw. Ant 938 ft. TL: N40 23 05 W99 27 30. Stereo. Hrs opn: 18. Box 83111, Lincoln (68501); 1800 N. 33rd St., Lincoln (68503). (402) 472-3611. FAX: (402) 472-1785. Licensee: Nebraska Educational Telecommunications Commission. Net: APR, NPR; Neb. Pub. Wash atty: Dow, Lohnes & Albertson. Format: Classical, news, info. News staff one; news progmg 30 hrs wkly. Target aud: General; 35 plus. Spec prog: Jazz 2 hrs, folk 2 hrs, American Indian one hr wkly. ■ Steve Robinson, gen mgr; Kathryn Stephens, prom mgr; Frank Hoffman, progmg dir; Bill Ramsay, chief engr.

KRVN(AM)—Feb 1, 1951: 880 khz; 50 kw-U, DA-N. TL: N40 31 03 W99 23 20. Hrs opn: 24. Box 880, 1007 S. Bridge St. (68850). (308) 324-2371. FAX: (308) 324-5786. Licensee: Nebraska Rural Radio Assn. (group owner). Net: ABC/E. Rep: Katz. Wash atty: Jerome Boros of Rosenman & Colin. Format: C&W, farm. News staff 4; news progmg 30 hrs wkly. Target aud: General; Nebraska farm/ranch families and consumers. Spec prog: Relg 6 hrs wkly. ■ Otto Geiger, pres; Eric Brown, gen mgr; Gordon Bennett, gen sls mgr; Dewey Nelson, prom mgr; Charles Brogan, progmg dir & pub affrs dir; Don Colvin, mus dir; James Struck, news dir; Vern Killion, chief engr. ■ Rates: $160; 160; 100; 30.

KRVN-FM—Nov 1, 1962: 93.1 mhz; 100 kw. Ant 320 ft. TL: N40 41 50 W99 47 17. Stereo. Hrs opn: 24. Dups AM 1%. Net: NBC. Format: Adult contemp, MOR. News staff one. Target aud: General; contemporary young adults, older residents. ■ Pam Hird, opns dir & progmg dir; Ed Bennett, rgnl sls mgr; Dave Thorell, prom mgr; Frank Snyder, news dir; Vern Killion, engrg dir. ■ Rates: $30; 30; 20; 20.

Lincoln

KEZG(FM)—Listing follows KLIN(AM).

*KFBN(FM)—Not on air, target date unknown: 88.5 mhz; 4.7 kw-V. Ant 390 ft. 1084 E. 28th St., Independence, MO (64052). Licensee: Community Family Broadcasting Inc.

KFGE(FM)—Not on air, target date unknown: 105.3 mhz; 3 kw. Ant 328 ft. TL: N40 49 12 W96 39 29. 3416 Neerpark Dr., (68506). Licensee: Lincoln Broadcasting Inc.

KFOR(AM)—Listing follows KFRX(FM).

KFRX(FM)—May 2, 1965: 102.7 mhz; 100 kw. Ant 500 ft. TL: N40 49 12 W96 39 29 (TL: N45 46 51 W96 22 52). Stereo. Box 80209 (68501); Suite 11, 6900 Van Dorn (68506). (402) 483-5100. FAX: (402) 483-4095. Licensee: KFOR/KFRX Broadcasting Inc. (acq 12-1-89; $6.6 million with co-located AM; FTR 10-9-89). Net: ABC/FM. Rep: Katz. Wash atty: Winston & Strawn. Format: CHR. News progmg 2 hrs wkly. Target aud: 18-49; women. ■ Ed May Jr., CEO; Bryce Pringle, CFO; Kathy Hietbrink, gen mgr; Brad Hartman, stn mgr; Brad King, opns dir & progmg dir; Jim Keck, gen sls mgr; Sonny Valentine, mus dir; Mike Elliott, chief engr. ■ Rates: $37; 35; 36; 30.

KFOR(AM)—Co-owned with KFRX(FM). March 4, 1924: 1240 khz; 1 kw-U. TL: N40 49 12 W96 39 29. Hrs opn: 24. Prog sep from FM. Net: ABC/I. Format: Adult contemp. News staff 3; news progmg 20 hrs wkly. Target aud: 30 plus. ■ Brad Hartman, opns mgr; Jill Foree (asst.), adv dir; Scott Young, progmg dir; Cathy Blythe, mus dir. ■ Rates: $70; 35; 36; 30.

KHAT(AM)—Listing follows KIBZ(FM).

KIBZ(FM)—Feb 23, 1973: 106.3 mhz; 3 kw. Ant 213 ft. TL: N40 48 48 W96 42 25. Stereo. Hrs opn: 24. Suite C, 5143 S. 48th St. (68516). (402) 483-1517. Licensee: Rock Steady Inc. (acq 4-1-93; $550,000; FTR 4-26-93). Format: AOR/current rock. News progmg one hr wkly. Target aud: 35-64. ■ Doug Agnew, exec vp & gen mgr.

KHAT(AM)—Co-owned with KIBZ(FM). Dec 21, 1965: 1530 khz; 5 kw-D, DA. TL: N40 43 31 W96 39 02. Box 6066, 4949 Yankee Hill Rd. (68506). FAX: (402) 487-1579. (Acq 11-5-93; $500; FTR 11-29-93).

KLDZ(FM)—March 6, 1975: 95.1 mhz; 50 kw. Ant 287 ft. TL: N40 58 49 W96 41 45. Stereo. Hrs opn: 24. Suite 311, 1230 O St. (68508-1402). (402) 476-3222. FAX: (402) 476-1300. Licensee: Radio One Lincoln Inc. Group owner: Raymond A. Lamb (acq 4-27-92; $765,000; FTR 5-18-92). Rep: Christal. Wash atty: Tierney & Swift. Format: Oldies. News staff one; news progmg 2 hrs wkly. Target aud: 25-54. ■ Roger Dodson, pres; Steve Heston, stn mgr; Dallas Michaels, opns mgr; Paige Turner, prom mgr; Dan Evans, mus dir; Dave Davis, chief engr. ■ Rates: $40; 40; 40; 25.

KLIN(AM)—August 1947: 1400 khz; 1 kw-U. TL: N40 49 29 W96 39 20 (CP: TL: N40 49 12 W96 39 29). Hrs opn: 24. 4343 O St. (68510); Box 30181 (68503). (402) 475-4567. FAX: (402) 479-1411. Licensee: KLIN Inc. Group owner: Warner Stns. (acq 9-71). Net: CBS, CNN, Mutual, ABC TalkRadio. Format: News/talk. News staff 4; news progmg 80 hrs wkly. Target aud: 35-64; upper income, business owner, educated with high disposable income. ■ Norton E. Warner, pres; Lisa Warner, stn mgr, opns dir, sls dir, natl sls mgr & rgnl sls mgr; H. Fred Monnich, mktg dir; Jane Monnich, news dir; Teri Lindstrom, pub affrs dir; Bill Seier, chief engr.

KEZG(FM)—Co-owned with KLIN(AM). Sept 1, 1968: 107.3 mhz; 100 kw. Ant 551 ft. TL: N40 43 38 W96 36 49. Stereo. Hrs opn: 24. Net: Unistar. Format: Adult contemp. Target aud: 25-54; middle-to-upper income, households, in-office and in-store lstng. ■ Jim Stevens, prom dir, progmg dir & mus dir; Van Coker, adv dir; Lisa Warner, adv mgr; Mike Whitney, progmg mgr; Walt Brady, asst mus dir.

KMEM(AM)—October 1949: 1480 khz; 5 kw-D, 1 kw-N, DA-2. TL: N40 47 47 W96 34 56. Stereo. Commerce Court. 1230 O St. (68508). Licensee: Radio One Nebraska Inc. Group owner: Radio One Broadcasting Inc. (acq 5-27-93; $200,000; FTR 6-14-93). Format: MOR, big band. ■ Steve Heston, gen mgr.

***KRNU(FM)**—Feb 23, 1970: 90.3 mhz; 100 w. Ant 180 ft. TL: N40 49 11 W96 42 11. Stereo. Hrs opn: 7 AM-1 AM. Avery Bldg., Room 203, Univ. of Nebraska (68588); Box 82422 (68501). (402) 472-3054; (402) 472-3396. FAX: (402) 472-8403. Licensee: Univ. of Nebraska. Net: ABC/C, MBS. Wash atty: Dow, Lohnes & Albertson. Format: Alternative, progsv. News progmg 10 hrs wkly. Spec prog: Jazz 6 hrs wkly. ■ Martin Massengale, pres; Larry Walklin, gen mgr; Richard Alloway, stn mgr & progmg dir; Jerry Renaud, news dir; William Ramsay, chief engr. ■ KUON-TV affil.

KTGL(FM)—(Beatrice). Nov 26, 1962: 92.9 mhz; 100 kw. Ant 809 ft. TL: N40 31 06 W96 46 07. Stereo. Hrs opn: 24. Suite 208, 3201 Pioneers Blvd., Lincoln (68502). (402) 483-6814. FAX: (402) 489-9607. Licensee: ERM Associates (acq 3-9-93; $2.2 million; FTR 3-29-93). Rep: Katz & Powell. Format: Classic rock. News staff one; news progmg 3 hrs wkly. Target aud: 18-49. ■ C.T. Robinson, pres; Julie Gade, gen mgr; Peg Jones, gen sls mgr & mktg dir; Bill Barker, progmg dir; Tim Cawley, news dir; Jim Haze, pub affrs dir; Jim Droege, chief engr.

***KUCV(FM)**—Jan 1, 1968: 90.9 mhz; 16 kw. Ant 600 ft. TL: N40 46 28 W96 39 10 (CP: Ant 718 ft., TL: N40 31 06 W96 46 07). Stereo. Box 83111, 1800 N. 33rd St. (68501). (402) 472-3611. FAX: (402) 472-1785. Licensee: Nebraska Educational Telecommunications Commission (acq 8-88). Net: NPR, APR, AP; Neb. Pub. Format: Class, news. News progmg 30 hrs wkly. Target aud: General. Spec prog: Jazz 5 hrs wkly. ■ Steve Robinson, gen mgr; Frank Hoffman, progmg dir.

KYNN(FM)—June 22, 1958: 101.9 mhz; 100 kw. Ant 1,132 ft. TL: N40 47 09 W96 23 07 (CP: Ant 981 ft.). Stereo. Suite 102, 14344 "Y" St., Omaha (68137). (402) 896-4477. FAX: (402) 896-9121. Licensee: KLMS-KFMQ Inc. Group owner: Midwest Communications Inc. Format: Country. ■ Peter Tanz, gen mgr; Jeff Woodbury, sls dir; Mike Moore, progmg dir; John Gaeta, chief engr.

KZKX(FM)—See Seward.

***KZUM(FM)**—1978: 89.3 mhz; 1.5 kw. Ant 174 ft. TL: N40 48 47 W96 42 24. Stereo. Hrs opn: 6 AM-2 AM. Suite 1025, 941 O St., (68508-3608). (402) 474-5086. Licensee: Sunrise Communications Inc. Format: Div, jazz, urban contemp. News progmg 11 hrs wkly. Target aud: General; the unserved and underserved population. Spec prog: Sp 4 hrs, rock/progsv 15 hrs, new age 8 hrs, blues 13 hrs, folk 8 hrs, gospel 3 hrs wkly ■ George Trevors, chmn; Richard Noble, gen mgr; Caroline Tetschner, opns dir, gen sls mgr, mktg dir, prom dir & adv dir; Ken Ringlein, opns mgr, rgnl sls mgr, prom mgr & adv mgr; Eli Rhodes, chief opns & chief engr; Michelle Moser, dev mgr. ■ Rates: $9; 9; 9; 9.

McCook

KBRL(AM)—Sept 26, 1947: 1300 khz; 5 kw-D, DA. TL: N40 11 31 W100 39 06. Box 333, 802 West C (69001). (308) 345-5400. FAX: (308) 345-4720. Licensee: Ron Crowe & Associates (acq 7-19-89; $42,000; FTR 8-7-89). Net: MBS; Kan. Agri. Format: Contemp country. News staff one; news progmg 12 hrs wkly. Target aud: 25-54. ■ Ron Crowe, pres, gen mgr & gen sls mgr; Kerry Ferguson, news dir; Ron Fritz, chief engr. ■ Rates: $8.70; 8.70; 8.70; 8.70.

KICX-FM—Co-owned with KBRL(AM). Jan 31, 1979: 96.1 mhz; 6 kw. Ant 380 ft. TL: N40 10 19 W100 41 05. Stereo. Hrs opn: 18. Format: Adult contemp. News staff one. Spec prog: Farm 6 hrs wkly.

***KNGN(AM)**—June 23, 1961: 1360 khz; 1 kw-D. TL: N40 11 45 W100 41 57. Box 240, 411 E. 6th St. (69001). (308) 345-2006. Licensee: Lutheran Church-Missouri Synod (acq 8-89; FTR 8-7-89). Net: Jubilee. Format: Relg. News progmg 7 hrs wkly. Target aud: 25-49; female, married, with children. ■ Lowell Highby, gen mgr, progmg dir & mus dir; Linda Lacey, asst mus dir & pub affrs dir; Ron Fritz, chief engr.

KZMC-FM—May 1, 1981: 105.3 mhz; 100 kw. Ant 622 ft. TL: N40 11 18 W100 48 37. Stereo. Hrs opn: 24. Box 218, 106 W. 8th St. (69001-0218). (308) 345-1981; (308) 345-1987. FAX: (308) 345-7202. Licensee: AmFirst Bank, National Association (acq 12-18-91; $180,000; FTR 1-13-92). Net: Unistar. Format: Rock. News staff one; news progmg 15 hrs wkly. Target aud: 18-54. Spec prog: Relg one hr wkly. ■ Van Korell (AmFirst Bank), pres; Lewis Tapia, gen mgr, opns mgr, gen sls mgr, progmg dir & mus dir; Jenny Cartwright, dev dir; John Allen, news dir; Tom Toenjes, chief engr.

Merriman

***KRNE-FM**—Aug 29, 1991: 91.5 mhz; 92 kw. Ant 964 ft. TL: N42 40 38 W101 42 36. Stereo. Box 83111, 1800 N. 33rd St., Lincoln (68501). (402) 472-3611. Licensee: Nebraska Educational Telecommunications Commission. Net: APR, NPR. Format: Educ, class, news/talk. News staff 3. Target aud: General. ■ Jack McBride, gen mgr; Steve Robinson, stn mgr; Dave Holmquist, dev dir; Kathryn Stephens, prom dir; Frank Hoffman, progmg dir; Nancy Finkel, news dir; Ralph Sanchez, chief engr.

Milford

KUHG(FM)—Not on air, target date unknown: 98.1 mhz. Ant 981 ft. TL: N40 48 00 W97 36 00. c/o 8801 E. 63rd St., Kansas City, MO (64133). Licensee: Bott Broadcasting Co. (acq 5-21-92).

Nebraska City

KNCY(AM)—June 29, 1959: 1600 khz; 500 w-D, 31 w-N, DA-2. TL: N40 40 27 W95 53 08. Box 278, Suite 1, 722 Central Ave. (68410). (402) 873-3348. FAX: (402) 873-7882. Licensee: Sunrise Broadcasting of Nebraska (group owner; acq 7-90; $675,000 with co-located FM; FTR 7-9-90.) Net: MBS. Rep: Soderlund, Farmakis. Wash atty: Rosenman & Colin. Format: MOR, oldies, news/talk. News staff 2; news progmg 21 hrs wkly. Target aud: 18-80; local residents, farmers, business owners, workers, students. Spec prog: Farm 6 hrs, sports 6 hrs wkly. ■ Joerg Klebe, pres; David J. Messing, vp, gen mgr & chief engr; Brad Fossberg, opns mgr, progmg dir & mus dir; Myron Hahn, gen sls mgr; Jody Pohlman, mktg mgr; Sandra Adkins, prom mgr; Laura Steinman, news dir. ■ Rates: $16; 16; 16; 16.

KNCY-FM—Sept 20, 1977: 97.7 mhz; 26 kw. Ant 300 ft. TL: N40 40 06 W95 56 40. Stereo. Dups AM 100%. ■ Rates: Same as AM.

Norfolk

KEXL(FM)—Listing follows WJAG(AM).

KNEN(FM)—April 6, 1979: 94.7 mhz; 100 kw. Ant 531 ft. TL: N41 55 16 W97 36 20. Stereo. Box 937, 300 Madison Ave. (68702). (402) 379-3300. Licensee: Central Radio Inc. (acq 6-82; $500,000; FTR 6-28-82). Net: ABC/I. Rep: Farmakis. Wash atty: John Wilner. Format: Adult contemp. News staff 2; news progmg 20 hrs wkly. Target aud: 25-54; young to middle-aged. Spec prog: Farm 10 hrs wkly. ■ Gene A. Koehn, pres & gen mgr; Ellen Denney, gen sls mgr; Kevin Rahfeldt, progmg dir; Jill Otto, mus dir; Sandy Connors, news dir. ■ Rates: $18.50; 18.50; 18.50; 18.50.

***KPNO(FM)**—Sept 23, 1992: 90.9 mhz; 50 kw. Ant 351 ft. TL: N42 06 16 W97 20 11. Stereo. Hrs opn: 24. Kensington Bldg., 114 No. 4 (68701). Licensee: The Praise Network Inc. Net: Moody, Skylight. Format: Relg, inspirational. News progmg 14 hrs wkly. Target aud: 25-54; family-oriented adults. ■ Herb Roszhart Jr., CEO; Ron Nealeigh, sr vp.

***KXNE-FM**—May 29, 1990: 89.3 mhz; 42.3 kw. Ant 984 ft. TL: N42 14 15 W97 16 41. Box 83111, Lincoln (68501); 1800 N. 33rd St. (68503). (402) 472-3611. FAX: (402) 472-1785. Licensee: Nebraska Educational Telecommunications Commission. Net: APR, NPR. Format: Classical. News progmg 30 hrs wkly. Target aud: General. Spec prog: Jazz 5 hrs wkly. ■ Steve Robinson, gen mgr; Kathryn Stephens, prom mgr; Frank Hoffman, progmg dir; Steve York, mus dir.

WJAG(AM)—July 27, 1922: 780 khz; 1 kw-U (L-WBBM). TL: N42 01 54 W97 29 47. Stereo. Box 789, 309 Braasch Ave. (68701). (402) 371-0780. FAX: (402) 371-6303. Licensee: WJAG Inc. Net: MBS. Rep: McGavren Guild; Howard Anderson Co. Wash atty: Fletcher, Heald & Hildreth. Format: C&W. News staff 2; news progmg 7 hrs wkly. Target aud: 30 plus. Spec prog: Farm. ■ Jerry Huse, pres; Robert G. Thomas, vp & gen mgr; Mark Smith, opns mgr & progmg dir; Don Grant, gen sls mgr; Jim Fischer, prom dir; J. Alan Johnson, mus dir; Jim Curry, news dir; Tony Wortman, chief engr.

KEXL(FM)—Co-owned with WJAG(AM). Aug 1, 1971: 106.7 mhz; 100 kw. Ant 1,027 ft. TL: N41 55 59 W97 40 49. Stereo. Dups AM 5%. Format: Adult contemp. News staff 2; news progmg 12 hrs wkly. Target aud: 18-49.

North Platte

KELN(FM)—Listing follows KOOQ(AM).

***KJLT(AM)**—July 1, 1957: 970 khz; 5 kw-D, 55 w-N. TL: N41 09 30 W100 52 36. Box 709 (69103). (308) 532-5515. FAX: (308) 532-5516. Licensee: Tri-State Broadcasting Assn Inc. (acq 7-1-57). Net: MBS, USA; Skylight. Format: Relg. Spec prog: Sp one hr wkly. ■ John L. Townsend, pres & gen mgr; Roger Olsen, prom dir; Gary Hofer, chief engr.

KJLT-FM—Sept 24, 1979: 94.9 mhz; 63 kw. Ant 200 ft. TL: N41 09 14 W100 46 23. Stereo. Licensee: Tri-State Broadcasting Association Inc. (acq 3-22-90; $85,000; FTR 4-16-90). Net: CBS Spectrum. Format: Adult contemp.

KODY(AM)—July 5, 1930: 1240 khz; 1 kw-U. TL: N41 09 14 W100 46 23. Box 1085 (69103); 305 E. Fourth St. (69101). (308) 532-3344. FAX: (308) 534-6651. Licensee: Central Nebraska Broadcasting Inc. (acq 9-87; $300,000; FTR 6-8-87). Net: CBS, Moody, NBC Talknet, Westwood One. Rep: Katz & Powell, Anderson, Art Moore. Format: News/talk. News staff one; news progmg 20 hrs wkly. Target aud: 25 plus; middle to upper income. ■ John C. Mitchell, pres; Rob Mandeville, gen

Broadcasting & Cable Yearbook 1994
B-227

mgr; John P. Kelley, opns mgr; Steve White, progmg dir; George Keltz, news dir.

KXNP(FM)—Co-owned with KODY(AM). June 7, 1982: 103.5 mhz; 100 kw. Ant 479 ft. TL: N41 12 49 W100 43 48. Stereo. Hrs opn: 24. Prog sep from AM. (308) 534-6650. FAX: (308) 534-6651. Net: Jones Satellite Audio. Format: Contemp country. ■ John Kelley, progmg dir.

KOOQ(AM)—January 1966: 1410 khz; 5 kw-D, 1 kw-N, DA-N. TL: N41 10 30 W100 45 07. Hrs opn: 24. Box 248, 1301 E. 4th St. (69103). (308) 532-1120. FAX: (308) 532-0458. Licensee: Robert E. Schmidt. Group owner: Beach-Schmidt Group (acq 3-20-91; grpsl; FTR 4-8-91). Net: ABC/E. Rep: Eastman, Intermountain. Format: Oldies. News staff one; news progmg 8 hrs wkly. Target aud: 30-55; baby boomers. Spec prog: Farm 4 hrs wkly. ■ Don Clonch, gen mgr; John Cox, opns mgr; Gretchen Engstrom, gen sls mgr; Gary Essels, chief engr. ■ Rates: $15; 15; 15; 15.

KELN(FM)—Co-owned with KOOQ(AM). February 1979: 97.1 mhz; 100 kw. Ant 458 ft. TL: N41 14 20 W100 41 43. Stereo. Hrs opn: 24. Prog sep from AM. Net: ABC/FM. Format: Adult contemp. Target aud: 25-40. ■ Rates: $13; 13; 13; 13.

***KPNE-FM**—July 1, 1991: 91.7 mhz; 16.5 kw-H, 81 kw-V. Ant 59 ft.-H, 289 ft.-V. TL: N41 01 21 W101 09 13. Stereo. Box 83111, 1800 N. 33rd St., Lincoln (68501). (402) 472-3611. Licensee: Nebraska Educational Telecommunications Commission. Net: APR, NPR. Format: Educ, class, news/talk. News staff 3. ■ Jack McBride, gen mgr; Steve Robinson, stn mgr; Jeff Smith, opns mgr; Frank Hoffman, progmg dir; Nancy Finken, news dir; Ralph Sanchez, chief engr.

KXNP(FM)—Listing follows KODY(AM).

O'Neill

KBRX(AM)—November 1955: 1350 khz; 1 kw-D. TL: N42 27 34 W98 39 23. Hrs opn: 6 AM-5 PM. Box 150, 251 N. Jefferson (68763). (402) 336-1612. FAX: (402) 336-3585. Licensee: Ranchland Broadcasting Co. Inc. (acq 7-1-61). Net: ABC/I; Mid-American Ag. Rep: Farmakis. Wash atty: John Wilner. Format: C&W. Spec prog: Farm 12 hrs, Ger 6 hrs wkly. ■ Gilbert L. Poese, pres, progmg dir & news dir; Scott Poese, gen mgr; Terry Downing, mus dir; Jim Droege, chief engr.

KBRX-FM—December 1973: 102.9 mhz; 100 kw. Ant 500 ft. TL: N42 26 06 W98 33 39. Stereo. Hrs opn: 24. Dups AM 100%. Format: Country 24 hours. News staff one; news progmg 6 hrs wkly. Target aud: 25-60. Spec prog: Farm 12 hrs, Ger 6 hrs wkly.

Ogallala

KMCX(FM)—1975: 106.5 mhz; 100 kw. Ant 300 ft. TL: N41 08 02 W101 41 42. Stereo. Hrs opn: 6 AM-midnight. 113 W. 4th St. (69153). (308) 284-2051. Licensee: Midwest Broadcasting Inc. Co. (acq 8-20-92; $125,000; FTR 9-7-92). Net: ABC/D; Brownfield, Mid-American Ag. Rep: Katz & Powell. Format: Country. News staff one; news progmg 10 hrs wkly. Target aud: General; cross section of 25-54. Spec prog: Farm 2 hrs wkly. ■ Don Keck, pres; Steve Tedman, chief engr. ■ Rates: $12; 12; 12; 12.

KOGA(AM)—Jan 23, 1955: 930 khz; 5 kw-U, DA-2. TL: N41 08 32 W101 42 48. Stereo. Box 509 (69153). (308) 284-3633. FAX: (308) 284-3517. Licensee: Ogallala Broadcasting Co. Net: ABC/I. Rep: Eastman, Art Moore. Format: Oldies. Spec prog: Farm 10 hrs wkly. ■ Ray H. Lockhart, pres & gen mgr; Robert Exom, chief engr.

KOGA-FM—November 1978: 99.7 mhz; 100 kw. Ant 805 ft. TL: N41 03 50 W101 20 16. Stereo. Prog sep from AM. Net: ABC/C. Format: Adult contemp.

Omaha

KCRO(AM)—March 1922: 660 khz; 1 kw-D. TL: N41 18 47 W96 00 36. 3615 Dodge St. (68131). (402) 422-1600. FAX: (402) 422-1602. Licensee: RadiOmaha Inc. (acq 4-19-79). Net: USA. Wash atty: Gardner, Carton & Douglas. Format: Christian contemp, inspirational. Target aud: 25-54. ■ Samuel W. Smulyan, pres; Jack N. Marsella, vp; Paul Rehm, gen mgr & gen sls mgr; Gene Piatt, progmg dir & mus dir. ■ Rates: $20; 18; 20; 16.

KEFM(FM)—Oct 21, 1983: 96.1 mhz; 100 kw. Ant 1,458 ft. TL: N41 04 15 W96 13 30. Stereo. 105 S. 70th St. (68132). (402) 558-9696. FAX: (402) 558-3036. Licensee: Webster Communications Co. Rep: McGavren Guild. Format: Adult contemp. ■ John W. Webster, pres, vp & gen mgr; Richard McCormick, gen sls mgr; Holly Dunning, prom mgr; Dwight Lane, progmg dir; Steve Albertsen, mus dir; Rick Vincent, news dir; James Leedham, chief engr.

KESY(AM)—Mar 2, 1957: 1420 khz; 1 kw-D, 330 w-N, DA-2. TL: N41 11 59 W95 54 34. 4807 Dodge St. (68132). (402) 556-6700. FAX: (402) 556-9427. Licensee: OMA Inc. (acq 3-2-93; with co-located FM; FTR 3-22-93). Net: ABC/D. Rep: McGavren Guild. Format: Soft adult contemp. ■ John Biddinger, pres; Dana Webb, gen mgr; Kisha Stevens, opns mgr; Tim McGaffin, gen sls mgr; Chuck Ramold, chief engr.

KESY-FM—May 12, 1972: 104.5 mhz; 100 kw. Ant 1,040 ft. TL: N41 18 25 W96 01 37. Stereo. Dups AM 100%.

KEZO(AM)—March 1942: 1490 khz; 1 kw-U. TL: N41 14 06 W95 57 57. Stereo. Hrs opn: 24. 11128 John Galt Blvd. (68137). (402) 592-5300. FAX: (402) 592-4538. Licensee: Narragansett Radio L.P. Group owner: Narragansett Capital Inc. (acq 5-9-88). Rep: Major Mkt. Format: Classic rock. News staff one. Target aud: 18-49. ■ Manuel Broussard, gen mgr; Taylor Walet, gen sls mgr; Barb Huehns, prom mgr; Randy Chambers, progmg dir; Craig Evans, news dir; John Bible, chief engr.

KEZO-FM—May 15, 1961: 92.3 mhz; 100 kw. Ant 1,250 ft. TL: N41 18 40 W96 01 37. Stereo. Dups AM 100%.

KFAB(AM)—1924: 1110 khz; 50 kw-U, DA-N. TL: N41 07 11 W96 00 06. Stereo. 5010 Underwood Ave. (68132). (402) 556-8000. FAX: (402) 556-8937. Licensee: Henry Broadcasting Co. Inc. (group owner; acq 12-86; $22 million with co-located FM; FTR 9-22-86). Net: NBC, NBC Talknet. Rep: Christal. Format: News/talk. News staff 8; news progmg 41 hrs wkly. Target aud: 35-64. ■ Charlton H. Buckley, pres; Paul Aaron, gen mgr; Lisa Obermyer, gen sls mgr; Don Watson, progmg dir & news dir; Butch Dulaney, chief engr. ■ Rates: $100; 45; 50; 35.

KGOR(FM)—Co-owned with KFAB(AM). 1959: 99.9 mhz; 115 kw. Ant 1,230 ft. TL: N41 18 25 W96 01 37. Stereo. Prog sep from AM. Format: Oldies. ■ Joni Woodruff, gen sls mgr; John Wagner, progmg dir. ■ Rates: $60; 50; 55; 30.

***KGBI-FM**—May 17, 1966: 100.7 mhz; 100 kw. Ant 1,161 ft. TL: N41 03 10 W96 11 35. Stereo. Hrs opn: 24. 9th & William Sts. (68108). (402) 449-2900. FAX: (402) 449-2825. Licensee: Grace College of the Bible. Net: Moody, Skylight. Format: Relg, talk. News staff one; news progmg 28 hrs wkly. Target aud: 25-54; conservative, evangelical. ■ Neal McBride, pres; Kenneth Brownlee, vp; Tom Sommerville, stn mgr; Jim Meyers, mus dir; Marty Stacy, news dir & pub affrs dir; Mark Krumwiede, chief engr.

KGOR(FM)—Listing follows KFAB(AM).

***KIOS-FM**—September 1969: 91.5 mhz; 55 kw. Ant 408 ft. TL: N41 17 15 W95 59 37. Stereo. 3230 Burt St. (68131). (402) 557-2777. Licensee: Douglas County School District 001. Net: NPR, APR. Wash atty: Cohn & Marks. Format: Class, educ, jazz. Spec prog: Black one hr, jazz 10 hrs wkly. ■ Wilson W. Perry, stn mgr; Bev Traub, dev dir; Robert Coate, progmg dir; Richard Dennis, chief engr.

KISP(FM)—See Blair.

KKAR(AM)—March 1925: 1290 khz; 5 kw-U, DA-N. TL: N41 11 20 W96 00 21. 1001 Farnam (68102). (402) 342-2000. FAX: (402) 345-3652. Licensee: Aegeus Inc. (acq 8-4-93; $470,000; FTR 8-23-93). Net: CBS Spectrum, Unistar, AP. Rep: Banner. Format: News/talk. News staff 2. Target aud: General. ■ Robert H. Dean, pres; Marty Riemenschneider, gen mgr; Mark Evans, opns mgr & progmg dir; Cathy Roach, gen sls mgr; Roger Olson, news dir.

KKCD(FM)—Aug 11, 1990: 105.9 mhz; 5.2 kw. Ant 346 ft. TL: N41 18 16 W96 01 41. Hrs opn: 24. Suite 301, 6910 Pacific St. (68106). (402) 554-1059. FAX: (402) 554-4309. Licensee: Vantage Communications Inc. Net: AP. Rep: Eastman. Wash atty: Corbett; Leventhal, Senter & Lerman. Format: Classic rock. News staff one; news progmg 10 hrs wkly. Target aud: 25-54. Spec prog: Jazz 4 hrs, blues one hr, reggae one hr wkly. ■ Diane Landen, pres; John Ginzkey, gen mgr; Dawn Villone, gen sls mgr; Bruce McGregor, progmg dir; John Gaeta, chief engr. ■ Rates: $35; 30; 35; 20.

***KVNO(FM)**—Aug 27, 1972: 90.7 mhz; 3 kw. Ant 640 ft. TL: N41 18 32 W96 01 37. Stereo. Engineering 202, 60th & Dodge (68182). (402) 559-5866. FAX: (402) 554-2440. Licensee: University of Nebraska Board of Regents. Format: Class, jazz. News staff one; news progmg 2 hrs wkly. Target aud: General. Spec prog: Ger one hr, Sp 2 hrs wkly. ■ Howard Lowe, gen mgr; James Payne, opns mgr; Debbi Aliano, dev dir & sls dir; Barry Anderson, mktg mgr; Mark Ford, progmg dir; Bill Jenks, mus dir; Steve Adair, news dir; Dave Kline, chief engr.

WOW(AM)—Apr 2, 1923: 590 khz; 5 kw-U. TL: N41 19 00 W95 59 52. 615 N. 90th St. (68114). (402) 390-2059. FAX: (402) 390-0540. Licensee: Great Empire Broadcasting Inc. (group owner; acq 9-16-83). Net: ABC/I. Rep: Torbet. Format: C&W. ■ Mike Lynch, pres; Ken Fearnow, gen mgr; Bill Calvert, gen sls mgr; Scott Parker, progmg dir; Morris James, news dir; Paul Sjodin, chief engr.

WOW-FM—1959: 94.1 mhz; 100 kw. Ant 508 ft. TL: N41 18 47 W96 00 36. Stereo. Dups AM 28%.

Orchard

KGRD(FM)—June 14, 1987: 105.3 mhz; 100 kw. Ant 495 ft. TL: N42 20 39 W98 25 03. Stereo. Hrs opn: 17. Box 247 (68764). (402) 338-5350. FAX: (402) 338-5350. Licensee: The Praise Network Inc. (acq 10-16-91). Net: USA, Moody, Skylight. Format: Family oriented Christian progmg. News progmg 10 hrs wkly. Target aud: 25-54; family oriented. Spec prog: Farm one hr wkly. ■ Herb Roszhart, pres, gen mgr, gen sls mgr, progmg dir & chief engr; Todd Gunnarson, opns mgr; Karen Barnes, mus dir. ■ Rates: $5.50; 5.50; 5.50; 5.50.

Ord

KNLV(AM)—July 15, 1965: 1060 khz; 1 kw-D. TL: N41 34 16 W98 55 29. 205 S. 16th St. (68862). (308) 728-3263. Licensee: KNLV Inc. (acq 6-1-74). Net: ABC/D; Brownfield. Rep: Howard Anderson. Format: Country. News progmg 7 hrs wkly. Target aud: 18-54; males & females ag oriented. Spec prog: Farm 8 hrs, Pol/Czeck/Bohemian 5 hrs wkly. ■ Dean W. Misko, pres; Lloyd D. Zikmund, vp; Larry D. Schultz, gen mgr, progmg dir, mus dir & chief engr; Rod Teply, gen sls mgr. ■ Rates: $9; 9; 9; 9.

KNLV-FM—July 10, 1981: 103.9 mhz; 3.85 kw. Ant 379 ft. TL: N41 34 16 W98 55 29. Stereo. Dups AM 100%.

Plattsmouth

KOTD(AM)—Oct 26, 1970: 1000 khz; 250 w-D, DA. TL: N41 01 35 W95 54 00. Hrs opn: Sunrise-sunset. Box 509 (68084). (402) 298-8000. FAX: (402) 296-2124. Licensee: Platte Broadcasting Co. Inc. Net: ABC, SMN; Brownfield. Format: MOR. News staff one. Target aud: 35-64. Spec prog: Polka 4 hrs, Ger 2 hrs, Pol 2 hrs, farm 6 hrs wkly. ■ Charles Warga, pres, gen mgr & gen sls mgr; Steve Warga, stn mgr & progmg dir; John Madr, mus dir; Mark Workhoven, news dir; John Marr, pub affrs dir; Rick Kreifels, chief engr. ■ Rates: $10; 10; 10; 10.

KOTD-FM—July 1993. 106.9 mhz; 6 kw. Ant 328 ft. TL: N41 01 35 W95 54 00. Stereo. Hrs opn: 6 AM-midnight. Platte Broadcasting Co. 625 1st Ave. (68048). (402) 296-2124. FAX: (402) 296-2124. (Acq 12-10-93; FTR 1-11-93).

Sargent

KNJP(FM)—Not on air, target date unknown: 92.1 mhz; 100 kw. Ant 761 ft. TL: N41 41 29 W99 21 57. Hrs opn: 24. 1211 10th Ave., Central City (68826). Licensee: Sandhills Giant Inc.

Scottsbluff

KMOR(FM)—Aug 4, 1978: 92.9 mhz; 100 kw. Ant 1,023 ft. TL: N41 50 23 W103 49 36. Stereo. Hrs opn: 24. Box 532, 2002 Char Ave. (69361). (308) 632-5667. FAX: (308) 635-1905. Licensee: Tracy Corp. Net: AP. Rep: Eastman; Art Moore. Wash atty: Michael Glaser. Format: CHR. News staff one; news progmg 7 hrs wkly. Target aud: 18-45. ■ Michael Tracy, pres & gen mgr; Scott Cannon, opns dir; Julie Marshell, gen sls mgr; June Jerger, mktg mgr & prom mgr; Mark Jensen, progmg mgr; Lee Judd, news dir; Bob Hinze, chief engr. ■ Rates: $14.22; 14.22; 13.30; 13.30.

KNEB(AM)—Jan 1, 1948: 960 khz; 1 kw-D, 500 w-N, DA-2. TL: N41 50 41 W103 38 09. Box 239 (69363-0239). (308) 632-7121. FAX: (308) 635-1071. Licensee: Panhandle Broadcasting Inc. Group owner: Nebraska Rural Radio Assn. (acq 8-1-84). Net: ABC/I. Rep: Katz. Format: C&W. Spec prog: Farm 18 hrs, Sp 5 hrs wkly. ■ Otto Geiger, pres; Marty Martinson, gen mgr; Barbara Martinson, gen sls mgr; Dennis Ernest, progmg dir; Kevin Mooney, news dir; Les Proctor, chief engr. ■ Rates: $30; 30; 20; 15.

KNEB-FM—Dec 25, 1960: 94.1 mhz; 100 kw. Ant 680 ft. TL: N41 42 04 W103 40 49. Stereo. Dups AM 10%. Format: Farm, C&W. Spec prog: Farm 18 hrs wkly. ■ Steve Voos, prom mgr. ■ Rates: Same as AM.

KOAQ(AM)—See Terrytown.

KOLT(AM)—Feb 15, 1930: 1320 khz; 5 kw-D, 1 kw-N, DA-N. TL: N41 51 37 W103 41 53. Box 660 (69363). (308) 635-1320. Licensee: Tracy Corp. V (acq 2-25-92;

$37,000; FTR 3-23-92). Net: CBS. Rep: Torbet. Wash atty: Michael Glaser. Format: Talk. News staff 2; news progmg 80 hrs wkly. Target aud: 39 plus. Spec prog: Farm 10 hrs wkly. ■ Michael Tracy, pres & gen mgr; Scott Cannon, opns mgr & progmg dir; Larry Patrick, gen sls mgr; June Jerger, mktg dir & prom dir; Lee Judd, news dir. ■ Rates: $11.75; 10.15; 10.15; 10.15.

Seward

KZKX(FM)—Nov 12, 1976: 96.9 mhz; 100 kw. Ant 610 ft. TL: N41 07 26 W96 50 03. Stereo. Suite 96, 4435 "O" St., Lincoln (68510). (402) 488-9601. FAX: (402) 489-9989. Licensee: C.T. Robinson (acq 10-15-92; $2.85 million; FTR 11-23-92). Net: ABC/D. Rep: D & R Radio. Wash atty: Jim Gammon. Format: Country. News staff one; news progmg 15 hrs wkly. Target aud: 25-54. ■ C.T. Robinson, pres; Julie Gade, gen mgr; Charlie Thomas, progmg dir; Carol Daniels, news dir; Mike Elliott, chief engr.

Sidney

KSID(AM)—June 2, 1952: 1340 khz; 1 kw-U. TL: N41 07 50 W102 58 15. Hrs opn: 24. Box 37, Legion Park (69162). (308) 254-5803. Licensee: KSID Radio Inc. (acq 1962). Net: ABC/I. Rep: Art Moore. Format: Country. Target aud: General. Spec prog: Farm 5 hrs wkly. ■ Elizabeth Young, pres & gen mgr; David S. Young, vp; David Young, engrg mgr.

KSID-FM—Sept 13, 1974: 98.7 mhz; 62 kw. Ant 368 ft. TL: N41 11 03 W103 11 37. Stereo. Dups AM 30%. Format: Adult contemp.

Superior

KRFS(AM)—Mar 17, 1959: 1600 khz; 500 w-D. TL: N40 01 30 W98 04 38. Hrs opn: 6 AM-11 PM. R.R. 2, Box 149 (68978). (402) 879-4741. Licensee: Superior Broadcasting Inc. (acq 8-90; $120,000 with co-located FM; FTR 8-20-90). Net: ABC/D; Brownfield. Format: Country. News progmg 11 hrs wkly. Target aud: 25-55; general. Spec prog: Farm 5 hrs, gospel 3 hrs, relg 3 hrs wkly. ■ Herbert Hoeflicker, pres, prom mgr, progmg dir, mus dir & chief engr; Ruby Hoeflicker, vp & stn mgr; Richard Disney, news dir.

KRFS-FM—Feb 25, 1977: 103.9 mhz; 2 kw. Ant 59 ft. TL: N40 01 30 W98 04 38 (CP: Ant 220 ft., TL: N40 06 20 W98 06 20). Stereo. Dups AM 100%. News opn: 16. Dups AM 100%. Wash atty: Sidley & Austin. Format: Country, farm.

Terrytown

KCMI(FM)—Mar 1, 1981: 96.9 mhz; 100 kw. Ant 692 ft. TL: N41 42 08 W103 41 00. Stereo. Hrs opn: 19. Box 401, 209 E. 15th, Scottsbluff (69363-0401). (308) 632-5264; (308) 635-0104. Licensee: Christian Media Inc. Net: USA. Format: Relg. News progmg 12 hrs wkly. Target aud: 25 plus. Spec prog: Class 4 hrs wkly. ■ Dwayne Kizzier, pres; Dale H. Brown, gen mgr; Linda Landrigan, prom mgr; Glenn Hascall, progmg dir; Bill Bauer, chief engr. ■ Rates: $8.60; 8.60; 8.60; 8.60.

KOAQ(AM)—June 15, 1961: 690 khz; 1 kw-D, 64 w-N, DA-1. TL: N41 50 02 W103 39 20. Stereo. Hrs opn: 24. Box 1263, 2002 Char Ave., Scottsbluff (69361). (308) 635-2690. FAX: (308) 635-1905. Licensee: Tracy Corp. IV (acq 12-86; $164,000; FTR 11-10-86). Net: Jones Satellite Audio, AP. Rep: Eastman, Intermountain, Art Moore. Wash atty: Michael Glaser. Format: Oldies. News staff 2; news progmg 21 hrs wkly. Target aud: 25-54; adults. Spec prog: Farm 5 hrs wkly. ■ Michael Tracy, pres & gen mgr; Larry Patrick, gen sls mgr; June Jerger, prom dir; Scott Cannon, progmg dir; Mark Jensen, mus dir; Lee Judd, news dir; Bob Hinze, chief engr. ■ Rates: $11.75; 10.15; 10.15; 10.15.

Valentine

KVSH(AM)—Mar 6, 1961: 940 khz; 5 kw-D, 19.6 w-N. TL: N42 51 54 W100 31 07. Hrs opn: 16. 126 W. Third St. (69201). (402) 376-2400. Licensee: Heart City Radio Corp. (acq 6-90; $235,000; FTR 6-4-90). Net: ABC/I. Wash atty: Dick Hildreth. Format: MOR. News staff one; news progmg 24 hrs wkly. Target aud: General; 35-60. ■ Dave Otradovsy, pres; Dave Otradovsky, gen mgr; Wallace Bazyn, gen sls mgr; Mike Burge, progmg dir & chief engr. ■ Rates: $7; 7; 7; 7.

Wayne

KTCH(AM)—Mar 18, 1968: 1590 khz; 2.5 kw-D, 33.4 w-N, DA-2. TL: N42 14 03 W97 03 19. Hrs opn: 6 AM-11 PM. Box 413, W. Hwy. 35 (68787). (402) 375-3700. FAX: (402) 375-5402. Licensee: KTCH Inc. (acq 6-1-78). Net: ABC/D; Brownfield, Mid-America Ag. Rep: Farmakis;

O'Malley. Format: Country. News staff one; news progmg 15 hrs wkly. Target aud: 30-64. Spec prog: Farm 20 hrs wkly. ■ Don Dolejs, pres; Mark Ahmann, gen mgr & stn mgr; Dan Baddorf, opns dir, progmg dir & mus dir; Sandy Bartling, rgnl sls mgr; Matt Turner, news dir. ■ Rates: $25; 7.50; 7.50; 4.

KTCH-FM—Oct 19, 1975: 104.9 mhz; 3 kw. Ant 300 ft. TL: N42 14 03 W97 03 19. Stereo. Hrs opn: 6 AM-11 PM. Dups AM 100%. ■ Tom Schmitz, engrg dir. ■ Rates: Same as AM.

***KWSC(FM)**—Oct 13, 1971: 91.9 mhz; 350 w. Ant 96 ft. TL: N42 14 30 W97 00 48. Wayne State College (68787). (402) 375-7000. Licensee: Wayne State College. Net: AP, Westwood One. Format: AOR. News progmg 3 hrs wkly. Target aud: 18 plus. Spec prog: Black 4 hrs, jazz 2 hrs, heavy metal 2 hrs, blues 2 hrs wkly. ■ Renee Klein, gen mgr; Bruce Nelson, progmg dir; Margee Nagel, news dir; Earl Norman, chief engr.

West Point

KWPN(AM)—Mar 17, 1985: 840 khz; 5 kw-D. TL: N41 47 06 W96 40 39. Stereo. Box 84 (68788), 435 N. Monitor (68788). (402) 372-5423. FAX: (401) 372-5425. Licensee: Kelly Communications Inc. Net: ABC/D. Wash atty: Baraff, Koerner, Olender & Hochberg. Format: Full service. News staff 2; news progmg 9 hrs wkly. Target aud: General; 18 plus. Spec prog: Farm 14 hrs. ■ David M. Kelly, pres & gen mgr; Sharon J. Kelly, progmg dir & mus dir; James C. Droege, chief engr.

KWPN-FM—Aug 1, 1988: 107.9 mhz; 6 kw. Ant 328 ft. TL: N41 47 06 W96 40 39. Stereo. Dups AM 100%. Target aud: 25-49.

Winnebago

KSUX(FM)—June 1, 1990: 105.7 mhz; 50 kw. Ant 463 ft. TL: N42 20 33 W96 31 13. Stereo. Hrs opn: 24. 2000 Indian Hills Dr., Sioux City, IA (51104). (712) 239-2100. FAX: (712) 239-3346. Licensee: Flagship Communications L.P. (acq 11-20-91; $450,000 for CP). Net: UPI. Format: Country. Spec prog: Farm. ■ Tom Spies, gen mgr; Denny Bullock, gen sls mgr; John W. McReynolds, progmg dir; Sam Seldon, chief engr.

York

KAWL(AM)—September 1954: 1370 khz; 500 w-D, 176 w-N. TL: N40 50 30 W97 35 16. Hrs opn: 24. Rt. 4, Box 121A (68467). (402) 362-4433. FAX: (402) 362-6501. Licensee: Central Nebraska Broadcasting Co. Inc. (acq 6-1-91; $530,000; with co-located FM; FTR 7-1-91). Net: NBC; Mid-American Ag, Browfield. Rep: Farmakis. Format: C&W. News staff one; news progmg 10 hrs wkly. Target aud: General; 30 plus. Spec prog: Bargain counter 3 hrs, farm 7 hrs, women 3 hrs wkly. ■ Tom Robson, gen mgr; Kent Kopetzky, news dir; James Droege, chief engr. ■ Rates: $12; 12; 12; 8.

KTMX(FM)—Co-owned with KAWL(AM). Sept 1, 1970: 104.9 mhz; 25 kw. Ant 328 ft. TL: N40 50 30 W97 35 16. Stereo. Hrs opn: 24. Prog sep from AM. Format: Adult contemp. News staff one; news progmg 3 hrs wkly. Target aud: General; 25-54. ■ Rates: $16; 16; 16; 12.

Nevada

Boulder City

KRRI(FM)—Licensed to Boulder City. See Las Vegas.

Carson City

KBUL(FM)—Nov 30, 1984: 98.1 mhz; 75.9 kw. Ant 2,273 ft. TL: N39 15 32 W119 42 06 (CP: 72.5 mhz, ant 2,286 ft.). Stereo. Hrs opn: 24. 2450 Wrondel Way, Reno (89502-3773). (702) 827-0980. FAX: (702) 827-9105. Licensee: Citadel Communications Corp. (group owner; acq 5-29-92). Rep: Christal. Format: C&W. News staff one; news progmg 4 hrs wkly. Target aud: 25-54. ■ Larry Wilson, pres; Debbie Raborn, vp & gen mgr; Gerry Schlegel, gen sls mgr; Matt Bowers, prom dir; Tom Jordan, progmg mgr & mus dir; Adrienne Abbott, news dir; Dave Collins, pub affrs dir; Martin Stabbert, chief engr.

KIZS(FM)—Nov 25, 1970: 94.7 mhz; 86.6 kw. Ant 2,072 ft. TL: N39 15 30 W119 42 36. Stereo. Suite 208, 255 W. Moana, Reno (89509). (702) 829-1964. Licensee: Sapphire Broadcasting Inc. Group owner: Crown Broadcasting Inc. (acq 11-89; $1.5 million; FTR 11-13-89). Wash atty: Arent, Fox, Kintner, Plotkin & Kahn. Format: Hot country. Target aud: General. ■ Thomas P. Gammon, pres; Sean Tayler, chief engr.

KKNK(AM)—Not on air, target date unknown: 750 khz; 10 kw-U, DA-2. TL: N39 12 50 W119 38 28. Box 1888 (89702). Licensee: Caballero Radio West Inc. (acq 10-28-91; $37,500 for CP, with CP KKNC(AM) Sun Valley; FTR 11-18-91).

***KNIS(FM)**—Oct 15, 1989: 91.3 mhz; 67 kw. Ant 2,165 ft. TL: N39 15 30 W119 42 36. Stereo. Hrs opn: 24. 6363 Hwy. 50 E. (89701). (702) 883-5647. Licensee: Western Inspirational Broadcasters Inc. (acq 10-15-89). Net: UPI. Format: Contemp Christian, educ, talk. News progmg 16 hrs wkly. Target aud: 24-44. ■ Tom Hesse, gen mgr; Bill Feltner, opns dir & progmg dir; Joseph Torsitano, chief engr.

KPTL(AM)—May 14, 1955: 1300 khz; 5 kw-D, 500 w-N, DA-N. TL: N39 09 59 W119 43 37. 1960 Idaho (89701). (702) 884-8000. FAX: (702) 882-3961. Licensee: MB Broadcasting Corp. (acq 10-89; $600,000; FTR 10-2-89). Net: ABC/I. Rep: Katz & Powell. Wash atty: Fisher, Wayland, Cooper & Leader. Format: Adult contemp, news/talk. News staff 2; news progmg 14 hrs wkly. Target aud: 35-54. Spec prog: Sp 4 hrs wkly. ■ Craig E. Swope, gen mgr; Paula Schofield, gen sls mgr; David Piel, mktg dir; Fred James, progmg dir; Howard Cadot, chief engr. ■ Rates: $16; 12; 14; 6.

KWNZ(FM)—Licensed to Carson City. See Reno.

East Las Vegas

KOWA Exp stn—(experimental synchronous AM station, operates simultaneously with primary KOWA facility at Laughlin). 870 khz; 300 w-D, 500 w-N, DA-N. Suite 208, 2235 E. Flamingo Rd. (89119). (702) 369-6004. FAX: (702) 369-4195. Licensee: Million Dollar Broadcasting Inc. ■ Paul Bowman, pres & gen mgr; Vivian Bowman, vp.

Elko

KELK(AM)—Dec 7, 1948: 1240 khz; 1 kw-U. TL: N40 50 37 W115 44 58. Box 5566, 1800 Idaho St. (89802). (702) 738-1240. FAX: (702) 753-5556. Licensee: Elko Broadcasting Co. (acq 11-1-74). Net: ABC/I. Wash atty: Gardner, Carton & Douglas. Format: Full svc adult contemp. News staff one; news progmg 5 hrs wkly. Target aud: 25-54. upscale, family oriented, white collar workforce. ■ Paul G. Gardner, pres, gen mgr, progmg dir & chief engr; Lin Anderson, opns dir; Valorie Hurtt, sls dir; Tony Joe, mus dir; Lori Gilbert, news dir. ■ Rates: $16; 15; 16; 15.

KLKO(FM)—Co-owned with KELK(AM). May 1982: 93.5 mhz; 3 kw. Ant -314 ft. TL: N40 50 37 W115 44 58. Stereo. Prog sep from AM. Format: Classic rock. News staff one. Spec prog: Rush Limbaugh 15 hrs wkly.

***KNCC(FM)**—1992: 91.5 mhz; 50 w. Ant 741 ft. TL: N40 49 16 W115 42 04. Rebroadcasts *KUNR(FM) Reno. Univ. of Nevada System, 901 Elm St. (89801). (702) 738-8493. Licensee: Northern Nevada Community College. Format: Classical.

KRJC(FM)—October 1981: 95.3 mhz; 450 w. Ant 761 ft. TL: N40 54 35 W115 49 05. Stereo. Box 1626, 1859 Manzanita Dr. (89801-1626). (702) 738-9895. FAX: (702) 753-8085. Licensee: Holiday Broadcasting of Elko. Group owner: Carlson Communications International. Net: UPI. Format: C&W. ■ Ralph J. Carlson, pres; Darrell Calton, gen mgr & gen sls mgr.

Ely

KDSS(FM)—Dec 22, 1984: 92.7 mhz; 320 w. Ant 941 ft. TL: N39 14 46 W114 55 39. 685 Lyons Ave. (89301). (702) 289-6474. FAX: (702) 289-3767. Licensee: Stubbs Broadcasting Co. Inc. (acq 11-30-92; $26,000; FTR 12-21-92). Format: Adult contemp. Target aud: 18-50. Spec prog: Relg one hr wkly. ■ Don Stubbs, vp, gen mgr & stn mgr; Dianne Stubbs, progmg dir; Jim Liebsack, chief engr. ■ Rates: $7; 7; 7; 6.

KELY(AM)—July 8, 1950: 1230 khz; 250 w-SH. TL: N39 15 45 W114 51 46. 807 Ave. F (89301). (702) 289-2077. FAX: (702) 289-4467. Licensee: Reed Communications Inc. (acq 12-9-86). Net: UPI. Format: C&W. ■ Bart Reed, gen mgr & progmg dir.

KELY-FM—Nov 1, 1986: 101.7 mhz; 480 w. Ant 804 ft. TL: N39 14 46 W114 55 39. Stereo. Dups AM 20%. Format: CHR. ■ Darren Pierson, mus dir.

Fallon

***KVCE(FM)**—Sept 8, 1986: 89.5 mhz; 378 w. Ant 116 ft. TL: N39 29 22 W118 51 26. 1445 Lucas Rd. (89406). (702) 867-3005. Licensee: Fallon Educ Broadcasting

Foundation. Format: Btfl mus, educ, relg. ■ T. Plants, gen mgr; Jim Hardy, chief engr.

KVLV(AM)—May 9, 1957: 980 khz; 5 kw-D. TL: N39 29 47 W118 48 50. 1155 Gummow Drive (89406). (702) 423-2243. FAX: (702) 423-8889. Licensee: Lahontan Valley Broadcasting Co. Net: AP; Great Basin Net. Format: C&W, farm. News progmg 10 hrs wkly. Target aud: 25 plus. ■ Mike McGinness, gen mgr & gen sls mgr; Deanna McGinness, progmg dir; Lynn L. Pearce, mus dir & news dir; Lester Pearce, chief engr. ■ Rates: $9; 9; 9; na.

KVLV-FM—Nov 26, 1966: 99.3 mhz; 2.9 kw. Ant 250 ft. TL: N39 29 47 W118 48 50. Stereo. Prog sep from AM. Format: Adult contemp.

AMERICAN RADIO BROKERS, INC.
MOST TRUSTED NAME IN MEDIA BROKERAGE
CHESTER P. COLEMAN / PRESIDENT
FOR THE BEST STATIONS FOR SALE FROM THIS AREA
CALL — 415/441-3377
1255 POST STREET / SUITE 625 / SAN FRANCISCO, CA 94109

Gardnerville-Minden

KGVMs(FM)—Sept 19, 1985: 99.3 mhz; 3 kw. Ant -816 ft. TL: N38 57 35 W119 50 36. Stereo. Box 2109, Hwy. 395, 1504 Main St. (89410). (702) 782-2211; (702) 782-2212. FAX: (702) 782-5486. Licensee: Carson Valley Radio Inc. Net: CNN. Format: Soft adult contemp. ■ Lloyd W. Higuera, gen mgr; Terry Reiswig, gen sls mgr; Caroline Higuera, progmg dir.

Henderson

KDOL(AM)—May 1956: 1280 khz; 5 kw-D, 28-N. TL: N36 03 13 W114 58 30. Hrs opn: 24. 740 N. Valle Verde Dr. (89015). (702) 435-5735. FAX: (702) 435-7027. Licensee: S&R Broadcasting Inc. (acq 10-16-90; $600,000; FTR 11-5-90). Rep: Lotus Hispanic. Wash atty: Rosenman & Colin. Format: Sp. News progmg 10 hrs wkly. Target aud: General; Hispanic, above-average income, high home ownership. ■ Paul R. Ruttan, pres & gen mgr; Scott Gentry, gen sls mgr; Luis Bonilla, news dir; Warren Brown, chief engr. ■ Rates: $30; 30; 30; 25.

KMZQ-FM—Nov 28, 1982: 100.5 mhz; 98 kw. Ant 1,180 ft. TL: N36 00 28 W115 00 20. Stereo. Suite F, 2880 E. Flamingo Rd., Las Vegas (89121). (702) 731-5100. FAX: (702) 734-1950. Licensee: Commonwealth Broadcasting of Northern California. Group owner: Commonwealth Broadcasting Co. (acq 2-20-89; $6.5 million; FTR 2-20-89). Format: Adult contemp. News staff one; news progmg 10 hrs wkly. Target aud: 25-49. ■ Jim Donahoe, gen mgr; Tom Carrell, gen sls mgr; Jeff Cochran, progmg dir; Trace Shannon, news dir; Jay Pierce, chief engr. ■ Rates: $70; 60; 60; 40.

KWNR(FM)—July 18, 1972: 95.5 mhz; 100 kw h, 61 kw v. Ant 1,120 ft. TL: N36 00 30 W115 00 20 (CP: 91.8 kw, ant 1,200 ft., TL: N36 00 31 W115 00 22). Suite B-200, 1515 E. Tropicana Bldg., Las Vegas (89119). (702) 798-4004. FAX: (702) 798-3076. Licensee: Southwest Radio Las Vegas Inc. (acq 8-88; $2.75 million; FTR 8-29-88). Rep: Banner. Format: Country. News staff one; news progmg 3 hrs wkly. Target aud: 18-54. ■ Mike Ginsburg, gen mgr; Rick White, gen sls mgr; Gary Moss, progmg dir & mus dir; Roy West, news dir; Jay Pierce, chief engr.

KXTZ(FM)—Feb 10, 1970: 94.1 mhz; 100 kw. Ant 1,210 ft. TL: N36 00 26 W115 00 24. Stereo. Hrs opn: 24. 2300 Paseo del Prado D-204, Las Vegas (89102); 307 Water St. (89015). (702) 367-9494; (702) 564-6066. FAX: (702) 565-3593; (702) 367-4846. Licensee: Parker Communications-Las Vegas. Group owner: Parker Communications. Rep: D & R Radio. Wash atty: Crowell & Moring. Format: Easy adult contemp. News staff one; news progmg 4 hrs wkly. Target aud: 25-54. ■ John B. Parker, pres; Deanne Shehan, gen mgr; Dave McKay, stn mgr; Laura Sable, prom mgr; Joe Sands, chief engr. ■ Rates: $50; 60; 60; 40.

Incline Village

KZAK(FM)—Licensed to Incline Village. See Reno.

Indian Springs

KPXC(FM)—Not on air, target date unknown: 99.3 mhz; 6 kw. Ant -167 ft. TL: N36 33 09 W115 36 08. 3481 Jewel Cave Dr., Las Vegas (89122). Licensee: Claire B. Benezra (acq 3-19-91; FTR 4-8-91).

LAUREN A. COLBY
301-663-1086
COMMUNICATIONS ATTORNEY
Special Attention to
Difficult Cases

Las Vegas

***KCEP(FM)**—October 1973: 88.1 mhz; 10 kw. Ant -39 ft. TL: N36 10 51 W115 08 43 (CP: 10 kw, ant 1,079 ft.). Stereo. 330 W. Washington St. (89106). (702) 648-4218. FAX: (702) 647-0803. Licensee: Operation Opportunities - Clark County. Format: Black. ■ Lewis Conner Jr., gen mgr.

KDOL(AM)—See Henderson.

KDWN(AM)—Apr 7, 1975: 720 khz; 50 kw-U, DA-N. TL: N36 04 22 W114 58 20. One Main St. (89101). (702) 385-7212. FAX: (702) 385-6094. Licensee: Radio Nevada Inc. Net: AP. Rep: Roslin. Format: News, talk. News progmg 30 hrs wkly. Target aud: 35 plus; middle & upper middle class. ■ A. J. Williams, pres; Claire Reis, gen mgr; C. B. Benezra, gen sls mgr; C. Williams, progmg dir; M. Messina, chief engr.

***KEDB(FM)**—Not on air, target date unknown: 88.7 mhz; 112 w. Ant 1,469 ft. Chapel of Las Vegas, 800 N. Rancho Dr. (89106). Licensee: Education Committee Calvary Chapel of Las Vegas. ■ Robert L. Purcell, chief engr.

KEDG(FM)—March 1989: 103.5 mhz; 100 kw. Ant 1,158 ft. TL: N36 00 29 W115 00 20. Suite 650, 1455 E. Tropicana, (89119). (702) 795-1035. FAX: (702) 798-1738. Licensee: George Tobin (acq 5-10-91; $2 million; FTR 6-3-91). Format: Mod rock. News staff one. Target aud: 18-34. ■ Dax Tobin, gen mgr; John Griffin, mus dir; Karen Lynne, news dir & pub affrs dir; Joe Sands, chief engr.

KENO(AM)—1940: 1460 khz; 5 kw-D, 1 kw-N, DA-N. TL: N36 06 16 W115 12 16 (CP: 30 kw-D, TL: N36 12 44 W115 09 43). 4660 S. Decatur Blvd. (89103). (702) 876-1460. FAX: (702) 876-6685. Licensee: Lotus Communications Corp. (group owner; acq 6-1-65). Rep: Christal. Format: Sports play-by-play, CNN. ■ Howard A. Kalmenson, pres; Ton Bonnici, gen mgr; Jesse Leeds, gen sls mgr; Michael Lyles, chief engr.

KOMP(FM)—Co-owned with KENO(AM). Sept 1, 1966: 92.3 mhz; 100 kw. Ant 1,520 ft. TL: N35 56 50 W115 03 01 (CP: 22.9 kw, ant 3,844 ft.). Stereo. Prog sep from AM. Format: AOR. ■ Marty Belter, mus dir; Sharon Gwin, news dir.

KEYV(FM)—Sept 1, 1977: 93.1 mhz; 24.5 w. Ant 3,724 ft. TL: N35 58 02 W115 36 06. Stereo. Suite P120, 101 Convention Center Dr. (89109). (702) 732-7753. FAX: (702) 732-4890. Licensee: Broadcast Associates Inc. (acq 8-3-93; $2.25 million; FTR 8-23-93). Rep: D & R Radio. Format: New age. News progmg 3 hrs wkly. Target aud: 25-49; upscale, well educated with disposable income. ■ Andrew Molasky, pres.

KFMS(AM)—(North Las Vegas). 1954: 1410 khz; 5 kw-U, DA-N. TL: N36 00 50 W115 09 35. Stereo. Hrs opn: 24. Box 15223, Las Vegas (89114); Suite P-120, 101 Convention Ctr. Dr., Las Vegas (89109). (702) 732-7753. FAX: (702) 732-4890. Licensee: Broadcast Assoc. (acq 8-28-72). Rep: Katz. Wash atty: Miller & Fields. Format: C&W. News staff 2; news progmg 5 hrs wkly. Target aud: General; adults 25-54. ■ Steve Gold, CEO & pres; Hank Thornley, sr vp & rgnl sls mgr; Catherine Gold, vp & natl sls mgr; Doug Shane, gen mgr & vp opns; Teddy Brown, opns dir, progmg dir & progmg mgr; Gina Burton, sls dir; Eric Patrick, prom dir; J.C. Simon, mus dir; Joe McCarthy, news dir; Ted Marvelle, pub affrs dir; Mark Nocte, chief engr.

KFMS-FM—March 22, 1963: 101.9 mhz; 100 kw. Ant 1,181 ft. TL: N36 00 28 W115 00 20. Stereo. Dups AM 100%.

***KILA(FM)**—July 18, 1972: 90.5 mhz; 100 kw. Ant 1,269 ft. TL: N36 00 29 W115 00 20. Stereo. Hrs opn: 24. 2201 S. 6th St. (89104). (702) 731-5452. FAX: (702) 731-1992. Licensee: Faith Communications Corp. (acq 12-31-71). Wash atty: Cohn & Marks. Format: Relg, adult contemp. News progmg 5 hrs wkly. Target aud: 25-44; young families. ■ Jack French, pres & gen mgr; Brad Staley, vp & opns dir; Chris Staley, progmg dir & news dir; Tim Hunt, chief engr.

KKLZ(FM)—Listing follows KMTW(AM).

KKVV(AM)—May 1, 1990: 1060 khz; 5 kw-D, 43 w-N. TL: N36 09 22 W115 15 24. Hrs opn: 6 AM-12 AM. 3185 S. Highland Dr., Suite 13 (89109). (702) 731-5588. Licensee: Carl J. Auel and Patricia A. Jones (acq 11-8-93; $17,000; FTR 11-29-93). Net: USA, CBN. Format: Relg, talk. News staff one; news progmg 6 hrs wkly. Target aud: General. Spec prog: Black 2 hrs wkly. ■ James E. Auel, pres; Jane A. Filler, vp; Rebecca Chapman, gen mgr, gen sls mgr & prom mgr; Carl J. Auel, dev dir; Warren Brown, engrg dir. ■ Rates: $15; 15; 15; na.

KLAV(AM)—June 1947: 1230 khz; 1 kw-U. TL: N36 11 20 W115 08 40. Hrs opn: 24. Suite 6201, 2000 S. Las Vegas Blvd. (89104). (702) 796-1230. FAX: (702) 385-2261. Licensee: WAGI Inc. Net: CNN. Wash atty: Robert Olender. Format: News/talk, sports, Sp. News staff one; news progmg 20 hrs wkly. Target aud: 25-54; serves all of Las Vegas's population. Spec prog: Black 6 hrs, Ger one hr, gospel one hr, It one hr, relg one hr, Chinese 6 hrs, Isreali one hr, Greek one hr, Persian/Iranian 6 hrs, Hawaiian one hr wkly. ■ Dave Wagenvoord, CEO; Marvin Chupack, CFO; Lola Wagenvoord, stn mgr; Hannah O'Brien, mktg dir; Walt Reno, progmg dir & asst mus dir; Don Jaye, progmg mgr, news dir & pub affrs dir. ■ Rates: $50; 40; 50; 30.

KLUC-FM—Listing follows KXNO(AM).

KMTW(AM)—1947: 1340 khz; 1 kw-U. TL: N36 09 22 W115 15 24. Hrs opn: 24. 4305 S. Industrial Rd., (89103). (702) 739-9600. Licensee: Southern Nevada Radio Inc. (acq 7-16-85; $2.5 million with co-located FM; FTR 6-17-85). Net: Unistar. Rep: D & R Radio. Format: CNN Headline news. Target aud: 25-54. ■ Terry McRight, gen mgr & gen sls mgr; Lin Aubuschon, prom dir; Bob Edwards, progmg dir; Warren Brown, chief engr. ■ Rates: $40; 40; 40; 20.

KKLZ(FM)—Co-owned with KMTW(AM). Jan 26, 1984: 96.3 mhz; 100 kw. Ant 1,170 ft. TL: N36 00 29 W115 00 20. Stereo. Hrs opn: 24. Prog sep from AM. Format: Classic rock. News staff one. Target aud: 25-44; baby boomers. ■ Marre McAllister, mus dir; Dennis Mitchell, news dir. ■ Rates: $90; 85; 70; 50.

***KNPR(FM)**—Mar 24, 1980: 89.5 mhz; 100 kw. Ant 1,532 ft. TL: N35 56 50 W115 03 01 (CP: 98.3 kw). Stereo. 5151 Boulder Hwy. (89122). (702) 456-6695. Licensee: Nevada Public Radio Corp. Net: NPR, APR. Wash atty: Dow, Lohnes & Albertson. Format: Class, news. Target aud: 35-54. ■ Lamar Marchese, gen mgr; Jay Volney, opns dir; Barbara Huffstetler, dev dir; John Stark, progmg dir; Gale Gilbreath, chief engr.

KNUU(AM)—(Paradise). Feb 21, 1962: 970 khz; 5 kw-D, 500 w-N, DA-2. TL: N36 04 23 W115 15 05. Suite 101, 2001 E. Flamingo Rd., Las Vegas (89119). (702) 735-8644. FAX: (702) 735-8184. Licensee: CAT Broadcasting Corp. (acq 4-1-87). Net: CBS, MBS, NBC Talknet, UPI, Wall Street. Format: News/talk. ■ Douglas Trenner, pres & gen mgr; Diana Hale, gen sls mgr; Glen Charles, news dir; Pat O'Gara, chief engr.

KOMP(FM)—Listing follows KENO(AM).

KORK(AM)—June 1953: 920 khz; 5 kw-D, 500 w-N, DA-2. TL: N36 11 25 W115 10 35. 4660 S. Decatur (89103). (702) 876-1460. FAX: (702) 876-6685. Licensee: Lotus Broadcasting Corp. (acq 11-4-92; $1,425,000; with co-located FM; FTR 11-23-92). Net: ABC/I. Format: Big band, nostalgia. Target aud: 35 plus. ■ Howard Kalmenson, pres; Tony Bonnici, gen mgr; Jesse Leeds, gen sls mgr; Sara Beth Cutter, prom mgr; Chris Davis, progmg dir; Mike Liles, chief engr. ■ Rates: $65; 55; 65; 40.

KXPT(FM)—Co-owned with KORK(AM). Nov 29, 1961: 97.1 mhz; 50 kw. Ant 1,950 ft. TL: N35 56 44 W115 02 31 (CP: 15 kw, ant 1,919 ft.). Stereo. Prog sep from AM. Net: ABC/FM. Rep: Banner. Format: CHR. Target aud: 12-34. ■ Larry Wells, progmg dir. ■ Rates: Same as AM.

KOWA(AM)—See Laughlin.

KRBO(FM)—Not on air, target date unknown: 105.1 mhz; 50 kw. Ant 1,614 ft. TL: N36 19 46 W115 21 49. Suite 660, 1920 N St. NW, Washington, DC (20036). Licensee: Patmor Broadcasting Group.

KRLV(FM)—Aug 18, 1987: 106.5 mhz; 100 kw. Ant 1,155 ft. TL: N36 00 30 W115 00 20. Stereo. 1064 E. Sahara Ave. (89104). (702) 796-4040. FAX: (702) 796-6347. Licensee: Wescom of Nevada Inc. (acq 8-2-89; $3.5 million; FTR 6-26-89). Rep: Major Mkt. Format: Adult contemp. News staff one. Target aud: 25-54. ■ Dale Matteson, pres; Tom Chase, prom dir & progmg dir; Jay Pierce, chief engr.

KRRI(FM)—(Boulder City). Sept 1, 1982: 105.5 mhz; 3.7 kw. Ant 1,588 ft. TL: N35 59 45 W114 51 51. Stereo. Hrs opn: 24. 2255A Renaissance Dr., Las Vegas (89119); Box 60097 (89006). (702) 293-5774; (702) 597-5350. Licensee: Rock 'n Roll Inc. Net: NBC, Westwood One, CBS, ABC. Wash atty: Miller & Fields. Format: Oldies Rock 'n' Roll. News staff 3; news progmg 3 hrs wkly. Target aud: 25-54; baby boomers. ■ Art Ferraro, pres, gen mgr & vp opns; Jodi Lawrence, gen sls mgr; Mugs McGuire, vp prom; Art Kevin, progmg dir & news dir; Joe Sands, chief engr.

***KUNV(FM)**—Apr 21, 1981: 91.5 mhz; 15 kw. Ant 1,100 ft. TL: N36 00 28 W115 00 20. Stereo. Hrs opn: 24 Univ. of Nevada, 4505 S. Maryland Pkwy. (89154). (702) 895-3877. FAX: (702) 895-4857. Licensee: Univ. of Nevada Board of Regents. Format: Div, jazz, alt. News progmg 10 hrs wkly. Target aud: General. Spec prog: Fr one hr, Sp 9 hrs, West Indian 3 hrs, blues 4 hrs, Farsi one hr, folk 4 hrs, world music 5 hrs, electronic 2 hrs, community affrs 10 hrs, women's mus 2 hrs, Broadway one hr, German one hr wkly. ■ Suzanne Scott Weiss, gen mgr & opns mgr; Jennifer Gilroy, dev dir; Brett McGlasson, progmg dir & pub affrs dir; Ian Scott Swirnow, Suzanne Scott Weiss, Kay Tuma, mus dirs; Gordie Allsum, chief engr.

KXNO(AM)—(North Las Vegas). 1956: 1140 khz; 10 kw-D, 2.5 kw-N, DA-N. TL: N36 16 03 W115 02 41. 3510 W. Hacienda, Las Vegas (89118). (702) 736-9383. FAX: (702) 736-1443. Licensee: Nationwide Communication Inc. Group owner: Nationwide Mutual Insurance Co. (acq 3-85). Rep: McGavren Guild. Format: AOR. ■ Clark Polock, pres; Keith A. Gerst, vp & gen mgr; Bob Berzins, progmg dir & mus dir.

KLUC-FM—Co-owned with KXNO(AM). 1956: 98.5 mhz; 97 kw. Ant 1,181 ft. TL: N36 00 29 W115 00 20. Stereo. Net: ABC/C. Rep: McGavren Guild. Format: Top-40. ■ Jerry Dean, progmg dir; John Naven, news dir.

KXPT(FM)—Listing follows KORK(AM).

Laughlin

KOWA(AM)—Aug 15, 1986: 870 khz; 10 kw-D, 1 kw-N, DA-2. TL: N35 10 10 W114 38 10. Stereo. Hrs opn: 24. Suite 209, 2235 E. Flamingo Rd., Las Vegas (89119). (702) 369-6004. FAX: (702) 369-4195. Licensee: Million Dollar Broadcasting (acq 9-1-91; $750,000). Net: AP. Rep: Torbet. Format: Classic country. Target aud: 35 plus. ■ Paul Bowman, pres; Vivian Bowman, exec vp; Phil Zieghery, opns dir; Paul Baumann, mus dir; Gordon Alsum, chief engr. ■ Rates: $25; 23; 25; 15.

Mesquite

KIPP(FM)—Not on air, target date unknown: 97.5 mhz; 100 kw. Ant 981 ft. TL: N36 51 21 W114 17 58. 1391 W. 320 N., St. George, UT (84770). Licensee: A.G.P. Inc.

North Las Vegas

KFMS(AM)—Licensed to North Las Vegas. See Las Vegas.

KJUL(FM)—April 1989: 104.3 mhz; 100 kw. Ant 1,181 ft. TL: N35 58 02 W115 30 06. Stereo. Suite E, 2880 E. Flamingo Rd., Las Vegas (89121). (702) 732-2200. FAX: (702) 731-1211. Licensee: Eight Chiefs Inc. (acq 7-20-93; $1.7 million; FTR 8-23-93). Format: Nostalgia. News progmg one hr wkly. Target aud: 35-64. ■ Bill Dimeolo, gen mgr; Doug James, progmg dir & mus dir; Dan Peluso, chief engr.

KVEG(AM)—1986: 840 khz; 50 kw-D, 25 kw-N, DA-2. TL: N36 23 53 W114 54 57. Stereo. Hrs opn: 24. 3333 Cambridge St., Las Vegas (89109-2806). (702) 731-5200. FAX: (702) 731-4200. Licensee: K-G Communications Inc. (acq 4-29-91; FTR 5-20-91). Wash atty: Baraff, Koerner, Olender & Hochberg. Format: 24-hr talk/sports. News staff 16. Target aud: 21 plus; male, sports audience. ■ Jules Kutner, chmn; Jerry Kutner, pres & progmg dir; Craig Bowers, gen mgr; Perry Johnstone, natl sls mgr; Carol Sweetman, prom mgr; Tim Neveritt, news dir; Jerry Heckerman, chief engr. ■ Rates: $35; 30; 35; 35.

KXNO(AM)—Licensed to North Las Vegas. See Las Vegas.

Pahrump

KFBI(FM)—1989: 107.5 mhz; 24.5 kw. Ant 3,715 ft. TL: N35 58 02 W115 30 06. Stereo. Hrs opn: 24. Suite P119, 101 Convention Ctr. Dr., Las Vegas (89109). (702) 791-1964. FAX: (702) 791-3326. Licensee: Americom Las Vegas L.P. Group owner: Americom (acq 9-19-89; $4 million; FTR 10-9-89). Rep: McGavren Guild. Wash atty: Rodger Metzler. Format: Howard Stern all morning, Classic Rock all day. News staff one. Target aud: 18-54. ■ Tom Quinn, CEO, chmn & pres; Scott Seidenstricker, vp, gen mgr & natl sls mgr; Bill Tod, progmg dir.

Panaca

***KLNR(FM)**—May 1989: 91.7 mhz; 100 w. Ant 3,424 ft. TL: N37 50 38 W114 34 40. 5151 Boulder Hwy., Las Vegas (89122). (702) 456-6695. FAX: (702) 458-2787. Licensee: Nevada Public Radio Corp. Net: NPR. Format: Class, news. ■ Lamar Marchese, gen mgr.

Paradise

KNUU(AM)—Licensed to Paradise. See Las Vegas.

Reno

KCBN(AM)—Listing follows KRNO-FM.

KHIT(AM)—See Sun Valley.

KHIT-FM—Oct 12, 1966: 104.5 mhz; 25 kw. Ant 2,930 ft. TL: N39 18 48 W119 52 59. Stereo. Hrs opn: 24. 2900 Sutro St. (89512). (702) 853-5448; (702) 853-1045. FAX: (702) 853-2960. Licensee: Lotus Radio Corp. (group owner; acq 3-30-93; $600,000 with KHIT[AM] Sun Valley; FTR 4-19-93). Rep: D & R Radio. Format: Country. News staff one; news progmg 3 hrs wkly. Target aud: 25-54. ■ Howard Kalmenson, pres; Carol Flynn, gen mgr; Martin Flynn, gen sls mgr; Dan Mason, progmg dir; Pat Frisch, news dir & pub affrs dir. ■ Rates: $22; 22; 22; 18.

KHTZ(AM)—Listing follows KODS(FM).

KNDE(FM)—See Sparks.

KNEV(FM)—Dec 25, 1953: 95.5 mhz; 60 kw. Ant 2,270 ft. TL: N39 15 34 W119 42 16 (CP: 2,280 ft.). Stereo. 2450 Wrondell Way (89502). Licensee: Citadel Communications Corp. (group owner; acq 4-13-93; $500,000; FTR 5-3-93). Net: ABC/E. Format: Easy listening. Target aud: General. Spec prog: Jazz 2 hrs, relg one hr wkly.

***KNIS(FM)**—See Carson City.

KODS(FM)—(Camelian Bay, Calif). 1970: 103.7 mhz; 6.3 kw. Ant 2,985 ft. TL: N39 18 16 W119 53 00. Stereo. Dups AM 100%. FAX: (702) 825-3183. (Acq 1985). Net: Unistar. Rep: CBS Radio.

KHTZ(AM)—(Truckee, Calif). Co-owned with KODS(FM). Target date unknown: 1400 khz; 1 kw-U. TL: N39 17 17 W120 06 07 (CP: COL: Sparks, NV, TL: N39 22 10 W120 08 36). Suite 208, 255 W. Moana Ln., Reno, NV (89509). (702) 829-1964. FAX: (702) 825-3183. Licensee: Americom (group owner; acq 10-1-82). ■ Tom Quinn, pres; Fred Giles, chief engr.

KOH(AM)—Oct 25, 1928: 630 khz; 5 kw-D, 1 kw-N, DA-N. TL: N39 34 25 W119 50 48. Hrs opn: 24. Suite 116, 1575 Delucchi Ln. (89502). (702) 828-8240. FAX: (702) 828-8246. Licensee: Olympic Broadcasters Inc. (acq 11-7-90; $2 million with co-located FM; FTR 11-26-90). Net: CBS, ABC. Rep: Katz. Format: News/talk. News staff 3. Target aud: 25-65. ■ Bill Rademaker, pres; Jamie Clark, vp; Magda Martinez, gen mgr; Johanna Marshall, gen sls mgr; Don Darne, prom dir; Ross Mitchell, progmg dir; Howard Dupree, news dir; Dave Herold, pub affrs dir; Shawn Taylor, chief engr.

KTHX(FM)—Co-owned with KOH(AM). Aug 12, 1986: 101.7 mhz; 1.3 kw. Ant 426 ft. TL: N39 35 03 W119 47 52. Prog sep from AM. Format: AAA, eclectic rock. ■ Bruce Van Dyke, progmg dir; Don Darne, mus dir.

KOZZ(AM)—Jan 29, 1955: 1450 khz; 1 kw-U. TL: N39 33 26 W119 47 47. 2900 Sutro St. (89512); Box 9870 (89507). (702) 329-9261. FAX: (702) 323-1450. Licensee: Lotus Radio Corp. Group owner: Lotus Communications Corp. (acq 9-67). Net: AP. Rep: D & R Radio. Format: Classic rock. News staff one. Target aud: 25-49. ■ Howard A. Kalmenson, pres; Carol J. Flynn, vp & gen mgr; Martin Flynn, gen sls mgr; Harry Reynolds, progmg dir; Jake Armer, news dir & pub affrs dir; Jack Parker, chief engr.

KOZZ-FM—September 1969: 105.7 mhz; 75 kw. Ant 2,120 ft. TL: N39 15 34 W119 42 21. Stereo. Dups AM 100%. (Acq 1-1-78). ■ Cindy Calloway, prom dir; Bryan Pryor, mus dir. ■ Rates: $40; 40; 40; 28.

KPLY(AM)—See Sparks.

KQLO(AM)—1946: 920 khz; 5 kw-D, 1 kw-N, DA-N. TL: N39 33 18 W119 45 17 (CP: TL: N39 30 35 W119 42 59). 2395 Tampa St. (89512). (702) 333-0123. FAX: (702) 333-0101. Licensee: Pacific Telecom Inc. (acq 8-29-89; grpsl; FTR 9-18-89). Net: NBC. Rep: Banner. Format: News/talk & info. ■ Roy Robinson, pres & gen mgr; Hank Laduke, opns mgr; Mike Weaver, chief engr.

KWNZ(FM)—(Carson City). Co-owned with KQLO(AM). June 27, 1972: 97.3 mhz; 87.1 kw. Ant 2,126 ft. TL: N39 15 21 W119 42 37. Stereo. Licensee: Pacific Telecom Inc. (acq 8-29; grpsl; FTR 9-18-89). Format: Adult contemp. ■ Ray Kalusa, progmg dir.

***KRNC(FM)**—Not on air, target date September 1994: 89.5 mhz; 5 kw. Ant -3 ft. 7000 Dandini Blvd. (89512). Licensee: Board of Regents of the University of Nevada, acting on behalf of Truckee Meadows Community College.

KRNO-FM—July 1974: 106.9 mhz; 37 kw. Ant 2,956 ft. TL: N39 18 38 W119 53 01. Stereo. Hrs opn: 24. Box 10630 (89510); 475 E. Moana Ln. (89502). (702) 826-1355. FAX: (702) 826-7671. Licensee: A & A Broadcasting Corp. (acq 7-90; $224,103 with co-located AM; FTR 7-9-90). Rep: Torbet. Wash atty: Fisher, Wayland, Cooper & Leader. Format: Adult contemp, soft hits. News staff one; news progmg 18 hrs wkly. Target aud: 25-54; women. ■ Lorraine Arms, pres & gen mgr; John Murphy, natl sls mgr & rgnl sls mgr; Don Schrader, prom dir; Laurie Adamson, progmg dir & mus dir; Dave Williams, news dir; Jim Lincioni, chief engr.

KCBN(AM)—Co-owned with KRNO-FM. Oct 30, 1963: 1230 khz; 1 kw-U. TL: N39 30 42 W119 42 48. Hrs opn: 24. Prog sep from FM. Net: CNN. Format: Nostalgia, MOR. News staff one. Target aud: General; men.

KROW(AM)—Oct 13, 1970: 780 khz; 50 kw-U, DA-N. TL: N39 40 41 W119 48 06. Hrs opn: 24. 2450 Wrondell Way (89502). (702) 827-0980. FAX: (702) 827-9105. Licensee: Citadel Communications Corp. (group owner; acq 5-18-92; $12.5 million grpsl; FTR 6-8-92). Net: ABC/I. Rep: Christal. Format: Classic country. News staff 4; news progmg 28 hrs wkly. Target aud: General; adults 35-64. Spec prog: Sports, Sp 2 hrs wkly. ■ Larry Wilson, pres; Debbie Raborn, gen mgr; Gerry Schleget, gen sls mgr; Matt Bowers, prom mgr; Buddy Van Arsdale, progmg dir & mus dir; Adrienne Abbott, news dir; Dick DeWitt, pub affrs dir; Martin Stabbert, chief engr.

KRZQ-FM—(Tahoe City, Calif). Apr 5, 1985: 96.5 mhz; 4 kw. Ant 2,965 ft. TL: N39 18 47 W119 52 59. Stereo. Hrs opn: 24. 4600 Kietzke Ln., D-136, Reno, NV (89502). (702) 827-0965. FAX: (702) 827-8641. Licensee: Mid-South Broadcasting (acq 10-22-91; FTR 11-11-91). Rep: Major Mkt. Format: Modern rock. News progmg 3 hrs wkly. Target aud: 18-34. Spec prog: Metal shop 2 hrs wkly. ■ John P. Smith, pres; Daniel Cook, gen mgr & gen sls mgr; Rob Brooks, progmg dir; Max Volume, mus dir; Fred Giles, chief engr.

KTHX(FM)—Listing follows KOH(AM).

***KUNR(FM)**—Oct 7, 1963: 88.7 mhz; 20 kw. Ant 2,169 ft. TL: N39 15 34 W119 42 16. Stereo. Rm. 106, Educ. Bldg., Univ. of Nevada (89557). (702) 784-6591. FAX: (702) 784-4050. Licensee: Univ. of Nevada Board of Regents. Net: NPR, APR. Format: Class, news/talk, jazz. News progmg 30 hrs wkly. Target aud: General. Spec prog: Folk 2 hrs, ethnic 9 hrs wkly. ■ Marianne Murray, stn mgr; JoAnn Newbury, dev mgr; Carol Baker, prom mgr; David Gordon, progmg dir; Rex Gunderson, news dir; Joe Vermes, chief engr.

KWNZ(FM)—Listing follows KQLO(AM).

KXEQ(AM)—July 1946: 1340 khz; 1 kw-U. TL: N39 32 22 W119 46 53. Suite 101, 2001 E. Flamingo Rd., Las Vegas (89119). (702) 827-1313. Licensee: Rolando Collantes (group owner; acq 10-16-91; $30,000; FTR 11-4-91). Net: AP. Format: Relg. ■ Juan Morales, gen mgr & progmg dir; Dennis Silver, chief engr.

KXTO(AM)—Not on air, target date unknown: 1550 khz; 2.5 kw-D, 94 w-N. TL: N39 34 39 W119 50 52. 4604 Hurford Terrace, Encino, CA (91436). Licensee: First Broadcasting of Nevada Inc.

KZAK(FM)—(Incline Village) June 10, 1983: 100.1 mhz; 760 w. Ant 2,955 ft. TL: N39 18 38 W119 55 14. Stereo. Hrs opn: 24. 4012 Kietzke Ln. (89502). (702) 826-1986. FAX: (702) 826-2099. Licensee: New World Enterprises Inc. (acq 12-6-90; $1.33 million; FTR 12-31-90). Rep: Eastman. Wash atty: Imlay & Frerett. Format:

Broadcasting & Cable Yearbook 1994
B-231

Rock/AOR. News progmg 2 hrs wkly. Target aud: 18-34; general. ■ Dave Newman, pres & gen mgr; Greg Newman, prom dir; Todd Janes, adv mgr; Katie Foxx, progmg dir; Chris Paine, mus dir; Ric Karou, chief engr.

KZSR(FM)—Not on air, target date unknown: 92.9 mhz; 45 kw. Ant 2,653 ft. TL: N39 18 09 W119 27 46. Box 1241, Suess Path, Quogue, NY (11959). (203) 749-9673. Licensee: Susan Lundborg.

Sparks

KNDE(FM)—Listing follows KPLY(AM).

KPLY(AM)—Aug 9, 1960: 1270 khz; 5 kw-U, DA-2. TL: N39 32 03 W119 39 44. Hrs opn: 24. 4012 Kietzke Ln., Reno (89502). (702) 826-1986. FAX: (702) 826-2099. Licensee: New World Enterprises Inc. (acq 3-10-93; $750,000 with co-located FM; FTR 3-29-93). Net: ABC/I, MBS, NBC. Rep: Katz & Powell. Wash atty: Kaye, Scholer, Fierman, Hays & Handler. Format: Sports & info, talk. News staff one; news progmg 5 hrs wkly. Target aud: 25-54; primarily men who are interested in sports. ■ David T. Newman, pres & gen mgr; Todd James, gen sls mgr; Bob Ramsey, progmg dir; Katie Fox, pub affrs dir; Rick Karav, chief engr.

KNDE(FM)—Co-owned with KPLY(AM). July 1, 1983: 100.9 mhz; 2.9 kw. Ant 203 ft. TL: N39 22 04 W119 47 07. Stereo. Hrs opn: 24. Prog sep from AM. Format: Light AOR. News staff one; news progmg 2 hrs wkly. Target aud: 25-54.

KSRN(FM)—Not on air, target date unknown: 92.1 mhz; 440 w. Ant 804 ft. TL: N39 32 03 W119 39 44. Box 1033, Reno (89504). Licensee: Comstock Broadcasters Inc.

Sun Valley

KHIT(AM)—Jan 1, 1984: 1590 khz; 5 kw-D. TL: N39 24 57 W119 42 51. Hrs opn: 24. 2900 Sutro St., Reno (89512). Box 9870, Reno (89507). (702) 329-9261. FAX: (702) 323-1450. Licensee: Lotus Radio Corp. (group owner; acq 3-30-93; $600,000 with KHIT[FM] Reno; FTR 4-19-93). Rep: D & R Radio. Format: Country. News staff one; news progmg 3 hrs wkly. Target aud: 25-54. ■ Howard Kalmenson, pres; Carol J. Flynn, gen mgr & natl sls mgr; Martin Flynn, gen sls mgr; Cindy Calloway, prom dir; Dan Mason, progmg dir; Jim McClain, mus dir; Pat Frisch, news dir & pub affrs dir; Jack Parker, chief engr. ■ Rates: $30; 25; 30; 20.

KKNC(AM)—Not on air, target date unknown: 730 khz; 500 w-U. TL: N39 41 30 W119 46 45. Box 700, Folsom, CA (95630). Licensee: Cabellero Radio West Inc. (acq 10-28-91; $37,500 for CP, with CP KKNK(AM) Carson City; FTR 11-18-91).

Tonopah

KHWK(FM)—July 29, 1982: 92.7 mhz; 1 kw. Ant 970 ft. TL: N38 04 22 W117 13 16. Stereo. Hrs opn: 24. Box 1669 Station House Complex, 1100 Erie Main (89049); Box 1708 (89049). (702) 482-5724; (702) 482-5725. FAX: (702) 482-3832. Licensee: Western Adventures Radio Network (acq 3-16-92; $240,000 FTR 4-6-92). Format: AOR, adult contemp. News progmg 11 hrs wkly. Target aud: General; 12-54, tourists & travelers, residents. Spec prog: Classic rock, big band, country, oldies. ■ Dimitri Karambellas, pres & stn mgr; Lisa Douglas, gen sls mgr; Ron Payne, chief engr.

*KTPH(FM)—October 1988: 91.7 mhz; 100 w. Ant 1,433 ft. TL: N38 03 07 W117 13 30. 5151 Boulder Hwy., Las Vegas (89122). (702) 456-6695. Licensee: Nevada Public Radio Corp. Net: NPR. Format: Class, news. ■ Lamar Marchese, pres & gen mgr.

Virginia City

KNKQ(AM)—Not on air, target date unknown: 1160 khz; 5 kw-D. TL: N39 18 40 W119 39 43. c/o Box 2842, Steamboat Springs, CO (80477). Licensee: A. M. Renaissance Inc.

Wendover

KYOU(FM)—Not on air, target date unknown: 102.3 mhz; 93.8 kw. Ant 1,292 ft. TL: N41 05 10 W114 33 02. Box 1093 (89883). Licensee: Gerald L. Pugh (acq 11-30-92; $74,880; FTR 12-21-92).

Winchester

KZTY(AM)—Not on air, target date unknown: 620 khz; 500 w-D, 450 w-N, DA-2. TL: N36 03 40 W115 17 40. 2340 Sawtelle Blvd., West Los Angeles, CA (90064). Licensee: Winchester Broadcasting.

Winnemucca

KWNA(AM)—Jan 28, 1955: 1400 khz; 1 kw-U. TL: N40 57 23 W117 42 48. Hrs opn: 5 AM-midnight (Mon-Fri); 6 AM-midnight (Sat); 7 AM-midnight (Sun). Box 1400, 5130 E. Weikel Dr. (89446). (702) 623-5203. FAX: (702) 625-1011. Licensee: Sheen Broadcasting Co. (acq 9-15-81; $200,000; FTR 9-28-81). Net: ABC/I. Rep: Art Moore. Wash atty: Gardner, Carton & Douglas. Format: Adult contemp. News staff one; news progmg 12 hrs wkly. Target aud: General. Spec prog: Farm 2 hrs wkly. ■ Torrey Sheen, pres, gen mgr & chief engr; Kris Cook, gen sls mgr; Joyce Sheen, news dir.

KWNA-FM—Apr 3, 1982: 92.7 mhz; 60 w. Ant 2,120 ft. TL: N41 00 40 W117 45 59. Stereo. Hrs opn: 5 AM-midnight (Mon-Fri); 6 AM-midnight (Sat); 7 AM-midnight (Sun). Prog sep from AM. Format: C&W.

New Hampshire

Belmont

WCNH(FM)—Not on air, target date unknown: 93.3 mhz; 300 w. Ant 1020 ft. TL: N43 23 52 W71 33 03. Stereo. Box 422, Washington (03280-0422). Licensee: RadioWorks Inc. (acq 8-11-93; $104,836.89; FTR 8-30-93). Wash atty: Arent, Fox, Kintner, Plotkin & Kahn. ■ Lindsay Collins, pres; Stuart Richter, gen mgr; Brit Johnson, gen sls mgr.

Berlin

WMOU(AM)—1947: 1230 khz; 1 kw-U. TL: N44 27 32 W71 10 16. Hrs opn: 24. Box 489, 38 Glen Ave. (03570). (603) 752-1230. FAX: (603) 752-3117. Licensee: New England Broadcasting Inc. (acq 4-15-89). Net: ABC/I, AP, Unistar. Wash atty: Holme, Roberts & Owen. Format: Oldies. News staff one; news progmg 6 hrs wkly. Target aud: 25-54; local residents of northern N.H. Spec prog: Fr 3 hrs, talk 2 hrs, swap shop 3 hrs wkly. ■ Stephen E. Powell, pres; Jack O'Brien, gen mgr, progmg dir & mus dir; Jeanne Brockway, opns dir; Robert R. Powell, gen sls mgr & prom dir; Bob Barbin, news dir. ■ Rates: $18; 16; 16; 12.

WZPK(FM)—October 1952: 103.7 mhz; 22.5 kw. Ant 3,870 ft. TL: N44 16 14 W71 18 15. Stereo. Prog sep from AM. Box 489, 38 Glen Ave (03570). (603) 752-1230. FAX: (603) 752-3117. Licensee: New England Broadcasting Inc. Net: AP. Format: Hot adult contemp. News staff one; news progmg one hr wkly. Target aud: 25-49; New England residents. ■ Jack O'Brien, gen mgr & progmg dir. ■ Rates: $60; 40; 50; 30.

Campton

WVFM(FM)—Not on air, target date unknown: 105.7 mhz; 125 w. Ant 2,001 ft. TL: N43 57 32 W71 33 23. Stereo. Hrs opn: 24. Box 530, MT County Realty Bldg., Town Square, Waterville Valley (03215). (603) 236-8311, ext. 5560. FAX: (603) 236-4174. Licensee: White Mountain Radio. Wash atty: Gurman, Kurtis, Blask & Freedman. Format: CHR. Target aud: 25-54. ■ Darrel Clark, gen mgr.

Claremont

WTSV(AM)—1948: 1230 khz; 1 kw-U. TL: N43 22 15 W72 19 42. Box 1230, Rt. 12 & 103 (03743). (603) 542-7735. FAX: (603) 542-8721. Licensee: DynaCom Corp. Group owner: Cayuga/Northstar Radio Group (acq 11-84; $575,000; with co-located FM; FTR 9-10-84). Net: ABC/I. Rep: Roslin. Wash atty: Haley, Bader & Potts. Format: Nostalgia. News staff 2; news progmg 15 hrs wkly. Target aud: 35 plus. ■ Jeffrey Shapiro, pres & gen mgr; Will Stanley, gen sls mgr; Ken Barlow, progmg dir; Robert Lipman, news dir; Bob Smith, chief engr.

WHDQ(FM)—Co-owned with WTSV(AM). 1948: 106.1 mhz; 9.51 kw. Ant 1,068 ft. TL: N43 23 48 W72 18 01. Stereo. Prog sep from AM. Box 5106, West Lebanon (03784). Format: Adult rock. Spec prog: Blues 3 hrs wkly. ■ Will Stanley, vp sls; Dave Ashton, mus dir.

Concord

*WEVO(FM)—Aug 4, 1981: 89.1 mhz; 50 kw. Ant 385 ft. TL: N43 12 53 W71 33 28. Stereo. Hrs opn: 24. 207 N. Main St. (03301). (603) 228-8910. Licensee: New Hampshire Public Radio Inc. Net: NPR, APR. Format: Class, news. News staff 4; news progmg 36 hrs wkly. Target aud: 25-54; well educated males & females. Spec prog: Jazz 9 hrs, folk 5 hrs, world music 2 hrs wkly. ■ Mark Handley, pres; Mark Handley, Tricia Brooks (asst), gen mgrs; Larry Beavers, opns dir; Cathy Ives, sls dir; Janice Bailey, progmg mgr; Erik Nycklemoe, news dir.

WJYY(FM)—Sept 15, 1983: 105.5 mhz; 1.55 kw. Ant 456 ft. TL: N43 16 46 W71 30 15. Stereo. Hrs opn: 24. Box 1517 (03302-1517); 7 Perley St. (03301). (603) 228-9036; (603) 485-8104. FAX: (603) 224-7280. Licensee: RadioWorks Inc (group owner; acq 12-1-93). Rep: Eastman. Format: Adult rock. News staff one; news progmg 6 hrs wkly. Target aud: 25-44. ■ Stuart Richter, gen mgr; Brit Johnson, gen sls mgr; John Reynolds, progmg dir; Denise Vozella, news dir.

WKXL(AM)—June 15, 1946: 1450 khz; 1 kw-U. TL: N43 11 39 W71 33 17. Hrs opn: 18. Box 875 (03302-0875). 37 Redington Rd. (03301). (603) 225-5521; (603) 224-1450. FAX: (603) 224-6404. Licensee: Capitol Broadcasting Corp. Inc. (acq 6-80; $1.5 million with co-located FM; FTR 6-16-80). Net: CBS. Rep: New England. Wash atty: Fisher, Wayland, Cooper & Leader. Format: Div. News staff 2; news progmg 30 hrs wkly. Target aud: 35 plus; adults in Concord & contiguous towns. ■ Richard W. Osborne, pres & gen mgr; Donald A. Shapiro, CFO; Gardner F. Hill, opns mgr & progmg dir; J.W. Patrick Chaloux, vp sls; Patrick Chaloux, prom dir; Don Duncklee, mus dir; Randi Goldberg, news dir; Peter Stohrer, chief engr. ■ Rates: $37; 33; 37; 33.

WKXL-FM—Mar 7, 1972: 102.3 mhz; 3 kw. Ant 285 ft. TL: N43 13 00 W71 34 34. Stereo. Hrs opn: 5:30 AM-midnight. Dups AM 98%. Rep: New England. Wash atty: Fisher, Wayland, Cooper & Leader. ■ Rates: Same as AM.

WNHA(AM)—Not on air, target date unknown: 1140 khz; 10 kw-D, DA. TL: N43 09 39 W71 35 06. 4853 Manor Hill Dr., Syracuse, NY (13215). Licensee: Concord Broadcasting Assn.

*WSPS(FM)—1974: 90.5 mhz; 200 w. Ant 110 ft. TL: N43 11 37 W71 34 29. Hrs opn: 7 PM-midnight. St. Paul's School (03301). (603) 225-3341. Licensee: St. Paul's School. Format: Div. Target aud: General. ■ Heather Handley, gen mgr; Mike McCormack, stn mgr.

*WVNH(FM)—Not on air, target date unknown: 91.1 mhz; 1 kw. Ant 98 ft. TL: N43 18 34 W71 26 57. 67 Old Loudon Rd. (03301). Licensee: Capitol City Education Foundation.

Conway

WBNC(AM)—Dec 21, 1955: 1050 khz; 1 kw-D, 63 w-N. TL: N43 58 48 W71 06 36. E. Main St. (03818). (603) 447-5988. Licensee: North Country Radio Inc. (acq 3-23-59). Net: AP. Format: Adult contemp. Spec prog: Jazz 5 hrs wkly. ■ Lawrence H. Sherman, pres; Joan T.B. Sherman, gen sls mgr; George Cleveland, progmg dir; Frank DiFruscio, news dir; Deaen Luttrell, pub affrs dir; Charles E. Osgood, chief engr.

WMWV(FM)—Co-owned with WBNC(AM). June 23, 1967: 93.5 mhz; 3 kw. Ant 420 ft. TL: N43 56 46 W71 08 24. Stereo. Dups AM 98%.

WMLY(FM)—Not on air, target date unknown: 104.5 mhz; 3 kw. Ant 328 ft. TL: N43 55 34 71 05 46. Box 99, Franklin (03235). Licensee: Northeast Communications Corp. (group owner; acq 7-27-89; $89,000; FTR 8-14-89).

WMWV(FM)—Listing follows WBNC(AM).

Derry

WDER(AM)—October 1983: 1320 khz; 5 kw-D, 1 kw-N, DA-2. TL: N42 51 59 W71 17 14. Box 465, 8 Lawrence Rd. (03038). (603) 434-9302. FAX: (603) 434-1035. Licensee: Spacetown Communications Corp. Format: Contemp Christian. ■ Adam C. Gureckis Sr., pres & gen mgr; Gail Rehse, stn mgr; Bill Carozza, mus dir; Peter Gureckis, chief engr.

Dover

WOKQ(FM)—August 1970: 97.5 mhz; 50 kw. Ant 500 ft. TL: N43 13 26 W70 58 18. Stereo. Box 576 (03820). (603) 749-9750. FAX: (603) 749-1459. Licensee: Fuller-Jeffrey Broadcasting Corp. of New England. Group owner: Fuller-Jeffrey Broadcasting Companies Inc. (acq 6-23-77). Net: UPI. Rep: McGavren Guild. Format: Country. ■ Robert Fuller, pres; Martin Lessard, vp & gen mgr; Cliff Blake, opns mgr & progmg dir; Jan Leavitt, gen sls mgr; Mike Martel, prom mgr; Dan Lunnie, mus dir; Roger Wood, news dir; Gene Terwilliger, chief engr. ■ Rates: $175; 175; 175; 110.

WTSN(AM)—August 1956: 1270 khz; 5 kw-U, DA-2. TL: N43 11 01 W70 51 14. Hrs opn: 24. Box 400, 101 Back Rd. (03820-0400). (603) 742-1270. FAX: (603) 742-

0448. Licensee: Garrison City Broadcasting Inc. (acq 3-18-83). Net: ABC/I, NBC Talknet. Rep: Roslin. Wash atty: Gardener, Carton & Douglas. Format: News/talk, sports. News staff 3. Target aud: 25-54; very affluent. ■ Jerome Lipman, vp & gen mgr; Paul LeBlanc, opns mgr & chief engr; B.J. Hickman, gen sls mgr; Connie Hiller, mktg dir; Steve Dore, prom dir; James Gelinas, progmg dir; Donald Briand, news dir; Mike Pomp, pub affrs dir. ■ Rates: $42; 30; 32; 28.

Durham

*WUNH(FM)—July 15, 1963: 91.3 mhz; 17.5 kw. Ant 250 ft. TL: N43 09 23 W70 56 26. Stereo. Hrs opn: 18. Memorial Union Bldg., Univ. of New Hampshire (03824). (603) 862-2541; (603) 862-2087. FAX: (603) 862-3952. Licensee: Univ. of New Hampshire. Net: AP. Format: Progsv. News progmg one hr wkly. Target aud: General. Spec prog: Black 3 hrs, class 2 hrs, jazz 5 hrs, Pol 2 hrs, reggae 2 hrs, folk 4 hrs wkly. ■ Jeff Noel, gen mgr, dev mgr, sls dir, mktg mgr & prom mgr; Angela Coraccio, progmg mgr; Matt Saunders, mus dir; Steve Coviello, asst mus dir; Donna Hyatt, Glenn Hauser, news dirs; Angela Coraccio, Matt Travis, pub affrs dirs; Wayne Scott, chief engr.

Exeter

WERZ(FM)—Listing follows WMYF(AM).

WMYF(AM)—June 4, 1966: 1540 khz; 5 kw-D. TL: N42 59 23 W70 56 14. Box 1540 (03833). (603) 772-4757. FAX: (603) 772-8464. Licensee: Precision Media Corp. Group owner: Precision Media L.P. (acq 7-23-87; $5.2 million with co-located FM; FTR 6-22-87). Net: SMN. Rep: McGavren Guild. Format: Stardust. ■ Tim Montgomery, pres; Al Perry, gen mgr; Tom Fucci, stn mgr; Pete Falconi, opns mgr & progmg dir; Wendy Larson, gen sls mgr; Jon Collins, news dir; Bob Perry, chief engr.

WERZ(FM)—Co-owned with WMYF(AM). Sept 21, 1972: 107.1 mhz; 5.2 kw. Ant 351 ft. TL: N43 01 38 W70 52 51. Prog sep from AM. Format: Contemp hits. ■ Stella Mars, mus dir.

*WPEA(FM)—1964: 90.5 mhz; 115 w. Ant 170 ft. TL: N42 58 44 W70 57 00. Stereo. Box 2652, Phillips Exeter Academy (03833). (603) 772-4311. FAX: (603) 778-9563. Licensee: Trustees of Phillips Exeter Academy. Format: Classic rock. Target aud: General; students. Spec prog: Class 2 hrs, Christian mus 2 hrs wkly. ■ Mike Wilson, gen mgr; John Englund, stn mgr.

Farmington

WRHF(FM)—Not on air, target date unknown: 106.5 mhz; 376 w. Ant 935 ft. TL: N43 19 48 W71 01 11. Box 326, Pinkham Notch Rd., Jackson (03846). Licensee: Stephen E. Powell.

Franklin

WFTN(AM)—Oct 30, 1966: 1240 khz; 1 kw-U. TL: N43 27 16 W71 38 33. Box 941, Babbitt Rd. (03235). (603) 934-2500. FAX: (603) 924-2933. Licensee: Northeast Communications Corp. (group owner; acq 9-30-74). Net: ABC/E. Format: Oldies. ■ Jeff Fisher, pres; Fred Caruso, progmg dir & mus dir.

WFTN-FM—Apr 10, 1987: 94.1 mhz; 6 kw. Ant 328 ft. TL: N43 28 23 W71 37 36 20. Stereo. Format: Adult contemp.

Gorham

WJTK(FM)—Not on air, target date unknown: 107.1 mhz; 6 kw. Ant 157 ft. Box 326, Pinkham Notch Rd., Jackson (03846). Licensee: Gladys E. Powell.

Hampton

WZEA(FM)—Not on air, target date unknown: 102.1 mhz; 3 kw. Ant 328 ft. TL: N42 53 51 W70 53 02. Box 280, North Hampton (03862). Licensee: Coastal Broadcasting Corp.

Hanover

WDCR(AM)—Mar 4, 1958: 1340 khz; 1 kw-U. TL: N43 41 59 W72 16 47. Hrs opn: 21. Box 957, Robinson Hall (03755). (603) 646-3313; (603) 643-7625. FAX: (603) 643-7655. Licensee: Trustees of Dartmouth College. Net: NBC. Rep: New England. Format: Div, Black, progsv. News progmg 4 hrs wkly. Target aud: General. Spec prog: Class 8 hrs, jazz 6 hrs, reggae 9 hrs, metal 3 hrs wkly. ■ Amt Ertel, gen mgr; Winona LaCoss, stn mgr; Tim Hoehn, natl sls mgr; Laura Daniels, rgnl sls mgr; Charlotte Flower, progmg dir; Brad Byrd, mus dir; Diego Prange, asst mus dir; Adrienne Kim, news dir; Ted Schuerzinger, pub affrs dir; Grant Bosse, engrg dir; Gary Savoie, chief engr.

WFRD(FM)—Co-owned with WDCR(AM). Feb 19, 1976: 99.3 mhz; 3.4 kw. Ant 285 ft. TL: N43 39 14 W72 17 43. Stereo. Hrs opn: 24. Prog sep from AM. Format: AOR. Target aud: 18-45. Spec prog: Metal 2 hrs, blues 2 hrs, alternative one hr wkly.

*WEVH(FM)—Not on air, target date unknown: 91.3 mhz; 150 w. Ant 1,240 ft. TL: N43 42 30 W72 09 16. 207 N. Main St., Concord (03301). (603) 228-8910. FAX: (603) 224-6052. Licensee: New Hampshire Public Radio Inc. ■ Mark Handley, gen mgr; Janice Bailey, news dir; Cathy Ives, pub affrs dir; Erik Nycklemoe, Larry Beavers, chiefs engr.

WFRD(FM)—Listing follows WDCR(AM).

WGXL(FM)—Listing follows WTSL(AM).

WNBX(FM)—See Lebanon.

WTSL(AM)—October 1950: 1400 khz; 1 kw-U. TL: N43 41 03 W72 17 46. Stereo. Hrs opn: 5:30 AM-midnight. Box 1400, The Mall, Lebanon (03766-0526). (603) 448-1400. FAX: (603) 448-1755. Licensee: RJ Communications Inc. (acq 12-14-92; $665,000 with co-located FM; FTR 1-11-93). Net: ABC/E, CBS. Rep: Kettell-Carter. Wash atty: Cohn & Marks. Format: Adult contemp, news/talk. News staff 3; news progmg 20 hrs wkly. Target aud: 35 plus. ■ Scott Roberts, pres; Tom Barney, gen mgr; Bob Sherman, gen sls mgr; Ray Reed, progmg dir; Mary Rozak, news dir; Ira Wilner, chief engr.

WGXL(FM)—Co-owned with WTSL(AM). Jan 12, 1987: 92.3 mhz; 3 kw. Ant 326 ft. TL: N43 39 17 W72 17 41. Stereo. Prog sep from AM. Format: Adult contemp. News progmg 3 hrs wkly. Target aud: 20 plus.

Haverhill

WYKR-FM—Feb 19, 1990: 101.3 mhz; 3 kw. Ant 39 ft. TL: N44 06 49 W71 58 54. Stereo. Hrs opn: 6 AM-10 PM. Box 1013, Woodsville (03785); Box 1100, Rt. 5, Historic Brick School House, Wells River, VT (05081). (802) 757-2773. FAX: (802) 757-8001. Licensee: Puffer Broadcasting Inc. Net: Drake-Chenault. Rep: Roslin. Wash atty: John Wilner. Format: Country. Target aud: 25 plus. Spec prog: Farm one hr wkly. ■ Stephen Puffer, pres, gen mgr, gen sls mgr & prom mgr; David Labounty, progmg dir, mus dir & news dir.

Henniker

*WNEC-FM—Feb 9, 1971: 91.7 mhz; 120 w. Ant -210 ft. TL: N43 10 34 W71 49 22. Hrs opn: 17. New England College, Danforth Library (03242). (603) 428-2278; (603) 428-2211. Licensee: New England College. Net: ABC/I, CBS/FM. Format: Progsv. News progmg one hr wkly. Target aud: 18-25; college students. Spec prog: Classic rock 3 hrs, blues 3 hrs, folk 3 hrs, country 3 hrs, jazz 3 hrs, world music 3 hrs wkly. ■ Megan Collier, gen mgr & asst mus dir; Clyde Hoey, progmg dir; Jon Kovar, pub affrs dir; Pete Stohrer, chief engr.

WNNH(FM)—Nov 17, 1989: 99.1 mhz; 6 kw. Ant 712 ft. TL: N43 09 17 W71 47 44. Stereo. Hrs opn: 24. 501 South St., Concord (03304). (603) 225-1160. FAX: (603) 225-5938. Licensee: Clark Broadcasting of New Hampshire Inc. Rep: D & R Radio. Wash atty: Verner, Liipfert, Bernhard, McPherson & Hand. Format: Oldies. News staff 2; news progmg 20 hrs wkly. Target aud: 25-54; mass appeal. ■ Clark F. Smidt, CEO, pres & gen mgr; Paul J. Fuller, stn mgr & gen sls mgr; Peter St. James, opns mgr; Bill York, rgnl sls mgr; Konrad Kayne, prom dir; Jim Kenton, mus dir; Dave B. Emerson, news dir; Bob Smith, engrg dir; Gary Hammond, engrg mgr; Larry Beavers, chief engr. ■ Rates: $50; 40; 40; 30.

Hillsboro

WRCI(FM)—Oct 1, 1989: 107.7 mhz; 3 kw. Ant -276 ft. TL: N43 06 53 W71 56 20. Stereo. Dups WJJY(FM) Concord 100%. Box 1517, 7 Perley St., Concord (03302-1517). (603) 478-1077. FAX: (603) 224-7280. Licensee: RadioWorks Inc acq 12-1-93). Rep: Eastman. Format: Adult contemp. News staff one; news progmg 8 hrs wkly. Target aud: 25-54. ■ Stuart Richter, stn mgr; Brit Johnson, gen sls mgr; Denise Vozella, news dir; Peter Stohrer, chief engr.

Hinsdale

WYRY(FM)—Licensed to Hinsdale. See Keene.

Jackson

WZJN(FM)—Not on air, target date unknown: 99.5 mhz; 465 w. Ant 833 ft. TL: N44 07 58 W71 09 25. Box 176 (03846). Licensee: Jackson Radio Partnership.

Keene

*WEVN(FM)—Not on air, target date unknown: 90.7 mhz; 1.5 kw. Ant 938 ft. 207 N. Main St., Concord (03301). Licensee: New Hampshire Public Radio Inc.

WKBK(AM)—May 1959: 1220 khz; 1 kw-U. TL: N42 55 50 W72 17 56. 13 Lamson St. (03431). (603) 352-6113. FAX: (603) 357-4582. Licensee: Roberts Communications Inc. (acq 6-25-91; grpsl; FTR 7-15-91). Net: ABC/C. Rep: Savalli. Format: Local talk. News staff one; news progmg 7 hrs wkly. Target aud: General. ■ Brent Myers, vp & gen mgr; Dave Packer, vp opns & vp prom; Dan Mitchell, vp progmg; Paul Scheuring, news dir. ■ Rates: $22; 18; 22; 18.

WKNE(AM)—June 2, 1927: 1290 khz; 5 kw-U, DA-1. TL: N42 56 56 W72 18 22. Box 466, Stanhope Ave. (03431). (603) 352-9230. FAX: (603) 357-3926. Licensee: L. B. New Hampshire Inc. (acq 11-88; $5.5 million with co-located FM; FTR 9-26-88). Net: CBS. Rep: Kadetsky. Format: MOR. News staff 2. Target aud: 25 plus. Spec prog: Big band 4 hrs wkly. ■ Richard Lightfoot, pres; Michael Trombly, gen mgr & chief engr; Gary James, stn mgr; Donald Gibb, vp sls; Ray Brewer, news dir.

WKNE-FM—May 1964: 103.7 mhz; 12.2 kw. Ant 991 ft. TL: N43 02 00 W72 22 04. Stereo. Prog sep from AM. Rep: Kadetsky. Format: Adult hit radio. News staff 2; news progmg 2 hrs wkly. Target aud: 18-49. ■ Gary James, progmg dir & mus dir.

*WKNH(FM)—November 1975: 91.3 mhz; 274 w. Ant 79 ft. TL: N42 55 29 W72 16 42 (CP: 91.7 mhz, 192 w, ant 363 ft.). Stereo. Hrs opn: 24. Elliot Hall, Keene State College (03431). (603) 358-2417. FAX: (603) 358-2257. Licensee: Bd of Trustees, University System of New Hampshire. Format: Progsv. News progmg 3 hrs wkly. Target aud: General; anyone who seeks to hear an alternative to what is offered. Spec prog: Class 4 hrs, folk 6 hrs, jazz 3 hrs, blues 3 hrs, reggae 4 hrs, Greek 2 hrs, new age 2 hrs, Irish 2 hrs wkly. ■ Carmen Darkangelo, gen mgr; Michael Colby, gen sls mgr & prom mgr; Jason Bersani, progmg dir; Adam Dobrowolski, asst mus dir; William Trafton, news dir; Mike Wakefield, chief engr.

WXOD(FM)—See Winchester.

WYRY(FM)—(Hinsdale). June 30, 1987: 104.9 mhz; 1.55 kw. Ant 456 ft. TL: N42 46 33 W72 27 19 (CP: 725 w, ant 669 ft.). Stereo. Hrs opn: 24. 30-10 Winchester, Keene (03431). (603) 357-5000; (603) 363-8880. FAX: (603) 357-1583. Licensee: Tri-Valley Broadcasting Corp. (acq 8-86). Net: SMN. Rep: Roslin. Wash atty: Reddy, Beyley & Martin. Format: Country. News staff 3; news progmg 10 hrs wkly. Target aud: 25-49; upscale adults & business decision makers. ■ Michael T. Decker, vp & gen mgr; Mark Johnson, news dir. ■ Rates: $30; 24; 30; 18.

Laconia

WEMJ(AM)—April 9, 1961: 1490 khz; 1 kw-U. TL: N43 32 29 W71 27 45. Box 1490 (03247). (603) 524-6050. FAX: (603) 528-6397. Licensee: Tole Broadcast Assocs. (acq 12-88; $800,000; FTR 12-19-88). Net: CBS, MBS. Rep: D & R Radio. Format: All talk. ■ Robert Tole, pres, gen mgr & gen sls mgr; Chris Michaels, progmg dir & news dir; John Kozel, chief engr.

WLNH-FM—Nov 22, 1965: 98.3 mhz; 1.9 kw. Ant 413 ft. TL: N43 35 46 W71 29 55 (CP: 3.8 kw, ant 412 ft.). Box 7326, Village W., Gilford (03247). (603) 524-1323. FAX: (603) 528-5185. Licensee: WLNH Radio Inc. Group owner: Sconnix Broadcasting Co. (acq 6-25-75). Format: Hot adult contemp. ■ Scott McQueen, pres; Carl DeProspo, gen mgr; Craig Sikofki, gen sls mgr; Paul Ciliano, progmg dir; Richard Wholey, chief engr. ■ Rates: $35; 22; 29; 11.

WLNH(AM)—Aug 22, 1922: 1350 khz; 5 kw-D, 112 w-N. TL: N43 30 27 W71 31 00. Prog dups FM 100%.

Lancaster

WLGW(AM)—Not on air, target date unknown: 1490 khz; 1 kw-U. TL: N44 29 42 W71 33 10 (CP: TL: N44 29 41 W71 35 37). Box 111 (03584). (603) 788-4778. FAX: (603) 788-4035. Licensee: Michael Beattie. ■ Michael Beattie, pres.

WLGW-FM—Not on air, target date Unknown: 102.3 mhz; 6 kw. Ant -66 ft. TL: N44 33 20 W71 34 30.

New Hampshire

Lebanon

WGXL(FM)—See Hanover.

WHDQ(FM)—See Claremont.

WNBX(FM)—Dec 18, 1990: 100.5 mhz; 6 kw. Ant 689 ft. TL: N43 37 17 W72 10 30. Hrs opn: 24. 19 Boas Ln., Wilton, CT (06897); Suite 300; 1 Court St. (03766). (603) 448-0500; (203) 762-9425. FAX: (203) 431-8473. Licensee: Radio South Burlington Inc. Jackson Group. Net: MBS, Daynet, ABC, NBC Talknet. Rep: The Northeast Co. Wash atty: Cohn & Marks. Format: News/talk, pub affrs. News staff 3; news progmg 20 hrs wkly. Target aud: 25 plus; upscale adults. ■ Dennis Jackson, chmn; Bob Vinikoor, stn mgr. ■ Rates: $25; 25; 25; 25.

Lisbon

WLTN-FM—Sept 1, 1991: 96.7 mhz; 6 kw. Ant 295 ft. TL: N44 13 11 W71 52 07 Stereo. Prog sep from AM. Box 349, 20 Main St., Littleton (03561). Licensee: Profile Broadcasting Co. Inc. Net: ABC/I. New England. Format: Classic rock, oldies. News staff 2; news progmg 7 hrs wkly. Target aud: 21-54. ■ Judith F. Aydelott, vp; Brad Bailey, gen mgr & vp sls; Vicki MacKay, opns dir; Jackie Scott, prom dir. ■ Rates: Same as AM.

Littleton

WLTN(AM)—Oct 10, 1963: 1400 khz; 1 kw-U. TL: N44 18 47 W71 46 08. Box 349, 20 Main St. (03561). (603) 444-3911. FAX: (603) 444-7186. Licensee: Profile Broadcasting Co. (acq 7-1-75). Net: ABC/I. Rep: New England. Format: News/talk, sports. News staff 2; news progmg 40 hrs wkly. Target aud: 21-65. ■ Peter C. Aydelott, pres & gen mgr; Vicky Mackay, opns mgr; Brad Bailey, gen sls mgr; Jackie Scott, progmg dir; Todd Lambert, mus dir; Jim Clothey, news dir; Charles Ryan, chief engr. ■ Rates: $20.60; 20.60; 20.60; 16.80.

WMTK(FM)—Feb 23, 1985: 106.3 mhz; 390 w. Ant 1,256 ft. TL: N44 21 14 W71 44 23. Stereo. Hrs opn: 24. Box 106, Thayers Inn, 136 Main St. (03561-0106). (603) 444-5106. Licensee: White Mountain FM Inc. Rep: Roslin. Wash atty: Fletcher, Heald & Hildreth. Format: Classic rock. News staff one. Spec prog: Blues power hour, Dead Zone. ■ Tom Pancoast, CEO; Rick DeFabio, gen mgr; Chris Miller, progmg dir; Jennifer James, news dir; Ira Wilner, chief engr. ■ Rates: $25; 18; 20; 15.

Madbury

WWNH(AM)—May 20, 1989: 1340 khz; 250 w-U. TL: N43 10 22 W70 55 00. Hrs opn: 24. Box 69, Rt. 155, Dover (03820). (603) 742-8575. FAX: (603) 743-6444. Licensee: Harvest Broadcasting. Net: UPI, USA, Moody. Format: MOR. News progmg 3 hrs wkly. Target aud: General; 29 plus. Spec prog: Family 24 hrs wkly. ■ Brian Dodge, CEO, pres, gen mgr, gen sls mgr & engrg dir; Liz Dodge, vp; Barbara Winson, chief opns & prom dir; Ernie Jenkins, progmg dir, mus dir & news dir. ■ Rates: $25; 25; 25; 25.

Manchester

WFEA(AM)—Mar 8, 1932: 1370 khz; 5 kw-U, DA-2. TL: N42 54 26 W71 27 45. 500 Commercial St. (03101). (603) 669-5777. FAX: (603) 669-4641. Licensee: Saga Communications of New England Inc. (group owner; acq 6-2-92); grpsl, including co-located FM). Net: CBS. Rep: McGavren Guild. Wash atty: Gary Smithwick. Format: MOR, nostaglia. News staff one; news progmg 10 hrs wkly. Target aud: 35 plus; "modern maturity" market. Spec prog: Fr 2 hrs wkly. ■ Ed Christian, CEO; Raymond C. Garon, gen mgr; Tom Kallechey, opns dir & progmg dir; Andy Orcutt, gen sls mgr. ■ Rates: $40; 30; 30; 20.

WZID(FM)—Co-owned with WFEA(AM). 1948: 95.7 mhz; 14.5 kw. Ant 930 ft. TL: N42 59 02 W71 35 22. Prog sep from AM. Format: Adult contemp. Target aud: 25-54. ■ Sally Dionne, news dir; Dan Guy, chief engr. ■ Rates: $125; 115; 115; 100.

WGIR(AM)—October 1941: 610 khz; 5 kw-D, 1 kw-N, DA-2. TL: N43 00 57 W71 28 48. Box 610 (03105). (603) 625-6915. FAX: (603) 625-9255. Licensee: Knight Radio Inc. Group owner: Knight Quality Group Stns. (acq 4-91). Net: ABC. Rep: Banner, Knight. Format: News/talk, sports. ■ Norman Knight, pres; Al Cappannelli, progmg dir; Dan Pierce, news dir; Warren Small, chief engr.

WGIR-FM—June 5, 1963: 101.1 mhz; 11.5 kw. Ant 1,027 ft. TL: N42 58 54 W71 35 21. Stereo. Prog sep from AM. Box 101 (03105). Format: AOR. ■ Jon Erdahl, opns mgr & progmg dir; Karen Andersen, mus dir.

*WLMW(FM)—Not on air, target date unknown: 90.7 mhz; 15 w. Ant 886 ft. 134 Hollis Rd., Amherst (03031). Licensee: Knowledge For Life.

WOKQ(FM)—See Dover.

*WRND(FM)—Not on air, target date unknown: 91.7 mhz; 1 w-H, 100 w-V. Ant 13 ft. TL: N43 00 50 W71 27 58. 2321 Elm St. (03104). Licensee: Notre Dame College.

WZID(FM)—Listing follows WFEA(AM).

Meredith

WWSS(FM)—Nov 16, 1988: 101.5 mhz; 3 kw. Ant 302 ft. TL: N43 38 28 W71 29 53. Stereo. Box 505, Rt. 3, Ladd Hill (03253). Licensee: Latchkey Broadcasting Inc. ■ Gary Howard, pres; Keith Murray, gen mgr.

Moultonborough

WSCY(FM)—May 31, 1993: 106.9 mhz; 150 w. Ant 1,961 ft. TL: N43 46 09 W71 18 52. Stereo. Box 577 (03254). (603) 253-8080. Licensee: Northeast Communications Corp. (group owner; acq 5-4-93; $399,072; FTR 5-24-93). Format: Hot country. ■ Jeff Fisher, pres; Jane Thurston, stn mgr.

Mt. Washington

WHOM(FM)—July 9, 1958: 94.9 mhz; 48 kw. Ant 3,760 ft. TL: N44 16 13 W71 18 13 (CP: Ant 46 ft.). Stereo. 477 Congress St., Portland, ME (04101). (207) 773-0200. FAX: (207) 773-5770. Licensee: Northland Broadcasting Inc. Group owner: Barnstable Broadcasting Inc. (acq 1-12-87; $7 million; FTR 12-8-86). Rep: Republic. Format: Easy lstng. News staff one; news progmg 7 hrs wkly. Target aud: 35-64; professionals with active lifestyles. ■ David Gingold, pres; Judy Sher, gen mgr; Barbara Cole, natl sls mgr; Tim Moore, progmg dir; Charle Goode, chief engr.

Nashua

WHOB(FM)—Oct 19, 1987: 106.3 mhz; 3 kw. Ant 100 ft. TL: N42 44 07 W71 23 37 (CP: 950 w. Ant 541 ft.). Stereo. Hrs opn: 24. 55 Lake St. (03060). (603) 889-1063. FAX: (603) 882-0688. Licensee: Gateway Broadcast Assoc. (acq 1987). Rep: Torbet. Wash atty: Cole, Raywid & Braverman. Format: Adult contemp, CHR. News staff one; news progmg 5 hrs wkly. Target aud: 18-49. ■ Mario DiCarlo, pres & gen mgr; Mike Bradley, stn mgr; Norman Kruglak, gen sls mgr; Paula Stone, progmg dir & mus dir; Joan Stylianos, news dir; Gary Hammond, chief engr.

WSMN(AM)—Mar 9, 1958: 1590 khz; 5 kw-U, DA-1. TL: N42 44 40 W71 29 52. Hrs opn: 18. Box 548, 502 W. Hollis St. (03061). (603) 882-5107. Licensee: 1590 Broadcasting Corp. (acq 4-23-59). Net: Moody. Rep: New England. Format: Oldies. News staff 2; news progmg 21 hrs wkly. Target aud: General. Spec prog: Fr 3 hrs, Pol one hr wkly. ■ Maurice R. Parent, gen mgr & prom mgr; John Halbert, progmg dir; Frank Palazzi, mus dir; Kevin Bowland, chief engr.

New London

WNTK-FM—Nov 30, 1992: 99.7 mhz; 840 w. Ant 613 ft. Hrs opn: 24. Box 2295 (03257). (603) 448-0500. FAX: (603) 526-9464. Licensee: Koor Communications Inc. Net: MBS, ABC TalkRadio, Daynet. Rep: Northeast Co. (Boston). Format: Talk. ■ Dennis Jackson, CEO, pres & gen mgr; Robert L. Vinikoor, stn mgr; Rush Limbaugh, progmg dir; Russ McAlister, chief engr.

Newport

WNTK(AM)—Aug 11, 1960: 1020 khz; 10 kw-D. TL: N43 21 52 W72 10 45. Box 2295, 250 Newport Rd., New London (03257); Box 249, Meadowbrook Rd., Norwich VT (05055). (603) 526-9464; (603) 448-0500. Licensee: KOOR Communications (acq 8-88; $250,000; FTR 8-29-88). Net: ABC TalkRadio, MBS. Rep: The Northeast Co. (Boston). Wash atty: Fisher, Wayland, Cooper & Leader. Format: Talk. News staff 2; news progmg 25 hrs wkly. Target aud: 25-54; informed adults. ■ Robert L. Vinikoor, pres & gen mgr; Luka Andrews, news dir; Janine Zabriskie, pub affrs dir; Russ McAlister, chief engr. ■ Rates: $16; 16; 16; 12.

WXXK-FM—1971: 101.7 mhz; 3 kw. Ant 2,006 ft. TL: N43 23 45 W72 17 40 (CP: Ant 1,115 ft.). Stereo. Hrs opn: 24. 25 Pine St., Claremont (03743). (603) 543-1511. FAX: (603) 543-1706. Licensee: Mountain View Broadcasting Inc. (acq 9-27-89; $2 million; FTR 10-16-89). Net: CNN, Unistar, Moody. Wash atty: Arent, Fox, Kintner, Plotkin & Kahn. Format: Contemp country. News staff one. Target aud: 25-54. ■ Robert Frisch, pres; John Gales, gen mgr;

Jane Dearden, gen sls mgr; John B. Gales, mktg mgr; Mike Walker, progmg dir & mus dir; Chris Frey, news dir; Doug Danzing, pub affrs dir & engrg mgr. ■ Rates: $32; 27; 32; 24.

Peterborough

WNHQ(FM)—June 1971: 92.1 mhz; 250 w. Ant 1,120 ft. TL: N42 51 28 W71 52 52. Stereo. Hrs opn: 24. Box 59, Granite Bank, Suite 3, Jones Rd., Milford (03055). (603) 672-9292. FAX: (603) 672-4114. Licensee: Peterborough Broadcasting Co. Inc. Net: CNN. Rep: Kettell-Carter. Format: Adult contemp. News staff one; news progmg 20 hrs wkly. Target aud: 25-54. ■ William (Bill) R. Williamson, exec vp & gen mgr; Tony Gerard, progmg dir; Laura Hallahan, news dir.

Plymouth

*WPCR-FM—Sept 29, 1974: 91.7 mhz; 215 w. Ant 95 ft. WPCR, Plymouth State College (03264). (603) 535-2242. FAX: (603) 535-2783. Licensee: Plymouth State College. Net: AP. Format: AOR. ■ Tim Williams, gen mgr; Michael Davidson, chief opns; Amy Watson, progmg dir; C.J. Walsh, mus dir; Fred Portnoy, chief engr.

WPNH(AM)—Nov 10, 1965: 1300 khz; 5 kw-D. TL: N43 46 32 W71 42 20. 2 High St. (03264). (603) 536-2500. FAX: (603) 536-4610. Licensee: Pemigewasset Broadcasters Inc. Group owner: Close Communications (acq 8-87; $1.32 million; FTR 8-3-87). Net: NBC. Rep: Kettell-Karter. Format: Quality rock. News staff one; news progmg 10 hrs wkly. Target aud: 18-49. Spec prog: Breakfast with the Bands 6 hrs, country 4 hrs wkly. ■ Elmer (Hal) Close, pres; Jim Riley, opns mgr, progmg dir & mus dir; Peter Petengill, gen sls mgr & stn mgr; Peter Kadetsky, rgnl sls mgr; Sue Ryan, news dir; Kevin Bowland, chief engr.

WPNH-FM—Oct 1, 1975: 100.1 mhz; 2.35 kw. Ant 364 ft. TL: N43 45 41 W71 38 59 (CP: 4.9 kw, ant 358 ft.). Stereo. Dups AM 75%. Format: Classic rock.

Portsmouth

WCQL(AM)—Dec 5, 1960: 1380 khz; 1 kw-U, DA-N. TL: N43 03 48 W70 47 09. Hrs opn: 24. 1555 Islington St. (03801). (603) 430-9500. FAX: (603) 430-9501. Licensee: Sunshine Group Broadcasting Inc. (acq 3-13-89; $1 million; FTR 2-13-89). Format: Sports/talk. Target aud: 25-54. ■ George Silverman, pres & gen mgr; Mark White, gen sls mgr; Scott Mason, progmg dir.

WERZ(FM)—See Exeter.

WHEB(FM)—Jan 14, 1964: 100.3 mhz; 31 kw. Ant 161 ft. TL: N43 03 02 W70 45 59 (CP: Ant 446 ft. TL: N43 03 05 W70 46 09). Stereo. Box 120 (03802). (603) 436-7300. FAX: (603) 430-4415. Licensee: Knight Broadcasting of New Hampshire Inc. Group owner: Knight Quality Group Stations (acq 1-22-59). Net: UPI. Rep: Banner. Format: Rock 'n roll. News staff 3; news progmg 2 hrs wkly. Target aud: 18-49. ■ Scott Knight, pres; Robert A. Knight, gen mgr; Shari Soffen, gen sls mgr; Glenn Stewart, progmg dir; Scott Laudani, mus dir; Kenneth Neenan, chief engr.

WMYF(AM)—See Exeter.

Rochester

WWEM(FM)—Oct 21, 1979: 96.7 mhz; 3 kw. Ant 328 ft. TL: N43 17 14 W70 56 49 (CP: 5.8 kw, ant 98 ft., TL: N43 23 40 W71 02 22). Stereo. Hrs opn: 24. Box 130, 113 Rochester Hill Rd. (03867). (603) 332-0930. FAX: (603) 332-0800. Licensee: Bear Broadcasting Co. (group owner; acq 6-90; $1.8 million with co-located AM; FTR 6-4-90). Net: Unistar. Rep: D & R Radio. Wash atty: Wiley, Rein & Fielding. Format: Adult contemp. News staff 3; news progmg 12 hrs wkly. Target aud: 25-54. ■ Philip Urso, pres; Thom Fucci, gen mgr; Liz Richards, news dir; Bob Perry, chief engr. ■ Rates: $40; 40; 40; 30.

WZNN(AM)—Co-owned with WWEM(FM). 1947: 930 khz; 5 kw-U, DA-N. TL: N43 17 13 W70 56 55. Hrs opn: 24. Prog sep from FM. Net: CNN. Format: News/talk. Target aud: 25-64; decision-makers, heads of businesses, households.

Salem

WNNW(AM)—Jan 10, 1977: 1110 khz; 5 kw-D, DA-D. TL: N43 45 42 W71 16 13. Box 1110 (03079); 462 Merrimack St., Methuen, MA (01844). (508) 894-1110; (508) 686-9966. FAX: (508) 687-1180. Licensee: Costa Communications (acq 6-17-88). Net: CNN. Rep: Roslin. Wash atty: Bryan, Cave, McPheeters & McRoberts. Format: Sp. News progmg 25 hrs wkly. Target aud: Spanish-speaking of all ages. ■ Pat Costa, gen mgr; David

Martinez, opns mgr & progmg mgr; James Metcalfe, gen sls mgr; Johnny MacKenzie, mus dir; Luis Pena, news dir; Linda Fernandez, pub affrs dir; Bob Perry, chief engr.

Winchester

WKBK(AM)—See Keene.

WXOD(FM)—Oct 15, 1991: 98.7 mhz; 6 kw. Ant 328 ft. TL: N42 49 56 W72 23 34. Stereo. Hrs opn: 24. Box 707, 13 Lamson St., Keene (03431). (603) 352-6113. FAX: (603) 357-4582. Licensee: Roberts Communications Inc. (acq 6-25-91; grpsl; FTR 7-15-91). Net: ABC/C. Format: Oldies. News staff 4. Target aud: 25-54. ■ Brent Myers, pres & stn mgr; Dave Packer, vp opns, vp prom, vp progmg & mus dir; Patrick M. Thomas, exec vp; Paul Scheuring, news dir; Dan Shaw, pub affrs dir; Bob Smith, chief engr. ■ Rates: $29; 24; 29; 24.

Wolfeboro

WASR(AM)—April 1970: 1420 khz; 5 kw-D. TL: N43 31 W71 13 12. Hrs opn: 5 AM-8 PM. Box 900, Varney Rd. (03894-0900). (603) 569-2232; (603) 279-8009. FAX: (603) 569-1900. Licensee: Radio Wolfeboro Inc. Net: ABC/E, AP. Format: MOR, news. News staff 4; news progmg 35 hrs wkly. Target aud: 25-54. ■ Alan W. Severy, pres & gen mgr; Dave Allison, opns mgr & mus dir; Sharon J. Severy, gen sls mgr; Charles Katt, prom mgr. ■ Rates: $25; 20; 20; na.

WLKZ(FM)—Feb 1, 1985: 104.9 mhz; 3 kw. Ant 300 ft. TL: N43 37 07 W71 13 17 (CP: 380 w, ant 912 ft.). Stereo. Hrs opn: 24. 21 Production Pl., No. 15, Gilford (03246-6622). (603) 524-0105. FAX: (603) 293-0699. Licensee: The Fifth Estate Inc. Net: Unistar. Rep: McGavren Guild. Format: Oldies. News staff 2; news progmg 5 hrs wkly. Target aud: 25-54; baby boomers. ■ Jay Williams, pres; Dirk Nadon, gen mgr, stn mgr & progmg mgr; Chris Conley, news dir; Gene Tewilleger, chief engr. ■ Rates: $22; 16; 18; 14.

New Jersey

Asbury Park

WHTG(AM)—See Eatontown.

WJLK(AM)—1926: 1310 khz; 2.5 kw-D, 1 kw-N, DA-2. TL: N40 13 47 W74 05 27. Box 880, Press Plaza, 605 Mattison (07712). (908) 774-7700. FAX: (908) 988-0777. Licensee: D & F Broadcasting Inc. (acq 3-6-89; $12.5 million with co-located FM; FTR 3-6-89). Net: AP. Format: Oldies, news. ■ Charles Cohn, vp; Garry Guida, progmg dir; Joe Bishop, news dir; Lou Ludovici, chief engr.

WJLK-FM—Nov 20, 1947: 94.3 mhz; 100 w. Ant 98 ft. TL: N40 13 45 W74 05 24 (CP: 1.3 kw, ant 498.5 ft.). Stereo. Prog sep from AM. Format: CHR. ■ WMOD-TV affil.

Atlantic City

WAYV(FM)—April 1961: 95.1 mhz; 50 kw. Ant 331 ft. TL: N39 22 51 W74 27 04. Stereo. 8025 Black Horse Pike, West Atlantic City (08232). (609) 484-8444. Licensee: Radio WAYV Inc. Rep: D & R Radio. Format: Adult contemp. ■ Vi Trofa, gen mgr; John Gilbert, prom mgr; Mark Hunter, progmg dir & mus dir; Mike Ferriola, chief engr.

WFPG(AM)—1940: 1450 khz; 1 kw-U. TL: N39 22 42 W74 26 53. Hrs opn: 24. 2707 Atlantic Ave. (08401). (609) 348-4646; (609) 348-1450. FAX: (609) 348-1752. Licensee: H & D Broadcasting L.P. (acq 8-1-86; with co-located FM). Net: CBS. Rep: Eastman. Format: Talk. News staff one; news progmg 24 hrs wkly. Target aud: 25 plus; the population of South Jersey. Spec prog: Black 2 hrs, class 2 hrs, Broadway 2 hrs wkly. ■ Barry Dickstein, pres; Dick Taylor, gen mgr; Tom Reagan, gen sls mgr; Joe Bonanni, rgnl sls mgr; John Speeney, progmg dir; Laura Tortella, news dir; Bob Kees, chief engr.

WFPG-FM—September 1962: 96.9 mhz; 50 kw. Ant 400 ft. TL: N39 22 42 W74 26 53. Hrs opn: 24. Prog sep from AM. (609) 348-4646; (609) 348-9374. FAX: (609) 348-1752. Rep: Eastman. Format: Lite favorites/lite adult contemp. News staff one; news progmg 3 hrs wkly. Target aud: 25-54; today's active adults. ■ Mike Morgan, mktg mgr; Sharon Rattay, prom mgr; Rich Fennessy, progmg dir; Marlene Aqua, mus dir.

WMGM(FM)—June 14, 1961: 103.7 mhz; 50 kw. Ant 400 ft. TL: N39 23 38 W74 30 34. Stereo. 1601 New Rd., Linwood (08221). (609) 653-1400. FAX: (609) 927-7014. Licensee: South Jersey Radio Inc. Group owner: Green Group. Rep: McGavren Guild. Format: Adult contemp. ■ Howard L. Green, pres; Dick Irland, gen mgr; Joe de Groot, gen sls mgr; Dave Sherman, progmg dir; Al Horner, mus dir; Jeff Whitaker, news dir; Mark Moss, chief engr.

WMID(AM)—May 30, 1947: 1340 khz; 1 kw-U. TL: N39 22 35 W74 27 08 (CP: 870 w). Hrs opn: 24. Box 5000 (08404); 1825 Murray Ave. (08401). (609) 344-0300. FAX: (609) 348-4442. Licensee: Amcom Inc. (acq 1-83; grpsl; FTR 1-17-83). Net: NBC, NBC Talknet. Rep: Banner. Format: Music of 40s, 50s & 60s, talk. News staff 2; news progmg 10 hrs wkly. Target aud: 45-64; mature, affluent adults. ■ Bill Musser, gen mgr; Tom McNally, opns dir & progmg dir; Scott Fisher, sls dir; Will Stuart, prom mgr; Frank Lario, mus dir; Bob Allen, news dir; Charles McCraw, chief engr. ■ Rates: $40; 37; 40; 37.

WMID-FM—See Pleasantville.

***WNJN(FM)**—Not on air, target date unknown: 89.7 mhz; 25 w-H, 6 kw-V. Ant 272 ft-H, 276 ft-V. TL: N39 27 40 W74 41 06. NJN Radio, CN777, Trenton (08625-0777). (609) 777-5030. Licensee: New Jersey Public Broadcasting Authority. Wash atty: Schartz, Woods & Miller. Format: News, talk, adult contemp. News staff 5; news progmg 13 hrs wkly. Target aud: General. ■ Harvey Fisher, CEO; George Hoover, exec vp & engrg dir; Prince Wooten, gen mgr, sls dir & mus dir; Hope Koseff, opns mgr, prom mgr & asst mus dir; Susan Sands, dev mgr, rgnl sls mgr & adv mgr; Lamont King, progmg dir; Jackie Anderson, news dir; Larry Will, chief engr.

WOND(AM)—See Pleasantville.

WSKR(FM)—(Petersburg). August 1991: 102.7 mhz; 3.3 kw. Ant 295 ft. TL: N39 12 18 W74 39 33. Hrs opn: 24. 2 Oak Ave., Wenonah (08090). (609) 390-2552. FAX: (609) 464-0743. Licensee: Joseph Donald Powers. Format: Sports. ■ Joseph D. Poweck, CEO; James F. Quinn, gen mgr.

WUSS(AM)—Jan 1, 1955: 1490 khz; 1 kw-U. TL: N39 22 23 W74 26 18. Box 7539, 1507 Atlantic Ave. (08401). (609) 345-7134. FAX: (609) 345-4286. Licensee: Jim Cuffee (acq 2-13-89; $350,000; FTR 2-13-89). Net: Moody, Westwood One. Rep: Katz & Powell. Format: Urban contemp. News staff one; news progmg 5 hrs wkly. Target aud: 18-54; Afro-Americans. Spec prog: Jazz 2 hrs, Sp 6 hrs, gospel 3 hrs wkly. ■ James Cuffee, pres; Larry Hayes, gen mgr. ■ Rates: $30; 30; 30; 30.

Avalon

WWOC(FM)—Mar 29, 1976: 94.3 mhz; 3 kw. Ant 300 ft. TL: N39 07 48 W74 47 20. Stereo. Hrs opn: 24. 1575 Rt. 9, Swainton (08210). (609) 465-9400. FAX: (609) 465-4956. Licensee: DiDonato Enterprises (acq 12-92). Format: Classical. ■ John J. DiDonato, CEO; Jack Moore, gen mgr & gen sls mgr; Paul Richards, mus dir; Howard Berger, pub affrs dir.

Belvidere

WRNJ-FM—Oct 15, 1992: 107.1 mhz; 3.9 kw. Ant 395 ft. TL: N40 55 33 W75 12 16. Box 1000, 100 Rt. 46, Hackettstown (07840). (908) 689-8000. Licensee: Radio New Jersey. Net: SMN. Wash atty: Mullin, Rhyne, Emmons & Topel; Roberts & Eckard. Format: Country. News staff 4; news progmg 4 hrs wkly. Target aud: 20 plus. ■ Lawrence J. Tighe Jr., CEO, pres & vp engrg; Norman Worth, exec vp, gen mgr & vp progmg; Pat Layton, stn mgr; George Beckenthal, vp opns; Charles Rieger, opns dir; Mike Hunt, vp dev; Edward Gorham, vp sls & vp adv; Oliver Guzman, vp prom; Nancy Eik, mus dir; Liz Bowen, news dir; Diedre Bryant, pub affrs dir. ■ Rates: $36; 30; 36; 26.

Berlin

***WNJS-FM**—Aug 21, 1992: 88.1 mhz; 1 w-H, 120 w-V. Ant 328 ft. TL: N39 43 41 W74 50 39 (CP: 2 w-H, 8.5 w-V, ant 377 ft.). Hrs opn: 18. NJN Radio, CN707, Trenton (08625-0777). (609) 777-5030. Licensee: New Jersey Public Broadcasting Authority (acq 3-6-91; FTR 3-25-91). Wash atty: Schwartz, Woods & Miller. Format: News/talk, adult contemp, div. News staff 5; news progmg 13 hrs wkly. Target aud: General. ■ Harvey Fisher, CEO; George Hoover, exec vp & engrg dir; Prince Wooten, gen mgr dev dir, sls dir, adv dir & mus dir; Hope Koseff, opns mgr, prom mgr & asst mus dir; Susan Sands, dev mgr, rgnl sls mgr & adv mgr; Ramond Rosser, progmg dir; Jackie Anderson, news dir; Larry Will, chief engr.

Blackwood

***WDBK(FM)**—June 7, 1979: 91.5 mhz; 100 w. Ant 87 ft. TL: N39 47 06 W75 02 19. Box 200 (08012). (609) 227-7200. Licensee: Camden County College. Format: Top-40. ■ Elle Manzano, gen mgr.

Blairstown

WHCY(FM)—Oct 21, 1973: 106.3 mhz; 340 w. Ant 859 ft. TL: N41 02 51 W74 58 22 Stereo. Hrs opn: 24. Box 428 (07825). (908) 362-8221; (717) 421-5171. FAX: (908) 362-9419. Licensee: Clearview Broadcasting Corp. (acq 11-84; $620,000; FTR 11-26-84). Format: Hot country. News staff one. Target aud: 25-54; baby boomers. Spec prog: Relg one hr wkly. ■ Rick Musselman, gen mgr; Paul LaFever, opns dir; Ken Stoudt, chief engr. ■ Rates: $29; 25; 29; 22.

Brick Township

***WBGD(FM)**—June 1975: 91.9 mhz; 150 w. Ant 72 ft. TL: N40 06 17 W74 07 34. Stereo. Brick Memorial High School, 2001 Lanes Mill Rd. (08724). (908) 477-2800. FAX: (908) 840-9089. Licensee: Brick Township Bd. of Educ. Format: Educ, div. Target aud: General. ■ Cliff Cowen, gen mgr.

Bridgeton

***WNJB(FM)**—Not on air, target date unknown: 89.3 mhz; 1 w-H, 3 kw-V. Ant 203 ft. TL: N39 27 35 W75 09 28. NJN Radio, CN777, Trenton (08625-0777). (609) 777-5030. Licensee: NJ Public Broadcasting Authority. Wash atty: Schwartz, Woods & Miller. Format: News/talk, adult contemp, div. News staff 5; news progmg 13 hrs wkly. Target aud: General. ■ Harvey Fisher, CEO; George Hoover, exec vp & engrg dir; Prince Wooten, gen mgr, sls dir & mus dir; Hope Koseff, opns mgr, prom mgr & asst mus dir; Susan Sands, dev mgr, rgnl sls mgr & adv mgr; Lamont King, progmg dir; Jackie Anderson, news dir; Larry Will, chief engr.

WSNJ(AM)—August 1937: 1240 khz; 1 kw-U. TL: N39 27 40 W75 12 21. Hrs opn: 5:30 AM-12:05 AM. Box 69, 1969 Old Burlington Rd. (08302). (609) 451-2900. FAX: (609) 453-9440. Licensee: Cohanzick Broadcasting Corp. (acq 1971). Net: MBS. Wash atty: Reed, Smith, Shaw & McClay. Format: Div. News staff one; news progmg 10 hrs wkly. Target aud: 25 plus; adults. Spec prog: Big band, MOR, news/talk, farm 10 hrs wkly. ■ Edward L. Bold, pres, gen mgr, gen sls mgr & chief engr; Katherine M. Bold, exec vp; Fred Sharkey, progmg dir; Bruce Sloan, mus dir; Robert Wanner, news dir; Lynn Timberman, pub affrs dir. ■ Rates: $216; 216; 216; 216.

WSNJ-FM—1946: 107.7 mhz; 15.2 kw. Ant 486 ft. TL: N39 27 40 W75 12 21. Stereo. Hrs opn: 5:30 AM-12:05 AM.

Bridgewater

WBRW(AM)—Dec 23, 1971: 1170 khz; 500 w-D, DA. TL: N40 33 30 W74 35 52. 2 Oak Ave., Wenonah (08090). Licensee: Somerset Valley Broadcasting Co.

Camden

***WKDN-FM**—July 23, 1968: 106.9 mhz; 38 kw. Ant 600 ft. TL: N39 54 33 W75 06 00. Stereo. 2906 Mt. Ephraim Ave. (08104). (609) 854-5300; (215) 922-0282. Licensee: Family Stations Inc. (group owner; acq 7-23-68). Wash atty: Dow, Lohnes & Albertson. Format: Relg. News progmg 5 hrs wkly. Target aud: General; families. Spec prog: Class 2 hrs wkly. ■ McDonald Martin, opns mgr; Richard Archut, chief engr.

WSSJ(AM)—September 1925: 1310 khz; 1 kw-D, 250 w-N. TL: N39 57 28 W75 06 54. Sixth & Market St. (08101). (609) 365-5600. FAX: (215) 563-1310. Licensee: WSSJ Broadcasting Ltd. (acq 9-84; $850,000; FTR 4-16-84). Net: MBS. Format: Adult contemp, oldies. Spec prog: It 2 hrs, Sp 10 hrs, gospel/relg 8 hrs wkly. ■ Pat Delsi, pres & gen mgr; Paul Douglas, gen sls mgr; Eileen Del Signore, prom mgr; Dave Michaels, mus dir; Dean Paul, chief engr.

WTMR(AM)—Nov 1, 1948: 800 khz; 5 kw-D, 500 w-N. TL: N39 54 33 W75 06 00. 2775 Mt. Ephraim Ave. (08104). (609) 962-8000. Licensee: Gore Overgaard Broadcasting Inc. (acq 9-86; $30,000; FTR 8-11-86). Format: Relg. ■ Louise Bessler, stn mgr; William Gravino, progmg dir; Michael Roberts, mus dir.

Canton

WNNN(FM)—Jan 15, 1972: 101.7 mhz; 3 kw. Ant 263 ft. TL: N39 25 51 W75 20 13. Box 132, Salem (08079); 81 Woodstown Rd. (08079). (609) 935-1762. FAX: (609) 935-3338. Licensee: PJC Broadcasters Inc. (acq 7-1-78). Net: ABC/E. Format: Relg. News staff 4. Target aud: 18-54. ■ Gloria Jennings, pres, gen mgr & gen sls mgr; Ben Ferguson, vp & chief engr; Elizabeth Cassidy, progmg dir.

Cape May

WSJL(FM)—June 3, 1967: 102.3 mhz; 3.2 kw. Ant 292 ft. TL: N39 00 33 W74 52 13. Stereo. Hrs opn: 24. 509 Rio Grande Ave., Rio Grande (08242). (609) 886-1144. Licensee: Lighthouse Broadcasting Co. (acq 3-83). Net: USA. Format: Relg. Target aud: 25-54; loyal, responsive, heavy with women. Spec prog: Class one hr wkly. ■ Nancy Schumacher, pres; Ken Manri, stn mgr, gen sls mgr, progmg dir & chief engr. ■ Rates: $12.50; 12.50; 12.50; 12.50.

Cape May Court House

WBNJ(FM)—Sept 5, 1985: 105.5 mhz; 3.3 kw. Ant 295 ft. TL: N39 07 32 W74 49 26. Stereo. Suite 108, 223 N. Main St., (08210). (609) 465-2044. Licensee: Avalon Group (acq 6-30-92; $850,000; FTR 7-20-92). Net: ABC/D, Jones Satellite Audio. Format: Hit country. News staff one. Target aud: 25-54; middle to upper income. ■ Don Greth, pres; Marc S. Mason, gen mgr & adv mgr; Nick Harris, prom dir & mus dir; Joanne Silvani, progmg dir & asst mus dir; Marsha Peles, news dir & pub affrs dir; Richard Arsenault, chief engr. ■ Rates: $216; 216; 216; 144.

Cherry Hill

***WEEE(FM)**—Jan 7, 1985: 89.5 mhz; 100 w. Ant 171 ft. TL: N39 51 33 W74 57 00. Box 1610, Delran (08075). (609) 424-8981. FAX: (215) 872-8865. Licensee: Broadcast Learning Center Inc. (acq 11-25-86; $175,000; FTR 10-27-86). Format: Educ, relg. Target aud: General. Spec prog: Arts 10 hrs wkly. ■ Tom Moffit Sr, pres; William Fenton, gen mgr; Lynne Gold, progmg dir.

Delaware Township

***WDVR(FM)**—Feb 19, 1990: 89.7 mhz; 3 kw. Ant 301 ft. TL: N40 26 56 W74 56 40. Stereo. Hrs opn: 18. Box 191, Rt. 604, Sergeantsville (08557-0191). (609) 397-1620; (609) 397-1339. Licensee: Penn-Jersey Educational Radio Corp. Format: Div. News progmg 2 hrs wkly. Target aud: 30 plus. Spec prog: American Indian 2 hrs, class 4 hrs, folk 6 hrs, gospel one hr, jazz 11 hrs, polka 2 hrs, relg 12 hrs, oldies 13 hrs, country 15 hrs wkly. ■ Frank W. Napurano, pres & gen mgr; Charles W. Loughery, Robert Wick, exec vps; Linda Fleming, opns mgr; Virginia Napurano, prom mgr; William Fleming, mus dir; Charles W. Loughery, chief engr.

Dover

WDHA-FM—Feb 22, 1961: 105.5 mhz; 3 kw. Ant 564 ft. TL: N40 51 19 W74 30 42. Stereo. Hrs opn: 24. Box 1250, Morristown (07962-1250); Horsehill Rd., Cedar Knolls (07927). (201) 538-1250. FAX: (201) 538-6804. Licensee: Signal Communications of NJ Ltd. (acq 12-14-90); grpsl; FTR 1-7-91). Net: Unistar. Rep: Katz. Wash atty: Wiley, Rein & Fielding. Format: AOR. Target aud: 18-49. ■ Steve Scola, gen mgr; Leonard Black, progmg dir; Susan Young, news dir. ■ Rates: $150; 100; 125; 75.

Dover Township

***WWNJ(FM)**—January 1989: 91.1 mhz; 10 kw. Ant 165 ft. TL: N39 58 07 W74 04 19. Stereo. Hrs opn: 5:30 AM-midnight. Dups WWFM(FM) Trenton 100%. Box B, Trenton (08690). (609) 587-8989. FAX: (609) 586-4533. Licensee: Mercer County Community College Board of Trustees (acq 11-4-91). Net: American Public Radio Net.; Mercer County Community College Public Radio Net. Wash atty: Rosenman and Colin. Format: Class. ■ George Schwartz, gen mgr; Alice Weiss, progmg dir; Jack Perlstein, mus dir; Walt Gradzki, Phil Joiner (asst), chiefs engr.

East Orange

***WFMU(FM)**—1958: 91.1 mhz; 1.44 kw Ant 360 ft. TL: N40 47 15 W74 04 19 (CP: Ant 505 ft., TL: N40 47 19 W74 15 20). Stereo. Hrs opn: 24. 580 Springdale Ave. (07019). (201) 678-8264. Licensee: Upsala College. Format: Div, free form. News progmg one hr wkly. Target aud: General. Spec prog: International 15 hrs wkly. ■ Ken Freedman, gen mgr; David Newgarden, progmg dir; Dan Andreana, chief engr.

Eatontown

WHTG(AM)—Nov 1, 1957: 1410 khz; 500 w-D. TL: N40 16 10 W74 04 19. 1129 Hope Rd., Asbury Park (07712). (908) 493-2000. FAX: (908) 493-0813. Licensee: WHTG Inc. (acq 8-1-85). Rep: Katz. Format: Big band, MOR. ■ Faye B. Gade, pres & gen mgr; Richard K. Swetits, opns mgr & chief engr; Richard Swetits, gen sls mgr; Matt Pinfield, progmg dir.

WHTG-FM—Oct 11, 1961: 106.3 mhz; 3.9 kw. Ant 328 ft. TL: N40 16 10 W74 04 19. Stereo. Prog sep from AM. Format: AOR. ■ Rich Robinson, progmg dir; Rob Kopcho, mus dir.

Egg Harbor City

WRDR(FM)—Sept 23, 1971: 104.9 mhz; 10 kw. Ant 508 ft. TL: N39 32 49 W74 38 19. Stereo. Box 295, 300 Philadelphia Ave. (08215). (609) 965-1055. FAX: (609) 965-3026. Licensee: Rodio Radio Inc. Net: AP. Format: Big band, nostalgia. News staff one; news progmg 12 hrs wkly. Target aud: 35 plus. Spec prog: Relg 4 hrs wkly. ■ James N. Rodio, pres; John DeMasi, gen mgr & gen sls mgr; Robert Canavan, prom mgr & progmg dir. ■ Rates: $25; 20; 25; 12.

Elizabeth

WJDM(AM)—March 11, 1970: 1530 khz; 500 w-D. TL: N40 38 56 W74 14 32 (CP: 1 kw-D). 9 Caldwell Place (07201). (908) 965-1530. FAX: (908) 965-1535. Licensee: Radio Elizabeth Inc. Format: Oldies. Target aud: 35-64. Spec prog: Ger 2 hrs, Pol 3 hrs, Irish 2 hrs, Sp 2 hrs wkly. ■ John Quinn, pres & gen mgr; Fran Engwall, opns mgr; Zim Barstein, gen sls mgr; Don Newmuller, chief engr.

Ewing

WIMG(AM)—Licensed to Ewing. See Trenton.

Flemington

***WCVH(FM)**—April 1974: 90.5 mhz; 78 w. Ant 449 ft. TL: N40 33 25 W74 54 18. Stereo. Hrs opn: 15. Rt. 31 (08822). (908) 782-9595. FAX: (908) 788-6745. Licensee: Hunterdon Central High School. Format: Div. Spec prog: Class 10 hrs, talk 2 hrs wkly. ■ David R. Kelber, gen mgr; John Anastasio, opns dir; Arthur Silver, chief engr.

WJHR(AM)—Not on air, target date Summer 1994: 1040 khz; 4.7 kw-D, 1 kw-N, DA-2. TL: N40 30 18 W74 58 37. Stereo. 16 Doe Run, Pittstown (08867). (908) 730-7959. Licensee: Hunterdon Mercury Communications Inc. Wash atty: Verner, Liipfert, Bernhard, McPherson & Hand. ■ Charles A. Hecht, pres & gen mgr.

Florence

WIFI(AM)—1985: 1460 khz; 5 kw-D, DA. TL: N40 04 53 W74 47 41. 2025 Burlington Columbus Rd., Burlington (08016). (609) 499-2131. FAX: (609) 499-4905. Licensee: Real Life Broadcasting. Format: News/talk. ■ Michael Venditti, gen mgr; Joan Venditti, opns dir.

Franklin

WSUS(FM)—Feb 28, 1965: 102.3 mhz; 590 w. Ant 745 ft. TL: N41 08 37 W74 32 21. Stereo. Box 102, 75 Main Street (07416). (201) 827-2525. FAX: (201) 827-5772. Licensee: WSUS Communications Inc. (acq 10-71). Net: MBS. Format: Adult contemp. ■ Jay Edwards, pres & gen mgr; Rosanne Francone, gen sls mgr; Dave Margolotti, progmg dir & mus dir.

Franklin Lakes

***WRRH(FM)**—Feb 22, 1963: 102.3 mhz; 10 kw. Ant 253 ft. TL: N41 00 00 W74 11 15. Licensee: Bergen County Community Broadcast Foundation (acq 12-31-92; $100,000; FTR 1-25-93).

Freehold Township

***WRLJ(FM)**—Not on air, target date unknown: 89.7 mhz; 1.26 kw-V. Ant 151 ft. TL: N40 11 21 W74 21 06. Box 88, 25 E. George St. (07728). Licensee: Faith Broadcasters Inc. Format: Adult contemporary, Christian music/talk. Target aud: General. ■ Andrew Stamat, pres.

Glassboro

***WGLS-FM**—January 1964: 89.7 mhz; 120 w. Ant 150 ft. TL: N39 42 32 W75 07 12 (CP: 158 w-H, 640 w-V, ant 164 ft.). Stereo. Rowan College of N.J. (08028-1701). (609) 863-7336. Licensee: Rowan College of N.J. Net: ABC/C, AP. Format: Div, educ. ■ Frank Hogan, stn mgr; Al Miller, chief engr.

Hackensack

WWDJ(AM)—1921: 970 khz; 5 kw-U, DA-2. TL: N40 54 40 W40 01 42. 167 Main St. (07601); Box 970, (07602).

(201) 343-5097. Licensee: H.E., L.P. Group owner: Communicom Co. of America L.P. (acq 7-7-93; grpsl; FTR 8-2-93). Net: ABC/D. Format: Contemp Christian. Target aud: 25-44. ■ Shirley Walker-Carter, gen mgr; Keith Stevens, progmg dir & mus dir; Sharon Davis, news dir; Stuart Engelke, chief engr.

Hackettstown

***WNTI(FM)**—Dec 5, 1957: 91.9 mhz; 5.6 kw. Ant 510 ft. TL: N40 51 07 W74 52 35. Stereo. 400 Jefferson St. (07840). (908) 852-4545; (908) 852-1400, ext. 391. FAX: (908) 850-9508. Licensee: Centenary College. Format: Rock, div, progsv. News progmg 2 hrs wkly. Target aud: 15 plus. Spec prog: Big band 4 hrs, blues 5 hrs, heavy metal 6 hrs, reggae 3 hrs, oldies 3 hrs, jazz 5 hrs wkly. ■ Eric Slater, gen mgr; Beth Grosinski, stn mgr & news dir; Paul Mason, opns mgr & mus dir; Tamiko Sciam, progmg dir; Jerry Balderson, asst mus dir; Billie Christie, pub affrs dir; Art White, chief engr.

WRNJ(AM)—Aug 26, 1976: 1000 khz; 2.5 kw-D, DA. TL: N40 50 47 W74 48 16. Box 1000 (07840). (908) 850-1000. FAX: (908) 850-0001. Licensee: Radio New Jersey Corporation. Net: ABC/E. Wash atty: Mullin, Rhyne, Emmons & Topel. Format: Adult contemp, MOR. News staff 3. Target aud: 25-50 plus; upwardly mobile. Spec prog: Talk 10 hrs wkly. ■ Lawrence J. Tighe Jr., pres & chief engr; Norman Worth, gen mgr & gen sls mgr; Chuck Reiger, progmg dir & mus dir; Liz Bohen, news dir. ■ Rates: $32; 28; 32; 28. ■ WRNJ(TV) affil.

Hammonton

WONZ(AM)—May 11, 1961: 1580 khz; 1 kw-D, 7 w-N. TL: N39 37 33 W74 47 44. Box 618 (08037). (609) 561-1900; (609) 653-1400. FAX: (609) 927-7014. Licensee: South Jersey Radio Inc. Group owner: The Green Group (acq 1-31-91; $100,000; FTR 2-18-91). Net: ABC/E, MBS. Format: News/talk. ■ Howard L. Green, pres; Dan Merrlo, chief engr.

Hazlet

***WCNJ(FM)**—May 24, 1979: 89.3 mhz; 100 w. Ant 260 ft. TL: N40 25 37 W74 11 40. Stereo. Box 90, Keyport (07735). (908) 888-0029. Licensee: WVRM Inc. Format: Relg, Sp. News staff one; news progmg one hr wkly. Target aud: 25-49. ■ Steve Liadis, pres & gen sls mgr. ■ Rates: $4; 4; 4; 4.

Lakewood

WOBM(AM)—Nov 20, 1970: 1160 khz; 5 kw-D, 8.9 kw-N, DA-2. TL: N40 08 09 W74 13 48. Hrs opn: 24. 46 Clayton Rd., Howell (07731). (908) 364-4400. FAX: (908) 269-9292. Licensee: North Shore Broadcasting Corp. (acq 6-8-81). Net: AP. Rep: Katz. Wash atty: Blair, Joyce & Silva. Format: Familiar music of the 40s, 50s, & 60s. News staff 8; news progmg 14 hrs wkly. Target aud: 25-54; educated. ■ Glenn Jones, gen mgr; Kevin Buckelew, opns mgr & progmg dir; Stuart Greenblatt, pub affrs dir; Rick St. James, chief engr.

WOBM-FM—See Toms River.

Lawrenceville

***WRRC(FM)**—Sept 23, 1989: 107.7 mhz; 17 w. Ant 36 ft. TL: N40 16 44 W74 44 15. Stereo. Hrs opn: 16. WRRC–Rider College, Student Ctr., 2083 Lawrenceville Rd. (08648). (609) 896-5211, ext. 536; (609) 896-5369. FAX: (609) 896-8029. Licensee: Rider College Board of Trustees. Format: Alternative. News staff 3; news progmg 4 hrs wkly. Target aud: 16-21; high school & college students. Spec prog: Black 10 hrs, heavy metal 10 hrs wkly. ■ Anthony Coleman, gen mgr & progmg dir; Jennifer Zipf, prom dir; Rob Buchanon, Claudia Testa, mus dirs; Patti Lewis, chief engr.

Lincroft

***WBJB-FM**—Jan 13, 1975: 90.5 mhz; 11 kw. Ant 135 ft. TL: N40 19 19 W74 07 57. Stereo. Hrs opn: 6 AM-midnight. Brookdale Community College, 765 Newman Springs Rd. (07738). (908) 224-2252; (908) 224-2490. Licensee: Board of Trustees of Brookdale Community College. Net: NPR, APR, AP. Wash atty: Dow, Lohnes & Albertson. Format: Jazz. News progmg 16 hrs wkly. Target aud: 25-54. Spec prog: Haitian 3 hrs, bluegrass 3 hrs, Sp 4 hrs, blues 3 hrs wkly. ■ Cheryl Cummings, stn mgr; Michael Ferrell, opns mgr; McKinley G. Gaines, progmg dir; Matthew T. Hughes, mus dir; Jack Christie, pub affrs dir; Michael L. Ferrell, chief engr.

Stations in the U.S.   New Jersey

Long Branch

WZVU(FM)—June 1, 1960: 107.1 mhz; 2.3 kw. Ant 371 ft. TL: N40 18 17 W73 59 08. Stereo. 156 Broadway (07740). (908) 222-1071. FAX: (908) 222-0439. Licensee: K&K Broadcasting (acq 1-89; $3.9 million; FTR 1-16-89). Net: CNN. Rep: Katz; Katz Suburban. Format: Oldies. News staff one; news progmg 3 hrs wkly. Target aud: 25-54; female. ■ Donald L. Kelly, pres; Jim Davis, exec vp; Jeff Clark, opns mgr; Merrily Morris, gen sls mgr. ■ Rates: $85; 65; 75; 55.

LAUREN A. COLBY
301-663-1086
COMMUNICATIONS ATTORNEY
Special Attention to Difficult Cases

Madison

*****WMNJ(FM)**—Sept 15, 1980: 88.9 mhz; 8 w. Ant 75 ft. TL: N40 45 30 W74 25 48. Stereo. Hrs opn: 24. Drew Univ., 26 Madison Ave. (07940). (201) 408-4753; (201) 408-5021 (REQUESTS). FAX: (201) 408-3939. Licensee: WMNJ Inc. (acq 9-25-89). Format: Alt/progsv, classic rock, div. News progmg 28 hrs wkly. Spec prog: Black 6 hrs, class 2 hrs, jazz 2 hrs, relg 2 hrs, blues 4 hrs, show tunes 6 hrs wkly. ■ Hardy Spire, pres; Vanessa Allen, gen mgr.

Mahwah

*****WRPR(FM)**—July 15, 1980: 90.3 mhz; 100 w. Ant 30 ft. TL: N41 04 51 W74 10 34. Stereo. Hrs opn: 18. 505 Ramapo Valley Rd. (07430). (201) 825-7449. FAX: (201) 327-9032. Licensee: Ramapo College of New Jersey. Format: College contemporary. News staff 4; news progmg 10 hrs wkly. Target aud: 18-24; college students. Spec prog: Pub affrs 12 hrs wkly. ■ Andre Perry, gen mgr; Anthony Nurse, stn mgr; Adolphe Holmes, chief engr.

Manahawkin

*****WAGB(FM)**—Not on air, target date unknown: 90.7 mhz; 1 w-H, 950 w-V. Ant 50 ft. Box 191, Sergeantsville (08557). Licensee: Penn-Jersey Ed Radio Corp.

WJRZ-FM—July 4, 1976: 100.1 mhz; 3 kw. Ant 499 ft. TL: N39 47 53 W74 12 12. Stereo. Hrs opn: 24. Box 1000, 1001 Beach Ave. (08050); Box 100, 22 W. Water St., Toms River (08753). (609) 597-1100; (908) 349-1100. FAX: (609) 597-4400; (908) 505-8700. Licensee: Jersey Shore Broadcasting Corp. Net: AP, Interep. Rep: D & R Radio. Wash atty: Roberts & Eckard. Format: Adult contemp. News staff 2; news progmg 4 hrs wkly. Target aud: 18-54. ■ Joseph Knox Jr., pres & gen mgr; Lance DeBock, Brent McNally, vps; Lance DeBock, vp opns & progmg mgr; Brent McNally, vp sls & vp engrg; Joanne Voss, prom dir; Rick Sweeney, prom mgr; Charlie Maxx, mus dir; Bill Mead, news dir; Mike Moran, engrg mgr; Bill Clanton, chief engr. ■ Rates: $60; 40; 50; 30.

Margate City

WTTH(FM)—Nov 19, 1991: 96.1 mhz; 2.3 kw. Ant 371 ft. TL: N39 21 02 W74 26 55. Stereo. Suite 201, 2922 Atlantic Ave., Atlantic City (03401). (609) 348-4040. FAX: (609) 348-1303. Licensee: Margate Communications L.P. Format: Urban & adult contemp. News progmg 3 hrs wkly. Target aud: 25-49. Spec prog: Gospel 5 hrs, relg one hr wkly. ■ Don Brooks, gen mgr, gen sls mgr & progmg dir. ■ Rates: $23; 23; 23; 14.

Millville

WBSS-FM—Feb 2, 1962: 97.3 mhz; 50 kw. Ant 203 ft. TL: N39 25 19 W75 01 14 (CP: Ant 466 ft., TL: N39 19 15 W75 46 17). Stereo. 205 W. Pkwy. Dr., Pleasantville (08232). (609) 645-8400. FAX: (609) 272-9490. Licensee: Wintersrun Communications Inc. Group owner: Beasley Broadcasting. Format: Contemp hit. Target aud: General. ■ Joseph J. Mitchell, gen mgr; Sonny Spear, gen sls mgr; Joe Chiapanna, prom mgr; Nick Giorno, progmg dir; Bob Burke, mus dir; Don Powers, chief engr.

WREY(AM)—December 1953: 1440 khz; 1 kw-D, 65 w-N, DA-2. TL: N39 25 19 W75 01 14. Box 2365, 115 S. 6th St., South Vineland (08360). (609) 692-5611; (609) 327-4141. FAX: (609) 696-2937. Licensee: Quinn Broadcasting Inc. (acq 12-5-91; $410,000 with WIBG(AM) Ocean City; FTR 1-6-92). Net: ABC/C. Format: Sp. ■ Jim Quinn, pres; Tommy Rodriguez, gen mgr & progmg dir.

Morristown

*****WJSV(FM)**—Feb 22, 1971: 90.5 mhz; 124 w. Ant 17 ft. TL: N40 50 10 W74 29 16. Stereo. Hrs opn: 8 AM-10 PM Mon-Fri. 50 Early St. (07960). (201) 292-2168; (201) 292-2166. Licensee: Morris School District Board of Education. Format: AOR. News staff one; news progmg 3 hrs wkly. Target aud: General. Spec prog: News/talk 3 hrs, sports 3 hrs wkly. ■ Virginia Lyttle, gen mgr & stn mgr; Daniel Barrett, chief opns; Howard Steyn, vp mktg & news dir; Patrich Coyle, mus dir; Heather Hamilton, engrg mgr, asst mus dir & pub affrs dir; Paul A. Werner Sr., chief engr.

WMTR(AM)—Dec 12, 1948: 1250 khz; 5 kw-D, 1 kw-N, DA-2. TL: N40 48 45 W74 27 36 (CP: 5 kw-N). Stereo. Box 1250 (07962-1250); 55 Horsehill Rd., Cedar Knolls (07927). (201) 538-1250. FAX: (201) 538-6804. Licensee: Northern New Jersey Radio L.P. (acq 12-14-90; grpsl; FTR 1-7-91). Net: BRN, AP. Rep: Katz. Wash atty: Wiley, Rein & Fielding. Format: Big band, nostalgia. News staff 3. Target aud: 25-54. ■ Burke Ross, pres; Beth Colon, gen sls mgr; Chris Edwards, progmg dir; Michael Quinn, news dir. ■ Rates: $80; 60; 70; 40.

Mount Holly

WWJZ(AM)—November 1992: 640 khz; 50 kw-D, 950 w-N, DA-2. TL: N40 05 28 W74 50 30. Box 81 (08060). (609) 267-2346. FAX: (609) 261-7246. Licensee: Mt. Holly Radio Co. ■ Edgar H. Cramer, gen mgr.

Netcong

*****WPFR(FM)**—Not on air, target date unknown: 88.1 mhz; 2.2 kw-V. Ant 134 ft. Suite 1, 3108 Fulton Ave., Sacramento, CA (95821). Licensee: Family Stations Inc.

New Brunswick

WCTC(AM)—Dec 12, 1946: 1450 khz; 1 kw-U. TL: N40 29 32 W74 25 11. Stereo. Hrs opn: 24. Box 100, Broadcast Center (08903); Tony Marano Broadcast Center, 78 Veronica Ave., Somerset (08873). (908) 249-2600. FAX: (908) 249-9010. Licensee: Raritan Valley Broadcasting Co. Group owner: Greater Media Inc. (acq 5-1-57). Net: ABC/E, NBC Talknet. Rep: Katz. Format: News/talk. News staff 6; news progmg 15 hrs wkly. Target aud: 35-54. Spec prog: Pol 2 hrs, Hungarian one hr, Jewish one hr wkly. ■ Frank Kabela, pres; Andrew J. Santoro Jr., gen mgr; Jack Shreve, opns mgr; Tony Odachowski, gen sls mgr; Julie Mickelsen, prom dir; Bruce Johnson, news dir; Lee Robinson, pub affrs dir; John Stanley, chief engr.

WMGQ(FM)—Co-owned with WCTC(AM). 1947: 98.3 mhz; 1 kw. Ant 525 ft. TL: N40 28 33 W74 29 34. Stereo. Hrs opn: 24. Rep: Katz. Format: Adult contemp. News progmg 3 hrs wkly. Target aud: 25-45. ■ Joe DeRose, progmg dir.

*****WRSU-FM**—April 1974: 88.7 mhz; 1.365 kw. Ant 150 ft. TL: N40 28 00 W74 26 15. Stereo. Hrs opn: 24. 126 College Ave. (08903). (908) 932-7800. FAX: (908) 932-1768. Licensee: Board of Governors, Rutgers Univ. Format: Var/div. News prgmg 6 hrs wkly. Target aud: 15-30; college students, div group of young adults. Spec prog: Black 7 hrs, class 2 hrs, jazz 2 hrs, country 8 hrs, Indian 2 hr, Pol one hr, Sp 2 hrs, Irish one hr, folk one hr, Pakistani one hr, new age one hr, Hungarian one hr, Israeli one hr, Greek one hr, gay 2 hrs wkly. ■ Stuart Hothem, gen mgr; Tim Espar, stn mgr; Neil Martin, prom dir; Kevin Czaplinski, progmg dir; Paul Weinstein, mus dir; Kristin DeMarco, news dir; Greg Nelson, chief engr.

Newark

*****WBGO(FM)**—Feb 7, 1948: 88.3 mhz; 10 kw. Ant 431 ft. TL: N40 44 11 W74 10 15. Hrs opn: 24. 54 Park Place (07102). (201) 624-8880. FAX: (201) 824-8888. Licensee: Newark Public Radio Inc. (acq 12-77). Net: NPR, AP. Wash atty: Baker & Hostetler. Format: Jazz. News staff 2; news progmg 5 hrs wkly. Target aud: General. ■ Samuel McGhee, chmn; Cephas Bowles, gen mgr; Gary Lue, opns mgr; Paula Hunchar, dev dir; Michelle Adams, rgnl sls mgr; Thurston Briscoe, progmg dir; Gary Walker, mus dir; Steve Inskeep, news dir & pub affrs dir.

*****WFME(FM)**—1947: 94.7 mhz; 38 kw. Ant 570 ft. TL: N40 47 18 W74 15 19. Stereo. 289 Mt. Pleasant Ave., West Orange (07052). (201) 736-3600; (212) 736-3600. FAX: (201) 736-1275. Licensee: Family Stations Inc. (group owner; acq 3-10-66). Format: Christian educ. Target aud: General. ■ Harold Camping, pres; Art Thompson, gen mgr; Les Englehart, stn mgr; Mike Lobaito, pub affrs dir; Charles Menut, chief engr.

WHTZ(FM)—June 1, 1961: 100.3 mhz; 7.8 kw. Ant 1,220 ft. TL: N40 44 54 W73 59 10. 767 Third Ave., New York, NY (10017); 333 Meadowlands Pkwy., Secaucus, NJ (07094). (212) 239-2300; (212) 826-6161. FAX: (212) 826-2172. Licensee: Shamrock Broadcasting Inc. Group owner: Shamrock Holdings Inc. (acq 6-4-93; grpsl; FTR 6-21-93). Rep: Christal. Format: CHR. ■ Alan Goodman, vp & gen mgr; Steve Kingston, opns mgr & progmg dir; Marty Wall, prom mgr; Frankie Blue, mus dir; David Reaves, chief engr.

WNJR(AM)—1947: 1430 khz; 5 kw-U, DA-N. TL: N40 42 32 W74 14 31. Stereo. Hrs opn: 24. Suite 345, One Riverfront Plaza, North Newark (07102). (201) 642-8000. FAX: (201) 642-5208. Licensee: N. John Douglas. Group owner: Douglas Broadcasting Inc. (acq 10-21-91; $6.75 million; FTR 11-11-91). Rep: Katz. Wash atty: Hopkins & Sutter. Format: Multicultural. News staff one; news progmg 2 hrs wkly. Target aud: 25-54. ■ Herb Leskowitz, gen mgr; Wilson Sampson, gen sls mgr.

WNWK-FM—August 1992: 105.9 mhz; 2.4 kw. Ant 722 ft. TL: N40 45 04 W73 58 25. 449 Broadway, New York, NY (10013). (212) 966-1059. FAX: (212) 966-9580. Licensee: Multicultural Broadcasting Inc. ■ Guy Gerow, chmn; Emil Antonoff, pres; Evelyn Jose, exec vp; Stephen LeBow, vp; Otto Miller, Kim Rogers (asst), gen mgrs; Mark Buniak, mus dir; Danny Andreana, chief engr.

WSKQ(AM)—December 1948: 620 khz; 5 kw-U, DA-2. TL: N40 47 51 W74 21 36. Stereo. 26 W. 56th St., New York, NY (10019). (201) 994-2994. FAX: (201) 541-9236. Licensee: Spanish Broadcasting System Inc. (group owner; acq 10-1-83; $3.2 million; FTR 8-22-83). Rep: Caballero. Format: Sp. ■ Raul Alarcon, pres; Alfredo Alozo, gen mgr; Mickie Reyes, gen sls mgr; George Meyer, progmg dir; Dan Lohse, chief engr.

Newton

WNNJ(AM)—Dec 15, 1953: 1360 khz; 1 kw-D, 75 w-PSSA. TL: N41 02 29 W74 44 19 (CP: 2 kw-D, 320 w-N, DA-2). Hrs opn: 6 AM-10 PM. Box 40, 40 Yates Ave. (07860). (201) 383-3400. Licensee: Group M Communications Inc. (acq 9-17-79). Net: NBC, AP. Wash atty: Haley, Bader & Potts. Format: Oldies, solid gold. News staff 3; news progmg 10 hrs wkly. Target aud: 25-54. Spec prog: Relg 2 hrs, pub affrs 2 hrs wkly. ■ Michael B. Levine, pres, vp sls & gen sls mgr; Marvin J. Strauzer, exec vp, vp & gen mgr; Larry Bear, opns dir & progmg dir; Zim Barstein, prom mgr; Paul Mencher, news dir; Michael Levine, chief engr. ■ Rates: $60; 37; 60; 22.

WNNJ-FM—Oct 15, 1961: 103.7 mhz; 3.5 kw. Ant 757 ft. TL: N41 11 33 W74 45 13. Stereo. Prog sep from AM. Format: Adult hit radio. Target aud: 12-49. ■ Ron Naldi, mus dir; Bill Scott, pub affrs dir. ■ Rates: $70; 45; 70; 15.

North Cape May

WJNN(FM)—Not on air, target date unknown: 106.7 mhz; 3 kw. c/o Jeanne T. Haefner, 10 S. Dennis Blvd., Cape May Court House (08210). (609) 886-0100. Licensee: Jeanne T. Haefner.

Oakland

WVNJ(AM)—Dec 13, 1993: 1160 khz; 10 kw-D, 2.5 kw-N, DA-2. TL: N41 03 26 W74 15 00. Stereo. 1086 Teaneck Rd., Teaneck (07666). (201) 837-0400. FAX: (201) 837-9664. Licensee: Bursam Communications Corp. (acq 11-9-92; $350,000; FTR 11-30-92). Net: AP, SMN. Format: Multicultural. Target aud: 35 plus. ■ Len Mirelson, gen mgr.

Ocean Acres

WQNJ(FM)—Summer 1992: 98.5 mhz; 6 kw. Ant 328 ft. TL: N39 45 06 W74 15 39. Hrs opn: 24. 703 Millcreek Rd., Manahawkin (08050). (609) 597-6700. FAX: (609) 597-0639. Licensee: Seaira Inc. Format: Adult contemp. ■ Pat Parson, gen mgr, Charles Purgavie, gen sls mgr.

Ocean City

WIBG(AM)—Not on air, target date unknown: 1020 khz; 500 w-D. TL: N39 19 05 W74 37 09. 957 Asbury Ave. (08226). (609) 399-1555. Licensee: Enrico S. Brancadora (acq 12-1-92; $140,000; FTR 12-21-92). Format: Oldies.

WKOE(FM)—Oct 1, 1972: 106.3 mhz; 3 kw. Ant 308 ft. TL: N34 13 40 W74 40 57. Stereo. 2707 Atlantic Ave., Atlantic City (08401). (609) 348-4646. FAX: (609) 348-1752. Licensee: Ocean Communications (acq 8-22-86). Net: UPI. Format: Adult contemp. News staff 2. Target aud: 25-54.

WKTU(FM)—April 1983: 98.3 mhz; 3 kw. Ant 300 ft. TL: N34 12 18 W74 39 33 (CP: Ant 328 ft.). Stereo. Hrs opn: 24. 618 West Ave., 2nd Fl. (08226). (609) 398-7600. FAX: (609) 398-4311. Licensee: Atlantic Morris Broadcasting Inc. (group owner; acq 12-1-86; $550,000; FTR 10-13-86). Format: Oldies. Target aud: 25-54. ■ Loryn Deane, gen mgr; Ed Connolly, gen sls mgr; Mike Russell, progmg dir; Jerry Beebe, news dir; Rick Arsenault, chief engr.

*****WRTQ(FM)**—Not on air, target date Mar 1994: 91.3 mhz; 82 w-H, 10.5 kw-V. Ant 384 ft. TL: N39 19 15 W74 46 17. Stereo. Hrs opn: 24. Dups WRTI (FM) Philadelphia, PA 100%. Broad & Montgomery Sts., Philadelphia, PA (19122). (215) 204-8405. FAX: (215) 204-4870. Licensee: Temple Univ. of the Commonwealth System of Higher Education. Net: NPR, AP; Radio Pa. Wash atty: Arent, Fox, Kintner, Plotkin & Kahn. Format: Jazz. News staff 2; news progmg 15 hrs wkly. Target aud: 25-49. Spec prog: Caribbean 4 hrs, Sp 4 hrs wkly. ■ W. Thedore Eldredge, gen mgr; Tobias Poole, opns mgr & chief engr; Valorie Jarrell, dev dir & sls dir; Monika Morris, prom dir; Bill Clark, progmg dir; Kim Berry, mus dir; Audrey Foltz, news dir. ■ Rates: $75; 50; 75; 50.

Parsippany-Troy Hills

WXMC(AM)—Jan 13, 1973: 1310 khz; 1 kw-D, 100 w-N, DA. TL: N40 51 51 W74 21 06 (CP: 360 w-N). Hrs opn: 24. Box 5487, One Percypenny Ln. (07054). (201) 335-1310. FAX: (201) 575-5294. Licensee: James Chladek (acq 1-15-93; $200,000; FTR 2-8-93). Net: AP. Rep: Williams. Format: Soft adult contemp. News staff one. Target aud: 25 plus. Spec prog: Jazz 8 hrs, Irish music 2 hrs wkly. ■ James Chaladek, CEO; Otto Gust, vp progmg, mus dir & chief engr; Lou Steele, news dir. ■ Rates: $34; 29; 34; 24.

Paterson

WPAT(AM)—May 3, 1941: 930 khz; 5 kw-U, DA-2. TL: N40 50 59 W74 10 59. Stereo. 1396 Broad St., Clifton (07013). (201) 345-9300. FAX: (201) 471-1386; TWX: 710-989-7010. Licensee: Park Radio of Greater New York Inc. Group owner: Park Communications Inc. (acq 10-85; $49 million with co-located FM; FTR 10-14-85). Net: AP. Format: Easy lstng. ■ Gene Hobicorn, gen mgr; Ken MacKenzie, opns mgr; Harry Mitchell, natl sls mgr; Ralph Sanabria, progmg dir; Debbie Sheehan, news dir; Gerald Corby, chief engr.

WPAT-FM—Mar 29, 1957: 93.1 mhz; 5.3 kw. Ant 1,420 ft. TL: N40 42 43 W74 00 49 (CP: 21.88 kw, ant 338 ft.). Stereo. Dups AM 100%.

Pemberton

*****WBZC(FM)**—Not on air, target date unknown: 88.9 mhz; 120 w-H, 2.5 kw-V. Ant 171 ft. County Rt. 530 (08068). Licensee: Burlington County College.

Petersburg

WSKR(FM)—Licensed to Petersburg. See Atlantic City.

Piscataway

*****WVPH(FM)**—May 1976: 90.3 mhz; 200 w. Ant 7 ft. TL: N40 32 45 W74 28 25. 100 Behmer Rd. (08854-4173). (908) 981-0700, ext. 2246. FAX: (908) 981-0082. Licensee: Board of Education, Piscataway High School. Format: Ed, progsv, talk. ■ Maureen McVeigh-Berzok (advisor), James McGarry (advisor), gen mgrs; John Stanley, engrg mgr.

Plainfield

WERA(AM)—Sept 16, 1961: 1590 khz; 500 w-U, DA-2. TL: N40 34 39 W74 24 10. Hrs opn: 24. 120 W. 7th St. (07060). (908) 755-1590. FAX: (908) 755-1992. Licensee: Tri-County Broadcasting Corp. Net: AP. Rep: Katz. Wash atty: Booth, Freret & Imlay. Format: Oldies, news/talk, sports. News staff 3; news progmg 15 hrs wkly. Target aud: 25-49. Spec prog: Black 3 hrs, Pol 2 hrs, Sp 2 hrs wkly. ■ Henry J. Behre, pres & gen mgr; Barbara Ballard, opns mgr; Steven Gortvay, gen sls mgr; Robert Morris, mus dir; Mike Kennedy, news dir; Robert Balfour, chief engr. ■ Rates: $35; 30; 35; 30.

Pleasantville

WMGM(FM)—See Atlantic City.

WMID-FM—1974: 99.3 mhz; 3.4 kw. Ant 289 ft. TL: N39 22 35 W74 27 08. Stereo. Hrs opn: 24. 1825 Murray Ave., Atlantic City (08401); Box 8000, Atlantic City (08404). (609) 344-0300. FAX: (609) 348-4442. Licensee: Amcom Inc. (acq 2-16-83; grpsl; FTR 1-17-85). Rep: Banner. Format: Classic rock. News staff 2; news progmg 2 hrs wkly. Target aud: 25-54; homeowners. ■ Bill Musser, gen mgr; Tom McNally, opns dir & progmg dir; Scott Fisher, sls dir; Will Stuart, prom mgr; Frank Lario, mus dir; Bob Allen, news dir; Charles McCraw, chief engr. ■ Rates: $40; 35; 40; 35.

WOND(AM)—July 1950: 1400 khz; 1 kw-U. TL: N39 23 26 W74 30 47. Rebroadcasts WONZ (AM) Hammonton 100%. 1601 New Rd., Linwood (08221). (609) 653-1400. Licensee: South Jersey Radio Inc. Group owner: Green Group (acq 7-15-55). Net: ABC/E, MBS. Rep: McGavren Guild. Format: News/talk. Spec prog: Philadelphia Phillies & Eagles. ■ Howard L. Green, pres; Dick Irland, gen mgr; Joe de Groot, gen sls mgr; Jeff Whitaker, news dir; Mark Moss, chief engr.

Point Pleasant

WADB(FM)—Oct 4, 1968: 95.9 mhz; 4 kw. Ant 240 ft. TL: N40 10 17 W74 01 39. Stereo. Hrs opn: 24. Broadcast Center, 1731 F St., South Belmar (07719-3051). (908) 681-3800; (908) 892-4300. FAX: (908) 681-9298. Licensee: Seawood Broadcasters Inc. (acq 12-7-92; $4 million; FTR 1-4-93). Net: UPI. Format: Adult soft contemp. News progmg 14 hrs wkly. Target aud: 35 plus; Monmouth/Ocean counties of N.J. Spec prog: Help Yourself one hr wkly. ■ Arthur Shadek, pres; Raymond Fodge, stn mgr, progmg dir & chief engr; Bud Heck, gen sls mgr; Phil Painter, pub affrs dir. ■ Rates: $64; 48; 64; 32.

Pomona

*****WLFR(FM)**—Oct 16, 1984: 91.7 mhz; 1.35 kw. Ant 135 ft. TL: N39 28 45 W74 32 23 (CP: 900 w). Stereo. Hrs opn: 8 AM-1 AM. Stockton State College (08240). (609) 652-4780. FAX: (609) 748-5523. Licensee: Stockton State College. Format: Alternative. News progmg 3 hrs wkly. Target aud: General. Spec prog: Class 4 hrs, jazz 10 hrs wkly. ■ Lori McArdle, gen mgr; Joe Maida, progmg dir; Bill Smith, mus dir; Jason Clark, asst mus dir; Richard Arsenault, chief engr.

Pompton Lakes

WGHT(AM)—Oct 3, 1964: 1500 khz; 1 kw-D, DA. TL: N40 58 51 W74 17 06. Box 1500, 1976 Lincoln Ave. (07442). (201) 839-1500. Licensee: Mariana Broadcasting Inc. (acq 7-8-93; $475,000; FTR 8-23-93). Format: Adult contemp. News staff one; news progmg 10 hrs wkly. Target aud: 20-60; general. Spec prog: Relg 2 hrs, big band one hr, polka one hr wkly. ■ Lee Novak, pres, gen mgr, gen sls mgr & prom mgr; Tom Niven, vp opns, progmg dir & news dir; Don Lawshe, chief engr. ■ Rates: $23; 23; 23; na.

Princeton

WHWH(AM)—Sept 7, 1963: 1350 khz; 5 kw-U, DA-2. TL: N40 22 00 W74 44 38. Hrs opn: 24. Box 1350 (08542); 221 Witherspoon St. (08542). (609) 924-3600. FAX: (609) 924-1725. Licensee: Nassau Broadcasting Co. Net: ABC/E, UPI, NBC Talknet, Wall Street, Unistar. Rep: Katz. Format: Lite adult contemp, news/talk. News staff 4; news progmg 36 hrs wkly. Target aud: 35 plus. Spec prog: Princeton University football & basketball. ■ Louis F. Mercatanti, CEO & chmn; John Morris, pres; G. Daniel Henrickson, CFO; Joan Gerberding, exec vp & gen mgr; Mark O'Brien, opns mgr; Cynthia Morgan, gen sls mgr; Gregg Stiansen, natl sls mgr; Hal Stein, mktg dir, prom mgr & adv dir; Mike Davidson, progmg dir & mus dir; Gary Block, pub affrs dir; Josh Hadden, chief engr. ■ Rates: $54; 48; 46; 46.

WPRB(FM)—October 1955: 103.3 mhz; 14 kw. Ant 731 ft. TL: N41 17 00 W74 41 20. Stereo. Box 342 (08542). (609) 258-3655. Licensee: Princeton Broadcasting Service Inc. Net: ABC/D. Format: Progsv, class. Spec prog: Jazz 20 hrs, C&W 2 hrs, Asian Indian 2 hrs wkly. ■ Sean Murphy, gen mgr & progmg dir; Karim Momin, gen sls mgr; Jen Moyse, mus dir; Marianne Apostolides, news dir; Jon Wood, chief engr. ■ Rates: $30; 30; 30; 30.

WPST(FM)—See Trenton.

Princeton Junction

*****WWPH(FM)**—November 1975: 107.9 mhz; 17 w. Ant 36 ft. TL: N40 18 20 W74 37 16. Box 248, 346 Clarksville Rd. (08550). (609) 799-3143, ext. 60. FAX: (609) 936-9226. Licensee: West Windsor Plainsboro Rgnl Bd. of Educ. Format: Variety. News progmg 5 hrs wkly. Target aud: 14-30; people looking for something different. ■ Glen Allison, gen mgr; Brian Novack, opns dir.

Salem

WJIC(AM)—Licensed to Salem. See Wilmington, Del.

WNNN(FM)—See Canton.

South Belmar

WADB(FM)—See Point Pleasant.

South Orange

*****WSOU(FM)**—Apr 14, 1948: 89.5 mhz; 2 kw. Ant 370 ft. TL: N40 44 44 W74 14 50 (CP: 2.8 kw, ant 313 ft., TL: N40 44 29 W74 14 42). Stereo. 400 S. Orange Ave. (07079). (201) 761-9520. FAX: (201) 761-7593. Licensee: Seton Hall Univ. Format: Hard rock, heavy metal. News progmg 7 hrs wkly. Target aud: 18-24; working class males. Spec prog: Black 3 hrs, Sp one hr, jazz one hr, Pol 2 hrs, Armenian 2 hrs, Arabic 2 hrs, Jewish 2 hrs, Lithuanian 2 hrs, Irish 2 hrs, Filipino 2 hrs wkly. ■ Michael A. Collazo, gen mgr; Mark Schmidt, stn mgr; Steve LiBrizzi, opns dir; Nancy J. Coughlin, sls dir, mktg dir & adv dir; Anya Feldman, prom dir; Kathy Pellicoro, progmg dir; Wayne Pighini, mus dir; Jenn Tonetti, news dir; Steve Edwards, pub affrs dir; Tom Parnham, chief engr. ■ Rates: $50; 50; 50; 50.

Stirling

WKMB(AM)—February 1972: 1070 khz; 250 w-D. TL: N40 40 35 W74 28 36. 1390 Valley Rd. (07980). (908) 647-4400. Licensee: K&M Broadcasters Inc. Format: Popular country. ■ Herbert P. Michels, pres; Alice Dunne, gen mgr, progmg dir & news dir; William Michels, gen sls mgr; Kevin Howard, mus dir; Ronald Michaels, chief engr. ■ Rates: $41; 35; 41; 35.

Sussex

*****WNJP(FM)**—Not on air, target date unknown: 88.5 mhz; 500 w. Ant 600 ft. TL: N41 08 37 W74 32 17. NJN Radio, CN777, Trenton (08625-0777). (609) 777-5030. Licensee: New Jersey Public Broadcasting Authority. Wash atty: Schwartz, Woods & Miller. Format: News/talk, adult contemp. News staff 5; news progmg 13 hrs wkly. Target aud: General. ■ Harvey Fisher, CEO; George Hoover, exec vp & engrg dir; Prince Wooten, gen mgr; Hope Koseff, opns mgr, prom mgr & asst mus dir; Susan Sands, dev mgr, rgnl sls mgr, mktg mgr & adv mgr; Lamont King, progmg dir; Jackie Anderson, news dir; Larry Will, chief engr.

Teaneck

*****WFDU(FM)**—Aug 30, 1971: 89.1 mhz; 550 w. Ant 550 ft. TL: N40 57 39 W73 55 23. Stereo. 1000 River Rd. (07666). (201) 692-2806. FAX: (201) 692-2807. Licensee: Fairleigh Dickinson University. Format: Jazz, C&W, ethnic, progsv. News progmg 3 hrs wkly. Target aud: General. ■ Carl J. Kraus, gen mgr, stn mgr & chief engr.

Toms River

WJRZ(AM)—Not on air, target date unknown: 1550 khz; 6 kw-D, 3 kw-N, DA-2. TL: N39 59 27 W74 15 33. Stereo. Hrs opn: 24. Box 100, 22 W. Water St. (08754). (908) 349-1100; (609) 597-1100. FAX: (908) 505-8700; (609) 597-4400. Licensee: Knox Broadcasting Group Inc. (acq 12-28-90; $198,375; FTR 1-14-91). Net: AP. Rep: D & R Radio, Interep. Wash atty: Roberts & Eckard. Format: News/talk. Target aud: General. ■ Joseph Knox Jr., gen mgr; Brent McNally, gen sls mgr; Lance DeBock, progmg dir; Bill Mead, news dir; Mike Moran, engrg mgr; Bill Clanton, chief engr.

WOBM-FM—March 1, 1968: 92.7 mhz; 1.4 kw. Ant 485 ft. TL: N39 52 30 W74 09 52. Stereo. Box 927 (08754). (908) 269-0927. FAX: (908) 269-9292. Licensee: Seashore Broadcasting Corp. Net: AP. Format: Adult contemp. ■ Roy G. Simmons, pres; Glenn Jones, gen mgr & gen sls mgr; Kevin Buckelew, opns mgr & progmg dir; Cathie Plescia, prom mgr; Jeff M. Rafter, mus dir; Doug Doyle, news dir; Rick St. James, chief engr.

Trenton

WBUD(AM)—Jan 20, 1947: 1260 khz; 5 kw-D, 1 kw-N, DA-2. TL: N40 15 56 W74 45 27 (CP: 2.5 kw-N). Box 5698, 218 Ewingville Rd. (08638). (609) 882-4600; (800) 876-9599. FAX: (609) 883-6684. Licensee: Press Broadcasting Co. (acq 3-27-83; $12 million with co-located FM; FTR 3-27-89). Net: AP, ABC TalkRadio. Rep: McGavren Guild. Wash atty: Dow, Lohnes & Albertson. Format: MOR, news/talk, nostalgia. News staff 5; news progmg 25 hrs wkly. Target aud: 35 plus. ■ Bob McAllan, pres; John Dziuba, vp & gen mgr; Jay Sorensen, opns mgr;

Barbara Rabinowitz, gen sls mgr; Tracie Ambrose, prom dir; Perry Simon, progmg mgr.

WKXW(FM)—Co-owned with WBUD(AM). Aug 27, 1962: 101.5 mhz; 18 kw. Ant 810 ft. TL: N40 17 00 W74 41 20 (CP: 19 kw, ant 803 ft.). Stereo. Prog sep from AM. Box 5698, 218 Ewingville Rd. (08638); 600 Essex Rd., Neptune (07754). (908) 922-4700; (800) 678-9599. FAX: (908) 922-3085. Net: AP. Format: Oldies, talk. News staff 5. Target aud: General; NJ residents. ■ Eric Scott, news dir; Bill Smith, chief engr.

WCHR(FM)—Listing follows WTTM(AM).

WIMG(AM)—(Ewing). 1923: 1300 khz; 5 kw-D, 1 kw-N, DA-2. TL: N40 17 16 W74 52 23. Box 9078, Trenton (08650). (609) 695-1300. Licensee: Morris Broadcasting Co. of New Jersey Inc. (acq 12-3-93; $45,000; FTR 12-20-93). Format: Gospel. Spec prog: Black 7 hrs, It one hr, Ger one hr wkly. ■ Michael Morris, pres; John Forsythe, gen mgr & gen sls mgr; Charlie Geter, progmg dir; Art White, chief engr.

WKXW(FM)—Listing follows WBUD(AM).

***WNJT-FM**—May 20, 1991: 88.1 mhz; 30 w. Ant 787 ft. TL: N40 16 58 W74 41 11. Hrs opn: 18. NJN Radio, CN777 (08625-0777). (609) 777-5030. Licensee: New Jersey Public Broadcasting Authority. Wash atty: Schwartz, Woods & Miller. Format: News/talk, adult contemp, div. News staff 5; news progmg 13 hrs wkly. Target aud: General. ■ Harvey Fisher, CEO; George Hoover, exec vp & engrg dir; Prince Wooten, gen mgr; Hope Koseff, opns mgr, prom mgr & asst mus dir; Susan Sands, dev mgr, rgnl sls mgr, mktg mgr & adv mgr; Lamont King, progmg dir; Jackie Anderson, news dir; Larry Will, chief engr.

WPST(FM)—Jan 19, 1949: 97.5 mhz; 50 kw. Ant 470 ft. TL: N40 14 05 W74 46 02. Stereo. Box 9750 (08650-1750); 221 Witherspoon St., Princeton (08542). (609) 924-3600. FAX: (609) 924-1725. Licensee: Nassau Broadcasting Co. (acq 12-1-64). Rep: Katz. Format: CHR. News staff 4; news progmg 2 hrs wkly. Target aud: 18-49. ■ John Morris, pres; Joan Gerberding, gen mgr & stn mgr; Hal Stein, mktg dir & adv dir; Michael Morris, prom mgr; Michelle Stevens, progmg dir; Rick Eby, chief engr.

***WTSR(FM)**—Sept 1966: 91.3 mhz; 1.5 kw. Ant 35 ft. TL: N40 16 17 W74 46 55. Stereo. Hrs opn: 18. Radio Stn. WTSR(FM), Kondall Hall, Trenton State College (08650-4700). (609) 771-3200; (609) 771-2554. Licensee: Trenton State College Radio System. Net: UPI. Format: Alternative, folk, jazz. News progmg 15 hrs wkly. Target aud: 13-28; people who listen to alternative music formats. Spec prog: Gospel 8 hrs, pub affrs 8 hrs, oldies 3 hrs wkly. ■ Dr. David A. Rogosky, gen mgr.

WTTM(AM)—Apr 11, 1941: 920 khz; 1 kw-U, DA-1. TL: N40 15 19 W74 51 44 (CP: 1.4 kw-D). Stereo. Hrs opn: 24. 333 W. State St. (08618). (609) 695-8515; (215) 946-8666. FAX: (609) 695-6706. Licensee: Great Scott Broadcasting Co. (group owner; acq 4-15-63). Net: BRN, ARN, CNN. Wash atty: Cohn & Marks. Format: News/talk. News staff 2; news progmg 2 hrs wkly. Target aud: 25-54; appeals to a responsive cross-section of adults. Spec prog: Black 6 hrs, Ger 2 hrs, Pol 2 hrs, Sp 6 hrs wkly. ■ Faye Scott, pres; Graham Satherlie, exec vp; Mark Mostontt, gen sls mgr; Dan Shaw, progmg dir; Ron Simpson, chief engr. ■ Rates: $25; 25; 25; 25.

WCHR(FM)—Co-owned with WTTM(AM). Aug 7, 1965: 94.5 mhz; 50 kw. Ant 492 ft. TL: N40 11 22 W74 50 47. Stereo. Prog sep from AM. Net: USA, Moody. Format: Relg, btfl mus. ■ Chuck Zulker, gen mgr; Geoff Howell, news dir; Tony Henry, pub affrs dir. ■ Rates: Same as AM.

***WWFM(FM)**—Sept 6, 1982: 89.1 mhz; 3 kw. Ant 180 ft. TL: N40 15 30 W74 38 59. Stereo. Hrs opn: 5:30 AM-midnight. Box B (08690). (609) 587-8989. FAX: (609) 586-4533. Licensee: Mercer County Community College Board of Trustees. Net: APR. Wash atty: Rosenman & Colin. Format: Class. ■ George Schwartz, gen mgr; Alice Weiss, progmg dir; Jack Perlstein, mus dir; Walt Gradzki, Phil Joiner (asst), chief engrs.

Tuckerton

WTUC(FM)—Not on air, target date unknown: 99.7; 520 Hillcrest Dr., Neshanic Station (08853). Licensee: Richard Lee Harvey.

Union Township

***WKNJ-FM**—January 1980: 90.3 mhz; 8.7 w. Ant 88 ft. TL: N40 40 35 W74 14 02. Stereo. Kean College, Morris Ave., Union (07083). (908) 527-2336. Licensee: Board of Trustees of Kean College. Format: New mus. Spec prog: Black 2 hrs, jazz 8 hrs, new age 8 hrs wkly. ■ Robin Lanzafama, gen mgr; Chris Arnone, stn mgr; Lori Kerrigan, progmg dir; Constance Jasper, mus dir.

Upper Montclair

***WMSC(FM)**—Dec 9, 1974: 101.5 mhz; 10 w. Ant 623 ft. TL: N40 51 53 W74 12 03. Stereo. Hrs opn: 7 AM-1 AM. Student Center Annex, Rm. 110, Montclair State College (07043). (201) 655-4257; (201) 655-4256. FAX: (201) 655-7433. Licensee: Board of Trustees, Montclair State College. Format: Alternative/progsv. News progmg 5 hrs wkly. Target aud: Under 35. Spec prog: Black 4 hrs, gospel 2 hrs, jazz 2 hrs, Sp 2 hrs, sports 3 hrs wkly. ■ Mike Hyde, gen mgr; Melanie Berry, opns dir; Kathleen Dillon, sls dir; Darrin King, prom dir; Christopher Miguel, progmg dir & asst mus dir; Chris Damon, mus dir; Stuart Weissman, news dir; Jenn Nolan, pub affrs dir; Al Reising, engrg dir; Mike Noone, chief engr.

Villas

WFNN(FM)—February 1992: 98.7 mhz; 3 kw. Ant 292 ft. TL: N39 00 33 W74 52 13. Rt. 47, Cape May Court House (08210). (609) 886-9100. FAX: (609) 889-9229. Licensee: Marc Scott Communications Inc. (acq 7-90; $175,000; FTR 7-16-90). Format: Adult contemp. ■ Marc Scott, pres; Bill Huf, gen mgr.

Vineland

WMIZ(AM)—Aug 19, 1959: 1270 khz; 500 w-D, 350 w-N, DA-2. TL: N39 29 53 W75 04 31 (CP: 360 w-D, 210 w-N). Box 689, 638 Landis Ave. (08360). (609) 692-8888; (609) 692-7111. FAX: (609) 696-2568. Licensee: Clear Communications Inc. (acq 8-1-86; $400,000; FTR 5-12-86). Format: Sp. News staff one; news progmg 8 hrs wkly. Target aud: Hispanic. ■ Charles McCreery, pres; David C. Fiedler, gen mgr & adv dir; Ben Garcia, stn mgr & progmg dir; David Schmidt, chief engr. ■ Rates: $15; 12; 15; 10.

WVLT(FM)—Co-owned with WMIZ(AM). October 1968: 92.1 mhz; 3 kw. Ant 328 ft. TL: N39 29 53 W75 04 31. Stereo. Prog sep from AM. Net: ABC. Format: Adult contemp. Target aud: 25-54; baby boomers. ■ Dave Fiedler, gen sls mgr; Kevin Hilley, prom mgr; Joe Palti, progmg dir; Mike Alfie, news dir. ■ Rates: $29; 26; 29; 20.

Washington Township

WNJC(AM)—July 29, 1946: 1360 khz; 5 kw-D, 1 kw-N, DA-2. TL: N39 47 23 W75 06 11 (CP: TL: N39 47 24 W75 06 04). Hrs opn: 6 AM-midnight. R.R. 4, Box 600, Suite 101, 150 N. Delsea Dr., Sewell (08080). (609) 232-7077. FAX: (609) 232-9093. Licensee: Vineland Broadcasting Inc. Group owner: Gus Cawley & Co. (acq 8-1-86; $250,000; FTR 5-12-86). Net: ABC/E. Wash atty: Bechtel & Cole. Format: Talk. News staff 3; news progmg 20 hrs wkly. Target aud: 30 plus; 52% women, upper income. Spec prog: Collegiate and professional sports, Governor's monthly prog, relg 6 hrs wkly. ■ Gus Cawley, pres, gen mgr & progmg dir; Bo Baxter, mus dir; Glen Chaplin, news dir; Dave Schmidt, engrg dir. ■ Rates: $45; 35; 40; 30.

Wayne

***WPSC-FM**—Nov 1, 1988: 88.7 mhz; 200 w. Ant 299 ft. TL: N40 59 46 W74 16 51. Stereo. Hrs opn: 20. Hobart Hall, 300 Pompton Rd. (07470). (201) 595-2454; (201) 595-3319. FAX: (201) 595-2483. Licensee: William Paterson College of New Jersey (acq 7-90; $1; FTR 7-16-90). Net: AP. Format: CHR. News progmg 10 hrs wkly. Target aud: 18-40. Spec prog: Black 4 hrs wkly, jazz 5 hrs, big band 2 hrs, metal 4 hrs, alternative 12 hrs, dance 8 hrs, relg one hr wkly. ■ Arnold Speert, pres; John Kiernan, stn mgr & chief engr; Kevin Serio, opns mgr & sls dir; Richard Rossillo, dev dir & gen sls mgr; Joseph Pardavilla, prom dir; Richard Kaminski, progmg dir; Marc Steiner, mus dir; Steve Greenfield, asst mus dir; Kristine Novak, news dir; Cheryl Laudadio, pub affrs dir.

West Long Branch

***WMCX(FM)**—May 2, 1974: 88.9 mhz; 1 kw. Ant 85 ft. TL: N40 16 44 W74 00 26. Stereo. Monmouth College, Cedar & Norwood Ave. (07764). (908) 571-3400. FAX: (908) 571-4407. Licensee: Monmouth College. Net: AP. Format: AOR. ■ Loral Milton, gen mgr; Mike Farrell, chief engr.

Wildwood

WCMC(AM)—Nov 25, 1951: 1230 khz; 1 kw-U. TL: N39 00 09 W74 48 46. 3010 New Jersey Ave. (08260). (609) 522-1416. FAX: (609) 729-9264; (609) 522-0800. Licensee: Vinrah of New Jersey Inc. Net: SMN. Rep: D & R Format: MOR. News staff 2; news progmg 20 hrs wkly. Target aud: 30 plus. ■ Arthur G. Camiolo, vp & gen mgr; Ray Marcolongo, stn mgr; Andrea Corun, gen sls mgr; Jim MacMillin, progmg dir.

WZXL(FM)—Co-owned with WCMC(AM). Dec 17, 1959: 100.7 mhz; 38 kw. Ant 350 ft. TL: N39 07 28 W74 45 56. Stereo. Prog sep from AM. Rep: D & R Radio. Format: AOR. News staff one; news progmg 7 hrs wkly. Target aud: 18-49. ■ Steve Raymond, progmg dir.

Wildwood Crest

WDOX(FM)—Aug 15, 1993: 93.1 mhz; 3.3 kw. Ant 291 ft. TL: N39 00 33 W74 52 13. Stereo. Hrs opn: 24. Two Oak Ave., Wenonah (08090). (609) 464-0467. FAX: (609) 464-0743. Licensee: Joseph Donald Powers (acq 7-92; $40,000; FTR 6-22-92). Format: Btfl music. Target aud: 40 plus. ■ Don Powers, vp engrg. ■ Rates: $18; 18; 18; 10.

Zarephath

WAWZ(FM)—Aug 22, 1954: 99.1 mhz; 37 kw. Ant 570 ft. TL: N40 36 42 W74 34 14. Stereo. Box 37 (08890). (908) 469-0991. FAX: (908) 231-1968. Licensee: Pillar of Fire Inc. (group owner). Net: AP. Format: Relg. News staff one. ■ Donald J. Wolfram, pres; S. Rea Crawford, gen mgr; Allen Lewis Lewicki, opns dir; Ron Habegger, chief engr.

New Mexico

Alamo Community

***KABR(AM)**—August 1983: 1500 khz; 1 kw-D. TL: N34 25 01 W107 30 04. Box 907, Magdalena (87825). (505) 854-2632; (505) 854-2641. FAX: (505) 854-2545. Licensee: Alamo Navajo Community School. Format: Country, rock, educ. News staff one; news progmg 10 hrs wkly. Target aud: General; Native Americans, local ranchers, tourists, teachers & health professionals. Spec prog: American Indian 10 hrs wkly. ■ Marcel Kerkmans, pres; Patsy Apachito, stn mgr.

Alamogordo

KINN(AM)—June 10, 1957: 1270 khz; 1 kw-D, 500 w-N. TL: N32 53 13 W105 57 04. Hrs opn: 24. Box 618, 501 S. Florida (88310). (505) 437-4440. FAX: (505) 434-2586. Licensee: KINN Inc. (acq 6-90; $10; FTR 6-11-90). Net: ABC/I, SMN. Wash atty: Baraff, Koerner, Olender & Hochberg. Format: Adult contemp. News progmg 22 hrs wkly. Target aud: 24-50; military & civil svc personel employed in high-tech jobs. ■ Robert Vaughn, pres, gen mgr & gen sls mgr; Nick Tafoya, progmg dir & mus dir; John Richards, news dir.

KZZX-FM—Co-owned with KINN(AM). 1979: 105.5 mhz; 6 kw. Ant 157 ft. TL: N32 53 13 W105 57 04 (CP: 105.3 mhz, 2.23 kw, ant 524 ft.). Stereo. Hrs opn: 24. Prog sep from AM. Format: Country. News progmg 22 hrs wkly. Target aud: 20-55.

KPSA(AM)—June 28, 1950: 1230 khz; 1 kw-U. TL: N32 53 46 W105 56 42. Hrs opn: 24. Box 720, Cuba Ave. & Canyon Rd. (88310). (505) 437-1505; (505) 437-1230. FAX: (505) 437-5566. Licensee: Cottonwood Communications Corp. (group owner; acq 10-7-77; $282,000). Net: MBS. Wash atty: Jones, Waldo, Holbrook & McDonough. Format: Modern country, talk. News staff 2; news progmg 10 hrs wkly. Target aud: 22 plus; active adults, community-oriented. Spec prog: Big band 6 hrs, farm one hr, gospel 8 hrs, relg 4 hrs wkly. ■ Bob Flotte, pres & gen mgr; Bev Flotte, gen sls mgr; Amanda Jolley, prom dir; T.J. Curry, progmg dir & mus dir; Mike Shinabery, news dir; Ken Hathaway, chief engr. ■ Rates: $18.65; 15.65; 18.65; na.

KPSA-FM—(La Luz). Jan 17, 1987: 92.7 mhz; 3 kw. Ant 192 ft. TL: N32 98 15 W105 59 21 (CP: 103.7 mhz, 50.2 kw, ant 1,338 ft., TL: N33 10 45 W105 53 53). Stereo. Hrs opn: 24. Prog sep from AM. Format: Lite adult contemp, oldies blend. News staff 2. Target aud: 21 plus; active adults, demo 21-54. ■ Bob Flotte, CFO, natl sls mgr & pub affrs dir; Casey Jones, progmg mgr; Kelly Lynch, mus dir; Ken Hathaway, engrg dir. ■ Rates: Same as AM.

KYEE(FM)—July 21, 1980: 94.3 mhz; 3 kw. Ant -492 ft. TL: N32 56 42 W105 56 47. Stereo. Box 1848, N. Florida Ave. (88311). (505) 434-1414. FAX: (505) 434-2213. Licensee: William F. Burt (acq 11-88; $230,000; FTR 12-19-88). Net: NBC. Format: CHR. News staff 2; news progmg 5 hrs wkly. Target aud: 18-44; young adults. ■ William F. Burt, pres & gen mgr; Donnie L. Burt, vp; Lori Swinford, gen sls mgr & adv dir.

KZZX-FM—Listing follows KINN(AM).

Albuquerque

KABQ(AM)—1947: 1350 khz; 5 kw-D, 500 w-N, DA-N. TL: N35 06 02 W106 40 34. Box 4486, Suite 2200, 1400 Central S.E. (87196). (505) 243-1744. Licensee: Albuquerque Corp. Group owner: The Gomez Group (acq 1971). Net: SIS. Rep: Lotus. Format: Sp. News progmg 6 hrs wkly. Target aud: General. ■ Ed Gomez, pres, gen sls mgr & news dir; Jim Gomez, gen mgr, opns mgr, progmg dir & mus dir; Carlos Gomez, pub affrs dir; Jim Hogg, chief engr.

KALY(AM)—(Los Ranchos de Albuquerque). 1982: 1240 khz; 1 kw-U. TL: N35 11 03 W106 36 50. Stereo. Box 10246, 9100 2nd St. N.W., Albuquerque (87184). (505) 898-1868; (505) 898-2027. FAX: (505) 898-2228. Licensee: Septien and Associates Inc. (acq 5-21-92; $460,000; FTR 6-15-92). Net: CRC. Rep: Lotus. Format: Sp. News staff one; news progmg 2 hrs wkly. Target aud: 25-49. ■ G. Septien, pres & gen mgr; Enrique Del-Real, gen sls mgr; Joseph Andrade, prom dir & progmg dir; Jesus Jose "Rafa" Portillo, mus dir. ■ Rates: $35; 35; 35; na.

KAMX(AM)—Feb. 22, 1971: 1520 khz; 1 kw-D. TL: N35 04 35 W106 40 37. Suite 290, 5700 Harper Dr. N.E. (87109). (505) 828-1600. Licensee: Coastal Communications of Albuquerque Inc. (acq 9-1-85; $2.12 million with co-located fm; FTR 5-20-85). Rep: Banner. Format: Adult contemp. ■ Don Robertson, gen mgr; David Ianni, gen sls mgr; Scott Kerr, progmg dir; Rob Ramseyer, chief engr.

KAMX-FM—Apr 27, 1979: 107.9 mhz; 22.5 kw. Ant 4,130 ft. TL: N35 12 43 W106 26 57. Stereo. Hrs opn: 24. Dups AM 100%. Target aud: 18-49.

***KANW(FM)**—October 1950: 89.1 mhz; 20 kw. Ant 4,152 ft. TL: N35 12 44 W106 26 57. Stereo. 2020 Coal Ave. S.E. (87106). (505) 242-7163. Licensee: Board of Educ of the City of Albuquerque. Net: ABC/C, American Urban. Format: Educ, urban contemp. Spec prog: Class 6 hrs, Sp 6 hrs, Indian 2 hrs, post modern 3 hrs wkly. ■ Michael Brasher, gen mgr; Leigh-Ann Gerow, progmg dir & mus dir; Judy Valdez, news dir & pub affrs dir; Bill Pace, chief engr.

KASY(FM)—Apr 20, 1988: 103.3 mhz; 22 kw. Ant 4,069 ft. TL: N35 12 50 W106 27 00. Stereo. 3800 Carlisle Blvd. N.E. (87107). (505) 881-2000. FAX: (505) 881-2266. Licensee: Guadalajara Chili Pepper Co. Rep: Katz Hispanic. Format: Country. Target aud: 18-49. ■ Ray Moran, gen mgr; Rick Parrish, gen sls mgr; Bruce Aglear, progmg dir & mus dir.

KDAZ(AM)—1959: 730 khz; 1 kw-D, 76 w-N, DA-2. TL: N35 00 31 W106 42 52. Box 4338, 5010 4th St. NW (87107). (505) 345-7373. FAX: (505) 345-5669. Licensee: Pan American Broadcasting Co. (acq 12-1-71). Net: CBN, SMN, USA. Wash atty: Gammon & Grange. Format: Contemp praise, Christian talk. Target aud: 18-45; three cultures-Indian, Hispanic, Angelo. ■ Belarmino R. Gonzales, pres, gen mgr & gen sls mgr; Annette Garcia, progmg dir; Jeremy Reynalds, mus dir; Jim Hogg, chief engr.

KDEF(AM)—September 1953: 1150 khz; 5 kw-D, 500 w-N, DA-2. TL: N35 12 06 W106 35 54. 2117 Menaul Blvd. N.E. (87107). (505) 837-1217. FAX: (505) 837-1219. Licensee: KCST Inc. (acq 8-15-92 LMA; FTR 7-1-91). Rep: Katz & Powell. Format: All sports. Target aud: General. ■ Ivan Braiker, CEO & gen mgr; Henry Tafoyo, vp opns, vp progmg & progmg dir; Gary Herron, opns dir.

***KFLQ(FM)**—Feb 20, 1983: 91.5 mhz; 22.5 kw. Ant 4,060 ft. TL: N35 12 51 W106 27 02. Stereo. Hrs opn: 24. 3801 Urbank N.E. (87111). (505) 296-9100. FAX: (505) 296-6262. Licensee: Family Life Broadcasting System (group owner; acq 1982). Net: Moody, USA. Format: Relg. News staff one; news progmg 3 hrs wkly. Target aud: 25-49. Spec prog: Sp 3 hrs wkly. ■ Warren Bolthouse, pres; Dan Rosecrans, stn mgr; Rod Robison, dev dir; Warren Bonesteel, prom mgr; Jon Webber, news dir; Steve Friis, chief engr.

KHFM(FM)—November 1954: 96.3 mhz; 20 kw. Ant 4,110 ft. TL: N35 12 44 W106 26 58. Stereo. 9910 Indian School Rd. N.E. (87112). (505) 294-9696. FAX: (505) 294-5600. Licensee: New Mexico Classical Radio Inc. (acq 11-87; $850,000; FTR 11-9-87). Rep: CMBS. Format: Class. News progmg 2 hrs wkly. Target aud: Upscale, affluent professionals. ■ Peter Besheer, pres; Michael Langner, gen mgr; Kip Allen, progmg dir & mus dir; Barbara DeKins, pub affrs dir; Mike Langner, engrg dir. ■ Rates: $37; 37; 37; 29.

KJBO(AM)—(Los Ranchos de Albuquerque). Dec 16, 1987: 1050 khz; 1 kw-D, 500 w-N, DA-1. TL: N34 59 46 W106 44 13. Hrs opn: 24. City Centre, Suite 590 W., 6400 Uptown Blvd. N.E., Albuquerque (87110). (505) 880-1118. Licensee: KNXX Inc. Format: Juke box oldies. Target aud: 25-54; info oriented professionals & investors. ■ Bobby Box, gen mgr.

KKIM(AM)—Apr 15, 1972: 1000 khz; 10 kw-D. TL: N35 10 14 W106 37 51. 307 Los Ranchos N.W. (87107). (505) 898-5185. FAX: (505) 898-5186. Licensee: Guardian Communications Inc. (group owner; acq 6-25-90; grpsl; FTR 5-21-90). Format: Christian, country. Target aud: 25-54. Spec prog: Black 2 hrs, country one hr wkly. ■ Mark McNeil, pres; Richard David, vp; Barry McCoy, gen mgr; Rodney Groomer, gen sls mgr; Bill Pace, chief engr. ■ Rates: $18; 18; 18; na.

KKJY-FM—December 1974: 100.3 mhz; 22.5 kw. Ant 4,110 ft. TL: N35 12 51 W106 27 02. Stereo. 5000 Marble Ave. N.E. (87110). (505) 262-1866. FAX: (505) 268-5563. Licensee: MBC Southwest Inc. (acq 7-87; $3.3 million; FTR 6-8-87). Rep: Torbet. Format: Jazz, new age. News progmg 39 hrs wkly. Target aud: 25-54; adults, high income professional and technical. ■ Bud Healey, gen mgr & gen sls mgr; Les Reed, opns mgr & progmg dir; Linda Martinez, progmg mgr; Joan Jamison, mus dir; Susan Dean, pub affrs dir; Bill Pace, chief engr. ■ Rates: $25; 25; 25; 20.

KKOB(AM)—Apr 5, 1922: 770 khz; 50 kw-U, DA-N. TL: N35 12 09 W106 36 41. Hrs opn: 24. Box 1351, 77 Broadcast Plaza S.W. (87103-1351). (505) 243-4411. FAX: (505) 764-2567. Licensee: U.S. Entertainment Corp. Group owner: Fairmont Communications Corp. (acq 6-90; $16 million with co-located FM; FTR 6-18-90). Net: ABC/I, NBC Talknet. Rep: McGavren. Wash atty: Haley, Bader & Potts. Format: MOR. ■ Mark Hubbard, pres; Jim Pidcock, gen mgr; Linda Land, gen sls mgr; Gary Diamond, chief engr.

KKOB-FM—Aug 1, 1967: 93.3 mhz; 21.5 kw. Ant 4,150 ft. TL: N35 12 42 W106 26 59. Stereo. Hrs opn: 24. Prog sep from AM. Box 1351, 93 Broadcast Plaza (87103-1351). Format: Adult contemp. ■ Jim Pidcock, gen mgr; John Forsythe, progmg dir; David Allen, mus dir.

***KLYT(FM)**—Sept 11, 1976: 88.3 mhz; 1.8 kw. Ant 4,000 ft. TL: N35 12 48 W106 27 00 (CP: Ant 4,172 ft.). Stereo. No. 2, 3107 Eubank N.E. (87111). (505) 293-8300. FAX: (505) 296-1331. Licensee: Christian Broadcasting Academy Inc. Net: USA. Format: Contemp Christian hit. ■ Randy Rich, pres & gen mgr; Bill Long, vp; Heidi Chavez, gen sls mgr; Peter Benson, progmg dir; Bill Pace, chief engr.

KMGA(FM)—Listing follows KQEO(AM).

KQEO(AM)—1947: 920 khz; 1 kw-D, 500 w-N, DA-N. TL: N35 06 00 W106 40 04. 5095 Ellison N.E. (87109). (505) 345-9071. FAX: (505) 345-8360. Licensee: SpaceCom Inc. (acq 10-17-90; $750,000 with co-located FM; FTR 11-5-90). Rep: Banner. Format: Oldies. Target aud: 25-54. ■ Walt Richi, pres; Doyle Peterson, gen mgr.

KMGA(FM)—Co-owned with KQEO(AM). Nov 11, 1963: 99.5 mhz; 19.5 kw. Ant 4,134 ft. TL: N35 12 44 W106 26 58. Stereo. Dups AM 15%. Net: Unistar. Rep: Katz. Format: Light contemp. Target aud: 25-54; upscale, business professionals & families. ■ Walt Richi, gen mgr.

KRLL(AM)—May 14, 1956: 1580 khz; 10 kw-D, 47 w-N. TL: N35 05 38 W106 40 48. Rebroadcasts KZKL-FM Rio Rancho 100%. 1561 Univ. N.E. (87102). (505) 242-0626. FAX: (505) 242-0627. Licensee: Territorial Communications Inc. (acq 10-1-92; $600,000 with KZKL-FM Rio Rancho; FTR 11-2-92). Net: CNN, Unistar. Rep: Christal. Format: 50s and 60s music. Target aud: 30-50. ■ Martin Balk, pres; Craig Parker, gen sls mgr; Dave Scott, progmg dir; Craig Collins, mus dir; Jim Schwar, news dir.

KRST(FM)—Listing follows KRZY(AM).

KRZY(AM)—June 1956: 1450 khz; 1 kw-U. TL: N35 06 26 W106 35 20 (CP: 1090 khz, 50 kw-LS, DA-2). Box 3280 (87190). (505) 884-5833. FAX: (505) 888-2406. Licensee: Commonwealth Broadcasting of Northern California. Group owner: Commonwealth Broadcasting Co. (acq 1-89; $8.1 million with co-located FM; FTR 1-23-89). Net: MBS. Rep: Katz. Format: C&W. ■ Dex Allen, pres; Cindy Weiner, gen mgr; Jim Patrick, progmg dir; Bill Pace, chief engr.

KRST(FM)—Co-owned with KRZY(AM). Sept 15, 1965: 92.3 mhz; 22.5 kw. Ant 4,110 ft. TL: N35 12 55 W106 27 02. Stereo. (505) 884-5770. Format: C&W.

***KUNM(FM)**—Oct 17, 1966: 89.9 mhz; 13.6 kw. Ant 4,070 ft. TL: N35 12 44 W106 26 57. Stereo. Hrs opn: 24. Onate Hall, Univ. of New Mexico (87131). (505) 277-4806. FAX: (505) 277-8004. Licensee: Regents of the Univ. of New Mexico. Net: NPR. Wash atty: Dow, Lohnes & Albertson. Format: Div. News staff one; news progmg 39 hrs wkly. Target aud: 25-54. Spec prog: Class 12 hrs, Black 3 hrs, Sp 9 hrs, Indian 3 hrs wkly. ■ Jane Bloom, gen mgr; Mary Ciwz, dev dir; David House, mus dir; Marcos Martinez, news dir; Ken Hjelmstad, chief engr.

KWQK(FM)—Not on air, target date unknown: 101.3 mhz; 4.1 kw. Ant 403 ft. TL: N35 04 00 W106 46 56. 408 Hillside Ave., Santa Fe, NM (87501). Licensee: FM Radio Partners L.P.

KXKS(AM)—Dec 16, 1969: 1190 khz; 10 kw-D. TL: N35 03 04 W106 38 34. Stereo. 6320 Zuni S.E. (87108). (505) 265-8331. FAX: (505) 266-3836. Licensee: Continental Broadcasting Corp of N.M. (acq 6-4-82; $325,000; FTR 6-14-82). Net: AP, UPI. Rep: Caballero. Format: Sp. News staff one; news progmg 14 hrs wkly. Target aud: 25 plus; Hispanic. ■ Jose Molina, chmn; Alfredo Jesus Morales, pres; Salvador Trevino, exec vp; Kelly Cunningham-Munson, gen mgr; Alex Bozzo, stn mgr; Kirk Munson, gen sls mgr & rgnl sls mgr; Hector Velez, progmg dir; Felipe Mendoza, news dir; Bob Henry, chief engr.

KZKL-FM—See Rio Rancho.

KZRR(FM)—June 25, 1961: 94.1 mhz; 100 kw. Ant 4,130 ft. TL: N35 12 44 W106 26 58. Stereo. 2700 San Pedro N.E. (87110). (505) 889-8899. FAX: (505) 889-0002. Licensee: Twin Peaks Radio (group owner; acq 6-4-93; grpsl; FTR 6-28-93). Net: Westwood One, NBC the Source. Rep: Eastman. Format: AOR. ■ Milt McConnell, vp & gen mgr; Frank Jaxon, opns mgr; Tim Gannon, gen sls mgr; Joan Abrams, prom mgr; Phil Mahoney, mus dir; Bill Pace, chief engr.

KZSS(AM)—Co-owned with KZRR(FM). March 28, 1928: 610 khz; 5 kw-U, DA-N. TL: N35 01 56 W106 39 48. Dups FM 100%.

Angel Fire

KAFR(FM)—Jan 15, 1990: 99.1 mhz; 5.743 kw. Ant 1,377 ft. TL: N36 22 33 W105 14 12. Stereo. Hrs opn: 18. Box 520, Agra Fria Business Ctr. (87710); Box 5030-350, Livermore, CA (94550). (505) 377-3576; (505) 377-2596. FAX: (505) 377-3578. Licensee: Moreno Valley Broadcasting. Format: Classic rock, country. Target aud: 35 plus; intelligent. Spec prog: Jazz 4 hrs, relg 8 hrs wkly. ■ Kenneth Lamson, CEO & chief engr; Francis O'Connell, pres, gen mgr, prom mgr & mus dir; Brian Edlund, asst mus dir.

Armijo

KUCU(FM)—Dec 17, 1991: 107.1 mhz; 50 kw. Ant 304 ft. TL: N35 03 15 W106 51 31 (CP: 60 kw, 2,365 ft.). Stereo. Hrs opn: 24. 2117 Manaul Blvd. N.E., Albuquerque (87107). (505) 837-1217. FAX: (505) 837-1219. Licensee: KCST Inc. (acq 8-15-92 LMA; FTR 7-1-91). Rep: Katz & Powell. Format: Country, class rock. News progmg 4 hrs wkly. Target aud: 25-54. ■ Ivan Braiker, CEO & gen mgr; Kathy Fix, rgnl sls mgr; Sherry Blowers, prom dir; Henry Tafoya, progmg dir. ■ Rates: $35; 25; 35; 20.

Artesia

KSVP(AM)—Nov 14, 1946: 990 khz; 1 kw-D, 250 w-N. TL: N32 49 29 W104 23 59. Hrs opn: 24. 317 W. Quay (88210). (505) 746-2751. FAX: (505) 748-3748. Licensee: Pecos Valley Broadcasting Co. (acq 1993; $150,000 with co-located FM; FTR 9-13-93). Net: MBS, ABC/I, ABC TalkRadio, Daynet. Rep: Katz & Powell. Wash atty: Cohn & Marks. Format: Talk. News staff one; news progmg 18 hrs wkly. Target aud: General. Spec prog: Sp 15 hrs, farm one hr wkly. ■ Sam F. Beard, pres; Gene Dow, gen mgr; Lana Faber, news dir. ■ Rates: $15; 15; 15; 15.

KTZA(FM)—Co-owned with KSVP(AM). May 9, 1969: 92.9 mhz; 100 kw. Ant 1,089 ft. TL: N32 47 39 W104 12 27. Stereo. Hrs opn: 24. Prog sep from AM. Net: Unistar, ABC/D. Format: C&W. News progmg 3 hrs wkly. Target aud: 25-54. ■ Rates: Same as AM.

Aztec

KCQL(AM)—Sept 4, 1959: 1340 khz; 1 kw-U. TL: N36 49 17 W107 59 58. Stereo. Hrs opn: 24. 303 Ash (87410); Box 2000, Farmington (87499). (505) 325-1716. FAX: (505) 325-1744. Licensee: Frank Elwood and Wanda Jean Elwood (acq 2-5-87; $216,000; FTR 11-24-86). Net: NBC. Rep: Hix. Format: Oldies. News progmg 14 hrs wkly. Target aud: 18-54. Spec prog: Sp 6 hrs wkly. ■ John Lockmiller, gen mgr; Kevin O'Neill, opns dir & progmg dir; Dan Kelly, chief engr. ■ Rates: $18; 10; 18; 10.

Stations in the U.S.   New Mexico

KWYK-FM—Jan 2, 1978: 94.9 mhz; 100 kw. Ant 433 ft. TL: N32 47 39 W104 12 27. Stereo. Hrs opn: 5 AM-midnight. 1515 W. Main, Farmington (87401). (505) 325-1996. FAX: (505) 327-2019. Licensee: Basin Broadcasting Co. Format: Adult contemp. News staff one; news progmg 15 hrs wkly. Target aud: 18-40; mainstream population. Spec prog: Jazz 3 hrs wkly. ■ Kerwin Gober, gen mgr; Sybil Tibbets, gen sls mgr; Steve Simmons, progmg dir; James A. Doiron, chief engr.

Bayard

KNFT(AM)—July 4, 1968: 950 khz; 5 kw-D. TL: N32 46 51 W108 11 58. Box 1410, Silver City (88062). (505) 388-1958. FAX: (505) 388-5000. Licensee: Hunter Enterprise & Investments (acq 10-23-91; $50,000 with colocated FM; FTR 11-11-91). Net: AP. Format: Nostalgia. ■ Paul Hunter, pres; John Ricketts, gen mgr; Thomas Martinez, progmg dir; Bob Cosgrove, chief engr.

KNFT-FM—June 15, 1981: 102.9 mhz; 3 kw. Ant 135 ft. TL: N32 50 40 W108 14 18 (CP: 29.14 kw, ant 491 ft.). Prog sep from AM. Format: C&W.

Belen

KARS(AM)—Oct 7, 1961: 860 khz; 250 w-D, 186 w-N. TL: N34 41 43 W106 46 13. Hrs opn: 5 AM-10 PM. Box 860, 208 N. 2nd St. (87002). (505) 864-7447. Licensee: Brooks Broadcasting Co. (acq 6-25-71). Net: ABC/E. Rep: Lotus, Art Moore. Format: C&W, Sp, news. News staff one; news progmg 30 hrs wkly. Target aud: 25 plus. ■ Cliff Somers, gen mgr & gen sls mgr; Al Miller, mus dir; Ron Travis, news dir; Bill Pace, chief engr. ■ Rates: $14; 14; 14; 14.

KARS-FM—1982: 97.7 mhz; 1.8 kw. Ant 381 ft. TL: N34 45 02 W106 39 55 (CP: 100 kw, ant 873 ft., TL: N34 47 55 W106 48 59). Stereo. Hrs opn: 5 AM-10 PM. Dups AM 18%. (Acq 7-85; $250,000; FTR 7-22-85). Format: C&W, news. News progmg 17 hrs wkly.

Bloomfield

KKFG(FM)—1988: 104.5 mhz; 100 kw. Ant 1,086 ft. TL: N36 38 33 W107 46 54. Box 2000, Farmington (87499). (505) 335-1716. FAX: (505) 335-6797. Licensee: J. Thomas Development of New Mexico Inc. Format: Hot country. ■ Jeff Thomas, pres; John Lockmiller, gen mgr; Elizabeth Lockmiller, gen sls mgr; Dan Kelley, progmg dir; Kevin O'Neill, mus dir.

Carlsbad

KAMQ(AM)—June 10, 1938: 1240 khz; 1 kw-U. TL: N32 23 43 W104 14 48. Box 1538 (88220). (505) 887-7563. FAX: (505) 887-7000. Licensee: James B. Hughes/Donald G. Hughes (acq 6-23-79). Net: AP. Format: Pure gold. ■ Jim Hughes, pres; Don Hughes, gen mgr; Kathy York, progmg dir & news dir; Frank Nymeyer, chief engr.

KCDY(FM)—Co-owned with KAMQ. July 1989: 104.1 mhz; 100 kw. Ant 676 ft. TL: N32 34 22 W104 05 32. Prog sep from AM. Format: Adult contemp.

KATK(AM)—May 17, 1950: 740 khz; 1 kw-D, 500 w-N. TL: N32 27 02 W104 12 47. 714 N. Canyon (88220). (505) 885-2151; (505) 885-4024. FAX: (505) 887-5691. Licensee: Radio Carlsbad Inc. (acq 8-26-92; $520,868 with co-located FM; FTR 9-14-92). Net: ABC. Format: Sp. News staff one; news progmg 3 hrs wkly. Target aud: General; bilingual Hispanics. ■ Cindy Swayze, gen sls mgr & mktg mgr; Scott Vera, progmg dir; Steve Swayze, chief engr. ■ Rates: $25; 15; 25; 15.

KATK-FM—Sept 15, 1966: 92.1 mhz; 3 kw. Ant 190 ft. TL: N32 27 02 W104 12 47. Stereo. Prog sep from AM. (800) 926-8255. Net: ABC/C. Format: Country. Target aud: 18-54 plus; Hispanic. Spec prog: Hispanic. ■ Steve Swayze, gen mgr; Frank Nymeyer, progmg dir & mus dir. ■ Rates: $25; 15; 15; 25.

KCCC(AM)—July 1, 1966: 930 khz; 1 kw-D, 60 w-N. TL: N32 24 20 W104 11 21. 1011 W. Mermod St. (88220). (505) 887-5521. FAX: (505) 887-2671. Licensee: Kolob Broadcasting Co. Net: MBS. Format: C&W, Sp, news/talk. ■ Marion Jenkins, pres; Nick Jenkins, gen mgr & gen sls mgr; Frank Nymeye, chief engr.

KCDY(FM)—Listing follows KAMQ.

KRHT(FM)—Not on air, target date unknown: 106.1 mhz; 50 kw. Ant 492 ft. TL: N32 34 22 W104 05 32. 1011 W. Mermod (88220). Licensee: Kolob Broadcasting Co. Inc.

Clayton

KLMX(AM)—Nov 10, 1949: 1450 khz; 1 kw-U. TL: N36 26 39 W103 11 24. Box 547 (88415). (505) 374-2555. Licensee: Johnson County Broadcasters Inc. (acq 11-10-78). Net: MBS. Format: Top-40 country. ■ Avis Green Tucker, pres; Jim McCollum, vp, gen mgr & chief engr; Janet Dillon, gen sls mgr; Paula Maestas, progmg dir & news dir.

Clovis

KCLV(AM)—February 1953: 1240 khz; 1 kw-U. TL: N34 22 40 W103 12 17. Box 1907 (88101-1907). 2112 Thornton (88101). (505) 763-4401. FAX: (505) 769-2564. Licensee: Zia Broadcasting Co. (acq 7-1-71). Net: SMN. Format: Country. ■ Lonnie D. Allsup, pres; Jimmy L. Davis, gen mgr; L. Patrick Davidson, gen sls mgr; Roy Norman, prom mgr, progmg dir, mus dir & news dir; Gary Jackson, chief engr.

KCLV-FM—Jan 8, 1970: 99.1 mhz; 74.2 kw. Ant 230 ft. TL: N34 23 18 W103 11 07. Stereo. Hrs opn: 24. Prog sep from AM. (Acq 11-12-81). Net: SMN, ABC/I. Format: Country. Target aud: 18-49. Spec prog: Farm 6 hrs wkly.

KERC(FM)—November 1982: 107.5 mhz; 100 kw. Ant 550 ft. TL: N34 11 34 W103 16 44. Stereo. Box 1785, 4901 N. Prince St. (88101). (505) 763-7109. FAX: (505) 763-7059. Licensee: Hi-Plains Broadcasting Inc. (acq 12-12-93). ■ Jim Day, pres & gen mgr; Janet Paterson, gen sls mgr.

KICA(AM)—1933: 980 khz; 1 kw-U, DA-N. TL: N34 23 21 W103 18 31. Box 7000 (88101). (505) 762-6200. FAX: (505) 762-8000. Licensee: Southwestern Broadcasting Corp. (acq 10-31-90; $30,000; FTR 11-19-90). Rep: Savalli Bcst Sls. Format: Sp. Spec prog: Farm 12 hrs wkly. ■ Tom Crane, pres; Len Vohs, gen mgr; Tina Hagy, progmg dir, mus dir & news dir; Charlie Minnis, chief engr.

KTQM-FM—Listing follows KWKA(AM).

KWKA(AM)—1971: 680 khz; 500 w-U, DA-1. TL: N34 21 48 W103 13 05. Hrs opn: 24. Box 869, Swift Plant Rd. (88102). (505) 762-4411. Licensee: Curry County Broadcasting Inc. (acq 10-24-80; $350,000; FTR 11-10-80). Net: MBS. Rep: Roslin. Wash atty: Fletcher, Heald & Hildreth. Format: Oldies. News staff one; news progmg 3 hrs wkly. Target aud: 25 plus. Spec prog: Farm 3 hrs wkly. ■ C. Hewel Jones, pres, gen mgr & gen sls mgr; Robert D. Coker, vp; Pam Atherton, progmg dir & mus dir; Tia Butts, news dir; Gary Jackson, chief engr. ■ Rates: $15; 13.05; 15; 13.05.

KTQM-FM—Co-owned with KWKA(AM). Mar 1, 1963: 99.9 mhz; 100 kw. Ant 360 ft. TL: N34 21 48 W103 13 05. Stereo. Hrs opn: 24. Prog sep from AM. Format: Adult contemp. Target aud: 18-49; young affluent. ■ Pam Atherton, opns dir; Gary Jackson, engrg dir. ■ Rates: $18.75; 13.50; 18.75; 13.50.

NEW FM—Not on air, target date unknown: 102.3 mhz; 25 kw. Ant 328 ft. TL: N34 20 36 W103 06 17. c/o Quarters 6306-C, U.S.A.F. Academy, Colorado Springs, CO (80840). Licensee: Karen Ann Mainieri.

Corrales

KIVA(AM)—July 15, 1985: 1310 khz; 5 kw-D, 500 w-N, DA-N. TL: N35 12 00 W106 35 59. Stereo. 10316 Edith Blvd. N.E., Albuquerque (87113). (505) 897-6937. Licensee: Broadcast Media Enterprises Inc. (acq 8-3-93; $850,000 with KZRQ[FM] Santa Fe; FTR 8-23-93). Format: Big band/nostalgia. ■ Craig Parker, gen mgr.

KSVA(FM)—Not on air, target date unknown: 95.1 mhz; 3 kw. Ant -531 ft. TL: N35 14 42 W106 36 18. 906 Ortega N.W., Albuquerque (87114). Licensee: LV Broadcasting Educational Foundation.

Deming

KOTS(AM)—March 10, 1954: 1230 khz; 1 kw-U. TL: N32 15 05 W107 45 28. Box 470, 1700 S. Gold (88031). (505) 546-9011; (505) 546-9342. Licensee: Luna County Broadcasting Co. (acq 3-14-90). Net: AP. Format: Country. News staff one; news progmg 2 hrs wkly. Target aud: General. Spec prog: Farm 5 hrs, Sp 8 hrs wkly. ■ Ernest F. Hurt, pres; Candie G. Sweetser, stn mgr. ■ Rates: $5.35; 5.35; 5.35; 5.35.

KDEM(FM)—Co-owned with KOTS(AM). Apr 15, 1977: 94.3 mhz; 3 kw. Ant 195 ft. TL: N32 15 05 W107 45 28. Stereo. Prog sep from AM. Net: SMN. Format: AOR. News staff one; news progmg one hr wkly. Target aud: 18-34. ■ Rates: Same as AM.

Dulce

*KCIE(FM)—Not on air, target date unknown: 90.5 mhz; 100 kw. Ant 1,535 ft. TL: N36 59 00 W106 58 12. Box 306 (87528). Licensee: Jicarilla Apache Tribe.

Espanola

KDCE(AM)—1963: 950 khz; 4.2 kw-D, 90 w-N. TL: N36 00 08 W106 03 59. 403 W. Pueblo Dr. (87532). (505) 753-2201. FAX: (505) 753-8685. Licensee: Richard L. Garcia Broadcasting Inc. (acq 11-29-82; $625,000; FTR 11-8-82). Net: CNN. Rep: Lotus. Format: Sp. ■ Richard Garcia, pres, gen mgr & gen sls mgr; Ray Casias, progmg dir.

KIOT(FM)—July 6, 1981: 102.3 mhz; 1.1 kw. Ant 636 ft. TL: N35 54 01 W105 53 40 (CP: 9 kw, ant 538 ft.). Stereo. Hrs opn: 24. 418 Cerrillos Rd., Santa Fe (87501). (505) 983-1111. FAX: (505) 989-7232. Licensee: Wizard Broadcasting Co. (acq 05-90; $400,000; FTR 10-22-90). Net: BBC. Wash atty: Jones, Waldo. Format: Div. News staff one. Target aud: 25-49; hip adults who like diversity and have disposable income. Spec prog: Gospel 4 hrs wkly. ■ Elliot McDowell, CEO; Bill Sims, pres; Ellen Cavanaugh, opns mgr; Mitch Berg, opns mgr; Mary Fahr, gen sls mgr; Stacia Saunders, prom mgr; Gary Wolter, progmg dir; Bill Pace, chief engr. ■ Rates: $20; 18; 20; 18.

Eunice

KYRK(FM)—Not on air, target date unknown: 100.9 mhz; 3 kw. Ant 295 ft. 2015 Peyton, Las Vegas, NV (89104). Licensee: Mark C. Nolte.

Farmington

KENN(AM)—Nov 1951: 1390 khz; 5 kw-D, 1.3 kw-N, DA-N. TL: N36 42 27 W108 08 50. Box 1558 (87499). (505) 325-3541. Licensee: Kennland Broadcasting. Group owner: Regional Radio (acq 3-15-54). Net: ABC/I, NBC Talknet, MBS. Rep: Eastman, Intermountain Net. Wash atty: Pepper & Corazzini. Format: Adult contemp. News staff one; news progmg 12 hrs wkly. Target aud: 25-54; upper middle class. ■ Kenny Kendrick, pres; Phil Marquez, gen mgr; Beth Jones, progmg dir & mus dir; Leon Reisinger, chief engr. ■ Rates: $16.50; 15; 16.50; 15.

KRWN(FM)—Co-owned with KENN(AM). 1974: 92.9 mhz; 30 kw. Ant 430 ft. TL: N36 41 45 W108 13 23 (CP: 62 kw. Ant 394 ft.). Stereo. Hrs opn: 24. Prog sep from AM. Box 1047 (87401). (505) 327-4449. Licensee: Music Men Inc. Net: SMN. Rep: Art Moore. Format: Classic rock. Target aud: 18-49. ■ Rates: $16.50; 13.50; 16.50; 11.50.

KISZ-FM—See Montezuma, Colo.

KNDN(AM)—Aug 1, 1957: 960 khz; 5 kw-D, 163 w-N. TL: N36 43 48 W108 13 47. Hrs opn: 6 AM-10 PM. 1515 W. Main (87401). (505) 325-1996. FAX: (505) 327-2019. Licensee: Basin Broadcasting Co. Format: Navajo Indian. Target aud: General; Navajo Indian reservation. ■ Jim Gober (owner), gen mgr; Wilbert Begay, progmg dir; James A. Doiron, chief engr. ■ Rates: $12.50; 10; 10; 5.

*KNMI(FM)—Mar 18, 1980: 88.9 mhz; 6.22 kw. Ant 360 ft. TL: N36 40 16 W108 13 54. Stereo. Hrs opn: 19. Box 1230, 2103 W. Main St. (87401). (505) 325-0255. Licensee: Navajo Missions Inc. Net: CBN. Wash atty: John S. Logan. Format: Relg, 70% music, 30% talk. News progmg 9 hrs wkly. Target aud: General. ■ James Baker, CEO; Dave Katzer, chmn; Patrick R. Wells, gen mgr, opns mgr, progmg dir & mus dir; Olive Iles, mktg dir; Matthew Joyce, news dir; Mark A. Frederick, chief engr.

KPCL(FM)—Dec 14, 1988: 95.7 mhz; 100 kw. Ant 394 ft. TL: N36 41 44 W108 13 11. Stereo. Box 232 (87499); 1105 W. Apache (87401). (505) 327-7202. Licensee: Voice Ministries of Farmington Inc. Net: Moody, Skylight, USA. Format: Relg. News staff one; news progmg 3 hrs wkly. Target aud: General; relg audience. Spec prog: Class one hr, Navajo 7 hrs wkly. ■ Fareed W. Ayoub, pres, gen mgr & mus dir.

KRAZ(FM)—Listing follows KRZE(AM).

KRWN(FM)—Listing follows KENN(AM).

KRZE(AM)—July 1, 1958: 1280 khz; 5 kw-D. TL: N36 49 03 W108 05 47. 120 S. Commercial St. (87401). (505) 325-1716. Licensee: J. Thomas Development of New Mexico Inc. (acq 12-18-91; with co-located FM). ■ Jeff Thomas, pres; Homer Perky, gen mgr; Dan Kelley, opns dir & chief engr; John Casey, progmg dir, mus dir & news dir.

KRAZ(FM)—Co-owned with KRZE(AM). Not on air, target date unknown: 96.9 mhz; 100 kw. Ant 1,010 ft. TL: N36 39 49 W108 12 55. Stereo. Prog sep from AM.

***KSJE(FM)**—November 1990: 90.9 mhz; 15 kw. Ant 390 ft. TL: N36 41 52 W108 13 14. Stereo. Hrs opn: 10 AM-11 PM. 4601 College Blvd. (87402). (505) 599-0231. FAX: (505) 599-0385; (505) 599-0472. Licensee: San Juan College. Format: Div, class. Target aud: 25-65. ■ James C. Henderson, pres; James L. Burgess, gen mgr; Constance Gotsch, progmg dir; Christine Arrasmith, pub affrs dir; Ron Nott, chief engr.

KTRA(FM)—Feb 19, 1987: 102.1 mhz; 100 kw. Ant 1,033 ft. TL: N36 48 52 W107 53 32. Stereo. Hrs opn: 19. Box 478, 607 E. Apache (87401). (505) 326-6553; (505) 326-6556. FAX: (505) 326-6555. Licensee: Dewey Matthew Runnels (acq 2-19-87). Net: ABC. Format: Country. News progmg 8 hrs wkly. Target aud: 25-54. ■ Matthew Runnels, pres; Joe Primrose, gen mgr, dev mgr & mktg mgr; Dave Schaefer, opns mgr, progmg dir & mus dir; Tim Ternes, gen sls mgr & adv mgr; Johnny Johnson, prom mgr; Ron Friday, pub affrs dir; Rick Hudson, chief engr. ■ Rates: $14.95; 11.50; 14.95; 9.20.

KWYK-FM—See Aztec.

Gallup

KGAK(AM)—Feb 9, 1945: 1330 khz; 5 kw-D, 1 kw-N, DA-N. TL: N35 32 34 W108 44 11. 401 E. Coal Ave. (87301). (505) 863-4444. Licensee: Gallup Broadcasting Co. (acq 9-1-67). Net: MBS, CBS. Rep: Savalli, Gillis. Format: Country, Indian. News staff 2; news progmg 14 hrs wkly. Target aud: 30-55. ■ Jack B. Chapman, pres & gen mgr; Ted Foster, gen sls mgr & progmg dir; John McBreen, news dir.

KQNM(FM)—Co-owned with KGAK(AM). Aug 15, 1975: 93.7 mhz; 62 kw. Ant 161 ft. TL: N35 36 22 W108 41 26. Stereo. Prog sep from AM. Net: CBS Spectrum. Format: CHR. News progmg 8 hrs wkly. Target aud: 25-44.

KGLP(FM)—Not on air, target date unknown: 91.7 mhz; 100 w. Ant 1,145 ft. TL: N35 36 13 W108 40 45. 910 Monterey Ct. (87301). (505) 863-6155. Licensee: Gallup Public Radio. ■ Roger Des Prez, pres.

KGLX(FM)—March 1, 1989: 99.1 mhz; 100 kw. Ant 500 ft. TL: N35 32 26 W108 44 36 (CP: 99.1 mhz, ant 1,241 ft.). Stereo. Hrs opn: 24. 219 W. Aztec (87301). (505) 863-9391. FAX: (505) 863-9393. Licensee: Skywest Communications Inc. (acq 2-18-93; FTR 3-8-93). Net: SMN. Format: Country. News progmg 14 hrs wkly. Target aud: 25-54. ■ Thomas C. Troland, CEO, gen mgr, stn mgr & engrg dir; Chip Begay, opns mgr & progmg dir; Mary Ann Hinshaw, sls dir; Gary Smart, adv dir & news dir; Regina Begay, mus dir & chief engr. ■ Rates: $14; 14; 14; 14.

KKJI(FM)—Not on air, target date unknown: 106.1 mhz; 26 kw. Ant 185 ft. TL: N35 32 27 W108 44 32. East Rock Rd., Allentown, PA (18103). Licensee: MBC Communications Southwest Inc.

KKOR(FM)—Listing follows KYVA(AM).

KQNM(FM)—Listing follows KGAK(AM).

KYVA(AM)—July 15, 1959: 1230 khz; 1 kw-U. TL: N35 32 02 W108 42 22. Stereo. Hrs opn: 24. Box 420 (87305-0420); 405-407 S. Second St. (87301). (505) 863-6851; (505) 722-9155. FAX: (505) 863-2429. Licensee: KKOR/KYVA Inc. (acq 3-77). Net: ABC/C. Rep: Katz & Powell; Art Moore. Wash atty: Fletcher, Heald & Hildreth. Format: Oldies. News staff one; news progmg 12 hrs wkly. Target aud: 35-54; mature with buying power. Spec prog: American Indian 6 hrs, Sp 2 hrs wkly. ■ George M. Malti, pres; Sammy Chioda, vp, gen mgr & gen sls mgr; Bill Lee, opns dir & prom mgr; Steven Chavez, mus dir; Sharon Maize, news dir; Rex Lee, chief engr.

KKOR(FM)—Co-owned with KYVA(AM). Oct 6, 1974: 94.5 mhz; 100 kw. Ant 1,388 ft. TL: N35 28 03 W108 14 25. Stereo. Hrs opn: 24. Prog sep from AM. Net: ABC/D. Format: Adult contemp. News staff one; news progmg 10 hrs wkly. Target aud: 25-44; young families with buying power.

Grants

KAGP(FM)—Not on air, target date unknown: 105.5 mhz; 100 kw. Ant 1,489 ft. 874 Rockrimmon Rd., Stamford (06903). Licensee: Margaret Everson.

KMIN(AM)—Sept 1, 1956: 980 khz; 1 kw-U. TL: N35 09 05 W107 52 31. Hrs opn: 24. 733 Roosevelt (87020). (505) 285-5598. FAX: (505) 285-5575. Licensee: Davis Broadcasting Co. Inc. (acq 3-1-84; $105,000; FTR 2-20-84). Net: Unistar. Format: Country. Target aud: 25-54; active, working adults. ■ Dorothy Davis, pres; Deborah Bustos, gen mgr; Bernie Bustos, progmg dir; Don Davis, chief engr. ■ Rates: $8.50; 8.50; 8.50; 4.

KZNM(FM)—June 1991: 100.9 mhz; 10 kw. Ant 223 ft. TL: N35 07 09 W107 54 08. Stereo. Hrs opn: 24. 733 Roosevelt (87020). (505) 285-5598. FAX: (505) 285-5575. Licensee: Don R. Davis. Net: Drake-Chenault. Format: Adult contemp. News staff one; news progmg 2 hrs wkly. Target aud: General 18-49. ■ Don R. Davis, pres & chief engr; Deborah Bustos, gen mgr; Bernie Bustos Jr., opns mgr, progmg dir & mus dir. ■ Rates: $7.50; 7.50; 7.50; 6.

Hobbs

KHOB(AM)—Aug 7, 1954: 1390 khz; 5 kw-D, 500 w-N, DA-N. TL: N32 44 21 W103 10 48. Box 454, 3301 Bensing Rd. (88240). (505) 397-1390. FAX: (505) 392-2500. Licensee: American Asset Management Inc. (acq 2-28-90; $55,500; FTR 3-19-90). Format: Sp. ■ Manuel Tersero, gen mgr; Claudia Baeza, progmg dir.

KKEL(AM)—Aug 8, 1938: 1480 khz; 5 kw-D, 1 kw-N, DA-N. TL: N32 42 57 W103 07 28. Box 777, 1515 N. Dal Paso (88240). (505) 393-3137. FAX: (505) 397-6088. Licensee: Robert D. Coker & Judy Coker. Net: MBS. Format: Oldies. Target aud: 25-54. Spec prog: Local sports. ■ Bob Coker, gen mgr, gen sls mgr & progmg dir; Frank Nymeyer, chief engr.

KLMA(FM)—Not on air, target date unknown: 96.5 mhz; 3 kw. Ant 91 ft. 110 S. Willow (88240). Licensee: Perla Acosta Ojeda.

KOKN(FM)—June 1, 1994: 102.9 mhz; 100 kw. Ant 518 ft. TL: N32 43 26 W103 34 34. Stereo. Box 720, Alamogordo (88310). Licensee: Cottonwood Communications Corp. (group owner). Wash atty: Jones, Waldo, Holbrook & McDonough. ■ Bob Flotte, pres.

KPER(FM)—August 1965: 95.7 mhz; 36 kw. Ant 255 ft. TL: N32 43 28 W103 09 03. Stereo. Box 2276 (88240). (505) 393-1551. Licensee: Arroyo Broadcasting. Net: SMN. Format: Country. Target aud: 25-54. ■ Robert D. Coker, gen mgr & gen sls mgr; Tim McGonigal, progmg dir; John Sanders, chief engr.

KYKK(AM)—July 17, 1971: 1110 khz; 5 kw-D. TL: N32 48 59 W103 13 56. Hrs opn: 6 AM-sunset. 619 N. Turner (88240). (505) 397-4969. FAX: (505) 393-4310. Licensee: Noalmark Broadcasting Corp. (group owner; acq 8-8-77). Net: ABC/I. Rep: Katz & Powell. Format: Country crossover. News staff one; news progmg one hr wkly. Target aud: 25-54; men. Spec prog: Talk 18 hrs wkly. ■ William Nolan, pres; Paul J. Starr, gen mgr & gen sls mgr; Harry Harlan, opns mgr, mktg dir & progmg dir; Anthony Garya, chief engr. ■ Rates: $10; 10; 10; 10.

KZOR(FM)—Co-owned with KYKK(AM). March 1975: 94.1 mhz; 100 kw. Ant 400 ft. TL: N32 48 59 W103 13 56. Stereo. Format: Adult contemp. Target aud: 18-44; female. ■ Rates: Same as AM.

Kirtland

KMYI(FM)—Not on air, target date unknown: 102.9 mhz; 96 kw. Ant 1,020 ft. TL: N36 48 40 W107 53 49. 3207 Espacio St., Farmington (87401). Licensee: Jeff and Joella Thomas, joint tenants.

La Luz

KPSA-FM—Licensed to La Luz. See Alamogordo.

Las Cruces

KASK(FM)—Dec 12, 1974: 103.1 mhz; 3 kw. Ant -111 ft. TL: N32 18 21 W106 46 43. Stereo. Suite 908, First National Tower (88001). (505) 524-2103. FAX: (505) 524-7488. Licensee: KASK Inc. (acq 1-1-77). Format: Adult contemp, eclectic. News progmg 7 hrs wkly. Target aud: 25-54; upscale adults. ■ Logan D. Matthews, pres & gen mgr; Rudy Tellez, gen sls mgr & progmg dir. ■ Rates: $11; 11; 11; 11.

KGRT(AM)—Dec 15, 1955: 570 khz; 5 kw-D, 155 w-N. TL: N32 18 33 W106 49 24. Hrs opn: 24. Box 968 (88004); 3401 W. Picacho (88005). (505) 524-8588. FAX: (505) 524-8580. Licensee: Sunrise Broadcasting Inc. (acq 12-30-88; with co-located FM; FTR 12-19-88). Net: ABC/D. Rep: Katz & Powell. Format: Country. News staff one. Target aud: 25 plus. Spec prog: Farm one hr wkly. ■ Allen Lumeyer, vp & gen mgr; Brian Hartz, progmg dir; Paul Kelley, mus dir; Jack Nixon, news dir; Doug Hanz, chief engr. ■ Rates: $12; 12; 12; 8.

KGRT-FM—Sept 8, 1966: 103.9 mhz; 3 kw. Ant 150 ft. TL: N32 18 33 W106 49 24. Stereo. Format: Country. Target aud: 25-54. ■ Rates: $15; 15; 15; 12.

KMVR(FM)—See Mesilla Park.

KOBE(AM)—April 1947: 1450 khz; 1 kw-U. TL: N32 18 07 W106 48 08. Drawer X (88004); 1832 W. Amador (88001). (505) 523-1450. Licensee: Rainbow Communications Corp. (acq 4-21-87). Net: ABC TalkRadio, CBS, NBC Talknet. Rep: Katz. Format: Relg, Sp, news, talk. News staff one; news progmg 25 hrs wkly. Target aud: 35 plus. ■ Miles Yeagly, pres; Frank Anglin, gen mgr & vp opns; Bob Pritchett, progmg dir; Laura Fernandez, news dir; Steve Jenkens, chief engr.

KROL(FM)—Not on air, target date unknown: 99.5 mhz; 100 kw. Ant 1,023 ft. TL: N32 31 33 W107 12 21. Stereo. Hrs opn: 24. Box 2104 (88004-2104). 4855 River Heights Dr. (88005). Licensee: STL Broadcasting Corp. Wash atty: Fisher, Wayland, Cooper & Leader. Format: Religious. Target aud: 25-54. Spec prog: Sp 15 hrs wkly. ■ Robert N. Mathis, pres; Jay Holland, sls dir; Jim Doiron, chief engr.

***KRUX(FM)**—Sept. 20, 1989: 91.5 mhz; 1 kw. Ant -194 ft. TL: N32 17 03 W106 45 00. Hrs opn: 7 AM- 2 AM. c/o Box C C 30004-NMSU, Corbett Center, University Park (88003). (505) 646-2597; (505) 646-3505. Licensee: Board of Regents New Mexico State Univ. Format: Alternative. Target aud: General. Spec prog: World beat 2 hrs, rap 2 hrs, heavy metal 2 hrs, new age 2 hrs, dance 2 hrs, blues/big band 2 hrs, imports 2 hrs, regional bands 2 hrs wkly. ■ Timothy Zura, gen mgr; Ian MacGillivray, prom dir & adv dir; Michele Lino, progmg dir; David Hyatt, Rebecca Jackson, mus dirs; Sioux Lhyn Shutt, asst mus dir; Dona Beth Smith, pub affrs dir; Greg Whitfield, Colleen Koenig, engrg dirs.

***KRWG(FM)**—Oct 3, 1964: 90.7 mhz; 100 kw. Ant 350 ft. TL: N32 15 24 W106 58 34. Stereo. Box 3000 (88003). (505) 646-4525. FAX: (506) 646-1924. Licensee: Regents of New Mexico State Univ. Net: NPR. Format: Class, jazz, news. News staff 2; news progmg 39 hrs wkly. Target aud: 18-60. Spec prog: Sp 15 hrs, bluegrass/folk 8 hrs wkly. ■ Colin Gromatzky, gen mgr & progmg dir; Susan Johnson, dev dir & prom dir; Thomas Huizenga, mus dir; Robert Nosbisch, news dir; Michael Doiron, James McCarten, chiefs engr. ■ KRWG-TV affil.

Las Vegas

KBAC(FM)—Nov 10, 1989: 98.1 mhz; 97 kw. Ant 1,037 ft. TL: N35 22 20 W105 22 02. Stereo. Hrs opn: 24. 740A Saint Michael's Dr., Santa Fe (87501); 3939 San Pedro N.E., Albuquerque (87110). (505) 471-7110. FAX: (505) 473-1557. Licensee: Masada Ltd. Wash atty: Hopkins & Sutter. Format: New rock. Target aud: 30-45. Spec prog: Jazz 5 hrs, world 5 hrs wkly. ■ Barbara McNally, vp; Armida Santa Cruz, progmg dir & pub affrs dir.

***KEDP(FM)**—September, 1968: 91.1 mhz; 72 w. Ant -215 ft. TL: N35 35 46 W105 13 18. Stereo. Hrs opn: 6 AM-midnight. New Mexico Highlands Univ. (87701). (505) 454-3366; (505) 454-3190. Licensee: Board of Regents, New Mexico Highlands Univ. Format: Classic rock, progsv, AOR. News staff one. College students & local young audience. Spec prog: Black 15 hrs, country 11 hrs, jazz 6 hrs, industrial 6 hrs, Sp 5 hrs, folk 2 hrs wkly. ■ Scott Fairhurst, stn mgr.

KFUN(AM)—Dec 25, 1941: 1230 khz; 1 kw-U. TL: N35 35 48 W105 12 21. Box 710, Radio Heights (87701). (505) 425-6766. FAX: (505) 425-6767. Licensee: KFUN/KLVF Inc. (acq 4-19-91; $400.000). Net: ABC/E. Format: Sp, C&W. News progmg 11 hrs wkly. Target aud: General. ■ Dennis D. Mitchell, pres & chief engr. ■ Rates: $7.50; 7.50; 7.50 7.50.

KLVF(FM)—Co-owned with KFUN(AM). June 19, 1973: 100.7 mhz; 10 kw. Ant -77 ft. TL: N33 35 48 W105 12 21. Stereo. Prog sep from AM. Format: Adult contemp. Target aud: 24-49. ■ Dennis D. Mitchell, gen mgr.

KNMX(AM)—Oct 1, 1980: 540 khz; 5 kw-D, DA. TL: N35 34 25 W105 10 17. Hrs opn: Sunrise-sunset. 615 E. Lincoln Ave. (87701). (505) 425-3555. FAX: (505) 425-3557. Licensee: San Miguel Broadcasting Co. Rep: Caballero. Format: Sp. News staff one; news progmg 15 hrs wkly. Target aud: 25-55; Hispanic. ■ Carlos D. Lopez, pres, gen mgr, sls dir & progmg dir; Anabelle Rael Lopez, opns dir. ■ Rates: $15; 15; 15; 15.

Lordsburg

KXKK(FM)—July 4, 1986: 97.7 mhz; 250 w. Ant -134 ft. TL: N32 34 57 W108 25 29 (CP: 97.9 mhz, 94 kw, ant 2,007 ft.). Stereo. R.R. 1, Box 80-10, Warren, VT (05674). Licensee: Interstate 10 Broadcasting of NM Inc. (acq 8-1-87). ■ John W. Krehbiel, pres & gen mgr; Robert Smith, gen sls mgr.

Los Alamos

KBOM(FM)—Mar 19, 1987: 106.7 mhz; 15.5 kw. Ant 1,948 ft. TL: N35 47 15 W106 31 35. Stereo. Hrs opn: 24. 2600 Entrada, Santa Fe (87505). (505) 471-1067. FAX: (505) 471-1087. Licensee: Tesuque Radio Inc. (acq 8-27-92; $560,000; FTR 9-21-92). Format: Oldies. News progmg 7 hrs wkly. Target aud: 25-54; mainstream audience with all socioeconomic cells represented. ■ Cindy Tingley, progmg dir; Al Greiner, chief engr.

KEFE(FM)—Not on air, target date unknown: 107.5 mhz; 100 kw. Ant 300 ft. 86 Alice Ave., Jensen Beach, FL (34957). Licensee: KREL Inc.

KRSN(AM)—Dec 9, 1949: 1490 khz; 1 kw-U. TL: N35 53 46 W106 17 21. Hrs opn: 5 AM-midnight. Box 1176, 400 N. Mesa (87544). (505) 662-4342. FAX: (505) 662-6740. Licensee: Community Broadcasting (group owner; acq 11-1-56). Rep: Katz. Format: Adult contemp, talk. News staff one; news progmg 14 hrs wkly. Target aud: 35-54; upper-class professionals. ■ Dean K. Burns, pres & gen mgr; Dale Burns, gen sls mgr; Gary Marshall, prom mgr, progmg dir & mus dir; Bill Frost, chief engr.

KTMN(FM)—June 1956: 98.5 mhz; 100 kw. Ant 1,781 ft. TL: N35 53 08 W106 23 14. Stereo. 1718 W. Alameda, Santa Fe (87501). (505) 983-5866. FAX: (505) 984-2012. Licensee: Pinon Property Inc. (acq 10-19-93; $650,000; FTR 11-8-93). Format: AOR. Spec prog: Class 10 hrs wkly. ■ Jim Leavy, gen mgr; Fred Seva, gen sls mgr; Rob Ramsire, chief engr.

Los Lunas

KOYT(FM)—Not on air, target date unknown: 102.5 mhz; 50 kw. Ant 492 ft. TL: N34 04 00 W106 46 53. 3512 Palomas N.E., Albuquerque (87110). (505) 298-8312. Licensee: Enchantment Media Inc. (acq 9-16-92; $68,500; FTR 11-9-92).

KZPY(FM)—Not on air, target date unknown: 106.3 mhz; 100 kw. Ant 656 ft. TL: N34 48 51 W106 50 29. 1205 Nakomis N.E., Albuquerque (87112). Licensee: Patricia Benns Komorowski.

Los Ranchos de Albuquerque

KALY(AM)—Licensed to Los Ranchos de Albuquerque. See Albuquerque.

KJBO(AM)—Licensed to Los Ranchos de Albuquerque. See Albuquerque.

Lovington

KLEA(AM)—Dec 25, 1952: 630 khz; 500 w-D. TL: N32 56 30 W103 19 12. Hrs opn: 24. Box 877, Country Club Rd. (88260). (505) 396-2244. FAX: (505) 396-3355. Licensee: Lea County Broadcasting Co. Net: AP. Format: Country. Target aud: 25-54. Spec prog: Sp 6 hrs wkly. ■ Iva Lea Barton, pres; Susan Coe, gen mgr, gen sls mgr & news dir; Michael Barr, mus dir; Frank Nymeyer, chief engr. ■ Rates: $10; 8.50; 10; 7.

KLEA-FM—October 1965: 101.7 mhz; 3 kw. Ant 280 ft. TL: N32 56 30 W103 19 12 (CP: 25 kw). Stereo. Hrs opn: 24. Dups AM 100%. ■ Rates: Same as AM.

Maljamar

*****KMTH(FM)**—Feb 14, 1985: 98.7 mhz; 100 kw. Ant 710 ft. TL: N32 54 55 W103 46 31. Stereo. Hrs opn: 19. Dups KENW(FM) 100%. Eastern New Mexico Univ., Portales (88130). (505) 562-2112. FAX: (505) 562-2590. Licensee: Eastern New Mexico Univ. Net: NPR, CNN, APR. Format: Class, btfl mus, news. Target aud: General. ■ Everett L. Frost, pres; Duane W. Ryan, gen mgr & stn mgr; Anthony Chapple, opns dir; Mark Hazlett, dev dir & mktg dir; Tom Bartsch, progmg dir. ■ KENW-TV affil.

KWMW(FM)—Jan 17, 1990: 105.1 mhz; 100 kw. Ant 917 ft. TL: N32 52 40 W103 41 13. Box 29 (88264). (505) 676-5969. FAX: (505) 676-5969. Licensee: M.T.D. Inc. Format: Country. ■ Mike Warren, gen mgr & Dave Warren, progmg dir.

Mesilla Park

KMVR(FM)—June 1, 1974: 104.9 mhz; 3 kw. Ant -32 ft. TL: N32 18 07 W106 48 08. Stereo. Drawer X, Las Cruces (88004); 1832 W. Amador Ave., Las Cruces (88005). (505) 526-2496. FAX: (505) 523-3918. Licensee: Rainbow Communications Corp. (acq 4-21-87). Rep: Katz. Format: Adult contemp. News staff one; news progmg one hr wkly. Target aud: 18-49. ■ Miles Yeagley, pres; Frank Anglin, gen mgr; J.T. Stevens, progmg dir; Laura Fernandez, news dir; Steve Jenkins, chief engr.

Milan

KOFK(AM)—Sept 1, 1989: 1130 khz; 5 kw-D. TL: N35 05 51 W107 52 19. 813 Seville Loop, Grants (87020). Licensee: Fred E. Rodarte & Danny Almanza. ■ Fred E. Rodarte, pres.

Pine Hill

*****KTDB(FM)**—Apr 24, 1972: 89.7 mhz; 15 kw. Ant 300 ft. TL: N34 57 59 W108 25 31 (CP: Ant 288 ft.). Box 40, Pine Hill (87357). (505) 775-3215. FAX: (505) 775-3551. Licensee: Ramah Navajo School Board. Format: C&W. Spec prog: Navajo. ■ Bernard J. Bustos, gen mgr & chief engr; Barbara Maria, prom mgr & mus dir; Irene Beaver, progmg dir.

Portales

*****KENW-FM**—Sept 1, 1979: 89.5 mhz; 100 kw. Ant 185 ft. TL: N34 10 27 W103 21 03. Stereo. Eastern New Mexico Univ. (88130). (505) 562-2112. FAX: (505) 562-2590. Licensee: Eastern New Mexico University. Net: NPR, APR, CNN; N.M. Pub. Format: Div. News staff one; news progmg 3 hrs wkly. Target aud: General. ■ Everett L. Frost, pres; Duane W. Ryan, gen mgr & stn mgr; Anthony Chapple, opns dir; Mark Hazlett, dev dir; Tom Bartsch, progmg dir. ■ KENW-TV affil.

KSEL(AM)—February 1950: 1450 khz; 1 kw-U. TL: N34 11 51 W103 19 24. Box 886, Clovis Hwy. (88130). (505) 359-1759. FAX: (505) 356-0724. Licensee: James G. Boles. Group owner: Boles Broadcasting (acq 12-88; $75,000; FTR 12-5-88). Net: NBC. Format: Adult contemp, country & oldies. Spec prog: Farm 15 hrs wkly. ■ Jim Boles, pres & gen mgr; Steve Richie, gen sls mgr; Doug Mykelz, prom mgr; Suzanne Abbey, progmg dir; Mona Boles, mus dir; Jerry Airhart, news dir; Larry Ahlstrom, chief engr.

KSEL-FM—March 1980: 95.3 mhz; 6 kw. Ant 300 ft. TL: N34 11 51 W103 19 24. Stereo. Dups AM 100%. Format: Adult contemp. ■ Rates: $20; 20; 20; 15.

Raton

*****KNJU(FM)**—Not on air, target date unknown: 90.9 mhz; 100 w. Ant -581 ft. 52 Broadcast Center, Portales (88130). Licensee: Eastern New Mexico Univ.

KRTN(AM)—1948: 1490 khz; 1 kw-U. TL: N36 53 10 W104 26 35. Box 638, 1128 State St. (87740). (505) 445-3652. FAX: (505) 445-2911. Licensee: Raton Broadcasting Co. (acq 2-66). Format: Div. News staff one; news progmg 35 hrs wkly. Target aud: General. ■ Mark A. Roper, pres, gen mgr, gen sls mgr & prom mgr; Flolene Roper, progmg dir; Debbie Tomscoe, mus dir; Robert Schaefer, chief engr.

KRTN-FM—April 1982: 94.3 mhz; 3 kw. Ant -531 ft. TL: N36 53 08 W104 26 33 (CP: 5.5 kw, ant 1,443 ft.). Stereo. Dups AM 80%. 1128 State St. (87740).

Rio Rancho

KZKL-FM—Nov 2, 1984: 101.7 mhz; 3.2 kw. Ant 99 ft. TL: N35 11 35 W106 28 15. 10316 Edith Blvd. N.E., Albuquerque (87113). (505) 897-6937. FAX: (505) 898-5081. Licensee: Territorial Communications Inc. (acq 10-1-92; $600,000; with KZKL[AM] Albuquerque; FTR 11-2-92). Rep: Christal. Format: Oldies. ■ Martin Balk, pres; Craig Parker, gen mgr; Brenda Cowle, gen sls mgr; Dave Scott, progmg dir & mus dir.

Roswell

KBCQ(FM)—Listing follows KCKN(AM).

KBIM(AM)—May 1953: 910 khz; 5 kw-D, 500 w-N, DA-N. TL: N33 26 26 W104 31 35. Box 2308, 1301 N. Main St. (88201). (505) 623-9100. FAX: (505) 623-4775. Licensee: King Broadcasting Co. Inc. Net: SMN. Rep: Roslin. Wash atty: Dow, Lohnes & Albertson. Format: Oldies. News staff one; news progmg 11 hrs wkly. Target aud: 25-54. ■ John King, pres & gen mgr; Betty King, gen sls mgr; Ken Bass, progmg dir & chief engr; Jim Stringer, news dir. ■ Rates: $17; 15; 15; 13.

KBIM-FM—June 1959: 94.9 mhz; 100 kw. Ant 1,880 ft. TL: N33 03 20 W104 49 12. Stereo. Prog sep from AM. Net: ABC/I. Format: Soft adult contemp. News progmg 15 hrs wkly. Target aud: 25 plus. ■ Ken Bass, opns dir & engrg dir; Betty King, sls dir & progmg dir. ■ Rates: Same as AM.

KCKN(AM)—Dec 20, 1965: 1020 khz; 50 kw-U, DA-2. TL: N33 27 53 W104 29 58. Stereo. Hrs opn: 5 AM-midnight. Box 670, Old Clovis Highway (88202). (505) 622-6450. FAX: (505) 622-9041. Licensee: Roswell Radio Inc. (group owner; acq 12-28-92; $600,000 with co-located FM; FTR 1-25-93). Net: ABC/E, Mutual, NBC Talknet. Rep: Eastman. Format: Country, relg, news/talk. News staff 2; news progmg 5 hrs wkly. Target aud: 18-54; urban country listeners, young professionals. ■ Tim Dill, opns dir; Lee Cook, gen sls mgr; Carolyn Abbey, mus dir; Kaylin Huffman, news dir; Don Niccum, chief engr.

KBCQ(FM)—Co-owned with KCKN(AM). Oct 15, 1977: 97.1 mhz; 100 kw. Ant 300 ft. TL: N33 24 05 W104 22 45. Stereo. Hrs opn: 5 AM-midnight. Prog sep from AM. Format: Adult contemp. Target aud: 24-55. ■ Tim Dill, opns mgr; Jim Kapp, mus dir.

KCRX(AM)—Mar 15, 1927: 1430 khz; 5 kw-D, 1 kw-N, DA-N. TL: N33 26 11 W104 36 18. Hrs opn: 24. Box 2052, Casarez Broadcasting Plaza, 905 Avenida Del Sumbre (88202-2052). (505) 622-7677. FAX: (505) 622-7677. Licensee: Rosendo Casarez Jr. Format: Sp language. News staff one; news progmg 10 hrs wkly. Target aud: 25-54; adult Hispanics. ■ Rosendo Casarez Jr., pres, opns dir & gen sls mgr; Paul Denney, progmg dir; Marcos Delaney, mus dir; Nestor Daniel, news dir. ■ Rates: $3; 3; 3; 3.

KEND(FM)—May 30, 1990: 106.5 mhz; 52 kw. Ant 135 ft. TL: N33 23 05 W104 43 22. Stereo. Hrs opn: 24. Box 388, Hwy 70 W., Buena Vida (88201). (505) 625-2098. Licensee: Shelia Roe. Format: Contemp Country. News progmg 6 hrs wkly. Target aud: 18-34; successful men & women. Spec prog: Farm one hr wkly. ■ Jim C. Moore, opns mgr; Bob Park, sls dir; Daryll Bunkfield, prom dir; Ken Bass, chief engr. ■ Rates: $10; 8; 10; 5.

KMOU(FM)—Listing follows KRSY(AM).

KRDD(AM)—1963: 1320 khz; 1 kw-D. TL: N33 24 14 W104 28 12. Box 1615 (88201). (505) 624-2663. Licensee: Trinnie (acq 3-31-92). Net: CBS Spectrum. Format: Sp. ■ Raul Castro, stn mgr; Carlos Espinoza, prom mgr & progmg dir; Jessie Carrillo, news dir.

KRSY(AM)—May 1947: 1230 khz; 1 kw-U. TL: N33 25 00 W104 30 40. Hrs opn: 24. Box 1981, 815 E. 19th St. (88201). (505) 622-0290. FAX: (505) 622-0303. Licensee: Ramar Communications Inc. (acq 2-2-87). Net: SMN; Rep: Katz & Powell. Format: Modern country. Target aud: 25-54. Spec prog: Farm 6 hrs, talk 15 hrs wkly. ■ Matthew Runnels, pres & stn mgr. KJTV(TV) affil. ■ Rates: $15; 12; 15; 10.

KMOU(FM)—Co-owned with KRSY(AM). August 1992: 104.7 mhz; 50 kw. Ant 409 ft. TL: N33 34 53 W104 31 51. Stereo. Hrs opn: 24. Format: Modern country.

KSFX(FM)—Mar 15, 1991: 100.5 mhz; 100 kw. Ant 122 ft. TL: N33 28 54 W104 39 12. Hrs opn: 24. 5206 W. Second St. (88201). (505) 625-1005; (505) 623-4000 (STUDIO). Licensee: Roswell FM Joint Venture. Rep: Katz & Powell. Format: Classic rock, AOR. Target aud: 25-49; mainstream upscale. Spec prog: Jazz 4 hrs wkly. ■ Warren Scott, gen mgr; Nora Chamberlin, opns mgr; Leslie Ramerez, sls dir & adv dir; Tony Clayton, progmg mgr; Penny Banks, pub affrs dir; Michael Montgomery, chief engr.

*****KWFL(FM)**—Dec 21, 1989: 99.5 mhz; 3 kw. Ant 73 ft. TL: N33 23 34 W104 31 28. Stereo. Hrs opn: 24. Box 2672, Petroleum Bldg., Suite 814, 200 W. First (88202). (505) 623-9433; (505) 623-9450. Licensee: Roswell Christian Radio Inc. Net: Moody. Format: Relg. Target aud: Christian community. ■ James C. Teel Jr., pres & gen mgr.

Ruidoso

KBUY(AM)—November 1959: 1360 khz; 5 kw-D, 199 w-N. TL: N33 19 35 W105 40 02. Hrs opn: 18. Box 39, 2818 Sudderth (88345). (505) 257-7333. FAX: (505) 258-5001. Licensee: Walton Stations New Mexico Inc. Group owner: Walton Stations (acq 10-22-82; $475,000 with co-located FM; FTR 11-15-82). Wash atty: Cohn & Marks. Format: C&W. News progmg 14 hrs wkly. Target aud: General. Spec prog: Sp 4 hrs wkly. ■ John B. Walton Jr., pres; Jerry Wright, gen mgr; Pete Esquibel, gen sls mgr; Phil Wright, progmg dir; Bill Wyatt, mus dir. ■ Rates: $10.50; 10.50; 10.50; 10.50.

New York

KWES(FM)—Co-owned with KBUY(AM). 1982: 93.5 mhz; 25 kw. Ant 58 ft. TL: N33 23 12 W105 40 14. Stereo. Dups AM 100%. FAX: (505) 258-5860.

Ruidoso Downs

KRUI(AM)—April 1984: 1490 khz; 1 kw-U. TL: N33 19 17 W105 35 24. Box 2010, 105 Sierra Ln. (88346). (505) 378-8111. FAX: (505) 378-8111. Licensee: MTD Inc. (acq 12-88; $20,000; FTR 12-19-88). Net: ABC/E. Format: Country. ■ Mike Warren, gen mgr, gen sls mgr & chief engr; Pam Warren, stn mgr; Dave Warren, progmg dir.

Santa Fe

KKSS(FM)—March 1969: 97.3 mhz; 94 kw. Ant 1,876 ft. TL: N35 46 50 W106 31 55 (CP: 100 kw, ant 1,631 ft.). 226 Third Ave., Nashville, TN (37201). (505) 265-1431. FAX: (505) 268-7807. Licensee: SunGroup Broadcasting of New Mexico Inc. Group owner: SunGroup Inc. Rep: Eastman. Format: CHR. ■ Frank A. Woods, pres; Arthur D. Tek, vp; Mary Ellen Merrigan, gen mgr; Roger Ayers, gen sls mgr; Roy Jaynes, progmg dir; Steve Bridges, chief engr.

KLSK(FM)—Nov 24, 1983: 104.1 mhz; 100 kw. Ant 1,876 ft. TL: N35 46 50 W106 31 35. Stereo. Hrs opn: 24. Suite 104, 2700 San Pedro N.E., Albuquerque (87110). (505) 883-6655. FAX: (505) 883-9064. Licensee: Twin Peaks Radio (group owner; acq 6-4-93; grpsl; FTR 6-28-93). Rep: Christal. Wash atty: Daniel Brenner. Format: Classic rock mus from 60s, 70s, 80s. News staff one. Target aud: 25-54. ■ Peter Baumann, pres; Milt McConnell, vp, gen mgr & vp progmg; Frank Jackson, opns mgr, news dir & pub affrs dir; Heidi O'Donnol, sls dir; Marc Sternhagen, gen sls mgr; Debi Loving, natl sls mgr; Wayne Beall, rgnl sls mgr; Doug Bird, mktg dir; Laurie Larson, mus dir; Bill Price, chief engr.

KNYN(FM)—Aug 15, 1965: 95.5 mhz; 19 kw. Ant 1,850 ft. TL: N35 53 08 W106 23 14. Stereo. Licensee: Plaza Broadcasting Inc. (acq 6-21-93; $525,000; FTR 7-5-93). Net: Unistar, MBS. Format: Country. ■ Jim Leary, gen mgr.

KOLT-FM—Nov 2, 1983: 105.9 mhz; 100 kw. Ant 1,936 ft. TL: N35 46 49 W106 31 35. Stereo. Radio Station KOLT-FM, 3700 Rio Grande Blvd. N.W. Albuquerque (87107). (505) 884-5778. FAX: (505) 883-5658. Licensee: The Braiker Family (acq 3-3-93; $1.4 million; FTR 3-22-93). Rep: Christal, Katz. Format: Country. News staff one; news progmg 2 hrs wkly. Target aud: 18-34. ■ Cindy Weiner, gen sls mgr; Joyce Rocha, prom dir; Jim Patrick, progmg dir; Sammy Cruise, mus dir; Gretchen Hall, news dir. ■ Rates: $50; 40; 40; 20.

***KSFR(FM)**—Mar 19, 1990: 90.7 mhz; 3 kw. Ant 199 ft. TL: N35 40 41 W105 59 29. Stereo. Hrs opn: 15. Box 4187, S. Richards Ave. (87502). (505) 438-1319. Licensee: Santa Fe Community College. Format: Fine arts, educ, jazz. News progmg 3 hrs wkly. Target aud: General. Spec prog: American Indian one hr, poetry 4 hrs, opera 6 hrs wkly. ■ Barzon Bond, stn mgr; Bill Dunning, progmg dir; Bill Frost, chief engr.

KSWV(AM)—June 1966: 810 khz; 5 kw-D. TL: N35 39 17 W106 00 05. 121 Sandoval (87501). (505) 989-7441. FAX: (505) 989-7607. Licensee: La Voz Broadcasting Co. (acq 12-20-90; $150,000). Rep: Katz. Format: Sp local info & mus. News staff one. Target aud: 25-54. ■ Celina V. Gonzales, pres; George Gonzales, gen mgr; Anthony Gonzales, progmg dir.

KTRC(AM)—Feb 20, 1947: 1400 khz; 1 kw-U. TL: N35 41 16 W105 56 04. Box 2227-87504, 1311 Calle Naba (87501). (505) 982-2666. FAX: (505) 988-3437. Licensee: Santa Fe Broadcasting Co. Inc. (acq 10-1-68). Net: ABC/I. Format: Nostalgia. Target aud: 35 plus. ■ Bill Mitchell, pres; Bill Hanrahan, vp, gen mgr, gen sls mgr, progmg & chief engr; Larry Myers, mus dir; Cec Hanrahan, pub affrs dir. ■ Rates: $14; 12; 14; 10.

KVSF(AM)—1935: 1260 khz; 5 kw-D, 1 kw-N. TL: N35 40 36 W105 58 21. 1311 Calle Nava (87501). (505) 982-2666. FAX: (505) 988-3437. Licensee: James T. Davis CPA Trustee Format: News/talk. ■ Bill Sims, gen mgr; Deborah Martinez, news dir.

KZRQ(FM)—Sept 28, 1985: 105.1 mhz; 100 kw. Ant 1,937 ft. TL: N35 47 15 W106 31 35. Stereo. 10316 Edith Blvd. NE, Albuquerque (87113). (505) 897-6937. FAX: (505) 898-5081. Licensee: Broadcast Media Enterprises Inc. (acq 8-3-93; $850,000 with KIVA[AM] Corrales; FTR 8-23-93). Net: ABC, SMN. Rep: Torbet. Format: AOR. ■ Craig Parker, gen mgr; Brenda Towle, gen sls mgr.

KZXA(FM)—Not on air, target date unknown: 94.7 mhz; 35 kw. Ant 2,916 ft. TL: N36 14 50 W105 39 15. 7354 Ruthven Rd., Norfolk, VA (23505). Licensee: John Strelitz.

Santa Rosa

KSSR(AM)—Nov 2, 1960: 1340 khz; 1 kw-U. TL: N34 56 40 W104 39 00. Hrs opn: 6 AM-8 PM. Box 427, 2818 Will Rogers Dr. (88435). (505) 472-5777. Licensee: J. Michael Esquibel. Format: Adult contemp, country. Target aud: General. Spec prog: Sp 15 hrs, class one hr wkly. ■ Michael Esquibel, gen mgr, progmg dir, mus dir, news dir & chief engr.

Silver City

KSCQ(FM)—Nov 28, 1989: 94.5 mhz; 6 kw. Ant 1,840 ft. TL: N32 50 40 W108 14 18 (CP: 570 w, ant 1,028 ft.). Stereo. Hrs opn: 24. Box 1351 (88062); 1872 Hwy. 180 E. (88061). (505) 538-3396; (505) 388-4116. FAX: (505) 388-1759. Licensee: Avila Beach Ltd. Group owner: John L. Alsip. Net: AP. Format: Adult contemp. News progmg 10 hrs wkly. Target aud: 25-49; baby boomers. Spec prog: Classic rock. ■ John L. Alsip, pres & opns dir; Arlene Schadel, gen mgr, sls dir, mktg dir & adv dir; John Alsip, progmg dir & mus dir; Dennis Wells, chief engr. ■ Rates: $7; 7; 7; 7.

KSIL(AM)—Sept 15, 1946: 1340 khz; 1 kw-U. TL: N32 46 53 W108 16 11. Box 590, 1640 Corbin St. (88061). (505) 538-2951. FAX: (505) 388-1106. Licensee: KSIL Radio Ltd. (acq 10-4-90; $200,000; FTR 10-22-90). Net: ABC/C. Rep: Katz & Powell. Wash atty: Haley, Bader & Potts. Format: Coyote rock. Target aud: 25-49. Spec prog: Sp 13 hrs wkly. ■ Ben Noe, progmg dir & mus dir; John Gojkovich, news dir; Cleve Prince, chief engr.

Socorro

KLSC(FM)—Not on air, target date unknown: 92.9 mhz; 6 kw. Ant -177 ft. Box 30570, Albuquerque (87190). Licensee: William H. Pace.

KMXQ(FM)—July 1, 1987: 92.7 mhz; 3 kw. Ant -234 ft. TL: N34 02 43 W106 54 21 (CP: 104.7 mhz, 100 kw, ant 1,822 ft.). Stereo. Box 699, 834 Hwy. 60 W. (87801). (505) 835-1286. FAX: (505) 835-2015. Licensee: H & HSB Corp. Group owner: The Holt Corporations. Net: ABC/D. Rep: Banner. Format: Country. News staff one; news progmg 6 hrs wkly. Target aud: 12 plus. Spec prog: Sp 3 hrs, Indian one hr wkly. ■ Arthur Holt, pres; Frankie H. Naranjo, gen mgr, chief opns, gen sls mgr & vp engrg; Penny M. Naranjo, dev mgr, prom mgr, vp progmg & asst mus dir; John Gonzales, mus dir, news dir & engrg dir. ■ Rates: $6.15; 4.25; 4.25; 4.

Taos

KKIT(AM)—Dec 23, 1961: 1340 khz; 1 kw-U. TL: N36 23 22 W105 35 09. Box 737 (87571). (505) 758-2231. FAX: (505) 758-4266. Licensee: Sam Inc. (acq 4-1-65). Net: ABC/I; Intermountain. Format: Var, Sp. ■ Stewart Jones, pres; Stuart C. Jones, gen sls mgr & progmg dir; Don Laine, news dir; Jacob Miller, chief engr.

KTAO(FM)—January 1978: 101.5 mhz; 3 kw. Ant -416 ft. TL: N36 25 00 W105 37 04 (CP: 1.05 kw, ant 2,824 ft.). Stereo. Box 1844, Blueberry Hill Rd. (87571). (505) 758-1017. Licensee: Taos Communications Corp. (acq 1-78). Net: AP. Format: Adult rock. News staff one; news progmg 10 hrs wkly. Target aud: 25-49. Spec prog: Country 5 hrs, jazz 5 hrs, Sp 3 hrs wkly. ■ Brad Hockmeyer, pres, gen mgr, progmg dir & mus dir; Sara Allen, chief engr.

Texico

KWXN(FM)—Not on air, target date unknown: 96.5 mhz; 4 kw. Ant 390 ft. TL: N34 20 36 W103 06 17. c/o 4501 N. Tamiami Trail, Naples, FL (33940). Licensee: North Plains Broadcasting Corp.

Thoreau

KXTC(FM)—Oct 21, 1991: 99.9 mhz; 100 kw. Ant 1,210 ft. TL: N35 36 13 W107 40 45. Stereo. Hrs opn: 24. 2495 E. Aztec, Gallup (87301). (505) 722-4442. FAX: (505) 722-7745. Licensee: Dewey Matthew Runnels (acq 7-89; $30,733; FTR 7-31-89). Net: ABC/E. Wash atty: Gardner, Carton & Douglas. Format: Country. Target aud: 18 plus. ■ Dewey Matthew Runnels, gen mgr; F. Lee Winslow, stn mgr & gen sls mgr; Kit Barrett, progmg dir. ■ Rates: $23; 20; 23; 10.

Truth or Consequences

KCHS(AM)—September 1944: 1400 khz; 1 kw-U. TL: N33 08 26 W107 13 55. Box 351, 1747 E. 3rd (87901). (505) 894-2400. FAX: (505) 894-3998. Licensee: Myrna Baird dba Bairdland Broadcasting (acq 6-18-92). Net: AP. Format: Town & country. News staff 3. Target aud: General; area residents. Spec prog: Sp 12 hrs, relg 11 hrs wkly. ■ Myrna Baird, pres & gen mgr. ■ Rates: $13; 13; 13; 13.

KSNM(FM)—Nov 1, 1984: 98.7 mhz; 100 kw. Ant 2,643 ft. TL: N32 58 15 W107 13 26. Stereo. Hrs opn: 24. Box 987 (87901); Box 880, Suite E-7, 755 S. Telshor, Las Cruces (88004-0880). (505) 894-3987; (505) 522-3987. FAX: (505) 522-1502. Licensee: Sierra Industries Inc. Net: ABC/E. Format: Classic rock, AOR. News staff one. Target aud: 25-49, 18-35 secondary; consumers in a building & acquisitions mode with disposable income. Spec prog: Aggie NMSU sports 4 hrs wkly. ■ William Grindell, chmn; Jeff Lyon, gen mgr; Teresa Frederick, prom dir; Adam West, progmg dir; Steve Jenkins, chief engr. ■ Rates: $14.50; 12; 14.50; 11.50.

Tse Bonito

KHAC(AM)—Mar 21, 1967: 880 khz; 10 kw-D, 430 w-N. TL: N35 38 41 W109 01 13. Box F, Window Rock, AZ (86515). (505) 371-5587. FAX: (505) 371-5588. Licensee: Western Indian Ministries (group owner). Format: Relg, Navajo. News staff one; news progmg 3 hrs wkly. Target aud: General; Indian. ■ Jim Maioramo, gen mgr; Laurence Harper, opns dir; David Mouttet, gen sls mgr; Dave Hilder, news dir; Bill Hume, chief engr.

Tucumcari

KTNM(AM)—1941: 1400 khz; 1 kw-U. TL: N35 10 15 W103 42 25. Box 668, 902 S. Date St. (88401). (505) 461-0522; (505) 461-1400. Licensee: Quay Broadcasters Inc. (acq 6-20-84; $524,000; FTR 7-16-84). Net: ABC, NBC Talknet, MBS. Wash atty: Cohn & Marks. Format: C&W, talk. News staff one; news progmg 20 hrs wkly. Target aud: General. Spec prog: Sp 18 hrs wkly. ■ John M. Dunn, pres; Wayne Kirkpatrick, gen mgr; Becky Burczyk, gen sls mgr; Diane Paris, prom mgr; Greg Carnefix, progmg dir; Dawn Dennis, news dir; Don Niccum, chief engr. ■ Rates: $24; 18.75; 20; na.

KQAY-FM—Co-owned with KTNM(AM). Jan 19, 1968: 92.7 mhz; 3 kw. Ant 64 ft. TL: N35 10 15 W103 42 25. Stereo. Prog sep from AM. Net: SMN. Format: Adult contemp. News staff one.

White Rock

KNLA(FM)—1991: 101.1 mhz; 3 kw. Ant 53 ft. TL: N35 53 46 W106 17 21 (CP: 750 w, ant 1,729 ft., TL: N35 53 08 W106 23 14). Stereo. Box 1176, 400 N. Mesa Rd. (87544). (505) 661-1011. FAX: (505) 662-6740. Licensee: Torjaq Radio Inc. Net: SMN. Wash atty: Fisher, Wayland, Cooper & Leader. Format: Oldies. News progmg 7 hrs wkly. Target aud: 25-54. ■ Dean Burns, pres & gen mgr; Tony Fitch, prom mgr & progmg dir; Bill Frost, chief engr.

Zuni

***KSHI(FM)**—Apr 6, 1978: 90.9 mhz; 100 w. Ant 100 ft. TL: N35 05 18 W108 47 22. Stereo. Box 339 (87327). (505) 782-4811. FAX: (505) 782-2700. Licensee: Zuni Communications Authority. Format: CHR, educ. News progmg 7 hrs wkly. Target aud: 18-34; primarily Indian. Spec prog: Indian 20 hrs wkly. ■ Duane Chimoni, gen mgr.

New York

Albany

WABY(AM)—1934: 1400 khz; 1 kw-U. TL: N42 41 21 W73 47 37. 12 Dennis Terrace, Schenectady (12303); Box 12521 (12212). (518) 456-6101. FAX: (518) 456-6377. Licensee: Bendat Communications & Broadcasting Inc. (acq 2-20-91; grpsl; FTR 3-11-91). Net: Unistar. Rep: D & R Radio. Wash atty: William Potts. Format: MOR. News staff 2; news progmg 2 hrs wkly. Target aud: 45 plus; mature adults. ■ Paul Bendat, pres & progmg dir; Beth Kline, gen sls mgr; Bill Edwardson, mus dir; Don Fields, news dir; Bob Blanchard, chief engr. ■ Rates: $100; 110; 110; 70.

WKLI(FM)—Co-owned with WABY(AM). 1972: 100.9 mhz; 3 kw. Ant 300 ft. TL: N42 43 54 W73 52 56 (CP: ant 286 ft.). Stereo. Prog sep from AM. Rep: D & R Radio.

Format: Adult contemp. News staff 2. Target aud: 25-54; upscale women. ■ Chris Holmberg, mus dir.

***WAMC(FM)**—Oct 1, 1958: 90.3 mhz; 10 kw. Ant 1,970 ft. TL: N42 38 14 W73 10 07. Stereo. Hrs opn: 24. 318 Central Ave. (12206). (518) 465-5233. FAX: (518) 432-0991. Licensee: WAMC. Group owner: WAMC/Northeast Public Radio (acq 7-1-82). Net: NPR, APR, UPI. Wash atty: Dow, Lohnes & Albertson. Format: Class, news, info. News staff 5; news progmg 48 hrs wkly. Target aud: General. Spec prog: Jazz 19 hrs, folk/bluegrass 8 hrs wkly. ■ Alan S. Chartock, chmn; Kathleen Taylor, dev dir; David Galletly (asst exec), progmg dir; Michael Carrese, news dir; Jim Scholefield, chief engr.

***WCDB(FM)**—Mar 1, 1978: 90.9 mhz; 100 w. Ant 222 ft. TL: N42 41 16 W73 49 19. Stereo. Hrs opn: 24. Campus Center 316, 1400 Washington Ave. (12222). (518) 442-5158. FAX: (518) 442-5622. Licensee: State Univ. of New York. Format: Alternative rock, jazz & urban contemp. News progmg 15 hrs wkly. Target aud: 15-55; students & surrounding community. Spec prog: Reggae 2 hrs, metal 2 hrs, world 2 hrs, local show one hr wkly. ■ Brian Perlis, gen mgr.

WGNA(AM)—June 14, 1924: 1460 khz; 5 kw-U, DA-N. TL: N42 37 21 W73 48 09. Hrs opn: 24. Box 800 New Loudon, 800 New Loudon Rd., Suite 4200, Latham (12110). (518) 782-1474. FAX: (518) 782-1486. Licensee: WGNA Broadcasting Inc. Group owner: Barnstable Broadcasting Inc. (acq 7-28-88). Rep: Katz. Format: Country. Target aud: 25-54. ■ Dave Gingold, pres; Al Vicente, vp & gen mgr; John Shea, gen sls mgr; Ruth Tietz, prom mgr; Jon Allen, progmg dir; Bill Earley, mus dir; Lynne Richarde, news dir; Jack Shafer, chief engr.

WGNA-FM—December 1973: 107.7 mhz; 12.5 kw. Ant 984 ft. TL: N42 38 18 W73 59 51. Dups AM 100%. (Acq 12-29-86). Net: Unistar. Rep: Katz. Wash atty: Kaye Scholer. News staff one; news progmg 18 hrs wkly. Target aud: General; 25-54. ■ Ruth Tietz, vp mktg; Jon Allen, vp progmg.

WGY(AM)—See Schenectady.

WHAZ(AM)—See Troy.

WHRL(FM)—Sept 1, 1966: 103.1 mhz; 3 kw. Ant 328 ft. TL: N42 39 46 W73 40 37. Stereo. Box 333 (12201). (518) 283-1123. Licensee: Regal Broadcasting Corp. Net: MBS. Rep: Torbet. Format: Lite jazz, new age. Target aud: 21-54; upscale arrivers. Spec prog: Black 2 hrs wkly. ■ Robert L. Hill, pres & gen mgr; Robert Costello, gen sls mgr.

WKLI(FM)—Listing follows WABY(AM).

WPTR(AM)—May 1948: 1540 khz; 50 kw-U, DA-1. TL: N42 44 01 W73 51 49. Hrs opn: 24. Box 12279, 4243 Albany St. (12212). (518) 456-1144; (518) 456-1540, NEWS. FAX: (518) 456-1149. Licensee: Albany Broadcasting Co. Inc. (acq 3-87). Net: ABC/E, CNN, MBS. Rep: Torbet. Format: News, sports. News staff 7; news progmg 90 hrs wkly. Target aud: 35-64; educated, upscale and interested in business news. ■ John Kelly, pres & gen mgr; Michael Morgan, opns mgr; Mike Collins, gen sls mgr; Barbara Borini, prom dir; Randy Gorbman, progmg dir; Steve Janack, news dir; Paul Thurst, chief engr.

WPYX(FM)—Sept 16, 1980: 106.5 mhz; 15.3 kw. Ant 902 ft. TL: N42 38 09 W74 00 05. Stereo. 1054 Troy-Schenectady Rd., Latham (12110). (518) 785-9800. FAX: (518) 785-0122. Licensee: CAP-TOWN Broadcasting. Group owner: The Griffin Group/Broadcast Division (acq 12-86; grpsl; FTR 10-20-86). Net: ABC/R. Rep: McGavren Guild. Wash atty: Arent, Fox, Kintner, Plotkin & Kahn. Format: Rock (AOR). Target aud: 25-54. ■ Merv Griffin, pres; Robert Ausfeld, gen mgr; John Hirsch, gen sls mgr; Jeff Gillis, prom dir; Ed Levine, progmg dir; John Cooper, mus dir; Brian Szewczyk, chief engr.

WQBK(AM)—See Rensselaer.

WROW(AM)—Sept 30, 1947: 590 khz; 5 kw-D, 1 kw-N, DA-2. TL: N42 34 25 W73 47 12. Hrs opn: 24 341 Northern Blvd. (12204). (518) 436-4841. FAX: (518) 465-1857. Licensee: Albany Broadcasting Co. Inc. (acq 4-22-93; $5 million with co-located FM; FTR 5-17-93). Net: AP, ABC/D. Rep: Christal. Format: Btfl mus. News progmg 8 hrs wkly. Target aud: 35 plus; affluent, educated, white collar, upwardly mobile, homeowners. Spec prog: Gospel 3 hrs wkly. ■ Gary Pease, pres; Jake Russell, vp & gen mgr; Bill Gagliardi, gen sls mgr; Larry Mossey, prom mgr; Jim Gagliardi, progmg dir; Joe Condon, mus dir; Dave DeMoulpied, news dir; Daniel Kelleher, chief engr.

WROW-FM—October 1966: 95.5 mhz; 12 kw. Ant 1,020 ft. TL: N42 38 11 W74 00 00. Stereo. Dups AM 95%. Format: Soft adult contemp. News staff 2. Target aud: 35-54.

WTRY(AM)—See Troy.

WTRY-FM—See Rotterdam.

Alfred

***WALF(FM)**—1971: 89.7 mhz; 200 w. Ant 73 ft. TL: N42 15 17 W77 47 13. Stereo. Box 548 (14802). (607) 871-2287; (607) 871-2200. Licensee: Alfred University. Net: ABC/I. Format: Div. ■ Shannon Evans, stn mgr; Eric Pardu, Cindy Dearborn, mus dirs; Dick Weeks, chief engr.

***WETD(FM)**—Mar 19, 1973: 90.9 mhz; 360 w. Ant 282 ft. TL: N42 15 37 W77 47 51. Stereo. Alfred State College, Orvis Activities Ctr. (14802). (607) 587-3527; (607) 587-4651. Licensee: State Univ. of New York. Format: Rock/AOR. ■ Dick Weeks, chief engr.

Amherst

WUFO(AM)—1948: 1080 khz; 1 kw-D. TL: N42 56 46 W78 49 43. 89 LaSalle Ave., Buffalo (14214). (716) 834-1080. FAX: (716) 837-1438. Licensee: Sheridan Broadcasting (group owner; acq 3-1-72). Net: American Urban. Format: Urban contemp, relg. Target aud: 25-54; Black adults, lower to middle class, strong work ethics. ■ Ron Davenport, pres; Lenore Williams, opns mgr, prom mgr, progmg dir, mus dir & news dir; Shelia Brown, gen sls mgr. ■ Rates: $35; 35; 35; na.

Amsterdam

WBUG(AM)—Aug 16, 1961: 1570 khz; 1 kw-D, 207 w-N. TL: N42 54 38 W74 13 04. Hrs opn: 24. Box 570, Rt. 30 S. (12010). (518) 843-1570. Licensee: William H. Walker III (acq 6-90; $150,000; FTR 5-28-90). Format: C&W. News staff 2; news progmg 10 hrs wkly. Target aud: 25 plus. ■ Bud Walker, gen mgr; Jim Cuozzo, stn mgr & news dir; Wendy Bynum, gen sls mgr; Jeannete Relyea, natl sls mgr; Patrick Iorio, rgnl sls mgr; Thom Williams, progmg dir; Frank Alford, mus dir; Jennifer Weir, pub affrs dir; Emile Plotkin, chief engr.

WCSS(AM)—Apr 8, 1948: 1490 khz; 1 kw-U. TL: N42 57 40 W74 10 35. Hrs opn: 24. 6 Genessee Lane (12010). (518) 843-2500. FAX: (518) 842-0315. Licensee: Gateway Broadcasting Corp. (group owner; acq 12-23-88; $900,000; FTR 1-23-89). Net: ABC/I. Format: Full svc MOR. News staff 2; news progmg 17 hrs wkly. Target aud: 25 plus; adults interested in news, pub affrs & mus. Spec prog: Pol 5 hrs, Sp 3 hrs wkly. ■ Joseph Isabel, pres; Philip Spencer Jr., gen mgr; Dan Kielbasa, gen sls mgr; Mark Scott, vp prom; John Becker, news dir; Lloyd Smith, chief engr. ■ Rates: $11; 11; 11; na.

WKOL(FM)—Co-owned with WCSS(AM). Aug 1, 1975: 97.7 mhz; 790 w. Ant 623 ft. TL: N42 59 05 W74 10 49 (CP: 2.1 kw, ant 388 ft., TL: N43 02 11 W74 10 34). Stereo. Prog sep from AM. Net: ABC/C. Rep: Christal. Format: Adult contemp. News staff 2; news progmg one hr wkly. Target aud: 18-45; General. ■ Joseph Isabel, CEO, chmn & CFO; Phillip Spencer Jr., stn mgr & pub affrs dir; Mark Scott, progmg dir; Lloyd Smith, engrg dir. ■ Rates: Same as AM.

Arlington

WDSP(FM)—December 1989: 96.9 mhz; 3 kw. Ant 1,010 ft. TL: N41 43 11 W73 59 45 (CP: 500 w, ant 233 ft.). Stereo. Rebroadcasts WDST(FM) Woodstock. Box 367, 118 Tinker St., Woodstock (12498). (914) 679-7266; (914) 485-9378. FAX: (914) 679-5395. Licensee: CHET-5 Broadcasting of Poughkeepsie Inc. Group owner: CHET-5 Broadcasting. Format: Alternative new music. News progmg 5 hrs wkly. Target aud: 25-54; upscale professionals. ■ Gary H. Chetkof, chmn, pres & gen mgr; Ike Phillips, vp sls & vp mktg; Fred Bluefox, progmg dir.

Attica

WBTF(FM)—Nov 9, 1977: 101.7 mhz; 3 kw. Ant 295 ft. TL: N42 50 51 W78 21 01. Stereo. 438 E. Main St., Batavia (14020-2594). (716) 344-1490. Licensee: John T. King II, trustee (acq 1-25-86; $500,000; FTR 11-18-85). Format: Country. News staff 2; news progmg 3 hrs wkly. Target aud: 25-54; blue collar, housewives. ■ Jack King, pres; Marty Mercurio, gen mgr; Judy Figliulo, gen sls mgr; Wayne Schmidieker, progmg dir.

Auburn

WAUB(AM)—Dec 24, 1959: 1590 khz; 500 w-D, 1 kw-N, DA-2. TL: N42 54 34 W76 36 09. Box 160, Experimental Rd. (13021). (315) 253-3040. FAX: (315) 253-8399. Licensee: Morgan Media Inc. (acq 1-10-92; $120,000; FTR 2-10-92). Net: CBS, Sun. Format: Adult contemp. News staff 2; news progmg 22 hrs wkly. Target aud: General; community residents. Spec prog: Pol 2 hrs, sports 4 hrs, public affairs 10 hrs wkly. ■ Richard E. Morgan, pres & gen mgr; Mark P. Shayler, prom mgr; Francis A. Ciccoricco, chief engr.

***WDWN(FM)**—Oct 31, 1972: 88.9 mhz; 250 w. Ant 102 ft. TL: N42 56 40 W76 32 33 (CP: 89.1 mhz, 3 kw). Stereo. Franklin St. (13021). (315) 255-1743, ext. 282. Licensee: Cayuga County Community College (acq 10-72). Format: AOR. ■ Lawrence Poole, pres; Steven Keeler, gen mgr; Stephen Roder, chief engr.

WMBO(AM)—Jan 26, 1927: 1340 khz; 1 kw-U. TL: N42 57 05 W76 35 05. 1340 Corporate Dr. (13021). (315) 253-7355. FAX: (315) 253-6268. Licensee: Great Scott Broadcasting Ltd. Group owner: Great Scott Broadcasting (acq 12-19-86). Net: MBS. Format: Golden oldies. ■ Faye Scott, pres; Lynn Cook, gen mgr; Becky Palmer, progmg dir; Bill Covert, chief engr.

WPCX(FM)—Co-owned with WMBO(AM). May 20, 1949: 106.9 mhz; 14 kw. Ant 941 ft. TL: N42 48 05 W76 26 14. Stereo. Prog sep from AM. Format: Mod country. ■ Bob Paris, progmg dir.

Avon

WEZO(FM)—Not on air, target date unknown: 93.3 mhz; 2.1 kw. Ant 381 ft. TL: N42 54 53 W77 39 36. Licensee: The Lincoln Group Ltd.

WYSL(AM)—Jan 23, 1987: 1030 khz; 1 kw-D. TL: N42 51 16 W77 42 39. Box 236, 5620 S. Lima Rd. (14414). (716) 226-3000. FAX: (716) 226-3000. Licensee: Radio Livingston Ltd. Net: ABC/D, ABC TalkRadio, CNN. Rep: Dome. Format: News/talk. News staff 3; news progmg 10 hrs wkly. Target aud: General; 35 plus. Spec prog: Jazz 2 hrs wkly. ■ Robert C. Savage, pres & gen mgr; Robert D'Angelo, opns mgr & progmg dir; Karen Klehamer, gen sls mgr; George Frederick, prom mgr; Dave Tubbs, mus dir; Mike Morgan, news dir; Karen Shillinger, pub affrs dir; Jerry Whitney, chief engr. WOKR(TV) affil. ■ Rates: $28; 18; 24; 18.

Babylon

WBAB-FM—Aug 27, 1958: 102.3 mhz; 3 kw. Ant 268 ft. TL: N40 47 58 W73 20 08. Stereo. Hrs opn: 24. 555 Sunrise Hwy., West Babylon (11704-6009). (516) 587-1023. Licensee: Liberty Broadcasting of New York Inc. (acq 1-21-93; $16 million with WGBB(AM) Freeport; FTR 2-15-93). Net: AP. Format: AOR. ■ Mike Cravin, pres, CFO & gen mgr; Debbi Buglisi, stn mgr; Janet Nauman, vp dev; Pat Bendik, dev mgr; Charles Cirelli, gen sls mgr; Morgan Thomas, prom dir; Steve Morris, prom mgr; Jeff Levine, progmg dir; Ralph Tortona, mus dir; Tracy Burgess, news dir; Dennis Ciapura, vp engrg; Chris Tobin, chief engr.

WNYG(AM)—Jan 1, 1958: 1440 khz; 1 kw-D, 38 w-N. TL: N40 42 32 W73 21 53. 404 Rt. 109 (11704). (516) 661-4000. FAX: (516) 587-5400. Licensee: Babylon Bay Shore Broadcasting Corp. (acq 2-5-58). Format: Oldies. Target aud: 27 plus. Spec prog: Country 2 hrs, It 4 hrs wkly. ■ Muriel Horenstein, pres & gen mgr; Larry Walsh, gen sls mgr; Carol Lucas, prom mgr; Jim Pierce, progmg dir & mus dir; Joel Martin, news dir; John Blake, chief engr.

Baldwinsville

***WBXL(FM)**—Jan 29, 1975: 90.5 mhz; 195 w. Ant 195 ft. TL: N43 09 47 W76 18 47. Stereo. Hrs opn: 7 AM-11 PM. Baker High School, E. Oneida St. Complex (13027). (315) 638-6010; (315) 638-6000. Licensee: Baldwinsville Central School District. Format: Noncommercial div. ■ Allen B. Jenner, gen mgr; Adam Matthews, vp progmg; Amy Coomes, mus dir; Al Jenner, engrg dir.

WFBL(AM)—Feb 25, 1959: 1050 khz; 2.5 kw-D, DA. TL: N43 10 46 W76 20 19. Stereo. Box 1050 (13027). (315) 635-3971. FAX: (315) 635-3490. Licensee: Buckley Broadcasting Corp. (group owner; acq 8-20-80; $700,000; with co-located FM; FTR 8-11-80). Net: CBS. Rep: D & R Radio. Format: Music of your life. Target aud: 25-54; well-educated professionals with disposable income. ■ Richard Buckley, pres; Doug Fleniken, vp & gen mgr; Judith Kelly, gen sls mgr; Allen Poppoon, prom mgr; Jim Tate, mus dir; Rick Laxton, news dir; Al Jenner, chief engr.

WSEN-FM—Co-owned with WFBL(AM). Nov 10, 1967: 92.1 mhz; 25 kw. Ant 300 ft. TL: N43 10 46 W76 20 19. Stereo. Hrs opn: 24. Dups AM 100%.

New York Directory of Radio

Ballston Spa

WZRQ(FM)—May 27, 1968: 102.3 mhz; 4.1 kw. Ant 386 ft. TL: N42 52 44 W73 51 47. Stereo. Hrs opn: 24. 316 Canal Square, Schenectady (12305). (518) 381-1180. FAX: (518) 393-0316. Licensee: DJA Radio Inc. (acq 11-6-92; $400,000; FTR 11-16-92). Rep: D & R Radio. Wash atty: Fisher, Wayland, Cooper & Leader. Format: AOR. Target aud: 18-49. ■ David Arkara, pres; Carolyn Holochuck, CFO & opns mgr; Lee Abrams, progmg dir; Pat Dawsey, mus dir; Jack Shafer, chief engr.

Batavia

WBTA(AM)—Feb 6, 1941: 1490 khz; 500 w-D, 1 kw-N. TL: N42 58 37 W78 11 12. 438 E. Main St. (14020). (716) 344-1490. FAX: (716) 344-1441. Licensee: Radio Batavia Inc. (acq 1-25-86; $504,000; FTR 11-18-85). Net: ABC/I. Format: News. News staff 3; news progmg 25 hrs wkly. Target aud: Older, upscale adults. Spec prog: Farm 10 hrs, sports 9 hrs, talk 15 hrs wkly. ■ Jack King, pres; Marty Mercurio, gen mgr; Judy Figliulo, gen sls mgr; Jerry Warner, progmg dir; Wayne Stone, mus dir & engrg mgr; Mary Klime, news dir. ■ Rates: $34.50; 29.50; 29.50; 21.

***WGCC-FM**—Nov 13, 1985: 90.7 mhz; 880 w. Ant 164 ft. TL: N43 01 03 W78 08 18. Stereo. One College Rd. (14020). (716) 343-0055, ext. 284 (Business); (716) 343-9422 (Request). FAX: (716) 343-0055, ext. 553. Licensee: Genesee Community College Board of Trustees. Format: Serious rock. News staff 2; news progmg 6 hrs wkly. Target aud: 13-30; high school & college youth. ■ Chuck Platt, pres & chief engr; Pat Boyle, gen mgr; Ted Ranieri, opns dir & progmg dir; Alise Tepedino, dev dir & prom mgr; John La Varnway, mus dir; Maria Lamanna, Deanna King, news dirs.

Bath

WABH(AM)—Nov 2, 1962: 1380 khz; 500 w-D. TL: N42 20 11 W77 17 34 (CP: 5 kw-D, 350 w-N). Hrs opn: 19. Box 72, E. Washington St. Ext. (14810). (607) 776-3326. FAX: (607) 776-6161. Licensee: Pembrook Pines Mass Media Inc. Group owner: Pembrook Pines Inc. (acq 4-13-90; with co-located FM; FTR 5-7-90). Net: CBS. Format: Adult contemp, contemp hit, oldies. Target aud: General. Spec prog: Farm one hr wkly. ■ Robert Pfuntner, pres; Bob Penrod, gen mgr & gen sls mgr; James F. Clark Jr., opns mgr & news dir; John Lyke, progmg dir; Jim Reed, chief engr. ■ Rates: $12; 12; 12; 10.

WVIN-FM—Co-owned with WABH(AM). Oct 10, 1971: 98.3 mhz; 3 kw. Ant 351 ft. TL: N42 19 06 W77 21 27 (CP: 2.75 kw, ant 341 ft.). Stereo. Hrs opn: 19. Dups AM 100%.

WCIK(FM)—Aug 29, 1983: 103.1 mhz; 790 w. Ant 532 ft. TL: N42 20 07 W77 27 27. Stereo. Hrs opn: 24. Box 506, 7634 Campbell Creek Rd., Bath (14810). (607) 776-4151. Licensee: Family Life Ministries Radio Inc. Format: Christian. News progmg 8 hrs wkly. Target aud: 25-55; general. ■ Dick Snavely, pres & gen mgr; Rick Snavely, vp, stn mgr & progmg dir; Jim Travis, chief engr.

WVIN-FM—Listing follows WABH(AM).

Bay Shore

WBZO(FM)—February 1993: 103.1 mhz; 3 kw. Ant 285 ft. TL: N40 45 04 W73 12 52. Stereo. Hrs opn: 24. 1265 Sunrise Hwy. (11706); Box 1030 (11706). (516) 666-3900. FAX: (516) 665-0329. Licensee: Shore Media Inc. Wash atty: Verner & Liipfert. Format: Oldies. News staff one; news progmg 25 hrs wkly. Target aud: General. ■ Estee Hollander, pres; Ron Gold, gen mgr; Karen Stripp, sls dir; Dennis Falcone, prom dir; Flo Federman, news dir; John Blake, chief engr. ■ Rates: $50; 50; 50; 40.

Beacon

WBNR(AM)—Dec 17, 1959: 1260 khz; 1 kw-D, 500 w-N, DA-2. TL: N41 29 32 W73 58 43. Stereo. Hrs opn: 24. Box 511, 475 South Ave. (12508). (914) 831-1260; (914) 562-1260. FAX: (914) 838-2109. Licensee: Beacon Broadcasting Corp. (group owner; acq 6-1-79). Net: Unistar. Rep: Banner. Wash atty: Rothman Gordon. Format: Oldies. News staff 2. Target aud: 35 plus. Spec prog: Religious one hr wkly. ■ Robert E. Lessner, CEO & chmn; Alford H. Lessner, pres & gen mgr; Robert A. Outer, exec vp & vp sls; Joseph P. Daily, vp opns & progmg dir; Bob Corsino, gen sls mgr; Maggie Carbaugh, rgnl sls mgr; Rich Ball, mus dir; Dawn Spicer, news dir; Dave Rozek, engrg dir & chief engr. ■ Rates: $29; 27; 29; 27.

WGNY-FM—See Newburgh.

WSPK(FM)—See Poughkeepsie.

Big Flats

WGMM(FM)—April 1989: 97.7 mhz; 1.30 kw. Ant 482 ft. TL: N42 09 43 W77 02 15. 3037 Palmer Rd. (14814). (607) 562-8455. Licensee: Culver Communications of Big Flats Inc. Format: Oldies. Target aud: 25-54. ■ Margaret E. Greene, pres; Brigid Langendorfer, gen mgr; Bob Michaels, progmg dir.

Binghamton

WAAL(FM)—Listing follows WKOP(AM).

***WHRW(FM)**—Mar 1, 1966: 90.5 mhz; 1.45 kw. Ant -47 ft. TL: N42 05 24 W75 58 05. Stereo. Hrs opn: 24. Box 2000, Binghamton Univ. (13902-6000). (607) 777-2137. Licensee: State Univ. of New York. Format: Alternative. News progmg 3 hrs wkly. Spec prog: Sp 20 hrs wkly. ■ Jason Frademan, gen mgr; Isabelle Osterlund, progmg dir; Jason Fradin, news dir; Stephanie Linder, pub affrs dir; Tom Siglin, chief engr.

WHWK(FM)—Listing follows WNBF(AM).

WINR(AM)—1946: 680 khz; 1 kw-D, 500 w-N, DA-2. TL: N42 06 53 W75 51 16. Hrs opn: 24. 3646 George F. Hwy., Endwell (13760). (607) 754-2454. FAX: (607) 775-4246. Licensee: Titus Broadcasting Systems Inc. (acq 11-87; FTR 11-16-87). Net: CBS, FNN. Rep: Roslin. Wash atty: Fisher, Wayland, Cooper & Leader. Format: MOR, news/talk. News staff one; news progmg 10 hrs wkly. Target aud: 35 plus; adult demographics. ■ Dr. Paul Titus, pres & gen mgr; Mary Fronek, opns mgr & prom mgr; Bruce Sohigian, gen sls mgr; Wally Roper, rgnl sls mgr; Tony Russell, news dir; Sherm Clapman, chief engr. ■ Rates: $15; 11; 13.50; 7.50.

***WJIK(FM)**—Not on air, target date unknown: 91.5 mhz; 1.5 kw. Ant 328 ft. 308 Harry L Dr., Johnson City (13790). Licensee: Arrowhead Ministries Inc.

WKOP(AM)—June 1947: 1360 khz; 5 kw-D, 500 w-N, DA-2. TL: N42 04 03 W75 54 20. Box 997, 122 State St. (13902). (607) 722-3437. FAX: (607) 722-3438. Licensee: Butternut Broadcasting Inc. Group owner: Regional Group Inc. (acq 3-27-90; with co-located FM; FTR 4-16-90). Net: MBS, ABC/E, Unistar, BRN. Rep: Eastman. Format: Business news. Spec prog: Ger one hr, Irish one hr wkly. ■ Richard Sutton, gen mgr.

WAAL(FM)—Co-owned with WKOP(AM). March 1954: 99.1 mhz; 7.1 kw. Ant 1,089 ft. TL: N42 03 22 W75 56 39. Stereo. (607) 772-8850. Net: ABC/FM. Format: CHR. ■ Don Morgan, progmg dir; Mike Orzel, mus dir.

WMRV(AM)—See Endicott.

WNBF(AM)—1928: 1290 khz; 5 kw-U, DA-2. TL: N42 03 31 W75 57 14. Box 414 (13902). (607) 772-8400. Licensee: American Radio Systems (group owner; acq 9-15-93; with co-located FM; FTR 10-4-93). Net: NBC, NBC Talknet. Rep: Katz. Format: News/talk. News staff 3. Target aud: 35-64. ■ Steve Dodse, CEO; Joe Winn, CFO; Roger Conklin, vp & gen mgr; Kal Barmada, gen sls mgr; Roger Neal, progmg dir; Bill Berg, mus dir; Bernard Fionti, news dir; Lawrence Hodge, chief engr.

WHWK(FM)—Co-owned with WNBF(AM). September 1956: 98.1 mhz; 10 kw. Ant 960 ft. TL: N42 03 34 W75 57 06. Stereo. Prog sep from AM. Format: Country. News staff 2. Target aud: 25-54. ■ Cathy Lewis, gen sls mgr; John Davison, progmg dir & mus dir; Dave Freeman, news dir.

***WSKG-FM**—Oct 22, 1975: 89.3 mhz; 10.2 kw. Ant 942 ft. TL: N42 03 22 W75 56 39. Stereo. Hrs opn: 24. Box 3000 (13902). (607) 729-0100. FAX: (607) 729-7328. Licensee: WSKG Public Telecommunications Council. Net: NPR, AP, APR. Wash atty: Dow, Lohnes & Albertson. Format: Class, news. News staff 4; news progmg 33 hrs wkly. Target aud: General. Spec prog: Jazz. ■ Michael J. Ziegler, pres; June M. Smith, vp; Katherine Bacon, prom mgr; Donna Hill, progmg mgr; Kelly Farewell, mus dir; Peter Iglinski, news dir; Charles F. Mulvey, vp engrg; Mark Polovick, chief engr. ■ *WSKG(TV) affil.

***WSQX-FM**—Not on air, target date unknown: 91.5 mhz; 560 w. Ant 843 ft. Box 3000 (13902). Licensee: WSKG Public Telecommunications Council.

Blue Mountain Lake

***WXLH(FM)**—November 1992: 91.3 mhz; 78 w. Ant 1,729 ft. TL: N43 52 18 W74 24 02. Hrs opn: 24. Rebroadcasts WSLU(FM) Canton 100%. c/o Radio Station WSLU(FM), St. Lawrence University, Canton (13617). (315) 379-5356. Licensee: St. Lawrence University. Wash atty: Donald Martin. Format: Div. News staff 2; news progmg 35 hrs wkly. Target aud: General. Spec prog: Gospel, jazz, classical, folk, public affrs. ■ Ellen Rocco, gen mgr.

Boonville

WBRV(AM)—June 22, 1955: 900 khz; 1 kw-D, 52 w-N. TL: N43 30 47 W75 21 46. Hrs opn: 24. 7606 State St., Lowville (13367). (315) 942-4311; (315) 376-8566. FAX: (315) 376-8560. Licensee: The Atwood Broadcasting Corp. (acq 6-22-78). Net: USA. Wash atty: Richard Zaragosa. Format: C&W. News progmg 18 hrs wkly. Target aud: General. ■ David R. Atwood, pres & gen mgr; George Capron, progmg dir; Stephen Douglass, news dir; Bob Thayer, chief engr. ■ Rates: $14; 14; 14; 14.

WBRV-FM—Jan 31, 1989: 101.3 mhz; 720 w. Ant 348 ft. TL: N43 26 53 W75 20 48. Stereo. Hrs opn: 24. Format: C&W. News progmg 10 hrs wkly. Target aud: General. Spec prog: Farm 3 hrs, relg 3 hrs wkly. ■ Nancy Atwood, sr vp. ■ Rates: Same as AM.

Brentwood

***WXBA(FM)**—June 21, 1975: 88.1 mhz; 180 w. Ant 90 ft. TL: N40 46 19 W73 15 19. Stereo. Hrs opn: 10 AM-8 PM. Ross High School, 1st & 5th Aves. (11717). (516) 434-2581; (516) 434-2330. FAX: (516) 434-2528. Licensee: Brentwood Public School District. Format: Educ, div, news/talk. News staff 2; news progmg 3 hrs wkly. Target aud: General. Spec prog: Black 5 hrs, Sp 5 hrs wkly. ■ Jerrold Steiner, gen mgr; Robert Ottone, stn mgr; Chris Bagielto, prom dir; Steve Colon, progmg dir; Yvonne Sing, mus dir; Kristen McQuillan, (asst) mus dir; Christopher Teves, news dir; Dawn Shannon, pub affrs dir; Frank Stehle, chief engr.

Brewster

WPUT(AM)—July 3, 1958: 1510 khz; 1 kw-D. TL: N41 24 34 W73 37 29. Box 105.5, Route 292, Patterson (12563). (914) 878-3334. Licensee: Tri-Valley Broadcasting Corp. (acq 6-1-86; grpsl; FTR 2-3-86). Net: CNN. Format: Country. News staff 2; news progmg 8 hrs wkly. Target aud: 35 plus. ■ Ronald Graiff, pres & chief engr; Winifred Graiff, gen mgr; Al Matthews, progmg dir; Janice Berliner, news dir.

Briarcliff Manor

WXPS(FM)—Apr 8, 1960: 107.1 mhz; 3 kw. Ant 325 ft. TL: N41 02 15 W73 50 35 (CP: 1.8 kw, ant 417 ft., TL: N41 02 15 W73 50 35). Stereo. Hrs opn: 24. 11 Skyline Dr., Hawthorne (10532). (914) 592-7451. Licensee: WestLand Communicators Inc. (acq 1-11-89; $5 million; FTR 1-30-89). Rep: Banner. Format: Adult contemp, rock. News staff 2. Target aud: 25-49; upscale, young, suburban families. ■ Michael Kakoyiannis, pres, gen mgr & progmg dir; Rosemary Corporale, prom mgr; Janet Bardini, mus dir; Glen Crespo, news dir; Paul Sanchez, chief engr. ■ Rates: $75; 65; 65; 50.

Bridgehampton

WAFV(FM)—Not on air, target date unknown: 102.5 mhz; 4.5 kw. Ant 112 ft. Box 612, Southold (11971). Licensee: Peconic Bay Broadcasting Corp.

Bridgeport

WTKW(FM)—Nov 9, 1992: 99.5 mhz; 3 kw. Ant 318 ft. TL: N43 09 07 W75 56 05 (CP: 2.85 kw). Stereo. Hrs opn: 24. 555 Rt. 31, Box 489 (13030-0489). (315) 633-0047. FAX: (315) 633-0161. Licensee: Francis G. Toce. Net: AP. Wash atty: James Oyster. Format: Classic Rock. News staff one; news progmg 3 hrs wkly. Target aud: 25-54 plus; stable, peak-earning males/females. ■ Francis G. Toce, pres; Mike Healy, gen mgr & natl sls mgr; Dave Alexander, prom dir; Ed Levine, progmg dir & mus dir; Frank Toce, chief engr. ■ Rates: $56; 50; 56; 40.

Brockport

WASB(AM)—Feb 15, 1970: 1590 khz; 1.8 kw-U, DA-2. TL: N43 11 44 W77 57 05. 6675 Fourth Section Rd. (14420). (716) 637-7040. Licensee: David L. Wolfe (acq 1-15-91; $27,500; FTR 1-28-91). Format: Christian. Target aud: All ages; rural audience, Western Rochester and suburbs. ■ Dr. David L. Wolfe, stn mgr; Gail Reed, progmg dir; Randy Orbaker, chief engr. ■ Rates: $18; 16; 18; 16.

***WBSU(FM)**—Jan 14, 1981: 89.1 mhz; 7.338 kw. Ant 160 ft. TL: N43 12 45 W77 57 17. Stereo. Hrs opn: 20. Seymour Union (14420). (716) 395-2580. Licensee: State Univ. of N.Y. Net: AP. Format: Div, educ, jazz. News progmg 4 hrs wkly. Target aud: General. Spec prog: Black 6 hrs, class 14 hrs, reggae 2 hrs, club/dance 2 hrs wkly. ■ John Van de Wetering, pres; Warren Kozireski, gen mgr; Bernard Lynch, chief engr.

Brooklyn

***WKRB(FM)**—Licensed to Brooklyn. See New York.

***WNYE(FM)**—See New York.

Brookville

***WCWP(FM)**—April 1965: 88.1 mhz; 100 w. Ant 190 ft. TL: N40 49 00 W73 35 49. Stereo. Long Island Univ., C.W. Post Campus (11548). (516) 299-2626. FAX: (516) 626-9730. Licensee: Long Island Univ. (acq 8-90; FTR 8-13-90). Format: AOR, variety. ■ Robert Clifford, gen mgr & stn mgr.

Buffalo

WBEN(AM)—Sept 8, 1930: 930 khz; 5 kw-U, DA-N. TL: N42 58 42 W78 57 27. Hrs opn: 24. 2077 Elmwood Ave. (14207). (716) 876-0930. FAX: (716) 875-6201. Licensee: Algonquin Broadcasting Corp. (acq 3-1-78). Net: CBS, MBS. Rep: D & R Radio. Format: News/talk. News staff 10. Target aud: 35-64; general. ■ Larry Levite, pres & gen mgr; Larry Robb, gen sls mgr; Peter Kates, mktg mgr; Cheryl Klocke, prom mgr; Kevin Keenan, progmg dir; Roger Christian, mus dir; Tom Wenger, news dir; Dave May, chief engr.

WMJQ(FM)—Co-owned with WBEN(AM). Nov 11, 1946: 102.5 mhz; 110 kw. Ant 1,340 ft. TL: N42 39 33 W78 37 33. Stereo. Hrs opn: 24 Prog sep from AM. Net: NBC the Source. Format: Contemp hit/Hot adult contemp. Target aud: 18-49. ■ Rob Lucas, opns dir & progmg dir; Dave May, vp engrg.

***WBFO(FM)**—Jan 7, 1959: 88.7 mhz; 24 kw. Ant 240 ft. TL: N43 00 13 W78 45 54 (CP: 20 kw, ant 253 ft.). 3435 Main St. (14214). (716) 829-2880; (716) 829-2555. FAX: (716) 829-2277. Licensee: State Univ. of New York. Net: NPR. Format: Jazz, news. News staff 2; news progmg 50 hrs wkly. Target aud: General; educated professionals. Spec prog: Blues 6 hrs, bluegrass 3 hrs, class one hr, Polish 3 hrs wkly. ■ Jennifer Roth, gen mgr; Mark Wozniak, opns dir; Mary Ann Rogers, dev mgr; Bert Gambini, sls dir; David Benders, progmg dir; Lydia Kulbida, asst mus dir; Mark Scott, news dir; S&B Communications, chief engr.

WBLK(FM)—See Depew.

***WBNY(FM)**—1982: 91.3 mhz; 100 w. Ant 115 ft. TL: N42 55 59 W78 52 59. Stereo. 1300 Elmwood (14222). (716) 878-5104; (716) 878-3080. FAX: (716) 878-6600. Licensee: State Univ. of N.Y. Format: New music, alternative rock. News progmg 6 hrs wkly. Target aud: General. Spec prog: Black 12 hrs, jazz 3 hrs, reggae 3 hrs, heavy metal 3 hrs, folk 3 hrs wkly. ■ John Hans, gen mgr; Dave Hawthorne, gen sls mgr; Kris Kraus, prom dir; Stephanie Workman, progmg dir; Celeste , mus dir; Jennifer Lyons, chief engr.

WBUF(FM)—1947: 92.9 mhz; 93 kw. Ant 580 ft. TL: N42 38 12 W78 42 58. Stereo. 715 Delaware Ave. (14209). (716) 882-4300. FAX: (716) 882-1515. Licensee: Lincoln Group Ltd. (group owner). Rep: McGavren Guild. Format: Adult contemp. News staff one; news progmg one hr wkly. Target aud: 25-54; women. ■ Albert Wertheimer, pres; Jack Palvino, exec vp; Chris Whittingham, opns mgr & mus dir; Ken Dobmeier, gen sls mgr; Ellen Carroll, prom mgr; Mark McCormick, news dir; Kathy McCarthy, pub affrs dir; Craig Kingcaid, chief engr.

WDCX(FM)—February 1963: 99.5 mhz; 110 kw. Ant 640 ft. TL: N42 38 07 W78 46 05 (CP: 17 kw, ant 430 ft.). Stereo. 625 Delaware (14202). (716) 883-3010. FAX: (716) 883-3606. Licensee: Kimtron Inc. Group owner: Crawford Broadcasting Co. Format: Relg. Target aud: General. ■ Donald B. Crawford, pres; Nevin W. Larson, gen mgr; Milton Ellis, gen sls mgr; Randy S. Kershner, progmg dir; Terry Simson, mus dir. ■ Rates: $32; 32; 32; 32.

WECK(AM)—See Cheektowaga.

***WFBF(FM)**—1989: 89.9 mhz; 20 kw. Ant 59 ft. TL: N42 49 26 W78 45 20. c/o Houghton College, 910 Union Rd., West Seneca (14224). (716) 674-8244; (800) 543-1495. Licensee: Family Stations Inc. (group owner). Format: Relg. ■ Walt Pickut, gen mgr.

WGR(AM)—May 22, 1922: 550 khz; 5 kw-U, DA-2. TL: N42 46 04 W78 50 39. Stereo. Hrs opn: 24. 464 Franklin St. (14202). (716) 881-4555. FAX: (716) 884-2931. Licensee: Rich Communications Corp. (acq 5-1-87; $5.25 million with co-located FM; FTR 5-4-87). Net: ABC/I. Rep: Katz. Wash atty: Fisher, Wayland, Cooper & Leader. Format: News/talk. News staff 15; news progmg 168 hrs wkly. Target aud: 25-54. Spec prog: Black one hr, relg 2 hrs wkly. ■ Melinda R. Rich, pres; Jim Meltzer, exec vp & gen mgr; Chuck Finney, chief opns & progmg dir; Ken Casseri, gen sls mgr & natl sls mgr; Chris Ma, rgnl sls mgr; Brian Dickman, prom mgr; Craig Edwards, news dir; Mary Davis, pub affrs dir; Doug Wolf, chief engr. ■ Rates: $150; 70; 70; 70.

WGR-FM—Sept 14, 1959: 96.9 mhz; 12.5 kw. Ant 790 ft. TL: N42 43 06 W78 33 48 (CP: 15.5 kw). Stereo. Prog sep from AM. Net: Unistar. Format: Classic rock. News staff one; news progmg 18 hrs wkly. Target aud: 18-34. ■ Bill Saurer, rgnl sls mgr; Heidi Kramer, prom mgr; John Hager, progmg dir; Nickie Cyr, mus dir; Jolene Baller, news dir; Anita West, pub affrs dir.

WHTT-FM—Oct 3, 1954: 104.1 mhz; 50 kw. Ant 500 ft. TL: N42 49 50 W78 47 54. Stereo. Hrs opn: 24. Buffalo Hilton, 120 Church St. (14202). (716) 854-1120. FAX: (716) 855-3385. Licensee: Pyramid Broadcasting (group owner; acq 1986). Rep: Major Mkt. Format: Oldies. Spec prog: Pol 10 hrs wkly. ■ Richard Balsbaugh, pres; Ronald Rice, vp & gen mgr; Darren Neaverth, gen sls mgr; Tara Wells-Regan, prom mgr; Tom Schuh, progmg dir & mus dir; Bill Stachowiak, chief engr.

WHTT(AM)—September 1947: 1120 khz; 1 kw-D. TL: N42 49 50 W78 47 54. Dups FM 100%.

WJYE(FM)—Nov 11, 1966: 96.1 mhz; 50 kw. Ant 480 ft. TL: N42 53 10 W78 52 25. Stereo. Hrs opn: 24. 1700 Rand Bldg. (14203). (716) 856-3550. FAX: (716) 852-0537. Licensee: EBE Buffalo (acq 8-90; grpsl; FTR 8-2-90). Rep: D & R Radio. Format: Adult contemp. News staff one; news progmg 23 hrs wkly. Target aud: 25-54. Spec prog: Relg 2 hrs wkly. ■ Robert L. Williams, pres & gen mgr; Donna Vullo, gen sls mgr; Joe Chille, progmg dir & mus dir; Bill Stachowiak, chief engr. ■ Rates: $125; 150; 125; 50.

WMJQ(FM)—Listing follows WBEN(AM).

WNED(AM)—Oct 14, 1924: 970 khz; 5 kw-U, DA-1. TL: N42 44 41 W78 00 00. 140 Lower Terrace (14202). (716) 845-7000. FAX: (716) 845-7043. Licensee: Western N.Y. Public Broadcasting Assoc. (acq 8-14-76). Net: APR, AP. Format: News, jazz. ■ J. Michael Collins, pres; Richard J. Daly, vp; Peter Goldsmith, stn mgr; Leon Thomas Lewek, news dir.

WNED-FM—June 6, 1960: 94.5 mhz; 105 kw. Ant 710 ft. TL: N42 38 13 W78 46 05. Prog sep from AM. Format: Class. ■ Peter Goldsmith, progmg dir.

WUFX(FM)—Listing follows WWWS(AM).

WWKB(AM)—1925: 1520 khz; 50 kw-U, DA-1. TL: N42 46 10 W78 50 34. Hrs opn: 24. 695 Delaware Ave. (14209). (716) 884-5101. FAX: (716) 881-5249. Licensee: Empire State Broadcasting Corp. Group owner: Price Communications Corp. Stations (acq 1-2-86; $2 million; FTR 10-7-85). Net: ABC, BRN. Rep: D & R Radio, Target. Wash atty: Mullin, Rhyne, Emmons & Topel. Format: Talk, sports. News staff 4; news progmg 20 hrs wkly. Target aud: 25-54. Spec prog: Pol one hr wkly, relg 5 hrs wkly. ■ Robert Price, pres; Al Green, stn mgr; Emily Eberhardt, prom mgr; Ken Casey, progmg dir; Tom Atkins, chief engr. ■ Rates: $50; 30; 30; 30.

WWWS(AM)—1934: 1400 khz; 1 kw-U. TL: N42 55 33 W78 50 28. 425 Franklin St. (14202). (716) 885-1400. FAX: (716) 882-8810. Licensee: Metroplex Communications Inc., an Ohio Corp. Group owner: Metroplex Communications Inc. (acq 2-5-92; no financial consideration, with co-located FM; FTR 2-24-92). Format: Oldies. Target aud: 35-54. ■ Jim Meltzer, pres & gen mgr; Ken Casseri, gen sls mgr; Tom Burns, progmg dir; Bill Meyers, chief engr.

WUFX(FM)—Co-owned with WWWS(AM). 1947: 103.3 mhz; 49 kw. Ant 340 ft. TL: N42 55 33 W78 50 28. Stereo. Prog sep from AM. Rep: Torbet. Format: Classic rock. News staff one; news progmg 6 hrs wkly. Target aud: 25-34; pin-striped rock and roll listeners. ■ Kelly McInnis, prom mgr; Ken Carson, progmg dir & mus dir.

WYRK(FM)—Nov 14, 1962: 106.5 mhz; 50 kw. Ant 390 ft. TL: N42 53 10 W78 52 25. Stereo. 500 Rand Bldg. (14203). (716) 852-7444. Licensee: American Radio Systems License Corp. Group owner: American Radio Systems (acq 9-15-93; FTR 10-4-93). Rep: Christal. Format: Country. ■ Ralph Christian, vp & gen mgr; Connie Nitkowski, adv mgr; Ken Johnson, progmg dir; Paul Prusakowski, chief engr.

Canajoharie

***WCAN(FM)**—October 1988: 93.3 mhz; 6 kw. Ant 268 ft. TL: N42 53 46 W74 35 45. Stereo. Hrs opn: 24. Rebroadcasts WAMC(FM) Albany 100%. 318 Central Ave., Albany (12206). (518) 465-5233; (800) 323-9262. FAX: (518) 432-0991. Licensee: WAMC. Group owner: WAMC/Northeast Public Radio. Net: UPI, APR, NPR. Format: Class, news, info. News progmg 48 hrs wkly. Target aud: General. Spec prog: Jazz 18 hrs, folk/bluegrass 8 hrs wkly. ■ Alan Chartock (exec dir), CEO; Alan Chartock, chmn; Kathleen Taylor, dev dir; David Galletly (asst exec), progmg dir; Michael Carrese, news dir; Jim Scholefield, chief engr.

Canandaigua

WCGR(AM)—1962: 1550 khz; 250 w-D. TL: N42 52 52 W77 15 02. Box 155, 3007 Townline Rd. (14424). (716) 394-1550. FAX: (716) 394-2301. Licensee: Canadaigua Broadcasting Co. Net: ABC/E. Format: Oldies. News staff 2; news progmg 25 hrs wkly. Target aud: General. Spec prog: Talk 6 hrs wkly. ■ Jim Herendeen, gen mgr, progmg dir & mus dir; Scott Hamula, gen sls mgr; Ed Pevear, news dir; Ken Haight, chief engr.

WLKA(FM)—Co-owned with WCGR(AM). July 16, 1974: 102.3 mhz; 3.4 kw. Ant 282 ft. TL: N42 51 47 W77 19 22. Stereo. Prog sep from AM. Format: Adult contemp. News progmg 10 hrs wkly. Target aud: 25-54. Spec prog: New age 6 hrs wkly. ■ Dean Amsler, mus dir.

***WCIY(FM)**—December 1992: 88.9 mhz; 70 w. Ant 1,059 ft. TL: N42 44 29 W77 25 23. Stereo. Hrs opn: 24. Box 506, 7634 Campbell Creek Rd., Bath (14810). (607) 776-4151. Licensee: Family Life Ministries Radio, Inc. Net: USA. Wash atty: Bill Crispen. Format: Relg, educ, news. News staff one. Target aud: 25-55; general, Christian. ■ Dick Snavely, pres & gen mgr; Rick Snavely, vp & stn mgr; Jim Travis, chief engr.

WLKA(FM)—Listing follows WCGR(AM).

Canton

WNYS(AM)—Not on air, target date unknown: 750 khz; 5 kw-D, 1 kw-N, DA-2. TL: N44 29 06 W75 13 27. c/o Townline Rd., Canandaigua (14424). Licensee: Canton Broadcasting Assocs.

***WSLU(FM)**—December 1964: 89.5 mhz; 40.3 kw. Ant 299 ft. TL: N44 32 01 W75 05 50. Hrs opn: 24. St. Lawrence University (13617). (315) 379-5356. FAX: (315) 379-5373. Licensee: St. Lawrence University. Net: NPR, APR. Wash atty: Donald Martin. Format: Div. News staff 2; news progmg 35 hrs wkly. Target aud: General. Spec prog: Gospel, jazz, class, folk, public affrs. ■ Ellen Rocco, gen mgr; Peter Euler, chief opns; Kathleen Brandt, dev dir; Jacqueline Sauter, progmg dir; Martha Foley, news dir; Robert G. Sauter, chief engr.

WVNC(FM)—July 1984: 96.7 mhz; 2.6 kw. Ant 310 ft. TL: N44 32 01 W75 05 50 (CP: Ant 230 ft.). Stereo. Hrs opn: 24. Box 136 (13617); 56 Park St. (13617). (315) 379-9777. FAX: (315) 379-9778. Licensee: B&B Broadcasting Inc. (acq 9-19-86). Net: CBS. Wash atty: Eugene Smith. Format: Adult contemp, sports. News staff one; news progmg 20 hrs wkly. Target aud: 25-54; white collar, upwardly mobile. Spec prog: Relg 4 hrs wkly. ■ David Button, pres, gen mgr & gen sls mgr; Shannon Steele, progmg dir & mus dir; Ed Thomas, asst mus dir; Greg Lapinski, news dir & pub affrs dir; Bob Sauter, chief engr. ■ Rates: $17.50; 14; 16.50; 8.

WXQZ(FM)—Not on air, target date Spring 1993: 101.5 mhz; 2.4 kw. Ant 364 ft. TL: N44 32 01 W75 05 50. Stereo. Box 136, 56 Park St. (13617). Licensee: David T. Button and Ann D.G. Button. Wash atty: Eugene Smith. ■ David Button, pres, gen mgr & gen sls mgr; Rick Pendleton, progmg dir.

Cape Vincent

WKGG(FM)—Not on air, target date unknown: 102.7 mhz; 3 kw. Ant 328 ft. TL: N44 06 58 W76 20 21. 214 Colorado Ave., Watertown (13601). Licensee: Cape Al Broadcasting Ltd.

***WMHI(FM)**—Oct 1, 1990: 94.7 mhz; 3 kw. Ant 284 ft. TL: N44 02 42 W76 15 37. Stereo. Hrs opn: 24. 4044 Makyes Rd., Syracuse (13215); Fox Creek Rd. & Rte. 12E, Cape Vincent (13618). (315) 649-3060. Licensee: Mars Hill Broadcasting Co. Inc. (group owner). Net: Moody. Wash atty: Wiley, Rein & Fielding. Format: Relg. News progmg 6 hrs wkly. Target aud: General; Christian families. ■ Glenn H. Burdick, pres; Clayton Roberts, vp; Gordon Bell, gen mgr; Kevin Tubbs, opns mgr; Ron Zorn, mus dir; Clayton R. Roberts, chief engr.

Carthage

WTOJ(FM)—Nov 1, 1984: 103.1 mhz; 3 kw. Ant 500 ft. TL: N43 57 16 W75 43 45. Stereo. 199 Wealtha Ave., Watertown (13601). (315) 782-1240. FAX: (315) 782-0312. Licensee: Clancy-Mance Communications Inc. (group owner; acq 6-20-88; grpsl; FTR 6-20-88). Net: Unistar. Rep: Roslin. Format: Adult contemp. News progmg 6 hrs wkly. Target aud: 25-54. ■ David W. Mance,

Catskill

WCKL(AM)—Feb 6, 1970: 560 khz; 1 kw-D, DA. TL: N42 12 00 W73 50 07. Box 445 (12414); Route 9G, Hudson (12534). (518) 828-5006; (518) 943-5464. FAX: (518) 828-1080. Licensee: Straus Communications in the Hudson Valley Inc. Group owner: Straus Media Group (acq 10-91; $335,000 with co-located FM; FTR 11-11-91). Net: CNN. Format: MOR. News staff 2; news progmg 2 hrs wkly. Target aud: 45 plus; Hudson Valley upscale adults. Spec prog: German one hr, Irish 2 hrs wkly. ■ Eric P. Straus, pres & gen mgr; Errol Hanson, CFO; R. Peter Straus, exec vp; Jeanne Straus, vp; James Brady, gen sls mgr; Paul Edwards, prom dir; Bill Williamson, progmg dir; Kate Capra, news dir; Barbara Kenton, pub affrs dir; Bud Williamson, chief engr.

WCTW(FM)—Co-owned with WCKL(AM). September 1990: 98.5 mhz; 2.1 kw. Ant 393 ft. TL: N42 12 00 W73 50 07. Stereo. Hrs opn: 24. Prog sep from AM. Format: Adult contemp. Target aud: 25-54. ■ Bob Johnson, progmg dir.

Cazenovia

*****WITC(FM)**—April 1978: 88.9 mhz; 129 w. Ant 33 ft. TL: N42 55 53 W75 51 15. Hrs opn: Noon-midnight. Box 5025, Cazenovia College, Seminary St. (13035). (315) 655-8536. FAX: (315) 655-2190. Licensee: Cazenovia College. Format: Div. News progmg 3 hrs wkly. Target aud: 15-35. Spec prog: News/talk 3 hrs, alternative 10 hrs wkly. ■ Paul MacArthur, stn mgr.

Champlain

WCHP(AM)—Aug 20, 1985: 760 khz; 25 kw-D, DA. TL: N44 56 44 W73 25 48. Box 888, McCrea Rd. (12919). (518) 298-2800. Licensee: Champlain Radio Inc. (acq 1-31-91; FTR 2-18-91). Format: Relg, talk. Target aud: 25 plus. Spec prog: Fr, Sp. ■ Robert A. Jones, vp & chief engr; Teri Billiter, gen mgr; Carl J. Auel, gen sls mgr.

Chateaugay

WYUL(FM)—Not on air, target date unknown: 94.7 mhz; 1.7 kw. Ant 610 ft. TL: N44 49 41 W73 58 43. Martz Communications Group, 5595 Liberty Rd., Chagrin Falls, OH (44022). Licensee: Vector Broadcasting Inc. Group owner: Martz Communications Group.

Cheektowaga

WECK(AM)—August 1956: 1230 khz; 1 kw-U. TL: N42 55 27 W78 46 41. 1700 Rand Bldg., Buffalo (14203). (716) 856-3550. FAX: (716) 852-0537. Licensee: EBE Communications Ltd. (acq 1-91; grpsl; FTR 8-20-90). Net: NBC. Rep: D & R Radio. Format: MOR. News staff 2; news progmg 14 hrs wkly. Target aud: 35-64. ■ Robert L. Williams, pres & gen mgr; Donna Vullo, gen sls mgr; Madonna Comerate, prom mgr; Joe Chille, progmg dir; Maryalice Demler, news dir; Skip Edmunds, chief engr.

Cherry Valley

WJIV(FM)—1949: 101.9 mhz; 8.9 kw. Ant 1,027 ft. TL: N42 47 36 W74 41 41. Stereo. Hrs opn: 24. Box 507, E. Hill Rd. (13320); 3 Computer Dr. W., Suite 126, Albany (12205). (607) 264-3062; (518) 437-1251. FAX: (518) 437-1252; (607) 264-8277. Licensee: WJIV Radio Inc. (acq 3-30-81; $300,000; FTR 12-8-80). Net: UPI. Wash atty: Cohen & Berfield. Format: Christian. Target aud: 25-54 plus. ■ Floyd Dykeman, pres & gen mgr; Walter Braemer, mktg dir; Bob Cain, progmg dir; Martin Braemer, mus dir; Ann Cardinale, pub affrs dir; Kevin Smith, chief engr. ■ Rates: $25; 25; 25; 25.

Clifton Park

WWCP-FM—November 1985: 96.7 mhz; 3 kw. Ant 328 ft. TL: N42 52 44 W73 51 47. Stereo. 433 State St., Schenectady (12305). (518) 382-5400. FAX: (518) 370-5394. Licensee: Capital Broadcasting Inc. (acq 8-20-87; $900,000; FTR 5-25-87). Net: NBC the Source. Format: Hot adult contemp. News staff one; news progmg 6 hrs wkly. Target aud: 25-54. ■ John T. Ahern, pres; Jeff Weber, gen mgr; Sandy Taylor, gen sls mgr; Nikki Donovan, progmg dir. ■ Rates: $30; 27; 30; 30.

Clinton

*****WHCL-FM**—Feb 18, 1963: 88.7 mhz; 270 w. Ant 97 ft. TL: N43 03 04 W75 24 24. Stereo. Hrs opn: 24. Box 82, Minor Theatre, 198 College Hill Rd. (13323). (315) 859-4215; (315) 859-4200. FAX: (315) 853-3891. Licensee: The Trustees of Hamilton College. Format: Div, progressive, AOR. News progmg 5 hrs wkly. Target aud: General. Spec prog: Class 9 hrs, jazz 9 hrs, relg 2 hrs, reggae 10 hrs, rap 14 hrs, sports 4 hrs wkly. ■ Steve Reynolds, gen mgr. ■ Rates: $10; 10; 15; 20.

Clyde

WRCD(FM)—Not on air, target date unknown: 93.7 mhz; 2.3 kw. Ant 364 ft. TL: N43 03 03 W76 51 48. 1735 Birchwood Dr., Farmington (14425). Licensee: Katharine Ingersoll et al, dba Kic Radio Ltd.

Cobleskill

WSCM(AM)—July 1, 1981: 1190 khz; 1 kw-D. TL: N42 41 26 W74 26 40. Box 370, Rt. 7 E. (12043). (518) 234-3400. FAX: (518) 234-3400. Licensee: Barry Sims. Group owner: SHO Radio Group (acq 12-7-89; $250,000; FTR 12-25-89). Net: MBS. Format: Adult contemp. News staff one; news progmg 14 hrs wkly. Target aud: 30 plus. Spec prog: Country 3 hrs, farm one hr, relg 3 hrs wkly. ■ Gael Joyal, stn mgr & progmg dir; Tim Powers, sls dir; Jim MacLaren, mus dir; Mike Carey, news dir; Ken Ruhland, chief engr. ■ Rates: $11.50; 11.50; 11.50; na.

WSHQ(FM)—Sept 1, 1986: 103.5 mhz; 50 kw. Ant 492 ft. TL: N42 58 21 W74 29 30. Stereo. Box 370, Kenyon Bldg., Rt. 7 (12043). (518) 234-3400; (518) 393-2305. FAX: (518) 234-4685; (518) 393-0316. Licensee: Barry W. Sims, receiver. Wash atty: Haley, Bader & Potts. Format: Adult contemp. Target aud: 25-54. ■ Timothy J. Powers, gen mgr & gen sls mgr; Walter Fritz, progmg mgr & mus dir; Mike Carey, news dir; Walter Fritz, Mike Carey, pub affrs dirs; Ken Ruhland, chief engr.

Conklin

WXEJ(FM)—Not on air, target date unknown: 100.5 mhz; 3.5 kw. Ant 433 ft. TL: N42 01 00 W75 44 38. c/o 1755 York Ave. 8D, New York (10028). Licensee: Cheryl Busch.

Copenhagen

WWLF-FM—Not on air, target date unknown: 106.7 mhz; 200 w. Ant 1,227 ft. TL: N43 52 47 W75 43 11. 6481 Newport Rd., Warners (13164). Licensee: Tia A. Soliday.

Corning

*****WAOI(FM)**—Not on air, target date unknown: 91.1 mhz; 12.6 kw. Ant 177 ft. Box 3000, Binghampton (13902). Licensee: WSKG Public Telecommunications Council.

WCBA(AM)—November 1948: 1350 khz; 2 kw-D. TL: N42 07 01 W77 02 25. Hrs opn: 20. Box 1047 (14830); 2309 Davis Rd. (14830). (607) 962-4646. FAX: (607) 962-1138. Licensee: Eolin Broadcasting Inc. (acq 6-8-90; $790,000 with co-located FM; FTR 6-4-90). Net: Unistar, CNN. Wash atty: Haley, Bader & Potts. Format: MOR, btfl music, big band. Target aud: 50 plus. ■ Robert Eolin, pres; Jack Horn, gen mgr & gen sls mgr; Dee Eolin, opns mgr & pub affrs dir; Edd Harnas, mus dir; Rick Taylor, chief engr.

WCBA-FM—February 1989: 98.5 mhz; 2 kw. Ant 393 ft. TL: N42 09 38 W77 02 19. Stereo. Hrs opn: 20. Format: Adult contemp.

*****WCEB(FM)**—1979: 91.9 mhz; 10 w-H. Ant 1,784 ft. TL: N42 07 10 W77 05 02. Corning Community College (14830). (607) 962-9360. FAX: (607) 962-9456. Licensee: Corning Community College. Format: AOR. Spec prog: Oldies 6 hrs wkly. ■ Nicole Darmstadt, stn mgr.

WCLI(AM)—November 1949: 1450 khz; 1 kw-U. TL: N42 09 43 W77 02 15. 99 W. 1st St. (14830). (607) 962-2424. FAX: (607) 937-5000. Licensee: Pro Radio Inc. (acq 6-1-93). Net: MBS. Rep: Roslin, Rgnl Reps. Format: News/talk. News staff 2; news progmg 20 hrs wkly. Target aud: 25-64. ■ Victor Michael, pres & chief engr; Van Michael, gen mgr, mktg mgr & prom mgr; Skip Spencer, opns mgr; Jan Dockstader, gen sls mgr; Doug Guyer, mus dir; Jeff Murray, news dir; Dave Pal, pub affrs dir. ■ Rates: $15; 13; 15; 12.

WNKI(FM)—Co-owned with WCLI(AM). May 1947: 106.1 mhz; 40 kw. Ant 532 ft. TL: N42 09 43 W77 02 15. Stereo. Prog sep from AM. Rep: Roslin. Format: Adult contemp, CHR. News staff 2; news progmg 3 hrs wkly. Target aud: General; 18-54. ■ Victor Michael, CEO; Doug Guyer, prom mgr. ■ Rates: $24; 21; 24; 20.

Cornwall

WRWD(AM)—Nov 22, 1969: 1170 khz; 1 kw-D, DA. TL: N41 26 24 W74 04 25. Rebroadcasts WRWD-FM Highland. Box 1073, Highland (12528). (914) 691-2800. FAX: Telex: 650-175-9279. Licensee: William H. Walker III (acq 12-9-92; $25,000; FTR 1-4-93). Net: ABC/I, CBS Spectrum. Format: Adult contemp, oldies. Spec prog: Irish one hr, German one hr, It 2 hrs wkly. ■ William H. Walker III, gen mgr.

Cortland

WKRT(AM)—Nov 15, 1947: 920 khz; 1 kw-D, 500 w-N, DA-N. TL: N42 33 22 W76 09 17. Hrs opn: 24. 292 Tompkins St. (13045). (607) 756-2828. FAX: (607) 756-2953. Licensee: Cayuga Radio Partners L.P. Group owner: Cayuga/Northstar Radio Group (acq 4-92; $1 million with co-located FM; FTR 11-18-91). Net: ABC/E. Rep: Roslin. Format: Oldies. News progmg 7 hrs wkly. Target aud: General; 35-64. Spec prog: Farm 5 hrs wkly. ■ Bill Goddard, gen mgr; Sonny King, progmg dir; Greg Thomas, news dir; Bud Williamson, chief engr.

WYYS(FM)—Co-owned with WKRT(AM). Nov 15, 1947: 99.9 mhz; 24 kw. Ant 710 ft. TL: N42 33 22 W76 09 17. Stereo. Hrs opn: 24. Prog sep from AM. Rep: Katz. Format: CHR. News staff 2; news progmg 7 hrs wkly. Target aud: 18-49. ■ Dave Ashton, opns mgr; Wally McCarthy, progmg dir & mus dir.

*****WSUC-FM**—Nov 17, 1976: 90.5 mhz; 241 w. Ant -110 ft. TL: N42 35 53 W76 11 13. Stereo. Hrs opn: 24. Brockway Hall, Graham Ave. (13045). (607) 753-2936; (607) 753-4818. FAX: (607) 753-2807. Licensee: State Univ. of New York. Net: AP. Format: Div/rock. Target aud: 12-50. Spec prog: Class 4 hrs, jazz 4 hrs, Grateful Dead 3 hrs, heavy metal 7 hrs, dance/rap 7 hrs wkly. ■ Colleen Oczek, gen mgr; Tania Azurco, progmg dir; Scott Moore, chief engr.

WYYS(FM)—Listing follows WKRT(AM).

Dansville

WDNY-FM—March 1990: 93.9 mhz; 570 w. Ant 741 ft. TL: N42 30 45 W77 38 07. Stereo. Hrs opn: 19. 129 Main St. (14437). (716) 335-9369. FAX: (716) 335-5585. Licensee: Dan-Way-Coa Broadcasting Co. Inc. Format: Adult contemp, talk. Spec prog: Relg one hr, big band 3 hrs, sports 4 hrs wkly. ■ Dorothy Hotchkiss, gen mgr; Dan Carpenter, progmg dir.

WDNY(AM)—Oct 20, 1978: 1400 khz; 1 kw-U. TL: N42 32 19 W77 40 57. Hrs opn: 19. Dups FM 100%. (Acq 4-13-92; $290,000; FTR 5-4-92).

Delhi

WDHI(FM)—Mar 16, 1992: 100.3 mhz; 770 w. Ant 643 ft. TL: N42 22 40 W74 50 23. Stereo. Hrs opn: 16. Box 58, Rt. 206, Walton (13856); 95 Main St. (13753). (607) 746-6000. FAX: (607) 746-6000. Licensee: Delaware County Broadcasting Corp. (group owner). Net: USA. Rep: Savalli. Format: Soft hits. ■ Amos F. Finch, vp, gen mgr & vp mktg; Terry Doyle, mus dir & news dir; John D. Clark, pub affrs dir; Philip Vessey, chief engr. $16; 13; 14.50; 13.

Depew

WBLK(FM)—December 1964: 93.7 mhz; 50 kw. Ant 400 ft. TL: N45 53 10 W78 52 25. Stereo. 712 Main St., Buffalo (14202). (716) 852-5955. FAX: (716) 852-6605. Licensee: WBLK Broadcasting Corp. Net: CBS Spectrum. Rep: D & R Radio. Format: Urban contemp. News staff one. Format: General. Spec prog: Gospel. ■ Franklin W. Lorenz, pres; Mark Plimpton, gen mgr & gen sls mgr; Eric Faison, progmg dir & mus dir; Lou St. James, news dir; Tom Atkins, chief engr.

Deposit

WIYN(FM)—Jan 16, 1991: 94.7 mhz; 770 w. Ant 642 ft. TL: N42 01 43 W75 28 25. Stereo. Hrs opn: 16. Suite 2, 113 Front St. (13754). (607) 467-5400. FAX: (607) 467-3175. Licensee: Delaware County Broadcasting Corp. (group owner). Net: Jones Satellite Audio. Rep: Savalli. Wash atty: Fisher, Wayland, Cooper & Leader. Format: Lite adult contemp. News staff one; news progmg 15 hrs wkly. Target aud: 28-55. ■ Myra Youmans, pres; Amos F. Finch, vp, gen mgr & vp mktg; D. Lee VerNooy, gen sls mgr & prom mgr; John D. Clark, progmg dir; Matt Brannon, mus dir; Kevin Faigle, news dir; Philip Vessey, chief engr. ■ Rates: $15.50; 12.50; 14; 12.50.

Stations in the U.S.   New York

DeRuyter

WVOA(FM)—1948: 105.1 mhz; 42 kw. Ant 540 ft. TL: N42 46 58 W75 50 28. Stereo. 7095 Myers Rd., East Syracuse (13057). (315) 656-2231. FAX: (315) 656-2259. Licensee: Forus Communications of N.Y. Inc. Group owner: Forus Communications (acq 10-81; $242,500; FTR 10-26-81). Format: Relg. Target aud: 18-40. Spec prog: Black 17 hrs, It one hr, Pol 2 hrs, class one hr, Sp one hr wkly. ■ Simon Rosen, pres; James Wall, gen mgr; Alan Higgins, mus dir.

Dundee

WFLR(AM)—Oct 1, 1956: 1570 khz; 5 kw-D, 442 w-N. TL: N42 32 40 W76 59 35. Hrs opn: 24. 30 Main St. (14837). (607) 243-7158; (607) 243-7070. FAX: (607) 243-7662. Licensee: Lakes Country Communications Corp. (acq 10-1-88; FTR 12-16-85). Net: MBS, Unistar, Motor Racing Net. Format: Country, news/talk. News staff 2. Target aud: 25-55. ■ John B. Johnson, pres; Harold Johnson, vp; Eric C. Bateman, opns mgr; Connie Prior, opns mgr; John Weidemer, gen sls mgr; Mark Feiock, prom dir & mus dir; Eric Bateman, progmg dir; Richard Evans, news dir; Ronald Tomion, chief engr. ■ Rates: $10; 9; 9; 9.

WFLR-FM—Aug 20, 1968: 95.9 mhz; 780 w. Ant 600 ft. TL: N42 32 40 W76 59 35. Stereo. Hrs opn: 24. Dups AM 50%. Format: Adult contemp, news/talk. News progmg 35 hrs wkly. Target aud: 21-49. ■ Rates: Same as AM.

Dunkirk

WDOE(AM)—Dec 24, 1949: 1410 khz; 1 kw-D, 500 w-N, DA-N. TL: N42 27 51 W79 21 21. Box 209, Willow Rd., (14048). (716) 366-1410; (716) 366-8580. FAX: (716) 366-1416. Licensee: North County Broadcasting Inc. (acq 12-31-91; $650,000 with WCQA(FM) Fredonia; FTR 1-20-92). Net: ABC/E, ABC/I, Daynet, Drake-Chenault. Format: Adult contemp, MOR, news. News staff 2; news progmg 12 hrs wkly. Target aud: 25-54. Spec prog: Pol 6 hrs, Sp 2 hrs wkly. ■ E. Michael Boyle, pres; Michael J. Felice, vp & gen mgr; Daniel C. Fischer, stn mgr; Doug Fearman, opns mgr; Charles Telford, gen sls mgr; David Rowley, news dir.

East Aurora

WNUC(FM)—See Wethersfield Township.

East Hampton

WEHM(FM)—Mar 1, 1993: 96.7 mhz; 4.3 kw. Ant 383 ft. TL: N40 59 37 W72 10 19. Hrs opn: 24. 34 Pantigo Rd. (11937). (516) 329-0010; (516) 329-0967. FAX: (516) 329-5004. Licensee: East Hampton Broadcasting Group Inc. (acq 9-24-92; $300,000; FTR 11-9-92). Net: AP. Wash atty: Roseman & Colin. Format: Adult contemp, jazz, news/talk. News staff 3; news progmg 20 hrs wkly. Target aud: 24-54; slightly upscale audience that wants to be kept informed. Spec prog: Local issue talk progs 5 hrs, Sp one hr wkly. ■ Michael P. Schulhof, CEO; Leonard I. Ackerman, pres; Jeffrey Shulman, CFO; Paul H. Conroy, gen mgr & stn mgr; Devera Lynn, prom dir; Steve Richards, progmg dir; Peter Elia, mus dir; Aaron Brodbar, chief engr.

East Syracuse

WSIV(AM)—Licensed to East Syracuse. See Syracuse.

Ellenville

WELV(AM)—December 1964: 1370 khz; 5 kw-D. TL: N41 44 19 W74 23 48. 22 N. Main St. (12428). (914) 647-5678. FAX: (914) 647-5008. Licensee: Straus Broadcasting Inc. Group owner: Straus Media Group (acq 12-4-84; $780,000). Net: ABC/E. Format: News/talk. News staff 2; news progmg 10 hrs wkly. Target aud: 30-64. Spec prog: Relg 2 hrs, Paul Harvey/Talk of the Town 3 hrs wkly. ■ Eric P. Straus, pres & gen mgr; Eric Hanson, exec vp; R. Peter Straus, sr vp; Jeanne H. Straus, vp; Debbie Springfield, gen sls mgr; Bob Mangles, progmg dir; Jackson Allen, news dir; Bud Williamson, chief engr.

WWWK(FM)—Co-owned with WELV(AM). August 1970: 99.3 mhz; 100 w. Ant 1,627 ft. TL: N41 41 06 W74 21 23 (CP: 116 w, ant 1,630 ft.). Stereo. Hrs opn: 24. Rebroadcasts WCTW(FM) Catskill 60%. Wash atty: Wiley, Rein & Fielding. Format: Adult contemp. News staff one; news progmg 10 hrs wkly. Target aud: 25-54; upscale adults. ■ Bob Johnson, opns mgr & progmg dir; Debbie Springfield, sls dir; Ed Bishop, mus dir; Kate Capra, news dir; Bob Williamson, engrg dir.

Elmira

*WCIH(FM)—July 31, 1989: 90.3 mhz; 7 kw. Ant 400 ft. TL: N41 53 59 W76 51 52 (CP: Ant 151 ft.). Stereo. Hrs opn: 24. Box 506, 7634 Campbell Creek Rd., Bath (14810). (607) 776-4151. Licensee: Family Life Ministries Inc. Net: USA. Format: Christian. News progmg 8 hrs wkly. Target aud: 25-59; general Christian public. ■ Dick Snavely, pres & gen mgr; Rick Snavely, vp, stn mgr & progmg dir; Jim Travis, chief engr.

*WECW(FM)—Jan 19, 1959: 107.7 mhz; 6 w. Ant -312 ft. TL: N42 05 52 W76 48 53. Stereo. Elmira College (14901). (607) 735-1885; (607) 735-1800. Licensee: Elmira College. Net: ABC/FM. Format: Classic rock, top-40. Target aud: 18-30. Spec prog: French 6 hrs wkly. ■ Kyle Wagner, gen mgr.

WEHH(AM)—See Elmira Heights-Horseheads.

WELM(AM)—April 1947: 1410 khz; 5 kw-D, 1 kw-N, DA-N. TL: N42 07 11 W76 48 37. Stereo. 1705 Lake St. (14901). (607) 733-5626; (607) 732-1400. FAX: (607) 733-5627. Licensee: Pembrook Pines Elmira Ltd. Group owner: Pembrook Pines Inc. (acq 10-1-77). Net: CBS. Wash atty: Baraff, Koerner, Olender & Hochberg. Format: Oldies. News staff one; news progmg 10 hrs wkly. Target aud: 25 plus. Spec prog: Jazz 2 hrs, Pol 3 hrs, blues 3 hrs, relg one hr wkly. ■ Robert J. Pfuntner, pres & gen mgr; David Crum, gen sls mgr; Jeff Whittaker, prom mgr; Donna Van De Bogart, progmg dir; Pat Salois, mus dir; Drew Guild, news dir; Judy Bloodgood, pub affrs dir; Robert Gauss, chief engr. ■ Rates: $13; 10; 13; 10.

WLVY(FM)—Co-owned with WELM(AM). Aug 1, 1966: 94.3 mhz; 3 kw. Ant 497 ft. TL: N42 07 49 W76 47 23. Stereo. Prog sep from AM. Net: Westwood One, CBS. Rep: Torbet. Format: CHR. News staff one; news progmg 5 hrs wkly. Target aud: 18-36. Spec prog: Relg one hr wkly. ■ Donna Van De Bogart, opns dir, opns mgr & chief opns; Mike Strobel, mus dir. ■ Rates: $15; 13; 15; 10.

WENY(AM)—1939: 1230 khz; 1 kw-U. TL: N42 04 30 W76 46 55. Box 208 (14902). (607) 739-0344. Licensee: WENY Inc. Group owner: Green Group (acq 9-21-61). Net: NBC, NBC Talknet, MBS, ABC TalkRadio. Format: News/talk. Target aud: 30 plus. ■ Patrick M. Parish, gen mgr; Joel Clawson, stn mgr; John Herrick, news dir; Jim Appleton, chief engr.

WENY-FM—Aug 15, 1965: 92.7 mhz; 700 w. Ant 561 ft. TL: N42 01 55 W76 47 02. Stereo. Prog sep from AM. Net: ABC/D. Format: Adult contemp. ■ WENY-TV affil.

WIQT(AM)—See Horseheads.

WLVY(FM)—Listing follows WELM(AM).

WNKI(FM)—See Corning.

WQIX(FM)—See Horseheads.

Elmira Heights-Horseheads

WEHH(AM)—July 4, 1956: 1590 khz; 500 w-D, 480 w-N, DA-N. TL: N42 08 47 W76 48 41. Hrs opn: 24. 200 Latta Brook Rd., Horseheads (14845). (607) 962-3800. Licensee: Latta Brook Broadcasting (acq 10-5-82; $150,000; FTR 10-18-82). Net: ABC/I. Rep: Savalli. Format: Big band, jazz, MOR. News progmg 2 hrs wkly. Target aud: 25-49; upscale adults. Spec prog: Polka 2 hrs wkly. ■ Bob Ealoin, gen mgr; Mike Owens, mus dir; Jack Dolphin, news dir; Mark Saia, chief engr.

Endicott

WMRV(AM)—September 1947: 1430 khz; 5 kw-U, DA-N. TL: N42 04 56 W76 01 53. Stereo. Hrs opn: 24. Box 8651, Endwell (13762); IBM/FCU Bldg., 3301 Country Club Rd., Endwell (13760). (607) 785-3351. FAX: (607) 754-7852. Licensee: Beacon Broadcasting Corp. (group owner; acq 10-87; $4.5 million with co-located FM; FTR 10-19-87). Net: Unistar. Rep: Banner. Wash atty: Rothman & Gordon. Format: Solid gold. News staff 2. Target aud: 35 plus. ■ Alford H. Lessner, pres; Jack Devlin, gen mgr; Wayne Gordon, gen sls mgr; Dana Potter, progmg dir & mus dir; Mark Simonson, news dir; Sherman Clapman, chief engr.

WMRV-FM—1969: 105.7 mhz; 35 kw. Ant 570 ft. TL: N42 08 20 W75 59 58. Stereo. Prog sep from AM. Format: Adult contemp. Target aud: 25-54. ■ Pete Bucky, prom mgr; Ray Keller, progmg dir.

Endwell

WRGG(FM)—Not on air, target date unknown: 107.5 mhz; 3 kw. Ant 328 ft. 314 Skye Island Dr., Endicott (13760). Licensee: Maurice Battisti.

Essex

WDOT(FM)—Not on air, target date unknown: 101.3 mhz; 487 w. Ant 804 ft. TL: N44 22 30 W73 29 15 (CP: 1 kw, ant 797 ft.). Box 967, SMK Enterprises Inc., Burlington, VT (05402). Licensee: Essex FM Radio Partnership.

Fort Ann

*WNGX(FM)—Not on air, target date unknown: 91.7 mhz; 1 kw. Ant 1,194 ft. TL: N43 27 37 W73 32 46. 43 George St. (12827). Licensee: Christian Theater of the Air Inc. (acq 3-17-93; FTR 4-5-93).

Fort Plain

WBUG-FM—Mar 1, 1990: 101.1 mhz; 1.25 kw. Ant 718 ft. TL: N42 52 44 W74 47 07. Stereo. Hrs opn: 24. Rebroadcasts WBUG(AM) Amsterdam. Box 570, Rte 30 S. (12010). (518) 843-1570. Licensee: William H. Walker III. Group owner: Walker Broadcasting (acq 1-23-92; FTR 2-17-92). Format: C&W. News staff 2; news progmg 10 hrs wkly. Target aud: 25 plus. ■ Bud Walker, gen mgr; Jim Cuozzo, stn mgr & news dir; Wendy Bynum, gen sls mgr; Jeannete Relyea, natl sls mgr; Pat Iorio, rgnl sls mgr; Thom Williams, progmg dir; Frank Alford, mus dir; Barb O'Neill, pub affrs dir; Emile Plotkin, chief engr.

Frankfort

WKLL(FM)—Licensed to Frankfort. See Utica.

Fredonia

WCQA(FM)—April 1989: 96.5 mhz; 660 w. Ant 686 ft. TL: N42 22 02 W79 23 12. Stereo. Hrs opn: 24. Box 209, Willow Rd., Dunkirk (14048). (716) 366-8580; (716) 366-1410. FAX: (716) 366-1416. Licensee: North County Broadcasting Inc. (acq 12-31-91; $660,000 with WDOE(AM) Dunkirk; FTR 1-20-92). Net: SMN. Format: Adult contemp, news. News progmg 12 hrs wkly. Target aud: 25-54. ■ E. Michael Boyle, pres; Michael J. Felice, gen mgr; Daniel C. Fischer, stn mgr; Doug Fearman, opns mgr; Chuck Telford, gen sls mgr; David Rowley, news dir.

*WCVF-FM—July 6, 1978: 88.9 mhz; 130 w. Ant 125 ft. TL: N42 27 08 W79 20 14. Stereo. Hrs opn: 24. McEwen Hall, State Univ. of New York (14063). (716) 673-3420; (716) 673-3428. FAX: (716) 673-3427. Licensee: State Univ. of New York. Net: AP, NPR. Format: Div, progressive. News progmg 15 hrs wkly. Target aud: 18-20; campus and community of Fredonia. Spec prog: Black 8 hrs, reggae 3 hrs, It 3 hrs, folk 3 hrs wkly. ■ Bill Gropper, stn mgr.

Freeport

WGBB(AM)—August 1924: 1240 khz; 1 kw-U. TL: N40 38 44 W73 34 38. 555 Sunrise Hwy., West Babylon (11704-6009). (516) 587-1023. Licensee: Liberty Broadcasting of New York Inc. (acq 1-21-93; $16 million with WBAB-FM Babylon; FTR 2-15-93). Net: ABC/D, CNN, AP. Rep: Major Mkt. Format: Adult contemp. News staff 2; news progmg 27 hrs wkly. ■ Mike Cravin, pres; Gary Tee, stn mgr; Pat Bendik, dev mgr; Charles Cirelli, gen sls mgr; Tracy Burgess, news dir; Brenda Baron, pub affrs dir; Dennis Ciapura, vp engrg; Chris Tobin, chief engr.

Friendship

*WCID(FM)—1989: 89.1 mhz; 7 kw. Ant 492 ft. TL: N42 07 04 W78 10 48. Stereo. Hrs opn: 24. Box 506, 7634 Campbell Creek Rd., Bath (14810). (607) 776-4151. Licensee: Family Life Ministries Radio Inc. Format: Christian. News progmg 8 hrs wkly. Target aud: 25-59; General. ■ Dick Snavely, pres & gen mgr; Rick Snavely, vp, stn mgr & progmg dir; Jim Travis, chief engr.

Fulton

WBBS(FM)—Aug 1, 1961: 104.7 mhz; 50 kw. Ant 310 ft. TL: N43 12 53 W76 23 44 (CP: Ant 492 ft.). Stereo. 500 Plumb St, Bridgewater Pl., Syracuse (13204). (315) 472-9797. FAX: (315) 472-2323. Licensee: NewCity Communications of Fulton Inc. Group owner: NewCity Communications Inc. (acq 6-17-93; $3.75 million; FTR 7-5-93). Rep: Select. Format: Country. ■ Ronald J. Tarsi, gen mgr; Alan Furst, opns dir & progmg dir; Joel Delmonico, gen sls mgr; Conrad Trautmann, chief engr.

WZZZ(AM)—Aug 19, 1949: 1300 khz; 1 kw-D. TL: N43 17 36 W76 26 31. R.R. 7, 1300 Radio Park, Lake Shore Rd., (13069). (315) 593-1313. FAX: (315) 598-8952. Licensee: Peter E. Hunn (acq 3-88). Net: UPI. Format: MOR, talk. News staff one; News progmg 3 hrs wkly. Target aud: General; hometown listeners. Spec prog: Farm one hr, Irish one hr, fishing one hr, polka 8 hrs, relg 3 hrs wkly. ■ Peter Hunn, pres, gen mgr, progmg dir, mus dir & news dir; Carol Hunn, gen sls mgr & prom mgr; Gary Kimball, chief engr. ■ Rates: $13; 13; 13; na.

Garden City

***WBAU(FM)**—July 31, 1972: 90.3 mhz; 1.1 kw. Ant 157 ft. TL: N40 43 24 W73 35 18. Stereo. Box 365, Adelphi Univ., South Ave. (11530). (516) 877-6400; (516) 877-6903. Licensee: Adelphi Univ. Format: Alternative rock, div. News staff 3; news progmg 5 hrs wkly. Target aud: 18-34; young adults. Spec prog: It 2 hrs, jazz 4 hrs, Pol 2 hrs, Irish 2 hrs, folk 2 hrs wkly. ■ Ken Norian, gen mgr; Jason Mello, stn mgr; Jeff Sperber, mus dir; Henry Ahner, asst mus dir; Lydia Sinischalci, news dir; John Schmidt, chief engr.

WDRE-FM—1988: 92.7 mhz; 1 kw. Ant 521 ft. TL: N40 45 26 W73 42 52. Stereo. 1600 Stewart Ave., Westbury (11590). (516) 832-9400. FAX: (516) 832-9414. Licensee: Jarad Broadcasting. Rep: Roslin. Wash atty: Keck, Mahin & Cate. Format: AOR, modern rock. News staff one; news progmg 2 hrs wkly. Target aud: 18-34. ■ Ron Morey, pres; Dan Zako, gen mgr & gen sls mgr; Tom Calderone, opns mgr & progmg dir; Roy Seransky, rgnl sls mgr; John Moschitta, Nancy Cambino, prom mgrs; Noreen Bendix, news dir; John Caracciolo, chief engr. ■ Rates: $120; 110; 120; 110.

***WHPC(FM)**—Oct 12, 1972: 90.3 mhz; 500 w. Ant 213 ft. TL: N40 43 47 W73 35 33. Stereo. Nassau Comm. College, One Education Dr. (11530). (516) 572-7438. Licensee: Nassau Community College Board of Trustees. Format: Soft music, news/talk. News progmg 5 hrs wkly. Target aud: 20-65. Spec prog: Pol one hr, Irish one hr wkly. ■ Jim Green, progmg dir.

Geneseo

***WGSU(FM)**—Feb 18, 1963: 89.3 mhz; 1.8 kw. Ant 11 ft. TL: N42 47 51 W77 49 13. Stereo. Hrs opn: 7 AM-2 AM. Dept. of Communications, Bldg. Blake-B, State Univ. College (14454). (716) 245-5586. Licensee: State Univ. of New York. Format: Educ, rock. News progmg 7 hrs wkly. Target aud: 12-55; college, immediate community. Spec prog: Classical 3 hrs, farm one hr, jazz 14 hrs, consumer info 2 hrs, science 2 hrs, govt one hr, health one hr, cultural info 5 hrs wkly. ■ Steven B. Konick, gen mgr; Mark Nagi, stn mgr; Kristen Bauer, opns dir; Adam Lamanna, vp sls; Linda Kelso, prom dir; Joe Guisto, mus dir; Carin Weisman, news dir; Amy Hogan, pub affrs dir; Jeantet Fields, engrg dir.

Geneva

***WEOS(FM)**—Mar 30, 1971: 89.7 mhz; 1.5 kw. Ant -7 ft. TL: N42 51 27 W76 59 21. Stereo. Hrs opn: 24. Hobart/William Smith Colleges (14456); 51 St. Clair St. (14456). (315) 781-3456; (315) 781-3897. FAX: (315) 781-3916. Licensee: The Colleges of the Seneca. Net: APR, NPR. Format: Jazz, progsv, news/talk. News staff one; news progmg 40 hrs wkly. Target aud: College age & up. Spec prog: Blues 12 hrs, reggae/world 20 hrs, metal 4 hrs, new age 5 hrs, folk 10 hrs, gospel 3 hrs, rap/R&B 18 hrs wkly. ■ Richard Hersh, pres; Michael R. Black, gen mgr, dev mgr, gen sls mgr, mktg dir & adv mgr; Andrew Sevin, opns dir & progmg dir; Sharon Best, vp dev; John Pittman, prom dir; Julie Kotok, mus dir; Joe Wyatt, Aaron Redalen, asst mus dirs; Kevin Shatter, news dir; Tracy Goldblatt, pub affrs dir; Jeff Pfeiffer, chief engr. ■ Rates: $15; 13; 15; 12.

WFLK(FM)—1974: 101.7 mhz; 3 kw. Ant 125 ft. TL: N42 51 34 W77 00 29. Stereo. Box 1017 (14456). (315) 781-1101. Licensee: M B Communications Inc. Format: Super hit country. Target aud: 25-49. ■ Dawn Smith, gen mgr.

WGVA(AM)—1947: 1240 khz; 1 kw-U. TL: N42 51 37 W77 00 59. 3568 Lenox Rd. (14456). Box 98, Waterloo (13165). (315) 781-7000. Licensee: Lake County Radio Consultant (acq 2-23-93; $350,000 with co-located FM; FTR 3-22-93). Net: ABC/I. Wash atty: James Oystar. Format: Oldies. News staff one. Target aud: 35 plus. ■ Robert Martin, pres, gen mgr, gen sls mgr, news dir & pub affrs dir; Mike Smith, progmg dir & mus dir. ■ Rates: $12; 10; 12; 8.

Glens Falls

WBZA(AM)—May 28, 1959: 1230 khz; 1 kw-U. TL: N43 19 43 W73 38 58. Box 928, Everts Ave. (12801). (518) 792-2151; (518) 584-0607. Licensee: Northway Broadcasting Inc. (acq 8-26-92; $800,000). Net: MBS. Format: MOR, talk. News staff one; news progmg 6 hrs wkly. Target aud: 35 plus. Spec prog: Religious 3 hrs wkly. ■ Clay Ashworth, gen mgr & gen sls mgr; Jessica Bennette, prom mgr; Steve Willet, progmg dir; Debbie Hoy, news dir; Kevin Smith, chief engr. ■ Rates: $25; 20; 20; 10.

WENU(FM)—See Hudson Falls.

***WGFR(FM)**—January 1977: 92.1 mhz; 10 w. Ant 62 ft. TL: N43 18 44 W73 38 58. Adirondack Community College, Queensbury (12804). (518) 793-6188. Licensee: Board of Trustees of Adirondack Community College. Format: AOR. ■ Don Racette, stn mgr; Ronald Pesha, gen sls mgr & chief engr; Matt Tardy, progmg mgr; Josh Greene, mus dir.

WMJR(FM)—See Hudson Falls.

WWSC(AM)—Dec 18, 1946: 1450 khz; 1 kw-U. TL: N43 18 59 W73 37 23. Hrs opn: 24. 217 Dix Ave. (12801). (518) 793-4444. FAX: (518) 792-3374. Licensee: Normandy Broadcasting Corp. (acq 7-1-59). Net: ABC/E. Format: Adult contemp, news/talk. Target aud: 30 plus; people who want full-service radio. Spec prog: Farm one hr, big band, oldies. ■ Christopher P. Lynch, pres, gen mgr & gen sls mgr; Steve Tefft, prom mgr, progmg dir & mus dir; Mike Hare, news dir; Rich Redmond, chief engr. ■ Rates: $360; 255; 255; 189.

WYLR-FM—Co-owned with WWSC(AM). September 1967: 95.9 mhz; 240 w. Ant 918 ft. TL: N43 18 17 W73 45 07. Stereo. Prog sep from AM. Net: ABC/R. Format: Classic rock. ■ Christopher P. Lynch, gen mgr, opns mgr & sls dir; Tom Jacobson, prom dir, progmg dir & news dir. ■ Rates: $276; 276; 276; 276.

Gloversville

WENT(AM)—July 1, 1944: 1340 khz; 1 kw-U. TL: N43 01 30 W74 21 10. Hrs opn: 5:30 AM-midnight. Box 831, Harrison St. Ext. (12078). (518) 725-7175. Licensee: Whitney Radio Broadcasting Inc. (acq 12-15-86; $700,000; FTR 11-3-86). Net: NBC, CBS. Format: Full svc adult contemp. News staff 2; news progmg 14 hrs wkly. Target aud: 30 plus. Spec prog: Talk one hr wkly. ■ Jack Scott, pres & gen mgr; Jon W. Clark, vp; Nina Webb, gen sls mgr; Steve Savage, prom mgr; Tim Murphy, mus dir; Tom Roehl, news dir; Anne Kearney, pub affrs dir; Lloyd Smith, chief engr.

Gouverneur

WIGS(AM)—July 15, 1964: 1230 khz; 1 kw-U. TL: N44 19 47 W75 27 20. Box 239 (13642). (315) 287-1230. FAX: (315) 287-1230. Licensee: RGR Broadcasting of Gouverneur Inc. Group owner: RGR Broadcasting Inc. (acq 12-27-84; grpsl; FTR 11-5-84). Net: MBS. Format: Adult contemp, relg, sports. Spec prog: Farm one hr wkly. ■ Bryant Sandburg, gen mgr.

WGIX-FM—Co-owned with WIGS(AM). Dec 5, 1967: 95.3 mhz; 3 kw. Ant 220 ft. TL: N44 19 47 W75 27 20. Stereo. Dups AM 100%.

Greece

***WGMC(FM)**—Nov 11, 1973: 90.1 mhz; 2.05 kw. Ant 46 ft. TL: N43 14 40 W77 41 36. Stereo. Hrs opn: 19. 750 Maiden Ln., Rochester (14515). (716) 621-9233. FAX: (716) 621-8692. Licensee: Greece Central School District. Net: Mutual. Wash atty: Dow, Lohnes & Albertson. Format: Jazz. News progmg 5 hrs wkly. Target aud: 25-50; upscale, educated, mus lovers. Spec prog: Folk 4 hrs, Polish one hr, Sp 10 hrs, Lithuanian one hr, Turkish one hr, blues 3 hrs, new age 3 hrs, fusion 5 hrs wkly. ■ Dr. Duane Ruppert, gen mgr; Eric Gruner, opns mgr, progmg dir & mus dir; Charyll Monk, dev dir & pub affrs dir; Al Holmes, chief engr.

Hamilton

***WRCU-FM**—Mar 22, 1970: 90.1 mhz; 1.9 kw. Ant 155 ft. TL: N42 48 38 W75 31 58. Stereo. Colgate Univ. (13346). (315) 824-1212. Licensee: Colgate Univ. Net: AP. Format: Progsv. News progmg 6 hrs wkly. Spec prog: Jazz 12 hrs, class 4 hrs, Black 10 hrs wkly. ■ Scott Keller, gen mgr & chief engr; Jim Terhune (faculty advisor), progmg dir.

Hampton Bays

WWHB(FM)—Nov 20, 1980: 107.1 mhz; 3 kw. Ant 280 ft. TL: N40 52 10 W72 34 38. Stereo. 260 W. Montauk Hwy. (11946). (516) 728-9229. FAX: (516) 728-9249. Licensee: South Fork Broadcasting Corp. (acq 4-24-84; $1.8 million; FTR 5-7-90). Net: NBC the Source, Westwood One. Rep: Roslin. Format: CHR, top-40. News progmg 3 hrs wkly. Target aud: 18-40. Spec prog: Local public affrs. ■ Eddie Simon, pres; J. Russ Williams, gen mgr; Rich Mastroberte, gen sls mgr; Liz Barett, progmg dir; Selina Silecchia, news dir; John Carraciola, chief engr.

Hempstead

WHLI(AM)—July 22, 1947: 1100 khz; 10 kw-D, DA. TL: N40 41 06 W73 36 38. Suite 306, 1055 Franklin Ave., Garden City (11530). (516) 294-8400. FAX: (516) 746-0025. Licensee: Long Island Broadcasting Inc. Group owner: Barnstable Broadcasting Inc. (acq 12-15-84; $5 million with co-located FM; FTR 9-24-84). Net: AP. Rep: Katz. Format: Big band, MOR. News staff 2. Target aud: 35 plus. ■ David Gingold, pres; Jane Bartsch, gen mgr; Karen Hecht, natl sls mgr; Kathy Dulanto, rgnl sls mgr; Donna Vaughan, prom mgr; Dean Anthony, progmg dir; Janell Tuebner, news dir; Chris Tobin, chief engr.

WKJY(FM)—Co-owned with WHLI(AM). July 22, 1947: 98.3 mhz; 3 kw. Ant 328 ft. TL: N40 41 08 W73 36 37. Stereo. Hrs opn: 24. Prog sep from AM. Format: Adult contemp. News staff one. Target aud: 25-54. ■ Donna Vaughan, prom dir & news dir; Tony Florentino, progmg dir.

***WRHU(FM)**—June 9, 1959: 88.7 mhz; 470 w. Ant 200 ft. TL: N40 43 03 W73 36 12. Stereo. Hrs opn: 7 AM-3 AM. 126 Memorial Hall, Hofstra Univ. (11550). (516) 463-5668; (516) 463-5667. FAX: (516) 564-4297. Licensee: Hofstra Univ. Wash atty: Scott Cinnamon. Format: Class, jazz, progsv. News progmg 11 hrs wkly. Target aud: General. Spec prog: Radio theatre 3 hrs, C&W 3 hrs, Ir 4 hrs, pub affrs 4 hrs, big band 9 hrs, R&B 2 hrs, It 4 hrs, Pol 3 hrs, Sp one hr wkly. ■ Sue Zizza, gen mgr, dev dir, mktg dir & prom dir; Brian McKinley, stn mgr; Kristi Jasberg, progmg dir; Jen Murphy, mus dir; Dave Mock, news dir; John Caracciolo, chief engr.

Henderson

WLKC(FM)—1991: 100.7 mhz; 3 kw. Ant 328 ft. TL: N43 49 13 W76 05 29 (CP: 6 kw). 199 Wealtha Ave., Watertown (13601). (315) 786-9552. FAX: (315) 782-0312. Licensee: Jefferson Broadcasting Inc. Format: Country. ■ Glen Curry, gen mgr; Jack Freer, opns mgr.

Henrietta

***WBER(FM)**—Licensed to Henrietta. See Rochester.

***WITR(FM)**—Mar 7, 1975: 89.7 mhz; 910 w. Ant 154 ft. TL: N43 05 08 W77 40 05. Stereo. Hrs opn: 24. Box 20563, Rochester (14602-0563). 32 Lomb Memorial Dr., Rochester (14623-5604). (716) 475-2000. FAX: (716) 475-4988. Licensee: Rochester Institute of Technology. Format: Progsv, alternative. Target aud: General. Spec prog: Rap 5 hrs, dance 3 hrs, reggae 5 hrs wkly. ■ Marc Moisa, gen mgr; Garrett Johnson, prom dir; Nathan Bergman, progmg dir; Al Wixson, mus dir; Jen Rother, news dir; Kristen Marshall, pub affrs dir; Ethan Funk, engrg dir.

Herkimer

***WVHC(FM)**—Not on air, target date unknown: 91.5 mhz; 350 w-V. Ant -115 ft. Reservoir Rd. (13350). Licensee: Herkimer County Community College.

WYUT(AM)—October 1956: 1420 khz; 1 kw-D. TL: N43 03 40 W75 01 44. Stn currently dark. Box 511, 114 N. Prospect St. (13350). Licensee: Robert E. Remmell, receiver (acq 2-27-92; with co-located FM).

WYUT-FM—Apr 28, 1979: 92.7 mhz; 3 kw. Ant 299 ft. TL: N43 03 50 W75 01 44. Stereo. Stn currently dark.

Highland

WRWD-FM—Oct 3, 1989: 107.3 mhz; 330 w. Ant 968 ft. TL: N41 41 58 W74 00 11. Stereo. Box 1073, 296 State Route 299 (12528). (914) 691-2800. FAX: (914) 691-3846. Licensee: Walker Broadcasting Co. Net: AP, ABC/E. Format: C&W. News staff 5; news progmg 25 hrs wkly. Target aud: 18 plus. Spec prog: Farm one hr wkly. ■ William H. Walker, pres; Bud Walker, gen mgr; Wendy Bynum, gen sls mgr; Jeannete Relyea, natl sls mgr; Sharon Pucher, prom mgr; Thom Williams, progmg dir; Caroline Barden, mus dir; Richard Flaherty, news dir; Dan Gorham, pub affrs dir; Emile Plotkin, chief engr. ■ Rates: $60; 50; 55; 35.

Homer

WXHC(FM)—1991: 101.5 mhz; 1.3 kw. Ant 489 ft. TL: N42 41 12 W76 11 54. Hrs opn: 24. Box 386, 12 S. Main St. (13077). (607) 749-9942. FAX: (607) 749-2374. Licensee: John Eves. Wash atty: Fisher, Wayland, Cooper & Leader. Format: Adult contemp. News staff one; news progmg 10 hrs wkly. Target aud: 25-54. Spec prog: Bluegrass 2 hrs, relg one hr wkly. ■ John Eves, pres; Bruce Eves, exec vp; Patricia Eves, vp; John Briggs, vp opns & mus dir; Duane Andrews, rgnl sls mgr; Beth Mowins, news dir; Tim Backer, chief engr. ■ Rates: $168; 144; 168; 120.

Honeyoye Falls

WFUD(FM)—Not on air, target date unknown: 107.3 mhz; 3 kw. Ant 328 ft. TL: N42 51 54 W77 26 50. 1728 Maplewood Dr., Farmington (14425). Licensee: Honeoye Falls Radio Inc.

Hoosick Falls

WNGN(FM)—July 4, 1991: 97.5 mhz; 450 w. Ant 1,115 ft. TL: N42 51 47 W73 13 56. R.D. 1, Box 36, The Kings Rd., Buskirk (12028). (518) 686-0975; (518) 686-1NGN. FAX: (518) 686-0975 Licensee: Brian Andrew Larson. Net: Moody, CBN, USA. Format: Gospel, contemp Christian. News progmg 17 hrs wkly. Target aud: 25-65; adult, conservative, fundamentalist Christian. ■ Brian A. Larson, CEO, pres & stn mgr; Dean Aiken, mus dir; Peter Morton, chief engr. ■ Rates: $28; 25; 28; 20.

Hornell

WCKR(FM)—Listing follows WLEA(AM).

WHHO(AM)—1949: 1320 khz; 5 kw-D. TL: N42 17 32 W77 40 27. Hrs opn: 6 AM-midnight. Box 726, Monpond Bldg., 1484 Beech St. (14843). (607) 324-2000. FAX: (607) 324-2001. Licensee: Bilbat Radio Inc. (acq 6-10-83; $450,000; with co-located FM; FTR 5-30-83). Net: Daynet. Format: MOR, div, talk. News staff 2; news progmg 14 hrs wkly. Target aud: 25-54. Spec prog: Farm. ■ Richard Lyons, pres & gen mgr; William H. Berry, CFO & gen sls mgr; Ralph Van, opns mgr, pub affrs dir & chief engr; Bill Fleishman, prom mgr; Lynn O'Brien, progmg dir; Brian Hurlburt, mus dir; Bat Lyons, news dir. ■ Rates: $27; 27; 27; 27.

WKPQ(FM)—Co-owned with WHHO(AM). 1946: 105.3 mhz; 43 kw. Ant 530 ft. TL: N42 17 32 W77 40 27. Stereo. Hrs opn: 5:30 AM-midnight. Prog sep from AM. (607) 324-2002. Net: ABC/C. Format: CHR, adult contemp. Target aud: 18-44. ■ Rates: Same as AM.

WLEA(AM)—September 1951: 1480 khz; 2.5 kw-D. TL: N42 17 15 W77 38 47. Hrs opn: 18. Box 127B, Ashbaugh Hill Rd. (14843). (607) 324-1480. FAX: (607) 324-5415. Licensee: PMJ Communications Inc. (acq 10-18-90; $538,000; with co-located FM; FTR 11-19-90). Net: ABC/I. Format: Oldies, news, talk. News staff 2; news progmg 16 hrs wkly. Target aud: 35 plus. Spec prog: Farm 2 hrs wkly. ■ Kevin Doran, gen mgr; Mary Margaret Doran, prom mgr; Glenn Lee, mus dir; John Mark, news dir.

WCKR(FM)—Co-owned with WLEA(AM). June 1981: 92.1 mhz; 1.25 kw. Ant 512 ft. TL: N42 20 38 W77 37 36. Stereo. Hrs opn: 19. Prog sep from AM. R.D. One, Ashbaugh Hill Rd. (14843). (607) 324-4141. Net: USA. Format: Country. News staff 2; news progmg 11 hrs wkly. Target aud: 21 plus.

Horseheads

WEHH(AM)—See Elmira Heights-Horseheads.

WIQT(AM)—April 1966: 820 khz; 5 kw-D, 1 kw-N, DA-2. TL: N42 09 14 W76 50 47. Box 288 (14845); 111 N. Main St., Elmira (14901). (607) 737-1314. FAX: (607) 737-1319. Licensee: Chemung County Radio Inc. Net: ABC/E. Rep: Katz and Powell. Format: Oldies, sports, country. News staff 2; news progmg 5 hrs wkly. Target aud: 25-54; baby boomers. ■ Ron Ferro, gen mgr; David Rockwell, prom mgr & progmg dir; Bill Russell, news dir; Jim Appleton, chief engr.

WQIX(FM)—Co-owned with WIQT(AM). July 4, 1970: 100.9 mhz; 3 kw. Ant 245 ft. TL: N42 12 00 W76 51 30. Stereo. Prog sep from AM. Net: ABC/E. Rep: Katz & Powell. Format: Country. Target aud: General. ■ George K, prom mgr.

WLNL(AM)—May 7, 1967: 1000 khz; 5 kw-D. TL: N42 09 14 W76 50 47. 111 W. Franklin St. (14845). (607) 739-3717. Licensee: Love Church Ministries Inc. (acq 10-24-91; $256,000; FTR 11-11-91). Net: USA. Format: Adult contemp, relg, news/talk. News progmg 7 hrs wkly. Target aud: General; Christian families. ■ James R. Pierce, pres & gen mgr; Robert L. Rundall, vp; Richard Ryerson, opns dir; Kevin Knight, gen sls mgr. ■ Rates: $6; 5; 6; na.

WQIX(FM)—Listing follows WIQT(AM).

Houghton

***WJSL(FM)**—Jan 18, 1979: 90.3 mhz; 6 kw. Ant 217 ft. TL: N42 22 39 W78 10 45. Stereo. Hrs opn: 5 AM-midnight. Rebroadcast WMHR(FM) Syracuse, 55%. Box 438, Campus Center, Genesse St. (14744). (716) 567-9425; (716) 567-9575. FAX: (716) 567-9248. Licensee: Houghton College Radio Corp. Format: Relg, adult contemp. Target aud: General. Spec prog: Class 5 hrs wkly. ■ David L. Manney, gen mgr; Dr. Fred Trexler, chief engr.

Hudson

WHUC(AM)—1947: 1230 khz; 1 kw-U. TL: N42 15 13 W73 45 45. Hrs opn: 5:30 AM- 11 PM. Box 123 (12534); Union Turnpike (12534). (518) 828-3341; (518) 828-4042. FAX: (518) 828-3341; (518) 828-4042. Licensee: Colgreene Broadcasting Co. (acq 1-1-58). Net: MBS. Rep: Roslin. Format: Full service, adult contemp. News staff 2; news progmg 4 hrs wkly. Target aud: 25-54; local people in Columbia & Greene counties. Spec prog: Pol one hr, Afro-American talk one hr, health talk one hr, news/talk one hr, Italian hour one hr, relg 3 hrs wkly. ■ Abert Heit, pres; John Verdon, gen mgr & vp adv; Marvin St. John, asst mus dir; Jack Mabb, news dir; Bud Williamson, chief engr. ■ Rates: $20; 20; 20; 12.

WRVW(FM)—Co-owned with WHUC(AM). Jan 20, 1969: 93.5 mhz; 3 kw. Ant -15 ft. TL: N42 15 13 W73 45 45. Stereo. Hrs opn: 6 AM-11 PM. Dups AM 3%. Net: MBS. Format: Oldies. News progmg 3 hrs wkly. Baby boomers, weekenders from New York City. ■ Steve Whateley, prom mgr, progmg dir & mus dir; Bud Williamson, vp engrg. ■ Rates: Same as AM.

***WHVP(FM)**—Not on air, target date unknown: 91.1 mhz. Stereo. Rebroadcasts WFGB(FM) Kingston 90%. Box 777, 199 Tuytenbridge Rd., Lake Katrine (12449). (914) 336-6199. FAX: (914) 336-7205. Licensee: Sound of Life Inc. Format: Christian. News progmg 3 hrs wkly. Target aud: General; Christians, Catholics, church goers. Spec prog: Black one hr, Sp one hr wkly. ■ Dennis Newcomer, pres; Bruce Winchel, gen mgr; Jeanmarie Elsner, prom mgr; Roger Thayer, progmg dir; Frank Amodeo, mus dir; Donna Quiles, pub affrs dir; John Katonah, chief engr.

WRVW(FM)—Listing follows WHUC(AM).

Hudson Falls

WENU(FM)—Sept 19, 1983: 101.7 mhz; 4.6 kw. Ant 180 ft. TL: N43 22 40 W73 39 56. Stereo. Hrs opn: 24 Quaker Village Bldg. No. 3, 76 Quaker Rd., Queensbury (12804). (518) 793-7733. Licensee: Bradmark Broadcasting Co. (acq 4-1-86; grpsl; FTR 1-6-86). Net: NBC. Format: Adult contemp. News staff one. Target aud: 25-54. ■ Donald W. Heckman, pres & gen mgr; Jean Heckman, exec vp; Rolly Merrill, gen sls mgr; Jay Scott, progmg dir; Ken Ruhland, chief engr. ■ Rates: $28; 26; 28; 22.

WMJR(FM)—June 26, 1967: 107.1 mhz; 280 w. Ant 844 ft. TL: N43 17 22 W73 44 35. Stereo. Box 928, Everts Ave., Glens Falls (12801). (518) 792-2151; (518) 584-0607. Licensee: Northway Broadcasting Inc. (group owner; acq 8-26-86; $800,000 grpsl; FTR 3-12-90). Net: MBS. Format: Adult contemp. News staff one; news progmg 4 hrs wkly. Target aud: 25-49. ■ Clay Ashworth, gen mgr; Steve Willet, progmg dir; Debbie Hay, pub affrs dir; Kevin Smith, chief engr.

Huntington

WGSM(AM)—Sept 1, 1951: 740 khz; 25 kw-D, DA. TL: N40 51 04 W73 26 16. Stereo. Hrs opn: 24. Box 697, 900 Walt Whitman Rd., Melville (11747). (516) 423-6740. FAX: (516) 423-6750. Licensee: WGSM Radio Inc. Group owner: Greater Media Inc. (acq 5-12-65). Net: AP. Rep: Major Mkt. Format: Big band. News staff 4. Target aud: 35-64. ■ Frank Kabela, pres; Paul Fleishman, gen mgr; Ben Mevorach, prom mgr, progmg dir & news dir; Jim Beery, chief engr.

Hyde Park

WCZX(FM)—Aug 18, 1970: 97.7 mhz; 300 w. Ant 1,030 ft. TL: N41 43 11 W73 59 45. Stereo. Hrs opn: 24. Box 416, Pendell Rd., Poughkeepsie (12601). (914) 471-1500. FAX: (914) 454-1204. Licensee: Valley Communications Inc. (acq 2-25-92; assumption of debt; FTR 3-16-92). Rep: Katz. Wash atty: Martin Leader. Format: Oldies. News staff one; news progmg 10 hrs wkly. Target aud: 25-54. ■ Jode Millman, gen mgr; Bill Palmeri, opns mgr & progmg dir; Stan Beinstien, gen sls mgr; Victor Goodman, natl sls mgr; Bob Miller, prom dir; Scott Carlin, mus dir; Brian Jones, news dir; Marc Stuart, pub affrs dir; David Groth, vp engrg. ■ Rates: $40; 30; 40; 30.

WHVW(AM)—July 4, 1963: 950 khz; 500 w-D, 57 w-N. TL: N41 44 46 W73 54 46. Hrs opn: 24. 507 Violet Ave. (12538). (914) 471-9500. FAX: (914) 454-9555. Licensee: Joseph-Paul Ferraro (acq 3-9-92; $350,000; FTR 3-30-92). Net: MBS, SMN. Format: Country (old & new). News staff 2. Target aud: 39-49. Spec prog: Ger one hr, It one hr, Irish one hr wkly. ■ J.P. Ferraro, pres & progmg dir; Al Weiner, gen mgr; Cathi Chapman, gen sls mgr; Ron Lyon, news dir. ■ Rates: $34; 30; 34; 26.

Irondequoit

WMAX-FM—March 1992: 106.7 mhz; 3.5 kw. Ant 627 ft. TL: N43 11 27 W77 37 11. Stereo. Hrs opn: 24. 412 State St., Rochester (14608). (716) 232-8870. Licensee: Auburn Cablevision Inc. Format: Rock. Target aud: 25-49; upscale, educated. ■ Mintum S. Osborne, vp; Alan Bishop, gen mgr; Tim Burke, gen sls mgr, natl sls mgr & rgnl sls mgr; Lori Baister, mktg mgr & prom mgr; Rick MacKenzie, progmg dir & mus dir; Jim Kelly, news dir; Nanette Levin, pub affrs dir. ■ Rates: $50; 50; 50; 35.

Islip

WLIX(AM)—1960: 540 khz; 250 w-D, 218 w-N. TL: N40 45 04 W73 12 52. Hrs opn: 5 AM-midnight. 138 W. Main St., Bayshore (11706). (516) 968-5400. FAX: (516) 968-5458. Licensee: Living Communications Inc. (acq 10-13-76). Format: Christian. Target aud: 25-44. ■ David R. Swanson, pres; Lloyd Parker, vp; Brad Crook, gen sls mgr; Jerry Williams, progmg dir; Kevin Egland, pub affrs dir; John Bennett, chief engr.

Ithaca

WHCU(AM)—Jan 23, 1923: 870 khz; 5 kw-D, 1 kw-N, DA-N. TL: N42 21 49 W76 36 20. Hrs opn: 24. Box 69, 1751 Hanshaw Rd. (14850). (607) 272-6400. FAX: (607) 257-6497. Licensee: Eagle Broadcasting Co. Inc. (acq 5-86). Net: CBS, AP, Unistar, MBS. Rep: Christal. Wash atty: Richard Carr. Format: News/talk, sports. News staff 3; news progmg 40 plus hrs wkly. Target aud: 25-64. ■ Kenneth Cowan, pres & gen mgr; Susan Johnston, vp sls & gen sls mgr; Jim Alo (local), rgnl sls mgr; Tom Joseph, progmg dir; Gerry Angel, mus dir; Roy Ives, news dir; Joe Scaglione, chief engr.

WYXL(FM)—Co-owned with WHCU(AM). Sept 1, 1947: 97.3 mhz; 26 kw. Ant 879 ft. TL: N42 27 54 W76 22 23. Stereo. Prog sep from AM. Format: Adult contemp. Target aud: 25-54. ■ Dave Smith, progmg dir & mus dir.

***WICB(FM)**—Jan 14, 1947: 91.7 mhz; 5.5 kw. Ant 105 ft. TL: N42 25 07 W76 29 39. Stereo. Hrs opn: 24. Ithaca College, Roy H. Park School of Communications (14850). (607) 274-3142, (607) 274-1040. FAX: (607) 274-1061. Licensee: Ithaca College. Net: ABC/D. Format: Modern rock. News progmg 6 hrs wkly. Target aud: 18-34; young audience with taste for innovative mus. Spec prog: Jazz 16 hrs, Black 20 hrs, folk 2 hrs, blues 2 hrs, reggae 2 hrs, world beat 2 hrs wkly. ■ Christopher Wheatley, gen mgr; Dave Allen, chief engr.

WQNY(FM)—Listing follows WTKO(AM).

***WSQG-FM**—Not on air, target date unknown: 90.9 mhz; 5 kw. Ant 294 ft. TL: N42 34 55 W76 33 22. Stereo. Hrs opn: 24 Box 3000, Binghamton (13902). (607) 729-0100. FAX: (607) 729-7328. Licensee: WSKG Public Telecommunications Council. Net: AP, NPR, APR. Wash atty: Dow, Lohnes & Albertson. Format: Div, class, news. News staff 4; news progmg 33 hrs wkly. Target aud: General. Spec prog: Jazz 8 hrs, folk/bluegrass 7 hrs wkly. ■ Michael Ziegler, pres; June M. Smith, vp; Judy V. Siggins, vp mktg; Katherine Bacon, prom mgr; Donna Hill, progmg mgr; Kelly Farewell, mus dir; Peter Iglinski, news dir; Charles F. Mulvey, Mark Polovick (assoc), vps engrg.

WTKO(AM)—April 1956: 1470 khz; 5 kw-D, 1 kw-N, DA-N. TL: N42 23 32 W76 28 29. Box 10 (14850); 317 N. Aurora St. (14850). (607) 272-9040; (607) 272-1470. FAX: (607) 277-1736. Licensee: Gilmore Communications (acq 6-7-89). 3,400,000). Net: ABC/I, NBC Talknet,

CNN. Rep: Torbet. Wash atty: Wiley, Rein & Fielding. Format: News/talk, sports. News staff 3; news progmg 55 hrs wkly. Target aud: 25-54; upper income & college educated. Spec prog: Relg one hr wkly. ■ Jim Gilmore, pres & gen mgr; Rhoda Gilmore, Wendy Pateruiti, Domm Sadowy, vps; Dave Vieser, opns dir; Wendy Paternti, vp sls & gen sls mgr; Lisa Johnson, prom mgr; Geoff Dunn, progmg dir & news dir; Ken Rohland, chief engr. ■ Rates: $24; 20; 24; 15.

WQNY(FM)—Co-owned with WTKO(AM). 1948: 103.7 mhz; 5 kw. Ant 876 ft. TL: N42 23 13 W76 40 10. Stereo. Format: Classic Rock 'n Roll. News progmg one hr wkly. Target aud: 18-49; highly educated, liberal college group with a large percent of Ph.Ds. Spec prog: Blues 3 hrs, jazz 2 hrs wkly. ■ Nancy Herrick, natl sls mgr, rgnl sls mgr & prom dir; Tracy Summers, progmg dir. ■ Rates: Same as AM.

WVBR-FM—June 7, 1958: 93.5 mhz; 3 kw. Ant 250 ft. TL: N42 25 42 W76 26 57. Stereo. 227 Linden Ave. (14850-4799). (607) 273-4000. Licensee: Cornell Radio Guild Inc. Net: NBC, AP, Westwood One. Rep: Katz. Format: Full svc AOR. News progmg 10 hrs wkly. Target aud: 18-49; highly educated listeners. Spec prog: Country 4 hrs, Black 4 hrs, oldies 10 hrs, heavy metal 4 hrs, folk 7 hrs, comedy 2 hrs, sports 4 hrs, album cuts 4 hrs wkly. ■ Andrew Ettinger, pres, gen mgr & vp opns; Boaz Kochman, opns mgr; Eddie Negron, vp dev; Mike Crandall, gen sls mgr; Jeremy Schulman, prom dir; Kelly Roth, progmg dir; Mike Dahan, mus dir; Dana Hill, news dir; John B. Hill, chief engr.

WYXL(FM)—Listing follows WHCU(AM).

WYYS(FM)—See Cortland.

Jamestown

***WCOT(FM)**—December 1992: 90.9 mhz; 10 kw. Ant 492 ft. TL: N42 00 26 W79 04 05. Stereo. Box 506, 7634 Campbell Creek Rd., Bath (14810). (607) 776-4151. Licensee: Family Life Ministries Radio Inc. Format: Educ, relg, news. News progmg 8 hrs wkly. Target aud: General; 25-59. ■ Dick Snavely, pres & gen mgr; Rick Snavely, vp; Jim Travis, chief engr.

WHUG(FM)—Listing follows WKSN(AM).

WJTN(AM)—Dec 1924: 1240 khz; 500 w-D, 1 kw-N. TL: N42 06 18 W79 15 28. Hrs opn: 24. Box 1139, 2 Orchard Rd. W.E. (14702-1139). (716) 487-1151. FAX: (716) 664-9326. Licensee: James Broadcasting Inc. Group owner: Goldman Group (acq 1955). Net: ABC/E, MBS, BRN, Alia Spanish. Rep: Roslin, Rgnl Reps. Format: Adult contemp, talk. News staff 3; news progmg 16 hrs wkly. Target aud: 35 plus; adults seeking full svc progmg. Spec prog: It one hr, Sp one hr, Swedish one hr, farm one hr wkly. ■ Simon Goldman, pres; Merrill Rosen, vp & gen mgr; Dennis Webster, opns mgr; Larry Saracki, gen sls mgr; Stephen E. Shulman, progmg dir; Hap Hazard, news dir; Wayne Goff, chief engr.

WWSE(FM)—Co-owned with WJTN(AM). October 1947: 93.3 mhz; 26.5 kw. Ant 643 ft. TL: N42 05 06 W79 17 23. Stereo. Hrs opn: 24. Prog sep from AM. Net: Unistar. Format: Adult contemp. News progmg 7 hrs wkly. Target aud: 18-44. ■ Merrill Rosen, gen sls mgr.

WKSN(AM)—Jan 26, 1948: 1340 khz; 500 w-D, 1 kw-N. TL: N42 05 46 W79 14 48. Box 1199, 202 Front St. (14701). (716) 664-2313. FAX: (716) 488-1471. Licensee: Derrick Publishing Co. (acq 12-31-86). Net: CBS. Rep: Dome. Format: Solid gold. ■ E. Michael Boyle, pres; Michael J. Felice, vp & gen mgr; Daniel C. Fischer, stn mgr; Chuck Telford, gen sls mgr; Gary McIntrye, progmg mgr; Bruce Baker, mus dir; Tim Johnson, news dir; Burton O. Waterman, chief engr.

WHUG(FM)—Co-owned with WKSN(AM). Feb 1, 1965: 101.7 mhz; 3.3 kw. Ant 300 ft. TL: N42 07 55 W79 13 09. Stereo. Prog sep from AM. Net: ABC. Format: Hot country.

***WNJA(FM)**—1991: 89.7 mhz; 6 kw. Ant 754 ft. TL: N42 02 48 W79 05 26. Box 1263, Horizon Plaza, Buffalo (14240). (716) 845-7000. FAX: (716) 845-7043. Licensee: Western New York Public Broadcasting Association. Format: News, jazz. ■ Richard J. Daly, vp & stn mgr.

***WUBJ(FM)**—Not on air, target date unknown: 88.1 mhz; 265 w. Ant 558 ft. State University Plaza, Albany (12246). Licensee: State University of New York.

WWSE(FM)—Listing follows WJTN(AM).

Jeffersonville

***WJFF(FM)**—Feb 12, 1990: 90.5 mhz; 3.7 kw. Ant 629 ft. TL: N41 48 58 W74 47 15. Stereo. Hrs opn: 18. Box 797, Rt. 52 E. (12748). (914) 482-4141; (914) 482-4153. FAX: (914) 482-WJFF. Licensee: Radio Catskill. Net: NPR, APR. Wash atty: Haley, Bader & Potts. Format: Class, news, rock. News progmg 39 hrs wkly. Target aud: General; 25-60. Spec prog: Folk 8 hrs, jazz 15 hrs, pub affrs 8 hrs wkly. ■ Barbara Gref, pres; Glen Wooddell, vp; Elizabeth Popovich, stn mgr; Earle Nietzel, chief engr.

WPDA(FM)—Not on air, target date unknown: 106.1 mhz; 1.6 kw. Ant 627 ft. TL: N41 48 57 W74 45 42. 10 Circular Rd., Poughkeepsie (12601). Licensee: Bambi Broadcasting.

Johnstown

WENT(AM)—See Gloversville.

WIZR(AM)—1964: 930 khz; 1 kw-D. TL: N42 59 54 W74 21 31. Stereo. Hrs opn: 24. Box 146, 178 E. State St. (12095). (518) 762-4631. FAX: (518) 762-0105. Licensee: Hometown Broadcasting Corp. (acq 12-83; $275,000; FTR 11-21-83). Net: SMN. Wash atty: Fisher, Wayland, Cooper & Leader. Format: Big band. News staff 2. Target aud: 25-45. ■ Matthew Mataraso, pres; Joseph D. Caruso, vp, gen mgr & gen sls mgr; Linda L. Caruso, adv dir; Jeff Simonson, news dir; Dave Abdoo, chief engr. ■ Rates: $10; 10; 10; 7.

WSRD(FM)—Co-owned with WIZR(AM). June 26, 1968: 104.9 mhz; 6 kw. Ant 300 ft. TL: N43 03 14 W74 25 27. Hrs opn: 24. Prog sep from AM. Format: Pure gold. Target aud: 45 plus. ■ Rates: Same as AM.

Kingston

***WAMK(FM)**—March 1988: 90.9 mhz; 940 w. Ant 1,486 ft. TL: N42 04 35 W74 06 26. Stereo. Hrs opn: 24. Rebroadcasts WAMC(FM) Albany 100%. 318 Central Ave., Albany (12206). (518) 465-5233; (800) 323-9262. FAX: (518) 432-0991. Licensee: WAMC. Group owner: WAMC/Northeast Public Radio. Net: APR, NPR, UPI. Format: Class, news, info. News progmg 48 hrs wkly. Target aud: General. Spec prog: Jazz 17 hrs, folk/bluegrass 8 hrs wkly. ■ Alan Chartock (exec dir), CEO; Alan Chartock, chmn; Kathleen Taylor, dev dir; David Galletly, progmg dir; Michael Carrese, news dir; Jim Scholefield, chief engr.

WBPM(FM)—Listing follows WGHQ(AM).

WDST(FM)—See Woodstock.

***WFGB(FM)**—January 1985: 89.7 mhz; 3.1 kw. Ant 1,486 ft. TL: N42 04 35 W74 06 26. Stereo. Hrs opn: 24. Box 777, Lake Katrine (12449). (914) 336-6199. FAX: (914) 336-7205. Licensee: Sound of Life Inc. Format: Relg. News progmg 3 hrs wkly. Target aud: General. Spec prog: Black one hr, Sp one hr wkly. ■ Dennis Newcomer, pres; Bruce Winchell, gen mgr; Roger Thayer, mus dir.

***WFRH(FM)**—Sept 1993: 91.7 mhz; 950 w. Ant 272 ft. TL: N41 59 04 W74 02 56. Hrs opn: 24. 60 Butternut Knolls, West Shokin (12494). Licensee: Family Stations Inc. (group owner). Format: Rgnl. ■ Harold Company, pres; Art Thompson, gen mgr; Don Elmendorf, stn mgr.

WGHQ(AM)—Mar 4, 1956: 920 khz; 5 kw-D, 77 w-N, DA-1. TL: N41 53 09 W73 58 15. Hrs opn: 24. Box 1880, 82 John St. (12401). (914) 331-8200. FAX: (914) 331-8292. Licensee: Historic Hudson Valley Radio Inc. (acq 1975). Net: NBC, SMN. Wash atty: Koteen & Naftalin. Format: MOR, news/talk. News staff one; news progmg 20 hrs wkly. Target aud: 30 plus. Spec prog: Relg 3 hrs wkly. ■ Walter C. Maxwell, pres & gen mgr; Jean Fitzgerald-Maxwell, gen sls mgr; Dan Hartman, news dir. ■ Rates: $33; 20; 23; 20.

WBPM(FM)—Co-owned with WGHQ(AM). Dec 13, 1965: 94.3 mhz; 1.1 w. Ant 554 ft. TL: N41 53 44 W73 59 32. Stereo. Hrs opn: 24. Prog sep from AM. Format: Contemp hit. Target aud: 18-49; women. ■ Jean Fitzgerald-Maxwell, gen mgr & progmg mgr. ■ Rates: $35; 24; 23; 22.

WKNY(AM)—Aug 1, 1939: 1490 khz; 1 kw-U. TL: N41 56 11 W74 00 30. Box 1398, 718 Broadway (12401). (914) 331-1490. Licensee: CHET-5 Broadcasting L.P. Group owner: CHET-5 Broadcasting (acq 2-12-93; $1.65 million with WDST[FM] Woodstock; FTR 3-8-93). Net: CBS. Format: Adult contemp. News staff 3; news progmg 26 hrs wkly. Target aud: 25-54; 60% female. Spec prog: Ger one hr, Pol one hr, Irish one hr wkly. ■ Gary H. Chetkof, chmn & pres; David Ocker, vp & gen mgr; Rick Albano, gen sls mgr; Ward Todd, progmg dir; Henry Ellenbogen, chief engr. ■ Rates: $32; 22; 28; 10.

Lake Luzerne

WBAR-FM—Not on air, target date unknown: 94.7 mhz; 300 w. Ant 892 ft. TL: N43 19 08 W73 45 10. 20 Liberty Ave., Whitesboro (13492). Licensee: Capital Media Corp. (acq 9-25-92; $271,000; FTR 11-9-92). ■ Paul Lotters, gen mgr.

Lake Placid

WIRD(AM)—Nov 21, 1961: 920 khz; 5 kw-D, 250 w-N. TL: N44 15 36 W74 01 22. Hrs opn: 24. Box 831, 332 Main St., Suite 105 (12946). (518) 523-3341. FAX: (518) 523-1349. Licensee: Adirondack Network Systems Inc. (acq 12-88; $1 million; FTR 1-16-89). Net: CBS. Wash atty: John Tierney & Assoc. Format: Adult contemp. News staff one; news progmg 4 hrs wkly. Target aud: 25-54. ■ Donald A. Nardiello, pres; Dan Nardiello, vp; Kathryn Nardiello, vp opns & prom mgr; Jim Williams, gen sls mgr, mktg dir & adv mgr; Bob Mac, progmg dir & mus dir; Sandy Caligore, news dir; Donald A. Nardiello Jr., chief engr. ■ Rates: $17.25; 14.95; 12.65; 12.65.

WLPW(FM)—Co-owned with WIRD(AM). October 1979: 105.5 mhz; 3 kw. Ant -236 ft. TL: N44 15 36 W74 01 22. Stereo. Dups AM 80%. Format: Adult contemp.

Lake Ronkonkoma

***WSHR(FM)**—January 1966: 91.9 mhz; 2.8 kw-H. Ant 141 ft. TL: N40 50 00 W73 06 01. Stereo. 212 Smith Rd. (11779). (516) 467-0424. Licensee: Board of Education, Sachem Central School District at Holbrook (acq 1967). Format: Jazz. Target aud: General. ■ Stuart Harris, gen mgr & chief engr.

Lake Success

WYNY(FM)—Licensed to Lake Success. See New York.

Lancaster

WXRL(AM)—1964: 1300 khz; 2.4 kw-D, 2.5 kw-N, DA-2. TL: N42 52 58 W78 37 54. Hrs opn: 18. Box 170, 5426 William St. (14086). (716) 681-1313. FAX: (716) 681-7172. Licensee: Dome Broadcasting Inc. (acq 11-1-70). Net: MBS. Format: Country. Spec prog: Relg 6 hrs, Ger 2 hrs, Pol 5 hrs, Sp 2 hrs wkly. ■ Louis A. Schriver, pres, gen mgr & mktg dir; Joan C Schriver, exec vp; Dave Saunders, opns dir & news dir; Lynn Carol Schriver, opns mgr & asst mus dir; Linda Sukennik, prom dir; Beverly Sionko, prom mgr; Joan Schriver, progmg dir; Louis E. Schriver, progmg mgr; Joan Marshall, mus dir; William Stachowiak, chief engr. ■ Rates: $30; 25; 30; 10.

Liberty

WVOS(AM)—1947: 1240 khz; 1 kw-U. TL: N41 46 54 W74 43 49. Hrs opn: 5 AM-11 PM. Box 150 (12754); Old Rt. 17, Ferndale (12734). (914) 292-5533. FAX: (914) 292-5534. Licensee: Mountain Broadcasting Corp. (acq 8-90; $485,000; FTR 8-13-90). Net: ABC/I. Wash atty: Fisher, Wayland, Cooper & Leader. Format: Country. News staff 2; news progmg 17 hrs wkly. Target aud: 25-54. Spec prog: Talk 2 hrs, Sp 2 hrs wkly. ■ Shirley R. Blabey, pres; Eugene H. Blabey, gen mgr; Christine Lanza, gen sls mgr; Mike Sakell, progmg dir & chief engr; Kristen Speranza, news dir.

WVOS-FM—Dec 1964: 95.9 mhz; 6 kw. Ant 328 ft. TL: N41 45 09 W74 43 01 Stereo. Hrs opn: 24. Dups AM 98%. ■ Christine Lanza, sls dir.

Little Falls

WLFH(AM)—June 10, 1952: 1230 khz; 1 kw-U. TL: N43 02 33 W74 51 31. Hrs opn: 24. Box 4490, Utica (13504); 341 S. 2nd St. (13365). (315) 823-1230; (315) 866-1230. FAX: (315) 823-1231. Licensee: Roser Communications Network Inc. (acq 8-90; $100,000; FTR 8-13-90). Net: SMN. Rep: Katz. Wash atty: Fisher, Wayland, Cooper & Leader. Format: Country. News staff one; news progmg 16 hrs wkly. Target aud: 25-54. ■ Kenneth Roser Jr., pres & gen mgr; Gary Van Veghten, opns mgr & mus dir; Gene Conte, progmg dir; Bill Fowler, news dir; Ken Ruhland, chief engr. ■ Rates: $10; 8; 8; 7.

WOWB(FM)—Dec 20, 1990: 105.5 mhz; 3 kw. Ant 466 ft. TL: N42 59 27 W74 55 06 (CP: 2.9 kw). Stereo. Hrs opn: 24. Box 4490, Utica (13504). (315) 823-1230; (315) 866-1230. FAX: (315) 823-1231. Licensee: Towpath Communications Ltd. Net: SMN. Rep: Katz. Wash atty: Pepper & Corazzini. Format: Adult contemp. Target aud: 25-54. ■ Kenneth Roser Jr., pres & gen mgr; Gary Van Veghten, opns mgr & mus dir; William Fowler, news dir; Ken Rhuland, chief engr. ■ Rates: $16; 16; 16; 16.

Stations in the U.S. New York

Lockport

WLVL(AM)—May 8, 1947: 1340 khz; 1 kw-U, DA-D. TL: N43 10 30 W78 42 39. Box 477, 320 Michigan St. (14095). (716) 433-5944. FAX: (716) 433-6588. Licensee: Culver Communications Inc. (acq 9-81; $549,500; FTR 10-5-81). Net: CNN. Format: Oldies, news/talk. News staff 2; news progmg 18 hrs wkly. Target aud: 30-65; adult Lockport area citizens. Spec prog: Farm 6 hrs, Dial A Deal 6 hrs, It 2 hrs wkly. ■ Richard C. Greene, pres, gen mgr & progmg dir; Paula Falsioni, gen sls mgr; Tom Porharaska, news dir; Tom Foley, chief engr. ■ Rates: $28; 22; 24; 15.

Loudonville

*WVCR-FM—Apr 26, 1963: 88.3 mhz; 360 w. Ant 860 ft. TL: N42 38 13 W74 00 06 (CP: 1.36 kw). Stereo. Siena College (12211). (518) 783-2986; (518) 783-2990. FAX: (518) 783-2990. Licensee: Siena College. Format: Rock, urban contemp, heavy metal. Spec prog: Polish 3 hrs, Sp 6 hrs wkly. ■ Shannon Woods, gen mgr; Arnold Abate, prom mgr; Jose Aponte, Steven Doellefeld, progmg dirs; Andrea Wedler, Gail Calvert, mus dirs.

Lowville

WLLG(FM)—Apr 1, 1987: 99.3 mhz; 1 kw. Ant 520 ft. TL: N43 45 12 W75 33 50. Stereo. Hrs opn: 24 7606 N. State St. (13367). (315) 376-8566; (315) 376-8549. Licensee: Lowville Radio Inc. Net: USA. Format: Adult contemp, oldies, MOR. News staff one; news progmg 18 hrs wkly. Target aud: General. ■ David R. Atwood, pres & progmg dir; Nancy Atwood, gen mgr; Stephen Douglass, news dir; Robert Thayer, chief engr. ■ Rates: $14; 14; 14; 14.

Malone

WICY(AM)—Nov 4, 1946: 1490 khz; 1 kw-U. TL: N44 50 46 W74 16 07. Hrs opn: 18. Porter Rd. (12953). (518) 483-1100. FAX: (518) 483-1382. Licensee: L.C.C. Media Inc. (acq 9-1-89; $150,000; FTR 9-11-89). Net: NBC. Rep: Rgnl Reps. Wash atty: Arter & Hadden. Format: Adult contemp. News staff 2; news progmg 15 hrs wkly. Target aud: 25-54. Spec prog: Country 3 hrs, farm one hr wkly. ■ J.M. Coughlin Jr., pres; Monte Coughlin, gen mgr, gen sls mgr & news dir; Noelia Carter, prom mgr & progmg dir; Kevin Andrews, mus dir; Erling Svenson, chief engr. ■ Rates: $16; 16; 16; na.

*WSLO(FM)—February 1989: 90.9 mhz; 200 w. Ant 354 ft. TL: N44 49 46 W74 22 31. Hrs opn: 24. Rebroadcasts WSLU(FM) Canton 100%. St. Lawrence University, Romoda Dr., Canton (13617). (315) 379-5356. Licensee: St. Lawrence University. Wash atty: Donald Martin. Format: Div. News staff 2; news progmg 35 hrs wkly. Target aud: General. Spec prog: Gospel, classical, jazz, folk, public affrs. ■ Ellen Rocco, gen mgr.

WVNV(FM)—May 1, 1993: 96.5 mhz; 2.4 kw. Ant 361 ft. TL: N44 49 37 W74 22 46. Stereo. Hrs opn: 20. Box 719, Porter Rd. (12953-0719). (518) 483-1100; (518) 483-1101. FAX: (518) 483-1382. Licensee: L.C.C. Media Inc. (acq 3-9-92; $38,369 for CP; FTR 4-6-92). Rep: Rgnl Rep. Wash atty: Arter & Hadden. Format: Country. News staff 2; news progmg 2 hrs wkly. Target aud: 18-54. ■ James M. Coughlin Jr., CEO, chmn, pres & CFO; Richard Lauigne, vp; James N. Coughlin Jr., gen mgr; Noel Carter, stn mgr & gen sls mgr; Mary Howard, progmg dir; Kevin Andrews, mus dir; Erling Svenson, chief engr. ■ Rates: $20.65; 20.65; 20.65; 12.

Manlius

WAQX-FM—Aug 23, 1978: 95.7 mhz; 25 kw. Ant 300 ft. TL: N43 00 25 W76 05 38. Stereo. Hrs opn: 24. 1064 James St., Syracuse (13203). (315) 472-0200. FAX: (315) 472-1146. Licensee: Pilot Communications of Syracuse Inc. (acq 10-10-90; $3.85 million; FTR 9-10-90). Net: ABC/R. Rep: Banner. Wash atty: Fisher, Wayland, Cooper & Leader. Format: AOR. News progmg 3 hrs wkly. Target aud: 25-54. Spec prog: Public service one hr wkly. ■ James L. Leven, CEO, chmn & pres; William Fleming, CFO; Michael Sehiefer, stn mgr & gen sls mgr; Lisa Walker, prom mgr; Steve Brill, progmg dir; Dave Frisina, mus dir; Jim Marco, chief engr. ■ Rates: $125; 100; 125; 80.

Massena

WMSA(AM)—Oct 12, 1945: 1340 khz; 1 kw-U. TL: N44 54 14 W74 53 01. Hrs opn: 5:30 AM-10:15 PM. Box 210, Rt. 420 Winthrop Rd. (13662). (315) 769-3594. FAX: (315) 769-3299. Licensee: 1340 Communications Inc. (acq 9-80; $210,000; FTR 9-1-80). Net: ABC/E. Rep: Torbet. Format: Adult contemp. News staff one; news progmg 16 hrs wkly. Target aud: 18 plus. Spec

News, sports. ■ Donald Alexander, pres; James Brett, vp; Victor Perry, gen mgr, sls dir, progmg dir & chief engr; James McCaffrey, natl sls mgr & rgnl sls mgr; Sandy Cook, mus dir; Paul Haggett, news dir & pub affrs dir; Mike Ring, engrg dir. ■ Rates: $25; 20; 25; 20.

WYBG(AM)—Aug 18, 1958: 1050 khz; 1 kw-D, 500 PSA. TL: N44 53 42 W74 56 05. Box 298, 162 E. Orvis (13662). (315) 764-0554. FAX: (315) 764-0118. Licensee: Wade Communications Inc. (acq 8-15-88; $450,000; FTR 8-15-88). Net: CNN. Format: Adult contemp, gold. News staff 2. Target aud: 25-49; baby boomers. Spec prog: "Bill of Fare" food show one hour, CFL Football, NHL hockey, relg 2 hrs wkly. ■ Curran Wade, pres & gen mgr; Bob Kampf, mus dir; Don Despaw, news dir; Robert Sauter, chief engr. ■ Rates: $15; 15; 15; 15.

Mechanicville

WMVI(AM)—Oct 19, 1981: 1160 khz; 5 kw-D, 570 w-N. TL: N42 55 12 W73 42 08. Stn currently dark. Box 569, 35 N. Main St. (12118). Licensee: Mechanicville Broadcasting Inc. ■ John Farina, pres.

WXLE(FM)—Not on air, target date unknown: 104.5 mhz; 5 kw. TL: N42 52 44 W73 51 47. 940 Rt. 146, Clifton Park (12065). (518) 383-1045. Licensee: Foley Broadcasting Ltd. (acq 3-4-93; FTR 3-22-93). ■ Ragan Henry, CEO; Don Kidwell, pres; Susan Cline, gen mgr; Mark Adamz, opns mgr; Bryan Jester, mktg dir & prom dir; Ron Michals, mus dir; Matt Humphreys, pub affrs dir.

Middletown

WALL(AM)—Aug 6, 1942: 1340 khz; 1 kw-U. TL: N41 27 21 W74 26 22 (CP: 660 w). Hrs opn: 24. One Broadcast Plaza (10940). (914) 343-7400. FAX: (914)-343-1201. Licensee: Atlantic Morris Broadcasting Inc. (group owner). Net: AP, NBC Talknet. Rep: Banner. Wash atty: Hogan & Hartson. Format: News/talk. News staff 4; news progmg 30 hrs wkly. Target aud: 35-64; educated, upscale families. Spec prog: Relg 3 hrs, farm one hr wkly. ■ Donald G. Schwartz, gen mgr; Andrea Cetera, gen sls mgr; Ray Arthur, progmg dir; Lynn Thompson, pub affrs dir. ■ Rates: $36; 30; 36; 26.

WKOJ(FM)—Co-owned with WALL(AM). Nov 11, 1966: 92.7 mhz; 3 kw. Ant 300 ft. TL: N41 27 21 W74 26 22 Stereo. Prog sep from AM. Format: AOR. News staff one; news progmg 3 hrs wkly. Target aud: 18-44; younger, mobile, upscale families. Spec prog: New music 2 hrs wkly. ■ Gary Sanders, progmg dir. ■ Rates: $38; 32; 38; 30.

*WOSR(FM)—Feb 3, 1992: 91.7 mhz; 1.8 kw. Ant 630 ft. TL: N41 36 04 W74 33 13. Stereo. Hrs opn: 24. Rebroadcasts WAMC(FM) Albany 100%. 318 Central Ave., Albany (12206). (518) 465-5233; (800) 323-9262. Licensee: WAMC. Group owner: WAMC/Northeast Public Radio. Net: NPR, APR, UPI. Format: Class, news, info. News progmg 48 hrs wkly. Target aud: General. Spec prog: Folk/bluegrass 8 hrs, jazz 18 hrs wkly. ■ Alan Chartock, chmn; Kathleen Taylor, dev dir; David Galletly (asst exec), progmg dir; Michael Carrese, news dir; Jim Scholefield, chief engr.

Mineola

WTHE(AM)—Jan 1, 1964: 1520 khz; 1 kw-D, 250 w-CH. TL: N40 44 45 W73 37 29. 260 E. Second St. (11501). (516) 742-1520. Licensee: Bursam Communications Corp. Group owner: Universal Broadcasting Corp. (acq 7-11-69). Format: Relg, Black gospel. News progmg 6 hrs wkly. Target aud: General. Spec prog: Ger one hr, polka one hr, Haitian 3 hrs, Sp 10 hrs wkly. ■ Paul W. Ploener, gen mgr; J.K. Jefferson, asst mus dir; Bruce Clark, chief engr. ■ Rates: $36; 36; 36; na.

Monroe

*WLJP(FM)—Not on air, target date unknown: 89.3 mhz; 200 w. Ant 1,023 ft. TL: N41 22 42 W74 08 16. Stereo. Rebroadcasts WFGB(FM) Kingston 100%. Box 777, 199 Tuytenbridge Rd., Lake Katrine (12449). (914) 336-6199. FAX: (914) 336-7205. Licensee: Sound of Life Inc. Format: Relg. News progmg 3 hrs wkly. Target aud: General. Spec prog: Black one hr, Sp one hr wkly. ■ Dennis Newcomer, pres.

Montauk

WBEA(FM)—Feb 19, 1993: 94.7 mhz; 6 kw. Ant 328 ft. TL: N41 01 57 W71 58 31. Box 7162, 249 Montauk Hwy., Amagansett (11930). (516) 267-7800. FAX: (516) 267-1018. Licensee: C&S Radio-South Fork L.P. Net: Unistar. Format: Adult Contemp. News staff one. Target aud: 25-45; upscale Hamptons at-work & NY City 2nd home

owners. ■ Derrick Cephas, pres; Zoe Kamitses, vp & gen mgr; Jaeques Ditte, progmg mgr; Steve Ardolina, mus dir; Bob Makson, chief engr.

WVZC(FM)—Not on air, target date unknown: 94.9 mhz; 3 kw. Ant 125 ft. TL: N41 02 07 W71 56 44. c/o Women Broadcasters Inc., 235 E. 73rd St. #9A, New York (10021). Licensee: Women Broadcasters Inc.

Monticello

WSUL-FM—Apr 16, 1977: 98.3 mhz; 3.0 kw. Ant 360 ft. TL: N41 39 38 W74 41 14 (CP: 1.1 kw, ant 553 ft.). Stereo. Hrs opn: 24. Box 983, 250 Broadway (12701). (914) 794-9898; (914) 794-0248. FAX: (914) 794-0125. Licensee: Reynolds Communications Inc. (acq 12-19-86). Net: NBC, AP. Wash atty: Wilkinson, Barker, Knowes & Quinn. Format: Adult contemp. News staff one. Target aud: 25-54. Spec prog: Relg one hr wkly. ■ William Reynolds, pres, vp & gen mgr; Fred Mulharin, opns mgr & progmg dir; Helena Manzione, gen sls mgr; Eddie Wilson, mus dir; Matt Rielly, news dir; A.J. Cole, pub affrs dir; David Groth, chief engr. ■ Rates: $37.65; 34.50; 37.65; 20.

WVOS-FM—See Liberty.

WXTM(FM)—Not on air, target date unknown: 99.7 mhz; 6 kw. Ant 328 ft. TL: N41 39 24 W74 43 40. Stereo. 117 Highland Lake Rd., Highland Lake (12743); 711 E. 134th St., Bronx NY (10454). (718) 292-1310. FAX: (718) 292-2835. Licensee: Larry Fishman. Format: Classic Rock, oldies.

Montour Falls

WNGZ(FM)—June 1973: 104.9 mhz; 1 kw. Ant 480 ft. TL: N42 15 05 W76 52 53. Stereo. Hrs opn: 24. 108 E. Gray St., Elmira (14901). (607) 733-3777. Licensee: Northeastern Broadcasting Inc. (acq 7-25-89; grpsl; FTR 10-2-89). Rep: Katz & Powell. Format: Classic rock. News staff one. Target aud: 20-49; baby boomers, young adults. ■ Guy Nichols, CEO & vp; Edward Valenta, pres; Bill Miller, gen mgr, prom dir & progmg dir; Joseph Fazzary, gen sls mgr; Jim Miller, mus dir; Cheryl Quinch, news dir; Steve Shimmer, chief engr. ■ Rates: $35; 30; 35; 25.

Morristown

WNCQ-FM—Not on air, target date unknown: 102.9 mhz; 2.4 kw. Ant 367 ft. TL: N44 34 02 W75 37 16. Rd. #2, Gifford Rd., Watertown (13601). (315) 393-3793. Licensee: Northstar Broadcasting Corp. Group owner: Cayuga/Northstar Radio Group. ■ Bruce Danziger, gen mgr.

Mt. Hope

*WXHD(FM)—Not on air, target date January 1994: 90.1 mhz; 1.1 kw. Ant 680 ft. TL: N41 26 05 W74 34 34. Box 709, Otisville, NY (10963); 4143 Cionashaugh Lakes, Milford, PA (18337). (717) 686-2930. Licensee: Shawangunk Communications. Wash atty: Haley, Bader & Potts. Format: Alternative/current events. Target aud: General. ■ Peter Maynard, chmn; Thomas S. Mondell, pres.

Mount Kisco

WVIP(AM)—Oct 27, 1957: 1310 khz; 5 kw-D, 33 w-N, DA-2. TL: N41 11 37 W73 44 22. Radio Circle (10549). (914) 241-1310. FAX: (914) 666-7509. Licensee: VIP Broadcasting Corp. (acq 7-22-66). Net: ABC/I. Rep: Katz. Format: MOR, news. News staff 3; news progmg 15 hrs wkly. Target aud: General; 45 plus. Spec prog: Class one hr wkly. ■ Martin Stone, pres; Damien Mass, progmg dir; Lisa Wiernick, news dir. ■ Rates: $60; 40; 50; na.

WVIP-FM—Jan 15, 1964: 106.3 mhz; 3 kw. Ant 440 ft. TL: N41 11 56 W73 41 37. Stereo. Licensee: Impulse Broadcasting Corp. (acq 9-15-93; $1.25 million; FTR 10-18-93). Net: Unistar. Format: Adult contemp, news. News progmg 5 hrs wkly. Target aud: 25-54.

Nanuet

WLIR(AM)—See Spring Valley.

New City

WRKL(AM)—July 4, 1964: 910 khz; 1 kw-D, DA. TL: N41 10 52 W74 02 53. Hrs opn: 5 AM-8 PM. Box 910, Rt. 202, Rockland County, Pomona (10970). (914) 354-2000. Licensee: Rockland Communicators Inc. (acq 12-85; $1.11 million; FTR 10-21-85). Rep: Banner; Katz. Wash atty: Fisher, Wayland, Cooper & Leader. Format: News/talk. News staff 6; news progmg 38 hrs wkly. Target aud: 30 plus; adults who live in Rockland County. Spec prog: Black 2 hrs, gospel one hr, jazz 2 hrs, relg 2 hrs wkly. ■ Bobbi Lewis, pres, stn mgr & pub affrs dir; Morton M. Siegel, vp & gen mgr; Richard DeMaria, gen sls mgr; Susan Tolve, news dir; Jeff Baker, chief engr. ■ Rates: $58; 40; 58; 40.

New Paltz

WBWZ(FM)—Nov 19, 1992: 93.3 mhz; 350 w. Ant 1328 ft. TL: N41 41 58 W74 00 11. Hrs opn: 24. Box 984 (12561). (914) 255-9300. FAX: (914) 255-9118. Licensee: New Paltz Broadcasting Co. Format: Z rock. Target aud: 18-34; late baby boom/post boom generation. ■ Betty Walker, gen mgr; Hal Robinson, gen sls mgr; Bill Rock, prom mgr. ■ Rates: $40; 35; 40; 30.

***WFNP(FM)**—Sept 1, 1990: 88.7 mhz; 230 w. Ant 1,289 ft. TL: N41 43 09 W73 59 47 (CP: COL: Rosendale). Stereo. Hrs opn: 7 PM-5 AM. SUB, Room 413, State Univ. of N.Y. (12561). (914) 257-3041. FAX: (914) 257-3099. Licensee: State Univ. of New York, Albany. Net: ABC. Format: Progressive. News progmg 3 hrs wkly. Target aud: General; demographic-specific programs. Spec prog: Black 10 hrs, jazz 4 hrs, Sp 3 hrs, reggae 5 hrs, Third World 3 hrs, news/talk 5 hrs wkly. ■ Lee H. Kobus, pres & opns mgr; Stephanie Salsberg, gen mgr; Jeff Martin, progmg dir; Will C. Robedee, chief engr.

New Rochelle

WVOX(AM)—1950: 1460 khz; 500 w-D. TL: N40 55 42 W73 46 30. Hrs opn: 6 AM-sunset. One Broadcast Forum (10801). (914) 636-1460. FAX: (914) 636-2900. Licensee: Hudson-Westchester Radio Inc. (acq 5-1-68). Net: Unistar, AP. Wash atty: Ray Kraus. Format: MOR, news/talk. News staff one; news progmg 50 hrs wkly. Target aud: 24 plus; community minded. Spec prog: Black one hr, gospel one hr, relg 3 hrs wkly. ■ William O'Shaughnessy, CEO, pres & mus dir; Cindy Gallagher, CFO & exec vp; Judy Fremont, sr vp & gen mgr; Andy Largent, opns mgr; Jami Sherwood, dev dir; Jean Satoris, gen sls mgr & prom dir; Amy Tortolani, news dir. ■ Rates: $175; 115; 146; 140.

WRTN(FM)—Co-owned with WVOX(AM). 1953: 93.5 mhz; 3 kw. Ant 325 ft. TL: N40 57 45 W73 50 32. Stereo. Hrs opn: 24. Prog sep from AM. Format: MOR, big band, jazz, society. News staff one; news progmg 14 hrs wkly. Target aud: 35 plus; upscale, highly educated, affluent and influential. ■ Judy Fremont, vp sls; Frank Hadsu, Roger Cucci, chiefs engr. ■ Rates: $110; 72; 90; na.

DATABASES - MAILING LABELS

★ RADIO/TELEVISION US/CANADA
99.7% Deliverable - System Updated Daily
Over 25 Selection Options. Accurate Formats, Market Size, Station Audiences, States, Networks, Random Lists, Execs by Name, Secondary Formats, Ethnic Stations, Delete/Add Markets or Stations

★ DATABASE AUDITS
We Correct, Update and Maintain Your Database

★ RADIOSCAN
All US Radio on Your PC - Includes Powerful Software
Instant Station Data on Screen - Reports in 10 Seconds
Station Lists for Each of 585 Markets
Rolls Royce of all Radio Database Systems
Ideal for Syndicators, Networks, all Vendors
Reasonably Priced

The CENTER For RADIO INFORMATION
19 Market Street, Cold Spring, NY 10516
PH: (800) 359-9898 FAX: (914) 265-2715

New York

WABC(AM)—Oct. 7, 1971. 770 khz; 50 kw-U. TL: N40 52 50 W74 04 12. 17th Fl., 2 Penn Plaza (10121). (212) 613-3800. FAX: (212) 947-1340. Licensee: Capital Cities/ABC Inc. Group owner: Capital Cities/ABC Broadcast Group (acq 1986; grpsl; FTR 4-15-85). Net: ABC/I, ABC TalkRadio. Rep: Banner. Format: Talk. Spec prog: "The Money Show" 26 hrs, real estate 3 hrs wkly. ■ Don Bouloukos, pres & gen mgr; Denise McIntee, opns dir; Stephanie McNamara, gen sls mgr; Stephanie McNamara (local sls), Duke Broadsky, Tim McCarthy, rgnl sls mgrs; Paulette Pettit, prom dir & pub affrs dir; John Mainelli, progmg dir; Bob Bucci, news dir; Bill Krause, chief engr.

WPLJ(FM)—Co-owned with WABC(AM). Jan 18, 1960: 95.5 mhz; 6.7 kw. Ant 1,335 ft. TL: N40 44 54 W73 59 10. Stereo. Prog sep from AM. (212) 613-8900. Licensee: WPLJ-FM Radio Inc. (acq 6-27-86). Net: ABC/R. Format: Top-40. ■ Mitch Dolan, pres & gen mgr; Scott Shannon, progmg dir; Mike Preston, mus dir; Naomi DiClementi, news dir. ■ WABC-TV affil.

WADO 1280 AM

WADO(AM)—Mar 12, 1934: 1280 khz; 5 kw-U, DA-1. TL: N40 49 35 W74 04 35. Hrs opn: 24. Kent, 17th Fl., 666 3rd Ave. (10017). (212) 687-9236. FAX: (212) 599-2161; (201) 438-6230. Licensee: Spanish Radio Network (acq 10-16-90; FTR 11-5-90). Rep: Katz Hispanic. Format: Sp, btfl mus, news/talk. News staff 13; news progmg 50 hrs wkly. Target aud: 25-54; Hispanics in the N.Y. metropolitan area. ■ Louis Wolfson III, chmn; Mark Blank, pres; Herbert M. Levin, sr vp; Carlos A. Rubio, gen mgr; Karen Cole-Reich, natl sls mgr; Joaquin Salz (local), rgnl sls mgr; Antonio Guillet Jr., prom dir; Daniel Ortiz, progmg dir; Jose Ramon Cotti, news dir; Richard Ross, chief engr. ■ Rates: $315; 285; 245; 185.

WAXQ(FM)—Dec 1, 1956: 104.3 mhz; 7.8 kw h, 5.6 kw v. Ant 1,220 ft. TL: N40 44 54 W73 59 10. Stereo. 1180 Ave. of the Americas (10036). (212) 730-9626. FAX: (212) 302-7824. Licensee: GAF Broadcasting Co. (acq 4-16-92). Net: AP, Wall Street, Unistar. Rep: Katz & Powell. Wash atty: Fleischman & Walsh. Format: Rock. News staff one. ■ Samuel Heyman, pres; Randy Bongarten, sr vp; David Lebow, gen sls mgr; Mario Mazza, progmg dir; Rik Malone, mus dir; Warren Dean, news dir; Richard Koziol, chief engr.

***WBAI(FM)**—January 1960: 99.5 mhz; 5.4 kw-H, 3.9 kw-V. Ant 1,220 ft. TL: N40 44 54 W73 59 10. Stereo. Hrs opn: 24. WBAI-Pacifica, 19th Fl., 505 8th Ave. (10018). (212) 279-0707. FAX: (212) 564-5359. Licensee: Pacifica Foundation. Group owner: Pacifica Foundation Inc. dba Pacifica Radio (acq 1-9-60). Format: Div, educ, news/talk. News staff 2; news progmg 5 hrs wkly. Target aud: General; New York metropolitan area. Spec prog: American Indian one hr, Black 10 hrs, class 5 hrs, folk 2 hrs, jazz 5 hrs, Sp 3 hrs wkly. ■ Valerie Van Isler, gen mgr; Darla Kashian, dev dir; Samuri Marksman, progmg dir; Anthony Sloan, mus dir; Amy Goodman, news dir; Mario Murillo, pub affrs dir; William Wells, chief engr.

WBBR(AM)—Feb 13, 1934: 1130 khz; 50 kw-U, DA-N. TL: N40 48 39 W74 02 24. 15th Floor, 499 Park Ave. (10022). (212) 318-2340. FAX: (212) 980-2341. Licensee: Bloomberg Communications Inc. (acq 11-4-92; $13.58 million; FTR 11-23-92). Net: NBC, SMN. Rep: Eastman. Format: Business news. ■ Michael Bloombery, gen mgr; Fran Sharp, gen sls mgr; Bob Leverone, news dir; Jon Fram, chief engr.

WBLS(FM)—Listing follows WLIB(AM).

WCBS(AM)—1924: 880 khz; 50 kw-U. TL: N40 51 35 W73 47 09. Hrs opn: 24. 51 W. 52d St. (10019). (212) 975-4321. FAX: (212) 975-4674. Licensee: CBS Inc. Group owner: CBS Broadcast Group. Net: CBS. Rep: CBS Radio. Format: All news. ■ Dan Griffin, vp & gen mgr; Robin Sloan, gen sls mgr; Richard Landesman, natl sls mgr; Jan Kramer, prom dir; Harvey Nagler, progmg dir & news dir; Ed Schwartz, chief engr.

WCBS-FM—1941: 101.1 mhz; 6.8 kw. Ant 1,353 ft. TL: N40 44 54 W73 59 10. Prog sep from AM. Format: Oldies. ■ Marie Mason, vp & gen mgr; Nancy Dobrow, gen sls mgr; Renee Casis, prom mgr; Joe McCoy, progmg dir; Dennis Falcone, mus dir; Al Meredith, news dir; Bob Sagendorf, chief engr.

WEVD
NEW YORK'S AM STEREO
GREATER 1050

WEVD(AM)—Aug 28, 1922: 1050 khz; 50 kw-U, DA-1. TL: N40 48 26 W74 04 11. Stereo. Hrs opn: 24. 770 Broadway (10003-9564). (212) 777-7900. Licensee: Forward Broadcasting Inc. Net: MBS, NBC, BRN. Format: News/talk. News progmg 12 hrs wkly. Target aud: 25-54. ■ Tom Bird, gen mgr; Ken Sperber, gen sls mgr; Bob August, progmg dir; Gary R'Nel, news dir; George Levites, chief engr.

WFAN(AM)—1930: 660 khz; 50 kw-U. TL: N40 51 35 W73 47 09. Stereo. Hrs opn: 24. Kaufman-Astoria Studios, 34-12 36th St., Astoria (11106). (718) 706-7690. FAX: (718) 361-9234. Licensee: Infinity Broadcasting Corp. of New York. Group owner: Infinity Broadcasting Corp. (acq 2-25-92; $70 million; FTR 4-92). Net: NBC, Unistar, CBS. Rep: D & R Radio. Format: Sports information. News staff 34. Target aud: 25-49; sports fans. ■ Mel Karmazin, pres; Joel Hollander, gen mgr; Lee Davis, gen sls mgr; Mark Chernoff, progmg dir; Sue Guzman, news dir; Ed Knapp, chief engr.

***WFUV(FM)**—July 1947: 90.7 mhz; 50 kw. Ant 215 ft. TL: N40 51 37 W73 53 03 (CP: Ant 500 ft., TL: N40 51 44 W73 53 00). Stereo. Hrs opn: 24. Keating Hall, Fordham University, Bronx (10458). (718) 365-9070. FAX: (718) 365-9815. Licensee: Fordham University, Executive Committee, Board of Trustees. Net: ABC/I, APR. Wash atty: Renouff & Polivy. Format: Div, acoustic/folk. News staff 2; news progmg 16 hrs wkly. Target aud: 35 plus; intelligent and sophisticated music listeners. Spec prog: Country 3 hrs, Fr 3 hrs, Ger 2 hrs, It 2 hrs, Pol 2 hrs, Sp 4 hrs, Indian 2 hrs, Ukrainian one hr, Irish 7 hrs, Middle Eastern 2 hrs, big band 2 hrs, opera 2 hrs, oldies 3 hrs, doo-wop 3 hrs wkly. ■ Ralph M. Jennings, Ginger Calder, gen mgrs; Monique J. Fortune, dev dir; Chuck Singleton, progmg dir; Liz Opoka, mus dir; Robert S. Jewell, chief engr.

***WHCR-FM**—February 1985: 90.3 mhz; 8 w. Ant 266 ft. TL: N40 49 09 W73 56 59. Hrs opn: 18. WHCR/City College of NY, 138th & Convent Ave. (10031). (212) 650-7481. FAX: (212) 650-8101. Licensee: City College of New York. Format: Jazz, Sp, Black. News progmg 70 hrs wkly. Target aud: Community of Harlem. ■ David Buschler, chmn; Linda Prout, pres; Frank Allen, progmg dir; Pedro J. Polanco, chief engr.

WHTZ(FM)—See Newark, N.J.

WINS(AM)—1924: 1010 khz; 50 kw-U, DA-1. TL: N40 48 16 W74 06 25 (CP: TL: N40 48 39 W74 02 24). 888 Seventh Ave. (10106). (212) 315-7000. Licensee: Westinghouse Broadcasting Co. (group owner; acq 7-26-62). Net: ABC/D, ABC/I, CNN, CNBC. Rep: Group W. Format: All news. Target aud: General. ■ Scott Herman, vp & gen mgr; Carey Davis, gen sls mgr; Steve Swenson, progmg dir; Steve Holt, news dir; Ken Nealy, chief engr.

***WKCR-FM**—October 1941: 89.9 mhz; 1 kw. Ant 849 ft. TL: N40 42 43 W74 00 49 (CP: 630 w, ant 1,419 ft.). Stereo. Hrs opn: 24. 208 Ferris Booth Hall, Columbia Univ. (10027). (212) 854-5223. FAX: (212) 854-6972. Licensee: Trustees of Columbia Univ. Net: AP. Format: variety/div. News progmg 6 hrs wkly. Target aud: General. Spec prog: Jazz, class, news/talk, bluegrass, R&B, International, Black 10 hrs, country 10 hrs, Por 2 hrs, Sp 15, Irish 2 hrs, It 2 hrs, folk 5 hrs, gospel 2 hrs, arts 3 hrs wkly. ■ Janet Balis, gen mgr & stn mgr; Ryan Deussing, opns dir; Hank Torbert, prom dir; Peter Smith, progmg dir & mus dir; Luxman Nathan, news dir; Marsha Goodman, pub affrs dir; William Wells, chief engr.

WKDM(AM)—1927: 1380 khz; 5 kw-D, DA. TL: N40 49 13 W74 04 09. Suite 1406, 570 7th Ave. (10018). (212) 594-1380. FAX: (201) 939-3772. Licensee: United Broadcasting Co. of New York (acq 12-4-60). Rep: Katz. Format: Sp. Spec prog: Community svc. ■ Gerald Hroblak, pres; Geno Heinemeyer, stn mgr; Art Gordon, gen sls mgr; Raul Lopez Bastidas, progmg dir; Hector Aquilaro, news dir; Richard Ross, chief engr.

***WKRB(FM)**—(Brooklyn). May 28, 1978: 90.9 mhz; 10 w. Ant 136 ft. TL: N40 34 36 W73 56 04. Stereo. Hrs opn: 24. Kingsborough Community College, 2001 Oriental Blvd. (11235). (718) 934-9572; (718) 368-5604. FAX: (718) 368-5357. Licensee: Kingsborough Community College. Net: Unistar. Format: Urban contemp. Target aud: General; young adults. Spec prog: Jazz one hr, Russian 2 hrs, gospel one hr, comedy/drama one hr, talk 2 hrs wkly. ■ Leon Goldstein, pres; Stephen Castellano, gen mgr; Dave Frankel, opns mgr; James Glanz, chief engr.

WLIB(AM)—1942: 1190 khz; 10 kw-D, DA. TL: N40 47 48 W74 06 06. 801 Second Ave. (10017). (212) 661-3344. FAX: (212) 922-9460. Licensee: Inner City Broadcasting Corp. Group owner: Inner City Broadcasting (acq 7-72). Net: ABC/C. Rep: McGavren Guild. Format: All Black news, talk. Spec prog: Caribbean music. ■ Pierre M. Sutton, chmn; David Lampel, pres & gen mgr; Reggie Thom, gen sls mgr; Bonnie Sutton, prom mgr; Mark Riley, progmg dir; Jeff Barnes, mus dir; Wayne Gillman, news dir; David Schwartz, chief engr.

WBLS(FM)—Co-owned with WLIB(AM). Sept 15, 1965: 107.5 mhz; 5.4 kw-H, 3.8 kw-V. Ant 1,220 ft. TL: N40 44 54 W73 59 10. Hrs opn: 24. Prog sep from AM. Format:

Black, urban contemp. ■ William Froelich, gen sls mgr; Quincy McCoy, progmg dir; Pierre Bradshaw, mus dir.

WLTW(FM)—Jan 26, 1961: 106.7 mhz; 7.8 kw v, 5.4 kw h. Ant 1,220 ft. TL: N40 44 54 W73 59 10. Stereo. 1515 Broadway (10036). (212) 258-7000. Licensee: Viacom Broadcasting Inc. (group owner) Net: AP. Rep: Katz. Format: Adult contemp. ■ Rona Landy, gen mgr; John Cahill, gen sls mgr; Louise Cecchini, natl sls mgr; Kurt Johnson, progmg dir; Rasa Kaye, news dir; Robert Tarsio, chief engr.

WMCA(AM)—1925: 570 khz; 5 kw-U, DA-1. TL: N40 45 10 W74 06 15 (CP: 50 kw-D, 30 kw-N). Hrs opn: 24. Suite 201, 201 Rt. 17 N., Rutherford, NJ (07070-2574). (201) 507-5700. Licensee: Salem Media. Group owner: Salem Communications (acq 9-15-89; $13 million; FTR 8-14-89). Format: Relg, talk. Target aud: General. Spec prog: Jewish 10 hrs wkly. ■ Edward G. Atsinger III, pres; Joe D. Davis, gen mgr; Carl Miller, opns mgr & progmg dir; Odila D'Astoli, gen sls mgr; Andrew Andersen, news dir & pub affrs dir; Fred Gleason, chief engr.

WMXV(FM)—Dec 14, 1953: 105.1 mhz; 7.8 kw-H, 5.5 kw-V. Ant 1,220 ft. TL: N40 44 54 W73 59 10. Stereo. Hrs opn: 24. 485 Madison Ave. (10022). (212) 752-3322; (212) 752-3586. FAX: (212) 223-6496. Licensee: Bonneville Holding Company. Group owner: Bonneville International Corp. (acq 12-14-53). Net: AP. Rep: McGavren Guild. Wash atty: Wilkinson, Barker, Knauer & Quinn. Format: Adult contemp. News staff 2. Target aud: 25-54. ■ Mark Bench, vp & gen mgr; Michael Valentino, vp sls; Joseph Sebolao, natl sls mgr; Doug Knopper, mktg dir & prom dir; Gloria Mastrianni, prom mgr; Robert Dunphy, vp progmg; David Isreal, mus dir; Liz White, news dir; Jim Stagnitto, chief engr.

WNEW(FM)—August 1958: 102.7 mhz; 7.8 kw. Ant 1,220 ft. TL: N40 44 54 W73 59 10. Stereo. Hrs opn: 24. 655 3rd Ave. (10017). (212) 286-1027. Licensee: Group W Radio. Group owner: Westinghouse Broadcasting Co. (acq 12-89; grpsl; FTR 12-11-89). Net: Unistar. Rep: Group W. Format: Rock (AOR). ■ Burt Stanier, chmn; Jim Thompson, pres; Mike Craven, exec vp; Kevin Smith, vp & gen mgr; Scott Muni, opns dir; Jill Colombo, gen sls mgr; Neil Barry, mktg mgr & prom mgr; Pat St. John, progmg dir; Lorraine Caruso, mus dir; Donna Fiducia, news dir; Marty Martinez, pub affrs dir; John Rosso, chief engr.

***WNYC(AM)**—July 8, 1924: 820 khz; 10 kw-D, 1 kw-N, DA. TL: N40 45 10 W74 06 15. One Centre St. (10007). (212) 669-7800. Licensee: City of New York Municipal Broadcasting. Net: APR, NPR. Format: News/talk, info. ■ Thomas B. Morgan, pres; Lawrence J. Orfaly, gen mgr & vp progmg; Ernie Dachel, vp opns; Polly Runyon, vp dev; Deborah Thomas, vp mktg; Scott Bonden, progmg mgr; Dick Hinchliffe, news dir.

***WNYC-FM**—Sept 21, 1943: 93.9 mhz; 5.4 kw. Ant 1,418 ft. TL: N40 42 43 W74 00 49. Stereo. Hrs opn: 24. Dups AM 20%. Format: News, class. Spec prog: Drama & literature 5 hrs wkly. ■ John Schaefer, mus dir. ■ *WNYC-TV affil.

***WNYE(FM)**—November 1938: 91.5 mhz; 20 kw. Ant 430 ft. TL: N40 41 21 W73 58 37. 112 Tillary St., Brooklyn (11201). (718) 935-4480. FAX: (718) 855-8863. Licensee: Board of Education, City of New York. Format: Educ, instructional. News progmg 2 hrs wkly. Target aud: General. Spec prog: Black 20 hrs, jazz 5 hrs, Pol 5 hrs, Indo-Caribbean 10 hrs, sports 10 hrs wkly. ■ Dr. Kenneth L. Bates, gen mgr; Terence M. O'Driscoll, stn mgr & progmg dir; Troy Holman, chief opns; H. Cooper, chief engr. ■ WNYE-TV affil.

***WNYU-FM**—May 3, 1973: 89.1 mhz; 8.3 kw. Ant 256 ft. TL: N40 51 26 W73 54 48. Stereo. Hrs opn: 4 PM-1 AM, Mon-Fri. 721 Broadway, 11th Fl. (10003). (212) 998-1660. FAX: (212) 998-1652. Licensee: New York Univ. Net: ABC. Format: Educ, progsv rock. Spec prog: Dance mus 13 hrs, Black 5 hrs, reggae 2 hrs, oldies 3 hrs wkly. ■ Julie Canning, gen mgr; Gabe Shuldiner, prom mgr; Ida Hakkila, progmg dir; Paul Cheevers, mus dir & asst mus dir; John Reigart, chief engr.

WOR(AM)—Feb 22, 1922: 710 khz; 50 kw-U, DA-1. TL: N40 47 30 W74 05 38. 1440 Broadway (10018). (212) 642-4500. FAX: (212) 642-4486. Licensee: Buckley-WOR Broadcasting Corp. Group owner: Buckley Broadcasting Corp. (acq 12-89; $25.1 million; FTR 12-11-89). Net: ABC/E, NBC Talknet, MBS. Rep: McGavren Guild. Format: Info, news/talk. Target aud: 35-64. Spec prog: Relg 10 hrs wkly. ■ Rick Buckley, pres; Joseph Bilotta, exec vp; Bob Bruno, vp & gen mgr; Paul Stewart, opns mgr & chief engr; Vince Gardino, gen sls mgr; Tom Hantzarides, natl sls mgr; Martin Woolfe, prom dir & adv dir; Ed Walsh, progmg dir & news dir.

WPLJ(FM)—Listing follows WABC(AM).

WQCD(FM)—1945: 101.9 mhz; 5.3 kw. Ant 1,420 ft. TL: N40 42 23 W74 00 49 (CP: Ant 1,355 ft.). Stereo. Hrs opn: 24. Room 2812, 220 E. 42nd St. (10017). (212) 210-2800. FAX: (212) 210-2771. Licensee: Tribune New York Radio Inc. Group owner: Tribune Broadcasting Co. Rep: Christal. Format: Jazz. News staff one; news progmg 4 hrs wkly. Target aud: 25-54. ■ Ray Gardella, vp & gen mgr; Shirley Maldonado, opns mgr; Joe Loece, gen sls mgr; Russ King, mktg mgr; Steve Williams, mus dir; Doug O'Brian, news dir; Andy Bater, chief engr. ■ WPIX(TV) affil.

WQEW(AM)—Dec 3, 1936: 1560 khz; 50 kw-U, DA-2. TL: N40 42 59 W73 55 04. Stereo. 3rd Fl., 122 5th Ave. (10011). (212) 633-7600. FAX: (212) 633-7666. Licensee: Interstate Broadcasting Co. Group owner: New York Times Co. (acq 2-1-44). Net: BRN. Rep: Major Market. Wash atty: Koteen & Naftalin. Format: Standard music. News staff one; news progmg 14 hrs wkly. Target aud: 25-64; educated & affluent. Spec prog: Jazz 2 hrs wkly. ■ Warren G. Bodow, pres & gen mgr; Simona McCray, exec vp & gen sls mgr; Stephanie Feuer, prom mgr; Stan Martin, progmg dir; Larry Yount, news dir; Herb Squire, chief engr. ■ Rates: $240; 160; 190; 160.

WQXR-FM—Co-owned with WQEW(AM). Nov 8, 1939: 96.3 mhz; 7.8 kw h, 5.5 kw v. Ant 1,220 ft. TL: N40 44 54 W73 59 10. Stereo. Hrs opn: 24. Format: Class.

WQHT(FM)—1940: 97.1 mhz; 6.7 w. Ant 1,338 ft. TL: N40 44 54 W73 59 10. Stereo. 16th Fl., 1372 Broadway (10018). (212) 840-0097. FAX: (212) 391-7830. Licensee: Emmis Broadcasting Corp. of New York. Group owner: Emmis Broadcasting Corp. Rep: D & R Radio. Format: Top-40. News staff one; news progmg 6 hrs wkly. Target aud: General. ■ Judy Ellis, vp & gen mgr; Jeff Dinetz, gen sls mgr; Rocco Macri, mktg mgr & adv mgr; Steve Smith, progmg dir; Tracy Cloherty, mus dir; Lisa Glassberg, news dir; Jim McGivern, chief engr.

WQXR-FM—Listing follows WQEW(AM).

WRKS-FM—1941: 98.7 mhz; 7.8 kw-H, 5.5 kw-V. Ant 1,220 ft. TL: N40 44 54 W73 59 10 (CP: 5.9 kw, ant 1,361 ft.). Hrs opn: 24. Stereo. 1440 Broadway (10018). (212) 642-4300. FAX: (212) 768-7957. Licensee: Summit-New York Broadcasting Corp. Group owner: Summit Communications Group Inc. (acq 12-89; $50 million; FTR 12-11-89). Net: NBC the Source, Unistar. Rep: D & R Radio. Wash atty: Dow, Lohnes & Albertson. Format: Urban contemp. News staff 3. Target aud: 18-49. ■ Charles Warfield, vp & gen mgr; Michelle Massaro, gen sls mgr; Wendi Caplan, prom dir & adv dir; Vinny Brown, progmg dir; Toya Beasley, mus dir; Bob Slade, news dir; Milta McLean-Dennis, pub affrs dir; Harry Leon, chief engr.

***WSIA(FM)**—(Staten Island). Aug 31, 1981: 88.9 mhz; 10 w. Ant 650 ft. TL: N40 35 51 W74 06 53. Stereo. Hrs opn: 20. 2800 Victory Blvd. (10314). (718) 982-3050. Licensee: College of Staten Island. Format: Div, jazz, rock. ■ Greg Adamo, gen mgr; Jen Rubin, prom dir; Ed Hicks, progmg dir; Ollie Siebelt, mus dir; Tom Deignan, news dir; John Correa, chief engr.

WSKQ(AM)—See Newark, N.J.

WSKQ-FM—1950: 97.9 mhz; 7.6 kw H, 5.4 kw V. Ant 1,220 ft. TL: N40 44 54 W73 59 10. Stereo. 26 W. 56th St. (10019). (212) 541-9200. FAX: (212) 541-9236. Licensee: Spanish Broadcasting System of New York Inc. Group owner: Spanish Broadcasting System Inc. Net: Unistar. Rep: Herbert Groskin. Format: Spanish. Target aud: General. ■ Alfredo Alonzo, gen mgr & progmg dir; Bob August, stn mgr; Gary R'Nel, news dir; George Levites, chief engr.

WWRL(AM)—Aug 26, 1926: 1600 khz; 5 kw-U, DA-2. TL: N40 47 44 W74 03 18. 41-30 58th St., Woodside (11377). (718) 335-1600. FAX: (718) 651-9749. Licensee: Sydney L. Small (acq 9-28-89; $1.98 million; FTR 10-16-89). Net: American Urban, MBS, NBC. Wash atty: Rubin, Winston, Diercks, Harris & Cooke. Format: Gospel, Black, talk. Target aud: 24-54; African-American. ■ Sydney L. Small, pres; Vince Sanders, vp & gen mgr; Ian Wilson, rgnl sls mgr; Errol Williams, mktg dir & prom dir; Van Jay, progmg dir; Joe Hanneman, chief engr.

***WWRV(AM)**—May 1, 1972: 1330 khz; 5 kw-U, DA-1. TL: N40 32 45 W74 12 11. Hrs opn: 24. Box 2908, Radiovision Christiana Management., Paterson, NJ (07509). (201) 881-8700. FAX: (201) 881-8324. Licensee: Radio Vision Christiana Management Corp. (acq 4-25-89; $13 million; FTR 5-15-89). Format: Relg, Sp. Target aud: General. ■ David J. Greco, vp & gen mgr; Jose Lastra, sls dir; Jack Maldonado, prom dir; E. Riveria, progmg dir; Bob Janney, chief engr.

WXRK(FM)—Listing follows WZRC(AM).

WYNY(FM)—(Lake Success). 1940: 103.5 mhz; 5.4 kw. Ant 1,417 ft. TL: N40 42 43 W74 00 49. Stereo. Hrs opn: 24. 9th Fl., 1700 Broadway, New York (10019). (212) 237-2900. FAX: (212) 237-2682. Licensee: WYNY-FM Inc. Net: NBC. Rep: D & R Radio. Wash atty: Levanthal, Senter & Lerman. Format: Country. News staff one. Target aud: 25-54. ■ Perry L. Lewis, Lee Simonson (vice), chrs; Barry Mayo, pres; Nathan W. Pearson Jr., CFO; Steven B. Candullo, gen mgr; Frank J. Vulpi, gen sls mgr; Scott Lazare, natl sls mgr; Jim Furgeson, Dave Cervini, prom mgrs; Jim Furgeson, adv mgr; Fred Horton, progmg mgr; Theda Sandiford, mus dir; Shelli Sonstein, news dir & pub affrs dir; Alan Kirschner, chief engr.

WZRC(AM)—1925: 1480 khz; 5 kw-U, DA-2. TL: N40 50 42 W74 01 12. 600 Madison Ave. (10022). (212) 935-5170. FAX: (212) 832-9544. Licensee: Hit Radio. Group owner: Infinity Broadcasting Corp. (acq 9-15-81). Rep: Caballero. Format: Z-Rock. Target aud: 12-34. ■ Mel Karmazin, pres; Tom Chiusano, gen mgr; Ed Moir, gen sls mgr; Peggy Panosh, prom mgr; Mark Chernoff, progmg dir; Richard Herby, chief engr.

WXRK(FM)—Co-owned with WZRC(AM). 1951: 92.3 mhz; 7.6 kw h, 5.4 kw v. Ant 1,220 ft. TL: N40 44 54 W73 59 10. Stereo. Prog sep from AM. (212) 750-0550. Licensee: Sagittarius Broadcasting Corp. Net: ABC/R, NBC the Source. Rep: Torbet. Format: Classic rock. ■ Tom Chiusano, vp; Robert Benjamin, mus dir.

Newark

WACK(AM)—Oct 19, 1957: 1420 khz; 5 kw-D, 500 w-N, DA-2. TL: N43 01 08 W77 04 41. Hrs opn: 24. Box 1420, 187 Vienna Rd. (14513). (315) 331-1420. Licensee: Pembrook Pines Inc. (group owner; acq 11-1-72). Net: CNN, MBS, Unistar. Wash atty: Baraff, Koerner, Olender & Hochberg. Format: Adult contemp, sports. News progmg 14 hrs wkly. Target aud: 25-54; active, affluent, upscale audience. Spec prog: Farm 5 hrs wkly. ■ Robert Pfuntner, pres; John Tickner, gen mgr & prom mgr; Ted Bertot, opns mgr; John Derleth, rgnl sls mgr; Mike Keenan, progmg dir & mus dir; Heather Hosey, news dir; Nolan Stephany, chief engr. ■ Rates: $25; 20; 25; 15.

Newburgh

WBNR(AM)—See Beacon.

WGNY(AM)—Feb 25, 1933: 1200 khz; 10 kw-D, DA. TL: N41 29 57 W74 03 54 (CP: 2.5 kw, TL: N41 32 07 W74 06 41). Hrs opn: 24. Box 2307, 429 Little Britain Rd. (12550). (914) 561-2131. FAX: (914) 561-2138. Licensee: Sunrise Broadcasting of New York Inc. Group owner: Sunrise Broadcasting Corp. (acq 8-90; $10,000; with co-located FM; FTR 8-20-90. Net: Unistar, AP, CNN. Wash atty: Rosenman & Colin. Format: MOR, news/talk. News staff 4; news progmg 168 hrs wkly. Target aud: General. Spec prog: Relg 4 hrs wkly. ■ Joerg Klebe, pres; Robert A. DeFelice, vp, gen mgr & natl sls mgr; Terry Donovan, prom dir & progmg dir; Roger Clark, news dir; Nick Morreli, pub affrs dir; Shawn McGrath, chief engr. ■ Rates: $33; 31; 28; 18.

WGNY-FM—Oct 29, 1966: 103.1 mhz; 6 kw. Ant 275 ft. TL: N41 28 22 W74 08 22. Stereo. Prog sep from AM. Format: Adult contemp. News staff one. ■ Tricia Liggan, dev dir. ■ Rates: $43; 39; 42; 33.

Niagara Falls

WHLD(AM)—May 20, 1940: 1270 khz; 5 kw-D, 147 w-N, DA-2. TL: N43 00 18 W78 59 35. Hrs opn: 19. 2692 Staley Rd., Grand Island (14072). (716) 773-1270. FAX: (716) 773-1498. Licensee: Butler Communications Corp. (acq 5-13-80; grpsl; FTR 6-2-80). Net: AP, USA. Wash atty: Shaw & McClay. Format: Big band, ethnic, relg. News staff 2. Target aud: 35 plus. Spec prog: Black 18 hrs, Pol 19 hrs, Sp 15 hrs, Irish one hr, Greek one hr, It 8 hrs, Arab 15 hrs, Ukrainian 3 hrs wkly. ■ Paul Butler, pres & gen mgr; Eugene Hegedus, vp; Michael Brummer, opns dir & news dir; Bill Stachowiak, chief engr. ■ Rates: $18; 18; 15; 10.

WJJL(AM)—Dec 21, 1947: 1440 khz; 1 kw-D, 55 w-N. TL: N43 04 43 W79 00 40. Hrs opn: 6 AM-midnight. 1224 Main St. (14301). (716) 285-5795; (716) 284-1440. FAX:

(716) 284-6000. Licensee: M.J. Phillips Communications Inc. (acq 10-20-92; $225,000; FTR 11-23-92). Wash atty: Leonard S. Joyce. Format: Old time rock & roll. News staff one. News progmg 3 hrs wkly. Target aud: 25-54; baby boomers. Spec prog: Black 2 hrs, It 4 hrs, news/talk 5 hrs wkly. ■ M. John Phillips, Dennis Westberg, presdts; Susan Bertozzi, vp opns; Sal Paonessa, opns dir; Dennis Westberg, sls dir; Earl Morgan, adv dir; Mark Phillips, progmg dir; Kathy Denman, news dir; Bill Stackowiak, engrg dir. ■ Rates: $25; 20; 25; 20.

WJYE(FM)—See Buffalo.

WKSE(FM)—Jan 1, 1946: 98.5 mhz; 46 kw. Ant 420 ft. TL: N43 00 18 W78 59 35. Stereo. 695 Delaware Ave., Buffalo (14209). (716) 884-5101. FAX: (716) 882-2048. Licensee: Empire State Broadcasting Corp. Group owner: Price Communications Corp. Stations (acq 9-86; $2.35 million; FTR 7-7-86). Net: ABC. Rep: D & R Radio Wash atty: Mullin, Rhyne, Emmons & Topel. Format: CHR. News staff 3. Target aud: 12 plus. ■ Robert Price, pres; Al Green, stn mgr & vp sls; Emily Eberhardt, prom mgr; Sue O'Neil, mus dir; Tom Atkins, chief engr. ■ Rates: $150; 100; 100; 80.

North Creek

***WXLG(FM)**—Not on air, target date unknown: 89.9 mhz; 200 w. Ant 1,994 ft. TL: N43 40 22 W74 02 58. Hrs opn: 24. Rebroadcasts WSLU(FM) Canton 100%. St. Lawrence University, Romoda Dr., Canton (13617). Licensee: St. Lawrence University. Wash atty: Donald Martin. Format: Div. News staff 2; news progmg 35 hrs wkly. Target aud: General. Spec prog: Gospel, jazz, classical, folk, public affrs. ■ Ellen Rocco, gen mgr.

North Syracuse

WKRL(AM)—Aug 1, 1959: 1200 khz; 1 kw-U, DA-N. TL: N43 09 06 W76 07 58. Hrs opn: 24. Box 100, Syracuse (13217-3149). (315) 633-0047; (315) 735-4490. FAX: 1-800 909-0094. Licensee: Syracuse Broadcasting Corp. (acq 12-10-90; $1 million with co-located FM; FTR 1-7-91). Net: CNN; CBS. Rep: Eastman. Format: CNN Headline News, talk. News staff 10; news progmg 168 hrs wkly. Target aud: 25-54; white-collar executives. ■ Laurence Levite, pres; Bob Wood, vp, gen mgr, opns dir, progmg dir & mus dir; Paul Reilly, news dir. ■ Rates: $40; 40; 40; 30.

WKRL-FM—March 1972: 100.9 mhz; 6 kw. Ant 164 ft. TL: N43 09 06 W76 07 58. Stereo. Prog sep from AM. Format: Soft adult contemp. News progmg 2 hrs wkly. ■ Mimi Griswold, progmg dir. ■ Rates: $50; 50; 50; 30.

Norwich

WCHN(AM)—January 1953: 970 khz; 1 kw-D. TL: N42 30 24 W75 29 29. Hrs opn: 5 AM-1 AM. Box 552, 43 Hale St. (13815). (607) 334-2218. FAX: (607) 334-9867. Licensee: Cooney Communications Corp. (acq 9-17-81). Net: NBC. Format: Solid gold. News progmg 20 hrs wkly. Target aud: 25-54; baby boomers. Spec prog: Farm 2 hrs wkly. ■ Matthew T. Cooney Jr., pres & gen mgr; Kim Stevens, opns mgr & progmg dir; Matt Dowling, mus dir; Jeff Bishop, news dir; Ken Ruhland, chief engr.

WKXZ(FM)—Co-owned with WCHN(AM). 1961: 93.9 mhz; 26 kw. Ant 680 ft. TL: N42 32 52 W75 27 07. Stereo. Prog sep from AM. Net: NBC. Format: Adult contemp. News progmg 10 hrs wkly. Target aud: 25-54; growing families. Spec prog: Solid gold 4 hrs wkly.

Noyack

***WSUF(FM)**—Not on air, target date unknown: 89.9 mhz; 3 kw. Ant 165 ft. 5151 Park Ave., Fairfield, CT (06432). Licensee: Sacred Heart University Inc.

Nyack

***WNYK(FM)**—May 5, 1982: 88.7 mhz; 14 w. Ant 55 ft. TL: N41 04 59 W73 55 45. Nyack College, One South Blvd. (10960). (914) 358-1828; (914) 358-1710, ext. 510. Licensee: Nyack College. Format: Contemp Christian. ■ Mr. Schroeder, pres; Donald Jehlen, gen mgr.

Ogdensburg

WPAC(FM)—Listing follows WSLB(AM).

WPFE(FM)—Not on air, target date unknown: 98.7 mhz; 3 kw. Ant 328 ft. TL: N44 37 51 W75 24 47. Box 57, Clayton (13624). Licensee: Thomas Turck.

WSLB(AM)—1940: 1400 khz; 1 kw-U. TL: N44 42 21 W75 27 55. Box 239, 2315 Knox St. (13669). (315) 393-1100. FAX: (315) 393-6673. Licensee: The Wireless Works Inc. (group owner; acq 8-12-72). Net: NBC, NBC Talknet. Wash atty: Fisher, Wayland, Cooper & Leader. Format: Adult contemp. News staff 3; news progmg 20 hrs wkly. Target aud: 25-49; community connected, active, mature, responsible & responsive. ■ Patricia Tocatlian, pres & gen mgr; Rick DeFranco, opns mgr; Jim Stagnitti, sls dir; John Winter, natl sls mgr; John Astolfi, mus dir; Jack Miller, news dir; Roger Osterhout, chief engr. ■ Rates: $25; 20; 25; 20.

WPAC(FM)—Co-owned with WSLB(AM). July 1981: 92.7 mhz; 3 kw. Ant 310 ft. TL: N44 42 21 W75 27 55. Stereo. Prog sep from AM. Format: Top-40. News staff 3; news progmg 7 hrs wkly. Target aud: 18-34; young, educated, active, oriented to recreation, travel & self development. ■ Patricia C. Tocatlian, opns mgr; Tony DeFranko, mus dir. ■ Rates: $38; 38; 38; 38.

Olean

WHDL(AM)—February 1929: 1450 khz; 1 kw-U. TL: N42 04 39 W78 28 32. Hrs opn: 24. 3219 W. State Rd. (14760). (716) 372-0161. FAX: (716) 372-0164. Licensee: Arrow Communications of N.Y. Inc. (group owner; acq 8-21-89; $1 million with co-located FM; FTR 9-11-89). Net: ABC/C. Format: Oldies. News staff 2; news progmg 6 hrs wkly. Target aud: 25-54. ■ Paul Rothfuss, CEO; Dan Farr, pres & gen mgr; John Morton, gen sls mgr; Rich Stevenson, prom dir; Scott McKenzie, progmg dir; Nick Pircio, news dir; Doug Bushnell, chief engr.

WPIG(FM)—Co-owned with WHDL(AM). Feb 1, 1949: 95.7 mhz; 43 kw. Ant 740 ft. TL: N42 02 08 W78 26 47. Stereo. Hrs opn: 24. Prog sep from AM. Net: ABC. Format: Contemp country.

WMNS(AM)—May 20, 1957: 1360 khz; 1 kw-D, 30 w-N. TL: N42 06 24 W78 23 28. Hrs opn: 6 AM-1 AM. 118 W. Henley St. (14760). (716) 372-6660. FAX: (716) 372-8700. Licensee: Erin Communications Inc. (group owner; acq 12-17-79). Net: CBS. Rep: Mkt 4, Dome. Wash atty: Baraff, Koerner, Olender & Hochberg. Format: News/talk. News staff 2. Target aud: 35 plus. ■ Jack Murphy, pres; Elaine Murphy, gen mgr; Gary Nease, progmg dir; Kathleen Donovan, news dir; Jim Linn, chief engr.

WMXO(FM)—Co-owned with WMNS(AM). Nov 1, 1978: 101.5 mhz; 1.55 kw. Ant 405 ft. TL: N42 06 24 W78 23 28. Stereo. Prog sep from AM. Format: Adult contemp. Target aud: 25-54.

***WOLN(FM)**—March 1993: 91.3 mhz; 115 w. Ant 656 ft. Rebroadcasts WBFO(FM) Buffalo. c/o WBFO(FM), 3435 Main St., Buffalo (14214). (716) 829-2880. FAX: (716) 829-2277. Licensee: State Univ. of New York. Format: National public radio news and jazz. Target aud: Educated professionals. ■ Jennifer Roth, gen mgr.

WPIG(FM)—Listing follows WHDL(AM).

Oneida

WMCR(AM)—Sept 26, 1956: 1600 khz; 1 kw-D, 20 w-N. TL: N43 05 04 W75 41 35. 237 Genesee St. (13421). (315) 363-6050. Licensee: Warren Broadcasting Co. Inc. (acq 1-1-69). ■ Vivian Warren, pres; William Warren, vp.

WMCR-FM—September 1972: 106.3 mhz; 390 w. Ant 718 ft. TL: N43 02 48 W75 39 58.

Oneonta

WDOS(AM)—Dec 1, 1947: 730 khz; 1 kw-D. TL: N42 27 29 W75 00 20. Box 649, Rt. 23, Southside (13820). (607) 432-1500. FAX: (607) 432-8952. Licensee: Ultimate Broadcasting Network Inc. (acq 3-2-92; with co-located FM). Net: ABC/I. Wash atty: Haley, Bader & Potts. Format: Adult full svc, country, news/talk. News staff 2; news progmg 10 hrs wkly. Target aud: General; adult. Spec prog: Big band 7 hrs, nostalgia 2 hrs, relg 7 hrs wkly. ■ Janet Laytham, exec vp, gen mgr & progmg dir; George Wells, chief opns; Brian Levis, gen sls mgr; Bob Caims, news dir; Ken Ruhland, chief engr.

WSRK(FM)—Co-owned with WDOS(AM). Jan 26, 1970: 103.9 mhz; 850 w. Ant 520 ft. TL: N42 25 33 W75 02 47 (CP: 2.05 kw). Stereo. Hrs opn: 5 AM-midnight. Prog sep from AM. Format: Adult contemp. News progmg 5 hrs wkly. Target aud: Adults; 25-54 males & females. Spec prog: Class 2 hrs wkly.

***WONY(FM)**—1975: 90.9 mhz; 177 w. Ant -72 ft. TL: N42 28 02 W75 03 40. Hrs opn: 24. Alumni Hall, SUCO Campus (13820). (607) 436-2711. Licensee: State University of New York. Format: Educ, div. Spec prog: Black 3 hrs, class 3 hrs, jazz 6 hrs, Broadway 3 hrs, rock/metal 3 hrs, hardcore 3 hrs wkly. ■ Mike Goldstein, gen mgr & progmg dir.

***WRHO(FM)**—Jan 1, 1970: 89.7 mhz; 150 w. Ant 150 ft. TL: N42 27 24 W75 04 28. Stereo. Hrs opn: 18. Dewar Hall, Hartwick Colleges (13820). (607) 431-4555; (607) 431-4556. Licensee: Hartwick College. Net: AP. Format: AOR, classic rock, progressive. News progmg 4 hrs wkly. Target aud: General; teenagers, college students & young adults. Spec prog: Folk 5 hrs, jazz 4 hrs, Sp 2 hrs, world beat 2 hrs, children's 2 hrs wkly. ■ Michael Coniaris, CEO, pres & stn mgr; Otto Sonder, chmn; Suzanne Smith, vp sls & sls dir; Matt Cantore, mktg dir; Lynne Shepardson, prom dir & pub affrs dir; Marlee Fickes, prom mgr; Brad Parmerter, progmg dir; T. J. Allard, Erik Sprague, mus dirs; Sid Werthan, Noel Liddy, asst mus dirs; Lori Noel, news dir; John Van Ryn, engrg dir; Larry Nienart, chief engr.

***WSQC-FM**—Not on air, target date unknown: 91.7 mhz; 570 w-H, 2.3 kw-V. Ant 528 ft. TL: N42 25 27 W75 02 33. Box 3000, Binghamton (13902). (607) 729-0100. Licensee: WSKG Public Telecommunications Council. Wash atty: Dow, Lohnes & Albertson. Format: Class, news. ■ Michael J. Ziegler, pres; Judy V. Siggins, vp mktg; Katherine Bacon, prom mgr; Donna Hill, progmg mgr; Kelly Farewell, mus dir; Peter Iglinski, news dir; Charles F. Mulvey, vp engrg; Mark Polovick, chief engr.

WSRK(FM)—Listing follows WDOS(AM).

WZOZ(FM)—Nov 28, 1972: 103.1 mhz; 2 kw. Ant 360 ft. TL: N42 25 28 W75 04 36. 172 Main St. (13820). (607) 432-1030. FAX: (607) 432-4128. Licensee: The Wireless Works Inc. (group owner; acq 10-87). Net: AP. Rep: Katz. Format: Rock 'n roll. News staff 2; news progmg 8 hrs wkly. Target aud: 25-54; pop music fans. Spec prog: Jazz 3 hrs wkly. ■ Jeff Coffin, gen mgr; Ed Ryan, opns mgr & news dir.

Ossining

***WDFH(FM)**—March 1994: 90.3 mhz; 2 kw. Ant -7 ft. TL: N41 09 59 W73 51 22. Hrs opn: 24. 21 Brookside Ln., Dobbs Ferry (10522). Licensee: Westchester Council for Public Broadcasting Inc. Wash atty: Carter, Ledyard & Milbum. Format: Progsv, AOR, news. Target aud: 18-39. Spec prog: Pub affrs 20 hrs wkly. ■ Marc Sophos, chmn, pres, gen mgr, progmg dir & chief engr; Jonathan Shulman, Marvin Holverstott, vps; Robert C. Martin, opns mgr; Tom O'Hanlan, prom dir; Stephen Farenga, mus dir; Bryan Levine, asst mus dir; Jim Carney, news dir & pub affrs dir.

***WOSS(FM)**—Feb 22, 1972: 91.1 mhz; 10 w. Ant 100 ft. TL: N41 09 36 W73 51 38 (CP: 91.9 mhz, 16.42 w, ant 69 ft.). 29 S. Highland Ave. (10562). (914) 941-3512. Licensee: Board of Education, Union Free School District 1. Format: Div. Target aud: General. ■ Ken Ward, progmg dir; George Legg, chief engr.

Oswego

WBBS(FM)—See Fulton.

WGES(FM)—Listing follows WSGO(AM).

***WNYO(FM)**—Not on air, target date unknown: 88.9 mhz; 100 w. Ant 10 ft. TL: N43 27 07 W76 32 40. State University Plaza, Albany (12246). Licensee: State University of New York.

***WRVO(FM)**—Jan 6, 1969: 89.9 mhz; 24 kw. Ant 430 ft. TL: N43 25 14 W76 32 39. Stereo. State Univ. College, Lanigan Hall (13126). (315) 341-3690. Licensee: State Univ. of N.Y. Net: APR, NPR, AP. Format: News. Target aud: 25-55. Spec prog: Jazz 19 hrs wkly ■ William D. Shigley, gen mgr & stn mgr; Jane Kelly, opns dir; William Foley, dev dir; John B. Hurlbutt, progmg dir; Christopher Ulanowski, news dir; Robert Hanson, chief engr.

WSGO(AM)—1960: 1440 khz; 1 kw-D, 42 w-N. TL: N76 28 00 W43 24 56. Hrs opn: 24. Box 4045, Rt. 481 & Dutch Ridge Rd. (13126). (315) 343-1440. FAX: (315) 343-1449. Licensee: Gessner Communications Inc. Net: MBS. Format: Big band, nostalgia. News staff 2; news progmg 15 hrs wkly. Target aud: 40 plus. Spec prog: Barbershop one hr wkly, Pol one hr wkly. ■ Robert C. Gessner, pres; William Sutter, opns dir & chief engr; James Lowery, gen sls mgr; Karen Gessner, mktg dir & progmg dir; Steven Westcott, news dir. ■ Rates: $12; 8; 10; 6.

WGES(FM)—Co-owned with WSGO(AM). Mar 15, 1973: 105.5 mhz; 3 kw. Ant 450 ft. TL: N43 24 56 W76 27 54. Stereo. Hrs opn: 24. Dups AM 15%. Net: Unistar; MBS. Format: Adult contemp. Target aud: 24-50. ■ Susan Gessner-Carey, opns mgr.

WZOS(FM)—1991: 96.7 mhz; 3 kw. Ant 328 ft. TL: N63 29 12 W76 23 10. Stereo. Hrs opn: 24. Suite 211, 38 E. Bridge St. (13126-2122). (315) 342-9600. FAX: (315) 342-1202. Licensee: Binder-Johnson Broadcasting Inc.

Stations in the U.S.   New York

(acq 5-15-92; $234,000; FTR 6-8-92). Rep: Rgnl Reps. Format: Soft hits. News staff one; news progmg 6 hrs wkly. Target aud: 25-54; women 32-49. Spec prog: Religion 2 hrs, pub affrs 2 hrs wkly. ■ E.C. "Chip" Binder, pres & gen mgr; Christopher M. Johnson, vp; Tammy L. Briggs, opns mgr; Patricia North, gen sls mgr. ■ Rates: $14; 12; 12; 8.

WZZZ(AM)—See Fulton.

Owego

WEBO(AM)—July 27, 1957: 1330 khz; 5 kw-D, 50 w-N. TL: N42 06 19 W76 16 22. Hrs opn: 5 AM-10 PM. Executive Inn Bldg. 3, Suite 2, One Delaware Ave., Endicott (13760). (607) 748-9131. FAX: (607) 748-0061. Licensee: WEBO Radio Inc. (acq 9-28-93; with co-located FM; FTR 10-25-93). Rep: Eastman. Format: Classic Country. News staff 2. Target aud: 35 plus. Spec prog: Relg 6 hrs wkly. ■ Steven Gilinsky, CEO, pres, gen mgr, progmg dir & mus dir; Michael T. McKilligan, vp; Don Webb, vp sls; Don Perkins, vp engrg. ■ Rates: $10; 10; 10; 10.

WGRG(FM)—Co-owned with WEBO(AM). Sept 3, 1972: 101.7 mhz; 1.15 kw. Ant 450 ft. TL: N42 01 48 W76 12 33 (CP: 1 kw, ant 558 ft.). Stereo. Prog sep from AM. Format: Contemp hit. Target aud: 18-49; emphasis on females. ■ Rates: $20; 20; 20; 20.

Palmyra

WZXV(FM)—Not on air, target date unknown: 99.7 mhz; 3 kw. Ant 328 ft. TL: N43 06 14 W77 20 44. 1777 Rt. 332, Farmington (14425). (315) 597-9574. Licensee: Palmyra Broadcasting Corp. Format: Christian worship.

Patchogue

WALK(AM)—May 20, 1952: 1370 khz; 500 w-D, 102 w-N. TL: N40 45 14 W72 59 14. Hrs opn: 24. Box 230 (11772). (516) 475-5200. Licensee: American Media Inc. (group owner; acq 12-23-86). Net: AP. Rep: D & R Radio. Format: Adult contemp. ■ Alan Beck, pres; Bill Edwards, stn mgr; Bob Bernstein, gen sls mgr; Gene Michaels, progmg dir; Susan Murphy, news dir; Tony Gervasi, chief engr.

WALK-FM—December 1952: 97.5 mhz; 39 kw. Ant 544 ft. TL: N40 50 41 W73 02 01. Stereo. Dups AM 100%.

WBLI(FM)—Dec 1, 1958: 106.1 mhz; 25 kw. Ant 492 ft. TL: N40 50 32 W73 01 35. Stereo. 3090 Rt. 112, Medford (11763). (718) 895-9310; (516) 732-1061. FAX: (516) 732-3848. Licensee: WBLI Inc. Group owner: Beck-Ross Communications Inc. (acq 1-14-71). Net: AP. Rep: Katz. Format: Adult contemp. News staff one; news progmg 5 hrs wkly. Target aud: 25-54; adults, leaning towards women. ■ Martin F. Beck, chmn; Jim Champlin, pres; Herb Usenheimer, vp & gen mgr; Len T. Rothberg, vp opns; Samantha Baltzer, vp sls; Jessica Surbeck, prom dir; Bill Terry, vp progmg; Michael Larkin, mus dir; Ken Rhodes, news dir; John Bachman, chief engr. ■ Rates: $225; 215; 220; 125.

WLIM(AM)—Dec 1, 1951: 1580 khz; 10 kw-D, 37 w-N, DA-N. TL: N40 47 45 W72 59 32 (CP: 1 kw-D, 500 w-N, DA-N). Woodside Ave. (11772). (516) 475-1580. FAX: (516) 475-1627. Licensee: Long Island Music Broadcasting Corp. (acq 7-8-81). Net: ABC/D. Rep: Katz. Format: Big band. ■ Jack Ellsworth, pres & gen mgr; George Drake, vp & chief engr; Dorothy Ellsworth, opns mgr.

Patterson

WMJV-FM—Jan 17, 1982: 105.5 mhz; 1.5 kw. Ant 460 ft. TL: N41 31 18 W73 38 06. Stereo. Box 105.5, Rt. 292 (12563). (914) 878-3307; (203) 748-1055. Licensee: Tri-Valley Broadcasting Corp. (acq 6-16-86; grpsl; FTR 2-3-86). Format: Adult contemp. News staff 2; news progmg 4 hrs wkly. Target aud: 25-54. ■ Ronald Graiff, pres & chief engr; Winifred Graiff, gen mgr; Al Matthews, progmg dir; Janice Berliner, news dir.

Pattersonville

*WPGL(FM)—Not on air, target date unknown: 90.7 mhz; 30 w. Ant 653 ft. Box 777, Lake Katrine (12449). Licensee: Sound of Life Inc.

Paul Smiths

*WPSA(FM)—Jan 10, 1973: 89.1 mhz; 10 w. Ant 1,679 ft. TL: N44 26 04 W74 15 04 (CP: 98.3 mhz, ant -7 ft., TL: N44 26 06 W4 15 05). c/o Jeff Walter, Box 118 (12970). (518) 327-6891. FAX: (518) 327-6060. Licensee: Paul Smiths College of Arts & Sciences. Format: Educ, social, MOR. ■ Jeff Walter, gen mgr.

Pawling

WMJV-FM—See Patterson.

Peekskill

WLNA(AM)—1948: 1420 khz; 5 kw-D, 1 kw-N, DA-2. TL: N41 18 31 W73 55 00. Box 188 (10566). (914) 737-1124. FAX: (914) 737-0441. Licensee: Radio Terrace Inc. (acq 9-82; $4.2 million with co-located FM; FTR 9-13-82). Net: AP. Rep: Katz. Format: News, talk, adult contemp. News staff 4; news progmg 21 hrs wkly. Target aud: 25-54. ■ Gary B. Pease, pres; Jake Russell, vp & gen mgr; Steve Patron, opns mgr; Dave Papandrea, gen sls mgr; Tanya Hansen, news dir; Dan Kelleher, chief engr.

WHUD(FM)—Co-owned with WLNA(AM). Oct 24, 1958: 100.7 mhz; 50 kw. Ant 500 ft. TL: N41 20 18 W73 53 41. Prog sep from AM. Format: Soft adult contemp. News progmg 6 hrs wkly. Target aud: Upscale adults. Spec prog: Oldies 5 hrs wkly. ■ Jim Valle, opns mgr; Michael Bennett, news dir.

Penn Yan

WYLF(AM)—1988: 850 khz; 1 kw-D, 500 w-N. TL: N42 39 41 W77 07 14. Hrs opn: 6 AM-2 hrs after local sunset. 100 Main St. (14527). (315) 536-0850; (716) 394-2795. FAX: (315) 536-3299. Licensee: M.B. Communications (acq 10-88). Net: SMN. Wash atty: James Oyster. Format: Big band, nostalgia. Target aud: 35 plus. ■ Russ Kimble, pres, gen mgr & news dir; Don Radigan, opns mgr; Mary Ann Hurlburt, gen sls mgr; Dutch Wignall, prom dir; Dave Allison, progmg dir; James Travis, chief engr. ■ Rates: $14; 14; 14; na.

Peru

*WXLU(FM)—1991: 88.3 mhz; 200 w. Ant 1,109 ft. TL: N44 34 26 W73 40 29. Hrs opn: 24. Rebroadcasts WSLU(FM) Canton 100%. St. Lawrence University, Romoda Dr., Canton (13617). (315) 379-5356. Licensee: St. Lawrence University. Wash atty: Donald Martin. Format: Div. News staff 2; news progmg 35 hrs wkly. Target aud: General. Spec prog: Gospel, jazz, classical, folk, public affrs. ■ Ellen Rocco, gen mgr.

Plainview

*WPOB-FM—September 1973: 88.5 mhz; 125 w. Ant 150 ft. TL: N40 46 53 W73 27 36 (CP: Ant 259 ft. TL: N40 47 48 W73 27 44). 50 Kennedy Dr. (11803-4098). (516) 937-6375. Licensee: Plainview-Old Bethpage Central School District. Format: Educ, AOR. News progmg 2 hrs wkly. Target aud: General. ■ David Israel, opns dir; Steven Bielik, prom mgr; Adam Weinstock, progmg dir; Dan Steinbok, mus dir; Steve Bielik, pub affrs dir.

Plattsburgh

WAEE(FM)—Not on air, target date unknown: 103.5 mhz; 3 kw. Ant 328 ft. Box 100 A, Rt. One, Peru (12972). Licensee: John T. Ryan.

*WCFE-FM—Jan 14, 1991: 91.9 mhz; 380 w. Ant 852 ft. TL: N44 46 27 W73 36 48 (CP: 190 w, ant 2,200 ft.). Stereo. Hrs opn: 24. Box 617, One Sesame St. (12901). Licensee: Northeast N.Y. Public Telecommunications Council Inc. Net: NPR, APR. Wash atty: Dow, Lohnes & Albertson. Format: Jazz, class, news/talk. News staff one; news progmg 27 hrs wkly. Target aud: General; Clinton, Franklin, Essex Counties, NY and Burlington County, VT Spec prog: Div 20 hrs, folk 7 hrs, blues 4 hrs, drama 2 hrs, loc public affairs 10 hrs wkly. ■ Gerald K. Bates, pres & gen mgr; Bruce Longstreet, stn mgr; Earl Baucom (asst), chief opns; Jane Ashley, rgnl sls mgr; Bill Barton, mus dir; Marco Werman, news dir & pub affrs dir; Claude Pine, chief engr. ■ WCFE-TV affil.

WEAV(AM)—Feb 3, 1935: 960 khz; 5 kw-U, DA-2. TL: N44 34 27 W73 26 54. 3206 Rt. 9 (Lakeshore), Peru (12972). (518) 561-0960. Licensee: Plattsburgh Broadcasting Corp. Rep: Katz & Powell. Format: Adult contemp. News staff one. Target aud: General. ■ Judy Bissell, pres; George F. Bissell Jr., pres/vp; Tom Lavin, sls dir; Ben Everest, progmg dir & news dir; Bob Muschara, mus dir; Bob Broadwell, chief engr.

WGFB(FM)—Co-owned with WEAV(AM). Feb 3, 1960: 99.9 mhz; 100 kw. Ant 984 ft. TL: N44 46 13 W73 36 47. Stereo. Prog sep from AM. Format: Adult contemp.

WIRY(AM)—Jan 30, 1950: 1340 khz; 1 kw-U. TL: N44 41 49 W73 28 40. 301 Cornelia St. (12901). (518) 563-1340. FAX: (518) 563-1343. Licensee: WIRY Inc. (acq 1-1-59). Net: Westwood One. Rep: Roslin. Format: Adult contemp. News staff one; news progmg 3 hrs wkly. Target aud: 18 plus. ■ Donald L. Pelkey, pres; Annette E. Devan, gen mgr; Gordon R. Little, progmg dir & news dir; Robert E. Broadwell, chief engr. ■ Rates: $26; 23; 26; 23.

WNWX(AM)—June 15, 1968: 1070 khz; 5 kw-D. TL: N44 36 14 W73 27 18. 388 Shelburne Rd., Burlington, VT (05401); 115 Latham Mills Rd., Peru (12972). (802) 862-8255. FAX: (802) 862-8255. Licensee: Hometown Broadcasting Inc. (acq 10-9-90; $287,500; FTR 10-29-90). Net: ABC TalkRadio. Rep: New England. Format: News. News staff 6; news progmg 20 hrs wkly. Target aud: 25 plus; upscale, mature, information & issues oriented. Spec prog: Occult 8 hrs, financial 6 hrs, shop radio 3 hrs wkly. ■ Louis Manno, pres & progmg dir; Gregg Neavin, gen mgr; James O. Condon, news dir; Russ Kinsley, chief engr.

*WPLT(FM)—April 1979: 93.9 mhz; 10 w. Ant 156 ft. TL: N44 41 40 W73 28 00. Stereo. Hrs opn: 7 AM-2:30 PM. State Univ. of N.Y., Angell College Center 110 (12901). (518) 564-2727; (518) 564-3694. FAX: (518) 564-3994; (518) 564-3205. Licensee: State University of N.Y. Format: Alternative. Target aud: 18-24. Spec prog: Heavy metal 10 hrs, classic rock 12 hrs, Black 9 hrs, relg 3 hrs wkly. ■ Bruce McDonald, stn mgr; Danna Turner, opns dir; Leigh Gibson, gen sls mgr; Jennie B. Eckhaus, prom dir; Greg Kaulm, progmg dir; Matt Martens, mus dir; Jen Mesiano, asst mus dir & pub affrs dir; Jason Keller, Steve Migliore, news dirs; Bob Richter, chief engr.

Port Henry

WMNM(FM)—Sept 5, 1982: 92.1 mhz; 18 kw. Ant 10 ft. TL: N44 01 38 W73 28 54 Stereo. Hrs opn: 24. Box 150, Rt. 7 S., Middlebury, VT (05753). (802) 388-9236; (802) 388-9323. Licensee: Pro-Radio Inc. (acq 8-31-89; $520,000; FTR 9-25-89). Rep: New England. Wash atty: Mullin, Rhyne, Emmons, Topel. Format: Jazz. News staff one; news progmg 7 hrs wkly. Target aud: 25-54; upscale adults. ■ Mark Brady, pres, gen mgr, sls dir & prom dir; Mary Brady, exec vp; Jim Knight, progmg dir & mus dir; Neil Langer, chief engr. ■ Rates: $18; 14; 18; 12.

Port Jervis

WDLC(AM)—July 4, 1953: 1490 khz; 1 kw-U. TL: N41 21 49 W74 40 41. Hrs opn: 24. Box 920, 18 Neversink Dr. (12771). (914) 856-5185. FAX: (914) 856-4757. Licensee: Port Jervis Broadcasting Co. (acq 3-28-85). Format: MOR, C&W. News staff 2. Target aud: 25-54. ■ Robert I. Wein, pres & gen mgr; Eileen Wein, stn mgr; Cindy Nelson, progmg dir; Mark West, mus dir; Paul Lester, news dir; Bud Williamson, chief engr.

WTSX(FM)—Co-owned with WDLC(AM). Oct 30, 1970: 96.7 mhz; 3 kw. Ant 300 ft. TL: N41 22 24 W74 43 49. Stereo. Hrs opn: 24. Prog sep from AM. Format: Adult contemp. News staff 2. Target aud: 25-54 ■ Jack Wilder, pub affrs dir.

*WRPJ(FM)—Oct 1991: 88.9 mhz; 500 w. Ant 590 ft. TL: N41 25 36 W74 34 45. Stereo. Rebroadcasts WFGB(FM) Kingston 100%. Box 777, 199 Tuytenbridge Rd., Lake Katrine (12449). (914) 336-6199. FAX: (914) 336-7205. Licensee: Sound of Life Inc. Format: Relg. News progmg 3 hrs wkly. Target aud: General. Spec prog: Black one hr, Sp one hr wkly. ■ Dennis Newcomer, pres.

WTSX(FM)—Listing follows WDLC(AM).

Potsdam

WPDM(AM)—Apr 30, 1955: 1470 khz; 1 kw-D. TL: N44 38 38 W75 03 32. Box 348 (13676). (315) 265-5510. FAX: (315) 265-4040. Licensee: St. Lawrence Radio Inc. Net: ABC/I, AP. Wash atty: Cohn & Marks. Format: Country. News progmg 10 hrs wkly. Target aud: 25 plus. ■ Jane A. Kyle, pres; William Solomon, vp & gen mgr; Derry Loucks, gen sls mgr; Jim Hill, progmg dir & mus dir; Robert LaRue, news dir; Charlie Lyons, chief engr. ■ Rates: $18.55; 10.65; 13.85; 10.35.

WSNN(FM)—Co-owned with WPDM(AM). Oct 15, 1968: 99.3 mhz; 3 kw. Ant 155 ft. TL: N44 38 38 W75 03 32. Prog sep from AM. Format: Adult contemp. News staff one; news progmg 10 wkly. Target aud: 25-54. ■ Rates: $18.55; 10.65; 10.65; 10.35.

*WTSC-FM—Nov 3, 1963: 91.1 mhz; 700 w. Ant 155 ft. TL: N44 39 45 W75 00 07. Stereo. Hamlin-Powers Bldg., Clarkson University (13699). (315) 268-7658. Licensee: Knight & Day Inc. Net: ABC/FM. Format: Div. ■ Frank Durango, gen mgr.

New York Directory of Radio

Poughkeepsie

WEOK(AM)—October 1949: 1390 khz; 5 kw-D, DA. TL: N41 43 14 W73 54 29. Hrs opn: 24. Box 416 (12602-0416). (914) 471-1500. FAX: (914) 454-1204. Licensee: Chrismol Corp. (acq 1971). Net: ABC/D. Format: MOR. News staff 3. Target aud: 35 plus. Spec prog: Farm 2 hrs, Pol one hr, relg 2 hrs, talk 5 hrs, Sinatra spec 2 hrs wkly. ■ Rob Dyson, pres; Michael J. Harris, exec vp & gen mgr; Stan Beinstein, gen sls mgr; Victor Goodman, natl sls mgr; Chris Lucas, prom dir & progmg dir; Lane Bajardi, news dir; Marc Stewart, pub affrs dir; Dave Groth, chief engr.

WPDH(FM)—Co-owned with WEOK(AM). December 1962: 101.5 mhz; 4.5 kw. Ant 1,540 ft. TL: N41 43 09 W73 59 47. Stereo. Hrs opn: 24. Prog sep from AM. Net: ABC/R. Format: AOR. Spec prog: Metal shop 2 hrs, flashback 2 hrs wkly. ■ Scott Carlin, prom mgr; Bill Palmeri, progmg dir; Greg O'Brien, mus dir.

WKIP(AM)—June 1940: 1450 khz; 1 kw-U, DA-D. TL: N41 42 18 W73 53 16. Box 1450 (12602); Tucker Dr. (12603). (914) 471-2300. FAX: (914) 471-2683. Licensee: WKIP Broadcasting Corp. (acq 4-26-86; $1.1 million; FTR 2-17-86). Net: ABC/I, ABC TalkRadio, Unistar, AP, MBS, NBC Talknet. Rep: Banner. Wash atty: Cohn & Marks. Format: News/talk. News staff one; news progmg 30 hrs wkly. Target aud: 35-64. ■ Richard D. Novik, pres; Steve Berner, gen mgr & vp sls; Joe Ryan, vp opns, prom mgr & progmg dir; Larry Matarasso, news dir; Bill Draper, chief engr. ■ Rates: $40; 30; 35; 25.

WPDH(FM)—Listing follows WEOK(AM).

***WRHV(FM)**—Sept 5, 1990: 88.7 mhz; 230 w. Ant 1,289 ft. TL: N41 43 09 W73 59 47. Box 17, Schenectady (12301). (518) 356-1700. FAX: (518) 356-0173. Licensee: WMHT Educational Telecommunications Inc. Net: APR. Wash atty: Schwartz, Woods & Miller. Format: Class. News progmg 3 hrs wkly. Target aud: 35-54; class mus lovers. Spec prog: Jazz 2 hrs, ethnic one hr wkly. ■ W. Donn Rogosin, pres & gen mgr; Glenda Bullock, prom mgr; Karen Perretta, progmg dir; Derk Van Rijsewijk, chief engr.

WRNQ(FM)—June 30, 1989: 92.1 mhz; 2.15 kw. Ant 384 ft. TL: N41 40 36 W73 49 14. Stereo. Hrs opn: 24. Box 9200, Tucker Dr. (12602). (914) 471-2300. Licensee: Dutchess Communications Corp. (acq 12-19-89; $49,000; FTR 1-8-90). Net: Unistar. Rep: Banner. Wash atty: Cohn & Marks. Format: Adult contemp. News staff 2. Target aud: 25-54; women 30-49. ■ Richard Novik, pres; Donald Verity, vp & gen mgr; John Steffanci, prom mgr; Joe Ryan, progmg dir; Mary Kaye Dolan, news dir; Bill Draper, chief engr. ■ Rates: $45; 30; 40; 25.

WSPK(FM)—Dec 7, 1947: 104.7 mhz; 7.4 kw. Ant 1,250 ft. TL: N41 29 19 W73 56 52. Stereo. Box 1703 (12601); Box 511, 475 South Ave., Beacon (12508). (914) 462-5800; (914) 831-8000. FAX: (914) 838-2109. Licensee: Beacon Broadcasting Corp. (group owner; acq 9-11-70). Net: ABC/FM. Rep: Banner. Wash atty: Rothman Gordon. Format: CHR. News staff 2. Target aud: 18-44. Spec prog: Black one hr wkly. ■ Robert E. Lessner, CEO; Alford H. Lessner, pres & gen mgr; Robert A. Outer, vp & gen sls mgr; Joseph P. Daily, vp opns; Robert Corsino, natl sls mgr; Maggie Carbaugh, rgnl sls mgr; Stew Schantz, progmg dir; Brett Richards, mus dir; Dawn Spicer, news dir; David Rozek, engrg dir & chief engr. ■ Rates: $92; 69; 92; 69.

***WVKR-FM**—1976: 91.3 mhz; 1 kw. Ant 85 ft. TL: N41 41 13 W73 53 43 (CP: 3.7 kw, ant 820 ft.). Stereo. Hrs opn: 24. Box 166, Vassar College (12601). (914) 437-5475. FAX: (914) 437-7187. Licensee: Vassar College. Format: Div, jazz, progsv, Black. News staff 10; news progmg 5 hrs wkly. Target aud: General. Spec prog: Classical 3 hrs, folk 5 hrs, Pol 5 hrs, Sp 3 hrs, techno 8 hrs, metal 3 hrs, new age 6 hrs wkly. ■ Kristin Romey, gen mgr; Scott Martin, progmg dir; Blair Carty, Ben Goldberg, mus dirs; Matt Donovan, Lee Swedowski, asst mus dirs; Dave Ludmar, Nomi Ernst, news dirs; Lisa Buckley, pub affrs dir.

Pulaski

WSCP(AM)—See Sandy Creek-Pulaski.

WSCP-FM—January 1987: 101.7 mhz; 2.5 kw. Ant 364.1 ft. TL: N43 36 32 W75 58 23. Box 226, 7890 N. Jefferson St. (13142). (315) 298-6505. FAX: (315) 298-6181. Licensee: Wheat Hill Broadcasters Inc. Format: C&W. ■ Linda Braunitzer, gen mgr; Fred Lewis Cantey, progmg dir; Craig Cantey, mus dir; Gail Rice, news dir.

Ravena

WEMX(FM)—Not on air, target date unknown: 94.5 mhz; 3 kw. Ant 328 ft. TL: N42 33 23 W73 52 05. 4433 Wells Parkway, University Park, MD (20782). Licensee: WRAV Inc. (acq 1-23-92).

Remsen

WADR(AM)—Dec 12, 1966: 1480 khz; 5 kw-D, 50 w-N. TL: N43 19 31 W75 10 29. Hrs opn: 24. Rebroadcasts WRNY(AM) Rome 100%. Box 67, Muck Rd., Rome (13440). (315) 336-5600. FAX: (315) 336-4030. Licensee: Adirondack Broadcasting Inc. (acq 1-13-93; $350,000 with co-located FM; FTR 2-8-93). Net: MBS, Unistar. Rep: Eastman. Wash atty: Baraff, Koerner, Olender & Hochberg. Format: Adult standards, sports. News progmg 3 hrs wkly. Target aud: 35-64. ■ Norma Eilenberg, pres; Jack Moran, gen mgr & natl sls mgr; Ginny Kukulech, rgnl sls mgr; Dave Silvers, progmg dir; Larry Fiorenza, news dir; Kerry Jayne, chief engr. ■ Rates: $10.25; 10.25; 10.25; na.

WUUU(FM)—Co-owned with WADR(AM). Dec 1, 1982: 93.5 mhz; 6 kw. Ant 300 ft. TL: N43 19 31 W75 10 29. Stereo. Prog sep from AM. Format: Oldies. News progmg one hr wkly. Target aud: 25-54.

Rensselaer

WQBK(AM)—Dec 3, 1961: 1300 khz; 5 kw-U, DA-2. TL: N42 35 23 W73 44 37. Box 1300, Albany (12201). (518) 462-5555. FAX: (518) 462-0784. Licensee: Maximum Media Inc. Net: CBS, ABC TalkRadio, NBC Talknet, Wall Street. Rep: Banner. Format: News/talk. News staff 2. Target aud: 35 plus. Spec prog: Auto repair one hr, money mgmt 3 hrs, real estate one hr wkly. ■ William P. Hunt, exec vp & vp; Dawn Weiss, prom mgr; William Brady, progmg dir; Richard Dalbec, chief engr.

WQBK-FM—Dec 1, 1972: 103.9 mhz; 3 kw. Ant 300 ft. TL: N42 35 06 W73 46 29 (CP: 6 kw). Stereo. Hrs opn: 24. Prog sep from AM. Smultz Rd., Glenmont (12077). Net: CBS Spectrum, Unistar, NBC, Daynet, NBC Talknet. Format: Classic rock, AOR. News progmg 4 hrs wkly. Target aud: 18-49. Spec prog: Jazz 2 hrs wkly. ■ Jim Sussman, progmg dir.

Riverhead

WRCN-FM—Listing follows WRHD(AM).

WRHD(AM)—Aug 8, 1963: 1570 khz; 1 kw-D, 500 w-N, DA-2. TL: N40 54 48 W72 39 16. Box 666, 72 W. Main St. (11901). (516) 727-1570. FAX: (516) 727-8629. Licensee: East Shore Broadcasting Corp. (acq 9-13-89; $5.2 million; with co-located FM; FTR 10-2-89). Net: SMN. Rep: Katz. Wash atty: Haley, Bader & Potts. Format: Country. News staff one; news progmg 12 hrs wkly. Target aud: 25-64. Spec prog: Pub affrs 3 hrs wkly. ■ Gary J. Starr, pres; David Feinblatt, gen mgr; Matt Mangas, opns mgr; Dick Newman, gen sls mgr; Dianne Polite, prom dir; Al Hobbs, progmg mgr; Kevin Thompson, mus dir; Bob Clifford, news dir; Bob Anderson, chief engr. ■ Rates: $30; 30; 30; 30.

WRCN-FM—Co-owned with WRHD(AM). Aug 14, 1962: 103.9 mhz; 1.5 kw. Ant 466 ft. TL: N40 51 07 W72 45 55 Stereo. Prog sep from AM. Net: Unistar. Format: Rock/AOR. News progmg 4 hrs wkly. Target aud: 18-49. ■ Matt Mangus, progmg dir; Samantha Stevens, asst mus dir; Bob Clifford, pub affrs dir. ■ Rates: $125; 125; 125; 125.

WRIV(AM)—June 1955: 1390 khz; 1 kw-D, 64 w-N. TL: N40 55 22 W72 38 52. Hrs opn: 6 AM-midnight. Box 1390 (11901). (516) 727-1390. FAX: (516) 369-WRIV. Licensee: Crystal Coast Communications (acq 10-87). Net: ABC/I. Rep: Savalli. Format: MOR. News staff one; news progmg 14 hrs wkly. Target aud: 35-64. Spec prog: Farm 8 hrs, Pol 4 hrs wkly. ■ Bruce Tria, gen mgr; Bob Fanning, news dir; Robert Makson, chief engr. ■ Rates: $28; 22; 26; 18.

Rochester

WBBF(AM)—Listing follows WBEE-FM.

WBEE-FM—Feb 1961: 92.5 mhz; 50 kw. Ant 500 ft. TL: N43 10 37 W77 28 39. Stereo. 500-B Forman Bldg. (14604). (716) 423-2900. FAX: (716) 325-5139. Licensee: WBBF Inc. Group owner: Heritage Media Corp. (acq 12-86; grpsl; FTR 11-17-86). Net: Unistar. Rep: Katz. Wash atty: Akin, Gump, Auer & Feld. Format: Country. News staff 2; news progmg 4 hrs wkly. Target aud: 25-54. ■ William M. Cloutier, pres & gen mgr; Bob Barnett, opns mgr & progmg dir; Gloria Smith, gen sls mgr; Mary Ellen Marshall, news dir; David Lane, chief engr. ■ Rates: $200; 150; 150; 100.

WBBF(AM)—Co-owned with WBEE-FM. 1947: 950 khz; 1 kw-U, DA-2. TL: N43 06 25 W77 35 51. Hrs opn: 24. Prog sep from FM. Format: Nostalgia. News staff one; news progmg 3 hrs wkly. Target aud: 35 plus; high income empty-nesters. ■ Todd Blide, progmg dir. ■ Rates: $40; 40; 40; 25.

***WBER(FM)**—(Henrietta). 1974: 90.5 mhz; 2.5 kw. Ant 417 ft. TL: N43 02 00 W77 25 11 (CP: 50 kw). Stereo. 2596 Baird Rd., Penfield (14526). (716) 381-4353. FAX: (716) 381-9074. Licensee: Cooperative Educational Services (BOCES), Monroe No. 1. Format: Alternative rock, Spanish. News staff one; news progmg 5 hrs wkly. Target aud: 18-24. Spec prog: Heavy metal 4 hrs wkly. ■ Andrew Chinnici, gen mgr & progmg dir; Edward Zebrowski, opns dir & news dir; Al Holmes, chief engr.

WCMF-FM—June 9, 1960: 96.5 mhz; 50 kw. Ant 457 ft. TL: N43 08 07 W77 35 02. Stereo. Suite 300, 3136 S. Winton Rd. (14623-2906). (716) 272-7260. FAX: (716) 272-7892. Licensee: American Radio Systems License Corp. Group owner: American Radio Systems (acq 9-15-93; with co-located AM; FTR 10-4-93). Format: AOR. News staff one; news progmg 10 hrs wkly. ■ Steve Dodge, pres; Suzanne McDonald, gen mgr; Tish Robinson, gen sls mgr; Stan Main, progmg dir; Rich Gaenzler, news dir; Jerry Whitney, chief engr.

WCMF(AM)—February 1947: 990 khz; 5 kw-D, 2.5 kw-N, DA-2. TL: N43 13 54 W77 52 00. Dups FM 100%.

WDKX(FM)—Apr 6, 1974: 103.9 mhz; 800 w. Ant 540 ft. TL: N43 09 17 W77 36 16. Stereo. Hrs opn: 24. 683 E. Main St. (14605). (716) 262-2050. FAX: (716) 262-2626. Licensee: Monroe County Broadcasting Co. Ltd. Wash atty: Mullin, Rhyne, Emmons & Topel. Format: Urban contemp. News staff 2; news progmg 6 hrs wkly. Target aud: General. Spec prog: Jazz 4 hrs. ■ Andrew A. Langston, CEO, gen mgr & gen sls mgr; Gloria M. Langston, pres, stn mgr & pub affrs dir; Andre Marcel, exec vp, opns dir, prom dir, progmg dir & mus dir; Camilla Maas, sr vp; Tom Gabruk, news dir; Mike Bostic, chief engr.

WHAM(AM)—July 11, 1922: 1180 khz; 50 kw-U. TL: N43 04 55 W77 43 30. 207 Midtown Plaza (14604). (716) 454-4884. FAX: (716) 454-5081. Licensee: WVOR Inc. Group owner: The Lincoln Group Ltd. Net: CBS. Format: Adult contemp. Spec prog: Farm 5 hrs wkly. ■ Albert Wertheimer Jr., pres; Jack Palvino, exec vp & vp; Jack Murphy, gen mgr; Jeff Howlett, stn mgr; Bob Longo, opns mgr & news dir; Arnie Rothschild, vp sls & vp mktg; Arnie Rothschild, gen sls mgr; Craig Kingcaid, chief engr.

WVOR-FM—Co-owned with WHAM. 1962: 100.5 mhz; 50 kw. Ant 480 ft. TL: N43 02 00 W77 25 17. Stereo. Box 40340, 1700 Midtown Tower (14604). (716) 454-3942. Net: AP. Rep: McGavren Guild. ■ Arnie Rothschild, gen sls mgr; Craig Kincaid, chief engr.

WHTK(AM)—Nov 22, 1947: 1280 khz; 5 kw-U, DA-N. TL: N43 05 54 W77 35 00. Hrs opn: 24. 30 N. Union St. (14607-1345). (716) 454-2600. FAX: (716) 454-1779. Licensee: Kiss Limited Partnership. Group owner: Pyramid Broadcasting (acq 5-90; FTR 5-21-90). Rep: Major Mkt. Wash atty: David Tillotson. Format: Talk. Target aud: 18-54; women. ■ Bill Schoening, gen mgr; Armand Miale, rgnl sls mgr; John Irey, progmg dir; Cat Collins, mus dir; Joan Bradenburg, news dir.

WPXY-FM—Co-owned with WHTK(AM). Sept 14, 1959: 97.9 mhz; 50 kw. Ant 456 ft. TL: N43 08 08 W77 35 02. Stereo. Format: CHR.

***WIRQ(FM)**—January 1960: 94.3 mhz; 10 w-H. Ant 485 ft. TL: N43 12 59 W77 35 46. Stereo. Hrs opn: 1 PM-8 PM Mon-Fri, Sept-June. 260 Cooper Rd. (14617). (716) 336-3066; (716) 342-6468. Licensee: Board of Education, Irondequoit Central School District. Format: Progsv mus. News progmg one hr wkly. Target aud: 13-45. Spec prog: Top 35 count-down 3 hrs, Progsv pioneers 3 hrs, techno 3 hrs wkly. ■ Greg Moore, gen mgr.

WJZR(FM)—Jan 22, 1993: 105.9 mhz; 3 kw. Ant 180 ft. TL: N43 09 35 W77 34 44. Stereo. Hrs opn: 24. Fedder Industrial Park, 1237 E. Main St. (14609). (716) 288-5020. FAX: (716) 288-5165. Licensee: North Coast Radio Inc. Net: AP. Wash atty: Cohn & Marks. Format: Adult contemp, jazz, urban contemp. News progmg 14 hrs wkly. Target aud: 25 plus. Spec prog: News review one hr wkly. ■ Lee Rust, pres, stn mgr & progmg mgr; Dawn Carmell, gen sls mgr; Eric Moon, asst mus dir; Denise Gaines, pub affrs dir; Michael Rostic, engrg dir. ■ Rates: $50; 30; 50; 30.

WKLX(FM)—1939: 98.9 mhz; 50 kw. Ant 560 ft. TL: N43 10 14 W77 40 23. Stereo. 500 B. Forman Bldg. (14604). (716) 423-2900. FAX: (716) 325-5139. Licensee: WBBF Inc. Group owner: Heritage Media Corp. (acq 7-20-93; $4.3 million; FTR 8-9-93). Net: Unistar. Rep: Katz. Wash atty: Akin, Gump, Haver & Feld. Format: Oldies. News

Stations in the U.S.   New York

staff one. Target aud: 25-54; upscale. ■ William M. Cloutier, pres & gen mgr; Gloria Smith, gen sls mgr; Harlan Spollio, prom dir; Al Brock, progmg dir; Pete Gallivan, news dir; David Lane, chief engr. ■ Rates: $150; 150; 150; 75.

WPXY-FM—Listing follows WHTK(AM).

WRMM-FM—Nov 14, 1966: 101.3 mhz; 27 kw. Ant 640 ft. TL: N43 10 14 W77 40 23. Stereo. Suite 300, 3136 S. Winton Rd. (14623-2906). (716) 272-7260. FAX: (716) 272-7892. Licensee: American Radio Systems License Corp. Group owner: American Radio Systems (acq 9-15-93; FTR 10-4-93). Format: Soft rock. News staff one; news progmg 2 hrs wkly. Target aud: 25-54; baby boomers. ■ Steve Dodge, pres; Suzanne McDonald, gen mgr; Tish Robinson, gen sls mgr; Stan Main, progmg dir; Rich Gaenzler, news dir; Jerry Whitney, chief engr.

WRQI(FM)—See South Bristol Township.

***WRUR-FM**—Mar 6, 1966: 88.5 mhz; 970 w. Ant 120 ft. TL: N43 07 40 W77 37 49 (CP: 2 kw, ant 232 ft.). Stereo. CPU Box 277356, River Station (14627-7356). (716) 275-6400. Licensee: Univ. of Rochester Broadcasting Corp. Net: AP. Format: Class, new music, jazz. Target aud: General. Spec prog: Black 13 hrs, folk 15 hrs, Sp 3 hrs wkly. ■ Richard P. Miller Jr., pres; Brian J. Thompson, vp; Bernard Sklanka, gen mgr & pub affrs dir; John F. Andres, opns dir; James Venetsanakos, sls dir & adv dir; Jessica Cleaver, prom dir; Michele Locurcio, progmg dir; Christopher Margeson, asst mus dir; Ethan Corona, news dir; Marc Spencer, chief engr.

WVOR-FM—Listing follows WHAM.

WWWG(AM)—Sept 11, 1925: 1460 khz; 5 kw-U, DA-N. TL: N43 06 34 W77 34 20. 2 Cambridge, 1840 S. Winton (14618). (716) 461-9212. FAX: (716) 461-0348. Licensee: Brandon Radio Inc. Group owner: American General Media (acq 1977). Format: Relg. Spec prog: Black 18 hrs, Ger 2 hrs, It 4 hrs, Sp 3 hrs wkly. ■ Anthony Brandon, pres; Christopher Scribani, gen mgr & gen sls mgr; Jerry Whitney, chief engr.

***WXXI(AM)**—1936: 1370 khz; 5 kw-U, DA-N. TL: N43 06 01 W77 34 23. Box 21, 280 State St. (14601). (716) 325-7500. FAX: (716) 258-0339. Licensee: WXXI Public Broadcasting Council. Net: NPR. Format: News/talk, jazz. ■ William J. Pearce, pres & gen mgr; Adele McCarthy, prom dir; Ernest Lowell, progmg mgr; Alex Crichton, mus dir; Paul Baker, news dir; John Bell, chief engr.

***WXXI-FM**—December 1974: 91.5 mhz; 45 kw. Ant 400 ft. TL: N43 08 07 W77 35 03. Stereo. Hrs opn: 24. Prog sep from AM. Net: AP, APR. Wash atty: Schwartz, Woods & Miller. Format: Class. ■ Ruth Phinney, progmg mgr; Laurie Dishman, mus dir. ■ WXXI-TV affil.

WYSL(AM)—See Avon.

Rome

WFRG-FM—See Utica.

WKDY(FM)—Listing follows WRNY(AM).

WODZ(AM)—September 1946: 1450 khz; 1 kw-U. TL: N43 12 18 W75 28 48. Hrs opn: 24. 6490 Thomas Rd., Oriskany (13424). (315) 736-5225. Licensee: WFRG Inc. Format: Oldies. ■ Christine Hillard, gen mgr.

WODZ-FM—August 1968: 96.1 mhz; 7.4 kw. Ant 600 ft. TL: N43 02 14 W75 26 40. Stereo. Hrs opn: 24. Dups AM 100%. Spec prog: Farm show.

WRNY(AM)—Oct 12, 1959: 1350 khz; 500 w-D, 60 w-N. TL: N43 12 18 W75 29 08. Hrs opn: 24. Box 67, Muck Rd. (13440). (315) 336-5600; (315) 733-0428. FAX: (315) 336-4030. Licensee: Promedia Communications Inc. (acq 3-15-69). Net: MBS, SMN, ESPN. Rep: Eastman. Wash atty: Baraff, Koerner, Olender & Hochberg. Format: Sports, adult standards. News staff one. Target aud: 25 plus. Spec prog: Black 3 hrs wkly. ■ Norma Eilenberg, pres; Jack Moran, gen mgr; Dave Silvers, opns mgr; Ginny Kukulech, gen sls mgr; Dave McGrath, prom mgr; Phil Allen, progmg dir; Larry Fiorenza, news dir; Kerry Jayne, chief engr.

WKDY(FM)—Co-owned with WRNY(AM). May 1, 1983: 102.5 mhz; 27 kw. Ant 649 ft. TL: N43 02 14 W75 26 40. Stereo. Hrs opn: 24. Prog sep from AM. FAX: (315) 831-2605. Net: Unistar. Format: Hot country. News staff one. Target aud: 25-54. Spec prog: Pub affrs one hr wkly. ■ Jack Moran, natl sls mgr; Ginny Kukulech, rgnl sls mgr; Phil Allen, mus dir; Larry Fiorenza, asst mus dir.

WRUN(AM)—See Utica.

Rotterdam

WTRY-FM—Dec 15, 1986: 98.3 mhz; 3 kw. Ant 328 ft. TL: N42 44 43 W74 04 10. Stereo. Hrs opn: 24. 1054 Troy-Schenectady Rd., Latham (12110). (518) 785-9800. FAX: (518) 785-0211. Licensee: Cap-Town Broadcasting Inc. Group owner: The Griffin Group/Broadcast Division (acq 6-14-93; $650,000; FTR 7-5-93). Net: Unistar. Rep: McGavren Guild. Wash atty: Arent, Fox, Kintner, Plotkin & Kahn. Format: Oldies. Target aud: 35-54. ■ Merv Griffin, pres; Robert Ausfeld, exec vp & gen mgr.

Sag Harbor

WLNG(AM)—Aug 13, 1963: 1600 khz; 500 w-D. TL: N40 59 53 W72 18 21. Box 2000 (11963). (516) 725-2300. Licensee: Mainstreet Broadcasting Co. Net: MBS. Rep: Mkt 4. Format: Oldies, top-40. ■ Paul Sidney, pres, gen mgr & progmg dir.

WLNG-FM—Apr 13, 1969: 92.1 mhz; 5.3 kw. Ant 350 ft. TL: N40 58 19 W72 20 54. Dups AM 100%

St. Bonaventure

***WSBU(FM)**—April 13, 1975: 88.3 mhz; 165 w. Ant 90 ft. TL: N42 04 45 W78 29 07. Stereo. Hrs opn: 24. Box O (14778). (716) 375-2307. FAX: (716) 375-2583. Licensee: St. Bonaventure University. Net: AP, Westwood One. Format: AOR. News progmg 6 hrs wkly. Target aud: General; primarily students. Spec prog: Jazz 2 hrs, class 2 hrs, folk one hr, relg one hr, reggae one hr, progressive 10 hrs, top-40 4 hrs, sports 3 hrs wkly. ■ Sister Alice Gallin, pres; Tim Sauda, stn mgr.

Salamanca

WGGO(AM)—June 18, 1957: 1590 khz; 5 kw-D. TL: N42 10 24 W78 41 07. Box 62 (14779). (716) 945-1515. Licensee: Michael Washington Jr. and Mary E. Washington (acq 10-14-92; $550,000 with co-located FM; FTR 11-23-92). Net: ABC/I. Format: Adult contemp, oldies. Spec prog: Country 5 hrs, Pol one hr wkly. ■ Michael Washington, pres, gen mgr & progmg dir; Sue Washington, vp & gen sls mgr; Susan Ash, mus dir; Robert Hand, news dir; Steve Arrowsmith, chief engr.

WQRT(FM)—Co-owned with WGGO(AM). Oct 15, 1988: 98.3 mhz; 1.6 kw. Ant 430 ft. TL: N42 06 32 W78 36 28. Stereo. (716) 945-1515. Net: ABC/I. Format: Country. ■ Zeke Cory Jr., prom mgr, progmg dir, mus dir & news dir.

Sandy Creek-Pulaski

WSCP(AM)—Aug 8, 1974: 1070 khz; 2.5 kw-D. TL: N43 36 19 W76 07 48. Box 226, 7890 Jefferson St. Pulaski (13142). (315) 298-6505. FAX: (315) 298-6181. Licensee: Wheat Hill Broadcasting Inc. (acq 7-11-86). Net: MBS. Format: C&W. ■ Fred Lewis, gen mgr & progmg dir; Linda Braunitcer, gen sls mgr; Craig Cantey, mus dir.

Saranac Lake

WNBZ(AM)—Sept 11, 1927: 1240 khz; 1 kw-U. TL: N44 18 58 W74 07 08. Hrs opn: 5:30 AM-11 PM. Box 211, Colony Court Ext. (12983). (518) 891-1544; (518) 891-3636. FAX: (518) 891-1545. Licensee: WNBZ Inc. (acq 3-1-63). Net: ABC/I. Rep: New England. Wash atty: Arent, Fox, Kintner, Plotkin & Kahn. Format: Adult contemp, news/info. News staff one; news progmg 36 hrs wkly. Target aud: General; local community. ■ James Rogers III, pres, gen mgr & gen sls mgr; John Gagnon, progmg dir & news dir; Roy Kristofferson, mus dir; Keela Rogers, pub affrs dir; Chris Brescia, chief engr. ■ Rates: $11; 11; 11; 11.

WSLK(FM)—Co-owned with WNBZ(AM). July 12, 1989: 101.7 mhz; 2.2 kw. Ant 388 ft. TL: N44 20 27 W74 07 37. Hrs opn: 6 AM-11 PM. Prog sep from AM. Net: Unistar. Format: Oldies. News progmg 2 hrs wkly. Target aud: 25-49. ■ Stephen Borst, opns mgr. ■ Rates: Same as AM.

***WSLL(FM)**—July 1, 1989: 90.5 mhz; 200 w. Ant 355 ft. TL: N44 20 28 W74 07 43. Rebroadcasts WSLU(FM) Canton 100%. St. Lawrence University, Romoda Dr., Canton (13617). (315) 379-5356. Licensee: St. Lawrence University. Format: Div. News staff 2; news progmg 35 hrs wkly. Target aud: General. Spec prog: Gospel, jazz, class, folk, public affrs. ■ Ellen Rocco, stn mgr.

Saratoga Springs

WBGG(AM)—March 23, 1964: 900 khz; 250 w-U. TL: N43 04 24 W73 48 07. Hrs opn: 24. Box 3090 (12866); 316 Canal Sq. Schenectady (12305). (518) 581-0900. FAX: (518) 581-0911. Licensee: William H. Walker III (acq 10-21-92; $30,000; FTR 9-21-92). Net: Unistar. Rep: Schubert Radio Sales. Wash atty: Fisher, Wayland, Cooper & Leader. Format: Contemp country. News staff 2; news progmg 20 hrs wkly. Target aud: 25-54. Spec prog: Farm one hr wkly. ■ David Arcara, pres, gen mgr & stn mgr; Earl Kent, gen sls mgr; Jeanette Relyea, natl sls mgr; Tom Williams, progmg dir & mus dir; Barbara O'Neill, news dir. ■ Rates: $35; 30; 32; 25.

***WSPN(FM)**—Sept 9, 1974: 91.1 mhz; 253 w. Ant 98 ft. TL: N43 05 55 W73 47 10. Stereo. Hrs opn: 24. Skidmore College (12866). (518) 584-7378; (518) 584-5770. FAX: (518) 584-7378. Licensee: Skidmore College. Net: AP. Format: Classic rock, progsv, jazz. Target aud: All ages. Spec prog: Folk 3 hrs, Pol 3 hrs, blues 9 hrs, world mus 3 hrs wkly. ■ Donald F. Jones, gen mgr; Steve Ensdorff, vp opns; Todd Strauss, vp prom; Racheal Heath, vp progmg; Johnathan Drout, mus dir; Meri Haitken, asst mus dir; Alex Duff, vp engrg.

Schenectady

WGY(AM)—Feb 20, 1922: 810 khz; 50 kw-U. TL: N42 47 37 W74 00 36. 1430 Balltown Rd. (12309). (518) 381-4800. Licensee: Dame Media Consultants Inc. Group owner: Pennsylvania Broadcasting Associates I, II, III (acq 10-28-93; $5.1 million with co-located FM; FTR 11-15-93). Net: CBS, AP. Rep: Eastman. Wash atty: Latham & Watkins. Format: Full svc adult contemp. News staff 6; news progmg 23 hrs wkly. Target aud: 25-54. Spec prog: Jazz 8 hrs, farm 3 hrs, gospel one hr wkly. ■ Guyon W. Turner, CEO & chmn; Gilbert J. Hoban, vp & gen mgr; Richard Berkson, gen sls mgr; Jim Millo, natl sls mgr; Tom Parker, prom dir; Kelly Carls, progmg dir & pub affrs dir; Jack Riccardi, mus dir; Greg Stet, news dir; Roger Brace, chief engr.

WGY-FM—April 1940: 99.5 mhz; 14.5 kw. Ant 925 ft. TL: N42 38 13 W73 59 48. Stereo. Hrs opn: 24. Prog sep from AM. Net: CBS Spectrum. Format: Oldies. News staff one; news progmg 3 hrs wkly. ■ Sue Wraymond, news dir & pub affrs dir.

***WMHT-FM**—June 8, 1972: 89.1 mhz; 11 kw. Ant 930 ft. TL: N42 38 13 W74 00 06. Stereo. Box 17 (12301); 17 Fern Ave. (12306). (518) 356-1700. FAX: (518) 356-0173. Licensee: WMHT Educational Telecommunications. Net: AP. Format: Class. Spec prog: Jazz one hr wkly. ■ Donn Rogosin, pres & gen mgr; Derk Van Rijsewijk, chief engr. ■ WMHT(TV) affil.

***WRUC(FM)**—May 9, 1975: 89.7 mhz; 100 w. Ant -88 ft. TL: N42 49 04 W73 55 45. Stereo. College Ctr., Union College (12308). (518) 388-6151. Licensee: Trustees of Union College. Net: AP. Format: Alt. News staff one; news progmg one hr wkly. Target aud: General; 18 plus. Spec prog: It one hr, Sp 3 hrs, jazz 15 hrs, sports 4 hrs wkly. ■ Steven Kinne, gen mgr; Kerry Ivers, prom mgr.

WTRY(AM)—See Troy.

WTRY-FM—See Rotterdam.

WVKZ(AM)—April 15, 1942: 1240 khz; 1 kw-U. TL: N42 48 37 W73 59 04. Hrs opn: 24. 433 State St., (12305). (518) 382-5400. FAX: (518) 370-5394. Licensee: Capital Broadcasting (acq 9-21-87). Format: Talk, news, sports. News staff one; news progmg 10 hrs wkly. Target aud: 25 plus. Spec prog: Italian, Polish, Irish one hour, relg one hour, Black 5 hrs wkly. ■ John T. Ahern, pres; Jeff Weber, gen mgr; Sandy Taylor, gen sls mgr; Nikki Donovan, progmg dir; John Shafer, chief engr. ■ Rates: $20; 17; 20; 15.

Schoharie

WMYY(FM)—1991: 97.3 mhz; 885 w. Ant 885 ft. TL: N42 37 51 W74 16 01 (CP: 1.98 w, ant 577 ft.). Stereo. Hrs opn: 24. Rebroadcasts WHAZ(AM) Troy 100%. 424 Albany-Shaker Rd., Albany (12211-1807). (518) 437-9700. FAX: (518) 437-9730. Licensee: Capital Media Corp. (acq 2-14-92; $525,000; FTR 2-17-92). Net: USA. Format: Contemp Christian. Target aud: 18-54. ■ Paul F. Lotters, pres & gen mgr; Rae Lee Robinson, stn mgr; Steven L. Klob, sls dir, mktg dir, prom dir & adv dir; Rex P. Gregory, progmg dir, mus dir & news dir; John W. Shafer, chief engr.

Seneca Falls

WSFW(AM)—Oct 1, 1968: 1110 khz; 1 kw-D. TL: N42 54 55 W76 46 28. Hrs opn: Sunrise-sunset. Box 608, One Water St. (13148-0608). (315) 568-9888. FAX: (315)

New York

568-9889. Licensee: BJR Broadcasting Corp. (acq 6-29-87; $370,000; with co-located FM; FTR 4-20-87). Net: CNN, Unistar. Rep: Rgnl Reps. Wash atty: Borsari & Paxson. Format: Adult contemp. News staff one; news progmg 7 hrs wkly. Target aud: General. Spec prog: lr 2 hrs, lt 2 hrs, rock/heavy metal 4 hrs, big band 2 hrs, oldies 3 hrs, relg 4 hrs wkly. ■ Brien B. Rogers, pres & gen mgr; Joan C. Rogers, vp sls; Gregory Cotterill, news dir; James Travis, chief engr. ■ Rates: $13; 13; 13; 12.

WSFW-FM—Nov 1, 1968: 99.3 mhz; 3 kw. Ant 303 ft. TL: N42 54 55 W76 46 28. Stereo. Hrs opn: 5:30 AM-midnight. Dups AM 100%. ■ Rates: Same as AM.

Sidney

WCDO(AM)—1983: 1490 khz; 1 kw-U. TL: N42 19 24 W75 22 57. 75 Main St. (13838). (607) 563-3588; (607) 563-3589. FAX: (607) 563-7805. Licensee: CDO Broadcasting Inc. Group owner: Clancy-Mance Communications (acq 3-8-86; $180,000 with co-located FM; FTR 1-13-86). Net: MBS. Format: Adult contemp. News staff one; news progmg 15 hrs wkly. Target aud: 25-54. ■ David Mance, pres; Craig Harris, vp & gen mgr; Greg Davie, gen sls mgr; Wayne Roberts King, progmg dir, mus dir & pub affrs dir; Jim Tomeo, asst mus dir; Rob Ray, news dir; Ken Ruhland, chief engr. ■ Rates: $14; 14; 14; 14.

WCDO-FM—May 1982: 100.9 mhz; 970 w. Ant 577 ft. TL: N42 17 33 W75 22 03 (CP: 1.88 kw,). Format: Adult contemp, oldies. News staff one; news progmg 15 hrs wkly. Target aud: 25-54. ■ Greg Davie, sls dir; Craig Harris, gen sls mgr. ■ Rates: Same as AM.

Smithtown

*WFRS(FM)—Oct 17, 1988: 88.9 mhz; 1.5 kw H, 1.45 kw V. Ant 433 ft. TL: N40 48 27 W73 10 48. Stereo. Hrs opn: 24. 3200 Expressway Dr. South, Central Islip (11722). (516) 234-4151. Licensee: Family Stations Inc. (group owner; acq 9-27-83). Net: Family Stations. Wash atty: Irwin, Campbell, & Crowe. Format: Nondenominational Christian educ. news progmg 5 hrs wkly Target aud: General. ■ Bruce Clark, stn mgr, opns mgr & chief engr; Ken Grimball, pub affrs dir.

WMJC(FM)—May 21, 1957: 94.3 mhz; 3 kw. Ant 300 ft. TL: N40 48 07 W73 17 06 (CP: 1.25 kw-H, 1.12 kw-V, ant 462 ft, TL: N40 48 55 W73 10 44). Stereo. Hrs opn: 24. Box 697, 900 Walt Whitman Rd., Melville (11747). (516) 423-6740. FAX: (516) 423-6750. Licensee: Greater Media Inc. (group owner; acq 1961). Net: AP. Format: Soft adult contemp. News staff 4; news progmg 2 hrs wkly. Target aud: 25-54. Spec prog: Folk 2 hrs, jazz 2 hrs wkly. ■ Frank Kabela, pres; Paul Fleishman, gen mgr; Martin Woolf, prom dir; Jack Kratoville, progmg dir; Ben Mevorach, news dir; Jim Beery, chief engr.

Sodus

WNNR-FM—1991: 103.5 mhz; 3 kw. Ant 243 ft. TL: N43 16 05 W77 09 40. Box 1420, Newark (14513). (315) 331-9667. FAX: (315) 331-7101. Licensee: Waynco Radio (acq 8-90; $10,000; FTR 8-19-90). Format: Classic rock. ■ John Pickner, gen mgr.

South Bristol Township

WRQI(FM)—1948: 95.1 mhz; 9.5 kw. Ant 994 ft. TL: N42 44 47 W77 25 35 (CP: 50 kw, ant 426 ft, TL: N42 51 02 W77 25 42). Stereo. Hrs opn: 24. Suite 2695, 349 W. Commercial St., East Rochester (14445). (716) 586-2263. FAX: (716) 586-0098. Licensee: Great Lakes Wireless Talking Machine Co. (acq 7-23-86; $2.1 million; FTR 11-25-85). Rep: D & R Radio. Format: Classic rock, AOR. News staff one; news progmg 2 hrs wkly. Target aud: 25-49. Spec prog: Regional news one hr wkly. ■ Steve Chartrand, pres & gen mgr; Orest Hrywnak, opns mgr & mktg dir; Mark Squires, gen sls mgr; Boy Payne, mus dir; Maria Dauis, news dir; Jerry Whitney, chief engr.

South Glens Falls

WSTL(AM)—Sept. 1988: 1410 khz; 1 kw-D, 126 w-N. TL: N43 16 07 W73 40 14. Stereo. Hrs opn: 24. Quaker Village Bldg. No. 3, 76 Quaker Rd., Queensbury (12804). (518) 793-7733. Licensee: Bradmark Broadcasting Co. (acq 4-1-86; grpsl; FTR 1-6-86). Net: NBC. Format: Country. Target aud: 25-54. ■ Donald W. Heckman, pres; Rolly Merrill, gen sls mgr; Jay Scott, progmg dir; Ken Ruhland, chief engr. ■ Rates: $14; 12; 14; 10.

Southampton

WHFM(FM)—October 1971: 95.3 mhz; 5 kw. Ant 354 ft. TL: N40 56 05 W72 23 15. Stereo. 56 Jagger Ln. (11968). (516) 283-9500; (516) 587-1032. FAX: (516) 283-9506.

Licensee: Faircom Southampton Inc. Group owner: Faircom Inc. Net: Unistar. Rep: Katz. Format: Adult contemp. Target aud: 25-49; upscale. ■ Jeff Levine, progmg dir; Samantha Ryan, news dir; Bob Makson, chief engr.

*WPBX(FM)—March 3, 1979: 91.3 mhz; 1 kw. Ant 165 ft. TL: N40 53 17 W72 26 43 (CP: 88.3 mhz, 5.88 kw-H, 25 kw-V). Stereo. Hrs opn: 24. WPBX/LIU, Southampton College (11968). (516) 283-8555; (516) 287-8290. Licensee: Long Island Univ. (acq 8-90; FTR 8-13-90). Net: APR. Format: Jazz, class, progsv. News progmg 6 hrs wkly. Spec prog: Public affairs one hr wkly. ■ Alexandra McCarty, gen mgr; Rob Herbst, stn mgr; Robert Anderson, chief engr.

Southold

WBAZ(FM)—July 3, 1985: 101.7 mhz; 5.5 kw. Ant 341 ft. TL: N40 58 43 W72 19 27. Stereo. Box 1200, 44210 County Rd. 48 (11971). (516) 765-1017. FAX: (516) 765-1662. Licensee: Peconic Bay Broadcasting Corp. Net: Unistar, CNN. Format: Lite Contemp. News staff one; news progmg 9 hrs wkly. Target aud: 25-64. ■ Joseph J. Sullivan Jr., pres & gen mgr; Chris Conley, news dir; Robert A. Anderson, chief engr. ■ Rates: $38; 38; 38; 10.

Southport

WOKN(FM)—Sept 15, 1993: 99.5 mhz; 1.27 kw. Ant 485 ft. TL: N42 07 49 W76 47 23. Hrs opn: 24. Business Office, 1561 Cedar, Elmira (14904); 2999 Olcott Rd., Big Flats (14814). Licensee: Nancy Nicastro. Wash atty: Bechtel & Cole. Format: Country. News progmg one hr wkly. Target aud: 18-49. ■ Nancy E. Nicastro, pres & gen mgr; Donna VanDeBogart, opns dir; Jared Lampman, gen sls mgr; Mark Hills, Donna Chiaramonte, mktg mgrs; Drew Guild, news dir; James Reed, chief engr.

Spencer

*WCII(FM)—Oct 1, 1989: 88.5 mhz; 6 kw. Ant 485 ft. TL: N42 06 54 W76 29 52 (CP: 20 kw, ant 590 ft.). Stereo. Hrs opn: 24 Box 506, 7634 Campbell Creek Rd., Bath (14810). (607) 776-4151. Licensee: Family Life Ministries Radio Inc. Format: Christian. News progmg 8 hrs wkly. Target aud: 25-55; general public. Spec prog: Country one hr wkly. ■ Dick Snavely, pres & gen mgr; Rick Snavely, vp, stn mgr & progmg dir; Jim Travis, chief engr.

Spring Valley

WLIR(AM)—Sept 15, 1965: 1300 khz; 500 w-D, 83 w-N, DA-2. TL: N41 05 48 W74 00 18. Box 489, Nanuet (10952). (914) 624-1300. FAX: (914) 624-2809. Licensee: Talkline Broadcasting Corp. (acq 5-10-93; FTR 5-17-93). Format: Jewish mus and talk. Target aud: 25-54; upscale. Spec prog: Hebrew 2 hrs, Yiddish 2 hrs wkly. ■ Zev J. Brenner, CEO & pres; Philip W. Plack, gen mgr; Gary Shifs, opns dir; Gary B. Duglin, opns mgr & gen sls mgr; Jeff Allen, progmg dir; Yaakov Spivak, news dir; Michael Lobaito, chief engr. ■ Rates: $75; 60; 75; 35.

Springville

WFWC(AM)—Apr 20, 1986: 1330 khz; 1 kw-U, DA-2. TL: N42 29 53 W78 41 10. Hrs opn: 17. 51 Franklin St. (14141). (716) 592-9500. FAX: (716) 592-9522. Licensee: Lloyd B. Lane (acq 7-2-91; $127,450; FTR 7-22-91). Net: ABC/E. Format: Country. News staff one; news progmg 10 hrs wkly. Target aud: 25-54; adults. Spec prog: Farm 5 hrs, relg 2 hrs wkly. ■ Lloyd Lane, gen mgr; Peter Regan, gen sls mgr; Skip Tillinghast, progmg dir & mus dir; Fred Haier, news dir; Bill Spitzman, chief engr. ■ Rates: $14; 14; 14; na.

Staten Island

*WSIA(FM)—Licensed to Staten Island. See New York.

Stillwater

WSSV(FM)—Oct 3, 1988: 101.3 mhz; 3.66 kw. Ant 413 ft. TL: N43 00 43 W73 40 59. Stereo. Box 828, 493 Broadway, Saratoga Springs (12866); 480 Broadway, Saratoga Springs (12866). (518) 587-6000. FAX: (518) 583-1212. Licensee: Voice of Saratoga Inc. Net: CNN. Rep: Katz & Powell. Wash atty: Gardner, Carton & Douglas. Format: Adult contemp. News progmg 6 hrs wkly. Target aud: 25-54; upscale. ■ I. Hanigan, pres & gen mgr; Larry Williams, prom mgr & mus dir; Charles Taylor, progmg dir & news dir.

Stony Brook

*WUSB(FM)—June 27, 1977: 90.1 mhz; 4 kw. Ant 223 ft. TL: N40 54 59 W73 07 27. Stereo. Hrs opn: 24. Stony Brook Union S.U.N.Y. (11794-3263). Box 303 (11790). (516) 632-6500; (516) 632-6498. FAX: (516) 632-7519; (516) 689-1663. Licensee: State University of N.Y. Format: Educ, class, div. News progmg 20 hrs wkly. Target aud: 18-49; progsv & musically adventurous. Spec prog: Black 12 hrs, Pol one hr, Sp 3 hrs, Chinese one hr, Korean one hr, class 14 hrs, folk 15 hrs, jazz 20 hrs, Greek one hr wkly. ■ Norman L. Prusslin, gen mgr; Frank Burgert, chief engr.

Syosset

*WKWZ(FM)—July 24, 1973: 88.5 mhz; 125 w. Ant 90 ft. TL: N40 49 48 W73 28 57 (CP: Ant 259 ft.). S. Woods Rd. (11791). (516) 364-5675; (516) 364-5746. Licensee: Syosset Central School District. Format: Div. Spec prog: C&W 6 hrs, class 6 hrs, jazz 12 hrs wkly. ■ Jack B. DeMasi, gen mgr; Eric Britton, stn mgr; Roy Dippel, chief engr.

Syracuse

*WAER(FM)—April 1, 1947: 88.3 mhz; 6 kw. Ant 300 ft. TL: N43 02 01 W76 07 53 (CP: 50 kw-H, 39.56 kw-V, ant 277 ft, TL: N43 00 50 W76 06 52). Stereo. Hrs opn: 20. 215 University Place (13244-2110); Box 7088, University Station (13210). (315) 443-4021. FAX: (315) 443-2148. Licensee: Syracuse University. Net: MBS, NPR. Wash atty: Arter & Hadden. Format: Jazz, sports, news. News staff 4; news progmg 20 hrs wkly. Target aud: 25-49. Spec prog: Gospel 3 hrs, blues 3 hrs, world music 4, new age 3 hrs hrs wkly. ■ David R. Anderson, gen mgr; Marion Hureldt, opns dir; Robert Stein, dev dir; Joe Lee, progmg dir; Jim Johnston, news dir; Nick Marasco, chief engr.

WAQX-FM—See Manlius.

WBBS(FM)—See Fulton.

*WCNY-FM—Dec 4, 1971: 91.3 mhz; 18.6 kw. Ant 740 ft. TL: N42 56 42 W76 01 28. Stereo. Hrs opn: 5 AM-midnight. Box 2400 (13220-2400). (315) 453-2424. FAX: (315) 451-8824. Licensee: Public Broadcasting Council of Central New York. Net: NPR. Wash atty: Haley, Bader & Potts. Format: Class. Target aud: General. Spec prog: Bluegrass 3 hrs, jazz 7 hrs wkly. ■ Richard Russell, CEO & pres; Thomas A. Burton, dev dir; Paul Dunn, prom dir; Don Dolloff, progmg dir; Hugh Cleland, chief engr. ■ *WCNY-TV affil.

WDCW(AM)—Feb 4, 1922: 1390 khz; 5 kw-U, DA-N. TL: N43 05 30 W76 05 19. Radio Station WDCW(AM), 1022 Willis Ave. (13204). (315) 484-9000. Licensee: Kimtron Inc. Group owner: Crawford Broadcasting Co. (acq 7-21-93; $425,000; FTR 8-9-93). Net: Unistar. Format: Christian.

WFBL(AM)—See Baldwinsville.

WHEN(AM)—Apr 14, 1941: 620 khz; 5 kw-D, 1 kw-N, DA-N. TL: N43 05 35 W76 11 19. Stereo. Hrs opn: 24. Box 6975 (13217). (315) 457-6110. FAX: (315) 457-1605. Licensee: Park Broadcasting. Group owner: Park Communications Inc. (acq 6-76). Net: ABC/I, CBS. Rep: Major Mkt; Eastman. Format: Talk radio. Spec prog: Syracuse Chiefs, Buffalo Bills. ■ Richard Carr, gen mgr; Chris Davis, opns dir; Mike Schaefer, gen sls mgr; Rod Carr, news dir; Roy Taylor, chief engr.

WHEN-FM—Sept 1, 1958: 107.9 mhz; 50 kw. Ant 490 ft. TL: N42 57 21 W76 06 36. Stereo. Hrs opn: 24. Prog sep from AM. 620 Old Liverpool Rd. (13217). Net: ABC/D. Format: Hit country.

*WJPZ-FM—Jan 30, 1985: 89.1 mhz; 100 w. Ant 120 ft. TL: N43 02 01 W76 07 53. Stereo. Hrs opn: 24. Box 239, 316 Waverly Ave. (13210). (315) 443-4689; (315) 443-2106. FAX: (315) 443-4379. Licensee: WJPZ Board of Directors. Net: AP. Wash atty: Gardner, Carton & Douglas. Format: CHR. Target aud: 12-34; women and teenagers. Spec prog: Black 12 hrs, pub svc 13 hrs wkly. ■ Tim McRuby, gen mgr. ■ Rates: $52; 36; 52; 52.

WKRL(AM)—See North Syracuse.

WKRL-FM—See North Syracuse.

*WMHR(FM)—Mar 9, 1969: 102.9 mhz; 20 kw. Ant 780 ft. TL: N42 58 00 W76 12 01. Stereo. 4044 Makyes Rd. (13215). (315) 469-5051. Licensee: Mars Hill Broadcasting Co. Inc. Group owner: Mars Hill Broadcasting Co. Net: Moody. Wash atty: Wiley, Rein & Fielding. Format: Relg. News progmg 6 hrs wkly. Target aud: General. Christian family. ■ Glenn H. Burdick, pres; Clayton Roberts, vp & chief engr; Gordon Bell, gen mgr; Kevin Tubbs, opns mgr; Ron Zom, mus dir.

WNDR(AM)—Listing follows WNTQ(FM).

WNTQ(FM)—1956: 93.1 mhz; 97 kw. Ant 659 ft. TL: N42 56 47 W76 01 32. Stereo. Box 93Q, Teall Station (13217). (315) 446-9090. FAX: (315) 446-1614. Licensee: Orange Communications. Group owner: Osborn Communications Corp. (acq 4-87; $6.5 million with co-located AM; FTR 11-24-86). Rep: McGavren Guild. Format: CHR. Target aud: 18-49. Spec prog: Black 6 hrs wkly. ■ Frank Osborn, pres; Bill McMartin, gen mgr; George Sample, gen sls mgr; Dave Edwards, progmg dir; Rob Wagman, mus dir; Bill Ryall, chief engr.

WNDR(AM)—Co-owned with WNTQ(FM). 1946: 1260 khz; 5 kw-U, DA-2. TL: N43 09 10 W76 11 35. Prog sep from FM. Net: CBS. Format: Country. Spec prog: Soundoff 10 hrs, Black one hr wkly.

WOLF(AM)—Apr 27, 1940: 1490 khz; 1 kw-U, DA-D. TL: N43 03 30 W76 10 00 (CP: 1510 khz, 50 kw-D, DA, TL: N42 57 42 W76 06 13). Stereo. Hrs opn: 24. Box 1490 (13201). (315) 472-0222. FAX: (315) 472-0224. Licensee: WOLF Radio Inc. (acq 10-5-82). Wash atty: James L. Oyster. Format: Black, urban contemp. ■ Butch Charles, pres; Craig L. Fox, gen mgr; Craig Fox, chief engr.

WSIV(AM)—(East Syracuse). Dec 6, 1955: 1540 khz; 1 kw-D. TL: N43 05 40 W76 02 00. 7095 Myers Rd., East Syracuse (13057). (315) 656-2231. FAX: (315) 656-2259. Licensee: Forus Communications of N.Y. Inc. Group owner: Forus Communications (acq 10-12-79). Format: Christian. Spec prog: Black 4 hrs, Sp one hr, It one hr, farm one hr, Pol one hr wkly. ■ Simon Rosen, pres; James Wall, gen mgr; Alan Higgins, news dir.

WSYR(AM)—1922: 570 khz; 5 kw-U, DA-2. TL: N42 59 13 W76 09 09. Stereo. Hrs opn: 24. Bridgewater Place, 500 Plum St. (13204). (315) 472-9797. FAX: (315) 472-2323. Licensee: NewCity Communications of Syracuse Inc. Group owner: NewCity Communications Inc. (acq 9-82). Net: NBC, NBC Talknet, APR. Rep: Katz. Format: Full svc news/talk. News progmg 35 hrs wkly. Target aud: 25-54. Spec prog: Farm 12 hrs wkly. ■ Ron Tarsi, gen mgr; Joel Delmonico, gen sls mgr; Carole Fargo, mktg dir; Dee Collins, prom dir; Alan Furst, progmg dir; John Butler, news dir; Nia Carter, pub affrs dir; Conrad Trautmann, chief engr.

WYYY(FM)—Co-owned with WSYR(AM). 1946: 94.5 mhz; 100 kw. Ant 650 ft. TL: N42 56 40 W76 07 08. Stereo. Prog sep from AM. Format: Adult contemp. News progmg 5 hrs wkly. ■ Robin Adams, natl sls mgr; Tim Kuhl, mktg mgr; Tom O'Brien, progmg dir.

WVOA(FM)—See DeRuyter.

WYYY(FM)—Listing follows WSYR(AM).

WZZZ(AM)—See Fulton.

Ticonderoga

***WANC(FM)**—Sept 6, 1982: 103.9 mhz; 1.55 kw. Ant 380 ft. TL: N43 49 55 W73 24 28. Stereo. Hrs opn: 24. Rebroadcasts WAMC(FM) Albany 100%. 318 Central Ave., Albany (12206). (518) 465-5233; (800) 323-9262. Licensee: WAMC. Group owner: WAMC/Northeast Public Radio (acq 8-90; $400,000; FTR 8-13-90). Net: NPR, APR, UPI. Format: Class, jazz, news. News staff 2. Target aud: General. ■ Alan Chartock, chmn; Kathleen Taylor, sls dir; David Galletly, progmg dir; Michael Carrese, news dir.

WIPS(AM)—July 1955: 1250 khz; 1 kw-D. TL: N43 51 16 W73 23 24. Hrs opn: 6 AM-sunset. 517 Lake George Ave. (12883). (518) 585-2868. FAX: (518) 585-2869. Licensee: Empire State Radio. Net: ABC/I. Rep: Eastman. Format: Full svc adult contemp. News staff one; news progmg 24 hrs wkly. Target aud: 25-54. Spec prog: Farm 6 hrs wkly. ■ Dave Downing, gen mgr, news dir & chief engr; Dave F. Thomas, progmg dir.

Troy

WFLY(FM)—August 1948: 92.3 mhz; 17 kw. Ant 850 ft. TL: N42 38 16 W73 59 55. Box 12279, Albany (12212); 4243 Albany St., Albany (12205). (518) 456-1144. FAX: (518) 456-1633. Licensee: Albany Broadcasting Co. Inc. (acq 2-87). Net: ABC/C. Rep: Torbet. Format: CHR, top-40. News staff 7. Target aud: 18-49. ■ John F. Kelly, pres & gen mgr; Mike Collins, gen sls mgr; Barbara Borini, prom mgr; Mike Morgan, progmg dir; Shawn Scott, mus dir; Steve Janack, news dir; Paul Thurst, chief engr.

WGNA-FM—See Albany.

WHAZ(AM)—August 1922: 1330 khz; 1 kw-U. TL: N42 46 35 W73 41 10. Hrs opn: 24. 424 Albany-Shaker Rd., Albany (12211); 30 Park Ave., Cohoes (12047). (518) 437-9700; (518) 237-1330. FAX: (518) 437-9730. Licensee: Capital Media Corporation (acq 9-24-87). Net: USA. Wash atty: Mullin, Rhyne, Emmons & Topel. Format: Adult contemp Christian. Target aud: 18 plus; young to middle-aged. Spec prog: Christian rock 3 hrs wkly. ■ Paul F. Lotters, pres & gen mgr; Steven L. Klob, dev mgr, gen sls mgr, mktg dir, prom dir & adv dir; Rex P. Gregory, progmg dir, mus dir, news dir & pub affrs dir; John Shafer, chief engr. ■ Rates: $28; 28; 28; 28.

WPYX(FM)—See Albany.

***WRPI(FM)**—Nov 1, 1957: 91.5 mhz; 10 kw. Ant 450 ft. TL: N42 41 14 W73 42 22. Stereo. Hrs opn: 6 AM-2 AM. One WRPI Plaza (12180). (518) 276-6248. Licensee: Rensellaer Polytechnic Institute. Format: Div. Target aud: Open minded, educated listeners. Spec prog: Black 8 hrs, country 2 hrs, Indian 2 hrs, Greek 2 hrs, women's mus 2 hrs, Chinese 2 hrs, African one hr, Folk 2 hrs wkly. ■ Matt Perry, chmn; Kevin Neves, vp.

WTRY(AM)—Apr 15, 1940: 980 khz; 5 kw-U, DA-N. TL: N42 46 56 W73 50 07. 1054 Troy-Schenectady Rd., Latham (12110). (518) 785-9800; (518) 785-9061. FAX: (518) 785-0122. Licensee: CAP-TOWN Broadcasting. Group owner: The Griffin Group/Broadcast Division (acq 12-86; grpsl; FTR 10-20-86). Net: Unistar. Rep: McGavren Guild. Wash atty: Arent, Fox, Kintner, Plotkin & Kahn. Format: Oldies. Target aud: 35-54. ■ Merv Griffin, pres; Robert Ausfeld, gen mgr; John Hirsch, gen sls mgr; John Knott, prom dir; Darcy Wells, news dir; Brian Szewczyk, chief engr.

Trumansburg

WPIE(AM)—Jan 15, 1990: 1160 khz; 990 w-D, 220 w-N, DA-2. TL: N42 32 42 W76 42 39 (CP: 5 kw-D, 0.31 kw-N, DA-2, U). Hrs opn: 24. Box 1160 (14886). (607) 387-3185. FAX: (607) 387-3474. Licensee: Pembrook Pines Ithaca Ltd. (acq 3-3-93; $150,000; FTR 3-22-93). Net: ABC/E. Wash atty: Bechtel & Cole. Format: Country News staff one; news progmg 18 hrs wkly. Target aud: 30 plus; mature, upscale adults. ■ William Sitzman, gen mgr; Joe Loverro, gen sls mgr; Jerry Ladd, rgnl sls mgr; Tom Vartanian, progmg dir; Sean Walker, asst mus dir; Kevin Walker, news dir; Bill McKinnon, engrg dir. ■ Rates: $14; 14; 14; 14.

Tupper Lake

WRGR(FM)—Feb 29, 1980: 102.3 mhz; 150 w. Ant 1,446 ft. TL: N44 09 35 W74 28 34. Stereo. Hrs opn: 24. Box 1030 (12986). (518) 359-9747. Licensee: RGR Broadcasting of Tupper Lake Inc., debtor in possession. Group owner: RGR Broadcasting Inc. (acq 9-10-87). Net: SMN. Format: Adult contemp. News progmg 2 hrs wkly. Target aud: General. Spec prog: Relg one hr, big band 2 hrs wkly. ■ Roy Edmonds, gen mgr, gen sls mgr, progmg dir & chief engr; Reid Knapp, opns mgr, mus dir & pub affrs dir; David Naone, news dir. ■ Rates: $9.60; 9.60; 9.60; 7.40.

Utica

WEIF(FM)—Not on air, target date unknown: 100.7 mhz; 1.16 w. Ant 551 ft. TL: N43 09 12 W75 09 32. 139 Main St., Clayville (13322). Licensee: Clara Crocco.

WFRG-FM—Listing follows WRUN(AM).

WIBX(AM)—Dec 5, 1925: 950 khz; 5 kw-U, DA-1. TL: N43 06 16 W75 20 20. Hrs opn: 24. Box 950 (13503). (315) 736-9313. FAX: (315) 736-0720. Licensee: 950 Communications Corp. (group owner; acq 11-91). Net: CBS, MBS, AP. Rep: Torbet. Format: Talk, news, info. News staff 5. Target aud: 35-64; middle-upper income adults. Spec prog: Pol 3 hrs, farm 14 hrs wkly. ■ Don Alexander, pres; Thomas L. Yourchak, gen mgr; George Carpenter, gen sls mgr; Jim McCaffrey, rgnl sls mgr; John Swann, progmg dir & news dir. ■ Rates: $50; 35; 40; 25.

WLZW(FM)—Co-owned with WIBX(AM). Jan 1, 1972: 98.7 mhz; 25 kw. Ant 660 ft. TL: N43 08 39 W75 10 45. Stereo. Hrs opn: 24. Prog sep from AM. Net: CBS Spectrum. Format: Lite adult contemp. News staff 6; news progmg 65 hrs wkly. Target aud: 35-64; mid-upper income and educational levels. ■ Randy Jay, progmg dir; Jeanne Ashley, mus dir. ■ Rates: $50; 60; 55; 35.

WKDY(FM)—See Rome.

WKLL(FM)—(Frankfort). Feb 12, 1990: 94.9 mhz; 50 kw. Ant 276 ft. TL: N43 03 26 W75 07 24. 1013 Rt. 5, Suite 200, Utica (13502). (315) 798-4092. FAX: (315) 733-3403. Licensee: Raivine Broadcasting Inc. (acq 10-90; $165,000. FTR 10-29-90). Net: ABC/R. Rep: D & R Radio. Format: AOR. ■ Bob Raide, chmn & chief engr; Ed Levine, pres; Pamela Levine, vp; Luann Losito, stn mgr; Bruce Layman, gen sls mgr; Geoff Storm, prom dir; Mimi Griswold, progmg dir.

WLFH(AM)—See Little Falls.

WLZW(FM)—Listing follows WIBX(AM).

WOUR(FM)—Listing follows WUTQ(AM).

***WPNR-FM**—November 1977: 90.7 mhz. 450 w. Ant 30 ft. TL: N43 05 35 W75 16 21. Stereo. c/o Utica College, Burstone Rd. (13502). (315) 792-3069. Licensee: Syracuse Univ.-Utica Branch. Format: Urban contemp, new wave. Spec prog: Class 10 hrs, jazz 14 hrs, Reggae 5 hrs wkly. ■ Michael Simpson, pres; Sue Szczerbra, gen mgr; John Bunkfeld, chief engr.

WRCK(FM)—Listing follows WTLB(AM).

WRNY(AM)—See Rome.

WRUN(AM)—Apr 24, 1948: 1150 khz; 5 kw-D, 1 kw-N, DA-2. TL: N43 10 31 W75 21 03. Broadcast House, Thomas Rd., Oriskany (13424). (315) 736-5225. Licensee: Oneida Communications Inc. Group owner: Altdoerffer Group (acq 3-1-85). Net: NBC, NBC Talknet, Unistar, BRN. Rep: Banner. Format: News/talk. News staff one; news progmg 50 hrs wkly. Target aud: General. Spec prog: Pol one hr, relg 12 hrs, Sp one hr wkly. ■ Christine Hillard, gen mgr.

WFRG-FM—Co-owned with WRUN(AM). Oct 10, 1948: 104.3 mhz; 100 kw. Ant 500 ft. TL: N43 03 27 W75 25 04. Stereo. Prog sep from AM. Net: Unistar. Rep: Banner. Format: Adult contemp. News staff one; news progmg one hr wkly. Target aud: 25-54.

***WRVN(FM)**—Not on air, target date unknown: 91.9 mhz; 212 w. Ant -82 ft. TL: N43 06 02 W75 13 57. Rebroadcasts WRVO(FM) Oswego 100%. c/o WRVO(FM), State Univ. College, Lanigan Hall, Oswego (13126). (315) 341-3690. Licensee: State University of New York. ■ William D. Shigley, gen mgr.

WTLB(AM)—1946: 1310 khz; 5 kw-D, 500 w-N, DA-2. TL: N43 03 24 W75 16 42. Box 781 (13503). (315) 797-1330. FAX: (315) 738-1073. Licensee: H & D Entertainment Inc. (acq 6-12-92; with co-located FM). Net: ABC/D, ABC TalkRadio. Rep: Eastman. Format: Oldies. Target aud: 25-54. ■ Ed Carey, gen mgr; Bill Flack, gen sls mgr; Kym Carmichael, prom mgr; James Reitz, progmg dir; A. Scott Burton, mus dir; Oakree Kuchenbacker, news dir; David Doughty, chief engr.

WRCK(FM)—Co-owned with WTLB(AM). Apr 23, 1962: 107.3 mhz; 50 kw. Ant 499 ft. TL: N43 08 40 W75 10 32. Stereo. Prog sep from AM. Format: Current hit rock.

***WUNY(FM)**—Oct 30, 1985: 89.5 mhz; 6.3 kw. Ant 777 ft. TL: N43 08 38 W75 10 40. Stereo. Hrs opn: 5 AM-midnight. Box 2400, 506 Old Liverpool Rd., Syracuse (13220-2400). (315) 453-2424. FAX: (315) 451-8824. Licensee: Public Broadcasting Council of Central N.Y. Net: NPR. Wash atty: Haley, Bader & Potts. Format: Classical. Target aud: General. ■ Richard W. Russell, CEO & pres; Thomas Burton, dev dir; Paul Dunn, prom dir; Don Dolloff, progmg dir; Hugh Cleland, chief engr. ■ *WCNY-TV affil.

WUTQ(AM)—Jan 29, 1962: 1550 khz; 1 kw-D. TL: N43 06 48 W75 15 25. Mayro, 239 Genesee St. (13501). (315) 797-0803; (315) 797-7292. FAX: (315) 797-7813. Licensee: Bendat Communications & Broadcasting Inc. (acq 2-20-91; grpsl; FTR 3-11-91). Net: CNN. Rep: D & R Radio. Wash atty: Haley, Bader & Potts. Format: Classic MOR. News staff one. Spec prog: It 2 hrs, Polish 4 hrs, relg 5 hrs wkly. ■ Patty Gallacher, gen sls mgr; Catherine Kellogg, progmg dir; Andy Cleary, news dir; Bob Blanchard, chief engr.

WOUR(FM)—Co-owned with WUTQ(AM). June 1967: 96.9 mhz; 16 kw. Ant 790 ft. TL: N43 08 46 W75 10 40. Stereo. Prog sep from AM. Net: Westwood One, CNN. Format: Rock (AOR). News staff one; news progmg 17 hrs wkly. Target aud: General; adults 25-49. Spec prog: Jazz 2 hrs wkly. ■ Jerry Kraus, prom mgr; Peter Hirsch, progmg dir; Alison Ryan, mus dir.

Valhalla

***WARY(FM)**—Oct 3, 1973: 88.1 mhz; 171 w. Ant 403 ft. TL: N41 04 13 W73 47 25 (CP: 400 w). Hrs opn: 16. 75 Grasslands Rd. (10595). (914) 285-6752. Licensee: Westchester Community College. Wash atty: Haley, Bader & Potts. Format: AOR. Target aud: 12-24. Spec prog: Misc. pub svc 10 hrs wkly. ■ Peter Kanze, stn mgr; David Rozek, chief engr.

Vestal

WMXW(FM)—June 2, 1989: 103.3 mhz; 6 kw. Ant 1,014 ft. TL: N42 03 22 W75 56 39. Stereo. Hrs opn: 24. 400 Plaza Dr., Vestal (13850). (607) 729-3131. FAX: (607) 729-1036. Licensee: Mix Radio Inc. Rep: Katz & Powell. Format: Spectrum adult contemp. News staff one. Target aud: 25-54. ■ David Mitchell, pres & gen mgr; Peter

New York

Zolnowski, opns mgr, prom dir, progmg dir & mus dir; Karyn Smith, gen sls mgr; Chris O'Connor, news dir & pub affrs dir. ■ Rates: $45; 42; 44; na.

Vorheesville

WCDA(FM)—May 24, 1991: 96.3 mhz; 200 w. Ant 1,118 ft. TL: N42 37 01 W74 00 46. Hrs opn: 24. Box 12369, Albany (12212); Star Plaza East, Suite 222, 2050 Western Ave., Guilderland (12084). (518) 456-9600. FAX: (518) 456-8980. Licensee: Kriscott Broadcasting Inc. Format: Country. News staff 2; news progmg 3 hrs wkly. Target aud: 18-49. ■ R. Bryan Jackson, pres; Allen F. Maikels, CFO; Robert N. Putnam Jr., gen mgr; Bruce Smith, natl sls mgr; Earl Kent, rgnl sls mgr; A.J. Roberts, prom dir; Bryan Jackson, progmg dir; Kevin Richards, mus dir; Kris Smith, news dir; Joe Gallagher, pub affrs dir. ■ Rates: $50; 35; 40; 25.

Walton

WDLA(AM)—May 30, 1951: 1270 khz; 5 kw-D, 100 w-N. TL: N42 08 08 W75 04 52. Box 58, Rt. 206 (13856). (607) 865-4321. FAX: (607) 865-4189. Licensee: Delaware County Broadcasting Corp. (group owner). Net: USA, Jones Satellite Audio. Rep: Savalli. Format: Country. News staff 2; news progmg 15 hrs wkly. Target aud: 28-55; general. Spec prog: Farm 2 hrs wkly. ■ Myra Youmans, pres; Amos F. Finch, vp & gen mgr; D. Lee VerNooy, prom mgr; John D. Clark, progmg dir & news dir; Ronald Galley, mus dir; Philip Vessey, chief engr. ■ Rates: $16; 13; 14.50; 13.

WDLA-FM—Nov 16, 1973: 92.1 mhz; 690 w. Ant 656 ft. TL: N42 08 10 W75 04 48. Prog sep from AM. ■ Rates: $17; 14; 15.50; 14.

Warrensburg

WKBE(FM)—1991: 100.5 mhz; 185 w-H. Ant 1,312 ft. TL: N43 25 12 W73 45 39. 292 Bay Rd., Queensbury, NY (12804). (518) 798-8654. FAX: (518) 798-8663. Licensee: Karamatt Broadcasting Inc. ■ Kate Desantis, pres; Rick Knight, stn mgr.

Warsaw

WCJW(AM)—May 16, 1973: 1140 khz; 1 kw-D, DA-D. TL: N42 43 35 W78 06 47. Hrs opn: Sunrise-sunset. Box 251, 3258 Merchant Rd. (14569). (716) 786-8131. FAX: (716) 786-2241. Licensee: Lloyd Lane Inc. (acq 9-1-84). Net: USA. Wash atty: Fisher, Wayland, Cooper & Leader. Format: Country. News staff 2; news progmg 10 hrs wkly. Target aud: General. Spec prog: Farm 6 hrs wkly. ■ Lloyd Lane, pres & gen mgr; Seth Fenton, opns mgr; Scott Cramer, news dir. ■ Rates: $14; 14; 14; na.

*WCOU(FM)—Not on air, target date unknown: 88.3 mhz; 7 kw. Ant 492 ft. TL: N42 49 36 W78 12 25. Box 506, Bath (14810). Licensee: Family Life Ministries Radio Inc.

Warwick

WTBQ(AM)—July 24, 1969: 1110 khz; 250 w-D. TL: N41 16 51 W74 21 46. Stn currently dark. 62 Main St., Florida, NY (10921). Licensee: Sturr Communications Corp. (acq 7-9-93; $184,481.45; FTR 8-2-93).

Waterloo

WNYR-FM—Apr 19, 1989: 98.5 mhz; 3 kw. Ant 328 ft. TL: N42 48 22 W76 50 47. Hrs opn: 24. 3568 Lenox Rd., Geneva (14156). (315) 781-7000. FAX: (315) 781-7700. Licensee: Lake Country Broadcasting. Wash atty: James Oystar. Format: Adult contemp. News staff one; news progmg 5 hrs wkly. Target aud: 25-54. ■ Robert Martin, pres, gen mgr & gen sls mgr; George Kimble, vp; Mike Smith, progmg dir & news dir. ■ Rates: $13; 11; 13; 8.

Watertown

WATN(AM)—Feb 3, 1941: 1240 khz; 1 kw-U. TL: N43 58 49 W75 56 12. 199 Wealtha Ave. (13601). (315) 782-1240. FAX: (315) 782-0312. Licensee: Clancy-Mance Communications (group owner; acq 6-20-88; grpsl; FTR 6-20-88). Net: ABC/E, Unistar, NBC Talknet. Rep: Roslin. Format: MOR. ■ David W. Mance, pres & gen mgr; Ted Ford, gen sls mgr; Jack Freer, progmg dir; Robert Kurtz, chief engr.

WCIZ(FM)—Listing follows WNCQ(AM).

*WJNY(FM)—July 24, 1986: 90.9 mhz; 7.09 kw. Ant 449 ft. TL: N43 51 44 W75 43 40. Stereo. Hrs opn: 5 AM-midnight. Dups WCNY-FM Syracuse. Box 2400, Syracuse (13220-2400). (315) 453-2424. FAX: (315) 451-8824. Licensee: Public Broadcasting Council of Central N.Y.

Inc. Net: NPR. Wash atty: Haley, Bader & Potts. Format: Classical. Spec prog: Folk 3 hrs, jazz 5 hrs wkly. ■ Richard W. Russell, CEO & pres; Thomas Burton, dev dir; Paul Dunn, prom dir; Don Dolloff, progmg dir; Hugh Cleland, chief engr. ■ WCNY-TV affil.

WNCQ(AM)—Nov 2, 1959: 1410 khz; 5 kw-D, 1 kw-N, DA-N. TL: N43 57 08 W75 52 33. R.D. 2, Gifford Rd. (13601). (315) 782-6540. FAX: (315) 788-0656. Licensee: Watertown Radio Associates. Group owner: Cayuga/Northstar Radio Group (acq 5-88; $1.55 million with co-located FM; FTR 5-2-88). Net: SMN. Rep: Katz. Format: Country. ■ Bruce Danziger, gen mgr; David Luyk, gen sls mgr; Ted Bilodeau, progmg dir; Andy Graham, news dir; Mike Ring, chief engr.

WCIZ(FM)—Co-owned with WNCQ(AM). Nov 22, 1968: 97.5 mhz; 41 kw. Ant 285 ft. TL: N43 57 23 W75 50 45 (CP: 100 kw). Stereo. Prog sep from AM. Format: AOR.

*WRVJ(FM)—Not on air, target date unknown: 91.7 mhz; 3 kw. Ant 328 ft. TL: N43 58 18 W75 54 41. Rebroadcasts WRVO(FM) Oswego 100%. c/o WRVO(FM), State Univ. College, Lanigan Hall, Oswego (13126). (315) 341-3690. Licensee: State University of New York. ■ William D. Shigley, gen mgr.

*WSLJ(FM)—1992: 88.9 mhz; 200 w. Ant 454 ft. TL: N43 57 23 W75 50 28. Hrs opn: 24. Rebroadcasts WSLU(FM) Canton 100%. St. Lawrence University, Romoda Dr., Canton (13617). Licensee: St. Lawrence Univ. Wash atty: Donald Martin. Format: Div. News staff 2; news progmg 35 hrs wkly. Target aud: General; Spec prog: Gospel, jazz, classical, folk, public affrs. ■ Ellen Rocco, gen mgr.

WTNY(AM)—Apr 29, 1941: 790 khz; 1 kw-U, DA-N. TL: N43 56 44 W75 56 54. Stereo. Hrs opn: 24. 134 Mullin St. (13601). (315) 788-0790. FAX: (315) 788-4379. Licensee: 790 Communications Corp. Group owner: Black River Broadcasting (acq 1980). Net: CBS, Unistar, MBS. Rep: Torbet. Wash atty: Dow, Lohnes & Albertson. Format: MOR. News staff 3; news progmg 20 hrs wkly. Target aud: 25 plus. Spec prog: Farm 3 hrs wkly. ■ Don Alexander, pres; George Neher, opns mgr & progmg dir; James W. Riley, gen sls mgr; Robert Paterson, prom mgr; Brian Ashley, news dir; Michael Ring, chief engr.

WTNY-FM—Aug 25, 1986: 93.5 mhz; 4 kw. Ant 330 ft. TL: N44 03 20 W75 57 15. Stereo. Hrs opn: 24. Prog sep from AM. (315) 782-9300. Format: CHR. News staff 3; news progmg 2 hrs wkly. Target aud: 18-34. ■ Dick O'Neil, progmg dir; Beth Hall, mus dir.

Watkins Glen

WGMF(AM)—June 22, 1968: 1490 khz; 400 w-U. TL: N42 21 11 W76 52 13. 421 N. Franklin St. (14891). (607) 535-2779. FAX: (607) 733-3777. Licensee: Northeastern Broadcasting Inc. (acq 7-25-89; grpsl; FTR 10-2-89). Net: ABC/C, MBS. Rep: D & R Radio. Format: Gold based adult oriented rock. News staff 2 Target aud: 20-49; baby boomers. Spec prog: Jazz 3 hrs wkly. ■ William Miller Jr., pres & gen mgr; Lee Potter, gen sls mgr; James Potent, prom mgr & progmg dir; Sherral Clinch, news dir; Stephen Skimeri, chief engr.

WNGZ(FM)—See Montour Falls.

Waverly

WATS(AM)—See Sayre, Pa.

WAVR(FM)—October 1974: 102.3 mhz; 1.5 kw. Ant 400 ft. TL: N42 03 48 W76 31 28. Stereo. 204 Desmond St., Sayre, PA (18840). (717) 888-7745. FAX: (717) 888-9005. Licensee: Wats Broadcasting Inc. Net: UPI. Format: Adult contemp. Target aud: 25-54. ■ Charles C. Carver Jr., pres, gen mgr & news dir; Peg Davis Croft, vp, stn mgr & gen sls mgr; Barbara Caum, progmg dir; Lawrence Brown, chief engr.

Webster

WDCZ(FM)—Feb 15, 1993: 102.7 mhz; 1.5 kw. Ant 456 ft. TL: N43 10 37 W77 28 39. 2494 Browncroft Blvd., Rochester (14625). (716) 264-1027. Licensee: Kimtron Inc. Group owner: Crawford Broadcasting Co. (acq 11-25-92; $950,000; FTR 12-21-92). Format: Relg. ■ Nevin Larson, Terry Simpson (asst), gen mgrs.

*WFRW(FM)—October 1988: 88.1 mhz; 11.5 kw. Ant 337 ft. TL: N43 04 18 W77 05 35. Stereo. Hrs opn: 24. 117C E. Miller St., Newark, (14513). (315) 331-7482; (800) 543-1495. Licensee: Family Stations Inc. (group owner). Wash atty: Dow, Lohnes & Albertson. Format: Relg. News progmg 4 hrs wkly. Target aud: General. ■ Harold Camping, pres & gen mgr; Richard Van Dyk, CFO; Scott Smith, vp & dev dir; Steve Marsille, stn mgr

& opns mgr; Craig Hulsebos, progmg mgr; Phyllis Johnson, mus dir.

*WMHN(FM)—Feb 29, 1988: 89.3 mhz; 1 kw. Ant 75 ft. TL: N43 13 45 W77 26 52. Stereo. Hrs opn: 24. 675 Holt Rd. (14580). (716) 872-1100; (315) 469-5051. Licensee: Mars Hill Broadcasting Co. Inc. (group owner). Net: UPI, USA. Format: Relg. News progmg 13 hrs wkly. Target aud: General; Christian families. ■ Glenn H. Burdick, pres; Gordon Bell, gen mgr; Wayne Taylor, stn mgr; Kevin Tubbs, opns mgr & progmg dir; Ron Zorn, mus dir; Clayton R. Roberts, chief engr.

Wellsville

WLSV(AM)—Oct 31, 1955: 790 khz; 1 kw-D, 41 w-N. TL: N42 04 37 W77 55 47. 82 Railroad Ave. (14895). (716) 593-6070. FAX: (716) 593-6212. Licensee: Erin Communications (group owner; acq 11-1-90; $225,000). Net: NBC. Wash atty: Baraff, Koerner, Olender & Hochberg. Format: Country. Target aud: General. ■ Jack Murphy, pres; Rodney Biehler, progmg dir & mus dir; Mike Baldwin, news dir; Ralph Van Derlindon, chief engr.

WJQZ(FM)—Co-owned with WLSV(AM). Feb 3, 1986: 93.5 mhz; 3 kw. Ant 466 ft. TL: N42 09 26 W77 55 26. Stereo. Prog sep from AM. (Acq 10-16-90; $400,000; FTR 11-5-90). Format: Adult contemp. Target aud: 25-54. ■ Rick Whitwood, progmg dir & mus dir; Jim Linn, chief engr.

Westhampton

WMRW(FM)—Nov 18, 1993: 98.5 mhz; 6 kw. Ant 282 ft. Rebroadcasts WDRE-FM Garden City 100%. 11 Main St., Riverhead (11901). (516) 369-9850. Licensee: Rose Communications Corp. Format: Modern rock. ■ Ron Reeve, gen mgr.

Westhampton Beach

WRCN-FM—See Riverhead.

Westport

WADQ(FM)—Not on air, target date unknown: 102.5 mhz; 6 kw. Ant -33 ft. TL: N44 11 03 W73 27 47. Stereo. Box 1085, Ridgefield, CT (06877-0842). (203) 438-1211. FAX: (203) 431-8473. Licensee: Westport Broadcasting. Wash atty: Cohn & Marks. ■ Dennis Jackson, chmn; Jonathan M. Becker, pres.

Wethersfield Township

WNUC(FM)—1948: 107.7 mhz; 11.5 kw. Ant 800 ft. TL: N42 37 23 W78 17 16. Stereo. 5500 Main St., Buffalo (14221). (716) 626-1077. FAX: (716) 626-1395. Licensee: Casciani Communications Inc. (acq 10-88). Net: Unistar. Wash atty: Kaye, Schuler, Fierman, Hays & Nandler. Format: Hot Country. News staff one. Target aud: 25-54. ■ John Casciani, pres & gen mgr; David Polito, gen sls mgr; Dan Kelley, progmg dir. ■ Rates: $46; 40; 40; 30.

White Plains

WFAS(AM)—Aug 11, 1932: 1230 khz; 1 kw-U. TL: N41 01 32 W73 49 39. Box 551 (10602); Secor Road, Hartsdale (10530). (914) 693-2400. FAX: (914) 693-4489. Licensee: CRB of Westchester Inc. Group owner: CRB Broadcasting Corp. (acq 9-9-86; with co-located FM). Net: AP. Rep: Katz. Format: All news, talk, info. News staff 7; news progmg 46 hrs wkly. Target aud: General. ■ Kevin Collins, gen mgr; Bill Goode, prom mgr; Mark Mitchell, progmg dir; Sue Richard, mus dir; Gene Lisansky, news dir; Randy Schall, chief engr.

WFAS-FM—Sept 1, 1947: 103.9 mhz; 600 w. Ant 669 ft. TL: N41 01 32 W73 49 39. Stereo. Prog sep from AM. Format: Adult contemp. Target aud: 25-54.

WXPS(FM)—See Briarcliff Manor.

Whitehall

WNYV(FM)—July 14, 1990: 94.1 mhz; 3 kw. Ant 328 ft. TL: N43 28 37 W73 26 56. Stereo. Hrs opn: 5:30 AM-midnight. Box 141 (12887); Box 210, Poultney, VT (05764). (802) 287-9030; (802) 287-9031. FAX: (802) 287-9030. Licensee: Pine Tree Broadcasting. Format: Adult contemp, country, oldies. News staff one; news progmg 18 plus hrs wkly. Target aud: 30-55; local, family oriented, mobile. Spec prog: Pol one hr, relg 2 hrs, big band 3 hrs, farm one hr, school news, local sports/events & fundraisers 3 hrs wkly. ■ Michael Leech, pres; Judith E. Leech, gen mgr & gen sls mgr; Rob Roy, progmg dir & mus dir; Joel Williams, news dir; Neil Langer, chief engr. ■ Rates: $10.20; 8.50; 10.20; 8.50.

Woodside

WWRL(AM)—See New York.

Woodstock

WDST(FM)—April 29, 1980: 100.1 mhz; 2.9 kw. Ant 308 ft. TL: N41 59 04 W74 02 56. Stereo. Box 367, 118 Tinker St. (12498). (914) 679-7266. FAX: (914) 679-5395. Licensee: CHET-5 Broadcasting L.P. Group owner: CHET-5 Broadcasting (acq 2-12-93; $1.65 million with WKNY[AM] Kingston; FTR 3-8-93). Net: CBS Spectrum. Format: Alternative adult contemp. Spec prog: Jazz 15 hrs, class 15 hrs wkly. ■ Gary H. Chetkof, chmn, pres & gen mgr; Ike Phillips, vp sls & vp mktg; Freddy Bluefox, progmg dir; Jeanne Atwood, mus dir; David Groth, chief engr.

Wurtsboro

WZAD(FM)—Sept 1, 1990: 97.3 mhz; 620 w. Ant 718 ft. TL: N41 36 04 W74 33 17. Stereo. Hrs opn: 24. Box 978, 137 Sullivan St. (12790); Box 423, Route 17 M, New Hampton (10958). (914) 888-0077; (914) 374-0077. FAX: (914) 888-0021; (914) 374-3015. Licensee: WZAD Inc. Net: SMN. Wash atty: Akin, Gump, Strauss, Hauer & Feld. Format: Oldies. News staff one; news progmg 5 hrs wkly. Target aud: 25-54; upscale, educated. ■ Richard Landy, pres; Bruce Allen, gen mgr; Mollie Morrow, gen sls mgr; Henry Cotterill, progmg dir, mus dir & chief engr; Jennifer Fogarty, news dir; Paul Di Marco, pub affrs dir. ■ Rates: $24; 20; 24; 20.

Yonkers

WRTN(FM)—See New Rochelle.

North Carolina

LAUREN A. COLBY
301-663-1086
COMMUNICATIONS ATTORNEY
Special Attention to Difficult Cases

Aberdeen

WEEB(AM)—See Southern Pines.

WIOZ-FM—See Southern Pines.

WQNX(AM)—January 1982: 1350 khz; 2.5 kw-D, 28 w-N, DA-2. TL: N35 07 20 W79 24 57. Box 1350 (82315). (919) 944-1350. FAX: (919) 944-8182. Licensee: Goss Capital Broadcasting (acq 1987; $128,000; FTR 4-20-87). Net: NBC, Sun. Rep: Carolina. Format: News, talk. ■ T.O. Calcott, gen mgr; N.M. Calcott, gen sls mgr.

Ahoskie

WQDK(FM)—Sept. 2, 1968: 99.3 mhz; 3 kw. Ant 300 ft. TL: N36 16 46 W77 01 59. Stereo. Hrs opn: 24. Rte 1, Box 13-B (27910); 179 Lovers Ln., Elizabeth City (27909). Licensee: Ray-D-O Biz Inc. (acq 5-27-92; FTR 2-17-92). Net: Agri-Net, Ray Sports. Format: Country. Spec prog: Farm 7 hrs wkly. ■ William Ray Owner, chmn; Lisa Ray Owner, exec vp; Don Upchurch, opns mgr & news dir.

WRCS(AM)—Apr 25, 1948: 970 khz; 1 kw-D. TL: N36 16 46 W77 01 59. Rt. 1, Box 13 B (27910). (919) 332-3101. Licensee: WRCS-AM 970 Inc. (acq 5-4-92; $150,000; FTR 5-25-92). Rep: Carolina. Format: Black, gospel. ■ James R. Wiggins, gen mgr & gen sls mgr; Linda Futrell, opns mgr; Rodney Bland, chief engr.

Albemarle

WABZ-FM—Feb 1958: 100.9 mhz; 1.8 kw. Ant 541 ft. TL: N35 22 40 W80 11 38. Stereo. Hrs opn: 24. Box 608, 115 W. South St. (28002). (704) 982-1009. FAX: (704) 983-1009. Licensee: Piedmont Crescent Communications (acq 8-2-88; $675,000; FTR 8-22-88). Net: USA. Rep: Dora-Clayton. Wash atty: Tharrington, Smith & Hargrove. Format: Relg. News progmg 12 hrs wkly. Target aud: 35-54; female. ■ Robert Hilker, CEO; William Rollins, pres; Robert Brown, gen mgr; Kent Little, stn mgr, sls dir, mktg dir & adv dir; Matt Smith, prom mgr, progmg dir, mus dir, news dir & pub affrs dir; Ken Kennedy, chief engr. ■ Rates: $14; 10; 12; 10.

WXLX(AM)—July 1947: 1010 khz; 1 kw-D. TL: N35 22 40 W80 11 38. Dups WZKY 100%. Box 550 (28002). (704) 983-1580. Licensee: Norman Communications Inc. (acq 3-3-93; $20,000; FTR 3-22-93). Rep: Carolina. Format: Talk. ■ Bill Norman, Suzy Norman, gen mgrs.

WZKY(AM)—July 9, 1956: 1580 khz; 1 kw-D, 167 w-N. TL: N35 21 38 W80 10 39. Stereo. Hrs opn: 24. Box 550 (28002-0550). (704) 983-1580. Licensee: Norman Communications Inc. (acq 6-1-80; $200,000; FTR 6-16-80). Net: CBS; N.C. News Net. Format: Oldies, news/talk. Target aud: 30 plus. ■ William Norman Jr., pres, gen mgr, gen sls mgr & news dir; Susi Norman, mus dir. ■ Rates: $15; 12; 12; 7.

Asheboro

WKRR(FM)—November 1948: 92.3 mhz; 100 kw. Ant 1,275 ft. TL: N35 22 40 W80 11 38. Stereo. 192 E. Lewis St., Greensboro (27406). (919) 274-8042. FAX: (919) 274-1269. Licensee: Dick Broadcasting Co. (group owner; acq 4-84). Rep: Katz. Format: Classic rock. Target aud: 18-49. ■ Allen Dick, pres & gen mgr; Jamey Kerr, gen sls mgr; Juliette Brown, prom mgr; Bruce Wheeler, progmg dir; John Amberg, mus dir; Chris Demm, news dir; Tom Cauldwell, chief engr.

WKXR(AM)—May 24, 1947: 1260 khz; 5 kw-D, 500 w-N, DA-2. TL: N35 43 26 W79 48 21. Hrs opn: 5 AM-midnight. 1115 Eastview Dr. (27203). (919) 625-2187. FAX: (919) 629-1741. Licensee: Randolph Broadcasting Inc. (acq 8-4-86; $500,000; FTR 7-7-86). Format: Country. News staff 8; news progmg 8 hrs wkly. Target aud: 18 plus. Spec prog: Farm one hr, gospel 5 hrs wkly. ■ Edward F. Swicegood II, pres, gen mgr & gen sls mgr; Larry Reid, progmg dir & mus dir; Add Penfield, news dir. ■ Rates: $12; 7; 9; 8.

WZOO(AM)—May 3, 1971: 710 khz; 1 kw-D, DA. TL: N35 45 50 W79 50 04. Box 460 (27204). (919) 672-0985. Licensee: Faith Enterprises Inc. (acq 11-15-86). Net: N.C. News Net. Format: Southern gospel. ■ D.W. Long, pres; Huey Turner, gen mgr & gen sls mgr; Max Parrish, chief engr.

Asheville

*****WCQS(FM)**—1975: 88.1 mhz; 260 w. Ant 1,132 ft. TL: N35 31 39 W82 29 49. Stereo. Hrs opn: 24. 73 Broadway (28801). (704) 253-6875. FAX: (704) 253-6700. Licensee: Western N.C. Public Radio Inc. (acq 1984). Net: APR, NPR. Wash atty: Cohn & Marks. Format: Class, jazz, news. News staff one; news progmg 35 hrs wkly. Target aud: General. Spec prog: Folk 11 hrs wkly. ■ Ed Subkis, gen mgr; Sandra Norbo, dev mgr & sls dir; Barbara Sayer, progmg dir; Richard J. Kowal, mus dir; David Hurand, news dir; Jobie F. Sprinkle, chief engr. ■ Rates: $16; 8; 16; 8.

WFGW(AM)—See Black Mountain.

WISE(AM)—1939: 1310 khz; 5 kw-D, 1 kw-N, DA-N. TL: N35 37 09 W82 34 21. Stereo. 90 Lookout Rd. (28804). (704) 253-1310. FAX: (704) 253-5619. Licensee: United Broadcasting Enterprises (acq 2-25-93; $15,000 with WTZQ[AM] Hendersonville; FTR 4-12-93). Net: SMN. Format: Nostalgia. ■ Glen Wilcox, pres; R.L. Sink, gen mgr; Dave Hogan, progmg dir; Jim Moody, chief engr.

WKJV(AM)—August 1947: 1380 khz; 5 kw-D, 1 kw-N, DA-N. TL: N35 36 24 W82 35 30. Hrs opn: 6 AM-11 PM. 70 Adams Hill Rd. (28806); Box 1611 (28816). (704) 252-1380. FAX: (704) 259-9427. Licensee: Anchor Baptist Broadcasting Association (group owner; acq 10-15-92; $295,000). Net: USA; N.C. News Net. Format: Classic gospel, news/talk. News staff one; news progmg 12 hrs wkly. Target aud: General. ■ Randy C. Barton, pres; Robin Baker, news dir; Lamar Owen, engrg mgr & chief engr.

WKSF(FM)—Listing follows WWNC(AM).

*****WLFA(FM)**—1975: 91.3 mhz; 440 w. Ant 3,340 ft. TL: N35 36 02 W82 39 07. Box 3172 (28802); 4611 Whitehall Dr. N.W., Huntsville (35816). (800) 849-8930; (704) 251-1991. Licensee: Greater Asheville Religious Educational Association. Format: Relg, talk. ■ Dr. Kenneth D. Brantley, pres & gen mgr; Ethan Hess, prom mgr & news dir; Allen Henderson, progmg dir & mus dir; Richard Cooper, chief engr.

WMIT(FM)—See Black Mountain.

WMYI(FM)—See Greenville.

WSKY(AM)—Apr 11, 1947: 1230 khz; 1 kw-U. TL: N35 35 43 W82 33 57. Hrs opn: 20. Box 2020 (28802); One N.W. Pack Square (28801). (704) 253-4451. FAX: (704) 253-7683. Licensee: Radio Asheville Inc. Net: CBS. Rep: T N. Format: Adult contemp. Target aud: 25-55. Spec prog: Gospel 6 hrs, jazz 6 hrs wkly. ■ Zeb Lee, pres & gen mgr; Brian Lee, prom mgr, progmg dir & mus dir; Kevin Briggs, news dir; John Randolph, chief engr.

WWNC(AM)—Feb 22, 1927: 570 khz; 5 kw-U, DA-N. TL: N35 35 49 W82 36 20. Hrs opn: 24. Box 6447 (28816). (704) 253-3835. FAX: (704) 255-7850. Licensee: Pine Trails Broadcasting Co. Inc. Group owner: Heritage Broadcast Group Inc. (acq 10-11-89; $25,500,000 with co-located WKSF FM; FTR 10-30-89). Net: ABC/I, MBS. Rep: McGavren Guild. Format: Full service, country. News staff 3; news progmg 20 hrs wkly. Target aud: 25-54. Spec prog: Farm one hr, gospel 3 hrs, relg 3 hrs wkly. ■ Jim Cullen, CEO & chmn; Steve Humphries, pres; John Hogan, gen mgr; Diane Augram, gen sls mgr; Frank Byrd, progmg dir; Peggy Fry, mus dir; Bill McClement, news dir; Terry Shinn, chief engr. ■ Rates: $112; 85; 90; 65.

WKSF(FM)—Co-owned with WWNC(AM). August 1947: 99.9 mhz; 53 kw. Ant 2,672 ft. TL: N35 25 32 W82 45 25. Stereo. Hrs opn: 24. Prog sep from AM. Net: ABC/C, ABC/FM, Unistar. Rep: McGavren Guild. Format: Hot adult contemp. News progmg 3 hrs wkly. Target aud: 25-44. ■ J.J. Cooke, progmg dir; Nikki Thomas, mus dir. ■ Rates: $105; 80; 90; 75.

Atlantic

WTKF(FM)—Not on air, target date unknown: 107.3 mhz; 6 kw. Ant 328 ft. TL: N34 53 01 W76 30 21. R.R. 3, Box 135, Beaufort (28516). Licensee: Down East Radio Co.

Banner Elk

WZJS(FM)—Aug 5, 1989: 100.7 mhz; 550 w. Ant 758 ft. TL: N36 11 12 W81 51 56 (CP: 1.1 kw). Box 132, Boone (28607). (704) 733-1200. FAX: (704) 264-2412. Licensee: Smith Communications. Net: Unistar. Format: Country. ■ Omer Tomlinson, gen mgr; Jason Forbin, news dir; Stoney Owen, chief engr.

Bayboro

WKZF(FM)—Apr 5, 1990: 97.9 mhz; 2.75 kw. Ant 341 ft. TL: N35 07 55 W76 52 32. Stereo. Hrs opn: 6 AM-midnight. Box K, Alma (31510). (912) 632-4411. FAX: (919) 633-9779. Licensee: Carolina Community Broadcasting Inc. (acq 3-11-92; $375,000; FTR 4-6-92). Target aud: 18-64; general. ■ Rates: $20; 15; 15; 10.

Beaufort

WBTB(AM)—Nov 30, 1954: 1400 khz; 1 kw-U. TL: N35 42 50 W76 38 51. Hrs opn: 24. Box 940 (28516). (919) 247-6343. FAX: (919) 247-7343. Licensee: Down East Radio Communications (acq 5-01-93; grpsl; FTR 7-1-91). Net: Moody. Format: Talk, relg. News progmg 14 hrs wkly. Target aud: 25 plus; adult Christians and Christian families. ■ Casey Warrington, gen mgr & progmg dir; Bob Kellner, opns mgr; Julie Naegelen, gen sls mgr; Dave Gemoske, chief engr.

Beech Mountain

WECR(FM)—Not on air, target date unknown: 102.3 mhz; 730 w. Ant 279 ft. 1211 N. Church St., Mountain City, TN (37683). Licensee: Frances G. Atkinson.

Belhaven

WKJA(FM)—Oct 15, 1980: 92.1 mhz; 31 kw. Ant 613 ft. TL: N35 29 29 W76 43 10 (CP: 101.1 mhz, 28 kw, ant 633 ft., TL: N35 18 12 W76 45 50). Stereo. Hrs opn: 24. Box 153, SR 1718 Banjo Creek (27810); Box 1126, 307 Johnson Blvd., Jacksonville (28540). (919) 964-9292. FAX: (919) 964-9294. Licensee: Winfas of Belhaven Inc. (group owner: acq 6-25-92; $594,000; FTR 7-20-92). Net: MBS. Rep: D & R Radio. Format: Oldies. News progmg 3 hrs wkly. Target aud: 35-44; baby-boomers. ■ W.S. Foster Jr., chmn; Roger Ingram, pres; Jewel Chesson, stn mgr; Margie Lester, gen sls mgr; Bill Lester, progmg dir & mus dir. ■ Rates: $10; 10; 10; 10.

Belmont

WCGC(AM)—Dec 11, 1954: 1270 khz; 5 kw-D, 500 w-N, DA-2. TL: N35 15 05 W81 03 26. Stereo. Hrs opn: 24. Box 888, 510 W. Wilkinson Blvd. (28012). (704) 825-2812; (704) 825-8224. FAX: (704) 825-2383. Licensee: James B. Mintzer (acq 5-25-89; $330,000; FTR 6-12-89). Net: NBC, MBS, Westwood One. Format: News/talk. News staff 2; news progmg 8 hrs wkly. Target aud: General. ■ James B. Mintzer, pres, gen mgr & gen sls mgr; Jim Huggins, mktg dir, progmg dir & news dir; Dusty Rhodes, mus dir; Bruce Musso, chief engr. ■ Rates: $18; 12; 18; 8.

Dusty Rhodes, mus dir; Bruce Musso, chief engr. ■ Rates: $18; 12; 18; 8.

Benson

WPYB(AM)—Sept 1, 1961: 1130 khz; 1 kw-D. TL: N35 21 40 W78 34 45. Box 215 (27504). (919) 894-3009. Licensee: Benson Broadcasting Co. Format: C&W, gospel. ■ Bob Johnson, pres & gen mgr; Amelda Johnson, adv mgr; Dorothy Hood, mus dir; Bill Lambert, chief engr.

Black Mountain

WFGW(AM)—May 27, 1962: 1010 khz; 50 kw-D (19 kw-CH), DA-2. TL: N35 36 19 W82 21 00. Hrs opn: 24. Box 159, 1330 U.S. Hwy. 70 (28711). (704) 669-8477. FAX: (704) 669-6983. Licensee: Blue Ridge Broadcasting Corp. Wash atty: Fisher, Wayland, Cooper & Leader. Format: Relg, MOR, oldies. Spec prog: Black one hr, classical one hr wkly. ■ B. Graham, chmn; T.W. Wilson, pres; Edna Edwards, gen mgr & dev mgr; Rob Schermerhorn, opns mgr; John Baker, Edna Edwards, prom mgrs; John Baker, progmg dir; Kevin Auman, mus dir; Tim Neese, chief engr.

WMIT(FM)—Co-owned with WFGW(AM). 1941: 106.9 mhz; 36 kw. Ant 3,090 ft. TL: N35 44 06 W82 17 10. Stereo. Dups AM 75%. Format: Relg, news, MOR. ■ Colin O'Brien, progmg dir.

WZQR(AM)—Feb 26, 1966: 1350 khz; 1 kw-D. TL: N35 37 19 W82 19 02. Hrs opn: 17. Box 1368, 109 Charlotte St. (28711). (704) 669-5441; (704) 669-5013. Licensee: Don Taylor (acq 9-20-93; FTR 10-11-93). Net: USA, CBN. Rep: Keystone (unwired net). Wash atty: Lee Peltzman. Format: Country. News staff one; news progmg 15 hr wkly. Target aud: General. ■ Don Taylor, pres, gen mgr, gen sls mgr & progmg dir; Ed McDade, chief engr. ■ Rates: $48; 48; 48; 18.

Blowing Rock

WVIO(AM)—1983: 1510 khz; 1 kw-D. TL: N36 08 56 W81 39 48. Box 2533 (28605); Mystery Hill, Hwy 321 (28605). (704) 262-1186. FAX: (704) 262-3292. Licensee: High Country Visitor's Info Net Inc. (acq 10-89; $1,550,000; FTR 9-25-89). Format: Vistor's info and Christian programing. Spec prog: Class 2 hrs, C&W 3 hrs wkly. ■ Wayne Underwood, pres & gen mgr; Morris Hatton, gen sls mgr; Ted Bell, progmg dir.

Boiling Springs

***WGWG(FM)**—Jan 22, 1974: 88.3 mhz; 4.7 kw. Ant 220 ft. TL: N35 15 03 W81 40 03 (CP: 50 kw, ant 302 ft.). Stereo. Hrs opn: 15. Box 876, College Circle (28017). (704) 434-2349. FAX: (704) 434-6246. Licensee: Gardner-Webb University. Format: Btfl mus, class, jazz. News progmg 10 hrs wkly. Target aud: General. Spec prog: Country 5 hrs, Sp one hr, farm one hr wkly. ■ Chris White, pres; M. Allen Setzer, gen mgr; Steve Smith, chief engr.

Boone

***WASU-FM**—May 18, 1972: 90.5 mhz; 340 w. Ant -120 ft. TL: N36 12 58 W81 40 55. Stereo. A.S.U., Wey Hall (28608). (704) 262-3170. Licensee: Appalachian State Univ. Net: Westwood One. Format: Classic rock, AOR, jazz. News progmg 2 hrs wkly. Target aud: 18-30; college students & area residents. Spec prog: Urban contemp 6 hrs, blues 2 hrs, Christian rock 3 hrs, country 8 hrs wkly. ■ Carl Tyrie, gen mgr; Larry Cornelison, chief engr.

WATA(AM)—September 1950: 1450 khz; 1 kw-U. TL: N36 12 59 W81 42 06. Stereo. Box 72 (28607). (704) 264-2411. FAX: (704) 264-2412. Licensee: WATA Inc. Net: CNN. Format: MOR. News staff one. ■ Roland Potter, pres; Omer Tomlinson, gen mgr; Jim Jernigan, progmg dir; Keith Pittman, mus dir; Don Scott, news dir; Stanley Owen, chief engr.

Brevard

WGCR(AM)—Sept 16, 1985: 720 khz; 10 kw-D. TL: N35 15 10 W82 40 28. Stereo. Box 720, Everette Rd., Pisqah Forest (28768). (704) 884-9427. FAX: (704) 883-9427. Licensee: Anchor Baptist Broadcasting Association (acq 2-87). Net: USA; N.C. News Net. Format: Relg, news. News staff one; news progmg 15 hrs wkly. Target aud: General. Spec prog: Gospel. ■ Randy C. Barton, pres & gen mgr; Suzanne M. Horton, gen sls mgr; Kristie Johnson, prom mgr; Randy Eubanks, progmg dir; Robin Baker, news dir; Lamar Owen, chief engr.

WRAQ(AM)—July 6, 1950: 1240 khz; 1 kw-U. TL: N35 13 23 W82 42 20. 207 E. Main Brevard St. (28712). (704) 884-6092. FAX: (704) 883-9329. Licensee: River City Communications Inc. (acq 9-28-93; $60,000; FTR 10-18-93). Net: CBS. Format: Full service, talk. News progmg 18 hrs wkly. Target aud: General. Spec prog: Jazz 8 hrs wkly. ■ Frank Kinney, pres; Tad Fogel, gen mgr & adv dir; Pat Ryan, opns mgr; Jim Moody, chief engr. ■ Rates: $10; 10; 10; 8.

Bryson City

WBHN(AM)—Oct 1, 1967: 1590 khz; 500 w-D. TL: N35 25 41 W83 26 18. Box 1309 (28713). (704) 488-2682. FAX: (704) 488-3594. Licensee: Starcast South Inc. Group owner: Starcast Stations (acq 10-84; $355,000; FTR 10-15-84). Net: ABC/E. Format: C&W. ■ Jack Mullen Sr., pres; Dan Lynch, gen mgr; Bill Estes, opns mgr; Sandy Serjak, gen sls mgr; Phyllis Hutchinson, mus dir; Jack Mullen II, chief engr.

Buie's Creek

***WCCE(FM)**—Oct 7, 1974: 90.1 mhz; 3 kw. Ant 105 ft. TL: N35 24 36 W78 44 21 (CP: 22.39 kw-H, 22 kw-V, ant 459 ft.). Stereo. Hrs opn: 5:45 AM-11:30 PM. Box 1030 (27506). (919) 893-1745. Licensee: Campbell Univ. Net: AP. Format: Btfl music, div, relg. News staff one; news progmg 10 hrs wkly. General. Spec prog: Bluegrass 4 hrs, big band 6 hrs wkly. ■ Travis Autry, gen mgr, mus dir & news dir; Carolyn Bowden, opns mgr, progmg dir & pub affrs dir; Ron McLamb, dev dir; Walter L. Johnson, chief engr.

Burgaw

WKXB(FM)—Dec 13, 1964: 99.9 mhz; 100 kw. Ant 520 ft. TL: N34 30 03 W78 04 45 (CP: 984 ft. TL: N34 30 07 W78 04 58). Stereo. (919) 259-5836. Licensee: Sea-Comm Inc. (acq 2-22-93; $600,000; FTR 3-15-93). Net: MBS. Format: CHR. News staff 2; news progmg 3 hrs wkly. Target aud: 18-49. ■ Bob Casey, progmg dir; Patrick Joyce, news dir.

WVBS(AM)—June 21, 1963: 1470 khz; 1 kw-D. TL: N34 32 05 W77 54 31. Suite B100, 201 N. Front St., Wilmington (28401); Box 1691 (28402). (919) 259-5836. Licensee: Jones-Eastern Radio Inc. (group owner: acq 5-14-87). Net: MBS. Rep: Christal. Format: Country, relg. ■ C.J. Jones, pres & gen mgr; David Weinfeld, gen sls mgr; Ron Stauffer, chief engr.

Burlington

WBBB(AM)—September 1941: 920 khz; 5 kw-D, DA-D. TL: N36 05 50 W79 29 03. Box 1119 (27216). (919) 584-0126. FAX: (919) 584-0739. Licensee: Curtis Media Group. Group owner: Curtis Media Group (acq 3-1-90). Net: MBS. Rep: McGavren Guild. Format: News/talk. News staff one; news progmg 5 hrs wkly. Target aud: 35 plus; upscale. ■ Don Curtis, CEO & pres; Joe Bell, exec vp; Jack Weinlein, gen mgr & sls dir; Dave Wright, stn mgr; Deirdre Brandt, opns mgr; Lesa Layno, news dir & pub affrs dir; Larry Allen, chief engr.

WPCM(FM)—Co-owned with WBBB(AM). December 1946: 101.1 mhz; 100 kw. Ant 910 ft. TL: N35 56 31 W79 26 33 (CP: Ant 1,189 ft.). Stereo. Hrs opn: 24. Prog sep from AM. Net: Moody. Format: Country, bluegrass. Target aud: 25-54. ■ Jim Howe, opns mgr.

Burlington-Graham

WBAG(AM)—1946: 1150 khz; 1 kw-D, 48 w-N. TL: N36 06 48 W79 27 00. Hrs opn: 5 AM-12 midnight. Box 2450, 236 N. Mebane St. (27216). (919) 226-1189. Licensee: Sumner Broadcasting Co. Inc. (acq 1993; $100,000; FTR 9-01-93). Net: NBC, MBS. Format: News/talk, sports. News staff 2; news progmg 25 hrs wkly. ■ Wayne L. Sumner, pres; David A. Wright, sr vp, gen mgr & progmg dir; Pat Bell, opns mgr; R. Gailes Stuckey, gen sls mgr; Ralph Snow, news dir; Larry Allen, chief engr. ■ Rates: $10; 10; 10; 10.

WSML(AM)—See Graham.

WZZU(FM)—1946: 93.9 mhz; 100 kw. Ant 1,269 ft. TL: N35 52 16 W79 09 38. Stereo. Suite 120, 1000 Park Forty Plaza, Durham (27712). (919) 834-1051. Licensee: Prism Radio Partners (acq 1993). $3.8 million Net: AP. Wash atty: David Tillotson. Format: Classic Rock. News staff one. Target aud: 25-49; men. Spec prog: UNC sports. ■ Bill Phalen, CEO; Tom Goodrich, CFO; John Duff, exec vp; Ron Stone, gen mgr; Carrie Butler, gen sls mgr; Brian Illes, progmg dir & mus dir; John W. Brett, news dir; Ben Brinitzer, chief engr. ■ Rates: $150; 100; 125; 50.

Burnsville

WKYK(AM)—May 28, 1967: 940 khz; 5 kw-D, 250 w-N, DA-N. TL: N35 55 32 W82 16 20. Stereo. Hrs opn: 5 AM-midnight. Box 744, Mark Group Bldg., 401 Sawmill Rd. (28714). (704) 682-3798; (704) 682-3510. FAX: (704) 682-6227. Licensee: Mark Media Inc. Group owner: The Mark Group (acq 4-10-69). Net: NBC. Format: Contemp country. News staff one; news progmg 15 hrs wkly. Target aud: 18-55; young adults and adults. Spec prog: Gospel 15 hrs wkly. ■ J. Arnell Sink, CEO; J. Ardell Sink, pres; Remelle K. Sink, exec vp; Michael Sink, vp, gen mgr, gen sls mgr & chief engr; Sally Root, prom mgr; Dave Doar, progmg dir, news dir & pub affrs dir. ■ Rates: $15; 15; 15; 10.

Camp Lejeune

WWOF(AM)—Sept 8, 1980: 1580 khz; 10 kw-D. TL: N34 43 27 W77 19 27 (CP: 830 khz; 10 kw-D, 2.5 kw-N, 10 kw-CH, DA-N). 1309 Lejeune Blvd., Jacksonville (28540). (919) 347-4114. FAX: (919) 347-5655. Licensee: Word of Faith of Jacksonville Inc. (acq 7-5-89; $54,000; FTR 7-24-89). Format: Contemporary MOR, relg. ■ James Ricky Osborne, pres; Leonard Stenson, gen mgr & mus dir; Jim Smith, chief engr.

Canton

WPTL(AM)—Aug 3, 1963: 920 khz; 500 w-D, 38 w-N. TL: N35 31 15 W82 48 24. Box 909, 131 Pisgah Dr. (28716). (704) 648-3576; (704) 648-3577. FAX: (704) 648-3577. Licensee: Skycountry Broadcasting Inc. (acq 3-1-78). Net: NBC. Format: C&W, relg. News progmg 8 hrs wkly. Target aud: 25 plus; adult family. ■ William Reck, pres; Clifford Hannah, gen mgr & progmg dir; Linda Reck, stn mgr; Shirley Rickman, gen sls mgr; Terry Shinn, chief engr. ■ Rates: $8; 8; 8; 8.

WWIT(AM)—July 12, 1954: 970 khz; 5 kw-D. TL: N35 31 58 W82 51 58. Hrs opn: 5:30 AM-8 AM. Box 1369, New Clyde Hwy. (28716). (704) 648-3588. Licensee: Green Communications Co., Inc. (acq 9-6-91). Net: SMN. Wash atty: Miller & Fields. Format: Oldies- 50s, 60s, 70s. News progmg 10 hrs wkly. Target aud: 28-50. Spec prog: Relg 7 hrs wkly. ■ Daniel Greene Jr., pres; Denise Sutton-Cloer, vp, gen mgr & progmg dir; Ken Woodward, chief engr. ■ Rates: $9; 8; 9; 8.

Carolina Beach

WLGX(FM)—Not on air, target date unknown: 106.7 mhz; 1.8 kw. Ant 253 ft. 14339 Tunsberg Terrace, Midlothian, VA (23113). Licensee: Kenneth R. Noble II.

WMYT(AM)—July 1, 1989: 1180 khz; 10 kw-D, DA. TL: N34 09 03 W78 04 48. Box 1092, Salem, VA (24153); 716 Princess St. Wilmington (28401). (919) 762-5343; (703) 389-3631. FAX: (703) 389-8968. Licensee: Gulfstream Radio. Wash atty: Booth, Freret & Imlay. Format: Relg. Target aud: General. Spec prog: Black 15 hrs wkly. ■ David H. Moran, pres & gen mgr; Sharon M. Moran, gen sls mgr & prom mgr; Cheryl Sparks, progmg dir; Paul Knight, chief engr.

Chadbourn

WVOE(AM)—Apr 23, 1962: 1590 khz; 1 kw-D. TL: N34 21 05 W78 50 38. Rte. 3, Box 39B (28431). (919) 654-5621. Licensee: Ebony Enterprises Inc. Format: Urban contemp, Black, gospel. Target aud: General; white & blue collar workers, housewives, students, senior citizens. ■ Willie J. Walls, pres & stn mgr; Ronald Johnson, gen sls mgr; Martha McKoy, prom mgr & news dir; Beulah Foxworth, progmg dir & mus dir; Gene West, chief engr.

Chapel Hill

WCHL(AM)—Jan 25, 1953: 1360 khz; 5 kw-D, 1 kw-N, DA-N. TL: N35 56 18 W79 01 36. Stereo. Box 2127 (27515). (919) 942-8765. FAX: (919) 942-8675. Licensee: Village Broadcasting Inc. Group owner: Village Companies. Net: MBS. Format: News/Talk. ■ James A. Heavner, pres; Kyle Caddell, gen mgr; Robert Boyd, gen sls mgr; Larry Stone, progmg dir & mus dir; Sabrina Smith, news dir; Paul Boone, chief engr.

WDCG(FM)—See Durham.

WRTP(AM)—December 1973: 1530 khz; 10 kw-D, DA. TL: N35 58 07 W79 00 10. 3013 Guess Rd., Durham (27705); Box 15400, Durham (27704). (919) 471-1530; (919) 929-9787. Licensee: WRTP Inc. (acq 4-1-89). Net: CBN. Format: Relg. News progmg 3 hrs wkly. Target aud: General. ■ Billie O. Leathers, pres; L.L. Leathers, gen mgr & sls dir; David Moore, stn mgr, gen sls mgr & vp mktg; Bettye Johnson, prom mgr; Mark Parker, progmg dir & mus dir; Leah Beth Gingrich, pub affrs dir; Jim Davis, chief engr.

***WUNC(FM)**—Nov 3, 1952: 91.5 mhz; 100 kw. Ant 810 ft. TL: N35 52 07 W79 10 06. Stereo. CB 6230, Swain

Stations in the U.S.

North Carolina

Hall, Univ. of N.C. (27599-6230). (919) 966-5454; (919) 962-9862. FAX: (919) 966-5955. Licensee: Univ. of North Carolina at Chapel Hill. Net: NPR, APR. Wash atty: Schwartz, Woods & Miller. Format: News, class, jazz. ■ Thomas W. Davis, gen mgr; Craig Curtis, progmg dir; David C. Wright, chief engr.

*WXYC(FM)—Mar 18, 1977: 89.3 mhz; 400 w. Ant 280 ft. TL: N35 54 15 W79 02 50. Stereo. Box 51, Carolina Union (27599). (919) 962-7768. Licensee: Student Educational Broadcasting Inc. Format: Contemp alternative. Target aud: General. ■ Bob Boster, gen mgr; Howard Hoyt, chief engr.

WZZU(FM)—See Burlington-Graham.

Charlotte

WAQQ(FM)—Listing follows WAQS(AM).

WAQS(AM)—1941: 610 khz; 5 kw-D, 1 kw-N, DA-2. TL: N35 17 53 W80 53 40. 400 Radio Rd. (28216). (704) 399-6195. FAX: (704) 393-5361. Licensee: Tenori Broadcasting Corp. (acq 1-17-89; $8.5 million with co-located FM; FTR 1-30-89). Format: Oldies, sports. News staff 4; news progmg 7 hrs wkly. Target aud: 18 plus; male, sports oriented. ■ Steve Adams Sr., pres; Larry Williams, gen mgr; Darlene Skipper, prom mgr; Shea Griffin, progmg dir; Mike Griffin, chief engr. ■ Rates: $50; 50; 50; 50.

WAQQ(FM)—Co-owned with WAQS(AM). July 21, 1962: 95.1 mhz; 100 kw. Ant 1,542 ft. TL: N35 21 44 W81 09 19. Stereo. (Acq 10-75). ■ Darlene Skipper, prom dir; Anne Kelly, progmg dir; Eddie Munster, mus dir; Frank Laseter, news dir. ■ Rates: $50; 50; 50; 40.

WBT(AM)—Apr 10, 1922: 1110 khz; 50 kw-U, DA-N. TL: N35 07 56 W80 53 23. Stereo. One Julian Price Pl. (28208). (704) 374-3500. FAX: (704) 374-3885. Licensee: Jefferson-Pilot Communications Co. (group owner; acq 9-45). Net: NBC. Rep: Banner. Format: Adult contemp.■ Bill Blackwell, pres; Rick Jackson, vp & gen mgr; Larry Rideaux, gen sls mgr; Sandra Mann, prom mgr; Mary June Rose, progmg dir; John Stokes, news dir; William R. White, chief engr.

WBT-FM—Aug 15, 1962: 107.9 mhz; 97 kw. Ant 1,692 ft. TL: N35 21 51 W81 11 13. Stereo. Prog sep from AM. Format: CHR, adult contemp. ■ Mike Donovan, progmg dir.

WCGC(AM)—See Belmont.

WCNV(AM)—Jan 18, 1955: 1480 khz; 5 kw-U, DA-2. TL: N35 17 05 W80 52 34. Hrs opn: 24. 1480 Pompano Rd. (28216). (704) 391-9070. Licensee: Christ Covenant Presbyterian Church (acq 9-1-92; $10; FTR 9-21-92). Net: NBC News, Talknet, AP. Rep: Katz & Powell. Wash atty: Fisher, Wayland, Cooper & Leader. Format: All news. News staff 3; news progmg 25 hrs wkly. Target aud: 35-54; male oriented, upscale professionals. ■ Tom Lamprecht, gen mgr; Ted Spangler, stn mgr. ■ Rates: $40; 35; 35; 25.

*WFAE(FM)—June 29, 1981: 90.7 mhz; 100 kw. Ant 760 ft. TL: N35 15 06 W80 41 12. Stereo. Hrs opn: 24. Suite 91, One University Pl. (28262). (704) 549-9323. Licensee: University Radio Foundation Inc. (acq 4-2-93; $22,630; FTR 4-26-93). Net: NPR, APR, AP. Format: News magazine, contemp jazz. News staff 3; news progmg 42 hrs wkly. ■ Fred Dabney, chmn; Roger Sarow, pres & gen mgr; Debra Peterson, CFO; Joe Brant, opns dir; Tony Reevy, dev dir; Lou Meux, sls dir; Catherine Smith, prom dir; Paul Stribling, mus dir; Kathleen Merritt, news dir; Jobie Sprinkle, engrg dir.

WGIV(AM)—November 1947: 1600 khz; 1 kw-D, 500 w-N, DA-N. TL: N35 14 57 W80 51 41. 601 S. Kings Dr. (28204). (704) 342-2644. FAX: (704) 343-9820. Licensee: Ardman Broadcasting (acq 6-20-88; grpsl; FTR 6-20-88). Net: SMN; N.C. News Net. Rep: D & R Radio; Katz. Wash atty: Leventhal, Senter & Lerman. Format: Gospel. Target aud: Black 25 plus. ■ Perry L. I Lewis, chmn; Barry Mayo, pres; Nathan W. Pearson Jr., CFO; Wayne Brown, gen mgr; Matt Ross, gen sls mgr; Mr. Chris Crawford (local), natl sls mgr; Angela Flemming, prom mgr; Michael Saunders, progmg dir; Frankie Darceol, mus dir; Valerie Moore, news dir; Phil Woods, engrg dir.

WGSP(AM)—Aug 23, 1958: 1310 khz; 1 kw-D, DA. TL: N35 15 23 W80 51 52 (CP: 1.6 kw, DA-N). 4209-F Stuart Andrew Blvd. (28217). (704) 527-9477. FAX: (704) 527-9210. Licensee: Willis Family Broadcasting Inc. (group owner; acq 3-4-92; $550,000 grpsl; FTR 3-23-92). Net: ABC/D, ABC/E. Format: Inspirational gospel. ■ Traci Siegel, gen mgr.

WHVN(AM)—Dec 6, 1928: 1240 khz; 1 kw-U, DA-1. TL: N35 12 00 W80 48 39. Box 18614 (28217); 5732 N. Tyron St. (28213). (704) 596-1240. FAX: (704) 596-6939. Licensee: WHVN Inc. Group owner: GHB Radio Group (acq 7-11-83). Net: ABC/I. Format: Southern gospel. News progmg 13 hrs wkly. Target aud: General; Christian. ■ George Buck, pres; Tom Gentry, gen mgr & prom mgr; Roger Matney, gen sls mgr; Scott Scarbrough, progmg dir; Brant Hart, mus dir & news dir; Steward Albert, chief engr. ■ Rates: $26; 20; 22; 18.

WMXC(FM)—1972: 104.7 mhz; 96 kw. Ant 1,210 ft. TL: N35 15 06 W80 41 12. Stereo. Hrs opn: 24. Box 30247 (28230). (704) 372-1104. FAX: (704) 335-4996. Licensee: E.Z. Communications Inc. (group owner; acq 4-1-72). Net: AP. Rep: Major Mkt. Format: Adult contemp. News staff 2. Target aud: 25-54. ■ Alan Box, pres; Dianne Earley, gen mgr; Sally Mitchener, gen sls mgr; Kathy O'Neill, prom mgr; Don Schaeffer, progmg dir; Charlie Davis, news dir; Scott Walker, pub affrs dir; Gary Morgan, chief engr.

WOGR(AM)—May 7, 1964: 1540 khz; 2.5 kw-D, DA. TL: N35 13 45 W80 58 32 (CP: TL: N35 16 26 W80 51 50). Box 16408, 1501 N. I-85 Service Rd. (28297). (704) 393-1540; (704) 393-1588. FAX: (704) 525-8638. Licensee: Victory Christian Center Inc. (acq 7-27-88). Net: USA. Wash atty: Gardner, Carton & Douglas. Format: Relg. Target aud: General. ■ Robyn Gool, pres; Wayne Hammond, gen mgr; William Crutchfield, opns mgr; Doris Massey, gen sls mgr & prom mgr; June Davis, news dir; David Anthony, chief engr.

WPEG(FM)—See Concord.

WSOC-FM—1947: 103.7 mhz; 100 kw. Ant 1,040 ft. TL: N35 15 41 W80 43 38 (CP: Ant 1,059 ft.). Stereo. Box 34665 (28234). (704) 570-9762. FAX: (704) 335-4996. Licensee: EZ Communications Inc. (group owner; acq 12-10-92; FTR 1-11-93). Rep: Christal. Format: Contemp country. ■ Gary Brobst, gen mgr, gen sls mgr & prom mgr; Tad Griffin, progmg dir; Scott Hollingsworth, chief engr.

WYFQ(AM)—Oct 14, 1933: 930 khz; 5 kw-D, 1 kw-N, DA-N. TL: N35 16 00 W80 54 05. 8030 Arrowridge Rd. (28273-5604). (704) 552-0601. Licensee: Bible Broadcasting Network Inc. (group owner; acq 2-6-92; $475,000; FTR 2-24-92). Format: Traditional Christian. News progmg 3 hrs wkly. Target aud: General. ■ Carl Redemann, gen mgr.

WYHC(FM)—Not on air, target date unknown: 98.9 mhz; 84 w-V. Ant 135 ft. TL: N35 16 37 W80 50 02. 6707-C Fairview Rd. (28210-3354). (704) 362-0400. FAX: (704) 362-2279. Licensee: MHS Holdings L.P. Target aud: General. ■ Marc Silverman, gen mgr.

Cherry Point

WCPQ(AM)—See Havelock.

WMSQ(FM)—See Havelock.

Cherryville

WCSL(AM)—June 28, 1967: 1590 khz; 1 kw-D, 42 w-N. TL: N35 22 28 W81 24 23. Box 370 (28021). (704) 435-3297. FAX: (704) 482-4680. Licensee: Calvin R. Hastings (acq 10-19-83; $300,000; FTR 10-31-83). Net: N.C. News Net. Format: Oldies. Spec prog: Farm one hr, loc sports 3 hrs wkly. ■ Calvin Hastings, pres & gen mgr; Calvin Minnix, gen sls mgr & prom mgr; Milton Baker, progmg dir; Amy Carpenter, news dir; Don Strawn, chief engr.

China Grove

WRNA(AM)—Nov 17, 1980: 1140 khz; 1 kw-D, 250 w-CH, DA-D. TL: N35 34 20 W80 35 21. Hrs opn: 6 am-2 hrs past sunset. Box 8146, Kannapolis (28083). (704) 857-1101; (704) 857-1140. FAX: (704) 857-0680. Licensee: South Rowan Broadcasting Co. Net: CNN. Format: Relg. Target aud: General. ■ Carl Ford, pres, gen mgr & progmg mgr; Judy Hunter, sls dir; Ted Fuller, chief engr. ■ Rates: $8; 8; 8; 4.

Claremont

WCXN(AM)—Sept 5, 1985: 1170 khz; 10 kw-D. TL: N35 43 34 W81 08 52. Box 909, 3289 WCXN Radio Rd. (28610-0909). (704) 459-9803; (704) 872-WCXN. Licensee: WCXN Inc. Group owner: Baker Family Stations. Net: USA. Format: Relg. Target aud: General. Spec prog: Bluegrass, gospel. ■ Edward A. Baker, pres; Donald W. Lee, gen mgr; Carolyn Lee, progmg dir; Larry Schropp, chief engr.

THE WHITTLE AGENCY
Media Brokerage
Gary Whittle

12716 Lindley Drive • Raleigh, NC 27614
(919) 848-3596 • FAX: (919) 848-0519

Clinton

WCLN(AM)—Sept 27, 1975: 1170 khz; 5 kw-D. TL: N35 01 21 W78 20 58. Box 28 (28328). (919) 592-6403. Licensee: Gospel Good News Inc. Net: ABC/E; N.C. Net. Rep: TN. Format: Christian. Spec prog: Farm 3 hrs wkly. ■ Kathy Klaus, gen mgr.

WCLN-FM—June 11, 1967: 107.1 mhz; 3 kw. Ant 299 ft. TL: N34 58 40 W78 18 15 (CP: 13 kw, ant 453 ft.). Stereo. Dups AM 90%. Licensee: Willis Broadcasting Corp.

WRRZ(AM)—May 4, 1947: 880 khz; 1 kw-D. TL: N34 58 40 W78 18 15. Box 378, Hwy 701 Business S. (28328). (919) 592-2165. FAX: (919) 592-8556. Licensee: WRRZ Radio Co. Inc. (acq 12-30-83). Net: N.C. News. Rep: T N. Wash atty: Tharrington, Smith & Hargrove. Format: C&W. News progmg 4 hrs wkly. Target aud: 25 plus. Spec prog: Black 5 hrs, relg 6 hrs wkly. ■ D. Patrick Dixon, pres, gen mgr & chief engr; Joyce Dixon, gen sls mgr; Dave Denton, prom mgr, mus dir & news dir. ■ Rates: $6.95; 6.95; 6.95; 6.95.

Columbia

WRSF(FM)—Licensed to Columbia. See Elizabeth City.

Concord

WEGO(AM)—Mar 5, 1943: 1410 khz; 1 kw-D. TL: N35 24 29 W80 36 41. Box 126 (28026). (704) 788-9346. FAX: (704) 782-4213. Licensee: Concord Kannapolis Communications Inc. (acq 12-18-91; $198,000; FTR 1-13-91). Net: N.C. News Net. Format: Pure Gold. ■ Bob Brown, gen mgr, prom mgr & progmg dir; Woody Cain, news dir.

WPEG(FM)—June 15, 1962: 97.9 mhz; 95 kw. Ant 1,608 ft. TL: N35 21 44 W81 09 19. Stereo. Hrs opn: 24. 520 Hwy. 29 N. (28025); Sales Office, 601 S. Kings Dr., Charlotte (28204). (704) 786-9111; (704) 342-2644. FAX: (704) 788-7628. Licensee: Broadcasting Partners of Charlotte Inc. (acq 6-20-88; grpsl; FTR 6-20-88). Net: Unistar Radio Net. Rep: Katz. Format: Urban contemp. News staff one; news progmg 20 hrs wkly. Target aud: 12 plus; blacks. Spec prog: Gospel 6 hrs, mix show 8 hrs wkly. ■ Perry L. Lewis, chmn; Barry Mayo, pres; Nathan W. Pearson Jr., CFO; Wayne K. Brown, gen mgr; Matt Ross, gen sls mgr; Chris Crawford (local), rgnl sls mgr; Angela Fleming, prom dir; Michael Saunders, progmg dir; Phil Woods, engrg dir.

Cullowhee

*WWCU(FM)—Jan 15, 1977: 90.5 mhz; 330 w. Ant -827 ft. TL: N35 18 40 W83 10 34. Stereo. Box 2728, Moore Bldg, WCU (28723). (704) 227-7173. Licensee: Western Carolina Univ. Format: AOR. News progmg 5 hrs wkly. Target aud: 18-30; university students and faculty. Spec prog: Christian rock 4 hrs wkly. ■ James Holt, gen mgr; Eddie Foxx, opns mgr; Bill McManus, prom dir; Brad Smith, progmg dir; Valerie Knox, news dir; Tim Warner, chief engr.

Dallas

WAAK(AM)—Jan 1, 1963: 960 khz; 1 kw-D, 500 w-N, DA-N. TL: N35 18 03 W81 10 13. Box 477 (28034). (704) 922-3411. Licensee: Cana Broadcasting (acq 7-24-85; $250,000; FTR 9-24-84). Format: Gospel. ■ Billy Martin, pres, gen mgr & gen sls mgr.

*WSGE(FM)—Oct 27, 1980: 91.7 mhz; 3 kw. Ant 140 ft. TL: N35 18 40 W83 10 34. Stereo. Hrs opn: 6 AM-midnight. Box 95, Gaston College, Rm 114, Ray Craig Clrm. Bldg., 201 Hwy 321 S. (28034-1499). (704) 922-6334; (704) 922-6333. FAX: (704) 922-6440. Licensee: Gaston College Bd of Trustees. Net: AP. Format: Btfl mus, big band, class. News progmg 11 hrs wkly. Target aud: General. Spec prog: Educ 6 hrs, jazz 5 hrs, instructional 10 hrs wkly. ■ Hattie Leeper, pres; Ben Hicks, stn mgr; Tracey Stewart, chief engr.

Davidson

***WDAV(FM)**—Sept 1, 1973: 89.9 mhz; 100 kw. Ant 807 ft. TL: N35 26 55 W80 50 24. Stereo. Hrs opn: 24. Box 1540, (28036). (704) 892-8900. FAX: (704) 892-2079. Licensee: Trustees of Davidson College. Net: APR. Wash atty: Arent, Fox, Kintner, Plotkin & Kahn. Format: Class. News progmg 2 hrs wkly. Target aud: General. ■ John Clark, gen mgr; Casey Jacobus, mktg dir; Ted Weiner, mus dir; Larry Schropp, chief engr.

Dobson

WYZD(AM)—Oct 10, 1978: 1560 khz; 1 kw-D. TL: N36 23 36 W80 44 05. Box 797, 131 1/2 Atkin St. (27017). (919) 386-8134. Licensee: Dobson Broadcasting Inc. Net: N.C. News Net. Format: Gospel. ■ John Comber, gen mgr & progmg dir; Don Mussel, chief engr.

Dunn

WCKB(AM)—Dec 7, 1946: 780 khz; 1 kw-D. TL: N35 17 30 W78 35 45. Stereo. Hrs opn: Sunrise-sunset. Box 789, Hwy 421 S. (28335). (919) 892-3133. FAX: (919) 892-3135. Licensee: Charles Fowler (acq 9-15-89; $216,000; FTR 10-2-89). Net: N.C. News Net. Rep: T-N. Format: Southern & black gospel. News progmg 6 hrs wkly. Target aud: 25 plus; mature audience with local concerns. Spec prog: Farm 3 hrs wkly. ■ Charles Fowler, pres; Ronald Tart, gen mgr, gen sls mgr, prom mgr & adv dir; Margie Taylor, progmg dir & mus dir; Lottie Henderickson, pub affrs dir; Bill Lambert, chief engr. ■ Rates: $8.50; 8.50; 8.50; 8.50.

WRCQ(FM)—May 17, 1971: 103.5 mhz; 48 kw. Ant 502 ft. TL: N35 03 09 W78 38 54. Stereo. Hrs opn: 24. Box 2008, Suite 700, 225 Green St., Fayetteville (28302-2008). (919) 484-2107. FAX: (919) 484-2683. Licensee: Metropolitan Broadcasting Associates, L.P. (acq 3-1-91; $2 million; FTR 9-5-89). Wash atty: Pepper & Corzinni. Format: Rock (AOR). News staff one; news progmg one hr wkly. Target aud: 18-49. ■ Steve Garchik, pres; Ronald D. Walton, gen mgr; Graham Bennett, natl sls mgr; Gina Lewis, rgnl sls mgr; Panama Jack, prom mgr; Kevin Culbreth, progmg mgr; Marc Owens, mus dir; Ann Thomas, news dir; Van Clough, chief engr. ■ Rates: $60; 40; 70; 50.

Durham

WDCG(FM)—Listing follows WDNC(AM).

WDNC(AM)—Apr 9, 1934: 620 khz; 5 kw-D, 1 kw-N, DA-2. TL: N36 02 10 W78 58 07. Hrs opn: 24. Suite 120, 1000 Park Forty Plaza (27713). (919) 361-0620. FAX: (919) 361-1051. Licensee: Durham Herald Co. Inc. (acq 12-30-86). Net: NBC Talknet, CNN, ESPN, NBC. Rep: D & R Radio. Format: MOR, news/talk, sports. News staff 3. Target aud: 35-64. ■ D.J. Mitsch, gen mgr; Steve McCall, gen sls mgr; Susan Hite, prom mgr; Barry Brown, progmg dir; Tom Britt, news dir; Ben Brinitzer, chief engr.

WDCG(FM)—Co-owned with WDNC(AM). February 28, 1948: 105.1 mhz; 100 kw. Ant 1,141 ft. TL: N35 52 20 W79 09 29. Stereo. Net: ABC. Format: CHR. Target aud: 18-49. ■ Bill Cahill, progmg dir; Sean Sellers, mus dir.

WDUR(AM)—1947: 1490 khz; 1 kw-U. TL: N35 58 03 W78 53 18. Hrs opn: 24. Simulcast with WFXC(FM). Suite 116, 5400 S. Miami Blvd., Morrisville (27560). (919) 941-0700. FAX: (919) 941-1074. Licensee: Ballston Trust Services L.C. Group owner: Pinnacle Broadcasting Co. (acq 12-22-92; grpsl; FTR 1-18-93). Net: SMN. Rep: Eastman, Katz. Wash atty: Wilmer, Cutler & Pickering. Format: Urban adult contemp. News progmg one hr wkly. Target aud: 25-54; Black adults. Spec prog: Pub affrs 4 hrs wkly. ■ Phil Marella, pres; Jon C. Jones, vp & gen mgr; Jim Davis, chief engr. ■ Rates: $70; 60; 70; 20.

WFXC(FM)—Co-owned with WDUR(AM). May 15, 1971: 107.1 mhz; 1.2 kw. Ant 490 ft. TL: N35 58 41 W78 48 59 (CP: 2.6 kw, ant 502 ft.). Stereo. Hrs opn: 24. Dups AM 100%. Net: SBN, SMN.

***WNCU(FM)**—Not on air, target date unknown: 90.7 mhz; 50 kw. Ant 433 ft. TL: N36 03 32 W78 57 13. Box 19363 (27707). Licensee: North Carolina State Univ.

WSRC(AM)—Oct 14, 1954: 1410 khz; 5 kw-D, 290 w-N, DA-2. TL: N36 01 44 W78 51 00. 3202 Guess Rd. (27705-2647). (919) 477-7999. FAX: (919) 477-9811. Licensee: Durham Christian Radio Inc. Group owner: Willis Broadcasting Corp. (acq 6-2-87). Format: Relg. News staff one. ■ L.E. Willis, Sr., pres; Anthony Lee, gen mgr & gen sls mgr; Harold Jackson, progmg dir, mus dir & news dir.

WTIK(AM)—1945: 1310 khz; 5 kw-D, 1 kw-N, DA-2. TL: N36 01 30 W78 54 08. Hrs opn: 24. 707 Leon St. (27702). (919) 220-3226. Licensee: W&W Broadcasting Co. (acq 9-1-56). Net: Moody. Format: C&W, relg, sports. News staff 2. Target aud: 24-54. ■ H.L. Welch, pres; H.L. Welch Jr., gen mgr; Austin Rigsbee, gen sls mgr; Jeff Gibson, prom mgr & progmg dir; Julie McLamb, mus dir; Stephen Roberts, news dir.

***WXDU(FM)**—November 1983: 88.7 mhz; 1.18 kw. Ant 103 ft. TL: N36 02 08 W79 04 48. Stereo. Box 4706, Duke Stn. (27706); Bivens Bldg., East Campus, Duke Univ. (27708). (919) 684-2957. Licensee: Duke Univ. Format: Div. News progmg 2 hrs wkly. Target aud: General. Spec prog: Jazz 18 hrs wkly. ■ Brian Harris, gen mgr; Kate Melcher, prom mgr; Ben Butler, progmg dir; Matt Walter, mus dir; Jim Besch, Jeremy Steckler, Bryan Perry, asst mus dirs; Katherine Conrad-Saydah, news dir; Lisa Linn, pub affrs dir; Tom Leverton, chief engr.

WZZU(FM)—See Burlington-Graham.

Eden

WCLW(AM)—Aug 16, 1970: 1130 khz; 1 kw-D, DA-3. TL: N36 31 21 W79 45 55. 123 The Blvd. (27288). (910) 627-9259. FAX: (910) 623-9935. Licensee: John Correa dba Newave Broadcasting (acq 6-24-92; $45,000; FTR 7-13-92). Format: Oldies, contemp hits. News staff 4; news progmg 4 hrs wkly. Target aud: 25-49. Spec prog: Hispanic 6 hrs wkly. ■ John Correa, pres & gen mgr; John Martin, progmg dir.

WLOE(AM)—Dec 20, 1946: 1490 khz; 1 kw-U. TL: N36 30 21 W79 46 18. Hrs opn: 6 AM-10 PM. Dups WMYN, Madison-Mayodan 100%. Box 311, Madison (27025). (919) 427-9696; (919) 548-9207. FAX: (919) 548-4636. Licensee: Mayo Broadcasting Corp. (acq 6-90; $100,000; FTR 6-4-90). Net: NBC; N.C. News Net. Rep: Keystone (unwired net); Rgnl Reps.Format: Info/talk, oldies. News progmg 30 hrs wkly. Target aud: General; 25 plus. Spec prog: Sports 20 hrs wkly. ■ Richard D. Hall, pres; Mike Moore, gen mgr & gen sls mgr; Annette Moore, stn mgr & pub affrs dir; Scotty Irving, mus dir; Tim Walker, chief engr. ■ Rates: $18; 18; 18; 18.

WNEU(FM)—March 20, 1949: 94.5 mhz; 100 kw. Ant 981 ft. TL: N36 20 48 W79 54 30. Stereo. 164 S. Main St., High Point (27260); Box 2208, High Point (27261). (910) 272-0995. FAX: (910) 882-4422. Licensee: WWMY FM Broadcasting. Format: Country. ■ Ivan E. Braiker, gen mgr; Brenda Blackerby, gen sls mgr; Nick Allen, progmg dir; Leanne Petty, news dir; Stuart Smith, chief engr.

WWMO(AM)—Aug 16, 1970: 830 khz; 50 kw-D, 1.9 kw-N, DA-2. TL: N36 32 08 W79 47 43. 234 E. Meadow Rd. (27288-3416). (919) 623-9966. FAX: (919) 627-0830. Licensee: Stone Broadcasting Corp. (acq 3-16-80). Format: Relg. ■ V.C. Stone, pres & gen mgr.

Edenton

WBXB(FM)—June 18, 1976: 100.1 mhz; 50 kw. Ant 302 ft. TL: N36 07 11 W76 35 29. Stereo. Box 765, 1001 Paradise Rd. (27932). (919) 482-2224; (919) 482-3200. FAX: (919) 482-5290. Licensee: Willis Family Broadcasting Inc. (group owner; acq 3-4-92; $550,000 grpsl; FTR 3-23-92). Net: American Urban. Rep: T-N. Format: Contemp gospel, relg. News progmg 8 hrs wkly. Target aud: General. ■ Bishop L.E. Willis Sr., pres; Calvin Pruden, gen mgr; Terry Love, progmg dir; Jerry Zachary, mus dir; Angelo Cooper, asst mus dir; Karen Hayes, news dir; Keyneisha Powell, pub affrs dir; Mike Chandler, chief engr.

WERX-FM—Listing follows WZBO(AM).

WZBO(AM)—November 1955: 1260 khz; 1 kw-D, 34 kw-N. TL: N36 05 00 W76 36 00. Box 950 (27932). (919) 482-2103. FAX: (919) 482-5591. Licensee: Lawrence F. Loesch & Margaret A. Loesch (acq 3-12-90; $400,000 with co-located FM; FTR 4-2-90). Net: Sun, UPI, NBC; N.C. News Net. Rep: TN. Wash atty: Tharrington, Smith & Hargrove. Format: MOR, talk, sports, big band. News staff one; news progmg 12 hrs wkly. Target aud: 35 plus; Edenton residents, business owners, professionals, NASCAR fans, community svc groups. ■ Rick Loesch, pres & gen mgr; Margaret Loesch, exec vp; Barry Kennedy, opns mgr & chief engr; Roselind Shields, gen sls mgr; Uchenna Bulliner, progmg dir; Brent Todd, mus dir; Morris Parker, news dir.

WERX-FM—Co-owned with WZBO(AM). March 14, 1983: 102.5 mhz; 26 kw. Ant 689 ft. TL: N36 05 00 W76 36 00. Stereo. Prog sep from AM. Net: Sun, UPI. Format: Rock/AOR. Target aud: 18-49; moderate to high income, mobile professionals & families with children. Spec prog: Flashback; in concert; off the record; BBC classic tracks.

Elizabeth City

WCNC(AM)—September 1939: 1240 khz; 1 kw-U. TL: N36 18 38 W76 13 56. Box 1246, 911 Parsonage St. Extended (27906-1246). (919) 335-4379. FAX: (919) 338-1561. Licensee: Albemarle Broadcasting Co. Net: AP. Format: Oldies. News staff 2; news progmg 10 hrs wkly. Target aud: 35 plus. Spec prog: Gospel 18 hrs wkly. ■ J.L. Lamb Jr., pres & chief engr; D.S. Barclay, gen sls mgr; Tom Cherry, progmg dir; Jeff Mercer, mus dir; Bill Winslow, news dir. ■ Rates: $11; 11; 11; 11.

WGAI(AM)—Nov 2, 1947: 560 khz; 1 kw-D, 500 w-N, DA-2. TL: N36 20 20 W76 14 50. Stereo. Hrs opn: 24. Box 1408, 179 Lovers Ln. (27909). (919) 335-4371. FAX: (919) 335-2496. Licensee: William S. Ray (acq 6-86; $400,000; FTR 2-17-86). Net: CNN; Agri Net. Format: Adult contemp. News staff 3; news progmg 30 hrs wkly. Target aud: General. Spec prog: Farm 7 hrs, black 12 hrs wkly. ■ William Ray, pres; Lisa Ray, vp adv; Mickie Pruden, engrg mgr. ■ Rates: $15; 15; 15; 15.

WKJX(FM)—Aug 21, 1984: 96.7 mhz; 3 kw. Ant 286 ft. TL: N36 18 26 W76 16 03. Stereo. Hrs opn: 24. 903 Halstead Blvd. (27909). (919) 338-0196; (919) 338-0197. FAX: (919) 338-0082. Licensee: North Carolina Radio Service Inc. Net: NBC; N.C. News Net. Rep: T-N. Format: Country. Target aud: 18-55. ■ James Bond, pres; Patricia Hill, vp, gen mgr, gen sls mgr & prom mgr; Connie Duncan, opns mgr & progmg mgr; Sean Evans, mus dir; Dave Eldridge, news dir; Doug Pickell, pub affrs dir. ■ Rates: $12; 12; 12; 7.

WKOC(FM)—Nov 30, 1973: 93.7 mhz; 100 kw. Ant 997 ft. TL: N36 32 57 W76 11 21. Stereo. Suite 100, 168 Business Park Dr., Virginia Beach, VA (23462). (804) 671-1000. FAX: (804) 671-1212. Licensee: Benchmark Radio Acquisition Fund IV Ltd. Group owner: Benchmark Communications Radio (acq 3-5-93; $2.6 million; FTR 3-22-93). Net: ABC/C. Rep: D & R Radio. Format: Adult rock. News staff one; news progmg 2 hrs wkly. Target aud: 25-54. ■ Mark Kanak, gen mgr; Nancy Bergaa, gen sls mgr; Lauren MacLash, progmg dir; Larry Brooks, news dir; Ben Shaner, chief engr. ■ Rates: $100; 80; 90; 50.

WRSF(FM)—(Columbia). June 13, 1983: 105.7 mhz; 100 kw. Ant 613 ft. TL: N35 53 18 W76 13 50 (CP: Ant 987 ft.). Stereo. Hrs opn: 24. Box 1418, 2401 S. Croatan Hwy, Nags Head (27959). (919) 441-1024; (800) 553-4494. FAX: (919) 441-2109. Licensee: Jones-Eastern Radio Inc. (group owner; acq 5-87). Net: MBS. Format: Country. News staff one; news progmg 5 hrs wkly. Target aud: 18-54; young & mid-range adults. ■ C.J. Jones, CEO & pres; Carolyn Jones, exec vp; Jim Lackey, gen mgr; Jerry Barco, opns mgr; Mary Stenger, gen sls mgr; Gary Dean, prom dir; Randy Gill, progmg dir & mus dir; Gem Meyer, news dir; Jim Mills, chief engr. ■ Rates: $24; 22; 24; 16.

***WRVS-FM**—Mar 18, 1986: 89.9 mhz; 41 kw. Ant 280 ft. TL: N36 16 55 W76 12 44. Stereo. Campus Box 800; Williams Hall, 1704 Wheatsville Rd. (27909). (919) 335-3517. FAX: (919) 335-7408. Licensee: Elizabeth City State Univ. Format: Urban contemp, informational, educ. News staff one; news progmg 5 hrs wkly. Target aud: 18-24; young adult, college. Spec prog: Jazz 19 hrs, Black 15 hrs, gospel 19 hrs wkly. ■ E. V. Wilkins, chmn; Jimmy R. Jenkins, pres; Edith Thorpe, gen mgr; Glen Mason, prom dir; Ben Fagan, progmg dir & mus dir; Kimberley Pierce, news dir & pub affrs dir; Ben Shaner, chief engr.

Elizabethtown

WBLA(AM)—Aug 3, 1956: 1440 khz; 5 kw-D, 189 w-N. TL: N34 37 38 W78 37 23. Hrs opn: 19. Box 458, 512 Peanut Rd. (28337). (919) 862-3184; (919) 862-2000. FAX: (919) 862-2000. Licensee: Sound Business Inc. (acq 11-1-90; $550,000 with co-located FM; FTR 10-29-90). Net: N.C. News Net. Format: Oldies. News progmg 5 hrs wkly. Target aud: 25-54. Spec prog: Farm 5 hrs, black gospel/relg 8 hrs wkly. ■ Lee Hauser, pres, gen mgr & gen sls mgr; Arthur Deberry, vp; Tony Denton, stn mgr; Catherine DeVane, rgnl sls mgr; Dan Greenfield, progmg dir & mus dir; Sam Garfield, chief engr. ■ Rates: $14; 11.50; 14; 9.

WGQR(FM)—Co-owned with WBLA(AM). December 1989: 105.7 mhz; 6 kw. Ant 387 ft. TL: N34 37 38 W78 37 23. Stereo. Hrs opn: 19. Dups AM 90%. Net: N.C. News Net, Tar Heels Sports Net. ■ Rates: Same as AM.

Elkin

WJOS(AM)—1949: 1540 khz; 1 kw-D, 500 w-CH. TL: N36 14 55 W80 52 26. Drawer 1038 (28621). (919) 835-9567. FAX: (919) 835-5248. Licensee: Tri-County

Broadcasting Co. (acq 12-1-54). Net: ABC/I. Format: Gospel. ■ Leon Reece, gen mgr; John Wishon, stn mgr; Kristi Vestal, news dir; Stony Owens, chief engr.

WIFM-FM—Co-owned with WJOS(AM). 1949: 100.9 mhz; 600 w. Ant 709 ft. TL: N36 11 33 W80 50 59. Format: Oldies. ■ Alan Combs, progmg dir.

Elon College

***WSOE(FM)**—November 1978: 89.3 mhz; 500 w. Ant 104 ft. TL: N36 06 25 W79 30 22. Stereo. Box 6000, Elon College (27244). (910) 584-2465. Licensee: Elon College. Format: Div, progressive. ■ Don Grady, gen mgr.

Erwin

***WUAW(FM)**—May 11, 1990: 88.3 mhz; 3 kw. Ant 207 ft. TL: N35 20 15 W78 39 49. Stereo. Hrs opn: 24. Box 210, Route One, Triton H.S., Rm. 710, 2nd Flr., Secondary Rd. 1726 (28339). (919) 897-8121, ext. 125. (919) 897-8070. Licensee: Central Carolina Community College. Format: Educ, CHR, country. News progmg 7 hrs wkly. Spec prog: Black. ■ Dr. Marvin Joyner, pres; Anthony Ross Harrington, gen mgr, progmg dir & mus dir; Walter L. "Toby" Johnson Jr., chief engr.

Fair Bluff

WJHB(AM)—July 1988: 1480 khz; 1 kw-D. TL: N34 19 23 W79 00 07. Hrs opn: 13. Stn currently dark. Box 774, Hwy 76 E. (28439). Licensee: Amsan Broadcasting Co. (acq 7-5-89; FTR 7-10-89). ■ Don Amsan, pres & gen mgr.

WWIR(FM)—Not on air, target date unknown: 105.3 mhz; 1.3 kw. Ant 479 ft. TL: N34 20 21 W79 06 10. Box 17964, Raleigh (27619). Licensee: Great American Media Ltd. I.

Fairmont

WFMO(AM)—July 13, 1953: 860 khz; 1 kw-D. TL: N34 31 03 W79 06 19. Box 665 (28340). (919) 628-6781. FAX: (919) 628-6648. Licensee: Pro Media Inc. Group owner: Clark-Pittman Group (acq 12-31-86; $600,000 with co-located FM; FTR 11-10-86). Net: N.C. News Net. Rep: T N. Format: Southern Gospel. Spec prog: Farm 10 hrs, Black 5 hrs wkly. ■ James C. Clark, pres & gen mgr; John W. Pitman, vp & gen sls mgr; Bill Sellars, progmg dir; Bill Sellers, news dir; Steve Poole, chief engr.

WSTS(FM)—Co-owned with WFMO(AM). August 1975: 100.9 mhz; 3 kw. Ant 300 ft. TL: N34 31 03 W79 06 19 (CP: 50 kw, ant 492 ft.). Stereo. Prog sep from AM. Net: USA. Format: Classic rock. ■ Ray Bauer, mus dir.

Fairview

WMIY(AM)—Not on air, target date unknown: 880 khz; 1.1 kw-D, DA. TL: N35 32 52 W82 28 16. 314 N. Park Circle, Kansas City, MO (64116). Licensee: Michael Glinter.

Farmville

WGHB(AM)—Dec 12, 1959: 1250 khz; 5 kw-D, 2.5 kw-N, DA-2. TL: N35 36 17 W77 34 29. Hrs opn: 5:45 AM-11 PM. Box 229, Hwy. 121 N. (27828). (919) 753-4121. FAX: (919) 753-4123. Licensee: Rivercity Radio Inc. (acq 5-1-91; $325,000; FTR 3-25-91). Net: USA. Rep: T N. Format: Southern gospel/relg, talk. News progmg 8 hrs wkly. Target aud: 25-54. ■ Frank Canale, pres; Tommy Williams, gen mgr, gen sls mgr, prom mgr & mus dir; Doug Farris, chief engr.

WRQR(FM)—Mar 24, 1974: 94.3 mhz; 1.95 kw. Ant 407 ft. TL: N35 36 25 W77 28 05. Stereo. Box 1546, 200 Blacksmith Ln., Greenville (27835). (919) 830-0944. FAX: (919) 830-0047. Licensee: Steven Cohen (acq 3-23-91). Net: N.C. News. Rep: T N. Wash atty: Cole, Raywid & Braverman. Format: Beach & oldies. Target aud: 25-54. ■ John Moore, pres, gen mgr, stn mgr & sls dir; Ann Bryan, opns mgr; Jeff Diamond, progmg dir & pub affrs dir; Al Cannon, mus dir & chief engr. ■ Rates: $18; 15; 18; 15.

Fayetteville

WAZZ(FM)—See Laurinburg.

WFAI(AM)—1947: 1230 khz; 1 kw-U. TL: N35 04 15 W78 52 45. Box 649 (28302); 1108-R Ramsey St. (28301). (919) 483-0393. Licensee: WFAI Radio Inc. (acq 1-31-91; $75,000; FTR 2-18-91). Net: CNN; N.C. News Net. Format: News/talk. Spec prog: Sports 20 hrs wkly. ■ Henry W. Hoot, vp & gen mgr; Les Mosher, progmg dir; Paul Brian, pub affrs dir; Steve McDaniel, chief engr.

WFLB(AM)—1947: 1490 khz; 1 kw-U. TL: N35 03 45 W78 54 30. Box 530, 1338 Bragg Blvd. (28302). (919) 323-0925. FAX: (919) 323-0434. Licensee: Kat Broadcasting. Group owner: KAT Broadcasting Corp. Net: MBS; Southern Farm. Format: Relg. ■ Curt Nunnery, stn mgr.

WFNC(AM)—1940: 640 khz; 10 kw-D, 1 kw-N. TL: N35 04 46 W78 55 58. Hrs opn: 24. Box 35297, 1009 Drayton Rd. (28303). (919) 864-5222. FAX: (919) 864-3065. Licensee: Cape Fear Broadcasting (group owner). Net: CBS. Rep: Katz. Format: News/talk. News staff 4; news progmg 20 hrs wkly. Target aud: 35 plus. ■ Victor W. Dawson, pres; John G. Dawson, gen mgr; Paul Michels, opns mgr; John Dawson, gen sls mgr; Jeff Thompson, progmg dir & news dir; Terry Jordan, chief engr.

WQSM(FM)—Co-owned with WFNC(AM). 1947: 98.1 mhz; 100 kw. Ant 850 ft. TL: N35 04 46 W78 55 58. Stereo. Prog sep from AM. Format: Adult contemp. Target aud: General. ■ Katy Rollins, gen sls mgr; Cheryle Rivas, prom mgr; Kent Layton, progmg dir; Don Wood, mus dir; Sue Runyan, news dir.

***WFSS(FM)**—Dec 7, 1977: 91.9 mhz; 100 kw. Ant 440 ft. TL: N35 04 22 W78 53 27 Stereo. Hrs opn: 18. 1200 Murchison Rd. (28301). (919) 486-1381. FAX: (919) 486-1516. Licensee: Fayetteville State Univ. Board of Trustees. Net: NPR. Wash atty: May & Dunne Chartered. Format: Jazz. News progmg 30 hrs wkly. Target aud: 18 plus; minorities, professionals, high school graduates to college graduates. Spec prog: Reggae 5 hrs, Sp 5 hrs wkly. ■ Robert L. Collins, gen mgr & chief engr; C. John Malzone, dev dir; R. Patrice Gilliam, prom dir; Janet G. Wright, progmg dir; Jimmy Miller, mus dir; Joseph C. Ross, news dir.

WIDU(AM)—Jan 20, 1958: 1600 khz; 1 kw-D, 25 w-N. TL: N35 02 58 W78 51 33 (CP: 5 kw-D, DA). Drawer 2247 (28302); 145 Rowan St. (28301). (919) 483-6111. FAX: (919) 483-6601. Licensee: Charles W. Cookman (acq 1-17-89). Rep: Roslin. Format: Black gospel, talk. ■ Wes Cookman, pres; Troy Williams, gen mgr; Sandra Larson, gen sls mgr; Andre DeLoach, progmg dir & mus dir; Richard Bowden, news dir; Van Clough, chief engr.

WQSM(FM)—Listing follows WFNC(AM).

WZFX(FM)—(Whiteville). Feb 21, 1962: 99.1 mhz; 100 kw. Ant 1,000 ft. TL: N34 44 05 W78 47 25. Stereo. Box 710 (28302). (919) 486-4991. FAX: (919) 486-6720. Licensee: Joyner Communications Inc. Group owner: Atlantic Broadcasting Group. Net: ABC/E. Rep: D & R Radio. Format: Urban contemp. News staff one; news progmg 2 hrs wkly. Target aud: 18-49. ■ David Weil, pres; Lynn Carraway, vp & gen mgr; Sonny Pagan, gen sls mgr; Bobby Jeffers, progmg mgr; Omega Jones, mus dir; Simone Enoch, news dir; Van Clough, chief engr.

Forest City

WAGY(AM)—Oct 15, 1958: 1320 khz; 1 kw-D, 500 w-N, DA-N. TL: N35 21 19 W81 52 52. Hrs opn: 16. Box 280, 1110 Oak St. (28043). (704) 245-9887. FAX: (704) 287-2429. Licensee: WAGY Inc. (acq 12-13-85; $310,000; FTR 11-4-85). Net: CNN. Rep: Midsouth. Format: C&W. News staff one; news progmg 7 hrs wkly. Target aud: General. Spec prog: Black one hr wkly. ■ Ray Riffle, chmn; Dale Riffle, pres; Grace Riffle, vp; Jay Engle, gen mgr; Wayne Dobbins, gen sls mgr; David Perry, prom mgr, progmg dir & mus dir; Patrick D. Nanney, news dir; Ed McDade, Jim Moody, engrg mgrs. ■ Rates: $8.80; 7.90; 8.80; na.

WBBO-FM—Sept 10, 1947: 93.3 mhz; 87.2 kw. Ant 2,030 ft. TL: N35 16 19 W82 14 00. Stereo. Suite 493, 37 Villa Rd., Greenville, SC (29615). (803) 233-9393. FAX: (803) 763-9393. Licensee: Rutherford County Radio. Format: Jazz, new age. ■ Jodi Freytag, gen mgr & gen sls mgr; Mike Murphy, progmg dir; Diane Swift, news dir; Tim Warner, chief engr.

WWOL(AM)—Sept 10, 1947: 780 khz; 1 kw-D. TL: N35 21 02 W81 54 04. 1263 W. Main St. (28043). (704) 245-0078. Licensee: Holly Springs Baptist Church (acq 3-1-90; $150,000; FTR 3-19-90). Wash atty: Maupin, Taylor, Ellis & Adams. Format: Southern gospel preaching and music. News progmg 2 hrs wkly. Target aud: General. ■ Wade H. Huntley, pres & stn mgr; Nancy Skipper, opns mgr; Ray Davis, progmg dir & mus dir; Henry E. Melton, chief engr. ■ Rates: $6.75; 6.25; 6.75; 6.25.

Franklin

WAJA(AM)—May 24, 1979: 1480 khz; 5 kw-D. TL: N35 10 58 W83 21 27 (CP: 13 w-N). 427 E. Main St. (28734-2646). (704) 369-5033. FAX: (704) 369-3197. Licensee: Macon Broadcasting Co. (acq 12-19-89; $133,000; FTR 1-8-90). Net: CNN. Format: Relg, C&W, var. ■ Carroll Lee, gen mgr; Grace Lee, gen sls mgr & news dir; Tony Angel, progmg dir & mus dir; Ronnie Evans, chief engr.

***WFQS(FM)**—Mar 31, 1989: 91.3 mhz; 265 w. Ant 2,304 ft. TL: N35 10 24 W83 34 52. Stereo. Hrs opn: 24. Rebroadcasts WCQS(FM) Asheville 100%. c/o 73 Broadway, Asheville (28801). (704) 253-6875. FAX: (704) 253-6700. Licensee: Western N.C. Public Radio Inc. Net: APR, NPR. Wash atty: Cohn & Marks. Format: Class, jazz, news. News staff one; news progmg 35 hrs wkly. Target aud: General. Spec prog: Folk 11 hrs wkly. ■ Edward Subkis, gen mgr; Sandra Norbo, dev mgr & sls dir; Barbara Sayer, progmg dir; Richard J. Kowal, mus dir; Dave Hurand, news dir; Jobie F. Sprinkle, chief engr. ■ Rates: $16; 8; 16; 8.

WFSC(AM)—May 5, 1957: 1050 khz; 1 kw-D. TL: N35 12 42 W83 22 07. Hrs opn: 18. Box 470, 1325 Radio Hill Rd. (28734). (704) 524-4418; (704) 524-5395. FAX: (704) 369-8070. Licensee: Cross Country Communications Inc. (acq 5-1-87; $650,000 with co-located FM; FTR 5-4-87). Net: ABC/I; N.C. News Net. Wash atty: Fletcher, Heald & Hildreth. Format: Country. News staff one; news progmg 3 hrs wkly. Spec prog: Gospel 14 hrs wkly. ■ Brenda Wooten, gen mgr; Jo Zachary, gen sls mgr; Randy Raby, mus dir; Nancie Wilson, news dir; Rick Cruse, chief engr. ■ Rates: $9; 9; 9; 9.

WRFR(FM)—Co-owned with WFSC(AM). Sept 1, 1965: 96.7 mhz; 6 kw. Ant -200 ft. TL: N35 12 42 W83 22 07. Stereo. Hrs opn: 18 Prog sep from AM. (704) 524-5395. Net: NC News Net. Format: Adult contemp. ■ Rates: $11.40; 11.40; 11.40; 11.40.

Fuquay-Varina

WCRY(AM)—1949: 1460 khz; 5 kw-D, 122 w-N, DA-2. TL: N35 36 37 W78 48 14. Hrs opn: 24. Box 489 (27526). (919) 552-2263; (919) 552-9332. FAX: (919) 552-8795. Licensee: Pinehurst Broadcasting Corp. (acq 10-1-93; $80,000; FTR 10-18-93). Net: NBC Talknet, CBS, ABC, Daynet, BRN; N.C. News Net. Wash atty: McNain & Sanford. Format: News/talk. Target aud: 25-64. ■ Dane' Adams, pres & gen mgr; Ann Adams, exec vp; Doug Crouch, opns mgr; Donna Alters, gen sls mgr; Mike Jordan, prom mgr; Steve Adams, progmg dir & news dir; Dr. Jim Davis, chief engr.

WNND(FM)—Dec 1, 1980: 103.9 mhz; 1.2 kw. Ant 493 ft. TL: N35 38 43 W78 43 29 (CP: 10.1 kw, ant 522 ft., TL: N35 37 42 W78 44 58). Stereo. Suite 295, 2000 Regency Pkwy., Cary (27511). (919) 481-1039. Licensee: Ceder Raleigh L.P. Net: NBC. Format: Easy lstng. ■ Michelle Clements, gen mgr.

Garner

WHEV(AM)—Aug 11, 1969: 1000 khz; 1 kw-D. TL: N35 43 50 W78 36 12. Box 755, 1423 Creech Rd. (27529). (919) 833-4487. Licensee: Henry E. Vail (acq 10-1-87). Net: USA. Format: Country. Target aud: 25 plus. ■ Henry E. Vail, gen mgr & progmg dir; Henry Edwards, mus dir; Robert Weaver, chief engr. ■ Rates: $12; 9; 9; na.

Gaston

WLGQ(FM)—Nov 28, 1988: 97.9 mhz; 1.35 kw. Ant 488 ft. TL: N36 27 38 W77 33 52. Stereo. Hrs opn: 24. Drawer Q, 1730 Birdsong St., Roanoke Rapids (27870). (919) 537-9790. FAX: (919) 535-2686. Licensee: Draper Communications. Net: NBC, N.C. Net, Va. News Net. Rep: T N. Format: Adult contemp. News staff one; news progmg 2 hrs wkly. Target aud: 21-54. ■ Johnny Draper, pres; Al Haskins, gen mgr; Russ Barrett, opns dir; Nell Haskins, gen sls mgr; Bobby Tuggles, prom mgr & mus dir; Mark Mathews, news dir; Gary Harrison, chief engr. ■ Rates: $13.50; 10; 12; 8.50.

Gastonia

WAAK(AM)—See Dallas.

WCKZ-FM—September 1947: 101.9 mhz; 99 kw. Ant 987 ft. TL: N35 13 56 W81 16 35. Stereo. Box 36609 (28236); 2303 W. Morehead St., Charlotte (28208). (704) 342-4102. FAX: (704) 333-3460. Licensee: BPI Charlotte License Subsidiary Inc. Group owner: Broadcasting Partners Inc. (acq 12-3-93; $3 million; FTR 1-3-94). Net: ABC/FM. Rep: D & R Radio. Wash atty: Gregg Skall. Format: Urban/contemp. News staff one. Target aud: 18-34; young adults. ■ Christine Remme, gen mgr; Tim Patterson, prom mgr & progmg dir; Alan Lane, chief engr.

WGAS(AM)—See South Gastonia.

WGNC(AM)—March 1939: 1450 khz; 1 kw-U. TL: N35 16 32 W81 12 04. Hrs opn: 24. Box 1884 (28053-1884). (704) 868-8222. FAX: (704) 482-4680. Licensee: KTC Broadcasting Inc. (acq 10-3-89; $125,000; FTR 10-23-

89). Net: CNN; N.C. News Net. Format: Adult comtemp, oldies, talk. News staff one; news progmg 5 hrs wkly. Target aud: 18-49. ■ Calvin R. Hastings, pres, gen mgr & gen sls mgr; Harold Watson, sls dir, prom mgr & adv dir; Milton Baker, progmg dir & mus dir; Amy Carpenter, news dir & pub affrs dir; Don Strawn, chief engr. ■ Rates: $11.50; 10.00; 11.50; 10.

WLTC(AM)—Mar 8, 1948: 1370 khz; 5 kw-D. TL: N35 15 40 W81 08 45. Box 3927, 304 N. New Hope Rd. (28052). (704) 865-1079. Licensee: Ford Broadcasting. Net: USA. Wash atty: Maupin, Taylor, Ellis & Adams. Format: Southern gospel. News progmg 22 hrs wkly. Target aud: 30 plus. Spec prog: Gospel 10 hrs wkly. ■ Carl Ford, pres, gen sls mgr, progmg dir, mus dir & news dir; Andrea Frieze, gen mgr.

Goldsboro

WEQR(FM)—Feb 2, 1972: 102.3 mhz; 6 kw. Ant 292 ft. TL: N35 23 54 WL78 00 38. Suite 200, 200 W. Ash St. (27530). (919) 736-1699. FAX: (919) 734-1908. Licensee: Southern Broadcasters Inc. Net: CNN. Format: Adult contemp. ■ Webster A. James, vp & vp mktg; Brad Hood, stn mgr; Warren Henderson, opns mgr & progmg dir; Ken Plummer, news dir; Don Price, chief engr.

WFMC(AM)—Nov 11, 1951: 730 khz; 1 kw-D, 98 w-N. TL: N35 22 25 W78 00 41. Stereo. Hrs opn: 18. Box 2006, Hwy 117 S. (27533). (919) 734-4211. Licensee: WEG Broadcasting Corp. (acq 11-1-84; $600,000; FTR 10-8-84). Net: Unistar; Southern Farm; N.C. News Net. Format: Variety, country. News staff one; news progmg 10 hrs wkly. Target aud: 18 plus. ■ Robert Y. Wooten, pres, gen mgr, gen sls mgr & progmg dir; Anne B. Walters, mus dir; Bonnie Edward, news dir; Bill Wiggs, chief engr. ■ Rates: $8; 8; 8; 7.

WGBR(AM)—1939: 1150 khz; 5 kw-D, 1 kw-N, DA-2. TL: N35 23 52 W78 00 32. Stereo. Hrs opn: 24. Box 207, 914 W. Grantham St. (27533). (919) 736-1150. FAX: (919) 736-3876. Licensee: New Age Communications L.P. Group owner: Great American Media (acq 2-15-89; $2.2. million with co-located FM; FTR 3-6-89). Net: ABC/I; N.C. News. Format: News, talk. News staff one; news progmg 11 hrs wkly. Target aud: 25 plus. Spec prog: Farm 6 hrs wkly. ■ Donald W. Curtis, pres; Rick Heilmann, gen mgr; Bill Kirby, gen sls mgr; Wayne Alley, progmg dir; Bill Justice, news dir; Lew Graves, chief engr. ■ Rates: $12; 12; 12; 7.50.

WKTC(FM)—Co-owned with WGBR(AM). 1946: 96.9 mhz; 100 kw. Ant 1,056 ft. TL: N35 23 52 W78 08 07. Stereo. Prog sep from AM. (919) 734-3336. Net: N.C. News. News progmg 2 hrs wkly. Target aud: 25-54. ■ Mike Sleyman, progmg dir; Donna James, mus dir.

WSSG(AM)—Oct 22, 1955: 1300 khz; 1 kw-D, 50 w-N. TL: N35 24 08 W78 01 20. Hrs opn: 16. 116 W. Mulberry St. (27530). (919) 734-1300. Licensee: Creative Broadcasting Co. (acq 9-1-92; $100 & assumption of seller's note, $114,750; FTR 8-10-92). Net: USA, Moody. Format: Southern gospel. News progmg 12 hrs wkly. Target aud: General. ■ Willie Strickland, pres; Don Smith, gen mgr. ■ Rates: $9; 9; 9; 9.

Graham

WBAG(AM)—See Burlington-Graham.

WSML(AM)—Dec 2, 1967: 1200 khz; 10 kw-D, 1 kw-N, DA-N. TL: N36 08 01 W79 28 14. Box 900, 120 E. Pine St. (27253). (919) 228-1200; (919) 227-4254. FAX: (919) 227-4254. Licensee: Alamance Broadcasting Co. Inc. Group owner: Gray Broadcasting (acq 7-1-85; $100; FTR 5-13-85). Net: ABC/I. Rep: Dora Clayton. Wash atty: Miller & Fields. Format: Relg, news, talk. Spec prog: Black 18 hrs wkly. ■ Ted J. Gray Jr., pres & gen mgr; Joey Gray, gen sls mgr; Olin Campbell, progmg dir; Larry Ingold, mus dir; Jim Davis, chief engr. ■ Rates: $10; 10; 10; na.

WZZU(FM)—See Burlington-Graham.

Granite Falls

WYCV(AM)—Feb 22, 1963: 900 khz; 500 w-D, 251 w-N. TL: N35 47 10 W81 25 00. Hrs opn: 5 AM-10:15 PM. Box 486, Hwy 321-A S. of Granite Falls (28630). (704) 396-3361; (704) 396-3362. FAX: (704) 396-9193. Licensee: Freedom Broadcasting Corp. Group owner: Marvin L. Sizemore (acq 4-29-92). Net: USA. Wash atty: Smithwick & Belendiuk. Format: Relg. News progmg 2 hrs wkly. Target aud: 25-60. Spec prog: Gospel. ■ Marvin L. Sizemore, pres; Ted Fuller, chief engr. ■ Rates: $6; 6; 6; 3.

Greensboro

WGLD(AM)—May 22, 1948: 1320 khz; 5 kw-U, DA-2. TL: N36 09 01 W79 54 48. Hrs opn: 24. Suite 400, 4000 Piedmont Pkwy., High Point (27265). (910) 885-2100. FAX: (910) 887-0104. Licensee: MHD Inc. (acq 4-23-93; $3.5 million with WWWB[FM] High Point; FTR 5-17-93). Net: Unistar. Rep: Major Mkt. Format: MOR. Target aud: 40 plus. ■ Bernard Mann, pres; Edward L. Weiss, gen mgr; Mike Fenley, progmg mgr; Pam McGann, news dir; Steve Warford, chief engr.

WJMH(FM)—See Reidsville.

WKEW(AM)—Feb 16, 1942: 1400 khz; 1 kw-U. TL: N36 04 00 W79 47 49. Box 13588 (27415); 708 Summit Ave. (27405). (919) 273-3631. Licensee: WKEW Partners (acq 12-8-82). Net: ABC/I, MBS. Format: News/talk. Target aud: 35 plus. Spec prog: Black 10 hrs wkly. ■ William P. Mitchell, gen mgr, gen sls mgr & prom mgr; Bill Ayers, mus dir; Janet Jones, news dir; Larry Allen, chief engr.

WKSI(FM)—Listing follows WPET(AM).

WMAG(FM)—See High Point.

WMQX(AM)—(Winston-Salem). Mar 25, 1937: 1340 khz; 1 kw-U. TL: N36 04 26 W80 15 19. Hrs opn: 24. Box 593, (27102). (919) 723-9393. FAX: (919) 722-5697. Licensee: Max Radio of Greensboro Inc. (acq 10-6-93; $2.5 million with co-located FM; FTR 10-25-93). Rep: D & R Radio. Format: Oldies. Target aud: 25-54. Spec prog: Relg 6 hrs wkly. ■ Jeff Silver, vp & gen mgr; Matt Allen, progmg dir; Ed Kasovic, chief engr.

WMQX-FM—(Winston-Salem). April 1947: 93.1 mhz; 100 kw. Ant 1,050 ft. TL: N36 16 33 W79 56 27. Stereo. Hrs opn: 24. Dups AM 100%.

***WNAA(FM)**—1979: 90.1 mhz; 10 kw. Ant 467 ft. TL: N36 04 58 W79 46 08. Stereo. Hrs opn: 24. Suite 200, Price Hall, NC A&T State Univ. (27411-1135). (910) 334-7936. Licensee: North Carolina Agricultural & Technical State University. Format: Black, urban comtemp, jazz, gospel. News staff one; news progmg 7 hrs wkly. Target aud: 35-45; general. Spec prog: Blues 3 hrs, reggae 4 hrs, oldies 2 hrs wkly. ■ Tony Welborne, gen mgr, stn mgr & prom mgr; Yvonne Anderson, opns mgr, progmg dir & mus dir; Teresa Styles, news dir; Judith Malik, pub affrs dir; Larry Allen, chief engr.

WPET(AM)—1954: 950 khz; 500 w-D. TL: N36 02 16 W79 47 42. Box 16924 (27416-0924); 221 W. Meadowview Rd. (27406). (919) 275-9738. FAX: (919) 275-6236. Licensee: Bahakel Communications (group owner; acq 5-87). Rep: Eastman. Format: Relg. Target aud: 25-54. ■ Cy N. Bahakel, pres; Stan Thomas, gen mgr; Dave Compton, opns mgr & progmg dir; Larry Allen, chief engr. ■ Rates: $20; 15; 15; na.

WKSI(FM)—Co-owned with WPET(AM). Jan 9, 1958: 98.7 mhz; 100 kw. Ant 1,000 ft. TL: N36 02 16 W79 47 42. Stereo. Hrs opn: 24. Prog sep from AM. (919) 275-9895. Format: CHR. Target aud: 18-49. ■ Chuck Finley, opns mgr & progmg dir; Ray Barber, gen sls mgr; Nancy Lee Jones, prom mgr. ■ Rates: $70; 40; 50; 15.

***WQFS(FM)**—January 1970: 90.9 mhz; 1.9 kw. Ant 200 ft. TL: N36 05 39 W79 53 21. Stereo. Box 17714 (27410). (919) 316-2352. FAX: (919) 316-2951. Licensee: Guilford College Bd of Trustees. Format: Progsv. News staff one; news progmg 4 hrs wkly. Target aud: 15-50. Spec prog: Class 2 hrs, Black 4 hrs, jazz 4 hrs, women's music 2 hrs, Sp 2 hrs, blues 7 hrs, reggae 9 hrs, acoustic jazz 2 hrs, hardcore 2 hrs, dance 6 hrs wkly. ■ Jennifer Fuller, gen mgr; Tanya Stigler, prom mgr; Ken Allen, progmg dir; Louisa Sparenta, Becky Browning, mus dirs; Paul Mosca, news dir; Geremy Pickens, chief engr.

WQMG(AM)—Oct 5, 1962: 1510 khz; 1 kw-D, 250 w-CH. TL: N36 03 42 W79 47 35. Hrs opn: Sun up-Sundown. Box 14702 (27415-4702); 1060 Gatewood Ave. (27405). (919) 272-5121. Licensee: North State Broadcasting Co. (acq 12-75). Rep: Banner. Format: Black gospel. Target aud: Black adults 25-54. ■ M. Rees Poag, pres; Lisa Powell, gen mgr; Irish Gaymon, stn mgr & progmg dir; George Majett, mus dir; Larry Allen, chief engr.

WQMG-FM—July 8, 1962: 97.1 mhz; 100 kw. Ant 1,289 ft. TL: N36 05 09 W79 45 38 (CP: N35 56 43 W79 51 44). Stereo. Dups AM 95%. (919) 275-1657. Licensee: Murray Hill Broadcasting Co. (acq 8-11-78). Net: ABC. Format: Urban contemp. News staff one. Target aud: Black adults 18-34. ■ Brian Wallace, progmg dir; Jackson Brown, mus dir.

***WUAG(FM)**—July 20, 1964: 103.1 mhz; 18.1 w. Ant 230 ft. TL: N36 03 51 W79 48 37 (CP: Ant 259 ft.). Stereo. Taylor Bldg., Univ. of N.C. at Greensboro (27412). (919) 334-5450. Licensee: U. of N.C. at Greensboro, Bd of Trustees. Format: Progsv rock. News staff one; news progmg 2 hrs wkly. Target aud: 12-40; high school and college students. Spec prog: Jazz 3 hrs, relg 3 hrs, rap & dance 3 hrs, blues 3 hrs, metal 3 hrs wkly. ■ Jack Fagan, gen mgr; Kelly Henderson, mus dir; Eric Layton, news dir; Woodrow McDougald, chief engr.

WWBG(AM)—Not on air, target date unknown: 1470 khz; 3.5 kw-D, 5 kw-N, DA-2. TL: N36 12 46 W79 54 46. 1108 Grecade St. (27408). Licensee: Triad Network Inc.

Greenville

WNCT(AM)—1940: 1070 khz; 10 kw-U, DA-N. TL: N35 36 14 W77 25 29. Hrs opn: 24. Box 7167 (27835). (919) 757-0011. Licensee: Park Communications Inc. (group owner; acq 1962). Net: CBS, MBS, ABC. Rep: Major Mkt. Format: Talk, news, sports. News staff one. Target aud: General. Spec prog: Farm 10 hrs wkly. ■ Rick Prusator, vp; Bob Manning, gen mgr; Joe Mule, gen sls mgr; Stacy Roberts, progmg dir; Roy McCory, chief engr.

WNCT-FM—Dec 22, 1963: 107.9 mhz; 100 kw. Ant 1,800 ft. TL: N35 21 55 W77 23 38. Stereo. Hrs opn: 24. Net: ABC/E. Format: Easy listening. ■ WNCT-TV affil.

WOOW(AM)—October 1959: 1340 khz; 1 kw-U. TL: N35 36 58 W77 22 14. Box 8361, 304 Evans St. (27834). (919) 757-0365. FAX: (919) 757-1793. Licensee: The Minority Voice Inc. (acq 8-24-88). Wash atty: Tharrington, Smith & Hargrove. Format: Black, urban contemp, talk. News staff one; news progmg 5 hrs wkly. Target aud: 35-45; older Afro-American adult community. Spec prog: Jazz 5 hrs wkly. ■ Jim Rouse, pres; Roger Johnson, gen mgr; William Clark, gen sls mgr; Abdul Rouse, progmg dir; T. L. Davis, mus dir; Lynette Riddick, news dir; Eugene Underwood, chief engr.

***WZMB(FM)**—Feb 2, 1982: 91.3 mhz; 282 w. Ant 134 ft. TL: N35 36 01 W77 21 53. Stereo. Hrs opn: 24. East Carolina Univ., Mendenhall Student Center (27858). (919) 757-6656. Licensee: East Carolina Univ. Media Board (acq 2-82). Net: AP. Format: Progsv rock. News progmg 6 hrs wkly. Target aud: 18-24; university students. Spec prog: Black 14 hrs, class 3 hrs, reggae 7 hrs, jazz 3 hrs, blues 3 hrs, contemp Christian 3 hrs wkly. ■ Beth Arthur, gen mgr; Paul Meador, mus dir; Ray Randall, news dir; Macon Dail, chief engr.

Grifton

WTND(FM)—Sept 11, 1989: 99.5 mhz; 16.5 kw. Ant 830 ft. TL: N35 12 07 W77 11 15. Stereo. 207 Glenbernie Dr., Newbern (28560). (919) 636-0995. FAX: (919) 633-0718. Licensee: Taylor Communications Corp. (acq 11-23-92; $1.4 million; FTR 12-14-92). Format: Hot country. ■ Bruce Wilson, gen mgr; Steve Kelly, progmg dir.

Hamlet

WJSG(FM)—Aug 25, 1991: 104.3 mhz; 2.5 kw. Ant 489 ft. TL: N34 48 44 W79 43 38. 418 Airport Rd., Rockingham (28379). (919) 895-3787. FAX: (919) 895-8811. Licensee: Jackson Broadcasting Co. Format: Christian country. ■ Sherrell Jackson, pres & gen mgr.

Hatteras

WVAV(FM)—Not on air, target date unknown: 94.3 mhz; 6 kw. Ant 197 ft. TL: N35 15 38 W75 35 02. 2557-E Mountain Lodge, Birmingham, AL (35216). Licensee: Hurricane Communications.

WYND-FM—Not on air, target date unknown: 97.5 mhz; 50 kw. Ant 492 ft. TL: N35 15 42 W75 33 20. 1359 Black Meadow Rd., Spotsylvania, VA (22553). (703) 972-2690. FAX: (703) 972-1309. Licensee: Pamlico Sound Co. Inc. Wash atty: Richard J. Hayes Jr. ■ Richard J. Hayes Jr., pres.

Havelock

WCPQ(AM)—June 16, 1962: 1330 khz; 1 kw-D. TL: N34 55 24 W76 56 37. Box 247 (28532). (919) 447-0101. FAX: (919) 447-0103. Licensee: Richard V. Goines (acq 8-19-86; $30,598 with co-located FM; FTR 7-7-86). Net: ABC/E. Rep: Southern. Format: Adult contemp. ■ Rick Goines, pres, gen mgr & gen sls mgr; Rich Bryant, mus dir; Tom Robertson, chief engr.

WMSQ(FM)—Co-owned with WCPQ(AM). Nov 12, 1971: 104.9 mhz; 3 kw. Ant 186 ft. TL: N34 55 24 W76 56 37 (CP: 2.9 kw, ant 310 ft.). Stereo. Dups AM 100%.

Henderson

WCBQ(AM)—See Oxford.

WHNC(AM)—June 20, 1945: 890 khz; 1 kw-D. TL: N36 21 04 W78 22 35. Box 1240, Norlina Rd. (27536). (919)

438-8111. FAX: (919) 430-8474. Licensee: Rigel Inc. (acq 8-1-78). Net: Unistar. Rep: Southern. Format: 40s, 50s, 60s with selected songs of the 70s & 80s, country. News staff one. Target aud: 35 plus; middle-age secure people. Spec prog: Black gospel 7 hrs wkly. ■ Roy O. Rodwell, pres; Peg Bonnabeau Turner, vp & gen mgr; Sylvia Thompson Edwards, opns dir; Suzanne Farnam, prom mgr & adv dir; Bill Harris, progmg dir & mus dir; Bob Harrison, news dir; Paul Leggett, pub affrs dir; Frank White, chief engr. ■ Rates: $7; 7; 7; na.

WIZS(AM)—May 1, 1955: 1450 khz; 1 kw-U. TL: N36 19 31 W78 24 36. Hrs opn: 5 AM-midnight. Box 192, Studio & Transmitter Bldg., Radio Lane (27536); Box 556, Office, 220 White Oak Dr. (27536). (919) 492-3001; (919) 438-8218. FAX: (919) 492-5594. Licensee: Rose Farm and Rentals Inc. (acq 6-1-89; $265,000; FTR 6-19-89). Net: N.C. News Net. Rep: T-N. Format: Country. News staff one; news progmg 8 hrs wkly. Target aud: 18-55; fans of top 60 country music. Spec prog: Religious 6 hrs, Sp 6 hrs, farm 2 hrs wkly. ■ John D. Rose III, pres; David Collier Jr., stn mgr; Kemp Collins, sls dir; Mike Elliott, prom dir & mus dir; Donna D. Young, progmg mgr & pub affrs dir; John Rose, news dir & chief engr. ■ Rates: $9.60; 9.20; 9.60; 4.60.

WYFL(FM)—1948: 92.5 mhz; 100 kw. Ant 1,020 ft. TL: N36 13 23 W78 12 07. Stereo. 120 E. Belle St. (27536). (919) 492-9511. Licensee: Bible Broadcasting Network (group owner; acq 10-3-81; $335,000; FTR 9-14-81). Net: AP. Format: Relg. Target aud: General. ■ Lowell Davey, pres; Bryant Nelson, gen mgr; Harold Richards, news dir; Ron Muffley, chief engr.

Hendersonville

WHKP(AM)—Oct 24, 1946: 1450 khz; 1 kw-U. TL: N35 20 20 W82 27 20. Box 2470, 1450 7th Ave. E. (28793). (704) 693-9061. Licensee: Radio Hendersonville Inc. (acq 6-4-86). Net: ABC/I, AP. Wash atty: Tharrington, Smith & Hargrove. Format: MOR. News staff one; news progmg 25 hrs wkly. Target aud: 25 plus; middle-to-upper income. ■ Art Cooley, pres & gen mgr; Richard Rhodes, vp sls & sls dir; Al Hope, vp progmg & progmg dir; Allen Reese, news dir; Norman Lyda, vp engrg & chief engr. ■ Rates: $26; 14; 17; 7.

WMYI(FM)—Licensed to Hendersonville. See Greenville, S.C.

WTZQ(AM)—Dec 25, 1964: 1600 khz; 5 kw-D, 500 w-N, DA-2. TL: N35 18 07 W82 27 30. 717 Greenville Hwy. (28792). (704) 692-1600. Licensee: United Broadcasting Enterprises Inc. (acq 2-25-93; $15,000 with WISE[AM] Asheville; FTR 4-12-93). Net: AP; N.C. News. Rep: Carolina. Format: Btfl mus. News staff one; news progmg 10 hrs wkly. Target aud: 35 plus; mature adult market. ■ Glen Wilcox, pres; R.L. Sink, gen mgr & gen sls mgr; Steve Murphy, opns mgr; Randy Houston, dev dir; Dave Hogan, progmg mgr; Tracy Peltier, news dir; Edward McDade, chief engr.

Hertford

WKJE(FM)—Not on air, target date unknown: 104.9 mhz; 3 kw. Ant 281 ft. TL: N36 10 45 W76 21 12. E. Rock Rd., Allentown, PA (18103). Licensee: Maranatha Broadcasting Co. Inc.

Hickory

***WAAE(FM)**—Not on air, target date unknown: 90.3 mhz; 150 w. Ant 245 ft. Licensee: University Radio Foundation Inc.

WEZC(FM)—Jan 20, 1959: 102.9 mhz; 31 kw. Ant 1,545 ft. TL: N35 24 26 W81 07 47. Stereo. Suite 210, 301 S. McDowell St., Charlotte (28281). (704) 335-1029. FAX: (704) 372-3208. Licensee: Trumper Communications of North Carolina Ltd. (acq 4-20-93; $6 million; FTR 5-10-93). Net: Unistar. Rep: Katz. Format: Adult contemp. News staff one. Target aud: 25-54. ■ Pat Reedy, gen mgr; Mike Berlak, opns mgr & progmg dir; Melinda Holt, gen sls mgr; Art Bussure, chief engr.

WHKY(AM)—June 10, 1940: 1290 khz; 5 kw-D, 1 kw-N, DA-N. TL: N35 43 42 W81 17 54. Hrs opn: 5 AM-midnight. 526 Main Ave. S.E. (28601). (704) 322-5115. FAX: (704) 322-8256. Licensee: Long Family Partnership (acq 3-16-87). Net: ABC/D; N.C. News. Rep: T-N. Wash atty: Hardy & Carey. Format: News/talk. News staff 2; news progmg 50 hrs wkly. Target aud: 35-54. ■ Thomas E. Long, gen mgr & chief engr; Jeff Long, stn mgr, prom mgr & progmg dir; Jim Carr, gen sls mgr; Louanne Kincaid, news dir; Susie Woods, pub affrs dir. WHKY-TV affil. ■ Rates: $14; 12; 13; 11.

WIRC(AM)—Dec 5, 1948: 630 khz; 1 kw-D, 57 w-N. TL: N35 43 07 W81 18 36. Box 938 (28603). (704) 521-9575. Licensee: Westcom Ltds. (acq 1985; $2,570,000 with co-located FM; FTR 6-10-85). Net: ABC. Rep: Roslin. Format: C&W. News staff one. Target aud: 25 plus. Spec prog: Relg 7 hrs, sports 5 hrs wkly. ■ Jerry Oakley, pres; Maynard Taylor, gen mgr; Jess Parks, gen sls mgr; J.J. Michaels, progmg dir; Eric Scott, mus dir; Dave Hardin, news dir; Larry Schropp, chief engr.

WXRC(FM)—Co-owned with WIRC(AM). Dec 7, 1962: 95.7 mhz; 100 kw. Ant 1,276 ft. TL: N35 42 32 W81 31 32. Stereo. Prog sep from AM. 3440-B Saint Vardell Ln., Charlotte (28217). (704) 338-9600. FAX: (704) 324-9329. Net: NBC the Source. Rep: Katz & Powell. Format: AOR. Target aud: 18-49.

***WPAR(FM)**—Dec 3, 1985: 88.1 mhz; 10 kw. Ant 300 ft. TL: N35 43 34 W81 08 52. Stereo. Hrs opn: 24. Box 909, Claremont (28610). (704) 459-9803. Licensee: Positive Alternative Radio Inc. Net: CBN. Format: Southern gospel, educational. ■ Donald W. Lee, gen mgr; Robert Barnett, mus dir.

WXRC(FM)—Listing follows WIRC(AM).

WYCV(AM)—See Granite Falls.

High Point

WGOS(AM)—July 1947: 1070 khz; 1 kw-D. TL: N35 54 58 W80 01 00. Hrs opn: Sunrise-sunset. 6223 Old Mendenhall Rd. (27263). (919) 434-5024. Licensee: Ritchy Broadcasting Co. Inc. (acq 8-6-79). Format: Oldies, golden country, southern gospel. Target aud: General. ■ Simon Ritchy, pres & progmg dir; Lynn Ritchy, gen mgr & gen sls mgr; Max Parrish, stn mgr & chief engr; D. W. Long, mus dir. ■ Rates: $12; 8; 10; na.

WHPE-FM—November 1947: 95.5 mhz; 100 kw. Ant 440 ft. TL: N35 55 10 W80 01 47. Stereo. 1714 Tower Ave. (27260). (919) 889-9473. Licensee: Bible Broadcasting Network (group owner; acq 10-74). Net: AP. Format: Relg. ■ Lowell Davey, pres; Jud Mast, gen mgr; Michael Raley, stn mgr.

WJMH(FM)—See Reidsville.

WMAG(FM)—Listing follows WMFR(AM).

WMFR(AM)—Oct 15, 1935: 1230 khz; 1 kw-U. TL: N35 57 20 W80 00 22. Hrs opn: 5:30 AM-1 AM. Box 2208 (27261); Radio Bldg., 164 S. Main St., 8th Fl. (27260). (910) 885-2191. FAX: (910) 882-4422. Licensee: Voyager Communications V Inc. (group owner; acq 10-25-91; with co-located FM). Net: ABC/I. Rep: Christal. Format: News/talk. ■ Jack McCarthy, pres; Ivan Braiker, gen mgr; Dennis Elliott, progmg dir; Larry Craven, news dir; Stuart Smith, chief engr.

WMAG(FM)—Co-owned with WMFR(AM). 1946: 99.5 mhz; 100 kw. Ant 1,500 ft. TL: N35 52 13 W79 50 25. Stereo. Hrs opn: 24. Prog sep from AM. (910) 882-0995. Format: Adult contemp. Target aud: 25-54. ■ Stan Bernstein, prom mgr; Kim Carson, mus dir; Leanne Petty, news dir.

WOKX(AM)—June 1953: 1590 khz; 1 kw-D, 26 w-N. TL: N35 57 41 W80 02 13. Box 1198 (27261); Suite 203, 327 N. Main (27620). (919) 882-1590; (919) 883-8852. Licensee: Key Broadcasting Inc. (acq 8-90; $135,000; FTR 8-13-90). Net: CBN. Format: Contemp Christian mus. News progmg 3 hrs wkly. Target aud: General. ■ Joel Key, pres; Deb Metcalf, gen mgr & prom mgr; Brad Wright, opns mgr; Buddy Poole, gen sls mgr; Max Parrish, chief engr. ■ Rates: $12; 12; 12; na.

***WWIH(FM)**—Sept 19, 1981: 90.3 mhz; 10 w. Ant 150 ft. TL: N35 58 19 W79 59 38. Stereo. Box 3071, High Point College, 933 Montlieu Ave. (27261). (919) 841-9000. Licensee: High Point College Bd of Trustees. Format: Progsv. News staff one. Target aud: 18-24; college students. ■ Kyle Pyke, gen mgr.

WWWB(FM)—June 1953: 100.3 mhz; 100 kw. Ant 1,049 ft. TL: N35 58 09 W79 49 29. Stereo. Box 11028 (27265-0265); Suite 400, 4000 Piedmont Pkwy. (27265). (910) 885-2100. FAX: (910) 887-0104. Licensee: MHD Inc. (acq 4-23-93; $3.5 million with WGLD[AM] Greensboro; FTR 5-17-93). Net: Unistar. Rep: Major Mkt. Format: Adult contemp. Target aud: 25-54. ■ Bernard Mann, pres; Edward L. Weiss, gen mgr; Mike Fenley, progmg dir; Pam McGann, news dir; Steve Warford, chief engr.

Hope Mills

WCCG(FM)—Not on air, target date unknown: 103.5 mhz; 3 kw. Ant 328 ft. TL: N34 56 20 W78 51 48. 1866 Geiberger Dr., Fayetteville (28303). Licensee: James E. Carson.

Icard Township

WUIV(AM)—Mar 29, 1981: 1580 khz; 5 kw-D, DA. TL: N35 43 07 W81 28 06. Stn currently dark. Box 940, c/o Radio Station WNNC, Newton (28658). (704) 464-4041. Licensee: Jim Jacumin. ■ Jim Jacumin, pres; Dave Lingafelt, gen mgr.

Jacksonville

WFXZ(FM)—November 1993: 92.3 mhz; 35 kw. Ant 236 ft. TL: N34 29 38 W77 29 18. 2616 Northwoods Dr. (28540). Licensee: Ferguson Radio Company Inc. ■ Mike Ferguson, CEO.

WJCV(AM)—Oct 10, 1968: 1290 khz; 1 kw-D. TL: N35 45 51 W77 23 18. Box 1216 (28546). (919) 347-6141. Licensee: Caleb Communications Inc. (acq 8-79). Net: ABC/C. Format: Southern gospel. ■ Michael Bland, gen mgr; Melvin Bland, progmg dir.

WJNC(AM)—Oct 16, 1945: 1240 khz; 1 kw-U. TL: N34 44 56 W77 24 51. Box 1691, 907 Lejeune Blvd. (28540). (919) 455-2202. FAX: (919) 455-2244. Licensee: WJNC Inc. (acq 12-86). Net: NBC, NBC Talknet, Westwood One. Format: Beach/oldies, news/talk. News staff one. Target aud: 25 plus. Spec prog: Relg 6 hrs wkly. ■ Glenn Hargett, pres, gen mgr & news dir; Jay Lawrence, opns dir & mus dir; Wanda Turner, sls dir & gen sls mgr; Andy Andrews, pub affrs dir; Don Brown, chief engr.

WKOO(FM)—Apr 28, 1965: 98.7 mhz; 100 kw. Ant 1,015 ft. TL: N34 29 38 W77 29 18. Stereo. Hrs opn: 24. Box 1126, 307 Johnson Blvd. (28540); Box 1126 (28541). (919) 455-5300. FAX: (919) 455-3112. Licensee: Winfas Inc. (acq 1-1-82; $1.15 million; FTR 11-30-81). Net: MBS. Rep: D & R Radio. Wash atty: Gary Smithwick. Format: Oldies. News staff one; news progmg 3 hrs wkly. Target aud: 25-54; middle to upper-income adults. ■ Larry W. Nichols, chmn; Roger Ingram, pres; W.S. Foster Jr., vp; Ronald S. Brown, gen mgr; Teresa Allen, gen sls mgr; Ben Ball, prom mgr, progmg dir & mus dir; Polly Framton, news dir; Don Brown, chief engr.

WLAS(AM)—June 21, 1954: 910 khz; 5 kw-U, DA-N. TL: N34 47 31 W77 29 40. Stereo. 535 Bellfork Rd. (28541). (919) 455-9528. Licensee: Eckhardt Broadcasting Corp. (acq 3-30-92; $160,000; FTR 4-20-92). Net: CBS, Sun. Rep: T-N. Format: News/talk. News staff one; news progmg 20 hrs wkly. Target aud: 18-49 male; 25-49 adult. Spec prog: Sports. ■ Keith Eckhardt, pres; Steve Peterson, opns dir; Jim Ervin, gen sls mgr; Julia Ladouy, news dir; Jim Smith, chief engr.

WXQR(FM)—Mar 14, 1966: 105.5 mhz; 3 kw. Ant 315 ft. TL: N34 47 31 W77 29 40 (CP: 19 kw, ant 794 ft.). Stereo. Box 1356 (28541-1356). 500 New Ridge St. (28541). (910) 455-2177. FAX: (910) 455-0330. Licensee: Marine Broadcasting Corp. Net: ABC. Format: AOR. ■ Sidney Popkin, pres; William Waldron, gen mgr & gen sls mgr; Kris Kelly, progmg dir, mus dir & news dir; Allen Bucklew, chief engr.

Kannapolis

WRFX(FM)—October 1964: 99.7 mhz; 100 kw. Ant 1,044 ft. TL: N35 33 45 W80 42 40 (CP: 84 kw, ant 1,056 ft.). Stereo. 915 E. Fourth St., Charlotte (28204). (704) 338-9970. FAX: (704) 342-3813. Licensee: Kiss Ltd Partnership. Group owner: Pyramid Broadcasting (acq 12-1-88). Rep: McGavren Guild. Format: Classic rock, AOR. Target aud: 18-34 adults. Spec prog: Talk 3 hrs wkly. ■ Jack Daniel, vp, gen mgr & progmg dir; Randy Brazell, opns mgr; Macon Moye, gen sls mgr; Fred McFarlin, mus dir; Robert Raiford, news dir; Bill Elliott, chief engr.

WRKB(AM)—Dec 11, 1960: 1460 khz; 500 w-D, 194 w-N. TL: N35 29 14 W80 36 18. Box R, 910 Fairview St. (28082). (704) 938-1460. FAX: (704) 857-0680. Licensee: Cabarrus Communications Inc. (acq 3-87). Net: CBN. Rep: Select. Format: Southern gospel. Spec prog: Black 5 hrs, Greek one hr wkly. ■ John Stiles, gen mgr & chief engr; Ken Mayfield, opns mgr; Mike Harding, gen sls mgr.

Kill Devil Hills

WCXL(FM)—January 1993: 104.1 mhz; 100 kw. Ant 463 ft. TL: N35 52 51 W75 39 31. Hrs opn: 24. Box 1221, Nags Head (27959). (903) 441-6638. Licensee: Ray-D-O Biz Inc. (acq 4-14-93; $1.003 million; FTR 5-10-93). Wash atty: Reed, Smith, Shaw & McClay. Format: Classic hits. News staff one. Target aud: 18-54. ■ J. Gary Ratcliff, pres, CFO & gen mgr.

King

WKTE(AM)—Dec 4, 1963: 1090 khz; 1 kw-D. TL: N36 17 48 W80 22 18. Stereo. Box 465 (27021); Goff Rd. (27021). (919) 983-3111. FAX: (919) 722-1499. Licensee: Booth-Newsom Broadcasting Inc. (acq 3-1-86; $105,000; FTR 1-6-86). Net: Sun; Southern Farm. Format: C&W, talk. Spec prog: Farm 2 hrs wkly. ■ P.W. Booth, pres; Rodney T. Booth, gen mgr, gen sls mgr & mus dir; Ron Wishon, prom mgr & progmg dir; Gary Tilton, chief engr.

Kings Mountain

WKMT(AM)—Mar 12, 1953: 1220 khz; 1 kw-U. TL: N35 15 59 W81 19 23. Stereo. Box 1220, Hwy. 161, N. (28086). (704) 739-1220. FAX: (704) 739-4900. Licensee: Bridges Broadcasting Co. Inc. (acq 6-1-89; $170,000; FTR 5-29-89). Net: NBC; N.C. News. Format: Country, relg. News staff 2; news progmg 6 hrs wkly. Target aud: 21-75. General; Spec prog: blue-collar, middle-income adults. ■ Jonas R. Bridges, pres & gen mgr; Hugh Dover, dev dir; Jim Arp, prom mgr; Doris Bridges, progmg dir; Jerry Bedsole, mus dir; Gene Austin, news dir.

Kinston

WELS(AM)—September 1950: 1010 khz; 1 kw-D, 75 w-N. TL: N35 15 45 W77 37 35 (CP: TL: N35 17 02 W77 39 55). Box 3384, 313 N. Queen St. (28501). (919) 523-5151. FAX: (919) 523-9357. Licensee: Farmers Broadcasting Service Inc. Net: N.C. News Net, Tobacco. Rep: Clayton-Davis. Format: Southern black gospel. Target aud: 25-54; middle income. ■ William S. Page, pres; David Cavileer, vp & gen mgr; Kris Richards, opns mgr, mus dir & pub affrs dir; Asheley Moseley, gen sls mgr. ■ Rates: $19; 19; 19; 19.

WKGK(FM)—Co-owned with WELS(AM). Nov 21, 1990: 102.9 mhz; 3 kw. Ant 295 ft. TL: N35 17 03 W77 39 53. Hrs opn: 17. Prog sep from AM. Net: ABC. Rep: T-N. Format: Country. Target aud: Middle-upper income, married, working, college grads.

WQDW(AM)—May 1954: 1230 khz; 1 kw-U. TL: N35 15 31 W77 36 33. Stn currently dark. Box 3384 (28501). (919) 523-5151. Licensee: CSP Communications (acq 6-90; FTR 6-18-90).

WQDW-FM—Sept 15, 1976: 97.7 mhz; 3 kw. Ant 248 ft. TL: N35 15 30 W77 36 19 (CP: 1.58 kw, ant 451 ft. TL: N35 15 31 W77 36 33). Stn currently dark.

WRNS-FM—Oct 12, 1968: 95.1 mhz; 95 kw. Ant 1,499 ft. TL: N35 06 18 W77 20 15. Stereo. Hrs opn: 24. Box 182, Rt. 2, Banks School Rd. (28501). (919) 522-4141. FAX: (919) 523-4877. Licensee: Ballston Trust Services L.C. Group owner: Pinnacle Broadcasting Co. (acq 12-22-92; grpsl; FTR 1-18-93). Net: ABC, Unistar. Rep: McGavren Guild. Wash atty: Wiemer, Cutler & Pickering. Format: Country. News staff one. Target aud: 25-54. ■ Philip D. Marella, pres; Ed Ferreri, CFO; Roy F. Sova, vp & gen mgr; Edward Hawkins, opns dir; Rich Goldstein, gen sls mgr; Cynthia Grady, prom dir; Mark Reid, adv dir & progmg dir; Wayne Carlyle, mus dir; Jim Barbour, news dir; Don Price, chief engr.

WRNS(AM)—Feb 28, 1937: 960 khz; 5 kw-D, 1 kw-N, DA-N. TL: N35 16 59 W77 39 01. Hrs opn: 24. Dups FM 100%. Net: ABC/C.

Laurinburg

WAZZ(FM)—Listing follows WEWO(AM).

WEWO(AM)—Sept 1, 1947: 1460 khz; 5 kw-U, DA-2. TL: N34 47 00 W79 30 40. Box 529 (28353). (919) 276-1460; (919) 276-2965. FAX: (919) 276-9787. Licensee: Curtis Media Group (group owner; acq 6-14-91; grpsl; FTR 7-1-91). Net: Unistar; N.C. News Net. Format: Oldies, talk. News progmg 5 hrs wkly. Target aud: 25-54; baby boomers who like Rush Limbaugh. ■ Don Curtis, pres; Joe Bell, exec vp; Michael Whalen, gen mgr; Tom Sherman, opns mgr; Dee Ana Christian, sls dir; Helen Hoover, progmg dir; Van Clough, chief engr.

WAZZ(FM)—Co-owned with WEWO(AM). May 1, 1951: 96.5 mhz; 100 kw. Ant 650 ft. TL: N34 29 34 W79 12 50 (CP: Ant 985 ft.). Stereo. Box 470, Wachovia Building, 224 Green St., Fayetteville (28302). Format: Top 40/Hot adult contemp. Target aud: 25-44. ■ Alan Hoover, progmg dir & mus dir.

WLNC(AM)—Jan 2, 1962: 1300 khz; 500 w-D. TL: N34 47 00 W79 26 22. Box 1748, 1300 Lila Dr. (28352). (919) 276-1300. Licensee: Fox Broadcasting Inc. (acq 2-1-90; $325,000). Net: ABC/C. Rep: T-N. Format: Adult contemp. News staff one; news progmg 8 hrs wkly. Target aud: General. Spec prog: Gospel 4 hrs wkly. ■ Fred Fox, pres & gen mgr; Dee Anna Christian, gen sls mgr; Jim Quick, mus dir; Sandy Callan, news dir. ■ Rates: $14; 11.25; 11.25; 11.25.

Leaksville

WLOE(AM)—See Eden.

WNEU(FM)—See Eden.

Leland

WAAV(AM)—Licensed to Leland. See Wilmington.

Lenoir

WJRI(AM)—Mar 15, 1947: 1340 khz; 1 kw-U. TL: N35 53 47 W81 33 57. Box 1350 (28645). (704) 754-5361. Licensee: WJRI Inc. (acq 11-01-91). Net: AP; N.C. News. Wash atty: Tharrington, Smith & Hargrove. Format: Adult contemp, country, oldies. News staff one; news progmg 7 hrs wkly. Target aud: Baby boomers. ■ Donnie Goodale, pres, gen mgr & gen sls mgr; Patty Guthrie, gen mgr; Charley Little, progmg dir & mus dir; Elbert Greenway, news dir; Olan Harmon, chief engr. ■ Rates: $13; 12; 13; 12.

WKGX(FM)—Feb 13, 1969: 1080 khz; 5 kw-D. TL: N35 54 38 W81 33 35. Stereo. Hrs opn: 12. Box 1080, 309 Creekway Dr. (28645). (704) 754-4180; (704) 754-6650. Licensee: Furniture City Broadcasters Inc. Format: Country, oldies. News staff one; news progmg 6 hrs wkly. Target aud: 24-55; older, mature wise spenders. Spec prog: Trading post show 5 hrs wkly ■ R.L. Bush Jr., pres; Gene Crawley, gen mgr; Barbara Verble, progmg dir; Jim Raab, chief engr. ■ Rates: $10; 9; 10; na.

WKVS(FM)—Sept 27, 1993: 103.3 mhz; 550 w. TL: N35 58 31 W81 33 05. Box 1678 (28645). (704) 758-1033. Licensee: Foothills Broadcasting Inc. Format: Country. ■ John Beall, gen mgr; Reta Thorn, stn mgr.

Lewisville

WSGH(AM)—Fall 1986: 1040 khz; 10 kw-D, DA. TL: N36 08 06 W80 30 14. Rte 2, Box 362, East Bend (27018). (919) 773-0869; (919) 699-8036. FAX: (919) 699-8036. Licensee: Winston-Salem Greensboro High Point Area Radio Inc. Group owner: Baker Family Stations. Net: USA. Format: Relg, gospel mus. Target aud: General. ■ Vernon H. Baker, pres; Kevin R. Warren, gen mgr; Mitzie Tilley, mus dir & pub affrs dir. ■ Rates: $12.75; 12.75; 12.75; 12.75.

Lexington

WLXN(AM)—Sept 22, 1946: 1440 khz; 5 kw-D, 1 kw-N, DA-N. TL: N35 49 55 W80 17 12. 200 Radio Dr. (27292). (704) 246-2716. FAX: (704) 246-2800. Licensee: Davidson County Broadcasting Co. Inc. Net: CNN; N.C. Net. Rep: T N. Format: News/talk, sports. News staff one; news progmg 30 hrs wkly. Target aud: 35 plus; those interested in news & sports. ■ Greeley N. Hilton Jr., gen mgr; Hal McGee, opns dir; Kirby Vale, news dir & pub affrs dir; Allan Godwin, engrg dir.

WWGL(FM)—Co-owned with WLXN(AM). Aug 24, 1949: 94.1 mhz; 100 kw. Ant 485 ft. TL: N35 58 12 W80 12 54 (CP: Ant 1,050 ft.). Stereo. Prog sep from AM. (704) 246-2716. Net: CNN. Format: Relg. ■ Greeley N. Hilton Sr., pres; Don Matney, sls dir & progmg dir; Hal V. McGee, chief engr.

Lillington

WLLN(AM)—Feb 12, 1979: 1370 khz; 5 kw-D, 49 w-N, DA-2. TL: N35 23 16 W78 48 22. Box 1209 (27546). (910) 892-9322. FAX: (910) 892-9322. Licensee: Christian Purities Fellowship Inc. (acq 4-12-91; $155,000; FTR 4-29-91). Net: N.C. Net. Format: Classical Christian. ■ Dr. Hubert Spence, gen mgr; Martin Ausdennore, news dir; Toby Johnson, chief engr.

Lincolnton

WLON(AM)—Aug 28, 1953: 1050 khz; 1 kw-D, 231 w-N. TL: N35 29 28 W81 16 03. Box 430, 1366 Startown Road (28093). (704) 735-8071. Licensee: Startown Broadcasting Inc. (acq 8-12-88). Net: AP; N.C. News Net. Rep: Dora-Clayton. Format: Oldies, adult contemp. News staff 2; news progmg 15 hrs wkly. Target aud: 25 plus. Spec prog: Gospel 5 hrs wkly. ■ Calvin R. Hastings, pres, gen mgr & gen sls mgr; Milton Baker, progmg dir & mus dir; Amy Carpenter, news dir; Don Strawn, chief engr. ■ Rates: $13.20; 11; 13.20; 11.

Louisburg

WYRN(AM)—Sept 12, 1958: 1480 khz; 500 w-D. TL: N36 06 46 W78 16 50. Box 463 (27549). (919) 496-3105. FAX: (919) 496-5864. Licensee: Franklin Broadcasting Co. Inc. (acq 3-1-69). Net: N.C. Net. Rep: T N. Format: Country, oldies. News staff one. Target aud: 25 plus. Spec prog: Black. ■ Mollie B. Evans, gen mgr, gen sls mgr & prom mgr; Charlie M. Evans Jr, mus dir; Marcia Good, news dir; Lou Parrish, chief engr.

WHLQ(FM)—Co-owned with WYRN(AM). Dec 5, 1989: 102.5 mhz; 6 kw. Ant 328 ft. TL: N36 07 12 W78 22 48. Stereo. Hrs opn: 5:30 AM-midnight. Format: Oldies with mellow adult contemp. News progmg 6 hrs wkly. Spec prog: News, birthday celebration, country exchange, sports.

Lumberton

WAGR(AM)—Nov 27, 1954: 1340 khz; 1 kw-U. TL: N34 35 58 W79 00 33. Hrs opn: 24. Box 1165 (28359); S. Chestnut St. Ext. (28358). (919) 739-3394. FAX: (919) 671-1812. Licensee: Arthur DeBerry & Associates (acq 10-25-93; $350,000 with co-located FM; FTR 11-15-93). Net: NBC. Format: Country. News progmg 10 hrs wkly. Target aud: 25-54. ■ Arthur DeBerry, pres; Lee Hauser, gen mgr; George Gilpin, opns mgr.

WJSK(FM)—Co-owned with WAGR(AM). July 19, 1964: 102.3 mhz; 3 kw. Ant 270 ft. TL: N34 35 58 W79 00 33. Stereo. Hrs opn: 24. Prog sep from AM. Format: Oldies. News progmg 6 hrs wkly.

WKML(FM)—Dec 1, 1960: 95.7 mhz; 100 kw. Ant 1,064 ft. TL: N34 46 56 W79 04 42. Stereo. Hrs opn: 24. Box 2563, Fayetteville (28302); Suite 500, 230 Donaldson St. (28301). (919) 483-9565. FAX: (919) 483-6008. Licensee: Beasley Broadcasting of Eastern N.C. Inc. Group owner: Beasley Broadcast Group (acq 1981). Net: ABC/E. Rep: McGavren Guild. Wash atty: Tharrington, Smith & Hargrove. Format: C&W. News staff 2; news progmg 5 hrs wkly. Target aud: 25-54. ■ George G. Beasley, pres; J. Daniel Highsmith, vp & gen mgr; Stewart Thrower, gen sls mgr; Nancy Roberts, prom mgr; Mac Edwards, progmg dir; Andy Brown, mus dir; Titus Miller, chief engr.

WTSB(AM)—Nov 27, 1954: 580 khz; 500 w-D, 67 w-N. TL: N34 35 58 W79 00 33 (CP: N34 35 15 W78 59 30). 1510 W. 5th St. (28358). (919) 618-9580. Licensee: Beasley Broadcasting of Eastern North Carolina Inc. Group owner: Beasley Broadcast Group (acq 6-2-93; FTR 6-21-93). Net: CNN; Southern Farm. Format: News/talk. Spec prog: Farm 8 hrs, sports 15 hrs, Lumbee 2 hrs wkly. ■ Sam Floyd, pres & gen mgr; Sandra Diaz, gen sls mgr; Dale Edwards, mus dir; Todd Miller, chief engr.

Manteo

WVOD(FM)—Mar 28, 1986: 99.1 mhz; 50 kw. Ant 491 ft. TL: N35 50 44 W75 38 50. Stereo. Hrs opn: 24. Box 2059 (27954). (919) 473-1993. FAX: (919) 473-1757. Licensee: Orbit Communications Inc. Net: CBS. Format: Adult contemp. News staff 2. Target aud: 29-65. Spec prog: Class 6 hrs, jazz 4 hrs, Broadway/big band 3 hrs, beach mus 4 hrs wkly. ■ Jennifer J. Frost, pres; Larry Wayne, stn mgr & news dir; Mary Ann Williams, gen sls mgr; Glen Johnston, mus dir; Phyllis Theil, pub affrs dir; John Kerner, chief engr. ■ Rates: $16; 16; 16; 16.

Marion

WBRM(AM)—May 9, 1949: 1250 khz; 5 kw-D, 62 w-N. TL: N35 40 59 W82 02 08. Box 219, 137 N. Garden St. (28752). (704) 652-9500. Licensee: WBRM Inc. (acq 12-1-88; $450,000). Net: AP. Format: Country. News staff one; news prgmg 9 hrs wkly. Target aud: 25-55; mature. Spec prog: Gospel 5 hrs, relg 7 hrs wkly. ■ Annette Bryant, pres & gen mgr; Kevin Estes, opns mgr; Keith Pittman, mus dir; Van McKinney, news dir. ■ Rates: $9; 9; 9; 9.

Mars Hill

*WVMH-FM—1974: 90.5 mhz; 250 w. Ant 230 ft. TL: N35 49 30 W82 33 00. Stereo. Box 1161-C, Blackwell Hall (28754). (704) 689-1232. Licensee: Mars Hill College. Format: Div. News progmg 7 hrs wkly. College students. ■ Jeff Davis, gen mgr; Jobie Sprinkle, chief engr.

Marshall

WHBK(AM)—Sept 20, 1956: 1460 khz; 500 w-D, 139 w-N. TL: N35 48 01 W82 40 34. 351 Skyway Dr. (28753). (704) 649-3914. Licensee: Southern Broadcasting Inc. (acq 10-22-91; $145,000). Net: AP. Format: Southern gospel. Spec prog: Farm 3 hrs wkly. ■ Bruce Philips, pres; Ricky Seay, gen mgr.

Mayodan

WMYN(AM)—July 15, 1957: 1420 khz; 1 kw-D, 70 w-N, DA-2. TL: N36 24 58 W79 59 29. Hrs opn: 6 AM-10 PM. 100% simulcast with WLOE. Box 311, (27025). (919) 548-9207; (919) 427-9696. FAX: (919) 548-4636. Licensee: Mayo Broadcasting Corp. (acq 1982). Net: NBC; N.C. Net. Rep: Keystone (unwired net). Format: Info/talk, oldies, sports. News staff one; news progmg 30 hrs wkly. Target aud: 25 plus. ■ Richard Hall, pres; Mike Moore, gen mgr, gen sls mgr, adv mgr, progmg mgr & news dir; Annette Moore, stn mgr; Scotty Irving, mus dir; Tim Walker, chief engr. ■ Rates: $18; 18; 18; 18.

Mebane

*WGSB(AM)—Dec 7, 1973: 1060 khz; 1 kw-D, DA. TL: N36 03 28 W79 16 36. 407 N. Second St. (27302). (919) 563-8927. Licensee: Great Speckled Bird Broadcasting Co. Inc. (acq 6-90; $129,000; FTR 6-4-90). Wash atty: McNair. Format: Southern gospel. News progmg 3 hrs wkly. Target aud: General. ■ James L. Christopher, pres & gen mgr; Scott Durham, stn mgr, progmg dir, mus dir, pub affrs dir & chief engr.

Mint Hill

WNOW(AM)—Aug 1, 1987: 1030 khz; 10 kw-D, DA. TL: N35 08 30 W80 36 05. Box 23509, Charlotte (28212). (704) 332-8764; (704) 822-9669. FAX: (704) 332-8779. Licensee: NOW Radio Inc. Group owner: Baker Family Stations. Format: Contemp Christian hit radio. ■ Virginia L. Baker, pres; Russ Douglass, gen mgr, gen sls & progmg dir; Tammy Moore, prom mgr & news dir; Leisa Miller, mus dir; Mike Miranda, chief engr.

Mocksville

WDSL(AM)—October 1964: 1520 khz; 5 kw-D, 1 kw-CH. TL: N35 52 50 W80 32 26. Box 1123 (27028-1123). (704) 634-2177; (704) 634-9375. FAX: (704) 634-5025. Licensee: WDSL Radio Inc. (acq 10-26-90; $52,000; FTR 11-19-90). Net: USA. Rep: T N. Format: Country, oldies. News progmg 10 hrs wkly. Target aud: General. Spec prog: Gospel 18 hrs, bluegrass 10 hrs, Black gospel one hr wkly. ■ Ouida B. Watts, pres, gen sls mgr, progmg dir, mus dir & new dir; Jeff L. Watts, gen mgr & chief engr. ■ Rates: $9.50; 9.50; 9.50; 9.50.

Monroe

WDEX(AM)—December 1983: 1430 khz; 2.5 kw-U, DA-2. TL: N34 59 04 W80 36 14. Box 1050, 105D Cedar St. (28110); Box 2956, Thomasville, GA (31799). (704) 289-9444; (912) 226-8468. Licensee: Geneva C. Mills (acq 1-14-91; FTR 1-28-91). Net: NBC. Format: Oldies. News staff one; news progmg 7 hrs wkly. Target aud: 25-55. ■ Geneva Mills, pres; Anne Long, opns mgr & gen sls mgr; Scott Carter, chief engr.

WIXE(AM)—May 3, 1968: 1190 khz; 1 kw-D. TL: N34 57 41 W80 32 40. Box 1007 (28110). (704) 289-2525. Licensee: Monroe Broadcasting Co. (acq 11-20-90; $250,000). Net: AP. Rep: T N. Wash atty: Steven Yelverton. Format: C&W, gospel. News staff one; news progmg 10 hrs wkly. Target aud: 18-55. ■ James E. Reddish, pres, gen mgr & news dir; Archie W. Morgan, gen sls mgr; Frank Funderburk, progmg dir, progmg mgr & chief engr; Bob Paxton, chief engr.

WMAP(AM)—July 1947: 1060 khz; 1 kw-D. TL: N34 58 45 W80 30 48. Stereo. Box 159, 2004 Walkup Ave. (28110). (704) 283-9321. FAX: (704) 283-9623. Licensee: Roldan Broadcasting (acq 11-18-89). Rep: T N. Format: CHR, adult contemp, talk. Spec prog: Relg 10 hrs wkly. ■ Adoll Roldan, pres; Jim Hill, gen mgr, gen sls mgr & news dir; Ray Scott, progmg dir & mus dir.

Mooresville

WHIP(AM)—1950: 1350 khz; 1 kw-D, DA-D. TL: N35 35 56 W80 48 50 (CP: TL: N35 36 04 W80 48 51). Hrs opn: 6 AM-6:30 PM. Box 600, Statesville Hwy. 115 (28115). (704) 664-9447. Licensee: Mooresville Media Inc. (acq 8-76). Net: USA. Format: Oldies. New progmg 13 hrs wkly. Target aud: 25-45. Spec prog: Black 6 hrs, relg 6 hrs wkly. ■ Glenn Hamrick, pres; Martha Hamrick, vp; John Withrow, gen sls mgr & progmg dir; Eugene Jones, chief engr. ■ Rates: $7; 6.30; 7; na.

Morehead City

WMBL(AM)—July 29, 1947: 740 khz; 1 kw-D, 14 w-N. TL: N34 44 18 W76 48 40. Box 1019, 601 Little Nine Dr. (28557). (919) 247-2002. FAX: (919) 726-3188. Licensee: WMBL Inc. (acq 9-8-92; $25,000; FTR 10-5-92). Net: N.C. News. Format: Big band, Sinatra. Target aud: 35-65; older, upscale adults. ■ Gene Gray, pres & gen mgr; Ryan Walker, progmg dir; Jay Cobb, news dir; Eddie Harrell, chief engr. ■ Rates: $9; 8; 9; 8.

*WOTJ(FM)—Dec 12, 1988: 90.7 mhz; 60 kw. Ant 405 ft. TL: N34 44 03 W76 46 58. Stereo. Hrs opn: 24. 4723 Country Club Rd. (28557). (919) 240-1600; (919) 726-1044. Licensee: Grace Christian School. Net: USA. Wash atty: Dennis Begley. Format: Relg. News progmg 8 hrs wkly. Target aud: General; family. Spec prog: Farm one hr wkly. ■ Clyde I. Ebron, pres; Michael D. Ebron, gen mgr, mktg mgr & progmg dir; Mark Patten, opns mgr; Terry Hardway, prom mgr & adv mgr; Alesia Robinson, mus dir, news dir & pub affrs dir; Eddie Harrel, chief engr.

WRHT(FM)—Dec 20, 1972: 96.3 mhz; 100 kw. Ant 492 ft. TL: N34 44 18 W76 48 40. Stereo. Box 1019, 601 Little Nine Dr. (28557). Licensee: Eastern Carolina Broadcasting Co. Inc. (acq 3-90; $1.2 million). Net: CNN. Wash atty: Waydorf & Van Bergh. Format: CHR. News progmg 7 hrs wkly. Target aud: 18-49; young active adults & military personnel. ■ Gene Gray, pres & gen mgr; Jay Cobb, opns mgr; Luther Griffin, gen sls mgr; J.T. Bosch, prom mgr; Ryan Walker, progmg dir; Gina Gray, mus dir; Jeff Garner, engrg dir. ■ Rates: $16; 12; 16; 12.

Morganton

WCIS(AM)—Mar 1, 1988: 760 khz; 500 w-D. TL: N35 47 40 W81 43 12. Stereo. Box 1806 (28680-1806). (704) 433-1498; (704) 433-1499. Licensee: W.F.M. Inc. (acq 10-1-93). Net: USA. Format: Southern gospel. News staff one; news progmg 5 hrs wkly. ■ John L. Whisnant Sr., pres; John L. Whisnant Jr., gen mgr & gen sls mgr; Jeffrey K. Whisnant, opns mgr; Cliff Gupton, vp sls & pub affrs dir; Alan C. Shuford, progmg dir, mus dir & news dir. ■ Rates: $8.50; 8.50; 8.50; 8.50.

WMNC(AM)—Sept 23, 1947: 1430 khz; 5 kw-D, 1 kw-N, DA-N. TL: N35 45 09 W81 43 03. Hrs opn: 24. Box 969, 1103 N. Green St. (28680-0969). (704) 437-0521; (704) 437-0009. FAX: (704) 433-8855. Licensee: Cooper Broadcasting Co. (acq 9-23-47). Net: CBS; Southern Farm. Format: Modern country. Spec prog: Farm 2 hrs wkly. ■ Josie L. Speas, pres; Joe Cooper, gen mgr; Elizabeth Cooper, gen sls mgr; Dave Garwood, progmg dir; John Tudor, news dir & chief engr.

WMNC-FM—Aug 3, 1963: 92.1 mhz; 6 kw. Ant 327 ft. TL: N35 45 09 W81 43 19. Stereo. Prog sep from AM. Format: Adult contemp, oldies.

WSVM(AM)—See Valdese.

Mount Airy

WPAQ(AM)—February 1948: 740 khz; 10 kw-D, 1 kw-CH. TL: N36 32 04 W80 35 48. Box 907 (27030). (910) 786-6111. FAX: (910) 789-7792. Licensee: Ralph D. Epperson. Net: AP. Format: MOR, country, bluegrass. Spec prog: Farm 2 hrs, community affrs one hr wkly. ■ Ralph D. Epperson, pres & chief engr; Kelly D. Epperson, gen mgr; Lucy Bowman, gen sls mgr; Mary Ruth Flynn, prom mgr; Steve Eastman, news dir.

WSYD(AM)—Oct 4, 1951: 1300 khz; 5 kw-D, 1 kw-N, DA-N. TL: N36 30 12 W80 35 35. Box 1678, City View Dr. (27030). (919) 786-2147; (919) 786-9793. FAX: (919) 789-9858. Licensee: Surry County Broadcasters Inc. (acq 5-4-93; $119,000; FTR 5-24-93). Net: AP, SMN. Format: Adult contemp. News staff one; news progmg 8 hrs wkly. Target aud: General. ■ Selbert M. Wood, pres; Bob Cockerham, vp, stn mgr, progmg dir & mus dir; Bonnie Monday, gen sls mgr; Ronald Johnson, news dir; Tim Walker, chief engr. ■ Rates: $9.50; 8.50; 9.50; 5.

Mount Olive

WDJS(AM)—Dec 27, 1961: 1430 khz; 1 kw-D. TL: N35 12 16 W78 03 06. Box 429, N. Center St. (28365). (919) 658-9751. Licensee: The Mount Olive Broadcasting Co. Format: Relg, div. Spec prog: Black 3 hrs, gospel 10 hrs wkly. ■ James H. Mayo, gen mgr, gen sls mgr & chief engr; Ann W. Mayo, progmg dir.

Moyock

WMYK(FM)—Oct 17, 1974: 92.1 mhz; 18 kw. Ant 384 ft. TL: N36 41 39 W76 02 57. Stereo. Suite 400, 645 Church St., Norfolk, VA (23510-2809). (804) 622-4600. FAX: (804) 624-6515. Licensee: Virginia Urban Radio Inc. (acq 1-22-92). Rep: TN. Format: Urban. Target aud: 18-34; males 18-49. ■ Diane Breathwait, gen mgr; Morris Baxter, progmg dir.

Murfreesboro

WYCM(AM)—March 20, 1965: 1080 khz; 1 kw-D. TL: N36 26 24 W77 08 10. Box 38 (27855). (919) 398-4111. Licensee: C 'n' W Inc. (acq 3-1-93; $170,000 with co-located FM; FTR 3-22-93). Net: Moody; N.C. Net. Rep: T N. Format: Relg. Spec prog: Farm 10 hrs wkly. ■ Bruce Whitehead, pres; Sammy Doughtie, gen mgr; Bill Coleman, chief engr.

WBCG(FM)—Co-owned with WYCM(AM). Oct 11, 1970: 98.3 mhz; 3 kw. Ant 302 ft. TL: N36 23 24 W77 08 10. Stereo. Prog sep from AM. Format: Urban contemp.

Murphy

WCNG(FM)—Oct 23, 1990: 102.7 mhz; 3 kw. Ant 426 ft. TL: N35 04 00 W83 59 58 (CP: Ant 236 ft.). Stereo. Hrs opn: 5 AM-11 PM. Box 280 (28906). (704) 837-9264; (704) 837-2151. FAX: (704) 837-9264. Licensee: Cherokee Broadcasting Co. Inc. Format: Adult contemp, news. ■ Dennis Blakemore, pres, gen sls mgr & prom mgr; Jane Blakemore, gen mgr & progmg dir; Skip Ballard, mus dir; Elvia Blakemore, news dir; Max Blakemore, chief engr. ■ Rates: $7.50; 6; 7; 6.

WCVP(AM)—Oct 12, 1958: 600 khz; 1 kw-D, 20 w-N. TL: N35 03 33 W83 59 56 (CP: TL: N35 04 00 W83 59 58). Hrs opn: 6 AM-11 PM. Box 280 (28906). (704) 837-2151; (704) 837-2152. FAX: (704) 837-9264. Licensee: Max M. Blakemore. Format: MOR, news. Target aud: All ages. Spec prog: Farm 3 hrs wkly. ■ Max M. Blakemore, pres & chief engr; Jane Blakemore, gen mgr, stn mgr & progmg dir; Dennis Blakemore, gen sls mgr & prom mgr; Skip Ballard, mus dir; Elvia Blakemore, news dir. ■ Rates: $8; 6; 8; 6.

WKRK(AM)—Aug 8, 1958: 1320 khz; 5 kw-D, 62 w-N. TL: N35 06 42 W84 00 31. Hrs opn: 6 AM-10 PM. 631 Andrews Rd. (28906). (704) 837-6200. FAX: (704) 837-4332. Licensee: Childress Broadcasting Corp. of Murphy. Net: NBC; N.C. News Net. Rep: Rgnl Reps. Format: C&W, news/talk. News staff 2; news progmg 14 hrs wkly. Target aud: General. Spec prog: Farm 2 hrs, pub affrs 3 hrs wkly. ■ Paul V. Ridenhour, pres, gen mgr & news dir; William Yonce, opns mgr; Susan Ridenhour Ferguson, gen sls mgr & prom mgr; Eric Sneed, mus dir; Ron Evans, chief engr. ■ Rates: $8; 8; 8; na.

Nags Head

WNHW(FM)—Apr 4, 1990: 92.5 mhz; 18.5 kw. Ant 203 ft. TL: N35 59 17 W75 38 42. Stereo. Hrs opn: 24. 2402 Wrightsville Ave. (27959). FAX: (919) 480-1500. Licensee: Coastal Broadcasting Co. Inc. Net: CNN, AP. Format: Country. News staff one. Target aud: 25-54. Spec prog: Gospel 3 hrs wkly. ■ Kenneth L. Mann, pres, gen mgr & gen sls mgr; Jeff Goodrich, opns mgr, progmg dir & mus dir.

New Bern

WIKS(FM)—August 1977: 101.9 mhz; 100 kw. Ant 1,020 ft. TL: N35 12 07 W77 11 15. Stereo. 207 Glenbumie Dr. (28561). (919) 633-1500. Licensee: WIKS-FM Inc. Group owner: Taylor Broadcasting (acq 12-31-88). Net: ABC/C. Rep: D & R Radio. Format: Urban contemp. Spec prog: Gospel 4 hrs, jazz 2 hrs wkly. ■ Steve Taylor, pres; Mike Binkley, vp & gen mgr; B.K. Kirkland, progmg dir; Jeff Kenney, mus dir; George Mimbs, chief engr.

WLOJ(AM)—July 5, 1953: 1490 khz; 1 kw-U. TL: N35 07 59 W77 03 56. Hrs opn: 24. Box 15060, 1319 S. Glenburnie Rd. (28560). (919) 633-1144; (919) 633-1490. FAX: (919) 636-1744. Licensee: CTC Media Group Inc. (acq 11-15-90; $75,000). Net: UPI, USA. Wash atty: Jimmy Young. Format: Relg, MOR, Black. News staff 6. Target aud: General; 35 plus. ■ Benita Afflerbach, pres; David W. Pierce, gen mgr; David Barbee, gen sls mgr; Sandra Henderson, prom mgr & Randy Field, progmg dir; Rick Tyler, mus dir; Rick Taylor, news dir; Bill Dixon, chief engr. ■ Rates: $10; 9; 10; 7.

WNOS(AM)—Apr 23, 1942: 1450 khz; 1 kw-U. TL: N35 06 03 W77 04 33. 1331 S. Glenburnie Road (28562). (919) 638-8888. FAX: (919) 638-8899. Licensee: RRR Broadcasting of New Bern Inc. (acq 9-9-89; $111,000; FTR 9-5-89). Net: SMN. Rep: T-N. Format: Big band. News progmg 5 hrs wkly. Target aud: 35 plus; mature, retired and semi-retired adults. Spec prog: Farm 3 hrs wkly. ■ Lee Thompsen, pres, gen mgr & chief engr; Leann Thompsen, gen sls mgr. ■ Rates: $9.50; 7.50; 8.50; 4.

WSFL(AM)—January 1973: 1380 khz; 5 kw-D. TL: N35 07 29 W77 00 06. Dups FM 100%. Box 3436 (28564). (803) 771-4838. Licensee: W & B Media Inc. Group owner: Beasley Broadcasting (acq 7-10-91; $500,000 with co-owned FM; FTR 7-29-91). Net: Unistar. Rep: Eastman.

WSFL-FM—July 20, 1968: 106.5 mhz; 100 kw. Ant 915 ft. TL: N35 02 27 W77 21 11. Stereo. Dups AM 100%. Box 3436 (28564). Rep: Eastman. Format: Classic based Rock & Roll. Target aud: 25-34. ■ Webster James, vp & gen mgr; Jay Lopez, opns dir, progmg dir & mus dir; Wilbur Vitols, natl sls mgr; Vinnie Kice, asst mus dir.

***WTEB(FM)**—June 4, 1984: 89.3 mhz; 100 kw. Ant 522 ft. TL: N35 06 32 W77 06 10. Stereo. Hrs opn: 24. 800 College Ct. (28562). (919) 638-3434. Licensee: Bd of Trustees, Craven Community College. Net: NPR, APR. Format: Classical, jazz, news & info. News progmg 32 hrs wkly. Spec prog: Folk 2 hrs wkly. ■ Kathleen Beal, gen mgr; Karen Harrison, dev dir; Jeanne Kennedy, prom mgr; Charles Wethington, progmg dir; Sefton Wiggs, mus dir; Francine Sawyer, news dir; J. Howard Jones, chief engr.

New Hope

WAUG(AM)—July 20, 1987: 750 khz; 500 w-D. TL: N35 47 28 W78 37 10. Stereo. Box 14815, Raleigh (27620); 1315 Oakwood Ave., Raleigh (27610). (919) 516-4750. FAX: (919) 516-4425. Licensee: Saint Augustine's College, Trustee and Communications Committee. Net: CNN, Natl Black. Format: Black. News staff one; news progmg 25 hrs wkly. Target aud: 35 plus; Black adults. Spec prog: Jazz 3 hrs wkly. ■ Prezell R. Robinson, pres; J.M. Holloway Jr., gen mgr; Charles Harrison, gen sls mgr; Alvin Waples, progmg dir; James W. Davis, chief engr.

Newland

WJTP(AM)—Aug 14, 1978: 1130 khz; 1 kw-D. TL: N36 04 39 W81 54 59. Rt. 4, Box 48 Hwy. 181 (28657). (704) 733-0188. FAX: (704) 733-0189. Licensee: J.T. Parker Broadcasting Corp. Net: ABC/I. Format: Country. News progmg 2 hrs wkly. Target aud: 25-54; middle class, blue collar. Spec prog: Gospel 10 hrs, relg 5 hrs wkly. ■ J.T. Parker Jr., pres; Mary Burleson, stn mgr, progmg dir & mus dir; John Fry, dev mgr & mktg mgr; Susie Fry, sls dir; Mitch Sandidge, chief engr. ■ Rates: $10; 10; 10; na.

Newport

WKQT(FM)—Sept 4, 1983: 103.3 mhz; 100 kw. Ant 600 ft. TL: N34 45 06 W76 52 57 (CP: Ant 980 ft.). Box 1407, Morehead City (28557). (919) 247-1033. FAX: (919) 247-7068. Licensee: New East Communications Inc. (acq 12-2-92; $262,581; FTR 12-21-92). Net: ABC/R. Format: Adult contemp. ■ Henry Hinton, gen mgr; Curt Smith, gen sls mgr; Rob Thaler, progmg dir; Dave Gernoske, chief engr.

Newton

WNNC(AM)—June 18, 1948: 1230 khz; 1 kw-U. TL: N35 40 20 W81 14 12. Stereo. Hrs opn: 5 AM-midnight. Box 940, 1666 Radio Stn. Rd. (28658). (704) 464-4041. FAX: (704) 464-9662. Licensee: Newton-Conover Communications Inc. (acq 8-76). Net: MBS. Rep: Carolina. Format: Adult contemp. News staff one. Target aud: 25-49. Spec prog: Black 2 hrs, jazz 3 hrs wkly. ■ Dave Lingafelt, pres, gen mgr & chief engr; Ken Reed, gen sls mgr; Janet Lingafelt, progmg dir; Bob Davis, mus dir; Al Mainess, news dir. ■ Rates: $14; 11.75; 11.75; 11.75.

North Wilkesboro

WKBC(AM)—June 1947: 800 khz; 1 kw-D, 308 w-N. TL: N36 11 18 W81 08 07. Hrs opn: 24. Box 938, 400 C St. (28659). (910) 667-2221; (910) 838-1186. FAX: (910) 667-3677. Licensee: Wilkes Broadcasting Co. Net: NBC. Format: Country, gospel. Spec prog: Bluegrass 2 hrs wkly. ■ Robert Brown, pres & gen mgr; Dave Brown, gen sls mgr; Cindy Norris, prom mgr, progmg dir & mus dir; Ed Racey, news dir; Stoney Owen, chief engr. ■ Rates: $8; 8; 5.90; 5.90.

WKBC-FM—July 1962: 97.3 mhz; 100 kw. Ant 1,350 ft. TL: N36 04 34 W81 07 44. Stereo. Prog sep from AM. Net: NBC. Format: Adult contemp.

Old Fort

WDLF(FM)—Feb 5, 1991: 104.3 mhz; 2.55 kw. Ant 348 ft. TL: N35 36 27 W82 11 58. Stereo. Hrs opn: 24. Box 1069, 104 Brown Dr., Marion (28752). (704) 659-2000. FAX: (704) 652-7491. Licensee: McDowell Communications Associates. Net: N.C. News Net. Wash atty: Reddy, Begley & Martin. Format: Adult contemp, oldies, news. News staff 2; news progmg 10 hrs wkly. Target aud: 25-54. Spec prog: Relg 2 hrs, talk/news 5 hrs wkly. ■ William Shaw, gen mgr & gen sls mgr; Bill Nowland, opns mgr; Bert Lindsay, progmg dir; Dave Thomas, mus dir; Yvonne Jackson, pub affrs dir; Jobie Sprinkle, chief engr. ■ Rates: $12; 12; 12; 8.

Oriental

WNBR(FM)—Not on air, target date unknown: 94.1 mhz; 11 kw. Ant 485 kw. TL: N35 00 02 W76 49 58. Apt. A, 100 Glendale Ave., La Grange (28551). Licensee: Conner Media Corp.

Oxford

***WAFP(FM)**—Not on air, target date unknown: 91.1 mhz; 5 kw. Ant 272 ft. Box 889, Blacksburg, VA (24063). Licensee: Granville-Vance Community Radio Inc.

WCBQ(AM)—June 9, 1949: 1340 khz; 1 kw-U. TL: N36 18 27 W78 34 37. Stereo. Hrs opn: 18. Box 336, One Broadcast Ctr., 601 Henderson St. (27565). (919) 693-4121; (919) 693-1340. FAX: (919) 693-9054. Licensee: Radio Granville Inc. (acq 2-76; $100,000). Net: USA, NBC; N.C. News Net. Rep: T-N. Format: Southern gospel. News progmg 10 hrs wkly. Target aud: General. Spec prog: Farm, professional & college sports, talk/news. ■ Anita C. Woodlief, pres, gen mgr, opns mgr, gen sls mgr & mus dir; F. Roger Page Jr., vp; Nat Smith, progmg dir & asst mus dir; David Boyton, chief engr. ■ Rates: $9; 9; 8; 6.

Paw Creek

WWFQ(AM)—Not on air, target date unknown: 820 khz; 2.5 kw-U, DA-2. TL: N35 13 42 W80 58 21. 2613 Craig Ave., Concord (28025). Licensee: Paw Creek Broadcasting Inc.

Pinehurst

WEEB(AM)—See Southern Pines.

WIOZ(AM)—Mar 25, 1980: 550 khz; 1 kw-D, 260 w-N, DA-2. TL: N35 09 04 W79 28 40. Hrs opn: 24. Box 1677, Corner of Short & Long Sts., Southern Pines (28387). (919) 692-6887. FAX: (919) 692-6849. Licensee: Muirfield Broadcasting Inc. (acq 12-28-83). Net: SMN. Format: Easy listening. News staff 2; news progmg 18 hrs wkly. Target aud: General. ■ Walker Morris, pres; Bob Dellert, gen mgr; Rich Rushforth, opns mgr & progmg dir; Patty Tighe, prom mgr; Gene Dennis, news dir.

WIOZ-FM—See Southern Pines.

Plymouth

WPNC-FM—December 1979: 95.9 mhz; 2.6 kw. Ant 350 ft. TL: N35 50 48 W76 45 22. Stereo. Rt. 3, Box 251 (27962). Licensee: D & T Communications. Format: Country. ■ Diane Scout Flowers, gen mgr. ■ Rates: $10.50; 7.50; 8.50; 5.50.

WPNC(AM)—Sept 11, 1959: 1470 khz; 5 kw-D. TL: N35 50 48 W76 45 22. Stn currently dark. (919) 355-3702.

Raeford

WMFA(AM)—Apr 25, 1963: 1400 khz; 1 kw-U. TL: N35 58 43 W79 12 32. 1085 E. Central Ave. (28376). (910) 875-6235. Licensee: W & V Broadcasting Enterprises Inc. (acq 6-2-93; $12,000; FTR 6-21-93). Wash atty: Steve Yelverton. Format: Gospel. ■ Rev. James Ross, pres; Gary Davis, gen mgr; Archie Swindle, opns mgr & progmg dir; Angenette McAllister, mktg dir.

Raleigh

WCLY(AM)—Aug 15, 1962: 1550 khz; 1 kw-D, 7 w-N. TL: N35 45 37 W78 39 27. 647 Maywood Ave (27603). (919) 821-1550. Licensee: Antelope Broadcasting Inc. (acq 8-31-92; $270,000; FTR 9-21-92). Net: Natl Black. Rep: Katz & Powell. Format: Relg. Target aud: 25-65; primarily Black. ■ Robert F. Bell, pres; Benny Moore, gen mgr.

***WCPE(FM)**—July 17, 1978: 89.7 mhz; 100 kw. Ant 679 ft. TL: N35 56 26 W78 28 45. Stereo. Hrs opn: 24. Box 828, 1928 Chalks Rd., Wake Forest (27588). (919) 556-5178. Licensee: Educational Information Corp. Format: Class. Target aud: 35 plus; classical music listeners. ■ Deborah S. Proctor, CEO, pres, gen mgr & engrg dir; Barbara N. Mulvaney, opns mgr; Frances T. Casey, mktg mgr & prom mgr; Charles Stegall, progmg dir; Thomas D. Heaton, mus dir; Jay Stevens, pub affrs dir; John E. Taffee, engrg mgr.

WCRY(AM)—See Fuquay-Varina.

WDCG(FM)—See Durham.

WHEV(AM)—See Garner.

WKIX-FM—Listing follows WYLT(AM).

***WKNC-FM**—September 1965: 88.1 mhz; 3 kw. Ant 260 ft. TL: N35 47 15 W78 40 14. Stereo. Hrs opn: 24. Box 8607, N.C. State Univ. Mail Ctr. (27695-8607). (919) 515-2401. FAX: (919) 515-5133. Licensee: North Carolina State Univ. Net: AP. Format: Rock, urban contemp. News progmg 5 hrs wkly. Target aud: 16-24; high-school & college students of all demographics. Spec prog: Progsv/new wave 12 hrs, Christian rock 3 hrs, jazz 3 hrs, blues 3 hrs, thrash metal 9 hrs, talk one hr, international 3 hrs, reggae one hr wkly. ■ Paul Williams, gen mgr; Traer Scott, opns dir; Krista Navjobs, gen sls mgr; Rich Palmer, prom dir; Alan Wathins, progmg dir; Zachary Lanier, mus dir; Justin Scranton, Garrich Tarver, asst mus dirs; Erin Roe, news dir; Jeff Leagan, pub affrs dir; Sam Mullis, chief engr.

WLLE(AM)—Dec 1, 1981: 570 khz; 500 w-D, 54 w-N. TL: N35 45 37 W78 39 27. Box 190, 522 E. Martin St. (27601). (919) 833-3874. Licensee: Special Markets Media Inc. Format: Black. ■ Prentice Monroe, pres; Henry Monroe, gen sls mgr, progmg dir & mus dir; Cash Michaels, news dir.

WPJL(AM)—March 1939: 1240 khz; 1 kw-U. TL: N35 46 25 W78 37 09. Stereo. Box 27946, 515 Bart St. (27611). (919) 834-6401. Licensee: WPJL Inc. (acq 7-86; $600,000; FTR 4-21-86). Net: CBN, USA. Format: Full-time Christian. News progmg 10 hrs wkly. Target aud: 25-54; Evangelical Christian community of greater Raleigh area. Spec prog: Black gospel. ■ William C. Suttles, pres & gen mgr; Bill Suttles, gen sls mgr; Eddie Thomas, mus dir; James Davis, chief engr. ■ Rates: $18; 18; 18; 9.

WPTF(AM)—Sept 22, 1924: 680 khz; 50 kw-U, DA-N. TL: N35 47 38 W78 45 41. Stereo. Hrs opn: 24. 3012 Highwoods Blvd. (27604). (919) 876-0674. FAX: (919) 790-6457. Licensee: First State Communications. Net: ABC/I, CNN, Wall Street; Southern Farm. Rep: McGavren Guild. Format: Div, news/talk. News progmg 20 hrs wkly. Target aud: 35-64. Spec prog: Farm 10 hrs wkly. ■ Joe Bell, gen mgr; Scott Farkas, gen sls mgr; Mary Jo Tumey, prom mgr; Mike Edwards, progmg dir; Mike Blackman, news dir; Gary Leibisch, chief engr. ■ Rates: $140; 80; 115; 65.

WQDR(FM)—Co-owned with WPTF(AM). August 1949: 94.7 mhz; 96 kw. Ant 1,679 ft. TL: N35 40 35 W78 32 09. Stereo. Hrs opn: 24. Prog sep from AM. (919) 876-6464. Net: ABC/E; Southern Farm. Format: Modern country. News progmg 2 hrs wkly. Target aud: 25-54. ■ Walker Sturdivant, gen mgr; Robert Cordle, gen sls mgr. WPTF-TV affil. ■ Rates: $130; 100; 120; 70.

WQOK(FM)—(South Boston, Va). Oct 1, 1960: 97.5 mhz; 100 kw. Ant 981 ft. TL: N36 20 52 W78 40 00. Stereo. Hrs opn: 24. The Forum, Suite 609, 8601 Six Forks Rd., Raleigh, NC (27615). (919) 848-9736. FAX: (919) 848-4724. Licensee: U.S. Radio L.P. Group owner: U.S. Radio L.P. (acq 6-1-89). Net: ABC/C. Rep: D & R Radio. Wash atty: Dan Van Horn. Format: Urban contemp. News staff one; news progmg 20 hrs wkly. Target aud: General; upwardly mobile with discretionary income. Spec prog: Jazz 2 hrs, gospel 9 hrs wkly. ■ John Broomfield, gen mgr; Gaynell Nichols, opns mgr; Lesley griffin, rgnl sls mgr; Cy Young, progmg dir; Marva Williams, news dir; Lewis Parrish, chief engr. ■ Rates: $140; 120; 140; 80.

WRAL(FM)—1947: 101.5 mhz; 96 kw. Ant 1,820 ft. TL: N35 40 35 W78 32 09. Stereo. Box 10100, 711 Hillsborough St. (27605). (919) 890-6101. Licensee: Capitol Broadcasting Co. Inc. (group owner; acq 1946). Net: AP; N.C. Net., Tobacco. Rep: Katz. Format: Adult contemp. Target aud: 25-54. ■ Jim Goodman, pres; Larry Adams, vp & gen mgr; Rob Hankin, gen sls mgr; Corey Scott, progmg dir; Dan Meyers, mus dir; Keith Harrison, chief engr. ■ WRAL-TV affil.

WRDU(FM)—(Wilson). Mar 1, 1961: 106.1 mhz; 100 kw. Ant 1,348 ft. TL: N35 45 36 W78 11 04. Stereo. Hrs opn: 24 Suite 300, 4110 Wake Forest Rd., Raleigh (27609). (919) 876-1061. FAX: (919) 876-2929. Licensee: Voyager Communications Inc. (group owner; acq 9-1-84; grpsl). Net: The Source. Rep: Major Mkt. Format: Rock. News staff 2; news progmg 3 hrs wkly. Target aud: 18-49. Spec prog: Jazz 5 hrs wkly. ■ Carl Venters Jr., chmn; Jack McCarthy, pres; George King, CFO; Phil Zachary, vp & gen mgr; Terry Swaim, gen sls mgr; Desiree McGee, natl sls mgr; Steve Thanhauser, rgnl sls mgr; Bob Walton, progmg dir; Tom Guild, mus dir; Lizz Wall, news dir; Cy

Fohr, pub affrs dir; Carl Davis, vp engrg; Don Smith, chief engr. ■ Rates: $175; 145; 160; 75.

***WSHA(FM)**—Nov 18, 1968: 88.9 mhz; 25.5 kw. Ant 115 ft. TL: N35 46 15 W78 38 10 (CP: 9 kw, ant 525 ft.). Stereo. Hrs opn: 6 AM-midnight. 118 E. South St. (27611). (919) 546-8432; (919) 546-8430. FAX: (919) 546-8437. Licensee: Shaw University Net: APR. Format: Jazz. News staff one; news progmg 13 hrs wkly. Target aud: General. Spec prog: Spanish 3 hrs, African 2 hrs, Caribbean 5 hrs, World Music 4 hrs, blues 8 hrs, gospel 20 hrs wkly. ■ Talbert O. Shaw, pres; Emeka Emekauwa, gen mgr; Christine Harrison, dev dir; Rashad Muhaimin, progmg dir; Beverley Pearce, mus dir; Nadine Clipper, news dir & pub affrs dir; David Wright, chief engr.

WTRG(FM)—(Rocky Mount). November 1947: 100.7 mhz; 100 kw. Ant 1,968 ft. TL: N35 49 53 W78 08 50. Stereo. Suite 709, 3100 Smoketree Court (27604); Box 40187 (27629). (919) 876-1007. FAX: (919) 876-8578. Licensee: Joyner Advertising Inc. (group owner; acq 9-24-90; 5.6 million; FTR 9-24-90). Net: AP, ABC. Rep: D & R Radio. Wash atty: Latham & Watkins. Format: Oldies. News staff 2; news progmg 6 hrs wkly. Target aud: 25-54; upscale adults. ■ Tom Joyner, pres & gen mgr; Kevin Buncum, vp sls; Linda Charlton, vp mktg; Lisa Joyner, vp prom; Randall C. Bliss, progmg dir; Mike Smith, mus dir; Lowell Shumaker, news dir; Jerry Brown, vp engrg. ■ Rates: $110; 95; 110; 35.

WYLT(AM)—1947: 850 khz; 10 kw-D, 5 kw-N, DA-N. TL: N35 48 04 W78 48 51. Stereo. Hrs opn: 24. 5706 New Chapel Hill Rd. (27607). (919) 851-2711. FAX: (919) 851-7219. Licensee: Alchemy Communications (acq 8-7-89; $7.7 million with co-located FM; FTR 9-25-89). Net: MBS, Unistar. Rep: CBS Radio. Format: MOR, sports. ■ Cathy Hasty, prom mgr; Rick Freeman, progmg dir & news dir; John Low, mus dir; Jon Hardee, chief engr.

WKIX-FM—Co-owned with WYLT(AM). 1947: 96.1 mhz; 100 kw. Ant 985 ft. TL: N35 41 07 W78 43 14. Stereo. Prog sep from AM. Net: Unistar. Format: Soft rock.

WZZU(FM)—See Burlington-Graham.

Red Springs

WYRU(AM)—June 15, 1970: 1160 khz; 5 kw-D, 250 w-N. TL: N35 50 19 W79 10 36. Hrs opn: 17.25. Box 711, Red Springs Industrial Park (28377). (919) 843-5946; (919) 738-2312. Licensee: Lumbee Regional Development Association Inc. (acq 7-1-87). Net: Southern Farm. Format: Oldies, top-40, gospel. News staff 2. Target aud: 24-54. Spec prog: Farm 5 hrs wkly. ■ Gene Hanrahan, gen mgr, gen sls mgr & prom mgr; Al Stone, progmg dir; George McPhaul, mus dir; Chris Johnson, news dir; Stephen Poole, chief engr.

Reidsville

WJMH(FM)—Sept 6, 1948: 102.1 mhz; 66 kw. Ant 1,065 ft. TL: N36 13 20 W79 41 47 (CP: 99.2 kw. Ant 1,203 ft.). Stereo. Hrs opn: 24. 4002 E. Spring Garden, Greensboro (27407); Box 19990, Greensboro (27419). (919) 855-6500. FAX: (919) 855-6530. Licensee: Beasley Broadcast Group (group owner). Net: ABC/E. Rep: D & R Radio. Format: Churban. Target aud: 18-40; young, upscale. ■ George G. Beasley, pres; Brian Beasley, gen mgr; Brian Douglas, progmg dir; J.D. Dunning, mus dir; Pam Gibson, news dir; Ed Kasovic, chief engr.

WREV(AM)—1948: 1220 khz; 1 kw-D, 67 w-N. TL: N36 23 19 W79 38 51 (CP: 10 kw-D, DA). 5608 US 29 Business (27320-8972). (919) 349-2986. Licensee: MHR Broadcasting Inc. (acq 11-76). Net: ABC/I; N.C. Net, Tobacco. Rep: TN. Wash atty: Ben Gangine. Format: C&W, news/talk. News staff one; news progmg 30 hrs wkly. Target aud: 25 plus. Spec prog: Black 7 hrs, gospel 7 hrs, farm 10 hrs wkly. ■ C. Tony Mullins, gen mgr & gen sls mgr; Von Heffinger, opns mgr & news dir; Moon Mullins, progmg dir & mus dir; Tim Walker, chief engr. ■ Rates: $7.50; 7.50; 7.50; 6.50.

Roanoke Rapids

WCBT(AM)—November 1940: 1230 khz; 1 kw-U. TL: N36 26 45 W77 39 51. Box 70, 1730 Birdsong St. (27870). (919) 537-4184. FAX: (919) 535-2686. Licensee: WCBT Radio Inc. (acq 9-69). Net: N.C. News. Rep: TN. Format: Oldies. ■ Johnny Draper, pres; Ken Pepper, gen mgr; Russ Barrett, opns mgr; Bobby Tuggle, mus dir; Larry Powell, chief engr.

***WPGT(FM)**—Dec 8, 1972: 90.1 mhz; 1 kw. Ant 175 ft. TL: N36 28 02 W77 39 06. 515 Becker Dr. (27870). (919) 537-8333. Licensee: Roanoke Christian School. Format: Relg. Target aud: General. ■ Clyde R. Alderman, pres; Alice Johnson, gen mgr; Gary Wilson, progmg dir; Doug Brown, chief engr.

WPTM(FM)—1973: 102.3 mhz; 6 kw. Ant 300 ft. TL: N36 30 12 W77 44 47 (CP: 5.4 kw, ant 344 ft.). Stereo. Hrs opn: 24. Box 910 (27870); Box 631, 616 Aurelian Springs Rd., Weldon (27870). (919) 536-3115. FAX: (919) 536-3045. Licensee: Moran Communications. Group owner: Tim Moran (acq 1977). Net: ABC/E; Southern Farm. Wash atty: Ginsberg, Feldman & Bress. Format: Country. News staff 3; news progmg 14 hrs wkly. Target aud: 25-54; females—spendable income, decision-makers. Spec prog: Farm 15 hrs, relg 3 hrs wkly. ■ Tim Moran, CEO; Charles Beaver, gen mgr; Frank White, stn mgr & chief engr; David Perkins, chief opns & progmg dir; Cleve Baker, sls dir; Frank Marucca, rgnl sls mgr; Wade Nelms, Sam Medlin, Susan Jones, news dirs.

***WZRU(FM)**—Not on air, target date March 1994: 88.5 mhz; 28.2 kw. Ant 162 ft. TL: N36 28 08 W77 39 02. Stereo. Hrs opn: 24. 230 B, Roanoke Ave. (27870-1916). (919) 537-9999. FAX: (919) 537-3333. Licensee: Better Life Inc. Net: NPR. Format: Btfl music, class, div. News staff 2. ■ Brian Lewis, gen mgr & stn mgr.

Robbinsville

WCVP-FM—1987: 95.9 mhz; 60 w. Ant 2,008 ft. TL: N35 15 28 W83 47 44. Hrs opn: 5:30 AM-10 PM M-F, 6 AM-10 PM Sat., 7 AM-10 PM Sun. Box 756, 129 North (28771). (704) 479-8080; (704) 479-2296. FAX: (704) 479-2296. Licensee: Cherokee Broadcasting Co. Net: AP. Format: C&W. Target aud: General. ■ Dennis G. Blakemore, pres, gen mgr, gen sls mgr, prom mgr & chief engr; Elvia Blakemore, progmg dir; Bishop Holder, mus dir. ■ Rates: $7; 6; 7; 6.

Rockingham

WAYN(AM)—September 1946: 900 khz; 1 kw-U, DA-2. TL: N34 55 30 W79 44 35. Hrs opn: 6 AM-10 PM. Box 519, 1223 Rockingham Rd. (28379). (919) 895-4041. Licensee: WAYN Inc. (acq 7-1-64). Net: NBC; N.C. News. Wash atty: Cohn & Marks. Format: Adult contemp & info. News progmg 20 hrs wkly. Target aud: 25-49; event-conscious adults. ■ William Futterer, pres, gen mgr & gen sls mgr; Jim Smith, progmg dir & news dir; Mary Futterer Morgan, mus dir; Gene Shaw, chief engr.

WLWL(AM)—Oct 27, 1969: 770 khz; 5 kw-D. TL: N34 55 30 W79 47 11. Box 1536 (28379). (919) 997-2526. Licensee: Sandhills Broadcasting Co. Inc. Net: UPI; N.C. Net. Format: Beach/oldies. News staff one; news progmg 7 hrs wkly. Target aud: 25-60. ■ Robert E. Perkins, pres & chief engr; Keith Davis, gen mgr; Pam Dillman, gen sls mgr & prom mgr; Beth Roberts-Sessons, progmg dir & mus dir; Ralph Ganner, news dir; Cathy Bruce, pub affrs dir.

***WRSH(FM)**—May 1973: 91.1 mhz; 10 w. Ant 60 ft. TL: N34 57 03 W79 42 56 (CP: 339.7 w, ant 161 ft.). Richmond Sr. High School, U.S. Hwy, No. 1 N (28379). (919) 997-9815. FAX: (919) 997-9816. Licensee: Richmond County Bd of Educ. Format: Educ. ■ Kim Newton, gen mgr.

Rocky Mount

WEED(AM)—Sept 10, 1933: 1390 khz; 5 kw-D, 2.5 kw-N, DA-N. TL: N35 57 41 W77 49 32. Box 2666, One WEED Rd. (27802). (919) 443-5976. FAX: (919) 443-5977. Licensee: Radio Station WEED Inc. Net: ABC/C. Format: Contemp. ■ Charles O'Johnson, gen mgr.

WRSV(FM)—Co-owned with WEED(AM). 1949: 92.1 mhz; 1.7 kw. Ant 380 ft. TL: N35 57 03 W77 53 37. Prog sep from AM. (919) 937-6111. Format: Black. ■ Angela Smith, progmg dir & mus dir.

***WESQ(FM)**—January 30, 1992: 90.9 mhz; 6 kw. Ant 627 ft. TL: N35 48 40 W77 44 33. North Carolina Wesleyan College 3400 N. Wesleyan Blvd. (27804). (919) 985-5236. Licensee: North Carolina Wesleyan College. Format: Educ. ■ Tim McDowell, CEO.

WFXK(FM)—See Tarboro.

WRMT(AM)—Dec 15, 1958: 1490 khz; 1 kw-U. TL: N35 55 57 W77 49 49. Box 4005 (27803-0005). (919) 442-8092. FAX: (919) 977-6664. Licensee: E. Wayne Gibson (acq 5-7-90; FTR 5-21-90). Net: CBS; N.C. News Net. Rep: TN. Format: Oldies. Target aud: 30 plus. ■ R. Gordon Finney, pres & gen mgr; Allen Garrett, progmg dir; Rob Lynn, mus dir; Gary Sabar, chief engr.

WSAY-FM—Co-owned with WRMT(AM). Dec 18, 1989: 98.5 mhz; 3 kw. Ant 328 ft. TL: N35 56 28 W77 44 43. Licensee: Radio Triangle East Co. Net: NBC. Format: Country. ■ Gordon Finney, gen sls mgr.

WRSV(FM)—Listing follows WEED(AM).

WSAY-FM—Listing follows WRMT(AM).

WTRG(FM)—Licensed to Rocky Mount. See Raleigh.

Rose Hill

WBSY(FM)—January 1993: 104.7 mhz; 2.8 kw. Ant 256 ft. TL: N34 55 41 W78 03 22. Box 608 (28458). (919) 289-2031; (919) 289-2032; (919) 289-3957. Licensee: Duplin County Broadcasters. Net: ABC-E Format: Upbeat country, super gospel (positive music). News staff one. Target aud: 25+; general. ■ Jeff Wilson Sr., pres; Jeff B. Wilson, gen mgr, gen sls mgr & news dir; Teresa Morgan, progmg dir & mus dir; Dave DeMos, chief engr.

WEGG(AM)—1971: 710 khz; 250 w-D. TL: N34 51 50 W78 02 22. Hrs opn: Day time. Box 608 (28458); R.R. #2, U.S. 117 (28458). (919) 289-2031; (919) 289-3957. Licensee: Duplin County Broadcasters. Net: ABC/E; Southern Farm. Rep: Keystone (unwired net), Carolina. Format: Gospel/relg, Black. Spec prog: Farm 9 hrs, bluegrass gospel 10 hrs wkly. ■ Jeff B. Wilson Sr., gen mgr & gen sls mgr; Teresa Morgan, progmg dir & mus dir; Jeff B. Wilson, news dir; Dave Demos, chief engr.

Roxboro

WRXO(AM)—1949: 1430 khz; 1 kw-D, 65 w-N. TL: N36 22 04 W78 59 58. Hrs opn: 6 AM-sunset. Box 1176, 2026 Hurdle Mills Rd. (27573). (919) 599-0266. FAX: (919) 599-9411. Licensee: Roxboro Broadcasting Co. (acq 5-8-92). Net: NBC; N.C. News Net., Tobacco. Wash atty: Jim Edmundson. Format: Oldies. News staff one; news progmg 7 hrs wkly. Target aud: 25 plus. Spec prog: Black 4 hrs, farm 8 hrs wkly. ■ David Bradsher, pres, gen mgr, gen sls mgr & adv mgr; David Bradsher Jr., progmg dir & mus dir; David H. Rust, news dir; Conrad Kimbrough, chief engr. ■ Rates: $11.45; 9.40; 11.45; 7.40.

WKRX(FM)—Co-owned with WRXO(AM). 1958: 96.7 mhz; 3 kw. Ant 300 ft. TL: N36 22 04 W78 59 58. Stereo. Hrs opn: 5 AM-11 PM. Dups AM 20%. Format: Country. Spec prog: Bluegrass mus 6 hrs, farm 4 hrs wkly. ■ Rates: Same as AM.

Rutherfordton

WCAB(AM)—Oct 19, 1966: 590 khz; 500 w-D, 228 w-N. TL: N35 23 48 W81 55 34. Hrs opn: 6 AM-midnight. Box 511, Old Whiteside Rd. (28139). (704) 287-3356. Licensee: Isothermal Broadcasting Corp. (acq 8-1-84; $275,000; FTR 7-16-84). Net: ABC/I; N.C. Net. Rep: Dora-Clayton. Format: Country, news, sports. News progmg 25 hrs wkly. Target aud: 35 plus; adult consumers. ■ James H. Bishop, pres & gen mgr; Malcolm Watson, stn mgr & gen sls mgr; Leabron Rogers, opns mgr & mus dir; Jim Moody, chief engr. ■ Rates: $9; 9; 9; na.

St. Pauls

NEW FM—Not on air, target date unknown: 106.9 mhz; 3 kw. Ant 328 ft. Box 68, Pembroke (28372). Licensee: Lumbee Regional Development Association Inc.

WKKE(AM)—Aug 1, 1966: 1080 khz; 5 kw-D. TL: N35 47 34 W78 58 55 (CP: 50 kw-D, DA-D). Box 286 (28384). (919) 865-3555. Licensee: Ferriss Yarnell Locklear (acq 7-22-92; $73,989; FTR 8-10-92). Net: USA. Rep: Savalli. Format: Southern gospel. ■ Mike Flannagan, pres, gen mgr, gen sls mgr & chief engr; Randall Cowan, progmg dir, mus dir & news dir. ■ Rates: $25; 20; 25; na.

Salisbury

***WNDN-FM**—unknown: 91.1 mhz; 10 w-H. Ant 754 ft. TL: N35 41 23 W80 29 05. 2613 Craig Ave., Concord (28027). Licensee: New Horizons Foundation Inc. (acq 4-15-92; donation; FTR 5-11-92).

WRDX(FM)—Listing follows WSTP(AM).

WSAT(AM)—June 1947: 1280 khz; 1 kw-U, DA-N. TL: N35 40 30 W80 30 30. Drawer 99, 1525 Jake Alekander Blvd. (28145). (704) 633-0621. FAX: (704) 633-0622. Licensee: Mid Carolina Broadcasting Co. Net: ABC/I, ABC/E, Motor Racing Net. Format: Oldies, sports, big band. News staff 2; news progmg 21 hrs wkly. Target aud: 25-64; people that can afford high ticket items. ■ Harry L. Welch, pres & gen mgr; Mike Mangan, opns dir, gen sls mgr, prom mgr, adv dir & mus dir; E.L. Sherman, dev dir; Mike Shannon, progmg dir; Russ McIntire, news dir; Melanie Chilson, pub affrs dir; Larry Schrapp, chief engr.

WSTP(AM)—Jan 1, 1939: 1490 khz; 1 kw-U. TL: N35 41 12 W80 30 15. Hrs opn: 24. Box 4157, 1105 Statesville Blvd. (28145). (704) 636-3811. FAX: (704) 637-1490. Licensee: WSTP Inc. (acq 10-20-56). Net: MBS, BRN, ARN; N.C. News Net. Format: News/info, talk, sports. Target aud: 35-64. ■ Tom Harrell, pres & gen mgr; Phil Kehr, opns mgr & prom mgr; Don Parden, gen sls mgr;

Kent Bernhardt, progmg dir; Howard Platt, news dir; Gene Jones, chief engr.

WRDX(FM)—Co-owned with WSTP(AM). Mar 16, 1946: 106.5 mhz; 100 kw. Ant 1,003 ft. TL: N35 44 11 W80 38 52. Stereo. Hrs opn: 24. Prog sep from AM. (704) 636-9739. Format: Rhythm & beach. News progmg 3 hrs wkly. Target aud: 35-54; upscale movers and shakers. ■ John Hook, mus dir.

Sanford

***WDCC(FM)**—1971: 90.5 mhz; 3 kw. Ant 148 ft. TL: N35 28 19 W79 08 36. 1105 Kelly Dr. (27330). (919) 775-5401. Licensee: Central Carolina Community College. Format: Top-40, C&W. ■ Jerry M. Farmer, gen mgr; Toby Johnson, chief engr.

WFJA(FM)—Listing follows WWGP(AM).

WWGP(AM)—1946: 1050 khz; 1 kw-D, 161 w-N. TL: N35 26 28 W79 12 54. Box 3457 (27331). (919) 775-3525. Licensee: WWGP Broadcasting Corp. (acq 7-1-58). Net: ABC/E. Format: Modern country. Spec prog: Farm 7 hrs wkly. ■ Richard K. Feindel, vp & gen mgr; Pete Saunders, gen sls mgr; Blair Cameron, mus dir; Margaret Murchison, news dir; Toby Johnson, chief engr.

WFJA(FM)—Co-owned with WWGP(AM). 1950: 105.5 mhz; 2.25 kw. Ant 377 ft. TL: N35 26 28 W79 12 54. (919) 776-9352. Net: ABC/C. Format: Classic rock. ■ Steve Stewart, progmg dir.

WXKL(AM)—Oct 2, 1952: 1290 khz; 1 kw-D, 44 w-N. TL: N35 27 01 W79 09 30. Hrs opn: 6 AM-8 PM. Box 1290, 115 W. Main St. (27330-5919). (919) 774-1080; (919) 774-1290. Licensee: WGSE Inc. (acq 9-12-91). Net: N.C. News Net. Format: Relg, oldies, Black. News progmg 6 hrs wkly. Target aud: General. ■ Jimmy Johnson, pres & chief engr; James Thomas, exec vp; Dolphus Pearson, vp sls. ■ Rates: $16; 11; 16; 11.

Scotland Neck

WWRT(FM)—Not on air, target date unknown: 95.5 mhz; 3 kw. Ant 328 ft. TL: N36 02 34 W77 32 17. Box 425 (27874). (919) 826-3114. Licensee: WYAL Radio Inc. ■ John Laurino, pres.

WYAL(AM)—Apr 3, 1960: 1280 khz; 5 kw. TL: N36 08 03 W77 25 53. Box 425 (27874). (919) 826-3114. Licensee: WYAL Radio Inc. Net: N.C. Net., Tobacco. Rep: T N. Format: Relg. Spec prog: Farm 2 hrs wkly. ■ John Laurino, pres; John Hall, gen mgr, gen sls mgr & progmg dir.

Selma

WBZB(AM)—Aug 4, 1964: 1090 khz; 1 kw-D. TL: N35 31 45 W78 18 10. Box 1 (27576). (919) 965-3753. Licensee: Waters & Brock Communications Inc. (acq 12-86). Net: N.C. News. Rep: T N. Format: Country, gospel. Spec prog: Black 6 hrs, farm 5 hrs wkly. ■ Gerald Waters, pres & gen mgr; Mike Coats, progmg dir; Brian Bowman, news dir.

Semora

WQVA(FM)—Not on air, target date unknown: 106.7 mhz; 6 kw. Ant 328 ft. TL: N36 29 24 W79 00 36. Box 223, 302 S. Lamar St., Roxboro (27573). Licensee: Semora Broadcasting Inc.

Shallotte

WCCA(FM)—Sept 20, 1986: 106.3 mhz; 6 kw. Ant 328 ft. TL: N34 02 50 W78 16 12. Stereo. Hrs opn: 24 Box 1550 (28459). (919) 754-9840. FAX: (919) 754-2456. Licensee: Sound Business of Coastal North Carolina Inc. (acq 10-16-93; $200,000; FTR 11-8-93). Net: AP. Format: Oldies/beach music. Target aud: 25 plus; mature professionals. Spec prog: Relg 2 hrs, beach music 6 hrs wkly. ■ Lee Hauser, pres & gen mgr; Ron Franklin, opns mgr; Marty Callaghan, mus dir; Dick Lee, news dir; Harold Bland, chief engr. ■ Rates: $16; 16; 16; 14.

WLTT(FM)—Oct 31, 1977: 103.7 mhz. 25 kw. Ant 328 ft. TL: N33 59 55 W78 22 25. Hrs opn: 24. Suite 7, 109 Causeway Dr., Ocean Isle (28469); Suite 200, 3366 Riverside Dr., Columbus, OH (43221). (919) 579-9301; (614) 538-0660. FAX: (919) 579-5095; (614) 538-0670. Licensee: PCG of the Golden Strand Inc. (acq 1-13-93; FTR 2-8-93). Net: ABC. Format: Adult contemp. News staff one; news progmg 7 hrs wkly. Target aud: 25-54; upscale female. ■ John E. Rayl, CEO & chmn; Mark Manafo, pres; John Sines, stn mgr & gen sls mgr; Mark S. Manafo, chief opns; Harold Bland, chief engr.

WVCB(AM)—June 11, 1964: 1410 khz; 500 w-D. TL: N33 58 20 W78 23 02. Box 314, 4640 Main St. (28459). (919) 754-4512. Licensee: John G. Worrell (acq 3-1-84; $30,000; FTR 1-30-84). Net: N.C. News. Format: Relg. News progmg 12 hrs wkly. Target aud: General. ■ John Worrell, gen mgr; Rhonda Worrell, stn mgr & progmg dir.

Shelby

WADA(AM)—July 9, 1958: 1390 khz; 1 kw-D, 500 w-N, DA-N. TL: N35 19 28 W81 32 00. Stereo. Box 2266 (28151); McBrayer Springs Rd. (28150). (704) 482-1390. FAX: (704) 487-4856. Licensee: WADA Inc. (acq 10-1-86; $287,846; FTR 6-2-86). Net: ABC/C, ABC/I. Format: Country. News staff one; news progmg 6 hrs wkly. Target aud: 25-54; middle and professional. Spec prog: Gospel 5 hrs wkly. ■ Debbie Clary, pres, gen mgr & gen sls mgr; Ann Clary, prom mgr; John Erick, progmg dir; Dave Thomas, mus dir; Christine Grant, news dir; Don Strawn, chief engr. WBTV(TV) affil. ■ Rates: $13; 8; 10.25; 6.

WBT(AM)—See Charlotte.

WOHS(AM)—Aug 21, 1946: 730 khz; 1 kw-D, 168.4 w-N. TL: N35 17 27 W81 34 05. Box 1590, (28151). (704) 482-4510. FAX: (704) 482-4680. Licensee: Harold R. & Billie B. Watson (acq 12-1-86; $210,000; FTR 10-20-86). Net: MBS; N.C. News Net. Format: Adult contemp, oldies. ■ Calvin R. Hastings, pres; Harold R. Watson, gen mgr, gen sls mgr & prom mgr; Milton Baker, progmg dir & mus dir; Amy Carpenter, news dir & pub affrs dir; Don Strawn, chief engr. ■ Rates: $16.80; 16.80; 16.80; 16.80.

WWMG(FM)—1948: 96.1 mhz; 100 kw. Ant 1,738 ft. TL: N35 21 44 W81 09 19. Stereo. Hrs opn: 24. 1437 E. Morehead St., Charlotte (28204-2925). (704) 338-9600. FAX: (704) 334-9525. Licensee: The Dalton Group Inc. (acq 7-26-93; $4.5 million; FTR 6-21-93). Net: CBS. Rep: Katz. Format: Oldies. News staff one; news progmg 4 hrs wkly. Target aud: 25-54. Spec prog: Motown, beach music. ■ Bill Dalton, pres; Richard F. Harlow, vp & gen mgr; Cheryl Hoffman, gen sls mgr & natl sls mgr; Lynn Henderson, prom mgr; Keith Abrams, progmg dir & mus dir; Bill Curtis, news dir & pub affrs dir; Gary Hattaway, chief engr.

Siler City

WNCA(AM)—Aug 19, 1952: 1570 khz; 1 kw-D, 290 w-N. TL: N35 43 40 W79 29 18. Hrs opn: 24. Box 429, Hwy. U.S. 64 W. (27344). (919) 742-2135; (919) 663-2843. Licensee: Chatham Broadcasting Co. Inc. of Siler City (acq 3-1-62). Net: N.C. News Net. Rep: T-N. Format: Adult contemp, oldies, news/talk. News staff 2; news progmg 30 hrs wkly. Target aud: 25-55; rural, agri-oriented, blue-collar. Spec prog: Gospel, relg 12 hrs, farm 5 hrs, loc sports 6 hrs, Sp 3 hrs wkly. ■ Barry Hayes, pres, gen mgr & engrg mgr; Renee Kennedy, opns dir, sls dir & news dir. ■ Rates: $7.50; 7.50; 7.50; 7.50.

Smithfield

WBZB(AM)—See Selma.

WMPM(AM)—1950: 1270 khz; 5 kw-D. TL: N35 31 33 W78 20 01. Box 240, 1270 Buffalo Rd. (27577). (919) 934-2434; (919) 989-6412. FAX: (919) 989-6388. Licensee: Carolina Broadcasting Svc. (acq 12-1-58). Net: CBS. Rep: T-N. Format: Country, gospel. News staff 5; news progmg 20 hrs wkly. Target aud: 30 plus; general. Spec prog: Farm. ■ Ellis C. Barbour, pres; Carl E. Lamm, gen mgr, progmg dir & mus dir; Travis Lamm, gen sls mgr; Mickey Lamm, news dir; Larry Barnes, pub affrs dir; Lewis V. Parrish, chief engr.

South Gastonia

WGAS(AM)—Aug 14, 1959: 1420 khz; 500 w-D. TL: N35 12 53 W81 10 31. Box 250, Gastonia (28052). (704) 865-5796. Licensee: MGM Broadcasting Corp. Rep: T-N. Format: MOR, Christian. Spec prog: Black 5 hrs wkly. ■ Glenn F. Mace, pres, gen mgr, vp engrg & chief engr; Carroll Henderson, stn mgr, gen sls mgr, prom mgr & progmg dir; Bill Davis, rgnl sls mgr; Carroll Henderson, Amy Mace, mus dirs; Linda Sherrin, news dir & pub affrs dir.

Southern Pines

WEEB(AM)—Nov 15, 1947: 990 khz; 10 kw-D, 5 kw-CH, 500 w-N. TL: N35 11 37 W79 24 42. Hrs opn: 24. Box 1855 (28388). (919) 692-7440. FAX: (919) 692-7372. Licensee: Pinehurst Broadcasting Corp. (acq 8-31-91; $275,000; FTR 6-10-91). Net: ABC/I, AP, NBC Talknet, Daynet, ARN; N.C. Net. Rep: Keystone (unwired net), T N. Wash atty: Maupin, Taylor, Ellis & Adams. Format: News/talk. News progmg 26 hrs wkly. Target aud: 25 plus. ■ Dane Adams, CFO; Steve Adams, vp, progmg dir, mus dir & news dir; Helen Sansone, gen mgr, opns mgr, dev mgr, gen sls mgr & natl sls mgr; Chuck Britt, chief engr. ■ Rates: $18; 14; 18; 10.

WIOZ-FM—Aug 14, 1973: 107.1 mhz; 3 kw. Ant 300 ft. TL: N35 09 57 W79 25 12 (CP: 106.9 mhz, 50 kw, ant 492 ft., TL: N35 09 04 W79 28 40). Stereo. Box 1677, Corner of Short & Long Sts. (28387). (919) 692-2107. FAX: (919) 692-6849. Licensee: Muirfield Broadcasting Inc. (acq 12-28-83). Net: MBS. Format: Btfl mus. News staff 2; news progmg 18 hrs wkly. ■ Walker Morris, pres; Bob Dellert, gen mgr; Rich Rushforth, opns mgr; Patty Tighe, prom dir; Gene Dennis, news dir.

Southport

WSFM(FM)—Apr 15, 1978: 107.5 mhz; 32 kw. Ant 594 ft. TL: N34 03 02 W77 57 20. Stereo. Hrs opn: 24. Box FM 107, First Union Bldg., 201 N. Front St., Wilmington (28402). (919) 251-0001. FAX: (919) 251-8004. Licensee: Sea Communications Inc. (acq 12-29-87). Net: NBC the Source. Rep: McGavren Guild. Format: Classic rock. News staff one; news progmg one hr wkly. Target aud: 18-49; young, upwardly mobile professionals. ■ Eric Jorgenson, pres; Dennis K. Deason, gen mgr; Brenda Jo Williams, vp sls; Doug Carsile, prom mgr; John Stevens, progmg dir; Brian Bolick, news dir; Paul Knight, chief engr. ■ Rates: $30; 35; 30; 20.

Sparta

WCOK(AM)—April 1967: 1060 khz; 800 w-D. TL: N36 28 55 W81 05 35. Box 637 (28675). (919) 372-8231. FAX: (919) 372-5863. Licensee: Sparta-Independence Radio Corp. (acq 3-76). Format: C&W, top-40, relg. Target aud: General. ■ Foy Hefner, pres & gen mgr; Judy Halsey, opns mgr & prom mgr; Jonathan Johnson, mus dir; Randy McKenzie, chief engr. ■ Rates: $5.25; 5.25; 5.25; 5.

Spindale

WGMA(AM)—October 1982: 1520 khz; 500 w-D. TL: N35 21 00 W81 56 18. Box 805, 301 W. Main (28160). (704) 287-5151; (704) 287-5150. Licensee: Moonglow Broadcasting Inc. Format: Southern gospel. News staff one; news progmg 20 hrs wkly. Target aud: 30-50; adults. ■ Billy D. Martin, pres & gen mgr; Barbara Martin, exec vp; Frances Anderson, vp; Beverly Bailey, gen sls mgr & prom dir; Paige Snyder, progmg dir; Tracey Martin, mus dir; Steve Martin, news dir; Don Lovelace, chief engr.

***WNCW(FM)**—Oct 13, 1989: 88.7 mhz; 17 kw. Ant 3,054 ft. TL: N35 44 5 W82 17 10. Stereo. Hrs opn: 6 AM-2 AM. Box 804 (28160). (704) 287-8000; (704) 286-3636. FAX: (704) 287-8012. Licensee: Isothermal Community College. Net: APR, NPR. Wash atty: Schwartz, Woods & Miller. Format: Triple A, news. News staff one; news progmg 31 hrs wkly. Target aud: 35-49; educated adults. Spec prog: Blues 4 hrs, jazz 5 hrs, folk 12 hrs, drama 3 hrs, gospel 2 hrs wkly. ■ Burr Beard, stn mgr; George Scheibner, opns mgr; Billie Jordan, dev dir; Will Johnson, dev mgr; Greg Hils, progmg dir; Bill Buchinsky, mus dir; Wandalu Greene, news dir; Jim Liverett, chief engr.

Spring Lake

WCIE(AM)—May 22, 1963: 1450 khz; 1 kw-U. TL: N35 11 00 W78 57 45. 1200 Hwy. 210 N. (28390). (813) 859-1465. Licensee: Evangel Christian School (acq 7-7-88). Rep: Southern. Format: Contemp Christian. News progmg 10 hrs wkly. Target aud: 18-49. ■ Karl Strader, pres; Jeff Davis, gen mgr; Donna Lynn, prom mgr; Mike Farrell, progmg dir; Kevin Wallace, mus dir; Rodger Roth, chief engr.

Spruce Pine

WTOE(AM)—Dec 24, 1955: 1470 khz; 5 kw-D, 100 w-N. TL: N35 54 24 W82 06 21. Hrs opn: 6 AM-midnight. Box 668, Highway 19-E (28777). (704) 765-7441. FAX: (704) 765-7442. Licensee: Mountain Valley Media Inc. Group owner: The Mark Group (acq 9-27-91; $140,000). Net: CBS; N.C. News Net. Format: Easy classic rock. News staff one; news progmg 12 hrs wkly. Target aud: 24-54; young adults. Spec prog: Relg 8 hrs wkly. ■ Remelle K. Sink, pres & gen mgr; J. Ardell Sink, exec vp; Bruce Ikard, opns mgr, progmg dir & pub affrs dir; Michael Sink, gen sls mgr & chief engr; Sally Root, prom dir. ■ Rates: $9; 8.50; 9; 4.

Statesville

WAME(AM)—Oct 7, 1957: 550 khz; 500 w-D. TL: N35 47 43 W80 51 17. 212 Signal Hill Dr. (28677). (704) 872-0956. FAX: (704) 872-0957. Licensee: Statesville Family Radio Corp. Group owner: GHB Radio Group (acq 4-22-86; $210,000; FTR 3-31-86). Net: CBS. Rep: T-N. Format: Gospel, news/talk. News staff one; news progmg 60 hrs wkly. Target aud: 35-64; adult, family oriented. Spec prog: Local & pro sports. ■ Wendell Echols, pres; Tom Gentry, gen mgr; Dave Arnold, gen sls mgr, mktg dir & adv mgr; Angela L. Henley, prom mgr & mus dir; David L. Wise, progmg dir; Dave Wise, news dir; Jim McJunkin, chief engr. ■ Rates: $10; 8; 9; 6.

WFMX(FM)—Listing follows WSIC(AM).

WSIC(AM)—May 3, 1947: 1400 khz; 1 kw-U. TL: N35 48 09 W80 53 30. Stereo. Hrs opn: 24. 1117 Radio Rd. (28677). (704) 872-6345. Licensee: Adventure Communications Inc. (group owner; acq 9-11-89; $2,500,000 with co-located FM; FTR 9-11-89). Net: NBC Talknet, NBC. Rep: Rgnl Reps; T-N.Format: MOR, talk. News staff one; news progmg 21 hrs wkly. Target aud: 35 plus; upscale. Spec prog: Relg 6 hrs wkly. ■ Mike Shott, pres; Mike Buxser, vp & gen mgr; Bill Blevins, opns mgr; Bonnie Hageman, gen sls mgr; Rita Kelly, mus dir; April McIntyre, news dir; Jeff Watts, chief engr. ■ Rates: $45; 44; 44; 30.

WFMX(FM)—Co-owned with WSIC(AM). May 3, 1947: 105.7 mhz; 100 kw. Ant 1,517 ft. TL: N35 49 55 W80 42 13. Stereo. Hrs opn: 24. Prog sep from AM. (704) 872-6348. Net: ABC/D. Format: C&W. News progmg 5 hrs wkly. Target aud: 25-54; adults—mid- to upper-income.

WTDR(FM)—Mar 16, 1961: 96.9 mhz; 100 kw. Ant 1,550 ft. TL: N35 31 57 W80 47 47. Stereo. Suite 210, 301 S. McDowell St., Charlotte (28209). (704) 333-9690. FAX: (704) 332-8805. Licensee: Trumper Communications Inc. (group owner; acq 9-21-89; $7 million; FTR 10-9-89). Rep: Christal. Format: Country. News staff one; news progmg 3 hrs wkly. Target aud: 25-54; middle- to upper-income adults. ■ Jeff Tromper, CEO; Pat Reedy, gen mgr & natl sls mgr; Ron Ellis, opns mgr & progmg dir; Bill Ramsey, gen sls mgr; Jackie Holt, prom mgr; Allison West, mus dir; Mark Rumsey, news dir; Art Bussure, chief engr.

Swan Quarter

***WHYC(FM)**—Mar 8, 1981: 88.5 mhz; 3 kw. Ant 293 ft. TL: N35 26 29 W76 13 09. Stereo. Rt. One, Box 155-A (27885). (919) 926-7201. Licensee: Hyde County Board of Ed. Format: Div, news/talk, ed. News staff one; news progmg 10 hrs wkly. Target aud: General; Eastern North Carolina population. Spec prog: Black 8 hrs, class 4 hrs, country 8 hrs, farm 2 hrs, jazz 8 hrs, adult contemp 24 hrs, btfl music 8 hrs, big band 8 hrs, Christian 4 hrs, contemp hit 8 hrs, oldies 16 hrs wkly. ■ Paul Avery, pres, gen mgr, gen sls mgr & progmg dir; Harvey Mason, chief engr.

Sylva

WRGC(AM)—Nov 8, 1957: 680 khz; 1 kw-D, 250 w-N, DA-N. TL: N35 23 35 W83 11 38. Hrs opn: 6 AM-11 PM. R.R. One, Box 1044 (28879); R.R. One, Box 322, Old Asheville Hwy. (28779). (704) 586-2221; (704) 586-9742. Licensee: WMSJ Inc. (acq 1962). Net: AP. Wash atty: Pepper & Corazzini. Format: Country. News staff one; news progmg 14 hrs wkly. Target aud: General. Spec prog: Gospel 10 hrs, talk 5 hrs wkly. ■ James B. Childress, CEO & pres; Tony V. Childress, vp, gen mgr, natl sls mgr, rgnl sls mgr & prom mgr; J.R. Carroll, opns mgr & mktg dir; Jeff Bryson, progmg dir; Brandon Stephens, mus dir & news dir; Suzannah H. Wells, asst mus dir; Traci Haskett, pub affrs dir; Tim Warner, chief engr. ■ Rates: $15; 15; 15; 9.

Tabor City

WTAB(AM)—July 1, 1954: 1370 khz; 5 kw-D, 109 w-N. TL: N34 09 00 W78 51 40. Hrs opn: 6 AM-midnight. Box 127 (28463). (919) 653-2131. Licensee: Great American Media Inc. (group owner; acq 5-86; $575,000; FTR 5-5-86). Net: N.C. News Net. Format: C&W, Black, gospel. News progmg 7 hrs wkly. Target aud: General. Spec prog: Swap shop, farm 8 hrs wkly. ■ Don Curtis, pres; Joe Bell, exec vp; Buddy Womack, chief engr.

WYNA(FM)—Co-owned with WTAB(AM). June 1964: 104.9 mhz; 1.5 kw. Ant 400 ft. TL: N34 09 00 W78 51 40. Stereo. Hrs opn: 5:30 AM- 1:30 AM. Prog sep from AM. Box 1407, Whiteville (28472). (919) 653-4841; (919) 642-9132. FAX: (919) 653-5146. Rep: T-N. Format: Country, talk. News progmg 4 hrs wkly. Target aud: 25-54. Spec prog: Beach 6 hrs wkly.

Tarboro

WCPS(AM)—January 1947: 760 khz; 1 kw-D. TL: N35 55 40 W77 34 15. Box 100, 3403 Main St. (27886). (919) 823-2191. FAX: (919) 823-2043. Licensee: Coastal Plains Media Inc. Group owner: Curtis Media Group (acq 12-18-87). Net: N.C. News. Rep: Southern, T-N. Format: MOR, relg, news/talk. News progmg 11 hrs wkly. Target aud: General. ■ Donald W. Curtis, pres; Rick Heilman, gen mgr; Sam Adams, progmg dir & mus dir; Charley Burlew, pub affrs dir; Doug Farris, chief engr.

WFXK(FM)—September 1952: 104.3 mhz; 100 kw. Ant 987 ft. TL: N35 48 40 W77 44 33. Stereo. Hrs opn: 24. Suite 116, 5400 S. Miami Blvd. Morrisville (27560). (919) 941-0700. FAX: (919) 941-1074. Licensee: Great American East Inc. Group owner: Osborn Communications Corp. (acq 12-19-88). Net: ABC/D. Rep: D & R Radio. Format: Adult contemp. News staff one; news progmg 3 hrs wkly. Target aud: 25-54. ■ Mark Hubbard, pres; Chris Jones, stn mgr & gen sls mgr; Michael Propst, mus dir; Mike Edwards, news dir; Gary Liebisch, chief engr.

Taylorsville

WACB(AM)—May 2, 1964: 860 khz; 250 w-D. TL: N35 55 57 W81 10 19. Hrs opn: Sunrise-sunset. 209 Main Ave., Dr. S.E. (28681). (704) 632-4621. Licensee: Apple City Broadcasting Co. Inc. (acq 9-24-93; $70,239; FTR 10-11-93). Format: Modern country. News staff 2; news progmg 4 hrs wkly. Target aud: general. Spec prog: Gospel 12 hrs wkly. ■ Norris Keever, pres; Roger Brown, exec vp; Sarah Keever, Mary Alice Brown, vps; Stuart Norfleet, stn mgr, opns dir & prom dir; Joyce Jolly, gen sls mgr; Jon Stephens, mus dir; Rick Fox, news dir; Wes Elder, chief engr. ■ Rates: $8.60; 8.60; 8.60; na.

WTLK(AM)—June 17, 1962: 1570 khz; 1 kw-D, 248 w-N. TL: N35 55 45 W81 09 44. Box 847, Tower Rd. (28681). (704) 632-4214. Licensee: International Broadcasting Co. Inc. acq 12-79). Net: Moody; N.C. News. Rep: T-N. Format: C&W. ■ Claudetta M. Potts, pres; Jay Douglas Blackburn, stn mgr & chief engr; Joyce B. Jolly, gen sls mgr; Pete Ray, prom mgr; Richard Fox, news dir.

Thomasville

WFAZ(FM)—April 1949: 98.3 mhz; 1.68 kw. Ant 429 ft. TL: N35 57 41 W80 02 13. Stereo. Box 6667, 1607 Country Club Dr., High Point (27262). (919) 887-0983. FAX: (919) 887-3055. Licensee: Hi Toms Broadcasting (acq 4-1-84). Net: MBS; N.C. News Net. Rep: T-N. Format: MOR, oldies. Target aud: 25-54. ■ William C. Boyce Jr., pres; Jim Poston, gen mgr; Ru Rose, opns mgr; Buddy Poole, gen sls mgr; Max Parrish, chief engr.

WTNC(AM)—September 1947: 790 khz; 1 kw-D, 50 w-N. TL: N35 53 40 W80 05 39. Box 1920, 726 Salem St. (27360). (919) 472-0790. Licensee: Radio Crusade Inc. Group owner: Willis Broadcasting Corp. (acq 1-24-86; $230,000; FTR 11-11-85). Net: Natl Black. Format: Gospel, inspirational. Target aud: 18-49; older, mature audience. ■ Alvin Roks, gen mgr; Tonio Gallimore, progmg dir & mus dir; Max Parrish, chief engr.

Topsail Beach

WZXS(FM)—Sept 12, 1993: 103.9 mhz; 21.5 kw Ant 328 ft. TL: N34 29 38 W77 29 18. Stereo. Hrs opn: 24. Drawer 127, Hwy. 117, Holly Ridge (28445). (919) 329-3667. FAX: (919) 329-3669. Licensee: Topsail Broadcasting Inc. Net: ABC, SMN. Wash atty: McNair & Sanford. News progmg 6 hrs wkly. Target aud: 45 plus; upper income and affluent retirees. ■ Sidney Williams, pres; Jackson F. Lee, CFO & sls dir; Hiram B. Williams, sr vp; Charles P. Wenk, gen mgr; Jim Kelso, stn mgr & pub affrs dir; Donald R. Brown, chief engr. ■ Rates: $5.75; 5.75; 5.75; 5.75.

Troy

WJRM(AM)—Dec 8, 1961: 1390 khz; 1 kw-D. TL: N35 21 43 W79 51 38. Box 549, Biscoe Rd. (27371). (910) 576-1390. FAX: (910) 572-2025. Licensee: Montgomery Broadcasting Inc. (acq 6-1-62). Net: AP. Format: Country. ■ John Wallace, gen mgr; William Norman, stn mgr; Jim Smith, opns mgr.

Tryon

WTYN(AM)—Oct 1, 1954: 1160 khz; 10 kw-D, 500 w-N, DA-N. TL: N35 14 07 W82 14 27. 116 N. Trade St. (28782). (704) 859-5800. Licensee: Anchor Baptist Broadcasting Association (acq 6-9-93; $153,644; FTR 6-28-93). Net: ABC, MBS. Wash atty: Tharrington, Smith & Hargrove. Format: Christian. News staff one; news progmg 25 hrs wkly. Target aud: 25 plus; middle-to-upper income. Spec prog: Jazz 3 hrs, class 2 hrs wkly. ■ Randy Barton, pres, gen mgr, opns mgr & progmg dir; Richard Rhodes, sls dir; Larry Owen, chief engr. ■ Rates: $10; 10; 10; 8.

Valdese

WSVM(AM)—Oct 6, 1961: 1490 khz; 1 kw-U. TL: N35 44 03 W81 34 04. Hrs opn: 5 AM-10 PM. Box 99, S. Praley St. (28690). (704) 874-0000. FAX: (704) 874-3316. Licensee: JBF Communications Inc. (acq 11-30-89; $225,000; FTR 12-18-89). Net: N.C. News. Format: Country. News progmg 4 hrs wkly. Spec prog: Gospel 4 hrs, sports 15 hrs wkly. ■ Jim Bishop, pres & gen mgr; Matt Lytle, stn mgr & gen sls mgr; Vicki Ollis, progmg mgr; Kelly Williams, mus dir; Ed Logan, chief engr. ■ Rates: $9; 7; 9; 6.25.

Wadesboro

WADE(AM)—July 23, 1947: 1340 khz; 500 w-U. TL: N34 57 01 W80 03 23. Hrs opn: 16. One Radio St. (28170). Licensee: Inspirational Deliverance Center Inc. (acq 6-8-93; $27,500; FTR 6-28-93). Format: Country, relg, urban contemp. Spec prog: Farm one hr wkly. ■ Clark Ratliffe, pres, gen mgr, prom mgr, progmg dir & mus dir; Dave Thomas, gen sls mgr; York David Anthony, chief engr. ■ Rates: $8; 8; 8; 8.

WRPL(FM)—Not on air, target date 1994: 93.5 mhz; 3 kw. Ant 328 ft. TL: N35 04 42 W80 17 08. Stereo. Hrs opn: 24. 208 S. Rutherford St. (28170). (704) 694-3969. FAX: (704) 694-3969. Licensee: WRPL Partnership. Wash atty: Fletcher, Heald & Hildreth. Target aud: 18-55. ■ Allen Lyon, pres & gen mgr; David Anthony, chief engr.

Wake Forest

WFTK(AM)—Sept 1, 1989: 1030 khz; 50 kw-D, DA. TL: N36 10 43 W78 45 30. Stereo. 211 W. C St., Butner (27509). (919) 781-1030; (919) 575-6644. Licensee: Vernon H. Baker. Group owner: Baker Family Stations. Format: Relg. Target aud: 25-54; middle-class families. ■ Vernon H. Baker, pres; Max Mathis, gen mgr; Robert Reuther, progmg dir; J. D. Watson, chief engr. ■ Rates: $22; 22; 22; na.

Wallace

WLSE(AM)—May 13, 1953: 1400 khz; 1 kw-U. TL: N34 45 29 W78 00 00. Hrs opn: 5:30 AM-midnight. Box 520, Hwy. 117 N. (28466). (919) 285-2187. Licensee: J G & J Broadcasting Inc. (acq 10-24-91; $230,000 with co-located FM; FTR 11-18-91). Net: NBC; N.C. News Net. Rep: T-N. Format: C&W. News progmg 2 hrs wkly. Target aud: 25-54. Spec prog: Black 6 hrs, farm 20 hrs wkly. ■ Mack Jones, pres & gen mgr; Teri Pope, gen sls mgr. ■ Rates: 8.70; 8.70; 8.70; 8.70.

WZKB(FM)—Co-owned with WLSE(AM). July 20, 1972: 94.3 mhz; 3 kw. Ant 300 ft. TL: N34 45 29 W78 00 00. Stereo. Format: Oldies, adult contemp. ■ Jim Smith, chief engr. ■ Rates: Same as AM.

Wanchese

WOBR(AM)—May 29, 1970: 1530 khz; 1 kw-D, DA. TL: N35 51 52 W75 39 01. Box 400, Hwy. 345 (27981). (919) 473-3434. Licensee: WOBR Inc. (acq 8-82; $110,000; FTR 8-9-82). Format: News/talk, vacation information. Target aud: General; tourists in the area. ■ William T. Smith, pres; Pat Cahill, gen mgr & gen sls mgr; John Harper, progmg dir & mus dir; Greg Clark, news dir; Don Small, chief engr.

WOBR-FM—June 1, 1973: 95.3 mhz; 25 kw. Ant 324 ft. TL: N35 51 53 W75 39 01 (CP: TL: N35 51 52 W75 39 01). Stereo. Prog sep from AM. Net: ABC, AP. Format: Adult contemp. News staff one; news progmg 3 hrs wkly. Target aud: 25-54. Spec prog: Jazz 2 hrs wkly. ■ Dan Banks, gen sls mgr.

Washington

WCZI(FM)—December 1988: 98.3 mhz; 1.3 kw. Ant 490 ft. TL: N35 29 14 W77 02 42. Stereo. Box 874, Greenville (27835-0874); 3219 Landmark St., Greenville (27889-2165). (919) 756-9898. Licensee: New East Communications Inc. (acq 7-26-89; $640,000; FTR 8-14-89). Net: Unistar. Wash atty: Tharrington, Smith & Hargrove. Format: News/talk. Target aud: 25-54; upscale, affluent audience. ■ Henry Hinton, pres & gen mgr; Kirk Smith, gen sls mgr; David Horn, progmg dir; Gene Brown, chief engr.

WDLX(FM)—Listing follows WRRF(AM).

WRRF(AM)—Mar 3, 1942: 930 khz; 5 kw-D, 1 kw-N, DA-N. TL: N35 31 34 W77 04 43. Box 1707 (27889). (919) 946-2162. Licensee: Tar Heel Broadcasting System. Net: ABC/I; N.C. Net. Rep: Banner. Wash atty: Tharrington, Smith & Hargrove. Format: Talk. News staff one; news progmg 21 hrs wkly. Target aud: 35 plus. ■ W. R.

Roberson Jr., chmn; C. Zoph Potts, pres & gen mgr; W. Riley Roberson, sr vp; Mark Storie, gen sls mgr; Gary Jackson, progmg dir; Doug Moreland, asst mus dir; Jan Hasty, news dir; John Wilroy, chief engr. ■ Rates: $35; 32; 35; 25.

WDLX(FM)—Co-owned with WRRF(AM). Jan 20, 1961: 93.3 mhz; 100 kw. Ant 1,940 ft. TL: N35 21 55 W77 23 38. Stereo. Hrs opn: 24. Prog sep from AM. U.S. Hwy. 17 S. (27889). Net: ABC/FM. Format: Adult contemp. News staff one; news progmg 12 hrs wkly; Target aud: 18-49. ■ W.R. Robertson Jr., CEO; Mark Storie, gen sls mgr; Gary Jackson, progmg dir; Doug Moreland, mus dir; Frank Gurnez, pub affrs dir; John Wilroy, engrg mgr. WITN-TV affil. ■ Rates: $40; 35; 40; 28.

WTOW(AM)—Sept 6, 1961: 1320 khz; 500 w-D. TL: N35 32 07 W77 04 04. 903 Hackney Ave. (27889). (919) 975-1320; (919) 946-1016. FAX: (919) 975-1322. Licensee: James Rouse (acq 2-1-93; $775,000; FTR 2-22-93). Net: USA. Format: Country, relg. News staff one; news progmg 7 hrs wkly. Target aud: 24-55; loyal listeners. Spec prog: Black 5 hrs; southern gospel 13 hrs wkly. ■ Mahalla Phelps, pres; William Clark, gen mgr; Ray Phelps, prom mgr; Polly Phelps, progmg dir; Michael Williams, mus dir; Anita Rogers, news dir; Gene Brown, chief engr.

Waxhaw

WLWW(FM)—Not on air, target date Apr 1, 1994: 106.1 mhz; 3 kw. Ant 111 ft. TL: N34 53 01 W80 47 37. Stereo. Hrs opn: 24. Box 258, c/o Jeffrey C. Sigmon, York (29745). (803) 684-4241; (803) 684-3405. FAX: (803) 684-4242. Licensee: Union County Communications Inc. ■ Jeffrey C. Sigmon, pres & gen mgr.

Waynesville

WHCC(AM)—August 1947: 1400 khz; 1 kw-U. TL: N35 30 14 W82 58 25. Hrs opn: 18. Box 659 (28786). (704) 456-8661. FAX: (704) 456-4316. Licensee: Media Mart Inc. (acq 8-3-93; $480,000 with co-located FM; FTR 8-30-93). Net: N.C. News Net. Rep: Keystone (unwired net). Format: News/talk. Target aud: General. Spec prog: Relg 3 hrs wkly. ■ Vann Campbell, CEO & gen mgr; Bob Garland, opns dir, prom dir, progmg dir, news dir & pub affrs dir; Betty Jo Nichols, sls dir; Kelvin Chappell, mus dir.

WQNS(FM)—Co-owned with WHCC(AM). October 1979: 104.9 mhz; 100 w. Ant 1,640 ft. TL: N35 34 07 W82 54 27. Stereo. Hrs opn: 24. Prog sep from AM. 139 1/2 Main St. (28786). Net: CNN. Format: C&W.

Weldon

WSMY(AM)—1957: 1400 khz; 1 kw-U. TL: N36 24 43 W77 37 06. Box 910, Roanoke Rapids (27870); 1616 Aurelian Springs Rd. (27890). (919) 536-3115. FAX: (919) 536-3045. Licensee: Moran Communications (acq 11-27-90; FTR 1-7-91). Net: ABC/I. Rep: Southern. Format: Urban, relg. News staff one; news progmg 12 hrs wkly. Target aud: 18 plus; affluent adults. ■ Tim Moran, pres; Amy Moran, vp, gen sls mgr & prom mgr; Joe Taylor, gen mgr; David Perkins, opns mgr, progmg dir & mus dir; Susan Mahne, news dir; Mickel Pruden, chief engr. ■ Rates: $10; 10; 10; na.

Wendell-Zebulon

WETC(AM)—June 16, 1959: 540 khz; 5 kw-D, 500 w-N, DA-2. TL: N35 52 06 W78 25 56 (CP: 8 kw-D). Hrs opn: 7 AM-1 PM. 1604 U.S. 64, Zebulon (27597). (919) 269-2240. FAX: (919) 269-5003. Licensee: East Wake Broadcasting Corp. (acq 2-7-92; assumption of debt; FTR 3-2-92). Format: Country, gospel, news/talk. Spec prog: Sp, farm 5 hrs wkly. ■ Lewis V. Parish, pres & chief engr; Richard A. Beck, stn mgr & progmg dir; Aaron Pitt, news dir.

West Jefferson

WKSK(AM)—May 27, 1959: 580 khz; 1 kw-D, 34 w-N. TL: N36 24 39 W81 29 48. Stereo. Hrs opn: 6 AM-9 PM (Mon-Sat), 7 AM-7 PM (Sun). Box 729, Hwy. 194 N. (28694). (919) 246-6001. Licensee: Caddell Broadcasting (acq 6-1-78). Net: AP. Format: C&W. News staff one; news progmg 16 hrs wkly. Target aud: General. Spec prog: Farm 3 hrs, gospel 5 hrs, Sp one hr wkly. ■ Jan Caddell, pres & gen mgr; Linda Shaffer, adv mgr; Jeff Brown, progmg dir; S. Huggins, mus dir; Michael Powers, news dir; Stoney Owen, chief engr. ■ Rates: $9; 9; 9; 9.

Whiteville

WENC(AM)—July 14, 1946: 1220 khz; 5 kw-D, 152 w-N. TL: N34 18 30 W78 43 00. Hrs opn: 6 AM-10 PM. 1220 Radio Station Rd. (28472). (919) 642-9291. Licensee: Hara Broadcasting Co. (acq 10-26-93; $135,000; FTR 11-8-93). Net: N.C. News. Rep: T-N. Format: Adult contemp. News staff one; news progmg 10 hrs wkly. Target aud: 25-54; women. Spec prog: Farm 5 hrs, relg 4 hrs wkly. ■ Doug Tyler, gen mgr, gen sls mgr & prom mgr; Dick Reus, progmg dir & mus dir; Mitch Kokai, news dir; Eddie Harrell, chief engr. ■ Rates: $7.20; 7.20; 7.20; 7.20.

WTXY(AM)—Jan 1, 1976: 1540 khz; 1 kw-D. TL: N34 19 23 W78 42 47. Box 1038, 501 W. Virgil St. (28472). (919) 642-8214. FAX: (919) 640-1540. Licensee: Stanley Broadcasting System Inc. (acq 2-2-87; $80,000; FTR 12-22-86). Net: UPI; Southern Farm. Format: Oldies, news/talk. News staff 2; news progmg 6 hrs wkly. Target aud: General. Spec prog: Farm 2 hrs, relg 10 hrs wkly. ■ Thos. V. Stanley Jr., pres, gen mgr, prom mgr, mus dir & vp progmg; John H. Stanley, execvp; Hilda Williamson, opns mgr; Mary Alice Stanley, news dir; Buddy Wommack, chief engr. ■ Rates: $7; 5; 5; 4.

WZFX(FM)—Licensed to Whiteville. See Fayetteville.

Wilkesboro

***WSIF(FM)**—Apr 6, 1977: 94.7 mhz; 10 w. Ant -151 ft. TL: N36 08 12 W81 11 02. Stereo. Box 120, Collegiate Dr. (28697). (919) 651-8723. FAX: (919) 651-8749. Licensee: Wilkes Community College. Format: Educational. ■ Dr. A.G. Stanley, gen mgr.

WWWC(AM)—Jan 26, 1970: 1240 khz; 1 kw-U. TL: N36 09 00 W81 09 42. Box 580, 602 W. Main St. (28697). (919) 667-1241. Licensee: Tomlinson Broadcasting Corp of Wilkes County (acq 9-1-83; $410,000; FTR 9-12-83). ■ Billy G. Tomlinson, pres; Jeff Wilson, gen mgr.

Williamston

WHTE(FM)—Aug 1, 1962: 103.7 mhz; 50 kw. Ant 331 ft. TL: N35 51 27 W77 02 34 (CP: 100 kw, ant 980 ft.). Stereo. Suite C101, 408 W. Arlington Blvd., Greenville (28801). (919) 355-2234. FAX: (919) 355-2234. Licensee: WHTE Inc. (acq 8-12-91). Format: CHR. ■ David Mack, gen mgr.

WIAM(AM)—March 1951: 900 khz; 1 kw-D, 258 w-N. TL: N35 51 27 W77 02 34. Box 590 (27892). (919) 792-4161. Licensee: Lifeline Ministries Inc. (acq 6-18-90; FTR 7-9-90). Net: N.C. News. Rep: T-N. Format: Relg, Southern gospel. Target aud: General. ■ Johnny Bryant, pres, gen mgr & progmg dir; Will Jackson, mus dir; Doug Ferris, chief engr.

Wilmington

WAAV(AM)—(Leland). Dec 20, 1957: 980 khz; 5 kw-U, DA-N. TL: N34 14 54 W78 00 09. Suite B, 211 N. Second St., Wilmington (28401). (919) 763-4000. FAX: (919) 763-4041. Licensee: Hara Broadcasting Inc. Net: NBC, MBS, ABC TalkRadio, Sun. Rep: Katz. Format: News/talk. News staff 2. Target aud: 35 plus. ■ Donn Ansell, pres, gen mgr & gen sls mgr; Audre Lelong, opns mgr; Chuck Agresta, progmg dir; Mark Boyer, pub affrs dir; Paul Knight, chief engr.

WBMS(AM)—Dec 24, 1946: 1340 khz; 1 kw-U. TL: N34 12 35 W77 56 53. Box 718 (28402). (919) 763-4633. FAX: (919) 251-0534. Licensee: H&N Holdings NC Inc. (acq 12-6-93; $140,000; FTR 12-20-93). Format: Talk, sports. ■ S. Frank McNeil, pres; Rachel Currie, gen mgr; Thomas McLaurin, adv mgr; Kenny Grady, progmg dir; Paul Knight, chief engr.

WGNI(FM)—Mar 1, 1970: 102.7 mhz; 100 kw. Ant 981 ft. TL: N34 03 00 W78 04 56. Stereo. 1890 Dawson St. (28403-2359). (919) 763-6511. FAX: (919) 763-5926. Licensee: Cape Fear Broadcasting (group owner; acq 5-1-84). Format: Adult contemp. ■ Hannah Gage, gen mgr; Monica Johnson, gen sls mgr; Mike Farrow, progmg dir; Mark Boyer, news dir; Terry Jordan, chief engr.

***WHQR(FM)**—Apr 24, 1984: 91.3 mhz; 10 kw. Ant 1,142 ft. TL: N34 07 51 W78 11 16. Stereo. 1026 Greenfield St. (28401). (910) 343-1640. FAX: (910) 251-8693. Licensee: Friends of Public Radio Inc. Net: NPR. Format: Class. Spec prog: Jazz 20 hrs wkly. ■ Bruce Deschamps, pres; Michael A. Titterton, gen mgr; Elizabeth Becka, gen sls mgr; Sam Burke, mus dir; Paul Knight, chief engr.

***WKQK(FM)**—Not on air, target date unknown: 90.5 mhz; 1 kw. Ant 328 ft. TL: N34 10 55 W78 02 46. Box 203A, Rt. One, Castleton (22716). Licensee: Coastal Community Radio Inc.

WKXB(FM)—See Burgaw.

WMFD(AM)—Apr 15, 1935: 630 khz; 1 kw-U, DA-2. TL: N34 14 37 W78 18 31. Suite 512, 333 Fayetteville St. (28402). (919) 763-6363. FAX: (919) 251-0534. Licensee: Specialized Communications Inc. (acq 9-3-92; $106,000; FTR 9-21-92). Net: CBS. Rep: Banner. Format: Easy lstng, 40s, 50s & 60s. News staff one; news progmg 3 hrs wkly. Target aud: 30 plus; upscale audience. ■ Sandra Franklin, gen mgr; Tony Woodrich, progmg dir; Paul Knight, chief engr. ■ Rates: $7.50; 7.50; 7.50; 6.50.

WMNX(FM)—Feb 24, 1970: 97.3 mhz; 100 kw. Ant 602 ft. TL: N34 16 34 W78 09 09. Stereo. Hrs opn: 24. 189 Dawson St. (28401-5052). (919) 763-6511. Licensee: Cape Fear Radio Co. (acq 11-18-92; $950,000; FTR 12-7-92). Format: Urban contemp. News staff one. Target aud: 18 plus. ■ Monica Johnson, gen sls mgr; Rod Cruze, progmg dir; Mark Boyer, news dir.

WUOY(FM)—Not on air, target date unknown: 104.5 mhz; 4.5 kw. Ant 377 ft. TL: N34 16 15 W77 57 23. Beatriz G.S. De McComas, 2495 Greenwell Court (28403). Licensee: Beatriz Garcia Suarez De McComas.

WVBS(FM)—See Burgaw.

WWIL(AM)—Aug 25, 1963: 1490 khz; 1 kw-U. TL: N34 13 52 W77 57 18. Box 957 (28402-0701). (910) 763-2452. FAX: (910) 251-0534. Licensee: Family Radio Network Inc. (acq 10-28-92; $35,000; FTR 11-23-92). Rep: Blair. Format: Adult contemp Christian. ■ Jim Stephens, gen mgr.

WWQQ-FM—Mar 31, 1969: 101.3 mhz; 50 kw. Ant 525 ft. TL: N34 13 31 W77 59 17 (CP: 40 kw, ant 544 ft.). Stereo. Hrs opn: 24. Suite 101, 721 Market St. (28401). (910) 763-9977. FAX: (910) 762-0456. Licensee: HVS Partners (group owner; acq 2-88; grpsl; FTR 2-29-88). Net: ABC/D. Format: Country. News staff one. Target aud: 25-54. ■ D. Chuck Langley, gen mgr; Judy Miller, gen sls mgr; Liz Zadeits, prom mgr; Tom Burton, progmg dir & mus dir; Babita Hariani, news dir. ■ Rates: $65; 50; 52; 40.

Wilson

***WAHD(FM)**—May 1990: 90.5 mhz; 3.8 kw. Ant 100 ft. TL: N35 47 48 W78 18 31. Suite 512, 333 Fayetteville St. Mall, Raleigh (27602). (919) 833-6259. Licensee: Mega Educational Communications Inc. (acq 6-6-89; $10,000; FTR 6-26-89). Format: Contemp hit. ■ Oscar Eatmon, pres.

WGTM(AM)—July 18, 1937: 590 khz; 5 kw-U, DA-2. TL: N35 43 04 W78 03 33. Box 3837, Hwy. 42 W. (29895). (919) 243-2188. FAX: (919) 237-8813. Licensee: Celestine L. Willis. Group owner: Willis Broadcasting Corp. (acq 12-15-89; $375,000; FTR 3-3-86). Format: Contemp gospel. ■ Thomas Ward, gen mgr & gen sls mgr; Edgar Suggs, progmg dir.

WLLY(AM)—1961: 1350 khz; 1 kw-D, 79 w-N. TL: N35 43 24 W77 55 16. Box 3587, 210 Beacon St. (27895). (919) 237-5171. FAX: (919) 237-5172. Licensee: Family Media Inc. (acq 1-27-92; $100; FTR 2-17-92). Net: USA. Format: Relg. ■ Michael R. Bland, pres, gen mgr, gen sls mgr & prom mgr; Jack Townsend, chief engr.

WRDU(FM)—Licensed to Wilson. See Raleigh.

WVOT(AM)—June 1948: 1420 khz; 1 kw-D, 500 w-N, DA-N. TL: N35 44 08 W77 53 02. Box 2528, (27893). (919) 243-5157. Licensee: Career Communications Inc. (acq 8-1-90; $213,254; FTR 8-20-90). Net: MBS; N.C. Net. Rep: T-N. Format: Adult contemp, oldies. News progmg 25 hrs wkly. Target aud: 25-55. ■ Rick Mendelson, pres & gen mgr; Bill Benjamin, vp sls & gen sls mgr; Mark Miller, progmg dir; Junior Norfleet, mus dir; Sam Garfield, chief engr. ■ Rates: $15.75; 11.50; 13.75; 8.

Windsor

WDRP(FM)—Dec 5, 1988: 98.9 mhz; 6 kw. Ant 350 ft. TL: N35 54 25 W77 00 32. Box 567 (27893). (919) 794-3130. Licensee: PS&W Enterprises Inc. Net: SMN. Format: Southern gospel. ■ J. Rodney Williford, pres; Johnny Bryant, gen mgr; A. Dean Roebuck, progmg dir & mus dir; Doug Ferris, chief engr.

Wingate

***WRCM(FM)**—June 14, 1993: 91.9 mhz; 17.7 kw. Ant 515 ft. TL: N35 03 33 W80 40 14. Hrs opn: 24. Box 17069, Charlotte (28270). 1092 Radio Rd., Indian Trail (28079). (704) 821-9293, (704) 570-9200. FAX: (704) 821-9285. Licensee: Columbia Bible College Broadcasting Co. Net: AP. Wash atty: Rini & Coran. Format: Contemp Christian. Target aud: 25-49. ■ Ken E. Mayfield, gen mgr;

Stations in the U.S.

Rodney Baucom, progmg dir; Shelly Mitchell, asst mus dir; Karen Wycoff, pub affrs dir; Don Strom, chief engr.

Winston-Salem

*NEW FM—Not on air, target date Nov 1, 1994: 89.3 mhz; 2.5 kw. 1249 Trade St. (27101). (919) 777-1560; (919) 777-1550. Licensee: Triad Family Network Inc. ■ Philip T. Watson, pres, gen mgr & gen sls mgr; Kurt Myers, prom mgr; John Hill, progmg dir; Wally Decker, mus dir; Larry Schropp, chief engr.

WAAA(AM)—Oct 28, 1950: 980 khz; 1 kw-D, 69.3 w-N. TL: N36 09 15 W80 16 34. Box 11197 (27116-1197); 4950 Indiana Ave. (27106). (910) 767-0430. FAX: (910) 767-0433. Licensee: Media Broadcasting Corp. (acq 9-1-56). Rep: Roslin. Format: Black. ■ Ms. Mutter D. Evans, pres & gen mgr; Mark Raymond, progmg dir & mus dir; Ed Kasovic, chief engr.

WBFJ(AM)—Oct 1, 1960: 1550 khz; 1 kw-D. TL: N36 06 33 W80 14 47. Stereo. Hrs opn: Sunrise-sunset. 1249 Trade St. (27101). (919) 721-1560. FAX: (919) 777-1550. Licensee: Word of Life Broadcasting Inc. (acq 6-29-83). Net: USA. Format: Adult contemp Christian. Target aud: 25-49. Spec prog: Sp one hr wkly. ■ Philip T. Watson, pres, gen mgr & gen sls mgr; Kurt Myers, prom mgr; John Hill, progmg dir; Wally Decker, mus dir; Larry Schropp, chief engr.

*WFDD-FM—Mar 13, 1961: 88.5 mhz; 22 kw. Ant 345 ft. TL: N35 58 12 W80 12 54 (CP: TL:N35 55 1.5 W80 17 37). Stereo. Hrs opn: 24. Box 8850, 56 Wake Forest Rd. (27109). (919) 759-8850. FAX: (919) 759-5193. Licensee: Trustees of Wake Forest Univ. Net: APR, NPR. Wash atty: Fletcher, Heald & Hildreth. Format: Class, news. News progmg 29 hrs wkly. Target aud: General; educated/public radio. Spec prog: Jazz 16 hrs, folk 6 hrs wkly. ■ Cleve Callison, stn mgr; Marissa Melton, chief opns; Joan Hatfield, dev dir; Bob Workmon, mus dir; Paul Brown, news dir; Tom Caldwell, chief engr.

WKTE(AM)—See King.

WKZL(FM)—1972: 107.5 mhz; 100 kw. Ant 500 ft. TL: N36 06 43 W80 06 11 (CP: Ant 1,194 ft., TL: N36 13 25 W80 06 06). Stereo. 192 E. Lewis St., Greensboro (27406-1459). (919) 274-8042. FAX: (919) 274-1629. Licensee: Dick Broadcasting Co. Inc. of Tennessee (acq 11-23-92; $6.5 million with WGFX(FM) Gallatin, TN; FTR 12-14-92). Rep: Katz. Format: CHR. News staff one; news progmg 3 hrs wkly. Target aud: 25-49; women. ■ Allen Dick, pres & gen mgr; David Henderglaht, CFO; Tom Jackson, opns mgr & progmg dir; James Kerr, gen sls mgr; Andy Steele, prom mgr; Jeff McHugh, mus dir; Terrie Knight, news dir; Tom Caldwell, chief engr.

WMAG(FM)—See High Point.

WMQX(AM)—Licensed to Winston-Salem. See Greensboro.

WMQX-FM—Licensed to Winston-Salem. See Greensboro.

WPIP(AM)—Not on air, target date unknown: 880 khz; 900 w-D. TL: N36 06 33 W80 14 47. 1711 Appletree Ln., Fort Mill, SC (29715). Licensee: Michael Glinter.

WSJS(AM)—Apr 17, 1930: 600 khz; 5 kw-D, 5 kw-N, DA-2. TL: N36 07 00 W80 21 26. Stereo. Box 3018, 875 W. 5th St. (27102). (919) 727-8826. Licensee: Newmarket Media of North Carolina. Group owner: NewMarket Media Corp. (acq 5-29-87). Net: MBS, NBC, NBC Talknet, Wall Street. Rep: McGavren Guild. Format: News/talk. News staff 5; news progmg 4 hrs wkly. Target aud: 25-64. ■ Steve Robertson, CEO; Peter M. Schulte, pres; Howard Nemenz, vp & gen mgr; Tom Hamilton, gen sls mgr; Stacey Propps, prom mgr; Paul Johnson, progmg dir; Bob Costner, news dir; Allen Boaz, chief engr.

WTQR(FM)—Co-owned with WSJS(AM). Dec 1, 1947: 104.1 mhz; 100 kw. Ant 1,420 ft. TL: N36 22 28 W80 22 31. Stereo. Prog sep from AM. Net: MBS. Format: Modern country. News staff 5; news progmg 2 hrs wkly. Target aud: 25-54. Spec prog: NASCAR, Bluegrass 2 hrs wkly. ■ Paul Johnson, dev mgr; Jo Ramsey, natl sls mgr; Dale Mitchell, progmg mgr; Danny Hall, mus dir.

WSMX(AM)—October 1964: 1500 khz; 10 kw-D (1-kw-CH), DA. TL: N36 06 34 W80 12 42. Hrs opn: Sunrise-sunset. Box 16056 (27115); 500 Kinard Dr. (27105). (919) 761-1545; (919) 724-7050. Licensee: Gospel Media Inc. (acq 6-82). Format: Relg, gospel. News progmg 12 hrs wkly. Target aud: 25 & older. Spec prog: Country 3 hrs wkly. ■ Bishop Sylvester D. Johnson, pres; Sarah Bailey, gen mgr & progmg dir; Ray Testerman, chief engr.

*WSNC(FM)—1982: 90.5 mhz; 125 w. Ant 92 ft. TL: N36 05 36 W80 13 53 (CP: 10 kw, ant 194 ft. TL: N36 05 24 W80 13 20). Stereo. Box 13095 (27110). (919) 750-2304. FAX: (919) 750-2459. Licensee: Winston-Salem State Univ. Format: Div, educ, jazz. News progmg 20 hrs wkly. Target aud: 12-70; African-Americans. Spec prog: Class 4 hrs wkly. ■ Dr. Brian Blount, gen mgr; Joe Watson, opns mgr; Jo Daniels II, chief engr.

WTOB(AM)—Apr 22, 1947: 1380 khz; 5 kw-D, 2.5 kw-N, DA-2. TL: N36 08 53 W80 19 11. Stereo. Hrs opn: 18. 8025 N. Point Blvd. (27106). (919) 759-0363. Licensee: Gary Sbordone (acq 11-87; $450,000; FTR 11-30-87). Net: CNN; N.C. News Net. Wash atty: Timothy Welch. Format: News. Target aud: 35 plus; affluent audience. ■ Gary Sbordone, pres; Dave Plyler, vp, gen mgr, gen sls mgr & progmg dir; Greg Epperson, opns mgr; Jack Pilaria, prom mgr; Ray Testerman, chief engr.

WTQR(FM)—Listing follows WSJS(AM).

WWWB(FM)—See High Point.

*WXRI(FM)—Not on air, target date unknown: 91.5 mhz; 20 kw. Ant 69 ft. TL: N36 08 06 W80 22 32. c/o Box 889, Blacksburg, VA (24060). Licensee: Positive Alternative Radio Inc. (group owner; acq 5-21-92). ■ Vernon H. Baker, pres.

Yanceyville

WYNC(AM)—Nov 9, 1979: 1540 khz; 2.5 kw-D. TL: N36 24 52 W79 20 06. Box 670, 545 Firetower Rd. (27379). (919) 694-1540. FAX: (919) 694-1670. Licensee: Semora Broadcasting Inc. (acq 12-9-91; $102,041; FTR 1-6-92). Net: Westwood One. Format: News/talk. News staff one. Target aud: General; rural Caswell county & Danville, VA. Spec prog: Gospel 16 hrs wkly. ■ Harry Myers, pres & gen mgr; Jeff Moore, vp opns & vp progmg; David Henderson, vp sls & gen sls mgr; Eric Pennebaker, pub affrs dir; Tim L. Walker, chief engr. ■ Rates: $6; 6; 6; na.

North Dakota

Arthur

KCQV(FM)—Not on air, target date unknown: 96.7 mhz; 5 kw. Ant 361 ft. TL: N47 05 42 W97 18 01. Box 194 (58006). Licensee: Mid-Valley Broadcasting Co.

Belcourt

*KEYA(FM)—October 1975: 88.5 mhz; 19 kw. Ant 263 ft. TL: N48 50 37 W99 45 02. Stereo. Hrs opn: 19. Box 190, Media Bldg., Hospital Rd. (58316). (701) 477-5686; (701) 477-3527. FAX: (701) 477-3252. Licensee: Belcourt School District No. 7. Format: Country, pub affrs. News staff one; news progmg 2 hrs wkly. Target aud: General; members of the Turtle Mountain Band of Chippewa Indians. Spec prog: Contemp Native American artists one hr, old-time fiddle mus 8 hrs, Chippewa 3 hrs wkly. ■ Michael V. Vann, pres; Vicky Short, gen mgr; David E. Garcia III, dev dir; Kimberly Thomas, progmg dir; Carla Schroeder, mus dir; Logan J. Davis, news dir; John Aasen, chief engr.

Beulah

KHOL(AM)—Oct 5, 1978: 1410 khz; 1 kw-D, 180 w-N. TL: N47 17 15 W101 45 46. Hrs opn: 6 AM-9 PM. Box 819, Hwy. 21 (58523). (701) 873-2215. FAX: (701) 873-2363. Licensee: Mercer Broadcasting Inc. Net: ABC/I, N.D. Net, American Agri. Format: C&W. News staff one; news progmg 14 hrs wkly. Target aud: 24-65; general. Spec prog: Loc sports , farm 6 hrs, relg 7 hrs, polka-fest 2 hrs wkly. ■ Alice Bolinske, pres; Sheri Schaper, gen mgr, vp opns, vp adv, progmg dir & mus dir; Robyn Skalsky, vp sls & gen sls mgr; Nolan Dix, news dir; Hope Doppong, pub affrs dir; Larry Rosenau, vp engrg. ■ Rates: $7.75; 7.75; 7.75; 7.75.

KPVZ(FM)—Not on air, target date unknown: 97.9 mhz; 6 kw. Ant 328 ft. TL: N47 17 58 W101 47 02. 127 Manvel Place, Grafton (58237). Licensee: Patricia L. Leighton.

Bismarck

*KBMK(FM)—Not on air, target date unknown: 101.5 mhz; 100 kw. Ant 1,151 ft. 23 Brookwood Ct., Princeton, NJ (08540). Licensee: J B Broadcasting Inc.

KBMR(AM)—Aug 15, 1958: 1130 khz; 50 kw-D, DA. TL: N46 50 04 W100 31 19 (CP: 710 khz (night), 4 kw-N, DA-3). Stereo. 3500 E. Rosser Ave. (58501). (701) 255-1234. FAX: (701) 222-1131. Licensee: Anderson Broadcasting Company (acq 4-1-65). Net: NBC. Rep: McGavren Guild. Wash atty: Borsari & Baxton. Format: C&W. News staff one; news progmg 2 hrs wkly. Target aud: 25 plus. Spec prog: Farm 4 hrs wkly. ■ Alvin L. Anderson, pres, gen mgr & chief engr; Roswell Henke, gen sls mgr; Darrell Anderson, prom mgr; Marv Allen, progmg dir; Shannon Dean, mus dir; Gus Becker, news dir. ■ Rates: $28; 24; 28; 16.

KQDY(FM)—Co-owned with KBMR(AM). Sept 13, 1968: 94.5 mhz; 100 kw. Ant 1,117 ft. TL: N46 51 31 W100 41 38. Stereo. Hrs opn: 24. (701) 258-9400. Net: CNN. Format: Contemp country. News progmg 4 hrs wkly. Target aud: 18-49. ■ John Kerzman, gen sls mgr; Darrell Anderson, progmg dir; Dean August, mus dir. ■ Rates: Same as AM.

*KCND(FM)—Sept 1, 1981: 90.5 mhz; 100 kw. Ant 1,250 ft. TL: N46 35 17 W100 48 07. Stereo. Hrs opn: 20. 1814 N. 15th St. (58501). (701) 224-1700; (800) 359-5566. FAX: (701) 224-0555. Licensee: Prairie Public Broadcasting Inc. Net: NPR. Format: Class, jazz, news. News staff 2; news progmg 40 hrs wkly. Target aud: General. Spec prog: Easy listening 8 hrs, folk 5 hrs wkly. ■ Steve Leyland, pres; Bill McGinley, stn mgr; Roger Lockbeam, opns mgr; Donald Hoffman, mus dir; David Thompson, news dir; Gary Stegmiller, chief engr.

KFYR(AM)—1925: 550 khz; 5 kw-U, DA-N. TL: N46 51 12 W100 32 37. Stereo. Box 1738 (58502). (701) 258-5555. Licensee: Meyer Broadcasting Co. (group owner). Net: ABC/I. Rep: Banner. Format: Adult contemp. ■ Tom Barr, vp; Dan Brannan, gen mgr; Syd Stewart, gen sls mgr; Sid Hardt, mus dir; Jeff Alexander, news dir; Herbert R. Leupp, chief engr. ■ Rates: $35.50; 35.50; 33; 18.50.

KYYY(FM)—Co-owned with KFYR(AM). Aug 15, 1966: 92.9 mhz; 100 kw. Ant 1,180 ft. TL: N46 36 19 W100 48 30. Stereo. Prog sep from AM. (701) 224-9393. Format: CHR. ■ Bob Beck, progmg dir; Brett Heartz, news dir.

KKCT(FM)—Not on air, target date unknown: 97.5 mhz; 100 kw. Ant 324 ft. Box 186-C, Rt. One, New Ulm, MN (56073). Licensee: James and Konnie Bartels.

KLXX(AM)—(Bismarck-Mandan). 1925: 1270 khz; 1 kw-D, 250 w-N. TL: N46 48 37 W100 50 10. Box 1377, Bismarck (58502). (701) 663-6411. FAX: (701) 663-8790. Licensee: Missouri River Broadcasting Inc. (acq 8-19-92; $395,000; FTR 9-7-92). Net: Unistar. Format: Oldies. Spec prog: Sports 6 hrs wkly. ■ James Ingstad, pres; Bob Denver, gen mgr; Terry A. Fleck, gen sls mgr; Dean Mastel, progmg dir & mus dir; Shelley Kincade, news dir; Larry Johnson, chief engr.

KQDY(FM)—Listing follows KBMR(AM).

KYYY(FM)—Listing follows KFYR(AM).

Bismarck-Mandan

KLXX(AM)—Licensed to Bismarck-Mandan. See Bismarck.

KBYZ(FM)—Co-owned with KLXX(AM). June 1, 1985: 96.5 mhz; 100 kw. Ant 1,000 ft. TL: N46 35 25 W100 47 47. Net: Unistar. Rep: D & R Radio, Roslin. Format: Adult contemp. News staff one. Target aud: 25-54.

Bottineau

KBTO(FM)—Nov 9, 1980: 101.9 mhz; 52 kw. Ant 492 ft. TL: N48 51 10 W100 20 01. Stereo. Hrs opn: 24. Box 12, Highway 5 W. (58318). (701) 228-5151. Licensee: Standef Broadcasting Corp. of N.D. (acq 4-92). Net: ABC/E; AgriAmerica. Format: C&W. ■ Ed Stanley, pres & gen mgr; Stan Edwards, gen sls mgr & mus dir; Jay McKay, chief engr.

Bowman

KPOK(AM)—Aug 9, 1980: 1340 khz; 1 kw-U. TL: N46 10 48 W103 22 12. Hrs opn: 18. Box 477, Dakota Western Insurance, 122 S. Main (58623). (701) 523-3883. Licensee: Tri-State Communications Inc. Net: NBC, Unistar, Westwood One, MBS. Format: Modern country. News staff one; news progmg 14 hrs wkly. Target aud: 25-54. Spec prog: Farm 2 hrs wkly. ■ Larry Kemnitz, pres; Brian Fisher, gen mgr; Mark Mosbrucker, opns dir; Pam Fisher, gen sls mgr; Pamela Fisher, prom dir; Beau Casey, progmg dir; Ty Dixon, mus dir; Emily Lambourn, news dir; Kelly Olson, pub affrs dir; Bill Spitzer, chief engr.

Carrington

KDAK(AM)—Oct 16, 1961: 1600 khz; 500 w-D, 90 w-N. TL: N47 25 43 W99 05 03. Hrs opn: 6 AM-7 PM. Box 50, 859 Main St. (58421). (701) 652-3151. FAX: (701) 652-2916. Licensee: Christensen Broadcasting (acq 5-1-85). Net: ABC/C; N.D. News Net. Format: C&W. Target aud: 30 plus. ■ Randy Christensen, pres, gen mgr & sls dir; Tim Fitterer, progmg dir & mus dir.

Devils Lake

KDLR(AM)—Jan 25, 1925: 1240 khz; 1 kw-U. TL: N48 06 42 W98 50 43. Box 190; 400 12th Ave. (58301). (701) 662-2161. FAX: (701) 662-2222. Licensee: Dakota Rose Broadcasting Inc. (acq 7-1-88). Net: MBS; American Agri., N.D. Net. Rep: Katz & Powell. Format: Country, news. News staff one. Target aud: 25 plus; general. Spec prog: Minn. Twins & Vikings. ■ Dale Alwin, pres, gen mgr & gen sls mgr; Bob Schmalseldt, progmg dir; Roger Graphenpeen, mus dir; Mike Walters, news dir; Cole Grace, chief engr.

KDVL(FM)—Co-owned with KDLR(AM). Jan 1, 1967: 102.5 mhz; 100 kw. Ant 471 ft. TL: N47 59 16 W98 55 59. Stereo. Prog sep from AM. Net: SMN. Format: Adult contemp. Target aud: 18-49.

KZZY-FM—March 1984: 103.5 mhz; 100 kw. Ant 433 ft. TL: N47 59 28 W98 56 57. Stereo. Hrs opn: 24. Box 882, 318 W. Walnut St. (58301). (701) 662-7563. FAX: (701) 662-7564. Licensee: Double Z Broadcasting Inc. (acq 4-11-90). Net: ABC/I. Rep: Group W. Format: C&W. News staff one. ■ Larry Larson, pres, gen mgr & gen sls mgr; Curt Teigen, opns mgr & progmg dir; Rob Hendricks, mus dir; Lloyd Kuehn, news dir; Dean Johnson, chief engr.

Dickinson

KDIX(AM)—1947: 1230 khz; 1 kw-U. TL: N46 53 44 W102 47 06. Box 1368 (58602). (701) 225-5133. Licensee: Starrdak Inc. (acq 4-1-93; $250,000; FTR 3-29-93). Net: CBS. Format: Adult contemp. ■ Lee Leiss, gen mgr; Rod Kleinjan, gen sls mgr, progmg dir & mus dir; Bob Stockbert, chief engr.

***KDPR(FM)**—Oct 12, 1987: 89.9 mhz; 12.5 kw. Ant 488 ft. TL: N46 43 34 W102 54 56. Stereo. Hrs opn: 20. 1814 N. 15th St., Bismarck (58501). (701) 224-1700; (800) 359-5566. FAX: (701) 224-0555. Licensee: Prairie Public Broadcasting Inc. Net: NPR. Format: Class, jazz, news. News staff 2; news progmg 40 hrs wkly. Target aud: General. Spec prog: Easy listening 8 hrs, folk 6 hrs wkly. ■ Steve Leyland, pres; Bill McGinley, stn mgr; Roger Lockbeam, opns mgr; Donald Hoffman, mus dir; David Thompson, news dir; Gary Stegmiller, chief engr.

KLTC(AM)—July 4, 1978: 1460 khz; 5 kw-U, DA-N. TL: N46 50 54 W102 49 49. Box 1478 (58602). (701) 227-1876. FAX: (701) 227-1901. Licensee: Western Media Inc. Net: ABC; American Agri. Rep: Hyett/Ramsland. Format: C&W. News staff 2; news progmg 3 hrs wkly. Target aud: General. ■ Ray David, pres & gen mgr; Rick Thompson, gen sls mgr; Helmuth Beck, progmg dir; Paul Quinn, mus dir; Jean Ashmore, asst mus dir; Darlene Keller, pub affrs dir; Earl Ackerman, chief engr.

KRRB(FM)—Aug 15, 1983: 92.1 mhz; 630 w. Ant 571 ft. TL: N46 55 24 W102 43 35 (CP: 1.55 kw). Stereo. 129-3rd Ave. E. (58601). (701) 227-1222. FAX: (701) 227-1959. Licensee: Roughrider Broadcasting Co. Net: SMN. Rep: Hyett/Ramsland. Format: Adult contemp. News staff one. Target aud: 18-45. ■ Ray David, pres; Larry Bolinske, gen mgr & gen sls mgr; Ron Lampheare, news dir; Earl Ackerman, chief engr.

KRRD(FM)—Co-owned with KRRB(FM). Not on air, target date unknown: 99.1 mhz; 100 kw. Ant 712 ft. TL: N46 43 34 W102 54 56.

Fargo

***KDSU(FM)**—Jan 17, 1966: 91.9 mhz; 100 kw. Ant 991 ft. TL: N47 00 48 W97 11 37. Stereo. Hrs opn: 18. Box 5347 (58105); Ceres Hall, Rm. 111, North Dakota State Univ. (58105). (701) 237-8322; (701) 237-8215. FAX: (701) 241-1893. Licensee: North Dakota State Univ. Net: NPR. Format: Talk, jazz. News staff one; news progmg 45 hrs wkly. Target aud: General; 24 plus. Spec prog: Folk, Sp. ■ Dr. J.L. Ozburn, pres; Roger W. Grimm, gen mgr, mktg dir & prom dir; Paula Larson, dev dir; Karen Severtsen-Olson, progmg dir & mus dir; James R. Hetland, chief engr.

KFGO(AM)—Mar 14, 1948: 790 khz; 5 kw-U, DA-N. TL: N46 04 05 W96 48 05. Stereo. Box 2966, 1020 S. 25 St. (58103-2966). (701) 237-5346. FAX: (701) 235-4042. Licensee: KFGO Inc. Net: ABC/E, ABC/R; Minn. Pub. Rep: CBS Radio. Format: C&W. News staff 3; news progmg 30 hrs wkly. Target aud: General. Spec prog: Farm 20 hrs, national sports 20 hrs wkly. ■ Bruce Thom, pres; Richard C. Voight, vp & gen mgr; Jack Hasbrouck, gen sls mgr; Robert Escen, natl sls mgr; Tina Rene, mktg dir; John Quick, progmg dir; Bob Harris, mus dir; Paul Jurgens, news dir; Sandy Buttweiler, pub affrs dir; Ken Bartz, chief engr. ■ Rates: $26; 19; 15; 7.

KFGO-FM—Feb 23, 1984: 101.9 mhz; 100 kw. Ant 866 ft. TL: N47 00 48 W97 11 37 (CP: Ant 987 ft.). Stereo. (Acq 3-86; $1.2 million; FTR 3-31-86). Format: Country. ■ Brad Rivers, progmg dir. ■ Rates: $10; 10; 10; 7.

***KFNW(AM)**—(West Fargo). Oct 28, 1955: 1200 khz; 10 kw-D, 1 kw-N, DA-N. TL: N46 48 06 W96 52 57. Hrs opn: 5:30 AM-11 PM. Box 6008, Fargo (58108). (701) 282-5910. FAX: (701) 282-5781. Licensee: Northwestern College. Group owner: Northwestern College Radio Network. Net: Skylight. Wash atty: John Wilner. Format: Relg. News staff one. ■ Harv Hendrickson (exec dir), gen mgr; Gary Herr, stn mgr; Phil Kvamme, news dir; Bob Benjamin, chief engr.

***KFNW-FM**—Mar 12, 1965: 97.9 mhz; 100 kw. Ant 350 ft. TL: N46 48 07 W96 52 58. Stereo. Hrs opn: 24. Dups AM 25%.

KPFX(FM)—Jan 4, 1993: 107.9 mhz; 100 kw. Ant 713 ft. TL: N46 32 41 W96 37 33. Stereo. Hrs opn: 24. Suite 201, 2501 13th Ave. S.W. (58103); Box 9919 (58106). (701) 237-4500; (701) 237-4949. FAX: (701) 237-9774. Licensee: Nan E. Carlisle & Jitendra R. Patel. Rep: Christal. Format: Classic rock. Target aud: 25-49; skews male. ■ Nan Carlisle, pres & gen mgr; Nancy Odney, gen sls mgr & natl sls mgr; Tim Richards, progmg mgr & mus dir; Lee Baxter, asst mus dir; Dave Justus, news dir; Robbie Daniels, pub affrs dir; Ken Bartz, chief engr.

KQWB(AM)—Mar 26, 1960: 1550 khz; 10 kw-D, 5 kw-N, DA-N. TL: N46 58 33 W96 35 02. Box 1301 (58107). (218) 236-7900. Licensee: Fargo-Moorhead Radio Inc. Group owner: Brill Media Company Inc. (acq 5-21-84; grpsl; FTR 4-16-84). Net: AP, Unistar. Rep: D & R Radio. Format: Oldies, talk. Target aud: 25-54. ■ Jim Lakoduk, gen mgr; Doug Gray, gen sls mgr; Mark Nicholls, progmg dir; Jim Davis, mus dir; Tina Rene, news dir; Ken Barts, chief engr. ■ Rates: $12; 12; 12; 12.

KQWB-FM—(Moorhead, Minn). November 1966: 98.7 mhz; 100 kw. Ant 460 ft. TL: N46 45 35 W96 36 26. Stereo. Box 1301, Fargo, ND (58107). (218) 236-7900. Licensee: Fargo-Moorhead Radio Inc. Group owner: Brill Media Company Inc. (acq 4-84; grpsl; FTR 4-16-84). Net: Unistar. Rep: D & R Radio. Format: Classic rock. ■ Jim Lakoduk, pres & gen mgr; Doug Gray, gen sls mgr; Mark Nicholls, progmg dir; Jim Davis, mus dir; Jennifer St. John, news dir.

KVOX(AM)—See Moorhead, Minn.

KVOX-FM—See Moorhead, Minn.

WDAY(AM)—May 22, 1922: 970 khz; 5 kw-U, DA-N. TL: N46 52 43 W96 53 05. Stereo. Hrs opn: 24. Box 2466, 301 S. 8th St. (58108). (701) 241-5350. (701) 241-5373. Licensee: Forum Communications Co. Inc. (group owner). Net: NBC, NBC Talknet, ABC/I, MBS. Rep: Katz. Format: Adult comtemp, news/talk, farm. News staff 3; news progmg 35 hrs wkly. Target aud: 25-54. Spec prog: Larry King. ■ William Marcil Sr., CEO & pres; Julia Puhlman, opns dir & prom dir; Lori Becker, mktg dir, progmg dir & mus dir; Mark Swartzell, news dir; Steve Tschida, pub affrs dir; Marty Berlinger, chief engr.

WDAY-FM—1965: 93.7 mhz; 100 kw. Ant 1,040 ft. TL: N47 00 43 W97 11 58. Stereo. Hrs opn: 24. Prog sep from AM. Format: Adult contemp. News staff 2; news progmg one hr wkly. Target aud: 18-49. ■ Mark Gemar, sls dir; Mark Malleck, prom dir & progmg dir; Gregg Olson, mus dir. ■ WDAY-TV affil.

Four Bears

***KMHA(FM)**—April 1983: 91.3 mhz; 100 kw. Ant 380 ft. TL: N47 44 23 W102 43 24. Stereo. HCR 3, Box One, New Town (58763). (701) 627-3333. Licensee: Fort Berthold Communications Enterprise. Format: Div. Target aud: Ranchers, farmers, Native Americans. Spec prog: American Indian-Mandan/Hidatsa/Arikara 4 hrs, country 8 hrs, farm one hr wkly. ■ Nina Fox, stn mgr & gen sls mgr; Gary Bell, chief engr.

Grafton

KXPO(AM)—July 12, 1958: 1340 khz; 1 kw-U. TL: N48 23 53 W97 26 56. Hrs opn: 6 AM-midnight. 856 12th St. W. (58237). (701) 352-0431. FAX: (701) 352-0436. Licensee: KGPC Co. (acq 12-12-72). Net: ABC; American Ag Network. Wash atty: Sam Miller. Format: Country. News staff 2; news progmg 15 hrs wkly. Target aud: 30-70. Spec prog: Farm 18 hrs, gospel 5 hrs, relg 4 hrs, Sp 2 hrs, oldies 4 hrs wkly. ■ Del Nygard, pres, gen mgr, gen sls mgr & adv mgr; Kathy Johnson, prom mgr; Brian James, progmg dir & news dir; John Sunberg, mus dir; John Asand, chief engr. ■ Rates: $10.35; 8.75; 8.25; 5.75.

KXPO-FM—Sept 17, 1984: 100.9 mhz; 3 kw. Ant 125 ft. TL: N48 23 53 W97 26 56. Hrs opn: 6 AM-midnight. (701) 352-3460. News staff one; news progmg 15 hrs wkly. Spec prog: Farm 18 hrs, gospel 4 hrs, relg 3 hrs, Sp 2 hrs, old-time music 4 hrs wkly. ■ Kathy Daniels, prom mgr; Larry Nelson, progmg dir; Brian James, mus dir. ■ Rates: $9; 7.20; 7.20; 5.

Grand Forks

KCNN(AM)—See East Grand Forks, Minn.

***KFJM(AM)**—Oct 22, 1923: 1370 khz; 1 kw-D, 250 w-N. TL: N47 55 55 W97 04 14. Hrs opn: 24. Box 8117 (58202-8117). (701) 777-2577. Licensee: Univ. of North Dakota. Net: NPR. Format: Adult alternative & acoustic, jazz, news. News staff 2; news progmg 23 hrs wkly. Target aud: General; well-educated adults. Spec prog: Polka 3 hrs, blues 2 hrs, folk 4 hrs wkly. ■ Tom Duval, gen mgr; Hoyt Carter, opns mgr; Kirsten Beck, dev dir; Bob Bertsch, prom dir; Mary Hawkins, progmg dir; Mike Olson, mus dir; Scott Karnik, news dir; Christine Paige, pub affrs dir; John Aasen, engrg dir.

***KFJM-FM**—May 30, 1976: 89.3 mhz; 38 kw. Ant 215 ft. TL: N47 55 55 W97 04 14. Stereo. Prog sep from AM. Format: Class, news. News staff 2; news progmg 31 hrs wkly. Target aud: General; well-educated, slightly older than average. Spec prog: New age 4 hrs wkly.

KJKJ(FM)—Aug 1, 1985: 107.5 mhz; 100 kw. Ant 500 ft. TL: N48 07 24 W97 04 20. Stereo. Hrs opn: 24. Box 1203, Mill Square, 301 N 3rd St. #301 A (58201). (701) 746-1417. FAX: (701) 746-1410. Licensee: Jeffrey J. Hoberg (acq 5-15-90; $300,000; FTR 6-4-90). Net: Unistar. Format: AOR. News progmg 5 hrs wkly. Target aud: 18-49. ■ Justin Hoberg, pres; Jeff Hoberg, gen mgr; Pat McLean, stn mgr; Michael Cross, progmg dir; Ken Bartz, chief engr.

KKXL(AM)—1941: 1440 khz; 1 kw-D, 500 w-N. TL: N47 57 52 W97 01 46. Stereo. Hrs opn: 24. Box 997, 505 University Ave. (58206-0997). (701) 775-0575. FAX: (701) 775-0579. Licensee: Excel Broadcasting Corp. Net: AP, Unistar. Rep: Torbet. Format: Country. News staff one; news progmg 10 hrs wkly. Target aud: 25-54; farm community. Spec prog: Farm 18 hrs wkly. ■ Troy Ramage, pres; Mike Pederson, gen mgr; John Vasichek, stn mgr; Kathy Loff, sls dir; Suzan Johnson, prom dir; Mike Hergert, progmg dir; Dave Schroeder, chief engr. ■ Rates: $17.65; 17.65; 16.45; 14.10.

KKXL-FM—March 1975: 92.9 mhz; 63 kw. Ant 385 ft. TL: N47 57 52 W97 01 46. Stereo. Prog sep from AM. (Acq 10-85; $8,000,000 FTR 7-1-85). Format: CHR. News staff one; news progmg 2 hrs wkly. Target aud: 18-34. ■ Rick Acker, progmg dir; Shawn Reese, mus dir. ■ Rates: $20; 16.50; 17.65; 16.50.

KNOX(AM)—Sept 7, 1947: 1310 khz; 5 kw-U, DA-N. TL: N47 50 39 W97 01 30. Hrs opn: 24. Box 13638, (58208-3638). (701) 775-4611. FAX: (701) 772-0540. Licensee: Radio Grand Forks Associates L.P. (acq 2-87). Net: ABC/E, NBC Talknet; MNN. Rep: Katz. Format: MOR, farm, news/talk. News staff 3; news progmg 80 hrs wkly. Target aud: 35 plus. ■ Justin Hoberg, gen mgr & gen sls mgr; Linn Hodgson, rgnl sls mgr; Dennis Johnson, prom mgr & mus dir; Ron West, progmg dir; Doug Barrett, news dir; Dave Schroeder, chief engr.

KNOX-FM—Feb 4, 1967: 94.7 mhz; 100 kw. Ant 325 ft. TL: N48 00 20 W97 04 18. Stereo. Prog sep from AM. Net: SMN, ABC/C. Format: Oldies. News progmg 20 hrs wkly. Target aud: 25-54. ■ Denny Johnson, progmg dir.

KQHT(FM)—(Crookston, Minn). March 1986: 96.1 mhz; 100 kw. Ant 413 ft. TL: N47 50 43 W96 50 22. Stereo. 2501 DeMers Ave., Grand Forks, ND (58201). (701) 746-1413. FAX: (701) 775-0991. Licensee: CD Broadcasting Corp. (group owner; acq 7-14-89; $507,500; FTR 7-31-89). Rep: Torbet. Format: CHR. Target aud: 18-49. ■ Chris Dahl, CEO; Jim Gilbertson, CFO; Mel Paradis, exec vp; Dave Salo, gen mgr & gen sls mgr; Jay Murphy, progmg dir; Josh Jones, mus dir & news dir; Scott Rand, chief engr.

KYCK(FM)—See Crookston, Minn.

Harvey

KHND(AM)—July 21, 1981: 1470 khz; 1 kw-D, 160 w-N. TL: N47 45 23 W99 55 06. 718 Lincoln Ave. (58341). (701) 324-4848. FAX: (701) 324-5235. Licensee: Prairie Communications Inc. (acq 2-15-83). Net: ABC; Dakota News, American Agri. Format: Country. Spec prog: Big Band 3 hrs, Polka 3 hrs wkly. ■ Norman Weckerly, pres; Todd Lewis, gen mgr & gen sls mgr; Rusty Nichols, progmg dir & mus dir; Rick Jensen, news dir; Jay McKay, chief engr.

Stations in the U.S. North Dakota

Hettinger

KNDC(AM)—Mar 1, 1954: 1490 khz; 1 kw-U. TL: N46 01 11 W102 41 33. Hrs opn: 5:45 AM-10 PM. Box 151, 505 2nd Ave. S. (58639). (701) 567-2421; (701) 567-2889. FAX: (701) 567-2425. Licensee: Hettinger Broadcasting Co. (acq 11-67). Net: ABC/I; American Agri., N.D. Net. Format: C&W. Target aud: 24-52; rural residents. ■ Allen R. McIntyre, pres, gen mgr, news dir & chief engr; Paul Rymer, mus dir. ■ Rates: $6.50; 6.50; 5.95; 5.95.

Jamestown

***KPRJ(FM)**—Not on air, target date unknown: 91.5 mhz; 18.6 kw. Ant 354 ft. Box 3240, Fargo (58108). Licensee: Prairie Public Broadcasting Inc.

KQDJ(AM)—Aug 12, 1954: 1400 khz; 1 kw-U. TL: N46 53 37 W98 41 20. Box 1170, 205 First Ave. S. (58401). (701) 252-1400. FAX: (701) 252-1402. Licensee: Sorenson Broadcasting Corp. (group owner; acq 1-83; $500,000; FTR 1-31-83). Net: CBS. Rep: Katz & Powell. Format: Adult contemp. Spec prog: Farm 6 hrs wkly. ■ Dean Sorenson, pres; Neil Cary, gen mgr & gen sls mgr; Dave Gandy, natl sls mgr; Randy Allen, progmg dir & mus dir; Wayne Byers, news dir.

KYNU(FM)—Co-owned with KQDJ(AM). Aug 25, 1984: 95.5 mhz; 100 kw. Ant 398 ft. TL: N46 51 52 W98 40 11. Stereo. Hrs opn: 5:15 AM-midnight. Prog sep from AM. Format: C&W.

KSJB(AM)—1937: 600 khz; 5 kw-U, DA-1. TL: N46 49 03 W98 42 34. Box 1840 (58402-1840); 212 First Ave. S. (58401). (701) 252-3570. FAX: (701) 252-1277. Licensee: Chesterman Communications Inc. (acq 8-20-90; $850,000 with co-located FM; FTR 9-10-90). Net: ABC/E; American Agri. Rep: Torbet. Format: C&W. Spec prog: Farm 12 hrs wkly. ■ C. Kenneth Kjeldseth, vp & gen mgr; Ole Olson, progmg dir; Kaye Hier, mus dir; Harvey Van Erem, chief engr.

KSJZ(FM)—Co-owned with KSJB(AM). 1968: 93.3 mhz; 57 kw. Ant 256 ft. TL: N46 49 03 W98 42 34. Stereo. Net: Unistar. Format: Adult contemp. ■ Kurt Sayler, mus dir.

KYNU(FM)—Listing follows KQDJ(AM).

Langdon

KNDK(AM)—June 27, 1967: 1080 khz; 1 kw-D. TL: N48 46 25 W98 21 50. Hrs opn: 16. Rt. 5, Box 9 (58249). (701) 256-1080. FAX: (701) 256-5151. Licensee: KNDK Inc. (acq 12-1-87). Net: ABC/I; American Agri. Wash atty: Haley, Bader & Potts. Format: News/talk, country. News staff one; news progmg 42 hrs wkly. Target aud: 25 plus. Spec prog: Farm 12 hrs, relg 6 hrs wkly. ■ Bob Simmons, pres, gen mgr & gen sls mgr; Diane Simmons, vp; Jake Kulland, progmg dir; Bruce Allen, news dir; Ken Bartz, chief engr. ■ Rates: $6.90; 6.90; 6.90; 6.90.

KNDK-FM—Jan 15, 1992: 95.7 mhz; 6 kw. Ant 328 ft. TL: N48 45 18 W98 21 38. (Acq 11-20-91; $90,000; FTR 12-16-91).

Lisbon

KQLX(AM)—November 1984: 890 khz; 1 kw-D. TL: N46 26 43 W97 39 07. Stereo. 1206 S. Main (58054). (701) 683-5287. FAX: (701) 683-4432. Licensee: Sheyenne Valley Broadcasting Inc. Net: American Agri. Format: C&W. ■ Robert Hein, pres; Bruce Dougherty, gen mgr & news dir; Terry Loomis, gen sls mgr & prom mgr; Jay Haaland, progmg dir & mus dir; Stan Mueller, chief engr.

KQLX-FM—Oct 24, 1986: 106.1 mhz; 50 kw. Ant 249 ft. TL: N46 26 43 W97 39 07 Stereo. Dups AM 95%.

Mandan

KLXX(AM)—See Bismarck.

KNDR(FM)—June 21, 1977: 104.7 mhz; 100 kw. Ant 852 ft. TL: N46 35 11 W100 48 20. Stereo. Box 516 (58554). (701) 663-2345. FAX: (701) 663-2347. Licensee: Central Dakota Enterprise. Net: Moody, Skylight, USA. Format: Relg. Target aud: General. ■ Dan Seifert, chmn; Ken Van Beck, vp; Brad Bales, gen mgr; Darlene Vander Vorst, gen sls mgr & adv dir; Mike Kopp, news dir; Bruce Vadnais, chief engr.

Mayville

KMAV(AM)—Oct 20, 1967: 1520 khz; 2.5 kw-D. TL: N47 29 45 W97 21 03. Hrs opn: Sunrise-sunset. Box 216 (58257). (701) 786-2335. FAX: (701) 786-2268. Licensee: R & J Broadcasting (acq 7-7-93; $200,000 with co-located FM; FTR 8-2-93). Net: ABC; N.D. Net, American Agri. Format: Country. News staff one; news progmg 15 hrs wkly. Target aud: 25-55. ■ Jim Berkemeyer, pres; Rich Haraldson, exec vp; Dan Keating, gen mgr & progmg dir; Jim Birkemeyer, sls dir; Kay Hoselton, news dir; Dean Johnson, chief engr. ■ Rates: $10; 10; 10; 10.

KMAV-FM—Jan 10, 1977: 105.5 mhz; 3 kw. Ant 121 ft. TL: N47 29 45 W97 21 03. Stereo. Dups AM 100%.

Minot

KBQQ(FM)—Listing follows KTYN(AM).

KCJB(AM)—September 1950: 910 khz; 5 kw-D, 1 kw-N, DA-2. TL: N40 11 57 W101 17 37. Box 1686, 3425 S. Broadway (58702). (701) 852-0361. FAX: (701) 838-9360. Licensee: Reiten Broadcasting (acq 1974). Net: CBS. Rep: Katz. Wash atty: Fisher, Wayland, Cooper & Leader. Format: Full service/country. News staff 3; news progmg 25 hrs wkly. Target aud: 25 plus. Spec prog: Farm 4 hrs hrs wkly, local sports play by play, various local talk segments. ■ David Reiten, pres; J. Davis, stn mgr; Charlie Ferguson, gen sls mgr; Teri Thomas, progmg dir; Stephanie Stevens, mus dir; John Williams, news dir; Bob Turneau, chief engr.

KYYX(FM)—Co-owned with KCJB(AM). Nov 15, 1966: 97.1 mhz; 100 kw. Ant 984 ft. TL: N48 03 02 W101 20 29. Stereo. Hrs opn: 24. Prog sep from AM. (58702). Format: Hot Country. News staff one; news progmg 6 hrs wkly. Target aud: 18-49; young families. ■ KXMC-TV affil.

KHRT(AM)—Nov 17, 1957: 1320 khz; 2.5 kw-D, 310 w-N. TL: N48 11 48 W101 14 30. Box 1210, Old Hwy. 52 S.E. (58702). (701) 852-3789. FAX: (701) 852-8498. Licensee: Faith Broadcasting Inc. (acq 9-1-82; $188,248; FTR 8-30-82). Net: CBN, IBN. Format: Relg. News staff one; news progmg 10 hrs wkly. Target aud: 25-54; large families, loyal, upper-income professionals. Spec prog: Farm one hr, Christian 2 hrs, gospel 3 hrs, Lite Show 6 hrs wkly. ■ Richard Leavitt, pres, gen sls mgr & progmg dir; Craig Cerkowniak, gen mgr & mus dir; Aaron Stadel, news dir; John Valker, chief engr. ■ Rates: $9; 9; 8; 8.

KIZZ(FM)—Sept 7, 1968: 93.7 mhz; 98 kw. Ant 571 ft. TL: N48 12 56 W101 19 05. Stereo. Hrs opn: 24. Box 2188, 216 S Broadway (58702). (701) 852-2494. FAX: (701) 838-8195. Licensee: DCP Broadcasting Corp. of Minot (acq 5-21-93; $450,000; FTR 6-14-93). Net: ABC/C. Rep: Banner. Format: Adult contemp. News staff one; news progmg 3 hrs wkly. Target aud: 25-54. ■ Rick Stensby, gen mgr; Doug Corbet, gen sls mgr; Jeff Bliss, progmg dir; Ray Roberts, chief engr. ■ KMOT-TV affil.

***KMPR(FM)**—Nov 23, 1983: 88.9 mhz; 100 kw. Ant 930 ft. TL: N48 03 03 W101 23 24. Stereo. Hrs opn: 19.5. 1814 N. 15th St., Bismarck (58501). (701) 224-1700; (800) 359-5566. FAX: (701) 224-0555. Licensee: Praire Public Broadcasting Inc. Net: NPR. Format: Class, news & jazz. News staff 2; news progmg 40 hrs wkly. Target aud: General. Spec prog: Easy listening 8 hrs, folk 6 hrs wkly. ■ Steve Leyland, pres; Bill McGinley, stn mgr; Roger Lockbeam, opns mgr; Donald Hoffman, mus dir; Dave Thompson, news dir; Gary Stegmiller, chief engr.

KRRZ(AM)—Oct 28, 1929: 1390 khz; 5 kw-D, 1 kw-N. TL: N48 12 45 W101 14 30. Box 10 (58702). (701) 852-4646. FAX: (701) 852-1390. Licensee: CD Broadcasting of Minot. Group owner: CD Broadcasting Corp. Net: Unistar, NBC Talknet; N.D. Net. Rep: Torbet. Format: Oldies. Target aud: 25-54. ■ Rick Stensby, gen mgr & gen sls mgr; Rick Anthony, progmg dir; Dave Dunsmorr, chief engr.

KZPR(FM)—Co-owned with KRRZ(AM). July 8, 1985: 105.3 mhz; 100 kw. Ant 579 ft. TL: N48 03 13 W101 26 03. Stereo. Hrs opn: 24. Prog sep from AM. 216 S. Broadway (58701). FAX: (701) 852-1390. (Acq 10-1-89.) Net: Unistar; American Agri. Format: C&W. News progmg 4 hrs wkly. Spec prog: Farm 4 hrs wkly. ■ Christopher Dahl, pres; Linda Mahlum, prom mgr; Troy Nelson, mus dir.

KTYN(AM)—Sept 13, 1968: 1430 khz; 5 kw-D, 210 w-N. TL: N48 09 15 W101 18 25. Hrs opn: 24. Box 637 (58702); 815 31st Ave. S.W. (58701). (701) 852-0301; (701) 852-0453. FAX: (701) 852-4400. Licensee: Kitten Radio Inc. Net: SMN, ABC. Rep: Torbet. Format: Big band, MOR. News progmg 9 hrs wkly. Target aud: 35 plus. Spec prog: Relg. ■ Justin Hoberg, pres; Steve Williams, gen mgr & prom mgr; Steven Williams, gen sls mgr; Allison Bostow, pub affrs dir; R. David Adams, chief engr. ■ Rates: $10; 9; 10; 8.

KBQQ(FM)—Co-owned with KTYN(AM). April 1984: 99.9 mhz; 100 kw. Ant 500 ft. TL: N48 10 57 W101 31 57. Stereo. Prog sep from AM. Net: SMN. Format: Oldies, Rock (AOR), classic rock. News progmg 4 hrs wkly. Target aud: 25-54; adult upper middle class with teens at home. ■ Scott Andrews, progmg dir. ■ Rates: $11; 10; 11; 9.

KYYX(FM)—Listing follows KCJB(AM).

KZPR(FM)—Listing follows KRRZ(AM).

Oakes

KDDR(AM)—July 31, 1959: 1220 khz; 1 kw-D, 327 w-N. TL: N46 07 23 W98 05 21. 412 Main Ave. (58474). (701) 742-2187. FAX: (701) 742-2009. Licensee: James D. Ingstad. Group owner: James Ingstad Broadcasting Inc. (acq 2-1-93; $85,000; FTR 2-22-93). Net: ABC/I; American Agri., N.D. Net. Wash atty: Fletcher, Heald & Hildreth. Format: Country, news. News staff 2; news progmg 10 hrs wkly. Target aud: 28-59; farm/agriculture. Spec prog: Farm 15 hrs wkly. ■ Larry Gemar, rgnl sls mgr, prom mgr & adv mgr; Lu Finnell, progmg mgr & news dir; Ken Bartz, chief engr.

KSSZ-FM—June 6, 1986: 92.7 mhz; 4 kw. Ant 151 ft. TL: N46 07 23 W98 05 34 (CP: 92.5 mhz, 100 kw, ant 800 ft. TL: N45 45 27 W98 18 34). 3301 S. University Dr., Fargo (58104). (701) 239-0414. FAX: (701) 239-0468. Licensee: CERM Broadcasting Corp. (acq 10-18-88; grpsl; FTR 1-23-89). Net: ABC/I. Format: CHR. ■ Ron Frisch, gen mgr.

Rugby

KZZJ(AM)—Aug 21, 1961: 1450 khz; 1 kw-U. TL: N48 21 14 W99 59 31. Box 105 (58368). (701) 776-5254. Licensee: Rugby Broadcasters Inc. (acq 7-6-89; $10,000; FTR 7-24-89). Net: ABC/C; American Agri. Format: Modern country. Spec prog: Farm 20 hrs wkly. ■ Richard Ivers, pres.

Tioga

KTGO(AM)—Feb 27, 1967: 1090 khz; 1 kw-D. TL: N48 23 30 W102 56 12. Box 457 (58852); 301 S.E. 2nd St. (58852). (701) 664-3322. Licensee: Tioga Broadcasting Corp. Net: ABC/I; American Agri. Format: C&W. ■ David Guttormson, pres, gen mgr & gen sls mgr; Claudia Rust, stn mgr; Kathy Reynolds, prom mgr, progmg dir & mus dir; Ron Gilbertson, news dir; Mike Thompson, chief engr.

Valley City

KOVC(AM)—Oct 19, 1936: 1490 khz; 1 kw-U. TL: N46 54 48 W98 01 02. Hrs opn: 19. Box 994, 232 Third St. N.E. (58072). (701) 845-1490. FAX: (701) 845-2903. Licensee: Ingstad Broadcasting Inc. Group owner: James Ingstad Broadcasting Inc. Net: ABC/I; American Agri. Format: Country. Target aud: 25 plus. ■ Tim Ost, gen mgr; Susan Stoudt, gen sls mgr; Dave Reed, prom dir & progmg dir; Jason Hunt, mus dir; Paul Titchenal, chief engr.

KOVC-FM—Aug 1, 1983: 101.1 mhz; 3 kw. Ant 319 ft. TL: N46 54 24 W97 58 20. Stereo. Prog sep from AM. Net: SMN. Format: Oldies. Target aud: 25-54. ■ Dave Reed, opns mgr; Jason Hunt, asst mus dir.

Wahpeton

KBMW(AM)—(Breckenridge, Minn). Aug 28, 1948: 1450 khz; 1 kw-U. TL: N46 16 41 W96 35 19. 605 Dakota Ave., Wahpeton, ND (58075). (701) 642-8747. FAX: (701) 642-9501. Licensee: W-B Broadcasting Inc. (acq 10-25-90). Net: ABC/I. Format: Country. News staff one; news progmg 28 hrs wkly. Target aud: 25-54; general. ■ Dean Aamodt, stn mgr & gen sls mgr; Ken Donovan, progmg dir; Curt Martin, mus dir; Gary Rogers, news dir; Ken Berndt, chief engr. ■ Rates: $22; 22; 22; 20.

KGWB(FM)—May 21, 1989: 107.1 mhz; 3 kw. Ant 302 ft. TL: N46 16 02 W96 31 52 (CP: 106.9 mhz, 50 kw, ant 492 ft.). Stereo. Hrs opn: 24. Box 127 (58074); 100 S. 4th St. (58075). (701) 642-6625. FAX: (701) 642-2911. Licensee: Guderian Broadcasting Inc. Wash atty: Miller & Fields. Format: Adult contemp. News staff one; news progmg 5 hrs wkly. Target aud: 25-54. ■ Dean Aamodt, gen mgr, gen sls mgr & adv mgr; Billy Dablow, prom mgr & progmg dir; Jay Easley, mus dir; Brian Downey, news dir; Ken Berndt, chief engr.

West Fargo

***KFNW(AM)**—Licensed to West Fargo. See Fargo.

Williston

KDSR(FM)—Feb 28, 1985: 101.1 mhz; 98 kw. Ant 800 ft. TL: N48 03 30 W104 00 00. Stereo. Hrs opn: 18. Box 1487, 910 E. Broadway (58801). (701) 572-4478. FAX: (701) 572-1419. Licensee: Robert H. Miller (acq 5-28-92; $115,102; FTR 6-22-92). Net: Unistar, CNN. Wash atty: Booth, Freret & Imlay. Format: Modern country. News progmg 7 hrs wkly. Target aud: 18-84; city, farm, ranch & rural. Spec prog: Farm, local news. ■ Robert H. Miller, pres, gen mgr, vp mktg, mus dir & news dir; Ron Anderson, gen sls mgr; Rhonda Woodhams, progmg dir; Bernie Arcand, Gary Farber, chiefs engr.

KEYZ(AM)—1948: 660 khz; 5 kw-U, DA-2. TL: N48 14 20 W103 39 01. Stereo. Hrs opn: 24. Box 2048, 410 E. 6th (58802-2048). (701) 572-5371. FAX: (701) 572-7511. Licensee: Charles L. Scofield. Group owner: Scofield Broadcasting Co. (acq 1951). Net: ABC/I; American Agri. Rep: Art Moore. Format: Country, news/talk. News staff one. Target aud: 25-54. Spec prog: Relg 5 hrs wkly. ■ Charles Scofield, pres & chief engr; John Scofield, gen mgr; Bill Hanson, gen sls mgr; Barry Arnold, prom dir, adv dir, progmg dir & mus dir; Dean McMartin, news dir; Earl Gross, pub affrs dir.

KYYZ(FM)—Co-owned with KEYZ(AM). Dec 1, 1979: 96.1 mhz; 100 kw. Ant 873 ft. TL: N48 02 52 W103 59 01. Stereo. Hrs opn: 24. Prog sep from AM. Net: ABC. Rep: Art Moore, Intermountain Net, Eastman. Format: Classic rock, contemporary hit. ■ Lyla Samenko, gen sls mgr; Chris Treager, prom dir; Lee Halvorson, progmg dir.

KPPR(FM)—Nov. 20, 1986: 89.5 mhz; 10.5 kw. Ant 492 ft. TL: N48 08 30 W103 53 34. Stereo. Hrs opn: 20. 1814 N. 15th St., Bismarck (58501). (701) 224-1700; (800) 359-5566. FAX: (701) 224-0555. Licensee: Prairie Public Broadcasting. Net: NPR. Format: Jazz, class, news. News staff 2; news progmg 40 hrs wkly. Target aud: General. Spec prog: Easy listening 8 hrs, folk 6 hrs wkly. ■ Dennis Falk, pres; Bill Miller, stn mgr; Roger Lockbeam, opns dir; Donald Hoffman, mus dir; David Thompson, news dir; Gary Stegmiller, chief engr.

KYYZ(FM)—Listing follows KEYZ(AM).

Wishek

KDRQ(AM)—July 24, 1982: 1330 khz; 500 w-D, 214 w-N. TL: N46 15 04 W99 30 13 (CP: 5 kw-U, DA-2, TL: N46 15 02 W99 30 17). Box 747, 107 Beaver Ave. (58495). Licensee: Stolle Communications Inc. (acq 9-12-90; $100,000; FTR 10-1-90). Wash atty: Frank Jasso. ■ Chris J. Stulee, pres; Gary F. Weber, exec vp & gen mgr.

Ohio

LAUREN A. COLBY
301-663-1086
COMMUNICATIONS ATTORNEY
Special Attention to
Difficult Cases

Ada

WONB(FM)—Oct 18, 1991: 94.9 mhz; 3 kw. Ant 328 ft. TL: N40 45 58 W83 50 14. Stereo. Hrs opn: 19. Freed Ctr. (45810). (419) 772-1194; (419) 772-2469. FAX: (419) 772-1856. Licensee: Ohio Northern Univ. Format: New age, contemp jazz, alternative. News progmg 8 hrs wkly. Target aud: General. Spec prog: Relg 8 hrs, gospel 6 hrs wkly. ■ Dr. DeBow Freed, pres; John Green, CFO; G. Richard Gainey, gen mgr; Kyle McPeck, progmg mgr; Chris Putt, mus dir; Bryan Gulbis, asst mus dir; Sean Bratton, news dir; Jan Hafer, pub affrs dir; Ric Corcoran, chief engr.

Akron

WAKR(AM)—Oct 16, 1940: 1590 khz; 5 kw-U, DA-N. TL: N41 01 14 W81 30 20. 1735 S. Hawkins Ave. (44320). (216) 869-9800. FAX: (216) 864-6799. Licensee: Gordon-Thomas Communications Inc. Group owner: Rubber City Radio Group Inc. (acq 10-6-93; $9.3 million with co-located FM; FTR 10-25-93). Net: Moody, UPI. Rep: McGavren Guild. Format: Adult contemp. News staff 7; news progmg 40 hrs wkly. Target aud: 25-54. Spec prog: Sports 14 hrs wkly. ■ Peter Acquaviva, vp & gen mgr; Harve Alan, opns mgr; Joyce Lagios, prom mgr; Bob Allen, mus dir; Larry States, news dir; Glenn Foldessy, chief engr.

WONE-FM—Co-owned with WAKR(AM). October 1947: 97.5 mhz; 12 kw. Ant 900 ft. TL: N41 03 57 W81 34 59. Stereo. Format: AOR, classic rock. Target aud: 18-49. ■ Jim Bickle, prom mgr; Harve Alan, progmg dir; J.D. Kunes, mus dir.

WAPS(FM)—Oct 4, 1955: 89.1 mhz; 1.7 kw. Ant 71 ft. TL: N41 03 19 W81 31 36 (CP: 91.3 mhz, 800 w, ant 151 ft.). Stereo. Hrs opn: 18. 65 Steiner Ave. (44301). (216) 434-1661, ext. 3182 OR 3186; (216) 376-1117. FAX: (216) 434-9515. Licensee: Board of Education, Akron City School District. Format: Modern rock, jazz, weekend speciality & ethnic programs. Target aud: College educated white collar adults & ethnic minorities. Spec prog: Ger 2 hrs, It 2 hrs, Pol one hr, Irish 2 hrs, East Indian one hr, Hungarian one hr, Arabic 2 hrs, Slovenian 2 hrs, Polka 3 hrs, Reggae 2 hrs, Sp one hr, student public affairs one hr wkly. ■ Phil Hoffman, gen mgr; Bill Gruber, opns dir; Pam Empkey, pub affrs dir; Jim Morgan, chief engr.

WCUE(AM)—See Cuyahoga Falls.

WHLO(AM)—October 1944: 640 khz; 5 kw-D, 500 w-N, DA-2. TL: N41 04 47 W81 38 45. Stereo. Hrs opn: 24. 2780 S. Arlington, (44312). (216) 668-4774. FAX: (216) 668-4009. Licensee: Mortensen Broadcasting Co. (group owner; acq 12-86). Net: ABC/D. Format: Contemp Christian. News staff one; news progmg 7 hrs wkly. Target aud: 25-44. ■ Jack Mortenson, pres; Garry Meeks, gen mgr & gen sls mgr; Ed Bostic, progmg dir; Brian Brooks, pub affrs dir; Dave Johnson, chief engr. ■ Rates: $23; 23; 23; 18.

WJMP(AM)—See Kent.

WKDD(FM)—Listing follows WSLR(AM).

WNIR(FM)—See Kent.

WONE-FM—Listing follows WAKR(AM).

WQMX(FM)—(Medina). 1960: 94.9 mhz; 16.2 kw. Ant 880 ft. TL: N40 04 58 W81 38 00. Stereo. Hrs opn: 24. Suite 107, 3610 W. Market St., Akron (44333). (216) 434-6499. Licensee: Gordon-Thomas Communications. Group owner: Rubber City Radio Group Inc. (acq 7-21-88). Rep: Banner. Wash atty: Verner, Liipfert, Bernhard, Mcpherson & Hand. Format: Country. News staff 2 Target aud: 25-54; upwardly mobile adults. ■ Thomas Mandel, CEO, pres & gen mgr; Dominic Rizzo, gen sls mgr; Paul Christopherson, natl sls mgr; Elisa Cefalu, prom dir; Steve Cherry, progmg dir; Bill Shiel, mus dir; Joyce Johnson, news dir; Al Hruska, chief engr.

WSLR(AM)—1926: 1350 khz; 5 kw-U, DA-1. TL: N41 10 05 W81 30 45. 1867 W. Market St. (44313). (216) 836-4700. FAX: (216) 836-5321. Licensee: OBC Broadcasting Inc. Group owner: Barnstable Broadcasting Inc. (acq 9-84). Net: ABC/E. Rep: Katz. Format: C&W. ■ Andy Graham, vp & gen mgr; Mason Ingles, gen sls mgr; Gina Massey, progmg dir & mus dir; Ton Erickson, news dir; Don Kreiger, chief engr.

WKDD(FM)—Co-owned with WSLR(AM). 1950: 96.5 mhz; 50 kw. Ant 475 ft. TL: N41 12 05 W81 31 25. Stereo. Format: CHR. ■ Neil Sullivan, progmg dir & mus dir.

WZIP(FM)—Dec 10, 1962: 88.1 mhz; 3.3 kw. Ant 810 ft. TL: N41 05 00 W81 37 57. Stereo. Hrs opn: 24. 1004 Guzzetta St. (44325-1004). (216) 972-7105. FAX: (216) 972-5521. Licensee: University of Akron. Net: ABC/I. Format: Urban contemp, rock. Target aud: 18-34. Spec prog: Polka 3 hrs, pub affrs 2 hrs, gospel 3 hrs wkly. ■ Thomas G. Beck, gen mgr; Blake Thompson, chief engr.

Alliance

WDPN(AM)—Sept 2, 1953: 1310 khz; 1 kw-D, 500 w-N, DA-2. TL: N40 55 34 W81 07 41. Hrs opn: 24. Box 2356, 393 Smyth Ave. N.E. (44601). (216) 821-1111; (216) 454-1310. FAX: (216) 821-0379. Licensee: D.A. Peterson Inc. Net: ABC/I. Rep: Katz. Format: News/talk. News staff 2; news progmg 3 hrs wkly. Target aud: General. Spec prog: Relg 4 hrs, polka 2 hrs wkly. ■ D.A. Peterson, pres; Dick Elliott, gen mgr; Trisha Jay Ferruccio, gen sls mgr; Mary Ann McAlister, prom mgr; Zack Stevens, progmg dir; Marlene Chipko, news dir; Bruce Harlan, chief engr.

WZKL(FM)—Co-owned with WDPN(AM). April 1947: 92.5 mhz; 50 kw. Ant 500 ft. TL: N40 47 24 W81 06 26. Stereo. Hrs opn: 24. Prog sep from AM. Format: Oldies. News progmg 4 hrs wkly. Target aud: 25-54. ■ Donald A. Peterson III, rgnl sls mgr; Bruce Harlan, engrg dir.

WRMU(FM)—Oct 17, 1970: 91.1 mhz; 2.8 kw. Ant 190 ft. TL: N40 54 16 W81 06 45. Stereo. Mount Union College, 1972 Clark Ave. (44601). (216) 823-2414; (216) 823-3777. Licensee: Mount Union College. Net: Jazz, class, talk. News progmg 11 hrs wkly. ■ Charles Morford, gen mgr; Charles R. Morford, stn mgr; Samuel Shimp, chief engr.

WZKL(FM)—Listing follows WDPN(AM).

Archbold

WBCY(FM)—Dec 1, 1992: 89.5 mhz; 3 kw. Ant 180 ft. TL: N41 30 33 W84 17 50 (CP: 20 kw, ant 328 ft.). c/o WBCL(FM), 1025 W. Rudisill Blvd., Fort Wayne, IN (46807). (219) 745-0576. FAX: (219) 745-2001. Licensee: Taylor University Inc. (acq 6-24-92). Format: Relg. ■ Char Binkley, Linda Richards (asst), gen mgrs.

WMTR-FM—Mar 1968: 96.1 mhz; 3.8 kw. Ant 400 ft. TL: N41 32 31 W84 16 08. Stereo. Hrs opn: 24. 303 N. Defiance St. (43502). (419) 445-9050. FAX: (419) 445-3531. Licensee: Nobco Inc. Net: Unistar, Westwood One; Agri Bcstg. Rep: Rgnl Reps. Wash atty: Hogan & Hartson. Format: Oldies. News staff one; news progmg 8 hrs wkly. Target aud: 25-54. ■ Max E. Smith Sr., pres & gen mgr; Max E. Smith Jr., stn mgr; Mark Knapp, mus dir; Larry Christy, news dir; Jack Didier, chief engr. ■ Rates: $13; 11; 13; 11.

Ashland

WNCO(AM)—1949: 1340 khz; 1 kw-U. TL: N40 50 25 W82 21 18. Hrs opn: 24. Box 311, 2435 Mansfield Rd. (44805). (419) 289-2605; (419) 526-5825. FAX: (419) 289-0304. Licensee: Ashland Broadcasting Corp. (acq 3-1-65). Net: SMN. Rep: Rgnl Reps. Wash atty: Arent, Fox, Kintner, Plotkin & Kahn. Format: Stardust, MOR, big band. News staff 2; news progmg 20 hrs wkly. Target aud: 35 plus. Spec prog: Farm 3 hrs wkly. ■ Walter Stampfli, pres & gen mgr; Dean Stampli, exec vp; Dean Stampfli, opns mgr; Martin Larson, gen sls mgr; Darla Stampfli, prom dir; Ron Kolman, progmg dir; Al Lawrence, news dir; Mike Hayward, chief engr. ■ Rates: $33; 27; 33; 22.

WNCO-FM—May 1947: 101.3 mhz; 50 kw. Ant 500 ft. TL: N40 50 25 W82 21 18. Stereo. Hrs opn: 24. Prog sep from AM. Net: MBS. Format: Country. News staff 3; news progmg 14 hrs wkly. Target aud: 25 plus. ■ Ron Kolman, opns dir; Martin Larsen, sls dir; Dean Stampfli, mktg dir; Darla Stampfli, prom mgr & pub affrs dir; Matt Appleby, mus dir. ■ Rates: $33; 31; 33; 29.

WRDL(FM)—Aug 24, 1967: 88.9 mhz; 3 kw. Ant 171 ft. TL: N40 51 41 W82 19 11. Stereo. Hrs opn: 6 AM-1 AM. 401 College Ave. (44805). (419) 289-5678; (419) 289-5140. Licensee: Ashland University. Net: MBS. Format: Rock, educ. News progmg 7 hrs wkly. Target aud: General; 18-35. Spec prog: Christian contemp 7 hrs, Jazz 5 hrs, oldies 4 hrs wkly. ■ Dr. G. William Benz, pres; Jay Pappas, gen mgr & vp progmg; Jeff Putz, prom mgr; Mike Bell, progmg dir; Tami Laubie, mus dir; Jennifer Brewer, asst mus dir; Georgia Wentler, news dir; Scott Paxson, chief engr. WRDL-TV-2.

Ashtabula

WFUN(AM)—November 1937: 970 khz; 5 kw-D, 1 kw-N, DA-2. TL: N41 48 52 W80 46 45. Hrs opn: 24. Box 738, 3226 Jefferson Rd. (44004). (216) 993-2126. Licensee: Radio Enterprises of Ohio Inc. Net: AP. Wash atty: Hopkins & Sutter. Format: Adult contemp, oldies, news. News staff 2; news progmg 20 hrs wkly. Target aud: Socially conscious, community-oriented listeners. Spec prog: Pro, college, high school sports. ■ Richard D. Rowley, pres; David Rowley, vp; Jeff Leppard, opns dir & progmg dir; Werner Poegel, gen sls mgr; Ron Ellis, mus dir; Bob Rundy, news dir; Brian Wolf, chief engr.

WREO-FM—Co-owned with WFUN(AM). 1949: 97.1 mhz; 50 kw. Ant 500 ft. TL: N41 48 58 W80 46 52. Stereo. Hrs opn: 24. Prog sep from AM. Format: Adult contemp. Target aud: 25-49; professionals.

WPHR—Not on air, target date unknown: 98.3 mhz; 2 kw. Ant 403 ft. TL: N41 51 39 W80 40 46. c/o 1321 Shepherd St. N.W., Washington, DC (20011). Licensee: Andrea L. Johnson.

WREO-FM—Listing follows WFUN(AM).

WZOO-FM—See Edgewood.

Athens

WATH(AM)—Oct 25, 1950: 970 khz; 1 kw-D, 160 w-N. TL: N39 20 40 W82 06 21. Stereo. Hrs opn: 24. Box 210, 300 N. Columbus Rd. (45701). (614) 593-6651; (614) 593-7982. FAX: (614) 594-3488. Licensee: WATH Inc. Group owner: Target Broadcast Group Inc. (acq 9-5-73). Net: CBS, NBC Talknet. Rep: Rgnl Reps. Wash atty: Pepper & Corazzini Format: MOR. News staff 3; news progmg 20 hrs wkly. Target aud: 35 plus. Spec prog: C&W 6 hrs, farm 4 hrs, big band 15 hrs wkly. ■ David W. Palmer, pres; Robert E. Lambert, vp & gen mgr; Daniel Harlett, gen sls mgr; Dave Palmer, progmg dir; Bob Beyette, mus dir; Kirk Greenfield, news dir; Joe Stack, chief engr. ■ Rates: $18; 14; 16; 12.

WXTQ(FM)—Co-owned with WATH(AM). Sept 16, 1964: 105.5 mhz; 6 kw. Ant 305 ft. TL: N39 21 18 W82 05 32. Stereo. Hrs opn: 24. Prog sep from AM. Net: NBC the Source, MBS. Format: CHR-live. News progmg 5 hrs wkly. Target aud: 18-34. ■ Jamie West, opns dir; John Chambers, mus dir. ■ Rates: Same as AM.

*WOUB(AM)—Sept 14, 1957: 1340 khz; 500 w-D, 1 kw-N. TL: N39 19 45 W82 05 29. 9 S. College St. (45701). (614) 593-4554. FAX: (614) 593-0240. Licensee: Ohio University. Net: ABC/I, NPR, APR. Format: News, talk, progsv. Spec prog: Black 8 hrs wkly. ■ Joseph Welling, gen mgr; Tim Myers, progmg dir.

*WOUB-FM—Dec 13, 1949: 91.3 mhz; 50 kw. Ant 500 ft. TL: N39 18 50 W82 08 54. Stereo. Prog sep from AM. Format: Class, jazz. ■ *WOUB-TV affil.

WXTQ(FM)—Listing follows WATH(AM).

Bainbridge

*WKHR(FM)—May 6, 1977: 88.3 mhz; 125 w. Ant 144 ft. TL: N41 23 42 W81 18 25 (CP: 1 kw.). Stereo. Kenston High School, 17425 Snyder Rd., Chagrin Falls (44023). (216) 543-9646; (216) 543-8835. Licensee: Kenston Local School District. Format: Alternative, big band, blues. Target aud: 18 plus. Spec prog: Metal, reggae, world, classic rock, now music. ■ Scott McVay, gen mgr; John Alan, stn mgr; Heather Lupca, prom dir; Cris Schneider, mus dir; Adam Mark, news dir; Gary Posti, pub affrs dir; William Weisinger, chief engr.

Barnesville

WBNV(FM)—July 1, 1991: 93.5 mhz; 6 kw. Ant 489 ft. TL: N39 54 10 W81 12 37. Stereo. Hrs opn: 6 AM-midnight. Box 293, 175 E. Main St. (43713-0293). Box 338, 4988 Skyline Dr., Cambridge (43725). (614) 425-5777; (614) 432-5605. FAX: (614) 432-1991. Licensee: W. Grant Hafley. Rep. Rgnl Reps. Format: Oldies. News progmg 15 hrs wkly. Target aud: 25-54. ■ W. Grant Hafley, gen mgr; David L. Wilson, opns mgr; Carl J. Harriman, gen sls mgr; D.J. Helriggle, progmg dir & mus dir; William R. Arnett, news dir; Susan G. Howell, pub affrs dir; John W. McCance, chief engr.

Batavia

*WOBO(FM)—July 30, 1981: 88.7 mhz; 15.5 kw. Ant 428 ft. TL: N39 03 43 W84 05 50. Stereo. Box 388, Owensville (45160). (513) 732-3232. Licensee: Educational Community Radio Inc. Format: Variety. ■ William Fiedler, pres & stn mgr; Richard Lahke, progmg dir; Susan Strong, mus dir; Fred Luecke, chief engr.

Beavercreek

WYMJ-FM—June 18, 1972: 103.9 mhz; 1.15 kw. Ant 522 ft. TL: N39 44 12 W84 09 25. Stereo. Hrs opn: 24. 699 N. Valley Rd. (45385). (513) 429-9080. Licensee: Tri-City Radio L.P. (acq 7-89; $3 million). Net: AP, Unistar. Rep: Torbet. Format: Oldies. News staff one. Target aud: 25-54; baby boomers. ■ Alan D. Gray, pres; Peter Coughlin, vp & gen mgr; Deborah Sumner (local), vp sls; Andrea Rees, prom mgr; Ron Scott, progmg dir; Scott Wallace, chief engr.

Bellaire

WOMP(AM)—Dec 2, 1947: 1290 khz; 1 kw-D, 33 w-N. TL: N40 02 09 W80 46 16. Hrs opn: 24. Box 448, Rt. 214, 56325 High Ridge Rd. (43906). (614) 676-5661. FAX: (614) 676-2742. Licensee: WSTV Inc. (acq 12-30-92; $575,000 with co-located FM; FTR 1-25-93). Net: ABC TalkRadio, ABC/D, Daynet, CNN. Rep: Rgnl Reps. Format: News, talk. News staff one; news progmg 30 hrs wkly. Target aud: 35 plus; affluent, educated adults. Spec prog: Polish 2 hrs, Czech 2 hrs wkly. ■ Bill Chesson, gen mgr; Howard Monroe, opns mgr & news dir; Ben Bain, gen sls mgr; Greg Harper, chief engr.

WOMP-FM—1947: 100.5 mhz; 48 kw. Ant 518 ft. TL: N40 02 09 W80 46 16. Stereo. Hrs opn: 24. Prog sep from AM. Net: Unistar. Format: CHR. Target aud: 12-24. ■ Joyee Nicholson, opns mgr; Steve Kline, progmg dir; Scott Fiest, mus dir.

Bellefontaine

WBLL(AM)—1951: 1390 khz; 500 w-D, 81 w-N. TL: N40 22 05 W83 44 02. Hrs opn: 24 1501 Rd. 235 (43311-9506). (513) 592-1045. FAX: (513) 592-3299. Licensee: V-Teck Communications Inc. (acq 12-2-87; grpsl; FTR 10-19-87). Net: Agri Bcstg. Rep: Rgnl Reps. Format: Country. Target aud: General. Spec prog: Relg. 6 hrs wkly. ■ Lou Vito, pres & gen mgr; Robert Wagner, opns dir; Dan Weldy, gen sls mgr & mktg dir; Brian Moore, prom dir; Bill Tipple, news dir; Dave Garwood, pub affrs dir; Bill Bowin, chief engr.

WPKO-FM—Co-owned with WBLL(AM). July 15, 1969: 98.3 mhz; 1.3 kw. Ant 430 ft. TL: N40 22 05 W83 44 02. Stereo. Hrs opn: 24. Format: Adult Contemp, urban contemp. News progmg 5 hrs wkly. Target aud: 25-49. Spec prog: Open house party (Sat & Sun PM). ■ Chris Oaks, progmg dir; Brian Moore, mus dir.

Bellevue

WNRR(FM)—Apr 4, 1973: 92.1 mhz; 3 kw. Ant 161 ft. TL: N41 16 30 W82 50 00. Stereo. Hrs opn: 24. 108 1/2 E. Main (44811). (419) 483-2511. Licensee: Bellevue Community Broadcasting Inc. (acq 1978). Net: Sun, USA; Agri. Format: CHR, hot adult contemp. News staff 2; news progmg 5 hrs wkly. Target aud: 18-49; upscale. Spec prog: Relg 3 hrs wkly. ■ Jean Ladd, pres; Robert Ladd, stn mgr & chief engr; Chris Armatige, gen sls mgr; Bob Ladd, progmg dir & news dir; Jeff Schlett, mus dir. WO2B4, WO6BK TV affils. ■ Rates: $12.50; 12.50; 12.50; 12.50.

Belpre

*WCVV(FM)—1986: 89.5 mhz; 3 kw. Ant 199 ft. TL: N39 17 11 W81 34 13. Stereo. Hrs opn: 24. Box 405 (45714). (614) 423-5895; (614) 423-8535. Licensee: Belpre Educ Broadcasting Foundation. Format: Christian, news. Target aud: General. ■ Clay Sloan, stn mgr; Felix Washington, chief opns; Ralph Matheny, chief engr.

*WMBP(FM)—May 1991: 91.7 mhz; 170 w. Ant 344 ft. TL: N39 20 46 W81 29 55. Box 568 (45714). (614) 423-5673. FAX: (614) 423-5673. Licensee: Lower Ohio Valley Educational Corp. Format: Christian contemp. ■ Tony Atkins, gen mgr; Larry Romans, progmg dir.

WNUS(FM)—Sept 12, 1981: 107.1 mhz; 2.3 kw. Ant 370 ft. TL: N39 18 36 W81 35 49. Stereo. Hrs opn: 24. Box 428 (45714). (614) 423-8213. FAX: (614) 295-4389. Licensee: WNUS Inc. (acq 5-24-93; $575,000 with WLTP[AM] Parkersburg, WV; FTR 6-14-93). Net: CNN. Rep: Dome. Wash atty: Bill Berton. Format: Country. News staff one; news progmg 2 hrs wkly. Target aud: 25 plus. ■ Ron Bishop, gen mgr; Missy Martin, prom mgr; William Benns IV, progmg dir; Doug Hess, news dir; Ralph Matheny, chief engr. ■ Rates: $20; 15; 17; 10.

Berea

*WBWC(FM)—Mar 2, 1958: 88.3 mhz; 100 w. Ant 40 ft. TL: N41 22 19 W81 50 52 (CP: 91.5 mhz, 3 kw, ant 259 ft.). Stereo. Baldwin-Wallace College, 275 Eastland Rd. (44017). (216) 826-2145; (216) 826-8525. FAX: (216) 826-2329. Licensee: Baldwin-Wallace College. Net: AP. Format: Alt mus. News progmg 10 hrs wkly. Target aud: General; alt mus listeners. Spec prog: Blues 5 hrs, class 5 hrs, jazz 5 hrs, Serbian 5 hrs, world 5 hrs, new age 5 hrs, industrial 5 hrs, avante garde 5 hrs, heavy metal 10 hrs wkly. ■ Dave Bobco, chief engr.

Bowling Green

*WBGU(FM)—November 1951: 88.1 mhz; 450 w. Ant 178 ft. TL: N41 22 33 W83 38 34. Hrs opn: 24. Dept. of Telecommunications, 322 W. Hall, Bowling Green State Univ. (43403). (419) 372-8800; (419) 372-2138. FAX: (419) 372-0202. Licensee: Bowling Green State Univ. Format: Div, jazz, black. News progmg 7 hrs wkly. Target aud: General. Spec prog: Progsv, urban contemp, country 4 hrs, classical 3 hrs, folk 4 hrs, Sp 4 hrs wkly. ■ Paul Olscamp, pres; Bruce Klopfenstein, gen mgr; Tobin J. Klinger, stn mgr; Cathy Carr, prom dir; Dawn Blackford, progmg dir; Nick DiFonzo, mus dir; Beth Tigue, news dir; Nick Shanta, pub affrs dir; Chuck Konecky, chief engr. ■ *WBGU-TV affil.

WJYM(AM)—December 1964: 730 khz; 1 kw-D, DA. TL: N41 31 57 W83 33 55. Hrs opn: 6 AM-midnight. 8761 Fremont Pike, Perrysburg (43551). (419) 352-4649. Licensee: Jimmy Swaggart Ministries (acq 10-14-76). Net: USA. Format: Relg. News progmg 3 hrs wkly. Target aud: 25-49. ■ Todd Hostetler, gen mgr; Becky Vassar, opns dir & progmg dir; Richard E. Dewese, chief engr. ■ Rates: $12; 12; 12; 12.

WRQN(FM)—June 1964: 93.5 mhz; 4.1 kw. Ant 397 ft. TL: N41 27 28 W83 39 33. 1315 Dussel Drive, Maumee (43537). (419) 891-1551; (419) 891-0935. FAX: (419) 891-1563. Licensee: ABS Toledo Partners L.P. Group owner: ABS Communications Inc. (acq 5-26-89; $2,685,000; FTR 1-16-89). Net: Unistar. Rep: Banner. Format: Oldies. News progmg 4 hrs wkly. Target aud: 25-54. Spec prog: Pub svc one hr wkly. ■ Ken Brown, Jon Sinton, presdts; John Alkire, stn mgr & opns mgr; Clyde Roberts, gen sls mgr; Leslie Verbal, prom mgr; Joe Siragusa, progmg dir & mus dir; Margie Szar, news dir & pub affrs dir; Dave Fuller, chief engr.

Bryan

WQCT(AM)—December 1962: 1520 khz; 500 w-D, 250 w-CH. TL: N41 28 43 W84 34 49. Simulcast with WBNO(FM). Box 603 (43506). (419) 636-3175; (419) 636-4577. FAX: (419) 636-4570. Licensee: Williams County Broadcasting System Inc. (group owner; acq 2-67). Net: ABC/C; Agri Bcstg. Format: Adult contemp, local talk. Spec prog: Professional, collegiate, & local sports. ■ Carl Shipley, pres; Luke Thaman, gen mgr & gen sls mgr; J.B. Orendoroff, opns mgr, news dir & chief engr; Gwen Takacs, natl sls dir.

WBNO-FM—Co-owned with WQCT(AM). June 30, 1966: 100.9 mhz; 6 kw. Ant 299 ft. TL: N41 28 44 W84 34 50. Dups AM 100%. News staff one; news progmg 27 hrs wkly. Target aud: General; local oriented. ■ J.B. Orendoroff, progmg dir. ■ Rates: $8.80; 8.80; 8.80; 8.80.

Buchtel

WAIS(AM)—Dec 3, 1984: 770 khz; 1 kw-D. TL: N39 25 56 W82 12 02. 15751 U.S Rt. 33 S., Nelsonville (45764). (614) 753-2154. FAX: (614) 753-4965. Licensee: Nelsonville TV Cable Inc. Net: ABC. Wash atty: Frank Jazzo. Format: Country. News staff 3; news progmg 21 hrs wkly. Target aud: 18-54. ■ Eugene Edwards, pres & gen mgr; Don Bedell, progmg dir; Mark King, mus dir; Bob Eby, news dir; Hubert Dalton, chief engr. ■ Rates: $13; 11.70; 13; 11.70.

Bucyrus

WBCO(AM)—Dec 22, 1962: 1540 khz; 500 w-D, DA. TL: N40 45 47 W82 56 05. Stereo. Box 789 (44820-0789). (419) 562-2222. Licensee: Brokensword Broadcasting Co. (acq 4-87; grpsl; FTR 4-13-87). Net: Unistar; Agri Bcstg. Rep: Rgnl Reps, Farmakis. Wash atty: Vorys, Sater, Seymour & Pease. Format: Adult contemp, news/talk. News staff 2; news progmg 17 hrs wkly. Target aud: 30-60. Spec prog: Farm 8 hrs, relg 4 hrs wkly. ■ Thomas P. Moore, pres & progmg dir; J. LaVonne Moore, execvp; John Cavinee, gen mgr; Donna Brause, stn mgr; Jim Radke, chief opns, progmg mgr, mus dir & pub affrs dir; Dave Jones, gen sls mgr; Debbie Gifford, prom mgr; Cheryl Lynn, news dir; Bill Bowin, chief engr. ■ Rates: $12.30; 9.80; 9.80; 9.80.

WQEL(FM)—Co-owned with WBCO(AM). Sept 5, 1964: 92.7 mhz; 3 kw. Ant 300 ft. TL: N40 45 45 W82 55 50. Stereo. Prog sep from AM. Net: CBS. Format: Classic rock. Target aud: 25-54. Spec prog: Relg 2 hrs wkly. ■ Rates: $12.25; 10; 10; 10.

Byesville

WUFA(FM)—Not on air, target date unknown: 97.7 mhz; 3 kw. TL: N39 53 44 W81 35 07. c/o Coshocton Broadcasting Co., 114 N. Sixth St., Coshocton (43812). (614) 622-1560. Licensee: Coshocton Broadcasting Co. (group owner).

Cadiz

WCDK(FM)—Aug 28, 1985: 106.3 mhz; 6 kw. Ant 360 ft. TL: N40 15 14 W80 50 35. Stereo. Hrs opn: 24. B7-116 Bantam Ridge Rd., Wintersville (43952). (614) 266-2700. Licensee: McGraw Broadcasting. Group owner: McGraw Group Stations (acq 9-90). Net: Jones Satellite Audio. Rep: Dome. Wash atty: Fisher, Wayland, Cooper & Leader. Format: Kuttin' edge kountry. News staff one; news progmg 5 hrs wkly. Target aud: General; 25-54. Spec prog: OSU football, local football, environmental minute. ■ Richard McGraw, pres, gen mgr, adv dir & engrg mgr; Todd Elliott, stn mgr, prom dir & progmg dir; Dave Hemmilrick, opns mgr; Cindy Smook, sls dir; Karen McGraw, mktg dir; Dave Himmelrick, news dir & pub affrs dir; Don Thomas, chief engr. ■ Rates: $18; 18; 18; 15.

Caldwell

WWKC(FM)—July 1, 1989: 104.9 mhz; 3 kw. Ant 300 ft. TL: N39 48 47 W81 56 38. Box 19, 310 East St. (43724); Box 338, 4988 Skyline Dr. Cambridge (43725). (614) 732-5777; (614) 432-5605. Licensee: W. Grant Hafley (acq 8-23-89; $15,000; FTR 9-18-89). Net: MBS; Agri Bcstg. Rep: Rgnl Reps. Format: Country. Target aud: 25-54. ■ W. Grant Hafley, gen mgr; David L. Wilson, opns mgr; Carl J. Harriman, gen sls mgr; Jeffrey P. Jirles, progmg dir; Jack Uplinger, mus dir; Bill Arnett, news dir; Rebecca A. McFerren, David L. Jacobs, pub affrs dirs; John W. McCance, chief engr.

Cambridge

WCMJ(FM)—Listing follows WILE(AM).

WILE(AM)—Apr 9, 1948: 1270 khz; 1 kw-D. TL: N40 02 24 W81 38 50. Box 338, 4988 Skyline Dr. (43725). (614) 432-5605. Licensee: AVC Communications Inc. (acq 5-5-83). Net: MBS. Rep: Rgnl Reps. Format: MOR. Target aud: 25-54. ■ W. Grant Hafley, gen mgr; David L. Wilson, opns mgr; Carl J. Harriman, gen sls mgr; Jeffrey P. Jirles, progmg dir; Jack Uplinger, mus dir; Bill Arnett, news dir; Rebecca A. McFerren, David L. Jacobs, pub affrs dirs; John McCance, chief engr.

WCMJ(FM)—Co-owned with WILE(AM). October 1964: 96.7 mhz; 1.3 kw. Ant 420 ft. TL: N40 02 24 W81 38 50. Stereo. Prog sep from AM. Format: Adult contemp. Target aud: 18-49. ■ D.J. Helriggle, progmg dir & mus dir.

***WOUC-FM**—May 11, 1987: 89.1 mhz; 5 kw. Ant 500 ft. TL: N40 05 32 W81 17 19. Stereo. Hrs opn: 18. Ohio Univ., Telecommunications Center, Athens (45701). (614) 593-4554. FAX: (614) 593-0240. Licensee: Ohio University. Net: APR, NPR. Format: Classical, jazz, news. News staff 2. ■ Joseph Welling, gen mgr; Tim Myers, progmg dir; Mark Smith, mus dir; Nancy Burton, news dir; David Wiseman, engrg mgr. ■ WOUC-TV affil.

Campbell

WASN(AM)—Oct 16, 1955: 1330 khz; 500 w-D, 1 kw-N, DA-2. TL: N40 58 30 W80 35 15. Hrs opn: 24. 401 N. Blaine Ave., Youngstown (44505). (216) 746-1330; (216) 746-1234. FAX: (216) 746-1311. Licensee: WVBR Inc. (acq 4-18-90; $230,000; FTR 5-7-90). Net: Motor Racing Net. Wash atty: Reddy, Martin & Begley. Format: All-sports, all-day. News staff one. Target aud: 25-54; adult males. Spec prog: It 2 hrs, Pol one hr, Golden Age radio 5 hrs wkly. ■ Ray Travaglini, pres; Sandy Petruso, vp; Larry K. Ward, gen mgr & gen sls mgr; Kelly Salandro, opns mgr & news dir; David Price, prom dir & progmg mgr; Carmen Carcelli, adv mgr; Wes Boyd, John Urchak, engrg dirs. ■ Rates: $18; 13; 15; 12.

WHOT-FM—See Youngstown.

Canton

WCER(AM)—1947: 900 khz; 500 w-D, 78 w-N. TL: N40 49 17 W81 25 34. Stereo. 4537 22nd St. N.W. (44708). (216) 478-6666. FAX: (216) 478-6651. Licensee: Melodynamic Broadcasting Corp. (acq 7-11-91; $85,000; FTR 7-29-91). Net: UPI, USA. Format: MOR. ■ Jack Ambrozic, gen mgr; Ron Riegler, opns mgr.

WDPN(AM)—See Alliance.

WHBC(AM)—Mar 9, 1925: 1480 khz; 5 kw-U, DA-2. TL: N40 43 15 W81 26 28. Stereo. Box 9917 (44711). (216) 456-7166. FAX: (216) 456-7199. Licensee: Beaverkettle Co. (acq 12-11-67). Net: ABC/E. Rep: Christal. Wash atty: Cohn & Marks. Format: MOR. News staff 6; news progmg 27 hrs wkly. Target aud: 25 plus. Spec prog: Farm one hr wkly. ■ William A. Chambers, pres & gen mgr; Raymond Hexamer, gen sls mgr; Kayleigh Kriss, prom dir & pub affrs dir; Doug Lane, progmg dir; Amanda Wilson, news dir; Wm. C. Glasser, chief engr.

WHBC-FM—Feb 2, 1948: 94.1 mhz; 50 kw. Ant 500 ft. TL: N40 53 53 W81 19 07. Stereo. Prog sep from AM. Format: Adult contemp. News staff 6; news progmg 5 hrs wkly. Target aud: 25-54.

WINW(AM)—Apr 14, 1966: 1520 khz; 1 kw-D, DA. TL: N40 50 41 W81 21 02. Hrs opn: Sunrise-sunset. 4111 Martindale Rd. N.E. (44705). (216) 492-5630. FAX: (216) 492-5633. Licensee: Canton/Akron Radio Inc. (acq 6-27-89). Rep: Eastman, Rgnl Reps. Format: MOR, adult contemp. Target aud: 35-54; professionals. ■ James Embrescia, pres; Pat Bammerlin, stn mgr; Lisa Rodman, opns mgr; Todd Downerd, prom dir; Dave Nicholas, progmg dir; Dale Lamm, chief engr. ■ Rates: $23; 23; 13; na.

WRQK(FM)—Co-owned with WINW(AM). March 1, 1961: 106.9 mhz; 27.5 kw. Ant 340 ft. TL: N40 49 17 W81 25 34. Stereo. Hrs opn: 24. Prog sep from AM. Format: Rock. Target aud: 18-49. ■ Pat Bammerlin, gen mgr; Scott Hughes, progmg dir. ■ Rates: Same as AM.

WRCW(AM)—Aug 11, 1946: 1060 khz; 5 kw-D, DA. TL: N40 50 04 W81 25 46. 4601 Hills and Dales Rd. N.W. (44708). (216) 477-8585. Licensee: Arcey Broadcasting (acq 3-42-82; $450,000; FTR 3-1-82). Format: Adult contemp, talk. ■ R.D. Colaner, pres, gen mgr & chief engr; W. Swartz, gen sls mgr; M.A. Hohler, prom mgr; Sam Collins, progmg dir & mus dir.

WRQK(FM)—Listing follows WINW(AM).

WTOF-FM—Nov 19, 1961: 98.1 mhz; 36 kw. Ant 570 ft. TL: N40 53 24 W81 25 34. Stereo. Hrs opn: 24. 2780 S. Arlington Rd., Akron (44312). (216) 452-4009; (216) 645-7777. Licensee: Mortenson Broadcasting Co. (group owner). Net: USA. Format: Relg, Christian country. Target aud: 25-64. Spec prog: Black 3 hrs, farm one hr wkly. ■ Jack Mortenson, pres; Tom Bishop, gen mgr, stn mgr & gen sls mgr; Dave Johnson, opns dir & chief engr; Greg Morrison, progmg dir & mus dir. ■ Rates: $19; 15; 19; 13.

WZKL(FM)—See Alliance.

Castalia

WGGN(FM)—January 1975: 97.7 mhz; 1.25 kw. Ant 725 ft. TL: N41 23 48 W82 47 31 Stereo. Hrs opn: 18. 3809 Maple Ave. (44824); Box 2397, Sandusky (44870). (419) 684-5311. FAX: (419) 684-5378. Licensee: Christian Faith Broadcasting Inc. (group owner). Net: USA, CBN. Wash atty: May & Dunne Chartered. Format: AC Christian. Target aud: General; 25-49. ■ Shelby Gilliam, pres; Rusty Yost, gen mgr & chief engr; Jeff Ferback, gen sls mgr; Jennifer Enlow, prom dir & mus dir. ■ Rates: $7.50; 7.50; 7.50; 7.50.

Cedarville

***WCDR-FM**—Dec 1, 1962: 90.3 mhz; 30 kw. Ant 354 ft. TL: N39 45 46 W83 53 05. Stereo. Hrs opn: 24. Box 601, 251 N. Main St. (45314). (513) 766-7815; (513) 766-5595. FAX: (513) 766-2760. Licensee: The Cedarville College. Net: CNN. Wash atty: Cohen & Berfield. Format: Relg, talk. News staff one; news progmg 16 hrs wkly. Target aud: 35-54. ■ Paul H. Dixon, pres & exec vp; Martin Clark, vp; Paul Gathany, gen mgr; Jon Skillman, opns mgr; Mark Kordic, mktg dir; Eric Johnson, mus dir; Chad Bresson, news dir; John Tocknell, chief engr.

Celina

WCSM(AM)—Sept 11, 1963: 1350 khz; 500 w-D, 11 w-N, DA-1. TL: N40 32 17 W84 35 20. Hrs opn: 6 AM-sunset. Box 492, Meyers & Schunck Roads (45822). (419) 586-5134. Licensee: Hayco Broadcasting Inc. (acq 1977). Net: ABC/D; Agri Bcstg. Format: Adult contemp. News staff one; news progmg 20 hrs wkly. Target aud: 18-49. Spec prog: Farm 5 hrs wkly. ■ John H. Coe, pres & gen mgr; Sue Heiser, gen sls mgr; Jim Hyatt, mus dir; Tony Felts, news dir; Dan Dietz, chief engr.

WCSM-FM—1968: 96.7 mhz; 3 kw. Ant 328 ft. TL: N40 33 08 W84 30 46. Hrs opn: 24. Prog dups AM 100%.

WKKI(FM)—Dec 18, 1960: 94.3 mhz; 2.2 kw. Ant 448 ft. TL: N40 33 08 W84 30 46. 126 W. Fayette St. (45822). (419) 586-7715; (419) 645-4193. FAX: (419) 586-1074. Licensee: The Sonshine Corp. dba Radio Station WKKI (acq 5-22-92; $325,000; FTR 6-15-92). Net: Unistar. Rep: Roslin, Rgnl Reps. Format: Adult contemp. News staff one; news progmg 6 hrs wkly. Target aud: 25-54. Spec prog: Contemp Christian 2 hrs, farm one hr wkly. ■ Ralph A. Guamieri Jr., pres; Virginia J. Guamieri, gen mgr; Patricia Dixon, opns mgr; Brett Johnson, progmg dir; Shari Hartsock, news dir; Dan Dietz, chief engr.

Centerville

***WCWT-FM**—Sept 20, 1971: 101.5 mhz; 10 w. Ant 110 ft. TL: N39 37 39 W84 09 57 (CP: Ant 194 ft.). 500 E. Franklin (45459). (513) 439-3557. FAX: (513) 439-3574. Licensee: Centerville City Board of Education. Format: Classic rock. Target aud: General. ■ Ken Carper, gen mgr; Jeff Dunn, progmg dir.

Chardon

WATJ(AM)—Feb 14, 1969: 1560 khz; 1 kw-D, DA. TL: N41 34 03 W81 11 33. Hrs opn: 8 AM-5 PM. Box 776, 11106 Aquilla Rd., Geneva (44024). (216) 286-1560. Licensee: Music Express Broadcasting Corp. (acq 3-7-89; $150,000; FTR 1-30-89). Format: Community radio. News progmg 3 hrs wkly. Target aud: 25-55. ■ Warren Jones, pres; Bruce A. Berger, gen mgr; Mark Lelland, sls dir.

Chillicothe

WBEX(AM)—September 1947: 1490 khz; 1 kw-U. TL: N39 19 56 W82 59 50. Hrs opn: 24. Box 244, 23 Pohlman Rd. (45601). (614) 773-2244. FAX: (614) 773-0933. Licensee: Guaranty Broadcasting Corp. (acq 9-20-93; with co-located FM; FTR 10-11-93). Net: CBS, CBS Spectrum, MBS. Rep: Rgnl Reps. Format: Oldies, news/talk. News staff 2; news progmg 10 hrs wkly. Target aud: 30-50. ■ Michael Adams, pres; Dan Latham, gen mgr; Mike Smith, news dir; Mac Porter, chief engr. ■ Rates: $26; 22; 26; 19.

WKKJ(FM)—Co-owned with WBEX(AM). July 1, 1961: 93.3 mhz; 50 kw. Ant 335 ft. TL: N39 19 52 W82 59 49. Stereo. Hrs opn: 24. Prog sep from AM. Net: SMN. Rep: Agri Bcstg. Format: Country. Target aud: 24-54. ■ Rates: Same as AM.

WCHI(AM)—Oct 1, 1951: 1350 khz; 1 kw-D, 250-N. TL: N39 19 13 W82 57 03. Hrs opn: 24. Box 94, 45 W. Main St. (45601). (614) 775-1350. FAX: (614) 774-4494. Licensee: Wyandot Radio Corp. (acq 10-2-89; $90,000; FTR 10-23-89). Net: NBC, NBC Talknet, Unistar. Format: News, talk. News staff 2 Target aud: 35 plus. ■ Dave Smith, pres & gen mgr; John Rose, vp opns; Bill Forthofer, vp sls; Bobbi Daily, prom mgr; Brian Cross, vp progmg; Lee Stevens, mus dir; Bob Neal, news dir; Steve Streitenberger, chief engr.

WFCB(FM)—Co-owned with WCHI(AM). Dec 22, 1978: 94.3 mhz; 25 kw. Ant 266 ft. TL: N39 19 52 W82 59 49. Stereo. Hrs opn: 24. Prog sep from AM. (614) 773-3000. (Acq 7-83; $285,000; FTR 7-25-83). Net: NBC the Source, Westwood One. Format: Top-40. Target aud: 18-54. ■ Kent Smith, gen mgr.

WKKJ(FM)—Listing follows WBEX(AM).

***WOHC(FM)**—May 1, 1992: 90.1 mhz; 2 kw-V. Ant 393 ft. TL: N39 20 45 W83 11 15. Stereo. Hrs opn: 24. 251 N. Main St., Cedarville (45314). (513) 766-7815; (513) 766-5595. FAX: (513) 766-2760. Licensee: The Cedarville College. Net: CNN. Wash atty: Cohen & Berfield. Format: Relg, info, educ. News progmg 16 hrs wkly. Target aud: 35-54; information-oriented Christians and/or church members.

***WOUH(FM)**—October 1992: 91.9 mhz; 750 w. Ant 649 ft. TL: N39 19 46 W82 48 08. 9 S. College St., Athens (45701). (614) 593-4949. Licensee: Ohio Univ. Format: News, classical, jazz. Spec prog: Public affairs. ■ Tim Myers, stn mgr.

***WVXC(FM)**—Jan 15, 1988: 89.3 mhz; 2.5 kw. Ant 115 ft. TL: N39 20 45 W83 11 15. Stereo. Xavier Univ., 3800 Victory Pkwy., Cincinnati (45207). (513) 745-3738. Licensee: Xavier University. Net: APR, NPR. Format: Div, educ. News staff 3; news progmg 29 hrs wkly. Educated, socially conscious middle & upper middle class. ■ Dr. James C. King, gen mgr; George Zahn, opns mgr & progmg dir; Jo Huntington, gen sls mgr; Mike Boberg, prom mgr; Mark Keefe, mus dir; Lorna Jordan, news dir; Jay Crawford, chief engr.

Cincinnati

WAKW(FM)—Nov 21, 1961: 93.3 mhz; 50 kw. Ant 500 ft. TL: N39 12 22 W84 33 23. Stereo. Box 24G, 6275 Collegevue Place (45224). (513) 542-3442. Licensee: Pillar of Fire Inc. (group owner). Net: AP, CBN, Moody. Format: Relg. Target aud: General. ■ Gerald Croucher, opns mgr; Bob Lewis, progmg dir; Nancy Huffine, mus dir; Victor Wong, pub affrs dir; Joe Stenger, chief engr.

WCIN(AM)—October 1953: 1480 khz; 5 kw-D, 500 w-N, DA-1. TL: N39 09 19 W84 30 03 (CP: 114 w). 106 Glenwood Ave. (45217). (513) 281-7180. FAX: (513) 281-6125. Licensee: Junior Broadcasting Co. (acq 2-3-93; $425,000; FTR 2-22-93). Net: Unistar. Format: Oldies, Black. News staff 2; news progmg 30 hrs wkly. Target aud: 25-64; affluent, upscale, $50,000 plus income. ■ John C. Thomas, pres & gen mgr; Joe Sears, gen sls mgr; Michelle Ward-Gilliam, prom mgr; Lincoln Ware, progmg mgr; Bonna King, news dir; Joe Strenger, chief engr.

WCKY(AM)—Sept 16, 1929: 1530 khz; 50 kw-U, DA-N, (LSS-Sacramento, CA). TL: N39 03 55 W84 36 27. 219 McFarland St. (45202). (513) 241-6565. Licensee: Pathfinder Communications Corp. Group owner: Federated Media (acq 12-22-75). Net: CBS, NBC, NBC Talknet. Rep: McGavren Guild. Format: News/talk. News staff 3; news progmg 30 hrs wkly. Target aud: 35-64; information-oriented, white-collar, above-average income. ■ John Dille Jr., pres; Thomas J. Severino, gen mgr; Bruce Still, opns mgr; Lisa Schackman, gen sls mgr; Michelle Dickinson, prom mgr; Steve Nicholl, progmg dir; Ric Owen, mus dir; Don Herman, news dir; Ted Kendrick, chief engr.

WIMJ(FM)—Co-owned with WCKY(AM). Aug 19, 1964: 92.5 mhz; 16 kw. Ant 910 ft. TL: N39 07 19 W84 32 52. Prog sep from AM. (513) 721-5678. (Acq 4-16-77). Format: Adult contemp. News staff one. Target aud: 25-54; educated, working women 35-54; dual income families. ■ Jon Horton, gen sls mgr.

WCVG(AM)—See Covington, Ky.

WEBN(FM)—Listing follows WLW(AM).

WGRR(FM)—See Hamilton.

Stations in the U.S. Ohio

***WGUC(FM)**—Sept 21, 1960: 90.9 mhz; 15 kw. Ant 960 ft. TL: N39 07 27 W84 31 18. Stereo. Hrs opn: 24. 1223 Central Pkwy. (45214). (513) 556-4444. Licensee: U. of Cincinnati. Net: NPR, APR, Ohio Educ Bcstg. Format: Class. News staff one; news progmg 10 hrs wkly. Target aud: 35 plus; well-educated. Spec prog: Jazz 12 hrs wkly. ■ Ann Santen, gen mgr; Jeff Krys, opns dir; Chris Phelps, dev dir & mktg dir; Andrea Taylor, sls dir; Dick Bailey, progmg dir; Brent Reider, chief engr.

WIMJ(FM)—Listing follows WCKY(AM).

WIZF(FM)—See Erlanger, Ky.

***WJVS(FM)**—Apr 7, 1976: 88.3 mhz; 175 w. Ant 105 ft. TL: N39 17 21 W84 24 52. Stereo. 3254 E. Kemper Rd. (45241). (513) 771-8810. Licensee: Great Oaks Joint Vocational School District (acq 1976). Format: Adult contemp. News staff one. ■ Joanne Easley, gen mgr; David Angelino, progmg dir.

WKRQ(FM)—1947: 101.9 mhz; 16 kw. Ant 876 ft. TL: N39 06 58 W84 30 05. Stereo. 1906 Highland Ave. (45219). (513) 763-5500. FAX: (513) 763-5541. Licensee: Great American TV & Radio Inc. Group owner: Great American Broadcasting (acq 1982). Rep: Katz. Format: Top-40. ■ Dave Crowl, pres; Jim Bryant, vp & gen mgr; Mike Fredrick, gen sls mgr; Von Freeman, prom dir; Jimmy Steel, progmg dir; Dennis Rooney, news dir; Tom Oliver, chief engr. ■ WKRC-TV affil.

WLW(AM)—Mar 22, 1922: 700 khz; 50 kw-U. TL: N39 21 11 W84 19 30. 1111 St. Gregory St. (45202). (513) 241-9597. FAX: (513) 852-1004. Licensee: Jacor Broadcasting of Cincinnati Inc. Group owner: Jacor Communications Inc. (acq 7-86; grpsl; FTR 8-11-86). Net: ABC/I. Rep: Eastman. Format: Full svc adult contemp, news/talk. ■ David Martin, pres & gen mgr; John Phillips, opns mgr; Rich Porter, gen sls mgr; Bill Wills, progmg dir; Kathy Lehr, news dir; Al Kenyon, chief engr.

WLWA(AM)—1922: 550 khz; 5 kw-D, 1 kw-N, DA-2. TL: N39 00 29 W84 26 39. 1111 St. Gregory St. (45202). (513) 241-9597. FAX: (513) 651-4555. Licensee: Jacor Broadcasting Corp. Group owner: Jacor Communications Inc. (acq 4-8-93; $1.6 million; FTR 4-26-93). Net: ABC/I. Rep: Eastman. Format: Info. station. ■ David Martin, pres & gen mgr; John Phillips, opns mgr; Al Kenyon, chief engr.

WEBN(FM)—Co-owned with WLW(AM). Aug 27, 1967: 102.7 mhz; 16.6 kw. Ant 876 ft. TL: N39 07 31 W84 29 57. Stereo. Prog sep from AM. (513) 621-9326. FAX: (513) 749-3299. (Acq 2-86; $8 million; FTR 2-17-86). Format: AOR. Spec prog: Class 4 hrs wkly. ■ Jaqui Brumm, gen mgr; Larry Hemsath, gen sls mgr; Tom Owens, progmg dir; Tony Tolliver, mus dir; Craig Kopp, news dir; Jay Crawford, chief engr.

WOFX(FM)—See Fairfield.

WRRM(FM)—Oct 1, 1959: 98.5 mhz; 17.5 kw. Ant 807 ft. TL: N39 07 19 W84 32 52. Stereo. Suite 1200, 205 W. Fourth St. (45202). (513) 241-9898. Licensee: Radio Cincinnati Inc. Group owner: Susquehanna Radio Corp. (acq 1-72). Rep: Christal. Format: Adult contemp. ■ A.W. Carlson, pres; Gordon Obarski, vp; Dan Swensson, gen mgr; Joe Schildmeyer, gen sls mgr; Greg Lonneman, prom mgr; Pat Holiday, progmg dir; Steve Crum, chief engr.

WSAI(AM)—June 7, 1923: 1360 khz; 5 kw-U, DA-N. TL: N39 14 51 W84 31 52. Hrs opn: 24. 2601 W. Eighth St. (45204). (513) 471-9465. Licensee: Booth American Co. (group owner; acq 3-82; grpsl; FTR 4-5-82). Net: MBS. Rep: Major Mkt. Wash atty: Dow, Lohnes & Albertson. Format: Sports Talk. News staff 2. Target aud: 18-64; men who love sports. ■ John L. Booth II, pres; Jim Wood, gen mgr; James Gnau, gen sls mgr; Terry Coker, natl sls mgr; Frank Callahan, rgnl sls mgr; Hal L. Van Tassel, prom mgr; Jim McKnight, progmg dir; Fred Slezak, news dir; Benny Massey, pub affrs dir; Glenn Simmons, chief engr.

WWNK-FM—Co-owned with WSAI(AM). 1955: 94.1 mhz; 32 kw. Ant 600 ft. TL: N39 06 18 W84 33 24. Stereo. Hrs opn: 24. Prog sep from AM. Format: Adult contemp. ■ Dickie Shannon, mus dir.

WTSJ(AM)—1947: 1050 khz; 1 kw-D, 278 w-N. TL: N39 04 50 W84 31 18. Hrs opn: 24. Suite 33, 800 Compton Rd. (45231). (513) 931-8080. Licensee: Guardian Communications Inc. (group owner; acq 5-7-90; grpsl; FTR 5-21-90). Net: USA. Format: Christian country. News staff 3; news progmg 10 hrs wkly. Target aud: 24-54; family oriented young adults. ■ Mark McNeil, pres; Richard David, gen mgr & gen sls mgr; Dave Johnson, progmg dir & mus dir; Joe Stenger, chief engr.

WUBE(AM)—1927: 1230 khz; 1 kw-U. TL: N39 06 27 W84 30 09. Hrs opn: 24. 225 E. Sixth St. (45202). (513) 721-1050. FAX: (513) 421-7460. Licensee: National Radio Partners Group owner: American Media Inc. (acq 1-2-91; with co-located FM). Net: CBS Spectrum. Rep: Christal. Format: Country. News staff one. Target aud: 25-54. ■ Alan Beck, pres; George Toulles, vp & gen mgr; David Brandeburg, gen sls mgr; Twana Burns, prom mgr; Tim Closson, progmg dir; Duke Hamilton, mus dir; Eric Boulanger, news dir.

WUBE-FM—July 20, 1949: 105.1 mhz; 14 kw. Ant 920 ft. TL: N39 07 31 W84 29 57. Stereo. Dups AM 100%.

***WVXU(FM)**—May 4, 1971: 91.7 mhz; 26.1 kw. Ant 683 ft. TL: N39 07 31 W84 29 57. Stereo. Xavier Univ., 3800 Victory Pkwy. (45207). (513) 745-3738. Licensee: Xavier University. Net: APR, NPR, AP, CNN; Ohio Radio Net. Format: Jazz, new age, news/talk. Target aud: 25-49; middle & upper class men & women. ■ James C. King, gen mgr; George Zahn, opns dir & progmg dir; Jo Strauss, dev dir; Mike Borerg, prom mgr; Mark Keefe, mus dir; Lorna Jordan, news dir; Jay Crawford, chief engr.

WWNK-FM—Listing follows WSAI(AM).

WYGY(FM)—See Hamilton.

Circleville

WNRJ(AM)—1974: 1540 khz; 1 kw-D, DA. TL: N39 38 21 W82 57 30. 122 1/2 S. Court St. (43113). (614) 474-3344. Licensee: Tel Lease Inc. Net: Agri Bcstg. Rep: Rgnl Reps. Format: News/talk. ■ Robert G. Casagrande, gen mgr; Kriste Kellar, prom mgr; Linda Snyder, mus dir; Mark Litton, chief engr.

WAHC(FM)—Co-owned with WNRJ(AM). Oct 1, 1965: 107.1 mhz; 3 kw. Ant 328 ft. TL: N39 39 52 W82 51 04. (614) 792-2911. Format: CHR. ■ Chris Forgy, gen mgr; John Fields, progmg dir.

Cleveland

WABQ(AM)—1947: 1540 khz; 1 kw-D. TL: N41 30 10 W81 37 57. 8000 Euclid Ave. (44103). (216) 231-8005. FAX: (216) 421-0738. Licensee: WABQ Inc. (acq 8-15-80; $600,000; FTR 9-1-80). Format: Relg. News progmg 4 hrs wkly. Target aud: 25-64; adult African American church-going audience. Spec prog: Full time gospel. ■ John Linn, pres & gen mgr; Denver Wilborn, vp opns & progmg mgr; Dick Statterwaite, chief engr.

WCLV(FM)—Apr 1, 1960: 95.5 mhz; 31 kw. Ant 610 ft. TL: N41 26 32 W81 29 28. Stereo. Hrs opn: 24. 26501 Emery Industrial Pkwy. (44128). (216) 464-0900. Licensee: Radio Seaway Inc. (acq 11-1-62). Net: Concert Music Network. Rep: CMBS. Wash atty: Hogan & Hartson. Format: Classical. News staff one; news progmg 9 hrs wkly. Target aud: 35 plus; high-income, college graduates & professionals. ■ Robert D. Conrad, CEO; C. K. Patrick, chmn & stn mgr; Robert D.K. Conrad, pres; Richard G. Marschner, CFO; Robert Conrad, vp, prom mgr & progmg dir; Richard Marschner, gen mgr & adv mgr; John Simna, mus dir; T. Bianchi, news dir; Richard Agnes, chief engr. ■ Rates: $80; 55; 80; 55.

***WCPN(FM)**—Sept 8, 1984: 90.3 mhz; 50 kw. Ant 500 ft. TL: N41 22 18 W81 42 48. Stereo. Hrs opn: 19. Joseph E. Cole Bldg. for Continuing Education, 3100 Chester Ave. (44114). (216) 432-3700. Licensee: Cleveland Public Radio. Net: APR, NPR. Wash atty: Cohn & Marks. Format: News, jazz. News staff 4; news 45 hrs wkly. Target aud: General. Spec prog: Ger one hr, Hungarian one hr, Lithuanian one hr, Pol one hr, Slovak one hr, Slovenian one hr, Serbian one hr, Ukrainian one hr wkly. ■ Susan Turben, chmn; Kathryn Jensen, pres & gen mgr; Jim Goldurs, opns mgr; David Kanzeg, progmg dir; Harvey Zay, mus dir; Anabelle Singh, news dir; James Young, chief engr.

***WCRF(FM)**—Nov 23, 1958: 103.3 mhz; 25.5 kw. Ant 660 ft. TL: N41 17 48 W81 39 27. Stereo. Hrs opn: 24. 9756 Barr Rd. (44141). (216) 526-1111. Licensee: Moody Bible Institute of Chicago. (group owner). Net: Moody, USA. Wash atty: J. Southmayd. Format: Relg, inspirational. Target aud: General. ■ Dr. Joseph Stowell III, pres; Richard Lee, stn mgr; Gary Bittner, mus dir; Michael Fletcher, pub affrs dir; Doug Hainer, chief engr.

***WCSB(FM)**—May 10, 1976: 89.3 mhz; 1 kw. Ant 190 ft. TL: N41 30 12 W81 40 30. Stereo. Cleveland State Univ., Rhodes Tower, Suite 956 (44115). (216) 687-3523. Licensee: Cleveland State Univ. Format: Alternative. News progmg 7 hrs wkly. Target aud: General. Spec prog: Black 20 hrs, Ger one hr, jazz 12 hrs, Pol one hr, Arabic one hr, Czech one hr, Hungarian one hr, Celtic one hr, Sp 12 hrs, Indian 3 hrs, Slovenian one hr wkly. ■ William Kennedy, gen mgr; Lou Ziegter, prom dir; Wendell Clayton, prom mgr; Jim Szatkowski, adv dir; John Xorxes, mus dir; Christina White, news dir & pub affrs dir; Mark Manolio, chief engr.

WDOK(FM)—Listing follows WRMR(AM).

WENZ(FM)—July 14, 1959: 107.9 mhz; 70 kw. Ant 750 ft. TL: N41 28 03 W81 17 25. Stereo. Hrs opn: 24. 1510 Euclid Ave. (44115). (216) 348-0108. FAX: (216) 348-3658. Licensee: Ardman Broadcasting Corp. (group owner; acq 11-87; $4,700,000; FTR 11-23-87). Net: Unistar, NBC the Source. Rep: Torbet. Wash atty: Ginsburg, Feldman & Bress. Format: Modern rock. News staff one. Target aud: 18-34. ■ Myer Feldman, pres; William H. Scull, vp & gen mgr; Paul Lorko, sls dir; Marshall Goudy, prom mgr; Rick Lorko, progmg dir; Sean Robertson, mus dir; Vic Gideon, news dir; Barry Thomas, chief engr.

WERE(AM)—July 6, 1949: 1300 khz; 5 kw-U, DA-1. TL: N41 20 28 W81 44 29. Hrs opn: 24. 1041 Huron Rd. (44115). (216) 696-1300. FAX: (216) 781-0267. Licensee: Metroplex Communications Inc., an Ohio Corp. Group owner: Metroplex Communications Inc. (acq 2-5-92; no financial consideration, with co-located FM; FTR 2-24-92). Net: MBS, CNN. Rep: McGavren Guild. Format: News/talk, sports. News staff 4; news progmg 30 hrs wkly. Spec prog: Black 6 hrs, It one hr, Pol 2 hrs, relg 2 hrs, Slovak one hr, Czech one hr wkly. ■ Matt Mills, pres & gen mgr; Harvey Simms, gen sls mgr; John Ciulla, prom mgr; Sam Cappas, chief engr.

WNCX(FM)—Co-owned with WERE(AM). Oct 23, 1948: 98.5 mhz; 16 kw. Ant 960 ft. TL: N41 20 28 W81 44 29. Stereo. Hrs opn: 24. Prog sep from AM. (216) 861-0100. Net: ABC. Format: Classic rock. News staff one; news progmg one hr wkly. Spec prog: Black 2 hrs, jazz 2 hrs wkly. ■ Mike Graham, gen sls mgr; Doug Podell, progmg dir; Bill Louis, mus dir.

WGAR-FM—July 1948: 99.5 mhz; 50 kw. Ant 500 ft. TL: N41 22 18 W81 43 04. Stereo. Suite 530, 5005 Rockside Rd., Independence (44131). (216) 328-9950. FAX: (216) 328-9951. Licensee: Nationwide Communications Inc. Net: ABC/E. Rep: McGavren Guild. Format: Contemp country. News staff 3. Target aud: 25-54. ■ Steve Berger, pres; Mickey Franko, exec vp; John Blassingame, gen mgr; Denny Nugent, opns mgr, mktg dir & adv dir; Donna Gamblin, natl sls mgr; Betty Roth, rgnl sls mgr; Sanaa Julien, prom dir; Chuck Collier, mus dir; Ed Richards, news dir; Jim Syzmanski, pub affrs dir; Mark Kreiger, chief engr.

WHK(AM)—July 28, 1921: 1420 khz; 5 kw-U, DA-N. TL: N41 21 30 W81 40 03. Suite 200, 1660 W. 2nd St. (44113). (216) 781-1420. Licensee: Shamrock Broadcasting Inc. Group owner: Shamrock Broadcasting Inc. (acq 6-21-93; with co-located FM; FTR 7-5-93). Net: NBC. Rep: Katz. Format: Business news radio. ■ Walt Tiburski, gen mgr; Sandy Lyon, gen sls mgr; Gaye Ramstrom, natl sls mgr; Paul Cox, news dir; Mike Knisely, chief engr.

WMMS(FM)—Co-owned with WHK(AM). Nov 11, 1948: 100.7 mhz; 34 kw. Ant 600 ft. TL: N41 21 30 W81 40 03. Stereo. Prog sep from AM. (216) 781-9667. Net: NBC the Source. Format: AOR. ■ Mark Bishop, prom mgr; Michael Luczak, progmg dir; Brad Hansen, mus dir.

WJMO(AM)—See Cleveland Heights.

WJMO-FM—See Cleveland Heights.

WKNR(AM)—December 1930: 1220 khz; 50 kw-U, DA-1. TL: N41 18 26 W81 41 21. Stereo. 9446 Broadview Rd. (44147-2397). (216) 838-1220. Licensee: CV Radio Associates L.P. (acq 6-30-90; FTR 4-2-89). Net: ABC/E. Rep: Eastman. Format: All Sports. Target aud: 25-54; male sports fans. ■ Frank Mancini, James R. Glass (asst), gen mgrs; Phil McDonald, gen sls mgr; Geoff Belzer, prom mgr; Jack Callaghan, news dir; John Hovanec, chief engr.

WLTF(FM)—Listing follows WWWE(AM).

WMJI(FM)—Dec 6, 1948: 105.7 mhz; 27 kw. Ant 900 ft. TL: N41 23 09 W81 41 23 (CP: 15.5 kw, ant 1,020 ft.). Stereo. Hrs opn: 24. Sixth Fl., 310 Lakeside Ave. (44113). (216) 623-1105. Licensee: Legacy Broadcasting Partners L.P. (acq 1-16-91). Net: NBC, AP. Rep: Katz. Format: Oldies. News staff 4; news progmg 5 hrs wkly. Target aud: 25-54. ■ Dean Thacker, exec vp & gen mgr; John Gorman, opns mgr; Gaye Ramstrom, natl sls mgr; Errol Dengler, vp mktg; Shane Hollett, prom dir; John Webster, news dir; Wayne Boggs, chief engr.

WMMS(FM)—Listing follows WHK(AM).

WNCX(FM)—Listing follows WERE(AM).

WQAL(FM)—1948: 104.1 mhz; 11 kw. Ant 1,060 ft. TL: N41 22 45 W81 43 12. Stereo. Hrs opn: 24. 1621 Euclid Ave. (44115-2138). (216) 696-6666. FAX: (216) 348-0104. Licensee: WIN Communications Inc./M.L. Media. Group owner: WIN Communications Inc. (acq 8-26-88). Rep: Banner. Wash atty: Wiley, Rein & Fielding. Format:

Adult contemp. News staff one. Target aud: 25-49; women. ■ David Uribach, vp & gen mgr; Larry Gawthrop, gen sls mgr; Steve Legerski, prom mgr; Dave Ervin, progmg dir; Sally Spitz, news dir; Dave MacKenzie, chief engr.

WRDZ(AM)—Apr 3, 1950: 1260 khz; 5 kw-U, DA-2. TL: N41 17 10 W81 38 34. Stereo. Hrs opn: 24. 8200 Snowville Rd. (44141). (216) 526-8989; (216) 253-1260. FAX: (216) 526-9781. Licensee: Gore-Overgaard Broadcasting Inc. (acq 8-1-88; $845,000; FTR 8-1-88). Net: USA. Wash atty: Haley, Bader & Potts. Format: Inspirational/adult contemp Christian. News progmg 5 hrs wkly. Target aud: 25-54; Christian church-going, family-oriented adults. Spec prog: Sp 17 hrs, It 4 hrs, Romanian one hr, Serbian one hr wkly. ■ Harold W. Gore, CEO; Cordell Overgaard, pres; Tony Lupo, vp & gen mgr; Lisa Lupo, stn mgr; Bil Webb, prom dir, progmg dir & mus dir; Don McGoun, asst mus dir; Mike Reynolds, pub affrs dir; Wayne Boggs, chief engr. ■ Rates: $20; 20; 20; 20.

WRMR(AM)—1926: 850 khz; 10 kw-D, 5 kw-N, DA-2. TL: N41 19 00 W81 43 51. Stereo. Hrs opn: 24. One Radio Ln. (44114). (216) 696-0123. Licensee: Independent Group L.P. Net: CNN. Rep: Major Mkt. Format: Nostalgia-Music of Your Life. News staff one; news progmg 3 hrs wkly. Target aud: 45 plus. Spec prog: Greek one hr; Jewish 2 hrs, Irish one hr, Ukranian one hr, Czech one hr wkly. ■ Tom Embrescia, CEO, pres & gen mgr; Sue Wilson, vp opns; Fred Embrescia, vp dev; Chris Madori, vp sls; Andrea Hess, prom dir; Jim Davis, vp progmg; Mark DiMarino, news dir; Ted Alexander, chief engr. ■ Rates: $75; 75; 75; 40.

WDOK(FM)—Co-owned with WRMR(AM). Apr 30, 1950: 102.1 mhz; 12 kw. Ant 1,004 ft. TL: N41 23 02 W81 42 06. Stereo. Prog sep from AM. Format: Soft adult contemp. News progmg one hr wkly. Target aud: 25-54. ■ Tom Embrescia, chmn; Sharon Day, natl sls mgr; Janet Pierce, rgnl sls mgr; Andrea Hess, prom mgr; Sue Wilson, progmg dir; Bobby Thomas, mus dir. ■ Rates: $225; 225; 225; 100.

***WRUW-FM**—Feb 26, 1967: 91.1 mhz; 1 kw. Ant 270 ft. TL: N41 31 14 W81 35 03 (CP: 14.5 kw, ant 276 ft.). Stereo. 11220 Bellflower Rd. (44106). (216) 368-2208. Licensee: Case Western Reserve Univ. Format: Div. Spec prog: Jazz 15 hrs, Pol 3 hrs, classical 4 hrs, folk 12 hrs, public affairs 5 hrs, reggae 7 hrs wkly. ■ Ben Winter, gen mgr; Crys Gee, prom dir; Sean Carney, progmg dir; Wade Tolleson, mus dir; Chuck Poulton, chief engr.

WWWE(AM)—1923: 1100 khz; 50 kw-U. TL: N41 16 50 W81 37 22. Hrs opn: 24. Western Reserve Bldg., 8th Floor, 1468 W. 9th St. (44113). (216) 696-4444. FAX: (216) 781-5143. Licensee: Booth American Co. (group owner; acq 6-90; $10 million plus trade of WRMR-AM). Net: ABC/I. Rep: Christal. Wash atty: Dow, Lohnes & Albertson. Format: News/talk, sports. News staff 9; news progmg 25 hrs wkly. Target aud: 35-64. ■ John L. Booth II, pres; Roger R. Turner, vp & gen mgr; Dave Popovich, opns mgr; Corrine L. Bomba, Debbie Fragapane, prom mgrs; Jay Clarke, progmg dir; Ed Coury, news dir; Ray Davis, pub affrs dir; Dave Szucs, chief engr.

WLTF(FM)—Co-owned with WWWE(AM). May 4, 1960: 106.5 mhz; 11.3 kw. Ant 1,036 ft. TL: N41 22 45 W81 43 12. Stereo. Prog sep from AM. Format: Adult contemp. News staff 9; news progmg 3 hrs wkly. Target aud: 25-54. ■ Debi Fargapane, mktg mgr.

WZAK(FM)—May 26, 1963: 93.1 mhz; 27.5 kw. Ant 620 ft. TL: N41 16 50 W81 37 22. Stereo. Hrs opn: 24. Suite 401, 2510 St. Clair Ave. (44114). (216) 621-9300. FAX: (216) 771-4164. Licensee: Zapis Communications Corp. Rep: D & R Radio. Wash atty: Bryan, Cave, McPheeters & McRoberts. Format: Urban contemp. Target aud: 18-49; Black adults. ■ Xenophon Zapis, pres & gen mgr; Lee Zapis, vp opns & vp prom; Michael Hilber, vp sls; George Cohn, natl sls mgr; Christina Grannetti, prom dir; Lynn Tolliver Jr., progmg dir; Bobby Bush, mus dir; Kim Johnson, pub affrs dir; Alfred Warmus, chief engr.

Cleveland Heights

WJMO(AM)—1947: 1490 khz; 1 kw-U. TL: N41 30 48 W81 36 05. Hrs opn: 24. 11821 Euclid Ave., Cleveland (44106). (216) 795-1212. FAX: (216) 791-9035. Licensee: Zebra Broadcasting Corp. ($4.25 million with co-located FM; FTR 6-14-93). Net: ABC/FM. Rep: Major Mkt. Wash atty: Arent, Fox, Kintner, Plotkin & Kahn. Format: Solid gold soul. News staff 2; news progmg 4 hrs wkly. Target aud: 25-54; Black adults. ■ Gerald J. Hroblak, pres; Art Dawson, CFO; Curtis E. Shaw, vp & gen mgr; Paul Guy, gen sls mgr; Sharon Williams, prom mgr; Ken Allen, progmg dir; Armetta Landrum, news dir & pub affrs dir; Jerry Goforth, chief engr. ■ Rates: $50; 40; 50; 30.

WJMO-FM—Nov 23, 1960: 92.3 mhz; 40 kw. Ant 548 ft. TL: N41 30 01 W81 33 59. Stereo. Prog sep from AM. 2156 Lee Rd. (44118). (216) 371-3534. FAX: (216) 371-0174. Format: CHR. News staff one; news progmg 2 hrs wkly. Target aud: 18-34; mass appeal, young adults. ■ Curtis E. Shaw, vp; Kathy Franseen, gen sls mgr; Marie Griffen-Gallo, prom mgr; Keith Clark, progmg dir; Don Jackson, mus dir. ■ Rates: $1.50; 1.50; 1.50; 1.50.

Clyde

***WHVT(FM)**—December 1986: 90.5 mhz; 370 w. Ant 170 ft. TL: N41 17 45 W82 58 26 (CP: 2.6 kw, ant 154 ft.). 144 Lemon St. (43410). (419) 547-8251. Licensee: Clyde Educ. Broadcasting Foundation. Format: Educ, relg. ■ James Lewis, pres; Jim Waugh, gen mgr.

WNCG(FM)—July 16, 1981: 100.9 mhz; 3 kw. Ant 300 ft. TL: N41 14 57 W82 54 47. Stereo. Hrs opn: 24. Box 66, 109 N. Main St. (43410). (419) 547-8792. FAX: (419) 547-6649. Licensee: S&S Communications Group Inc. (acq 2-7-92; $280,000; FTR 3-2-92). Net: ABC. Rep: Rgnl Reps. Wash atty: Irwin, Campbell & Crowe. Format: Classic hits. News progmg 2 hrs wkly. Target aud: 25-54. ■ Kent D. Smith, chmn & engrg dir; David L. Searfoss, pres & sls dir; Maria L. Smith, stn mgr; Mark Stewart, progmg dir; Sandy Beach, news dir. ■ Rates: $43; 41; 43; 32.

WNRR(FM)—See Bellevue.

Coal Grove

WXVK(FM)—Feb 1, 1990: 97.1 mhz; 3 kw. Ant 472 ft. TL: N38 25 27 W82 32 04. Box 2288, 134 Fourth Ave., Huntington, WV (25724-2288). (304) 525-7788; (304) 523-9700. FAX: (304) 525-6281. Licensee: Adventure Three Communications Inc. (group owner; acq 3-18-93; $260,000; FTR 4-5-93). Format: Hot country. News staff one; news progmg 9 hrs wkly. Target aud: General; adults 35 plus with 80% or disposable income. ■ Toufie Kassab, gen mgr; Greg Evans, progmg dir; Elliot Gerringer, chief engr. ■ Rates: $24; 24; 24; 24.

Columbus

WBNS(AM)—1922: 1460 khz; 5 kw-D, 1 kw-N, DA-N. TL: N39 57 06 W82 54 23. Hrs opn: 24. 175 S. Third St. (43215). (614) 460-3850. FAX: (614) 460-3757. Licensee: RadiOhio Inc. (acq 1933). Net: CBS. Rep: Banner. Format: Adult contemp, MOR. Spec prog: Ohio State football & basketball. ■ Dana Harmon, vp & gen mgr; Ed Douglas, opns mgr, progmg dir & mus dir; Tom Pierce, gen sls mgr; Karen Reddington, prom mgr; Sharon Rich, news dir; Ron McGrew, chief engr.

WBNS-FM—June 1959: 97.1 mhz; 26 kw. Ant 660 ft. TL: N39 58 16 W83 01 40 (CP: 20.5 kw, ant 800 ft.). Stereo. Prog sep from AM. Format: Oldies. ■ WBNS-TV affil.

WBZX(FM)—Listing follows WMNI(AM).

WCKX(FM)—See London.

WCOL-FM—1947: 92.3 mhz; 22 kw. Ant 754 ft. TL: N39 58 16 W83 01 40. Stereo. 195 E. Broad (43215). (614) 221-7811. Licensee: Nationwide Communications Inc. (group owner; acq 11-24-93; $15 million with co-located FM; FTR 12-13-93). Net: Unistar. Rep: Christal. Format: Oldies. ■ David Van Stone, gen mgr; Jason Roberts, mus dir; Angela Summers, news dir; John Baumann, chief engr.

WCOL(AM)—1922: 1230 khz; 1 kw-U. TL: N39 56 31 W83 01 20. Stereo. Dups FM 100%.

WLVQ(FM)—Listing follows WTVN(AM).

WMNI(AM)—Apr 26, 1958: 920 khz; 1 kw-D, 500 w-N, DA-2. TL: N39 53 32 W83 02 51. Hrs opn: 24. 1458 Dublin Rd. (43215). (614) 481-7800. FAX: (614) 481-8070. Licensee: North American Broadcasting Co. Net: MBS, NBC; Agri Bcstg. Rep: Eastman. Wash atty: Hogan & Hartson. Format: Country. News staff 3; news progmg 20 hrs wkly. Target aud: 35 plus. Spec prog: Farm 2 hrs, relg 2 hrs wkly. ■ Norma J. Mnich, CEO; Matthew Mnich, pres; Mark E. Jividen, vp & gen mgr; Thomas R. Simkins, vp sls & gen sls mgr; Greg Moebius, prom dir & prom mgr; Steve Cantrell, progmg dir; Joe Cunningham, mus dir; Mark Nuce, news dir; Kathryn Dillard, pub affrs dir; Bill Bowin, chief engr.

WBZX(FM)—Co-owned with WMNI(AM). April 26, 1962: 99.7 mhz; 20 kw. Ant 784 ft. TL: N39 58 16 W83 01 40. Stereo. Hrs opn: 24. Prog sep from AM. Rep: Eastman. Format: Rock. Target aud: 18-49. ■ Hal Fish, progmg dir; Ronnie Hunter, mus dir; Mark Howell, news dir.

WNCI(FM)—July 1961: 97.9 mhz; 175 kw. Ant 560 ft. TL: N39 58 10 W83 00 10. Stereo. One Nationwide Plaza, 2nd Fl. (43215). (614) 224-9624. Licensee: Nationwide Communications Inc. (group owner). Rep: Major Mkt. Wash atty: Fletcher, Heald & Hildreth. Format: Adult contemp. ■ Steven Berger, pres; Dan S. Morris, gen mgr; Katie Corbett-Cyr, gen sls mgr; Dan Bowen, prom mgr & mus dir; Dave Robbins, progmg dir; Jeff Gulick, chief engr.

***WOSU(AM)**—Apr 24, 1922: 820 khz; 5 kw-D, 790 w-N, (L-WBAP Ft. Worth, Tex). TL: N40 01 44 W82 03 22 (CP: 1 kw-N). Hrs opn: 5 AM-11 PM, Mon-Fri; 6 AM-midnight Sat-Sun. 2400 Olentangy River Rd. (43210). (614) 292-9678. FAX: (614) 292-0513. Licensee: Ohio State Univ. Net: NPR, AP, APR; Ohio Radio Network. Wash atty: Dow, Lohnes & Albertson. Format: News, pub affrs. News staff 12; news progmg 114 hrs wkly. Target aud: 25 plus. Men & women 25 yrs & older. Spec prog: Black one hr, bluegrass 12 hrs wkly. ■ Dale K. Ouzts, gen mgr; Sam Eiler, stn mgr; Gary May, opns dir; Joyce Schreiber, dev dir; Don Scott, mktg dir; Joe Banicki, prom mgr; Howard R. Ornstein, progmg dir; Christina Morgan, news dir; Larry W. Reynolds, chief engr.

***WOSU-FM**—Dec 13, 1949: 89.7 mhz; 13.3 kw. Ant 938 ft. TL: N39 56 16 W83 01 16. Stereo. Hrs opn: 24. Prog sep from AM. Net: APR, AP. Format: Class mus. News progmg 3 hrs wkly. Target aud: 25 plus; men & women 25 & older. ■ David B. Carwile, progmg dir; Bev Ervine, asst mus dir. ■ *WOSU-TV affil.

WRFD(AM)—(Columbus-Worthington). Sept 27, 1947: 880 khz; 9 kw-D. TL: N40 09 32 W83 00 36. Box 802, N. High at Powell Rd. (43085). (614) 885-5342. FAX: (614) 885-6322. Licensee: Salem Media of Ohio Inc. Group owner: Salem Communications Corp. (acq 2-1-82; $1,800,000; FTR 12-21-81). Net: USA. Format: Relg, farm. ■ Edward Atzinger III, pres; Bill Caridas, gen mgr & progmg dir; Mike Reed, gen sls mgr; Doug Leonard, chief engr.

WRZR(FM)—(Johnstown). June 16, 1975: 103.1 mhz; 3 kw. Ant 444 ft. TL: N40 13 44 W82 39 32. Stereo. 1150 Morse Rd., Columbus (43229); 44 S. Main St., Johnstown (43031). (614) 846-1031; (614) 967-6776. FAX: (614) 436-1486. Licensee: Ragan Henry Communications Group L.P. Group owner: Ragan Henry Broadcast Group Inc. (acq 6-89). Rep: D & R Radio. Format: Rock. News staff one. Target aud: 18-49; upscale, professional; homeowners with disposable incomes. ■ Regan Henry, CEO; Don Kidwell, pres; Susan Cline, gen mgr; Bryan Jester, mktg dir & prom dir; Ron Michals, mus dir; Matt Humphreys, pub affrs dir.

WSNY(FM)—Listing follows WVKO(AM).

WTVN(AM)—1924: 610 khz; 5 kw-U, DA-N. TL: N39 52 26 W82 58 36. 1301 Dublin Rd. (43215-7009). (614) 486-6101. FAX: (614) 487-2559. Licensee: Great American Broadcasting (group owner; acq 7-24-54). Net: ABC/I. Rep: Katz. Wash atty: Koteen & Naftalin. Format: Adult contemp. News staff 8; new progmg 30 hrs wkly. Target aud: 25-54; leaning male. ■ Perry A. Frey, pres & gen mgr; Bobby Hatfield, opns mgr; John Potter, gen sls mgr; Jan Chamberlin, prom mgr; Mike Perkins, progmg dir; John Lane, mus dir; Dave Claborn, news dir; Liz Evans, pub affrs dir; Greg Savoldi, chief engr.

WLVQ(FM)—Co-owned with WTVN(AM). April 1, 1959: 96.3 mhz; 40 kw. Ant 550 ft. TL: N39 58 16 W83 01 40. Stereo. Prog sep from AM. (614) 488-9696. Format: Rock. News staff one; news progmg 15 hrs wkly. Target aud: 18-44; leaning male. ■ Tom Thon, vp & gen mgr; Gary Mincer, gen sls mgr; Annie Vian, prom mgr; Bob Neumann, progmg dir; Jo Robinson, mus dir; Kristy Kemper, news dir.

WVKO(AM)—Nov 21, 1951: 1580 khz; 1 kw-D, 250 w-N, DA-2. TL: N40 02 50 W83 03 44. Hrs opn: 24. 4401 Carriage Hill Ln. (43220). (614) 451-2191. Licensee: Franklin Communications Inc. Group owner: Saga Communications Inc. (acq 5-14-82; $2,500,000; FTR 1-18-82). Rep: McGavren Guild. Format: Urban contemp. ■ Al Fetch, pres & gen mgr; Bill Brooks, gen sls mgr; Sam Nelson, progmg dir; James Evans, news dir; John Marocchi, chief engr.

WSNY(FM)—Co-owned with WVKO(AM). Nov 11, 1948: 94.7 mhz; 22 kw. Ant 753 ft. TL: N39 58 16 W83 01 40. Stereo. Prog sep from AM. Format: Adult contemp. ■ Christine Graves, gen sls mgr; Colleen McCann, prom mgr; Don Hallett, progmg dir; Bob Nunnally, mus dir; Clark Donley, news dir.

Columbus-Worthington

WRFD(AM)—Licensed to Columbus-Worthington. See Columbus.

Stations in the U.S. | Ohio

Conneaut

*WGOJ(FM)—Apr 5, 1964: 105.5 mhz; 3 kw. Ant 295 ft. TL: N41 51 42 W80 31 01 (CP: 6 kw). Stereo. Hrs opn: 24. Box 725 (44030). (216) 599-7252. Licensee: Bible Broadcasting Inc. (acq 1979). Format: Christian. Target aud: General. ■ Roger P. Hogle, pres & gen mgr; Robert Jackson (asst), stn mgr; Jonathon Pulaski, pub affrs dir; Floyd Huston, chief engr.

WWOW(AM)—Oct 25, 1959: 1360 khz; 500 w-D. TL: N41 55 32 W80 32 32. 239 Broad St. (44030). (216) 593-2233. FAX: (216) 593-4470. Licensee: Contemporary Media Inc. (acq 1-1-80). Net: UPI. Format: Country. Spec prog: Farm one hr wkly. ■ Doyle Flurry, pres; Sally Terry, gen mgr; Ken Vaughn, news dir; Ron Terry, chief engr.

Cortland

WKTX(AM)—Apr 1, 1985: 830 khz; 1 kw-D. TL: N41 22 53 W80 43 12. 178 N. Mecca (44410). (216) 638-2425. FAX: (216) 221-3638. Licensee: Nationality Broadcasting (acq 10/91). Net: AP. Format: Greek, nostalgia, oldies. ■ Miklos Kossanyi, pres; Attila Kossanyi, vp; Maria Kossanyi, stn mgr; Jack Cory, progmg dir.

Coshocton

WTNS(AM)—Nov 9, 1947: 1560 khz; 1 kw-D. TL: N40 16 30 W81 49 37. 114 N. 6th St. (43812). (614) 622-1560. FAX: (614) 622-7940. Licensee: Coshocton Broadcasting Co. (group owner; acq 9-86; $560,652.82; FTR 9-22-86). Net: AP. Format: Country. ■ Bruce Wallace, pres & gen mgr; Tom Thompson, gen sls mgr; Brad Haynes, mus dir; Debbie Hill, news dir; Jay Drummond, chief engr.

WTNS-FM—April 25, 1968: 99.3 mhz; 1.2 kw. Ant 440 ft. TL: N40 16 30 W81 49 37. Format: Adult contemp.

Covington

WPTW(AM)—See Piqua.

Crestline

WAPQ(FM)—Licensed to Crestline. See Mansfield.

Crooksville

WYBZ(FM)—Oct 26, 1990: 107.3 mhz; 3 kw. Ant 328 ft. TL: N39 47 23 W82 05 39 (CP: Ant 302 ft.). Stereo. Hrs opn: 24. Box 4310, Zanesville (43702). (614) 453-6004. FAX: (614) 453-5865. Licensee: Rick N. Sabine, Walter D. Winner, Edgar Davis and David A. Ringer (acq 12-26-90; $60,000; FTR 1-14-91). Net: CNN, Unistar. Wash atty: Smithwick & Belenduick. Format: Oldies. News staff one; news progmg 9 hrs wkly. Target aud: 25-55. ■ Rick Sabine, pres, gen mgr, gen sls mgr & chief engr; Robert Stolz, news dir.

Cuyahoga Falls

*WCUE(AM)—1950: 1150 khz; 5 kw-U, DA-2. TL: N41 12 05 W81 31 25. Hrs opn: 24. 4075 Bellaire Ln., Peninsula (44264). (216) 920-1150. Licensee: Family Stations Inc. (group owner; acq 10-22-86). Net: UPI. Wash atty: Dow, Lohnes & Albertson. Format: Relg. News progmg 4 hrs wkly. Target aud: 25 plus; Christians. Spec prog: Class 2 hrs wkly. ■ Harold Camping, pres; P. Michael Zeimann, stn mgr; Curt Flick, chief engr.

WKDD(FM)—See Akron.

WQAL(FM)—See Cleveland.

Dayton

WDAO(AM)—March 1, 1955: 1210 khz; 1 kw-D. TL: N39 43 36 W84 12 23. 4309 W. Dr. Martin Luther King Jr. Way (45417). (513) 263-9326. FAX: (513) 263-6100. Licensee: Johnson Communications Inc. (acq 1-88; $725,000; FTR 1-18-88). Rep: Christal. Format: Urban contemp. ■ Jim Johnson, vp & gen mgr; Micheal Ecton, prom mgr, progmg dir & mus dir; Gene Simmons, chief engr.

*WDPR(FM)—1976: 89.5 mhz; 6 kw. Ant 270 ft. ST *WDPS(FM) Dayton. TL: N39 45 26 W84 12 24. Stereo. 126 N. Main St. (45402). (513) 496-3850. FAX: (513) 496-3852. Licensee: Dayton Public Radio Inc. (acq 6-1-85). Format: Class, jazz. ■ John E. Kohnlee, pres; William L. Combs, gen mgr; Charles W. Wilson, mus dir.

*WDPS(FM)—1976: 89.5 mhz; 200 w. Ant 198 ft. TL: N39 45 26 W84 12 24. Hrs opn: 9:15 AM-4:30 PM. 441 River Corridor Dr. (45402). (513) 223-5999. FAX: (513) 228-8286. Licensee: Dayton Public Schools (acq 1976). Format: Educ, jazz. News progmg 2 hrs wkly. Spec prog: Black 5 hrs, Celtic 2 hrs, folk 4 hrs, pub affrs 6 hrs wkly. ■ Dale White, pres; Michael Reisz, gen mgr, progmg dir; mus dir & news dir; Tobi Weatherspoon, asst mus dir; Tom Nornhold, chief engr.

WFCJ(FM)—See Miamisburg.

WGTZ(FM)—See Eaton.

*WGXM(FM)—October 1974: 97.3 mhz; 129 w. Ant 100 ft. TL: N39 43 37 W84 11 33 (CP: 98.1 mhz). Stereo. 2251 Timber Lane (45414). (513) 275-8434. Licensee: Northridge Local School Dist. Bd. of Educ. Format: C&W, educ, adult contemp. ■ William Howell, gen mgr.

WHIO(AM)—Feb 9, 1935: 1290 khz; 5 kw-U, DA-N. TL: N39 40 41 W84 07 53. Stereo. Box 1206, 1414 Wilmington Ave. (45420). (513) 259-2111. FAX: (513) 259-2168; (513) 259-2024. Licensee: WHIO Inc. Group owner: Cox Broadcasting. Net: NBC Talknet, AP. Rep: D & R Radio. Wash atty: Dows, Lohnes & Albertson. Format: Full svc news/talk. Target aud: 35-64. ■ Chuck Browning, gen mgr; Brent Millar, gen sls mgr; Jackie Heitman, mktg dir; Wes Minter, progmg dir; Jim Barrett, news dir; Ron Gaier, chief engr.

WHKO(FM)—Co-owned with WHIO(AM). 1946: 99.1 mhz; 50 kw. Ant 1,060 ft. TL: N39 44 03 W84 14 50. Stereo. Prog sep from AM. Format: Country. ■ Don Cristi, progmg dir. ■ WHIO-TV affil.

WING(AM)—May 24, 1921: 1410 khz; 5 kw-U, DA-N. TL: N39 40 56 W84 09 33. 717 E. David Rd. (45429). (513) 294-5858. FAX: (513) 297-5233. Licensee: Great Trails Broadcasting Corp. (group owner; acq 5-39). Net: NBC, SMN. Rep: Katz. Wash atty: Michael Bader. Format: CNN News. News staff one; news progmg 10 hrs wkly. Target aud: 25-54; vanguard of baby boomers. ■ David Macejko, vp & gen mgr; Allyson Berry, prom mgr; Louis Kaplan, progmg dir; Kim Faris, news dir; Will Bevis, chief engr.

WLQT(FM)—See Kettering.

WMMX(FM)—September 1964: 107.7 mhz; 50 kw. Ant 420 ft. TL: N39 43 36 W84 12 23. Stereo. Suite 200, 101 Pine St. (45402). (513) 224-1137. FAX: (513) 224-3667. Licensee: American Radio Systems License Corp. Group owner: American Radio Systems (acq 9-15-93; FTR 10-4-93). Rep: Eastman. Format: Adult contemp. Target aud: 25-54. ■ Glen Bell, pres; Deborah Parenti, gen mgr; Josh Gertzog, gen sls mgr; Teresa Strong, prom mgr; Randy James, progmg dir; Dean Taylor, mus dir; Darrel Gray, news dir; Jeff Bennett, chief engr.

WONE(AM)—March 20, 1949: 980 khz; 5 kw-U, DA-N. TL: N39 40 43 W84 10 01. Stereo. Hrs opn: 24. Suite 200, 101 Pine St. (45402). (513) 224-1137. FAX: (513) 224-3667. Licensee: American Radio Systems License Corp. Group owner: American Radio Systems (acq 9-15-93; with co-located AM); FTR 10-4-93). Net: ABC/I. Rep: Eastman. Format: Sports, talk. News staff 3; news progmg 18 hrs wkly. Target aud: 35-64. ■ Deborah Parenti, vp & gen mgr; Randy James, opns mgr; Jennifer A. Jacques, gen sls mgr; Lora Lewis, prom mgr; Lee Riley, progmg dir & mus dir; Jeff Bennett, chief engr.

WTUE(FM)—Co-owned with WONE(AM). 1959: 104.7 mhz; 50 kw. Ant 418 ft. TL: N39 43 19 W84 12 36. Stereo. Hrs opn: 24. Prog sep from AM. Rep: Eastman. Format: AOR. News staff one; news progmg 2 hrs wkly. Target aud: 18-49. ■ Tom Carroll, progmg dir; John Beaulieu, mus dir.

*WQRP(FM)—See West Carrollton.

WTUE(FM)—Listing follows WONE(AM).

*WWSU(FM)—April 4, 1977: 106.9 mhz; 10 w. Ant 150 ft. TL: N39 46 57 W84 03 43. 044 University Center, 3640 Colonel Glenn Hwy. (45435). (513) 873-5554. Licensee: Wright State University. Format: Prog rock. News progmg 3 hrs wkly. Target aud: 15-26; college & high school students. Spec prog: Black 6 hrs, class 3 hrs, relg 2 hrs wkly. ■ Pete Ziehler, gen mgr; Greg Short, progmg dir; Martin Stajkowski, chief engr.

De Graff

*WDEQ-FM—Sept 1, 1967: 103.3 mhz; 10 w. Ant 23 ft. TL: N40 18 48 W83 55 06. Moore St. (43318). (513) 585-5981. Licensee: Riverside Local Board of Education. Format: Educ. ■ James A. Grove, gen mgr & stn mgr.

Defiance

WDFM(FM)—June 25, 1985: 98.1 mhz; 50 kw. Ant 500 ft. TL: N41 17 28 W84 32 17. Stereo. Hrs opn: 24. 118 Clinton St. (43512). (419) 782-9336. Licensee: Wolfe Communications Inc. Net: ABC/D. Wash atty: Fletcher, Heald & Hildreth. Format: Adult contemp. Target aud: 18-49. ■ Robert R. Wolfe, pres, gen mgr & chief engr; Frances E. Wolfe, gen sls mgr. ■ Rates: $22.31; 20.28; 22.31; 15.21.

WONW(AM)—1949: 1280 khz; 1 kw-D, 500 w-N, DA-N. TL: N41 14 44 W84 23 50. Hrs opn: 5 AM-midnight. 2110 Radio Dr. (43512); 709 N. Perry St., Napoleon (43545). (419) 782-8126; (419) 782-7776. FAX: (419) 784-4154. Licensee: Maumee Valley Broadcasting Inc. (acq 6-87). Net: MBS; Agri Bcstg. Rep: Rgnl Reps. Wash atty: Miller & Fields. Format: C&W. News staff 2. Target aud: General. Spec prog: Rush Limbaugh, Ger 4 hrs wkly. ■ C. Richard McBroom, CEO & pres; Robert E. McLimans, sr vp & gen mgr; Connie Bechtol, vp & gen sls mgr; Joe Chontos, opns mgr; Joseph Chontos, progmg dir & mus dir; Denny Gordon, news dir. ■ Rates: $13.75; 11; 12; 9.50.

WZOM(FM)—Aug 25, 1989: 105.9 mhz; 3 kw. Ant 347 ft. TL: N41 13 23 W84 22 36. Stereo. Hrs opn: 24. 2110 Radio Dr. (43512); 709 N. Perry St., Napoleon (43545). (419) 784-1059. FAX: (419) 784-4154. Licensee: Maumee Valley Broadcasting Inc. (acq 2/1/93). Net: SMN. Rep: Rgnl Reps. Format: Oldies. News staff 2; news progmg 15 hrs wkly. Target aud: 25-54; upscale adults, baby boomers. Spec prog: Relg 6 hrs wkly. ■ C. Richard McBroom, CEO & pres; Robert E. McLimans, sr vp & gen mgr; Connie Bechtol, vp & gen sls mgr; Robert E. Limans, gen mgr; Rick Small, opns mgr; John Clark, progmg dir. ■ Rates: $16; 13.75; 13.75; 13.75.

Delaware

WCEZ(FM)—June 21, 1991: 107.9 mhz; 6 kw. Ant 285 ft. TL: N40 17 57 W83 02 45. Stereo. Hrs opn: 24. Suite 335, One Campus View Blvd., Columbus (43235). (614) 848-3108. FAX: (614) 433-7108. Licensee: Radio Delaware Inc. (acq 3-7-91; FTR 4-1-91). Rep: Katz & Powell, Rngl Reps. Format: Easy listening. Target aud: 35-64; people with high school/college aged children & more diposable income. Spec prog: Broadway shows one hr, jazz 3 hrs wkly. ■ Jim Shaheen Sr., CEO, chmn, pres, CFO & gen mgr; Jim Shaheen Jr., opns mgr, vp prom & progmg dir; Tim Stinson, gen sls mgr; Joe Ternovan, chief engr. ■ Rates: $35; 30; 35; 30.

WDLR(AM)—Jan 18, 1961: 1550 khz; 500 w-D, 29 w-N, DA-2. TL: N40 17 56 W83 02 46. 501 Bowtown Rd. (43015). (614) 363-1107. Licensee: Radio Delaware Inc. (acq 2-74). Net: CNN; Agri Bcstg. Rep: Rgnl Reps. Format: All news. News staff 2; news progmg 126 hrs wkly. Target aud: 25 plus. ■ Jim Shaheen, pres & gen mgr; Sherry Fisher, news dir; Gary Cope, chief engr.

*WSLN(FM)—April 28, 1952: 98.7 mhz; 100 w. Ant 105 ft. TL: N40 17 46 W84 22 36. Stereo. Ohio Wesleyan Univ., 40 Slocum Hall (43015). (614) 369-4431. FAX: (614) 368-3314. Licensee: The Trustees of Ohio Wesleyan University. Net: ABC/FM. Format: Progvs rock (AOR), Black, jazz. ■ Stacey Colley, gen mgr; David Barash, chief engr.

Delphos

WDOH(FM)—Dec 16, 1972: 107.1 mhz; 3 kw. Ant 300 ft. TL: N40 49 55 W84 21 11. Stereo. Box 100, 111 E. 2nd St. (45833). (419) 642-3963. FAX: (419) 692-5896. Licensee: Vogel Roach Corp. Net: CBS. Format: Country. Spec prog: Farm 8 hrs wkly. ■ David P. Roach, pres & gen mgr; William J. Lyons, gen sls mgr; Bob Ulm, progmg dir & news dir; Dave Morris, chief engr.

Delta

WMHE(FM)—Not on air, target date unknown: 106.5 mhz; 3 kw. Ant 328 ft. TL: N41 35 13 W83 54 11. Stn currently dark. 4029 Deepwood Ln., Toledo (43614). Licensee: Toledo Radio Inc. (acq 8-3-93; $149,920.86; FTR 8-23-93).

Dover

WJER-FM—Licensed to Dover. See Dover-New Philadelphia.

Dover-New Philadelphia

WJER-FM—(Dover). Aug 29, 1968: 101.7 mhz; 3 kw. Ant 280 ft. TL: N40 33 50 W81 31 05. Stereo. Hrs opn: 24. 646 Blvd., Dover (44622). (216) 343-7755. FAX: (216) 364-4538. Licensee: WJER Radio Inc. (acq 3-9-77). Format: Adult contemp. Spec prog: Farm 2 hrs wkly. ■ Gary Petricola, pres; Bob Scanlon, vp & gen mgr; Dan Pitzo, gen sls mgr; Steve Anderson, progmg dir; Steve Kelley, mus dir; Matt Ritzert, news dir; Bruce Whitsel, chief engr.

Broadcasting & Cable Yearbook 1994
B-285

Ohio

Directory of Radio

WJER(AM)—Feb 10, 1950: 1450 khz; 1 kw-U. TL: N40 30 46 W81 27 24. Dups FM 100%. Net: AP. Rep: Rgnl Reps.

East Liverpool

WOHI(AM)—Dec 1, 1949: 1490 khz; 1 kw-U. TL: N40 37 47 W80 36 09 (CP: 660 w-U). Box 2050, 15655 St. Rt. 170 (43920). (216) 385-1490. Licensee: Constrander Corp. (acq 10-71). Net: ABC/E, SMN. Rep: Rgnl Reps. Wash atty: Dow, Lohnes & Albertson. Format: Oldies, talk, sports. News staff 2; news progmg 21 hrs wkly. Target aud: General. Spec prog: Big band 4 hrs, gospel one hr wkly. ■ Frank Mangano, pres; Ron Aughinbaugh, vp, gen mgr & gen sls mgr; Jim Martin, prom mgr, progmg dir & mus dir; John Rambo, news dir; Jan Nicholson, chief engr. ■ Rates: $16; 15.50; 16; 11.25.

WELA(FM)—Co-owned with WOHI(AM). Apr 15, 1959: 104.3 mhz; 50 kw. Ant 330 ft. TL: N40 37 48 W80 36 10. Stereo. Prog sep from AM. Format: Country. News progmg 14 hrs wkly. ■ Kalen Boyd, prom mgr, progmg dir & mus dir. ■ Rates: $17; 16; 17; 15.

Eaton

WCTM(AM)—January 1979: 1130 khz; 250 w-D, DA. TL: N39 44 55 W84 35 02. 320 Woodside Dr., West Alexandria (45381). (513) 456-3200. FAX: (513) 456-4200. Licensee: Western Ohio Broadcasting Service Inc. Net: USA, Ind Bcstrs, Sun; Agri Bcstg. Rep: Rgnl Reps. Format: Btfl mus, big band, farm. Target aud: 30-60. ■ Stanley Coning, pres & gen mgr; John Baumann, mus dir & chief engr.

WGTZ(FM)—Nov 28, 1960: 92.9 mhz; 31.6 kw. Ant 600 ft. TL: N39 50 10 W84 24 16. Stereo. 717 E. David Rd., Dayton (45429). (513) 294-5858. FAX: (513) 297-5233. Licensee: Great Trails Broadcasting Corp. (group owner). Rep: Katz. Wash atty: Michael Bader. Format: CHR. News staff one; news progmg 6 hrs wkly. Target aud: 18-49; contemp Middle America. ■ David Majecko, vp & gen mgr; Dan Covey, gen sls mgr; Allyson Berry, prom mgr; Louis Kaplan, progmg dir; Shawn Roberts, mus dir; Kim Faris, news dir; Will Bevis, chief engr.

Edgewood

WZOO-FM—Jan 23, 1989: 102.5 mhz; 5.8 kw. Ant 328 ft. TL: N41 49 44 W80 49 28. Stereo. Hrs opn: 24. Box 102, 217 Park Pl., Ashtabula (44004); Box 289, Ashtabula (44004). (216) 997-1025. FAX: (216) 993-1025. Licensee: Bulmer Communications of Ashtabula Inc. Group owner: Bulmer Communications Group. Wash atty: Miller & Miller. Format: Hot adult contemp. Target aud: General; mass-appeal adult. ■ John Bulmer, pres; Mike Anthony, gen mgr & gen sls mgr; Mark Allen, progmg dir; John Edwards, mus dir; Carolyn Behr, news dir.

Elyria

WEOL(AM)—Oct 1948: 930 khz; 1 kw-U, DA-2. TL: N41 16 10 W82 00 21. Stereo. Box 4006, 538 Broad St. (44036). (216) 322-3761. FAX: (216) 322-1536. Licensee: Elyria-Lorain Broadcasting Co. Net: ABC/E. Rep: Torbet, Rgnl Reps. Wash atty: Putbrese, Hunsaker & Ruddy. Format: MOR, div, news. News staff 4; news progmg 14 hrs wkly. Target aud: 35 plus. Spec prog: Sp 4 hrs wkly. ■ Gary L. Kneisley, pres & gen mgr; Bill Hatheway, sls dir; Mike James Whitmore, progmg dir; Craig Adams, news dir; Glenn Smith, chief engr.

WNWV(FM)—Co-owned with WEOL(AM). Oct 1948: 107.3 mhz; 50 kw. Ant 466 ft. TL: N41 16 10 W82 00 16. Stereo. Prog sep from AM. Format: Smooth jazz, fresh hits. News progmg 2 hrs wkly. Target aud: 25-54; upscale. ■ Charlie Schnell, gen sls mgr; Steve Hibbaro, progmg dir.

Englewood

WZJX(FM)—Not on air, target date unknown: 94.5 mhz; 6 kw. Ant 328 ft. TL: N39 57 17 W84 18 25. 1831 Bartley Rd., Dayton (45414). Licensee: Englewood Broadcasting Inc.

Fairborn

WGNZ(AM)—Sept 1, 1968: 1110 khz; 1.65 kw-D, DA. TL: N39 41 15 W83 57 55. Box 1110 (45324). (513) 878-9000. FAX: (513) 878-8595. Licensee: L & D Communications (acq 12-83). Net: USA. Wash atty: Miller & Fields. Format: Relg. Target aud: General; listeners who like family radio. ■ Norman Livingston, pres; Tim Livingston, gen mgr; Larry Williams, mus dir. ■ Rates: $12; 12; 12; 12.

WYMJ-FM—See Beavercreek.

Fairfield

WCNW(AM)—Feb 14, 1964: 1560 khz; 5 kw-D, DA. TL: N39 20 20 W84 31 30. 8686 Michael Ln. (45014). (513) 829-7700. Licensee: Vernon R. Baldwin Inc. (group owner; acq 6-11-84; $700,000 FTR 3-19-84). Format: Relg. ■ Vernon R. Baldwin, pres & gen mgr; Kenneth Brown, gen sls mgr; Mark Mitchell, progmg dir; Jeff Perkins, mus dir; Jim Wagner, chief engr.

WOFX(FM)—1925: 94.9 mhz; 10.5 kw. Ant 1,056 ft. TL: N39 12 01 W84 31 22. Stereo. Hrs opn: 24. Suite 300E, 250 W. Court St., Cincinnati (45202). (513) 241-9500. FAX: (513) 241-8896. Licensee: WOFX-FM Inc. (group owner, acq 6-1-92; FTR 5-4-92). Rep: Katz. Wash atty: Akin, Gump, Strauss, Hauer & Feld. Format: Classic rock. News staff one; news progmg 4 hrs wkly. Target aud: 25-44. ■ Carey Merz, pres & gen mgr; Randy Grossert, sls dir; Matt Gutbeod, natl sls mgr; Tracy Cox, prom mgr; Tom O'Brien, progmg dir; Ken Snyder, mus dir; Don Jensen, news dir; Dean Brown, chief engr.

Findlay

WFIN(AM)—Dec 15, 1941: 1330 khz; 1 kw-D, 79 w-N. TL: N41 00 36 W83 38 04. Stereo. Hrs opn: 24. Box 1507, 551 Lake Cascades Pkwy. (45840). (419) 422-4545. FAX: (419) 422-6736. Licensee: Blanchard River Broadcasting Co. Group owner: Findlay Publishing Co. (acq 1949). Net: ABC/I, NBC Talknet, Mutual. Rep: Rgnl Reps. Format: News/talk. News staff 2. Target aud: 45 plus. Spec prog: Farm 7 hrs, sports 12 hrs wkly. ■ Edwin L. Heminger, chmn; Kurt P. Kah, pres; David Glass, vp; Sandy Kozlevcar, stn mgr & gen sls mgr; Kelly Green, progmg dir; Tom Sheldon, news dir; Jim Hall, pub affrs dir; Dennis Rund, chief engr.

WKXA-FM—Co-owned with WFIN(AM). 1948: 100.5 mhz; 20 kw. Ant 440 ft. TL: N40 55 00 W83 35 45. Stereo. Hrs opn: 24. Prog sep from AM. Format: CHR. Target aud: 18-49. ■ Jerry Wise, prom mgr; Pat McCauley, progmg dir & mus dir.

WHMQ(FM)—See North Baltimore.

WKXA-FM—Listing follows WFIN(AM).

*WLFC(FM)—Nov 1, 1973: 88.3 mhz; 155 w. Ant 66 ft. TL: N41 03 11 W83 39 13. Stereo. Hrs opn: 6 AM-midnight. 1000 N. Main St. (45840). (419) 424-4571. Licensee: University of Findlay. Net: UPI. Format: Rock/AOR. News progmg 3 hrs wkly. Target aud: 18-40. ■ James G. Greenwood, chmn & mus dir; Michelle Fisher, gen mgr; Dawn Hopkins, progmg dir; Carla Bauman, news dir; Kris Campana, pub affrs dir.

Fort Shawnee

WBUK(FM)—1991: 107.5 mhz; 3 kw. Ant 328 ft. TL: N40 40 04 W84 01 41. Box 1484, Lima (45802). (419) 222-1075. FAX: (419) 222-3794. Licensee: Hutchko Partnership. ■ Jake Phillips, gen mgr.

Fostoria

WFOB(AM)—Dec 9, 1952: 1430 khz; 1 kw-U, DA-2. TL: N41 06 11 W83 24 00. Stereo. Box W, 101 N. Main St. (44830). (419) 435-5666. FAX: (419) 435-6611. Licensee: Tri-County Broadcasting Inc. (acq 4-11-89). Net: CBS. Rep: Rgnl Reps. Wash atty: Baker & Hostetler. Format: Adult contemp, talk. News staff 3; news progmg 15 hrs wkly. Target aud: General. Spec prog: Sp 3 hrs wkly. ■ Greg Peiffer, pres; Carol Boos, adv mgr; Gus Sierra, progmg dir; Sam Shriver, news dir; Jack Didier, chief engr. ■ Rates: $18; 14; 13; 13.

WBVI(FM)—Co-owned with WFOB(AM). 1946: 96.7 mhz; 3 kw. Ant 330 ft. TL: N41 06 01 W83 28 41. Stereo. Hrs opn: 24. Prog sep from AM. Format: Box 1624 (45839-1624). (419) 422-9284. Net: Jones Satellite Audio. Format: Soft adult contemp. Target aud: 25-54. ■ Rates: $19; 19; 19; na.

Fredericktown

WWBK(FM)—Sept 14, 1987: 98.3 mhz; 3 kw. Ant 300 ft. TL: N40 34 27 W82 30 27. Stereo. 155 N. Main St. (43019). (614) 694-1577. FAX: (614) 694-1578. Licensee: Bohmar Communications Inc. (acq 3-30-92; $325,000; FTR 4-20-92). Net: SMN. Format: Country. News staff one; news progmg 14 hrs wkly. Target aud: 25-49. ■ Arlene Bohack, pres & gen mgr; Mark E. Bohack, progmg dir & chief engr; David Bevington, news dir.

Fremont

WFRO(AM)—December 1949: 900 khz; 500 w-D, 286.9-N, DA-2. TL: N41 19 35 W83 05 04. Hrs opn: 24. 905 W. State St. (43420). (419) 332-8218. FAX: (419) 332-9341. Licensee: Wolfe Broadcasting Corp. Format: Adult contemp, top 40. Spec prog: Farm 4 hrs, jazz 10 hrs wkly. ■ Margaret R. Wolfe, pres; Thomas J. Wolfe, gen mgr & progmg dir; Larry Ziebold, mus dir; Art Smith, news dir; Mike Nargis, chief engr. ■ Rates: $14.45; 14.45; 14.45; 14.45.

WFRO-FM—Dec 15, 1946: 99.1 mhz; 20 kw. Ant 195 ft. TL: N41 20 58 W83 07 10. Dups AM 100%. ■ Rates: Same as AM.

Gahanna

*WCVO(FM)—Oct 13, 1972: 104.9 mhz; 3 kw. Ant 320 ft. TL: N40 04 16 W82 48 35. Stereo. Hrs opn: 24. Box 7, 4400 Reynoldsburg-New Albany Rd., New Albany (43054). (614) 855-9171. FAX: (614) 855-9280. Licensee: Christian Voice of Central Ohio. Net: USA. Format: Relg, talk. News progmg 15 hrs wkly. Target aud: General; Christian, politically aware, mid-age professionals. ■ John Hull, chmn; Bob Roller, pres; Dan Franks, gen mgr, opns dir, prom mgr & news dir; Greg Johnston, progmg dir; Michael Buckingham, mus dir; Ron Frank, chief engr.

Galion

WQLX(FM)—Nov 8, 1974: 102.3 mhz; 3 kw. Ant 300 ft. TL: N40 45 25 W82 47 21. 1466 N. Market (44833). (419) 468-4664. FAX: (419) 462-5642. Licensee: Malone Broadcasting Inc. Format: Adult contemp. ■ Ray Malone, gen mgr.

WGLX(AM)—Co-owned with WQLX(FM). Aug 21, 1972: 1570 khz; 250 w-U, DA-2. TL: N40 45 30 W82 47 18. Stn currently dark.

Gallipolis

WJEH(AM)—June 19, 1950: 990 khz; 1 kw-D. TL: N38 48 21 W82 12 23. Stereo. Hrs opn: 24. Box 448, 117 Portsmouth Rd. (45631). (614) 446-3543. FAX: (614) 446-3001. Licensee: Wagner Broadcasting Corp. (acq 6-1-67). Rep: Rgnl Reps. Wash atty: Dean, George, Hill & Welch. Format: Country. News staff one; news progmg 10 hrs wkly. Target aud: 25-54. ■ Ruth Wagner Pellegrinon, pres; Tim Maxwell, gen mgr & gen sls mgr; Kris Cockran, news dir; Bill Henry, chief engr. ■ Rates: $20; 16; 20; 14.

WMGG(FM)—Co-owned with WJEH(AM). Dec 15, 1961: 105.5 mhz; 50 kw. Ant 500 ft. TL: N38 48 19 W82 13 36. Stereo. Hrs opn: 24. Prog sep from AM. Format: Classic rock. Target aud: 24-49. ■ Eric Turner, progmg dir & mus dir.

Gambier

*WKCO(FM)—1975: 91.9 mhz; 266 w. Ant 190 ft. TL: N40 22 25 W82 23 45. Stereo. Hrs opn: 19. Box 312, Kenyon College (43022). (614) 427-5412. Licensee: Kenyon College. Format: Variety, progsv. News progmg 8 hrs wkly. Target aud: 18-25; college population. Spec prog: Class 3 hrs, Black 10 hrs, folk 5 hrs, jazz 3 hrs wkly. ■ Chris Egan, gen mgr; Scott Gosnell, vp prom; Mary Giallanza, vp progmg; Karen Rocket, mus dir; David Lilley, news dir & pub affrs dir.

Geneva

WKKY(FM)—Nov 2, 1987: 104.9 mhz; 3 kw. Ant 380 ft. TL: N41 49 16 W80 59 42. Stereo. Hrs opn: 24. Box 406, 95 W. Main St. (44041). (216) 466-1049. FAX: (216) 466-3138. Licensee: Ray-Mar Broadcasting Co. (acq 3-15-90; $441,965; FTR 4-2-90). Format: Country. News staff one; news progmg 6 hrs wkly. Target aud: 25-54. Spec prog: Pub affrs 2 hrs wkly. ■ Warren Jones, pres; Neil Hershberger, gen mgr; Joseph Popely, gen sls mgr; Garth Cornell, progmg dir; Mike Reilley, news dir; Harold Barnard, chief engr.

Georgetown

WAXZ(FM)—Apr 19, 1976: 97.7 mhz; 1.6 kw. Ant 390 ft. TL: N38 52 03 W83 48 44. Stereo. 8354 Fryer Rd. (45121). (513) 378-6151. FAX: (800) 933-0977. Licensee: Richard L. Plessinger. Group owner: Plessinger Radio Group (R.L. Plessinger Holding Co). Net: ABC/E; Ohio Net., Agri Bcstg. Format: Modern country. Spec prog: Farm 10 hrs wkly. ■ Steve Parton, gen mgr & progmg dir; George Morgan III, mus dir; Scott Lanter, news dir; Jim Gray, chief engr.

Stations in the U.S. — Ohio

Gibsonburg

WYHK(FM)—Jan 24, 1989: 95.7 mhz; 3.5 kw. Ant 433 ft. TL: N41 28 19 W83 25 05. Stereo. Hrs opn: 24. Box 6, Perrysburg (43552); 1201 Fremont Pike, Woodville (43469). (419) 837-9696; (419) 243-9957. Licensee: Buddy and Carolyn J. Carr. Format: Country. News staff one. Target aud: 20-40. Spec prog: Mexican 8 hrs wkly. ■ Buddy Carr, pres & gen mgr; Carolyn Carr, prom mgr; Ron Flick, chief engr.

Granville

*****WDUB(FM)**—Feb 7, 1962: 91.1 mhz; 100 w. Ant 171 ft. TL: N40 04 16 W82 31 24. Stereo. Slayter Hall, Denison Univ. (43023). (614) 587-3008; (614) 587-6382. Licensee: Denison University. Net: UPI. Format: Progsv, classic rock. News progmg 7 hrs wkly. Target aud: General; college students, faculty & local residents. Spec prog: Black 5 hrs, class 5 hrs, jazz 10 hrs wkly. ■ Brendan Higgins, gen mgr; Keith Chapman, mus dir; Tony Facemyre, asst mus dir; Maria Hess, chief engr.

Greenfield

WVNU(FM)—Not on air, target date unknown: 97.5 mhz; 2.75 kw. Ant 305 ft. TL: N39 23 51 W83 26 52. c/o Danny M. Watson, 2300 E. Kemper Rd., Cincinnati (45241). Licensee: Danny M. Watson.

Greenville

*****WDPG(FM)**—Not on air, target date unknown: 89.9 mhz; 50 kw. Ant 403 ft. 1514 W. Dorothy Ln., Dayton (45409). Licensee: Dayton Public Radio Inc.

WLSN(FM)—Oct 26, 1990: 106.5 mhz; 50 kw. Ant 482 ft. TL: N40 08 49 W84 36 36. Stereo. Hrs opn: 24. 5209 Horatio-Harris Cr. Rd. (45331). (513) 548-8655. FAX: (513) 548-9900. Licensee: Treaty City Broadcasting Corp. Wash atty: Reddy, Begley & Martin. Format: Easy favorites. Target aud: 25-54. ■ Nicholas F. Bodi, pres, gen mgr & chief engr. ■ Rates: $15; 15; 15; 12.50.

Grove City

WWCD(FM)—Aug 21, 1990: 101.1 mhz; 6 kw. Ant 328 ft. TL: N39 48 50 W83 03 19. Stereo. Hrs opn: 24. 1721 S. High St., Columbus (43207). (614) 444-9923; FAX: (614) 445-4413. Licensee: Ingleside Radio Inc. (acq 7-91; $2 million for CP; FTR 7-29-91). Wash atty: David Irwin. Format: Progsv. Target aud: General. Spec prog: Reggae 2 hrs, Celtic one hr wkly. ■ Terry Mowery, gen mgr; John McKinley, chief engr. ■ Rates: $45; 40; 40; 40.

Hamilton

WGRR(FM)—April 15, 1961: 103.5 mhz; 19.3 kw. Ant 790 ft. TL: N39 16 24 W84 31 37. Stereo. 3656 Edwards Rd., Cincinnati (45208). (513) 321-8900. FAX: (513) 321-1175. Licensee: Dalton Group Inc. (acq 6-87). Format: Oldies. Target aud: 25-54. ■ David O'Donnell, gen mgr; Jim Richards, gen sls mgr; Marty Thompson, progmg dir & mus dir; Tony Michaels, news dir; Larry Fiebig, chief engr.

*****WHSS(FM)**—May 12, 1975: 89.5 mhz; 190 w. Ant 282 ft. TL: N39 25 51 W84 37 40. Hrs opn: 7:45 AM-5 PM. Hamilton High School, 1165 Eaton Rd. (45013). (513) 887-4832; (513) 887-4818. Licensee: Hamilton City Schools Board of Education. Format: Rock, educ. News staff one; news progmg 3 hrs wkly. Target aud: 12 plus; general. Spec prog: Heavy metal one hr, dance/hip hop one hr, alt one hr, pub affrs 5 hrs wkly. ■ David P. Spurrier, gen mgr & stn mgr; Don McDonald, opns dir; Tim McVay, dev dir; Cassandra Price, prom dir; David Spurrier, progmg dir; Michelle Tribby, mus dir; Kendra Sawyer, asst mus dir; Dwayne Spiers, news dir; Todd Matthews, engrg dir; Robert Wilson, chief engr.

WMOH(AM)—Aug 15, 1944: 1450 khz; 1 kw-U. TL: N39 24 10 W84 31 54. Stereo. 2081 Fairgrove Ave. (45011). (513) 863-1111. FAX: (513) 863-6856. Licensee: Miami River Broadcasting (acq 12-30-85). Net: MBS. Rep: Rgnl Reps. Format: News, talk. News staff 2; news progmg 25 hrs wkly. Target aud: 35-49. Spec prog: Professional, collegiate & local sports. ■ Kurt F. Kah, pres; Terry Kah, stn mgr & gen sls mgr; Kert Radel, progmg dir; Teri Horsley, news dir; Dennis Rund, chief engr. ■ Rates: $20; 20; 20; 20.

WYGY(FM)—May 26, 1958: 96.5 mhz; 19.5 kw. Ant 810 ft. TL: N39 21 11 W84 19 30. Stereo. Hrs opn: 24. 225 E. 6th St. Cincinnati (45013). (513) 721-1050. FAX: (513) 421-2105. Licensee: National Radio Partners Ltd. Group owner: American Media Inc. (acq 12-17-92; $3.25 million; FTR 1-11-93). Net: Unistar. Rep: D & R Radio. Format: Young country. Target aud: 18-34. ■ George Toulas, gen mgr.

Harrison

WNLT(FM)—Sept 1, 1991: 104.3 mhz; 3 kw. Ant 328 ft. TL: N39 15 02 W84 50 10. 10555-B Harrison Ave. (45030). (513) 829-9658. Licensee: Vernon R. Baldwin Inc. (group owner). Format: Adult contemp Christian mus. ■ Vernon R. Baldwin, pres; Kenny Brown, gen sls mgr.

Heath

WHTH(AM)—Oct 16, 1970: 790 khz; 1 kw-D, DA-1. TL: N40 03 05 W82 28 08. Hrs opn: 6 AM-9 PM. Box 1057, 1000 N. 40th St., Newark (43055). (614) 522-8171. Licensee: Runnymede Corp. Net: UPI, CNN. Rep: Katz & Powell. Format: Country. Target aud: 25-54. ■ J. Thomas Swank, gen mgr; Bryan Richards, progmg dir & mus dir.

WNKO(FM)—See Newark.

Hillsboro

WSRW(AM)—July 15, 1956: 1590 khz; 500 w-D. TL: N39 09 58 W83 36 25. Box 9, State Rt. 247 (45133). (513) 393-1590. FAX: (513) 393-1611. Licensee: Highland Broadcasting Co. (acq 7-59). Net: AP. Rep: Rgnl Reps. Format: Country, gospel. News staff 4; news progmg 5 hrs wkly. Target aud: 35-54; general. ■ Tom Archibald, pres, gen mgr & progmg dir; Willard Parr, stn mgr; Gayle Fender, sls dir; Bill Cornetet, news dir; LaRue Turner, chief engr.

WSRW-FM—1962: 106.7 mhz; 50 kw. Ant 300 ft. TL: N39 09 58 W83 36 25. Stereo. Dups AM 80%. Format: Country. News staff one; news progmg 8 hrs wkly.

Holland

WPOS-FM—Sept 1, 1966: 102.3 mhz; 6 kw. Ant 312 ft. TL: N41 37 32 W83 42 41. Stereo. Hrs opn: 24. Box 457, 7112 Angola Rd. (43528). (419) 865-5551. Licensee: Maumee Valley Broadcasting Assoc. (acq 8-1-65). Net: AP. Format: Relg. ■ Ray Turkington, gen mgr; Bonnie Turkington, mus dir.

Hubbard

WRBP(FM)—Not on air, target date unknown: 101.9 mhz; 3 kw. Ant 328 ft. TL: N41 05 29 W30 30 05. 100 S. Third St., Columbus (43215). Licensee: Stop 26-Riverbend Productions Inc.

Ironton

WIRO(AM)—September 1951: 1230 khz; 1 kw-U. TL: N38 32 22 W82 40 17. Hrs opn: 18. Box 292, Radio Plaza (45638). (614) 532-1922; (606) 836-3151. FAX: (614) 532-0137. Licensee: Tri Radio Broadcasting Inc. (acq 2-26-62). Rep: Keystone (unwired net), Rgnl Reps. Format: Oldies. News progmg 5 hrs wkly. Target aud: 18-49; yuppy market. Spec prog: Relg 7 hrs wkly. ■ Gene McCoy, pres; Wayne Thomas, gen mgr, stn mgr & gen sls mgr; Ron Pritchard, progmg dir & mus dir; Ken Auble, chief engr. ■ Rates: $24; 24; 24; 24.

WMLV(FM)—Co-owned with WIRO(AM). July 1, 1973: 107.1 mhz; 3 kw. Ant 125 ft. TL: N38 32 22 W82 40 17. Hrs opn: 18. Prog sep from AM. Format: Easy lstng. News progmg 3 hrs wkly. Target aud: 35 plus; affluent, middle-aged. Spec prog: Relg 2 hrs wkly. ■ T. Michael Martin, progmg dir & mus dir. ■ Rates: Same as AM.

*****WOUL-FM**—Oct 12, 1987: 89.1 mhz; 50 kw. Ant 400 ft. TL: N38 31 23 W82 39 20. Stereo. Ohio University, 9 S. College St., Athens (45701). (614) 593-1771; (614) 593-1000. FAX: (614) 593-0240. Licensee: Ohio University. Net: APR, NPR. Format: Class, arts & news. News staff 2. ■ N. Joseph Welling, gen mgr; Tim Myers, progmg dir; Mark Smith, mus dir; Nancy Burton, news dir; Joseph Berman, chief engr.

Jackson

WCJO(FM)—1971: 97.7 mhz; 3 kw. Ant 300 ft. TL: N39 01 45 W82 35 51. Box 551, 287 E. Main St. (45640). (614) 286-3023. FAX: (614) 281-4121. Licensee: Jackson County Broadcasting Inc. (group owner; acq 4-22-93; $260,000; FTR 5-10-93). Format: Country. ■ Lewis E. Davis, gen mgr; Rob Tomblin, chief opns.

WLMJ(AM)—December 1953: 1280 khz; 1 kw-D. TL: N39 02 18 W82 35 26. Box 551 (45640). (614) 286-2141. Licensee: Jac-Vin Religious Broadcasters Inc. (acq 10-27-93; $45,000; FTR 11-15-93). Rep: Keystone (unwired net), Rgnl Reps. Format: Southern gospel. ■ Tyrone Hemry, news dir & chief engr.

Jefferson

*****WCVJ(FM)**—1978: 90.9 mhz; 5.5 kw. Ant 372 ft. TL: N41 37 48 W80 45 46. Stereo. Box 112 (44047). (216) 294-3854. Licensee: Agape School Inc. Format: Christian educ. ■ Myron J. Hubler, pres; Sarah Hubler, gen mgr; Pastor Porter, progmg dir; Mike Hubler, chief engr.

Johnstown

WRZR(FM)—Licensed to Johnstown. See Columbus.

Kent

WJMP(AM)—March 1964: 1520 khz; 1 kw-D, DA. TL: N41 09 35 W81 18 19. Box 2170, Akron (44309-2170). (216) 673-2323. Licensee: Media-Com Inc. (acq 1971). Format: Oldies. ■ Richard M. Klaus, pres; Robert Klaus, vp; William B. Klaus, stn mgr; Janet DiGiacomo, news dir; Bob Sassman, chief engr.

WNIR(FM)—Co-owned with WJMP(AM). Feb 19, 1962: 100.1 mhz; 1.95 kw. Ant 390 ft. TL: N40 13 44 W82 39 32. Net: CBS. Rep: Katz. Wash atty: Baker & Hostetler. Format: Talk.

*****WKSU-FM**—1950: 89.7 mhz; 50 kw. Ant 390 ft. TL: N41 09 03 W81 20 19. Stereo. 1613 E. Summit St. (44242). (216) 672-3114. FAX: (216) 672-4107. Licensee: Kent State Univ. Net: APR, NPR, AP. Wash atty: Dow, Lohnes & Albertson. Format: Class, in-depth news. News staff 4; news progmg 35 hrs wkly. Target aud: 25-49; college grad, professional & upper income. Spec prog: Folk 12 hrs wkly. ■ John E. Perry, gen mgr; Allen E. Bartholet, dev dir; Robert J. Burford, prom dir; Eric Hammer, progmg dir; Charles Andrews, mus dir; Lennord Will, news dir; Ron Bartlebaugh, engrg dir.

WNIR(FM)—Listing follows WJMP(AM).

Kenton

WKTN(FM)—June 20, 1963: 95.3 mhz; 3 kw. Ant 270 ft. TL: N40 38 41 W83 33 59. Stereo. Hrs opn: 5:45 AM-midnight. Box 213, 112 N. Detroit St. (43326). (419) 675-2355. FAX: (419) 673-1096. Licensee: Radio General Ltd. (acq 5-12-77). Net: AP; Agri Bcstng. Wash atty: Arent, Fox, Kintner, Plotkin & Kahn. Format: Adult contemp. News staff one; news progmg 10 hrs wkly. Target aud: 25-54. Spec prog: Farm 2 hrs wkly. ■ Keith P. Gensheimer, pres & gen mgr; Quentin White, gen sls mgr; Amy Downey, progmg dir; Susan Gensheimer, mus dir; Mark Wamack, news dir; Robert Morris, chief engr.

Kettering

*****WDPR(FM)**—See Dayton.

*****WKET(FM)**—May 5, 1975: 98.3 mhz; 10 w. Ant 150 ft. TL: N39 41 46 W84 09 43. 3301 Shroyer Rd. (45429). (513) 296-7669; (513) 296-7670. FAX: (513) 296-1740. Licensee: Kettering City School Dist. Format: Educ, classic rock, AOR. Target aud: 13-18; high school students. ■ Karl Bremer, stn mgr; Ken Paul, prom dir; Janine Clingman, progmg dir; Jim Sutherland, mus dir; Beth Schlotterbeck, news dir; Tiffany Hamiel, pub affrs dir; Pat Schurr, engrg mgr.

WLQT(FM)—Feb 20, 1962: 99.9 mhz; 50 kw. Ant 500 ft. TL: N39 44 07 W84 14 10. Stereo. One Dayton Ctr., Suite 2050, One S. Main St., Dayton (45402). (513) 331-5100. Licensee: Liggett Broadcast Inc. (group owner; acq 8-26-92; $3.35 million; FTR 9-14-92). Format: Adult contemp. News staff one. Target aud: 25-54. Spec prog: Jazz 4 hrs wkly. ■ James Jenskn, pres; Donald Griffin, gen mgr; Madonna Friend, rgnl sls mgr; Scott Barrett, progmg dir; Charles Van Sant, news dir. ■ Rates: $150; 150; 150; 150.

Lancaster

*****WFCO(FM)**—August 1988: 90.9 mhz; 200 w. Ant 223 ft. TL: N39 40 49 W82 35 51. Stereo. Hrs opn: 24. 1332 E. Main St. (43130). (614) 654-8556; (614) 536-7231. Licensee: Lancaster Educational Broadcasting Foundation. Net: Bible Bcstg Net. Format: Relg. Target aud: 40 plus. ■ James Rauch, gen mgr & engrg mgr; Elden Fox, John McKinley, chiefs engr.

WHOK(FM)—Listing follows WLOH(AM).

WLOH(AM)—Oct 1948: 1320 khz; 1 kw-D, 28 w-N. TL: N39 44 21 W82 37 48. Hrs opn: 24. 2300 N. Memorial Dr. (43130). (614) 653-4373. FAX: (614) 653-0702. Licensee: WHOK Inc. (acq 5-72). Net: AP, CNN, Unistar, MBS. Rep: Interep, D & R. Wash atty: Covington & Burling. Format: All talk-local & CNN. News staff 2; news progmg 24 hrs wkly. Target aud: General; Fairfield, Franklin and surrounding county residents. Spec prog:

Cleveland Cavaliers, Cincinnati Reds. ■ William M. France, pres; William France Jr., vp; Stanley C. Robinson, gen mgr & gen sls mgr; Cheryl Ballou, mktg dir; Stephanie Beougher, progmg dir & news dir; Mark Hiner, chief engr. ■ Rates: $12; 10; 12; 8.

WHOK(FM)—Co-owned with WLOH(AM). December 1958: 95.5 mhz; 50 kw. Ant 492 ft. TL: N39 40 32 W82 40 34. Stereo. Hrs opn: 24. Prog sep from AM. Suite 2000, 6172 Busch Blvd, Columbus (43229). (614) 341-9595; (614) 847-9595. FAX: (614) 847-4022. Net: AP. Format: Country. News progmg 2 hrs wkly. Target aud: 25-54. ■ William France Jr., gen mgr; Mark Hanson, gen sls mgr; Kristy Good, prom dir; Maxwell Raines, progmg dir; Mark Clark, mus dir. ■ Rates: $110; 100; 110; 50.

WSWZ(FM)—Oct 7, 1989: 103.5 mhz; 6 kw. Ant 328 ft. TL: N39 43 58 W82 35 43. Stereo. Hrs opn: 24. 115 W. Wheeling St. (43130). (614) 687-4949; (614) 687-4686. FAX: (614) 687-0346. Licensee: Skyway Broadcasting Inc. (acq 3-29-89). Net: CBS. Wash atty: Lauren Colby. Format: Oldies. News staff one; news progmg 4 hrs wkly. Target aud: 25-54. ■ John Garber, pres & gen mgr; Richard Schorr, gen sls mgr; Steve Edwards, progmg dir; Rick Ervin, chief engr.

Lebanon

WMMA(FM)—Not on air, target date unknown: 97.3 mhz; 3 kw. Ant 328 ft. Hrs opn: 24. Box 27, 950 W. Main St. (45036-0027). (513) 932-0080; (513) 932-2504. Licensee: McMurray Communications. Wash atty: Tierney & Swift. ■ Marilyn A. McMurray, pres, gen sls mgr & mktg dir; Michael A. McMurray, vp & gen mgr; Walter Biggs, chief engr.

Lima

WCIT(AM)—Aug 22, 1963: 940 khz; 250 w-D, DA-2. TL: N40 43 21 W84 05 04. Stereo. Hrs opn: 24. 1301 N. Cable Rd. (45802). (419) 228-9248. FAX: (419) 228-5085. Licensee: Allen Broadcasting Co. (acq 7-22-86; $1.1 million; FTR 6-2-86). Net: CBS, MBS. Rep: Roslin. Wash atty: Thompson, Hine & Flory. Format: News/talk. News staff 2; news progmg 30 hrs wkly. Target aud: 35-54; affluent, community involved. Spec prog: Morning exchange 5 hrs wkly. ■ Martin D. Gould, pres; Diane Kahn, exec vp; Stephanie M. Skylar, stn mgr; David F. Amos, vp opns & progmg dir; Anne Nashif, news dir. ■ Rates: $24; 24; 24; 24.

WLSR(FM)—Co-owned with WCIT(AM). Nov 25, 1970: 104.9 mhz; 3 kw. Ant 260 ft. TL: N40 43 21 W84 05 04 (CP: Ant 286 ft.). Stereo. Prog sep from AM. Net: NBC. Format: AOR. Target aud: 25-54. ■ David F. Amos, mus dir; Kellie Houser, pub affrs dir. ■ Rates: $15; 15; 15; 15.

***WGLE(FM)**—Dec 2, 1981: 90.7 mhz; 50 kw. Ant 420 ft. TL: N40 39 15 W84 06 36. Stereo. Hrs opn: 24. Box 30, 136 N. Huron St., Toledo (43692). (419) 243-3091. FAX: (419) 243-9711. Licensee: The Public Broadcasting Foundation of Northwest Ohio. Net: APR, NPR. Format: Class, pub affrs. Target aud: 35 plus. ■ Thomas Fairhurst, chmn; Shirley E. Timonere, pres & gen mgr; Allen Mazurek, opns mgr; Jamie Pierman, prom mgr; Thomas K. Paine, progmg dir; William Engelke, mus dir; Dan Niedzwiecki, chief engr. ■ WGTE-TV affil.

WIMA(AM)—Dec 5, 1948: 1150 khz; 1 kw-U, DA-2. TL: N40 40 47 W84 06 34. 667 W. Market St. (45802). (419) 223-2060. FAX: (419) 229-3888. Licensee: Lima Broadcasting Co. (acq 5-86). Net: ABC/I. Rep: Katz. Format: Adult contemp. Target aud: 35 plus. Spec prog: Farm 3 hrs wkly. ■ Les C. Rau, pres & gen mgr; Art Versnick, gen sls mgr; Eric Hanson, prom mgr, progmg dir & mus dir; Tom Watkins, news dir; Mark Gierhart, chief engr.

WIMT(FM)—Co-owned with WIMA(AM). December 1948: 102.1 mhz; 11 kw. Ant 1,060 ft. TL: N40 38 03 W84 12 29. Stereo. Prog sep from AM. Net: ABC/E. Format: Country. ■ Jack Wheelbarger, gen sls mgr; Steve Lewis, prom mgr, progmg dir & mus dir.

WLSR(FM)—Listing follows WCIT(AM).

***WTGN(FM)**—Sept 27, 1966: 97.7 mhz; 6 kw. Ant 300 ft. TL: N40 45 26 W84 08 12. Stereo. 1600 Elida Rd. (45805). (419) 227-2525. Licensee: Associated Christian Broadcasting. Net: AP. Format: Relg. ■ Wesley Lytle, pres; Scott Young, gen mgr; Charlie Wisener, progmg dir; Rick Corcoran, chief engr.

WYRX(FM)—Not on air, target date unknown: 93.1 mhz; 3 kw. Ant 328 ft. TL: N40 45 47 W84 10 59. 420 Elliot Dr., Rome, GA (30165). Licensee: Limaland Radio Inc. (acq 5-15-92; $37,000; FTR 6-8-92).

WZOQ(FM)—See Wapakoneta.

Logan

WLGN(AM)—Dec 1967: 1510 khz; 1 kw-D, 250 w-CH. TL: N39 31 47 W82 23 10. Stereo. Hrs opn: Sunrise-sunset. Box 429, One Radio Ln. (43138). (614) 385-2151. FAX: (614) 385-4022. Licensee: Logan Broadcasting Co. (acq 12-29-83; $310,000; FTR 12-19-83). Rep: Rgnl Reps. Format: Adult contemp. News staff one; news progmg 10 hrs wkly. Target aud: 18-54. ■ Roger L. Hinerman, pres, gen mgr & gen sls mgr; Mike Diamond, mus dir; Bill Morgan, news dir; Jerry Carmean, chief engr. ■ Rates: $10; 9; 10; 9.

WLGN-FM—Dec 10, 1965: 98.3 mhz; 3 kw. Ant 240 ft. TL: N39 31 47 W82 23 10. Stereo. Hrs opn: 24. Prog sep from AM. Format: Country. News progmg 25 hrs wkly. ■ Roger L. Hinerman, CEO; Bill Morgan, vp prom; Mike Diamond, vp progmg. ■ Rates: Same as AM.

London

WCKX(FM)—Not on air, target date unknown: 106.3 mhz; 6 kw. Ant 328 ft. TL: N39 53 05 W83 25 23. Stereo. 510 E Mound St., Columbus (43215-5539). (614) 464-0020. Licensee: Sunrise Broadcasting of Ohio Inc. Group owner: Sunrise Broadcasting Corp. Rep: Roslin. Format: Urban contemp, Black. ■ Vince Fruge, gen mgr & vp mktg; Phil Madre, gen sls mgr; John Tyson, prom mgr; Frank Kelly, progmg dir; Kim Jones, news dir; Kirt Tuckerman, chief engr.

Lorain

***WNZN(FM)**—Not on air, target date unknown: 89.1 mhz; 2.2 kw. Ant 374 ft. TL: N41 18 34 W82 26 31. 511 W. 26th St. (44052). Licensee: Spanish Cultural Network.

WRKG(AM)—December 1969: 1380 khz; 500 w-D, 67 w-N. TL: N41 25 48 W82 09 07. Suite 107, 300 Washington Ave. (44052). (216) 244-1380. FAX: (216) 244-1381. Licensee: Victory Radio Inc. Group owner: Vernon R. Baldwin Inc. (acq 12-26-89; $300,000; FTR 1-22-90). Format: Country Gospel. News staff 2. Target aud: 35 to 64. ■ Jim Lewis, mus dir.

WZLE(FM)—Co-owned with WRKG(AM). July 1975: 104.9 mhz; 1.3 kw. Ant 499 ft. TL: N41 25 29 W82 08 58. Stereo. (Acq 4-18-88; $820,000; FTR 8-22-88). Net: ABC/D. Format: Relg. Spec prog: Greek one hr wkly. ■ Vernon Baldwin, pres; Leonard Howser, stn mgr & progmg dir; Jim Lewis, gen sls mgr; Ron Cox, mus dir; John Paul Jones, chief engr.

Loudonville

WBZW(FM)—Licensed to Loudonville. See Wooster.

Manchester

WAGX(FM)—1992: 101.3 mhz; 3 kw. Ant 299 ft. TL: N38 40 58 W83 39 45. Box 492 (45144). (606) 564-8474. Licensee: Jewell Schaeffer Broadcasting Inc. Format: Oldies, adult contemp. ■ James P. Wagner, pres & gen mgr.

Mansfield

WAPQ(FM)—(Crestline). Dec 10, 1990: 98.7 mhz; 1.8 kw. Ant 418 ft. TL: N40 46 08 W82 46 03. Stereo. Hrs opn: 24. 2282 Village Mall Dr., Mansfield (44906). (419) 747-9870; (419) 747-9898. FAX: (419) 747-2679. Licensee: Mid-American Radio Group Inc. (acq 4-5-93; $475,000; FTR 4-26-93). Rep: Katz & Powell. Format: Adult AOR. News staff one. Target aud: 25-54; mainstream adult music enthusiasts. ■ Barry F. Gerber, pres; Adam Vetter, gen mgr & gen sls mgr; Kathy Riddle, prom mgr; Tim Kelly, asst mus dir; Maura Tyner, news dir; John Dight, pub affrs dir; Bill Bowin, chief engr. ■ Rates: $23; 21; 21; 21.

WMAN(AM)—Dec 4, 1939: 1400 khz; 1 kw-U. TL: N40 46 13 W82 32 36. Hrs opn: 24. Box 8, 1400 Radio Ln. (44901). (419) 529-2211. FAX: (419) 529-2516. Licensee: Treasure Radio Associates L.P. (acq 4-16-87; $2,000,000; FTR 5-4-87). Net: ABC/E, NBC, MBS, CBS, Westwood One. Rep: Eastman. Format: Talk, news & info. News staff 3; news progmg 30 hrs wkly. Target aud: 35 plus; upscale, active mgmt/exec. Spec prog: Black one hr wkly. ■ Harrison Fuerst, pres; Gary Gunton, gen mgr; Diana Coon, gen sls mgr; Rusty Cates, progmg dir; Kathy Linn, mus dir; Ron Allen, news dir.

WYHT(FM)—Co-owned with WMAN(AM). Oct 18, 1962: 105.3 mhz; 50 kw. Ant 370 ft. TL: N40 46 09 W82 32 23 (CP: 17.5 kw, ant 217 ft.). Stereo. Format: Top-40. ■ Kathy Lynn, progmg dir.

WNCO-FM—See Ashland.

***WOSV(FM)**—June 27, 1989: 91.7 mhz; 750 w. Ant 450 ft. TL: N40 42 33 W82 29 11. Hrs opn: 24. Rebroadcasts WOSU-FM Columbus 100%. 2400 Olentangy River Rd., Columbus (43210). (614) 292-9678. Licensee: Ohio State University. Net: APR, AP. Wash atty: Dow, Lohnes & Albertson. Format: Class. News progmg 3 hrs wkly. Target aud: 25 plus. ■ Dale K. Ouzts, gen mgr; Sam Eiler, stn mgr; Gary May, opns mgr; Joyce Schreiber, dev dir; Deb Whitney, rgnl sls mgr; Joe Banicki, prom mgr; Don Scott, adv dir; David B. Carwile, progmg dir; Larry Reynolds, chief engr. ■ WOSU-TV, WPBO-TV affil.

WRGM(AM)—See Ontario.

***WVMC(FM)**—March 1979: 90.7 mhz; 10 w. Ant 235 ft. TL: N40 43 19 W82 31 52 (CP: 834 w). Hrs opn: 24. 500 Logan Rd. (44907). (419) 756-5651. FAX: (419) 756-7470. Licensee: Mansfield Christian School Board. Net: USA, Moody. Format: Relg. Target aud: 35-64; middle income adults, mostly female. ■ Craig Hamm, gen mgr; Rick Cruz, chief engr.

WVNO-FM—Aug 11, 1962: 106.1 mhz; 40 kw. Ant 545 ft. TL: N40 45 50 W82 37 04. Stereo. Hrs opn: 24. 2900 Park Ave. W. (44906). (419) 529-5900. FAX: (419) 529-2319. Licensee: Johnny Appleseed Broadcasting Co. Rep: Rgnl Reps. Format: Adult contemp. News staff 5. Target aud: 25-54. ■ Gunther S. Meisse, pres & gen mgr; Jim Holmes, opns mgr; Glenn Cheesman, gen sls mgr; James Holmes, progmg dir; Steve Nelson, news dir & pub affrs dir; Wayne Flick, chief engr.

WYHT(FM)—Listing follows WMAN(AM).

Mariemont

WAQZ(FM)—See Milford.

Marietta

WBRJ(AM)—Aug 4, 1964: 910 khz; 5 kw-D, 61 w-N, DA-2. TL: N39 26 07 W81 28 01. 233 Pennsylvania Ave. (45750). (614) 373-0910. FAX: (614) 373-0914. Licensee: Tschudy Communications Corp. (group owner; acq 5-88.) Net: AP; Agri Bcstg. Rep: Dome, Rgnl Reps. Format: News, talk. Spec prog: Farm 3 hrs wkly. ■ Earl Judy, pres; Sonnie Thomas, opns mgr; David Sheaffer, gen sls mgr; Kim Lynch, progmg dir; Rick Williams, chief engr.

WEYQ(FM)—Co-owned with WBRJ(AM). Dec 1, 1964: 102.1 mhz; 25 kw. Ant 400 ft. TL: N39 25 07 W81 28 34 (CP: 11 kw, ant 492 ft.). Stereo. Net: CBS Spectrum. Format: CHR.

***WCMO(FM)**—Oct 1, 1960: 98.5 mhz; 40 w. Ant 105 ft. TL: N39 25 07 W81 26 32. Marietta College (45750). (614) 374-4802. FAX: (614) 376-4896. Licensee: Marietta College. Format: AOR. ■ Ralph Machesen, gen mgr.

WEYQ(FM)—Listing follows WBRJ(AM).

WMOA(AM)—Sept. 8, 1946: 1490 khz; 1 kw-U. TL: N39 25 07 W81 28 34. Hrs opn: 24. Box 708, 925 Lancaster St. (45750). (614) 373-1490; (614) 373-1498. FAX: (614) 373-1717. Licensee: Quiet Radio Inc. (acq 9-9-85; $600,000; FTR 6-3-85). Net: ABC/I. Wash atty: Lee Schubert. Format: Easy lstng, news, talk. News staff 2; news progmg 5 hrs wkly. Target aud: 35 plus; mature, middle-class to affluent. Spec prog: Farm one hr, jazz 6 hrs, relg one hr, sports 15-20 hrs wkly. ■ John A. Wharff Jr., pres & gen mgr; Mike Cullums, vp opns, news dir & pub affrs dir; John Wharff III, gen sls mgr; Scott Weston, vp prom; Ed Erjavec, vp progmg; Carrol S. Wharff, mus dir; Ralph Matheny, chief engr. ■ Rates: $8; 6; 7; 5.

***WMRT(FM)**—Nov 13, 1975: 88.3 mhz; 9.2 kw. Ant 205 ft. TL: N39 25 07 W81 26 32. Stereo. Marietta College (45750). (614) 374-4800. Licensee: Marietta College. Format: Class, news/talk, jazz. ■ Craig Nelson, gen mgr.

WXIL(FM)—See Parkersburg, W.Va.

Marion

WDIF(FM)—Feb 27, 1975: 94.3 mhz; 3 kw. Ant 300 ft. TL: N40 36 27 W83 14 14. Stereo. Box 10000, 355 E. Center St. (43302). (614) 387-9343. FAX: (614) 387-9346. Licensee: Scantland Communications. Net: ABC/C. Rep: Rgnl Reps. Format: Adult contemp. News staff 3; news progmg 10 hrs wkly. Target aud: 25-54; upscale adult females. Spec prog: Jazz 2 hrs wkly. ■ George Scantland, pres; Ray Reynolds, gen mgr & gen sls mgr; Keith Burke, opns mgr & progmg dir; Mike Messina, rgnl sls mgr & adv dir; Tammy Kelly, prom dir & mus dir; Sherry Abel, news dir; Greg Hodges, engrg dir. ■ Rates: $35; 28.50; 35; 11.

WMRN(AM)—Dec 23, 1940: 1490 khz; 1 kw-U. TL: N40 36 54 W83 07 54. Box 518 (43302). (614) 383-1131. FAX: (614) 387-3697. Licensee: Marion Radio Co. Group owner: Burbach Broadcasting Group (acq 12-27-85; $2,800,000; FTR 11-4-85). Net: Moody. Format: Adult contemp. Spec prog: Farm 5 hrs wkly. ■ Nick Galli, pres; Diane Glassmeyer, gen mgr; Jeff Boudrie, gen sls mgr; Scott Shawver, progmg dir; Rob Baxter, chief engr.

WMRN-FM—April 1953: 106.9 mhz; 25 kw. Ant 340 ft. TL: N40 36 54 W83 07 54. Stereo. Prog sep from AM. Format: Contemp country.

Marysville

WUCO(AM)—Dec 1, 1983: 1270 khz; 500 w-U, DA-2. TL: N40 14 46 W83 19 50. Hrs opn: 24. 107 N. Main St. (43040). (614) 644-1160. FAX: (513) 644-1617. Licensee: Union Broadcasting Co., an Ohio Corp. (acq 6-9-92; $35,000; FTR 6-29-92). Net: ABC, SMN; Agri-Net. Format: Real country. News staff one; news progmg 6 hrs wkly. Target aud: 25-54. ■ Charles Chamberlain, pres; Charles Hutchinson, CFO; Richard Riggs, vp; Mike Ramsey, gen mgr; Don Gabriel, prom mgr & news dir. ■ Rates: $24; 20; 22; 18.

WWHT(FM)—Feb 6, 1991: 105.7 mhz; 6 kw. Ant 100 ft. TL: N40 18 23 W83 19 44. Stereo. Hrs opn: 24. 126 W. 5th St. (43040). (513) 642-2048. FAX: (614) 442-2001. Licensee: Tel Lease Inc. Net: ABC. Format: Adult contemp. News staff one; news progmg 5 hrs wkly. Target aud: 18-34. ■ Robert Casagrande, vp & gen mgr; Mark Litton, opns dir, opns mgr & chief engr; Robert Miller, gen sls mgr; Rob Morris, progmg dir; Dave Riley, mus dir; Paige Turner, news dir.

Massillon

WTIG(AM)—Aug 1, 1957: 990 khz; 250 w-D, 119-N, DA-2. TL: N40 49 56 W81 33 40. Box 573, Suite 200, 35 N. Erie St. (44648). (216) 837-9900. FAX: (216) 837-9844. Licensee: WTIG Inc. (acq 1991; FTR 8-12-85). Net: CBS. Format: Sports, oldies. News staff one; news progmg 10 hrs wkly. Target aud: 25-54; male. Spec prog: Sports/talk 20 hrs wkly. ■ Ray Jeske, pres, gen mgr & gen sls mgr; Paul Russell, opns dir, progmg dir, mus dir & news dir; Kate Ruda, pub affrs dir; Bob Sassaman, chief engr. ■ Rates: $15; 8; 15; 4.

Maumee

***WYSZ(FM)**—Not on air, target date unknown: 89.3 mhz; 6.3 kw. Ant 321 ft. TL: N41 38 55 W83 42 22. 9035 Salisbury Rd., Mouclova (43542). Licensee: Side By Side Inc.

McConnelsville

WJAW(FM)—unknown: 100.9 mhz; 928 w. Ant 577 ft. TL: N39 33 24 W81 51 06. Box 547 (43756). (614) 373-1490. Licensee: Quiet Radio Inc (acq 6-4-91; $7,671; FTR 6-24-91). Format: Soft hits. ■ Bob Crock, gen mgr.

Medina

WQMX(FM)—Licensed to Medina. See Akron.

Miamisburg

WFCJ(FM)—Jan 7, 1961: 93.7 mhz; 50 kw. Ant 492 ft. TL: N39 39 36 W84 18 50. Stereo. Hrs opn: 24. Box 93.7, Dayton (45449); 7333 Manning Rd. (45342). (513) 866-2471. FAX: (513) 866-2062. Licensee: Miami Valley Christian Broadcasting Association Inc. Net: Moody, Skylight, USA. Wash atty: Miller & Fields. Format: Relg. News progmg 10 hrs wkly. Target aud: 35-54; evangelical Christians. ■ Wilbur Powell, pres; Clair D. Miller, vp & gen mgr; Shelly Sutton, mktg dir; Bill Nance, progmg dir & news dir; John Graham, chief engr. ■ Rates: $17; 13; 17; 13.

Middleport-Pomeroy

WMPO(AM)—Aug 28, 1959; 1390 khz; 5 kw-D, 120 w-N. TL: N39 00 35 W82 04 14. Box 71, Bradbury Rd., Middleport (45760). (614) 992-6485. Licensee: ET Broadcasting Inc. (acq 12-20-89; $600,000; FTR 1-16-89). Net: ABC/E. Rep: Rgnl Reps. Format: Country. Target aud: 35 plus. Spec prog: Relg 6 hrs, farm one hr, gospel 18 hrs wkly. ■ Lenny Eliason, pres & gen mgr; Kathy Malesick, gen sls mgr; Tom Payne, progmg dir; Joe Stack, chief engr. ■ Rates: $9; 9; 9; 9.

WMPO-FM—Aug 27, 1973: 92.1 mhz; 4.7 kw. Ant 113 ft. TL: N39 03 30 W82 02 31. Stereo. Hrs opn: 19. Prog sep from AM. News progmg 3 hrs wkly. Target aud: 25-54. Spec prog: Relg 6 hrs wkly. ■ Brian Collins, progmg dir. ■ Rates: Same as AM.

Middletown

WPFB(AM)—Sept 1, 1947: 910 khz; 1 kw-D, 100 w-N. TL: N39 30 57 W84 21 05. Hrs opn: 24. 4505 Central Ave. (45044). (513) 422-3625. FAX: (513) 424-9732. Licensee: Radio Station WPFB Inc. Group owner: WPAY/WPFB Inc. Net: AP, SMN. Rep: Roslin. Format: Music of Your Life. News staff 2; news progmg 26 hrs wkly. Target aud: 25-55; baby boomers. Spec prog: Radio Movie of the Week 2 hrs wkly. ■ Douglas L. Braden, pres & gen mgr; Mark Evar, opns mgr; Ed Ganzmann, news dir; Jim Wagner, chief engr.

WPFB-FM—July 1, 1959: 105.9 mhz; 34 kw. Ant 590 ft. TL: N39 30 57 W84 21 05. Stereo. Hrs opn: 24. (513) 422-3625. Net: SMN, MBS. Format: Country. Target aud: 25-54.

Milford

WAQZ(FM)—Aug 1, 1969: 107.1 mhz; 3 kw. Ant 299 ft. TL: N39 06 16 W84 20 10 (CP: 1.2 kw, ant 315 ft.). Stereo. 1591 Boyle Rd., Hamilton (45013). (513) 248-1072. Licensee: Richard L. Plessinger. Group owner: Plessinger Radio Group (R.L. Plessinger Holding Co.) (acq 1-20-87; $1,287,330; FTR 12-15-86). Format: Rock. ■ Steve Parton, gen mgr; Jim Grey, chief engr.

Millersburg

WKLM(FM)—1988: 95.3 mhz; 3 kw. Ant 328 ft. TL: N40 29 07 W81 50 40. Stereo. Hrs opn: 5:30 AM-midnight. 7368 County Rd. 623 (44654). (216) 674-1953. FAX: (216) 674-9556. Licensee: Coshocton Broadcasting Co. (group owner; acq 7-10-90; $490,000; FTR 8-6-90). Net: ABC. Format: Adult contemp. News staff one; news progmg 12 hrs wkly. Target aud: General. Spec prog: Loc sports. ■ Bruce Wallace, pres; Tom Thompson, gen sls mgr; Mark Lonsinger, progmg dir & mus dir; Mellisa Patterson, news dir; Rick Morrison, chief engr.

Montpelier

WLZZ(FM)—1991: 104.5 mhz; 3 kw. Ant 328 ft. TL: N41 30 54 W89 39 43. Hrs opn: 24. Bryan (43506). Licensee: Lake Cities Broadcasting Corp. Net: ABC/E. Format: Country. News staff one; news progmg 12 hrs wkly. Target aud: 25-54. ■ Tom Andrews, CEO, chmn & pres; William Kerner, exec vp; Brad Perk, gen mgr; John Hendricks, progmg mgr; Steven Smith, news dir.

Morrow

***WLMH(FM)**—1970: 89.1 mhz; 100 w. Ant 200 ft. TL: N39 20 51 W84 08 13. 605 Welch Rd. (45152). (513) 899-3884. Licensee: Little Miami Local Schools. Format: Educ, oldies, classic rock. ■ Eric Ettensohn, gen mgr, opns mgr & chief engr.

Mount Vernon

WMVO(AM)—Nov 26, 1953: 1300 khz; 500 w-D, DA. TL: N40 24 17 W82 26 23. Box 348 (43050). (614) 397-1000. Licensee: Jonathon L. and Juliet S. Zelkowitz (acq 7-8-93; with co-located FM; FTR 8-2-93). Net: ABC Talk-Radio, CNN. Rep: Rgnl Reps. Format: MOR, news/talk. Spec prog: C&W 3 hrs, relg 7 hrs wkly. ■ Jonathon Zelkowitz, pres & gen mgr; Juliet Zelkowitz, vp; Ron Staats, progmg dir, mus dir & news dir; David Lane, chief engr.

WQIO(FM)—Co-owned with WMVO(AM). May 26, 1951: 93.7 mhz; 37 kw. Ant 565 ft. TL: N40 24 18 W82 26 20. Stereo. Prog sep from AM. Net: CNN. Format: Contemp hit. Spec prog: Hit Music 4 hrs wkly. ■ Sheri Wharton, progmg dir; Eric Sider, mus dir.

***WNZR(FM)**—May 1, 1986: 90.9 mhz; 100 w. Ant 193 ft. TL: N40 22 14 W82 28 05. Stereo. Hrs opn: 6 AM-midnight. 800 Martinsburg Rd. (43050). (614) 397-1244, ext. 3550; (614) 392-9090. Licensee: Mt. Vernon Nazarene College. Net: AP. Wash atty: Fisher, Wayland, Cooper & Leader. Format: Adult contemp Christian. News staff one. Target aud: 25-50; Christian adults. ■ E. LeBron Fairbanks, pres; Mervin Ziegler, vp; Mitch Barber, stn mgr, prom dir, vp progmg, mus dir & news dir; Jeremy Johnson, opns mgr; Scott Wolfe, dev mgr & progmg dir; Dave Henry, chief engr.

WQIO(FM)—Listing follows WMVO(AM).

Napoleon

WNDH(FM)—June 1972: 103.1 mhz; 3 kw. Ant 300 ft. TL: N41 18 00 W84 09 22. Stereo. Hrs opn: 5 AM-midnight. 709 N. Perry St. (43545). (419) 592-8060. FAX: (419) 592-1085. Licensee: Maumee Valley Broadcasting Inc. Net: CBS, CBS Spectrum; Agri Bcstg. Rep: Rgnl Reps. Wash atty: Miller & Fields. Format: Adult contemp. News staff 2 Target aud: General. Spec prog: Ger polka 10 hrs wkly. ■ C. Richard McBroom, CEO & pres; Robert E. McLimans, sr vp, gen mgr, opns dir & mus dir; Connie Bechtol, gen sls mgr; Joel Miller, (asst) mus dir; Dave Kleck, news dir. ■ Rates: $15.25; 12; 13.25; 10.50.

Nelsonville

WSEO(FM)—September 1990: 107.7 mhz; 3 kw. Ant 328 ft. TL: N39 27 38 W82 13 09. Stereo. Hrs opn: 24. 15751 U.S. Route 33 S. (45764). (614) 753-2154. FAX: (614) 753-4965. Licensee: Nelsonville TV Cable Inc. Net: SMN. Wash atty: Frank Jazzo. Format: New country. News staff 3; news progmg 15 hrs wkly. Target aud: 12-34. ■ Eugene R. Edwards, gen mgr; Don Bedell, progmg dir; Mark King, mus dir; Bob Eby, news dir; Hubert Dalton, chief engr. ■ Rates: $9.10; 8.40; 9.10; 8.40.

New Boston

WIOI(AM)—Sept 2, 1959: 1010 khz; 1 kw-D, 22 w-N. TL: N38 43 48 W82 57 10. Box 478, Wheelersburg (45694); 8212 Old Gallia Pike, Wheelersburg (45694). (614) 574-6255. FAX: (614) 574-6895. Licensee: Shawnee Broadcasting (acq 9-1-82; $250,000; FTR 6-28-82). Format: Easy lstng ■ Jim Rowland, gen mgr; Gary Rae, progmg dir & news dir; James Hedrick, chief engr.

New Concord

***WMCO(FM)**—Jan 28, 1961: 90.7 mhz; 1.3 kw. Ant 84 ft. TL: N39 59 46 W81 43 18. Stereo. Hrs opn: 6 AM-12 PM. Stormont St. (43762). (614) 826-8375; (614) 826-8379. FAX: (614) 826-8404. Licensee: Muskingum College. Format: Div, educ. News progmg 10 hrs wkly. Target aud: General. Spec prog: Jazz 20 hrs, class 6 hrs, country 12 hrs wkly. ■ Jeffrey D. Harman, gen mgr; Kathy German, opns mgr; Anita McDonald, dev mgr; Jeff Beitzel, mus dir; Crystal Miller, news dir; George Alfman, chief engr.

New Lexington

WWJM(FM)—May 1, 1978: 106.3 mhz; 1.7 kw Ant 627 ft. TL: N39 46 37 W82 09 54 Stereo. Hrs opn: 24. 210 S. Jackson St. (43764). (614) 342-1988. FAX: (614) 342-1036. Licensee: Perry County Broadcasting Co. Net: AP, Westwood One. Format: CHR., AOR, classic rock. News staff one; news progmg 2 hrs wkly. Target aud: 12-44; young to middle-aged. ■ Charles W. Edwards, chmn; Charles T. Edwards, pres & gen mgr; Tina M. Edwards, gen sls mgr; Michelle West, prom mgr & pub affrs dir; Chuck Edwards, progmg dir; Jim Ferguson, mus dir; Dave Frye, news dir; Mark Bohach, chief engr. ■ Rates: $15.50; 15.50; 15.50; 14.50.

New Philadelphia

WJER(AM)—See Dover-New Philadelphia.

***WKRJ(FM)**—Not on air, target date unknown: 91.5 mhz; 3 kw. Ant 217 ft. TL: N40 29 26 W81 25 31. 1935 E. Main St., Kent (44242). Licensee: Kent State University.

WNPQ(FM)—Feb 2, 1969: 95.9 mhz; 3 kw. Ant 400 ft. TL: N40 35 51 W81 29 32. Stereo. 125 Johnson Dr., Uhrichsville (44683). (614) 922-2700. FAX: (614) 922-2702. Licensee: Tuscarawas Broadcasting Co. ■ James Natoli Jr., pres & chief engr; Allison Best, gen mgr & gen sls mgr; Karen Cox, prom mgr; Mike Adams, progmg dir; Scott Davidson, mus dir; Jeff Shreve, news dir.

Newark

WCLT(AM)—Jan 4, 1949: 1430 khz; 500 w-D, 48 w-N. TL: N40 02 02 W82 24 08. Hrs opn: 24. Box 899, 674 Jacksontown Rd. S.E. (43058-0899). (614) 345-4004. FAX: (614) 345-5775. Licensee: WCLT Radio Inc. (acq 1-1-58). Net: MBS, NBC; ABN. Rep: Rgnl Reps. Format: News/talk. News staff 2; news progmg 12 hrs wkly. Target aud: General. ■ Robert H. Pricer, CEO; Douglas C. Pricer, pres & gen mgr; Chris Emde, gen sls mgr; Tim Bubb, progmg dir & news dir; Jeff Irwin, mus dir; Jon Hartmeyer, chief engr. ■ Rates: $21; 17; 19; 7.

WCLT-FM—Aug 7, 1947: 100.3 mhz; 50 kw. Ant 390 ft. TL: N40 02 02 W82 24 08. Stereo. Hrs opn: 24. Prog sep from AM. Format: Country. Target aud: 25-54. ■ Amanda Black, prom dir; Russ Shafer, progmg dir; Greg Jeffries, mus dir. ■ Rates: $46; 37; 46; 28.

WHTH(AM)—See Heath.

WNKO(FM)—Dec 8, 1972: 101.7 mhz; 3 kw. Ant 280 ft. TL: N39 59 38 W82 30 13. Stereo. Hrs opn: 24. Box 1057, 1000 N. 40th St. (43055). (614) 522-8171. Licensee: Runnymede Corp. Net: UPI, CNN. Rep: Katz & Powell. Format: Hot adult contemporary. News staff 2 Target

Ohio

aud: 25-45. ■ Charles Franks, pres; Tom Swank, gen mgr & gen sls mgr; Mark McKay, prom mgr, progmg dir & mus dir; Joe Case, news dir; John Franks, chief engr. ■ Rates: $16; 13; 15; 11.

Niles

WNRB(AM)—Nov 1, 1963: 1540 khz; 500 w-D, DA. TL: N41 07 56 W80 45 40. Box 625 (44446); (216) 652-0106. FAX: (216) 652-9354. Licensee: WN Broadcasting Inc. Net: MBS. Format: Urban contemp. ■ Robert Doane, pres; Dominic Baragona, gen mgr; Gary Zocolo, opns mgr; Della Pizzati, gen sls mgr; Chris Patrick, news dir.

WNCD(FM)—Co-owned with WNRB(AM). May 15, 1988: 106.1 mhz; 3 kw. Ant 328 ft. TL: N41 15 52 W80 45 35. Box 626 (44446). Format: AOR.

North Baltimore

WHMQ(FM)—July 30, 1990: 107.7 mhz; 3 kw. Ant 328 ft. TL: N41 07 04 W83 32 38. Stereo. Hrs opn: 24. Box 108, 1624 Tiffin Ave., Findlay (45839); Box 289, Corp Headquarters, Ashtabula (44004). (419) 425-1077. FAX: (419) 422-4329. Licensee: Bulmer Communications of Findlay Inc. Group owner: Bulmer Communications Group. Wash atty: Miller & Miller. Format: Contemp country. Target aud: General. ■ John A. Bulmer, pres; Mark Mackey, gen mgr; Todd Mitchell, progmg dir & mus dir; Rich Ryder, news dir.

North Ridgeville

WJTB(AM)—Sept 16, 1984: 1040 khz; 5 kw-D. TL: N41 22 37 W82 00 27. 105 Lake Ave., Elyria (44035). (216) 327-1844. Licensee: Taylor Broadcasting Co. Net: UPI. Format: Urban contemp. ■ James Taylor, pres, gen mgr, gen sls mgr & progmg dir.

Norwalk

WVAC(AM)—March 18, 1968: 1510 khz; 500 w-D, DA. TL: N41 16 45 W82 39 23. Hrs opn: Sunrise-sunset. Box 547, 202 Old State Rd. (44857). (419) 668-8151. FAX: (419) 668-9557. Licensee: Firelands Broadcasting Inc. (acq 8-79). Net: CNN. Wash atty: Fred Polner. Format: Adult 40s, 50s, 60s. News staff one; news progmg 2 hrs wkly. Target aud: 40 plus. ■ James R. Westerhold, pres & gen mgr; David Smith, news dir; Ken Wilde, chief engr. ■ Rates: $10; 10; 10; na.

WLKR-FM—Co-owned with WVAC(AM). Sept 17, 1962: 95.3 mhz; 3 kw. Ant 300 ft. TL: N41 16 49 W82 39 27. Stereo. Hrs opn: 5:45 AM-midnight. Prog sep from AM. Net: ABC/I. Format: MOR, adult contemp. News progmg 3 hrs wkly. Target aud: General. Spec prog: Farm 3 hrs wkly. ■ Gail Krafczinski, mus dir; Scott Truxell, asst mus dir; David Smith, pub affrs dir. ■ Rates: $18; 17; 16.50; 6.

Oak Harbor

WJZE(FM)—August 1993: 97.3 mhz; 1.15 kw. TL: N41 29 51 W83 16 12. Suite 2, 1600 Woodville Rd., Millbury (43447). (419) 836-1973. Licensee: Oak Harbor Community Broadcasting Inc. Format: Jazz. ■ Jim Lorenzen, gen mgr.

Oberlin

*****WOBC-FM**—November 1951: 91.5 mhz; 440 w. Ant 124 ft. TL: N41 17 39 W82 13 26 (CP: 88.3 mhz, 3.5 kw). Stereo. Hrs opn: 24. Wilder Hall (44074). (216) 775-8107; (216) 775-8139. FAX: (216) 775-8886. Licensee: Oberlin College Student Network Inc. Net: AP. Wash atty: Holland & Knight, Harold McCombs. Format: Div, educ. News progmg 5 hrs wkly. Target aud: General. Spec prog: Black 20 hrs, class 15 hrs, folk 4 hrs, gospel 3 hrs, jazz 15 hrs, Sp 8 hrs, reggae 6 hrs, world 8 hrs wkly. ■ David Seubert, CEO & stn mgr; Brent Haynie, CFO; Todd Hutlock, vp opns; Peter Flint, vp dev; Anna Wislocki, vp prom; Lara Utian, vp progmg; Leah Hunter, mus dir; Kris Markle, news dir; Alex Samuel, pub affrs dir; Jerry Goforth, chief engr.

WOBL(AM)—Dec 24, 1971: 1320 khz; 1 kw-U, DA-2. TL: N41 16 05 W82 12 40. Hrs opn: 24. Box 277 (44074); 45624 Rt. 20 E. (44074). (216) 774-1320. FAX: (216) 774-1336. Licensee: WOBL Inc. (acq 9-17). Net: AP; Agri Bcstg. Format: Contemp C&W. News staff one; news progmg 14 hrs wkly. Target aud: 25-50; middle income laborers & managers evenly split between males & females. Spec prog: Farm 5 hrs, relg one hr wkly. ■ Doug Wilber, gen mgr, gen sls mgr & prom dir; Tim Cole, opns mgr & mus dir; Kevin Keane, news dir; Tracey Liston, chief engr. ■ Rates: $20; 18; 20; 16.

Ontario

WRGM(AM)—July 17, 1987: 1440 khz; 1 kw-D, DA. TL: N40 46 05 W82 37 04. Stereo. Hrs opn: 24. 2900 Park Ave. W., Mansfield (44906). (419) 529-5900. FAX: (419) 529-2319. Licensee: GSM Media Corp. Net: ABC/D. Rep: Commercial, Rgnl Reps. Format: Btfl mus. News staff 5. Target aud: 35 plus. ■ Gunther Meisse, pres & gen mgr; Glenn Cheesman, gen sls mgr; Jim Holmes, progmg dir & mus dir; Steve Nelson, news dir; Wayne Flick, chief engr.

Ottawa

WQTL(FM)—Feb 4, 1977: 106.3 mhz; 3 kw. Ant 297 ft. TL: N41 01 22 W84 03 40. Stereo. Hrs opn: 24. Box 5, 147 Court St. (45875). (419) 523-4020. Licensee: M.M. Group Inc. (group owner; acq 4-13-86; $408,553; FTR 1-20-86). Net: NBC The Source, Westwood One, Agri Bcstg. Format: Classic rock. News staff one, Agri news progmg 3 hrs wkly. Target aud: 18-49; affluent, upscale adults. Spec prog: Farm. ■ Robert Maccini, stn mgr. ■ Rates: $24; 20; 24; 20.

Oxford

*****WMUB(FM)**—1950: 88.5 mhz; 30 kw. Ant 475 ft. TL: N39 33 26 W84 47 35 (CP: 25.5 kw, ant 499 ft.). Stereo. Miami Univ. (45056). (513) 529-5885. Licensee: President & Trustees of Miami University. Net: NPR, AP, APR. Format: Big band, jazz, news. News staff 2. Target aud: General. Spec prog: Folk 5 hrs wkly. ■ John D. Bortel, gen mgr; Jim Haskins, opns mgr; Herb Day, mktg mgr; Robert Long, news dir; David Walrod, chief engr.

WOXY(FM)—Dec 24, 1959: 97.7 mhz; 3 kw. Ant 255 ft. TL: N39 28 44 W84 45 51 (CP: Ant 321 ft.). Stereo. 5120 College Corner Pike (45056). (513) 523-4114. Licensee: Balogh Broadcasting Co. Inc. (acq 7-21-81; $375,000 FTR 8-10-81). Format: Modern rock. ■ Douglas Balogh, pres & gen mgr; Steve Baker, stn mgr; Chris Adryan, gen sls mgr; Phil Manning, progmg dir; Julie Maxwell, news dir.

Painesville

WBKC(AM)—Apr 25, 1956: 1460 khz; 1 kw-D, 500 w-N, DA-2. TL: N41 44 20 W81 14 09. Hrs opn: 24. One Radio Pl. (44077). (216) 352-1460. FAX: (216) 357-7701. Licensee: Consolidated Investment Corp. (acq 3-3-92). Net: AP. Wash atty: Pepper & Corazzini. Format: News/talk, adult contemp. News staff 3; news progmg 40 hrs wkly. Target aud: 35 plus. Spec prog: Local affiliate for Cleveland Browns, Indians & Cavaliers. ■ Donald D. Smith, pres; Daniel Smith, CFO; Clarence V. Bucaro, exec vp & gen mgr. ■ Rates: $19; 14; 14; 8.

Parma

WCCD(AM)—May 31, 1973: 1000 khz; 500 w-D, DA. TL: N41 19 11 W81 46 07. Box 33250, Cleveland (44133). (216) 237-3300. FAX: (216) 237-3301. Licensee: Guardian Communications Inc. (group owner; acq 5-7-90; grpsl; FTR 5-21-90). Net: USA. Format: Relg. News staff one. Spec prog: Sp one hr wkly. ■ Mark McNeil, pres; Candy Hermann, gen mgr; Richard David, gen sls mgr & prom mgr; Kevin McArthur, progmg dir, mus dir & news dir; Jim Pogras, chief engr.

Paulding

WERT-FM—Aug 14, 1989: 99.7 mhz; 3 kw. Ant 328 ft. TL: N41 03 32 W84 35 30. Box 487, Van Wert (45891). (419) 238-1220. FAX: (419) 238-2578. Licensee: Community Broadcasting Inc. (acq 5-1-90). Net: SMN. Rep: Rgnl Reps. Format: Adult contemp. ■ Mona Kennedy, gen mgr; Peni Hellar, gen sls mgr; J.P. Steffan, mus dir.

Piqua

WPTW(AM)—Nov 1947: 1570 khz; 250 w-U. TL: N40 08 14 W84 16 00. Stereo. 1625 Covington Ave. (45356). (513) 773-3513. FAX: (513) 773-4345. Licensee: WPTW Radio Inc. (acq 11-1-59). Net: Unistar, ABN. Rep: Rgnl Reps. Wash atty: Miller & Fields. Format: Adult standards. News staff 2. Target aud: 35 plus. Spec prog: Farm 4 hrs wkly. ■ Richard Hunt, pres; Dave Dexter, vp & gen mgr; Mark Earhart, gen sls mgr; Brian DeMay, progmg dir; Lorna Vaniekerk, news dir; Donald Kuether, chief engr.

WCLR(FM)—Co-owned with WPTW(AM). Nov 30, 1960: 95.7 mhz; 50 kw. Ant 476 ft. TL: N40 13 02 W84 17 35. Stereo. Format: Easy contemp.

Pomeroy

WMPO(AM)—See Middleport-Pomeroy.

Port Clinton

WXKR(FM)—Oct 4, 1961: 94.5 mhz; 30 kw. Ant 640 ft. TL: N41 29 51 W83 16 12. Stereo. Hrs opn: 24. 611 Lemoyne Rd., Northwood (43619-1811). (419) 693-9957. FAX: (419) 697-2490. Licensee: Venice Broadcasting Inc. (acq 5-4-90; $2,370,238; FTR 5-21-90). Net: ABC. Rep: Major Mkt. Wash atty: Fletcher, Heald & Hildreth. Format: Classic rock. News progmg one hr wkly. Target aud: 25-49; men. Spec prog: Sp one hr wkly. ■ Venice Michel, pres; Dennis C. Lemon, gen mgr; Sophie Frye, dev dir; Stuart B. Roberts, gen sls mgr; Trisha Wendel, prom dir; Michael E. Ryan, progmg dir & mus dir; Julie Weitman, news dir; Jim Stevens, chief engr. ■ Rates: $50; 40; 50; 15.

Portsmouth

WNXT(AM)—Aug 30, 1951: 1260 khz; 5 kw-D, 1 kw-N, DA-2. TL: N38 48 38 W82 59 21. Hrs opn: 24. Box 1228, 405 Masonic Bldg. Chillicothe (45662). (614) 353-1161. FAX: (614) 353-8080. Licensee: Staradio Corp. (group owner; acq 10-85; $427,500; FTR 5-21-85). Net: ABC/I. Rep: Rgnl Reps. Wash atty: Jack Whitley. Format: Country. News staff one; news progmg 25 hrs wkly. Target aud: 24-60; office workers. Spec prog: Larry King. ■ Jack W. Whitley, pres; Jerry McKeown, gen mgr; Jan Morton, gen sls mgr; Mary Ruth Charles, prom mgr; Larry Dale Mullins, progmg dir, mus dir & chief engr; Sam McKibben, news dir.

WNXT-FM—Sept 15, 1965: 99.3 mhz; 2.25 kw. Ant 536 ft. TL: N38 43 20 W83 00 05. Stereo. Prog sep from AM. Format: Classic rock. News staff one; news progmg one hr wkly. Target aud: 18-34. ■ Jerry McKeown, stn mgr; Chris Hollis, progmg dir & mus dir. ■ Rates: $13; 11; 11; 7.

*****WOHP(FM)**—Feb 18, 1992: 88.3 mhz; 1 kw. Ant 643 ft. TL: N38 43 20 W83 00 05. Hrs opn: 24. Dups WCDR(FM) Cedarville 100%. 251 N. Main St., Cedarville (45314). (513) 766-7815; (513) 766-5595. FAX: (513) 766-2760. Licensee: The Cedarville College. Net: CNN. Wash atty: Coher & Berjold. Format: Relg, talk. News staff one; news progmg 16 hrs wkly. Target aud: 35-54. ■ Paul H. Dixon, pres; Paul Gathany, gen mgr; Jon Skillman, opns mgr; Mark Kordic, mktg dir; Eric Johnson, mus dir; Chad Bresson, news dir; John Tecknell, chief engr.

*****WOSP(FM)**—May 25, 1993: 91.5 mhz; 110 w. Ant 1,207 ft. TL: N38 45 42 W83 03 41. Hrs opn: 24. Rebroadcasts WOSU-FM Columbus 100%. 2400 Olentangy River Rd., Columbus (43210). Net: APR, AP. Wash atty: Dow, Lohnes & Albertson. Format: Class. News progmg 3 hrs wkly. Target aud: 25 plus. ■ Dale K. Ouzts, gen mgr; Sam Eiler, stn mgr; Gary May, opns dir; Joyce Schreiber, dev dir; Don Scott, mktg dir; Joe Banicki, prom dir; Dave Carwile, progmg dir; Bev Ervine, (asst) mus dir; Larry Reynolds, chief engr. ■ WOSU-TV & WPBO-TV affils.

WPAY(AM)—April 15, 1935: 1400 khz; 1 kw-U. TL: N38 44 06 W82 59 33. 1009 Gallia St. (45662-4140). (614) 353-5176. FAX: (614) 353-1715. Licensee: WPAY Inc. Group owner: WPAY/WPFB Inc. (acq 2-1-57). Net: CBS. Format: Solid Gold. News staff one; news progmg 10 hrs wkly. Target aud: 18-65; young, affluent & upwardly mobile adults. Spec prog: Gospel 6 hrs wkly. ■ Douglas Braden, pres; Frank Lewis, gen mgr & gen sls mgr; Jim Schuler, prom mgr, progmg dir & mus dir; Jim Hufferd, news dir; Jerry Eves, chief engr.

WPAY-FM—June 15, 1948: 104.1 mhz; 100 kw. Ant 1,000 ft. TL: N38 43 20 W83 00 05. Stereo. Dups AM 10%. Net: Unistar, CBS. Format: Country. ■ John Boswell, opns dir.

Proctorville

*****WMEJ(FM)**—Jan 25, 1986: 91.9 mhz; 3.5 kw. Ant 220 ft. TL: N38 27 14 W82 25 05. Stereo. Hrs opn: 24. Box 7575, Huntington, WV (25777). (614) 867-5333. Licensee: Maranatha Broadcasting Inc. Wash atty: Russell C. Powell. Format: Easy listening Christian music. News progmg 9 hrs wkly. Target aud: General. ■ Paul S. Warren, pres; Marilyas Warren, stn mgr; Fred Damron, chief engr.

Reading

*****WMKV(FM)**—Not on air, target date unknown: 89.3 mhz; 340 w. Ant 239 ft. 11100 Springfield Pike, Cincinnati (45246). Licensee: Southwestern Ohio Seniors' Services Inc.

Stations in the U.S. — Ohio

Ripley

WAOL(FM)—Not on air, target date unknown: 99.5 mhz; 3 kw. Ant 328 ft. TL: N38 45 14 W83 50 24. 8354 Fryer Rd., Georgetown (45121). (800) 933-0977. Licensee: James Philip Gray. ■ Steve Parton, gen mgr.

St. Mary's

WKKI(FM)—See Celina.

WZOQ(FM)—See Wapakoneta.

Salem

WSOM(AM)—June 2, 1965: 600 khz; 1 kw-D, 45 w-N, DA-2. TL: N40 49 47 W80 55 54. Box 530, 465 E. State St. (44460). (216) 337-9544. Licensee: Reach Radio Inc. (acq 12-26-91; $6 million with co-located FM; FTR 1-13-92). Rep: Banner. Format: Nostalgia. News staff one; news progmg 3 hrs wkly. Target aud: 35 plus. Spec prog: Farm 2 hrs wkly. ■ Albert L. Wertheimer, CEO; Jack Palvino, exec vp; Mark Levy, gen mgr; Chuck Stevens, opns dir & progmg dir; Pam Allen, gen sls mgr; Kathy Velez, rgnl sls mgr; Bambi Vail, prom mgr; Burton Lee, mus dir; Melinda Michaels, asst mus dir; Marianne Graff, news dir; A.J. McCloud, pub affrs dir; Jim Dacey, chief engr.

WQXK(FM)—Co-owned with WSOM(AM). Nov 25, 1958: 105.1 mhz; 88 kw. Ant 430 ft. TL: N40 53 06 W80 49 50 (CP: N40 53 08 W80 49 55). Stereo. Prog sep from AM. Net: Unistar. Format: Country. News staff one; news progmg 4 hrs wkly. Target aud: 25-54.

Sandusky

WCPZ(FM)—Listing follows WLEC(AM).

WGGN(FM)—See Castalia.

WLEC(AM)—Dec 7, 1947: 1450 khz; 1 kw-U. TL: N41 26 29 W82 41 10. Hrs opn: 24. 1640 Cleveland Rd. (44870). (419) 626-2000. FAX: (419) 625-1348. Licensee: Erie Broadcasting Inc. (acq 5-24-90; $1.5 million; FTR 6-18-90). Net: MBS, CBS, NBC Talknet. Rep: Rgnl Reps. Format: MOR. News progmg 2 hrs wkly. Target aud: 35 plus. Spec prog: Relg 6 hrs, black 6 hrs, farm 2 hrs wkly. ■ James Embrescia, pres; Jeffrey A. Storey, stn mgr & gen sls mgr; Mark Fogg, progmg dir; Vicki Taylor, news dir. ■ Rates: $50; 50; 50.

WCPZ(FM)—Co-owned with WLEC(AM). Aug 15, 1959: 102.7 mhz; 50 kw. Ant 141 ft. TL: N41 26 29 W82 41 12. Stereo. Prog sep from AM. (419) 625-1010. Format: Contemp hits. Target aud: 18-54. ■ Todd Lewis, rgnl sls mgr; Randy Hugg, mus dir. ■ Rates: Same as AM.

*WVMS(FM)—Not on air, target date unknown: 89.5 mhz; 2.12 kw-H, 5.36 kw-V. Ant 69 ft. 820 N. LaSalle Dr., Chicago, IL (60610). Licensee: The Moody Bible Institute of Chicago.

Shadyside

WEEL(FM)—Sept 1, 1990: 95.7 mhz; 850 w. Ant -626 ft. TL: N40 03 41 W80 45 08. Hrs opn: 24. 98 16th St. Wheeling, WV (26003). (304) 233-9335; (304) 233-7560. FAX: (304) 233-7563. Licensee: Adventure Three Inc. (group owner; acq 1-15-91; $1; FTR 2-4-91). Net: SMN. Format: Good time rock-n-roll. ■ Lil Goddard, gen mgr.

Shelby

WSWR(FM)—Dec 1, 1981: 100.1 mhz; 3 kw. Ant 300 ft. TL: N40 56 42 W82 39 42. Stereo. 47 E. Main St. (44875). (419) 347-9797. FAX: (419) 347-1776. Licensee: The Petroleum V. Nasby Corp. (acq 12-1-81). Net: AP. Format: Oldies. Spec prog: Farm 12 hrs wkly. ■ Tim Moore, pres, gen mgr & gen sls mgr; Scott Roller, progmg dir; Jeff Swank, news dir; Bill Bowen, chief engr.

Sidney

WMVR(AM)—Nov 1, 1963: 1080 khz; 250 w-D, DA. TL: N40 18 04 W84 12 21. Box 889, 2929 Russell Rd. (45365). (513) 498-1055. FAX: (513) 498-2277. Licensee: Dean Miller Broadcasting (acq 1967). Net: MBS, ABC TalkRadio. Rep: Rgnl Reps. Format: Adult contemp. News staff 2; news progmg 21 hrs wkly. Target aud: 21-59; rural. Spec prog: Farm 10 hrs wkly. ■ Dean Miller, pres; Doug Short, gen sls mgr & prom mgr; Jack Michaels, progmg dir & mus dir; Joe Neaves, news dir; Dan Deitz, chief engr.

WMVR-FM—1965: 105.5 mhz; 3 kw. Ant 155 ft. TL: N40 18 04 W84 12 21. Stereo. Hrs opn: 24. Dups AM 100%. ■ Jack Michaels, gen mgr.

Springfield

WAZU(FM)—August 1958: 102.9 mhz; 50 kw. Ant 160 ft. TL: N39 57 11 W83 52 07 (CP: Ant 492 ft.). Stereo. 717 E. David Rd. Dayton (45429). (513) 294-5858. FAX: (513) 297-5233. Licensee: Osborn of Ohio Inc. Group owner: Osborn Communications Corp. (acq 12-88; $2.6 million; FTR 12-19-88). Format: Classic rock. ■ David Macejko, gen mgr; Dan Covey, gen sls mgr; Allison Berry, prom mgr; Louis Kaplan, progmg dir.

WBLY(AM)—1947: 1600 khz; 1 kw-D, 34 w-N. TL: N39 57 11 W83 52 07. 1529 Miracle Mile Rd. (45503). (513) 399-4955. FAX: (513) 399-8767. Licensee: Ray Corp. Net: MBS. Rep: Rgnl Reps. Format: News, talk, sports. ■ Ronald Yontz, pres, gen mgr & gen sls mgr; Dell Grim, progmg dir; Daryl Bauer, news dir; Craig Robinson, chief engr.

*WEEC(FM)—Dec 15, 1961: 100.7 mhz; 50 kw. Ant 469 ft. TL: N39 57 44 W83 51 49. Stereo. Hrs opn: 24. 2348 Troy Rd. (45504). (513) 399-7837. Licensee: World Evangelistic Enterprise Corp. Net: USA, AP, Moody. Format: Relg. News progmg 12 hrs wkly. Target aud: General. Spec prog: Black one hr, farm one hr wkly. ■ Mike Maddex, pres; Larry Correll, stn mgr & progmg dir; Charles Steger, chief engr.

WIZE(AM)—Nov 1, 1940: 1340 khz; 1 kw-U. TL: N39 56 33 W83 47 15. 1529 Miracle Mile (45503). (513) 399-4955. Licensee: Staggs Broadcasting Inc. (acq 3-23-92; $300,000; FTR 5-25-92). Net: ABC/I. Format: Adult contemp. Spec prog: Jazz 2 hrs wkly. ■ Jerry Staggs, gen mgr; Mike Manley, opns mgr; Doug Montanus, gen sls mgr; Michael Manley, progmg dir; Janet Baver, mus dir; Gerry Allen, news dir; Gene Simmons, chief engr.

*WUSO(FM)—Feb 20, 1966: 89.1 mhz; 10 w-H. Ant 1,109 ft. TL: N39 56 09 W83 48 43. Wittenberg University (45501). (513) 327-7026; (513) 327-7030. Licensee: Wittenberg Univ. Format: Alt. Target aud: Wittenberg students. Spec prog: Jazz 6 hrs, class 3 hrs, blues 3 hrs, urban contemp 9 hrs wkly. ■ Michael DeAmicis, gen mgr; John Montag (faculty Advisor), progmg dir; Mark Jedow, chief engr.

Steubenville

WDIG(AM)—Sept 25, 1973: 950 khz; 1 kw-D, DA. TL: N40 26 49 W80 34 06. Box 970 (43952). (614) 264-1760. FAX: (614) 264-7771. Licensee: Romano R. Cionni Sr. (acq 4-13-89; $116,000; FTR 5-1-89). Net: SMN. Format: Oldies. Spec prog: It 3 hrs wkly. ■ John Holley, gen mgr.

WKWK-FM—See Wheeling, W.Va.

WRKY(FM)—Listing follows WSTV(AM).

WSTV(AM)—Nov 4, 1940: 1340 khz; 1 kw-U. TL: N40 26 49 W80 34 06. 320 Market St. (43952). (614) 283-4747. FAX: (614) 283-3655. Licensee: WSTV Inc. Group owner: Associated Communications Corp. (acq 3-22-79). Net: NBC Talknet, MBS. Rep: Rgnl Reps. Wash atty: Fleischman & Walsh. Format: News, talk. News staff 3; news progmg 20 hrs wkly. Target aud: 35 plus. ■ Myles P. Berkman, pres; William B. Chesson, vp & gen mgr; Joyce Nicholson, prom mgr & progmg dir; Charles Calabrese, news dir; Greg Harper, chief engr. ■ Rates: $45; 40; 40; 35.

WRKY(FM)—Co-owned with WSTV(AM). May 1, 1947: 103.5 mhz; 16 kw. Ant 879 ft. TL: N40 20 32 W80 37 14. Stereo. Prog sep from AM. Format: CHR. News progmg 2 hrs wkly. Target aud: 18-44. ■ Steve Kline, prom mgr & progmg dir; Scott Feist, mus dir. ■ Rates: $55; 55; 55; 45.

Streetsboro

*WSTB(FM)—September 1973: 91.5 mhz; 300 w. Ant 125 ft. TL: N41 14 12 W81 19 32. Hrs opn: 7 AM-9 PM. Box 2542, 1900 Annalane Dr. (44241). (216) 626-4906. FAX: (216) 626-9350. Licensee: Streetsboro City Schools. Net: MBS. Format: Heavy Rock/Metal. News staff one; news progmg 4 hrs wkly. Target aud: 16-34. ■ Robert L. Long, gen mgr; William Weisinger, chief engr.

Struthers

*WKTL(FM)—Sept 6, 1965: 90.7 mhz; 15 kw. Ant 23 ft. TL: N41 03 06 W80 35 56. Struthers High School, 111 Euclid Ave. (44471). (216) 755-1435. Licensee: Struthers Board of Education. Format: Div. Spec prog: Hungarian one hr, Lithuanian one hr, Irish one hr, C&W 4 hrs, Greek one hr, Croatian one hr, Slovak 2 hrs, Sp one hr, Ukranian one hr, Pol 14 hrs wkly. ■ Sharon Fedor Chalfin, gen mgr; Peter Suszczynski, chief engr.

Swanton

NEW FM—Not on air, target date unknown: 107.3 mhz; 3 kw. Ant 328 ft. Suite 496, 1251 S. Renold Rd., Toledo (43615). Licensee: Welch Communications Inc.

Sylvania

WWWM-FM—Nov 29, 1968: 105.5 mhz; 2.15 kw. Ant 390 ft. TL: N41 38 48 W83 36 22 (CP: 2.7 kw). Stereo. Box 167581, Oregon (43616); 2965 Pickle Rd., Toledo (43616). (419) 691-1470. TWX: (419) 693-0396. Licensee: Midwestern Broadcasting Co. (acq 3-72). Rep: Banner. Format: Adult contemp, oldies. News staff 2; news progmg 5 hrs wkly. Target aud: 25-54. ■ Lewis W. Dickey, pres; Gil Rosenwald, exec vp & gen mgr; Sharon Avaritt, stn mgr & adv dir; Christopher Feighan, gen sls mgr; Jeff Schwartz, natl sls mgr; Rob Crider, rgnl sls mgr; Jeff Donofrio, prom dir; Ron Finn, progmg dir & mus dir; Wendy Sheridan, news dir; Casey McMichaels, pub affrs dir; Peter Walkowiak, chief engr.

Tiffin

*WHEI(FM)—Sept 13, 1972: 89.9 mhz; 15.1 w. Ant 52 ft. TL: N41 06 59 W83 10 03. Hrs opn: 6:30 AM-midnight. Heidelberg College, Founder's Hall (44883). (419) 448-2283; (419) 448-2282. Licensee: Heidelberg College. Format: Progsv/alternative. ■ Dr. Gary Dickerson, gen mgr; Rob Stiltner, stn mgr.

WTTF(AM)—Dec 19, 1959: 1600 khz; 500 w-D, 20 w-N, DA-1. TL: N41 07 32 W83 13 45. 185 S. Washington St. (44883). (419) 447-2212. Licensee: WTTF Inc. Net: ABC/E; Agri Bcstg. Wash atty: Miller & Miller. Format: Adult contemp, oldies. News staff 2; news progmg 18 hrs wkly. Target aud: General. Spec prog: Farm 3 hrs wkly. ■ Richard J. Wright, pres, gen mgr & chief engr; Robert E. Wright, prom dir & progmg dir; Jack Kagy, news dir; Deanna White, pub affrs dir. ■ Rates: $14.40; 14.40; 14.40; 14.40.

WTTF-FM—July 11, 1963: 103.7 mhz; 50 kw. Ant 492 ft. TL: N41 08 20 W83 14 45. Stereo. Dups AM 100%. ■ Rates: Same as AM.

Toledo

WCWA(AM)—Apr 10, 1938: 1230 khz; 1 kw-U. TL: N41 38 13 W83 33 52. Suite 400, 124 N. Summit St. (43604-1064). (419) 248-2627. Licensee: Reams Broadcasting Corp. (acq 1964). Rep: Eastman. Format: Stardust. Spec prog: Ger one hr, Pol one hr, relg 3 hrs, sports 15 hrs wkly. ■ Brian McNeill, pres; Nancy Dymond, vp & gen mgr; Ron Steinman, gen sls mgr; Tom Staudt, prom mgr; Ron Sobczak, progmg dir; Beth Daniels, news dir; Denny Moon, chief engr.

WIOT(FM)—Co-owned with WCWA(AM). October 1949: 104.7 mhz. Ant 540 ft. TL: N41 40 23 W83 25 31. Stereo. Hrs opn: 24. Prog sep from AM. (419) 248-3377. Net: NBC The Source. Format: Rock (AOR). Spec prog: Jazz 2 hrs wkly. ■ Lyn Casye, progmg dir; Don Davis, mus dir.

*WGTE-FM—May 2, 1976: 91.3 mhz; 13.5 kw. Ant 949 ft. TL: N41 39 27 W83 25 55. Stereo. Hrs opn: 24. Box 30, 136 N. Huron St. (43697). (419) 243-3091. Licensee: The Public Broadcasting Foundation of Northwest Ohio. Net: APR, NPR. Wash atty: Schwartz, Woods & Miller. Format: Class, pub affrs. News staff one; news progmg 23 hrs wkly. Target aud: General. ■ Shirley E. Timonere, CEO, pres & gen mgr; Thomas Fairhurst, chmn; Jos A. Campbell III, stn mgr; Allen Mazurek, opns mgr & progmg mgr; Johnetta McCollough, dev dir; Kathleen Kozy, prom mgr; Joseph Campbell III, progmg dir; William Engelke, mus dir; Dan Niedzwiecki, engrg dir; Kenneth Zuercher, chief engr. ■ WGTE-TV affil.

WIOT(FM)—Listing follows WCWA(AM).

WJYM(AM)—See Bowling Green.

WKKO(FM)—Listing follows WTOD(AM).

WLQR(FM)—Listing follows WSPD(AM).

*WOTL(FM)—Mar 24, 1988: 90.3 mhz; 700 w. Ant 377 ft. TL: N41 38 48 W83 36 22. Stereo. 716 N. Westwood Ave. (43607). (419) 537-1505; (609) 854-5300. Licensee: Family Stations Inc. (group owner). Format: Relg. Target aud: General. ■ Harold Camping, pres; Mike Zeiman, gen mgr; Wayne E. Stoffel, stn mgr.

WSPD(AM)—Apr 15, 1921: 1370 khz; 5 kw-U, DA-N. TL: N41 36 03 W83 32 11. Stereo. 125 S. Superior St. (43602). (419) 244-8321. FAX: (419) 244-7631. Licensee: Toledo Broadcasting Inc. (acq 12-11-86; $15.5 million with co-located FM). Net: CBS, NBC Talknet. Rep: Christal. Wash atty: Dow, Lohnes & Albertson. Format:

Ohio

News/talk. News staff 7; news progmg 34 hrs wkly. Target aud: 25 plus. Spec prog: Relg 5 hrs, farm 3 hrs wkly. ■ Ron Kempff, gen mgr; Chuck Buckenmeyer, gen sls mgr; Tim Corbin, natl sls mgr; Andi Roman, progmg dir; Dave Brannen, news dir; Bill Rossini, chief engr. ■ Rates: $75; 55; 50; 31.

WLQR(FM)—Co-owned with WSPD(AM). Aug 11, 1946: 101.5 mhz; 19.1 kw. Ant 810 ft. TL: N41 41 00 W83 24 29. Stereo. Prog sep from AM. Rep: Christal. Wash atty: Dow, Lohnes & Albertson. Format: Adult contemp. News progmg one hr wkly. Target aud: 25-54. Spec prog: Jazz 6 hrs wkly. ■ Steve Kendall, progmg dir; Elizabeth Gray, news dir. ■ Rates: $85; 92; 87; 25.

WTOD(AM)—June 16, 1946: 1560 khz; 5 kw-D, DA. TL: N41 36 59 W83 37 22. 3225 Arlington Ave. (43614). (419) 385-2507. FAX: (419) 385-2902. Licensee: Booth American Co. (group owner; acq 8-17-57). Net: ABC/I. Rep: Major Mkt. Format: Classic & contemp country. Spec prog: Pol 4 hrs wkly. ■ John Booth, pres; Clyde Roberts, gen mgr; Gary Shores, progmg dir; Trisha Courtney, news dir; Dave Fuller, chief engr.

WKKO(FM)—Co-owned with WTOD(AM). Dec 7, 1956: 99.9 mhz; 50 kw. Ant 50 ft. TL: N41 40 05 W83 27 01. Stereo. Prog sep from AM. (419) 385-2536. Format: Country. ■ Pam Rumpf, prom mgr; Gary Stores, progmg dir; Gary Outlaw, mus dir. ■ Rates: Sold in combination with AM.

WVKS(FM)—Oct 14, 1957: 92.5 mhz; 50 kw. Ant 480 ft. TL: N41 31 55 W83 35 37. Stereo. 4665 W. Bancroft St. (43615). (419) 531-1681. FAX: (419) 536-9271. Licensee: Noble Broadcast of Toledo. Group owner: Noble Broadcast Group (acq 9-1-88; $16.7 million) Rep: McGavren Guild; Rgnl Reps.Wash atty: Haley, Bader & Potts. Format: CHR. News staff one; news progmg one hr wkly. Target aud: 18-49; educated, employed adults, mostly female; families including teens. ■ John Lynch, pres; Andrew Stuart, gen mgr; Bill Clark, gen sls mgr; Greg Brady, prom dir; Mike Wheeler, progmg dir; Stacey Latona, news dir; Gary Fullhart, chief engr. ■ Rates: $100; 85; 95; 25.

WVOI(AM)—Nov 28, 1966: 1520 khz; 1 kw-U, DA-2. TL: N41 44 15 W83 35 19. Box 5408 (43613); 6695 Jackman Rd., Temperance, MI (48182). (419) 243-7052; (313) 847-0628. FAX: (313) 847-0629. Licensee: God's Way Communications Inc. (acq 2-1-93; $125,000; FTR 2-22-93). Net: American Urban; Unistar. Rep: Roslin; Rgnl Reps.Format: Relg, urban. News staff one. Target aud: 25-59; older established audience. Spec prog: Relg (church ministry). ■ Kirt McReynolds, CEO, pres, gen mgr, prom dir & progmg dir; Crystal Sampson, vp; Kris Rose (asst stn mgr), stn mgr; Kris Rose, opns mgr & vp prom; Dr. Marjorie Holt, vp dev; Dana Cumberland, sls dir & mktg mgr; Kris Rose, Shawn Kevin Powers, news dirs; Kris Rose, Shawn Kevin Powers, pub affrs dirs; David Coller, chief engr.

WWWM(AM)—October 1954: 1470 khz; 1 kw-U, DA-2. TL: N41 37 55 W83 28 45. Box 167581, Oregon (43616); 2965 Pickle Rd., Toledo (43616). (419) 691-1470. FAX: (419) 691-0396. Licensee: The Midwestern Broadcasting Co. (acq 3-15-65). Net: Unistar, SMN. Rep: D & R Radio. Format: Adult contemp, Black. News staff one. Target aud: 25-54; urban sound for adults. ■ Lewis W. Dickey, pres; Gil Rosenwald, gen mgr; Sharon Avaritt, stn mgr; Christopher Feigaan, gen sls mgr; Jeff Donofrio, prom dir; Ron Finn, progmg dir; Mark Roberts, news dir; Peter Walkowiak, chief engr.

WWWM-FM—See Sylvania.

***WXTS-FM**—Feb 1975: 88.3 mhz; 1 kw. Ant 125 ft. TL: N41 41 40 07 W83 33 15. Stereo. Hrs opn: 24. 2400 Collingwood (43620). (419) 244-6875. FAX: (419) 729-8425. Licensee: Toledo Board of Education. Format: Jazz. Target aud: 28-55. Spec prog: Blues 5 hrs wkly. ■ John Kuschell, gen mgr; Robin Wheatley, prom dir; Johnathan Turner, mus dir; Art Glauner, chief engr.

***WXUT(FM)**—Nov 4, 1990: 88.3 mhz; 100 w-H. Ant 190 ft. TL: N41 39 26 W83 36 57. Stereo. Hrs opn: Mon-Wed 8 PM-2 AM, Thur-Fri 8 PM-4 AM, Sat 9 AM-4 AM, Sun 9 AM-2 AM. Student Union, Suite 2515, 2801 W. Bancroft St. (43606). (419) 537-4172; (419) 537-4761. FAX: (419) 537-2210. Licensee: Univ. of Toledo. Format: Div, educ, progsv. News progmg 4 hrs wkly. Target aud: General. Spec prog: Black 14 hrs, folk 2 hrs, jazz 4 hrs, heavy metal 4 hrs, comedy 2 hrs, R&B 2 hrs, reggae 4 hrs wkly. ■ Terrance Teagarden, gen mgr; Daniel Beck, stn mgr; Peggy Stierman, prom dir; Alex Clarkson, progmg dir; Dennis Burke, mus dir; Jennifer Clarke, news dir; Johnny Trippe, pub affrs dir; Gary Homza, chief engr.

Troy

WCLR(FM)—See Piqua.

WTRJ(FM)—1991: 96.9 mhz; 3 kw. Ant 315 ft. TL: N40 01 41 W84 11 28. Stereo. Hrs opn: 24. Box 819, 315 Public Sq., S.W. Suite 2D (45373). (513) 339-2505. FAX: (513) 339-6924. Licensee: WTRJ Broadcasting Inc. Net: SMN. Wash atty: Lauren A. Colby. Format: News, adult contemp. News staff 4. Target aud: 24-55. ■ William R. Coffey, pres & gen mgr; Sue Seitz, pub affrs dir. ■ Rates: $10; 9; 9; 6.

Uhrichsville

WBTC(AM)—Dec 13, 1963; 1540 khz; 250 w-D. TL: N40 25 26 W81 21 47. 125 Johnson Dr. (44683). (614) 922-2700; (614) 254-9000. FAX: (614) 922-2702. Licensee: Tuscarawas Broadcasting Co. Net: CBS. Rep: Rgnl Reps. Format: Talk, news/talk, oldies. News staff one; news progmg 2 hrs wkly. Target aud: 30-55. Spec prog: Relg 2 hrs wkly. ■ James Natoli Jr., pres, gen sls mgr & chief engr; Jim Natoli Jr., stn mgr; Ken Courtright, progmg dir & news dir; Allen Little, mus dir; Marge Durgle, pub affrs dir. ■ Rates: $8.50; 7.50; 6.75; na.

WTUZ(FM)—May 1, 1990: 99.9 mhz; 6 kw. Ant 328 ft. TL: N40 26 21 W81 25 01. Stereo. Box 191 (44683); 2695 Possom Hollow Rd. S.E., New Philadelphia (44663). (216) 339-2222. FAX: (216) 339-5441. Licensee: WTUZ Radio Inc. Net: Unistar, CNN. Wash atty: Smithwick & Belendiuk. Format: Country. News staff one; news progmg 7 hrs wkly. Target aud: General. Spec prog: Farm one hr, relg one hr wkly. ■ Edward A. Schumacher, pres & gen mgr; Laura Everett, gen sls mgr; Pat Smith, prom mgr; Bob Jacobs, progmg dir; Stacy McGuire, news dir; Don Graff, chief engr. ■ Rates: $16.25; 14; 16.25; 8.25.

Union City

WTGR(FM)—February 1994: 97.5 mhz; 6 kw. Ant 328 ft. TL: N40 11 32 W84 47 58. Box 889, Baker Family Stations, Blacksburg, VA (24063). (703) 552-4252. Licensee: State Line Radio. ■ Vernon H. Baker, gen mgr.

University Heights

***WUJC(FM)**—May 13, 1969: 88.7 mhz; 850 w. Ant 321 ft. TL: N41 29 24 W81 31 54. Stereo. Hrs opn: 6 AM-2 AM. c/o John Carroll Univ., 20700 N. Park Blvd., Cleveland (44118). (216) 397-4437; (216) 397-4438. FAX: (216) 397-4439. Licensee: John Carroll University. Wash atty: David Tillotson. Format: Div, modem, progsv. News progmg one hr wkly. Target aud: General. Spec prog: Black 3 hrs, class 4 hrs, It 2 hrs, jazz 4 hrs, relg 12 hrs wkly. ■ Dave Reese, gen mgr; Adrienne D'Ambrosio, stn mgr; Charlie Hickey, opns mgr; Mike Halkovich, dev dir; Shannon Jones, prom dir; Ed Douglas, progmg dir; Cheryl Botchick, mus dir; Jennifer Manley, news dir; Cornelius Gould, chief engr.

Upper Arlington

WRVF(FM)—May 25, 1989: 98.9 mhz; 3 kw. Ant 328 ft. TL: N39 58 16 W83 01 40. Stereo. Suite 250, 1650 Watermark Dr., Columbus (43215). (614) 488-4321. FAX: (614) 486-8022. Licensee: Tri-City Radio Ltd. Partnership (acq 8-91). Net: CNN. Rep: Eastman. Wash atty: Rosenman & Colin. Format: Country. News staff one. Target aud: 25-54; upscale, educated, active & responsive. ■ Alan Gray, gen mgr; Dave Barlow, gen sls mgr; Gregg Jordan, prom mgr; Rob Ellis, progmg dir; Terri Silver, news dir.

Upper Sandusky

***WXML(FM)**—Dec 26, 1993: 90.1 mhz; 3 kw-V. Ant 328 ft. TL: N40 50 10 W83 14 11. Stereo. Hrs opn: 6:30 AM-9 PM. Box 158, 1800 E. Wyandot Ave. (43351). (419) 294-2900. Licensee: Kayser Broadcast Ministries Inc. Net: Skylight. Wash atty: Verner, Liipfert, Bernard, McPherson & Hand. Format: Relg. News progmg 8 hrs wkly. Target aud: General. ■ Daniel L. Kayser, CEO, pres, CFO, gen mgr & stn mgr; Richard Johnson, vp; Mike Hayward, Francis Hensel, chiefs engr.

WYNT(FM)—Oct 1, 1986: 95.9 mhz; 3 kw. Ant 299 ft. TL: N40 49 30 W83 15 06. Stereo. Hrs opn: 19. Box 316 (43351). (419) 294-4903. FAX: (419) 294-4960. Licensee: U.S. Communications Inc. Net: NBC; Agri Bcstg. Format: Adult contemp, country crossover. Spec prog: Farm 6 hrs wkly. ■ Forest Whitehead, pres & gen mgr.

Directory of Radio

Urbana

WKSW(FM)—Aug 1, 1965: 101.7 mhz; 2.2 kw. Ant 397 ft. TL: N40 02 57 W83 46 06. Stereo. 2963 Derr Rd., Springfield (45503). (513) 399-5300. FAX: (513) 399-3661. Licensee: Champaign Communications Inc. (acq 11-16-70). Wash atty: Fletcher, Heald, Hildreth. Format: Country. News staff one; news progmg 7 hrs wkly. Target aud: 25-54; above-average income, blue-collar. ■ Robert Miller, pres; Roger C. Mackall, vp & gen mgr; Bruce Douglas, prom mgr; Nick Roberts, progmg dir & mus dir; Beth Anderson, news dir; Gene Simmons, chief engr. ■ Rates: $21; 20; 20; 15.

Van Wert

WBYR(FM)—Oct 1, 1962: 98.9 mhz; 50 kw. Ant 450 ft. TL: N40 53 33 W84 31 40. Stereo. Box 11160, Ft. Wayne, IN (46856); 347 W. Berry St., Ft. Wayne, IN (46802). (219) 420-9890. FAX: (219) 420-3299. Licensee: Atlantic Resources Corp. Net: Unistar. Rep: Eastman. Format: Classic rock. News staff one. Target aud: 25-49. ■ Paul Cheney, CEO; Joseph T. Conway, pres & gen mgr; Joesph T. Conway, gen sls mgr; John Robertson, progmg dir. ■ Rates: $70; 65; 75; 30.

WERT(AM)—Nov 27, 1958: 1220 khz; 250 w-U. TL: N40 52 19 W84 33 15. Hrs opn: 5:30 AM-11:00 PM. Box 487 (45891). (419) 238-1220. FAX: (419) 238-2578. Licensee: Community Broadcasting Inc. (acq 4-25-90; $155,000; FTR 5-14-90). Net: Agri Bcstg. Rep: Rgnl Reps. Wash atty: Pepper & Corazzini, Robert Thompson. Format: Oldies. News staff 7; news progmg 30 hrs wkly. Target aud: 25-54. Spec prog: Gospel 3 hrs, Sp one hr wkly. ■ Dale Profit, pres; Mona Kennedy, gen mgr; Peni Heller, gen sls mgr; J.P. Steffan, progmg dir; Donna Grube, news dir. ■ Rates: $14; 10; 8; 5.

Wapakoneta

WZOQ(FM)—July 1, 1964: 92.1 mhz; 3 kw. Ant 320 ft. TL: N40 39 20 W84 06 54. Stereo. Hrs opn: 24. Box 1487, Lima (45802); 710 N. Cable Rd, Lima (45805). (419) 222-9292. FAX: (419) 222-3755. Licensee: WZOQ Inc. (group owner; acq 1-26-93; grpsl; FTR 2-15-93). Net: ABC/C. Rep: McGavren Guild. Format: Contemp hit. News staff 1; news progmg 21 hrs wkly. ■ William Glover, vp & gen mgr; Tom Gallagher, progmg dir; Mike Carpenter, news dir; Dan Dietz, chief engr.

Warren

WANR(AM)—Apr 7, 1971: 1570 khz; 500 w-D,116 w-N, DA-1. TL: N41 12 22 W80 50 29. Hrs opn: 19. 119 W. Market St. (44481); Box 727 (44482-0727). (216) 382-3223; (216) 394-1501. Licensee: W-A Broadcasting Corp. (acq 11-30-90; $47,000; FTR 12-31-90). Net: ABC/C. Rep: Torbet. Format: News/talk, urban contemp. News staff one; news progmg 3 hrs wkly. Target aud: 18-54. ■ Craig Waffen, pres & gen sls mgr; Jack N. Alpern, CFO, sr vp, gen mgr & prom mgr; James Geogiades, chief opns & chief engr; Michael Vaughn, news dir. ■ Rates: $25; 20; 25; 20.

WRRO(AM)—Nov 11, 1941: 1440 khz; 5 kw-U, DA-2. TL: N41 09 52 W80 50 47. Box 1440 (44482). (216) 373-1440. FAX: (216) 373-1572. Licensee: Robin E. Best (acq 12-4-92; $460,000; FTR 12-21-92). Net: ABC/I. Rep: Rgnl Reps. Format: Oldies. ■ Robin E. Best, pres.

Washington Court House

WOFR(AM)—February 1952: 1250 khz; 500 w-D. TL: N39 32 59 W83 27 10. Box 260, 1535 N. North St. (43160). (614) 335-0941. FAX: (614) 335-6869. Licensee: Rodgers Broadcasting Corp. (group owner). Net: Agri Bcstg. Format: C&W. Spec prog: Farm 5 hrs wkly. ■ David A. Rogers, pres; Anthony Hays, gen mgr, gen sls mgr & mus dir; Laura Kunkel, news dir; Steve Stritenberger, chief engr.

WCHO-FM—Co-owned with WOFR(AM). December 1968: 105.5 mhz; 3 kw. Ant 300 ft. TL: N39 32 59 W83 27 10. Dups AM 70%.

Wauseon

WMTR-FM—See Archbold.

WZJU(FM)—Not on air, target date unknown: 96.9 mhz; 3 kw. Ant 328 ft. TL: N41 33 43 W84 09 10. 2637 N. Richmond St., Arlington, VA (22207). Licensee: Steamboat Radio Partners.

Stations in the U.S.   Ohio

Waverly

WXIC(AM)—1954: 660 khz; 1 kw-D. TL: N39 07 50 W83 00 46. Box 227, 6655 St. Rt. 220 W. (45690). (614) 947-2166. FAX: (614) 447-4600. Licensee: Crystal Communications Corp. (acq 7-1-79). Net: ABC/I. Rep: Keystone (unwired net), Rgnl Reps. Format: Southern gospel mus. News staff one; news progmg 16 hrs wkly. Target aud: Gospel music lovers. ■ Gerald E. Davis, pres; Bryan Chaffins, gen mgr & gen sls mgr; Rick Schweinsberg, progmg dir & mus dir; Rick Smith, chief engr. ■ Rates: $8; 6; 8; na.

WXIZ(FM)—Co-owned with WXIC(AM). March 1971: 100.9 mhz; 920 w. Ant 500 ft. TL: N39 13 17 W82 59 33. Stereo. Net: ABC/C. Format: Country. News staff one; news progmg 10 hrs wkly. Target aud: 25-50. ■ Steve Nibert, gen sls mgr; Wayne Montgomery, progmg dir & mus dir; Tim Hughes, news dir. ■ Rates: $6.20; 5.10; 6.20; 5.10.

Wellston

WYPC(AM)—1953: 1330 khz; 500 w-D, 50 w-N. TL: N39 06 22 W82 34 44. Hrs opn: 5 AM-midnight. Box 606, 287 E. Main, Jackson (45640). (614) 286-3023. FAX: (614) 286-6679. Licensee: Jackson County Broadcasting Inc. (group owner; acq 9-14-70). Net: CBS, Unistar. Format: Country. Target aud: 18-45. ■ Lewis E. Davis, pres & gen mgr; John Pelletier, gen sls mgr; Rod Tomlin, progmg dir; Tina Merry, mus dir; Mindy Ferguson, news dir; Tyrone Hemry, chief engr. ■ Rates: $4.10; 4.10; 4.10; 4.10.

WKOV-FM—Co-owned with WYPC(AM). July 17, 1971: 96.7 mhz; 16.5 kw. Ant 430 ft. TL: N39 01 45 W82 33 51. Stereo. Hrs opn: 24. Dups AM 10%. Wash atty: Fletcher, Heald & Hildreth. Format: Adult contemp. News staff one; news progmg 21 hrs wkly. Target aud: 20-55. ■ Rates: $7.60; 6.80; 7.60; 5.50.

West Carrollton

***WQRP(FM)**—Apr 9, 1977: 88.1 mhz; 4 kw. Ant 295 ft. TL: N39 42 59 W84 15 24 (CP: 4 kw, ant 295 ft.). Stereo. Hrs opn: 24. 2673 S. Dixie Dr., Dayton (45409). (513) 298-4044; (513) 298-6987. FAX: (513) 298-4816. Licensee: Southwestern Ohio Public Radio Inc. Net: USA. Format: Relg. Target aud: 24-50. Spec prog: Black 12 hrs, Ger 5 hrs, Hungarian 3 hrs wkly. ■ Harold F. Parshall, pres, gen mgr & chief engr; Angela Jones, prom mgr & mus dir; Brad Pyle, progmg dir.

WROU(FM)—Not on air, target date unknown: 92.1 mhz; 890 w. Ant 597 ft. TL: N39 43 15 W84 15 39. 581 W. Spring Valley Rd., Centerville (45459). (216) 222-9768. Licensee: Ronita Bernice Hawes-Saunders.

West Chester

***WLHS(FM)**—Sept 3, 1976: 89.9 mhz; 100 w. Ant 338 ft. TL: N39 19 40 W84 22 04. Hrs opn: 9 AM-5 PM. 5050 Tylersville Rd. (45069). (513) 874-4699. Licensee: Lakota School District. Format: Educ. ■ C. Kay Taylor Watson, gen mgr.

West Union

WRAC(FM)—Dec 15, 1981: 103.1 mhz; 3.3 kw. Ant 417 ft. TL: N38 51 25 W83 36 38 (CP: 3.3 kw, ant 426 ft.). Stereo. Hrs opn: 37. Box 103, 106 S. West St. (45693). (513) 544-9722. FAX: (513) 544-5523. Licensee: Ohio River Broadcasting Assoc Inc. (acq 9-21-81; $4,820; FTR 10-12-81). Net: Unistar. Rep: Rgnl Reps. Format: Adult contemp, C&W, gospel. News staff one; news progmg 5 hrs wkly. Target aud: General. Spec prog: Farm 10 hrs wkly. ■ Virginia M. Purdy, pres & gen mgr; Ted Foster, progmg dir, mus dir & news dir; Bill Donnemeyer, chief engr. ■ Rates: $9; 9; 9; 5.

***WVXM(FM)**—1990: 89.5 mhz; 4 kw. Ant 330 ft. TL: N38 51 36 W83 36 42. Stereo. Xavier University, 3800 Victory Pkwy., Cincinnati (45207). (513) 745-3738. FAX: (513) 745-1004. Licensee: Xavier Univ. Net: NPR; Ohio Educ Bcstg. Format: Jazz, CNN News, nostalgia. News staff 3; news progmg 35 hrs wkly. Target aud: 25-49; mid to upscale working audience. Spec prog: Black one hr, class 5 hrs wkly. ■ J.C. King, gen mgr; Mike Boberg, prom mgr; George Zahn, progmg dir; Mark Keefe, mus dir; Lorna Jordan, news dir; Jay Crawford, chief engr.

Westerville

***WOBN(FM)**—Oct 8, 1958: 101.5 mhz; 28 w. Ant 40 ft. TL: N40 07 28 W82 56 15. Stereo. Cowan Hall, Otterbein College (43081). (614) 823-1557; (614) 823-1725. FAX: (614) 823-5998. Licensee: Otterbein College. Format: Rock, class rock, progsv. News progmg 3 hrs wkly. Target aud: General; Westerville & Otterbein College community. Spec prog: Black 2 hrs, jazz one hr, relg 4 hrs, heavy metal 2 hrs wkly. ■ Latina Duffy, gen mgr. ■ WOCC-TV affil.

Wilberforce

***WCSU-FM**—Dec 15, 1962: 88.9 mhz; 1 kw. Ant 150 ft. TL: N39 42 57 W83 52 27. Stereo. Central State Univ. (45384). (513) 376-6371. Licensee: Central State University. Format: Urban contemp, jazz. News progmg 3 hrs wkly. Target aud: 12-49; African-Americans. ■ J.C. Logan, gen mgr; Jahan Culbreath, mus dir; Stephan Lane, chief engr.

Willoughby-Eastlake

WELW(AM)—Jan 25, 1965: 1330 khz; 500 w-D. TL: N41 38 56 W81 25 19. Hrs opn: 24. Box 1330, 36913 Stevens Blvd., Willoughby (44094). (216) 946-1330. FAX: (216) 953-0320. Licensee: Harris Broadcasting Inc. (acq 9-11-90; FTR 10-1-90). Wash atty: Arent, Fox, Kintner, Plotkin & Kahn. Format: Btfl mus, div, oldies. News staff 2; news progmg 5 hrs wkly. Target aud: 35 plus; community adults. Spec prog: It one hr, Hungarian one hr, Croation 4 hrs, Irish one hr, Pol 2 hrs, relg 4 hrs, Slovenian 4 hrs, sports 10 hrs wkly. ■ Ray Somich, pres, gen mgr & progmg dir; Camilla D'Andrea, stn mgr; Mark Tromba, opns dir; Van Lane, gen sls mgr; Bruce Totten, prom mgr; Kelly McGinty, news dir; Bob Meyer, chief engr.

Wilmington

WKFI(AM)—Dec 5, 1964: 1090 khz; 1 kw-D, DA. TL: N39 26 12 W83 51 21. Box 1 (45177). (513) 382-1608. FAX: (513) 382-1665. Licensee: Marion Brechner (acq 12-21-90; FTR 1-14-91). Net: ABC/E, MBS, NBC, APR. Wash atty: Cohn & Marks. Format: Farm, talk, country. News staff one. Target aud: General. Spec prog: Big band 5 hrs wkly. ■ Rick Johnston, gen mgr & gen sls mgr; Jim Rankin, prom dir; Eric Ferguson, progmg dir; Karla Burton, mus dir & news dir; Ted Ryan, chief engr. ■ Rates: $25; 25; 25; na.

WSWO(FM)—Co-owned with WKFI(AM). 1974: 102.3 mhz; 3 kw. Ant 300 ft. TL: N39 21 54 W83 46 08. Stereo. Prog sep from AM. (513) 382-1023. Net: ABC/E. Format: Adult contemp. News progmg 22 hrs wkly. ■ Greg Hamm, mus dir.

Wooster

WBZW(FM)—(Loudonville). March 1990: 107.7 mhz; 6 kw. Ant 328 ft. TL: N40 36 58 W82 05 34. Stereo. Hrs opn: 24. Box 932, Wooster (44691); 127 N. Water St. (44842). (419) 994-5511. Licensee: The Charter Broadcast Group Ltd. Net: Jones Satellite Audio. Wash atty: Donald E. Martin. Format: Oldies News staff one; news progmg 20 hrs wkly. Target aud: 25-54; money demo. Spec prog: Relg 5 hrs wkly. ■ Donald E. Martin, chmn; Esther Martin, exec vp; Sara Bontempo, stn mgr, opns dir & sls dir; Richard Morrison, chief engr. ■ Rates: $18; 16; 18; 14.

***WCWS(FM)**—April 1968: 90.9 mhz; 1.05 kw. Ant 230 ft. TL: N40 48 34 W81 56 18. Stereo. Hrs opn: 10 AM-midnight. Wishart Hall, College of Wooster (44691). (216) 287-2240. Licensee: The College of Wooster. Net: AP. Format: Div, CHR. Target aud: General; college students and people of the surrounding area. Spec prog: Class 12 hrs, jazz 8 hrs, classic rock 16 hrs, urban contemp 3 hrs, heavy metal 4 hrs, reggae 3 hrs wkly. ■ Kate Kilbane, gen mgr; Amy Diefenbach, prom mgr; John Mallon, progmg dir; Bob Carpenter, mus dir.

***WKRW(FM)**—Not on air, target date unknown: 89.3 mhz; 2.1 kw. Ant 318 ft. TL: N40 46 28 W81 55 05. Licensee: Kent State Univ.

WKVX(AM)—1947: 960 khz; 1 kw-D, 32 w-N. TL: N40 47 31 W81 54 17. Stereo. Hrs opn: 24. Box 384, 186 S. Hillcrest Dr. (44691). (216) 264-5122. FAX: (216) 264-3571. Licensee: WWST Corp. Group owner: Dix Communications. Net: AP, SMN. Rep: Rgnl Reps. Format: Oldies. ■ Ken Nemeth, gen mgr; Craig Walton, gen sls mgr; David Peppler, progmg dir; Alan B. Lang, news dir; Wayne Fick, chief engr. ■ Rates: $17; 12.50; 17; 12.50.

WQKT(FM)—Co-owned with WKVX(AM). 1947: 104.5 mhz; 52 kw. Ant 330 ft. TL: N40 47 31 W81 54 17. Stereo. Hrs opn: 24. Prog sep from AM. Net: SMN. Format: C&W. Spec prog: Farm 2 hrs wkly. ■ Rates: $28; 22; 28; 22.

Xenia

WBZI(AM)—Nov 11, 1963: 1500 khz; 500 w-D. TL: N39 42 48 W83 54 48. Hrs opn: Sunrise-sunset. Box 99, 600 Kinsey Rd. (45385). (513) 372-3531; (513) 426-2433. FAX: (513) 372-8484. Licensee: Dayton Area Radio Inc. Group owner: Baker Family Stations. Net: USA; Agri Bcstg, Agri-Net. Format: Country, relg. News progmg 14 hrs wkly. Target aud: 25-64; upper income, married, home owners. Spec prog: Gospel 6 hrs wkly. ■ Vern Baxter, CEO; Al Pichot, gen mgr, gen sls mgr & pub affrs dir; Joe Hardin, news dir; Winston Hawkins, chief engr. ■ Rates: $35; 30; 35; 25.

WGNZ(AM)—See Fairborn.

WZLR(FM)—Mar 3, 1967: 95.3 mhz; 3 kw. Ant 300 ft. TL: N39 37 54 W83 53 49. Stereo. Prog sep from AM. 1930 N. Lakeman Ave., Bellbrook (45305). (513) 848-8828. Licensee: Clear 95 Inc. (acq 9-1-93; $800,000; FTR 10-4-93). Net: SMN, Unistar. Format: C&W. ■ Dave Dexter, gen mgr.

Yellow Springs

***WYSO(FM)**—Feb 8, 1958: 91.3 mhz; 10 kw. Ant 410 ft. TL: N39 45 46 W83 53 05. Stereo. Hrs opn: 24. Union Bldg., Antioch College (45387). (513) 767-6420. Licensee: Antioch Univ. Net: APR, NPR; Ohio Educ Bcstg. Format: News, eclectic. News staff one; news progmg 44 hrs wkly. Spec prog: Jazz 18 hrs, class 10 hrs, C&W 2 hrs, Pol 2 hrs, Indian one hr, blues 16 hrs, bluegrass/country 10 hrs wkly. ■ Brian Gibbons, gen mgr; Ruth Yellowhawk, progmg dir; Scott Wallace, chief engr.

Youngstown

WASN(AM)—See Campbell.

WBBG(FM)—Listing follows WBBW(AM).

WBBW(AM)—Feb 20, 1949: 1240 khz; 1 kw-U. TL: N41 04 50 W80 38 54. 418 Knox St. (44502). (216) 744-4421. Licensee: H & D Communications L.P. Group owner: H & D Broadcast Group (acq 5-13-88). Net: CNN. Rep: Christal. Format: News/talk. News staff 4; news progmg 140 hrs wkly. Target aud: General. Spec prog: It 6 hrs wkly. ■ Larry Weiss, gen mgr; Kelley McGrath, gen sls mgr; Amy Garvin, prom mgr; Jeff Kelly, progmg dir; Don Ferguson, news dir; George Drapp, chief engr.

WBBG(FM)—Co-owned with WBBW(AM). June 1959: 93.3 mhz; 50 kw. Ant 280 ft. TL: N41 04 50 W80 38 54. Stereo. Prog sep from AM. Format: Oldies. Target aud: 25-54.

WGFT(AM)—May 9, 1976: 1500 khz; 500 w-D, 250 w-CH, DA. TL: N41 06 26 W80 34 57. 131 W. Boardman St. (44503). (216) 744-5115. Licensee: WGFT Inc. Group owner: Spart Communications (acq 1985). Format: Relg. News progmg 4 hrs wkly. Target aud: General; families. Spec prog: Black 4 hrs wkly. ■ Timothy DeCapua, pres; Rebecca Reichard, stn mgr & prom mgr; Calvin Penny, progmg dir; Linda Thompson, mus dir; Brian Collins, pub affrs dir; Tom Zocolo, chief engr. ■ Rates: $15; 15; 15; 15.

WHOT(AM)—Sept 7, 1939: 1390 khz; 9.5 kw-U, DA-N. TL: N41 01 22 W80 38 46 (CP: TL: N41 07 17 W80 42 05 (day), N41 00 13 W80 38 16 (night)). Stereo. Hrs opn: 24. 4040 Simon Rd. (44512). (216) 783-1000. FAX: (216) 783-0060. Licensee: WHOT Inc. Group owner: The Jet Broadcasting Co. (acq 4-18-90; FTR 5-7-90). Format: Music of Your Life. News staff 2; news progmg 3 hrs wkly. Target aud: 50 plus. ■ Myron Jones, CEO; John Kanzius, chmn & gen mgr; Joe Martin, sls dir; Tom Meister, prom dir; Tom Pappas, progmg dir; Bruce Robertson, news dir; Jack Aye, chief engr.

WHOT-FM—November 1959: 101.1 mhz; 24 kw. Ant 711 ft. TL: N41 03 28 W80 38 24 (CP: 25 kw, ant 694 ft.). Stereo. Rep: Rgnl Reps, Christal. Wash atty: Reddy, Begley & Martin. Format: CHR. ■ John Kanzius, pres; Donna Palowitz, gen sls mgr; J.Timothy Foley, natl sls mgr & rgnl sls mgr; Tom Pappas, vp mktg & prom dir.

WHTX(FM)—Listing follows WRQQ(AM).

WKBN(AM)—1926: 570 khz; 5 kw-U, DA-N. TL: N40 59 07 W80 36 02. Hrs opn: 24. 3930 Sunset Blvd. (44501). (216) 782-1144. FAX: (216) 782-3504. Licensee: WKBN Broadcasting Corp. Net: CBS, MBS, NBC Talknet. Rep: Katz. Format: News, sports, talk. Spec prog: Polka 2 hrs, Croation 2 hrs wkly. ■ J.D. Williamson II, pres; William E. Kelly Jr., gen mgr; Dan Rivers, opns dir; Brad Marshall, gen sls mgr; Pete Gabriel, prom mgr; Jim Hartzler, chief engr.

Oklahoma | Directory of Radio

WKBN-FM—Aug 26, 1947: 98.9 mhz; 4.5 kw. Ant 1,370 ft. TL: N41 03 24 W80 38 44. Stereo. Prog sep from AM. Net: CBS Spectrum. Format: Soft contemp. ■ Don Guthrie, progmg dir; Jim Michaels, mus dir. ■WKBN-TV affil.

WNCD(FM)—See Niles.

WNRB(AM)—See Niles.

WRQQ(AM)—(Farrell, Pa). Oct 3, 1954: 1470 khz; 1 kw-D, 500 w-N, DA-N. TL: N41 11 58 W80 31 22. Hrs opn: 24. 401 N. Blaine, Campbell (44505). (216) 746-1330. FAX: (216) 746-1311. Licensee: National Communications System Inc. (acq 3-26-93; $328,000 with co-located FM; FTR 4-12-93). Rep: Katz & Powell. Format: Oldies. News staff one; news progmg one hr wkly. Target aud: 25-54. Spec prog: High school sports 12 hrs wkly. ■ Kelly Holtzclaw, pres; Larry Ward, gen mgr; Kelly Salandro, news dir.

WHTX(FM)—(Sharpsville, Pa). Co-owned with WRQQ(AM). Dec 28, 1976: 95.9 mhz; 3 kw. Ant 328 ft. TL: N41 13 05 W80 33 43. Stereo. Hrs opn: 24. Dups AM 95%. Format: Country, rock. News progmg one hr wkly.

WRRO(AM)—See Warren.

*****WYSU(FM)**—September 1969: 88.5 mhz; 50 kw. Ant 499 ft. TL: N41 03 28 W80 38 42. Stereo. Youngstown State Univ. (44555). (216) 742-3363. FAX: (216) 742-1501. Licensee: Youngstown State University. Net: APR, NPR. Wash atty: Dow, Lohnes & Albertson. Format: Classical, jazz, news. News progmg 24 hrs wkly. Target aud: General. Spec prog: Folk 3 hrs, Broadway one hr wkly. ■ Robert W. Peterson, gen mgr; Gary Sexton, opns mgr & progmg dir; Catherine Cala, dev dir; Ann Cliness, pub affrs dir; William C. Panko, chief engr.

*****WYTN(FM)**—May 1991: 91.7 mhz; 3 kw. Ant 299 ft. TL: N41 03 28 W80 38 42. Stereo. Hrs opn: 24. 1140 E. Midlothian Blvd. (44502). (216) 783-9986. Licensee: Family Stations Inc. (group owner). Net: UPI. Wash atty: Dow, Lohnes & Albertson. Format: Relg. Target aud: 25 plus; Christians. Spec prog: Class 2 hrs wkly. ■ David Ficere, gen mgr; Mike Zeimann, rgnl sls mgr; Curt Flick, chief engr.

Zanesville

*****WCVZ(FM)**—Jan 5, 1983: 92.7 mhz; 3 kw. Ant 304 ft. TL: N39 56 55 W81 57 48 (CP: Ant 407 ft.). Stereo. 2477 E. Pike (43701-4626). (614) 455-3181. FAX: (614) 455-6195. Licensee: Christian Voice of Central Ohio Inc. Net: USA. Format: Relg, talk. ■ Bob Roller, pres & gen mgr; Carl Sullivan, stn mgr; Austin Taylor, progmg dir & mus dir; Neil Snelling, news dir; Farris Whilhite, chief engr.

WHIZ(AM)—July 8, 1924: 1240 khz; 1 kw-U. TL: N39 55 42 W81 59 06. Stereo. Hrs opn: 24. 629 Downard Rd. (43701). (614) 452-5431. FAX: (614) 452-6553. Licensee: Southeastern Ohio Broadcasting System Inc. (acq 6-47). Net: NBC, NBC Talknet. Rep: Roslin; Rgnl Reps. Wash atty: J. Richard Carr. Format: Adult contemp, news/talk. News staff 10; news progmg 30 hrs wkly. Target aud: General; 25-54. Spec prog: Sports: Cincinnati Reds, Ohio State football/basketball, Cleveland Browns & local high-school football/basketball. Farm progmg 2 hrs wkly. ■ Mrs. W.O. Littick, pres; Allan Land, vp & gen mgr; Pete Petonlak, opns mgr, mktg mgr & progmg dir; Robin Smith, gen sls mgr; George Hlotis, news dir; C.E. Hartmeyer, chief engr. ■ Rates: $16.25; 16,25; 16.25; 13.

WHIZ-FM—Dec 16, 1961: 102.5 mhz; 50 kw. Ant 490 ft. TL: N39 55 42 W81 59 06. Stereo. Hrs opn: 24. Dups AM 20%. Net: NBC Talknet. Format: Easy lstng, talk. News progmg 12 hrs wkly. Target aud: General; 25 plus. Spec prog: Relg one hr, sports 3 hrs wkly. ■ Steve Oliver, opns mgr & progmg dir. WHIZ-TV affil. ■ Rates: $14.75; 14.75; 14.75; 11.30.

*****WOUZ(FM)**—Not on air, target date unknown: 90.1 mhz; 3 kw. Ant 279 ft. TL: N39 48 50 W81 57 21. c/o Ohio University, 9 S. College St., Athens (45701). Licensee: Ohio University.

WYBZ(FM)—See Crooksville.

Oklahoma

Are You Ready To Cash In On Communications?
NF&A
Norman Fischer & Associates, Inc.
Media Brokerage • Appraisals • Management Consultants
1209 Parkway • Austin, Texas 78703 • (512) 476-9457

Ada

KADA(AM)—September 1934: 1230 khz; 1 kw-U. TL: N34 47 06 W96 40 44. Box 609, 1019 N. Broadway (74820). (405) 332-1212. FAX: (405) 332-0128. Licensee: KADA Broadcasting Inc. Net: Okla. Net. Format: Country. News staff 2; news progmg 5 hrs wkly. Target aud: 25-54. Spec prog: Gospel. ■ Katherine Hoover, pres; Roger Harris, gen mgr; Brenda Revels, gen sls mgr; Buddy Kessinger, prom mgr & progmg mgr; Colin Boyd, mus dir; Michael Wilder, news dir; Preston Walker, chief engr.

KADA-FM—1979: 96.7 mhz; 3 kw. Ant 299 ft. TL: N34 42 31 W96 44 24. Stereo. Prog sep from AM. Licensee: KADA Broadcasting Inc. (acq 7-88). Net: Unistar, CNN. Format: Adult contemp, oldies. Spec prog: Jazz 7 hrs wkly. ■ Rates: $7.50; 5; 6; 4.

KEOR(AM)—See Atoka.

KTLS(FM)—April 15, 1971: 93.3 mhz; 100 kw. Ant 630 ft. TL: N34 54 06 W96 40 37. Stereo. Suite No. 2, 1610 Arlington (74820). (405) 332-2211. FAX: (405) 436-1629. Licensee: Oklahoma Broadcasting Co. (acq 5-23-90; $503,425; FTR 6-18-90). Net: ABC/C. Rep: Katz. Format: Adult contemp. News staff one; news progmg 4 hrs wkly. Target aud: 25-54. ■ Randy May, gen mgr; Kenny Morrisson, gen sls mgr; Mike Hall, prom mgr & progmg dir; Kevin Christopher, mus dir; Rick Cody, news dir; Mark McGenee, chief engr.

Altus

KEYB(FM)—Dec 25, 1988: 107.9 mhz; 6 kw. Ant 190 ft. TL: N34 38 19 W99 21 47. Stereo. Hrs opn: 24. Box 1077, 219 E. Commerce (73522). (405) 482-1555. FAX: (405) 482-8353. Licensee: Paul E. Wilmes (acq 12-6-90; FTR 12-31-90). Net: MBS. Rep: Riley. Wash atty: Gardner, Carton & Douglas. Format: Country. News progmg 3 hrs wkly. Target aud: 25-54. Spec prog: Farm 2 hrs wkly. ■ Paul Wilmes, chmn; Gayle Ledbetter, gen mgr, mktg mgr & prom mgr; H. G. Milner, gen sls mgr; Cliff Miller, progmg dir; Ken Austin, engrg mgr.

*****KKVO(FM)**—1985: 90.9 mhz; 400 w. Ant 121 ft. TL: N34 42 44 W99 19 03. Box 797 (73522). (405) 477-4110. Licensee: Altus Educational Broadcasting Foundation. Format: Relg. ■ Peter Galloway, gen mgr.

KRKZ(FM)—Listing follows KWHW(AM).

KWHW(AM)—April 2, 1947: 1450 khz; 1 kw-U. TL: N34 37 35 W99 20 10. Box 577 (73522). (405) 482-1450. Licensee: Altus Radio Inc. Group owner: Community Service Radio Group. Net: ABC/E, Okla. Net. Format: C&W, farm. Spec prog: Sp 16 hrs wkly. ■ Galen Gilbert, pres; Jimmy Young, gen mgr; Dick Fontana, progmg dir; Tony Quest, mus dir; Keith Dobson, news dir; Don Smith, chief engr.

KRKZ(FM)—Co-owned with KWHW(AM). April 1, 1974: 93.5 mhz; 45 kw. Ant 528 ft. TL: N34 37 35 W99 20 10. Stereo. Prog sep from AM. (Acq 6-1-84). Format: CHR.

Alva

KALV(AM)—Oct 18, 1956: 1430 khz; 500 w-U, DA-2. TL: N36 49 06 W98 38 38. Stereo. Hrs opn: 6 AM-12 AM. Box KALV, Rt. 1, Box 53 (73717). (405) 327-1430; (405) 327-1431. FAX: (405) 327-1433. Licensee: Alvaomni Inc. (acq 1-88; $366,000; FTR 10-31-88). Net: ABC/I; Okla. News. Format: Contemp country. News staff one; news progmg 8 hrs wkly. Target aud: 45-70; loc residents. Spec prog: Farm 4 hrs, class one hr, relg 7 hrs wkly. ■ Douglas Williams, pres; Randy Mitchel, gen mgr & gen sls mgr; Charlotte Brucks, dev dir; Cat Stephenson, news dir; Bill Reid, chief engr.

KTTL(FM)—Not on air, target date unknown: 94.3 mhz; 50 kw. Ant 492 ft. TL: N36 47 06 W98 33 01. Box 69, Dover, NH (03820). (603) 742-8575. Licensee: Women, Handicapped Americans and Minorities for Better Broadcasting Inc.

KVNR(FM)—Not on air, target date unknown: 104.7 mhz; 100 kw. Ant 981 ft. TL: N36 35 57 W98 14 56. 654 India St., Suite D, San Diego, CA (92101). Licensee: Quantum Broadcasting Co. (acq 11-13-91; $15,000 for CP; FTR 12-2-91).

KXLS(FM)—Licensed to Alva. See Enid.

Anadarko

KRPT(AM)—Dec 17, 1970: 850 khz; 500 w-D, DA. TL: N35 06 58 W98 17 45. Box 1360, 115 W. Broadway (73005). (405) 247-6682. FAX: (405) 247-5778. Licensee: Anadarko Broadcasting Co. Net: ABC/D; Okla. Agri. Format: Country. News staff 2; news progmg 10 hrs wkly. Target aud: 25 plus. Spec prog: American Indian one hr, relg 2 hrs, bluegrass 2 hrs wkly. ■ Karen Thomasson, vp & gen mgr; Rene Strong, gen sls mgr; Larry LaLiverte, mus dir & news dir.

KRPT-FM—September 1981: 103.7 mhz; 86 kw. Ant 987 ft. TL: N34 56 30 W98 22 34. Stereo. Dups AM 100%. ■ Rates: $21; 14; 18; 13.

Ardmore

KICM(FM)—See Healdton.

KKAJ(AM)—September 1935: 1240 khz; 1 kw-U. TL: N34 10 54 W97 08 48. Stereo. Hrs opn: 24. Box 429 (73402); 1205 Northglen (73401). (405) 226-0421. FAX: (405) 226-0464. Licensee: Chuckle Broadcasting Co. (acq 5-20-93; $430,000 with co-located FM; FTR 4-12-93). Net: ABC; Okla. News Net. Rep: Statnets. Format: Country. Target aud: 25 plus. Spec prog: Farm 2 hrs wkly, Oklahoma Sooners football, Dallas Cowboys, Rush Limbaugh, high school football/basketball. ■ Ken Taishoff, pres; Bob Clark, exec vp, gen mgr & gen sls mgr; Becky Fincher, opns dir; Donna Foster (local), rgnl sls mgr; Al Hamilton, prom dir, progmg dir & pub affrs dir; Donna Foster, adv mgr; Steve Foster, mus dir; Rob Carter, asst mus dir; Kriss Roberts, news dir; Bill Gilliland, chief engr. ■ Rates: $26; 20; 26; 20.

KKAJ-FM—June 24, 1974: 95.7 mhz; 100 kw. Ant 449 ft. TL: N34 05 56 W97 10 54. Stereo. Hrs opn: 24. Dups AM 100%. News staff one; news progmg 4 hrs wkly. Target aud: Rural area adults. ■ Donna Foster, rgnl sls mgr; Al Hamilton, pub affrs dir; John Orr, engrg mgr. ■ Rates: Same as AM.

KRDM(FM)—Jan 1, 1989: 96.5 mhz; 3 kw. Ant 328 ft. TL: N34 12 48 W97 11 45. Stereo. Stn currently dark. 1908 12th Ave. N.W. (73401). Licensee: Versace Comm. Inc. (acq 9-88; $220,297; FTR 1-23-89). ■ Robert Versace, pres & gen mgr; Hal Smith, chief engr.

Atoka

KEOR(AM)—Jan 29, 1968: 1110 khz; 5 kw-D, DA. TL: N34 25 08 W96 11 24. Box 810, Hwy. 75 N. (74525). (405) 889-3392; (405) 889-3393. FAX: (405) 889-3393. Licensee: Ballard Broadcasting of Okla. (acq 12-31-83; $243,170; FTR 10-19-87). Net: ABC/E. Format: Relg. News staff one; news progmg 14 hrs wkly. Target aud: General. ■ Drew Ballard, pres; John Clemmetsen, gen mgr. ■ Rates: $8; 8; 8; na.

KHKC-FM—Co-owned with KEOR(AM). June 15, 1984: 103.1 mhz; 3 kw. Ant 454 ft. TL: N34 25 05 W96 11 25. Stereo. Prog sep from AM. 4410 10th St., Lubbock, TX (74416). Net: ABC/E. Format: Country. News staff 3; news progmg 15 hrs wkly. ■ Ricky Chase, gen mgr & progmg dir; James Cunningham, chief engr. ■Rates: $8; 8; 8; 8.

KTLS(FM)—See Ada.

Bartlesville

KRIG(FM)—(Nowata). Sept. 25, 1993: 94.3 mhz; 3.5 kw. Ant 429 ft. TL: N36 44 35 95 45 17. Stereo. Hrs opn: 24. Suite 1A. 1740 S.E. Washington Blvd, Bartlesville, OK (74006); Box 877, Bartlesville, OK (74005). (918) 333-7943. FAX: (918) 333-7986. Licensee: KRIG Radio Homer H. Hilson, Jr. & Bruce H. Campell (acq 9-16-91). Net: ABC/Satelite Music Network. Wash atty: Cohn & Marks. Format: Real country. Target aud: 25-54. ■ Bruce H. Campbell, vp & gen mgr; Jim Ford, news dir. ■ Rates: $25; 15; 20; 10.

KWON(AM)—April 1942: 1400 khz; 1 kw-U. TL: N36 45 53 W95 57 35. Stereo. Hrs opn: 24. Box 1100 (74005); 1200 S.E. Frank Phillips Blvd. (74003). (918) 333-1400;

(918) 336-1001. FAX: (918) 336-6939. Licensee: KYFM Radio Inc. (acq 10-15-92; $250,000; FTR 11-16-92). Net: CBS. Okla. Net. Wash atty: Fletcher, Heald & Hildreth. Format: Country, news/talk. News staff one; news progmg 25 hrs wkly. Target aud: 25-54. ■ Galen Gilbert, pres; Timothy Akers, vp; Lynne Akers, gen sls mgr; Todd Mathes, news dir. ■ Rates: $14; 8; 14; 3.

KYFM(FM)—Co-owned with KWON(AM). Nov 6, 1961: 100.1 mhz; 950 w. Ant 492 ft. TL: N36 44 04 W95 51 18. Stereo. Hrs opn: 24. (acq 6-1-83; $1.1 million; FTR 6-20-83). Net: ABC/E, Unistar. Format: Adult contemp. News staff one; news progmg 15 hrs wkly. Target aud: 25-49; mid-upper class income. Spec prog: Relg 5 hrs wkly. ■ Rates: $15; 9; 15; 5.

Bethany

KNTL(FM)—Licensed to Bethany. See Oklahoma City.

Bixby

KBXT(FM)—Not on air, target date January 1994: 105.5 mhz; 25 kw. Ant 328 ft. TL: N35 51 41 W95 46 03. 7715 S. Oxford Ave., Tulsa (74136). Licensee: John M. Singer. Wash atty: Meyer, Faller, Weisman & Rosenberg. ■ Robert Cauthon, chief engr.

Blackwell

KLOR-FM—See Ponca City.

KOKB(AM)—October 1952: 1580 khz; 1 kw-D, 49 w-N. TL: N36 48 35 W97 15 50. Hrs opn: 6 AM-9 PM. Box 70, One Radio Tower Rd. (74631). (405) 363-4567. FAX: (405) 363-4568. Licensee: Moore Communications (acq 10-15-90; $130,000). Net: ABC/E, NBC Talknet, Sun. Rep: Okla. Net. Format: News/talk. News progmg 30 hrs wkly. Target aud: 35-75; adult, upper-middle income. Spec prog: Gospel 11 hrs wkly. ■ Donald Moore, pres, gen mgr, gen sls mgr & chief engr; Don Moore, prom mgr; Gary Tyler, progmg dir; Sheryl Moore, news dir.

Bristow

KREK(FM)—Nov 14, 1978: 104.9 mhz; 2.6 kw. Ant 351 ft. TL: N35 47 11 W96 27 35. Stereo. Box 1280 (74010). (918) 367-5501. Licensee: Big Chief Broadcasting Co. of Bristow Inc. Net: ABC/I. Format: C&W. ■ Clifford W. Smith, pres & gen mgr; Deanna Smith, mus dir.

Broken Arrow

KCMA(FM)—Dec 23, 1970: 92.1 mhz; 27 kw. Ant 656 ft. TL: N36 06 38 W96 01 57. Stereo. Hrs opn: 6 AM-midnight. Suite 760, 2021 S. Lewis Ave., Tulsa (74104-5715). (918) 747-9999. FAX: (918) 747-7345. Licensee: KCMA Inc. (acq 3-4-86). Rep: CMBS. Wash atty: Pepper & Corazzini. Format: Classical. Target aud: General. Spec prog: Jazz 7 hrs wkly. ■ John K. Major, pres; Thomas H. Shealy, gen mgr & gen sls mgr; James Fellow, opns mgr; James Fellows, mus dir; Richard Hardy, chief engr.

*KNYD(FM)—Aug 19, 1986: 90.5 mhz; 100 kw. Ant 1,638 ft. TL: N36 01 15 W95 40 32. Stereo. Box 1924, Tulsa (74101); 11717 S. 129th E. Ave. (74011). (918) 455-5693. Licensee: Creative Educational Media Inc. (acq 1985). Format: Positive easy gospel. Target aud: General. Spec prog: Talk 5 hrs wkly. ■ David Ingles, pres; Kim Spence, prom mgr; David Warren, progmg dir & mus dir; Greg Thomas, engrg dir; Roger King, chief engr.

Broken Bow

KKBI(FM)—January 1983: 106.1 mhz; 50 kw. Ant 1621 ft. TL: N34 14 45 W94 46 58 Stereo. Hrs opn: 24. Box 1016, 617 S. Park Dr. (74728-1016). (405) 584-3388; (405) 584-3372. FAX: (405) 584-3341. Licensee: Care-Phil Communications (acq 11-89; $562,500; FTR 11-27-89). Net: SMN. Wash atty: Fletcher, Heald & Hildreth. Format: Country. News progmg 12 hrs wkly. Target aud: 24-55. Spec prog: Farm 2 hrs wkly. ■ Carole Williams, gen mgr & stn mgr; Dave Smulyan, gen sls mgr & prom dir; Debra DeMoss, progmg dir & mus dir; Dale Gorsuch, chief engr. ■ Rates: $12; 10.65; 12; 8.65.

Byng

KYKC(FM)—Not on air, target date unknown: 100.1 mhz; 50 kw. Ant 492 ft. TL: N34 43 43 W96 42 45. 1806 Melody Ln., Ada (74820). Licensee: Central Oklahoma Communications Co.

Chickasha

KWCO(AM)—Nov 1946: 1560 khz; 1 kw-D, 250 w-N, DA-N. TL: N35 00 58 W97 56 15. Hrs opn: 5:30 AM-midnight. Box 1268, 500 Country Club Rd. (73018). (405) 224-1560. FAX: (405) 224-2890. Licensee: Brewer Broadcasting Corp. Net: ABC/C. Format: Adult contemp. News staff one; news progmg 16 hrs wkly. Target aud: 18 plus. ■ Bob Martin, pres, gen mgr, gen sls mgr & news dir; Jack G. Brewer, vp; Ted Turner, opns mgr, progmg dir & chief engr; Brent Caldwell, mus dir. ■ Rates: $20; 18; 20; 15.

KXXK(FM)—Co-owned with KWCO(AM). Nov 4, 1966: 105.5 mhz; 3 kw. Ant 195 ft. TL: N35 00 58 W97 56 15 (CP: 3.27 kw, Ant 443 ft.). Stereo. Dups AM 100%. ■ Ted Turner, opns dir. ■ Rates: Same as AM.

Claremore

*KRSC-FM—Aug 4, 1980: 91.3 mhz; 2.2 kw. Ant 364 ft. TL: N36 19 06 W95 38 18. Stereo. Hrs opn: 6 AM-midnight. Rogers State College (74017). (918) 341-7510, ext. 201; (918) 341-6100. FAX: (918) 342-5966. Licensee: Rogers State College. Format: Big band, adult contemp, classic rock. Target aud: College and community, young and older adults. Spec prog: Folk 5 hrs, gospel 4 hrs, jazz 5 hrs, progressive 12 hrs, blues 6 hrs, country 5 hrs wkly. ■ Alan Lambert, stn mgr & chief engr; Chip Rodgers, dev dir; Ron Yates, progmg dir. ■ KRSC-TV affil.

*KTFR(FM)—Not on air, target date unknown: 100.7 mhz; 3 kw. Ant 328 ft. TL: N36 21 47 W95 29 55. 1825 S. 129th E. Ave., Tulsa (74108). Licensee: Educational Broadcasting Corp.

KTRT(AM)—Jan 17, 1958: 1270 khz; 1 kw-U, DA-N. TL: N36 17 59 W95 37 16. 11330 E. 21st St., Tulsa (74129). (918) 234-1270. FAX: (918) 341-1411. Licensee: Oklahoma Sports Properties Inc. (acq 8-6-90; $71,000; FTR 8-27-90). Net: ABC/D, ARN. Rep: Riley. Wash atty: Arent, Fox, Kintner, Plotkin & Kahn. Format: Talk. News progmg 4 hrs wkly. Target aud: 35 plus; upscale adults. ■ Fred M. Weinberg, pres, gen mgr & progmg dir; Keith Brown, gen sls mgr; Bill Wolf, chief engr. ■ Rates: $15; 10; 15; 5.

Clinton

KCLI(FM)—April 9, 1978: 95.5 mhz; 50 kw. Ant 492 ft. TL: N35 27 04 W98 58 19. Stereo. Hrs opn: 24. 700 Frisco (73601). (405) 323-5254. FAX: (405) 323-1892. Licensee: Clinton Broadcasting Co. (acq 2-23-89). Net: SMN. Format: Adult contemp. News progmg 8 hrs wkly. Target aud: 18-49; 2 paycheck families interested in loc news & weather. Spec prog: Sp 3 hrs, sports 6 hrs wkly. ■ Ray David, pres; Rod Knodel, gen mgr, gen sls mgr, prom mgr & engrg mgr; Vivian Knodel, progmg dir. ■ Rates: $10.50; 10.50; 10.50; 10.50.

KSWR(FM)—Listing follows KXOL(AM).

KXOL(AM)—April 15, 1949: 1320 khz; 1 kw-D, 108 w-N. TL: N35 28 53 W98 59 14. 1730 Neptune Dr. (73601). (405) 323-0617. FAX: (405) 323-0717. Licensee: Custer Broadcasting Inc. (acq 5-13-91; with co-located FM; FTR 5-27-91). Net: ABC/D, MBS, Okla. Net. Wash atty: Fletcher, Heald & Hildreth. Format: Talk. News staff one. Target aud: General. Spec prog: Sports. ■ D. Linda Neidy, gen mgr; D'Linda Neidy, gen sls mgr; Dennis Burton, progmg dir, mus dir & chief engr; Sabrina Valenti, news dir. ■ Rates: $12; 10; 12; na.

KSWR(FM)—Co-owned with KXOL(AM). September 1968: 106.9 mhz; 100 kw. Ant 285 ft. TL: N35 28 53 W98 59 14. Stereo. Hrs opn: 24. Prog sep from AM. Net: ABC/E. Format: Country. News staff one; news progmg 16 hrs wkly. Target aud: 18-65. ■ Rates: $8; 6; 8; na.

Comanche

KDDQ(FM)—April 1, 1982: 96.7 mhz; 3 kw. Ant 300 ft. TL: N34 26 12 W97 54 47. Stereo. Hrs opn: 24. Box 700, Terry & Tucker Roads, Duncan (73533). (405) 252-6090; (405) 439-6379. FAX: (405) 252-2340. Licensee: Harold E. Cochran (acq 8-15-88; $150,000). Format: Country. News staff one; news progmg 4 hrs wkly. Target aud: 25-54; females with $27,000 annual income. Spec prog: Gospel 2 hrs wkly. ■ Harold E. Cochran, pres, gen mgr, stn mgr & adv mgr; Scott Mitchell, opns dir, sls dir, prom dir, news dir & pub affrs dir; Harry Ellis, chief engr. ■ Rates: $7; 7; 7; 6.

Cordell

KCDL(FM)—Sept 1, 1988: 99.3 mhz; 3 kw. Ant 200 ft. TL: N35 17 35 W99 01 38. Box 26B, Rt. 2 (73632). (405) 832-3805. Licensee: Richard L. Adams, receiver. Format: Country. News staff 2. Target aud: All ages. Spec prog: Gospel 2 hrs wkly. ■ Don Wrightsman, gen mgr.

Cushing

KUSH(AM)—1953: 1600 khz; 1 kw-D, 70 w-N. TL: N35 59 11 W96 42 37. Box 791, Hwy. 33 (74023). (918) 225-0922. FAX: (918) 225-0925. Licensee: Cimarron Valley Broadcasters Inc. (acq 3-4-65). Net: ABC/I. Format: Country. ■ Don Kelly, pres & news dir; Edith Kelly, gen mgr; Tim Wilbur, prom mgr, progmg dir & mus dir.

Duncan

KRHD(AM)—Oct 31, 1947: 1350 khz; 250 w-D, 100 w-N. TL: N34 40 43 W97 58 05. Stereo. Hrs opn: 6 AM-midnight. 1701 Pine St. (73533-2937). (405) 255-1350. FAX: (405) 252-1023. Licensee: Duncan Broadcasting Co. Inc. Group owner: R.H. Drewry Group. Net: ABC/E; Okla. News. Format: CHR, country. News staff one; news progmg 20 hrs wkly. Target aud: General. ■ R.H. Drewry, pres; Larry Patton, vp; Melvin Jones, gen mgr & stn mgr; David Altom, progmg dir; David Oltom, mus dir; Derrick McMillin, chief engr. ■ Rates: $7; 7; 7; 7.

KRHD-FM—Dec 31, 1975: 102.3 mhz; 3 kw. Ant 207 ft. TL: N34 40 43 W97 58 05. Stereo. Prog sep from AM. Net: ABC/E. Format: Oldies. News staff one; news progmg 10 hrs wkly. Target aud: 25-54. ■ Rates: Same as AM.

Durant

*KHIB(FM)—Feb 1, 1972: 91.9 mhz; 323 w. Ant 135 ft. TL: N34 00 30 W96 22 30. Stereo. Hrs opn: 12. Box 4129, Stn. A, Southeastern Oklahoma State Univ., 5th & University (74701). (405) 924-0121, ext. 2480; (405) 924-0149. Licensee: Southeastern Oklahoma State Univ. Format: Contemp hit, progsv. News progmg 3 hrs wkly. Target aud: 18-25; college, high school students & area residents. Spec prog: Jazz one hr, relg one hr wkly. ■ Ben A. Chappell, pres; Tina R. Vercelli, gen mgr & progmg dir; Mike Helberg, Lori Roan, mus dirs; Debee' Nichols, news dir; Keith Edge, pub affrs dir; Steven Wyatt, chief engr.

KLAK(FM)—Jan 6, 1986: 97.5 mhz; 45 kw. Ant 513 ft. TL: N33 47 14 W96 33 00. Stereo. Suite 255, 101 E. Main St., Dennison, TX (75020). (903) 463-6800. FAX: (903) 463-9816. Licensee: Stansell Communications Inc. (group owner; acq 4-27-87). Net: SMN. Format: Adult contemp. News staff one; news progmg 7 hrs wkly. Target aud: 18-54; people who like personality adult contemp. ■ Jim Stansell, pres; Bill Harrison, vp & gen mgr; Karen Savage, gen sls mgr; Bob McKinzie, progmg dir; Steve Comer, chief engr.

KLBC(FM)—Listing follows KSEO(AM).

KSEO(AM)—May 1947: 750 khz; 250 w-D. TL: N34 00 07 W96 25 19. Box 190 (74702); 1418 N. First (74701). (405) 924-3100. Licensee: Durant Broadcasting Corp. (acq 3-83; grpsl; FTR 3-7-83). Net: SMN; Okla. News. Format: Adult contemp, gold. ■ Steve Landtroop, pres & gen mgr; Carolyn Corbin, gen sls mgr; Bob Sullins, progmg dir.

KLBC(FM)—Co-owned with KSEO(AM). November 1958: 107.1 mhz; 6 kw. Ant 365 ft. TL: N34 00 07 W96 25 19. Stereo. Prog sep from AM. Net: SMN. Format: Country.

Edmond

*KCSC(FM)—April 1966: 90.1 mhz; 100 kw. Ant 430 ft. TL: N35 39 38 W97 28 15. Stereo. Hrs opn: 24. Univ. of Central Okla., 100 N. University Dr. (73034-0202). (405) 341-2980, ext. 2415; (405) 460-5272. FAX: (405) 341-4964. Licensee: University of Central Oklahoma. Net: AP, APR. Format: Class. News progmg 5 hrs wkly. Target aud: 35 plus; educated, affluent. ■ Bradford Ferguson, gen mgr; Kent Anderson, opns mgr; Jovanna Bracket, dev dir; Larry Iverson, chief engr.

*KOKF(FM)—September 1977: 90.9 mhz; 100 kw. Ant 480 ft. TL: N35 33 59 W97 28 28. Stereo. 7700 N. Council Rd, Oklahoma City (73132). (405) 728-7717. FAX: (405) 728-7521. Licensee: RDM Broadcasting Enterprises (acq 1-85). Wash atty: May & Dunne. Format: Christian hit radio, top-40, div. Target aud: 12-34; 18-34 day, 12-24 night. Spec prog: Rap 3 hrs, party mix 4 hrs, adult singles talk 2 hrs wkly. ■ Ron Dryden, pres; Greg Griffin, gen mgr & progmg mgr; Ken Farley, progmg dir; Jim Bowman, chief engr. ■ Rates: $50; 25; 30; 25.

KTNT-FM—Licensed to Edmond. See Oklahoma City.

El Reno

KZUE(AM)—Sept 9, 1962: 1460 khz; 500 w-D. TL: N35 30 30 W97 54 00. 2715 S. Radio Rd. (73036). (405) 262-1886. FAX: (405) 262-1886. Licensee: Clark Broadcasting Ltd. (acq 10-1-79). Net: ABC/I. Rep: Keystone (unwired net). Format: Spanish. Spec prog: Farm 7 hrs, Indian one hr wkly. ■ Nancy Galvan, gen mgr.

Elk City

KADS(AM)—Oct 1932: 1240 khz; 1 kw-U. TL: N35 22 51 W99 24 25. Box 949 (73648). (405) 243-5237. FAX: (405) 225-0463. Licensee: I Vestar Inc. Net: ABC/I; Okla. News. Format: Talk. Spec prog: Farm 8 hrs wkly. ■ Joe Tilton, pres, gen mgr & chief engr; Larry Acker, gen sls mgr.

KECO(FM)—July 20, 1982: 96.5 mhz; 100 kw. Ant 500 ft. TL: N35 24 22 W99 29 54. Stereo. Box 945 (73648); 220 S. Pioneer Rd. (73644). (405) 225-9696. FAX: (405) 225-9699. Licensee: Paragon Broadcasting Inc. (acq 9-16-92; $260,000; FTR 10-19-92). Net: SMN. Wash atty: Bryan, Cave, McPheeters & McRoberts. Format: Country. News staff one. Target aud: General. ■ C.C. Killian, chmn; Mary Ann Killian, exec vp; Brooks Brewer, vp & gen sls mgr; Stephanie Brewer, prom mgr; Robin Dykes, progmg dir & mus dir; Guy Baker, chief engr. ■ Rates: $20; 16.80; 20; 9.35.

KTIJ(FM)—Not on air, target date unknown: 98.5 mhz; 100 kw. Ant 1,089 ft. TL: N34 58 39 W99 24 35. Stn currently dark. Box 69, Dover, NH (03820). (603) 742-8575. Licensee: Women, Handicapped Americans and Minorities for Better Broadcasting Inc. ■ David Reeder, vp.

Enid

***KBVV(FM)**—Oct 1, 1986: 91.1 mhz; 300 w. Ant 297 ft. TL: N36 23 48 W97 52 38. Stereo. Hrs opn: 24. 901 S. Cleveland (73703). (405) 237-6480. Licensee: Wesley Byrd and Cliff Woolsey. Net: Moody. Format: Btfl mus, relg, gospel. Target aud: General. ■ Wesley Byrd, pres & gen mgr; Betsy Byrd, mus dir; Ken Isbell, chief engr.

KCRC(AM)—1926: 1390 khz; 1 kw-U, DA-1. TL: N36 25 11 W97 52 28. Box 952 (73702); 316 E. Willow (73701). (405) 237-1390. FAX: (405) 242-1390. Licensee: Chisolm Trail Broadcasting Co. (acq 6-1-83; $1.38 million; FTR 6-20-83). Net: ABC/C; Okla. Net. Rep: Savalli. Format: Rock. Target aud: General. Spec prog: Polka one hr, talk 5 hrs wkly. ■ Hiram Champlin, pres & gen mgr; Tom Tucker, opns mgr & prom mgr; Sandy Holmes, gen sls mgr; Alan Clepper, progmg dir; Ricky Roggow, mus dir & news dir; Hal Smith, chief engr.

KNID(FM)—Co-owned with KCRC(AM). May 1, 1967: 96.9 mhz; 100 kw. Ant 550 ft. TL: N36 32 14 W98 00 36. Stereo. Prog sep from AM. (405) 237-5643. Net: ABC/C; Okla. Net. Format: Country. Target aud: 18-54.

KGWA(AM)—1950: 960 khz; 1 kw-U, DA-1. TL: N36 26 13 W97 55 16. Box 960 (73702); 300 N. Van Buren (73703). (405) 234-4230; (405) 234-2971. FAX: (405) 237-3233. Licensee: Hammer Williams Broadcasting Inc. (acq 12-1-93; $435,000 with co-located FM; FTR 12-20-93). Net: CBS, NBC Talknet, Daynet. Wash atty: Putbrese, Hunsaker & Ruddy. Format: News/talk. News staff one; news progmg 15 hrs wkly. Spec prog: Farm 3 hrs wkly. ■ Allan Page, pres & gen mgr; Allen Page, gen sls mgr; Keith Hillyard, progmg dir; April Craddock-Danahy, news dir; Scott Clark, chief engr. ■ Rates: $18; 18; 18; 8.

KOFM(FM)—Co-owned with KGWA(AM). March 1982: 103.1 mhz; 25 kw. Ant 298 ft. TL: N36 26 14 W97 55 15. Stereo. Hrs opn: 6 AM-1 AM. Prog sep from AM. Box 5736 (73702). (405) 234-6371. Format: Country. ■ Zolli Page, pres. ■ Rates: Sama as AM.

KNID(FM)—Listing follows KCRC(AM).

KOFM(FM)—Listing follows KGWA(AM).

KXLS(FM)—(Alva). Feb 1, 1981: 99.7 mhz; 100 kw. Ant 850 ft. TL: N36 35 41 W98 15 38. Stereo. Hrs opn: 24. Suite 997, 205 W. Maple, Enid (73701). (405) 242-5958. FAX: (405) 242-6081. Licensee: Lesso Inc. (group owner; acq 8-26-83). Net: MBS; Mid-America Ag. Format: Adult contemp. New progmg 2 hrs wkly. Target aud: 25-49. ■ Larry Steckline, pres; Frank Baker, gen mgr; Keet Eaton, prom mgr; Bert E. Chambers, progmg dir & mus dir; Wayne LaMunyon, news dir; Bill Nolan, chief engr. ■ Rates: $22; 22; 22; 22.

Eufaula

KCES(FM)—June 15, 1967: 102.3 mhz; 3 kw. Ant 150 ft. TL: N35 22 25 W95 34 00. Hrs opn: 7 AM-10 PM. Box 1290, Rt. 4 (74432). (918) 689-3663. Licensee: Harmon Davis. Net: Okla. News Net. Format: C&W. Spec prog: Gospel 3 hrs, bluegrass 3 hrs, relg 5 hrs wkly. ■ Harmon Davis, pres & gen mgr; Clark Davis, progmg dir; Leo Roth, chief engr.

Frederick

***KSYE(FM)**—July, 1992: 91.5 mhz; 100 kw. Ant 390 ft. TL: N34 21 52 W98 50 04. Stereo. Hrs opn: 24. 411 Ryan Plaza Dr., Arlington, TX (76011). (817) 792-3800. Licensee: Criswell Center for Biblical Studies (group owner). Format: Inspirational, educ. Target aud: General. ■ Dr. Richard Melick, pres; Ronald L. Harris, stn mgr; David Briggs, engrg dir.

KTAT(AM)—1948: 1570 khz; 250 w-D. TL: N34 23 30 W99 01 51. Box 1088 (73542). (405) 335-5923. FAX: (405) 335-5532. Licensee: Breckenridge Broadcasting Co. (acq 12-18-90; $60,000 with co-located FM; FTR 1-7-91). Net: ABC/I; Okla. Net. Format: C&W. Spec prog: Farm 2 hrs wkly. ■ Randy Muirhead, gen mgr; Rick Whitworth, chief engr.

KYBE(FM)—Co-owned with KTAT(AM). Aug 15, 1982: 95.9 mhz; 3 kw. Ant 207 ft. TL: N34 23 30 W99 01 51. Stereo. Prog sep from AM. Format: Adult contemp.

Goodwell

***KPSU(FM)**—September 1977: 91.7 mhz; 380 w. Ant 121 ft. TL: N36 35 41 W101 38 10. Box 430, (73939). (405) 349-2414. Licensee: Panhandle State University. Format: Div. Target aud: College age. ■ Dr. Charles R. Meek, pres; Russell A. Guthrie, gen mgr; Greg Crane, stn mgr; Janet Mann, progmg dir.

Grove

KGVE(FM)—Dec 12, 1980: 99.3 mhz; 6 kw. Ant 325 ft. TL: N36 36 49 W94 45 53. Stereo. Hrs opn: 18. Box 1749, N. Cherokee (74344). (918) 786-2211. Licensee: Caleb Corp. (acq 4-1-92; FTR 3-16-92). Net: AP; Okla. News Net. Format: C&W. News staff one. Target aud: General. ■ Larry J. Hestand, pres; Janell M. Hestand, vp, opns dir & progmg dir; Janell Hestand, mus dir; Chris Weatherred, asst mus dir; Bill Van Ness, news dir. ■ Rates: $6; 6; 6; 6.

Guthrie

KOKC(AM)—Nov 16, 1955: 1490 khz; 1 kw-U. TL: N35 52 56 W97 23 24. Hrs opn: 24. Box 1490 (73044). (405) 282-1490. Licensee: OKC Ltd. (acq 6-1-87; $122,000; FTR 6-1-87). Net: AP, SMN. Format: Classic country. News staff 6; news progmg 3 hrs wkly. Target aud: 25-64. Spec prog: Farm one hr, gospel 5 hrs, black 2 hrs, relg 2 hrs wkly. ■ Larry Jones, chmn; W.E. Macabee, pres; George Griffith, gen mgr & progmg dir; Mike Chambers, opns mgr & mus dir; Danny Fellos, sls dir; Pat Oliver, prom dir; Tommy McClure, engrg dir. ■ Rates: $12; 12; 12; 6.

Guymon

KGYN(AM)—Dec 12, 1948: 1210 khz; 10 kw-U, DA-N. TL: N36 40 34 W101 22 58. Stereo. Hrs opn: 24. Box 130, 2300 N. Lelia (73942). (405) 338-1210. FAX: (405) 338-8255. Licensee: Telns Broadcasting Co. Inc. (acq 9-5-86; $400,000; FTR 8-4-86). Net: ABC/E; Okla. News. Wash atty: Arnold & Porter. Format: Adult contemp, country. News staff one; news progmg 12 hrs wkly. Target aud: 25-65; broad based listenership due to full service progmg. Spec prog: Farm 8 hrs, gospel 3 hrs, relg 10 hrs wkly. ■ Ed Smith, pres & gen mgr; T.N. Miller, gen sls mgr; Bill Weldon, progmg dir; Chris Strong, news dir; Jim Stanford, chief engr. ■ Rates: $16.70; 16.70; 16.70; na.

KKBS(FM)—Dec 25, 1983: 92.7 mhz; 11.5 kw. Ant 485 ft. TL: N36 42 43 W101 27 27. Stereo. Hrs opn: 24. Box 1756, 2143 Hwy. 64 N. (73942). (405) 338-5493; (405) 338-5494. FAX: (405) 338-0717. Licensee: MLS Communications Inc. (acq 8-7-90; 8-27-90). Net: SMN. Wash atty: Jerry D. Sokolosky. Format: Country. News staff 5; news progmg 17 hrs wkly. Target aud: 24-66; working people, 2 income families, farmers. Spec prog: Markets 5 hrs wkly. ■ Marsha Strong, pres, gen mgr, gen sls mgr & prom mgr; Stacey Johnson, opns dir, progmg dir & news dir; Smokey King, chief engr.

Healdton

KICM(FM)—Nov 11, 1984: 105.7 mhz; 50 kw. Ant 632 ft. TL: N34 02 27 W97 20 00. Stereo. Hrs opn: 24. Box 1487, Ardmore (73402); Suite 501, 115 W. Broadway, Ardmore (73401). (405) 226-5105. Licensee: Lake Country Communications Inc. (acq 10-1-88). Net: CBS. Rep: Roslin. Wash atty: Vince Curtis, Fletcher, Herald & Hildreth. Format: Progsv country. News staff one; news progmg 8 hrs wkly. Target aud: 18-49; middle, upper-middle class listeners. ■ Pat Ownbey, pres, gen mgr & news dir; Gary Cook, vp; Jim Fischer, gen sls mgr & prom mgr; Terry Bell, progmg dir & mus dir. ■ Rates: $16; 14; 16; 14.

Heavener

KPRV-FM—Oct 1, 1989: 92.5 mhz; 790 w. Ant 640 ft. TL: N34 53 54 W94 34 30. Stereo. Hrs opn: 5 AM-10 PM. Rt. 2, Box 147-A, Poteau (74953); Box 368, Poteau (74953). (918) 647-3221. Licensee: LeRoy Billy. Net: CBS; Okla. News Net. Wash atty: Robert Allen. Format: Country. News progmg 24 hrs wkly. Target aud: 24-54. Spec prog: Gospel 12 hrs wkly. ■ LeRoy Billy, vp, gen mgr, stn mgr & gen sls mgr; David Billy, progmg dir & mus dir; Larry Johnson, chief engr.

Henryetta

KCKI(FM)—Dec 20, 1966: 99.5 mhz; 100 kw. Ant 984 ft. TL: N35 50 02 W96 07 28. Stereo. Suite 204, 1502 S. Boulder, Tulsa (74119). (918) 584-0995. FAX: (918) 582-4740. Licensee: Boulder Broadcasting Inc. (acq 11-85). Net: Unistar. Rep: Schubert. Wash atty: Koteen & Naftalia. Format: Contemp country. News staff one; news progmg 9 hrs wkly. Target aud: 25-54. ■ Tommy Bascocu, pres; Jeff Sattler, gen mgr; Doug Wood, gen sls mgr; Sydney Shapshard, prom mgr & news dir; Steve Hunter, progmg dir; Troy Langham, chief engr.

KDLB(AM)—July 19, 1956: 1590 khz; 500 w-D. TL: N35 25 45 W95 58 12. 6741 E. 51st Place, Tulsa (74145). Licensee: Fisher Broadcasting Inc. (acq 1-14-86). ■ Fred Weinberg, gen mgr.

***KVAZ(FM)**—Dec 26, 1985: 91.5 mhz; 250 w. Ant 178 ft. TL: N35 21 56 W96 00 34. Rt. One, Box 65A, Weleetka (74880). (918) 652-2132. Licensee: Henryetta Educational Broadcasting Foundation. Net: USA. Format: Educ, relg. Spec prog: Jewish one hr wkly. ■ Carl Van Meter, pres & gen mgr; Wayne Tucker, chief engr.

Hobart

KTJS(AM)—June 21, 1947: 1420 khz; 1 kw-D, 360 w-N. TL: N35 02 57 W99 05 48. Hrs opn: 19. Box 311, 1515 N. Broadway (73651). (405) 726-5656. Licensee: Alfred Ray Fuchs (acq 6-26-90). Net: ABC/E; Okla. News Net. Format: Country. News progmg 19 hrs wkly. Target aud: 30 plus; agri-related businessmen. Spec prog: Relg 15 hrs wkly. ■ A.R. Fuchs, pres, gen mgr & chief engr; Gene Williams, gen sls mgr; Eddie Williams, progmg dir & mus dir; Paul Shields, news dir.

KQTZ(FM)—Co-owned with KTJS(AM). May 28, 1979: 105.9 mhz; 100 kw. Ant 1,020 ft. TL: N34 52 15 W99 17 36. Stereo. Prog sep from AM. Net: Unistar. Format: Adult contemp, top-40. News progmg 2 hrs wkly. Contemporary adults during the day, rockers at night. ■ Chad Fuchs, mus dir.

Holdenville

KRAF(AM)—Oct 23, 1963: 1370 khz; 500 w-D, 77 w-N. Ant 200 ft. TL: N35 03 24 W96 22 49. Hrs opn: 24. Box 978 (74848). (405) 379-2370. Licensee: Hughes County Broadcasting (acq 6-4-92; $165,000; with with co-located FM; FTR 6-22-92). Net: USA. Format: Farm, talk, country. News progmg 12 hrs wkly. Target aud: 24-54; rural. ■ George Chambers, gen mgr & chief engr; Bryant Ellis, opns dir; Derek Devilla, gen sls mgr; Shawn Martin, progmg dir; Roy Davis, mus dir.

KXKY(FM)—Co-owned with KRAF(AM). Nov 30, 1991: 106.5 mhz; 4.5 kw. Ant 203 ft. TL: N35 03 24 W96 22 49. Stereo. Hrs opn: 24. Dups AM 100%. (Acq 6-4-92; with KRAF(AM)).

KWSH(AM)—See Wewoka.

Hugo

KIHN(AM)—October 1948: 1340 khz; 1 kw-U. TL: N34 00 15 W95 29 20. Hrs opn: 16. Box 430, Hwy. 70 E. (74743). (405) 326-6411. Licensee: Little Dixie Broadcasting Co. Format: Var. News staff one. Target aud: General. Spec prog: Gospel 5 hrs, farm 3 hrs wkly. ■ Leeta Henson, gen mgr. ■ Rates: $7.50; 7.50; 7.50; 7.50.

KITX(FM)—June 1983: 95.5 mhz; 50 kw. Ant 492 ft. TL: N33 54 56 W95 28 00. Stereo. Hrs opn: 24. Box 886, Hwy. 70 W. (74743); Box 1280, Hwy. 271 N., Paris, TX (75460). (405) 326-2555; (903) 784-6952. FAX: (405) 326-2623. Licensee: Harold E. Cochran (acq 5-84; $340,000; FTR 5-21-84). Net: CNN. Format: C&W, news. News staff one; news progmg 22 hrs wkly. Target aud: General. Spec prog: Farm 2 hrs, gospel 3 hrs wkly. ■ Harold E. Cochran, pres & gen mgr; Hal Cochran, adv mgr; Larry Cochran, progmg dir; Stixx Frierson, mus dir; Bob Walling, news dir. ■ Rates: $10; 8; 10; 8.

Idabel

KBEL(AM)—June 3, 1948: 1240 khz; 1 kw-U. TL: N33 52 54 W94 49 10. Box 418 (74745). (405) 286-7601. Licensee: Curtis L. Cochran (acq 8-23-90; $240,000 with co-located FM; FTR 9-10-90). Net: ABC/C; Okla. News Net. Format: Southern gospel. News progmg 7 hrs wkly. Target aud: 25 plus. Spec prog: OU, OSU, Idabel football, McCurtan County basketball, Dallas Cowboys. ■ Curt Cochran, gen mgr & stn mgr; Doug Cochran, vp opns, progmg dir, mus dir & chief engr. ■ Rates: $8.80; 8.80; 8.80; 7.65.

KBEL-FM—Oct 1, 1973: 96.7 mhz; 3 kw. Ant 300 ft. TL: N33 52 54 W94 49 10. Stereo. Prog sep from AM. Format: Country. Target aud: 15-50; country audience. Spec prog: OU, OSU, Dallas Cowboys, McCurtain County basketball.

KKBI(FM)—See Broken Bow.

Ketchum

KGND(FM)—May 26, 1989: 107.5 mhz; 50 kw. Ant 492 ft. TL: N36 41 18 W95 11 30. Stereo. Hrs opn: 24. Box 419, 410 E. Illinois, Vinita (74301). (918) 256-7224; (918) 256-8742. Licensee: Leemay Broadcasting Co. Inc. Net: ABC/E, Okla. Net. Format: Adult contemp, sports. Target aud: 25-54. ■ Jack Lee, pres & gen mgr. ■ Rates: $9; 8; 7; 6.

Lahoma

KMKZ(FM)—Not on air, target date unknown: 95.7 mhz; 5.6 kw. Ant 338 ft. 1802 Marksdale, Colwich, KS (67030). Licensee: Donald W. McCoy.

Langston

***KALU(FM)**—March 3, 1975: 90.7 mhz; 10 w. Ant 77 ft. TL: N35 56 37 W97 15 40. Hrs opn: 8 AM-midnight. Box 837 (73050). (405) 466-2231. Licensee: Langston Univ. Format: Div. ■ Lester V. LeSure, gen mgr.

Lawton

KBXD(FM)—Nov 1, 1982: 95.3 mhz; 6 kw. Ant 302 ft. TL: N34 34 36 W98 28 30. Stereo. Hrs opn: 24. Box 7953, Suite C, 1421 Great Plains Blvd. (73506-1953). (405) 536-9530. FAX: (405) 536-FAXX. Licensee: Broadco of Texas Inc. (acq 3-9-92; trade and joint venture agreement for KMGZ(FM); FTR 4-6-92). Net: Unistar. Rep: Roslin. Wash atty: Waysdorf & Van Bergh. Format: CHR. News progmg one hr wkly. Target aud: 18-34. ■ Chuck Morgan, pres, gen mgr & gen sls mgr; Michelle Tribble, mktg dir; Rick Walker, prom dir; Scott Stalker, progmg dir; Ken Saunders, mus dir; Fred Morton, vp engrg. ■ Rates: $20; 14; 17; 11.

KBZQ(FM)—May 1 1992: 99.5 mhz; 3.428 kw. Ant 276 ft. TL: N34 34 36 W98 28 30. Stereo. Hrs opn: 24. PO Box 6888, 1421 Great Plains Blvd., Suite D (73505). (405) 536-0995. FAX: (405) 536-3299. Licensee: William R. Fritsch Jr. (acq 3-9-92; trade and joint venture agreement for KBZQ(FM); FTR 4-6-92). Net: Unistar, CNN. Wash atty: Waysdorf & Van Bergh. Format: Soft Adult Contemp. News progmg one hr wkly. Target aud: 25-49; Baby-boomers, upscale white collar workers. ■ Rick Fritsch, gen mgr; Linda Haight, natl sls mgr; Alicia Thomas, progmg dir; Fred R. Morton Jr., chief engr. ■ Rates: $8; 6; 6; 4.

***KCCU(FM)**—July 13, 1989: 89.3 mhz; 2 kw. Ant 463 ft. TL: N34 37 26 W98 16 15. Stereo. Hrs opn: 24. Admin. Bldg., 2800 W. Gore Blvd. (73505). (405) 581-2425. Licensee: Cameron University. Net: NPR, APR. Format: Btfl mus, jazz, news. News staff 5; news progmg 40 hrs wkly. Target aud: General. ■ Mark Norman., gen mgr; Shirley Allen, dev dir; Mark Koonce, dev mgr; Mike Leal, progmg dir; Doug Swanson, news dir; Charles Thurston, chief engr.

KKRX(AM)—May 27, 1956: 1050 khz; 250 w-D, DA. TL: N34 35 27 W98 21 10. Box 1050 (73502). (405) 355-1050. FAX: (405) 355-1050. Licensee: Ella Louise Downing, trustee (acq 3-8-93; with co-located FM; FTR 3-29-93). Rep: D & R Radio. Format: News/talk, solid gold rock. Spec prog: Ger one hr wkly. ■ Bill Shoemate, gen mgr; Eric Sharum, progmg dir.

KKRX-FM—Oct 23, 1970: 98.1 mhz; 100 kw. Ant 202 ft. TL: N34 35 27 W98 21 10. Stereo. Hrs opn: 24. Prog sep from AM. Wash atty: Eugene T. Smith. Format: Classic rock.

KLAW(FM)—Jan 1, 1965: 101.5 mhz; 100 kw. Ant 600 ft. TL: N34 33 00 W98 32 20. Stereo. Hrs opn: 24. Box 569 (73502); 626 D Ave. S.W. (73501). (405) 357-2860. FAX: (405) 357-2880. Licensee: KLAW Broadcasting Inc. (acq 11-1-78). Net: ABC/E. Rep: Katz. Format: C&W. News staff one; news progmg 4 hrs wkly. Target aud: General. ■ Ron Rogers, pres; Robert Payton, vp, gen mgr & gen sls mgr; Frank Seres, opns mgr, progmg dir & chief engr; Jessie Amos, mus dir; Stacy Brown, news dir & pub affrs dir. ■ Rates: $40; 40; 40; 30.

KSWO(AM)—May 1, 1941: 1380 khz; 1 kw-U, DA-2. TL: N34 35 24 W98 21 44. Box 709 (73502). (405) 355-1380. FAX: (405) 355-7300. Licensee: Oklahoma Quality Broadcasting Co. Group owner: R.H. Drewry Group (acq 5-1-45). Net: CNN, NBC Talknet. Rep: Roslin. Format: News/talk. Target aud: 35 plus. ■ R. H. Drewry, pres; Larry Patton, gen mgr; Ninfa Brandt, gen sls mgr; John Brandt, progmg dir & mus dir; Derrick McMillan, chief engr. ■ KSWO-TV affil.

***KVRS(FM)**—Dec 1989: 90.3 mhz; 1 kw-V. Ant 151 ft. TL: N34 37 32 W98 31 43. Stereo. Hrs opn: 24. 11 Winding Creek Rd. (73505). (405) 536-8886. FAX: (405) 536-8891. Licensee: Lawton Educational Broadcasting Foundation. Net: Moody. Format: Relg. News progmg 14 hrs wkly. Target aud: General. ■ Harold Wilson, chmn; Kim Shahan, exec vp; Clint Herring Jr., vp engrg.

KVRW(FM)—March 13, 1992: 107.3 mhz; 50 kw. Ant 492 ft. TL: N34 36 27 W98 16 26. Stereo. Hrs opn: 24. 6210 N.W. Oak (73505). (405) 536-2242; (405) 536-4399. FAX: (405) 536-1073. Licensee: Arthur Patrick. Net: Jones Satellite Audio. Wash atty: Lukas, McGowan, Nace and Gutierrez. Format: Oldies. News progmg one hr wkly. Target aud: 25-54. ■ Arthur Patrick, CEO & gen mgr; Steve Polone, opns dir & progmg dir; Mike Miller, sls dir, prom dir & adv dir; John Johnson, chief engr.

KZCD(FM)—June 8, 1987: 94.3 mhz; 3 kw. Ant 328 ft. TL: N34 34 24 W98 28 40. (94.1 mhz, 50 kw, 349 ft.). Stereo. Hrs opn: 24. Suite 6, 5108 W. Gore St. (73505). (405) 357-9494. Licensee: Communicorp Inc. (acq 8-87). Net: Jones Satellite Audio. Wash atty: May & Dunne. Format: Hot country. News staff one; news progmg 2 hrs wkly. Target aud: 18-54. ■ James L. Gardner, pres, gen mgr & chief engr; Joyce Wade, gen sls mgr; Brian Cypert, progmg dir. ■ Rates: $15; 13; 14; 10.

Lindsay

KBLP(FM)—Oct 1, 1988: 105.1 mhz; 850 w. Ant 564 ft. TL: N34 54 01 W97 33 56. Stereo. Hrs opn: 6 AM-11 PM. 204 S. Main (73052). (405) 756-2040. FAX: (405) 756-3137. Licensee: South Central Oklahoma Broadcasting & Advertising. Net: Okla. Net. Format: Country. News staff 2; news progmg 21 hrs wkly. Target aud: 21-65; working consumers. ■ Charlie Jones, pres & gen mgr; Keith Humphries, gen sls mgr.

Locust Grove

KEMX(FM)—Feb 14, 1991: 94.5 mhz; 2.3 kw. Ant 367 ft. TL: N36 15 05 W95 13 21. Stereo. Hrs opn: 24. Rebroadcasts KXOJ-FM Tulsa-Sapulpa 100%. Box 1250, Sapulpa (74067); Old Frankoma Rd., Sapulpa (74067). (918) 224-2620. FAX: (918) 224-4984. Licensee: KXOJ Inc. (group owner; acq 4-29-92; grpsl). Net: UPI. Format: Contemp Christian music. Target aud: 18-35; young married or single Christians. ■ Mike Stephens, pres & gen mgr; Joy Stephens, vp; David Stephens, stn mgr, sls dir, mktg dir & adv dir; Seth Andrews, prom dir; Randall Nance, progmg dir; Bill Davis, chief engr. ■ Rates: $13.75; 13.75; 13.75; 13.75.

Lone Grove

KYNZ(FM)—May 25, 1988: 106.7 mhz; 5.5 kw. Ant 335 ft. TL: N34 14 09 W97 14 48. Stereo. Hrs opn: 24. Box 1609, Ardmore (73402); 700 1/2 N. Commerce, Ardmore (73401). (405) 226-8475. FAX: (405) 226-7118. Licensee: SSS Communications Inc. Net: Unistar. Format: Adult contemp. Target aud: 18-49. ■ Scott Benton, gen mgr, progmg dir & chief engr.

Madill

KMAD(AM)—May 20, 1962: 1550 khz; 250 w-D. TL: N34 06 24 W96 46 30. Box 576 (73446). (405) 795-2345. Licensee: Radio Station KMAD (acq 7-25-74). Net: ABC/I; Okla. News. Rep: Riley. Format: C&W. Spec prog: Farm 2 hrs wkly. ■ Glen "Sky" Corbin, gen mgr; Scott Corbin, gen sls mgr; Sky Corbin, progmg dir & mus dir; Pat Corbin, news dir; Glenn Corbin, chief engr.

KMAD-FM—June 1, 1985: 102.3 mhz; 3 kw. Ant 233 ft. TL: N34 06 24 W96 46 30.

Marlow

KFXI(FM)—December 1986: 92.1 mhz; 100 kw. Ant 718 ft. TL: N34 42 30 W98 03 13 (CP: Ant 387 ft.). Stereo. Hrs opn: 24. Box 433, Lawton (73502). (405) 658-9292. FAX: (405) 658-2561. Licensee: Austin Broadcast Services Inc. Net: MBS, SMN; Wash atty: Southmayd & Miller. Format: Country. Target aud: 25-55. Spec prog: Gospel 4 hrs wkly. ■ K.D. Austin, pres & gen mgr; Sherry Lynn, gen sls mgr; James Keith, progmg dir; James Wilson, chief engr.

McAlester

KMCO(FM)—Listing follows KNED(AM).

KNED(AM)—March 14, 1950: 1150 khz; 1 kw-D, 500 w-N, DA-N. TL: N34 56 12 W95 43 59. Stereo. Hrs opn: 24. Box 1068 (74502-1068). (918) 423-1460. FAX: (918) 423-7119. Licensee: Little Dixie Radio Inc. (acq 2-16-63). Net: ABC/E. Format: C&W. Target aud: 45 plus. ■ Francis Stipe, pres & gen mgr; Roslyn Stipe, stn mgr & opns mgr; Kari Klusak, gen sls mgr; Lee Anderson, progmg dir & mus dir; Fred Ingraham, chief engr.

KMCO(FM)—Co-owned with KNED(AM). November 1965: 101.3 mhz; 100 kw. Ant 494 ft. TL: N34 59 13 W95 42 10. Stereo. (918) 426-1050. Net: Moody. Format: C&W. ■ Sheila Dean, gen sls mgr; Tom Dolph, news dir.

KTMC(AM)—Mar 3, 1946: 1400 khz; 1 kw-U. TL: N34 57 00 W95 45 00. Hrs opn: 24. Box 848 (74502); 2020 N. A St. (74501). (918) 423-1400. Licensee: Trayne Communications Inc. (acq 3-9-89; $152,500; FTR 2-13-89). Net: USA; SMN. Format: Real country, relg, news/talk. Target aud: 25-55; older, middle-aged, mature & retired adults. Spec prog: Gospel 5 hrs wkly. ■ Thomas H. Payne, pres & news dir; Bill Eustis, gen mgr; Hal Smith, chief engr. ■ Rates: $17; 11.90; 11.90; na.

KTMC-FM—June 24, 1987: 104.9 mhz; 1.5 kw. Ant 454 ft. TL: N34 58 08 W95 46 21. Stereo. Prog sep from AM. (918) 426-5300. (Acq 2-18-89; $300,000; FTR 2-20-89). Net: NBC, Unistar. Format: Adult contemp. News progmg 10 hrs wkly. Target aud: young professionals to middle age. Spec prog: Gospel 2 hrs, relg 5 hrs wkly. ■ Judith Sorrell, vp mktg & vp prom; Thomas H. Payne, vp progmg. ■ Rates: $17; 14.30; 14.30; 11.90.

Miami

KVIS(AM)—February 1948: 910 khz; 1 kw-U, DA-1. TL: N36 53 27 W94 47 00. Hrs opn: 24. Box 1555 (74355). (918) 542-1818; (918) 542-3301. Licensee: Eagle Braodcasting Inc. (acq 2-15-91; with co-located FM; FTR 3-11-91). Net: CBN; Brownfield. Wash atty: Latham & Watkins. Format: Relg. News staff one; news progmg 9 hrs wkly. Target aud: General. ■ Terry R. Millikin, gen mgr & gen sls mgr; Robert Suman, progmg dir & mus dir; Kim Barnes, news dir; Rusty Wynn, chief engr. ■ Rates: $9; 7.50; 9; 7.50.

KGLC(FM)—Co-owned with KVIS(AM). December 1975: 100.9 mhz; 3.6 kw. Ant 273 ft. TL: N36 53 27 W94 47 01. Stereo. Dups AM 100%. ■ Kevin Barnes, mus dir. ■ Rates: Same as AM.

Midwest City

KTLV(AM)—April 1973: 1220 khz; 250 w-D, DA. TL: N35 23 50 W97 27 04. 3336 S.E. 67th St., Oklahoma City (73135). (405) 672-1220; (405) 672-3886. FAX: (405) 672-5858. Licensee: First Choice Broadcasting Inc. (acq 6-19-92). Format: Black Christian, Sp. Target aud: 24 plus. ■ Dale Williams, pres, gen mgr & progmg dir.

Moore

***KMSI(FM)**—Mar 26, 1991: 88.1 mhz; 30 kw-V. Ant 597 ft. TL: N35 12 07 W97 35 18. Stereo. Hrs opn: 20. Box 1924, Tulsa (74101); 1105 N. Main, New Castle (73065). (405) 387-3688. Licensee: Creative Educational Media Corp Inc. Format: Positive easy gospel. Target aud: General. Spec prog: Talk 5 hrs wkly ■ David Ingles, pres; Kim Spence, prom mgr; David Warren, progmg dir & mus dir; Greg Thomas, engrg dir; Roger King, chief engr.

WWLS(AM)—Sept 26, 1922: 640 khz; 1 kw-U, DA-N. TL: N35 17 21 W97 30 08. 4000 W. Indian Hills Rd. (73069). (405) 360-7000. FAX: (405) 364-1557. Licensee: Fox Broadcasting Co. (acq 1-18-89; $550,000; FTR 2-6-89). Net: AP. Rep: H.R. Stone. Format: All sports. ■ John Fox, pres & gen mgr; Tony Sellars, opns mgr & progmg dir.

Muskogee

KBIX(AM)—May 1, 1936: 1490 khz; 1 kw-U. TL: N35 46 06 W95 21 14. Hrs opn: 24. Box 1269 (74402-1269). (918) 682-1331. FAX: (918) 682-6775. Licensee: D&E Broadcasting Inc. (acq 10-26-93; $110,000; FTR 11-8-93). Net: MBS; Okla. Net. Format: News/talk info. News progmg 11 hrs wkly. Target aud: 25-54. ■ Dick Embody, gen mgr; Mick Reed, progmg dir; Gregg Mashburn, news dir.

KHJM(FM)—See Taft.

KHTT(FM)—February 1972: 106.9 mhz; 100 kw. Ant 1,005 ft. TL: N35 51 41 W95 46 03. Stereo. Hrs opn: 24. Suite 711, 7030 S. Yale, Tulsa (74136). (918) 492-2020. FAX: (918) 496-2681. Licensee: Renda Broadcasting Corp. Group owner: Renda Broadcasting Corp.-Renda Radio Inc. (acq 4-15-93; $1.6 million; FTR 5-3-93). Net: ABC/FM, NBC. Rep: Major Mkt. Format: Hot contemp hit. News staff one; news progmg 10 hrs wkly. Target aud: 12-44; teens & young adults. ■ Tony Renda, pres; Mark Clark, prom dir; Mike Ring, vp progmg & mus dir; Kitt Smith, news dir; Dennis Orcutt, chief engr.

KMMY(FM)—Jan 19, 1984: 97.1 mhz; 100 kw. Ant 1,274 ft. TL: N35 17 05 W95 25 26. Stereo. Box 9700 (74402). (918) 682-9700. FAX: (918) 682-6775. Licensee: KMMY Inc. (acq 9-15-93; $500,000; FTR 10-11-93). Format: Country News staff one. Target aud: 21-49; middle, upper-middle class. Spec prog: Farm 5 hrs wkly. ■ David Stephens, stn mgr.

Norman

***KGOU(FM)**—Sept 25, 1970: 106.3 mhz; 3 kw. Ant 300 ft. TL: N35 17 22 W97 21 30. Stereo. Hrs opn: 5 AM-midnight. 780 Van Vleet Oval (73019). (405) 325-3388. FAX: (405) 325-7129. Licensee: University of Oklahoma. Net: NPR. Wash atty: Dow, Lohnes & Albertson. Format: Class, jazz, news. News staff 2; news progmg 47 hrs wkly. Target aud: 25-54. Spec prog: Blues 10 hrs, new age 4 hrs wkly. ■ Karen Holp, gen mgr; Jay Childs, opns mgr; Rachel Jacquemain, dev dir; Michael F. Jackson, mus dir; Steve Carmody, news dir; David White, chief engr.

KNOR(AM)—November 1949: 1400 khz; 1 kw-U. TL: N35 13 04 W97 24 37. Hrs opn: 5 AM-midnight (Mon-Fri), 6 AM-midnight (Sat-Sun). 115 W. Gray St. (73069). (405) 321-1400. FAX: (405) 321-6820. Licensee: Voice of Norman Inc. (acq 7-8-92; $190,000; FTR 7-27-92). Net: ABC/I, NBC; Okla. News Net. Wash atty: Reed, Smith, Shaw & McClay. Format: Oldies, news/talk. News staff one. Target aud: 25-54; middle-upper class adults. ■ Bruce Morain, pres; Don Mayes, exec vp, gen mgr, mktg dir & prom dir; Larry Rhodes, chief opns, progmg dir & mus dir; Tim Lashar, gen sls mgr & adv mgr; Steve Ellis, news dir; Steve Holderby, chief engr. ■ Rates: $14; 10; 12; 8.

Nowata

KRIG(FM)—Licensed to Nowata. See Bartlesville.

Oklahoma City

KATT-FM—Oct 17, 1960: 100.5 mhz; 97 kw. Ant 1,191 ft. TL: N35 35 22 W97 29 03. Stereo. 4045 N.W. 64th (73116). (405) 848-0100. Licensee: CAT Communications Inc. (acq 6-28-93; FTR 8-2-93). Net: NBC the Source. Format: AOR. ■ Larry Bastida, gen mgr; Tricia York, gen sls mgr; Chris Baker, prom mgr; Brad Copeland, progmg dir; Kelly Davis, mus dir.

KBYE(AM)—1946: 890 khz; 1 kw-D. TL: N35 33 59 W97 28 28. Box 20700 (73156). (405) 478-2100. Licensee: SCI Inc. (acq 2-4-91; $315,000; FTR 2-18-91). Format: Relg. ■ Virginia LaFara, gen mgr, progmg dir & mus dir; Bill Gilliland, chief engr.

KEBC(FM)—June 6, 1967: 94.7 mhz; 98 kw. Ant 1,387 ft. TL: N35 32 58 W97 29 50. Stereo. Hrs opn: 24. 5101 S. Shields (73129). (405) 631-7501. FAX: (405) 631-6372. Licensee: Independence Broadcasting Inc. Group owner: Independence Broadcasting Corp. (acq 12-1-88; $3,900,000; FTR 12-19-88). Net: ABC/E. Format: Country. News staff 2. Target aud: 25-54. ■ Don Boyles, gen mgr; J. Robert Dark, gen sls mgr; Erik Logan, Mark Andrews, progmg dirs; Dave Dotson, Al Hamilton, mus dirs; Randy Mullinax, chief engr. ■ Rates: $50; 50; 50; 50.

KJYO(FM)—Listing follows KTOK(AM).

KMGL(FM)—Nov 25, 1965: 104.1 mhz; 100 kw. Ant 1,425 ft. TL: N35 32 58 W97 29 18. Stereo. Hrs opn: 24. Box 14818, 1200 E. Britton Rd. (73113). (405) 478-5104. FAX: (405) 478-0448. Licensee: Renda Broadcasting (group owner; acq 4-88). Rep: Eastman. Format: Adult contemp. ■ Tony Renda, pres; Rob Adair, vp & gen mgr; Carol Simmons, gen sls mgr; Jeff Roberts, prom mgr; Steve O'Brien, progmg dir; Brenda Bennett, mus dir; Bob Glover, news dir; Dennis Orcutt, chief engr.

KNTL(FM)—(Bethany). Oct 29, 1965: 104.9 mhz; 3 kw. Ant 299 ft. TL: N35 29 58 W97 37 08. Hrs opn: 24. 2809 N. MacArthur, Oklahoma City (73127). (405) 789-1140. FAX: (405) 789-1289. Licensee: Broadcast Equities Inc. (acq 3-90; $1 million; FTR 1-15-90). Net: AP. Format: Adult contemp, Christian. News progmg 4 hrs wkly. Target aud: 25-54. ■ Pat Robertson, chmn; Mark Barth, pres; Tom McCoy, gen mgr; Rick Woodward, gen sls mgr & adv mgr; Leanne Flask, prom mgr; Dave Riley, progmg mgr & mus dir; Gary Hughes, pub affrs dir; Hal Smith, chief engr. ■ Rates: $35; 25; 30; 20.

***KOCC(FM)**—Nov 3, 1980: 88.9 mhz; 4.3 kw. Ant 502 ft. TL: N35 36 48 W97 28 30. Stereo. Hrs opn: 6 AM-midnight. Box 11000 (73136-1100); 2501 E. Memorial Rd. (73111). (405) 425-5622. FAX: (405) 425-5625. Licensee: Oklahoma Christian University of Science & Arts (acq 3-26-89). Net: AP. Format: Adult contemp. News progmg 5 hrs wkly. Target aud: 18-35; young adults, recent college graduates, college students. Spec prog: Jazz 6 hrs, relg 8 hrs, pub affrs 4 hrs wkly. ■ Larry Jurney, gen mgr; Robin Powell, vp mktg & vp adv; Judy Henbest, vp prom & pub affrs dir; Wes Frye, vp progmg; Eric Blankenship, mus dir; Dennis Orcutt, chief engr.

KOMA(AM)—Dec 24, 1922: 1520 khz; 50 kw-U, DA-N. TL: N35 20 00 W97 30 16. Stereo. Box 6000 (73153); 820 S.W. Fourth St., Moore (73160). (405) 794-4000. FAX: (405) 793-0514. Licensee: Diamond Broadcasting Inc. (group owner; acq 9-88; grpsl; FTR 8-8-88). Net: CBS. Rep: CBS Radio. Format: Oldies. News staff 2 Target aud: 25-54. ■ Vance Harrison Jr, gen mgr; Clif Wilson, gen sls mgr; Ashley Paige, prom mgr; Kent Jones, progmg dir; Michael Dean, mus dir; Steve Bennett, news dir; Dennis Pharr, chief engr.

KOMA-FM—1964: 92.5 mhz; 98 kw. Ant 984 ft. TL: N35 32 52 W97 29 29. Stereo. Hrs opn: 24. 110 N.E. 48th St., Moore (73160). (405) 794-4000. FAX: (405) 793-0514. Licensee: Wilks-Schwartz Broadcasting (acq 5-15-89; $3,500,000; FTR 4-10-89). Rep: Torbet. Format: Oldies. Target aud: 25-54. ■ Randy Mullinax, gen mgr; Kent Jones, progmg dir.

KRXO(FM)—Co-owned with KOMA(AM). February 1986: 107.7 mhz; 99 kw. Ant 991 ft. TL: N35 32 58 W97 29 18. Stereo. Prog sep from AM. Format: Classic rock. ■ Mansoor Khaleeluddin, prom mgr; Dan Balla, progmg dir.

KOQL(FM)—March 16, 1962: 101.9 mhz; 100 kw. Ant 1,390 ft. TL: N35 32 58 W97 29 50. Stereo. Hrs opn: 24. Suite 550, 9400 N. Broadway (73114). (405) 478-7000. FAX: (405) 478-1688. Licensee: Entertainment Communications Inc. Group owner: Entercom (acq 10-31-88; $4.15 million; FTR 12-5-88). Rep: D & R Radio. Format: Oldies. Target aud: 35-44. ■ Joe Field, pres; David Griffin, gen mgr; Sandy McAlister, gen sls mgr; Donnie Campbell, rgnl sls mgr; Leslie Spears, prom dir; John Brent, progmg dir; Fred Hendrickson, mus dir; Ron Williams, news dir; Don Owen, chief engr. ■ Rates: $75; 75; 75; 25.

KQCV(AM)—1948: 800 khz; 2.5 kw-D, 500 w-N, DA. TL: N35 27 53 W97 28 46 (CP: TL: N35 24 45 W97 40 26). 1919 N. Broadway (73103). (405) 521-1412. FAX: (405) 521-1391. Licensee: Bott Broadcasting (group owner; acq 1-76). Format: Relg, news/talk. Target aud: 35-64; family oriented, mature. ■ Richard P. Bott, pres & exec vp; Robin Jones, gen mgr.

***KROU(FM)**—See Spencer.

KRXO(FM)—Listing follows KOMA(AM).

KTNT-FM—(Edmond). June 28, 1962: 97.9 mhz; 6 kw. Ant 300 ft. TL: N35 34 11 W97 30 01. Stereo. Hrs opn: 24. 110 NE 48th St., Oklahoma City (73105-2006). (405) 524-4979; (405) 478-7111. FAX: (405) 524-5029. Licensee: Life Broadcasting Inc. (acq 9-6-91; FTR 10-28-91). Rep: Katz & Powell. Wash atty: Birch, Horton, Bittner & Cherot. Format: Contemporary jazz, new age. News progmg 3 hrs wkly. Target aud: 35-49 primary, 25-34 secondary; young, professional, upscale, $30,000 plus income - buyers. Spec prog: Relg 5 hrs wkly. ■ Porter Davis, pres; Randy Jacobs, gen sls mgr; Terri Davis, prom dir; Ken Jones, progmg dir; Stephani Stewart, mus dir; Cynthia Ryan, news dir; Brian Roth, chief engr. ■ Rates: $30; 35; 30; 25.

KTOK(AM)—Jan 29, 1927: 1000 khz; 5 kw-U, DA-2. TL: N35 21 29 W97 27 48. Box 1000 (73101); 50 Penn Pl., Fl. K (73118). (405) 840-5271. FAX: (405) 840-4025. Licensee: Clear Channel Radio Inc. (group owner; acq 8-5-92). Net: ABC/I, MBS; Okla. News. Rep: Christal. Format: News/talk. News staff 12. ■ L. Lowry Mays, CEO; Mark Mays, CFO; R. Miles Chandler, vp & gen mgr; Mike Elder, opns mgr & progmg dir; Nan Lawrie, gen sls mgr; Mike Wahl, mktg dir; Jerry Bohren, news dir; Mike Downs, chief engr.

KJYO(FM)—Co-owned with KTOK(AM). April 9, 1961: 102.7 mhz; 98 kw. Ant 900 ft. TL: N35 32 52 W97 29 29 (CP: Ant 984 ft.). Stereo. Prog sep from AM. Net: ABC/E. Format: Contemp hits. ■ Buddy Howell Jr., gen sls mgr; Mike Wahl, prom dir; Mike McCoy, progmg dir; Stacy Barton, news dir.

KVSP(AM)—1946: 1140 khz; 1 kw-D. TL: N35 23 14 W97 29 56. 1528 N.E. 23rd St. (73111). (405) 427-5877. Licensee: Perry Broadcasting Co. Inc. (acq 3-3-93; $375,000; FTR 3-22-93). Net: American Urban. Rep: Banner. Format: Urban contemp. ■ Darnell Swift, gen mgr, progmg dir & mus dir; Russell Perry, gen sls mgr; Mike Fields, chief engr.

KXXY(AM)—1922: 1340 khz; 1 kw-U. TL: N35 29 28 W97 30 33. Stereo. Hrs opn: 24. 101 N.E. 28th St. (73105). (405) 528-5543. FAX: (405) 524-5823. Licensee: NewMarket Media Corp. (group owner; acq 5-29-87). Rep: McGavren Guild. Wash atty: Kaye, Scholer, Fierman, Hayes & Handler. Format: C&W. News staff one; news progmg 3 hrs wkly. Target aud: 25-54. Spec prog: Oklahoma City 89ers baseball, Oklahoma City Calvary pro basketball, Tulsa University football, New Orleans Saints football. ■ Pete Schulte, pres; Bill Hurley, gen mgr; Rickey Rudy, mktg dir & prom mgr; Jay Phillips, progmg dir; Bill Reed, mus dir; Nate Webb, news dir; Britt Lockhart, chief engr. ■ Rates: $180; 140; 150; 50.

KXXY-FM—October 1964: 96.1 mhz; 100 kw. Ant 1,167 ft. TL: N35 32 58 W97 29 18 (CP: Ant 256 ft.). Stereo. Dups AM 100%.

KYIS(FM)—June 1969: 98.9 mhz; 100 kw. Ant 1,108 ft. TL: N35 33 36 W97 29 07. Stereo. Hrs opn: 24. Suite 800, 3545 N.W. 58th St. (73112). (405) 942-3399. FAX: (405) 948-1028. Licensee: Desert Communications III Inc. (acq 1-3-92). Net: AP. Format: Hot adult contemp. News staff one. Target aud: 25-54; female. ■ Bill LeGrand, gen mgr; Lisa Scott, gen sls mgr; David Shuler, prom dir & adv dir; Jon Zellner, progmg dir; Amy Johns, news dir & pub affrs dir; Chuck DePacpe, chief engr.

WKY(AM)—January 1920: 930 khz; 5 kw-U, DA-N. TL: N35 33 43 W97 30 27. Stereo. Hrs opn: 24. Box 14930 (73113); 400 E. Britton Rd. (73114). (405) 478-2930. FAX: (405) 478-7739. Licensee: Gaylord Broadcasting Co. (group owner; acq 8-1-28). Net: Torbet. Rep: Cristal. Wash atty: Reed, Smith, Shaw & McClay. Format: Easy listening. Target aud: 35 plus. ■ Edward L. Gaylord, pres; Jim Fisher, gen mgr; Maria Bernal, gen sls mgr; B.J. Wexler, progmg dir; Jay Perkey, chief engr.

Okmulgee

KOKL(AM)—October 1937: 1240 khz; 1 kw-U. TL: N35 36 31 W95 58 19. Hrs opn: 6 AM-10 PM. Box 756, 410 W. 6th (74447). (918) 756-3646; (918) 756-5400. FAX: (918) 756-1800. Licensee: Brewer Communications Inc. (acq 6-1-73). Net: ABC/I. Rep: Keystone (unwired net). Format: Country, Gospel. News staff one; news progmg 8 hrs wkly. Target aud: 35 plus; Religious, black, white and Native American women. ■ James R. Brewer, pres; Paul Brown, chief opns; Delores Van Stratton, dev dir; Thomas Morrow, progmg dir & mus dir; Jerry Morris, asst mus dir; Jim Daxon, news dir; William Davis, chief engr. KGLB-TV affil. ■ Rates: $16.50; 13.75; 16.50; 9.75.

KTHK(FM)—May 24, 1976: 94.3 mhz; 3 kw. Ant 300 ft. TL: N35 36 31 W95 58 19 (CP: 94.1 mhz; 18.07 kw. Ant 817 ft.). 7030 S. Yale, Suite 302, Tulsa (74136). (918) 496-0941. Licensee: Integrated Broadcasting Co. (acq 8-2-89; $1,400,000; FTR 8-21-89). Format: Country. ■ Jan Dean, gen mgr.

Owasso

KQLL-FM—Oct 1, 1981: 106.1 mhz; 100 kw. Ant 1,315 ft. TL: N36 31 36 W95 39 12. Stereo. Hrs opn: 24. Rebroadcasts KQLL(AM) Tulsa. Suite 400, 5314 S. Yale Ave, Tulsa (74135). (918) 481-1061. FAX: (918) 481-1773. Licensee: Truth Publishing Co. (acq 1-13-92; with KQLL[AM] Tulsa). Rep: Banner. Format: Oldies. ■ John Dille, III, pres; Bill Paddock, gen mgr; Dave Simons, gen sls mgr; Julie Meylink, prom dir; Paul Langston, progmg dir; Julie Jennings, news dir.

Pauls Valley

KVLH(AM)—December 1947: 1470 khz; 1 kw-D, DA. TL: N34 42 15 W97 15 19. Box 610 (73075). (405) 238-3314. FAX: (405) 238-5959. Licensee: Washita Broadcasting Inc. (acq 12-88; $381,000; FTR 1-23-89). Net: ABC/D, ABC/E; Okla. Net. Format: C&W. News staff one; news progmg 18 hrs wkly. Target aud: General. Spec prog: Farm 6 hrs, news 18 hrs, gospel 5 hrs wkly. ■ Mark Rawlings, pres & gen mgr; Kelly Rawlings, opns dir & prom dir; Mike Laird, progmg dir & mus dir; Tony Malaska, news dir; Hal Smith, chief engr.

KGOK(FM)—Co-owned with KVLH(AM). October 1978: 97.7 mhz; 3 kw. Ant 303 ft. TL: N34 39 32 W97 09 33. Stereo. Format: Oldies, classic rock. News staff one; news progmg 19 hrs wkly.

Pawhuska

KXVQ(AM)—Oct 19, 1963: 1500 khz; 5 kw-D, 500 w-CH, DA-D. TL: N36 40 00 W96 21 48. Hrs opn: Sunrise-sunset. 513 Kihekah (74056). (316) 943-1133; (918) 287-1500. Licensee: Ed Toles. Net: ABC/I; Okla. Net. Format: Country, bluegrass. News progmg 15 hrs wkly. Target aud: 42-55 plus. Spec prog: Farm 5 hrs, American Indian 5 hrs, gospel 10 hrs wkly. ■ Edward R. Toles, pres; Larry Wagnon, chief engr. ■ Rates: $8; 8; 8; na.

Perry

KASR(AM)—July 6, 1986: 1020 khz; 400 w-D, 250-w, DA-2. TL: N36 15 35 W97 13 01. Hrs opn: 24. Box 1086, 615 Delaware St. (73077). Licensee: Starlight Broadcasting Inc. (acq 2-24-93; $150,000 with co-located FM; FTR 3-15-93). ■ James Dunn, pres; John Deken, exec vp & gen mgr; Harry Gilstrap, vp opns & engrg dir; Jack Bush, prom mgr & news dir; Sean Anderson, mus dir. ■ Rates: $9; 8; 9; 6.

KASR-FM—Nov 24, 1988: 105.1 mhz; 6 kw. Ant 328 ft. TL: N36 14 15 W97 21 59. Stereo. Hrs opn: 24. Prog sep from AM. (405) 336-1020. Wash atty: Baraff, Koerner, Olender & Hochberg. Format: AC light. News staff one; news progmg 5 hrs wkly. Target aud: General.

Ponca City

KIXR(FM)—June 1986: 100.1 mhz; 3 kw. Ant 299 ft. TL: N36 47 19 W97 02 53. Stereo. Hrs opn: 24. Box 2631 (74602); 2nd Floor, 100 S. Pine (74601). (405) 765-5491. FAX: (405) 762-8329. Licensee: Kix Communications Inc. (acq 4-2-86; FTR 4-28-86). Format: Chr. News staff one; news progmg 4 hrs wkly. Target aud: 18-45. ■ Scott Taylor, gen mgr & gen sls mgr; Steve Taylor, opns mgr, mus dir & chief engr; Kari Arthur, pub affrs dir. ■ Rates: $14; 9; 14; 9.

KLOR-FM—Dec 1965: 99.3 mhz; 3 kw. Ant 300 ft. TL: N36 46 59 W97 04 15. Stereo. 122 N. 3rd St. (74601). (405) 762-9930. Licensee: Pioneer Communications Inc. (acq 7-21-81). Net: CBS Spectrum. Format: Classic rock. News staff one. Target aud: 18-55. ■ Mary Jane Kelly, pres & gen mgr; Kathleen Kelly, gen sls mgr; Dave Michaels, progmg dir & mus dir; Roger Allen, news dir. ■ Rates: $14.50; 14.50; 14.50; na.

***KLVV(FM)**—December 1992: 88.7 mhz; 11.5 kw. Ant 479 ft. TL: N36 41 25 W97 10 20. Stereo. Hrs opn: 24. Box 14 (74602); Rte 1 Box 215 (74601). (405) 767-1400. FAX: (405) 765-1700. Licensee: The Love Station Inc. Format: Adult contemp, Christian music/teaching. News progrmg 7 hrs wkly. Target aud: 25-45; young Christian adults. ■ Doyle Brewer, CEO, chmn, pres & gen mgr; Cleve Powell, vp; Tony Weir, progmg dir & mus dir; David Land, chief engr.

KOKB(AM)—See Blackwell.

KPNC-FM—June 5, 1979: 100.9 mhz; 3 kw. Ant 285 ft. TL: N36 39 56 W97 04 20. Stereo. Hrs opn: 24. Box 2509 (74602); 1000 Bourgell Rd. (74602). (405) 765-2485; (405) 767-1101. FAX: (405) 767-1103. Licensee: KPNC Broadcasting Co. (acq 7-20-90). Net: ABC/E, SMN; Okla. News Net. Format: Country. News progmg 20 hrs wkly. Target aud: 25-54; working middle class. Spec prog: Farm 5 hrs wkly. ■ Ken Greenwood, chmn; Bill Coleman, vp & gen mgr; Joe Garland, opns dir, progmg dir & chief engr; Illene Ozment, sls dir; Danny Diamond, mus dir.

WBBZ(AM)—1927: 1230 khz; 1 kw-U. TL: N36 41 46 W97 03 07. Stereo. Hrs opn: 5 AM-midnight. Box 588, 1601 E. Oklahoma (74602). (405) 765-6607. FAX: (405) 762-6397. Licensee: Ponca City Publishing Co. (acq 1949). Net: MBS. Format: Adult contemp, sports, news/information. News staff one; news progmg 12 hrs wkly. Target aud: 35 plus. Spec prog: Class 5 hrs, gospel 2 hrs; relg 4 hrs; big band 2 hrs wkly. ■ Allan Muchmore, CEO; Kathy Adams, gen mgr; Tom Muchmore, mus dir & chief engr; Phil Turney, news dir; Randy Bishop, pub affrs dir. ■ Rates: $12.50; 11; 12.50; 12.50.

Poteau

KBSY(FM)—Oct 18, 1969: 107.3 mhz; 100 kw. Ant 1,810 ft. TL: N34 57 50 W94 22 34. Stereo. 3108 Jenny Lind Rd., Fort Smith, AR (72901). (501) 782-1992. FAX: (501) 782-4999. Licensee: Landmark Communications Inc. (acq 7-10-89; $900,000). Wash atty: Gardner, Carton & Douglas. Format: Adult contemporary. Target aud: 25-49; upwardly mobile middle & upper class, 55% female, 45% male. ■ Kaye Michael, gen mgr. ■ Rates: $20; 18; 20; 14.

KPRV(AM)—Nov 25, 1953: 1280 khz; 1 kw-D. TL: N35 01 08 W94 39 22. Hrs opn: 14. Box 368, Hwy. 59 S. (74953). (918) 647-3221. Licensee: LeRoy Billy. Net: CBS; Okla. Net. Wash atty: Robert Allen. Format: Country. News progmg 24 hrs wkly. Target aud: 24-54. Spec prog: Gospel 12 hrs wkly. ■ LeRoy Billy, gen mgr & gen sls mgr; David Billy, progmg dir, mus dir & pub affrs dir; Larry Johnson, chief engr. ■ Rates: $7.50; 7.50; 7.50; 7.50.

KZBB(FM)—1967: 97.9 mhz; 100 kw. Ant 2,000 ft. TL: N35 04 19 W94 40 46. 9001 Rogers Ave., Ft. Smith, AR (72903). (501) 452-0105. FAX: (501) 484-7808. Licensee: Arklahoma Communications Co. (acq 1-21-93; $355,000; FTR 2-15-93). Net: Unistar. Format: CHR-A/C mix. News progmg one hr wkly. Target aud: 18-49; upscale. ■ Eldon Coffman, pres; Larry Tate, gen mgr; Judy Sorrell, gen sls mgr; Dennis Snow, progmg mgr. ■ Rates: $21; 20; 20; 15.

Pryor

KMYZ-FM—July 3, 1969: 104.5 mhz; 78 kw. Ant 1,250 ft. TL: N36 18 04 W95 19 29. Stereo. c/o 149 Penn Ave., Scranton, PA (18503); Suite 801, 5810 E. Skelly Dr., Tulsa (74135). (918) 665-3131; (800) 522-9018. FAX: (918) 663-6622. Licensee: Shamrock Communications Inc. (group owner; acq 4-14-84). Net: NBC the Source. Format: Rock. ■ Rick Cohn, gen mgr; Truman Criss, gen sls mgr; D.C. Roberts, prom dir; Mel Myers, progmg dir; Tim Smith, mus dir; Joe Hancock, chief engr.

KMYZ(AM)—July 3, 1950: 1570 khz; 1 kw-D. TL: N36 18 04 W95 19 29. Dups FM 100%.

Roland

KYUC(FM)—Not on air, target date unknown: 92.3 mhz; 930 w. Ant 571 ft. TL: N35 28 24 W94 30 42. 2201 N. 58th St., Fort Smith, AR (72904). Licensee: Sequoyah Communications Corp.

Sallisaw

KKID(AM)—Sept 16, 1968: 1560 khz; 250 w-D. TL: N35 26 34 W94 46 33. Box 666 (74955). (918) 775-9109. Licensee: Hendren-McChristian Communications. (group owner; acq 6-8-92; $1.2 million; grpsl; FTR 6-29-92). Net: ABC/I; Format: C&W. News progmg 6 hrs wkly. Target aud: 18 plus. ■ Kim Hendren, pres; Norman D. McChristian, gen mgr; Tony Demaree, gen sls mgr. ■ Rates: $6.50; na; na; na.

KKUZ-FM—Co-owned with KKID(AM). May 18, 1972: 95.9 mhz; 30 kw. Ant 600 ft. TL: N35 24 29 W94 41 13 Stereo. Dups AM 100%. 1912 Church St., Barling (72927); HC-61, Box 565, Railroad St. (74955-9413). (501) 484-9833. ■ Billy D. Sexton, gen sls mgr; N.D. McChristian, chief engr. ■ Rates: $8.50; na; na; na.

Sand Springs

KTOW(AM)—July 22, 1961: 1340 khz; 500 w-D, 1 kw-N. TL: N36 09 40 W96 03 10 (CP: TL: N36 07 58 W96 05 36). 8886 W. 21st St. (74063). (918) 245-0254; FAX: (918) 245-0255 (CALL FIRST). Licensee: Music Sound Radio (acq 11-7-79). Net: MBS. Format: Relg. News staff one; news progmg one hr wkly. Target aud: 18-34; general. ■ Joe Bowen, pres; Tim Barraza, gen mgr; Tony Barrow, progmg dir. ■ Rates: $25; 25; 25; 25.

KTOW-FM—June 1989: 102.3 mhz; 1.7 kw. Ant 436 ft. TL: N36 12 39 W96 06 03. Format: Urban contemp. ■ Rates: $35; 35; 35; 35.

Sapulpa

KXOJ(AM)—June 15, 1962: 1550 khz; 2.5 kw-D, 47 w-N, DA-1. TL: N36 01 08 W96 05 55. Stereo. Box 1250 (74067); Old Frankoma Rd. (74066). (918) 224-2620. FAX: (918) 224-4984. Licensee: KXOJ, Inc. (acq 5-2-73). Net: UPI. Format: Conservative relg. News progmg 2 hrs wkly. Target aud: 35 plus. ■ Mike Stephens, pres & gen mgr; David Stephens, opns mgr, sls dir & mktg dir; Seth Andrews, dev dir & prom dir; Mark Dames, progmg dir; Srth Andrews, mus dir; Bill Davis, chief engr.

KXOJ-FM—Feb 22, 1977: 100.9 mhz; 2 kw. Ant 360 ft. TL: N36 03 38 W96 06 03. Stereo. (918) 224-1550. Format: Contemp Christian music.

Seminole

KIRC(FM)—Nov 1, 1978: 105.5 mhz; 2.35 kw. Ant 367 ft. TL: N35 12 53 W96 44 26 (CP: 4.56 kw). Stereo. Hrs opn: 24 120 E. Main St., Shawnee (74801-6906); One Radio Rd. (74818). (405) 382-0105; (405) 275-5670. FAX: (405) 382-6639. Licensee: One Ten Broadcast Inc. (acq 9-6-91). Format: Country. News staff 9; news progmg 2 hrs wkly. Target aud: General; 12-55. Spec prog: Area tribes one hr wkly. ■ Herman Jones, pres, gen mgr & progmg dir; Linda Jones, vp; Granville Higley, chief engr. ■ Rates: $11.75; 10.75; 11.75; 8.75.

KRAF(AM)—See Holdenville.

KWSH(AM)—See Wewoka.

Shawnee

KABH(FM)—Not on air, target date unknown: 95.1 mhz; 100 kw. Ant 1,417 ft. 10841 E. 28th St., Independence, MO (64052). Licensee: Bott Communications Inc.

KGFF(AM)—Dec 10, 1930: 1450 khz; 1 kw-U. TL: N35 21 39 W96 53 41. Hrs opn: 24. Box 9 (74802); 2610 Bryan N. (74801). (405) 273-4390; (405) 273-2222. FAX: (405) 273-4530. Licensee: Overland Communications Inc. (acq 6-5-92; $150,000; FTR 6-22-92). Net: ABC/I, CBS, MBS; Okla. News Net, Texas State Net. Format: Adult contemp. News staff 2; news progmg 20 hrs wkly. Target aud: 25-54; general. Spec prog: Relg 2 hrs wkly, sports/talk, Oklahoma Univ. Sooners, Dallas Cowboys, Paul Harvey. ■ Dan Overland, CEO; Neil O'Donnell, gen mgr & gen sls mgr; Mike Askins, opns dir & progmg dir; Shari Jalee, prom dir & pub affrs dir; Trey Davis, news dir; Michael Askins, chief engr. ■ Rates: $7.50; 7.50; 7.50; 7.50.

Spencer

***KROU(FM)**—January 28, 1993: 105.7 mhz; 4 kw. Ant 328 ft. TL: N35 35 22 W97 29 03. Stereo. Hrs opn: 5 AM-Midnight. Dups KGOU(FM) 100%. 780 Van Vleet Oval, Norman (73019). (405) 325-3388. Licensee: Univ. of Oklahoma. Net: NPR. Wash atty: Dow, Lohnes & Albertson. Format: Class, jazz, news. News staff 2; news progmg 47 hrs wkly. Target aud: 25-54; adults. Spec prog: Blues 10 hrs, new age 4 hrs wkly. ■ Karen Holp, gen mgr; Jay Childs, opns dir; Rachel Jacquemain, dev dir; Michael F. Jackson, mus dir; Steve Carmody, news dir; David White, chief engr.

Stillwater

KGFY(FM)—Feb 6, 1967: 105.5 mhz; 4.9 kw. Ant 400 ft. TL: N36 10 31 W97 00 51. Stereo. Hrs opn: 24. 217 S. Washington St. (74074). (405) 372-6000; (800) 377-6016. FAX: (405) 372-6002. Licensee: Gentry Media (acq 3-20-93; $275,000; FTR 6-14-93). Net: ABC/E. Rep: Katz & Powell. Wash atty: Fletcher, Heald & Hildreth. Format: Country. News progmg 5 hrs wkly. Target aud: 25-54; young, college community & upscale educated people. Spec prog: Contemp Christian 4 hrs wkly. ■ Frank Gentry, pres, gen mgr & adv dir; Toni Coleman, opns dir; Chuck Pearson, sls dir & prom dir; John Ellis, mktg dir & pub affrs dir; Steve Dunn, progmg dir; Susan Ray, mus dir; Casey Kindrick, news dir; Frank Gilley, chief engr. ■ Rates: $18; 16; 18; 16.

***KOSU-FM**—Dec 29, 1955: 91.7 mhz; 100 kw. Ant 1,010 ft. TL: N36 06 33 W97 11 43. Stereo. Oklahoma State Univ., 302 P.M. Bldg. (74078). (405) 744-6352. Licensee: Oklahoma State Univ. Net: NPR. Format: Class, educ. News staff 3; news progmg 40 hrs wkly. Spec prog: American Indian one hr wkly. ■ John Campbell, pres; Craig Beeby, gen mgr & dev dir; Susan Anderson, opns dir & progmg dir; Paula Price, mus dir; Paul Sund, news dir; Dan Schroeder, chief engr.

KSPI(AM)—June 1, 1947: 780 khz; 250 w-D. TL: N36 04 56 W97 03 13. Stereo. Box 2288 (74076); 215 W. 9th St. (74074). (405) 372-7800. FAX: (405) 372-3112. Licensee: Stillwater Publishing Co. Net: MBS. Format: Btfl mus, big band. News staff one; news progmg 12 hrs wkly. Target aud: 30 plus. ■ J.R. Bellatti, pres; Leon Matthews, gen mgr & gen sls mgr; Judy Morton, prom dir; Jack Lorenz, adv dir; Jim Randolph, progmg dir & mus dir; Michael Varnum, asst mus dir; Sean Kelly, news dir & pub affrs dir; Dan Schroeder, chief engr. ■ Rates: $8.70; 8.70; 8.70; na.

KSPI-FM—Nov 1, 1947: 93.7 mhz; 16 kw. Ant 886 ft. TL: N36 06 31 W97 11 46. Stereo. Hrs opn: 18. Prog sep from AM. Net: MBS. Format: Classic rock. News progmg 11 hrs wkly.

Sulphur

KFXT(FM)—Nov 11, 1979: 100.9 mhz; 3 kw. Ant 300 ft. TL: N34 32 57 W96 58 34 (CP: 50 kw, ant 492 ft.). Stereo. Hrs opn: 24. RR 2, Box 1200 (73086-9802). (405) 658-9292. Licensee: Central Oklahoma Radio Group (acq 10-1-90). Net: MBS. Wash atty: Southmayd & Miller. Format: Country. News staff one; news progmg 5 hrs wkly.

Broadcasting & Cable Yearbook 1994
B-299

Target aud: 25-52. ■ Ken Austin, pres & gen mgr; Bob Urioste, gen sls mgr; Jack Steel, mus dir; Francie Holmes, pub affrs dir; James Wilson, chief engr.

Taft

KHJM(FM)—Mar 20, 1990: 100.3 mhz; 6 kw. Ant 380 ft. TL: N35 48 42 W95 34 12. Stereo. Hrs opn: 24. First National, Severs Bldg., Suite 910, 215 N. State St., Muskogee (74401); Box 2416 (74402). (918) 682-2233. FAX: (918) 682-2233. Licensee: Taft Broadcasting Inc. (acq 9-5-90; $30,000; FTR 9-24-90). Net: USA. Format: Relig, Christian country mus, gospel. News progmg 14 hrs wkly. Target aud: 25-55. Spec prog: Farm one hr wkly. ■ Bryant W. Ellis, pres; George Chambers, exec vp & chief engr; Roy Davis, progmg dir. ■ Rates: $17; 17; 17; 10.

Tahlequah

KTLQ(AM)—August 1957: 1350 khz; 1 kw-D, 61 w-N. TL: N35 53 43 W94 57 12. Hrs opn: 6 AM-midnight. Box 719, 517 S. Muskogee Ave. (74465). (918) 456-2511. FAX: (918) 456-3231. Licensee: Demaree Communications Inc. (acq 1-1-89; grpsl; FTR 1-16-89). Net: CNN, Unistar. Format: Country. News staff one; news progmg 6 hrs wkly. Target aud: 30-60. Spec prog: American Indian one hr wkly. ■ Paul Demaree, pres; Martha Demaree, gen mgr; Scott Pettus, gen sls mgr & prom mgr; Henry McCray, progmg dir & news dir; Phil Cooper, mus dir; Dayne McChristen, chief engr. ■ Rates: $12; 12; 12; 12.

KEOK(FM)—Co-owned with KTLQ(AM). Aug 20, 1966: 101.7 mhz; 3 kw. Ant 300 ft. TL: N35 53 43 W94 57 12. Stereo. Hrs opn: 18 Dups AM 75%. News staff 4; news progmg 4 hrs wkly. Target aud: 25-50. ■ Henry McCray, opns dir; Martha Demaree, gen sls mgr & prom mgr. ■ Rates: Same as AM.

Tishomingo

KTSH(FM)—Not on air, target date unknown: 106.3 mhz; 25 kw. Ant 328 ft. TL: N34 11 15 W96 43 28. Licensee: Ballard Broadcasting of Oklahoma Inc.

Tonkawa

***KAYE-FM**—June 1, 1976: 90.7 mhz; 1.2 kw. Ant 67 ft. TL: N36 40 42 W97 17 50. Stereo. Hrs opn: 7:30 AM-11:30 PM (Mon-Fri). 1220 E. Grand (74653). (405) 628-6446; (405) 628-6200. FAX: (405) 628-6209. Licensee: Northern Oklahoma College. Format: AOR. News progmg 6 hrs wkly. Target aud: Teens-25. Spec prog: R&B one hr, CHR 2 hrs, classic rock 2 hrs wkly. ■ Dr. Joe Kinzer, pres; Sally Nesselrode, gen mgr; Mark Schultz, progmg dir; J.D. Shaklee, mus dir; Ray Larson, chief engr.

Tulsa

KAKC(AM)—July 15, 1938: 1300 khz; 5 kw-D, 1 kw-N, DA-2. TL: N35 59 40 W95 51 27. 5801 E. 41st St., Suite 900 (74135). (918) 664-2810. FAX: (918) 665-0555. Licensee: Clear Channel Radio Licenses Inc. (group owner; acq 8-5-92). Net: CNN. Rep: Christal. Format: News, sports. News staff one; news progmg 100 hrs wkly. Target aud: General; 25-54. ■ L. Lowry Mays, pres; Jim Smith, vp & gen mgr; Allen McLaughlin, gen sls mgr; Jennifer Stewart, prom mgr; Phil Stone, progmg dir; Janine Burns, news dir; Steve Davis, chief engr.

KMOD-FM—Co-owned with KAKC(AM). Oct 10, 1959: 97.5 mhz; 100 kw. Ant 1,800 ft. TL: N36 11 46 W96 05 53. Stereo. Format: AOR. ■ Bruce Simms, natl sls mgr; Jennifer Stewart, prom dir; Janine Burns, mus dir.

KBEZ(FM)—March 1964: 92.9 mhz; 100 kw. Ant 1,319 ft. TL: N36 11 26 W96 05 50. Stereo. Suite 711, 7030 S. Yale Ave. (74136). (918) 496-9336. FAX: (918) 495-1850. Licensee: Renda Broadcasting Corp. (group owner; acq 6-8-90; grpsl; FTR 6-25-90). Rep: Eastman. Format: Soft Adult Contemp. Target aud: 25-54. Spec prog: Big band 5 hrs wkly. ■ Tim Van Maren, opns mgr.

KCFO(AM)—1946: 970 khz; 2.5 kw-D, 1 kw-N, DA-2. TL: N36 11 46 W96 02 22. Hrs opn: 18. 3737 S. 37th W. Ave. (74107). (918) 445-1186. Licensee: Friendship Broadcasting Ltd. (acq 8-1-90; $953,000; FTR 7-2-90). Net: USA. Format: Relg, talk, progsv. News progmg 3 hrs wkly. Target aud: 25-54; women. Spec prog: Sp one hr wkly. ■ Ray Clatworthy, pres; Kenneth Staley, gen mgr; Robert Cauthon, chief engr.

KGTO(AM)—1946: 1050 khz; 1 kw-D. TL: N36 09 40 W96 03 10. No. 1100, 1638 S. Carson (74119). (918) 585-5555. Licensee: The Kravis Co. Net: CNN, Unistar. Rep: Republic. Format: Big band. Target aud: 35-54. ■ George R. Kravis, pres; Linda Tabor, vp & gen mgr; Bob Tomarkin, gen sls mgr; John Hart, progmg dir; Cathy Carroll, news dir; Morgan Bear, chief engr.

KRAV(FM)—Co-owned with KGTO(AM). Nov 21, 1962: 96.5 mhz; 100 kw. Ant 137 ft. TL: N36 11 46 W96 05 53. Stereo. Prog sep from AM. Format: Adult contemp. News staff 2; news progmg 2 hrs wkly. Target aud: 25-54.

KMOD-FM—Listing follows KAKC(AM).

KQLL(AM)—Jan 22, 1934: 1430 khz; 5 kw-U, DA-N. TL: N36 14 10 W95 56 50. Suite 400 5314 S. Yale Ave., Owasso, (74135). (918) 481-1061. FAX: (918) 481-1773. Licensee: Truth Publishing Co. (acq 1-13-92; with KQLL-FM Owasso). Rep: Banner. Format: Sports. Target aud: 25-54. ■ Bill Paddock, gen mgr; Dave Simons, gen sls mgr; Julie Meylink, progmg dir.

KRAV(FM)—Listing follows KGTO(AM).

KRMG(AM)—Dec 31, 1949: 740 khz; 50 kw-D, 25 kw-N, DA-2. TL: N36 04 50 W96 17 09. Stereo. Hrs opn: 24. 7136 S. Yale (74136). (918) 493-7400. Licensee: Newcity Communications Corp. (group; acq 7-87). Net: NBC Talknet, ABC/I. Rep: Katz. Format: Adult contemp, div, talk. News staff 7. Target aud: General; 25 plus. ■ Rod B. Krebs, gen mgr; Tom Holiday, gen sls mgr; Michael DelGiorno, progmg dir; Wayne Smith, chief engr.

KWEN(FM)—Co-owned with KRMG(AM). 1961: 95.5 mhz; 96 kw. Ant 1,328 ft. TL: N36 11 46 W95 05 53. Stereo. Prog sep from AM. (918) 494-9500. TWX: 510-601-8539. (Acq 1986; grpsl; FTR 4-28-86). Net: AP. Format: Contemp country. ■ Brad West, opns dir; Wayne Blackmon, gen sls mgr; Vivian Steele, prom mgr; Dave Block, progmg dir; Kevin Meyer, mus dir.

KTFX(FM)—Nov 1, 1966: 103.3 mhz; 100 kw. Ant 1,278 ft. TL: N36 09 40 W95 53 06. Stereo. Hrs opn: 24. Communications Bldg, 8107 E. Admiral Pl. (74115). (918) 836-5512; (918) 836-5839. Licensee: Central Broadcast Co. (acq 9-1-77). Format: C&W. News staff 2; news progmg 18 hrs wkly. Target aud: 18-34; contemporary Yuppie country listener. Spec prog: Farm 2 hr, Elvis Presley one hr wkly. ■ William Haydon Payne, pres & chief engr; Travis Reeves, stn mgr; Mike Rogers, dev dir; Bill Payne, sls dir & mus dir; Kelly Lindholm, vp mktg & adv dir; Will Payne, vp prom; Jim Richards, progmg dir, news dir & pub affrs dir.

KTOW(AM)—See Sand Springs.

KTRT(AM)—See Claremore.

KVOO(AM)—Jan 23, 1925: 1170 khz; 50 kw-U, DA-N. TL: N36 08 49 W95 48 27. Stereo. Hrs opn: 24. Box 52548, 4590 E. 29th. (74114). (918) 743-7814. FAX: (918) 743-7613. Licensee: Tulsa Great Empire Broadcasting Inc. Group owner: Great Empire Broadcasting Inc. (acq 6-1-90). Net: ABC. Rep: Schubert. Wash atty: Dow, Lohnes & Albertson. Format: C&W. News staff 7; news progmg 24 hrs wkly. Target aud: 35 plus. Spec prog: Farm 5 hrs, gospel 2 hrs, call-in talk show 2 hrs wkly. ■ Mike Oatman, CEO; Mike Lynch, pres; Danny Jenkins, CFO; Mike Demarco, gen mgr; Billy Parker, opns mgr; Rick Clary, gen sls mgr; Andy Oatman, progmg dir; Brian Gann, news dir; Larry White, chief engr. ■ Rates: $65; 60; 50; 42.

KVOO-FM—Nov 16, 1973: 98.5 mhz; 100 kw. Ant 1,229 ft. TL: N36 11 26 W96 05 50. Stereo. Hrs opn: 24. Prog sep from AM. Target aud: 25-54.

KWEN(FM)—Listing follows KRMG(AM).

***KWGS(FM)**—Oct 19, 1947: 89.5 mhz; 50 kw. Ant 1,067 ft. TL: N36 01 15 W95 40 32. Stereo. Hrs opn: 24. 600 S. College (74104). (918) 631-2577. Licensee: The University of Tulsa. Net: NPR, APR. Wash atty: Pellegrin & Levine. Format: News & information. News staff one; news progmg 84 hrs wkly. Target aud: General. Spec prog: International news 50 hrs wkly. ■ Frank Christel, gen mgr; Bill Nole, opns dir & progmg dir; Brad Newman, chief engr.

KXOJ(AM)—See Sapulpa.

Vinita

KITO-FM—Apr 9, 1981: 96.1 mhz; 50 kw. Ant 492 ft. TL: N36 34 56 W95 01 35. Stereo. Hrs opn: 24. Box 961, 402 N. Wilson St. (74301). (918) 256-2255. FAX: (918) 256-2633. Licensee: DLB Broadcasting Inc. Net: AP. Format: C&W. News progmg 28 hrs wkly. Target aud: General; traditional country music fans. ■ Dave Boyd, pres, gen mgr & progmg dir; Leona Boyd, gen sls mgr; Gavin Boyd, mus dir; Verna Altebaumer, news dir; William E. Davis, chief engr. ■ Rates: $9.95; 9.35; 9.95; 9.35.

KITO(AM)—Dec 7, 1954: 1470 khz; 500 w-D, 88 w-N. TL: N36 38 44 W95 07 35. Box 961 (74301). (918) 256-7224. FAX: (918) 256-8081. Licensee: Leemay Broadcasting Services Rep: Mkt 4. Format: Country, sports. News staff one. Target aud: 30-50.

Wagoner

KXTD(AM)—Mar 1, 1966: 1530 khz; 5 kw-D, DA. TL: N35 58 30 W95 29 30. Stereo. Sports Radio Inc., 4000 W. Indian Hills Rd. Norman (73072). (405) 364-8118. Licensee: Sportsradio Inc. (acq 9-13-90; $75,000; FTR 10-1-90). Rep: Keystone (unwired net). Format: Sports News progmg 18 hrs wkly. Target aud: 25-49. ■ John Fox, gen mgr; Tony Sellers, opns mgr.

Watonga

KIMY(FM)—Dec 12, 1987: 93.5 mhz; 3 kw. Ant 190 ft. TL: N35 54 17 W98 23 09. Stereo. Hrs opn: 5 AM-11 PM. Box 221, 5.5 miles N. of Hwy 33 & Hwy 8 intersection (73772). (405) 623-4777; (405) 623-2494. FAX: (405) 623-4549. Licensee: Vera L. Dunn. Group owner: KIMY Radio Inc. Net: SMN; Cowboy Sports Network, OK State Univ. Format: Country. News staff 2; news progmg 4 hrs wkly. Target aud: General; 25-54. Spec prog: Farm one hr, gospel 4 hrs, news/talk 7 hrs wkly. ■ Vera Dunn, pres; James W. Dunn, vp; Ron Gabe, gen mgr, gen sls mgr & adv mgr; Bob DeLong, prom mgr; Mike Sullins, chief engr. ■ Rates: $12; 11; 12; 11.

Weatherford

KWEY(AM)—June 1, 1970: 1590 khz; 1 kw-D, DA. TL: N35 33 33 W98 43 11. Box 587, Hwy 54 N. (73096). (405) 772-5939. FAX: (405) 772-1590. Licensee: Wright Broadcasting Systems Inc. (acq 7-17-91; $407,435 with co-located FM; FTR 8-5-91). Net: ABC/I; Okla. Agrinet. Wash atty: Putbrese & Hunsacker. Format: C&W. News staff one. Target aud: 25 plus. ■ G. Harold Wright, CEO; Ray Michaels, progmg dir & engrg dir; Dianne Mathews, mus dir; Michael Dodson, news dir.

KWEY-FM—Aug 18, 1977: 97.3 mhz; 70 kw. Ant 385 ft. TL: N35 33 02 W98 43 59. Stereo. Prog sep from AM. Net: ABC/C. News staff one; news progmg 10 hrs wkly. ■ Rates: $21; 14; 18; 13.

Wewoka

KWSH(AM)—July 1951: 1260 khz; 1 kw-U, DA-N. TL: N35 10 10 W96 32 30. Box 1260 (74884). (405) 382-1260; (405) 257-5441. Licensee: The Five Bells Inc. (group owner; acq 9-28-93; FTR 10-18-93). Net: ABC/I, ABC/C; Okla. News Net. Format: Country. Target aud: 21-61. Spec prog: Black one hr, American Indian one hr wkly. ■ Jean Bell, pres; Jerry Spencer, gen mgr & engrg mgr; Evelyn Hammon, gen sls mgr; Don Coker, prom mgr & pub affrs dir; Garry Walker, progmg dir, mus dir & news dir. ■ Rates: $6.45; 5.45; 6.45; 5.45.

Wilburton

KZUD(FM)—Not on air, target date unknown: 103.7 mhz; 6 kw. Ant 272 ft. TL: N34 55 11 W95 19 03 (CP: 90 kw, ant 905 ft.). Licensee: Blue Mountain Broadcasting.

Woodward

KMZE(FM)—Sept 15, 1984: 92.1 mhz; 2.15 kw. Ant 1,099 ft. TL: N36 16 06 W99 26 56. Stereo. #D 2728 Williams Ave. (73801). (405) 256-3692. FAX: (405) 256-5821. Licensee: FM 92 Broadcasters Inc. (acq 8-17-89; $24,600; FTR 9-5-89). Format: Adult contemp. ■ Dwaine T. Martin, pres; Kevin Grice, gen mgr; Tim Mascarenas, gen sls mgr.

KSIW(AM)—September 1947: 1450 khz; 1 kw-U. TL: N36 25 42 W99 24 10. Hrs opn: 18. Box 1246, 1922 22nd St. (73802). (405) 256-7455; (405) 256-1450. Licensee: Fuchs Communications Inc. (acq 10-22-87). Net: ABC/I. Format: C&W. News staff one. Target aud: 40 plus. Spec prog: Farm & relg. ■ H. Gene Fuchs, pres, gen mgr & chief engr; Sam Brittain, gen sls mgr; Jack Casey, news dir. ■ Rates: $12; 9; 9; 9.

KWFX(FM)—Co-owned with KSIW(AM). Nov 1, 1974: 93.5 mhz; 3 kw. Ant 150 ft. TL: N36 25 42 W99 24 10 (CP: 100.1 mhz, 100 kw, ant 981 ft. TL: N36 22 39 W99 25 05). Stereo. Hrs opn: 19. Prog sep from AM. (405) 256-5939. Net: Unistar. Format: Adult contemp. Target aud: 25-45; affluent, predominantly females. ■ Rates: $10; 10; 10; 10.

KWDQ(FM)—Jan 9, 1990: 102.3 mhz; 2.35 kw. Ant 355 ft. TL: N36 24 02 W99 25 44. Suite B, 1517 Down Ave. (73801). (405) 254-9103. FAX: (405) 254-9102. Licensee: Classic Communications Inc. (acq 3-20-92). Format: Classic rock. ■ Rick Carnahan, pres; Sherry House,

Stations in the U.S. — Oregon

gen mgr; Ladonna Cross, gen sls mgr; B.K. Blaze, progmg dir, mus dir & news dir; Rick Camaha, chief engr.

KWFX(FM)—Listing follows KSIW(AM).

KWOX(FM)—Dec 16, 1983: 101.1 mhz; 100 kw. Ant 1,204 ft. TL: N36 16 06 W99 26 56. Stereo. Hrs opn: 24. K-101, 101 Centre, Williams & Downs (73801). (405) 256-4101; (405) 254-2034. FAX: (405) 256-3825. Licensee: Omni Communications Corp. Net: ABC/E, Unistar, NBC, Westwood One. Format: Country. News staff 2; news progmg 5 hrs wkly. Target aud: General. Spec prog: Farm 10 hrs wkly. ■ J. Douglas Williams, pres; Karen Lambhan, sr vp; C.J. Montgomery, gen mgr & chief opns; Jim Vincent, gen sls mgr; Kevin Grice, prom dir; Becky Myles, mus dir; Tony Wright, asst mus dir; Jay Roper, news dir & pub affrs dir; Bill Reid, chief engr. ■ Rates: $32; 28; 30; 26.

Oregon

LAUREN A. COLBY
301-663-1086
COMMUNICATIONS ATTORNEY
Special Attention to
Difficult Cases

Albany

KHPE(FM)—Listing follows KWIL(AM).

KRKT(AM)—1959: 990 khz; 250 w-D. TL: N44 35 43 W123 07 54. Hrs opn: 24. 1207 E. Ninth St. (97321). (503) 926-8628. Licensee: M3X Corp. (acq 3-73). Net: ABC/I. Rep: McGavren Guild. Wash atty: Fisher, Wayland, Cooper & Leader. Format: C&W. News staff one; news progmg 10 hrs wkly. Target aud: 25-54. ■ Gary M. Grossman, pres & gen mgr; Bill O'Brian, opns mgr & progmg dir; Bill Nielsen, vp sls & gen sls mgr; Larry Rogers (local), rgnl sls mgr; Mike Bell, prom dir; David Allen, mus dir; Rick Rogers, news dir; Dave Wooten, chief engr. ■ Rates: $26; 20; 24; 18.

KRKT-FM—June 1978: 99.9 mhz; 100 kw. Ant 1,069 ft. TL: N44 38 46 W123 16 11. Stereo. Dups AM 100%. ■ Rates: $22; 20; 22; 19.

KSHO(AM)—See Lebanon.

KWIL(AM)—Jan 14, 1941: 790 khz; 1 kw-U, DA-2. TL: N44 37 54 W123 00 57. Hrs opn: 24. Box 278 (97321). (503) 926-2233. FAX: (503) 926-3925. Licensee: Albany Radio Corp. (acq 7-1-57). Net: CBN. Format: Christian. ■ David M. Winchester, gen mgr; Jack Lute, gen sls mgr; Ed Knox, progmg dir; Jim Tsalapinas, mus dir; Ray Dammon, chief engr.

KHPE(FM)—Co-owned with KWIL(AM). Jan 12, 1969: 107.9 mhz; 100 kw. Ant 1,160 ft. TL: N44 38 46 W123 16 11. Stereo. Hrs opn: 24. Prog sep from AM. Format: Contemp Christian.

Altamont

KCHQ(FM)—Not on air, target date unknown: 101.3 mhz; 60 kw. Ant 882 ft. TL: N45 05 32 W121 26 35. Suite A, 12550 Brookhurst St., Garden Grove, CA (92640). (714) 636-5040. Licensee: Western States Broadcasting (acq 11-2-88; $10,000 FTR 12-5-88). ■ William L. Zawila, pres; Jay Stevens, vp.

Ashland

KCMX(AM)—1946: 580 khz; 1 kw-U, DA-N. TL: N42 09 46 W122 38 51. Box 159, 1438 Rossanley Dr., Medford (97501). (503) 779-1550. FAX: (503) 776-2360. Licensee: Rogue Valley Broadcasting Inc. Group owner: Johnson Communications (acq 10-22-93; $585,000 with co-located FM; FTR 11-8-93). Net: ABC; Rep: Eastman. Wash atty: Dow, Lohnes & Albertson. Format: News/talk. News staff one; news progmg 24 hrs wkly. Target aud: 30 plus; white male, affluent, businessmen. Spec prog: Farm 3 hrs wkly. ■ Karen Johnson, pres & gen sls mgr; Bob Johnson, gen mgr; John Greider, vp progmg; Robin Lawson, news dir; Ron Santos, pub affrs dir; Don Bennett, chief engr. ■ Rates: $8; 8; 8; 5.

KCMX-FM—July 20, 1978: 101.9 mhz; 31.5 kw. Ant 1,457 ft. TL: N42 17 54 W122 44 59 (CP: 31.62 kw, ant 1,426 ft.). Stereo. Hrs opn: 24. Prog sep from AM. Net:

ABC. Rep: Eastman. Format: Adult contemp. News staff one; Target aud: 25-64. ■ Rates: Same as AM.

***KSJK(AM)**—See Talent.

***KSMF(FM)**—Nov 7, 1987: 89.1 mhz; 2.3 kw. Ant 1,340 ft. TL: N42 17 54 W122 44 59. Stereo. 1250 Siskiyou Blvd. (97520). (503) 552-6301. FAX: (503) 552-6773. Licensee: State of Oregon, State Board of Higher Education. Net: APR, NPR. Wash atty: Arter & Hadden. Format: New age, jazz, news. News staff one; news progmg 37 hrs wkly. Target aud: General. Spec prog: Blues 6 hrs, folk 3 hrs, pub affairs 7 hrs wkly. ■ Ronald Kramer, gen mgr; Keith Henty, chief opns; Paul Westhelle, dev dir; John Baxter, progmg dir; Pat Daly, mus dir; Annie Hoy, news dir; John Holt, engrg mgr.

***KSOR(FM)**—April 1969: 90.1 mhz; 38 kw. Ant 2,657 ft. TL: N42 41 30 W123 13 44. Stereo. Southern Oregon State College, 1250 Siskiyou Blvd. (97520). (503) 552-6301. FAX: (503) 552-6773. Licensee: Oregon State Board of Higher Education. Net: APR, NPR. Wash atty: Arter & Hadden. Format: Class, news. News staff one; news progmg 27 hrs wkly. Target aud: General. Spec prog: Pub affairs 7 hrs wkly. ■ Ronald Kramer, gen mgr; Keith Henty, chief opns; Paul Westhelle, dev dir & prom mgr; John Baxter, progmg dir; Pat Daly, mus dir; Annie Hoy, news dir; John Holt, engrg mgr.

Astoria

KAST(AM)—1922: 1370 khz; 1 kw-U, DA-N. TL: N46 10 30 W123 50 50. Hrs opn: 5 AM-12 AM. 1006 W. Marine Drive (97103). (503) 325-2911. Licensee: Youngs Bay Broadcasting (acq 11-1-84; grpsl; FTR 1-30-84). Net: ABC/I. Format: New/talk, sports. News progmg 50 hrs wkly. Target aud: 35 plus. Spec prog: Rush Limbaugh, Larry King, Bruce Williams, Paul Harvey. ■ Jim Servino, gen mgr; Tom Freel, progmg dir. ■ Rates: $18; 18; 18; 18.

KAST-FM—May 10, 1981: 92.9 mhz; 99 kw. Ant 541 ft. TL: N46 10 54 W123 48 19. Stereo. Format: Soft rock. News progmg 14 hrs wkly. Target aud: 18-49. ■ Rates: $20; 20; 20; 20.

***KMUN(FM)**—April 1983: 91.9 mhz; 3 kw. Ant 1,060 ft. TL: N46 15 46 W123 53 09. Stereo. Hrs opn: 5 AM-1 AM. Box 269, 1445 Exchange St. (97103). (503) 325-0010. Licensee: Tillicum Foundation. Net: NPR. Wash atty: Haley, Bader & Potts. Format: Class, jazz, news/talk. News progmg 12 hrs wkly. Target aud: General. Spec prog: Folk 18 hrs, children's 6 hrs, Sp 5 hrs, Amer Indian 2 hrs, Black 2 hrs, Fr 2 hrs wkly. ■ Doug Sweet, CEO & gen mgr; Jan Faber, pres; Pearl Linteau, opns dir; Trudy Nydell, dev dir; Scott Wills, engrg mgr.

KVAS(AM)—1950: 1230 khz; 1 kw-U. TL: N46 11 15 W123 49 30. Hrs opn: 24. 1490 Marine Dr. (97103). (503) 325-6221. Licensee: Lower Columbia Broadcasting Co. Group owner: Farmer Stations (acq 6-11-90; grpsl; FTR 7-2-90). Net: CBS. Rep: Tacher. Format: Top 40 country. News staff one; news progmg 7 hrs wkly. Target aud: 25-54; 35 plus females with some college, kids. Spec prog: Scandinavian one hr wkly. ■ Chuck Farmer, pres & chief engr; Dave Heick, gen mgr & gen sls mgr; Jack McGee, progmg dir; Jim Hagen, mus dir; Scott Keith, news dir.

Baker City

KBKR(AM)—1939: 1490 khz; 1 kw-U. TL: N44 47 18 W117 48 35. Hrs opn: 24. Box 907, 2510 E. Cove Ave., La Grande (97850). (503) 523-4431. Licensee: Grande Radio Inc. (group owner; acq 5-16-88). Net: ABC/I, Jones Satellite Audio. Rep: Katz & Powell; Tacher. Wash atty: Denise Moline. Format: Oldies, news/talk. News staff one; news progmg 22 hrs wkly. Target aud: 25-54. Spec prog: Farm 4 hrs, Christian 4 hrs wkly. ■ Bryan Christle, pres, gen mgr, gen sls mgr & vp adv; Linda Wagoner, opns mgr; Bill Christle, mktg dir; Jamie Stewart, progmg dir, mus dir & chief engr; John Russell, news dir. ■ Rates: $10.50; 9.50; 9.50; 7.50.

KKBC-FM—Co-owned with KBKR(AM). Feb 1981: 95.3 mhz; 3 kw. Ant -200 ft. TL: N44 47 18 W117 48 35 (CP: 25 kw). Prog sep from AM. Format: Country. Target aud: 18-49. ■ Bill Christle, gen mgr. ■ Rates: $13.50; 11.50; 11.50; 10.50.

KCMB(FM)—June 26, 1988: 104.7 mhz; 100 kw. Ant 1,747 ft. TL: N45 07 26 W117 46 48. Stereo. 1009-C Adams Ave., La Grande (97850); Box 781, 1911 Court, La Grande (97814). (503) 963-3405; (503) 523-3400. FAX: (503) 963-5090. Licensee: Clare Marie Ferguson. Net: ABC. Rep: Eastman, Target. Format: Country. Target aud: 25-54. ■ Clare Marie Ferguson, pres; Randy McKone, gen mgr; Mark Adams, progmg dir; Lonnie Shurtleff, chief engr. ■ Rates: $24; 22; 22; 22.

WILLIAM A. EXLINE, INC

MEDIA BROKERS
CONSULTANTS

4340 Redwood Highway
Suite F 230
San Rafael, California 94903
TEL (415) 479-3484
• **FAX (415) 479-1574**

KKBC-FM—Listing follows KBKR(AM).

Banks

KDBX(FM)—June 1990: 96.3 mhz. 2 kw. Ant 397 ft. TL: N45 39 57 W123 00 35. Hrs opn: 24. 448 S. 1st, Millsboro (97123). (503) 693-9200. FAX: (503) 693-9294. Licensee: Common Ground Broadcasting. Format: Contemp Christian music. ■ Bob Fogal, pres & gen mgr.

Beaverton

KKCW(FM)—February 1984: 103.3 mhz; 100 kw. Ant 1,654 ft. TL: N45 31 22 W122 45 12. Stereo. Hrs opn: 24. Suite 790, 888 S.W. 5th Ave., Portland (97204). (503) 222-5103. FAX: (503) 222-0030. Licensee: Trumper Communications of Portland Ltd. Group owner: Trumper Communications Inc. (acq 12-3-86; $7,500,000; FTR 11-24-84). Rep: D & R Radio. Format: Soft rock, adult contemp. News staff 3. Target aud: 25-54. ■ Jeffery Trumper, pres; Ronald S. Saito, vp & gen mgr; Bill Minckler, opns mgr & progmg dir; Jack Hutchison, gen sls mgr; Shannon Dugan, prom mgr; John Erickson, news dir; Martin Soehrman, chief engr.

Bend

KBND(AM)—1938: 1110 khz; 25 kw-D, 5 kw-N, DA-N. TL: N44 06 25 W121 14 39. Box 5037 (97708); 2600 N.E. Studio Rd. (97701). (503) 382-5263. FAX: (503) 388-0456. Licensee: Central Oregon Broadcasting (acq 4-27-90). Net: CBS. Rep: Intermountain Net, Eastman, Art Moore. Wash atty: Dow, Lohnes, & Albertson. Format: News/talk. Target aud: 25-54; upscale, professionals. ■ Jim Torrey, pres; Mike Cheney, gen mgr; Daryl Delaney, gen sls mgr; Frank Bonacquisti, progmg dir; Janet Navarra, news dir; James Boyd, chief engr. ■ Rates: $16; 15; 14; 13.

KLRR(FM)—(Redmond). Co-owned with KBND(AM). June 17, 1985: 107.5 mhz; 100 kw. Ant 985 ft. TL: N44 04 41 W121 19 57. Stereo. Format: Adult contemp, jazz. Target aud: 25-54; upscale, professional women. ■ Doug Donoho, progmg dir. ■ Rates: $26; 24; 22; 20.

KGRL(AM)—Feb 4, 1960: 940 khz; 10 kw-D, 60 w-N, DA-2. TL: N44 04 50 W121 16 51. Box 5068 (97708); 1500 N.E. Butler Mkt. Rd. (97708). (503) 382-5611. FAX: (503) 389-7885. Licensee: Oak Broadcasting Inc. (acq 1-17-90; grpsl; FTR 2-12-90). Net: CNN. Rep: Katz & Powell. Format: Sports, sportstalk, news. News staff 2. Target aud: 25 plus. ■ Bill Hosier, gen mgr; Kerry O'Donnell, progmg dir; James Boyd, chief engr.

KXIQ(FM)—Co-owned with KGRL(AM). December 1974: 94.1 mhz; 100 kw. Ant 1,028 ft. TL: N44 04 41 W121 19 57. Stereo. Prog sep from AM. Rep: Katz & Powell. Format: AOR. News staff 2; news progmg one hr wkly. Target aud: 18-49. ■ Sean Lisle, progmg dir; Kristi Miller, mus dir.

KICE(FM)—July 4, 1973: 100.7 mhz; 50 kw. Ant 598 ft. TL: N44 02 48 W121 31 53 (CP: 100 kw). Stereo. Box 751, 969 S.W. Colorado (97709). (503) 388-3300. FAX: (503) 388-3303. Licensee: Sequoia Communications Inc. (acq 6-13-79). Net: ABC/E. Rep: Major Mkt. Format: C&W. News staff 2; news progmg 11 hrs wkly. Target aud:

Broadcasting & Cable Yearbook 1994

Oregon Directory of Radio

25 plus; middle to upper income consumers. ■ Richard Behrendt, pres; Sam. D. Kirkaldie, gen mgr; Mike Holmes, gen sls mgr, prom mgr & adv mgr; R.L. Garrigus, progmg dir & news dir; James Boyd, chief engr. ■ Rates: $20.75; 16; 17.75; 16.

KLRR(FM)—Listing follows KBND(AM).

KNLR(FM)—Dec 31, 1984: 97.5 mhz; 97 kw. Ant 536 ft. TL: N44 04 38 W121 19 49. Stereo. Box 7408 (97708). (503) 389-8873. FAX: (503) 389-5291. Licensee: Terry A. Cowan. Net: USA. Format: Contemp Christian. ■ Terry A. Cowan, gen mgr, progmg dir & chief engr.

***KOAB-FM**—Not on air, target date unknown: 91.3 mhz; 25 kw. Ant 604 ft. TL: N44 04 41 W121 19 57. 7140 S.W. McAdam, Portland (97219). (503) 293-1905. Licensee: Oregon Public Broadcasting (acq 9-20-93; grpsl; FTR 10-11-93). ■ Howard Paine, chief engr. ■ *KOAB-TV affil.

KQAK(FM)—Sep 5, 1986: 105.7 mhz; 35 kw. Ant 592 ft. TL: N44 04 40 W121 19 48 (CP: 40 kw). Stereo. Hrs opn: 24. 854 N.E. 4th St. (97701). (503) 383-3825. FAX: (503) 383-3403. Licensee: JJP Broadcasting Inc. (acq 9-21-90; $250,000; FTR 10-15-90). Net: SMN. Format: Pure gold. Target aud: 25-54; baby boomers, upscale adults. ■ Clifton Topp, gen mgr & gen sls mgr; Lynae Chase, prom dir; Sam Pence, progmg dir; James Boyd, chief engr.

KTWS(FM)—Dec 21, 1990: 98.3 mhz; 7 kw. Ant 706 ft. TL: N44 04 41 W121 19 57. Stereo. Hrs opn: 24. Rebroadcasts KTWI(FM) Warm Springs 100%. 20450 Empire St. (97701). (503) 389-9500. Licensee: Confederation Tribes of the Warm Reservation of Oregon. Group owner: Confederation Tribes of Warm Springs (acq 12-11-89; grpsl; FTR 1-1-90). Rep: McGavren Guild. Wash atty: Fisher, Wayland, Cooper & Leader. Format: Classic rock. News staff one; news progmg 7 hrs wkly. Target aud: 25-54. Spec prog: Portland Trailblazer basketball. ■ Ken Smith, pres; John Stolz, gen mgr; Steve Moan, adv mgr; Grayson Colefax, news dir.

KXIQ(FM)—Listing follows KGRL(AM).

Brookings

KURY(AM)—May 2, 1958: 910 khz; 1 kw-D. TL: N42 04 32 W124 18 52. Box 1029 (97415); 605 R.R. (97415). (503) 469-2111; (503) 469-2112. FAX: (503) 409-6397. Licensee: KURY Radio Inc. (acq 11-1-64). Rep: Intermountain Net, Eastman, Art Moore. Wash atty: Blooston, Mordkofsky, Jackson & Dickens. Format: MOR. News staff one; news progmg 3 hrs wkly. Target aud: General. Spec prog: Gospel one hr wkly. ■ Vern Garvin, pres, gen mgr & stn mgr; Bill Dwinell, progmg dir & mus dir; Lee Garvin, chief engr.

KURY-FM—May 1977: 95.3 mhz; 3 kw. Ant 90 ft. TL: N42 04 32 W124 18 52 (CP: 8.7 kw, ant 1,164 ft.). Stereo. Hrs opn: 16. Dups AM 100%.

Brownsville

KGAL-FM—April 1, 1991: 102.3 mhz; 6 kw. Ant 961 ft. TL: N44 26 11 W122 59 05. Stereo. Hrs opn: 24. Box 749, Albany (97321); 36991 KGAL Dr., Lebanon (97355). (503) 451-5425; (503) 926-8683. FAX: (503) 451-5429. Licensee: Eads Broadcasting Corp. Net: SMN; N.W. Net. Rep: Major Mkt, MMNW. Wash atty: Crowell & Moring. Format: Oldies. News progmg 5 hrs wkly. Target aud: 25-54. ■ Richard B. Eads, pres; Richard C. Eads, vp & gen mgr; Bobby Dee, opns mgr & progmg dir; Charlie Eads, gen sls mgr; Pat Clarke, mus dir; Sparks Scott, chief engr. ■ Rates: $17; 14; 16; 13.

Burns

KZZR(AM)—Sept 28, 1957: 1230 khz; 1 kw-U. TL: N43 33 49 W119 03 22. Hrs opn: 6 AM-11 PM. Box 877 Fairgrounds Rd. (97720). (503) 573-2055. FAX: (503) 573-5223. Licensee: Warren D. Evans. Net: ABC/I. Rep: Mkt 4, Moore. Format: C&W, news. News staff one. Target aud: 18-55. Spec prog: Farm 6 hrs wkly. ■ Warren D. Evans, pres; Stan Swol, gen mgr, opns mgr, gen sls mgr & news dir; Randy Parks, prom mgr, progmg dir & mus dir; James Boyd, chief engr. ■ Rates: $19; 19; 19; 19.

Cave Junction

KCNA(FM)—Apr 30, 1985: 102.7 mhz; 100 kw. Ant 1,976 ft. TL: N42 15 30 W123 39 38. 139 S.E. J St., Grants Pass (97526). (503) 474-7564. FAX: (503) 474-9650. Licensee: Sound Broadcasting Corp. (acq 5-18-89; grpsl; FTR 6-12-89). Net: Unistar. Format: Oldies. ■ Charles Knerr, pres, gen mgr, gen sls mgr, progmg dir & mus dir; Eric Anthony, news dir; Rocky Shryock, chief engr.

Coos Bay

KHSN(AM)—Mar 15, 1928: 1230 khz; 1 kw-U. TL: N43 22 11 W124 12 54. Hrs opn: 24. Box 180, Hall Bldg., 320 Central (97420). (503) 267-2121. FAX: (503) 267-5229. Licensee: Bay Broadcasting Corp. (acq 12-5-89; grpsl; FTR 12-25-89). Net: ABC/C. Rep: Eastman/Intermountain Net; Art Moore, Inc.Format: MOR. News staff one; news progmg 25 hrs wkly. Target aud: 35-54. Spec prog: Jazz 2 hrs wkly. ■ Laurence Goodman, pres; Craig Finley, gen mgr & prom mgr; Bill McGuire, gen sls mgr; Mikel Chavez, progmg mgr; Dave Cooper, news dir; Martin Abts, chief engr. ■ Rates: $15.50; 14.50; 15.50; 12.50.

KOOS(FM)—See North Bend.

KRSR(AM)—Dec 7, 1956: 1420 khz; 1 kw-D. TL: N43 21 45 W124 11 33. 580 Kingwood Ave. (97420). (503) 269-2022. Licensee: Joel W. Lemon, Harry Abel Jr. and Dan Seleshanko (acq 7-1-93; $70,000 with co-located FM; FTR 8-2-93). Format: News, talk.

KRSR-FM—Nov 1, 1979: 106.5 mhz; 3 kw. Ant 400 ft. TL: N43 23 26 W124 14 31 (CP: 4 kw, ant 545 ft.). Stereo. Prog sep from AM. Licensee: KLYTT, an Oregon General Partnership (acq 10-25-93; $64,400; FTR 11-8-93). ■ James Baker, pres & gen mgr; Diana Whitson, gen sls mgr; J.J. Jensen, progmg dir, mus dir & news dir; Tim Hishizer, chief engr.

***KSBA(FM)**—Nov 4, 1988: 88.5 mhz; 2.2 kw. Ant 532 ft. TL: N43 23 26 W124 04 46. Stereo. 1250 Siskiyou Blvd., Ashland (97520). (503) 552-6301. FAX: (503) 552-6773. Licensee: Oregon State Board of Higher Education. Net: APR, NPR. Wash atty: Arter & Hadden. Format: Jazz, news, new age. News staff one; news progmg 37 hrs wkly. Target aud: General. Spec prog: Blues 6 hrs, folk 3 hrs, pub affairs 7 hrs wkly. ■ Ronald Kramer, gen mgr; Keith Henty, chief opns; Paul Westhelle, dev dir & prom mgr; John Baxter, progmg dir; Pat Daly, mus dir; Annie Hoy, news dir; John Holt, engrg mgr.

KYTT-FM—November 1978: 98.7 mhz; 31 kw. Ant 551 ft. TL: N43 23 26 W124 07 46 (CP: 12.8 kw, ant 962 ft.). Stereo. Hrs opn: 24. 580 Kingwood (97420). (503) 269-2022. FAX: (503) 267-0114. Licensee: K Light Inc. (acq 3-1-89). Net: USA. Format: Contemp Christian. News progmg 8 hrs wkly. ■ Rick Stevens, gen mgr, opns mgr, progmg dir & mus dir; Mike Hadley, gen sls mgr; Jordan McKenzie, news dir; Dan Selishanko, chief engr.

Coquille

KWRO(AM)—Feb 1, 1949: 630 khz; 5 kw-D. TL: N43 10 17 W124 11 54. Box 250 (97423); 1270 W. 13th (97423). (503) 396-2141. FAX: (503) 396-2143. Licensee: Coquille River Broadcasters Inc. (acq 3-87). Net: CBS Spectrum. Rep: McGavren Guild. Format: Oldies. ■ William G. Williamson, pres; Connie Williamson, gen mgr & gen sls mgr; Jack Jensen, progmg dir; Ken James, mus dir; Kevin Mack, news dir; James Boyd, chief engr.

KSHR-FM—Co-owned with KWRO(AM). Nov 1, 1981: 97.3 mhz; 61 kw. Ant 856 ft. TL: N43 14 51 W124 06 46. Stereo. Prog sep from AM. Net: CNN. Rep: McGavren Guild. Format: Adult contemp.

Corvallis

***KBVR(FM)**—Oct 26, 1965: 88.7 mhz; 340 w. Ant -80.6 ft. TL: N44 33 50 W123 16 30. Stereo. Oregon State Univ., M.U. East, Snell Hall (97331). (503) 737-2008. Licensee: State Board of Higher Education. Format: Jazz, urban contemp, alt rock. Spec prog: Classical 3 hrs, Sp one hr wkly. ■ Emory Creel, stn mgr; Dean Harrison, Adam Althouse, vps prom; Kim Gentry, progmg dir; Chris Joy, Tanya Zeller, Guy Paupaw, mus dirs; Matt Fitzgerald, news dir; Rick Brand, chief engr.

KEJO(FM)—Listing follows KFLY(AM).

KFAT(FM)—Listing follows KLOO(AM).

KFLY(AM)—August 1955: 1240 khz; 1 kw-U. TL: N44 35 44 W123 14 54. Box K (97339); 2786 N.E. Belvue St. (97333). (503) 754-6633. FAX: (503) 754-6725. Licensee: Madgekal Broadcasting Co. (acq 8-77). Net: ABC/C, ABC/E. Rep: McGavren Guild. Format: Memory music. News staff 2; news progmg 15 hrs wkly. Target aud: 40 plus. ■ Mario Pastega, pres; Bob Holt, gen mgr, opns mgr, prom mgr & mus dir; Weldon Greig, news dir; Dick Linn, chief engr. ■ Rates: $15; 12; 15; 12.

KEJO(FM)—Co-owned with KFLY(AM). Oct 1, 1966: 101.5 mhz; 28 kw. Ant 98 ft. TL: N44 35 44 W123 14 54. Stereo. (503) 758-5356. Net: ABC/FM. Format: Easy rock. News staff 2; news progmg 10 hrs wkly. Target aud: 25-39; females. ■ Rates: $16; 13; 16; 13.

KLOO(AM)—Aug 23, 1947: 1340 khz; 1 kw-U. TL: N44 33 25 W123 16 22. Hrs opn: 24. Box 965, 1221 S.W. 15th (97339). (503) 753-4493; (503) 753-6666. FAX: (503) 752-0404. Licensee: Pacific Broadcasting Co. (acq 1-11-83). Net: CBS, MBS. Rep: IMN/Eastman, Art Moore. Wash atty: Barry Wood. Format: Oldies, news/talk. News progmg 12 hrs wkly. Target aud: 35-54. ■ Donald Smullin, pres; Larry Blair, vp, gen mgr, gen sls mgr, adv dir & progmg dir; Debby Baker, opns mgr, prom dir & mus dir; Dave Daniels, news dir & pub affrs dir; Robin O'Kelly, chief engr. ■ Rates: $18; 14; 18; 14.

KFAT(FM)—Co-owned with KLOO(AM). January 1973: 106.1 mhz; 100 kw. Ant 1,140 ft. TL: N44 38 45 W123 16 13. Stereo. Hrs opn: 24. Prog sep from AM. Format: C&W. ■ Larry Blair, vp mktg. ■ Rates: Same as AM.

***KOAC(AM)**—Dec 7, 1922: 550 khz; 5 kw-U, DA-2. TL: N44 38 12 W123 11 33. Hrs opn: 5 AM-midnight. 239 Covell Hall, Oregon State Univ. (97331). (503) 737-4311. FAX: (503) 737-4314. Licensee: Oregon Public Broadcasting (acq 9-20-93; grpsl; FTR 10-11-93). Net: APR, NPR. Format: Class, new age, news/talk. News staff 5; news progmg 40 hrs wkly. Target aud: 25-54; college educated with an interest in news & music. Spec prog: Jazz 12 hrs wkly. ■ Maynard Orme, pres; Virginia Breen, gen mgr; Robert McBride, mus dir; David Christensen, asst mus dir; Morgan Holm, news dir; Lynn Clendenin, pub affrs dir; Roger Dominigues, chief engr. ■ *KOAC-TV affil.

Cottage Grove

KCGR(FM)—Not on air, target date unknown: 100.5 mhz; 6 kw. Ant 115 ft. 321 Main St. (97424). Licensee: Thornton Pfleger Inc.

KNND(AM)—August 1953: 1400 khz; 1 kw-U. TL: N43 47 10 W123 04 40. 321 Main St. (97424). (503) 942-2468. Licensee: Robert L. & Diane C. O'Renick (acq 12-3-89). Net: AP. Rep: Art Moore. Wash atty: Dow, Lohnes & Albertson. Format: C&W, news/talk. News staff one; news progmg 20 hrs wkly. Target aud: General. Spec prog: Relg 3 hrs wkly. ■ Diane C. O'Renick, pres & gen sls mgr; Robert L. O'Renick, gen mgr; Wayne Clark, progmg dir & news dir; Ted Hicks, chief engr. ■ Rates: $11.25; 10; 10; 6.50.

Creswell

KZZK-FM—Sept 1, 1983: 95.3 mhz; 625 kw. Ant 1,207 ft. TL: N44 00 04 W123 06 45. Stereo. Box 1123, Eugene (97440); Suite 303, 44 W. Broadway (97401). (503) 686-9530. FAX: (503) 686-9534. Licensee: JED Broadcasting Co. of Oregon Ltd. (acq 3-14-90; grpsl; FTR 4-2-90). Rep: Target. Format: AOR. News staff one; news progmg 2 hrs wkly. Target aud: 18-34. Spec prog: Blues 2 hrs, women 2 hrs, Grateful Dead 2 hrs, Veterans of Foreign Wars one hr, loc musicians one hr wkly. ■ David Miller, pres & gen mgr; B.J. O'Brien, gen sls mgr; Jordan Seaman, progmg dir; Phil Potter, mus dir & news dir; Chris Murray, chief engr. ■ Rates: $25; 25; 25; 25.

Dallas

KWIP(AM)—Licensed to Dallas. See Salem.

Eagle Point

***KEPO(FM)**—Feb 3, 1976: 92.1 mhz; 10 w. Ant 50 ft. TL: N42 28 21 W122 47 48. Box 198 (97524). (503) 826-3364. Licensee: School District 9. Format: Contemp. ■ Michael Remick, pres.

Enterprise

KWVR(AM)—June 1, 1960: 1340 khz; 1 kw-U. TL: N45 26 14 W117 17 30. 220 W. Main St. (97828-1244). (503) 426-4577. FAX: (503) 426-4578. Licensee: Wallowa Valley Radio Broadcasting Corp. (acq 9-1-84; grpsl; FTR 7-2-84). Net: ABC. Rep: Art Moore. Format: Country. News staff one; news progmg 11 hrs wkly. Target aud: General. Spec prog: Farm 4 hrs, Rush Limbaugh 15 hrs AM, wkly. ■ Lee D. Perkins, pres & gen mgr; Carol-Lee Perkins, opns mgr; Dave Nelson, progmg dir & mus dir; Steve Franko, pub affrs dir.

KWVR-FM—1986: 92.1 mhz; 3 kw. Ant -626 ft. TL: N45 19 01 W117 13 14. Hrs opn: 24. Dups AM 100%.

Eugene

KDBS(AM)—1992: 840 khz; 1 kw-D, 220 w-N. TL: N44 05 48 W123 04 18. 2100 W. 11th Ave. (97402). (503) 686-6165. FAX: (503) 686-3048. Licensee: Bjomstad Broadcasting. Net: NBC, Unistar, MBS. Format: Talk.

News staff one; news progmg 12 hrs wkly. Target aud: 35 plus. ■ Paul C. Bjornstad, gen mgr; Ken Sturdevant, opns mgr; Jim Tarrey, gen sls mgr; Bob Duval, rgnl sls mgr; Fred Webb, news dir & pub affrs dir; Chris Murray, chief engr.

KDUK(AM)—Nov 9, 1949: 1280 khz; 5 kw-D, 1 kw-N, DA-N. TL: N44 04 47 W123 04 12. Stereo. 75 Centennial Loop (97401). (503) 345-8888. FAX: (503) 686-0329. Licensee: Pacific Telecommunications Inc. (acq 10-89; grpsl; FTR 9-18-89). Rep: McGavern Guild. Format: Cool gold, sports. ■ Roy Robinson, pres; Neil Olsson, gen mgr; Chuck Rogers, progmg dir & chief engr.

KDUK-FM—(Florence). Nov 21, 1983: 104.7 mhz; 63 kw. Ant 2,326 ft. TL: N44 17 35 W123 32 15. Stereo. (Acq 9-89; grpsl; FTR 9-18-89). Format: AOR. ■ Greg Adams, prom dir & progmg dir; Al Scot, mus dir.

KKNU(FM)—See Springfield-Eugene.

KKXO(AM)—Sept 7, 1954: 1450 khz; 1 kw-U. TL: N44 04 54 W123 06 34. Suite 200, 925 Country Club Rd. (97401). (503) 484-9400. FAX: (503) 344-9424. Licensee: McKenzie River Broadcasting Co. (acq 3-87). Net: Unistar. Rep: Eastman, Major Mkt. Format: MOR. News staff one; news progmg 2 hrs wkly. Target aud: 25-54. ■ John Tilson, pres; Bob Oxarart, gen mgr & gen sls mgr; Dennis Nakata, news dir; Chris Murray, chief engr. ■ Rates: $14; 11; 11; 7.

KMGE(FM)—Co-owned with KKXO(AM). Oct 10, 1965: 94.5 mhz; 100 kw-H, 43 kw-V. Ant 1,299 ft. TL: N44 00 05 W123 06 48. Stereo. Prog sep from AM. (Acq 3-87; $950,000; FTR 9-29-86). Format: Adult contemp. Target aud: 18-49.

***KLCC(FM)**—Feb 17, 1967: 89.7 mhz; 81 kw-h, 54 kw-v. Ant 1,161 ft. TL: N44 00 05 W123 06 48. Stereo. Hrs opn: 5 AM-1 AM. Rebroadcasts KLCO (FM) Newport 100%. 4000 E. 30th Ave. (97405). (503) 726-2224; (503) 726-2222. FAX: (503) 744-3962. Licensee: Lane Community College. Net: AP, NPR. Format: Jazz, news. News staff one; news progmg 50 hrs wkly. Target aud: 25-54. Spec prog: Sp 5 hrs, folk 12 hrs, Black 3 hrs, blues 4 hrs, world 3 hrs, electronic 6 hrs wkly. ■ Jerry Moskus, pres; Steve Barton, gen mgr; Don Hein, opns dir & progmg dir; Paula Chan, dev dir & sls dir; Gayle Chisholm, mktg mgr & prom mgr; Michael Canning, mus dir; Tripp Sommer, news dir & pub affrs dir; John Bredesen, chief engr.

KMGE(FM)—Listing follows KKXO(AM).

KORE(AM)—See Springfield-Eugene.

KPNW(AM)—Feb 12, 1962: 1120 khz; 50 kw-U, DA-1. TL: N43 57 24 W123 02 10. Box 1120 (97440); 1345 Olive St. (97401). (503) 485-1120. FAX: (503) 484-5769. Licensee: McCoy Broadcasting Co. (acq 7-91; $4.1 million grpsl; FTR 7-15-91). Net: ABC/I. Rep: Katz. Format: News/talk. News staff 2. Target aud: 25 plus. Spec prog: Sports. ■ Craig McCoy, pres; Dave Woodward, gen mgr; Doug Grant, gen sls mgr; Jerry Allen, progmg dir; Tom Adams, news dir; Tony Mulder, chief engr.

KPNW-FM—November 1968: 99.1 mhz; 100 kw. Ant 1,945 ft. TL: N44 06 56 W122 59 56. Stereo. Prog sep from AM. Format: Oldies. Target aud: 25-54; working women. ■ Dave Marias, progmg dir.

***KRVM(FM)**—Dec 8, 1947: 91.9 mhz; 1.9 kw. Ant -36 ft. TL: N44 03 44 W123 06 17 (CP: 1.12 kw, ant 98 ft.). Stereo. Hrs opn: 20. Suite 237, 1574 Coburg Rd. (97401). (503) 687-3370; (503) 687-3147. FAX: (503) 687-3573. Licensee: School District 4 J, Lane County. Net: NPR. Format: AAA, AOR, blues. News progmg 3 hrs wkly. Target aud: General. Spec prog: Black 2 hrs, country one hr, folk 3 hrs wkly. ■ Carl Sundberg, gen mgr; Jason Parker, progmg dir; John Ethredge, mus dir; Carl Sundberg, Don Farel, chiefs engr.

KUGN(AM)—July 4, 1946: 590 khz; 5 kw-D, 1 kw-N, DA-N. TL: N44 05 48 W123 04 18 (CP: 5 kw-N, TL: N44 06 03 W123 03 06). Stereo. Hrs opn: 24. 4222 Commerce St. (97402). (503) 485-5846. FAX: (503) 485-0969. Licensee: Combined Communications Inc. (acq 7-24-89; grpsl; FTR 8-14-89). Net: CBS, MBS, NBC. Rep: Torbet, Art Moore. Wash atty: Dow, Lohnes & Albertson. Format: Adult contemp, div, news/talk. News staff 5; news progmg 28 hrs wkly. Target aud: General; 25 plus. ■ Chas Chackel, pres & gen mgr; Larry Miller, gen sls mgr; Dan Spice, progmg dir; Rick Little, news dir; Ted Hicks, chief engr.

KUGN-FM—Dec 26, 1958: 97.9 mhz; 100 kw. Ant 1,230 ft. TL: N44 00 08 W123 06 50. Stereo. Prog sep from AM. Format: Country. News staff 2; news progmg 12 hrs wkly.

***KWAX(FM)**—Apr 4, 1951: 91.1 mhz; 20 kw. Ant 1,013 ft. TL: N44 00 07 W123 06 53 (CP: 21.5 kw-H, 12.5 kw-V, ant 1,050 ft. TL: N44 00 04 W123 06 45). Stereo. Hrs opn: 24. 2365 Bonnie View Dr. (97401). (503) 343-2123. Licensee: State Bd of Higher Educ. Net: APR. Format: Class. News progmg 7 hrs wkly. Target aud: 35 plus. ■ Paul C. Bjornstad, gen mgr.

***KWVA(FM)**—May 27, 1993: 88.1 mhz; 500 w. Ant 56 ft. TL: N44 00 07 W123 06 53. Suite 4, EMU, Univ. of Oregon (97403). (503) 346-4091. Licensee: Associated Students of Univ. of Oregon (acq 6-29-92; FTR 7-20-92). Format: Div, progsv, urban contemp. Target aud: 3-30; intelligent, bright, charming, attractive. Spec prog: Black 20 hrs, folk 4 hrs, jazz 4 hrs, Sp 4 hrs, blues 4 hrs, children's 4 hrs wkly. ■ J.D. Pierson, gen mgr & stn mgr; Chris Scholz, prom dir; Gil Hansen, adv dir; John Thomas, progmg dir; Scott Drew, mus dir; Kristin Robisson, asst mus dir; Ami Mezahav, news dir; Tim Carvey, chief engr.

KZEL-FM—Apr 22, 1962: 96.1 mhz; 100 kw. Ant 1,093 ft. TL: N44 00 04 W123 06 45. Stereo. 270 Oakway Ctr. (97401-2313). (503) 342-7096. FAX: (503) 484-6397. Licensee: Noula Pappas (acq 1-84; $1,050,000; FTR 1-30-84). Net: Westwood One. Rep: Christal. Format: Classic rock. News staff one; news progmg 6 hrs wkly. Target aud: 18-44. ■ Rick Cavagnaro, gen mgr; Mike Groshong, gen sls mgr; Ken Martin, progmg dir; Debi Starr, mus dir; Mark Ramey, news dir.

KZZK(AM)—(Springfield). June 12, 1962: 1320 khz; 1 kw-D, 40 w-N. TL: N44 05 25 W123 06 43. Box 1123, Eugene (97440); 44 W. Broadway, Suite 303, Eugene (97401). (503) 686-9530. FAX: (503) 686-9534. Licensee: JED Broadcasting Co. of Oregon Ltd. (acq 3-14-90; grpsl; FTR 4-2-90). Format: AOR. Target aud: 25 plus. ■ David Miller, pres; B.J. O'Brien, gen sls mgr; Jordan Seaman, progmg dir; Barbara Dellenback, news dir; Chris Murray, chief engr. ■ Rates: $15; 15; 15; 15.

Florence

KCST(AM)—May 5, 1985: 1250 khz; 1 kw-D, 68 w-N. TL: N44 00 38 W124 05 37. Box 20000, 1231 18th St. (97439). (503) 997-9136. FAX: (503) 997-9165. Licensee: Coast Broadcasting Co. Inc. Group owner: Farmer Stations (acq 11-84; $1738.57; FTR 11-5-84). Format: Adult contemp. ■ Chuck Farmer, pres; Jon Thompson, gen mgr & gen sls mgr; Rick Vann, progmg dir, mus dir & news dir.

KCST-FM—October 1992: 106.9 mhz; 2.3 kw. Ant 508 ft. TL: N43 57 19 124 04 26. Format: MOR.

KDUK-FM—Licensed to Florence. See Eugene.

Gleneden Beach

KSHL(FM)—December 1992: 97.5 mhz; 17 kw. Ant 843 ft. TL: N44 45 22 W124 02 57. Box 1180, Newport (97365). (503) 265-6477. Licensee: Stephanie Linn. Format: Modern country. ■ Dick Linn, gen mgr.

Gold Beach

KGBR(FM)—December 1984: 92.7 mhz; 265 w. Ant 1,030 ft. TL: N42 23 50 W124 21 50 (CP: 42.06 kw, ant 2,700 ft. TL: N42 23 44 W124 21 47). Hrs opn: 5 AM-11 PM (Mon-Fri), 6 AM-10 PM (Sat-Sun). Box 787, BetGar Bldg., Suite E, 360 N. Ellensburg (97444). (503) 247-7211; (503) 247-7418. FAX: (503) 247-4155. Licensee: St. Marie Communications Inc. (acq 3-87; $60,000; FTR 11-16-87). Net: N.W. Net. Rep: Art Moore. Wash atty: Lester Spillane. Format: Country, adult contemp. News staff 2; news progmg 4 hrs wkly. Target aud: 25-54. ■ Dale L. St. Marie, pres & gen mgr. ■ Rates: $8.25; 7.20; 7.20; 5.50.

Gold Hill

KRWQ(FM)—Aug 11, 1980: 100.3 mhz; 30 kw. Ant 970 ft. TL: N42 27 07 W123 03 20. Stereo. Hrs opn: 24. Box 388, 86 Fourth St. (97525). (503) 855-1587. Licensee: Hill Radio Inc. Net: AP. Rep: McGavren Guild. Format: Contemp country. News staff 2. Target aud: 18-54. ■ Duane E. Hill, pres, gen mgr & gen sls mgr; Jim Zinn, opns dir & progmg dir; Judy Austin, prom dir & mus dir; Duane Hill, adv mgr; Brian Bishop, news dir; Russ Jump, chief engr.

Grants Pass

KAGI(AM)—Dec 16, 1939: 930 khz; 5 kw-D, 1 kw-N, DA-N. TL: N42 25 24 W123 20 04 (CP: 1.5 kw-N). 1250 Siskiyou Blvd., Ashland (97520). (503) 552-6301. FAX: (503) 552-6773. Licensee: Southern Oregon State College (acq 7-11-91; FTR 7-29-91). Net: NPR, APR. Wash atty: Arter & Hadden. Format: Jazz, New Age, News. News staff one. Target aud: General. ■ Ronald Kramer, gen mgr; Keith Henty, chief opns; Paul Westheve, dev dir; John Baxter, progmg dir; Pat Daly, mus dir; Annie Hoy, news dir.

KAJO(AM)—Aug 15, 1957: 1270 khz; 5 kw-D, 48 w-N. TL: N42 26 16 W123 21 27. Stereo. Hrs opn: 5 AM-11 PM. Box 230 (97526). (503) 476-6608. Licensee: Grants Pass Broadcasting Corp. Net: AP. Format: MOR. News staff 2; news progmg 22 hrs wkly. Target aud: 35 plus. ■ Jim Wilson, pres; Carl Wilson, gen mgr & progmg dir; Matt Wilson, gen sls mgr; B.J. Calvert, prom dir & mus dir; Mike Carmichael, news dir; Marvin Pangburn, chief engr.

KYJC-FM—Oct 2, 1981: 96.9 mhz; 32 kw. Ant 2,058 ft. TL: N42 22 56 W123 16 29 skf-fm(CP: 74 kw). Stereo. Hrs opn: 20. Suite 10, 1257 N. Riverside St., Medford (97501). (503) 772-0322. FAX: (503) 772-4233. Licensee: Encore Broadcasting Corp. (acq 3-6-91; $63,634; with KYJC(AM) Medford; FTR 7-29-91). Format: Hot country. News progmg 9 hrs wkly. Target aud: 25-54; affluent middle America. ■ Van Sias, pres & gen mgr; Richard Bauemfiend, sls dir; Angie Chapman, mus dir. ■ Rates: $22; 17; 20; 15.

Gresham

***KMHD(FM)**—January 1984: 89.1 mhz; 7.08 kw. Ant 986 ft. TL: N45 30 58 W122 43 59. 26000 S.E. Stark (97030). (503) 661-8900. FAX: (503) 669-6999. Licensee: Mt. Hood Community College. Format: Jazz. ■ Paul Kreider, pres; John M. Rice, gen mgr; Tom Costello, stn mgr; Jon Kettering, mus dir; John Ghormley, news dir; Wendell Bates, chief engr.

KMUZ(AM)—Licensed to Gresham. See Portland.

Harbeck-Fruitdale

KLDR(FM)—May 3, 1991: 98.3 mhz; 185 w. Ant 2,096 ft. TL: N42 22 56 W123 16 29. Stereo. Hrs opn: 24. Rebroadcasts KAJO(AM) Grants Pass. Box 230, Grants Pass (97526). (503) 476-6608. FAX: (503) 476-6608. Licensee: Grants Pass Broadcasting Corp. Net: AP. Format: Adult contemp. News staff 2; news progmg 10 hrs wkly. Target aud: 25-54. ■ Jim Wilson, pres; Carl Wilson, gen mgr, progmg dir & mus dir; Matt Wilson, gen sls mgr; B.J. Calvert, prom dir; Mike Carmichael, news dir; Marvin Pangburn, chief engr.

Hermiston

KOHU(AM)—Feb 6, 1956: 1360 khz; 4.3 kw-D, 500 w-N, DA-N. TL: N45 51 57 W119 18 45. Hrs opn: 5 AM-midnight. Box 145, Cooney Ln. (97838). (503) 567-6500. FAX: (503) 567-6068. Licensee: Hermiston Broadcasting Co. (acq 7-66). Net: CBS. Rep: Farmakis, Target. Wash atty: Fisher, Wayland, Cooper & Leader. Format: C&W. News staff one; news progmg 10 hrs wkly. Target aud: General; two county local audience. Spec prog: Sp 4 hrs wkly. ■ Robert Chopping, pres; Harmon Springer, gen mgr; Steve Bertelson, gen sls mgr; Todd Nevard, progmg dir & mus dir; Tamara Chorey, news dir; Dave Hebert, chief engr. ■ Rates: $10; 9; 10; 9.

KQFM(FM)—Co-owned with KOHU(AM). Sept 18, 1978: 99.3 mhz; 3 kw. Ant 300 ft. TL: N45 51 57 W119 18 45. Stereo. Hrs opn: 5 AM-midnight. Prog sep from AM. Format: Adult contemp. News staff one; news progmg 5 hrs wkly. Target aud: 25-49; young adult. ■ Rates: Same as AM.

Hillsboro

KUIK(AM)—1954: 1360 khz; 5 kw-U, DA-N. TL: N45 29 13 W122 54 31. Hrs opn: 24. Box 566 (97123); Bldg. 3355, N.E. Cornell Rd. (97124). (503) 640-1360. FAX: (503) 640-6108. Licensee: Dolphin Communications Inc. (group owner; acq 8-1-78). Net: MBS. Rep: Target. Format: News/talk. News staff one; news progmg 24 hrs wkly. Target aud: 25-54. Spec prog: Sp 17 hrs, relg 2 hrs wkly. ■ Don McCoun, pres, gen mgr & gen sls mgr; Lisa Dupre, opns mgr, prom mgr & progmg dir; Steve James, news dir; Joe Allen, chief engr.

Hood River

KIHR(AM)—Oct 17, 1950: 1340 khz; 1 kw-U. TL: N45 42 07 W121 32 10. Box 360 (97031). (503) 386-1511. FAX: (503) 386-7155. Licensee: Columbia Gorge Broadcasters Inc. (acq 4-1-67). Net: MBS. Rep: Art Moore. Format: C&W. Spec prog: Class 3 hrs, Spanish 2 hr wkly. ■ Greg Walden, pres & gen sls mgr; Mylene Walden, gen mgr; Bill Robertson, mus dir; Mark Bailey, news dir; Paul Walden, chief engr.

KCGB(FM)—Co-owned with KIHR(AM). Dec 4, 1978: 105.5 mhz; 3 kw. Ant -460 ft. TL: N45 42 07 W121 32 10. Prog sep from AM. Format: CHR.

Oregon Directory of Radio

John Day

KJDY(AM)—Dec 13, 1963: 1400 khz; 1 kw-U. TL: N44 25 17 W118 57 09. Hrs opn: 24. Box 399, 413 N.W. Bridge St. (97845). (503) 575-1185. FAX: (508) 575-1185. Licensee: Blue Mountain Broadcasting Co. (acq 11-87; $150,000; FTR 11-9-87). Net: ABC/I. Rep: Eastman, Art Moore. Wash atty: J. Dominic Monahan. Format: C&W. News staff one. ■ Phil Gray, gen mgr; Pat Robinson, vp sls; Issac Blair, progmg dir; Ruth Harris, news dir; J. Kelly Carlson, vp engrg.

Junction City

KZTU(AM)—Not on air, target date unknown: 650 khz; 10 kw-D, 1 kw-N, DA-2. TL: N44 19 36 W123 00 02. c/o Jerry J. Collins, 25485 Boots Rd., Monterey, CA (93940). (408) 372-8383. Licensee: Jerry J. Collins.

Keizer

KYKN(AM)—1951: 1430 khz; 5 kw-U. TL: N44 55 36 W122 57 19. Hrs opn: 24. Box 1430, Salem (97308); 4205 Cherry Ave, N.E., Salem (97303). (503) 390-3014. Licensee: Willamette Broadcasting (acq 9-19-91). Net: NBC Talknet, NBC, MBS. Rep: Tacher. Format: News/talk. News staff 3; news progmg 46 hrs wkly. Target aud: 25-54. $30-60K income, homeowners, white collar. Spec prog: Portland Trailblazers, OSU Beavers, Gospel 3 hrs wkly. ■ Michael Frith, pres, gen mgr & gen sls mgr; Joe Borenstein, natl sls mgr; Fritz Wenzel, progmg dir & news dir; Dick Linn, chief engr. ■ Rates: $21.50; 21.50; 21.50; 18.50.

Klamath Falls

KAGO(AM)—July 19, 1923: 1150 khz; 5 kw-D, 1 kw-N, DA-N. TL: N42 12 56 W121 47 56. Hrs opn: 24. Box 1150, One Radio Hill (97601). (503) 882-2551. Licensee: Key Broadcasting (acq 6-3-91; with co-located FM; FTR 6-24-91). Net: CBS, MBS, NBC. Rep: Eastman, Art Moore. Wash atty: Dan Alpert. Format: News/talk. News staff one; news progmg 25 hrs wkly. Target aud: 35-65; upscale, professional. Spec prog: Farm 3 hrs, Sp 5 hrs wkly. ■ William R. Garrard, pres & gen mgr; A.J. Krisik, CFO; Greg Dourian, rgnl sls mgr; George Fedla, mktg dir; Kelly Clark, prom mgr; Michael Garrard, progmg mgr & mus dir; Sean Adams, asst mus dir; Jeff Mullins, news dir; Merrill Frink, engrg dir. ■ Rates: $13; 12; 13; 10.

KAGO-FM—Oct 15, 1973: 99.5 mhz; 26.5 kw. Ant 360 ft. TL: N42 12 56 W121 47 56 (CP: 100 kw. Ant 994 ft. TL: N42 13 08 W121 48 56). Stereo. Hrs opn: 24. Prog sep from AM. FAX: (503) 883-6141. Format: Adult contemp. Spec prog: Jazz 5 hrs wkly. ■ Greg Dourian, sls dir, mktg mgr & adv mgr; George Fedla, prom dir; Mike Garrard, progmg dir; Sean Gordon, asst mus dir. ■ Rates: Same as AM.

KFLS(AM)—1946: 1450 khz; 1 kw-U. TL: N42 12 19 W121 46 04. Stereo. Hrs opn: 24. Box 1450, 1338 Oregon Ave. (97601). (503) 882-4656. FAX: (503) 884-2845. Licensee: Wynne Broadcasting Co. Inc. (acq 1-1-71). Net: ABC. Rep: Tacher. Format: Oldies. Target aud: 35 plus. ■ Robert Wynne, pres & gen mgr; Floyd Wynne, vp; Maryann Christensen, gen sls mgr; Ian Crawford, progmg dir; Brian Bicknell, news dir; Merrill Frink, chief engr.

KKRB(FM)—Co-owned with KFLS(AM). April 1, 1983: 106.9 mhz; 100 kw. Ant 1,200 ft. TL: N42 13 26 W121 49 02. Stereo. Prog sep from AM. Format: Adult contemp. ■ Randy Adams, progmg dir.

KLAD(AM)—September 1955: 960 khz; 5 kw-U. TL: N42 09 42 W121 39 01. Hrs opn: 24. Suite 201, 4509 S. 16th St. (97603); Box 339 (97601). (503) 882-8833. FAX: (503) 882-8836. Licensee: B&B Broadcasting (group owner; acq 4-18-90; FTR 5-7-90). Net: ABC/D. Rep: McGavren Guild. Format: Country. News staff one; news progmg 3 hrs wkly. Target aud: 25-54; mature with spendable income. Spec prog: Farm one hrs wkly. ■ Robert Barron, pres; Scott Allen, stn mgr; Red Allen, opns mgr; Glenn Garrett, prom dir, progmg dir, mus dir & pub affrs dir; Niki Renshaw, news dir; James Boyd, chief engr.

KLAD-FM—July 19, 1974: 92.5 mhz; 63 kw. Ant 2,188 ft. TL: N42 05 51 W121 37 58. Dups AM 100%. Net: McGavren Guild.

***KSKF(FM)**—Nov 10, 1989: 90.9 mhz; 2 kw. Ant 2,260 ft. TL: N42 05 50 W121 37 59 (CP: Ant 2,252 ft.). Stereo. 1250 Siskiyou Blvd., Ashland (97520). (503) 552-6301. FAX: (503) 552-6773. Licensee: State of Oregon, State Board of Higher Education. Net: APR, NPR. Wash atty: Arter & Hadden. Format: New age, jazz, news. News staff one; news progmg 37 hrs wkly. Target aud: General. Spec prog: Blues 6 hrs, folk 3 hrs, pub affairs 7 hrs wkly. ■ Ronald Kramer, gen mgr; Keith Henty, opns dir; Paul Westhelle, dev dir & prom mgr; John Baxter, progmg dir; Pat Daly, mus dir; Annie Hoy, news dir; John Holt, engrg mgr.

***KTEC(FM)**—Dec 19, 1950: 89.5 mhz; 250 w. Ant 184 ft. TL: N42 12 59 W121 47 57 (CP: Ant 597 ft. TL: N42 13 26 W121 49 02). Stereo. Hrs opn: 9 AM-midnight. 3201 Campus Dr., Oregon Institute of Tech (97601). (503) 885-1840. Licensee: Oregon State Board of Higher Education. Format: Alt. Spec prog: Class 2 hrs wkly. ■ Pete Belfonti, gen mgr, progmg dir & mus dir; Tony Skujins, chief engr.

La Grande

***KEOL(FM)**—Oct 1973: 91.7 mhz; 310 w. Ant -750 ft. TL: N45 19 16 W118 05 26. Stereo. Hrs opn: 24. KEOL-FM, 1410 L Ave. (97850). (503) 962-3397; (503) 962-3698. Licensee: Eastern Oregon State College. Group owner: Oregon State Board of Higher Education. Format: Div, AOR, CHR. Target aud: 14-25; College students & local youth. Spec prog: Black 12 hrs, class 4 hrs, jazz 6 hrs, heavy metal 20 hrs, reggae 7 hrs wkly. ■ Rachel Steen, stn mgr; Dennis Quinn, progmg dir & news dir; Mark O'Neil, mus dir; John Hilmer, chief engr. ■ KEOL-TV affil.

KLBM(AM)—1938: 1450 khz; 1 kw-U. TL: N45 19 45 W118 04 00. Hrs opn: 24. Box 907, 2510 E. Cove Ave. (97850). (503) 963-4121. Licensee: Grande Radio Inc. (group owner; acq 1-14-85; grpsl; FTR 11-19-84). Net: ABC/I, Jones Satellite Audio. Rep: Katz & Powell; Tacher. Wash atty: Denise Moline. Format: Oldies, news/talk. News staff one; news progmg 22 hrs wkly. Target aud: 25-54. Spec prog: Farm 4 hrs, Christian 4 hrs wkly. ■ Bryan Christle, pres, gen sls mgr & vp adv; Bill Christle, gen mgr & mktg dir; Linda Wagoner, opns mgr; Jamie Stewart, progmg dir, mus dir & chief engr; John Russell, news dir. ■ Rates: $10.50; 9.50; 9.50; 7.50.

KUBQ(FM)—Co-owned with KLBM(AM). Aug 15, 1977: 98.7 mhz; 2.25 kw. Ant 1,942 ft. TL: N45 26 26 W117 53 31. Stereo. Hrs opn: 24. Prog sep from AM. Format: Adult contemp. Target aud: 18-49. ■ Bryan Christle, vp prom. ■ Rates: $13.50; 11.50; 13.50; 10.50.

KWRL(FM)—Sept 27, 1988: 100.1 mhz; 3 kw. Ant 90 ft. TL: N45 20 54 W118 07 04. Stereo. Hrs opn: 24. Box 370 (97850). (503) 963-7911. FAX: (503) 963-7619. Licensee: Richard J. and Deborah A. Freeman (acq 3-28-90; $215,000; FTR 4-16-90). Net: CNN, Unistar. Rep: Tacher. Wash atty: Matt McCormick. Format: Adult contemp. ■ Rick Freeman, pres, gen mgr & gen sls mgr; James Harsin, progmg dir; Ken Johnson, chief engr.

Lake Oswego

KKBK(FM)—Aug 1, 1977: 106.7 mhz; 94 kw. Ant 879 ft. TL: N45 27 17 W122 32 58 (CP: 96 kw, ant 997 ft.). Stereo. Hrs opn: 24. Suite 302, 9500 S.W. Barbur Blvd., Portland (97219). (503) 245-1433. FAX: (503) 244-7621. Licensee: BayCom Oregon. Group owner: BayCom Partners L.P. (acq 6-11-93; $2,625,010; FTR 7-5-93). Net: ABC/FM. Rep: D & R Radio. Wash atty: Haley, Bader & Potts. Format: Classical. Target aud: 25-49; women. ■ Bill Failing, gen mgr; Cindy Hanson, progmg dir.

KPHP(AM)—June 1948: 1290 khz; 5 kw-U, DA-N. TL: N45 28 27 W122 39 33. Hrs opn: 24. Suite 102, 4700 S.W. Macadam St., Portland (97201). (503) 242-1950; (503) 242-1290. FAX: (503) 242-0155. Licensee: Crawford Broadcasting Co. Group owner: Donald B. Crawford (acq 7-91; $450,000; FTR 7-29-91). Format: Relg, talk. News staff one; news progmg 12 hrs wkly. Target aud: 25-54. ■ Donald Crawford, pres; David Harms, gen mgr & gen sls mgr; Sandy Snavely, prom dir & pub affrs dir; John Springsteel, adv mgr; Matt Williams, mus dir; Joe Allen, chief engr.

Lakeview

KQIK(AM)—Dec 5, 1956: 1230 khz; 1 kw-U. TL: N42 12 30 W120 21 39. Hrs opn: 24. HC 64, Box 46 (97630). (503) 947-3351. FAX: (503) 947-3375. Licensee: KQIK Limited (acq 6-30-93; $182,000 with co-located FM; FTR 7-26-93). Net: ABC/D. Rep: Tacher. Format: C&W. Target aud: General. Spec prog: Farm 10 hrs, This, That & the Other one hr wkly. ■ Art Collins, gen mgr, gen sls mgr & progmg dir; Vickie Price, stn mgr & mus dir; Nancy Haufle, news dir; Cole Malcomb, chief engr.

KQIK-FM—Co-owned with KRIT(AM). 1987: 93.5 mhz; 284 w. Ant 1,000 ft. TL: N42 12 18 W120 19 39. Stereo. Hrs opn: 24. Dups AM 100%. News progmg 5 hrs wkly.

Lebanon

KSHO(AM)—1950: 920 khz; 1 kw-U, DA-1. TL: N44 34 30 W122 55 15. Hrs opn: 24. Box 749, Albany (97321); 36991 KGAL Dr., Lebanon (97355). (503) 451-5425; (503) 926-8683. FAX: (503) 451-5429. Licensee: Eads Broadcasting Corp. (acq 10-1-81; $425,000; FTR 10-5-81). Net: SMN; N.W. Net. Rep: Major Mkt. Wash atty: Crowell & Moring. Format: MOR. News staff one; news progmg 7 hrs wkly. Target aud: 35 plus; mature adults. Spec prog: Farm one hr wkly. ■ Richard B. Eads, pres; Richard C. Eads, vp & gen mgr; Charlie Eads, gen sls mgr; Bobby Dee, progmg dir; Dave Allison, mus dir; Sparks Scott, chief engr. ■ Rates: $18; 14; 16; 12.

KXPC(FM)—Apr 8, 1974: 103.7 mhz; 100 kw. Ant 1099 ft. TL: N44 30 17 W122 57 20. Stereo. Hrs opn: 24. Suite 10, 743 Main St. (97355). (503) 451-1037; (503) 928-1926. FAX: (503) 258-5479. Licensee: Spotlight Media Corp. (acq 6-88). Rep: Katz & Powell. Wash atty: Larry Movshin. Format: Country hit radio. News progmg one hr wkly. Target aud: 18-44. ■ Michael Gelfand, pres; Jeffrey L. Schneider, gen mgr; Lynne Keller, gen sls mgr; Lee Melton, progmg mgr; Jeff Ryan, chief engr. ■ Rates: $24; 20; 24; 16.

Lincoln City

KBCH(AM)—May 27, 1955: 1400 khz; 1 kw-U. TL: N44 59 27 W123 58 45. Box 820 (97367). (503) 994-2181. FAX: (503) 994-2004. Licensee: Oceanlake Broadcasting Co. (acq 7-31-90). Net: SMN. Rep: Tacher. Format: MOR. Spec prog: Farm 2 hrs wkly. ■ Hal D. Fowler, pres, gen sls mgr & rgnl sls mgr; Bruce Holt, progmg dir; Dave Humphrey, news dir; Joe Figuth, chief engr.

KCRF-FM—Licensed to Lincoln City. See Newport.

KNJM(FM)—Not on air, target date unknown: 95.1 mhz; 24.5 kw. Ant 709 ft. TL: N44 53 24 W123 58 51. Apt. 11K, 432 S. Curson St., Los Angeles, CA (90036). Licensee: Elite Broadcasting Inc. (acq 5-26-93; $17,500; FTR 6-21-93).

McMinnville

KLYC(AM)—June 18, 1949: 1260 khz; 1 kw-U, DA-N. TL: N45 13 19 W123 10 21. Box 1099, 1975 Calvin Ct. (97128). (503) 472-1260. FAX: (503) 472-3243. Licensee: Bohnsack Strategies Inc. (acq 10-2-90; $120,000; FTR 10-22-90). Net: CNN. Rep: Target. Format: Adult contemp, oldies. News staff one. Target aud: 25-54. Spec prog: Sp 3 hrs wkly. ■ Larry Bohnsack, pres & gen mgr; Eve Fuller, news dir.

***KSLC(FM)**—Jan 17, 1972: 90.3 mhz; 320 w. Ant -46 ft. TL: N45 12 06 W123 11 52. Stereo. Hrs opn: 6 AM-3 PM. Box 365, 900 S. Baker St. (97128). (503) 472-3851; (503) 434-2550. FAX: (503) 472-3851. Licensee: Linfield College. Net: MBS. Format: Alt rock. News staff one; news progmg 3 hrs wkly. Target aud: 12-25; young people looking for new music. Spec prog: Black 2 hrs, heavy metal 7 hrs wkly. ■ James Longhurst, gen mgr; Andy Schleuter, vp sls; Brian MacKinnon, mus dir; Cort Goebel, asst mus dir; Gene Sugano, news dir.

Medford

KBOY-FM—Listing follows KRVC(AM).

***KCIA(FM)**—Not on air, target date unknown: 91.7 mhz; 1.25 kw. Ant -508 ft. TL: N42 20 13 W122 51 44. Box A, Dove Bible Institute, Phoenix (97535). (503) 535-8141. Licensee: Dove Bible Institute (acq 4-13-93; FTR 5-3-93).

KCMX(AM)—See Ashland.

KCMX-FM—See Ashland.

KCNA(FM)—See Cave Junction.

KMED(AM)—1922: 1440 khz; 5 kw-D, 1 kw-N. TL: N42 18 36 W122 48 41. Hrs opn: 24. Box 388, 86 Fourth St., Gold Hill (97525). (503) 773-1440. Licensee: Crater Broadcasting Inc. (acq 1-85; $180,000; FTR 1-7-85). Net: Unistar. Rep: McGavren Guild. Format: MOR. Spec prog: Farm 5 hrs wkly. ■ Duane Hill, pres, gen mgr & gen sls mgr; Jim Zinn, progmg dir; Rick Boyd, news dir; Russ Jump, chief engr.

KOPE(FM)—Aug 19, 1991: 103.5 mhz; 100 kw. Ant 1,023 ft. TL: N42 17 10 W123 00 21. Stereo. Hrs opn: 24. 744 E. Pine St., Central Point (97502). (503) 664-5673. FAX: (503) 664-8261. Licensee: Medford Judeo-Christian Outreach Inc. Net: Daynet, USA. Wash atty: Miller & Fields. Format: News/talk. Target aud: 35 plus. ■ Ann Masters, pres; Alan Corbeth, vp, gen mgr, stn mgr & progmg dir; Stephanie Smith, opns mgr; Yuta Stenscaard, sls dir; Gary Stamps, mktg dir; David Masters, adv dir; Lisa Truchin, adv mgr; Brian Saylor, chief engr. ■ Rates: $19; 12; 19; 9.

KRVC(AM)—May 31, 1954: 730 khz; 1 kw-D, 74 w-N. TL: N42 18 36 W122 48 41. Suite 9, 1425 N. Market Blvd., Sacramento (95834). (503) 779-2244. Licensee: KBoy Radio Inc. (acq 8-30-79). Rep: McGavren Guild. Format: AOR. Spec prog: Jazz 3 hrs wkly. ■ Bob Esty, pres; Richard Jenkins, gen mgr; Lee Melton, gen sls mgr; Bill Scott, progmg dir; Bob Jeffries, mus dir; Carol Scott, news dir; Mike McGuire, chief engr.

KBOY-FM—Co-owned with KRVC(AM). February 1958: 95.7 mhz; 100 kw. Ant 935 ft. TL: N42 27 07 W23 03 20 (CP: 60 kw, ant 751 ft.). Stereo. Dups AM 100%. 2729 Jacksonville Hwy. (97501). FAX: (503) 772-6282. ■ Bob Esty, gen mgr.

KTMT(AM)—(Phoenix). Apr 7, 1962: 880 khz; 1 kw-U. TL: N42 18 36 W122 48 41. Hrs opn: 24. Box 159, 1438 Rossanley Dr., Medford (97501). (503) 779-1550. FAX: (503) 776-2360. Licensee: Sierra Cascade Communications Inc. Group owner: Johnson Communications (acq 6-29-84). Net: ABC, CNN. Rep: Torbet; Art Moore.Wash atty: Dow, Lohnes & Albertson. Format: News/talk. News staff one; news progmg 153 hrs wkly. Target aud: 25 plus; affluent white collar males-business owners. ■ Robert R. Johnson, gen mgr; Karen Johnson, gen sls mgr; John Greider, progmg mgr; Robin Lawson, news dir; Don Bennett, chief engr. ■ Rates: $8; 5; 5; 5.

KTMT-FM—Oct 15, 1970: 93.7 mhz; 31 kw. Ant 7,580 ft. TL: N42 04 55 W122 43 07. Stereo. Hrs opn: 24. Dups AM 100%. Format: Adult CHR. News staff one; news progmg 3 hrs wkly. Target aud: 18-54; young adults & older adults who feel young. ■ Robert R. Johnson, vp; Lori Littrell, prom dir; Charles Snyder, progmg dir & mus dir. ■ Rates: $25; 25; 25; 18.

KYJC(AM)—October 1947: 610 khz; 5 kw-U, DA-2. TL: N42 23 15 W122 46 11. Stereo. Hrs opn: 20. Suite 10, 1257 N. Riverside (97501). (503) 772-0322. FAX: (503) 772-4233. Licensee: Frederick A. Danz (acq 7-9-91; $63,634 with KYJC-FM Grants Pass; FTR 7-29-91). Net: SMN. Rep: Major Mkt. Wash atty: Liebowitz & Spencer. Format: Hot country. News progmg 14 hrs wkly. Target aud: 25-54; affluent middle America. Spec prog: Sp 3 hrs wkly. ■ Van Sias, pres, prom mgr & vp engrg; Michael Perry, progmg mgr; Anjie Chapman, mus dir. ■ Rates: $16; 13; 15; 11.

Milton-Freewater

KLKY(FM)—Sept 10, 1992: 97.9 mhz; 50,000 kw. Ant 705 ft. TL: N44 54 22 W124 37 25 (CP: 8 kw, ant 1,112 ft.). Stereo. Hrs opn: 24. 14 E. Main St, Walla Walla WA (99362). (509) 529-6242. FAX: (509) 529-5534. Licensee: Alexandra Communications (acq 10-2-92; $50,000; FTR 11-9-92). Format: Adult Contemp. Target aud: General. ■ Thomas Hodgins, chmn, pres & stn mgr.

Milwaukie

KZRC(AM)—February 1988: 1010 khz; 4.5 kw-D. TL: N45 29 35 W122 24 40 (CP: 500 w-N, TL: N45 29 03 W122 24 40 (night)). Stereo. Box 40588, Portland (97240). (503) 226-4772. Licensee: KXYQ Broadcasting Co. Inc. (acq 3-31-92; $1.3 million with KXYQ(FM) Salem; FTR 4-20-92). Net: ABC/FM, SMN. Format: Z-Rock. Target aud: 18-34. ■ John E. Grant, pres; Aaron Olson, stn mgr; Mike Everhart, chief engr.

Newport

KCRF-FM—(Lincoln City). Nov 1, 1981: 96.7 mhz; 610 w. Ant 670 ft. TL: N44 52 30 W123 59 03 (CP: 30 kw, ant 627 ft.). Stereo. Box 820, Lincoln City (97367). (503) 994-5273. (acq 7-25-90). Net: AP. Rep: Mkt 4, McGavren Guild. Format: Soft contemp.

KCLM(FM)—Not on air, target date unknown: 92.7 mhz; 12 kw. Ant 472 ft. TL: N44 45 52 W123 52 53. 407 Third St. N.E., Washington, DC (20002). Licensee: Charlotte McNaughton.

KCRF-FM—Listing follows KBCH(AM).

***KLCO(FM)**—Sept 11, 1990: 90.5 mhz; 3.2 kw. Ant 256 m. TL: N44 45 22 W124 02 57. Stereo. Hrs opn: 5 AM-1 AM. Rebroadcasts KLCC(FM) Eugene 100%. 4000 E. 30th Ave., Eugene (97405). (503) 726-2224; (503) 726-2212. FAX: (503) 744-3962. Licensee: Lane Community College. Net: NPR, APR. Format: News, jazz, div. News staff one; news progmg 60 hrs wkly. Target aud: 25-54. Spec prog: Sp 5 hrs, black 3 hrs, folk 12 hrs, blues 4 hrs, world 3 hrs, electronic 6 hrs wkly. ■ Jerry Moskus, pres; Steve Barton, gen mgr; Don Hein, opns dir & progmg dir; Paula Chan, dev dir & sls dir; Gayle Chisholm, mktg mgr & prom mgr; Michael Canning, mus dir; Tripp Sommer, news dir & pub affrs dir; John Bredensen, chief engr.

KNPT(AM)—June 28, 1948: 1310 khz; 5 kw-D, 1 kw-N, DA-N. TL: N44 37 40 W123 59 15. Hrs opn: 24. Box 1430, 906 S.W. Alder St. (97365). (503) 265-2266. FAX: (503) 265-6397. Licensee: Central Coast Broadcasting Co. Inc. (acq 2-87; $450,000; FTR 12-22-86). Net: ABC/I, NBC Talknet. Rep: Major Mkt. Format: Adult standards, talk. News staff 2; news progmg 21 hrs wkly. Target aud: 34 plus. Spec prog: Relg 2 hrs wkly. ■ Joan Carman Heffner, pres; George M. Carman, vp; David J. Miller, gen mgr; Vern Morris, gen sls mgr; Johnny Randolph, progmg dir; Howard Wright, mus dir; Bill Hall, news dir. ■ Rates: 13.60; 9.20; 13.60; 6.40.

KYTE(FM)—Co-owned with KNPT(AM). Oct 25, 1976: 102.7 mhz; 66 kw. Ant 881 ft. TL: N67 45 24 W124 02 47. Stereo. Hrs opn: 24. Prog sep from AM. 3478 N. Coast Hwy., Lincoln City (97367). (503) 265-2266; (503) 996-6800. Net: ABC/E. Format: Adult contemp. News progmg 13 hrs wkly. Target aud: 24-49. Spec prog: Oldies 6 hrs, jazz 4 hrs, blues 2 hrs wkly. ■ Vern Morris, rgnl sls mgr. ■ Rates: Same as AM.

KZUS(AM)—See Toledo.

North Bend

KACW(FM)—October 1990: 107.3 mhz; 100 kw. Ant 521 ft. TL: N73 24 55 W124 10 18. Stereo. Hrs opn: 24. Box 308 (97459). (503) 756-5108. Licensee: Big Bay Radio Inc. Net: CBS. Format: Adult contemp. Target aud: 25-49. ■ Steve Walker, gen mgr; Cindi Miller, gen sls mgr; Dave Walker, progmg dir & mus dir; Robin O'Kelly, chief engr.

KBBR(AM)—December 1950: 1340 khz; 1 kw-U. TL: N43 25 52 W124 12 23. Box 308 (97459). (503) 756-5108. Licensee: Big Bay Radio Inc. (acq 12-1-59). Net: CBS. Rep: Katz & Powell, Tacher. Format: Country. ■ Steve Walker, pres & gen mgr; Cindi Miller, gen sls mgr; Dave Walker, progmg dir & mus dir; Matt Jarvis, news dir; Robin O. Kelly, chief engr.

KOOS(FM)—Dec 10, 1979: 94.9 mhz; 56 kw. Ant 502 ft. TL: N43 23 26 W124 07 46. Stereo. Hrs opn: 24. Box 180, Hall Bldg., 320 Central, Coos Bay, (97420). (503) 267-2121. FAX: (503) 267-5229. Licensee: Bay Broadcasting Corp. (acq 12-5-89; grpsl; FTR 12-25-89). Net: ABC/I. Rep: IMN/Eastman, Art Moore.Format: C&W. News staff one; news progmg 18 hrs wkly. Target aud: 25 plus. ■ Laurence Goodman, pres; Craig Finley, gen mgr, natl sls mgr & rgnl sls mgr; Bill McGuire, gen sls mgr; Mikel Chavez, progmg dir; Dave Cooper, news dir; Martin Abts, chief engr. ■ Rates: $15.50; 14.50; 15.50; 12.50.

Nyssa

KGZH(FM)—Not on air, target date unknown: 98.7 mhz; 100 kw. Ant 354 ft. TL: N43 25 03 W116 51 15. R.R. 4, Box 54, Vincennes, IN (47591). (812) 324-2200. Licensee: Robert M. Mason.

Oakridge

***KAVE(FM)**—Oct 22, 1990: 92.1 mhz; 580 w-H. Ant -817 ft. TL: N43 44 34 W122 26 03. Hrs opn: 8. 200 N. Monroe, Eugene (97401); Oakridge High School, 47997 W. First St. (97463). (503) 687-3370; (503) 782-2231. FAX: (503) 687-3573. Licensee: School District 4J Lane County. Format: CHR, country. Target aud: General. ■ Carl Sundberg, chief opns & chief engr; D. Gillespie, progmg dir.

Ontario

KSRV(AM)—Nov 23, 1946: 1380 khz; 5 kw-D, 1 kw-N, DA-N. TL: N44 02 45 W116 58 24. Hrs opn: 24. Box 129, 1725 N. Oregon St. (97914). (503) 889-8651. FAX: (503) 889-8733. Licensee: KSRV Inc. Net: ABC/E, NBC Talknet; N.W. Net. Rep: Art Moore. Wash atty: Dow, Lohnes & Albertson. Format: Country. News staff one; news progmg 15 hrs wkly. Target aud: 25 plus. Spec prog: Farm 15 hrs wkly. ■ David Capps, pres; Vicki L. Swain, gen mgr; Barb Cowgill, sls dir; Helen Dickensen, prom dir; Mike Hansell, progmg dir; Doug Cooper, news dir.

KSRV-FM—July 4, 1977: 96.1 mhz; 100 kw. Ant 450 ft. TL: N44 01 50 W117 04 36. Stereo. Hrs opn: 24. Dups AM 80%. (503) 889-9600. Format: Country.

Oregon City

KFXX(AM)—July 4, 1947: 1520 khz; 50 kw-D, 10 kw-N, DA-2. TL: N45 24 44 W122 34 37. Hrs opn: 24. 4614 S.W. Kelly Ave., Portland (97201). (503) 223-1441. FAX: (503) 223-6909. Licensee: Apogee Communications Inc. (group owner; (acq 1992; $5,500,000 with co-located FM; FTR 11-9-92). Rep: D & R Radio. Format: Sports/talk. News staff one. ■ Jim Johnson, gen mgr; Bob Hogan, gen sls mgr; Julie Miele, prom mgr; Kevin Touh, progmg dir; Mike Turner, news dir; Larry Holtz, chief engr.

KGON(FM)—See Portland.

Pendleton

***KRBM(FM)**—April 18, 1970: 90.9 mhz; 25 kw. Ant 587 ft. TL: N45 35 21 W118 59 53. Stereo. Hrs opn: 19. Box 100, Morrow Hall, 2411 N.W. Carden Ave., (97801). (503) 276-1260; (503) 276-7952. FAX: (503) 276-6119. Licensee: Oregon Public Broadcasting (acq 9-20-93; grpsl; FTR 10-11-93). Net: APR, NPR; Ore. Pub. Bcstg Radio Net. Format: Class, jazz, AOR. News progmg 50 hrs wkly. Target aud: Teens to adults. ■ Blaine T. Hanks, gen mgr.

KTIX(AM)—1941: 1240 khz; 1 kw-U. TL: N45 39 49 W118 47 19. Stereo. Hrs opn: 24. Box 640, 1000 S.W. 6th St. (97801). (503) 278-2500. FAX: (503) 276-6842. Licensee: Agpal Broadcasting Inc. (group owner; acq 5-81). Net: ABC/I. Rep: McGavren Guild. Format: Adult contemp, news/talk. News staff one; news progmg 21 hrs wkly. Target aud: 25-54; upscale adults. ■ Andrew Harle, pres; Kathi Zollman, gen mgr; Cheri Schuler, gen sls mgr; Jeff Walker, progmg dir & mus dir; Kevin Cook, news dir; Dave Herbert, chief engr.

KWHT(FM)—Co-owned with KTIX(AM). May 1, 1984: 103.5 mhz; 100 kw. Ant 720 ft. TL: N45 47 51 W118 22 17. Stereo. Prog sep from AM. Box 640, 1000 S.W. 6th St. (97801); 515 N. Wilbur, Walla Walla, WA (99362). (503) 278-2500; (509) 522-1383. FAX: (503) 276-6842. (acq 12-83; $55,223; FTR 12-19-83). Net: ABC/I. Format: Country. Target aud: 25-54.

KUMA(AM)—Aug 25, 1955: 1290 khz; 5 kw-U, DA-N. TL: N45 40 25 W118 44 48. Hrs opn: 24. Box 340 (97801). (503) 276-1511. FAX: (503) 276-1480. Licensee: Round-Up Radio Inc. (acq 7-1-93; $340,000 with co-located FM; FTR 7-26-93). Net: NBC. Rep: Moore. Format: MOR, news. News staff 2; news progmg 40 hrs wkly. Spec prog: Sp one hr wkly. ■ Dave Capps, pres; Ron Shirtlift, gen mgr & chief engr; Kevin McCow, progmg dir; Angela Pursel, news dir.

KUMA-FM—Oct 1, 1978: 107.7 mhz; 27.5 kw. Ant 610 ft. TL: N42 35 19 W118 59 45 (CP: 100 kw, ant 1,128 ft.). Stereo. Prog sep from AM. Format: Oldies.

KWHT(FM)—Listing follows KTIX(AM).

Phoenix

KDOV(AM)—Jan 2, 1977: 1300 khz; 20 kw-U, DA-N. TL: N42 17 44 W122 48 15. Box 396 (97535). (503) 535-6833. FAX: (503) 535-6833. Licensee: Dove Communication Network Inc. (acq 10-24-91). Net: NBC. Rep: Major Market. Format: New/talk, Christian. News staff 4; news progmg 30 hrs wkly. Target aud: 25-54. ■ Perry Atkinson, gen mgr & opns mgr; Paul Wesner, gen sls mgr; Bob Dennis, news dir; Russ Jump, vp engrg. ■ Rates: $15; 14; 14; 13.

KROG(FM)—Not on air, target date unknown: 105.1 mhz; 52 kw. Ant 545 ft. TL: N42 25 41 W123 00 04. Box 250, Barstow, CA (92312). (619) 256-2121. Licensee: Bear Creek Broadcasting Inc. (acq 4-8-92; $343,500; FTR 4-27-92). ■ Steven Hess, gen mgr.

KTMT(AM)—Licensed to Phoenix. See Medford.

Portland

KBBT(AM)—Oct 18, 1925: 970 khz; 5 kw-U, DA-N. TL: N45 30 56 W122 43 56. Stereo. Hrs opn: 24. 2040 S.W. 1st Ave. (97201). (503) 222-1011. FAX: (503) 222-2047. Licensee: Henry Broadcasting Co. (group owner; acq 4-1-82). Rep: Eastman. Format: Alt rock. Target aud: 18-49. ■ Charlton Buckley, CEO; Dave McDonald, gen mgr; Mickie Hall, gen sls mgr; Craig Ramos, rgnl sls mgr; Annette Nauman, prom mgr & pub affrs dir; Dave Numme, progmg dir; Troy Daniels, mus dir; Joe Allen, chief engr.

KUFO(FM)—Co-owned with KBBT(AM). May 1, 1977: 101.1 mhz; 100 kw. Ant 1,640 ft. TL: N45 30 58 W122 43 59. Stereo. Hrs opn: 24. Prog sep from AM. Format: AOR. ■ Michelle Dodd, mus dir.

KBMS(AM)—See Vancouver, Wash.

KBNP(AM)—1949: 1410 khz; 5 kw-D, 250 w-N. TL: N45 28 24 W122 39 36. Hrs opn: 24. Paulson Investment, Suite 430, 811 S.W. Front Ave. (97204). (503) 223-6769. FAX: (503) 223-4305. Licensee: 2nd Amendment Foundation (acq 8-8-90; $320,000; FTR 8-27-90). Net: BRN; N.W. Net. Format: Business news & info. News staff 6;

news progmg 163 hrs wkly. Target aud: General; corporates & individuals concerned with how-to's of making & keeping money. ■ Keith Lyons, gen mgr, gen sls mgr & progmg dir; Christopher Piper, mktg mgr, prom mgr & adv dir; James Boyd, chief engr. ■ Rates: $65; 55; 45; 25.

AMERICAN RADIO BROKERS, INC.
MOST TRUSTED NAME IN MEDIA BROKERAGE
CHESTER P. COLEMAN / PRESIDENT
FOR THE BEST STATIONS FOR SALE FROM THIS AREA
CALL — 415/441-3377
1255 POST STREET / SUITE 625 / SAN FRANCISCO, CA 94109

***KBOO(FM)**—June 1968: 90.7 mhz; 25.5 kw. Ant 1,266 ft. TL: N45 29 20 W122 41 40. Stereo. Hrs opn: 24. 20 S.E. 8th St. (97214). (503) 231-8032. FAX: (503) 231-7145. Licensee: KBOO Foundation (acq 8-5-75). Wash atty: Haley, Bader & Potts. Format: Div. News staff one; news progmg 5 hrs wkly. Target aud: General. Spec prog: Black 18 hrs, class 18 hrs, country 3 hrs, Sp 10 hrs, Indian one hr, women's 4 hrs, ethnic 4 hrs, world 3 hrs, bluegrass/folk 8 hrs, African/reggae 10 hrs, folk 8 hrs wkly. ■ Alan Baily, stn mgr; Chris Merrick, progmg dir; Brandon Lieberman, mus dir; Larry Rothman, Emily Harris, news dirs; Kathleen Stephenson, pub affrs dir; Michael Johnson, chief engr.

***KBPS(AM)**—Mar 23, 1923: 1450 khz; 1 kw-U. TL: N45 31 38 W122 29 03. Hrs opn: 24. 515 N.E. 15th Ave. (97232). (503) 280-5828. Licensee: School District No. 1. Net: APR. Format: Class, educ, news/talk. News progmg 13 hrs wkly. Spec prog: Jazz 8 hrs, Sp one hr wkly. ■ Patricia Green Swenson, gen mgr; Darryl Conser, mus dir; Tom Cauthers, chief engr.

***KBPS-FM**—Aug 1983: 89.9 mhz; 8.7 kw. Ant 964 ft. TL: N45 30 58 W122 43 59. Stereo. Hrs opn: 24. Prog sep from AM. Format: Class. News progmg 5 hrs wkly. ■ Darryl Conser, opns dir.

***KBVM(FM)**—Dec 8, 1989: 88.3 mhz; 1.85 kw. Ant 1,434 ft. TL: N45 29 23 W122 41 47 (CP: Ant 1,404 ft.). Stereo. Hrs opn: 24. Box 5888, 5000 N. Willamette, No.44 (97228-5888). (503) 283-7455. FAX: (503) 283-7355. Licensee: Metro Catholic Broadcasting Inc. Format: Div, relg, btfl mus. Target aud: General; those who want to listen to positive family-oriented programs. Spec prog: Sp 2 hrs wkly. ■ Ric Schmidt, gen mgr; David Firth, progmg dir.

KEX(AM)—Dec 24, 1926: 1190 khz; 50 kw-U, DA-N. TL: N45 25 20 W122 33 57. Stereo. 4949 S.W. Macadam Ave. (97201). (503) 225-1190; (503) 585-1190. TWX: 910-464-8066. Licensee: Great American TV and Radio Co. Group owner: Great American Broadcasting (acq 4-84; grpsl; FTR 4-2-84). Net: ABC/I. Rep: Katz. Wash atty: Koteen & Naftalin. Format: Full svc adult contemp. News progmg 25 hrs wkly. ■ Dave Milner, pres & gen mgr; Duane Link, opns dir & progmg dir; Gerry Vitort, gen sls mgr; Kerry Riley, prom dir; J. D. Fort, mus dir; Jim Howe, news dir; Byron Swanson, chief engr.

KKRZ(FM)—Co-owned with KEX(AM). May 1946: 100.3 mhz; 95 kw. Ant 1,433 ft. TL: N45 31 22 W122 45 07. Stereo. (503) 226-0100. Net: ABC/R. Format: CHR. Target aud: 18-49. ■ Bill Ashenden, gen mgr; Robert Dove, rgnl sls mgr; Allison Jansky, prom mgr; Ken Benson, progmg dir; Kim Mathews, mus dir.

KEZF(AM)—(Tigard). June 28, 1993: 1040 khz; 2.2 kw-D, 200 w-N. TL: N45 28 24 W122 39 36. Hrs opn: 24. 622 Parkmeadow Loop N, Keizer (97303). The Oaks Park, Portland (97219). (503) 231-2772. Licensee: Educational Media Foundation Inc. (acq 4-25-90; $45,000; FTR 5-14-90). Wash atty: Fisher, Wayland, Cooper & Leader. Format: Contemp Christian. Target aud: 25-35; Judeo/Christian females. ■ Richard Jenkins, pres & gen mgr; Sabrina Alvarez, stn mgr.

KGON(FM)—December 1967: 92.3 mhz; 100 kw. Ant 920 ft. TL: N45 20 23 W122 41 47. Stereo. Hrs opn: 24. Rep: D & R Radio. Format: Rock (AOR). ■ Dick Sheetz, progmg dir.

KINK-FM—Dec 24, 1968: 101.9 mhz; 100 kw. Ant 1,673 ft. TL: N45 31 21 W122 44 46. Stereo. Hrs opn: 24. 1501 S.W. Jefferson St. (97201). (503) 226-5080. FAX: (503) 226-4578. Licensee: Portland Radio Inc. (acq 7-2-92; $11.5 million; FTR 5-18-92). Net: AP. Rep: Major Mkt; Major Mkt.Format: Adult album rock & jazz. News staff 3. Target aud: 25-44. ■ Paul Clithero, gen mgr; Lisa Decker Grindell, gen sls mgr; Martha Nielson, prom mgr; Carl Widing, progmg dir; Jan Wilkerson, news dir; Lee McCormick, chief engr.

KINK(AM)—March 25, 1922: 620 khz; 5 kw-U, DA-N. TL: N45 36 05 W122 41 09. Stereo. Hrs opn: 24. Dups KINK-FM 100%.

KKBK(FM)—See Lake Oswego.

KKCW(FM)—See Beaverton.

KKEY(AM)—July 4, 1954: 1150 khz; 5 kw-D, 47 w-N, DA-1. TL: N45 38 34 W122 36 49. Box 5757, Portland (97228); 5500 E. Fourth Plain Blvd., Vancouver, WA (98661). (503) 222-1150; (206) 693-5407. FAX: (503) 760-2035. Licensee: Western Broadcasting. Net: Westwood One, MBS, NBC, Daynet. Format: Talk. News progmg 6 hrs wkly. Target aud: 35-65. Spec prog: It one hr, jazz 15 hrs, Romanian one hr, Scandinavian one hr wkly. ■ Florinda J. Weagant, pres & gen mgr; Steve Bradley, prom mgr; Ronald Hudson, chief engr.

KKRZ(FM)—Listing follows KEX(AM).

KKSN-FM—April 1, 1980: 97.1 mhz; 100 kw. Ant 1,266 ft. TL: N45 29 20 W122 41 40. Stereo. 5005 S.W. Macadam (97201). (503) 226-9791. FAX: (503) 243-3299. Licensee: Heritage Media Corp. (group owner; acq 8-88; $5,750,000; FTR 8-15-88). Net: Unistar. Rep: Christal. Wash atty: Sydley & Austin. Format: Oldies. News staff 2. Target aud: 25-54. ■ Harry Williams, pres & gen mgr; Lynn Keller, gen sls mgr; Susette Seales, prom mgr; Robert Harlow, progmg dir; Michael Belfonzo, progmg mgr; Chris Burns, news dir; Gary Hilliard, chief engr.

KMUZ(AM)—(Gresham). Sept 28, 1956: 1230 khz; 1 kw-U. TL: N45 29 35 W122 24 40. Hrs opn: 24. Port of Camas/Washougal, Suite A, 24 A St., Washougal WA (98671). (206) 835-3000; (503) 667-1000. FAX: (206) 835-3400. Licensee: Pacific Northwest Broadcasting Corp. (acq 3-17-92; $82,000; FTR 4-6-92). Net: ABC. Format: News/talk, adult contemp. News staff one; news progmg 60 hrs wkly. Target aud: 21-54; middle to upper income. ■ Bill King, gen mgr; Marshall Moss, progmg dir; Gary Hilliard, chief engr.

KMUZ-FM—(Camas, Wash). Nov. 1, 1992: 94.7 mhz; 3 kw. Ant 223 ft. TL: N45 35 54 W122 22 38. Stereo. Hrs opn: 24 Port of Camas/Washougal, Suite A, 24 A Street, Washougal, WA (98671). (Group owner; acq: 1-92). Wash atty: Pepper & Corazzini. Format: Soft adult contemp. News staff one. Target aud: 25-54. ■ R. L. Schwary, CEO; William F. King, pres; Marshall H. Moss, opns dir; Bill King, gen sls mgr; Louise Dunn, natl sls mgr; Kat Stevens, prom dir; Angie Buss, news dir. ■ Rates: $34; 30; 28; 26.

***KOPB-FM**—1962: 91.5 mhz; 70 kw-H, 21 kw-V. Ant 1,558 ft. TL: N45 31 22 W122 45 07. Stereo. 7140 S.W. Macadam Ave. (97219). (503) 293-1905. FAX: (503) 293-1919. Licensee: Oregon Public Broadcasting (acq 9-20-93; grpsl; FTR 10-11-93). Net: APR, NPR. Format: News, jazz, classical, world beat. News staff 5; news progmg 44 hrs wkly. Target aud: 34-54. ■ Maynard Orme, CEO; Debbi Hint, sr vp; Virginia Breen, vp & vp progmg; Jim Lewis, vp dev; Kim Duncan, prom dir & adv dir; Robert McBride, mus dir; Morgon Holm, news dir; Larry Bently, vp engrg. ■ *KOPB-TV affil.

KPDQ(AM)—July 30, 1947: 800 khz; 1 kw-D, 500 w-N. TL: N45 28 45 W122 44 55. 5110 S.E. Stark St. (97215). (503) 231-7800. FAX: (503) 238-7202. Licensee: Salem Media of Oregon Inc. Group owner: Salem Communications Corp. (acq 8-86; grpsl; FTR 7-28-86). Net: MBS. Format: Relg. ■ Edwin Attsinger, pres; Darrell E. Kennedy, gen mgr; Lew Davies, opns dir; Dennis Hayes, gen sls mgr; David Moore, prom dir; Joe Alcorn, mus dir; Allan Garren, chief engr.

KPDQ-FM—1961: 93.7 mhz; 97 kw. Ant 1,269 ft. TL: N45 29 20 W122 41 40. Stereo. Prog sep from AM.

KPHP(AM)—See Lake Oswego.

***KRRC(FM)**—May 1958: 107.5 mhz; 8 w. Ant -49 ft. TL: N45 28 52 W122 37 33. Reed College, 3203 S.E. Woodstock (97202). (503) 771-2180. Licensee: The Reed Institute (acq 1959). Format: Div. News progmg 6 hrs wkly. Target aud: 17-21; Reed College student body. Spec prog: Black 10 hrs, class 4 hrs, country 2 hrs, Fr 2 hrs, jazz 10 hrs, Sp 2 hrs wkly.

KUFO(FM)—Listing follows KBBT(AM).

KUPL(AM)—Nov 12, 1923: 1330 khz; 5 kw-U, DA-1. TL: N45 27 13 W122 32 45. Hrs opn: 24. 6400 S.W. Canyon Ct. (97221). (503) 297-3311. FAX: (503) 297-8249. Licensee: BayCom Partners (acq 10-20-93; $23 million with co-located FM; FTR 11-8-93). Net: AP. Rep: Banner; Art Moore.Wash atty: Baker & Hostetler. Format: Country. ■ Larry Leser, CEO & pres; Edward T. Hardy, vp & gen mgr; Mark Benecke, natl sls mgr; Mike Atterberry (local), rgnl sls mgr; Tawny Reckamp, prom mgr; Bill Bradley, progmg dir; Neal Penland, news dir; Ken Broeffle, chief engr.

KUPL-FM—1948: 98.5 mhz; 100 kw. Ant 1,104 ft. TL: N45 27 13 W122 32 45. Stereo. Hrs opn: 24. News staff 3.

KWJJ(AM)—Jan 17, 1925: 1080 khz; 50 kw-D, 10 kw-N, DA-2. TL: N45 33 26 W122 29 08. 931 S.W. King Ave. (97205). (503) 228-4393. TWX: 910-464-8094. Licensee: Roy H. Park Broadcasting. Group owner: Park Communications Inc. (acq 2-11-73). Net: ABC/E. Rep: D & R Radio. Format: Country. News staff 2. Target aud: 25-54. Spec prog: Hockey. ■ Roy H. Park, pres; Rick Prusator, vp; Daniel S. Volz, gen mgr; Stephanie Fredrickson, opns mgr; Mark Durkin, gen sls mgr; Jeanne James, prom dir; Robin Mitchell, progmg dir; Kelly McCrae, mus dir; Roger Pike, news dir; Christopher Cullen, chief engr.

KWJJ-FM—1968: 99.5 mhz; 50 kw. Ant 1,266 ft. TL: N45 29 20 W122 41 40. Stereo. Dups AM 55%.

KXL(AM)—1926: 750 khz; 50 kw-D, 20 kw-N, DA-2. TL: N45 24 05 W122 26 47. Box 14957 (97214). (503) 231-0750. FAX: (503) 235-4446. Licensee: Alexander Broadcasting Co. Inc. (acq 6-7-58). Net: CBS, NBC Talknet, AP, ABC TalkRadio. Rep: McGavren Guild. Format: News/talk. News staff 16; news progmg 56 hrs wkly. Target aud: 25-54. ■ Lester M. Smith, chmn; Irv Karl, pres; Ray G. Watson, vp & gen mgr; Dennis M. Kelly, opns mgr & news dir; Tim McNamara, gen sls mgr; Robyn Skone, mktg dir; Angie Levsrenz, prom dir; Bob Kellogg, pub affrs dir; Larry Wilson, chief engr.

KXL-FM—June 18, 1965: 95.5 mhz; 100 kw. Ant 990 ft. TL: N45 29 23 W122 41 47. Stereo. Hrs opn: 24. Prog sep from AM. Format: Adult contemp.

Prineville

KRCO(AM)—Feb 1, 1950: 690 khz; 1 kw-D, 77 w-N. TL: N44 20 30 W120 54 10. Box K (97754). (503) 447-6239. FAX: (503) 447-4724. Licensee: High Lakes Broadcasting (acq 2-1-79). Net: MBS. Rep: Tatcher. Format: C&W. ■ John Kendall, pres & gen sls mgr; Brian Williams, progmg dir & mus dir; Boone Elliott, news dir.

KIJK(FM)—Co-owned with KRCO(AM). April 8, 1981: 95.1 mhz; 100 kw. Ant 472 ft. TL: N44 18 32 W120 55 47. Stereo. Format: Soft adult contemp.

Redmond

KLRR(FM)—Licensed to Redmond. See Bend.

KPRB(AM)—October 1952: 1240 khz; 1 kw-U. TL: N44 16 38 W121 11 57. Hrs opn: 24. Box 1240 (97756); 706 S.W. 12 St (97756). (503) 548-5101; (800) 521-5755. FAX: (503) 548-6987. Licensee: Stewart Broadcasting Inc. (acq 6-22-92; $710,000; with co-located FM; FTR 7-13-92). Net: ABC/I, SMN. Rep: Intermountain Net, Eastman; Target.Wash atty: Arent, Fox, Kintner, Plotkin & Kahn. Format: Country. News staff one; news progmg 8 hrs wkly. Target aud: 25-54. ■ Sande Stewart, pres; Norm Louvau, exec vp & stn mgr; Andrew Untermeyer, sls dir; Colleen Robbins, mktg mgr & vp prom; Michael Cook, progmg dir; Andy Kahn, mus dir; Jim Malloy, news dir & pub affrs dir; Gary Fuller, chief engr. ■ Rates: $28; 23; 28; 20.

KSJJ(FM)—Co-owned with KPRB(AM). Feb 4, 1981: 102.9 mhz; 100 kw. Ant 400 ft. TL: N44 10 25 W121 16 29. Stereo. Hrs opn: 24. Dups AM 90%. ■ Rates: Same as AM.

Reedsport

KDUN(AM)—June 2, 1961: 1030 khz; 10 kw-D, 63 w-N. TL: N43 44 17 W124 04 30. Hrs opn: 24 Box 147, 365 Hawthorne St. (97467). (503) 271-3674; (503) 271-2674. Licensee: KDUN Radio Inc. (acq 3-72). Net: CNN. Rep: Art Moore. Format: MOR, country. News staff one; news progmg 20 hrs wkly. Target aud: General. ■ Lyle Irons, pres, gen mgr & news dir; Ellie Irons, progmg dir; Robin O'Kelly, chief engr. ■ Rates: $9; 9; 9; 7.

KRBZ(FM)—1993: 99.5 mhz; 6 kw. Ant 236 ft. Box 599 (97467). (503) 271-3300. Licensee: Fafara Partners. Format: Adult contemp, CHR. ■ Rodney Fafara, gen mgr.

KSYD(FM)—March 1990: 92.1 mhz; 2.78 kw-H. Ant 335 ft. TL: N43 43 21 W124 05 20. 200 N. Monroe, Eugene (97401). (503) 687-3370. FAX: (503) 687-3573. Licensee: School District 4J, Lane County. Format: Adult contemp, Black, modern rock. Target aud: 12-40. ■ Carl Sundberg, gen mgr & chief engr.

Stations in the U.S.

Oregon

Rogue River

KRRM(FM)—Not on air, target date unknown: 94.7 mhz; 130 w. Ant 2,043 ft. Box 1091, Grants Pass (97526). Licensee: Shirley M. Bell.

Roseburg

KQEN(AM)—Sept 19, 1950: 1240 khz; 1 kw-U. TL: N43 11 44 W123 21 33. Box 5180; (97470). (503) 673-6641. FAX: (503) 673-7598. Licensee: Markham Broadcasting Inc. (acq 7-86; $119,113; FTR 5-12-86). Net: ABC/E. Rep: Katz, Tacher. Wash atty: Haley, Bader & Potts. Format: MOR. News staff 2; news progmg 4 hrs wkly. Target aud: General; 35 plus. ■ Patrick A. Markham, pres; Dan Hern, gen mgr & gen sls mgr; Mike Carter, opns mgr & progmg dir; Dave Hansen, prom mgr; Kevin Mack, news dir; Jim Macke, chief engr. ■ Rates: $13; 10; 13; 8.

KRNR(AM)—June 1935: 1490 khz; 1 kw-U. TL: N43 13 39 W123 20 42. Hrs opn: 24. Box 910 (97470). (503) 673-5553. Licensee: Douglas County Tricasters Inc. (acq 3-1-61). Net: CBS. Rep: IMN, Moore. Format: C&W, news/talk. Target aud: 25 plus. ■ V. Faye Johnson, pres; John L. Pundt, gen mgr; Wayne B. Hoobler, chief engr. ■ Rates: $14.25; 12.75; 14.25; 10.75.

KRSB-FM—Oct 1, 1970: 103.1 mhz; 2.75 kw. Ant 308 ft. TL: N43 12 24 W123 21 47 (CP: 25.5 kw, ant 676 ft. TL: N43 13 59 W123 19 22). Stereo. Box 5180 (97470). (503) 672-6641. FAX: (503) 673-7598. Licensee: Brooke Communications (acq 4-30-89). Rep: Katz, Tacher. Wash atty: Haley, Bader & Potts. Format: Contemp country. News staff 2; news progmg 15 hrs wkly. Target aud: 18-34. ■ Patrick A. Markham, pres; Dan Hern, gen sls mgr; Dave Hansen, prom mgr; Mike Carter, progmg dir; Brian Prawitz, news dir; Jim Macke, chief engr. ■ Rates: $13; 10; 13; 8.

***KSRS(FM)**—December 1990: 91.5 mhz; 2 kw. Ant 305 ft. TL: N43 12 24 W123 21 47. Stereo. Hrs opn: 5 AM-2 AM. 1250 Siskiyou Blvd., Ashland (97520). (503) 552-6301. FAX: (503) 552-6773. Licensee: State of Oregon Acting By and Through the State Board of Higher Education. Net: NPR, APR, AP. Wash atty: Arter & Hadden. Format: Class, news. ■ Ronald Kramer, gen mgr; Keith Henty, opns dir; Paul Westhelle, dev dir & prom mgr; John Baxter, progmg dir; Pat Daly, mus dir; Annie Hoy, news dir; John Holt, engrg mgr.

KTBR(AM)—November 1955: 950 khz; 1 kw-D. TL: N43 10 08 W123 22 28. 2726 Diamond Lake Blvd. (97470). (503) 672-4427. Licensee: K/S Riggs Broadcasting Inc. (acq 8-01-92; $280,000; FTR 8-01-92). Rep: Major Mkt. Format: Classic rock, oldies. ■ Susan Riggs, pres & progmg dir; Keith Riggs, gen mgr.

St. Helens

KOHI(AM)—March 2, 1960: 1600 khz; 1 kw-D, 500 w-CH. TL: N45 51 18 W122 49 29 (CP: TL: N45 51 15 W122 49 11). Hrs opn: 6 AM-10 PM. Box 398, St. Helens Prof. Ctr. Suite D, 530 N. Columbia River Hwy & Pittsburg Rd. (97051). (503) 397-1600. Licensee: Volcano Broadcasting (acq 5-21-82; $150,000; FTR 6-14-82). Net: UPI. Rep: Keystone (unwired net), Tacher. Format: Country, country rock, talk. News staff one; news progmg 7 hrs wkly. Target aud: 35 plus. ■ Kenneth E. Karge, pres; Forrest W. Smith, vp, gen mgr & gen sls mgr; Jan Carlson, progmg dir, mus dir & news dir; Mike Mowery, chief engr. ■ Rates: $11; 11; 11; na.

Salem

KBZY(AM)—May 1957: 1490 khz; 1 kw-U. TL: N44 57 03 W123 02 43. Box 14900 (97309); 4340 Commercial St. S.E. (97302). (503) 362-1490. Licensee: Capital Broadcasting Inc. (acq 6-15-82; $365,000; FTR 7-5-82). Net: ABC/E, Mutual. Rep: Roslin, Tacher. Format: Adult contemp. News staff 2; news progmg 25 hrs wkly. Target aud: 25-54. ■ Roy Dittman, pres & gen mgr; Warren Franklin, vp & gen sls mgr; Jim Adams, progmg dir & mus dir; Steve Kay, news dir; Ken Lewetag, chief engr.

KCCS(AM)—Dec 12, 1961: 1220 khz; 1 kw-D, 171 w-N. TL: N44 58 57 W123 00 17. Hrs opn: 24. 4303 Market St. N.E. (97301). (503) 364-1000; (503) 588-1003. FAX: (503) 364-1022. Licensee: Christian Center of Salem (acq 12-15-71). Net: CBN, Moody. Format: Contemp relg. News progmg 14 hrs wkly. Target aud: 25-54; family. ■ Rev. Dale Albritton, pres; Earl Allbritton, gen mgr & gen sls mgr; Dan Sheets, progmg dir & mus dir; Brent Anderson, asst mus dir; Ken Lewetag, engrg dir.

KSLM(AM)—1934: 1390 khz; 5 kw-D, 1 kw-N. TL: N44 56 32 W123 04 17. Box 631 (97308). (503) 363-1390. FAX: (503) 363-5688. Licensee: K-Salem Communications (acq 4-6-92; $151,000; FTR 5-11-92). Net: CBS.

Rep: Group W, Farmakis. Format: Solid Gold. Spec prog: Farm 2 hrs wkly. ■ Greg Fabos, gen mgr & gen sls mgr; Doc Nelson, opns mgr & progmg dir; Ken Lewetag, chief engr.

KWIP(AM)—(Dallas). April 15, 1955: 880 khz; 5 kw-D, 1 kw-N. TL: N44 55 45 W123 17 22. Stereo. Box 469 Dallas (97338). (503) 623-0245. FAX: (503) 623-6733. Licensee: Jupiter Communications Corp. (acq 6-10-91; $21,000; FTR 7-1-91). Rep: Art Moore. Format: Hit-based adult contemp. News staff one; news progmg 8 hrs wkly. Target aud: 21-54; families and professionals. Spec prog: Talk 5 hrs wkly. ■ Diana Burns, gen mgr; Maria Theresa Porras, progmg dir.

KXYQ(AM)—July 3, 1970: 105.1 mhz; 100 kw. Ant 1,840 ft. TL: N45 00 28 W122 20 05. Stereo. Suite 1150, 111 S.W. 5th Ave., Portland (97204). (503) 226-6731. Licensee: KXYQ Broadcasting Co. Inc. (acq 3-31-92; $1.3 million with KZRC(AM) Milwaukie; FTR 4-20-92). Net: ABC/E. Rep: Banner. Format: Top-40. ■ Denise Swanson, gen mgr & gen sls mgr; Big Jim Ryan, progmg dir; Mike Everhart, chief engr.

KYKN(AM)—See Keizer.

Seaside

KSWB(AM)—July 12, 1968: 840 khz; 1 kw-D, 500 w-N. TL: N45 58 55 W123 55 02. Stn currently dark. Box 24 (97138). Licensee: Monte Corp. (acq 1-15-92; $130,000 with co-located FM; FTR 2-10-92). ■ Robert Gilbert, pres; Kenneth E. Karge, gen mgr.

KQEM(FM)—Co-owned with KSWB(AM). Not on air, target date unknown: 94.7 mhz; 3 kw. Ant 213 ft. TL: N45 58 45 W123 55 02.

Sisters

KPXA(FM)—Not on air, target date unknown: 104.1 mhz; 1.3 kw. Ant 709 ft. TL: N44 09 04 W121 34 31. 730 Winchester Dr., Burlingame, CA (94010). Licensee: Schuyler H. Martin (acq 3-29-91; FTR 4-15-91).

Springfield

***KQFE(FM)**—March 7, 1989: 88.9 mhz; 2 kw. Ant 418 ft. TL: N44 02 01 W123 00 25. Suite 4, 5120 Franklin Blvd. (97403). (503) 726-9156. FAX: (503) 746-2101. Licensee: Family Stations Inc. (group owner). Format: Relg. ■ Ken Seydlitz, gen mgr; Linda Seydlitz, stn mgr; Thad McKinney, rgnl sls mgr.

KZZK(AM)—Licensed to Springfield. See Eugene.

Springfield-Eugene

KKNU(FM)—Dec 18, 1958: 93.1 mhz; 100 kw-horiz, 33.3 kw-V. Ant 985 ft. TL: N44 00 05 W123 06 48 Stereo. Suite 200, 925 Country Club Rd. (97401). (503) 484-9400. FAX: (503) 344-9424. Licensee: McKenzie River Broadcasting Co. Inc. (acq 11-17-92; $1.01 million with KEED(AM) Eugene; FTR 12-14-92). Wash atty: Koteen & Naftalin. Format: New Country News staff one. Target aud: 18-49; young, country life group. ■ John Q. Tilson III, pres; Cary Rolfe, progmg dir & mus dir; Chris Murray, chief engr.

KORE(AM)—September 1927: 1050 khz; 5 kw-D, 149 w-N. TL: N44 04 07 W123 01 45. Hrs opn: 24. 2080 Laura St. (97477-2197). (503) 747-5673. FAX: (503) 746-0680. Licensee: Support Christian Broadcasting Inc. (acq 8-87). Net: USA. Format: Christian. ■ Larry Knight, gen mgr; Darrel Wilson, gen sls mgr; Darren Bailey, progmg dir; Sonny Starr, mus dir; John Brambora, news dir; Robin O'Kelly, chief engr.

KPNW(AM)—See Eugene.

KUGN(AM)—See Eugene.

KZZK(AM)—See Eugene.

Stayton

KCKX(AM)—June 1, 1987: 1460 khz; 1 kw-D, 15 w-N. TL: N44 48 10 W122 44 03. Hrs opn: 24. 1460 N. First St. (97383-1212). (503) 769-1460. FAX: (503) 769-4085. Licensee: Spotlight Communications Inc. (acq 8-1-92; $83,000; FTR 8-17-92). Net: Jones Satellite Audio. Format: Modern country. News progmg 3 hrs wkly. Target aud: 25 plus; men & women with varied professions. Spec prog: Portland Trailblazers-NBA Basketball, farm 15 hrs wkly. ■ Don Craig, pres, gen mgr, gen sls mgr, prom mgr & adv dir; Betty Craig, exec vp; Todd Craig, vp & stn mgr; Gail Boger, opns dir; Todd Graig, rgnl sls mgr; Denise Sampson, mktg dir; John Zolkoske, progmg dir & pub affrs dir; Ross Shelton, engrg dir. ■ Rates: $24; 24; 24; na.

Sweet Home

KFIR(AM)—Aug 7, 1968: 1370 khz; 1 kw-D, 72 w-N. TL: N44 24 52 W122 44 22. Box 400, 28041 Pleasant Valley Rd. (97386). (503) 367-5115. Licensee: Galaxy Broadcasting Corp. (acq 2-1-87). Net: ABC/E. Format: Modern country. News progmg 8 hrs wkly. Target aud: 25 plus. ■ Bob Ratter, gen mgr, gen sls mgr & progmg dir; Brad Lee, mus dir & news dir; Dick Linn, chief engr.

KSKD(FM)—Co-owned with KFIR(AM). Sept 20, 1989: 107.1 mhz; 9 kw. Ant 2,476 ft. TL: N44 28 59 W122 34 55. Stereo. Hrs opn: 24. Dups AM 100%. (503) 367-8107. Format: Adult contemp, Christan (K-Love). Target aud: 18-49. ■ Bob Ratter, adv mgr; Izzy Great, progmg dir.

Talent

***KSJK(AM)**—October 1960: 1230 khz; 1 kw-U. TL: N42 13 27 W122 44 33. Southern Oregon State College, 1250 Siskiyou Blvd., Ashland (97520). (503) 552-6301. FAX: (503) 552-6773. Licensee: Oregon State Board of Higher Education (acq 7-28-89). Net: APR. Wash atty: Arter & Hadden. Format: News/info. News staff one; news progmg 5 hrs wkly. Target aud: 25-49. Spec prog: Spanish 6 hrs wkly. ■ Ronald Kramer, gen mgr; Keith Henty, chief opns; Paul Westhelle, prom mgr; John Baxter, progmg dir; Pat Daly, mus dir; Annie Hoy, news dir; John Holt, engrg mgr.

The Dalles

KACI(AM)—June 1955: 1300 khz; 1 kw-D, 54 w-N. TL: N45 34 54 W121 07 53. Box 516, Williams Bldg., Fourth and Washington (97058). (503) 296-2211. FAX: (503) 296-2213. Licensee: Nugent Broadcasting Co. (acq 9-1-77). Net: ABC/I. Rep: Eastman, Art Moore. Wash atty: Dow, Lohnes & Albertson. Format: Bright adult contemp. News staff one; news progmg 4 hrs wkly. Target aud: 25-54. Spec prog: Relg one hr wkly. ■ Burns Q. Nugent, CEO; Joan F. Nugent, pres & gen mgr; Alex King, news dir. ■ Rates: $15; 10; 15; 6.

KACI-FM—Feb 1, 1985: 97.7 mhz; 5 kw. Ant 890 ft. TL: N45 38 56 W121 16 20. Stereo. Hrs opn: 18. Dups AM 100%. ■ Rates: Same as AM.

KMCQ(FM)—Nov 28, 1968: 104.5 mhz; 100 kw. Ant 2,001 ft. TL: N45 42 41 W121 07 07. Stereo. Box 104, 719 E. 2nd (97058). (503) 298-5116; (503) 298-5117. FAX: (503) 298-5119. Licensee: Mid Columbia Broadcasting Inc. (acq 1983; FTR 12-31-84). Net: CBS Spectrum. Rep: McGavren Guild. Format: Adult contemp. News staff one; news progmg 19 hrs wkly. Target aud: 25-54. Spec prog: Jazz 6 hrs, oldies 6 hrs, blues 2 hrs wkly. ■ Frank Diegmann, pres; John Huffman, gen mgr & prom mgr; Linda Griswold, sls dir; Shannon Milburn, progmg dir & mus dir; Gene Gillette, news dir; Holly Kier, pub affrs dir; James Boyd, chief engr. ■ Rates: $16.50; 12; 16.50; 12.

KODL(AM)—Oct 12, 1940: 1440 khz; 5 kw-D, 1 kw-N, DA-N. TL: N45 35 31 W121 11 57. Box 741, 2112 Scenic Dr. (97058). (503) 296-2101. FAX: (503) 296-3766. Licensee: Larson-Wynn Inc. (acq 9-1-74). Net: CNN; N.W. Net. Rep: Uni-Rep, Tacher. Format: C&W. Spec prog: Farm 4 hrs, Sp 2 hrs wkly. ■ Al Wynn, pres & gen mgr; Tom Wilds, gen sls mgr, progmg dir & mus dir; Jake Grossmiller, news dir.

Tigard

KEZF(AM)—Licensed to Tigard. See Portland.

Tillamook

KMBD(AM)—August 1947: 1590 khz; 5 kw-D, 1 kw-N, DA-N. TL: N45 27 24 W123 52 36. Box 40, 170 W. 3rd St. (97141). (503) 842-4422. FAX: (503) 842-2755. Licensee: Oregon Eagle Inc. (acq 12-29-86; $250,000 grpsl; FTR 10-26-86). Net: ABC/E. Rep: Art Moore. Format: Adult contemp, C&W. ■ Van Moe, pres, gen mgr, progmg dir & mus dir; Joyce Moe, gen sls mgr; Barbara Trout, news dir; Jim Garling, chief engr.

KTIL-FM—Co-owned with KMBD(AM). May 1986: 104.1 mhz; 6.5 kw. Ant 150 ft. TL: N45 27 24 W123 52 36. (acq 12-29-87). Format: Sports.

Toledo

KZUS(AM)—Sept 26, 1960: 1230 khz; 1 kw-U. TL: N44 37 47 W123 56 35. Box 456, 304 S.W. Coast Hwy., Newport (97365). (503) 265-5000. FAX: (503) 265-9576. Licensee: Agpal Broadcasting Inc. (group owner; acq 3-14-90; grpsl; FTR 4-2-90). Net: CBS. Rep: McGavren Guild. Wash atty: Haley, Bader & Potts. Format: Country. Target aud: 25-54. ■ Andrew Harle, pres; Cheryl Harle, gen mgr & gen sls mgr; Bill Johnstone, rgnl sls mgr; Bruce Meyers, prom mgr; Ken Lovejoy, progmg dir & mus dir; James Boyd, chief engr.

KZUS-FM—December 1980: 100.7 mhz; 3 kw. Ant 430 ft. TL: N48 38 40 W124 00 52. Stereo. Dups AM 100%. Box 568 (97391). ■ Cheryl Harle, vp; Bill Johnson, gen sls mgr.

Tri City

KKMX(FM)—Nov 11, 1989: 104.3 mhz; 5.6 kw. Ant 1,384 ft. TL: N43 00 13 W123 21 26. Stereo. Hrs opn: 18. Box 5043, Roseburg (97470). (503) 863-7707. Licensee: Tri City Communications Inc. Format: Adult contemp. ■ Christine Mackey, gen mgr.

Troutdale

KZTW(AM)—Not on air, target date unknown: 860 khz; 20 kw-D, 500 w-N, DA-2. TL: N45 35 16 W122 17 34. c/o Jerry J. Collins, 25485 Boots Rd., Monterey, CA (93940). (408) 372-8383. Licensee: Jerry J. Collins.

Umatilla

KLWJ(AM)—June 1980: 1090 khz; 2.5 kw-D. TL: N45 52 46 W119 20 37 (CP: 1100 khz, 10 kw-D, 710 w-N, DA-N). Box 1410, Powerline Rd. (97882). (503) 567-2102. Licensee: Umatilla Broadcasting Inc. Net: USA, IBN. Format: Relg, news/talk. Target aud: General. Spec prog: Black one hr, farm one hr, Sp one hr wkly. ■ Darrell Marlow, pres; John Marlow, gen mgr, gen sls mgr, progmg dir, mus dir & news dir; Steve Thompson, chief engr.

Waldport

KORC(AM)—July 1, 1988: 820 khz. 1000 w-D, 15 w-N. TL: N44 26 05 W124 01 20 Box 1419, 235 S.W. Arrow, Suite 3 (97394). (503) 563-5100. FAX: (503) 563-5116. Licensee: Jarvis Communications Inc. (acq 7-21-92; FTR 8-10-92). Format: Big band, easy listening. ■ Matt Jarvis, gen mgr; Jim Biggs, chief engr.

Warm Springs

KTWI(FM)—Jan 18, 1986: 96.5 mhz; 100 kw. Ant 1,092 ft. TL: N44 50 24 W121 13 56. Stereo. Rebroadcasts KTWS(FM) Bend 100%. 20450 Empire Blvd., Bend (97701). (503) 389-9500. FAX: (503) 388-5448. Licensee: Confederation Tribes of Warm Springs. (group owner). Rep: McGavren Guild. Format: Classic rock. News staff one; news progmg 7 hrs wkly. Target aud: 25-54. ■ Ken Smith, pres; John Stolz, gen mgr & sls dir; Steve Moan, adv dir; Brook Snavley, news dir.

*__KWSO(FM)__—Sept 22, 1986: 91.9 mhz; 3.3 kw. Ant 203 ft. TL: N44 50 24 W121 13 56. Stereo. Box 489 (97761). (503) 553-1968; (503) 553-1969. FAX: (503) 553-3348. Licensee: Confederation Tribes of Warm Springs (group owner). Format: Div, Native American news & music. News progmg 16 hrs wkly. Target aud: General. Spec prog: Country 15 hrs, black 2 hrs; blues one hr, reggae one hr wkly. ■ Mike Villabobos, stn mgr; Ken Miller, progmg dir; Sue Ryan, news dir & pub affrs dir.

West Klamath

KWSA(AM)—Dec 1, 1987: 1070 khz; 5 kw-D, 1 kw-CH. TL: N42 11 38 W121 46 27. 1415 La Verne Klamath Falls (97603). (503) 884-3257. FAX: (503) 883-3341. Licensee: Western States Broadcasting Co. Format: Nostalgia. ■ William L. Zawila, pres; Jay Stevens, vp & gen mgr.

Winston

KGRV(AM)—Feb 12, 1984: 700 khz; 25 kw-D, 500 w-N. TL: N43 03 26 W123 23 48. Hrs opn: 5:45 AM-midnight. Box 1598, 196 S.E. Main St. (97496). (503) 679-8185. FAX: (503) 679-6456. Licensee: Pacific Cascade Communications Corp. (acq 4-15-85). Net: Moody, USA. Format: Relg. Target aud: 25-54. ■ Bill Simmons, gen mgr; Phil Morrow, rgnl sls mgr; John Scott Welch, progmg dir; Kyle Bailey, pub affrs dir; Paul Brown, engrg mgr. ■ Rates: $9; 9; 9; 8.

Woodburn

KWBY(AM)—July 10, 1964: 940 khz; 250 w-D, 200 w-N. TL: N45 10 37 W122 50 58. Hrs opn: 5 AM-midnight. Box 158, 1585 H N. Pacific Hwy. (97071). (503) 981-9400. FAX: (503) 981-3561. Licensee: Donald D. Coss (acq 10-18-91; $300,000; FTR 11-4-91). Net: MBS. Format: Classic country/western, Sp. News staff one; news progmg 35 hrs wkly. Target aud: 35-60. Spec prog: Relg 5 hrs, farm 3 hrs wkly. ■ Donald Coss, pres, gen mgr,

gen sls mgr; Todd Dennis, progmg dir & mus dir; Joe Allen, chief engr. ■ Rates: $25; 20; 25; 18.

Pennsylvania

Allentown

WAEB(AM)—1949: 790 khz; 1 kw-U, DA-2. TL: N40 37 05 W75 26 58 (day), N40 39 37 W75 30 50 (night) (CP: 3.8 kw-D, 5 kw-N, DA-2, TL (night): N40 39 33 W75 30 48). 700 N. Fenwick St. (18103). (215) 434-4424. FAX: (215) 434-2285. Licensee: CRB Broadcasting Corp. (group owner; acq 7-16-82 grpsl; FTR 6-14-82). Net: CBS, MBS. Rep: Katz. Format: News/talk. News staff 5; news progmg 28 hrs wkly. Target aud: 35-64. ■ Richard Lewis, gen mgr; Doug Hillard, gen sls mgr; Chris Bailey, progmg dir; Mathew Kerr, news dir; Harry Simons, chief engr. ■ Rates: $82; 62; 54; 38.

WAEB-FM—June 30, 1961: 104.1 mhz; 50 kw. Ant 500 ft. TL: N40 43 13 W75 35 44. Stereo. Prog sep from AM. Format: CHR. News staff one. Target aud: 18-44. ■ Brian Check, progmg dir. ■ Rates: $110; 110; 115; 70.

*__WDIY(FM)__—Not on air, target date unknown: 89.3 mhz; 120 w-V. Ant 245 ft. Box 1456 (18105). Licensee: Lehigh Valley Community Broadcasters Association Board of Directors.

WFMZ(FM)—July 1947: 100.7 mhz; 11 kw. Ant 1,073 ft. TL: N40 33 54 W75 26 26. Stereo. East Rock Rd. (18103). (215) 797-4530. Licensee: Maranatha Broadcasting Corp. (acq 1965). Rep: Torbet. Format: Easy lstng. ■ Dave Hinson, gen mgr.

WHOL(AM)—Sept 12, 1948: 1600 khz; 500 w-D, 100 w-N, DA-2. TL: N40 35 33 W75 28 42. Hrs opn: 6 AM-midnight. 1125 Colorado St. (18103). (215) 434-4801. Licensee: Lehigh Valley Broadcasting Associates Inc. (acq 11-1-85; $500,000; FTR 8-5-85). Net: USA, CBN. Format: Contemp Christian. Target aud: 18-65. Spec prog: Spanish 13 hrs wkly. ■ Leigh J. Murray, pres & gen mgr; Mary Ruth Seybold, gen sls mgr; Michael Smitreski, progmg dir; John Steiner, mus dir; George Motter, chief engr. ■ Rates: $24; 24; 24; 17.

WKAP(AM)—September 1948: 1320 khz; 5 kw-D, 1 kw-N, DA-2. TL: N40 37 40 W75 29 09. Suite 400, 961 Marcon Blvd. (18103). (215) 264-4040. FAX: (215) 266-6464. Licensee: WKAP/Holt Corporation of Pennsylvania. Group owner: The Holt Corporations (acq 12-15-88). Net: SMN. Rep: D & R Radio. Wash atty: Kaye, Schoeler, Fierman, Hays & Handler. Format: MOR. News staff one; news progmg 2 hrs wkly. Target aud: Women 25-54. ■ Arthur Holt, CEO & pres; Phyllis Holt, chmn; Christine Burger, CFO & exec vp; Bernie Fahrmann, gen mgr; Edwin Baumer, news dir; George Friel, chief engr. ■ Rates: $20; 20; 20; 20.

*__WMUH(FM)__—Feb 6, 1966: 91.7 mhz; 500 w. Ant -3 ft. TL: N40 35 52 W75 30 38. Stereo. Box 2806, Muhlenberg College (18104). (215) 821-3456; (215) 821-3239. FAX: (215) 821-3234. Licensee: Muhlenberg College. Net: NPR. Format: Div. News progmg 13 hrs wkly. Target aud: General. Spec prog: Black 4 hrs, Pol 3 hrs, Sp 4 hrs, East Indian 3 hrs, classical 6 hrs, jazz 14 hrs wkly. ■ Arthur Taylor, CEO; Jane A. Swanson, gen mgr; Heather Nicholas, stn mgr; Robert Friedman, opns mgr; Neil Hever, dev dir; Brian Olson, prom dir; Anthony Torre, progmg dir; Gina Steward, mus dir; Carolyn Blazovsky, news dir.

WXKW(AM)—May 24, 1923: 1470 khz; 5 kw-U, DA-N. TL: N40 38 10 W75 29 06. Stereo. Box 9595 (18105); Suite 400, 1541 Alta Dr., Whitehall (18052). (215) 821-9559; (215) 434-9511. FAX: (215) 821-9504. Licensee: Harold G. Fulmer III. Group owner: HGF Media Group (acq 12-1-80; $1,500,000; FTR 10-27-80). Net: ABC/I. Rep: D & R Radio. Format: Country. News staff one; news progmg 10 hrs wkly. Target aud: 25-54. Spec prog: Pol 3 hrs wkly. ■ Harold G. Fulmer III, pres; Thomas L. Harpster, gen mgr; Les Baer, stn mgr & progmg dir; Ed Baumer, news dir; George Friel, chief engr.

WYNS(AM)—(Lehighton). Apr 12, 1962: 1160 khz; 4.5 kw-D, 1 kw-N, DA-2. TL: N40 49 03 W75 41 31. Hrs opn: 5:30 AM-midnight. Box 115, 308 Upper Nis Hollow Dr., Lehighton (18235). (215) 377-1160. FAX: (215) 377-9117. Licensee: Valley Broadcasting Co. Net: ABC/E. Format: Oldies. News staff one; news progmg 11 hrs wkly. Target aud: 25-54; double income; middle class, blue collar. ■ Martin H. Philip, pres; Betty Straubinger, vp, gen mgr, gen sls mgr, prom mgr & progmg dir; Adrian Nothstein, mus dir; Karliene Zack, pub affrs dir; George Motter, chief engr. ■ Rates: $19; 16; 18.50; 10.50.

WZZO(FM)—See Bethlehem.

Altoona

WALY(FM)—(Bellwood). Mar 28, 1970: 103.9 mhz; 3 kw. Ant 984 ft. TL: N40 34 04 W79 26 26. Stereo. 104 Lakemont Park Blvd., Altoona (16602). (814) 944-2221. Licensee: S & P Broadcasting Ltd. Partnership. Group owner: S & P Broadcasting Co. (acq 2-17-89; $1,000,000; FTR 3-6-89). Net: AP. Rep: Katz; Dome. Format: Adult contemp. News staff one; news progmg 2 hrs wkly. ■ John A. Piccirillo, pres & gen mgr; Roger Cory, opns dir; K.C. O'Day, progmg dir & mus dir.

WFBG(AM)—Oct 30, 1924: 1290 khz; 5 kw-D, 1 kw-N, DA-N. TL: N40 27 20 W78 23 50. Stereo. Hrs opn: 24. Box 2005, Hilltop, Logan Blvd. (16602). (814) 941-9800. FAX: (814) 943-2754. Licensee: Logan Broadcasting Inc. Group owner: Empire Radio Partners Ltd. (acq 12-24-90; $2.1 million with co-located FM; FTR 1-14-91). Net: Unistar. Rep: Christal. Format: Adult contemp. News staff 2; news progmg 2 hrs wkly. Target aud: 25-54. ■ Carol Logan, pres & gen mgr; Steve Kelsey, opns mgr; Cindy Kline, sls dir; Rich Deleo, news dir; Troy Barnharts, chief engr.

WFGY(FM)—Co-owned with WFBG(AM). Oct 17, 1960: 98.1 mhz; 30 kw. Ant 1,020 ft. TL: N40 34 01 W78 26 31. Stereo. Hrs opn: 24. Prog sep from AM. Net: CBS. Format: Contemp country. News staff one. Target aud: 25-64. ■ Polly Ogg, prom dir, progmg dir & mus dir; Rich Deleo, pub affrs dir.

WHPA(FM)—See Hollidaysburg.

WPRR(FM)—Listing follows WVAM.

WRTA(AM)—June 12, 1946: 1240 khz; 1 kw-U. TL: N40 30 26 W78 25 15. Hrs opn: 19. Box 728, 1417-19 12th Ave. (16603). (814) 943-6112. FAX: (814) 944-9782. Licensee: Altoona Trans-Audio Corp. (acq 4-56). Net: ABC TalkRadio, Sun, NBC Talknet, ABC/I, ARN, Daynet. Wash atty: Pepper & Corazzini. Format: Talk, news. News staff 2; news progmg 13 hrs wkly. Target aud: 35 plus. ■ David R. Wolf, pres & gen mgr; Rod Wolf, gen sls mgr; Cem Maier, rgnl sls mgr; Charlie Weston, progmg dir & mus dir; Mike Morning, chief engr. ■ Rates: $23; 23; 23; 9.75.

WVAM(AM)—July 1948: 1430 khz; 5 kw-D, 1 kw-N, DA-N. TL: N40 29 42 W78 24 06. 2727 W. Albert Dr. (16602). (814) 944-9456. FAX: (814) 944-0250. Licensee: Music Broadcasting Inc. Group owner: Music Broadcasting Group (acq 12-88). Net: CBS Spectrum. Rep: Torbet. Format: C&W. Spec prog: Pol one hr wkly. ■ Gary Gunton, pres; Eric Donaldson, vp & gen mgr; Robin Jackson, gen sls mgr; Jim O'Brien, prom mgr; Michael Jaye, progmg dir & mus dir; Dave Bithell, news dir; John Super, chief engr.

WPRR(FM)—Co-owned with WVAM. July 1976: 100.1 mhz; 3 kw. Ant 30 ft. TL: N40 29 42 W78 24 06 (CP: Ant 311 ft.). Stereo. Prog sep from AM. Format: Contemp hit. ■ Dave McCall, prom mgr; Scott St. John, progmg dir & mus dir.

Ambridge

WMBA(AM)—May 1957: 1460 khz; 500 w-U, DA-2. TL: N40 35 08 W80 12 11. Hrs opn: 24. 761 Merchant St. (15003). (412) 266-1110. FAX: (412) 266-4929. Licensee: Donn Communications Inc. (acq 11-86; $270,000; FTR 7-7-86). Net: CNN. Wash atty: Barry Wood. Format: Talk. News staff 3. Target aud: 35-54. Spec prog: It one hr, Croation one hr wkly. ■ Donn R. Wuycik, pres, gen mgr, gen sls mgr & progmg dir; Al Goehring, news dir; Tom Zhender, chief engr. ■ Rates: $13; 13; 13; na.

Annville-Cleona

WWSM(AM)—Aug 4, 1968: 1510 khz; 5 kw-D, DA. TL: N40 17 44 W76 27 46. Stn currently dark. Box 15, Lebanon (17042). Licensee: Patrick H. Sickafus (acq 10-14-93; $1; FTR 11-1-93). ■ John Anspach, pres; Dorotha J. Sullivan, stn mgr; Tina Bechtold, gen sls mgr; Matthew Popecki, progmg dir; Tom Roy, news dir; William Margut, chief engr.

Apollo

WAVL(AM)—Dec 13, 1947: 910 khz; 5 kw-D, DA. TL: N40 35 01 W79 31 34. Box 277 (15613). (412) 478-4020. Licensee: Tri-Borough Broadcasting Co. Net: USA. Format: Relg, news. ■ Alice Clifton, pres; Robert Dain, stn mgr, gen sls mgr & progmg dir; Carman Tubby, pub affrs dir; Ray Jenkins, chief engr.

Avis

WQBR(FM)—Aug 11, 1989: 99.9 mhz; 450 w. Ant 823 ft. TL: N41 13 42 W77 22 21. Stereo. Box 999, McElhatton (17745). (707) 769-2327. FAX: (707) 769-7746. Licensee: Maximum Impact Communications Inc. (acq 9-9-93; $270,000; FTR 10-4-93). Format: Country. Target aud: General. ■ Karyn O'Brien, opns mgr; Joseph J. Kalie, gen sls mgr.

Barnesboro

WNCC(AM)—Oct 15, 1950: 950 khz; 500 w-D. TL: N40 40 47 W78 44 26. Suite 627, 616 Main St., Johnstown (15901). (814) 536-9270. FAX: (814)536-5855. Licensee: Eagle Broadcasting Group Inc. (acq 1-25-93; $10; FTR 2-15-93). Format: Christian. ■ Jane Allison Lee, gen mgr.

Beaver Falls

WBVP(AM)—May 25, 1948: 1230 khz; 1 kw-U. TL: N40 44 16 W80 17 47. Hrs opn: 24. Box 719, 1316 Seventh Ave. (15010); Box 719 (412) 846-4100; (412) 761-6600. FAX: (412) 843-7771. Licensee: Baltimore Radio Show Inc. (group owner; acq 5-29-90; $2,910,000; with co-located FM; FTR 6-11-90). Net: ABC TalkRadio, ABC/I; Radio Pa. Format: All news, talk. News staff 2. Target aud: 35 plus. Spec prog: Big Band 4 hrs, Black 2 hrs, relg 6 hrs wkly. ■ Harry Shriver, pres; Jim Harris, gen mgr & gen sls mgr; John Nuzzo, opns mgr; Brandon Davis, prom dir; Carl Anderson, progmg dir; Chris Gaffney, news dir; Harold Sproul, chief engr.

WWKS(FM)—Co-owned with WBVP(AM). May 1960: 106.7 mhz; 47 kw. Ant 520 ft. TL: N40 44 16 W80 17 47 Stereo. Prog sep from AM. Box 719, 1316 7th Ave. (15010); Box 15887, Pittsburgh (15244). (412) 761-6600; (412) 846-4100. FAX: (412) 843-7771. Net: ABC/FM. Format: Adult rock hits. Target aud: 25-49. ■ Jim Harris, stn mgr.

***WGEV(FM)**—Nov 15, 1965: 88.3 mhz; 15 w. Ant 240 ft. TL: N40 46 21 W80 18 33. Hrs opn: 18. Geneva College (15010). (412) 846-5100; (412) 847-6678. FAX: (412) 847-6672. Licensee: Geneva College, Board of Trustees. Net: ABC/E. Format: Christian contemp hit. News progmg 2 hrs wkly. Target aud: 14-24; college plus surrounding community. ■ Pete Croisant, gen mgr; Scott Swietzer, stn mgr; Todd Hughes, chief opns; Scott Ransey, gen sls mgr; Scott Ramsey, prom dir & adv dir; Heather Nutter, progmg dir; Emily Jo Di Mattia, mus dir; Elizabeth Robinson, news dir; Jennifer Smith, pub affrs dir; Mark Schaefer, engrg mgr; John Schaefer, chief engr.

***WITX(FM)**—June 19, 1986: 90.9 mhz; 100 w. Ant 167 ft. TL: N40 47 05 W80 20 36. Box 928, 3700 High St. Extension (15010). (412) 846-8738. Licensee: Beaver Falls Educational Broadcasting Foundation. Format: Relg. ■ Rev. Kenneth Manypenny, pres.

WWKS(FM)—Listing follows WBVP(AM).

Beaver Springs

WWBV(FM)—Feb 21, 1993: 106.1 mhz; 175 w. Ant 1,312 ft. TL: N40 42 04 W77 12 50. Stereo. Hrs opn: 24. R.D. 2, Box 503A, Mifflinburg (17844). (717) 966-0098. FAX: (717) 966-4622. Licensee: Marnu Inc. (acq 3-1-92; $50,000 for CP, with WWBE(FM) Mifflenburg; FTR 3-16-92). Wash atty: Lauren A. Colby. Format: Adult contemp. News staff 2; news progmg 2 hrs wkly. Target aud: 25-54. ■ Pryor Neuber Jr., gen mgr & pub affrs dir; Paul Hartman, gen sls mgr; Lisa Richards, prom dir; Barry Seidel, news dir; William Margut, engrg dir; Roger Allvord, chief engr. ■ Rates: $17.50; 15.25; 17.50; 14.25.

Bedford

WAYC(AM)—Aug 5, 1974: 1310 khz; 2.5 kw-D, 85 w-N. TL: N40 02 37 W78 30 11. Hrs opn: 24. Box 1, 134 E. Pitt St. (15522). (814) 623-1000. FAX: (814) 623-9692. Licensee: Cessna Communications Inc. (acq 3-22-93; $350,000 with WOOX(FM) Bedford; FTR 3-29-93). Net: Unistar, NBC Talknet, NBC, MBS; Radio Pa. Wash atty: Duncan, Weinberg, Miller & Pembroke. Format: News/talk. News staff one. Target aud: 30 plus. Spec prog: Relg 3 hrs wkly. ■ Jay B. Cessna, pres & gen sls mgr; John H. Cessna, vp, gen mgr & progmg dir; Christopher K. Collins, opns mgr; George H. England, sls dir; Keith P. Bagley, news dir; John T. MacAlarney, chief engr. ■ Rates: $8; 8; 8; 8.

WAYC-FM—Aug 15, 1988: 107.5 mhz; 370 w. Ant 1,309 ft. TL: N40 00 46 W78 33 12. Stereo. Rep: Dome. Format: Adult rock 'n roll. Target aud: 18-44. ■ Rates: $8; 8; 8; 8.

WBFD(AM)—July 2, 1955: 1600 khz; 5 kw-D, 28 w-N. TL: N40 00 45 W78 29 54. Hrs opn: 24. Box 672 134 E. Pitt St. (15522). (814) 623-5131. FAX: (814) 623-9692. Licensee: Sherwood B. Hawley. Net: USA. Wash atty: Duncan, Weinberg, Miller & Pembroke. Format: Country gospel, relg. Target aud: 35 plus. Spec prog: Talk 10 hrs wkly. ■ Rosemary Hawley, gen mgr; Paul D. Imgrund, opns mgr & progmg dir; Gina Montgomery, gen sls mgr; John T. MacAlarney, chief engr. ■ Rates: $4; 4; 4; 4.

WOOX(FM)—Dec 22, 1966: 100.9 mhz; 19 kw. Ant 1,279 ft. TL: N40 00 46 W78 33 12. Stereo. Hrs opn: 24. Box 1 (15522); 134 E. Pitt St. 2nd Floor (15522). (814) 623-1000. FAX: (814) 623-9692. Licensee: Cessna Communications Inc. (acq 3-22-93; $350,000 with WAYC[AM] Bedford; FTR 3-29-93). Net: NBC, Unistar. Radio Pa. Rep: Dome. Format: Oldies. Target aud: General; 25-59. ■ Jay B. Cessna, pres; John H. Cessna, vp & gen mgr; Christopher K. Collins, opns mgr; Linda Hoffman, gen sls mgr; Chris Collins, mus dir; John T. McAlarney, chief engr. ■ Rates: $8; 8; 8; 8.

Bellefonte

WBLF(AM)—Aug 1, 1958: 970 khz; 1 kw-D, 61 w-N. TL: N40 54 12 W77 46 06. Box 88 107 N. Allegheny St. (16823). (814) 355-4751. FAX: (814) 355-4752. Licensee: Clark-Richards Broadcasting (acq 4-8-93; $105,000; FTR 4-26-93). Net: SMN. Format: Country. ■ Jay Richards, gen mgr; A.J. O'Donald, news dir; J.G. Daugherty, chief engr.

***WTLR(FM)**—See State College.

WZWW(FM)—Licensed to Bellefonte. See State College.

Bellwood

WALY(FM)—Licensed to Bellwood. See Altoona.

Benton

WDLE(FM)—Oct 4, 1985: 95.9 mhz; 3 kw. Ant 328 ft. TL: N41 10 16 W76 24 37. Box B, 3rd St. (17814). (717) 925-2583. FAX: (717) 779-4888. Licensee: Holt Associates Group Inc. Group owner: The Holt Corporations (acq 5-13-87). Net: SMN. Rep: Banner. Format: Country. Target aud: 25-54. ■ Michelle Metzger, gen mgr; Bernard Fuhrman, gen sls mgr; Nancy Faye, progmg dir; Rob Thomas, chief engr.

Berwick

WKAB(FM)—Feb 14, 1992: 103.5 mhz; 2 kw. Ant 387 ft. TL: N41 05 11 W76 16 41. Third & Pine Sts. (18603). (717) 759-3570. FAX: (717) 759-3438. Licensee: 4M Broadcasting (acq 6-8-92; $350,000; FTR 6-29-92). Net: SMN. Format: Adult contemp, oldies. News staff one; news progmg 2 hrs wkly. Target aud: 25-54; females at work, 18-39 men on weekends. ■ Robert J. Moisey, pres; Janice L. Banko, stn mgr; Joseph Talmon, opns mgr; Joe Talmon, progmg mgr; Joe Anthony, news dir; Robin Thomas, chief engr. ■ Rates: $15; 12; 15; 10.

WSQV(AM)—Aug 1, 1957: 1280 khz; 1 kw-D, 175 w-N. TL: N41 04 36 W76 15 32. 545 W. Front St. (18603). (717) 752-4546. Licensee: Heritage Broadcasting (acq 4-29-91; $160,000; FTR 5-20-91). Format: Oldies. ■ Russ Grebe, progmg dir; Ron Schacht, chief engr.

Bethlehem

WGPA(AM)—Feb 14, 1946: 1100 khz; 250 w-D. TL: N40 37 27 W75 21 19. 528 N. New St. (18018). (215) 866-8074. Licensee: Joseph Timmer dba Timmer Broadcasting Co. (acq 6-19-92; $100,000; FTR 7-13-92). Format: Adult contemp, country, oldies. News staff one; news progmg 3 hrs wkly. Target aud: General. Spec prog: Ger 2 hrs, Pol 2 hrs, polka 5 hrs, Sp one hr wkly. ■ Joe Timmer, pres & gen mgr; Robert Wolken, opns mgr & news dir; Bob Hartel, mktg mgr; Carl Raub, mus dir.

***WLVR(FM)**—May 3, 1973: 91.3 mhz; 185 w. Ant 60 ft. TL: N40 36 22 W75 22 42. Stereo. Hrs opn: 7 AM-4 AM. Lehigh Univ., 29 Trembley Dr. (18015-3066). (215) 758-4187; (215) 758-4161. FAX: (215) 758-6132. Licensee: Lehigh University. Format: Div. News progmg one hr wkly. Target aud: General. Spec prog: Black 12 hrs, class 8 hrs, reggae 6 hrs, jazz 12 hrs hrs wkly. ■ James Carrier, gen mgr; Tom Wolfe, progmg dir; Chris Newmyer, mus dir; Laura Dreger, pub affrs dir; Dave Horoschak, chief engr.

WZZO(FM)—Feb 14, 1946: 95.1 mhz; 30 kw. Ant 631 ft. TL: N40 37 13 W75 17 37. Stereo. Box 9595, Allentown (18105); Suite 400, 1541 Alta Dr., Whitehall (18052). (215) 821-9559. Licensee: CRB Broadcasting of Pennsylvania (acq 7-12-93; $9.375 million; FTR 11-22-93). Rep: Katz. Format: AOR. ■ Arthur H. Holt, pres; Thomas L. Harpster, gen mgr & gen sls mgr; Rob Heckman, prom mgr; Rick Strauss, progmg dir; Todd Heft, mus dir; George Friel, chief engr.

Blairsville

WLCY(FM)—April 15, 1985: 106.3 mhz; 2.4 kw. Ant 363 ft. TL: N40 31 10 W79 13 26. Stereo. Hrs opn: 24. Route 22 at 119 (15717). (412) 459-8888. FAX: (412) 459-8980. Licensee: Longo Media Group Inc. (acq 11-1-89; $485,000; FTR 11-20-89). Net: Jones Satellite Audio. Format: Adult contemp. News staff 2; news progmg 2 hrs wkly. Target aud: 25-54. ■ John Longo, pres; Tony Michaels, stn mgr; Dow Carnahan, opns mgr; J.R. Howard, gen sls mgr; Cheryl Tomaselli, prom dir; Ken Hawk, progmg mgr; Kristen Henigen, pub affrs dir; Dick Ruby, chief engr. ■ Rates: $20; 20; 20; 20.

Bloomsburg

***WBUQ(FM)**—Sept 16, 1986: 91.1 mhz; 1 kw. Ant 500 ft. TL: N41 00 29 W76 26 51. Stereo. Hrs opn: 18. Bloomsburg Univ., 1250 MCHS (17815). (717) 389-4686; (717) 389-BU91. Licensee: Bloomsburg Univ. of Pennsylvania. Format: New music, classic rock, progsv. Target aud: College & area high school students. Spec prog: Metal 15 hrs, talk one hr, jazz 3 hrs wkly. ■ Tom Joseph, pres; Matt Kolara, gen mgr; Tim Martin, prom dir & adv dir; John Elick, mus dir; Deena Eberhart, asst mus dir; John Richardson, news dir; Michael DePietropaolo, pub affrs dir; Jeff Tate, chief engr.

WCNR(AM)—Sept 26, 1947: 930 khz; 1 kw-D, 23 w-N. TL: N41 01 14 W76 25 16. Hrs opn: 18. Box 38, 125 W. Main St. (17815). (717) 784-1200; (717) 784-9300. Licensee: Columbia Montour Broadcasting Co. Inc. (acq 4-30-66). Net: Motor Racing Net. Rep: Dome, Rgnl Reps. Format: Modern country. News staff one; news progmg 15 hrs wkly. Target aud: 25-54. Spec prog: Farm 3 hrs, relg 4 hrs, NASCAR racing 6 hrs, Penn State sports 6 hrs wkly. ■ Joe Darlington, pres, gen mgr & gen sls mgr; Leon Ricci, mus dir; Tracy Green, news dir; Jim Slifer, pub affrs dir; Tom Blackledge, chief engr.

WHLM(FM)—September 1956: 106.5 mhz; 36.5 kw. Ant 570 ft. TL: N40 59 42 W76 29 51. Stereo. Box 260, 107 W. Main St. (17815). (717) 784-5500. FAX: (717) 784-1004. Licensee: Magee Industrial Enterprises Inc. Net: Unistar. Rep: Banner. Format: CHR. News staff 2; news progmg 15 hrs wkly. Target aud: 18-49. Spec prog: Religious 3 hrs wkly. ■ Harry "Mike" Katerman, pres; Robert W. Sweppenheiser, gen mgr; Joe D'Andrea, gen sls mgr; Doug Farley, mus dir; Tim Vincent, news dir; Ted Koppen, chief engr.

WJMW(AM)—Co-owned with WHLM(FM). 1947: 550 khz; 1 kw-U, DA-2. TL: N40 59 38 W76 29 23. Prog sep from FM. Rep: Banner. Format: Country. Target aud: 25-54.

Boalsburg

WVCV(FM)—Not on air, target date unknown: 92.9 mhz; 265 w. Ant 1,102 ft. TL: N40 45 08 W77 45 16. c/o Raul Delerme, 202 Erinway, Unit 203, Reisterstown, MD (21136). (301) 833-3916. Licensee: Boalsburg Broadcasting Co.

Boyertown

WBYN(FM)—Oct 31, 1960: 107.5 mhz; 29.9 kw. Ant 611 ft. TL: N40 24 15 W75 39 09 (CP: 50 kw). Stereo. Hrs opn: 24. 280 Mill Street (19512). (215) 369-7777. FAX: (215) 269-7780. Licensee: WDAC Radio Co. (acq 11-5-91; $3 million; FTR 12-2-91). Net: Moody, USA. Wash atty: Jones, Waldo. Format: Southern/Country Gospel music, teachings & talk. Target aud: Evangelical Christians. ■ Richard Crawford, pres; Paul Hollinger, gen mgr; Joe Hartman, stn mgr; Cindy Fronheiser, prom dir; Wilmer Borneman, chief engr. ■ Rates: $47.36; 47.36; 46.36; 47.36.

Braddock

WCXJ(AM)—June 1947: 1550 khz; 1 kw-D, 4 w-N. TL: N40 24 47 W79 51 13. Hrs opn: 5 AM-midnight. 7138 Kelly St., Pittsburgh (15208). (412) 243-3050. FAX: (412) 243-0644. Licensee: Homewood-Brushton Revitalization & Development Corp. (acq 11-4-91; $112,500; FTR 12-2-91). Net: American Urban. Format: Urban contemporary, relg, talk. News staff one; news progmg 6 hrs wkly. Target aud: 25-54. ■ Lester Cain, chmn; Del King, gen mgr, stn mgr, gen sls mgr, progmg dir & chief engr; Dave Beasley, opns mgr; Helen Hurst, dev dir; Deborah Parker, news dir & pub affrs dir. ■ Rates: $24; 20; 24; 15.

WRRK(FM)—June 1959: 96.9 mhz; 44.7 kw. Ant 530 ft. TL: N40 24 42 W79 55 53. Stereo. Hrs opn: 24. Suite

Pennsylvania

780, 7 Parkway Ctr., Pittsburgh (15220). (412) 922-9290. FAX: (412) 928-9290. Licensee: WHYW Associates. Net: ABC. Rep: Major Mkt. Wash atty: Dow, Lohnes & Albertson. Format: Classic rock. ■ Greg Frischling, gen mgr & stn mgr; Theresa Sullivan, gen sls mgr; Vicki Capocconi, prom dir; Bill Knight, progmg dir & mus dir; Ted Lewcwyzk, chief engr.

Bradford

WESB(AM)—Apr 1947: 1490 khz; 1 kw-U. TL: N41 27 54 W78 37 01. Box 545, 1490 St. Francis Dr. (16701). (814) 368-4141. Licensee: Radio Station WESB Inc. Net: NBC, AP, CBS. Rep: Dome. Wash atty: Baraff, Koerner, Olender & Hochberg. Format: Adult contemp. News staff 2. Target aud: 35 plus. ■ T.R. Bromeley, pres; Donald J. Fredeen, vp & gen mgr; Peggy Austin, sls dir; Frank Williams, progmg dir & mus dir; Lori Maze, news dir.

WBRR(FM)—Co-owned with WESB(AM). Dec 1, 1987: 100.1 mhz; 970 w. Ant 535 ft. TL: N41 58 12 W78 42 03. Stereo. Prog sep from AM. Acq 10-87; $21,000; FTR 10-12-87. Net: SMN. Format: Oldies. Target aud: 25-54.

Brockway

WVCQ(AM)—Not on air, target date unknown: 800 khz; 500 w-U, DA-2. TL: N41 15 32 W78 47 47. 611 W. Cliveden St., Philadelphia (19119). Licensee: Tri-County Broadcasters.

Brookville

WMKX(FM)—Aug 22, 1981: 95.9 mhz; 2 kw. Ant 418 ft. TL: N41 07 21 W79 03 51. Stereo. Hrs opn: 24. 51 Pickering St. (15825). (814) 849-8100. FAX: (814) 849-4585. Licensee: Strattan Broadcasting Inc. (acq 2-84; $170,000; FTR 2-27-84). Rep: Commercial. Wash atty: Robert L. Olender. Format: Adult contemp. News staff one; news progmg 5 hrs wkly. Target aud: General; 25-54. Spec prog: Jazz 3 hrs, rock classics 6 hrs, oldies 8 hrs wkly. ■ James W. Farley, pres & gen mgr; Diana Farley, gen sls mgr; Robin Commons, progmg dir & news dir; Joseph D. Powers, chief engr. ■ Rates: $11; 11; 11; 11.

Brownsville

WASP(AM)—Aug 3, 1968: 1130 khz; 5 kw-D, DA. TL: N40 02 33 W79 54 20. Box 270 (15417); Blaine Rd., off Rt. 88, California (15419). (412) 785-3450. FAX: (412) 938-7824. Licensee: The Humes Broadcasting Corp. (acq 5-1-84; FTR 3-26-84). Net: AP, USA. Rep: Commercial. Format: News/talk. News staff one. Target aud: Adults 35-64. ■ James J. Humes, pres & gen mgr; Kim Smith, opns mgr & news dir; Salvatore V. Glorioso, sls dir, mktg dir & prom mgr; Jim Schlosser, progmg dir & mus dir; Lee Crowthers, chief engr. ■ Rates: $12; 10; 12; na.

Burnham

WVNW(FM)—Not on air, target date unknown: 96.7 mhz; 450 w. Ant 850 ft. TL: N40 35 10 W77 41 40. Box 1244, Lewiston (17044). Licensee: Pauline S. Hain.

Butler

WBUT(AM)—March 14, 1949: 1050 khz; 500 w-D, 65 w-N. TL: N40 53 51 W79 53 22. Box 1645, 1768 No. Main St., Ext. (16001). (412) 287-5778. FAX: (412) 282-9188. Licensee: WBUT Inc. (acq 7-14-78). Net: MBS. Rep: Dome. Format: Adult contemp. ■ Robert C. Brandon, pres & gen mgr; Robert A. Cupp, progmg dir; Shirley A. Minehart, Robert A. Cupp, mus dirs; Cathy Martin, news dir; R.C. Brandon, chief engr.

WLER-FM—Co-owned with WBUT(AM). Mar 14, 1949: 97.7 mhz; 2.3 kw. Ant 374 ft. TL: N40 53 51 W79 53 22. Stereo. Prog sep from AM. Net: Westwood One.

WISR(AM)—Sept 26, 1941: 680 khz; 250 w-D. TL: N40 52 39 W79 54 09. Box 151, 357 N. Main St. (16003-0151). (412) 283-1500. FAX: (412) 283-3015. Licensee: Butler Broadcasting Inc. Net: AP. Rep: Keystone (unwired net), Commercial. Format: Adult contemp, news/talk. Target aud: 25-54. Spec prog: Farm 10 hrs, jazz 3 hrs, country one hr wkly. ■ Joel W. Rosenblum, pres & gen mgr; David Wood, gen sls mgr; Dave Malarkey, mus dir & news dir; John Hook, chief engr. ■ Rates: $10; 10; 10; na.

WLER-FM—Listing follows WBUT(AM).

California

*****WVCS(FM)**—September 1973: 91.9 mhz; 3 kw. Ant 160 ft. TL: N40 02 57 W79 54 01. Stereo. Hrs opn: 24. California Univ. of PA, 428 Hickory St. (15419). (412) 938-4330; (412) 938-4105. FAX: (412) 938-5959. Licensee: Student Activities Association Inc. (acq 6-3-78). Net: Westwood One, AP. Format: Top 40. News progmg 5 hrs wkly. Target aud: 18-25; students at California Univ. Spec prog: Contemp Christian 6 hrs, urban contemp 12 hrs, rap 4 hrs, alternative 6 hrs, metal 5 hrs wkly. ■ Bob Cross, stn mgr; Tom Grimm, opns mgr & chief engr; Ryan Fedor, gen sls mgr; Bob Greer, prom dir; Casey McCerey, progmg dir; Chris Ostien, mus dir; Rick Cumings, news dir.

LAUREN A. COLBY
301-663-1086
COMMUNICATIONS ATTORNEY
Special Attention to Difficult Cases

Canonsburg

WWCS(AM)—Nov 28, 1957: 540 khz; 7.5 kw-D, 500 w-N, DA-2. TL: N40 17 22 W80 11 07 (CP: 5 kw-D, 500 w-N, DA-2). Hrs opn: 24. Box WWCS, Pittsburgh (15241). (412) 531-9927. FAX: (412) 531-8800. Licensee: Birach Broadcasting Corp. (acq 6-28-92; $475,000; FTR 6-22-92). Net: CBN. Format: International music, BBC news. ■ Sima Birach Sr., gen mgr; Jay Reynolds, stn mgr; Ian McGrath, pub affrs dir; Sima Birach, chief engr.

Canton

WHGL(AM)—See Troy.

WHGL-FM—Aug 30, 1978: 100.3 mhz; 3.9 kw. Ant 846 ft. TL: N41 44 32 W76 50 08. Stereo. Hrs opn: 24. Box 100, 170 Redington Ave., Troy (16947). (717) 297-0100. Licensee: Cantroair Communications (acq 7-1-88; grpsl; FTR 6-22-87). Net: ABC/C. Format: Country. News staff one. Target aud: 25-54. ■ David Bernstein, pres; Mike Powers, vp, gen mgr, vp progmg & progmg dir; Bob Gisler, gen sls mgr; Georgia Pepper, prom mgr; Kenny Lane, mus dir; Jay Curtis, news dir; Rob Thomas, chief engr.

Carbondale

WCDL(AM)—January 1950: 1440 khz; 5 kw-D. TL: N41 33 28 W75 29 11. 43 Seventh Ave. (18407). (717) 282-2770. FAX: (717) 876-1561. Licensee: S&P Broadcasting Ltd. III. Group owner: S&P Broadcasting Co. (acq 7-17-90; $1,750,000 with co-located FM; FTR 8-6-90). Rep: Eastman. Format: MOR, big band. News progmg 4 hrs wkly. Target aud: 45 plus; local residents. Spec prog: Local sports 8 hrs, Pol 8 hrs, It 3 hrs, Slavic 2 hrs, relg 3 hrs wkly. ■ Ron Swanson, CEO & pres; Bob Van Derheyden, vp & gen mgr; Jim Brando, progmg dir & news dir; Dave Swartz, chief engr. ■ Rates: $20; 15; 20; na.

WSGD-FM—Co-owned with WCDL(AM). 1965: 94.3 mhz; 1.1 kw. Ant 770 ft. TL: N41 32 37 W75 27 44. Stereo. Hrs opn: 24. Prog sep from AM. 1 Montage Rd, Moosic (18507). (717) 341-9494. FAX: (717) 344-3661. Format: Oldies. News staff one; news progmg 4 hrs wkly. Target aud: 35-64. Spec prog: Community affairs. ■ Erika Allen, news dir. ■ Rates: $45; 35; 45; 25.

Carlisle

*****WDCV-FM**—Jan 1972: 88.3 mhz; 450 w. Ant 150 ft. TL: N40 12 09 W77 11 46. Stereo. Hrs opn: 7 AM-2 AM. HUB 640, Box 4888, Dickinson College (17013-0928). (717) 245-1444; Licensee: Board of Trustees, Dickinson College. Format: Div. News staff 5; news progmg 9 hrs wkly. Spec prog: Jazz 6 hrs, Ger one hr, Sp one hr, funk/rap 15 hrs, Russian one hr, politics one hr, blues 6 hrs wkly. ■ Jeffrey Foster, Jay Gordon, gen mgrs; Matt Diorio, Rees Hunt, prom dirs; Chris Diorio, progmg dir; Johanna Lipschur, news dir.

WHYL(AM)—1948: 960 khz; 5 kw-D, DA. TL: N40 11 34 W77 10 28. Box WHYL, 1703 Walnut Bottom Rd. (17013). (717) 249-1717. FAX: (717) 258-4638. Licensee: Zeve Broadcasting Co. (acq 3-17-89; grpsl; FTR 3-20-89). Net: CNN. Rep: D & R Radio Format: Country. News staff one. Target aud: 55 plus; older, mature adults. Spec prog: Polka 2 hrs wkly. ■ Lincoln Zeve, pres & gen mgr; Glenn Stoner, progmg dir; Curt Cleland, chief engr.

WHYL-FM—1959: 102.3 mhz; 3 kw. Ant 328 ft. TL: N40 17 23 W77 08 10. Stereo. Hrs opn: 24. Dups AM 100%. Target aud: 25-54. ■ Lee Adams, opns mgr & prom mgr.

WIOO(AM)—July 8, 1965: 1000 khz; 1 kw-D. TL: N40 09 30 W77 11 49. Hrs opn: Sunrise-sunset. 180 York Rd. (17013). (717) 243-1200. Licensee: Harold Swidler. Net: ABC/I; Radio Pa. Format: Adult contemp. News staff 2; news progmg 15 hrs wkly. Target aud: 21 plus. Spec prog: Relg 5 hrs wkly. ■ Harold Swidler, pres, gen mgr & gen sls mgr; Ben Barber, prom mgr, progmg dir & mus dir; David Payne, news dir, Charles Bean, chief engr.

Carnegie

WPLW(AM)—July 1962: 1590 khz; 1 kw-D, DA. TL: N40 25 40 W80 05 09 (CP: 5 kw-D). Hrs opn: 6 AM-sunset. 201 Ewing Ave., Pittsburgh (15205). (412) 922-0550. FAX: (412) 922-0553. Licensee: Hickling Broadcasting Corp. (acq 10-75). Wash atty: Baraff, Koerner, Olender & Hochberg. Format: Christian contemp, gospel. Target aud: General. Spec prog: Pol 2 hrs, other ethnic 2 hrs wkly. ■ Robert Hickling, pres, gen mgr & gen sls mgr; Dolores Hickling, progmg dir & mus dir; Ed Zawatski, engrg dir. ■ Rates: $26; 26; 26; na.

Cashtown

WFKJ(AM)—Dec 17, 1988: 890 khz; 1 kw-D. TL: N39 52 59 W77 20 43. Box 115 (17310); 3425 Chambersburg Rd., Biglerville (17307). (717) 334-8911. FAX: (717) 334-8914. Licensee: Jesus is Lord Ministries. Net: USA, CBN, Moody. Format: Relg. News staff 2; news progmg 10 hrs wkly. Target aud: General. Spec prog: Black 2 hrs, country 8 hrs, children 14 hrs wkly. ■ Michael H. Yeager, pres; Rev. Michael H. Yeager, gen mgr; Fred Bream, stn mgr; Kenneth Martin, gen sls mgr & progmg dir; Donna Martin, mus dir & news dir. ■ Rates: $6; 6; 6; 6.

Central City

WYSN(FM)—Oct 19, 1972: 101.7 mhz; 725 w. Ant 643 ft. TL: N40 06 42 W78 51 33. Stereo. Hrs opn: 24. R.D. 1, Box 1330, Cannel Dr., Somerset (15501). (814) 467-8669. Licensee: Norlin Broadcasters Inc. (acq 5-14-88). Net: CNN, Unistar. Wash atty: Booth, Freret & Imlay. Format: MOR. News staff 4. Target aud: 35-64. Spec prog: Relg 5 hrs wkly. ■ Ronald W. Lorence, pres, gen mgr & chief engr; Norma J. Lorence, gen sls mgr; Brad J. Lorence, prom mgr & progmg dir.

Chambersburg

WCBG(AM)—1956: 1590 khz; 5 kw-D, 1 kw-N, DA-N. TL: N39 54 15 W77 37 39 45. Hrs opn: 24. Box 92, Mercersburg (17236); 8737 Kuhn Bridge Rd., Greencastle (17225). (717) 267-1590. FAX: (717) 597-9210. Licensee: M. Belmont VerStandig Inc. Group owner: VerStandig Broadcasting (acq 1993; $1.6 million with WGLL[FM] Mercersburg; FTR 9-6-93). Net: ABC/D. Rep: Dome. Wash atty: Haley, Bader & Potts. Format: Superstars of today and yesterday, sports. News staff one. Target aud: 25-54; dual paycheck. Spec prog: Classic rock 6 hrs wkly. ■ John Verstanding, pres; Marge Martin, exec vp & gen mgr; Brad Christman, progmg dir & news dir.

WCHA(AM)—Aug 11, 1946: 800 khz; 1 kw-D, 196 w-N. TL: N39 55 41 W77 41 44. Stereo. Box 479 (17201). (717) 264-7121. FAX: (717) 263-9649. Licensee: Chambersburg Broadcasting Co. Net: ABC/E. Format: Country. News staff one; news progmg 10 hrs wkly. Target aud: 25-54. ■ John S. Booth, chmn; Margaret Booth Ehle, pres; Matt Kellam, gen mgr; Rich Bateman, gen sls mgr; Rick Alexander, progmg dir; Lisa Kline, news dir; Jeff Baker, Stan Shaeffer, chiefs engr.

WIKZ(FM)—Co-owned with WCHA(AM). Apr 15, 1948: 95.1 mhz; 50 kw-H, 42 kw-V. Ant 449 ft. TL: N39 55 41 W77 41 44. Stereo. Prog sep from AM. Wash atty: Borsari & Paxson. Format: Adult contemp. Target aud: 25-44. ■ Donna Rosenberry, natl sls mgr; Lisa Harding, prom mgr; Rick Alexander, mus dir.

Charleroi

WESA(AM)—1947: 940 khz; 250 w-D, 5 w-N, U. TL: N40 07 24 W79 53 45. Hrs opn: 24. 10 Chamber Plaza (15022). (412) 483-6551; (412) 391-7902. FAX: (412) 483-9251. Licensee: Farr Communications (acq 5-15-85; grpsl; FTR 3-25-85). Net: ABC/C. Rep: Commercial Media Sls. Format: Adult contemp, talk. News staff 2; news progmg 4 hrs wkly. Target aud: general; Mon Valley area. Spec prog: Croation one hr, Polish 2 hrs wkly. ■ Rita R. Resick, pres; David L. Waugaman, stn mgr; Ted Mathews, progmg dir; Cliff Gorski, news dir; Cliff Ewing, chief engr. ■ Rates: $15; 10; 10; 8.

WESA-FM—July 10, 1967: 98.3 mhz; 6 kw. Ant 300 ft. TL: N40 07 24 W79 53 45. Stereo. Hrs opn: 24. Dups AM 100%. ■ Rates: $21; 21; 21; 15,

Chester

WCZN(AM)—October 1947: 1590 khz; 3.2 kw-D, 1 kw-N, DA-N. TL: N39 52 39 W75 27 22. Stereo. Hrs opn: 24. 12 Kent Rd., Aston (19014); Box 1590, Chester Heights (19017). (215) 358-1400. FAX: (215) 358-1845. Licensee: Lloyd B. Roach Inc. (acq 11-12-85; $600,000). Net: CNN. Wash atty: Hopkins, Sutter, Hamel & Park. Format: Adult standard. Target aud: 25-64; blue collar and middle management. Spec prog: Black 4 hrs, gospel 4 hrs wkly. ■ Lloyd B. Roach, CEO; John Rafal, gen mgr; Jon Rafal, vp opns; Al Edmundson, pub affrs dir; Larry H. Will, vp engrg. ■ Rates: $30; 30; 40; 25.

*WDNR(FM)—Apr 22, 1977: 89.5 mhz; 10 w. Ant 117 ft. TL: N39 51 42 W75 21 20. Stereo. Hrs opn: 20. Box 1000, Widener Univ., One University Place (19013). (215) 499-4439. FAX: (215) 876-9751. Licensee: Widener Univ. Format: Div, Black, progsv. Target aud: 16-30; high school & college age population. Spec prog: Jazz 2 hrs, blues 2 hrs, oldies 2 hrs wkly. ■ Frederica Rodner, gen mgr; Tom Runtagh, opns dir; John Dymoski, gen sls mgr; prom dir, progmg dir & mus dir; Ken Smith, chief engr.

WVCH(AM)—Apr 4, 1948: 740 khz; 1 kw-D. TL: N39 52 38 W75 24 24 (CP: 50 kw-D, 450 w-N, DA-1). Box 102, Springhouse (19477). (215) 279-9000. FAX: (215) 279-9002. Licensee: WVCH Communications Inc. (acq 10-74). Net: Moody, USA. Wash atty: Wiley, Rein & Fielding. Format: Relg. Target aud: General. ■ Thomas H. Moffit, pres & gen sls mgr; Ted Boyda, opns dir & news dir; Warren Racine, chief engr.

Clarendon

WOVU(FM)—Not on air, target date unknown: 106.9 mhz; 4.7 kw. Ant 371 ft. Box 247, Tyrone (16686). Licensee: Cary H. and Betty F. Simpson (group owner).

Clarion

WCCR(FM)—Listing follows WWCH(AM).

*WCUC-FM—April 1977: 91.7 mhz; 2.3 kw. Ant 323 ft. TL: N41 12 33 W79 22 43. Stereo. G55 Becker Hall, Clarion Univ. of Pa. (16214). (814) 226-2330. Licensee: Clarion Univ. of Pa. (acq 6-76). Net: MBS. Format: Variety. Spec prog: Black 6 hrs, country 6 hrs, jazz 3 hrs, new wave 9 hrs wkly. ■ Henry L. Fueg, gen mgr; Paul Levy, progmg dir; Milburn Cooper, chief engr.

WWCH(AM)—June 12, 1960: 1300 khz; 1 kw-D. TL: N41 10 34 W79 20 22. Box 688, 725 Wood St. (16214). (814) 226-8600; (814) 226-4500. FAX: (814) 226-5898. Licensee: Clarion County Broadcasting Corp. Net: USA. Rep: Dome. Wash atty: Frederick Polner. Format: C&W. News staff one; news progmg 10 hrs wkly. Target aud: General. Spec prog: Relg 8 hrs wkly. ■ William S. Hearst, pres, gen mgr, gen sls mgr & prom mgr; Ron Smith, opns mgr; Wayne Brosios, progmg dir & mus dir; Frank Stacey, news dir; Michael Kunkle, pub affrs dir; Scott Mathewson, chief engr.

WCCR(FM)—Co-owned with WWCH(AM). June 28, 1985: 92.7 mhz; 3 kw. Ant 400 ft. TL: N41 14 41 W79 15 42. Stereo. Hrs opn: 6 AM-1 AM. Prog sep from AM. Format: Classic rock. News progmg 8 hrs wkly. Target aud: 25-54. ■ William Hearst, progmg dir; Ron Smith, mus dir.

Clearfield

WCPA(AM)—1947: 900 khz; 2.5 kw-D, 500 w-N, DA-2. TL: N41 02 32 W78 26 54. 110 Healy Ave. (16830). (814) 765-5541. FAX: (814) 765-6333. Licensee: Clearfield Broadcasters Inc. Net: ABC/I. Rep: Dome. Format: News/talk, sports. Target aud: General. ■ Carl A. Falvo, pres; Bob Day, progmg dir; Meg Stevens, news dir; Thomas Wonderling, chief engr.

WQYX(FM)—Co-owned with WCPA(AM). July 12, 1967: 93.5 mhz; 3 kw. Ant 98 ft. TL: N41 02 32 W78 26 54. Stereo. Prog sep from AM. Format: Hot adult contemp. ■ Scott Powell, progmg dir & mus dir.

Coatesville

WCOJ(AM)—Nov 29, 1949: 1420 khz; 5 kw-U, DA-N. TL: N40 01 21 W75 48 53. Hrs opn: 5 AM-midnight. Box 1408 (19320). (215) 384-2100. FAX: (215) 384-3804. Licensee: Liberty Cable Inc. (acq 3-16-92; FTR 4-6-92). Net: CNN. Format: Adult contemp, news/talk. News staff 2; news progmg 14 hrs wkly. Target aud: 25-55. Spec prog: Relg 8 hrs wkly. ■ H. Fitzgerald Lenfest, pres; Dave Heffline, exec vp; Art Douglas, gen mgr, stn mgr, opns mgr & progmg dir; George Hall, gen sls mgr; Bill Gillan, mus dir; Kevin Woodward, news dir; Margie McCue, pub affrs dir; Ralph Spence, chief engr.

Columbia

WNZT(AM)—May 10, 1984: 1580 khz; 500 w-D, 15 w-N. TL: N40 00 53 W76 28 13. Box 270 (17512). (717) 684-4804. FAX: (717) 299-0064. Licensee: The Hadley Media Corp. (acq 6-20-85; $80,900; FTR 5-6-85). Net: ABC TalkRadio, Daynet, USA. Format: News/talk. News progmg 20 hrs wkly. Target aud: 35 plus; professional head of household & family. Spec prog: Sports 4 hrs wkly. ■ Theodore R. Byrne, pres, gen mgr & gen sls mgr; Larry Kay, news dir & chief engr. ■ Rates: $20; 20; 20; na.

Connellsville

WCVI(AM)—Apr 23, 1947: 1340 khz; 1 kw-U. TL: N40 01 27 W79 36 35. Hrs opn: 24. 133 E. Crawford Ave. (15425). (412) 628-4600. FAX: (412) 628-5188. Licensee: Mar Com Broadcasting Inc. (acq 8-29-85; $500,000; FTR 7-15-85). Net: ABC/E. Dome. Format: Adult contemp. Target aud: 25-64. ■ Geoffrey Kelly, pres & gen mgr; Norman Jones, news dir; Chuck Leavens, chief engr.

Corry

WWCB(AM)—Apr 2, 1955: 1370 khz; 1 kw-D, 500 w-N, DA-N. TL: N41 56 10 W79 39 20. Box 4 (16407). (814) 664-8694. FAX: (814) 664-2168. Licensee: Corry Communications Corp. (acq 1-22-89; $140,000; FTR 1-15-90). Net: Unistar, Motor Racing Net. Format: Div. Target aud: General. Spec prog: Country 10 hrs wkly. ■ William Hammond III, pres; Ron Smith, gen sls mgr; Hal Martin, prom mgr; Bruce Lewis, progmg dir & news dir; Bruce Hullihen, chief engr. ■ Rates: $9.50; 9.50; 9.50; 9.50.

Coudersport

WFRM(AM)—May 1953: 600 khz; 1 kw-D, 46 w-N. TL: N41 45 11 W78 00 03. Box 309, S. Main St. (16915). (814) 274-8600; (814) 642-9396. FAX: (814) 274-0760. Licensee: Farm & Home Broadcasting Co. Group owner: Allegheny Mountain Network Stns. Net: MBS, SMN. Rep: Dome. Wash atty: Borsari & Paxson. Format: MOR. News staff 4; news progmg 16 hrs wkly. Target aud: General. Spec prog: Farm 2 hrs wkly. ■ Cary H. Simpson, pres; John Salter, gen mgr, adv mgr, progmg mgr & mus dir; Gerri Miller, opns mgr & news dir; Robert H. Lynn, chief engr. ■ Rates: $12; 8; 12; 6.

WFRM-FM—Sept 18, 1985: 96.7 mhz; 1.45 kw. Ant 666 ft. TL: N41 45 11 W78 00 03. Stereo. Hrs opn: 24 Prog sep from AM. Net: SMN. Format: Adult rock. News progmg 9 hrs wkly. ■ John Salter, gen sls mgr. ■ Rates: Same as AM.

Covington

WDKC(FM)—Not on air, target date unknown: 101.5 mhz; 1.45 kw. TL: N41 37 15 W77 08 13. RD 1, Box 460, Cogan Station (17728). Licensee: Kennedy Broadcasting Inc. ■ John A. Kennedy Jr., gen mgr.

Cresson

WBXQ(FM)—November 1981: 94.3 mhz; 350 w. Ant 958 ft. TL: N40 27 55 W78 31 17. Hrs opn: 24. 4000 Fifth Ave., Altoona (16602). (814) 886-7777; (814) 944-9420. FAX: (814) 944-9350. Licensee: Sounds Good Inc. Net: ABC/FM. Rep: Banner. Format: Album rock. News staff one; News progmg 7 hrs wkly. Target aud: 18-54; males. ■ Ed Sherlock, CEO, pres, stn mgr & sls mgr; Mike Thomas, opns mgr, prom mgr, progmg dir & mus dir; Jay Randall, asst mus dir; Anglea DeLuca, pub affrs dir; Clyde May, engrg dir. ■ Rates: 20; 20; 20; 20.

Curwensville

WOKW(FM)—Aug 1, 1989: 102.9 mhz; 350 w. Ant 959 ft. TL: N41 04 29 W78 31 58. Stereo. Hrs opn: 24. Box 589, R.R. Old Town Rd., Clearfield (16830). (814) 765-4955. FAX: (814) 765-7038. Licensee: Raymark Broadcasting Co. Inc. Net: SMN. Wash atty: Steptoe & Johnson. Format: Adult contemp. News staff one; news progmg 14 hrs wkly. Target aud: 21-54. Spec prog: Oldies 2 hrs wkly. ■ Mark E. Harley, pres & gen mgr; Yvonne Lehman, exec vp & sls mgr; Dennis Wood, progmg dir; Dan Litten, news dir; Fred Shetler, chief engr. ■ Rates: $11; 11; 11; 11.

Dallas

WDLS(FM)—May 29, 1989: 93.7 mhz; 750 w. Ant 679 ft. TL: N41 15 43 W75 58 04 (CP: 1.45 kw). Stereo. Box U (18612); 1895 W. Mountain Rd. Plymouth (18651-4336). (717) 779-3399; (717) 822-3911. FAX: (717) 779-4888. Licensee: Mountain Broadcasting. Net: Westwood One, Interstate; Agri-Net. Rep: D & R Radio. Wash atty: Bechtel & Cole. Format: Country. News staff one; news progmg 6 hrs wkly. Target aud: General. Spec prog: Farm 3 hrs wkly. ■ Ronald Schacht, pres & chief engr; Mike McCormack, gen mgr & sls dir; Carl Krupa, opns dir & prom mgr; Nancy Faye, mus dir; Jim Gannon, pub affrs dir.

Danville

*WPGM(AM)—June 1963: 1570 khz; 2.5 kw-D. TL: N40 59 10 W76 37 37. 8 E. Market St. (17821). (717) 275-1570. FAX: (717) 275-4071. Licensee: Montrose Broadcasting Corp. (group owner; acq 1-6-64). Net: AP. Format: Relg, btfl mus. News staff one. Target aud: General; families. ■ Lawrence H. Souder, pres; Bradley T. Miller, chief engr.

*WPGM-FM—Sept 6, 1968: 96.7 mhz; 340 w. Ant 760 ft. TL: N40 59 16 W76 32 51. Stereo. Dups AM 75%.

Doylestown

WBUX(AM)—1948: 1570 khz; 5 kw-D, 500 w-N, DA-2. TL: N40 19 34 W75 09 40 (CP: 950 w-N). Hrs opn: 24. Box 2187, Ricketts Rd. (18901). (215) 345-1570. FAX: (215) 348-1936. Licensee: Network Broadcasting Corp. (acq 3-14-91; $1 million; FTR 4-1-91). Format: Hits of the 70s. News progmg 14 hrs wkly. Target aud: 25-54; mature, middle to upper income. ■ Joseph Wesley, CEO; Mike Deardorff, gen mgr; Kevin Moore, progmg dir; Ron Simpson, chief engr. ■ Rates: $42; 42; 42; 32.

DuBois

WCED(AM)—February 1941: 1420 khz; 5 kw-D, 500 w-N, DA-N. TL: N41 08 31 W78 48 07. Box 1087, 80 N. Park Pl. (15801). (814) 371-6100; (814) 371-8300. FAX: (814) 371-7724. Licensee: Tri-County Broadcasting Co. (acq 11-20-88; grpsl; FTR 1-9-89). Net: ABC/I; Radio Pa. Rep: Dome. Wash atty: Baraff, Kogrner, Olender & Hochberg. Format: Oldies. News staff 2; news progmg 20 hrs wkly. Target aud: 25 plus. ■ E. Michael Boyle, pres; Michael Felice, gen mgr; Dave Anthony, stn mgr; Gary Stormer, gen sls mgr, prom mgr & mus dir; Tom Rogers, news dir; Gene Williams, chief engr. ■ Rates: $12; 10; 10; 10.

WOWQ(FM)—Co-owned with WCED(AM). 1948: 102.1 mhz; 28.2 kw. Ant 664 ft. TL: N41 02 43 W78 42 11. Stereo. Hrs opn: 24. Prog sep from AM. Format: Country. News staff 2; news progmg 10 hrs wkly. Target aud: 18 plus. Spec prog: Polish 3 hrs wkly. ■ Rates: $18; 14; 14; 14.

WDBA(FM)—Nov 12, 1975: 107.3 mhz; 50 kw. Ant 499 ft. TL: N41 11 28 W78 41 27. Stereo. Hrs opn: 24. 28 W. Scribner Ave. (15801). (814) 371-1330. FAX: (814) 375-5650. Licensee: Dan, Debbie, Charles and Joyce Brownlee (acq 10-6-93; $360,000; FTR 10-25-93). Net: USA, Skylight. Wash atty: Reddy, Begley & Martin. Format: Inspirational. News progmg 6 hrs wkly. Target aud: 25-65; family oriented adults with desire to make a difference. Spec prog: Class one hr, children 2 hrs wkly. ■ Daniel Brownlee, pres; Daniel Brownlee, Dan Kennard (asst.), gen mgrs; Gerald Meloon, stn mgr & chief engr; Dan Kennard, mus dir & news dir; Mark Flanagan, asst mus dir. ■ Rates: $11; 8; 9; 6.

WOWQ(FM)—Listing follows WCED(AM).

East Stroudsburg

*WESS(FM)—March 10, 1971: 90.3 mhz; 1.37 kw. Ant -165 ft. TL: N40 59 55 W75 10 21. Stereo. McGarry Communications Ctr., East Stroudsburg University (18301). (717) 424-3134; (717) 424-3512. FAX: (717) 424-3777. Licensee: East Stroudsburg Univ., Board of Trustees/Student Activities (acq 3-79). Format: Div, alt. Spec prog: Black 3 hrs, class 4 hrs, jazz 6 hrs, folk 3 hrs wkly. ■ Rob McKenzie, pres; Griff Lewis, chief engr.

Easton

WEST(AM)—Feb 17, 1936: 1400 khz; 1 kw-U. TL: N40 40 23 W75 12 30. Stereo. Hrs opn: 24. Box 81, 436 Northampton St. (18042). (215) 250-9600. Licensee: TMZ Broadcasting Co. (group owner; acq 2-13-89; grpsl; FTR 2-27-89). Net: NBC, SMN. Rep: McGavren Guild. Wash atty: Fleishman & Walsh. Format: MOR. News staff 2; news progmg 20 hrs wkly. Target aud: General. ■ Ira Rosenblatt, vp & vp opns; Paige Lamers, pres; Brian Nagy, gen sls mgr; Susan Ferguson, prom mgr; Tony Rogers, progmg dir; Mike Moore, news dir; Bob Kratz, chief engr.

WLEV(FM)—Co-owned with WEST(AM). 1948: 96.1 mhz; 50 kw. Ant 500 ft. TL: N40 35 55 W75 25 12. Stereo. Hrs opn: 24. Prog sep from AM. Box 25096, Lehigh Valley (18002-5096). Format: Adult contemp.

WIPI(AM)—May 1956: 1230 khz; 1 kw-U, DA-2. TL: N40 42 30 W75 13 00. Box 190, 107 W. Paxinosa Rd. W. (18044-0190). (215) 258-6155. FAX: (215) 253-3384. Licensee: Cape Media Inc. Group owner: Roth Communications. Rep: Torbet. Format: Oldies (50's, 60's & 70's). ■ Mike Marder, gen mgr; Jeff Frank, gen sls mgr; Jamie Sommers, prom mgr; Karl Baker, news dir; George Mottor, chief engr.

WODE-FM—Co-owned with WIPI(AM). June 1950: 99.9 mhz; 50 kw. Ant 449 ft. TL: N40 42 30 W75 13 00. Stereo. Prog sep from AM. Format: Top-40. ■ Joey Mitchel, progmg dir & mus dir.

***WJRH(FM)**—March 1953: 104.9 mhz; 10 w. Ant 23 ft. TL: N40 41 53 W75 12 30. Stereo. Hrs opn: 15. Box 9473, Farinon Ctr., Lafayette College (18042). (215) 250-5316; (215) 250-5318. FAX: (215) 250-5318. Licensee: Lafayette College. Net: AP. Format: Progsv, class rock. News staff one; news progmg 40 hrs wkly. Target aud: General; college students. Spec prog: Jazz 9 hrs, reggae 6 hrs, metal 6 hrs, Sp 6 hrs wkly. ■ Ralph Davis, opns mgr; Ray Gilbert, gen sls mgr; Brian Berkey, prom dir; D.C. Jackson, progmg dir; Tom Volpe, Becca Wall, Kim VanCleave, mus dirs; Annette Costigan, news dir; Nils Steffensen, chief engr.

WLEV(FM)—Listing follows WEST(AM).

WODE-FM—Listing follows WIPI(AM).

Ebensburg

WJRV(AM)—See Loretto.

WQKK(FM)—July 15, 1962: 99.1 mhz; 50 kw. Ant 500 ft. TL: N40 24 41 W78 46 29 (CP: 24 kw, ant 713 ft.). Stereo. 160 Clearview Ave., State College (16803). (814) 238-5085. Licensee: Tele-Media Broadcasting of Johnstown-Altoona. Group owner: TMZ Broadcasting Co. (acq 4-20-93; $450,000; FTR 5-10-93). Net: SMN. Rep: Dome. Format: Oldies. ■ Robert Schmidt, gen mgr; Helen L. Walker, stn mgr; John T. Walko, news dir; Robert Lynn, chief engr.

WRDD(AM)—May 25, 1961: 1580 khz; 1 kw-D. TL: N40 29 33 W78 42 54. Stereo. Hrs opn: Sunrise-sunset. Suite 627, 616 Main St., Johnstown (15901). (814) 536-9270. FAX: (814) 536-5855. Licensee: Eagle Broadcasting Group (acq 11-89; $35,000). Net: USA. Format: MOR, relg, talk. News progmg 4 hrs wkly. Target aud: General; church goers. ■ J. Richard Lee, pres; Jane Allison Lee, gen mgr; Bob Folckemer, gen sls mgr; Clyde May, chief engr. ■ Rates: $3.25; 3.25; 3.25; 3.25.

Edinboro

***WFSE(FM)**—April 3, 1979: 88.9 mhz; 3 kw. Ant 312 ft. TL: N41 52 41 W80 10 40. Stereo. Hrs opn: 24. 104 Compton Hall, Edinboro U. of Pa. (16444). (814) 732-2526; (814) 732-2889. FAX: (814) 732-2427. Licensee: Edinboro University. Net: AP. Format: Alternative/modern rock. News progmg 18 hrs wkly. Target aud: 18-25; college students with community interest. Spec prog: Sports (football/basketball), black 15 hrs, relg 4 hrs, loc news 3 hrs, swing 2 hrs wkly. ■ Foster F. Diebold, CEO; Anthony Peyronell, chmn; James Driscoll, Robert Gibson, Robert Radencic, gen mgrs; Doug Fumo, James Steinhoff, prom mgrs; Karen Idzik, progmg dir; Willie Coleman, Mike Drahuschak, mus dirs; Robert Radencic, asst mus dir; Angelique Vallot, news dir; Ric Pogson, chief engr.

WXTA(FM)—Oct 15, 1988: 97.9 mhz; 10 kw. Ant 505 ft. TL: N41 57 59 W80 40 10. Stereo. Hrs opn: 24. 4910 Richmond St., Erie (16509). (814) 864-4835. FAX: (814) 864-4837. Licensee: Win Capp Broadcasting Inc. (acq 8-16-89 $900,000). Net: Unistar. Rep: Torbet. Wash atty: Mullin, Rhyne, Emmons & Topel. Format: Country. Target aud: 25-54; general. ■ Robert M. Winters, pres; Jim Kozlowski, gen mgr; Bill Shannon, opns mgr; Chris Atkins, mus dir. ■ Rates: $40; 30; 35; 25.

Elizabethtown

WPDC(AM)—May 1958: 1600 khz; 500 w-D, 79 w-N. TL: N40 10 16 W76 35 50. Hrs opn: 24. 939 Radio Rd. (17022). (717) 367-1600; (717) 533-3525. Licensee: JVJ Communications Inc. (acq 10-1-84; $125,000; FTR 10-15-84). Net: UPI, USA; Radio Pa. Format: CHR, sports. News staff one; news progmg 5 hrs wkly. Target aud: 25-54. Spec prog: Farm 4 hrs wkly. ■ Vincent Grande, pres & gen mgr; Bill Wilson, vp opns; Kathryn Ferree, gen sls mgr; John Weiss, prom mgr & adv mgr; Mike O'Reilly, progmg dir; Lindsay Weller, mus dir; Bob Walter, news dir; John Hess, chief engr. ■ Rates: $16; 16; 16; 16.

WRKZ(FM)—(Hershey). April 30, 1964: 106.7 mhz; 14 kw. Ant 499 ft. TL: N40 10 16 W76 35 50. Stereo. Hrs opn: 24. Box Z, Hershey (17033). (717) 367-7700. FAX: (717) 367-9322. Licensee: TMZ Broadcasting Co. Group owner: Tele-Media Broadcasting Co. of Hershey (acq 2-27-89; grpsl; FTR 2-27-89). Net: ABC/E. Rep: Torbet. Wash atty: Fleishman & Walsh. Format: Contemp country. Target aud: 25-34. ■ Nancy Tulli, gen mgr & gen sls mgr; Brad Slick, opns dir; Jennifer Kuzo, prom mgr; Steve Wagner, news dir; Bob Kratz, chief engr.

***WWEC(FM)**—Aug 25, 1990: 88.3 mhz; 100 w. Ant 373 ft. TL: N40 08 83 W76 35 38. Stereo. Hrs opn: 18. Elizabethtown College, One Alpha Dr. (17022-2298). (717) 361-1413. FAX: (717) 361-1180. Licensee: Elizabethtown College. Wash atty: Blair, Joyce & Silva. Format: Div, progsv, news/talk. News progmg 40 hrs wkly. Target aud: General; college students, high school, churches, community. Spec prog: Class 3 hrs, jazz 2 hrs; relg 4 hrs; adult contemp 15 hrs wkly. ■ Prof. Donald E. Smith, gen mgr; Steve Rutter, chief engr.

Elizabethville

WYGL-FM—Dec 7, 1989: 100.5 mhz; 1.2 kw. Ant 515 ft. TL: N40 37 24 W76 49 54. Stereo. Hrs opn: 24. Box 654, 2 W. Main St. (17023); Box 1240, Rt. 204 & State School Rd., Selinsgrove (17870). (717) 362-3025; (800) 326-9488. FAX: (717) 374-7444; (717) 362-3079. Licensee: SunAir Communications Inc. Group owner: Air Communications (acq 3-1-90; $225,000; FTR 3-26-90). Net: ABC/E. Wash atty: Kaye, Scholer, Fierman, Hays & Handler. Format: Contemp country. News staff one; news progmg 8 hrs wkly. Target aud: 25-54. ■ David Bernstein, pres; Greg Adair, vp & gen mgr; Scott West, opns dir, progmg dir & mus dir; Scott Richards, gen sls mgr & adv mgr; Chuck Edwards, mktg dir & prom dir; Dawn Marie, news dir & pub affrs dir; Harry Bingaman, chief engr. ■ Rates: $19; 19; 19; 14.25.

Ellwood City

WKST-FM—July 4, 1968: 92.1 mhz; 6 kw. Ant 299 ft. TL: N40 52 13 W80 17 15. Stereo. 219 Savannah-Gardner, New Castle (16101). (412) 654-5501. FAX: (412) 654-3101. Licensee: Great Scott Broadcasting Ltd. Group owner: Great Scott Broadcasting. Net: MBS. Format: Adult contemp. ■ Faye Scott, pres; Sharon Kennedy-Clifton, gen mgr; Lawrence Rispoli, progmg dir & mus dir; Ken Hlebovy, news dir; Don Danko, chief engr.

Emporium

WLEM(AM)—Mar 2, 1958: 1250 khz; 2.5 kw-D, 30 w-N. TL: N41 30 22 W78 13 26 (CP: 650 khz, 5 kw-D). Hrs opn: 16. 145 E. Fourth (15834). (814) 486-3712; (814) 486-0491. FAX: (814) 486-1772. Licensee: Emporium Broadcasting Co. (acq 1-27-71). Net: NBC, Westwood One, Unistar. Rep: Dome, Rgnl Reps. Wash atty: Bryan, Cave, McPheeters & McRoberts. Format: Adult contemp, oldies, country. News staff one; news progmg 3 hrs wkly. Target aud: 25-65 plus. ■ Suzanne Spotts Smith, pres; Jeannine A. Barnett, gen mgr; Steve Kelly, opns mgr, progmg dir, mus dir & news dir; Mike Brennan, gen sls mgr; Robert Davis, chief engr.

WQKY(FM)—Co-owned with WLEM(AM). May 20, 1985: 99.3 mhz; 3 kw. Ant 492 ft. TL: N41 30 22 W78 13 26 (CP: 1 kw, ant 548 ft, TL: N41 29 32 W78 15 19). Stereo. Dups AM 100%. Spec prog: Relg 2 hrs wkly.

Ephrata

WIOV-FM—Nov 9, 1962: 105.1 mhz; 25 kw. Ant 700 ft. TL: N40 10 27 W76 09 31. Stereo. Box 430 (17522). (717) 738-1191. FAX: (717) 738-1661. Licensee: WIOV Inc. Group owner: Brill Media Company Inc. (acq 12-84). Net: ABC/E. Rep: Banner. Format: Country. ■ Mitch Carroll, pres, gen mgr & gen sls mgr; Joe O'Donnell, opns mgr, prom mgr, progmg dir & mus dir; Bill Quay, asst mus dir; Jeff Werner, news dir; Casey Allyn, pub affrs dir; Tom Moyer, chief engr.

***WRTL(FM)**—Not on air, target date Mar 1994: 90.7 mhz; 650 w. Ant 848 ft. Stereo. Hrs opn: 24. Dups WRTI (FM) Philadelphia, PA 100%. Broad and Montgomery Sts., Philadelphia (19122). (215) 204-8405. FAX: (215) 204-4870. Licensee: Temple University of the Commonwealth System of Higher Education. Net: NPR, AP; Radio Pa. Wash atty: Arent, Fox, Kintner, Plotkin & Kahn. Format: Jazz. News staff 2; news progmg 15 hrs wkly. Target aud: 25-49. ■ W. Theodore Eldredge, gen mgr; Tobias Poole, opns mgr & chief engr; Valorie Jarrell, dev mgr & sls dir; Monika Morris, prom dir; Bill Clark, progmg mgr; Kim Berry, mus dir; Audrey Foltz, news dir. ■ Rates: $75; 50; 75; 50.

Erie

***WEFR(FM)**—January 1992: 88.1 mhz; 3 kw. Ant 236 ft. TL: N41 59 02 W80 10 38. Stereo. Hrs opn: 24. 3108 Fulton Ave., Sacramento, CA (95821). (916) 481-8191. FAX: (916) 481-0410. Licensee: Family Stations Inc. (group owner). Net: UPI. Format: Relg. Target aud: General. ■ Harold Camping, pres; Scott L. Smith, vp; Michael Zeimann, gen mgr.

***WERG(FM)**—Dec 1, 1972: 89.9 mhz; 3 kw. Ant -125 ft. TL: N42 07 30 W80 05 42. Stereo. Hrs opn: 20. Gannon Univ., University Square (16541). (814) 871-7496; (814) 459-9374. Licensee: Gannon Univ. Net: UPI. Format: College progsv hits, Black. News staff 4; news progmg 5 hrs wkly. Target aud: 12-30. Spec prog: It 3 hrs, Pol 3 hrs, Sp 3 hrs, gospel 3 hrs, reggae 4 hrs wkly. ■ Tom Weber, gen mgr; Jen Markham, Tim Miller, news dirs; Dr. John Duda, chief engr. ■ WETG-TV 66 affil.

WEYZ(AM)—See North East.

WFGO(FM)—Not on air, target date unknown: 94.7 mhz; 1.1 kw. Ant 538 ft. TL: N42 02 31 W80 03 57. c/o Peninsula Broadcasting Corp., 717 State St., Suite 700 (16501). Licensee: Peninsula Broadcasting Corp.

WFLP(AM)—1947: 1330 khz; 5 kw-U, DA-2. TL: N42 03 18 W80 02 24. 2953 W. 12th St. (16505). (814) 835-5000. FAX: (814) 835-8395. Licensee: Heart Broadcasting Inc. (acq 1993). Net: ABC/I. Rep: Katz, Eastman. Format: Music of Your Life. News staff 2; news progmg 8 hrs wkly. Target aud: 35-64. Spec prog: Gospel 4 hrs, Pol one hr wkly. ■ Christopher J. Hagerty, pres & gen mgr; Michael Malpiedi, mktg dir, vp adv & adv dir; John Gallagher, prom mgr, progmg dir & mus dir; Kim Young, news dir; Robert Mallery, chief engr.

WJET(FM)—Oct 15, 1951: 102.3 mhz; 6 kw. Ant 670 ft. TL: N42 02 31 W80 03 57. Stereo. 1635 Ash St. (16503). (814) 453-5000. FAX: (814) 459-0838. Licensee: The Jet Broadcasting Co. (group owner; acq 10-86; $850,000; FTR 9-16-85). Rep: Banner, Dome, Rgnl Reps. Wash atty: Reddy, Begley & Martin. Format: Adult rock. News staff 2; news progmg 5 hrs wkly. Target aud: 18-49; active young adults. ■ Myron Jones, CEO; John Kanzius, pres; Robert Bach, gen sls mgr; Neal Sharpe, prom dir & progmg dir; Marsha McKinnon, news dir; Mike Kobylka, chief engr. ■ WJET-TV affil.

WLKK(AM)—1951: 1400 khz; 1 kw. TL: N42 07 28 W80 03 54. Hrs opn: 24. 18 W. Ninth St. (16501). (814) 456-7034. FAX: (814) 456-0292. Licensee: KDC Inc. (acq 1-89; $380,000). Net: NBC Talknet, MBS. Wash atty: Kaye, Scholer, Fierman, Hays & Handler. Format: News/talk. News staff 2. Target aud: 25-54. ■ Tim DeCapua, gen mgr; Allan Carpenter, opns mgr & prom mgr; Laith Wardi, gen sls mgr; Kim Young, news dir; Mark Himmler, chief engr.

***WMCE(FM)**—Feb 2, 1989: 88.5 mhz; 250 w. Ant 367 ft. TL: N42 05 24 W79 57 12. Stereo. Hrs opn: 18. Baldwin Hall, 501 E. 38th St. (16546). (814) 824-2260; (814) 824-2261. FAX: (814) 824-2590. Licensee: Mercyhurst College. Wash atty: Gammon & Grange. Format: Classical, class rock, div. News progmg 6 hrs wkly. Target aud: General. Spec prog: Black 4 hrs, Pol 3 hrs, relg 2 hrs, Sp 3 hrs, Irish one hr, folk 2 hrs wkly. ■ John Leisering, gen mgr; John Danknich, stn mgr; Joanna Shirey, prom mgr; Jennifer Trinidad, progmg dir; Jim Bean, mus dir; Jay Kennedy, pub affrs dir; Rick Pogson, chief engr.

WMXE(FM)—May 1, 1969: 103.7 mhz; 50 kw. Ant 499 ft. TL: N42 05 25 W79 56 37. Stereo. One Broadcast Park, North East (16428). (814) 725-4000. FAX: (814) 725-5401. Licensee: Rambaldo Communications Inc. (acq 9-15-93; FTR 10-18-93). Format: Adult contemp. ■ Richard Rambaldo, pres & gen mgr.

WPSE(AM)—Apr 21, 1935: 1450 khz; 1 kw-U. TL: N42 08 11 W80 02 25. Penn State-Behrend, Station Rd. (16563-1450). (814) 898-6171; (814) 898-6495. FAX: (814) 898-6015. Licensee: Board of Trustees, Pennsylvania State Univ. (acq 12-23-89). Net: CBS, BRN. Format: Business news, sports. News progmg 10 hrs wkly. Target aud: General. Spec prog: Pol 3 hrs wkly. ■ Fred Anzivino, gen mgr; Mike Rectenwald, vp sls; Mike Kobylka, chief engr.

***WQLN-FM**—Jan 7, 1973: 91.3 mhz; 35 kw. Ant 500 ft. TL: N42 02 35 W80 03 59. Stereo. Hrs opn: 15. 8425 Peach St. (16509). (814) 864-3001. FAX: (814) 864-4077. Licensee: Public Broadcasting of Northwest Pennsylvania Inc. Net: NPR, APR. Wash atty: Dow, Lohnes & Albertson. Format: Class, jazz, news. News progmg 24 hrs wkly. Target aud: General. Spec prog: Sp one hr, pub affrs 5 hrs, new age 2 hrs, call in show 3 hrs wkly. ■ Paul

Stankavich, CEO; Ronald Daugherty, vp; Pat Combine, dev dir; Joseph Mosier, prom dir; Thomas McLaren, progmg dir; Dennis Spagnolo, engrg dir. ■ *WQLN(TV) affil.

WRIE(AM)—1941: 1260 khz; 5 kw-U, DA-2. TL: N42 03 18 W80 02 24. Hrs opn: 24. 471 Robison Rd. W. (16509). (814) 868-5355. FAX: (814) 868-1876. Licensee: K&K Radio Broadcasting (acq 4-1-85; $230,000; FTR 2-27-89). Net: SMN. Rep: Christal. Format: Oldies. ■ Donald L. Kelly, pres; Dawn Kelly, gen mgr; Carolyn Buckel, gen sls mgr; Ron Arlen, progmg dir; Paul Davies, mus dir; Dave Benson, news dir; Rick Pogson, chief engr.

WXKC(FM)—Co-owned with WRIE(AM). 1949: 99.9 mhz; 50 kw. Ant 492 ft. TL: N42 05 24 W79 57 12. Stereo. Hrs opn: 24. Prog sep from AM. Format: Adult contemp.

WRKT(FM)—See North East.

WXKC(FM)—Listing follows WRIE(AM).

Everett

WSKE(AM)—Mar 15, 1963: 1040 khz; 10 kw-D, 4 kw-CH. TL: N40 00 26 W78 21 44. Stereo. Box 187 (15537-0187); 151 E. First Ave. (15537-0171). (814) 652-2600. FAX: (814) 652-9347. Licensee: Radio Everett Inc. (acq 7-1-67). Net: ABC/I. Wash atty: Lauren Colby. Format: Country. Target aud: 25-54. Spec prog: Bluegrass 3 hrs wkly. ■ Melvin Bakner, pres; Sandra (King) Bakner, gen mgr; Martin M. Bakner, progmg dir; Bob Resconsin, chief engr. ■ Rates: $7.75; 7.75; 7.75; 6.75.

WSKE-FM—Mar 15, 1988: 104.3 mhz; 6 kw. Ant 968 ft. TL: N40 00 04 W78 24 04. Stereo. Hrs opn: 18. Dups AM 100%. ■ Rates: Same as AM.

Fairless Hills

WKXW(FM)—See Trenton, N.J.

Farrell

WHTX(FM)—See Youngstown, Ohio.

WRQQ(AM)—Licensed to Farrell. See Youngstown, Ohio.

Folsom

***WRSD(FM)**—Jan 5, 1983: 94.9 mhz; 1.4 kw. Ant 20 ft. TL: N39 53 12 W75 20 01. Ridley School District Admin. Bldg. (19033). (215) 586-0861. Licensee: Ridley School District. Format: Adult contemp. ■ Michael Iannacci, gen mgr; Daniel Deaver, stn mgr; John Tideck, chief engr.

Franklin

WFRA(AM)—Apr 13, 1958: 1450 khz; 1 kw-U. TL: N41 23 27 W79 48 43. Hrs opn: 6 AM-midnight. Box 908, 1411 Liberty St. (16323). (814) 432-2188. (814) 432-2189. FAX: (814) 437-9372. Licensee: Northwestern Pennsylvania Broadcasting Co. Inc. Net: Moody. Wash atty: Reddy, Bigley & Martin. Format: MOR, news. News staff one; news progmg 12 hrs wkly. Target aud: 45 plus. ■ Robert H. Sauber, pres & chief engr; Thomas J. Sauber, gen mgr, progmg dir & mus dir; Douglas W. Metheney, gen sls mgr; Paul Joseph, news dir. ■ Rates: $15; 11; 15; 9.

WFRA-FM—Mar 5, 1971: 99.3 mhz; 7.3 kw. Ant 600 ft. TL: N41 26 16 W79 55 29. Stereo. Hrs opn: 6 AM-midnight. Prog sep from AM. Format: The best mix of today's hits and great oldies. News progmg 4 hrs wkly. Target aud: 18-44. ■ Rates: $19; 14; 19; 13.

Freeland

WQEQ(FM)—April 2, 1976: 103.1 mhz; 730 w. Ant 679 ft. TL: N41 01 06 W75 54 28. Stereo. RD1 Walnut St. (18224). (717) 636-2346. FAX: (717) 636-2877. Licensee: Friendship Communications Inc. (acq 4-84; $450,000; FTR 3-19-84). Format: Oldies. News staff 3; news progmg 9 hrs wkly. Target aud: 18-54; general. ■ Susan Bock, pres & gen mgr; Sammy Esposito, gen sls mgr & adv mgr; Tom Emanski, prom mgr; Tony Pacelli, progmg dir & mus dir; Tom Ragan, news dir.

Gettysburg

WGET(AM)—Aug 27, 1950: 1320 khz; 1 kw-D, 500 w-N, DA-2. TL: N39 50 30 W77 13 25. Hrs opn: 24. Box 3179, 775 Old Harrisburg Rd. (17325). (717) 334-3101. FAX: (717) 334-5822. Licensee: Times and News Publishing Co. Net: MBS, CBS, NBC Talknet; Radio Pa. Rep: Banner. Wash atty: Hogan & Hartson. Format: Adult contemp, news/talk. News staff 3; news progmg 40 hrs wkly. Target aud: 35-64; mainstream mature adults. Spec prog: Farm 12 hrs wkly. ■ Philip Jones, pres; Rod Burnham, vp & gen mgr; Fred Snyder, opns mgr; Al Potena, gen sls mgr; Dave Jackson, progmg dir; Larry Rhoten, news dir; Larry Angle, chief engr. ■ Rates: $28; 21; 24; 18.

WGTY(FM)—Co-owned with WGET(AM). July 5, 1962: 107.7 mhz; 16 kw. Ant 829 ft. TL: N39 51 23 W76 56 57. Stereo. Hrs opn: 24. Prog sep from AM. Format: Country. Target aud: 25-54. ■ John Pellegrini, progmg dir & mus dir. ■ Rates: $95; 80; 88; 56.

***WZBT(FM)**—Oct 23, 1976: 91.1 mhz; 180 w. Ant 380 ft. TL: N39 50 15 W77 14 09 (CP: 180 w, ant 380 ft.). Box 435, Gettysburg College (17325). (717) 337-6315; (717) 337-6314. FAX: (717) 337-6314. Licensee: Gettysburg College. Format: Progsv. Target aud: General. Spec prog: Class 3 hrs, folk 6 hrs, jazz 2 hrs, Sp one hr wkly. ■ Larry Angle, chief engr.

Glen Mills

***WZZE(FM)**—May 20, 1975: 97.3 mhz; 18 w. Ant 180 ft. TL: N39 55 15 W75 29 58 (CP: Ant 184 ft.). Glen Mills Schools, Concordville (19331). (215) 459-8100. Licensee: Glen Mills Schools (acq 2-28-84). Net: ABC/E. Format: CHR. ■ C.D. Ferrainola, pres; Mark Smith, opns mgr; Dave Schmidt, chief engr.

Grantham

***WVMM(FM)**—Sept 29, 1989: 90.7 mhz; 100 w. Ant 300 ft. TL: N40 09 34 W76 59 00. Messiah College (17027). (717) 766-7093. Licensee: Messiah College. Format: Contemp Christian. Target aud: General. Spec prog: Jazz 10 hrs, class 4 hrs wkly. ■ Deborah Adkins, gen mgr; Julie Ondrasia, progmg dir; Ron Loomis, mus dir; Pat Schmidt, news dir; Mat Wells, chief engr.

Greencastle

WKSL(FM)—May 6, 1967: 94.3 mhz; 2.5 kw. Ant 469 ft. TL: N39 47 29 W77 40 30 (CP: 1.82 kw, ant 423 ft.). Stereo. Box 10, 203 S. Antrim Way (17225). (717) 597-7151. FAX: (717) 597-1142. Licensee: Benjamin F. Thomas. Net: AP. Format: Country. News staff one; news progmg 18 hrs wkly. Target aud: 35 plus; mature adults. Spec prog: Farm 6 hrs wkly. ■ Benjamin F. Thomas Sr., pres; Robert L. Thomas, gen mgr & gen sls mgr; Larry Flood, mus dir; Donald Aines Jr., news dir; Jeff Hollinshead, chief engr.

Greensburg

WHJB(AM)—Oct 28, 1934: 620 khz; 2.5 kw-D, 500 w-N, DA-2. TL: N40 18 14 W79 35 50. Hrs opn: 24. 245 Brown St. (15601). (412) 834-0600; (412) 242-3303 FAX: (412) 836-3425. Licensee: WHJB Group. (acq 6-88; grpsl; FTR 10-27-86). Net: Unistar, MBS, Talknet; Radio Pa. Format: Adult contemp, MOR, oldies, talk. News staff one; news progmg 19 hrs wkly. Target aud: Adults. Spec prog: Pol 4 hrs wkly. ■ Melvin A. Goldberg, pres & gen mgr; Barry Banker, opns mgr, prom mgr, mus mgr & news mgr; Richard Ruby, chief engr.

WSSZ(FM)—Co-owned with WHJB(AM). July 8, 1968: 107.1 mhz; 1.6 kw. Ant 450 ft. TL: N40 18 57 W79 39 22. Stereo. Prog sep from AM. Format: Classic hits. News staff one; news progmg one hr wkly. ■ Dennis Elliot, progmg dir.

Greenville

WEXC(FM)—Listing follows WGRP(AM).

WGRP(AM)—Sept 19, 1959: 940 khz; 1 kw-D, DA. TL: N41 23 10 W80 24 35. Box 189 (16125). (412) 588-8900. FAX: (412) 588-1043. Licensee: Greenville Broadcasting Co. Net: ABC/D. Rep: Commercial Media. Format: Adult contemp. ■ Merle G. Anderson, pres & chief engr; Gary L. Fleming, gen mgr, opns mgr & gen sls mgr; David Hixson, news dir.

WEXC(FM)—Co-owned with WGRP(AM). July 1965: 107.1 mhz; 3 kw. Ant 240 ft. TL: N41 23 10 W80 24 35. Prog sep from AM. Format: Top-40.

***WTGP(FM)**—Sept 3, 1971: 88.1 mhz; 1.1 kw. Ant 6 ft. TL: N41 24 51 W80 24 50. Stereo. Hrs opn: 9 AM-12 midnight. Thiel College, 75 College Ave. (16125). (412) 589-2210; (412) 589-2730. Licensee: Thiel College. Format: Div, progsv. Target aud: 18-23; Thiel college students, faculty & staff. Spec prog: Relg one hr wkly. ■ Kevin Evans, gen mgr; Kevin A. Ankeny, stn mgr.

Grove City

WRKU-FM—Sept 10, 1962: 95.1 mhz; 19 kw. Ant 805 ft. TL: N41 15 08 W80 21 28. Stereo. Hrs opn: 24. Suite A, 4800 Belmont Ave., Youngstown, OH (44505). (216) 759-0579. FAX: (216) 759-1368. Licensee: Beasley Broadcasting. Group owner: Beta Broadcasting (acq 12-86). Format: AOR. News staff one; news progmg 2 hrs wkly. Target aud: 18-34. ■ Sandra Doolittle, gen mgr & opns mgr; John Clarke, stn mgr & chief engr; David Kardaz, dev dir; Joe V. Kat, mktg dir; John Thomas, progmg dir; Brian Gartland, mus dir; Michelle Sloan, news dir.

***WSAJ(AM)**—April 1920: 1340 khz; 100 w-U. TL: N41 09 30 W80 11 30. Grove City College (16127). (412) 458-3303. Licensee: Grove City College. Format: Jazz. Spec prog: Class 2 hrs, jazz 2 hrs wkly. ■ Everett C. DeVelde, gen mgr.

***WSAJ-FM**—September 1968: 91.1 mhz; 200 w. Ant 450 ft. TL: N41 09 20 W80 04 47. Stereo. Format: Big band, class, jazz.

Hampton Township

WEEP(AM)—Licensed to Hampton Township. See Pittsburgh.

Hanover

WHVR(AM)—Jan 9, 1949: 1280 khz; 5 kw-D, 500 w-N, DA-2. TL: N39 49 11 W77 00 25. Box 234 (17331). (717) 637-8023. FAX: (717) 637-9006. Licensee: Radio Hanover Inc. Net: UPI. Format: MOR. ■ Barbara McLaughlin, gen sls mgr; Pat Case, progmg dir; Sue Kervin, news dir.

WYCR(FM)—(York-Hanover). Co-owned with WHVR(AM). Dec 22, 1962: 98.5 mhz; 10.5 kw. Ant 928 ft. TL: N39 51 30 W76 56 52. Stereo. Prog sep from AM. Format: Contemp hit.

Harrisburg

WCMB(AM)—February 1948: 1460 khz; 5 kw-U, DA-N. TL: N40 15 42 W76 54 40. Hrs opn: 24. Box 3433 (17105); 360 Poplar Church Rd., Camp Hill (17011). (717) 763-7020. FAX: (717) 763-1978. Licensee: Gemini Broadcasting Corp. (acq 8-22-89; grpsl; FTR 9-11-89). Net: CBS, MBS, Wall Street. Rep: McGavren Guild. Wash atty: Fisher, Wayland, Cooper & Leader. Format: News/talk. News staff 4; news progmg 3 hrs wkly. Target aud: General. Spec prog: Gospel 2 hrs, public svc 2 hrs wkly. ■ Brian E. Danzis, pres & gen mgr; Randy L. Gaeckler, gen sls mgr; Sandra D. Fenton, prom dir.

WIMX-FM—Co-owned with WCMB(AM). July 1965: 99.3 mhz; 3 kw. Ant 328 ft. TL: N40 15 44 W76 54 37 (CP: 6 kw). Stereo. Prog sep from AM. Net: Westwood One. Format: Adult contemp. News progmg 2 hrs wkly. Target aud: 25-49. ■ Ed August, mus dir.

WHP(AM)—1924: 580 khz; 5 kw-U, DA-N. TL: N40 18 11 W76 57 07. Stereo. Hrs opn: 24. Box 6477 (17110); Suite 100, 600 Corporate Cir. (17110). (717) 540-8800. FAX: (717) 540-9271. Licensee: PA Broadcasting Assoc. III (acq 3-12-92; with co-located FM). Net: ABC, NBC Talknet. Format: News/Talk. News staff 8. Target aud: 35-64. ■ J. Albert Dame, pres; Terry Kile, gen mgr; Rolla Lehman, gen sls mgr; Mark Dame, mktg dir; Kathy Stone, prom dir & adv dir; Bill Richardson, news dir; John Lane, chief engr.

WRVV(FM)—Co-owned with WHP(AM). 1946: 97.3 mhz; 17 kw. Ant 840 ft. TL: N40 20 44 W76 52 09. Stereo. Hrs opn: 24. Prog sep from AM. Box 6477 (17110). Format: Rock, adult contemp. Target aud: 25-54. ■ Chris Tyler, opns mgr & progmg dir; Stephanie Pedrick, gen sls mgr.

***WHPN(FM)**—Not on air, target date unknown: 88.1 mhz; 260 w. Ant 217 ft. TL: N40 15 41 W76 52 48. c/o WXPN(FM), Wayne Hall, 3905 Spruce St., Philadelphia (19104). (215) 898-6677. Licensee: Trustees of University of Pennsylvania (acq 12-18-92; $5,000; FTR 1-18-93). ■ Mark Fuerst, gen mgr.

WHTF(FM)—See Starview.

WIMX-FM—Listing follows WCMB(AM).

***WITF-FM**—Apr 1, 1971: 89.5 mhz; 5.9 kw. Ant 1,361 ft. TL: N40 20 45 W76 52 06. Stereo. 1982 Locust Ln. (17109). (717) 236-6000. FAX: (717) 236-4628. Licensee: WITF Inc. Net: NPR, APR. Format: Class, news/talk. News staff 2; news progmg 40 hrs wkly. ■ Stewart Cheifet, pres & gen mgr; Wick Woodford, stn mgr; Michael Greenwald, vp dev; Joe Krushinsky, dev mgr; Lynn Fauth, sls dir; June Knight, vp mktg; Mitzi Dodson, progmg dir; Richard Strawson, mus dir; Ed Arke, news dir; John Bosak, chief engr. ■ *WITF-TV affil.

WKBO(AM)—1922: 1230 khz; 1 kw-U. TL: N40 15 11 W76 53 08. 600 Corporate Cir., Suite 100 (17110). (717) 540-8200. Licensee: Dame Media (acq 6-80). Net: Unistar. Rep: Banner. Format: All news. News staff 6. Target aud: 35-54; well educated, upscale professionals. ■ J.

Pennsylvania

Albert Dame, pres; John W. Dame, gen mgr; Bill Rehkopf, opns mgr & news dir; Rolla Lehman, gen sls mgr; John Lane, chief engr.

WNNK-FM—Listing follows WTCY(AM).

WRVV(FM)—Listing follows WHP(AM).

WTCY(AM)—May 28, 1945: 1400 khz; 1 kw-U. TL: N40 14 58 W76 52 03. Hrs opn: 24. Box 104, 3400 N. 6th St. (17108). (717) 238-1402. Licensee: June Broadcasting Inc. (acq 3-9-93; $12 million with co-located FM; FTR 3-29-93). Net: ABC/C, SMN. Rep: Christal. Format: Urban adult contemp. News staff 2; news progmg 2 hrs wkly. Target aud: 25-54. Spec prog: Gospel. ■ Philip Giordano, CEO; Jim Sack, CFO; David C. Savadove, vp & gen mgr; Joseph Dalto, opns mgr & gen sls mgr; Debbie Maiocco, natl sls mgr; Joe Ostrander, prom mgr; Don Davis, progmg dir; Lauren Rooney, news dir; Tom Walker, chief engr. ■ Rates: $50; 40; 45; 25.

WNNK-FM—Co-owned with WTCY(AM). 1962: 104.1 mhz; 22.5 kw. Ant 725 ft. TL: N40 18 59 W76 57 04. Stereo. Hrs opn: 24. Dups AM 100%. Net: AP. ■ Ron Giovanniello, Karen Richards, rgnl sls mgrs; John O'Dea, progmg dir; Scott Shaw, mus dir. ■ Rates: $175; 150; 165; 100.

WWKL(FM)—Sept 30, 1962: 94.9 mhz; 25 kw. Ant 699 ft. TL: N40 18 57 W76 57 02. Stereo. 3605 Vartan Way (17110). (717) 541-9515. FAX: (717) 233-0503. Licensee: Barnstable Corp. Group owner: Barnstable Broadcasting Inc. Net: Unistar. Rep: Banner. Format: Oldies. News staff one. Target aud: 30 plus. ■ David Gingold, pres; Chris Wegmann, vp; Gary Kurtz, gen sls mgr; Jill Parnes, prom mgr; Denny Alexander, progmg dir; Jay Smith, news dir; George Wright, chief engr.

Havertown

***WHHS(FM)**—Dec 6, 1949: 107.9 mhz; 14 w. Ant 161 ft. TL: N39 58 59 W75 18 10. 200 Mill Rd. (19083). (215) 446-7111. Licensee: School District of Haverford Township. Format: Div. ■ Nicholas Rotoli, gen mgr; Mike Levistine, news dir; C. Vecchio, chief engr.

Hawley

WYCY(FM)—Not on air, target date unknown: 105.3 mhz; 2.9 kw. Ant 479 ft. TL: N41 35 01 W75 10 30. 2801 Westgate Dr., Easton (18042). Licensee: Banner Broadcasting Corp. (acq 3-18-93; $80,000; FTR 4-5-93).

Hazleton

WAZL(AM)—Dec 19, 1932: 1490 khz; 1 kw-U. TL: N40 56 24 W75 58 04. Box 326, (18201). (717) 454-4002. FAX: (717) 454-4008. Licensee: 4 M Broadcasting Inc. (acq 8-2-93; $750,000 with co-located FM; FTR 8-23-93). Net: ABC/D, Moody. Rep: Katz & Powell. Format: Adult contemp, oldies. News staff one; news progmg 11 hrs wkly. Target aud: 12 plus. Spec prog: Big band 5 hrs wkly. ■ Bob Moisey, pres; San Banko, gen mgr; Bill Waschko, opns mgr; Scott McAndrews, progmg dir; Mark Michaels, mus dir; L. A. Tarone, news dir; Bob Schacht, chief engr.

WZMT(FM)—Co-owned with WAZL(AM). 1949: 97.9 mhz; 19.5 kw. Ant 722 ft. TL: N41 04 55 W75 56 55 (CP: 27.5 mhz, ant 659 ft.). Stereo. Prog sep from AM. (FTR 8-30-93). Net: ABC/D. Format: Adult contemp, oldies. News staff one; news progmg 4 hrs wkly. Target aud: 25 plus.

Hershey

WRKZ(FM)—Licensed to Hershey. See Elizabethtown.

Hollidaysburg

WHPA(FM)—Dec 1, 1978: 104.9 mhz; 280 w. Ant 1,417 ft. TL: N40 29 15 W78 21 09. Stereo. Box 464 (16648); R.D. 4, Box 210 (16648). (814) 695-4441. FAX: (814) 696-9522. Licensee: WHPA/WKMC Inc. (acq 11-1-88). Net: CNN. Rep: Roslin. Format: Adult contemp, oldies. News staff one; news progmg 28 hrs wkly. Target aud: 25-54; adults with significant income. ■ David G. Mitchell, pres; Donald L. Ambrose, vp & gen mgr; John Hodgens, gen mgr; Jan Brooks, mktg mgr; Ray Keller, progmg dir; Joyce Kavanaugh, news dir; Cindy Shope, pub affrs dir; Gary S. Magill, chief engr. ■ Rates: $40; 36; 34; 30.

WKMC(AM)—See Roaring Spring.

Homer City

WCCS(AM)—Oct 25, 1983: 1160 khz; 10 kw-D, 1 kw-N, DA-1. TL: N40 34 18 W79 10 12. Hrs opn: 24. Box 1020, Indiana (15701); R.D. 2, Old Rt. 119 S (15748). (412) 479-1160. FAX: (412) 479-3500. Licensee: Raymark Broadcasting Co. Inc. Net: SMN. Rep: Commercial. Format: Adult contemp. News staff 2; news progmg 14 hrs wkly. Target aud: 25-49. Spec prog: Polish 3 hrs, oldies 9 hrs wkly. ■ Mark E. Harley, pres; Mark A. Bertig, stn mgr & gen sls mgr; Jack Benedict, opns dir; Holly Wolfe, progmg dir & pub affrs dir; Bernie Smith, news dir; Fred Shetler, chief engr. ■ Rates: $14.10; 14.10; 14.10; 14.10.

Honesdale

WWCC(AM)—September 1972: 1590 khz; 2.5 kw-D. TL: N41 33 13 W75 15 18. Box 1104, 575 Grove St. (18431). (717) 253-1616; (717) 253-9922. FAX: (717) 253-6297. Licensee: WDNH Broadcasting Corp. (acq 6-8-88). Net: USA. Rep: Dome. Wash atty: Schwartz, Woods & Miller. Format: C&W, news/talk. News staff one; news progmg 14 hrs wkly. Target aud: General; mass appeal. ■ Edward K. Histed, CEO, pres, gen mgr & progmg dir; Peter Ward, sls dir; Denny Talarico, news dir & pub affrs dir; George Guida, chief engr.

WDNH-FM—Co-owned with WWCC(AM). Oct 12, 1981: 95.3 mhz; 3 kw. Ant 256 ft. TL: N41 34 23 W75 11 30. Stereo. Hrs opn: 24. Prog sep from AM. (717) 253-9595. Net: USA. Format: Hot adult contemp. News staff one; news progmg 6 hrs wkly. Target aud: 25-54.

Hughesville

WMRE(AM)—Aug 4, 1985: 1190 khz; 1 kw-D, 17 w-N. TL: N41 12 34 W76 44 56 (CP: 1200 khz, 10 kw-D, 250 w-N, DA-2). Rebroadcasts WJSA (AM) Jersey Shore 100%. 220 S. Russel Ave., Williamsport (17701). (717) 323-8200. FAX: (717) 323-5075. Licensee: North Penn Broadcasting Inc. Group owner: HGF Media Group (acq 5-31-90; $150,000; FTR 6-18-90). Net: Unistar. Format: Relg. News staff 2; news progmg 3 hrs wkly. Target aud: General. ■ Vic Michael, gen mgr; Randy Lapriola, gen sls mgr; Holiday Owens, prom dir; Mark Williams, vp progmg; Jeff Thomas, progmg dir; Shaun Carey, mus dir; Liz Brady, news dir. ■ Rates: $25; 20; 25; 15.

Huntingdon

WHUN(AM)—Mar 2, 1947: 1150 khz; 5 kw-D, 36 w-N. TL: N40 27 18 W77 58 50. 400 Washington St. (16652). (814) 643-3340. FAX: (814) 643-7379. Licensee: Huntingdon Broadcasters Inc. Net: ABC, AP. Format: Real country. News staff one; news progmg 15 hrs wkly. Target aud: 35 plus. Spec prog: Sports. ■ Joseph F. Biddle II, CEO; Josephine B. McMeen, pres; Kathleen R. Biddle, gen mgr; Virginia Oakman, vp opns & natl sls mgr; Joseph Biddle, opns mgr; Terry Barnhart, gen sls mgr; Terry Bittner, progmg dir & mus dir; Mike Ellenberger, chief engr.

WLAK(FM)—Co-owned with WHUN(AM). Sept 12, 1967: 103.5 mhz; 160 w. Ant 1,427 ft. TL: N40 29 51 W78 08 00. Stereo. Prog sep from AM. Format: Hot adult contemp. Target aud: 18-44.

***WKVR-FM**—March 1978: 92.3 mhz; 10 w. Ant -376 ft. TL: N40 30 00 W78 00 52. Stereo. Hrs opn: 19. Box 1005, Ellis Hall, Juniata College (16652). (814) 643-5031. FAX: (814) 643-4477. Licensee: Juniata College Board of Trustees. Net: ABC/I. Format: Class rock, progsv, AOR. News progmg 4 hrs wkly. Target aud: 18-25; college students. Spec prog: Class 2 hrs, folk 2 hrs, jazz 3 hrs, Black 10 hrs, contemp Christian 3 hrs, reggae 3 hrs wkly. ■ Erik Werner, stn mgr; Scott Newcomer, sls dir & gen sls mgr; Tim Miller, mus dir; Deb Miller, news dir; Keith Noll, pub affrs dir; Fred Smithbower, chief engr.

WLAK(FM)—Listing follows WHUN(AM).

WQHG(FM)—Mar 30, 1992: 106.3 mhz; 6 kw. Ant 154 ft. TL: N40 29 11 W77 59 35. Stereo. Hrs opn: 24. Box 260-A, Fairgrounds Rd., R.D. 4 (16652). (814) 643-9620. FAX: (814) 643-9625. Licensee: Huntingdon County Broadcasting Inc. Net: Jones Satellite Audio, CNN. Format: Adult contemp. News staff one. Target aud: women 25-49, men 25-54; above average educ, income & status. ■ Mary Lou Maierhofer, pres; Lou Maierhofer, gen mgr; Jeff Speck, chief opns; William Germann, sls dir; Diane Huggler, progmg dir; John Super, chief engr. ■ Rates: $14.10; 11.76; 14.10; 12.

Indiana

WCCS(AM)—See Homer City.

WDAD(AM)—Nov 4, 1945: 1450 khz; 1 kw-U. TL: N40 37 01 W79 07 55. Hrs opn: 24. Box 668, 21 N. 5th St. (15701). (412) 349-1450. FAX: (412) 349-6842. Licensee: RMS Media Management Inc. Net: CBS. Rep: Dome. Wash atty: Pepper & Corazzini. Format: Adult contemp. News staff one. Target aud: 35 plus. Spec prog: Relg 2 hrs wkly. ■ Dick Sherry, pres & gen mgr; Marty Chapman, gen sls mgr; Chuck Clark, progmg dir; Chauncey Ross, news dir; Joe Shupienis, chief engr.

WQMU(FM)—Co-owned with WDAD(AM). Aug 14, 1968: 103.1 mhz; 3 kw. Ant 170 ft. TL: N40 37 01 W79 07 55 (CP: 2.4 kw). Stereo. Hrs opn: 24. Prog sep from AM. Format: Classic rock. Target aud: 21-41. ■ Mike Cavanaugh, progmg dir.

***WIUP-FM**—Oct 1969: 90.1 mhz; 1.6 kw. Ant 88 ft. TL: N40 36 57 W79 09 40. Stereo. Hrs opn: 7 AM-2 AM. Indiana Univ. of Pa., 121 Stouffer Hall (15705). (412) 357-3210; (412) 357-5652. Licensee: Indiana University of Pennsylvania. Format: Div. News progmg 11 hrs wkly. Target aud: General. Spec prog: Black 14 hrs, class 15 hrs, jazz 15 hrs, gospel one hr, jazz 15 hrs, new age 4 hrs, radio drama one hr wkly. ■ B. Gail Wilson, gen mgr; Ken Ciroli, chief engr. ■ *WIUP-TV affil.

WQMU(FM)—Listing follows WDAD(AM).

Jackson Township

***WRTY(FM)**—Aug 23, 1991: 91.1 mhz; 3.5 kw. Ant 862 ft. TL: N41 02 40 W75 22 45. Stereo. Hrs opn: 24. Dups WRTI(AM) Philadelphia, 100%. 100 Annenberg Hall, Temple University, Philadelphia (19122). (215) 204-8405. FAX: (215) 204-4870. Licensee: Temple University. Net: NPR, AP; Radio Pa. Wash atty: Arent, Fox, Kintner, Plotkin & Kahn. Format: Jazz. News staff 2; news progmg 15 hrs wkly. Target aud: 25-49. Spec prog: Caribbean 4 hrs, Sp 4 hrs wkly. ■ W. Theodore Eldredge, gen mgr; Tobias Poole, opns mgr & chief engr; Valorie Jarrell, dev dir & prom mgr; Monika Morris, sls dir; Bill Clark, progmg dir & mus dir; Audrey Foltz, news dir. ■ Rates: $75; 50; 75; 50.

Jeannette

WBCW(AM)—Jan 28, 1974: 1530 khz; 1 kw-D, 250 w-CH. TL: N40 19 17 W79 35 30. 111 S. Fourth St. (15644). (412) 527-5656. Licensee: Central Westmoreland Broadcasting Co. Net: ABC/I. Format: Talk, top-40. News staff one. Spec prog: Pol 5 hrs, farm one hr, Slovenian 4 hrs wkly. ■ Verna M. Calisti, pres & gen mgr; Jacqueline Rae Calisti, mus dir; John M. Orange, chief engr.

Jenkintown

WIBF-FM—Nov 1, 1960: 103.9 mhz; 340 w. Ant 1,000 ft. TL: N40 02 26 W75 14 20. Hrs opn: 24. Suite A-1, 100 Old York Rd. (19046). (215) 884-9400. FAX: (215) 884-2608. Licensee: Jarad Broadcasting Co. (acq 9-23-92; $3.4 million; FTR 11-9-92). Rep: Groskin; Media Communications. Wash atty: Erwin G. Krasnow. Format: Modern rock. News staff 2. Target aud: Adult. Spec prog: Por 4 hrs, Ger 6 hrs, Jewish 14 hrs, Fr one hr, It 6 hrs, Pol 2 hrs, Ukrainian 2 hrs, Russian one hr, Hungarian one hr wkly. ■ Ronald J. Worey, pres; Ted Utz, gen sls mgr; John Caracciolo, gen mgr; Joe Ruyak, gen sls mgr; John Caracciolo, chief engr.

Jersey Shore

WJSA(AM)—July 10, 1979: 1600 khz; 1 kw-D, 20 w-N. TL: N41 13 32 W77 16 01. Hrs opn: 24. 262 Allegheny St. (17740). (717) 398-7200. FAX: (717) 398-7201. Licensee: Covenant Broadcasting Co. Net: Moody, USA. Format: Relg. News progmg 14 hrs wkly. Target aud: 25-54. Spec prog: Class one hr, gospel 2 hrs wkly. ■ John K. Hogg Jr., gen mgr; Larry Schutzke, gen sls mgr; David J. Bauman, progmg dir; Liz Brady, news dir. ■ Rates: $10; 7.50; 8.75; 5.

WJSA-FM—Nov 1, 1984: 93.5 mhz; 3 kw. Ant 144 ft. TL: N41 14 00 W77 12 09. Stereo. Hrs opn: 24. Dups AM 100%. ■ Rates: Same as AM.

WWWD(FM)—Aug 20, 1979: 97.7 mhz; 3 kw. Ant 300 ft. TL: N41 13 14 W77 16 39 (CP: 6 kw, ant 295 ft.). Stereo. Hrs opn: 24. 2401 Reach Rd., Williamsport (17701). (717) 323-7118. FAX: (717) 326-1043. Licensee: S&P Broadcasting LP. Group owner: S&P Broadcasting Co. (acq 1-18-89; grpsl; FTR 12-19-8). Rep: Katz. Format: Oldies. Target aud: 25-49. ■ Ron Swanson, pres; Darrell Alva, gen mgr; Scott Masteller, opns mgr; Bryan May,

Stations in the U.S.

Johnsonburg

WKBI-FM—See St. Marys.

Johnstown

WCRO(AM)—September 1947: 1230 khz; 1 kw-U. TL: N40 19 55 W78 54 46. Suite 627, 616 Main St. (15901-2127). (814) 536-9270. FAX: (814) 536-5855. Licensee: Eagle Broadcasting Group Inc. (acq 2-6-91). Net: SMN. Format: Christian, talk. ■ Jay Richard Lee, pres; Jane Allison Lee, gen mgr; Bob Folckemer, opns mgr, progmg dir & mus dir; Clyde May, chief engr.

*****WFRJ(FM)**—June 6, 1986: 88.9 mhz; 900 w. Ant 1,063 ft. TL: N40 22 15 W78 59 02. Hrs opn: 24. 1770 William Penn Ave. (15909). (814) 322-3144. Licensee: Family Stations Inc. (group owner). Format: Conservative Christian. News progmg 6 hrs wkly. Target aud: General. ■ Harold Camping, pres; Mike Ziman, gen mgr; Gary Johnson, stn mgr.

WGLU(FM)—Sept 1, 1974: 92.1 mhz; 300 w. Ant 1,043 ft. TL: N40 22 15 W78 59 02. Stereo. Hrs opn: 24. Box 986, Landmark Bldg., 516 Main St. (15901-0986). (814) 536-7825. FAX: (814) 539-5570. Licensee: P.A.C. Media Inc. (acq 8-12-87); $451,000; FTR 8-10-87). Net: NBC the Source. Rep: Christal. Format: Contemp hit. News staff one; news progmg one hr wkly. Target aud: 18-49. ■ Warren S. Diggins, pres; David Banks, exec vp; Ralph T. Lovette, gen mgr; Keith Whistler, gen sls mgr; Keith Whistler, Jeadie Feather, rgnl sls mgrs; Kim Meyers, prom mgr; Rich Adams, progmg dir; Mitch Edwards, mus dir; Chris Harvey, engrg mgr; Brian Chase, engrg mgr. ■ Rates: $50; 40; 50; 35.

WJAC(AM)—Apr 1925: 850 khz; 10 kw-U, DA-1. TL: N40 10 54 W78 53 20. 109 Plaza Dr. (15905). (814) 255-4186. FAX: (814) 255-6145. Licensee: Winston Radio Inc. (acq 1993; $2,153,788 with co-located FM; FTR 9-6-93). Net: NBC, Unistar. Rep: McGavren Guild; Dome. Format: Real country. Target aud: 25 plus. ■ Michael F. Brosig Sr., CEO, chmn & gen mgr; Bill Creager, gen sls mgr; Sharon Honkys, prom dir; Jack Michaels, progmg dir; Brian Wolfe, mus dir; Rick Shepard, news dir; Jim Boxler, chief engr.

WKYE(FM)—Co-owned with WJAC(AM). Aug 1949: 95.5 mhz; 57 kw. Ant 1,060 ft. TL: N40 22 18 W78 58 57. Stereo. Prog sep from AM. Format: Adult contemp. Target aud: 25-54.

WMTZ(FM)—Listing follows WNTJ(AM).

WNTJ(AM)—August 1946: 1490 khz; 1 kw-U. TL: N40 19 25 W78 53 49. Box 370 (15907-0370). (814) 535-8554. Licensee: Pennsylvania Broadcasting Associates II (acq 6-12-90); $1.35 million with co-located FM; FTR 7-2-90). Net: CBS, Unistar. Rep: Roslin. Format: News/talk. ■ Alison Dame, gen mgr; Bill Bingler, gen sls mgr; Brian Cleary, progmg dir; Tom Sclafani, news dir; Bill Caramana, chief engr.

WMTZ(FM)—Co-owned with WNTJ(AM). Aug 14, 1973: 96.5 mhz; 50 kw. Ant 489 ft. TL: N40 19 45 W78 53 54. Stereo. Prog sep from AM. FAX: (814) 535-8557. Net: CBS Spectrum. Rep: Banner. Wash atty: Latham Watkins. Format: New country. News staff one; news progmg one hr wkly. Target aud: 12-54. ■ Brian Cleary, opns dir; Yvonne Brooks, pub affrs dir.

WQKK(FM)—See Ebensburg.

Kane

WLMI(FM)—Sept 17, 1984: 103.9 mhz; 3 kw. Ant 300 ft. TL: N41 39 34 W78 48 42. Stereo. Hrs opn: 24. Box 868, 27 Fraley St. (16735). (814) 837-9711; (814) 837-9745. FAX: (814) 837-6154. Licensee: Beech Tree Broadcasting Co. (acq 12-2-92); $245,000; FTR 12-21-92). Net: SMN. Wash atty: Verner, Liipfert, Bernhard, McPherson & Hand. Format: Country. News staff one; news progmg 8 hrs wkly. Target aud: 25-49; families. ■ Charles W. Crouse, pres, gen mgr & progmg dir; Virginia Crouse, vp & mktg mgr; Joseph Disque, prom mgr; Barry Morgan, natl sls mgr; Chuck Crouse, news dir; Scott McGuire, pub affrs dir. ■ Rates: $12; 12; 12; 9.50.

WQLE(AM)—June 7, 1954: 960 khz; 1 kw-D, 48 w-N. TL: N41 38 55 W78 48 10. Stereo. Stn currently dark. Box 518 (16735). Licensee: Walter R. Pierre (acq 12-11-91; $63,500; FTR 1-6-92). Wash atty: Earl Stanley. ■ Robert Wall, opns dir.

Kittanning

WTYM(AM)—1948: 1380 khz; 1 kw-D, 28 w-N. TL: N40 47 19 W79 32 05. R.D. 7, Box 371 (16201). (412) 543-1380. FAX: (412) 543-1140. Licensee: Vernal Enterprises Inc. (acq 7-22-92); $85,000; FTR 6-15-92). Wash atty: Baraff, Koerner, Olender & Hochberg. Format: Oldies, sports. News staff one; news progmg 12 hrs wkly. Target aud: 20-55. Spec prog: Relg 4 hrs wkly. ■ Larry L. Schrecongost, pres & gen mgr; Nancy W. Schrecongost, vp; Amanoa R. Wojcik, opns mgr; Becky Everson, news dir; Ken Snyder, chief engr. ■ Rates: $15; 15; 15; na.

Lancaster

WDAC(FM)—Dec 13, 1959: 94.5 mhz; 19 kw. Ant 810 ft. TL: N39 53 46 W76 14 22. Stereo. Hrs opn: 24. Box 3022 (17604); for UPS, Fed-Ex only: 683 Lancaster Pike, New Providence (17560). (717) 284-4123. FAX: (717) 284-4123. Licensee: WDAC Radio Co. Net: Moody, USA, AP. Rep: Savalli, Dome. Wash atty: Wiley, Rein & Fielding. Format: Btfl Christian mus, teachings & talk. News staff 2; news progmg 8 hrs wkly. Target aud: 25-49; Evangelical Christians. Spec prog: Farm 16 hrs wkly. ■ Paul Hollinger, CEO; Richard Crawford, pres; Paul R. Hollinger, gen mgr; John Eby, stn mgr; John White, gen sls mgr, natl sls mgr & rgnl sls mgr; Sylvia Hollinger, prom mgr; John E. Eby, progmg dir & mus dir; Greg Barton, news dir; Ralph Haneman, chief engr. ■ Rates: $54; 41; 54; 41.

*****WFNM(FM)**—May 1973: 89.1 mhz; 100 w. Ant 150 ft. TL: N40 02 43 W76 19 14. Stereo. Hrs opn: 20. Box 90, Franklin and Marshall College (17604). (717) 291-4096. FAX: (717) 399-4437. Licensee: Franklin and Marshall College. Format: Adult contemp., div, rock(AOR). News progmg 4 hrs wkly. Target aud: 13-35. Spec prog: Black 6 hrs, sports talk 2 hrs, class 2 hrs, jazz 8 hrs wkly. ■ David Mann, pres & gen mgr; Rich Quinlan, progmg dir; Dan Ralph, mus dir; Norm Elrod, asst mus dir; Will Miller, Chris McNally, news dirs; Cecille Cabigon, pub affrs dir; Nelson Keperling, chief engr.

*****WJTL(FM)**—Aug 27, 1984: 90.3 mhz; 4.7 kw. Ant 198 ft. TL: N40 04 13 W76 17 19 (CP: 11.8 kw, ant 495 ft.). Stereo. Box 1614 (17608). (717) 392-3690. Licensee: Creative Ministries Inc. (acq 11-30-90); $500,000; FTR 12-31-90). Net: USA. Wash atty: Fisher, Wayland, Cooper & Leader. Format: Contemp Christian. ■ Fred McNaughton, stn mgr; John Shirk, progmg dir; Kent Hayburn, mus dir; Roy Landis, chief engr.

WLAN(AM)—Aug 9, 1946: 1390 khz; 5 kw-D, 1 kw-N, DA-2. TL: N40 03 12 W76 20 26. Stereo. 252 N. Queen St. (17603). (717) 295-9700. FAX: (717) 295-7329. Licensee: Peoples Broadcasting Co. Group owner: Altdoerffer Group. Net: CBS. Rep: D & R Radio. Format: Contemp Christian. News staff one; news progmg 15 hrs wkly. Target aud: 25-54. ■ Samuel M. Altdoerffer, CEO; Chuck Lontine, vp & gen mgr; John Fraunfelter, gen sls mgr; Scott Shannon, progmg dir; Garett Micheals, mus dir; Chadrick Bruske, asst mus dir; Ellen Wascou, news dir; Troy Becker, chief engr.

WLAN-FM—January 1948: 96.9 mhz; 50 kw. Ant 500 ft. TL: N40 02 52 W76 27 25. Stereo. Prog sep from AM. Net: ABC/FM, ABC/R. Format: Adult contemp, top-40. News staff 4; news progmg 10 hrs wkly. Target aud: 18-54. Spec prog: Penn State sports.

*****WLCH(FM)**—Sept 14, 1987: 91.3 mhz; 160 w. Ant 135 ft. TL: N40 04 13 W76 17 19. 2nd Floor, 30 N. Ann St. (17602). (717) 295-7760; (717) 295-7996. Licensee: Spanish American Civic Association for Equality Inc. Format: Sp, educ, div. Target aud: Hispanics of all ages. ■ Enid Vazquez, gen mgr; Sol Velazquez, Enid Vazquez-Pereira, gen sls mgrs; Maria del Valle, progmg mgr & mus dir; Sol Velazquez, news dir; Nelson Kepperling, chief engr. ■ Rates: $15; 15; 15; 15.

WLPA(AM)—1922: 1490 khz; 600 w-U. TL: N40 03 38 W76 18 59. Stereo. Hrs opn: 24. Box 4368 (17604); 24 S. Queen St. (17603). (717) 653-0800; (717) 222-1013. FAX: (717) 653-0122. Licensee: Hall Communications Inc. (group owner); acq 2-13-77). Net: CNN; Radio Pa. Format: News. News staff 3. Target aud: General. Spec prog: Relg 2 hrs, sports 20 hrs wkly. ■ Robert M. Hall, chmn; Arthur J. Rowbotham, pres; William S. Baldwin, sr vp & gen mgr; Dan Knighton, opns mgr; Glenn Brooks, gen sls mgr & rgnl sls mgr; Edd Monskie, chief engr.

WROZ(FM)—Co-owned with WLPA(AM). 1944: 101.3 mhz; 50 kw. Ant 1,289 ft. TL: N40 02 04 W76 37 08. Stereo. Hrs opn: 24. Prog sep from AM. Format: Soft adult contemp. Target aud: 18-49. Spec prog: Relg 2 hrs wkly.

Lansdale

WNPV(AM)—Oct 17, 1960: 1440 khz; 2.5 kw-D, 500 w-N, DA-2. TL: N40 14 18 W75 19 00. Hrs opn: 6 AM-10 PM. Box 1440 (19446). (215) 855-8211. FAX: (215) 368-0180. Licensee: WNPV Inc. (acq 10-1-80). Net: AP, MBS; Radio Pa. Format: MOR, news, talk. News staff 2; news progmg 20 hrs wkly. Target aud: 30 plus. Spec prog: Big band 4 hrs, gospel 2 hrs, It one hr, relg 5 hrs wkly. ■ John G. Skibbe, pres; Phillip N. Hunt, vp & gen mgr; Bob Burton, gen sls mgr; Darryl Bergel, progmg dir; Jenny Robinson, news dir; Dave McCrork, chief engr. ■ Rates: $32; 21.50; 22; 18.

Lansford

WLSH(AM)—Dec 24, 1952: 1410 khz; 5 kw-D, DA. TL: N40 50 40 W75 50 37. Box D (18232). (717) 645-3123. FAX: (717) 645-2159. Licensee: East Penn Broadcasting Inc. Group owner: HGF Media Group (acq 1-69; $300,000; FTR 1-16-89). Net: UPI. Format: Adult contemp. Spec prog: Swing years, polkas, memory music, Pol 3 hrs wkly. ■ Harold G. Fulmer III, pres; Mick Haggerty, gen mgr; Bill Lokatas, chief engr.

Latrobe

WCNS(AM)—Aug 11, 1956: 1480 khz; 500 w-D, 1 kw-N, DA-N. TL: N40 16 12 W79 23 13. Hrs opn: 24. 317 Depot St. (15650). (412) 537-3338. FAX: (412) 539-9798. Licensee: Longo Media Group (acq 1-89). Net: Unistar, CNN. Format: Adult contemp. News staff 3; news progmg 15 hours wkly. Target aud: General; 25-54. Spec prog: Relg 2 hrs wkly. ■ John Longo, pres & gen mgr; Dow Carnahan, opns mgr; Donna Longo, dev mgr; J.R. Howard, gen sls mgr; Cheryl Tomaselli, prom mgr; Rhonda Riener, news dir; Chuck Campbell, pub affrs dir; Dick Ruby, chief engr. ■ Rates: $20; 20; 20; 20.

WQTW(AM)—1952: 1570 khz; 1 kw-D, 220 w-N. TL: N40 18 07 W79 21 26. Box 208 (15650). (412) 628-2800. Licensee: L. Stanley Wall (acq 4-84); $66,000; FTR 4-23-84). Format: MOR, oldies. Prog Pol 5 hrs wkly. ■ L. Stanley Wall, pres; Chris Molten, gen mgr & gen sls mgr; Joey Kaye, progmg dir; Debbie Larson, mus dir; Al Colisti, chief engr.

Lebanon

WADV(AM)—July 4, 1976: 940 khz; 1 kw-D, 5 w-N. TL: N40 22 22 W76 21 53. Stereo. Hrs opn: 19. Box 940, 720 E. Kercher Ave. (17042). (717) 273-2611. FAX: (717) 273-7293. Licensee: F.D.K. Inc. (acq 1-2-92; $50,000; FTR 1-20-92). Net: Moody. Format: Southern gospel. News staff one; news progmg 18 hrs wkly. Target aud: 25 plus; loyal, exclusive. ■ Fred Krug, pres, gen mgr & gen sls mgr; Charles Devine, opns mgr, progmg dir & mus dir; Craig Senior, news dir; Craig Baker, chief engr. ■ Rates: $21; 17; 21; 7.

WLBR(AM)—Nov 13, 1946: 1270 khz; 5 kw-D, 1 kw-N, DA-2. TL: N40 21 35 W76 27 30. Hrs opn: 5 AM-1 AM. Box 1270, Rt. 72 N. (17042). (717) 272-7651. FAX: (717) 274-0161. Licensee: Lebanon Broadcasting Co. Net: ABC/I; Radio Pa. Rep: Katz & Powell; Dome. Wash atty: Kenkel & Assoc. Format: Full service, talk. News staff 2. Target aud: 25 plus. ■ Lester P. Etter, pres; Robert D. Etter, vp & progmg dir; Edward J. Burris, gen mgr; Mickey Santora, gen sls mgr; Greg Lyons, mus dir; Henry Homan, news dir; Glenn Waybright, chief engr.

WQIC(FM)—Co-owned with WLBR(AM). January 1948: 100.1 mhz; 3 kw. Ant 270 ft-H, 265 ft-V. TL: N40 21 37 W76 27 31. Stereo. Hrs opn: 5 AM-1 AM. Prog sep from AM. Format: CHR. News staff 2. Target aud: 18-40. ■ Hank Bastian, opns mgr, progmg dir & mus dir.

WWSM(AM)—See Annville-Cleona.

Lehighton

WYNS(AM)—Licensed to Lehighton. See Allentown.

Pennsylvania

Directory of Radio

Levittown-Fairless Hills

WBCB(AM)—Dec 8, 1957: 1490 khz; 1 kw-U. TL: N40 10 08 W74 50 08. Hrs opn: 24. 200 Magnolia Dr., Levittown (19054). (215) 949-1490. FAX: (215) 949-3671. Licensee: Progressive Broadcasting Co. (acq 11-13-92; $550,000; FTR 11-30-92). Net: USA. Format: Adult contemp. News staff one. Target aud: 25-34. ■ Pasquale T. Deon Sr., pres; Merrill Reese, gen mgr; William Dollman, stn mgr; Jim Heston, gen sls mgr; M.J. Klein, pub affrs dir; John Packard, chief engr. ■ Rates: $30; 25; 30; 20.

Lewisburg

*****WGRC(FM)**—April 22, 1988: 91.3 mhz; 5 kw. Ant 89 ft. TL: N40 59 58 W76 52 24. Stereo. Hrs opn: 24. Creamery Building, Suite 202, 150 Buffalo Rd. (17837). (717) 523-1190. FAX: (717) 523-1114. Licensee: Salt and Light Media Ministries Inc. Net: Moody, Skylight. Wash atty: Miller & Miller. Format: Contemp Christian. News progmg 16 hrs wkly. Target aud: 25-49; young to middle-aged adult. ■ Larry Weidman, gen mgr & mus dir; Eric Reinholt, progmg dir; Terry Diener, news dir; Harry Bingaman, chief engr.

WTGC(AM)—Sept 9, 1957: 1010 khz; 1 kw-D, 13 w-N. TL: N40 29 11 W77 59 35. Hrs opn: 24. Box 592, 101 Armory Blvd. (17837). (717) 523-3271; (717) 524-7000. FAX: (717) 523-9510. Licensee: Town, Gown and Country Radio (acq 6-28-76). Wash atty: Mullin, Rhyne, Emmons & Topel. Format: Country, contemp. News staff 2; news progmg 2 hrs wkly. Target aud: 25-54; professional, affluent men & women. Spec prog: Southern gospel 12 hrs wkly. ■ Louis J. Maierhofer, gen mgr; Andrea S. Delaney, opns mgr; Paul Hartman, gen sls mgr & adv mgr; Lisa Richards, progmg dir; Ray Swartz, mus dir; Barry Seidel, news dir; John Super, engrg dir; Roger Allvord, chief engr.

WUNS(FM)—Co-owned with WTGC(AM). Oct 18, 1990: 96.3 mhz; 3 kw. Ant 418 ft. TL: N40 56 40 W76 52 45. Stereo. Hrs opn: 18. Dups AM 80%. Format: Adult contemp. Target aud: 24-49; professional, affluent and youthful women. ■ Pryor Neuber Jr., progmg dir; Skip Hurst, mus dir.

*****WVBU-FM**—October 1965: 90.5 mhz; 500 w. Ant -120 ft. TL: N40 57 18 W76 52 46. Stereo. Hrs opn: 8 AM-2 AM. Box C-3956, Bucknell University (17837). (717) 524-3489; (717) 524-1326. FAX: (717) 524-3760. Licensee: Bucknell University. Format: Div, rock, progrsv. News progmg 7 hrs wkly. Target aud: 18-23; college students. Spec prog: Jazz 3 hrs, dance/club 6 hrs, prison request 2 hrs, modern/new age one hr wkly. ■ Lisa Bell, stn mgr; Christy Schiano, opns dir; Fred Koczwara, dev mgr; Mark Fadden, Brian Vettoso, gen sls mgrs; Eric Langheim, prom dir; Liz Shaw, progmg dir; Christopher Ebbesen, mus dir; John Shuttleworth, Kyle Smith, chiefs engr.

Lewistown

WCHX(FM)—July 1, 1987: 105.5 mhz; 3 kw. Ant 817 ft. TL: N40 39 43 W77 34 28 (CP: 465 w, ant 816 ft.). Stereo. Hrs opn: 24. Box 1055, Burnham (17009); 114 N. Logan, Burnham (17009). (717) 242-1500. FAX: (717) 242-3764. Licensee: Mifflin County Communications Inc. Net: ABC/E. Wash atty: Wilkinson, Barker, Knauer, Quinn. Format: Adult contemp. News staff one; news progmg 10 hrs wkly. Target aud: 24-55; mature, affluent, middle & upper class adults. ■ Russell Crawford Jr., pres; David E. Semler, gen mgr; Roger A. Herto, gen sls mgr; Larry Wise, mus dir; Jerry Boyer, news dir; Harry S. Hain, chief engr. ■ Rates: $15; 15; 15; 8.

WIEZ(AM)—June 1, 1941: 670 khz; 5.4 kw-D. TL: N40 36 30 W77 34 45. 12 1/2 E. Market St. (17044). (717) 248-6757. FAX: (717) 248-6759. Licensee: Mifflin County Broadcasting Co. (acq 8-1-78). Net: ABC/I. Rep: Dome. Format: Oldies. News staff 2; news progmg 12 hrs wkly. Target aud: 25-54; adults who control the area's disposable income. ■ Frank P. Troiani, pres & gen mgr; Peter Herman, gen sls mgr; Jeff Stevens, prom mgr; progmg dir & mus dir; Nils Frederiksen, news dir; Dave Supplee, chief engr.

WMRF-FM—Co-owned with WIEZ(AM). Oct 1, 1964: 95.9 mhz; 3.9 kw. Ant 407 ft. TL: N40 36 30 W77 34 45. Stereo. Hrs opn: 18. Prog sep from AM. Net: CNN. Format: Adult CHR. News staff 2; news progmg 8 hrs wkly. Target aud: 18-44; young adults.

WKVA(AM)—Dec 4, 1949: 920 khz; 1 kw-D, 500 w-N, DA-N. TL: N40 34 45 W77 34 18. Hrs opn: 5 AM-midnight. Box 911, One Juniata St. (17044). (717) 242-1493. FAX: (717) 242-3779. Licensee: Central Pennsylvania Broadcasting Co. (acq 3-1-51). Net: AP; Radio Pa. Format: Country. News staff 2; news progmg 31 hrs wkly. Target aud: 25-54. ■ Robert L. Wilson, pres & gen mgr; Kimberly Sprout, stn mgr & dev dir; Ed Fisher, opns mgr & progmg dir; Steven Pechter, gen sls mgr & adv dir; Ron Dawson, mktg dir; Tom Scott, prom mgr; Tina DiDomizio, mus dir; Missi Bair, news dir; John Dillon, chief engr. ■ Rates: $16; 16; 16; 16.

WMRF-FM—Listing follows WIEZ(AM).

Lincoln University

*****WLIU(FM)**—Aug 1, 1975: 88.7 mhz; 10 w. Ant 100 ft. Lincoln University (19352). (215) 932-8300, ext. 555. Licensee: Lincoln University. Format: Div. ■ Lisa Bacon, pres & gen mgr.

Linesville

WVCC(FM)—May 4, 1970: 101.7 mhz; 3 kw. Ant 300 ft. TL: N41 40 48 W80 27 12. Stereo. Hrs opn: 24. Box 307 (16424). (814) 683-4000. FAX: (814) 683-4000. Licensee: Arthur W. Cervi. Net: SMN. Format: MOR. ■ A.W. Cervi Sr., pres; A. W. Cervi Jr., gen mgr & progmg dir; C. Stopp, news dir.

Lock Haven

WBPZ(AM)—Feb 20, 1947: 1230 khz; 1 kw-U. TL: N41 08 03 W77 28 09. Hrs opn: 24. Box 420, 738 Bellefonte Ave. (17745). (717) 748-4038. FAX: (717) 748-0092. Licensee: Lipez Broadcasting Corp. (acq 3-27-86). Net: UPI. Rep: Keystone (unwired net), Dome. Format: Oldies. News staff one; news progmg 10 hrs wkly. Target aud: General. Spec prog: Local sports. ■ John Lipez, pres & gen mgr; Randy Dorey, progmg dir & mus dir; Dan Adams, news dir; Dennis Sherman, chief engr.

WSNU(FM)—Co-owned with WBPZ(AM). September 1965: 92.1 mhz; 3 kw. Ant 255 ft. TL: N41 08 49 W77 29 16. Stereo. Hrs opn: 24. Prog sep from AM. Format: Adult contemp. News staff one; news progmg 6 hrs wkly. Target aud: 21-48.

Loretto

WJRV(AM)—Dec 7, 1963: 1400 khz; 1 kw-U. TL: N40 30 12 W78 38 10. Box 68 (15940). (814) 472-4900. FAX: (814) 472-4908. Licensee: Stevens Broadcasting Co. Inc. (acq 7-28-92; FTR 8-17-92). Format: Soft adult rock. News staff one; news progmg 7 hrs wkly. Target aud: 25-54; females 25-54 plus, males 30 plus. Spec prog: Farm one hr wkly. ■ Tom Stevens, CEO, pres & gen mgr. ■ Rates: $7; 7; 7; 7.

Mansfield

WMPA(FM)—Not on air, target date unknown: 92.3 mhz; 540 w. Ant 764 ft. TL: N41 53 43 W77 04 21. 15th & Hamilton Sts., Allentown (18102). Licensee: Penn Central Broadcasting Inc. Group owner: Harold G. Fulmer III (acq 4-24-92; $3,000 for CP; FTR 5-18-92).

*****WNTE(FM)**—Sept 15, 1968: 89.5 mhz; 115 w. Ant -320.4 ft. TL: N41 48 22 W77 04 27. Box 84, South Hall, Mansfield University (16933). (717) 662-4650 Licensee: Mansfield University of Pa. (acq 9-15-78). Net: AP. Format: AOR, top-40. Target aud: 17-25; college students/community. Spec prog: Black 5 hrs, jazz 2 hr wkly. ■ Joe Healey, gen mgr; Jennifer Holt, sls dir; Marc Sanders, prom dir; Ben Nevin, progmg dir; Mitchell Hellman, mus dir; Robert Weigand, engrg dir; Robert Wiegand, engrg mgr. ■ Rates: $12; 12; 12; 12.

Marietta

*****WRFH(FM)**—Not on air, target date unknown: 88.7 mhz; 4.1 kw. Ant 679 ft. TL: N40 04 29 W76 48 01. 246 Front St. (17547). Licensee: People's United Christian Way Church of Faith, Hope and Love Inc.

Martinsburg

WJSM(AM)—Feb 27, 1968: 1110 khz; 1 kw-D. TL: N40 18 14 W78 15 59. Box 87, Rt. 2 (16662); Box 2258, Altoona (16603). (814) 793-2188. Licensee: Martinsburg Broadcasting Inc. (acq 10-1-89). Net: CBN. Wash atty: Harold McCombs. Format: Relg. News staff one; news progmg 10 hrs wkly. Target aud: general. Spec prog: Farm one hr wkly. ■ Larry S. Walters, pres, gen mgr, progmg dir & news dir; Deborah J. Walters, opns mgr; Byrle R. Ritchey Jr., rgnl sls mgr; Gary G. Dull, prom dir; Hap Ritchey, prom mgr, adv mgr & mus dir; Bill Reed, asst mus dir; Matthew Lightner, engrg dir; J. Terry MacAlamey, chief engr.

WJSM-FM—Apr 19, 1965: 92.7 mhz; 330 w. Ant 984 ft. TL: N40 17 37 W78 15 38.

WKMC(AM)—See Roaring Spring.

Masontown

*****WRIJ(FM)**—Nov 1990: 106.9 mhz; 3 kw. Ant 328 ft. TL: N39 47 15 W79 59 20. Stereo. Hrs opn: 24. Rebroadcasts WAIJ(FM) Grantsville 100%. Box 540, He's Alive Corp. Offices, 34 Springs Rd., Grantsville, MD (21536). (301) 895-3292; (412) 324-9218. FAX: (301) 895-3293. Licensee: He's Alive Inc. (group owner). Net: USA. Wash atty: Lee Peltzman. Format: Gospel, Christian adult contemp. Target aud: 18-35. ■ Dewayne Johnson, pres; Wally Weeks, gen mgr & stn mgr; Mark Van Ouse, progmg mgr; Rick Williams, chief engr.

McConnellsburg

WVFC(AM)—December 1976: 1530 khz; 1 kw-D, 250 w-CH. TL: N39 55 23 W77 59 08. Box 1530, Rt. 16 (17233). (717) 485-3117. Licensee: Fulton County Radio (acq 1-12-76). Format: C&W. News staff one; news progmg 20 hrs wkly. Target aud: 25-65. Spec prog: Farm one hr wkly. ■ Arthur Greiner, pres; Teresa Guyer, gen sls mgr; Michelle Hollenshead, prom mgr; Steve Ward, progmg dir, mus dir & news dir; Harry Taylor, chief engr.

McKean

WJET(FM)—See Erie.

McKeesport

WEDO(AM)—1947: 810 khz; 1 kw-D. TL: N40 21 52 W79 48 49. Midtown Plaza Mall, 414 5th Ave. (15132). (412) 664-4431. Licensee: 810 Inc. (acq 5-72). Format: Talk, variety. Spec prog: Relg one hr, health 2 hrs, psychic one hr wkly. ■ Judith Baron, pres; John James, gen mgr; Bill Korch, progmg dir & news dir; Richard Ruby, chief engr.

WIXZ(AM)—April 1947: 1360 khz; 5 kw-D, 1 kw-N, DA-N. TL: N40 24 30 W79 55 40. Hrs opn: 6 AM-1 AM. Box 1360, 400 Lincoln Hwy., East McKeesport (15035). (412) 823-1100. Licensee: Serena Communications Inc. (acq 7-16-85; $1,420,000; FTR 12-17-84). Net: SMN. Format: Country, div. News staff 3; news progmg 20 hrs wkly. Target aud: 25-54. Spec prog: Oldies 9 hrs wkly. ■ Alan C. Serena, pres & gen mgr; Tim E. Charpie, gen sls mgr; Annie Carter, progmg dir; Michael D. Manko, mus dir & news dir; Dick Ruby, chief engr.

Meadville

*****WARC(FM)**—Feb 3, 1963: 90.3 mhz; 150 w. Ant 86 ft. TL: N41 38 55 W80 08 45. Stereo. Box C, Allegheny College (16335). (814) 332-3376; (814) 332-2305. Licensee: Allegheny College. Net: AP. Format: Alternative, div. News progmg one hr wkly. Spec prog: Black 8 hrs, class 10 hrs, jazz 4 hrs wkly. ■ Carleton Garrett, gen mgr; Mike Keeley, opns dir; Mike Hanson, mus dir; Daniel Winsor, chief engr.

WMGW(AM)—1947: 1490 khz; 1 kw-U. TL: N41 37 53 W80 10 37. Box 397, Downtown Mall (16335). (814) 724-1111. FAX: (814) 333-9628. Licensee: Great Circle Broadcasting Co. Group owner: Music Broadcasting Group (acq 4-13-83; grpsl; FTR 4-2-84). Net: ABC/I, AP. Format: Adult contemp. News staff one; news progmg 5 hrs wkly. Target aud: 25-54. ■ Gary Gunton, pres & gen mgr; Mark Kilburn, gen sls mgr; Ray Horner, prom mgr, progmg dir & mus dir; Todd Hart, news dir; John McWilliams, chief engr.

WZPR(FM)—Co-owned with WMGW(AM). 1947: 100.3 mhz; 20 kw. Ant 587 ft. TL: N41 37 53 W80 10 37. Stereo. Prog sep from AM. Net: ABC/D, ABC/E. Format: Country. ■ Ray Horner, mus dir.

Mechanicsburg

WTPA(FM)—Nov 1, 1978: 93.5 mhz; 1.75 kw. Ant 620 ft. TL: N40 10 38 W76 52 38 (CP: 1.25 kw, ant 718 ft.). Stereo. Box 9350, Harrisburg (17108); 970 W. Trindle Rd., Mechanicsburg (17055). (717) 697-1141. FAX: (717) 697-1149. Licensee: Quaker State Broadcasting Corp. (acq 6-15-82; $650,000; FTR 7-5-82). Rep: Banner. Wash atty: Wilkinson, Barker, Knauer & Quinn. Format: AOR. News staff one; news progmg 5 hrs wkly. Target aud: 18-49. ■ Michael Brandon, CEO & gen mgr; John Butler, gen sls mgr; Jeff Kauffman, progmg dir; Chris James, mus dir; Ed Coffey, news dir; Rich Hill, chief engr.

Media

WPLY(FM)—November 1982: 100.3 mhz; 35 kw. Ant 600 ft. TL: N39 35 29 W75 25 22 (CP: 9.2 kw, ant 1,145 ft.). Stereo. Hrs opn: 24. 1001 Baltimore Pike (19063). (215) 565-8900. FAX: (215) 565-7823. Licensee:

Greater Media Radio Co. Rep: D & R Radio. Wash atty: E. William Henry. Format: Adult top 40. News staff one. Target aud: 25-54. ■ Daniel M. Lerner, CEO & chmn; Lynn Bruder, gen mgr; Tom Interrante, sls dir; Eric Johnson, prom mgr; Garett Michaels, progmg dir; Sherry Lee Stevens, news dir; Doug Fearn, chief engr.

Mercer

WLLF(FM)—January 1985: 96.7 mhz; 1.4 kw. Ant 485 ft. TL: N41 18 43 W80 16 39. Stereo. Hrs opn: 6 AM-10 PM. Box 358 (16137). (412) 662-5361. Licensee: Mercer County Broadcasting. Format: Classic rock, relg. Peggy Engrao, pres; Albert Zippay, gen mgr. ■ Rates: $10; 10; 10; 7.

WWIZ(FM)—October 1972: 103.9 mhz; 3 kw. Ant 300 ft. TL: N41 12 10 W80 21 30. Stereo. Box 1120, Hermitage (16148). (412) 981-4580. FAX: (412) 981-9050. Licensee: GBS Communications (acq 8-85; $850,000; FTR 7-15-85). Net: Moody. Format: C&W. Target aud: 25-54. ■ Karl Brandt, pres & gen mgr; Dan Brandt, progmg dir; Andy Brandt, mus dir; Lisa Pavel, news dir; John Clarke, chief engr.

Mercersburg

WSRT(FM)—March 23, 1976: 92.1 mhz; 3.3 kw. Ant 295 ft. TL: N39 48 34 W77 48 22 (CP: 2.7 kw, ant 465 ft.). Stereo. Hrs opn: 24. Box 92 (17236); 8737 Kuhn Bridge Rd., Greencastle (17225). (717) 597-9200; (717) 267-1590. FAX: (717) 597-9210. Licensee: M. Belmont VerStandig Inc. Group owner: VerStandig Broadcasting (acq 10-1-93; $1.6 million with WCBG[AM] Chambersburg; FTR 9-6-93). Net: ABC/D. Format: Adult contemp. News staff one; news progmg 6 hrs wkly. Target aud: 25-54; double income households. ■ John D. Yarstandig, pres; Marge Martin, gen mgr; Barry Starliper, stn mgr; Randall Ackerman, gen sls mgr; Dennis Hughes, progmg dir & mus dir; Brad Christman, news dir; Chris Snively, chief engr. ■ Rates: $22.50; 22.50; 22.50; 22.50.

Mexico

WJUN(AM)—Sept 8, 1955: 1220 khz; 1 kw-D, 40 w-N. TL: N40 32 07 W77 20 34. Box 209, Old Rt. 22 E. (17056). (717) 436-2135. FAX: (717) 436-8155. Licensee: WJUN Inc. (acq 11-16-89; grpsl; FTR 12-19-88). Net: NBC; Radio Pa. Format: Adult contemp. News staff one; news progmg 12 hrs wkly. Target aud: 25-54. Spec prog: Gospel 3 hrs, relg 6 hrs wkly. ■ Douglas George, pres; Curt Dreibelbis, gen mgr & gen sls mgr; Mindi Dee, mus dir; Dan Roland, news dir; John Hess, chief engr.

WJUN-FM—July 4, 1989: 92.5 mhz; 3 kw. Ant 1,302 ft. TL: N40 28 38 W77 23 12. Stereo. Hrs opn: 24. Prog sep from AM. Format: Country. Spec prog: Farm one hr wkly. ■ Mel Thomas, progmg dir.

Meyersdale

WQZS(FM)—Not on air, target date unknown: 93.3 mhz; 630 w. Ant 964 ft. TL: N39 47 49 W79 10 05. R.D. 3, Box 194 (15552). (814) 634-0882. Licensee: Roger Wahl. ■ Kevin Gardner, gen mgr.

Middletown

*WMSS(FM)—Sept 7, 1978: 91.1 mhz; 1.35 w. Ant -69 ft. TL: N40 11 52 W76 43 30. Hrs opn: 9 AM-9 PM. 214 Race St. (17057). (717) 948-9136. FAX: (717) 948-3329. Licensee: Middletown Area School District. Net: Radio Pa. Format: CHR, progsv, educ. News progmg 3 hrs wkly. Target aud: General. Spec prog: Sports 5 hrs, class 2 hrs, jazz 2 hrs, relg 6 hrs wkly. ■ John Wilsbach, gen mgr; Steve Leedy, dev dir; Maureen Denis, dev mgr; Paul Yoder, progmg mgr; Trish Arnold, mus dir; Mike Fisher, pub affrs dir; Tim Starliper, engrg dir; Randy Miller, chief engr.

Mifflinburg

WWBE(FM)—1975: 98.3 mhz; 3 kw. Ant 403 ft. TL: N40 53 27 W76 59 54. Stereo. Hrs opn: 24. Box 503A, R.R. #2 (17844). (717) 966-0098. FAX: (717) 966-4622. Licensee: Marnu Inc. (acq 3-1-92; $725,000 with WWBV[FM] Beaver Springs; FTR 3-16-92). Wash atty: Lauren A. Colby. Format: Contemporary country. News staff 2; news progmg 2 hrs wkly. Target aud: 25-54. ■ Pryor Neuber Jr., gen mgr & pub affrs mgr; Lisa Richards, opns mgr, prom dir & progmg dir; Paul Hartman, gen sls mgr; Barry Seidel, news dir; William Margut, engrg dir; Roger Allvord, chief engr. ■ Rates: $17.50; 15.25; 17.50; 14.25.

Mifflintown

*WQJU(FM)—Oct 15, 1985: 107.1 mhz; 500 w. Ant 1,117 ft. TL: N40 37 13 W77 28 42. Hrs opn: 24. Rebroadcasts WTLR(FM) State College, 100%. 2020 Cato Ave., State College (16801). (814) 237-9857. Licensee: Central Pennsylvania Christian Institute (acq 1-22-93; $132,500; FTR 2-15-93). Net: Moody, USA. Wash atty: Shanis & Peltzman. Format: Relg. Target aud: 25-49; young adults, family oriented. ■ Kenneth Krater, pres; Garry Sutley, gen mgr; Doreen Crandell, opns mgr & mus dir.

Millersburg

WQLV(FM)—Feb 24, 1992: 98.9 mhz; 780 w. Ant 895 ft. TL: N40 30 18 W77 07 03. Hrs opn: 24. 309 Peachtree Dr., Gratz (17030). (717) 692-2193; (717) 365-3161. FAX: (717) 692-2080. Licensee: Hepco Communications Inc. Format: Soft adult contemp. News staff one; news progmg 6 hrs wkly. Target aud: 25-60. Spec prog: High school sports 6 hrs wkly. ■ James F. Hepler, pres & gen mgr; Maggie Leuschner, gen sls mgr; Beverly Amsler, news dir. ■ Rates: $18; 12; 15; 10.

Millersville

*WIXQ(FM)—1978: 91.7 mhz; 129 w. Ant 69 ft. TL: N39 59 53 W76 21 20. Hrs opn: 7 AM-3 AM. Millersville University (17551). (717) 872-3518. Licensee: Millersville University. Format: Alternative progsv, Black, class. News progmg one hr wkly. Target aud: 18-24; college students. Spec prog: Jazz 2 hrs wkly. ■ Vince D'Ambrosio, stn mgr; Denise Ditmore, opns mgr; Steve Gallo, sls dir; Michelle Arizmendi, prom dir; Rich Thomas, progmg dir; Matt Conn, mus dir; Karen Applegate, news dir; Steve Weaver, pub affrs dir; Nelson Keperling, chief engr.

Milton

WMLP(AM)—Oct 27, 1955: 1380 khz; 1 kw-D, 18 w-N. TL: N40 59 52 W76 52 17. Box 334 (17847); R.R. 3, Rt. 15, Lewisburg (17837). (717) 568-1380. FAX: (717) 568-1300. Licensee: WMLP Inc. (acq 8-1-61). Net: MBS, NBC Talknet. Rep: Dome. Format: Oldies, talk. News staff one; news progmg 11 hrs wkly. Target aud: 35 plus. ■ Joseph Kesnow, pres; John H. Yingling, vp, stn mgr & gen sls mgr; Donald C. Steese, gen mgr, progmg dir & mus dir; Kathy Coup, news dir; Harry Bingaman, chief engr. ■ Rates: $10; 8; 8; 8.

WOEZ-FM—Co-owned with WMLP(AM). Oct 1, 1967: 100.9 mhz; 640 w. Ant 690 ft. TL: N40 57 06 W76 45 03. Stereo. Hrs opn: 5 AM-1 AM. Prog sep from AM. Format: Lite adult contemp. Target aud: 25-54. ■ Rates: $15; 18; 15; 6.

Monroeville

WXVX(AM)—Sept 27, 1964: 1510 khz; 1 kw-D, DA. TL: N40 26 03 W79 46 54. One Progressive Alley (15146). (412) 856-4123. Licensee: Barua Communications of Monroeville Inc. (acq 8-14-80). Net: Westwood One. Format: Alternative rock, new age, progsv, AOR. Target aud: 18-34; middle class and higher income households. Spec prog: Loc music, in-house countdown show, new mus exclusives. ■ Paul Goodman, gen mgr & mus dir; Lon Wilson, gen sls mgr; Randy Dietrichs, chief engr.

Montrose

*WPEL(AM)—May 30, 1953: 1250 khz; 1 kw-D. TL: N41 51 16 W75 51 50. Hrs opn: 6 AM-sunset. Box 248, 9 Locust St. (18801). (717) 278-2811. FAX: (717) 278-1442. Licensee: Montrose Broadcasting Corp. (group owner). Net: AP. Wash atty: Gammon & Grange. Format: Relg, btfl mus. News progmg 7 hrs wly. Target aud: General; families. Spec prog: Ukrainian one hr, class one hr, farm one hr wkly. ■ Larry Souder, pres & gen mgr; Lloyd Sheldon, opns mgr; LaVerne Sollick, prom dir; Robert Brigham, chief engr.

*WPEL-FM—June 5, 1961: 96.5 mhz; 57 kw. Ant 459 ft. TL: N41 51 16 W75 51 50. Stereo. Hrs opn: 24. Dups AM 50%. Net: Moody. News progmg 12 hrs wkly.

Mount Carmel

WSPI(FM)—Not on air, target date unknown: 99.7 mhz; 790 w. Ant 646 ft. TL: N40 49 09 W76 27 45. 612 N. Shamokin St., Shamokin (17872). (717) 644-0700. Licensee: H & P Communications Ltd. (acq 12-28-92; $24,000; FTR 1-25-93). Format: Adult contemp. ■ Rebecca Boedker, gen mgr; Gary Surak, gen sls mgr; Mary Ann Donlin, prom dir; Rick Ricigliano, progmg dir & mus dir; Bill Lakatas Jr., chief engr.

Mount Pocono

WPMR(AM)—April 8, 1981: 960 khz; 1 kw-D, 24 w-N, DA-2. TL: N41 04 14 W75 23 33. Hrs opn: 24. Rebroadcasts WPMR-FM Tobyhanna. Box 132, Mountain Dr., (18344). (717) 839-3939. FAX: (717) 839-9875. Licensee: Tiab Communications Corporation (acq 4-15-92; $198,000). Wash atty: Denise B. Moline, P.C. Format: AOR. News staff 2; news progmg one hr wkly. Target aud: 18-34; males. ■ Jeff Woehrle, gen mgr & chief engr; Kitty Moyer, opns mgr; Carole Gehring, gen sls mgr; Chris Debello, rgnl sls mgr; Kelly Lockwood, prom dir; Robin Lee, progmg dir; Patrick Butler, mus dir; Mason Hall, news dir; Kim Kalina, pub affrs dir. ■ Rates: $38.50; 28.50; 38.50; 28.50.

Mount Union

WXMJ(FM)—May 24, 1989: 99.5 mhz; 300 w. Ant 1,440 ft. TL: N40 24 53 W77 54 13. Stereo. 112 W. Shirley St. (17066). (814) 542-8648. FAX: (814) 542-8649. Licensee: Bardcom Inc. Net: AP. Format: Adult contemp. News staff one; news progmg 7 hrs wkly. Target aud: 25-54; community minded adults. Spec prog: Relg 2 hrs wkly. ■ Ron Rabena, pres & chief engr; Brian Williams, gen mgr; Andrew Hunter, gen sls mgr; Tom Sheeder, prom mgr & progmg dir; Ron Rabena, Tom Sheeder, mus dirs. ■ Rates: $30; 30; 30; 30.

Mountaintop

WBHT(FM)—Not on air, target date unknown: 97.1 mhz; 250 w. Ant 1,102 ft. TL: N41 10 57 W75 52 22. 37 Race St., Wilkes-Barre (18702-3636). (717) 824-9702. Licensee: Fairview Communications Inc. Wash atty: Cohn & Marks. ■ Bob Crawford, pres; C. Morgan Jr., CFO.

Muncy

WHTO(FM)—Licensed to Muncy. See Williamsport.

Murrysville

*WRWJ(FM)—Dec 1, 1993: 88.1 mhz; 100 w. Ant 220 ft. TL: N40 29 40 W80 01 08. Hrs opn: 24. Rebroadcasts WAIJ(FM) Grantsville, MD. 1000 Springs Rd., Grantsville, MD (21536). (301) 895-3292; (800) 437-2548. FAX: (301) 895-3293. Licensee: He's Alive Inc. Net: USDA. Format: Gospel/Christian adult contemp. Target aud: 18-35; general. ■ Dewayne Johnson, pres & gen mgr; Wally Weeks, stn mgr; June Justice, opns dir; Monte Palmer, progmg dir; Scott Reppert, mus dir; Martha Reppert, news dir; Claire Saulpaw, pub affrs dir; Marty White, engrg mgr; Bruce Herget, chief engr.

Nanticoke

WNAK(AM)—February 1947: 730 khz; 1 kw-D, 38 w-N. TL: N41 13 10 W75 59 28. Stereo. 84 S. Prospect St. (18634). (717) 735-0730. FAX: (717) 735-4844. Licensee: Seven-Thirty Broadcasters Inc. (acq 3-28-66). Net: NBC, AP. Rep: Katz & Powell. Format: MOR, btfl mus. News staff one; news progmg 9 hrs wkly. Target aud: 35 plus. Spec prog: Relg 8 hrs wkly. ■ Harold F. Detweiler, pres; R.W. Neilson, vp & gen mgr; Charmaine Grove, gen sls mgr. ■ Rates: $28; 28; 28; na.

*WSFX(FM)—Oct 25, 1987: 89.1 mhz; 100 w. Ant 50 ft. TL: N41 11 42 W75 59 28. Stereo. Luzerne County Community College, Prospect St. & Middle Rd. (18634). (717) 821-0934. Licensee: Luzerne County Community College. Format: Div. News staff 3. Target aud: 16-25; college age alternative mus audience. ■ Thomas J. Moran, pres; Kathy Bozinski, gen mgr; Ron Rino, stn mgr; Gary Blais, chief engr.

WYOS(FM)—Oct 31, 1973: 92.1 mhz; 760 w. Ant 663 ft. TL: N41 15 43 W75 58 04. Stereo. Hrs opn: 24. One Broadcast Plaza, Wilkes-Barre (18703). (717) 288-7575. FAX: (717) 288-7577. Licensee: Frank & Maley Inc. (acq 11-87). Rep: Roslin. Format: Oldies. News staff one; news progmg 5 hrs wkly. Target aud: 25-54. Spec prog: Pol 3 hrs wkly. ■ Joseph A. Frank, pres; Rick Malyk, gen mgr; Vince Clark, prom mgr & progmg mgr; Mary-

Pennsylvania

beth Rockwell, news dir & pub affrs dir; Tom Sommers, chief engr.

New Castle

WBZY(AM)—Aug 25, 1968: 1200 khz; 5 kw-D, 1 kw-N, DA-N. TL: N40 56 22 W80 23 38. 1906 Wilmington Rd. (16105). (412) 656-1200. FAX: (412) 656-6397. Licensee: WBZY Radio (acq 12-29-86; $600,000; FTR 11-10-86). Net: AP. Rep: Shelley Katz. Format: Adult contemp, oldies. News staff 2; news progmg 7 hrs wkly. Target aud: 34 plus. Spec prog: Ger one hr, Greek one hr wkly. ■ Robert McCracken, gen mgr & gen sls mgr; Carol King, progmg dir & mus dir; Joan Hemming, news dir; Bill King, chief engr.

WKST(AM)—Oct 23, 1938: 1280 khz; 5 kw-D, 1 kw-N, DA-N. TL: N40 57 15 W80 19 03. 219 Savannah-Gardner Rd. (16101). (412) 654-5501. FAX: (412) 654-3101. Licensee: Great Scott Broadcasting Ltd. Group owner: Great Scott Broadcasting. Net: ABC/C. Rep: Dome, Rgnl Reps. Format: Full service. News staff 2. Target aud: 30 plus. Spec prog: Black one hr, class one hr wkly. ■ Faye Scott, pres; Sharon Kennedy-Clifton, gen mgr; Lawrence Rispoli, progmg dir; Gary West, mus dir; Ken Hlebovy, news dir; Vicky Schooley, pub affrs dir; Terry Dalton, engrg dir; Don Danko, chief engr. ■ Rates: $26; 21; 26; 18.

New Kensington

WGBN(AM)—October 1940: 1150 khz; 1 kw-D, 70 w-N, DA-1. TL: N40 34 24 W79 46 58. Hrs opn: 24. Suite 200, 955 4th Ave (15068). (412) 337-3588. FAX: (412) 337-1318. Licensee: Pentecostal Temple Development Corp. (acq 11-3-92; FTR 11-23-92). Net: USA. Rep: Dome. Wash atty: Fletcher, Heald & Hildreth. Format: Gospel. News staff one; news progmg 19 hrs wkly. Target aud: 30 plus; older upscale. Spec prog: Pol 3 hrs, It 2 hrs, Irish 2 hrs, relg 2 hrs wkly. ■ Lauren Mann, CEO, pres, gen mgr, gen sls mgr & prom mgr; Randy Dietterich, chief engr.

WQKB(FM)—Aug 17, 1967: 100.7 mhz; 17 kw. Ant 850 ft. TL: N40 29 43 W80 00 18. Stereo. Hrs opn: 24. 1715 Grandview Ave., Pittsburgh (15211). (412) 821-6140. Licensee: E Z Communications (acq 8-1-88). Net: ABC/FM. Rep: D & R Radio. Wash atty: Rosennan & Colin. Format: Country. News staff one. Target aud: Women 18-49. ■ Alan Box, pres; Tex Meyer, gen mgr; Diane Battista, gen sls mgr; Maureen Mihm, prom mgr; Bill Macky, progmg dir & mus dir; Chris Hudak, chief engr.

WXRB(FM)—See Pittsburgh.

New Wilmington

*****WWNW(FM)**—Jan 31, 1968: 88.9 mhz; 110 w. Ant -39 ft. TL: N41 07 08 W80 19 49. Stereo. Box 89, Westminster College (16172). (412) 946-7242. Licensee: Westminster College Board of Trustees. Net: ABC/I. Format: Top-40. Spec prog: Classical 6 hrs wkly. ■ David L. Barner, gen mgr.

Norristown

WNAP(AM)—Aug 6, 1946: 1110 khz; 4.8 kw-D, DA. TL: N40 08 05 W75 18 48. Box 11, Philadelphia (19128); 2311 Old Arch Rd., Norristown (19401). (215) 272-7600. FAX: (215) 272-7593. Licensee: George H. Buck. Group owner: GHB Radio Group (acq 12-15-87; $725,000; FTR 4-2-84). Net: USA. Rep: Mkt 4. Format: Gospel mus. Target aud: General. ■ Fred Blain, gen mgr; Maurice Crawford, progmg dir; Dave McCork, chief engr.

North East

WEYZ(AM)—Nov 24, 1966: 1530 khz; 1 kw-D, 250 w-CH, DA-1. TL: N42 12 05 W79 51 43. 2953 W. 12th St., Erie (16505). (814) 835-5000. Licensee: Heart Broadcasting Inc. (acq 5-21-92; $155,831; FTR 6-15-92). Net: CNN, Unistar. Rep: Eastman. Wash atty: Fletcher, Heald & Hildreth. Format: News/Talk. News progmg 50 hrs wkly. Target aud: 25-54. Spec prog: Sports 4 hrs, PSA one hr wkly. ■ Christopher J. Hagerty, pres & gen mgr. ■ Rates: $12; 12; 12; na.

WRKT(FM)—Mar 29, 1970: 100.9 mhz; 6 kw. Ant 252 ft. TL: N42 12 05 W79 51 43 (CP: 4.2 kw, ant 797 ft., TL: N42 11 51 W79 45 10). Stereo. Hrs opn: 24. One Broadcast Park (16428). (814) 725-4000. FAX: (814) 725-5401. Licensee: Rambaldo Communications Inc. (acq 1-26-89; FTR 2-13-89). Rep: Eastman. Wash atty: Fletcher, Heald & Hildreth. Format: Rock/AOR. News staff one; news progmg one hr wkly. Target aud: 25-54.

Spec prog: PSA one hr, NFL 4 hrs wkly. ■ Richard Rambaldo, pres, gen mgr & gen sls mgr; Ron Kline, prom mgr, progmg dir & mus dir; Debbie Ireland, news dir; Brian Wolfe, chief engr.

Northumberland

WAFH(FM)—Not on air, target date unknown: 107.3 mhz; 2 kw. Ant 377 ft. Box 293, Road No. 2, Sunbury (17801). Licensee: William P. Zurick.

Oil City

WKQW(AM)—Dec 1, 1986: 1120 khz; 1 kw-D. TL: N41 23 45 W79 39 53. 234 Elm St. (16301). (814) 676-8254. FAX: (814) 677-4272. Licensee: Stephen M. Olszowka. Net: CNN, Unistar. Format: Adult contemp. News staff one; news progmg 4 hrs wkly. Target aud: 25-54. ■ Stephen M. Olszowka, pres & gen mgr; Joe Barr III, news dir. ■ Rates: $10; 10; 10; na.

WKQW-FM—September 1992: 96.3 mhz; 6 kw. Ant 328 ft. TL: N41 23 45 W79 39 53. Hrs opn: 24. Format: Oldies. ■ Rates: $14; 14; 14; na.

WOYL(AM)—Feb 14, 1946: 1340 khz; 1 kw-U, DA-D. TL: N41 25 04 W79 42 53. Box 1127, 746 Orange St. (16301). (814) 676-5744. Licensee: Fidelity Communications Inc. (acq 7-16-82; grpsl; FTR 8-2-82). Net: NBC. Rep: Dome, Keystone (unwired net). Format: Adult contemp, talk. Spec prog: C&W 3 hrs, farm one hr wkly. ■ Samuel Shapiro, pres; Sam Gordon, gen mgr & progmg dir.

WRJS(FM)—Co-owned with WOYL(AM). May 1, 1957: 98.5 mhz; 20 kw. Ant 299 ft. TL: N41 25 04 W79 72 53. Stereo. Prog sep from AM. Net: NBC. Format: C&W.

Oliver

WASP-FM—June 11, 1993: 94.9 mhz; 205 w. Ant 1,240 ft. TL: N39 52 11 W79 38 22. Stereo. Box 789, Uniontown (15401); 159-B Morgantown St., Uniontown (15401). (412) 785-3450; (412) 430-0949. FAX: (412) 938-7824. Licensee: The Humes Broadcasting Corp. Format: Country. News staff one. Target aud: 25-54. ■ James J. Humes, pres & gen mgr; Kim Smith, opns mgr & news dir; Salvatore V. Glorioso, sls dir, mktg dir & prom dir; Jim Schlosser, progmg dir & mus dir; Jack Rees, chief engr. ■ Rates: $12; 10; 12; 6.

Olyphant

WKQV(FM)—1991: 95.7 mhz; 300 w. Ant 1,010 ft. TL: N41 26 10 W75 43 45. 673 E. Drinker St., Dunmore (18512). (717) 969-0750. Licensee: Northeast Radionet L.P. Format: Talk, classic rock. ■ Robert Woody, gen mgr; Kim Hall, stn mgr.

WMXH(AM)—July 20, 1987: 750 khz; 1.6 kw-D. TL: N41 28 34 W75 29 41. Hrs opn: Sunrise-sunset. 211 S. Main St., Taylor (18517-1817). (717) 562-0750; (717) 562-0825. Licensee: Carmen V. Nardone Inc. (acq 2-23-93; $103,000; FTR 3-15-93). Format: News, MOR. Target aud: 30 plus, middle class, middle aged men and women. Spec prog: Polka 7 hrs wkly. ■ Robert C. Cordaro, pres; Carmen Nardone, pres; Ed Kanuik, gen sls mgr. ■ Rates: $12; 12; 12; na.

Palmyra

WCTX(FM)—Sept 22, 1959: 92.1 mhz; 3 kw. Ant 300 ft. TL: N40 19 35 W76 36 33 (CP: 3.3 kw). Stereo. Box 231, N. Railroad St. (17078); Box 617, Hershey (17033). (717) 838-1318; (717) 534-1894. FAX: (717) 838-1319. Licensee: Clinton Broadcasting (acq 4-14-93). Net: ABC/FM. Format: Btfl mus. News staff one; news progmg 7 hrs wkly. Target aud: 25-54. Spec prog: Relg 6 hrs, Sp one hr wkly. ■ Hugh J. Clinton, pres; Robert Stevens, vp & gen mgr; Joseph S. Shiffer, gen sls mgr; John Montis, prom mgr; Robert D. Moore, progmg dir & news dir; Dave Weit, mus dir; Gary Gauver, chief engr. ■ Rates: $27; 24; 27; 22.

Patton

WBRX(FM)—1991: 94.7 mhz; 1 kw. Ant 551 ft. TL: N40 42 03 W78 37 26. Rt. 1, Box 756A (16668). (814) 674-5150. Licensee: WRG Altoona L.P. (acq 2-21-90; $450,000; FTR 3-12-90). ■ Paul Gregg, gen mgr.

Philadelphia

KYW(AM)—1921: 1060 khz; 50 kw-U, DA-1. TL: N40 06 12 W75 14 56. Independence Mall E. (19106). (215) 238-4700. FAX: (215) 238-4545. Licensee: Group W Radio Inc. Group owner: Westinghouse Broadcasting Company Inc. Net: NBC, ABC, CNN. Rep: Group W. Format: All news. ■ Bill Korn, chmn; Dan Mason, pres; John Waugaman, vp; Roy Shapiro, gen mgr; Blaise Howard, stn mgr & gen sls mgr; Mark Helms, progmg dir; Bill Roswell, Scott Herman, news dirs; Jan Kowalczyk, chief engr.

WMMR(FM)—Co-owned with KYW(AM). April 20, 1942: 93.3 mhz; 18 kw. Ant 827 ft. TL: N39 57 09 W75 10 05. Stereo. Hrs opn: 24. (215) 238-8000. FAX: (215) 238-4737. Licensee: Westinghouse Broadcasting Co. (group owner; acq 12-89; grpsl; FTR 12-11-89). Net: Unistar. Rep: AOR. Spec prog: Sports/rock mornings. ■ Charles B. Fee, vp & gen mgr; Rick Feinblatt, gen sls mgr; John Kubiak, prom mgr; Joseph Bonadonna, progmg dir. ■ KYW-TV affil.

WBEB-FM—Listing follows WPHY(AM).

WDAS(AM)—1923: 1480 khz; 5 kw-D, 1 kw-N, DA-2. TL: N39 59 53 W75 12 43. Hrs opn: 24. Belmont Ave. & Edgely Dr. (19131). (215) 581-2100. FAX: (215) 877-3931. Licensee: Unity Broadcasting Network Inc. (acq 1979). Net: American Urban, NBC. Rep: McGavren Guild. Format: Black gospel, relg, talk. ■ Eugene Jackson, CEO; Kernie Anderson, gen mgr; Chris Squire, stn mgr; Jeff Taylor, natl sls mgr; Lillian Jones, rgnl sls mgr; E. Steven Collins, prom dir; Clarence Blair, progmg dir; Rick Greene, mus dir; Martin Connely, pub affrs dir; William Sullivan, chief engr.

WDAS-FM—1959: 105.3 mhz; 3.3 kw. Ant 870 ft. TL: N40 02 30 W75 14 24 (CP: 16.3 kw). Stereo. Prog sep from AM. Format: Black adult contemp. News staff 3. Target aud: 25-54. ■ Joe Tamburro, progmg dir; Pat Jackson, mus dir.

WFLN-FM—Mar 1, 1949: 95.7 mhz; 50 kw. Ant 500 ft. TL: N40 03 33 W75 14 20. Stereo. Hrs opn: 24. 8200 Ridge Ave. (19128). (215) 482-6000. Licensee: Marlin Ltd. Broadcasting Inc. Group owner: Marlin Broadcasting Inc. (acq 2-88; $15 million; FTR 2-22-88). Rep: CMBS. Wash atty: Sidley & Austin. Format: Class. News progmg 3 hrs wkly. Target aud: 25-54; professional, upscale executives. ■ Howard P. Tanger, pres; Denise McDevitt, vp; Edward Berger, gen sls mgr & natl sls mgr; Dave Conant, progmg dir; Terry Peyton, mus dir; Henry Varlack, pub affrs dir; Jim Perry, chief engr. ■ Rates: $200; 200; 200; 200.

WHAT(AM)—1925: 1340 khz; 1 kw-U. TL: N40 00 06 W75 12 35. Suite 220, 2471 N. 54 St. (19131). (215) 581-5161. FAX: (215) 581-5185. Licensee: KBT Communications Inc. (acq 7-17-89; $1,650,000; FTR 7-31-89). Format: Afro-American classics, talk, jazz. Target aud: 25-54. Spec prog: Gospel 12 hrs wkly. ■ W. Cody Anderson, pres & gen mgr; Donna Clark, gen sls mgr; John Heal, chief engr.

*****WHYY-FM**—1954: 90.9 mhz; 13.5 kw. Ant 920 ft. TL: N40 02 30 W75 14 24. Stereo. Hrs opn: 5 AM-midnight. 150 N. 6th St. (19106). (215) 351-9200; (215) 351-9204. FAX: (215) 351-6278. Licensee: WHYY Inc. Net: NPR, APR, PPTN. Wash atty: Schwartz, Woods & Miller. Format: News, info. News staff 7; news progmg 40 hrs wkly. Target aud: 35-49. Spec prog: New age 10 hrs, class 9 hrs, folk 4 hrs, jazz 3 hrs wkly. ■ M. Lynn Herrick Sharp, chmn; David Othmer, vp; Kingsley Smith, opns mgr; Robert Altman, vp dev; Tim Roll, gen sls mgr; Nessa Forman, vp prom; Neil Tickner, news dir; Bill Weber, vp engrg; Jay Goldman, engrg mgr; Ron Barron, chief engr. ■ WHYY-TV.

WIOQ(FM)—1941: 102.1 mhz; 27 kw. Ant 650 ft. TL: N40 02 40 W75 14 30 (CP: Ant 669 ft.). Stereo. Hrs opn: 24. Suite 201, 2 Bala Plaza, Bala Cynwyd (19004). (215) 667-8100. FAX: (215) 668-4657. Licensee: Professional Broadcasting Inc. Group owner: EZ Communications Inc. Net: CNN. AP. Format: CHR, adult contemp. Target aud: 18-34; females & teens. Spec prog: Relg, pub affrs. ■ Alan Box, pres; Gil Rozzo, gen mgr; Val Lavigna, rgnl sls mgr; Mark Gullett, prom dir; Jefferson Ward, progmg dir; Glenn Kalina, mus dir; Ben Hill, chief engr.

WIP(AM)—March 16, 1922: 610 khz; 5 kw-U, DA-1. TL: N39 51 56 W75 06 43. 441 N. 5th St. (19123). (215) 922-5000. FAX: (215) 922-2434. Licensee: Infinity Broadcasting Corp. of Philadelphia. Group owner: Infinity Broadcasting Corp. (acq 8-12-93; FTR 8-30-93). Net: Mutual, Westwood One. Rep: Katz. Format: Sports. ■ Cecil Forster, vp & gen mgr; Tom Bigby, stn mgr; David Helfrich, prom mgr; Bill Rinier, chief engr.

WYSP(FM)—Co-owned with WIP(AM). August 1971: 94.1 mhz; 16 kw. Ant 900 ft. TL: N40 02 30 W75 14 24. Stereo. Suite 424, One Bala Cynwyd Plaza, Bala Cynwyd (19004). (215) 668-9460. FAX: (215) 667-9738. Licensee: Infinity Broadcasting Corp. (acq 11-1-81; grpsl; FTR 9-28-81). Net: ABC. Rep: Torbet. Format: Classic rock. ■ Ken Stevens, gen mgr; Sam Benrubi, gen sls mgr; Robert Avicolli, prom mgr; Tim Sabean, progmg dir; Andre Gardner, mus dir; Steve Trevelise, news dir; Richard Bagge, chief engr.

WJJZ(FM)—Nov 11, 1959: 106.1 mhz; 22 kw. Ant 740 ft. TL: N40 04 58 W75 10 54. Stereo. Suite 580E, 3 Bala Plaza, Bala Cynwyd (19004). (215) 667-3939. FAX: (215) 667-1082. Licensee: Malrite Guaranteed Partnership Inc. Group owner: Malrite Communications Group Inc. (acq 4-15-87). Rep: Eastman. Format: Jazz. ■ Mark Thomas, vp & gen sls mgr; Dia Davidson, prom mgr; Bernie Kimble, progmg dir & mus dir; Kellie Hansbrough, news dir; Don Melnyk, chief engr.

***WKDU(FM)**—1970: 91.7 mhz; 110 w. Ant 155 ft. TL: N39 57 36 W75 11 27. Stereo. Hrs opn: 24. 3210 Chestnut St. (19104). (215) 895-5920. FAX: (215) 895-5922. Licensee: Drexel Univ. Format: Progsv, alternative rock. Target aud: General. Spec prog: International 12 hrs, R&B 3 hrs, gospel 4 hrs, Israeli 3 hrs, new age 2 hrs, metal 4 hrs, Black 8 hrs wkly. ■ Chris Marlowe, gen mgr; John Paul, prom dir.

WMGK(FM)—Listing follows WPEN(AM).

WMMR(FM)—Listing follows KYW(AM).

WOGL(AM)—1922: 1210 khz; 50 kw-U. TL: N39 58 46 W74 59 13. WCAU-AM CBS Inc., City Ave & Monument Rd. (19131). (215) 668-5800. FAX: (215) 668-5888. Licensee: CBS Inc. Group owner: CBS Broadcast Group (acq 8-58). Net: CBS. Rep: CBS Radio. Format: Oldies. Spec prog: Sports. ■ Steve Carver, vp & gen mgr; Dennis Begley, gen sls mgr; Joanne Tombrakos, natl sls mgr; Kevin Jones, rgnl sls mgr; Tommy McCarthy, mus dir; Jennifer Stephens, news dir & pub affrs dir; Ken Tankel, chief engr.

WOGL-FM—May 16, 1944: 98.1 mhz; 12.5 kw. Ant 1,000 ft. TL: N40 02 31 W75 14 11. Stereo. Prog sep from AM. (215) 668-5900. FAX: (215) 668-5939. Target aud: 25-54. ■ WCAU-TV affil.

***WPEB(FM)**—May 15, 1981: 88.1 mhz; 10 w. Ant 100 ft. TL: N39 57 33 W75 12 54. Suite 7B, 3901 W. Market St. (19104). (215) 386-3800. Licensee: West Philadelphia Educational Broadcasting Corp. Format: Div. News progmg one hr wkly. Target aud: General. Spec prog: Class 2 hrs, jazz 17 hrs, R&B 18 hrs, talk 16 hrs, rap 16 hrs, reggae 12 hrs, ethnic 12 hrs, gospel 10 hrs, children's 8 hrs wkly. ■ Sister Atikah H. Bey, pres; Kentu Malik, mus dir.

WPEN(AM)—April 1929: 950 khz; 5 kw-U, DA-N. TL: N39 58 28 W75 16 30. Stereo. Hrs opn: 24. Third Floor W., One Bala Cynwyd Plaza, Bala Cynwyd (19004). (215) 667-8500. FAX: (215) 664-9610. Licensee: Greater Philadelphia Radio Inc. Group owner: Greater Media Inc. (acq 1-6-75). Net: Unistar. Rep: Major Mkt. Format: Adult standards, big band, nostalgia. News staff 4. Target aud: 35 plus. ■ Dean Tyler, vp & gen mgr; Julian Breen, opns mgr; Ed McCusker, Marc Taub, gen sls mgrs; Kim Romano, natl sls mgr; Ann Letizi, prom dir; Ed Klein, mus dir; Elaine Soncini, news dir; Lynn Sturdivant, pub affrs dir; Larry Paulausky, chief engr.

WMGK(FM)—Co-owned with WPEN(AM). 1942: 102.9 mhz; 8.5 kw. Ant 1,140 ft. TL: N40 02 21 W75 14 13. Stereo. Hrs opn: 24. Prog sep from AM. Format: Soft rock. Target aud: 25-54; women. ■ Mike Weinstein, gen sls mgr.

WPGR(AM)—July 11, 1947: 1540 khz; 50 kw-D, DA. TL: N40 02 46 W74 14 15 (CP: COL: Bala Cynwyd, PA, 50 kw-D, 500-N). 200 Monument Rd., Bala Cynwyd (19004). (215) 664-6780. FAX: (215) 664-8529. Licensee: All-Star Radio Inc. (acq 3-13-92; $800,000; FTR 4-6-92). Rep: Roslin. Wash atty: Taylor, Thiemann & Aitken. Format: Oldies. News staff one. Target aud: 25-54. ■ Marina Kats, pres; Eric Farber, vp & gen mgr; Tom Lucidon, gen sls mgr; John Bloodwell, prom dir & pub affrs dir; Jerry Blavat, progmg dir; Michael Vindetti, chief engr. ■ Rates: $50; 50; 50; 30.

WPHE(AM)—See Phoenixville.

WPHY(AM)—1922: 560 khz; 5 kw-U, DA-2. TL: N40 05 59 W75 15 47. Stereo. Hrs opn: 24. 4118 Franklin Way, Lafayette Hill (19444). (215) 941-9560. Licensee: Pennsylvania Media Associates. Rep: Salem Radio Rep. Wash atty: Borsari & Paxson. Format: Relg. News staff one; news progmg 2 hrs wkly. Target aud: 50 plus. ■ Jay Davis, gen mgr. ■ Rates: $100; 100; 100; 100.

WBEB-FM—Co-owned with WPHY(AM). May 13, 1963: 101.1 mhz; 12.5 kw. Ant 1,010 ft. TL: N40 02 21 W75 14 13 (CP: 14 kw, ant 940 ft.). Stereo. Hrs opn: 24. 10 Presidential Blvd., Bala Cynwyd (19004). FAX: (215) 667-6795. Licensee: WEAZ Radio Inc. Format: Adult contemp. Target aud: 25-54. ■ Meg DeLone, gen mgr; Mark Hamlin, progmg mgr.

***WRTI(FM)**—July 9, 1953: 90.1 mhz; 12.5 kw. Ant 1,010 ft. TL: N40 02 21 W75 14 13. Stereo. Hrs opn: 24. Annenberg Hall, 13th & Diamond St. (19122). (215) 204-8405. FAX: (215) 204-4870. Licensee: Temple University. Net: AP, NPR; Radio Pa. Wash atty: Arent, Fox, Kintner, Plotkin & Kahn. Format: Jazz. News staff 2; news progmg 15 hrs wkly. Target aud: 25-49; interested in jazz. Spec prog: Caribbean 4 hrs, Sp 4 hrs wkly. ■ W. Theodore Eldredge, gen mgr; Tobias Poole, opns mgr & chief engr; Valorie Jarrell, dev dir & sls dir; Monika Foltz, prom mgr; Bill Clark, progmg dir; Kim Berry, mus dir; Audrey Foltz, news dir. ■ Rates: $75; 50; 75; 50.

WTEL(AM)—1925: 860 khz; 10 kw-D, DA. TL: N40 09 15 W75 22 10 (CP: 500 w-N, DA-2). 555 Cityline Ave., Bala Cynwyd (19004). (215) 677-2870. FAX: (215) 677-4515. Licensee: Beasley Broadcasting of Eastern Pennsylvania Inc. Group owner: Beasley Broadcast Group (acq 9-9-86; $2.4 million; FTR 8-11-86). Rep: Katz Hispanic. Format: Sp contemp. News staff one; news progmg 3 hrs wkly. Target aud: 18-54. Spec prog: Ger 5 hrs, It 5 hrs, Pol 7 hrs, Portuguese 3 hrs wkly. ■ George Beasley, pres; Raul G. Lahee, gen mgr; Rafael Grullon, progmg dir; Bill Stallman, chief engr. ■ Rates: $75; 65; 75; 60.

WXTU(FM)—Co-owned with WTEL(AM). September 1958: 92.5 mhz; 15.5 kw. Ant 900 ft. TL: N40 02 21 W75 14 13. Stereo. Prog sep from AM. (215) 667-9000. Licensee: Beasley Broadcasting of Eastern Pennsylvania Inc. Group owner: Beasley Broadcast Group (acq 7-83; $6 million; FTR 7-11-83). Net: MBS. Format: Contemp country. ■ Bruce Bewley, vp; Rich Marcton, gen sls mgr; Keith Gate, prom mgr; John Mart, progmg dir; Mike Brophy, mus dir.

WTMR(AM)—See Camden, N.J.

WURD(AM)—July 23, 1958: 900 khz; 1 kw-D, 42 w-N, DA-2. TL: N39 55 05 W75 13 19. Box 233, Bldg. 10, 5301 Tacony St. (19137). (215) 533-8900. FAX: (215) 533-5679. Licensee: Willis Family Broadcasting Inc. (group owner; acq 3-4-92; grpsl; FTR 3-23-92). Net: MBS. Format: Gospel. Spec prog: It 3 hrs wkly. ■ Bishop L.E. Willis Sr., pres; Walter Stewart, progmg dir; Mike Chandler, chief engr.

WUSL(FM)—1961: 98.9 mhz; 18 kw. Ant 830 ft. TL: N40 02 31 W75 14 11. Stereo. Hrs opn: 24. 440 Domino Ln. (19128). (215) 483-8900. FAX: (215) 483-5930. Licensee: Tak Communications Inc. (group owner; acq 4-8-87). Rep: Katz. Wash atty: Dow, Lohnes & Albertson. Format: Urban contemp. News staff 2; news progmg 4 hrs wkly. Target aud: 18-49. ■ Bartley D. Walsh, pres & gen mgr; Marty Conn, gen sls mgr; Jacqui Allen, prom mgr; Dave Allan, progmg dir; Ladonna Monet, mus dir; Lorraine Ballard-Morrill, news dir; Lehronda Upshur, pub affrs dir; Charles Benner, chief engr.

WWDB(FM)—1957: 96.5 mhz; 19 kw. Ant 866 ft. TL: N40 02 21 W75 14 13. Stereo. Hrs opn: 24. 166 E. Levering Mill Rd., Bala Cynwyd (19004). (215) 668-4400. Licensee: Panache Broadcasting L.P. (group owner; acq 3-87; grpsl; FTR 10-20-86). Net: ABC/D, ABC/I, Wall Street. Rep: Banner. Wash atty: Latham & Watkins. Format: Talk. Target aud: 18 plus; general. Spec prog: Nostalgia 10 hrs wkly. ■ Charles D. Schwartz, CEO, pres & gen mgr; David Rimmer, opns mgr & progmg dir; Daniel Sullivan, gen sls mgr; Becki West, rgnl sls mgr; Jeff Oddo, prom dir; Paul Perrello, news dir; Chris Sarris, chief engr.

***WXPN(FM)**—April 1957: 88.5 mhz; 2.8 kw. Ant 918 ft. TL: N40 02 36 W75 14 33. Stereo. Hrs opn: 24. Wayne Hall, 3905 Spruce St. (19104-6005). (215) 898-6677. FAX: (215) 898-0707. Licensee: Trustees of the Univ. of Pennsylvania. Net: NPR, APR. Wash atty: Cohn & Marks. Format: Adult alternative. Target aud: 18-35. Spec prog: Drama 4 hrs, children's 5 hrs wkly. ■ Mark Fuerst, gen mgr; Vincent Curren, opns dir; Michael Morrison, progmg dir; Scott Fowler, chief engr.

WXTU(FM)—Listing follows WTEL(AM).

WYSP(FM)—Listing follows WIP(AM).

WYXR(FM)—February 1965: 104.5 mhz; 12.5 kw. Ant 1,008 ft. TL: N40 02 30 W75 14 24. Stereo. Hrs opn: 24. Suite 100 W., One Bala Plaza, Bala Cynwyd (19004). (215) 668-0750. FAX: (215) 668-8253. Licensee: Kiss L.P. Wash atty: Katz Radio Group. Format: Adult contemp. News staff one. Target aud: 25-54. ■ Jeffrey Specter, vp & gen mgr; Sil Scaglione, gen sls mgr; Scott Musgrave, natl sls mgr; Holly Hawkins, prom dir; John Cook, progmg dir; Anne Gress, mus dir; Joe Prokolyshun, asst mus dir; Michelle Pollino, news dir; Jerry Abear, pub affrs dir; Michael Guidotti, chief engr.

WZZD(AM)—1924: 990 khz; 50 kw-D, 10 kw-N, DA-2. TL: N40 06 14 W75 16 16. Stereo. Hrs opn: 24. 117 Ridge Pike, Lafayette Hill (19444); Box 26098 (19128). (215) 828-6965. FAX: (215) 828-8879. Licensee: H.E., L.P. Group owner: Communicom Co. of America L.P. (acq 7-7-93; grpsl; FTR 8-2-93). Format: Contemp Christian. News progmg one hr wkly. Target aud: 24-49. ■ Rich Kylberg, pres; Jennifer E. Downing, gen mgr; Mike Fernandez, progmg dir; Stu Engelke, chief engr. ■ Rates: $40; 40; 40; 20.

Philipsburg

WPHB(AM)—June 1, 1956: 1260 khz; 5 kw-D, 34 w-N. TL: N40 53 39 W78 11 51. R.R. 1, Box 38 (16866). (814) 342-2300. FAX: (814) 342-WPBH. Licensee: Moshannon Valley Broadcasting Inc. (acq 7-16-82; $274,000; FTR 8-9-82). Net: NBC Talknet, MBS; Radio Pa. Format: Relg, C&W. Spec prog: Bluegrass 5 hrs wkly. ■ C. Dean Sharpless, pres & chief engr; Sheldon Sharpless, gen mgr, gen sls mgr & prom mgr; Scott Sharpless, progmg dir, mus dir & news dir.

WPHB-FM—Mar 1989: 105.9 mhz; 4.8 kw. Ant 216 ft. TL: N40 59 08 W78 06 41. Stereo. Hrs opn: 5 AM-5 PM. Dups AM 50%. Format: Country. ■ C. Dean Sharpless, gen mgr; Sheldon Sharpless, opns mgr.

Phoenixville

WPHE(AM)—Aug 23, 1978: 690 khz; 1 kw-D, DA. TL: N40 08 08 W75 33 37. Box 46327, Philadelphia (19160). (215) 223-7532. FAX: (215) 223-3329. Licensee: Salvation Broadcasting Co. (acq 12-1-88). Net: AP. Rep: Caballero. Format: Sp, relg, div. News staff one; news progmg 5 hrs wkly. Spec prog: Por 3 hrs wkly. ■ Sarrail Salva, pres & gen mgr; Josean Cintron, sls dir; Isabel Salva, prom dir; Angel Luis Guzman, progmg dir; Ron Simpson, chief engr.

Pittsburgh

KDKA(AM)—Nov 2, 1920: 1020 khz; 50 kw-U. TL: N40 33 33 W79 57 11. Stereo. One Gateway Ctr. (15222). (412) 575-2200. FAX: (412) 575-6956. Licensee: Group W Radio. Group owner: Westinghouse Broadcasting Co. Net: NBC. Rep: Select. Format: News/talk. News staff 9. ■ Ted Jordan, gen mgr; Mike Frohm, gen sls mgr; Judy Yanke-Fritzges, prom mgr; Rich Cook, news dir; Jerry Kalke, chief engr.

KQV(AM)—Nov 19, 1919: 1410 khz; 5 kw-U, DA-2. TL: N40 31 17 W80 00 34. 411 7th Ave. (15219). (412) 562-5900; (412) 562-5960 (NEWSROOM). FAX: (412) 562-5936 (BUSINESS); (412) 562-5903 (NEWS). Licensee: Calvary Inc. (acq 12-1-82; $1,750,000; FTR 1-3-83). Net: CBS, MBS, Wall Street, CNN. Rep: Torbet. Format: All news. News staff 24; news progmg 154 hrs wkly. Target aud: 35 plus; affluent, information oriented adults. Spec prog: 190 play-by-play bcsts: CBS Major League Baseball, playoffs & World Series, NFL, Notre Dame football, Duquesne University basketball. ■ Robert W. Dickey, pres & gen mgr; Judith Ross, gen sls mgr; Erik Selby, prom mgr; Frank Gottlieb, progmg dir & news dir; Steven Conti, chief engr.

WAMO-FM—Listing follows WYJZ(AM).

WBZZ(FM)—July 19, 1948: 93.7 mhz; 41 kw. Ant 550 ft. TL: N40 26 28 W80 01 32. Stereo. 1715 Grandview Ave. (15211). (412) 381-8100. FAX: (412) 381-2943. Licensee: EZ Communications Inc. (group owner). Rep: Banner. Wash atty: Rainer Krauss. Format: Top-40. Target aud: 18-34; adults. Spec prog: Relg 2 hrs wkly. ■ Alan Box, pres; Edward (Tex) Meyer, vp, gen mgr & stn mgr; Cassidy Haus, gen sls mgr; Lori Campbell, prom dir; Buddy Scott, progmg dir; John Cline, Jeff Tyson, mus dirs; Shelley Duffy, news dir; Chris Hudak, chief engr.

WCXJ(AM)—See Braddock.

WDSY-FM—Listing follows WEEP(AM).

***WDUQ(FM)**—Dec 15, 1949: 90.5 mhz; 25 kw. Ant 480 ft. TL: N40 25 52 W80 00 26. Stereo. Hrs opn: 24. Des Places Communications, Duquesne Univ. (15282-0001). (412) 434-6030. FAX: (412) 434-5061. Licensee: Duquesne Univ. Net: NPR. Wash atty: Arter & Hadden. Format: Jazz, news, public issues. News staff 2. Target aud: General. ■ Judy D. Jankowski, gen mgr; Mary Lloyd, dev dir & adv dir; Tony Mowod, prom mgr; David Becker, progmg dir; Evelyn Hawkins, mus dir; Kevin Gavin, news dir; Chuck Leavens, chief engr.

WDVE(FM)—May 10, 1962: 102.5 mhz; 55 kw. Ant 820 ft. TL: N40 29 38 W80 01 09. Stereo. 200 Fleet St. (15220). (412) 937-1441. FAX: (412) 937-0323. Licensee: Broadcast Alchemy L.P. (acq 10-14-91; $54 million grpsl; FTR 10-14-91). Net: NBC the Source. Rep: Christal. Format: AOR. News staff one; news progmg 5 hrs wkly. Target aud: 18-49. ■ Bob Roof, gen mgr; Gene Romano, opns mgr & progmg dir; Jack Dibrell, gen sls mgr; Anthony Alfonsi, prom dir; Cris Winter, mus dir; Lou Galzerano, chief engr.

WEDO(AM)—See McKeesport.

WEEP(AM)—(Hampton Township). 1947: 1080 khz; 50 kw-D, DA. TL: N40 36 17 W79 57 37. 320 Fort Dequesne Blvd., Pittsburgh (15222). (412) 471-9950. FAX: (412) 471-9958. Licensee: Entertainment Communications Inc. Group owner: Entercom. Net: Unistar. Rep: Republic. Format: Classic country. ■ Joe Armao, vp & gen mgr; Cassidy Hauf, gen sls mgr; Nanci Rich, prom mgr; Ellen Gamble, news dir; Cliff Bryson, chief engr.

WDSY-FM—Co-owned with WEEP(AM). September 1962: 107.9 mhz; 50 kw. Ant 500 ft. TL: N40 28 20 W79 59 41 (CP: 17.7 kw, ant 827 ft.). Stereo. 320 Ft. Duquesne Blvd. (15222). Format: Modern country.

WJAS(AM)—Oct 19, 1921: 1320 khz; 5 kw-U, DA-N. TL: N40 25 11 W79 54 38. Broadcast Plaza, 1459 Crane Ave. (15220-4098). (412) 531-4800. FAX: (412) 531-4068. Licensee: Renda Broadcasting Corp. (group owner; acq 7-16-85; $700,000; FTR 12-17-84). Net: CNN, Unistar. Rep: Eastman. Format: Big band, nostalgia, MOR. News staff one. Target aud: 35 plus; older upscale. Spec prog: Big band jump, Frank Sinatra 2 hrs wkly. ■ Anthony F. Renda, pres; Judy Reich, gen mgr; Stephen Granato, opns dir; Fern Bathurst, gen sls mgr; Rob Heming, prom dir; Don Piazza, progmg dir; Robert LaFore, chief engr.

WSHH(FM)—Co-owned with WJAS(AM). March 8, 1948: 99.7 mhz; 10.5 kw. Ant 928 ft. TL: N40 27 47 W80 00 17. Stereo. (Acq 11-83; $2.7 million; FTR 11-14-83). Format: Soft adult contemp. Target aud: 25-54; white collar, upscale office workers, professionals, managers. Spec prog: Pub affrs one hr wkly. ■ Nancy Ackerman, natl sls mgr; Rob Heming, mktg dir; Stephen Granato, progmg dir.

WLTJ(FM)—April 4, 1942: 92.9 mhz; 47 kw. Ant 890 ft. TL: N40 29 38 W80 01 09. Suite 780, 7 Parkway Ctr. (15220). (412) 922-9290. Licensee: Saul Frischling. Group owner: WPNT Inc. (acq 4-84; $3 million; FTR 3-19-84). Rep: D & R Radio. Format: Adult contemp. News staff 2. Target aud: 25-54; affluent, professional, working public. ■ Saul Frischling, pres; Greg Frischling, gen mgr; Theresa Sullivan, gen sls mgr; Scott Kornblum, prom mgr; John Gallagher, progmg dir; Rich Charles, news dir; Roy Humphrey, chief engr.

WORD-FM—Listing follows WPIT(AM).

WPIT(AM)—1947: 730 khz; 5 kw-D. TL: N40 29 02 W79 59 34. Suite 625, Seven Park Ctr. (15220). (412) 937-1500. FAX: (412) 937-1576. Licensee: Salem Media of Pennsylvania Inc. (acq 12-2-92; $6.5 million; FTR 12-21-92). Net: Moody, USA. Format: Christian. Target aud: 44 plus. ■ Chuck Gratner, gen mgr.

WORD-FM—Co-owned with WPIT(AM). 1948: 101.5 mhz; 48 kw. Ant 505 ft. TL: N40 29 02 W79 59 34. Stereo. Format: Contemp Christian. Target aud: 25-49. ■ Chuck Bratner, gen mgr; Joe Fern, progmg dir; Randy Detrich, chief engr.

WPLW(AM)—See Carnegie.

***WPTS-FM**—Aug 26, 1984: 98.5 mhz; 10 w. Ant 550 ft. TL: N40 26 39 W79 57 12 (CP: 92.1 mhz, 16 w, ant 462 ft.). Stereo. Univ. of Pittsburgh, 411 William Pitt Union (15260). (412) 648-7990. Licensee: University of Pittsburgh (acq 8-26-84). Net: AP. Format: Eclectic contemp progsv. News staff 3; news progmg 10 hrs wkly. Target aud: General. ■ Ron Asbury, gen mgr; Allison Hollihan, stn mgr; Chad DeVinney, news dir; Roy Humphrey, chief engr.

***WQED-FM**—Jan 25, 1973: 89.3 mhz; 43 kw. Ant 500 ft. TL: N40 26 46 W79 57 51. Stereo. Hrs opn: 20. 4802 5th Ave. (15213). (412) 622-1436. FAX: (412) 622-7073. Licensee: QED Communications Inc. Net: AP, APR. Format: Classical. Target aud: General; hip, young, educated, fun-loving, classical mus listeners. Spec prog: Arts magazine one hr wkly. ■ Donald C. Korb, pres; Jim Cunningham, stn mgr; Ted Sohier, opns mgr; Kweilin Nassar, gen sls mgr; Anthony Marino, prom dir; Susan Johnson, progmg mgr; Jack O'Donnell, engrg dir.

***WRCT(FM)**—April 1974: 88.3 mhz; 100 w. Ant 53 ft. TL: N40 26 39 W79 56 37 (CP: 1.5 kw). Stereo. Hrs opn: 24. One WRCT Plaza, 5020 Forbes Ave. (15213). (412) 621-0728; (412) 621-9728. FAX: (412) 268-6549. Licensee: Carnegie Mellon Student Government Corp. Wash atty: Putbrese, Hunsacker & Ruddy. Format: Div, educ. News progmg 10 hrs wkly. Target aud: General. Spec prog: Black 12 hrs, classical 3 hrs, country 3 hrs, folk 3 hrs, Pol 20 hrs, experimental 12 hrs, jazz 18 hrs wkly. ■ Ralph Pleshur, gen mgr; Dave Bulebush, prom mgr; Steve Snyder, Matt Drown, mus dirs; Sam Minter, news dir; Ivan Bou, pub affrs dir; Mark Yeck, chief engr.

WRRK(FM)—See Braddock.

WSHH(FM)—Listing follows WJAS(AM).

WTAE(AM)—May 1922: 1250 khz; 5 kw-U, DA-N. TL: N40 23 50 W79 57 43. 400 Ardmore Blvd. (15221). (412) 731-1250. FAX: (412) 244-4596. Licensee: Hearst Corp. Group owner: Hearst Broadcasting Group (acq 1931). Net: ABC/E, MBS. Rep: Katz. Format: News/talk. ■ James Carter, vp & gen mgr; Colleen Walsh, prom dir; Tom Clendening, progmg dir; John Poister, news dir; Kurt Haase, chief engr.

WVTY(FM)—Co-owned with WTAE(AM). Aug 8, 1960: 96.1 mhz; 50 kw. Ant 500 ft. TL: N40 23 49 W79 57 43 (CP: 43.7 kw, ant 522 ft.). Stereo. Prog sep from AM. (412) 731-0996. Format: Adult contemp. ■ WTAE-TV affil.

WWCS(AM)—See Canonsburg.

WWSW(AM)—1932: 970 khz; 5 kw-U, DA-2. TL: N40 30 30 W80 00 30. Hrs opn: 24. One Allegheny Square (15212). (412) 323-5300. Licensee: Shamrock Broadcasting Co. Inc. (group owner; acq 3-5-84; grpsl; FTR 1-30-84). Net: ABC/D. Rep: McGavren Guild. Format: Golden Oldies. News staff one. ■ Michael S. Crusham, vp & gen mgr; Gary Marince, opns mgr & progmg dir; Speed Marriott, gen sls mgr; Linda Guiler, natl sls mgr; Chris Ostranden, prom mgr; Kenny Woods, mus dir; Rose Douglas, news dir; Victor Pasquarelli, chief engr.

WWSW-FM—1940: 94.5 mhz; 50 kw. Ant 810 ft. TL: N40 27 48 W80 00 18. Stereo. Prog dups AM 100%. ■ Bill Clark, CEO; Marty Loughman, pres; Gary Marince, opns mgr.

WXRB(FM)—Feb 4, 1963: 104.7 mhz; 50 kw. Ant 500 ft. TL: N40 34 24 W79 46 58 (CP: 19 kw). Stereo. Suite 300, 320 Fort Duquesne Blvd. (15222). (412) 471-9950. FAX: (412) 471-9958. Licensee: Entertainment Communications Inc. (group owner; acq 2-19-93; $4 million; FTR 3-8-93). Rep: Katz & Powell. Format: Country. News staff one; news progmg 5 hrs wkly. Target aud: 35-64; white collar, working females. ■ Joe Armao, gen mgr; Chris Decarlo, mus dir.

***WYEP-FM**—Apr 30, 1974: 91.3 mhz; 18.2 kw. Ant 265 ft. TL: N40 24 42 W79 55 33. Stereo. Hrs opn: 24. Box 66, Woodland Road (15232). (412) 362-9937. FAX: (412) 661-3764. Licensee: Pittsburgh Community Broadcasting Corp. Net: APR. Format: Adult alternative. News progmg 26 hrs wkly. Target aud: 25-49. Spec prog: Blues 7 hrs, bluegrass 4 hrs, international/world 3 hrs, Caribbean 3 hrs, Celtic one hr wkly. ■ Peter Rosenfeld, pres; Heidi Rinkacs, gen mgr; Mary Pam Sprague, opns dir; Robert Addleman, mktg dir; J. Mikel Ellcessor, progmg dir; Rosemary Welsch, mus dir; Bill Hansen, chief engr.

WYJZ(AM)—Aug 1, 1948: 860 khz; 1 kw-D, DA. TL: N40 29 27 W79 58 55. Suite 1500, 411 Seventh Ave. (15219). (412) 471-2181. FAX: (412) 391-3559. Licensee: Sheridan Broadcasting Corp. (group owner; acq 3-1-73). Net: American Urban. Rep: D & R Radio. Format: MOR. ■ Ronald R. Davenport, chmn; Alan Lincoln, gen sls mgr; David Calabrese, prom mgr; Stephanie Butler, mus dir; Tene Croom, news dir; Bob Sharkey, chief engr.

WAMO-FM—Co-owned with WYJZ(AM). 1960: 105.9 mhz; 72 kw. Ant 440 ft. TL: N40 29 27 W79 58 55. Stereo. Prog sep from AM. Format: Urban contemp.

Pittston

WARD(AM)—June 21, 1953: 1550 khz; 10 kw-D, 500 w-N, DA-2. TL: N41 20 45 W75 47 08. Box 1550 (18640); 83 Foote Ave., Duryea (18642). (717) 655-5521. FAX: (717) 883-0959. Licensee: Ward Broadcasting Corp. (acq 1-28-75). Net: ABC TalkRadio, CNN. Rep: Savalli Bcst Sls. Format: News/talk. Spec prog: Pol 6 hrs wkly. ■ James F. Ward, pres; Buz Boback, gen mgr & gen sls mgr; Samuel M. Liguori, progmg dir & news dir; Robert Schacht, chief engr.

WSKS(FM)—November 1983: 102.3 mhz; 3 kw. Ant 71 ft. TL: N41 18 20 W75 45 38. Stereo. 302 Hwy. 315 (18460). (717) 655-6893. FAX: (717) 655-6862. Licensee: Futuremark Communications (acq 3-7-90). Net: ABC/C. Rep: Eastman. Format: Top-40. Target aud: 18-49. ■ Tony Lee, stn mgr; Dave Valenti, opns mgr; Tommy Frank, progmg dir.

Port Allegany

WHKS(FM)—1991: 94.9 mhz; 530 w. Ant 1090 ft. TL: N41 48 36 W78 23 10. Stereo. Hrs opn: 24. 219 N. Main St. (16743). 817 N. Main St. (16743). (814) 642-7004; (814) 642-9491. FAX: (814) 642-9491. Licensee: L-Com Inc. Net: Jones Satellite Audio, CNN, Radio PA. Format: Soft hits, adult contemp. News progmg 2 hrs wkly. Target aud: General; 35-54. Spec prog: Relg 2 hrs wkly. ■ David F. Lent, pres, opns mgr, gen sls mgr, progmg mgr & news dir; Cathy L. Lent, vp; James G. Linn, chief engr. ■ Rates: $7; 4; 6; 3.

Port Matilda

WXXZ(FM)—Not on air, target date unknown: 107.9 mhz; 350 w. Ant 469 ft. TL: N40 45 19 W78 05 07. R.D. 1, Box 124 (16870). Licensee: Steven S. Seltzer and Jeane B. Singer (acq 10-27-93; $20,000; FTR 11-8-93).

Portage

WHYM(AM)—Aug 25, 1960: 1470 khz; 466 w-D, 88 w-N. TL: N40 22 57 W78 39 29. Hrs opn: 24. 609 Main St. (15946). (814) 736-8000. Licensee: H & B Broadcasting Inc. (acq 4-11-90; $60,000; FTR 5-7-90). Net: CBS, MBS, NBC Talknet, Unistar; Radio Pa. Wash atty: Reddy, Begley & Martin. Format: Oldies, talk. News progmg 12 hrs wkly. Target aud: 35-55; baby boomers, middle-aged, middle-upper income. Spec prog: Polka 14 hrs wkly. ■ Bill Henderson, pres, gen mgr, gen sls mgr, prom mgr & news dir; Earl Garber, chief engr. ■ Rates: $10.70; 9.60; 10.25; 9.60.

WZGO(FM)—Co-owned with WHYM(AM). Nov 15, 1990: 105.7 mhz; 3 kw. Ant 321 ft. TL: N40 22 59 W78 39 31. Stereo. Hrs opn: 24. 434 Swank Bldg., Johnstown (15901). (814) 536-1057. Format: Country. News progmg 10 hrs wkly. Target aud: 18-54; country mix, middle to upper income. ■ George H. Buck, vp; Tom Strauss, mus dir & pub affrs dir; Amy Smith, news dir. ■ Rates: $24; 20; 24; 16.

Pottstown

WPAZ(AM)—Oct 1, 1951: 1370 khz; 1 kw-D. TL: N40 16 35 W75 37 44. Hrs opn: 6 AM-7 PM. 224 Maugers Mill Rd. (19464). (215) 326-4000. FAX: (215) 326-7984. Licensee: Faye Scott. Group owner: Great Scott Braodcasting. Net: ABC/D. Format: Lite hits. News staff 2; news progmg 8 hrs wkly. Target aud: 25 plus; most affluent people. Spec prog: Country one hr, Pol one hr, relg 12 hrs, Ger one hr wkly. ■ Faye Scott, pres; Graham Satherlie, gen mgr; Jay Warren, progmg dir; Donna Solinger, news dir; Terry Dalton, chief engr. ■ Rates: $25; 25; 25; na.

WRFY-FM—See Reading.

Pottsville

WAVT-FM—Listing follows WPPA(AM).

WPAM(AM)—1946: 1450 khz; 1 kw-U. TL: N40 41 27 W76 11 39. Hrs opn: 18. Box 629, Lawton's Hill (17901). (717) 622-1450; (717) 622-1451; (717) 622-1452. FAX: (717) 628-4779. Licensee: Curran Communications (acq 1-76). Net: MBS. Wash atty: Blair, Joyce & Silva. Format: Oldies. News staff 2; news progmg 20 hrs wkly. Target aud: 25-59; young adults to senior citizens. Spec prog: Polka show 3 hrs, Irish one hr wkly. ■ James J. Curran, pres & gen mgr; John J. Curran, vp; Jo Hoffman, gen sls mgr; Al Kovy, prom dir, vp progmg, mus dir & news dir; Andy Pavelko, chief engr. ■ Rates: $11; 11; 11; 10.

WPPA(AM)—May 9, 1946: 1360 khz; 5 kw-D, 500 w-N, DA-2. TL: N40 41 56 W76 11 43. Hrs opn: 24. Box 540, 212 S. Centre St. (17901). (717) 622-1360; (717) 622-1362. FAX: (717) 622-2822. Licensee: Pottsville Broadcasting Co. Group owner: The Tidmore Group. Net: CBS. Rep: PRO Radio, Dome. Format: MOR. ■ A.V. Tidmore, pres; Argie D. Tidmore, gen mgr; Les Blankenhorn, opns mgr; William Tidmore, gen sls mgr & adv mgr; Vince Angelo Jr., progmg mgr & mus dir; Jim Smith, news dir; Milt Seltzer, chief engr.

Stations in the U.S. — Pennsylvania

WAVT-FM—Co-owned with WPPA(AM). Nov 20, 1948: 101.9 mhz; 50 kw. Ant 540 ft. TL: N40 49 50 W76 12 32. Stereo. Prog sep from AM. Net: CBS Spectrum. Format: CHR. ■ James A. Bowman, stn mgr, gen sls mgr & adv mgr; Skip Carr, opns mgr, progmg mgr & mus dir.

Punxsutawney

WECZ(AM)—Mar 18, 1953: 1540 khz; 5 kw-D, 1 kw-CH. TL: N40 57 36 W79 00 08. Box 458 (15767). (814) 938-6000. FAX: (814) 938-4237. Licensee: Renda Radio Inc. (group owner; acq 6-1-81; $512,000; FTR 5-11-81). Net: Unistar, ABC/I. Format: MOR. Target aud: 45 plus. ■ Anthony F. Renda, pres; Chris Lash, gen mgr; Larry McGuire, progmg dir; Rick Sparks, news dir.

WPXZ-FM—Co-owned with WECZ(AM). Dec 12, 1973: 105.5 mhz; 3 kw. Ant 300 ft. TL: N40 57 36 W79 00 08. Stereo. Prog sep from AM. Format: Adult contemp. Target aud: 35-64.

Radnor Township

*****WYBF(FM)**—August 1991: 88.5 mhz; 700 w-V. Ant 223 ft. TL: N40 03 22 W75 22 30. Dups WXVU(FM) Villanova. Eagle & King of Prussia (19087). (215) 971-8360. Licensee: Cabrini College. Format: Alternative. ■ Jerry Zurek (faculty), chmn.

Reading

WBYN(FM)—See Boyertown.

WEEU(AM)—1931: 850 khz; 1 kw-U, DA-N. TL: N40 21 28 W75 59 03. Stereo. 34 N. 4th St. (19601-3996). (215) 376-7335; (215) 372-1698. FAX: (215) 376-7756. Licensee: WEEU Broadcasting Co. (acq 12-46). Net: ABC/I, AP. Rep: McGavren Guild. Wash atty: Cohn & Marks. Format: Adult contemp, talk. News staff 2; news progmg 6 hrs wkly. Target aud: 30 plus; mature. Spec prog: Farm 2 hrs, Ger 2 hrs wkly. ■ James C. Flippin, pres; Dave Kline, gen mgr, gen sls mgr, mktg mgr, prom mgr & adv mgr; Charlie Adams, prom dir; Jo Painter, progmg dir & pub affrs dir; Bill Brosey, mus dir; Lew Runkle, news dir; John Engle, chief engr. ■ Rates: $50; 40; 40; 8.50.

WIOV(AM)—Sept 1, 1946: 1240 khz; 1 kw-U. TL: N40 19 28 W75 56 31. 436 Tenn Ave., Sinking Spring (19608). (215) 484-4653. FAX: (215) 678-9298. Group owner: Brill Media Company Inc. (acq 8-81; $1.5 million; FTR 8-17-81). Net: CBS. Format: Country. ■ Mitch Carroll, pres; Larry Blazick, gen sls mgr.

WRAW(AM)—September 1922: 1340 khz; 1 kw-U. TL: N40 19 27 W75 55 10. Stereo. Hrs opn: 24. 1265 Perkiomen Ave. (19602). (215) 376-1340. FAX: (215) 376-1270. Licensee: US Radio L.P. (group owner; acq 4-8-90; grpsl; FTR 10-23-89). Net: CBS. Rep: Torbet. Wash atty: Arent, Fox, Kintner, Plotkin & Kahn. Format: MOR. Target aud: 45 plus. Spec prog: Class one hr, Pol 3 hrs, Sp 3 hrs, big band 5 hrs, gospel one hr, relg one hr wkly. ■ Mike Shannon, vp & gen mgr; Mike Rubright, gen sls mgr; Bob Minnich, progmg dir & mus dir; Susan Sheetz, news dir; John Arndt, chief engr. ■ Rates: $153; 135; 153; 68.

WRFY-FM—Co-owned with WRAW(AM). Sept 23, 1962: 102.5 mhz; 19 kw. Ant 807 ft. TL: N40 19 19 W75 53 41. Stereo. Rep: Torbet. Format: CHR. News staff 2. Target aud: 18-49. ■ Al Burke, progmg mgr; Mike Browne, mus dir. ■ Rates: Same as AM.

*****WXAC(FM)**—1967: 91.3 mhz; 219 w. Ant -23 ft. TL: N40 21 39 W75 54 37. Stereo. Albright College (19612-5234). (215) 921-7545; (215) 921-7683. Licensee: Albright College. Format: Progsv, alternative. Spec prog: Sp 6 hrs, reading for the blind 5 hrs, NAACP 3 hrs wkly. ■ Syd Sklar, stn mgr; Xi Yu, chief engr.

Red Lion

WGCB(AM)—Oct 22, 1950: 1440 khz; 1 kw-D. TL: N39 54 17 W76 34 49. Box 88 (17356). (717) 244-5360. Licensee: John N. Norris (acq 5-5-93; $2.825 million with co-located FM; FTR 5-24-93). Format: Relg. Spec prog: Farm one hr, Dutch one hr wkly. ■ John H. Norris, pres; Geneva Stamper, stn mgr; Fred Wise, chief engr.

WGCB-FM—October 1960: 96.1 mhz; 50 kw. Ant 500 ft. TL: N39 54 17 W76 34 51. Stereo. Dups AM 100%. ■ WGCB-TV affil.

Renovo

WMHU(FM)—Not on air, target date unknown: 93.1 mhz; 3 kw. Ant 328 ft. TL: N41 19 43 W77 43 15. North Penn Broadcasting Inc., 15th & Hamilton St., Allentown (18102). Licensee: North Penn Broadcasting Inc. (acq 8-29-90; $125,000; FTR 9-24-90). ■ Jay Kennedy, gen mgr.

Reynoldsville

WDSN(FM)—Feb 14, 1990: 99.5 mhz; 3 kw. Ant 328 ft. TL: N41 08 41 W78 52 41. Stereo. Hrs opn: 24. 51 W. Long Ave., Dubois (15801). (814) 375-5260. FAX: (814) 375-5262. Licensee: Priority Communications Inc. (acq 11-6-90; $275,000; FTR 11-26-90). Net: MBS. Rep: Commercial. Wash atty: Pepper & Corazzini. Format: Adult contemp. News staff one; news progmg 18 hrs wkly. Target aud: 25-54. ■ Jay M. Philippone, pres & gen mgr; Pete Frechio, opns mgr, progmg dir & mus dir; Michael Brennen, sls dir. ■ Rates: $15; 13; 13; 8.

Ridgebury

WMKB(FM)—1991: 96.9 mhz; 1.55 kw. Ant 430 ft. TL: N41 55 43 W76 46 58. 3136 Lake Rd., Horseheads, NY (14902). (607) 739-3717. Licensee: Lighthouse Ministries (acq 11-30-93; FTR 12-20-93). ■ James R. Pierce, gen mgr.

Ridgway

WKBI(AM)—See St. Marys.

WKBI-FM—See St. Marys.

Riverside

WLGL(FM)—Oct 25, 1990: 92.3 mhz; 440 w. 833 ft. TL: N40 57 30 W76 42 53. Stereo. Hrs opn: 5 AM-1 AM. Dups WYGL-AM, Selinsgrove. Box 510, Riverside (17868); 14 Spruce St., Selinsgrove (17870). (717) 374-1155; (800) 326-9488. Licensee: Cantroair Communications Co. Group Owner: Air Communications (Wiggle Network) Net: ABC/I; Radio Pa. Wash atty: Kaye, Scholer, Fierman, Hays & Handler. Format: Contemp hot country. News staff 4; news progmg 5 hrs wkly. Target aud: 25-54. ■ David Bernstein, pres; Greg Adair, gen mgr; Scott West, opns dir & mus dir; Scott Richards, gen sls mgr & adv dir; Scott Bernstein, mktg dir; Mike Daniels, prom dir; Ross Merante, progmg dir; Shelly Marks, asst mus dir; Doug Preston, news dir; Harry Bingaman, chief engr. ■ Rates: $12.50; 10; 11.50; 9.

Roaring Spring

WHPA(FM)—See Hollidaysburg.

WKMC(AM)—May 1, 1955: 1370 khz; 5 kw-D, 38 w-N, DA-2. TL: N40 19 26 W78 23 40. Stereo. Box 464, Hollidaysburg (16648); R.D. 4, Box 210, Scoth Valley Rd. (16648). (814) 695-4441. FAX: (814) 696-9522. Licensee: WHPA/WKMC Inc. (acq 1-1-88). Net: CNN. Rep: Roslin. Format: Big band, nostalgia. News staff one; news progmg 2 hrs wkly. Target aud: 45 plus; mature, loyal listeners. ■ David G. Mitchell, pres; Donald L. Ambrose, vp & gen mgr; John Hodgens, gen sls mgr; Jan Brooks, mktg dir; Ray Keller, progmg dir; Calib James, mus dir; Joyce Kavanaugh, news dir; Gary Magill, chief engr. ■ Rates: $22; 22; 22; 18.

Russell

WRLP(FM)—Nov 11, 1984: 103.1 mhz; 2.1 kw. Ant 351 ft. TL: N41 57 48 W79 09 42. Stereo. Box 609 (16345). (814) 757-8751. Licensee: Magnum Broadcasting Inc. (acq 5-18-92; $200,000; FTR 6-15-92). Rep: Hugh Wallace. Format: AOR. ■ Michael Stapleford, pres & gen mgr.

St. Marys

WKBI(AM)—July 23, 1950: 1400 khz; 1 kw-U. TL: N41 24 56 W78 33 56. Box 466, Melody Rd. (15857). (814) 834-2821; (814) 834-2822. FAX: (814) 834-4319. Licensee: Elk-Cameron Broadcasting Co. Group owner: Allegheny Mountain Network Stns. Net: SMN; Allegheny Mtn. Net. Rep: Dome. Wash atty: Borsari & Paxson. Format: Classic hits from the 50s, 60s & 70s. News staff one; news progmg 10 hrs wkly. Target aud: 35-55. ■ Cary H. Simpson, pres; John Salter, gen mgr, gen sls mgr & prom mgr; John Allen Kuhn, progmg dir; Phil Leslie, mus dir; Bob Lynn, chief engr.

WKBI-FM—August 1966: 94.3 mhz; 2.9 kw. Ant 339 ft. TL: N41 24 56 W78 33 56. Stereo. Hrs opn: 20. Prog sep from AM. Net: Unistar. Format: Adult contemp. Target aud: General. ■ John Salter, opns mgr.

WKYN(FM)—Apr 22, 1986: 97.5 mhz; 32 kw. Ant 617 ft. TL: N41 36 06 W78 34 58 (CP: 20 kw, ant 754 ft.). Stereo. Hrs opn: 24. HCR 1, Box 109, Bootjack Rd., Ridgeway (15853). (814) 772-9700. FAX: (814) 772-9750. Licensee: WKYN Inc. Net: ABC/FM. Rep: Rgnl Reps, Commercial. Format: AOR. Target aud: 25-54; programmed for adults, featuring mass appeal hit music. ■ Robert Michael Stevens, pres & gen mgr; Ashley Rachael Stevens, vp & sls dir; Bill Kaltwasser, chief engr.

Salladasburg

WFRY(FM)—1989: 95.5 mhz; 3.9 kw. Ant 239 ft. TL: N41 14 00 W77 12 09. Stereo. Hrs opn: 24. 220 S. Russell Ave., Wiliamsport (17701). (717) 323-8200. FAX: (717) 323-5075. Licensee: North Penn Broadcasting Inc. Group owner: HGF Media Group (acq 3-20-89; $982,000; FTR 3-20-89). Net: Unistar. Format: Hot country. News staff 2; news progmg 3 hrs wkly. Target aud: 25-54. ■ Harold G. Fulmer, chmn; Vic Michael, gen mgr; Randy Lapriola, gen sls mgr & mktg mgr; Mark Williams, vp progmg; Jeff Thomas, progmg dir; Shaun Carey, mus dir; Liz Brady, news dir; Dave Mason, chief engr.

Sayre

WATS(AM)—June 1950: 960 khz; 5 kw-D. TL: N41 59 48 W76 30 03. 204 Desmond St. (18840). (717) 888-7745. FAX: (717) 888-9005. Licensee: WATS Broadcasting Inc. (acq 10-17-86). Net: UPI. Format: Adult contemp. News progmg 4 hrs wkly. Target aud: 25-54. Spec prog: Farm one hr wkly. ■ Charles C. Carver Jr., vp, gen mgr & news dir; Peg Croft, gen sls mgr; Barbara Caum, progmg dir; Lawrence Brown, chief engr.

WAVR(FM)—See Waverly, N.Y.

Schnecksville

*****WXLV(FM)**—Sept 23, 1983: 90.3 mhz; 670 w. Ant 177 ft. TL: N40 39 52 W75 36 40 (CP: 420 w, ant 230 ft.). Stereo. 4525 Education Park Dr. (18078). (215) 799-4141; (215) 799-1145. FAX: (215) 799-1527. Licensee: Lehigh County Community College. Format: Div. Target aud: General; all segments of the community. Spec prog: Class 13 hrs, jazz 6 hrs, Pol 6 hrs, blues 4 hrs, new wave 6 hrs wkly. ■ Brian Barton, gen mgr; Mike Adamcik, chief engr.

Scottdale

WLSW(FM)—Dec 21, 1971: 103.9 mhz; 325 w. Ant 780 ft. TL: N40 00 51 W79 31 01. Stereo. Box 763, Connellsville (15425). (412) 628-2800. Licensee: L. Stanley Wall. Net: MBS. Format: Adult contemp. Spec prog: 50s & 60s oldies 6 hrs wkly. ■ L. Stanley Wall, pres; Chris Molten, gen mgr & gen sls mgr; Christopher Sky, progmg dir; Debbie Larson, mus dir; Al Colisti, chief engr.

Scranton

WARD(AM)—See Pittston.

WARM(AM)—1940: 590 khz; 5 kw-U, DA-2. TL: N41 28 44 W75 52 51. Hrs opn: 24. Rte Box 590, Rt. 3, Wilkes Barre Scranton Hwy., Avoca (18641). (717) 655-2271. FAX: (717) 457-8737. Licensee: WARM Broadcasting Co. Group owner: Susquehanna Radio Corp. (acq 6-15-58). Net: NBC, NBC Talknet, AP. Rep: McGavren Guild. Format: Adult contemp, MOR, new/talk. News staff 7; news progmg 30 hrs wkly. Target aud: 35 plus. Spec prog: Sports. ■ Arthur Carlson, pres; Jim Loftus, gen mgr; Tim Durkin, gen sls mgr; Christine Grieco, prom mgr; George Gilbert, progmg dir; Stan Philips, mus dir; Jerry Heller, news dir; Bob Lenio, chief engr.

WBAX(AM)—See Wilkes-Barre.

WEJL(AM)—Nov 29, 1922: 630 khz; 500 w-D, 32 w-N. TL: N41 24 35 W75 40 41. 149 Penn Ave. (18503). (717) 346-6555. FAX: (717) 346-6038. Licensee: The Scranton Times. Group owner: Shamrock Communications Inc. Net: ABC/I, Unistar. Rep: Christal. Format: Original hits of the 40s, 50s & 60s. ■ Jim Davey, gen mgr; Phil Cummings, progmg dir & news dir; Ron Schact, chief engr.

WEZX(FM)—Co-owned with WEJL(AM). Nov 1, 1967: 106.9 mhz; 190 w. Ant 1,266 ft. TL: N41 25 41 W75 44 50 (CP: 380 w). Stereo. Prog sep from AM. (717) 961-1842. Format: AOR. ■ Jack Mayers, prom mgr; Jim Rising, Dave Lonoun, progmg dirs; Jim Rising, mus dir.

WGBI(AM)—Jan 12, 1925: 910 khz; 1 kw-D, 500 w-N. TL: N41 22 56 W75 41 51. 305 Hwy. 315, Pittston (18640). (717) 883-9850. FAX: (717) 883-9851. Licensee: Lackazerne Inc. (acq 2-2-93; $3 million with co-located FM; FTR 3-1-93). Net: CBS. Rep: Torbet. Format: Adult contemp. ■ Gerald Getz, gen mgr; Mike Remley, gen sls mgr; Nancy Kaman, progmg dir.

Pennsylvania

WGGY(FM)—Co-owned with WGBI(AM). Dec 25, 1948: 101.3 mhz; 7 kw. Ant 1,110 ft. TL: N41 25 38 W75 44 53. Stereo. Prog sep from AM. Format: Top-40. ■ Bob De Mono, gen sls mgr; Mark Lindow, progmg dir.

WICK(AM)—Apr 17, 1954: 1400 khz; 1 kw-U. TL: N41 25 05 W75 39 43. Stereo. 1049 N. Sekol Rd. (18504). (717) 344-1221. FAX: (717) 344-0996. Licensee: Lancom Inc. (acq 9-11-78). Net: ABC/D. Format: Btfl mus. ■ Douglas V. Lane, pres & gen mgr; Phil Bullwinkel, gen sls mgr; Lou Schwass, progmg dir; Jean Wilding, news dir.

WWDL-FM—Co-owned with WICK(AM). Nov 26, 1964: 104.9 mhz; 270 w. Ant 1,092 ft. TL: N41 26 06 W75 43 35. Stereo. Prog sep from AM. Licensee: Lane Broadcasting Corp. Format: Adult contemp. ■ Paula Deignan, progmg dir.

WILK(AM)—See Wilkes-Barre.

WKRZ-FM—See Wilkes-Barre.

WMGS(FM)—See Wilkes-Barre.

WUSR(FM)—Not on air, target date unknown: 99.5 mhz; 302 w. Ant 1,014 ft. TL: N41 26 09 W75 43 33. Linden & Monroe Sts. (18510). Licensee: Univ. of Scranton.

*****WVIA-FM**—Apr 23, 1973: 89.9 mhz; 5 kw. Ant 1,250 ft. TL: N41 10 55 W75 52 17. Stereo. Hrs opn: 24. Public Broadcasting Ctr., 70 Old Boston Rd., Pittston (18640-9606). (717) 655-2808; (717) 826-6144. FAX: (717) 655-1180. Licensee: N.E. Pa. Educ TV Assoc. Net: NPR, APR; Pa. Pub. Format: Class, jazz, news. News progmg 24 hrs wkly. ■ A. William Kelly, pres; Erika Funke, gen mgr, stn mgr & progmg dir; Larry Vojtko, opns dir; Ray Boyle, vp dev; Judy Sedlak, sls dir; Rory Giavenucci, prom mgr; George Graham, mus dir; William Myers, chief engr. ■ *WVIA-TV affil.

*****WVMW-FM**—Sept. 1974: 91.5 mhz; 100 w. Ant -185 ft. TL: N41 25 57 W75 38 06. Stereo. Hrs opn: 14. Marywood College, 2300 Adams Rd. (18509). (717) 348-6202; (717) 348-6272. FAX: (717) 348-1817. Licensee: Marywood College. Net: AP. Format: College top 100. News staff 2; news progmg 7 hrs wkly. Target aud: 15-25; young adults. Spec prog: Black 2 hrs, class 7 hrs, jazz 10 hrs wkly. ■ Tina Butler, gen mgr & stn mgr; Janice Inzillo, progmg dir & mus dir; John Wharton, news dir; George Graham, chief engr.

WWDL-FM—Listing follows WICK(AM).

WYCK(AM)—See Wilkes-Barre.

Selinsgrove

*****WQSU(FM)**—September 1967: 88.9 mhz; 12 kw. Ant 620 ft. TL: N40 57 06 W75 45 03. Stereo. Hrs opn: 7:30 AM-2 AM. Susquehanna University (17870). (717) 372-4100. Licensee: Susquehanna University. Net: AP. Format: AOR, educ. News progmg 7 hrs wkly. Target aud: 18-34. Spec prog: Farm 3 hrs, jazz 18 hrs, relg 3 hrs wkly. ■ Robert L. Gross, gen mgr & progmg dir; Harry Bingaman, chief engr.

WYGL(AM)—Jan 16, 1967: 1240 khz; 1 kw-U. TL: N40 48 59 W76 52 13. Hrs opn: 24. Dups WLGL-FM, Riverside. Box 1240, R.D. 1, Rt. 204 & State School Rd. (17870). (717) 374-1155; (717) 286-4487. FAX: (717) 374-7444. Licensee: Sunair Communications. Group owner: Air Communications (Wiggle Network) (acq 3-15-84; $322,350; FTR 3-19-84). Net: ABC/E. Wash atty: Kaye, Scholer, Fierman, Hays & Handler. Format: Contemp country. News staff one; news progmg 8 hrs wkly. Target aud: 25-54. ■ David Bernstein, pres; Greg Adair, gen mgr; Scott West, opns dir & mus dir; Scott Richards, gen sls mgr; Scott Bernstein, mktg dir; Mike Daniels, prom dir; Shelly Marks, asst mus dir; Doug Preston, news dir; Harry Bingaman, chief engr. ■ Rates: $19; 19; 19; 14.25.

Sellersville

*****WBYO(FM)**—March 1991: 88.9 mhz; 100 w. Ant 436 ft. TL: N40 23 02 W75 21 02 (CP: 900 w). Stereo. Hrs opn: 6 AM-midnight. Box 186 (18960). (215) 674-8002. Licensee: Bux-Mont Educational Radio Assn. Wash atty: Schwartz, Woods & Miller. Format: Adult contemp, relg. News staff one; news progmg 10 hrs wkly. Target aud: General. Spec prog: Gospel 10 hrs wkly. ■ Charles W. Loughery, pres & gen mgr; David Baker, stn mgr; Dennis Grafton, engrg mgr.

Shamokin

WISL(AM)—January 1948: 1480 khz; 1 kw-D, 250 w-N, DA-2. TL: N40 45 53 W76 31 18. Rock & Sunbury Sts. (17872). (717) 648-6831. FAX: (717) 648-1617. Licensee: Laurel (acq 1-12-93; $300,000; FTR 2-1-93). Net: UPI. Format: Oldies. Spec prog: Pol 2 hrs wkly. ■ James P. O'Leary, pres; John C. Berry, gen mgr; John Berry, gen sls mgr, prom mgr & news dir; Tom Caroll, progmg dir; Tom Kutza, mus dir.

WISL-FM—1968: 95.3 mhz; 1.25 w. Ant 505 ft. TL: N40 45 36 W76 32 19. Stereo. Box P (17872). Licensee: Northeast Broadcasting of Northumberland Inc. (acq 1992). Net: UPI. Format: Classic rock. ■ John Berry, gen sls mgr & prom dir; Tom Carroll, progmg mgr.

Sharon

WPIC(AM)—Oct 25, 1938: 790 khz; 1 kw-D, 51 w-N. TL: N41 13 10 W80 28 25. Hrs opn: 24. Box 211, 2030 Pine Hollow Blvd. (16146). (412) 346-4113. FAX: (412) 981-4545. Licensee: Sharon Broadcasting Co.Inc. Group owner: Regional Group Inc. (acq 1959). Net: ABC/I. Rep: Eastman. Format: News/talk, sports. News staff 2; news progmg 22 hrs wkly. Target aud: 35 plus. Spec prog: Pol 6 hr, lt 2 hrs, relg 2 hrs, infomercials 12 hrs wkly. ■ Tom Klein, CEO, vp & gen mgr; Scott Kennedy, opns mgr; Ira J. Fmura, gen sls mgr; Roxy Gurlea, natl sls mgr; Dave Hanahan, progmg dir, mus dir & pub affrs dir; Joe Biro, news dir; Charles Ring, chief engr. ■ Rates: $20; 15; 15; 12.

WYFM(FM)—Co-owned with WPIC(AM). Oct 25, 1947: 102.9 mhz; 44 kw. Ant 455 ft. TL: N41 13 10 W80 28 25. Stereo. Prog sep from AM. 3622 Belmont Ave. Youngstown, OH (44505). Net: ABC/C. Format: Adult contemp. News staff 2; news progmg 5 hrs wkly. Target aud: 25-54. ■ Scott Kennedy, progmg dir; John Batcho, mus dir; Lynn Davis, mus dir; Mark Morris, pub affrs dir. ■ Rates: $45; 45; 45; 45.

Sharpsville

WHTX(FM)—Licensed to Sharpsville. See Youngstown, Ohio.

Shenandoah

WMBT(AM)—March 19, 1963: 1530 khz; 2.5 kw-D, 250 W-CH. TL: N40 49 30 W76 13 33. Box 1530 (17976). (717) 462-2759. Licensee: WMBT Broadcasting Inc. (acq 9-86). Net: AP, Westwood One. Format: Oldies. News staff one; news progmg 14 hrs wkly. Target aud: 25 plus. ■ Uzal Martz Jr., pres; Ron Sotak, gen mgr; Frank Jordan, stn mgr & progmg mgr; Jeff Rudloff, rgnl sls mgr; Vicki Terwilliger, news dir; Julian Milewski, chief engr. ■ Rates: $15; 9; 9; na.

Shippensburg

WSHP(AM)—Dec 5, 1961: 1480 khz; 500 w-D, 20 w-N. TL: N40 02 17 W77 32 23. Box 1480, 891 W. King St. (17257). (717) 532-4105. Licensee: Town Radio Inc. Net: Radio Pa. Format: Oldies, country, bftl music. Target aud: 30 plus. Spec prog: Class 5 hrs wkly. ■ Arthur K. Greiner, pres & gen mgr; Nancy Goshorn, prom mgr; Jason Wert, progmg dir & mus dir; Drew Jefferies, news dir; Harry Taylor, chief engr.

*****WSYC-FM**—February 1975: 88.7 mhz; 100 w. Ant 155 ft. TL: N40 03 32 W77 31 20 (CP: TL: N40 04 30 W77 31 15). Stereo. Cumberland Union Bldg. (17257). (717) 532-6006. Licensee: Shippensburg University. Net: Westwood One. Format: AOR. News progmg 5 hrs wkly. Target aud: 16-25; college & area high school students. ■ Mike Elliott, gen mgr.

Shiremanstown

WWII(AM)—June 1987: 720 khz; 2 kw-D. TL: N40 11 28 W76 57 09. Stereo. Hrs opn: 6 AM-sunset. 8 W. Main St. (17011). (717) 731-9944. FAX: (717) 731-4002. Licensee: Hensley Broadcasting. Net: CBN. Format: Relg. News staff one; news progmg 2 hrs wkly. Target aud: General. Spec prog: Ger one hr, gospel 2 hrs, polka 7 hrs, big band 2 hrs wkly. ■ Dean Lebo, gen mgr, gen sls mgr, prom mgr & mus dir; Tom Sullivan, progmg dir; Bob Foor, news dir; Judy Byra, pub affrs dir; Carl Kuehn, chief engr. ■ Rates: $15; 13; 13; na.

Slippery Rock

*****WRSK(FM)**—Sept 20, 1991: 88.1 mhz; 100 w. Ant 79 ft. TL: N41 03 43 W80 02 35. Hrs opn: 14. Box C-211, University Union, E. Central Loop (16057). (412) 738-2655; (412) 738-2931. Licensee: Slippery Rock Univ. Net: ABC, AP. Format: Classic rock, progsv, AOR. News progmg 14 hrs wkly. Target aud: 18-24; on & off campus students. Spec prog: Relg one hr, campus info one hr, sports one hr wkly. ■ Tori Verts, gen mgr; Wayne Miller, prom mgr; Werner Ullrich, chief engr.

Smethport

WQRM(FM)—January 1990: 106.3 mhz; 1.2 kw. Ant 731 ft. TL: N41 48 36 W78 23 10. Stereo. 208 Fulton St. (16749). (814) 887-1977. FAX: (814) 834-2821. Licensee: Farm & Home Broadcasting Co. Group owner: Allegheny Mountain Network Stns. Net: SMN; Allegheny Mtn. Net. Rep: Dome. News staff one; news progmg 6 hrs wkly. Target aud: 18-54. ■ Cary Simpson, pres; John Salter, gen mgr; Ted Simpson, gen sls mgr; Erik Lane, progmg dir; Bob Maynard, mus dir; Robert H. Lynn, chief engr.

Somerset

WADJ(AM)—June 15, 1981: 1330 khz; 5 kw-D, 35 w-N, DA-1. TL: N39 59 33 W79 05 41. Hrs opn: 24. Box 1330, R.D. 1, Cannel Dr. (15501). (814) 443-1677; (814) 443-1330. Licensee: NorLin Broadcasters Inc. Net: CNN, NBC Talknet; Radio Pa. Wash atty: Booth, Freret & Imlay. Format: Oldies. News progmg 7 hrs wkly. Target aud: 18-35. ■ Ronald W. Lorence, pres, gen mgr & chief engr; Norma J. Lorence, gen sls mgr; Brad J. Lorence, progmg dir.

WVSC(AM)—Jan 15, 1951: 990 khz; 10 kw-D, 75 w-N, DA-2. TL: N40 01 31 W79 05 42. Hrs opn: 5:30 AM-11 PM. Box 231 (15501). (814) 445-4186. Licensee: Ridge Communications Inc. (acq 5-11-70). Net: ABC/I. Rep: Dome, Rgnl Reps. Format: C&W. News staff one; news progmg 20 hrs wkly. Target aud: 25-49. ■ I. Richard Adams, pres & gen mgr; Gerald Chabol, gen sls mgr; Jerry Lyons, progmg dir; Harold Showman, mus dir & chief engr; Pam Tokar-Ickes, news dir. ■ Rates: $19.25; 17.50; 19.25; 17.50.

WVSC-FM—June 15, 1966: 97.7 mhz; 3 kw. Ant 265 ft. TL: N40 01 31 W79 05 42 (CP: 3.5 kw, ant 430 ft.). Prog sep from AM. Format: Adult contemp. ■ Rates: Same as AM.

South Waverly

WLGK(FM)—Not on air, target date unknown: 96.1 mhz; 940 w. Ant 590 ft. Lordstown Meadow Farm, Weaver Rd., Waverly, NY (14892). Licensee: William F. Shaughnessy.

South Williamsport

WFXX(AM)—Feb 22, 1957: 1450 khz; 1 kw-U. TL: N41 14 06 W76 58 50. Box 5057 (17701). (717) 323-3608. FAX: (717) 323-8882. Licensee: PAC Communications (acq 6-24-83; $475,000; FTR 8-20-83). Net: NBC The Source. Format: All sports. ■ David W. Banks, pres; Warren Biggins, vp; Josef Wagner, gen mgr; Ted Minier, progmg dir & mus dir; Jeff Lyon, news dir.

WZXR(FM)—Co-owned with WFXX(AM). June 1, 1968: 99.3 mhz; 210 w. Ant 1,230 ft. TL: N41 12 35 W76 57 20 (CP: 4.2 kw, ant 394 ft., TL: N41 16 59 W76 50 11). Stereo. Prog sep from AM. Format: AOR.

Spangler

WCCZ(FM)—Sept 30, 1991: 97.3 mhz; 2.15 kw. Ant 393 Ft. TL: N40 38 26 W78 47 45 (CP: 2.25 kw, ant 344 ft.). Stereo. Hrs opn: 24. Box 400, Intersection Rt. 219 & Rt. 271 (15775). (814) 948-4653. FAX: (814) 948-4315. Licensee: WKYN Inc. (acq 7-26-93; $167,500; FTR 8-23-93). Net: USA. Rep: Commercial. Format: Oldies. News staff 2; news progmg 14 hrs wkly. Target aud: 21-54. ■ Mark E. Harley, pres; Roger Peebles, Nichole Kruise, news dirs; Fred Shetler, chief engr. ■ Rates: $10; 10; 10; 10.

Starview

WHTF(FM)—Nov 22, 1971: 92.7 mhz; 1.42 kw. Ant 699 ft. TL: N40 04 29 W76 48 01. Stereo. Hrs opn: 24. 1360 Copenhaffer Rd., York (17404). (717) 266-6606. Licensee: Starview Media Inc. (acq 8-83; $525,000). FTR 8-15-83). Net: NBC The Source, ABC. Rep: McGavren Guild. Format: AOR. Target aud: 25-49. ■ Douglas George, pres; Dave Powers, gen mgr & progmg dir; Joni Beck, gen sls mgr; Carol Seidel, prom mgr; Mike Tyler, mus dir; Mike Snyder, news dir; John Hess, chief engr.

State College

WBHV(FM)—Listing follows WMAJ(AM).

WBLF(AM)—See Bellefonte.

WFGI(FM)—Oct 23, 1991: 94.5 mhz; 940 w. Ant 581 ft. TL: N40 54 04 W77 50 20. Stereo. Rebroadcasts WFGY(FM) Altoona, 99%. Bldg 100, Suite 250, 2743 Perimeter Pkwy., Augusta, GA (30909); 307 Benner

Stations in the U.S.

Pike, State College (16801). (814) 237-9800. FAX: (814) 237-2477. Licensee: WGGY Inc. (acq 12-24-91). ■ Lynn Deppen, gen mgr; Kelly Krause, opns mgr; Todd Taylor, gen sls mgr.

WGMR(FM)—See Tyrone.

WMAJ(AM)—1945: 1450 khz; 1 kw-U. TL: N40 48 32 W77 50 28. Hrs opn: 24. Box 888 (16804); 421 E. Beaver (16801). (814) 237-4959. FAX: (814) 234-1659. Licensee: Nittany Broadcasting. Group owner: Burbach Broadcasting Group (acq 1988). Net: CBS, NBC Talknet. Rep: Katz. Format: News/talk. News staff 3; news progmg 49 hrs wkly. Target aud: 30 plus; college educated, upscale. Spec prog: Sports. ■ Nick Galli, pres; John Fredorickson, gen mgr; Timothy Molnar, opns mgr; Dana Schulte, gen sls mgr; Tim Molnar, progmg dir; Patrick Boland, news dir. ■ Rates: $17.50; 15; 15; 12.

WBHV(FM)—Co-owned with WMAJ(AM). 1965: 103.1 mhz; 3 kw. Ant -55 ft. TL: N40 48 32 W77 50 28. Stereo. Hrs opn: 24. Prog sep from AM. (814) 237-9103. Net: CBS, NBC Talknet. Rep: Katz. Format: CHR. Target aud: 18-34; college aged youth, young adults. ■ Dave Dallon, progmg dir; Ronnie Fox, mus dir. ■ Rates: $25.50; 20.60; 25.50; 17.50.

*WPSU(FM)—Dec 6, 1953: 91.1 mhz; 870 w-H, 850 w-V. Ant -78 ft-H, -83 ft-V. TL: N40 48 32 W77 50 28 (CP: 91.5 mhz, 1.7 kw, ant 1,197 ft.). Stereo. Hrs opn: 18. Suite 202, 123 S. Burrowes St. (16802). (814) 865-1877. Licensee: Pennsylvania State U. Net: NPR. Format: Div, class, jazz. News progmg 35 hrs wkly. Target aud: General; Penn State students & the surrounding communities. Spec prog: Black 11 hrs, gospel 2 hrs, reggae 3 hrs, blues 3 hrs, new age 3 hrs, oldies 3 hrs, folk 10 hrs wkly. ■ David Dzikowski, stn mgr; Carl Fisher, chief engr. ■ WPSX-TV affil.

WQWK(FM)—Listing follows WRSC(AM).

WRSC(AM)—May 29, 1961: 1390 khz; 2.0 kw-D, 1 kw-N, DA-N. TL: N40 48 50 W77 53 30. 160 Clearview Ave. (16803). (814) 238-5085. Licensee: Telemedia Broadcasting (acq 2-13-89); grpsl; FTR 2-27-89). Net: ABC/I. Rep: Torbet; Dome. Wash atty: Fleishman & Walsh. Format: Adult contemp, news. News staff 3; news progmg 15 hrs wkly. Target aud: 35 plus. Spec prog: Classical 3 hrs wkly. ■ Robert Tudek, chmn; Robert H. Schmidt, gen mgr; Jonas Hunter, opns mgr; Rob Wilson, gen sls mgr; Bob Martin, rgnl sls mgr; Mary Lou Miller, prom dir; David Price, progmg mgr; Amy Williams, news dir. ■ Rates: $32; 24; 24; 20.

WQWK(FM)—Co-owned with WRSC(AM). Apr 1965: 97.1 mhz; 3 kw. Ant 403 ft. TL: N40 48 27 W77 56 29. Stereo. Prog sep from AM. Format: Classic rock. News staff one; news progmg one hr wkly. Target aud: 18-49. ■ Mike Donovan, progmg dir; Pat Urban, mus dir. ■ Rates: Same as AM.

*WTLR(FM)—Jan 1, 1978: 89.9 mhz; 25 kw. Ant 584 ft. TL: N40 53 52 W77 51 49. Stereo. Hrs opn: 24. 2020 Cato Ave. (16801). (814) 237-9857. Licensee: Central Pennsylvania Christian Institute Inc. Format: Relg. ■ Kenneth Krater, pres; Garry T. Sutley, gen mgr; Doreen Crandell, stn mgr; Mark D. Van Ouse, chief engr.

WZWW(FM)—(Bellefonte). Sept 15, 1986: 95.3 mhz; 933 w. Ant 577 ft. TL: N40 53 32 W77 51 49 (CP: 794 w., ant 636 ft.). Stereo. Hrs opn: 24. 863 Benner Pike, State College (16801). (814) 231-0953. FAX: (814) 231-0950. Licensee: Talleyrand Broadcasting Inc. Net: Unistar. Rep: Katz & Powell. Format: Adult contemp. News staff 2; news progmg 7 hrs wkly. Target aud: 25-54; upscale families. Spec prog: Sports 3 hrs wkly. ■ Dan Barker, pres; Walter D. Barker, gen mgr; Jeff Brown, opns dir, prom mgr & progmg dir; Dan Madio, gen sls mgr; Warren Keeney, chief engr. ■ Rates: $29.50; 23.75; 29.50; 23.75.

Stroudsburg

WVPO(AM)—1947: 840 khz; 250 w-D. TL: N40 58 26 W75 11 43. 22 S. 6th St. (18360). (717) 421-2100. FAX: (717) 421-2040. Licensee: Keystone Broadcasting Co. Inc. Group owner: Commonwealth Broadcasting Company Inc. (acq 10-15-93; FTR 11-8-93). Net: AP. Format: News & info, adult contemp. News staff 2. Target aud: 35 plus. Spec prog: Ger one hr, Pol one hr wkly. ■ Howard McAnany, pres; Susan T. LaRose, gen mgr; Mike Beckenbach, progmg dir; Bob Matthews, news dir; Steve Boyer, chief engr. ■ Rates: $24; 24; 24; na.

WSBG(FM)—Co-owned with WVPO(AM). Oct 1, 1964: 93.5 mhz; 550 w. Ant 764 ft. TL: N40 56 56 W57 09 29. Stereo. Prog sep from AM. Format: CHR. Target aud: 18-40. ■ Steve Ettman, progmg dir. ■ Rates: $37.50; 37.50; 37.50; 18.75.

Summerdale

*WJAZ(FM)—Jan 10, 1991: 91.7 mhz; 140 w. Ant 683 ft. TL: N40 18 16 W76 55 53. Stereo. Hrs opn: 24. Dups WRTI-FM Philadelphia 100%. 100 Annenberg Hall, Temple University, Philadelphia (19122). (215) 204-8405. FAX: (215) 204-4870. Licensee: Temple University of the Commonwealth System of Higher Education (acq 12-88; $5,000; FTR 12-5-88). Net: NPR, AP; Radio Pa. Wash atty: Arent, Fox, Kintner, Plotkin & Kahn. Format: Jazz. News staff 2; news progmg 18 hrs wkly. Target aud: 25-49. Spec prog: Caribbean 4 hrs, Sp 4 hrs wkly. ■ W. Theodore Eldredge, gen mgr; Tobias Poole, opns mgr & chief engr; Valorie Jarrell, dev mgr; Monika Morris, prom mgr; Bill Clark, progmg dir; Kim Berry, mus dir; Audrey Foltz, news dir. ■ Rates: $75; 50; 75; 50.

Sunbury

WKOK(AM)—1933: 1070 khz; 10 kw-D, 1 kw-N, DA-N. TL: N40 52 46 W76 49 18. Stereo. Hrs opn: 5 AM-1 AM. Box 1070 (17801); RD# 2, County Line Rd., Selinsgrove (17870). (717) 286-5838; (717) 743-1841. FAX: (717) 743-7837. Licensee: Sunbury Broadcasting Corp. (acq: 5/33). Net: CBS. Rep: Roslin; Dome. Wash atty: Wilkinson, Barker, Knauer & Quinn. Format: Adult contemp. News staff 3; news progmg 23 hrs wkly. Target aud: 25-54. Spec prog: Farm 3 hrs wkly. ■ Roger S. Haddon, pres; Joseph A. McGranaghan, exec vp & gen mgr; Jack Richards, opns mgr; Marvin Benfer, vp sls; Ron Mackley, mktg mgr; Lynn Hall, prom mgr; Rob Senter, mus dir; Mark Lawrence, news dir; John W. Keller Jr., chief engr. ■ Rates: $13.25; 11.50; 11.75; 6.25.

WQKX(FM)—Co-owned with WKOK(AM). Sept 15, 1948: 94.1 mhz; 16 kw. Ant 879 ft. TL: N40 47 07 W76 41 51. Stereo. Prog sep from AM. Format: CHR. ■ Tom Morgan, progmg dir; Aaron Collins, mus dir; Terry Ford, asst mus dir; Ann Blugis, news dir; Donna Shannon, pub affrs dir. ■ Rates: $19.50; 17.50; 18.50; 11.50.

Susquehanna

WKGB-FM—Feb 11, 1989: 92.5 mhz; 6 kw. Ant 709 ft. TL: N42 03 10 W75 42 07 (CP: 1.3 kw). Stereo. Hrs opn: 24. 495 Court St., Binghamton, NY (13904). (607) 723-2925; (607) 723-9542. FAX: (607) 723-5268. Licensee: K.G. Broadcasting Inc. (acq 12-26-90; FTR 1-14-91). Net: NBC the Source. Rep: D & R Radio. Wash atty: Carr, Morris & Graeff. Format: AOR, classic rock. News progmg one hr wkly. Target aud: 25-49; baby boomers who grew up with rock and roll of the 60s & 70s. Spec prog: Jazz 2 hrs, farm one hr wkly. ■ Ben Smith, pres, gen mgr & pub affrs dir; Kevin Fitzgerald, opns mgr & chief engr; Joe Kane, gen sls mgr; Todd McCarthy, progmg dir.

Swarthmore

*WSRN-FM—Dec 31, 1939: 91.5 mhz; 110 w. Ant 140 ft. TL: N39 54 18 W75 21 16. Stereo. Swarthmore College, 500 College Ave. (19081-1397). (215) 328-8340. FAX: (215) 328-8000. Licensee: Swarthmore College. Format: Div. ■ James R. Deane, gen mgr; Jacob Anderson, opns mgr; Graham Richmond, mus dir; Leif Kirschenbaum, chief engr.

Sweet Valley

*WRGN(FM)—Oct 15, 1984: 88.1 mhz; 500 w. Ant 239 ft. TL: N41 17 54 W76 07 28 (CP: Ant 302 ft.). RD3 Hunlock Creek (18621). (717) 477-3688. FAX: (717) 477-2310. Licensee: Gospel Media Institute Inc. Format: Relg. ■ Burl F. Updyke, pres, gen mgr & chief engr; Burl Updike, gen sls mgr; Shirley J. Updyke, progmg dir; Tim Madeira, news dir.

Tamaqua

WMGH-FM—June 14, 1965: 105.5 mhz; 1.3 kw. Ant 485 ft. TL: N40 47 14 W76 01 59. Stereo. Box 105 (18252). (717) 668-2992. FAX: (717) 645-2159. Licensee: East Penn Broadcasting Inc. Group owner: HGF Media Group (acq 2-28-87; $300,000; FTR 12-15-86). Format: Adult contemp. ■ Harold G. Fulmer, pres; Mick Haggerty, gen mgr & progmg dir; Mark Marek, gen sls mgr; Mike Berzowski, prom mgr; Tom Tkach, news dir; Joe Manjack, chief engr.

Tarentum

WQKB(FM)—See New Kensington.

Tioga

WPHD(FM)—May 23, 1991: 94.7 mhz; 820 w. Ant 895 ft. TL: N41 54 36 W77 00 40. Stereo. Hrs opn: 24. Suite 2, 303 W. Church St., Elmira, NY (14901). Suite 106, 4359 S. Howell Ave., Milwaukee, WI (53207). (717) 733-6600; (717) 662-7474. FAX: (607) 733-2112. Licensee: Europa Communications Inc. (acq 5-22-92). Net: NBC the Source. Rep: D & R Radio. Wash atty: Harry Cole. Format: AOR. News staff one; news progmg 3 hrs wkly. Target aud: 21-44; emphasis on males. Spec prog: New age 2 hrs, Christian rock one hr, alternative/modern 2 hrs, metal 3 hrs, jazz 2 hrs. ■ Kevin M. Fitzgerald, CEO, gen mgr & chief engr; Patrick L. LoPeman, exec vp & opns dir; Benjamin J. Smith, vp; Sandi Kirk, gen sls mgr & prom dir; Dom Milone, progmg dir; Todd McCarthy, mus dir; Ben P. Smith, asst mus dir & pub affrs dir; Glen Pitcher, news dir. ■ Rates: $10; 8; 10; 5.

Titusville

WTIV(AM)—Nov 27, 1955: 1230 khz; 1 kw-U. TL: N41 37 00 W79 41 34. Hrs opn: 6 AM-midnight. Box 184, WTIV Building, 150 W. Central Ave. (16354). (814) 827-3651. FAX: (814) 827-1679. Licensee: Robert H. Sauber. Net: MBS. Rep: Commercial Media Sales. Wash atty: Reddy, Begley & Martin. Format: Lite adult contemp. News progmg 13 hrs wkly. Target aud: 22-54; mixed. ■ Robert H. Sauber, gen mgr & chief engr; Thomas J. Sauber, opns dir & progmg dir; Doug Metheney, gen sls mgr. ■ Rates: $11.15; 11.15; 11.15; 11.15.

Tobyhanna

WPMR-FM—Jan 15, 1993: 107.9 mhz; 5.7 kw. Ant 564 ft. TL: N41 07 04 W75 22 43. Stereo. Hrs opn: 24. Box 132, Mountain Dr., Mt. Pocono (18344). (717) 839-3939. FAX: (717) 839-9875. Licensee: Tiab Communications Corp. Wash atty: Denise B. Moline P.C. Format: AOR. News staff 2. Target aud: 18-34; male. ■ Jeff Woehrle, chmn, gen mgr & chief engr; Kathleen Moyer, opns mgr; Carole Gehring, gen sls mgr; Chris DeBello, rgnl sls mgr; Kelly Lockwood, prom dir; Robin Lee, progmg dir; Patrick Butler, mus dir; Mason Hall, news dir; Kim Kalina, pub affrs dir. ■ Rates: $38.50; 28.50; 38.50; 28.50.

Towanda

WTTC(AM)—1959: 1550 khz; 500 w-D. TL: N41 45 55 W76 29 10. 214 Main St. (18848). (717) 265-2165; (717) 265-2166. Licensee: Twin Tier Broadcasting Inc. (acq 11-1-65). Net: Motor Racing Net. Format: Adult contemp, country, oldies. News progmg 5 hrs wkly. Target aud: General. ■ Michael DiSisti, pres; Joel Crayton, gen mgr & gen sls mgr; Richard Hollenback, progmg dir & mus dir.

WTTC-FM—Nov 1959: 95.3 mhz; 3 kw. Ant 125 ft. TL: N41 45 55 W76 29 10. Hrs opn: 6 AM-11 PM. Dups AM 100%.

Troy

WHGL(AM)—Mar 3, 1982: 1310 khz; 500 w-D, 72 w-N. TL: N41 46 51 W76 49 09. Box 100, 170 Redington Ave. (16947). (717) 297-0100. Licensee: Cantroair Communications (acq 7-1-88); grpsl; FTR 6-22-87). Net: ABC/C. Format: Country. News staff one. Target aud: 25-54. ■ David Bernstein, pres; Mike Powers, vp, gen mgr & vp progmg; Bob Gisler, gen sls mgr; Georgia Pepper, prom mgr; Kenny Lane, mus dir; J. Curtls, news dir; Rob Thomas, chief engr.

WHGL-FM—See Canton.

Tunkhannock

WEMR(AM)—June 13, 1986: 1460 khz; 5 kw-D, 1.25 kw-N, DA-2. TL: N41 33 46 W75 58 11. Hrs opn: 18. R.R. 3, Box 1460 (18657). (717) 836-1460; (717) 836-1077. FAX: (717) 836-2432. Licensee: Endless Mountain Broadcasting Inc. Net: AP. Format: Country. News staff one; news progmg 2 hrs wkly. Target aud: 24-54; blue collar workers. Spec prog: Farm one hr, relg 3 hrs wkly. ■ Norman Werkheiser, pres; Jim Petrie, gen mgr & sls dir; Aldo Cardoni, progmg dir & mus dir; Dan Miller, news dir; Robert Graham, chief engr. ■ Rates: $20; 16; 20; 12.

WYMK(FM)—Co-owned with WEMR(AM). Oct 10, 1990: 107.7 mhz; Ant 1,161 ft. TL: N41 31 29 W76 04 13. Stereo. Hrs opn: 24. Prog sep from AM. (717) 945-7571. Format: Rock 'n roll favorites. News staff one; news progmg one hr wkly. Target aud: 25-35; young, mobile, white & blue collar workers, $20,000 plus income.

Pennsylvania

Tyrone

WTRN(AM)—Jan 12, 1955: 1340 khz; 1 kw-U. TL: N40 39 37 W78 15 21. Hrs opn: 24. Box 247, Washington Ave. & 1st St. (16686). (814) 684-3200. FAX: (814) 684-1220. Licensee: Allegheny Mountain Network Stns. (group owner). Net: Allegheny Mtn. Net. Rep: Dome. Wash atty: Borsari & Paxson. Format: Top-40. News progmg 16 hrs wkly. Target aud: General. ■ Cary H. Simpson, pres; William E. Moses, gen mgr & gen sls mgr; Jean Dixon, prom mgr; Richard Saupp, progmg dir; Craig Shaffer, mus dir; Joyce Nowlin, news dir; Robert H. Lynn, chief engr. ■ Rates: $12; 10; 12; 8.

WGMR(FM)—Co-owned with WTRN(AM). Aug 15, 1961: 101.1 mhz; 8.5 kw. Ant 1,171 ft. TL: N40 55 10 W77 58 28. Stereo. Hrs opn: 24. Prog sep from AM. Box 204, Suite 203, 204 E. Calder Way, State College (16801). (814) 238-0717; (814) 238-0792. FAX: (814) 234-3533. Net: SMN. Format: Country. ■ Peter Szebin, prom mgr; John F. Simpson, mus dir. ■ Rates: $22; 22; 22; 22.

Union City

WCTL(FM)—Apr 23, 1967: 106.3 mhz; 3.4 kw. Ant 430 ft. TL: N42 00 04 W79 52 33. Stereo. Hrs opn: 24. 10912 Rt. 19, Waterford (16441). (814) 438-7686. FAX: (814) 438-7688. Licensee: Inspiration Time Inc. (acq 3-72). Net: USA, CBN. Wash atty: Wiley, Rein & Fielding. Format: Relg. News progmg 20 hrs wkly. Target aud: 25-54; Christian families. Spec prog: Children's 2 hrs wkly. ■ Ronald Fuhrman, pres; Joel Natalie, gen mgr & progmg dir; Bob Smith, gen sls mgr; Mark Shearer, prom mgr; Tim Matthews, mus dir; Donna Shearer, pub affrs dir; Mel Burger, chief engr. ■ Rates: $16; 16; 16; 12.

Uniontown

WMBS(AM)—July 15, 1937: 590 khz; 1 kw-U, DA-N. TL: N39 51 35 W79 44 44. 82 W. Fayette St. (15401). (412) 438-3900. FAX: (412) 438-2406. Licensee: Fayette Broadcasting Corp. Net: CBS. Format: Adult contemp/country. Spec prog: Farm one hr, Pol 2 hrs wkly. ■ Simon Rider, pres & gen mgr; Steve Marsinko, gen sls mgr; James Morgan, progmg dir; Raymond E. Hice, mus dir; Dave Bridges, news dir; Larry Campbell, chief engr.

WPQR-FM—Dec 20, 1968: 99.3 mhz; 3 kw. Ant 300 ft. TL: N39 53 09 W79 46 29. Stereo. Hrs opn: 5 AM-1 AM. 133 E. Crawford Ave., Connellsville (15425). (412) 437-2813. Licensee: Kel Com Broadcasting Inc. (acq 5-21-87; FTR 12-1-86). Net: ABC/E. Rep: Dome. Format: Adult contemp. ■ Geoffrey Kelly, pres; David Zinkhann, gen mgr; Chuck Leavens, chief engr.

Upton

WSRT(FM)—See Mercersburg.

Villanova

*****WXVU(FM)**—August 1991: 89.1 mhz; 710 w-V. Ant 223 ft. TL: N40 03 22 W75 22 30. Box 105, Tolentine Hall, Villanova Univ. (19085). (215) 519-7200; (215) 519-7201. Licensee: Villanova Univ. in the State of Pennsylvania. Format: Alternative. News progmg 3 hrs wkly. Target aud: 15-25; youngsters. ■ Dave Seminars, gen mgr & stn mgr; Craig Remar, vp prom; Christine Connolly, Ellen Bruno, mus dirs.

Warminster

*****WRDV(FM)**—Sept 6, 1976: 89.3 mhz; 200 w. Ant 88 ft. TL: N40 12 19 W75 06 27 (CP: 100 w-H, 1 kw-V, ant 118 ft.). Hrs opn: 19. Box 2012, Township Bldg., Henry & Gibson Ave. (18974). (215) 674-8002; (215) 674-3278. Licensee: Bux-Mont Educ. Radio Assoc. (acq 3-80). Format: Big band, oldies. Target aud: General. Spec prog: C&W 4 hrs, bluegrass 3 hrs, folk 3 hrs, reggae 3 hrs, new age 3 hrs, jazz 3 hrs wkly. ■ Ron Michael, pres; Todd H. Allen, vp & gen mgr; Todd Allen, prom mgr; Dan Lennon, progmg dir; Chuck Warren, mus dir; Charles W. Loughery, chief engr.

Warren

WNAE(AM)—Dec 31, 1946: 1310 khz; 5 kw-D, 94 w-N. TL: N41 48 50 W79 10 04. Hrs opn: 6 AM-midnight. Box 824, 310 2nd Ave. (16365). (814) 723-1310. FAX: (814) 723-3356. Licensee: Kinzua Broadcasting Co. (acq 1974). Net: UPI, Radio Pa. Rep: Commercial. Format: Adult contemp. News staff one; news progmg 21 hrs wkly. Target aud: General. ■ W. LeRoy Schneck, pres & gen mgr; Mark Silvis, progmg dir; Robert Seiden, news dir; Richard Gilson, chief engr. ■ Rates: $14.15; 7.80; 7.80; 7.80.

WRRN(FM)—Co-owned with WNAE(AM). March 1948: 92.3 mhz; 50 kw. Ant 410 ft. TL: N41 48 50 W79 10 04. Stereo. Dups AM 17%. Format: EZ lstng. News staff one; news progmg 100 hrs wkly. Target aud: General. ■ Richard Gilson, vp. ■ Rates: Same as AM.

Washington

WJPA(AM)—Feb 1, 1941: 1450 khz; 1 kw-U. TL: N40 11 23 W80 14 02. Hrs opn: 24. 98 S. Main St. (15301). (412) 222-2110. FAX: (412) 228-2299. Licensee: Washington Broadcasting Co. Net: MBS; Radio Pa. Format: Oldies. News staff 2. ■ Michael S. Siegel, pres & gen mgr; Bob Gregg, gen sls mgr & chief engr; Sue Sobrasky, prom mgr; Pete Povich, progmg dir; Margie Konstantinou, mus dir; Jim Jefferson, news dir.

WJPA-FM—Sept 26, 1964: 95.3 mhz; 2.15 kw. Ant 390 ft. TL: N40 11 23 W80 14 02 (CP: 4.2 kw). Stereo. Hrs opn: 24. Dups AM 100%.

WKZV(AM)—August 1968: 1110 khz; 1 kw-D, DA. TL: N40 13 16 W80 14 34. 80 E. Chestnut St. (15301). (412) 228-6678. Licensee: U.S. North Broadcasting Inc. (acq 11-9-92; $100,000; FTR 11-30-92). Net: ARN. Rep: Dome. Format: Country. News staff 2; news progmg 3 hrs wkly. Target aud: 35 plus. Spec prog: Pol 3 hrs wkly. ■ Helen Suspinski, pres; Michael Panjuscek, gen mgr; Gerge Lasko, gen sls mgr; Barbara Wallace, news dir; Goerge Lasko, chief engr. ■ WTRF-TV affil.

*****WXJX(FM)**—Nov 26, 1972: 92.1 mhz; 10 w. Ant 59 ft. TL: N40 10 15 W80 14 25 (CP: 390 w, ant 62 ft.). Stereo. One S. Lincoln St. (15301). (412) 222-4400; (412) 223-6039. Licensee: Washington & Jefferson College. Format: Progsv. ■ John Unice, pres; David Kuhn, gen mgr.

Waynesboro

WHGT(AM)—Aug 19, 1953: 1380 khz; 1 kw-D. TL: N39 44 20 W77 36 10. 33 E. Main St. (17268). (717) 762-3138; (717) 263-0369. FAX: (717) 762-7153. Licensee: HJV Ltd. Group owner: VerStandig Broadcasting (acq 10-19-81; grpsl; FTR 11-16-81). Net: AP. Format: Contemp country. Target aud: 25-54. ■ Marge Martin, gen mgr; Stacy Drake, progmg dir & mus dir; Chris Snively, chief engr.

WAYZ-FM—Co-owned with WHGT(AM). Feb 3, 1959: 101.5 mhz; 50 kw-H, 48 kw-V. Ant 230 ft. TL: N39 49 44 W77 33 10. Stereo. Dups AM 100%. ■ John D. Ver Standig, pres; Michelle Pfirman, news dir.

Waynesburg

WANB(AM)—Sept 27, 1956: 1580 khz; 1 kw-D. TL: N39 52 11 W80 08 02. First Federal Bldg., 25 E. High St. (15370). (412) 627-5555. Licensee: Joseph F. Hennessey. Net: AP. Rep: Dome. Format: C&W. News staff 5. Target aud: 20 plus. Spec prog: Talk 5 hrs wkly. ■ Joseph F. Hennessey, pres; Judy Rostoka, gen mgr; Drew Gordon, mus dir; Lori Salva-Houy, news dir; Allen Fox, chief engr. ■ Rates: $12; 11; 11; 10.

WANB-FM—April 21, 1978: 103.1 mhz; 550 w. Ant 620 ft. TL: N39 52 11 W80 08 02. Stereo. Dups AM 100%.

*****WCYJ-FM**—July 6, 1979: 88.7 mhz; 18 w. Ant -33 ft. TL: N39 53 59 W80 11 07. Waynesburg College 51 W. College St. (15370). (412) 852-3310. FAX: (412) 852-3270. Licensee: Waynesburg College (acq 7-3-79). Format: Alternative. ■ William Molzon, gen mgr.

Wellsboro

WNBT(AM)—May 13, 1955: 1490 khz; 1 kw-U. TL: N41 44 41 W77 17 35. Hrs opn: 24. Box 98, 33 East Ave. (16901). (717) 724-1490. FAX: (717) 724-6971. Licensee: Farm & Home Broadcasting Co. Group owner: Allegheny Mountain Network Stns. Net: ABC/I; Radio Pa. Rep: Dome. Wash atty: Borsari & Paxson. Format: CHR/lite rock. News staff one; news progmg 10 hrs wkly. Target aud: 25-55. ■ Cary Simpson, pres; Steve Worthington, opns dir, prom mgr, progmg dir, mus dir & news dir; Al Harer, sls dir, mktg mgr & prom mgr; Robert H. Lynn, chief engr.

WNBT-FM—July 2, 1969: 104.5 mhz; 50 kw. Ant 380 ft. TL: N41 44 17 W77 21 50. Stereo. (717) 662-7100. Net: Unistar. News staff one; news progmg 2 hrs wkly. Target aud: 18-55. ■ Steve Worthington, asst mus dir.

West Chester

WCHE(AM)—Oct 4, 1963: 1520 khz; 250 w-D. TL: N39 58 06 W75 37 59. 119 W. Market St. (19382). (215) 692-3131. FAX: (215) 692-3133. Licensee: Tri-State Radio Inc. (acq 3-3-93; $198,000; FTR 3-22-93). Net: MBS. Format: Talk. News staff one; news progmg 20 hrs wkly. Target aud: 24-64. ■ Horace Gross, pres; Gene Boyd, gen mgr; Mark Crouch, gen sls mgr, prom mgr, mus dir & chief engr; Bill Thomas, progmg dir; Lucinda Law, news dir.

WCOJ(AM)—See Coatesville.

West Hazleton

WXPX(AM)—1982: 1300 khz; 5 kw-D, 500 w-N, DA-2. TL: N40 56 26 W76 00 07. R.D. 1 Walnut St., Freeland (18224). (717) 636-2346. Licensee: Friendship Communications Inc. (acq 4-84; $320,000; FTR 3-19-84). Net: ABC/I; Radio Pa. Rep: Dome. Format: Country. News staff 3; news progmg 28 hrs wkly. Target aud: General; affluent, educated. Spec prog: Big band 4 hrs, talk 2 hrs wkly, local sports. ■ Susan Bock, gen mgr; Tom Emanski, prom mgr; Tom Ragan, news dir; Robert Schacht, chief engr.

Whitneyville

WLIH(FM)—Mar 15, 1987: 107.1 mhz; 3.3 kw. Ant 299 ft. TL: N41 46 13 W77 12 08. Stereo. Hrs opn: 18. Box 97, Wellsboro (16901); R.R. 2, Box 257 (16901). (717) 724-4272. Licensee: Good Christian Radio Broadcasting Inc. Net: USA. Format: Relg. Target aud: General. ■ Robert Makin, pres; Warren Berg, vp; Carol Makin, gen mgr, adv mgr & progmg mgr.

Wilkes-Barre

WARD(AM)—See Pittston.

WARM(AM)—See Scranton.

WBAX(AM)—May 1, 1922: 1240 khz; 1 kw-U. TL: N41 15 13 W75 54 25. One Broadcast Plaza, (18703). (717) 288-7575. FAX: (717) 288-7577. Licensee: WBAX Inc. (acq 2-28-86). Net: CNN. Rep: Torbet. Format: MOR, big band. News staff one; news progmg 5 hrs wkly. Target aud: 50 plus; mature individuals who like the music of the 30s, 40s & 50s. Spec prog: Frank Sinatra Sundays, polka, sports. ■ Joseph A. Frank, pres; Rick Malyk, gen mgr; Vince Clark, progmg dir; Marybeth Rockwell, news dir; Tom Sommers, chief engr. ■ Rates: $20; 20; 20; 12.

*****WCLH(FM)**—Feb 6, 1972: 90.7 mhz; 175 w. Ant 1,020 ft. TL: N41 10 58 W75 52 21. Stereo. Hrs opn: 8 AM-2 AM. S. River & W. South St. (18766). (717) 831-5907. Licensee: Wilkes University. Net: AP. Format: Div, educ, progsv new mus. Target aud: 12-44. Spec prog: Heavy metal 18 hrs, classic rock 9 hrs, jazz 3 hrs wkly. ■ David Bradbury, gen mgr; Jarrod Norton, stn mgr; Jon Erik Kosleski, opns dir; Matt Brenner, vp dev; Eric Freeman, prom dir; Miri Lynn Steinmetz, progmg dir; Marisa Rae, mus dir; Eric Bailey, asst mus dir; Joseph Glynn, chief engr.

WEJL(AM)—See Scranton.

WGBI(AM)—See Scranton.

WGGY(FM)—See Scranton.

WICK(AM)—See Scranton.

WILK(AM)—Feb 13, 1947: 980 khz; 5 kw-D, 1 kw-N, DA-N. TL: N41 13 42 W75 56 53. Stereo. 305 Hwy. 315, Pittston (18640). (717) 883-9800. FAX: (717) 883-1360. Licensee: Keymarket of N.E. Pennsylvania. Group owner: Keymarket Communications (acq 8-31-89; $350,000; FTR 7-24-89). Net: ABC/E, MBS, CNN. Rep: Katz. Format: News, talk. News staff 15; news progmg 108 hrs wkly. Target aud: 15-54. ■ Barry Drake, pres; Mike Remely, gen mgr & gen sls mgr; Nancy Kaman, progmg dir & news dir; Ronald F. Balonis, chief engr.

WKRZ-FM—Co-owned with WILK(AM). 1947: 98.5 mhz; 8.7 kw. Ant 1,171 ft. TL: N41 11 56 W75 49 06. Stereo. Prog sep from AM. (717) 883-9850. Net: NBC the Source. Format: Adult contemp. ■ Gerald Getz, gen mgr & gen sls mgr.

WMGS(FM)—1946: 92.9 mhz; 5.3 kw. Ant 1,384 ft. TL: N41 10 58 W75 52 26. Stereo. Hrs opn: 24. Box 930, Wilkes Barre Scranton Hwy., Avoca (18641). (717) 655-2271. FAX: (717) 457-8737. Licensee: WARM Broadcasting Co. Group owner: Susquehanna Radio Corp. (acq 3-12-85; $2 million; FTR 3-11-85). Rep: McGavren Guild. Format: Adult contemp. Spec prog: Jazz 2 hrs wkly. ■ Jim Loftus, gen mgr; Tim Dunkin, gen sls mgr & natl sls mgr; Christine Coneco, prom dir; Mike Edwards, progmg dir; Stan Phillips, mus dir; Bob Lenco, chief engr.

WNAK(AM)—See Nanticoke.

*****WRKC(FM)**—Sept 18, 1968: 88.5 mhz; 440 w. Ant -470 ft. TL: N41 14 57 W75 52 26. Stereo. Hrs opn: 7 AM-2 AM. King's College (18711). (717) 826-5821; (717) 826-5931. FAX: (717) 825-9049. Licensee: King's College. Net: ABC/I. Format: Jazz, AOR, reading for the blind.

Stations in the U.S.

Target aud: General; people who need wide-ranging svcs. ■ Thomas Carten, pres & gen mgr; Chris Vail, vp opns; Judy Vail, dev dir; Jan Souther, mktg dir; Bart Sommers, prom dir; Kim Hayes, progmg dir; Bob Schacht, chief engr.

WWDL-FM—See Scranton.

WYCK(AM)—1923: 980 khz; 5 kw-D, 1 kw-N. TL: N41 15 42 W75 42 35. 305 Hwy. 315, Pittston (18640). Licensee: Key Market of North PA. (acq 12-11-92; $77,000; FTR 1-11-93). Format: News, talk, sports. ■ Gerald Getz, vp & gen mgr.

Williamsport

WFXX(AM)—See South Williamsport.

WHTO(FM)—(Muncy). Aug 11, 1983: 103.9 mhz; 1.3 kw. Ant 460 ft. TL: N41 16 59 W76 50 11 (CP: 93.3 mhz). Stereo. Hrs opn: 24. 220 S. Russell Ave., Williamsport (17701). (717) 323-8200. FAX: (717) 323-5075. Licensee: Pro Marketing Inc. (acq 5-87). Net: ABC/FM. Rep: Christal. Format: Adult contemp, CHR. News staff 2. Target aud: 18-54; adult oriented, mass appeal. ■ Victor A. Michael Jr., pres, gen mgr & adv dir; Mark Williams, vp, opns mgr & prom dir; Lori L. Michael, stn mgr; Mike Wright, dev dir; Randy Laprilla, sls dir; Van Michael, mktg dir; Mark Williams, Shawn Carey (ass't), progmg dirs; Shawn Carey, mus dir & pub affrs dir; Liz Brady, news dir; Victor Michael, chief engr. ■ Rates: $25; 23.50; 25; 20.

WILQ(FM)—Listing follows WLYC(AM).

WKSB(FM)—Listing follows WRAK(AM).

WLYC(AM)—June 1951: 1050 khz; 1 kw-D, 36 w-N. TL: N41 15 44 W77 01 59. Hrs opn: 6 AM-10 PM. Box 1176, 353 Pine St. (17703). (717) 322-4676; (800) 326-9376. FAX: (717) 323-3332. Licensee: Pennsylvania Radio. Group owner: Lamco Communications Inc. (acq 6-81). Net: ABC/I. Rep: Roslin, Dome. Wash atty: Koteen & Naftalin. Format: Nostalgia, MOR. News staff 3. Target aud: 35 plus; greater Lycoming County area. Spec prog: Jazz. ■ Robert J. Cunnion, pres & gen mgr; James Cameron, gen sls mgr; Mike Yoder, progmg dir; Neal Bowes, mus dir; Vanessa Hunter, news dir; John H. Ellis, chief engr. ■ Rates: $26.40; 24.20; 25.30; 7.50.

WILQ(FM)—Co-owned with WLYC(AM). July 31, 1949: 105.1 mhz; 9.2 kw. Ant 1,135 ft. TL: N41 11 43 W76 58 18. Stereo. Hrs opn: 24. Prog sep from AM. Net: ABC/I. Format: Country. Target aud: 25 plus; adults in a 10 county area. ■ Barabara Evans, progmg dir; Doug Herendeen, mus dir. ■ Rates: $47.60; 43.80; 45.70; 20.

WRAK(AM)—Apr 10, 1930: 1400 khz; 1 kw-U. TL: N41 14 22 W77 02 27. Hrs opn: 24. Box 3638, 1559 W. 4th St. (17701). (717) 327-1400. Licensee: Pennsylvania Broadcasting Associates L.P. (acq 3-19-87; grpsl; FTR 10-27-86). Net: CNN, NBC. Format: News/talk. News staff 2; news progmg 91 hrs wkly. Target aud: 25 plus. ■ J. Albert Dame, pres; Jim Dabney, gen mgr & gen sls mgr; Anne Dame, adv dir; Ken Sawyer, progmg dir & news dir; Skip Smith, chief engr.

WRAK-FM—Aug 16, 1989: 107.9 mhz; 180 w. Ant 1,292 ft. TL: N41 12 39 W76 57 17. Stereo. Box 3638, 1559 W. 4th St. (17701). (717) 327-1400. FAX: (717) 327-8156. Licensee: Bald Eagle Broadcast Associates Inc. Net: NBC, MBS. Rep: Banner. Format: News/talk. News staff 2. Target aud: 25 plus; professionals. Spec prog: Class one hr, jazz one hr, comedy one hr, blues 3 hrs, relg one hr, sports 2 hrs wkly.

WKSB(FM)—Co-owned with WRAK(AM). Apr 1, 1948: 102.7 mhz; 53 kw. Ant 1,270 ft. TL: N41 11 21 W76 58 53. Stereo. Hrs opn: 24. Prog sep from AM. Format: Adult contemp. News staff 2. Target aud: 25-54. ■ Tom Benson, progmg dir & mus dir.

*****WRLC(FM)**—Apr 5, 1976: 91.7 mhz; 740 w-H. Ant -298 ft. TL: N41 14 42 W76 59 50. Stereo. Hrs opn: 19. Mass Communication Dept., Lycoming College, College Place (17701). (717) 321-4054; (717) 321-4060. FAX: (717) 321-4090. Licensee: Lycoming College (acq 1-76). Format: Div, progsv. News progmg 5 hrs wkly. Target aud: Varied; Lycoming College and its surrounding communities. Spec prog: Class one hr, gospel 2 hrs, children's 2 hrs, BBC World News 10 hrs, pub affrs 2 hrs, Christian rock 3 hrs, jazz 3 hrs, blues 2 hrs wkly. ■ Brad Nason (faculty advsr), gen mgr; Karen Tepsic, mus dir; Skip Smith, chief engr.

*****WWAS(FM)**—Sept 3, 1980: 88.1 mhz; 100 w. Ant -58 ft. TL: N41 14 11 W77 01 26. Stereo. Hrs opn: 7 AM-midnight, M-Th; 7 AM-6 PM, F. Lifelong Education Center, One College Ave. (17701). (717) 327-4521; (717) 326-3761, ext. 7214. FAX: (717) 327-4503. Licensee: Pennsylvania College of Technology (acq 3-14-90). Format:

AOR. News progmg 2 hrs wkly. Target aud: 18-24; college students. Spec prog: Jazz 2 hrs, alternative 2 hrs, rap 2 hrs, urban contemp 2 hrs, sports 2 hrs wkly. ■ Thomas Speicher, gen mgr; Michael Gruver, stn mgr & progmg mgr; Jon Kratzer, prom dir; Troy Mills, mus dir; Andrea Slater, asst mus dir; Mike Juran, news dir & pub affrs dir; N. Clifford Smith Jr., chief engr.

WWPA(AM)—May 22, 1949: 1340 khz; 1 kw-U. TL: N41 13 45 W77 00 45. Hrs opn: 24. 2401 Reach Rd. (17701). (717) 323-7118. FAX: (717) 326-1043. Licensee: S&P Broadcasting L.P. Group owner: S&P Broadcasting Co. (acq 10-18-89; grpsl; FTR 11-6-89). Net: CBS. Rep: Katz. Format: Talk. News staff one; news progmg 20 hrs wkly. Target aud: 35 plus. Spec prog: Sports. ■ Ron Swanson, pres; Darrell Alva, gen mgr; Scott Masteller, opns mgr & progmg mgr; Bryan May, prom dir; Dave Swartz, chief engr. ■ Rates: $14; 12; 14; 10.

WWWD(FM)—See Jersey Shore.

WZXR(FM)—See South Williamsport.

Windber

WBEM(AM)—May 18, 1964: 1350 khz; 2.5 kw-D. TL: N40 13 32 W78 44 03. Box 5547, 1724 Scalp Ave., Johnstown (15904). Licensee: Jotocon Communications Inc. (acq 4-1-89). Net: ABC/E, ABC TalkRadio, Radio Pa. Format: MOR, talk. Target aud: 35-64. ■ J. Thomas Conners, pres & gen sls mgr; David Rod Wolf, gen mgr; Ryan C. Coplan, progmg dir & news dir; Tim Molnar, mus dir; Mike Conners, chief engr.

York

WARM-FM—Listing follows WSBA(AM).

WHTF(FM)—See Starview.

WOYK(AM)—March 1932: 1350 khz; 5 kw-D, 1 kw-N, DA-N. TL: N39 56 00 W76 49 06. Hrs opn: 24. 1360 Copenhaffer Rd. (17404). (717) 266-6606. Licensee: Starview Media Inc. (acq 12-87). Net: MBS, ABC/I, Motor Racing Net. Rep: McGavren Guild. Format: Classic C&W. News staff one; news progmg 10 hrs wkly. Target aud: 35-64; adults, blue collar & agricultural. ■ Douglas George, pres; Tim Michaels, gen mgr & gen sls mgr, progmg dir & news dir; Andrea Lelii, prom mgr; Chuck Edwards, mus dir; John Hess, chief engr. ■ Rates: $20; 20; 20; 10.

WQXA(AM)—1948: 1250 khz; 1 kw-D. TL: N39 59 56 W76 41 43. Stereo. Hrs opn: 24. 1614 Druck Valley Rd. (17405). (717) 755-1049. FAX: (717) 757-7876. Licensee: Penn Central Broadcasting. Group owner: HGF Media Group (acq 12-16-83). Rep: D & R Radio. Format: Oldies, talk. News progmg 10 hrs wkly. Target aud: 25-54. Spec prog: High school football/basketball, Philadelphia Phillies. ■ Harold G. Fulmer, pres; Fred Bohn, gen mgr; Bill Cox, opns mgr; Bill Lakatas, chief engr.

WQXA-FM—1948: 105.7 mhz; 25 kw. Ant 705 ft. TL: N39 59 56 W76 41 43. Stereo. Prog sep from AM. (717) 757-9402. Format: Hot adult contemp. Target aud: 18-49.

WSBA(AM)—Sept 1, 1942: 910 khz; 5 kw-D, 1 kw-N, DA-2. TL: N39 59 53 W76 44 42. Hrs opn: 24. Box 910 (17405). (717) 764-1155. FAX: (717) 252-4708. Licensee: Susquehanna Radio Corp. (group owner). Net: AP. Rep: Eastman. Format: News/talk. News staff 9. Spec prog: Black 3 hrs, farm 4 hrs wkly. ■ Arthur W. Carlson, pres; Chris J. Huber, vp & gen mgr; Jim Horn, opns mgr & progmg dir; Tom Ranker, gen sls mgr; Yvonne Bland, mktg mgr; Gary Taylor, prom mgr; Cathy Clark, news dir; Dave Russell, pub affrs dir; Steve Johnston, chief engr.

WARM-FM—Co-owned with WSBA(AM). Sept 1, 1962: 103.3 mhz; 6.4 kw. Ant 1,305 ft. TL: N40 01 38 W76 36 08. Stereo. Prog sep from AM. Format: Adult contemp. ■ Kelly West, progmg dir.

*****WVYC(FM)**—Nov 18, 1976: 88.1 mhz; 370 w. Ant 97 ft. TL: N39 56 49 W76 43 47. Stereo. Hrs opn: 18. Student Union Bldg., York College of Pennsylvania (17403-3426). (717) 846-7788, ext. 311; (717) 845-7413. Licensee: York College of Pennsylvania. Net: AP. Format: Educ, progsv, rock. News staff one; news progmg 3 hrs wkly. Target aud: 14-24; new music lovers. Spec prog: Class 8 hrs, jazz 8 hrs, Sp one hr wkly. ■ Dr. George Waldner, pres; David Schneier, gen mgr; Thomas Gibson, chief engr.

York-Hanover

WYCR(FM)—Licensed to York-Hanover. See Hanover.

Rhode Island

Block Island

WBLQ(FM)—Oct 3, 1988: 99.3 mhz; 4.6 kw. Ant 177 ft. TL: N41 10 30 W71 34 10. Stereo. Hrs opn: 24. Box 3357, 140 Point Judith Rd., Narragansett (02882). (401) 782-4555. FAX: (401) 783-6161. Licensee: WCRN Inc. Format: Adult contemp, local info. News staff one; news progmg 7 hrs wkly. Target aud: 18 plus; total community. ■ Dr. Richard H. Bolt, chmn; Andy Gambardella, pres & gen mgr; Dina Grills, opns dir & news dir; Joe Hevrin, gen sls mgr; Rick Edwards, progmg dir & chief engr. ■ Rates: $30; 19; 19; 10.

WVBI(FM)—Feb 1, 1994: 95.9 mhz; 6 kw. Ant 174 ft. TL: N41 10 21 W71 33 52. Hrs opn: 24. Box 1240, Block Island (02807). (203) 261-5555. Licensee: Bantam Broadcasting Co. Inc. Format: Classical. General. Spec prog: New age 4 hrs, folk 4 hrs, big band 4 hrs, relg 2 hrs wkly. ■ Tim English, pres & gen mgr. ■ Rates: $15; 15; 15; 15.

Bristol

*****WQRI(FM)**—April 1989: 88.3 mhz; 100 w. Ant 75 ft. TL: N41 38 49 W91 15 34. Old Ferry Road (02809). (401) 254-3283. FAX: (401) 254-3485. Licensee: Roger Williams College. Net: AP. Format: AOR. ■ Tony Ferrara, gen mgr; Gordon Kent, progmg dir; Rebecca Starr, asst mus dir.

Coventry

*****WCVY(FM)**—Oct 19, 1978: 91.5 mhz; 200 w. Ant 36 ft. TL: N41 41 10 W71 35 37. Stereo. 40 Reservoir Rd. (02816-9532). (401) 821-8540. Licensee: Coventry Public Schools. Format: Top-40. News staff 5; news progmg 5 hrs wkly. Target aud: 12-30. Spec prog: Sports 2 hrs wkly. ■ Ken Grady, stn mgr; Dan Fisher, progmg dir; Eric Lichtenberg, mus dir; Gisele Laliberty, news dir; Steve Jurczyk, chief engr.

East Greenwich

WARV(AM)—See Warwick.

East Providence

WHIM(AM)—April 15, 1947: 1110 khz; 5 kw-D, 250 w-N, DA-N. TL: N41 49 40 W71 22 09. 75 Oxford St., Providence (02905). (401) 781-9979. FAX: (401) 781-9329. Licensee: Bear Broadcasting Co. (group owner; acq 2-89; $700,000; FTR 2-20-89). Net: ABC, CNN. Rep: D & R Radio. Format: Country. ■ Philip Urso, pres & gen mgr; Dick Allen, gen sls mgr, progmg dir & mus dir; Mike Montecalro, news dir; Randy Place, chief engr.

Hope Valley

WJJF(AM)—Oct 7, 1985: 1180 khz; 1.8 kw-D. TL: N41 31 36 W71 44 35. Stereo. 26 Woody Hill Rd. (02832). (401) 539-1180. FAX: (401) 539-0645. Licensee: Astro Broadcasting System. Net: USA. Format: Country, loc news. ■ John J. Fuller, pres, gen mgr, gen sls mgr & chief engr. ■ Rates: $11; 11; 11; na.

Kingston

*****WRIU(FM)**—Feb 16, 1964: 90.3 mhz; 3.44 kw. Ant 415 ft. TL: N41 29 52 W71 31 42. Stereo. Hrs opn: 24. Rm. 362, Memorial Union Bldg. (02881). (401) 789-4949. FAX: (401) 792-4349. Licensee: University of R.I. Net: AP. Format: Div, jazz, progsv. Spec prog: Class 15 hrs, folk 15 hrs, gospel 5 hrs, heavy metal 6 hrs, blues 3 hrs, reggae 7 hrs, Black 17 hrs, Sp 3 hrs wkly. ■ Andrea Reynhout, gen mgr; Phil Dorian, sls dir; Mark Brosman, progmg dir; Andrew Reynhout, mus dir & chief engr; Ted Daniels, news dir.

Middletown

WOTB(FM)—Oct 6, 1978: 100.3 mhz; 3.35 kw. Ant 295 ft. TL: N41 33 55 W71 17 07 (CP: 6 kw, ant 302 ft.). Stereo. Box 367, Newport (02840). (401) 846-6900. FAX: (401) 846-1598. Licensee: Perry Communications of Rhode Island Inc. (acq 1-86; $100,000; FTR 1-6-86). Net: AP. Format: Jazz. ■ Bernard Perry, pres; William Lancaster, gen mgr & gen sls mgr; Bill Gray, progmg dir; John King, chief engr.

Narragansett Pier

WPJB(FM)—July 15, 1990: 102.7 mhz; 5 kw. Ant 148 ft. TL: N41 23 24 W71 29 02. Stereo. Hrs opn: 19. Box 5555, Wakefield (02880). (401) 789-9780; (401) 539-8502. Licensee: Full Power Radio of Narragansett Inc. Net: USA. Wash atty: Arthur V. Belendiuk. Format: Adult contemp. Target aud: 25-54. Spec prog: Class, big band. ■ John Fuller, pres & gen mgr; Steve Russell, progmg dir. ■ Rates: $13.50; 13.50; 13.50; 13.50.

Newport

WADK(AM)—Nov 6, 1948: 1540 khz; 1 kw-D. TL: N41 30 13 W71 18 43. Box 367 (02840). (401) 846-1540. FAX: (401) 846-1598. Licensee: Newport Broadcasting L.P. (acq 12-10-91). Net: ABC/E. Format: Talk, news. ■ Bernard Perry, pres & progmg dir; William Lancaster, gen mgr & gen sls mgr; John King, chief engr.

Pawtucket

WICE(AM)—Feb 12, 1950: 550 khz; 1 kw-D, 500 w-N, DA-N. TL: N41 54 15 W71 25 54 (CP: 5 kw-D, 3.4 kw-N, DA-2). Stereo. 100 John St., Cumberland (02864). (401) 725-9000. FAX: (401) 725-9002. Licensee: TransNet Stations Inc. (acq 5-90; $775,000; FTR 4-23-90). Net: Unistar, MBS, BBC, CBS, FNN. Rep: Republic. Format: Oldies, news, sports. News staff one; news progmg 40 hrs wkly. Target aud: 25-54. Spec prog: Pol one hr, relg 2 hrs wkly. ■ Carl Grande, pres; Chuck Stevens, gen sls mgr; Charles Avia, news dir; Norman Allabaugh, chief engr.

Portsmouth

***WJHD(FM)**—Apr 3, 1972: 90.7 mhz; 360 w. Ant 80 ft. TL: N41 36 06 W71 16 20. Portsmouth Abbey School, Cory's Ln. (02871). (401) 683-4756; (401) 683-1617. Licensee: The Order of St. Benedict. Format: Div. Spec prog: Opera (Sun night), rock. ■ Kate Carter, gen mgr; Father Jeffries, progmg dir & chief engr.

Providence

WALE(AM)—Apr 12, 1961: 990 khz; 50 kw-D, 500 w-N, DA-D. TL: N41 57 18 W71 35 39. 311 Westminster St. (02903). (401) 521-0990. FAX: (401) 521-5077. Licensee: North American Broadcasting Co. (acq 7-20-89; $1.05 million; FTR 5-8-89). Rep: McGavren Guild. Format: Talk. News staff 8; news progmg 65 hrs wkly. Target aud: 25 plus. Spec prog: Black, gospel, Italian 2 hrs, relg 4 hrs, Sp 2 hrs, Hispanic 2 hrs, Haitian one hr wkly. ■ Frank Battaglia, pres; Chris Trudeau, gen mgr & prom mgr; Frances Battaglia, gen sls mgr; Rob Michaels, progmg dir; Joan Douglas, news dir; Ken Torres, chief engr.

WBRU(FM)—Feb 21, 1966: 95.5 mhz; 20 kw. Ant 546 ft. TL: N41 49 40 W71 22 09 (CP: 50 kw, ant 492 ft., TL: N41 48 28 W71 28 12). Stereo. Hrs opn: 24. 88 Benevolent St. (02906). (401) 272-9550. FAX: (401) 272-9278. Licensee: Brown Broadcasting Service Inc. Net: AP, NBC the Source. Rep: Major Mkt. Wash atty: Arent, Fox, Fintner, Plotkin & Kahn. Format: Jazz, alternative rock, reggae. News progmg one hr wkly. Target aud: 18-34; highly educated professionals. Spec prog: Black 18 hrs. ■ Eric Schultz, pres; Jason Bordoff, vp & gen mgr; Randy Hershoff, sls dir; Mike Osborne, progmg dir; Laura Gardner, news dir; Craig Healy, chief engr.

WCTK(FM)—Listing follows WNBH(AM).

***WDOM(FM)**—Mar 15, 1966: 91.3 mhz; 125 w. Ant 130 ft. TL: N41 50 39 W71 26 14. Stereo. Hrs opn: 18. Providence College (02918). (401) 865-2460; (401) 865-2091. FAX: (401) 865-2057. Licensee: Providence College. Net: MBS. Format: Div, class, progsv. News progmg one hr wkly. Target aud: General; college students and professionals. Spec prog: Urban contemp 16 hrs, metal 6 hrs, country 2 hrs, classic rock 3 hrs, sports 2 hrs wkly. ■ Edward L. Wilson, gen mgr; Stacie Jontos, prom dir; Andrew DiGiovani, Lisa MacRae, mus dirs; Lisa Champagne, news dir; Ken Milligan, pub affrs dir; Craig Healy, chief engr.

***WELH(FM)**—Not on air, target date 1994: 88.1 mhz; 25 w-H, 150 w-V. Ant 98 ft. TL: N41 51 30 W71 19 04. 216 Hope St. (02906). (401) 421-8100. FAX: (401) 751-7674. Licensee: The Wheeler School. Wash atty: Bechtel & Cole. Format: Progressive. Target aud: 16-34. ■ Lauren Nocera, gen mgr; Kathy Kraig, opns mgr; Nick Hapmann, progmg dir; John Corrigan, chief engr.

WHJJ(AM)—Sept 6, 1922: 920 khz; 5 kw-U, DA-N. TL: N41 46 53 W71 19 55. Hrs opn: 24. 115 Eastern Ave., East Providence (02914). (401) 438-6110. FAX: (401) 438-3520. Licensee: Rhode Island Radio Inc. Group owner: The Griffin Group/Broadcast Division (acq 4-89; grpsl; FTR 3-6-89). Net: NBC, NBC Talknet. Rep: Katz. Wash atty: Arent, Fox, Kintner, Plotkin & Kahn. Format: News/talk. Target aud: 35-54. ■ James Corwin, gen mgr; Mark Gosziminski, rgnl sls mgr; Michele Maker, prom dir; John Carpilio, progmg dir & news dir; Mark Fisher, chief engr.

WHJY(FM)—Co-owned with WHJJ(AM). March 14, 1966: 94.1 mhz; 50 kw. Ant 546 ft. TL: N41 49 40 W71 22 09. Stereo. Prog sep from AM. Format: AOR. News staff one. Target aud: 18-34; adults. ■ Barbara Cash, gen sls mgr; Bill Weston, progmg dir.

WLKW(AM)—June 2, 1922: 790 khz; 5 kw-U, DA-N. TL: N41 50 03 W71 21 56. Stereo. 1502 Wampanoag Tr., East Providence (02915). (401) 831-7979. FAX: (401) 433-5967. Licensee: Telemedia Communications. Group owner: TMZ Broadcasting Co. (acq 2-89; grpsl; FTR 2-27-89). Rep: McGavren Guild. Format: Class. News staff 2; news progmg 15 hrs wkly. Target aud: 25-64; upper class, affluent, college educated. ■ Ira Rosenblatt, pres; Carol Carson, gen mgr; Bill George, opns mgr; Bob Carson, gen sls mgr; Kerri Fitzgerald, prom mgr; Norm Dagolinzer, progmg dir; Jeff Lalumiere, chief engr.

WWLI(FM)—Co-owned with WLKW(AM). July 11, 1948: 105.1 mhz; 50 kw. Ant 500 ft. TL: N41 48 22 W71 28 12. Stereo. Prog sep from AM. (401) 272-1105. Format: Adult contemp, classic rock, oldies. News staff 2; news progmg 17 hrs wkly. Target aud: 25-54; mid to upper income professionals-general appeal format.

WNBH(AM)—(New Bedford, Mass). May 21, 1921: 1340 khz; 1 kw-U. TL: N41 37 21 W70 55 07. Hrs opn: 24. Box 3201, 737 County St., New Bedford, MA (02740). (508) 996-3371. FAX: (508) 990-3453. Licensee: Hall Communications Inc. (group owner; acq 10-1-66). Net: ABC/E. Rep: D & R Radio. Wash atty: Arent, Fox, Kintner, Plotkin & Kahn. Format: Oldies. News staff one. Target aud: 25-54. ■ Robert M. Hall, chmn; Arthur J. Robotham, pres; Tom Devoe, stn mgr, natl sls mgr & rgnl sls mgr; Jack Peterson, progmg dir; Russ Baldwin, news dir; David Goldstein, chief engr.

WCTK(FM)—(New Bedford, Mass). Co-owned with WNBH(AM). Dec 9, 1946: 98.1 mhz; 47.3 kw. Ant 508 ft. TL: N41 37 21 W70 55 07. Stereo. Hrs opn: 24. Box 4980, East Providence, RI (02916); 2374 Post Rd., Warwick, RI (02886). (401) 732-5400. FAX: (401) 732-5404. Rep: D & R Radio. Format: Country. News progmg 3 hrs wkly. Target aud: 25-54. Spec prog: Pol 2 hrs wkly. ■ Bernadette Coelho, prom mgr; Mike Macoy, progmg dir; Don Nelson, mus dir; David Goldstein, chief engr.

WPRO(AM)—Oct 16, 1931: 630 khz; 5 kw-U, DA-N. TL: N41 46 28 W71 19 23. 1502 Wampanoag Trail, East Providence (02915). (401) 433-4200. FAX: (401) 433-5967. Licensee: Tele-Media Broadcasting Company of America (acq 3-19-93; $6 million with co-located FM; FTR 4-19-93). Net: ABC/I. Rep: Banner. Format: Adult contemp, news/talk. ■ Ira Rosenblatt, vp; Carol Carson, gen mgr; Mike Wheeler, gen sls mgr; Jim Candy, rgnl sls mgr; Rosemary Mulligan, prom mgr; Artie Tefft, progmg dir; Jeff Lalumiere, chief engr.

WPRO-FM—April 1949: 92.3 mhz; 39 kw. Ant 550 ft. TL: N41 48 18 W71 28 24 (CP: 45.4 kw, ant 489 ft.). Stereo. Prog sep from AM. Net: ABC/C. Format: CHR. ■ Donna Leach, rgnl sls mgr; David Simpson, progmg dir; Tony Mascaro, mus dir.

WRCP(AM)—1947: 1290 khz; 5 kw-U, DA-2. TL: N41 51 21 W71 26 41. Hrs opn: 24. 1110 Douglas Ave., North Providence (02904). (401) 273-7000. FAX: (401) 273-7008. Licensee: Neto Communications Inc. (acq 12-29-86; $1,353,350; FTR 11-10-86). Format: Portuguese, Sp. News staff one; news progmg 25 hrs wkly. Target aud: General; Portuguese speaking, all ages. ■ Manuel Fernando Neto, pres; Jose Da Paz, stn mgr, prom mgr, progmg dir & mus dir; Vasco Vargas, gen sls mgr; Francisco Borges, news dir; James Andrews, chief engr.

WRIB(AM)—June 16, 1946: 1220 khz; 1 kw-D, 166 w-N. TL: N41 49 15 W71 23 07. 200 Water St., East Providence (02914). (401) 434-0406. FAX: (401) 434-0409. Licensee: Carter Broadcasting Corp. (acq 12-24-86; $378,841; FTR 9-15-86). Format: Relg, Sp. Spec prog: It 5 hrs, Pol 2 hrs, Armenian one hr, Greek one hr wkly. ■ John Pierce, gen mgr; Craig Healy, chief engr.

WSNE(FM)—See Taunton, Mass.

WWBB(FM)—June 7, 1968: 101.5 mhz; 13.5 kw. Ant 951 ft. TL: N41 52 13 W71 17 47 (CP: 2.2 kw, ant 380 ft.). Stereo. Suite 202, 1445 Wampanoag Trail, East Providence (02915). (401) 433-1000. FAX: (401) 433-5512. Licensee: Radio Station Management Inc. (acq 1993; grpsl; FTR 9-20-93). Rep: Major Mkt. Format: Oldies. ■ Michael Schwartz, pres; Matt Chase, vp & gen mgr; Christopher Gardiner, prom mgr; John Morgan, progmg dir; Daria Bruno, pub affrs dir; Randy Place, chief engr.

WWLI(FM)—Listing follows WLKW(AM).

Smithfield

***WJMF(FM)**—Aug 1, 1974: 88.7 mhz; 225 w. Ant 130 ft. TL: N41 55 13 W71 32 26. Stereo. Hrs opn: 7 AM-2 AM. Box 6, Bryant College, 1150 Douglas Pike (02917). (401) 232-6044; (401) 232-6150. FAX: (401) 232-6413. Licensee: Bryant College of Business Administration. Format: Progsv, rock/AOR. News staff one; news progmg 12 hrs wkly. Target aud: 16-30; from teenagers to young executives. ■ Scott Terrien, gen mgr; Chris Hinckley, progmg dir; Ferdinand Torres, mus dir; Chris Urian, asst mus dir; Peter Gosselin, news dir; Bill Lange, pub affrs dir; Bryan Palmieri, chief engr.

Wakefield-Peacedale

WUAE(FM)—Not on air, target date unknown: 99.7 mhz; 3 kw. Ant 328 ft. TL: N41 25 31 W71 34 59. 494 Woonasquatucket Ave., North Providence (02911). Licensee: Amerzine Broadcasting L.P.

Warwick

WARV(AM)—Aug 12, 1959: 1590 khz; 5 kw-U, DA-2. TL: N41 43 40 W71 27 46. Hrs opn: 6 AM-midnight. 19 Luther Ave., (02886). (401) 737-0700. Licensee: Blount Communications (group owner; acq 7-7-78). Net: USA, Moody, CBN, IBN. Format: Relg. Spec prog: Black 2 hrs, Sp one hr, French 2 hrs wkly. ■ William A. Blount, pres, gen mgr & progmg dir; Deborah C. Blount, exec vp; David O. Young, vp; Jennifer Hayden, opns mgr; Gary Todd, gen sls mgr; Eleanor Hubbard, news dir; Lincoln Hubbard, chief engr. ■ Rates: $14; 14; 14; 14.

West Warwick

WKRI(AM)—Aug 12, 1956: 1450 khz; 1 kw-U. TL: N41 41 38 W71 31 26. Hrs opn: 18. 1585 Centreville Rd., Warwick (02886). (401) 821-6200; (401) 822-1450. FAX: (401) 821-9574. Licensee: DBH Broadcasting Inc. (acq 10-30-89; $350,000; FTR 7-3-89). Net: CNN. Format: Adult contemp, big bands 40s, 50s, 60s, Sp. News staff one. Target aud: 35 plus. Spec prog: Talk, Fr one hr, It 3 hrs, Polish 2 hrs wkly. ■ Roger E. Bouchard, pres; Lorraine E. Corey, gen mgr, gen sls mgr & adv dir; Christine Flyntz, opns mgr; John Parente, news dir; Joe Mattias, chief engr. ■ Rates: $22; 18; 20; 15.

Westerly

WERI(AM)—July 1949: 1230 khz; 1 kw-U. TL: N41 21 57 W71 50 11. Box 325 (02891); 19 Railroad Ave. (02891). (401) 596-7728. Licensee: Westerly Broadcasting Co. (acq 1967). Net: NBC, MBS. Rep: D & R Radio. Wash atty: Wiley, Rein & Fielding. Format: MOR, news/talk. News staff 3. Target aud: 35-64. ■ Natale Urso, pres; Philip Urso, gen mgr; Mike Kelley, stn mgr; Mark Urso, progmg dir & news dir; Randy Place, chief engr.

WWRX-FM—Co-owned with WERI(AM). Oct 17, 1967: 103.7 mhz; 37 kw. Ant 570 ft. TL: N41 34 22 W71 37 55. Stereo. Prog sep from AM. Net: ABC/R. Format: Classic rock. News staff one. Target aud: 25-49. ■ Rick Everett, progmg dir; Mike Montecalvo, news dir.

Wickford

WOTB(FM)—See Middletown.

Woonsocket

WNRI(AM)—Nov 28, 1954: 1380 khz; 2.5 kw-D. TL: N42 00 58N 71 29 30W. Stereo. 786 Diamond Hill Rd. (02895). (401) 769-6925; (401) 274-4270. FAX: (401) 769-0601. Licensee: American Independent Radio Inc. (group owner; acq 2-14-83; $265,000; FTR 3-7-83). Net: CNN. Format: Adult contemp. Target aud: 35 plus. Spec prog: Fr 4 hrs, Pol 2 hrs, Por 2 hrs wkly. ■ Roger E. Bouchard, pres & gen mgr; Donna Gallant, gen sls mgr; Bob Mandeville, prom mgr; Roger Bouchard, progmg dir & mus dir; Glee Violette, news dir & pub affrs dir; David A. St. Onge, chief engr. ■ Rates: $22; 18; 22; 18.

WOON(AM)—Nov 11, 1946: 1240 khz; 1 kw-U. TL: N41 59 35 W71 30 33 (CP: TL: N41 59 34 W71 30 20). One Social St. (02895). (401) 762-1240. Licensee: Woonsocket Broadcasters L.P. (acq 7-14-90; $600,000). Net: CBS. Format: Variety, news, sports, oldies. News progmg 17 hrs wkly. Target aud: General. Spec prog: Fr 3 hrs, Pol 6 hrs wkly. ■ Dave Richards, pres, gen mgr, gen sls mgr, adv mgr & chief engr; Lisa Wolf, progmg mgr & mus dir; Bill Cranford, news dir.

WWKX(FM)—July 1, 1949: 106.3 mhz; 1.5 kw. Ant 518 ft. TL: N41 59 43 W71 26 54 (CP: Ant 520 ft.). Stereo. 8 N. Main St., Attleboro, MA (02703). (508) 222-1320; (508) 222-1321. FAX: (508) 761-9239. Licensee: Ten

Mile Communications Inc. (acq 9-26-90; $2.4 million; FTR 10-8-90). Net: Unistar. Rep: Christal. Wash atty: Arent, Fox, Kintner, Plotkin & Kahn. Format: CHR. Target aud: 18-34. ■ Peter H. Ottmar, pres; Gene Lombardi, vp; Joseph Lembo, gen sls mgr; Scotty Snipes, progmg dir; Tom Naylor, mus dir; Grady Moates, chief engr.

South Carolina

LAUREN A. COLBY
301-663-1086
COMMUNICATIONS ATTORNEY
Special Attention to Difficult Cases

Abbeville

WZLA-FM—Jan 1, 1990: 92.9 mhz; 6 kw. Ant 243 ft. TL: N34 11 13 W82 19 28. Stereo. Hrs opn: 24. Box 548, 116 N. Main St. (29620). (803) 459-5785; (803) 223-9300. FAX: (803) 459-9391. Licensee: Shelley Reid. Net: SMN. Wash atty: Fletcher, Heald & Hildreth. Format: Oldies. Target aud: 25-65. Spec prog: Gospel 5 hrs wkly. ■ Shelley Reid, pres, gen mgr, prom mgr & progmg dir; Ray Lorrick, gen sls mgr; Jim Zippo, mus dir; Bob Beirman, chief engr. ■ Rates: $10; 10; 10; 7.

Aiken

WAJY(FM)—See New Ellenton.

WKXC-FM—August 1966: 99.5 mhz; 22.5 kw. Ant 728 ft. TL: N33 38 44 W21 55 40. Stereo. BTC 995, Suite 499, 802 E. Martintown Rd., North Augusta (29841). (803) 279-2099. FAX: (803) 279-3664. Licensee: GHB of Augusta Inc. Group owner: GHB Radio Group (acq 4-6-92; $3.8 million; FTR 4-27-92). Format: Country. ■ Coni E. Sanson, gen mgr; Coni E. Sansom, stn mgr; Mark Haddoen, gen sls mgr; Bob Rally, prom mgr, progmg dir & mus dir; Jill Kelly, Steve Smith, news dirs; Earl Welch, chief engr.

*****WLJK(FM)**—1990: 89.1 mhz; 10 kw. Ant 1,374 ft. TL: N33 24 18 W81 50 15. 1101 George Rogers Blvd., Columbia (29201). (803) 737-3420. FAX: (803) 737-3552. Licensee: South Carolina Educational TV Commission. Net: NPR, APR, AP. Wash atty: Dow, Lohnes & Albertson. Format: Fine arts. ■ Henry J. Cauthen, pres & gen mgr; Ronald L. Schoenherr, sr vp; Jesse Bowers, vp; Al Jackson, news dir; Charlton Bowers, vp engrg; Paul Zweimiller, engrg mgr.

WRXR-FM—Sept 17, 1966: 96.3 mhz; 15 kw. Ant 889 ft. TL: N33 41 10 W81 55 43 (CP: 25.2 kw, ant 699 ft.). 753 Broad St., Augusta (30901). (706) 722-9696. FAX: (706) 722-4300. Licensee: J & L Broadcasting Inc. (acq 3-30-92; $1.5 million; FTR 4-20-92). Format: Classic rock. ■ Jeff Wilks, gen mgr.

Allendale

WDOG(AM)—Jan 1, 1966: 1460 khz; 1 kw-D. TL: N33 01 22 W81 19 58. Hwy 125 N.W. (29810). (803) 584-3500. FAX: (803) 584-7714. Licensee: Good Radio Broadcasting Inc. Net: ABC/E; S.C. Net. Format: C&W. Black. ■ H. Carl Gooding, pres, gen mgr & gen sls mgr; Rick Gooding, prom mgr; Jim Lowe, progmg dir & mus dir; Lisa Gooding, news dir; Carl Gooding, chief engr.

WDOG-FM—Aug 29, 1983: 93.5 mhz; 3 kw. Ant 300 ft. TL: N33 01 22 W81 19 58. Stereo. Dups AM 100%.

Anderson

WAIM(AM)—April 1935: 1230 khz; 1 kw-U. TL: N34 31 52 W82 36 50. 2203 Old Williamston Road (29621). (803) 226-1511; (803) 225-1230. FAX: (803) 226-1513. Licensee: Palmetto Broadcasting Co. Inc. (acq 9-15-92; $80,000; FTR 10-19-92). Net: CNN. Format: News, talk. News progmg 10 hrs wkly. Target aud: 25-64. ■ Rick Driver, gen mgr, gen sls mgr, progmg dir & mus dir. ■ Rates: $12; 7; 10; 5.

WANS(AM)—June 1, 1949: 1280 khz; 5 kw-D, 1 kw-N, DA-N. TL: N34 32 17 W82 41 28. Watson Village Shopping Ctr. (29624). (803) 224-6733. FAX: (803) 224-6733. Licensee: FM 103 Inc. Net: SMN. Rep: Christal. Format: Hot adult contemp. News staff one. Target aud: 25-34 plus; active, affluent, young adult yuppies or the young at heart. ■ Matt Phillips, pres & gen mgr; Jeanette Phillips, vp.

WJMZ-FM—Aug 1, 1963: 107.3 mhz; 100 kw. Ant 1,008 ft. TL: N34 42 06 W82 36 20. Stereo. Drawer B-35, 84 Villa Rd., Greenville (29615). (803) 235-1073. FAX: (803) 297-8490. Licensee: AM-COM General Corp. Format: Urban contemp. ■ Sam Church, gen mgr; Paul Jackson, progmg mgr; Bob Herman, chief engr.

WROQ(FM)—1947: 101.1 mhz; 100 kw. Ant 994 ft. TL: N34 38 51 W82 16 13. Stereo. Suite 314, 555 N. Pleasantburg Dr., Greenville (29607). (803) 231-6237. Licensee: ABS Greenville Partners. Group Owner: ABS Communications Inc. (acq 10-20-89; grpsl; FTR 11-6-89). Net: ABC/R. Rep: D & R Radio. Format: Classic rock. Target aud: 18-49; baby-boomers. ■ Bob Bellin, gen mgr.

WTBI(AM)—See Pickens.

Andrews

WGTN-FM—Licensed to Andrews. See Georgetown.

Atlantic Beach

WMIW(AM)—Not on air, target date unknown: 1190 khz; 690 w-D. TL: N33 50 10 W78 51 08. 314 N. Park Circle, Kansas City, MO (64116). (816) 454-4419. Licensee: Michael B. Glinter.

Bamberg

WWBD(FM)—Licensed to Bamberg. See Bamberg-Denmark.

Bamberg-Denmark

WRIT(AM)—June 23, 1957: 790 khz; 1 kw-D, 100 w-N. TL: N33 18 50 W81 04 43. Box 244, Bamberg (29003). (803) 245-1138. Licensee: Gaston Broadcasting Inc. (acq 1-13-93; $55,000; FTR 2-8-93). Net: S.C. Net. Format: Adult contemp. Spec prog: Farm one hr wkly. ■ Eddie Gaston, gen mgr.

WWBD(FM)—(Bamberg). May 1967: 92.1 mhz; 3 kw. Ant 300 ft. TL: N33 18 50 W81 04 43 (CP: Ant 310 ft.). Stereo. Rt. 78, Bamberg (29003). (803) 245-2411. FAX: (803) 245-3737. Licensee: Branch Communications Inc. (acq 10-6-93; $200,000; FTR 10-25-93). Format: C&W. ■ Bob Clary, gen mgr.

Barnwell

WBAW(AM)—Oct 12, 1953: 740 khz; 1 kw-D. TL: N33 13 25 W81 21 25. Box 447, 1001 Jackson (29812). (803) 259-3507. FAX: (803) 259-2691. Licensee: Radio WBAW Inc. (acq 8-30-56). Net: MBS; S.C. Net. Rep: T N. Format: Adult contemp. ■ Drew Wilder, pres, gen mgr & progmg dir; B.J. Funderburk, opns mgr; Randy Russell, news dir; Fayne Anderson, chief engr. ■ Rates: $12.25; 12.25; 12.25; 12.25.

WBAW-FM—Aug 31, 1966: 99.1 mhz; 25 kw. Ant 328 ft. TL: N33 13 25 W81 21 35. Stereo. Format: Adult contemp, urban contemp. News staff one; news progmg 15 hrs wkly. Target aud: General.

Batesburg

WBLR(AM)—May 10, 1956: 1430 khz; 5 kw-D, 142 w-N. TL: N33 54 58 W81 31 42. Box 410 (29006). (803) 532-9500. Licensee: Durst Broadcasting Co. Inc. (acq 5-21-93; $40,000; FTR 6-14-93). Net: ABC/E; S.C. Net. Format: Pop country. News progmg 10 hrs wkly. Target aud: General. Spec prog: Black 2 hrs, relg 5 hrs, sports 10 hrs wkly. ■ Ken Durst, pres & chief engr; Marie Riser, gen mgr; Roy Anick, progmg dir. ■ Rates: $9; 8; 9; 8.

WKWQ(FM)—Aug 5, 1965: 93.1 mhz; 6 kw. Ant 400 ft. TL: N33 54 02 W81 24 25. Stereo. 1205 D Ave., West Columbia (29169). (803) 739-6905. FAX: (803) 739-6910. Licensee: Willis Broadcasting Corp. Format: Urban adult contemp. ■ L.E. Willis, pres; Brenda Olds, gen mgr; Johnny Green, progmg dir; John George, chief engr.

Beaufort

*****WAGP(FM)**—Oct 10, 1987: 88.7 mhz; 6 kw. Ant 297 ft. TL: N32 24 25 W80 47 39 (CP: 6 kw). Stereo. Hrs opn: 24. Box 119 (29901). (803) 525-1859. FAX: (803) 525-1859. Licensee: The Christian Broadcasting Corp. of Beaufort. Net: Moody. Format: Relg. News progmg 20 hrs wkly. Target aud: General; evangelical Christians. ■ Carl J. Broggi, pres; Charles Smith Jr., gen mgr.

WBEU(AM)—March 1954: 960 khz; 1 kw-D. TL: N32 26 18 W80 42 38. Box 21379, Hilton Head (29925); Rt. One, Box 156, Hwy 170/278, Ridgeland (29936). (803) 521-9870. FAX: (803) 521-9877. Licensee: Tri City Broadcasting Co. Inc. Group owner: DeDominicis Broadcasting (acq 8-89). Net: ABC/E. Rep: Eastman. Format: Div. News staff one; news progmg 3 hrs wkly. Target aud: 35-64. ■ Enzo DeDominicis, pres; Mark Robertson, gen mgr, progmg dir, mus dir & pub affrs dir; Kathy Allen, gen sls mgr; Robert Smith, prom dir; Marty Foglia, chief engr. ■ Rates: $10; 7; 8; 5.

WYKZ(FM)—Co-owned with WBEU(AM). Aug 8, 1962: 98.7 mhz; 100 kw. Ant 1,001 ft. TL: N32 19 50 W80 56 19. Stereo. Hrs opn: 24. Prog sep from AM. Wash atty: Arent, Fox, Kinter, Plotkin & Kahn. Format: Lite adult contemp. Target aud: 25-54; female. ■ Enzo DiDominicus, CEO; Mark Robertson, opns dir & vp progmg; Charlie Bryant, prom mgr. ■ Rates: $32; 28; 30; 25.

*****WJWJ-FM**—Aug 1, 1980: 89.9 mhz; 47 kw. Ant 1,100 ft. TL: N32 42 44 W80 40 49. Hrs opn: 6 AM-1 AM. Box 1165, 105 S. Ribaut Rd. (29901). (803) 524-0808. FAX: (803) 524-1016. Licensee: South Carolina Educational TV. Net: NPR. Format: Class, news/public affairs, div. News progmg 25 hrs wkly. Target aud: General. ■ Michael Brannon, gen mgr.

WOCW(FM)—See Parris Island.

WVGB(AM)—1959: 1490 khz; 1 kw-U. TL: N32 26 08 W80 41 54. Box 1477, 806 Monson St. (29902). (803) 524-4700; (803) 524-9742. Licensee: Vivian Broadcasting Inc. (acq 1-21-83; $61,000). Format: Adult contemp, relg, rhythm & blues. News progmg 3 hrs wkly. Target aud: 18-65; African American. Spec prog: Community progmg, sports. ■ Vivian M. Galloway, pres, gen mgr, vp opns & vp sls; Patricia Heyward, mus dir; Marti Foglia, chief engr.

WYKZ(FM)—Listing follows WBEU(AM).

Belton

*****WAFZ(FM)**—Not on air, target date unknown: 88.5 mhz; 50 kw. Ant 91 ft. 17 N., Toccoa Falls, GA (30598). Licensee: Toccoa Falls College.

WHPB(AM)—October 1956: 1390 khz; 1 kw-D. TL: N34 30 38 W82 28 40. Box 490, 9400 Belton-Homer Path Hwy. (29627). (803) 338-7786. FAX: (803) 338-9472. Licensee: CG & B Broadcasting Inc. (acq 4-2-93; $130,000; FTR 4-19-93). Format: Relg. News staff 2. Target aud: General. ■ Bonnie Fleming, pres, gen mgr & gen sls mgr; Bobbie Jean White, prom mgr & mus dir; Stan Woodward, chief engr. ■ Rates: $4.25; 4.25; 4.25; na.

Belvedere

*****WUOZ(FM)**—Not on air, target date unknown: 88.3 mhz; 4.5 kw. Ant 1,387 ft. TL: N33 24 29 W81 50 36. c/o WRAF-FM, Box780, Toccoa Falls College, Toccoa Falls, GA (30598). (706) 886-6831. Licensee: Toccoa Falls College. ■ Paul L. Alford, CEO, pres & gen mgr.

Bennettsville

WBSC(AM)—June 1947: 1550 khz; 10 kw-D, 5 kw-N, DA-N. TL: N34 40 52 W79 42 04. 226 Radio Rd. (29512). (803) 479-7121. Licensee: Big Bend Broadcasting Corp. (acq 9-23-62). Net: SMN. Rep: Dora-Clayton. Format: Pure Gold, oldies, gospel. Spec prog: Black 15 hrs wkly. ■ A.K. Harmon, vp & gen mgr; Richard Gehm, chief engr. ■ Rates: $8.90; 8.90; 8.90; 8.90.

Bishopville

WAGS(AM)—Feb 24, 1954: 1380 khz; 1 kw-D. TL: N34 12 35 W80 13 34. Hrs opn: 6 AM-6 PM. 142 Wags Dr. (29010). (803) 484-5415. Licensee: The A. L. Group (acq 3-9-92; $22,000; FTR 4-6-92). Net: USA. Rep: TN. Format: Country. News staff one; news progmg 7 hrs wkly. Target aud: 25-60. Spec prog: Live remotes- parades, civic events, festivals 2 hrs, relg 5 hrs, sports 6 hrs wkly. ■ Argent Landrum, pres; Arie Landrum, gen mgr, dev mgr & progmg mgr; Harold Bledsoe, chief opns; Grady Brown, vp sls; Robert E. Perkins, engrg dir. ■ Rates: $9; 9; 9; na.

WKHT(FM)—Not on air, target date unknown: 93.7 mhz; 3 kw. Ant 328 ft. TL: N34 16 26 W80 20 13. Box 305, Sumter (29151). (803) 775-0627; (803) 484-6207. FAX: (803) 484-5728. Licensee: JKRC Central Communications Ltd. ■ Mike Mullin, stn mgr; Curtis Carpenter, progmg dir & mus dir; Ernie Dee, news dir; John George, chief engr.

Blackville

WAAN(FM)—Not on air, target date unknown: 97.9 mhz; 6 kw. Ant 328 ft. 100 Wexford Place, Athens, GA (30606). Licensee: Dallas M. Tarkenton.

Bluffton

WLOW(FM)—June 22, 1988: 106.9 mhz; 50 kw. Ant 492 ft. TL: N32 13 17 W80 49 05 (CP: 100 kw, ant 849 ft.). Stereo. Hrs opn: 24. One St. Augustine Pl., Hilton Head Island (29928). (803) 785-9569. Licensee: DHA Broadcasting Inc. (acq 10-16-90; $100,000; FTR 11-5-90). Net: MBS. Rep: Katz & Powell. Format: Big band, jazz. News staff one; news progmg 5 hrs wkly. Target aud: 35 plus; general. ■ Lee Simmons, CEO, chmn, pres & chief engr; Fred Germann, gen mgr & gen sls mgr; Kevin Coan, chief opns & progmg dir; Harry Gilman, rgnl sls mgr; Dick Conrad, prom mgr & mus dir. ■ Rates: $45; 45; 45; 30.

Blythwood

WBAJ(AM)—Not on air, target date unknown: 880 khz; 1.6 kw-D, DA. TL: N34 05 42 W81 03 50. 314 N. Park Circle, Kansas City, MO (64116). (816) 454-4419. Licensee: Michael B. Glinter

Bowman

NEW FM—Not on air, target date unknown: 94.5 mhz; 3 kw. Ant 328 ft. Box 610, Goose Creek (29445). Licensee: Radio Bowman Inc.

Branchville

WGFG(FM)—Not on air, target date unknown: 105.1 mhz; 6 kw. Ant 100 ft. Box 1546, Orangeburg (29115). Licensee: Eagle of Orangeburg Inc.

Bucksport

WGTR(FM)—Not on air, target date unknown: 107.9 mhz; 36 kw. Ant 571 ft. 3428 Lakeshore Dr., Florence (29501). Licensee: Atlantic Broadcasting Co. Inc. (acq 1993; $50,000; FTR 9-13-93).

Burnettown

WVAA(AM)—Sept 28, 1968: 1510 khz; 1 kw-D, 250 w-CH. TL: N34 30 55 W81 50 58. Box 816, Langley (29834). (803) 593-2033. Licensee: Robert S. Cannella (acq 11-87). Format: Gospel, talk & sports. ■ David Hadarits, gen mgr.

Camden

WCAM(AM)—July 23, 1948: 1590 khz; 1 kw-D, 27 w-N. TL: N34 13 36 W80 40 45. Stereo. Hrs opn: 6 AM-11 PM. Box 753 (29020). (803) 438-9002; (800) 438-2454. Licensee: Kershaw Radio Corp. (acq 8-87; $75,000; FTR 5-5-86). Net: ABC/E; S.C. Net. Format: MOR. Target aud: 45 plus. ■ Gary M. Davidson, pres; Chris Johnson, gen mgr & gen sls mgr; Angie Goodman, prom mgr; Phil Rogers, progmg dir & mus dir; Dave McIntosh, news dir; Fayne Anderson, chief engr.

WPUB-FM—Co-owned with WCAM. December 1974: 94.3 mhz; 3.3 kw. Ant 299 ft. TL: N34 13 31 W80 40 44. Stereo. Format: Adult contemp. Target aud: 25-55.

Cayce

WHKZ(FM)—Licensed to Cayce. See Columbia.

WTGH(AM)—Aug 22, 1958: 620 khz; 1 kw-D, 125 w-N. TL: N33 57 45 W81 03 27. 1303 State St. (29033). (803) 796-9533. FAX: (803) 796-7706. Licensee: Midland Communications Co. Inc. Net: American Urban. Format: Relg. Target aud: General. ■ Isaac Heyward, pres; C.L. Lorick Jr., stn mgr; C.L. Lorick, gen sls mgr; Alvin Lorick, progmg dir; Sheila Stewart, news dir; John Scott, chief engr.

***WYFV(FM)**—Oct 10, 1990: 88.7 mhz; 150 w. Ant 141 ft. TL: N33 55 22 W81 04 42. Hrs opn: 24. 1801 Charleston Hwy., Suite B (29033). (803) 739-1294. Licensee: Bible Broadcasting Network (group owner; acq 6-26-90; FTR 7-23-90). Format: Bible preaching & teaching, conservative Christian mus, children's progs. ■ Thomas R. Williams, gen mgr.

Charleston

WAVF(FM)—See Hanahan.

WEZL(FM)—Oct 3, 1970: 103.5 mhz; 100 kw. Ant 659 ft. TL: N32 49 04 W79 50 08 (CP: Ant 987 ft.). Stereo. Box Z (29402). (803) 884-2534. FAX: (803) 884-1218. Licensee: Apollo Radio of Charleston. Group owner: Apollo Radio Ltd. (acq 3-29-90; $8.1 million; FTR 4-16-90). Net: MBS. Format: C&W. ■ Ron Raybourne, v gen mgr; Jeff Kautz, gen sls mgr; Cynthia Murray, prom mgr; T.J. Phillips, progmg mgr; Gary Griffin, mus dir; Dan Gregory, news dir.

***WFCH(FM)**—Not on air, target date unknown: 88.5 mhz; 29.6 kw. Ant 305 ft. TL: N32 49 04 W79 50 08. Box 1505, Mount Pleasant (29465). 1209-B Venning Rd., Mount Pleasant (29464). (803) 881-9450. Licensee: Family Stations Inc. (group owner). Format: Relg. ■ Dick Elton, opns mgr.

WKYB(AM)—(Hemingway). Apr 28, 1967: 1000 khz; 10 kw-D, 5 kw-CH. TL: N33 41 55 W79 27 32. c/o Legare, Hare & Smith, Box 578, Charleston (29402). (803) 722-7773. Licensee: Robert D. Fogel.

WOKE(AM)—1946: 1340 khz; 1 kw-U. TL: N32 49 07 W79 57 43. Box 30547, 1715 Sam Rittenberg Blvd. (29417). (803) 763-1340. Licensee: Weaver Broadcasting Corp. (acq 7-20-55). Net: CNN. Format: Btfl mus, oldies, news/talk. News progmg 10 hrs wkly. Target aud: High school to senior citizens. Spec prog: Sports 20 hrs, relg 9 hrs, class 4 hrs, gospel 2 hrs wkly. ■ Harry C. Weaver, pres, gen mgr & gen sls mgr; Ruth H. Weaver, exec vp; Wally Momeier, opns mgr & chief engr; Buck Clayton, progmg dir. ■ Rates: $11.50; 10; 10; 10.

WPAL(AM)—1947: 730 khz; 1 kw-D, 100 w-N. TL: N32 46 22 W80 00 58. Hrs opn: 24. Box 30999, 1717 Wappoo Rd. (29417). (803) 763-6330. FAX: (803) 769-4857. Licensee: WPAL Inc. (acq 1-1-80). Net: Roslin. Format: Black, gospel. Target aud: Black community. Spec prog: Jazz 9 hrs wkly. ■ William Saunders, pres & gen mgr; Juanita W. LaRoche, gen sls mgr; Tanya Smith, prom mgr; Don Kendricks, Jay Jackson, progmg dirs; Don Kendricks, Jay Jackson, mus dirs; Donzella Hendrix, news dir; Willie Bennett, chief engr. ■ Rates: $41.18; 35.30; 41.18; 31.77.

***WSCI(FM)**—1973: 89.3 mhz; 97 kw. Ant 540 ft. TL: N32 47 49 W79 50 27. Stereo. Box 801, Mount Pleasant (29464). (803) 881-1160. Licensee: S.C. Educational TV Commission. Net: NPR. Format: Fine arts. Spec prog: Black 3 hrs, jazz 15 hrs wkly. ■ Henry J. Cauthen, pres; William D. Hay, vp; Marcie Byars-Warnock, stn mgr; Taylor Lewis, progmg dir; Charlton Bowers, chief engr.

WSSX-FM—1945: 95.1 mhz; 100 kw. Ant 361 ft. TL: N32 49 20 W79 58 45 (CP: Ant 1,000 ft.). Stereo. One Orange Grove Rd., Mt. Pleasant (29407). (803) 556-5660. Licensee: Dixie Communications (acq 9-3-93; $400,000; FTR 9-27-93). Net: ABC/R, Westwood One. Rep: Katz. Format: Adult contemp, Top-40. News staff one. Target aud: 18-34. ■ Joel Farman, pres; Steve Judy, gen mgr; Bruce Roberts, chief engr.

WSUY(FM)—Listing follows WTMA(AM).

WTMA(AM)—1939: 1250 khz; 5 kw-D, 1 kw-N, DA-N. TL: N32 49 20 W79 58 45. Box 30909 (29417). (803) 556-1250. FAX: (803) 763-0304. Licensee: Jett Communications Inc. (acq 6-12-89; $575,000; FTR 6-12-89). Net: ABC TalkRadio, NBC, NBC Talknet, ARN. Rep: Katz. Format: News/talk. News staff one. Target aud: 25-54. ■ Hugh Jett, vp, gen mgr & gen sls mgr; Scott Cason, prom mgr; Dan Moon, progmg dir; Mike Robertson, news dir; Bruce Roberts, chief engr.

WSUY(FM)—Co-owned with WTMA(AM). Apr 4, 1990: 100.7 mhz; 2 kw. Ant 400 ft. TL: N32 49 20 W79 58 45 (CP: 100.5 mhz, 25 kw, ant 328 ft.). Stereo. Hrs opn: 24. (803) 556-5660. Licensee: Southern Communications Inc. (acq 7-3-90; $502,858; FTR 7-23-90). Rep: Katz. Format: Adult contemp. ■ Hugh Jett, pres & gen mgr; Steve Judy, vp & gen sls mgr; David Sousa, progmg dir & mus dir; Tom Kennedy, news dir; Bruce Roberts, chief engr.

WUJM(AM)—(Goose Creek). 1948: 1450 khz; 1 kw-U. TL: N32 48 15 W79 57 43. 108 Stephanie Dr., Goose Creek (29445). (803) 824-8943. Licensee: Jones Eastern Charleston Inc. Group owner: Jones-Eastern Radio Inc. (acq 6-19-87). Net: Moody. Format: Christal. Format: Nostalgia. News staff 2. Target aud: 18-49. ■ C.J. Jones, pres & gen mgr; Arnold Baynard, gen sls mgr; Bob Casey, progmg dir; Paul Jackson, mus dir; Jim Gooden, news dir; Don Powers, chief engr.

WXLY(FM)—See North Charleston.

WXTC(AM)—May 14, 1930: 1390 khz; 5 kw-U, DA-N. TL: N32 49 26 W80 00 06. Stereo. Hrs opn: 24. 478 E. Bay St. (29403). (803) 722-7611. FAX: (803) 577-7726. Licensee: EBE Communications L.P. (acq 10-87). Rep: McGavren Guild. Wash atty: Haley, Bader & Potts. Format: Adult contemp. News staff one. Target aud: 25-54. ■ Ken Patch, pres & gen mgr; Karen Hagan, gen sls mgr; Beth McClellan, rgnl sls mgr; John Quincy, progmg dir; Gary Robinson, chief engr.

WXTC-FM—Apr 1, 1948: 96.9 mhz; 100 kw. Ant 1,750 ft. TL: N32 55 28 W79 41 58. Stereo. Dups AM 100%.

WYBB(FM)—See Folly Beach.

WZJY(AM)—See Mt. Pleasant.

Cheraw

WCRE(AM)—July 1953: 1420 khz; 1 kw-D, 97 w-N. TL: N34 41 12 W79 53 42. Hrs opn: 6 AM-8 PM. Box 631 (29520). (803) 537-7887. Licensee: De Hope Communications Inc. (acq 1-1-88). Net: ABC/E, MBS; S.C. Net. Format: Adult contemp. Target aud: 25 plus. Spec prog: Black 5 hrs, farm 2 hrs wkly. ■ Albert W. De Hope III, pres & gen mgr; Kay Walters, prom dir; Rob Eastwood, progmg dir; Dave Raley, chief engr. ■ Rates: $12; 12; 12; 12.

WJMX-FM—July 17, 1979: 103.3 mhz; 44 kw. Ant 525 ft. TL: N34 30 19 W79 54 15 (CP: 50 kw, ant 492 ft.). Stereo. Box 103000, 181 E. Evans St., Florence (29501). (803) 667-9569. Licensee: Atlantic Broadcasting Co. (acq 1-1-85). Net: AP. Rep: McGavren Guild. Format: CHR with classic hits. News staff one; news progmg one hr wkly. Target aud: 18-34. ■ Fred Avent, pres; Harold Miller, vp & gen mgr; Theresa Miller, gen sls mgr & prom mgr; Tom Brockway, progmg dir; Jay Lewis, mus dir; Alan Hovermale, chief engr.

Chester

WBZK-FM—Aug 30, 1969: 99.3 mhz; 7.6 kw. Ant 603 ft. TL: N34 47 29 W81 16 01. Stereo. Hrs opn: 5 AM-midnight. Rebroadcasts WBZK (AM) York 92%. Box 398, 625 Hwy. 321 Bypass, York (29745). (803) 684-4241; (803) 581-9930. FAX: (803) 684-4242. Licensee: Chester County Broadcasting Corp. Net: NBC the Source. Format: Adult contemp, oldies. News progmg 6 hrs wkly. Target aud: 22-50. Spec prog: Gospel 6 hrs wkly. ■ C. Curtis Sigmon, pres & gen mgr; Jeff Sigmon, opns mgr, progmg dir & mus dir; J.B. Ferrell, news dir; Curtis Sigmon, chief engr. ■ Rates: $26; 24; 26; 20.

Chesterfield

WVSZ(FM)—Not on air, target date unknown: 107.3 mhz; 3 kw. Ant 328 ft. Box 125 (29709). Licensee: D, D & D Broadcasters of Chesterfield.

Clearwater

WSLT(FM)—April 1987: 98.3 mhz; 2.8 kw. Ant 484 ft. TL: N33 28 07 W81 52 26. Stereo. Hrs opn: 24. Suite 499, 802 E. Martintown Rd., BTC 995, North Augusta (29841). (803) 279-2099. FAX: (803) 279-3664. Licensee: GHB of Clearwater Inc. (acq 1-29-93; $750,000; FTR 2-22-93). Net: AP. Format: Btfl mus. ■ Conie Sansom, pres; Mark Haddon, gen sls mgr; Chuck Whittaker, progmg dir; Bob Raleigh, mus dir; Earl Welch, chief engr.

Clemson

WCCP(AM)—July 27, 1969: 1560 khz; 1 kw-D, 500 w-CH. TL: N34 42 04 W82 49 30. Hrs opn: 6 AM-8 PM. Box 1560, 202 Lawrence Rd. (29633). (803) 654-1560; (803) 654-5400. FAX: (803) 654-9328. Licensee: Golden Corners Broadcasting Inc. (acq 9-28-89; $100,000; FTR 10-16-89). Net: Sun. Format: News, talk, sports. News staff one; news progmg 35 hrs wkly. Target aud: 35-58; older yuppies. ■ George W. Clement, pres & gen mgr; Faye Clement, vp & stn mgr; Tommy Powell, progmg dir & news dir.

***WSBF-FM**—Mar 16, 1961: 88.1 mhz; 3 kw. Ant 200 ft. TL: N34 40 42 W82 49 15. Stereo. Box 2156, Clemson Univ., Rm. 800, University Union (29632). (803) 656-4010. FAX: (803) 656-4011. Licensee: Clemson Univ. Net: Westwood One. Format: Alternative. News staff 5. Target aud: 16-25. ■ Rebecca Townsend, gen mgr & progmg dir; Shari Altman, Johannah Johnson, prom dirs; David Attaway, Julie Gelin, mus dirs; Kristie Gantt, news dir; Mike Kloss, chief engr.

Clinton

WPCC(AM)—Sept 11, 1957: 1410 khz; 1 kw-D, 100 w-N. TL: N34 26 42 W81 53 24. Box 1455, Greenwood Hwy. (29325). (803) 833-1410; (803) 833-1423. FAX: (803) 833-2467. Licensee: Laurens County Communications Inc. (acq 12-83; $90,000; FTR 12-5-83). Rep: Keystone (unwired net). Format: Popular country, news & sports. News staff one; news progmg 10 hrs wkly. Target aud: General. ■ A. Cruickshanks, pres; Diana Evatt, gen mgr & gen sls mgr; Jim Blackwell, progmg dir & news dir; Jim Warren, chief engr. ■ Rates: $10.50; 10.50; 10.50; 10.50.

Columbia

WARQ(FM)—Listing follows WVOC(AM).

WCOS(AM)—1939: 1400 khz; 1 kw-U. TL: N34 00 18 W81 00 43. Box 748 (29202); 2440 Millwood Ave. (29205). (803) 256-7348. FAX: (803) 779-7572. Licensee: Benchmark Radio Acquisition Fund V L.P. Group owner: Benchmark Communications Radio (acq 1993; $10 million with co-located FM; FTR 9-13-93). Net: ABC/I. Rep: McGavren Guild. Format: Classic country. ■ Jimmy Collins, gen mgr.

WCOS-FM—March 1951: 97.5 mhz; 100 kw. Ant 981 ft. TL: N34 08 23 W81 03 22. Stereo. Prog sep from AM. Format: Modern country.

WCTG(AM)—Jan 1, 1994: 840 khz; 50 kw-D, DA. TL: N34 12 42 W80 50 05. Stereo. Box 23840 (29223). (803) 799-8484. Licensee: Radio 840 Inc. Format: Christian country. News staff 2; news progmg 3 hrs wkly. Target aud: General. ■ Steven Brisker, pres & gen mgr; Rosemary Brisker, mus dir; Chaka Brisker, news dir; Peter V. Gurelkis, chief engr.

WHKZ(FM)—(Cayce). July 11, 1974: 96.7 mhz; 3.3 kw. Ant 443 ft. TL: N34 00 04 W81 02 05. Stereo. 2334 Airport Blvd., West Columbia (29170). (803) 796-8896. FAX: (803) 796-8189. Licensee: Benchmark Radio Acquisition Fund V L.P. Group owner: Benchmark Communications Radio (acq 1993; $2.7 million; FTR 9-6-93). Format: Country. News staff one; news progmg 3 hrs wkly. Target aud: 25-44; professionals and young adults. Spec prog: Jazz 2 hrs wkly. ■ Jimmy Collins, gen mgr.

***WLTR(FM)**—July 1, 1976: 91.3 mhz; 96 kw. Ant 761 ft. TL: N34 07 07 W80 56 12. Stereo. 1101 George Rogers Blvd. (29201). (803) 737-3420. FAX: (803) 737-3552. Licensee: South Carolina Educ. TV Commission. Net: NPR, APR, AP. Wash atty: Dow, Lohnes & Albertson. Format: Fine arts. News staff 5. ■ Henry J. Cauthen, pres & gen mgr; Ronald L. Schoenherr, sr vp; Jesse Bowers, vp; Al Jackson, news dir; Charlton Bowers, vp engrg; Paul Zweimiller, engrg mgr.

WMFX(FM)—(St. Andrews). Jan 23, 1985: 102.3 mhz; 3 kw. Ant 322 ft. TL: N34 05 55 W81 04 48. Stereo. Box 210271, Columbia (29221); Suite 207, 1345 Garner Ln., Columbia (29210). (803) 772-4980. FAX: (803) 798-6801. Licensee: BTMI Inc., receiver (acq 5-14-92). Rep: D & R Radio. Format: Classic rock. News progmg one hr wkly. Target aud: 18-49. ■ Dennis Murphy, pres & gen mgr; Benji Norton, progmg dir; Dan Wuori, mus dir; Andrea James, news dir; Burt Smith, chief engr.

***WMHK(FM)**—Aug 30, 1976: 89.7 mhz; 100 kw. Ant 420 ft. TL: N34 04 33 W81 04 16 (CP: Ant 1,397 ft.). Stereo. Box 3122 (29230). (803) 754-5400. Licensee: Columbia Bible College Broadcasting Co. Net: UPI, Skylight, Moody. Format: Relg. News staff 2; news progmg 8 hrs wkly. Target aud: 25-49. ■ David Morrison, gen mgr; Cindy Elmore, prom dir; Linda White, progmg dir; Carolyn Walter, news dir; Rashie Kennedy Jr., chief engr.

WNOK-FM—Listing follows WOIC(AM).

WOIC(AM)—Jan 1, 1947: 1230 khz; 1 kw-U, DA-N. TL: N33 59 25 W81 02 41. Box 50568, 1717 Gervais St. (29201). (803) 771-0105. FAX: (803) 799-4367. Licensee: Voyager Communications V Inc. Group owner: Voyager Communications (acq 10-25-91; with co-located FM). Rep: Katz. Format: Black, gospel. News staff one; news progmg 10 hrs wkly. Target aud: General. Spec prog: Jazz 6 hrs wkly. ■ Margaret Fort, gen mgr; Don Hambrick, stn mgr & progmg dir; Gwen Foushee, news dir; Tony Gervaisi, chief engr.

WNOK-FM—Co-owned with WOIC(AM). July 15, 1959: 104.7 mhz; 100 kw. Ant 1,014 ft. TL: N34 09 06 W80 54 36. Stereo. Prog sep from AM. Net: ABC/R. Format: CHR. ■ Gray Frakes, prom mgr; Johnathon Rush, progmg dir; T.J. McKay, mus dir; Kathy Scott, news dir.

WOMG(AM)—June 30, 1954: 1320 khz; 5 kw-D, 2.5 kw-N, DA-N. TL: N34 00 16 W81 04 15. Box 565 (29202); 910 Comanchee Trail, West Columbia (29169). (803) 796-9975. FAX: (803) 796-5502. Licensee: Price Columbia Co. Ltd. Group owner: Price Broadcasting Co. (acq 5-88). Rep: Torbet. Wash atty: Fletcher, Heald & Hildreth. Format: Oldies. News staff one; news progmg 3 hrs wkly. Target aud: 25-54. Spec prog: Sports. ■ Mike Steinhilper, gen mgr; Karl Hess, gen sls mgr; Hunter Herring, progmg dir & mus dir; Michael Hart, news dir; John George, engrg mgr; Willie Bennett, chief engr. ■ Rates: $50; 35; 40; 20.

WOMG-FM—Apr 15, 1989: 103.1 mhz; 3 kw. Ant 300 ft. TL: N34 03 05 W81 00 07. Stereo. ■ Rates: Same as AM.

WQXL(AM)—June 15, 1945: 1470 khz; 5 kw-D, 138 w-N. TL: N34 01 44 W81 02 23. Box 3277 (29230-3277). (803) 779-7911; (803) 742-1470. FAX: (803) 779-7911. Licensee: Covenant Communications Inc. (acq 7-3-89). Net: USA, CBN. Format: Adult contemp Christian. Target aud: 25-49; Black females. ■ John Lastinger, pres; Bill Deas, opns mgr, vp progmg & mus dir; Fayne Anderson, chief engr. ■ Rates: $16; 14; 16; 14.

WSCQ(FM)—(West Columbia). Aug 5, 1975: 100.1 mhz; 5.9 kw. Ant 331 ft. TL: N34 04 08 W81 04 16. Stereo. 1440 Knox Abbott Dr., West Columbia (29169). (803) 796-9060. FAX: (803) 791-9100. Licensee: WSCQ Inc. (acq 9-1-89; $4.2 million; FTR 9-25-89). Net: CBS Spectrum. Rep: Republic. Format: Lite Rock. ■ Dennis Waldrop, gen mgr & gen sls mgr; Dennis Adams, progmg dir; Theresa Riley, news dir; Fayne Anderson, chief engr.

WTCB(FM)—See Orangeburg.

***WUSC-FM**—Jan 17, 1977: 90.5 mhz; 2.5 kw. Ant 233 ft. TL: N34 00 02 W81 01 19 (CP: Ant 253 ft.). Stereo. Hrs opn: 24. Drawer B, Univ. of South Carolina (29208). (803) 777-5124. FAX: (803) 777-6482. Licensee: University of South Carolina. Format: Alternative. Spec prog: Jazz 3 hrs, Black 6 hrs, blues 3 hrs, folk 3 hrs, reggae 3 hrs, class 3 hrs wkly. ■ Jennifer Dougherty, stn mgr; Kathy Rimmer, prom mgr; Brian Mouzan, progmg dir; Andy Uhrich, mus dir; Brian Poust, asst mus dir; Michael Wright, pub affrs dir; Cecily McKinney, chief engr.

WVOC(AM)—July 10, 1930: 560 khz; 5 kw-U, DA-N. TL: N34 02 00 W81 08 32. Stereo. Hrs opn: 24. Box 21567 (29221); 56 Radio Ln. (29210). (803) 772-5600. FAX: (803) 798-5255. Licensee: Clayton Radio Inc. (acq 12-5-90; $2.55 million with co-located FM; FTR 12-31-90). Net: CBS, NBC Talknet, CNN; S.C. Net. Rep: Banner. Format: News, talk. News staff 7; news progmg 40 hrs wkly. Target aud: 25-54. ■ Rick Dames, pres & gen mgr; Jennifer McDonald, gen sls mgr; David Adare, progmg dir; Dianne Chase, news dir; John George, engrg mgr.

WARQ(FM)—Co-owned with WVOC(AM). Feb 6, 1971: 93.5 mhz; 3 kw. Ant 443 ft. TL: N34 02 00 W80 58 56. Stereo. Hrs opn: 24. Prog sep from AM. Format: Adult contemp. News staff one; news progmg 5 hrs wkly. Target aud: 25-54. ■ Jodie Gaimari, gen sls mgr; Chuck McKay, progmg dir; Lyn Scott, mus dir.

Conway

***WHMC-FM**—Sept 15, 1985: 90.1 mhz; 30 kw. Ant 706 ft. TL: N33 57 05 W79 06 31. 1103 George Rogers Blvd., Columbia (29201); Mount Holyoke College, 3 Carr Lab, Columbia (01075). (803) 737-3200. Licensee: South Carolina Educational Television Commission. Net: NPR. Format: Fine arts. ■ Henry J. Cauthen, pres; Jesse Bowers, vp.

WJXY(AM)—Feb 23, 1977: 1050 khz; 5 kw-D, 473 w-N, DA-2. TL: N33 50 56 W79 05 03. Stereo. Hrs opn: 24. Box 1207, 1750 Radio Ln. (29526). (803) 397-4212. FAX: (803) 397-3668. Licensee: Downs Satellite Broadcasting of South Carolina Inc. (acq 2-16-93; $400,000 with co-located FM; FTR 3-8-93). Net: S.C. Net. Format: Southern gospel. News staff one. ■ Bob Chrysler, CEO, vp & gen mgr; Paul H. Downs, pres; Danny Graham, opns mgr & prom mgr; Jim Turner, gen sls mgr; Sandra Diaz, natl sls mgr; Julianna Brown, adv dir; Bo Graham, progmg dir; Mike Green, news dir; Robert Smith, chief engr. ■ Rates: $8; 6; 7; 5.

WJXY-FM—Oct 1990: 93.9 mhz; 6 kw. Ant 328 ft. TL: N33 51 15 W79 01 16. Stereo. Hrs opn: 24. Prog sep from AM. (803) 397-1939. Format: Country. News progmg 2 hrs wkly. Target aud: 25-64. ■ Bob Chrysler, exec vp; Steve Stewart, progmg dir; David Joyner, mus dir; Mike Green, pub affrs dir. ■ Rates: $35; 27; 32; 18.

WPJS(AM)—August 1945: 1330 khz; 5 kw-D, 500 w-N, DA-N. TL: N33 50 57 W79 04 11. Box 961 (29526). (803) 248-9040. FAX: (803) 248-6365. Licensee: Beasley Communications of South Carolina Inc. Group owner: Beasley Broadcast Group (acq 1985; $1,850,000; FTR 4-2-84). Net: MBS. Rep: T N. Format: Black. Target aud: 12 plus. Spec prog: Sports, oldies, relg. ■ T. J. Parrish, gen mgr; Claudine Schofield, prom mgr; Cheryl Hall, news dir; Buddy Womack, chief engr.

WYAV(FM)—July 1964: 104.1 mhz; 100 kw. Ant 600 ft. TL: N33 35 27 W79 02 53 (CP: 12.2 kw, ant 981 ft.). Stereo. 1571 Trade St., Myrtle Beach (29577). (803) 448-1041. FAX: (803) 626-5988. Licensee: Ballston Trust Services L.C. Group owner: Pinnacle Broadcasting Co. (acq 12-22-92; grpsl; FTR 1-18-93). Format: Adult CHR. News staff one; news progmg one hr wkly. Target aud: 18-49. ■ Philip Marella, pres; Edward Ferreri, CFO; Roy Sova, gen mgr & vp sls; George Rossi, stn mgr; Scott Harris, vp progmg; Tank Sherman, progmg dir; Booker Madison, mus dir; Bob Smith, chief engr.

Darlington

WDAR(AM)—1955: 1350 khz; 1 kw-D. TL: N34 18 58 W79 53 17. Florence 122 Asbury Ave. (29532). (803) 393-8999. FAX: (803) 395-0013. Licensee: MEG Associates Ltd. (acq 6-16-93; with co-located FM; FTR 7-12-93). Net: ABC/D. Format: Classic rock. News staff one; news progmg 4 hrs wkly. Target aud: 25 plus. ■ Harley Lampman, gen mgr; Neal Hunter, opns dir; Woody Lynch, sls dir; Cathie Gilberth, pub affrs dir; Gale Gilberth, engrg dir & chief engr. ■ Rates: $24; 20; 22; 18.

WDAR-FM—December 1965: 105.5 mhz; 4 kw. Ant 400 ft. TL: N34 18 58 W79 53 17 (CP: 1.8 kw). Stereo. Dups AM 100%.

Dillon

WDSC(AM)—May 22, 1946: 800 khz; 1 kw-D, 382 w-N. TL: N34 22 11 W79 24 08. Hrs opn: 24. Box 231 (29536). (803) 774-9000. FAX: (803) 774-6721. Licensee: Metropolitan South Broadcasting Assoc. L.P. (acq 1993; $800,000 with co-located FM; FTR 9-13-93). Format: All sports. Target aud: General. ■ Mark L. Cooper, gen mgr & gen sls mgr. ■ Rates: $12; 12; 12; 10.

WZNS(FM)—Co-owned with WDSC(AM). Feb 16, 1954: 92.9 mhz; 100 kw. Ant 1,801 ft. TL: N34 21 53 W79 19 49. Stereo. Hrs opn: 24. Prog sep from AM. Net: NBC. Format: Classic rock. Spec prog: Jazz one hr wkly. ■ Rates: $40; 40; 40; 40.

Dorchester Terrace-Brentwood

WTMZ(AM)—Licensed to Dorchester Terrace-Brentwood. See North Charleston.

Due West

***WECE(FM)**—Not on air, target date unknown: 88.5 mhz; 20 kw. Ant 518 ft. Box 205, Erskine College (29639). (803) 379-2131. Licensee: Erskine College.

Easley

WLWZ(AM)—March 1951: 1360 khz; 1 kw-D. TL: N34 50 20 W82 38 24. Suite 625, 15 South St., Greenville (29601). (803) 235-4600. FAX: (803) 370-3403. Licensee: Voyager Communications V Inc. Group owner: Voyager Communications (acq 10-25-91; with co-located FM). Net: AP, SBN. Rep: D & R Radio. Wash atty: Harrington, Smith & Hargrove. Format: Urban Contemp. News staff one. ■ Carl Venters, chmn; Jack McCarthy, pres; George King, CFO; Curtis E. Downey, vp & gen mgr; Roger Moore, progmg dir; Rocky Valentine, mus dir; Ted McCall, chief engr.

WLWZ-FM—1964: 103.9 mhz; 3 kw. Ant 328 ft. TL: N34 50 21 W82 31 37. Stereo. Dups AM 100%.

Elloree

WORG(FM)—Licensed to Elloree. See Elloree-Santee.

Elloree-Santee

WMNY(AM)—1961: 1370 khz; 5 kw-D, 177 w-N, DA-2. TL: N33 30 07 W80 32 14. Stereo. Hrs opn: 6 AM-10 PM. Box 189, Rt. 1, Santee (29142-9718). (803) 854-2671. Licensee: Clarence E. Jones. Net: USA. Format: Tourist info radio. News progmg 112 hrs wkly. Target aud: 45-80; tourists & newcommer residents. ■ Clarence E. Jones, gen mgr & chief engr.

WORG(FM)—(Elloree). Co-owned with WMNY(AM). May 1988: 100.3 mhz; 25 kw. Ant 328 ft. TL: N33 21 42 W80 41 05. Stereo. Hrs opn: 16. Format: News/talk.

Florence

WDSC(AM)—See Dillon.

WFLU(AM)—Not on air, target date unknown: 1120 khz; 1 kw-D, DA. TL: N34 14 43 W79 44 15. 314 N. Park Circle, Kansas City, MO (64116). (816) 454-4419. Licensee: Michael Glinter.

WJMX(AM)—July 13, 1947: 970 khz; 5 kw-D, 3 kw-N, DA-N. TL: N34 13 47 W79 48 07. Stereo. Hrs opn: 24. Box 103000, Florence Bus & Tech Center, 181 E. Evans St. (29501-3000). (803) 667-9569; (803) 665-0970. FAX: (803) 664-2869. Licensee: Atlantic Broadcasting Co. Inc. (acq 1-1-85; $725,000; FTR 11-19-84). Net: AP, NBC Talknet, EFN, Daynet, ARN; S.C. Net. Rep: McGavren Guild. Format: News/talk. News staff one. Target aud: 25-54. Spec prog: Big band 3 hrs. ■ Fred C. Avent, pres; Harold Miller, vp & gen mgr; Dave Allan Graham, opns mgr; Theresa Miller, gen sls mgr & prom mgr; Tom Brockway, progmg dir; Bob Smith, chief engr.

***WLPG(FM)**—Not on air, target date unknown: 91.7 mhz; 10-kw-H, 9.2 kw-V. Ant 492 ft. 3213 Huxley Dr., Augusta (30909). Licensee: South Carolina Radio Fellowship.

WOLS(AM)—Nov 18, 1937: 1230 khz; 1 kw-U. TL: N34 13 48 W79 44 49. 151 S. Dargan St. (29503). (803) 665-1230. FAX: (803) 665-8786. Licensee: WOLS Broadcasting Corp. Group owner: GHB Radio Group (acq 9-13-88). Net: USA. Format: Southern gospel. Target aud: 21-101 within a 30 mile radius. ■ Geo. H. Buck Jr., pres; Frank Bumgardner, gen mgr & gen sls mgr; Hal Boykin, progmg dir & mus dir.

WYNN(AM)—Nov 5, 1958: 540 khz; 250 w-U. TL: N34 13 05 W79 48 22. Hrs opn: 24. Box 100531 (29501-0531). (803) 662-6364. FAX: (803) 669-2654. Licensee: Forjay Broadcasting (acq 4-16-72; $512,000; FTR 7-13-81). Net: American Urban. Rep: Schubert. Wash atty: Scott Johnson. Format: Black gospel, jazz, blues, Black classics. News staff one; news progmg 12 hrs wkly. Target aud: 35 plus; Black. ■ James N. Maurer, pres & natl sls mgr; Paige Smith, opns mgr; Pansy Lowe, gen sls mgr; Ollie Williams, progmg dir & mus dir; Daniel Tindal, asst mus dir. ■ Rates: $40; 40; 40; 40.

WYNN-FM—Oct 1, 1964: 106.3 mhz; 1.1 kw. Ant 507 ft. TL: N34 14 03 W79 46 52 (CP: 1.7 kw). Stereo. Hrs opn: 24. Prog sep from AM. Format: Urban contemp. News staff one; news progmg one hr wkly. Target aud: 12-34. ■ Fred Brown, progmg dir; Tony Tee, mus dir. ■ Rates: $46; 46; 46; 46.

WZNS(FM)—See Dillon.

Folly Beach

WYBB(FM)—July 4, 1988: 98.1 mhz; 50 kw. Ant 500 ft. TL: N32 39 57 W80 03 11. Stereo. Hrs opn: 24. 59 Windermere Blvd., Charleston (29407). (803) 769-4799. FAX: (803) 769-4797. Licensee: L.M. Communications of South Carolina Inc. Group owner: L.M. Communications Inc. (acq 5-17-88). Rep: Eastman. Format: Classic rock. Target aud: 25-49; men 25-44. ■ Lynn Martin, pres; Ken French, gen mgr; Taft Moore, opns dir; Jeff Stein, gen sls mgr; Stacie Kendrick, prom dir & pub affrs dir; Wayne Long, chief engr.

Fountain Inn

WFIS(AM)—October 1956: 1600 khz; 1 kw-D, 25 w-N. TL: N34 42 28 W82 13 40. Hrs opn: 6 AM-9 PM. Box 156, 1318 N. Main St. (29644). (803) 963-5991. Licensee: Golden Strip Broadcasting (acq 3-1-88). Net: UPI; S.C. Net. Rep: Rgnl Reps. Format: Country, talk. News staff one; news progmg 3 hrs wkly. Target aud: 25-49; working adults. Spec prog: Gospel 3 hrs, Black 2 hrs wkly. ■ Steven D. Blair, pres, gen mgr & news dir; Jerry Wickline, gen sls mgr; B.J. Hart-Landers, progmg dir & mus dir; Kevin Raper, chief engr. ■ Rates: $12; 10; 12; 5.

Gaffney

WAGI-FM—Listing follows WEAC(AM).

WEAC(AM)—Sept 28, 1962: 1500 khz; 1 kw-D, 500 w-CH. TL: N35 05 18 W81 38 40. Box 1210, 340 Providence Rd. (29342). (803) 489-9066. FAX: (803) 489-9069. Licensee: Gaffney Broadcasting Inc. Net: NBC; S.C. Net. Format: Oldies, news/talk, Black. News staff one. ■ E. Raymond Parker, pres; Bright G. Parker, vp; Ronald Owenby, gen mgr; Dennis Fowler, news dir; Craig S. Turner, chief engr.

WAGI-FM—Co-owned with WEAC(AM). 1959: 105.3 mhz; 100 kw. Ant 1,190 ft. TL: N35 25 05 W81 46 32. Stereo. (Acq 1-15-71). Format: C&W, gospel. News progmg 5 hrs wkly. Spec prog: Talk 10 hrs, Clemson, Univ. of S.C. sports, racing, local sports.

WFGN(AM)—1948: 1180 khz; 2.5 kw-D. TL: N35 02 59 W81 38 42. Hrs opn: 6 AM-8 PM. Box 1388 (29342). (803) 489-9430. Licensee: Hope Broadcasting Inc. (acq 8-7-90; $160,000; FTR 8-27-90). Net: ABC/C. Format: Relg. ■ Eddie Leroy Bridges Jr., pres; Charles Montgomery, opns mgr; Rev. Eula Miller, gen sls mgr.

***WYFG(FM)**—Oct 12, 1982: 91.1 mhz; 100 kw. Ant 574 ft. TL: N35 06 57 W81 46 42. Hrs opn: 24. 6150 Cannons Campground Rd., Cowpens (29330). (803) 487-5836. Licensee: Bible Broadcasting Network (group owner). Format: Relg. News staff one. Target aud: General. ■ Lowell Davey, pres; Scott Curtis, gen mgr.

Georgetown

WGTN(AM)—July 1, 1949: 1400 khz; 1 kw-U. TL: N33 23 31 W79 19 21. Hrs opn: 24. Drawer 1400, Indian Hut Rd. (29442). (803) 546-1400. FAX: (803) 546-3297. Licensee: Georgetown Broadcasting (acq 12-19-91; $350,000 with co-located FM; FTR 1-13-92). Net: ABC. Format: Adult contemp. News staff one; news progmg 10 hrs wkly. Target aud: 25-54; upscale adult; business, professional and technical. Spec prog: Black 2 hrs, gospel 2 hrs, relg one hr wkly. ■ Chris Ling, gen mgr, gen sls mgr, mktg mgr, adv mgr & progmg dir; Dan Hoffman, opns mgr & dev mgr; Ken Wilmott, news dir; Buddy Womack, chief engr. ■ Rates: $17; 15; 17; 13.

WGTN-FM—(Andrews). Aug 19, 1985: 100.9 mhz; 3 kw. Ant 328 ft. TL: N33 24 24 W79 27 07. Stereo. Hrs opn: 24. Dups AM 80%. (Acq 9-10-90). Spec prog: Gospel 5 hrs, relg 2 hrs wkly. ■ Rates: Same as AM.

WSCA(FM)—Sept 1, 1990: 93.7 mhz; 3 kw. Ant 328 ft. TL: N33 16 09 W79 17 49 (CP: 6 kw). Stereo. Hrs opn: 24. Box 2020, 936 Front St. (29440). (803) 527-9882. FAX: (803) 527-2308. Licensee: VBX Communications Inc. (acq 4-1-92; $160,000). Net: SMN. Format: Classic rock. News staff one; news progmg 3 hrs wkly. Target aud: 25-49; career-orientated, college-educated adults. ■ C.A. Pasey, CEO & gen sls mgr; George B. Wilkes III., vp; Maria DeBacco, opns mgr & mus dir; Buddy Wennacr, chief engr. ■ Rates: $13; 11; 13; 11.

WSYN(FM)—May 1, 1973: 106.5 mhz; 50 kw. Ant 530 ft. TL: N33 26 20 W79 08 11. Stereo. Hrs opn: 24. Box 14770, Surfside Beach (29587). (803) 651-7869. FAX: (803) 651-3197. Licensee: Sunny Broadcasters Inc. (acq 4-24-91; $1.1 million; FTR 5-13-91). Net: CNN. Format: Oldies. ■ Richard Laughridge, pres; Barry Brown, gen mgr; David Lewis, gen sls mgr; Joe Johnson, progmg dir; Frank Barnhill, news dir.

WWXM(FM)—Sept 25, 1971: 97.7 mhz; 50 kw. Ant 492 ft. TL: N33 25 58 W70 16 16 (CP: 100 kw, 500 ft.). Stereo. Hrs opn: 24. Box 2908, Suite 301, 350 Wesley St., Myrtle Beach (29578). (803) 236-9800. FAX: (803) 236-9121. Licensee: Coastline Communications of Carolina Inc. (acq 12-88; $2.5 million; FTR 12-19-88). Wash atty: Fletcher, Heald & Hildreth. Format: CHR, hot adult contemp. News staff one; news progmg 2 hrs wkly. Target aud: 18-49. ■ Jerome Bresson, pres; Tom Atkinson, gen mgr; Mike Parnell, progmg dir; Greg Fry, mus dir; Calvin Hicks, news dir; Harold Bland, chief engr.

Goose Creek

WSSP(FM)—May 19, 1983: 94.3 mhz; 6 kw. Ant 479 ft. TL: N33 00 06 W79 55 51. Stereo. 108 Stephanie Dr. (29445). (803) 824-8943. FAX: (803) 824-8940. Licensee: Jones-Eastern of Charleston Inc. Group owner: Jones-Eastern Radio Inc. (acq 6-87). Net: Moody. Rep: Christal. Format: Nostalgia, stardust. Target aud: 18-49. ■ John Magliola, pres; Mary Russell, mus dir; Willie Bennett, chief engr.

WUJM(AM)—Licensed to Goose Creek. See Charleston.

Gray Court

WSSL-FM—Licensed to Gray Court. See Greenville.

Greenville

WDAB(AM)—See Travelers Rest.

***WEPR(FM)**—Sept 3, 1972: 90.1 mhz; 85 kw. Ant 1,184 ft. TL: N34 56 26 W82 24 38. Stereo. 1101 George Rogers Blvd., Columbia (29201). (803) 737-3420. FAX: (803) 737-3552. Licensee: South Carolina Educ. TV Commission. Net: AP, NPR, APR. Wash atty: Dow, Lohnes & Albertson. Format: Fine arts. ■ Henry J. Cauthen, pres & gen mgr; Ronald L. Schoenherr, sr vp; Jesse Bowers, vp; Al Jackson, news dir; Charlton Bowers, vp engrg; Paul Zweimiller, engrg mgr. *WRLK-TV Columbia.

WESC(AM)—March 1947: 660 khz; 50 kw-D, 10 kw-CH. TL: N34 53 10 W82 28 03. Box 660 (29602). (803) 242-4660. FAX: (803) 271-5029. Licensee: Broadcasting Co. of the Carolinas (acq 4-58; $15 million; FTR 11-23-87). Net: ABC/E. Rep: Banner. Format: Country. News staff one; news progmg 3 hrs wkly. Target aud: 25-54. ■ Allen Power, gen mgr; Wayne Sumner, gen sls mgr; John Landrum Mozingo, progmg dir; Tommy Gentry, mus dir; Don Gowens, chief engr.

WESC-FM—March 1948: 92.5 mhz; 100 kw. Ant 2,000 ft. TL: N35 08 16 W82 36 31. Stereo. Hrs opn: 24. Dups AM 100%. 223 W. Stone Ave. (29609).

WFBC(AM)—1933: 1330 khz; 5 kw-U, DA-N. TL: N34 51 18 W82 25 24. Hrs opn: 24. 505 Rutherford St. (29609); Box 1330 (29602). (803) 271-9200. FAX: (803) 242-1567. Licensee: Multimedia Inc. Group owner: Multimedia Broadcasting Co. Net: NBC, NBC Talknet, ABC/D, MBS. Rep: Katz. Wash atty: Dow, Lohnes & Albertson. Format: News/talk. News staff 2; news progmg 30 hrs wkly. Target aud: 25-54. Spec prog: Furman University football and basketball, Atlanta Braves baseball. ■ Pat A. Servodidio, pres; Ray Cal, gen mgr; Jim Burnside, opns mgr; Gene Kendrick, gen sls mgr; Mike Whitaker, natl sls mgr; Mike Gallagher, progmg mgr; Jerry Massey, chief engr.

WFBC-FM—1947: 93.7 mhz; 100 kw. Ant 1,850 ft. TL: N35 06 40 W82 36 17. Stereo. Hrs opn: 24. Prog sep from AM. Net: ABC/D, NBC. Rep: Katz. Format: Oldies. News staff 2; news progmg one hr wkly. Target aud: 25-54. ■ Bruce Cole, progmg dir; Steve Chris, mus dir.

WHYZ(AM)—(Sans Souci). May 26, 1966: 1070 khz; 50 kw-D, 1.5 kw-N, DA-2. TL: N34 55 05 W82 27 21. Stn currently dark. Box 4309, Hwy 25-Bypass (29611). Licensee: Greenville Family Broadcasters Inc. (acq 8-16-89; $730,000; FTR 9-7-87). ■ Steven Brisker, CEO & pres; Pandora Bonner, gen mgr.

***WLFJ(FM)**—May 1983: 89.3 mhz; 41 kw. Ant 1,100 ft. TL: N34 56 26 W82 24 44. Stereo. Hrs opn: 24. 2420 Wade Hampton Blvd. (29615). (803) 292-6040; (803) 292-5683. FAX: (803) 292-8428. Licensee: Radio Training Network Inc. (acq 8-31-89). Net: AP. Format: Contemp Christian. News progmg 9 hrs wkly. Target aud: 18-49. ■ Jim Campbell, pres; Allen Henderson, gen mgr; David Irvine, prom mgr; Ben Birdsong, progmg dir; Peter Lloyd, mus dir; Ted McCall, chief engr.

WMUU(AM)—Sept 15, 1949: 1260 khz; 5 kw-D, 29 w-N. TL: N34 53 16 W82 23 27. 920 Wade Hampton Blvd. (29609). (803) 242-6240. FAX: (803) 370-3829. Licensee: WMUU Inc. (acq 3-27-75). Net: AP. Format: Relg. ■ Jim Dickson, gen mgr; Paul Wright, gen sls mgr, prom mgr, progmg dir & mus dir; Joe Norris, chief engr.

WMUU-FM—Aug 15, 1960: 94.5 mhz; 100 kw. Ant 1,200 ft. TL: N34 56 29 W82 24 41. Stereo. Prog sep from AM. Net: AP, Wall Street. Format: Btfl mus. Spec prog: Class 14 hrs, relg 20 hrs wkly. ■ Paul Wright, sls dir; Charlie Koelsh, mus dir; Joe Norris, engrg dir.

WMYI(FM)—(Hendersonville, N.C). April 15, 1958: 102.5 mhz; 20 kw. Ant 1,778 ft. TL: N35 13 22 W82 32 57. Stereo. Hrs opn: 24. Suite 801, National Bank Plaza, 7 N. Laurens St., Greenville, SC (29601-2744). (803) 235-1025. Licensee: Capstar Communications of South Carolina (WMYI) Inc. Group owner: SFX Broadcasting Inc. (acq 12-23-92; $10.25 million; FTR 1-18-93). Rep: Republic. Format: Adult contemp. News staff one. ■ George R. Francis Jr., pres; John D. Cullen, sr vp & gen mgr; Barbara Allen, gen sls mgr; Van McClenneghan, natl sls mgr; Sandra Dill, prom dir; Loyd Ford, progmg dir; Roxanne Walker, news dir; Jim Graham, chief engr.

WPCI(AM)—Feb 8, 1954: 1490 khz; 1 kw-U. TL: N34 51 38 W82 24 31. 840 Hwy. 25 Bypass (29609); 400 Mayberry St. (29601). (803) 370-1490. FAX: (803) 370-1490. Licensee: Hunter Broadcast Group (acq 12-88; $15,000; FTR 2-20-89). Net: BRN. Format: Business Radio. ■ Randy Mathena, pres; Ken Lucking, gen mgr; Ted A. McCall, chief engr.

***WPLS-FM**—Sept 1980: 96.5 mhz; 4 w. Ant 66 ft. TL: N34 55 27 W82 26 13. Stereo. Hrs opn: 9 AM-1 PM (Mon-Fri). Box 28573, Furman Univ., 3300 Poinsett Hwy. (29613). (803) 294-3045; (803) 294-3577. FAX: (803) 294-3580. Licensee: Furman Univ. Format: Progsv. Target aud: 18-24; college students. Spec prog: Classic rock 2 hrs, rap 2 hrs, talk shows 3 hrs, new age 2 hrs, jazz 2 hrs, dance 2 hrs, relg 2 hrs, syndicated 2 hrs wkly. ■ William F. Marion, gen mgr; Jeff Montgomery, opns mgr & progmg dir; Brett Paden, prom dir; Richard Hubbard, prom mgr; Tiffiny Douglas, adv dir; Simon Crowe, Jason Kriese, mus dirs; Todd Nickelsen, asst mus dir; Julie Yoder, pub affrs dir; Ted McCall, chief engr. ■ Rates: $5; 5; 5; 5.

WSSL(AM)—1950: 1440 khz; 5 kw-U, DA-N. TL: N34 52 06 W82 28 04. Hrs opn: 24. Box 100 (29602); Nations Bank Plaza, 8 Laurens St. (29601). (803) 242-1005; (803) 235-1025. FAX: (803) 271-3830; (803) 233-7827. Licensee: SFX Broadcasting of S.C. Inc. (acq 11-89; grpsl; FTR 8-7-89). Net: AP, Unistar. Rep: McGavren Guild. Wash atty: Fisher, Wayland, Cooper & Leader. Format: Country. News staff 2; news progmg 4 hrs wkly. Target aud: 25-54. ■ Steve Hicks, pres; John Cullen, sr vp & gen mgr; Barbara Allen, gen sls mgr; Sandra Dill, prom mgr; Loyd Ford, progmg dir; John Crenshaw, mus dir; Allen Bookout, news dir; Jim Graham, chief engr.

WSSL-FM—(Gray Court). November 1960: 100.5 mhz; 100 kw. Ant 1,240 ft. TL: N34 34 19 W82 06 41. Hrs opn: 24. Dups AM 100%.

***WTBI-FM**—June 1991: 91.7 mhz; 3 kw. Ant 328 ft. TL: N34 49 43 W82 26 59. Hrs opn: 18. 3931 White Horse Rd. (29611). (803) 855-1916. Licensee: Tabernacle Baptist Bible College. Net: S.C. Net. Format: Relg music, educational, gospel. News staff one; news progmg 4 hrs wkly. Target aud: General. ■ Harold B. Sightler, pres; Pierre Allston, vp & gen mgr; Angela Huneycutt, progmg dir & mus dir.

Greenwood

WCRS(AM)—Sept 1, 1941: 1450 khz; 1 kw-U. TL: N34 12 34 W82 09 05. Hrs opn: 24. Box 1247 (29648); 637 E. Durst Ave. (29649). (803) 223-8553; (803) 223-6264. FAX: (803) 223-8554. Licensee: Eaton Broadcasting Inc. (acq 9-22-82). Net: NBC. Rep: Rgnl Reps. Format: MOR. News staff one; news progmg 20 hrs wkly. Target aud: 35 plus. ■ W.P. Eaton, pres & vp gen mgr; Fred Moore, gen mgr; Tom Karel, progmg dir; Charles M. Sparks, chief engr.

WSCZ(FM)—Co-owned with WCRS(AM). Apr 28, 1965: 96.7 mhz; 4.1 kw. Ant 390 ft. TL: N34 12 34 W82 09 05. Stereo. Hrs opn: 24. Prog sep from AM. Net: ABC/E. Format: Modern country. Target aud: 18 plus.

WLMA(AM)—Apr 15, 1953: 1350 khz; 1 kw-D, 85 w-N, DA-1. TL: N34 13 06 W82 08 00. Stereo. Box 1396 (29648); 2410 Kateway Rd. (29646). (803) 223-5945; (803) 942-0004. Licensee: Morradio Inc. (acq 10-5-92; $90,000; FTR 11-9-92). Net: Natl Black. Format: Urban contemp. News staff one; news progmg 5 hrs wkly. Target aud: 18-45; responsible adults with purchasing power.

WMTY(AM)—June 20, 1973: 1090 khz; 780 w-D. TL: N34 09 46 W82 11 41. Stereo. 370 Burnett (29646); Box 459 (29648). (803) 223-4300; (803) 223-9689. FAX: (803) 223-4096. Licensee: United Community Enterprises Inc. Net: ABC/C; S.C. Net. Wash atty: Lawrence J. Bernard Jr. Format: Urban contemp. Target aud: 18-34; Black. Spec prog: Gospel 7 hrs wkly. ■ Wally Mullinax, pres; Betty K. Black, gen mgr; Stan Woodward, progmg dir & chief engr; Angela Austin, mus dir. ■ Rates: $19.75; 15.25; 19.75; 15.25.

WMTY-FM—March 1989: 103.5 mhz; 25 kw. Ant 328 ft. TL: N34 09 46 W82 11 41. Stereo. Hrs opn: 5 AM-12:30 AM. Dups AM 100%. Target aud: 18-34. ■ Rates: Same as AM.

WSCZ(FM)—Listing follows WCRS(AM).

Greer

WCKI(AM)—Mar 3, 1955: 1300 khz; 1 kw-D. TL: N34 55 39 W82 15 42. Box 709 (29652). (803) 877-8458. Licensee: Sira-Pack Radio Inc. (acq 5-4-64). Rep: Dora-Clayton. Format: Southern gospel. News progmg one hr wkly. Target aud: 25-54; working people who spend money. ■ Ronald T. Pack, pres; Allen Lovelace, gen mgr; Arlene C. Pack, gen sls mgr; Ronald Pack, progmg dir & mus dir; Thomas Moore, pub affrs dir.

WLYZ(FM)—Not on air, target date unknown: 103.3 mhz; 2.7 kw. Ant 495 ft. TL: N34 59 13 W82 09 56. 153 Henson St., Spartanburg (29302). Licensee: Greer Communications L.P.

WPJM(AM)—June 15, 1949: 800 khz; 1 kw-D, 438 w-N. TL: N34 56 59 W82 14 43. 305 N. Tryon St. (29651). (803) 877-1112. Licensee: Robert F. Bell (acq 12-29-89; $125,000; FTR 1-15-90). Net: S.C. Net. Format: Oldies. Target aud: General. ■ John A. Salter Jr., pres; Bobby Cohen, gen mgr; Norma Latta, progmg dir.

Hampton

WBHC(AM)—Sept 1957: 1270 khz; 1 kw-D. TL: N32 50 39 W81 07 28. Box 666 (29924). (803) 943-2831. Licensee: Hampton County Broadcasters Inc. (acq 10-83; $220,000; FTR 10-3-83). Net: MBS. Format: Relg. ■ Carl Gross, pres & gen mgr; Jim Daniel, progmg dir & news dir; Gene Todd, chief engr.

WBHC-FM—Sept 1970: 103.1 mhz; 3 kw. Ant 328 ft. TL: N32 50 39 W81 07 28. Stereo. Prog sep from AM. Net: S.C. Net. Format: Country. News staff one; news progmg 11 hrs wkly. Spec prog: Relg 6 hrs, oldies 14 hrs, urban contemp 20 hrs wkly.

Hanahan

WAVF(FM)—Mar 11, 1985: 96.1 mhz; 538 w. Ant 1,443 ft. TL: N32 49 04 W79 50 08. Stereo. Hrs opn: 24. 1417 Remount Rd., Charleston (29406). (803) 554-4401. FAX: (803) 566-0814. Licensee: Cordes Street Communications Inc. Rep: Christal. Format: Rock (AOR). ■ Haywood B. Bartlett Jr., pres & gen mgr; Barbara E. Cameron, gen sls mgr; Jude E. Sloan, prom dir; Dave Rossi, progmg dir; Willie Bennett, chief engr.

Hardeeville

WLVH(FM)—Aug 30, 1992: 101.1 mhz; 50 kw. Ant 476 ft. TL: N32 05 48 W81 19 17. Stereo. Hrs opn: 24. Box 727, Savannah, GA (31402); 24 W. Henry St., Savannah, GA (31401). (912) 232-3322; (912) 231-1011. FAX: (912) 232-6144. Licensee: Savannah Radio Partners (acq 12-30-92; $601,730; FTR 1-25-93). Net: Unitstar. Rep: Banner. Format: Adult urban contemp. Target aud: 25-49; affluent Black adults. ■ Thomas Birch, chmn; Raymond Quinn, pres; Daniel Gorby, gen mgr; Jeff Roper, opns mgr; Walt Rosen, sls dir; Martin Foglia, chief engr.

Hartsville

WHSC(AM)—Oct 1, 1946: 1450 khz; 1 kw-U. TL: N34 21 15 W80 04 20. Hrs opn: 5:30 AM-midnight. Box 940, S. Fifth St. (29550). (803) 332-8101. Licensee: Hartsville Broadcasting Co. Inc. Net: ABC/E; Tobacco, S.C. Net. Wash atty: Reddy, Begley & Martin. Format: Country. News staff one; news progmg 12 hrs wkly. Target aud: 19-49; those with buying power. Spec prog: Farm 3 hrs, gospel 3 hrs, relg 6 hrs, big band 3 hrs, oldies 6 hrs wkly. ■ Hugh Campbell, pres & gen mgr; O. B. Lyles, gen sls mgr; Betty Sue Wilkie, prom mgr; Howard Garland, progmg dir; Samantha Lyles, mus dir; Doug Carter, chief engr. ■ Rates: $7.25; 7.25; 7.25; 6.50.

WHSC-FM—Nov 19, 1992: 98.5 mhz; 3 kw. Ant 328 ft. TL: N34 21 16 W80 04 06. ■ Hugh Campbell, gen mgr.

WTNI(AM)—Dec 4, 1972: 1490 khz; 1 kw-U. TL: N34 21 47 W80 04 28. 430 W. Lincoln Ave. (29550). (803) 383-2100. Licensee: J&J Broadcasting Inc. (acq 11-2-90; $28,528; FTR 11-19-90). Format: Traditional gospel. ■ Patricia Jackson, gen mgr; James A. Jackson, chief engr.

Hemingway

WKYB(AM)—Licensed to Hemingway. See Charleston.

*WLGI(FM)—July 1, 1984: 90.9 mhz; 50 kw. Ant 505 ft. TL: N33 43 09 W79 19 50. Stereo. Hrs opn: 15. Box 69, Rt. 2 (29554). (803) 558-9544; (803) 558-2977. FAX: (803) 558-2921. Licensee: Louis G. Gregory Baha'i Institute. Wash atty: Reddy, Begley & Martin. Format: Div, gospel, jazz. Target aud: 15-25; Black, rural. ■ Stephen Kozlow, stn mgr; Ernest Hilton, mus dir; Laurie C.J. Cohen, Dan McCoy, asst mus dirs; Laurie "C.J" Cohen, pub affrs dir; Greg Kintz, chief engr.

Hilton Head Island

WFXH(FM)—Listing follows WHHR(AM).

WHHR(AM)—Feb 14, 1983: 1130 khz; 1 kw-D, 500 w-N, DA-N. TL: N32 12 01 W80 43 27. Stereo. Box 7665 (29928). (803) 785-9447. FAX: (803) 686-3699. Licensee: Adventure Communications Inc. (group owner; acq 2-11-91; $300,000 with co-located FM; FTR 3-11-91). Net: AP. Format: Talk. News staff one; news progmg 5 hrs wkly. Target aud: 35 plus. ■ Jerry Stevens, gen mgr; Bill Triebold, opns mgr.

WFXH(FM)—Co-owned with WHHR(AM). July 14, 1973: 106.1 mhz; 10.5 kw. Ant 794 ft. TL: N32 19 50 W80 56 19. Stereo. Prog sep from AM. Format: Btfl mus.

WIJY(FM)—February 1988: 107.9 mhz; 50 kw. Ant 485 ft. TL: N32 13 17 W80 49 05. Box 6988, 1036 Wm. Hilton Pkwy. (29938). (803) 785-3001. FAX: (803) 686-8798. Licensee: WIJY Inc. (acq 1-12-90; $2,063,000; FTR 2-12-90). Net: Unistar. Format: Adult contemp. News staff one. Target aud: 35-55. Spec prog: Jazz 4 hrs wkly. ■ Howard Raycroft, gen mgr; Roger Clark, gen sls mgr; Brad Tholen, progmg dir; John Ihrig, Brad Tholen, news dirs; Martin Foglia, chief engr. ■ Rates: $30; 26; 28; 20.

WSHG(FM)—(Ridgeland). July 15, 1986: 104.9 mhz; 3 kw. Ant 300 ft. TL: N32 26 10 W80 55 23 (CP: 16 kw, ant 410 ft.). Stereo. R.R. 1, Box 135-C, Ridgeland (29936-9801). (803) 726-5444. FAX: (803) 726-5059. Licensee: Mattox-Guest Broadcasting Inc. (acq 4-15-93; $375,000; FTR 5-3-93). Net: CBS Spectrum. Format: Southern. Format: Adult contemp. Spec prog: Beach 3 hrs, oldies 4 hrs wkly. ■ Tex Lowther (owner), CEO; William J. Pennington Jr., pres; William J. Pennington III, gen mgr & chief engr; Bill Breland, opns mgr; Jake Phillips, gen sls mgr; Bob Laurence, progmg dir; Deborah Carter, news dir.

Holly Hill

WJBS(AM)—Dec 1, 1972: 1440 khz; 1 kw-D, 98 w-N. TL: N33 20 23 W80 26 18. Box 1087 (29059). (803) 496-5352. Licensee: Eugene Schoebinger (acq 7-1-85). Format: C&W, community involvement. News staff one; news progmg 14 hrs wkly. Spec prog: Black 17 hrs, fishing/hunting 2 hrs, farm 2 hr wkly. ■ Eugene Schoebinger, gen mgr, gen sls mgr & news dir; Elise Schoebinger, prom mgr; Peggy Hold, progmg dir; Bert Rickenbacker, chief engr. ■ Rates: $8; 8; 8; 4.

Homeland Park

WRIX(AM)—Sept 1, 1986: 1020 khz; 10 kw-D. TL: N34 28 14 W82 38 03. Watson Village Shopping Center, Anderson (29624). (803) 225-9999. FAX: (803) 224-6733. Licensee: AM 1020 Inc. Net: S.C. Net. Format: Relg. Spec prog: Black 7 hrs wkly. ■ Matt Phillips, pres & gen mgr; Paul Lindsey, mus dir; Dave Reddick, chief engr.

Honea Path

WRIX-FM—June 10, 1977: 103.1 mhz; 6 kw. Ant 392 ft. TL: N34 23 43 W82 29 49. Stereo. Hrs opn: 24. Watson Village, Anderson (29624). (803) 224-9749. FAX: (803) 224-6733. Licensee: FM 103 Inc. Net: ABC; S.C. Net. Rep: Southern. Wash atty: Lawrence J. Bernard Jr. Format: C&W. Spec prog: Talk 20 hrs wkly. ■ Matt Phillips, pres & gen mgr; Dann Scott, mus dir; Joel Kay, news dir; Dave Reddick, chief engr.

James Island

WWRJ(AM)—Not on air, target date unknown: 1200 khz; 10 kw-D, 1 kw-N, DA-2. TL: N32 45 11 W80 04 09. 613 S. La Grange Rd., La Grange, IL (60525). (312) 352-2275. Licensee: J&K Broadcasters.

Johnsonville

WRHA(FM)—Not on air, target date unknown: 105.1 mhz; 3 kw. Ant 321 ft. TL: N33 47 00 W79 28 02. Box 4203, Wilmington, NC (28406). Licensee: Waccamaw Neck Broadcasting Co. (acq 3-18-92; $20,823 for CP; FTR 4-6-92).

Johnston

WJES(AM)—June 12, 1961: 1190 khz; 1 kw-D. TL: N33 50 18 W81 49 48. Drawer I (29832). (803) 275-4444. Licensee: Edgefield-Saluda Radio Co. Inc. Net: ABC/D; S.C. Net. Rep: Keystone (unwired net). Format: Adult contemp. ■ Mike Casey, pres & gen mgr; Frank Davis, progmg dir.

WKSX(FM)—Co-owned with WJES(AM). Aug 26, 1985: 92.7 mhz; 3 kw. Ant 268 ft. TL: N33 42 11 W79 49 08 (CP: 1.79 kw, ant 577 ft.). Stereo. Dups AM 95%. Licensee: Edgefield-Saluda Radio Co. Inc. (acq 4-85; $3,585.75; FTR 4-8-85).

Kershaw

WKSC(AM)—Dec 21, 1961: 1300 khz; 500 w-D. TL: N34 33 30 W80 33 34. 502 W. Church St. (29067). (803) 475-8585. Licensee: Kershaw Broadcasting Corp. Format: Southern gospel. ■ Jess B. Tatum, pres & chief engr; Johnny Shack, gen mgr.

Kingstree

WDKD(AM)—July 1949: 1310 khz; 5 kw-D, 67 w-N. TL: N33 42 11 W79 49 08. Hrs opn: 6 AM-11 PM. Box 1125, Hwy. 52 N. (29556). (803) 382-2361. Licensee: Davidson Communications (acq 6-30-75). Net: ABC/I; S.C. Net. Format: Talk, C&W. News staff one; news progmg 10 hrs wkly. Target aud: 35 plus. ■ Gary Davidson, pres; Charles Westbrook, gen mgr; Samella Barr, progmg dir; Barry Bradley, news dir; Fane Anderson, chief engr.

WWKT-FM—Co-owned with WDKD(AM). May 28, 1966: 99.3 mhz; 3 kw. Ant 289 ft. TL: N33 42 11 W79 49 08. Stereo. Prog sep from AM. Net: ABC/I. Format: Urban contemp.

Ladson

*WKCL(FM)—Jan 11, 1982: 91.5 mhz; 100 kw. Ant 305 ft. TL: N33 00 24 W80 05 17. Hrs opn: 24. Box 809, 362 College Park Rd. (29456). (803) 553-1525. FAX: (803) 553-0636. Licensee: Chapel of the Holy Spirit and Holy Spirit Bible College. Net: Unistar. Format: Contemp MOR. Target aud: General; baby boomers. ■ Carl L. Wiggins Sr., pres.

WRLQ(FM)—Not on air, target date unknown: 106.3 mhz; 3 kw. Ant 100 ft. 5081 Rivers Ave., North Charleston (29418). Licensee: Thomas B. Daniels.

Lake City

WRIP(AM)—Oct 9, 1953: 1260 khz; 5 kw-D, 55 w-N. TL: N33 51 42 W79 44 15. Hrs opn: 6 AM-6 PM. Box 1177, 925 E. Main St. (29560). (803) 394-2088; (803) 665-1230. FAX: (803) 665-8786. Licensee: GHB of Lake City

South Carolina

Inc. (group owner; acq 5-28-92; $35,000; FTR 6-15-92). Net: S.C. Net. Rep: T-N. Wash atty: Dennis Begley. Format: Christian. News staff one; news progmg 5 hrs wkly. Target aud: General. Spec prog: Local news. ■ George H. Buck Jr., pres; Frank Bumgardner, gen mgr & gen sls mgr. ■ Rates: $7; 5; 7; 4.

WWFN(FM)—May 11, 1977: 100.1 mhz; 1.3 kw. Ant 482 ft. TL: N33 51 42 W79 44 15. Stereo. Box 1177, 925 E. Main St. (29560). (803) 394-8008. Licensee: Florence County Broadcasting Co. Group owner: Suburban Radio Group (acq 10-29-93; $450,000; FTR 11-15-93). ■ Judy Hundley, gen mgr.

Lancaster

WAGL(AM)—Aug 7, 1962: 1560 khz; 50 kw-D, DA. TL: N34 49 53 W80 52 08. Stereo. Box 28, 101 S. Woodland Dr. (29720). (803) 283-8431. Licensee: Palmetto Broadcasting System Inc. Net: NBC. Format: Modern country. ■ B.L. Phillips Jr., pres, gen mgr & gen sls mgr; Veronica Pentz, prom mgr; Kim Davis, progmg dir; Bob Thomas, mus dir; Jim Wall, news dir; Pete Gilmore, chief engr. ■ Rates: $17; 17; 17; na.

WRHM(FM)—July 27, 1964: 107.1 mhz; 3 kw. Ant 500 ft. TL: N34 48 05 W80 47 51. Stereo. Box 307, 142 N. Confederate Ave., Rock Hill (29731). (803) 324-1071; (803) 286-1071. FAX: (803) 324-2860. Licensee: Our Three Sons Broadcasting (acq 10-1-87). Net: ABC; S.C. Net. Format: Country, local news and sports. News staff 3. Target aud: 25-54. ■ Bill Rice, opns mgr & mus dir; Allan M. Miller, rgnl sls mgr; Ron Tollison, progmg dir, news dir & chief engr.

Laurens

WLBG(AM)—Mar 1, 1947: 860 khz; 1 kw-U. TL: N34 30 13 W82 01 06. Box 1289, 104 Hillcrest (29360). (803) 984-3544. Licensee: Southeastern Broadcast Assocs. Inc. (acq 8-5-83). Format: Urban contemp. News progmg 4 hrs wkly. Target aud: 30 plus; Black. Spec prog: Gospel 18 hrs wkly. ■ Emil J. Finley, pres; Chris Burgin, gen mgr; Keith Michaels, mus dir; Harold Ward, chief engr.

Leesville

WBLR(AM)—See Batesburg.

Lexington

WLGO(AM)—1984: 1170 khz; 10 kw-D. TL: N33 58 17 W81 16 43. 145 Branham View Rd. (29072-2335). (803) 359-1170. FAX: (803) 359-1095. Licensee: A A R C Inc. Format: Black gospel. ■ Rev. Douglas Franklin, gen mgr; Art James, opns mgr; Wanda Sightler, progmg dir & mus dir; Milton Holiday, chief engr.

Loris

WLSC(AM)—August 1958: 1240 khz; 1 kw-U. TL: N34 02 41 W78 53 39. Hrs opn: 6 AM-midnight. Box 578, Hwy. 701 S. (29569). (803) 756-1183. Licensee: JARC Broadcasting Inc. (acq 8-15-88). Net: S.C. Net. Rep: Keystone (unwired net). Format: Country. Target aud: 21-54. ■ Chris Poulos, pres; Jerry D. Jenrette, gen mgr; Jerry Jenrette, progmg dir.

WVCO(FM)—Not on air, target date unknown: 105.9 mhz; 2.65 kw. Ant 495 ft. TL: N34 02 32 W78 54 39. Box 437, Conway (29526). Licensee: Robert Lee Rabon.

Manning

WYMB(AM)—July 15, 1957: 1410 khz; 1 kw-D, 128 w-N. TL: N33 41 22 W80 16 16 (CP: 920 khz; 2.3 kw-D, 1 kw-N, DA-N, TL: N33 41 22 W80 16 16). Box 400 (29102). (803) 435-8388. FAX: (803) 435-2788. Licensee: Clarendon County Broadcasting Corp. (acq 5-15-68). Net: AP, CBS Spectrum. Rep: McGavren Guild. Format: Adult contemp. ■ Betty T. Roper, pres; Carl D. Roach, gen mgr & chief engr; Christine Harvin, gen sls mgr; Matt Scherry, progmg dir.

WHLZ(FM)—Co-owned with WYMB(AM). April 16, 1973: 92.5 mhz; 100 kw. Ant 1,207 ft. TL: N33 32 05 W79 59 15. Stereo. Prog sep from AM. Format: Country.

Marion

WKSY(FM)—August 1991: 100.5 mhz; 21.5 kw. Ant 354 ft. TL: N34 19 36 W79 32 35. 2014 N. Irby St., Florence (29502). (803) 667-1200. Licensee: Holder Media Inc. (acq 7-12-91; $625,000 for CP; FTR 7-29-91). Format: Country. ■ Hugh Holder, pres; Harmon Jernigan, opns mgr.

WLXP(FM)—Sept 18, 1970: 94.3 mhz; 3 kw. Ant 499 ft. TL: N34 11 14 W79 31 23. Stereo. Hrs opn: 24. Box 1103, American Legion Rd. (29571). (803) 423-9147; (803) 423-7236. FAX: (803) 423-6497. Licensee: Winfas of Belhaven Inc. (group owner; acq 6-25-92; FTR 7-20-92). Net: USA. Rep: T-N. Wash atty: Gary Smithwick. Format: Christian country. News staff one; news progmg 8 hrs wkly. Target aud: 18-54; country listening demo who prefers positive messages. ■ Larry Nichols, chmn; Roger Ingram, pres; W.S. Foster Jr., exec vp; David Solomon, gen mgr, gen sls mgr & progmg mgr; Rita Garcia, dev dir; Ron Brown, natl sls mgr; Derek Frerrichs, progmg dir; Clay McCarghley, news dir; Buddy Wommack, chief engr. ■ Rates: $17; 15.50; 16; 14.

McClellanville

WZJQ(FM)—Not on air, target date unknown: 98.9 mhz; 50 kw. Ant 492 ft. TL: N33 11 20 W79 33 25. 1729 Heritage Park Rd., Charleston (29407). Licensee: Gilchrist Communications Inc.

Moncks Corner

WMCJ(AM)—December 1963: 950 khz; 500 w-D. TL: N33 12 18 W80 03 11. Box 67 (29461). (803) 761-6010. FAX: (803) 761-6979. Licensee: Berkeley Broadcasting Corp. (acq 1984). Net: S.C. Net. Rep: Clayton-Davis. Format: Black, relg. ■ Clary K. Butler, pres & chief engr; Dorothy M. Mitchum, vp & gen mgr; Susanna Footman, news dir.

Mt. Pleasant

WJUK(FM)—June 1, 1985: 104.5 mhz; 28 kw. Ant 656 ft. TL: N32 47 15 W79 51 00. Stereo. Hrs opn: 24. Suite 1600, 4995 LaCross Rd., Charleston (29406). (803) 566-1100. FAX: (803) 529-1933. Licensee: Low-country Media Inc. (acq 9-3-93; $850,000; FTR 9-27-93). Net: SMN. Rep: Katz & Powell. Format: Country. ■ Buddy Barton, gen mgr; Charlie Lindsay, progmg dir; Bruce Roberts, chief engr.

WZJY(AM)—May 21, 1982: 1480 khz; 1 kw-D, 44 w-N. TL: N32 48 59 W79 50 18. Hrs opn: 24. 424 Broadway St. (29464). (803) 881-2482. FAX: (803) 884-3259. Licensee: Mount Pleasant Communications Inc. (acq 8-87; $115,000; FTR 8-31-87). Net: CNN. Format: Relg. News staff one; news progmg 28 hrs wkly. Target aud: General. Spec prog: Gospel. ■ Edward L. Johnson, pres; Micah A. Fields, gen mgr & opns mgr; Sam Dennis, gen sls mgr, asst mus dir & news dir; Edwin Wright, prom dir, progmg dir, mus dir & pub affrs dir; Joe Papp, chief engr. ■ Rates: $96; 72; 132; 106.

Mullins

WJAY(AM)—June 1, 1949: 1280 khz; 5 kw-D, 270 w-N. TL: N34 11 30 W79 18 55. Hrs opn: 18. Box 1005, U.S. Hwy. 76 (29574). (803) 423-1140; (803) 423-2829. Licensee: Mullins & Marion Broadcasting Co. Net: ABC/C, Sun; S.C. Net, Tobacco. Rep: T-N. Format: Country, talk. News progmg 8 hrs wkly. Target aud: General. Spec prog: Farm 10 hrs wkly. ■ James F. Ramsey, pres, gen mgr, gen sls mgr & chief engr; Jack Brown, progmg dir & news dir. ■ Rates: $4.50; 4.50; 4.50; 4.50.

WCIG(FM)—Co-owned with WJAY(AM). April 5, 1975: 107.1 mhz; 3 kw. Ant 328 ft. TL: N34 11 30 W79 18 55. Stereo. Hrs opn: 18. Prog sep from AM. Net: S.C. Net. Format: Urban contemp, relg. ■ Eugene Brantley, opns mgr, progmg dir, mus dir & news dir. ■ Rates: $6; 6; 6; 6.

Murrell's Inlet

WRNN(FM)—Apr 7, 1991: 94.5 mhz; 6 kw. Ant 420 ft. TL: N33 36 04 W79 03 05. Stereo. Hrs opn: 24. Box 1112, Myrtle Beach (29578). (803) 238-1125. FAX: (803) 238-1805. Licensee: Kings Road Radio Inc. (acq 5-22-92; $322,000; FTR 6-15-92). Format: News/talk. ■ Scott O'Neil, pres.

Myrtle Beach

WJYR(FM)—Jan 11, 1965: 92.1 mhz; 50 kw. Ant 325 ft. TL: N33 42 56 W78 52 57. Stereo. Hrs opn: 24. 706 21st Ave. N. (29577). (803) 448-3189; (803) 448-9292. FAX: (803) 626-2508. Licensee: Hirsh Broadcasting Group L.P. (acq 1-6-89; $2 million; FTR 1-23-89). Net: Unistar. Rep: Banner. Wash atty: Cohn & Marks. Format: Easy lstng. Target aud: General; adults 18 plus. Spec prog: Big band, classical. ■ Tony Hirsh, pres; Scott Norton, gen mgr; Kelli Dixon, opns mgr & progmg dir; Don Westcott, rgnl sls mgr; Bob Smith, chief engr.

Directory of Radio

WKZQ(AM)—Apr 24, 1965: 1520 khz; 5 kw-D, DA. TL: N33 42 20 W78 58 23. Box 2389, 130 Ocala St. (29578). (803) 448-4739. Licensee: Grand Strand Broadcasting Corp. Format: Rock & roll. News staff one; news progmg 2 hrs wkly. Target aud: 12-38. ■ Thomas J. Rogers, pres; William S. Hennecy, gen mgr; Jim Savel, gen sls mgr; Johnny Diaz, progmg dir; Bill Files, chief engr.

WKZQ-FM—July 3, 1969: 101.7 mhz; 50 kw. Ant 601 ft. TL: N33 56 14 W78 57 53. Stereo. Hrs opn: 24. Dups AM 100%. Format: Rock.

New Ellenton

WAJY(FM)—December 1989: 102.7 mhz; 3 kw. Ant 328 ft. TL: N33 30 47 W81 38 05. Hrs opn: 24. Box 5550, Aiken (29804); 640 Old Airport Rd., Aiken (29801). (803) 641-1027. FAX: (803) 642-9444. Licensee: GRR Marketing Inc. (acq 3-15-91; $829,539; FTR 4-1-91). Net: NBC. Format: All talk. News progmg 7 hrs wkly. Target aud: 25-55. ■ Greg Ryberg, pres; Taylor Garnett, exec vp; Bobby Saul, vp, gen mgr & sls dir; Dave Wrenn, opns dir; David Wrenn, chief engr. ■ Rates: $17; 15; 17; 12.

Newberry

WKDK(AM)—October 1946: 1240 khz; 1 kw-U. TL: N34 17 24 W81 37 10. Hrs opn: 17. Box 753, 3000 Hazel (29108). (803) 276-2957. Licensee: Newberry Broadcasting Co. (acq 1951). Net: ABC/E; S.C. Net. Rep: Dora-Clayton. Format: Adult contemp, oldies. ■ James F. Coggins, pres; James P. Coggins, gen mgr, gen sls mgr, progmg dir & mus dir; Marcia Coggins, prom mgr; Jim Murray, news dir; E.R. Gilliam Sr., chief engr.

WKMG(AM)—May 22, 1968: 1520 khz; 1 kw-D. TL: N34 15 12 W81 35 44. Box 16A-2 (29108). (803) 276-2507. FAX: (803) 276-2507. Licensee: Service Radio Co. Inc. Net: ABC/E. Format: Adult contemp. ■ Ken Durst, gen mgr, news dir & chief engr; Cornell Blakely, opns mgr & progmg dir; Shotsie McCutchin, gen sls mgr; Roy Amick, mus dir.

WNMX(FM)—July 10, 1989: 106.3 mhz; 25 kw. Ant 328 ft. TL: N34 19 38 W81 32 42. Stereo. Hrs opn: 24. Box 1036, 1207 Nance St. (29108). (803) 276-1063. FAX: (803) 276-9839. Licensee: Professional Radio Inc. Net: CNN. Format: Urban contemp. News staff 4; news progmg 2 hrs wkly. Target aud: 25-54; early 20s to 40 plus, goers, doers, buyers. ■ Tony Brooks, pres; Mike Brooks, stn mgr, gen sls mgr & mus dir; Antonio Stevens, progmg dir. ■ Rates: $20; 16; 16; 12.

North Augusta

WGUS(AM)—Licensed to North Augusta. See Augusta, Ga.

WKZK(AM)—May 9, 1962: 1600 khz; 500 w-D. TL: N34 09 03 W82 23 34. Hrs opn: Sunrise-sunset. Box 1454, Augusta, GA (30903); 2 Milledge Rd., Augusta, GA (30904). (706) 738-9191. Licensee: Gospel Radio Inc. (acq 9-22-83; $190,000; FTR 10-10-83). Net: American Urban. Rep: Dora-Clayton. Format: Black gospel & relg. Target aud: Black adults. ■ Mildred Hunnicutt, pres; Walter Robinson, gen mgr & chief engr; Garfield Turner, progmg dir & mus dir. ■ Rates: $16; 15; 16; 15.

WTHB(AM)—See Augusta, Ga.

North Charleston

WBUB(FM)—Licensed to North Charleston. See St. George.

WTMZ(AM)—(Dorchester Terrace-Brentwood). Nov 17, 1960: 910 khz; 500 w-U, DA-N. TL: N34 09 03 W82 23 34. Hrs opn: 24. Box 30909, Charleston (29417). (803) 556-5660. Licensee: Equico Capital Corp. (acq 6-19-92; $900,000 with WDXZ[FM] Mt. Pleasant; FTR 7-20-92). Format: Talk radio. ■ Hugh Jett, gen mgr.

WXLY(FM)—July 17, 1962: 102.5 mhz; 100 kw. Ant 1,000 ft. TL: N32 47 44 W79 50 27. Stereo. Hrs opn: 24. Suite 201, 950 Houston Northcutt Blvd., Mt. Pleasant (29464). (803) 881-9591. FAX: (803) 881-0666. Licensee: Charleston Signa Corp. Group owner: Bloomington Broadcasting Corp. Net: Unistar. Rep: Eastman. Format: Pure gold-oldies. Target aud: 25-54. ■ Sylvia Brown, gen mgr; Jeff Kautz, gen sls mgr; Cynthia Marry, prom mgr; T.J. Phillips, progmg dir; Gary Griffin, mus dir; Willie Bennett, chief engr. ■ Rates: $42; 35; 42; 15.

***WYFH(FM)**—July 7, 1984: 90.7 mhz; 50 kw. Ant 492 ft. TL: N32 58 23 W80 13 54. Stereo. 10870 Dorchester Rd., Summerville (29485). (803) 875-9095. Licensee: Bible Broadcasting Network (group owner). Net: Bible Bcstg

Net. Format: Relg, Christian. ■ Lowell Davey, pres; Dewey Godwin, gen mgr; Joe Papp, chief engr.

North Myrtle Beach

WGSN(AM)—April 1, 1983: 900 khz; 500 w-U, DA-2. TL: N33 49 26 W78 45 59. Box 4059, 429 Pine Ave. (29582). (803) 249-5451. FAX: (803) 249-7823. Licensee: Ocean Drive Communications Inc. (acq 10-27-93; $2 million with co-located FM; FTR 11-8-93). Net: ABC/I. Format: Adult contemp. ■ Matt Sedota, pres.

WNMB(FM)—Co-owned with WGSN(AM). Aug 15, 1972: 105.5 mhz; 3 kw. Ant 355 ft. TL: N33 49 19 W78 46 18. Stereo. (803) 249-3441. News staff one. Target aud: 25-54.

Orangeburg

WIGL(FM)—Oct 10, 1987: 102.9 mhz; 3 kw. Ant 300 ft. TL: N33 27 53 W80 56 42. Stereo. Box 1546, 504 River Dr., Rowsville (29133). (803) 536-1710. Licensee: Eagle Radio. Group owner: Eagle Communications (acq 12-3-87). Net: CNN, Unistar. Rep: Dora-Clayton. Format: Country. News staff one; news progmg 10 hrs wkly. Target aud: 25-54. Spec prog: Relg. ■ Charlie Boswell, pres & gen mgr; Russ T. Fender, progmg dir; Ed Noyes, chief engr.

WJZS(AM)—Dec 9, 1964: 1150 khz; 5 kw-D, 500 w-N, DA-2. TL: N33 31 26 W80 53 08. Hrs opn: 24. 178 Middleton St. (29115). (803) 531-1150. FAX: (803) 534-4835. Licensee: O'Brien Broadcast Services Inc. (acq 2-4-93; $80,000; FTR 2-22-93). Net: ABC. Format: News, talk. News progmg 23 hrs wkly. Target aud: 25-54. Spec prog: Farm 3 hrs wkly. ■ Melissa O'Brien, pres & gen mgr; Michael O'Brien, chief opns; John Bocock, gen sls mgr & mktg dir; Bob Fee, prom dir, progmg dir & mus dir; J. Michael Thomas, engrg dir. ■ Rates: $14; 10; 14; 3.

WKSO(FM)—September 1973: 103.9 mhz; 3 kw. Ant 299 ft. TL: N33 26 23 W80 41 11 (CP: 9.2 kw, ant 531 ft.). Stereo. 645 Church St., Suite 400, Norfolk, VA (23510). (803) 739-6905. FAX: (803) 739-6910. Licensee: Orangeburg Broadcasting Inc. Group owner: Willis Broadcasting Corp. Format: Urban contemp. ■ L.E. Willis, pres; Donzella Hendrix, gen mgr, gen sls mgr, prom mgr, progmg dir & mus dir; Michael Thomas, chief engr.

WPJK(AM)—Nov 3, 1958: 1580 khz; 1 kw-D. TL: N33 28 43 W80 52 46. 175 Cannon Bridge Rd. (29115). (803) 534-4848. Licensee: Radio Orangeburg Partnership (acq 6-86). Net: USA. Format: Relg, urban contemp. ■ Bose Gowdy, pres, gen mgr & chief engr; Rev. Pinckney Palmer Jr., opns mgr; Pat Glaster, gen sls mgr; Billy Dash, progmg dir, mus dir & news dir.

***WSSB-FM**—Mar 15, 1985: 90.3 mhz; 90 kw. Ant 225 ft. TL: N33 29 55 W80 50 30. Stereo. Hrs opn: 24. Box 7656 (29117). (803) 536-8196. FAX: (803) 533-3652. Licensee: South Carolina State University. Format: Black, urban contemp, gospel. News staff one; news progmg 7 hrs wkly. Target aud: 8-65. Spec prog: Jazz 10 hrs, reggae 4 hrs, blues 2 hrs, rap 4 hrs wkly. ■ Gil Harris, gen mgr; Dawna Diggs, progmg dir & news dir; Marion White, mus dir; Ken Durst, chief engr.

WTCB(FM)—July 6, 1967: 106.7 mhz; 100 kw. Ant 787 ft. TL: N33 46 52 W80 55 14. Stereo. Box 5106, Columbia (29250); 1801 Charleston Hwy., Cayce (29033). (803) 796-7600. FAX: (803) 796-9291. Licensee: Radio South Carolina Inc. Group owner: Bloomington Broadcasting Corp. (acq 9-19-89; $4,345,000; FTR 8-28-89). Rep: Christal. Format: Adult contemp. Target aud: 25-54; affluent, upscale young adults. ■ William L. McElveen, pres & gen mgr; Ken Watts, gen sls mgr; Billy Mac, prom mgr; Doug Spets, progmg dir; Ed Noyes, chief engr. ■ Rates: $90; 80; 85; 45.

Pageland

WMAP-FM—Feb 22, 1975: 102.3 mhz; 3 kw. Ant 280 ft. TL: N34 45 53 W80 15 43. Stereo. Box 5 (29728); Rt. One, Mt. Croghan (29727). (803) 623-6170. FAX: (803) 623-6170. Licensee: Roldan Broadcasting Corp. (acq 6-15-89; $560,000; FTR 6-19-89). Rep: T N. Format: CHR. News staff one; news progmg one hr wkly. Spec prog: Black 2 hrs, relg 5 hrs wkly. ■ Adolf Roldan, pres; James Roldan, prom mgr; Larry Schropp, chief engr.

Pamplico

WMXT(FM)—Nov 1, 1990: 102.1 mhz 50 kw. Ant 500 ft. TL: N34 04 56 W79 37 19 (CP: Ant 492 ft.). Stereo. Hrs opn: 24. Box 13468, 2704 S. Irby St., Florence (29505).
(803) 661-5000. FAX: (803) 661-0888. Licensee: Pamplico Broadcasting L.P. (acq 11-20-89). Net: ABC/FM. Rep: Rgnl Reps. Wash atty: Fletcher, Heald & Hildreth. Format: Adult contemp. News staff 2; news progmg 3 hrs wkly. Target aud: 25-54. ■ Edward F. Seeger, gen mgr; John Peace, opns mgr & progmg dir; Kenny Bilton, gen sls mgr; Earl Taylor, prom dir; Brad Means, news dir; Jerry Smith, chief engr. ■ Rates: $42; 36; 42; 25.

Parris Island

WOCW(FM)—July 1985: 92.1 mhz; 3 kw. Ant 284 ft. TL: N32 21 37 W80 35 37 (CP: 6 kw, ant 328 ft., TL: N32 21 26 W80 35 27). Stereo. Hrs opn: 24. Box 2387, Beaufort (29901-2387). (803) 524-9236; (803) 524-9210. FAX: (803) 524-1120. Licensee: O.C. Welch Broadcasting Corp. (acq 8-30-90; $387,500; FTR 9-3-90). Format: Oldies. News staff one; news progmg 4 hrs wkly. Target aud: 25-54; resort/active lifestyle. ■ O.C. Welch III, chmn & pres; Jane Welch, vp; Robert Gainey, gen mgr & gen sls mgr; Jon Allen, progmg dir & progmg mgr; Joe Speed, news dir; C.B. Gaffney, chief engr. ■ Rates: $20; 20; 20; 15.

Pawley's Island

WDAI(FM)—Oct 2, 1993. 98.5 mhz; 6 kw. Ant 328 ft. TL: N33 32 07 W79 03 50. Stereo. Hrs opn: 24. 700 J S. Kings Hwy., Surfside Beach (29575). (803) 238-0985. FAX: (803) 238-5882. Licensee: Carocom Media. Net: AP. Format: Full service adult contemp. News staff one; news progmg 6 hrs wkly. Target aud: 25-54. Spec prog: Sports 10 hrs wkly. ■ Ron McKay, gen mgr; Martha Prince, gen sls mgr; Darlene Skipper, news dir.

WSEA(FM)—Not on air, target date unknown: 100.3 mhz; 3 kw. Ant 328 ft. TL: N33 26 20 W79 08 11. Licensee: Audrey R. Morris.

Pickens

WTBI(AM)—Aug 3, 1967: 1540 khz; 10 kw-D. TL: N34 51 37 W82 43 25. Box 837 (29671). (803) 878-0348. Licensee: Tabernacle Christian Schools (acq 11-83; $150,000; FTR 11-83). Net: S.C. Net. Format: Christian. ■ Dr. Harold B. Sightler, pres; Pierre Allston, Charles Creager Sr. (asst), gen mgrs; Charles Creager Sr., gen sls mgr; Angela Honeycutt, prom dir.

Port Royal

WNCK(FM)—July 15, 1988: 99.7 mhz; 100 kw. Ant 1,250 ft. TL: N32 25 10 W80 28 30. Stereo. Hrs opn: 24. One St. Augustine Pl., Hilton Head Island (29928). (800) 768-7500; (803) 785-9569. FAX: (803) 842-3369. Licensee: Barnacle Broadcasting Ltd. Format: American music classics. News staff one; news progmg 3 hrs wkly. ■ Lee Simmons, pres; Fred Germann, gen mgr; Harry Gillman, gen sls mgr. ■ Rates: $30; 47; 28; 24.

Ravenel

WMGL(FM)—February 1986: 101.7 mhz; 3 kw. Ant 482 ft. TL: N32 46 44 W80 10 37 (CP: 6.5 kw, ant 689 ft., TL: N32 38 59 W80 19 00). Stereo. Hrs opn: 24. Suite 4, 60 Markfield Dr., Charleston (29407). (803) 556-8881. FAX: (803) 769-0876. Licensee: Southwind Communications Inc. (acq 8-13-92; $400,000; FTR 8-31-92). Net: ABC/C. Rep: Katz & Powell. Wash atty: Cole, Raywid & Braverman. Format: New adult contemp. News staff 2; news progmg 6 hrs wkly. Target aud: 25-54; upscale adults. ■ Bill Lucas, pres; Anthony Keith, opns mgr. ■ Rates: $30; 20; 30; 10.

Ridgeland

WNFO(AM)—1964: 1430 khz; 1 kw-D, 880 w-N. TL: N32 28 07 W81 00 15 (CP: 630 w-D). 9B Wanderer Ln., Hilton Head Island (29928). Licensee: Walter M. Cruza (acq 7-9-91; $22,500; FTR 7-29-91). Format: Vistor Info. ■ Chip Chambers, gen mgr; Stu Wright, prom mgr.

WSHG(FM)—Licensed to Ridgeland. See Hilton Head Island.

Rock Hill

WAGL(AM)—See Lancaster.

WAVO(AM)—May 18, 1948: 1150 khz; 1 kw-D, 2.6 kw-N. TL: N34 57 02 W81 00 16. Hrs opn: 24. Box 1024 (29731); 456 Pineview Rd. (29730). (803) 596-1240. FAX: (803) 329-1177, ext. 408. Licensee: WHVN Inc. Group owner: GHB Radio Group (acq 2-4-92; $115,000; FTR 2-24-92). Net: ABC, Moody, USA. Format: Relg. News staff one;
news progmg 15 hrs wkly. Target aud: 25-54; career-oriented. ■ Tom Gentry, stn mgr & gen sls mgr; Scott Scarbrough, progmg dir; Brant Hart, mus dir; Stu Albert, chief engr. ■ Rates: $15; 10; 11.50; 9.50.

WBZK(AM)—See York.

WBZK-FM—See Chester.

***WNSC-FM**—Jan 3, 1978: 88.9 mhz; 100 kw. Ant 600 ft. TL: N34 50 24 W81 01 07. Stereo. 1101 George Rogers Blvd., Columbia (29201). (803) 737-3420. Licensee: South Carolina Educational Television Commission. Net: NPR; SECA. Format: Fine arts. ■ Henry J. Cauthen, pres & gen mgr; Jesse Bowers, vp.

WRHI(AM)—Dec 14, 1944: 1340 khz; 1 kw-U. TL: N34 54 51 W81 00 42. Box 307 (29731); 142 N. Confederate Ave. (29730). (803) 324-1340. FAX: (803) 324-2860. Licensee: Our Three Sons Broadcasting (acq 10-1-84). Net: ABC, NBC Talknet; S.C. Net. Format: Adult contemp—emphasis on news, sports. News staff 3. Target aud: 25-50. ■ Allan M. Miller, Manning M. Kimmel, gen mgrs; Bill Rice, opns mgr, progmg dir & mus dir; Carl East, news dir; Ron Tallison, chief engr. ■ Rates: $14; 12; 14; 10.

St. Andrews

WMFX(FM)—Licensed to St. Andrews. See Columbia.

St. George

WBUB(FM)—(North Charleston). Jan 5, 1971: 107.5 mhz; 100 kw. Ant 984 ft. TL: N33 05 11 W80 22 33. Stereo. Suite 1600, 4995 Lacross Rd. (29406). (803) 566-1100. Licensee: Lowcountry Media Inc. (acq 7-14-91; $1.0 million with WQIZ(AM) St. George; FTR 7-29-91). Rep: McGavren Guild. Format: Country. News staff one. Target aud: 25-54. ■ C.A. Barton, vp & gen sls mgr; Charlie Lindsey, progmg dir; Jim Gooden, news dir; Bruce Roberts, chief engr.

WQIZ(AM)—Aug 23, 1962: 810 khz; 5 kw-D. TL: N33 08 51 W80 33 47. Box 903 (29477). (803) 563-2337. FAX: (803) 529-1933. Licensee: Lowcountry Media Inc. (acq 7-14-91; $1.5 million with WBUB(FM) North Charleston; FTR 7-29-91). Format: Gospel. ■ Ron Hoover, pres; Buddy Barton, gen mgr; Bob Brown, stn mgr; Sabrena Gerideau, mus dir; Bruce Roberts, chief engr.

St. Matthews

WQKI(AM)—Aug 15, 1975: 710 khz; 1 kw-D, DA. TL: N33 37 04 W80 46 50. Box 777 (29135). (803) 874-2777; (803) 534-2777. FAX: (803) 874-2777. Licensee: Robert & Lucille Newsham (acq 12-20-89; $210,000; FTR 1-8-90). Net: AP. Rep: Dora-Clayton, New England. Format: Urban contemp. ■ Robert W. Newsham, pres & gen mgr; Andy Henderson, mus dir; Ron Shuler, news dir.

St. Stephen

WTUA(FM)—May 1990: 106.1 mhz; 3 kw. Ant 328 ft. TL: N33 29 36 W79 53 21. Box 1103 (29479). (803) 567-2091. FAX: (803) 567-3088. Licensee: George Wells. Format: Gospel. ■ Terris Greene, gen mgr.

Saluda

WJRQ(FM)—May 23, 1987: 92.1 mhz; 3 kw. Ant 328 ft. TL: N34 02 48 W81 47 01. Stereo. Rt. One, Box 22 (29138). (803) 445-2277. FAX: (803) 445-3333. Licensee: Durst Broadcasting Co. Inc. (acq 4-86; $5,301.22; FTR 3-17-86). Net: Unistar. Format: Country. Spec prog: Farm 2 hrs wkly. ■ W.K. Durst, pres & gen mgr; Liz Durst, gen sls mgr; Roy Amick, prom mgr, mus dir & news dir; Bill Ladneck, progmg dir; Ken Durst, chief engr.

Sans Souci

WHYZ(AM)—Licensed to Sans Souci. See Greenville.

Scranton

WSQN(FM)—1991: 102.9 mhz; 2.9 kw. Ant 466 ft. TL: N34 00 39 W79 45 24. Box 103000, Florence (29501). (803) 667-9569. FAX: (803) 673-7390. Licensee: Scranton Communications Inc. Format: Soft contemp. ■ Harold Miller, gen mgr.

Seneca

WSNW(AM)—June 1, 1949: 1150 khz; 1 kw-D. TL: N34 41 11 W82 59 27. Hrs opn: Sunrise-sunset. Box 793 11071 N. Station Rd. (29679). (803) 882-2388. FAX: (803) 882-1837. Licensee: Blue Ridge Broadcasting Co.

Inc. Net: CBS Spectrum. Format: Btfl mus, big band. News staff one; news progmg 12 hrs wkly. Target aud: 45 plus; Mature adults, retired community. ■ C. Wayne Gallimore, pres; Dianne G. Dorris, vp; Francis A. Gaillard, stn mgr & progmg dir; Kyle Sims, prom mgr, news dir & pub affrs dir; Ted McCall, chief engr. ■ Rates: $7.50; 6.50; 7.50; na.

WBFM(FM)—Co-owned with WSNW(AM). June 6, 1953: 98.1 mhz; 100 kw. Ant 905 ft. TL: N34 41 11 W82 59 27. Stereo. Hrs opn: 5:30 AM-midnight. Net: CBS. Format: Oldies, adult contemp. News staff one; news progmg 6 hrs wkly. Target aud: 25-54; female oriented. ■ Francis Gaillard, opns mgr. ■ Rates: $42; 28; 28; 28.

Simpsonville

WFIS(AM)—See Fountain Inn.

Socastee

WMYB(FM)—Not on air, target date unknown: 99.5 mhz; 14.5 kw. Ant 430 ft. TL: N33 49 30 W78 51 47. 11560 Rolling Green Ct., Reston, VA(22091). Licensee: Puritan Radiocasting Co. (acq 1-30-91; FTR 2-18-91).

South Congaree

WFMV(FM)—Not on air, target date unknown: 95.3 mhz; 3 kw. Ant 328 ft. 820 Royal Tower, Irmo (29063). Licensee: Glory Communications.

Spartanburg

WASC(AM)—Jan 15, 1968: 1530 khz; 1 kw-D, 250 w-CH. TL: N34 56 58 W81 57 33. Box 5686 (29304); 840 Wofford (29301). (803) 585-1530. FAX: (803) 573-7790. Licensee: New South Broadcasting Corp. (acq 2-9-76). Net: Natl Black, ABC/C. Rep: Group W Radio Sls. Format: Black. ■ Sam E. Floyd, pres; K. Joseph Sessoms, gen mgr & chief engr; Lou Broadus, progmg dir & mus dir.

WORD(AM)—September 1940: 910 khz; 5 kw-D, 1 kw-N, DA-2. TL: N34 59 05 W81 57 55 (CP: 3.6 kw-D, 890 w-N, TL: N35 01 10 W82 00 36). Box 1330, Greenville (29602); 505 Rutherford St. (29602). (803) 271-9200. FAX: (803) 242-1567. Licensee: Multimedia Inc. (group owner; acq 4-3-90; $65,000; FTR 4-23-90). Net: NBC; ABC; MBS; NBC Talknet. Rep: Katz. Wash atty: Dow, Lohnes & Albertson. Format: News/talk. News staff 2; news progmg 30 hrs wkly. Target aud: 25-54. Spec prog: Furman University football and basketball, Atlanta Braves baseball, Spartanburg High School football. ■ Pat A. Servodidio, pres; Ray Cal, gen mgr; Jim Burnside, opns mgr; Gene Kendrick, gen sls mgr; Tony Brooks, rgnl sls mgr; Bruce Cole, mktg dir; Mike Gallagher, progmg mgr; Jerry Massey, chief engr.

WSPA(AM)—Feb 17, 1930: 950 khz; 5 kw-U, DA-N. TL: N34 58 35 W81 59 20. Box 1717, 224 East Main St. (29304). (803) 585-9500; (803) 585-9999. FAX: (803) 594-4608. Licensee: Spartan Radiocasting Co. (group owner). Net: CBS. Rep: McGavren Guild. Format: News/talk. News staff 2. Target aud: 35-64. ■ Walter J. Brown, CEO; Nick Evan, pres; Jack West, gen mgr; Greg McKinney, opns mgr; Rhita Nance, gen sls mgr; Dave Welchel (asst.), prom dir; Dave Welchel, mus dir; Craig Turner, chief engr.

WSPA-FM—Aug 29, 1946: 98.9 mhz; 100 kw. Ant 1,910 ft. TL: N35 10 12 W82 17 27. Stereo. Prog sep from AM. Net: AP. Format: Lite adult contemp. Spec prog: Class 2 hrs, relg 3 hrs wkly. ■ Jack Sapp, opns mgr; Rod Duckett, gen sls mgr; Bob Lowry, mus dir. ■ WSPA-TV affil.

WYYR(AM)—Sept 1, 1952: 1400 khz; 1 kw-U. TL: N34 58 26 W81 55 37. Box 5416 (29304). 340 Gardner Rd. (29304). (803) 573-1400. FAX: (803) 583-3786. Licensee: Associated Broadcasting Corp. (group owner; acq 10-4-90; $95,000; FTR 10-29-90). Net: ABC/E, USA. Format: Gospel. News staff one; Target aud: General. Spec prog: Ger 2 hrs wkly. ■ T.C. Lewis, CEO & chmn; Joyce Lewis, vp; Scott Davis, stn mgr, progmg dir & mus dir; Steve Boiter, news dir; Lee Griffin Jr., pub affrs dir; Don Gowens, vp engrg.

Summerton

WLJI(FM)—Not on air, target date unknown: 95.5 mhz; 6 kw. Ant 328 ft. Box 1552, Rt. 4, Manning (29102). Licensee: Summer Town Partners.

Summerville

WAZS(AM)—June 7, 1963: 980 khz; 1 kw-D, 131 w-N. TL: N33 01 56 W80 11 58. Box 859 (29484); U.S. Hwy. 78 W. (29483). (803) 875-4411. Licensee: Radio Summerville Inc. (acq 2-22-91). Net: NBC. Format: Country. News staff one; news progmg 9 hrs wkly. Target aud: 24 plus. ■ W. L. Phillips, pres & gen mgr; Wayne Lanier, gen sls mgr; Audreyette Phillips, progmg dir & mus dir; Phil Rodgers, news dir; Berry Walters, chief engr.

WWWZ(FM)—May 10, 1974: 93.5 mhz; 1.1 kw. Ant 459 ft. TL: N32 56 55 W80 12 32 (CP: 1.5 kw). Box 30669, Charleston (29407). (803) 556-9132. Licensee: Millenium Communications of Charleston Inc. (acq 1-1-81; $1,050,000; FTR 4-2-84). Net: Natl Black. Rep: PRO Radio. Format: Urban contemp. ■ Cliff Fletcher, pres, gen mgr & mus dir; Dean Mutter, gen sls mgr; George Hamilton, progmg dir; Patrice Smith, news dir; Gary Robbins, chief engr.

Sumter

WDXY(AM)—May 23, 1960: 1240 khz; 1 kw-U. TL: N33 54 16 W80 19 25. Box 1269 (29151). (803) 775-2321. FAX: (803) 773-4856. Licensee: Raymond F. Reich. Rep: Southern. Wash atty: Reddy, Begley & Martin. Format: MOR. News staff one; news progmg 6 hrs wkly. Target aud: 35 plus. ■ Raymond Reich, pres & gen mgr; Barbara Hill, sls mgr; Jim O'Neill, mus dir; Cheryl Hall, news dir; Tommy Dubose, chief engr. ■ Rates: $24; 18; 24; 18.

WICI(FM)—Not on air, target date unknown: 94.7 mhz; 3 kw. Ant 328 ft. 294 Bultman Dr. (29150). Licensee: Iris Communications Inc.

WQMC(AM)—March 16, 1940: 1290 khz; 1 kw-U, DA-N. TL: N33 55 16 W80 16 59. Hrs opn: 16. Box 1569 (29151). (803) 775-1290. FAX: (803) 773-3687. Licensee: Morris College. Format: Gospel. News staff one; news progmg 4 hrs wkly. Target aud: General; working adults & retirees. Spec prog: Farm 2 hrs, class 15 hrs, third world 2 hrs wkly. ■ Janet Clayton, gen mgr; Robert Edwards, sls dir; Samuel Lewis, progmg dir.

*WRJA-FM—Aug 25, 1975: 88.1 mhz; 98 kw. Ant 1,000 ft. TL: N33 52 32 W80 16 14. Stereo. 1101 George Rogers Blvd., Columbia (29201). (803) 773-5546; (803) 737-3420. FAX: (803) 775-1059. Licensee: South Carolina Educational TV Commission. Net: NPR. Format: Fine arts. ■ Henry J. Cauthen, pres; Tom Fowler, stn mgr; Alfred Turner, progmg dir; Paul Zweimiller, chief engr.

WSSC(AM)—Apr 27, 1953: 1340 khz; 1 kw-U. TL: N33 55 45 W80 19 29. Hrs opn: 6 AM-midnight. 201 Oswego Rd. (29150). (803) 778-2355. FAX: (803) 773-4875. Licensee: Mid Carolina Communications Inc. (acq 4-8-77). Net: NBC; S.C. Net. Format: Oldies. Target aud: 25-54. ■ Charles A. Barton, pres; Bob Burr, gen mgr, gen sls mgr, progmg dir & mus dir.

WWDM(FM)—1961: 101.3 mhz; 100 kw. Ant 1,322 ft. TL: N33 52 52 W80 16 14. Stereo. Hrs opn: 24. Box 9127 (29290). (803) 776-1013; (803) 495-2258. FAX: (803) 695-8608. Licensee: Threshold Broadcasting Co. Net: Unistar. Rep: D & R Radio. Format: Urban contemp. News staff one; news progmg 6 hrs wkly. Target aud: 18-49. ■ John Marshall, pres; Billie Grooms, gen mgr; Alex Snipes, gen sls mgr; Andre Carson, progmg dir & mus dir; Brenda Jones, news dir; John Scott, chief engr.

Surfside Beach-Garden City

WYAK(AM)—June 27, 1980: 1270 khz; 5 kw-D, 500 w-N, DA-2. TL: N33 34 32 W79 02 29. Hrs opn: 24. Box 15401, Surfside Beach (29587); Hwy. 707, Murrells Inlet (29576). (803) 651-7936. FAX: (803) 651-6840. Licensee: Multi-Market Radio of Myrtle Beach Inc. (acq 4-16-93; grpsl; FTR 5-3-93). Net: MBS. Rep: Christal. Wash atty: Fisher, Wayland, Cooper & Leader. Format: Country. News staff one; news progmg 4 hrs wkly. Target aud: 25-54. ■ Gary Morris, gen mgr; Mark Kravetz, gen sls mgr; Dave Priest, progmg dir, mus dir & news dir; Tab Allen, pub affrs dir; Buddy Womack, chief engr.

WYAK-FM—April 4, 1977: 103.1 mhz; 6 kw. Ant 325 ft. TL: N33 34 32 W79 02 29 (CP: 12.5 kw). Stereo. Hrs opn: 24. Dups AM 100%.

Travelers Rest

WDAB(AM)—Oct 12, 1964: 1580 khz; 5 kw-D. TL: N34 56 55 W82 26 38. Box 25276, Greenville (29616). (803) 834-2898. FAX: (803) 834-2997. Licensee: Dabney-Adamson Broadcasting Inc. (acq 3-31-93; $180,000; FTR 4-19-93). Net: USA. Format: All news. ■ Michael Adamson, pres, gen mgr, progmg dir & news dir; Don Goings, chief engr. ■ Rates: $11; 10; 11; na.

WBCU-AM 1460
Union County's Radio Station

Union

WBCU(AM)—Aug 27, 1949: 1460 khz; 1 kw-U, DA-N. TL: N34 43 10 W81 39 44. Hrs opn: 6 AM-10 PM. Box 70, 210 E. Main (29379). (803) 427-2411. FAX: (803) 427-2412. Licensee: Broadcasting Co. of Union Inc. (acq 10-52). Net: ABC; S.C. Net. Rep: Dora-Clayton. Format: Contemporary country. News staff 2; news progmg 24 hrs wkly. Target aud: 30 plus; working class adult buyers. Spec prog: Sports 10 hrs, news/talk 10 hrs wkly. ■ Douglas M. Sutton Jr., pres, gen mgr & gen sls mgr; Philip M. Hobbs, opns mgr & progmg dir; Robert Colson, mus dir; William Christopher, news dir & pub affrs dir; Danny Taylor, chief engr. ■ Rates: $8; 7.60; 7; 5.

Walhalla

WGOG(AM)—Apr 15, 1959: 1000 khz; 1 kw-D. TL: N34 44 29 W83 04 18. Hrs opn: 8 AM-5:30 PM. Box 10 (29691). (803) 638-3616. FAX: (803) 638-7975. Licensee: Appalachian Broadcasting Co. Inc. (acq 12-1-84; $455,000; FTR 9-24-84). Net: NBC. Rep: T N, Midsouth. Format: Gospel, relg. News staff 2; news progmg 6 hrs wkly. Target aud: 25-64; emphasis on women. ■ Luzanne M. Griffith, pres & gen mgr; Marvin Hill, gen sls mgr; Jeff Grant, mus dir; Dick Mangrum, news dir; Jim Graham, chief engr. ■ Rates: $10.50; 8; 10.50; na.

WGOG-FM—Sept 1, 1991: 96.3 mhz; 6 kw. Ant 328 ft. TL: N34 51 33 W83 03 31. Hrs opn: 24. (Acq 3-22-91; FTR 4-15-91). Net: S.C. Net. Format: Adult contemp, oldies. News progmg 15 hrs wkly. Target aud: 25-54; more male, average age 45, income $40,000 plus. ■ Luzanne Griffith, pres; Marvin Hill, stn mgr & gen sls mgr; George Allgood, prom mgr & progmg dir; Dough Stephens, mus dir; Dick Mangrum, news dir; Jim Graham, chief engr. ■ Rates: $15.75; 11.50; 15.75; 9.20.

Walterboro

WALD(AM)—August 1947: 1080 khz; 2.5 kw-D. TL: N32 52 52 W80 41 24. Box 1621 (29488). (803) 538-4000. FAX: (803) 538-4001. Licensee: Holiday Communications Inc. (acq 6-3-93; $140,000; FTR 6-21-93). Net: ABC; S.C. Net. Format: Gospel. ■ D. Holiday, gen mgr.

WONO(FM)—Dec 13, 1991: 93.7 mhz; 6 kw. Ant 345 ft. TL: N32 49 54 W80 43 30. Hrs opn: 24. Box 1105, 724 S. Jeffries Blvd. (29488). (803) 549-1543; (803) 549-2000. FAX: (803) 549-2711. Licensee: Greene Communications of S.C. Inc. (acq 7-20-93; $220,000; FTR 8-9-93). Wash atty: Fisher, Wayland, Cooper & Leader. Format: Country. News staff one; news progmg 5 hrs wkly. Target aud: 25-54; adults. ■ Terry O'Quinn, CEO & mus dir; Daniel Greene Jr., gen mgr & opns mgr; Heather S. Simmons, stn mgr, sls dir, natl sls mgr, rgnl sls mgr & adv mgr; Karen A. Nettles, progmg dir & progmg mgr; Marc Haley, news dir & pub affrs dir; Klein Beach, chief engr. ■ Rates: $15; 15; 15; 12.

WPAL-FM—September 1968: 100.9 mhz; 3 kw. Ant 300 ft. TL: N32 52 52 W80 41 24. Stereo. 1717 Wappol Rd., Charleston (29407). (803) 763-6330. FAX: (803) 769-4857; (803) 852-5588. Licensee: William Saunders (acq 11-30-93; $150,000; FTR 12-20-93). Format: Urban contemp. ■ William Saunders, gen mgr; Tanya Smith, gen sls mgr; Donzella Hendricks, news dir; Kline Beach, chief engr.

Wedgefield

WIBZ(FM)—Mar 1, 1985: 95.5 mhz; 3 kw. Ant 300 ft. TL: N33 51 14 W80 31 47. Stereo. Hrs opn: 24. Box 1269, 51 Commerce St., Sumter (29150). (803) 773-1859. FAX: (803) 773-4856. Licensee: Raymond F. Reich (acq 10-1-91; $220,200; FTR 10-28-91). Net: ABC/D. Rep: Rgnl Reps. Wash atty: Reddy, Begley & Martin. Format: Adult contemp. News staff one. Target aud: 18-49. ■ Raymond Reich, pres & gen mgr; Barbara Hill, gen sls mgr; Don Vandervort, progmg dir; Tommy Dubose, chief engr. ■ Rates: $24; 18; 24; 18.

West Columbia

WHKZ(FM)—See Columbia.

Stations in the U.S.

WSCQ(FM)—Licensed to West Columbia. See Columbia.

WTGH(AM)—See Cayce.

Williston

WAAW(FM)—Not on air, target date unknown: 94.7 mhz; 2.11 kw. Ant 561 ft. TL: N33 28 33 W81 32 57. Box 580, Yarmouth Rd., Yarmouth, ME (04096). Licensee: Bay Communications Inc. ■ Robert J. Cole, pres.

Woodruff

WJKI(AM)—July 7, 1967: 1510 khz; 1 kw-D, 250 w-N. TL: N34 45 22 W82 03 18. Box 576 (29388). (803) 476-8189. FAX: (803) 476-3902. Licensee: Jackie Cooper Media Inc. (acq 6-1-89). Net: ABC/D. Format: Relg. Target aud: General. Spec prog: Black 12 hrs wkly. ■ Furman Boyce, pres & gen mgr; Donna Stokes, stn mgr. ■ Rates: $8; 8; 8; na.

York

WBZK(AM)—April 19, 1956: 980 khz; 3.15 kw-D, 291 w-N, DA-2. TL: N34 59 50 W81 15 09. Hrs opn: 5 AM-midnight. Box 398, Hwy. 321 Bypass (29745). (803) 684-4241; (803) 684-9941. FAX: (803) 684-4242. Licensee: York-Clover Broadcasting Co. Inc. Net: NBC the Source. Rep: Rgnl Reps. Format: Beach & oldies. News progmg 6 hrs wkly. Target aud: 22-50. Spec prog: Farm one hr, Black 4 hrs wkly. ■ C. Curtis Sigmon, pres, gen mgr & chief engr; Jeff Sigmon, opns dir, progmg dir & mus dir; Bruce Ferrell, news dir. ■ Rates: $19; 15; 19; 13.

South Dakota

LAUREN A. COLBY
301-663-1086
COMMUNICATIONS ATTORNEY
Special Attention to Difficult Cases

Aberdeen

KGIM(AM)—September 1933: 1420 khz; 1 kw-D, 232 w-N. TL: N45 29 07 W98 29 46. Box 306, 349 Berkshire Plaza (57401). (605) 229-3632. FAX: (605) 229-4849. Licensee: ALROX Inc. (acq 6-4-82; $195,000; FTR 6-21-82). Net: NBC. Rep: Katz & Powell. Wash atty: Fisher, Wayland, Cooper & Leader. Format: Country, news. News staff one; news progmg 30 hrs wkly. Target aud: General; 25 plus. Spec prog: Farm 12 hrs wkly. ■ Allen D. Rau, pres & gen mgr; Phil Duchscher, gen sls mgr; Bill Hild, prom mgr & mus dir; Scott Solberg, progmg dir; Doug Haynie, news dir. ■ Rates: $22; 22; 22; 19.

KKAA(AM)—Sept 12, 1974: 1560 khz; 10 kw-D, 5 kw-N, DA-2. TL: N45 25 05 W98 28 36. 3980 South Dakota St. (57401). (605) 225-1560. FAX: (605) 225-4564. Licensee: CD Broadcasting Corp. (group owner; acq 9-18-90; $850,000 with co-located FM; FTR 10-8-90). Net: SMN. Rep: Christal. Format: C&W. Spec prog: Farm 13 hrs wkly. ■ Deb O'Donnell, gen mgr; J.D. Harris, progmg dir; Mike Johnson, mus dir; Jim Monk, news dir.

KQAA(FM)—Co-owned with KKAA(AM). September 1979: 94.9 mhz; 100 kw. Ant 1,383 ft. TL: N45 06 32 W97 53 30 (CP: Ant 430 ft., TL: N45 25 05 W98 28 36). Stereo. Box 1770 (57401). (605) 226-0950. (Acq 5-87). Format: Oldies. ■ Pat Clark, progmg dir.

KSDN(AM)—April 16, 1947: 930 khz; 5 kw-D, 1 kw-N, DA-2. TL: N45 25 29 W98 31 03. Box 1930, Hwy. 281 (57402). (605) 225-5930. FAX: (605) 225-8290. Licensee: Green Bay Broadcasting Co. (acq 1975). Net: ABC; American Agri. Rep: McGavren Guild. Format: Adult contemp. Spec prog: Farm 15 hrs wkly. ■ William C. Laird, pres; Mike Levsen, stn mgr; Gene Reich, news dir; Doug Moore, chief engr.

KSDN-FM—Nov 18, 1979: 94.1 mhz; 100 kw. Ant 440 ft. TL: N45 25 27 W98 31 00. Stereo. Box 36 (54305). Format: Rock.

Belle Fourche

KBFS(AM)—July 22, 1959: 1450 khz; 1 kw-U. TL: N44 40 02 W103 51 22. Stereo. Hrs opn: 24. Box 787 (57717); 721 State St. (57717). (605) 892-2571. Licensee: KBFS Inc. Group owner: Lovcom Inc. (acq 6-1-83; $350,000; FTR 6-20-83). Net: SMN. Rep: Eastman/Intermountain. Format: Country, sports, news. News progmg 20 hrs wkly. Target aud: 25-54. Spec prog: Farm 10 hrs wkly. ■ Karl W. J. Grimmelmann III, gen mgr & gen sls mgr.

Brookings

KBRK(AM)—July 28, 1955: 1430 khz; 1 kw-D, 100 w-N. TL: N44 18 13 W96 46 10 (CP: N44 18 12 W96 46 01). 227 22nd Ave. S. (57006). (605) 692-1430. FAX: (605) 692-4441. Licensee: Dakota Broadcasting Inc. Group owner: Radio One Broadcasting. Net: NBC. Format: Big band, MOR, oldies. Spec prog: Farm 9 hrs wkly. ■ Raymond Lamb, chmn; Roger Dodson, pres; Chris Jesson, CFO; Tom Coughlin, gen mgr; Michael Quinn, progmg dir & mus dir; Dellas Cole, news dir; Robert Cook Jr., chief engr. ■ Rates: $10; 7.50; 7.50; 7.50.

KBRK-FM—Aug 10, 1968: 93.7 mhz; 36 kw. Ant 571 ft. TL: N44 20 22 W96 09 16. Hrs opn: 24. Prog sep from AM. Format: Adult contemp. Target aud: 20-45.

***KESD(FM)**—July 1967: 88.3 mhz; 50 kw. Ant 623 ft. TL: N44 20 10 W97 13 41. Stereo. South Dakota State Univ., 414 E. Clark St., Vermillion (57069). (605) 677-5861. Licensee: State Board of Directors for Educational TV. Net: NPR, APR, CMN. Format: News, classical. News staff 4. Target aud: 35-65; upscale, higher educated and arts-oriented. ■ Larry Roher, progmg dir; Janice Lehmkuhl, mus dir; Mike Johnson, chief engr. ■ *KESD-TV affil.

KJJQ(AM)—(Volga). May 6, 1981: 910 khz; 500 w-D, 1 kw-N, DA-2. TL: N44 15 01 W96 57 22. Box 790, 111 Main Ave., Brookings (57006). (605) 692-9125. FAX: (605) 692-6434. Licensee: CD Broadcasting of Brookings, S.D. Inc. Group owner: CD Broadcasting Corp. (acq 10-1-89; with co-located FM; FTR 9-7-89). Net: ABC/I; American Agri., S.D. News. Rep: Torbet. Format: Country. News staff one. ■ Mel Paradis, pres; Mark Tollefson, gen mgr; Garret Lysiak, chief engr. ■ Rates: $20; 18; 15; 10.

KKQQ(FM)—(Volga). Co-owned with KJJQ(AM). April 15, 1984: 102.3 mhz; 25 kw. Ant 234 ft. TL: N44 15 01 W96 57 22 (CP: 25 kw, ant 243 ft.). Stereo. Prog sep from AM. Format: Classic rock. Target aud: 18-49.

***KSDJ(FM)**—1993: 90.7 mhz. 1 kw. Ant 148 ft. TL: N44 19 01 W96 47 02. Hrs opn: 24. Box 057, USU (57007). Licensee: South Dakota State University. Format: Div, progsv, AOR. News staff one. Target aud: 17-22; college students that have a taste for new music. ■ Robert Wagner, CEO; Mark Sebert, gen mgr, stn mgr, dev dir & engrg dir.

Canton

KIXK(FM)—Not on air, target date unknown: 102.5 mhz; 3 kw. Ant 243 ft. TL: N43 17 05 W96 32 49. 100 Wexford Pl., Athens, GA (30606). Licensee: Dallas M. Tarkenton. Group owner: Contemporary Communications.

Custer

KFCR(AM)—May 1, 1988: 1490 khz; 830 w. TL: N43 43 03 W103 35 00. 437 Montgomery St. (57730). (605) 673-5327. Licensee: Mount Rushmore Broadcasting Inc. (acq 5-6-92; FTR 5-25-92). Net: SMN. Format: Country. ■ Conrad Slettom, gen mgr, gen sls mgr & progmg dir.

KACP(FM)—Co-owned with KFCR(AM). Not on air, target date unknown: 105.1 mhz; 6.5 kw. Ant 1,312 ft.

Deadwood

KDSJ(AM)—July 2, 1947: 980 khz; 5 kw-D, 1 kw-N, DA-N. TL: N44 22 57 W103 39 44. 745 Main (57732). (605) 578-1826. FAX: (605) 578-1033. Licensee: Goldrush Broadcasting (acq 7-1-82). Net: ABC/I; S.D. News Net. Format: Oldies, Top 40. Target aud: 25-50. ■ Al Decker, pres & gen mgr; Dwight Wagner, adv mgr; Bill Spitzer, chief engr. ■ Rates: $10; 10; 10; 8.

KSQY(FM)—Sept 4, 1982: 95.1 mhz; 100 kw. Ant 1,707 ft. TL: N44 19 49 W103 50 10. Stereo. Hrs opn: 24. Box D, 666 Main St. (57732); Creamery Mall, Suite D, 201 Main St., Rapid City (57701). (605) 578-3533; (605) 348-2217. FAX: (605) 348-9877. Licensee: Associated Investors Inc. (acq 1982). Net: Westwood One. Rep: Roslin. Wash atty: Roberts & Eckard. Format: AOR. News staff one; news progmg 2 hrs wkly. Target aud: 25-54; young, active adults within a 5 state region. Spec prog: Jazz 2 hrs wkly. ■ Houston Haugo, pres; Cynthia S. McNeill, gen mgr & gen sls mgr, mktg mgr & prom mgr; Jack Daniels, progmg dir; Jim Kallas, mus dir; Tom Collins, news dir; Bill Spitzer, chief engr. ■ Rates: $25; 23; 23; 18.

South Dakota

Faith

KPSD(FM)—June 1, 1989: 97.1 mhz; 100 kw. Ant 1,525 ft. TL: N45 03 14 W102 15 47. Box 5000, Dakota & Cherry Sts., Vermillion (57069). (605) 677-5861. Licensee: South Dakota Board of Directors for Educational Telecommunications. Format: Class, jazz, folk. ■ Don Checots, gen mgr.

Gregory

KVCX(FM)—May 8, 1982: 101.5 mhz; 100 kw. Ant 640 ft. TL: N43 07 41 W99 26 10. Stereo. Box 101, 220 W. Fifth St. (57533); 3434 W. Kilbourn Ave, Milwaukee WI (53208). (605) 835-8777. Licensee: Wisconsin Voice of Christian Youth Inc. (group owner; acq 4-87). Net: USA, Moody. Format: Relg. ■ Dr. Randall Melchert, pres; Vic Eliason, gen mgr; Dale Waters, opns mgr & prom mgr; Jim Schneider, progmg dir; Andrew Eliason, chief engr.

Hot Springs

KZMX(AM)—July 4, 1958: 580 khz; 500 w-D, 310 w-N. TL: N43 27 24 W103 28 34 (CP: 2.3 kw-D). Box 611 (57747). (605) 745-3637. Licensee: Mt. Rushmore Broadcasting Inc. (acq 5-20-93; $45,000 with co-located FM; FTR 6-14-93). Net: ABC/I. Format: Lite & easy. Spec prog: Farm 6 hrs wkly. ■ Tom McKee, progmg dir; Tony Roerick, chief engr.

KZMX-FM—Feb 10, 1981: 96.7 mhz; 3.4 kw. Ant 440 ft. TL: N43 26 34 W103 27 27. Stereo. Dups AM 100%.

Huron

KIJV(AM)—July 1, 1947: 1340 khz; 1 kw-U. TL: N44 20 46 W98 12 34. Hrs opn: 24. Box 1407, 1726 Dakota Ave. S. (57350). (605) 352-8621. Licensee: Dakota Broadcasting Co. Inc. Group owner: Radio One Broadcasting Inc. Net: AP. Format: MOR. News staff one. Target aud: 35 plus. ■ Raymond Lamb, CEO & chmn; Roger Dodson, pres; Bonita Tate, gen mgr; Ken Lindblad, progmg dir & mus dir; Monica Steele, news dir. ■ Rates: $14.50; 12.50; 12.50; 12.50.

KZNC(FM)—Co-owned with KIJV(AM). Nov 1, 1972: 92.1 mhz; 3 kw. Ant 184 ft. TL: N44 20 46 W98 12 34 (CP: 99.1 mhz, 91 kw, ant 804 ft., TL: N45 04 47 W98 37 09). Stereo. Format: Hot country. Target aud: 25-54. ■ Mike Jaqua, progmg dir. ■ Rates: $12.50; 10.50; 10.50; 10.50.

KOKK(AM)—Jan 13, 1976: 1210 khz; 5 kw-D, 1 kw-N, DA-2. TL: N44 21 44 W98 09 09. Hrs opn: 5:30 AM-midnight. Box 931, 1835 Dakota S. (57350). (605) 352-1933. FAX: (605) 352-0911. Licensee: Dakota Communications Ltd. Net: ABC/I. Rep: Katz & Powell. Format: C&W. News staff one; news progmg 20 hrs wkly. Target aud: 25 plus. Spec prog: Farm 5 hrs wkly. ■ Duane Butt, Barbra Butt, CEOs; Linda Marcus, gen mgr & gen sls mgr; Tim Omodt, chief opns & progmg dir; Jeff Duffy, mus dir; Mike Dramstad, news dir; Paul Derby, chief engr. ■ Rates: $8.50; 8.50; 8.50; 8.50.

KZKK(FM)—Not on air, target date unknown: 105.1 mhz; 6 kw. Ant 154 ft. TL: N44 21 44 W98 09 09. 1835 Dakota Ave. S. (57350). Licensee: Dakota Communications Ltd.

KZNC(FM)—Listing follows KIJV(AM).

Lemmon

KBJM(AM)—Apr 1, 1966: 1400 khz; 1 kw-U. TL: N45 55 05 W102 11 55. Hrs opn: 6 AM-9 PM. Box 540, 500 First Ave. E. (57638). (605) 374-5747. Licensee: Media Associates Inc. (acq 1-17-91; $108,240; FTR 2-4-91). Net: CNN. Rep: Keystone (unwired net), Walton. Format: C&W, oldies. Spec prog: Farm 10 hrs wkly. ■ Mike Schweitzer, pres & gen mgr; Robert Kelley, vp; Mike Shweitzer, stn mgr; Kevin Senger, gen sls mgr; Kathy Hess, prom mgr; Pat Sorenson, progmg dir & mus dir; Tim Kochel, chief engr. ■ Rates: $4.50; 4.50; 4.50; 4.50.

Little Eagle

***KAEN(FM)**—Not on air, target date unknown: 89.5 mhz; 90 kw. Ant 324 ft. Box 32 (57642). Licensee: Seventh Generation Media Services Inc.

Lowry

***KSQD-FM**—Not on air, target date unknown: 91.9 mhz; 100 kw. Ant 725 ft. TL: N45 16 34 W99 59 03. 414 E. Clark St., Vermillion (57069). Licensee: State Board of Directors for Educational Television. ■ Greg Schnirring, stn mgr.

Madison

KJAM(AM)—Dec 3, 1959: 1390 khz; 500 w-D, 62 w-N. TL: N44 00 37 W97 10 18. Hrs opn: 18. Box D, 101 S. Egan Ave. (57042). (605) 256-4515. Licensee: Madison Broadcasting Co. Inc. (acq 3-75). Net: AP. Rep: Roslin. Format: C&W, news/talk. Target aud: 21 plus. Spec prog: Farm 11 hrs wkly. ■ John A. Goeman, pres, gen mgr & chief engr; Dave Borman, gen sls mgr; Lorin Larsen, prom dir; Tom Roubik, progmg dir & mus dir; Dean Gehrels, news dir. ■ Rates: $24.65; 24.65; 24.65; 24.65.

KJAM-FM—Dec 17, 1967: 103.1 mhz; 6 kw. Ant 321 ft. TL: N43 59 08 W97 07 42. Stereo. Hrs opn: 18. Net: AP. Format: Country. News staff 2; news progmg 20 hrs wkly. Target aud: 21 plus. ■ Rates: Same as AM.

Martin

***KZSD-FM**—July 3, 1991: 102.5 mhz; 100 kw. Ant 754 ft. TL: N43 26 06 W101 33 14. Box 5000, Dakota & Cherry Sts., Vermillion (57069). (605) 677-5861. Licensee: South Dakota Board of Directors for Educational Telecommunications. Format: Class, jazz, folk. ■ Don Checots, gen mgr.

Milbank

KCGN-FM—(Ortonville, Minn). Sept 23, 1983: 101.5 mhz; 100 kw. Ant 1,001 ft. TL: N45 22 29 W97 02 20. Stereo. Box 101, Milbank, SD (57252). (605) 432-9571. FAX: (605) 432-9573. Licensee: C.G.N. Corp. (acq 4-27-86). Format: Christian, adult contemp. Target aud: 25 plus. Spec prog: Farm 6 hrs wkly. ■ Verlyn Menning, chmn & gen mgr; Alice Blum, sls dir & adv dir; Dean Robinson, progmg dir & news dir; Vicki Limberg, mus dir; Al Gilbertson, chief engr.

KMSD(AM)—Mar 20, 1975: 1510 khz; 5 kw-D. TL: N45 11 42 W96 38 18. Box 1005 (57252). (605) 432-5516. FAX: (605) 432-6325. Licensee: Success Broadcasting Corp. (acq 1-5-93; $540,000 with co-located FM; FTR 1-25-93). Net: ABC/I; S.D. Net., American Agri. Format: Oldies, news, talk. News staff one; news progmg 7 hrs wkly. Target aud: General. Spec prog: Farm 6 hrs wkly. ■ Daniel D. Scrensen, pres & stn mgr; Neil Bagas, news dir & pub affrs dir. ■ Rates: $12.75; 12.75; 12.75; na.

KPHR(FM)—Co-owned with KMSD(AM). Feb 4, 1991: 104.3 mhz; 100 kw. Ant 981 ft. TL: N45 10 31 W96 59 15. Stereo. Hrs opn: 24. Prog sep from AM. (605) 432-5518. FAX: (605) 432-4231. Format: Classic rock. Target aud: 18-45. Spec prog: Sports 5 hrs wkly. ■ Rates: $12.75; 12.75; 12.75; 12.75.

Mitchell

KMIT(FM)—Mar 10, 1975: 105.9 mhz; 100 kw. Ant 449 ft. TL: N43 41 25 W98 00 27. Stereo. Hrs opn: 24. Box 520, Suite 204, 119 E. 3rd Ave. (57301). (605) 996-9667. FAX: (605) 996-0013. Licensee: Mitchell Broadcasting Inc. (acq 9-1-84; FTR 12-31-84). Net: ABC/I, Unistar. Format: Country, oldies. News staff 2. Target aud: 25-54. Spec prog: Farm 18 hrs wkly. ■ Gordon Thomsen, pres; Tim Grivna, vp; Tim Smith, gen mgr; Terry Imus, sls dir; Sue Stulc, prom mgr; Joel VanDover, progmg dir; Rod Pattison, mus dir; Wayne Menning, news dir; Gerald Calhoun, chief engr. ■ Rates: $24.30; 20.70; 18.70; 17.50.

KORN(AM)—1947: 1490 khz; 1 kw-U. TL: N43 42 14 W97 59 57. Box 921 (57301). (605) 996-1490. FAX: (605) 996-6680. Licensee: Korn Palace Broadcasting Inc. (acq 11-1-75). Net: MBS, Westwood One. Format: Oldies. News staff one; news progmg 9 hrs wkly. Target aud: 35 plus; mature adults. Spec prog: Farm 10 hrs wkly. ■ Joseph R. Shields, pres, gen mgr, gen sls mgr & chief engr; J.P. Skelly, progmg dir; Doug Cunningham, mus dir; John Haglund, news dir.

KQRN(FM)—Co-owned with KORN(AM). Aug 17, 1980: 107.3 mhz; 100 kw. Ant 450 ft. TL: N43 41 46 W98 03 35. Stereo. Hrs opn: 5:30 AM-1 AM. Prog sep from AM. Format: Adult contemp, rock/AOR. News staff one; news progmg 4 hrs wkly Target aud: 18-35.

Mobridge

KOLY(AM)—Aug 10, 1956: 1300 khz; 5 kw-D, 111 w-N. TL: N45 32 07 W100 20 45. Hrs opn: 24. Box 400, 118 E. 3rd St. (57601). (605) 845-3654. FAX: (605) 845-3656. Licensee: Mobridge Broadcasting Corp. Net: ABC/E. Rep: Shelley & Katz. Format: Oldies. News staff one; news progmg 21 hrs wkly. Target aud: General. Spec prog: Farm, American Indian. ■ Nadine Coleman Gill, CEO & pres; Darrell Gill, gen mgr & gen sls mgr; John Schreier, progmg dir & mus dir; Sharon Martin, news dir; Rolland Cory, chief engr.

KOLY-FM—Oct 1, 1973: 99.5 mhz; 56 kw. Ant 560 ft. TL: N45 31 50 W100 20 30 (CP: 100 kw, ant 361 ft., TL: N45 32 07 W100 20 45). Stereo. Dups AM 5%. Net: ABC/R. Format: Adult contemp, country. Spec prog: American Indian one hr wkly. ■ Scott Harper, opns dir; Cindy Dafnis, opns mgr; Scott Huber, adv mgr.

Pierpont

***KDSD-FM**—Apr 1, 1984: 90.9 mhz; 70 kw. Ant 1,057 ft. TL: N45 29 55 W97 40 35. Stereo. 414 E. Clark (57069). (605) 677-5861. FAX: (605) 677-5010. Licensee: S.D. Board of Educational Telecommunications. Net: APR, NPR; S.D. Pub. Format: Div. ■ Larry Roher, progmg dir; Diane Johns, mus dir; Tom Sorensen, news dir; Mike Johnson, chief engr.

Pierre

KCCR(AM)—Feb 4, 1959: 1240 khz; 1 kw-U. TL: N44 21 02 W100 19 08. Hrs opn: 5:30 AM-midnight. Box 309, 106 W. Capitol (57501). (605) 224-1240. FAX: (605) 224-0095. Licensee: Sorenson Broadcasting Corp. (group owner; acq 3-1-72). Net: CBS, NBC Talknet. Rep: Katz & Powell, O'Malley Communications. Format: MOR, adult contemp, info. News staff 2; news progmg 14 hrs wkly. Target aud: 25 plus; well-educated, upper income, politically aware business people, retirees, housewives. ■ Dean Sorenson, pres; Carol Breck, gen mgr; Fred Smith, opns mgr; Carl Osterkamp, gen sls mgr; Chris Helsa, chief engr.

KLXS-FM—Co-owned with KCCR(AM). April 15, 1981: 95.3 mhz; 3 kw. Ant 299 ft. TL: N44 22 15 W100 24 17 (CP: 50 kw, ant 289 ft.). Stereo. Prog sep from AM. Net: SMN. Format: Oldies.

KGFX(AM)—1927: 1060 khz; 10 kw-D, 1 kw-N, DA-2. TL: N44 17 12 W100 20 18. Hrs opn: 24. Box 1197, 214 W. Pleasant Dr. (57501). (605) 224-8686. FAX: (605) 224-8984. Licensee: James River Broadcasting. Group owner: Robert Ingstad Broadcast Properties (acq 11-15-68). Net: ABC/I; S.D. News Net, American Ag. Wash atty: Fisher, Wayland, Cooper & Leader. Format: C&W. Target aud: 25-54. Spec prog: Farm 18 hrs wkly. ■ Robert E. Ingstad, pres; Mark A. Swendsen, gen mgr; Charlie Hale, progmg dir.

KGFX-FM—Jan 4, 1982: 92.7 mhz; 3 kw. Ant 245 ft. TL: N44 22 15 W100 24 17. Stereo. Hrs opn: 20. Prog sep from AM. Format: Classic rock. Target aud: 18-34. ■ Paul Rollie, progmg dir.

KLXS-FM—Listing follows KCCR(AM).

Rapid City

KBHB(AM)—See Sturgis.

***KBHE-FM**—1984: 89.3 mhz; 9.8 kw. Ant 410 ft. TL: N44 03 09 W103 14 38. Stereo. 3650 Skyline Dr. (55701). (605) 394-2551. Licensee: S.D. Board of Educational Telecommunications. Net: APR, NPR; S.D. Pub. Format: Div. Spec prog: Sioux one hr wkly. ■ Michelle Van Maanen, news dir; Mike Johnson, chief engr.

KGGG-FM—Listing follows KIMM(AM).

KIMM(AM)—Mar 16, 1962: 1150 khz; 5 kw-D, 500 w-N, DA-N. TL: N44 04 35 W103 08 49. Box 8205, Metropolitan Federal Plaza, 2nd Fl., 9th & Josephs Sts. (57709). (605) 348-1100. FAX: (605) 348-8121. Licensee: Tom Ingstad Broadcasting. Group owner: Tom Ingstad Broadcasting Group (acq 1-1-85; $2,275,000 with co-located FM; FTR 1-7-85). Net: ABC/E. Rep: Christal. Wash atty: Fisher, Wayland, Cooper & Leader. Format: News/ talk. News staff 2; news progmg 8 hrs wkly. Target aud: 25-54. Spec prog: Farm one hr wkly. ■ Tom Ingstad, pres; Ted Peiffer, gen mgr & gen sls mgr; Gary Paterson, chief opns; Marla Christenson, sls dir; Steve Kinder, progmg dir; Patti Pavlish, news dir; Gary Peterson, chief engr. ■ Rates: $32; 25; 30; 20.

KGGG-FM—Co-owned with KIMM(AM). April 11, 1977: 100.3 mhz; 100 kw. Ant 450 ft. TL: N44 04 14 W103 15 01. Stereo. Hrs opn: 24. Prog sep from AM. Net: ABC/R. Format: CHR. News staff one; news progmg 3 hrs wkly. Target aud: 18-49. ■ Jack Lundy, opns mgr & progmg dir; Dave Michaels, mus dir. ■ Rates: $35; 30; 30; 28.

KIQK(FM)—Listing follows KTOQ(AM).

KKLS(AM)—June 7, 1959: 920 khz; 5 kw-D, 100-N. DA-2. TL: N44 03 43 W103 10 29. Stereo. Box 460, 2100 S. Seventh St. (57709). (605) 343-6161. FAX: (605) 343-9012. Licensee: Southern Minnesota Broadcasting Co. (group owner; acq 8-15-88). Net: Unistar. Rep: McGavren Guild. Format: Oldies. ■ Roger Currier, gen mgr; Lia Green, gen sls mgr; Kevin Phillips, progmg dir; Rich Peterson, news dir; Bill Spitzer, chief engr.

KKMK(FM)—Co-owned with KKLS(AM). 1971: 93.9 mhz; 100 kw. Ant 650 ft. TL: N44 02 48 W103 14 46. Stereo. Prog sep from AM. Net: CNN. Format: Adult contemp. ■ Trent Taylor, progmg dir; Carla Shotts, news dir.

KLMP(FM)—Oct 1, 1968: 97.9 mhz; 100 kw-H. Ant 390 ft. TL: N44 02 46 W103 14 41. Stereo. Hrs opn: 24. Box 523, 4040 Tower Rd. (57709). (605) 342-6822; (605) 342-3384. FAX: (605) 348-4316. Licensee: Fischer Broadcasting Inc. (acq 6-23-92). Net: Moody, USA. Format: Gospel. Target aud: General.

KOTA(AM)—November 1936: 1380 khz; 5 kw-U, DA-N. TL: N44 02 00 W103 11 15. Stereo. Hrs opn: 24. Box 1760, 518 St. Joe (57709). (605) 342-2000. FAX: (605) 342-7305; FAX: (605) 348-5693. Licensee: Duhamel Broadcasting Enterprises (group owner; acq 5-54). Net: CBS. Rep: Katz, Art Moore. Wash atty: Fisher, Wayland, Cooper & Leader. Format: Adult contemp, news/talk. News staff 2. Target aud: 35 plus. Spec prog: Farm 15 hrs wkly. ■ William F. Duhamel, pres & gen mgr; Dennis Goodman, stn mgr; Jim Shaw, progmg dir; Bob Burnell, news dir; Frank Etherington, chief engr. ■ KOTA-TV affil.

KOUT(FM)—Not on air, target date unknown: 98.7 mhz; 100 kw. Ant 515 ft. TL: N44 01 50 W103 15 34. 120 Nebraska St. (57701). Licensee: Crystal Broadcast Partners.

KRCS(FM)—See Sturgis.

***KTEQ(FM)**—Aug 7, 1971: 91.3 mhz; 750 w. Ant 300 ft. TL: N44 04 08 W103 15 03. Stereo. Hrs opn: 21. Old Gym, SDSM&T, 501 E. St. Joe (57701). (605) 394-2231. Licensee: Tech Educational Radio Council. Format: Div, alternative. News staff one. Target aud: 15-80. Spec prog: Class 3 hrs, country 6 hrs, Black 6 hrs, jazz 15 hrs, hardcore 3 hrs, new age 3 hrs, new wave 6 hrs wkly. ■ Mike Ray, Cody Schell (asst), gen mgrs; Kevin Lein, asst mus dir; Tony Jacobson, chief engr.

KTOQ(AM)—Sept 26, 1953: 1340 khz; 1 kw-U. TL: N44 04 06 W103 10 11. Hrs opn: 24. Box 1680, 306 E. St. Joseph St. (57709). (605) 343-0888. FAX: (605) 342-3075. Licensee: Tom-Tom Communications Inc. (acq 12-7-78). Net: NBC; Midwest Radio. Rep: Katz & Powell. Wash atty: Hopper & Kanouff. Format: MOR. News staff 2; news progmg 3 hrs wkly. Target aud: 35 plus; upscale, mature men & women. Spec prog: American Indian, farm 3 hrs wkly. ■ Tom Kearns, pres, gen mgr & prom mgr; Steve Blake, gen sls mgr; Phil Amundson, progmg dir; Abner Hunter George, news dir; Gary Peterson, chief engr. ■ Rates: $26; 26; 26; 20.

KIQK(FM)—Co-owned with KTOQ(AM). Jan 7, 1992: 104.1 mhz; 100 kw. Ant 515 ft. TL: N44 01 50 W103 15 34. Stereo. Hrs opn: 24. Prog sep from AM. (605) 343-0888; (605) 341-5425. Rep: Katz. Wash atty: Hopper & Kanouff. Format: Country. News staff one; news progmg 3 hrs wkly. Target aud: 18-65. ■ Bob Look, prom dir, progmg dir & mus dir; Karen Kinney, news dir. ■ Rates: $42; 42; 42; 34.

Redfield

KQKD(AM)—December 1962: 1380 khz; 500 w-D, 140 w-N, DA-2. TL: N44 53 53 W98 30 23. Hrs opn: 19. R.R. 2, Box 110 (57469). (605) 472-1380. FAX: (605) 472-3255. Licensee: Victoria Broadcasting System Inc. (acq 5-79). Net: CBS, NBC Talknet. Rep: Keystone (unwired net). Format: Country, news/talk. News staff one; news progmg 12 hrs wkly. Target aud: 25-65. ■ Steve Kaiser, pres, gen mgr & chief engr; Barb Johnson, opns mgr & gen sls mgr; Daryl Roos, progmg dir & news dir; Robin Stahl, mus dir.

KQKD-FM—Apr 7, 1991. 103.7 mhz; 50 kw. Ant 324 ft. TL: N45 07 39 W98 27 14. Stereo. Hrs opn: 5:30 AM-midnight. Prog sep from AM. Format: Country. News staff one. Target aud: 25-49.

Reliance

KPLO-FM—Jan 1986: 94.5 mhz; 95 kw. Ant 1,000 ft. TL: N43 57 55 W99 36 11. Stereo. Hrs opn: 24. Box 1197, Pierre (57501). (605) 224-8686. FAX: (605) 224-8984. Licensee: MAS Communications Inc. (acq 4-22-92; $250,000; FTR 5-11-92). Rep: Banner. Format: Country. Target aud: 25 plus. Spec prog: Farm 5 hrs wkly. ■ Mark Swendsen, pres & gen mgr; Gary McQuistion, gen sls mgr; Charlie Hale, progmg dir; Paul Titchenal, chief engr.

***KTSD-FM**—1984: 91.1 mhz; 100 kw. Ant 1,480 ft. TL: N43 57 55 W99 35 56. Stereo. HC5 Box 24, 414 E. Clark St. (57069). (605) 473-5643. FAX: (605) 677-5861. Licensee: S.D. Board of Educational Telecommunications. Net: APR, NPR. Format: Div. Spec prog: Sioux one hr wkly. ■ Larry Rohere, progmg dir; Janis Lemkuhl, mus dir; Michelle Van Maanen, news dir.

St. Francis

***KINI(FM)**—See Crookston, Neb.

Salem

KIKN(FM)—Nov 4, 1993: 100.5 mhz; 100 kw. Ant 981 ft. TL: N43 29 18 W97 26 34. Stereo. Hrs opn: 24. Southern Minnesota Broadcasting Co., 122 4th St. S.W., Rochester, MN (55902). (507) 286-1010. Licensee: Southern Minnesota Broadcasting Co. (group owner; acq 2-25-93; $150,000; FTR 3-22-93). ■ Gregory D. Gentling Jr., pres; Don Jacobs, gen mgr; Gary Michaels, opns mgr & progmg dir; Dave Engebretson, rgnl sls mgr; Ben Davis, prom mgr & mus dir; Mike Langford, chief engr.

Sioux Falls

***KAUR(FM)**—Oct 9, 1972: 89.1 mhz; 680 w. Ant 184 ft. TL: N43 31 37 W96 44 18. Stereo. Hrs opn: 10 AM-midnight. Box 751, KAUR-FM, Augustana College (57197). (605) 336-5287. Licensee: Augustana College Association. Net: ABC/FM. Format: Rock, jazz. Spec prog: Relg-Christian rock 12 hrs wkly. ■ Joshua Westgaurd, gen mgr; Kathy Hansen, progmg dir.

***KCFS(FM)**—July 1985: 94.5 mhz; 2.35 kw. Ant 190 ft. TL: N43 31 57 W96 44 20 (CP: 94.5 mhz). 1501 S. Prairie Ave. (57105-1699). (605) 331-6692. Licensee: Sioux Falls College. Net: MBS. Format: Top-40, contemp Christian. Spec prog: Urban 6 hrs wkly. ■ Gerry Schlenker, gen mgr; Terry Harris, stn mgr.

KCGN(AM)—June 13, 1970: 1520 khz; 500 w-D. TL: N43 33 28 W96 47 46. 305 W. 14th St. (57102). (605) 335-8800. FAX: (605) 335-8428. Licensee: CGN Corp. (acq 6-15-93). Net: USA. Format: Contemp Christian. Target aud: 25-50. ■ Verlyn Menning, pres; Beth Hubley, opns dir & sls dir; Doug Mashek, prom dir; Dean Robinson, progmg dir; Vicki Limberg, mus dir; Steve Twiselton, engrg dir. ■ Rates: $6; 6; 6; 6.

***KCSD(FM)**—July 1, 1985: 90.9 mhz; 2.35 kw. Ant 190 ft. TL: N43 31 57 W96 44 20. Stereo. Hrs opn: 24. 1501 S. Prairie Ave. (57105-1699). (605) 331-6694. FAX: (605) 331-6692. Licensee: Sioux Falls College. Net: NPR, S.D. Pub. Format: Class. News staff one; news progmg 44 hrs wkly. Target aud: 25 plus; educated males & females. Spec prog: Folk 5 hrs, jazz 10 hrs wkly. ■ Terry L. Harris, stn mgr; Paulette Pippert, news dir.

KDLO-FM—See Watertown.

KELO(AM)—1937: 1320 khz; 5 kw-U, DA-N. TL: N43 29 17 W96 38 14. Stereo. Hrs opn: 24. 500 S. Phillips (57102). (605) 331-5350. FAX: (605) 336-0415. Licensee: Midcontinent Broadcasting of South Dakota Inc. Group owner: Midcontinent Media Inc. (acq 1952). Net: AP. Rep: Banner. Wash atty: Dow, Lohnes & Albertson. Format: Adult contemp. Target aud: 25-54. ■ N. Larry Bentson, chmn; W. Thomas Simmons, vp & gen mgr; Leigh Anglin, gen sls mgr; Al Helgeson, prom mgr; Warren West, progmg dir; Jack Taylor, news dir; Scott Schmidt, chief engr.

KELO-FM—July 11, 1965: 92.5 mhz; 100 kw. Ant 1,900 ft. TL: N43 31 07 W96 32 05. Stereo. Hrs opn: 24. Prog sep from AM. Format: Lite adult contemp. ■ KELO-TV affil.

KKLS-FM—Listing follows KXRB(AM).

***KNWC(AM)**—Mar 25, 1961: 1270 khz; 2.5 kw-U, DA-2. TL: N43 29 19 W96 47 08. Hrs opn: 6 AM-midnight. Box 23, Rt. 3 (57106). (605) 339-1270. FAX: (605) 339-1271. Licensee: Northwestern College. Group owner: Northwestern College Radio Network. Format: Relg mus. News staff one; news progmg 24 hrs wkly. Target aud: 35-54. ■ Donald Ericksen, pres; David Martin, gen mgr, stn mgr, opns dir & progmg dir; Jeff Rupp, news dir; Scott Merry, pub affrs dir; Ted Miller, chief engr.

***KNWC-FM**—March 28, 1969: 96.5 mhz; 100 kw. Ant 1,600 ft. TL: N43 31 07 W96 32 05. Stereo. Hrs opn: 24. Dups AM 25%.

KPAT(FM)—Listing follows KSOO(AM).

KRRO(FM)—Listing follows KWSN(AM).

***KRSD(FM)**—May 11, 1985: 88.1 mhz; 2 kw. Ant 183 ft. TL: N43 31 37 W96 44 18. Stereo. Hrs opn: 24. Box 737, Augustana College (57197). (605) 335-6666. FAX: (605) 335-1259. Licensee: Minnesota Public Radio. Net: NPR, APR. Format: Class, news. News staff one. Target aud: General. ■ William H. Kling, pres; Valerie Arganbright, gen mgr; Cara Hirsch, news dir; Vince Fuhs, chief engr.

KSOO(AM)—1926: 1140 khz; 10 kw-D, 5 kw-N, DA-N. TL: N43 28 47 W96 41 04. 2600 S. Spring Ave. (57105). (605) 339-1140. FAX: (605) 339-2735. Licensee: T&J Broadcasting Inc. Group owner: Tom Ingstad Broadcasting Group (acq 7-25-90; $2.4 million with co-located FM; FTR 8-13-90). Net: ABC/I, NBC Talknet. Rep: Christal. Format: MOR. ■ Thomas E. Ingstad, pres; Tom Theis, gen mgr; Rick Knobe, progmg dir; Gene Hetland, news dir; Vince Fuhs, chief engr.

KPAT(FM)—Co-owned with KSOO(AM). Oct 1, 1973: 97.3 mhz; 60 kw. Ant 221 ft. TL: N43 35 48 W96 38 20. Stereo. (605) 339-9999. Net: ABC/C. Format: Adult contemp. ■ Barb Andrewski, gen sls mgr; Jim Donnelly, progmg dir.

KTWB(FM)—May 5, 1990: 101.9 mhz; 34 kw. Ant 580 ft. TL: N43 45 11 W96 53 22. Stereo. Hrs opn: 24. Suite 202, 330 North Main (57102). (605) 334-3300; (605) 334-1019. FAX: (605) 334-7309. Licensee: Kirkwood Broadcasting Inc. Rep: Banner. Wash atty: Leventhal, Senter & Lerman. Format: Country. News staff one; news progmg 10 hrs wkly. Target aud: 25-44. ■ Lee O. Axdahl, pres & gen mgr; Robert L. Christensen, opns mgr; Kim Feddersen, sls dir; Bill Daniels, prom mgr & mus dir; Norm Anderson, progmg dir; Bryan Bjerke, news dir. ■ Rates: $30; 22; 30; 22.

KWSN(AM)—May 6, 1948: 1230 khz; 1 kw-U. TL: N43 32 30 W96 46 50 (CP: TL: N43 33 21 W96 49 10). Hrs opn: 24. 1704 S. Cleveland (57103). (605) 335-6500. Licensee: XMT Group Inc. (acq 4-1-90; $1.8 million with co-located FM; FTR 3-9-90). Net: CBS. Rep: Katz. Wash atty: Fisher, Wayland, Cooper & Leader. Format: Full svc, news/talk. News staff 2; news progmg 27 hrs weekly. Target aud: 25-54; adults with disposable income, business leaders. ■ Barry Schloss, pres & chief engr; Mike Costanzo, gen mgr; Frank Hanford, gen sls mgr; Steve Thompson, progmg dir; Steve Thomson, news dir. ■ Rates: $20; 15; 20; 12.

KRRO(FM)—Co-owned with KWSN(AM). May 6, 1969: 103.7 mhz; 50 kw. Ant 187 ft. TL: N43 29 20 W96 45 40. Stereo. Hrs opn: 24. Prog sep from AM. Format: Classic rock. News staff 2; news progmg 12 hrs wkly. Target aud: 25-49; young adults, family-rearing age with disposable income. ■ Frank Hanford, prom mgr & adv mgr; Chris King, progmg dir; Michelle Thury, mus dir. ■ Rates: $30; 25; 25; 20.

KXRB(AM)—February 1969: 1000 khz; 10 kw-D, DA. TL: N43 29 13 W96 35 48. Hrs opn: 14. 3205 S. Meadow (57106). (605) 361-0300. FAX: (605) 361-5410. Licensee: Southern Minn. Broadcasting (group owner; acq 4-78). Net: MBS. Rep: McGavren Guild, Hyett/Ramsland. Wash atty: Dennis Kelly. Format: Country, farm. News staff one; news progmg 5 hrs wkly. Target aud: 25-54. ■ Greg Gentling, pres; Don Jacobs, gen mgr; Dave Engebretson, gen sls mgr; Ratt Reno, progmg dir; Charlie Walker, mus dir; Craig Mattick, news dir; Tony Randall, chief engr. ■ Rates: $20; 20; 20; 17.

KKLS-FM—Co-owned with KXRB(AM). March 1975: 104.7 mhz; 100 kw. Ant 705 ft. TL: N43 43 46 W97 05 10 (CP: Ant 984 ft.). Stereo. Prog sep from AM. Format: Adult contemp, oldies. ■ Dave Engebretson, rgnl sls mgr; Dave Roberts, prom dir.

Sisseton

KBWS-FM—Dec 28, 1983: 102.9 mhz; 100 kw. Ant 496 ft. TL: N45 36 52 W97 24 51. Stereo. Box 8, Eden (57232). (605) 486-4581. FAX: (605) 486-4582. Licensee: Lake Region News Corp. Net: CNN. Format: Country. Target aud: General. ■ Jack Adams, pres; Larry Ingalls, sr vp; Randy Peterson, gen mgr & rgnl sls mgr; Lee McCoy, progmg dir; Mike LaBelle, mus dir; Robert Spotts, chief engr.

***KSWS(FM)**—Not on air, target date unknown: 89.3 mhz; 3 kw. Ant 374 ft. Box 509, Agency Village (57262). Licensee: Sisseton Wahpeton Sioux Tribe of Lake Traverse Reservation.

Spearfish

***KBHU-FM**—Oct 18, 1974: 89.1 mhz; 100 w. Ant 55 ft. TL: N44 29 48 W103 52 13. Stereo. Hrs opn: 18. Box 9665, E.Y. Berry Library, Black Hills State Univ. (57799). (605) 642-6737; (605) 642-6255. Licensee: Black Hills State College. Net: Westwood One. Format: Adult contemp, alternative. News progmg 3 hrs wkly. Target aud: 12-24; high school/college age students. ■ Clifford Trump, pres; Dan Brookings, prom mgr, progmg dir & mus dir; Cal Crooks, chief engr.

KEZV(FM)—July 19, 1985: 101.1 mhz; 100 kw. Ant 1,604 ft. TL: N44 19 40 W103 50 14 (CP: Ant 1,817 ft., TL: N44 19 36 W103 50 12). Stereo. Box 1013 (57783-7013); 2827 E. Colorado Blvd. (57783-1013). (605) 642-5747. FAX: (605) 342-7305. Licensee: Duhamel Broadcasting Enterprises (group owner; acq 3-16-92; $525,000; FTR 3-30-92). Net: AP. Format: Lite rock. Target aud: 35 plus. ■ Dennis Goodman, gen mgr & gen sls mgr; Don Grant, opns mgr.

KSLT(FM)—Feb 17, 1984: 107.3 mhz; 100 kw. Ant 1,702 ft. TL: N44 19 36 W103 50 12. Stereo. Hrs opn: 24. Box 845, 2910 Fourth Ave. (57783). (605) 642-7792. FAX: (605) 642-8872. Licensee: The Word in Music Inc. Net: AP. Format: Contemp Christian. Target aud: 25-49. Spec prog: Educ 12 hrs wkly. ■ Mark Pluimer, pres; John Derrek, gen mgr; Kerry Dean Liebelt, mus dir; Tony Roerick, chief engr. ■ Rates: $11; 9; 11; 9.

Sturgis

KBHB(AM)—Sept 27, 1962: 810 khz; 21 kw-D. TL: N44 25 24 W103 25 37. Box 99, Hwy. 79 N. (57785). (605) 347-4455. FAX: (605) 347-5120. Licensee: CD Broadcasting Corp. (group owner; acq 7-14-89; $900,000 with co-located FM; FTR 7-31-89). Net: MBS, AP; American Agri. Rep: Katz & Powell. Format: C&W, farm. News staff one; news progmg 17 hrs wkly. ■ Dana Caldwell, gen mgr; Dean Kinney, progmg dir; Bob Looby, mus dir; Dave Maschoff, news dir; Steve Neave, chief engr.

KRCS(FM)—Co-owned with KBHB(AM). Dec 5, 1972: 93.1 mhz; 100 kw. Ant 1,059 ft. TL: N44 19 58 W103 32 20. Stereo. Prog sep from AM. Net: MBS. Format: C&W. News progmg 14 hrs wkly.

Vermillion

***KAOR(FM)**—September 1986: 91.1 mhz; 120 w. Ant 107 ft. TL: N42 47 01 W96 55 26. Stereo. Hrs opn: 18. Mass Communications Dept., Univ. of South Dakota (57069). (605) 677-5477. Licensee: The Univ. of South Dakota. Net: AP. Wash atty: Cohen & Marks. Format: Rock (AOR), classic rock, progsv. News progmg 2 hrs wkly. Target aud: 16-30; university-age students & faculty. ■ Bonnie Brown, gen mgr; Tim Salmi, mus dir.

KOSZ(AM)—Nov 16, 1967: 1570 khz; 500 w-D. TL: N42 47 32 W97 00 03. Box 282, 1407 Cherry St. (57069). (605) 624-2662. FAX: (605) 624-2664. Licensee: Culhane Communications Inc. (acq 5-6-93; $340,000 with co-located FM; FTR 5-24-93). Net: SMN. Format: C&W, farm. Target aud: 18 plus. ■ Debora Kribell, gen mgr; Randy Eichelberg, progmg dir & mus dir; Kevin Culhane, news dir; Mike Johnson, chief engr.

KVHT(FM)—Co-owned with KOSZ(AM). Nov 16, 1967: 106.3 mhz; 3 kw. Ant 255 ft. TL: N42 47 32 W97 00 03 (CP: 6 kw). Stereo. Format: Contemp hit. Target aud: 12-45.

***KUSD(AM)**—May 20, 1922: 690 khz; 1 kw-D, 21 w-N, DA-2. TL: N42 47 53 W96 55 39. Box 5000, 414 E. Clark St. (57069). (605) 677-5861. FAX: (605) 677-5010. Licensee: S.D. Board of Educational Telecommunications. Net: NPR, APR; S.D. Pub. Format: Class, news & pub affrs, jazz. Spec prog: Sioux one hr wkly. ■ Larry Rohrer, gen mgr; Ross King, progmg dir; Diane Johns, mus dir; Tom Sorenson, news dir; Wayne Nelson, chief engr.

***KUSD-FM**—Oct 1, 1967: 89.7 mhz; 50 kw-H, 21.5 kw-V. Ant 518 ft. TL: N43 03 00 W96 47 12 (CP: 32 kw, ant 663 ft.). Stereo. Dups AM 99%. ■ *KUSD-TV affil.

KVHT(FM)—Listing follows KOSZ(AM).

Volga

KJJQ(AM)—Licensed to Volga. See Brookings.

KKQQ(FM)—Licensed to Volga. See Brookings.

Watertown

KDLO-FM—Mar 1, 1968: 96.9 mhz; 100 kw. Ant 1,571 ft. TL: N44 57 57 W97 35 22. Stereo. Hrs opn: 24. 1311 9th Ave S.W. (57201). (605) 882-1597. FAX: (605) 886-6757. Licensee: Midcontinent Broadcasting. Group owner: Midcontinent Media Inc. Net: AP. Rep: Banner. Format: C&W. News staff one. Target aud: 25-54. ■ Tom Simmons, vp & gen mgr; Jim Kaiser, opns mgr & progmg dir; Ann Florey, sls dir; Jason Brown, news dir; Scott Smit, chief engr. KDLO-TV.

KIXX(FM)—Listing follows KWAT(AM).

KSDR(AM)—Apr 16, 1961: 1480 khz; 1 kw-D, 53 w-N. TL: N44 55 58 W97 06 19. Hrs opn: 6 AM- midnight. Box 1480, Suite 300, 3 E. Kemp (57201). (605) 886-5747; (605) 882-1480. FAX: (605) 886-2121. Licensee: Lake Region Broadcasting Co. (acq 12-16-85). Net: ABC/I. Wash atty: Richard Swift. Format: Oldies. News staff 3; news progmg 15 hrs wkly. Target aud: 25-54; young adults. ■ Bob Faehn, gen mgr; Jim Aesoph, opns mgr & progmg dir; Judy Swenson, gen sls mgr; Chris Wookey, prom dir; Jon Klein, mus dir; Reed Peterson, news dir; Gerry Calhoun, chief engr.

KSDR-FM—Mar 10, 1992: 92.9 mhz; 97 kw. Ant 977 ft. TL: N45 10 31 W96 59 15. Stereo. Hrs opn: 24. Net: ABC/I; Tribune. Wash atty: Tierney & Swift. Format: C&W. News staff one; news progmg 12 hrs wkly. Target aud: General; regional country stn with wide variety of ages. Spec prog: Farm 8 hrs, sports 8 hrs wkly. ■ Dorene Foster, asst mus dir.

KWAT(AM)—Mar 8, 1940: 950 khz; 1 kw-U, DA-N. TL: N44 52 12 W97 06 49. Hrs opn: 5 AM-midnight. Box 950 (57201). (605) 886-8444. FAX: (605) 886-9306. Licensee: Sorenson Broadcasting Corp. (group owner); acq 6-1-76). Net: CBS. Rep: Katz. Format: MOR, news, farm. Target aud: 35 plus. ■ Dean Sorenson, pres; Dean Johnson, vp, gen mgr & gen sls mgr; Bruce Erlandson, opns mgr; Perry Miller, mus dir; David Law, news dir.

KIXX(FM)—Co-owned with KWAT(AM). Sept 29, 1968: 96.1 mhz; 97 kw. Ant 977 ft. TL: N45 10 31 W96 59 15. Stereo. Hrs opn: 6 AM-1 AM. Box 96 (57201). (605) 886-9306. Net: Unistar. Rep: Katz. Format: Adult contemp. Target aud: 25-54. ■ Curt Crawford, progmg dir.

Winner

KWYR(AM)—Sept 27, 1957: 1260 khz; 5 kw-D, 146 w-N. TL: N43 22 57 W99 54 38. Hrs opn: 24. 346 Main St. (57580). (605) 842-3333. FAX: (605) 842-3875. Licensee: Midwest Radio Corp. (acq 11-23-58). Net: ABC/I. Format: Country. News staff one; news progmg 14 hrs wkly. Target aud: 25-60. ■ Steve Clark, pres & gen mgr; John Driscoll, vp & gen sls mgr; Steve Ammerman, opns mgr; Rita Steele, prom dir; Tom Engstran, progmg dir; Grant Giessinger, mus dir; Tim Bormanno, news dir; Mike Cooney, chief engr.

KWYR-FM—Nov 25, 1971: 93.7 mhz; 100 kw. Ant 560 ft. TL: N43 17 46 W99 52 02. Stereo. Prog sep from AM. (605) 842-3693. FAX: (605) 842-3875. Net: ABC/E. Format: Adult contemp. News progmg one hr wkly. Target aud: 18-45; females. ■ Rich Rahn, chief engr.

Yankton

KKYA(FM)—Listing follows KYNT(AM).

KYNT(AM)—March 15, 1955: 1450 khz; 1 kw-U. TL: N42 53 30 W97 25 10. Hrs opn: 5 AM-midnight. Box 628, 202 W. 2nd (57078). (605) 665-7892. FAX: (605) 665-0818. Licensee: Sorenson Broadcasting Corp. (group owner); acq 7-1-73). Net: MBS. Rep: Katz & Powell, O'Malley. Format: Oldies, news/talk. News staff one; news progmg 25 hrs wkly. Target aud: General. Spec prog: Farm 5 hrs, polka one hr, Pol one hr wkly. ■ Dean Sorenson, pres; Bill Holst, gen mgr; Scott Kooistra, opns mgr & progmg dir; Neil Lipetsky, gen sls mgr; Mike Frederick, mus dir; Dave Skalka, news dir; Troy Cowman, chief engr. ■ Rates: $20; 15; 15; 12.

KKYA(FM)—Co-owned with KYNT(AM). May 25, 1982: 93.1 mhz; 100 kw. Ant 469 ft. TL: N42 43 49 W97 24 13. Stereo. Hrs opn: 5 AM-midnight. Prog sep from AM. Format: Modern country. News staff one; news progmg 10 hrs wkly. Spec prog: Farm 5 hrs wkly. ■ Dave Lee, progmg mgr; Fred Michaels, mus dir. ■ Rates: $25; 20; 20; 15.

WNAX(AM)—November 1922: 570 khz; 5 kw-U, DA-N. TL: N42 54 47 W97 18 54. 1609 E. Hwy. 50 (57078). (605) 665-7442. FAX: (605) 665-8788. Licensee: Roy H. Park Broadcasting of the Midwest Inc. Group owner: Park Communications Inc. (acq 12-68). Net: CBS, ABC/E; MNN. Rep: McGavren Guild. Wash atty: Wiley, Rein & Fielding. Format: Country, news. News staff one; news progmg 23 hrs wkly. Target aud: 25 plus; farmers & agribusinesses. Spec prog: Relg 16 hrs, sports 10 hrs, weather 15 hrs wkly. ■ Roy H. Park, pres; Rick Prusator, vp; Jerry Bretey, gen mgr; Tim Powers, opns mgr; Cindy Weiland, gen sls mgr; Jim Reimler, mus dir; Jerry Oster, news dir; Terry Morley, chief engr. ■ Rates: $195; 150; 135; 110.

WNAX-FM—Aug 9, 1973: 104.1 mhz; 97 kw. Ant 981 ft. TL: N42 38 24 W97 03 21. Stereo. Prog sep from AM. (Acq 10-1-91; $675,000; FTR 10-28-91). Net: ABC/C. Format: Oldies. ■ Bob Baron, gen mgr; Joe Bouza, gen sls mgr; Charlie Stone, progmg dir.

Tennessee

LAUREN A. COLBY
301-663-1086
COMMUNICATIONS ATTORNEY
Special Attention to
Difficult Cases

Adamsville

WEAB(AM)—Dec 20, 1978: 960 khz; 500 w-D. TL: N35 14 00 W88 21 35. Box 559 (38310). Licensee: Bible Belt Broadcasting Inc. (acq 6-22-86; $78,000; FTR 3-24-86). ■ Bill L. Brown, pres.

Alamo

WCTA(AM)—October 1983: 810 khz; 250 w-D, DA. TL: N35 47 59 W89 07 20. Box 246 (38001); 114 N. Johnson (38001). (901) 696-5591; (901) 696-2781. Licensee: Gary Morris Reasons (acq 10-10-90; $75,000; FTR 10-29-90). Net: NBC. Format: Adult contemp. News staff one; news progmg 2 hrs wkly. Target aud: 30 plus. ■ Gary M. Reasons, pres; Billy H. Williams, gen mgr, gen sls mgr, prom mgr & mus dir; Rita Reasons, progmg mgr; Kathey Williams, news dir; Kirt Harnack, chief engr. ■ Rates: $12.50; 10.50; 12.50; na.

WWGM(FM)—Aug 10, 1989: 93.1 mhz; 25 kw. Ant 328 ft. TL: N35 43 31 W89 03 25. Rt. 1, Box 281, Bells (38006); Box 2767, Jackson (38302). (901) 664-9393. FAX: (901) 663-3993. Licensee: Good News Network Inc. (acq 8-20-92; $471,057; FTR 9-7-92). Net: CNN. Wash atty: Eugene Smith. Format: Southern gospel. News staff one; news progmg 3 hrs wkly. Target aud: 24-54; upscale women. ■ Jim Williams, gen mgr; Bob Faulkner, opns mgr; Jimmy Williams, sls dir; Ron Haney, prom dir. ■ Rates: $10.50; 10.25; 10.50; 9.50.

Alcoa

WBCR(AM)—Aug 25, 1957: 1470 khz; 1 kw-D. TL: N35 47 47 W83 56 17. Box 130 (37701). (615) 983-0890. FAX: (615) 984-1470. Licensee: Blount County Broadcasting Co. (acq 9-12-60). Net: ABC/D. Format: Adult contemp, news/talk. ■ Win Maxwell, dev dir.

*WYLV(FM)—Feb 14, 1993: 89.1 mhz; 80 w-H., 3 kw-V. Ant 102 ft. TL: N35 47 47 W83 56 17. Stereo. Hrs opn: 24. Box 70089, Tazewell Pike Office Park, Suite 101, 3214 Tazewell Pike, Knoxville (37918-7000). (615) 689-1000. Licensee: Foothills Broadcasting Inc. Format: Contemp gospel. ■ John Hanna, gen mgr; Larry Richmond, opns mgr; Dave Berry, chief engr.

Algood

WATX(AM)—Oct 5, 1981: 1590 khz; 1 kw-D, 500 w-N. TL: N36 11 02 W85 25 03. Hrs opn: 6 AM-9 PM. 259 S. Willow Ave., Cookeville (38501). (615) 528-9289. Licensee: Manna Broadcasting Co. Inc. (acq 9-17-90; FTR 10-8-90). Net: CBN. Format: News/talk, relg. News staff 2; news progmg 34 hrs wkly. Target aud: General. Spec prog: Gospel. ■ Joe Wilmouth, pres; Kevin Paul, gen mgr, gen sls mgr, vp prom & vp adv; Gail Desantis, adv mgr; Bill Penn, progmg dir & mus dir; Alston Stinent, chief engr. ■ Rates: $8; 6; 8; 6.

Ardmore

WSLV(AM)—September 1968: 1110 khz; 2.5 kw-D. TL: N34 59 35 W86 51 22. Box 96, Stateline Rd. (38449). (615) 427-2178. FAX: (615) 427-2179. Licensee: B&E Broadcasting Inc. (acq 1-13-89; $85,000; FTR 1-30-89). Net: USA. Format: Southern gospel. Target aud: 25 plus; agricultural & factory workers, housewives. Spec prog: Country 10 hrs wkly. ■ Ernie Ashworth, pres & gen mgr; Mark Ashworth, gen sls mgr, progmg dir & mus dir; John Parker, prom mgr; Harold Starks, chief engr.

Arlington

WGSF(AM)—Licensed to Arlington. See Memphis.

Ashland City

WQSV(AM)—July 14, 1982: 790 khz; 500 w-U. TL: N36 17 08 W87 04 58. Box 619, 208 N. Main St. (37015). (615) 792-6789. Licensee: Sycamore Valley Broadcasting Inc. (acq 12-20-91; $55,000; FTR 1-13-92). Net: ABC/D; Tenn. Radio Net. Format: Christian country. News progmg 11 hrs wkly. Target aud: General. ■ Betty Albright, CEO & pres; Richard Albright, gen mgr, stn mgr & sls mgr; Gary Kaye, mus dir & pub affrs dir. ■ Rates: $8; 7.50; 7.50; 6.

Athens

WJSQ(FM)—Listing follows WLAR(AM).

WLAR(AM)—May 15, 1946: 1450 khz; 1 kw-U. TL: N35 26 44 W84 36 43. Hrs opn: 24. Box 986, 2110 Oxnard Rd. (37303). (615) 745-1000. Licensee: James C. Sliger (acq 4-18-83; $200,000; FTR 5-9-83). Format: Contemp country. Spec prog: Farm 2 hrs wkly. ■ James C. Sliger, gen mgr & chief engr; William P. Atkins, gen sls mgr; Randy Sliger, progmg dir & mus dir; Hayward Armstrong, news dir.

WJSQ(FM)—Co-owned with WLAR(AM). Dec 1, 1979: 101.7 mhz; 7.5 kw. Ant 528 ft. TL: N35 31 19 W84 27 29. Stereo. Hrs opn: 24. Prog dups AM. Net: AP.

WYXI(AM)—Oct 5, 1966: 1390 khz; 2.5 kw-D, 62 w-N. TL: N35 26 48 W84 34 19. Hrs opn: 6 AM-7:30 PM. Box 1390, 112 E. Madison Ave. (37371-1390). (615) 745-1390; (615) 745-2391. FAX: (615) 745-4439. Licensee: Cornerstone Broadcasting Inc. (acq 9-11-86; $75,000; FTR 7-21-86). Net: ABC/E. Rep: Midsouth. Format: MOR, news/talk. News staff one; news progmg 10 hrs wkly. Target aud: 25-64; mature middle class. Spec prog: Black one hr, relg 8 hrs wkly. ■ Mark Lefler, pres, gen mgr & sls dir; Bob Ketchersid, vp, stn mgr, progmg dir & news dir. ■ Rates: $6.18; 6.18; 6.18; 6.18.

Bartlett

WJWL(FM)—May 1994: 92.9 mhz; 6 kw. Ant 328 ft. TL: N35 10 20 W89 56 40. Hrs opn: 24. 2205 Poplar Ave., Memphis (38104). (901) 726-9727. FAX: (901) 726-9727. Licensee: Belz Broadcasting Co. ■ Julianne P. Belz, pres.

Baxter

WBXE(FM)—Not on air, target date unknown: 93.7 mhz; 25 kw. Ant 328 ft. Box 22, Hilham, TN (38568). Licensee: Joel R. Upton.

Bells

WNWS(AM)—See Brownsville.

Benton

WBIN(AM)—May 18, 1977: 1540 khz; 1 kw-D. TL: N35 11 15 W84 38 13. Box K (37307). (615) 338-2864. FAX: (615) 338-9180. Licensee: Stonewood Communications Corp. Net: ABC; Tenn. Net. Format: Southern traditional gospel. ■ W.J. Woody, pres & gen mgr; Andrew Bell, stn mgr & chief engr.

WBIN-FM—Not on air, target date 1994: 93.1 mhz; 6 kw. Ant 307 ft. TL: N35 04 48 W84 42 25. Stereo. Hrs opn: 6 AM-midnight. Net: ABC. Format: MOR. Spec prog: Public affairs 2 hrs, talk, University of Tennessee sports, local sports wkly.

Berry Hill

WVOL(AM)—December 1951: 1470 khz; 5 kw-D, 1 kw-N, DA-2. TL: N36 12 01 W86 46 47. Box 70085, 1320 Brick Church Pike (37207). (615) 227-1470. FAX: (615) 227-2740. Licensee: Phoenix of Nashville Inc. Group owner: Phoenix Holdings Inc. (acq 5-16-80). Net: Natl Black. Rep: Republic. Format: Classic soul. News staff one. Target aud: 25-54; Black adults. Spec prog: Gospel 19 hrs wkly. ■ Samuel Howard, pres; Scott Peters, gen mgr; Clarence Kilcrease, progmg dir; Clinton Hooper, chief engr.

Blountville

WGOC(AM)—Sept 20, 1967: 640 khz; 10 kw-D, 810 w-N, DA-N. TL: N36 31 19 W81 25 25. Stereo. 640 Radio Way (37617). (615) 323-0640. FAX: (615) 323-1864. Licensee: J.T. Parker Broadcasting. Net: NBC. Rep: Dora-Clayton. Format: Top gun country. News staff one; news progmg 12 hrs wkly. Target aud: 25-54; $35,000 household income, family of 3. Spec prog: Relg 16 hrs wkly. ■ J.T. Parker, pres; John E. Fry, gen mgr & stn mgr; Susie Fry, gen sls mgr; Fred Williams, Jim Smith, progmg dirs;

Fred Williams, mus dir; Jim Smith, asst mus dir & pub affrs dir; Ned Michaels, news dir; Mitch Sandidge, chief engr. ■ Rates: $14; 14; 14; 14.

*WPGB(FM)—Not on air, target date Fall 1994: 88.3 mhz; 1 kw. Ant 1,811 ft. TL: N36 27 30 W82 05 30 (CP: COL: Kingsport, ant 2,139 ft.). Box 889, Blacksburg, VA (24060). (703) 552-4252. Licensee: Blountsville Educational Association. Format: Relg/educ. ■ Virginia L. Baker, pres.

Bolivar

WMOD(FM)—Jan 27, 1975: 96.7 mhz; 3 kw. Ant 300 ft. TL: N35 15 00 W88 53 28. Stereo. Hrs opn: 24. Box 438, 100 E. Market St. (38008). (901) 658-7328. Licensee: West Tennessee Radio Inc. (acq 1-3-87). Net: SMN; Tenn. Radio Net. Rep: Midsouth. Format: Country. ■ D. Haley Smith, pres & gen mgr; Kirk Harnack, chief engr. ■ Rates: $9.50; 8.50; 9.50; 6.

Brentwood

WYOR(AM)—Sept 4, 1985: 560 khz; 500 w-D, DA. TL: N35 54 32 W86 46 13. 3765 N. Chapel Rd., Franklin (37064). (615) 791-9967. Licensee: Down Home Broadcasting Co. Inc. (acq 9-3-92; $150,000; FTR 10-5-92). Net: BRN. Format: Blues. Target aud: General. ■ Mae Hutchins, pres; Josh Hutchins, progmg dir & mus dir; Ellery Queen, news dir; John Almond, chief engr. ■ Rates: $8; 8; 8; 6.

Bristol

WBCV(AM)—Aug 18, 1962: 1550 khz; 5 kw-D. TL: N36 33 58 W82 09 30. Box 68 (37621); 26 6th St. (37620). (615) 968-5221. Licensee: Sunshine Broadcasters (acq 6-80; $200,000; FTR 7-21-80). Format: Relg. News progmg 3 hrs wkly. Target aud: General. ■ Jennings Dotson, CEO, pres, gen mgr & gen sls mgr; Newl K. Dotson, exec vp; Christopher J. Dotson, sr vp & prom mgr; Ruth O. Dotson, progmg dir & mus dir; Cecil Reed, news dir; Larry Morelock, pub affrs dir; Bernard Leonard, chief engr. ■ Rates: $6; 6; 6; na.

*WHCB(FM)—Aug 10, 1984: 91.5 mhz; 1.5 kw. Ant 2,326 ft. TL: N36 26 03 W82 08 03 (CP: 1.52 kw, ant 2,345 ft.). Stereo. Hrs opn: 24. Box 2061 (37621-2061); 4045 Weaver Pike, Bluff City (37618). (615) 878-6279. FAX: (615) 878-6520. Licensee: Appalachian Educational Communication Corp. Net: Moody, USA. Format: Talk, educ, Christian. News progmg 14 hrs wkly. Target aud: General. Spec prog: Class one hr, Appalachian culture 2 hrs, farm one hr, folk one hr, Sp one hr, Jewish one hr wkly. ■ Kenneth C. Hill, pres & gen mgr; Janet R. Hill, prom mgr & pub affrs dir; Mark Ferguson, progmg mgr; Pat Jenkins, chief engr.

WKPT(AM)—See Kingsport.

WOPI(AM)—(Bristol, Va). June 15, 1929: 1490 khz; 1 kw-U. TL: N36 35 45 W82 09 42. Hrs opn: 24. 3245 W. State St., Bristol, TN (37620). (615) 764-5131. Licensee: Joe Morrell Inc. (acq 4-16-90; FTR 5-7-90). Net: ABC/E. Format: Btfl music, big band, country. Target aud: 30 plus. Spec prog: Bluegrass 4 hrs wkly. ■ Joe Morrell, pres & gen mgr; Robyn Sproles, progmg dir & mus dir; Dennis Wenk, vp engrg.

WQUT(FM)—See Johnson City.

WXBQ(AM)—See Bristol, Va.

WXBQ-FM—1945: 96.9 mhz; 67 kw. Ant 2,200 ft. TL: N36 25 59 W82 08 11. Stereo. Box 1389, 901 E. Valley Dr., Bristol, VA (24201). (703) 669-8112. FAX: (703) 669-0541. Licensee: Bristol Broadcasting Inc. Group owner: Nininger Stations. Net: ABC/I. Rep: McGavren Guild. Format: Country. Target aud: 25-54. ■ W. L. Nininger, pres & gen mgr; Winnie Quaintence, gen sls mgr; Bill Hagy, prom mgr & progmg dir; Reggie Neel, mus dir; George Dixon, news dir; Chuck Lawson, chief engr.

Brownsville

WNWS(AM)—Oct 14, 1963: 1520 khz; 250 w-D. TL: N35 36 30 W89 14 40. Hrs opn: Sunrise-sunset. Box 198, 42 S. Washington Ave. (38012). (901) 772-3700. Licensee: The Wireless Group Inc. (group owner; acq 4-80; $320,000 with co-located FM; FTR 3-31-80). Net: CNN. Format: News. ■ Carlton Veirs, pres & gen mgr; Kim Bishop, progmg dir.

WTBG(FM)—Co-owned with WNWS(AM). Nov 9, 1965: 95.3 mhz; 5 kw. Ant 150 ft. TL: N35 36 30 W89 14 40. Stereo. Prog sep from AM. Net: ABC/E. Wash atty: Baker, Worthington, Stansberry & Woolf. Format: Country, news/talk. News staff one. Target aud: 25-54.

Calhoun

WXSE(FM)—Not on air, target date unknown: 104.1 mhz; 3 kw. Ant 325 ft. TL: N35 18 15 W84 49 55 (CP: 6 kw, ant 328 ft.). 1995 Keith St. N.W., Cleveland (37311). Licensee: Randal W. Sliger (acq 7-19-93; $200,000 with WCLE[AM] Cleveland; FTR 8-9-93).

Camden

WFWL(AM)—Sept 18, 1956: 1220 khz; 250 w-D, 140 w-N. TL: N36 03 10 W88 05 15. Hrs opn: 24. Box 662, 117 Vicksburg Ave. (38320). (901) 584-7570; (901) 584-4444. FAX: (901) 642-2222. Licensee: Benton County Broadcasting Inc. (acq 6-3-77). Net: ABC/E; Tenn. Net. Rep: Keystone (unwired net); Midsouth. Wash atty: Miller & Fields. Format: C&W. Target aud: 25-49; adult. Spec prog: Gospel 8 hrs wkly. ■ Ray Smith, pres; Ron Lane, gen mgr; John Latham, gen sls mgr; Jim Hart, prom mgr, progmg dir & mus dir; Flash Metton, news dir; Dave Hacker, engrg mgr. ■ Rates: $12.50; 12.50; 12.50; 12.50.

WRJB(FM)—June 20, 1976: 98.3 mhz; 3 kw. Ant 300 ft. TL: N36 03 25 W88 06 10. Stereo. Hrs opn: 24. Box 508, 117 Vicksburg (38320). (901) 584-4444; (901) 584-7570. FAX: (901) 642-2222. Licensee: Valley Wide Broadcasting Inc. Net: ABC/E. Rep: Southern. Format: Adult contemp. News progmg 4 hrs wkly. Target aud: 20-50. Spec prog: Gospel 4 hrs wkly. ■ Ray Smith, pres; John Latham, gen mgr, gen sls mgr & vp adv; Virginia Latham, stn mgr; Terry Hudson, progmg dir; Jim Hart, asst mus dir; Paul Hacher, chief engr. ■ Rates: $4; 4; 4; 3.50.

Carthage

WRKM(AM)—June 20, 1959: 1350 khz; 1 kw-D, 91 w-N. TL: N36 14 42 W85 56 44. Hrs opn: 19. Box 179, 104-Z Country Ln. (37030). (615) 735-1350; (615) 449-7024. FAX: (615) 735-0381. Licensee: Wood Broadcasting Inc. (acq 11-1-87). Net: Tenn. Radio Net. Format: Southern gospel. News staff one; news progmg 8 hrs wkly. Target aud: 35 plus. ■ Judy Wood, gen mgr, gen sls mgr & progmg dir; Dennis Banka, prom dir & mus dir; Kevin Chase, news dir; Carl Campbell, chief engr. ■ Rates: $10; 4; 5; 4.

WUCZ-FM—Co-owned with WRKM(AM). July 18, 1975: 104.1 mhz; 6 kw. Ant 300 ft. TL: N36 18 43 W85 57 08. Stereo. Hrs opn: 24. Prog sep from AM. Net: SMN. Format: Country. News progmg 14 hrs wkly. Target aud: General. ■ Judy Wood, opns mgr. ■ Rates: $10; 8.75; 10; 7.75.

Celina

WVFB(FM)—Not on air, target date unknown: 101.5 mhz; 6 kw. Ant 328 ft. TL: N36 33 15 W85 36 39. Stereo. Box 427, 150 Worsham Ln., Monticello, KY (42633). Licensee: Elizabeth Bernice Whittimore (acq 5-5-93; $14,000; FTR 5-24-93).

Centerville

WNKX(AM)—Nov 16, 1955: 1570 khz; 5 kw-D. TL: N35 45 29 W87 27 35. Hrs opn: 24. Box 280, #150 Hwy. 50 E. (37033). (615) 729-5191; (615) 729-9600. FAX: (615) 729-5467. Licensee: Hickman County Broadcasting Inc. (acq 6-27-91; $140,000 with co-located FM; FTR 7-15-91). Net: Tenn. Radio Net. Rep: Dora-Clayton; Midsouth. Wash atty: McCampbell & Young. Format: Country. News staff one; news progmg 10 hrs wkly. Target aud: 18-65; general. Spec prog: Farm one hr, gospel 5 hrs wkly. ■ Steve Turner, CEO, vp, gen mgr, stn mgr & opns mgr; Charles Galbreath, pres; Susan Mobley, mktg mgr; Rhonda Taylor, prom mgr & pub affrs dir; Terry Durham, progmg dir, mus dir & news dir; Jeff Perrigo, chief engr. ■ Rates: $10; 8; 8; 8.

WNKX-FM—May 1974: 96.7 mhz; 3 kw. Ant 300 ft. TL: N35 49 39 W87 34 02. Stereo. Hrs opn: 24. Dups AM 100%. News staff 6. ■ Rhoda Taylor, dev mgr & mktg dir; Steve Turner, sls dir & progmg mgr; Susan Mobley, prom dir & adv dir. ■ Rates: Same as AM.

Chattanooga

*WAWL-FM—See Red Bank.

WDEF(AM)—Dec 31, 1940: 1370 khz; 5 kw-U, DA-N. TL: N35 02 25 W85 20 22. 3300 S. Broad St. (37408). (615) 785-1200. FAX: (615) 785-1264. Licensee: Roy H. Park Broadcasting of Tennessee Inc. Group owner: Park Communications Inc. (acq 2-64). Net: CBS; Tenn. Radio. Rep: Major Mkt. Format: EZ Listening. News staff 2; news progmg 21 hrs wkly. Target aud: 35-54; adults with modern lifestyle. Spec prog: Various sports. ■ Dorothy H. Park, CEO & chmn; Wright M. Thomas, pres; Randel N. Stair, CFO; Rick Pursator, vp; Gary Downs, gen mgr; Jeff Fontana, gen sls mgr; Danny Howard, progmg dir; Chuck Stevens, mus dir; Anita Bray, news dir; Phil Langston, chief engr.

WDEF-FM—Sept 15, 1964: 92.3 mhz; 100 kw. Ant 1,180 ft. TL: N35 08 06 W85 19 25. Stereo. Hrs opn: 24. Dups AM 21%. Net: CBS. News staff 2; news progmg 21 hrs wkly. Target aud: 35-54; upscale adults. ■ WDEF-TV affil.

WDOD(AM)—April 13, 1925: 1310 khz; 5 kw-U, DA-N. TL: N35 04 54 W85 20 14. Hrs opn: 24. Box 4232, Old Baylor School Rd. (37405). (615) 266-5117. FAX: (615) 265-6433. Licensee: WDOD of Chattanooga Inc. Group owner: Bahakel Communications (acq 6-62). Rep: Banner. Format: Big band, country, talk. News staff 2; news progmg 10 hrs wkly. Target aud: 35 plus; parents of the baby boom generation. ■ Cy N. Bahakel, pres; Bill McKay, gen mgr; James Phillips, mus dir; S. Parks Hall, chief engr.

WDOD-FM—February 1960: 96.5 mhz; 100 kw. Ant 1,080 ft. TL: N35 09 39 W85 19 11. Stereo. Prog sep from AM. Net: ABC/E. Format: Country. Target aud: 25-54; upscale, contemporary adults.

*WDYN-FM—June 1, 1968: 89.7 mhz; 100 kw. Ant 205 ft. TL: N35 10 17 W85 18 58. Stereo. Hrs opn: 24. 1815 Union Ave. (37404). (615) 493-4382. Licensee: Tennessee Temple University. Format: Relg. News progmg 2 hrs wkly. Target aud: General; conservative Christians. ■ Dr. Roger Stiles, pres; Tommy L. Sneed, gen mgr & stn mgr; Dee D. Decker, opns dir, progmg dir & mus dir; Joy Ray, pub affrs dir; Glenn Morgan, chief engr.

WFLI(AM)—See Lookout Mountain.

WFXS(FM)—Listing follows WNOO(AM).

WGOW(AM)—1936: 1150 khz; 5 kw-D, 1 kw-N, DA-N. TL: N35 04 05 W85 20 04. Box 11202 (37401). (615) 756-6141. Licensee: Radio Chattanooga Inc. Group owner: Bloomington Broadcasting Corp. (acq 5-1-78). Net: AP, MBS, Sun, NBC Talknet. Rep: Christal. Wash atty: Reddy, Begley & Martin. Format: News/talk. ■ Donald J. Newberg, pres & gen mgr; Danny Brown, vp & gen sls mgr; Bill Lockhurt, progmg dir; Mike Murrell, chief engr.

WSKZ(FM)—Co-owned with WGOW(AM). Nov 1960: 106.5 mhz; 100 kw. Ant 1,080 ft. TL: N35 09 42 W85 19 06. Stereo. Prog sep from AM. Format: CHR. ■ Scott Chase, progmg mgr & mus dir; Mike Murrell, engrg dir.

WJOC(AM)—July 4, 1948: 1490 khz; 1 kw-U. TL: N35 03 07 W85 16 24. 805 Chickamauga Ave., Rossville, GA (30741). (706) 861-0800. Licensee: Bobby E. Godgiben. Format: Southern gospel. ■ John Godgiben, gen mgr.

WJTT(FM)—See Red Bank.

WLMX-FM—See Rossville, Ga.

*WMBW(FM)—Aug 1, 1969: 88.9 mhz; 100 kw. Ant 1,505 ft. TL: N34 57 43 W85 22 40. Stereo. Hrs opn: 24. Box 73026, 1920 E. 24th St. Pl. (37407). (615) 629-8900. FAX: (615) 629-0021. Licensee: Moody Bible Institute of Chicago (group owner; acq 5-18-73). Net: USA, Moody. Wash atty: Jeff Southmayd. Format: Educ, relg. News staff 2. Target aud: General. ■ Dr. Joseph Stowell, pres; Dean Sippel, gen mgr & stn mgr; Linda Wells, opns dir; Andrew Napier, mus dir; Doug Baker, news dir; Bernie Miller, pub affrs dir; F.L. Pierce, chief engr.

WMOC(AM)—Oct 5, 1961: 1450 khz; 1 kw-U. TL: N35 02 54 W85 16 26. 2701 E. 47th St. (37407). (615) 867-1450. Licensee: Grace Media Inc. (acq 1-25-93; $307,174; FTR 2-15-93). Format: Southern gospel. Spec prog: Black 15 hrs wkly. ■ Bob Wilkens, pres; Marge Fryar, gen mgr & mus dir; S. Parks Hall, chief engr.

WNOO(AM)—June 1951: 1260 khz; 5 kw-D. TL: N35 03 08 W85 16 22. Box 5156, 1108 Hendricks (37406); Suite 102, 1200 Mountain Creek Rd. (37405). (615) 698-8617; (615) 875-0659. FAX: (615) 875-3306. (615) 629-0244. Licensee: Tennessee Communications L.P., debtor in possession (acq 9-1-89; grpsl; FTR 8-28-89). Rep: Banner. Format: Black. News staff one; news progmg 15 hrs wkly. Target aud: 25-54; mature Black adults. ■ Fred J. Webb, pres & gen mgr; Cherri McIntyre, vp opns & opns mgr; Karen Conner (local), gen sls mgr; Frank St. James, progmg dir & mus dir; Charlotte Logan, asst mus dir; Jamie Hancock, news dir; Jamie Hamcock, pub affrs dir; Thomas Cook, chief engr. ■ Rates: $15; 15; 15; 15.

WFXS(FM)—(Soddy-Daisy). Co-owned with WNOO(AM). July 14, 1977: 102.3 mhz; 3 kw. Ant 287 ft. TL: N35 11 45 W85 13 45. Stereo. Prog sep from AM. Format: Classic rock, AOR. Target aud: 18-54; baby boomers. ■ Ray W. Skates, prom mgr; John Thomas, progmg dir; Angela Richardson, news dir. ■ Rates: $30; 30; 30; 30.

Tennessee

WSKZ(FM)—Listing follows WGOW(AM).

*WSMC-FM—See Collegedale.

WTYR(AM)—(Soddy-Daisy). May 23, 1970: 1550 khz; 1 kw-D. TL: N35 13 47 W85 12 12. 120 Jane Manor Circle, Soddy-Daisy (37379). (615) 332-8112. Licensee: Greg B. Schaffer (acq 5-22-92; $35,000; FTR 6-15-92). Format: Hits of 50s, 60s & 70s. Target aud: 25-54; high school and college graduates. ■ Greg Schaeffer, gen mgr. ■ Rates: $156; 156; 156; na.

*WUTC(FM)—March 1980: 88.1 mhz; 50 kw-H. Ant 750 ft. TL: N35 12 28 W85 16 46 (CP: 30 kw, ant 895 ft.). Stereo. Hrs opn: 24. 615 McCallie Ave. (37403). (615) 755-4790. Licensee: Board of Trustees of Univ. of Tenn. Net: APR, NPR. Format: Jazz. Target aud: General. ■ Dr. John McCormack, stn mgr; Mark Colbert, progmg dir; Richard Winham, mus dir.

Church Hill

WMCH(AM)—May 8, 1954: 1260 khz; 1 kw-D. TL: N36 31 15 W82 44 54. Box 128, 112 W. Main (37642). (615) 357-5601. Licensee: Wallace Broadcasting Inc. Net: USA. Format: Full-time gospel. ■ Bettye Jo Russell, pres, gen mgr & gen sls mgr; Shane Farrell, mus dir; Mike Jackson, news dir; Darrell Smith, chief engr.

Clarksville

*WAPX-FM—Oct 1, 1984: 91.7 mhz; 3 kw. Ant 160 ft. TL: N36 32 13 W87 21 24. Stereo. Hrs opn: 18. Box 4627, Austin Peay State Univ. (37044). (615) 648-7205; (615) 648-7378. Licensee: Austin Peay State Univ. Net: AP. Format: Alternative, AOR. News progmg 8 hrs wkly. Target aud: 18-34; college students and young professionals. Spec prog: Black 6 hrs, jazz 6 hrs wkly. ■ Dr. Oscar C. Page, pres; David von Palko, gen mgr; James Trodglen, stn mgr; Susan Budzyna, opns mgr; Angie Bosio, progmg dir; David Terrell, mus dir; Julie Clark, asst mus dir; Leighton Brown, news dir; Dale Howard, chief engr.

WCTZ(AM)—Jan 24, 1980: 1550 khz; 2.5 kw-D, 250 w-N, DA-N. TL: N36 32 12 W87 22 24. Box 1550, 305 N. Riverside Dr. (37041-1550). (615) 645-1550. FAX: (615) 645-1015. Licensee: Bayard H. Walters. Group owner: The Cromwell Group Inc. (acq 10-17-91). Net: MBS, NBC Talknet. Wash atty: Pepper & Corazzini. Format: Country. Target aud: 24-56; country music lovers. ■ Bayard Walters, pres; Larry Trimmer, srvp; Sears Hallatt, gen mgr; Watt Hariston, chief engr.

WDXN(AM)—Nov 12, 1954: 540 khz; 1 kw-D, 54.5 w-N. TL: N36 32 28 W87 19 33. Hrs opn: 19. Box 887, 117 W. Dunbar Cave Rd. (37040). (615) 645-2411. FAX: (615) 647-7232. Licensee: Tenn-Aire Communications Inc. (acq 6-01-93; $140,000; FTR 4-12-93). Net: ABC/E. Rep: T N. Format: Contemp country. News staff 2; news progmg 36 hrs wkly. Target aud: 25-54. Spec prog: Farm 3 hrs, gospel 3 wkly. ■ Jack Mayer, gen mgr; Lon Sosh, gen sls mgr, adv dir & adv mgr; Susan Ash, mus dir; Stefanie Silvey, news dir; Leslie Hartman, pub affrs dir; J. C. Morrow, chief engr.

WJZM(AM)—Oct 19, 1941: 1400 khz; 1 kw-U. TL: N36 30 57 W87 20 57. Hrs opn: 24. Box 648, 411 Madison St. (37041). (615) 645-6414. FAX: (615) 551-8432. Licensee: Ted Young and Trent C. Knott (acq 12-22-92; $344,206 with WTWL(FM) McKinnon; FTR 1-25-93). Net: AP. Format: News, sports, talk. News progmg 8 hrs wkly. Target aud: 25-60; blue collar, working women, businessmen. Spec prog: Relg. ■ Len Sosh, pres; Charles Boyd, gen mgr & progmg dir; Trent Knott, gen sls mgr; Jeff Lyon, mus dir; Amy Scott, news dir; Watt Hairston, chief engr.

Cleveland

WALV(FM)—Listing follows WBAC(AM).

WBAC(AM)—June 18, 1945: 1340 khz; 1 kw-U. TL: N35 09 54 W84 51 13. Box 1059 (37364-1059). (615) 476-7593. FAX: (615) 472-5290. Licensee: Thomason Broadcasting (acq 10-18-76). Net: MBS. Format: MOR. Spec prog: Black one hr wkly. ■ Clyde Thomason, pres & gen mgr; Cordel Whitlock, vp; Robert G. Gault, news dir; Charles Daugherty, chief engr.

WALV(FM)—Co-owned with WBAC(AM). Feb 27, 1980: 95.3 mhz; 3.5 kw. Ant 436 ft. TL: N35 09 54 W84 51 13. Stereo. Prog sep from AM. (615) 472-4053. Format: Adult contemp.

WCLE(AM)—May 2, 1957: 1570 khz; 5 kw-D, 84 w-N. TL: N35 10 55 W84 50 55. 1995 Keith St. N.W. (37311). (615) 472-6511. Licensee: Randal W. Sliger (acq 7-19-93; $200,000 with WCLE-FM Calhoun; FTR 8-9-93). Net: NBC. Rep: Keystone (unwired net); Midsouth. Wash atty: Greg Skall. Format: C&W. News staff 2; news progmg 14 hrs wkly. ■ George Wyatt, gen mgr & gen sls mgr; Kathy Usury, prom dir; George Carpenter, progmg dir & mus dir; Tom Rowland, news dir; Jim Sliger, chief engr. ■ Rates: $11; 9; 11; 7.

*WSMC-FM—See Collegedale.

WUSY(FM)—Aug 1, 1961: 100.7 mhz; 100 kw. Ant 1,191 ft. TL: N35 12 26 W85 17 10. Stereo. Box 8799, Chattanooga (37414). (615) 892-3333. FAX: (615) 899-7224. Licensee: Colonial Broadcasting (acq 5-19-83). Net: Unistar. Format: Contemp country. ■ Sammy George, gen mgr; Charles Sells, gen sls mgr & prom mgr; Bob Sterling, progmg dir & mus dir; Shedd Johnson, news dir; Andre Johnson, chief engr.

Clinton

*WDVX(FM)—Not on air, target date unknown: 89.9 mhz; 200 w. Ant 1,960 ft. Box 808, Rt. 1, Duff (37729). Licensee: Communities Communications Inc.

*WYFC(FM)—July 4, 1966: 95.3 mhz; 540 w. Ant 669 ft. TL: N36 04 21 W84 01 18. Stereo. Hrs opn: 24. 7901 Old Clinton Pike, Powell (37849). (615) 938-7843. Licensee: Bible Broadcasting Network. (group owner; acq 8-18-89; $450,000; FTR 9-5-89). Rep: Eastman. Format: Traditional Christian. ■ Lowell Davey, pres; Damon Rose, gen mgr.

WYSH(AM)—November 1960: 1380 khz; 1 kw-D, 500 w-N, DA-N. TL: N36 06 48 W84 08 30. Hrs opn: 24. Box 329 (37717). (615) 457-1380. Licensee: Clinton Broadcasters Inc. (acq 6-10-91; $138,000; FTR 11-19-90). Net: Tenn. Net. Rep: Keystone (unwired net). Format: C&W. News progmg 5 hrs wkly. Target aud: 25-54; families: blue collar to upper income. Spec prog: Relg 15 hrs wkly. ■ Ronald C. Meredith Jr., pres & gen mgr; Denise Meredith, opns mgr & progmg dir; Wendall Eads, gen sls mgr; Candi Bryant, prom dir; Tom Bryant, mus dir; Bob Wallace, chief engr. ■ Rates: $6; 6; 6; 5.

Coalmont

WSGM(FM)—Not on air, target date unknown: 104.7 mhz; 1 kw. Ant 548 ft. TL: N35 20 22 W85 46 10. Stereo. Hrs opn: 6 AM-11 PM. Box 1269, Tracy City (37387); Fire Tower Rd., Tracy City (37387). (615) 592-7777; (615) 692-7777. Licensee: Cumberland Communication Corp. Wash atty: Donald Martin. Format: Div, relg. News progmg 30 hrs wkly. Target aud: General; interested in community affairs. ■ Dr. Byron Harbolt, pres; Jerry Fletcher, vp, gen mgr, gen sls mgr & progmg mgr; Nancy Fletcher, adv mgr & pub affrs dir; Y.B. Ashley, news dir; Phil Patton, chief engr.

Collegedale

*WSMC-FM—November 1961: 90.5 mhz; 100 kw. Ant 554 ft. TL: N35 01 20 W85 04 32 (CP: 1,029 ft., N35 15 20 W 85 13 34). Stereo. Box 870 (37315). (615) 238-2905. Licensee: Southern College. Net: APR, NPR. Format: Class, news. Target aud: 25-54. ■ Donald Sahly, pres; Doug Walter, gen mgr & chief engr; Myrna Ott, opns dir; Jeff Lemon, dev dir; Jeanette Hart, sls dir; Dan Landrum, progmg dir; Jeremy Francisco, mus dir.

Collierville

WCRV(AM)—Oct 1, 1966: 640 khz; 50 kw-D, 480 w-N, DA-N. TL: N34 59 35 W89 53 58. Hrs opn: 24. 4990 Poplar Ave., Memphis (38117). (901) 763-4640. FAX: (901) 763-4920. Licensee: Bott Broadcasting (group owner). Format: Relg, news/talk. Target aud: 35-64; family oriented, mature. ■ Richard P. Bott, pres & vp; Mark Loeffel, gen mgr.

WPLX(AM)—Licensed to Collierville. See Memphis.

Colonial Heights

*WZMC(AM)—Dec 31, 1984: 870 khz; 10 kw-D. TL: N36 27 40 W82 27 12. Hrs opn: Sunrise-sunset. Box 870, Milligan College (37682). (615) 461-8787; (615) 461-8962. FAX: (615) 461-8755. Licensee: Milligan College (acq 11-21-91; $115,000; FTR 12-16-91). Rep: Target. Format: News. News staff 3; news progmg 60 hrs wkly. Target aud: 25-55. Spec prog: Relg 5 hrs wkly.

Columbia

*WAYM(FM)—Not on air, target date unknown: 88.7 mhz; 3.5 kw. Ant 508 ft. TL: N35 49 27 W86 49 28. Box 061275, Fort Myers, FL (33906). Licensee: Southwest Florida Community Radio Inc. (acq 3-13-91; FTR 4-1-91).

WKOM(FM)—Listing follows WKRM(AM).

WKRM(AM)—Nov 25, 1946: 1340 khz; 1 kw-U. TL: N35 36 38 W87 03 22. Box 1377 (38401); 315 W. 7th St. (38401). (615) 388-3636. FAX: (615) 381-3636. Licensee: Robert M. McKay III (acq 12-26-89). Net: CBS. Rep: Southern. Format: Country. News staff one; news progmg 8 hrs wkly. Target aud: 25-54. Spec prog: Black one hr, relg 4 hrs wkly. ■ R. M. McKay Jr., pres; R. M. McKay III, gen mgr; Jerry Twilla, gen sls mgr & prom mgr; Randy Barlow, news dir; Roger Peters, chief engr.

WKOM(FM)—Co-owned with WKRM(AM). Jan 1, 1967: 101.7 mhz; 3 kw. Ant 300 ft. TL: N35 37 04 W87 02 34. Stereo. Prog sep from AM. (Acq 9-1-72). Format: Pure Gold. News staff one; news progmg 3 hrs wkly. Target aud: 30-50.

WMCP(AM)—Nov 12, 1956: 1280khz; 5 kw-D, 500 w-N, DA-N. TL: N35 37 08 W86 58 52. Box 711, 1st Farmer & Merchants Bank Bldg., 816 S. Garden (38401). (615) 388-3241. FAX: (615) 381-2510. Licensee: Maury County Boosters Corp. (acq 12-79). Net: ABC/E; Tenn. Radio Net. Format: C&W, farm. News staff one; news progmg 13 hrs wkly. Target aud: Adults 18 plus. ■ Edna Williford, pres & gen mgr; Mack Shaw, vp & gen sls mgr; Tom Williford, progmg dir & news dir; Mike Williams, mus dir; M. Keith Williford, chief engr. ■ Rates: $10; 10; 10; 10.

WMRB(AM)—Aug 14, 1982: 910 khz; 500 w-D, 88 w-N. TL: N35 36 24 W87 01 30. 609 W. Seventh St. (38401). (615) 381-7100. FAX: (615) 381-7101. Licensee: B & B Broadcasting (group owner; acq 4-15-93; $50,000; FTR 5-3-93). Net: USA. Rep: Dora Clayton. Format: Adult contemp. ■ Randy Benderman, gen mgr; Michael Bridges, opns mgr. ■ Rates: $20; 15; 20; 15.

Cookeville

WGSQ(FM)—Listing follows WPTN(AM).

WHUB(AM)—July 20, 1940: 1400 khz; 1 kw-U. TL: N36 10 25 W85 30 40. Hrs opn: 20. Box 1420 (38503); 136 E. Spring St. (38501). (615) 526-2131. FAX: (615) 528-3635. Licensee: WHUB Inc. Net: CBS. Rep: Midsouth. Format: Country. News staff one; news progmg 18 hrs wkly. Target aud: General. Spec prog: Farm 3 hrs wkly. ■ M. Luke Medley, pres; Stacey Mott, gen mgr; Martin Medley, gen sls mgr; Gene Davidson, progmg dir; Mike Dyer, mus dir; Austin Stinnett, chief engr. ■ Rates: $10; 9; 10; 8.

WHUB-FM—Mar 26, 1964: 98.5 mhz; 50 kw. Ant 492 ft. TL: N36 08 34 W85 28 02. Stereo. Hrs opn: 20. Prog sep from AM. Net: CBS Spectrum. Format: Adult contemp. News progmg 8 hrs wkly. ■ Rates: $16; 15; 16; 14.

WPTN(AM)—July 10, 1962: 780 khz; 1 kw-D. TL: N36 09 30 W85 31 15. Box 3146, 698 S. Willow (38501). (615) 526-7144. FAX: (615) 528-8400. Licensee: Cookeville Radio General Partnership (acq 1-11-89; $2.5 million with co-located FM; FTR 8-7-89). Net: ABC/I. Rep: Katz. Wash atty: Haley, Bader & Potts. Format: News/talk. News staff 2; news progmg 14 hrs wkly. Target aud: General. ■ John Casey, chmn; Bob Williamson, pres; Dave Thomas, gen mgr & gen sls mgr; Dave Johnson, prom dir; Kerry Massey, progmg dir; Jim Herrin, news dir; Michelle Spencer, pub affrs dir; Austin Stinnett, chief engr. ■ Rates: $5; 5; 5; na.

WGSQ(FM)—Co-owned with WPTN(AM). Mar 8, 1963: 94.7 mhz; 100 kw. Ant 1,319 ft. TL: N36 10 26 W85 20 37. Stereo. Hrs opn: 24. Prog sep from AM. Net: ABC/C. Format: C&W. News staff 2; news progmg 28 hrs wkly. Target aud: General. ■ Dave Thomas, vp, vp sls & natl sls mgr; Michael Bandy, prom dir; Kimberly Vance, progmg mgr; Phillip Gibbons, mus dir. ■ Rates: $30; 30; 30; 30.

*WTTU(FM)—May 22, 1972: 88.5 mhz; 2.25 kw. Ant 168 ft. TL: N36 10 26 W85 30 12 (CP: 2 kw-H, ant 164 ft.). Stereo. Box 5113, University Ctr., Dixie Ave. (38505). (615) 372-3169. FAX: (615) 372-6138. Licensee: Tennessee Technological Univ. Format: Progsv. News progmg 2 hrs wkly. Spec prog: Black 3 hrs, jazz 3 hrs, contemp Christian 6 hrs, metal 3 hrs, reggae 3 hrs, blues 3 hrs, Christian metal 3 hrs wkly. ■ Joe Doyle, mus dir.

*WWOG(FM)—Not on air, target date unknown: 90.9 mhz; 3 kw. Ant 697 ft. TL: N36 11 05 W85 22 30. c/o 2034 N. Hwy. 39, Somerset, KY (42501). Licensee: Somerset Educational Broadcasting Foundation.

Copperhill

WLSB(AM)—Dec 2, 1958: 1400 khz; 1 kw-U. TL: N34 59 25 W84 23 02. Hrs opn: 6 AM-10 PM. Box 430 (37317). (615) 496-3311. Licensee: Copper Basin Broadcasting Inc. (acq 12-1-62). Format: Country, gospel. ■ Robert P. Schwab Sr., pres & gen mgr; Barry Newman, opns mgr; Donald Rutherford, mus dir.

Covington

WKBL(AM)—Aug 16, 1954: 1250 khz; 1 kw-D, 106 w-N. TL: N35 35 10 W89 38 35. Hrs opn: 6 AM-10 PM. 101 WKBL Dr. (38019). (901) 476-7129. FAX: (901) 476-7120. Licensee: Royce D. Wilson (acq 4-1-82; $380,000 with co-located FM; FTR 3-29-82). Net: Tenn. Net. Format: Gospel, relg. News staff 2; news progmg 14 hrs wkly. Target aud: General. Spec prog: Black 12 hrs wkly. ■ Royce Wilson, gen mgr, progmg dir & news dir; Don Wilson, gen sls mgr & mus dir; Dee May, chief engr. ■ Rates: $6; 6; 6; 6.

WKBL-FM—Aug 31, 1965: 93.5 mhz; 6 kw. Ant 328 ft. TL: N35 35 12 W89 38 21. Stereo. Hrs opn: 6 AM-10 PM. Format: Super country. ■ Rates: Same as AM.

Cowan

WZYX(AM)—Mar 10, 1957: 1440 khz; 5 kw-D, 100 w-N. TL: N35 09 39 W86 01 51. Stereo. Hrs opn: 24. Box 398, 540 W. Cumberland St. (37318-0398). (615) 967-7471. Licensee: Tims Ford Broadcasting Co. (acq 6-1-80). Net: MBS, NBC Talknet, Westwood One, NBC. Rep: Midsouth. Format: Country, oldies, adult contemp. News staff one; news progmg 15 hrs wkly. Target aud: 35-55; middle-of-the-road working people. Spec prog: Talk, gospel 10 hrs, farm 2 hrs wkly. ■ Joe Brewer, pres, gen mgr & mus dir; Mary Lou Garner, vp, prom mgr & pub affrs dir; Chuck Moye, gen sls mgr; Jeff Pennington, progmg dir & asst mus dir; Dale D. Moore, news dir; Tom Wiseman, chief engr. ■ Rates: $8; 8; 8; na.

Crossville

WAEW(AM)—1952: 1330 khz; 1 kw-D. TL: N35 56 59 W85 02 08 (CP: TL: N35 57 01 W85 02 09). Box 1110, Tenth St. (38557). (615) 484-5115; (615) 484-9014. FAX: (615) 456-1195. Licensee: Crossville Radio Inc. (acq 9-2-88). Net: Moody. Rep: MidSouth. Format: Talk. News staff one; news progmg 4 hrs wkly. Target aud: 25-54. ■ Ed Whiteaker, pres, gen mgr & gen sls mgr; Tony Wick, progmg dir & mus dir; Lee Lawson, news dir; Gunther Muhsemann, chief engr. ■ Rates: $8; 8; 8; 8.

WCSV(AM)—June 15, 1968: 1490 khz; 1 kw-U. TL: N35 56 46 W85 02 13 (CP: TL: N35 57 01 W85 02 09). Box 591 (38557); 716 Miller Ave. (38555). (615) 484-5168. Licensee: Samuel T. Ames (acq 8-21-92; $5,160; FTR 9-7-92). Net: ABC/E. Rep: Keystone (unwired net), Midsouth. Format: C&W. News staff one; news progmg 3 hrs wkly. Target aud: General. Spec prog: Relg 5 hrs, nostalgia 5 hrs, oldies 2 hrs, bluegrass 2 hrs wkly. ■ James P. Young, pres, gen mgr & news dir; Rita L. Young, vp & gen sls mgr; John M. Cunningham, chief engr. ■ Rates: $14; 9.50; 12; 7.

WEGE(FM)—June 15, 1990: 102.5 mhz; 6 kw. Ant 984 ft. TL: N36 01 22 W85 00 07 (CP: 3.16 kw, ant 922 ft.). Stereo. Box 2525 (38557); 716 Miller Ave. (38555). (615) 456-9343. Licensee: Mountain Top Broadcasters Inc. Format: Country. Spec prog: Relg 5 hrs, nostalgia 5 hrs, oldies 2 hrs, bluegrass one hr wkly. ■ James P. Young, pres, gen mgr & news dir; Rita L. Young, vp & gen sls mgr; John M. Cunningham, chief engr.

WXVL(FM)—May 12, 1967: 99.3 mhz; 6 kw. Ant 259 ft. TL: N35 57 01 W85 02 09. Stereo. Box 1110, 510 10th St. (38557). Licensee: Crossville Radio Inc. Format: Adult contemp. ■ Ed Whittaker, gen mgr.

Dayton

WDNT(AM)—Dec 6, 1957: 1280 khz; 1 kw-D, 345 w-N. TL: N35 28 12 W85 02 15. Box 290, 3931 Raga Cty Hwy. (37321). (615) 775-2331. FAX: (615) 775-9368. Licensee: Dayton Broadcasting Co. (acq 12-30-86). Format: C&W. ■ George Johnson, pres; Rick Dye, gen mgr; Sue Jackson, stn mgr; Krystal Tylley, news dir & pub affrs dir; George C. Hudson, chief engr. ■ Rates: $8.50; 8; 8.50; 7.

WDNT-FM—July 1, 1976: 104.9 mhz; 420 w. Ant 699 ft. TL: N35 29 31 W85 02 59 (CP: 1.15 kw, ant 535 ft., TL: N35 26 57 W85 02 59). Stereo. (615) 775-5750. FAX: (615) 775-9368. Format: Modern country. News staff 2; news progmg 15 hrs wkly. Target aud: 21 plus; working adults. ■ Rates: Same as AM.

WREA(AM)—Sept 8, 1979: 1520 khz; 5 kw-D. TL: N35 30 40 W85 00 36. Hrs opn: Sunrise-sunset. 3269 Market St. (37321). (615) 775-5000. Licensee: Jackson Broadcasting Corp. (acq 10-3-85). Format: Oldies, relg. News progmg 3 hrs wkly. Target aud: Baby boomers. ■ Wade Brock, pres & chief engr; Jim Graw, gen mgr, prom mgr, progmg dir, mus dir & news dir; Marilyn Graw, stn mgr, gen sls mgr, adv dir & asst mus dir; Dorothy Anderson, rgnl sls mgr & adv mgr. ■ Rates: $8; 8; 8; na.

Dickson

WDKN(AM)—Jan 1, 1955: 1260 khz; 5 kw-D. TL: N36 06 31 W87 22 14. Box 607, 106 E. College St. (37055). (615) 446-4000. Licensee: Edmission & Eubank Communications Inc. (acq 6-29-87; $220,000; FTR 5-18-87). Wash atty: McCampbell & Young. Format: C&W. News progmg 3 hrs wkly. Target aud: General. Spec prog: Relg 12 hrs. ■ Tommy Edmisson, pres & gen mgr; Oscar Eubank, vp & chief engr; Jackie Vares Rhodes, gen sls mgr; Bill McColluga, progmg dir; Gordon Rhodes, mus dir. ■ Rates: $9; 9; 9; 9.

WQZQ(FM)—Apr 27, 1964: 102.5 mhz; 50 kw. Ant 500 ft. TL: N36 06 31 W87 22 14. Stereo. Hrs opn: 24. Box 171097, Nashville (37217). 1824 Murfreesboro Rd., Nashville (37217). (615) 399-1029. FAX: (615) 399-1023. Licensee: Montgomery Broadcasting (acq 1990). Rep: Katz & Powell. Wash atty: Pepper & Corazzini. Format: Easy listening. Target aud: 35 plus; mature, well-educated, affluent. ■ Bayard H. Walters, pres; Larry Trimmer, vp, gen mgr & progmg dir; Melodie Houston, chief opns; Melodie Huston, news dir; Watt Hairston, chief engr.

WYYB(FM)—May 1, 1992: 93.7 mhz; 6 kw. Ant 215 ft. TL: N36 04 32 W87 15 44. Hrs opn: 24. Box 607, 106 E. College St. (37055). FAX: (615) 446-9681. Licensee: Edmission & Eubank Communications Inc. Wash atty: McCambell & Young (Bob Stone). Format: Soft Spectrum music, local sports, country, news/talk. News progmg 3 hrs wkly. Target aud: General. ■ Oscar Eubank, chmn & chief engr; Tommy Edmisson, pres, gen mgr, dev dir & sls dir; Leroy Kennell, sr vp; Jackie Rhodes, opns mgr, gen sls mgr & adv dir; Gordon Rhodes, progmg mgr & mus dir. ■ Rates: $12; 12; 12; 12.

Donelson

WAMB(AM)—Licensed to Donelson. See Nashville.

WAMB-FM—Licensed to Donelson. See Nashville.

Dresden

WGNN(FM)—Apr 10, 1992: 95.1 mhz; 6 kw. Ant 328 ft. TL: N36 15 50 W88 40 03. Box 789 (38225). (901) 364-5253. FAX: (901) 364-5253. Licensee: Dresden Broadcasting Inc. Format: Gospel. ■ John Latham, gen mgr; Rodney Minyard, progmg dir.

Dunlap

WSDQ(AM)—Nov 1, 1980: 1190 khz; 5 kw-D. TL: N35 21 41 W85 22 33. Suite B, 712 Old York Hwy. N. (37327). (615) 949-4114. FAX: (615) 949-5143. Licensee: Tollye Wayne Tittsworth (acq 6-4-84). Net: ABC/E; Tenn. Radio Net. Format: C&W, Top-40. Spec prog: Farm one hr, gospel 7 hrs wkly. ■ Tollye Wayne Tittsworth, pres, gen mgr, prom mgr & news dir; Ruth Tittsworth, gen sls mgr, progmg dir & mus dir; Ed Harmon, chief engr.

Dyersburg

WASL(FM)—Listing follows WTRO(AM).

***WKNQ(FM)**—Oct 30, 1992. 90.7 mhz; 100 kw. Ant 373 ft. TL: N36 06 00 W89 29 12. Stereo. Hrs opn: 24. Rebroadcasts WKNO(FM) Memphis 100%. Box 241880, Memphis (38124); 900 Getwell Rd. (38111). (901) 458-2521. FAX: (901) 458-2221. Licensee: Mid-South Public Communication Foundation. Net: APR, NPR. Wash atty: Schartz, Woods & Miller. Format: Class, news. News staff one; news progmg 46 hrs wkly. Target aud: 35 plus. ■ Michael LaBonia, pres; Dan Campbell, gen mgr; Darel Snodgrass, opns dir & progmg mgr; Charles McLarty, dev dir; Becky Kelly, dev mgr; Jim Eikner, gen sls mgr; Joel Hurd, prom mgr; Everette Rice, news dir; Pamela Poletti, pub affrs dir; Russ Abernathy, engrg dir; Pat Lane, chief engr.

WTRO(AM)—July 13, 1946: 1450 khz; 1 kw-U. TL: N36 03 02 W89 22 07. Hrs opn: 24. Box 100, Radio Rd. (38025); One Radio Rd. (38024). (901) 285-1450; (901) 285-1339. FAX: (901) 287-0100. Licensee: Dr. Pepper/Pepsi Cola Bottling Co. of Dyersburg Inc. (acq 1991). Net: ABC/C. Wash atty: Bryan, Cave, McPheeters & McRoberts. Format: Country. ■ W. E. Burks, pres; Charles W. Maxey, exec vp & gen mgr; Steve Guttery, opns mgr & progmg dir; Dave Parker, gen sls mgr; Linda Graves, prom mgr; Earl Danials, mus dir; Wayne Doles, news dir; Dave Hacker, chief engr.

WASL(FM)—Co-owned with WTRO(AM). July 1, 1968: 100.1 mhz; 26 kw. Ant 676 ft. TL: N36 04 14 W89 23 52. Stereo. Hrs opn: 24. Prog sep from AM. Net: Tenn. Radio. Format: Hot adult contemp. News progmg 5 hrs wkly. Target aud: 18-54. ■ Amy Maxey, prom mgr.

East Ridge

WOGT(FM)—Nov 9, 1990: 107.9 mhz; 3 kw. Ant 328 ft. TL: N34 56 37 W85 18 01. Hrs opn: 24. Box 11202, Chattanooga (37401). (615) 756-6141. FAX: (615) 266-1652. Licensee: Radio Chattanooga Inc. Group owner: Bloomington Broadcasting Corp. (acq 8-11-93; $1.3 million; FTR 8-30-93). Format: Oldies. ■ Donald J. Newberg, gen mgr; Dan Brown, gen sls mgr; John Wailin, progmg dir; Bill Lockheart, news dir; Mike Murrell, chief engr.

Elizabethton

WBEJ(AM)—July 1946: 1240 khz; 1 kw-U. TL: N36 20 07 W82 13 03. Hrs opn: 24. 626 1/2 E. Elk Ave. (37643). (615) 542-2184. FAX: (615) 542-2185. Licensee: CB Radio Inc. (acq 9-24-82; $335,000; FTR 10-18-82). Net: Unistar. Format: Country. News staff one; news progmg 3 hrs wkly. Target aud: 25-49. ■ Don Crisp, pres; Cleo Reed, gen mgr; David A. Miller, opns dir, progmg dir & mus dir; Barton Edens, gen sls mgr; Bernard Leonard, chief engr. ■ Rates: $10; 9; 10; 9.

WUSJ-FM—May 17, 1968: 99.3 mhz; 420 w. Ant 2,148 ft. TL: N36 25 53 W82 08 16. Stereo. Box 5188 EKS, Johnson City (37603). (615) 926-3121. FAX: (615) 929-8799. Licensee: Eaton P. Govan III & Berton B. Cagle Jr. (acq 4-86). Net: NBC. Rep: D & R Radio. Format: Country. News staff 3. Target aud: 25-54. ■ Eaton P. Govan III, pres & gen mgr; Roger Bouldin, opns dir & chief engr; Ben Cagle, gen sls mgr; Liz McCarter, prom mgr; Kevin Tanner, progmg dir; Nancy Ensor, Bob Love, news dirs.

Englewood

WENR(AM)—Apr 21, 1967: 1090 khz; 1 kw-D. TL: N35 25 35 W84 30 57. Drawer 670, Hwy. 39 (37329). (615) 887-1090; (615) 458-4400. Licensee: M & H Broadcasting Inc. (group owner; acq 10-27-92; $75,000; FTR 11-30-92). Net: Tenn. Net. Format: Relg, country. ■ J.B. Mull, gen mgr; Bob Thomas, gen sls mgr & progmg dir; Robert Wallace, chief engr.

Erwin

WEMB(AM)—May 17, 1956: 1420 khz; 5 kw-D. TL: N36 06 58 W82 26 49. Box 280, Asheville Hwy. S. (37650). (615) 743-6123; (615) 743-6124. FAX: (615) 743-6124. Licensee: WEMB Inc. (acq 4-1-61). Net: ABC/E; Tenn. Net. Rep: Midsouth. Format: C&W, div. News staff one; news progmg 3 hrs wkly. Spec prog: Bluegrass 2 hrs, big band 2 hrs, gospel 10 hrs wkly. ■ J.E. True Jr., pres; Jim Crawford, gen mgr; Charles W. Ray, progmg dir, mus dir & chief engr; Kathy Thornberry, news dir.

WXIS(FM)—Co-owned with WEMB(AM). Nov 21, 1968: 103.9 mhz; 2.5 kw. Ant 2,600 ft. TL: N36 08 15 W82 23 00. Stereo. Prog sep from AM. Format: AOR. News staff one. ■ Todd Ambros, mus dir; Ken Silvers, asst mus dir.

Etowah

WDRZ-FM—1977: 103.1 mhz; 50 kw. Ant 492 ft. TL: N35 27 24 W84 40 43. 2500 Executive Park N., Cleveland (37312); Box 4492, Cleveland (37320). (615) 339-1103. Licensee: BVACK Broadcasting Co. Inc. (acq 7-28-83; $259,000 with co-located AM; FTR 8-15-83). Net: CBN. Format: Contemp Christian. ■ Vardaman White, pres; Crystle White, gen mgr; Steve Chelehe, gen sls mgr; Jim Long, chief engr.

WCPH(AM)—Co-owned with WDRZ-FM. 1955: 1220 khz; 1 kw-D, 108 w-N. TL: N35 19 15 W84 30 34. Stn currently dark.

Fairview

WPFD(AM)—May 28, 1982: 850 khz; 500 w-D. TL: N36 00 29 W87 08 38. Hrs opn: 6 AM-sunset. 1074 Hwy. 96 N. (37062). (615) 799-8585. Licensee: Robert Lee Martin, trustee. Format: Country. Target aud: 18-54. ■ Sam Warden, pres; Chuck Hussey, gen mgr; John Almon, chief engr. ■ Rates: $6.50; 6.50; 6.50; na.

Farragut

WTNN(AM)—Nov 10, 1988: 670 khz; 500 w-D. TL: N35 53 12 W84 14 48. Stereo. 13206 Buttermilk Rd., Knoxville (37932). (615) 531-2297; (615) 690-8807. FAX: (615) 531-2297. Licensee: Barry Frank Cummings. Net: USA. Format: Jazz, talk. News staff one. Target aud: 25-54; upscale adults. ■ Barry Frank Cummings M.D., pres; Ken Crostwait, gen mgr; Barry Shelton, progmg dir. ■ Rates: $15; 15; 15, na.

Fayetteville

WEKR(AM)—Oct 1, 1948: 1240 khz; 1 kw-U. TL: N35 09 28 W86 35 25. Hrs opn: 4:30 AM-10 PM. Box 638, 7 Old Boonshill Rd. (37334). (615) 433-3545; (615) 433-4487. FAX: (615) 438-0620. Licensee: Hopkins Broadcasting System Inc. (acq 6-27-91; $213,000; FTR 7-15-91). Net: MBS, NBC Talknet, MRN; Tenn. Radio Net. Format: C&W. News staff one; news progmg 5 hrs wkly. Target aud: 25 plus; general. Spec prog: Farm one hr wkly. ■ Claude Hopkins, CEO; Lee Maddox, gen mgr, gen sls mgr, progmg dir & mus dir; Ernest Tucker, chief opns; Don Counts, prom mgr; Eddie Tucker, news dir; Ernest J. Tucker, chief engr. ■ Rates: $9; 7; 7; 7.

WYTM-FM—Mar 27, 1970: 105.5 mhz; 3 kw. Ant 295 ft. TL: N35 07 37 W86 34 47 (CP: 2.25 kw, ant 495 ft.). Stereo. Hrs opn: 5 AM-midnight. Box 717, Milano Rd. (37334). (615) 433-1531. FAX: (615) 433-4110. Licensee: Time Broadcasters Inc. Format: Country. ■ Joseph D. Young, pres & gen mgr; Jerry Raby, opns mgr; Don Roden, chief engr.

Franklin

WAKM(AM)—Mar 18, 1953: 950 khz; 1 kw-D, 80 w-N. TL: N35 57 25 W86 50 03. Hrs opn: 18. Box 469, 222 Mallory Stn. Rd. (37065). (615) 794-1594. FAX: (615) 794-1595. Licensee: Franklin Radio Associates Inc. (acq 10-1-82; $310,600; FTR 10-18-82). Net: UPI; Tenn. Radio Net. Format: Country crossover. News staff one; news progmg 14 hrs wkly. Target aud: 24 plus. Spec prog: NASCAR racing 4 hrs wkly. ■ James H. Hayes, chmn & CFO; Tom Lawrence, pres, gen mgr & gen sls mgr; Charles C. Dibrel Sr., exec vp; William W. Ewin Jr., sr vp & vp opns; Dibrell Williams, vp, vp prom, vp progmg & mus dir; Linda Jackson Carden, sls dir; Jim Hayes, engrg mgr. ■ Rates: $12.50; 10; 10; 7.50.

WIZO(AM)—Feb 1, 1969: 1380 khz; 5 kw-D, 500 w-N, DA-N. TL: N35 54 22 W86 54 21. Hrs opn: 18. 1811 Carters Creek Pike (37064). (615) 791-1380. FAX: (615) 791-1346. Licensee: A.J. Communications Inc. (acq 10-22-91; $160,000; FTR 11-11-91). Net: CNN. Wash atty: Pepper & Corazzini. Format: Classic rock, oldies, div. News staff one; news progmg 7 hrs wkly. Target aud: 18-65; those who enjoy the hits of the 40s, 50s, 60s & 70s. Spec prog: Sports 6 hrs, gospel 3 hrs, relg 3 hrs wkly. ■ Alice Jackson, pres, gen sls mgr & news dir; Jan Carroll, pub affrs dir; Gary Brown, chief engr.

WRLT-FM—Nov 16, 1961: 100.1 mhz; 3 kw. Ant 1,134 ft. TL: N36 02 06 W86 50 54. Stereo. Hrs opn: 24. Suite 100, 131 2nd Ave. N., Nashville (37201-1917). (615) 242-5600. FAX: (615) 242-9877. Licensee: GMX Communications of Tennessee Inc. (acq 10-1-88; grpsl). Net: ABC/C. Rep: Dora-Clayton. Wash atty: Fisher, Wayland, Cooper & Leader. Format: Progsv adult AOR. News staff one; news progmg 5 hrs wkly. Target aud: 25-49; sophisticated music lovers. Spec prog: Jazz 7 hrs, blues 3 hrs, new age 2 hrs wkly. ■ Ned Horton, pres, gen mgr & progmg dir; John Conlon, opns dir; John Moseley, gen sls mgr; James Wade, prom dir; Michael Parks, progmg mgr & mus dir; Pat Reilly, news dir; Mark Alan, pub affrs dir; Gibson Prichard, engrg dir. ■ Rates: $40; 35; 40; 30.

Gallatin

WGFX(FM)—Dec 1, 1960: 104.5 mhz; 49 kw. Ant 1,312 ft. TL: N36 16 05 W86 47 16. Stereo. Hrs opn: 24. Box 101604, Nashville (37224); 506 2nd Ave. S., Nashville (37210). (615) 244-9533; (615) 737-1045. FAX: (615) 259-1271. Licensee: Dick Broadcasting Co. Inc. of Tennessee (acq 11-23-92; $6.5 million with WKZL(FM) Winston-Salem, NC; FTR 12-14-92). Net: NBC the Source. Rep: Katz. Wash atty: Kaye, Scholer, Fierman, Hays & Handler. Format: Classic rock. Target aud: 18-49. ■ Allen Dick, pres; Stephen E. Dickert, vp, gen mgr, vp opns & gen sls mgr; Kidd Redd, opns dir & progmg dir; Pat Ervin, opns mgr & prom dir; Steve Dickert, natl sls mgr; Paul Lyle, rgnl sls mgr; Mark Hale, adv dir; John Nagarya, mus dir; Harry Magee, news dir; Dave Hodge, chief engr.

WHIN(AM)—Aug 2, 1948: 1010 khz; 5 kw-D. TL: N36 26 00 W86 28 00. Stereo. 1625 Hwy. 109 N. (37066). (615) 451-0450; (615) 452-9446. FAX: (615) 451-0451. Licensee: WHIN Inc. (acq 10-84). Rep: Midsouth. Format: Country. News staff one; news progmg 14 hrs wkly. Target aud: 25-54; upper middle to lower middle income. Spec prog: Black 2 hrs, Farm 5 hrs wkly. ■ Jack Williams, pres, gen mgr, progmg dir & mus dir; Paul Martin, gen sls mgr; Ivan Davis, chief engr.

***WVCP(FM)**—Jan 4, 1979: 88.5 mhz; 1 kw. Ant 390 ft. TL: N36 28 02 W86 28 35. Stereo. Hrs opn: 6 AM-10 PM M-F, 7 AM-11 PM Sat & Sun. Suite A-201, 1360 Nashville Pike (37066). (615) 451-1640. Licensee: Volunteer State Comm. College. Net: AP. Format: Div, CHR. Spec prog: Black 8 hrs, class 15 hrs, metal 10 hrs, jazz 15 hrs wkly. ■ Hal R. Ramer, pres; Howard Espravnik, gen mgr; John Robbins, prom mgr & progmg dir; Darren Futch, mus dir; James Milliner, chief engr.

Gatlinburg

WDLY(FM)—January 1983: 105.5 mhz; 650 w. Ant 964 ft. TL: N35 42 13 W83 33 57. Stereo. Hrs opn: 24. Box 4340, 415 Middle Creek Rd., Sevierville (37864-4340). (615) 453-2844. FAX: (615) 429-2601. Licensee: Dolly-Wood Broadcasting Co. (acq 5-31-90; grpsl; FTR 6-18-90). Net: CBS; Tenn. Radio Net. Rep: Rgnl Reps. Format: Contemp country. News staff one. Target aud: 25-49; local adults, tourists, C&W lovers. ■ Gary Voss, gen mgr; Clydia Millard, rgnl sls mgr; Jim Meadows, prom mgr & mus dir; Charles Primm, news dir. ■ Rates: $25; 20; 20; 16.

Germantown

WAQK(FM)—Not on air, target date unknown: 107.5 mhz; 3 kw. Ant 328 ft. TL: N35 07 46 W89 45 30. 79 S. Mendenhall Rd., Memphis (38117). Licensee: Omni Broadcasting Corp.

WNWZ(AM)—Licensed to Germantown. See Memphis.

WOGY-FM—Licensed to Germantown. See Memphis.

Graysville

WAYB-FM—Not on air, target date unknown: 95.7 mhz; 55 kw. Ant 721 ft. TL: N35 30 44 W85 07 53. 4 Rockhaven Ln., Signal Mountain (37377). Licensee: Richard C. Wagner.

Greeneville

WGRV(AM)—1946: 1340 khz; 1 kw-U. TL: N36 10 10 W82 50 52. Hrs opn: 24. Box 278, 1004 Arnold Rd. (37744). (615) 638-4147. Licensee: Radio Greeneville Inc. Net: NBC; Tenn. Radio Net. Rep: Midsouth. Format: Modern country. News staff 3. ■ P. Ronald Metcalfe, pres & gen mgr; Ray Smith, opns mgr; Leroy Moon, gen sls mgr; Ron Metcalfe, progmg dir; Nathan Humbard, mus dir; Bobby Rader, news dir; Ray C. Elliott, chief engr. ■ Rates: $11.50; 9.25; 11.50; 9.25.

WIKQ(FM)—Co-owned with WGRV(AM). 1956: 94.9 mhz; 100 kw. Ant 1,090 ft. TL: N36 04 34 W82 41 28. Stereo. Hrs opn: 24. Prog sep from AM. (615) 639-1831. Net: SMN. Format: Adult contemp. News staff 2. Target aud: 25-49. ■ Rates: $20; 18.75; 20; 17.75.

WSMG(AM)—Dec 1, 1961: 1450 khz; 1 kw-U. TL: N36 10 30 W82 50 18. Box 727 (37744). (615) 638-3188. FAX: (615) 638-3180. Licensee: Burley Broadcasters Inc. (acq 10-1-72). Net: ABC/E. Format: C&W. Spec prog: Bluegrass 2 hrs wkly. ■ Darrell Bryan, pres, gen mgr, progmg dir & mus dir; Kathy Knight, gen sls mgr & prom mgr; Brian Cutshaw, news dir; Walt Stone, chief engr.

Harriman

WLIQ(FM)—Jan 21, 1981: 92.7 mhz; 1.25 kw. Ant 440 ft. TL: N35 56 05 W84 34 09 (CP: 790 w, ant 663 ft.). Stereo. Box 432 (37748). (615) 882-6500. FAX: (615) 882-3376. Licensee: W.O. Powers (acq 1-16-91; $1; FTR 2-10-92). Format: Country. ■ Orville Bailey, gen mgr; Donnie Halls, stn mgr; Ben Harold, progmg dir; Bob Wallace, chief engr.

Harrogate

***WLMU(FM)**—Aug 5, 1987: 91.3 mhz; 190 w. Ant 284 ft. TL: N36 35 10 W83 39 54. Stereo. Hrs opn: 6 AM-10 PM. Box 2025, Sigmon Communications Ctr., Hwy. 25E, (37752). (615) 869-4676; (615) 869-4825. Licensee: Lincoln Memorial University. Net: AP. Format: Adult contemp, oldies. News progmg 7 hrs wkly. Target aud: 25-54; businesses in the tri-state area. Spec prog: Gospel 4 hrs wkly. ■ Scott Miller, pres; Earl Brooks, exec vp; Marion Alexander, gen mgr; Michael R. Peace, stn mgr; Mike Peace, opns mgr, news dir & pub affrs dir; Scott Ogan, prom mgr & progmg dir; Scott Ogan, Steve Spicer, mus dirs; Bernard Leonard, engrg dir; David Laws, chief engr.

WSVQ(AM)—Nov 10, 1980: 740 khz; 1 kw-D. TL: N36 34 32 W83 39 37. Box 2025, Cumberland Gap Pkwy. (37752). (615) 869-4705. FAX: (615) 869-4825. Licensee: Pine Hills of Tenn, Inc. (acq 7-86). Net: ABC/E. Rep: Rgnl Reps. Format: Gospel. News staff 5. Target aud: 25-54. ■ Scott Miller, pres; Marion Alexander, gen mgr; Jay Don Gibson, gen sls mgr; Rusty Peace, prom mgr, progmg dir & mus dir; Scott Ogan, news dir; Bernie Leonard, chief engr. ■ Rates: $8; 7; 8; 5.

WXJB-FM—Aug 15, 1991. 96.5 mhz; 6 kw. Ant 325 ft. TL: N36 34 44 W83 34 42. Stereo. Hrs opn: 24. Box 719 (37752); 2118 Cumberland Ave., Middlesboro, KY (40965). (615) 869-2266; (606) 248-0001. FAX: (606) 248-6397. Licensee: Cumberland Broadcasters Inc. (acq 12-4-91; $90,000; FTR 1-6-92). Net: SMN, ABC/D; Ky. Net., Tenn. Net. Rep: Rgnl Reps. Wash atty: Bechtel & Cole. Format: Country. News staff 2; news progmg 25 hrs wkly. Target aud: 25-54; community-oriented adults. Spec prog: Farm 2 hrs, gospel 2 hrs, relg 2 hrs wkly. ■ Warren Pursifull, pres & gen mgr; Ben Harold, opns mgr; Jeff Hendrickson, sls dir; Rhonda Raines, mktg mgr, prom dir & mus dir; Jimmy Pursifull, adv dir; Dominica Reynolds, progmg dir; Terry Michael, news dir; Bernard Leonard, chief engr. ■ Rates: $6; 5; 5; 6.

Hartsville

WJKM(AM)—Sept 1, 1966: 1090 khz; 1 kw-D. TL: N36 23 17 W86 09 55. Box 1090, Marlene St. (37074). (615) 374-2111. Licensee: Blanton-Gosser-White Broadcasters Inc. (acq 5-11-87; $140,000; FTR 4-13-87). Rep: Keystone (unwired net). Format: C&W, relg, bluegrass. ■ Howard Gosser, gen mgr & gen sls mgr; Jerry Richmond, progmg dir & mus dir.

Henderson

***WFHC(FM)**—May 22, 1967: 91.5 mhz; 3 kw. Ant 300 ft. TL: N35 27 50 W88 41 10. Stereo. Hrs opn: 16. 158 E. Main (38340). (901) 989-6691; (901) 989-6749. FAX: (901) 989-6065. Licensee: Freed-Hardeman University. Format: Jazz, new age. News progmg 3 hrs wkly. Target aud: General; young adults to senior citizens. Spec prog: Gospel 5 hrs, blues 4 hrs wkly. ■ Milton Sewell, pres; Ray Eaton, gen mgr; P.J. Hicks, sls dir & mktg dir; Deborah Hicks, progmg dir; Chris Manel, mus dir; John Rickard, chief engr. ■ Rates: $3; 2; 3; 2.

WFKX(FM)—Feb 1, 1984: 95.9 mhz; 3 kw. Ant 300 ft. TL: N35 29 52 W88 42 29 (CP: 6 kw). Stereo. Hrs opn: 24. 425 E. Chester, Jackson (38301). (901) 427-9616. FAX: (901) 427-9302. Licensee: Wolfe Communications Inc. Wash atty: John Borsari. Format: Urban contemp, Black. Target aud: 18-34; the general Black population and contemporary women. ■ James E. Wolfe Jr., chmn, pres, gen mgr & stn mgr; Denise La Salle, vp; Dave Shaw, vp opns, opns dir & progmg dir; Steve Smith, gen sls mgr & adv mgr; Kimberly Kaye, mus dir; Jeffrey Butler, asst mus dir; Jefferson Jones, news dir; Kirk Hornac, chief engr. ■ Rates: $21; 19; 21; 19.

WHHM-FM—Nov 19, 1990: 107.7 mhz; 6 kw. Ant 328 ft. TL: N35 27 23 W88 37 36. Stereo. Hrs opn: 5 AM-11 PM. Box 203, 111 E. Main St. (38340). (901) 989-5981. Licensee: Chester County Broadcasting Co. Inc. (acq 7-2-93; FTR 8-2-93). Net: ABC/D, Tenn. Net. Rep: Midsouth. Wash atty: McFadden, Evans & Sill. Format: Hot country. News staff one; news progmg 5 hrs wkly. Target aud: 12 plus. Spec prog: Gospel 10 hrs, rock 6 hrs wkly. ■ Wanda Smith, pres, gen mgr, stn mgr, gen sls mgr & progmg mgr; Ted Charles, mus dir; Mike Whited, news dir; Mike Gideon, chief engr. ■ Rates: $10; 8; 10; 8.

Hendersonville

WQQK(FM)—Oct 16, 1970: 92.1 mhz; 3 kw. Ant 462 ft. TL: N36 17 50 W86 45 11 Stereo. Box 70085, 1320 Brick Church Rd., Nashville (37207). (615) 227-1470. FAX: (615) 227-2740. Licensee: Phoenix of Hendersonville Inc. (acq 5-17-82; $1.35 million; FTR 6-7-82). Net: ABC/C. Format: Urban contemp. News staff one. Target aud: 18-49; upscale professionals. Spec prog: Gospel 2 hrs, jazz 6 hrs, blues 6 hrs wkly. ■ Samuel H. Howard, pres; Scott Peters, gen mgr; Ernie Allen, news dir; Clinton Hooper, chief engr.

Hohenwald

WMLR(AM)—July 4, 1970: 1230 khz; 1 kw-U. TL: N35 31 22 W87 32 40. 184 Switzerland Rd. (38462). (615) 796-5966. FAX: (615) 796-5259. Licensee: Lewis County Broadcasting Co. Net: ABC/E. Format: C&W. ■ Julia Lane, gen mgr; David Lynn, mus dir; Revis Hobbs, chief engr.

Humboldt

WHMT(AM)—July 5, 1972: 1190 khz; 420 w-D. TL: N35 50 41 W88 54 08. Box 488, 2603 Spangler Park Dr. (38343). (901) 784-1190. FAX: (901) 784-4033. Licensee: Boyd Enterprises Inc. (acq 3-84; FTR 3-19-84). Net: ABC/E. Format: Pure gold. Target aud: 25-54. ■ F. Darrell Boyd, pres & gen mgr; F. Darrell Boyd II, gen sls mgr & news dir.

WLSZ(FM)—Co-owned with WHMT(AM). Jan 19, 1989: 105.3 mhz; 3 kw. Ant 328 ft. TL: N35 50 41 W88 54 08. Stereo. Hrs opn: 24. Dups AM 60%. (901) 784-1053. Format: Adult contemp.

WZDQ(FM)—Sept 1, 1964: 102.3 mhz; 6 kw. Ant 305 ft. TL: N35 45 45 W88 51 42. Stereo. Hrs opn: 24. Suite A, 378 Carriage House Dr., Jackson (38305). (901) 664-2102; (800) 951-2102. FAX: (901) 664-9875. Licensee: Quality Broadcasting of Tenn. Inc. Group owner: Quality Broadcasting Inc. (acq 4-3-87). Net: ABC, Westwood One. Rep: Rgnl Reps. Format: Adult contemp. Target aud: 25-54; middle to upper class adults. ■ Tom McAfee, vp, gen mgr & gen sls mgr; Brad Douglass, opns mgr, progmg dir & mus dir; David Hopper, news dir & pub affrs dir; Kirk Harnack, chief engr.

Huntingdon

WJPJ(AM)—Oct 21, 1975: 1530 khz; 1 kw-D. TL: N36 00 04 W88 26 02. Box 747, 207 W. Main St. (38344). (901) 986-9746. Licensee: Radio WJPJ (acq 4-1-91; $25,000; FTR 4-1-91). Format: Christian/Southern gospel. News staff 2. Target aud: General. ■ Howard E. Dickinson, gen mgr; Lynn Dickinson, stn mgr & gen sls mgr.

WTKB-FM—Not on air, target date unknown: 93.7 mhz; 6 kw. Ant 328 ft. TL: N35 57 05 W88 27 47. Box 565, 2052 Main St., Milan (38358). (901) 686-9852. Licensee: Big Tenn Communications Co. Inc. (acq 7-3-91; $15,000 for CP; FTR 7-29-91). ■ Brad McCoy, gen mgr.

WVHR(FM)—November 1979: 100.9 mhz; 6 kw. Ant 300 ft. TL: N35 57 05 W88 27 47. Stereo. Box 23 (38344). Box 114, 114 Baker (38344). (901) 986-2205. FAX: (901) 986-8557. Licensee: Milan Broadcasting Co. Inc. (acq 5-1-91; $150,000; FTR 5-27-91). Net: NBC; Tenn. Radio Net. Format: Country. ■ Jerry Vandiver, gen mgr & sls dir; Michael Ray, progmg dir; Dave Hacker, chief engr.

Jackson

WDXI(AM)—Oct 31, 1948: 1310 khz; 5 kw-D, 1 kw-N, DA-N. TL: N35 39 50 W88 49 20. Hrs opn: 24. One Radio Park (38301); Box 3845 (38303-3845). (901) 427-9611; (901) 424-1310. FAX: (901) 424-1321. Licensee: Gerald W. Hunt (acq 1-15-93; $480,000 with co-located FM; FTR 2-8-93). Net: SMN. Rep: D&R Radio. Format: C&W. News staff one; news progmg 10 hrs wkly. Target aud: 25 plus. Spec prog: Farm 12 hrs, gospel 16 hrs, sports 16 hrs wkly. ■ Gerald W. Hunt, gen mgr; Kirk Harnack, chief engr. ■ Rates: $18; 15; 18; 10.

WMXX-FM—Co-owned with WDXI(AM). May 9, 1979: 103.1 mhz; 35 kw. Ant 577 ft. TL: N35 32 39 W88 47 18. Stereo. Prog sep from AM. Format: Adult contemp. News progmg 5 hrs wkly. Target aud: 25-54. Spec prog: Oldies 15 hrs wkly. ■ Courtney James, mus dir. ■ Rates: Same as AM.

***WKNP(FM)**—Dec 17, 1990: 90.1 mhz; 17 kw. Ant 528 ft. TL: N35 38 46 W88 49 57. Stereo. Hrs opn: 24. Rebroadcasts WKNO(FM) Memphis, 100%. Box 241880, Memphis (38124); 900 Getwell Rd., Memphis (38111). (901) 458-2521. FAX: (901) 458-2221. Licensee: Memphis Community Telecommunications Foundation. Net: APR, NPR. Wash atty: Schwarz, Woods & Miller. Format: Class, news. News staff one; news progmg 36 hrs wkly. Target aud: 35 plus. ■ Michael LaBonia, pres; Dan Campbell, gen mgr; Darel Snodgrass, opns mgr & progmg mgr; Charles McLarty, dev dir; Becky Kelly, dev mgr; Jim Eikner, gen sls mgr; Joel Hurd, prom mgr; Everette Rice, news dir; Russ Abernathy, engrg dir; Pat Lane, chief engr. ■ *WKNO-TV affil.

WMXX-FM—Listing follows WDXI(AM).

WNWS-FM—August 1993: 101.5 mhz; 3 kw. Ant 300 ft. TL: N35 38 59 W88 46 11. Stereo. Hrs opn: 24. 101 Main St., 3rd Fl. (38301). (901) 423-8316. Licensee: Jackson Broadcasters L.P. Net: MBS, CBS; Unistar. Format: News/talk. News staff 2; news progmg 25 hrs wkly. Target aud: 25 plus; upscale adults. ■ Carlton Viers, gen mgr; Steve Hemann, opns dir; Dave Gluett, opns mgr; Dave McCulley, sls dir; Mary Ellen Cheatham, news dir; James Rambo, pub affrs dir.

WQCR(AM)—Nov 14, 1954: 1460 khz; 1 kw-D, 128 w-N. TL: N35 38 37 W88 46 24. Hrs opn: 24. Suite A, 378 Carriage House Dr. (38305). (901) 664-2102. FAX: (901) 664-9875. Licensee: Quality Broadcasting of TN Inc. Group owner: Quality Broadcasting of TN. Net: Moody, USA. Rep: Rgnl Reps. Format: Relg, talk. News progmg 14 hrs wkly. Target aud: General. ■ Tom McAfee, vp, gen mgr, gen sls mgr & chief engr; Becky Howard, mus dir.

WTJS(AM)—1931: 1390 khz; 5 kw-D, 1 kw-N, DA-N. TL: N35 38 50 W88 50 00. Hrs opn: 24. Box 1119 (38302); 122 Radio Rd. (38301). (901) 427-3316. FAX: (901) 427-4576. Licensee: Currzy Broadcasting Corp. Group owner: Osborn Communications Corp. (acq 1991; with co-located FM; FTR 4-15-91). Net: ABC/E, ABC/I. Format: Big band/talk. Spec prog: Black 2 hrs wkly. ■ Don Hodges, gen mgr; Ron Malone, opns mgr; Abe Sandoval, sls dir; Jim Sykes, mus dir; Carl Martin, chief engr.

WTNV(FM)—Co-owned with WTJS(AM). 1947: 104.1 mhz; 100 kw. Ant 655 ft. TL: N35 38 46 W88 49 57. Stereo. Prog sep from AM. Net: ABC/FM. Format: Country.

Jamestown

WCLC(AM)—Oct 28, 1957: 1260 khz; 1 kw-D. TL: N36 26 10 W84 55 42. Box 1509 (38556). (615) 879-8188. FAX: (615) 879-9252. Licensee: Jamestown Broadcasting Co. Format: Modern country. Spec prog: Farm 2 hrs, bluegrass 3 hrs wkly. ■ Bob Lyles, gen mgr, progmg dir & news dir; Jim Cady, gen sls mgr; Robert Huddleston, chief engr.

WCLC-FM—1985: 105.1 mhz; 1.1 kw. Ant 605 ft. TL: N36 26 31 W84 55 28. Stereo. Dups AM 100%.

WDEB(AM)—Jan 12, 1968: 1500 khz; 1 kw-D, 500 w-CH. TL: N36 25 49 W84 56 32. Hrs opn: Sunrise-sunset. Box 69 (38556); Hwy. 52 W. (38556). (615) 879-8164; (615) 879-9332. FAX: (615) 879-9336. Licensee: BAZ Broadcasting (acq 4-1-72). Net: ABC/E; Tenn. Radio. Rep: Midsouth. Format: Country, relg. News staff 3; news progmg 10 hrs wkly. Target aud: 18-54; household members who spend money in the mkt place. Spec prog: Farm 3 hrs wkly. ■ N. A. Baz, pres, gen mgr, stn mgr, prom dir & adv dir; Jean Baz, vp & gen sls mgr; Gary Crocket, progmg dir; Kevin R. Baz, mus dir; Gunther Muhsemann, chief engr. ■ Rates: $5; 4.50; 4.50; 4.

WDEB-FM—Oct 10, 1972: 103.9 mhz; 1.6 kw. Ant 450 ft. TL: N36 25 55 W84 56 33. Stereo. Hrs opn: 5 AM-midnight. Dups AM 80%. Format: Modern country. Spec prog: Gospel 24 hrs wkly. ■ Jean Baz, sls dir; N. A. Baz, rgnl sls mgr, mktg mgr, prom mgr & news dir. ■ Rates: $5; 5; 5; 5.

Jasper

WWAM(AM)—Mar 2, 1987: 820 khz; 5 kw-D. TL: N35 04 23 W85 37 39. Stereo. Box 279 (37347). (615) 942-5611. Licensee: Patton Broadcasting Co. Net: USA. Format: Gospel, news/talk. News progmg 5 hrs wkly. Target aud: 25-49. Spec prog: Bluegrass one hr, a cappella one hr wkly. ■ Phil Patton, gen mgr, progmg dir & chief engr; Jim Walker, gen sls mgr; Calvin McNabb II, mus dir.

Jefferson City

WJFC(AM)—Nov 1, 1961: 1480 khz; 500 w-D. TL: N36 06 15 W83 29 10. Hrs opn: 6 AM-6 PM. Box 430, 1179 North Hwy. 92 (37760). (615) 475-3800; (615) 475-3825. FAX: (615) 475-3800. Licensee: DeFuniak Communications Inc. (acq 12-22-86). Net: SMN. Wash atty: Timothy K. Brady. Format: Country. News staff one; news progmg 10 hrs wkly. Target aud: 25 plus; Jefferson, Grainger & Hamblen counties. Spec prog: Gospel 16 hrs, farm one hr, relg 4 hrs wkly. ■ Chuck Ketron, gen mgr; Michael Scott Walker, stn mgr; Jeff Cutshaw, progmg mgr & mus dir; Ed Martin, chief engr.

WNDD(FM)—Co-owned with WJFC(AM). Feb 1, 1976: 99.3 mhz; 3 kw. Ant 654 ft. TL: N36 04 28 W83 34 56. Hrs opn: 24. Net: SMN. Format: Soft Jazz. News staff one; news progmg 17 hrs wkly. Spec prog: Gospel 4 hrs, relg 2 hrs wkly.

Jellico

WEKX(FM)—Not on air, target date unknown: 102.7 mhz; 630 w. Ant 1,008 ft. TL: N36 37 55 W84 08 31. Box 1027, Williamsburg (40769). Licensee: Fate Lamont McCanally.

WJJT(AM)—Feb 1, 1972: 1540 khz; 1 kw-D, 500 w-CH. TL: N36 34 13 W84 08 43. Hrs opn: 12. Box 210, Mobile Home, Newcomb Pike (37762). (615) 784-5991; (615) 784-9444. Licensee: Trio Broadcasting Corp. Net: ABC/C; Tenn. Radio Net. Format: Gospel. News staff one; news progmg 20 hrs wkly. Target aud: 25-60. ■ Roger Martin, pres; Marvin Douglas, gen mgr; Emmitt Gibson, gen sls mgr, prom mgr & mus dir; Tim Zecchini, progmg dir & news dir; Dave Smith, chief engr. WBIR-TV affil. ■ Rates: $3.75; 3.75; 3.75; na.

Johnson City

WETB(AM)—Oct 1, 1947: 790 khz; 5 kw-D, 72 w-N. TL: N36 19 43 W82 24 39. Hrs opn: 6 AM-11 PM. Box 4127 (37602); 231 Brandenwood Dr. (37601). (615) 928-7131. Licensee: Mountain Signals Inc. (acq 12-5-90; FTR 12-31-90). Net: USA. Format: Southern Gospel. News staff one; news progmg 3 hrs wkly. Target aud: General. ■ Paul Gobble Jr., pres & gen mgr; Steve Nelson, stn mgr & news dir; Gary Ward, opns mgr; Loretta Gouge, gen sls mgr; Scott Onks, progmg dir & mus dir; Bob Morrison, chief engr. ■ Rates: $15; 15; 15; 15.

***WETS(FM)**—Feb 26, 1974: 89.5 mhz; 66 kw. Ant 2,273 ft. TL: N36 26 02 W82 08 08. Stereo. Hrs opn: 24. Box 70630, Eastern Tenn. State Univ. (37614-0630). (615) 929-6440. FAX: (615) 929-6449. Licensee: East Tenn. State Univ. Net: NPR, APRN. Format: Class, jazz, news/talk. News progmg 22 hrs wkly. Target aud: General. Spec prog: Folk 14 hrs, blues 12 hrs wkly. ■ Roy Nicks, pres; Wayne Winkler, gen mgr & opns dir; Phil Leonard, progmg dir; Ron Wickman, mus dir; Trevor Swoyer, chief engr.

WJCW(AM)—Dec 13, 1938: 910 khz; 5 kw-D, 1 kw-N, DA-N. TL: N36 24 37 W82 27 13. Hrs opn: 24. Box 8668, Gray (37615); WJCW Rd., Gray (37615). (615) 477-3127. FAX: (615) 477-4747. Licensee: Tri-Cities Radio Corp. Group owner: Bloomington Broadcasting Corp. (acq 12-1-82; $3.4 million with co-located FM; FTR 12-7-81). Net: CBS, MBS, ABC. Rep: Katz. Wash atty: Reddy, Begley & Martin. Format: News/talk, sports, MOR. News staff 4; news progmg 30 hrs wkly. Target aud: 25 plus; primary 35-54, secondary 25-49—mid- to upper-income. Spec prog: Relg 4 hrs wkly. ■ Ken Maness, pres & gen mgr; Bobbie Kabool, gen sls mgr & prom mgr; Bobbie kabool, progmg dir; Art Countiss, news dir; Al F. LeFevere, chief engr. ■ Rates: $23; 18; 18; 6.

WQUT(FM)—Co-owned with WJCW(AM). March 1, 1948: 101.5 mhz; 100 kw. Ant 1,500 ft. TL: N36 16 07 W82 20 21. Stereo. Prog sep from AM. Net: CBS, Unistar. Format: CHR, rock. News progmg 3 hrs wkly. Target aud: 18-39. ■ Don Raines, gen sls mgr; Rufus Hurt, progmg dir; Steve Mann, mus dir. ■ Rates: $48; 48; 48; 20.

WKTP(AM)—See Jonesborough.

WQUT(FM)—Listing follows WJCW(AM).

WTFM(FM)—See Kingsport.

Jonesborough

WKTP(AM)—October 1958: 1590 khz; 1.6 kw-D, 5 kw-N, DA-2. TL: N36 19 54 W82 28 27. Hrs opn: 24. Rebroadcasts WKPT(AM) Kingsport. Box WKPT, Kingsport (37662); 222 Commerce St., Kingsport (37660). (615) 246-9578; (615) 926-9800. FAX: (615) 246-6261. Licensee: Holston Valley Broadcasting Corp. Group owner: The Home News Co. (acq 1-25-90; $90,000; FTR 3-5-90). Net: ABC/E, AP; Tenn. Radio Net. Rep: Eastman. Wash atty: Cordon & Kelly; Wiley, Rein & Fielding. Format: Country, btfl music. News staff one. Target aud: 35 plus. ■ George Devault, pres & gen mgr; N. David Widener, exec vp & stn mgr; Mike Padgett, gen sls mgr; Steve Howard Smith, prom mgr & progmg dir; Duane Nelson, news dir; Harold Dougherty, vp engrg; John O. Davis, engrg dir. ■ WKPT-TV affil.

WUSJ-FM—See Elizabethton.

Karns

WWZZ(FM)—Jan 8, 1989: 93.1 mhz; 1.2 kw. Ant 515 ft. TL: N35 58 59 W84 04 37 (CP: 2.4 kw, ant 512 ft., TL: N35 57 46 W84 01 23). Suite 600, 1900 N. Winston Rd. (37919). (615) 531-2000. FAX: (615) 531-0101. Licensee: WCKS Broadcasting Ltd. (acq 5-30-90). Format: Contemporary Hit/Top-40. ■ Michael J. Benns, pres, gen mgr & gen sls mgr; Clay Gish, opns dir, progmg dir & mus dir.

Kingsport

***WCSK(FM)**—Nov 5, 1984: 90.3 mhz; 195 w. Ant 23 ft. TL: N36 31 37 W82 35 12. Stereo. 1800 Legion Dr. (37664). (615) 378-8470. Licensee: Kingsport Bd. of Ed. Format: Educ, classical, div. ■ Gerhard G. Ruetz, gen mgr; Jerry Ruetz, progmg dir; Gary Smith, chief engr.

WJCW(AM)—See Johnson City.

WKCV(AM)—Not on air, target date unknown: 1090 khz; 10 kw-D. TL: N36 31 16 W82 25 28. King College, 1350 King College Rd., Bristol (37620). (615) 968-1187. FAX: (615) 968-4456. Licensee: Tadlock Radio Inc.

WKIN(AM)—October 1951: 1320 khz; 5 kw-D, 500 w-N, DA-N. TL: N36 33 59 W82 33 22. Box 8668, Gray (37615). (615) 477-1000. FAX: (615) 477-4747. Licensee: Tri-Cities Radio Corp. (acq 12-8-92; $500,000 with co-located FM; FTR 1-4-93). Net: AP. Rep: Torbet. Format: C&W. ■ Ken Maness, pres & gen mgr; Bobbie Kabol, opns mgr; Art Countiss, news dir; Al LeFevere, chief engr.

WKOS(FM)—Co-owned with WKIN(AM). Feb 21, 1970: 104.9 mhz; 1 kw. Ant 475 ft. TL: N36 33 13 W82 27 00 (CP: 2.74 kw, ant 492 ft.). Stereo. Prog sep from AM. Net: ABC/C. Format: Top-40. ■ Bob Gordon, opns mgr; Mike Patterson, natl sls mgr.

WKPT(AM)—July 14, 1940: 1400 khz; 1 kw-U. TL: N36 32 37 W82 31 21. Stereo. Hrs opn: 24. Box WKPT (37662); 222 Commerce St. (37660). (615) 246-9578. FAX: (615) 249-9836; TWX: 810-574-5180. Licensee: Holston Valley Broadcasting Corp. Group owner: The Home News Co. (acq 6-1-66). Rep: Eastman. Wash atty: Wiley, Rein & Fielding, Cordon & Kelly. Format: Btfl mus. News staff one. Target aud: 35 plus. ■ George Devault, pres & gen mgr; N. David Widener, exec vp & stn mgr; Mike Padgett, gen sls mgr; Steve Howard Smith, prom mgr & progmg dir; Duane Nelson, news dir; Harold Dougherty, vp engrg; John O. Davis, engrg dir.

WTFM(FM)—Co-owned with WKPT(AM). February 1948: 98.5 mhz; 100 kw. Ant 1,260 ft. TL: N36 31 36 W82 35 14. Stereo. Hrs opn: 24. Prog sep from AM. Box WTFM (37662). Net: ABC/E. Format: Adult contemp. Target aud: 25-54. ■ N. David Widener, gen sls mgr; Morris Fleischer, prom mgr; Mark McKinney, progmg dir. ■ WKPT-TV affil.

WQUT(FM)—See Johnson City.

WTFM(FM)—Listing follows WKPT(AM).

Kingston

WBBX(AM)—July 1978: 1410 khz; 500 w-D. TL: N35 52 49 W84 30 56. Box 389, 705 Greenwood St. (37763). (615) 376-6954. FAX: (615) 376-6954. Licensee: Pilgrim Pathway Inc. (acq 6-30-92; $35,000; FTR 7-27-92). Format: Gospel. News progmg 2 hrs wkly. Target aud: General. ■ Grant Carter, pres. ■ Rates: $42; 36; 42; na.

Knoxville

WEMG(AM)—January 1960: 1430 khz; 5 kw-D. TL: N36 00 16 W83 53 14. 12844 S. Halsted St., Chicago, IL (60628). (312) 468-1060. Licensee: Word of Faith Fellowship Inc. (acq 2-11-87). Net: SRN. Format: Urban contemp, Christian. ■ Richard Singleton, pres; Gwen Singleton, gen mgr & mus dir; Darryl Cannon, gen sls mgr; John Claiborne, progmg dir; Jim Sloan, chief engr.

WEZK(AM)—Listing follows WIMZ-FM.

WEZK-FM—April 10, 1967: 97.5 mhz; 96 kw. Ant 1,296 ft. TL: N36 00 36 W83 55 57. Stereo. Box 27100 (37927). (615) 525-7380. FAX: (615) 637-7801. Licensee: South Central Communications Corp. (group owner). Rep: D&R Radio. Format: Soft adult contemp. Target aud: 25-54; educated, above-average income. ■ John D. Engelbrecht, chmn; Steve Edwards, pres; Craig Jacobus, gen mgr; Nancy F. Wilson, natl sls mgr; Chris Conley, progmg dir; Jim Kelly, mus dir; John Wilkerson, news dir & pub affrs dir; Frank Folsom, chief engr.

WHJM(AM)—June 1, 1988: 1180 khz; 10 kw-D, 2.6 kw-CH. TL: N35 58 48 W83 49 09. 802 S. Central St. (37902-1207). (615) 546-4653; (615) 637-7133. Licensee: Morgan Broadcasting Co. Net: MBS, NBC. Format: Big band. News progmg 7 hrs wkly. Target aud: 30 plus; young, married with small children. ■ Harry J. Morgan, pres & gen mgr; Horton Davis, gen sls mgr; Gerry Morgan, progmg dir & mus dir; Jodie Ritchie, chief engr.

WIMZ-FM—October 1949: 103.5 mhz; 100 kw. Ant 1,723 ft. TL: N36 08 06 W83 43 29. Stereo. Suite 200, 901 E. Summit Hill Dr. (37915). (615) 525-6000. FAX: (615) 637-3350. Licensee: South Central Communications Corp. (group owner; acq 2-23-93; $3.5 million with co-located AM; FTR 3-15-93). Net: NBC the Source. Rep: Christal. Format: AOR. ■ Steve Edwards, pres; Craig JAcobus, gen mgr; April Cureton, prom mgr; Jim Pemberton, progmg dir; Billy Kidd, mus dir; Colvin Idol, news dir; Bob Glenn, chief engr.

WEZK(AM)—Co-owned with WIMZ-FM. Jan 21, 1941: 1240 khz; 1 kw-U. TL: N35 57 17 W83 57 04. Dups FM 100%. 825 N. Central (37917). (615) 525-7380.

WITA(AM)—Sept 1, 1960: 1490 khz; 1 kw-U. TL: N35 58 11 W83 57 56. 7212 Kingston Pike (37919). (615) 588-2974; (615) 588-2975. Licensee: F.W. Robbert Broadcasting Co. (group owner: acq 12-83; $675,000; FTR 11-14-83). Net: USA, CBN. Format: Relg. Target aud: General. Spec prog: Black 8 hrs wkly. ■ Fred Westenberger, pres; Gail Scott, gen mgr & gen sls mgr; Dennis Gann, progmg dir & chief engr. ■ Rates: $9; 9; 9; 9.

WIVK(AM)—Mar 23, 1953: 990 khz; 10 kw-U, DA-N. TL: N36 02 37 W83 53 54. Stereo. Hrs opn: 24. 6711 Kingston Pk. (37919); Box 11167 (37939). (615) 588-6511. FAX: (615) 588-3725. Licensee: Dick Broadcasting Co. (group owner). Net: ABC/I, NBC Talknet, ESPN, BRN. Rep: Katz. Format: News/talk. News staff 8; news progmg 28 hrs wkly. Target aud: 25-54. ■ James A. Dick, chmn; James A. Dick Jr., pres; Bobby Denton, sr vp, gen mgr & gen sls mgr; Les Acree, opns mgr & progmg dir; Kent Stephens, mktg mgr; Mickey Dearstone, prom mgr & mus dir; David Foulk, news dir; Cleve Hays, chief engr.

WIVK-FM—Dec 16, 1965: 107.7 mhz; 91 kw. Ant 2,053 ft. TL: N35 48 41 W83 40 10. Stereo. Hrs opn: 24. Net: ABC/I. Format: C&W. ■ Gail Robeson, gen sls mgr.

***WKCS(FM)**—December 1952: 91.1 mhz; 250 w. Ant 73 ft. TL: N35 59 36 W83 55 24. 2509 Broadway N.E. (37917). (615) 594-1240. FAX: (615) 594-1228. Licensee: Fulton High School. Format: Adult contemp. ■ Alan Johnson, gen mgr; Scott Wyrick, chief engr.

WKGN(AM)—Sept 28, 1947: 1340 khz; 1 kw-U. TL: N35 57 20 W83 58 14. Stereo. Box 10005 (37939). (615) 546-7900. Licensee: Triple S Enterprises Inc. (acq 11-26-91; $50,000; FTR 12-16-91). Net: Westwood One. Rep: Roslin, Midsouth. Format: Urban contemp, news. Target aud: 18-34; young, mobile adults. Spec prog: Gospel 15 hrs, relg 5 hrs, medicine/health one hr wkly. ■ Robert Stewart, pres & gen mgr; Jack Bean, progmg dir; David Shirk, news dir; Ed Martin, chief engr.

WKNF-FM—See Oak Ridge.

WKNL(AM)—Not on air, target date unknown: 760 khz; 2.5 kw-D. TL: N36 02 34 W84 02 51. 314 N.E. Park Cir., Kansas City, MO (64116). Licensee: Tennessee Broadcasting Co. (acq 3-14-90; $10,000; FTR 4-2-90).

WKXV(AM)—February 1953: 900 khz; 1 kw-D, 258 w-N. TL: N35 58 52 W83 59 15. 5106 Middlebrook (37921). (615) 558-0900. Licensee: Ratel Broadcasting Co. Inc. Format: Relg, southern gospel. ■ Ted H. Lowe Sr., pres; Ted H. Lowe Jr., gen mgr & gen sls mgr; Danny Scarbrough, mus dir; Sonny Morrell, news dir; Frank Folsom, chief engr.

WMYU(FM)—See Sevierville.

WNDD(FM)—See Jefferson City.

WOKI-FM—(Oak Ridge). Apr 20, 1974: 100.3 mhz; 100 kw. Ant 2,001 ft. TL: N36 11 53 W84 13 51. Stereo. Suite 600, 1900 Winston Rd., Knoxville (37919). (615) 531-2000. FAX: (615) 531-0101. Licensee: Oak Ridge FM Inc. Net: ABC/FM, CBS. Rep: D & R Radio. Format: Country. Target aud: General; 25-54. ■ John W. Pirkle, pres; Bill Hays, vp, gen mgr & gen sls mgr; Bob Anderson, prom mgr; Ray Edwards, progmg dir & mus dir; Jerry C. Howell, news dir; Ernest O. Sutton Jr., chief engr. ■ Rates: $75; 60; 60; 60.

WQBB-FM—November 1991: 104.5 mhz; 6 kw. Ant 394 ft. TL: N36 00 36 W83 55 57 (CP: 2.80 kw, ant 485 ft.). 1114 W. Clinch Ave. (37916). (615) 546-1040. FAX: (615) 546-1045. Licensee: McDonald Communications Inc. Net: CNN. Rep: Roslin. Format: Adult standard. News staff one; news progmg 2 hrs wkly. Target aud: 35 plus; female. Spec prog: Public affairs 2 hrs wkly. ■ Elizabeth Richards, pres; Jim Staley, gen mgr; B. R. Staley, opns mgr; Jim Richards, sls dir; Eddy Roy, progmg dir; Bob Wallace, chief engr.

WQBB(AM)—(Powell). Aug 15, 1984: 1040 khz; 10 kw-D. TL: N36 02 34 W84 02 51. Stereo. Dups FM 100%.

WRJZ(AM)—Feb 12, 1927: 620 khz; 5 kw-U, DA-N. TL: N35 59 24 W83 50 15. Hrs opn: 24. Suite 101, 3214 Tazewell Pike (37918). (615) 656-6262; (615) 687-1395. FAX: (615) 687-1195. Licensee: Tennessee Media Associates (acq 10-84). Net: USA, Moody. Format: Relg. News progmg 5 hrs wkly. Target aud: 25-54. ■ Thomas H. Moffit Jr., pres; John T. Hanna, gen mgr & gen sls mgr; Larry Richmond, opns mgr, progmg dir & mus dir; Dave Berry, chief engr.

***WUOT(FM)**—October 1949: 91.9 mhz; 100 kw. Ant 1,580 ft. TL: N36 00 19 W83 56 23. Stereo. Hrs opn: 24. U. of Tennessee, 232 Communications Bldg. (37996-0322). (615) 974-5375. FAX: (615) 974-3941. Licensee: U. of Tennessee. Net: APR, NPR. Format: Class, jazz. News staff 2; news progmg 14 hrs wkly. ■ Lauren Murphy, stn mgr; S.D. Williamson, opns mgr; Norris Dryer, progmg dir; Kim Smith, news dir; Tim Berry, chief engr.

WUTK(AM)—Jan 16, 1989: 850 khz; 50 kw-D, DA. TL: N36 04 12 W83 58 19. Stereo. University of Tenn., P-103 Andy Holt Tower (37996). (615) 974-4291. FAX: (615) 974-2814. Licensee: University of Tenn. (acq 8-31-88). Net: CBS, CNN. Format: All news. News staff 5; news progmg 98 hrs wkly. Target aud: 25 plus; educated, informed adults. ■ Kimberly Wall, news dir; Milton Jones, chief engr. ■ Rates: $15; 10; 15; 5.

***WUTK-FM**—Jan 4, 1982: 90.3 mhz; 800 w. Ant 23 ft. TL: N35 57 09 W83 55 34. Stereo. Prog sep from AM. Format: New rock. Target aud: 18-24; students. ■ Jim Schwan, progmg dir.

***WYFC(FM)**—See Clinton.

La Follette

WLAF(AM)—May 17, 1953: 1450 khz; 1 kw-U. TL: N36 22 52 W84 07 32. Drawer 1409, 107 N. 5th St. (37766). (615) 566-1450; (615) 562-3557. FAX: (615) 562-5764. Licensee: Stair Co. Inc. (acq 12-15-88; $125,000; FTR 1-16-89). Net: Tenn. Radio Net. Format: C&W, gospel. Spec prog: Bluegrass 7 hrs wkly. ■ Jim Stair, pres; Bill Waddell, vp & gen mgr; Jim Freeman, stn mgr, prom mgr & progmg dir; Jerry Monday, adv mgr; Harold Branam, mus dir; Glenda Blackwell, news dir; Ray Brown, chief engr.

WQLA(AM)—Sept 1, 1983: 960 khz; 1 kw-D. TL: N36 22 02 W84 08 50. Box 1530, Woodson Mall, Jacksboro Pike (37766). (615) 566-1000. FAX: (615) 457-5900. Licensee: Cherokee Communications Corp. (acq 6-12-90; $400,000 with co-located FM; FTR 7-9-90). Net: CNN. Rep: Roslin. Format: Southern gospel. News staff 2; news progmg 12 hrs wkly. Target aud: General. ■ Cliff Jennings, pres, gen mgr & gen sls mgr; Barbara Nulf, opns mgr & mktg dir; Frank Scott, progmg dir & news dir; Bob Wallace, chief engr. ■ Rates: $6; 6; 6; 6.

WQLA-FM—Sept 1, 1982: 104.9 mhz; 1.1 kw. Ant 499 ft. TL: N36 21 08 W84 05 20 (CP: 900 w). Stereo. Prog sep from AM. Licensee: La Follette Broadcasters. Format: C&W, sports. Target aud: 18 plus. ■ Barbara Nulf, adv dir & progmg dir. ■ Rates: $10; 10; 10; 10.

Lafayette

WEEN(AM)—Nov 3, 1958: 1460 khz; 1 kw-D, 138 w-N. TL: N36 32 06 W86 00 27. Box 160 (37083). (615) 666-2169. Licensee: Lafayette Broadcasting Inc. Net: Tenn. Radio. Format: Country. Spec prog: Farm 5 hrs wkly. ■ Billie G. Speck, pres & gen mgr; Steve Speck, gen sls mgr, progmg dir & news dir; Teresa Wilson, mus dir; Ivon Davis, chief engr.

Lawrenceburg

WDXE(AM)—July 21, 1951: 1370 khz; 1 kw-D, 44 w-N. TL: N35 15 25 W87 18 24. 122 N. Military Ave. (38464). (615) 762-4411. FAX: (615) 762-4789. Licensee: H-M-S Broadcasting Co. (acq 1-1-74). Net: ABC/D; Tenn. Radio. Rep: Midsouth. Format: C&W. ■ Milton D. Griffin, stn mgr; Mike Harris, prom mgr, progmg dir & mus dir; Jack Cheatwood, news dir; Phillip Kemper, chief engr.

WDXE-FM—Aug 28, 1964: 95.9 mhz; 3 kw. Ant 290 ft. TL: N35 15 25 W87 18 24. Prog sep from AM. Format: Adult contemp. ■ Jack Cheatwood, progmg dir.

WLLX(FM)—Listing follows WWLX(AM).

WWLX(AM)—June 21, 1987: 590 khz; 750 w-D, 133 w-N. TL: N35 12 18 W87 19 39 (CP: 600 w). Stereo. Box 156 (38464). (615) 762-6200. FAX: (615) 762-6200. Licensee: Roger W. Wright dba Prospect Communications. Net: ABC/I. Format: C&W. ■ Roger Wright, pres, gen mgr & chief engr; Janet Wright, gen sls mgr & prom mgr; Dan Hollander, progmg dir & mus dir; Sheryl Bryant, news dir.

WLLX(FM)—Co-owned with WWLX(AM). May 1991: 97.5 mhz; 2.3 kw. Ant 535 ft. TL: N35 12 18 W87 19 39. Stereo. Hrs opn: 19. Box 156, 1208 N. Locust Ave. (38464). News staff one. Target aud: 25-54. ■ Roger Wright, opns mgr, pub affrs dir & chief engr; Carol Cox, gen sls mgr & adv mgr; Janet Wright, mktg mgr & prom mgr; Dan Hollander, mus dir; Jan Stutts, news dir. ■ Rates: $9; 7; 9; 7.

Lebanon

WANT(FM)—Listing follows WCOR(AM).

WCOR(AM)—October 1949: 900 khz; 500 w-D, 136 w-N. TL: N36 12 25 W86 16 03. 510 Trousdale Ferry Pike (37087). (615) 444-0900. FAX: (615) 443-4235. Licensee: WCOR Inc. (acq 4-93; $16,000; FTR 3-15-93). Wash atty: Tierney & Swift. Format: Country. Target aud: General. ■ Susan H. Bay, pres & gen mgr; Gary Brown, chief engr.

WANT(FM)—Co-owned with WCOR(AM). Not on air, target date May 1, 1994: 98.9 mhz; 5 kw. Ant 320 ft. TL: N36 12 24 W86 16 02. Stereo. Hrs opn: 24. 510 Trousdale Ferry Pk. (37087). (615) 449-3699. FAX: (615) 443-4235. Licensee: Bay-Pointe Broadcasting Co. Inc. Net: SMN. ■ Clyde Harville, opns mgr; Cindy Peel, adv mgr; Jeff St. John, progmg dir & mus dir.

***WFMQ(FM)**—Dec 15, 1966: 91.5 mhz; 500 w. Ant 100 ft. TL: N36 12 13 W86 18 01. Stereo. Box 609 (37087). (615) 444-2562. Licensee: Cumberland University. Format: Classical. Spec prog: Jazz 4 hrs, Sp 3 hrs wkly. ■ Dr. Ray Phillips, pres; Quentin Lane, sr vp; Jim Henderson, gen mgr; Carl Campbell, chief engr.

WQDQ(AM)—1979: 1200 khz; 10 kw-D, 500 w-N, DA-N. TL: N36 11 28 W86 19 44. Box 40333, Nashville (37204). (615) 832-4653. Licensee: Wilson County Broadcast Svcs Inc. Format: MOR. Spec prog: Class 3 hrs, farm 2 hrs, jazz 3 hrs wkly. ■ P.L. Severy, pres & gen mgr; Herb Tarlick, gen sls mgr; Buck Fenton, mus dir; Wally Bileau, news dir; Gary Brown, chief engr.

WYHY(FM)—Aug 31, 1962: 107.5 mhz; 58 kw. Ant 1,234 ft. TL: N36 15 50 W86 47 38. Stereo. Hrs opn: 24. 810 Division St., Nashville (37203). (615) 256-6556. FAX: (615) 256-1752. Licensee: Legacy Broadcasting Partners of Nashville. Net: ABC/C. Rep: Eastman/Katz. Wash atty: Hogan & Hartson. Format: CHR. News staff one; news progmg 4 hrs wkly. Target aud: 18-34. ■ John King, gen mgr; Cameron Atkins, opns mgr & chief engr; Tom Peace, Billy Brown, mus dirs; Rhett Walker, news dir.

Lenoir City

WBLC(AM)—June 15, 1965: 1360 khz; 1 kw-D. TL: N35 47 32 W84 17 45. Box 100 (37771). (615) 986-8021. Licensee: Lauderdale/McKeehan Christian Broadcasting Corp. Format: Relg. ■ Earl Lauderdale, pres & gen mgr; Robert Van McKeehan, vp & gen sls mgr.

WLIL(AM)—May 30, 1950: 730 khz; 1 kw-D, 280 w-N. TL: N35 46 12 W84 16 47. Box 340, Broadway at Grand (37771). (615) 986-7561. FAX: (615) 986-1716. Licensee: WLIL Inc. Group owner: Wilkerson Broadcasting Group. Net: CNN. Rep: Keystone (unwired net). Format: Country. News staff one; news progmg 30 hrs wkly. Target aud: General. Spec prog: Black one hr, farm 4 hrs, gospel 18 hrs wkly. ■ Arthur Wilkerson, pres; Glenn A. McNish, vp, stn mgr, gen sls mgr & news dir; Sue Wilkerson, progmg dir; Norman Rhyne, mus dir; Bob Crane, chief engr.

WLIL-FM—Sept 19, 1967: 93.5 mhz; 6 kw. Ant 165 ft. TL: N35 46 12 W84 16 47. Dups AM 80%. Box 340, 406 E. Broadway (37771). News staff one; news progmg 41 hrs wkly. Target aud: General.

Lewisburg

WAXO(AM)—Sept. 1, 1980: 1220 khz; 1 kw-D. TL: N35 25 42 W86 46 22. 217 W. Commerce St. (37091). (615) 359-6641. FAX: (615) 359-6642. Licensee: Marshall County Radio Corp. (acq 9-1-82; $250,000; FTR 8-23-82). Net: USA. Format: Country. Spec prog: Gospel 12 hrs wkly. ■ Bob Smartt, pres, gen mgr, gen sls mgr, progmg dir & news dir; Dale Howard, chief engr.

WJJM(AM)—May 15, 1947: 1490 khz; 1 kw-U. TL: N35 26 58 W86 46 55. Box 2025, 344 E. Church St. (37091). (615) 359-4511. Licensee: Martha M. Lingner, executrix (acq 7-19-89). Net: ABC; Tenn. Radio. Rep: Keystone (unwired net). Format: Country. Target aud: 25-65. ■ Martha M. Lingner, pres; Pamela Meredith, gen mgr; Doug Cheek, gen sls mgr; Amy Biggerstaff, prom mgr & mus dir; Pam Meredith, progmg dir; Fred Mustain, news dir; Sam Wiley, chief engr. ■ Rates: $4.50; 4.25; 4.25; 4.25.

WJJM-FM—Feb 20, 1969: 94.3 mhz; 3 kw. Ant 115 ft. TL: N35 27 03 W86 46 57. Stereo. Hrs opn: 17. Dups AM 100%. ■ Doug Cheek, adv dir; Amy Biggustalf, progmg dir. ■ Rates: Same as AM.

Lexington

WDXL(AM)—July 1954: 1490 khz; 1 kw-U. TL: N35 38 05 W88 23 34. Hrs opn: 24. Box 170, Smith St. (38351). (901) 968-3500; (901) 968-9990. FAX: (901) 968-0380. Licensee: Lexington Broadcast Service Inc. (acq 1955). Net: ABC/E, Jones Satellite Audio. Format: Country. News staff one; news progmg 10 hrs wkly. Target aud: 30 plus. Spec prog: Black 4 hrs, gospel 10 hrs wkly. ■ Mary Enochs, pres; Dan Hughes, gen mgr & gen sls mgr; Don Enochs, opns dir; Barney Beatty, chief engr. ■ Rates: $4; 4; 4; 4.

WZLT(FM)—Co-owned with WDXL(AM). September 1964: 99.3 mhz; 5 kw. Ant 150 ft. TL: N35 38 05 W88 23 34. Stereo. Hrs opn: 24. Prog sep from AM. (901) 968-3500. Target aud: General. ■ Steve James, progmg dir & news dir. ■ Rates: $6; 6; 6; 6.

Livingston

WLIV(AM)—Nov 26, 1956: 920 khz; 1 kw-D. TL: N36 22 28 W85 18 20. Box 359, 1024 W. Main (38570). (615) 823-1226. FAX: (615) 823-6005. Licensee: WLIV Inc. (acq 9-1-65). Net: NBC; Tenn. Radio. Rep: Keystone (unwired net), Midsouth. Format: Mod country. News staff 2; news progmg 7 hrs wkly. Target aud: General. Spec prog: Farm 2 hrs, relg 15 hrs wkly. ■ Larry E. Nunn, gen mgr; Carolyn Peterman, stn mgr; Roger Ealey, progmg dir; Austin Stinnett, chief engr. ■ Rates: $7.25; 6.25; 7.25; 6.25.

WCSD(FM)—Co-owned with WLIV(AM). December 1966: 95.9 mhz; 2.85 kw. Ant 472 ft. TL: N36 22 28 W85 18 20 (CP: 12 kw). Stereo. Prog sep from AM. 1283 Bunker Hill Rd., Cookville (38501). (615) 528-7001. FAX: (615) 372-8088. Net: NBC the Source. Format: Btfl mus. News staff 2; news progmg 7 hrs wkly. Target aud: General. ■ Larry Nunn, stn mgr; Jack Johnson, news dir. ■ Rates: Same as AM.

Lobelville

WIST(FM)—October 1974: 94.3 mhz; 21 kw. Ant 758 ft. TL: N35 46 21 W87 52 05 (CP: 94.5 mhz, 50 kw, ant 262 ft.). Stereo. Hrs opn: 24. Box 460, 127 Main St. (37097). (615) 593-2294. FAX: (615) 593-2971. Licensee: Ohio Broadcast Associates (acq 9-9-93; $235,000; FTR 10-4-93). Net: SMN; Tenn. Radio. Rep: Midsouth. Wash atty: Lawrence J. Bernard Jr. Format: Country, southern gospel. News staff one. Target aud: General. Spec prog: Farm one hr, oldies 18 hrs wkly. ■ Glen Powers, gen mgr; John Edwards, opns mgr. ■ Rates: $6; 6; 6; 5.50.

Lookout Mountain

WFLI(AM)—Feb 20, 1961: 1070 khz; 50 kw-D, 2.5 kw-N, DA-2. TL: N35 02 42 W85 21 44. 621 O'Grady Dr., Chattanooga (37419). (615) 821-3555. FAX: (615) 821-3557. Licensee: WFLI Inc. Net: ABC/D. Format: Relg. ■ William E. Benns Jr., pres; Ying Hua Benns, gen mgr; Bob Broome, gen sls mgr; Mike Way, progmg dir & mus dir; Mike King, news dir; Jeff Gregory, chief engr.

Loretto

WKNI(AM)—See Lexington, Ala.

Loudon

WLOD(AM)—Jan 1, 1983: 1140 khz; 1 kw-D. TL: N35 43 35 W84 20 49. Box 465, 405 Mullberry St. (37774). (615) 458-9563; (615) 458-4621. Licensee: Loudon Broadcasters Inc. (acq 9-85). Net: USA. Format: Country classics & bluegrass. News staff 2. Target aud: 35 plus. Spec prog: Gospel 12 hrs wkly. ■ Doyle Lowe, pres, gen mgr, gen sls mgr & pub affrs dir; Pete Egler, mus dir; Wes Hall, news dir; Chip Lynn, engrg mgr.

WNOX(FM)—Jan 5, 1989: 99.1 mhz; 3 kw. Ant 300 ft. TL: N35 47 10 W84 17 24 (CP: 6 kw). Stereo. Hrs opn: 24. 108-A W. Inskip Rd., Knoxville (37912). (615) 281-9999. FAX: (615) 688-0375. Licensee: C-K Inc. (acq 5-30-91; $185,000; FTR 6-17-91). Format: Soft jazz. ■ Chuck Ketron, gen mgr.

WXST(FM)—May 20, 1991: 105.3 mhz; 6 kw. Ant 328 ft. TL: N35 48 40 W84 16 02. Stereo. Hrs opn: 24. Suite 2, 620 Campbell Stn. Rd., Knoxville (37922). (615) 675-4105. FAX: (615) 675-4859. Licensee: Tellico Sound Ltd. Net: SMN. Wash atty: Robert Stone. Format: Oldies. News progmg 3 hrs wkly. Target aud: 25-50; baby boomers. ■ Deborah H. Greenwood, pres; Mike Beverly, gen mgr & news dir; Brian McKinley, opns mgr; Don Tonkin, chief engr. ■ Rates: $26; 24; 26; 18.

Madison

WHNK(AM)—1958: 1430 khz; 5 kw-D, 1 kw-N, DA-N. TL: N36 16 19 W86 42 53. c/o Gary Stevens, receiver, 49 Locust Ave., New Canaan, CT (06840). (203) 966-6465. Licensee: GMX Communications of Tennessee Inc. (acq 10-1-88; grpsl).

WRLT-FM—See Franklin.

Madisonville

WRKQ(AM)—July 12, 1967: 1250 khz; 500 w-D, 86 w-N. TL: N35 30 29 W84 22 45. Hrs opn: 6 AM-6 PM. Box 489, Hwy. 411 S. (37354). (615) 442-1446. Licensee: Monroe Area Broadcasters Inc. (acq 4-14-92; $1; FTR 5-4-92). Net: USA. Rep: Midsouth. Format: Country, gospel. News staff one; news progmg 12 hrs wkly. Target aud: General. Spec prog: Gospel 12 hrs wkly. ■ Norman Lee, pres; Rick Hood, gen mgr, gen sls mgr, mus dir & news dir; Sandra Sprague, progmg dir; Jim Long, chief engr. ■ Rates: $5; 5; 5; 5.

WYGO(FM)—Nov 15, 1992: 99.5 mhz; 2.51 kw. Ant 515 ft. TL: N35 30 20 W84 27 21. Hrs opn: 24. Box 875, 137 College St. (37354). (615) 442-4636. FAX: (615) 442-2750. Licensee: Major Broadcasting Corp. Format: Adult contemp. Target aud: 18-54. ■ Mike Anderson, pres & gen mgr. ■ Rates: $6; 5; 6; 4.50.

Manchester

WFTZ(FM)—Nov 16, 1992: 101.5 mhz; 3 kw. Ant 345 ft. TL: N35 23 51 W86 08 39. Stereo. Hrs opn: 24. Box 1015, 1025 Hillsboro Blvd. (37355). (615) 723-1015. FAX: (615) 728-8001. Licensee: Phase Two Communications Inc. (acq 10-21-91). Net: ABC. Wash atty: Timothy K. Brady. Format: Adult contemp. News staff one; news progmg 4 hrs wkly. Target aud: 25-45; white collar, educated. ■ Roger H. Dotson, CEO, pres & opns mgr; Roger Dotson, gen mgr; Marsha T. Dotson, gen sls mgr; Peggy Artley, prom dir; Edward L. Knott, progmg dir; Wayne D. Hudgens, asst mus dir, news dir & pub affrs dir; Jim Gilmore, chief engr. ■ Rates: $9.50; 8; 9.50; 8.

WMSR(AM)—Apr 7, 1957: 1320 khz; 5 kw-D, 79 w-N. TL: N35 28 03 W86 05 42. 914 Oakdale St. (37355). (615) 728-3526. FAX: (615) 728-3527. Licensee: WMSR Inc. Net: UPI. Format: C&W, farm, relg. ■ Russell Daniel, gen mgr, prom mgr & mus dir; Cindy Whaley, progmg dir.

WWTN(FM)—June 20, 1962: 99.7 mhz; 100 kw. Ant 2,033 ft. TL: N35 28 03 W86 05 42. Stereo. Penthouse, 1808 W. End Ave., Nashville (37203). (615) 254-9986. FAX: (615) 329-3246. Licensee: American General Media-Nashville Inc., debtor-in-possession. Group owner: American General Media. Format: News, talk. ■ Ron Hale, gen mgr; Bill Buntin, gen sls mgr; Greg Ruff, progmg dir; Holly Connes, news dir.

Martin

WCMT(AM)—June 8, 1957: 1410 khz; 700 w-D, 58 w-N. TL: N36 21 45 W88 50 56. Hrs opn: 24. Box 318, 733 N. Lindell (38237). (901) 587-9527. FAX: (901) 587-5079. Licensee: Thunderbolt Broadcasting Co. (acq 3-1-80; FTR 2-18-80). Net: AP, MBS, NBC. Rep: Howard Weiss; Midsouth. Wash atty: May & Dunne. Format: Adult country, news/talk. News staff one; news progmg 10 hrs wkly. Target aud: 25-54; baby boomers. Spec prog: Gospel 8 hrs wkly. ■ Paul F. Tinkle, CEO; Jimmy Smith, vp; Cindy Prince, opns mgr; Barbara Roberts, prom dir; Chris Chandler, progmg dir & mus dir; Trace Sharp, news dir; Brad Hosford, chief engr.

WCMT-FM—Sept 26, 1968: 101.7 mhz; 6 kw. Ant 328 ft. TL: N36 21 45 W88 50 56. Stereo. Hrs opn: 24. Prog sep from AM. (901) 587-9526. Wash atty: Pepper & Corazzini. Format: Adult contemp mix. News progmg 25 hrs wkly. Spec prog: Relg 6 hrs wkly. ■ Jimmy Smith, exec vp; Paul F. Tinkle, mktg mgr & adv dir.

***WUTM(FM)**—Sept 1, 1971: 90.3 mhz; 185 w. Ant 250 ft. TL: N36 20 28 W88 51 39. Stereo. Gooch Hall, Rm. 305, Univ. of Tenn. at Martin (38238). (901) 587-7550; (901) 587-7095. Licensee: Univ. of Tennessee. Net: UPI. Format: Jazz, classical. News staff one; news progmg 5 hrs wkly. Target aud: General; university community. Spec prog: Black 15 hrs wkly. ■ Dr. Gary Steinke, stn mgr; Gene Evans, chief engr.

Maryville

WBCR(AM)—See Alcoa.

WCGM(AM)—1989: 1120 khz; 500 w-D. TL: N35 45 08 W83 35 04. Stereo. Stn currently dark. 366 Glasscock Ave., Alcoa (37701). Licensee: Dove Inc. ■ Jody Ritchie, pres; Brian Holliday, gen mgr, gen sls mgr & progmg dir.

WGAP(AM)—Aug 13, 1947: 1400 khz; 1 kw-U. TL: N35 45 41 W83 58 57. Hrs opn: 24. Box 4939, 316 Court St. (37803-0607). (615) 983-4310. Licensee: WGAP Broadcasting Corp. (acq 11-18-82; $585,000; FTR 11-29-82). Net: AP. Rep: Rgnl Reps. Format: Country. News staff 2; news progmg 18 hrs wkly. Target aud: 25 plus; general. ■ James A. Calkin Jr., pres; Harry N. Plumlee, gen mgr & chief engr; David Paine, gen sls mgr; Norman Plumlee, prom mgr, progmg dir & mus dir; Glenn Morton, news dir. ■ Rates: $22.50; 18.75; 22.50; 12.50.

WGAP-FM—Feb 2, 1990: 95.7 mhz; 3 kw. Ant 328 ft. TL: N35 49 53 W84 01 25. Stereo. Hrs opn: 24. FAX: (615) 983-4314. Licensee: Gateway Broadcasting Corp. Target aud: General. ■ Harry N. Plumlee, pres, gen mgr & chief engr; David Paine, gen sls mgr; Sam Truan, progmg dir & mus dir; Glenn Morton, news dir. ■ Rates: $22.50; 18.75; 22.50; 12.50.

McKenzie

WHDM(AM)—Jan 29, 1954: 1440 khz; 500 w-D. TL: N36 07 46 W88 29 50. Box 128, 143 Main St. (38201). (901) 352-3371; (901) 352-3372. Licensee: Richard E. Bennett (acq 7-88). Format: Country, relg, news. News staff one; news progmg 77 hrs wkly. Target aud: 25 plus. ■ Richard Bennett, pres & gen mgr; Barbara King, gen sls mgr; Sandi Wilkes, prom mgr; Jim Norris, progmg dir & mus dir; Jim Potts, news dir; David Hacker, chief engr.

WWYN(FM)—Feb 11, 1963: 106.9 mhz; 100 kw. Ant 892 ft. TL: N35 54 06 W88 46 55. Stereo. 68 Federal Dr., Jackson (38305). (901) 664-5524. FAX: (901) 664-5545. Licensee: Rainbow Media Inc. (acq 9-28-89; $200,010; FTR 10-16-89). Net: MBS. Format: Modern country. News staff one. Target aud: General. ■ Ed Dobson, pres; Don Benefield, gen mgr; Rusty McDaniels, opns mgr; Steve Hilliard, gen sls mgr; Shane Conner, prom mgr & progmg dir; Phyllis Oliver, news dir; Dave Hacker, chief engr. ■ Rates: $20; 18; 20; 16.

McKinnon

WTWL(FM)—Not on air, target date unknown: 101.5 mhz; 790 w. Ant 607 ft. TL: N36 24 39 W87 58 06. Box 648, Clarksville (37041-0648). (615) 645-6414. Licensee: Ted Young and Trent C. Knott (acq 12-22-92; $344,206 with WJZM(AM) Clarksville; FTR 1-25-93). ■ Trent Knott (owner), chmn.

McMinnville

WAKI(AM)—1947: 1230 khz; 1 kw-U. TL: N35 41 42 W85 46 33. Box 31, 100 Mullican St. (37110). (615) 473-6535. FAX: (615) 473-8566. Licensee: Durham Broadcasting Co. Inc. (acq 1967). Net: SMN. Wash atty: Timothy K. Brady. Format: Country, adult contemp, talk. News staff one; news progmg 24 hrs wkly. Target aud: General; 18-45. Spec prog: Farm 2 hrs wkly. ■ Aaron Durham, pres & gen sls mgr; Mark Bradford Durham, vp; Earl Dugan, gen mgr; Dwayne McDowell, progmg dir; Jay Walker, news dir; Homer Wilson, chief engr. ■ Rates: $7; 6; 7; 5.

WBMC(AM)—May 1, 1955: 960 khz; 500 w-D. TL: N35 40 00 W85 46 00. Box 759, 103 S. High St. (37110). (615) 473-2104. Licensee: Cumberland Valley Broadcasting Co. (acq 2-14-86). Net: AP, ABC. Format: Country, top-40, gospel. News staff one; news progmg 10 hrs wkly. Target aud: General. Spec prog: Farm 5 hrs wkly. ■ Thorold Ramsey, pres & gen mgr; Rob Jones, gen sls mgr; Patrick Ramsey, prom mgr & progmg dir; Jeff Edwards, mus dir & news dir; Homer Wilson Jr., chief engr.

WTRZ-FM—Co-owned with WBMC(AM). Jan 23, 1964: 103.9 mhz; 5.3 kw. Ant 130 ft. TL: N35 40 00 W85 46 00. Stereo. Prog sep from AM. Format: Top-40. News staff one; news progmg 10 hrs wkly. Target aud: 18-40. ■ Rob Jones, sls dir & prom mgr; Dave Chappell, progmg dir; Jeff Edwards, mus dir.

Memphis

KJMS(FM)—Listing follows KWAM.

KSUD(AM)—See West Memphis, Ark.

KWAM(AM)—1946: 990 khz; 10 kw-D, 450 w-N, DA-2. TL: N35 08 04 W90 05 38. Box 11839, 80 N. Tillman (38111). (901) 323-2679. FAX: (901) 320-1749. Licensee: KWAM Inc. (acq 1951). Rep: Republic. Format: Gospel. News staff one; news progmg 6 hrs wkly. Target aud: 25 plus; general. ■ David Brown, gen mgr & opns mgr; G.W. Albright, gen sls mgr; Michael McKinney, progmg dir.

KJMS(FM)—Co-owned with KWAM. March 10, 1965: 101.1 mhz; 100 kw. Ant 347 ft. TL: N35 08 01 W90 05 38. Stereo. Prog sep from AM. (901) 323-0101. Net: ABC/FM. Format: Black, urban contemp. News staff one; news progmg 8 hrs wkly. Target aud: 18-49.

WBBP(AM)—Apr 11, 1964: 1480 khz; 5 kw-D, 100 w-N. TL: N35 03 18 W90 05 15. Hrs opn: 24. 2272 Central Ave. (38104). (901) 278-7878; (800) 238-5576. FAX: (901) 276-9229. Licensee: Bountiful Blessings Inc. (acq 10-25-90; $462,000; FTR 11-19-90). Format: 24-hr gospel. ■ Bishop G. E. Patterson, pres & gen mgr; Freddie Henderson, opns mgr; James Chambers, prom mgr & progmg dir; Rob Herring, chief engr.

WCRV(AM)—See Collierville.

WDIA(AM)—June 7, 1947: 1070 khz; 50 kw-D, 5 kw-N, DA-2. TL: N35 16 05 W90 01 03. Hrs opn: 24. Box 3584, 112 Union Ave. (38103). (901) 529-4300. FAX: (901) 529-9557. Licensee: Ragan Henry Communications Group L.P. Group owner: Ragan Henry Broadcast Group Inc. (acq 5-2-88; $13 million with co-located FM; FTR 5-2-88). Net: CBS. Rep: McGavren Guild. Format: Black adult contemp, news/talk. Target aud: 25-54; Black adults. Spec prog: Gospel. ■ Rick Caffey, gen mgr; Bobby O'Jay, progmg dir; Bev Johnson, news dir; Alonzo Pendleton, chief engr.

WHRK(FM)—Co-owned with WDIA(AM). Jan 1, 1961: 97.1 mhz; 100 kw. Ant 530 ft. TL: N35 13 23 W90 02 33. Stereo. Hrs opn: 24. Prog sep from AM. (901) 529-4397. Net: NBC the Source. Format: Urban contemp. Target aud: 18-49. ■ Bobby O'Jay, opns dir; Verta Hathaway, prom mgr.

WEGR(FM)—Listing follows WREC(AM).

***WEVL(FM)**—May 1, 1976: 89.9 mhz; 13 kw. Ant 300 ft. TL: N35 08 05 W89 45 38. Stereo. Hrs opn: 20. Box 40952 (38174-0952). (901) 528-0560; (901) 528-0561. Licensee: Southern Communication Volunteers Inc. Format: Variety, educ. News progmg 2 hrs wkly. Target aud: General. Spec prog: Jazz 15 hrs, Black 10 hrs, C&W 15 hrs, blues 22 hrs, live music one hr, class one hr, Sp 3 hrs, Indian one hr, reggae 4 hrs, African one hr, Klezmer one hr, Celtic 5 hrs, Polka 2 hrs, Jewish 2 hrs, bluegrass 4 hrs wkly. ■ Les Edwards, pres; Judy Dorsey, stn mgr & opns dir; Chris Monroe, dev dir; Brian Craig, mktg dir & progmg dir; Dorothy Simon, prom dir; Mike Shearin, mus dir; Vicki Davis, pub affrs dir; Robert Benjamin, chief engr.

WGKX(FM)—Jan 10, 1968: 105.9 mhz; 100 kw. Ant 994 ft. TL: N35 10 28 W89 50 41. Stereo. Hrs opn: 24. 5900 Poplar Ave. (38119). (901) 767-6532. FAX: (901) 767-9531. Licensee: KIX Broadcasting Inc. Group owner: Barnstable Broadcasting Inc. (acq 7-85; grpsl; FTR 4-1-85). Format: Country. News staff one; news progmg one hr wkly. Target aud: 25-54. Spec prog: Weather, traffic, sports, PSAs, public progmg. ■ John Bibbs, pres & gen mgr; Chris Butterick, gen sls mgr; Bill Jones, progmg dir; Jon Conlon, mus dir; Regina Burns, news dir; Doug Gossett, chief engr.

WGSF(AM)—(Arlington). Aug 19, 1986: 1210 khz; 10 kw-U, DA-N. TL: N35 18 27 W89 38 21 (CP: COL: Bartlett). Stereo. Box 548, 11958 Hwy. 70, Arlington (38002). (901) 867-9473; (901) 458-8255. FAX: (901) 452-0034. Licensee: Arlington Broadcasting Co. Inc. Net: USA, CBN. Format: Christian contemp mus. Target aud: 25-46; committed Christians with income $25,000 & up. ■ Fred Flinn, pres & gen mgr; Allen Bray, opns mgr; Linda Blair, gen sls mgr; Jay Ralls, mus dir; Rob Herring, chief engr. ■ Rates: $25; 18; 25; 15.

WHBQ(AM)—Mar 18, 1925: 560 khz; 5 kw-D, 1 kw-N, DA-2. TL: N35 15 12 W90 02 51. Hrs opn: 24. 5900 Poplar Ave. (38119). (901) 458-8255. FAX: (901) 452-0034. Licensee: Flinn Broadcasting Corp. (acq 10-1-88). Net: Unistar. Rep: Republic. Format: Sports. ■ George S. Flinn, pres; John Bibbs, gen mgr; Bill Jones, progmg dir; Doug Gossett, chief engr.

WHRK(FM)—Listing follows WDIA(AM).

WJCE(AM)—March 1925: 680 khz; 10 kw-D, 5 kw-N, DA-N. TL: N35 13 23 W90 02 33. Stereo. 5904 Ridgeway Ctr. Pkwy. (38120). (901) 767-0104. FAX: (901) 767-0582. Licensee: Keymarket Communications (group owner; acq 12-88). Rep: Major Mkt. Format: Urban Gold. News staff 2. Target aud: 25-54; active, affluent adults. ■ Barry Drake, pres; Curt Peterson, gen mgr; Jim Kirkland, opns dir & progmg dir; Ken Miller, gen sls mgr; Kathy Jowers, prom mgr; Kay Manley, mus dir; Ronda Cloud, news dir; Bob Mayben, chief engr.

WRVR-FM—Co-owned with WJCE(AM). Sept 15, 1968: 104.5 mhz; 100 kw. Ant 751 ft. TL: N35 09 17 W89 49 20. Stereo. Prog sep from AM. (Acq 3-81). Format: Adult contemp.

***WKNO-FM**—Mar 1, 1972: 91.1 mhz; 100 kw. Ant 580 ft. TL: N35 09 17 W89 49 20. Stereo. Hrs opn: 24. Box 241880 (38124); 900 Getwell Rd. (38111). (901) 458-2521. FAX: (901) 458-2221. Licensee: Mid-South Public Communications Foundation. Net: APR, NPR. Wash atty: Schwarz, Woods & Miller. Format: Class, news. News staff one. Target aud: 35 plus. ■ Michael LaBonia, pres; Dan Campbell, gen mgr; Darel Snodgrass, opns mgr & progmg mgr; Charles McLarty, dev dir; Juanita Homer, dev mgr; Jim Eikner, gen sls mgr; Lee Hill, prom mgr; Charles Billings, mus dir; Everette Rice, news dir; Pamela Poletti, pub affrs dir; Russ Abernathy, engrg dir; Pat Lane, chief engr. ■ *WKNO-TV affil.

WLOK(AM)—Mar 1, 1956: 1340 khz; 1 kw-U. TL: N35 07 01 W90 00 59. Hrs opn: 24. Box 69 (38101); 363 S. Second St. (38103). (901) 527-9565. FAX: (901) 525-4322. Licensee: Gilliam Communications Inc. (acq 1-12-77). Net: American Urban, Unistar. Rep: Katz & Powell. Format: Black. News staff one. Target aud: 25-54. ■ H.A. Gilliam Jr., pres & gen mgr; Michael Anderson, gen sls mgr; Sandra Hayes, prom dir & progmg dir; Delsa Fleming, mus dir; Rick Taylor, news dir; Rob Herring, chief engr. ■ Rates: $40; 40; 40; 40.

WMC(AM)—Jan 21, 1923: 790 khz; 5 kw-U, DA-N. TL: N35 10 09 W89 53 12 (CP: TL: N35 10 07 W89 53 05). Stereo. 1960 Union Ave. (38104). (901) 726-0555. FAX: (901) 726-5847. Licensee: Ellis Communications (group owner; acq 10-7-93; $65 million with co-located FM-TV; FTR 10-25-93). Net: ABC/I, NBC Talknet. Rep: Banner. Wash atty: Baker & Hostetler. Format: News/talk. News staff 6. Target aud; 35 plus. Spec prog: Sports, farm 11 hrs wkly. ■ Bert Ellis, pres; Sidney Mendelson, gen mgr; Cindy Horton, prom dir; Jim Cassel, progmg dir; Paul Davis, news dir; Mike Schwartz, chief engr. ■ WMC-TV affil.

WMC-FM—May 22, 1947: 99.7 mhz; 300 w. Ant 970 ft. TL: N35 10 09 W89 53 12. Stereo. Hrs opn: 24. Prog sep from AM. Net: NBC the Source. Format: Adult contemp. News staff 2. Target aud: 20-40. ■ Steve Conley, progmg dir; Will Pendarvis, mus dir; Craig Robbins, news dir.

WNWZ(AM)—(Germantown). October 1955: 1430 khz; 2.5 kw-U, DA-N. TL: N35 04 20 W89 51 40 (day), N35 12 50 W89 47 46 (night) (CP: 2.8 kw-U, DA-2, TL: N34 59 22 W89 51 45 (one-site)). 6080 Mount Mariah Rd. Ext., Memphis (38115). (901) 767-0104. Licensee: Flinn Broadcasting Corp. (acq 9-22-93; $695,000; FTR 10-11-93). Net: MBS. Rep: Eastman. Format: Adult contemp. News staff one; news progmg 7 hrs wkly. Target aud: 25-54. ■ Ed Winton, pres & gen mgr; David Beveridge, opns mgr; Kirk Harnach, gen sls mgr.

WOGY-FM—(Germantown). Apr 15, 1977: 94.3 mhz; 3 kw. Ant 300 ft. TL: N35 04 20 W89 51 40 (CP: 25 kw, ant 472 ft., TL: N34 59 22 W89 51 45). Stereo. 5904 Ridgeway Pkwy., Memphis (38120). (901) 795-8831. Licensee: Ardman Broadcasting Corp. of Tenn. Group owner: Ardman Broadcasting Corp. Format: Easy lstng. News progmg 7 hrs wkly. Target aud: 35-64; adults with discretionary income.

WPLX(AM)—(Collierville). April 1987: 1170 khz; 1 kw-D. TL: N35 01 28 W89 42 21 (CP: COL: Germantown). 4554 Fleming Rd. (38017). (901) 853-0801. FAX: (901) 853-4410. Licensee: Pollack Supply Inc. (acq 5-8-91; $114,000; FTR 5-27-91). Net: SMN. Format: Country. News staff 2; news progmg 8 hrs wkly. Target aud: General. ■ Steve Kelly, progmg dir & news dir; Rob Herring, chief engr.

***WQOX(FM)**—Apr 8, 1974: 88.5 mhz; 30 kw. Ant 430 ft. TL: N35 09 17 W89 49 20. Stereo. Hrs opn: 6 AM-10 PM, Mon-Sat. Craigmont High School, 3333 Covington Pike (38128). (901) 385-4317; (901) 722-4444. FAX: (901) 722-4402. Licensee: Board of Ed, Memphis City Schools. Format: Adult contemp, educ, pub affrs. News progmg 4 hrs wkly. Target aud: General. Spec prog: Sports 6 hrs, Black 5 hrs, folk 3 hrs, jazz/blues 10 hrs wkly. ■ Bob Taylor, gen mgr & mus dir; Jim Futrel, opns mgr; Sherman Austin, progmg dir; Robert Thomas, pub affrs dir; Harry Gibson, chief engr.

WREC(AM)—September 1922: 600 khz; 5 kw-U, DA-2. TL: N35 11 51 W90 00 31. Hrs opn: 24. Box 2099, 203 Beale St. (38103). (901) 578-1160; (901) 578-1103. FAX: (901) 525-8054. Licensee: NewMarket Media Corp. (group owner; acq 3-87). Net: CBS, MBS, Unistar. Prog Farm, Tenn. Radio Net. Rep: McGavren Guild. Wash atty: Kaye Scholar. Format: Full svc, news, sports & info. News staff one; news progmg 3 hrs wkly. Target aud: 35 plus; upscale, professional-skews males 70%. Spec prog: Farm 3 hrs wkly. ■ Pete Schulte, CEO; Steve Robertson, chmn; Steve Watts, CFO; Sherri Sawyer, gen mgr; Phil Morgan, gen sls mgr; Diane Hampton, mktg dir; Toni Bell, prom mgr; Fred Cook, progmg dir; Alan Tynes, mus dir; Bill Dries, news dir; Gary Condrey, chief engr.

WEGR(FM)—Co-owned with WREC(AM). March 1967: 102.7 mhz; 100 kw. Ant 970 ft. TL: N35 10 52 W89 49 56. Stereo. Hrs opn: 24. Prog sep from AM. Net: ABC/R. Format: Classic rock. News staff 2; news progmg one hr wkly. Target aud: 25-54; 25-34 core audience-60% male, 40% female. Spec prog: Rockline, flashback. ■ Tim Spencer, opns mgr & progmg dir; Jimmy Wilmer, gen sls mgr; Drake Hall, progmg mgr; Zeke Logan, mus dir; Bev Hart, news dir.

Stations in the U.S. Tennessee

WRVR-FM—Listing follows WJCE(AM).

***WSMS(FM)**—July 1975: 91.7 mhz; 25 kw. Ant 394 ft. TL: N35 09 17 W89 51 28. Stereo. Memphis State Univ., Dept of Theater & Comm. Arts (38152). (901) 678-3176. FAX: (901) 678-4331. Licensee: Memphis State Univ. (acq 1979). Format: Progsv, jazz, talk. News staff one; news progrmg 2 hrs wkly. Target aud: 18-49; upscale, college-educated. Spec prog: Sports. ■ Robert McDowell, gen mgr; Teresa Curtis, progmg dir; Malvin Massey, mus dir; Eddy Arnold, chief engr. ■ Rates: $15; 15; 15; 15.

WXSS(AM)—February 1984: 1030 khz; 50 kw-D, 1 kw-N, DA-N. TL: N35 10 59 W89 56 17. 2265 Central Ave. (38104-5516). (901) 272-3004. FAX: (901) 272-0747. Licensee: Willis Family Broadcasting Inc. (group owner; acq 3-4-92; grpsl; FTR 3-23-92). Format: Gospel. ■ Chuck Woodson, gen mgr; Ray Price, progmg dir & mus dir; Jerry Campbell, chief engr.

WYKL(FM)—(Millington). Apr 12, 1960: 98.1 mhz; 100 kw. Ant 1,240 ft. TL: N35 28 03 W90 11 27 (CP: Ant 768 ft.). Stereo. 88 Union Ave., Memphis (38103). (901) 529-0098. FAX: (901) 529-4431. Licensee: Barnstable Broadcasting Inc. (group owner; acq 3-9-93; $4.25 million; FTR 3-29-93). Net: ABC/C. Rep: Christal. Format: CHR. News staff one; news progmg 3 hrs wkly. Target aud: 12-34; young adults, upwardly mobile with average income. ■ Craig McKee, gen mgr & gen sls mgr; John Doyle, prom mgr; Howard Cassel, mus dir; Art Mehring, news dir; Robert Benjamin, chief engr.

***WYPL(FM)**—Apr 17, 1991: 89.3 mhz; 2.75 kw. Ant 194 ft. TL: N35 08 02 W90 00 00. Stereo. Hrs opn: 18. Memphis Public Library, 1850 Peabody Ave. (38104). (901) 725-8833. FAX: (901) 272-5104. Licensee: Cossitt Library. Group owner: Memphis Shelby City Public Library and Information. Wash atty: Ready, Bagley & Martin. Format: Information. Target aud: General. ■ Steven C. Terry, stn mgr & chief engr; Mary M. Guth, dev dir; Jackie Nerren, mktg dir; Bob Baker, pub affrs dir.

Milan

WKBJ(AM)—Apr 27, 1955: 1600 khz; 2.5 kw-D, 71 w-N. TL: N35 55 37 W88 44 27. 21 Gibson Hwy. (38358). (901) 986-0242; (901) 686-3311. FAX: (901) 986-8557. Licensee: Milan Broadcasting Co. (acq 8-31-90; $80,000; FTR 9-24-90). Net: Tenn. Net. Rep: Katz & Powell; Midsouth.Format: Oldies. News staff one. Target aud: 25 plus. Spec prog: Relg 15 hrs wkly. ■ Dr. James Hoppers, pres; Jerry Vandiver, opns mgr; Michael Ray, mus dir; Dave Hacker, chief engr. ■ Rates: $84; 75; 60; na.

WYNU(FM)—Dec 12, 1964: 92.3 mhz; 100 kw. Ant 991 ft. TL: N35 54 06 W88 46 55. Stereo. 115 Devonshire Sq., Jackson (38305). (901) 668-9201. FAX: (901) 664-7345. Licensee: Ohio Broadcast Associates (acq 10-29-93; $1.226 million; FTR 11-15-93). Format: Adult contemp. News staff one. ■ Jack Hendrickson, pres; Betty Eggenberger, gen mgr; Larry Wood, gen sls mgr; Julie Rhodes, prom mgr; Dave James, mus dir; Steve Bowers, news dir; Dave Hacker, chief engr.

Millington

WMPS(AM)—June 22, 1962: 1380 khz; 2.5 kw-D, 1 kw-N, DA-2. TL: N35 18 56 W89 55 23. 6960 Bucknell Rd. (38053). (901) 873-1380. Licensee: David Grayson Life Changing Ministries (acq 4-8-93; $360,000; FTR 4-26-93). Net: CBN. Rep: Bolton. Format: Contemp Christian. ■ David Grayson, gen mgr; Dave Church, chief engr.

WYKL(FM)—Licensed to Millington. See Memphis.

Minor Hill

WYBM(FM)—Sept 2, 1983: 92.1 mhz; 1.2 kw. Ant 460 ft. TL: N35 07 18 W87 11 17. Stereo. Box 127, Pulaski (38478). (615) 363-0133. FAX: (615) 424-9604. Licensee: Hometown Broadcasting Inc. (acq 9-3-93; $211,027.80; FTR 9-27-93). Net: ABC/I. Format: Oldies. ■ Bill Moore, pres.

Monterey

WKXD(FM)—Mar 3, 1986: 106.9 mhz; 25 kw. Ant 731 ft. TL: N36 07 13 W85 14 44. Stereo. Hrs opn: 24. 259 S. Willow Ave., Cookeville (38501). (615) 526-6860. Licensee: JWC Broadcasting (acq 10-16-91; $590,000; FTR 11-4-91). Net: USA. Format: Adult contemp. News staff one. Target aud: 18-49; young, adult & affluent audiences. ■ Kevin Paul, CEO, gen mgr, opns mgr, dev mgr & gen sls mgr; Connie Neal, prom mgr; Bill Penn, progmg dir; Gordon Stack, asst mus dir; Brian Welch, news dir; Julie Sotis, pub affrs dir; Austin Stinnett, chief engr. ■ Rates: $10; 10; 10; 10.

Morristown

WCRK(AM)—October 1947: 1150 khz; 5 kw-D, 500 w-N, DA-N. TL: N36 14 11 W83 18 33. Hrs opn: 24. Box 220, 204 Brown Ave. (37814). (615) 586-9101. Licensee: WCRK Inc. (acq 11-22-60). Net: AP. Rep: Rgnl Reps. Format: Adult contemp, MOR. News staff one. Target aud: 25-54. ■ John P. Hart, pres; Howell Ashford, vp; Mark Ashford, gen mgr; Ed Arnold, mus dir & pub affrs dir; Rick Brooks, news dir; Dan Trombley, Leon Duncan, engrg mgrs; Frank Folsom, chief engr.

WJDT(FM)—See Rogersville.

WMTN(AM)—Oct 19, 1957: 1300 khz; 5 kw-D, 100 w-N. TL: N36 12 15 W83 19 57. Box 70 (37815); 510 W. Economy Rd. (37814). (615) 586-7993; (615) 586-9696. FAX: (615) 235-7012. Licensee: Franklin Communications Corp. (acq 11-84; $1.1 million with co-located FM; FTR 9-24-84). Net: Sun, ABC; Tenn. Radio Net. Format: C&W, news/talk. News staff 2; news progmg 2 hrs wkly. Target aud: 25-64; farmers & factory workers. Spec prog: Farm 5 hrs, gospel 5 hrs wkly. ■ Terry Bond, gen mgr; Marcella Stuart, rgnl sls mgr; Robin Keith, prom mgr; Tim Crews, progmg dir; Sharon Case, mus dir; Rod Bramblett, news dir; Bob Wallace, chief engr.

WMXK(FM)—Co-owned with WMTN(AM). May 31, 1964: 95.9 mhz; 1.1 kw. Ant 771 ft. TL: N36 13 40 W83 19 58. Stereo. Prog sep from AM. Format: Adult contemp. News staff 2; news progmg 3 hrs wkly. Target aud: 18-54; middle to upper income. Spec prog: Jazz one hr, relg 2 hrs wkly. ■ Marcella Stuart, sls dir; Cookie Larkin, prom dir; Robin Keith, progmg dir & asst mus dir.

Mt. Carmel

WRVX(AM)—Not on air, target date unknown: 1200 khz; 10 kw-D, 250 w-N, DA-2. TL: N36 33 55 W82 41 34. 5224 Foxfire Pl., Kingsport (37664). Licensee: Carmel Communications Corp.

Mt. Pleasant

WXRQ(AM)—Dec 15, 1981: 1460 khz; 1 kw-D, 170 w-N. TL: N35 31 21 W87 11 34. Hrs opn: 6 AM-8 PM. Box 31, 209 Bond St. (38474). (615) 379-3119. FAX: (615) 379-3129. Licensee: New Life Broadcasting Inc. (acq 1-17-89; $75,000; FTR 1-30-89). Net: USA. Format: Christian. Spec prog: Black 4 hrs wkly. ■ Donald Paul, pres & gen mgr; Rick Hancock, prom mgr; Eric Kennedy, progmg dir; Kevin Kidd, chief engr.

Mountain City

WMCT(AM)—Dec 8, 1967: 1390 khz; 1 kw-D. TL: N36 29 23 W81 47 12. Hrs opn: 6 AM-6 PM. 1211 N. Church St., (37683). (615) 727-6701; (615) 727-9454. Licensee: Johnson County Broadcasting Co. Net: ABC/E; Tenn. Net. Rep: Keystone (unwired net), Midsouth. Format: C&W. ■ Fran Atkinson, pres & gen mgr; Jim Gilley, gen sls mgr & news dir; Kevin Parsons, prom mgr & mus dir; Lester Morley, progmg dir; Bob Morrison, chief engr. ■ Rates: $8; 8; 8; na.

Murfreesboro

WGNS(AM)—Jan 1, 1947: 1450 khz; 1 kw-U. TL: N35 50 26 W86 23 27. Stereo. Hrs opn: 24. Box 1450 (37133-1450); Broadcast Plaza, 306 S. Church St. (37130). (615) 893-5373. Licensee: The Rutherford Group Inc. (acq 1984; FTR 10-15-84). Net: BRN, UPI. Rep: Keystone (unwired net), Midsouth. Format: News/talk, sports. News progmg 80 hrs wkly. Target aud: 25 plus; active adults, "movers and shakers" in economic and education groupings. Spec prog: Black 6 hrs, farm 3 hrs, relg 6 hrs wkly. ■ Bart Walker, pres & gen mgr; Lee Ann Walker, vp & prom mgr; Bobbie Hayes, opns mgr; Van Cowart, dev dir; Dan Russell, sls dir; Scott Walker, mktg dir; Bryan Barrett, news dir; Matt Lane, pub affrs dir; Gary Brown, chief engr.

***WMOT(FM)**—Apr 9, 1969: 89.5 mhz; 50 kw. Ant 210 ft. TL: N35 51 00 W86 21 00. Stereo. Box 3, Middle Tenn. State U. (37132). (615) 898-2800; (615) 255-9071. FAX: (615) 898-2774. Licensee: Middle Tenn. State Univ. Net: NPR. Format: Jazz. News staff 2; news progmg 20 hrs wkly. Target aud: 24-49 plus; general. ■ John L. High, gen mgr; John Egly, opns mgr; Laura McComb, dev dir; Greg Lee Hunt, progmg dir; Randy O'Brien, Shawn Jacobs (producer), news dirs; Gary Brown, chief engr.

WMTS(AM)—Nov 1, 1953: 810 khz; 5 kw-D. TL: N35 50 14 W86 25 00. Box 860 (37130). (615) 893-6611. FAX: (615) 895-2633. Licensee: Colonial Broadcasting of Tenn. (acq 4-1-81; $1.23 million; FTR 3-30-81). Net: ABC/D; Tenn. Radio. Rep: Southern. Format: Modern country. Spec prog: Farm 3 hrs wkly. ■ Bob Corlew, pres; Phil Randolph, gen mgr; Neil Lancaster, gen sls mgr; Greg Nance, news dir.

WRMX(FM)—Aug 10, 1963: 96.3 mhz; 100 kw. Ant 827 ft. TL: N36 05 07 W86 26 22 (CP: 52 kw, ant 1,286 ft., TL: N36 15 50 W86 47 38). Stereo. Hrs opn: 24. United Artists Tower, Suite 901, 50 Music Sq. W., Nashville (37203). (615) 327-9636. FAX: (615) 327-0832. Licensee: Signature Broadcasting Inc. (acq 12-1-87). Wash atty: Rosenman & Colin. Format: Oldies. News staff one. Target aud: 25-54. ■ Richard Oppenheimer, pres; Michael Oppenheimer, gen mgr; Rick Steele, gen sls mgr; Bobby Knight, progmg dir; Margaret Hood, news dir; Carl Campbell, chief engr.

Nashville

WAMB(AM)—(Donelson). Apr 12, 1971: 1160 khz; 50 kw-D, 1 kw-N, DA-N. TL: N36 09 49 W86 42 55. Stereo. Hrs opn: 24. 1617 Lebanon Rd., Nashville (37210). (615) 889-1960. FAX: (615) 889-1973. Licensee: Great Southern Broadcasting Co. Inc. Net: MBS. Rep: Roslin. Wash atty: Tierney & Swift. Format: MOR, nostalgia, big band. Target aud: General. Spec prog: Jazz 3 hrs, Sp 6 hrs, business news 6 hrs wkly. ■ William O. Barry, pres & gen mgr; Will C. Baird Jr., vp & news dir; Beth Lane, opns mgr & prom mgr; Harry P. Stevenson, gen sls mgr; Ken Bramming, progmg dir; Bob Sticht, mus dir; Gary Brown, chief engr.

WAMB-FM—(Donelson). Nov 26, 1990: 106.7 mhz; 75 w. Ant 250 ft. TL: N36 09 49 W86 42 55. Stereo. Hrs opn: 24. Dups AM 100%. Target aud: 35 plus.

WENO(AM)—May 23, 1988: 760 khz; 1 kw-D. TL: N36 09 49 W86 42 55. Stereo. Hrs opn: Sunrise-sunset. 333 Murfreesboro Rd. (37210). (615) 242-4240. Licensee: WENO Inc. (acq 5-7-90; $300,000; FTR 5-21-90). Net: USA. Format: Relg. News progmg 6 hrs wkly. Target aud: 25-54. ■ Millard Reed, pres; Ray Richards, CFO; David Deese, gen mgr; John W. Hembree, stn mgr & gen sls mgr; Gregg Hutchins, mus dir; Tom Marshall, pub affrs dir; Dale Howard, chief engr. ■ Rates: $20; 20; 20; na.

***WNAZ-FM**—Co-owned with WENO(AM). May 23, 1967: 89.1 mhz; 1.4 kw. Ant 120 ft. TL: N36 08 33 W86 45 10. Stereo. Hrs opn: 24. Prog sep from AM. (615) 248-1689. Licensee: Trevecca Nazarene College Inc. Format: Relg. News progmg 3 hrs wkly. Target aud: 25-45; white collar professionals & their families. ■ Mark DeYoung, stn mgr & mus dir.

***WFSK(FM)**—May 15, 1973: 88.1 mhz; 700 w. Ant 6 ft. TL: N36 10 00 W86 48 17. Stereo. Hrs opn: 8 hrs. Fisk University, 1000 17th Ave. N. (37208-3051). (615) 329-8754. Licensee: Fisk University. Format: Div. Target aud: General; alternative music listeners. Spec prog: Black, jazz, relg, urban contemp, rap/house 18 hrs, oldies 3 hrs, ladies nite 3 hrs, reggae 3 hrs, mellow madness 13 hrs wkly. ■ Tryone Shelton, gen mgr; Wayne Miller, chief engr.

WGFX(FM)—See Gallatin.

WKDA(AM)—1948: 1240 khz; 1 kw-U. TL: N36 09 24 W86 46 15. Hrs opn: 24. Box 101604 (37224-1604). (615) 244-9533. FAX: (615) 244-5163. Licensee: Dick Broadcasting Co. (group owner; acq 8-1-76). Net: ABC/R, CNN. Rep: Katz. Format: News. News staff 2. Target aud: 25-54. Spec prog: Relg 2 hrs wkly. ■ Allen Dick, pres; Steve Dickert, gen mgr; Pat Ervin, opns mgr; Paul Lyle, gen sls mgr; Cindy Francis, progmg dir & news dir; David Hodge, chief engr.

WKDF(FM)—Co-owned with WKDA(AM). Jan 1, 1967: 103.3 mhz; 100 kw. Ant 1,233 ft. TL: N36 02 08 W86 50 56. Stereo. Prog sep from AM. Format: AOR. Target aud: General; 18-34. ■ Pat Ervin, prom mgr; Kidd Redd, progmg dir; John Nagarya, mus dir.

WLAC(AM)—Nov 24, 1926: 1510 khz; 50 kw-U, DA-N. TL: N36 16 15 W86 45 24. Hrs opn: 24. 10 Music Circle E. (37203). (615) 256-0555. FAX: (615) 242-4826. Licensee: Ward Broadcasting. Group owner: Fairmont Communications Corp. (acq 1987). Net: CBS, UPI, Wall Street; Rep: Banner. Wash atty: Haley, Bader & Potts. Format: News/talk, sports, relg. News staff 3; news progmg 18 hrs wly. Target aud: 35-64; professionals, business owners & managers. Spec prog: Black 20 hrs wkly. ■ Mark Hubbard, pres; Chris Karb, gen mgr; Ginny Underwood, gen sls mgr; Cori Dodson, prom mgr; Billy Shears, progmg dir; Bryan Sargent, mus dir; Jim Ellis, news dir; Watt Hairston, chief engr.

WLAC-FM—1953: 105.9 mhz; 100 kw. Ant 1,226 ft. TL: N30 02 08 W86 50 56. Stereo. Hrs opn: 24. Prog sep from AM. Net: ABC/FM. Format: Adult contemp. News staff one; news progmg 3 hrs wkly. Target aud: 25-54; upwardly mobile adults. Spec prog: Christian 6 hrs wkly. ■ Bryan Sargent, mus dir; Kris Kelly, news dir.

WMDB(AM)—Aug 15, 1983: 880 khz; 2.5 kw-D. TL: N36 12 43 W86 49 09. 3051 Stokers Ln. (37218). (615) 255-2876; (615) 254-8880. Licensee: Babb Broadcasting Co. Format: Gospel, R&B. Target aud: General. ■ Morgan Babb, pres, gen mgr & progmg dir; Michael Babb, gen sls mgr. ■ Rates: $30; 30; 30; na.

WMRO(AM)—Apr 23, 1967: 1560 khz; 10 kw-D, DA. TL: N36 12 32 W86 52 21. Box 65, Gallatin (37066-0065). Licensee: Lindsey Christian Broadcasting (acq 12-27-87).

WNAH(AM)—Dec 24, 1949: 1360 khz; 1 kw-U. TL: N36 11 30 W86 46 26. Hrs opn: 24. 44 Music Sq. E. (37203). (615) 254-7611. FAX: (615) 254-4565. Licensee: Hermitage Broadcasting Corp. Net: MBS. Format: Southern gospel. News progmg 5 hrs wkly. Target aud: 21-50. ■ V. T. Irwin Jr., pres; Hoyt M. Carter Jr., gen mgr, progmg dir & chief engr; Tony Cappuccilli, gen sls mgr; Bill Grist, prom mgr; Mike Brown, mus dir; Mike Perry, news dir.

***WNAZ-FM**—Listing follows WENO(AM).

WNQM(AM)—July 1, 1948: 1300 khz; 5 kw-U, DA-N. TL: N36 12 30 W86 53 38. Hrs opn: 5:30 AM-midnight. 1300 WWCR Ave. (37218). (615) 255-1300; (800) 238-5576. Licensee: WNQM Inc. Group owner: F.W. Robbert Broadcasting Co. Inc. (acq 1-83; $700,000; FTR 12-19-83). Format: Relg. Target aud: General. ■ Fred P. Werstenberger, pres; George McClintock, gen mgr & chief engr; Joe Brashier, progmg dir.

***WPLN(FM)**—Dec 17, 1962: 90.3 mhz; 80 kw. Ant 1,132 ft. TL: N36 02 08 W86 50 56. Stereo. 8th Ave. N. & Union (37203-3585). (615) 862-5810. Licensee: Public Library of Nashville & Davidson County. Net: NPR, AP, APR. Wash atty: Donald E. Martin. Format: Class, cultural, educ. News staff 2; news progmg 7 hrs wkly. Target aud: General. ■ Alvin Lewis Bolt, gen mgr; J. Gregory Pope, dev mgr; Dr. Calvert Bean, progmg dir; Suzanne Potter, mus dir; Carl N. Pedersen, chief engr.

WQQK(FM)—See Hendersonville.

WQZQ(FM)—See Dickson.

WRMX(FM)—See Murfreesboro.

***WRVU(FM)**—Dec 3, 1971: 91.1 mhz; 14.5 kw. Ant 457 ft. TL: N36 08 27 W86 51 56. Stereo. Hrs opn: 24. Box 9100-B, 128 Sarratt Student Ctr., Vanderbilt Univ. (37235). (615) 322-3691; (615) 322-7625. FAX: (615) 343-2582. Licensee: Vanderbilt Student Communications. Net: ABC/R. Format: Progsv rock. News progmg 6 hrs wkly. Target aud: 13-30. Spec prog: Black 3 hrs, Fr one hr, Ger one hr, jazz 18 hrs, Russian one hr, Sp one hr, Por one hr, bluegrass 3 hrs, reggae 3 hrs, blues 3 hrs wkly. ■ Joseph Helm, gen mgr; Doug Smallwood, Veronica Welbourne, progmg dirs; Doug Smallwood, mus dir; Brennan T. Price, news dir; Marc Pezzolla, chief engr.

WSIX-FM—1948: 97.9 mhz; 100 kw. Ant 1,140 ft. TL: N36 02 49 W86 49 49. Stereo. Hrs opn: 24. 21 Music Sq. W. (37203). (615) 664-2400. Licensee: Capstar Communications Inc. Group owner: SFX Broadcasting Inc. Rep: McGavern Guild. Format: Country. News staff 2; news progmg one hr wkly. Target aud: 25-54. ■ R. Steven Hicks, CEO; Geoff Armstrong, CFO; John King, gen mgr; Beth Murphy, gen sls mgr; Virginia Julian, natl sls mgr; Duncan Stewart, prom dir; Doug Baker, progmg dir; Al Voeks, news dir; Tracy Weaver, pub affrs dir; Mike Gideon, chief engr.

WSM(AM)—1925: 650 khz; 50 kw-U. TL: N35 59 50 W86 47 32. Stereo. Hrs opn: 24. 2644 McGavock Pike (37214). (615) 889-6595. FAX: (615) 871-6778. Licensee: WSM Inc. Group owner: Gaylord Broadcasting Co. Net: NBC. Rep: Christal. Format: Full service, country. News staff 12; news progmg 11 hrs wkly. Target aud: 35 plus; high school graduates, married homeowners, income $25,000 plus. Spec prog: Farm 6 hrs wkly. ■ Bob Meyer, gen mgr; John Padgett, gen sls mgr; Brent Stoker, prom mgr; Kyle Cantrell, progmg dir; Wade Jessen, mus dir; Jerry Dahmen, news dir & pub affrs dir; Hugh Hickerson, chief engr.

WSM-FM—Nov 1, 1962: 95.5 mhz; 100 kw. Ant 1,280 ft. TL: N36 08 27 W86 51 56. Stereo. Prog sep from AM. Format: Country. News staff 12; news progmg one hr wkly. Target aud: 25-54. ■ Lee Cory, progmg dir.

WVOL(AM)—See Berry Hill.

WYFN(AM)—Jan 7, 1927: 980 khz; 5 kw-U, DA-N. TL: N36 12 25 W86 40 25. 1940 Neely's Bend Rd., Madison (37115-3203). (615) 868-4458. TWX: 910-997-0501. Licensee: Bible Broadcasting Network (group owner; acq 1-31-91; $600,000; FTR 2-18-91). Net: ABC/E. Rep: McGavren Guild. Format: Relg. ■ David R. Mills, gen mgr; Watt Hairston, chief engr.

WZEZ(FM)—Apr 3, 1976: 92.9 mhz; 100 kw. Ant 1,086 ft. TL: N36 07 14 W86 58 07. Stereo. Hrs opn: 24. Box 40506 (37204-0506); 504 Rosedale Ave. (37211). (615) 259-9393; (615) 259-4567. FAX: (615) 259-4594. Licensee: South Central Communications Corp. (group owner). Rep: D & R Radio. Wash atty: Bryan, Cave, McPheeters & McRoberts. Format: Soft adult contemp. News progmg one hr wkly. Target aud: 25-54. ■ John David Engelbrecht, CEO & pres; Robert L. Shirel, CFO; Steve Edwards, vp & gen mgr; Jim Kennedy, opns mgr & progmg mgr; Rick Steele, rgnl sls mgr; Keith Kaufman, prom dir; Katherine Dunn, news dir; Clifton Harris, pub affrs dir; Clinton Hooper, chief engr. ■ Rates: $150; 150; 150; 50.

Newport

WLIK(AM)—Apr 9, 1954: 1270 khz; 5 kw-D, 500 w-N, DA-N. TL: N35 57 49 W83 12 31. Hrs opn: 6 AM-12 midnight. 640 W. Hwy 25/70 (37821). (615) 623-3095. FAX: (615) 623-3096. Licensee: WLIK Inc. Group owner: Wilkerson Broadcasting Group. Net: CNN. Format: C&W. Target aud: General. Spec prog: Relg 18 hrs wkly. ■ Arthur Wilkerson, pres & gen mgr; Dwight D. Wilkerson, vp, stn mgr, gen sls mgr & chief engr; Jim Cox, news dir. ■ Rates: $8; 8; 8; na.

WNPC(AM)—September 1978: 1060 khz; 1 kw-D. TL: N35 59 10 W83 10 46. Box 189 (37821); 377 Graham St. (37821). (615) 623-8743; (615) 623-8744. FAX: (615) 623-0545. Licensee: WNPC Inc. Net: ABC. Wash atty: Taylor & Zimsky. Format: Country. Target aud: 25-49. ■ Carroll Wayne Harris, gen mgr; Jim Phillips, mus dir; Ray Snader, news dir; Vonn Murrell, chief engr.

WNPC-FM—February 1993: 92.9 mhz; 3.1 kw. Ant 459 ft. TL: N35 57 27 W83 05 03. Stereo. Hrs opn: 24. Dups AM 90%. ■ Carroll Wayne Harris, pres; Teddy Harris, gen sls mgr; Bill Beason, prom dir & progmg dir; Jim Phillips, vp progmg; Brian Fredette, asst mus dir; Ray Snader, news dir. ■ Rates: $10; 10; 10; 10.

Oak Ridge

WATO(AM)—Feb 1, 1948: 1290 khz; 5 kw-D, 500 w-N, DA-2. TL: N36 03 02 W84 12 38. Box 6168 (37831). (615) 482-1290; (615) 483-1290. FAX: (615) 481-3570. Licensee: WATO Inc. (acq 9-29-93; $130,000; FTR 10-18-93). Net: ABC/D. Rep: Select, Midsouth. Format: News/talk, sports. ■ Ron Meredith, pres; David Clary, gen mgr & progmg dir; Wendall Eades, gen sls mgr; Mike McNeely, news dir; Bob Wallace, chief engr.

WKNF-FM—February 1967: 94.3 mhz; 2.5 kw. Ant 515 ft. TL: N35 56 28 W84 09 28. Stereo. Suite 600, 1900 N. Winston Rd., Knoxville (37932). (615) 531-2000. FAX: (615) 531-0101. Licensee: John W. Pirkle (acq 4-5-93; $507,801; FTR 4-26-93). Format: Classic country. ■ Johnathan W. Pirckle, pres & gen mgr; Glynn Pullen, gen sls mgr; Bill Cleary, progmg dir; Scott Wyrick, chief engr.

WOKI-FM—Licensed to Oak Ridge. See Knoxville.

Olive Hill

***WDNX(FM)**—Jan 10, 1975: 89.1 mhz; 100 kw. Ant 150 ft. TL: N35 12 30 W88 03 46. Stereo. Hrs opn: 15. WDNX, Rt. 2, 3730 Lonesome Pine Rd., Savannah (38372); R.R. 2, Box 212, HHA Administration Bldg., Savannah (38372). (901) 925-9236; (901) 925-3098. Licensee: Rural Life Foundation. Format: Easy lstng, educ, gospel, relg. News progmg 3 hrs wkly. Target aud: General. Spec prog: Classical 5 hrs, farm one hr wkly. ■ Charles Harris, chmn; Lester L. Dickman, pres; Judy Edwards, CFO; Steven Dickman, exec vp; Albert K. Nielsen, stn mgr, gen sls mgr, mktg mgr, adv mgr & pub affrs dir; Steve Dickman, dev mgr; Dennis Wentzloff, prom dir.

Oliver Springs

WXVO(FM)—Sept 15, 1989: 98.7 mhz; 6 kw. Ant 328 ft. TL: N36 01 31 W84 21 29. Box 987, Clinton (37717); 874 E. Tri-County Blvd. (37840). (615) 435-0987. Licensee: Charles E. Phillips. Format: Country. News progmg 4 hrs wkly. Target aud: 25 plus. ■ Charles E. Phillips, pres, gen mgr & news dir; Charles E. Peters, gen sls mgr; Charlotte Phillips, prom mgr; David Dotson, progmg dir & mus dir; Estle Cloud, chief engr.

Oneida

WOCV(AM)—Aug 1, 1959: 1310 khz; 1 kw-D. TL: N36 30 03 W84 29 24. Hrs opn: 6 AM- sunset. Box 4370, Rt. 1, Buffalo Rd. (37841). (615) 569-8598; (615) 569-9268. FAX: (615) 569-5572. Licensee: Oneida Broadcasters Inc. (acq 5-1-69). Net: ABC/E; Tenn. Radio Net. Format: Relg. News staff one; news progmg 20 hrs wkly. Target aud: 22-55. ■ George Guertin, pres; Charolett Guertin, vp; Hillard Mattie, gen mgr, opns dir & gen sls mgr; Kristy Mattie, progmg dir & mus dir; Paul Strunk, news dir; Darrel E. Smith, chief engr. ■ Rates: $4.80; 4.80; 4.80; na.

WBNT-FM—Co-owned with WOCV(AM). June 10, 1965: 105.5 mhz; 3 kw. Ant 280 ft. TL: N36 30 03 W84 29 24. Stereo. Dups AM 50%. Net: ABC/E; Tenn. Radio Net. Format: Adult contemp. News staff 2; news progmg 9 hrs wkly. ■ Hillard Mattie, prom mgr & adv mgr; Darrel Smith, engrg dir. ■ Rates: $3.15; 3.15; 3.15; na.

Paris

WAKQ(FM)—Listing follows WTPR(AM).

WMUF(AM)—May 9, 1980: 1000 khz; 5 kw-D, DA. TL: N36 18 50 W88 17 33. Box 1239, India Rd. (38242). (901) 644-9455. FAX: (901) 644-9595. Licensee: Benton-Weatherford Broadcasting Co. (acq 4-1-85). Net: USA. Format: Country. News staff one; news progmg 2 hrs wkly. Target aud: 25-54; people with disposable income. Spec prog: Farm 2 hrs wkly. ■ Gary D. Benton, pres & gen sls mgr; Frances Linsman, progmg mgr & mus dir; John Kent, news dir; Brad Hofford, chief engr.

WMUF-FM—Nov 1, 1991: 94.1 mhz; 3 kw. Ant 328 ft. TL: N36 18 50 W88 17 33. Stereo. Hrs opn: 24. Box 1239, India Rd. (38242). (901) 644-9456. Licensee: Benton-Weatherford Broadcasting Inc. of Tennessee (acq 3-15-91; FTR 4-8-91). Net: USA. Format: Adult contemp. ■ Gary D. Benton, pres. ■ Rates: $8; 8; 8; 7.

WTPR(AM)—May 7, 1947: 710 khz; 750 w-D. TL: N36 16 48 W88 17 39 (CP: TL: N36 16 47 W88 20 32). Stereo. 206 N. Brewer St. (38242). (901) 642-2621. FAX: (901) 644-9367. Licensee: WENK Broadcast Group Inc. Group owner: WENK Broadcast Group Inc. (acq 7-28-89; $575,000; FTR 8-14-89). Net: ABC/D; Tenn. Radio. Format: Oldies. News staff one; news progmg 12 hrs wkly. Target aud: 25-64. ■ Terry Hailey, pres & gen mgr; Ed Taylor, gen sls mgr; Bill McCutcheon, news dir; Brad Hosford, chief engr.

WAKQ(FM)—Co-owned with WTPR(AM). September 1967: 105.5 mhz; 6 kw. Ant 419 ft. TL: N36 16 45 W88 20 31. Stereo. Prog sep from AM. Format: CHR. News progmg 14 hrs wkly. Target aud: 12-34. ■ Richard Upton, mus dir.

Parsons

WKJQ(AM)—Oct 3, 1970: 1550 khz; 1 kw-D. TL: N35 39 26 W88 09 07. Box 576, Iron Hill Rd. (38363). (901) 847-3011. Licensee: Clenney Broadcasting Corp. (acq 4-1-89). Rep: Midsouth. Wash atty: Robert S. Stone. Format: Relg. Target aud: General. ■ Ralph D. Clenney, pres, gen mgr, gen sls mgr, progmg dir & chief engr; Dwight Lancaster, prom mgr; Steve Clenney, mus dir. ■ Rates: $3.30; 3.30; 3.30; na.

WKJQ-FM—June 4, 1990: 97.3 mhz; 6 kw. Ant 256 ft. TL: N35 39 39 W88 07 05. Stereo. Hrs opn: 24. Prog sep from AM. Format: Country. Target aud: 25-54. ■ Steve Clenney, opns dir & rgnl sls mgr; Ralph Clenney, adv mgr; Dwight Lancaster, news dir. ■ Rates: $3.80; 3.80; 3.80; 3.80.

Pikeville

WUAT(AM)—Dec 19, 1972: 1110 khz; 250 w-D. TL: N35 36 18 W85 11 14. Box 128, Spring St. (37367). (615) 447-2906. FAX: (615) 447-2669. Licensee: Charles Bownds Jr. ($74,000; FTR 11-23-92). Wash atty: Lukas, McGowan, Nace & Gutierrez. Format: Country. News staff 2; news progmg 7 hrs wkly. Spec prog: Farm 5 hrs, relg 15 hrs wkly. ■ Proctor Upchurch, pres; Charles M. Bownds, gen mgr, vp mktg & news dir; Joe Young, gen sls mgr; Joyce Forbes, progmg dir & pub affrs dir; Sharon Farley, mus dir; Austin Stinnett, chief engr. WUAT-TV affil. ■ Rates: $5; 5; 5; na.

Portland

WQKR(AM)—July 15, 1980: 1270 khz; 1 kw-D, 60 w-N. TL: N36 36 11 W86 32 01. Hrs opn: 5 AM-10 PM. 817 N. Broadway (37148). (615) 325-3250. FAX: (615) 325-3250. Licensee: Bravo Broadcasting Co. Inc. (acq 8-12-89). Net: UPI. Rep: Keystone (unwired net), Midsouth. Format: News, talk. News staff one. Target aud: General; 25-54. Spec prog: Country 2 hrs wkly. ■ Ron Simpson, pres, gen mgr & chief engr; Devita Simpson, vp sls; Bill Jones, prom mgr; Charlie Goad, progmg dir; Dr. Mike McDonald, news dir. ■ Rates: $8.40; 8.40; 8.40; 8.40.

Powell

WQBB(AM)—Licensed to Powell. See Knoxville.

Stations in the U.S.   Tennessee

Pulaski

WKSR(AM)—May 6, 1947: 1420 khz; 1 kw-U, DA-N. TL: N35 12 04 W87 03 20. Box 738 (38478). (615) 363-2505. Licensee: Pulaski Broadcasting Inc. (acq 4-4-80; $481,300; FTR 4-21-80). Format: Country. Target aud: 25-54. ■ Hershel Lake, pres; Ronnie Robe, gen mgr; Don Eastep, prom mgr; Ed Carter, progmg dir & mus dir; George Martin, news dir; Bill Wiseman, chief engr.

WINJ(FM)—Co-owned with WKSR(AM). Jan 12, 1970: 98.3 mhz; 3 kw. Ant 453 ft. TL: N35 08 47 W87 05 28. Stereo. Prog sep from AM. (Acq 1-1-84; $350,000; FTR 12-19-83). Format: Adult contemp. ■ Bob Plunkett, chief engr.

Red Bank

***WAWL-FM**—Sept 12, 1980: 91.5 mhz; 6 kw. Ant 951 ft. TL: N35 09 42 W85 19 06. Stereo. Hrs opn: 7 AM-11 PM. 4501 Amnicola Hwy., Chattanooga (37406). (615) 697-4470; (615) 697-4405. FAX: (615) 697-4740. Licensee: Chattanooga State Technical Community College. Net: AP. Format: Alternative. News staff one. Target aud: 18-34. ■ Bob Riley, gen mgr; Don Hixson, progmg dir & mus dir; Alan Baldwin, chief engr.

WJTT(FM)—November 1972: 94.3 mhz; 2.8 kw. Ant 331 ft. TL: N35 07 32 W85 17 23. Stereo. Hrs opn: 24. Suite A-154, 409 Chestnut St., Chattanooga (37402). (615) 265-9494. FAX: (615) 266-2335. Licensee: Jettcom Inc. (acq 10-27-86; $1,050,000; FTR 8-4-86). Rep: D & R Radio. Format: Urban contemp. Target aud: 18-49. Spec prog: Jazz 2 hrs, relg 4 hrs wkly. ■ Jim L. Brewer II, pres, vp & gen mgr; Wayne Collins, prom mgr & news dir; Keith Landecker, progmg dir; Tony Rankin, mus dir; Parks Hall, chief engr.

Ripley

WTRB(AM)—Dec 11, 1954: 1570 khz; 1 kw-D, 50 w-N. TL: N35 43 46 W89 32 33 (CP: 28 kw-D, 5 kw-N). Hrs opn: 17. Box 410, 372 S. Jefferson St. (38063). (901) 635-2221. FAX: (901) 635-2221. Licensee: Lauderdale Broadcasting Co. (acq 11-13-57). Net: ABC/E; Tenn. Radio. Rep: Keystone (unwired net), Midsouth. Format: C&W. Spec prog: Gospel 6 hrs wkly. ■ Ruth Dunn, pres & gen mgr; Don Paris, stn mgr & gen sls mgr; David Henderson, progmg dir & asst mus dir. ■ Rates: $6.30; 6.30; 6.30; 6.30.

WTRB-FM—Jan 1, 1993: 94.9 mhz; 6 kw. Ant 328 ft. TL: N35 48 28 W89 28 27. (901) 635-9490. Format: Hits of the 60s, 70s, 80s and today. Target aud: 18-50. Spec prog: News, community affairs, sports. ■ Don Paris, gen mgr; David Henderson, opns dir, mus dir, news dir & pub affrs dir; Todd Turner, chief engr. ■ Rates: $7.95; 7.95; 7.95; 6.15.

Rockwood

WOFE(AM)—May 12, 1957: 580 khz; 1 kw-D. TL: N35 49 40 W84 39 19. Box 387 (37854). (615) 354-0580. FAX: (615) 354-9658. Licensee: P & G Properties Inc. (acq 6-14-91; $120,000 with co-located FM; FTR 7-8-91). Format: C&W. News staff one; news progmg 12 hrs wkly. Target aud: General. Spec prog: Black one hr wkly. ■ Gary Wells, gen mgr & mus dir; Jody Wells, progmg dir; Dudley Evans, news dir; Randall Wells, chief engr. ■ Rates: $5; 4.50; 4.50; 4.50.

WOFE-FM—July 9, 1991: 105.7 mhz; 600 w. Ant 728 ft. TL: N35 51 41 W84 43 11 (CP: 925 w, ant 836 ft.). Dups AM 100%.

Rogersville

WJDT(FM)—Dec 1, 1990: 106.5 mhz; 6 kw. Ant 1,378 ft. TL: N36 22 51 W83 10 47. Stereo. Hrs opn: 24. Box 519, Morristown (37815-0519); 2387 Warren Dr., Morristown (37814). (615) 235-4640; (615) 993-3639. Licensee: C&S Broadcasting. Net: CNN. Wash atty: Larry D. Perry. Format: Country. News progmg 14 hrs wkly. Target aud: 21-60. ■ Clark Quillen, pres; David C. Quillen, opns dir; Chuck Morris, progmg dir; Bob Wallace, chief engr.

WRGS(AM)—Aug 20, 1954: 1370 khz; 1 kw-D, 40 w-N. TL: N36 24 58 W82 59 04. Burem Road (37857). (615) 272-2628. FAX: (615) 272-8338. Licensee: WRGS Inc. Net: ABC/E; Tenn. Net. Format: Country. News progmg 10 hrs wkly. Target aud: General. ■ C. Philip Beal, pres & gen mgr; Mavis Livingston, gen sls mgr; Steve Waller, progmg dir & mus dir; Charles Windham, chief engr.

St. Joseph

WJOR-FM—1991: 101.5 mhz; 3 kw. Ant 328 ft. TL: N35 00 42 W87 30 46. Box 187 (38481). (615) 845-4172; (205) 757-9455. Licensee: Radio Lawrence County Inc. (acq 5-6-92). Format: Country, gospel. ■ Brenda Chandler, pres & gen sls mgr; Raynom Chandler, vp; Raymon Chandler, gen mgr; Kay Chandler, prom dir & progmg dir; Kevin Kidd, chief engr.

Savannah

WKWX-FM—June 23, 1980: 93.5 mhz; 6 kw. Ant 300 ft. TL: N35 17 08 W88 10 03. Stereo. Box 40 (38372). (901) 925-9600. Licensee: Tennessee River Broadcasting. Net: UPI. Format: Adult contemp, country. ■ Granville Hinton, pres; Melvin Carnal, gen mgr; Loyd Stricklin, gen sls mgr & chief engr.

WORM(AM)—June 29, 1956: 1010 khz; 250 w-D, 27 w-N. TL: N35 14 24 W88 14 29. Box 550 (38372). (901) 925-4981. Licensee: Gerald W. Hunt. Net: Tenn. Net. Format: Pure gold. ■ Gerald W. Hunt, pres, gen mgr, gen sls mgr & chief engr; Greg Gurley, prom mgr & news dir; Dave Morgan, progmg dir; Randy Tucker, mus dir.

WORM-FM—Aug 25, 1966: 101.7 mhz; 3 kw. Ant 175 ft. TL: N35 14 24 W88 14 29. Stereo. Format: Country.

Selmer

WDTM(AM)—Oct 31, 1967: 1150 khz; 1 kw-D. TL: N35 11 27 W88 35 21. Box 388 (38375). (901) 645-6165. FAX: (901) 645-3970. Licensee: WDTM Inc. Net: ABC/E. Format: C&W. ■ David B. Jordan, pres & chief engr; Cindy Tucker, gen mgr; Tom Howell, gen sls mgr; Patty Cherry, progmg dir. ■ Rates: $4.45; 4.45; 4.45; na.

WSIB(FM)—Co-owned with WDTM(AM). January 1990: 93.9 mhz; 3 kw. Ant 328 ft. TL: N35 11 27 W88 35 21. Stereo. Hrs opn: 24. Format: Adult contemp. Target aud: 20-45.

WXOQ(FM)—June 15, 1986: 105.5 mhz; 3 kw. Ant 300 ft. TL: N35 13 11 W88 40 23. Stereo. Hrs opn: 24. 302 E. Poplar (38375). (901) 645-9880. FAX: (901) 645-9586. Licensee: Perry S. Smith. Net: Westwood One. Format: CHR. News staff 2. Target aud: General. ■ P. Stevens Smith, pres; Gerald Hunt, gen mgr & chief engr; Dave Morgan, progmg dir; Randy Tucker, mus dir.

Sevierville

WMYU(FM)—Feb 3, 1961: 102.1 mhz; 100 kw. Ant 1,979 ft. TL: N35 48 41 W83 40 08. Stereo. 8419 Kingston Pike, Knoxville (37919). (615) 693-1020. Licensee: Jacor Broadcasting of Knoxville. Group owner: Jacor Communications Inc. (acq 12-1-86). Net: CNN. Format: Adult contemp. News staff 3; news progmg 8 hrs wkly. Target aud: 25-49. ■ James Ridings, vp & gen mgr; Jeff Jacoby, gen sls mgr; Mary Deschamps, prom mgr; Larry Trotter, progmg dir; Ashley Adams, mus dir; Roger Hawkins, news dir; John Maples, chief engr. ■ Rates: $100; 80; 90; 70.

WSEV(AM)—April 23, 1955: 930 khz; 5 kw-D, 148 w-N. TL: N35 52 42 W83 33 18. Stereo. Hrs opn: 24. Simulcast WDLY(FM). 415 Middle Creek Rd. (37862). (615) 453-2844. FAX: (615) 429-2601. Licensee: DollyWood Broadcasting Co. Group owner: Orr & Earls Broadcasting Inc. (acq 5-31-90; $715,000; FTR 6-18-90). Net: CBS; Tenn. Net. Rep: Rgnl Reps. Format: Country, news/talk. News staff one; news progmg 6 hrs wkly. Target aud: 25 plus. ■ Gary Voss, gen mgr; Claudia Maillard, gen sls mgr; Jay Adams, prom dir; Dan Bell, mus dir; Charles Primm, news dir. ■ Rates: $21; 5.25; 15.75; 5.25.

Sewanee

***WUTS(FM)**—May 1972: 91.3 mhz; 200 w. Ant 658 ft. TL: N35 12 20 W85 55 07. University of the South, 735 University Ave. (37383). (615) 598-1112. FAX: (615) 598-1145. Licensee: Univ. of the South. Format: Div. progsv. News progmg one hr wkly. Target aud: General; college students. Spec prog: Black 2 hrs, class 4 hrs, country 2 hrs, jazz 4 hrs, blues 3 hrs, reggae 5 hrs, new age 4 hrs, Fr 2 hrs, soul 2 hrs, musicals 2 hrs, bluegrass 2 hrs, punk/hardcore 2 hrs wkly. ■ David Roark, gen mgr; Jefferson Parker, mus dir; Tim Mitchell, chief engr.

Seymour

WJBZ(FM)—March 31, 1991: 96.3 mhz; 3 kw. Ant 328 ft. TL: N35 54 32 W83 40 59. Hrs opn: 24. Box 2526, Knoxville (37901). (615) 577-4885. Licensee: Seymour Communications. Format: Southern gospel. ■ J. Bazzel Mull, pres; Elizabeth Mull, vp & gen mgr.

Shelbyville

WHAL(AM)—December 1946: 1400 khz; 1 kw-U. TL: N35 28 26 W86 26 45. Box 106, Horse Mountain Rd. (37160). (615) 684-1400. FAX: (615) 890-2417. Licensee: Lenk Broadcasting Co., Inc. Group owner: The Cromwell Group Inc. (acq 11-28-89). Net: ABC; Tenn. Net. Wash atty: Pepper & Corazzini. Format: MOR. Target aud: General; residents of the loc area. ■ Bayard Walters, pres; Larry Trimmer, sr vp & vp sls; Douglas Combs, gen mgr.

WYCQ(FM)—Co-owned with WHAL(AM). May 1, 1962: 102.9 mhz; 100 kw. Ant 820 ft. TL: N35 30 46 W86 25 12. Stereo. Hrs opn: 24. Prog sep from AM. 1824 Murfreesboro Rd., Nashville (37217). Net: Tenn. Agri. Format: Country. Target aud: 25-54; residents in middle Tennesse. Spec prog: Farm one hr wkly. ■ Larry Trimmer, stn mgr; Ricky Casteel, progmg dir; Melody Houston, news dir.

WLIJ(AM)—Dec 2, 1959: 1580 khz; 1 kw-D, 12 w-N. TL: N35 27 21 W86 27 09. Stereo. Hrs opn: 6 AM-6 PM. Box 7, 236 Woodland Dr. (37160); 3563 Hwy. 231 N. (37160). (615) 684-1514; (615) 684-1515. Licensee: Hopkins-Hall Broadcasting Inc. (acq 7-19-90; $110,000; FTR 8-6-90). Net: ABC. Wash atty: Cordon & Kelly. Format: Bluegrass, country. News staff one; news progmg 14 hrs wkly. Target aud: General. Spec prog: Black one hr, farm 3 hrs, relg 11 hrs wkly. ■ Nadine Hopkins, pres; Hal Ball, gen mgr, prom mgr & news dir; Dickie Overcast, vp sls & vp adv; Paul Hopkins, progmg dir & mus dir; Terry Hall, chief engr.

WYCQ(FM)—Listing follows WHAL(AM).

Signal Mountain

WVXA(FM)—Not on air, target date unknown: 98.1 mhz; 1 kw. Ant 794 ft. TL: N35 05 15 W85 21 50. c/o 1544 Heritage Landing Dr., Chattanooga (37405). Licensee: Radio One Management Group Inc. Group owner: Radio One Broadcasting Inc. (acq 4-30-93; $450,000; FTR 5-24-93).

Smithville

WJLE(AM)—April 11, 1964: 1480 khz; 1 kw-D, 34 w-N. TL: N35 55 31 W85 49 14. Hrs opn: 16. Rt. 1, Box 105 (37166). (615) 597-4265. FAX: (615) 597-6025. Licensee: Center Hill Broadcasting Corp. Net: ABC/E. Format: Country. News staff one; news progmg 14 hrs wkly. Target aud: General. Spec prog: Gospel 15 hrs wkly. ■ W.E. Vanatta, pres & gen mgr; Dwayne Page, progmg dir, mus dir & news dir; Homer Wilson Jr., chief engr. ■ Rates: $6.50; 6.50; 5; 5.

WJLE-FM—1970: 101.7 mhz; 3 kw. Ant 195 ft. TL: N35 55 31 W85 49 14. Hrs opn: 16. Dups AM 100%.

Smyrna

WRLG(FM)—Oct 7, 1993: 94.1 mhz; 4.3 kw. Ant 200 ft. TL: N35 59 43 W86 33 29. Stereo. Hrs opn: 24. Dups WRLT(FM) Franklin 99%. 131 Second Ave. N., Nashville (37201). (615) 242-5600; (615) 737-0100. FAX: (615) 242-9877. Licensee: Tuned In Broadcasting Inc. (acq 5-12-92; $22,000). Net: ABC/C. Wash atty: Fisher, Wayland, Cooper & Leader. Format: Adult alternative. News staff one; news progmg 3 hrs wkly. Target aud: 25-49. Spec prog: Jazz 2 hrs, modern rock 9 hrs, blues 2 hrs, reggae 3 hrs wkly. ■ Ned Horton, pres & gen mgr; Fred Buc, opns mgr; John Mosely, gen sls mgr; James Wade, prom dir; Michael Parks, mus dir; David Hall, asst mus dir; Pat Reilly, news dir; Gibson Prichard, chief engr. ■ Rates: $40; 30; 35; 25.

WZRS(AM)—Not on air, target date unknown: 710 khz; 250 w-D. TL: N35 58 31 W86 33 16. 240 N. Lowry St. (37167). (615) 355-4367. Licensee: Salvation Broadcasting Inc. (acq 4-16-93; $50,000; FTR 5-3-93). Format: Gospel. ■ Ron Eadx, stn mgr.

Soddy-Daisy

WFXS(FM)—Licensed to Soddy-Daisy. See Chattanooga.

WSDT(AM)—Feb 27, 1970: 1240 khz; 1 kw-U. TL: N35 16 16 W85 10 28. Box 1209 (37379). (615) 332-6666. Licensee: Lee College (acq 8-29-90). Net: ABC/I. Rep: David Carpenter. Format: Southern Gospel. Spec prog: Farm one hr wkly. ■ Lee College, pres; Bobby Godgiben, gen mgr; Parks Hall, chief engr.

WTYR(AM)—Licensed to Soddy-Daisy. See Chattanooga.

Broadcasting & Cable Yearbook 1994
B-349

Tennessee

South Pittsburg

WEPG(AM)—July 9, 1954: 910 khz; 5 kw-D, 950 w-N. TL: N35 00 57 W85 42 00. Box 8, Ash Ave. (37380). (615) 837-7577. Licensee: Jerry Nelson (acq 11-6-92). Net: AP. Rep: Keystone (unwired net). Format: Country. News staff one. Target aud: 24-54. ■ Jerry Nelson, pres; Johnny Ray, mus dir; Shannon Lynn, news dir. ■ Rates: $5; 4.50; 5; 4.

WKXJ(FM)—Nov 5, 1990: 97.3 mhz; 16 kw. Ant 856 ft. TL: N34 58 21 W85 37 58. Stereo. Hrs opn: 24. 1000 Monte Sano Blvd., Huntsville, AL (35801); Box 71, 97 Smith Ln. (37380). (615) 533-3131; (615) 837-5544. FAX: (615) 837-5684. Licensee: Marson Broadcasting Inc. (acq 11-89; $17,355; FTR 1-15-90). Format: Adult contemp. News staff 2; news progmg 20 hrs wkly. Target aud: 18-54. ■ M. Davidson Smith IV, pres; Robert A. Gay, vp; Laura Smith, sls dir; Trent Waters, prom mgr; Jay Hasting, progmg dir & mus dir; Bob Mayben, engrg dir.

Sparta

WSMT(AM)—April 26, 1953: 1050 khz; 1 kw-D. TL: N35 57 00 W85 28 50. Rt. 8, Box 13 (38583). (615) 836-1055; (615) 836-2824. FAX: (615) 836-2320. Licensee: Austin Broadcasting Corp. (acq 1-22-93; $375,000 with co-located FM; FTR 2-15-93). Net: AP. Format: Country, gospel, news. News staff one; news progmg 10 hrs wkly. Target aud: General; 25 plus. Spec prog: Relg 10 hrs wkly. ■ Bill Austin, gen mgr & opns mgr; Barbara Lacy, gen sls mgr; Dan Miller, progmg dir & news dir; Austin Stinnett, chief engr. ■ Rates: $10; 10; 10; 6.

WSMT-FM—Aug 2, 1964: 105.5 mhz; 3 kw. Ant 35 ft. TL: N35 57 00 W95 28 50. Stereo. Hrs opn: 24. Prog sep from AM. Format: Classic rock. Target aud: 25-54. ■ Duke Rice, mus dir. ■ Rates: $15; 15; 15; 12.

WTZX(AM)—Nov 26, 1971: 860 khz; 1 kw-D, 9.9 w-N. TL: N35 55 20 W85 26 50. Stereo. Hrs opn: 5 AM-10 PM. Box 210 (38583). Hwy. 70 S., (38583). (615) 738-2256. FAX: (615) 738-2259. Licensee: Robert W. Gallaher (acq 8-31-92; FTR 9-21-92). Format: Country. News staff one; news progmg 10 hrs wkly. Target aud: 18-49. Spec prog: Gospel 6 hrs wkly. ■ Robert W. Gallaher, pres & gen mgr; Jeff Howard, progmg dir & news dir; Homer Wilson, chief engr. ■ Rates: $7; 7; 7; 6.50.

Spencer

WWEE(FM)—Not on air, target date unknown: 98.7 mhz; 1.1 kw. Ant 548 ft. TL: N35 40 37 W85 32 05. Box 31, McMinnville (37110). Licensee: Van Buren Broadcasting Corp.

Spring City

WXQK(AM)—July 12, 1979: 970 khz; 500 w-D. TL: N35 39 59 W84 52 44. Box 290, Dayton (37321). (615) 775-2331; (615) 775-5750. FAX: (615) 775-9368. Licensee: Walter E. Hooper III (acq 9-13-90; FTR 10-1-90). Net: ABC/I. Format: Adult contemp, top-40. News staff one. ■ Walter Hooper, pres; Rick Dye, gen mgr & gen sls mgr.

WAYA(FM)—Co-owned with WXQK(AM). October 1989: 93.9 mhz; 2 kw. Ant 344 ft. TL: N35 42 06 W84 53 01.

Springfield

WDBL(AM)—July 24, 1950: 1590 khz; 1 kw-D, 30 w-N. TL: N36 29 43 W86 54 26 (CP: 710 w-D, TL: N36 29 42 W86 54 22). Box 606 (37172). (615) 384-5541. FAX: (615) 384-9325. Licensee: DBL Broadcasting. Group owner: Key Broadcasting Inc (acq 6-10-83; $530,000 with co-located FM; FTR 6-27-83). Net: ABC/E. Rep: Rgnl Reps. Format: Contemp country. News staff one; news progmg 16 hrs wkly. Spec prog: Black, farm 10 hrs, gospel 10 hrs wkly. ■ Terry E. Forcht, pres; John Crawford, gen mgr; Cristy Ray, news dir; Greg Happel, chief engr. ■ Rates: $18.80; 18.80; 18.80; 18.80.

WDBL-FM—Aug 31, 1964: 94.3 mhz; 3 kw. Ant 215 ft. TL: N36 29 43 W86 54 26 (CP: Ant 325 ft., TL: N36 29 42 W96 54 26). Stereo. Hrs opn: 19. Dups AM 100%.

WSGI(AM)—Dec 15, 1982: 1100 khz; 1 kw-D. TL: N36 31 00 W86 53 30. 5628 S. Hillview, Brentwood (37027); Box 909, 722 S. Main St. (37172). (615) 384-9744; (615) 367-2701. Licensee: F&M Broadcasting Inc. (acq 4-86). Net: USA. Format: Country, relg, news. News staff one. Target aud: General. Spec prog: Relg, farm 5 hrs, gospel 16 hrs wkly. ■ Fred Harron, chmn & pres; Billy Gray, gen mgr, gen sls mgr & prom dir; Adrian Marshall, vp progmg; Gary Brown, chief engr.

Static

WSBI(AM)—Apr 7, 1986: 1210 khz; 1 kw-D. TL: N36 37 22 W85 05 15. Hrs opn: 6 AM-4:30 PM. Box 316, Byrdstown (38549). (606) 387-6625. Licensee: State Line Broadcasting Inc. Net: USA. Format: Country. News staff one; news progmg 15 hrs wkly. Target aud: 25 plus. Spec prog: Gospel 5 hrs, bluegrass one hr, rock-n-roll classics one hr wkly. ■ Hank Thomas, gen mgr, gen sls mgr, progmg dir & mus dir; Judy Thomas, vp prom & vp adv; Jan Allred, news dir; Robert Huddleston, chief engr. ■ Rates: $4; 3; 4; na.

Surgoinsville

WEYE(FM)—November 1990: 104.3 mhz; 6 kw. Ant 300 ft. TL: N36 29 01 W82 50 31. Stereo. Burem Rd., Rogersville (37857); 111 Della St., Mt. Carmel (37642). (615) 272-3900. Licensee: C. Philip Beal (acq 2-15-91; $20,000; FTR 3-11-91). Net: ABC/E. Rep: Rgnl Reps. Wash atty: Bryan, Cave, McPheeters & McRoberts. Format: Oldies. ■ Phil Beale, stn mgr.

Sweetwater

WDEH(AM)—1955: 800 khz; 1 kw-D, 379 w-N. TL: N35 36 49 W84 27 33. Box 330 (37874). (615) 337-5025. FAX: (615) 579-4667. Licensee: Sweetwater Broadcasting Co. (acq 6-5-90; $375,000 with co-located FM; FTR 7-2-90). Format: All Gospel. ■ Rev. J. Bazzel Mull, pres, gen mgr, gen sls mgr & prom mgr; Jerry Thomas, progmg dir, mus dir & news dir.

WDEH-FM—September 1967: 98.3 mhz; 2.78 kw. Ant 135 ft. TL: N35 36 49 W84 27 33. Format: Country.

Tazewell

WCTU(FM)—October 1989: 94.1 mhz; 1.3 kw. Ant 492 ft. TL: N36 27 32 W83 35 07 (CP: 2.75 kw). Rt. 4, Box 215, Cumberland Pkwy. (37879). (615) 626-7145. Licensee: WFSM Inc. Format: Country. ■ Jim Stair, pres; Walter Stair, gen mgr, mus dir & news dir; Darryl Turner, progmg dir; Bob Wallace, Roy Steck, chiefs engr.

WNTT(AM)—July 1, 1960: 1250 khz; 500 w-D. TL: N36 27 09 W83 34 23. Hrs opn: 6 AM-sundown. Box 95, 115 Bluetop Rd. (37879). (615) 626-4203. Licensee: Caliborne Broadcasting Co. Net: CNN. Format: Country. News progmg 12 hrs wkly. Target aud: General. Spec prog: Gospel. ■ Charles E. Shoffner, CEO & gen sls mgr; Blanche Crawford, opns mgr; Don Gulley, progmg dir; Randy Brock, news dir; Hubert Turner, chief engr. ■ Rates: $4; $4; $4; na.

Tiptonville

WAAT(FM)—Not on air, target date unknown: 101.3 mhz; 25 kw. Ant 328 ft. 1729 Nailling, Union City (38261). Licensee: Wenk of Union City Inc.

Trenton

WWEZ(FM)—August 1980: 97.5 mhz; 25 kw. Ant 299 ft. TL: N35 58 45 W88 55 37 (CP: ant 328 ft., TL: N36 05 10 W88 54 39). Stereo. Hrs opn: 24. Prog sep from AM. Box 500 (38382). (901) 855-0098. FAX: (901) 855-1600. Licensee: Trenton Wireless Corp. Group owner: The Wireless Group Inc. (acq 11-1-86; $340,000 with co-located AM; FTR 7-28-86). Net: CNN. Format: Adult contemp, news, talk. Target aud: 25-60. Spec prog: High school sports 10 hrs, college football 10 hrs wkly. ■ Rates: $8; 6.50; 8; 6.

WTNE(AM)—Co-owned with WWEZ(FM). Dec 9, 1966: 1500 khz; 250 w-D. TL: N35 58 45 W88 55 37 (CP: TL: N35 58 52 W88 55 32). Stn currently dark. Net: CNN. Rep: Midsouch. Format: Adult contemp. News staff one; news progmg 4 hrs wkly. Target aud: general; Gibson County, news oriented people. Spec prog: Sports. ■ Carlton Veirs, pres; Steven Hemann, gen mgr, gen sls mgr, progmg dir, mus dir & news dir; Janet Buie, prom dir; Dave Hacker, chief engr. ■ Rates: Same as FM.

Tullahoma

WHVK(FM)—July 1, 1962: 93.3 mhz; 100 kw. Ant 981 ft. TL: N35 02 04 W86 22 52. Stereo. Hrs opn: 24. 137 McMurtrie Ln. N.W., Huntsville, AL (35806). (205) 721-9393; (800) 695-0093. FAX: (205) 721-9399. Licensee: Tennessee Valley Radio Inc. (acq 10-26-93; $2.5 milion; FTR 11-8-93). Rep: Banner. Wash atty: Fisher, Wayland, Cooper & Leader. Format: Country. Target aud: 25-49; baby boomers graduating high school 1965-80. ■ Ron Bailey, pres & gen mgr; Nona Carson, gen sls mgr; Storming Norman, asst mus dir; Carl Santpiere, chief engr. ■ Rates: $75; 75; 75; 50.

Union City

WENK(AM)—Oct 26, 1946: 1240 khz; 1 kw-U. TL: N36 25 28 W89 02 17. Stereo. Hrs opn: 24. 1729 Nailling Dr. (38261). (901) 885-1240. FAX: (901) 885-3405. Licensee: WENK of Union City Inc. Group owner: WENK Broadcast Group Inc. (acq 1-74). Net: Keystone (unwired net), Midsouth. Wash atty: Philip R. Hochberg. Format: Adult contemp, talk. Target aud: 25-54. ■ Terry Hailey, pres & gen mgr; Mary Bondurant, gen sls mgr; John Mech, prom mgr; James Cawley, news dir; Charles Holland, chief engr. ■ Rates: $9.85; 7.85; 9.85; 5.85.

WKWT(FM)—Sept 20, 1974: 104.9 mhz; 3 kw. Ant 298 ft. TL: N36 28 27 W88 56 42 (CP: 6 kw, ant 302 ft.). Stereo. Hrs opn: 24. Box 590, 709 S. First St. (38261). (901) 885-2014. Licensee: Twin States Broadcasting Inc. (acq 10-29-93; $400,000; FTR 11-15-93). Net: ABC/E; Tenn. Radio. Format: Country. News staff 2; news progmg 25 hrs wkly. Target aud: 18 plus. Spec prog: Farm 2 hrs, Black 5 hrs, gospel 7 hrs wkly. ■ Hal Dodd, pres; Larry Doxey, gen mgr, stn mgr & gen sls mgr; Scott Reeves, progmg dir & mus dir; Danny Carr, news dir; Charles Holland, chief engr. ■ Rates: $16; 14; 14; 10.

WLJJ(FM)—Not on air, target date unknown: 105.7 mhz; 6 kw. Ant 328 ft. 329 S. Second St. (38261). Licensee: Twin State Broadcasting Inc.

Wartburg

WECO(AM)—Aug 31, 1970: 940 khz; 5 kw-D. TL: N36 05 48 W84 35 31. Box 100 (37887). (615) 346-3900. FAX: (615) 346-7686. Licensee: Morgan County Broadcasting Co. Net: Unistar; Tenn. Net. Format: Country. ■ Carl Stump, pres, progmg dir & chief engr; Sandy Lavender, gen mgr & stn mgr; Ed Knight, gen sls mgr; Brad Byrd, news dir.

WECO-FM—August 1988: 101.3 mhz; 500 w. Ant 770 ft. TL: N36 05 25 W78 38 05. (Acq 1-30-89). News staff one. Target aud: 25-49.

Waverly

WVRY(FM)—Sept 26, 1972: 105.1 mhz; 50 kw. Ant 492 ft. TL: N36 05 16 W87 51 19. Stereo. Hrs opn: 24. Box 415, Browntown Rd. (37185). (615) 296-2456. Licensee: Mid-Cumberland Communications Inc. (acq 7-1-84; $340,000; with co-located AM; FTR 4-16-84). Net: Tenn. Radio. Rep: Midsouth. Wash atty: McNair & Sanford. Format: Oldies 60s, 70s, 80s. ■ Joe A. Copley, CEO, pres & gen mgr; Steve Kennedy, mus dir; David Hacker, chief engr.

WPHC(AM)—Co-owned with WVRY(FM). Sept 25, 1963: 1060 khz; 1 kw-D. TL: N36 04 57 W87 50 05. Format: C&W, news/talk.

Waynesboro

WTNR(AM)—Jan 31, 1970: 930 khz; 500 w-D. TL: N35 18 30 W87 44 44. Hrs opn: 12. Box 100, 100 Public Sq. South (38485). (615) 722-3631. FAX: (615) 722-3632. Licensee: Pioneer Radio Inc. (acq 8-14-87; $87,000; FTR 6-22-87). Net: CNN. Wash atty: Mullin, Rhyne, Emmons & Topel. Format: C&W. News progmg 13 hrs wkly. Target aud: General; working class & affluent country fans. Spec prog: Gospel. ■ Wayne C. Hall, pres, gen mgr, progmg dir & mus dir; Dan Mullin, gen sls mgr, prom mgr & news dir; Kevin Kidd, chief engr.

WTNR-FM—July 1991: 94.9 mhz; 6 kw. Ant 328 ft. TL: N35 14 04 W87 42 50 (CP: 25 kw). Stereo. Hrs opn: 24. Dups AM 100%. Licensee: Pioneer Radio Inc.

White Bluff

WQSE(AM)—July 18, 1982: 1030 khz; 1 kw-D, DA-N. TL: N36 08 03 W87 12 58. Box 489, c/o Bernie Bishop Broadcasting & Advertisement Co. (37187). (615) 446-5176. Licensee: Bernie Bishop Broadcasting & Advertisement Co.

Winchester

WCDT(AM)—Mar 8, 1948: 1340 khz; 1 kw-U. TL: N35 10 51 W86 05 34. Hrs opn: 24. 1201 S. College St. (37398). (615) 967-2201; (615) 967-2202. FAX: (615) 967-2246. Licensee: Franklin County Radio & Broadcasting Co. Inc. (acq 8-1-56). Net: Tenn. Radio. Rep: Midsouth. Format: Progsv country. News staff one; news progmg 15 hrs wkly. Target aud: General. Spec prog: Farm 15 hrs, oldies 6 hrs wkly. ■ George Willis Frassrand, pres; John T. Yarbrough, vp; Jack W. Vineyard, gen mgr; Pam Ledford, opns mgr, gen sls mgr & prom mgr; Al Tipps, adv mgr, progmg mgr & mus dir; Wayne Thomas, news dir; Tom Wiseman, chief engr. ■ Rates: $10.50; 9; 9; 7.

Woodbury

WBRY(AM)—Oct 24, 1963; 1540 khz; 500 w-D. TL: N35 49 53 W86 06 42. Box 7, 153 Mile Valley Rd. (37190). (615) 563-2313. FAX: (615) 563-2358. Licensee: DaSan Communications Inc. (acq 2-86; $110,000; FTR 12-16-85). Wash atty: John Kinkel. Format: Country, local news, talk. News staff one; news progmg 6 hrs wkly. Target aud: General. Spec prog: Gospel 16 hrs, farm one hr, loc sports 10 hrs wkly. ■ Dave Bunge, pres; Debbie Grizzle, mus dir; Homer Wilson, chief engr. ■ Rates: $5; 5; 5; na.

WLMM-FM—Co-owned with WBRY(AM). Not on air, target date Spring 1994: 104.9 mhz; 3 kw. Ant 328 ft. TL: N35 49 33 W86 09 28. Stereo. Hrs opn: 24. Wash atty: John Kenkel.

Texas

LAUREN A. COLBY
301-663-1086
COMMUNICATIONS ATTORNEY
Special Attention to Difficult Cases

Abilene

*KACU(FM)—June 2, 1986: 89.7 mhz; 33 kw. Ant 215 ft. TL: N32 28 34 W99 42 22. Stereo. Hrs opn: 5 AM-midnight (wkdy), 6 AM-midnight (wknd). ACU Station, Box 7568, 1600 Campus Court (79699). (915) 674-2441. FAX: (915) 674-2417. Licensee: Abilene Christian Univ. Net: NPR. Format: Adult contemp, class, news. News progmg 32 hrs wkly. Target aud: 35 plus; middle-to-upper income professionals. Spec prog: Jazz 3 hrs wkly. ■ Dutch Hoggatt, gen mgr; Kyle McAlister, stn mgr & progmg dir; Susan Robinson, dev dir; Jim Richard, chief engr.

*KAGN(FM)—June 26, 1986: 91.3 mhz; 300 w. Ant 592 ft. TL: N32 16 59 W99 44 57. Suite C-212, 209 S. Danville (79605). (915) 692-0770. Licensee: Criswell Center for Biblical Studies (group owner; acq 3-26-86). Format: Relg inspirational. ■ Dr. Richard Mellick, pres; Greg Kelly, gen mgr; David Briggs, chief engr.

KBBA(AM)—Aug 29, 1962: 1560 khz; 500 w-D. TL: N32 27 21 W99 47 59. Box 2135 (79604). (915) 672-8482. Licensee: Dynamic Broadcasting Co. (acq 4-1-82; $234,000; FTR 4-12-82). Format: Sp. Target aud: 18-49. Spec prog: Black 4 hrs wkly. ■ Jesse Olvera, gen mgr; Randy Jones, progmg dir & mus dir. ■ Rates: $17; 15; 17; na.

KBCY(FM)—See Tye.

KEAN(AM)—June 15, 1957: 1280 khz; 500 w-D, 226 w-N. TL: N32 26 30 W99 43 08. Hrs opn: 24. Box 3098, 3911 S. First St. (79605). (915) 676-7711. FAX: (915) 676-3851. Licensee: Radio SunGroup of Texas Inc. Group owner: SunGroup Inc. (acq 11-1-85; grpsl; FTR 9-23-85). Net: ABC/I. Rep: McGavren Guild. Format: Country. News progmg 4 hrs wkly. Target aud: 25-54; general. ■ John Biddinger, pres; John Southwood, Louis P. Murray, vps; Louis P. Murray, gen mgr & stn mgr; Lynne Wilson, gen sls mgr; Kelly Jay, progmg dir; Rudy Fernandez, mus dir; James Cameron, chief engr.

KEAN-FM—July 1, 1969: 105.1 mhz; 100 kw. Ant 810 ft. TL: N32 16 35 W99 35 39. Stereo. Hrs opn: 24. Dups AM 100%.

KEYJ-FM—Apr 30, 1961: 107.9 mhz; 100 kw. Ant 670 ft. TL: N32 17 06 W99 38 38. Stereo. Box 473 (79604). (915) 677-7225. Rep: Katz. Format: Classic rock, AOR. Target aud: 18-49.

KFXJ(FM)—Not on air, target date unknown: 92.5 mhz; 50 kw. Ant 492 ft. TL: N32 18 55 W99 59 24. Box 288, 26 Burbank Rd., Sutton, MA (01527). Licensee: American Indian Broadcasting Group (acq 4-16-90; $50,000; FTR 5-7-90).

*KGNZ(FM)—Mar 7, 1981: 88.1 mhz; 75 kw. Ant 710 ft. TL: N32 17 46 W99 43 01. Stereo. 542 Butternut (79602); 1001 Cedar Crest (79601). (915) 673-3045; (915) 677-8370. Licensee: Christian Broadcasting Co. Net: USA. Format: Adult contemp Christian. ■ Larry Jack Hill, pres & gen mgr; Randy Martinez, progmg dir; Gary Hill, mus dir; James Thompson, chief engr.

KHXS(FM)—Oct 6, 1989: 106.3 mhz; 4.6 kw. Ant 201 ft. TL: N32 28 34 W99 42 22. Suite 4, 720 Pine St. (79601-5129). (915) 672-5497. Licensee: Sure Broadcasting. Wash atty: Kaye Scholer, Bruce Elsen. Format: Easy lstng, big band. Target aud: 25-54. ■ David Boyll, gen mgr; James Thompson, chief engr. ■ Rates: $8; 8; 8; 8.

KNTS(AM)—Oct 1, 1936: 1470 khz; 5 kw-D, 1 kw-N, DA-N. TL: N32 29 26 W99 45 02. 4510-AS. 14th (79605). (915) 692-1064. FAX: (915) 698-6625. Licensee: Ovation Broadcasting Co. (acq 8-1-89; $950,000 with co-located FM; FTR 8-21-89). Net: MBS. Rep: Eastman. Format: News, talk, sports. ■ Jim Batson, pres; Mark Batson, gen mgr & gen sls mgr; John Michael Scott, opns mgr; Harvey Johnston, news dir.

KORQ-FM—September 1974: 100.7 mhz; 100 kw. Ant 1,260 ft. TL: N32 24 48 W100 06 25. Stereo. Box 473 (79604). (915) 677-7225. Net: Unistar. Format: Adult contemp. News progmg 5 hrs wkly. Target aud: 23-49; women. Spec prog: Oldies 2 hrs wkly. ■ Bourdon Wooten, CEO.

KYYD(AM)—June 19, 1948: 1340 khz; 1 kw-U. TL: N32 25 14 W99 43 54. Hrs opn: 24. Box 2201, 4542 Loop 322, #102 (79602). (915) 691-1022. Licensee: Wooten Broadcasting Inc. (acq 10-27-92; $2.9 million with co-located FM; FTR 11-23-92). Net: Moody; Texas State. Rep: Banner. Format: All Sports. ■ Suzanne Wooten, exec vp; Bourdon Wooten, gen mgr; Sharon Johnson, sls dir; John Scott, progmg dir & news dir; Kevin Bel, mus dir. ■ Rates: $30; 25; 25; 17.

Alamo

KJAV(FM)—Aug 17, 1980: 104.9 mhz; 3 kw. Ant 260 ft. TL: N26 12 49 W98 05 21. Box 252, McAllen (78502). (210) 781-5528. FAX: (210) 781-2730. Licensee: Paulino Bernal (acq 10-10-86; $475,000; FTR 9-8-86). Format: Relg. ■ Eloy Bernal, gen mgr & gen sls mgr.

Alamo Heights

KDRY(AM)—Licensed to Alamo Heights. See San Antonio.

KLUP(AM)—See Terrell Hills.

Alice

KBIC(FM)—Jan 1, 1974: 102.3 mhz; 3 kw. Ant 300 ft. TL: N27 46 35 W98 04 41. Stereo. 102 E. Main St. (78333). (512) 664-5555. Licensee: Christian Ministries of the Valley Inc. (acq 9-23-92; $250,000; FTR 11-9-92). Format: Christian. ■ Enrique Garza, pres & gen mgr.

KDSI(AM)—1947: 1070 khz; 1 kw-U, DA-N. TL: N27 46 39 W98 04 53. Hrs opn: 24. Box 731 (78333); Hwy. 281 N. (78332). (512) 664-1884; (800) 552-3070. FAX: (512) 664-1886. Licensee: Alice Radio Co. Inc. (group owner, acq 6-10-91; with co-located FM; FTR 7-13-92). Format: Sp. News staff 12; news progmg 2 hrs wkly. Target aud: 18-59. ■ Mike Smith, gen mgr & gen sls mgr; Pete Vasquez, progmg dir, mus dir & news dir.

KQNN(FM)—Co-owned with KDSI(AM). Jan 20, 1976: 92.1 mhz; 3 kw. Ant 300 ft. TL: N27 46 39 W98 04 53. Stereo. Prog sep from AM. Net: SMN. Format: Country.

Alpine

KALP(FM)—September 1986: 92.7 mhz; 2.37 kw. Ant 328 ft. TL: N30 19 09 W103 37 04. Hrs opn: 6 AM-10 PM. Box 9650 (79831). (915) 837-2346. Licensee: Rio Grande Broadcasting Co. Net: SMN. Format: C&W. ■ Gene Ray Hendryx, pres.

KVLF(AM)—Feb 27, 1947: 1240 khz; 1 kw-U. TL: N30 22 30 W103 39 36. Hrs opn: 6 AM-10 PM. Drawer 779 (79831); 500 Hendryx Ave. (79830). (915) 837-2144. Licensee: Big Bend Broadcasters. Format: Div. News progmg 21 hrs wkly. Spec prog: Sp 10 hrs wkly. ■ Gene Hendryx, pres; Ray Hendryx, gen mgr; Jerry Sotillo, gen sls mgr.

Are You Ready To Cash In On Communications?
NF&A
Norman Fischer & Associates, Inc.
Media Brokerage • Appraisals • Management Consultants
1209 Parkway • Austin, Texas 78703 • (512) 476-9457

Alvin

*KACC(FM)—Nov 1, 1993: 89.7 mhz; 5.6 kw. Ant 338 ft. TL: N29 24 01 W95 12 13. Stereo. Hrs opn: 18. 3110 Mustang Rd. (77511). (713) 388-4675. FAX: (713) 388-4910. Licensee: Alvin Community College. Format: Educ, CHR. News staff one. Target aud: General. ■ Cathy Forsythe, gen mgr; Mark Moss, chief opns & progmg dir; Jennie Blankenship, prom dir. ■ Rates: $50; 50; 50; 50.

KTEK(AM)—November 1981: 1110 khz; 2.5 kw, DA. TL: N29 22 51 W95 14 15. Suite 633, 24 E. Greenway Plaza, Houston (77046). (713) 270-5835. Licensee: Jim Runsdorf, liquidating agent. Group owner: Children's Broadcasting Corp. Net: CBN, USA. Rep: Marsh Radio Mktg.; Wash atty: Putbrese, Hunsaker & Ruddy. Format: Christian praise music/teaching. News progmg 6 hrs wkly. Target aud: 25-54; upscale families, 60% women, 40% male. Spec prog: Urdu-Hindi 3 hrs, Sp 2 hrs wkly. ■ Dick Marsh, pres; Jim Googowski, gen mgr; Iris Lefkoff, gen sls mgr; Marsha Lambeth, progmg dir & mus dir; Ken Pelletier, news dir; Rick Jones, chief engr.

Amarillo

*KACV-FM—Mar 15, 1976: 89.9 mhz; 100 kw. Ant 1,041 ft. TL: N35 20 33 W101 49 21. Stereo. Hrs opn: 6 AM-midnight. 2408 S. Jackson (79178); Box 447 (79109). (806) 371-5222; (806) 371-5228. FAX: (806) 371-5258. Licensee: Amarillo Junior College District. Net: ABC/C. Format: AOR. Spec prog: Class 16 hrs, jazz 12 hrs, Black 8 hrs wkly. ■ Joyce Herring, gen mgr; Jamey Karr, progmg dir; Donald H. Ford, chief engr.

KAEZ(FM)—Dec 6, 1991: 105.7 mhz; 6 kw. Ant 236 ft. TL: N35 12 28 W101 51 18. Hrs opn: 24. 1603 W. 8th Ave. (79101). (806) 372-3002. Licensee: KAEZ-FM Inc. Format: Adult contemp. ■ John Gay, CEO, Jon Wolfe, vp opns. ■ Rates: $17; 17; 17; 17.

KAKS(AM)—(Canyon). May 8, 1962: 1550 khz; 1 kw-D, 219 w-N. TL: N34 58 54 W101 57 18. Hrs opn: 6 AM-6 PM. Box 8580, Amarillo (79114). (806) 353-3500. FAX: (806) 353-1142. Licensee: Apollo Broadcasting Corp. (acq 10-18-91; $225,000 with co-located FM; FTR 11-4-91). Rep: D & R Radio. Format: CNN Headline News. Spec prog: Texas A & M football and basketball. ■ Rick Matchett, gen mgr & gen sls mgr; John Muesch, progmg dir.

KAKS-FM—(Canyon). Sept 30, 1985: 107.9 mhz; 96 kw. Ant 1,322 ft. TL: N35 20 33 W101 49 21 (CP: 95 kw, ant 1,371 ft., TL: N35 13 36 W102 00 24). Stereo. Hrs opn: 24. Suite 205, 2505 Lakeview, Amarillo (79109). (806) 353-3500. Net: Unistar. Rep: D & R Radio. Format: CHR. News staff one. Target aud: 18-44. ■ Rick Matchett, gen sls mgr; John Moesch, progmg dir & mus dir.

KARX(FM)—(Claude). Apr 12, 1992: 95.7 mhz; 100 kw. Ant 391 ft. TL: N35 06 16 W101 39 28. Stereo. Suite 6A, 3611 Soncy, Amarillo (79121). (806) 359-4000. Licensee: KARX Broadcasting Corp. of Texas (acq 4-29-92). Rep: D & R Radio. Format: Classic rock. News staff one; news progmg 10 hrs wkly. Target aud: 18-54. ■ Lu Lacy, CEO; Bill Lacy, exec vp, stn mgr, vp progmg & mus dir; Tim Guentz, vp engrg.

KATP(FM)—March 11, 1976: 101.9 mhz; 100 kw. Ant 935 ft. TL: N35 20 33 W101 49 21. Stereo. Hrs opn: 24. Suite 660, 7701 I-40 W. (79160). (806) 359-5999; (806) 359-5287. FAX: (806) 359-0136. Licensee: Meyer-Baldridge Radio Inc. Group owner: Meyer Communications Inc. (acq 2-16-93; $350,000; FTR 3-8-93). Rep: Katz & Powell. Format: Classic/album rock. Target aud: 18-49. ■ Ken E. Meyer, pres; Jonathon Hale, gen mgr; Johnathan Hale, gen sls mgr; Dale Miller, progmg dir & mus dir; Dennis Allen, pub affrs dir; Smokey King, chief engr. ■ Rates: $18; 18; 18; 12.

KBUY-FM—Listing follows KDJW(AM).

KDJW(AM)—1946: 1010 khz; 5 kw-D, 500 w-N, DA-2. TL: N35 11 03 W101 41 28. Hrs opn: 24. Box 5844, 5200 Amarillo Blvd. E. (79117). (806) 372-6543. FAX: (806) 379-7339. Licensee: Walton Communications Inc. (group owner). Rep: Banner. Format: Country. Target aud: 25-54; primarily female. ■ John B. Walton, pres; Dan Shanahan, gen mgr; Rick Mason, gen sls mgr; Dewayne Wells, prom dir, progmg dir & mus dir; April Stevens, news dir & pub affrs dir; A.C. Martin, engrg dir.

KBUY-FM—Co-owned with KDJW(AM). March 1946: 94.1 mhz; 100 kw. Ant 1,082 ft. TL: N35 20 33 W101 49 21. Stereo. Dups AM 100%. (806) 372-6544.

KGNC(AM)—May 19, 1922: 710 khz; 10 kw-U, DA-2. TL: N35 25 12 W101 33 20. Hrs opn: 24. Box 710 (79189-0710); 3505 Olsen Blvd. (79109). (806) 355-9801. FAX: (806) 354-8779; NEWS: (806) 354-9450. Licensee: Stauffer Communications Inc. (group owner; acq 1966). Net: CBS; Texas State Net. Rep: Katz. Wash atty: Dow, Lohnes & Albertson. Format: News/talk. News staff 3; news progmg 35 hrs wkly. Target aud: General; upscale adults & agricultural business listeners. Spec prog: Farm 11 hrs, relg 4 hrs wkly. ■ Bob Russell, gen mgr; Bob Reed, opns mgr & progmg dir; Doug Sullens, gen sls mgr; James Hunt, news dir & pub affrs dir; Farris Fincher, chief engr.

KGNC-FM—Dec 24, 1958: 97.9 mhz; 100 kw. Ant 1,285 ft. TL: N35 18 52 W101 50 47. Stereo. Hrs opn: 24. Prog sep from AM. Format: Country. News progmg one hr wkly. Target aud: 25-54; upscale adults. ■ Dan Gorman, gen sls mgr; Mary Lyn Halley, mktg mgr & prom mgr; Tim Butler, progmg mgr.

KIXZ(AM)—June 1947: 940 khz; 5 kw-D, 1 kw-N, DA-2. TL: N35 09 17 W101 45 28. Hrs opn: 24. Box 10940 (79116-1940). 1703 Avondale (79106). (806) 355-9777. FAX: (806) 355-5832. Licensee: Catalyst Radio Ltd. (acq 4-1-93; $2.45 million with co-located FM; FTR 10-19-92). Net: ABC/I, AP, Unistar. Rep: Banner. Wash atty: Akin, Gump, Hauger & Feld. Format: Nostalgia. News staff one; news progmg 8 hrs wkly. Target aud: General. Spec prog: Talk 2 hrs, gospel 6 hrs wkly. ■ Daryl Hayes, pres; Richard Haines, gen mgr & gen sls mgr; Debbie Davis, opns mgr; Jim Nash, prom mgr; David Emmons, progmg dir & mus dir; Jay Daniels, news dir; Smokey King, chief engr. ■ Rates: $14; 11; 14; 10.

KQAC(FM)—Co-owned with KIXZ(AM). October 1979: 98.7 mhz; 100 kw. Ant 480 ft. TL: N35 11 02 W101 58 11. Stereo. Hrs opn: 24. Prog sep from AM. Net: ABC. Rep: Banner. Format: Contemp country. News staff one; news progmg 2 hrs wkly. Target aud: General. ■ Richard Haines, gen sls mgr; Patrick Clarke, progmg dir; Patrick Clark, mus dir. ■ Rates: $35; 32; 35; 26.

*KJRT(FM)—Not on air, target date unknown: 88.3 mhz; 6 kw-V. Ant 289 ft. Box 469, 106 E. Texas St., Wheeler (79096). Licensee: Wheeler Educational Broadcasting Foundation.

KLCJ(AM)—Sept 15, 1955: 1360 khz; 500 w-D, 137 w-N. TL: N35 14 49 W101 49 13. 1759 Avondale Center (79106). (806) 353-4448. Licensee: New Life Communications Inc. (acq 1986). Net: Morningstar Radio. Format: Contemp Christian. News staff one; news progmg 12 hrs wkly. Target aud: 18-45; mature adults with money.

*KLMN(FM)—August 1989: 89.1 mhz; 620 w. Ant 413 ft. TL: N35 10 21 W101 57 13. Stereo. Hrs opn: 24. 910 S. Lamar (79106). (806) 376-5746. FAX: (806) 373-5702. Licensee: Maranatha Radio Inc. (acq 8-20-93; FTR 11-8-93). Net: Moody. Format: MOR inspirational, talk, news, educ. Target aud: 28 plus. ■ T. Kent Atkins, pres; Ken Haney, gen mgr, progmg dir & mus dir; George Whitaker, chief engr.

KMML-FM—March 1985: 96.9 mhz; 100 kw. Ant 550 ft. TL: N35 17 33 W101 50 48. Stereo. Hrs opn: 24. Box 7407, 803 S. Rusk (79114-7407). (806) 371-9797. FAX: (806) 371-9129. Licensee: Catalyst Broadcasting Ltd. (acq 11-30-93; $700,000; FTR 12-20-93). Rep: Banner. Wash atty: James L. Oyster. Format: Adult contemp. Target aud: 25-54. ■ Keith Adams, pres & gen mgr; Joe Geoffroy, opns mgr, progmg dir & mus dir; JoAnna Alexander, gen sls mgr; Gary Baggett, news dir; John Harold, chief engr. ■ Rates: $26; 26; 26; 22.

KPUR(AM)—Aug 1, 1949: 1440 khz; 5 kw-D, 1 kw-N, DA-N. TL: N35 07 20 W101 48 09. Stereo. Hrs opn: 24. Box 7407 (79114-7407). (806) 371-9797. FAX: (806) 371-9129. Licensee: Westwind Broadcasting Inc. (acq 10-29-92; $245,000 with KPUR-FM Canyon; FTR 11-23-92). Format: Talk, sports. ■ Keith Adams, pres & gen mgr; Susan Brofft, progmg dir & mus dir.

KPVY(FM)—Not on air, target date unknown: 100.9 mhz; 100 kw. TL: N35 17 33 W101 50 48. 1317 E. 14th St. (79102). Licensee: Mandujano Communications Inc.

KQAC(FM)—Listing follows KIXZ(AM).

KQFX(FM)—(Borger). March 1975: 104.3 mhz; 100 kw. Ant 590 ft. TL: N35 25 54 W101 36 47. Stereo. 3639B Wolfin Ave., Amarillo (79102). (806) 355-1044. FAX: (806) 352-6525. Licensee: South Central Broadcasting Inc. (acq 2-19-92; $350,000; FTR 3-9-92). Format: C&W. ■ John Wiggins, pres & progmg dir; John Fulton, gen mgr.

KQIZ-FM—November 1976: 93.1 mhz; 100 kw. Ant 700 ft. TL: N35 17 33 W101 50 48. Stereo. Hrs opn: 24. Box 7488 (79114). (806) 353-6662. Licensee: Wiskes-Abaris Communications KQIZ Partnership (acq 8-90; FTR 8-6-90). Rep: McGavren Guild. Format: CHR. Target aud: 18-44. Spec prog: Relg 2 hrs wkly. ■ Jack Higgins, pres; Larry Swikard, gen mgr; Stu Smoke, progmg dir; John Harrold, chief engr. ■ Rates: $26; 24; 26; 22.

KRGN(FM)—Oct 6, 1986: 103.1 mhz; 25 kw. Ant 300 ft. TL: N35 16 04 W101 53 06. Hrs opn: 24. 910 S. Lamar (79116). (806) 376-5746. FAX: (806) 373-5702. Licensee: La Voz Del Salvacion (acq 8-20-93; FTR 11-8-93). Net: USA. Format: MOR inspirational, talk, news, educ. News progmg 4 hrs wkly. Target aud: 28 plus; mature Christian, mainstream evangelical. ■ T. Kent Atkins, pres; Ken Haney, gen mgr; Kevin Haney, mus dir; George Whitaker, chief engr.

KRQA(FM)—Not on air, target date unknown: 99.7 mhz; 6 kw. Ant 328 ft. 3611 Soncy Suite 6-A (79121). Licensee: William R. Lacy.

*KYFA(FM)—Not on air, target date unknown: 91.9 mhz; 2.25 kw. Ant 292 ft. TL: N35 14 31 W101 48 43. Box 1818, Chesapeake, VA (23320). Licensee: Bible Broadcasting Network Inc.

KZIP(AM)—Sept 15, 1955: 1310 khz; 1 kw-D. TL: N35 11 02 W101 58 11. Hrs opn: 6 AM-10 PM. 1011 S. Jackson (79101). (806) 374-8555. FAX: (806) 371-0559. Licensee: Del Norte Inc. (acq 11-30-84; $270,000; FTR 12-19-83). Rep: Caballero. Format: Sp. News staff one; news progmg one hr wkly. Target aud: General. ■ George Veloz, pres, gen mgr & gen sls mgr; Ester Romero, natl sls mgr; Fermin Dimas, progmg dir; Lynn Martinez, chief engr. ■ Rates: $19; 19; 19; 19.

Amarillo Township

KCLP(AM)—Not on air, target date unknown: 1180 khz; 1 kw-D, 240 w-N, DA-2. TL: N35 15 54 W101 44 32. 6720 Lakeview Dr., Carmichael, CA (95608). (916) 967-0410. Licensee: Marlene V. Borman.

Andrews

KACT(AM)—Jan 12, 1955: 1360 khz; 1 kw-D. TL: N32 20 50 W102 33 23. Box 524 (79714). (915) 523-2845. Licensee: Zia Broadcasting Co. (acq 5-26-76). Net: SMN. Rep: Paul Miller. Format: Relg, C&W. ■ Lonnie Allsup, pres; Gerald Reid, gen mgr; Jimmy Davis, gen sls mgr; Delana Nock, news dir.

KACT-FM—1980: 105.5 mhz; 3 kw. Ant 210 ft. TL: N32 20 50 W102 33 23. Stereo. Dups AM 100%.

Anson

KKHR(FM)—June 1988: 98.1 mhz; 50 kw. Ant 292 ft. TL: N32 39 47 W99 51 13. Stereo. 2303 S. Danville, Abilene (79605). (915) 691-9898. FAX: (915) 691-9991. Licensee: Webster Broadcasting Inc. (group owner; acq 1-13-92; $475,000; FTR 2-10-93). Rep: Katz & Powell. Format: Classic rock, oldies. News staff one; news progmg 3 hrs wkly. Target aud: 18-54. ■ Suzy Dutton, CEO & vp; Dave Harrison, progmg dir; Gary Smith, chief engr. ■ Rates: $20; 15; 20; 15.

Arlington

KSNN(FM)—Licensed to Arlington. See Dallas.

Athens

KCKL(FM)—See Malakoff.

KLVQ(AM)—May 17, 1948: 1410 khz; 1 kw-U. TL: N32 10 20 W95 50 36. Hrs opn: 24. Box 489, Hwy. 31 E., Malakoff (75148). (903) 489-1238. FAX: (903) 489-2671. Licensee: Love Radio Co. Group owner: Routt Radio Companies Inc. (acq 8-88). Format: All news/talk. News staff one. Target aud: 35 plus. Spec prog: Black one hr, relg 8 hrs wkly. ■ Alan Routt, pres, gen mgr & gen sls mgr; Pat Isaacson, opns mgr & pub affrs dir; Tim Michaels, progmg dir & mus dir; Rich Flowers, news dir; Billy Rasco, chief engr. ■ Rates: $8.50; 7.60; 8.50; 7.

Atlanta

KALT(AM)—Oct 18, 1950: 900 khz; 1 kw-D. TL: N33 04 53 W94 10 56. Hrs opn: Sunrise-sunset. Box 1166, Hwy. 43 S. (75551). (903) 796-2817. FAX: (903) 796-6400. Licensee: Ark-La-Tex Broadcasting Co. (acq 1974). Net: SMN. Rep: Riley. Format: Country. News staff one; news progmg 8 hrs wkly. Target aud: General. Spec prog: Black 5 hrs wkly. ■ David Wommack Jr., pres & gen mgr. ■ Rates: $15; 11; 11; 11.

KPYN(FM)—Co-owned with KALT(AM). Dec 22, 1978: 99.3 mhz; 3 kw. Ant 235 ft. TL: N33 04 53 W94 10 56 (CP: 100.1 mhz, 50 kw, ant 472 ft.). Stereo. Hrs opn: 24. Dups AM 100%. News progmg 15 hrs wkly. ■ Rates: Same as AM.

Austin

KASE(FM)—Listing follows KVET(AM).

*KAZI(FM)—Aug 29, 1982: 88.7 mhz; 1.6 kw. Ant 351 ft. TL: N30 16 37 W97 49 34. Hrs opn: 24. Suite 203, 8906 Wall St., (78754). (512) 836-9544; (512) 836-9545. FAX: (512) 836-2246. Licensee: Austin Community Radio. Wash atty: Haley, Bader, & Potts. Format: Div, Black, jazz. News progmg 12 hrs wkly. Target aud: General; all ages, all ethnic groups. Spec prog: Reggae 6 hrs, blues 6 hrs, gospel 20 hrs wkly. ■ Garland Hampton, gen mgr; Sharon Jones, prom mgr; Marion Nicholson, progmg dir.

KEYI-FM—Listing follows KFON(AM).

KFGI-FM—See Luling.

KFIT(AM)—(Sunset Valley). Feb 1, 1967: 1060 khz; 2 kw-D, DA. TL: N30 19 13 W97 38 59. #375, 110 Wild Basin, Austin (78746); Box 160518, Austin (78716-0518). (512) 328-8400. FAX: (512) 328-8734. Licensee: KFIT Inc. (acq 6-25-91; $400,000; FTR 7-15-91). Net: NBC. Wash atty: Dow, Lohnes & Albertson. Format: Black, gospel. News staff 2. Target aud: 18-65. ■ Rev. Darrell Martin, gen mgr; Michael Kindle, gen sls mgr; Bill Woleben, chief engr. ■ Rates: $25; 30; 25; na.

KFON(AM)—1922: 1490 khz; 1 kw-U. TL: N30 15 13 W97 42 25. Stereo. Suite 505, 811 Barton Springs Rd. (78716). (512) 474-9233. Licensee: Mercury Broadcasting Co. Inc. (group owner; acq 1-8-92; $3 million with co-located FM; FTR 1-27-92). Net: SMN. Format: Talk. Target aud: General. ■ Van Archer, pres; David LaBrozzi, opns mgr; Carla Jenkins, Jon Meyer, gen sls mgrs; Bob McDonald, natl sls mgr; Ginny Schoggins, prom mgr; Debbie Beal, news dir; Steve Freeman, chief engr.

KEYI-FM—(San Marcos). Co-owned with KFON(AM). 1971: 103.5 mhz; 95.5 kw. Ant 1,256 ft. TL: N30 02 42 W97 52 50. Stereo. Prog sep from AM. Format: Adult contemp. News staff one. Target aud: 25-44; women. ■ Stan Webb, gen sls mgr; Bob McDonald, natl sls mgr; Ginny Schoggins, prom dir.

KGSR(FM)—(Bastrop). Nov 1986: 107.1 mhz; 46 kw. Ant 518 ft. TL: N30 06 58 W97 17 45. Stereo. Hrs opn: 24. Suite 700, 505 Barton Springs Rd., Austin (78704). (512) 472-1071. FAX: (512) 478-5100. Licensee: Central Texas Broadcasters Inc. (acq 5-87; $3 million; FTR 5-4-87). Rep: McGavren Guild. Format: Progsv, AOR. News staff one. Target aud: 25-44; upscale, active, educated adults. Spec prog: Jazz 6 hrs wkly. ■ Bruce G. Beasley, pres; Scott T. Gillmore, gen mgr; Tim Williams, gen sls mgr; Kathy Aubry, prom dir; Jody Denberg, progmg dir; Susan Castle, mus dir; Cecilia Nasti, news dir; Sky Skyler, pub affrs dir; Duncan Black, chief engr. ■ Rates: $100; 100; 100; 35.

KIXL(AM)—(Del Valle). Aug 8, 1959: 970 khz; 1 kw-U. TL: N30 19 13 W97 37 25. Hrs opn: 24. Suite 300, 3910 S. I-H 35, Austin (78704). (512) 444-3000. Licensee: KIXL Partners Ltd. (acq 12-88; $1.5 million; FTR 1-16-89). Net: CBN, Moody, USA. Wash atty: Roseman & Colin. Format: Contemp Christian. News progmg 10 hrs wkly. Target aud: 25-54; conservative, family-oriented adults. Spec prog: Black 6 hrs wkly. ■ Gene Bender, gen mgr; Angi Willis, gen sls mgr; Collin Lambert, progmg dir; Dick Pickens, chief engr. ■ Rates: $25; 15; 20; 12.

KJCE(AM)—(Rollingwood). Aug 12, 1958: 1370 khz; 5 kw-D, 500 w-N. TL: N30 18 16 W97 38 53. Bldg. B, Suite 350, 4301 Westbank Dr., Austin (78746). (512) 327-9595. FAX: (512) 329-6257. Licensee: Amaturo Group Ltd. (acq 10-4-90; grpsl; FTR 10-22-90). Format: Oldies. ■ Lon Bason, vp & gen mgr.

KKMJ-FM—Co-owned with KJCE(AM). Jan 5, 1968: 95.5 mhz; 100 kw-H, 87 kw-V. Ant 1,000 ft. TL: N30 19 23 W97 47 58. Stereo. Hrs opn: 24. (512) 327-9595. FAX: (512) 329-6252. Rep: Major Mkt. Format: Adult contemp. Target aud: 25-54. ■ Joel Burke, opns dir & progmg dir; Marcy Kimball, gen sls mgr; Carla McCown, prom mgr & pub affrs dir; Doc Burns, mus dir; Steve Bumpous, chief engr.

KLBJ(AM)—1939: 590 khz; 5 kw-D, 1 kw-N, DA-N. TL: N30 14 14 W97 37 44. 8309 N. I-35 (78753). (512) 832-4000. FAX: (512) 832-4063. Licensee: The LBJ Co. L.C. (acq 1943). Net: CBS, NBC Talknet, MBS, Wall Street. Rep: Eastman. Format: News/talk. ■ Ian Turpin, pres; Jim Gustafson, gen mgr; Bill Vance, opns mgr; Mark Caesar, progmg dir; Janet Evans, news dir; Bryan King, chief engr.

KLBJ-FM—1960: 93.7 mhz; 100 kw. Ant 1,050 ft. TL: N30 18 36 W97 47 33. Stereo. Prog sep from AM. Format: Rock (AOR). ■ Christine Card, natl sls mgr; Jeff Carol, progmg dir; Ed Mayberry, news dir.

***KMFA(FM)**—January 1967: 89.5 mhz; 65 kw. Ant 853 ft. TL: N30 19 20 W97 48 03. Stereo. Hrs opn: 19. Suite 100, 3001 N. Lamar (78705). (512) 476-5632. Licensee: Capitol Broadcasting Assn. Inc. Wash atty: Goldberg, Godles, Wiener & Wright. Format: Class. Target aud: General. ■ John N. Eddins Jr., gen mgr; Scott Dawes, progmg dir; Thomas B. Morris Jr., chief engr.

KPEZ(FM)—Aug 13, 1976: 102.3 mhz; 20 kw. Ant 685 ft. TL: N30 13 24 W97 49 39. Stereo. Suite 967, 811 Barton Springs Rd. (78704). (512) 474-9233. FAX: (512) 397-1400. Licensee: Clear Channel Radio Licenses Inc. Group owner: Clear Channel Communications Inc. (acq 7-24-92). Rep: Christal. Wash atty: Cohn & Marks. Format: Classic rock. News staff one. News progmg 3 hrs wkly. Target aud: 18-49; young adults with families, above average income, education. ■ Lowry Mays, pres; Stan Webb, vp & gen mgr; Jon Meyer, Carla Jenkins, gen sls mgrs; Bob McDonald, natl sls mgr; Jinny Schoggins, prom mgr; John Roberts, progmg dir; Jim Spector, mus dir; Karen Clauss, news dir; Gil Garcia, chief engr. ■ Rates: $90; 80; 80; 35.

KRGT(FM)—See Hutto.

KTXZ(AM)—See West Lake Hills.

***KUT(FM)**—Nov 10, 1958: 90.5 mhz; 100 kw. Ant 680 ft. TL: N30 18 51 W97 51 58. Stereo. Hrs opn: 24. Communications Bldg. B, Univ. of Texas (78712-1090). (512) 471-1631. Licensee: Univ. of Texas at Austin. Net: NPR. Wash atty: Cohn & Marks. Format: Div. News progmg 25 hrs wkly. Target aud: 26-54. ■ William S. Giorda, gen mgr; Leonora Siedo, opns mgr & progmg dir; Betsy Pilkington, dev mgr & prom mgr; Rollin Morehouse, mktg mgr; Cheryl Bateman, mus dir; David Penn, chief engr.

KVET(AM)—1946: 1300 khz; 5 kw-D, 1 kw-N, DA-2. TL: N30 22 31 W97 42 59. Stereo. Hrs opn: 24. Box 380 (78767). (512) 495-1300. FAX: (512) 495-9423. Licensee: KVET Broadcasting Inc. (acq 7-1-65). Net: ABC/I. Rep: Katz. Wash atty: Kaye, Scholer, Fierman, Hays & Handler. Format: Country. News staff 4. Target aud: 25-64. ■ Roy Butler, CEO; Ron Rogers, pres, gen mgr & natl sls mgr; Bob Cole, opns mgr & progmg mgr; Steve Wilder, gen sls mgr; Tony Luttrell, prom mgr; Steve Gary, mus dir; Jerry Johnson, news dir; David Matyis, chief engr.

KVET-FM—1950: 98.1 mhz; 100 kw. Ant 686 ft. TL: N30 13 24 W97 49 39. Stereo. Hrs opn: 24. 705 N. Lamar (78703). (512) 495-1300. FAX: (512) 495-9423. Licensee: Spur Austin L.P. Group owner: Spur Capital Inc. Net: Westwood One. Rep: Banner. Format: Classic country. Target aud: 18-34; women. ■ Ron Rogers, gen mgr; Bob Cole, opns mgr; Steve Wilder, gen sls mgr; Toni Luttrell, prom mgr; Bran Hansen, progmg dir; Steve Gary, mus dir; Jerry Johnson, news dir; Dave Matyis, chief engr. ■ Rates: $70; 70; 70; 60.

KASE(FM)—Co-owned with KVET(AM). Mar 30, 1969: 100.7 mhz; 100 kw. Ant 1,100 ft. TL: N30 19 10 W97 48 06. Stereo. Hrs opn: 24. Prog dups AM 100%. ■ Brad Hansen, progmg mgr.

***KVRX(FM)**—Not on air, target date unknown: 91.7 mhz; 2 kw. Ant 85 ft. 2500 Whitis Ave. (78705). Licensee: University of Texas at Austin.

Balch Springs

KSKY(AM)—Licensed to Balch Springs. See Dallas.

Ballinger

KRUN(AM)—August 1947: 1400 khz; 1 kw-U. TL: N31 43 31 W99 57 42. Box 351 (76821). (915) 365-5500. FAX: (915) 365-5516. Licensee: Central West Broadcasting Co. (acq 1-1-53). Net: Moody. Rep: Keystone (unwired net). Format: Country, adult contemp, farm. Target aud: General. Spec prog: Sp 4 hrs wkly. ■ Dean Smith, pres; Lynn Smith, gen mgr, progmg dir & chief engr; Joanne Barta, gen sls mgr.

KRUN-FM—August 1977: 103.1 mhz; 3 kw. Ant 300 ft. TL: N31 43 31 W99 57 42. Stereo. Dups AM 100%. Box 103 (76821).

Bandera

KEEP(FM)—July 11, 1981: 98.3 mhz; 1.43 kw. TL: N29 48 53 W99 04 55. Box 117731, Carrollton (75007). (210) 796-7971. Licensee: James G. Withers. Wash atty: Arent, Fox, Kintner, Plotkin & Kahn. Format: Contemp Christian. Target aud: 25-49. ■ James G. Withers, pres & gen mgr; Donna Graham, stn mgr; Gina M. Withers, progmg dir; Bill Watkins, news dir; Cefus Scarbeau, chief engr.

Bastrop

KGSR(FM)—Licensed to Bastrop. See Austin.

Bay City

KIOX(AM)—Aug 1, 1947: 1270 khz; 1 kw-U, DA-N. TL: N28 59 51 W95 54 42. Box 2340 (77404). (409) 245-4642. Licensee: N. Star Communications Inc. (acq 8-22-88). Format: Contemp hit country. News progmg 2 hrs wkly. Target aud: 21-55. Spec prog: Gospel 4 hrs wkly. ■ Hal Kemp, gen mgr & gen sls mgr; Kevin West, mus dir; Skeet Donahue, news dir; Ted Green, chief engr.

KMKS(FM)—July 27, 1984: 102.5 mhz; 50 kw. Ant 492 ft. TL: N28 58 12 W95 59 01. Stereo. Hrs opn: 24. Box 789, 1627 Seventh St. (77414). (409) 244-4242. FAX: (409) 245-0107. Licensee: Sandlin Broadcasting Co. Inc. Net: Drake Chenault-Jones. Format: Adult contemp. ■ Margaret K. Sandlin, pres & mktg mgr; Larry Sandlin, gen mgr & chief engr; Teresa Kaufmann, gen sls mgr, prom mgr & pub affrs dir; Darline Sandlin, progmg dir & mus dir. ■ Rates: $23; 23; 23; 19.

KXGJ(FM)—Not on air, target date unknown: 96.1 mhz; 50 kw. Ant 492 ft. TL: N28 50 36 W96 12 26. c/o Ammerman Enterprises Inc., 4800 Sugar Grove Blvd., Suite 400, Stafford (77477). Licensee: Ammerman Enterprises Inc. (acq 7-90; FTR 7-23-90).

Baytown

KWWJ(AM)—October 1947: 1360 khz; 1 kw-U, DA-2. TL: N29 46 28 W95 00 55 (CP: 5 kw-U, DA-2). Hrs opn: 24. Box 419 (77522); 4638 Decker Dr. (77520). (713) 424-7000. FAX: (713) 424-7588. Licensee: Salt of the Earth Broadcasting (acq 8-88). Net: American Urban, Natl Black. Rep: William Radio. Format: Relg. News staff one. Target aud: General. ■ Darrell E. Martin, pres, gen mgr & prom mgr; Robert Meyers, gen sls mgr & progmg dir; Michael Mosley, mus dir; Theresa Lavinze, pub affrs dir; Dave Biondi, chief engr.

Beaumont

KAYC(AM)—1938: 1450 khz; 1 kw-U. TL: N30 03 52 W94 07 12. Box 870, 3130 Blanchette (77704). (409) 833-9421. FAX: (409) 833-9296. Licensee: Petracom Inc. (group owner; acq 9-25-89; $1.2 million with co-located FM; FTR 10-16-89). Rep: McGavren Guild. Wash atty: Scott Johnson. Format: C&W. News staff one. Target aud: 25-54. ■ Henry Ash, chmn; Katie Wellman, gen mgr & stn mgr; Don Demartino, gen sls mgr; Jay Bernard, prom mgr; Von Cook, progmg dir & mus dir; Frank Dawson, asst mus dir; Richard Core, news dir; John Lackness, chief engr. ■ Rates: $40; 38; 40; 28.

KAYD(FM)—Co-owned with KAYC(AM). 1948: 97.5 mhz; 100 kw. Ant 1,099 ft. TL: N30 03 52 W94 07 12. Stereo. Dups AM 100%. Target aud: 18-49; active responsive decision makers.

KLTN(FM)—See Port Arthur.

KLVI(AM)—1924: 560 khz; 5 kw-U, DA-N. TL: N30 02 42 W93 52 07. Stereo. Hrs opn: 24. Box 5488 (77726); 27 Sawyer (77702). (409) 838-3911. FAX: (409) 838-3233; (409) 838-9993. Licensee: Gulfstar Broadcasting L.C. (acq 1-7-92; with KYKR-FM Beaumont). Net: ABC/I. Rep: McGavren Guild. Wash atty: Fisher, Wayland, Cooper & Leader. Format: News/talk. News staff 3; news progmg 5 hrs wkly. Target aud: 25-64; men and women, informed professionals. Spec prog: Farm 5 hrs, cajun 5 hrs, relg 2 hrs wkly. ■ R. Stevens Hicks, CEO, chmn & pres; Geoffery Armstrong, CFO; Jim Ray, vp & gen mgr; Jim Love, opns mgr; Glenn Hicks, gen sls mgr; Larry Crumpton (local), rgnl sls mgr; Amy Mattingly, prom mgr; Al Caldwell, progmg dir; Jack Pieper, news dir; Patrick Parks, chief engr. ■ Rates: $46; 42; 46; 34.

KQXY-FM—September 1966: 94.1 mhz; 100 kw. Ant 1,099 ft. TL: N30 06 56 W94 00 00. Stereo. Box 1716, 117 Nederland Ave., Nederland (77627). (409) 724-1292. FAX: (409) 724-7055. Licensee: Ninety-Four Point One Inc. (acq 12-3-93; $700,000 with KQHN(AM) Nederland; FTR 12-20-93). Rep: Christal. Format: Adult contemp. Target aud: 18-49; skewed female. ■ Laurie Harbison, gen mgr; Cindy Simon, natl sls mgr; Joe Arnold, prom mgr; Jay Jefferies, progmg dir; Richard Core, news dir; John Lackness, chief engr.

***KTXB(FM)**—Jan 23, 1990: 89.7 mhz; 9 kw. Ant 567 ft. TL: N30 09 27 W93 48 06. Hrs opn: 24. Suite 1327, 550 Fannin (77701). (409) 835-2141. Licensee: Family Stations Inc. (group owner). Format: Relg. ■ Harold Camping (owner), chmn; Doug Sarver, opns mgr.

***KVLU(FM)**—1974: 91.3 mhz; 40 kw. Ant 450 ft. TL: N30 06 40 W94 03 10. Stereo. Hrs opn: 24. Box 10064 (77710). (409) 880-8164. Licensee: Lamar University. Net: NPR. Format: Classical, jazz, news. Spec prog: Sp 5 hrs wkly. ■ George Beverly, gen mgr; Byron Balentine, progmg dir; Marge Wallace, news dir; Ken Wilson, chief engr.

KXTJ(FM)—July 10, 1967: 107.9 mhz; 100 kw. Ant 1,000 ft. TL: N30 02 09 W94 08 31. Stereo. Hrs opn: 24. Suite 1500, 1980 Post Oak Blvd., Houston (77056). (719) 993-0108. FAX: (719) 621-5325. Licensee: El Dorado 108 Inc. (acq 2-16-93; FTR 3-8-93). ■ Ken D. Wolt, gen mgr.

KYKR(FM)—Feb 1, 1966: 95.1 mhz; 100 kw. Ant 500 ft. TL: N30 08 57 W94 07 59. Stereo. Hrs opn: 24. Box 5488 (77726); 27 Sawyer St. (77702). (409) 838-3911. FAX: (409) 838-3233; (409) 838-9993. Licensee: Gulfstar Broadcasting (acq 11-25-92; $425,000; FTR 12-21-92). Rep: McGavren Guild. Wash atty: Fisher, Wayland, Cooper & Leader. Format: Country. News progmg 2 hrs wkly. Target aud: 18-54. ■ R. Steven Hicks, CEO, chmn & pres; Geoffrey Armstrong, CFO; Jim Ray, gen mgr; Jim Love, opns mgr; Glenn Hicks, gen sls mgr; Larry Crumpton (local), rgnl sls mgr; Amy Mattingly, prom mgr; Jimmy Lehn, progmg dir; Chrissie Roberts, mus dir; Patrick Parks, chief engr. ■ Rates: $65; 50; 65; 45.

KZXT(AM)—July 1947: 1380 khz; 1 kw-D, 127 w-N. TL: N30 02 09 W94 08 31. 1690 N. Major Dr., #101 (77713). Licensee: Modern World Media Inc., debtor-in-possession. ■ Mark White, pres & gen mgr; Gary Teany, gen sls mgr; Fred Ollie, progmg dir; Ernest Larkins, mus dir; Matt McKay, news dir; Richard Ryley, chief engr.

KZZB(AM)—May 1, 1947: 990 khz; 1 kw-U, DA-1. TL: N30 08 57 W94 07 59. Hrs opn: 24. 2531 Calder St. (77702); Box 20495 (77720). (409) 833-0990. FAX: (409) 835-0995. Licensee: Martin Broadcasting Inc. (group owner; acq 7-28-92; $70,000; FTR 8-17-92). Rep: Christal. Wash atty: Haley, Bader & Potts. Format: Gospel. News staff one. Target aud: 18-49. ■ Rev. Darrell Martin, pres & gen mgr; Juliet Marks, prom mgr; Kathy Hunter, news dir.

Beeville

KIBL(AM)—Oct 20, 1949: 1490 khz; 1 kw-U. TL: N28 23 08 W97 43 42. Hrs opn: 5 AM-10 PM. Box 700, 2300 S. Washington (78102). (512) 358-1490. FAX: (512) 358-3685. Licensee: Lovelace Assocs. Inc. (acq 11-1-79). Net: SIS; Texas Net. Wash atty: Gardner, Carton & Douglas. Format: C&W (5 AM-9 AM), Sp (9 AM-10 PM). Target aud: 18-64; our blend of Tejano, Conjunto & Marachi reaches all loc Hispanics. Spec prog: Relg 6 hrs wkly. ■ Ed Lovelace, pres; Dan Thompson, opns mgr, news dir & chief engr; Mike Rodriguez, gen sls mgr; Rene Rodriguez, progmg dir; Mac Serenil, mus dir. ■ Rates: $14; 12; 14; 9.

KIBL-FM—Dec 12, 1976: 104.9 mhz; 3 kw. Ant 300 ft. TL: N28 23 08 W97 43 42 (CP: 25 kw, ant 328 ft.). Stereo. Hrs opn: 5 AM-10 PM. Prog sep from AM. Format: Country. News staff one; news progmg 13 hrs wkly. Target aud: 18-64. Spec prog: Gospel 7 hrs, farm 6 hrs wkly. ■ Rich Wilson, progmg dir & mus dir. ■ Rates: Same as AM.

KYTX(FM)—October 1988: 97.9 mhz; 50 kw. Ant 492 ft. TL: N28 22 33 W97 58 58 (CP: 34 kw, ant 584 ft.). Box 1664 (78014). FAX: (512) 358-0601. Licensee: Hamon

Texas

Broadcasting Corp. Format: Golden oldies. ■ Sonja Carr, gen mgr; Mike Carr, opns mgr.

Bellville

KFRD(AM)—Aug 8, 1974: 1090 khz; 250 w-D. TL: N29 56 50 W96 15 54. Stn currently dark. Box 590209, Houston (77259-0209). (713) 480-9992. Licensee: New Ulm Broadcasting Co. Group owner: Bayport Broadcast Group (acq 4-17-90; $150,000). Format: Sp. ■ Roy Henderson, pres; Paul Mougel, gen mgr; Danial Fernandez, progmg dir; Steve Brightwell, chief engr.

Belton

KTON(AM)—Dec 1, 1961: 940 khz; 1 kw-D, DA. TL: N31 02 37 W97 25 46. Hrs opn: 24. Box 1387 (76513). (817) 939-9377. FAX: (817) 939-9458. Licensee: Sheldon Communications Inc. (acq 5-30-91; with co-located FM; FTR 6-24-91). Net: ABC/I. Format: Christian, gospel. ■ Mike Thatcher, gen mgr; Mark Ryan, prom mgr & progmg dir; Adrianne Harris, chief engr.

KOOC(FM)—Co-owned with KTON(AM). Apr 25, 1970: 106.3 mhz; 1.35 kw. Ant 489 ft. TL: N31 03 46 W97 31 54. Stereo. Box 607 (76522). (817) 547-8889. Net: ABC/FM. Format: Country. ■ Gaylon Christie, gen mgr; Troy Deneke, stn mgr & gen sls mgr.

Big Lake

KWGH-FM—Not on air, target date unknown: 103.9 mhz. TL: N31 11 30 W101 28 06. Box 3747, La Habra, CA (90632). Licensee: WMO Broadcasting.

Big Spring

KBST(AM)—Dec 23, 1936: 1490 khz; 1 kw-U. TL: N32 15 44 W101 27 37. Stereo. Box 1632, 608 Johnson (79720). (915) 267-6391. FAX: (915) 267-1579. Licensee: David Wrinkle dba KBST (acq 12-85; $525,000; FTR 10-14-85). Net: ABC/E. Rep: Riley. Format: Div. News staff 2. Target aud: 25 plus. ■ David Wrinkle, pres, gen mgr & gen sls mgr; Kelly Cole, progmg dir; Mike Henry, mus dir; Chris Sommer, news dir; George Franklin, chief engr.

KBST-FM—1961: 95.3 mhz; 8 kw. Ant 482 ft. TL: N32 13 20 W101 27 35 (CP: 95.9 mhz). Stereo. Dups AM 90%.

KBTS(FM)—Not on air, target date unknown: 94.3 mhz; 20 kw. Ant 374 ft. Box 1632 (79721). Licensee: David W. Wrinkle.

KBYG(AM)—1949: 1400 khz; 1 kw-U. TL: N32 13 22 W101 28 35. Hrs opn: 24. Box 1713 (79721); 2801 Wasson Rd. (79720). (915) 263-5294. FAX: (915) 263-8223; (806) 791-0527. Licensee: Ballard Drew (acq 4-9-90). Rep: Target, Katz. Format: Country. News staff 2; news progmg 25 hrs wkly. Target aud: 18 plus. Spec prog: Farm 2 hrs, relg 2 hrs wkly. ■ Bob Bell, gen mgr.

Bishop

KFLZ(FM)—June 15, 1980: 107.1 mhz; 3 kw. Ant 324 ft. TL: N27 39 10 W97 54 59. Stereo. Hrs opn: 24. 110 E. Main (78343). (512) 584-2532. FAX: (512) 584-3959. Licensee: Cismek Corp. (acq 5-26-87). Net: Hispano USA. Rep: Lotus Hispanic. Wash atty: J. Baraff. Format: Sp. News staff one. Target aud: 18-49; people with buying power. ■ Joe A. Cisneros, pres & vp sls; Hector Jaspuez, opns mgr; Bob Solis, progmg dir & mus dir; Paul McKay, chief engr.

Bloomington

KLUB(FM)—December 1992: 106.9 mhz; 6 kw. Ant 295 ft. TL: N28 42 16 W96 50 08. Stereo. Hrs opn: 24. 7439 Alverstone Way, San Antonio (78250). Licensee: Tschirhart Broadcasting Inc.

Boerne

KBRN(AM)—May 10, 1982: 1500 khz; 250 w-D. TL: N29 48 24 W98 43 41 (CP: N29 44 34 W98 41 36). Hrs opn: 6 AM-8 PM. 32830 I-10 W. (78006); Box 1766 (78006). Licensee: Boerne Radio Co. (acq 5-13-91; $30,000; FTR 5-27-91). Wash atty: Dunne & May. ■ Wade Andrews, pres.

Bonham

KFYN(AM)—May 1948: 1420 khz; 250 w-D, 148 w-N. TL: N33 34 40 W96 09 55. Box 248 (75418). (903) 583-3151. FAX: (903) 583-3357. Licensee: Bonham Broadcasting Co. (acq 11-28-75). Net: Texas State. Format: Country. Spec prog: Farm 6 hrs, relg 6 hrs, oldies rock 6 hrs wkly. ■ Roy Floyd, pres & gen mgr; Bob Holliday, gen sls mgr; John Wallis, progmg dir; Jeff Davis, mus dir; Jerry Anderson, news dir; Joe Johnson, chief engr.

KFYZ-FM—Co-owned with KFYN(AM). Nov 1, 1979: 98.3 mhz; 3 kw. Ant 300 ft. TL: N33 33 26 W96 13 13. Stereo. Dups AM 80%. Format: Div. Spec prog: Oldies rock 6 hrs wkly.

Borger

KQFX(FM)—Licensed to Borger. See Amarillo.

KQTY(AM)—Jan 10, 1947: 1490 khz; 1 kw-U. TL: N35 41 05 W101 23 20. Stereo. Hrs opn: 24. Box 165, 113 Union (79007). (806) 273-7533; (806) 273-5889. FAX: (806) 273-3727. Licensee: Zia Broadcasting (acq 12-1-79). Net: ABC/E, SMN. Format: Country. News progmg 15 hrs wkly. Target aud: 25-54; blue-collar workers with traditional values & beliefs. Spec prog: Relg 12 hrs wkly. ■ Lonnie Ausups, CEO; Jim Davis, gen mgr; George Grover, stn mgr, gen sls mgr, mktg dir, adv mgr & news dir; Donald Collett, prom mgr, progmg dir, mus dir & pub affrs dir; Gary Jackson, chief engr. ■ Rates: $10; 7.50; 6.75; 6.75.

Bowie

KRJT(AM)—May 29, 1959: 1410 khz; 500 w-D, DA. TL: N33 35 10 W97 48 23. Hrs opn: 6 AM-sunset. Box 1080, Montague Hwy. (76230). (817) 872-2288. FAX: (817) 872-2288. Licensee: Everett C. Mason (acq 9-20-78). Net: Texas State. Rep: Riley. Format: Country. News progmg 15 hrs wkly. Target aud: 25-54. Spec prog: Farm 4 hrs wkly. ■ Everett Mason, pres & gen mgr; Billy Jon Etter, progmg dir & mus dir; Bill Etter, news dir; Don Whan, chief engr. ■ Rates: $8.25; 8.25; 8.25; 8.25.

KRJT-FM—Nov 15, 1988: 100.7 mhz; 3.1 kw. Ant 459 ft. TL: N33 38 43 W97 49 08 (CP: 6.25 kw, ant 435 ft.). Stereo. Hrs opn: 18. Dups AM 100%. (Acq 9-30-87). Net: Texas State. Rep: Riley. Target aud: General. ■ Bill Etter, opns dir, prom dir, mus dir, news dir & pub affrs dir; Don Whan, engrg dir. ■ Rates: Same as AM.

Brady

KNEL(AM)—December 1935: 1490 khz; 1 kw-U. TL: N31 07 48 W99 19 21. Box 630, 117 S. Blackburn (76825). (915) 597-2119. Licensee: SEC/CESS Broadcasting Inc. (acq 11-1-83; $450,000 with co-located FM; FTR 10-31-83). Net: Texas State Net. Format: Country. News staff 2; news progmg 24 hrs wkly. Target aud: General. Spec prog: Farm 14 hrs, Spanish 12 hrs wkly. ■ Steve Everett, pres, gen mgr & gen sls mgr; Susan Abbott, progmg dir; Stan Cooper, chief engr.

KIXV(FM)—Co-owned with KNEL(AM). Aug 21, 1979: 95.3 mhz; 3 kw. Ant 299 ft. TL: N31 07 27 W99 21 34. Stereo. Prog sep from AM. Net: ABC/D. Format: Adult contemp. News staff 2; news progmg 36 hrs wkly. Target aud: 20-54. Spec prog: Spanish 12 hrs wkly.

Breckenridge

KBIL(AM)—January 1994: 1430 khz; 1 kw-D. TL: N32 45 00 W98 55 38 (CP: 500 w-N, DA-N). Box 711 (76424-0711). (817) 559-6543. Licensee: Buckaroo Broadcasting Inc. (acq 3-24-92; $100,000 with co-located FM; FTR 4-27-92). Net: NBC. Format: Contemp country. ■ Bill Jamar, pres; Dink Foree, gen mgr & gen sls mgr; Lydia Foree, progmg dir & pub affrs dir; Ron Cowan, news dir; Brent Morris, chief engr.

KROO(FM)—Co-owned with KBIL(AM). Aug 1, 1982: 93.5 mhz; 3 kw. Ant 268 ft. TL: N32 45 31 W98 56 00 (CP: 12.5 kw, ant 446 ft.). Stereo. Box 711, Suite 201, 101 E. Walker St. (76424). (817) 559-6543. FAX: (817) 559-6545. Licensee: Buckaroo Broadcasting Inc. Format: Country. ■ Dink Foree, gen mgr; Dale Brooks, gen sls mgr; Ron Cowan, news dir; Justin McClure, chief engr.

Brenham

KTTX(FM)—Listing follows KWHI(AM).

KULF(FM)—August 1988: 94.1 mhz; 6 kw. Ant 328 ft. TL: N30 08 31 W96 25 00. Stereo. Hrs opn: 24. 306 E. Main St. (77833). (409) 836-9411. FAX: (409) 836-9435. Licensee: May Broadcasting Inc. (acq 8-1-89). Wash atty: Fletcher, Heald & Hildreth. Format: Country. News staff one; news progmg 10 hrs wkly. Target aud: 18-49. Spec prog: Gospel 10 hrs wkly. ■ Roy May, pres, stn mgr & gen sls mgr; Jon Dee May, gen mgr, opns mgr & progmg dir; Kevin Fishbeck, news dir. ■ Rates: $12; 10; 12; 8.

KWHI(AM)—Apr 15, 1947: 1280 khz; 1 kw-D, 89 w-N. TL: N30 10 05 W96 25 20. Box 1280, 223 E. Main St. (77834). (409) 836-3655. FAX: (409) 830-8141. Licensee: Tom S. Whitehead (acq 5-1-47). Net: ABC/E. Format: C&W. News staff 2; news progmg 25 hrs wkly. Target aud: General. Spec prog: Polka 2 hrs wkly. ■ Tom S. Whitehead Jr., pres; Tom Dee Whitehead, vp, gen mgr & mktg dir; Keith R. Iwig, stn mgr, opns mgr & gen sls mgr; Keith Iwig, progmg dir; Rick Richards, mus dir; Kristi Kocian, pub affrs dir; Mark Whitehead, chief engr. ■ Rates: $19; 17; 18; 10.

KTTX(FM)—Co-owned with KWHI(AM). Sept 15, 1964: 106.1 mhz; 50 kw. Ant 492 ft. TL: N30 21 49 W96 34 33. Stereo. Dups AM 95%. Suite 100-B, 1673 Briarcrest, Bryan (77802). (409) 776-1061. FAX: (409) 774-7545. Format: Contemp country. News staff 2; news progmg 2 hrs wkly. Target aud: 18-35. ■ Don Dakota, opns mgr & progmg dir; Tom Dee Whitehead, prom dir; Jon Desperado, mus dir. ■ Rates: $27; 24; 28; 21.

Bridgeport

KBOC(FM)—Aug 2, 1982: 96.7 mhz; 3 kw. Ant 246 ft. TL: N33 13 28 W97 47 51 (CP: Ant 226 ft.). Stereo. Hrs opn: 5 AM-midnight. Box 156, FM 1658 (76426). (817) 683-5486; (817) 627-2378. Licensee: Community Broadcast Network (acq 5-3-93; $92,000; FTR 3-29-93). Format: Country, oldies. News staff 2; news progmg 15 hrs wkly. Target aud: 25-60; farmers, business men or women. Spec prog: Farm 8 hrs, gospel 6 hrs, relg 6 hrs, Sp one hr, talk (community) 5 hrs wkly. ■ Ted T. Haynes, CEO, gen mgr, vp sls, vp progmg & news dir; Candace Dalme, chief opns, prom mgr, adv mgr & engrg mgr; Pam Niblett, mus dir; Norman Phillips, chief engr. ■ Rates: $12.75; 12; 12.75; 12.

***KBTT(FM)**—Not on air, target date unknown: 90.5 mhz; 1 kw. Ant 98 ft. TL: N33 07 58 W97 40 48. 3108 Fulton Ave., Sacramento, CA (95821). Licensee: Family Stations Inc. (group owner).

Brownfield

KKUB(AM)—August 1949: 1300 khz; 1 kw-D. TL: N33 10 49 W102 14 51. Rt.1, Box 66, 1722 Tahoka Rd. (79316). (806) 637-4531; (806) 637-4610. Licensee: Brownfield Radio Inc. (acq 1-22-76). Net: Texas State. Rep: Riley. Format: Div. News staff one; news progmg 14 hrs wkly. Target aud: General. Spec prog: Sp 16 hrs wkly. ■ Lou Farr, pres; Jim Farr, stn mgr; Winnie Burnett, gen sls mgr; Chris Miller, news dir. ■ Rates: $10.35; 10.35; 10.35; 10.35.

KLZK(FM)—Nov 12, 1984: 103.9 mhz; 3 kw. Ant 320 ft. TL: N33 10 30 W102 17 20. c/o KICA-AM-FM, Box 7000, Clovis, NM (88101). Licensee: Southwestern Broadcasting Corp. (group owner; acq 5-21-90; $250,000; FTR 5-21-90). Format: C&W. ■ Tom Crane, pres & gen mgr; Brenda Boyd, gen sls mgr; Jack Denison, prom mgr, progmg dir & news dir; Robin Jenkins, mus dir; Charles E. Wilson, chief engr.

Brownsville

***KBNR(FM)**—Apr 10, 1984; 88.3 mhz; 3 kw. Ant 289 ft. TL: N25 55 10 W97 31 4. Stereo. Hrs opn: 6 AM-midnight Sun-Fri, 7 AM-midnight Sat. Box 5480. 216 W. Elizabeth (78523-5480). (210) 542-6933. FAX: (210) 542-0523. Licensee: World Radio Network Inc. Format: Relg, educ, Sp. News progmg 3 hrs wkly. Target aud: 20-45; Hispanic, middle & upper income. ■ Don Larson, stn mgr; Mardelle Brown, sls dir; Don Larson, Malcolm Brown, prom dirs; Lucy Castillo, progmg dir & mus dir; Paul Salzman, engrg dir.

KBOR(AM)—Feb 22, 1949: 1600 khz; 1 kw-U, DA-1. TL: N25 56 57 W97 33 15. Stereo. Hrs opn: 24. Box 3407, 1050 McIntosh (78523). (210) 544-1600; (210) 541-6348. FAX: (210) 542-4109; (210) 544-0311. Licensee: La Nueva KBOR Inc. (acq 1-1-88). Rep: Caballero. Wash atty: Fisher, Wayland, Cooper & Leader. Format: Sp. News staff 3. Target aud: General. ■ Edgar C. Trevino, pres & gen sls mgr; Hilda Trevino, gen mgr; David Carpinteyro, opns mgr & news dir; Samuel Guerra, progmg dir & mus dir; Severo Garza, chief engr.

KKPS(FM)—Jan 17, 1978: 99.5 mhz; 100 kw. Ant 1,034 ft. TL: N26 04 53 W97 49 44. Stereo. 901 E. Pike Blvd., Weslaco (78596). (512) 968-1548. FAX: (512) 968-3952. Licensee: Rio Grande Partners Ltd. (acq 5-21-93; $910,000; FTR 6-14-93). Net: ABC/R, Unistar. Rep: Torbet. Wash atty: Pepper & Corazzini. Format: Sp mus. News staff one. Target aud: 18-49; Hispanic females, young adults. ■ Jeffrey Millar, gen mgr; Greg Rambin, progmg dir.

KRIO(AM)—See McAllen.

KTEX(FM)—Jan 1975: 100.3 mhz; 100 kw. Ant 1,125 ft. TL: N26 03 13 W97 44 39. Stereo. Hrs opn: 24. Box 1808, Harlingen (78551); 3301 S. Expwy. 83, Harlingen (78550). (512) 423-5068. Licensee: Tate Communications Inc. (group owner; acq 4-87). Rep: Christal. Wash atty: Haley, Bader & Potts. Format: Country. Target aud: General. ■ Harvey J. Tate, chmn, pres & gen mgr; George Hochman, exec vp; Roger Kay, gen sls mgr; Charlie Kennedy, prom dir; Kenny Garcia, progmg dir; Sonny Laguna, mus dir; Debbie Del Rio, news dir & pub affrs dir; Ken Meek, chief engr.

Brownwood

KBWD(AM)—Aug 17, 1941: 1380 khz; 1 kw-D, 500 w-N. TL: N31 42 36 W98 57 36. Hrs opn: 18. Box 280, 801 Carnegie Blvd. (76801). (915) 646-3505. FAX: (915) 646-2220. Licensee: Brown County Broadcasting Co. Net: ABC/I. Format: Oldies, 50s, 60s, 70s. News staff 2; news progmg 8 hrs wkly. Target aud: 25-54. ■ Bill Jamar, pres; Don Dillard, gen mgr; Jim Laird, chief engr.

KOXE(FM)—Co-owned with KBWD(AM). May 17, 1975: 101.5 mhz; 100 kw. Ant 727 ft. TL: N31 43 45 W99 01 12. Stereo. Prog sep from AM. (915) 646-1015. Net: NBC. Format: C&W. Spec prog: Farm 3 hrs wkly.

KPSM(FM)—April 11, 1981: 99.3 mhz; 800 w. Ant 489 ft. TL: N31 43 10 W99 00 57. Stereo. Box 1522 (76804). (915) 646-3420. FAX: (915) 646-5993. Licensee: Word of Faith Christian Center of Brownwood Inc. (acq 1-22-93; $40,000; FTR 2-15-93). Net: CBN. Format: Christian contemp. ■ Jerry Martin, gen mgr.

KXYL(AM)—1953: 1240 khz; 1 kw-U. TL: N31 42 21 W98 59 45. Box 100, One Texas Ave. (76804). (915) 646-3535. FAX: (915) 646-5347. Licensee: Central Texas Communications Inc. (acq 1-7-93; $30,000 promissory note with co-located FM; FTR 2-1-93). Net: SMN; Texas State Net. Rep: Roslin. Format: Adult contemp, contemp hit. News staff one; news progmg 10 hrs wkly. Target aud: 25-49. Spec prog: Sp (Tex-Mex) music 16 hrs wkly, news/info. ■ Lynn Nabers, pres; Helen Lehman, gen mgr, gen sls mgr & prom mgr; Mike Woods, progmg dir; Mark Kasinger, news dir; Marion Bishop, chief engr. ■ Rates: $12; 12; 10; 8.

KXYL-FM—September 1965: 104.1 mhz; 74 kw-H. Ant 321 ft. TL: N31 42 16 W99 00 05. Stereo. Hrs opn: 24. Prog sep from AM. Format: Country. Target aud: 18-49.

Bryan

KAGC(AM)—Dec 27, 1977: 1510 khz; 500 w-D. TL: N30 41 21 W96 21 35. Box 4066 (77805); 202 East Carson St. (77801). (409) 779-1510. FAX: (409) 779-1587. Licensee: Divcon Associates Inc. (acq 3-87). Net: USA. Wash atty: Verner, Liipfert, Bernhard & Hand. Format: Contemp Christian. News staff one; news progmg 8 hrs wkly. Target aud: 25-54; upscale, higher income & conservative. Spec prog: Black 2 hrs wkly. ■ Bob Bell, pres & gen sls mgr; Judith S. Bell, gen mgr; James Cordray, opns mgr & mus dir; Terry Rosser, vp dev; Whitney Gortney, prom mgr; Bill Briscoe, progmg dir; Jere Smith, news dir; John Risenbrecht, pub affrs dir; Steve Sandlin, chief engr.

KBMA(FM)—Not on air, target date unknown: 99.5 mhz; 3 kw. Ant 328 ft. TL: N30 39 02 W96 20 57. c/o Felix Torres, 206 N. Parker St. (77804). (409) 779-3391. Licensee: Mexican-American Communications. ■ Felix Torres, gen mgr.

KKYS(FM)—July 28, 1984: 104.7 mhz; 50 kw. Ant 350 ft. TL: N30 42 59 W96 22 20. Stereo. Hrs opn: 24. Box 4132, Suite 26, 701 Villa Maria (77805). (409) 823-5597. FAX: (409) 823-7578. Licensee: Radio Sungroup of Bryan. Group owner: SunGroup Inc. (acq 10-5-89; grpsl; FTR 10-23-89). Rep: McGavren Guild. Format: CHR (adult). New progmg 15 hrs wkly. Target aud: 18-49; heavy office listening. ■ John Biddinger, pres; John Southwood, CFO; Greg Hale, sr vp, gen mgr, stn mgr & gen sls mgr; Sabrina Woodson, natl sls dir; Ron Elliott, progmg dir; Steve Bridges, chief engr. ■ Rates: $30; 30; 24; 18.

KORA-FM—Listing follows KTAM.

KTAM(AM)—Sept 10, 1947: 1240 khz; 1 kw-U. TL: N30 39 02 W96 20 59. Box 3069, 1240 Villa Maria (77801). (409) 776-1240. FAX: (409) 776-0123. Licensee: Clear Channel Radio Licenses Inc. (group owner; acq 8-5-92; with co-located FM). Net: ABC/C. Format: Oldies. Target aud: 25 plus. ■ L. Lowry Mays, CEO; Randal Mays, CFO; Mark Mays, exec vp; Benny Springer, vp & gen mgr; Harley Malone, gen sls mgr; Jason Hightower, prom dir; Bob Shannon, progmg dir; Jay Socol, news dir; Tom Fussell, chief engr. ■ Rates: $14; 12; 14; 8.

KORA-FM—Co-owned with KTAM. Apr 1, 1966: 98.3 mhz; 900 w. Ant 528 ft. TL: N30 39 02 W96 20 57 (CP: 2.3 kw). Stereo. Prog sep from AM. Net: MBS. Format: C&W. News staff 2; news progmg 10 hrs wkly. Target aud: 25-54.

KTSR(FM)—See College Station.

WTAW(AM)—See College Station.

Burkburnett

KYYI(FM)—June 1, 1989: 104.7 mhz; 100 kw. Ant 1,017 TL: N34 05 35 W98 52 44. Stereo. Hrs opn: 24. 4203 Callfield Rd., Wichita Falls (76308). (817) 691-1054. FAX: (817) 691-5855. Licensee: Y-104 Broadcasting Co. Inc. (acq 6-8-92; FTR 6-29-92). Rep: Katz. Wash atty: Cohn & Marks. Format: Young Country. ■ Mark Walker, opns dir; Chris Canyon, prom mgr; Jeff Chancey, chief engr.

Burnet

KBLK(FM)—Not on air, target date unknown: 92.5 mhz; 3 kw. Ant 299 ft. TL: N30 48 53 W98 17 28. 20707 Camelback, Lago Vista (78645). Licensee: Nolte Broadcasting Corp.

KHLB(AM)—Aug 19, 1963: 1340 khz; 1 kw-U. TL: N30 46 04 W98 13 49. Box 639, Marble Falls (78654). (210) 693-5551. FAX: (210) 693-5107. Licensee: Kirkman Group Inc. (acq 3-29-90). Net: ABC/I; Texas State. Format: News, info, adult contemp. ■ Ken Kirkman, gen mgr; Carl Geisler, opns mgr; Ellen Kirkman, gen sls mgr; Terry Wooten, progmg dir; Cliff McCormack, news dir; Brian King, chief engr.

KHLB-FM—Dec 15, 1978: 106.9 mhz; 2 kw. Ant 367 ft. TL: N30 44 12 W98 17 36. Stereo. Prog sep from AM. Format: C&W.

Caldwell

KHEN(FM)—Not on air, target date unknown: 95.1 mhz; 3 kw. Ant 328 ft. TL: N30 35 43 W96 38 30. Box 590209, c/o Bayport Broadcast Group, Roy E. Henderson, Houston (77259). Licensee: Roy E. Henderson. Group owner: Bayport Broadcast Group.

Cameron

KHLR(FM)—Apr 8, 1985: 103.9 mhz; 25 kw. Ant 695 ft. TL: N30 45 16 W96 54 30. Stereo. Hrs opn: 6 AM-midnight. Box 387, c/o KOKE(FM), Giddings (78942). (409) 542-0045; (817) 697-6541. Licensee: KCRM Broadcasting (acq 8-22-89; $372,000; FTR 9-11-89). Net: USA. Wash atty: Dow, Lohnes & Albertson. Format: Christian gospel. Target aud: 25-54; conservative, family-oriented adults. Spec prog: Farm one hr, Ger one hr, gospel 10 hrs wkly. ■ Bill Jamar, pres; Paul Jamar, vp & gen mgr; Jennifer Jamar, mus dir; Bill Woleben, chief engr. ■ Rates: $10; 10; 10; 8.

KJKS(FM)—Not on air, target date unknown: 101.3 mhz; 3 kw. Ant 328 ft. TL: N30 57 00 W96 54 03. 1303 N. Davis St. (76520). Licensee: Joseph Kent Smitherman. ■ Joe Smitherman, pres.

KMIL(AM)—September 1955: 1330 khz; 500 w-D, 97 w-N. TL: N30 50 48 W96 57 55. Drawer 832, 901 E. First (76520). (817) 697-6633. FAX: (817) 697-6330. Licensee: Milam Broadcasting Co. (acq 1-1-60). Net: MBS. Rep: Keystone (unwired net). Format: C&W, Sp. News staff 2; news progmg 15 hrs wkly. Target aud: General. Spec prog: Gospel 6 hrs, Czech 8 hrs wkly. ■ Eugene Smitherman, pres & chief engr; Joe Smitherman, gen mgr, sls dir & news dir; Robert Reed, prom mgr, progmg dir & mus dir. ■ Rates: $7.50; 7.50; 7.50; 7.50.

Canadian

KEZP(FM)—Feb 9, 1988: 103.1 mhz; 830 w. Ant 574 ft. TL: N35 49 10 W100 23 38 (CP: 94.9 mhz, 100 kw, ant 558 ft., TL: N35 48 56 W100 23 35). c/o Owensville Communications Co., 104 Juniper, Flat River, MO (63601); 1115 Texas Ave., Alexandria, VA (71301). (318) 445-1234. Licensee: KEZP Inc. Format: Oldies. ■ Taylor Thompson, gen mgr; Randy Reynolds, gen sls mgr.

Canyon

KAKS(AM)—Licensed to Canyon. See Amarillo.

KAKS-FM—Licensed to Canyon. See Amarillo.

KPUR-FM—Jan 12, 1981: 107.1 mhz; 5 kw. Ant 300 ft. TL: N35 05 09 W101 54 52. Stereo. Box 7407 (79114). (806) 371-9797. FAX: (806) 371-9129. Licensee: Westwind Broadcasting Inc. (acq 10-29-92; $245,000 with KPUR(AM) Amarillo; FTR 11-23-92). Format: Oldies. ■ Keith Adams, pres; Susan Brofft, opns mgr; Joanna Alexander, gen sls mgr; Farris Fincher, chief engr.

*****KWTS(FM)**—1971: 91.1 mhz; 100 w. Ant -9 ft. TL: N34 58 59 W101 55 10. Stereo. Box 1514, Wt. Station (79016). (806) 656-2911. FAX: (806) 656-2807. Licen-

see: West Texas State Univ. Format: CHR, rock. News staff 2. Target aud: 16-25. ■ RuNell Coons, pres; Leigh Browning, exec vp; Leonard S. Martinez, gen mgr & chief engr.

Carrizo Springs

KBEN(AM)—Aug 9, 1955: 1450 khz; 1 kw-U. TL: N28 31 15 W99 51 30. Box 335, 203 S. 4th St. (78834). (210) 876-2210; (210) 876-5489. FAX: (210) 876-2210. Licensee: Noelia S. Herbort, executrix. Group owner: The Herbort Stations (acq 2-87). Net: SIS; Texas State Net. Wash atty: Borsari & Paxson. Format: Sp, C&W. News staff one. Target aud: English & Spanish listeners; all ages. Spec prog: Farm 4 hrs wkly. ■ Noelia Herbort, CEO, gen mgr, vp dev & news dir; Lisa Jaime, opns mgr, vp adv, progmg dir & pub affrs dir; Richard Jaime, vp sls; Manny Martinez III, vp prom; Cindy L. Weed, mus dir; Juan Salgado, asst mus dir; Joe R. Gragg, vp engrg.

KCZO(FM)—1991: 92.1 mhz; 3 kw. Ant 296 ft. TL: N28 33 24 W99 53 49. Box 252, McAllen (78502). (210) 781-5528. Licensee: Paulino Bernal. Format: Christian. ■ Eloy Bernal, gen mgr.

Carthage

KGAS(AM)—October 1955: 1590 khz; 2.5 kw-D, 130 w-N. TL: N32 09 12 W94 18 52. 226 S. Shelby (75633). (903) 693-6668. FAX: (903) 693-7188. Licensee: Jerry T. Hanszen (acq 9-1-88). Net: ABC/E; Texas State Net. Rep: Miller. Format: Country. News staff 2; news progmg 10 hrs wkly. Target aud: General. Spec prog: Relg 10 hrs wkly. ■ Jerry T. Hanszen, gen mgr, mus dir & news dir; Jim Stanford, chief engr. ■ Rates: $13; 13; 13; 13.

KGAS-FM—Aug 1, 1992: 104.3 mhz; 6 kw. Ant 328 ft. TL: N32 08 11 W94 23 07. Dups AM 100%.

KTUX(FM)—Licensed to Carthage. See Shreveport, La.

Center

KDET(AM)—Feb 22, 1949: 930 khz; 1 kw-D, 36 w-N. TL: N31 50 03 W94 12 53. Box 934, 307 San Augustine St. (75935). (409) 598-3304. FAX: (409) 598-9537. Licensee: Center Broadcasting Inc. Net: AP; Texas Net. Rep: Riley. Format: Southern gospel. Spec prog: Black 10 hrs wkly. ■ Dan Dellinger, vp, gen mgr & chief engr; Jack McLendon, gen sls mgr; Mary McKay, progmg dir, mus dir & news dir.

KDET-FM—July 5, 1978: 102.3 mhz; 3 kw. Ant 300 ft. TL: N31 50 03 W94 12 53. Stereo. Prog sep from AM. Format: Country.

Childress

KCTX(AM)—May 8, 1947: 1510 khz; 250 w-D. TL: N34 25 41 W100 13 47. Hrs opn: 6:30 AM-6 PM. Box 297, U.S. Hwy. 83 S. (79201). (817) 937-2563. Licensee: Greenbelt Broadcasting (acq 12-19-91; $65,000; FTR 1-13-92). Net: Moody; Voice of the S.W. Format: Oldies. News staff 2; news progmg 8 hrs wkly. Target aud: 50 plus; older listeners, usually retired. Spec prog: Relg 10 hrs wkly. ■ W.J. Hubanks, gen mgr; Keith Hodo, opns mgr, mus dir & news dir; Allen Gregory, progmg dir; Bob Seagroves, chief engr.

KSRW(FM)—July 1, 1984: 96.1 mhz; 50 kw. Ant 520 ft. TL: N34 26 20 W100 13 10. Stereo. Box 1511 Ave. F N.W. (79201). (817) 937-6551; (817) 937-6316. Licensee: Eddie J. Leary (acq 10-4-93; $135,000; FTR 10-25-93). Net: ABC/6, Unistar. Rep: Riley. Format: Country. News staff 2; news progmg 20 hrs wkly. Target aud: General. Spec prog: Relg 5 hrs wkly. ■ Stephen R. White, pres, gen mgr & chief engr; Ed Leary, gen sls mgr; Mary R. White, prom mgr & news dir; Dusty Hansard, progmg dir & mus dir.

Clarksville

KCAR(AM)—Apr 27, 1956: 1350 khz; 500 w-D. TL: N33 36 41 W95 01 01. Hrs opn: 6 AM-6 PM. Box 609, 228 W. Main St. (75426). (903) 427-3861. FAX: (903) 427-5524. Licensee: Basso Broadcasting Inc. (acq 7-14-93; $120,000 with co-located FM; FTR 8-9-93). Net: AP; VSA Radio. Rep: Busby, Finch. Wash atty: Chris Imlay. Format: C&W. News progmg 10 hrs wkly. Target aud: 35 plus; rural, agricultural, low-income, middle-aged. Spec prog: Gospel 6 hrs, sports 10 hrs, farm 2 hrs wkly. ■ Mike Basso, pres, gen mgr, gen sls mgr & progmg dir; Gary Pinetta, news dir; Dale Gorsuch, chief engr. ■ Rates: $9; 8; 9; na.

Texas **Directory of Radio**

KGAP(FM)—Co-owned with KCAR(AM). Dec 11, 1990: 98.5 mhz; 6 kw. Ant 328 ft. TL: N33 35 47 W95 01 03. Stereo. Hrs opn: 6 AM-10 PM. Prog sep from AM. Format: Adult contemp. News progmg 2 hrs wkly. Target aud: 25-65.

Claude

KARX(FM)—Licensed to Claude. See Amarillo.

Cleburne

KCLE(AM)—April 1947; 1120 khz; 250 w-D. TL: N32 23 05 W97 23 46. 919 N. Main (76031). (817) 645-6643. FAX: (817) 645-6644. Licensee: Texas Country Connection Inc. (acq 8-87). Net: TSN. Rep: Keystone (unwired net). Wash atty: Fletcher, Heald & Hildreth. Format: C&W. News staff 2; news progmg 6 hrs wkly. Target aud: General. Spec prog: Farm 2 hrs wkly. ■ Gary Moss, gen mgr; Jimmy Aiken, progmg dir; Ed Pryor, chief engr. ■ Rates: $19; 17; 19; na.

Cleveland

KRTK(FM)—Jan 17, 1993: 97.1 mhz; 100 kw. Ant 981 ft. TL: N30 29 36 W95 12 11. Rebroadcasts KRTS(FM) Seabrook 100%. Suite 5100, 1600 Smith, Houston (77002). (713) 921-5787. FAX: (713) 651-0267. Licensee: Texas Classical Radio Inc. Format: Class. ■ George Stokes, exec vp & gen mgr.

Clifton

KWOW(FM)—1989: 103.3 mhz; 8.37 kw. Ant 574 ft. TL: N31 47 40 W97 27 17. Hrs opn: 24. 400 Bowden Dr., Waco (76710). (817) 776-1033. FAX: (817) 776-4505. Licensee: Bosque Broadcasting Corp. Net: Unistar, CNN. Wash atty: Blooston & Mordofsky. Format: Easy lstng. Target aud: 35-64. ■ Lawrence L. Bush Jr., pres; Bob Kirby, gen sls mgr; Larry Bush, chief engr.

Coahoma

KBYG-FM—Not on air, target date unknown: 105.5 mhz; 6 kw. Ant 91 ft. 2801 Wasson Dr., Big Spring (79720). Licensee: Drew Ballard.

Cockrell Hill

KRVA(AM)—Licensed to Cockrell Hill. See Dallas.

Coleman

KSTA(AM)—Nov 1, 1947: 1000 khz; 250 w-D. TL: N31 51 16 W99 25 36. Box 432, 2500 N. Neches (76834). (915) 625-4188. FAX: (915) 625-3917. Licensee: Coleman County Broadcasters Inc. (acq 10-11-90). Net: MBS; Texas Net, VSA. Format: C&W. News staff one. Target aud: General. Spec prog: Farm 14 hrs, Sp 5 hrs, gospel 7 hrs wkly. ■ Ross L. Jones, pres; Randy Turner, gen mgr & sls dir; Jerry Woods, progmg dir; Stan Cooper, chief engr. ■ Rates: $10; 8; 10; 6.

KSTA-FM—1974: 107.1 mhz; 3 kw. Ant 180 ft. TL: N31 51 16 W99 25 36. Stereo. Dups AM 100%. ■ Rates: Same as AM.

College Station

*****KAMU-FM**—Mar 30, 1977: 90.9 mhz; 32 kw. Ant 340 ft. TL: N30 37 48 W96 20 33 (CP: 2.4 kw-H, 32 kw-V). Stereo. Moore Communications Center, Texas A&M University (77843-4244). (409) 845-5611. Licensee: Texas A&M University. Net: NPR. Format: News, class. News progmg 37 hrs wkly. Spec prog: Sp 2 hrs, Black 3 hrs, folk 3 hrs, jazz 10 hrs, relg one hr wkly. ■ Rodney L. Zent, gen mgr; Larry Jackson, stn mgr; Randall Kowalik, opns mgr; Penny Zent, dev dir; Richard Howard, progmg dir; Wayne M. Pecena, chief engr.

KKYS(FM)—See Bryan.

KTAM(AM)—See Bryan.

KTSR(FM)—Listing follows WTAW(AM).

WTAW(AM)—Oct 2, 1922; 1150 khz; 1 kw-D, 500 w-N, DA-N. TL: N30 38 05 W96 21 20. Stereo. Hrs opn: 24. Box 3248, Bryan (77805); Suite 601, 1716 Briarcrest, Bryan (77802). (409) 846-1150. FAX: (409) 846-1933. Licensee: Bryan Broadcasting L.C. (acq 2-21-92) $500,000 with co-located FM; FTR 3-9-92). Net: CBS, MBS; Texas Agribus. Rep: Katz. Format: News/talk, sports. News staff 3; news progmg 58 hrs wkly. Target aud: 25-54. Spec prog: Farm 10 hrs wkly. ■ William R. Hicks, pres; Benjamin D. Downs, gen mgr; Sam Jones, sls dir; Randy Ricci, progmg dir; K.L. Wechler, mus dir; Brad Whellis, news dir; Mark Steptoe, engrg dir.

KTSR(FM)—Co-owned with WTAW(AM). Aug 8, 1964: 92.1 mhz; 3 kw. Ant 275 ft. TL: N30 38 05 W96 21 20. Stereo. Prog sep from AM. Format: Classic rock. News staff 2; news progmg 18 hrs wkly.

Colorado City

KVMC(AM)—June 16, 1950; 1320 khz; 1 kw-D. TL: N32 23 15 W100 53 33. Box 990 (79512). (915) 728-5224. Licensee: James G. Baum (acq 2-13-81; $395,000; FTR 3-9-81). Net: Texas State. Rep: Busby. Format: C&W. Spec prog: Farm 8 hrs wkly. ■ James G. Baum, pres, gen mgr & chief engr.

KAUM(FM)—Co-owned with KVMC(AM). March 29, 1983: 106.3 mhz; 3 kw. Ant 157 ft. TL: N32 23 15 W100 53 33. Stereo. Prog sep from AM. Format: Adult contemp.

Columbus

KULM(FM)—Sept 3, 1973: 98.3 mhz; 3 kw. Ant 253 ft. TL: N29 42 03 W96 34 24 (CP: 6 kw). Stereo. Hrs opn: 5:30 AM-10 PM. Box 111, 325 Radio Ln. (78934). (409) 732-5768. FAX: (409) 723-6377. Licensee: Wajama Productions Inc. (acq 11-19-90; $85,000; FTR 12-10-90). Net: Texas State Net. Format: C&W. Spec prog: Farm 4 hrs wkly. ■ Mark Canon, gen mgr.

Comanche

KCOM(AM)—Apr 1, 1962: 1550 khz; 250 w-D. TL: N31 53 54 W98 35 14. Hrs opn: 6 AM-7 PM. Box 9 (76442). (915) 356-2558. FAX: (915) 356-5757. Licensee: Arrowhead Broadcasting Inc. (acq 4-1-74). Net: Texas Radio Net. Format: C&W, Sp. Spec prog: Gospel 5 hrs wkly. ■ Roy E. Parker, pres; Betty Hayes, Tommy Wilhelm, stn mgrs; Tommy Wilhelm, opns mgr & mus dir. ■ Rates: $10; 10; 10.

Comfort

KATG(FM)—Not on air, target date unknown: 95.1 mhz; 50 kw. Ant 492 ft. TL: N29 54 08 W98 57 09. Bldg. B, Suite 350, 4301 W. Bank Dr., Austin (78746). (512) 329-0947. Licensee: Nancy K. Hinson Grubbs.

Commerce

KEMM(FM)—Dec 1, 1981: 92.1 mhz; 3 kw. Ant 300 ft. TL: N33 11 40 W96 01 20. Stereo. Box 1292, Rt. One, Hwy. 224, Greenville (75428). (903) 886-3120. FAX: (903) 455-3692. Licensee: Russell-Fields Inc. (acq 11-91; $230,000; FTR 12-16-91). Format: Country. News staff one; news progmg 5 hrs wkly. Target aud: 25-54; members of dual income families with kids. ■ Joe McHugh, pres; Gene Fields, gen mgr; Brad Marshall, gen sls mgr; Brad Blanchard, prom mgr; Ross Johnson, progmg dir & mus dir; Doug Ledbetter, news dir; Hugh Beavers, chief engr.

*****KETR(FM)**—Apr 7, 1975: 88.9 mhz; 100 kw. Ant 400 ft. TL: N33 14 17 W95 55 27. Stereo. Hrs opn: 24. Box 4504 East Texas Stn., Performing Arts Center, 2600 S. Neal (75429). (903) 886-5848. FAX: (903) 886-5522. Licensee: Board of Regents, East Texas State Univ. Net: APR, AP; Texas State Net. Format: Classic gold, jazz, news. News staff one; news progmg 7 hrs wkly. Target aud: 21-66. Spec prog: Jazz 10 hrs, bluegrass 5 hrs wkly. ■ Bill Oellermann, gen mgr; Rob Stanley Ernest, stn mgr & progmg dir; Freda Ross, news dir; Dave Sloan, chief engr. ■ Rates: $15; 4; 5; 4.

Conroe

KJOJ(AM)—Apr 16, 1951: 880 khz; 10 kw-D, 1 kw-N, DA-2. TL: N30 17 38 W95 25 55. Stereo. Box 73503, Houston (77273); 29801 I-45 N., Spring (77381). (409) 756-0107. Licensee: U.S. Radio L.P. (group owner; acq 12-31-91; $750,000; FTR 1-21-91). Net: ABC/D. Format: Christian. Target aud: 25 plus. ■ Hardy Brundage, gen mgr; Jackie Goudeau, progmg dir; Errol R. Coker, chief engr.

KKZR(FM)—Feb 14, 1965: 106.9 mhz; 95 kw. Ant 1,128 ft. TL: N30 20 02 W95 12 51. Stereo. Box 73503, Houston (77273-3503). (713) 260-3600. FAX: (713) 260-3628. Licensee: U.S. Radio L.P. Group owner: U.S. Radio Corp. (acq 7-19-89; $8,000,000; FTR 8-7-89). Net: USA. Format: Mainstream rock/roll. ■ Mike Ryan, gen mgr; Randy Schell, opns mgr; Mark Krueger, gen sls mgr.

KSSQ(FM)—Apr 13, 1981: 1140 khz; 5 kw-D, DA. TL: N30 20 40 W95 27 32. 300 E. Bryant Rd. (77301). (409) 441-1140. FAX: (409) 788-1140. Licensee: Martin Broadcasting Inc. Group Owner: (acq 2-10-92; $175,000; FTR 3-2-92). Net: SBN. Format: Gospel. News staff one. Target aud: 24-55. ■ Darrell Martin, stn mgr; George Nelson Jr., news dir; Dave Biondi, chief engr.

Copperas Cove

*****KNCT-FM**—See Killeen.

KOOV(FM)—Nov 21, 1977: 103.1 mhz; 760 w. Ant 630 ft. TL: N31 07 59 W97 54 17 (CP: 6.3 kw, ant 66 ft.). Stereo. Hrs opn: 24. Dups KOOC(FM) Belton. Box 607, 108 E. Ave. E. (76522). (817) 547-8889. FAX: (817) 547-2394. Licensee: Centroplex Communications Inc. (acq 12-19-91). Net: ABC/E. Rep: Schubert. Wash atty: Cohn & Marks. Format: Country. News staff 3; news progmg 13 hrs wkly. Target aud: 18-34; men and women. ■ Gaylon W. Christie, pres & gen mgr; Dennis James, stn mgr & gen sls mgr; James Harrison, opns dir & prom mgr; Joe Lombardi, progmg dir; Ben Bradshaw, mus dir; Chuck Kelly, news dir; Leroy Franklin, chief engr. ■ Rates: $25; 21; 25; 18.

Corpus Christi

*****KBNJ(FM)**—January 1985: 91.7 mhz; 5 kw. Ant 500 ft. TL: N27 46 43 W97 37 57. Stereo. Hrs opn: 24. Box 270068 (78427); 3766 Saturn Rd. (78413). (512) 855-0975; (512) 855-0976. FAX: (512) 855-0977. Licensee: World Radio Network Inc. (group owner; acq 6-5-84; $36,000; FTR 5-21-84). Net: Moody, USA. Format: Relg, educ, Sp & English. News progmg 7 hrs wkly. Target aud: General. ■ Abe C. Van Der Puy, pres; Jones H. Kinard, stn mgr; Stanley Swanson, chief engr.

KBSO(FM)—Not on air, target date unknown: 94.7 mhz; 3 kw. Ant 285 ft. TL: N27 49 50 W97 32 34. 107 Lost Creek, Portland (78374). Licensee: Reina Broadcasting Inc.

KCCT(AM)—June 1954: 1150 khz; 1 kw-D, 500 w-N, DA-2. TL: N27 48 01 W97 28 44. Stereo. Hrs opn: 24. Box 5278 (78465); 701 Benys (78408). (512) 289-0999. FAX: (512) 289-6215. Licensee: Radio KCCT Inc. (acq 8-15-74). Net: CRC. Rep: Caballero. Format: Sp. Target aud: 25-54; Hispanics. ■ Manuel Davila Sr., pres; Manuel Davila Jr., vp & gen mgr; Manual Davila Jr., gen sls mgr; Don Valdez, mus dir; Leopolda Luna, news dir; Paul Easter, chief engr.

KCTA(AM)—Oct 24, 1959: 1030 khz; 50 kw-D. TL: N27 56 01 W97 15 34. Box 898 (78403). (512) 883-1600. FAX: (512) 883-9303. Licensee: Broadcasting Corp of the Southwest (acq 1959). Net: USA. Format: Relg. Spec prog: Sp 6 hrs wkly. ■ Bill York, pres & gen mgr; David Freymiller, opns mgr & gen sls mgr; Chris Munson, progmg dir & mus dir; Paul Easter, chief engr.

KOUL(FM)—(Sinton). Co-owned with KCTA(AM). May 20, 1968: 103.7 mhz; 100 kw. Ant 941 ft. TL: N28 02 05 W97 26 10. Stereo. Prog sep from AM. Net: AP. Rep: McGavren Guild. Format: C&W. Spec prog: Relg. ■ Alec Drake, gen sls mgr & prom mgr; John Boudreau, progmg dir & mus dir; Russ Martin, news dir.

KDAE(AM)—(Sinton). 1954: 1590 khz; 1 kw-D, 500 w-N, DA-2. TL: N28 01 16 W97 28 14. Stereo. Box 31274, 1602 S. Brownlee, Corpus Christi (78404). (512) 882-4394. FAX: (512) 882-7055. Licensee: Stereo Broadcasting Corp. Net: CNN. Rep: McGavren Guild. Wash atty: Fisher, Wayland. Format: Btfl mus. News staff one; news progmg 2 hrs wkly. Target aud: 35-64. Spec prog: Farm 6 hrs wkly. ■ Stephen A. Dewalt, CEO; Michelle Tripp, prom mgr; Fred Hoffman, chief engr. ■ Rates: $50; 50; 50; 30.

KLTG(FM)—Co-owned with KDAE(AM). Sept 1, 1967: 96.5 mhz; 97 kw. Ant 869 ft. TL: N27 39 12 W97 33 55 (CP: Ant 955 ft., TL: N27 44 28 W97 36 08). Stereo. Prog sep from AM. (acq 9-28-90; grpsl; FTR 10-22-90). Format: Oldies. ■ Steve DeWalt, gen mgr; Chris Bailey, progmg dir. ■ Rates: $20; 20; 20; 10.

*****KEDT-FM**—Mar 2, 1982: 90.3 mhz; 100 kw. Ant 802 ft. TL: N27 39 12 W97 33 55. Stereo. Hrs opn: 24. Suite 38, 4455 South Padre Island Dr. (78468-1690). (512) 855-2213. FAX: (512) 855-3877. Licensee: South Texas Public Broadcasting System. Net: NPR. Wash atty: Schwartz, Woods & Miller. Format: Classical, news, jazz. News staff one; news progmg 37 hrs wkly. Target aud: General. Spec prog: Sp 4 hrs wkly. ■ Robert Valerius, chmn; Peter A. Frid, pres & gen mgr; Myra Lombardo, dev dir & mktg dir; Anita Hebert, sls dir; Marcy Hunter, prom dir; David Srebnik, progmg dir & mus dir; Duncan Lively, news dir; Mike Neibauer, chief engr.

KEYS(AM)—March 1941: 1440 khz; 1 kw-U, DA-N. TL: N27 47 02 W97 27 29. Box 9757 (78469). (512) 882-7411. FAX: (512) 882-9767. Licensee: Malkan Broadcast Associates. Rep: Banner. Format: Oldies. ■ Arnold Malkan, pres; Bryce Taylor, gen mgr; Mirta DeLaFuente, opns mgr; Susan Ludka, gen sls mgr; John Gifford, chief engr.

***KFGG(FM)**—Mar 11, 1991: 88.7 mhz; 5 kw. Ant 856 ft. TL: N27 44 28 W97 36 08. Stereo. Hrs opn: 24. Box 1177 (78403); 410 South Padre Island Dr. (78405). (512) 289-0887. FAX: (512) 289-7719. Licensee: Roloff Evangelistic Enterprises Inc. (acq 10-3-90; $40,000; FTR 10-29-90). Format: Christian. News progmg one hr wkly. Target aud: 35 plus. ■ Alfred Edge, pres; Bobby Glenn, exec vp; Jim Wilken, gen mgr, opns mgr & engrg mgr; Paul Easter, chief engr. ■ Rates: $4; 4; 4; 4.

KLTG(FM)—Listing follows KDAE(AM).

KMXR(FM)—January 1970: 93.9 mhz; 100 kw. Ant 840 ft. TL: N27 46 50 W97 38 03. Stereo. Hrs opn: 24. Box 3489, One Gaslight Sq. (78404). (512) 883-5576. FAX: (512) 883-5329. Licensee: Sparkling City Communications Inc. (acq 12-10-92; $693,000; FTR 1-11-93). Wash atty: Kaye, Scholer, Fierman, Hays & Handler. Format: Adult contemp. News staff one; news progmg 5 hrs wkly. Target aud: 25-54; mainly female upwardly mobile professionals. ■ Bob White, CEO, gen mgr & gen sls mgr; Barry Andrews, pres; Tom Kane, CFO; Lauri Pearson, prom dir; Jesse DeLeon, progmg dir; Jana Shaw, mus dir; Ken Sullivan, news dir; Steve West, chief engr. ■ Rates: $32; 36; 26; 18.

KNCN(FM)—(Sinton). July 1, 1972: 101.3 mhz; 100 kw. Ant 401 ft. TL: N27 55 24 W97 25 26. Stereo. Hrs opn: 24. Box 9781, Corpus Christi (78469); 5544 Leopard St., Corpus Christi (78408). (512) 289-1000. FAX: (512) 289-6228. Licensee: Tippie Communications of CC Inc. Group owner: Tippie Communications Inc. (acq 7-21-82; $610,000; FTR 7-26-82). Rep: Torbet. Wash atty: Bryan, Cave, McPheeters & McRoberts. Format: Rock (AOR). News staff one; news progmg one hr wkly. Target aud: 18-49; active adults. Spec prog: Coastal Bend Forum one hr, In Concert 2 hrs, Crossroads 2 hrs, In the Station one hr, Flashback 2 hrs wkly. ■ Richard M. Delaney, pres & stn mgr; Lynn Blackburn, gen sls mgr; Laura Stewart, prom mgr & news dir; Jamie Wood, adv dir; Tim Parker, progmg dir; Matthew Vaughn, mus dir; Paul Easter, chief engr. ■ Rates: $35; 35; 35; 25.

KOUL(FM)—Listing follows KCTA(AM).

KQTX(FM)—See Portland.

KRYS(AM)—1927: 1360 khz; 1 kw-U. TL: N27 48 01 W97 27 41. Hrs opn: 24. 702 McBride Ln. (78408). (512) 289-0111. FAX: (512) 289-5836. Licensee: Ranger Broadcasting Co. (acq 6-7-93; $3.2 million with co-located FM; FTR 7-5-93). Net: ABC/E, SMN. Rep: Banner. Format: Country, talk. Target aud: 25 plus. Spec prog: Sports. ■ Richard M. Hill, pres; Kent A. Cooper, exec vp; Kent Cooper, gen mgr & gen sls mgr; Rene Bosquez, sls dir; Terry Shannon, prom mgr, progmg mgr & news dir; Fred Hoffman, chief engr.

KRYS-FM—Dec 5, 1982: 99.1 mhz; 100 kw. Ant 1,049 ft. TL: N27 45 07 W97 38 18 (CP: 97 kw). Stereo. Dups AM 100%. ■ Darcy Kane, prom dir; Scott Ward, progmg dir; Glenn Michaels, mus dir; Suzi Camacho, pub affrs dir.

KSIX(AM)—September 1947: 1230 khz; 1 kw-U. TL: N27 48 19 W97 27 15. Stereo. Box TV-10, 301 Artesian (78403). (512) 883-7070. Licensee: Corpus Christi Broadcasting Co. Net: CBS, MBS. Format: News, sports, EZ lstng. ■ Vann M. Kennedy, pres & gen mgr; Vivian L. Mitchell, stn mgr; Walter Furley, news dir; Lester Waters, chief engr. ■ Rates: $21; 17; 21; 11.

KUNO(AM)—May 1950: 1400 khz; 1 kw-U. TL: N27 45 36 W97 26 14. Stereo. Hrs opn: 24. Drawer 4722 (78469); 1301 Horn Rd. (78416). (512) 851-1414. FAX: (512) 851-8409. Licensee: KDOS Inc. Group owner: Tichenor Media System Inc. (acq 2-21-89; $1.2 million; FTR 3-6-89). Net: SIS. Rep: Katz. Wash atty: Cohn & Marks. Format: Sp. News progmg 17 hrs wkly. Target aud: 25-64. ■ Luis A. Munoz, pres & gen mgr; Al Herrera, gen sls mgr & prom mgr; Victor Lara Ortegon, progmg dir; Virginia Costante, mus dir; Robert Mendes, news dir; Fred Hoffman, chief engr.

KWVS(FM)—See Kingsville.

KZFM(FM)—Dec 7, 1964: 95.5 mhz; 100 kw. Ant 994 ft. TL: N27 39 32 W97 34 10. Stereo. Box 9757 (78469). (512) 883-3516. Licensee: Malkan Broadcast Associates. Rep: Banner. Format: Contemp mass appeal. ■ Arnold Malkan, pres; Bryce Taylor, gen mgr; Susan Ludka, gen sls mgr; J.D. Gonzalez, mus dir; Bud Lockhart, news dir; John Gifford, chief engr.

Corsicana

KAND(AM)—May 17, 1937: 1340 khz; 1 kw-U. TL: N32 06 53 W96 27 47. Hrs opn: 5 AM-midnight. 609 W. 7th (75110). (903) 874-7421; (903) 874-1340. FAX: (903) 872-6623. Licensee: Kan-D Land Inc. (acq 6-1-68). Net: ABC/I; Texas State. Format: C&W. News staff one; news progmg 25 hrs wkly. Target aud: General. ■ Richard C. Parker, pres; Bob Belcher, gen mgr & progmg dir; Mike Nekvza, gen sls mgr; Roy Miller, mus dir; Dick Aldama, news dir.

KAND-FM—Nov 1, 1972: 107.9 mhz; 100 kw. Ant 842 ft. TL: N31 55 00 W96 33 24. Stereo. Dups AM 100%.

Crane

KAIR(FM)—Not on air, target date unknown: 101.3 mhz; 50 kw. Ant 328 ft. TL: N31 21 56 W102 20 22. Stereo. Hrs opn: 18. Rt. 6, Box 250, Byhalia, MS (38611); General Delivery (79731). Licensee: Albert L. Crain (acq 6-3-93).

KXOI(AM)—December 1959: 810 khz; 1 kw-D, 500 w-N, DA-1. TL: N31 28 39 W102 20 24. Hrs opn: 6 AM-midnight. Box 2344, Odessa (79760). (915) 332-5964; (915) 332-8058. FAX: (915) 337-2524. Licensee: Hispanic Outreach Ministries Inc. Format: Christian Sp. Target aud: General. ■ Rev. Pedro Emiliano, pres; Eli Emiliano, gen mgr & progmg dir; Don Cook, chief engr.

Crockett

KBHT(FM)—Nov 15, 1982: 93.5 mhz; 50 kw. Ant 479 ft. TL: N31 20 03 W95 47 13. Stereo. Hrs opn: 24. Box 1067, 3rd Floor, Woodworks Bldg., 101 S. Fourth (75835). (409) 544-9350. FAX: (409) 544-9695. Licensee: Nicol Broadcasting Ltd. (acq 9-7-93; $179,000; FTR 9-27-93). Net: CNN; Texas AP. Format: Soft adult contemp, oldies. Target aud: 30-59. Spec prog: Gospel 6 hrs wkly. ■ Tom Nicol, chmn; Lonnie Hunt, pres, gen mgr & gen sls mgr; Suzan Knox, prom mgr; Jim Walker, progmg dir & mus dir; Steve Sandlin, chief engr. ■ Rates: $15; 12; 15; 10.

KIVY(AM)—Jan 19, 1950: 1290 khz; 2.5 kw-D, 175 w-N. TL: N31 18 20 W95 27 06. Box 1109, 129 Radio Ln., Loop 304 (75835). (409) 544-2171; (409) 544-KIVY. FAX: (409) 544-4891. Licensee: James H. Gibbs dba Pioneer Broadcasting. Format: Music of Your Life, golden oldies. News progmg 35 hrs wkly. Target aud: General. ■ James H. Gibbs, pres & gen mgr; Dorothy Corbitt, gen sls mgr; Jim Gibbs, progmg dir. ■ Rates: $8; 8; 8; 8.

KIVY-FM—June 1, 1970: 92.7 mhz; 50 kw. Ant 497 ft. TL: N31 18 18 W95 27 06. Stereo. Dups AM 10%. Format: Country. ■ Rates: $10; 10; 10; 10.

Crystal City

KHER(FM)—Sept 5, 1985: 94.3 mhz; 3 kw. Ant 135 ft. TL: N28 39 57 W99 48 58. Box 743, Big Wells Hwy. (78839). (210) 374-2803; (210) 374-2203. Licensee: Acelga Broadcasting Co. Inc. Group owner: The Herbort Stations. Net: SIS; Texas State Net. Wash atty: Borsari & Paxson. Format: Sp, news/talk. News staff 2; news progmg 19 hrs wkly. Target aud: General; Hispanic population of area. Spec prog: Relg 2 hrs wkly. ■ Noelia Herbort, pres, gen mgr, adv mgr, news dir & pub affrs dir; Manny Martinez (local), vp sls; Manny Martinez, gen sls mgr & vp mktg; Rudy Gomez, progmg dir & progmg mgr; Joe Gragg, chief engr. ■ Rates: $10; 10; 10; 10.

Cuero

KQRO(AM)—Mar 18, 1949: 1600 khz; 500 w-U. TL: N29 04 25 W97 14 20. Hrs opn: 18. Box 864 (77954). (512) 275-3430; (512) 275-9111. FAX: (512) 275-6912. Licensee: Cuero Broadcasting Inc. Net: Texas State. Wash atty: Dominic Monahan. Format: C&W. News progmg 20 hrs wkly. Target aud: General. Spec prog: Sp 5 hrs, gospel 2 hrs, polka 3 hrs wkly. ■ John Bumgardner, CEO, gen mgr & stn mgr; Gayle Schumacker, gen sls mgr; Charles Smithey, chief engr. ■ Rates: $15; 10; 15; 7.50.

KQRO-FM—July 1989: 97.7 mhz; 3 kw. Ant 297 ft. TL: N29 04 25 W97 14 20. Dups AM 100%. U.S. Hwy. 87 S. at Radio Rd. (77954). Format: Country. ■ Rates: Same as AM.

Cypress

KYND(AM)—December 1991: 1520 khz; 3 kw-D, DA. TL: N30 01 36 W95 41 11. Box 19886, Houston (77224-9886); 740 Voss Rd., Houston (77024). (713) 373-1520. FAX: (713) 256-2531. Licensee: Matthew Provenzano. Format: Relg. Target aud: General. ■ Matt Provenzano, CEO.

Daingerfield

KEGG(AM)—August 1966: 1560 khz; 1 kw-D. TL: N33 01 35 W94 42 22. Box 600 (75638-0600). (903) 645-3928. Licensee: Network Communications Co. (acq 2-21-91; $50,000; FTR 3-11-91). Format: Country. News staff one; news progmg 3 hrs wkly. Target aud: General. Spec prog: Farm one hr wkly. ■ Quincy L. Ollison, chmn; Ruth Ollison, gen mgr & gen sls mgr; Vera Lewis, vp opns & pub affrs dir; Jera Lewis, progmg dir.

Dalhart

KXIT(AM)—1948: 1240 khz; 1 kw-U. TL: N36 05 45 W102 30 38. Hrs opn: 6 AM-10 PM. Box 1350 (79022). (806) 249-4747. FAX: (806) 249-6343. Licensee: Dalhart Broadcasters (acq 1953). Net: SMN; Texas Net. Format: Farm, C&W. ■ Robert J. Beller, pres, gen mgr & chief engr; Sheryl Muller, news dir.

KXIT-FM—1962: 95.9 mhz; 3 kw-H. Ant 171 ft. TL: N36 05 45 W102 30 38. Hrs opn: 6 AM-10 PM. Dups AM 70%.

Dallas

KAAM(AM)—1920: 1310 khz; 5 kw-D, 2 kw-N, DA-2. TL: N32 56 41 W96 56 25. Stereo. Suite 1200, 15851 Dallas Pkwy. (75248). (214) 770-7777. FAX: (214) 770-7747. Licensee: Bonneville International Corp. (group owner; acq 1978). Net: MBS. Rep: D & R Radio. Wash atty: Wilkinson, Barker, Knauer & Quinn. Format: Big bands & great singers. Target aud: 50 plus. ■ Thomas S. Glade, vp & gen mgr; Buz Powers, gen sls mgr; David Perez, natl sls mgr; Becky Young, rgnl sls mgr; Jamie Ramsey, prom mgr; Hugh Beavers, progmg dir; Vicki Robbins, pub affrs dir; Hue Beavers, chief engr.

KZPS(FM)—Co-owned with KAAM. Apr 1, 1948: 92.5 mhz; 100 kw. Ant 1,590 ft. TL: N32 35 22 W96 58 10. Stereo. Format: Classic rock. News staff 2. Target aud: Men 25-44; upscale young adults.

KAHZ(AM)—See Fort Worth.

***KCBI-FM**—May 19, 1976: 90.9 mhz; 100 kw. Ant 1,509 ft. TL: N32 35 22 W96 58 10. Stereo. Hrs opn: 24. 411 Ryan Plaza, Arlington (76011). (817) 792-3800. Licensee: Criswell Center Biblical Studies. (group owner). Net: USA. Wash atty: Midlen & Guillot. Format: Inspirational/traditional. News staff one; news progmg 4 hrs wkly. Target aud: 27 plus; Christian families. ■ Dr. Richard Melick, pres; Ronald L. Harris, gen mgr; David Briggs, engrg dir.

KDGE(FM)—(Gainesville). 1958: 94.5 mhz; 100 kw. Ant 1,896 ft. TL: N33 33 36 W96 57 35. Stereo. Hrs opn: 24. Suite 700, 1320 Greenway Dr., Irving (75038). (214) 580-9400. FAX: (214) 580-9450. Licensee: Edge Broadcasting Corp. (acq 6-26-89; $3,300,000; FTR 3-30-92). Rep: Katz & Powell. Wash atty: Gardere & Wynne. Format: Progsv, new rock. News staff one; news progmg one hr wkly. Target aud: 18-44; affluent generation X'ers. ■ Ed Wodka, CEO, pres, mktg dir & prom mgr; Bruce Garver, chmn; Kyle Drake, CFO; Joel Folger, stn mgr, progmg dir & pub affrs dir; Brian Brown, vp sls; Johnny Pegues, natl sls mgr; Alex Luke, mus dir; Andy Pickard, chief engr. ■ Rates: $200; 150; 200; 125.

KDMX(FM)—1965: 102.9 mhz; 99 kw. Ant 1,348 ft. TL: N32 34 54 W96 58 32. Hrs opn: 24. 1353 Regal Row (75247). (214) 688-0641. FAX: (214) 688-1029. Licensee: Nationwide Communications Inc. Group owner: Nationwide Mutual Insurance Co. (acq 2-13-91; grpsl; FTR 3-11-91). Format: Adult contemp. News progmg 3 hrs wkly. Target aud: 25-49; upper income females. ■ Chris McMurray, gen mgr; Marilyn Massucci, gen sls mgr; Tammy Bembenek, mktg dir; Pat McMahon, progmg dir; Steve Knoll, mus dir; Tammara Gant, pub affrs dir; John Adcock, chief engr.

KEGL(FM)—See Fort Worth.

***KERA(FM)**—July 11, 1974: 90.1 mhz; 95 kw. Ant 1,260 ft. TL: N32 34 43 W96 57 12. Stereo. 3000 Harry Hines Blvd. (75201). (214) 871-1390. FAX: (214) 754-0635. Licensee: North Texas Public Broadcasting. Net: NPR, APR. Format: Progsv, news/talk. ■ Richard J. Meyer, pres; Mark Boardian, stn mgr; Don Boswell, vp sls; Bobbi Wedlan, vp prom; Jeff Luchsinger, progmg dir; Jeff McCehan, news dir; John Allison, chief engr.

KESS(AM)—See Fort Worth.

KFJZ(AM)—See Fort Worth.

KGBS(AM)—1947: 1190 khz; 50 kw-D, 5 kw-N, DA-2. TL: N32 47 10 W96 57 00. Suite 1470, 3500 Maple at Turtle Creek (75219-3906). (214) 526-2580. Licensee: Greystone D/M L.P. (acq 10-24-91; $71,500; FTR 11-11-91). Net: NBC, NBC Talknet. Rep: Eastman. Format: Talk. ■ Don Walker, gen mgr; Vicki Knight, gen sls mgr;

Dan Bennett, progmg dir; Steve Mace, news dir; Norm Philips, chief engr.

KGGR(AM)—June 8, 1947: 1040 khz; 1 kw-D. TL: N32 46 45 W96 43 49. 3929 S. Polk (75224). (214) 372-9000. Licensee: C2M Inc. (acq 10-26-93; $605,250; FTR 11-8-93). Format: Relg, talk. Target aud: 18 plus. ■ Brother Alvin McCottry, CEO; Don Evans, progmg dir & mus dir; Cris Alexander, chief engr.

KHKS(FM)—See Denton.

KHVN(AM)—See Fort Worth.

KJMZ(FM)—Dec 25, 1965: 100.3 mhz; 100 kw. Ant 1,280 ft. TL: N32 35 07 W96 58 06. 17th Fl., 545 E. John Carpenter Fwy., Irving (75062). (214) 556-8100. FAX: (214) 988-1003. Licensee: Summit-Dallas Broadcasting Corp. Group owner: Summit Communications Group Inc. Rep: McGavren Guild. Format: Urban contemp. News staff one. Target aud: 18-49. ■ James Wesley, CEO; Mary Catherine Sneed, exec vp; Howard Tooele, vp & gen mgr; Steven Giles, stn mgr & natl sls mgr; Debbie Kessler, mktg dir; Tom Casey, progmg dir; Sandra Daniels, news dir; Ken Fine, chief engr.

KKDA(AM)—See Grand Prairie.

KKDA-FM—June 8, 1947: 104.5 mhz; 100 kw. Ant 1,585 ft. TL: N32 35 22 W96 58 10. Stereo. Box 530860, Grand Prairie (75053). (214) 263-9911. FAX: (214) 558-0010. Licensee: Service Broadcast Group (acq 5-76). Net: AP. Format: Urban contemp. ■ Hymen Childs, pres & gen mgr; Ken Johnson, gen sls mgr; Julia Atherton, prom mgr; Michael Spears, progmg dir; Norman Hall, news dir; Gerry Dalton, chief engr.

KLIF(AM)—June 26, 1922: 570 khz; 5 kw-U, DA-2. TL: N32 56 40 W96 59 25. Suite 1600, 3500 Maple Ave. (75219). (214) 526-2400. Licensee: KLIF Co. Group owner: Susquehanna Radio Corp. (acq 12-15-89). Net: NBC. Rep: Eastman/Intermountain Net. Format: Talk. Target aud: 25-54; men. ■ Larry Grogan, exec vp & sr vp; Dan Halyburton, vp & gen mgr; Mike Wade, progmg dir.

KLTY(FM)—See Fort Worth.

KLUV(FM)—1961: 98.7 mhz; 98 kw. Ant 1,584 ft. TL: N32 35 22 W96 58 10. Stereo. Suite 700, 4131 N. Central Expwy. (75204). (214) 826-9870. FAX: (214) 827-4365. Licensee: TK Communications Inc. (group owner; acq 10-27-82; $8.5 million; FTR 11-15-82). Rep: Major Mkt. Format: Oldies. News staff 2. Target aud: 35-44. ■ Bob Reich, pres; Dave Siebert, gen mgr; Olivia Lawrence, gen sls mgr; Shari Hanrahan, prom mgr; Chuck Brinkman, progmg dir; Jay Cresswell, mus dir; Kate Garvin, news dir; John Gaeta, chief engr.

KMRT(AM)—1952: 1480 khz; 5 kw-D, 1.9 kw-N, DA-2. TL: N32 39 42 W96 39 20. Suite 2000, 5956 Sherry Ln. (75225). (214) 691-1075. FAX: (214) 368-1075. Licensee: GCI Dallas II. Group owner: Granum Communications Inc. (acq 1-30-92; with KCDU(FM) Fort Worth). Net: Unistar, CNN. Rep: Christal. Format: New adult contemp, smooth jazz. News staff one; news progmg 14 hrs wkly. Target aud: 45-64; mature, upscale. ■ Herb McCord, pres; Skip Schmidt, gen mgr; Beth Davis, gen sls mgr; Kimberly Morgan, prom dir; Paul Goldstein, progmg dir; Rose Wright, news dir & pub affrs dir; Vance Henley, chief engr.

***KNON(FM)**—Aug 29, 1975: 89.3 mhz; 55 kw. Ant 850 ft. TL: N32 35 24 W96 58 21. Stereo. Box 710909 (75371). (214) 828-9500. Licensee: Agape Broadcasting Foundation Inc. Format: Community info, alt mus. ■ Rita Webb, progmg dir; Mike Doyal, chief engr.

KOAI(FM)—See Fort Worth.

KPBC(AM)—(Garland). 1990: 770 khz; 10 kw-D, 1 kw-N, DA-2. TL: N33 01 58 W96 34 31. Stereo. Box 561307, Dallas (75356); 3201 Royalty Row, Irving (75062). (214) 445-1700. FAX: (214) 438-6574. Licensee: Crawford Broadcasting Co. (group owner; acq 1979). Format: Christian country. Target aud: 25 plus; Christian adults. ■ Donald B. Crawford, pres; Paul Niven, gen mgr; Don Evans, progmg dir & mus dir; Cris Alexander, chief engr.

KPLX(FM)—See Fort Worth.

KRLD(AM)—October 1926: 1080 khz; 50 kw-U, DA-N. TL: N32 53 25 W96 38 44. 1080 Metromedia Pl. (75247). (214) 634-1080. FAX: (214) 637-3843. Licensee: Legacy Broadcasting Partnership II. Group owner: SFX Broadcasting Inc. (acq 3-20-91; grpsl; FTR 4-8-91). Net: CBS; Texas Net. Rep: Katz. Format: News, sports. News staff 39; news progmg 119 hrs wkly. Target aud: 25-54. ■ Charles Seraphin, gen mgr; Jerry Bolo, gen sls mgr; Tina Nelson, progmg dir; Eric Disen, chief engr.

KRRW(FM)—1965: 97.9 mhz; 99 kw. Ant 1,611 ft. TL: N32 35 15 W96 57 59. Stereo. Suite 1200, 4131 North Central Expressway (75204). (214) 528-5500. FAX: (214) 528-4314. Licensee: CBS Radio Network (acq 8-16-93). Rep: Katz. Format: All Rock & Roll oldies. ■ Clint Culp, vp & gen mgr; Bob Saunders, sls dir; Tim Trostle, mktg dir; Andy Lockridge, progmg dir; Neil Peden, chief engr.

***KRSM(FM)**—1975: 93.3 mhz; 33 w-H. Ant 148 ft. TL: N32 53 24 W96 48 03. 10600 Preston Rd. (75230). (214) 363-6491, ext. 151 & 139. Licensee: St. Mark's School of Texas. Format: Educ, AOR. ■ Mia Squilla, gen mgr; Josh Einsohn, mus dir; Gray Kinnay, chief engr.

KRVA(AM)—(Cockrell Hill). Sept 29, 1947: 1600 khz; 5 kw-D, 1 kw-N, DA-2. TL: N32 44 25 W96 42 38. Suite 1310, 3500 Maple Ave., Dallas (75219). (214) 528-1600. Licensee: Radio Plano Inc. (acq 3-27-90). Rep: Caballero. Wash atty: Cohn & Marks. Format: Spanish. News staff one. Target aud: General; 2nd & 3rd generation Hispanics. ■ Tony Rodriquez, pres; Jorge Infant Sr., gen mgr & natl sls mgr; Fernando Gonzalez, sls dir; Florentino Garcia, progmg dir, mus dir & news dir; George Whitaker, chief engr.

KSKY(AM)—(Balch Springs). Sept 30, 1941: 660 khz; 10 kw-D, 500 w-N, DA-N. TL: N29 22 51 W95 14 15. Suite 266, 4144 N. Central Expwy., Dallas (75204-2102). (214) 827-5759. FAX: (214) 827-7983. Licensee: Broadcasting Partners of Dallas (acq 10-13-88; grpsl; FTR 6-20-88). Wash atty: Levanthal, Senter & Lerman. Format: Relg, Black, sports. New progmg one hr wky. Target aud: 25-55. Spec prog: High school, college and pro sports 14 hrs wkly. ■ Perry L. Lewis, chmn; Bary Mayo, pres; Nathan W. Pearson Jr., CFO; Bill Simmons, gen mgr; Kathie Watson, gen sls mgr; Kathie Watson (local), natl sls mgr; Freda Wells, progmg dir; Dick Cox, news dir; Mike Van Hooser, engrg dir; Mike Vanhooser, chief engr.

KSNN(FM)—(Arlington). April 1949: 94.9 mhz; 100 kw. Ant 1,699 ft. TL: N32 35 22 W96 58 10. Stereo. Hrs opn: 24. c/o KYNG(FM), 12201 Merit Dr. #930, Dallas (75251). (214) 716-7800. FAX: (214) 716-7835. Licensee: Armadillo Broadcasting LP. Group owner: Alliance Broadcasting (acq 1993; FTR 9-6-93). Rep: Group W. Wash atty: Mintz, Levin, Cohn, Ferris, Glovsky & Popeo. Format: Country. News staff one; news progmg 3 hrs wkly. Target aud: 35-54. ■ John Hayes Jr., CEO & pres; Scott Savage, gen mgr; Ginger Keas (local), gen sls mgr; Lee Ann Longinotti, natl sls mgr; Christy Kelly, prom mgr; Dan Pearman, progmg dir; Mike Easterlin, mus dir; Joe Holstead, news dir; Bob Henke, chief engr.

KTXQ(FM)—See Fort Worth.

KVIL(AM)—See Highland Park.

KVIL-FM—See Highland Park.

***KVTT(FM)**—Jan 26, 1950: 91.7 mhz; 100 kw. Ant 786 ft. TL: N32 35 24 W96 58 21. Stereo. 11061 Shady Trail (75229). (214) 351-6655. Licensee: Research Educational Foundation (acq 3-29-76). Format: Relg, talk, educ. Spec prog: Sp 2 hrs, Korean 2 hrs, Vietnamese one hr, Cambodian one hr, Black 2 hrs wkly. ■ Stanley Thomas, pres; Raye Nell Thomas, gen mgr; Brandon Donnel, stn mgr; Devin Whickham, progmg dir; Todd Loney, chief engr.

KYNG(FM)—Apr 5, 1968: 105.3 mhz; 100 kw. Ant 1,558 ft. TL: N32 35 07 W96 58 06. Stereo. Hrs opn: 24. 12201 Merit Dr., #930 (75251). (214) 716-7800. FAX: (214) 716-7835. Licensee: Alliance Broadcasting Dallas L.P. Group owner: Alliance Broadcasting (acq 12-19-91; $11 million; FTR 1-13-92). Rep: Group W. Wash atty: Mintz, Levin, Cohn, Ferris, Glovsky & Popeo, P.C. Format: Young country. News staff one; news progmg 3 hrs wkly. Target aud: 18-44. ■ John Hayes Jr., CEO & pres; Scott Savage, gen mgr; Lee Ann Longinotti, natl sls mgr; Ginger Keas (local), rgnl sls mgr; Christy Kelly, prom mgr; Dan Pearman, progmg dir; Toni Trueblood, news dir; Bob Henke, chief engr.

KZPS(FM)—Listing follows KAAM.

WBAP(AM)—See Fort Worth.

WRR(FM)—1948: 101.1 mhz; 100 kw. Ant 1,510 ft. TL: N32 35 22 W96 58 10. Stereo. Hrs opn: 24. Box 159001 (75315-9001). (214) 670-8888. FAX: (214) 670-8394. Licensee: City of Dallas. Net: AP. Rep: CMBS. Wash atty: Kaye, Scholer, Fierman, Hays & Handles. Format: Classical. Target aud: 25-54; upscale. ■ Maurice Lowenthal, gen mgr; Mary Lou Rodriguez, stn mgr; Sue Swiggart, gen sls mgr; Bob Barbee, prom mgr; Kevin Connell, progmg dir; Jim Rhodes, chief engr.

Del Rio

KDLK(FM)—Listing follows KLKE(AM).

KLKE(AM)—1947: 1230 khz; 1 kw-U. TL: N29 25 46 W100 54 10. Hrs opn: 24. Box 1489, 107 Center Dr. (78841). (210) 775-9583. FAX: (210) 774-4009. Licensee: Forum Broadcasting (acq 10-22-76). Net: CNN. Format: Modern Country. News progmg 60 hrs wkly. Target aud: 25-54. ■ Larry Mariner, vp & gen mgr; Dave Allyn, prom mgr, progmg dir & mus dir; Dough Morin, chief engr.

KDLK(FM)—Co-owned with KLKE(AM). Aug 15, 1966: 94.3 mhz; 2.65 kw. Ant 200 ft. TL: N29 25 46 W100 54 18. Stereo. Prog sep from AM. Format: Adult contemp.

KTDR(FM)—Mar 31, 1986: 96.3 mhz; 100 kw. Ant 490 ft. TL: N29 32 25 W101 07 21. Stereo. Hrs opn: 24. Box 420848, 307 E. 8th St. (78842). (210) 775-6291; (210) 774-3696. FAX: (210) 775-6545. Licensee: Grande Broadcasting of Del Rio Inc. Net: ABC/FM. Wash atty: Harry Sells. Format: CHR, Sp. News staff one; news progmg 25 hrs wkly. Target aud: 18 plus. Spec prog: Relg 2 hrs wkly. ■ Dr. Alfredo Guiterrez, pres; Ginny McKnight, gen mgr; Roy Lombard, opns dir; Dave Daniels, dev mgr; Kevin Bass, gen sls mgr; Jaime Monzon, prom mgr; Melissa Ann, progmg dir; Frank Mendoza, news dir; Manny Gonzales, chief engr. ■ Rates: $16.50; 12.50; 18.50; 12.50.

KWMC(AM)—Aug 20, 1967: 1490 khz; 1 kw-U. TL: N29 22 17 W100 51 55. Hrs opn: 24. 903 E. Cortinas St. (78840); Box 1408 (78841-1408). (210) 775-3544. FAX: (210) 775-3546. Licensee: Faz Broadcasting Inc. (acq 7-4-88; $375,000; FTR 10-31-88). Net: SMN; Texas State Net. Format: C&W. News staff 2. Spec prog: Relg 5 hrs wkly. ■ Ramiro Faz, pres, gen mgr & progmg dir; Carlos Faz, stn mgr, opns mgr & gen sls mgr; Jim Weed, news dir; Alfredo Garza, chief engr. ■ Rates: $10; 8.50; 10; 7.

Del Valle

KIXL(AM)—Licensed to Del Valle. See Austin.

Denison

KJIM(AM)—See Sherman.

KTCY(FM)—Oct 17, 1983: 104.9 mhz; 50 kw. Ant 492 ft. TL: N33 42 10 W96 34 05. Stereo. Box 116780 (75011-6780). Licensee: Davis Family Trust (acq 10-20-92; $227,500; FTR 11-23-92). ■ Mark Manafo, pres; Sandi Davidson, gen mgr & gen sls mgr; Martha Hurd, progmg dir; Dick Wheeler, news dir; Ken Wilson, chief engr.

Denison-Sherman

KDSX(AM)—Sept 26, 1948: 950 khz; 500 w-U, DA-2. TL: N33 41 08 W96 32 28. 318 W. Chesnut, Sherman (75020). (903) 465-1600. FAX: (903) 463-3162. Licensee: Octavian Communications Corp. (acq 6-2-93; $350,000 with co-located FM; FTR 6-21-93). Net: ABC/C, ABC/E, ABC/I. Rep: Riley. Format: C&W. Spec prog: Sports 10 hrs wkly. ■ Charles Davis, pres; Mike Bradley, gen mgr & gen sls mgr; David Anderson, chief engr.

KDSQ(FM)—Co-owned with KDSX(AM). June 29, 1967: 101.7 mhz; 3 kw. Ant 276 ft. TL: N33 41 08 W96 32 28 (CP: 17.6 kw, ant 384 ft. TL: N33 38 11 W96 41 57). Stereo. Dups AM 100%.

Denton

KDNT(AM)—1938: 1440 khz; 5 kw-D, 500 w-N, DA-N. TL: N33 09 45 W97 06 18. 1440 Wheeler Dr. (76205). (817) 382-2552. FAX: (817) 383-1492. Licensee: Rodriguez Broadcasting. Net: ABC, Sun, Daynet, American; Texas State. Rep: Dean R. Minnick. Format: News, talk. News staff 2; news progmg 40 hrs wkly. Target aud: 25 plus. ■ Galen O. Gilbert, pres; Dean R. Minnick, exec vp, gen mgr, stn mgr, gen sls mgr & vp mktg; Dale Olson, opns mgr; Paul Jackson, news dir; Hal Whatley, chief engr. ■ Rates: $50; 50; 50; 50.

KDZR(FM)—September 1988: 99.1 mhz; 97 kw. Ant 1,168 ft. TL: N33 23 22 W97 33 53. Stereo. Hrs opn: 24. One Metro Sq., #205, 2655 Villa Creek Dr., Dallas (75234). (214) 406-1991. FAX: (214) 247-3962. Licensee: Broadcast House Inc. of Texas (acq 8-89; $6 million). Net: MBS. Format: Hard rock. News staff one; news progmg one hr wkly. Target aud: 25-54; affluent/educated adults. ■ Mike Scott, gen mgr; David Hynson, gen sls mgr; Mike Bass, progmg dir; Tommy Olcott, mus dir.

KHKS(FM)—1947: 106.1 mhz; 100 kw. Ant 1,584 ft. TL: N32 35 22 W96 58 10. Stereo. Suite 2000, 5659 Sherry Ln., Dallas (75225). (214) 691-1075. FAX: (214) 368-

1075. Licensee: Gannett Texas Broadcasting Inc. Group owner: Gannett Broadcasting (acq 1-2-86). Rep: D & R Radio. Wash atty: Reed, Smith, Shaw & McClay. Format: Jazz, new age. News staff one; news progmg 5 hrs wkly. Target aud: 25-54. Spec prog: Dow Jones Report.

***KNTU(FM)**—November 1969: 88.1 mhz; 100 kw. Ant 442 ft. TL: N33 17 24 W97 08 11 Stereo. Hrs opn: 6 AM-midnight. Box 13585 (76203); Smith Hall, UNT, 1105 W. Mulberry (76201). (817) 565-3459; (817) 565-3688. FAX: (817) 565-2518. Licensee: University of North Texas. Net: Texas State. Format: Class, jazz. News progmg 8 hrs wkly. Target aud: 18 plus. Spec prog: Class 14 hrs, Sp 6 hrs, new music 2 hrs, public affairs 9 hrs wkly. ■ Samuel J. Sauls, gen mgr; Russ Campbell, gen sls mgr & news dir; Frank Bonner, chief engr.

Devine

KTXX(FM)—Nov 17, 1982: 92.1 mhz; 3 kw. Ant 299 ft. TL: N29 07 58 W98 59 10. Stereo. Box 635 (78016). (210) 663-4456. FAX: (210) 663-5943. Licensee: Hamon Broadcasting Corp. Format: Country. Spec prog: Relg 18 hrs wkly. ■ Khan Hamon, gen mgr & stn mgr; Mike Carr, gen sls mgr, progmg dir & news dir; Jay Fletcher, chief engr.

Diboll

KAFX(AM)—Licensed to Diboll. See Lufkin.

KAFX-FM—Licensed to Diboll. See Lufkin.

Dimmitt

KDHN(AM)—Dec 22, 1963: 1470 khz; 500 w-D, 149 w-N. TL: N34 35 11 W102 18 35. 704 W. Cleveland, N. Hwy. 385 (79027). (806) 647-4161. Licensee: Collins Communications Co. (acq 12-12-84). Format: C&W, farm. News staff 2; news progmg 12 hrs wkly. Target aud: General. Spec prog: Sp 17 hrs wkly. ■ Wayne Collins, pres, gen mgr, news dir & chief engr; Terry Todd, vp sls & progmg dir.

KDIU(FM)—Co-owned with KDHN(AM). January 1992: 95.9 mhz; 3 kw. Ant 152 ft. TL: N34 35 11 W102 18 35. Dups AM 100%. ■ Terry Todd, sls dir.

Dumas

KDDD(AM)—May 1, 1948: 800 khz; 250 w-D. TL: N35 51 42 W101 55 50. Hrs opn: 6 AM-sundown. Box 555, 408 N. Dumas Ave. (79029). (806) 935-4141. FAX: (806) 935-3836. Licensee: Xtra Cattle Co. Inc. (acq 3-20-91; $350,000 with co-located FM; FTR 4-8-91). Net: ABC/I. Format: C&W. News staff one; news progmg 30 hrs wkly. Target aud: General; adult, hometown. Spec prog: Sp 16 hrs wkly. ■ Phil Haaland, pres; Dick Hoff, gen mgr & gen sls mgr; Forrest Green, chief engr. ■ Rates: $12; 10; 12; na.

KMRE(FM)—Co-owned with KDDD(AM). June 29, 1960: 95.3 mhz; 3 kw. Ant 260 ft. TL: N35 51 51 W101 55 45. Stereo. Dups AM 100%.

Eagle Pass

KEPS(AM)—August 1957: 1270 khz; 1 kw-D. TL: N28 43 45 W100 29 30. Box 1123, 127 Kilowatt Dr. (78852). (210) 773-9247. FAX: (210) 773-9500. Licensee: Eagle Pass Broadcasters Inc. (acq 8-1-64). Rep: Locust. Format: Tejano (Sp). News staff one. Target aud: 18-49; middle income, Texas-born Hispanics. ■ Bob Kitchmille, gen mgr; Rosa Delagarca, gen sls mgr; Jose Luis Borgas, news dir; Arturo Travino, chief engr.

KINL(FM)—Co-owned with KEPS(AM). Nov 2, 1971: 92.7 mhz; 3 kw. Ant 255 ft. TL: N28 43 45 W100 29 30. Stereo. Prog sep from AM. Format: C&W.

***KEPX(FM)**—Not on air, target date unknown: 89.5 mhz; 100 kw. Ant 187 ft. Box 3333, McAllen (78502). Licensee: World Radio Network Inc.

KINL(FM)—Listing follows KEPS(AM).

Eastland

KEAS(AM)—August 1953: 1590 khz; 500 w-D. TL: N32 23 47 W98 46 26. Box 590, 306 S. Seamen (76448). (817) 629-2621; (817) 629-8462. Licensee: WDS Broadcasting Co. (acq 1986; $225,000; FTR 3-17-86). Net: Moody. Format: Country. News staff 3; news progmg 8 hrs wkly. Target aud: 35-60; older audience. Spec prog: Gospel 6 hrs wkly. ■ Dan Staggs, pres, gen mgr & gen sls mgr; Mike Cockburn, prom mgr & news dir; Dobie Staggs, progmg dir; Davie Staggs, mus dir; Jim Stanford, chief engr.

KEAS-FM—Sept 1, 1986: 97.7 mhz; 3 kw. Ant 156 ft. TL: N32 23 47 W98 46 26. Stereo. Dups AM 100%.

KVMX(FM)—Nov 1, 1981: 96.7 mhz; 2.85 kw. Ant 306 ft. TL: N32 28 34 W98 50 20. Stereo. Hrs opn: 24. Box 550, 2010 W. Commerce (76448). (817) 629-8585. FAX: (817) 629-8935. Licensee: Luck Broadcasting Co. (acq 6-1-93; $100,000; FTR 7-19-93). Net: ABC/E. Rep: Riley. Format: Lite adult contemp. Target aud: General. ■ John E. Conner, pres; Elmer Luck, exec vp, gen mgr, stn mgr, vp prom & mus dir; Jeannette Luck, sr vp, progmg dir & pub affrs dir; Kenneth Luck, vp sls & news dir; Gary Smith, vp engrg. ■ Rates: $8.50; 7.50; 8.50; 5.

Edinburg

KBFM(FM)—February 1972: 104.1 mhz; 100 kw. Ant 990 ft. TL: N26 05 59 W97 50 16. Stereo. Box 3764, McAllen (78501). (512) 383-4961. Licensee: May Communications Inc. (acq 7-15-91; $3.5 million). Net: ABC/FM. Rep: D & R Radio. Format: CHR. News staff one; news progmg 2 hrs wkly. Target aud: 18-34; adult females. Spec prog: Community affairs. ■ Phil Giordano, pres; Jeffrey Hedgemon, vp & gen mgr; J.D. Gonzalez, opns mgr; Cynthia M. Ramos, gen sls mgr; Gary Rodriguez, prom mgr & news dir; Billy Santiago, progmg dir; Jackie Lin, mus dir; Paul Easter, chief engr. ■ Rates: $40; 35; 40; 35.

***KOIR(FM)**—Feb 5, 1983: 88.5 mhz; 3 kw. Ant 285 ft. TL: N26 07 49 W98 10 51. Stereo. Hrs opn: 5:45 AM-midnight. 4300 S. Business 281 (78539). (210) 383-3845. Licensee: Rio Grande Bible Institute Inc. Wash atty: Bryan, Cave, McPheeters & McRoberts. Format: Relg, educ, Sp. Target aud: General. ■ Gordon E. Johnson, pres; Javier Salinas, gen mgr & progmg dir; Don L. DeMonbrun, opns mgr; Jerry Jeske, chief engr.

KURV(AM)—October 1947: 710 khz; 1 kw-U, DA-2. TL: N26 19 43 W98 09 35. Hrs opn: 24. 2921 N. Closner (78539). (512) 383-2777. Licensee: Voice of Valley Agriculture (acq 1984; $1 million). Net: CBS, ABC TalkRadio; TSN. Wash atty: Wray Fitch. Format: Talk, news, sports. News staff 2; news progmg 30 hrs wkly. Target aud: 35-64. Spec prog: Farm 14 hrs wkly. ■ Davis Rankin, pres; Lance Hawkins, vp & gen mgr; Casey Hales, opns dir; Jane Smith, sls dir; Tom Vinger, progmg dir & news dir; Ken Meek, chief engr. ■ Rates: $52; 31; 33; 24.

KVLY(FM)—1974: 107.9 mhz; 100 kw. Ant 765 ft. TL: N26 15 01 W97 55 21. Stereo. 3307 S. Hwy. 281 (78539); Box 850 (78540). (210) 383-7478. FAX: (210) 380-1207. Licensee: Tippie Communications Inc. (group owner; acq 11-1-79). Rep: Torbet. Format: Adult contemp. Target aud: 25-54. ■ Henry B. Tippie, pres; Bob Scott, stn mgr; Kevin McRae, gen sls mgr; John Hagle, prom dir; Del Shaw, progmg dir; Jerry Jeske, chief engr.

Edna

KTMR(AM)—July 28, 1980: 1130 khz; 10 kw-D, DA. TL: N29 01 40 W96 40 05. Box 188 (77957). (512) 782-7133. Licensee: HZ Broadcasting Inc. Net: SIS. Rep: Caballero. Format: Sp. News staff one. Spec prog: Black 3 hrs, Sp 12 hrs wkly. ■ Johnny Francis, gen mgr & gen sls mgr; Joel Hernandez, progmg dir; Juan Francisco, news dir; Paul Easter, chief engr.

El Campo

KIOX-FM—September 1968: 96.9 mhz; 50 kw. Ant 420 ft. TL: N29 05 44 W96 27 25 (CP: 100 kw, ant 981 ft. TL: N28 53 35 W96 21 40). Box 2340, Bay City (77404). (409) 245-4642. FAX: (409) 245-6463. Licensee: North Star Communications Inc. (acq 3-30-90; $375,000; FTR 4-23-90). Format: Hot country. ■ Hal Kemp, gen mgr.

KULP(AM)—1948: 1390 khz; 500 w-D, 180 w-N. TL: N29 12 34 W96 15 50. Hrs opn: 6 AM-10 PM. Box 390 (77437). (409) 543-3303. FAX: (409) 543-0097. Licensee: Bar B Broadcasting Inc. (acq 7-1-68). Net: MBS. Rep: Jack Riley & Assoc. Format: Community radio. Target aud: 25 plus. Spec prog: Sp 14 hrs, Czech 5 hrs wkly. ■ Fred V. Barbee Jr., pres; Jerry Aulds, gen mgr; Paul Wright, opns mgr; Clint Robinson, mus dir; Al Kozel, news dir; Joe Miller, chief engr.

El Paso

KAMA(AM)—July 13, 1972: 750 khz; 10 kw-D, 1 kw-N, DA-1. TL: N31 46 21 W106 16 56. Hrs opn: 24. Suite 120, 4150 Pinnacle (79902). (915) 544-7600. FAX: (915) 532-0947. Licensee: Ballston Trust Services L.C. Group owner: Pinnacle Broadcasting Co. (acq 12-22-92; grpsl; FTR 1-18-93). Net: CNN. Rep: Caballero. Wash atty: Wilmer, Cutler & Pickering. Format: Sp. News staff one; news progmg 8 hrs wkly. Target aud: 25-54; women. ■ Phil Marella, pres; Ed Ferreri, CFO; Greg Heitzman, gen mgr; Bob Kennedy, opns mgr; Joe Torres, gen sls mgr; Carlos Teran, progmg dir; Terry Bustillos, mus dir; Jose Luis Torres, news dir; Cliff Gibson, chief engr. ■ Rates: $70; 60; 60; 50.

KAMZ(FM)—Co-owned with KAMA. Dec 30, 1975: 93.1 mhz; 100 kw. Ant 1,422 ft. TL: N31 47 34 W106 28 47. Stereo. Hrs opn: 24. Prog sep from AM. Net: Unistar. Rep: Eastman. Format: Classic rock. News staff one; news progmg 2 hrs wkly. Target aud: 25-54; 60% male, 40% female. ■ Pat Tepsick, gen sls mgr. ■ Rates: $75; 70; 60; 50.

KBNA(AM)—June 1947: 920 khz; 1 kw-D, 360 w-N, DA-N. TL: N31 45 41 W106 26 14. Suite 300 S., 2211 E. Missouri (79903). (915) 544-9797. FAX: (915) 544-1247. Licensee: Tichenor Media System Inc. (group owner; acq 10-31-85; $1.3 million with co-located FM; FTR 9-2-85). Rep: Katz Hispanic. Format: Sp. News staff one; news progmg 5 hrs wkly. ■ MacHenry Tichenor Jr., pres; Dan Wilson, gen mgr; Kathy Clark, gen sls mgr; Jose Luis Garcia, prom mgr; Pedro Skaggs, progmg dir & mus dir; Carlos Tarango, news dir; David L. Stewart, chief engr.

KBNA-FM—Aug 15, 1969: 97.5 mhz; 100 kw h, 48 kw v. Ant 1,088 ft. TL: N31 47 34 W106 28 47. Stereo. Dups AM 100%.

KELP(AM)—Apr 10, 1959: 1590 khz; 5 kw-D, 800 w-N. TL: N31 46 12 W106 25 37 (CP: TL: N31 44 38 W106 23 45). 6900 Commerce (79915). (915) 779-0016. Licensee: McClatchey Broadcasting (acq 2-14-84; $590,000; FTR 1-30-84). Format: Relg, Sp. Target aud: 25-54. ■ Arnie McClatchey, pres & gen mgr; Gary Rabah, progmg dir; Ron Haney, engrg dir.

KFNA(AM)—Sept 16, 1985: 1060 khz; 10 kw-D. TL: N31 48 41 W106 31 53. 3312 Bosham Dr. (79925-3002). (915) 833-1338. Licensee: K-Fina Results Inc. (acq 2-4-91; $100,000; FTR 2-18-91). Format: Sp, fine romantic mus. ■ Roberta Corral, gen mgr; Jose Martinez, news dir; Bruce Crow, chief engr.

KHEY(AM)—1947: 690 khz; 10 kw-U, DA-2. TL: N31 58 11 W106 21 15. Stereo. 2419 N. Piedras St. (79930). (915) 566-9301. FAX: (915) 566-0928. Licensee: U.S. Radio L.P. (group owner; acq 3-5-90; $8,425,000 with co-located fm; FTR 3-19-90). Net: ABC/I. Rep: Katz. Format: C&W. Spec prog: Farm 6 hrs wkly. ■ Rob Burton, vp & gen mgr; Joyce Marshall, gen sls mgr; Kim Gabbard, prom dir; Jim Hayes, progmg dir; John Hunter, mus dir; Sharon Bowman, news dir; Kevin Jenkins, chief engr.

KHEY-FM—Aug 1, 1974: 96.3 mhz; 100 kw. Ant 1,390 ft. TL: N31 47 47 W106 28 55. Stereo. Dups AM 100%.

KINT-FM—Listing follows KSVE(AM).

KLAQ(FM)—Listing follows KROD(AM).

KOFX(FM)—June 6, 1978: 92.3 mhz; 100 kw. Ant 1,860 ft. TL: N31 48 55 W106 29 20. Stereo. Hrs opn: 24. Suite 31-C, 5411 N. Mesa (79912). (915) 581-6663. FAX: (915) 581-0155. Licensee: ELP Broadcasting Associates L.P. (acq 8-25-86; $1 million; FTR 7-7-86). Net: Unistar. Rep: McGavren Guild. Wash atty: Dow, Lohnes & Albertson. Format: Adult contemp, classic hits. Target aud: 25-54; upscale. ■ Les Roberson, gen mgr; Leslie M. Morris, stn mgr; Denny Luell opns mgr & prom mgr; Doug Moser, gen sls mgr; Leslie M. Morris, natl sls mgr; Mike Preston, progmg dir & mus dir; Ron Haney, chief engr.

KPAS(FM)—See Fabens.

KPRR(FM)—Dec 5, 1969: 102.1 mhz; 100 kw. Ant 1,190 ft. TL: N31 47 34 W106 28 47. Stereo. Suite 216, 444 Executive Ctr. Blvd. (79902). (915) 532-6515. Licensee: Transcontinental Broadcasting Co. Group owner: Baton Rouge Broadcasting Co., Transcontinental Broadcasting Co. and WLIN Inc. (acq 8-11-86; $1.25 million; FTR 6-23-86). Rep: D&R Radio. Wash atty: Cohn & Marks. Format: CHR. ■ John Candelaria, vp & mus dir; Natalie Estrada (admin), gen mgr; John Lansdale, gen sls mgr; Shon Hodgkinson, progmg dir; Ed Miles, chief engr. ■ Rates: $80; 75; 75; 50.

KROD(AM)—June 1, 1940: 600 khz; 5 kw-U, DA-N. TL: N31 54 56 W106 23 33. Hrs opn: 24. Suite 120, 4141 Pinnacle (79902). (915) 544-8864. FAX: (915) 532-6342. Licensee: D & F Broadcasting (acq 3-89). Net: Texas State Net. Rep: D & R Radio. Format: Talk. News staff one; news progmg 3 hrs wkly. Target aud: 25-54; adult listeners who grew up on the roots of rock n' roll. Spec prog: Dallas Cowboys football, UTEP sports. ■ Charles Cohn, CEO; Brad Dubow, gen mgr; Will Douglas, opns mgr; Sheila Diamond, sls dir; Courtney Nelson, progmg dir; Ron Haney, chief engr. ■ Rates: $25; 25; 25; 15.

KLAQ(FM)—Co-owned with KROD(AM). Oct 1, 1978: 95.5 mhz; 88 kw. Ant 1,390 ft. TL: N31 47 47 W106 28 55. Stereo. Prog sep from AM. Format: AOR. Target aud: 18-49; adults who grew up on FM rock n' roll. ■ Will Douglass, progmg dir; Mike Ramsey, mus dir.

KSET(FM)—Nov 29, 1958: 94.7 mhz; 61 kw. Ant 1,080 ft. TL: N31 47 34 W106 28 49. Stereo. Suite 150, 4105 Rio Bravo (79902). (915) 533-2400. FAX: (915) 532-4970. Licensee: Magic Media Inc. (acq 9-30-93; $2.7 million; FTR 10-28-93). Rep: Republic. Format: Country. News staff one; news progmg 2 hrs wkly. Target aud: 18-49. ■ J.R. Phillips, pres & gen mgr; Brian Kennedy, vp; Ken Stice, gen sls mgr; Brad Hawkins, progmg dir; Ron Haney, chief engr.

KSVE(AM)—June 1958: 1150 khz; 1 kw-D, 380 w-N. TL: N31 45 15 W106 25 11. Stereo. 2501 N. Mesa (79902). (915) 534-0094. FAX: (915) 542-3580. Licensee: Paso Del Norte Broadcasting Corp. (acq 5-27-92; $1.02 million with co-located FM; FTR 9-14-92). Rep: Caballero. Format: Sp. Target aud: 18-64; Hispanic El Pasons. ■ Raul Rodriguez, gen mgr; Raul Rodriquez, gen sls mgr; Caesar Chavez, progmg dir & news dir; Bruce Crow, chief engr. ■ Rates: $36; 34; 35; 29.

KINT-FM—Co-owned with KSVE(AM). July 4, 1975: 93.9 mhz; 96.2 kw. Ant 1,207 ft. TL: N31 47 36 W106 28 50 (CP: Ant 1,420 ft.). Prog sep from AM. Net: ABC/FM. Rep: Christal. Wash atty: Hogan & Hartson. Format: CHR. Target aud: 12-54. ■ Eulises Munoz, prom mgr; Bob West, progmg dir; Angel Gonzalez, mus dir; Jamie Chavez, news dir. ■ Rates: $38; 36; 36; 29.

***KTEP(FM)**—Sept 14, 1950: 88.5 mhz; 100 kw. Ant 730 ft. TL: N31 47 17 W106 28 46. Stereo. Hrs opn: 6 AM-1 AM. Cotton Memorial, Univ. of TX-El Paso, 500 W. University Ave. (79968-0556). (915) 747-5152; (915) 747-5212. FAX: (915) 747-5641. Licensee: Univ. of Texas at El Paso. Net: APR, NPR. Format: Class, jazz, news. News staff one. Target aud: 35 plus; college educated, upper-income. Spec prog: Sp 7 hrs, Ger one hr, gospel 4 hrs wkly. ■ Louis H. Valles, gen mgr; Pat Piotrowski, opns mgr & mus dir; Sheela Wolford, dev dir; Louie Saenz, news dir; Ed Miles, chief engr.

KTSM(AM)—Aug 22, 1929: 1380 khz; 5 kw-D, 500 w-N. TL: N31 45 42 W106 24 36. 801 N. Oregon (79902). (915) 532-5421. FAX: (915) 544-5658; TWX: 910-964-1329. Licensee: Tri-State Broadcasting Co. Net: ABC TalkRadio, AP, CBS, MBS, NBC Talknet; Texas AP. Rep: D & R Radio. Format: News/talk. Target aud: General. ■ Richard E. Pearson, CEO; Karen Daniels, vp, gen mgr & natl sls mgr; Bill Tole, opns mgr; Steve Masters, rgnl sls mgr; Melissa Kerr, news dir; Cindy Collins, pub affrs dir; Oscar Medina, chief engr. ■ Rates: $90; 90; 90; 90.

KTSM-FM—June 11, 1962: 99.9 mhz; 87 kw. Ant 1,820 ft. TL: N31 48 19 W106 28 57. Stereo. Prog sep from AM. Net: ABC TalkRadio, AP, CBS, MBS, NBC Talknet. Format: Adult contemp. KTSM-TV affil.

***KVER(FM)**—Jan 1, 1993: 91.1 mhz; 140 w. Ant 1,118 ft. Stereo. Box 12008 (79913-0008). (915) 544-9190. Licensee: World Network Radio Inc. (group owner). Format: Sp religious & educ. ■ Adrian Carrera, stn mgr.

KVIV(AM)—Dec 3, 1949: 1340 khz; 1 kw-U. TL: N31 46 24 W106 24 52. 7157 Alemeda St. (79915). (915) 779-2141; (915) 779-2662. FAX: (915) 779-0923. Licensee: Dunn Broadcasting Co. (acq 3-13-92; $25,000; FTR 4-6-92). Net: CRC. Rep: Lotus. Wash atty: Dow, Lohnes, & Albertson. Format: Sp, relg. News staff 3; news progmg 7 hrs wkly. Target aud: Mexican-American. ■ John Dunn, pres; Sam A. Kobren, vp; Alfonso Cabrena, gen mgr; Richard Estrada, stn mgr; Fernando Sosa, progmg dir & mus dir; Horacio Lopez, news dir; Ron Haney, chief engr.

***KXCR(FM)**—May 1, 1985: 89.5 mhz; 3 kw. Ant 1,189 ft. TL: N31 47 34 W106 28 47. 2023 Myrtle St. (79901). (915) 542-2900. Licensee: Etcom Inc. Wash atty: Haley, Bader & Potts. Format: Contemp jazz. Target aud: 25-44. ■ Arturo Vasquez, chmn, pres & gen mgr; Pete Vega, opns mgr; Juanita Vasquez, progmg dir.

Electra

KWTA(FM)—Aug 1, 1990: 94.9 mhz; 50 kw. Ant 397 ft. TL: N34 01 00 W98 55 31. Stereo. Hrs opn: 18. Rt. 6, Box 250, Byhalia, MS (38611). Licensee: Albert L. Crain.

Elgin

KELG(AM)—Apr 22, 1981: 1440 khz; 550 w-U, DA-2. TL: N30 21 05 W97 21 25 (CP: COL: Manor, 800 w-D, 500 w-N, DA-2, TL: N30 19 36 W97 32 35). Hrs opn: 24. Suite 200, 7524 N. Lamar, Austin (78752). (512) 453-1491. FAX: (512) 453-6809. Licensee: Dynamic Radio Broadcasting Corp. (acq 9-17-85). Net: SIS. Rep: Caballero. Format: Sp. ■ Lorenza O. Garcia, pres; Jose Jaime Garcia Jr., gen mgr; Evelyn L. Garza, stn mgr; Cipriano Chapa, adv mgr; Memo Cuelliar, mus dir; Steve Freeman, chief engr. ■ Rates: $35; 30; 35; na.

KKLB(FM)—Not on air, target date unknown: 92.5 mhz; 1.6 kw. Ant 449 ft. TL: N30 19 00 W97 20 22. Suite 200, 7524 N. Lamar Blvd., Austin (78752). (512) 453-1491. FAX: (512) 453-6809. Licensee: Elgin FM L.P. Net: CNN. Rep: Caballero. Wash atty: Bechtel & Cole. ■ Lorenza O. Garcia, pres; Jose J. Garcia Jr., gen mgr; Cipriauo Chapa, adv dir; Steve Freeman, vp engrg.

Fabens

KPAS(FM)—Mar 24, 1979: 103.1 mhz; 3 kw. Ant 300 ft. TL: N31 35 42 W106 11 58. Stereo. Hrs opn: 18. Box 371010, El Paso (79937). (915) 851-3382. FAX: (915) 851-4360. Licensee: Algie A. Felder (acq 6-27-86; $375,000; FTR 5-12-86). Net: USA. Format: Relg (50% Sp, 50% Eng), inspirational, gospel. News progmg 6 hrs wkly. ■ Algie A. Felder (owner), pres. ■ Rates: $16; 16; 16; 16.

Fairfield

KNES(FM)—Dec 1, 1983: 92.1 mhz; 940 w. Ant 500 ft. TL: N31 41 52 W96 09 44. Stereo. Hrs opn: 24. Box 347, 627 W. Commerce (75840). (903) 389-5637. FAX: (903) 389-7172. Licensee: J&J Communications Inc. (acq 11-19-90; $209,000; FTR 12-10-90). Net: Jones Satellite Audio; Texas State Net. Rep: Riley. Format: Country. News staff one; news progmg 6 hrs wkly. Target aud: General. Spec prog: Farm 3 hrs, talk 15 hrs, black 3 hrs, gospel 3 hrs wkly. ■ Jerry Moon, pres, gen mgr & gen sls mgr; Judy Moon, vp mktg & vp adv; Buzz Russell, prom mgr, progmg dir, mus dir & news dir; John Easterwood, chief engr. ■ Rates: $15; 12; 12; 9.

Falfurrias

KPSO(AM)—Jan 1, 1953: 1260 khz; 500 w-D, 330 w-N. TL: N21 14 11 W98 10 22. Hrs opn: 6 AM-10 PM. 304 E. Rice (78355-3624). (512) 325-2112. Licensee: Brooks Broadcasting Corp. (acq 1975). Net: USA; Texas State. Wash atty: Baraff, Koerner, Olender & Hochberg. Format: Sp, country. News progmg 10 hrs wkly. Target aud: General. Spec prog: Gospel, relg. ■ Raymond Creely, pres, gen mgr, progmg dir & chief engr; Steve Cantu, gen sls mgr; Mauricio Lopez, mus dir. ■ Rates: $9.53; 7.18; 9.53; 3.59.

KPSO-FM—Nov 1, 1983: 106.3 mhz; 180 w. Ant 188 ft. TL: N21 14 11 W98 10 22. Stereo. Hrs opn: 6 AM-10 PM. Dups AM 100%.

Farwell

KICA-FM—Sept 15, 1984: 98.3 mhz; 6 kw. Ant 256 ft. TL: N34 23 22 W103 10 27. Stereo. Box 7000, 1000 Sycamore St. Clovis, NM (88101). (505) 762-7600. FAX: (505) 762-8800. Licensee: Southwestern Broadcasting Corp. (acq 2-15-91; $65,000; FTR 3-11-91). Net: ABC/D; Texas State Net. Rep: Riley. Format: Classic rock. Spec prog: Farm 5 hrs wkly. ■ Len Vohs, gen mgr; Kevin Kitaen, progmg dir; Gary Jackson, chief engr.

KIJN(AM)—Apr 17, 1958: 1060 khz; 5 kw-D. TL: N34 23 14 W103 01 51. Box 458 (79325). (806) 481-3318. Licensee: Best Broadcasting Co. Inc. (acq 1-12-66). Net: CBN, USA; VSA Radio. Wash atty: Gammon & Grange. Format: Relg. News progmg 6 hrs wkly. Target aud: General. Spec prog: Farm 3 hrs wkly. ■ Gil Patschke, pres, gen mgr & gen sls mgr; Don Labelle, opns mgr; Ken Burchard, progmg dir; Don LaBelle, chief engr.

KIJN-FM—Aug 1, 1985: 92.3 mhz; 100 kw. Ant 433 ft. TL: N34 32 26 W102 47 56. Stereo. Prog sep from AM. Format: Adult contemp, relg. News progmg 11 hrs wkly.

Ferris

KDFT(AM)—July 13, 1988: 540 khz; 1 kw-D, 220 w-N, DA-2. TL: N32 30 53 W96 34 46 (CP: COL: Desoto). Box 411540, Suite 217, 2303 W. Ledbetter, Dallas (75241). (214) 943-8391. FAX: (214) 943-8395. Licensee: Willis Family Broadcasting Inc. (group owner; acq 3-4-92; $2 million grpsl; FTR 3-23-92). Net: USA. Format: Relg. ■ Dr.E.L. Scott, progmg dir.

Floresville

KRIO-FM—June 15, 1977: 94.1 mhz; 22 kw. Ant 695 ft. TL: N29 11 03 W98 30 49. Stereo. Suite 330, 7800 N.W. I-10, San Antonio (78230). (210) 340-1234. FAX: (210) 340-1775. Licensee: April Communications Group Inc. (acq 3-1-91; $710,000). Wash atty: Bechtel & Cole. Format: Tejano (Sp). ■ John W. Barger, pres & gen mgr; Lee Woods, opns mgr; Larry Wilson, gen sls mgr; Robert Lopez, prom dir.

***KWCB(FM)**—Not on air, target date unknown: 89.7 mhz; 9 kw. Ant 138 ft. TL: N29 13 55 W98 03 05. 1905 Tenth St. (78114). Licensee: Wilson County Ed. Foundation Inc.

Floydada

KAWA(AM)—1951: 900 khz; 250 w-D. TL: N33 58 20 W101 21 00. Box 658 (79235). (806) 983-5704. FAX: (806) 983-5705. Licensee: R. L. Alldredge (acq 12-84; $133,570.74 with co-located FM; FTR 10-8-84). Net: Mutual. Rep: Paul Miller. Format: Country. News staff one; news progmg 8 hrs wkly. Target aud: General; contemporary music lovers. Spec prog: Farm news, mkt reports, college football, Sunday worship. ■ R.L. Alldredge, gen mgr; Darolyn Snell, progmg mgr. ■ Rates: $15; 11; 13; na.

KFLL(FM)—Co-owned with KAWA(AM). Apr 1, 1985: 95.3 mhz: 3 kw. Ant 240 ft. TL: N33 58 07 W101 21 13. Stereo. Dups AM 100%. Net: VSA. ■ Rates: Same as AM.

Fort Stockton

KFST(AM)—May 8, 1954: 860 khz; 250 w-U. TL: N30 52 37 W102 53 30. Hrs opn: 6 AM-8:30 PM. Rt. One, Box 165, Hwy. 385 S. (79735). (915) 336-2228; (915) 336-5834. FAX: (915) 336-5834. Licensee: Fort Stockton Radio Co Inc. (acq 1-1-86). Net: ABC/E; Texas State Net. Format: C&W. News staff 2; news progmg 6 hrs wkly. Target aud: General. Spec prog: Sp 20 hrs wkly. ■ Gail Garlitz, pres; Ken Ripley, exec vp, gen mgr & news dir; Fred Dutchover, sls dir & prom dir; Kevin Duncan, progmg dir & mus dir; Floyd Phillips, chief engr. ■ Rates: $8.50; 8.50; 8.50; 8.50.

KFST-FM—November 1974: 94.3 mhz; 3 kw. Ant 235 ft. TL: N30 52 37 W102 53 30. Stereo. Dups AM 100%. ■ Ken Ripley, vp; Fred Dutchover, dev dir & adv dir; Kevin Lake, progmg dir & mus dir. ■ Rates: Same as AM.

Fort Worth

KAHZ(AM)—April 1947: 1360 khz; 5 kw-D, 1 kw-N, DA-2. TL: N32 46 21 W97 24 48. 121 N.E. Loop 820, Hurst (76053). (817) 589-1100. FAX: (817) 590-9590. Licensee: Jim Runsdorf, liquidating agent. Group owner: Children's Broadcasting Corp. Net: CBN, USA. Format: Children & family pgmg. Target aud: children 2-12 yrs. ■ Dick Marsh, CEO & exec vp; Chris Dahl, chmn; Jim Gilbertson, CFO; Keith Whipple, gen mgr; Brad Lane, opns mgr, news dir & pub affrs dir; Phil Lawrence, gen sls mgr; Chris Doba, prom dir; Charlie Rohde, chief engr. ■ Rates: $100; 90; 95; 50.

KCYT(FM)—See Granbury.

KDMX(FM)—See Dallas.

KEGL(FM)—April 1959: 97.1 mhz; 99 kw. Ant 1,460 ft. TL: N32 34 43 W96 57 12. Stereo. Hrs opn: 24. Box 540397, Dallas (75354); One Xerox Center, 222 W. Las Colinas Blvd., #1400, Irving (75039). (214) 869-9700. Licensee: Eagle Radio Inc. Group owner: Sandusky Radio (acq 1-21-82; $8,315,000; FTR 3-8-82). Rep: Christal. Wash atty: Baker & Hostetler. Format: AOR. News staff one; news progmg 5 hrs wkly. ■ Norman Rau, pres; Donna Fadal, vp & gen mgr; Debi Nielson, gen sls mgr; Leslee Hunter, natl sls mgr; Cindy Coyle, prom dir; Brian Krysz, progmg dir; Duane Doherty, T.C. McGuire, mus dirs; Les Colinas, pub affrs dir; Chris Hudgins, chief engr.

KESS(AM)—1922: 1270 khz; 5 kw-U. TL: N32 43 36 W97 11 30. Stereo. Hrs opn: 24. 7700 John Carpenter Fwy., Dallas (75247). (214) 630-8531; (214) 263-0700. Licensee: Mark Rodriguez Jr. Broadcasting Inc. (acq 9-11-86; $3.5 million; FTR 4-28-86). Rep: Katz. Wash atty: Cohn & Marks. Format: Sp. News staff 2; news progmg 11 hrs wkly. ■ Mark Rodriquez Jr., pres & gen mgr; Carmen Aguilera, opns mgr; Pedro Gasc, gen sls mgr; Ermilo Oviedo, progmg dir; Ricardo Rojas, mus dir; Gonzalo Aquilera, news dir; Charles Staples, engrg mgr.

KLTY(FM)—Dec 24, 1964: 94.1 mhz; 100 kw. Ant 1,585 ft. TL: N32 35 22 W96 58 10. Stereo. Hrs opn: 24. 18th Fl., 909 E. Las Calinas Blvd., Irving (75039). (214) 401-3694. Licensee: Metroplex Broadcasting (acq 1976). Net: AP, ABC. Rep: Katz & Powell. Format: Adult contemp. ■ Pete Thomson, gen sls mgr; Jon Rivers, vp progmg; Scott Wilder, progmg dir & mus dir; Dave Tucker, news dir.

KFJZ(AM)—Feb 15, 1947: 870 khz; 500 w-D. TL: N32 45 42 W97 18 49. Box 7498 (76111); 2214 E. 4th St. (76102). (817) 336-7175. FAX: (817) 338-1205. Licensee: Garden City. Format: Sp. ■ Antonia Lujan, pres;

Jose Vasquez, gen mgr, gen sls mgr & prom mgr; April Whitt Horner, news dir; Hue Beavers, chief engr.

KGBS(AM)—See Dallas.

KHVN(AM)—Dec 6, 1946: 970 khz; 1 kw-D, 270 w-N. TL: N32 47 56 W97 17 43. 17th Fl., 545 E. John Carpenter Fwy., Irving (75062). (214) 556-8100. FAX: (214) 988-1003. Licensee: Summit-Dallas Broadcasting. Group owner: Summit Communications Group Inc. (acq 5-89; $14 million with co-located FM; FTR 12-5-88). Net: ABC/D, Unistar. Rep: McGavren Guild. Format: Gospel. News staff one; news progmg 3 hrs wkly. Target aud: 25-54. ■ Howard Toole, gen mgr; Buddy Howell, gen sls mgr; Drew Dawson, prom mgr; Warren Brooks, progmg dir; Ketrana Bryant, mus dir; Robert Ashley, news dir; Ken Fine, chief engr.

KJMZ(FM)—See Dallas.

KKDA-FM—See Dallas.

KLIF(AM)—See Dallas.

KLTY(FM)—Listing follows KESS(AM).

KLUV(AM)—See Dallas.

KOAI(FM)—Feb 8, 1965: 107.5 mhz; 25 kw. Ant 1,647 ft. TL: N32 35 07 W96 58 06. Stereo. Hrs opn: 24. Suite 2000, 5956 Sherry Ln., Dallas (75225). (214) 691-1075. FAX: (214) 368-1075. Licensee: GCI Dallas II. Group owner: Granum Communications Inc. (acq 6-21-92; with KCMZ(AM) Dallas). Rep: Christal. Format: Adult contemp, smooth jazz. Target aud: 25-64. ■ Herb McCord, pres; Skip Schmidt, gen mgr; Beth Davis, gen sls mgr; Clare Wynne, rgnl sls mgr; Kimberly Morgan, prom mgr; Paul Goldstein, progmg dir; Rose Wright, news dir; Vance Henry, engrg mgr.

KPLX(FM)—Dec 15, 1962: 99.5 mhz; 100 kw. Ant 1,680 ft. TL: N32 34 54 W96 58 32. Stereo. Suite 1600, 3500 Maple at Turtle Creek, Dallas (75219). (214) 526-2400. Licensee: Radio Metroplex Inc. Group owner: Susquehanna Media Co. (acq 1974). Rep: Eastman. Format: C&W. News progmg 6 hrs wkly. Target aud: 25-54. ■ Dan Halyburton, vp & gen mgr; Wayne Olson, opns mgr; Patrick Sbarra, gen sls mgr; Denise Maddox, natl sls mgr; Bob Waterman, rgnl sls mgr; Susan Fine, mktg mgr; Barbara Luchsinger, prom dir; Brad Chambers, progmg dir; Diana Underwood, mus dir; Steve Mace, news dir; Norman Philips, chief engr.

KRLD(AM)—See Dallas.

KRRW(FM)—See Dallas.

KRVA(AM)—See Dallas.

KSCS(FM)—Listing follows WBAP(AM).

KSKY(AM)—See Dallas.

KSNN(AM)—See Dallas.

*KTCU-FM—Oct 6, 1964: 88.7 mhz; 3 kw. Ant 320 ft. TL: N32 42 40 W97 22 00. Stereo. Hrs opn: 9:30 AM-midnight. Box 30793, Moudy Bldg., Rm. 149-S, Texas Christian U. (76129). (817) 921-7631; (817) 921-7634. Licensee: Board of Trustees, Texas Christian University. Net: AP. Format: New jazz, class, alternative. ■ John Freeman, gen mgr; Andrew Haskett, stn mgr; D. Green, chief engr.

KTNO(AM)—1945: 1540 khz; 50 kw-D, 1 kw-N, DA-2. TL: N32 39 05 W97 11 38 (CP: COL: University Park, 5 kw-N, DA-2, TL: N32 26 27 W96 22 29). Hrs opn: 19. 3105 Arkansas Ln. Arlington (76016). (817) 469-1540. FAX: (817) 261-2137. Licensee: Stuart Gaines Broadcasting Corp. (acq 5-7-92; $875,000; FTR 5-25-92). Rep: Select. Wash atty: Rosenman & Colin Format: Sp. News progmg 5 hrs wkly. Target aud: General; mature, relg-oriented. ■ Mary Gaines, pres & gen mgr; Tony Avalos, gen sls mgr; Bobby Pena, progmg dir; Jack Stuart, chief engr. ■ Rates: $70; 70; 70; 70.

KTXQ(FM)—Apr 10, 1962: 102.1 mhz; 100 kw. Ant 1,447 ft. TL: N32 34 54 W96 58 32. Stereo. Hrs opn: 24. Suite 1200, 4131 North Central Expy., Dallas (75204). (214) 528-5500; (214) 263-0804. FAX: (214) 528-4314. Licensee: CBS Inc. Group owner: CBS Broadcast Group (acq 8-85; grpsl; FTR 6-10-85). Net: CBS Spectrum. Rep: CBS Radio Reps. Format: AOR. News staff one; news progmg 5 hrs wkly. Target aud: 20-44. ■ Clint Culp, vp & gen mgr; Andy Lockridge, opns mgr & progmg dir; Haley Davis-Lenz, gen sls mgr; Jeff Wodka, natl sls mgr; Tim Trostle, prom mgr & adv mgr; Red Beard, mus dir; Jim White, news dir; Neal Peden, chief engr.

KYNG(FM)—See Dallas.

KZPS(FM)—See Dallas.

WBAP(AM)—May 2, 1922: 820 khz; 50 kw-U. TL: N32 36 38 W97 10 00. Stereo. One Broadcast Hill (76103).

(817) 429-2330; (817) 654-6100. FAX: (817) 654-4814. Licensee: WBAP-KSCS Operating Ltd. Group owner: Capital Cities/ABC Broadcast Group (acq 1974). Net: ABC/I. Rep: Banner. Format: Full svc MOR; news, sports, weather & traffic. News staff 7; news progmg 25 hrs wkly. Target aud: 25-54. Spec prog: Flagship stn for Texas Rangers & Dallas Mavericks; farm 6 hrs wkly, sports. ■ John Hare, gen mgr; Doug Sheldon, gen sls mgr; Robert Shiflet, prom mgr; Tyler Cox, progmg dir; Dan Potter, news dir; Clay Steely, chief engr.

KSCS(FM)—Co-owned with WBAP(AM). March 8, 1949: 96.3 mhz; 99 kw. Ant 1,610 ft. TL: N32 35 15 W96 57 59. Stereo. Prog sep from AM. Format: Country. ■ Victor Sansone, gen mgr; Paul Danitz, gen sls mgr; Shelly Duval, prom mgr; Paul Bottoms, news dir.

Franklin

KLTR(FM)—Not on air, target date unknown: 98.9 mhz; 3 kw. Ant 328 ft. TL: N31 02 58 W96 26 06. 839 Timber Cove, Seabrook (77586). Licensee: Franklin Community Broadcasting.

Fredericksburg

KNAF(AM)—November 1947: 910 khz; 1 kw-D, 174 w-N. TL: N30 17 12 W98 52 58. Box 311, (78624). (512) 997-2197. FAX: (512) 997-2198. Licensee: Fritz Broadcasting Co., inc. (acq 1-23-91; FTR 2-11-91). Net: Texas Net. Format: C&W. Spec prog: Farm 5 hrs, Ger 2 hrs wkly. ■ Jayson Fritz, pres & gen mgr; Jan Fritz, vp & gen sls mgr; Laverne Moldenhauer (local), rgnl sls mgr; Duane Weinheimer, progmg dir; John Scott, mus dir; Tom Mills, news dir; Ducan Black, chief engr. ■ Rates: $12; 10; 12; 6.

KONO-FM—Feb 18, 1971: 101.1 mhz; 98 kw. Ant 1,371 ft. TL: N29 50 26 W98 49 32. Stereo. Hrs opn: 24. Dups KONO(AM) San Antonio 100%. Suite 330, 7800 NW I-10, San Antonio (78230). (210) 340-1234. FAX: (210) 340-3118. Licensee: Gillespie Broadcasting Co. Rep: MajorMkt. Format: Oldies. News staff one; news progmg one hr wkly. Target aud: 25-64; total audience appeal. ■ John Barger, gen mgr; George Cooper, progmg dir & news dir.

Freeport

KBRZ(AM)—October 1952: 1460 khz; 500 w-D, 214 w-N. TL: N28 58 59 W95 20 00. Drawer AA (77541). (409) 233-2655. FAX: (409) 233-2556. Licensee: Coastal Broadcasting Inc. (acq 2-74). Net: ABC/E. Format: C&W. ■ Jim T. Payne, pres, gen mgr & adv dir; Tommy Ward, opns dir; Ron Brown, gen sls mgr; Rochelle Murray, prom dir; Kelly Mann, progmg dir & mus dir; Chris Van Martin, news dir; Guy Whealdon, chief engr.

KJOJ-FM—Co-owned with KBRZ(AM). 1987: 103.3 mhz; 100 kw. Ant 453 ft. TL: N28 48 57 W95 36 03. 304 Flag Lake Dr., Lake Jackson (77566). (409) 297-2103. Licensee: US Radio L.P. (group owner; acq 3-30-90; $2 million; FTR 11-13-89). Net: USA. Format: Country, oldies. Spec prog: Relg 4 hrs, Sp 10 hrs wkly. ■ Lon McVaigh, gen sls mgr.

Friona

KGRW(FM)—Not on air, target date unknown: 95.1 mhz; 3 kw. Ant 285 ft. TL: N34 39 28 W102 43 35. Rt. 6, Box 250, Byhalia, MS (38611). Licensee: Lois B. Crain.

Gainesville

KDGE(FM)—Licensed to Gainesville. See Dallas.

KGAF(AM)—1947: 1580 khz; 250 w-U, DA-N. TL: N33 37 42 W97 06 25. Box 368 (76241). (817) 665-5546. Licensee: First IV Media Inc. (acq 11-15-74). Format: C&W, adult contemp. Spec prog: Farm 2 hrs, sports 3 hrs wkly. ■ Richard Klement, pres; Tom Carson, gen mgr & news dir; Jody Shorwell, gen sls mgr; Brian Shannon, progmg dir; Frank Bonner, chief engr.

KPXG(FM)—Not on air, target date unknown: 107.9 mhz; 50 kw. TL: N33 52 09 W97 09 16. 750 N. 11th St., Monmouth, IL (61462). Licensee: 107.9 Inc.

Galveston

KGBC(AM)—May 1947: 1540 khz; 1 kw-D, 250 w-N, DA-N. TL: N29 18 51 W94 48 16. Pelican Island, Bradner & Todd (77554). (409) 744-4567. Licensee: Harbor Broadcasting Inc. (acq 12-20-64). Net: ABC/I. Rep: Savalli. Format: MOR, Black. Spec prog: Sp 5 hrs wkly. ■ Vandy Anderson, pres; Luke Stripling, chief engr.

*KHCB(AM)—Licensed to Galveston. See Houston.

KQQK(FM)—Feb 11, 1968: 106.5 mhz; 100 kw. Ant 1,322 ft. TL: N29 24 40 W94 57 04. Stereo. Hrs opn: 24. Suite 200, 6006 Bellaire Blvd. (77081). (713) 432-1065. FAX: (713) 664-1065. Licensee: KQQK Inc. (acq 5-19-89). Format: Bilingual Tejano hits. News staff 2; news progmg 3 hrs wkly. Target aud: 18-54; Assimilated Hispanics. ■ Edith L. Baker, pres & gen mgr; Ben Walker, opns dir & chief engr; Bob Proud, gen sls mgr; Mary Rose Garcia, prom mgr; Marco Arias, progmg dir; Abby Chavarilla, news dir. ■ Rates: $90; 80; 85; 70.

KRTX(FM)—November 1989: 104.9 mhz; 1.9 kw. Ant 403 ft. TL: N29 23 45 W94 44 10. Stereo. Washington Hotel, Suite 200, 2228 Mechanic St. (77550). (409) 762-2100; (409) 762-9283. Licensee: Irvin Davis, dba Galtex Broadcasting Inc. Net: Westwood One. Format: Adult contemp, rock. News staff 2. Target aud: 25-54; white collar upper-middle class. ■ Irvin Davis, pres; Al Mainwaring, gen mgr, opns mgr, prom mgr, progmg dir & mus dir; J. D. Pike, sls dir; Rick Jones (Systems I), chief engr.

Garland

KPBC(AM)—Licensed to Garland. See Dallas.

Gatesville

KRYL(FM)—Apr 6, 1976: 98.3 mhz; 3 kw. Ant 299 ft. TL: N31 23 52 W97 38 24 (CP: Ant 315 ft. TL: N31 23 52 W97 38 54). Stereo. Hrs opn: 24. Box 918, 715 N. Main St. (76528). (817) 865-8995; (817) 865-7960. Licensee: LDR Broadcasting Ltd. (acq 6-28-91; $125,000; FTR 7-15-91). Net: Texas State Net. Rep: Riley. Format: Country. News progmg 15 hrs wkly. Target aud: 18-49. Spec prog: Farm 5 hrs, relg 5 hrs wkly. ■ Max Rudolph, pres; Billy Ray, opns mgr; Danny Hull, mus dir; Leroy Franklin, chief engr.

Georgetown

KHFI-FM—Mar 1, 1972: 96.7 mhz; 100 kw. Ant 951 ft. TL: N30 19 20 W97 48 03. Stereo. Hrs opn: 24. Suite 967, 811 Barton Springs Rd., Austin (78704-1166). (512) 474-9233. FAX: (512) 397-1400. Licensee: Clear Channel Radio Licenses Inc. Group owner: Clear Channel Communications Inc. (acq 3-9-93; $3.5 million; FTR 3-29-93). Rep: Christal. Format: CHR. News staff one; news progmg one hr wkly. Target aud: 18-34; women. ■ L. Lowry Mays, pres; Stan Webb, vp & gen mgr; John Roberts, opns mgr; Judy Lakin, gen sls mgr; Bob McDonald, natl sls dir; Ginny Schoggins, prom mgr; Tracy Austin, progmg dir; Carey Edwards, mus dir; Karen Clauss, news dir; Gil Garcia, chief engr.

KNNC(FM)—Oct 31, 1991: 107.7 mhz; 25 kw. Ant 328 ft. TL: N30 42 17 W97 38 32. Hrs opn: 24. 1600 Nueces, Austin (78705). (512) 863-0077; (512) 472-1077. Licensee: Rees-Slaymaker Radio Partnership I L.P. (acq 6-27-91; $400,000). Rep: Katz & Powell. Wash atty: Jones, Waldo, Holbrook & McDonough. Format: Progsv, new rock. Target aud: 18-34. ■ Richard D. Rees, Eric E. Slaymaker, chrs; Chris Margiotta, gen sls mgr; Bruce Jones, Paul Kreigler, vp progmg; Paul Kreigler, progmg mgr; Melissa Spease, pub affrs dir; Cole McClellan, William Traue, chiefs engr.

KOPY(AM)—Dec 8, 1962: 1530 khz; 10 kw-D, 900 w-CH. TL: N30 38 47 W97 40 08. Stereo. Box 272, c/o Dan Kubiak, Rockdale (76567). Licensee: Lower Colorado River Authority (acq 9-23-93; $225,000; FTR 10-11-93).

Giddings

KOKE(FM)—Sept 1, 1984: 101.7 mhz; 3 kw. Ant 328 ft. TL: N30 09 56 W96 52 16 (CP: 101.5 mhz, 38.8 kw, ant 561 ft. TL: N30 00 54 W97 11 58). Stereo. Hrs opn: 24. Box 387, Spindletop Industrial Park, Hwy. 290 E. (78942). (409) 542-0045. FAX: (409) 542-1937. Licensee: Radio Lee County (acq 3-22-85). Net: USA. Wash atty: Dow, Lohnes & Albertson. Format: Christian gospel. News staff 2. Target aud: 25-54; conservative, family-oriented adults. Spec prog: Farm one hr, Ger one hr, gospel 10 hrs wkly. ■ Paul Mayes Jamar, pres; Brian Jamar, dev dir; Jennifer Jamar, mus dir; Bill Woleben, chief engr. ■ Rates: $10; 10; 10; 8.

KVYK(AM)—Not on air, target date unknown: 1600 khz; 500 w-D, 250 w-N, DA-2. TL: N30 09 56 W96 52 16. Box 387 (78942). (409) 542-0045. Licensee: Radio Lee County.

Gilmer

KFRO-FM—July 24, 1980: 95.3 mhz; 2 kw. Ant 572 ft. TL: N32 38 39 W94 54 49 (CP: 8 kw, ant 571 ft.). Stereo. Hrs opn: 24. Box 4299, Longview (75606-4299); 481 Loop 281 E., Longview (75601). (903) 663-3700. FAX: (903) 663-1033. Licensee: Curtis Broadcasting Stns Inc.

Texas

(acq 12-1-86). Rep: Katz & Powell. Wash atty: Kaye Scholer. Format: Oldies. Target aud: 25-49. Spec prog: Jazz 5 hrs wkly. ■ J.R. Curtis, pres & gen mgr; Mary Helen Bair, opns mgr; Marilyn Payne, gen sls mgr; Charlie Bush, progmg dir; Barry Davis, news dir; Rod Mathews, chief engr.

KHYM(AM)—June 17, 1973: 1060 khz; 10 kw-D. TL: N32 43 51 W95 02 35. 116 S. Kilgore St., Kilgore (75662). (903) 984-1062. Licensee: American Music Radio (acq 10-16-91; $10 plus assumption of notes; FTR 11-4-91). Net: USA, Texas State. Format: Relg. News staff one; news progmg 8 hrs wkly. Target aud: General; Christians. Spec prog: Black 4 hrs wkly. ■ Helen T. Jaylor, pres; Vern Coldiron, gen mgr & mus dir; Vicky Scott, opns mgr; Joe Powell, gen sls mgr & prom mgr; Jim Bowden, progmg dir & news dir; Wayne Shultice, chief engr. ■ Rates: $10; 10; 10; na.

Gladewater

KEES(AM)—1947: 1430 khz; 5 kw-D, 1 kw-N, DA-N. TL: N32 31 46 W94 52 50. 1430 W. Hwy. 80, Longview (75604). (903) 845-2291. Licensee: Williams Communications (acq 3-1-88). Net: ABC TalkRadio, NBC Talknet, Westwood One, AP. Rep: Riley. Format: News/talk. ■ Matthew L. Williams, gen mgr.

Gonzales

KCTI(AM)—Dec 17, 1947: 1450 khz; 1 kw-U. TL: N29 30 35 W97 24 51. 428 Saint Andrew St. (78629). (512) 672-3631. Licensee: Nugent Broadcasting Co. (acq 8-1-83). Net: ABC/D; Texas State Net. Format: Country. Target aud: General. Spec prog: Polka 5 hrs, farm 5 hrs, Spanish 6 hrs wkly. ■ Patrick Nugent, pres; Eddy Weems, gen mgr, gen sls mgr & chief engr; Randy Mikus, mus dir; Joe Haynes, news dir. ■ Rates: $8.25; 6.50; 8.25; 6.50.

KPJN(FM)—Co-owned with KCTI(AM). March 1986: 106.3 mhz; 3 kw. Ant 167 ft. TL: N29 30 35 W97 24 51. Dups AM 100%.

Graham

KSWA(AM)—1948: 1330 khz; 500 w-D. TL: N33 07 37 W98 35 35. Hrs opn: 12. Box 1507, 412 U.S. Hwy. 380 W. (76450). (817) 549-1330. FAX: (817) 549-8628. Licensee: KSWA Inc. (acq 12-7-67). Net: AP. Rep: Riley. Wash atty: Baraff, Koerner, Olender & Hochberg. Format: C&W. News staff one; news progmg 10 hrs wkly. Target aud: General. ■ James M. Jones, pres, gen mgr, gen sls mgr & chief engr; Karl Lentz, progmg dir; William Proffitt, mus dir. ■ Rates: $10.60; 8.80; 8.80; 8.80.

KWKQ(FM)—Co-owned with KSWA(AM). August 1975: 107.1 mhz; 3 kw. Ant 100 ft. TL: N33 07 37 W98 35 35. Stereo. Hrs opn: 18. Dups AM 100%. Net: AP. ■ Rates: Same as AM.

Granbury

KCYT(FM)—January 1990: 106.7 mhz; 100 kw. Ant 991 ft. TL: N32 15 07 W98 02 48. Stereo. Hrs opn: 6 AM-10 PM. Box 807 (76048). 500 Main St., Fort Worth (76102). (817) 579-0216; (817) 332-1067. FAX: (817) 332-5617. Licensee: First Heritage Broadcasting Corp. Wash atty: Gammon & Grange. Format: Big band, jazz, nostalgia. Target aud: 50 plus; music for grown-ups. ■ David J. Carter, pres; Ann Massengale, gen sls mgr & prom mgr; Frank Benton, mus dir.

KPAR(AM)—Mar 13, 1980: 1420 khz; 500 w-U, DA-2. TL: N32 27 43 W97 47 19. Box 1534, Hwy. 51 N. (76048). (817) 573-5546. FAX: (817) 573-8015. Licensee: James & Fran Parr (acq 11-17-87). Net: AP. Format: Country. News staff one; news progmg 21 hrs wkly. Target aud: General. Spec prog: Farm one hr wkly. ■ Fran Parr, gen mgr; James Parr, gen sls mgr & news dir; Diane Jones, progmg dir; Frank Parr, chief engr.

Grand Prairie

KKDA(AM)—Aug 1, 1957: 730 khz; 500 w-U. TL: N32 45 52 W96 59 36. Box 530860 (75053). (214) 263-9911. FAX: (214) 558-0010. Licensee: Service Broadcasting Corp. (acq 12-22-76). Net: AP. Format: Oldies. ■ Hymen Childs, pres; Chuck Smith, gen mgr; Ken Johnson, gen sls mgr; Julia Atherton, prom mgr; Willis Johnson, progmg dir; Lynn Haze, mus dir; Gerry Dalton, chief engr.

Greenville

KEMM(FM)—See Commerce.

KGVL(AM)—Mar 26, 1946: 1400 khz; 1 kw-U. TL: N33 10 02 W96 05 55. Stereo. Box 1015 (75403); 1517 Wolfe City Dr. (75401). (903) 455-1400. FAX: (903) 455-5485. Licensee: First Greenville Corp. (acq 7-31-84; $1.2 million; FTR 6-25-84). Net: ABC; Texas State. Rep: Riley. Wash atty: Dow, Lohnes & Albertson. Format: News, talk, sports. News staff 2; news progmg 15 hrs wkly. Target aud: 25 plus. Spec prog: Black one hr, farm, relg 6 hrs wkly. ■ William Andrews, chmn; John Butler, gen mgr; Mary Stanfield, opns mgr; JC Butten, gen sls mgr; Michael Brown, prom dir; Jim Patrick, progmg dir & mus dir; Scot Harrison, news dir; Vernon Hodek, chief engr. ■ Rates: $10; 8; 10; 5.

KIKT(FM)—Co-owned with KGVL(AM). Sept 15, 1978: 93.5 mhz; 3 kw. Ant 300 ft. TL: N33 11 00 W96 03 19. Stereo. Hrs opn: 24. Prog sep from AM. (903) 454-3282. Format: Country. News staff 2; news progmg 15 hrs wkly. Target aud: General. ■ Rates: $13; 10; 13; 8.

Groves

KTFA(FM)—Sept 17, 1983: 92.5 mhz; 50 kw. Ant 440 ft. TL: N30 01 45 W93 52 59. Stereo. Hrs opn: 24. Box 820, 2000 Roundbunch, Bridge City (77611). (409) 735-7174; (409) 722-9200. FAX: (409) 735-7177. Licensee: Voice Broadcasting Inc. Net: USA. Wash atty: Gammon & Grange. Format: Contemp Christian. News progmg 2 hrs wkly. Target aud: Females 25-44; Christian lifestyle orientation. ■ Ralph H. McBride, pres & gen mgr; Jeff Roberts, progmg dir; T.J. Fordelon, chief engr. ■ Rates: $15; 13; 14; 9.

Hallettsville

KFSL(FM)—Not on air, target date unknown: 99.9 mhz; 3 kw. Ant 328 ft. TL: N29 25 37 W96 49 12. 500 E. Fifth (77964). Licensee: Tom E. Donnelly.

KRJH(AM)—Sept 5, 1979: 1520 khz; 250 w-D. TL: N29 26 38 W96 57 22. Hrs opn: Sunrise to sunset. 111 N. Main St. (77964). (512) 798-4333. Licensee: Tom E. Donnelly (acq 1-1-83; FTR 1-17-83). Net: Texas State Net. Format: C&W. News staff one; news progmg 13 hrs wkly. Target aud: General. Spec prog: Farm 6 hrs, Czech 3 hrs, Ger 3 hrs wkly. ■ Tom E. Donnelly, gen mgr & chief engr; Chuck Stratman, progmg dir; Bob Roznovsky, mus dir; Vicki Causey, news dir. ■ Rates: $8; 7; 8; 7.

Hamilton

KCLW(AM)—May 22, 1948: 900 khz; 250 w-D. TL: N31 43 08 W98 08 39. 119 A N. Rice (76531). (817) 386-8804. FAX: (817) 386-5270. Licensee: Gary L. Moss (acq 5-24-91; $175,000 with co-located FM; FTR 6-17-91). Net: Unistar, USA. Rep: Riley. Format: Country, oldies, Sp. News staff one; news progmg 6 hrs wkly. Target aud: 18-65. Spec prog: Relg 6 hrs, farm 12 hrs wkly. ■ Saul Sanchez, chief engr.

Hamlin

KCDD(FM)—Jan 30, 1987: 103.7 mhz; 100 kw. Ant 985 ft. TL: N32 43 31 W100 04 19. Stereo. 3517 Grape, Abilene (79601). (915) 672-2336. FAX: (915) 672-2381. Licensee: Taylor County Broadcasting (acq 8-19-92; $320,000). Format: CHR. ■ George Chambers, pres; Jim Christopherson, gen mgr.

Harker Heights

KLFX(FM)—June 1987: 105.5 mhz; 930 w. Ant 587 ft. TL: N31 05 23 W97 35 55 (CP: 36 kw). Stereo. Box 2469 (76543); Suite 108, 2501 S. W.S. Young, Killeen (76542). (817) 628-5000. FAX: (817) 628-8840. Licensee: Mid-Texas Communications Inc. (acq. 11-89; grpsl). Net: ABC/C. Rep: Christal. Format: Classic rock. News staff one; news progmg 2 hrs wkly. Target aud: 18-49. ■ Ken Williams, vp; Tim Thomas, gen mgr; Laura Brodie, sls dir; Bill Waddington, prom dir, progmg dir & mus dir; Julia Hardge, news dir; Jerry White, chief engr.

KRMY(AM)—See Killeen.

Harlingen

KFRQ(FM)—January 1960: 94.5 mhz; 100 kw. Ant 1,158 ft. TL: N26 08 55 W97 49 17. Stereo. Hrs opn: 24. Box 8277, Weslaco (78596); 901 E. Pike, Weslaco (78596). (210) 968-1548; (201) 968-1549. FAX: (210) 968-1643; (210) 968-3952. Licensee: Rio Grande Partners L.P. (acq 11-1-88; $1.5 million; FTR 10-31-88). Rep: Torbet. Format: Country. News staff one. Target aud: 25-54. ■ Jeffrey B. Millar, gen mgr; Peggy McCormick, gen sls mgr; Joe Salinas, prom mgr; Greg Rambin, progmg dir; Alex Macina, news dir. ■ Rates: $50; 40; 45; 25.

KGBT(AM)—1941: 1530 khz; 50 kw-D, 10 kw-N, DA-N. TL: N26 22 29 W97 53 40. Stereo. Drawer 711 (78551-0711); 1519 W. Harrison (78550). (512) 423-3910. FAX: (512) 425-4930. Licensee: Tichenor Media Inc. Group owner: Tichenor Media Systems Inc. Rep: Katz Hispanic. Format: Sp. News staff 2. Target aud: 18 plus. ■ McHenry T. Tichenor, pres; Tony Solis, vp; Jose Luis Munoz, gen mgr & natl sls mgr; Joe M. Garza, gen sls mgr; Rogelio Botello Rios, progmg dir; Brenda Huerta, news dir; Sergio Pizano, chief engr.

KIWW(FM)—Co-owned with KGBT(AM). July 1975: 96.1 mhz; 100 kw. Ant 449 ft. TL: N26 10 34 W97 46 59. Stereo. Prog sep from AM. 2 Tichenor Ctr. (78551). (512) 423-3211. Format: Sp. Target aud: 18 plus.

*****KMBH-FM**—Apr 30, 1991: 88.9 mhz; 3 kw. Ant 298 ft. TL: N26 16 46 W97 30 06. Stereo. Hrs opn: 6 AM-midnight. Box 2147, 1701 Tennessee (78551). (210) 421-4111. Licensee: RGV Educational Broadcasting Inc. Net: NPR. Format: News, classical, jazz. News progmg 34 hrs wkly. Target aud: General. Spec prog: Sp 3 hrs wkly. ■ Darrell Rowlett, pres & gen mgr; John Harris III, vp; John Harris, stn mgr; Bobbie Barajas, progmg mgr; Brian Smith, chief engr. ■ KMBH(TV) affil.

Haskell

KVRP-FM—Apr 8, 1981: 95.5 mhz; 100 kw. Ant 531 ft. TL: N33 09 40 W99 48 57 (CP: Ant 1,046 ft.). Stereo. Hrs opn: 24. Box 1118, 1406 N. First (79521). (817) 864-8505; (800) 460-5877. FAX: (817) 864-8001. Licensee: Rolling Plains Broadcasting Corp. Net: Texas State Net. Rep: Banner. Format: CD Country. News staff one; news progmg 6 hrs wkly. Target aud: 35 plus. Spec prog: Farm 8 hrs wkly. ■ Kenneth Lane, pres, gen mgr & chief engr; Gary Barrett, stn mgr, gen sls mgr & prom mgr; Carl Shearer, progmg dir, asst mus dir & news dir; Ron McCandless, mus dir. ■ Rates: $17; 14; 17; 14.

Hemphill

KAWS(AM)—Feb 16, 1978: 1240 khz; 1 kw-U. TL: N31 21 07 W93 50 14. Box 1530, Hwy. 87 N. (75948). (409) 787-3150. FAX: (409) 787-2557. Licensee: Sabine Broadcasting Co. Format: Country, relg, gospel. News progmg 5 hrs wkly. Target aud: 25 plus. Spec prog: Farm 2 hrs wkly. ■ Grover C. Winslow, pres; Johnny Cryer, gen mgr, opns mgr & progmg mgr; Troy Suggs, gen sls mgr; Mark Phillips, mus dir; Candy Graham, news dir; Kenny Carter, engrg dir. ■ Rates: $11; 10.50; 11; 5.50.

Hempstead

KEZB(FM)—Not on air, target date unknown: 105.3 mhz; 6 kw. Ant 328 ft. 1500 N. Woodward Ave., Birmingham, MI (48009). Licensee: Farmers Communications. Group owner: Bayport Broadcast Group.

Henderson

KWRD(AM)—March 1956: 1470 khz; 5 kw-D. TL: N32 10 55 W94 47 49. Box 1400 (75653). (903) 657-2324. FAX: (903) 657-4520. Licensee: Wes Dean & Assocs. Inc. (acq 8-80; $240,000; FTR 8-25-80). Net: AP; Texas State Net. Format: C&W. News progmg 12 hrs wkly. Target aud: General. Spec prog: Farm 5 hrs wkly. ■ Chipper Dean, pres & gen mgr; Don Arber, opns mgr, prom mgr & news dir; Sharon Staehs, gen sls mgr & mktg mgr; Ronnie Powell, chief engr.

KGRI-FM—Co-owned with KWRD(AM). Aug 1, 1965: 99.9 mhz; 1.35 kw. Ant 420 ft. TL: N32 07 30 W94 48 00 (CP: 7.1 kw, ant 433 ft.). Prog sep from AM. ■ Sharon Staehs, adv mgr. ■ Rates: $13; 11; 13; 11.

Hereford

KPAN(AM)—August 1948: 860 khz; 250 w-U. TL: N34 47 33 W102 25 45. Hrs opn: 6 AM-midnight. Drawer 1757, 218 E. Fifth St. (79045). (806) 364-1860. FAX: (806) 364-5814. Licensee: KPAN Broadcasters. Group owner: Formby Stations. Net: Texas State Net. Format: Contemp country. News staff one; news progmg 20 hrs wkly. Target aud: General; adults all ages. Spec prog: Sp 15 hrs, farm 18 hrs wkly. ■ Clint Formby, pres; Buddy

Peeler, gen mgr & gen sls mgr; Jack Denver, mus dir; Bill Anderson , asst mus dir; Chip Formby, news dir & chief engr. ■ Rates: $9.10; 7.60; 7.60; 7.60.

KPAN-FM—Sept 1, 1965: 106.3 mhz; 7 kw. Ant 259 ft. TL: N34 47 33 W102 25 45 (CP: 25 kw, ant 220 ft.). Stereo. Hrs opn: 6 AM-midnight. Dups AM 100%. ■ Rates: Same as AM.

Highland Park

KVIL(AM)—Mar 1, 1960: 1150 khz; 1 kw-D, 6 w-N, DA-2. TL: N32 53 36 W96 55 33. Suite 1600, 9400 N. Central Expwy., Dallas (75231). (214) 691-1037. FAX: (214) 891-7975. Licensee: Infinity Broadcasting Corp. (group owner; acq 7-2-87). Net: AP. Rep: Torbet. Format: Adult contemp personality. ■ Ann Bradley, vp; Bob Cooper, gen mgr; Ken Reisor, gen sls mgr; Craig Zurek, natl sls mgr; Tricia Crisp, prom mgr; Bill Curtis, progmg dir; Alex O'Neal, mus dir; Peggy Sears, news dir; Bill Ryan, chief engr.

KVIL-FM—(Highland Park-Dallas). Aug 14, 1961: 103.7 mhz; 100 kw. Ant 1,571 ft. TL: N32 34 54 W96 58 32. Stereo. Hrs opn: 24. Dups AM 100%.

Highland Park-Dallas

KVIL-FM—Licensed to Highland Park-Dallas. See Highland Park.

Hillsboro

KHBR(AM)—May 21, 1948: 1560 khz; 250 w-D. TL: N32 01 00 W97 06 32. Box 569, 335 Country Club Rd. (76645). (817) 582-3431. Licensee: KHBR Radio Inc. (acq 1955). Net: Texas State Net. Rep: Miller. Format: Country. News staff 4. Target aud: General. Spec prog: Czech 2 hrs, relg 7 hrs wkly. ■ Roger Galle, pres; Rick Bailey, gen mgr, gen sls mgr, prom mgr, progmg dir & news dir; Damon Isbell, mus dir; Dave Kolar, chief engr.

KJNE(FM)—Oct 20, 1959: 102.5 mhz; 100 kw. Ant 450 ft. TL: N31 49 29 W97 09 33. Stereo. Box 7795, Waco (76714-7795); 8801 A Woodway Dr., Waco (76712). (817) 776-6333. Licensee: Sonance Waco L.C. (acq 12-1-93; $850,000; FTR 12-20-93). Rep: Blair. Format: Country. ■ R.J. Moran, pres; Susan Hughes, gen mgr; Harvey Brown, gen sls mgr; John Swan, prom mgr; Chuck Nance, progmg dir; Tom Barfield, mus dir; Liz Richards, news dir; Mike Jugert, chief engr.

Hondo

KRME(AM)—Feb 13, 1970: 1460 khz; 500 w-D, 226 w-N. TL: N29 21 42 W99 07 42. Hrs opn: 6 AM-10 PM. Box 447, 1605 Ave. K (78861). (210) 426-3367. FAX: (210) 426-3348. Licensee: Radio Medina Inc. Net: Texas State Net. Rep: Keystone (unwired net). Wash atty: Wray & Fitch. Format: Country, Sp. News staff one; news progmg 20 hrs wkly. Target aud: General. ■ William E. Berger, pres; Jeff Berger, gen mgr; Ronnie Mason, mus dir; Joe Gragg, chief engr. ■ Rates: $8.50; 8.50; 8.50; 8.50.

KRBH(FM)—Co-owned with KRME(AM). 1993: 98.5 mhz; 3 kw. Ant 272 ft. TL: N29 15 11 W99 07 29. Stereo. Hrs opn: 5 AM-10 PM. Format: Country, news.

Hooks

KLLI(FM)—Dec 22, 1985: 95.9 mhz; 1.4 kw. Ant 449 ft. TL: N33 27 25 W94 10 59 (CP: 11.3 kw, ant 485 ft.). Stereo. Hrs opn: 24. 4110 McKnight Rd., Texarkana (75501). (903) 832-5536. Licensee: Texarkana Broadcasting Inc. Rep: Katz & Powell. Format: Hot new country. News staff one. Target aud: 25-54; contemporary adults, upscale middle America. ■ John Mitchell, chmn; Bob Gipson, vp & gen mgr; Jay James, opns mgr; Rob Ryan, progmg dir; Chuck Zack, news dir; Norm Mason, chief engr.

Hornsby

***KOOP(FM)**—Not on air, target date unknown: 91.7 mhz; 3.13 kw. Ant 27 ft. 2500 Nueces St. (78705). Licensee: Texas Educational Broadcasting Cooperative Inc.

Houston

KBXX(FM)—January 1958: 97.9 mhz; 100 kw. Ant 1,920 ft. TL: N29 34 34 W95 30 36. Stereo. Suite 600, 6420 Richmond (77057). (713) 978-7328. Licensee: Cook Inlet Radio License Partnership L.P. (acq 6-8-92). Rep: Katz. Format: Adult contemp. ■ Carl Hamilton, pres; Jim Bell, gen mgr; Mark McMillen, gen sls mgr; Bob Wood, progmg dir; Chuck Shramek, news dir; Frank Rainey, chief engr.

KCOH(AM)—1953: 1430 khz; 1 kw-D. TL: N29 45 22 W95 16 37. 5011 Almeda (77004). (713) 522-1001. Licensee: KCOH Inc. (acq 9-27-76). Rep: Roslin. Format: Black. ■ John B. Coleman, pres; Mike Petrizzo, vp, gen mgr & gen sls mgr; Travis O. Gardner, prom mgr, progmg dir & mus dir; Michael Harris, news dir; Dave Biondi, chief engr.

KEYH(AM)—November 1974: 850 khz; 10 kw-D, DA. TL: N29 39 19 W95 40 19. 10250 Bissonnet, No. 400 (77036). (713) 995-8500. Licensee: Artlite Broadcasting Co. (acq 6-11-86). Rep: Lotus Hispanic. Format: Sp. Target aud: 24-65; Hispanic. ■ David Armstrong, exec vp, gen mgr, progmg dir & engrg dir; Teresa Aliaga, news dir.

***KHCB(AM)**—(Galveston). 1922: 1400 khz; 1 kw-U. TL: N29 17 24 W94 50 12. Hrs opn: 24. 2424 South Blvd., Houston (77098-5196). (409) 744-6343; (913) 520-7900. Licensee: Houston Christian Broadcasting Inc. (acq 12-4-90; $150,000). Format: Sp, relg. News staff one. Target aud: General. Spec prog: Chinese 10 hrs, Vietnamese 3 hrs wkly. ■ Bruce Munsterman, pres, stn mgr & progmg dir; Dolly Martin, progmg mgr, mus dir & news dir; Dan Wares, chief engr.

***KHCB-FM**—Mar 10, 1962: 105.7 mhz; 100 kw. Ant 1,614 ft. TL: N29 34 06 W95 29 57. Stereo. Hrs opn: 24. Dups AM 50%. Format: Relg. Spec prog: Sp 10 hrs wkly. ■ Bruce E. Munsterman, gen mgr; Bonnie C. BeMent, mus dir & news dir; Dan Wales, engrg dir.

KHMX(FM)—1961: 96.5 mhz; 100 kw. Ant 1,952 ft. TL: N29 34 34 W95 30 36. Stereo. Suite 2300, 1990 Post Oak Blvd. (77056). (713) 790-0965. FAX: (713) 297-0344. Licensee: Nationwide Communications Inc. Group owner: Nationwide Mutual Insurance Co. (acq 3-90; $30 million; FTR 3-19-90). Rep: Hillier, Newmark, Wechsler & Howard. Format: Adult contemp. News staff one; news progmg 4 hrs wkly. Target aud: 25-40. ■ Steve Berger, pres; Mickey Franco, vp; Don Peterson, gen mgr; Pat Paxton, opns mgr; John Brevot, gen sls mgr; Kirt Hayes, natl sls mgr; Joe Pogge, mktg dir; Geno Pearson, mus dir; Susan Lennon, news dir & pub affrs dir; Don Stevenson, chief engr.

KIKK(AM)—See Pasadena.

KIKK-FM—Oct 4, 1959: 95.7 mhz; 100 kw. Ant 1,971 ft. TL: N29 34 34 W95 30 36. Stereo. Hrs opn: 24. 6306 Gulfton Dr. (77081). (713) 772-4433. FAX: (713) 995-7956. Licensee: Group W (group owner; acq 10-20-93; FTR 11-8-93). Net: AP. Rep: Torbet. Format: Modern country. News staff 3. Target aud: 25-54. ■ Dickie Rosenfeld, vp; Rick Candea, gen mgr; Ron Bergess, gen sls mgr; Bob Presley, rgnl sls mgr; Joan Hays, prom mgr; Carl Geisler, progmg dir; Joe Ladd, mus dir; Dan Woodard, chief engr.

KILT(AM)—1948: 610 khz; 5 kw-U, DA-2. TL: N29 55 04 W95 25 33. 500 Lovett Blvd. (77006). (713) 526-3461. FAX: (713) 526-5458. Licensee: Westinghouse Broadcasting Co. (group owner; acq 12-89). Net: AP. Rep: Group W. Format: Country. ■ Dickie Rosenfeld, vp & gen mgr; Bob Presley, gen sls mgr; Rick Candea, progmg dir; Debbie Murray, mus dir; Jim Carola, news dir; Dan Woodard, chief engr.

KILT-FM—1961: 100.3 mhz; 100 kw. Ant 1,920 ft. TL: N29 34 34 W95 30 36. Stereo. Hrs opn: 24. Format: Country.

KKBQ(AM)—Oct 16, 1944: 790 khz; 5 kw-U, DA-2. TL: N29 54 54 W95 27 42. Stereo. Suite 2022, 11 Greenway Plaza (77046). (713) 961-0093. Licensee: Gannett Broadcasting (group owner; acq 12-3-84; grpsl; FTR 12-10-84). Rep: McGavren Guild. Format: CHR. ■ Don Troutt, gen mgr; Shelly Owens, vp sls; Kathy Armstrong, gen sls mgr; Tammy Easley, prom mgr; Dene Hallam, progmg dir; Jeff Garrison, mus dir; Alan Justice, news dir; June Garcia-Apel, pub affrs dir; Bob Stroupe, chief engr.

KKBQ-FM—See Pasadena.

KKRW(FM)—Jan 1, 1964: 93.7 mhz; 100 kw. Ant 1,779 ft. TL: N29 34 27 W95 29 37. Stereo. Suite 6937, 10333 Richmond Ave. (77042). (713) 780-0937. FAX: (713) 974-1905. Licensee: CBS Inc. Group owner: CBS Broadcast Group (acq 8-1-85; grpsl; FTR 6-10-85). Net: CBS Spectrum. Rep: CBS Radio. Format: Soft contemp. News staff one; news progmg 2 hrs wkly. Target aud: 25-54; upscale adults. Spec prog: Light jazz 4hrs wkly. ■ John D. Hiatt, vp & gen mgr; John Hufnagel, gen sls mgr; Michelle Kalanja, natl sls mgr; Sean Luce, rgnl sls mgr; Cathy Frank, prom mgr; Michele James, progmg dir; Betsy Ballard, news dir; Ray Nelson, chief engr. ■ Rates: $250; 250; 250; 150.

KKZR(FM)—See Conroe.

KLAT(AM)—July 31, 1961: 1010 khz; 5 kw-U, DA-2. TL: N29 53 47 W95 17 25. Stereo. Suite 400, 1415 N. Loop W. (77008). (713) 868-4344. FAX: (713) 868-5947. Licensee: Tichenor Media System Inc. (group owner). Net: AP. Rep: Katz Hispanic. Format: Sp. Target aud: 25-54. ■ Mac Tichenor, pres; Gary Stone, gen mgr; Dan Blanchard, gen sls mgr; Mario Garcia, prom mgr & news dir; Everardo V. Morales, progmg dir; Don Freestone, chief engr.

KLDE(FM)—Nov 1, 1964: 94.5 mhz; 100 kw. Ant 2,000 ft. TL: N29 34 34 W95 30 36. Stereo. 5353 W. Alabama (77056). (713) 622-5533. FAX: (713) 622-7479. Licensee: Entertainment Communications Inc. Group owner: Entercom (acq 6-5-69). Rep: D & R Radio. Format: Oldies. News staff one; news progmg 2 hrs wkly. Target aud: 25-54; baby boomers. Spec prog: Talk 2 hrs, relg one hr, pub affrs one hr wkly. ■ Joseph Field, pres; Steve Shepard, gen mgr; R.C. Rogers, opns mgr & progmg dir; Fran Epstein, gen sls mgr; Karl Trollinger, prom mgr; Colonel St. James, mus dir; Sheree Bernardi, news dir; Tony Robichaux, chief engr.

KLOL(FM)—Listing follows KTRH(AM).

KLVL(AM)—See Pasadena.

KMJQ(FM)—Listing follows KYOK(AM).

KNUZ(AM)—Feb 18, 1948: 1230 khz; 1 kw-U. TL: N29 45 26 W95 20 18. Hrs opn: 24. Box 188, 4701 Caroline (77004). (713) 525-2581. FAX: (713) 529-9117. Licensee: Texas Coast Broadcasters Inc. Net: ABC/E. Rep: Banner. Wash atty: Cohn & Marks. Format: Oldies. News staff 7. Target aud: 25 plus; mature, upscale, high-income. ■ David H. Morris, CEO & pres; Vesta F. Brandt, gen mgr & natl sls mgr; Ken Grant, opns dir & prom dir; Jim Livingston, vp sls; Jim Richards, progmg dir & mus dir; Wes Johnson, news dir; Alex Schneider, chief engr.

KQUE(FM)—Co-owned with KNUZ(AM). Oct 4, 1960: 102.9 mhz; 100 kw. Ant 1,049 ft. TL: N29 45 26 W95 20 18. Stereo. Prog sep from AM. Rep: Eastman. Format: MOR, oldies, big band. News staff 14; news progmg 14 hrs wkly. Target aud: Upscale adults. ■ Paul Berlin, opns mgr, progmg dir & mus dir; Vesta F. Brandt, gen sls mgr; Jim Livingston, rgnl sls mgr.

KODA(FM)—Nov 9, 1958: 99.1 mhz; 95 kw. Ant 1,920 ft. TL: N29 34 34 W95 30 36. Stereo. 4810 San Felipe Rd. (77056). (713) 622-1010. FAX: (713) 622-7369. Licensee: Capstar Media of Texas Inc. Group owner: SFX Broadcasting Inc. (acq 10-7-92; grpsl; FTR 11-16-92). Rep: Major Mkt. Format: Adult contemp. ■ Michael Black, vp & gen mgr; Dave Dillon, progmg dir; Eric Braum, chief engr.

***KPFT(FM)**—March 1970: 90.1 mhz; 100 kw. Ant 433 ft. TL: N29 55 26 W95 32 17. Stereo. 419 Lovett Blvd. (77006). (713) 526-4000. Licensee: Pacifica Foundation Inc. Group owner: Pacifica Foundation Inc. dba Pacifica Radio. Net: APR. Format: Div, news. News staff one; news progmg 30 hrs wkly. Target aud: General. Spec prog: Black 15 hrs, Ger 2 hrs, jazz 6 hrs, Sp 7 hrs, Hindi 3 hrs, Irish one hr wkly. ■ Barry Forbes, gen mgr; Margie Glaser, opns mgr; James Gladwin, dev dir; Garland Ganter, progmg dir; Kyle Huckins, news dir; Duane Burlison, chief engr.

KPRC(AM)—May 9, 1925: 950 khz; 5 kw-U, DA-N. TL: N29 48 14 W95 16 42. Hrs opn: 24. Suite 1170, 11767 Katy Fwy. (77079). (713) 588-4800. Licensee: Sunbelt Broadcasting Co. (acq 12-14-92; $3.5 million; FTR 1-11-93). Net: CBS, CNN, NBC Talknet; Texas Net. Rep: Banner, Eastman. Wash atty: Dow, Lohnes & Albertson. Format: News/talk. News staff 15; news progmg 32 hrs wkly. Target aud: 25-54. Spec prog: Gardening 7 hrs, home handyman 6 hrs, automotive 3 hrs. ■ Van Patrick, opns dir & gen sls mgr; Phil Stewart, natl sls mgr; Brian Hill, news dir; Chuck McCloud, chief engr. ■ KPRC-TV affil.

KQUE(FM)—Listing follows KNUZ(AM).

KRBE(AM)—Jan 17, 1968: 1070 khz; 10 kw-D, 5 kw-N, DA-2. TL: N29 59 33 W95 29 33. Stereo. Suite 700, 9801 Westheimer (77042). (713) 266-1000. FAX: (713) 954-2344. Licensee: KRBE License Investment Co. (group owner; acq 11-86; $25 million with co-located FM; FTR 10-6-86). Rep: D & R Radio. Format: Heavy metal. ■ Nancy Vaeth, vp & gen mgr; Billie Parrott, gen sls mgr; Tom Poleman, progmg dir; Chuck Underwood, chief engr.

KRBE-FM—Nov 8, 1959: 104.1 mhz; 100 kw. Ant 1,920 ft. TL: N29 34 34 W95 30 36. Stereo. Prog sep from AM. Format: CHR/Top-40. ■ Adam Cook, progmg dir.

KRTS(FM)—See Seabrook.

KTEK(AM)—See Alvin.

KTRH(AM)—Mar 29, 1930: 740 khz; 50 kw-U, DA-2. TL: N29 57 57 W94 56 32. Box 1520 (77251); 510 Lovett Blvd. (77006). (713) 526-5874; (713) 630-3622. FAX: (713) 630-3614. Licensee: KTRH License Corp. (acq 5-6-93; $49 million with co-located FM; FTR 5-24-93). Net: CBS. Rep: CBS Radio. Wash atty: Dow, Lohnes & Albertson. Format: News, sports. Target aud: 25-54. ■ Scott Ginsbero, pres; Dorsey McLeroy, CFO; Laura Morris, gen mgr; Pete Gardner, opns mgr & progmg dir; Richard Fennema, gen sls mgr; Steve Chambers, natl sls mgr; Mark Masepohl, rgnl sls mgr; Susan Coffman, mktg dir; Pam Kehoe, prom mgr; Joe Izbrand, news dir; Christi Woods, pub affrs dir; Errol Coker, chief engr.

KLOL(FM)—Co-owned with KTRH(AM). 1947: 101.1 mhz; 100 kw. Ant 1,920 ft. TL: N29 34 34 W95 30 36. Stereo. Prog sep from AM. (713) 526-6855. Format: AOR. News staff 2. Target aud: 18-54. ■ Pat Fant, vp & gen mgr; Muriel Funches, gen sls mgr; Alan Ecklund, natl sls mgr; Cathy White, rgnl sls mgr; Doug Harris, mktg dir; Jay Isbell, prom mgr; Sig Izbrand, adv dir; Ted Edwards, progmg dir; Dayna Steele, mus dir; Martha Martinez, news dir; Cindy Bennett, pub affrs dir; John Alan, chief engr.

***KTRU(FM)**—May 20, 1971: 91.7 mhz; 50 kw. Ant 492 ft. TL: N30 03 54 W95 16 10. Stereo. Box 1892 (77251); 6100 S. Main (77005). (713) 527-4098. Licensee: Rice Univ. Format: Div. News progmg 6 hrs wkly. Target aud: General. Spec prog: Class 8 hrs, jazz 6 hrs, reggae 6 hrs, folk 3 hrs, sixties 3 hrs, women's one hr, new age one hr wkly. ■ Eric W. Davis, gen mgr; David Cole, prom mgr; Brian Prince, progmg dir; H. R. Kawng, mus dir; Anu Bajaj, news dir; Craig Dial, chief engr.

***KTSU(FM)**—October 1973: 90.9 mhz; 18.5 kw. Ant 285 ft. TL: N29 43 25 W95 21 52. Stereo. Hrs opn: 24. Bell Bldg., 3100 Cleburne St. (77004). (713) 527-4354. Licensee: Board of Regents, Texas Southern Univ. Format: Educ, div. News staff one; news progmg 10 hrs wkly. Target aud: 25-54. Spec prog: Reggae 8 hrs wkly. ■ Dr. Joanne Horton, pres; Rick Roberts, gen mgr & mktg dir; Detria Ward, prom dir, progmg dir & mus dir; George Thomas, adv dir; Maurice Hopethompson, news dir; Dave Biondi, vp engrg & chief engr.

***KUHF(FM)**—Nov 6, 1950: 88.7 mhz; 100 kw. Ant 1,800 ft. TL: N29 34 28 W95 29 37. Stereo. Hrs opn: 24. University of Houston (77204-4061); Room 101, Comm Bldg., 3801 Cullen Blvd. (77004). (713) 743-0887. FAX: (713) 743-1818. Licensee: University of Houston. Net: NPR, APR. Wash atty: Dow, Lohnes & Albertson. Format: Class, news. News staff 3; news progmg 25 hrs wkly. Target aud: 25 plus. ■ John Gladney Proffitt, gen mgr; Howard Cornelsen, opns dir; Betty Morgan (publ & spec events), prom dir; Robert Stevenson, progmg dir; Debra Fraser-Alford, news dir; David Knodel, chief engr.

KXYZ(AM)—Aug 8, 1930: 1320 khz; 5 kw-U, DA-N. TL: N29 42 37 W95 10 29. Box 87190 (77287). (713) 472-2500. FAX: (713) 920-8930. Licensee: 13 Radio Corp. Group owner: Infinity Broadcasting Corp. (acq 4-21-83; $1.5 million; FTR 5-16-83). Rep: Caballero. Format: Contemp Sp, talk. ■ Mel Karmazin, pres; Hugo Cadelago, stn mgr; J.D. French, gen sls mgr; Alex Cabellero, progmg dir; Rolando Becerra, news dir; George Shank, chief engr.

KYOK(AM)—1955: 1590 khz; 5 kw-U, DA-N. TL: N29 50 38 W95 26 51. 24 Greenway, Suite 1590 (77046). (713) 623-0102; (713) 621-1590. FAX: (713) 623-0106. Licensee: Noble Broadcast of Houston Inc. Group owner: Noble Broadcast Group. Net: ABC/C, SMN. Rep: McGavren Guild. Format: Solid gold soul satellite. Target aud: General; 25-54. Spec prog: Talk 12 hrs wkly. ■ John T. Lynch, CEO; Ernest Jackson, vp; Aldie Beard, stn mgr; Selma Dodson, gen sls mgr; Bobrie Jefferson, prom dir; Carl Conner, progmg dir; Leroy Patterson, progmg mgr; Dave Rowland, chief engr.

KMJQ(FM)—Co-owned with KYOK(AM). Feb 1, 1964: 102.1 mhz; 100 kw. Ant 1,719 ft. TL: N29 34 27 W95 29 37. Stereo. Suite 1508, 24 Greenway Plaza (77046). Rep: Christal. Format: Urban contemp. Spec prog: Talk 3 hrs wkly.

KZFX(FM)—See Lake Jackson.

Howe

KHYI(FM)—Apr 1949: 95.3 mhz; 3.9 kw. Ant 413 ft. TL: N33 21 29 W96 36 03. Stereo. Hrs opn: 24. c/o KYNG(FM), 12201 Merit Dr. #930, Dallas (75251). (214) 716-7800. FAX: (214) 716-7835. Licensee: Maple Communications L.P. Rep: Group W. Wash atty: Mintz, Levin, Ferris, Glovsky & Popeo. Format: Country. News staff one; news progmg 3 hrs wkly. Target aud: 35-64. ■ John Hayes Jr., CEO & pres; Scott Savage, gen mgr; Ginger Keas (local), gen sls mgr; Lee Ann Longinotti, natl sls mgr; Christy Kelly, prom mgr; Dan Pearman, progmg dir; Joe Holstead, news dir; Bob Henke, chief engr.

Humble

KGOL(AM)—July 18, 1984: 1180 khz; 50 kw-D, 1 kw-N, DA-3. TL: N30 08 21 W95 17 24. Stereo. Suite 525, 525 N. Sam Houston Pkwy E., Houston (77060). (713) 999-1180; (800) 438-6311. FAX: (713) 999-0730. Licensee: Douglas Broadcasting Inc. (group owner; acq 11-30-93; $700,000; FTR 12-13-93). Format: Christian. News progmg 6 hrs wkly. Target aud: General. Spec prog: Sp 9 hrs wkly. ■ Michael Glinter, pres; Scott Ellis, progmg dir; David Anthony, chief engr.

***KSBJ(FM)**—July 6, 1982: 89.3 mhz; 100 kw. Ant 840 ft. TL: N30 12 26 W95 05 28. Stereo. Hrs opn: 24. Box 187 (77347); 327 Wilson Rd. (77338). (713) 446-5725. FAX: (713) 540-2198. Licensee: KSBJ Educational Foundation. Net: USA. Format: Contemp Christian. News staff 2; news progmg 4 hrs wkly. Target aud: 25-49; Christian adults. ■ Johnny Franks, pres; Tim McDermott, gen mgr; Susan O'Donnell, dev dir; Jeff Scott, prom dir; Tom Carter, progmg dir; Roger Clark, mus dir; Roger Greer, news dir; Lyn Hare, chief engr.

Huntington

KAQU(FM)—March 1, 1994: 101.9 mhz; 6 kw. Ant 328 ft. TL: N31 20 05 W94 38 13 (CP: 50 kw). Stereo. Hrs opn: 24. 218 Randall St., Pasadena (77506). Licensee: Huntington Broadcasting Corp. ■ E. Leon Phillips, pres.

Huntsville

KCEY(FM)—Not on air, target date Unknown: 99.7 mhz; 3 kw. Ant 328 ft. TL: N30 41 57 W95 38 24. Rt. 2, Box 213 (77340). Licensee: Helen Maryse Casey.

KSAM(AM)—Nov 3, 1938: 1490 khz; 1 kw-U. TL: N30 41 48 W95 33 08. Box 330, 3303 Interstate Rd. (77342). (409) 295-2651. Licensee: Walker County Communications Inc. Group owner: Formby Stns. (acq 1-1-82; $1 million with co-locted FM; FTR 1-25-82). Format: Country. News staff one; news progmg 3 hrs wkly. Target aud: General; 25-34. Spec prog: Black 4 hrs. ■ George Franz, pres & gen mgr; Danny McWilliams, opns dir & mus dir; Linda Hunt, gen sls mgr & prom dir; John Bradley, progmg dir; Wayne Sorge, news dir & pub affrs dir; Dave Hammer, chief engr. ■ Rates: $10; 10; 10; 10.

KSAM-FM—Aug 1, 1965: 101.7 mhz; 3.8 kw. Ant 420 ft. TL: N30 41 48 W95 33 08. Stereo. Hrs opn: 24. Prog sep from AM. Format: CHR. News staff one; news progmg 2 hrs wkly. Target aud: General; 18-49 ■ Danny McWilliams, progmg dir.

***KSHU(FM)**—October 1973: 90.5 mhz; 3 kw. Ant 255 ft. TL: N30 42 50 W95 32 58. Stereo. Hrs opn: 6 AM-1 AM. Box 2207 (77341); Sam Houston Ave. (77340). (409) 294-1354; (409) 294-1344. FAX: (409) 294-1888. Licensee: Sam Houston State Univ. Format: Class, jazz, AOR. News progmg 2 hrs wkly. Target aud: General; 18-45. Spec prog: Black 6 hrs wkly. ■ Donald Silcott, CEO & gen mgr; Darrel Roe, opns dir; Ron Mewis, mktg dir & prom mgr; Clay Marshall, news dir; Aimee Spillers, pub affrs dir; Jack Nichols, chief engr.

KVST(FM)—Not on air, target date unknown: 103.5 mhz; 3.6 kw. Ant 426 ft. TL: N30 36 03 W95 29 02 (CP: 103.7 mhz, 14.9 kw). 914 Champions, Lufkin (75901). Licensee: New Wavo Communications Group Inc. (acq 6-13-91; $125,000; FTR 7-1-91).

KYLR(AM)—Oct 4, 1982: 1400 khz; 250 w-D, 1 kw-N. TL: N30 43 07 W95 31 40. 1018 12th St. (77342-7525). (409) 295-1413. Licensee: James W. Standefer ($39,673; FTR 11-23-92). Net: ABC/I. Format: Oldies. News staff 2; news progmg 10 hrs wkly. Target aud: 25-54; upscale adults. Spec prog: Farm one hr, black 6 hrs wkly. ■ James W. Standefer, gen mgr; Pam Standefer, gen sls mgr.

Hutto

KRGT(FM)—February 1980: 92.1 mhz; 3 kw. Ant 300 ft. TL: N30 32 01 W97 35 12 (CP: Ant 238 ft.). Stereo. Hrs opn: 19. 2908 Overdale Rd., Austin (78723). Licensee: Austin Broadcasting Inc. (acq 3-17-93; $78,432; FTR 4-12-93). ■ Robert N. Simmons, gen mgr.

Jacksonville

***KBJS(FM)**—May 16, 1987: 90.3 mhz; 3 kw. Ant 266 ft. TL: N31 58 16 W95 15 51 (CP: 19 kw, ant 1,286 ft., TL: N32 03 40 W95 18 50). Stereo. Box 193, 406 Nacogdoches Rd. (75766). (903) 586-5257. FAX: (903) 586-4986. Licensee: East Texas Media Association Inc. Net: Moody. Format: Relg. Spec prog: Black one hr, Sp one hr wkly. ■ Bob Shivery, pres & gen mgr; Steve Comer, chief engr.

KEBE(AM)—Jan 12, 1947: 1400 khz; 1 kw-U. TL: N31 57 54 W95 15 58 (CP: 450 w-U). Hrs opn: 24. Box 1648, Radio Center, 402 S. Ragsdale (75766). (903) 586-2527. FAX: (903) 586-1394. Licensee: Waller Broadcasting, Inc. Net: ABC/E. Rep: Eastman. Wash atty: Fletcher Heald & Hildreth. Format: Country. News progmg 15 hrs wkly. Target aud: 25-54. Spec prog: Farm 9 hrs wkly. ■ Wm. Dudley Waller, pres & gen mgr; Jack Beazley, opns dir; Jim Hendrick, sls dir; Perry Andrews, prom mgr; Alan Mather, progmg dir; Gary Lesniewski, news dir; Hank Hardisty, chief engr.

KOOI-FM—Co-owned with KEBE(AM). Sept 9, 1967: 106.5 mhz; 100 kw. Ant 1,468 ft. TL: N32 03 40 W95 18 50. Stereo. Hrs opn: 24. Prog sep from AM. 621 Chase Dr., Tyler (75703). (903) 581-2376. Net: ABC; Texas Net. Format: Contemp EZ lstng. News staff 3. Target aud: 25-64; upscale adults. ■ Larry Bessler, mus dir.

KSIZ(FM)—Not on air, target date unknown: 102.3 mhz; 3 kw. Ant 328 ft. TL: N32 01 52 W95 17 56. 408 Alexander St. (75766). Licensee: Robert W. Shivery.

Jasper

KMIA(FM)—Dec 1, 1987: 100.7 mhz; 5.1 kw. Ant 299 ft. TL: N31 00 57 W93 59 13. Stereo. Hrs opn: 24. Box 590209, Roy E. Henderson, c/o Bayport Broadcast Group, Houston (77259). (713) 480-9992. FAX: (713) 286-1666. Licensee: Roy E. Henderson. Group owner: Bayport Broadcast Group (acq 2-23-90; $235,000; FTR 3-12-90). Net: ABC/D, AP, Westwood One; Texas AP. Format: Country. News staff one; news progmg 7 hrs wkly. Target aud: 21-54. Spec prog: Oldies 6 hrs, fishing report 2 hrs wkly. ■ Robert S. Eaves Jr., pres; Paul Mougel, gen mgr; Lloyd E. Persons, opns mgr; Annita Harrison, gen sls mgr; Ray Hilley, progmg dir; Ron Cummings, news dir; Robert McWhorter, chief engr.

KNKE-FM—Not on air, target date unknown: 107.3 mhz; 3 kw. Ant 298 ft. TL: N31 00 57 W93 59 13. 765 Hemphill St. (75951). Licensee: dba Rayburn Broadcasting Co.

KTXJ(AM)—Aug 6, 1948: 1350 khz; 5 kw-D, 37 w-N. TL: N30 55 11 W93 68 13. Box 2008 (75951). (409) 384-6801. FAX: (409) 384-3866. Licensee: KTXJ Radio Inc. Group owner: Community Service Radio Group (acq 8-1-79). Net: Unistar, ABC/D; Texas Net. Format: 40s, 50s and 60s. Spec prog: Farm 5 hrs wkly. ■ Jack Borgen, gen mgr; Robert Holcomb, opns mgr, progmg dir & mus dir; Craig Lester, news dir; Alan McKee, chief engr.

KWYX(FM)—Co-owned with KTXJ(AM). November 1964: 102.3 mhz; 3 kw. Ant 299 ft. TL: N30 55 11 W93 58 13 (CP: 102.7 mhz, 50 kw, ant 492 ft., TL: N31 09 12 W93 59 25). Stereo. Prog sep from AM. Format: Country.

Jefferson

KJTX(FM)—October 1990: 104.5 mhz; 1.75 kw. Ant 423 ft. TL: N32 48 13 W94 22 26. Stereo. Hrs opn: 24. Box 642 102 E. Harrison (75657). (903) 665-1150. FAX: (903) 665-1170. Licensee: Wisdom Ministries Inc. (acq 4-16-93; $140,000; FTR 5-3-93). Format: Gospel News progmg 2 hrs wkly. ■ Leroy Richardson, pres; Ray Lee Williams, opns mgr; Ray Lee Willard, progmg dir.

Johnson City

KFAN-FM—1991: 107.9 mhz; 37.2 kw. Ant 492 ft. TL: N30 11 49 W98 38 19. Stereo. Hrs opn: 24. Box 311, 210 Woodcrest, Fredericksburg (78624). (512) 997-2197. FAX: (512) 997-2198. Licensee: Fritz Broadcasting Co. Inc. Format: Progsv, AAA. Target aud: 25-49. ■ Jayson Fritz, pres & gen mgr; Jan Fritz, sr vp, gen sls mgr, vp mktg & pub affrs dir; Laverne Moldenhauer (local), rgnl sls mgr; Laverne Moldenhauer, adv mgr; J.D. Rose, progmg mgr; John Scott, mus dir; Tom Mills, news dir; Ducan Black, chief engr. ■ Rates: $20; 18; 20; 12.

Junction

KMBL(AM)—1953: 1450 khz; 1 kw-U. TL: N30 29 34 W99 45 41. Hrs opn: 24. 214 Pecan St. (76849). (915) 446-3371. Licensee: Murnic-Mead (acq 7-2-82; $95,000; FTR 7-26-82). Net: Unistar; Texas AP. Format: Country. News staff one; news progmg 6 hrs wkly. Target aud: General. Spec prog: Farm 6 hrs wkly. ■ Bob Meadows, pres, gen mgr & progmg dir. ■ Rates: $6; 5; 5; 3.

Keene

***KJCR(FM)**—June 13, 1974: 88.3 mhz; 23 kw. Ant 180 ft. TL: N32 24 19 W97 19 55. Stereo. Hrs opn: 6 AM-midnight. 300 N. College Dr. (76059). (817) 556-4788. FAX: (817) 556-4744. Licensee: Southwestern Adventist College (acq 6-13-74). Wash atty: Donald Martin. Format: Relg. News progmg 8 hrs wkly. Target aud: General; adult Christians. Spec prog: Class 4 hrs, gospel 2 hrs wkly. ■ Marvin E. Anderson, pres; Robert R. Mendenhall, gen mgr; Jeremy W. Woodruff, progmg dir; Karl E. Leukert, mus dir; John A. Williams, news dir; Walter M. Bolinger, chief engr. ■ Rates: $36; 36; 36; 36.

Kenedy-Karnes City

KAML(AM)—November 1954: 990 khz; 250 w-D. TL: N28 51 02 W97 52 48. Rt. One, Box 990, Kenedy (78119); Rt. 1, Box 990, Karnes City (78118). (512) 583-2990; (800) 390-2290. Licensee: Dorisann L. Eckols (acq 2-15-71). Rep: Dome. Format: Country. Spec prog: Farm 12 hrs, polka one hr wkly. ■ Steve Eckols, pres, gen mgr, gen sls mgr, prom mgr & chief engr.

Kermit

KERB(AM)—June 1950: 600 khz; 1 kw-D, DA. TL: N31 50 05 W103 08 10. Box 553, Odessa (79760). (915) 333-1227. Licensee: Mesa Entertainment Inc. (acq 11-4-91; $80,000 with co-located FM). Net: Texas Net. Rep: Keystone (unwired net). Format: Sp. ■ Pete Almanza, gen mgr; Don Cook, chief engr.

KERB-FM—1983: 106.3 mhz; 3 kw. Ant 276 ft. TL: N31 50 05 W103 08 10. Dups AM 100%.

Kerrville

KERV(AM)—Nov 5, 1948: 1230 khz; 990 w-U. TL: N30 04 14 W99 11 07. Stereo. Hrs opn: 24. Suite 333, 301 Junction Hwy. (78028). (512) 896-1230. FAX: (512) 792-5555. Licensee: Griffin Broadcasting Corp. (acq 5-10-89; $737,500 with co-located FM; FTR 5-29-89). Net: ABC/E, Unistar. Wash atty: Fisher, Wayland, Cooper & Leader. Format: MOR, news/talk. News staff 2; news progmg 25 hrs wkly. Target aud: 45 plus; educated professionals. Spec prog: Relg 2 hrs, gospel one hr, Sp one hr wkly. ■ Neal Griffin, pres; Rick Phipps, gen mgr & gen sls mgr; Bob Meadows, natl sls mgr & rgnl sls mgr; J.R. Blankenship, prom mgr; Steve Alex, progmg dir & mus dir; Bruce Clark, news dir; Ron Cole, chief engr. ■ Rates: $15; 15; 15; 14.

KRVL(FM)—Co-owned with KERV(AM). Sept 12, 1975: 94.3 mhz; 50 kw. Ant 492 ft. TL: N30 15 45 W99 07 59. Stereo. Hrs opn: 24. Prog sep from AM. (512) 792-5785. Net: ABC. Format: Contemp country. News staff 2; news progmg 15 hrs wkly. Target aud: 25-49. ■ Neil Griffin, CEO; Richard Griffin, pres; Steve Alex, vp progmg; Bruce Clark, asst mus dir; Ron Cole, vp engrg. ■ Rates: $22; 20; 22; 18.

KITE(FM)—Oct 1990: 92.3 3 kw. Ant 299 ft. TL: N30 07 04 W99 11 40 (CP: 92.3 mhz, 44 kw, ant 403 ft.). 115 Crestwood Dr. (78028-4830). (210) 792-4560. FAX: (210) 895-1431. Licensee: Ron Whitlock. Format: Light adult contemp. ■ Ron Whitlock, pres & gen mgr; Irene Vanwinkle, gen sls mgr & mus dir.

KRVL(FM)—Listing follows KERV(AM).

Kilgore

KKTX(AM)—Dec 26, 1936: 1240 khz; 1 kw-U. TL: N32 25 02 W94 51 15. 3607 Gilmer Rd., Longview (75604). (903) 297-3696. FAX: (903) 297-3699. Licensee: Noalmark Broadcasting Corp. (group owner; acq 7-1-76). Net: ABC/FM. Rep: Katz, Target. Format: Classic rock. Target aud: 18-49. ■ William C. Nolan Jr., pres; Jerome Orr, gen mgr.

KKTX-FM—Dec 23, 1976: 96.1 mhz; 32 kw. Ant 620 ft. TL: N32 24 25 W94 50 57. Stereo. Dups AM 100%. ■ Rates: $20; 18; 19; 14.

***KTPB(FM)**—Feb 4, 1991: 88.7 mhz; 10 kw-V. Ant 400 ft. TL: N32 20 14 W95 02 41. Stereo. Hrs opn: 19. 904 Houston, Kilgore (75662). (903) 983-8625. Licensee: Kilgore College. Net: APR. Format: Class. News staff one; news progmg 6 hrs wkly. Target aud: 35-50; higher socio-economic, educated. Spec prog: Jazz 4 hrs, new age 6 hrs, local concerts 2 hrs wkly. ■ John B. Dozier, gen mgr; Kathy Housby, opns dir & progmg dir; Kevin Kelley, mus dir; Jim Allen, news dir; N. Bryan Black, chief engr.

Killeen

KHHT(FM)—Aug 1, 1961: 93.3 mhz; 100 kw. Ant 1,948 ft. TL: N30 43 34 W97 59 23. Stereo. 8309 N. I-35, Austin (78753). (512) 832-4000. FAX: (512) 832-4063. Licensee: Genesis Broadcasting Inc. (acq 10-5-93; $2.5 million). Format: Hot country. Spec prog: Public Service 2 hrs wkly. ■ Jim Gustafson, stn mgr; Ed Mayberry, news dir; Bryan King, chief engr.

KIIZ-FM—Dec 10, 1990: 92.3 mhz; 3 kw. Ant 259 ft. TL: N31 06 33 W97 39 00. Stereo. Hrs opn: 24. Box 2469, Harker Heights (76543). (817) 699-5000. FAX: (817) 628-8840. Licensee: Conner Communications Inc. (acq 6-17-92). Net: ABC/C. Rep: Christal. Format: Urban. News progmg 2 hrs wkly. Target aud: 18-49. ■ Tim Thomas, gen mgr; Deserai Downs, progmg dir & mus dir; Julia Conner, news dir; Jerry White, chief engr.

KLFX(FM)—See Harker Heights.

***KNCT-FM**—Nov 23, 1970: 91.3 mhz; 50 kw. Ant 1,170 ft. TL: N30 59 12 W97 37 47. Stereo. Hrs opn: 24. Box 1800, Central Texas College, Hwy. 190 W. (76540-9990). (817) 526-1176. FAX: (817) 526-4000. Licensee: Central Texas College. Net: APR. Format: Btfl mus. News staff one; news progmg 11 hrs wkly. Target aud: 45 plus. Spec prog: Jazz 15 hrs wkly, big band 6 hrs wkly. ■ Max Rudolph, gen mgr; Jose Fajardo, stn mgr; Carolyn Vales, mktg mgr; Brodie Bashaw, progmg mgr; Steve Sullivan, chief engr. ■ KNCT(TV) affil.

KRMY(AM)—July 4, 1955: 1050 khz; 250 w-D. TL: N31 06 53 W97 42 00. 314 N. 2nd St. (76541). (817) 628-7070; (817) 634-5263. FAX: (817) 628-7071. Licensee: Mid-Texas Radio Communications Inc. (acq 11-89; grpsl; FTR 11-27-89). Net: ABC/C. Format: Ethnic. News progmg 2 hrs wkly. Target aud: 18-44. ■ Eugene Kim, pres.

Kingsville

KNGV(FM)—November 1981: 92.7 mhz; 3 kw. Ant 210 ft. TL: N27 32 07 W97 53 06. Box 671, 308 E. Kleberg (78363). (512) 592-4377; (512) 592-4378. FAX: (512) 592-7678. Licensee: Ohio Broadcast Associates. Net: SMN. Wash atty: Fletcher-Heald. Format: Oldies. News staff one; news progmg 5 hrs wkly. Target aud: 25-54. ■ Arnold Maulkin, chmn & pres; Lillian Katz, stn mgr; Marc Munroe, Sean Hall, progmg dirs; Sean Hall, news dir; John Gifford, chief engr.

***KTAI(FM)**—Feb 23, 1970: 91.1 mhz; 100 w. Ant 75 ft. TL: N27 31 24 W97 52 42. Stereo. Campus Box 178 (78363). (512) 595-3489. Licensee: Texas A&M Kingsville University. (group owner). Format: Variety. ■ Dr. Manuel Ibanez, pres; Mel Strait, gen mgr & chief engr; John Carreon, progmg dir.

KWVS(FM)—May 2, 1970: 97.5 mhz; 100 kw. Ant 1,000 ft. TL: N27 30 54 W97 51 58. Stereo. Hrs opn: 24. 1520 S. Port, Corpus Christi (78405). (512) 883-5987. FAX: (512) 883-3648. Licensee: Quality Broadcasting Corp. (acq 12-23-88; $800,000; FTR 1-23-89). Rep: D&R Radio. Wash atty: Barry Wood. Format: Classic rock, AOR, new age. News staff one; news progmg 3 hrs wkly. Target aud: 25-49; educated, affluent young adults. ■ Gary F. Maricle, pres, gen sls mgr, prom mgr & progmg dir; Jane St. John, mus dir; Dan King, news dir; Paul Easter, chief engr.

La Grange

KVLG(AM)—June 27, 1959: 1570 khz; 250 w-D, DA. TL: N29 52 58 W96 51 57. Box 609 (78945). (409) 968-3173; (409) 743-4050. FAX: (409) 968-6196. Licensee: Fayette Broadcasting Corp. Net: Texas State. Format: C&W. News staff one; news progmg 16 hrs wkly. Target aud: General. Spec prog: Ger one hr, Black one hr, farm 4 hrs, Polish/Czech 12 hrs, relg 5 hrs wkly. ■ Raymond G. Schindler, pres; George Keith, gen mgr; Dan Mueller, progmg dir & news dir; Mike Anders, chief engr.

KBUK(FM)—Co-owned with KVLG(AM). Dec 21, 1970: 104.9 mhz; 3 kw. Ant 203 ft. TL: N29 52 57 W96 51 58 (CP: Ant 328 ft.). Stereo. Dups AM 10%.

Lake Jackson

KBRZ(AM)—See Freeport.

KZFX(FM)—Apr 1963: 107.5 mhz; 100 kw. Ant 2,000 ft. TL: N29 17 16 W95 13 53. Stereo. Hrs opn: 24. #1100, 3050 Post Oak Blvd., Houston (77056). (713) 968-1000. FAX: (713) 986-1055. Licensee: Shamrock Broadcasting Co. Inc. (group owner; acq 9-86; FTR 6-16-86). Rep: Katz. Format: Classic rock. News staff 2; news progmg 5 hrs wkly. Target aud: 25-54; college grads from the 60s, 70s & 80s. ■ Bill Clark, CEO; Marty Laughman, pres; Mary Bennett, gen mgr; Kandice Armstrong, gen sls mgr; John Poche, natl sls mgr; Andrew Huang, mktg dir; Dan Michaels, progmg dir; Steve Robison, mus dir; Jackie Robbins, news dir & pub affrs dir; Mike Hudman, chief engr. ■ Rates: $300; 250; 350; 150.

Lamesa

KIOL-FM—Aug 13, 1987: 100.3 mhz; 100 kw. Ant 800 ft. TL: N32 23 47 W101 57 24. Stereo. Suite 2720, 6 Desta Dr., Midland (79705). (915) 570-8833. Licensee: Galen O. Gilbert. Group owner: Community Service Radio Group (acq 12-21-89; FTR 1-15-90). Format: Special blend. News staff one; news progmg one hr wkly. Target aud: 25-54; college-educated, upper-income families. Spec prog: Community theater, relg. ■ Charissa Boedecker, gen mgr & prom mgr; Clayton Allen, progmg dir; Jill Myers, news dir. ■ Rates: $15; 13; 15; 10.

KMMX(FM)—May 1, 1988: 104.7 mhz; 100 kw. Ant 920 ft. TL: N33 08 15 W101 54 48. Stereo. Hrs opn: 24. Suite 104, 10 Briercroft Park, Lubbock (79412). (806) 762-1047. FAX: (806) 762-8419. Licensee: West Texas Broadcasting Co. Inc. Rep: Banner. Wash atty: Lawrence J. Bernard. Format: Adult contemp. News staff one; news progmg 5 hrs wkly. Target aud: 25-54. ■ Mike Harlan, gen mgr; Steve Sever, gen sls mgr.

KPET(AM)—May 21, 1947: 690 khz; 250 w-U. TL: N32 42 27 W101 56 11. Hrs opn: 24. Box 1188, One Radio Rd. (79331). (806) 872-6511; (806) 872-6537. FAX: (806) 872-6514. Licensee: KPET Inc. (acq 8-7-91; $150,000). Net: ABC/D, SMN; Texas Net. Format: C&W. News staff one; news progmg 2 hrs wkly. Target aud: 18-65. ■ Bill Gerber, chmn, exec vp & vp opns; Don Sitton, gen mgr, opns dir, opns mgr, mus dir & news dir; Tommy Scarborough, gen sls mgr; Anthony Garza, chief engr.

Lampasas

KCYL(AM)—1948: 1450 khz; 1 kw-U. TL: N31 04 31 W98 11 02. Hrs opn: 5 AM-11 PM. Box 889 (76550). (512) 556-3671. Licensee: Ronald K. Witcher (acq 2-12-85). Net: Texas State Net. Format: C&W. News progmg 15 hrs wkly. Target aud: 30 plus. agriculture, farm & ranch. Spec prog: Farm 5 hrs, local news and community svc 14 hrs, sports 8 hrs wkly. ■ Ronnie Witcher, pres, gen mgr, stn mgr & chief engr; Charles Schaub, gen sls mgr; Robert McCormack, progmg mgr & asst mus dir. ■ Rates: $8; 7.50; 7.50; 7.50.

KUTZ(FM)—May 16, 1976: 98.9 mhz; 18.5 kw. Ant 1,860 ft. TL: N30 43 34 W97 59 23. Stereo. Hrs opn: 24. Suite 390, 12710 Research Blvd., Austin (78759). (512) 331-9191; (512) 390-5665. FAX: (512) 331-9933. Licensee: Shamrock Communications. (group owner; acq 6-88). Net: SMN. Rep: Torbet. Wash atty: Wilkinson, Barke, Konue & Quinn. Format: AOR (current, intensive). news progmg 2 hrs wkly. Target aud: 18-34; men. ■ Bill Lynett, pres; Mark Kiester, gen mgr & natl sls mgr; Malcolmm Ryke, opns dir; Susan Kelly, gen sls mgr; Daryl O'Neal, prom dir; Malcolmn Ryke, progmg dir; Kevin Stone, chief engr. ■ Rates: $50; 55; 60; 25.

Laredo

***KBNL(FM)**—July 27, 1985: 89.9 mhz; 100 kw. Ant 575 ft. TL: N27 35 21 W99 16 45. Stereo. Hrs opn: 24. Box 2425 (78044). (210) 724-9090. FAX: (210) 724-8019. Licensee: World Radio Network Inc. (group owner; acq 10-24-85). Format: Relg, Sp. News progmg 5 hrs wkly. Target aud: General. ■ Abe C. Van Der Puy, pres; Tom Narwold, gen mgr; Stanley Swanson, chief engr.

KDOS(AM)—Apr 20, 1990: 1490 khz; 1 kw-U. Hrs opn: 6 AM-midnight. Box 814 (78042); 505 Houston St. (78040). (210) 725-1490; (210) 725-1491. FAX: (210) 725-3424. Licensee: Miguel A. Villarreal Jr. (acq 1-17-90; $250,000; FTR 12-25-89). Rep: Caballero. Wash atty: Baraff, Koerner, Hoechberg & Olender. Format: Sp. News staff 2; news progmg 6 hrs wkly. Target aud: 18-54. ■ Miguel A. Villarreal Ibarra, pres & news dir; Miguel A. Villarreal Jr., gen mgr & gen sls mgr; Luis C. Villarreal, progmg dir; Deyla R. DeVillarreal, mus dir; Arturo Trevino, chief engr. ■ Rates: $35; 30; 35; 24.

***KHOY(FM)**—November 1985: 88.1 mhz; 1.8 kw. Ant 348 ft. TL: N27 31 14 W99 31 19. 1901 Corpus Cristi (78043). (210) 722-4167. Licensee: Diocesan Telecommunications Corp. Format: Sp, btfl mus, educ. News progmg 3 hrs wkly. Target aud: General. Spec prog: Class 4 hrs, jazz 4 hrs wkly. ■ Bennett McBride, gen mgr.

KJBZ(FM)—Dec 29, 1982: 92.7 mhz; 3 kw. Ant 289 ft. TL: N27 31 04 W99 31 20. Stereo. Hrs opn: 24. 902 E. Calton Rd. (780410). (210) 726-9393; FAX: (210) 724-9915. Licensee: Guerra Enterprises. Group owner: Encarnacion A. Guerra (acq 12-14-89; $750,000; FTR 1-8-90). Net: ABC/D. Rep: Katz. Wash atty: J. Jokovich. Format: Tejano. News staff one; news progmg 18 hrs wkly. Target aud: General; all ages. ■ Carny Guerra, pres, opns dir, vp sls, progmg dir & mus dir; Frank Mull, gen mgr, gen sls mgr, mktg dir & prom mgr; Rene Gonzalez, chief engr. ■ Rates: $25; 25; 25; 25.

KLAR(AM)—1956: 1300 khz; 1 kw-D, 500 w-N, DA-N. TL: N27 28 17 W99 28 47. Stereo. Hrs opn: 24. Box 1899, S. Lapata Hwy. at Norton (78044). (210) 723-7459. Licensee: Crystal Media Inc. (acq 7-1-86). Net: CNN. Format: News/talk. News staff 2; news progmg 18 hrs wkly. Target aud: 18-54; Hispanic & Anglo middle-, upper-middle-class. Spec prog: Tesano Tex-Mex music 8 hrs wkly. ■ Rafael Gomez, pres & adv dir; Jim Allen, gen sls mgr & natl sls mgr; Rick O'Neil, prom mgr, progmg dir, pub affrs dir & engrg dir; Frank Wagner, news dir; Renee Gonzalez, chief engr. ■ Rates: $15; 15; 15; 10.

KOYE(FM)—Listing follows KVOZ(AM).

KRRG(FM)—October 1982: 98.1 mhz; 100 kw. Ant 737 ft. TL: N27 31 14 W99 31 19. Stereo. 902 E. Calton Rd. (78041). (210) 724-9800. FAX: (210) 724-9813. Licensee: Encarnacion A. Guerra (acq 11-20-92; $1.2 million; FTR 12-21-92). Rep: D & R Radio. Format: Adult contemp, CHR. ■ Encarnacion A. Guerra, pres; Frank Mull, gen mgr & gen sls mgr; Mark McClain, progmg dir & mus dir.

KVOZ(AM)—Apr 15, 1952: 890 khz; 10 kw-D, 1 kw-N, DA-N. TL: N27 32 57 W99 22 21. Box 1638 (78044). (210) 723-4396. FAX: (210) 723-8575. Licensee: Border Broadcasting. Format: Spanish gospel. News staff one. Target aud: 18 plus. ■ W. I. Harpole, pres; Bob Kitzmiller, exec vp & gen mgr; Art Treveno, chief engr.

KOYE(FM)—Co-owned with KVOZ(AM). Feb 2, 1972: 94.9 mhz; 100 kw. Ant 1,000 ft. TL: N27 31 14 W99 31 19. Stereo. Prog sep from AM. Rep: Roslin. Format: Country. ■ Jim Scott, progmg dir & mus dir.

KZTQ(FM)—Not on air, target date unknown: 106.1 mhz; 3 kw. Ant 213 ft. TL: N27 33 12 W99 24 17. Licensee: Miguel A. Villarreal Jr. (acq 2-26-93; $122,500; FTR 3-15-93).

Levelland

KLVT(AM)—August 1949: 1230 khz; 1 kw-U. TL: N33 35 49 W102 23 09. Box 967, N. West Ave. (79336). (806) 894-3134. Licensee: James D. Peeler (acq 10-16-92; $400,000 with co-located FM; FTR 11-16-92). Net: AP; Texas State Net. Format: Country, Sp. ■ James D. Peeler, pres; Alva Lee Peeler, vp; Russ Nelson, gen mgr; Rex Clark, news dir.

KLVT-FM—Nov 8, 1983: 105.5 mhz; 3 kw. Ant 300 ft. TL: N33 34 54 W102 23 48. Stereo. Format: Country, Sp.

Liberty

KSHN-FM—Aug 29, 1991: 99.9 mhz; 26 kw. Ant 679 ft. TL: N30 03 05 W94 31 37. Stereo. Hrs opn: 19. 517 Travis (77575). (409) 336-5793. FAX: (409) 336-5250. Licensee: Trinity River Valley Broadcasting Co. (acq 11-77). Net: Texas State Net. Wash atty: Pepper & Corazzini. Format: Adult contemp, oldies, recurrent country. News staff 2; news progmg 36 hrs wkly. Target aud: Adult. Spec prog: Black 3 hrs wkly. ■ William R. Buchanan, pres & gen mgr; J.R. Austin, prom mgr & mus dir; Sam Sailer, adv mgr; Allen Wayne, asst mus dir; Wade Dove, news dir; Barbara Moss, pub affrs dir; Larry Hutson, chief engr. ■ Rates: $13; 13; 13; 13.

KPXE(AM)—Co-owned with KSHN-FM. Not on air, target date unknown: 1050 khz; 250 w-D, DA.

Littlefield

KZZN(AM)—1947: 1490 khz; 1 kw-U. TL: N33 56 17 W102 20 38. Box 192 (79339). (806) 385-4474. Licensee: Emil Macha (acq 10-29-92; $46,000; FTR 11-23-92). Net: USA; Tex. State Net., Tex. Agribus. Format: Country. Target aud: General; try to reach all ages. Spec prog: Farm 7 hrs, relg 5 hrs wkly. ■ Emil Macha, CEO, gen mgr, opns mgr, sls dir & chief engr; Sandra Macha, mus dir; Regina Boelyn, news dir. ■ Rates: $5; 5; 5; na.

Livingston

KETX(AM)—June 28, 1957: 1440 khz; 5 kw-D. TL: N30 44 23 W94 55 30. Hrs opn: 6 AM-midnight. Drawer 1236, U.S. 59 N. (77351). (409) 327-8916. Licensee: Harold J. Haley dba Polk County Broadcasting Co. Net: ABC; Texas State. Wash atty: Eugene T. Smith. Format: Country. News staff 2. Target aud: General. ■ Hal Haley, pres & gen mgr.

KETX-FM—Sept 1, 1970: 92.3 mhz; 50 kw. Ant 699 ft. TL: N30 44 23 W94 55 30 (CP: TL: N30 44 18 W94 55 23). Stereo. Dups AM 100%. ■ KETX-TV affil.

Llano

KLKM(FM)—1984: 104.7 mhz; 11 kw. Ant 459 ft. TL: N30 41 12 W98 34 15. Stereo. 1014 Hwy. 1431 W., Granite Shoals (78654). (915) 247-3729; (210) 598-2840. Licensee: Maxagrid Broadcasting Co. (acq 4-1-88). Wash atty: John Kenkel. Format: Adult contemp. News staff one; news progmg 10 plus hrs wkly. Target aud: 40 plus; upscale, retired, affluent. Spec prog: Big band 10 hrs wkly. ■ Shane Fox, pres; Bill Fox, gen mgr & gen sls mgr; Terry Wooden, progmg dir; Butch Case, news dir; Kevin Stone, chief engr.

Longview

KARW(AM)—1948: 1280 khz; 1 kw-D, 56 w-N. TL: N32 26 58 W94 43 38. Hrs opn: 6 AM-midnight. Box 7100 (75607). (903) 757-2020. FAX: (903) 757-6005. Licensee: Pinetree Media Inc. (acq 11-10-88; $225,000; FTR 12-19-88). Format: Urban. Target aud: 18-50; Black audience. ■ Janet Washington, pres & gen sls mgr; Eugene Washington, gen mgr; Dave Felder, prom dir, progmg dir & mus dir; Lavoyd Williams, news dir.

KFRO(AM)—Feb 6, 1935: 1370 khz; 1 kw-U, DA-N. TL: N32 30 07 W94 42 12. Stereo. Hrs opn: 24. Box 4299, Curtis Bldg., 481 E. Loop 281 E., (75606-4299). (903) 663-3700. FAX: (903) 663-1022. Licensee: Voice of Longview Inc. Net: CBS; Texas State. Rep: Katz & Powell. Wash atty: Kaye Scholer. Format: Oldies. News staff one; news progmg 30 hrs wkly. Target aud: 25-54; general. Spec prog: Black 3 hrs wkly. ■ James R. Curtis Jr., pres & gen sls mgr; Mary Helen Bair, opns mgr; Barry Davis, news dir; Lamar George, chief engr. ■ Rates: $20; 20; 20; 20.

KYKX(FM)—July 1, 1974: 105.7 mhz; 100 kw. Ant 1,005 ft. TL: N32 36 04 W94 52 15. Stereo. Hrs opn: 24. Box 5818, 1618 Judson Rd. (75608-5818). (903) 757-2662. FAX: (903) 757-2684. Licensee: Radio SunGroup of Texas Inc. Group owner: SunGroup Inc. (acq 11-1-85; grpsl; FTR 9-23-85). Net: ABC/I. Rep: McGavren Guild. Format: Modern country. News staff one; news progmg 6 hrs wkly. Target aud: General. ■ Ed Cearley, vp, gen mgr, stn mgr & natl sls mgr; Sherri Garrett, opns dir; Robert Taylor, gen sls mgr; Diane Day, Gary Walker, prom dirs; Ken Curtis, progmg dir & mus dir; Tony McCullogh, asst mus dir; Diane Bridges, news dir; Annett Justice, pub affrs dir; Steve Bridges, engrg dir & chief engr. ■ Rates: $67; 53; 67; 27.

Lorenzo

KKCL(FM)—Not on air, target date unknown: 98.1 mhz; 50 kw. Ant 431 ft. TL: N33 36 32 W101 43 45. Box 11472, Lubbock (79408). Licensee: American General Media-Lubbock. Group owner: American General Media (acq 5-87; $400,000; FTR 6-23-86). Format: Oldies. ■ Anthony S. Brandon, pres; Teri Wilson, gen mgr; Brian Roberts, progmg dir.

Los Ybanez

KYMI(FM)—December 1990: 107.9 mhz; 50 kw. Ant 459 ft. TL: N32 43 22 W102 01 50. Stereo. Hrs opn: 6 AM-midnight. Box 1143, Lamesa (79331). (806) 872-6553. FAX: (806) 872-6244. Licensee: Israel Ybanez (acq 3-8-90; FTR 4-2-90). Net: SMN, ABC. Format: Adult contemp, Sp. News staff 2; news progmg 3 hrs wkly. Target aud: 25-49. Spec prog: Farm 12 hrs, gospel 3 hrs, Sp, relg 3 hrs wkly. ■ Israel Ybanez, pres & vp opns; Larry Ybanez, gen mgr; Lorina Lara, opns mgr, dev dir, prom mgr & asst mus dir; Brock Whitten, chief opns & dev mgr; Kyann Amos, gen sls mgr; Floyd Phillips, chief engr.

Lubbock

***KAMY(FM)**—Oct 1, 1990: 90.1 mhz; 200 w. Ant 492 ft. TL: N33 30 08 W101 52 20. Stereo. Hrs opn: 24. 6401 University Ave. (79413). (806) 799-7104. FAX: (806) 799-7113. Licensee: Maranatha Radio Inc. (acq 8-20-93; FTR 11-8-93). Net: Skylight. Format: Christian, talk, news, educ. Target aud: 28 plus; Christian community of Lubbock. ■ T. Kent Atkins, pres; Randy Hays, gen mgr & chief engr; Ken Haney, mus dir.

KCAS(AM)—See Slaton.

KEJS(FM)—Not on air, target date unknown: 106.5 mhz; 34 kw. Ant 587 ft. TL: N33 30 08 W101 52 20. 4319 57th St. (79413). Licensee: Barton Broadcasting Co.

KFMX-FM—Listing follows KKAM.

KFYO(AM)—Sept 6, 1927: 790 khz; 5 kw-D, 1 kw-N, DA-3. TL: N33 27 50 W101 55 30. Stereo. Hrs opn: 24. Box 64670 (79464-4670). 14302 Slide Rd. (79424). (806) 794-7979. FAX: (806) 794-1660. Licensee: South Plains Broadcasting Co. Inc. Group owner: Seaton Stations (acq 2-1-79). Net: CBS; Texas State. Rep: Torbet. Wash atty: Borsari & Kump. Format: Full svc, country. News staff 2; news progmg 12 hrs wkly. Target aud: General. Spec prog: Farm 15 hrs, relg 6 hrs wkly. ■ Edward L. Seaton, pres; Danny Fletcher, gen mgr; Kim Bitar, gen sls mgr; Max Mott, prom mgr, progmg dir & news dir; Charles Kenny, chief engr. ■ Rates: $35; 20; 23; 16.

KZII-FM—Co-owned with KFYO(AM). Mar 10, 1982: 102.5 mhz; 100 kw. Ant 850 ft. TL: N33 31 05 W101 51 25. Stereo. Hrs opn: 24. Prog sep from AM. (Acq 2-1-85). Format: Contemp hit. News staff one; news progmg 5 hrs wkly. Target aud: 18-49. ■ Todd Chambers, prom dir; Chuck Luck, progmg dir; Jay Shannon, mus dir. ■ Rates: $36; 27; 34; 18.

KJAK(FM)—(Slaton). Feb 12, 1978: 92.7 mhz; 100 kw. Ant 584 ft. TL: N33 32 32 W101 50 14. Stereo. Hrs opn: 24. Box 3890, Lubbock (79452). (806) 745-6677. FAX: (806) 745-8140. Licensee: Williams Broadcasting Group (acq 6-19-81; $575,000; FTR 7-13-81). Format: Relg. Christians & those looking for answers to everyday problems. Spec prog: Sports 5 hrs wkly. ■ J. Douglas Williams, pres; Woody Van Dyke, gen mgr, gen sls mgr, prom mgr, mus dir & news dir; Roger Taylor, chief engr. ■ Rates: $20; 20; 20; 20.

KJBX(AM)—Sept 19, 1953: 580 khz; 500 w-D, 290 w-N, DA-2. TL: N33 32 00 W101 49 14. 6602 Quirt Ave. (79404). (806) 798-7995. FAX: (806) 798-7052. Licensee: Sonnance Lubbock (acq 7-93; $760,000 with co-located FM; FTR 9-20-93). Net: ABC/I. Rep: Christal. Format: Adult contemp. Target aud: 18-49; lean to female 25-49. ■ Scott Parsons, gen mgr; John Hart, mus dir; Cindy St. James, news dir; Roger Taylor, chief engr.

KRLB-FM—Co-owned with KJBX(AM). July 15, 1964: 99.5 mhz; 100 kw. Ant 817 ft. TL: N33 31 05 W101 51 25. Stereo. Box 53120 (79453). Format: Adult contemp. News staff one. ■ Alan Thomas, Cindy St. James, news dirs.

KKAM(AM)—Jan 1, 1955: 1340 khz; 1 kw-U. TL: N33 33 24 W101 51 46. Suite 300, 4413 82nd St. (79424-3366). (806) 798-7078. FAX: (806) 798-7052. Licensee: Sonance Lubbock L.C. (group owner; acq 10-7-92; $1 million with co-located FM; FTR 11-16-92). Net: NBC Talknet. Rep: Katz. Format: Stardust. ■ Scott Parsons, gen mgr; Edith Castillo, prom mgr & progmg dir; Kid Manning, mus dir; Jackie Montes, news dir; Roger Taylor, chief engr.

KFMX-FM—Co-owned with KKAM. Aug 1, 1966: 94.5 mhz; 100 kw. Ant 817 ft. TL: N33 31 05 W101 51 25. Stereo. Dups AM 1%. Net: NBC the Source. Format: AOR. ■ Wes Nessman, progmg dir.

KLFB(AM)—Nov 15, 1966: 1420 khz; 500 w-U, DA-N. TL: N33 36 49 W101 52 30. Hrs opn: 18. Box 5697 2700 Marshall St. (79417). (806) 765-8114. Licensee: Drew Ballard (acq 3-28-91; $40,000; FTR 4-15-91). Net: Texas Net. Rep: Caballero. Format: Sp. ■ Walter Ledesma, gen mgr & gen sls mgr; Helen Castro, prom mgr; Santos Perez, progmg dir; Bill Enloe, chief engr.

KLLL(AM)—May 14, 1947: 1590 khz; 1 kw-U, DA-2. TL: N33 31 16 W101 46 28. 1314 50th (79412). (806) 763-1911. FAX: (806) 770-5363. Licensee: Ballstrom Trust Services L.C. Group owner: Pinnacle Broadcasting Co. (acq 12-22-92; grpsl; FTR 1-18-93). Net: MBS. Rep: Eastman. Format: C&W. ■ Scott Harris, gen mgr; Jon Steele, opns mgr; Kim Bitar, gen sls mgr; Rick Gilbert, progmg dir; Jeff Scott, mus dir; Jay Prince Jones, news dir; Cliff Gibson, chief engr.

KLLL-FM—Mar 1, 1958: 96.3 mhz; 100 kw. Ant 817 ft. TL: N33 31 05 W101 51 25. Stereo. Dups AM 100%.

***KOHM(FM)**—January 1973: 89.1 mhz; 50 kw. Ant 525 ft. TL: N33 34 55 W101 53 25. Stereo. Box 43082 (79409). (806) 742-3716. Licensee: Texas Tech Univ. (acq 11-87). Net: NPR, BSN. Format: Class. ■ Clive J. Kinghorn, gen mgr; Sylvia Jones, stn mgr; Michael Croney, dev dir; Clinton Barrick, mus dir; Ben Price, pub affrs dir; Donald Patterson, chief engr. ■ *KTXT-TV affil.

KONE(FM)—1975: 101.1 mhz; 100 kw. Ant 750 ft. TL: N33 30 08 W101 52 20. Stereo. Box 6752 (79493); 3002 50th St. (79413). (806) 797-3377. Licensee: Texas Lotus Communications. Group owner: Lotus Communications Corp. (acq 6-20-83; $1.05 million; FTR 7-11-83). Net: Unistar. Rep: D&R Radio. Format: Hot country. News staff one; news progmg one hr wkly. Target aud: 18-49. ■ Holden Elliot, vp opns & rgnl sls mgr; Page Miller, vp prom; Jerry Brownlow, vp progmg & mus dir; Jim Spann, pub affrs dir; Bob Schnieder, vp engrg. ■ Rates: $35; 35; 35; 25.

KRLB-FM—Listing follows KJBX(AM).

KTNP(AM)—April 1953: 1460 khz; 1 kw-D, 250 w-N. TL: N33 32 53 W101 49 24. Hrs opn: 24. Box 93013 (79493); 5120 Magnolia Ave. (79404). (806) 763-6051. FAX: (806) 744-8363. Licensee: Cecilia G. Benavides (acq 3-85; $200,000; FTR 3-18-85). Format: Sp, Tejano. Target aud: General. ■ Rick Benavides, gen mgr; Albert Benavides, opns mgr; Ben Benavides, natl sls mgr; Joe Rodriguez, mus dir; Mike Rodriguez, news dir; Bob Schieder, chief engr. ■ Rates: $20; 18; 20; 18.

***KTXT-FM**—Apr 1, 1961: 88.1 mhz; 35 kw. Ant 423 ft. TL: N33 34 55 W101 53 25. Stereo. Box 43082, Texas Tech Univ. (79409). (806) 742-3916. Licensee: Texas Tech Univ. Format: Div. Spec prog: Black 6 hrs wkly. ■ Clive Kinghorn, gen mgr; Donald Patterson, chief engr. ■ *KTXT-TV affil.

KXTQ(AM)—Nov 1, 1946: 950 khz; 5 kw-D, 500 w-N, DA-2. TL: N33 34 53 W101 49 38. Hrs opn: 24. 904 E. Broadway (79403). (806) 747-2555. FAX: (806) 741-1757. Licensee: Ramar Development Inc. (acq 9-93; $362,500). Net: AP. Rep: Caballero. Format: Sp hit radio. ■ Brad Moran, gen mgr & gen sls mgr; Ben Gonzalez, progmg dir, mus dir & news dir.

KXTQ-FM—November 1963: 93.7 mhz; 100 kw. Ant 740 ft. TL: N33 30 57 W101 50 54. Stereo. Hrs opn: 24. Prog sep from AM. Net: AP. Format: Country.

***KYFT(FM)**—Oct 24, 1993: 90.9 mhz; 5 kw. Ant 236 ft. TL: N33 32 30 W101 49 16. 4216 50th St (79413). (806) 788-1909. Licensee: Bible Broadcasting Network Inc. (group owner). Format: Traditional christian mus & gospel hymns. ■ Dave Dixon, gen mgr.

KZII-FM—Listing follows KFYO(AM).

Lufkin

KAFX(AM)—(Diboll). June 2, 1957: 1260 khz; 1 kw-D, 109 w-N. TL: N31 10 14 W94 47 10 (CP: COL: Huntington, 500 w-U, TL: N31 13 44 W94 34 11). Hrs opn: 24. Box 588, 2714 S. Medford, Lufkin (75901). (409) 634-5596. FAX: (409) 639-5540. Licensee: Eagle of Texas Inc. Group owner: Eagle Communications (acq 1986). Net: Unistar. Rep: Christal. Format: Contemp hit. News staff one; news progmg 4 hrs wkly. Target aud: General. Spec prog: Gospel 7 hrs wkly. ■ John Hazlewood, gen mgr; Bill Stix, progmg dir; Don Steed, chief engr.

KAFX-FM—(Diboll). June 29, 1960: 95.5 mhz; 100 kw. Ant 567 ft. TL: N31 24 28 W94 45 53. Stereo. Hrs opn: 24. Dups AM 95%.

***KLDN(FM)**—May 2, 1991: 88.9 mhz; 50 kw. Ant 649 ft. TL: N31 24 28 W94 45 53. Stereo. Hrs opn: 24. One University Place, Shreveport, LA (71115). (318) 797-5150. FAX: (318) 797-5154. Licensee: Board of Supervisors of Louisiana State Univ. Net: NPR. Format: Class, news, jazz. Target aud: 28-40. ■ Jean Hardman, mktg dir; Mary Masters, progmg dir; Rod Matthews, chief engr.

KRBA(AM)—May 3, 1938: 1340 khz; 1 kw-U. TL: N31 21 51 W94 43 09. Hrs opn: 24. Box 1345, 121 Calder Sq. (75901). (409) 634-6661. FAX: (409) 632-5722. Licensee: Darrell E. Yates. Rep: Katz. Format: Country, Classic rock, relig, Sp. News staff one; news progmg 7 hrs wkly. Target aud: General. ■ Darrell E. Yates, pres; Shirley Yates, gen mgr; John Chaney, gen sls mgr; Keith Sims, progmg dir, mus dir & news dir; Melanie Quine, pub affrs dir. ■ Rates: $8; 7; 8; 5.

KUEZ(FM)—Co-owned with KRBA(AM). May 1, 1978: 99.3 mhz; 25 kw. Ant 699 ft. TL: N31 24 28 W94 45 53. Stereo. Hrs opn: 24. Prog sep from AM. Wash atty: Lee Peltzman. Format: Adult contemp. Target aud: 25-54.

***KSWP(FM)**—Aug 31, 1985: 91.1 mhz; 380 w. Ant 174 ft. TL: N31 23 17 W94 46 43 (CP: 90.9 mhz, 30 kw, ant 787 ft.). Stereo. Hrs opn: 6 AM-midnight. Rt. 8, Box 1150 (75904); Hwy. 69 N. at Holmes Rd. (75901). (409) 639-5673. FAX: (409) 639-5677. Licensee: Lufkin Educational Broadcasting Foundation. Net: USA. Format: Christian mus. Spec prog: Pub affrs talk show 2 hrs wkly. ■ Dwyane Calvert, pres; Billy Baldwin, gen mgr, progmg dir & mus dir; Brian Cameron, chief engr.

KUEZ(FM)—Listing follows KRBA(AM).

KYKS(FM)—July 9, 1976: 105.1 mhz; 100 kw. Ant 1,066 ft. TL: N31 22 08 W94 38 45. Stereo. Hrs opn: 24. Box 2209, 1206 S. 1st (75901). (409) 639-4455; (409) 639-4456. FAX: (409) 632-5957. Licensee: Gulfstar Broadcasting (acq 11-1-93). Net: AP. Rep: Eastman. Wash atty: Fletcher, Heald & Hildreth. Format: Country. News staff one. Target aud: 25-54. ■ Larry Gunter, gen mgr; Mary Ramos, gen sls mgr; Gary Roberts, progmg dir; Steve Ricks, mus dir; James McWain, chief engr.

Luling

KFGI-FM—Mar 22, 1987: 94.7 mhz; 100 kw. Ant 1,154 ft. TL: N30 02 42 W97 52 50. Stereo. Hrs opn: 24. Bldg. B, Suite 350, 4301 Westbank Dr., Austin (78746). (512) 327-9595; (512) 390-5344. FAX: (512) 329-6257. Licensee: New Thinking Inc. Net: SMN. Rep: D & R Radio. Format: Oldies. Target aud: 18-54. Spec prog: Pub affrs 2 hrs wkly. ■ Ion Bason, gen mgr; Joel Burke, progmg dir.

Lytle

***KXPZ(FM)**—Jan 20, 1990: 91.3 mhz; 3 kw. Ant 302 ft. TL: N29 14 39 W98 44 27. Stereo. Hrs opn: 7 AM-7 PM. 381 E. Ramsey, San Antonio (78216). (512) 340-9053. Licensee: The Stronghold Foundation Inc. Format: All music. Target aud: 18-34; youth & young adult. ■ James C. Baer, pres; Lyn Willoughby, chief engr.

Madisonville

KAGG(FM)—Dec 5, 1989: 96.1 mhz; 50 kw. Ant 500 ft. TL: N30 48 02 W96 07 00. Stereo. Hrs opn: 24. 4101 S. Texas, Bryan (77802). (409) 268-9696. FAX: (409) 846-0414. Licensee: Oara Inc. Group owner: Osburn/Reynolds Group (acq 8-16-89). Rep: Eastman. Wash atty: Fletcher, Heald & Hildreth. Format: Country. ■ Gary Koeffler, gen mgr; Serene Rognon, opns mgr; Susan Molitor, gen sls mgr; Bobby Bell, progmg dir; Cindy Sweatman, pub affrs dir; James McWain, chief engr.

KMVL(AM)—October 1989: 1220 khz; 500 w-D, 12 w-N. TL: N30 56 04 W95 52 52 (CP: TL: N30 57 56 W95 53 52). Hrs opn: 24. 102 W. Main (77864). (409) 348-9200; (409) 348-9201. FAX: (409) 348-9201. Licensee: Hunt Broadcasting (acq 7-17-91; FTR 8-5-91). Net: SMN, USA; Texas State. Format: Oldies, relg, local news/sports/talk. News staff one; news progmg 15 hrs wkly. Target aud: General. ■ Leon Hunt, gen mgr; Chester Leediker, chief engr. ■ Rates: $9; 6; 6; 6.

NEW AM—Not on air, target date unknown: 880 khz; 5 kw-D, 1 kw-N. Box 176J, R.R. 3, Denison (75020). Licensee: Madison County Radio Inc. (acq 5-9-83).

Malakoff

KCKL(FM)—Aug 8, 1983: 95.9 mhz; 6 kw. Ant 306 ft. TL: N32 08 48 W95 58 25 (CP: Ant 295 ft.). Stereo. Hrs opn: 24. Box 489, Hwy. 31 E. (75148). (903) 489-1238. FAX: (903) 489-2671. Licensee: Cedar Creek Radio Co. Inc. Group owner: Routt Radio Companies Inc. Net: Texas State Net. Format: Light country. News progmg 10 hrs wkly. Target aud: 25-54; country/city folk & 100,000 weekenders & visitors to Cedar Creek Lake. Spec prog: Relg 7 hrs wkly. ■ Alan Routt, pres, gen mgr & gen sls mgr; Pat Isaacson, opns mgr; Tim Michaels, progmg dir & mus dir; Rich Flowers, news dir; John Gee, chief engr. ■ Rates: $15; 13; 15; 10.

Marion

***KBIB(AM)**—Sept 21, 1989: 1000 khz; 250 w-D, DA. TL: N29 34 09 W98 09 47. Rt. 1, Box 95-C, Marion (78124). (210) 420-2083. Licensee: Hispanic Community College. Wash atty: Wiley, Rein & Fielding. Format: Relg, Sp. Target aud: General. ■ Pastor Ken Hutchinson, pres & gen mgr.

Marlin

KBBW(AM)—See Waco.

KEYR(FM)—Apr 2, 1977: 92.9 mhz; 3 kw. Ant 300 ft. TL: N31 19 31 W96 54 36. Stereo. Hrs opn: 24. Box 8093, Waco (76714); 1018 N. Valley Mills Dr., Waco (76710). (817) 772-0930. Licensee: KRZI Inc. (acq 1-27-89; $410,266; FTR 1-16-89). Net: Unistar. Rep: Roslin. Wash atty: Leventhal, Senter & Lerman. Format: Adult contemp. News staff one; news progmg one hr wkly. Target aud: 25-49. Spec prog: Black 4 hrs, relg 2 hrs wkly. ■ Van Goodall Jr., pres; Robert Lauck, gen mgr; Tyler Thosen, progmg dir; Roland Richter, news dir; Dave Fricker, chief engr. ■ Rates: $15; 14; 14; 8.

Marshall

***KBWC(FM)**—March 1977: 91.1 mhz; 100 w. Ant 110 ft. TL: N32 32 12 W94 22 29. Stereo. Hrs opn: 8 AM-midnight. 711 Wiley Ave. (75670). (903) 927-3307. FAX: (903) 927-3100. Licensee: Wiley College. Net: American Urban. Format: Black. Target aud: 18-34. ■ David L. Beckley, pres; Nela Gilbert, gen mgr; Clarice Watkins, progmg dir & mus dir; Wayne Wilkinson, chief engr.

KCUL(AM)—Oct 7, 1957: 1410 khz; 500 w-D, 90 w-N, DA-2. TL: N32 29 30 W94 21 52. Hrs opn: 5:30 AM-11 PM. Box 1326, (75671). 200 W. Interstate 20 (75670). (903) 935-1410. FAX: (903) 938-9730. Licensee: East Texas Stereo Inc. (acq 1-1-90). Net: USA; Format: Relg, news/talk. News staff one; news progmg 15 hrs wkly. Target aud: General. Spec prog: Farm 3 hrs wkly. ■ A.T. Moore, pres; H.A. Bridge Jr., exec vp, gen mgr & vp sls; Mark Sorenson, opns mgr & mus dir; Marion O'Neil, prom dir; John Gordon, news dir; A. T. Moore, chief engr. ■ Rates: $10; 8; 10; 8.

KCUL-FM—1988: 92.3 mhz; 3 kw. Ant 328 ft. TL: N32 32 26 W94 24 03. Stereo. Hrs opn: 5:30 AM-11 PM. Prog sep from AM. (Acq 3-12-90). Net: Texas State Net. Format: Oldies, news. Spec prog: Sports, farm 3 hrs wkly. ■ Rates: $12; 11; 12; 11.

KMHT(AM)—1947: 1450 khz; 1 kw-U. TL: N32 33 50 W94 21 04. Box 8428 (75671). (903) 935-6018. Licensee: Wiley College (acq 6-2-93; donated, with co-located FM; FTR 6-21-93). Format: News/talk. ■ Jerry Russell, CEO.

KZEY-FM—Co-owned with KMHT(AM). Sept 4, 1977: 103.9 mhz; 3 kw. Ant 300 ft. TL: N32 33 50 W94 21 04. Format: Urban contemp.

Mason

KOAX(FM)—Not on air, target date unknown: 97.9 mhz; 50 kw. Ant 492 ft. TL: N30 37 25 W99 25 41. Stereo. Box 590209, c/o Henderson, Houston (77259-0209). (309) 364-3903. Licensee: Laser Communications Inc.

McAllen

***KHID(FM)**—July 1992: 88.1 mhz; 2.1 kw. Ant 253 ft. TL: NN26 21 44 W98 19 26. Stereo. Hrs opn: 6 AM-midnight. Simulcasts KMBH-FM Harlingen. Box 2147, 1701 Tennessee St., Harlingen (78551). (210) 421-4111. FAX: (210) 421-4150. Licensee: RGV Educational Broadcasting Inc. Format: News, class & btfl mus. News progmg 34 hrs wkly. Target aud: General. Spec prog: Sp 3 hrs wkly. ■ Darrell Rowlett, pres & gen mgr; John Harris III, vp & stn mgr; Bobbie Barajas, progmg dir; Brian Smith, chief engr. ■ KMBH(TV) affil.

KIRT(AM)—See Mission.

KJAV(FM)—See Alamo.

KQXX(FM)—1964: 98.5 mhz; 100 kw. Ant 1,400 ft. TL: N26 05 59 W97 50 16. Stereo. 608 S. 10th St. (78501). (512) 686-2111. FAX: (512) 630-0886. Licensee: Bravo Broadcasting Co. Group owner: The Gomez Group (acq 10-4-66). Rep: Caballero. Format: Sp. ■ Edward L. Gomez, pres & vp mktg; Tina Compean, gen mgr, gen sls mgr, mktg mgr & mus dir; Marsiela Bracchini, adv mgr; Juan F. Vargas, progmg dir & news dir; Rick Butler, chief engr.

KRIO(AM)—1947: 910 khz; 5 kw-U, DA-4. TL: N26 17 52 W98 12 26. Hrs opn: 5:45 AM-midnight. 4300 S. Business 281, Edinburg (78539). (512) 686-3147; (512) 383-3845. FAX: (512) 380-8105. Licensee: Rio Grande Bible Institute Inc. (acq 5-30-86). Wash atty: Bryan, Cave, McPheeters & McRoberts. Format: Relg, educ, Sp. Target aud: General. ■ Gordon E. Johnson, pres; Javier Salinas, gen mgr & progmg dir; Don L. DeMonbrun, opns mgr; Jerry Jeske, chief engr.

KVLY(FM)—See Edinburg.

***KVMV(FM)**—March 1972: 96.9 mhz; 100 kw. Ant 1,160 ft. TL: N26 04 53 W97 49 44. Stereo. Hrs opn: 24. Box 3333 (78502); 715 E. Thomas Dr., Pharr (78577). (210) 787-9700. FAX: (210) 787-9783. Licensee: World Radio Network Inc. (group owner; acq 8-27-84). Net: Moody, USA, Skylight. Format: Relg. News staff one; news progmg 4 hrs wkly. Target aud: 30-65; general. ■ Abe C. Van Der Puy, pres; Ben Cummings, sr vp; Joe Fahl, stn mgr & progmg dir; Kevin Davis, mus dir; Dawn Autperle, news dir; Martha Phillips, pub affrs dir; David Riley, chief engr.

***KXGZ(FM)**—Not on air, target date unknown: 88.1 mhz; 2.1 kw. Ant 253 ft. TL: N26 21 44 W98 19 26. Hrs opn: 6 AM-midnight. Box 2147, 1701 E. Tennessee Ave., Harlingen (78550). Licensee: RGV Educational Broadcasting Inc. (acq 4-1-91; FTR 4-22-91). Format: News, class, jazz. Target aud: General. ■ John E. Harris III, stn mgr; Thelma Camacho, mktg mgr; Bobbie Balajas, progmg mgr; Brian Smith, chief engr.

McKinney

KRVA-FM—Aug 1, 1969: 106.9 mhz; 2.5 kw. Ant 351 ft. TL: N33 15 49 W96 35 54. Stereo. Hrs opn: 24. Suite 1310, 3500 Maple Ave., Dallas (75219). (214) 528-1600.

Memphis

KLSR(AM)—Apr 26, 1966: 1130 khz; 1 kw-D, DA. TL: N34 41 13 W100 30 23. Hrs opn: Sunrise-sunset. Box 400, 114 N. 7th (79245). (806) 259-3511. Licensee: Harold James Davis (acq 7-15-86; $78,348.49 with co-located FM; FTR 7-28-86). Net: CNN; Texas State Net, Texas Agribus. Wash atty: Cohn & Marks. Format: C&W, div, contemporary. Spec prog: Sp 6 hrs, Live from the 60s 3 hrs, relg 5 hrs wkly. ■ Donna Davis, pres & gen sls mgr; Joe Davis, gen mgr, progmg dir & chief engr; Hal Davis, news dir.

KLSR-FM—1982: 105.3 mhz; 61 kw. Ant 180 ft. TL: N34 41 W100 30 23. Stereo. Hrs opn: 6 AM-midnight. Dups AM 100%.

Mercedes

KTJN(FM)—Sept 10, 1982: 105.5 mhz; 3 kw. Ant 285 ft. TL: N26 13 50 W98 20 18. Stereo. Hrs opn: 24. Box 3407, 1050 McIntosh, Brownsville (78523). (210) 544-1600; (210) 541-6348. FAX: (210) 542-4109; (210) 544-0311. Licensee: La Nueva KBOR Inc. (acq 3-1-89; FTR 3-20-89). Rep: Caballero. Wash atty: Fisher, Wayland & Cooper. Format: Sp. News staff 3. Target aud: General. ■ Edgar C. Trevino, pres & gen sls mgr; Hilda Trevino, gen mgr; David Carpinteyro, news dir; Severo Garza, chief engr.

Merkel

KCWS(FM)—Nov 4, 1983: 102.7 mhz; 100 kw. Ant 1,486 ft. TL: N32 22 00 W99 58 42. Stereo. 4510-A S. 14 St., Abilene (79605). (915) 691-9292. Licensee: Ovation Broadcasting Co. (acq 8-1-89). Net: ABC/C. Format: Country.

KMXO(AM)—June 1, 1963: 1500 khz. 604 N. 2nd (79536). (915) 928-3060. Licensee: Ray R. Silva. Format: Christian, Sp.

Mesquite

*__KEOM(FM)__—Sept 4, 1984: 88.5 mhz; 61 kw. Ant 514 ft. TL: N32 45 46 W96 38 04. Stereo. Hrs opn: 5 AM-midnight. 2500 Memorial Pkwy. (75149). (214) 285-0297. FAX: (214) 329-6314. Licensee: Mesquite Independent School District. Net: Texas State. Format: Div, educ with AC music. Target aud: General; citizens of Mesquite & surrounding area. ■ James Griffin, stn mgr; Dennis Hevron, chief engr.

Mexia

KRQX(AM)—May 21, 1956: 1590 khz; 500 w-D, 128 w-N. TL: N31 41 10 W96 27 18. 919 E. Milan (76667). (817) 562-5328. FAX: (817) 562-6729. Licensee: First American Broadcasting Corp. (acq 6-19-86; $220,000 with co-located FM; FTR 2-24-86). Net: Texas State Net. Format: Country. ■ Matt Groveton, gen mgr; Linda Webb, gen sls mgr; Ray Boucher, progmg dir; Matt D. Groveton, news dir.

KYCX-FM—Co-owned with KRQX(AM). Aug 29, 1983: 104.9 mhz; 3 kw. Ant 301 ft. TL: N31 42 25 W96 31 23. Stereo. Prog sep from AM. Net: CBS. Format: C&W.

Midland

KBAT(FM)—1974: 93.3 mhz; 100 kw. Ant 500 ft. TL: N31 57 30 W102 03 59. Sterec. Hrs opn: 24. 3306 Andrews Hwy. (79703). (915) 520-9600. Licensee: KWEL Inc. Rep: Eastman. Format: AOR. News staff one; news progmg 2 hrs wkly. Target aud: 18-44. ■ Bob Hicks, pres; Bob Clark, opns mgr; Bill Wiggleton, gen sls mgr; Bob Gerhard, progmg dir; Dru Dawson, mus dir; Sandra Bundrick, news dir; Larry Mitchell, chief engr.

KCHX(FM)—Aug 15, 1988: 106.7 mhz; 100 kw. Ant 613 ft. TL: N31 54 53 W101 57 49. Stereo. Hrs opn: 24. Suite 2700, 6 Desta Dr. (79705-5519). (915) 570-8833. FAX: (915) 685-7870; (915) 685-7873. Licensee: Sonance Midland L.C. (group owner; acq 9-17-92; $700,000; FTR 11-16-92). Net: Unistar. Format: CHR, top 40. Target aud: General; 18-39. ■ Dale Hendry, gen mgr; Charlotte Hill, opns mgr; Andrew Adams, gen sls mgr; Clayton Allen, progmg dir & mus dir; Jill Meyers, pub affrs dir; Rodney Norris, chief engr. ■ Rates: $22; 19; 22; 16.

KCRS(AM)—Dec 20, 1935: 550 khz; 5 kw-D, 1 kw-N, DA-2. TL: N32 04 10 W102 01 46. Stereo. Hrs opn: 24. Box 4607, 1001 Midkiff Dr. (79701). (915) 560-0550. FAX: (915) 699-5064. Licensee: Midland Broadcasting Co. Group owner: Wendell Mayes Stn. (acq 8-1-57). Net: Texas State Net. Rep: McGavren Guild. Wash atty: Dow, Lohnes & Albertson. Format: C&W. News staff 2; news progmg 10 hrs wkly. Target aud: 25-54. Spec prog: Relg 4 hrs, farm 5 hrs, gospel 4 hrs wkly. ■ Wendell Mayes Jr., CEO & chmn; Parker M. Humes, pres; Dick Baze, opns mgr & prom mgr; Floyd Phillips, chief opns & chief engr; Charles R. Palmer, gen sls mgr; Robert Hallmark, prom dir, progmg dir & mus dir; Jerry Mayfield, asst mus dir; Jesse Grimes, news dir & pub affrs dir. ■ Rates: $17.50; 14; 17.50; 11.

KCRS-FM—May 25, 1976: 103.3 mhz; 100 kw. Ant 920 ft. TL: N32 05 11 W102 17 11. Dups AM 100%. (915) 699-5062. Net: NBC. ■ Rates: Same as AM.

KJBC(AM)—Aug 6, 1950: 1150 khz; 1 kw-D. TL: N31 58 55 W102 03 30. 1903 S. Lamesa Rd. (79701). (915) 684-5152. Licensee: Donald R. Kennedy (acq 9-17-92; $70,000; FTR 11-16-92). Net: CNN. Format: Traditional country, Spanish. ■ Don Kennedy, pres, gen mgr & gen sls mgr; Oscar Chavez, prom dir; William K. Ward, progmg dir; Gracie Rayos, mus dir; Adolfo Bustamante, asst mus dir.

KMND(AM)—Nov 27, 1963: 1510 khz; 500 w-D. TL: N31 37 48 W102 04 53. Box 61147, 2911 LaForce Blvd. (79711). (915) 563-5636. FAX: (915) 687-5428. Licensee: Bakcor Broadcasting Inc. Group owner: Bakke Communications Inc. (acq 5-82; $92,000; FTR 5-13-82). Net: ABC/I. Rep: Banner. Format: Oldies. Spec prog: Jazz one hr wkly. ■ Steve Pingel, pres, gen mgr & gen sls mgr; Max Howard, progmg dir; Jay Hendricks, news dir; Tommy Jenkins, mus dir.

KNFM(FM)—Co-owned with KMND(AM). Nov 2, 1959: 92.3 mhz; 100 kw. Ant 985 ft. TL: N32 05 51 W102 17 21. Stereo. Net: ABC/E. Format: C&W. ■ Julie Rich, progmg dir.

KQIP(FM)—See Odessa.

KQRX(FM)—Not on air, target date 1994: 95.1 mhz; 10.35 kw. Ant 505 ft. TL: N32 03 10 W102 17 38. Box 12, (79702). Licensee: Three Card Enterprises. (acq 4-24-90; FTR 7-16-90). Wash atty: Fletcher, Heald & Hildreth. ■ David Cardwell, pres.

KWEL(AM)—April 1957: 1070 khz; 2.5 kw-D. TL: N31 57 44 W102 04 07. 1110 E. Scharbauer Dr. (79705). (915) 687-0585. Licensee: Faustino Quiroz (acq 5-1-93; $140,000; FTR 4-5-93). Rep: Lotus. Format: Sp. News progmg 6 hrs wkly. Target aud: General. ■ Faustino Quiroz, CEO, gen mgr & gen sls mgr; Marcelino Hernandez, progmg dir.

Mineola

KJMC(AM)—Sept 12, 1963: 1510 khz; 500 w-D. TL: N32 41 02 W95 29 44. Stn currently dark. Licensee: Canton Broadcasters Inc.

KMOO-FM—Sept 1, 1977: 96.7 mhz; 3 kw. Ant 300 ft. TL: N32 45 04 W95 33 18. Hrs opn: 24. Box 628, Greenville Hwy. (75773). (903) 569-3823. Licensee: KMOO Inc. (acq 1-31-89; $340,000 with co-located AM; FTR 2-20-89). Net: SMN. Format: C&W. News staff one; news progmg 3 hrs wkly. ■ Sam Curry, pres, gen mgr & news dir; Alice Tomeslin, gen sls mgr; Josh Fuller, chief engr. ■ Rates: $14; 9; 9; 9.

Mineral Wells

KJSA(AM)—Dec 1, 1946: 1140 khz; 250 w-D. TL: N32 47 12 W98 05 53. Box 638, Number One Radio Rd. (76067). (817) 325-1140. FAX: (817) 328-1712. Licensee: Jerry Snyder and Assoc. (acq 5-1-83; with co-located FM; FTR 7-11-83). Net: AP. Format: Traditional country. News staff 2. Target aud: Upscale adults. ■ Jerry Snyder, pres; Rick Brumfield, gen mgr & gen sls mgr; Tami Brumfield, prom mgr, progmg dir & mus dir; Kym West, news dir; Robert Snyder, chief engr. ■ Rates: $12; 12; 12; 12.

KYXS-FM—Co-owned with KJSA(AM). March 1, 1970: 95.9 mhz; 25 kw. Ant 295 ft. TL: N32 48 42 W98 06 11. Stereo. Hrs opn: 24. Format: Modern country. Target aud: General. ■ Jerry Snyder, CEO; Glynda Snyder, vp opns; Tami Brumfield, vp prom.

Mirando City

KBDR(FM)—Not on air, target date unknown: 100.5 mhz; 42 kw. Ant N27 21 13 W99 13 50. Stereo. Hrs opn: 24. 1919 Victoria St., Laredo (78040-7704). (512) 724-1000. Licensee: Alderete Communications. Wash atty: Fisher, Wayland, Cooper & Leader. ■ Cynthia Alderete Earle, pres; Bruce Miller Earle, gen mgr & chief engr; Danny Garcia, opns mgr & progmg dir.

Mission

KIRT(AM)—Feb 23, 1958: 1580 khz; 1 kw-D, 302 w-N. TL: N26 17 36 W89 19 50. 608 S. 10th St., McAllen (78501). (512) 686-1580. Licensee: Rio Broadcasting Co. Group owner: Gomez Group (acq 8-1-70). Net: Texas State. Rep: Caballero. Format: Sp. ■ Edward L. Gomez, pres & gen mgr; Humberto Pedraza, gen sls mgr; Rosie Pedraza, prom mgr; Joe Moralez, progmg dir, mus dir & news dir; Lawson Campbell, chief engr.

KQXX(FM)—See McAllen.

KTJX(FM)—1989: 105.5 mhz; 3 kw. Ant 300 ft. TL: N26 13 50 W98 20 18. Stereo. Hrs opn: 24. Box 3407, 1050 McIntosh, Brownsville (78523). (210) 544-1600; (210) 541-6348. FAX: (210) 542-4109; (210) 544-0311. Licensee: La Nueva KBOR Inc. (acq 5-5-93; $350,000; FTR 2-8-93). Rep: JB Systems. Format: Sp, country, oldies. News staff 3. ■ Edgar C. Trevino, pres & gen sls mgr; Hilda Trevino, gen mgr; David Carpinteyro, news dir; Severo Garza, chief engr.

Monahans

KCDQ(FM)—Jan 9, 1984: 102.1 mhz; 100 kw. Ant 977 ft. TL: N31 57 55 W102 46 10. Stereo. Hrs opn: 24. Box 4716, Suite 404, 700 N. Grant, Odessa (79761). (915) 333-1927. FAX: (915) 580 9102. Licensee: FHL Communications Corp. (acq 10-91; $325,000; FTR 10-28-91). Net: ABC/FM. Rep: Christal. Format: Classic rock, country. Target aud: 25-49. Spec prog: Relg 3 hrs wkly. ■ Gordon Holcomb, pres, gen mgr & progmg mgr; Karen Carter, prom mgr & news dir.

KGEE(FM)—Licensed to Monahans. See Odessa.

KLBO(AM)—Mar 12, 1947: 1330 khz; 5 kw-D, 1 kw-N, DA-N. TL: N31 38 45 W103 00 04. Hrs opn: 24. Box 270, 1706 E. Sealy (79756). (915) 943-2588. FAX: (915) 943-7314. Licensee: KLBO Inc. (acq 12-27-89; $175,000; FTR 1-23-89). Net: AP, Jones Satellite Audio. Rep: Riley. Wash atty: Robert & Eckard. Format: Adult contemp, country, Sp. News staff one; news progmg 6 hrs wkly. Target aud: 25-54; general. Spec prog: Gospel 3 hrs wkly. ■ Bill Cole, gen mgr, gen sls mgr & progmg dir; Roger Holley, mus dir; Rex Thee, news dir; Floyd Phillips, chief engr. ■ Rates: $7; 7; 7; 6.

Mount Pleasant

KIMP(AM)—Oct 8, 1948: 960 khz; 1 kw-D, 75 w-N. TL: N33 09 54 W95 00 27. Box 990 (75455). (903) 572-8726. FAX: (903) 572-7232. Licensee: East Texas Broadcasting Inc. (acq 11-21-91; $850,000 with co-located FM; FTR 12-16-91). Net: CNN; Texas State Net. Format: C&W, Sp. News staff one; news progmg 14 hrs wkly. Target aud: General. ■ John Mitchell, pres; Bud Kitchens, vp, gen mgr & gen sls mgr; Ron Tracy, opns dir; Michael Gunn, progmg dir & mus dir; Clint Cooper, news dir; Norm Mason, chief engr. ■ Rates: $13; 12; 13; 11.

KPXI(FM)—Co-owned with KIMP(AM). Oct 8, 1961: 100.7 mhz; 100 kw. Ant 984 ft. TL: N33 04 36 W95 14 26. Stereo. Hrs opn: 24. Prog sep from AM. Format: Contemp country. News staff one; news progmg 2 hrs wkly. Target aud: 25-54. ■ Bud Kitchens, adv mgr; Steve Bailey, progmg dir; Mick Fulpham, mus dir. ■ Rates: $25; 22; 25; 21.

Muenster

KXGM-FM—Dec 23, 1991: 106.5 mhz; 6 kw. Ant 328 ft. TL: N33 38 34 W97 19 15. Stereo. Hrs opn: 24. 107 S. Commerce, Gainesville (76240). (817) 668-1065; (817) 668-1000. FAX: (817) 668-1001. Licensee: Gain-Air Co Inc. (acq 6-29-90; FTR 7-23-90). Net: USA. Rep: Roslin. Wash atty: Reddy, Beglin & Martin. Format: Adult contemp, news. News staff one; news progmg 8 hrs wkly. Target aud: 25-54; general. ■ Charley M. Henderson, pres; Pamela A. Henderson, vp; Dee Blanton, opns dir & news dir. ■ Rates: $18; 12; 18; 10.

Muleshoe

KMUL(AM)—July 6, 1956: 1380 khz; 1 kw-D. TL: N34 13 39 W102 44 10. Box 486 (79347). (806) 272-4273. Licensee: Southwestern Broadcasting Co. (acq 12-1-89; $200,000 with co-located FM; FTR 12-18-89). Format: C&W, Sp. Spec prog: Farm 3 hrs wkly. ■ Tom Crane, pres.

KKYC(FM)—Co-owned with KMUL(AM). Feb 6, 1966: 103.1 mhz; 2.9 kw-H. Ant 75 ft. TL: N34 13 29 W102 44 10 (CP: 3.6 kw, ant 403 ft., TL: N34 12 58 W102 43 42). Stereo. Dups AM 55%.

Nacogdoches

KEEE(AM)—March 27, 1947: 1230 khz; 1 kw-U. TL: N31 34 51 W94 40 16. Hrs opn: 24. Box 63-1111 (75963). (409) 564-4444. FAX: (409) 564-3392. Licensee: Tri-Com Broadcasting Inc. Group owner: Carolyn G. Vance Group (acq 6-87; $1,948,000 with co-located FM; FTR 6-22-87). Net: ABC, ARN, MBS, SMN; Texas State Net. Format: News/talk, sports. News staff one; news progmg 12 hrs wkly. Target aud: 25 plus. ■ Carolyn G. Vance, pres; Carolyn Gage, gen mgr; William R. Vance, opns mgr; Joe Ramos Jr., gen sls mgr; Danny Merrell, progmg dir.

KJCS(FM)—Co-owned with KEEE(AM). May 1967: 103.3 mhz; 100 kw. Ant 476 ft. TL: N31 34 51 W94 40 16. Stereo. Hrs opn: 24. Prog sep from AM. Net: ABC; Format: C&W. News progmg 15 hrs wkly. Target aud: 25-54. Spec prog: Gospel 6 hrs wkly. ■ Kirk Looney, chief engr.

***KSAU(FM)**—July 5, 1975: 90.1 mhz; 3.5 kw. Ant 450 ft. TL: N31 37 45 W94 40 44. Hrs opn: 10 AM-2 AM. Box 13048 (75962). (409) 568-4000. FAX: (409) 568-1331. Licensee: Stephen F. Austin State U. Format: Jazz, progsv, new age. Target aud: 18-54. Spec prog: Blues 2 hrs, world music/reggae 2 hrs, rap 2 hrs wkly. ■ Dr. Dan Angel, pres; Sherry Williford, gen mgr; Alan Clarke, chief engr.

KSFA(AM)—June 2, 1947: 860 khz; 1 kw-D, 500 w-N. TL: N31 36 40 W94 37 50. Stereo. 338 University Dr. (75961). (409) 560-6677. FAX: (409) 569-9669. Licensee: George B. Wilkes III (acq 11-27-91; $700,000; with co-located FM; FTR 12-16-91). News staff 2; news progmg 2 hrs wkly. Target aud: 25-54. ■ George Wilkes, pres; Steve Laukhuf, gen mgr; Rebecca Cooper, gen sls mgr.

KTBQ(FM)—Co-owned with KSFA(AM). July 15, 1967: 107.7 mhz; 50 kw. Ant 492 ft. TL: N31 42 30 W94 41 18. Stereo. Prog sep from AM. Format: Adult contemp. ■ Shelley Swanzy, opns dir; Steve Laukhuf, progmg dir.

KYKS(FM)—See Lufkin.

Navasota

KWBC(AM)—Sept 21, 1960: 1550 khz; 250 w-D. TL: N30 22 48 W96 06 01. Hrs opn: Sunrise-sunset. Box 1349, 114 Farquhar St. (77868). (409) 825-8448. Licensee: McMullen Broadcasting Co. (acq 1-16-92; $175,000 with co-located FM; FTR 2-10-92). Net: SMN. Format: Oldies. News progmg 5 hrs wkly. Target aud: 21-55. Spec prog: Black 3 hrs wkly. ■ Ulman D. McMullen, pres & gen mgr; Michele McNew, gen sls mgr & prom mgr; Chuck Clements, progmg dir & news dir; Steve Sandlin, chief engr.

KMBV(FM)—Co-owned with KWBC(AM). Mar 1, 1989: 92.5 mhz; 6 kw. Ant 263 ft. TL: N30 24 58 W96 04 43 Stereo. Hrs opn: 24. Dups AM 95%. Box 11291, College Station (77842). (409) 764-9250. News progmg one hr wkly. Target aud: 25-54. ■ Chuck Clements, opns mgr.

Nederland

KQHN(AM)—Jan 11, 1969: 1510 khz; 5 kw-D, DA-D. TL: N30 03 35 W93 58 49. Box 1716, 117 Nederland Ave. (77627). (409) 724-1292. FAX: (409) 724-7055. Licensee: Ninety-Four Point One Inc. (acq 12-3-93; $700,000 with KQXY-FM Beaumont; FTR 12-20-93). Format: All sports. Target aud: 18-49; male. Spec prog: Relg 4 hrs wkly. ■ Laurie Harbison, gen mgr; Cindy Simon, natl sls mgr; John Lackness, progmg dir; Ken Johnson, news dir. ■ Rates: $15; 15; 15; na.

New Boston

KNBO(AM)—Nov 16, 1969: 1530 khz; 2.5 kw-D. TL: N33 28 56 W94 25 25. Hrs opn: 6 AM-6 PM. Box 848, F.M. Rd. 992 (75570). (903) 628-2561; (903) 628-2562. Licensee: Bowie County Broadcasting Co. Inc. Format: MOR, relg, news. News progmg 50 hrs wkly. Target aud: General. Spec prog: Farm 7 hrs wkly. ■ Richard E. Knox, pres, gen mgr, adv dir & chief engr; Carmen Johnson, vp progmg & mus dir. ■ Rates: $8; 8; 8; na.

KZRB(FM)—July 1, 1991: 103.5 mhz; 3 kw. Ant 328 ft. TL: N33 28 00 W94 27 48. Stereo. Hrs opn: 24. Box 1055 (75570). (903) 628-6059. Licensee: B & H Broadcasting System Inc. (acq 4-16-93; $90,000; FTR 5-3-93). Net: CNN; Texas State Net. Format: Urban contemp. News progmg 9 hrs wkly. Target aud: 25-55. ■ Ray C. Bursey Jr., CEO, pres & gen mgr; Darian T. Cox, opns mgr.

New Braunfels

KGNB(AM)—Apr 1, 1950: 1420 khz; 1 kw-D, 196-N. TL: N29 39 45 W98 10 29. Hrs opn: 24. 1540 Loop 337 N. (78130). (210) 625-7311. FAX: (210) 625-7336. Licensee: New Braunfels Communications Inc. (acq 12-15-89; $975,000 with co-located FM; FTR 1-1-90). Net: ABC, MBS, Unistar, ABC/E. Wash atty: Southmayd & Miller. Format: News, talk, original hits. News staff 3; news progmg 26 hrs wkly. Target aud: 35 plus. Spec prog: Ger one hr, relg 2 hrs wkly. ■ Hal S. Widsten, pres, gen mgr & gen sls mgr; Kim L. Lamas, prom mgr; Wayne Fanning, progmg dir & mus dir; Don Ferguson, news dir; Tom Bray, chief engr.

KNBT(FM)—Co-owned with KGNB(AM). Nov 22, 1968: 92.1 mhz; 3 kw. Ant 300 ft. TL: N29 43 50 W98 07 15. Stereo. Hrs opn: 24. Prog sep from AM. Format: Country. Target aud: 25-54. Spec prog: Relg 3 hrs wkly.

Odem

KKHQ(FM)—Feb 18, 1985: 98.3 mhz; 3 kw. Ant 303 ft. TL: N27 53 31 W97 30 11. Stereo. Suite 208, 317 Peoples, Corpus Christi (78401). (512) 887-9903. FAX: (512) 888-6696. Licensee: Coastal Digital Broadcasting Ltd. (acq 10-8-92; $72,000; FTR 11-16-92). Format: AOR ■ Bill Woody, pres; Lynn Poyner, gen mgr; Henry Garcia, gen sls mgr; Gustavo Michael Hurtado, progmg dir; Belarmino Cruz, news dir; Tony Gonzales, chief engr.

Odessa

KADM(FM)—Not on air, target date unknown: 107.7 mhz; 49 kw. Ant 502 ft. Box 13185 (79768). Licensee: Ruben Velasquez.

KCDQ(FM)—See Monahans.

***KENT(AM)**—Jan 29, 1947: 920 khz; 1 kw-D, 500 w-N, DA-1. TL: N31 49 14 W102 25 42. Hrs opn: 24. Box 3509 (79760). (915) 332-5791. Licensee: Southwest Educational Media Foundation. Rep: Moody. Format: Relg, MOR. ■ T. Kent Atkins, pres, gen mgr & progmg dir; Harold Willis, stn mgr & opns dir; George Whitaker, chief engr.

***KENT-FM**—Sept 1, 1989: 90.5 mhz; 6.5 kw. Ant 453 ft. TL: N31 53 50 W102 33 57. Dups AM 50%. (Acq 6-26-89). Format: Relg.

KGEE(FM)—(Monahans). Nov 1, 1983: 99.9 mhz; 98 kw. Ant 574 ft. TL: N31 45 40 W102 31 28. Stereo. Hrs opn: 24. 1514 N. Grandview, Odessa (79768). (915) 561-5499. FAX: (915) 550-5499. Licensee: New Frontier Communications Inc. (acq 8-7-89; $1 million; FTR 8-28-89). Net: ABC/I. Rep: Katz. Wash atty: Jones, Waldo, Holbrook & McDonough. Format: C&W. News staff one. Target aud: 25-54; general. ■ Tommy Vascou, pres; Michelle Murrill, gen sls mgr & adv mgr; Mike Lawrence, progmg dir; Boomer Kingston, mus dir; Will Wallace, chief engr.

KKKK(FM)—July 1, 1977: 99.1 mhz; 100 kw. Ant 500 ft. TL: N31 50 50 W102 27 15. Stereo. Box 60375, Midland (79711); 12200 W. I-20 E. (79765). (915) 563-2266. FAX: (915) 563-2288. Licensee: Tower Power Corp. Net: USA. Format: Relg. Target aud: General; 25-54. Spec prog: Black 5 hrs wkly. ■ J. R. McClure, pres; Robby McClure, vp; Becky Hill, gen mgr & gen sls mgr; Debra Guinn, prom mgr; George Collins, progmg dir & mus dir; Don Cook, chief engr. ■ Rates: $13.50; 12; 13.50; 10.50.

KMRK-FM—Aug 23, 1991: 96.1 mhz; 50 kw. Ant 440 ft. TL: N31 46 12 W102 32 26. Stereo. Hrs opn: 6 AM-11 PM. 4000 Rasco (79764). (915) 363-9696; (915) 550-9127. FAX: (915) 550-9696. Licensee: Mid-Cities Corp. Net: Unistar, CNN. Rep: Caballero. Format: Sp. News progmg 2 hrs wkly. Target aud: 18-54; 2nd and 3rd generation Hispanics. ■ Edward L. Roskelley, pres, stn mgr, sls dir, news dir & pub affrs dir. ■ Rates: $23; 23; 23; 23.

KNDA(AM)—Sept 26, 1980: 1000 khz; 250 w-D. TL: N31 48 09 W102 22 57. Box 7319 (79760). Licensee: L&T Enterprises Inc. ■ Ruben Velasquez, pres; Wilma Velasquez, gen mgr; David Jimenez, gen sls mgr & prom mgr; Ramon Arroyo, progmg dir; Miquel Martinez, news dir; Tom Barnes, chief engr.

KNFM(FM)—See Midland.

***KOCV(FM)**—Jan 6, 1964: 91.3 mhz; 5 kw. Ant 300 ft. TL: N31 51 30 W102 23 00. Stereo. Hrs opn: 6:15 AM-11 PM. 201 W. University Blvd. (79764). (915) 335-6336. Licensee: Odessa College. Net: NPR. Format: Classical. Spec prog: Jazz 10 hrs, opera 4 hrs wkly. ■ Phillip Speegle, pres; Tracy Taylor, gen mgr; Tom Hughes, stn mgr; Al Harris, chief engr.

KODM(FM)—1965: 97.9 mhz; 100 kw. Ant 361 ft. TL: N31 47 40 W102 10 44. Stereo. Claydesta Plaza, 6 Desta Dr., Midland (79705). (915) 561-9800. FAX: (915) 366-0217. Licensee: D&F Communications L.P. (acq 12-8-88; $2.55 million; FTR 1-16-89). Format: Adult contemp. Target aud: 25-54; women. ■ Charlie Cohn, pres; Charlotte Hill, gen mgr; Dale Hendry, opns mgr; Jim Martin, gen sls mgr; Ben Ray, progmg dir; Geno Pearson, mus dir; Rodney Norris, chief engr.

KOZA(AM)—Jan 20, 1947: 1230 khz; 1 kw-U. TL: N31 49 52 W102 22 09. Box 553 (79760); 1300 S. Crane (79763). (915) 333-1230. FAX: (915) 333-1227. Licensee: Mesa Enterainment Inc. (acq 4-20-89). Format: Sp. News staff one. Target aud: 18-54. ■ Agustine Mesa, pres; Pete Almanza, gen mgr; Luis C. Mendoza, progmg dir, mus dir & news dir; Rodney Norris, chief engr.

KQIP(FM)—Jan 1961: 96.9 mhz; 100 kw. Ant 500 ft. TL: N32 05 13 W102 17 12. Stereo. Hrs opn: 24. 3306 Andrews Hwy., Midland (79703). (915) 520-9600. Licensee: KWEL Inc. (acq 4-1-93). Rep: Eastman. Format: Gold 60s & 70s. News staff one; news progmg 2 hrs wkly. Target aud: 25-54; men. ■ Bob Hicks, pres; Bob Clark, gen mgr & opns mgr; Bill Wiggleton, gen sls mgr; Larson Cooper, progmg dir; Dru Dawson, mus dir; Sandra Brendrick, news dir; Larry Mitchell, chief engr.

KRIL(AM)—June 1946: 1410 khz; 1 kw-U, DA-N. TL: N31 49 00 W102 21 00. Box 4312, 1410 Crane Hwy. (79760). (915) 332-6870; (915) 580-6870. FAX: (915) 332-6882. Licensee: Clyde Butter (acq 11-8-90; FTR 11-26-90). Net: Wall Street, NBC, CBS, MBS. Wash atty: David Jatlow. Format: Heavy news, information, classical, news/talk. News staff 3; news progmg 80 hrs wkly. Target aud: 25 plus; higher educational level, higher income level. Spec prog: Farm one hr, jazz 4 hrs wkly. ■ Clyde Butter, pres & gen mgr; Doug Cole, progmg dir; Harland Johnson, chief engr. ■ Rates: $18; 18; 18; 18.

KXOI(AM)—See Crane.

Orange

KIOC(FM)—Feb 28, 1977: 106.1 mhz; 100 kw. Ant 1,225 ft. TL: N30 09 31 W93 59 11. Stereo. 1725 Evangeline Dr., Vidor (77662). (713) 769-2475. Licensee: K-106 Inc. Rep: Banner, Katz. Wash atty: John Fiorinni. Format: Rock 40. Target aud: 12-44; super active young adults. ■ Ken Stephens, CEO & gen mgr; Elizabeth McGalin, sls dir; Mark Landis, progmg dir; Jack Daniels, mus dir; Branden Shaw, news dir; Dave Biondi, chief engr.

KKMY(FM)—1972: 104.5 mhz; 100 kw. Ant 440 ft. TL: N30 08 07 W93 50 39 (CP: 98 kw, ant 984 ft. TL: N30 08 04 W93 56 59). Stereo. 4945 Fannett Rd., Beaumont (77705). (409) 842-5569. FAX: (409) 842-0800. Licensee: Uno Broadcasting Corp. (group owner; acq 3-89). Net: AP, Unistar, CNN. Rep: Eastman. Format: Adult contemp. News staff one; news progmg 2 hrs wkly. Target aud: 25-54; productive working adults with or without children. Spec prog: All request oldies 17 hrs, jazz 6 hrs wkly. ■ Bob Tezak, pres; Steve Lewis, gen mgr; George F. Ferris, stn mgr, opns mgr & progmg dir; Alan Pace, gen sls mgr; Robert Brock, prom mgr & mus dir; Sidney Austin, news dir & pub affrs dir; Russ Ingram, chief engr. ■ Rates: $35; 35; 35; 27.

KOGT(AM)—August 1948: 1600 khz; 1 kw-U, DA-N. TL: N30 08 25 W93 45 11. Box 1667 (77631). (409) 883-4381. Licensee: G-Cap Communications Inc. (acq 8-7-92; $250,000; FTR 8-24-92). Net: Texas State. Format: C&W. ■ Gary Stelly, pres & gen mgr; Richard Corder, gen sls mgr; Glen Earle, news dir.

Ozona

KYXX(FM)—Nov 25, 1976: 94.3 mhz; 3 kw. Ant 300 ft. TL: N30 42 39 W101 07 34. Stereo. HC 65, Box 50, Sonora (76950). (915) 387-3553. Licensee: Sonora-Ozona Broadcasting Co. (acq 10-15-93; grpsl; FTR 11-8-93). Rep: Riley. Format: C&W. ■ Camille Cauthorn, gen mgr; Fred Key, gen sls mgr; Jeremy Gibson, progmg dir; George Chambers, chief engr.

Palestine

KLIS(FM)—June 15, 1970: 96.7 mhz; 3 kw. Ant 300 ft. TL: N31 46 48 W95 38 23. Stereo. Box 788, 1801 N. Queen (75802). (903) 729-0181. Licensee: Vista Broadcasting Co. Inc. Net: MBS. Format: Contemp hit. News staff one; news progmg 6 hrs wkly. Target aud: 18-49. Spec prog: Gospel 2 hrs wkly. ■ L. D. Harris, pres; Jeff Harley, sls dir; Dennis Lively, prom mgr & progmg dir; Mike Monday, mus dir; Marvin Crain, news dir. ■ Rates: $11; 10; 11; 10.

KNET(AM)—Jan 2, 1936: 1450 khz; 1 kw-U. TL: N31 46 26 W95 37 00. Hrs opn: 24. Box 649, Loop 256 & Moody St. (75802). (903) 729-6077. Licensee: North Star Communications Inc. (acq 5-89). Net: CNN. Wash atty: Andrews & Kurth. Format: News. News staff one; news progmg 168 hrs wkly. Target aud: 35 plus. Spec prog: Farm 2 hrs. ■ Clive Runnels, CEO; Bruce Griffin, CFO; Hal Kemp, vp & gen mgr; Ken Kuhl, stn mgr; Leslie Hoover, gen sls mgr; Kevin McAdams, prom mgr; Kevin Mason, news dir; Wayne Hall, chief engr. ■ Rates: $20; 20; 20; 15.

KYYK(FM)—Co-owned with KNET(AM). Aug 20, 1976: 98.3 mhz; 50 kw. Ant 492 ft. TL: N31 46 26 W95 37 00. Stereo. Hrs opn: 24. Format: Contemp country. News staff one; news progmg 2 hrs wkly. Target aud: 18-54.

***KTDN(FM)**—Feb 19, 1987: 91.5 mhz; 550 w. Ant 519 ft. TL: N31 43 55 W95 37 25. Stereo. c/o CRN, 411 Ryan Plaza Dr., Alington (76011). 408 Old Elkhart Rd. (75802). (903) 723-3900; (817) 792-3800. FAX: (817) 277-9929. Licensee: Criswell Center for Biblical Studies (group owner; acq 11-84; grpsl; FTR 11-4-85). Format: Relg, inspirational. ■ Ron Harris, gen mgr.

KYYK(FM)—Listing follows KNET(AM).

Pampa

KGRO(AM)—1947: 1230 khz; 1 kw-U. TL: N35 34 39 W100 57 08. Box 1779, 1701 N. Banks (79065). (806) 669-6809. Licensee: Pampa Broadcasters Inc. (acq 8-1-67). Net: ABC/E. Format: Adult contemp. News staff one; news progmg 20 hrs wkly. Target aud: 18-45. ■ James Hughes, pres; Darrell Sehorn, gen mgr & gen sls mgr; Doc Deweese, progmg dir & progmg mgr; Matt Parsons, mus dir; Mike Ehrle, news dir; Phil Grove, chief engr. ■ Rates: $12; 12; 12; 10.

KOMX(FM)—Co-owned with KGRO(AM). May 18, 1981: 100.3 mhz; 32 kw. Ant 300 ft. TL: N35 34 39 W100 57 08. Stereo. Prog sep from AM. Net: SMN; Texas State Net. Format: Country. Target aud: 20 plus. Spec prog: Farm 10 hrs wkly. ■ Rates: Same as AM.

Paris

KBUS(FM)—Listing follows KGDD(AM).

KGDD(AM)—September 1950: 1250 khz; 500 w-D, 95 w-N. TL: N33 43 21 W95 32 50. Stereo. Hrs opn: 24. 2775 N.E. Loop 286 (75460). (903) 785-1069. FAX: (903) 785-6874. Licensee: Webster Broadcasting Corp. Group owner: Webster Broadcasting (acq 10-22-91; $561,893 with co-located FM; FTR 11-11-91). Net: SMN. Format: Oldies. News progmg 10 hrs wkly. Target aud: 25 plus. Spec prog: Relg 4 hrs, farm 5 hrs wkly. ■ Anne Oliver, pres, progmg dir & mus dir; Eddie Anderson, gen mgr; Charles Fox, news dir.

KBUS(FM)—Co-owned with KGDD(AM). June 3, 1985: 101.9 mhz; 50 kw. Ant 500 ft. TL: N33 37 15 W95 32 50. Stereo. Hrs opn: 24. (903) 785-1068. Net: ABC/I. Format: Adult contemp. Spec prog: Oldies 6 hrs wkly.

KOYN(FM)—Oct 6, 1988: 93.9 mhz; 50 kw. Ant 492 ft. TL: N33 49 36 W95 27 49. Stereo. Hrs opn: 24. Suite A, 3305 N.E. Loop 286 (75460). (903) 784-1293. FAX: (903) 985-7176. Licensee: C&E Broadcasting Inc. Net: USA. Wash atty: Greg Skall. Format: Country. News staff 2; news progmg 3 hrs wkly. Target aud: 12 plus. ■ Janie Kirland, stn mgr; Janie Kirkland, gen sls mgr; James Wyatt, prom mgr; Jim Corley, progmg dir & mus dir; Dale Gorsuch, chief engr. ■ Rates: $17; 15; 17; 13.

KPLT(AM)—Nov 19, 1936: 1490 khz; 1 kw-U. TL: N33 38 07 W95 33 14. Box 9 (75461); 2305 S.E. 3rd St. (75460). (903) 784-3311. FAX: (903) 784-5758. Licensee: KPLT Inc. (acq 5-19-87). Net: Texas State Net. Rep: Target. Format: Modern country. News staff one; news progmg 4 hrs wkly. Target aud: General. Spec prog: Gospel 4 hrs wkly. ■ Jeff Methven, pres, gen sls mgr & chief engr; Mike Rogers, stn mgr; Mike Patterson, news dir.

KPLT-FM—Aug 14, 1966: 107.7 mhz; 35 kw. Ant 300 ft. TL: N33 38 07 W95 33 14. Stereo. (903) 784-3313. FAX: (903) 784-3311. Format: Country, adult contemp. News staff one; news progmg 3 hrs wkly. Target aud: 21-44.

Pasadena

KIKK(AM)—October 1957: 650 khz; 250 w-D. TL: N29 41 18 W95 10 29. 6306 Gulfton Dr., Houston (77081). (713) 772-4433; (713) 526-3461. FAX: (713) 995-7956. Licensee: Group W (group owner; acq 10-20-93; FTR 11-8-93). Net: AP. Rep: Torbet. Format: Classic country. Target aud: 35-64. ■ Dickie Rosenfeld, vp & gen mgr; Rick Candea, opns mgr; Ron Burgess, gen sls mgr; Joan Hays, prom mgr; Carl Geisler, progmg dir; Joe Ladd, mus dir; Dan Woodard, chief engr.

KIKK-FM—See Houston.

***KJIC(FM)**—February 1981: 88.1 mhz; 440 w. Ant 110 ft. TL: N29 40 02 W95 09 17. 2936 Oleander (77503). (713) 998-8800. Licensee: Community Radio Inc. Format: Relg. News progmg 7 hrs wkly. ■ Robert L. Vaughn, pres, gen mgr & mus dir; Sharon Vaughn, prom mgr & progmg dir; Rick Jones, chief engr.

KKBQ-FM—August 1962: 92.9 mhz; 100 kw. Ant 1,919 ft. TL: N29 34 34 W95 30 36. Stereo. Suite 2022, 11 Greenway Plaza, Houston (77046). (713) 961-0093. FAX: (713) 963-1293. Licensee: Station KKBQ. Group owner: Gannett Broadcasting (acq 12-3-84; grpsl; FTR 12-10-84). Rep: McGavren Guild. Wash atty: Reid, Smith & Shaw. Format: Fresh country. ■ Don Troutt, pres & gen mgr; Kathy Armstrong, gen sls mgr; Tammy Justice, prom mgr; Dene Hallam, progmg dir; Jeff Garrison, mus dir; Allen Justice, news dir; Bob Strupe, chief engr.

KLVL(AM)—May 5, 1950: 1480 khz; 1 kw-D, 500 w-N, DA-N. TL: N29 41 02 W95 11 09. 111 N. Ennis, Houston (77003). (713) 225-3207. FAX: (713) 225-2824. Licensee: Angeline V. Morales. Rep: Lotus. Format: Norteno musica, ranchera musica. Spec prog: Black 4 hrs wkly. ■ Gustavo Perez, gen mgr & gen sls mgr; Al Padron, progmg dir; Lupita Hurtado, mus dir; Rudi Cantu, news dir; David Biondi, chief engr.

Pearsall

KVWG(AM)—Nov 3, 1962: 1280 khz; 500 w-D. TL: N28 53 13 W99 06 40. Box K, Hwy. 1581, Oil Field Rd. (78061). (210) 334-3664. FAX: (210) 334-3470. Licensee: Pearsall Broadcasters Inc. Group owner: The Herbort Stations (acq 11-26-75). Net: SIS; Texas State Net. Format: Sp, C&W, farm. ■ Noelia S. Herbort, pres; Jesus Sifuentes Jr., gen mgr, gen sls mgr, prom mgr, mus dir & news dir; Robert Ortegon, progmg dir.

KVWG-FM—March 1984: 95.3 mhz; 3 kw. Ant 203 ft. TL: N28 53 13 W99 06 40. Stereo. Dups AM 100%.

Pecos

KIUN(AM)—Oct 23, 1935: 1400 khz; 1 kw-U. TL: N31 26 09 W103 30 14. Box 469 (79772). (915) 445-2497. FAX: (915) 445-4092. Licensee: Pecos Radio Co. (acq 6-15-78). Net: Texas State Net. Rep: Riley. Format: C&W, Sp. Target aud: General. Spec prog: Farm 3 hrs wkly. ■ Roy E. Parker, pres; Bill R. Cole, gen mgr; David Baeza, gen sls mgr; Art Corrales, progmg dir, mus dir & news dir; Floyd Phillips, chief engr. ■ Rates: $7.75; 7.75; 7.75; 7.75.

KPTX(FM)—Co-owned with KIUN(AM). Aug 3, 1981: 98.3 mhz; 3 kw. Ant 160 ft. TL: N31 26 09 W103 30 14. Stereo. Hrs opn: 6 AM-10 PM. Prog sep from AM. Net: ABC/E. Format: Country. ■ David Baeza, progmg dir. ■ Rates: Same as AM.

Perryton

KEYE(AM)—Nov 19, 1948: 1400 khz; 1 kw-U TL: N36 23 20 W100 49 37. Box 630 (79070). (806) 435-5458. FAX: (806) 435-5393. Licensee: Perryton Radio Inc. (acq 8-69). Net: Texas State Net. Rep: Miller. Format: C&W. Spec prog: Farm 2 hrs, relg 3 hrs wkly. ■ Sharon Garrison Ellzey, pres; Levita Joyner, gen mgr & prom mgr; Darin Clark, gen sls mgr & progmg dir; David Schwalk, news dir.

KEYE-FM—January 1978: 95.9 mhz; 3 kw. Ant 300 ft. TL: N36 21 54 W100 46 46. Stereo. Dups AM 100%. Format: Country.

Pharr

KVJY(AM)—February 1985: 840 khz; 5 kw-D, 1 kw-N, DA-2. TL: N26 19 00 W98 06 16. Stereo. Box 1808, 3301 S. Expressway 83, Harlingen (78551). (512) 423-5068. Licensee: Tate Communications Inc. (group owner). Net: ABC/E. Rep: Christal. Wash atty: Haley, Bader & Potts. Format: MOR. Target aud: General. ■ Harvey J. Tate, pres & gen mgr; Charlie Kennedy, opns dir; Rodger Kay, gen sls mgr; Ken Meek, chief engr.

Pittsburg

KXAL-FM—Dec 15, 1986: 103.1 mhz; 3.824 kw. Ant 328 ft. TL: N33 03 43 W95 04 36. Stereo. Hrs opn: 24. Drawer 502 (75686). (903) 577-1135. FAX: (903) 577-1150. Licensee: Camp-Titus Radio Co. Inc. Group owner: Ron Gray & Assoc. (acq 8-91). Net: ABC/E. Rep: Miller. Format: C&W. Spec prog: Farm 6 hrs, gospel 3 hrs, relg 6 hrs wkly. ■ Ron Gray, pres, gen mgr, stn mgr, vp sls & progmg mgr; Spencer Gray, opns dir; John Gray, news dir. ■ Rates: $10; 10; 10; 6.

Plains

***KPLN-FM**—Nov 14, 1977: 90.3 mhz; 220 w. Ant 135 ft. TL: N33 11 16 W102 49 20. Box 479 (79355). (806) 456-7401. FAX: (806) 456-4325. Licensee: Plains Independent School District. Format: Var. ■ Sue Banfield, gen mgr.

Plainview

KATX(FM)—Listing follows KVOP(AM).

KKYN(AM)—Oct 1, 1974: 1090 khz; 5 kw-D, 500 w-N, DA-2. TL: N34 05 32 W101 38 26. Hrs opn: 5 AM-midnight. Box 147, 3218 N. Quincy (79072). (806) 293-2661. FAX: (806) 293-5732. Licensee: Radio Music Box Co. L.C. (group owner; acq 12-27-88; $297,500 with co-located FM; FTR 1-23-90). Net: ABC/I. Rep: Banner. Format: C&W. Spec prog: Farm 12 hrs wkly. ■ Mike Fox, gen mgr & gen sls mgr; Tony St. James, progmg dir & mus dir; Wes Naron, news dir; David Carr, chief engr. ■ Rates: $12; 10; 12; 8.

KKYN-FM—1987: 103.9 mhz; 3 kw. Ant 300 ft. TL: N34 13 05 W101 42 02 (CP: 25 kw, ant 354 ft.). Stereo. Hrs opn: 5 AM-midnight. Dups AM 100%. News staff one; news progmg 3 hrs wkly. Target aud: 35-54, spreads to 65 plus. ■ Mike Fox, chmn, stn mgr & sls dir; Tony St. James, mktg dir, prom dir & pub affrs dir; Phil Hamilton, news dir. ■ Rates: $16; 10; 16; 10.

KVOP(AM)—Aug 14, 1944: 1400 khz; 1 kw-U. TL: N34 12 20 W101 42 59. Hrs opn: 24. Box 1420, 3218 N. Quincy (79072). (806) 296-2661. Licensee: Radio Music Box Co. Group owner: Radio Music Box Co., L.C. (acq 4-6-93; $250,000; FTR 4-26-93). Net: SMN; Texas State Net. Rep: Riley. Format: Country. News staff one; news progmg 7 hrs wkly. Target aud: 18-49; the male farm community. Spec prog: Farm 20 hrs, Sp 12 hrs wkly. ■ Mike Fox, pres, gen mgr & gen sls mgr; Tony St.James, progmg dir & mus dir; Wes Naron, news dir; David Carr, chief engr.

KATX(FM)—Co-owned with KVOP(AM). September 1961: 97.3 mhz; 100 kw. Ant 500 ft. TL: N34 15 45 W101 40 05. Stereo. Prog sep from AM. Format: Adult contemp. Target aud: 25-54. Spec prog: Farm 12 hrs.

***KWLD(FM)**—1952: 91.5 mhz; 370 w. Ant 150 ft. TL: N34 11 14 W101 43 32. Stereo. 1900 W. 7th St. (79072). (806) 296-5521; (806) 296-4915. Licensee: Wayland Baptist University. Net: USA. Format: CHR, Sp. News progmg 14 hrs wkly. Target aud: 15-25; high school through college, afternoon & evening. Spec prog: Class 5 hrs, C&W 15 hrs wkly. ■ Wallace Davis, pres; Steve Long, gen mgr; David Carr, chief engr.

Pleasanton

KBOP(AM)—Feb 8, 1951: 1380 khz; 4 kw-D, 160 w-N, DA-D. TL: N29 00 00 W98 31 50. Hrs opn: 5 AM-midnight. Box 39955, San Antonio (78218); 215 N. Main (78064). (210) 829-KBOP; (210) 569-2194. FAX: (210) 569-2196. Licensee: Reding Broadcasting Co. Inc. (acq 1-87; $515,000 with co-located FM; FTR 9-15-86). Net: Texas State Net. Rep: Riley. Format: C&W. News progmg 2 hrs wkly. Target aud: 25-55; middle & working class. Spec prog: Farm 3 hrs wkly. ■ L. W. Reding Jr., pres; Jesse Jones, gen mgr, opns mgr, gen sls mgr, mktg mgr & prom mgr; Bubba Reding, natl sls mgr & adv mgr; Warren Domke, news dir; Dick Schuh, chief engr.

KBUC(FM)—Co-owned with KBOP(AM). Feb 1, 1976: 98.3 mhz; 3 kw. Ant 300 ft. TL: N29 00 01 W98 31 49. Stereo. Hrs opn: 6 AM-10 PM. Prog sep from AM. ■ Jesse Jones, stn mgr.

Port Arthur

KALO(AM)—August 1934: 1250 khz; 5 kw-D, 1 kw-N, DA-N. TL: N29 57 04 W93 52 46. 7700 Gulfway Dr. (77642). (409) 963-1276. FAX: (409) 963-1640. Licensee: Clear Channel Radio Licenses Inc. (group owner; acq 8-5-92; with co-located FM). Net: Unistar, American Urban. Rep: Katz & Powell. Format: Black gold & gospel. Target aud: 25-54; Black middle class individuals. Spec prog: Fr 3 hrs, Cajun 4 hrs wkly. ■ L. Lowry Mays, pres; Ron Mathis, gen mgr; J. Moore, progmg dir. ■ Rates: $16; 12; 14; 8.

KHYS(FM)—Co-owned with KALO(AM). Apr 15, 1963: 98.5 mhz; 98 kw. Ant 1,952 ft. TL: N30 03 05 W94 31 37. Stereo. Prog sep from AM. Suite 1390-A, 5 Post Oak Park, Houston (77027). (713) 622-0010. FAX: (713) 622-1733. Net: ABC/C. Format: Urban contemp. ■ Jim Snowden, gen mgr & progmg dir; Aldie Beard, gen sls mgr.

KLTN(FM)—July 4, 1969: 93.3 mhz; 100 kw. Ant 420 ft. TL: N30 03 39 W93 58 49 (CP: Ant 1,952 ft., TL: N30 03 05 W94 31 37). Stereo. Hrs opn: 24. Box 5488, Beaumont (77726). (409) 838-3911. FAX: (409) 838-3233. Licensee: Gulfstar Broadcasting L.C. (acq 1-7-92; with KLVI(AM) Beaumont). Rep: Katz & Powell. Format: L &

A station w/Tischnerors (Sp). ■ Tom Boggess, gen mgr; Glen Hicks, gen sls mgr; Debbie Pletcher, prom mgr; Jim Love, progmg dir; Patrick Parks, chief engr.

KOLE(AM)—1947: 1340 khz; 1 kw-U. TL: N29 54 15 W93 56 10. 2950 Commerce (77642). (409) 842-5569. FAX: (409) 842-0800. Licensee: Uno Broadcasting Corp. (group owner; acq 12-13-83). Net: Texas Net. Rep: Eastman. Format: Oldies, big band, classic rock. Target aud: 25 plus. ■ Steve Lewis, gen mgr; Lee Gower, opns mgr, progmg dir & mus dir; Russ Ingram, chief engr.

Port Isabel

KVPA(FM)—Not on air, target date unknown: 101.1 mhz; 3 kw. Ant 300 ft. TL: N26 03 43 W97 12 55. 14 Poinsetta St., Brownsville (78520). Licensee: Matthew C. Trub.

Port Lavaca

KGUL(AM)—June 7, 1961: 1560 khz; 500 w-D. TL: N28 36 45 W96 40 07. Hrs opn: 6 AM-sunset. Box 386, 1 1/2 W. Hwy. 87 (77979). (512) 552-2951. FAX: (512) 552-2953. Licensee: Double R Radio Inc. (acq 7-31-81; grpsl; FTR 9-21-81). Format: Variety, Sp. Target aud: 35-65; adult Hispanic 25 plus. Spec prog: Top 40. ■ Paul Duenez, pres, gen mgr, gen sls mgr, mus dir & news dir; Robert Villafuerte, progmg dir.

KPLV(FM)—Licensed to Port Lavaca. See Victoria.

Port Neches

KUHD(AM)—June 13, 1959; 1150 khz; 500 w-D, 63 w-N, DA-2. TL: N30 04 45 W93 57 05. Hrs opn: Mon-Thurs. 6 AM-8PM, Fri 6 AM-midnight, Sat 5 AM-1 AM, Sun 6 AM-9 PM. 3185 Merriman (77651). (409) 727-2177; (409) 768-1768. Licensee: Under His Direction Inc. (acq 9-8-93; $75,000; FTR 9-27-93). Net: USA. Format: Relg, gospel. News staff one; news progmg 4 hrs wkly. Target aud: General. ■ Billy James Hargis, pres; Michael Devillier, gen mgr, gen sls mgr, progmg dir & mus dir; Lauri Grantham, prom dir & pub affrs dir; Aaron Kingston, asst mus dir; Jeremy Ryan, news dir; Ken Wilson, chief engr. ■ Rates: $9.25; 9.25; 9.25; 9.25.

Portland

KOUL(FM)—See Corpus Christi.

KQTX(FM)—Dec 15, 1979: 105.5 mhz; 1.9 kw. Ant 354 ft. TL: N27 47 48 W97 23 51. Stereo. Hrs opn: 24. 126 Sunrise Mall, Corpus Christi (78412). (512) 994-7700. FAX: (512) 994-7780. Licensee: Chitex Communications Inc. (acq 2-17-90; $525,000; FTR 3-5-90). Net: ABC/C. Rep: Christal. Format: Contemp mass appeal. Target aud: 18-49; general. ■ Daniel G. Donovan, pres & gen mgr. ■ Rates: $25; 25; 25; 25.

Post

KPOS-FM—May 1, 1991: 107.3 mhz; 50 kw. Ant 334 ft. TL: N33 13 28 W101 26 21. Box 98 (79356). (806) 495-2831. FAX: (806) 495-3924. Licensee: Boles Broadcasting. Net: SMN. Format: Country. Target aud: 25-54. Spec prog: American Country Countdown 4 hrs, Texas Tech sports 4 hrs, local high school sports 4 hrs wkly. ■ Jim Boles, gen mgr & stn mgr; Kathy Boles-Whitten, gen sls mgr; Thomas Zachary, prom mgr, progmg dir & mus dir; Janice Mason, news dir & pub affrs dir. ■ Rates: $5; 5; 5; 5.

KPOS(AM)—September 1955: 1370 khz; 1 kw-D, 158 w-N. TL: N33 13 28 W101 26 21. Hrs opn: 24. (800) 530-4435. ■ Rates: Same as FM.

Prairie View

***KPVU(FM)**—Nov 26, 1981: 91.3 mhz; 98.3 kw. Ant 410 ft. TL: N30 05 21 W95 59 46. Stereo. Box 156, Hilliard Hall (77446). (409) 857-4511; (409) 857-4515. Licensee: Prairie View A&M Univ. Format: Black, jazz, urban contemp. News staff one; news progmg 6 hrs wkly. Target aud: 18-55. Spec prog: Blues 4 hrs, gospel 4 hrs wkly. ■ Lori Gray, gen mgr & stn mgr; Carol Campbell, dev mgr & prom dir; Larry Coleman, progmg dir; Carol Means, news dir; Dave Claoras, chief engr.

Premont

KMFM(FM)—1989: 104.9 mhz; 3 kw. Ant 299 ft. TL: N27 22 19 W98 11 21. Box 252, McAllen (78502). (512) 781-5528. Licensee: Latin Broadcast Co. Format: Sp, relg. ■ Eloy Bernal, gen mgr; Pauline Bernal, stn mgr; Pauline Bernal Jr., progmg dir; Mario Perez, chief engr.

Quanah

KVDL(AM)—May 11, 1951: 1150 khz; 500 w-D, DA. TL: N34 18 58 W99 44 49. Hrs opn: 6 AM-sunset. Box 685 (79252). (817) 663-2773. Licensee: Glen A. Ingram (acq 11-7-89; with co-located FM; FTR 11-27-89). Format: C&W, Sp. Target aud: General. ■ Glen A. Ingram, pres, gen mgr, gen sls mgr & progmg dir; Ray Garza, stn mgr & opns dir.

KIXC-FM—Co-owned with KVDL(AM). Sept 1, 1982: 100.9 mhz; 3 kw. Ant 192 ft. TL: N34 18 58 W99 44 49. Stereo. Hrs opn: 24. Dups AM 100%. Box 29 (79252). (817) 663-6363. Net: USA.

Ralls

KCLR(AM)—May 31, 1963: 1530 khz; 5 kw-D, 1 kw-CH. TL: N33 40 00 W101 22 44. Box 340 (79357). (806) 253-9914. Licensee: Pete Rodriguez (acq 6-10-80; $215,000; FTR 6-2-80). Rep: Lotus. Format: Sp. ■ Pete Rodriguez, pres; Zelia Salas, gen mgr; Juan Salas, progmg dir; Charlie Wilson, chief engr.

Raymondville

KARU(FM)—Not on air, target date unknown: 105.7 mhz; 1.35 kw. Ant 420 ft. TL: N26 26 49 W97 42 02. c/o KRGE, Box 1290, Weslaco (78599). (210) 968-7777. Licensee: Christian Ministries of the Valley Inc. (acq 2-4-93; $18,000; FTR 3-1-93).

KSOX(AM)—June 1, 1957: 1240 khz; 1 kw-U. TL: N26 27 28 W97 46 55. Hrs opn: 6 AM-midnight. 345 S. 7th (78580). (210) 689-3333. FAX: (210) 689-3341. Licensee: Edgar L. Clinton Sr. (acq 9-1-69). Format: C&W. Target aud: 25-55. ■ Edgar L. Clinton Sr., gen mgr & progmg dir.

KSOX-FM—1979: 102.1 mhz; 17.9 kw. Ant 758 ft. TL: N26 38 09 W97 50 10. Stereo. Hrs opn: 6 AM-midnight. Dups AM 100%.

Refugio

KZTX(FM)—Oct 5, 1979: 106.1 mhz; 25 kw. Ant 299 ft. TL: N28 08 15 W97 12 45 Stereo. Hrs opn: 24. 3426 Hopecrest, San Antonio (78230). (512) 340-5144. Licensee: Mazal Broadcasting Co. of Corpus Christi Inc. (acq 5-25-89; $250,000; FTR 6-12-89). Format: Adult contemp. News progmg 5 hrs wkly. Target aud: 25-54. ■ Akiva N. Gerstein, pres, gen mgr, gen sls mgr, progmg dir & news dir.

Richmond

KMPQ(AM)—See Rosenberg-Richmond.

KMPQ-FM—See Rosenberg-Richmond.

Rio Grande City

KCTM(FM)—April 1985: 103.1 mhz; 1.41 kw. Ant 420 ft. TL: N26 25 47 W98 49 25. Stereo. Hrs opn: 5 AM-midnight. Rt. 2, Box 103-FM (78582-9805). (512) 487-8224. Licensee: Sound Investments Unlimited Inc. Rep: Caballero. Format: Bilingual. News progmg 5 hrs wkly. Target aud: 18-45. ■ Gustavo "Gus" Valadez Jr., pres, stn mgr & opns mgr.

Robstown

KGLF(AM)—Feb 22, 1963: 1510 khz; 500 w-D. TL: N27 47 40 W97 39 20. Box 260715, Corpus Cristi (78426-0715). (512) 387-1510. FAX: (512) 387-0288. Licensee: Tempest Broadcasting Corp. (acq 3-25-93; $75,000; FTR 4-21-93). Format: Clear country. ■ David Showalter, pres; Bert Salas, gen mgr; Dan Efpanoza, gen sls mgr; Justin Case, Bert Salas, progmg dirs.

***KLUX(FM)**—Mar 17, 1985: 89.5 mhz; 60 kw. Ant 954 ft. TL: N27 46 50 W97 38 03. Stereo. Hrs opn: 24. 1200 Lantana, Corpus Christi (78407). (512) 289-6437. FAX: (512) 289-7418. Licensee: Diocesan Telecommunications Corp. Net: USA. Format: Btfl mus, relg. News progmg 13 hrs wkly. Target aud: 35 plus. Spec prog: Sp 2 hrs wkly. ■ Robert E. Freeman, pres; Marty Wind Sr., vp & opns mgr; Chuck McDowell, opns dir & progmg dir; Marty Wind, chief engr.

KMIQ(FM)—July 23, 1989: 105.1 mhz; 3 kw. Ant 300 ft. TL: N27 40 39 W97 38 20. Stereo. Box 270547, Corpus Christi (78427). (512) 855-7123. Licensee: Cotton Broadcasting. Rep: Caballero. Wash atty: Baraff, Koerner, Olender & Hochberg P.C. Format: Tejano. News staff 2; news progmg 3 hrs wkly. Target aud: 18 plus. Spec prog: Relg 6 hrs wkly. ■ Humberto Lozano Lopez, pres; Carlos Lopez, gen mgr & progmg dir; Ernest R. Lopez, news dir; Homer Lopez, vp prom; Ed Sharp, prom mgr; Manuel "Manny L" Lopez, mus dir; Lupe Silva, news dir; Paul McKay, chief engr.

KSAB(FM)—Oct 13, 1966: 99.9 mhz; 96 kw. Ant 955 ft. TL: N27 44 28 W97 36 08. Stereo. Box 4722, Corpus Christi (78469); 1301 Home Rd. (78416). (512) 851-1414. FAX: (512) 851-8409. Licensee: KDOS Ltd. (acq 4-24-91; $600,000; FTR 5-13-91). Format: Sp. ■ Luis Munoz, gen mgr; Al Herrra, gen sls mgr; Victor Larra, progmg dir; Fred Hoffman, chief engr.

Rockdale

KRXT(FM)—Feb 27, 1989: 98.5 mhz; 6 kw. Ant 328 ft. TL: N30 38 32 W97 02 13. Stereo. Box 1560, W. Hwy. 79 (76567). (512) 446-6985. FAX: (512) 446-6987. Licensee: KRXT Inc. Net: ABC/E; Texas State Net. Wash atty: Michael Wilhelm. Format: Country. News staff one; news progmg 21 hrs wkly. Target aud: General. Spec prog: Sp 4 hrs wkly. ■ Charles W. McGregor, pres, stn mgr, gen sls mgr & news dir; Bill Gregory, progmg dir; Charles Taylor, pub affrs dir; George Bradshaw, chief engr. ■ Rates: $8.80; 8.80; 8.80; 8.80.

Rockport

KXCC(FM)—October 1986: 102.3 mhz; 2.5 kw. Ant 328 ft. TL: N28 00 03 W97 04 34 (CP: 50 kw, ant 371 ft.). 1602 Brownlee, Corpus Christi (78404). (512) 884-1029. Licensee: Coastal Bend Radio Active Inc. (acq 5-7-93; $400,000; FTR 5-31-93). Format: Classic rock. ■ Steve DeWalt, gen mgr; Janna Hensler, gen sls mgr; Charles Stewart, news dir; J.C. Faldo, chief engr.

KZTX(FM)—See Refugio.

Rollingwood

KJCE(AM)—Licensed to Rollingwood. See Austin.

Roma

***KBMI(FM)**—Apr 30, 1983: 97.7 mhz; 3 kw. Ant 298 ft. TL: N26 24 22 W99 00 37. Hrs opn: 18. Box 627 (78584); 100 S. Bethel St. (78584). (512) 849-3022. FAX: (512) 849-1701. Licensee: Grant Communications Group. Format: Sp, relg. Target aud: General; spanish speaking audience. ■ Robert Grant Smiley, chmn; Paul Swartzendruber, gen mgr & chief engr; Fernando Hernandez, opns mgr & progmg dir.

Rosenberg

KMPQ-FM—Licensed to Rosenberg. See Rosenberg-Richmond.

Rosenberg-Richmond

KMPQ(AM)—Nov 15, 1948: 980 khz; 1 kw-D. TL: N29 33 10 W95 47 00. Stereo. Hrs opn: 24. Suite 218, 6420 Richmond, Houston (77057). (713) 342-6601. FAX: (713) 341-1120. Licensee: Fort Bend Broadcasting Co. Inc. Group owner: Bayport Broadcast Group. Net: AP; Cadena QBS. Rep: Lotus. Format: Sp. ■ Roy Henderson, pres; Paul Mougel, gen mgr; Raul Gomez, gen sls mgr; Daniel Fernandez, progmg dir; Steve Brightwell, chief engr.

KMPQ-FM—(Rosenberg). Aug 8, 1968: 104.9 mhz; 4 kw. Ant 230 ft. TL: N29 33 10 W95 47 00 (CP: 1.35 kw, ant 505 ft., TL: N29 39 54 W95 45 28). Stereo. Hrs opn: 24. Prog sep from AM. Net: AP, CRC. Format: Sp. Target aud: 12 plus. ■ Mario Campos, progmg dir.

Round Rock

***KNLE-FM**—Aug 13, 1981: 88.1 mhz; 700 w. Ant 53 ft. TL: N30 30 33 W97 41 05. Stereo. No. 2, 11800 N. Lamar, Austin (78753). (512) 837-8801. FAX: (512) 836-5499. Licensee: Ixoye Productions Inc. Net: CNN. Format: Adult Christian contemp. ■ Randall Thomas, pres & chief engr; Sherland Priest, gen mgr; David Henninger, progmg dir.

KOPY(AM)—See Georgetown.

Rusk

KTLU(AM)—1955: 1580 khz; 840 w-D, 250 w-N. TL: N31 49 12 W95 10 19. Stereo. Hrs opn: 24. Box 475, 618 N. Main (75785). (903) 683-2257. Licensee: E.H. Whitehead. Net: SMN; Texas State Net. Format: Oldies. News staff one; news progmg 3 hrs wkly. Target aud: 35-65. Spec prog: Sp 4 hrs wkly. ■ E.H. Whitehead, pres; Robert Gonzalez, gen mgr, progmg dir, mus dir & news dir; Steve Comer, chief engr.

KWRW(FM)—Co-owned with KTLU(AM). July 1, 1981: 97.7 mhz; 1.4 kw. Ant 185 ft. TL: N31 49 12 W95 10 19 (CP: 14.5 kw). Stereo. Hrs opn: 24. Dups AM 100%.

San Angelo

KCRN(AM)—1947: 1340 khz; 1 kw-U. TL: N31 28 43 W100 27 50. Hrs opn: 24. 21 S. Chadbourne (76903). (915) 655-6917. Licensee: Criswell Center for Biblical Studies (group owner; acq 6-18-91; $350,000 with co-located FM; FTR 7-8-91). Format: Relg, educational. News staff one; news progmg 2 hrs wkly. Target aud: 18 plus. ■ Greg Kelly, stn mgr.

KCRN-FM—Feb 1, 1965: 93.9 mhz; 100 kw. Ant 710 ft. TL: N31 42 11 W100 19 20. Stereo. Hrs opn: 24. Prog sep from AM. Format: Inspirational. Target aud: 25 plus.

KDCD(FM)—June 1, 1980: 92.9 mhz; 100 kw. Ant 729 ft. TL: N31 26 08 W100 34 08. Stereo. 3298 Sherwood Way (76901). (915) 947-0899. Licensee: Regency Broadcasting Inc. (acq 8-10-92; $186,000; FTR 9-21-92). Rep: Miller. Format: Top-40. Target aud: 18-49. Spec prog: Class 3 hrs wkly. ■ Jack Auldridge, pres.

KELI(FM)—November 1986: 98.7 mhz; 100 kw. Ant 1,290 ft. TL: N31 22 01 W100 02 48. Stereo. Hrs opn: 24. Box 3834 (76902). (915) 655-5483. FAX: (915) 655-9675. Licensee: Earshot Broadcasting Inc. Net: Unistar. Rep: Katz & Powell. Format: Adult contemp. News staff one; news progmg 6 hrs wkly. Target aud: 25-54. Spec prog: Relg 4 hrs wkly. ■ Greg Thomas, pres & gen mgr; Sylvia K. Thomas, vp; Lee Swift, stn mgr; Kathy Keaton, gen sls mgr; Robin Lowe, prom mgr; Shawn Schlueter, news dir.

KGKL(AM)—Dec 4, 1928: 960 khz; 5 kw-D, 1 kw-N, DA-N. TL: N31 29 39 W100 24 55. Box 1878 (76902); 1301 S. Bryant (76903). (915) 655-7161. FAX: (915) 658-7377. Licensee: KGKL Inc. (acq 4-5-71). Net: ABC/I. Rep: Katz. Format: AC. News staff 3; news progmg 28 hrs wkly. Target aud: 35 plus. Spec prog: Farm 6 hrs wkly. ■ Reba Gloger, pres; Susan Moncrieff, vp; Perry L. Curnutt, gen mgr; Lee Swift, opns mgr; Ric Reyes, sls dir & adv mgr; Richard Aquirre, progmg mgr; Linda Stone, mus dir; John Lynch, news dir; Eddie Smith, chief engr.

KGKL-FM—Dec 24, 1965: 97.5 mhz; 100 kw. Ant 500 ft. TL: N31 29 46 W100 24 50. Stereo. Hrs opn: 24. Prog sep from AM. Net: ABC/I, AP. Wash atty: John B. Kenkel. Format: Modern country. News progmg 3 hrs wkly. Target aud: 25-54. ■ Lynn Cook, prom mgr; Linda Stone, progmg dir; Dan Springer, pub affrs dir.

KIXY-FM—Listing follows KXQZ(AM).

KSJT-FM—Oct 7, 1985: 107.5 mhz; 100 kw. Ant 656 ft. TL: N31 26 19 W100 34 18. Stereo. Hrs opn: 6 AM-midnight. 209 W. Beauregard (76903). (915) 655-1717. FAX: (915) 657-0601. Licensee: La Unica Broadcasting Co. Net: SIS. Rep: Lotus. Format: Sp. Target aud: 18-55. ■ Louis Perez, pres; Patagonia M. Mercedero, stn mgr; Minnie Magallan, gen sls mgr; Arturo Madrid, prom mgr; Bertha Aussenac, progmg dir & mus dir; George Reyes, chief engr.

KXQZ(AM)—Nov 28, 1954: 1260 khz; 1 kw-D, 250 w-N. TL: N31 29 14 W100 26 57. Stereo. Hrs opn: 24. Box 2191, KIXY Complex, 2824 Sherwood Way (76902). (915) 949-2112. FAX: (915) 944-0851. Licensee: Foster Communications Inc. (acq 4-9-84). Net: CNN, MBS, NBC Talknet, Unistar; Texas State Net. Rep: Torbet. Wash atty: Leventhal, Senter & Lerman. Format: News/talk. News staff 2; news progmg 20 hrs wkly. Target aud: 25-54. ■ Walton Foster, CEO & pres; Fred M. Key, CFO, gen mgr & vp prom; Don W. Griffis, sr vp; Dee Watkins, dev mgr & mktg mgr; Jay Michaels, gen sls mgr; John Raymond, progmg dir & pub affrs dir; Jeff Rottman, news dir; Gary Smith, chief engr.

KIXY-FM—Co-owned with KXQZ(AM). October 1966: 94.7 mhz; 100 kw. Ant 446 ft. TL: N31 29 14 W100 26 57. Stereo. Hrs opn: 24. Prog sep from AM. Net: CNN. Format: Top-40, adult contemp, mass appeal. Target aud: 18-49. ■ Bobby Ramos, prom dir; Mike Steele, progmg dir; Robert Elfman, pub affrs dir.

San Antonio

KAJA(FM)—Listing follows WOAI(AM).

KCHL(AM)—June 1960: 1480 khz; 2.5 kw-D, 90 w-N, DA-2. TL: N29 24 45 W98 24 52. Hrs opn: 15. 1211 W. Hein Rd. (78220-3301). Box 200880 (77220-0880). (512) 333-0050. FAX: (512) 333-0081. Licensee: Martin Broadcasting Inc. (group owner; acq 6-4-92; FTR 6-22-92). Net: Unistar. Rep: McGavren Guild. Wash atty: Latham & Watkins. Format: Gospel. News staff one. Target aud: 25-54. ■ Darrel Martin, gen mgr; Janice King, gen sls mgr, progmg dir & mus dir; Richard Igou, prom mgr; Bruce Earle, Richard Igou, chiefs engr. ■ Rates: $20; 20; 20; na.

KCOR(AM)—Feb 1, 1946: 1350 khz; 5 kw-U, DA-N. TL: N29 31 27 W98 37 05. 1115 W. Martin (78207). (210) 246-1350. FAX: (210) 224-2401. Licensee: Tichenor Media System Inc. (group owner). Rep: Katz. Format: Sp. ■ McHenry Tichenor, pres; Warren Tichenor, gen mgr; David Simmers, gen sls mgr; Jesse Rios, progmg dir; Ramiro Cordoba, news dir; Marvin Fiedler, chief engr.

KROM(FM)—Co-owned with KCOR(AM). June 1947: 92.9 mhz; 100 kw. Ant 1,016 ft. TL: N29 11 03 W98 30 49. Stereo. Suite 1400, 1777 N.E. Loop 410 (78217). (210) 829-1075. (Acq 3-9-93; $3.8 million; FTR 3-29-93). Format: Hot adult contemp. News staff one; news progmg 6 hrs wkly. Target aud: 25-44; female. ■ Cindy Rucker, vp mktg & vp prom; Rudy Roch, mus dir; Frank Cortez, pub affrs dir.

KCYY(FM)—Listing follows KKYX(AM).

KDIL(FM)—See Terrell Hills.

KDRY(AM)—(Alamo Heights). Nov 8, 1963: 1100 khz; 11 kw-D, 1 kw-N, DA-N. TL: N29 33 26 W98 22 35. Box 34478, Suite 202, 8100 Roughrider, San Antonio (78265). (512) 655-7757. Licensee: National Enterprises Inc. Format: Relg. Target aud: General. ■ Sam Morris Jr., pres & gen mgr; Robert Ritchey, chief engr.

KEDA(AM)—March 14, 1966: 1540 khz; 5 kw-D, 1 kw-N, DA-2. TL: N29 21 30 W98 21 05. Stereo. 510 S. Flores St. (78204). (512) 226-5254; (512) 226-5810. FAX: (512) 227-7937. Licensee: D & E Broadcasting Co. (acq 3-7-66). Net: Texas State. Rep: Caballero. Format: Tex Mex. News staff 2; news progmg 10 hrs wkly. Target aud: 25-54; men & women. Spec prog: Salsa 4 hrs wkly. ■ Manuel G. Dadila, pres; Alberto P. Dadila, vp, gen mgr, natl sls mgr, rgnl sls mgr & vp mktg; Madeline P. Dadila, vp opns; Ricardo P. Dadila, progmg dir & mus dir; Larry Tischart, chief engr. ■ Rates: $57; 57; 57; 50.

KENS(AM)—Nov 13, 1961: 1160 khz; 10 kw-D, 1 kw-N, DA-2. TL: N29 32 11 W98 41 08. Stereo. Hrs opn: 24 501 W. Quincy (78212). (210) 224-1166. FAX: (210) 225-2756. Licensee: Hispanic Radio Broadcasters (acq 9-8-90; $650,000; FTR 8-13-90). Net: ALIA Communications. Rep: Spanish Broadcast Systems, Riley. Wash atty: Haley, Bader & Potts. Format: Sp, contemp. Target aud: 18-49; mostly young females. ■ Lincoln Dellar, pres; P. Gilberto Esquivel, vp & gen mgr; Ramiro Torres, gen sls mgr; Fausto Avalos, progmg dir & mus dir; Francisco Wallan, news dir; Tom Bray, chief engr.

KFIT Exp Stn—Not on air, target date NA 1060 khz; 1 kw-d, DA. TL: N29 17 32 W98 31 57 Rebroadcasts KFIT (AM) Sunset Valley. Suite 375, 110 Wild Basin Rd., Austin (78746). (512) 328-8400. ■ Rev. Darrell Martin, gen mgr.

KISS-FM—Dec 1946: 99.5 mhz; 100 kw. Ant 1,112 ft. TL: N29 16 29 W98 15 52. Stereo. Suite 500, 8930 Four Winds Dr. (78239). (512) 646-0105. Licensee: KISS Radio of San Antonio Ltd. Group owner: Rusk Corp. (acq 7-9-93; $3.95 million with KLUP[AM] Terrell Hills; FTR 8-2-93). Net: CBS. Format: AOR. News staff one; news progmg 5 hrs wkly. Target aud: 25-54. ■ J.H. Jones II., pres; Caroline Devine, gen mgr; Susan Nieman, sls dir; Janis Maxymof, gen sls mgr; Carmen Del Chambre, mktg dir; Tracy Walker, prom mgr; Virgil Thompson, progmg dir; Debbie Alcocer, mus dir; Tom Scheppke, asst mus dir; Steve Hahn, news dir; Richard Schult, chief engr.

KKYX(AM)—1926: 680 khz; 50 kw-D, 10 kw-N, DA-N. TL: N29 30 03 W98 49 54. Stereo. Hrs opn: 24. Suite 500, 8122 Datapoint (78229). (210) 615-5400. FAX: (210) 615-5300. Licensee: NewCity Communications Inc. (group owner; acq 7-17-87). Net: UPI, ABC/D. Rep: Katz. Format: C&W. News progmg 3 hrs wkly. Target aud: 35-64. Spec prog: Pub affrs 2 hrs wkly. ■ Dick Ferguson, pres; Hugh Barr, gen mgr; Ben Reed, gen sls mgr; Cathy Gerloff, prom mgr; Carl Becker, progmg dir; Jerry King, mus dir; Chrissie Murnin, Ross Blake, news dirs; Paul Reynolds, chief engr.

KCYY(FM)—Co-owned with KKYX(AM). June 25, 1966: 100.3 mhz; 100 kw. Ant 985 ft. TL: N29 31 25 W98 43 25. Stereo. Hrs opn: 24. Prog sep from AM. (Acq 12-17-84; $8 million; FTR 12-17-84). Net: UPI. Target aud: 25-54. ■ Julie Wolse, prom mgr; Scott Huskey, progmg dir.

KONO(AM)—January 1927: 860 khz; 5 kw-D, 1 kw-N, DA-N. TL: N29 26 14 W98 25 19. Stereo. Hrs opn: 24. Suite 330, 7800 NW I-10 (78230). (210) 340-1234. FAX: (210) 340-3118. Licensee: Gillespie Broadcasting Co. (acq 6-25-93; $1.125 million; FTR 7-19-93). Rep: Major Mkt. Format: Oldies. News staff one; news progmg one hr wkly. Target aud: 25-54; total audience appeal. ■ John Barger, gen mgr; George Cooper, progmg dir & news dir.

KONO-FM—See Fredricksburg.

***KPAC(FM)**—Nov 7, 1982: 88.3 mhz; 100 kw. Ant 820 ft. TL: N29 31 25 W98 43 25. Stereo. Hrs opn: 24. Prog sep from FM. Suite 800, 8401 Datapoint Dr. (78229). (210) 614-8977. FAX: (210) 614-8983. Licensee: Texas Public Radio. Net: APR. Wash atty: Haley, Bader & Potts. Format: Classical. News progmg 3 hrs wkly. Target aud: General. ■ Joe Gwathmey, gen mgr; Corleen Farley, dev mgr; Tom Sittner, chief engr.

KQXT(FM)—Nov 19, 1967: 101.9 mhz; 100 kw. Ant 700 ft. TL: N29 25 08 W98 29 00. Stereo. Hrs opn: 24. 6222 N.W. Interstate 10 (78201). (210) 736-9700. FAX: (210) 736-9776. Licensee: Clear Channel Communications (group owner; acq 1-27-93; $8 million; FTR 3-8-93). Rep: Group W. Format: Soft adult contemp. News staff one; news progmg 2 hrs wkly. Target aud: 25-54. ■ L. Lowry Mays, CEO; Herb Hill, CFO; Mark Mays, sr vp; Bob Cohen, gen mgr; Anna Davis, sls dir; Weldon Crelia, natl sls mgr; Deanna Spruce, prom mgr; Mike Scott, progmg dir; Rosenda Burns, news dir; Dan Walthers, chief engr.

KROM(FM)—Listing follows KCOR(AM).

***KRTU(FM)**—Jan 22, 1976: 91.7 mhz; 3 kw. Ant 120 ft. TL: N29 27 51 W98 28 56. Stereo. 715 Stadium Dr. (78212). (512) 736-8159. Licensee: Trinity University. Format: Class, jazz. ■ Robert O. Blanchard, gen mgr; Scott B. Sowards, stn mgr; Robert Luk, chief engr.

KSAH(AM)—See Universal City.

KSJL-FM—May 5, 1964: 96.1 mhz; 100 kw. Ant 479 ft. TL: N29 38 00 W98 37 50 (CP: 99 kw, ant 328 ft.). Stereo. Hrs opn: 24. Suite 200, 217 Alamo Plaza (78205). (210) 271-9600. Licensee: Inner City Broadcasting of San Antonio. Group owner: Inner City Broadcasting. Net: SMN. Wash atty: Koteen & Naf. Format: AC, urban contemp. News staff one; news progmg 3 hrs wkly. Target aud: 25-54; females. Spec prog: Gospel 8 hrs, jazz 8 hrs, reggae 2 hrs wkly. ■ Charles Andrews Jr., pres & gen mgr; John Martinez, opns dir; Delia Alcocer, prom dir; Michael Andrews, progmg dir; Ric Ollervidez, mus dir; Jessica Chandler, news dir; Tom Sittner, chief engr.

KSLR(AM)—Dec 26, 1926: 630 khz; 5 kw-U, DA-2. TL: N29 23 24 W98 21 00. Hrs opn: 24. Suite 1200, 9601 McAllister (78216). (512) 344-8481. FAX: (512) 340-1213. Licensee: Communicom Co. of America L.P. (group owner; acq 7-7-93; grpsl; FTR 8-2-93). Net: USA. Format: Contemp Christian. News progmg 2 hrs wkly. Target aud: 25-49; women & young families. ■ Carl Dean, gen mgr & gen sls mgr; John Walk, opns mgr; Dave Gordon, progmg dir & mus dir. ■ Rates: $50; 40; 45; 35.

***KSTX(FM)**—Dec 1981: 89.1 mhz; 100 kw. Ant 656 ft. TL: N29 31 33 W98 43 21. Stereo. Hrs opn: 24. Suite 800, 8401 Datapoint Dr. (78229). (512) 614-8977. FAX: (512) 614-8983. Licensee: Texas Public Radio (acq 10-11-89). Net: NPR, APR. Wash atty: Haley, Bader & Potts. Format: News/info. News progmg 156 hrs wkly. Target aud: General. Spec prog: Jazz 6 hrs, variety talk 6 hrs wkly. ■ Joe N. Gwathmey, gen mgr & progmg dir; Corleen Farley, dev mgr; Thomas Sittner, chief engr.

***KSYM-FM**—Sept 15, 1966: 90.1 mhz; 3 kw. Ant 128 ft. TL: N29 26 50 W98 29 55. 1300 San Pedro Ave. (78284). (512) 733-2793. FAX: (512) 733-3393. Licensee: San Antonio College. Format: Alt, jazz. Spec prog: Black 3 hrs, jazz 19 hrs, Sp 4 hrs, Caribbean 5 hrs wkly. ■ Ken Shumate, pres; John Onderdonk, gen mgr; Rick Hernandez, chief engr.

KTFM(FM)—Listing follows KTSA(AM).

KTSA(AM)—May 9, 1922: 550 khz; 5 kw-U, DA-N. TL: N29 29 49 W98 24 52. Hrs opn: 24. Box 18128, 4050 Eisenhower Rd. (78218). (512) 599-5500. FAX: (512) 599-5588. Licensee: Waterman Broadcasting Corp. of Texas. Group owner: Waterman Broadcasting Corp. (acq 1965). Net: AP, ABC/D, CNN, MBS. Rep: Banner. Wash atty: Cohn & Marks. Format: News/talk. News staff 11; news progmg 35 hrs wkly. Target aud: 25-54. ■ Bernard Waterman, pres; Joe Ernest, gen mgr; Anne Schiller, opns mgr & news dir; Wendy Oliver, gen sls mgr; Jamie Allen, natl sls mgr; Brunella Bruni, prom dir; Eliza Sonneland, progmg dir; Leroy Dietrich, chief engr.

KTFM(FM)—Co-owned with KTSA(AM). 1969: 102.7 mhz; 100 kw-h, 70 kw-v. Ant 670 ft. TL: N29 25 09 W98 29 06. Stereo. Prog sep from AM. Format: CHR. News staff one. Target aud: 12 plus. ■ Joe Ernest, stn mgr; Mary Paizer, sls dir; Rick Upton, progmg dir; Steve Anthony, mus dir; Cindy Casiano, pub affrs dir.

KXTN(AM)—1948: 1310 khz; 5 kw-D, 280 w-N, DA-2. TL: N29 24 53 W98 20 36. 1777 N.E. Loop 410 (78217). (210) 829-1075. FAX: (512) 826-4706. Licensee: Tichenor Media System Inc. (group owner; acq 4-8-93; $11 million with co-located FM; FTR 4-26-93). Rep: McGavren Guild. Format: Sp. Target aud: 25-44; upscale Hispanic appeal. ■ Warren Tichenor, chmn; David Simmers, gen sls mgr; Rudy Rocha, progmg dir; Gilbert Aleman, mus dir; Alex Cruz, news dir; Bret Higgins, chief engr.

KXTN-FM—Dec 31, 1967: 107.5 mhz; 100 kw. Ant 1,514 ft. TL: N29 16 29 W98 15 52. Stereo. Prog sep from AM. Format: Tejano. Target aud: 25-49; contemporary Spanish, affluent, upscale.

*****KYFS(FM)**—Nov 7, 1982: 90.9 mhz; 3 kw. Ant 299 ft. TL: N29 31 05 W98 34 10. Hrs opn: 24. Suite 401, 8401 Datapoint Dr. (78229). (512) 615-8973. Licensee: Bible Broadcasting Network Inc. (group owner; acq 11-20-91; $75,000; FTR 12-9-91). Wash atty: Smithwick & Belenduck. Format: Relg. Target aud: 2 plus. ■ Jeff Apthorp, gen mgr.

KZEP-FM—Oct 1, 1966: 104.5 mhz; 100 kw. Ant 735 ft. TL: N29 25 09 W98 29 06. Stereo. Hrs opn: 24. 427 E. 9th (78215). (210) 226-6444. FAX: (210) 225-5736. Licensee: Texas Lotus Corp. Group owner: Lotus Communications Corp. Net: MBS. Rep: D & R Radio. Format: Classic rock. News staff one; news progmg 3 hrs wkly. Target aud: 25-54; males. ■ Howard Kalmenson, pres; Jay A. Levine, vp & gen mgr; Gary Isaacs, sls dir & natl sls mgr; Carrie Wood, prom dir; R.W. "Catfish" Crouch, progmg dir; Cody Robbins, mus dir; Alyce Ian, news dir; Ron Cole, chief engr.

KZEP(AM)—Jan 1, 1953: 1250 khz; 1 kw-U, DA-N. TL: N29 24 29 W98 26 39. Stereo. Hrs opn: 24. (Acq 3-4-83). Format: All sports (talk, play-by-play).

KZXS(AM)—May 10, 1984: 760 khz; 50 kw-D, 1 kw-N, DA-2. TL: N29 30 05 W98 18 33. Stereo. c/o WOAI(AM), 6222 N.W. I-10 (78201). (210) 734-7301; (210) 736-9700. FAX: (2100 735-8811. Licensee: Clear Channel Radio Licenses Inc. Group owner: Clear Channel Communications Inc. (acq 6-16-93; $800,000; FTR 7-5-93). Net: ABC/R, CBS Spectrum, NBC the Source. Rep: Eastman. Format: Talk. Target aud: 12-34. ■ William G. Hill, gen mgr.

WOAI(AM)—Sept 29, 1922: 1200 khz; 50 kw-U. TL: N29 30 05 W98 07 09. 6222 N.W. I-10 (78201). (210) 736-9700. FAX: (210) 735-8811. Licensee: Clear Channel Radio Licenses Inc. (acq 7-24-92). Net: NBC, CBS. Rep: Christal. Format: News/talk. ■ L. Lowry Mays, pres; William G. Hill, gen mgr; Betty Kocurek, gen sls mgr; Pat Rogers, progmg dir; Jim Forsyth, news dir; Dan Walthers, chief engr.

KAJA(FM)—Co-owned with WOAI(AM). 1951: 97.3 mhz; 100 kw. Ant 984 ft. TL: N29 25 20 W98 29 22. Stereo. Prog sep from AM. Format: Country. News staff 2; news progmg 2 hrs wkly. Target aud: 18-54. ■ Bob Cohen, gen mgr; Mike McDonald, gen sls mgr; Bob Norman, prom mgr; Randy Carroll, progmg dir.

San Augustine

KCOT(FM)—Not on air, target date unknown: 92.5 mhz; 150 w. Ant 139 ft. TL: N31 31 44 W94 05 59. 4201 Far Hills Dr., Austin (78731). FAX: (409) 275-3242. Licensee: San Augustine Cable TV Inc.

San Diego

KUKA(FM)—July 14, 1993: 105.9 mhz; 6 kw. Ant 328 ft. TL: N27 45 34 W98 10 50. Hrs opn: 24. c/o Armando Marroquin Jr., 1800 Country Club Dr., Laredo (78041); 810 Alviar, Alice (78332). (512) 668-6666; (512) 668-9393. FAX: (512) 668-6661. Licensee: Armando Marroquin Jr. (acq 9-16-92; $5,900; FTR 11-16-92). Format: Spanish. News staff one; news progmg one hr wkly. Target aud: 18-34. ■ Armando Marroquin Jr., pres; Dan Pena, gen sls mgr, vp opns, vp progmg & mus dir; Buddy Travis, rgnl sls mgr; Armando Pena, news dir; Paul Easter, vp engrg. ■ Rates: $10.50; 8.50; 10.50; 8.50.

San Juan

KUBR(AM)—1991: 1210 khz; 10 kw-D, 1 kw-N, DA-2. TL: N26 14 41 W98 05 25. Box 252, McAllen (78502). (210) 781-5528. Licensee: Paulino Bernal. ■ Eloy Bernal, gen mgr.

San Marcos

KEYI-FM—Licensed to San Marcos. See Austin.

*****KTSW(FM)**—Apr 15, 1992: 89.9 mhz; 10.5 kw. Ant 299 ft. TL: N29 39 20 W98 07 59. Stereo. Hrs opn: 6 AM-2 AM. Old Main 106, 601 University Dr. (78666-4616). (512) 245-3485. FAX: (512) 245-3708. Licensee: Southwest Texas State Univ. (acq 4-16-92; $150,000; FTR 5-11-92). Format: College alt, news/talk, sports. Target aud: 18-25; College students. ■ Bob Shrader, gen mgr; Joel Tarver, stn mgr; Devin Bendy, dev dir; John Scott, prom dir; Amy Herndon, progmg dir; Kent Frisbie, mus dir; Ina White, news dir; Arvin Wallace, pub affrs dir; Tim Walker, chief engr.

KUOL(AM)—1948: 1470 khz; 250 w-U, DA-N. TL: N29 53 53 W97 54 44. Hrs opn: 5:30 AM-midnight. Box 2150 (78667). Licensee: SMR Corp. (acq 6-30-93; FTR 7-26-93).

San Saba

KBAL(AM)—1954: 1410 khz; 800 w-D, 203 w-N. TL: N31 11 26 W98 42 55. Hrs opn: 24. Box 126 (76877). (915) 372-5225. FAX: (915) 372-5225. Licensee: Fletcher Broadcasting Inc. (acq 5-30-91; $42,000; FTR 6-24-91). Wash atty: Fletcher, Heald. Format: C&W. News staff 2; news progmg 6 hrs wkly. Target aud: General. Spec prog: Farm 2 hrs wkly. ■ Lloyd Moss, pres; Gary Moss, gen mgr; Jim Murphy, stn mgr; Beverly Hughes, rgnl sls mgr; Martha Umble, mus dir; Rick Hadley, news dir. ■ Rates: $19; 17; 19; na.

Seabrook

KRTS(FM)—Apr 23, 1984: 92.1 mhz; 33 kw. Ant 630 ft. TL: N29 27 57 W95 13 23. Stereo. Hrs opn: 24. Suite 5100, 1600 Smith, Houston (77002). (713) 921-5787. FAX: (713) 651-0267. Licensee: KRTS Inc. (acq 7-1-87). Net: Concert Music Net. Rep: Katz & Powell. Wash atty: Leventhal, Senter & Lerman. Format: Class. News progmg 5 hrs wkly. Target aud: General. ■ M.S. Stude, pres; David Nichols, CFO; George Stokes, exec vp & gen mgr; Tom Richards, gen sls mgr & progmg dir; Leonard Liss, gen sls mgr; Jenny Sommer, rgnl sls mgr; Gena Richerson, prom dir; Blanton Alspaugh, mus dir; Chris Collins, (asst) mus dir & pub affrs dir; Rynn Parker, chief engr. ■ Rates: $100; 75; 100; 50.

Seguin

KSMG(FM)—Sept 9, 1970: 105.3 mhz; 100 kw. Ant 1,240 ft. TL: N29 16 29 W98 15 52. Stereo. Hrs opn: 24. No. 500, 8930 Four Winds, San Antonio (78239). (512) 646-0105; (512) 590-1111. FAX: (512) 646-9736. Licensee: Rusk Corp. (group owner). Net: Unistar. Rep: CBS Radio. Format: Oldies, adult contemp. News staff 2. Target aud: 25-54. ■ J.H. Jones II, pres; Caroline Devine, gen mgr; Susan Nieman, gen sls mgr; Carmen Delchambre, prom mgr; Bill Conway, progmg dir; J.J. Rodriguez, mus dir; Stan Kelly, news dir; Megan Bishop, pub affrs dir; Richard Schuh, chief engr.

KWED(AM)—Sept 9, 1948: 1580 khz; 1 kw-D, 249 w-N. TL: N29 34 48 W97 59 05. Box 1600, 609 E. Court (78155). (512) 379-2234. FAX: (512) 379-2238. Licensee: Seguin Broadcasting Co. (acq 12-31-69). Net: Mutual. Format: Country, news/talk. News staff 2; news progmg 30 hrs wkly. Target aud: General. Spec prog: Farm 6 hrs wkly. ■ Albert H. Kaplan, pres; Stan McKenzie, opns mgr; Ed Engelhardt, gen sls mgr; Mark Howard, progmg dir; Terri Brotze, news dir; Dick Schuh, chief engr. ■ Rates: $18; 14; 16; 12.

Seminole

KIKZ(AM)—Apr 15, 1954: 1250 khz; 1 kw-D, 250 w-N. TL: N32 41 58 W102 38 12. Hrs opn: 24. 105 N.W. 11th St. (79360). (915) 758-5878. FAX: (915) 758-5474. Licensee: Gaines County Broadcasting Ltd. (acq 6-9-93; $193,276 with co-located FM; FTR 7-5-93). Net: ABC/C, MBS, ABC. Format: Progsv country. News staff one; news progmg 7 hrs wkly. Target aud: General. Spec prog: Sp 26 hrs, farm 5 hrs, Ger one hr, relg 6 hrs wkly. ■ Kenneth Ripley, Gail Garlitz, presidents; Carla Cook, gen mgr, gen sls mgr & prom mgr; Dan Curtis, progmg dir & mus dir; Audie Cox, news dir; George Chambers, chief engr.

KSEM-FM—Co-owned with KIKZ(AM). March 15, 1985: 106.3 mhz; 3 kw. Ant 174 ft. TL: N32 41 58 W102 38 12. Stereo. Hrs opn: 24. Dups AM 100%.

Seymour

KSEY(AM)—Oct 26, 1950: 1230 khz; 1 kw-U. TL: N33 35 49 W99 16 42. Box 471 (76380). (817) 888-1230. Licensee: Suncountry Broadcasting Inc. (acq 3-89). Format: C&W. ■ Wes Yeager, pres, gen mgr & gen sls mgr; Rick King, opns mgr & news dir; Richard Dormier, chief engr.

KSEY-FM—June 26, 1981: 94.3 mhz; 3 kw. Ant 112 ft. TL: N33 35 49 W99 16 42 (CP: 93.9 mhz, 50 kw, ant 492 ft., N33 42 00 W99 08 12). Stereo. Dups AM 100%. (817) 888-2861.

Sherman

KDSX(AM)—See Denison-Sherman.

KIKM-FM—Apr 1, 1969: 96.7 mhz; 3 kw. Ant 299 ft. TL: N33 42 10 W96 34 05. Stereo. Box 3068, 3405 Loy Lake Rd. (75091-3068). (903) 893-1151. FAX: (903) 893-1154. Licensee: Hunt Broadcasting Inc. (acq 9-15-92; $500,000; FTR 10-19-92). Net: AP, ABC. Rep: McGavren Guild. Format: Country. News staff one; news progmg 6 hrs wkly. Target aud: 25-54. ■ Jeff Pettiette, gen mgr; Barry Diamond, progmg dir; Gil Nelson, mus dir; Ray Canevari, news dir; Amy Chell, pub affrs dir; Bill Hughes, chief engr. ■ Rates: $15; 14; 15; 13.

KJIM(AM)—Dec 19, 1947: 1500 khz; 1 kw-D, DA. TL: N33 41 30 W96 33 29. Box 220 (75091). (903) 893-1197. Licensee: Harmon G. Husbands (acq 5-72). Net: MBS. Format: Southern Gospel. Spec prog: Farm 12 hrs, relg 12 hrs wkly. ■ Larry L. Henderson, pres, gen mgr & gen sls mgr; Ann Wilson, progmg dir & mus dir.

KWSM(FM)—Co-owned with KJIM(AM). December 1989: 104.1 mhz; 3 kw. Ant 328 ft. TL: N33 42 10 W96 34 05. Stereo. Hrs opn: 24. Prog sep from AM. Format: Classic hits. Target aud: 24-55.

KXEB(AM)—October 1936: 910 khz; 1 kw-U, DA-1. TL: N33 40 25 W96 35 40. Suite 139, 1402 Corinth St., Dallas (75214). (214) 426-6110. FAX: (214) 428-4378. Licensee: Pesa Broadcasting Inc. (acq 4-90; $250,000; FTR 4-2-90). Format: Spanish. ■ Carmen Hernandez, gen mgr; Salomon Carmona, gen sls mgr; Juan Navarro, progmg dir.

Silsbee

KKAS(AM)—Oct 13, 1959: 1300 khz; 500 w-D. TL: N30 21 02 W94 13 39. Box 455 (77656). (409) 385-2883; (409) 385-4101. Licensee: Jewel P. White (acq 12-1-64). Net: Texas State Net. Rep: Riley. Format: Country. News progmg 10 hrs wkly. Target aud: General. ■ Jewel Pat White, pres, gen mgr & chief engr.

KWDX(FM)—Co-owned with KKAS(AM). June 21, 1980: 101.7 mhz; 3 kw. Ant 200 ft. TL: N30 21 02 W94 13 39. Stereo. Dups AM 100%.

Sinton

KDAE(AM)—Licensed to Sinton. See Corpus Christi.

KNCN(FM)—Licensed to Sinton. See Corpus Christi.

KOUL(FM)—Licensed to Sinton. See Corpus Christi.

Slaton

KCAS(AM)—Jan 15, 1962: 1050 khz; 250 w-D. TL: N33 26 58 W99 39 18. Hrs opn: Sunrise-sunset. No. 10, Briercroft Office Park Lubbock (79412). (806) 744-1050; (806) 744-1057. Licensee: Vision Media Inc. (acq 10-4-90; $65,000; FTR 10-22-90). Net: USA. Wash atty: B. Geguine. Format: MOR, christian music. News progmg 8 hrs wkly. Target aud: 35 plus; affluent, mature. Spec prog: Gospel one hr, relg 4 hrs wkly. ■ Bill Stewart, pres; Mark S. Beneze, gen mgr & progmg dir; George Goretskie, gen sls mgr; Jim Spann, prom dir & pub affrs dir; B. Barnwell, chief engr. ■ Rates: $11; 10; 10; na.

KJAK(FM)—Licensed to Slaton. See Lubbock.

Snyder

KSNY(AM)—Dec 22, 1949: 1450 khz; 1 kw-U. TL: N32 43 33 W100 56 30. Box 1008, 1806 KSNY Dr. (79549). (915) 573-9322. FAX: (915) 573-7445. Licensee: Snyder Broadcasting Co. Group owner: Wendell Mayes Stns (acq 1952). Net: ABC; VSA. Wash atty: Dow, Lohnes & Albertson. Format: Country. News progmg 15 hrs wkly. Target aud: General. Spec prog: Sp 6 hrs wkly. ■ Paula J. Gilbert, pres & gen mgr; Donna Fowler, gen sls mgr & prom mgr; Paul Z. Gilbert, progmg dir & chief engr; Johnny Thomas, mus dir; Michael Howard, news dir. ■ Rates: $10; 10; 6.50; 6.50.

KSNY-FM—Sept 2, 1980: 101.7 mhz; 3 kw. Ant 295 ft. TL: N32 45 23 W100 54 09. Stereo. Prog dups AM 5%. Format: Classic rock. News progmg 5 hrs wkly. ■ Rates: Same as AM.

Somerset

KCHG(AM)—Mar 1, 1988: 810 khz; 250 w-D, DA. TL: N29 13 02 W98 31 00. Hrs opn: 6 AM-midnight. Box 18025 (78218). (210) 828-0810. FAX: (210) 804-1515. Licensee: A.G.A. Inc. (acq 4-10-89; $476,000; FTR 4-24-89). Net: CBN. Format: Relg. News progmg 10 hrs wkly. Target aud: 25-40; Christian females. Spec prog:

Spanish. ■ Myron Wade, gen mgr; Mary Wade, opns mgr, progmg dir & chief engr.

Sonora

KHOS(AM)—Apr 9, 1976: 980 khz; 1 kw-D, 260 w-N. TL: N30 33 08 W100 39 24. Hrs opn: 14. Box 50 (76950). (915) 387-3553; (915) 387-3554. FAX: (915) 387-3554. Licensee: Sonora-Ozona Broadcasting Co. (acq 10-15-93; grpsl; FTR 11-8-93). Net: Texas State Net. Format: C&W. News staff one; news progmg 13 hrs wkly. Target aud: General. Spec prog: Farm 2 hrs, gospel 5 hrs, relg 2 hrs, Sp 19 hrs wkly. ■ Gail Garlitz, pres; Camille J. Cauthorn, exec vp, gen mgr, gen sls mgr, progmg dir & news dir; Floyd Phillips, chief engr.

KHOS-FM—May 1979: 92.1 mhz; 3 kw. Ant 300 ft. TL: N30 33 33 W100 37 54. Stereo. Dups AM 100%.

South Padre Island

KJIB(FM)—Not on air, target date unknown: 92.7 mhz; 3 kw. Ant 279 ft. TL: N26 03 51 W97 13 02. Box 590209, Houston (77259-0209). (713) 480-9992. Licensee: Laser Communications Inc. (acq 1-10-91; $20; FTR 1-28-91).

KZSP(FM)—July 27, 1990: 95.3 mhz; 3 kw. Ant 353 ft. TL: N26 04 04 W97 13 16. Stereo. Hrs opn: 24. Box 685, Suite 205, 215 Queen Isabella Blvd., Port Isabel (78578). (512) 943-9500. FAX: (512) 943-4121. Licensee: Rio Bravo Broadcasting (acq 11-16-90; FTR 12-10-90). Format: Oldies. News progmg 2 hrs wkly. Target aud: 25-54; success-oriented adults. ■ Doug Stalker, gen mgr; Susan Stalker, rgnl sls mgr. ■ Rates: $5; 5; 5; 5.

Spearman

KRDF-FM—Nov 16, 1963: 98.3 mhz; 3 kw. Ant 220 ft. TL: N36 12 31 W101 08 31. Stereo. Hrs opn: 16. Box 307, 605 E. Kenneth Ave. (79081). (806) 659-2529. Licensee: Spearhead Broadcasting Inc. (acq 10-1-88). Net: ABC/E; Texas State Net. Format: Country. Target aud: General. Spec prog: Farm 18 hrs, Sp 7 hrs wkly. ■ George Young, pres, gen mgr, gen sls mgr & chief engr; Dwayne Smith, vp & news dir.

Stamford

KVRP(AM)—July 1947: 1400 khz; 1 kw-U. TL: N32 55 52 W99 47 00. Hrs opn: 24. Box 1118, 1406 N. First St., Haskell (79521). (817) 864-8505. FAX: (817) 864-8001. Licensee: Rolling Plains Broadcasting Corp. (acq 8-5-86). Net: Texas State Net. Rep: Banner. Format: CD country. News staff one; news progmg 5 hrs wkly. Target aud: 25 plus. Spec prog: Farm 8 hrs, relg 6 hrs, sp 20 hrs wkly. ■ Kenneth Lane, pres, gen mgr & chief engr; Gary Barrett, stn mgr, gen sls mgr & prom mgr; Carl Shearer, progmg dir, (asst) mus dir & news dir; Ron McCandless, mus dir. ■ Rates: $17; 14; 17; 14.

Stephenville

KCUB-FM—July 1, 1990: 98.3 mhz; 3 kw. Ant 328 ft. TL: N32 12 46 W98 15 19. Stereo. Hrs opn: 24. Suite 102, 471 Harbin Dr. (76401). (817) 968-7459. Licensee: Pyramid Broadcasting Inc. (acq 12-21-89; $40,000; FTR 1-8-90). Net: Unistar, ABC; Texas State Net. Format: Adult contemp, light rock, news. News staff 2; news progmg 7 hrs wkly. Target aud: 18-42; all important age group of today's buying public. ■ R. LaVance Carson, pres; Rick Bushman, Norma Savage, gen mgrs; Russell Huffman, progmg dir & mus dir; Janice Howell, news dir; Gary Graham, chief engr. ■ Rates: $20; 20; 20; 20.

KSTV(AM)—1947: 1510 khz; 500 w-D. TL: N32 12 08 W98 14 54. Box 289, 3209 W. Washington (Dublin Hwy.) (76401). (817) 968-2141. FAX: (817) 968-6221. Licensee: Cen-Tex Media Inc. (acq 3-1-85; $750,000 with co-located FM; FTR 10-1-84). Net: ABC/D, SMN. Format: Contemp country, news, talk. News staff one; news progmg 8 hrs wkly. Target aud: 25-54; general. Spec prog: Farm 5 hrs, relg 6 hrs wkly. ■ Charles H. Strickland, pres; Julia Gray, prom mgr; J. D. Evans, progmg dir; Doc Wesson, mus dir; Michael Isbell, news dir.

KSTV-FM—Aug 15, 1968: 105.7 mhz; 100 kw. Ant 492 ft. TL: N32 11 11 W98 17 26. Stereo. Hrs opn: 24. Dups AM 100%. Net: ABC.

Sulphur Springs

KDXE(FM)—Aug 30, 1982: 95.9 mhz; 6 kw. Ant 285 ft. TL: N33 09 07 W95 36 12. Stereo. Box 564, 306 Glover St. (75482). (903) 885-1546; (903) 885-1221. FAX: (903) 885-1101. Licensee: Gilbert Group Inc. Group owner: Community Service Radio Group. Net: CNN. Rep: Miller. Wash atty: Fletcher, Heald & Hildreth. Format: Country. News staff 3; news progmg 13 hrs wkly. Target aud: 18-60. ■ Galen Gilbert, pres; Bryan Friesth, gen mgr, gen sls mgr & prom mgr; Dave Kirkpatrick, progmg dir & news dir; Jesse Gilbert, chief engr. ■ Rates: $11.20; 10.40; 9.60; 8.80.

KSST(AM)—March 1947: 1230 khz; 1 kw-U. TL: N33 07 00 W95 35 05. Hrs opn: 4:30 AM-midnight. Box 284, Radio Rd. (75483). (903) 885-3111. FAX: (903) 885-4160. Licensee: Hopkins County Broadcasting Co. (acq 1948). Net: ABC/I; Texas State. Format: C&W, news. News staff 2; news progmg 30 hrs wkly. Target aud: 25-54. ■ William Bradford, CEO, pres, gen mgr & chief engr; Dwayne Grimes, opns dir & progmg dir; Jim Thompson, gen sls mgr; Kelly Grimes, prom dir & adv dir; Enola Gay, mus dir; Cecil Savage, news dir & pub affrs dir.

Sunset Valley

KFIT(AM)—Licensed to Sunset Valley. See Austin.

Sweetwater

KXOX(AM)—November 1939: 1240 khz; 1 kw-U. TL: N32 29 16 W100 23 31. Box 570 (79556). (915) 236-6655. Licensee: Stein Broadcasting Inc. (acq 1956). Net: Texas State Net. Format: C&W. Target aud: 25-54. Spec prog: Farm 5 hrs, Sp 8 hrs wkly. ■ Jack Stein, pres; Jeff Stein, gen mgr & prom mgr; Susan Bewley, gen sls mgr; Earl B. Ray, chief engr. ■ Rates: $6.85; 6.55; 6.55; 6.55.

KXOX-FM—Apr 7, 1976: 96.7 mhz; 2.9 kw. Ant 154 ft. TL: N32 29 16 W100 23 31. Stereo. Hrs opn: 18. Prog sep from AM. 1801 Hoyt Lane (79556). Net: SMN. Format: Oldies. News staff one. ■ Rates: $13.75; 9.35; 9.35; 9.35.

Tahoka

KZUB(FM)—Not on air, target date unknown: 95.3 mhz; 3 kw. Ant 328 ft. TL: N33 08 15 W101 54 48. 110 County Rd. 203, Cameron (76520). Licensee: Parity Radio Corp.

Taylor

KTAE(AM)—Apr 1, 1948: 1260 khz; 1 kw-D. TL: N30 36 19 W97 24 51. Box 1160, 121 1/2 E. 2nd St. (76574). (512) 352-3631. Licensee: KTAE Inc. Net: UPI. Rep: PRO, Riley. Format: Var, C&W. Spec prog: Sp 14 hrs, Black 14 hrs, farm 4 hrs wkly. ■ Gillis G. Conoley, pres; G. G. Conoley, gen mgr; John Wehby, gen sls mgr; Fred Switzer, progmg dir & news dir; Ed Lee, mus dir; Colman McCalan, chief engr.

Temple

KLTD(FM)—Not on air, target date unknown: 101.7 mhz; 3 kw. Ant 282 ft. Box 42 (76503). Licensee: Progressive Communications Inc.

KPLE(FM)—Listing follows KTEM(AM).

KTEM(AM)—Nov 25, 1936: 1400 khz; 1 kw-U. TL: N31 03 56 W97 23 57. Hrs opn: 24. Box 1230, 301 N. Main (76503). (817) 773-5252; (817) 773-1400. FAX: (817) 773-0115. Licensee: KTEM Radio Inc. Group owner: Formby Stations (acq 3-20-70). Net: CBS, NBC Talknet, Daynet, ARN, MBS, BRN; Texas Net. Format: News/talk. News staff 3; news progmg 30 hrs wkly. Target aud: 35 plus; older, upscale, educated. Spec prog: Sp 2 hrs, Czech 3 hrs wkly. ■ Clint Formby, pres; Jim Cooper, gen mgr & gen sls mgr; Dave Owens, progmg dir; Joyce Hauk, news dir; Kevin Randall, chief engr. ■ Rates: $12; 10; 12; 8.

KPLE(FM)—Co-owned with KTEM(AM). Apr 4, 1975: 104.3 mhz; 34 kw. Ant 597 ft. TL: N30 59 12 W97 37 47. Stereo. Hrs opn: 24. Prog sep from AM. (817) 773-5253; (817) 771-5753. Format: Country. News staff 2; news progmg 5 hrs wkly. Target aud: 25-54. ■ Terry Hunt, progmg dir; Mark McClain, mus dir. ■ Rates: $21; 18; 21; 15.

Terrell

KPYK(AM)—October 1947: 1570 khz; 250 w-U. TL: N32 44 35 W96 18 18 (day), N32 45 18 W96 18 58 (night) (CP: 600 w-D, 30 w-N, DA-1, TL: N32 44 39 W96 18 18). Box 157 (75160); Box 1412C, W. Moore (75160). (214) 524-5795. Licensee: Mohnkem Electronics Inc. (acq 2-21-92; $25,000 plus assumption of debt; FTR 3-16-92). Format: Christian country, btfl mus. News staff one. Target aud: General; country listeners looking for a better message. Spec prog: Sp 2 hrs wkly. ■ Len Mohnkern, pres, gen mgr, gen sls mgr & news dir; Chuck Mohnkern, progmg dir & mus dir. ■ Rates: $15; 12; 15; na.

KTLR-FM—May 23, 1979: 107.1 mhz; 3.1 kw. Ant 440 ft. TL: N32 46 19 W96 11 51. Stereo. 105 W. Moore Ave. (75160). (214) 563-1071; (214) 524-2323. FAX: (214) 563-8895. Licensee: Metro Broadcasters-Texas Inc. (acq 5-79). Net: ABC, SMN. Format: Traditional country, Tejano. Target aud: 25-54; white collar professionals, affluent, highly educated. Spec prog: Country gospel 4 hrs wkly. ■ Glenda Jones, CFO; Ken Jones, gen mgr; Scott Myers, progmg dir & asst mus dir; Sam Simms, news dir; Vernon Hodeck, chief engr. ■ Rates: $60; 60; 60; na.

Terrell Hills

KDIL(FM)—July 18, 1979: 106.7 mhz; 100 kw. Ant 1,030 ft. TL: N29 11 03 W98 30 49. Stereo. Hrs opn: 24. 8401 Datapoint Dr., No. 935, San Antonio (78229-5925). (512) 359-1067. FAX: (512) 359-8832. Licensee: Vision Communications Inc. (acq 2-18-87; grpsl; FTR 12-1-86). Net: CBS Spectrum. Rep: Katz. Wash atty: Latham & Watkins. Format: C&W. News staff one. Target aud: 35-64. Spec prog: jazz 4 hrs wkly.

KLUP(FM)—Oct 17, 1947: 930 khz; 5 kw-D, 1 kw-N, DA-N. TL: N29 31 06 W98 24 25. #500, 8930 Fair Winds Dr., San Antonio (78239). (512) 646-0105. FAX: (512) 646-9711. Licensee: KISS Radio of San Antonio Ltd. Group owner: Rusk Corp. (acq 7-9-93; $3.95 million with KISS-FM San Antonio; FTR 8-2-93). Rep: CBS Radio. Format: MOR. Target aud: 35-64; upper & middle income, empty nesters. ■ Caroline Devine, gen mgr; Susan Nieman, gen sls mgr; Carmen Del Chambre, prom mgr; Bill Conway, progmg dir; Cathy Hawkins, mus dir.

Texarkana

KCMC(AM)—Feb 26, 1932: 740 khz; 1 kw-U, DA-1. TL: N33 26 17 W94 08 33. Hrs opn: 24. Box 6397, 3225 Summerhill Rd. (75503). (903) 793-1137. FAX: (903) 793-0285. Licensee: KCMC Inc. (acq 1936). Net: CBS; Texas AP, Texas State Net, Texas Agribus. Rep: Katz & Powell. Format: Full time traditional country music & sports. News staff one; news progmg 8 hrs wkly. Target aud: 30 plus; blue collar, working class. Spec prog: Farm, gospel 15 hrs wkly. ■ Walter Hussman, pres; Doug Davis, gen mgr, gen sls mgr, prom mgr, progmg dir & mus dir; Al Hanna, news dir; George Hammond, chief engr. ■ Rates: $15; 15; 15; 8.

KTAL-FM—Co-owned with KCMC(AM). 1945: 98.1 mhz; 100 kw h, 61 kw v. Ant 1,360 ft. TL: N32 54 11 W94 00 22. Box 7428, Shreveport, LA (71107); 3150 N. Market St., Shreveport, LA (71137). (318) 425-2422. Format: AOR. ■ H. Lee Bryant, pres; Kyle B. Hamaoka, stn mgr. ■ KTAL-TV affil.

KHSP(AM)—1946: 1400 khz; 1 kw-U. TL: N33 26 28 W94 03 16. 1323 College Dr. (75503-3531). (903) 793-1109. FAX: (903) 794-4717. Licensee: Beat of His Heart Broadcasting Inc. (acq 3-12-91; $225,000 with co-located FM; FTR 4-1-91). Net: ABC/I; Texas State. Format: News, talk. ■ Jay Calhoun, gen mgr; Don Slayter, news dir; Juan Callum, chief engr.

KKYR(AM)—See Texarkana, Ark.

KKYR-FM—July 15, 1965: 102.5 mhz; 100 kw. Ant 445 ft. TL: N33 22 24 W94 01 00. Stereo. 2324 Arkansas Blvd., Texarkana, AR (75502). (501) 772-3771. FAX: (501) 772-0364. Licensee: Broadcasting Unlimited Inc. (acq 6-89). Net: AP. Rep: Banner. Format: Country. News staff one; news progmg 6 hrs wkly. Target aud: General. ■ Don R. Chaney, pres; Craig D. Reininger, gen mgr; Ed Torres, gen sls mgr; Gary Lawrence, progmg dir.

KRMD(AM)—See Shreveport, La.

KRMD-FM—See Shreveport, La.

KTAL-FM—Listing follows KCMC(AM).

KTWN(AM)—Oct 23, 1961: 940 khz; 2.5 kw-D, 11 w-N. TL: N33 24 28 W94 02 45. 303 W. Broad St. (75501). (903) 793-4671. FAX: (903) 793-4672. Licensee: KATQ Radio Inc. Net: ABC/E. Format: Big band. News progmg 2 hrs wkly. Target aud: 35 plus. Spec prog: Black gospel 2 hrs wkly, Paul Harvey, Rush Limbaugh. ■ John H. Bell, pres & gen mgr; Floyd Bell, vp; Hazel E. Cotton, news dir. ■ Rates: $12; 10; 12; 8.

KTWN-FM—See Texarkana, Ark.

***KTXK(FM)**—Feb 1, 1984: 91.5 mhz; 5.2 kw. Ant 335 ft. TL: N33 23 33 W94 14 44. Stereo. 2500 N. Robinson (75501). (903) 838-4541. FAX: (903) 832-5053. Licensee: Texarkana College. Net: APR, NPR. Format: Btfl mus, class, jazz. News staff one; news progmg 12 hrs wkly. Target aud: 35 plus; males & females. ■ Steve Mitchell, vp, gen mgr & adv dir; Jerry Atkins, progmg dir & mus dir; Alton Pettigrew, (asst) mus dir; Carl Spicher, chief engr.

Texas City

KYST(AM)—November 1947: 920 khz; 5 kw-D, 1 kw-N, DA-2. TL: N29 25 03 W94 56 12. Suite 500, 7322 S.W. Freeway, Houston (77074). (713) 779-9292. FAX: (713) 779-1651. Licensee: Hispanic Broadcasting Inc. (acq 10-1-93; $548,000; FTR 10-18-93). Format: Sp. ■ Skipper Jones, gen sls mgr; Manuel Velasquez, progmg dir, mus dir & news dir.

Tomball

KSEV(AM)—Dec 1, 1986: 700 khz; 25 kw-D, 1 kw-N, DA-2. TL: N30 11 34 W95 35 40. Suite 1170, 11767 Katy Freeway, Houston (77079). (713) 588-4800. FAX: (713) 588-4820. Licensee: Sunbelt Broadcasting Co. (acq 10-89; $47,164; FTR 10-2-89). Net: NBC, BRN. Format: Talk, business, sports. ■ Dan Patrick, pres, gen mgr & progmg dir; Bonny English, gen sls mgr; Chuck McLeod, chief engr.

Tulia

KTUE(AM)—November 1954: 1260 khz; 1 kw-D, 53 w-N. TL: N34 31 34 W101 46 56. Box 1260 (79088); 708 S. Hwy. 87 (79088). (806) 995-3531. Licensee: Amburn Communications (acq 10-88). Net: Texas State Net. Rep: Keystone (unwired net), Riley. Format: Modern country. News staff one; news progmg 10 hrs wkly. Target aud: General. Spec prog: Farm 10 hrs wkly. ■ Jay Amburn, pres, gen mgr, gen sls mgr, prom mgr & progmg dir; Bob Schnieder, chief engr.

KJMX(FM)—Co-owned with KTUE(AM). Apr 1, 1991: 104.9 mhz; 7.2 kw. Ant 187 ft. TL: N34 31 34 W101 46 56. (Acq 7-6-90; $7,500; FTR 8-6-90). Format: Adult contemp. Spec prog: Local sports.

Tye

KBCY(FM)—October 1983: 99.7 mhz; 100 kw. Ant 744 ft. TL: N32 24 39 W100 06 26. Stereo. Hrs opn: 24. Box 3337, Abilene (79604); Suite 14C, 241 Pine, Abilene (79601). (915) 673-5252. FAX: (915) 675-6449. Licensee: Tye Broadcasting Inc. (acq 12-85; $485,000; FTR 10-28-85). Rep: Schubert. Format: Country. News progmg 21 hrs wkly. Target aud: 25-49; upscale adults. Spec prog: Relg 5 hrs wkly. ■ Glen Hine, pres; J.R. Greeley, gen mgr; Jack Smith, gen sls mgr; Jaye Dylan, progmg dir; Gary Smith, chief engr.

Tyler

KDOK(FM)—Listing follows KGLD(AM).

KGLD(AM)—May 1956: 1330 khz; 1 kw-D, 500 w-N. TL: N32 22 35 W95 15 55. Hrs opn: 24. Box 1330 (75710); Suite 300, 1828 E.SE. Loop 323 (75701). (903) 593-2519; (903) 533-1330. FAX: (903) 597-4141. Licensee: Gleiser Communications Inc. (acq 7-29-91; $65,000; FTR 8-5-91). Net: SMN. Wash atty: Scott Johnson. Format: MOR. News staff one; news progmg 5 hrs wkly. Target aud: 35 plus. ■ Paul Gleiser, pres & gen mgr; Mike Harris, stn mgr; Sam Matthews, gen sls mgr; Ty Turner, prom mgr; Bill Atkins, progmg dir, mus dir & news dir; Steve Comer, chief engr. ■ Rates: $12; 10; 12; 8.

KDOK(FM)—Co-owned with KGLD(AM). November 1975: 92.1 mhz; 3 kw. Ant 280 ft. TL: N32 22 52 W95 20 52. Stereo. Prog sep from AM. FAX: (903) 533-1330. (Acq 6-30-93; $175,000; FTR 7-26-93). Format: Oldies. News staff one. Target aud: General.

***KGLY(FM)**—June 1988: 91.3 mhz; 12 kw. Ant 462 ft. TL: N32 21 06 W95 16 00. Stereo. Hrs opn: 24. Box 8525 (75711); 2721 E. Erwin (75708). (903) 593-5863. FAX: (903) 593-2663. Licensee: Educational Radio Foundation of East Texas Inc. Net: Moody, USA, Beethoven. Format: Relg. News progmg 3 hrs wkly. Target aud: 35 plus. Spec prog: Class 14 hrs wkly. ■ Phil Hook, chmn & opns dir; Shelley Chapin, gen mgr; Mike Harper, stn mgr; Todd Hinkie, mus dir; Sans Hawkins, chief engr.

***KVNE-FM**—Co-owned with KGLY(FM). Oct 15, 1983: 89.5 mhz; 100 kw. Ant 899 ft. TL: N32 32 21 W95 13 16 (CP: 96 kw). Stereo. Hrs opn: 24. Prog sep from KGLY(FM). Net: USA, Moody. Format: Relg. News progmg 6 hrs wkly. Target aud: 20-45; families. Spec prog: Gospel 2 hrs, children 4 hrs, Sp 2 hrs wkly. ■ Mike Harper, progmg dir; Shelley Chapin, progmg mgr.

KISX(FM)—See Whitehouse.

KKUS(FM)—Not on air, target date unknown: 104.1 mhz; 50 kw. Ant 492 ft. TL: N32 29 40 W95 28 55. 113 E. 7th St. (75701). Licensee: Tyler FM Inc.

KNUE(FM)—Dec 31, 1964: 101.5 mhz; 100 kw. Ant 1,074 ft. TL: N32 15 35 W94 57 02. Stereo. Hrs opn: 24. 3810 Brookside (75701). (903) 581-0606. FAX: (903) 581-2011. Licensee: Golden Eagle Broadcasters Inc. Group Owner: Broadcasters Unlimited Inc. (acq 2-15-83). Rep: Banner. Format: Country. News staff one; news progmg 4 hrs wkly. Target aud: General. ■ Don R. Chaney, CEO; Jim Bell, CFO; Terry Cooper, gen mgr; Richard Kelley, sls dir & mktg dir; Mike Gatons, gen sls mgr; John Moore, prom dir; Amy Austin, progmg dir; Chuck McKinley, mus dir; Dave Goldman, news dir; Roy Faubion, pub affrs dir; Wayne Blackwelder, engrg dir; Barry Hopson, chief engr.

KTBB(AM)—Aug 28, 1947: 600 khz; 5 kw-D, 2.5 kw-N, DA-2. TL: N32 16 18 W95 12 23. Stereo. Hrs opn: 24. Suite 317, 1828 E.S.E Loop 323 (75701). (903) 595-2631. FAX: (903) 592-9923. Licensee: KTBB Radio Inc. Group owner: Stansell Communications Inc. (acq 10-13-89; $605,000; FTR 7-3-89). Net: ABC/I, ABC TalkRadio; Texas State Net. Rep: D & R Radio. Wash atty: Fisher, Wayland, Cooper & Leader. Format: Full svc-news, talk, sports & info. News staff 7; news progmg 70 hrs wkly. Target aud: 35 plus. Spec prog: Gospel 5 hrs wkly. ■ Jim Stansell, pres & gen mgr; Jim Wallace, stn mgr; Paul Gleiser, gen sls mgr; Mike Edwards, progmg dir & news dir; Steve Comer, chief engr. ■ Rates: $40; 30; 35; 15.

KTYL-FM—Co-owned with KTBB(AM). February 1966: 93.1 mhz; 100 kw. Ant 459 ft. TL: N32 22 30 W95 14 40. Stereo. Hrs opn: 24. Prog sep from AM. Format: Adult contemp. News staff one; news progmg 10 hrs wkly. Target aud: 18-54. ■ Bill Davis, prom mgr; Dave Moreland, progmg dir; Janie Baker, mus dir; Laura Kay, news dir. ■ Rates: $55; 50; 50; na.

***KVNE-FM**—Listing follows KGLY(FM).

KYZS(AM)—1930: 1490 khz; 1 kw-U. TL: N32 22 30 W95 16 05. Stereo. Hrs opn: 24. Box 1490, Radio Station KYZS(AM) (75710). (903) 593-1490. Licensee: Blue Jay Production Inc. (acq 10-12-89). Net: NBC, MBS. Rep: Katz & Powell. Format: Talk. ■ Don Backus, gen mgr; Adam Johnson, progmg dir; Steve Comer, chief engr.

KZEY(AM)—1958: 690 khz; 1 kw-D, 92 w-N, DA-2. TL: N32 22 52 W95 20 52. Hrs opn: 24. Box 4248, Lake Park Dr. (75712). (903) 593-1744. FAX: (903) 593-2666. Licensee: Community Broadcast Group Inc. Net: AP. Format: Urban contemp. News staff one. Target aud: General. Spec prog: Gospel 16 hrs wkly. ■ Jerry Russell, pres & gen mgr; B.J. Williams, mus dir; Daryl Bowdre, news dir; Bill Hughes, chief engr. ■ Rates: $21.75; 19; 21.75; 16.

Universal City

KSAH(AM)—Nov 1, 1986: 720 khz; 10 kw-D, 1 kw-N, DA-2. TL: N29 31 51 W98 10 39. Stereo. Suite 803, 1777 N.E. Loop 410, San Antonio (78217). (512) 820-3503. Licensee: Ganadores Inc. Rep: Caballero. Format: Sp. News staff one; news progmg 2 hrs wkly. Target aud: 18-49. ■ Miguel Villarreral, pres; Dennis G. Roberts, gen mgr; Ray Torres, gen sls mgr; Lucy Ruiz, prom dir; Oscar Rios De La Renta, progmg dir; Ricardo Morin, news dir; Bill Haberer, chief engr. ■ Rates: $60; 60; 60; 50.

Uvalde

KUVA(FM)—Aug 20, 1984: 102.3 mhz; 3 kw. Ant 280 ft. TL: N29 11 46 W99 46 48. Stereo. 828 S. Getty (78801). (210) 278-1102. FAX: (210) 278-1479. Licensee: Marqueze Broadcasting Corp. (acq 9-1-92; $235,000; FTR 6-12-89). Format: Sp. Spec prog: Sp 19 hrs wkly.

KVOU(AM)—Apr 4, 1947: 1400 khz; 1 kw-U. TL: N29 11 16 W99 46 36. Hrs opn: 6 AM-midnight. Box 758, 1400 Batesville Rd. (78802-0758). (512) 278-2555; (512) 278-6095. FAX: (512) 278-9461. Licensee: Uvalde Broadcasters Inc. Net: ABC/E; Texas State Net, VSA Radio. Rep: Lotus. Format: Country, Sp. News staff one; news progmg 15 hrs wkly. Target aud: General. Spec prog: Farm 12 hrs wkly. ■ E. C. Stern Jr., vp, gen mgr & adv mgr; Zac Gray, progmg dir; Richard Morris, news dir; Tom Winkle, chief engr.

KYUF(FM)—Co-owned with KVOU(AM). Sept 9, 1976: 104.9 mhz; 3 kw. Ant 263 ft. TL: N29 11 16 W99 46 36. Stereo. Prog sep from AM. Format: C&W. News progmg 2 hrs wkly. Target aud: 25-54. ■ Wade Carpenter, progmg dir; Richard Morris, pub affrs dir.

Vernon

KVWC(AM)—July 1939: 1490 khz; 1 kw-U. TL: N34 09 12 W99 16 09. Hrs opn: 6 AM-10 PM. Box 1419, 302 E. Wilbarger (76385). (817) 552-6221. FAX: (817) 553-4222. Licensee: KVWC Inc. (acq 6-1-61). Net: AP. Rep: Riley. Format: MOR, farm, country. News staff one; news progmg 10 hrs wkly. Target aud: General; Wildarger & surrounding counties. Spec prog: Sp 4 hrs, gospel 16 hrs wkly. ■ Mike Klappenbach, pres, gen mgr & chief engr; Dan Hendrix, progmg dir. ■ Rates: $7.50; 7; 7; 7.

KVWC-FM—Apr 10, 1972: 102.3 mhz; 3 kw. Ant 138 ft. TL: N34 09 12 W99 16 09. Stereo. Dups AM 20%. Format: Btfl mus, adult contemp, MOR. ■ Rates: Same as AM.

Victoria

KAMG(AM)—August 1939: 1340 khz; 1 kw-U. TL: N28 49 49 W97 00 33. Stereo. Hrs opn: 24. Prog dups KPLV(FM) Port Lavaca 100%. Box 3487 (77903); 3613 N. Main St. (77901). (512) 576-2000. FAX: (512) 572-0014. Licensee: Independence Broadcasting Co. Group owner: Wendell Mayes Stations (acq 12-1-64). Net: ABC/D. Rep: McGavren Guild. Wash atty: Dow, Lohnes & Albertson. Format: Country. News progmg 5 hrs wkly. Target aud: 25-54. Spec prog: Farm one hr wkly. ■ Bob Woodman, CEO, pres & gen mgr; Wendell Mayes Jr., chmn; Cecil Parker, stn mgr; Gary Haus, progmg dir & mus dir; Sue Robbyns, pub affrs dir; Jim Koenig, chief engr.

KVIC(FM)—Co-owned with KAMG. Apr 8, 1976: 95.1 mhz; 100 kw. Ant 500 ft. TL: N28 46 55 W96 56 30. Stereo. Hrs opn: 24. (512) 576-6111. Net: ABC. News staff one. Target aud: 18-49. ■ Rick Shaw, prom dir, progmg dir & mus dir.

KEPG(FM)—Feb 2, 1989: 100.9 mhz; 2.7 kw. Ant 312 ft. TL: N28 47 20 W97 03 00. Box 3588 (77901). (512) 578-2751. Licensee: KEPG Inc. Format: Tejano, country, top-40. ■ Yolanda Dorrsett, gen mgr; Natie Padierna, gen sls mgr; Bilamino Cruz, progmg dir; Lee Lopez, chief engr.

KIXS(FM)—Dec 4, 1980: 107.9 mhz; 100 kw. Ant 362 ft. TL: N28 46 03 W96 59 11. Stereo. Box 1267 (77902). (512) 573-0777. FAX: (512) 578-0059. Licensee: Radio Victoria Inc. (acq 12-87). Net: AP. Rep: Katz. Format: C&W. ■ Bill Hooten, vp & gen mgr; Dave Winston, progmg dir; Charles Smithey, chief engr.

KPLV(FM)—(Port Lavaca). Aug 1, 1976: 93.3 mhz; 100 kw. Ant 450 ft. TL: N28 32 10 W96 43 20 (CP: Ant 318 ft.). Stereo. Box 3487, 3613 N. Main, Victoria (77901). (512) 576-2000. FAX: (512) 572-0014. Licensee: Coastal Wireless Co. (acq 11-87; $630,000; FTR 11-16-87). Rep: Target. Format: Country. News progmg 5 hrs wkly. Spec prog: Farm one hr wkly. ■ Rita Parker, gen mgr; Cecil Parker, gen sls mgr.

KTXN-FM—Sept 5, 1991. 98.7 mhz; 100 kw. Ant 253 ft. TL: N28 48 46 W97 03 45. Stereo. Hrs opn: 24. Box 2682 (77902); FM 1685 (77901). (512) 573-4366. Licensee: Cosmopolitan Enterprises of Victoria Inc. Format: Nostalgia. Target aud: 35 plus; adults with buying power who want neither country nor rock. ■ John J. Tibiletti, pres; Bob Nance, gen mgr, stn mgr & mus dir; Ron Sumbera, chief engr. ■ Rates: $10; 6; 8; 6.

KVIC(FM)—Listing follows KAMG.

KVLT(FM)—Dec 1, 1990: 92.3 mhz; 3 kw. Ant 298 ft. TL: N28 46 03 W96 59 11. Stereo. Hrs opn: 24. Suite 208, 2001 E. Sabine (77901). (512) 573-9176. FAX: (512) 573-9177. Licensee: Ellis Broadcasting (acq 6-15-92; $90,000; FTR 7-6-92). Rep: Katz & Powell. Wash atty: Pepper & Corazzini. Format: Light adult contemp. ■ John E. Ellis, pres & gen mgr; Bob Rice, gen sls mgr; Sandy Arocha, prom mgr.

***KXBJ(FM)**—Mar 1994: 89.3 mhz; 18.5 kw. Ant 302 ft. TL: N28 49 20 W96 58 20. Stereo. Rebroadcasts KSBJ(FM) Humble, 100%. Box 187, Humble (77347). Licensee: Educational Media Foundation of Victoria. Net: USA. Wash atty: Hardy & Carey. Format: Contemporary Christian music. News staff 3; news progmg 5 hrs wkly. Target aud: 25-54. ■ Tim McDermott, gen mgr; Buddy Holiday, stn mgr; Susan O'Donnell, dev dir; Jeff Scott Wurthmann, prom dir; Tom Carter, progmg dir; Roger Clark, mus dir; Roger Greer, (asst) mus dir; Tony Bano, engrg dir.

Waco

KBBW(AM)—April 1953: 1010 khz; 10 kw-D, 2.5 kw-N, DA-2. TL: N31 34 09 W97 00 00. 1019 Washington St. (76701). (817) 757-1010. FAX: (817) 752-5339. Licensee: Steve Williams dba American Broadcasting of Texas (acq 6-16-86; FTR 5-12-86). Net: USA. Format: Christian. News progmg 15 hrs wkly. Target aud: 25-54. ■ Steve Williams, pres & gen mgr; Bill Thrasher, opns dir & gen sls mgr; Randy James, prom mgr; Sean Eakin, progmg dir; Shelley Layne, mus dir; Don Daunis, news dir; Dave Fricker, chief engr.

KCKR(FM)—Sept 6, 1959: 95.5 mhz; 100 kw. Ant 1,100 ft. TL: N31 19 17 W97 20 41. Stereo. Hrs opn: 24. 4949

Franklin Ave. (76710). (817) 776-3900. FAX: (817) 776-3917. Licensee: Broadcasters Unlimited Inc. ($610,000; FTR 6-14-93). Net: MBS; Rep: Katz. Format: Country. News staff one. Target aud: 25-54. ■ Don Chaney, CEO, chmn & pres; Ray Eller, gen mgr; Sandy Culverhouse, opns dir; Art Opperman, prom mgr & progmg dir; Wendy Michaels, news dir; Kelly Lough, chief engr. ■ Rates: $25; 22; 25; 18.

KJNE(FM)—See Hillsboro.

KRZI(AM)—Oct 8, 1962: 1580 khz; 1 kw-D, 500 w-N, DA-2. TL: N31 31 04 W97 05 16. Hrs opn: 18. Box 8093 (76714); 1018 N. Valley Mills Dr. (76710). (817) 772-0930. FAX: (817) 772-1580. Licensee: KRZI Inc. (acq 9-22-86; $360,000; FTR 9-22-86). Net: Unistar. Rep: Roslin. Wash atty: Leventhal, Senter & Lerman. Format: News/talk News staff one; news progmg 2 hrs wkly. Target aud: 25-54. Spec prog: Black 4 hrs, Sp 14 hrs wkly. ■ Van Goodall Jr., pres; Robert Lauck, gen mgr; Roland Richper, news dir; Dave Fricker, chief engr.

***KWBU(FM)**—Mar 15, 1966: 107.1 mhz; 3 kw. Ant 190 ft. TL: N31 31 51 W97 09 10. Stereo. Hrs opn: 7 AM-midnight. Box 97368, Castellaw Communications Ctr., Baylor Univ. (76798). (817) 752-5015. FAX: (817) 755-1563. Licensee: Baylor Univ. Class, div. Spec prog: Jazz 10 hrs wkly.■ Herbert Reynolds, pres; Frank Fallon, gen mgr; Paul E. Wagenschein, chief engr.

KWTX(AM)—May 1, 1946: 1230 khz; 5 kw-D, 250 w-N, DA-2. TL: N31 31 42 W97 07 14. Hrs opn: 24. Box 2636 (76702). (817) 776-5989. FAX: (817) 751-0097. Licensee: KWTX Broadcasting Co. (group owner). Net: SMN. Rep: Katz. Format: Adult music. Target aud: 35 plus. Spec prog: Relg 2 hrs wkly. ■ Tom Pears, pres; Bill Knobler, gen mgr; Bob Bunch, gen sls mgr; Vern Pecore, progmg dir; Dave Emely, news dir; Bill Moore, chief engr.

KWTX-FM—Dec 1, 1970: 97.5 mhz; 97 kw. Ant 1,568 ft. TL: N31 19 19 W97 18 58. Stereo. Hrs opn: 24. Prog sep from AM. Format: CHR. Target aud: 18-49. ■ Tom Martens, progmg dir. ■ KWTX-TV affil.

WACO(AM)—July 22, 1922: 1460 khz; 1 kw-U, DA-N. TL: N31 31 01 W97 06 38. Hrs opn: 24. Box 21088 (76702). (817) 772-7100. FAX: (817) 772-8708. Licensee: SBG Communications of Texas Inc. Net: ABC/E; Texas State. Rep: McGavren Guild. Format: Hit Country. News progmg 4 hrs wkly. Target aud: 25-54; general. Spec prog: Farm 5 hrs wkly. ■ John Blake, gen mgr; Zack Owen, opns mgr & progmg mgr; Carl Ray, gen sls mgr; Greg Sax, mus dir; Ann Harder, news dir; Dave Fricker, chief engr.

WACO-FM—June 1960: 99.9 mhz; 90 kw. Ant 1,660 ft. TL: N31 20 15 W97 18 37. Stereo. Hrs opn: 24. Dups AM 90%. Net: ABC/I; Texas State Net. News progmg one hr wkly.

Waxahachie

KBEC(AM)—June 1955: 1390 khz; 500 w-D, 65 w-N, DA-2. TL: N32 25 30 W96 51 56 (CP: 480 w-D, 260 w-N, DA-2, TL:N32 26 45 W96 48 15). Hrs opn: 6 AM-11 PM. Box 558, 1937 Hwy. 3E North (75165). (214) 923-1390; (214) 938-1390. FAX: (214) 923-0811. Licensee: Faye and Richard Tuck Inc. (acq 6-55). Net: Texas State Net. Format: Classic country oldies. News staff 3; news progmg 15 hrs wkly. Target aud: 25-54. Spec prog: Farm 3 hrs, Sp 10 hrs, Pol 2 hrs wkly. ■ Richard Tuck, pres, gen mgr, sls dir & chief engr; Ken Roberts, stn mgr & progmg dir; Connie Poirier, mktg dir; Pat McDonald, prom mgr; Barry Wolverton, adv mgr; Sam Meyers, mus dir.

Weatherford

KZEE(AM)—Aug 12, 1956: 1220 khz; 500 w-D, 8 w-N. TL: N32 47 09 W97 47 55. Box 269 (76086). (817) 594-1220. FAX: (817) 599-9818. Licensee: TriStar Communications (acq 12-16-88). Net: Texas State Net. Format: Country. News staff one; news progmg 12 hrs wkly. Target aud: 25-65. Spec prog: Farm one hr, sports 8 hrs, talk 5 hrs wkly. ■ Jeff Helbing, gen mgr; Sam Booth, sls dir. WFAA-TV affil. ■ Rates: $13; 10; 10; na.

Wellington

KLSR(AM)—See Memphis.

Weslaco

KRGE(AM)—1926: 1290 khz; 5 kw-U, DA-N. TL: N26 12 36 W97 54 33. Hrs opn: 24. Box 1290, Mile 7 W. Hwy. 83 (78596). (210) 968-7777. Licensee: Christian Ministries of the Valley (acq 1-31-91; $300,000; FTR 2-18-91). Net: Unistar, ABC/R. Rep: Torbet. Format: Christian, Sp. News progmg 3 hrs wkly. Target aud: 18-34. ■ Enrique Garza, gen mgr.

KTJN(FM)—See Mercedes.

West Lake Hills

KTXZ(AM)—June 9, 1982: 1560 khz; 2.5 kw-U, DA-2. TL: N30 21 38 W97 39 11. Hrs opn: 24. Suite 101, 400 E. Anderson Ln., Austin (78752). (512) 834-1515. FAX: (512) 834-1631. Licensee: Scan Communications. Net: Unistar. Rep: Lotus. Format: Bilingual Tejano. News progmg 14 hrs wkly. Target aud: 18-54; Bilingual, Hispanic, male & female. Spec prog: Sunday Christian music 6 hrs wkly. ■ Bennett Spelce, pres; Douglas C. Raab, gen mgr & gen sls mgr; Ed "Mr. Fats" Fuentes, progmg dir; Allen Spelce, pub affrs dir; George Bradshaw, chief engr. ■ Rates: $25; 21; 25; 14.

Wharton

KANI(AM)—June 17, 1962: 1500 khz; 500 w-U, DA-N. TL: N29 19 22 W96 03 32. 215 E. Milam St. (77488). (409) 532-3800. Licensee: Ammerman Enterprises Inc. (acq 6-1-82; $250,000; FTR 6-14-82). Net: Texas State. Format: Gospel. Spec prog: Sp 3 hrs, Pol 6 hrs wkly. ■ Darrell Martin, pres & gen mgr; Sandra Stewart, gen sls mgr, progmg dir, mus dir & news dir; Dave Biondi, chief engr.

Wheeler

***KPDR(FM)**—Aug 31, 1986: 90.5 mhz; 10 kw. Ant 482 ft. TL: N35 25 57 W100 16 31. Stereo. Box 469 (79096). (806) 826-5737. FAX: (806) 826-3048. Licensee: Wheeler Educational Broadcasting Foundation. Net: USA. Wash atty: Don, Lohones & Albertson. Format: Relg, educ. News progmg 9 hrs wkly. Target aud: General. Spec prog: Sp 5 hrs wkly. ■ Ricky Pfeil, pres; Jim Turaville, opns dir & engrg dir; Darla Brown, prom dir.

Whitehouse

KISX(FM)—Aug 15, 1982: 107.3 mhz; 50 kw. Ant 500 ft. TL: N32 17 19 W95 11 56. Stereo. Hrs opn: 24. 3810 Brookside Tyler (75701). (903) 507-5477. FAX: (903) 581-2011. Licensee: Tyler Broadcasting Co. Group owner: Carolyn G. Vance Group. Net: MBS. Rep: Banner. Format: Top-40. Target aud: 18-44. ■ William Whitley, CEO; Michael Storm, gen mgr, progmg dir & mus dir; Mike Gatons, gen sls mgr; Dave Goldman, news dir; Wayne Blackwelder, chief engr.

Wichita Falls

KLLF(AM)—1948: 1290 khz; 5 kw-D, 250 w-N. TL: N33 57 38 W98 33 42. Hrs opn: 6 AM-midnight. 5080 Kiel Rd. (76305). (817) 855-3555. FAX: (817) 855-1070. Licensee: Brandon Broadcasting of Texas Inc. Group owner: American General Media (acq 4-1-83; $1 million; FTR 4-18-83). Net: NBC, Sun. Format: Relg, news/talk. Target aud: 25 plus; adults. Spec prog: Sp 18 hrs wkly. ■ Anthony Brandon, pres; L. Rogers Brandon, execvp; Jon R. Gibson, gen mgr & gen sls mgr; Rev. Brad Cosway, progmg dir; Hal Smith, chief engr. ■ Rates: $10; 20; 10; 15.

KWFS(FM)—Co-owned with KLLF(AM). 1961: 103.3 mhz; 100 kw. Ant 449 ft. TL: N33 53 47 W98 32 33 (CP: Ant 1,017 ft., TL: N34 05 35 W98 52 44). Stereo. Prog sep from AM. (Acq 6-12-91; $1.2 million; FTR 7-1-91). Rep: Christal. Format: Country News staff one. Target aud: 18-49; adults, male skew. ■ Jessie Cassity, prom mgr, progmg dir & mus dir. ■ Rates: $30; 25; 25; 15.

KLUR(FM)—Apr 14, 1963: 99.9 mhz; 100 kw. Ant 820 ft. TL: N33 54 04 W98 32 21. Stereo. Box 5344 (76307). (817) 691-2311. FAX: (817) 696-2255. Licensee: Klur Broadcasting Co. Net: ABC/I. Rep: Katz. Format: C&W. ■ Jim Marks, gen mgr; Jim Russell, progmg dir; Steve Randal, mus dir; Debbie Day, news dir; Leon Hoeffner, chief engr.

***KMOC(FM)**—July 9, 1987: 89.5 mhz; 3 kw. Ant 672 ft. TL: N33 54 04 W98 32 21 (CP: 10 kw). Box 41 (76307). (817) 767-3303. Licensee: Christian Service Foundation Inc. Net: Moody. Format: Christian. ■ Bill Striech, pres; Gary Forsythe, gen mgr; Lynda Stringer, progmg dir; Charles Neal, chief engr.

KNIN(AM)—November 1947: 990 khz; 10 kw-D, 1 kw-N, DA-2. TL: N33 55 40 W98 34 10. Stereo. Hrs opn: 24. Box 787 (76307); Spring Lake Rd. (76305). (817) 855-6924. FAX: (817) 855-4041. Licensee: Moran Broadcasting. Net: USA. Rep: Banner. Format: Country gospel. Target aud: 25-54. ■ R.J. Moran, pres; Randy Smith, gen mgr; Don Hightower, news dir; Eric Harley, prom mgr; J.J. MacKay, progmg dir & mus dir; Vernon Beck, chief engr.

KNIN-FM—May 12, 1975: 92.9 mhz; 100 kw. Ant 930 ft. TL: N33 54 04 W98 32 21. Stereo. Hrs opn: 24. Prog sep from AM. Net: Unistar. Format: CHR. Target aud: 18-49. ■ Eric Harley, mktg mgr; J.J. McKay, adv mgr.

KQXC(FM)—Not on air, target date unknown: 105.5 mhz; 3 kw. Ant 328 ft. TL: N33 53 50 W98 32 33. Licensee: Red River Communications Inc. (acq 10-28-91; $25,000 for CP; FTR 11-18-91).

***KTEO(FM)**—Not on air, target date unknown: 90.5 mhz; 6.5 kw. Ant 782 ft. TL: N33 53 23 W98 33 20. 3622 Kingside Dr., Dallas (75229). (817) 929-9450. Licensee: Red River Educational Media Foundation Inc. (acq 1-22-92; $1 for CP; FTR 2-10-92). ■ Charles E. Coldwell Jr., pres; Carl Singer, vp; David Briggs, chief engr.

KTLT(FM)—Nov 15, 1984: 106.3 mhz; 2.4 kw. Ant 423 ft. TL: N33 53 18 W98 34 08 (CP: 15.5 kw, ant 899 ft., TL: N33 53 23 W98 33 31). Stereo. Suite 820, 4245 Kemp Blvd. (76308). (817) 692-7106. FAX: (817) 696-0291. Licensee: Pegasus Broadcasting Inc. Net: AP. Rep: Christal. Format: Adult contemp. ■ Kenneth R. Schroder, pres, gen mgr & gen sls mgr; Chris Walters, progmg dir; Jerry Houston, news dir.

KWFS(FM)—Listing follows KLLF(AM).

KWFT(AM)—July 15, 1939: 620 khz; 5 kw-U, DA-N. TL: N33 55 07 W98 32 37. Box 420, 503 Radio Ln. (76307). (817) 322-4416. Licensee: North Texas Radio Inc. (acq 11-57). Net: CBS. Rep: Torbet. Format: MOR, news. News progmg 36 hrs wkly. Spec prog: Farm 13 hrs, relg 8 hrs wkly. ■ Don F. Whan, pres, gen sls mgr & chief engr; A.L. Pierce, Dick Mitchel, gen sls mgrs; Susie Bradshaw, prom mgr; Lonnie Padron, news dir.

Winfield

KALK(FM)—Sept 27, 1987: 97.7 mhz; 22.5 kw. Ant 328 ft. TL: N33 11 01 W95 12 32. Stereo. Hrs opn: 24. Jefferson Plaza, Suite 101, 106 S. Jefferson, Mt. Pleasant (75455). (903) 577-9770. FAX: (903) 577-9772. Licensee: Parker-Hill Communications Inc. (acq 12-19-90; $160,000; FTR 1-7-91). Net: Unistar. Wash atty: Haley, Bader & Potts. Format: Light adult contemp, classic rock. Target aud: 29-54. Spec prog: Gospel 5 hrs wkly. ■ Bob Hill, CEO & gen mgr; Donna R. Hill, pres, mktg dir & prom mgr; Mary O'Connell, stn mgr; Andy Fuller, progmg dir; Bill Hughes, chief engr. ■ Rates: $11.50; 9.50; 11.50; 7.50.

Winnsboro

KWNS(FM)—Sept 1, 1983: 104.9 mhz; 3 kw. Ant 282 ft. TL: N32 56 32 W95 18 53. Stereo. Hrs opn: 24. Box 54 (75494). (903) 342-3501. Licensee: Richard E. Foster (acq 11-1-89; $10,000; FTR 11-20-89). Net: USA. Texas State Net. Format: C&W, Southern gospel. News staff one. Target aud: 35-70. ■ Richard Foster, pres, gen mgr & progmg dir. ■ Rates: $12; 9; 7; 6.

Woodville

KVLL(AM)—Jan 4, 1968: 1490 khz; 1 kw-U, DA-1. TL: N30 44 52 W94 25 56. Hrs opn: 6 AM-10 PM. Box 459 185 Spring Valley Dr. (75979). (409) 283-3734. Licensee: Trinity Valley Broadcasting Co. (acq 4-25-75). Net: Texas State Net. Format: C&W. News staff one; news progmg 17 hrs wkly. Target aud: 18-55. Spec prog: Farm 2 hrs, gospel 2 hrs, relg 3 hrs wkly. ■ Kenneth Bond, pres, gen mgr, gen sls mgr & prom mgr; C.D. Woodrome, progmg dir & chief engr; David Sindle, mus dir; Melodey Raxles, news dir. ■ Rates: $9; 8; 9; 8.

KVLL-FM—Not on air, target date unknown: 94.7 mhz; 50 kw. Ant 492 ft. TL: N31 00 32 W94 24 14. Box 459 (75979). Licensee: Trinity Valley Broadcasting Co. Inc.

Yoakum

KYOC(FM)—January 1982: 92.5 mhz; 3 kw. Ant 300 ft. TL: N29 21 03 W97 11 32. Stereo. Hrs opn: 24. Box 776, 216 W. May (77995). (512) 293-6939. Licensee: Tom E. Donnelly (acq 8-1-88). Net: ABC, SMN. Format: Country. News progmg 12 hrs wkly. Target aud: General. Spec prog: Ger 2 hrs wkly. ■ Tom Donnelly, pres; David H. Huber, progmg dir; Chuck Stratman, mus dir. ■ Rates: $7.50; 7.50; 7.50; 6.

Utah

LAUREN A. COLBY
301-663-1086
COMMUNICATIONS ATTORNEY
Special Attention to
Difficult Cases

Blanding

KUTA(AM)—Sept 15, 1961: 790 khz; 1 kw-D, 113 w-N. TL: N37 39 13 W109 27 14. Hwy. 191 N. 6-1 (84511). (801) 678-2261. FAX: (801) 678-2262. Licensee: Mueller Broadcasting Inc. (acq 9-11-87). Net: CBS. Rep: Art Moore, Eastman. Format: Talk. Target aud: 25 plus. Spec prog: Navajo 5 hrs wkly. ■ Phil Mueller, pres & gen mgr.

Bountiful

KUTQ(FM)—Mar 15, 1988: 99.5 mhz; 39 kw. Ant 2,953 ft. TL: N40 36 29 W112 09 33. 3595 S. 1300 W., Salt Lake City (84119). (801) 264-8250. FAX: (801) 264-8978. Licensee: Bountiful Broadcasting Inc. Rep: Katz & Powell. Format: Contemp hit. News staff one; Target aud: 18-34; active adults. Spec prog: New age 2 hrs wkly. ■ Starley D. Bush, pres; Gary H. Waldron, gen mgr & progmg dir; Bruce Corrigan, gen sls mgr; Mark McKean, natl sls mgr; Gary Michaels, mus dir; Bill Traue, chief engr.

Brian Head

KREC(FM)—Nov 14, 1988: 98.1 mhz; 56 kw. Ant 2,526 ft. TL: N37 32 32 W113 04 05. Stereo. Hrs opn: 24. Box 747, Cedar City (84721); 7656 W. Hwy. 56, Cedar City (84720). (801) 586-9812. FAX: (801) 586-9889. Licensee: Brian Head Broadcasting Co. Net: Unistar. Format: Soft adult contemp. Target aud: 25-54. ■ Jeff Johnston, gen mgr & stn mgr; Mike Henrie, opns mgr; Trudy Collard, gen sls mgr; David Sanford, chief engr. ■ Rates: $11; 11; 11; 11.

Brigham City

KIDZ(FM)—Not on air, target date unknown: 100.7 mhz; 100 kw. Ant 1,328 ft. TL: N41 35 49 W112 14 58. Suite D-272, 5282 S. 320 W., Salt Lake City (84107). (801) 264-1075. FAX: (801) 269-8595. Licensee: U.S. Radio IV Inc. (group owner; acq 12-18-92; grpsl; FTR 1-18-93). ■ Bill Struck, gen mgr.

KSOS(AM)—Feb 19, 1948: 800 khz; 1 kw-D, 32 w-N. TL: N41 18 54 W112 04 03. #820, 385 24th St., Ogden (84401). (801) 546-1722. Licensee: First National Broadcasting Corp. (acq 1983; $450,000; FTR 2-21-83). Net: ABC/I; Intermountain, Art Moore. Format: C&W. Target aud: 25-54. Spec prog: Farm 8 hrs, Sp 2 hrs wkly. ■ Robert Boogalou, pres; Donald Steve, gen mgr; Kami Neilson, gen sls mgr, prom mgr & progmg dir; Brent Larson, mus dir & news dir; Lisa Erickson, chief engr.

KSOS-FM—Oct 20, 1972: 106.9 mhz; 68 kw. Ant 2,369 ft. TL: N41 15 27 W112 26 24. Stereo. David Eccles Bldg., 8th Fl., 385 24th St., Ogden (84401). Format: Adult contemp. Target aud: 25-54.

Cedar City

KBRE(AM)—1971: 940 khz; 10 kw-D. TL: N37 45 51 W113 06 15. 450 W. 400 S. (84720). (801) 586-5273. FAX: (801) 586-0458. Licensee: Kolob Broadcast Radio Enterprises Inc. (acq 10-14-93; $325,000 with co-located FM; FTR 11-1-93). Net: ABC/E, AP; Intermountain. Rep: Eastman/Intermountain. Format: Pure Gold. ■ Charles F. Hunter, pres; Jon C. Hunter, gen mgr, news dir & chief engr.

KBRE-FM—May 10, 1974: 94.9 mhz; 25.5 kw. Ant 1,681 ft. TL: N37 38 41 W113 22 28. Stereo. Prog sep from AM. Net: ABC/FM, AP. Format: Classic Rock. ■ Bob Tuttle, progmg dir.

*****KGSU-FM**—October 1966: 91.1 mhz; 10 kw. Ant -462 ft. TL: N37 38 55 W113 05 32. Stereo. Hrs opn: 6 AM-midnight (winter), 10 AM-10 PM (summer). 351 West Center (84720). (801) 586-7975. Licensee: Southern Utah University. Format: Contemp hit, educ. Target aud: General. Spec prog: Opera 3 hrs wkly. ■ Arthur Challis, gen mgr; Matt Barton, stn mgr & progmg dir; Aaron Goodman, vp sls, vp mktg & vp prom; Brooke Larsen, progmg mgr, mus dir & pub affrs dir; Heidi Swa, news dir; Lance Jackson, chief engr.

KSSD(FM)—Listing follows KSUB(AM).

KSUB(AM)—July 4, 1937: 590 khz; 5 kw-D, 1 kw-N, DA-N. TL: N37 41 55 W113 10 44. Hrs opn: 24. Box 819, 6200 W. Hwy. 16 (84721). (801) 586-5900. FAX: (801) 586-0437. Licensee: Southern Utah Broadcasting Co. (acq 1959). Net: CBS, AP. Rep: Art Moore; Target.Format: News/talk, sports, country. News staff one; news progmg 15 hrs wkly. Target aud: 35-65; adults. Spec prog: Relg, local talk, farm 6 hrs wkly. ■ Jerold Johnson, pres & gen mgr; Steve Miner, vp opns, vp progmg, mus dir & news dir; Rod Wray, vp dev, vp sls & vp mktg; Sheri Sorenson, pub affrs dir; Don Blanchard, vp engrg. ■ Rates: $10; 10; 10; 5.

KSSD(FM)—Co-owned with KSUB(AM). Oct 15, 1976: 92.5 mhz; 41.6 kw. Ant 1,690 ft. TL: N37 38 41 W113 22 28. Stereo. Hrs opn: 24. (801) 586-5773; (801) 674-0110. Net: Jones Satellite Audio. Format: Country. News prog 5 hrs wkly. ■ Tim Nesmith, progmg dir & mus dir. ■ Rates: Same as AM.

Centerville

KCPX(AM)—Dec 1, 1957: 1600 khz; 5 kw-D, 1 kw-N, DA-N. TL: N40 54 08 W111 55 40. Suite D, No. 272, 5282 S. 320 W., Salt Lake City (84107). (801) 264-1075. Licensee: U.S. Radio IV Inc. (group owner; acq 12-18-92; grpsl; FTR 1-18-93). Rep: D & R Radio. Format: Adult contemp. News progmg 8 hrs wkly. Target aud: 25-54. ■ Bill Struck, gen mgr; Chuck Condron, chief engr.

KUMT(FM)—Co-owned with KCPX(AM). Dec 24, 1979: 105.7 mhz; 7.3 kw. Ant 3,661 ft. TL: N40 39 35 W112 12 05 (CP: 25.5 kw). Stereo. Prog sep from AM. Format: Traditional Country. News progmg one hr wkly. ■ Greg Givens, progmg dir.

Coalville

KCUA(FM)—Not on air, target date unknown: 92.5 mhz; 110 w. Ant -1,059 ft. TL: N40 54 30 W111 25 03. 445 Marsac Ave., Park City (84060). (801) 963-8055. Licensee: Blair and Susan Feulner and Community Wireless of Park City Inc. (acq 6-16-92; $18,812; FTR 7-6-92).

Delta

KFMD(FM)—Sept 5, 1989: 95.7 mhz; 100 kw. Ant 7 ft. TL: N39 10 30 W112 24 20. Stereo. Station currently dark. Box 869 (84624). (801) 864-4500. FAX: (801) 896-9333. Licensee: TGWM Inc. (acq 2-16-89). ■ Morgan Skinner, gen mgr.

KNAK(AM)—Feb 25, 1974: 540 khz; 1 kw-D. TL: N39 20 12 W112 33 21. Hrs opn: 24. Box 636, (84624-0626). (801) 864-5111. FAX: (801) 835-2250. Licensee: KNAK Inc. (acq 7-1-92; FTR 7-20-92). Net: MBS. Rep: Art Moore. Format: Country. News staff one; news progmg 15 hrs wkly. Target aud: 20-50. Spec prog: Farm. ■ Douglas L. Barton, pres, stn mgr & chief engr; Troy Shelley, gen sls mgr; Larry Masco, progmg dir; Jeff Markworth, news dir. ■ Rates: $8; 7; 8; na.

Ephraim

*****KAGJ(FM)**—Not on air, target date unknown: 89.5 mhz; 100 w. Ant -354 ft. 150 College Ave. (84627). Licensee: Snow College.

Garland

KNFL(AM)—See Tremonton.

KNFL-FM—See Tremonton.

Heber City

KTMP(AM)—Oct 1, 1981: 1340 khz; 1 kw-U. TL: N40 30 02 W111 26 55. 418 S. 200 West (84032-2209). (801) 654-3244. Licensee: Creek Broadcasting Corp. (acq 5-15-86; $153,838; FTR 3-24-86). Net: SMN. Rep: Art Moore. Format: Country. Target aud: General. ■ Larry Mahoney, pres & chief engr; Sandy Mahoney, gen mgr, gen sls mgr & progmg dir; Paul Royal, prom mgr, mus dir & news dir.

Kanab

KONY-FM—1986: 101.1 mhz; 99 kw. Ant 786 ft. TL: N36 43 18 W112 12 57. Stereo. Hrs opn: 24. 248 S. 100 E. (84741). (801) 644-5101. Licensee: Red Rock Broadcasting Inc. (acq 8-13-92; $100,000; FTR 8-31-92). Net: Unistar. Format: Country. ■ Harold R. Hickman, pres; Carl Lamar, gen mgr; Jeannie Hunt, stn mgr.

Logan

KBLQ-FM—Listing follows KLGN(AM).

KLGN(AM)—March 1968: 1390 khz; 5 kw-D, 500 w-N, DA-N. TL: N41 44 04 W111 51 13. Box 3369, 810 W. 200 North (84321). (801) 752-1390. FAX: (801) 752-1392. Licensee: Sun Valley Radio Inc. Group owner: Western Communications Inc. (acq 12-27-91); $572,279.37 with co-located FM). Net: SMN. Rep: IMN, Eastman, Art Moore. Format: Country. Target aud: 25-54. ■ Kent Frandsen, pres; Jay Eubanks, gen mgr, gen sls mgr & prom mgr; Michael Carver, progmg dir; Sally White, news dir; Rick Hughes, chief engr.

KBLQ-FM—Co-owned with KLGN(AM). August 1977: 92.9 mhz; 50 kw. Ant 154 ft. TL: N41 52 18 W111 48 31. Stereo. Prog sep from AM. Net: Unistar. Format: Adult contemp. Target aud: General; 18-49. Spec prog: Gospel 8 hrs, jazz 4 hrs wkly. ■ Sally White, mus dir.

KNUC—See Smithfield.

*****KUSU-FM**—April 1953: 91.5 mhz; 90 kw. Ant 1,140 ft. TL: N41 53 11 W112 04 17. Stereo. KUSU-FM, Utah State Univ. (84322-8505). (801) 750-3138. Licensee: Utah State Univ. Net: APR, NPR. Format: Class, info. ■ Jerry L. Allen, gen mgr; Richard Meng, progmg dir; Lee Austin, news dir; Rick Hughes, chief engr.

KVFM(FM)—Listing follows KVNU(AM).

KVNU(AM)—Nov 20, 1938: 610 khz; 5 kw-D, 1 kw-N, DA-N. TL: N41 40 30 W111 56 06. Hrs opn: 24. Box 267, 1350 North 200 W. (84321). (801) 752-5141. Licensee: Reed Bullen. Net: ABC/I, NBC Talknet. Rep: Target, Eastman, Intermountain Net. Format: Adult contemp, talk. News staff one; news progmg 15 hrs wkly. Target aud: General. Spec prog: Farm 2 hrs, relg 3 hrs wkly. ■ Al Lewis, gen mgr; James Murdock, gen sls mgr; Daryl Sroufe, progmg dir; Jennie Christiansen, news dir; John Griffin, chief engr. ■ Rates: $18; 18; 18; 10.

KVFM(FM)—Co-owned with KVNU(AM). Nov 11, 1974: 94.5 mhz; 15.6 kw. Ant 1,148 ft. TL: N41 53 50 W111 57 39. Stereo. Hrs opn: 24. Prog sep from AM. (Acq 5-15-84; $408,000; FTR 2-27-84). Format: CHR. Target aud: 18-34. ■ Platte Clark, progmg mgr. ■ Rates: $17; 17; 17; 10.

Manti

KMTI(AM)—June 7, 1976: 650 khz; 10 kw-D, 1 kw-N, DA-2. TL: N39 17 39 W111 38 13. Hrs opn: 24. Box K, 1600 W. 500 N. (84642). (801) 835-7301. FAX: (801) 835-2252. Licensee: Sanpete County Broadcasting Co. Net: ABC/E. Rep: Art Moore. Wash atty: Rosenman & Colin. Format: Country. News staff one; news progmg 20 hrs wkly. Target aud: 25-50. Spec prog: Farm 6 hrs wkly. ■ Douglas Barton, pres, gen mgr & chief engr; Troy Shelley, gen sls mgr; Bruce Mehew, prom mgr; Larry Masco, progmg dir; Sam Penrod, mus dir; Jeff Markworth, news dir. ■ Rates: $10; 9; 10; 8.

KMXU(FM)—Co-owned with KMTI(AM). December 1978: 105.1 mhz; 63 kw. Ant 2,360 ft. TL: N39 19 23 W111 46 23. Stereo. Prog sep from AM. Format: Easy listening. ■ Rates: Same as AM.

Moab

*****KZMU(FM)**—April 1992: 89.7 mhz; 100 w. Ant -581 ft. TL: N38 32 47 W109 31 03. Stereo. Hrs opn: 24. Box 1079, 1734 Rocky Rd. (84532). (801) 259-4897. Licensee: Moab Public Radio. Format: Div/variety. News progmg 8 hrs wkly. Target aud: General. Spec prog: Asian one hr, American Indian 5 hrs, Black 3 hrs, Sp one hr, folk 6 hrs, blues 19 hrs wkly. ■ Alan Robinson, gen mgr.

Monticello

KUTA(AM)—See Blanding.

Murray

KMGR(AM)—Nov 8, 1948: 1230 khz; 1 kw-U. TL: N40 39 57 W111 54 26. Stereo. Hrs opn: 24. Suite D-272, 5282 S. 320 W., Salt Lake City (84107). (801) 570-1003. Licensee: US Radio II Inc. (group owner; acq 7-29-92; $400,000 with KMXB[FM] Orem; FTR 8-17-92). Net: Unistar, BRN. Rep: D & R Radio. Format: Adult contemp. ■ Bill Struck, gen mgr.

Nephi

KYKN-FM—May 9, 1991: 103.9 mhz; 6 kw. Ant -656 ft. TL: N39 42 54 W111 48 09. Stereo. Hrs opn: 24. Box 165 (84648). (801) 623-4010; (800) 316-4010. FAX: (801) 623-5035. Licensee: Charles D. Hall. Net: SMN. Rep:

Utah Directory of Radio

Target, IMN. Wash atty: Reddy, Beggly & Martin. Format: Country. News progmg 2 hrs wkly. Target aud: 25 plus. ■ Charles D. Hall, CEO.

North Salt Lake City

KFAM(AM)—Sept 22, 1981: 700 khz; 50 kw-D, 1 kw-N, DA-2. TL: N40 53 29 W111 56 28. Stereo. 1171 S.W. Temple, Salt Lake City (84101). (801) 295-0700; (801) 295-2300. Licensee: General Broadcasting Inc. Format: Btfl mus. News progmg 14 hrs wkly. Target aud: General; 30-65. ■ David R. Williams, pres; Howard Bogart, gen mgr; Scott Dean, mus dir; Larry Hunter, news dir; Troy German, chief engr.

Ogden

KBER(FM)—July 13, 1976: 101.1 mhz; 25 kw. Ant 3,740 ft. TL: N40 39 35 W112 12 05. Stereo. Hrs opn: 24. Suite 101.1, 19 E. 200 S., Salt Lake City (84111). (801) 372-3311. Licensee: Devine Media Inc. (acq 12-29-89; $1,838,750; FTR 1-22-90). Net: ABC. Rep: Torbet. Format: AOR. News staff one. Target aud: 18-34. ■ Chris DeVine, CEO; Susan Andrews, gen mgr & gen sls mgr; Emily Evans, prom dir; John Edwards, vp progmg; Cory Draper, progmg dir; Trudy Tillman, pub affrs dir; Fritz Ashuer, chief engr. ■ Rates: $75; 75; 75; 50.

KBZN(FM)—1978: 97.9 mhz; 26 kw. Ant 3,770 ft. TL: N40 39 35 W112 12 05. Suite 400727, 257 E. 200 S., Salt Lake City (84111). (801) 670-1001. FAX: (801) 364-8068. Licensee: Capitol Broadcasting Inc. (acq 4-5-91; FTR 4-29-91). Net: Unistar. Rep: CBS. Format: Jazz, new age. ■ John Webb, gen mgr.

KJOE(AM)—April 1948: 1490 khz; 1 kw-U. TL: N41 14 50 W111 58 46. Stereo. Hrs opn: 24. 1506 Gibson Ave. (84404). (801) 392-9550; (801) 328-9550. FAX: (801) 627-1515. Licensee: Abacus Broadcasting Corp. (acq 10-18-89; $700,000 with co-located FM; FTR 11-6-89). Rep: Schubert. Format: Rock. News staff one. Target aud: Adults. ■ Garrett W. Haston, pres; Gordon Holt, gen mgr; Jim Facer, gen sls mgr; Bill Allred, prom mgr; Mike Summers, progmg dir; Biff Raffe, mus dir.

KKBE-FM—Co-owned with KJOE(AM). June 1983: 95.5 mhz; 64 kw. Ant 2,368 ft. TL: N41 15 17 W112 14 14 (CP: 75 kw, ant 2,293 ft., TL: N41 15 27 W112 26 24). Stereo. Hrs opn: 24. Prog sep from AM. Format: New rock. Target aud: 15-35. ■ Bruce Jones, mus dir.

KKAT(FM)—Aug 1, 1964: 101.9 mhz; 26 kw. Ant 3,740 ft. TL: N40 39 35 W112 12 05. Stereo. 455 E. 400 S., Salt Lake City (84111). (801) 533-0102. Licensee: Apollo Radio of Salt Lake City. Group owner: Apollo Radio Ltd. (acq 4-90; $12 million; FTR 4-16-90). Rep: Katz. Wash atty: Latham Watkins. Format: Modern country. Target aud: 21-49. ■ Dana Horner, gen mgr; John Marks, vp opns & progmg dir; Darren Tucker, prom mgr; Jim Mickelson, mus dir; Ken Simmons, news dir; Chuck Condron, chief engr.

KKBE-FM—Listing follows KJOE(AM).

KLO(AM)—1924: 1430 khz; 5 kw-U, DA-N. TL: N41 10 44 W112 04 09 (CP: TL: N41 02 48 W112 01 38). Suite 727, 385 24th St. (84401). (801) 627-1430. FAX: (801) 627-0317. Licensee: KLO Broadcasting Co. Net: ABC/I. Rep: Intermountain. Format: Adult contemp, MOR. ■ John Webb, pres, gen mgr & gen sls mgr; Don Hill, progmg dir & mus dir; Arny Wheeler, news dir; Sam Stephens, chief engr.

KSVN(AM)—Jan 1, 1946: 730 khz; 1 kw-D, 66 w-N. TL: N41 11 17 W112 04 52. Hrs opn: 24. 4215 W. 4000 S., Hooper (84315). (801) 292-1799; (801) 731-4797. FAX: (801) 292-1799. Licensee: Azteca Broadcasting (acq 2-1-86). Net: CRC. Rep: Lotus. Format: Sp. ■ Alex Collantes, pres, gen mgr, gen sls mgr & progmg dir; Dennis Silver, news dir.

***KWCR-FM**—May 21, 1966: 88.1 mhz; 2 kw. Ant -470 ft. TL: N41 11 30 W111 56 37. Stereo. 3750 Harrison Blvd. (84408-2188). (801) 626-6450. FAX: (801) 626-6935. Licensee: Weber State College Board of Trustees. Format: Urban contemp. News progmg 4 hrs wkly. Target aud: 18-26; college students, teens & minorities. Spec prog: Black 12 hrs, Sp 12 hrs wkly. ■ Ira Cronin, gen mgr; Bob Wayman, opns mgr & gen sls mgr; Chaunteu Richardson, dev dir; Ryan Bennett, progmg dir; Derek Crimon, mus dir; Kathy Costello, news dir; Barry McClellon, engrg mgr; Bill Clapp, chief engr.

Orem

KMXB(FM)—Nov 15, 1978: 107.5 mhz; 45 kw. Ant 2,850 ft. TL: N40 16 48 W111 56 05. Stereo. Hrs opn: 24. Suite D-272, 5282 S. 320 W., Salt Lake City (84107). (801) 224-1075. FAX: (801) 269-8595. Licensee: U.S. Radio II Inc. (acq 7-29-92; $400,000 with KMGR[AM] Murray; FTR 8-17-92). Rep: D & R Radio. Format: Adult contemp. Target aud: 25-49. ■ Bill Struck, gen mgr; Lindsay Russell-Horner, sls dir & gen sls mgr; Karen Gallegos, prom mgr; Tom Connelly, progmg dir & mus dir; Robin Morales, news dir.

***KOHS(FM)**—Oct 1974: 91.7 mhz; 1.75 kw. Ant -831 ft. TL: N40 17 48 W111 41 04 (CP: Ant -869 ft., TL: N40 17 32 W111 40 56). Stereo. 175 S. 400 E. (84058). (801) 224-9236. Licensee: Alpine School District. Format: Post-modern. ■ Ken Seastrand, stn mgr.

KSRR(AM)—See Provo.

Park City

***KPCW(FM)**—July 2, 1980: 91.9 mhz; 105 w. Ant -23 ft. TL: N40 40 59 W111 31 22. Stereo. Box 1372, 445 Marsac Ave. (84060). (801) 649-9004. Licensee: Community Wireless of Park City. Net: CNN. Format: Adult contemp, class, news. Spec prog: Class 17 hrs, C&W 18 hrs, jazz 12 hrs wkly. ■ Blair Feulner, pres & gen mgr; Steve Lloyd, prom mgr; Beth Fratkin, progmg dir; Nan Chalat, news dir; Alan Cook, chief engr.

Payson

KTCE(FM)—Not on air, target date unknown: 92.3 mhz; 110 w. Ant 2,215 ft. TL: N40 05 27 W111 49 16. 1150 Inca Townhouse, Denver, CO (80204). Licensee: Moenkopi Communications Inc.

Pleasant Grove

***KPGR(FM)**—May 1976: 88.1 mhz; 115 w. Ant -1,128 ft. TL: N40 21 48 W111 43 30. 700 E. 200 S. (84062). (801) 785-5747; (801) 785-8700. Licensee: Alpine School District. Format: CHR. Target aud: 12-18; students. ■ Van L. Bulkley, gen mgr & chief engr.

Price

KARB(FM)—Listing follows KOAL(AM).

KOAL(AM)—October 1936: 750 khz; 10 kw-U, 6.8 kw-N, DA-N. TL: N39 34 02 W110 47 53. Box 875 (84501). (801) 637-1167. FAX: (801) 637-1177. Licensee: Eastern Utah Broadcasting Co. Net: ABC/I, MBS; Intermountain. Rep: Eastman/Intermountain. Format: Country. Spec prog: Farm 5 hrs wkly. ■ Thomas B. Anderson, pres & gen mgr; Eric Albrecht, chief engr.

KARB(FM)—Co-owned with KOAL(AM). July 1977: 98.3 mhz; 3 kw. Ant -145 ft. TL: N39 36 36 W110 48 52 (CP: 7 kw). Stereo. Net: ABC/FM.

KPRQ(FM)—Listing follows KRPX(AM).

KRPX(AM)—Sept 6, 1980: 1080 khz; 10 kw-D. TL: N39 33 43 W110 46 36. Stereo. 163 E. 100 N. (84501). (801) 637-1080. FAX: (801) 637-1126. Licensee: Michael J. Halloran (acq 6-90; grpsl; FTR 6-4-90). Rep: Target. Format: Adult contemp. News staff one; news progmg 5 hrs wkly. Target aud: General; mature adults. ■ Mike Halloran, pres, gen sls mgr & news dir; Ty Curtis, progmg dir; James M. Dart Jr., chief engr.

KPRQ(FM)—Co-owned with KRPX(AM). December 1985: 100.9 mhz; 3 kw. Ant 111 ft. TL: N39 32 42 W110 48 56. Stereo. Hrs opn: 24. Dups AM 100%. ■ Steve Laude, gen sls mgr.

Provo

***KBYU-FM**—Nov 1960: 89.1 mhz; 32 kw. Ant 2,913 ft. TL: N40 36 28 W112 09 33. Stereo. Box 26408, C302 Harris Fine Arts Ctr., Brigham Young Univ. (84602). (801) 378-3551. FAX: (801) 378-5300. Licensee: Brigham Young Univ. Net: APR, AP, NPR. Format: Class. News progmg 8 hrs wkly. Target aud: 35 plus. Spec prog: Relg 2 hrs wkly. ■ Thomas A. Griffiths, gen mgr; Walter Rudolph, stn mgr; Christine Nokleby, dev dir; Elizabeth King, prom dir; Daniel Cronenwett, progmg dir; Rob Millett, mus dir; Crystal Heer, asst mus dir; Duane Roberts, news dir; Lynn Edwards, chief engr. ■ *KBYU-TV affil.

***KEYY(AM)**—December 1949: 1450 khz; 1 kw-U. TL: N40 13 49 W111 41 12. Hrs opn: 24. Box KEYY (84603-3200); UPS only, 307 S. 1600 W. (84601). (801) 374-5210. Licensee: Biblical Ministries Worldwide (acq 5-10-88). Net: Moody. Wash atty: Haley, Bader & Potts. Format: Relg. News progmg 13 hrs wkly. Target aud: General. ■ Steven A. Barsuhn, gen mgr; Charlotte Bechtel, pub affrs dir; John Steel, chief engr.

KOVO(AM)—Sept 12, 1939: 960 khz; 5 kw-D, 1080 w-N, DA-N. TL: N40 12 44 W111 40 13. 651 W. 1560 S. (84601-5524). (801) 373-9600. Licensee: The Great Stock Co. (acq 3-13-90; $972,000; FTR 3-9-90). Net: ABC/E. Rep: D&R Radio. Format: Big band, nostalgia. News progmg 12 hrs wkly. Target aud: 35 plus; upper income affluent males & females 35-65. ■ Mary Katherine Veach, pres; Jesse Clinton Veach Jr., gen mgr; Benjamin Reed, opns mgr, progmg dir & mus dir; Varr Gailey, gen sls mgr; Bryan Freeman, mktg dir & prom dir; Dave Shaw, news dir; Ben Reed, Bill Ruhlman, pub affrs dirs; V. Ray Bishop, chief engr. ■ Rates: $15; 15; 15; 15.

KXRK(FM)—Co-owned with KOVO(AM). Feb 14, 1968: 96.1 mhz; 55 kw. Ant 2,620 ft. TL: N40 16 48 W111 56 05. Stereo. 651 W. 1560 S. (84601). (801) 373-8550. Licensee: ACME Broadcasting Inc. (acq 9-2-93; $925,000; FTR 9-27-93). Wash atty: Fletcher, Healdretts. Format: Rock/AOR. ■ Larsen Bennett, progmg dir.

KSRR(AM)—Nov 24, 1947: 1400 khz; 1 kw-U. TL: N40 12 52 W111 39 19 (CP: TL: N40 15 29 W111 42 24). Hrs opn: 24. Box 828, 1240 E. 800 N., Orem (84059). (801) 224-1400. Licensee: Positive Communications Inc. (acq 2-1-85). Net: ABC/I. Rep: Eastman. Format: Adult contemp. News progmg one hr wkly. Target aud: 18-54. ■ Robert H. Morey, gen mgr; Gordon W. Bullock, gen sls mgr; V. Ray Bishop, progmg dir, mus dir & chief engr.

KXRK(FM)—Listing follows KOVO(AM).

KZHT(FM)—January 1981: 94.9 mhz; 47 kw. Ant 2,798 ft. TL: N40 16 58 W111 56 11. Stereo. No. 19 E., 200 S, Suite 101, Salt Lake City (84111). (801) 322-3311. FAX: (801) 355-2117. Licensee: Stephen Marriott. Group owner: The Heusser Group (acq 5-90; grpsl; FTR 5-21-90). Rep: Christal. Format: CHR. News staff one. ■ Susan Andrews, gen mgr; Jeff Wheeler, gen sls mgr; Dave Hurtt, prom mgr; Sue Kelly, news dir; Fritz Ashauer, chief engr.

Richfield

KSVC(AM)—September 1947: 980 khz; 5 kw-D, 1 kw-N, DA-N. TL: N38 45 40 W112 04 35. Stereo. Hrs opn: 24. Box 848, 450 E. 400 S. (84701). (801) 896-4456. FAX: (801) 896-9333. Licensee: Sevier Valley Broadcasting Co. (acq 5-4-84). Net: ABC/I. Rep: Eastman; Target. Wash atty: Borsari & Paxson. Format: Country. News progmg 18 hrs wkly. Target aud: 18-54. Spec prog: Farm 14 hrs wkly. ■ Kent L. Colby, pres, gen mgr, gen sls mgr, mus dir & news dir; Kathy Bingham, rgnl sls mgr; Tyla Riddle, adv mgr; Mike Smith, chief engr. ■ Rates: $9.50; 9.50; 9.50; 8.

KKWZ(FM)—Co-owned with KSVC(AM). 1978: 93.7 mhz; 35.7 kw. Ant 3,014 ft. TL: N38 45 47 W112 04 42 (CP: 33.7 kw, ant 3,129 ft., TL: N38 50 02 W112 16 07). Stereo. Hrs opn: 24. Prog sep from AM. Format: Adult contemp. ■ Rates: Same as AM.

Roosevelt

KIFX(FM)—Dec 14, 1987: 98.5 mhz; 2.65 kw. Ant 1,853 ft. TL: N40 31 15 W109 42 17 (CP: 3.19 kw, ant 1,689 ft., TL: N40 32 16 W109 41 57). Stereo. Hrs opn: 24. Rt. 2, Box 2384, One Mile South Ballard (84066); South Ballard Rd. (84066). (801) 789-5011; (801) 722-5101. FAX: (801) 722-5012. Licensee: Evans Broadcasting Inc. (acq 5-31-91; $283,750; FTR 6-24-91). Net: SMN. Rep: Art Moore. Wash atty: Trot Tanner. Format: Adult contemp. News staff one; news progmg 5 hrs wkly. Target aud: 21-45. ■ Joseph L. Evans, pres & gen mgr; Teddie Evans, vp; Vickie Reary, opns dir; Earl Hawkins, gen sls mgr; Bob Watts, progmg dir; Fred Brown, news dir; Brian Leifsim, chief engr.

KNEU(AM)—Jan 6, 1978: 1250 khz; 5 kw-D, 129 w-N. TL: N40 17 13 W109 57 32. Hrs opn: 5 AM-11 PM. Rt. 2, Box 2384 (84066); One Mile South Ballard (84066). (801) 722-5011; (801) 789-5101. FAX: (801) 722-5012. Licensee: Country Gold Broadcasting (acq 2-84; $419,419; FTR 2-20-84). Rep: Art Moore. Format: C&W. News staff one; news progmg 10 hrs wkly. Target aud: 25-54. ■ Joseph L. Evans, pres & gen mgr; Earl Hawkins, gen sls mgr; Fred Brown, progmg dir, mus dir & news dir; Brian Leifson, chief engr.

Roy

***KANN(AM)**—September 1961: 1120 khz; 10 kw-D, 1 kw-N, DA-2. TL: N41 03 31 W112 04 10. Hrs opn: 24. Box 3880, Ogden (84409); 2500 W. 3700 S., Syracuse (84075). (801) 776-0249. Licensee: Faith Communications. Format: Relg. Target aud: 25-44; young families. ■ Jack French, pres; Bob Alzugarat, gen mgr; Rick Shelton, opns mgr; Chris Staley, progmg dir & mus dir; Tim Hunt, chief engr.

KRGQ-FM—September 1986: 107.9 mhz; 67 kw. Ant 2,383 ft. TL: N41 15 27 W112 26 24. 1975 W. 5300 S. (84067). (801) 773-1301. FAX: (801) 972-4243. Licensee: Kargo Broadcasting Co. Wash atty: Robert Olender. Format: Country. Target aud: General. ■ Gene Guthrie, pres, gen mgr, gen sls mgr & adv dir; Kurt Kelly, progmg dir; Penny Lane, mus dir; Lee Sands, pub affrs dir; Dennis Silver, chief engr. ■ Rates: $30; 30; 30; 30.

St. George

KDXU(AM)—July 3, 1957: 890 khz; 10 kw-U, DA-N. TL: N37 04 04 W113 31 04. Box 1890, 750 W. Ridgeview Dr. (84770). (801) 673-3579. FAX: (801) 673-8900. Licensee: Simmons Family Inc. (acq 11-10-86; $807,000; FTR 10-13-86). Net: ABC/I. Rep: Banner, Art Moore. Format: News/talk. News staff one; news progmg 3 hrs wkly. Target aud: 25-54. Spec prog: Relg 4 hrs wkly. ■ C. Craig Hanson, pres; Mark Crump, gen mgr; Marti Zohner, opns mgr; Don Shelline, gen sls mgr; Bryan Benware, prom mgr; Mike McGary, progmg dir & news dir; X.V. Kelly, pub affrs dir; Jed Wickinson, chief engr. ■ Rates: $14; 14; 14; 6.

KZEZ(FM)—Co-owned with KDXU(AM). June 15, 1973: 93.5 mhz; 3 kw. Ant -125 ft. TL: N37 06 54 W113 34 23. Stereo. Dups AM 5%. Format: Adult contemp. News progmg 3 hrs wkly. Target aud: 12-49. ■ Rates: Same as AM.

KONY(AM)—(Washington). June 6, 1982: 1210 khz; 10 kw-D, 250 w-N. TL: N37 08 38 W113 30 03. Hrs opn: 24. Box 2530, St. George (84771); 135 N. 900 E., St. George (84770). (801) 628-3643; (801) 673-1210. FAX: (801) 628-3643; (800) 289-KONY. Licensee: Red Rock Broadcasting Inc. (acq 5-5-87). Net: SMN. Format: Modern country. News progmg one hr. wkly. Target aud: 18-64. ■ Harold R. Hickman, pres; Carl Lamar, gen mgr & gen sls mgr; Rinda Hunter, stn mgr; David Combs, progmg dir & mus dir; Jed Wilkinson, chief engr. ■ Rates: $19; 17; 17; 16.

***KRDC-FM**—1975: 91.7 mhz; 105 w. Ant -312 ft. TL: N37 06 16 W113 33 55. Stereo. 225 S. 700 E. (84770). (801) 673-4811, ext. 331. Licensee: Dixie College. Format: Top-40. News progmg one hr wkly. Target aud: 14-25; college & high school students. Spec prog: Class 15 hrs, jazz 10 hrs wkly. ■ Larry Jewel, gen mgr.

KSGI(AM)—Oct 9, 1957: 1450 khz; 1 kw-U. TL: N37 05 02 W113 33 26. Stereo. Hrs opn: 24. Box 1450, 210 N. 1000 E. (84771); 341 S. Bluff St. (84770). (801) 628-1000. FAX: (801) 628-6636. Licensee: Bear River Communications Inc. (acq 11-16-88; FTR 12-19-88). Net: CBS, MBS, NBC Talknet. Rep: Banner. Format: Adult contemp, MOR. News staff 3; news progmg 26 hrs wkly. Target aud: 25-54. ■ Morgan Skinner, pres & gen mgr; Terry Teeters, sls dir; Fred Kueni, prom dir; Larry Jewell, progmg dir; Kent McGregor, news dir; Patrick O'Gara, engrg dir.

KSGI-FM—Not on air, target date unknown: 99.7 mhz; 100 kw. Ant 2,033 ft. c/o Ear Inc., 781 N. Valley Drive #34 (84770). Licensee: Ear Inc.

KVYS(FM)—Not on air, target date unknown: 95.9 mhz; 96.6 kw. Ant 1,965 ft. TL: N36 50 50 W113 29 28. 965 S. 400 E., Providence (84332). Licensee: Marvin Kent Frandsen.

KZEZ(FM)—Listing follows KDXU(AM).

AMERICAN RADIO BROKERS, INC.
MOST TRUSTED NAME IN MEDIA BROKERAGE
CHESTER P. COLEMAN / PRESIDENT
FOR THE BEST STATIONS FOR SALE FROM THIS AREA
CALL — 415/441-3377
1255 POST STREET / SUITE 625 / SAN FRANCISCO, CA 94109

Salt Lake City

KALL(AM)—1945: 910 khz; 5 kw-D, 1 kw-N, DA-2. TL: N40 30 48 W112 00 23. Stereo. Hrs opn: 24. 312 E. South Temple (84111). (801) 533-0102. FAX: (801) 521-5018. Licensee: Apollo Radio of Salt Lake City Inc. Group owner: Apollo Radio Ltd. (acq 10-30-92; $1.88 million; FTR 11-23-92). Net: MBS. Rep: Katz. Wash atty: Latham & Watkins. Format: Talk/news, sports. Target aud: 25-54. Spec prog: University of Utah football & basketball. ■ Dana Horner, vp & gen mgr; John Marks, vp opns; Bill Sauer, gen sls mgr; Darren Tucker, prom mgr; Bob Hendricks, progmg dir; Kevin Stanfied, news dir; Chuck Condron, chief engr.

KODJ(FM)—Co-owned with KALL(AM). Dec 1, 1968: 94.1 mhz; 40 kw. Ant 3,030 ft. TL: N40 36 22 W112 09 49. Stereo. Hrs opn: 24. Prog sep from AM. Format: Oldies. ■ KUTV(TV) affil.

KCNR(AM)—1923: 1320 khz; 50 kw-D, 200 w-N. TL: N40 38 36 W111 55 24. Stereo. 434 Bearcat Dr. (34115-2520). (801) 485-6700. FAX: (801) 487-5369. Licensee: Price Broadcasting Co. (group owner; acq 1-83). Net: NBC the Source. Rep: Katz. Format: Contemp lifestyle. News staff 5. ■ Larry Wilson, pres; Leonard Smart, gen mgr; Ken Robert, gen sls mgr; Amy Kelly, prom mgr; Brian Casey, progmg mgr; Trish Griffith, mus dir; Tim Lewis, news dir.

***KCPW(FM)**—Not on air, target date unknown: 88.3 mhz; 750 w. Ant -587 ft. TL: N40 45 33 W111 49 48. Box 1372, Park City (84060). Licensee: Community Wireless of Park City Inc.

KCPX(AM)—See Centerville.

KDYL(AM)—February 1945: 1280 khz; 5 kw-D, 500 w-N, DA-N. TL: N40 44 47 W111 54 42. Suite 700, 57 W. South Temple (84101). (801) 524-2600. FAX: (801) 521-9234. Licensee: Simmons Family Inc. (acq 5-12-82; $750,000; FTR 5-24-82). Net: SMN. Rep: CBS Radio. Format: MOR. Target aud: 35 plus. ■ Roy W. Simmons, chmn; G. Craig Hanson, pres; Stephen C. Johnson, gen mgr; Terry Mathis, gen sls mgr; Ken Bell, prom mgr; Scott MacNeil, progmg dir; Pete Peterson, chief engr.

KSFI(FM)—Co-owned with KDYL(AM). Dec 26, 1946: 100.3 mhz; 26 kw. Ant 3,740 ft. TL: N40 39 35 W112 12 05. Stereo. Prog sep from AM. (Acq 1-26-78). Format: Adult contemp. Target aud: General. ■ Lyle Morris, mus dir; Peggy Ijams, news dir.

KFAM(AM)—See North Salt Lake City.

KISN(AM)—Aug 1, 1938: 570 khz; 5 kw-U, DA-2. TL: N40 49 09 W111 55 56. Hrs opn: 24. Suite 800, 4001 S. 700 E. (84107). (801) 262-9797. FAX: (801) 262-9772. Licensee: Sun Mountain Broadcasting (acq 8-1-85; $4.5 million; FTR 6-3-85). Net: Utah Jazz Radio Net. Rep: McGavren Guild. Wash atty: Dow, Lomes & Albertson. Format: Sports radio. News staff one; news progmg 2 hrs wkly. Target aud: 25-54 men; upscale, well educated 35,000 plus income. ■ Ballard Smith, pres; Randy Rodgers, gen mgr; Jim Vandiver, gen sls mgr; Colin Thomas, prom mgr; Chris Tunis, progmg dir; Charla Haley, news dir; Gary Smith, chief engr. ■ Rates: $50; 50; 50; 75.

KISN-FM—Feb 1, 1961: 97.1 mhz; 26 kw. Ant 3,650 ft. TL: N40 39 35 W112 12 05. Stereo. Format: Adult contemp. ■ John Dimick, progmg dir; Jim Morales, mus dir. ■ Rates: $120; 90; 95; 40.

KKAT(FM)—See Ogden.

KKDS(AM)—(South Salt Lake). Sept 2, 1967: 1060 khz; 10 kw-D, 1 kw-N, DA-N. TL: N40 39 15 W111 55 30. Stereo. Box 57760, 1130 W. 5200 S., Salt Lake City (84123). (801) 262-5624. FAX: (801) 266-1510. Licensee: Holiday Broadcasting Co. Group owner: Carlson Communications International (acq 9-2-67). Format: Children's. Target aud: 2-12; kids & their parents. ■ Ralph J. Carlson, pres, gen mgr & gen sls mgr; Jeri Youngberg, progmg dir & mus dir; Ken Meyer, chief engr. ■ Rates: $32; 32; 32; 25.

KRSP-FM—Co-owned with KKDS(AM). Aug 21, 1968: 103.5 mhz; 27.5 kw. Ant 3,630 ft. TL: N40 39 37 W112 12 05. Stereo. Prog sep from AM. Suite 700, 57 W. South Temple (84101). (801) 262-5541. FAX: (801) 521-9234. Net: ABC/R. Format: AOR. Target aud: 18-34. ■ Craig Hanson, pres; Steve Johnson, gen mgr; Allen Hague, stn mgr; Steve Carlson, chief opns; Terri Mathis, Brent Carlson, gen sls mgrs; Evan Lake, mus dir; Pete Peterson, chief engr.

KLZX(AM)—Nov 15, 1955: 860 khz; 10 kw-D, 195.8 w-N, 3 kw-CH. TL: N40 42 47 W111 55 53. Stereo. 434 Bearcat Dr. (84115). (801) 485-6700. FAX: (801) 487-5369. Licensee: Citadel Communications Corp. (group owner). Net: AP, NBC the Source, CNN. Rep: Christal. Format: News (CNN Headline). News staff one. Target aud: 25-54. ■ Larry Wilson, chmn; Stuart Stanek, sr vp; Leonard Smart, gen mgr; Kenneth Roberts, gen sls mgr; Leonard Thomas, prom mgr; Brian Casey, progmg dir; Tricia Griffith, mus dir; Dan Bammes, news dir; Chuck Condron, chief engr.

KLZX-FM—July 31, 1965: 93.3 mhz; 26 kw. Ant 3,740 ft. TL: N40 39 35 W112 12 05. Stereo. Licensee: Citadel Associates L.P. Format: Classic rock.

KMGR(AM)—See Murray.

KODJ(FM)—Listing follows KALL(AM).

***KRCL(FM)**—Dec 3, 1979: 90.9 mhz; 16.5 kw. Ant 3,770 ft. TL: N40 39 35 W112 12 05. Stereo. Hrs opn: 24. 208 W. 800 S. (84101). (801) 363-1818. FAX: (801) 365-5725. Licensee: Listeners Community Radio of Utah Inc. Net: Pacifica News. Format: Div, educ. News progmg 3 hrs wkly. Target aud: General. Spec prog: Black 12 hrs, folk 12 hrs, world music 9 hrs, thrash & death metal 9 hrs, reggae 8 hrs, blues 5 hrs, new age 5 hrs, American Indian 3 hrs, relg/gospel 3 hrs, Asian 4 hrs, Sp one hr, Polynesian one hr, women's 7 hrs wkly. ■ Dave Young, gen mgr & stn mgr; Kris Liszkowski, dev dir; Donna Land Maldonado, progmg dir; Ken Pavia, mus dir; Lewis Downey, chief engr. ■ Rates: $10; 10; 10; 10.

KRGQ(AM)—(West Valley City). Nov 16, 1956: 1550 khz; 10 kw-D, 500 w-N. TL: N40 43 29 W112 00 43. Hrs opn: 24. 5065 W. 2100 S., Salt Lake City (84120); Box 539, Magna (84044). (801) 972-3449. FAX: (801) 972-3440. Licensee: Group Communications (acq 3-11-68). Wash atty: Robert Olender. Format: Sp. Target aud: General. Spec prog: Class 2 hrs, Ger one hr, relg 4 hrs wkly. ■ Sherwin Brotman, pres; Gene Guthrie, vp & gen sls mgr; Gene Guthrie, Kathy Wamsley (office), gen mgrs; Robin Tetrick, stn mgr; David B. Smith, vp progmg & mus dir; Dennis Silver, chief engr. ■ Rates: $20; 20; 20; 20.

KRSP-FM—Listing follows KKDS(AM).

KSFI(FM)—Listing follows KDYL(AM).

KSL(AM)—May 6, 1922: 1160 khz; 50 kw-U. TL: N40 46 46 W112 05 56. Stereo. Box 1160, Broadcast House, 55 N. 300 W. (84110-1160). (801) 575-7600. FAX: (801) 575-7625. Licensee: Bonneville International Corp. (group owner). Net: CBS, CNN. Rep: CBS. Format: Info, news, talk. ■ Bruce Reese, pres; William Murdoch, gen mgr; Richard Mecham, gen sls mgr; Gary Whiting, natl sls mgr; Jeri Openshaw, prom mgr; Al Henderson, progmg dir; Amanda Dickson, pub affrs dir; John Dehnel, chief engr. ■ KSL-TV affil.

KSOP(AM)—(South Salt Lake). Feb 1, 1955: 1370 khz; 5 kw-D, 500 w-N, DA-N. TL: N40 43 12 W111 55 42. Hrs opn: 24. Box 25548, Salt Lake City (84125); 1285 W. 2320 S., Salt Lake City (84119). (801) 972-1043. FAX: (801) 974-0868. Licensee: KSOP Inc. Rep: Major Mkt. Format: Modern country. Target aud: 25-54. ■ Greg Hilton, pres, gen mgr & gen sls mgr; Don Hilton, progmg dir; Debbie Turpin, mus dir; Dick Jacobson, news dir; Bill Traue, chief engr. ■ Rates: Sold in combination with FM.

KSOP-FM—Dec 10, 1964: 104.3 mhz; 25 kw. Ant 3,650 ft. TL: N40 39 35 W112 12 05. Stereo. Hrs opn: 24. Dups AM 100%.

KTKK(AM)—(Sandy). May 13, 1960: 630 khz; 1 kw-D, 500 w-N, DA-2. TL: N40 41 30 W111 55 30. Hrs opn: 24. 3595 S. 1300 W., Salt Lake City (84119). (801) 264-8250. FAX: (801) 264-8978. Licensee: D&B Broadcasting Co. (acq 12-1-63). Net: NBC. Rep: Katz & Powell. Format: Talk. Target aud: 35 plus. ■ Starley D. Bush, pres & gen mgr; Marge Bush, vp; John Harrington, opns mgr & progmg dir; John Linsmeier, gen sls mgr; Bill Traue, chief engr.

***KUER(FM)**—June 4, 1960: 90.1 mhz; 38 kw. Ant 2,900 ft. TL: N40 36 30 W112 09 34. Stereo. Univ. of Utah, 101 Wasatch Dr. (84112). (801) 581-6625. FAX: (801) 581-5426. Licensee: Univ. of Utah. Net: NPR, APR. Format: News, class, jazz. News staff 3. Spec prog: Gospel 3 hrs wkly. ■ John Greene, gen mgr; Gene Pack, mus dir; Doug Fabrizio, news dir; Garth Steck, chief engr.

***KUFR(FM)**—Dec 14, 1989: 91.7 mhz; 250 w. Ant -354 ft. TL: N40 48 59 W111 55 19. Hrs opn: 24. 290 Hegenberger Rd. Oakland, CA (94621); 3108 Fulton Ave., Sacramento, CA (95821). (801) 359-3147; (510) 568-6200. FAX: (916) 481-0410. Licensee: Family Stations Inc. (group owner). Format: Christian relg. ■ Harold Camping, pres; Roy Skogler, gen mgr; John Tefertiller, opns mgr; Thad McKinney, rgnl sls mgr.

KUMT(FM)—See Centerville.

KVRI(FM)—1947: 98.7 mhz; 40 kw. Ant 2,932 ft. TL: N40 36 30 W112 09 34. Stereo. 434 Bearcutd Dr. (84115). (801) 485-6700. FAX: (801) 487-5369. Licensee: Price Broadcasting. Format: CHR. ■ Brian Casey, progmg dir; Greg Smith, mus dir.

KXRK(FM)—See Provo.

Sandy

KTKK(AM)—Licensed to Sandy. See Salt Lake City.

Vermont

Smithfield

KNUC(FM)—February 1983: 103.9 mhz; 3 kw. Ant -116 ft. TL: N41 48 44 W111 47 31. Box 727, Logan (84323-0727). (801) 753-2200. Licensee: Logan River Media Corp. Net: AP. Rep: Roslin. Format: Rock. ■ Steve Skinner, stn mgr, progmg dir & mus dir; Pat O'Gara, chief engr.

South Salt Lake

KKDS(AM)—Licensed to South Salt Lake. See Salt Lake City.

KSOP(AM)—Licensed to South Salt Lake. See Salt Lake City.

Spanish Fork

KHQN(AM)—July 24, 1960: 1480 khz; 1 kw-D. TL: N40 04 30 W111 39 42. 8628 S. State St. (84660). (801) 798-3559. Licensee: Chris Warden (acq 9-9-82). Net: UPI. Format: New age, progsv, relg. Spec prog: Farm 4 hrs wkly. ■ Chris Warden, pres; Christine Warden, gen mgr.

Tooele

KTLE-FM—Sept 1, 1979: 92.1 mhz; 1.4 kw. Ant -35 ft. TL: N40 31 51 W112 17 50. Stereo. Hrs opn: 5 AM-10 PM. Box 608, Suite 104, 7 S. Main (84074). (801) 833-9211; (801) 539-8907. FAX: (801) 833 9210. Licensee: Local Broadcasters Inc. (acq 11-1-91; $30,000). Net: USA News, Jones Satellite Audio; UT Jazz Network. Format: Country, local news and sports (Utah Jazz). News staff one; new progmg 12 hrs wkly. Target aud: general. ■ Mary F. Kirigin, pres, gen mgr & gen sls mgr; John L. Kirigin, opns dir; Andrew Del Prete, progmg dir; Martin Harguindeguv, news dir; Margie Benson, pub affrs dir; Michael McKenzie, chief engr. ■ Rates: $9.50; 9; 9.50; 9.

KTUR(AM)—July 3, 1956: 1010 khz; 1 kw-D, 10 w-N. TL: N40 32 36 W112 18 33 (CP: 1010 khz, 50 kw-D). Hrs opn: Sunrise-sunset. 765 W. 400 S., Salt Lake City (84104). (801) 363-2416; (801) 363-1010. FAX: (801) 539-8373. Licensee: KTUR Inc. (acq 10-13-92; $100,000; FTR 11-16-92). Rep: Katz & Powell. Format: Sp.

Tremonton

KNFL(AM)—Feb 5, 1982: 1470 khz; 5 kw-D, 109 w-N. TL: N41 43 34 W112 12 33. Box 727, Logan (84323); 610 N. Main, Logan (84321). (801) 257-1987. Licensee: Evergreen Media Corp. (acq 1993; FTR 9-20-93). Format: News, sports, info. ■ Morgan Skinner, gen mgr; Pat O'Gara, chief engr.

KNFL-FM—July 1, 1983: 104.9 mhz; 3 kw. Ant -112 ft. TL: N41 43 34 W112 12 33 (CP: 105.1 mhz, 12.5 kw, ant 987 ft. TL: N41 44 53 W112 13 40). Stereo. Hrs opn: 24. Prog sep from AM. Format: Today's new country.

Vernal

KVEL(AM)—Jan 19, 1947: 920 khz; 4.5 kw-D, 1 kw-N, DA-N. TL: N40 29 30 W109 31 45. Hrs opn: 5 AM-midnight. Box 307, 2425 N. Vernal Ave. (84078). (801) 789-0920; (801) 789-1059. FAX: (801) 789-6977. Licensee: C.I.C Inc. (acq 7-12-93; $300,000 with co-located FM; FTR 8-2-93). Net: ABC/I; Intermountain Net. Rep: Eastman, Art Moore. Wash atty: Haley, Bader & Potts. Format: MOR. News staff one. Target aud: 30 plus; general. Spec prog: Farm 2 hrs, relg, Sp, public affrs one hr wkly. ■ George C. Hatch, pres; Steve Evans, gen mgr; Clay Johnson, progmg dir; Carl Stuart, news dir; Byron Colton, chief engr. ■ Rates: $19.50; 16.50; 19.50; 13.50.

KLCY-FM—Co-owned with KVEL(AM). May 1, 1975: 105.9 mhz; 3 kw. Ant 430 ft. TL: N40 24 50 W109 35 34 (CP: 7.4 kw). Format: Modern country. Target aud: 18-54.

Washington

KONY(AM)—Licensed to Washington. See St. George.

West Jordan

KLLB(AM)—1982: 1510 khz; 10 kw-D. TL: N40 33 06 W111 58 17. Suite 130, 406 W. South Jordan Pkwy. South Jordan (84095). (801) 576-8892. FAX: (801) 576-8801. Licensee: United Security Financial Inc. (acq 6-18-91; $180,001; FTR 7-8-91). Format: Gospel. ■ Darrell Cosby, gen mgr.

West Valley City

KRGQ(AM)—Licensed to West Valley City. See Salt Lake City.

Vermont

Barre

WSKI(AM)—See Montpelier.

WSNO(AM)—Oct 13, 1959: 1450 khz; 1 kw-U. TL: N44 11 40 W72 30 52. Hrs opn: 24. 41 Jacques St. (05641). (802) 476-4168. Licensee: Kimel Broadcast Group (group owner; acq 9-1-74). Net: CBS, MBS. Rep: Eastman. Format: Country. ■ William A. Noyes, gen mgr & news dir; Mike Donovan, gen sls mgr; Jay Taylor, progmg mgr & mus dir; Mike Raymond, chief engr.

WORK(FM)—Co-owned with WSNO(AM). Aug 5, 1974: 107.1 mhz; 1.5 kw. Ant 410 ft. TL: N44 09 30 W72 28 46. Prog sep from AM. Format: Adult contemp. ■ William A. Noyes, mus dir.

Bellows Falls

WBFL(FM)—November 1981: 107.1 mhz; 1 kw. Ant 530 ft. TL: N43 12 33 W72 19 58. Stereo. Hrs opn: 19. Box 107 (05101); Westminister Stn., U.S. Rt. 5 (05159). (802) 722-4890. FAX: (802) 722-3435. Licensee: WBFL Inc. (acq 7-9-92; $240,000; FTR 7-27-92). Net: Westwood One, MBS. Format: Classic rock, AOR. News staff one; news progmg 2 hrs wkly. Target aud: 18-49. Spec prog: Jazz 3 hrs wkly. ■ Ed Herlihy, pres; Bradley Weeks, gen sls mgr; Eric Anderson, prom mgr, progmg dir & mus dir; Mike Michaels, news dir; Roger Brace, chief engr. ■ Rates: $15; 12; 15; 12.

Bennington

WBTN(AM)—Sept 23, 1953: 1370 khz; 1 kw-D. TL: N42 54 19 W73 12 32. Box 560, U.S. Historic 7A N. (05201). (802) 442-6321. FAX: (802) 442-3112. Licensee: Catamount Broadcasters Inc. Net: AP. Wash atty: Lohnes & Culver. Format: MOR. Target aud: 30-54 plus. Spec prog: Farm 2 hrs, class one hr wkly. ■ Belva Chase Keyworth, pres & gen mgr; Robert Harrington, gen sls mgr & news dir; A. Paul Willey, chief engr.

WHGC(FM)—Co-owned with WBTN(AM). Nov 4, 1978: 94.3 mhz; 3 kw. Ant 110 ft. TL: N42 56 52 W73 10 36. Stereo. Hrs opn: 6 AM-midnight. Prog sep from AM. Format: Easy contemp. Target aud: 20-54; young parents.

Berlin

NEW AM—Not on air, target date unknown: 870 khz; 250 w-U, DA-1. TL: N44 11 22 W72 38 21. Hrs opn: 24. Box 69, Rt. 155, Dover, NH (03820). Licensee: Harvest Broadcasting. Group owner: Love Radio Network (acq 5-4-89). Net: Love Radio. Wash atty: Colby May. News progmg 3 hrs wkly. Target aud: General. Spec prog: Family 24 hrs wkly. ■ Brian Dodge, CEO, pres, gen mgr & engrg dir. ■ Rates: $25; 25; 25; 25.

Brattleboro

WKVT(AM)—Nov 29, 1959: 1490 khz; 1 kw-U. TL: N42 50 51 W72 34 56. Box 1490, Williams & Larkin Sts. (05301); 108 Williams St. (05301). (802) 254-2343. FAX: (802) 254-6683. Licensee: Brattleboro Broadcasters Inc. (acq 8-29-83; grpsl; FTR 8-1-83). Net: CBS, NBC Talknet, Daynet, AP. Rep: Kettell-Carter, Kettell-Carter/Boston. Format: Full svc, news/MOR/talk. News staff 2; news progmg 30 hrs wkly. Target aud: 35-64; news & info oriented adults. Spec prog: Farm one hr wkly. ■ David L. Underhill, pres & gen mgr; Linda M. Underhill, vp opns; James P. Miller, vp dev; Doug Tweedy, gen sls mgr; William Howard, mktg mgr; Diane Maggipinto, prom mgr; Rich Bryan, progmg dir; Tim Johnson, news dir; Virginia Yager, pub affrs dir; Mark Hutchins, vp engrg & chief engr. ■ Rates: $30; 24; 30; 20.

WKVT-FM—1980: 92.7 mhz; 6 kw. Ant 610 ft. TL: N42 53 45 W72 39 49. Stereo. Hrs opn: 20. Prog sep from AM. Net: AP, Unistar. Rep: Kettell Carter. Format: AOR, classic rock. News staff 2; news progmg 9 hrs wkly. Target aud: 18-44. ■ Rates: Same as AM.

WTSA(AM)—Apr 19, 1950: 1450 khz; 1 kw-U. TL: N42 52 13 W72 33 35. Hrs opn: 24. Box 819, 197 Western Ave. (05302). (802) 254-4577. FAX: (802) 257-4644. Licensee: Tri-State Broadcasters Inc. (acq 7-1-86; grpsl; FTR 5-26-86). Net: NBC, SMN. Rep: D & R Radio. Wash atty: Cohn & Marks. Format: Country. News staff one. Target aud: General. Spec prog: Red Sox Baseball. ■ John Kilduff, pres; Lawrence Smith, gen mgr, news dir & chief engr; Robert McCurdy, gen sls mgr; Sue McCurdy, prom mgr; Dan Taylor, progmg dir & mus dir. ■ Rates: $20; 20; 20; 20.

WTSA-FM—Dec 15, 1975: 96.7 mhz; 5.2 kw. Ant 167 ft. TL: N42 53 21 W72 36 47. Stereo. Prog sep from AM. Net: NBC, Unistar. Format: Adult contemp. Target aud: 12 plus. Spec prog: Oldies 16 hrs wkly. ■ Rates: Same as AM.

WXOD(FM)—See Winchester, N.H.

WYRY(FM)—See Keene, N.H.

Burlington

WEZF(FM)—July 19, 1968: 92.9 mhz; 46 kw. Ant 2,703 ft. TL: N44 31 40 W72 48 58. Stereo. Hrs opn: 24. 1500 Hegeman Ave., Colchester (05446). (802) 655-0093. FAX: (802) 655-0478. Licensee: Knight Radio Inc. Group owner: Knight Quality Group Stations (acq 5-14-84; $4,000,000; FTR 3-19-84). Net: Unistar. Rep: Banner. Wash atty: Pepper & Corazzini. Format: Adult contemp. News staff one; news progmg 7 hrs wkly. Target aud: 25-54. ■ Norman Knight, chmn; N. Scott Knight, pres; Thomas Pierce, exec vp & gen mgr; Karen Marshall, stn mgr & gen sls mgr; Warren Baker, opns mgr; Dave Symonds, progmg dir; Brent Jarvis, mus dir; MaryEllen O'Brien, news dir & pub affrs dir; Glenn Dudley, chief engr. ■ Rates: $70; 60; 60; 40.

WIZN(FM)—(Vergennes). Nov 15, 1983: 106.7 mhz; 50 kw. Ant 373 ft. TL: N44 18 40 W73 14 34. Stereo. Hrs opn: 24. Box 1067, Burlington (05402). (802) 860-2440. FAX: (802) 860-1818. Licensee: Burlington Broadcasters Inc. Group owner: Deer River Broadcasting Group (acq 8-85; $64,000; FTR 8-26-85). Rep: Katz. Format: Rock (AOR), live. Target aud: 18-49. Spec prog: Oldies 3 hrs, reggae one hr, progsv one hr, blues 3 hrs wkly. ■ Arthur J. La Vigne, pres; Steve Cormier, progmg dir; Mike Luoma, mus dir.

WJOY(AM)—Sept 14, 1946: 1230 khz; 1 kw-U. TL: N44 27 03 W73 11 51. Hrs opn: 24. Box 4489 (05406-4489). Joy Dr. (05403). (802) 658-1230. FAX: (802) 862-0786. Licensee: Hall Communications Inc. (group owner; acq 12-1-83; FTR 12-5-83). Net: Unistar. Rep: D & R Radio. Wash atty: Arent, Fox, Kintner, Plotkin & Kahn. Format: News, MOR. News staff 2. Target aud: General. ■ Robert M. Hall, chmn; Arthur J. Rowbotham, pres; Dan Dubonnet, gen mgr; R. J. Potter, news dir; Dennis Synder, chief engr.

WOKO(FM)—Co-owned with WJOY(AM). June 26, 1962: 98.9 mhz; 100 kw. Ant 307 ft. TL: N44 27 03 W73 11 51. Stereo. Hrs opn: 24. Prog sep from AM. Format: Country. ■ Rod Hill, progmg dir.

WKDR(AM)—Apr 19, 1954: 1390 khz; 5 kw-U, DA-N. TL: N44 29 47 W73 12 49. Stereo. Hrs opn: 24. 388 Shelburne Rd. (05401); 352 S. Cove Rd. (05401). (802) 863-8255. FAX: (802) 862-8255. Licensee: Hometown Broadcasting Inc. (acq 3-24-93; $300,000; FTR 4-12-93). Net: CNN, SMN. Rep: Eastman. Wash atty: Wiley, Rein & Fielding. Format: News/talk. News staff one; news progmg 2 hrs wkly. Target aud: 25-54; affluent, upscale baby boomer generation. ■ Louis Manno, pres; John C. Nichols, Louis Manno, gen mgrs; Gregg Neavin, gen sls mgr & prom mgr; Jim Condon, news dir; Russ Kinsley, chief engr. ■ Rates: $25; 25; 25; 25.

WNWX(AM)—See Plattsburgh, N.Y.

WOKO(FM)—Listing follows WJOY(AM).

*WRUV(FM)—Oct 3, 1965: 90.1 mhz; 460 w. Ant 145 ft. TL: N44 28 37 W73 11 59. Stereo. Hrs opn: 24. c/o Stn. Mgr. Billings Student Ctr., UVM (05405). (802) 656-4399. FAX: (802) 656-7719. Licensee: Univ. of Vermont & State Agricultural College. Format: Div, educ. Spec prog: Class 6 hrs, jazz 20 hrs, folk 9 hrs, reggae 15 wkly. ■ Mari Anne Paraskevas, stn mgr; Brian Marshal, chief engr.

WVMT(AM)—May 20, 1922: 620 khz; 5 kw-U, DA-N. TL: N44 29 47 W73 12 49. Stereo. Hrs opn: 24. Box 620, Malletts Bay Ave., Colchester (05446). (802) 655-1620. FAX: (802) 655-1329. Licensee: James Broadcasting Co. Inc. Group owner: Goldman Group (acq 2-1-63). Net: ABC/D, MBS, Westwood One. Rep: McGavren Guild, InterRep. Format: Sports, oldies, talk. News staff one; news progmg 14 hrs wkly. Target aud: 25-60. ■ Simon Goldman, pres; Paul S. Goldman, vp & gen mgr; George Goldring, gen sls mgr; John Hill, prom mgr; Mark Esbjerg, progmg dir & mus dir; Ernie Farrar, news dir; Michael Seguin, chief engr.

*WVPS(FM)—Oct 15, 1980: 107.9 mhz; 36 kw. Ant 2,640 ft. TL: N44 31 32 W72 48 54. Stereo. 107.9 Ethan Allen Ave., Colchester (05446). (802) 655-9451. Licensee: Vermont Public Radio. Net: NPR; Eastern Pub. Wash atty: Covington & Burling. Format: Class, jazz, news. Target aud: General. Spec prog: Switchboard call-in prog, 2 hrs wkly. ■ Mark Vogelzang, CEO, pres & gen mgr; Cindy Shuman, CFO & vp; Sam Sanders, opns mgr;

Fred Hill, dev dir; Christopher Wienk, progmg dir; Walter Parker, mus dir; Ira Wilner, chief engr.

Canaan

WXMX(FM)—Not on air, target date unknown: 94.1 mhz; 16 kw. Ant 387 ft. TL: N44 58 40 W71 44 13. Stereo. 5595 Liberty Rd., Chagrin Falls, OH (44022). (216) 498-1221. Licensee: Vector Broadcasting Inc. Group owner: Martz Communications Group (acq 6-5-89). Wash atty: Cohn & Marks. ■ Timothy D. Martz, pres.

Castleton

***WIUV(FM)**—Oct 1, 1976: 91.3 mhz; 227 w. Ant -235 ft. TL: N43 36 29 W73 10 54. Castleton State College (05735). (802) 468-5611, ext. 264; (802) 468-5686. Licensee: Board of Trustees. Format: Progsv, alternative. News progmg 6 hrs wkly. Target aud: General; smart people. Spec prog: Jazz 10 hrs, reggae 6 hrs, class 3 hrs, folk 4 hrs, Sp one hr, industrial one hr, acid-house one hr, country 2 hrs, blues 3 hrs, rap-urban 5 hrs wkly. ■ Tad Lemire, gen mgr; Kym Ringle, mus dir.

Colchester

***WWPV-FM**—Aug 10, 1973: 88.7 mhz; 100 w. Ant 82 ft. TL: N44 29 38 W73 09 51. St. Michaels College (04539). (802) 654-2338; (802) 654-2334. Licensee: Board of Trustees, St. Michaels College. Format: College AOR. ■ Bill Conlon, gen mgr; Matt Engels, progmg dir; Glen Dudley, chief engr.

Danville

WSHX(FM)—Not on air, target date unknown: 95.7 mhz; 230 w. Ant 1,174 ft. TL: N44 22 45 W72 13 13. 1000 Worcester Rd., Framingham, MA (01701). Licensee: Barry W. Sims, receiver (acq 3-18-92).

Derby Center

WMOO(FM)—Apr 1991: 92.1 mhz; 2.25 kw. Ant 619 ft. TL: N44 58 23 W72 04 30 Stereo. Hrs opn: 24. Box 92, Derby/Newport Rd. (05829). (802) 766-9236. FAX: (802) 766-8067. Licensee: Steele Communications Co. Net: Jones Satellite Audio, ABC/E. Rep: Roslin. Wash atty: Covington & Burling. Format: Oldies, classic hits. News staff one; news progmg 16 hrs wkly. Target aud: General. Spec prog: Community events 3 hrs wkly. ■ Thomas S. Steele, pres, vp progmg & chief engr; Carol J. Steele, CFO & mus dir; McDonnell Smith, vp sls; Alice B. Grow, news dir. ■ Rates: $18; 18; 18; 18.

Hartford

WGLV(FM)—Mar 15, 1992: 104.3 mhz; 2.7 kw. Ant 489 ft. TL: N43 39 15 W72 21 32. Stereo. Box 4723, Holiday Inn Dr., White River Jct. (05676-4723). (802) 295-6999. FAX: (802) 295-7275. Licensee: Family Broadcasting Inc. Group owner: Family Broadcasting Network (acq 5-9-91; $100,000; C.P. FTR 6-3-91). Net: Skylight, USA, CBN; See WGLY-FM & WMNV-FM. Wash atty: May & Dunne Format: Inspirational/Christian. Spec prog: Children 3 hrs, classical 5 hrs wkly. ■ Alexander D. McEwing, pres; Dan Parker, stn mgr; Leslie Bashaw, natl sls mgr; Karlo Salminen, progmg dir. ■ Rates: $10; 10; 10; 10.

Johnson

***WJSC-FM**—July 16, 1972: 90.7 mhz; 155 w. Ant -485 ft. TL: N44 38 29 W72 40 20. Stereo. WJCS, Box A-37 (05656). (802) 635-9572. Licensee: Vermont State College. Format: Alt, div. Spec prog: Class 3 hrs, C&W 3 hrs wkly. ■ Shane Chick, gen mgr.

Killington

WEBK(FM)—Aug 4, 1993: 105.3 mhz; 1.15 kw. Ant 2,578 ft. TL: N43 36 47 W72 49 14 Stereo. Hrs opn: 24. Box 34, HCR 70, Killington Mall, Killington Rd. (05751). Licensee: Killington Broadcasting Ltd. Wash atty: Verner, Liipfert, Bernhard, McPherson & Hand. Format: Classical rock, rock/AOR. New progmg one hr wkly. Target aud: 24-48; baby boomers. ■ Daniel W. Ewald, CEO, gen mgr, stn mgr, chief opns & vp progmg; Diane Ewald, sls dir & pub affrs dir; Britt Elwell, prom mgr & adv dir; Daniel Tolley, progmg dir & mus dir; Jane Crussman, progmg dir & (asst) mus dir; Michelle Bastian, news dir; Daniel Ewald, engrg mgr; Vince Diamond, chief engr. ■ Rates: $18; 16; 18; 23.

Lyndon

WGMT(FM)—May 19, 1990: 98.3 mhz; 190 w. Ant 1,990 ft. TL: N44 30 26 W71 53 21. Stereo. Hrs opn: 24. Rt. 114, Box 98, 98 Main St., East Burke (05832). (802) 626-9800. FAX: (802) 626-8500. Licensee: Vermont Broadcast Associates Inc. Net: CNN. Rep: Roslin. Wash atty: Bryan, Cave, McPheeters & McRoberts. Format: Adult contemp. News staff 2; news progmg 5 hrs wkly. Target aud: 18-49; families, more female, disposable income, mobile. ■ Bruce James, pres, gen mgr, prom dir & pub affrs dir; Richard Davis, vp; Rick Davis, opns dir; Mark Hilton, gen sls mgr; Lynn Beaudoin, natl sls mgr & rgnl sls mgr; Steve Merrill, progmg dir; Steve Chizmas, mus dir; Jan McCormick, news dir; Don Smith, engrg mgr; Roger Brace, chief engr. ■ Rates: $22; 18; 22; 18.

Lyndonville

***WWLR(FM)**—Feb 4, 1977: 91.5 mhz; 3 kw. Ant -75 ft. TL: N44 32 04 W72 01 36. Stereo. Lyndon State College (05851). (802) 626-8633; (802) 626-9371. Licensee: Board of Trustees, Vermont State Colleges. Format: Rock (AOR). Spec prog: Class 2 hrs, jazz 3 hrs wkly. ■ Mike Hatch, gen mgr; Todd Jordan, progmg dir; Tom Laffin, chief engr.

Manchester

WEQX(FM)—November 1984: 102.7 mhz; 1.35 kw. Ant 2,490 ft. TL: N43 09 58 W73 06 59. Stereo. Hrs opn: 24. Box 1027, Elm St. & Highland Ave. (05254). (802) 362-4800. FAX: (802) 362-5555. Licensee: Northshire Communications. Net: AP, ABC Rock. Wash atty: Verner, Lipfert, Bernhard, McPherson & Hand. Format: New rock, progsv AOR. News staff one; news progmg 5 hrs wkly. Target aud: 25-54. Spec prog: Jazz 4 hrs wkly. ■ A. Brooks Brown, pres, vp, gen mgr, news dir & chief engr; Susan Gosselin, gen sls mgr; Jim McGuinn, progmg dir. ■ Rates: $60; 50; 60; 50.

Middlebury

WFAD(AM)—Dec 24, 1965: 1490 khz; 1 kw-U. TL: N43 59 57 W73 09 35. Box 150 (05753). (802) 388-9323. Licensee: Pro-Radio Inc. (acq 2-6-91; $75,000; FTR 9-9-91). Net: CBS. Rep: New England. Wash atty: Mullin, Rhyne, Emmons & Topel. Format: Classic Country, big band, class. News progmg 15 hrs wkly. Target aud: 25-54. Spec prog: Farm one hr wkly, sports 10 hrs wkly. ■ Mark Brady, pres, gen mgr, gen sls mgr & mktg dir; Mary Brady, exec vp; Earl Parsons, progmg dir & mus dir; Jim Wright, pub affrs dir; Neil Langer, chief engr. ■ Rates: $18; 14; 18; 12.

WGTK(FM)—Apr 2, 1975: 100.9 mhz; 3 kw. Ant 300 ft. TL: N44 01 34 W73 09 44. Stereo. Hrs opn: 24. Box 590 (05753). (802) 388-4101; (802) 388-7101. FAX: (802) 388-1723. Licensee: Dynamite Radio Inc. (acq 3-28-91; $575,000; FTR 4-15-91). Wash atty: Gardner, Carton, Douglas. Format: Class rock. Target aud: 18-49; young professionals. ■ Anthony Neri, pres & gen mgr; Jeff Dickinson, vp opns & opns dir; Bob Catan, vp progmg; Gale Parmelee, mus dir; Neil Langer, chief engr. ■ Rates: $14; 14; 14; 12.

***WRMC-FM**—May 1949: 91.7 mhz; 100 w. Ant 90 ft. TL: N44 00 35 W73 10 45 (CP: 3 kw, ant 249 ft., TL: N44 01 34 W73 09 44). Stereo. Hrs opn: 24. Drawer 29, Middlebury College (05753). (802) 388-6323. Licensee: President and Fellows of Middlebury College. Net: AP. Format: Div. News staff 2; news progmg 8 hrs wkly. Target aud: General. Spec prog: Urban contemp 12 hrs, class 15 hrs, folk 15 hrs, relg one hr, Sp one hr wkly. ■ John DaMour, pres & gen mgr; Jesse Cunningham, progmg dir; John Coltits, mus dir; Rob Schlesinger, news dir.

Montpelier

WNCS(FM)—June 13, 1977: 104.7 mhz; 1.9 kw. Ant 2,093 ft. TL: N44 18 14 W72 37 18. Stereo. Box 551 (05601); 7 Main St. (05602). (802) 223-2396. Licensee: Montpelier Broadcasting Co. Inc. Group owner: Northeast Broadcasting Co. Inc. (acq 2-12-87). Format: AOR. News progmg 4 hrs wkly. Target aud: 25-40; above-average income & educated, baby boomers choosing the Vermont lifestyle. Spec prog: Class 4 hrs, jazz 5 hrs, world 2 hrs wkly. ■ Steven Silberberg, pres; Edward Flanagan, gen mgr; Candis Scott, gen sls mgr; Diane Manion, prom mgr; Steve Zind, progmg dir; Jody Petersen, news dir; Robert Kinzel, news dir; Tom Laffin, chief engr.

WORK(FM)—See Barre.

WSKI(AM)—Dec 7, 1947: 1240 khz; 1 kw-U. TL: N44 14 40 W72 32 47. Stereo. Box 487, 48 State St. (05602). (802) 223-5275. Licensee: Galloway Communications Inc. (acq 7-15-91; $400,000; FTR 7-29-91). Net: ABC/E. Format: Adult contemp. News progmg wkly. Target aud: 18-35. ■ Ed Flanagan, pres & gen mgr; Candis Scott, gen sls mgr; Tim Janowicz, prom mgr; Jim Severence, progmg dir & mus dir; Jerry Duchene, news dir; Tom Laffin, chief engr.

WSNO(AM)—See Barre.

Morrisville

WLVB(FM)—August 1993: 93.9 mhz; 5.4 kw. TL: N44 34 24 W72 38 11. Box 94, (05661); Box 550, Waterbury (05676). (802) 244-7321. Licensee: Radio Vermont Inc. Format: Country. ■ Eric Michaels, gen mgr.

Newport

WIKE(AM)—Oct 12, 1952: 1490 khz; 1 kw-U. TL: N44 56 28 W72 13 35. Hrs opn: 24. Box 377 (05855). (802) 334-6521. FAX: (802) 334-6522. Licensee: Northeast Kingdom Broadcasting. Group owner: Radio Management Associates Inc. (acq 9-1-79). Net: SMN. Rep: Katz & Powell. Format: Country. News progmg 4 hrs wkly. Target aud: 18 plus. Spec prog: Loc info/entertainment 5 hrs wkly. ■ Fred Gage, gen mgr & gen sls mgr; A. J. Cummings, progmg dir, mus dir & news dir; Charlie Ryan, chief engr. ■ Rates: $15; 11; 15; na.

Northfield

***WNUB-FM**—Dec 8, 1967: 88.3 mhz; 285 w. Ant -387 ft. TL: N44 08 32 W72 39 31. Stereo. Hrs opn: 6 AM-2 AM. Norwich Univ., Comm. Ctr., 7 Park Ave. (05663). (802) 485-2560; (802) 485-2437. Licensee: The Trustees of Norwich University. Net: AP. Format: AOR, top-40. News progmg 10 hrs wkly. Target aud: 14-40; listeners who enjoy 60s, 70s and 80s pop/rock music. Spec prog: Class 6 hrs, C&W 6 hrs, jazz 10 hrs wkly. ■ Scott C. Fields, gen mgr; Russ Fontaine, stn mgr & progmg dir; Chris Cook, Brandon Deacon, prom dirs; Steve Autiello, adv dir; Keith Silva, mus dir; Warren Fligg, Pierce Williams, asst mus dirs; Ritva Carlson, news dir; Chris Bradley, pub affrs dir; Iva Wilner, chief engr.

Plainfield

***WGDR(FM)**—May 11, 1973: 91.1 mhz; 800 w. Ant -350 ft. TL: N44 17 04 W72 26 28. Stereo. Box 336, Goddard College (05667). (802) 454-7762; (802) 454-8311, EXT. 269. FAX: (802) 454-1238. Licensee: Goddard College Corp. Format: Div. News staff 4; news progmg 15 hrs wkly. Target aud: Multiple. Spec prog: Folk 10 hrs, black 8 hrs, jazz 6 hrs, class 3 hrs, farm one hr, American Indian one hr wkly. ■ Stuart Bautz, gen mgr, dev mgr & progmg dir; Stuart Bautz, Louie Ducharme, opns dirs; Laura Paris, mus dir; Brendan Martin, (asst) mus dir; Russ Rollins, pub affrs dir; Brian Justin, Jr., chief engr.

Poultney

WVNR(AM)—Aug 1, 1981: 1340 khz; 1 kw-U. TL: N43 30 16 W73 13 11. Hrs opn: 5:30 AM-midnight. Box 210 (05764); Box 141, Whitehall, NY (12887). (802) 287-9031. Licensee: Pine Tree Broadcasting Co. (acq 4-86). Format: Adult contemp, country, oldies. News staff one; news progmg 3.25 hrs wkly. Target aud: 30-55; local, family oriented, mobile. Spec prog: Pol one hr, relg 2 hrs, big band 3 hrs, loc sports/events & fundraisers 3 hrs, school news one hr, farm one hr, pub affairs 5 hrs wkly. ■ Michael J. Leech, pres; Judith E. Leech, exec vp, gen mgr & gen sls mgr; Rob Roy, progmg dir & mus dir; Joel Williams, news dir; Helen Willis, pub affrs dir; Neil Langer, chief engr.

Randolph

WWWT(AM)—Nov 26, 1968: 1320 khz; 1 kw-D, 66 w-N. TL: N43 56 21 W72 38 13. Box 249 (05061); One Radio Dr. (05060). (802) 728-4411. Licensee: Stokes Communications Corp. (acq 11-1-80; $250,000; FTR 11-10-80). Net: SMN. Rep: Savalli. Wash atty: Fisher, Wayland, Cooper & Leader. Format: Country. News staff one; news progmg 5 hrs wkly. Target aud: 18-49. ■ Edward H. Stokes, pres; Margaret W. Stokes, gen mgr; Ken Worthington, gen sls mgr; David Goldsworthy, progmg dir.

WCVR-FM—Co-owned with WWWT(AM). Oct 25, 1982: 102.3 mhz; 3 kw. Ant 300 ft. TL: N43 57 20 W72 36 10 (CP: 11 kw, ant 466 ft.). Stereo. News progmg 6 hrs wkly. Target aud: 25-54.

Vermont

Randolph Center

*WVTC(FM)—Aug 29, 1983: 90.7 mhz; 300 w-H. Ant 203 ft. TL: N43 56 07 W72 36 10. Stereo. Hrs opn: Noon-2 AM. Vermont Technical College (05061). (802) 728-3464. Licensee: Vermont State Colleges, Vermont Technical College. Format: AOR, country. Target aud: General.

Rupert

WMNV(FM)—Apr 10, 1990: 104.1 mhz; 1.5 kw. Ant 249 ft. TL: N43 14 18 W73 13 42 (CP: 2.8 kw, ant 223 ft.). Stereo. Hrs opn: 14. Box 57 (05768). Licensee: Family Broadcasting Inc. Group owner: Family Broadcasting Network (acq 8-7-92; $55,000; FTR 8-24-92). Format: Relg. ■ Peter Morton, gen mgr.

Rutland

*WFTF(FM)—Jan 10, 1987: 90.5 mhz; 720 w. Ant -560 ft. TL: N43 37 09 W72 59 04. 2 Meadow Ln. (05701). (802) 775-0358. Licensee: Calvary Bible Church. Net: Moody. Format: Relg. ■ Dean Grossman, pres & gen mgr.

WHWB(AM)—June 1949: 970 khz; 1 kw-D. TL: N43 36 43 W73 01 37. Hrs opn: 24. Box 945 (05702). Licensee: Con Brio Broadcasting Inc. (acq 11-2-90; $325,000; FTR 11-19-90). Format: Country. ■ Raymond Lemire, pres & gen mgr.

WJJR(FM)—Mar 25, 1971: 98.1 mhz; 1.15 kw. Ant 2,953 ft. TL: N43 36 17 W72 49 14. Stereo. Hrs opn: 24. Box 30 (05702); 67 Merchants Row (05701). (802) 775-7500. FAX: (802) 775-7555. Licensee: Jewel Radio Inc. (acq 8-90; FTR 8-6-90). Rep: Eastman, Katz. Wash atty: Hogan & Hartson. Format: Adult contemp. News staff one; news progmg one hr wkly. Target aud: 25-54; in office-managerial professional. Spec prog: News/pub affrs one hr wkly. ■ Harrison M. Fuerst, pres; Samuel J. Gorruso, vp & gen mgr; Harry Weinhagen Jr., gen sls mgr; Terry Jarrosak, progmg dir; Nanci Gordon, news dir; F. Christopher McCormack, pub affrs dir; Neil Langer, chief engr. ■ Rates: $28; 28; 28; 28.

*WRVT(FM)—Jan 10, 1989: 88.7 mhz; 2.77 kw. Ant 1,328 ft. TL: N43 39 32 W73 06 25. 107 Ethan Allen Ave., Colchester (05446). (802) 665-9451. Licensee: Vermont Public Radio. Net: NPR. Wash atty: Covington & Burling. Format: Class, jazz, news. News progmg 18 hrs wkly. Target aud: General. Spec prog: Switchboard call-in, 2 hrs wkly. ■ Mark Vogelzang, CEO, pres & gen mgr; Cindy Shuman, CFO & exec vp; Sam Sanders, opns mgr; Fred Hill, dev dir; Christopher Wienk, progmg dir; Walter Parker, mus dir; Ira Wilner, chief engr.

WSYB(AM)—Dec 10, 1930: 1380 khz; 5 kw-D, 1 kw-N, DA-D. TL: N43 35 35 W72 59 25. Box 940 (05702-0940). 249 Dorr Dr. (05701). (802) 775-5597. FAX: (802) 775-6637. Licensee: H & D Limited Partnership. Group owner: H & D Broadcast Group (acq 4-1-89; grpsl; FTR 5-18-87). Net: NBC. Rep: McGavren Guild. Format: Adult contemp, oldies, news/talk. News staff 3; news progmg 7 hrs wkly. Target aud: 25-54. Spec prog: Polish one hr wkly. ■ Richard H. Vaughan, gen mgr; Sherri Birkheimer, natl sls mgr; Lisa Diamond, prom dir; Ed Kelly, progmg dir; Kris Pearson, news dir; Tom Elmore, chief engr. ■ Rates: $20; 15; 17; 11.

WZRT(FM)—Co-owned with WSYB(AM). 1974: 97.1 mhz; 1.15 kw. Ant 2,591 ft. TL: N43 36 17 W72 49 14. Stereo. Hrs opn: 24. Dups AM 30%. Net: McGavern Guild. Format: Adult contemp. News staff 2; news progmg 5 hrs wkly. Target aud: 18-49. ■ Richard H. Vaughan, vp; Sherri Birkheimer (local), rgnl sls mgr; Lisa Diamond, prom mgr; Ed Kelly, progmg dir; Kevin Smith, engrg dir. ■ Rates: $35; 32; 35; 30.

WYOY(FM)—October 1988: 94.5 mhz; 6 kw. Ant 389 ft. TL: N43 36 49 W73 01 33. Stereo. Hrs opn: 24. Box 945 (05702). (802) 747-4700; (802) 775-9999. FAX: (802) 747-1400. Licensee: Rutland Community Broadcasting Inc. (acq 6-28-93; $75,000; FTR 7-26-93). ■ Raymond Lemire, pres & gen mgr.

WZRT(FM)—Listing follows WSYB(AM).

St. Albans

WWSR(AM)—1930: 1420 khz; 1 kw-D, 110 w-N. TL: N44 50 12 W73 04 57. Hrs opn: 24. 102 Swanton Rd. (05478). (802) 524-2133. FAX: (802) 527-1450. Licensee: Kimel Broadcast Group Inc. (group owner; acq 9-59). Net: MBS. Rep: Republic. Format: Oldies, news/talk. News staff one; news progmg 20 hrs wkly. Target aud: General. ■ John O. Kimel, pres; David R. Kimel, vp; Paul Battaini, vp; Phil Knight, natl sls mgr & rgnl sls mgr; Steve Salls, prom mgr; Kenny Rodman, progmg dir; Matt Henry, mus dir; Richard Cowperthwait, news dir; Mike Raymond, chief engr. ■ Rates: $15; 13; 15; 9.

WLFE(FM)—Co-owned with WWSR(AM). April 1970: 102.3 mhz; 440 w. Ant 800 ft. TL: N44 46 56 W73 03 54. Stereo. Hrs opn: 24. Prog sep from AM. Format: Country. News staff one; news progmg 5 hrs wkly. Target aud: 18-54. ■ Rates: $18; 16; 18; 12.

St. Johnsbury

WSTJ(AM)—July 10, 1949: 1340 khz; 1 kw-U. TL: N44 25 06 W71 59 45. Hrs opn: 24. Box 249 (05819). (802) 748-2345. FAX: (802) 748-2361. Licensee: Northeast Kingdom Broadcasting Inc. Group owner: Radio Management Associates Inc. (acq 8-31-79). Net: ABC. Rep: Katz & Powell. Format: Adult contemp, news, info. Spec prog: Big band 3 hrs wkly. ■ Rick DeFabio, gen mgr. ■ Rates: $14; 12; 14; 10.

WNKV(FM)—Co-owned with WSTJ(AM). Aug 1, 1985: 105.5 mhz; 400 w. Ant 712 ft. TL: N44 24 38 W71 58 13. Stereo. Hrs opn: 24. Prog sep from AM. (802) 748-2362. Format: Country. News staff 2. Target aud: General.

South Burlington

WXXX(FM)—Nov 16, 1984: 95.3 mhz; 3 kw. Ant 225 ft. TL: N44 30 35 W73 11 05. Stereo. Box 9530, Malletts Bay Ave., Colchester (05446). (802) 655-9530. FAX: (802) 655-1329. Licensee: James Broadcasting Co. Inc. Group owner: The Goldman Group (acq 4-90; $3.95 million; FTR 5-21-90). Rep: McGavren Guild. Format: CHR. News staff one; news progmg one hr wkly. Target aud: 18-49. ■ Si Goldman, pres; Paul Goldman, gen mgr & gen sls mgr; Mark Esberg, opns mgr; Lisa Berigan, prom mgr; Ben Hamilton, progmg dir & mus dir; Ann Grady, news dir; Mike Seguin, chief engr.

Springfield

WCFR(AM)—May 26, 1954: 1480 khz; 5 kw-D. TL: N43 16 54 W72 29 21. Box 800 (05156). (802) 885-4555. FAX: (802) 885-3674. Licensee: Bernhardt Broadcasting Co. Inc. (acq 2-6-92; $365,000 with co-located FM; FTR 2-24-92). Net: SMN. Format: News, big band, MOR. News staff one; news progmg 7 hrs wkly Target aud: 45 plus. ■ Mike Bernhardt, pres; Frank P. Zezza, gen mgr; Bob Furman, gen sls mgr; Bill Salati, prom mgr; Bob Flynt, opns mgr, progmg dir & mus dir; Kathleen Marple, news dir; Ira Wilner, chief engr. ■ Rates: $12.50; 10; 12.50; 10.

WCFR-FM—Jan 1, 1972: 93.5 mhz; 3 kw. Ant 300 ft. TL: N43 16 54 W72 29 21. Stereo. Prog sep from AM. Format: Adult contemp. News progmg 10 hrs wkly. Target aud: 25-50. ■ Bob Furman, rgnl sls mgr; Sara Stretcher, adv mgr; Bob Flynt, progmg dir. ■ Rates: $25; 20; 25; 12.

Stowe

WVMX(FM)—Feb 28, 1977: 101.7 mhz; 43 w. Ant 2,653 ft. TL: N44 30 11 W72 41 35. Stereo. Box 1467 (05672). (802) 253-4877. Licensee: Sage Broadcasting of Vermont Inc. (acq 6-7-93; $750,000; FTR 7-5-93). Rep: New England. Format: Adult contemp, rock. Target aud: 25-49. ■ Frank Allen, gen mgr & progmg dir; Dave Johnson, mus dir. ■ Rates: $20; 19; 20; 17.

Sunderland

WJAN(FM)—May 1, 1991: 95.1 mhz; 48 w. Ant 2,398 ft. TL: N43 09 58 W73 07 02. Stereo. Hrs opn: 24. R.R. 1, Box 1118, Lincoln Ave., Manchester Center (05255). (802) 362-9500. FAX: (802) 362-1000. Licensee: Radio New England Ltd. Net: SMN. Format: Country. Target aud: 25-54. ■ Ronald Morlino, pres & chief engr; Samuel Stern, gen mgr; Fred Malone, sls mgr; Fran Kusala, prom mgr & progmg dir; Willy Clark, mus dir.

Vergennes

WIZN(FM)—Licensed to Vergennes. See Burlington.

WWGT(FM)—Not on air, target date unknown: 96.7 mhz; 3.4 kw. Ant 430 ft. 33 Pine Plain Rd., Wellesley, MA (02181). Licensee: Lakeside Broadcasting Corp.

Warren

WDEV-FM—Aug 11, 1989: 96.1 mhz; 3 kw. Ant 4,000 ft. TL: N44 07 37 W72 55 43. Stereo. Hrs opn: 24. Simulcasts WDEV(AM) Waterbury. Box 550, Waterbury (05676). (802) 244-7321. FAX: (802) 244-5266. Licensee: Radio Vermont Inc. (acq 10-15-92; $643,000 with WKDR[AM] Burlington; FTR 11-23-92). Net: SMN. Rep: Eastman. Wash atty: Wiley, Rein & Fielding. Format: News, sports, div. News staff one; news progmg 2 hrs wkly. Target aud: 25-54; affluent, upscale baby boomer generation. ■ Ken D. Squier, pres; Eric Michaels, gen mgr.

Waterbury

WDEV(AM)—July 16, 1931: 550 khz; 5 kw-D, 1 kw-N, DA-2. TL: N44 21 09 W72 45 06. Box 550 (05676). (802) 244-7321. FAX: (802) 244-5266. Licensee: Radio Vermont Inc. (acq 1969). Net: AP. Rep: Kettell-Carter. Format: News, sports, div. Spec prog: Farm 6 hrs, class one hr wkly. ■ Ken D. Squier, pres; Eric Michaels, gen mgr & progmg dir; Steve Barone, gen sls mgr; Jack Donovan, mus dir; Anson Tebbetts, news dir; Peter Dean, chief engr.

WGLY-FM—Feb 14, 1985: 103.3 mhz; 920 w. Ant 891 ft. TL: N44 25 22 W72 43 27. Stereo. Hrs opn: 24. Box 150, Rt. 2 W. (05676-0150). (802) 244-5683. FAX: (802) 244-5685. Licensee: Family Broadcasting Inc. Group owner: Family Broadcasting Network (acq 2-86; $227,000; FTR 12-2-85). Net: USA, CBN. See WGLV-FM & WMNV-FM. Wash atty: May & Dunne. Format: Contemp Christian. News progmg 16 hrs wkly. Target aud: General; 25-54, families. Spec prog: Children's 3 hrs wkly. ■ Alexander McEwing, pres & gen mgr; Leslie Bashaw, gen sls mgr; Karlo Salminen, progmg dir. ■ Rates: $15; 15; 15; 15.

Wells River

WYKR(AM)—Oct 3, 1976: 1100 khz; 5 kw-D. TL: N44 08 55 W72 04 02. Box 1100, Rt. 5, Historic Brick School House, Main St. (05081); Box 1013, Woodsville, NH (03785). (802) 757-2773; (802) 757-2774. FAX: (802) 757-8001. Licensee: Puffer Broadcasting Inc. (acq 10-3-77). Net: USA. Rep: Roslin. Wash atty: Richard J. Hayes, Jr. Format: Country. News progmg 9 hrs wkly. Target aud: 25 plus. Spec prog: Farm one hr, relg 2 hrs, class 2 hrs wkly. ■ Stephen J. Puffer, pres, gen sls mgr & prom mgr; Eugene Puffer, gen mgr; David Labounty, progmg dir & mus dir; Don Smith, chief engr. ■ Rates: $15; 15; 15; 15.

White River Junction

WNBX(FM)—See Lebanon, N.H.

WNHV(AM)—Feb 28, 1963: 910 khz; 1 kw-D, 84 w-N. TL: N43 37 19 W72 21 04. Rebroadcasts WTSV (AM) Claremont 100%. Box 910 (05001). (802) 295-3093. FAX: (802) 295-3095. Licensee: Dynacom Corp. Group owner: Cayuga/Northstar Radio Group (acq 9-15-93; $525,000 with co-located FM; FTR 10-11-93). Net: AP, MBS. Rep: D & R Radio. Format: Nostalgia. News staff 2; news progmg 25 hrs wkly. Target aud: 55 plus. Spec prog: Nostalgia, "music of your life," high school sports, Boston Celtics. ■ Jeffrey Shapiro, pres; William Stanley, exec vp; Geoffrey A. Blair, gen mgr; Tim Tobin, vp prom; Kenneth Barlow, progmg dir; Bob Lipman, pub affrs dir. ■ Rates: $19; 19; 19; 17.

WKXE-FM—Co-owned with WNHV(AM). Feb 1, 1969: 95.3 mhz; 3 kw. Ant 225 ft. TL: N43 39 14 W72 17 43. Stereo. Prog sep from AM. Net: AP. Format: Soft AC. News staff 2; news progmg 10 hrs wkly. Target aud: 35-54. Spec prog: Dialogue (talk) 2 hrs wkly. ■ Bob Lipman, news dir. ■ Rates: $33; 33; 33; 29.

WTSL(AM)—See Hanover, N.H.

Williston

*WTBC-FM—Not on air, target date unknown: 90.9 mhz; 1.5 kw. Ant 49 ft. TL: N44 28 06 W73 06 31. Rt. 2A (05495). (802) 878-8118. Licensee: Trinity Baptist High School. ■ Douglas A. Peacock, chief engr.

Wilmington

WVAY(FM)—June 1, 1989: 100.7 mhz; 135 w. Ant 1,460 ft. TL: N42 57 33 W72 55 22. Stereo. Hrs opn: 5:30 AM-1 AM. Box 850, Rt. 100, N. Commercial Ctr. West Dover (05356). (802) 464-1111. FAX: (802) 464-1112. Licensee: Rothschild Broadcasting Inc. Net: AP. Wash atty: Dan Alpert. Format: Adult alternative airplay. News progmg 2 hrs wkly. Target aud: 25-54. Spec prog: Jazz 2 hrs, teen show one hr wkly. ■ Robin Rothschild, pres & gen mgr; Robert Scherer, gen sls mgr; Sarah Kimball, prom mgr; Shawn Taylor, progmg dir & mus dir; Niel Langer, chief engr.

Windsor

*WVPR(FM)—Aug 13, 1976: 89.5 mhz; 1.78 kw. Ant 2,160 ft. TL: N43 26 17 W72 27 08. Stereo. 54 Main St. (05089). (802) 674-6772; (802) 655-9451. FAX: (802) 674-5095; (802) 655-2799. Licensee: Vermont Public Radio. Net: NPR. Format: Educ, class, news, jazz. News progmg 18 hrs wkly. Target aud: General. Spec prog: Folk

Stations in the U.S. | Virginia

6 hrs wkly. ■ Hilton Wick, chmn; Mark Vogelzang, pres & gen mgr; Cynthia Shuman, CFO; Christopher Wienk, opns dir, progmg dir & engrg dir; Fred Hill, dev dir & mktg dir; Robin Turnau, sls dir; Walter Parker, mus dir.

Woodstock

WMXR(FM)—Apr 18, 1989: 93.9 mhz; 670 w. Ant 682 ft. TL: N43 36 17 W72 28 03. Stereo. Hrs opn: 24. Box 404 (05091); Jct. Rts. 4 & 12, Taftsville (05073). (802) 457-9494. FAX: (802) 457-9496. Licensee: Robert and Shirley Wolf. Net: AP. Rep: Kettell-Carter. Format: Oldies, classic hits. News staff 3; news progmg 4 hrs wkly. Target aud: 25-49; reaches baby boomers in upscale mkt. ■ Robert J. Wolf, pres, gen mgr & chief engr; Ken Hayes, opns mgr & progmg dir; Ray Lemire, gen sls mgr; Shirley P. Wolf, prom mgr & adv mgr; Lisa Franklin, news dir & pub affrs dir.

Virginia

LAUREN A. COLBY
301-663-1086
COMMUNICATIONS ATTORNEY
Special Attention to Difficult Cases

Abingdon

WABN(AM)—Dec 10, 1956: 1230 khz; 1 kw-U. TL: N36 43 07 W81 56 55. Hrs opn: 6 AM-midnight. Box 1067, 769 Radio Dr. (24210). (703) 628-2147; (703) 628-4422. FAX: (703) 628-9847. Licensee: Legend Radio Group Inc. (acq 5-1-87; grpsl; FTR 5-18-87). Net: NBC, NBC Talknet; Va. News Net. Format: Adult contemp. News progmg 5 hrs wkly. Target aud: 25-54: business and professional, educated and concerned. Spec prog: Farm 5 hrs, Countdown America 3 hrs, talk 2 hrs, sports 5 hrs, relg 18 hrs wkly. ■ Craig Sutherland, pres & gen sls mgr; Craig Sutherland, Rita Sutherland, gen mgrs; Rita Sutherland, opns mgr, progmg dir & pub affrs dir; Lynn Rutledge, mus dir; Bob Dix, chief engr. ■ Rates: $21; 18; 21; 18.

WABN-FM—Dec 10, 1966: 92.7 mhz; 1.8 kw. Ant 371 ft. TL: N36 43 07 W81 56 55. Stereo. Hrs opn: 6 AM-midnight. Prog sep from AM. Net: NBC. Format: CHR. News progmg 2 hrs wkly. Target aud: 12 plus; progressive, contemporary and urban. Spec prog: Casey's Top 40 4 hrs wkly. ■ Rates: Same as AM.

Accomac

WVES(FM)—Aug 13, 1990: 99.3 mhz; 16.5 kw. Ant 400 ft. TL: N37 47 05 W75 36 16. Stereo. Hrs opn: 6 AM-midnight. Box 390 (23301). (804) 665-6500. FAX: (804) 665-6178. Licensee: Eastern Shore Broadcasting Inc. Format: Hot Country. Target aud: 25 plus. Spec prog: Jazz 3 hrs, talk 2 hrs wkly. ■ Charlie Walters, gen mgr, progmg dir & mus dir; Charlie Waters, gen sls mgr & prom mgr; Gus Buhalis, news dir; Earl McCleary, chief engr. ■ Rates: $9; 8; 9; 7.

Alexandria

WCPT(AM)—Licensed to Alexandria. See Washington, D.C.

Altavista

WKDE(AM)—Apr 29, 1962: 1000 khz; 1 kw-D. TL: N37 07 20 W79 17 20. Box 390, 200 Frazier Rd. (24517). (804) 369-5588; (804) 369-6006. FAX: (804) 369-1632. Licensee: DJ Broadcasting Corp. (acq 1-13-92; $300,000 with co-located FM; FTR 2-10-92). Net: UPI; Va. News Net. Format: Southern gospel. Target aud: General. ■ David Hoehne, pres; Lester Woodie, gen mgr & gen sls mgr; Dave Hoehne, progmg dir; Don Scholefield, chief engr. ■ Rates: $8.75; 8.75; 8.75; 8.75.

WKDE-FM—June 30, 1969: 105.5 mhz; 3 kw. Ant 328 ft. TL: N37 07 20 W79 17 20. Stereo. Prog sep from AM. (804) 528-5105. Format: C&W. Target aud: 25-54. Spec prog: Black 5 hrs, gospel 5 hrs wkly. ■ Rates: $10.75; 10.75; 10.75; 9.00.

Amherst

***WAMV(AM)**—Oct 1, 1976: 1420 khz; 1 kw-D, 47 w-N. Box H, c/o Dean of Student Activities, Sweet Briar College, Sweet Briar (24595). (804) 381-6184. FAX: (804) 381-6173. Licensee: Sweet Briar College. Format: Div. Spec prog: Class 4 hrs wkly. ■ Ann H. Richards, stn mgr.

WYYD(FM)—Jan 27, 1981: 107.9 mhz; 20.5 kw. Ant 1,768 ft. TL: N37 28 13 W79 22 30. Stereo. Hrs opn: 24. Box 4108, 8435 Timberlake Rd., Lynchburg (24502). (804) 237-4700. FAX: (804) 237-8070. Licensee: Winfas of Virginia Inc. Net: ABC; Va. News Net. Rep: McGavern Guild. Format: Country. News staff one. Target aud: 25-54; those with moderate expendable income. ■ Roger Ingram, pres; Barbara Rexrode, gen mgr; Sterling Slaughter, gen sls mgr; Nan Richards, prom mgr; Kenny Shelton, progmg dir; Robynn Jaymes, mus dir; Glen Reinheimer, chief engr. ■ Rates: $80; 60; 80; 40.

Appalachia

WAXM(FM)—See Big Stone Gap.

Appomattox

WLDJ(FM)—May 17, 1989: 102.7 mhz; 22 kw. Ant 745 ft. TL: N37 28 07 W79 00 27. Stereo. Box 6440, Lynchburg (24505); 1150 Main St., Madison Heights (24572). (804) 847-1266. FAX: (804) 845-4385. Licensee: L-R Radio Group Inc. (acq 11-20-92; $1.24 million; FTR 12-14-92). Format: CHR/top-40. Spec prog: New age 8 hrs wkly. ■ Jack Alix, pres.

WTTX(AM)—June 1, 1974: 1280 khz; 1 kw-D. TL: N37 22 19 W78 50 06. Box 637 (24522). (804) 352-2451. Licensee: CLL Inc. (acq 1-16-89; grpsl; FTR 1-16-89). Net: UPI. Format: Relg. ■ Terry Cooke, pres & gen mgr; Wayne Green, prom mgr & progmg dir; Jeff Worley, news dir; Glenn Rehmier, chief engr.

WTTX-FM—September 1976: 107.1 mhz; 3 kw. Ant 300 ft. TL: N37 22 19 W78 50 06. Dups AM 100%.

Arlington

WABS(AM)—Nov 7, 1946: 780 khz; 5 kw-D. TL: N38 53 44 W77 08 04. 5545 Lee Hwy. (22207). (703) 534-2000. FAX: (703) 534-3330. Licensee: Radio 780 Inc. (acq 11-10-77). Format: Contemp Christian. ■ Edwin Tornberg, pres; Steven R. Cross, vp & gen mgr; Dawn Dicker, progmg dir.

WAVA(FM)—Licensed to Arlington. See Washington, D.C.

WMZQ(AM)—Apr 7, 1947: 1390 khz; 5 kw-U, DA-2. TL: N38 54 15 W77 09 54. Stereo. 5513 Connecticut Ave. N.W., Washington, DC (20015). (202) 362-8330. FAX: (202) 966-2679. Licensee: Viacom Broadcasting Inc. (group owner; acq 8-1-84). Rep: Christal. Format: C&W. News staff one. Target aud: 25-54. ■ Charlie Ochs, vp & gen mgr; Gary McCartie, opns mgr; Nancy Bryant, gen sls mgr; Vasco Bramao, natl sls mgr; Janie Floyd, prom mgr; Mac Daniels, mus dir; Kim Leslie, news dir & pub affrs dir; Thomas Shedlick, chief engr.

Ashland

WPES(AM)—May 1, 1962: 1430 khz; 1 kw-U. TL: N37 44 46 W77 29 44 (CP: 5 kw-D, DA, TL: N37 44 45 W77 29 44). Hrs opn: Dawn-dusk. Box 148, 2320 Ashcake Rd. (23005). (804) 798-1010; (804) 345-1430. FAX: (804) 752-2163. Licensee: Calvary Communications Inc. (acq 7-89; $95,000). Net: USA, CBN, Moody. Format: Relg, news/talk. News progmg 7 hrs wkly. Target aud: General; 18-35. ■ Wallace Heflin, pres; Helen Lofton, stn mgr, gen sls mgr, adv mgr & progmg dir; Ed Burkhardt, chief engr. ■ Rates: $11.50; 10.50; 11.50; na.

WYFJ(FM)—Dec 7, 1967: 100.1 mhz; 3.3 kw. Ant 300 ft. TL: N37 19 14 W79 37 59 (CP: 6 kw). Stereo. Hrs opn: 24. 407 S. Washington Hwy. (23005). (804) 798-3248. Licensee: Bible Broadcasting Network (group owner; acq 2-1-80). Net: AP. Format: Relg. News progmg 9 hrs wkly. ■ Lowell Davey, pres; Randy Adams, gen mgr & stn mgr; Edward Burkhardt, chief engr.

Bassett

WCBX(AM)—Oct 1, 1960: 900 khz; 500 w-U, DA-2. TL: N36 46 47 W80 00 35 (CP: 1.8 kw-D, 500 w-N, DA-2). Box 192, Martinsville (24114). (703) 638-5235. FAX: (703) 638-5235. Licensee: Radio 1160 (acq 2-4-93; $50,000; FTR 4-19-93). Net: MBS. Format: Gospel. News staff one; news prgmg 12 hrs. Target aud: 25 plus. Spec prog: Bluegrass 4 hrs wkly. ■ Vernon H. Baker, pres; Kevin Warren, gen mgr. ■ Rates: $9.25; 9.25; 9.25; 9.25.

Bedford

WBLT(AM)—Feb 9, 1950: 1350 khz; 1 kw-D. TL: N37 20 50 W79 31 24. Box 506, 1201 Poplar St. (24523). (703) 586-8245. Licensee: Bedford Broadcasting Corp. Net: UPI; Va. News Net. Format: Adult contemp, oldies, news. News staff one; news progmg 20 hrs wkly. Target aud: General. Spec prog: Farm 5 hrs, church progmg 10 hrs wkly. ■ James E. Synan, pres; James W. Patterson, gen mgr, sls dir & progmg dir; Chris Patterson, opns dir; H. Watts Key, mus dir. ■ Rates: $7.50; 7.50; 7.50; na.

WYMY(FM)—Oct 20, 1992: 106.9 mhz; 180 w. Ant 1,276 ft. TL: N37 19 14 W79 37 59. 101A Turnpike Rd. (24523). (703) 586-7000. Licensee: Madison Broadcasting Group. Format: Hot country. ■ Hank Jarnigan, gen mgr; Jackie Howard, progmg dir.

Berryville

WAPP(FM)—May 19, 1980: 105.5 mhz; 3 kw. Ant 300 ft. TL: N39 07 03 W77 58 22. Stereo. Dups WESI(FM) Strasburg 100%. Box 1658, Winchester (22601); 210 W. King St., Strasberg (22657). (703) 465-9100. FAX: (703) 465-5350. Licensee: Signal Knob Radio Partners (acq 4-1-89). Net: Satellite Music Net. Format: Oldies ■ Candice Stover-McGowan, gen mgr; Jim McGowan, gen sls mgr; Keith Provost, progmg dir.

Big Stone Gap

WLSD(AM)—Aug 20, 1953: 1220 khz; 1 kw-D, 45 w-N. TL: N36 50 26 W82 44 14. Stereo. Drawer W, 2nd Fl., 1600 Intermont (24219). (703) 523-1700. FAX: (703) 523-3843. Licensee: Valley Broadcasting Inc. (acq 5-1-80; $359,000; FTR 5-12-80). Net: ABC/FM. Wash atty: Jerry Miller. Format: Relg. News staff one; news progmg 40 hrs wkly. Target aud: 19-60. ■ Don Wax, pres; Dale Kennedy, gen mgr; Jim Baker, progmg dir; Don Mussels, chief engr.

WAXM(FM)—Co-owned with WLSD(AM). Apr 8, 1975: 93.5 mhz; 2.45 kw. Ant 1,883 ft. TL: N36 54 50 W82 53 40. Stereo. Hrs opn: 24. Prog sep from AM. Net: ABC. Format: Country. News staff one; news progmg 40 hrs wkly. Target aud: 19-60. ■ Lamara Wax, vp; Dale Kennedy, stn mgr.

Blacksburg

WFNR(AM)—1973: 710 khz; 10 kw-D, DA. TL: N37 08 01 W80 21 17. 485 Tower Rd., Christiansburg (24073). (703) 382-6106. FAX: (703) 381-2932. Licensee: Travis Broadcasting Corp. (acq 8-11-92; $100,000; FTR 8-31-92). Net: UPI; Va. News Net. Format: News, talk. News progmg 7 hrs wkly. Target aud: General; 25 plus. ■ Bob Travis, pres; Karen Travis, gen sls mgr; Bill Lineberry, progmg dir. ■ Rates: $10.50; 9.50; 10.50; 7.

WJJJ(AM)—See Christiansburg.

WKEX(AM)—July 10, 1969: 1430 khz; 1 kw-D, 62 w-N. TL: N37 13 57 W80 26 40 (CP: 5 kw-U, DA-2). Box 11600 (24060). (703) 951-9539; (703) 961-1430. Licensee: Robert R. Smith Jr. (acq 8-1-85; $200,000; FTR 5-6-85). Net: USA; Agri-Net. Format: Standard popular and big band. News staff 4; news progmg 10 hrs wkly. Target aud: 21 plus; mature adults, all income levels, male and female equal. Spec prog: Country 4 hrs, bluegrass 2 hrs, gospel 6 hrs wkly. ■ Robert R. Smith Jr., pres, gen mgr & sls dir; Warren Stevenson, prom dir; Homer Johnson, asst mus dir; Carl Castello, news dir; Dan Leary, pub affrs dir; Tom Crockett, chief engr. ■ Rates: $6; 6; 6; 6.

***WUVT-FM**—Oct 23, 1969: 90.7 mhz; 3 kw. Ant 156 ft. TL: N37 13 28 W80 24 30. Stereo. 350 Squire Student Ctr. (24061). (703) 231-9881; (703) 231-6000. Licensee: Virginia Polytechnic Institute & State University. Format: Div. ■ A.J. Miller, gen mgr; Bryan McNamara, mus dir; Paul Duncan, chief engr.

WVVV(FM)—December 1964: 104.9 mhz; 3 kw. Ant 310 ft. TL: N37 09 11 W80 24 57. Stereo. Hrs opn: 24. Box 882 (24060); Box 30, 1780 N. Franklin, Christiansburg (24073). (703) 382-4993. FAX: (703) 381-0581. Licensee: New River Media Group Inc. (acq 9-8-93; $512,500 with WJJJ[AM] Christianburg; FTR 10-4-93). Net: ABC/F. Format: AOR, classic rock. News progmg 2 hrs wkly. Target aud: 18-34. ■ William R. Rollins, pres; Ralph N. Stewart, gen mgr; Ron Dayle, gen sls mgr; Kevin Walsh, progmg dir; Stevie Lynn, mus dir; Victor Kuehn, news dir. ■ Rates: $23; 20; 23; 20.

Broadcasting & Cable Yearbook 1994
B-383

Virginia

Blackstone

WKLV(AM)—1947: 1440 khz; 5 kw-D. TL: N37 03 14 W78 01 15. Hrs opn: 6 AM-6 PM. Drawer 192 (23824). (804) 292-4146. FAX: (804) 292-7669. Licensee: Denbar Communications Inc. (acq 7-26-91; $175,000 with co-located FM; FTR 6-10-91). Rep: Dora-Clayton. Format: Oldies, gospel. Target aud: 25-54. ■ Dennis Royer, pres; Barbara Royer, gen mgr.

WBBC-FM—Co-owned with WKLV(AM). Nov 17, 1975: 93.5 mhz; 1.8 kw. Ant 370 ft. TL: N37 03 14 W78 01 15. Dups AM 40%. Format: Oldies, Black. News progmg 3 hrs wkly. Target aud: 25-54; middle class, with two cars, homeowners. Spec prog: Sports 10 hrs wkly. ■ Gary Taggart, progmg dir.

Bluefield

WHYS(AM)—Nov 17, 1980: 1190 khz; 10 kw-D, DA. TL: N37 16 19 W81 19 05. Box 509 (24605). (703) 326-2207; (304) 327-7114. FAX: (304) 325-7850. Licensee: Bluefield Broadcasting Co. Inc. Net: SMN. Rep: Rgnl Reps. Wash atty: Gardner, Carton & Douglas. Format: Country. News staff 2; news progmg 18 hrs wkly. Target aud: 25 plus; working & retired adults with disposable income. ■ Frank Barnes Jr., pres & gen mgr; Dave Kirby, stn mgr; John Bowen, prom mgr & mus dir; Kurt Pickering, news dir; Keith Bowman, chief engr.

WBDY-FM—Co-owned with WHYS(AM). December 1970: 106.3 mhz; 3 kw. Ant 1,122 ft. TL: N37 15 30 W81 10 36. Stereo. Hrs opn: 24. Dups AM 98%. (800) 487-1063. News progmg 17 hrs wkly.

Bridgewater

WAMM-FM—Mar 3, 1989: 105.1 mhz; 6 kw. Ant 328 ft. TL: N38 24 30 W78 54 04. Stereo. Hrs opn: 24. Box 392, 3180 S. Main St., Harrisonburg (22801). (703) 433-9735. FAX: (703) 433-7438. Licensee: WRDJ Inc. (acq 1993; $10,000 with WHBG[AM] Harrisonburg; FTR 9-13-93). Net: Unistar. Format: Contemp country. Target aud: 25-54. ■ Robert L. Dean, pres, gen mgr & chief engr; Kenneth W. Dean, exec vp; Gene Hoover, opns dir & progmg dir; Ron Reedy, gen sls mgr. ■ Rates: $15; 10; 15; na.

Bristol

WBCV(AM)—See Bristol, Tenn.

WOPI(AM)—Licensed to Bristol. See Bristol, Tenn.

WQUT(FM)—See Johnson City, Tenn.

WXBQ(AM)—January 1947: 980 khz; 5 kw-D, 1 kw-N, DA-N. TL: N36 36 30 W82 09 36. Hrs opn: 24. Box 1389, 901 E. Valley Dr. (24201). (703) 669-8112. Licensee: Bristol Broadcasting Inc. Group owner: Nininger Stns. (acq 1972). Net: ABC/I. Rep: McGavren Guild. Wash atty: Fisher, Wayland & Cooper. Format: News/talk, sports. ■ W.L. Nininger, pres; Bill Blake, gen mgr; Steve Blevins, opns dir.

WXBQ-FM—See Bristol, Tenn.

WZAP(AM)—1946: 690 khz; 10 kw-D, 14 w-N. TL: N36 37 51 W82 09 53. Hrs opn: 6 AM-midnight. Box 369, 180 Wallace Pike (24203). (703) 669-6950; (703) 669-6900. FAX: (703) 669-0794. Licensee: RAM Communications Inc. (acq 1-1-77; $375,000). Net: USA. Rep: J.C. Gates. Wash atty: Brown, Finn & Nietert. Format: Relg. News progmg 8 hrs wkly. Target aud: General. ■ R. A. Morris, pres, gen mgr & gen sls mgr; Tommy Tester, prom mgr & progmg dir; Glen Harlow, mus dir; Al Morris, news dir; Tim Hickman, pub affrs dir; John Faniola, chief engr. ■ Rates: $10; 8; 10; 8.

Broadway

WLTK(FM)—Licensed to Broadway. See Broadway-Timberville.

Broadway-Timberville

WBTX(AM)—May 18, 1972: 1470 khz; 5 kw-D. TL: N38 37 24 W78 48 52. Box 337, 166 Main St., Broadway (22815). (703) 896-8933. FAX: (703) 896-1448. Licensee: Massanutten Broadcasting Co. Inc. Net: CBN. Wash atty: David Tillotson. Format: Southern gospel. News progmg 8 hrs wkly. Target aud: 25-54; young adult through elderly. ■ David Eshleman, pres & gen mgr; Jim Snavely, opns mgr, progmg dir, mus & news dir; Bill Fawcett, chief engr. ■ Rates: $14.50; 12.50; 14.50; na.

WLTK(FM)—(Broadway). Co-owned with WBTX(AM). Dec 18, 1989: 96.1 mhz; 2.6 kw. Ant 1,000 ft. TL: N38 33 50 W78 57 00. Stereo. Net: CBN. Format: Contemp Christian. News progmg 9 hrs wkly. Target aud: 18-34. ■ Brad Huddleston, opns dir; David M. Eshleman, gen sls mgr; Brian Charrette, mus dir. ■ Rates: $16.50; 13.50; 16.50; 13.

Buena Vista

WREL-FM—1981: 96.7 mhz; 3 kw. Ant 154 ft. TL: N37 46 09 W79 21 35 (CP: 10 kw, ant 492 ft., TL: N37 46 37 W79 12 18). Stereo. Drawer 902, Lexington (24450). (703) 463-2161. FAX: (703) 463-4093. Licensee: Equus Communications (acq 9-85; $158,000; FTR 6-10-85). Net: AP, MBS. Rep: Southern. Format: Rock, adult contemp. Spec prog: Farm 3 hrs wkly. ■ Kian Putbrese, pres & gen mgr; Anthony Vita, opns dir; Elsworth Neff, chief engr.

Buffalo Gap

WSKO(FM)—1988: 105.5 mhz; 3 kw. Ant 308 ft. TL: N38 10 55 W79 13 34. Stereo. Hrs opn: 24. Suite 200, 15 Campbell St., Luray (22835); 2304 W. Beverley, Staunton (24401). (703) 886-9325. Licensee: Tschudy Communications Corp. (group owner). Format: Hot adult contemp. ■ Earl Judy Jr., pres & gen mgr; Gary Kirtley, gen sls mgr; Jim Richards, progmg dir; Rick Williams, chief engr.

Cape Charles

WROX-FM—Licensed to Cape Charles. See Virginia Beach.

Cedar Bluff

WBBY(FM)—1989: 107.7 mhz; 550 w. Ant 751 ft. TL: N37 09 49 W81 46 06. Box 509, Bluefield (24605). (703) 326-2207. FAX: (304) 325-7850. Licensee: Bluefield Broadcasting Co. Inc. (group owner; acq 1993; $150,000; FTR 9-6-93). Format: Country. ■ Frank Barnes, gen mgr; John Bowen, progmg dir; Keith Bowen, chief engr.

WYRV(AM)—March 1985: 770 khz; 5 kw-D. TL: N37 05 05 W81 46 07. Hrs opn: Sunrise-sunset. Box 1206, Middle Creek Rd. (24609). (703) 964-9619. FAX: (703) 964-9610. Licensee: Cedar Bluff Broadcasting Inc. Format: Southern gospel. News staff one; news progmg 3 hrs wkly. Target aud: 30 plus. ■ Acie T. Rasnake, pres; H. David Taylor, gen mgr; Denise Rasnake, adv mgr; Kenneth A. Rasnake, mus dir; Acie Rasnake, chief engr.

Charlottesville

WCHV(AM)—1930: 1260 khz; 5 kw-D, 2.5 kw-N, DA-2. TL: N38 06 52 W78 27 18. Stereo. Hrs opn: 24. 1140 Rose Hill Dr. (22903). (804) 977-5566. FAX: (804) 977-0747. Licensee: Eure Communications (group owner; acq 4-21-88). Net: CNN. Rep: Christal. Format: Oldies. Target aud: 25-49. ■ W. Bradford Eure, pres & gen mgr; Jacquie Walker, progmg dir; Robert Alexander, chief engr.

WWWV(FM)—Co-owned with WCHV(AM). 1959: 97.5 mhz; 50 kw. Ant 450 ft. TL: N38 01 49 W78 25 07. Stereo. Hrs opn: 24. Format: Adult rock. Target aud: 18-49. ■ Mark Conner, prom mgr; Tom Bass, progmg dir; Debbie Gilbert, mus dir.

WCYK(AM)—See Crozet.

WCYK-FM—See Crozet.

WINA(AM)—Sept 1949: 1070 khz; 5 kw-U, DA-N. TL: N38 05 22 W78 30 14. Box 498 (22902). (804) 977-3030. FAX: (804) 977-3775. Licensee: Charlottesville Broadcasting Corp. (acq 1969). Net: CBS; Va. News Net. Format: MOR. Spec prog: Farm 4 hrs wkly. ■ Laurence E. Richardson, pres; Colin Rosse, exec vp & gen mgr; Barbara Marshall, gen sls mgr; Dann Miller, progmg dir; Sarah McConnell, news dir; Alan Williams, chief engr.

WQMZ(FM)—Co-owned with WINA(AM). Oct 1954: 95.1 mhz; 6 kw. Ant 145 ft. TL: N38 02 54 W78 28 12. Stereo. Prog sep from AM. Format: Adult contemp.

WKAV(AM)—October 1957: 1400 khz; 1 kw-U. TL: N38 01 49 W78 29 22. Hrs opn: 24. Box 498 (22902). (804) 977-3030. FAX: (804) 977-3775. Licensee: Charlottesville Broadcasting Corp. (acq 5-15-93; $115,000; FTR 5-24-93). Net: SMN. Format: Easy listening. Target aud: 25-54. ■ Laurence E. Richardson, pres; Colin Rosse, exec vp & gen mgr; Barbara Marshall, gen sls mgr; Dann Miller, progmg dir; Sarah McConnell, news dir; Alan Williams, chief engr. ■ Rates: $15; 12; 12; 12.

WQMZ(FM)—Listing follows WINA(AM).

Directory of Radio

***WTJU(FM)**—May 10, 1957: 91.1 mhz; 1.5 kw. Ant 305 ft. TL: N38 01 57 W78 31 21. Stereo. Hrs opn: 24. 711 Newcomb Hall Stn. (22904). (804) 924-0885. Licensee: Univ. of Virginia. Format: Multi-format, alternative rock, class., folk, pub affrs. ■ Jennifer Meyer, CFO, dev dir, mktg dir & prom dir; Charles Taylor III, stn mgr; Mike Firends, opns mgr; Charles W. Taylor III, chief opns; Tom Morgan, progmg dir; Steve Graziano, D.V. Schanck, Charley Curtis, mus dirs; Ann Whitfield, Terry Grant, Harold Timmeny, asst mus dirs; Roma Marling, pub affrs dir; Mike Friend, chief engr.

WUVA(FM)—June 22, 1979: 92.7 mhz; 220 w. Ant 3,000 ft. TL: N37 59 06 W78 28 51. Stereo. Hrs opn: 6 AM-1 AM. Stn. No. One (22904). (804) 924-3194. FAX: (804) 296-6397. Licensee: WUVA Inc. Net: ABC, Westwood One. Format: CHR. News staff 20; news progmg 20 hrs wkly. Target aud: 18-49. ■ Joseph Walker, CEO, exec vp & gen mgr; Daryl Lewis, chmn; Robert Shear, pres; Lisa Speakman, CFO; Cortland Putbrese, gen sls mgr; Fred Keel, progmg dir; Michael Neal, Valerie Cox, progmg mgrs; Beth Gaston, mus dir; Rahul Keshap, news dir; Charles Perry, chief engr. ■ Rates: $10; 9; 10; 7.

WVSY(FM)—(Ruckersville). Mar 29, 1990: 101.9; 6 kw. Ant 223 ft. TL: N38 13 06 W78 22 03. Hrs opn: 24. Box 7932, Charlottesville (22906). (804) 973-2200. FAX: (804) 973-7308. Licensee: Ridge Broadcasting Corp. (acq 8-90; FTR 8-20-90). Net: NBC, Westwood One. Wash atty: Borsari, Paxson. Format: Adult contemp. News progmg 5 hrs wkly. Target aud: 30 plus; middle to upper middle class. ■ Ronald H. Fries, vp; Susn McCurry, gen sls mgr; Ronald Fries, natl sls mgr & engrg dir; Bobbi Deshae, prom dir; Theresa Cates, progmg dir; Julie Freda, pub affrs dir. ■ Rates: $20; 15; 15; 10.

***WVTU(FM)**—Jan 8, 1991: 89.3 mhz; 195 w-H, 160 w-V. Ant 1,696 ft. TL: N38 03 58 W78 47 54 (CP: 3.2 kw). Stereo. Rebroadcasts WVTF(FM) Roanoke, 100%. 4235 Electric Rd. S.W., Roanoke (24014). (703) 231-8900. FAX: (703) 857-7578. Licensee: Virginia Tech Foundation Inc. Net: NPR, APR, Va. News Net. Wash atty: Dow, Lohnes & Albertson. Format: Educ, div. ■ Steve Mills, gen mgr; Seth Williamson, mus dir; Rick Mattoni, news dir; Paxton Durham, chief engr.

WWWV(FM)—Listing follows WCHV(AM).

Chase City

WFXQ(FM)—Feb 1, 1994: 99.9 mhz; 12 kw. Ant 469 ft. TL: N36 48 13 W78 21 02. (CP: 99.9 FM N36 48 17 W78 20 59). Stereo. Rt. 3, Box 1403 (23924). (804) 372-2700. Licensee: Patricia B. Wagstaff. Format: Country. ■ John W. Wagstaff Jr., CEO; Patricia B. Wagstaff, pres; Polly Davis, gen mgr.

WMEK(AM)—Jan 18, 1959: 980 khz; 500 w-D. TL: N36 48 22 W78 26 22. Box 697, Rt. 47 E. (23924). (804) 372-3141. Licensee: West Mecklenburg Broadcasting Inc. (acq 3-86; $180,000; FTR 3-3-86). Net: UPI. Rep: T-N. Format: Country, talk. News staff 2; news progmg 20 hrs wkly. Target aud: General. Spec prog: Black 3 hrs, gospel 5 hrs, farm 3 hrs wkly. ■ Lee Payne, pres & gen mgr; Darlene Jones, progmg dir.

Chatham

WKBY(AM)—June 8, 1966: 1080 khz; 1 kw-D. TL: N36 46 54 W79 23 29. Rt. 2, Box 105A (24531). (804) 432-8108. FAX: (804) 432-1523. Licensee: William L. Bonner (acq 11-15-90; $250,000; FTR 12-3-90). Format: Black. News staff one. ■ William L. Bonner, pres; Harold James, gen sls mgr; Vicky Pritchett, progmg dir & mus dir.

Chesapeake

***WFOS(FM)**—Sept 14, 1973: 88.7 mhz; 15 kw. Ant 172 ft. TL: N76 18 03 W36 43 18. Stereo. 1617 Cedar Rd. (23320-7111). (804) 547-1036; (804) 547-0134. FAX: (804) 436-9320. Licensee: Chesapeake School Board. Net: MBS. Format: Class, big band. Target aud: High school. ■ C. Fred Bateman, pres; Dave Desler, gen mgr & chief engr; Dennis McCurdy, progmg dir & news dir.

WJQI(AM)—1967: 1600 khz; 5 kw-D. TL: N36 48 10 W76 16 58. Suite 95, 5544 Greenwich Rd., Virginia Beach (23462). (804) 671-9490. FAX: (804) 456-5090. Licensee: Radio WJQI Inc. (acq 12-30-86). Net: Unistar. Rep: D & R Radio. Format: Adult contemp. ■ Aylett B. Coleman, pres; Scott Quesinberry, vp; Meredith Coleman, stn mgr; Jim Wiggins, gen sls mgr; Rick Dillow, prom mgr; Bill Campbell, progmg mgr; Jennifer Ashley, news dir & pub affrs dir; Mike Settles, chief engr.

WMYK(FM)—See Moyock, N.C.

Chester

WGGM(AM)—Sept 1964: 820 khz; 10 kw-D, 1 kw-N, DA-2. TL: N37 22 58 W77 25 21. Hrs opn: 24. 10600 Jefferson Davis Hwy., Richmond (23237). (804) 275-6161. Licensee: Hoffman Communications. Group owner: Hoffman Communications/Hoffman Media Inc. (acq 10-76). Net: CNN. Wash atty: Steve Yelverton. Format: Relg. Target aud: 25-49. ■ Hurbert Hoffman, pres; Paul Scott Bulifant, vp & gen mgr; Rob Witham, mus dir. ■ Rates: $15.50; 15.50; 15.50; 15.50.

WDYL(FM)—Co-owned with WGGM(AM). Dec 1968: 92.1 mhz; 3 kw. Ant 356 ft. TL: N37 22 58 W77 25 41 (CP: 93.1 mhz, 1.35 kw, ant 492 ft.). Stereo. Prog sep from AM. Format: Relg. ■ Rates: $17.50; 17.50; 17.50; 17.50.

Christiansburg

WBNK(FM)—1990: 100.7 mhz; 3 kw. Ant 328 ft. TL: N37 08 01 W80 21 17. Hrs opn: 17. 485 Tower Rd. (24073). (703) 382-4993. FAX: (703) 381-2932. Licensee: Valley Radio Corp. (acq 9-1-92). Net: Va. News Net. Format: Country. News progmg 7 hrs wkly. Target aud: 25 plus. ■ Bob Travis, pres; Karen Travis, gen mgr & gen sls mgr; Sandy Duke, prom mgr; Garret Fuller, progmg dir.

WJJJ(AM)—October 1954: 1260 khz; 2.5 kw-D, 28 w-N. TL: N37 09 11 W80 24 57. Hrs opn: 19. Box 30, 1780 N. Franklin (24073). (703) 382-4993; (703) 382-4994. FAX: (703) 381-0581. Licensee: Blacksburg-Christiansburg Broadcasting Co. (acq 9-8-93) $512,500 with WVVV[FM] Blacksburg; FTR 10-4-93). Net: ABC/D, BRN. Format: Oldies. News progmg 20 hrs wkly. Target aud: 30-54; business professionals. ■ W.R. Rollins, pres; Ralph N. Stewart, gen mgr; Ron Dayle, gen sls mgr; Kevin Walsh, progmg dir. ■ Rates: $12; 10; 12; 10.

WVVV(FM)—See Blacksburg.

Churchville

WBOP(FM)—Licensed to Churchville. See Harrisonburg.

WNLR(AM)—Mar 9, 1962: 1150 khz; 2.5 kw-D, 30 w-N. TL: N38 12 39 W79 07 53. Box 400 (24421). (703) 885-8600. FAX: (703) 886-3624. Licensee: Blue Ridge Broadcasting Inc. (acq 5-26-81). Net: Moody. Format: Relg, adult contemp. Target aud: General. ■ Alan J. Carter, pres & gen mgr; Tom Watson, gen sls mgr; Russ Whitesell, progmg dir, mus dir & news dir; Bill Fawcett, chief engr.

Claremont

WARO(AM)—Not on air, target date unknown: 670 khz; 20 kw-D. TL: N37 14 54 W76 55 02. 205 N. Evergreen St., Arlington (22203). Licensee: Ultimate High Fidelity Medium Inc. Wash atty: Harold McCombs, Jr./Holland & Knight.

Clarksville

WLCQ(FM)—Jan 1, 1984: 98.3 mhz; 17.5 kw. Ant 394 ft. TL: N36 44 24 W78 44 49 (CP: 25 kw, ant 328 ft.). Stereo. Hrs opn: 24. Box 983, 912 Virginia Ave. (23927). (804) 374-2157. FAX: (804) 374-0146. Licensee: Clarksville Broadcasting Co. Inc. Net: ABC/I. Rep: T N, Keystone (unwired net). Format: Adult contemp & oldies. News progmg 16 hrs wkly. Target aud: 25-54. ■ Robert R. Boyd, pres; Randy Jones, stn mgr, progmg dir & mus dir; Scott Poe, opns mgr & prom mgr; Melvina Wright, gen sls mgr; Dwain Rash, mktg dir; Jon Bennett, chief engr. ■ Rates: $14; 12; 14; 11.

Clifton Forge

WXCF(AM)—Oct 19, 1950: 1230 khz; 1 kw-U, DA-1. TL: N37 49 18 W79 48 46. Box 104, 1047 Ingalls St. (24422). (703) 862-5751. FAX: (703) 862-2120. Licensee: Impact Broadcasting (acq 2-1-85); grpsl; FTR 12-31-84). Net: CNN. Format: Country. Target aud: 18-54. ■ Gerald K. Gimmel, pres; T.G. Ailstock, gen mgr; Kevin Tanner, prom dir & news dir; Rita Kay, mus dir; Mark Smith, chief engr.

WXCF-FM—Nov 20, 1982: 103.9 mhz; 150 w. Ant 1,909 ft. TL: N37 54 12 W82 21 37. Stereo. Dups AM 100%.

Clinchco

WDIC(AM)—May 1961: 1430 khz; 5 kw-D, DA-1. TL: N37 08 42 W82 23 22. Hrs opn: 14. Box 412, Route 1, Clintwood (24228). (703) 835-8626. FAX: (703) 835-8627. Licensee: Richard E. Edwards (acq 1-84); $366,850; FTR 10-30-84). Net: SMN, ABC. Wash atty: Gary Smithwick. Format: Country. News staff one; news progmg 8 hrs wkly. Target aud: General. Spec prog: Farm one hr, relg 12 hrs wkly. ■ Richard W. Edwards, pres; Rufus E. Nickles, gen mgr, gen sls mgr & prom mgr; Betty N. Fleming, progmg dir & mus dir; Gerald Hibbitts, chief engr. ■ Rates: $4.70; 4.70; 4.70; 4.70.

WDIC-FM—July 2, 1989: 93.1 mhz; 2.5 kw. Ant 505 ft. TL: N37 08 42 W82 23 22. Stereo. Net: SMN, ABC. Format: Oldies. Target aud: 25-55. ■ Rufus E. Nickles, stn mgr; Betty N. Fleming, opns mgr, natl sls mgr, rgnl sls mgr & progmg mgr. ■ Rates: $6; 6; 6; 6.

Coeburn

WZQK(FM)—Apr 15, 1991: 99.7 mhz; 3 kw. Ant 2,850 ft. TL: N36 56 44 W82 29 50. Stereo. Box 150 (24230). (703) 395-3997. FAX: (703) 395-5477. Licensee: Preston Communications Group Inc. Net: USA. Format: Adult Contemp hit. Target aud: 18-44. ■ Preston L. Salyer, pres & gen mgr; Kevin Castle, opns mgr; Al LeFevere, chief engr.

Collinsville

WFIC(AM)—Mar 1, 1970: 1530 khz; 1 kw-D, 250 w-CH. TL: N36 42 56 W79 55 15. Box 475, Endless Rd. (24078). (703) 647-1530; (703) 647-1018. Licensee: Scotts Radio Enterprises Inc. (acq 1-88). Net: USA. Format: Bluegrass. ■ Lester L. Williams, pres & gen mgr; Angelo Summers, gen sls mgr; Pam Epperson, prom mgr; Earl Shelton, progmg dir; Troy Spencer, chief engr.

Colonial Beach

WGRQ(FM)—May 3, 1986: 95.9 mhz; 6 kw. Ant 524 ft. TL: N38 13 38 W77 06 58. Stereo. Hrs opn: 24. Box 689, Rt. 3, The Village Ctr., King George (22485). (703) 775-3744; (703) 899-6474. FAX: (703) 775-4402. Licensee: Telemedia Broadcasting Inc. Group owner: Capital Radio Holdings Inc. (acq 1-20-88). Net: SMN. Format: Hot adult contemp. News staff one; news progmg 3 hrs wkly. Target aud: 18-34; upwardly mobile young adults with above average income. ■ Carl W. Hurlebaus, pres; Thomas P. Cooper, gen mgr; Martin Green, progmg dir; Lori Kelly, news dir. ■ Rates: $25; 20; 23; 20.

Colonial Heights

WKHK(FM)—Licensed to Colonial Heights. See Richmond.

WSTK(AM)—Licensed to Colonial Heights. See Richmond.

Covington

WKEY(AM)—May 23, 1941: 1340 khz; 1 kw-U. TL: N37 46 09 W79 58 59. Hrs opn: 24. Box 710, 508 Oak St. (24426). (703) 962-1133. Licensee: WKEY Inc. (acq 6-1-73). Net: ABC/E. Rep: T-N. Wash atty: Fletcher, Heald & Hildreth. Format: C&W. News staff one; news progmg 12 hrs wkly. Target aud: 25 plus; younger country listeners. Spec prog: Black one hr wkly. ■ Eddy Croy, pres; Denny Tincher, gen mgr & gen sls mgr; Dwight Rohr, news dir; Ranny Mason, chief engr.

WIQO-FM—Co-owned with WKEY(AM). October 1964: 100.9 mhz; 3 kw. Ant -255 ft. TL: N37 46 00 W79 59 05. Hrs opn: 24. Net: ABC/FM. Format: Young adult contemp. Target aud: 20-45; young professionals. ■ Rates: $5; 5; 5; 4.

Crewe

WSVS(AM)—April 7, 1947: 800 khz; 5 kw-D, 275 w-N. TL: N37 11 43 W78 10 01. 800 Melody Ln. (23930). (804) 645-7734. FAX: (804) 645-9185. Licensee: ABS Communications (acq 12-16-92; $3 million with co-located FM; FTR 1-11-93). Net: MBS; Agrinet Farm. Format: C&W. Spec prog: Farm 10 hrs wkly. ■ Polly Davis, gen mgr; Gary Taggart, mus dir.

WKIK(FM)—Co-owned with WSVS(AM). June 9, 1949: 104.7 mhz; 100 kw-H, 84 kw-V. Ant 981 ft. TL: N37 10 15 W77 57 16. Stereo. Dups AM 95%. (804) 645-7735.

Crozet

WCYK(AM)—Mar 16, 1970: 810 khz; 1 kw-D. TL: N38 04 00 W78 41 42. Suite 2, 1705 Seminole Trail, Charlottesville (22901). (804) 978-4408. FAX: (804) 978-1109. Licensee: High Communications Partnership. Group owner: High Media Group (acq 9-18-89); grpsl; FTR 7-31-89). Net: ABC. Rep: Katz & Powell. Wash atty: Robert Levine. Format: Contemp country. Target aud: 25-54. ■ Terry Kile, pres; Kevin Dalton, gen mgr; Mark Garwood, chief opns mgr; John Sandy, mktg dir; Greg Breeden, prom dir; Gina Rogers, progmg dir; Mike Todd, mus dir; Jon Bennett, chief engr.

WCYK-FM—September 1980: 102.3 mhz; 4.9 kw. Ant 360 ft. TL: N38 04 47 W78 44 22. Stereo. Hrs opn: 24. Prog dups AM 100%.

Culpeper

WCUL(FM)—Listing follows WCVA(AM).

WCVA(AM)—February 1949: 1490 khz; 1 kw-U. TL: N38 29 04 W77 59 22. Hrs opn: 19. Box 699, One Radio Lane (22701). (703) 825-3900. FAX: (703) 825-4237. Licensee: Culpeper Media Inc. (group owner; acq 9-1-89); grpsl; FTR 7-3-89). Net: ABC/E, Unistar, Va. News Net. Format: Adult contemp. News staff one; news progmg 10 hrs wkly. Target aud: General. ■ William D. Cannon, chmn; Jeff Petagna, gen mgr & opns mgr; Loretta Jamason, mktg mgr; India Barton, prom mgr & mus dir; Winn Reise, news dir & pub affrs dir.

WCUL(FM)—Co-owned with WCVA(AM). Dec 4, 1971: 103.1 mhz; 3 kw. Ant 300 ft. TL: N38 29 04 W77 59 22 (CP: 3.3kw). Stereo. Prog sep from AM. Net: CNN, Unistar. Format: Mod country. ■ Cheri Alyse, mus dir.

*WPVB(FM)—Not on air, target date unknown: 89.9 mhz; 12 kw. Ant 255 ft. TL: N38 40 42 W77 47 18. Box 889, Blacksburg (24060). (703) 552-4252. Licensee: Positive Alternative Radio Inc. ■ Vernon H. Baker, pres & chief engr.

Danville

WAKG(FM)—Listing follows WBTM(AM).

WBTM(AM)—May 24, 1930: 1330 khz; 5 kw-D, 1 kw-N, DA-N. TL: N36 36 36 W79 25 47. Stereo. Hrs opn: 24. Box 1629 (24543); 710 Grove St. (24541). (804) 793-4411. FAX: (804) 797-3918. Licensee: Piedmont Broadcasting Corp. Net: ABC/E, NBC Talknet. Format: Adult contemp. News staff 2; news progmg 5 hrs wkly. Target aud: 24 plus; young working adults. ■ T. David Luther, CEO, pres & gen mgr; Ben Davenport, chmn; Louis Dibrell, sr vp; Mylene Duffy, gen sls mgr & natl sls mgr; Carol Meetze, prom mgr; Alex Vardavas, progmg dir; Linwood Duncan, news dir; Johnny Cole, chief engr.

WAKG(FM)—Co-owned with WBTM(AM). June 3, 1968: 103.3 mhz; 100 kw. Ant 630 ft. TL: N36 44 28 W79 23 05. Stereo. Hrs opn: 24. Prog sep from AM. (804) 797-4290. Format: Modern country. Target aud: 18-54. ■ Dave Harville, stn mgr; Philip Watlington, mus dir.

WDVA(AM)—June 29, 1947: 1250 khz; 5 kw-U, DA-N. TL: N36 34 53 W79 26 33. Stereo. Box 1598 (24543). (804) 797-1250. Licensee: Mitchell Communications Inc. (acq 6-28-93; $100,000; FTR 7-19-93). Format: Gospel. ■ Fletcher Hubbard, gen mgr; Robert Tucker, progmg dir.

WILA(AM)—Aug 25, 1957: 1580 khz; 1 kw-D. TL: N36 34 03 W79 22 50. Box 3444, 865 Industrial Ave. (24543). (804) 792-2133. FAX: (804) 792-2134. Licensee: Tol-Tol Communications Inc. (acq 12-29-92; $205,000; FTR 1-25-93). Net: American Urban. Rep: Savalli. Format: Black. Target aud: General. ■ Lawrence Toller, pres; Leon Toller, progmg dir & mus dir; Sharhonda Hasper, news dir; Tim Walker, chief engr. ■ Rates: $8; 8; 8; na.

WVOV(AM)—Sept 7, 1959: 970 khz; 1 kw-D. TL: N36 33 34 W79 22 02. Box 3325 (24543); 414 N. Main St. (24540). (804) 793-9700. FAX: (804) 793-9709. Licensee: Danville Christian Radio Ltd. (acq 8-87). Format: Southern gospel, relg. ■ Tony Johnson, pres; David Parsons, gen mgr & progmg mgr; Sandra Wood, mus dir; Charlie Jones, chief engr.

Deltaville

WLUD(FM)—Not on air, target date unknown: 92.3 mhz; 3 kw. Ant 328 ft. TL: N37 31 24 W76 29 41. 2567J Mountain Lodge Cir., Birmingham, AL (35216). Licensee: Deltaville Communications.

Dillwyn

WVXE(FM)—Not on air, target date unknown: 93.7 mhz; 6 kw. Ant 1,656 ft. Suite 700, 1200 Nineteenth St. N.W., Washington, DC (20036). Licensee: Dillwyn Radio Co.

Dublin

WKNV(AM)—1994: 810 khz; 350 w-D, DA. TL: N37 08 26 W80 36 49. c/o Box 889, Blacksburg (24060). (703) 552-4252. Licensee: Dublin Radio dba Edward A. Baker. Wash atty: Booth, Freret & Imlay. ■ Edward A. Baker, pres, gen mgr & chief engr.

Virginia

WPIN(FM)—Not on air, target date unknown: 91.5 mhz; 100 w-H, 90 w-V. Ant 1,204 ft. TL: N37 01 27 W80 44 47. Box 889, Blacksburg (24060). (703) 552-4252. Licensee: Positive Alternative Radio Inc. (acq 6-16-92).

Duffield

WDUF(AM)—Aug 12, 1986: 1120 khz; 1 kw-D. TL: N36 42 30 W82 47 30. Box 391, Rt. 5 (24244). (703) 431-4357. Licensee: Duffield Broadcasting Co. Format: Bluegrass, gospel, news. News staff one; news progmg 28 hrs wkly. Target aud: General; miners, industrial & agricultural workers, seniors. Spec prog: Lunchtime farm & home progmg. ■ Jay Marion Smith, stn mgr; Arlene Smith, chief opns.

Dumfries-Triangle

WPWC(AM)—Dec 22, 1961: 1480 khz; 1 kw-D, 500 w-N, DA-2. TL: N38 34 06 W77 20 20. Hrs opn: 14. Box 189, 214 S. Main St., Dumfries (22026). (703) 221-1124; (703) 221-1480. Licensee: Happy Broadcasting Co. Inc. (acq 6-1-74). Net: USA. Format: Country, gospel. News staff 3; news progmg 6 hrs wkly. Target aud: General. Spec prog: Black 4 hrs, farm 3 hrs, relg 6 hrs, Sp one hr wkly. ■ Raymond Woolfenden Sr., pres, gen mgr & gen sls mgr; Doris Woolfenden, CFO; Raynee Woolfenden, progmg dir, mus dir & news dir; Kevin Strom, chief engr. ■ Rates: $7.50; 7.50; 7.50; na.

Earlysville

WKTR(AM)—Feb 17, 1991: 840 khz; 8.2 kw-D, DA. TL: N38 15 57 W78 24 53. Box 309, Quinque (24060). (804) 296-3300. Licensee: Rural Radio Service. Group owner: Baker Family Stations. Wash atty: Booth, Freret & Imlay. Format: Relg. ■ Edward A. Baker, pres; Tina Deane, stn mgr.

Elkton

WPKZ(FM)—Mar 6, 1989: 98.5 mhz; 900 w. Ant 1,607 ft. TL: N38 23 36 W78 46 14. Box 337 (22827). (703) 298-2001. FAX: (703) 298-2001. Licensee: Stonewall Broadcasting Co. (acq 1-31-89). Format: Country. ■ Ernest Evans, sr vp; Brenda Merica, vp; George Hume, gen mgr, opns mgr & progmg mgr; Ellsworth Neff, chief engr.

Emory

*WEHC(FM)—Not on air, target date unknown: 90.7 mhz; 100 w. Ant 95 ft. TL: N36 46 20 W81 49 56. Administration Bldg. (24327). Licensee: Emory and Henry College.

Emporia

WEVA(AM)—Nov 4, 1952: 860 khz; 1 kw-D. TL: N36 41 56 W77 32 55. Box 1056, 700 Washington St. (23847). (804) 634-2133. FAX: (804) 634-5050. Licensee: Stone Broadcasting Corp. Net: CBS. Wash atty: Wilkinson, Barker, Knauer & Quinn. Format: Adult contemp. News progmg 7 plus hrs wkly. Target aud: 25 plus. Spec prog: Farm one hr wkly. ■ Willis L. Stone, pres, gen mgr & mus dir; Susan Epps, gen sls mgr. ■ Rates: $11; 11; 11; 11.

WEVA-FM—Not on air, target date unknown: 99.5 mhz; 2 kw. Ant 403 ft. TL: N36 39 20 W77 34 22. ■ Willis L. Stone, gen mgr, mus dir, news dir & chief engr; Susan Epps, prom dir.

Exmore

WKRE-FM—1972: 107.5 mhz; 50 kw. Ant 259 ft. TL: N37 42 01 W75 41 36. Stereo. Hrs opn: 24. Box 220 (23350); Box 810, Pocomoke City (21851). (804) 787-1100; (410) 957-4300. FAX: (804) 787-9572; (410) 957-4930. Licensee: Bay Star Communications, Inc. Net: NBC. Wash atty: Cohn & Marks. Format: Adult contemp, oldies. News progmg 10 hrs wkly. Target aud: 25-54. Spec prog: Black 6 hrs, gospel 6 hrs wkly. ■ Klein G. Leister, pres; James D. Layton, gen mgr; Bill LeCato, prom mgr, progmg dir & mus dir; Jim Trotter, news dir.

WPHG(FM)—Not on air, target date unknown: 106.1 mhz; 25 kw. Ant 328 ft. TL: N37 33 15 W75 49 38. c/o Seashore Broadcasting Co., 2212 Old Court Rd., Baltimore, MD (21208). Licensee: Seashore Broadcasting Co.

Fairfax

WDCT(AM)—Sept 25, 1955: 1310 khz; 5 kw-D, 500 w-N, DA-2. TL: N38 51 08 W77 18 57. Hrs opn: 6 AM-midnight. Box 1310 (22030); 3909 Oak St. (22030). (703) 273-4000; (703) 273-9328. FAX: (703) 273-1015. Licensee: Children's Radio Group of Washington D.C. Inc. Group owner: Children's Broadcasting Corp. (acq 7-88). Net: USA, Moody. Wash atty: Putbrese, Hunsaker & Rudy. Format: Talk, info, news, inspiration, & sports. News staff one; news progmg 10 hrs wkly. Target aud: 25-54; 60% female, 40% male. Spec prog: Iranian 3 hrs wkly. ■ Christopher T. Dahl, CEO & chmn; Christopher T.V. Dahl, pres; James G. Gilbertson, CFO; Richard V. Marsh, vp; David F. Reeder, gen mgr & gen sls mgr; Bob Appel, opns dir & progmg dir; Debbie Brown, dev dir; Judy Palmore, mktg dir; Shannon Burke, prom dir; David Howe, mus dir; Danny Johnson, news dir; Lee Bailey, pub affrs dir; Ron Depas, chief engr. ■ Rates: $45; 35; 40; 30.

Fairlawn

WCQR(AM)—Not on air, target date unknown: 890 khz; 2.5 kw-D. TL: N37 08 26 W80 36 49. Box 889, Blacksburg (24063). (703) 552-4252. Licensee: Positive Radio Group Inc. Group owner: Baker Family Stations.

Falls Church

WFAX(AM)—Licensed to Falls Church. See Washington, D.C.

Farmville

WFLO(AM)—August 1947: 870 khz; 1 kw-D. TL: N37 18 38 W78 23 13. Hrs opn: Sunrise-sunset. Box 367, Rt. 45 N. (23901). (804) 392-4195. Licensee: Colonial Broadcasting Co. Inc. (acq 4-71). Net: UPI, Motor Racing Net.; Va. News Net. Format: C&W, news/talk. News staff one; news progmg 4 hrs wkly. Target aud: 25 plus. Spec prog: Relg 10 hrs wkly. ■ John D. Wilson, pres; Henry Fulcher, vp; Gene Eike, gen mgr & chief engr; Francis Wood, opns dir; T. J. Fulcher, gen sls mgr; Tom Jenkins, mus dir; Elliott Irving, news dir. ■ Rates: $8.50; 8.50; 8.50; 8.50.

WFLO-FM—May 1961: 95.7 mhz; 40 kw. Ant 340 ft. TL: N37 18 38 W78 23 13. Stereo. Hrs opn: 5 AM-11 PM. Prog sep from AM. Format: Adult contemp. ■ Francis Wood, progmg mgr; Chris Hay, mus dir. ■ Rates: Same as AM.

*WLCX(FM)—1988: 90.1 mhz; 10 w. Ant 26 ft. TL: N37 18 15 W78 26 05. Box 2903, Longwood College (23909). (804) 395-2475. Licensee: Longwood Radio Assoc. Format: College rock. ■ Ross Homer, gen mgr.

WPAK(AM)—June 15, 1978: 1490 khz; 1 kw-U. TL: N37 18 47 W78 23 41. 446 Plank Rd. (23901). (804) 392-8114. FAX: (804) 392-1080. Licensee: Rick R. Darnell (acq 6-90; $10,000; FTR 6-18-90). Format: Urban contemp. Spec prog: Farm one hr, gospel 12 hrs wkly. ■ Rick Darnell, pres, gen mgr & gen sls mgr; Perlina Cokran, prom mgr; Reginald Foster, progmg dir & mus dir; Jim Granger, chief engr.

Ferrum

*WFFC(FM)—January 1989: 89.9 mhz; 100 w. Ant -40 ft. TL: N36 55 46 W80 01 27. Stereo. Hrs opn: 16. WFFC Radio, Ferrum College (24088). (703) 365-4482; (703) 365-4483. FAX: (703) 365-5589. Licensee: Ferrum College. Format: Class, progsv. ■ Chuck Bailey, mus dir; Gab Enriquez, asst mus dir; Doug Mason, Tommy Campbell (asst), news dirs; Trey Cherry, Matt Seymor, pub affrs dirs; Paxton Durham, chief engr.

Fieldale

WODY(AM)—1993: 1160 khz; 5 kw-D, 250 w-N, DA-2. TL: N36 42 36 W79 57 58. Box 889, Blacksburg (24060). (703) 552-4252. Licensee: Radio Eleven Sixty. Group owner: Baker Family Stations. Format: Relg. ■ Vernon H. Baker, pres & gen mgr.

Floyd

WGFC(AM)—Apr 20, 1985: 1030 khz; 1 kw-D. TL: N36 55 53 W80 16 34. Box 495 (24091). (703) 745-9811. Licensee: Gallimore Electronics Inc. Format: C&W. News progmg 10 hrs wkly. Target aud: Local community interest & general audience. Spec prog: Gospel 18 hrs, relg 6 hrs, bluegrass 18 hrs wkly. ■ Gerald W. Gallimore, pres & gen mgr; Anthony V Gallimore, vp; Anthony V. Gallimore, opns mgr & mus dir; Dale W. Gallimore, gen sls mgr & chief engr; Marie V. Gallimore, progmg dir. ■ Rates: $9; 8; 9; na.

Franklin

WLQM(AM)—Oct 13, 1956: 1250 khz; 1 kw-D. TL: N36 40 57 W76 55 43. Box 735 (23851). (804) 562-5650. Licensee: Franklin Broadcasting Corp. (acq 8-10-59). Net: SMN. Format: Country, farm. News staff one. Target aud: 25-49. Spec prog: Gospel 12 hrs wkly. ■ Peter E. Clark, pres, gen mgr, gen sls mgr & news dir; Michael Clark, natl sls mgr & vp adv; Earl Hundley, rgnl sls mgr; Helen Day, prom mgr & progmg dir; Gloria Worrell, mus dir; Mickle Pruden, chief engr. ■ Rates: $10; 10; 10; 10.

WLQM-FM—Not on air, target date unknown: 101.7 mhz; 6 kw. Ant 469 ft. TL: N36 41 17 W77 00 58. Dups AM 100%. FAX: (804) 562-2345. Licensee: Franklin Broadcasting Corp. ■ Rates: Same as AM.

Fredericksburg

WBQB(FM)—Listing follows WFVA(AM).

WFLS(AM)—July 15, 1960: 1350 khz; 1 kw-D, 37 w-N. TL: N38 18 46 W77 26 20. Hrs opn: 24. 616 Amelia St. (22401). (703) 373-1500. FAX: (703) 373-8450. Licensee: The Free Lance-Star Publishing Co. Net: AP. Format: Country. News staff 3; news progmg 12 hrs wkly. Target aud: General. ■ Charles S. Rowe, pres; J. William Poole, gen mgr; James T. Butler, gen sls mgr; Jon Reed, progmg dir; Carolyn Taylor, mus dir; Sheila Quinn, news dir; Gary Harrison, chief engr.

WFLS-FM—June 12, 1962: 93.3 mhz; 50 kw. Ant 492 ft. TL: N38 18 46 W77 26 20. Stereo. Hrs opn: 24. Dups AM 100%. News staff 3; news progmg 12 hrs wkly. Target aud: General.

WFVA(AM)—Sept 8, 1939: 1230 khz; 1 kw-U. TL: N38 16 50 W77 26 11. Hrs opn: 24. Box 269, 1914 Mimosa (22405). (703) 373-7721. FAX: (703) 899-3879. Licensee: Mid-Atlantic Network Inc. (group owner). Net: ABC/E, ABC Talk, Mutual, Va. News Net. Format: MOR. News staff 3; news progmg 15 hrs wkly. Target aud: 35 plus. Spec prog: Farm one hr wkly. ■ John P. Lewis, pres; David P. Lewis, Howard P. Lewis, vps; Tom Scheithe, gen mgr; Mark Clifford, opns mgr; Shawn Sloan, gen sls mgr; Kat Kammer, rgnl sls mgr; Michelle Carpenter, news dir; Chris Wilk, chief engr. ■ Rates: $18; 18; 18; 9.

WBQB(FM)—Co-owned with WFVA(AM). May 15, 1960: 101.5 mhz; 50 kw. Ant 492 ft. TL: N38 19 57 W77 23 41. Stereo. Hrs opn: 24. Prog sep from AM. Format: Adult contemp. News staff 3; news progmg 8 hrs wkly. Target aud: 25-44. Spec prog: Relg 2 hrs wkly.

WGRQ(FM)—See Colonial Beach.

*WJYJ(FM)—May 6, 1983: 90.5 mhz; 18.5 kw. Ant 560 ft. TL: N38 11 48 W77 33 45. Stereo. Hrs opn: 24. Box 905, Spotsylvania (22553); 830 Gunnery Hill Rd., Spotsylvania (22553). (703) 582-5371. Licensee: Educational Media Corp. (acq 3-86). Net: Moody. Va. News Net. Format: Contemp Christian mus, news/talk, educ. News staff one; news progmg 14 hrs wkly. Target aud: 25-44; persons seeking God. ■ Peter D. Stover, pres; Joseph F. Stover, vp; Robert D. Davis, stn mgr; Ted Schubel, news dir; Dave Roycraft, chief engr.

Front Royal

WFQX(FM)—Jan 17, 1973: 99.3 mhz; 3 kw. Ant 295 ft. TL: N39 00 11 W78 20 28. Stereo. Hrs opn: 24. 381 Spinning Wheel Lane, Winchester (22601). (703) 465-9369. FAX: (703) 662-8610. Licensee: SRO/Nova Inc. (acq 10-10-85; $450,000; FTR 8-12-85). Net: NBC The Source, Westwood One. Format: Hot adult contemp. News staff one; news progmg 2 hrs wkly. Target aud: 18-42. ■ Charles Wolf, CE & pres; David Ridgeway, gen mgr; Chuck Carroll, opns dir; Nikki Ciattei, gen sls mgr, prom dir & adv dir; Kevin Edmonston, mus dir; Jennifer Lee, news dir; Fran Little, chief engr. ■ Rates: $16; 13; 15; 11.

WFTR(AM)—Sept 19, 1948: 1450 khz; 1 kw-U. TL: N38 54 31 W78 10 37. Hrs opn: 24. Box 192, 1106 Elm St. (22630). (703) 635-4121. FAX: (703) 635-9387. Licensee: Straus Communications in Virginia Inc. Group owner: Straus Media Group. Net: CNN, NBC Talknet, Unistar. Format: News/talk. News staff 2; news progmg 20 plus hrs wkly. Target aud: 25-54. Spec prog: Relg 2 hrs wkly. ■ R. Peter Strauss, chmn; Mike O'Dell, gen mgr & gen sls mgr; Jim Lawrence, opns mgr & mus dir; Vicky Sine, prom mgr; Brian Brehm, progmg dir; Dave Partenheimer, news dir & pub affrs dir; Mike Hurst, chief engr. ■ Rates: $20; 20; 20; 20.

WFTR-FM—1981: 95.3 mhz; 4 kw. Ant 300 ft. TL: N38 58 29 W78 12 09. Stereo. Hrs opn: 24. Dups AM 100%. (800) 782-7361. FAX: (800) 329-2953. (Acq 1973). Format: Adult contemp. Spec prog: Washington Redskins football. ■ Rates: Same as AM.

Galax

WBOB(AM)—Feb 1, 1947: 1360 khz; 5 kw-D. TL: N36 39 48 W80 54 52. Box 270, 325 Poplar Knob Rd. (24333). (703) 236-2921. Licensee: Twin County Broadcasting Corp. (acq 4-19-85; $200,000; FTR 4-8-85). Net: CBS. Va. News Net. Format: Adult contemp. News progmg 11 hrs wkly. Target aud: 18 plus. Spec prog: Farm one hr wkly. ■ Deborah E. Sizer, pres, gen mgr & progmg dir; J. Brice Parks, gen sls mgr; Buford Kegley, mus dir.

WBRF(FM)—Dec 15, 1961: 98.1 mhz; 100 kw. Ant 1,756 ft. TL: N36 34 50 W80 58 23. Stereo. Box 838, 325 Poplar Knob Rd. (24333). (703) 236-9273; (703) 236-7198. FAX: (703) 236-7198. Licensee: Blue Ridge Radio Inc. (acq 4-19-85; FTR 12-31-84). Net: UPI; Va. News Net. Format: C&W. Target aud: General. Spec prog: Pub affrs one hr wkly. ■ Ralph D. Epperson, pres; Debbie Robinson, gen mgr & gen sls mgr; Sonya Carlan, progmg dir; Phipps Caudell, chief engr.

***WPRH-FM**—Not on air, target date 1994: 91.1 mhz; 1 kw-H, 940 w-V. Ant 495 ft. TL: N36 39 27 W80 54 22. Box 889, Blacksburg (24060). (703) 552-8073. FAX: (703) 951-5282. Licensee: Golden Rule Organization Workshop Inc. Net: USA. ■ Vernon H. Baker, pres.

Gate City

WGAT(AM)—July 24, 1959: 1050 khz; 1 kw-D, 266 w-N. TL: N36 37 59 W82 34 56. Hrs opn: 24. Suite 2, 117 E., Jackson (24251). (703) 386-7025. FAX: (703) 386-3600. Licensee: Tri-Cities Broadcasting Corp. (acq 11-28-90; $70,000; FTR 12-17-90). Net: USA. Rep: Regl Reps. Wash atty: Dow, Lohnes & Albertson. Format: Bluegrass, relg, news/talk. News progmg 10 hrs wkly. Target aud: 25 plus. ■ Carol McConnell, pres & gen mgr; Herman Long, vp, gen sls mgr & prom mgr; Michael Long, progmg dir, mus dir, news dir & chief engr. ■ Rates: $7; 7; 7; 7.

Gloucester

WXGM(AM)—Jan 20, 1957: 1420 khz; 740 w-D. TL: N37 24 36 W76 32 52. Stereo. Hrs opn: 6 AM-7 PM. Rt. 17 N., Box 634 (23061). (804) 693-2105; (804) 693-9946. FAX: (804) 693-2182. Licensee: WXGM Inc. (acq 7-91; FTR 6-22-81). Net: Agri-Net, Va. News Net. Rep: T-N. Wash atty: Verner, Liipfert, Bernhard, McPherson & Hand. Format: Adult Contemporary. News staff one; news progmg 7 hrs wkly. Target aud: 25-54. Spec prog: Farm 2 hrs, relg 2 hrs wkly. ■ Thomas W. Robinson, pres & gen mgr; Harvey King, opns mgr, progmg dir & mus dir; Joe Baker, gen sls mgr; Herman King, news dir & pub affrs dir; Will Sommers, chief engr. ■ Rates: $18; 15; 18; 12.

WXGM-FM—July 29, 1991: 99.1 mhz; 6 kw. Ant 328 ft. TL: N37 24 36 W76 32 52. Stereo. Hrs opn: 24. Dups AM 100%. ■ Rates: $20; 18; 20; 12.

Gretna

WMNA(AM)—Aug 11, 1956: 730 khz; 1 kw-D, 28 w-N, DA-2. TL: N36 55 31 W79 19 50. Hrs opn: 6 AM-10 PM. Box 730, Zion Rd. (24557). (804) 656-1234; (804) 432-4730. Licensee: Central Virginia Broadcasting Co. Net: USA; Agri-Net. Rep: T-N. Wash atty: Reddy, Begley & Martin. Format: Country. News staff one; news progmg 19 hrs wkly. Target aud: 18-55; family groups. Spec prog: Farm 8 hrs, Black 2 hrs, bluegrass 15 hrs, gospel 15 hrs wkly. ■ Lyle C. Motley, CEO, pres, gen mgr, stn mgr & gen sls mgr; J.G. Aylor, chmn; Elton J. Toler, vp; Charlotte Wells, progmg dir; Charlotte B. Wells, mus dir; Sherri Yeatts, news dir. ■ Rates: $5.30; 5.30; 5;30; 5;30.

WMNA-FM—Feb 28, 1959: 106.3 mhz; 3 kw. Ant 260 ft. TL: N36 55 31 W79 19 50. Hrs opn: 5:30 AM-10 PM. Dups AM 75%. Net: Agri-Net. Format: Diverse. ■ Rates: Same as AM.

Grundy

WNRG(AM)—Nov 16, 1955: 940 khz; 5 kw-D, 14 w-N. TL: N37 18 08 W82 07 04. Box 2045 (24614). (703) 935-2587. Licensee: Virginia-Kentucky Broadcasting Co. Net: UPI. Format: MOR, C&W. Spec prog: Farm 5 hrs wkly. ■ Herman G. Dotson, pres; David B. Jordan, gen mgr; Ronald F. Cole, gen sls mgr & progmg dir; Marie Fair, mus dir; Gary D. Street, chief engr.

WMJD(FM)—Co-owned with WNRG(AM). June 21, 1965: 97.7 mhz; 1.4 kw. Ant 490 ft. TL: N37 18 08 W82 07 04. Stereo. Prog sep from AM. Box 1060 (24614). (703) 935-2816. Net: Unistar. Format: Top-40, MOR. News staff one. ■ David B. Jordan, gen mgr; Ruth Bish, opns mgr; Jill Meade, news dir.

Hampden-Sydney

***WWHS-FM**—Oct 11, 1972: 92.1 mhz; 10 w. Ant 140 ft. TL: N37 14 19 W78 27 48. Stereo. Box 606, Hampden-Sydney College (23943). (804) 223-6009. Licensee: Pres & Board of Trustees of Hampden-Sydney College. Format: Progsv. News progmg 5 hrs wkly. Target aud: 18-25; college community. Spec prog: Blues 2 hrs, class 2 hrs, jazz 6 hrs, reggae 4 hrs wkly. ■ Nole Bumpas, gen mgr; Lane Seely, progmg dir.

Hampton

***WHOV(FM)**—Mar 5, 1964: 88.1 mhz; 2 kw-H, 8 kw-V, Ant 200 ft. TL: N37 01 03 W76 20 13. Stereo. Hrs opn: 17. Dept. of Mass Media Arts, Hampton Univ. (23668). (804) 727-5670; (804) 727-5408. FAX: (804) 727-5084. Licensee: Hampton Univ. Format: Black, jazz, urban contemp. News progmg 5 hrs wkly. Target aud: 18-54; young adults and adults. Spec prog: Gospel 5 hrs, Sp 9 hrs, blues 3 hrs, reggae 3 hrs wkly. ■ Leon Scott, pres; Jay Wright, gen mgr, gen sls mgr, adv mgr & progmg dir; Dana Mapson, opns mgr; Jennifer Neal, prom dir; Veda Howard, Jason Baker, mus dirs; Shalonela Miller, Joelynn Clouser, news dirs; Robert Grau, chief engr.

WOJY(AM)—July 1, 1948: 1490 khz; 1 kw-U. TL: N37 01 46 W76 22 35. Hrs opn: 24. 32 E. Mellen St. (23663). (804) 728-3607. FAX: (804) 728-1922. Licensee: Hampton Radio Inc. (acq 12-9-86; $485,000; FTR 10-20-86). Net: USA. Format: Southern gospel. News staff one; news progmg 14 hrs wkly. Target aud: 25-54. ■ Kevin Kelley, progmg dir.

WWDE-FM—June 1, 1962: 101.3 mhz; 50 kw. Ant 499 ft. TL: N36 49 41 W76 15 05. Stereo. Hrs opn: 24. 2101 Executive Dr. (23666). (804) 838-4295. FAX: (804) 838-8261. Licensee: Max Radio of Hampton Inc. (acq 11-18-92; FTR 11-30-92). Net: CBS Spectrum. Rep: Christal. Wash atty: Bryan, Cave, McPheeters & McRoberts. Format: Adult contemp. ■ Dick Lamb, Krissy Hoffman (exec sec), gen mgrs; Chris Wilson, prom mgr; Steve Shaw, mus dir; Laura Coffey, news dir; Ernie Warinner, chief engr.

Harrisonburg

WBOP(FM)—(Churchville). Mar 2, 1991: 106.3 mhz; 10 kw. Ant 328 ft. TL: N38 09 52 W79 08 24. Stereo. Suite 325, 1790-10 E. Market St., Harrisonburg (22801); 639 N. Main St., Mt. Crawford (22841). (703) 432-1063. Licensee: Peter Wayne Lechman. Wash atty: Jeff Southmayd. Format: Oldies based adult contemp. News staff one; news progmg 7 hrs wkly. Target aud: 25-54. ■ Tom Manley, gen mgr & gen sls mgr; Rich Randall, progmg dir & mus dir; Dan Wright, news dir. ■ Rates: $22; 18; 22; 18.

***WEMC(FM)**—1955: 91.7 mhz; 100 w. Ant 205 ft. TL: N38 28 16 W78 52 57 (CP: 1.85 kw, 304 ft., TL: N38 28 20 W78 52 57). Stereo. Hrs opn: 6 AM-1 AM. Eastern Mennonite College, 1200 Park Rd. (22801). (703) 432-4288; (703) 432-4287. FAX: (703) 432-4444. Licensee: Eastern Mennonite College Inc. Wash atty: Booth, Freret & Imlay. Format: Relg, educ, class. News progmg 15 hrs wkly. Target aud: Wide variety of all ages. Spec prog: Bluegrass 6 hrs, childrens 2 hrs, jazz 2 hrs, gospel 8 hrs wkly. ■ Douglas D. King, gen mgr, stn mgr & progmg dir; Steve Farrar, Chris Scott, mus dirs; Steve Farrar, asst mus dir & pub affrs dir; Kim Atkins, news dir; Harold D. Kuhns, chief engr.

WHBG(AM)—August 1956: 1360 khz; 4.7 kw-D, 20 w-N. TL: N38 24 30 W78 54 04. Stereo. Hrs opn: 24. Box 392, 3180 S. Main St. (22801). (703) 434-9424. FAX: (703) 433-7438. Licensee: WHBG Inc. (acq 1993; $10,000 with WRDJ-FM Bridgewater; FTR 9-13-93). Net: Unistar. Format: C&W. Target aud: 24-50. ■ Robert L. Dean, pres, gen mgr & chief engr; Gene Hoover, opns dir, progmg dir & news dir; Ron Ready, gen sls mgr. ■ Rates: $10; 7; 10; 7.

WKCY(AM)—May 11, 1967: 1300 khz; 5 kw-D. TL: N38 27 52 W78 50 53. Stereo. Box 1107, Suite 200-202, 207 University Blvd. (22801). (703) 434-1777. FAX: (703) 432-9968. Licensee: Mid Atlantic Network. (group owner; acq 3-17-89). Format: Country, talk. News staff one; news progmg 4 hrs wkly. Target aud: 25-54. Spec prog: Farm one hr wkly. ■ John P. Lewis, pres; Frank W. Kelley, gen mgr; Delena Kelley, gen sls mgr; Sue Snyder, prom dir; Dusty Rhodes, progmg dir; David Burman, news dir; Archie McKay, engrg dir. ■ Rates: $30; 26; 30; 18.

WKCY-FM—November 1980: 104.3 mhz; 50 kw. Ant 409 ft. TL: N38 23 40 W79 08 26. Stereo. Hrs opn: 24. Dups AM 100%. Net: Mid Atlantic Net. Target aud: 25-54.

***WMRA(FM)**—June 18, 1969: 90.7 mhz; 24.5 kw. Ant 710 ft. TL: N38 33 40 W78 56 56 (CP: 7.5 kw, ant 1,046 ft.). Stereo. 821 S. Main St. (22807). (703) 568-6221. FAX: (703) 568-6920. Licensee: Board of Visitors of James Madison University. Net: NPR, AP. Format: Class, news & info. News staff one. Spec prog: Folk 20 hrs wkly. ■ Brenda Hankey, gen mgr; Robert L. Howerton, dev dir; Sheila Rue, progmg dir; Steve Coghill, mus dir; Phil Picardi, news dir; Chuck Slott, pub affrs dir; William D. Fawcett, engrg dir.

WQPO(FM)—Listing follows WSVA(AM).

WSVA(AM)—June 9, 1935: 550 khz; 5 kw-D, 1 kw-N, DA-N. TL: N38 27 04 W78 54 29. Hrs opn: 24. Box 752, Rawley Pike (22801). (703) 434-0331. FAX: (703) 434-7087. Licensee: M. Belmont VerStandig Inc. Group owner: VerStandig Broadcasting (acq 4-17-87). Net: NBC Talknet, ABC/I; Va. News Net. Format: News/talk. News staff 5. Target aud: 35 plus. Spec prog: Farm 8 hrs wkly. ■ John D. VerStandig, pres; R. David Ridgeway, vp; Susan Mowbrary, gen mgr; Robert MacNeil, opns dir; Steve Knupp, progmg dir; Tim Allan, mus dir.

WQPO(FM)—Co-owned with WSVA(AM). Dec 3, 1946: 100.7 mhz; 50 kw. Ant 492 ft. TL: N38 27 08 W78 54 32 (CP: 3.8 kw, ant 1,617 ft., TL: N38 23 37 W78 46 14). Stereo. Hrs opn: 24. Prog sep from AM. Net: ABC/C. Format: CHR. News staff 3. ■ Steve Knupp, opns dir.

***WXJM(FM)**—September 1990: 88.7 mhz; 390 w. Ant 62 ft. TL: N38 26 22 W78 52 21. Stereo. Anthony Seeger Hall., James Madison Univ. (22807). (703) 568-6878; (703) 568-3425. FAX: (703) 568-6920. Licensee: Board of Trustees, James Madison Univ. (acq 9-1-89). Format: Alternative. Target aud: James Madison Univ. students. ■ Brenda Hankey, gen mgr; Steven Coghill, progmg dir; Don Mussell, chief engr.

Highland Springs

WCLM(AM)—May 18, 1959: 1450 khz; 960 kw-U. TL: N37 32 39 W77 20 47. 4719 Nine Mile Rd., Richmond (23223). (804) 236-0532. Licensee: Momentum Broadcasting Inc. (acq 4-88). Net: CNN. Format: Jazz. Target aud: 25-55; upscale, active, educated, consumer oriented. ■ Reggie Turner, pres; Wayne Williams, gen mgr; Bernie Braun, chief engr.

***WHCE(FM)**—Sept 29, 1980: 91.1 mhz; 3 kw. Ant 103 ft. TL: N37 32 18 W77 19 27. Box 99, Highland Springs Tech. Center, 100 Tech Dr. (23075). (804) 328-4075; (804) 328-4078. Licensee: Henrico County Schools. Format: CHR. News progmg 2 hrs wkly. Target aud: 12-20; teenagers, young adults. ■ Bob Kaufman, gen mgr & progmg dir; Keith Fields, chief engr.

Hillsville

WHHV(AM)—Sept 16, 1961: 1400 khz; 1 kw-U. TL: N36 45 W00 80 43 20. Hrs opn: 5 AM-10 PM. Box 648, 343 Virginia St. (24343). (703) 728-9114. Licensee: Magnum Communications Inc. (acq 7-1-83; $210,000; FTR 7-11-83). Net: ABC/E. Format: Modern country. News staff one; news progmg 16 hrs wkly. Target aud: General. Spec prog: Farm 2 hrs, bluegrass 17 hrs, gospel 15 hrs wkly. ■ Howard E. Espravnik, pres; Mary Jane Espravnik, vp; Herb Gardner, gen mgr; Scott Gardner, opns dir, progmg dir, mus dir & news dir; Joyce Gardner, gen sls mgr & adv dir; Elbert Marshall, chief engr. ■ Rates: $4; 4; 4; 4.

Hopewell

WHAP(AM)—Jan 16, 1949: 1340 khz; 1 kw-U. TL: N37 17 46 W77 18 50. Hrs opn: 24. Box 621, 150 S. Mesa Dr. (23860). (804) 458-8518. FAX: (804) 452-0661 Licensee: Connon Communications Corp. (acq 10-91). Net: CBS, MBS; Va. News Net. Wash atty: Cohn & Marks. Format: Talk, news, sports, country. ■ Howard H. Keller, gen mgr; Mark Dorroh, opns mgr; Paul Ferguson, mus dir; Jeff Loughridge, chief engr.

Hot Springs

WBHA(FM)—October 1989: 107.1 mhz 160 w. Ant 1,407 ft. TL: N38 01 53 W79 46 52. Stn currently dark. c/o Radio Stn WVMR, State Rt. 28, Dunmore (24934). (304) 799-6004. Licensee: Pocahontas Communications Cooperative Corp. (acq 11-23-93; $2,000; FTR 12-13-93). ■ Gibbs Kinderman, gen mgr.

WWES(AM)—Dec 20, 1982: 1 kw-D. TL: N37 58 46 W79 50 20. Stn currently dark. Box 929 (24445). Licensee: Koinonia Broadcasting Inc. ■ Clay Shelton Jr., pres, gen mgr & news dir; Betsy Harrison, gen sls mgr; Debbie Dickerson, prom mgr & mus dir; Chip Tyler, progmg dir; Bob Gauss, chief engr.

Ivanhoe

***NEW FM**—Not on air, target date unknown: 90.1 mhz; 250 w. Box 201 (24350). Licensee: Ivanhoe Civic League Inc.

Kilmarnock

WKWI(FM)—Sept 1, 1975: 101.7 mhz; 3 kw. Ant 328 ft. TL: N37 43 26 W76 23 27. Stereo. Hrs opn: 6 AM-10 PM. Box 819, Radio Rd. (22482). (804) 435-1414; (804) 435-1313. Licensee: Buffalo Broadcasters Inc. (acq 9-30-92; $715,000; FTR 11-16-92). Net: Va. News Net. Format: Adult contemp. Target aud: 25-64. Spec prog: Farm 2 hrs wkly. ■ Tom Davis, pres, gen mgr, sls dir, adv dir & news dir; C.D. Hathway, opns mgr; Whitney Mills, rgnl sls mgr; Bill Goss, mus dir; Rick Lee, chief engr. ■ Rates: $8; 8; 8; na.

Lawrenceville

WHFD(FM)—Sept 1, 1991: 98.9 mhz; 3 kw. Ant 154 ft. TL: N36 45 10 W77 51 49. Rt. 1, Box 16 (23868). (804) 848-2600. Licensee: William Carlton Link. Format: Country, bluegrass, gospel. ■ William Carlton Link, pres & gen mgr.

WLES(AM)—September 1959: 580 khz; 500 w-D. TL: N36 45 10 W77 51 49. Rt. 1, Box 16, Hwy. 58, E. (23868). (804) 848-2600. Licensee: Brunswick Broadcasting Co. (acq 1-66). Net: UPI; Va. News Net. Format: Country. ■ William Carlton Link, gen mgr; Linda Link, mus dir; Rich Clary, news dir; John Hart, chief engr.

Lebanon

WLRV(AM)—Oct 28, 1974: 1380 khz; 1 kw-D, 63 w-N. TL: N36 55 18 W82 06 16. R.R. 3, Box One, 303 W. Main St. (24266-9413). (703) 889-1380. FAX: (703) 889-1388. Licensee: J.T. Parker Broadcasting Corp. Net: NBC; Va. News Net. Format: Country, news/talk, sports. News staff one; news progmg 20 hrs wkly. Target aud: 25-54. ■ J. T. Parker Jr., pres; Wallace Nelms, gen mgr & gen sls mgr; Mike Lowe, progmg dir; D.J. Mathews, news dir; Mitch Sandidge, chief engr. ■ Rates: $10; 10; 10; 10.

WXLZ-FM—Feb 1, 1993: 107.3 mhz; 530 w. Ant 774 ft. TL: N36 50 38 W82 11 04. Stereo. Hrs opn: 24. Box 1299, Russell County Industrial Park., WXLZ Dr., Lebanon (24266). (703) 889-1073; (703) 762-0967. FAX: (703) 889-3677. Licensee: Yeary Broadcasting Inc. Net: CBS. Format: Country. News staff one; news progmg 3 hrs wkly. Target aud: 18 plus; students, farmers, miners, executives and rural residents. ■ Lannis Yeary, pres, gen mgr, gen sls mgr & prom mgr; Kevin Mays, opns mgr & news dir; Greg Hunter, prom dir; Robin Burten, progmg dir, mus dir & pub affrs dir; Elmo McCracken, chief engr. ■ Rates: $10.75; 10.75; 10.75; 10.75.

Leesburg

WAGE(AM)—March 6, 1958: 1200 khz; 5 kw-D, 1 kw-N, DA-N. TL: N39 06 36 W77 35 03. Hrs opn: 24. 711 Wage Dr. S.W. (22075). (703) 777-1200. FAX: (703) 777-7431. Licensee: Radio WAGE Inc. Group owner: Emmet Broadcasting Co. (acq 3-80). Net: MBS; Va. News Net. Wash atty: Cohn & Marks. Format: News, full svc adult contemp. News staff 2; news progmg 114 hrs wkly. Target aud: 25 plus. Spec prog: Farm 2 hrs wkly. ■ Grenville Emmet III, pres; Charles Thornton Jr., gen mgr & gen sls mgr; Anita Thornton, prom dir; Todd James, progmg dir, mus dir & pub affrs dir; Kathleen Hazelton, news dir; Fran Little, chief engr. ■ Rates: $29; 24; 29; 20.

Lexington

***WLUR(FM)**—Feb 27, 1967: 91.5 mhz; 225 w. Ant -75 ft. TL: N37 47 17 W79 26 36. Stereo. Hrs opn: 6:30 AM-2 AM. Reid Hall, Washington and Lee Univ. (24450). (703) 463-8443; (703) 463-8444. FAX: (703) 463-8045. Licensee: Washington & Lee Univ. Format: Div. News progmg 7 hrs wkly. Target aud: General; college students, city and county residents. ■ John D. Wilson, pres; Robert J. de Maria, gen mgr; Thomas Tinsley, chief engr.

***WMRL(FM)**—June 1992: 89.9 mhz; 100 w. Ant 196 ft. TL: N37 42 22 W79 26 11. Hrs opn: 24. Rebroadcasts WMRA(FM) Harrisonburg, 100%. 821 S. Main St., Harrisonburg (22807). Licensee: James Madison Univ. Net: NPR, APR. Format: Class, folk, news. News staff 2; news progmg 32 hrs wkly. Target aud: 35 plus. ■ Brenda Hankey, gen mgr; Beth Steventon, opns dir; Bob Howerton, dev dir; Holly Watts, mktg dir; Sheila Rue, progmg dir; Steve Coghill, mus dir; Phil Picardi, news dir; Chuck Slott, pub affrs dir; William D. Fawcett, engrg dir.

WREL(AM)—Nov 14, 1948: 1450 khz; 1 kw-U. TL: N37 46 00 W79 25 56. Drawer 902 (24450). (703) 463-2161. FAX: (703) 463-4093. Licensee: Equus Communications Inc. (acq 11-85; $198,825; FTR 9-2-85) Net: Agri-Net. Rep: Keystone (unwired net). Format: Modern country. Spec prog: Farm 3 hrs wkly. ■ Kemper Miller, gen mgr & gen sls mgr; Sandy Garrett, stn mgr; Anthony Vita, mus dir; Jim Bresnahan, news dir; Ellsworth Neff, chief engr. ■ Rates: $9; 6; 9; 6.

Louisa

WLSA(FM)—July 10, 1980: 105.5 mhz; 3.3 kw. Ant 325 ft. TL: N38 01 37 W78 01 05. Stereo. Hrs opn: 5 AM-midnight. Box 277, Rt. 22/33 W. (23093). (703) 967-1142. Licensee: Mid-Virginia Broadcasting Corp. (acq 5-84). Net: ABC/E. Format: Country. News progmg 2 hrs wkly. Spec prog: Farm 2 hrs, bluegrass 8 hrs, relg 3 hrs, gospel 3 hrs wkly. ■ J. David Watt, pres, gen mgr & gen sls mgr. ■ Rates: $16; 12; 16; 7.

Luray

WLCC(FM)—Listing follows WRAA(AM).

WRAA(AM)—October 1962: 1330 khz; 1 kw-D, 40 w-N. TL: N38 39 34 W78 29 28. Box 387, Hwy. 211 W. (22835). (703) 743-5167. FAX: (703) 743-9522. Licensee: Commonwealth Audio Visual Enterprises (acq 6-2-88; $585,000 with co-located FM). Net: UPI; Va. News Net., Agrinet Farm. Rep: Keystone (unwired net), T N. Wash atty: Tharrington, Smith & Hargrove. Format: Country. News staff one; news progmg 10 hrs wkly. Target aud: 18-49; middle to upper income, mobile. Spec prog: Relg 15 hrs wkly. ■ J. D. Cave, pres & gen mgr; J.D. Cave, gen sls mgr; John Natalie, progmg dir & mus dir; Jeff Stapleton, news dir; Bill Fawcett, chief engr. ■ Rates: $10.80; 10.80; 10.80; 10.80.

WLCC(FM)—Co-owned with WRAA(AM). Oct 16, 1979: 105.7 mhz; 440 w. Ant 1,079 ft. TL: N38 30 41 W78 29 15. Stereo. Prog sep from AM. Net: Va. News Net. Rep: T N. Format: Adult contemp. News staff one; news progmg 15 hrs wkly. Target aud: 18-54; working people with disposable income interested in music, news and sports. Spec prog: Farm one hr wkly. ■ John Natalie, opns mgr. ■ Rates: $15.84; 15.84; 15.84; 15.84.

WYFT(FM)—October 1980: 103.9 mhz; 3 kw. Ant 299 ft. TL: N38 38 17 W78 24 06 (CP: 6 kw). Stereo. 598 5th St. (22835). (703) 743-7602; (704) 523-5555. Licensee: Bible Broadcasting Network (group owner; acq 12-22-86). Format: Relg. Target aud: General. ■ Lowell Davey, pres; Mike Hager, gen mgr; Harold Richards, progmg dir & mus dir; Ron Muffley, chief engr.

Lynchburg

WBRG(AM)—Sept 6, 1956: 1050 khz; 1 kw-D, 100 w-N. TL: N37 25 15 W79 06 55. Box 1079 (24505); 520 Ragland Rd. (24572). (804) 845-5916. Licensee: Tri-County Broadcasting Inc. (acq 7-1-67). Format: Contemp Christian, talk. News progmg 10 hrs wkly. Target aud: 25-49. ■ Lucy Bowman, pres; Brent Epperson, gen mgr & gen sls mgr; Eric Powers, mus dir; Rob Branch, chief engr.

WGOL(FM)—Listing follows WLLL(AM).

WJJS(FM)—Listing follows WVLR(AM).

WKPA(AM)—July 7, 1988: 1170 khz; 3.5 kw-D, DA. TL: N37 27 50 W79 07 23. 942 Kyle Ave., Roanoke (24012); Box 1092, Salem (24153). (703) 343-5597; (703) 389-3631. FAX: (703) 345-4064. Licensee: Seven Hills Media Inc. Wash atty: Booth, Freret & Imlay. Format: Relg. Target aud: General. Spec prog: Black. ■ David H. Moran, pres & gen mgr; Sharon Moran, opns dir; Sharon M. Moran, prom mgr; Dorothy Durrett, mus dir; Robert Branch, chief engr.

WLLL(AM)—Nov 1, 1963: 930 khz; 5 kw-D, 49 w-N. TL: N39 24 02 W79 13 59. No. One Radio Lane (24501). (804) 385-9555. FAX: (804) 385-9466. Licensee: Douglas Broadcasting (acq 5-89; grpsl; FTR 8-4-86). Net: NBC; Va. News Net. Rep: Roslin. Format: News/talk, sports. News staff one. ■ Don Cuthrell, stn mgr.

WGOL(FM)—Co-owned with WLLL(AM). Sept 1, 1970: 97.9 mhz; 3 kw. Ant 240 ft. TL: N37 24 02 W79 13 59 (CP: 570 w, ant 1,925 ft, TL: N37 33 46 W79 11 38). Stereo. Prog sep from AM. Format: Oldies. ■ Sue Schamerhorn, gen sls mgr; Janet Rose, prom mgr; Todd Anders, news dir; Glen Reinhemier, chief engr.

WLVA(AM)—Apr 21, 1930: 590 khz; 5 kw-D, 1 kw-N, DA-2. TL: N37 25 39 W79 13 23. Stereo. Hrs opn: 24. Box 3338 (24503); 4119 Boonsboro Rd. (24503). (804) 384-5936. FAX: (804) 384-2203. Licensee: Madison Broadcasting Group Inc. (acq 2-15-91; $65,000; FTR 3-11-91). Net: SMS. Wash atty: Gammon & Grange. Format: Talk. News staff 2; news progmg 10 hrs wkly. Target aud: 35-55. ■ James M. Armstrong, CFO; Hank Jernigan, gen mgr; Jack Howard, opns mgr; Randy Graham, sls dir; Rob Branch, chief engr.

WLYK(FM)—1948: 100.1 mhz; 730 w. Ant 646 ft. TL: N37 20 56 W79 10 06 (CP: 20 kw, ant 328 ft., TL: N37 28 06 W79 05 50). Stereo. Hrs opn: 6 AM-midnight. Suite 9, 3727 Old Forest Rd. (24501). (804) 385-9496. FAX: (804) 385-6430. Licensee: CEBE Investments Inc. (acq 7-17-91; $450,000; FTR 8-5-91). Net: SMN. Rep: Banner. Format: Adult contemp. Target aud: 25-54. ■ Aylett Coleman, pres; Wayne Moss, gen mgr; Dale Cook, chief engr.

WMXQ(FM)—Not on air, target date unknown: 105.9 mhz; 6 kw. Ant 266 ft. TL: N37 25 37 W79 07 26. Box 2298 (24501). Licensee: Friendship Broadcasting Corp. Format: Talk.

***WRVL(FM)**—June 19, 1981: 88.3 mhz; 50 kw. Ant 1,082 ft. TL: N37 11 50 W79 21 07. Stereo. Hrs opn: 24. Box 25000, Candlers Mt. Rd. (24506). (804) 582-3688. FAX: (804) 582-2076. Licensee: Liberty Univ. Net: UPI. Wash atty: Harry Martin. Format: Educ, relg. News staff one; news progmg 8 hrs wkly. Target aud: 25 plus. ■ A. Pierre Guillermin, pres; Jerry Edwards, gen mgr; Ed Stewart, mus dir; Rob Branch, chief engr.

WVLR(AM)—Feb 22, 1962: 1320 khz; 1 kw-U. TL: N37 25 37 W79 07 26. Box 6440 (24505). (804) 847-1266. FAX: (804) 845-4385. Licensee: CRS Communications Inc. (acq 11-85; $752,250; FTR 9-30-85). Net: CBS. Rep: Katz & Powell. Format: Urban contemp. Spec prog: Gospel 19 hrs wkly. ■ Douglas E. Caton, pres; Mary Tinsley, gen mgr; Randy Graham, gen sls mgr; Jack Alix, prom mgr; Mario Anotoy, progmg dir & news dir; Lad Goins, mus dir; Paxton Durham, chief engr.

WJJS(FM)—Co-owned with WVLR(AM). Aug 1, 1964: 101.7 mhz; 3.4 kw. Ant 300 ft. TL: N37 25 37 W79 07 26. Stereo. Prog sep from AM. Net: NBC the Source. Format: Country. Target aud: 18-54; general. ■ Bill Showers, gen mgr; Lee Cameron, progmg dir; Darold Newton, mus dir; Marie Anstey, news dir.

WWOD(AM)—May 1947: 1390 khz; 5 kw-D, 1 kw-N, DA-N. TL: N37 26 24 W79 12 38. Stn currently dark. Box 1390, 2020 Mimosa Dr. (24505). Licensee: Lynchburg Independent Broadcasters Inc. Group owner: Bahakel Communications Ltd.

WYYD(FM)—See Amherst.

Manassas

WJFK-FM—Licensed to Manassas. See Washington, D.C.

WKDV(AM)—Oct 1, 1957: 1460 khz; 5 kw-U, DA-2. TL: N38 45 00 W77 30 49. Hrs opn: 24. Rebroadcasts WKDL (AM) 100%. Suite 100, 8555 16th St., Silver Spring, MD (20910). (301) 588-1050. FAX: (301) 588-2249. Licensee: Capital Kids' Radio Co. (acq 3-30-93; $305,000; FTR 4-19-93). Format: Modern country. ■ Virginia Carson, CEO; Lawrence Kessner, pres; David Eppler, sr vp; Joan Schultz, gen mgr; Michael Kelly, opns mgr; Charlene Meyer, prom dir; Kenneth Curtis, progmg dir.

WRCY(FM)—See Warrenton.

Marion

WMEV(AM)—Dec 12, 1948: 1010 khz; 1 kw-D, 30 w-N. TL: N36 51 23 W81 30 21. Hrs opn: 24. Box 968, Summit Broadcasting Bldg., One Radio Rd. (24354). (703) 783-3151; (703) 783-9400. FAX: (703) 783-3152. Licensee: Summit Broadcasting (acq 12-1-82; $650,000; FTR 12-6-82). Net: NBC. Format: Country. News progmg 3 hrs wkly. Target aud: 18 plus. Spec prog: Gospel 2 hrs, relg 12 hrs, motor racing network-Winston Cup Races. ■ Sam R. Russell, CEO, vp, gen mgr & gen sls mgr; Hugh S. Gwyn, pres; Jim Mabe, opns dir; Ken Heath, prom dir & pub affrs dir; Jim Love, mus dir; Lyle Musser, chief engr. ■ Rates: $32; 32; 32; 20.

WMEV-FM—June 21, 1961: 93.9 mhz; 100 kw. Ant 1,480 ft. TL: N36 54 08 W81 32 33. Stereo. Dups AM 90%. Spec prog: Motor Racing Network-Winston Cup Races. ■ Rates: $36; 36; 36; 18.

WOLD(AM)—Apr 25, 1962: 1330 khz; 5 kw-D, 31 w-N. TL: N36 49 11 W81 28 12. Box 31 (24354). (703) 783-7109. FAX: (703) 783-2064. Licensee: Emerald Sound Inc. (acq 1965). Net: MBS. Format: Modern country, relg. Target aud: 25-49. ■ Robert S. Dix, pres & gen mgr; Patricia Ann Dix, opns mgr; Kevin C. Soos, progmg dir & news dir; Don Miller, chief engr.

WOLD-FM—Mar 14, 1968: 102.3 mhz; 6 kw. Ant 1,312 ft. TL: N36 54 10 W81 32 27. Stereo. Hrs opn: 24. Prog sep from AM. Net: MBS. Format: CHR, adult contemp, oldies.

***WVTR(FM)**—Nov 22, 1991: 91.9 mhz; 4.5 kw. Ant 1,489 ft. TL: N36 44 52 W81 18 15. Rebroadcasts WVTF(FM)

Roanoke 100%. c/o WVTF, 4235 Electric Rd. S.W., Roanoke (24014). (703) 857-8900. Licensee: Virginia Tech Foundation Inc. Format: Class, news. ■ Steve Mills, stn mgr.

Martinsville

WHEE(AM)—Aug 4, 1954: 1370 khz; 5 kw-D, 500 w-N. TL: N36 41 09 W79 54 14. Drawer 3551 (24115); 40 Franklin St. (24112). (703) 632-9811; (703) 642-9812. FAX: (703) 632-9813. Licensee: Patrick Henry Broadcasting Corp. Net: CBS. Wash atty: Wilkinson, Barker, Knauer & Quinn. Format: Country, talk. News staff one; news progmg 3 hrs wkly. Target aud: 17-60; agriculture & mfg area audience. ■ Thomas W. Patterson, pres; Nan Wood, gen mgr, gen sls mgr & prom mgr; Andy Johnson, progmg dir; Temple Mays, Andy Johnson, mus dirs; Yvette Foster, Mike Spence, news dirs; T.L. Walker, chief engr. ■ Rates: $8; 8; 8; 8.

WMVA(AM)—December 1941: 1450 khz; 1 kw-U. TL: N36 42 00 W79 51 07. Hrs opn: 5 AM-11 PM. Box 3831 (24115); 1129 Chatham Rd. (24112). (703) 632-2152. FAX: (703) 632-4500. Licensee: Martinsville Radio Inc. Net: NBC, NBC Talknet, Motor Racing Net., Mutual, Va. News Net. Format: Adult contemp, news/talk. News staff one; news progmg 6 hrs wkly. Target aud: General; blue collar, factory workers. ■ H. P. Bluhm, pres, gen mgr & progmg dir; Cathleen Y. Bluhm, vp; Mike Evans, opns mgr & gen sls mgr; Ron Morris, mus dir; Bill Wyatt, news dir; Tim Walker, chief engr.

***WPIM(FM)**—Not on air, target date unknown: 90.5 mhz; 5.9 kw. Ant 326 ft. TL: N36 42 16 W79 50 06. Box 889, Martinsville Community Workshop, Blacksburg (24063). Licensee: Martinsville Community Workshop Inc.

WROV-FM—January 1950: 96.3 mhz; 13.8 kw. Ant 2,076 ft. TL: N36 43 00 W79 51 07. Stereo. Box 4005, 15th and Cleveland Ave., Roanoke (24015). (703) 343-4444. FAX: (703) 343-0616. Licensee: Lisa Broadcasting Inc. Group owner: Atlantic Broadcasting Group. Net: ABC/R. Rep: D & R Radio. Format: AOR. News staff one; news progmg 2 hrs wkly. Target aud: 18-49; general. ■ David Weil, pres; Mike Slenski, vp & gen mgr; Jim Colston, gen sls mgr; Lindsey Livesay, prom dir; Ellen Flaherty, progmg dir; Helen Cunningham, news dir; Cookie Miller, pub affrs dir; Walter Smith, chief engr.

Mechanicsville

WCDX(FM)—Oct 7, 1985: 92.7 mhz; 2.35 kw. Ant 367 ft. TL: N37 37 44 W77 23 06 (CP: 92.1 mhz, 4.5 kw, ant 771 ft.). Stereo. Suite 300, Richmond (23294); 2809 Emerywood Pkwy., Richmond (23294). (804) 672-9300. FAX: (804) 672-9314; (804) 672-9316. Licensee: Sinclair Telecable Inc. Wash atty: Mullin, Rhyme & Topel. Format: Urban contemp. Target aud: 18-44. ■ John L. Sinclair, pres; Ben Miles, vp & gen mgr; Larry Jones, gen sls mgr; Katie Prendergast, prom mgr & news dir; Aaron Maxwell, progmg dir; Eric Lee, mus dir; Jeff Loughbridge, chief engr.

Moneta

WBLU(AM)—November 1991: 880 khz; 1 kw-D. TL: N37 10 00 W70 37 50. Stereo. Hrs opn: 12. 16 Village Sq. (24121). (703) 297-1188. Licensee: JLR Communciations Inc. Wash atty: Julian Freret. Format: Nostalgia. Target aud: 35 plus; lake residents, mostly middle aged. Spec prog: Bluegrass. ■ Diane Newman, pres & gen mgr; Jeffrey Raynor, vp. ■ Rates: $7; 7; 7; 7.

Monterey

***WVLS(FM)**—Not on air, target date unknown: 91.9 mhz; 200 w. Ant 426 ft. State Rte. 28, Dunmore, WV (24934). Licensee: Pocahontas Communications Cooperative Corp.

Mount Jackson

WSVG(AM)—Apr 23, 1954: 790 khz; 1 kw-D, 40 w-N. TL: N38 46 15 W78 37 17. Box 425, State Rd. 796 (22842). (703) 477-2937. FAX: (703) 477-2937. Licensee: Shenandoah County Broadcasting (acq 10-84; $375,000; FTR 7-23-85). Net: UPI, SMN; Agri-Net, Va. News Net. Format: Oldies. Target aud: 18-54. ■ Earl Judy Jr, pres.

WSIG(FM)—Co-owned with WSVG(AM). Oct 1988: 96.9 mhz; 3 kw. Ant -29 ft. TL: N38 46 15 W78 37 17. Stereo. Prog sep from AM. Net: UPI; Va. News Net., Agri-Net. Format: Contemp country. News staff 4. Target aud: 18-54. Spec prog: Farm 3 hrs wkly. ■ Frank Young, progmg dir; J.R. Cood, mus dir.

Narrows

WNRV(AM)—August 1953: 990 khz; 5 kw-D. TL: N37 20 39 W80 46 36. 485 Tower Rd., Christiansburg (24073). (703) 921-1996. Licensee: WNRV Radio. Format: Bluegrass. ■ Becky Lolli, pres; Karen Travis, gen mgr; James Christianson, gen sls mgr; Jeff Williams, progmg dir; James R. Boult, chief engr.

WZFM(FM)—Not on air, target date unknown: 101.3 mhz; 5.7 kw. Ant -403 ft. TL: N37 21 01 W80 47 46. Licensee: Faye A. Nicholson (acq 12-3-92; FTR 12-21-92).

New Market

WEZI(FM)—Not on air, target date unknown: 103.3 mhz; 2.1 kw. Ant 544 ft. Box 387, Luray, CA (22835). Licensee: Commonwealth Audio Visual Enterprises Inc.

Newport News

WGH-FM—November 1948: 97.3 mhz; 74 kw. Ant 415 ft. TL: N36 57 47 W76 24 42. Stereo. Pembroke One, 281 Independence Blvd., Virginia Beach (23462). (804) 497-1310. Licensee: Susquehanna Radio Corp. (group owner; acq 1985). Rep: Eastman. Format: Contemp country. News staff one. Target aud: 25-34. ■ Arthur W. Carlson, pres; Bill Whitlow, gen mgr; W. Sandy Smith, gen sls mgr; Kurt Etheridge, prom mgr; Smokey Rivers, John Castleberry, progmg dirs; Mare Carmody, mus dir; Carol Lewis, pub affrs dir; Steve Johnson, chief engr.

WGH(AM)—October 1928: 1310 khz; 5 kw-U, DA-N. TL: N36 57 47 W76 24 42. Hrs opn: 24. Prog sep from FM. Format: Sports talk. Target aud: General. ■ Smokey Rivers, Tony Mercurio, progmg mgrs.

WNVZ(FM)—See Norfolk.

WTJZ(AM)—November 1947: 1270 khz; 1 kw-U, DA-N. TL: N37 01 52 W76 22 00. 553 Michigan Dr., Hampton (23669). (804) 723-1270. Licensee: Broadcasting Corp. of Va. (group owner; acq 3-8-86; $350,000; FTR 1-13-86). Net: Natl Black. Format: Gospel, inspirational. ■ Eric C. Reynolds, pres & gen mgr; Bill Gilcrest, gen sls mgr; James Phillips, progmg dir; Theresa Hopskin, mus dir; John Hart, chief engr.

Norfolk

WCMS(AM)—July 1, 1954: 1050 khz; 5 kw-D, 358 w-N, DA-2. TL: N36 49 44 W76 12 26. 900 Commonwealth Pl., Virginia Beach (23464). (804) 424-1050. FAX: (804) 424-3479. Licensee: WCMS Radio Norfolk Inc. (acq 7-1-61). Net: ABC/E. Rep: Eastman. Wash atty: Arent, Fox, Kintner, Plotkin & Khan. Format: Country. ■ Marjorie S. Crump, pres; Pam Hughes, gen mgr; Cynthia Russell, gen sls mgr; Janie Crowder, prom mgr; Mike Meehan, progmg dir & mus dir; Cheri Bass, news dir. ■ Rates: $130; 125; 120; 100.

WCMS-FM—Oct 1, 1962: 100.5 mhz; 50 kw. Ant 500 ft. TL: N36 49 44 W76 12 26. Stereo. Hrs opn: 24. Dups AM 100%. ■ Rates: Same as AM.

WFOG(FM)—See Suffolk.

WGH(AM)—See Newport News.

WGH-FM—See Newport News.

***WHRO-FM**—1990: 90.3 mhz; 23 kw. Ant 630 ft. TL: N36 48 32 W76 30 13. Stereo. Hrs opn: 18. 5200 Hampton Blvd. (23508). (804) 489-9476; (804) 489-9484. FAX: (804) 489-0007. Licensee: Hampton Roads Educational Telecommunications Assoc. Inc. Net: NPR, APR. Wash atty: Wayne Coy. Format: Class & fine arts. Target aud: 35 plus; well-educated, executives, leaders. ■ John R. Morison, CEO & pres; Kenneth Krall, CFO & exec vp; Lawrence Crum, sr vp; Raymond Jones, vp & gen mgr; Lisa M. Murray, opns mgr; Mita Vail, vp dev & vp mktg; Elizabeth Vickers, dev dir & sls dir; Rosalyn Teichroew, prom mgr; Betty Luse, pub affrs dir; Keith Massie, vp engrg; Herman Wood, chief engr. ■ *WHRO-TV affil.

***WHRV(FM)**—1974: 89.5 mhz; 23 kw. Ant 730 ft. TL: N36 48 32 W76 30 13. Stereo. Hrs opn: 24. 5200 Hampton Blvd. (23508). (804) 489-9476; (804) 489-9484. FAX: (804) 489-0007. Licensee: Hampton Roads Educational Telecommunications Assn. (acq 2-86). Net: NPR, APR. Wash atty: Wayne Coy. Format: News, pub affrs, jazz. News staff one; news progmg 80 hrs wkly. Target aud: 35 plus. Spec prog: Alternative 14 hrs, folk 7 hrs wkly. ■ John R. Morison, CEO & pres; Kenneth Krall, CFO & exec vp; Lawrence Crum, sr vp; Raymond Jones, vp & gen mgr; Lisa Murray, opns mgr; Mita Vail, vp dev & vp mktg; Elizabeth W. Vickers, sls dir; Donna Hudgins, mktg dir; Rosalyn Teichrow, prom mgr; Betty Luse, pub affrs dir; Keith Massie, vp engrg; Herman Wood, chief engr.

WLPM(AM)—See Suffolk.

WLTY(FM)—Listing follows WTAR(AM).

WMXN(FM)—Licensed to Norfolk. See Portsmouth.

WNIS(AM)—September 1952: 850 khz; 50 kw-D, 25 kw-N, DA-2. TL: N36 51 39 W76 21 13. 500 Dominion Tower, 999 Waterside Dr. (23510). (804) 640-8500. FAX: (804) 640-8552. Licensee: Sinclair Telecable Inc. (group owner; acq 9-87; $725,000; FTR 9-21-87). Net: ABC TalkRadio, MBS, NBC, NBC Talknet, Wall Street, Westwood One. Rep: Major Mkt. Format: News/talk. ■ John L. Sinclair, pres; Bob Sinclair, gen mgr; Ginger Power, gen sls mgr; Tony Macrini, progmg dir; Ken Johnson, news dir.

WNOR(AM)—1949: 1230 khz; 1 kw-U. TL: N36 50 03 W76 16 12. Suite 399, 870 Greenbrair Cir., Chesapeake (23320). (804) 366-9900. FAX: (804) 366-0022. Licensee: Tidewater Communications Inc. Group owner: Saga Communications Inc. (acq 9-15-86). Rep: McGavren Guild. Format: AOR/classic rock. ■ Joe Schwartz, pres, vp & gen mgr; Chris Xenakis, gen sls mgr; Harvey Kojan, progmg dir; Gigi Young, news dir.

WNOR-FM—1961: 98.7 mhz; 46 kw. Ant 520 ft. TL: N36 50 03 W76 16 12. Stereo.

***WNSB(FM)**—Mar 22, 1980: 91.1 mhz; 920 w-H. Ant 154 ft. TL: N36 50 55 W76 15 57 (CP: 18 kw, ant 299 ft. TL: N36 45 23 W76 23 06). Stereo. 2401 Corprew Ave. (23504). (804) 683-9672. FAX: (804) 683-2385. Licensee: Norfolk State Univ. Board of Visitors. Net: UPI. Format: Jazz. ■ Erwin K. Thomas, gen mgr; Edward Turner, stn mgr; Douglas Perry Jr., progmg dir.

WNVZ(FM)—July 1967: 104.5 mhz; 50 kw. Ant 480 ft. TL: N37 02 20 W76 18 30. Stereo. 5555 Greenwich Rd., Suite 104, Virginia Beach (23462). (804) 497-1067. FAX: (804) 456-5458. Licensee: Max Radio Inc. (group owner; acq 1993). Rep: Katz, Banner, Christal. Format: CHR. News staff one; news progmg 5 hrs wkly. Target aud: 18-34; females. ■ Larry Saunders, pres; Dick Lamb, vp & gen mgr; Michael D. Bump, vp sls; Pat Kimsey, Scott Blume, natl sls mgrs; Chris Wilson, prom dir; Don London, progmg dir; Larry Davis, mus dir; Ernie Warinner, chief engr.

WOJY(AM)—See Hampton.

WOWI(FM)—June 1948: 102.9 mhz; 50 kw. Ant 500 ft. TL: N36 45 23 W76 23 06. Stereo. Suite 201, 645 Church St. (23510). (804) 627-5800. FAX: (804) 627-4048. Licensee: Ten Chiefs Co. Group owner: U.S. Radio L.P. (acq 7-27-89; $8.3 million; FTR 8-28-89). Rep: McGavren Guild. Format: Urban contemp. News staff one. Target aud: 18-34. ■ Ragan A. Henry, CEO & chmn; Donald L. Kidwell, pres; Janet Armstead, gen mgr; Steve Crumbley, opns mgr & progmg mgr; Missy Teachman, gen sls mgr; Toni Bailey, prom mgr; Michael Mazone, mus dir; Cheryl Wilkerson, news dir; Doc Christian, pub affrs dir; Greg Gabriel, chief engr. ■ Rates: $150; 125; 160; 105.

WPCE(AM)—See Portsmouth.

WPMH(AM)—See Portsmouth.

WSVY(AM)—See Portsmouth.

WTAR(AM)—Sept 21, 1923: 790 khz; 5 kw-U, DA-1. TL: N37 04 23 W76 17 28. Stereo. Suite 201, 168 Business Park Dr., Virginia Beach (23462). (804) 671-1000. FAX: (804) 671-1010. Licensee: Benchmark Radio Acquisition Fund IV Ltd. Group owner: Benchmark Communications Radio (acq 1993; $4.5 million; FTR 2-15-93). Net: CBS, NBC, Unistar; Va. News Net. Rep: Katz. Format: News/talk. Spec prog: Sports, relg 2 hrs wkly. ■ Mark T. Kanak, gen mgr; Judi Sedell, sls dir; Mary Noel, natl sls mgr; Ted Baroody, prom dir; Pat Murphy, progmg mgr; John Zaun, chief engr.

WLTY(FM)—Co-owned with WTAR(AM). Sept 21, 1961: 95.7 mhz; 40 kw. Ant 881 ft. TL: N36 48 56 W76 28 00. Stereo. Prog sep from AM. Format: News/talk. ■ Cindy Butler, mktg mgr; Rick Shockley, progmg dir; Pat Murphy, pub affrs dir; Dan Case, engrg mgr.

WTJZ(AM)—See Newport News.

WWDE-FM—See Hampton.

WYFI(FM)—Oct 2, 1971: 99.7 mhz; 50 kw. Ant 456 ft. TL: N36 49 41 W76 15 05. Stereo. Suite 5, 4310 Indian River Rd., Chesapeake (23325). (804) 547-9423. Licensee: Bible Broadcasting Network (group owner; acq 12-24-70). Net: AP. Format: Relg. ■ Lowell Davey, pres; Jerry Endres, gen mgr.

WZAM(AM)—April 6, 1976: 1110 khz; 50 kw-D, DA. TL: N36 56 34 W76 31 56. Stn currently dark. Suite 100, 168 Business Park Dr., Virginia Beach (23462). Licensee:

Virginia

Hampton Roads Radio. ■ Steve Brisker, pres; Henderson Vaughan, gen mgr.

Norton

WNVA(AM)—March 1946: 1350 khz; 5 kw-D, 37 w-N. TL: N36 57 58 W82 35 17. Hrs opn: 24. Box 500 (24273). (703) 328-2244. FAX: (703) 328-0024. Licensee: Radio-Wise Inc. Net: Sun. Format: Country, relg, talk. News progmg 2 hrs wkly. Target aud: 25-65. Spec prog: For the People, gospel 15 hrs wkly. ■ R.L. Helms, pres; William G. Stallard, gen mgr; John Fawbush, progmg dir; Gerald Hibbitts, chief engr.

WNVA-FM—July 25, 1969: 106.3 mhz; 1.65 kw. Ant 613 ft. TL: N36 57 58 W82 35 17. Stereo. Hrs opn: 24. Prog sep from AM. Net: Unistar. Format: Adult contemp, country.

Onley-Onancock

WESR(AM)—Jan 23, 1958: 1330 khz; 5 kw-D, 51 w-N. TL: N37 43 02 W75 41 01. Box 460, Onley (23418). (804) 787-3200. FAX: (804) 787-3819. Licensee: Eastern Shore Radio Inc. (acq 6-1-87). Net: ABC. Rep: Dome, T N. Format: Talk. ■ Ben Ferguson, pres; Gloria Jennings, vp; Charles F. Russell, gen mgr & gen sls mgr; Kelley Drummond, progmg dir; Selicity Stokes, mus dir; Nancy Namoski, news dir; Dennis Copes, chief engr.

WESR-FM—1968: 103.3 mhz; 50 kw. Ant 320 ft. TL: N37 43 02 W75 41 01. Stereo. Prog sep from AM. Net: ABC. Format: Adult contemp.

Orange

WJMA(AM)—Sept 10, 1949: 1340 khz; 1 kw-U. TL: N38 15 14 W78 07 15. Box 271, 207 Spicers Mill Rd. (22960-0157). (703) 672-1000. FAX: (703) 672-0282. Licensee: Piedmont Communications Inc. (acq 2-18-93; $30,000 with co-located FM; FTR 3-8-93). Net: AP; Va. News Net. Format: Adult contemp. News staff one; news progmg 18 hrs wkly. Target aud: 18-49. Spec prog: Urban contemp 15 hrs wkly. ■ John Schick, gen mgr; Joe Boucher, prom dir & progmg dir; Sue Harlow, mus dir; Phil Goodwin, news dir; Laura Skelly, pub affrs dir. ■ Rates: $16; 12; 14; 12.

WJMA-FM—Nov 22, 1971; 96.7 mhz; 2.7 kw. Ant 343 ft. TL: N38 15 14 W78 07 15 (CP: 3.1 kw). Stereo. Dups AM 100%. ■ Rates: Same as AM.

Pearisburg

WNRV(AM)—See Narrows.

WZFM(FM)—See Narrows.

Pennington Gap

WSWV(AM)—June 1, 1959: 1570 khz; 2.3 kw-D, 191 w-N. TL: N36 44 02 W83 02 34. Hrs opn: 5 AM-11 PM. Box 630, 203 W. Morgan Ave. (24277). (703) 546-2520. FAX: (703) 546-1356. Licensee: Lee Broadcasting Corp. (acq 6-1-80). Net: NBC, American Net. Rep: Rgnl Reps. Format: Adult contemp, oldies, relg. Target aud: 24-54; young, working adults. ■ David Hartley, vp, gen mgr & mus dir; Mary Lou Clontz, opns mgr, natl sls mgr & rgnl sls mgr; Clyde Wardell, gen sls mgr & adv mgr; Keith Cowden, progmg dir; Sharon Crabtree, news dir; Wayne Sizemore, chief engr. ■ Rates: $7.35; 6.65; 7.35; 6.65.

WSWV-FM—1973: 105.5 mhz; 3.5 kw. Ant 276 ft. TL: N36 44 02 W83 02 34. Stereo. Dups AM 100%. ■ Rates: Same as AM.

Petersburg

WGCV(AM)—May 7, 1945: 1240 khz; 1 kw-U. TL: N37 14 01 W77 22 36. 2809 Enerywood Pkwy., Richmond (23294). (804) 733-4567. FAX: (804) 861-2066. Licensee: Sinclair Telecable Inc. (group owner; acq 5-28-92; $1.4 million with co-located FM; FTR 6-22-92). Net: Unistar. Rep: McGavren Guild. Format: Gospel. News staff one. ■ Bob Sinclair, pres; Cavell Phillips, mus dir; Jeff Loughridge, chief engr. ■ Rates: $10; 10; 10; 10.

WPLZ-FM—Co-owned with WGCV(AM). Oct 1, 1966: 99.3 mhz; 3 kw. Ant 328 ft. TL: N37 14 01 W77 22 36. Stereo. Prog sep from AM. (804) 748-4199; (804) 748-6161. Format: Urban contemp. Target aud: 25-54; Black adults. ■ Paul Scott, vp & gen mgr; Cavell Phillips, stn mgr; Michael Ogburn, opns mgr; Rick Killingsworth, sls dir; Martin Stith, prom mgr; Gwen Williams, news dir.

WSVV(FM)—December 1992: 100.3 mhz; 4.7 kw. Ant 328 ft. TL: N37 08 57 W77 24 54. 3267 S. Crater Rd. (23805). (804) 732-0300; (804) 768-0100. FAX: (804) 768-0487. Licensee: Sandra M. Adair Vaughan. Format: Adult contemp. Target aud: 25-45. ■ Sandra Adair Vaughan, pres & gen mgr; Mike Ogburn, stn mgr; Glenn Shockey, gen sls mgr; Leanard Ware, prom dir; Stefan Henderson, progmg dir.

*WVST(FM)—July 12, 1987: 91.3 mhz; 100 w. Ant 120 ft. TL: N37 14 15 W77 24 55 (CP: 2.2 kw, ant 167 ft.). Stereo. Hrs opn: 19. Box 9010, 130 Harris Hall, Virginia State Univ. (23806). (804) 524-5933; (804) 524-5932. FAX: (804) 524-5826. Licensee: Virginia State Univ. Net: American Urban. Format: Adult contemp, jazz, news/talk. Target aud: General; 20-60. Spec prog: Class 2 hrs wkly. ■ Nathanael Pollard Jr., pres; Clarence A. Hamler, stn mgr; Will Harris, progmg dir; Phil McIntyre, chief engr.

Portsmouth

WMXN(FM)—(Norfolk). Aug 3, 1962: 105.3 mhz; 50 kw. Ant 499 ft. TL: N36 48 43 W76 27 49. Stereo. 240 Corporate Blvd., Suite 105, Norfolk (23502-4948). (804) 466-1053. TWX: 710-882-7526. Licensee: WIN Communications Inc. (group owner). Net: ABC/D, MBS. Rep: Roslin. Format: Oldies. News staff one; news progmg one hr wkly. Target aud: 25-54. ■ George Sosson, pres; John Moen, gen mgr; Ralph Salarino, gen sls mgr; Paula Uaiden, prom mgr; Steve Labeau, progmg dir; Barbara Sommers, mus dir; Erin Fraser, news dir; Dave Ryan, chief engr.

WPCE(AM)—Jan 11, 1964: 1400 khz; 1 kw-U. TL: N36 49 45 W76 19 23. Hrs opn: 24. Suite 400, 645 Church St., Norfolk (23501). (804) 622-4600. FAX: (804) 624-6515. Licensee: Willis Family Broadcasting Inc. (group owner; acq 3-4-92; grpsl; FTR 3-23-92). Net: MBS, Natl Black. Format: Inspirational. ■ L. E. Willis, pres & gen mgr; Regina Williams, opns mgr; Terry Love, progmg dir & mus dir; Mike Chandler, chief engr.

WPMH(AM)—Jan 9, 1972: 1010 khz; 5 kw-D, 449 w-N, DA-2. TL: N36 49 20 W76 26 38. Box 1010 (23705); 2202 Jollif Rd., Chesapeake (23321). (804) 488-1010. Licensee: Chesapeake-Portsmouth Broadcasting Corp. Net: Moody. Format: Inspirational. ■ Stewart Epperson, pres; Les Litchfield, gen mgr.

WSVY(AM)—January 1942: 1350 khz; 5 kw-U, DA-2. TL: N36 53 00 W76 22 22. Hrs opn: 24. Suite 201, 645 Church St., Norfolk (23510). (804) 627-5800. FAX: (804) 627-4048. Licensee: U.S. Radio L.P. (group owner; acq 7-27-89; $400,000; FTR 8-14-89). Net: ABC/FM, ABC/R. Format: Adult contemp, Black. News staff 2; news progmg 6 hrs wkly. Target aud: 25-54. Spec prog: Gospel. ■ Janet Armstead, gen mgr; Missy Teachman, gen sls mgr; Tony Bailey, prom mgr; Steven Crumbley, progmg dir & mus dir; Cheryl Wilkerson, news dir; Greg Gabriel, chief engr. ■ Rates: $50; 30; 40; 25.

Pound

WDXC(FM)—Not on air, target date unknown: 102.3 mhz; 280 w. Ant 992 ft. TL: N37 09 07 W82 37 57 (CP: 35 kw, ant 1,315 ft.). Stereo. Hrs opn: 24. Box 877, Hwy. 23, Jenkins/Pound Mountain (24279). (703) 796-5411; (606) 832-4827. FAX: (703) 796-5412. Licensee: WDXC Radio Inc. (acq 6-90; FTR 6-4-90). Net: SMN. Wash atty: May & Dunne. Format: Country. Target aud: General. ■ Howard Cornett, pres; Jackie Cornett, exec vp; Don Nelson, vp sls; Jeff Mullins, progmg dir; Robert McCown, chief engr. ■ Rates: $12; 12; 12; 8.

Pulaski

WBLB(AM)—May 8, 1973: 1340 khz; 1 kw-U. TL: N37 03 57 W80 47 03. Hrs opn: 6 AM-11 PM. Box 150, 5 Radio Hill (24301). (703) 980-3411; (703) 980-6517. FAX: (703) 980-8320. Licensee: WBLB Inc. (acq 10-89; $125,000; FTR 11-13-89). Format: Southern gospel. Target aud: General. ■ Larry Nipper, pres & gen mgr; Mary K. Nipper, vp; Mike Woolwine, opns mgr, gen sls mgr, prom mgr, adv mgr & progmg mgr; Don Taylor, mus dir; Ervin Largen, chief engr. ■ Rates: $7; 6; 7; 6.

WPSK-FM—Dec 1, 1967: 107.1 mhz; 25 kw. Ant 1,207 ft. TL: N37 01 28 W80 44 47. Stereo. Hrs opn: 24. Box 351, 1006 Bob White Blvd. (24301). (703) 980-2702. FAX: (703) 980-0755. Licensee: New River Media Group Inc. (acq 1989). Net: ABC/D. Format: Country. ■ Ralph Davis, pres; Ed Sherman, gen mgr; Rusty Clark, opns dir; Scott Stevens, mus dir; Kandy Andrews, pub affrs dir; J.J. Largen, chief engr.

WPUV(AM)—May 31, 1946: 1580 khz; 5 kw-D, 1 kw-CH. TL: N37 02 34 W80 45 43. Box 29 (24301). (703) 980-1580. Licensee: Billy G. Hale (acq 11-13-90; FTR 12-3-90). Net: CBN. Format: Bluegrass, country gold. News progmg 7 hrs wkly. Target aud: General. Spec prog: Family progmg, contemp Christian music. ■ Billy G. Hale, pres, prom mgr & mus dir; Becky Hale, gen sls mgr; Don Crowder, progmg dir; Tom Crocket, chief engr. ■ Rates: $7; 7; 7; na.

Purcellville

WLPY(AM)—February 1994: 840 khz; 250 w-D, DA. TL: N39 08 15 W77 42 05. 769 E. Main St. (22132). (703) 338-5568. FAX: (703) 338-2647. Licensee: Philip Y. Hahn. Format: Loc news, country.

Quantico

WPWC(AM)—See Dumfries-Triangle.

Radford

WRAD(AM)—1950: 1460 khz; 5 kw-D, 500 w-N, DA-N. TL: N37 08 35 W80 34 38. Stereo. Hrs opn: 5 AM-11 PM. Box 1168, U.S. Rt. 11 (24141). (703) 639-2461. FAX: (703) 639-1725. Licensee: WRAD Broadcasting Co. Group owner: Dix Communications (acq 10-9-57). Net: AP. Format: C&W. Target aud: 25 plus. ■ Charles Dix, pres; Ray L. Hatley, gen mgr; Ann Dix-Manza, gen sls mgr; Bob Thomas, news dir; Irven Largen, chief engr. ■ Rates: $12; 12; 12; 8.

WRIQ(FM)—Co-owned with WRAD(AM). 1965: 101.7 mhz; 3 kw. Ant 66 ft. TL: N37 08 33 W80 34 39. Stereo. Prog sep from AM. ■ Rates: Same as AM.

*WVRU(FM)—Oct 9, 1978: 89.9 mhz; 500 w. Ant 15 ft. TL: N37 08 26 W80 33 11. Stereo. Box 6973 (24142). (703) 831-5171. FAX: (703) 831-5893. Licensee: Radford University. Format: Class, div. Spec prog: Jazz 12 hrs, Black 6 hrs, country one hr wkly. ■ Theodore S. McKosky Jr., gen mgr & prom mgr; Jenifer Keys, progmg dir; Kiley Thompson, mus dir; Stephanie Terry, news dir; Randy S. McCallister, chief engr.

Richlands

WGTH(FM)—Jan 3, 1977: 105.5 mhz; 450 w. Ant 800 ft. TL: N37 09 20 W81 46 11. Hrs opn: 24. Box 370 (24641). (703) 964-2502; (703) 964-4500. FAX: (703) 964-4500. Licensee: High Knob Broadcasters Inc. Format: Relg. News progmg 11 hrs wkly. Target aud: General. ■ Ron Brown, pres & gen mgr; Edythe Brown, vp; Doug Johnson, opns dir; Charlene Pinkerton, vp sls; Mike Luttrell, chief engr. ■ Rates: $6; 6; 6; 6.

WRIC(AM)—Oct 5, 1951: 540 khz; 1 kw-D, 97 w-N. TL: N37 05 01 W81 46 58. Hrs opn: 24. Box 838, Edgewater Dr. (24641). (703) 964-4066. FAX: (703) 963-4927. Licensee: Clinch Valley Broadcasting Corp. Net: ABC/E; Va. News Net. Wash atty: Wilkinson, Barker, Knauer & Quinn. Format: Adult contemp. News staff one; news progmg 11 hrs wkly. Target aud: 25-54; young adults. ■ Mary Lawson, pres; Sam F. Cooper, gen mgr; Rocky Smith, progmg dir; Paul Van Scott, mus dir; Patricia Higgins, news dir. ■ Rates: $10; 8; 10; 7.

WRIC-FM—November 1989: 100.7 mhz; 1.3 kw. Ant 705 ft. TL: N37 09 04 W81 53 56. Stereo. Hrs opn: 24. Prog sep from AM. Format: Classic rock. News progmg 2 hrs wkly. Target aud: 24-54; young adult professionals. ■ Rates: $9; 7.50; 9; 6.50.

Richmond

WCDX(FM)—See Mechanicsville.

WCLM(AM)—See Highland Springs.

*WCVE(FM)—May 6, 1988: 88.9 mhz; 8.3 kw. Ant 840 ft. TL: N37 34 00 W77 28 36. Stereo. Hrs opn: 24. 23 Sesame St. (23235). (804) 320-1301. FAX: (804) 320-8729. Licensee: Central Virginia Educational Telecommunications. Net: APR, NPR. Format: Class, jazz, news. News progmg 22 hrs wkly. Target aud: 35 plus. Spec prog: Folk 2 hrs, big band 2 hrs wkly. ■ Charles Sydnor, pres; Bill Miller, stn mgr; Steve Clark, chief opns; Amy Chown, dev dir; Jim Manning, prom mgr; Henry Wailes, mus dir; Stephanie Pyle, pub affrs dir; Sam Straus, chief engr. ■ WCVE-TV affil.

*WDCE(FM)—Sept 7, 1977: 90.1 mhz; 100 w. Ant 118 ft. TL: N37 34 48 W77 32 35. Stereo. Hrs opn: 24. Box 85, Univ. of Richmond, 28 W. Hampton Way (23173). (804) 289-8790. FAX: (804) 289-8996. Licensee: University of Richmond. Format: Prgrsv, div, new mus. News progmg 3 hrs wkly. Target aud: 15-30. Spec prog: Class 3 hrs, jazz 9 hrs, relg 3 hrs wkly. ■ Eric Radziejewski, gen mgr; Kristen Leigh Netsel, opns mgr & progmg dir; Gregory Eden, gen sls mgr; Jason Leder, prom mgr; Will Mason, mus dir; Jonothan Mercantini, news dir.

WDCK(FM)—(Williamsburg). July 29, 1963: 96.5 mhz; 50 kw. Ant 492 ft. TL: N37 25 43 W76 56 41. Stereo. Hrs opn: 24. Suite C, 9321 Midlothian Pike, Richmond

(23235); Rt. 249 E., Kentwood Square, Quinton (23141). (804) 320-9696. Licensee: Benchmark Radio Acquisition Fund III Ltd. Group owner: Benchmark Communications Radio (acq 2-11-93; $4.25 million; FTR 3-8-93). Rep: D & R Radio. Format: Oldies. News staff one; news progmg 5 hrs wkly. Target aud: 35-54. ■ John Crowley, gen mgr; Vonneva Carter, gen sls mgr; Eric Cunningham, prom dir; Sid Mills, progmg dir; Lanie O'dell, news dir; Jon Bennett, chief engr.

WFTH(AM)—June 16, 1964: 1590 khz; 5 kw-D, 19 w-N. TL: N37 30 02 W77 27 28. Box 24625 (23224). (804) 233-0765. Licensee: Tri-City Christian Radio Inc. (acq 3-22-90; $450,000; FTR 4-16-90). Format: Gospel. ■ Jack Johnson Jr., gen mgr, gen sls mgr & prom mgr.

WGCV(AM)—See Petersburg.

WGGM(AM)—See Chester.

WKHK(FM)—(Colonial Heights). Nov 17, 1972: 95.3 mhz; 13 kw. Ant 449 ft. TL: N37 20 22 W77 24 31. Stereo. Suite 590, 300 Arboretum Pl., Richmond (23236). (804) 330-5700. FAX: (804) 330-5714. Licensee: ABS Richmond Partners L.P. Group owner: ABS Communications Inc. (acq 12-5-88). Rep: Banner. Wash atty: Fisher, Wayland, Cooper & Leader. Format: Country. News staff one; news progmg 8 hrs wkly. Target aud: 25-54. ■ Eric Hauenstein, gen mgr; Marlene Earnest, gen sls mgr & mktg mgr; Yvonne Vesseis-Hagen, rgnl sls mgr; Dawn Erickson, prom dir; Mark Richards, progmg dir; Rick Campbell, mus dir; Chuck Deel, news dir; Tony Diggs, chief engr.

WLEE(AM)—September 1955: 1320 khz; 5 kw-D, DA. TL: N37 28 00 W77 27 08. Suite 300, 121 Wyck St. (23225). (804) 675-0300. FAX: (804) 276-3804. Licensee: Pearson Newco Inc. Group owner: Star Radio (acq 11-17-89; FTR 12-4-89). Net: CNN, ABC, NBC, MBS. Format: News/talk. News staff 3; news progmg 15 hrs wkly. Target aud: 35 plus. ■ Max H. Pearson, pres; Tony Booth, gen mgr & sls dir; Dick Harmon, opns mgr; Dick Harman, progmg dir & news dir; Jon Bennett, chief engr. ■ Rates: $25; 42; 48; na.

WMXB(FM)—Dec 23, 1961: 103.7 mhz; 18.5 kw. Ant 750 ft. TL: N37 30 31 W77 34 37. Stereo. Hrs opn: 24. Suite 200, 812 Moorefield Pk. Dr. (23236). (804) 560-1037. FAX: (804) 323-1524; (804) 330-4079. Licensee: Four Seasons Communications. Net: AP. Rep: Banner. Format: Adult contemp. News staff one; news progmg 8 hrs wkly. Target aud: 25-54; predominately female. ■ Robert J. Rich, gen mgr; Adam Stubbs, prom dir; Steve Davis, progmg dir; Leslie Taylor, news dir; Joe Wetherbee, chief engr. ■ Rates: $180; 160; 160; 70.

WPLZ-FM—See Petersburg.

WREJ(AM)—May 8, 1964: 1540 khz; 10 kw-D, DA-D. TL: N37 37 08 W77 25 27. Hrs opn: 6 AM- 9 PM. Box 25147 (23260); 6001 Wilkinson Rd. (23227). (804) 264-1540. FAX: (804) 264-2809. Licensee: 1540 Broadcasting Corp. (acq 7-29-79). Net: BRN, USA; Va. News Net. Rep: Roslin. Format: Urban contemp, Christian. News staff 3; news progmg 90 hrs wkly. Target aud: 35-64; individuals who are concerned about financial, civic and economic issues. Spec prog: Indian one hr, gospel one hr, Italian one hr wkly. ■ Charles Cummings, chmn; Walton Belle, pres; Herbert O. Pollard, gen mgr; Allan P. Brown, gen sls mgr; Sheri Andrews, news dir; Jeff Loughridge, chief engr. ■ Rates: $35; 35; 35; 25.

WRVA(AM)—Nov 2, 1925: 1140 khz; 50 kw-U, DA-1. TL: N37 24 13 W77 18 59. Hrs opn: 24. Box 1516 (23212). 200 N. 22nd St. (23223). (804) 780-3400. FAX: (804) 780-3427. Licensee: Clear Channel Radio Inc. (group owner; acq 6-26-92; grpsl; FTR 7-20-92). Net: CBS. Rep: Katz. Format: Adult contemp, news/talk. News staff 10; news progmg 24 hrs wkly. Target aud: 35 plus. Spec prog: Farm one hr wkly. ■ Carl McNeill, gen mgr; John T. Harding, opns mgr & news dir; Ken Wayland, gen sls mgr; Bob Walden, natl sls mgr; Betsy Moore, rgnl sls mgr; Kathy Nipps, prom mgr; Tim Farley, progmg dir; John Francioni, chief engr.

WRVQ(FM)—Co-owned with WRVA(AM). Aug 4, 1948: 94.5 mhz; 200 kw. Ant 455 ft. TL: N37 24 13 W77 18 59. Stereo. Prog sep from AM. Box 1394 (23211). (804) 649-9151. Net: ABC/C. Format: CHR. ■ Linda Forem, gen mgr; Lisa McKay, opns mgr & mus dir; Kim Pond, mktg dir; Dottie Brooks, prom dir; Treeda Smith, news dir; Alan Kass, chief engr.

WRVH(AM)—Nov 15, 1937: 910 khz; 5 kw-U, DA-N. TL: N37 36 52 W77 30 49. Hrs opn: 24. Dups FM 80%. c/o WRVA(AM), 200 N. 22nd St. (23212). (804) 780-3400. FAX: (804) 780-3427. Licensee: Clear Channel Radio Licenses Inc. Group owner: Clear Channel Communications Inc. (acq 8-10-93; $9.75 million with co-located FM; FTR 8-30-93). Net: Va. News Net. Rep: Katz. Format: AOR, classic rock, sports. ■ Bob Lind, exec vp; Claire Shaffner-Slade, gen mgr; Melba Powell, prom dir; Paul Shugrue, progmg dir; Rick Maybee, mus dir; John Heimerl, chief engr.

WRXL(FM)—Co-owned with WRVH(AM). Mar 4, 1949: 102.1 mhz; 140 kw. Ant 320 ft. TL: N37 36 52 W77 30 49 (CP: 20 kw, ant 786 ft.). Stereo. Hrs opn: 24. 3245 Basie Rd. (23228). (804) 756-6400. FAX: (804) 756-6444. Format: AOR, classic rock. Target aud: 25-44.

WRVQ(FM)—Listing follows WRVA(AM).

WRXL(FM)—Listing follows WRVH(AM).

WSTK(AM)—(Colonial Heights). 1955: 1290 khz; 5 kw-D, 41 w-N. TL: N37 15 30 W77 23 40. Hrs opn: 24. Box 10, Colonial Heights (23834); 1024 E. Washington St., Petersburg (23803). (804) 861-1290; (804) 768-1290. FAX: (804) 861-1294. Licensee: Fletcher Communications Inc. (acq 8-5-93; $395,000; FTR 8-23-93). Net: Unistar, CNN. Format: Nostalgia, the original hits of the 40s, 50s & 60s. News progmg 7 hrs wkly. Target aud: 35 plus; middle to upper middle class adults. Spec prog: The Sounds of Sinatra 2 hrs wkly. ■ S. David Fletcher, pres; Jeffrey A. Fletcher, vp, gen mgr & gen sls mgr; Gary Bernstein, opns dir, prom dir & progmg mgr; John Bennett, chief engr. ■ Rates: $15; 13.50; 15; 9.50.

WTMM(AM)—May 4, 1951: 990 khz; 1 kw-D, 1 w-N. TL: N37 31 40 W77 22 48. Hrs opn: 24. Box 6747, 4116 Fitzhugh Ave. (23230). Licensee: OptiCom Inc. (acq 9-90; $1 million; FTR 9-3-90). Format: Black, div. ■ John Galloway, pres & gen mgr.

WTVR(AM)—September 1926: 1380 khz; 5 kw-U, DA-2. TL: N37 37 13 W77 26 57. 3314 Cutshaw Ave. (23230). (804) 355-3217. FAX: (804) 355-8682. Licensee: Roy H. Park Broadcasting of Va. Inc. Group owner: Park Communications Inc. (acq 1967). Net: ABC/E. Format: Big band. Target aud: 35 plus; older, upscale. ■ Roy H. Park, pres; Reggie Jordan, gen mgr; Jean Massey, gen sls mgr; Scott Lindemulder, progmg dir & chief engr; Mike LeVay, mus dir.

WTVR-FM—February 1946: 98.1 mhz; 50 kw. Ant 1,004 ft. TL: N37 34 00 W77 28 36. Stereo. Prog sep from AM. Net: ABC/E. Format: Btfl music. ■ WTVR-TV affil.

WVGO(FM)—May 1957: 106.5 mhz; 7.6 kw. Ant 1,233 ft. TL: N37 30 14 W77 41 53. Stereo. Suite 401, 1011 Boulder Springs Dr. (23225). (804) 330-3106. FAX: (804) 330-4780. Licensee: Benchmark Radio Acquisition. Group owner: Benchmark Communications Radio (acq 5-17-91; $4 million; FTR 6-3-91). Net: AP, ABC. Rep: Torbet. Wash atty: Pepper & Corazzini. Format: Adult rock. Target aud: 25-54. ■ John Crowley, gen mgr; Buck Albritton, gen sls mgr; Steve Forrest, progmg dir; Jim Hatcher, news dir.

WXGI(AM)—Oct 1, 1947: 950 khz; 5 kw-D, 64 w-N. TL: N37 30 52 W77 30 28. Hrs opn: 5:30 AM-midnight. Box 8872, 701 German School Rd. (23225). (804) 233-7666. FAX: (804) 233-7681. Licensee: WXGI Inc. (acq 11-88). Net: NBC. Format: C&W, bluegrass. Target aud: 30 plus. Spec prog: Farm 2 hrs, relg 6 hrs wkly. ■ Jay D. Keatley, pres; David Holt, gen mgr; Bob Shannon, gen sls mgr & prom mgr; Jim Granger, chief engr. ■ Rates: $20; 20; 20; 20.

WYFJ(FM)—See Ashland.

Roanoke

WFIR(AM)—June 20, 1924: 960 khz; 5 kw-U, DA-N. TL: N37 15 20 W79 57 20. Box 150 (24002); 3509 Hounds Chase Ln. (24014). (703) 345-1511. FAX: (703) 342-2270. Licensee: Jim Gibbons Radio Inc. (acq 4-30-77). Net: CBS. Rep: Christal. Format: News/talk. News staff one. Target aud: 25 plus. ■ James L. Gibbons, pres; Terry Gibbons, gen mgr; Terrilynn Hardman, gen sls mgr; Bill Bratton, progmg dir; Jim Wilson, news dir; Roger Lide, chief engr.

WPVR(FM)—Co-owned with WFIR(AM). November 1948: 94.9 mhz; 100 kw. Ant 1,979 ft. TL: N37 11 41 W80 09 22. Stereo. Prog sep from AM. (703) 345-3841. Format: EZ lstng. Target aud: 25 plus. ■ Michael Gibbons, prom mgr & mus dir; Ronnie Stoots, progmg dir.

WJLM(FM)—See Salem.

WKBA(AM)—(Vinton). Oct 9, 1961: 1550 khz; 10 kw-D, DA. TL: N37 17 24 W79 55 22. Box 1092, Salem (24153); 2043 10th St. N.E., Roanoke (24012). (703) 343-5597; (703) 389-3681. FAX: (703) 389-8968. Licensee: Tinker Creek Broadcasters Inc. (acq 2-1-83). Wash atty: Booth, Freret & Imlay. Format: Relg. Target aud: General. Spec prog: Black 10 hrs wkly. ■ David H. Moran, pres & gen mgr; Sharon M. Moran, stn mgr & sls dir; Zeke Leonard, prom mgr; Dorothy Durrett, progmg dir; Ben Givavdan, chief engr.

***WPIR(FM)**—See Salem.

WPVR(FM)—Listing follows WFIR(AM).

***WRDJ(FM)**—Not on air, target date unknown: 90.3 mhz; 2.4 kw. Ant 1,345 ft. TL: N37 22 27 W79 46 08. 2023 Westvan Ave. N.E. (24012). Licensee: Visions Communications Inc. ■ Jack Alix, gen mgr.

WRIS(AM)—Feb 28, 1953: 1410 khz; 5 kw-D, 72 w-N. TL: N37 16 47 W79 59 29. Hrs opn: 20. Box 6099, 219 Luckett St. N.W. (24017). (703) 342-3131; (703) 345-0294. FAX: (703) 345-2650; (703) 342-0080. Licensee: WRIS Inc. (acq 5-9-64). Net: MBS, Moody, USA; Va. News Net. Rep: Torbet. Wash atty: Joyce-Silva Blair. Format: Relg. News staff one. Target aud: 35-75. ■ Lloyd Gouchenour, pres & gen mgr; Chris Thompson, gen sls mgr; Gary E. Cooper, progmg dir & news dir.

WROV(AM)—1946: 1240 khz; 1 kw-U. TL: N37 16 12 W79 58 14. Box 4005, 15th & Cleveland Ave. (24015). (703) 343-4444. FAX: (703) 343-0616. Licensee: Lisa Broadcasting Inc. Group owner: Atlantic Broadcasting Group (acq 6-1-89; $150,000; FTR 6-12-89). Net: ABC/D; Va. News Net. Rep: D & R Radio. Format: Oldies. News staff one; news progmg 4 hrs wkly. Target aud: 25-54. ■ David Weil, pres; Mike Slenski, vp, gen mgr & stn mgr; Bob Carmody, vp opns; Jim Colston, gen sls mgr; Lindsey Livesay, mktg dir; Jeff Dickerson, progmg dir; Helen Cunningham, news dir & pub affrs dir; Walter Smith, chief engr.

WROV-FM—See Martinsville.

WSLC(AM)—Oct 1, 1940: 610 khz; 5 kw-D, 1 kw-N, DA-2. TL: N37 18 11 W80 02 33. Stereo. Hrs opn: 24. Box 6002 (24017); 1002 Newman Dr., Salem (24153). (703) 387-0234; (703) 387-2283. FAX: (703) 389-0837. Licensee: Mel Wheeler Inc. (group owner; acq 10-1-76). Net: NBC. Rep: Katz. Wash atty: Pepper & Corazzini. Format: Country. News staff 2; news progmg 28 hrs wkly. Target aud: 25 plus; active working adults. ■ Mel Wheeler, pres; Herm Reavis, exec vp, gen mgr & gen sls mgr; Don Morrison, opns mgr & progmg dir; H. Lee, prom mgr; George Gillock, mus dir; J.W. Davis, vp engrg; J.J. Largen, chief engr.

WSLQ(FM)—Co-owned with WSLC(AM). Nov 1, 1947: 99.1 mhz; 200 kw. Ant 1,985 ft. TL: N37 11 42 W80 09 22. Stereo. Hrs opn: 24. Prog sep from AM. Net: ABC/FM. Format: Adult contemp. News progmg 3 hrs wkly. Target aud: 25-54; active working adults. ■ Dick Daniels, mus dir.

***WVTF(FM)**—Aug 1, 1973: 89.1 mhz; 100 kw. Ant 1,970 ft. TL: N37 11 56 W80 09 02. Stereo. Hrs opn: 5 AM-1 AM. Grand Pavilion, 4235 Electric Rd. S.W. (24014). (703) 857-8900. FAX: (703) 857-7578. Licensee: Virginia Tech Foundation Inc. (acq 1-1-82). Net: APR, NPR, Va. News Net. Wash atty: Dow, Lohnes & Albertson. Format: Class, jazz, talk. News staff 3; news progmg 39 hrs wkly. Target aud: General. ■ Steve Mills, gen mgr; Mike Stater, dev dir; Seth Williamson, mus dir; Rick Mattioni, news dir; Paxton Durham, chief engr.

WWWR(AM)—April 1957: 910 khz; 1 kw-D, 84 w-N. TL: N37 16 06 W79 54 46. 1848 Clay St. (24013). (703) 343-7109. FAX: (703) 343-2306. Licensee: Perception Media Group Inc. (acq 4-25-91; $150,000; FTR 5-13-91). Net: USA. Format: Adult contemp Christian. Target aud: 25-54. ■ Ben Peyton, pres; Lacey Raines, vp; Hal Mabe, gen mgr & gen sls mgr; Sandy Durrett, progmg dir; Bart Prater, chief engr. ■ Rates: $23; 18; 23; 7.

WXLK(FM)—Dec 17, 1960: 92.3 mhz; 93 kw. Ant 2,050 ft. TL: N37 11 56 W80 09 03. Stereo. 3934 Electric Rd. S.W. (24018). (703) 774-9200. Licensee: CEBE (acq 9-15-72). Net: Unistar. Rep: Torbet. Format: Contemp hit. ■ Aylett B. Coleman, pres; Wayne Moss, gen sls mgr; Tim Wright, prom mgr; Chris Taylor, progmg dir; Sally Sevareid, news dir; Dale Cook, chief engr.

Rocky Mount

WNLB(AM)—Dec 10, 1959: 1290 khz; 3.2 kw-D, 55 w-N. TL: N36 58 37 W79 53 45. Box 602, 722 Glennwood Dr. (24151). (703) 483-7011. FAX: (703) 483-7022. Licensee: WNLB Radio Inc. Net: UPI; Agri-Net. Rep: T N. Format: C&W. ■ Donny Brook, pres, gen mgr, gen sls mgr, progmg dir & mus dir; Glenn Lynch, news dir & chief engr.

WZBB(FM)—Co-owned with WNLB(AM). March 1989: 99.9 mhz; 3 kw. Ant 328 ft. TL: N36 58 37 W79 53 45 (CP: 1.2 kw, ant 722 ft., TL: N36 54 50 W79 57 07). Stereo. Hrs opn: 24. Prog sep from AM. (703) 489-9999. Net: Va. News Net. Format: Adult contemp. Target aud: 21 plus.

Glenn Lynch, progmg dir & mus dir; Donny Brook, news dir; Paxton Durham, chief engr.

WYTI(AM)—Mar 31, 1957: 1570 khz; 2.5 kw-D, 440 w-N. TL: N37 01 11 W79 53 09. Hrs opn: 5:30 AM-10 PM. Drawer 430, N. Main St. (24151). (703) 483-9955. FAX: (703) 483-7802. Licensee: WYTI Inc. (acq 1-71). Net: USA. Format: Traditional country, bluegrass, gospel. Target aud: 30 plus; general. Spec prog: NASCAR races, relg 10 hrs wkly. ■ William E. Jefferson, pres, gen mgr, gen sls mgr, adv mgr & mus dir; Susan Mullins, exec vp, opns mgr, prom mgr & news dir; Donnie Hutchinson, progmg dir & chief engr. ■ Rates: $3.92; 3.92; 3.92; 3.92.

WZBB(FM)—Listing follows WNLB(AM).

Ruckersville

WVSY(FM)—Licensed to Ruckersville. See Charlottesville.

Rural Retreat

WCRR(AM)—May 15, 1985: 660 khz; 550 w-D. TL: N36 55 17 W81 14 34. Box 660 (24368). (703) 686-4111. FAX: (703) 686-4112. Licensee: Highland Broadcasting Inc. Net: Unistar, UPI; Va. News Net. Wash atty: Pepper & Corazzini. Format: Country, relg. News staff one; news progmg 11 hrs wkly. Target aud: General. ■ Bob Smallwood, pres; Isom Sturgill, gen sls mgr. ■ Rates: $7; 6; 7; 6.

WCRR-FM—Sept. 2, 1991: 95.3 mhz; 6 kw. Ant 400 ft. TL: N36 55 17 W81 14 34. Stereo. Hrs opn: 24. Prog sep from AM. (703) 686-4112. Net: ABC/I. ■ Paul Sexton, vp mktg & vp adv; Alan Bell, prom dir & asst mus dir; Dawn Loggins, pub affrs dir. ■ Rates: Same as AM.

St. Paul

WXLZ(AM)—Nov 3, 1981: 1140 khz; 2.5 kw-D. TL: N36 52 15 W82 18 21. Hrs opn: Sunrise-sunset. Rebroadcasts WXLZ-FM Lebanon 80%. Box 250, Mew Rd., Castlewood (24224). (703) 762-5595. FAX: (703) 762-5596. Licensee: Yeary Broadcasting Inc. Net: CBS. Format: Country, relg. News staff one; news progmg 3 hrs wkly. Target aud: 25 plus; students, farmers, miners and rural area residents. Spec prog: Farm 2 hrs, gospel 15 hrs wkly. ■ Lannis Yeary, CEO & gen sls mgr; Donna Yeary, exec vp; Kevin Mays, opns mgr & news dir; Greg Hunter, prom dir; Robin Burton, progmg dir & mus dir. ■ Rates: $10.75; 10.75; 10.75; 10.75.

Salem

WJLM(FM)—Mar 7, 1969: 93.5 mhz; 5.8 kw. Ant 98 ft. TL: N37 16 47 W79 59 29. Stereo. Hrs opn: 24. Box 6099, 219 Luckett St. N.W., Roanoke (24017). (703) 342-3131. FAX: (703) 345-2650; (703) 342-0080. Licensee: WRIS Inc. Net: Westwood One, MBS. Rep: Torbet. Wash atty: Blair & Joyce. Format: Today's Hot Country. News progmg one hr wkly. Target aud: 24 plus. ■ Lloyd Gochenour, pres & gen mgr; Chris Thompson, sls dir, vp mktg & vp adv; Richard Freedman (acting dir), progmg dir; John Russell, mus dir; Gary E. Cooper, news dir.

***WPIR(FM)**—Not on air, target date 1994: 91.3 mhz; 3.3 kw-H, 3 kw-V. Ant 902 ft. TL: N37 22 23 W79 55 40. Box 889, Blacksburg (24063). (703) 552-4252. Licensee: Positive Alternative Radio Inc. (acq 5-90; FTR 5-21-90). Wash atty: Booth, Freret & Imlay. Format: Inspirational. ■ Vernon H. Baker, pres.

WTOY(AM)—Sept 7, 1956: 1480 khz; 5 kw-D. TL: N37 16 21 W80 04 52. 2614 Cove Rd. N.W., Roanoke (24017). (703) 362-9558. FAX: (703) 362-9544. Licensee: Ward Broadcasting Corp. (acq 3-2-92). Format: Adult urban contemp. ■ Irving L. Ward Sr., pres; Andrea Hicks, gen mgr; Dwayne Ellis, dev dir; Lynelle Hines, sls dir; Daniel Ellington, progmg dir; Tom Crocket, chief engr.

Saltville

WXMY(AM)—Nov 5, 1981: 1600 khz; 5 kw-D, 500 w-PSA. TL: N36 51 43 W81 43 29. Hrs opn: 6 AM-sunset. Box 1109089 (24370). (703) 496-5511. Licensee: Troy L. Rose (acq 7-7-93; $75,000; FTR 8-2-93). Net: CNN. Format: Country. Target aud: 25-54. Spec prog: Gospel 8 hrs wkly. ■ Troy Rose, pres & gen sls mgr; Henry Thomas, vp, stn mgr, progmg dir & mus dir; Troy Rose, Bill Keesee (asst), gen mgrs; Bob Bix, chief engr. ■ Rates: $6; 6; 6; na.

Smithfield

WKGM(AM)—Dec 18, 1974: 940 khz; 10 kw-D, 3.21 kw-N, DA-N. TL: N36 57 16 W76 37 48. Hrs opn: 20. Box 339 (23431); 13379 Great Spring Rd. (23430). (804) 357-9546; (804) 622-9546. FAX: (804) 365-0412. Licensee: WKGM Inc. Group owner: Baker Family Stations. Format: Relg. News progmg one hr wkly. Target aud: 25 plus. Spec prog: Farm 2 hrs, Ger 2 hrs, Sp one hr wkly. ■ Vernon H. Baker, pres; Larry W. Cobb, vp, gen sls mgr & chief engr; Robert Stallings, pub affrs dir.

South Boston

WHLF(AM)—Sept 1, 1947: 1400 khz; 1 kw-U. TL: N36 42 24 W78 55 28. Stereo. Hrs opn: 24. Box 526, 1210 Porter Ln. (24592). (804) 572-2988. FAX: (804) 572-1662. Licensee: JLC Properties Inc. (acq 4-1-93; $500,100 with co-located FM; FTR 4-19-93). Net: NBC; Va. News Net. Rep: T N. Wash atty: Dan Alpert. Format: loc news, sports, adult contemp. News staff one; news progmg 10 hrs wkly. Target aud: 25-54; Upwardly mobile, high spendable income. Spec prog: Gospel 7 hrs wkly. ■ John L. Cole III, CEO, pres, vp sls, vp mktg & vp adv; Catherine M. Cole, gen mgr, sls dir, prom dir & adv mgr; Jim Chandler, stn mgr & opns mgr; Paul Cordell, progmg dir; Chuck Vipperman, news dir & pub affrs dir; John Cole, chief engr. ■ Rates: $12; 10; 12; 8.

WJLC(FM)—Co-owned with WHLF(AM). Sept 1, 1992: 95.3 mhz; 6 kw. Ant 246 ft. TL: N36 43 59 W78 56 03. Stereo. Hrs opn: 24. Rebroadcasts WHLF (AM) South Boston 100%. Net: Va. News Net. Rep: T N; T N.Format: Adult contemp, local news, sports. News staff 2; news progmg 8 hrs wkly. Target aud: 25-54; those that have spendable inome. ■ Catherine M. Cole, gen mgr; Jim Chandler, stn mgr & dev dir; Paul Cordell, vp progmg & mus dir. ■ Rates: Same as AM.

WQOK(FM)—Licensed to South Boston. See Raleigh, N.C.

WSBV(AM)—1980: 1560 khz; 2.5 kw-D, DA-1. TL: N36 42 24 W78 52 28. Box 778, Hwy. 879, Plank Rd. (24592). (804) 572-4418. Licensee: Taylor Communications Inc. Format: Southern gospel, top-40. News progmg one hr wkly. Target aud: 40 plus. Spec prog: Farm one hr wkly. ■ Norman Hall, pres; Mary Hall, gen mgr; Claude McKinney, gen sls mgr & prom mgr; Linda Waller, progmg dir; Rhonda Thomas, mus dir & news dir; Johnny Cole, chief engr.

South Hill

WJWS(AM)—Nov 1, 1953: 1370 khz; 5 kw-D. TL: N36 44 39 W78 09 42. Hrs opn: 6 AM-6 PM. Box 216, Hwy. 47 N. (23970). (804) 447-8997; (804) 447-4007. Licensee: Old Belt Broadcasting Corp. (acq 7-1-64). Net: AP; Tobacco. Format: Black. News staff one. Target aud: General. ■ Norman L. Talley, CEO, pres & gen sls mgr; Nancy Talley, vp; Frank Malone, gen mgr; Robert Wilson, prom mgr & news dir; Freddie Hargrove, progmg dir & asst mus dir; Tom Stanley, chief engr.

WSHV(FM)—Co-owned with WJWS(AM). Dec 23, 1966: 105.5 mhz; 15 kw. Ant 328 ft. TL: N36 44 39 W78 09 42. Stereo. Prog sep from AM. FAX: (804) 447-4789. Rep: Tobacco Radio Net. Format: Country. ■ Frank Malone, gen sls mgr; Greg Thrift, prom mgr; Steve Howell, progmg dir & mus dir; Tom Stanley, chief engr.

Spotsylvania

WPLC(FM)—March 31, 1988: 99.3 mhz; 3 kw. Ant 291 ft. TL: N38 08 31 W77 41 38. Stn currently dark. 616 Amelia St., Fredericksburg (22401). (703) 373-1500. Licensee: The Free Lance-Star Publishing Co. of Fredericksburg, Va. (acq 4-19-93; $200,000; FTR 5-3-93). Format: Jazz, new age. Target aud: 25-49; affluent baby boomers. ■ J. William Poole, gen mgr.

Staunton

WANV(AM)—See Waynesboro.

WANV-FM—Sept 1984: 99.7 mhz; 3.25 kw. Ant 1,692 ft. TL: N38 09 55 W79 18 50. Stereo. Hrs opn: 24. 13 W. Beverley St. (24401). (703) 885-2455. FAX: (703) 943-9673. Licensee: WANV Ltd. (acq 11-30-93; $1.1 million with WANV(AM) Waynesboro; FTR 12-20-93). Net: Unistar. Wash atty: Jim Freeman. Format: Oldies. News staff 2; news progmg 10 hrs wkly. Target aud: 25-54. ■ Teresa Rogers, pres; Christopher Rodgers, gen sls mgr; L.A. Pete Brooks, news dir; Jerry Lee Dowd, chief engr.

WKDW(AM)—April 1954: 900 khz; 2.5 kw-D, 128 w-N. TL: N38 10 27 W79 04 12. Stereo. Hrs opn: 24. Box 2189, 704 Richmond Ave. (24401). (703) 886-2377. FAX: (703) 885-8662. Licensee: Clark Broadcasting Co. (acq 1-74; grpsl; FTR 5-11-87). Net: NBC, AP. Wash atty: Dow, Lohnes & Albertson. Format: Country. News staff 2; news progmg 15 hrs wkly. Target aud: 25-54. Spec prog: Farm progmg one hr wkly. ■ Scott Jackson, opns mgr; John Cappes, gen sls mgr; Mark Bowen, mktg mgr; Dave McCormick, prom mgr, progmg dir & mus dir; John Lewis, news dir; Bill Betlej, chief engr. ■ Rates: $25; 20; 25; 17.50.

WKDW-FM—May 29, 1959: 93.1 mhz; 2.8 kw. Ant 338 ft. TL: N38 10 27 W79 04 12 (CP: TL: N38 10 32 W79 04 12). Stereo. Dups AM 100%. (703) 886-2376. Format: AOR. News progmg 3 hrs wkly. Target aud: 18-49. ■ Joe Koontz, adv mgr. ■ Rates: Same as AM.

WNLR(AM)—See Churchville.

WTON(AM)—Mar 9, 1946: 1240 khz; 1 kw-U. TL: N38 08 30 W79 02 33. Box 1085 (24402-1085). (703) 885-5188. FAX: (703) 885-1240. Licensee: Ogden Broadcasting of Virginia Inc. Group owner: Ogden Newspapers Inc. (acq 11-1-82; $1,650,000; FTR 11-1-82). Net: ABC/E. Format: FM adult contemp, AM news/talk. ■ G. Ogden Nutting, pres; Robert S. Koon, vp; J. Gary Ratcliff, gen mgr; Brenda Benson, adv dir; Shan Harris, progmg dir.

WTON-FM—November 1990: 94.3 mhz; 330 w. Ant 2,263 ft. TL: N38 09 55 W79 18 51. Stereo. Hrs opn: 5 AM-12:30 AM. 304 W. Beverly St. (24402). Wash atty: Steptoe & Johnson. Format: Easy listening. News progmg 3 hrs wkly. Target aud: 35-64 plus. Spec prog: Big band 2 hrs wkly. ■ Gary Ratcliff, stn mgr; Shan Harris, progmg dir; Jim Mills, news dir & engrg dir; Kathy Jones, pub affrs dir; Fred Fleshacker, chief engr.

Strasburg

WBPP(FM)—Jan 1, 1987: 104.9 mhz; 3 kw. Ant 219 ft. TL: N39 01 22 W78 25 35. Stereo. Hrs opn: 24. Box 1658, Winchester (22601); 210 W. King St. (22657). (703) 465-9100. FAX: (703) 465-5350. Licensee: Signal Knob Radio Partners. Net: SMN. Format: Oldies. Target aud: 25-54; all income levels - blue & white collar workers. ■ Candice Stover-McGowan, gen mgr; Jim McGowan, gen sls mgr; Keith Provost, progmg dir.

Stuart

WHEO(AM)—Oct 12, 1959: 1270 khz; 5 kw-D. TL: N36 37 25 W80 15 50. Rt. 1, Box 75 (24171). (703) 694-3114. FAX: (703) 694-2241. Licensee: Mountain View Communications Inc. (acq 6-86). Net: UPI; Va. News Net. Format: Country, news. News staff one; news progmg 20 hrs wkly. Target aud: General. Spec prog: Farm 4 hrs, relg 10 hrs, loc news 10 hrs wkly. ■ Mike Mc Coll, gen mgr & gen sls mgr; Bill Whitt, progmg dir & mus dir; Mike Dunavant, news dir; Bruce Dollarhite, chief engr. ■ Rates: $7.65; 7.65; 7.65; na.

Suffolk

WAFX(FM)—Dec 12, 1983: 106.9 mhz; 100 kw. Ant 984 ft. TL: N36 48 16 W76 45 17. Stereo. Suite 555, 700 Monticello Ave., Norfolk (23510). (804) 624-9759. FAX: (804) 627-3291. Licensee: TWC II Corp. (acq 1-93; $460,000; FTR 1-11-93). Rep: CBS Radio. Format: Classic rock. News staff one; news progmg 2 hrs wkly. Target aud: 18-49. ■ Bob Longwell, pres; Joe Schwartz, gen mgr; Chris Xenakis, gen sls mgr; Phil Ryan, prom mgr; Mike Ferris, progmg dir; Nikky Reid, news dir; Paul Campbell, chief engr.

WFOG(FM)—Dec 1965: 92.9 mhz; 50 kw. Ant 480 ft. TL: N36 52 35 W76 23 28. Stereo. Hrs opn: 24. Harbour Pl., 215 Brooke Ave., Norfolk (23510); 5600 Greenbrooke Dr., Portsmouth (23701). (804) 622-6771; (804) 244-2222. FAX: (804) 624-9501. Licensee: Sunshine Wireless Co. Inc. (group owner; acq 4-11-89; $8 million; FTR 4-24-89). Net: Unistar. Rep: Banner. Wash atty: Winston & Strawn. Format: Soft adult contemp. News staff one; news progmg one hr wkly. Target aud: 35-54; adults 35-54, secondary women 25-54. Spec prog: Jazz 3 hrs, relg 2 hrs wkly. ■ Dan N. Cohen, pres; Jeffrey D. Greenhawt, sr vp; Jerry DelCore, gen mgr; Julie Paras (local), Karen Moeller (local), rgnl sls mgrs; Dana Clark Thornton, prom dir; Rich Hawkins, progmg dir; Glen Grey, news dir; Chuck Allen, pub affrs dir; Greg Gabriele, chief engr.

WLPM(AM)—Mar 17, 1940: 1450 khz; 1 kw-U. TL: N36 45 05 W76 32 55. Hrs opn: 5 AM-11 PM. 100 Bank St. (23434). (804) 539-2394. FAX: (804) 539-1800. Licensee: Johnson Media Inc. (acq 3-91). Net: SMN. Format: Gospel. News staff one. Target aud: General. Spec prog: Sports 8 hrs wkly. ■ Jim Johnson, pres. ■ Rates: $15; 15; 15; 15.

Tappahannock

WRAR(AM)—Nov 1, 1970: 1000 khz; 500 w-D. TL: N37 57 08 W76 48 57. Box 1023 (22560). (804) 443-4321; (804) 333-3000. FAX: (804) 443-1055. Licensee: Rappahanock Communications Inc. (acq 1-85). Net: ABC/I. Format: Talk. Spec prog: Farm 5 hrs wkly. ■ Danny C. Wadsworth, pres & gen mgr; Lin Wadsworth, vp & gen

Stations in the U.S. • **Virginia**

sls mgr; Paula Kidwell, progmg dir; Frank S. Miner, chief engr.

WRAR-FM—July 26, 1971: 105.5 mhz; 6 kw. Ant 328 ft. TL: N37 52 27 W76 43 37. Stereo. Dups AM 25%. Format: Adult contemp.

Tasley

WESR-FM—See Onley-Onancock.

Tazewell

WTZE(AM)—Apr 22, 1966: 1470 khz; 5 kw-D. TL: N37 07 11 W81 32 33. Box 69 (24651). (703) 988-4150. Licensee: Tazewell Broadcasting Co. Inc. (acq 4-1-66). Net: USA; Agri-Net. Format: C&W. ■ Fred W. Cox, pres & chief engr; Walter L. Wright, gen mgr & progmg dir; Yvonne Elswick, gen sls mgr.

WTZE-FM—Sept 1, 1968: 100.1 mhz; 4.2 kw. Ant 395 ft. TL: N37 08 00 W81 35 43. Stereo. Dups AM 100%. Net: Motor Racing Net. Target aud: 18-44; young adults.

Vinton

WKBA(AM)—Licensed to Vinton. See Roanoke.

WWFO(FM)—Not on air, target date unknown: 106.1 mhz; 3 kw. Ant 92 ft. TL: N37 17 01 W79 59 14. No. 24, 1930 New Hampshire Ave. N.W., Washington, DC (20009). Licensee: Michael Scott Copeland.

Virginia Beach

WCMS-FM—See Norfolk.

WJQI-FM—May 5, 1984: 94.9 mhz; 50 kw. Ant 499 ft. TL: N36 48 38 W76 16 57. Stereo. Hrs opn: 24. Suite 95, 5544 Greenwich Rd. (23462). (804) 671-9490. FAX: (804) 456-5090. Licensee: Radio WJQI Inc. Net: Unistar. Rep: D & R Radio Format: Adult contemp. News staff one; news progmg 5 hrs wkly. Target aud: 25-54. ■ Aylett Coleman, pres; Scott Quesinberry, vp; Meredith Coleman, stn mgr; Jim Wiggins, gen sls mgr; Rick Dillow, prom mgr; Bill Campbell, progmg dir; Jennifer Ashley, news dir & pub affrs dir; Mike Settles, chief engr.

WKOC(FM)—See Elizabeth City, N.C.

*****WODC(FM)**—Feb 12, 1989: 88.5 mhz; 300 w. Ant 150 ft. TL: N36 50 27 W76 04 54. Suite B, 3177 Virginia Beach Blvd. (23452). (804) 498-9632. FAX: (804) 340-1588. Licensee: Virginia Beach Educational Broadcasting Foundation. Format: Christian. Target aud: General. ■ Fritz Stegmann, pres; Anne Verebely, gen mgr, vp progmg & mus dir; Ann Norman, prom dir & prom mgr; John Vinson, asst mus dir; Steve Shrader, chief engr.

WROX-FM—(Cape Charles). 1986: 96.1 mhz; 50 kw. Ant 499 ft. TL: N37 15 47 W76 00 47. Stereo. 500 Dominion Tower, 999 Waterside Dr., Norfolk (23510). (804) 331-3160. FAX: (804) 622-9769. Licensee: Sinclair Communications Inc. (group owner; acq 9-28-93; $1,300,010; FTR 10-25-93). Format: Rock. Target aud: 25-54. ■ Bob Sinclair, gen mgr; Chris Blade, progmg dir.

Warrenton

WKCW(AM)—Dec 7, 1957: 1420 khz; 5 kw-D. TL: N38 45 05 W77 44 38. Box 740, Rts. 29 & 673 (22186). (703) 347-1420; (800) 727-9529. FAX: (703) 347-4666. Licensee: WKTF Inc. (acq 10-58). Fmt. Format: Traditional country & bluegrass. News staff one; news progmg 2 hrs wkly. Target aud: 35-65; mature adults with discretionary income. Spec prog: Farm one hr, relg 3 hrs wkly. ■ Joyce Crescente, pres; Barry H. Cohen, gen mgr & gen sls mgr; Marc Alan Felton, opns mgr & progmg dir; Tom Reeder, mus dir; Robert Hughes, chief engr. ■ Rates: $22; 19; 22; na.

WPRZ(AM)—Nov 21, 1957: 1250 khz; 5 kw-D, 32 w-N, DA-2. TL: N38 43 52 W77 46 42. Box 3220 (22186); 444 Hunton St. (22186). (703) 349-1250. Licensee: Praise Communications Inc. Net: USA, Moody. Format: Christian, MOR. ■ Steve W. Buchanan, pres; Sally Buchanan, gen mgr, progmg dir & mus dir; John H. Houser, chief engr. ■ Rates: $12; 10; 12; 10.

WQRA(FM)—Nov 2, 1978: 94.3 mhz; 2.1 kw. Ant 397 ft. TL: N38 40 42 W77 47 18. Stereo. Hrs opn: 24. Box 771, Rts. 29 & 744 (22186). (703) 347-9430; (703) 825-9000. FAX: (703) 349-1148. Licensee: Dettra Broadcasting Inc. Net: CBS, MBS; Va. News Net. Wash atty: Blair, Joyce & Silva. Format: Adult contemp. News staff 2; news progmg 10 hrs wkly. Target aud: 25-54. Spec prog: Gospel 5 hrs wkly.■ Mary Dettra, pres; John Dettra, exec vp; Larry James, stn mgr; Gloria Williams, gen sls mgr; Larry Jones, adv mgr; Tom Casey, progmg dir; Chuck Williams, news dir; William Fawcett, chief engr. ■ Rates: $24.90; 20.80; 21.90; 19.

WRCY(FM)—Mar 28, 1966: 107.7 mhz; 33 kw. Ant 1199 ft. TL: N38 44 31 W77 50 07. Stereo. Suite 901, 7900 Sudley Rd., Manassas (22110). (703) 631-2577 (METRO); (703) 369-1080 (LOCAL). FAX: (703) 369-6901. Licensee: First Virginia Communications Inc. Net: ABC/D. Wash atty: Kaye, Scholer, Fierman, Hayes & Handler. Format: Rock, country. Target aud: 25-49. ■ Sydney A. Abel, pres; Rick Scharf, gen mgr; Chris O'Brien, progmg dir. ■ Rates: $45; 35; 45; 35.

Warsaw

WNNT(AM)—July 3, 1949: 690 khz; 250 w-D, 10 w-N. TL: N37 56 39 W76 45 05. Stereo. Hrs opn: 16. Box 877, Islington Rd. (22572). (804) 333-4900; (804) 443-5500. FAX: (804) 333-4531. Licensee: Northern Neck Communications (acq 1963). Format: C&W. News progmg 5 hrs wkly. Target aud: 25 plus; general. Spec prog: Farm 5 hrs, Black 10 hrs, relg 8 hrs wkly. ■ Linwood Wadsworth, pres & gen mgr; William Martin, gen sls mgr & news dir; Mark Bryant, progmg dir & mus dir; Jim Thorne, chief engr.

WNNT-FM—Mar 1, 1967: 100.9 mhz; 3 kw. Ant 305 ft. TL: N37 56 39 W76 45 05. Stereo. Dups AM 100%.

Waynesboro

WANV(AM)—March 10, 1965: 970 khz; 5 kw-D, 1 kw-N, DA-2. TL: N38 05 12 W78 54 42. Hrs opn: 24. Box 1248, White Bridge Rd. (22980). (703) 942-1153. FAX: (703) 943-9673. Licensee: WANV Ltd. (acq 11-30-93; $1.1 million with WANV-FM Staunton; FTR 12-20-93). Net: SMN; Capitol Radio Net., Va. RFD. Format: Country. News staff one; news progmg 2 hrs wkly. Target aud: 25-54. Spec prog: Black 3 hrs, farm 2 hrs wkly. ■ Teresa Rogers, pres; Chris Rogers, gen mgr; Jerry Lee Dowd, prom mgr & chief engr. ■ Rates: $12.50; 10; 12.50; 9.

WAYB(AM)—Dec 19, 1947: 1490 khz; 1 kw-U. TL: N38 04 42 W78 53 47. c/o Phillip C. Showers, Rt. 2, Box 220, Forest (24551). (703) 943-9292. Licensee: Hometown Media Inc. (acq 12-6-93; $14,000; FTR 1-3-94). Format: Adult contemp.

*****WPVA(FM)**—Not on air, target date 1994: 90.1 mhz; 2.5 kw. Ant 984 ft. TL: N38 01 41 W78 52 22. Hrs opn: 18. Box 889, Blacksburg (24060). (703) 552-4252. FAX: (703) 951-5282. Licensee: Positive Alternative Radio Inc. (group owner). Net: USA. Wash atty: Booth, Freret & Imlay. Format: adult contemp, Christian mus.■ Vernon H. Baker, pres; George McNevlin, gen mgr.

West Point

WPTG(FM)—July 1991: 107.9 mhz; 6 kw. Ant 328 ft. TL: N37 30 04 W76 52 16. Stereo. Hrs opn: 24. 4007 Ironbound Rd., Williamsburg (23188). (804) 229-7400. Licensee: West Point Broadcasting Co. Inc. Net: CNN. Format: Country. ■ Gilbert Granger, pres; Charlie Thompson, gen mgr.

White Stone

WVZG(FM)—Not on air, target date unknown: 100.1 mhz; 3 kw. Ant 328 ft. TL: N37 37 22 W76 17 26. Licensee: Windmill Community General Partnership.

Williamsburg

*****WCWM(FM)**—Sept 28, 1959: 90.7 mhz; 1.6 kw. Ant 350 ft. TL: N37 16 05 W76 42 52. Stereo. Hrs opn: 24. Campus Center, College of William & Mary (23185). (804) 221-3288. Licensee: College of William & Mary. Net: Moody. Format: Div, alternative new mus, progsv. News progmg 3 hrs wkly. Target aud: General. Spec prog: Jazz 13 hrs, class 11 hrs, reggae 6 hrs, blues 3 hrs wkly. ■ Terri Anderson, gen mgr.

WDCK(FM)—Licensed to Williamsburg. See Richmond.

WMBG(AM)—Jan 1, 1958: 740 khz; 500 w-D, 8 w-N. TL: N37 16 37 W76 45 07. Hrs opn: 6 AM-9 PM. 4007 Ironbound Rd. (23188). (804) 229-7400; (804) 220-5555. FAX: (804) 229-9396. Licensee: Great Sounds Inc. Net: CNN. Format: Big band, oldies. News staff one. Target aud: 45 plus. Spec prog: Gospel 5 hrs wkly. ■ Gil Granger, pres, stn mgr & opns mgr; Bob Sheeran, gen sls mgr & mktg dir; Lisa Granger, prom mgr, mus dir, news dir & pub affrs dir; Bill Wilson, adv mgr; Jerry Lee Scott, chief engr. ■ Rates: $12; 10; 12; 8.50.

Winchester

WINC(AM)—June 15, 1941: 1400 khz; 1 kw-U. TL: N39 11 12 W78 09 06. Hrs opn: 24. 520 N. Pleasant Valley Rd. (22601); Box 3300 (22604). (703) 667-2224. FAX: (703) 722-3295. Licensee: Mid-Atlantic Network Inc. (group owner). Net: Unistar. Format: Adult contemp, talk. News staff 3; news progmg 6 hrs wkly. Target aud: 25-49; mid-to-upscale active adults. ■ John Lewis, pres; David Lewis, Howard Lewis, vps; Thomas Scheithe, gen mgr; Chuck Peterson, gen sls mgr; Pat Evans, progmg dir; Steve Edwards, news dir; Arch McKay, chief engr. ■ Rates: $48; 19; 48; 20.

WINC-FM—Oct 1946: 92.5 mhz; 22 kw. Ant 1,424 ft. TL: N38 57 21 W78 01 28. Stereo. Hrs opn: 24. Prog sep from AM. Format: Adult contemp. ■ Rates: $48; 48; 48; 20.

WNTW(AM)—Jan 27, 1961: 610 khz; 500 w-U, DA-2. TL: N39 11 53 W78 13 13. Hrs opn: 24. 381 Spinning Wheel Lane (22603). (703) 662-5101. FAX: (703) 662-8610. Licensee: Benchmark Radio Acquisition Fund II Ltd. Group owner: Benchmark Communications Radio (acq 4-24-91); $3.65 million with co-located FM; FTR 5-20-91). Net: CNN. Format: News/talk. Target aud: General. Spec prog: Sports. ■ David Ridgeway, gen mgr; Steve Gaines, gen sls mgr; Randy Woodward, progmg dir. ■ Rates: $7; 5; 7; 4.

WUSQ-FM—Co-owned with WNTW(AM). Dec 10, 1965: 102.5 mhz; 31 kw. Ant 630 ft. TL: N39 10 38 W78 15 53. Stereo. Net: ABC/E. Format: Modern country. News progmg one hr wkly. Target aud: 25-54, 35-64. ■ Wendy Robbins, prom mgr; Jennifer Woodward, progmg mgr; Steve Williams, mus dir; Susan Hawthorne, pub affrs dir. ■ Rates: $35; 29; 35; 27.

*****WTRM(FM)**—July 1986: 91.3 mhz; 6.1 kw. Ant 1,348 ft. TL: N39 10 59 W78 23 23. Stereo. Hrs opn: 24. Box 3438 (22604). (703) 869-4997. FAX: (703) 869-7179. Licensee: Timber Ridge Ministries Inc. Net: USA. Wash atty: Southmayd, Simpson & Miller. Format: Southern gospel. Target aud: General. ■ Leona Choy, pres; Richard Choy, vp, gen mgr & chief engr; Sheryl Rickard, news dir.

WUSQ-FM—Listing follows WNTW(AM).

Windsor

WSVY-FM—May 1990: 107.7 mhz; 3 kw. Ant 328 ft. TL: N36 48 58 W76 41 35. Stereo. Hrs opn: 24. Box 677 (23487). (804) 242-3213. Licensee: JH Communications Inc. Net: CNN, CBN. Format: Urban. Target aud: 25-34; women. Spec prog: Talk 5 hrs wkly. ■ Andy Booth, pres & chief engr.

Wise

WNVA-FM—See Norton.

Woodbridge

WCXR-FM—Licensed to Woodbridge. See Washington, D.C.

Woodstock

WAMM(AM)—Oct 9, 1981: 1230 khz; 1 kw-U. TL: N38 51 11 W78 31 30. Hrs opn: 6 AM-midnight. Box 392, Harrisonburg (22664). (703) 459-5700. FAX: (703) 433-7438. Licensee: Dean O'Connell Inc. (group owner). Net: SMN. Format: Country. News staff one; news progmg 9 hrs wkly. Target aud: 22-45; middle income. Spec prog: Farm 2 hrs wkly. ■ Robert Dean, pres, stn mgr & chief engr; Ron Reedy, gen sls mgr & adv mgr.

WAZR(FM)—Oct 18, 1985: 93.7 mhz; 10 kw. Ant -49 ft. TL: N38 50 23 W78 33 32 (CP: 93.7 mhz, 25 kw). Stereo. Hrs opn: 24. Box 10, 123 E. Court St. (22664); Box 10, Loudoun Mall, Winchester (22604). (703) 459-8810; (800) 296-8810. FAX: (703) 459-5834. Licensee: Ruarch Associates L.P. Net: SMN, ABC. Rep: Roslin. Wash atty: Borsari & Paxton. Format: Big band, MOR. News staff 2; news progmg 4 hrs wkly. Target aud: 25-65; affluent upwardly mobile & mature listeners.■Dr. Arthur D. Stamler, pres, stn mgr & news dir; Alan Arehart, opns mgr; Virginia I. Stamler, sls dir; Dick Getz, gen sls mgr; Mike Baptist, prom mgr; Phil Luttrell, progmg dir; Frank Crum, mus dir; Jon Wenger, pub affrs dir; Jack Farrance, chief engr. ■ Rates: $25; 18; 25; 15.

Wytheville

WYVE(AM)—Sept 21, 1949: 1280 khz; 2.5 kw-D, 164 w-N. TL: N36 57 54 W81 04 55. Stereo. Hrs opn: 6 AM-sunset. Box 534, 195 S. First St. (24382). (703) 228-3185; (703) 228-6803. FAX: (703) 228-9261. Licensee: Advent Communications. Net: UPI; Va. News Net. Rep: Dome. Format: C&W, loc news & sports. News staff one; news progmg 10 hrs wkly. Target aud: 25 plus; general. Spec prog: Gospel 4 hrs wkly. ■ Ralph Davis, CEO; Gary Hearl, CFO; David R. Roederer, vp & gen mgr; Don

Nickell, opns dir; David Roederer, gen sls mgr; Kevin Fore, mktg dir; Martha Vance, prom dir; Danny Gordon, news dir. ■ Rates: $6; 6; 6; na.

Yorktown

WXEZ(FM)—July 4, 1975: 94.1 mhz; 50 kw. Ant 500 ft. TL: N37 29 37 W76 26 30. Stereo. Hrs opn: 24. 4026 George Washington Hwy. (23692). (804) 898-9494. FAX: (804) 898-9401. Licensee: Eure Communications (group owner; acq 11-86; $1,950,000; FTR 11-10-86). Format: Easy listening. News staff 8. Target aud: 35-64. ■ Bill Eure, CEO; Wes Eure, gen mgr, gen sls mgr & progmg dir; Ernie Warner, chief engr. ■ Rates: $40; 40; 40; 20.

*WYCS(FM)—February 1966: 91.5 mhz; 1.3 kw-H, 20 kw-V. Ant 371 ft-H, 331 ft-V. TL: N37 12 15 W76 30 07. Stereo. Box 1469 (23692); 9300 George Washington Hwy. (23692). (804) 898-0357. FAX: (804) 898-0367. Licensee: York County School Board. Format: Adult contemp. News progmg 3 hrs wkly. Target aud: 25-40. Spec prog: Ger one hr, Sp one hr, Fr one hr wkly. ■ William M. Swartz, gen mgr, stn mgr & chief engr; Charles S. Teagle, mus dir.

Washington

WILLIAM A. EXLINE, INC
MEDIA BROKERS
CONSULTANTS

4340 Redwood Highway
Suite F 230
San Rafael, California 94903
TEL (415) 479-3484
• FAX (415) 479-1574

Aberdeen

KAYO(AM)—Aug 1, 1949: 1450 khz; 1 kw-U. TL: N46 56 59 W123 49 13. Box 188, 701 E. Heron (98520). (206) 532-1450. FAX: (206) 532-1456. Licensee: Kayo Broadcasting Co. (acq 4-1-84; grpsl; FTR 4-16-84). Net: ABC/I. Rep: Eastman, InterMountain, Art Moore. Format: Country. Target aud: 25-54. ■ Jack Comfort, gen mgr; Rhys Davis, opns mgr; Heidi Persson, gen sls mgr. ■ Rates: $20; 15; 20; 12.50.

KAYO-FM—1981: 99.3 mhz; 3 kw. Ant -17 ft. TL: N36 56 59 W123 49 13. Stereo. Dups AM 95%.

KDUX-FM—Listing follows KXRO(AM).

KGHO(AM)—See Hoquiam.

KGHO-FM—See Hoquiam.

KXRO(AM)—May 28, 1928: 1320 khz; 5 kw-D, 1 kw-N, DA-N. TL: N46 57 28 W123 48 26. Hrs opn: 5 AM-midnight. Box 47, 1308 Coolidge Rd. (98520). (206) 533-1320. FAX: (206) 532-0935. Licensee: Pioneer Broadcasting Co. (acq 4-10-80). Net: Moody, NBC. Rep: McGavren Guild. Wash atty: Covington & Burling. Format: Adult contemp. News staff one; news progmg 6 hrs wkly. Target aud: 25-54. ■ Richard Kale, CEO; Elizabeth Clapp, pres; Louis Wright, CFO; Roger Nelson, gen mgr & gen sls mgr; Randy Roadz, opns mgr & progmg mgr; Pat Anderson, mus dir; Liz Miller, news dir; Jay White, chief engr. ■ Rates: $17; 14; 16; 12.

KDUX-FM—Co-owned with KXRO(AM). Oct 4, 1964: 104.7 mhz; 48 kw. Ant 360 ft. TL: N46 56 00 W123 43 49. Stereo. Hrs opn: 5 AM-12 AM. Prog sep from AM. Net: Westwood One. Format: Rock. News staff one; news progmg 2 hrs wkly. Target aud: 18-49. ■ Rates: Same as AM.

Anacortes

KLKI(AM)—Dec 18, 1963: 1340 khz; 1 kw-U. TL: N48 29 44 W122 36 15. Hrs opn: 24. Box 96, 25th Commercial St. (98221). (206) 293-3141. Licensee: Island Broadcasting Inc. (acq 1965). Net: MBS, Unistar, Westwood One, NBC. Format: Adult contemp, sports, news. News staff one; news progmg 30 hrs wkly. Target aud: 25-60. Spec prog: Relg one hr wkly. ■ William Berry, gen mgr; Lynn McMullen, prom mgr; Jason Brooks, news dir; Bob Walther, chief engr. ■ Rates: $14.50; 14; 14.50; 11.

Asotin

KCLK(AM)—Mar 2, 1971: 1430 khz; 5 kw-D, 1 kw-N, DA-2. TL: N46 18 59 W117 02 24. Hrs opn: 24. Box 669, 1859 5th Ave., Clarkston (99403). (509) 758-3361. Licensee: Clarkston Broadcasters. Net: Moody. Rep: Tacher. Format: Country. News staff one. Target aud: 25 plus. ■ W.E. Lawrence, pres & gen mgr; Helen Warkentin, gen sls mgr; Gene Lawrence, progmg dir & mus dir; Reiny Baer, news dir. ■ Rates: $17; 17; 17; 17.

KCLK-FM—See Clarkston.

Auburn

KBSG(AM)—Aug 6, 1958: 1210 khz; 27 kw-D, 10 kw-N. TL: N47 18 20 W122 14 51 (CP: COL: Auburn-Federal Way). Stereo. Hrs opn: 24. Rebroadcasts KBSG (FM) Tacoma. 1730 Minor Ave., 20th Fl., Seattle (98101). (206) 343-9700; FAX: (206) 623-7677; (206) 343-0481. Licensee: KBSG Inc. Group owner: Viacom Broadcasting Inc. (acq 10-3-89; $1.5 million; FTR 10-23-89). Rep: Torbet. Format: Oldies. News staff one. Target aud: 25-54; adults. ■ Bill Figenshu, pres; Charles E. Maylin, gen mgr; Susan Seifert, gen sls mgr; Carol Stripling, mktg mgr; Jay Kelly, progmg mgr; Heidi May, mus dir; Kim Wilson, news dir; Clay Freinwald, chief engr.

*KGRG(FM)—December 1974: 89.9 mhz; 100 w. Ant 570 ft. TL: N47 18 43 W122 10 35 (CP: 250 w, ant 367 ft.). Stereo. Hrs opn: 24. 12401 S.E. 320th St. (98002). (206) 833-9111, ext. 431. FAX: (206) 939-5135. Licensee: Green River College. Wash atty: Akin, Gump, Strauss, Hauer & Feld. Format: Modern rock. News progmg 2 hrs wkly. Target aud: 17-34; teens & young adults. Spec prog: Local music 3 hrs, grunge 2 hrs wkly. ■ Toby Teneyck, gen mgr; Dave Wilson, mktg dir; Dave Mahar, prom mgr; Jon Shearer, progmg mgr; Terry Kelly, Kathie Crosby, mus dirs; Amy Roe, news dir; Matt Warren, pub affrs dir; Jon Kasprick, chief engr.

Bellevue

*KASB(FM)—Mar 22, 1971: 89.3 mhz; 10 w. Ant 289 ft. TL: N47 36 17 W122 11 47. 10416 S.E. Kilmarnock St. (98004-6698). (206) 455-6154. Licensee: Bellevue School District No. 405. Format: Alternative, AOR, news. Spec prog: News magazine 3 hrs, sports 6 hrs wkly. ■ Don O'Neill, pres; Juris Jansons, gen mgr.

*KBCS(FM)—Feb 3, 1973: 91.3 mhz; 1.2 kw. Ant 100 ft. TL: N47 35 07 W122 08 39. Stereo. 3000 Landerholm Circle S.E. (98007). (206) 641-2424. Licensee: Bellevue Community College. Format: Div. Spec prog: Sp 4 hrs wkly. ■ Harriet Baskas, opns mgr & chief engr; Caitlin Sullivan, progmg dir; Eric Thomas, mus dir.

KBLV(AM)—March 1958: 1540 khz; 5 kw-U, DA-N. TL: N47 35 29 W122 10 56. Suite 106, 14400 Bel-Red Rd., Bellevue (98007). (206) 957-1540. FAX: (206) 957-0714. Licensee: Classic Country Radio Inc. (acq 12-26-91; $75,000; FTR 1-13-92). Format: Country gold. News staff 2. Target aud: 25-65; working folks. Spec prog: Sports 6 hrs, western 6 hrs wkly. ■ Barbara Geesman, pres; Wes Geesman, gen mgr; Ruben Aker, stn mgr; Roy Newcomb, progmg dir; Larry Gruber, chief engr. ■ Rates: $10; 5; 10; 2.

KLSY-FM—November 1964: 92.5 mhz; 58 kw. Ant 2,342 ft. TL: N47 30 14 W121 58 29. Stereo. Suite 206, 12011 N.E. First St. (98005). (206) 454-1540. FAX: (206) 455-8849. Licensee: Bellevue Radio Inc. Group owner: Sandusky Radio. Rep: Christal. Format: Adult contemp. News staff 2. Target aud: 25-49; working women & families. ■ Norman Rau, pres; Gary Robb, vp & gen mgr; Bobby Irwin, opns dir & progmg dir; Bob Bordonaro, gen sls mgr; Bill Jensen, rgnl sls mgr; Laura Sieberns, Denise Hale, prom mgrs; Bob Brooks, mus dir; Dave Sloan, news dir; Jim Stevens, chief engr.

Bellingham

KAFE(FM)—Listing follows KPUG(AM).

KARI(AM)—See Blaine.

KGMI(AM)—1927: 790 khz; 5 kw-D, 1 kw-N, DA-N. TL: N48 41 09 W122 26 43. 2219 Yew St. Rd. (98226). (206) 734-9790. FAX: (206) 733-4551. Licensee: KGMI Inc. (acq 9-69). Net: ABC/I, NBC Talknet. Rep: Art Moore. Format: News/talk. News staff 4. Target aud: 35-54. ■ Ann Jones, pres; Rick Staeb, gen mgr; Dan King, natl sls mgr; Scott Brockett, prom mgr; Debbie Schuitema, progmg dir; Robert Kennedy, news dir; Will Vos, chief engr.

KISM(FM)—Co-owned with KGMI(AM). Mar 1960: 92.9 mhz; 50 kw. Ant 2,440 ft. TL: N48 40 48 W122 50 24. Stereo. Prog sep from AM. Format: Rock, classic rock. Target aud: 25-44. ■ Don Kurtis, natl sls mgr; Julie Marletto, progmg dir; John Napier, mus dir.

KPUG(AM)—Feb 29, 1948: 1170 khz; 10 kw-D, 5 kw-N, DA-N. TL: N40 46 34 W122 26 21. Hrs opn: 24. Box 1170 (98227); 2340 E. Sunset Dr. (98226). (206) 734-1170. FAX: (206) 734-5697. Licensee: San Juan Radio Inc. Net: MBS. Rep: McGavren Guild. Format: CNN Headline News. News staff 2; news progmg 24 hrs. Target aud: 25-54. ■ Michael Pollock, pres & gen mgr; Jim Tincker, gen sls mgr; Mark Edwards, progmg dir & mus dir; Bill Baker, news dir.

KAFE(FM)—Co-owned with KPUG(AM). July 2, 1965: 104.3 mhz; 60 kw. Ant 2,310 ft. TL: N48 40 48 W122 50 24. Stereo. Hrs opn: 24. Prog sep from AM. (206) 734-5233. Net: MBS. Format: Adult contemp.

*KUGS(FM)—Jan 29, 1974: 89.3 mhz; 100 w. Ant 384 ft. TL: N48 44 11 W122 28 47. Western Wash. Univ., 410 Viking Union Bldg. (98225). (206) 650-5847. FAX: (206) 738-6507. Licensee: Western Washington Univ. Format: Div. News staff 5; news progmg 5 hrs wkly. Spec prog: Class 5 hrs, country 5 hrs, Black 5 hrs, Sp 3 hrs, rock 15 hrs, blues 15 hrs, jazz 20 hrs wkly. ■ Dan Tritle, gen mgr; Matt Eidson, progmg dir; Doug Hildenbrandt, chief engr.

*KZAZ(FM)—Sept 1, 1991: 91.7 mhz; 120 w. Ant 334 ft. TL: N48 48 04 W122 27 40. Stereo. Hrs opn: 18. Bellingham Towers, Suite 270, 119 N. Commercial (98225). (206) 671-1912; (206) 738-9170. FAX: (206) 738-4605. Licensee: Northern Sound Public Radio. Net: NPR, APR. Wash atty: Haley, Bader & Potts. Format: Class, jazz, news. News progmg 40 hrs wkly. Target aud: General. Spec prog: Folk. ■ Patricia Karlock, gen mgr; Ted Askew, mus dir.

Bellingham-Ferndale

KBFW(AM)—Apr 4, 1958: 930 khz; 1 kw-D, 500 w-N, DA-N. TL: N48 47 52 W122 28 01 (CP: COL: Bellingham). Hrs opn: 24. Box D, 1919 Broadway, Bellingham (98227). (206) 734-8555. FAX: (206) 734-8557. Licensee: Bellingham Broadcasting Corp. (acq 7-29-85). Net: NBC. Rep: Tacher. Wash atty: Haley, Bader & Potts. Format: Country. News staff one; news progmg 5 hrs wkly. Target aud: 25-54. ■ Steven L. Smith, pres, gen mgr, prom mgr & chief engr; Chet Cory, opns mgr, progmg dir & news dir; Dave Lizer, gen sls mgr; Erin Lynne, mus dir. ■ Rates: $25; 22; 25; 18.

Blaine

KAFE(FM)—See Bellingham.

KARI(AM)—Feb 12, 1960: 550 khz; 5 kw-D, 2.5 kw-N, DA-2. TL: N48 57 15 W122 44 36. Hrs opn: 24. 4840 Lincoln Rd. (98230); Box 1037, Bellingham (98227). (206) 371-5500; (604) 536-7733. FAX: (206) 371-7617. Licensee: Birch Bay Broadcasting Co. Inc. Group owner: Ostrander-Wilson Stns. Net: USA. Wash atty: Cohn & Marks, Pepper & Corazzini. Format: Religious, news/talk. News progmg 15 hrs wkly. Target aud: 35 plus. Spec prog: Ger 2 hrs, farm 3 hrs, Ukrainian one hr, Sp one hr wkly. ■ George A. Wilson, pres; Don J. Bevilacqua, vp & gen mgr; Gary Nawman, opns mgr; Tim Toronchuk, gen sls mgr; Gary Nauman, progmg dir; Jim Scott, mus dir & chief engr; Jan Larsen, news dir.

Bremerton

KBRO(AM)—May 1947: 1490 khz; 1 kw-U. TL: N47 33 52 W122 39 26. Hrs opn: 24. Box 1277, Tacoma (98401). (206) 377-2325. FAX: (206) 922-3348. Licensee: KLDY Inc. (acq 2-4-93; $98,500; FTR 2-22-93). Format: Big band. News staff one; news progmg 20 hrs wkly. Target aud: 25-54; Kitsap County residents. Spec prog: Kitsap County news & information. ■ Josie Baine, pres & sls dir; Lee Jackson, opns mgr, mus dir & news dir; Gary Greenfield, chief engr. ■ Rates: $20; 15; 20; 10.

Stations in the U.S.   Washington

KRWM(FM)—Aug 22, 1964: 106.9 mhz; 100 kw. Ant 819 ft. TL: N47 36 57 W122 18 26. Stereo. Hrs opn: 24. Watermark Tower, Suite 300, 1109 First Ave., Seattle (98101). (206) 292-8600. FAX: (206) 292-6964. Licensee: The KKNW Co. Group owner: Brown Broadcasting Co. (acq 6-27-90; $10 million; FTR 6-4-90). Rep: CBS Radio. Wash atty: Reed, Smith, Shaw & McClay. Format: Soft adult contemp. News staff one. Target aud: 25-54.

Burien-Seattle

KGNW(AM)—Oct 10, 1970: 820 khz; 50 kw-D, 5 kw-N, DA-2. TL: N47 26 00 W121 28 02. Hrs opn: 24. Suite 550, 2815 2nd Ave., Seattle (98121). (206) 443-8200. FAX: (206) 443-1561. Licensee: Inspiration Media Inc. Group owner: Salem Communications Corp. (acq 12-12-86). Net: USA. Wash atty: Miller & Fields. Format: Relg, Christian talk. News progmg 3 hrs wkly. Target aud: 35 plus. Spec prog: Southern gospel, Black gospel, Talkline, Northwest Life, Women in Touch, Married Life. ■ Stuart Epperson, chmn; Edward G. Atsinger III, pres; Don Cartmell, Norm Olsen, vps; Richard Ulrich, gen mgr; Roger Grossenbacher, opns mgr & mus dir; Rob Evans, gen sls mgr; Dick Harris, chief engr.

Camas

KMUZ-FM—Licensed to Camas. See Portland, Ore.

Cashmere

KYSN(FM)—See Wenatchee.

KZPH(FM)—Not on air, target date unknown: 106.7 mhz; 2.45 kw. Ant 513 ft. TL: N47 30 35 W120 31 24. Box 920, Wenatchee (98807-0920). Licensee: Big Rock Inc. (acq 4-9-92; $34,000; FTR 5-4-92).

Centralia

*KCED(FM)—Licensed to Centralia. See Centralia-Chehalis.

KMNT(FM)—Licensed to Centralia. See Centralia-Chehalis.

Centralia-Chehalis

*KCED(FM)—(Centralia). Feb 17, 1975: 91.3 mhz; 1 kw. Ant -72 ft. TL: N46 42 54 W122 57 33. Stereo. 600 W. Locust St., Centralia (98531). (206) 736-9391, ext. 243. Licensee: Board of Trustees, Centralia College. Format: Educ, top-40, news. ■ Wade Fisher, gen mgr, progmg dir & pub affrs dir; Bill Schoelkopf, chief engr.

KELA(AM)—Nov 1, 1937: 1470 khz; 5 kw-D, 1 kw-N. TL: N46 41 47 W122 57 23. Hrs opn: 5 AM-midnight. 1635 S. Gold St., Centralia (98531); Box 827, Chehalis (98532). (206) 736-3321; (206) 748-3321. Licensee: KELA Corp. (acq 6-15-65). Net: NBC, Daynet. Rep: Tacher. Wash atty: Ogden, Murphy & Wallace. Format: News, talk, sports. News staff 2; news progmg 28 hrs wkly. Target aud: 35 plus. Spec prog: Big band 3 hrs, class 2 hrs wkly. ■ M.J. Chytil, pres; John DiMeo Jr., gen mgr; Larry Miner, gen sls mgr; Steve Richert, progmg dir; Steve George, mus dir; Jim Cook, news dir; William Tilton, chief engr. ■ Rates: $20; 18; 20; 16.

KMNT(FM)—(Centralia). Co-owned with KELA(AM). Aug 24, 1965: 102.9 mhz; 100 kw. Ant 1,057 ft. TL: N46 33 18 W123 03 27. Stereo. Hrs opn: 5 AM-midnight. Prog sep from AM. Format: Country. News staff 2; news progmg 7 hrs wkly. Target aud: 18 plus. Spec prog: Farm one hr wkly. ■ Steve Williams, mus dir. ■ Rates: $22; 18; 20; 16.

KITI(AM)—(Chehalis-Centralia). October 1954: 1420 khz; 5 kw-U, DA-2. TL: N46 42 08 W122 55 58. Hrs opn: 24. 1133 Kresky, Centralia (98531). (206) 736-1355. FAX: (206) 736-4761. Licensee: Premier Broadcasters Inc. Group owner: Premier Group (acq 10-77). Net: ABC/I. Rep: Intermountain Net, Eastman. Art Moore.Wash atty: Setner. Format: Adult contemp. News staff 2; news progmg 15 hrs wkly. Target aud: 25-54. ■ Derek Shannon, gen mgr; Peter Talbot, gen sls mgr; Roger Dale, progmg dir; Dave Pavlitich, mus dir; Scott Hodges, news dir; Harvey Brooks, chief engr. ■ Rates: $22; 20; 18; 9.

KMNT(FM)—Listing follows KELA(AM).

Chehalis

*KACS(FM)—Aug 18, 1993: 90.5 mhz; 3 kw. Ant 98 ft. TL: N46 43 13 W123 01 29. Stereo. Hrs opn: 24. Box 601 Suite B, 2401 N.E. Kresky (98532). (206) 740-9436. FAX: (206) 748-1596. Licensee: Chehalis Valley Educational Foundation. Net: Skylight. Wash atty: Don Martin. Target aud: 35-49. ■ Loren Olson, stn mgr.

KITI(AM)—See Centralia-Chehalis.

Chehalis-Centralia

KITI(AM)—Licensed to Chehalis-Centralia. See Centralia-Chehalis.

Chelan

KOZI(AM)—Mar 1, 1957: 1230 khz; 1 kw-U. TL: N47 50 50 W120 00 29. Hrs opn: 24. Box 819, 123 E. Johnson (98816). (509) 682-4033. FAX: (509) 682-4035. Licensee: Northcentral Broadcasting Co. (acq 12-15-69). Net: MBS. Rep: Target. Wash atty: Haley, Bader & Potts. Format: Adult contemp, talk, news. News staff 3; news progmg 32 hrs wkly. Target aud: General. Spec prog: Farm 3 hrs, Sp 4 hrs wkly. ■ Jerry E. Isenhart, pres & gen mgr; Ray Dobbs, stn mgr & gen sls mgr; Steve Byquist, progmg dir; Jennifer Martin, mus dir; Scott Brundage, news dir; Jerry Isenhart, vp engrg. ■ Rates: $23; 13; 18; 9.

KOZI-FM—Aug 26, 1981: 93.5 mhz; 590 w. Ant 1,040 ft. TL: N47 51 07 W119 52 18. Dups AM 100%. Target aud: General. ■ Rates: Same as AM.

Cheney

*KEWU-FM—Apr 3, 1964: 89.5 mhz; 10 kw. Ant 1,407 ft. TL: N47 34 43 W117 17 50. Stereo. Hrs opn: 6 AM-midnight. MS No. 104, Dept. of Radio-TV, Eastern Washington Univ. (99004-2495). (509) 359-4226. FAX: (509) 359-7028. Licensee: Eastern Washington Univ. Board of Trustees. Format: Jazz. ■ Marvin E. Smith, gen mgr; N. J. Brown, stn mgr; April Minister, news dir.

KEYF-FM—May 4, 1986: 101.1 mhz; 100 kw. Ant 1,965 ft. TL: N47 42 41 W111 51 31. Stereo. Hrs opn: 24. S. 6019 Crestline, Spokane (99223). (509) 448-1111. FAX: (509) 448-6523. Licensee: KEYF Corp. (acq 8-27-92; $1.825 million with KEYF(AM) Dishman; FTR 9-21-92). Rep: McGavren Guild. Format: Oldies. News staff one; news progmg 15 hrs wkly. Target aud: 25-54. ■ Norm Feuer, CEO; Terry Robinson, pres; Chris Garras, gen mgr; Brad Krueger, Chris Garras, gen sls mgrs; Scott Valentine, progmg dir; Scot Valentine, progmg mgr; Janean Jay, news dir; Jim Nichols, chief engr.

Clarkston

KCLK-FM—1974: 94.1 mhz; 100 kw. Ant 1,233 ft. TL: N46 27 27 W117 06 03. Stereo. Hrs opn: 24. Prog dups KCLK(AM) Asotin. Box 669, 1859 5th Ave. (99403). (509) 758-3361. Licensee: Clarkston Broadcasters. Net: MBS. Rep: Tacher. Format: Country. News staff one. Target aud: 25 plus. ■ W.E. Lawrence, pres, gen mgr & stn mgr; Helen Warkentin, gen sls mgr; Gene Lawrence, progmg dir & mus dir; Steve Franko, chief engr. ■ Rates: $17; 17; 17; 17.

KQQQ(AM)—See Pullman.

KRLC(AM)—See Lewiston, Idaho.

Colfax

KCLX(AM)—1950: 1450 khz; 1 kw-U. TL: N46 52 17 W117 22 37. Box 710, Almota Rd. (99111). (509) 397-3441. FAX: (509) 397-4752. Licensee: Dakota Communications (acq 9-17-85; $110,000; FTR 8-5-85). Net: MBS. Rep: Farmakis, Moore. Format: Country. News staff one; news progmg 9 hrs wkly. Target aud: 25 plus; agricultural-urban. Spec prog: Farm 5 hrs, sports 7 hrs wkly. ■ Robert G. Hauser, pres & gen mgr; Kim Rodgers, gen sls mgr; Dana Elder, prom mgr & progmg dir; Dennison Bird, mus dir; Phil Vandervort, news dir; Bill Gott, chief engr.

KRAO(FM)—Co-owned with KCLX(AM). Not on air, target date unknown: 102.3 mhz; 1.6 kw. Ant 433 ft. TL: N46 48 38 W117 20 34. Stereo.

College Place

*KGTS(FM)—Oct 5, 1963: 91.3 mhz; 4.6 kw. Ant 1,297 ft. TL: N45 59 20 W118 10 29. Stereo. Hrs opn: 24. 204 S. College Ave. (99324). (509) 527-2991. FAX: (509) 527-2611. Licensee: Walla Walla College. Net: USA. Format: Christian contemp. News staff one. Target aud: 35-49. ■ Neil Erik Andreason, pres; Kevin Krueger, gen mgr; Harry Watts, adv dir; Mark Trenchard, progmg mgr; Todd Brandenburg, chief engr.

Colville

KCVL(AM)—Nov 15, 1955: 1240 khz; 1 kw-U. TL: N48 31 15 W117 54 28. Hrs opn: 24. Box 111, Mantz & Ricky Rd. (99114). (509) 684-5032. Licensee: Tri-County Broadcasting (acq 1-20-81). Net: Unistar. Rep: Tacher. Format: Country. ■ Eric Carpenter, pres.

KCRK-FM—Co-owned with KCVL(AM). Oct 13, 1981: 92.1 mhz; 3 kw. Ant -780 ft. TL: N48 31 15 W117 54 28. Stereo. Hrs opn: 24. Prog sep from AM. (509) 684-5031. FAX: (509) 684-5034. Net: Unistar. Format: Adult contemp.

Davenport

KZQB(FM)—Not on air, target date unknown: 97.3 mhz; 3 kw. Ant 72 ft. TL: N47 39 12 W118 09 03. Box 159, Davenport Radio Partnership, Fayetteville, GA (30214). Licensee: Davenport Radio Partnership.

Dayton

KZHR(FM)—December 1992: 92.5 mhz; 54 kw. Ant 1,243 ft. TL: N46 19 14 W117 58 46. Box 1641, 103 E. Main St., Walla Walla (99362). (509) 525-3162. Licensee: KMEX Inc. (acq 10-22-91; $137,500 for CP; FTR 11-11-91). Format: Sp. ■ Robert Boggess, pres.

Deer Park

KAZZ(FM)—Sept 1983: 107.1 mhz; 9 kw. Ant 253 ft. TL: N48 01 45 W117 35 57. Stereo. Hrs opn: 24. Box 1369 (99006). (509) 276-8816. FAX: (509) 276-2790. Licensee: Barbara Kazmark (acq 4-1-86; $80,000; FTR 1-20-86). Net: SMN, MBS. Format: Country. ■ Earle Kazmark, gen mgr; Ron McGuire, progmg dir; Don Cary, chief engr. ■ Rates: $13; 13; 13; na.

Dishman

KEYF(AM)—Oct 3, 1984: 1050 khz; 5 kw-D, 335 w-N. TL: N47 35 58 W117 22 38. Hrs opn: 24. S. 6019 Crestline, Spokane (99223). (509) 448-1111. FAX: (509) 448-6523. Licensee: KEYF Corp. (group owner; acq 8-27-92; $1.825 million with KEYF-FM Cheney; FTR 9-21-92). Net: ABC/E. Rep: McGavren Guild Radio. Format: 50s & 60s oldies. Target aud: 25-54. ■ Terry Robinson, pres; Chris Garras, gen mgr; Jeff Johnson, gen sls mgr; Dave Mason, prom mgr & news dir; Scott Valentine, progmg dir; Keith Harvey, chief engr.

KWQL(FM)—Not on air, target date unknown: 106.5 mhz; 3 kw. Ant 328 ft. TL: N47 36 10 W117 16 13. Box 638, Pottstown, PA (19464). Licensee: Vera Broadcasting (acq 7-27-93; $20,000; FTR 8-23-93). ■ Mitchell Scott, pres.

East Wenatchee

KYSN(FM)—Licensed to East Wenatchee. See Wenatchee.

Eatonville

KJUN-FM—Not on air, target date unknown: 104.9 mhz; 6 kw. Ant 90 ft. Suite 350, 1001 22nd St. N.W., Washington, DC (20037). Licensee: Barbara J. Geesman.

Edmonds

KCIS(AM)—1954: 630 khz; 5 kw-D, 2.5 kw-N, DA-N. TL: N47 46 06 W122 21 06 (CP: TL: N47 46 06 W122 21 07). Hrs opn: 24. Rm. 19303 Fremont Ave. N., Seattle (98133); Box 330300, Seattle (98133). (206) 546-7350. FAX: (206) 546-7372. Licensee: Crista Ministries. Group owner: Crista Broadcasting. Net: USA, AP, MBN. Format: Christian teaching/inspirational mus, talk, sports. News staff 2; news progmg 40 hrs wkly. Target aud: 35-55. ■ James A. Gwinn, pres; Ron Kawamoto, gen mgr & gen sls mgr; Scott Thunder, vp progmg; Eric Kirchner, progmg dir; Kip Johns, mus dir; Bryan Hubert, chief engr.

KCMS(FM)—Co-owned with KCIS(AM). Mar 11, 1960: 105.3 mhz; 115 kw. Ant 722 ft. TL: N47 46 06 W122 21 07. Stereo. Prog sep from AM. Format: Adult contemp Christian mus. News staff 2; news progmg one hr wkly. Target aud: 25-44; general.

Ellensburg

*KNWR(FM)—Not on air, target date unknown: 90.7 mhz; 5 kw. Ant 2,552 ft. TL: N47 15 48 W120 23 31. Murrow Center, Wash. State Univ., KWSU Radio-TV Service, Pullman (99164-2530). (509) 335-6511. Licensee: Washington State Univ. Net: NPR, APR. Format: Class, news. News progmg 37 hrs wkly. Target aud: General. Spec prog: Jazz, folk. ■ Stanton E. Schmid (University Relations), vp; Dennis Haarsager (KWSU Radio-Television Services), gen mgr; Jean Palmquist (Dir of Radio), stn mgr; Jerry Miller, opns dir; Elizabeth Carroll, dev dir; Jean Palmquist, progmg dir; Dale Harrison, news dir; John Gray, engrg dir. ■ KWSU(TV) affil.

Broadcasting & Cable Yearbook 1994

Washington

KQBE(FM)—Nov 24, 1983: 103.1 mhz; 2 kw. Ant 1,273 ft. TL: N47 00 21 W120 30 55. Stereo. Box 1032, Suite 209, 4th & Pearl (98926). (509) 962-2823. FAX: (509) 962-2823. Licensee: Peak Communications Inc., debtor in possession (acq 5-1-89; $265,000; FTR 5-1-89). Net: SMN. Rep: Art Moore. Format: Adult contemp. News staff one; news progmg 3 hrs wkly. Target aud: 18-49. ■ Pat Peterson, pres; Jack Kelleher, gen mgr & gen sls mgr; Dennis Leach, opns mgr & prom mgr; James T. Peterson, progmg dir & mus dir; Robert Lowery, news dir. ■ Rates: $10; 9; 10; 7.

KXLE(AM)—1946: 1240 khz; 1 kw-U. TL: N47 00 00 W120 31 40. Hrs opn: 24. 1311 Vantage Hwy. (98926). (509) 925-1488. FAX: (509) 962-7882. Licensee: KXLE Inc. (acq 6-82). Net: ABC/E. Rep: Tacher. Wash atty: Haley, Bader & Potts. Format: News/talk. News staff 4. Target aud: General. ■ Sol M. Tacher, pres; Rich Carr, gen mgr & prom mgr; Chris Kennedy, progmg dir & news dir; Mike Fields, engrg mgr. ■ Rates: $22; 21; 22; 19.

KXLE-FM—1972: 95.3 mhz; 1.92 kw-H. 1,345 ft. TL: N46 53 16 W120 26 31. Stereo. Net: ABC/C. Rep: Tacher. Format: Country. Target aud: 18-59. ■ Steve Scellick, progmg dir. ■ Rates: Same as AM.

Enumclaw

KENU(AM)—Mar 1, 1992: 1330 khz; 500 w-D, 26 w-N. TL: N47 12 53 W121 58 19 (CP: 500 w-N, DA-N). 22712 S.E. 436th St. (98202-9038). (206) 825-5368. FAX: (206) 825-9667. Licensee: Country Gold Network Inc. (acq 2-28-92; $135,000; FTR 3-23-92). Rep: Tacher. Format: Country. ■ Wes Geesman, pres & gen mgr; Robert Reed, stn mgr; Brian Love, prom mgr; Emilio Cinco, progmg dir, mus dir & news dir; Tim Vik, chief engr.

Ephrata

KTBI(AM)—Aug 17, 1950: 810 khz; 50 kw-D. TL: N47 21 22 W119 28 56. Box 31000, Spokane (99223). (509) 754-2000; (509) 448-3155. FAX: (509) 448-3811. Licensee: TRMR Inc. Net: MBS, USA. Wash atty: Pepper & Corazzini. Format: Relg, talk. Target aud: 35 plus. Spec prog: Farm 15 hrs wkly. ■ Thomas W. Read, pres & gen mgr; Melinda Read, vp; Dewie Trostel, stn mgr; Reuben James, opns mgr; Nate Bridges, progmg dir; Jane McKee Johnson, mus dir; Jim Key, news dir; George Frese, engrg dir.

KULE(AM)—1952: 730 khz; 1 kw-D. TL: N47 18 55 W119 33 53. 910 Basin S.W. (98823). (509) 754-4661. Licensee: B&G Enterprises (acq 6-85; $95,000; FTR 6-17-85). Net: AP. Rep: Art Moore. Format: Country. ■ Tim Harrington, gen mgr & gen sls mgr; Bryan Jones, progmg dir & news dir; Jerry Isenhart, engrg mgr.

KULE-FM—Dec 25, 1982: 95.9 mhz; 1.5 kw. Ant 460 ft. TL: N47 19 14 W119 34 21 (CP: 92.3 mhz, 20 kw, ant 394 ft.). Stereo. Box 31000, Spokane (99223). (509) 754-2000. Licensee: Basin Street Broadcasting (acq 7-90; $1.2 million; FTR 7-23-90). Net: NBC, CBS. Format: Btfl mus. Spec prog: Classical 5 hrs, farm 5 hrs wkly. ■ Melinda Read, gen mgr.

Everett

KRKO(AM)—Aug 1, 1920: 1380 khz; 5 kw-U, DA-N. TL: N47 55 32 W122 11 19. Stereo. Hrs opn: 24. 7115 Larimer Rd. (98208). (206) 353-1380. FAX: (206) 355-5289. Licensee: S & R Broadcasting (acq 1987). Net: AP. Format: Pure gold oldies. News staff one; news progmg 6 hrs wkly. Target aud: 25-54; residents of Snohomish county. ■ Andrew P. Skotdal, gen mgr & gen sls mgr; Athan James, progmg dir; Moose Moran, mus dir; Renae O'Keefe, news dir; Butch McBride, chief engr.

***KSER(FM)**—Feb 9, 1991: 90.7 mhz; 1 kw. Ant 548 ft. TL: N47 51 45 W122 17 04. Stereo. Hrs opn: 6 AM-2 AM. Suite 150, 14920 Hwy. 99, Lynnwood (98037). (206) 742-4541; (206) 742-1146. FAX: (206) 742-4191. Licensee: Jack Straw Foundation. Net: APR. Wash atty: Haley, Bader & Potts. Format: Div. News staff one; news progmg 17 hrs wkly. Target aud: General. Spec prog: Class 4 hrs, folk 8 hrs, jazz 10 hrs, blues 8 hrs, world 10 hrs, CBC & BBC news 17 hrs, Celtic 6 hrs, popular 6 hrs wkly. ■ Stu Witmer, gen mgr & progmg dir; Jeni Greenlee, opns mgr; Joni Decker-Wright, mus dir; Ed Bremmer, news dir; Sandra Woodruff, chief engr.

KWYZ(AM)—July 21, 1957: 1230 khz; 1 kw-U. TL: N47 58 06 W122 12 04. Stereo. Box 1230 (98206-1230). (206) 348-1230. FAX: (206) 353-8710. Licensee: Quality Broadcasting Corp. (acq 3-29-93; $400,000; FTR 4-19-93). Net: NBC. Rep: Roslin. Format: Country. News progmg 15 hrs wkly. Target aud: 25-54. ■ Wes Geesman, pres; Denise Haddix, stn mgr; Roy Newcomer, progmg dir & mus dir; Denise Hadddix, news dir; Larry Gruber, chief engr. ■ Rates: $47; 37; 42; 27.

Ferndale

KNTR(AM)—May 1963: 1550 khz; 50 kw-D, 10 kw-N, DA-2. TL: N48 50 35 W122 36 05. Hrs opn: 6 AM-midnight. Box 308 (98248). (206) 384-5117; (206) 734-1550. Licensee: Help Ministries Inc. (group owner; acq 6-6-84). Net: USA. Format: Relg, talk. News progmg 4 hrs wkly. Target aud: 35-54; adult Christian. Spec prog: Sp one hr, Chinese one hr, Russian one hr wkly. ■ Richard Ellison, pres; Michael Ellison, exec vp; Marty Hamstra, gen mgr; Larry Vandergriend, stn mgr; Glenda Hamilton, vp opns; Larry Lee, progmg mgr; Ron Cowell, chief engr. ■ Rates: $19; 19; 19; 17.

Forks

KVAC(AM)—October 1967: 1490 khz; 1 kw-U. TL: N47 57 16 W124 23 20. Hrs opn: 24. Box 450 (98331). (206) 374-6233. Licensee: Ices' Inc. Net: MBS. Rep: Tacher. Format: Country. News progmg 2 hrs wkly. Target aud: General. Spec prog: NFL, Sonics, college & high school football, Mariners 20 hrs wkly, gospel 4 hrs wkly. ■ Don Ice, pres, gen mgr, gen sls mgr & mus dir.

KLLM(FM)—Co-owned with KVAC(AM). 1985: 103.9 mhz; 3 kw. Ant -75 ft. TL: N47 57 16 W124 23 20. Dups AM 100%.

Gig Harbor

***KGHP(FM)**—Aug 30, 1988: 89.9 mhz; 1.5 kw. Ant 190 ft. TL: N47 14 29 W122 46 14. Hrs opn: 12 AM-10 PM. 14105 Purdy Dr. N.W. (98332); 14015 62nd Ave. N.W. (98332). (206) 857-3513. FAX: (206) 857-3588. Licensee: Peninsula School District No. 401. Wash atty: Sidley & Austin. Format: Div. Target aud: General; diverse community audience. ■ Don Hofmann, gen mgr; Max Bice, chief engr.

Goldendale

KLCK(AM)—Sept 4, 1984: 1400 khz; 1 kw-U. TL: N45 49 14 W120 50 15. Box 305, 514 S. Columbus (98620). (509) 773-3300; (509) 773-3781. FAX: (509) 773-3301. Licensee: Klickitat Valley Broadcasting Svc Inc. Net: ABC, SMN. Rep: Tacher. Format: Country. ■ Colin Malcolm, pres, gen mgr & chief engr; Kevin Malcolm, progmg dir; Julian Notestine, news dir.

KYYT(FM)—Jan 6, 1992: 102.3 mhz; 1.8 kw. Ant 574 ft. TL: N45 48 02 W120 47 35. Box 149 (98620). (509) 773-9102. FAX: (509) 773-3301. Licensee: Colin B. Malcolm. Format: Country. ■ Cole B. Malcolm, gen mgr.

Grand Coulee

KEYG(AM)—1979: 1490 khz; 1 kw-U. TL: N47 52 58 W118 58 20. Hrs opn: 24. Drawer K (99133). (509) 633-2020. Licensee: Wheeler Broadcasting Inc. (acq 12-6-85). Net: ABC/D. Wash atty: Barry Friedman. Format: Country. News staff one; news progmg 4 hrs wkly. Target aud: 25 plus. Spec prog: Class 4 hrs, mus to remember 4 hrs, big band 4 hrs wkly. ■ Verl D. Wheeler, pres & gen mgr; Mark R. Wheeler, gen sls mgr; Dan Farrell, prom mgr; Joyce Fleischman, progmg dir; Sue Peters, mus dir; Robert Clayton, news dir; Dan Farrel, chief engr. ■ Rates: $25; 22; 25; 15.

KEYG-FM—Feb 10, 1984: 98.5 mhz; 25 kw-H. Ant 463 ft. TL: N47 52 58 W118 58 20 (CP: 100 kw-H, 85 kw-V, ant 994 ft., TL: N47 49 18 W118 58 20). Stereo. Hrs opn: 24. Prog sep from AM. Format: Adult contemp, oldies. ■ Verl D. Wheeler, CEO. ■ Rates: Same as AM.

Grandview

KARY-FM—Aug 21, 1989: 100.9 mhz; 6 kw. Ant -91 ft. TL: N46 14 03 W119 48 49. Stereo. Box 1310, Wine Country Rd., Prosser (99350). (509) 786-1310; (509) 882-3500. FAX: (509) 786-3300. Licensee: Prosser Grandview Broadcasters Inc. Net: CNN, Unistar. Rep: Tacher. Format: Country. News staff one; news progmg 14 hrs wkly. Target aud: 25-54. Spec prog: Sp, relg 8 hrs wkly. ■ Judith Rae Roach, pres & gen mgr; Sidney Lee Roach, opns mgr & chief engr; Karl Wyokoff, gen sls mgr.

Hoquiam

KGHO(AM)—Nov 16, 1961: 1490 khz; 1 kw-U. TL: N46 58 22 W123 51 10. 3102 Bay Ave. (98550). (206) 532-1200. FAX: (206) 533-4571. Licensee: Trinity Broadcasting Network Inc. (group owner; acq 12-27-88; grpsl; FTR 1-23-89). Format: MOR Christian. News progmg 5 hrs wkly. Target aud: 25-60; older, mature listener. ■ Paul Crouch, pres; Rick Moyer, gen mgr; Rod Henke, progmg dir; Nick Winter, chief engr.

KGHO-FM—Sept 3, 1965: 95.3 mhz; 1.15 kw. Ant 750 ft. TL: N46 55 53 W123 44 02. Stereo. Prog sep from AM. Format: Contemp Christian. Target aud: 16-45; on-fire Christians and people who need Jesus.

Kelso

KLOG(AM)—Oct 8, 1949: 1490 khz; 1 kw-U. TL: N46 07 00 W122 53 07. Stereo. Hrs opn: 24. Box 90, 506 Cowlite Way W. (98626). (206) 636-0110. FAX: (206) 577-6949. Licensee: Washington Interstate Broadcasters Inc. (acq 8-67). Net: NBC, MBS. Rep: Katz, Tacher. Wash atty: Richard Hayes. Format: Adult contemp. Target aud: 25-54. ■ Steve Hanson, pres & gen mgr; Rick Roberts, gen sls mgr; Bill Dodd, progmg dir; Ray Bartley, mus dir; Kirc Rolland, news dir; Brent Bradley, chief engr. ■ Rates: $21; 18; 21; 16.

KUKN(FM)—Co-owned with KLOG(AM). Aug 7 1991: 94.5 mhz; 3 kw. Ant 100 ft. TL: N46 12 54 W123 02 24 (CP: 6 kw). Stereo. Hrs opn: 24. Format: Country. News staff 2; news progmg 2 hrs wkly. ■ Steve Hanson, natl sls mgr & rgnl sls mgr; Tim Burr, prom dir; Dawn Feldhaus, pub affrs dir. ■ Rates: $21; 20; 21; 19.

Kennewick

KONA(AM)—Licensed to Kennewick. See Richland-Pasco-Kennewick.

KONA-FM—Licensed to Kennewick. See Richland-Pasco-Kennewick.

KTCR(AM)—Licensed to Kennewick. See Richland-Pasco-Kennewick.

***KTCV(FM)**—Licensed to Kennewick. See Richland-Pasco-Kennewick.

Kirkland

***KARR(AM)**—1964: 1460 khz; 5 kw-D, 2.5 kw-N, DA-2. TL: N47 40 24 W122 10 07. Hrs opn: 24. Box 883 (98033). (206) 828-6738. Licensee: Family Stations Inc. (group owner; acq 10-22-86; $50,000; FTR 8-11-86). Format: Relg. News progmg 5 hrs wkly. Target aud: General; conservative Christians & Evangelicals. Spec prog: Classical. ■ Harold Campig, pres; F. Van Eich, Scott Smith, vps; Scott Smith, vp dev; Bob Walther, chief engr.

KXRX(FM)—See Seattle.

Lacey

KLDY(AM)—June 1, 1986: 680 khz; 250 w-D. TL: N47 00 41 W122 49 53. Box 308, Help Ministries Inc., Ferndale (98248). (206) 491-6800; (800) 659-5539. FAX: (206) 380-4202. Licensee: Help Ministries Inc. (acq 4-22-91; $75,000; FTR 5-13-91). Net: AP, NBC, N.W. Net. Format: News & info. News staff 2; news progmg 30 hrs wkly. Target aud: 30 plus. Spec prog: Gardening 2 hrs, sports 9 hrs wkly. ■ Marty Hamstra, gen mgr; Larry Lee, gen sls mgr & news dir; Ron Cowell, chief engr.

KTOL(AM)—Sept. 22, 1983: 1280 khz; 1 kw-D, 500 w-N. TL: N47 03 44 W122 49 49. Stereo. Hrs opn: 24. Suite 200, 691 Sleater-Kinney Rd. S.E. (98538). (206) 438-1280; (206) 926-1450. FAX: (206) 438-1322; (206) 922-2495. Licensee: Bar-B Broadcasting Inc. (acq 10-25-91; $75,000; FTR 11-18-91). Format: Country Gold. News staff 2; news progmg 2 hrs wkly. Target aud: 25-65; working adults. Spec prog: Local sports 6 hrs, western 6 hrs wkly. ■ Barbara Geesman, pres; Wes Geesman, gen mgr & gen sls mgr; Kevin Atwood, stn mgr; Roy Newcomb, progmg dir; Larry Gruber, chief engr.

Lakewood

KDFL(AM)—Licensed to Lakewood. See Tacoma.

KLAY(AM)—Licensed to Lakewood. See Tacoma.

Long Beach

KKEE(FM)—May 1987: 94.3 mhz; 3 kw. Ant 233 ft. TL: N46 18 51 W124 03 07. Stereo. Hrs opn: 24. 1490 Marine Dr., Astoria, OR (97103); Box 1003, 9th and Hwy. 103, Long Beach (98631). (503) 325-6221; (206) 642-8555. Licensee: Lower Columbia Broadcasting Co. Inc. Group owner: Farmer Stations (acq 7-90; grpsl; FTR 7-2-90). Net: SMN. Rep: Tacher. Format: Oldies. News staff one; news progmg 6 hrs wkly. Target aud: 25-54; 35 plus female, some college students, kids. ■ Chuck Farmer, pres & chief engr; Dave Heick, gen mgr & gen sls mgr; Jack McGee, progmg dir; Scott Keith, news dir.

Longview

KBAM(AM)—Aug 15, 1955: 1270 khz; 5 kw-D, 83 w-N. TL: N46 10 58 W122 57 28. Box 96 (98632). (206) 423-1210. FAX: (206) 423-1378. Licensee: Armak Broadcasters Inc. (acq 4-1-65). Net: CBS. Rep: McGavren Guild. Format: Country. News staff one. ■ Howard "Terry" Kynaston, pres & gen mgr; Phil Roger, gen sls mgr; Steve Kaye, progmg dir; Kelly Guinn, news dir; Larry Wilson, chief engr. ■ Rates: $16; 15; 16; 13.

KEDO(AM)—May 1938: 1400 khz; 1 kw-U. TL: N46 08 57 W122 58 44. Hrs opn: 24. Broadcast Center, 1130 14th Ave. (98632). (206) 425-1500. FAX: (206) 423-1554. Licensee: Longview Broadcasting Co. Group owner: Premier Broadcasters Inc. (acq 5-85; $750,000; FTR 6-3-85). Net: ABC/I. Rep: Art Moore. Wash atty: S. Meredith Senter. Format: Adult contemp, news. News staff 2; news progmg 15 hrs wkly. Target aud: 25-54. Spec prog: Pub affrs 2 hrs wkly. ■ Derek Shannon, pres & gen mgr; Bob Hart, stn mgr; Peter Talbot, sls dir; Ron Moyer, prom mgr & progmg dir; Craig Martin, mus dir; Chris Lehman, news dir; Rod Etherton, chief engr. ■ Rates: $17; 13; 12; 7.

KLYK(FM)—Co-owned with KEDO(AM). July 7, 1962: 105.5 mhz; 315 w. Ant 859 ft. TL: N46 09 52 W122 51 13 (CP: 700 w.) Stereo. Hrs opn: 24. Prog sep from AM. Net: Westwood One. Format: Contemp Hit. Target aud: 18-49. ■ Bob Hart, progmg dir & mus dir. ■ Rates: $22; 18; 21; 12.

***KJVH(FM)**—1988: 89.5 mhz; 100 w. Ant 780 ft. TL: N46 09 52 W122 51 13. 1130 14th Ave. (98632). (206) 577-8288. Licensee: Family Stations Inc. (group owner). Format: Relg. ■ David Swiderski, gen mgr & stn mgr.

KLOG(AM)—See Kelso.

KLYK(FM)—Listing follows KEDO(AM).

KUKN(FM)—See Kelso.

***KZOE(FM)**—Oct 22, 1987: 90.3 mhz; 860 w. Ant -3 ft. TL: N46 10 12 W122 56 43 (CP: 500 w, ant 735 ft.). Stereo. Hrs opn: 24. 3609 Columbia Heights Rd. (98632). (206) 577-5433. Licensee: Columbia Heights Christian Academy. Net: UPI, Skylight. Wash atty: Reddy, Begley & Martin (Matthew McCormack). Format: Inspirational. News progmg 15 hrs wkly. Target aud: 25-54. ■ Melvin Doehne, pres; Danny Houle, gen mgr.

Lynden

KLYN(FM)—Nov 8, 1960: 106.5 mhz; 100 kw. Ant 718 ft. TL: N48 59 48 W122 38 52. Stereo. 1843 Front St. (98264). (206) 354-5596. FAX: (206) 354-7517. Licensee: Crista Ministries Inc. Group owner: Crista Broadcasting (acq 7-80). Net: AP. Format: Contemp Christian. Spec prog: Farm 6 hrs wkly. ■ James Gwinn, pres; Ron Kawamoto, gen mgr; Marvin Mickley, opns dir & progmg dir; Chuck Lee, gen sls mgr; Jim Bouma, mus dir; Bryan Hubert, chief engr. ■ Rates: $24; 21; 22; 18.

McCleary

KGY-FM—October 1992: 96.9 mhz; 2.33 kw. Ant 1,056 ft. TL: N47 05 08 W123 11 19. Hrs opn: 24. 1240 N. Washington St., Olympia (98501); Box 1249 (98507). (206) 943-1240. FAX: (206) 352-1222. Licensee: KGY Inc. Wash atty: Haley, Bader & Potts. Format: Classic rock. Target aud: 25-49. ■ Rates: $29; 22; 24; 15.

Medical Lake

KTSL(FM)—Mar 7, 1989: 101.9 mhz. 12 kw. Ant. 495 ft. TL: N47 41 30 W117 46 00. Stereo. Hrs opn: 24. Suite 124, 1212 Washington, Spokane (99201); Box 9978, Spokane (99209). (509) 326-9500. FAX: (509) 326-1560. Licensee: The Word in Music Inc. (group owner; acq 10-21-92; FTR 11-23-92) Net: AP. Wash atty: Fisher, Wayland, Cooper & Leader. Format: Contemp Christian. News staff one; news progmg one hr wkly. Target aud: 25-54. ■ Dale Turner, chmn; Mark Pluimer, pres; David Fitt, gen mgr; Steve Hafen, opns dir & progmg dir; H. Marshall Thompson, mus dir; Conrad Agte, chief engr. ■ Rates: $13; 11; 13; 11.

Mercer Island

***KMIH(FM)**—February 1970: 104.5 mhz; 14 w-H. Ant 233 ft. TL: N47 34 19 W122 12 55. Stereo. Hrs opn: 6 AM-11 PM. 9100 S.E. 42nd (98040-4107). (206) 236-3296. FAX: (206) 236-3358. Licensee: Mercer Island School District No. 400. Format: Educ, progsv, rock. Target aud: 15-35; young, progressive students. ■ N. De Vogel, gen mgr.

Mercer Island-Seattle

KIXI(AM)—Licensed to Mercer Island-Seattle. See Seattle.

Moses Lake

KBSN(AM)—November 1947: 1470 khz; 5 kw-D, 1 kw-N, DA-2. TL: N47 06 16 W119 17 32. Drawer B, 2241 W. Main (98837). (509) 765-3441. FAX: (509) 766-0273. Licensee: KSEM Inc. Net: ABC/I. Rep: Art Moore. Format: News/talk. News staff 2; news progmg 20 hrs wkly. Target aud: General. Spec prog: Farm 20 hrs, Sp 9 hrs wkly. ■ Ted R. Mason, gen mgr & gen sls mgr; Jim Davis, opns mgr; Gary Roberts, progmg dir; Andy Patrick, news dir; Will Vos, chief engr. ■ Rates: $12; 12; 12; na.

KDRM(FM)—Co-owned with KBSN(AM). Oct 1, 1980: 99.3 mhz; 3 kw. Ant 275 ft. TL: N47 05 54 W119 17 47. Stereo. Net: ABC/C. Format: Adult contemp. Target aud: 18-34. ■ Dale Roth, prom mgr & progmg dir.

KWIQ-FM—May 22, 1968: 100.3 mhz; 100 kw. Ant 194 ft. TL: N47 06 09 W119 14 26. Stereo. Hrs opn: 24. 11768 Kittleson Rd. (98832). Net: MBS. Format: Country. ■ Craig Shawn Caraway, prom dir.

Moses Lake North

KWIQ(AM)—Feb 20, 1956: 1020 khz; 2.5 kw-D, 500 w-N, DA-2. TL: N47 09 54 W119 21 38 (CP: 5 kw). Box 999 (98837). (509) 765-1761; (509) 765-1762. FAX: (509) 765-8901. Licensee: KWIQ Radio Inc. (acq 4-27-61). Net: Moody. Rep: Tacher. Format: Country. News staff one; news progmg 6 hrs wkly. Target aud: 18-54; bus & farm oriented listeners. Spec prog: Farm 20 hrs, Sp 4 hrs wkly. ■ Fran Lawrence, pres; William M. Gilbert, gen mgr, gen sls mgr & vp progmg; Craig Shawn Caraway, progmg dir; Ken Lacey, mus dir; Robin Kay, news dir; Kati Lynne, pub affrs dir; Dewey Trostel, chief engr.

Mount Vernon

KAPS(AM)—March 17, 1963: 660 khz; 10 kw-D, 1 kw-N. TL: N48 26 22 W122 20 45. Hrs opn: 24. Box 70 (98273). (206) 424-7676. FAX: (206) 424-1660. Licensee: Valley Broadcasters Inc. (acq 8-13-93; $182,000; FTR 8-30-93). Net: ABC/E. Rep: Eastman/Intermountain Net.; Art Moore.Format: Country. News staff 2. Target aud: General. ■ Jim Keane, pres; Jerry Keane, gen sls mgr; Ron Cowell, chief engr.

KBRC(AM)—Dec 11, 1946: 1430 khz; 5 kw-D, 1 kw-N, DA-N. TL: N48 25 22 W122 21 10. Stereo. Box 250, Suite 770, 2222 Riverside Dr., (98273). (206) 424-4278; (206) 424-1430. FAX: (206) 424-1016. Licensee: M.C. Radio Inc. Group owner: Pioneer Broadcasting (acq 4-8-83; $825,000; FTR 5-2-83). Net: ABC/D. Rep: Tacher. Wash atty: Covington and Burling. Format: Adult contemp. News staff 2. Target aud: 25-54; Hispanic population during Hispanic show, men & women of all walks of life. Spec prog: Sp 3 hrs wkly. ■ Elizabeth Clapp, CEO; Matthew Clapp, pres; Rich Franklin, gen mgr & gen sls mgr; Nan Hough, mktg dir; Jeff French, progmg dir & news dir; Wedge Michaels, mus dir; Paul Thompson, engrg mgr; Jay White, chief engr. ■ Rates: $25; 19; 24; 18.

***KSVR(FM)**—May 4, 1973: 90.1 mhz; 100 w. Ant 75 ft. TL: N48 26 13 W122 18 36. Hrs opn: 7:30 AM-midnight. 2405 College Way (98273). (206) 428-1198. Licensee: Skagit Valley College. Format: Progsv, div, Sp. Target aud: 15-25; males. Spec prog: Black 10 hrs, relg 10 hrs wkly. ■ Francisco Gamayo, gen mgr & opns mgr; Michael Enquist, sls dir & mktg mgr; Justin Sage, progmg dir; Joe Wilson, mus dir; Arn Lundquist, Howie Taylor, asst mus dirs; Mel Bratley, chief engr.

Naches

KYKA(FM)—Licensed to Naches. See Yakima.

Newport

KMJY(AM)—October 1986: 700 khz; 10 kw-D, 1 kw-N, DA-N. TL: N48 09 37 W117 01 48. Hrs opn: 6 AM-10 PM. Box 1740, Oldtown, ID (83822). (208) 437-5331. FAX: (208) 437-5887. Licensee: James E. and Helen G. Stargel. Net: CNN. Format: Modern country. Target aud: 25-55. ■ James Stargel, pres, gen mgr, gen sls mgr, progmg dir & mus dir.

KMJY-FM—December 1989: 104.9 mhz; 3 kw. Ant -33 ft. TL: N48 09 37 W117 01 49 (CP: 6 kw, ant 102 ft., TL: N48 12 16 W117 00 42). Stereo. Hrs opn: 6 AM-10 PM. Dups AM 100%.

***KUBS(FM)**—Sept 10, 1973: 91.5 mhz; 150 w. Ant -538 ft. TL: N48 10 23 W117 03 15. Box 70, Newport High School (99156). (509) 447-4931. Licensee: Newport Consolidated School District #56415. Format: Oldies, AOR, talk. Spec prog: Country 5 hrs, farm 2 hrs, jazz 2 hrs wkly. ■ Mitch Stratton, gen mgr.

Oak Harbor

KJTT(AM)—Dec 14, 1984: 1110 khz; 500 w-D. TL: N48 17 27 W122 42 28 (CP: 1520 khz, 1 kw-D, TL: N48 16 55 W122 42 26). Box 70, 6373 60th N.W. (98277). (206) 679-1110. FAX: (206) 679-5562. Licensee: Oak Harbor Communications Inc. (acq 4-8-93; $150,000; FTR 4-26-93). Net: AP. Rep: Tacher. Format: Oldies. ■ Pat O'Day, pres; Patrick Nolan, vp; David A. Bowden, gen mgr & progmg dir; Rick Bell, mus dir & chief engr; David Bowden, news dir.

Olympia

***KAOS(FM)**—Jan 1, 1973: 89.3 mhz; 1.5 kw. Ant -19 ft. TL: N47 04 22 W122 58 51. Stereo. Hrs opn: 24. CAB 301, TESC (98505). (206) 866-6000, ext. 6893. FAX: (206) 866-6797. Licensee: Evergreen State College. Format: Div. Spec prog: Jazz 6 hrs, class 2 hrs, C&W 10 hrs, women's 2 hrs, various Northwest tribes 3 hrs, rap 5 hrs, gay/lesbian 4 hrs, pub affrs 8 hrs, reggae 5 hrs, labor 3 hrs, blues 5 hrs, world beat 3 hrs, Fr 2 hrs, Sp 6 hrs wkly. ■ Michael Huntsberger, gen mgr; Juli Kelen, opns dir, progmg dir & pub affrs dir; Tom Freeman, dev dir & prom dir; Matt Johnston, mus dir; Jody Daisa, engrg mgr; Al Saari, chief engr.

KCPL(AM)—October 1956: 920 khz; 5 kw-D, 500 w-N, DA-2. TL: N47 01 52 W122 51 10. Stereo. Box 48 (98507); 2914 Yelm Hwy. (98501). (206) 491-9200. FAX: (206) 438-9462. Licensee: Natl. Communications Inc. (acq 10-81; $700,000; FTR 10-12-81). Net: AP. Rep: Roslin, Tacher. Format: Classic hits. ■ Ron Palmer, gen mgr & prom mgr; Larry Kammerer, gen sls mgr; Dan Mason, progmg mgr & mus dir; Jim Feehan, news dir; James Boyd, chief engr.

KGY(AM)—Apr 15, 1922: 1240 khz; 1 kw-U. TL: N47 03 31 W122 54 09. Box 1249, 1240 N. Washington St. (98507). (206) 943-1240. Licensee: KGY Inc. (acq 1-15-39). Net: AP. Format: Full svc adult contemp. News staff 3. ■ Barbara Kerry, pres; Richard Pust, gen mgr; Darrell Wray, gen sls mgr; Willie Kelley, progmg dir & mus dir; Jeanna Spain, asst mus dir; Bob Macleod, news dir; Cathy Bentley, pub affrs dir; Tom Trotzer, chief engr. ■ Rates: $29; 22; 24; 15.

KTOL(AM)—See Lacey.

KXXO(FM)—Jan 16, 1990: 96.1 mhz; 85 kw. Ant 2,100 ft. TL: N46 38 07 W122 28 01. Stereo. Hrs opn: 24. Box 7937 (98507); Rockway/Leland Bldg., 2nd Fl., 119 N. Washington Ave. (98501). (206) 943-9937; (206) 943-9629. FAX: (206) 352-3643. Licensee: Three Cities FM Inc. Wash atty: Young & Jatlow. Format: Soft adult contemp. News staff one; news progmg one hr wkly. Target aud: 25-49; rabid consumers. ■ David J. Rauh, pres & gen mgr; Toni C. Holm, sr vp, stn mgr & opns mgr; Brian B. Butler, gen sls mgr; John S. Foster, progmg dir; Casey Conley, news dir; Tim Vik, chief engr. ■ Rates: $45; 45; 45; 30.

Omak

KOMW(AM)—Sept 30, 1947: 680 khz; 5 kw-D. TL: N48 23 40 W119 32 00. Box 151 (98841); 320 Emery St. (98841). (509) 826-0100. FAX: (509) 826-3929. Licensee: North Cascades Broadcasting (acq 7-90; FTR 12-11-89). Net: ABC/I. Rep: Tacher. Format: Adult contemp. Target aud: 25 plus. Spec prog: Farm 2 hrs, Sp 2 hrs wkly. ■ John P. Andrist, pres, gen mgr, gen sls mgr & prom mgr; Denny Macleod, progmg dir & mus dir; John Evans, news dir; Jerry Robinson, chief engr.

KOMW-FM—Apr 10, 1978: 92.7 mhz; 3 kw. Ant -836 ft. TL: N48 23 40 W119 32 00. Stereo. Prog sep from AM. Format: Country. Spec prog: Farm one hr wkly.

Opportunity

KKPL(AM)—Listing follows KNFR(FM).

KNFR(FM)—April 1, 1961: 96.1 mhz; 56 kw. Ant 2,378 ft. TL: N47 34 11 W117 05 00. Stereo. 300 E. Third Ave., Spokane (99202). (509) 459-9800. FAX: (509) 459-9850. Licensee: Silverado Broadcasting Co. Net: Unistar. Format: Adult contemp. Target aud: 25-54. ■ Kosta Panidif, gen mgr. ■ Rates: $29; 26; 29; 17.

KKPL(AM)—Co-owned with KNFR(FM). November 1955: 630 khz; 1 kw-D, 32 w-N. TL: N47 36 55 W117 14 57 (CP: 840 khz; 50 kw-D, 250 w-N, DA-N). Net: CNN. Rep: Banner, Katz. Format: CNN Headline News. Target aud: General. ■ Rates: $7; 5; 7; 3.

KSVY(AM)—Licensed to Opportunity. See Spokane.

Othello

KRSC(AM)—Sept 1, 1957: 1400 khz; 1 kw-U. TL: N46 49 29 W119 11 26. Box 566 (99344). (509) 488-2791. Licensee: R.D. Leary (acq 5-1-88). Net: ABC/I. Rep: Farmakis, Tacher. Format: MOR. Target aud: General. Spec prog: Christian rock 14 hrs wkly. ■ R.D. Leary, pres; Linda G. Capps, gen mgr; Chuck Hart, progmg dir; Don Lockwood, chief engr.

KZLN-FM—February 1992: 97.5 mhz; 4.6 kw. Ant 656 ft. TL: N46 45 55 W119 16 49. Stereo. Hrs opn: 24. Box 2869, 126 E. Hemlock (99344). (509) 488-6089. FAX: (509) 488-3299. Licensee: P-N-P Broadcasting, Inc. Net: SMN. Rep: Tacher. Format: Oldies. Target aud: 25-54. ■ Duane J. Polich, pres, gen mgr, stn mgr & opns mgr; George Polich, sr vp; Bob Hauser, vp; Bill Gott, chief engr. ■ Rates: $10; 10; 10; 10.

Pasco

KEYW(FM)—June 30, 1986: 98.3 mhz; 3 kw. Ant 197 ft. TL: N46 08 48 W119 05 59. Stereo. Suite 111, 3900 W. Clearwater, Kennewick (99336). (509) 735-4539. FAX: (509) 735-9451. Licensee: United Broadcasting Inc. Net: Unistar. Format: Adult contemp, oldies. ■ Andrew Molasky, pres; Terry Bailey, gen mgr; Tami Jarrett, gen sls mgr; Katrina Marks, prom dir; Jim Swartz, progmg dir; Paul Drake, mus dir; Dave Herbert, chief engr.

KGDN(FM)—Licensed to Pasco. See Richland-Pasco-Kennewick.

***KOLU(FM)**—Sept 1, 1971: 90.1 mhz; 3.99 kw. Ant 93 ft. TL: N46 14 59 W119 09 10. Stereo. 4921 W. Wernett (99301). (509) 547-2021. Licensee: Riverview Baptist Christian Schools. Format: Relg. ■ Pastor J. Jowne, gen mgr; Juan Munoz, opns dir; Kent Gunnison, progmg dir & chief engr.

KORD(AM)—Licensed to Pasco. See Richland-Pasco-Kennewick.

Port Angeles

KAPY(AM)—June 16, 1961: 1290 khz; 1 kw-D, 149 w-N, DA-2. TL: N48 05 55 W123 24 21. Hrs opn: 24. Box 1290, 1772 Melody Ln. (98362). (206) 452-9228. Licensee: Strait Corp. (acq 10-16-78). Net: SMN. Rep: Art Moore. Format: Classic rock, adult contemp. News staff one; news progmg 10 hrs wkly. Target aud: 25-49; heavy buyers, strong family base. Spec prog: Relg 5 hrs wkly. ■ Tom Newcomb, pres, gen mgr, gen sls mgr, mus dir & chief engr; Jeff Allen, news dir. ■ Rates: $9; 6; 9; 4.

KONP(AM)—1945: 1450 khz; 1 kw-U. TL: N48 07 19 W123 26 13. Box 1450, 313 W. First (98362). (206) 457-1450. FAX: (206) 457-9114. Licensee: Radio Pacific Inc. Net: ABC/I. Rep: Tacher. Format: Adult contemp, news/talk, sports. News staff one; news progmg 15 hrs wkly. Target aud: 28-54. ■ George Buck, pres; Jim MacDonald, gen mgr; Terry MacDonald, gen sls mgr & prom mgr; Brennan Haselton, news dir; Kris Grier, chief engr. ■ Rates: $14.25; 12.75; 14.25; 11.25.

Prosser

KARY(AM)—Dec 14, 1956: 1310 khz; 5 kw-D, 66 w-N. TL: N46 14 03 W119 48 49. Box 1310, Wine Country Rd. (99350). (509) 786-1310; (509) 882-3500. Licensee: Prosser-Grandview Broadcasters Inc. (acq 9-24-64). Net: CNN, Unistar. Rep: Tacher. Format: Country. News staff one; news progmg 14 hrs wkly. Target aud: 25-54. Spec prog: Sp, relg 8 hrs wkly. ■ Judith Rae Roach, pres; Sid Lee Roach, gen mgr; Melba Fujiura, gen sls mgr.

KZXR(FM)—Sept 6, 1962: 101.7 mhz; 3.5 kw. Ant 865 ft. TL: N46 11 12 W119 45 13. Stereo. 1227 Hillcrest Dr. (99350). (509) 786-1017; (509) 786-4481. FAX: (509) 786-1181. Licensee: Bogart-Funk Enterprises Inc. (acq 12-9-92; $285,000; FTR 1-4-93). Net: MBS. Rep: Target. Wash atty: Sidley & Austin. Format: Adult contemp. News progmg 8 hrs wkly. Target aud: 18-49. ■ Eldon Bogart, pres, gen mgr, gen sls mgr, prom mgr & chief engr; Brian Tucker, mus dir.

Pullman

KHTR(FM)—Listing follows KQQQ(AM).

KQQQ(AM)—1938: 650 khz; 1 kw-D, 500 w-N, DA-N. TL: N46 43 38 W117 12 22. Hrs opn: 24. Box 1 (99163). (509) 332-6551. FAX: (509) 332-5151. Licensee: Radio Palouse (acq 12-74). Net: ABC TalkRadio, NBC, NBC Talknet, Daynet, IBN; N.W. Net. Rep: Eastman, IMN, Art Moore. Format: News/talk. News staff one; news progmg 12 hrs wkly. Target aud: General. Spec prog: Farm 3 hrs wkly. ■ Bill Weed, gen mgr; Rod Schwartz, gen sls mgr; Inger Brandal, news dir; Steve Franko, chief engr.

KHTR(FM)—Co-owned with KQQQ(AM). 1967: 104.3 mhz; 24 kw. Ant 1,669 ft. TL: N46 48 40 W116 54 55. Stereo. Prog sep from AM. Net: CBS Spectrum. Format: CHR. ■ Rod Schwartz, stn mgr; Jim Johnson, mus dir.

***KRFA-FM**—See Moscow, Idaho.

***KRLF(FM)**—July 1, 1991: 88.5 mhz; 420 w-V. Ant 794 ft. TL: N46 38 01 W117 05 13. Stereo. Hrs opn: 24. S.W. 345 Kimball (99163). (509) 332-3545. FAX: (509) 332-5433. Licensee: Living Faith Fellowship Educational Ministries. Wash atty: Gammon & Grange. Format: Christian adult contemp, inspirational, praise & worship. News progmg 11 hrs wkly. Target aud: 18-54. ■ Karl A. Barden, pres; Rodney J. Marshall, vp & gen mgr; Aaron Atkinson, opns mgr & asst mus dir; Curtis Troll, prom mgr & pub affrs dir; Kevin O. Hunter, progmg dir & mus dir; Francis Benjamin, engrg mgr.

***KWSU(AM)**—June 1922: 1250 khz; 5 kw-U. TL: N46 41 47 W117 14 44. Hrs opn: 6 AM-midnight. Murrow Communications Ctr., Washington State Univ. (99164-2530). (509) 335-6500. Licensee: Washington State Univ. Net: NPR. Format: News, classical. News staff 2; news progmg 60 hrs wkly. Target aud: General. Spec prog: Jazz 14 hrs wkly. ■ Dennis Haarsager, gen mgr; Jean Palmquist, stn mgr & progmg mgr; Elizabeth Carroll, dev dir; Barbara Hanford, prom mgr; Dale Harrison, news dir; John Gray, engrg dir. ■ KWSU-TV affil.

***KZUU(FM)**—Sept 21, 1979: 90.7 mhz; 800 w. Ant 105 ft. TL: N46 43 51 W117 09 08. Stereo. Hrs opn: 24. Compton Union Bldg., Third Fl. (99164-7204). (509) 335-2208. FAX: (509) 335-4636. Licensee: Washington State Univ. Board of Regents. Format: Div, alternative. News staff one; news progmg 5 hrs wkly. Target aud: 18-49; college students. Spec prog: Jazz 12 hrs, Black 12 hrs, folk 4 hrs, Sp 3 hrs, new mus 10 hrs, environmental protection 2 hrs wkly. ■ Dan Mahr, pres; Ben Rupp, stn mgr; Christy Snelson, opns mgr & news dir; Tammy Sortore, Dave Wick, mus dirs; Steve Franko, chief engr.

KZZL-FM—Nov. 1991: 99.5 mhz; 81.4 kw. Ant 1,059 ft. TL: N46 40 52 W116 58 19. Stereo. Hrs opn: 24. Box 710, Almota Rd., Colfax (99111). Licensee: P-N-P Broadcasting Inc. (acq 1993; $13,000; FTR 9-20-93). Wash atty: Dow, Lohnes & Albertson. Format: Country. News staff one; news progmg 2 hrs wkly. Target aud: 25 plus. ■ Duane J. Polich, pres; Bill Gott, vp & chief engr; Robert Hauser, stn mgr & sls dir; Hennison Bird, mus dir. ■ Rates: $13; 13; 13; 13.

Puyallup

KJUN(AM)—Dec 1, 1951: 1450 khz; 1 kw-U. TL: N47 10 41 W122 16 24 (CP: 1440 khz; 5 kw-D, 2 kw-N, DA-2). Hrs opn: 24. 6310 16th St. E., Tacoma (98424). (206) 926-1450; (800) 834-6531. FAX: (206) 922-2495. Licensee: Joy Broadcasting Inc. (acq 11-90; $750,000; FTR 8-20-90). Format: Country gold. News staff 2; news progmg 2 hrs wkly. Target aud: 25-65; working folks. Spec prog: Sports 6 hrs, C&W 6 hrs wkly. ■ Barbara Geesman, pres; Wes Geesman, gen mgr & gen sls mgr; Roy Newcomer, progmg dir & news dir; Larry Grouper, chief engr. ■ Rates: $10; 5; 10; 2.

Quincy

KWNC(AM)—Sept 10, 1957: 1370 khz; 1 kw-D, 500 w-PSA, 40 w-N. TL: N47 16 15 W119 51 13. Box 607, 305 S. Central (98848). (509) 787-4461. FAX: (509) 787-2682. Licensee: Jack Rabbit Broadcasting Co. (acq 12-10-91; $66,000; FTR 1-6-92). Net: MBS. Rep: Tacher. Format: Adult contemp. News staff one; news progmg 20 hrs wkly. Target aud: 35 plus; farm-oriented. Spec prog: Farm 5 hrs, Sp 7 hrs wkly. ■ Don Lockwood, gen mgr, news dir & chief engr. ■ Rates: $9; 9; 9; 9.

KWWW-FM—Aug 29, 1985: 96.7 mhz; 440 w. Ant 1,079 ft. TL: N47 19 13 W199 48 00. Stereo. 113 B St. S.W., Wenatchee (98848); Box 638, Suite 401, 5 S. Wenatchee Ave., Wenatchee (98807). (509) 787-4371; (509) 787-3693. FAX: (509) 663-1150. Licensee: Sans Inc. Net: SMN, Westwood One. Rep: Major Mkt. Format: CHR. Target aud: 18-49. ■ Kent Phillips, pres; David C. Herald, gen mgr, sls dir, gen sls mgr & prom mgr; Mike Gould, progmg mgr & news dir; Wayne Bowden, chief engr.

Raymond

KAPA(AM)—June 1950: 1340 khz; 1 kw-U. TL: N46 40 15 W123 46 27. Box 2009, Longview (98632-8153). Licensee: Blue Denim Music Inc. (acq 12-1-89; $130,000; FTR 12-4-89).

KSWW(FM)—Oct 26, 1984: 97.7 mhz; 230 w. Ant 920 ft. TL: N46 41 44 W123 46 16 (CP: 3.1 kw). Stereo. Hrs opn: 6 AM-midnight. Box 628, 205 Duryea St. (98577). (206) 942-5533. Licensee: Pacific Broadcasting Co. Net: CBS. Rep: Art Moore Inc.; Target Radio.Format: Adult contemp. News progmg 10 hrs wkly. Target aud: General. ■ Mary R. Gauger, pres; David E. Gauger, vp & gen mgr; Bob Coates, chief engr. ■ Rates: $11; 11; 11; 11.

Renton

KRIZ(AM)—Feb 2, 1982: 1420 khz; 1 kw-D, 500 w-N, DA-2. TL: N47 26 25 W122 12 09. 2600 S. Jackson St., Seattle (98144). (206) 323-3070. FAX: (206) 322-6518. Licensee: KRIZ Broadcasting Inc. (acq 2-84; $400,000; FTR 3-5-84). Net: Natl Black. Format: Black. Target aud: 18 plus. ■ Christopher H. Bennett, pres & stn mgr; Frank P. Barrow, progmg dir & mus dir; Rodney Sheffer, chief engr.

Richland

KALE(AM)—Licensed to Richland. See Richland-Pasco-Kennewick.

KEGX(FM)—Licensed to Richland. See Richland-Pasco-Kennewick.

***KFAE-FM**—Licensed to Richland. See Richland-Pasco-Kennewick.

KIOK(FM)—Licensed to Richland. See Richland-Pasco-Kennewick.

KORD-FM—Licensed to Richland. See Richland-Pasco-Kennewick.

Richland-Pasco-Kennewick

KALE(AM)—(Richland). April 1, 1950: 960 khz; 5 kw-D, 1 kw-N, DA-N. TL: N46 14 34 W119 10 48. Hrs opn: 24. 310 W. Kennewick, Kennewick (99336); Box K, TriCities (99302). (509) 586-2151. Licensee: Columbia Theater Co. (acq 7-1-70). Net: NBC. Rep: Tacher,D&R Radio. Wash atty: Haley, Bader & Potts. Format: Oldies. News staff one. Target aud: 25 plus; general. ■ Fred Danz, pres; Kathy Balcom, gen mgr; Greg Kronlund, progmg dir; Jolynn Winter, news dir; Dave Hebert, chief engr. ■ Rates: $17; 15; 17; 13.

KIOK(FM)—(Richland). Co-owned with KALE(AM). Oct 3, 1978: 94.9 mhz; 100 kw. Ant 1,250 ft. TL: N46 05 47 W119 11 36. Stereo. Prog sep from AM. Format: Top-40. ■ Heidi Romans, prom dir; Paul Walker, progmg dir; Jim O'Brien, mus dir; Karen Deatherage, pub affrs dir. ■ Rates: $30; 28; 30; 26.

KEGX(FM)—Listing follows KTCR(AM).

***KFAE-FM**—(Richland). July 1982: 89.1 mhz; 100 kw. Ant 1,148 ft. TL: N46 05 43 W119 11 41. Stereo. Hrs opn: 24. Murrow Communications Ctr., Washington State Univ., Pullman (99164-2530); Washington State Univ. at Tri-Cities, 100 Sprout Rd. (99352). (509) 335-6511; (509) 375-5323. FAX: (509) 335-3772. Licensee: Washington State Univ. Net: APR, NPR. Wash atty: Cohn & Marks. Format: Class, news. News staff one; news progmg 37 hrs wkly. Target aud: General. Spec prog: Folk, jazz 15 hrs wkly. ■ Dennis L. Haarsager, gen mgr; Jean Palmquist (Dir of Radio), stn mgr; Jerry Miller, opns mgr; Elizabeth Carroll, dev dir; Forrest Faubion (Underwriting), Barbara Hanford (Membership), dev mgrs; Bob Christiansen, mus dir; Dale Harrison, news dir; John Gray, engrg dir. KTNW-TV

KGDN(FM)—(Pasco). February 1992: 101.3 mhz; 6 kw. TL: N46 13 16 W119 11 20. Hrs opn: 24. Box 3258, Tri Cities (99302); Box 683, Spokane (99210). (509) 783-8600; (509) 534-6000. FAX: (509) 448-3811. Licensee: West Pasco Fine Arts Radio. Net: USA. Wash atty: Pepper & Corazzini. Format: Family-orientated talk. Target aud: 35 plus. ■ Thomas W. Read, gen mgr; William Glen, stn mgr; Robert Olafson, opns dir; Melinda Read, sls dir; Joseph Spinelli, progmg dir; Jane McKee, asst mus dir; Dick Joy, pub affrs dir; Bill Glenn, engrg dir; George Frese, chief engr.

KIOK(FM)—Listing follows KALE(AM).

KONA(AM)—(Kennewick). Jan 1948: 610 khz; 5 kw-U, DA-2. TL: N46 13 41 W119 04 07. Stereo. Hrs opn: 24. 2823 W. Lewis, Pasco (99301); Box 2623, Tri Cities (99302). (509) 547-1618. FAX: (509) 547-1618. Licensee: Tri-Cities Communications Inc. (acq 1-16-78). Net: ABC/I. Rep: Katz & Powell; Art Moore.Wash atty: Pepper & Corazzini. Format: Adult contemp, news. News staff 2; news progmg 25 hrs wkly. Target aud: 25-54. Spec prog: Farm 3 hrs, sports 8 hrs wkly. ■ Dean W. Mitchell, gen mgr; Dick Carstens, gen sls mgr; Kim Taylor, prom dir;

Greg Martin, progmg dir; Kent Johnson, news dir; Art Blum, chief engr. ■ Rates: $18; 15; 18; 14.

KONA-FM—(Kennewick). Aug 1, 1969: 105.3 mhz; 100 kw. Ant 1,180 ft. TL: N46 05 48 W119 11 36. Stereo. Hrs opn: 24. Prog sep from AM. Format: Lite adult contemp. News progmg 3 hrs wkly. Spec prog: Class 2 hrs, sports 3 hrs wkly. ■ Judy West, pub affrs dir.

KORD(AM)—(Pasco). July 28, 1956: 870 khz; 10 kw-U. TL: N46 13 41 W119 07 32. Stereo. Hrs opn: 24. Box 2485, Tri-Cities (99302-2485); 2621 W. A St. (99301). (509) 547-9791. FAX: (509) 547-8509. Licensee: 4-K Radio Partnership (acq 12-1-82; FTR 9-27-82). Net: ABC/D. Rep: Major Mkt; MMR-NW.Format: Country. News staff one; news progmg 3 hrs wkly. Target aud: 18-64. ■ Jeff Ripley, gen mgr; Kendell Huling, stn mgr; Ken Olson, gen sls mgr; John Ross, progmg dir; Jeff Turnbow, news dir; David Forsman, chief engr.

KORD-FM—(Richland). Oct 15, 1965: 102.7 mhz; 100 kw. Ant 1,100 ft. TL: N46 05 47 W119 11 36. Stereo. Dups AM 100%. News staff one; news progmg 4 hrs wkly. Spec prog: Farm 4 hrs wkly.

KTCR(AM)—(Kennewick). August 1945: 1340 khz; 1 kw-U. TL: N46 13 16 W119 11 20. Suite B-2, 830 N. Columbia Ctr. Blvd., Kennewick (99336). (509) 783-0783. FAX: (509) 735-8627. Licensee: KOTY-FM Inc. (acq 11-1-92; with co-located FM). Net: MBS, Talknet, BRN, Daynet. Rep: Christal. Format: News/talk. News staff 2; news progmg 40 hrs wkly. Target aud: 25-64. Spec prog: Sports. ■ C.T. Robinson, pres; Roger McDowell, gen mgr & natl sls mgr; Larry McKenzie, gen sls mgr; Jon McGann, progmg dir; Kevin Cole, news dir; Ron Sweatte, engrg dir; Bill Glenn, chief engr. ■ Rates: $14; 17; 13; 10.

KEGX(FM)—(Richland). Co-owned with KTCR(AM). June 10, 1992: 106.5 mhz; 100 kw. Ant 1,082 ft. TL: N46 05 51 W119 11 30. Stereo. Net: MBS. Format: Classic rock. News staff one; news progmg 2 hrs wkly. Target aud: 25-54.

***KTCV(FM)**—(Kennewick). Dec 10, 1984: 88.1 mhz; 320 w. Ant 92 ft. TL: N46 13 05 W119 12 17. Stereo. 5929 W. Metaline (99336). (509) 736-2517; (509) 736-2518. Licensee: Kennewick School District No. 17. Format: Alternative rock. ■ Marv Carstens, gen mgr; Dave Hebert, chief engr.

Rock Island

KXAA(FM)—Sept 19, 1990: 99.5 mhz; 450 w. Ant 167 ft. TL: N47 24 21 W120 17 11. Stereo. Hrs opn: 24. 800 N. Eastmont, East Wenatchee (98802). (509) 884-3322; (509) 663-9599. FAX: (509) 886-0142. Licensee: Sunbrook Wenatchee Ltd. Group owner: Sunbrook Communications (acq 7-90; $91,000; FTR 7-23-90). Rep: McGavren Guild. Wash atty: Fisher, Wayland, Cooper & Leader. Format: Oldies. News staff one; news progmg 10 hrs wkly. Target aud: 25-54. ■ Larry Roberts, pres; Dan Sollom, gen mgr; Dave Franklin, gen sls mgr; Gary Patrick, prom mgr, progmg dir & mus dir; Joe Bowers, chief engr. ■ Rates: $29; 19; 21; 14.

Roy

***KWFJ(FM)**—Not on air, target date unknown: 89.7 mhz; 1 kw. Ant 30 ft. Box 401 (98580). Licensee: Calvary Baptist Church.

Royal City

KQVN(FM)—Not on air, target date unknown: 96.3 mhz; 800 w. Ant 1,656 ft. Box 800, Granger (98932). Licensee: Northwest Chicano Radio Network Inc.

ARB AMERICAN RADIO BROKERS, INC.
MOST TRUSTED NAME IN MEDIA BROKERAGE
CHESTER P. COLEMAN / PRESIDENT
FOR THE BEST STATIONS FOR SALE FROM THIS AREA
CALL — 415/441-3377
1255 POST STREET / SUITE 625 / SAN FRANCISCO, CA 94109

Seattle

KBLE(AM)—1948: 1050 khz; 5 kw-D, 453.5 w-N. TL: N47 34 35 W122 21 52. Hrs opn: 6 AM-midnight. 114 Lakeside Ave. (98122). (206) 324-2000. Licensee: KBLE-AM Inc. Group owner: Ostrander-Wilson Stns. Wash atty: Pepper & Corazzini. Format: Relg. Spec prog: Ger one hr, Scandinavian 2 hrs, Sp 7 hrs wkly. ■ Laura W. McKenna, pres; George W. Boucher, gen mgr & gen sls mgr; Don Bevilacqua, natl sls mgr; Bud Harrington, mus dir; Bill Fanning, news dir; Sara Hildebrand, pub affrs dir; Terry Denbrook, chief engr.

KBSG-FM—See Tacoma.

KCMS(FM)—See Edmonds.

***KCMU(FM)**—1972: 90.3 mhz; 400 w. Ant 535 ft. TL: N47 36 58 W122 18 28. Stereo. Hrs opn: 24. 304 Communications Bldg., DS-55, Univ. of Washington (98195). (206) 543-5541. FAX: (206) 543-2720. Licensee: Regents of Univ. of Washington. Net: APR. Format: Progsv, div. News progmg 5 hrs wkly. Target aud: 18-44. ■ Christopher Knab, stn mgr; Terry Denbrook, chief opns & chief engr; Tom Mara, dev dir, sls dir, mktg dir, prom dir & adv dir; Don Yates, progmg dir & mus dir; Sheri Herndon, news dir.

KEZX(AM)—1926: 1150 khz; 5 kw-U, DA-N. TL: N47 35 11 W122 11 11. Hrs opn: 24. 4th & Vine Bldg., 2615 4th Ave., Suite 150 (98121). (206) 441-3699; (800) 863-3699. FAX: (206) 441-6322. Licensee: Roy H. Park Broadcasting of Washington Inc. Group owner: Park Communications Inc. Net: BRN. Rep: D & R Radio. Format: Business news. News staff 2; news progmg 10 hrs wkly. Target aud: 35-64; active, well educated adults with mid to upper income. ■ Roy Park, CEO; W. M. Thomas, pres; Rick Prusator, vp; Peg Dempsey, gen mgr & gen sls mgr; Wes Longino, opns mgr; Finn MacGinty, progmg dir; Jill Kenly, news dir & pub affrs dir; Stan MacLafferty, chief engr.

KEZX-FM—Nov 1, 1954: 98.9 mhz; 100 kw. Ant 1,110 ft. TL: N47 32 41 W122 06 28. Stereo. Hrs opn: 24. Prog sep from AM. Box 61309 (98121). (206) 441-6001. Net: CBS Spectrum, Unistar. Format: Contemp jazz, new adult contemp. News staff 2; news progmg 9 hrs wkly. Target aud: 25-54; younger active, mid to upper income adults. ■ Michael Eades, mus dir.

KGNW(AM)—See Burien-Seattle.

KING(AM)—1927: 1090 khz; 50 kw-U, DA-2. TL: N47 23 38 W122 25 25. Hrs opn: 24. Suite 400, 333 Dexter Ave. N. (98109). (206) 448-3666. FAX: (206) 448-0928. Licensee: Classic Radio Inc. (acq 2-92; $9.75 million with co-located FM). Net: ABC/D, MBS, Unistar. Rep: Major Mkt. Wash atty: Fletcher, Heald & Hildreth. Format: News/talk. News staff 6; news progmg 42 hr wkly. Target aud: 25-54; adults. ■ Jack Swanson, vp & gen mgr; Don Oylear, gen sls mgr; Roland Galli, natl sls mgr; Sara Breene, Marita Cabellon, rgnl sls mgrs; Kim Yokoyama, prom dir; Andy Ludlum, progmg dir; Tony Miner, news dir; Paul Vandegrift, chief engr.

KING-FM—1947: 98.1 mhz; 58 kw-H. Ant 2,342 ft. TL: N47 30 55 W122 58 29 Stereo. Hrs opn: 24. Prog sep from AM. (206) 448-3981. Licensee: Classic Radio Inc. Rep: Major Mkt, Major Mkt/NW. Format: Class. News progmg 5 hrs wkly. ■ Tom Dahlstrom, opns mgr; Don Oylear, gen sls mgr; Peter Newman, progmg dir; Tom Olsen, mus dir.

KIRO(AM)—1927: 710 khz; 50 kw-U, DA-N. TL: N47 23 55 W122 26 01. 2807 3rd Ave. (98121). (206) 728-7777. Licensee: KIRO Inc. Group owner: Bonneville International Corp. Net: CBS. Format: News, sports, talk. ■ Kenneth L. Hatch, pres; Joseph K. Abel, exec vp & gen mgr; Sonja Riveland, vp dev & vp mktg; Bill Aanenson, gen sls mgr; George Anderson, chief engr.

KIRO-FM—1946: 100.7 mhz; 100 kw. Ant 736 ft. TL: N47 38 01 W122 21 20. Stereo. Prog sep from AM. Box 21326 (98111-3326). (206) 728-5732. FAX: (206) 728-7261. Format: News/talk. News progmg 15 hrs wkly. Target aud: 25-54; women. Spec prog: Relg 2 hrs wkly. ■ Kevin P. Cooney, vp; Dave Ratener, chief engr. ■ KIRO-TV affil.

KISW(FM)—1950: 99.9 mhz; 100 kw. Ant 1,150 ft. TL: N47 32 41 W122 06 28. Stereo. 712 Aurora Ave. N. (98109). (206) 285-7625. FAX: (206) 282-7018. Licensee: Nationwide Communications Inc. Group owner: Nationwide Mutual Insurance Co. (acq 10-86; $12.95 million; FTR 6-16-86). Net: AP. Rep: McGavren Guild. Format: Rock/AOR. News staff 2; news progmg 3 hrs wkly. Target aud: 18-49; adults. ■ David Samp, gen mgr; John Keithan, gen sls mgr; Bob Nordberg (local), rgnl sls mgr; Cathy Keller, prom mgr; Steve Young, progmg dir; Kathy Faulkner, mus dir; Jim Kampmann, news dir; Buzz Anderson, chief engr.

KIXI(AM)—(Mercer Island-Seattle). 1947: 880 khz; 50 kw-D, 10 kw-N, DA-2. TL: N47 34 59 W122 10 52. Suite 206, 1211 N.E. First St., Bellevue (98005-3182). (206) 454-1540. FAX: (206) 455-8849. Licensee: Bellevue Radio Inc. (group owner; acq 11-15-91; $3.5 million; FTR 12-3-91). Rep: Christal. Format: MOR. News staff one; news progmg 2 hrs wkly. Target aud: 35 plus; mature active adults. ■ Gary Robb, vp & gen mgr; Bobby Irwin, opns dir & progmg dir; Bob Bordonaro, gen sls mgr; Bill Jensen, rgnl sls mgr; Laura Sieberns, Denise Hale, prom mgrs; Mike Webb, progmg mgr & mus dir; Dave Sloan, news dir; Jim Stevens, chief engr.

KJR(AM)—1921: 950 khz; 5 kw-U, DA-N. TL: N47 34 57 W122 21 46. Suite 100, 190 Queen Anne Ave. N. (98109). (206) 285-2295. FAX: (206) 286-2376. Licensee: Ackerley Communications Inc. (group owner; acq 1984). Net: NBC. Rep: D&R Radio. Format: Sports. News staff 2. Target aud: 25-54. ■ John Dresel, vp & gen mgr; Mitch Poll, natl sls mgr & rgnl sls mgr; Janet Magleby, mktg dir & prom mgr; Linda Connors, prom dir; Tom Lee, progmg dir; Bill Rice, news dir; Kelly Alford, chief engr.

KLTX(FM)—Co-owned with KJR(AM). May 25, 1960: 95.7 mhz; 100 kw. Ant 1,150 ft. TL: N47 32 41 W122 06 28. Stereo. (Acq 10-87; $8.7 million; FTR 10-19-87). Format: Adult contemp. Target aud: 30-44. ■ Sue Dyer, stn mgr; Scott Ingram, mus dir.

KKDZ(AM)—May 15 1993: 1250 khz; 5 kw-U, DA-N. TL: N47 33 41 W122 21 34. Hrs opn: 24. Arcade Bldg., Suite 150, 1334 First Ave. (98101-2003). (206) 382-1250. FAX: (206) 624-7956. Licensee: CMN Broadcasting Inc. (acq 1993; $1,132,142.80; FTR 9-13-93). Net: ABC/C. Wash atty: Haley, Bader & Potts. Format: Educ, news/talk. News staff 2; news progmg 25 hrs wkly. Target aud: Families with pre-teens. ■ Bill Koenig, pres & mktg dir; Bob Day, exec vp & gen mgr; John King, vp; Jodell Seagrave, vp sls; Annie Block, natl sls mgr; Danita Davis, prom dir; Rick Scott, progmg dir; Maura Gallucci, news dir.

KLSY-FM—See Bellevue.

KLTX(FM)—Listing follows KJR(AM).

KMPS(AM)—1922: 1300 khz; 5 kw-U, DA-N. TL: N47 35 09 W122 20 56. Box 24888 (98124); 113 Dexter Ave. N. (98109). (206) 443-9400. FAX: (206) 448-4038. (206) 441-1411. Licensee: EZ Seattle Inc. Growner owner: EZ Communications Inc. (acq 11-10-86). Net: AP. Rep: Eastman. Format: Country. ■ Fred Schumacher, Tim Murphy, vps; Fred Schumacher, gen mgr; Tony Thomas, progmg dir; Carll Ann Struder, mus dir; Don Riggs, news dir; George Bisso, chief engr.

KMPS-FM—July 8, 1961: 94.1 mhz; 57 kw. Ant 2,342 ft. TL: N47 30 14 W121 58 29. Stereo. Dups AM 100%.

KMTT(AM)—(Tacoma). August 1942: 850 khz; 10 kw-D, 1 kw-N, DA-2. TL: N47 13 56 W122 23 22. Stereo. Hrs opn: 24. Suite 1650, 1100 Olive Way, Seattle (98101-1827). 4301 S. Pine #651, Tacoma (98409). (206) 233-1037. FAX: (206) 233-8979. Licensee: Entertainment Communications Inc. Group owner: Entercom (acq 6-73; with co-located FM). Net: ABC/R. Rep: D & R Radio. Format: Adult contemp. News staff one; news progmg 3 hrs wkly. Target aud: 25-49. Spec prog: Mountain Green Report. ■ Joseph M. Field, pres; G. Michael Donovan, vp & gen mgr; Bryan Thomon, gen sls mgr; Sandy Stahl, prom dir; Chris Mays, progmg dir; Brad Dolbeer, mus dir; Reyton Mays, news dir; Marty Hadfield, engrg dir; John Price, chief engr.

KMTT-FM—(Tacoma). June 2, 1958: 103.7 mhz; 58 kw. Ant 2,343 ft. TL: N47 30 14 W121 58 29. Stereo. Hrs opn: 24. (206) 233-8984. FAX: (206) 473-5261. Format: Adult rock. ■ Rates: $85; 110; 100; 60.

KNDD(FM)—Mar 9, 1985: 107.7 mhz; 100 kw. Ant 1,194 ft. TL: N47 32 35 W122 06 25. Stereo. 1100 Olive Way (98101). (206) 622-3251. Licensee: Subsidiary of Viacom International (acq 12-29-92; traded in exchange for KHOW-AM-FM Denver; FTR 1-25-93). Format: Modern rock. News staff one. Target aud: 18-34; well educated active adults. ■ Anna Shreeve, gen mgr; Marco Collins, mus dir.

***KNHC(FM)**—Jan 25, 1971: 89.5 mhz; 30 kw. Ant 322 ft. TL: N47 41 26 W122 17 45. Stereo. Hrs opn: 24. 10750 30th Ave. N.E. (98125). (206) 281-6215. FAX: (206) 281-6929. Licensee: Seattle Public Schools. Net: AP. Wash atty: Wilmer, Cutler & Pickering. Format: CHR, educ. News progmg 9 hrs wkly. Target aud: 12-34. Spec prog: Black 4 hrs, gospel 6 hrs wkly. ■ Gregg Neilson, gen mgr, gen sls mgr & mktg dir; Judy Rudow, opns mgr & news dir; Jon McDaniel, prom mgr & mus dir; Lawrence Adams, progmg dir; Bob Walthers, chief engr. ■ Rates: $20; 20; 20; 20.

KOMO(AM)—1926: 1000 khz; 50 kw-U, DA-N. TL: N47 27 54 W122 26 27. Hrs opn: 24. 100 4th Ave. N. (98109). (206) 443-4010. FAX: (206) 443-6169. Licensee: Fisher Broadcasting Inc. (group owner). Net: ABC/I. Rep: Katz. Format: Full svc adult contemp. News staff 9; news progmg 11 hrs wkly. Target aud: 25-54. Spec prog: Univ. of Washington football, basketball play-by-play. ■ Patrick Scott, CEO & pres; John Behnke, chmn; Ralph Heyward, gen sls mgr; Phelps Fisher, vp mktg & mktg dir; Rob Dunlop, progmg dir & mus dir; Stan Orchard, news dir; Don Wilkinson, vp engrg & engrg dir. ■ KOMO-TV affil.

KPLZ(FM)—Listing follows KVI(AM).

KUBE(FM)—May 6, 1964: 93.3 mhz; 100 kw. Ant 1,291 ft. TL: N47 32 39 W122 06 29. Stereo. Suite 310, 120 Lakeside Ave. (98122). (206) 322-1622. FAX: (206) 726-9393. Licensee: Cook Inlet Radio License Partnership L.P. (acq 6-8-92). Rep: Major Mkt. Format: Contemp hits. ■ Michael O'Shea, vp & gen mgr; Michelle Grosenick, gen sls mgr; Lisa Groschell, prom mgr; Bob Case, progmg dir; Shelli Hart, mus dir; Ty Flint, news dir; Ernie Hopseker, chief engr.

KULL(AM)—1925: 770 khz; 50 kw-D, 5 kw-N, DA-2. TL: N47 23 38 W122 25 25. Hrs opn: 24. Suite 300, 15375 S.E. 30th Pl., Bellevue (98005); Box 91202, Bellevue (98009). (206) 649-0106. FAX: (206) 649-9246. Licensee: Heritage Media Corp. (group owner; acq 10-1-88; $12,008,000; FTR 10-31-88). Net: Unistar. Rep: Christal. Wash atty: Sidley & Austin. Format: Oldies. News staff one; news progmg one hr wkly. Target aud: 25-54. ■ John Rogers, pres & gen mgr; Chris Ackerman, gen sls mgr; Christi Taylor, natl sls mgr; Ken Moultrie, prom dir; Ray Randall, progmg dir; R.P McMurphy, mus dir; Mark Pierce, news dir; Robert Trimble, chief engr.

***KUOW(FM)**—Jan 16, 1952: 94.9 mhz; 100 kw. Ant 730 ft. TL: N47 36 58 W122 18 28. Stereo. Hrs opn: 24. Univ. of Washington (98195). (206) 543-2710. FAX: (206) 543-9285. Licensee: Univ. of Washington. Net: APR, NPR. Wash atty: Baker & McKenzie. Format: News, information. News staff 10; news progmg 60 hrs wkly. Target aud: 25-54. Spec prog: Sp 2 hrs, jazz 5 hrs wkly. ■ Wayne Roth, gen mgr; Dana Rehm, dev dir; Ross Reynolds, progmg dir; Dave Beck, mus dir; Marcie Sillman, news dir; Terry Denbrook, chief engr.

KVI(AM)—1929: 570 khz; 5 kw-U. TL: N47 25 19 W122 25 44. Tower Bldg., Suite 200, 7th Ave & Olive Way (98101). (206) 223-5700. FAX: (206) 292-1015. Licensee: KVI Inc. Group owner: Golden West Broadcasters (acq 7-1-59). Rep: Banner. Format: Talk radio. ■ J. Shannon Sweatte, vp & gen mgr; Bill Sigmar, gen sls mgr; Brian Jennings, progmg dir; Bill Dorweiler, chief engr.

KPLZ(FM)—Co-owned with KVI(AM). Sept 1, 1959: 101.5 mhz; 100 kw. Ant 1,150 ft. TL: N47 32 42 W122 06 29. Stereo. Format: Contemp hit radio. ■ Linda Brault, prom mgr; Casey Keating, progmg dir; Kent Phillips, news dir.

KXRX(FM)—1959: 96.5 mhz; 100 kw. Ant 1,223 ft. TL: N47 32 39 W122 06 32. Stereo. Hrs opn: 24. 7th Fl., 3131 Elliott Ave. (98121). (206) 283-5979. Licensee: Shamrock Broadcasting Inc. (group owner; acq 12-86). Rep: Katz. Wash atty: Leventhal, Senter & Lerman. Format: Adult rock. Target aud: 25-54. Spec prog: Sunday blues show. ■ Bill Clark, CEO; Marty Loughman, pres; Steve West, gen mgr; Lucy Rice, gen sls mgr; Randy Becker, natl sls mgr; Ken Cardwell, mktg dir; Bill Pugh, progmg dir; Lindsey Cipic, mus dir; Kate Ellison, asst mus dir; John Maynard, news dir; Stephen Hegg, pub affrs dir; Don Winget, chief engr.

KZOK(AM)—Sept 10, 1956: 1590 khz; 5 kw-U, DA-N. TL: N47 39 19 W122 31 06. Suite 304, 200 W. Mercer St. (98119). (206) 281-5600. FAX: (206) 281-5605. Licensee: CLG Media of Seattle Inc. (acq 11-20-92; grpsl; FTR 12-14-92). Rep: Eastman. Format: Classic rock. Target aud: 25-54. ■ Mike Fowler, gen mgr; Kevin O'Grady, Riki Pritcherd, gen sls mgrs; Jennifer Nichols, prom mgr; Dave Richards, progmg dir; Bob Hovanes, news dir; Allen Hartle, chief engr.

KZOK-FM—Dec 1964: 102.5 mhz; 100 kw. Ant 1,170 ft. TL: N47 32 35 W122 06 25. Stereo. Prog sep from AM. ■ Mike Fowler, vp.

Selah

KUTI(AM)—Licensed to Selah. See Yakima.

KYXE(AM)—Sept 13, 1983: 1020 khz; 5 kw-D, 500 w-N, DA-2. TL: N46 40 03 W120 30 49. Box 2888, Yakima (98907). (509) 457-1000. FAX: (509) 452-0541. Licensee: Tad Broadcasting Inc. (acq 5-90; grpsl; FTR 5-21-90). Net: MBS. Rep: Katz. Format: Spanish contemp. Spec prog: Farm 2 hrs wkly. ■ Roy Larson, gen mgr & gen sls mgr; Gilberto Dalvan, progmg dir; Manuel Rodriguez, news dir; Craig Siegenhaler, chief engr.

Shelton

KMAS(AM)—Sept 21, 1962: 1030 khz; 10 kw-D, 1 kw-N. TL: N47 13 17 W123 04 46. Hrs opn: 24. Box 760, 210 W. Cota St. (98584). (206) 426-1030. FAX: (206) 427-5268. Licensee: Sound Broadcasting Inc. (acq 4-1-87). Net: ABC/I. Rep: Art Moore. Format: Adult contemp. News staff 2; news progmg 20 hrs wkly. Target aud: 25-64. ■ Harold S. Greenberg, pres, gen mgr & gen sls mgr; Marian Greenberg, vp; Terry Allen, prom mgr; Deena Delco, progmg dir & mus dir; Barry Jenkins, news dir; Tony Wilson, pub affrs dir; Tom Trotzer, chief engr.

Silverdale

KITZ(AM)—Oct 14, 1948: 1400 khz; 1 kw-D, 890 w-N. TL: N47 37 45 W122 39 52. Box 1400 (98383); 7266 Tibardis Rd. N.W., Bremerton (98310). (206) 698-1400. FAX: (206) 698-1400. Licensee: Kitz Broadcasting Inc. (acq 4-16-91; $200,000; FTR 5-6-91). Net: ABC/D, Mutual, Sun. Rep: Tacher. Format: News/talk. News staff 2; news progmg 15 hrs wkly. Target aud: 25-54; general. Spec prog: Filipino one hr, relg 5 hrs, Black 2 hrs wkly. ■ Celia Johnson, pres; Fred Miles Watson, opns mgr; Lee Anders, news dir; Dale Mangels, chief engr.

AMERICAN RADIO BROKERS, INC.
MOST TRUSTED NAME IN MEDIA BROKERAGE
CHESTER P. COLEMAN / PRESIDENT
FOR THE BEST STATIONS FOR SALE FROM THIS AREA
CALL — 415/441-3377
1255 POST STREET / SUITE 625 / SAN FRANCISCO, CA 94109

South Bend

KAPA(AM)—See Raymond.

Spokane

***KAGU(FM)**—March 16, 1988: 88.7 mhz; 100 w. Ant -141 ft. TL: N47 40 06 W117 24 05. Stereo. E. 502 Boone Ave. (99258). (509) 328-4220. Licensee: Gonzaga Univ. Telecommunications Association (acq 12-4-91). Format: Adult contemp, new age. Spec prog: Class 2 hrs, jazz 2 hrs, folk 2 hrs, drama 2 hrs wkly. ■ Fr. Robert Lyons, gen mgr; Luara Lathrop, progmg dir.

KAQQ(AM)—1922: 590 khz; 5 kw-U. TL: N47 36 59 W117 22 12. 300 E. Third Ave. (99202). (509) 459-9800. FAX: (509) 624-5957. Licensee: Silverado Broadcasting Co. (group owner; acq 7-27-92; grpsl; FTR 8-17-92). Net: CNN. Rep: Major Mkt. Wash atty: Wiley, Rein & Fielding. Format: MOR. Target aud: 35-64. Spec prog: Farm 6 hrs wkly. ■ John Winkel, pres; Kosta Panidis, gen mgr & natl sls mgr; Jim Ostrander, gen sls mgr; Barry Watkins, prom dir & progmg dir; Steve Nelson, news dir; Keith Harvey, chief engr.

KISC(FM)—Co-owned with KAQQ(AM). May 1, 1966: 98.1 mhz; 94 kw. Ant 2,030 ft. TL: N47 34 53 W117 17 47. Stereo. Prog sep from AM. Format: Adult contemp. ■ Rob Harder, progmg dir.

KCDA(FM)—(Coeur d'Alene, Idaho). June 29, 1979: 103.1 mhz; 2.35 kw. Ant 4,400 ft. TL: N47 39 35 W116 57 12. Stereo. Hrs opn: 24. E. 300 Third Spokane, WA (99202). (509) 534-3636. FAX: (509) 459-9850. Licensee: Rook Broadcasting of Idaho Inc. (acq 9-83; $225,000; FTR 10-31-83). Net: SMN. Rep: Roslin. Wash atty: Pepper & Corazzini. Format: Country. News staff 2; news progmg one hr wkly. Target aud: 25-54; active and affluent. ■ John H. Rook, pres & prom dir; Clifford Rook, vp; Kim Cooper, gen mgr; Jeff Swartz, gen sls mgr; John Goes, progmg dir & pub affrs dir; John Rook, mus dir; Randy Anderson, news dir; Keith Harvey, chief engr. ■ Rates: $21; 18; 18; 12.

KDRK-FM—Listing follows KGA(AM).

KEEH(FM)—July 1, 1991: 104.7 mhz. 317 w. Ant 1,378 ft. Stereo. Hrs opn: 6 AM-11 PM. Suite 124, No. 1212 Washington (99201). (509) 326-9500. Licensee: Upper Columbia Media Association (acq 9-8-93; $148,000; FTR 10-4-93). Wash atty: Fisher, Wayland, Cooper, & Leader. Format: Christian. Target aud: General. ■ Larry Roberts, CEO, chmn & pres; Jon Dalvyuple, stn mgr; Art Lenz, engrg dir.

KEYF-FM—See Cheney.

KEZE-FM—Listing follows KJRB(AM).

KGA(AM)—1926: 1510 khz; 50 kw-U, DA-N. TL: N47 35 44 W117 22 15. Box 30013 (99223-3000). (509) 448-2311. FAX: (509) 448-7015. Licensee: Citadel Communications Corp. (group owner; acq 5-18-92; grpsl, including co-located FM; FTR 6-8-92). Net: ABC/I. Rep: Eastman, Moore. Format: Contemp country. Spec prog: Farm one hr wkly. ■ Steve Cody, Barbara Beddor (asst.), gen mgrs; Dean Allen, progmg dir; Tim Cotter, mus dir; Stephan Kaufman, news dir; Bill Gott, chief engr.

KDRK-FM—Co-owned with KGA(AM). 1965: 93.7 mhz; 56 kw. Ant 2,380 ft. TL: N47 34 13 W117 05 00. Stereo. Hrs opn: 24. (509) 448-8300. Rep: Eastman, Moore. ■ Gary Charles, mus dir.

KISC(FM)—Listing follows KAQQ(AM).

KJRB(AM)—1947: 790 khz; 5 kw-U, DA-N. TL: N47 36 16 W117 23 11. Stereo. Box 8007 (99203). E. 1601 57th (99223). (509) 448-1000; (509) 448-8888. FAX: (509) 448-4549. Licensee: Citadel Communications Corp. (group owner; acq 9-20-93; $125,000; FTR 10-11-93). Net: NBC, NBC Talknet. Rep: Katz. Format: Talk, sports. News staff one. Spec prog: GSL football & basketball, North Idaho Vandals football, GU basketball, Bloomsday & Jr. Bloomsday. ■ Lawrence Wilson, pres; Steve Cody, gen mgr; Gary Allen, opns mgr & progmg dir; Fay Mills, gen sls mgr; Barbara Beddor, natl sls mgr; Jamie Bowers, prom dir; Scott Carlon, news dir; Lee Fichtner, chief engr.

KEZE-FM—Co-owned with KJRB(AM). Nov 8, 1965: 105.7 mhz; 100 kw. Ant 1,910 ft. TL: N47 34 44 W117 17 46. Stereo. Prog sep from AM. (Acq 3-22-93; $2.75 million with co-located AM; FTR 4-12-93). Net: ABC. Format: Rock (AOR). ■ Gary Allen, mus dir; Belinda Simmons, asst mus dir; Scott Carlon, pub affrs dir.

KKZX(FM)—Listing follows KUDY(AM).

***KMBI(AM)**—July 12, 1959: 1330 khz; 5 kw-D. TL: N47 36 17 W117 21 27. Hrs opn: 6 AM-sunset. 5408 S. Freya (99223). (509) 448-2555. FAX: (509) 448-6855. Licensee: Moody Bible Institute. Group owner: The Moody Bible Institute of Chicago (acq 6-74). Format: Relg. Target aud: 35-64. ■ D. Gary Leonard, gen mgr; Michael A. Cornell, opns mgr; Gordon Canaday, chief engr.

***KMBI-FM**—Apr 22, 1968: 107.9 mhz; 56 kw. Ant 2,380 ft. TL: N47 34 15 W117 05 00. Stereo. Dups AM 30%.

KNJY(FM)—1988: 103.9 mhz; 3 kw. Ant 299 ft. TL: N47 41 52 W117 31 07 (CP: 5.5 kw). 211 Sprague (99202). (509) 535-7272. FAX: (509) 747-1650. Licensee: TCC Broadcasting (acq 1-3-92). Format: News/talk. ■ Tom Cock, gen mgr; Martha Lou Wheatly, progmg dir.

***KPBX-FM**—1970: 91.1 mhz; 56 kw. Ant 2,380 ft. TL: N47 34 13 W117 05 00. Stereo. Hrs opn: 24. 2319 N. Monroe St. (99205). (509) 328-5729. FAX: (509) 328-5764. Licensee: Spokane Public Radio Inc. Net: APR, NPR. Format: Class, news, pub affrs. News staff 3; news progmg 50 hrs wkly. Target aud: General; educated. Spec prog: Jazz, folk, world mus, new age/space, new mus. ■ Richard Kunkel, CEO, gen mgr, dev dir & progmg dir; Brian Flick, opns dir; Christie Bruntlett, Kathy Grabicki, sls dirs; Staci Erickson, Kathy Grabicki, mktg dirs; Julia Schauble, prom mgr; Verne Windham, mus dir; Doug Nadvornick, news dir & pub affrs dir; Ron Mahan, chief engr. ■ Rates: $17; 13; 17; 13.

KSBN(AM)—September 1921: 1230 khz; 1 kw-U. TL: N47 39 30 W117 25 08. Hrs opn: 24. 211 E. Sprague Ave. (99202); Box 2203 (99210). (509) 747-1955. FAX: (509) 747-1650. Licensee: T.C.C. Broadcasting (acq 9-90; $90,000; FTR 9-10-90). Net: BRN. Format: Business/financial. News staff 3. Target aud: 30-65; upscale; business owners. ■ Thomas C. Cock Jr., pres & gen mgr; Laurie J. Turner, vp opns; Martha Lou Wheatley, vp progmg & news dir; Conrad Agte, chief engr. ■ Rates: $25; 18; 20; 12.

***KSFC(FM)**—March 1973: 91.9 mhz; 100 w. Ant 92 ft. TL: N47 40 37 W117 27 31. Hrs opn: 7:30 AM-midnight. W. 3410 Fort George Wright Dr. (99204). (509) 533-3825; (509) 459-3825. FAX: (509) 533-3433. Licensee: Spokane Falls Community College. Format: AOR. Target aud: 18-27. ■ Richi Caldwell, gen mgr; Patrick Klausen, progmg dir; Mike Hale, mus dir; Sam Julagay, news dir; Larry Poole, chief engr.

KSPO(FM)—Dec 25, 1992: 96.9 mhz; 6 kw. Ant 535 ft. TL: N47 41 39 W117 20 03. Hrs opn: 24. Box 8238 (99203). (509) 534-6000. FAX: (509) 448-3811. Licensee: Melinda Boucher Read. Net: MBS, USA. Wash atty: Pepper & Corazzini. Format: Relg, talk. Target aud: 35 plus. ■ Joe Spinelli, gen mgr.

Stations in the U.S. Washington

KSVY(AM)—(Opportunity). Sept 1, 1962: 1550 khz; 10 kw-D, 2.5 kw-N, DA-N. TL: N47 36 39 W117 14 28. Hrs opn: 6 AM-10 PM. W. 933 Third Ave., Spokane (99204). (509) 924-1393. Licensee: Harold Orr (acq 12-85). Rep: Roslin. Format: Class. Target aud: General; adults. ■ Dick Wright, gen mgr; Jerry Anderson, progmg dir; Ron Mahan, chief engr. ■ Rates: $25; 25; 25; 15.

KTRW(AM)—1947: 970 khz; 5 kw-D, 1 kw-N, DA-N. TL: N47 36 59 W117 21 55. Hrs opn: 24. Suite 505, S. 140 Arthur (99202). (509) 536-9700. FAX: (509) 536-7622. Licensee: Louis Dearias, receiver (acq 4-29-92; grpsl, including co-located FM). Net: Unistar, SEN. Rep: Eastman. Format: All sports, talk. Target aud: 25-54. Spec prog: Dallas Cowboys, Washington Huskies, Greater Spokane League football & basketball. ■ Bryce Phillipy, gen mgr; Brian Paul, gen sls mgr; Daron Howard, prom mgr; Rob Potter, progmg dir; Lyn Daniels, news dir; Keith Harvey, chief engr. ■ Rates: $15; 10; 15; 10.

KZZU-FM—Co-owned with KTRW(AM). September 1955: 92.9 mhz; 81 kw. Ant 2,080 ft. TL: N47 35 42 W117 17 53. Stereo. Prog sep from AM. (509) 536-5555. Format: CHR. Target aud: 18-49. ■ Kendall Hopkins, progmg dir; Rob Potter, mus dir. ■ Rates: $60; 50; 60; 20.

KUDY(AM)—1965: 1280 khz; 5 kw-D, DA. TL: N47 36 27 W117 21 40. Hrs opn: Sunrise-sunset. S. 5106 Palouse Hwy. (99223-7128). (509) 448-1280. FAX: (509) 448-4043. Licensee: Carl T. Robinson (acq 12-7-92; $1.008 million with co-located FM; FTR 1-4-93). Rep: D & R Radio; Tacher. Wash atty: Arent, Fox, Kintner, Plotkin & Kahn. Format: Relg. News progmg one hr wkly. Target aud: General. ■ Terry A. McRight, pres; Chris Gavras, gen mgr; Bill Thompson, opns mgr; Ray O'Russa, progmg dir & mus dir; Brad Kemmer, news dir; Jim Nichols, chief engr. ■ Rates: $20; 20; 20; 20.

KKZX(FM)—Co-owned with KUDY(AM). Oct 10, 1975: 98.9 mhz; 100 kw. Ant 1,614 ft. TL: N47 35 35 W117 17 46. Stereo. Hrs opn: 24. Prog sep from AM. (509) 448-9900. Format: Classic rock. News progmg one hr wkly. Target aud: 25-54. Spec prog: Blues 2 hrs wkly. ■ John Langan, progmg dir; Steve Hawk, mus dir; C. Foster Kane, news dir. ■ Rates: $40; 40; 40; 25.

***KWRS(FM)**—Sept 16, 1991: 90.3 mhz; 100 w. Ant 61 ft. TL: N47 45 30 W117 25 00. Stereo. Hrs opn: 17. Stn. 40, Hardwick Union Bldg., Whitworth College (99251). (509) 466-3278; (509) 466-1000, ext. 4575. Licensee: Whitworth College. Format: New music. News staff one; news progmg 2 hrs wkly. Target aud: 15-35; mostly college & high school students. Spec prog: Jazz 9 hrs, AOR 2 hrs, Christian 6 hrs, political 2 hrs, beat 2 hrs, all female artists 2 hrs, country 2 hrs, reggae 2 hrs wkly. ■ Steve Radonick, gen mgr, opns dir & dev dir; Mike Struelens, sls dir; Jamie Bowers, prom dir; Crystal King, progmg dir; Johanna Richard, mus dir; Julie Gage, asst mus dir; Paul Spencer, news dir; Lee M. Rey, Bill Gott, chiefs engr.

KXLY(AM)—October 1922: 920 khz; 5 kw-U. TL: N47 36 30 W117 22 25. W. 500 Boone Ave. (99201). (509) 328-6292. FAX: (509) 325-0676. Licensee: Spokane Radio Inc. Group owner: Morgan Murphy Stns. (acq 3-21-62). Net: ABC TalkRadio, CBS, MBS, Wall Street. Rep: Torbet, Eastman. Format: All news. Spec prog: Farm 6 hrs wkly. ■ Elizabeth M. Burns, pres; Stephen R. Herling, vp; Robert Witter, gen mgr; Kim MacKelvie, gen sls mgr; Robin Riley, news dir; Tim Anderson, chief engr.

KXLY-FM—September 1959: 99.9 mhz; 37 kw. Ant 2,998 ft. TL: N47 55 18 W117 06 48. Stereo. Format: Btfl mus. ■ Ron Hatch, progmg dir. ■ KXLY-TV affil.

KZZU-FM—Listing follows KTRW(AM).

Sumner

KZIZ(AM)—1990: 1560 khz; 5 kw-D. TL: N47 12 48 W122 13 25. 2600 S. Jackson St., Seattle (98144). (206) 323-3070. FAX: (206) 322-6518. Licensee: KRIZ Broadcasting Inc. Net: Natl Black. Format: Urban contemp. Target aud: 12 plus; African-American. ■ Chris Bennett, gen mgr & gen sls mgr; Frank P. Barrow, progmg dir, mus dir & news dir; Rodney Schaffer, chief engr.

Sunnyside

KREW(AM)—September 1950: 1210 khz; 10 kw-D, 1 kw-N. TL: N46 19 49 W120 02 10. Hrs opn: 6 AM-10 PM. Box 149, 638 Decauter (98944). (509) 837-2277. FAX: (509) 837-3777. Licensee: Bennett Broadcasting Co. (acq 7-1-65). Net: CBS. Rep: Tacher. Format: MOR, news, Sp. News staff 2; news progmg 40 plus hrs wkly. Target aud: 25-55. Spec prog: Car racing, high school sports, Washington State University sports. ■ Don Bennett, pres & gen mgr; Larry Bennett, gen sls mgr; Alice Beneditti, progmg dir; Rich Robert, mus dir; Joe Just, news dir; Carl McDonald, chief engr. ■ Rates: $8.40; 8.40; 8.40; 8.40.

KREW-FM—Aug 1, 1974: 96.7 mhz; 3 kw. Ant -1 ft. TL: N46 19 10 W120 01 28. Stereo. Hrs opn: 6 AM-10 PM. Dups AM 30%. Format: C&W, news, sports. ■ Don Bennett, CEO; Alice Benetti, opns dir; Larry Bennett, vp sls & prom mgr; Joe Just, pub affrs dir. ■ Rates: $10.50; 10.50; 10.50; 11.25.

Tacoma

KBSG-FM—Oct 26, 1948: 97.3 mhz; 52 kw. Ant 2,391 ft. TL: N47 30 14 W121 58 29. Stereo. Hrs opn: 24. 20th Fl., 1730 Minor Ave., Seattle (98101). (206) 952-9700; (206) 343-9700. FAX: (206) 623-7677 (ADMIN/SALES); (206) 343-0481. Licensee: KBSG Inc. Group owner: Viacom Broadcasting Inc. Net: AP. Rep: Torbet. Format: Oldies. News staff one. Target aud: 25-54. ■ Bill Fishenshu, pres; Charles E. Maylin, gen mgr; Susan Seifert, gen sls mgr; Judi Yazzolino, natl sls mgr; Mitch Boyle, rgnl sls mgr; Carol Stripling, mktg mgr, prom dir & adv mgr; Jay Kelly, progmg dir; Kim Wilson, news dir; Clay Freinwald, chief engr.

***KBTC-FM**—June 1, 1949: 91.7 mhz; 7.9 kw. Ant 553 ft. TL: N47 18 15 W122 23 44. Stereo. Hrs opn: 14. 1101 S. Yakima Ave. (98405-4895). (206) 596-1600. FAX: (206) 596-1643. Licensee: State Board for Community and Technical Colleges. Format: Adult contemp. Spec prog: Sp 2 hrs, blues 2 hrs wkly. ■ Debbie Emond, stn mgr; Mel Jackson, pub affrs dir. ■ KBTC-TV affil.

KDFL(AM)—(Lakewood). September 1978: 1480 khz; 5 kw-D, 1 kw-N, DA-N. TL: N47 09 00 W122 24 38. Hrs opn: 7 AM-dusk. 5208 100 Street S.W., Tacoma (98499). (206) 582-0706. Licensee: Help Ministries Inc. (acq 4-5-93; $58,000; FTR 4-26-93). Format: Contemp Christian, talk. Target aud: General; handicapped, elderly. Spec prog: Ger 2 hrs, relg 12 hrs wkly. ■ Richard Ellison, pres; Marty Hamstra, gen mgr; Bud Henthorm, opns dir; Larry Lee, progmg dir.

KKMO(AM)—1922: 1360 khz; 5 kw-U. TL: N47 18 19 W122 26 33. Hrs opn: 24. Box 1277, KKMO Office/Studios (98401); 4501 Pacific Hwy. E. (98424). (206) 922-3345. Licensee: KAMT Inc. (acq 11-77; $1,250,000). Net: SMN. Format: Big band, Sp, Korean. Target aud: 35 plus. Spec prog: Ger 2 hrs, Japanese 10 hrs wkly. ■ James L. Baine, pres & gen mgr; Jennifer Wood, opns mgr; Josie Schilling, prom mgr; Lee Jackson, progmg dir; Gary Greenfield, chief engr.

KLAY(AM)—(Lakewood). 1978: 1180 khz. Suite B, 10025 Lakewood Dr. S.W., Tacoma (98499). (206) 581-0324. Licensee: Clay Frank Huntington. Format: Talk. ■ Clay Frank Huntington, pres.

KMTT(AM)—Licensed to Tacoma. See Seattle.

KMTT-FM—Licensed to Tacoma. See Seattle.

***KPLU-FM**—November 1966: 88.5 mhz; 58 kw. Ant 2,356 ft. TL: N47 28 50 W122 31 58. Stereo. Hrs opn: 24. 121st & Park (98447-0003). (206) 535-7758. FAX: (206) 535-8332. Licensee: Pacific Lutheran Univ. Net: APR, NPR. Wash atty: Arter & Hadden. Format: Jazz, news. News staff 6; news progmg 54 hrs wkly. Target aud: 25-54; upscale, highly educated professionals. Spec prog: Blues 9 hrs, car talk 2 hrs wkly. ■ Martin J. Neeb, gen mgr; Mel Baer, dev dir & mktg dir; Greg Coe, prom mgr; Roger Johnson, progmg dir; Joe Cohn, mus dir; Michael Marcotte, news dir; David Christian, chief engr.

KRPM-FM—May 1959: 106.1 mhz; 55 kw. Ant 699 ft. TL: N47 18 15 W122 23 44. Stereo. 15375 S.E. 30th Pl., Bellevue (98005). (206) 649-0106. FAX: (206) 649-9246. Licensee: Heritage Media Corp. (group owner). Net: Unistar. Rep: Christal. Wash atty: Sidley & Austin. Format: Contemp country. News staff 2; news progmg 20 hrs wkly. Target aud: 25-54. ■ John Rogers, pres & gen mgr; Ray Randall, opns mgr & progmg dir; Chris Ackerman, gen sls mgr; Christy Taylor, natl sls mgr; Ken Moultrie, prom mgr; R.P. McMurphy, mus dir; Mark Pierce, news dir; Andy Laird, vp engrg; Robert Trimble, chief engr.

***KUPS(FM)**—Feb 28, 1978: 90.1 mhz; 100 w. Ant 65 ft. TL: N47 15 48 W122 28 37. Stereo. Hrs opn: 8 AM-3 AM. 1500 N. Warner (98416). (206) 756-3277. (206) 756-3288. FAX: (206) 756-3500. Licensee: Univ. of Puget Sound. Format: Progsv. News staff one; news progmg 2 hrs wkly. Target aud: General. Spec prog: Black 12 hrs, world music 2 hrs, country 3 hrs, classic rock 8 hrs, reggae 11 hrs, metal 13 hrs, Hawaiian 3 hrs wkly. ■ Julie Leydelmeyer, gen mgr; Geoff Chackel, Bret Cullivan, sls dirs; Geoff Chackel, Bret Cullivan, mktg dirs; Steve Schultz, prom dir; Jason Stuck, progmg dir & mus dir; Keith Hirata, asst mus dir; Troy Hirsh, news dir; Dave Kerlin, chief engr.

***KVTI(FM)**—Nov 15, 1955: 90.9 mhz; 51 kw. Ant 422 ft. TL: N47 09 39 W122 34 35. Stereo. Hrs opn: 24. 4500 Steilacoom Blvd. S.W. (98499-4098). (206) 589-5884. FAX: (206) 589-5797. Licensee: Clover Park Technical College. Wash atty: Haley, Bader & Potts. Format: CHR, top-40. News progmg 2 hrs wkly. Target aud: 12-34; teens & young adults. Spec prog: Live music 3 hrs, talk 4 hrs wkly. ■ Alson E. Green Jr., pres; G. James Capelli, sr vp; John L. Mangan, gen mgr & progmg dir; Beth Valiant, mus dir; Nick Winter, chief engr.

Toppenish

KENE(AM)—May 16, 1954: 1490 khz; 1 kw-U. TL: N46 22 33 W120 19 18. Box 350 (98948-0350). (509) 865-5363; (509) 865-3900. Licensee: Good News and Music Broadcasting Co. (acq 1-23-87; $240,000; FTR 9-22-86). Net: Jones Satellite Audio. Rep: Roslin. Format: Country. News progmg 2 hrs wkly. Target aud: 25-58. Spec prog: Children one hr, farm one hr wkly. ■ Rick Knapp, pres & gen mgr; Joe Langdon, progmg dir & mus dir; Dave Hebert, chief engr. ■ Rates: $10; 7; 10; 5.

KXXS(FM)—Oct 31, 1977: 92.9 mhz; 17 kw. Ant 843 ft. TL: N46 30 15 W120 23 33. Stereo. Hrs opn: 24. Box 1280, Yakima (98907). (509) 457-8115; (509) 248-9393. FAX: (509) 453-3368. Licensee: Tad Broadcasting Inc. (acq 5-90; grpsl; FTR 5-21-90). Net: CNN. Rep: McGavren Guild. Wash atty: Cliff Harrington. Format: Hot country. Target aud: 25-54. ■ Dave Aamodt, gen mgr, stn mgr, gen sls mgr, natl sls mgr & rgnl sls mgr; Dennis Heinz, prom mgr; Jeff Howell, progmg dir, mus dir & news dir; Bob Maxwell, chief engr.

Tumwater

KVSN(AM)—August 1987: 1500 khz; 1 kw-D. TL: N47 00 26 W122 54 58. Box 4207 (98501); 2105 54th Ave. S.W., Olympia (98502). (206) 943-9834; (206) 481-1463. Licensee: Evergreen Broadcasting Inc. Net: USA, Moody. Wash atty: Gary Preble. Format: Relg. News staff one. Target aud: General. ■ Lawrence Adams, gen mgr; Don Trosper, opns mgr & asst mus dir; Tanya Parker, gen sls mgr & mktg mgr; Gregg Neilson, progmg dir; Jerome Wilen, news dir; Corrie Foss, pub affrs dir; Gary Foss, chief engr. ■ Rates: $11; 11; 11; na.

Twisp

KVLR(FM)—Not on air, target date unknown: 106.3 mhz; 220 w. Ant 1,633 ft. Box 626, Winthrop (98862). Licensee: Methow Radio.

Vancouver

KBMS(AM)—1955: 1480 khz; 1 kw-D, 2.5 kw-N, DA-N. TL: N45 36 06 W122 43 06. Suite 400, 601 Main St. (98660). (206) 699-1881. FAX: (206) 699-5370. Licensee: Chris Bennett Broadcasting Inc. Net: CBS Spectrum. Format: Urban contemp. ■ Chris Bennett, gen mgr & gen sls mgr; Angela Jenkins, stn mgr, progmg dir & mus dir; Richard Wilson, chief engr.

KKEY(AM)—See Portland, Ore.

KKSN(AM)—Sept 1, 1946: 910 khz; 5 kw-U, DA-2. TL: N45 33 28 W122 30 09. Hrs opn: 24. 5005 S.W. McAdam, Portland (97201). (503) 226-9791. FAX: (503) 243-3299. Licensee: Heritage Media Corp. (group owner; acq 8-15-88; $5.75 million; FTR 8-15-88). Rep: Christal. Format: Nostalgia. News staff one. Target aud: 35-64. ■ Harry Williams, pres & gen mgr; Michael Del Fonzo, opns mgr; Rocky Blumhagen, gen sls mgr; Debb Janes, news dir; Gary Hilliard, chief engr.

KKSN-FM—See Portland, Ore.

KVAN(AM)—Aug 10, 1963: 1550 khz; 10 kw-U, 500 w-N, DA-N. TL: N45 38 47 W122 30 51. Hrs opn: 24. Box 4507, 7710 N.E. Vancouver Mall Dr., (98662). (206) 944-1550. FAX: (206) 944-6679. Licensee: Vancouveradio Inc. (acq 7-12-93; $177,750; FTR 8-2-93). Rep: D & R Radio, Target. Wash atty: Haley, Bader & Potts. Format: News. ■ Richard A. Granger Sr., pres; Jeff Williams, gen mgr, progmg dir & news dir; Bill Cole, gen sls mgr.

Walla Walla

***KGTS(FM)**—See College Place.

KHSS(FM)—Nov 5, 1986: 100.9 mhz; 1.3 kw. Ant 1,374 ft. TL: N46 04 04 W118 20 21 (CP: 100.7 mhz, ant 1,414 ft., TL: N45 59 04 W118 10 08). Stereo. Hrs opn: 24. Whitman Towers Penthouse, 107 N. Second Ave. (99362). (509) 522-5412. FAX: (509) 522-5414. Licensee: KHSS Inc. (acq 4-10-91; $225,000; FTR 4-29-91). Net: SMN. Rep: Katz & Powell, Art Moore. Wash atty: Pepper & Corazzini. Format: AOR, classic rock. Target aud: 18-34. Spec prog: Relg 3 hrs wkly. ■ John R. Ramstad, pres & chief engr; Jim Bock, gen mgr, gen sls mgr, prom mgr, asst mus dir & news dir; Chris Robert, stn mgr & opns mgr; John Ramstad, progmg dir & mus dir. ■ Rates: $15; 12; 15; 10.

KNLT(FM)—Listing follows KUJ(AM).

KNSN(FM)—August 1977: 97.1 mhz; 50 kw. Ant 1,360 ft. TL: N45 59 04 W118 10 08 (CP: 64.8 kw). Stereo. Hrs opn: 24. Box 796, 11 S. Palouse (99362). (509) 525-3190. Licensee: Johnson Communications Inc. (acq 4-19-91; $105,400; FTR 5-13-91). Net: CNN. Format: C&W. News staff one. Target aud: 25 plus; businesses & mid to upper income level listeners. ■ Tim Kammer, opns mgr; Pierrie Dozios, prom mgr; Scott Hendericks, progmg dir & news dir. ■ Rates: $21; 17.75; 21; 14.

KSMX(AM)—Dec 6, 1956: 1320 khz; 1 kw-D. TL: N46 02 13 W118 21 07. Box 1641, 103 E. Main St. (99362). (509) 525-3162. Licensee: Ralph and Cheryl Broetje and Barry and Maria Delaluz Jenkins (acq 5-1-91; $180,159.60; FTR 5-20-91). Net: CRC. Format: Sp. ■ Salvatore Hernandez, progmg dir; Todd Branderberge, chief engr.

KTEL-FM—May 10, 1977: 93.3 mhz; 42 kw. Ant 1,378 ft. TL: N45 59 19 W118 10 28. Stereo. 112 N.E. 5th Ave., Milton-Freewater, OR (97862). (503) 938-6688. Licensee: ComCast Media Services Inc. Net: ABC/I. Rep: Katz & Powell, Farmakis, Tacher. Format: Adult contemp, country. News staff one. Target aud: General. Spec prog: Farm 2 hrs wkly. ■ Dennis Widmer, pres, gen mgr & prom mgr; Sherrie Lindemann, gen sls mgr; Bill Boggs, progmg dir, mus dir & news dir.

KTEL(AM)—October 1946: 1490 khz; 1 kw-U. TL: N46 20 33 W118 20 20. Dups FM 100%.

KUJ(AM)—1928: 1420 khz; 5 kw-U, DA-N. TL: N46 04 03 W118 24 08. Hrs opn: 24. Suite B-2, 830 N. Columbia Ctr. Blvd., Kennewick (99336); Rt. 5, Box 513 (99336). (509) 783-0783; (509) 529-8000. FAX: (509) 735-8627; (509) 525-3727. Licensee: KUJ L.P. (acq 1-1-81). Net: NBC Talknet, MBS, Daynet. Rep: Christal. Format: News/talk. News staff one; news progmg 8 hrs wkly. Target aud: 25 plus. ■ Norm Feller, CEO; C.T. Robertson, pres; Ken Welland, CFO; Roger McDowell, gen mgr & natl sls mgr; Larry McKenzie, gen sls mgr; Danny Mitchell, progmg dir; Kevin Cole, news dir; Jon Anderson, engrg dir; Ron Sweatte, chief engr. ■ Rates: $10; 8; 10; 6.

KNLT(FM)—Co-owned with KUJ(AM). Jan 1, 1980: 95.7 mhz; 100 kw. Ant 1,401 ft. TL: N45 59 04 W118 10 08. Stereo. Prog sep from AM. Net: Unistar. Format: Adult contemp. Target aud: 25-54.

***KWCW(FM)**—1971: 90.5 mhz; 160 w. Ant 96 ft. TL: N46 04 10 W118 19 54. Stereo. Whitman College (99362). (509) 527-5283. Licensee: The Associated Students of Whitman College Radio Committee. Net: ABC/FM. Format: Div, rock. ■ Gina Frazzini, gen mgr.

Wapato

***KSOH(FM)**—Mar 6, 1992: 89.5 mhz; 9.5 kw. Ant 974 ft. TL: N46 31 42 W120 31 16. 1006 S. Tenth St., Yakima (98901). (509) 248-4673. Licensee: Central Washington Education Foundation. Format: Btfl music, relg, news, talk. News progmg 9 hrs wkly. Target aud: General; families, singles needing courage, hope and answers to societal ills. ■ Paul E. Moore, pres, stn mgr, gen sls mgr, mktg dir & prom dir; Joe Mann, opns dir & progmg dir; Don Parks, mus dir; Georgina F. Moore, April Hardinge, news dirs; Ken Watson, engrg dir. ■ Rates: $48; 48; 48; 48.

Wenatchee

KKRT(AM)—Nov 17, 1956: 900 khz; 1 kw-D, 78 w-N. TL: N47 27 45 W120 19 24. Box 79 (98807). (509) 663-5186. FAX: (509) 663-8779. Licensee: Infinity Systems Inc. (acq 10-15-93; $250,000 with co-located FM; FTR 11-8-93). Rep: Major Mkt. ■ Doug Shirk, pres; Jon Bellizzi, gen mgr & gen sls mgr; Greg Roberts, opns mgr & progmg dir; Debi Campestrini, prom dir; Wayne Bowden, chief engr.

KKRV(FM)—Co-owned with KKRT(AM). May 1, 1976: 104.9 mhz; 6.3 kw. Ant 1,312 ft. TL: N47 28 44 W120 12 49. Stereo. Suite 411, 5 S. Wenatchee Ave. (98801). Format: AOR. Spec prog: Blues, Blues & more Blues. ■ Greg Roberts, vp progmg.

KPQ(AM)—December 1929: 560 khz; 5 kw-U, DA-N. TL: N47 27 12 W120 19 43. Hrs opn: 24. 32 N. Mission (98801). (509) 663-5121. FAX: (509) 664-6799. Licensee: Wescoast Broadcasting Co. (acq 9-7-77). Net: ABC/I. Rep: Tacher. Format: News/talk. Target aud: 35 plus. Spec prog: Farm 3 hrs. ■ Jim Wallace Jr., pres; H. Donald MacKinnon, stn mgr; Bob Clarke, gen sls mgr; Steve Hair, news dir; Wayne Bowden, chief engr.

KPQ-FM—December 1967: 102.1 mhz; 35 kw. Ant 2,655 ft. TL: N47 16 28 W120 25 30. Stereo. Hrs opn: 24. Prog sep from AM. Net: Unistar. Format: Adult contemp. Target aud: 25 plus.

KWWX(AM)—1948: 1340 khz; 1 kw-U. TL: N47 23 50 W120 16 25. Hrs opn: 24. Box 638, 304 S. Mission St. (98801). (509) 662-7135. Licensee: Sans Inc. Net: CRC. Rep: Major Mkt; Major Mkt NW.Format: Sp. News staff one; news progmg 10 hrs wkly. Target aud: General. ■ David C. Herald, pres, gen mgr, gen sls mgr & prom mgr; Ralph Ochoa, stn mgr, progmg dir & mus dir; Don Bernier, news dir; Wayne Millich, chief engr.

KYSN(FM)—(East Wenatchee). Dec 25, 1980: 97.7 mhz; 3 kw. Ant -150 ft. TL: N47 22 52 W120 17 16. Stereo. Hrs opn: 24. 800 N. Eastmont Ave., East Wenatchee (98802). (509) 884-1555. FAX: (509) 884-2994. Licensee: Sunbrook Wenatchee Ltd. (acq 2-26-93; $230,000; FTR 3-22-93). Net: MBS. Rep: Art Moore. Format: Country. News staff one; news progmg 20 hrs wkly. Target aud: 25-54. Spec prog: Farm one hr, relg one hr wkly. ■ Larry Roberts, pres; Brian L. Stephenson, gen mgr; Julie Pittsinger, gen sls mgr; Doug McDowell, progmg dir; Eric Granstrom, news dir; Wayne Bowden, chief engr. ■ Rates: $20; 20; 20; 18.

Wilson Creek

KVYF(FM)—Not on air, target date unknown: 103.3 mhz; 6 kw. Ant 328 ft. TL: N47 25 00 W119 12 30. c/o 11608 Blossomwood Ct., Moorpark CA (93021). Licensee: Wilson Creek Broadcasting Co. (acq 6-9-92).

Yakima

KATS(FM)—Listing follows KIT(AM).

KBBO(AM)—1947: 1390 khz; 5 kw-D, 500 w-N, DA-2. TL: N46 34 17 W120 27 15 (CP: 400 w-N). Hrs opn: 19. Box 9188 (98909); 2120 Riverside Rd. (98901). (509) 248-1390. FAX: (509) 453-6530. Licensee: Northwest Broadcast Representatives Inc. Group owner: B&B Broadcasting (acq 11-1-93; $218,750 with co-located FM; FTR 11-22-93). Net: AP, CBN. Rep: Major Mkt. Format: Relg. News staff one. Target aud: 35-64; family oriented. Spec prog: Black 2 hrs, Sp 2 hrs wkly. ■ Bob Barron, pres; Jack G. Anderson, gen mgr; Jack G. Andersen, gen sls mgr; Tom Berg, progmg dir & mus dir; Dean Heinen, chief engr.

KRSE(FM)—Co-owned with KBBO(AM). Aug 18, 1977: 105.7 mhz; 100 kw. Ant 584 ft. TL: N46 42 45 W120 37 46. Stereo. Hrs opn: 19. Prog sep from AM. Format: Soft adult contemp. Target aud: Upscale listener, primarily women, 25 plus.

***KDNA(FM)**—Dec 19, 1979: 91.9 mhz; 18.5 kw. Ant 920 ft. TL: N46 31 42 W120 31 03. Stereo. Box 800, 121 Sunnyside Ave., Granger (98932). (509) 854-1900; (509) 854-2222. FAX: (509) 854-2223. Licensee: Northwest Chicano Radio Network (acq 12-19-79). Format: Sp. News staff one; news progmg 8 hrs wkly. Target aud: General; Spanish speaking farm workers. Spec prog: Relg 6 hrs, jazz 4 hrs, Indian 2 hrs wkly. ■ Ricardo Garcia, gen mgr; Amelia Ramon, dev dir; Rosa Ramon, prom dir; Ezequiel M. Ramirez, progmg dir; Maria Estella Rebollosa, mus dir; Nelly Mares, news dir; Ninfa R. Gutierrez, pub affrs dir; Gabriel Martinez, chief engr.

KFFM(FM)—Listing follows KMWX(AM).

KIT(AM)—Apr 8, 1929: 1280 khz; 5 kw-D, 1 kw-N. TL: N46 34 19 W120 29 41. Stereo. Box 1280, 114 S. Fourth St. (98901). (509) 457-8115; (509) 248-1280. FAX: (509) 453-3368. Licensee: T & J Broadcasting Inc. Group owner: Tom Ingstad Broadcasting Group (acq 9-87; $1,550,000; FTR 9-7-87). Net: CBS, MBS, NBC. Rep: McGavren Guild. Wash atty: Cliff Harrington. Format: News/talk. News staff 2. Target aud: 25-64. Spec prog: Farm 6 hrs wkly. ■ Randy Holland, CEO; Tom Ingstad, pres; Dave Aamodt, gen mgr & gen sls mgr; Ric McClary, progmg dir & mus dir; Al Bell, news dir; Robert Maxwell, chief engr. ■ Rates: $40; 30; 30; 22.

KATS(FM)—Co-owned with KIT(AM). Dec 15, 1968: 94.5 mhz; 100 kw. Ant 850 ft. TL: N46 31 59 W120 30 14. Stereo. Prog sep from AM. (509) 457-1902. Rep: McGavren Guild. Format: Classic rock. News staff one. Target aud: 20-45; adults. ■ Darren Johnson, prom dir & progmg dir; Robert Maxwell, vp engrg.

KMWX(AM)—Oct 19, 1944: 1460 khz; 5 kw-U, 3.7 kw-N, DA-N. TL: N46 33 29 W121 27 02. Hrs opn: 24. Box 1460 (98907); 215 N. 4th St. (98901). (509) 248-1460. FAX: (509) 453-5550. Licensee: Northwest Broadcasting Co. (acq 1-16-78). Net: NBC. Rep: Katz & Powell. Wash atty: Pepper & Corazzini. Format: Oldies. News staff one; news progmg 2 hrs wkly. Target aud: 25-49. ■ Michael Mercy, pres; Dennis Green, vp; Dale Carpenter, gen mgr & gen sls mgr; Frank Taylor, progmg dir & mus dir; Lou Bartelli, news dir; Aaron Wasilewski, chief engr. ■ Rates: $20; 15; 20; 11.

KFFM(FM)—Co-owned with KMWX(AM). September 1970: 107.3 mhz; 100 kw. Ant 1,500 ft. TL: N46 38 27 W120 23 42. Stereo. Hrs opn: 24. Prog sep from AM. Format: CHR. News staff one; news progmg one hr wkly. Target aud: 18-34; adult females & males. ■ Dale Carpenter, natl sls mgr; Michael Jack Kirby, progmg dir & mus dir. ■ Rates: $32; 24; 32; 16.

***KNWY(FM)**—Not on air, target date unknown: 90.3 mhz; 5 kw. Ant 895 ft. TL: N46 31 57 W120 30 37. Licensee: Washington State University.

KRSE(FM)—Listing follows KBBO(AM).

KUTI(AM)—(Selah). 1955: 980 khz; 5 kw-D, 500 w-N, DA-N. TL: N46 36 46 W120 28 24. Hrs opn: 24. 706 Butterfield Rd., Yakima (98901). (509) 248-2900. FAX: (509) 452-9661. Licensee: Butterfield Broadcasting Corp. (acq 10-5-93; $425,100 with KXDD-FM Yakima; FTR 10-25-93). Net: ABC, AP. Rep: Tacher. Wash atty: Mullin, Rhyne, Emmons & Topel. Format: Country. News staff one; news progmg 11 hrs wkly. Target aud: 35-64. ■ Greg Smith, pres; Gary Myhre, gen mgr & gen sls mgr; Bob Reece, opns mgr & progmg mgr; Ron King, natl sls mgr & rgnl sls mgr; Brenda Houis, prom dir; Lee McClanathan, progmg dir & mus dir; Mike Bastinelli, news dir; Andy Thompson, chief engr. ■ Rates: $19; 17; 18; 9.

KXDD(FM)—July 1, 1971: 104.1 mhz; 61 kw. Ant 781 ft. TL: N46 30 48 W120 24 05 (CP: 100 kw, ant 1,447 ft., TL: N46 38 27 W120 23 42). Stereo. Prog sep from AM. Licensee: Butterfield Broadcasting Corp. (acq 10-5-93; $425,100 with KUTI[AM] Selah; FTR 10-25-93). Net: ABC/I, AP. Target aud: 18-54. ■ Chris Kelly, progmg dir; Bob Reece, mus dir; Curt Hutchinson, pub affrs dir. ■ Rates: $40; 27; 28; 15.

KYKA(FM)—(Naches). Oct 25, 1988: 96.9 mhz; 5.8 kw. Ant 36 ft. TL: N46 41 40 W120 41 01. Stereo. Hrs opn: 24. Box 2754, Yakima (98907). (509) 453-6296. FAX: (509) 575-4772. Licensee: Mathias Broadcasting Inc. Group owner: John Mathias (acq 12-88; $190,000; FTR 12-5-88). Net: Unistar. Rep: Tacher. Format: Oldies. Target aud: 25-54; upwardly mobile, two-income families. ■ Don Schrack, pres, stn mgr & gen sls mgr; Mike Nofsinger, opns mgr, prom dir, progmg dir, mus dir & pub affrs dir; Dean Heinen, chief engr. ■ Rates: $132; 72; 120; 72.

***KYSC(FM)**—Sept 1980: 88.5 mhz; 3 kw. Ant -254 ft. TL: N46 35 06 W120 31 41. Stereo. Hrs opn: 24. Yakima Valley Skills Ctr., 1116 S. 15th Ave. (98902). (509) 575-3333; (509) 575-3436. FAX: (509) 454-3522. Licensee: Yakima School District No. 7. Format: AOR, jazz. News staff one; news progmg 5 hrs wkly. Target aud: 16-40. Spec prog: Heavy metal 10 hrs, relg 3 hrs wkly. ■ John Schieche, pres; Randy Beckstead, gen mgr, dev dir & chief engr; Charlie Dickens, opns mgr; Jessica James, prom mgr; Josh Ellingsworth, progmg dir; Joe Rogers, mus dir; Brad Apple, asst mus dir; Annette Pressnell, news dir; Mari Tillett, pub affrs dir.

KYXE(AM)—See Selah.

KZTA(AM)—Oct 17, 1962: 930 khz; 1 kw-D, 127 w-N. TL: N46 36 48 W120 28 51. Hrs opn: 5 AM-midnight. Box 2489 (98907). (509) 248-4722. FAX: (509) 457-7241. Licensee: KZTA Broadcasting Inc. (acq 6-8-92; $250,000 with co-located FM; FTR 7-6-92). Rep: Caballero. Format: Sp. News progmg one hr wkly. Target aud: General; Hispanic. ■ Amador Bustos, pres; Ramon Duarte, gen mgr & progmg dir.

KZTA-FM—Dec 1, 1984: 99.3 mhz; 630 w. Ant 590 ft. TL: N46 31 53 W120 26 58 (CP: 99.7 mhz, 3.5 kw, ant 882 ft.). Stereo. Hrs opn: 5 AM-midnight. Prog sep from AM. Target aud: 25-54.

West Virginia

**LAUREN A. COLBY
301-663-1086
COMMUNICATIONS ATTORNEY
Special Attention to
Difficult Cases**

Barrackville

WMMN-FM—Not on air, target date unknown: 93.1 mhz; 2.6 kw. Ant 497 ft. TL: N39 31 23 W80 12 00. Box 64, Kingmont (26578). Licensee: Rosemary C. Fanctacia.

Beckley

WCIR-FM—Listing follows WIWS(AM).

WIWS(AM)—Nov 14, 1966: 1070 khz; 10 kw-D. TL: N37 45 18 W81 14 12. 118 Philpott Ln., Beaver (25813). (304) 252-6452. FAX: (304) 255-1044. Licensee: Southern Communications Corp. (acq 1976). Format: Visitor info. News progmg 80 hrs wkly. Target aud: 18-54; traveling motorists. ■ Ira W. Southern, chmn; R. Shane Southern, pres, gen mgr & gen sls mgr; Joe Hovanski, progmg mgr; Sharon Bleau, news dir.

WCIR-FM—Co-owned with WIWS(AM). June 1971: 103.7 mhz; 5 kw. Ant 1,485 ft. TL: N37 56 51 W81 18 32. Stereo. Hrs opn: 24. Prog sep from AM. Net: Unistar. Rep: Katz & Powell. Wash atty: Borsari & Payson. Format: Adult contemp. News staff 2; news progmg 2 hrs wkly. Target aud: 25-54. ■ Art Argyries, gen sls mgr; Joe Hovanski, progmg dir; Jeff Davis, mus dir; Keith Edwards, news dir.

WJLS(AM)—Mar 5, 1939: 560 khz; 5 kw-D, 500 w-N, DA-N. TL: N37 46 40 W81 09 40. Hrs opn: 24. Box AB, WJLS Bldg., 102 N. Kanawha St. (25801). (304) 253-7311; (304) 252-5656. FAX: (304) 253-3466. Licensee: Personality Stations Inc. Net: MBS. Rep: Dome, Savalli, Rgnl Reps. Wash atty: Reed, Smith, Shaw & McClay. Format: Relg. News staff 2; news progmg 4 hrs wkly. Target aud: 25-54. Spec prog: Sports 10 hrs wkly. ■ Nancy R. Smith, pres; William A. O'Brien, vp & gen mgr; Charlie Jennings, sls dir & prom dir; Margaret Lacy, mktg mgr; Sandi Smith, progmg dir & mus dir; Jerri Miller, news dir; Charles Marlow, chief engr.

WJLS-FM—Nov 6, 1946: 99.5 mhz; 34 kw. Ant 1,050 ft. TL: N37 35 23 W81 06 51. Stereo. Hrs opn: 24. Prog sep from AM. Rep: Savalli; Dome, Rgnl Reps. Format: Country. News progmg 10 hrs wkly. ■ Charlie Jennings, opns mgr, mktg dir, prom mgr & adv dir; Rick Janney, prom dir; Bob West, progmg dir; Greg White, asst mus dir; Jerri Miller, pub affrs dir.

WOAY(AM)—See Oak Hill.

*WVPB(FM)—May 1, 1974: 91.7 mhz; 10.5 kw. Ant 920 ft. TL: N37 53 46 W80 59 21. Stereo. Hrs opn: 24. 600 Capitol St., Charleston (25301). (304) 558-3000. FAX: (304) 558-4034. Licensee: West Virginia Educational Broadcasting Authority. Net: NPR, APR. Format: News, classical, jazz. News staff 2. Spec prog: Mountain stage 2 hrs wkly. ■ Barbara Herrick, gen mgr; Marilyn DiVita, dev mgr; Nancy Buckingham, prom mgr; Jeanne Fisher, progmg dir; Jim Wallace, news dir; Francis Fisher, chief engr.

WWNR(AM)—Aug 9, 1946: 620 khz; 1 kw-D, 500 w-N, DA-N. TL: N37 47 18 W81 14 18. Stereo. Box AE, 345 Prince St. (25801). (304) 253-8307; (304) 253-8308. FAX: (304) 252-6200. Licensee: Martine Broadcasting Inc. (acq 4-30-84; $360,000; FTR 12-19-83). Net: ABC/C. Rep: Katz. Format: News/talk. News staff 2; news progmg 34 hrs wkly. Target aud: 25-54; adults. Spec prog: HS & college sports. ■ Albert A. Martine, CEO, pres & gen mgr; Jim Martin, opns mgr, progmg dir & mus dir; John Hager, gen sls mgr; Bill Farthing, chief engr. ■ Rates: $12; 10; 11; 8.

Berkeley Springs

WCST(AM)—Sept 7, 1958: 1010 khz; 250 w-D, 17 w-N. TL: N39 37 00 W78 13 03. Box 10, Fulton St. (25411). (304) 258-1010. Licensee: Trump Broadcasting Inc. Net: ABC/E. Format: Country. ■ Conrad Trump, pres, gen mgr, gen sls mgr & news dir; Verg Ruppenthal, progmg dir & mus dir; Kevin McNamara, chief engr.

WCST-FM—December 1965: 93.5 mhz; 3 kw. Ant 70 ft. TL: N39 37 01 W78 13 00. Stereo. Hrs opn: 6 AM-10 PM. Dups AM 100%.

Bethany

*WVBC(FM)—Jan 1, 1967: 88.1 mhz; 1.1 kw. Ant 410 ft. TL: N40 12 58 W80 33 31. Stereo. Bethany House, Bethany College (26032). (304) 829-7853; (304) 829-7562. FAX: (304) 829-7108. Licensee: Bethany College. Net: UPI. Wash atty: Blair, Joyce & Silva. Format: Div, educ, progsv. News staff 2; news progmg 3 hrs wkly. Target aud.: 18-34; high school & college students, young adults. Spec prog: Christian rock 4 hrs, folk 2 hrs, classic rock 8 hrs, class 2 hrs wkly. ■ Patrick Sutherland, gen mgr & gen sls mgr; Derek Stubbs, prom mgr; David Chambers, progmg dir; Mish Paull, mus dir; David George, news dir; Russell Zorves, chief engr.

Bethlehem

WHLX(FM)—June 13, 1985: 105.5 mhz; 2.7 kw. Ant 313 ft. TL: N40 03 17 W80 42 26 (CP: 3 kw). Stereo. Box 6462, 27 Highland Ln., Wheeling (26003). (304) 232-7058. FAX: (304) 232-7051. Licensee: Bethlehem Radio Inc. (acq 4-84; $21,116.97; FTR 4-23-84). Format: Easy lstng. ■ Neil B. Fondas, pres & gen mgr; Richard Howard, opns mgr & gen sls mgr; Carl M. Robbins, chief engr.

Blennerhassett

WRRD(AM)—Not on air, target date unknown: 940 khz; 480 w-D, DA. TL: N39 17 32 W81 33 22. Box 1462, Jeffersonville, IN (47131). (812) 282-6142. Licensee: Minority Christian Radio of West Virginia. Net: CBN. Format: Relg. Target aud: General; Christian. ■ John W. Smith II, pres & gen sls mgr; Mary L. Smith, gen mgr; Angelia M. Pait, prom mgr; David B. Smith, progmg dir & mus dir; Darlene Smith, news dir; John W. Smith I, chief engr.

Bluefield

WHAJ(FM)—Listing follows WHIS(AM).

WHIS(AM)—June 27, 1929: 1440 khz; 5 kw-D, 500 w-N. TL: N37 16 33 W81 15 06. Stereo. 900 Bluefield Ave. (24701). (304) 327-7114. Licensee: Adventure Communications Inc. (group owner; acq 9-1-84; $2.1 million; FTR 7-30-84). Net: NBC Talknet. Format: News/talk. News staff one; news progmg 20 hrs wkly. Target aud: 35 plus; upper income, leaders of the community. ■ Mike Shott, pres; Paul McNeill, CFO; Frank Barnes, gen mgr; Dave Kirby, stn mgr; Ken Dietz, prom mgr & progmg dir; Kurt Pickering, news dir; Keith Bowman, chief engr. ■ Rates: $12; 12; 10; 8.

WHAJ(FM)—Co-owned with WHIS(AM). Apr 23, 1963: 104.5 mhz; 100 kw. Ant 1,200 ft. TL: N37 15 21 W81 10 55. Stereo. Prog sep from AM. Net: ABC/C, Unistar. Format: Adult contemp. News progmg one hr wkly. Target aud: 25-49. ■ Ken Dietz, progmg mgr; J. Patrick, mus dir. ■ Rates: $70; 70; 70; 70.

WKOY(AM)—May 18, 1948: 1240 khz; 1 kw-U. TL: N37 15 57 W81 11 20. Hrs opn: 24. Box 7204, Mercer Mall (24701). (304) 327-6124; (304) 327-8000. FAX: (304) 327-6125. Licensee: Mountain Broadcasting Corp. (acq 5-8-89; grpsl; FTR 5-29-89). Format: News/talk. News staff 8; news progmg 24 hrs wkly. Target aud: 30 plus. Spec prog: Relg 5 hrs wkly. ■ Earl Judy Jr., pres; Tina Etter, opns mgr; Linda Slater, gen sls mgr; Steve Stout, prom mgr, progmg dir, progmg mgr & pub affrs dir; Jeffery W. Sparks, mus dir & news dir; Jay Belt, engrg mgr. ■ Rates: $8.40; 8.40; 8.40; 8.40.

*WPIB(FM)—Not on air, target date 1994: 90.9 mhz; 740 w-H, 700 w-V. Ant 1,102 ft. TL: N37 15 26 W81 10 43. Box 889, Blacksburg, VA (24060). (703) 552-4252; (703) 552-8073. FAX: (703) 951-5282. Licensee: Positive Alternative Radio Inc. (acq 4-22-92). Net: USA. Format: Adult contemp, Christian. ■ Vernon H. Baker, pres; George McNerlin, gen mgr.

Bridgeport

WDCI(FM)—June 29, 1991: 104.1 mhz; 3 kw. Ant 328 ft. TL: N39 17 59 W80 17 30. Stereo. Hrs opn: 24. Box 371, Summit Park Rd. (26330). (304) 842-8644. FAX: (304) 842-8644. Licensee: Dolphin Communications Inc. Net: Jones Satellite Audio. Rep: Dome. Wash atty: Blair, Joyce & Silva. Format: Soft adult contemp. Target aud: 25-54. ■ Earl W. Stewart Jr., pres; Debra L. Stewart, vp; Richard B. Floyd, gen mgr & sls dir. ■ Rates: $7.50; 7.50; 7.50; 7.50.

Buckhannon

WBTQ(FM)—1984: 93.5 mhz; 2.75 kw. Ant 538 ft. TL: N38 56 03 W80 11 20. Stereo. Hrs opn: 24. Box 728, 157 S. Kanawha St. (26201). (304) 472-1400. FAX: (304) 472-1528. Licensee: Harlynn Inc. (acq 10-89). Net: ABC. Rep: Commercial; Dome.Wash atty: Dean George Hill. Format: Solid gold. Target aud: 25-49. Spec prog: Relg 4 hrs wkly. ■ Ron Roth, gen mgr; Phil Phillips, chief engr. ■ Rates: $6.60; 6; 6.60; 6.

WBUC(AM)—Dec 13, 1959: 1460 khz; 5 kw-D, 87 w-N. TL: N39 00 07 W80 15 50. Stereo. Drawer C, 1 1/2 miles W. on Hwy. 33 (26201). (304) 472-1460. FAX: (304) 472-1528. Licensee: Cat Radio Inc. (acq 9-4-86; $395,000; FTR 8-4-86). Net: SMN. Rep: Commercial, Rgnl Reps. Wash atty: Dean George Hill. Format: Country. Target aud: General. Spec prog: Relg 7 hrs wkly. ■ Phil Phillips, pres, gen mgr & chief engr; Vicky Lough, gen sls mgr; Joyce Philips, prom mgr; Vicky Phillips, mus dir; Nancy Boyce, news dir. ■ Rates: $7; 6.50; 7; na.

WBUC-FM—June 16, 1990: 101.3 mhz; 50 kw. Ant 497 ft. TL: N38 56 40 W80 10 46. Stereo. Hrs opn: 24. Net: SMN. Target aud: 25-54; upper middle class, white collar, craftsman. ■ Phil Phillips, progmg dir.

*WVPW(FM)—Sept 1968: 88.9 mhz; 14 kw. Ant 840 ft. TL: N39 02 04 W80 33 47. Stereo. 600 Capitol, Charleston (25301). (304) 558-3239. FAX: (304) 558-4034. Licensee: West Virginia Education Broadcasting Authority (acq 5-76). Net: NPR, APR. Format: News, classical, jazz. News staff 2. ■ Barbara Herrick, gen mgr; Marilyn DiVita, dev mgr; Nancy Buckingham, prom mgr; Jeanne Fisher, progmg mgr; Jim Wallace, news dir; Francis Fisher, chief engr.

*WVWC(FM)—Sept 5, 1977: 92.1 mhz; 10 w. Ant 85 ft. TL: N38 59 24 W80 13 10. Box 167 (26201-2999). (304) 473-8000; (304) 473-8035. FAX: (304) 472-2751. Licensee: West Virginia Wesleyan College. Format: Class rock, progsv. Target aud: 12-25; high school and college. Spec prog: Classic 2 hrs, Black 2 hrs, jazz 4 hrs, prgsv 4 hrs, heavy metal 4 hrs, Christian 4 hrs, new age 4 hrs wkly. ■ Geof Iverson, gen mgr & mus dir; Barb Plummer, opns mgr; J.B. Thornton, sls dir; Rod Gunter, prom dir & pub affrs dir; Bob Adams, progmg dir; Rob Adams, asst mus dir; Arnold Sayre, chief engr.

Charles Town

WXVA(AM)—May 28, 1962: 1550 khz; 5 kw-D. TL: N39 16 23 W77 51 56. Box 700 (25414). (304) 725-0402. FAX: (304) 728-7941. Licensee: Heritage Broadcasting Co. (acq 9-9-82; $400,000; FTR 9-27-82). Net: AP, Unistar. Format: Oldies. ■ Gene McCoy, pres; Linda Karl, opns dir; Shelly Drennen Brown, gen sls mgr; Tom Tucker, progmg dir; Andrea Starace, news dir; John Humphreys, chief engr.

WXVA-FM—Aug 28, 1966: 98.3 mhz; 3 kw. Ant 300 ft. TL: N39 16 23 W77 51 56. Stereo. Dups AM 3%. Net: AP. Format: Adult contemp. Spec prog: Big band 4 hrs wkly.

Charleston

WCAW(AM)—1946: 680 khz; 50 kw-D, 250 w-N, DA-2. TL: N38 19 15 W81 36 31. Hrs opn: 24. 4110 McCorkle Ave. S.E. (25304). (304) 925-4986; (304) 342-8131. Licensee: West Virginia Radio Corp. of Charleston (acq 7-14-93; $1.1 million with co-located FM; FTR 8-9-93). Net: ABC. Rep: Banner. Format: Country, sports. News staff one. Target aud: 25-54. ■ Gary Martins, gen mgr; Mark Allen, gen sls mgr; Paul Higginbotham, progmg dir; Dave Higginbotham, chief engr.

WVAF(FM)—Co-owned with WCAW(AM). Feb 1, 1965: 99.9 mhz; 50 kw. Ant 490 ft. TL: N38 19 15 W81 36 31. Stereo. Prog sep from AM. Format: Adult contemp. News progmg 13 hrs wkly. Target aud: Female skew. ■ Randi Daniels, gen mgr; Rick Johnson, progmg dir; Kevin Kasey, mus dir; Jenny Murray, news dir; Jeff Batten, chief engr.

WCHS(AM)—Sept 15, 1927: 580 khz; 5 kw-U, DA-N. TL: N38 21 49 W81 46 05. 1111 Virginia St. E. (25301). (304) 342-8131. FAX: (304) 344-4745. Licensee: West Virginia Radio Corp. of Charleston (acq 6-1-92; $1,743,836 with co-located FM; FTR 6-22-92). Net: CBS, MBS. Rep: Eastman. Format: News/talk, sports. News staff 2; news progmg 60 hrs wkly. Target aud: 25-54. ■ Gary Mertins, gen mgr; Don Cook, progmg dir; Jeff Batten, chief engr. ■ Rates: $24; 20; 22; 18.

WKWS(FM)—Co-owned with WCHS(AM). Sept 16, 1969: 96.1 mhz; 50 kw. Ant 360 ft. TL: N38 21 24 W81 36 19 (CP: Ant 550 ft., TL: N38 21 51 W81 46 05). Stereo. Prog sep from AM. Format: Hot country hits. Spec prog:

Fusion jazz 3 hrs wkly. ■ Doug Hammond, progmg dir. ■ Rates: Same as AM.

WCZR(AM)—1939: 1490 khz; 1 kw-U. TL: N38 21 28 W81 37 00. Hrs opn: 24. 136 High St. (25311). (304) 342-1490. FAX: (304) 342-4646. Licensee: Empire Broadcasting System (acq 4-7-88). Net: SMN. Rep: D & R Radio. Format: Rock and roll. ■ Don Cavaleri, pres; Jay Smith, gen mgr; Noel Richardson, chief engr.

WKAZ(FM)—See Miami.

WKWS(FM)—Listing follows WCHS(AM).

WQBE(AM)—Feb 16, 1957: 950 khz; 5 kw-D, 1 kw-N, DA-N. TL: N38 23 00 W81 42 52. Box 871, 4250 Washington St. W. (25323). (304) 744-9691. FAX: (304) 744-8562. Licensee: Bristol Broadcasting Co. Inc. Group owner: Nininger Stns. (acq 5-1-64). Net: ABC/I. Rep: McGavren Guild. Format: Country. Spec prog: Black one hr wkly. ■ W.L. Nininger, pres; John Gush, gen mgr & gen sls mgr; Jeff Whitehead, progmg dir; Roy Jones, mus dir; Greg Walsh, news dir; Ron Taylor, chief engr.

WQBE-FM—Feb 16, 1957: 97.5 mhz; 50 kw. Ant 500 ft. TL: N38 24 22 W81 43 26. (304) 744-7020. Format: Country.

WVAF(FM)—Listing follows WCAW(AM).

***WVPN(FM)**—May 8, 1979: 88.5 mhz; 50 kw. Ant 299 ft. TL: N38 22 32 W81 39 25. Stereo. Hrs opn: 24. 600 Capitol St. (25301). (304) 558-3000. FAX: (304) 558-4034. Licensee: West Virginia Educational Broadcasting Authority. Net: NPR, APR. Format: News, classical, jazz. News staff 2. Spec prog: Mountain stage 2 hrs wkly. ■ Barbara Herrick, gen mgr; Marilyn DiVita, dev mgr; Nancy Buckingham, prom mgr; Jeanne Fisher, progmg dir; Jim Wallace, news dir; Francis Fisher, chief engr.

WVSR(AM)—Nov 4, 1946: 1240 khz; 1 kw-U. TL: N38 21 26 W81 40 05. Box 3697 (25336); 817 Suncrest Pl. (25303). (304) 342-3136. FAX: (304) 342-3118. Licensee: Ardman Broadcasting Corp. (group owner; acq 8-90; grpsl). Net: AP. Rep: Katz. Format: CHR. News staff one; news progmg 5 hrs wkly. Target aud: 18-49. ■ Myer Feldman, pres; Tom Collins, gen mgr; Nancy Hurley, gen sls mgr; Bill Shahan, progmg dir; Burke Allen, mus dir; Carol Short, news dir; Noel Richardson, chief engr.

WVSR-FM—September 1964: 102.7 mhz; 50 kw. Ant 403 ft. TL: N38 21 26 W81 40 05. Stereo. Dups AM 100%.

Clarksburg

WHAR(AM)—Nov 28, 1946: 1340 khz; 1 kw-U. TL: N39 17 27 W80 18 56. Hrs opn: 24. 350 W. Main St. (26301). (304) 624-5525. FAX: (304) 624-5526. Licensee: Harrison Corp. (acq 7-25-61). Net: ABC/C. Rep: Roslin, Rgnl Reps. Wash atty: Pepper & Corazzini. Format: News/talk. News progmg 14 hrs wkly. Target aud: 35 plus; office workers. retirees, housewives. ■ James T. Fawcett, pres; Mark Mills, gen mgr; Bill Mahoney, prom mgr; Mike Shirley, progmg dir; Asa Gawthrop, chief engr.

WVHF-FM—Co-owned with WHAR(AM). 1975: 92.7 mhz; 660 w. Ant 600 ft. TL: N39 17 27 W80 18 56. Stereo. Hrs opn: 5:30 AM-1 AM. Prog sep from AM. (304) 624-5526. Net: ABC/C. Format: Adult contemp. News progmg 3 hrs wkly. Target aud: Female 25-45; office workers, housewives. ■ Bill Mahoney, prom dir. ■ Rates: $18.25; 15; 18.25; 15.

***WKJL(FM)**—Not on air, target date unknown: 88.1 mhz; Licensee: He's Alive Inc.

WKKW-FM—1973: 106.5 mhz; 50 kw. Ant 500 ft. TL: N39 11 14 W80 32 45. Stereo. Hrs opn: 24. 130 S. Second St. (26301). (304) 623-6546. FAX: (304) 623-6547. Licensee: West Virginia Radio Corp. of Clarksburg (acq 3-2-93; $1.2 million; FTR 3-22-93). Format: Country. ■ Dale B. Miller, gen mgr; Jim Dodril, gen sls mgr; Dave Harmon, mus dir; Ralph Messer, chief engr.

WOBG(AM)—Apr 12, 1936: 1400 khz; 1 kw-U. TL: N39 17 46 W80 18 16. Hrs opn: 24. Box 3190, Old Weatherservice Bldg., Old Rt. 50 E. (26301). (304) 624-1400. FAX: (304) 624-1402. Licensee: Hilber Corp. (acq 1-5-90; $100,000; FTR 1-22-90). Net: ABC/E. Rep: Katz & Powell; Commercial Media Sales.Wash atty: Shainis & Peltzman. Format: Golden oldies. Target aud: 25-54. Spec prog: Health talk. ■ Bob Hilber, pres & gen mgr; Sally Hilber, vp; Mike King, gen sls mgr; Dan Terango, progmg dir; Don Niles, mus dir; Barbara Scott, pub affrs dir; Asa Gawthrop, chief engr. ■ Rates: $24; 24; 24; 24.

WPDX(AM)—Aug 19, 1947: 750 khz; 1 kw-D. TL: N39 14 40 W80 23 05. Box 1920, 139 1/2 W. Main St. (26301). (304) 624-6425. FAX: (304) 622-3560. Licensee: Tschudy Broadcasting Corp. (group owner; acq 11-5-91; $405,000 with co-located FM; FTR 12-2-91). Net: CNN. Format: Country. Target aud: 18-49. ■ Earl Judy Jr., pres; Bill Dunn, gen mgr; Gary Hamrick, mus dir; John Lambert, news dir; Rick Williams, vp engrg. ■ Rates: $12; 10; 11; 9.

WPDX-FM—Aug 19, 1974: 104.9 mhz; 2.5 kw. Ant 321 ft. TL: N39 14 40 W80 23 05. Stereo. Dups AM 100%. ■ John Lambert, pub affrs dir. ■ Rates: Same as AM.

WVHF-FM—Listing follows WHAR(AM).

Danville

WZAC-FM—Oct 9, 1989: 92.5 mhz; 610 w. Ant 697 ft. TL: N38 05 01 W81 48 17. Stereo. Box 87 (25053). (304) 369-5201. FAX: (304) 369-5200. Licensee: Price Broadcasting Co. Format: Country. News progmg 7 hrs wkly. Target aud: General. ■ Wayne Price, gen mgr, gen sls mgr & chief engr; Steve Green, progmg dir & mus dir; Tim Buskirk, news dir.

Dunbar

WBES-FM—Oct 13, 1988: 94.5 mhz; 3 kw. Ant 328 ft. TL: N38 23 51 W81 43 09 (CP: 8.5 kw, ant 525 ft., TL: N38 25 11 W81 43 24). Stereo. Hrs opn: 24. Box 5307, Charleston (25361). (304) 345-9237. FAX: (304) 345-9248. Licensee: Ardman Broadcasting Corp. of West Virginia. Group owner: Ardman Broadcasting Corp. (acq 11-29-93; $1 million; FTR 12-13-93). Net: ABC/E, Moody, Westwood One. Rep: Katz & Powell, Dome, Rgnl Reps. Format: Easy lstng. Spec prog: Class 2 hrs wkly. ■ Mort Victorson, gen mgr; Mark Lockhart, prom mgr; Randy Mallory, progmg dir & mus dir; Greg Kirk, chief engr.

Elkins

***WCDE(FM)**—1975: 90.3 mhz; 100 w. Ant 90 ft. TL: N38 55 52 W79 50 49 (CP: 1 kw). Box J, Davis & Elkins College, 100 Sycamore St. (26241-3996). (304) 636-6800; (304) 636-1900. FAX: (304) 636-8624. Licensee: Davis and Elkins Board of Trustees. Format: AOR. Target aud: 15-35. Spec prog: Jazz 3 hrs, reggae 3 hrs, alternative 12 hrs wkly. ■ Jim Carl, gen mgr; Doug Kranch, chief engr.

WDNE(AM)—February 1948: 1240 khz; 1 kw-U. TL: N38 55 25 W79 51 33. Hrs opn: 21. Box 1337 (26241). (304) 636-1300. FAX: (304) 636-1300. Licensee: Marja Broadcasting Corp. (acq 12-1-55). Net: AP. Format: Country. News staff one. Target aud: 18 plus. ■ William G. Carr, pres & gen mgr; Bob Cowgill, gen sls mgr; Brian Moore, progmg dir; Gary Simmons, mus dir; Bill Rice, news dir; Dave Saffel, chief engr. ■ Rates: $14.15; 14.15; 14.15; 14.15.

WDNE-FM—June 15, 1985: 99.3 mhz; 3 kw. Ant 328 ft. TL: N38 51 53 W79 48 26. Stereo. Hrs opn: 21. Dups AM 100%. ■ Rates: Same as AM.

WELK(FM)—Oct 17, 1982: 94.7 mhz; 5 kw. Ant 728 ft. TL: N38 54 43 W79 47 19. Stereo. Hrs opn: 24. 228 Randolph Ave. (26241). (304) 636-8800. FAX: (304) 636-8801. Licensee: Elkins Radio Corp. Group owner: McGraw Group Stations. Net: Unistar. Wash atty: Fisher, Wayland, Cooper & Leader. Format: Adult contemp, top-40. ■ Richard H. McGraw, pres; Karen McGraw, vp & gen mgr; Mark Philips, gen sls mgr; Eric McGuire, prom dir; Brian Elliott, adv mgr; David Skidmore, progmg dir; Larry Smith, news dir; Chuck Snoderly, chief engr. ■ Rates: $23.50; 18.50; 18.50; 13.50.

Fairmont

WFGM(FM)—October 1975: 97.9 mhz; 32 kw. Ant 600 ft. TL: N39 25 04 W80 03 44. Stereo. Box 2798, 7002 Mountain Park Dr. (26555-2798). (304) 366-9880; (304) 366-9811. FAX: (304) 366-9881. Licensee: Dailey Corp. (acq 11-84; $650,000; FTR 12-3-84). Net: ABC/D. Rep: Dome, Rgnl Reps. Wash atty: Reddy, Begley & Martin. Format: CHR. News staff one; news progmg 6 hrs wkly. Target aud: 18-45; young professionals. Spec prog: Relg 3 hrs wkly. ■ Calvin Dailey Jr., pres; Randy Dailey, gen mgr; Mark Mayhugh, opns mgr & chief engr; Connie Brown, sls dir; Al Mayo, prom dir & news dir; Scott Martin, progmg dir; Jennifer Peplin, pub affrs dir.

WMMN(AM)—Dec 22, 1928: 920 khz; 5 kw-U, DA-N. TL: N39 28 03 W80 12 20. Box 1549 (26554). (304) 366-3700. FAX: (304) 366-3706. Licensee: Fantasia Broadcasting Inc. (acq 11-6-92; $80,000; FTR 11-30-92). Format: News/talk. ■ Nick Fantasia, pres & gen mgr.

WRLF(FM)—Listing follows WTCS(AM).

WTCS(AM)—January 1948: 1490 khz; 1 kw-U. TL: N39 28 19 W80 08 27. Box 1549, 450 Leonard Ave. (26554). (304) 366-3700. FAX: (304) 366-3706. Licensee: Fairmont Broadcasting Co. (acq 5-1-56). Net: NBC. Rep: Keystone (unwired net). Format: AOR. Target aud: 18-40. Spec prog: It 4 hrs wkly. ■ Nick Fantasia, pres, gen mgr & gen sls mgr; Gary Deavers, news dir; Bob Ice, chief engr.

WRLF(FM)—Co-owned with WTCS(AM). Aug 26, 1989: 94.3 mhz; 3 kw. Ant 328 ft. TL: N39 28 03 W80 12 20 (CP: 3.63 kw, ant 248 ft.). Stereo. Dups AM 90%.

Fisher

WELD(AM)—Aug 1, 1956: 690 khz; 2 kw-D. TL: N39 03 08 W79 00 21. Box 1A, HC 85 (26818). (304) 538-6062. FAX: (304) 538-7032. Licensee: South Branch Communications Inc. Net: AP. Rep: Dome, Keystone (unwired net). Wash atty: Reddy, Begley & Martin. Format: Country. News progmg 14 hrs wkly. Target aud: General. Spec prog: Farm 3 hrs, relg 10 hrs wkly. ■ Willard L. Earle, CEO & gen mgr; Edwin Allen, chief engr. ■ Rates: $10; 9; 10; na.

WYFY(FM)—Not on air, target date unknown: 103.7 mhz; 6 kw. Ant 328 ft. TL: N39 05 05 W79 01 47. Suite 5, 4310 Indian River Rd., Chesapeake, VA (23325). (804) 547-9423. Licensee: Bible Broadcasting Network Inc. ■ Jerry Endres, gen mgr.

Fort Gay

***WFGH(FM)**—June 4, 1973: 90.7 mhz; 7.8 kw. Ant 205 ft. TL: N38 07 58 W82 35 37. Hrs opn: 12. Box 410, Tolsia High School, One Rebel Dr. (25514). (304) 648-5752; (304) 648-5566. FAX: (304) 648-5447. Licensee: Wayne County Board of Education. Format: Adult contemp, country, relg. News staff 2; news progmg 15 hrs wkly. Target aud: General. Spec prog: Oldies. ■ Vernon R. Stanfill, gen mgr, opns dir & chief engr; Hazel Damron, prom mgr & progmg dir.

Frost

***WVMR(AM)**—Aug 17, 1981: 1370 khz; 5 kw-D. TL: N38 17 25 W79 55 52. State Rt. 28, Dunmore (24934). (304) 799-6004. FAX: (304) 799-6005. Licensee: Pocahontas Communications Cooperative Corp. Net: APR. Format: Country. News staff one; news progmg 10 hrs wkly. Target aud: General. Spec prog: Farm 5 hrs, relg 10 hrs, big band 3 hrs, bluegrass 4 hrs wkly. ■ Patricia Keller, pres; Gibbs Kinderman, gen mgr; Glenda Van Reenen, stn mgr; Doug Van Gundy, progmg dir; Janet Queen, mus dir; John Geiger, news dir; Jim Dolan, chief engr.

Grafton

WTBZ(AM)—January 1948: 1260 khz; 500 w-D. TL: N39 21 01 W80 02 40. Box 2 (26354). (304) 265-2000. FAX: (304) 265-0972. Licensee: Taylor-Barbour Broadcasting Inc. (acq 3-10-86; $40,000; FTR 10-14-85). Net: MBS. Rep: Dome, Keystone (unwired net). Format: Country. Spec prog: Farm 2 hrs, relg 8 hrs wkly. ■ Tom Friend, pres.

WTBZ-FM—Sept 10, 1979: 95.9 mhz; 3 kw. Ant 150 ft. TL: N39 21 16 W80 01 27. Stereo. (304) 265-2200. Licensee: Taylor-Barbour Broadcasting Inc. (acq 1-15-82). Rep: Commercial. Format: Country. Spec prog: Farm 2 hrs wkly. ■ Tom Friend, pres & gen mgr.

Green Valley

WAMN(AM)—January 1987: 1050 khz; 1.5 kw-D. TL: N37 18 20 W81 07 30 (CP: 1050 khz; 1.43 kw-D, 250 w-N). 145 Jackson St., Blacksburg, VA (24063). (304) 327-9266; (703) 552-4252. Licensee: WAMN Inc. Group owner: Baker Family Stations (acq 2-8-89). Format: Relg, talk. ■ Vernon H. Baker, pres; Bob Teachout, stn mgr & mus dir.

Hinton

WMTD(AM)—Jan 11, 1963: 1380 khz; 1 kw-D. TL: N37 40 49 W80 54 24. Hrs opn: 6 AM-sunset. 95 Pleasant St. (25951). (304) 466-1380. FAX: (304) 466-5779. Licensee: Bluestone Broadcasters Inc. (acq 1-1-64). Format: Country. News progmg 9 hrs wkly. Target aud: General. ■ Lonnie R. Mullins, pres & gen mgr.

WMTD-FM—Oct 1, 1985: 102.3 mhz; 160 w. Ant 1,007 ft. TL: N37 42 56 W80 56 55. Stereo. Dups AM 80%.

Huntington

WCMI(AM)—See Ashland, Ky.

WEMM(FM)—Sept 6, 1971: 107.9 mhz; 50 kw. Ant 500 ft. TL: N38 28 33 W82 15 00. Stereo. Hrs opn: 24. 703 3rd Ave. (25701). (304) 525-9366. FAX: (304) 525-0748. Licensee: Mortenson Broadcasting Co. (group owner). Net: USA. Format: Relg. News progmg 4 hrs wkly. Target aud: 35 plus; responsive, loyal, family oriented. ■ Jack M. Mortenson, pres; Clint McElroy, gen mgr; Bill Hammond, prom dir; Michael Fincham, progmg dir, mus dir & pub affrs dir; Gene Stephenson, engrg dir; David Johnson, chief engr. ■ Rates: $15; 15; 15; 15.

WHRD(AM)—1946: 1470 khz; 5 kw-D. TL: N38 24 22 W82 29 04. Stn currently dark. Box 1037, Beaver (25813). (304) 252-6452. Licensee: Southern Communications Corp. (acq. 8-27-91; $30,000; FTR 9-17-91). ■ Frank Flabeetz, gen mgr.

WKEE(AM)—July 1947: 800 khz; 5 kw-D, 185.3 w-N. TL: N38 23 35 W82 28 24. Stereo. Box 2288 (25724). (304) 525-7788. FAX: (304) 525-6281. Licensee: Adventure Communications Inc. (group owner; acq 10-87; grpsl; FTR 10-19-87). Net: CNN. Rep: D & R Radio. Wash atty: Alan Campbell. Format: EZ lstng. Target aud: 25-54. ■ Michael R. Shott, pres; Toufie Kassab, gen mgr; Richard T. Myhrwold, gen sls mgr; Paul Michaels, progmg dir & mus dir; Bill Cornwell, news dir; Greg Elliott, chief engr.

WKEE-FM—Nov 1947: 100.5 mhz; 53 kw. Ant 560 ft. TL: N38 23 35 W82 28 24. Stereo. Prog sep from AM. Net: Unistar. Format: Adult contemp, CHR. ■ Jedd Flowers, prom mgr; Dan Persiqehl, progmg dir; Gary Miller, mus dir.

***WMEJ(FM)**—See Proctorville, Ohio.

***WMUL(FM)**—Nov 1, 1961: 88.1 mhz; 1.15 kw. Ant -56 ft. TL: N38 25 26 W82 25 39. Stereo. Hrs opn: 6 AM-2 AM. Comm Bldg., Marshall Univ., 400 Hal Greer Blvd. (25755-2635). (304) 696-6640; (304) 696-6651 (Control Room). FAX: (304) 696-3333. Licensee: Univ. of West Virginia Board of Trustees (acq 10-5-90; grpsl; FTR 10-29-90). Net: ABC/FM. Wash atty: Blair, Joyce & Silva. Format: Div. News progmg 7 hrs wkly. Target aud: General. ■ Dr. J. Wade Gilley, pres; Dr. Chuck G. Bailey, gen mgr; Chuck Cook, chief opns; Denton Anderson, mus dir; Carol Elmore, news dir; Tom Irwin, chief engr.

WRVC(AM)—Oct 23, 1923: 930 khz; 5 kw-D, 1 kw-N, DA-N. TL: N38 24 11 W82 29 38. Box 1150, Coal Exchange Bldg., Suite 200, 401 11th St. (25701). (304) 523-8401. FAX: (304) 523-4848. Licensee: Fifth Avenue Broadcasting Co. Inc. (acq 6-1-70). Net: NBC. Rep: Banner. Wash atty: Arent, Fox, Kitner, Plotkin & Kahn. Format: Oldies. News staff one. Target aud: 35 plus; affluent. Spec prog: Relg 3 hrs wkly. ■ Tom Wolf, pres; Mike Kirtner, gen mgr; Mark Jesse, gen sls mgr; Jeff Crawford, progmg dir; Teresa Nichools, news dir; Bill Geyer, chief engr. ■ Rates: $7; 7; 7; na.

WRVC-FM—See Ashland, Ky.

WTCR(AM)—See Kenova.

WTCR-FM—May 1, 1966: 103.3 mhz; 50 kw. Ant 490 ft. TL: N38 25 11 W82 24 06. Rebroadcasts WTCR(AM) Kenova. Box 2186 (25722). (606) 739-8427. FAX: (606) 739-6009. Licensee: CRB Broadcasting of Kentucky. Group owner: CRB Broadcasting Corp. Net: ABC/I. Rep: Katz, Rgnl Reps. Format: Country. ■ Judy Jennings, gen mgr; Gloria Ward, gen sls mgr; Dave Poole, progmg dir; Davana Ferris, news dir; Scott Hensley, chief engr.

***WVWV(FM)**—Nov 24, 1978: 89.9 mhz; 8.1 kw. Ant 1,200 ft. TL: N38 29 42 W82 12 03. Stereo. Hrs opn: 24. 600 Capitol St., Charleston (25301). (304) 558-3000. FAX: (304) 558-4034. Licensee: West Virginia Educational Broadcasting Authority. Net: NPR, APR. Format: News, class, jazz. News staff 2. Spec prog: Mountain stage 2 hrs wkly. ■ Barbara Herrick, gen mgr; Marilyn DiVita, dev mgr; Nancy Buckingham, prom mgr; Jeanne Fisher, progmg dir; Jim Wallace, news dir; Francis Fisher, chief engr.

WZZW(FM)—(Milton). Oct 1, 1980: 106.3 mhz; 560 w. Ant 1,092 ft. TL: N38 30 21 W82 12 33 Stereo. Box 2324, Huntington (25724). (304) 743-9056. FAX: (304) 743-9991. Licensee: Peters Broadcasting Inc. Net: Unistar. Format: Classic rock. Target aud: 25-49; baby boomers. ■ Roscoe Peters, pres; Dick Findley, gen mgr; Mick Hallerun, opns mgr; Earl Buck, gen sls mgr; Mick Halleron, chief engr. ■ Rates: $20; 20; 20; 10.

Hurricane

WVKV(AM)—July 2, 1971: 1080 khz; 5 kw-D, DA. TL: N38 26 41 W82 00 54. Hrs opn: 10. Box 1080 (25526). (304) 562-9155. Licensee: Milliken Investment Corp. (group owner; acq 11-1-83; $200,000; FTR 2-6-84). Format: Relg/southern gospel. ■ James S. Milliken, pres, gen mgr & chief engr; Teresa Milliken, prom mgr.

Kenova

WTCR(AM)—August 1954: 1420 khz; 5 kw-D, 500 w-N, DA-N. TL: N38 24 42 W82 36 13. One Radio Park Rd., Catlettsburg, KY (41129); Box 2186, Huntington (25722). (606) 739-8427. FAX: (606) 739-6009. Licensee: CRB Broadcasting of Kentucky. Group owner: CRB Broadcasting Corp. Net: ABC/I. Rep: Katz, Rgnl Reps. Format: Country. News staff 2. Target aud: 25-54. ■ Judy Jennings, gen mgr; Gloria Ward, gen sls mgr; Dave Poole, progmg dir; Davana Ferris, news dir; Scott Hensley, chief engr.

Keyser

WKLP(AM)—Aug 31, 1965: 1390 khz; 1 kw-D, 74 w-N. TL: N39 26 12 W78 57 21. Hrs opn: 24. Drawer F, Rt. 46 E. (26726). (304) 788-1662. Licensee: Starcast Systems Inc. Group owner: Starcast Stations (acq 1-1-82; $300,000; FTR 1-11-82). Net: ABC/E. Format: MOR. Target aud: 35 plus. Spec prog: Big band. ■ Jack Mullen I, pres; Jack I Mullen II, gen mgr; Jay Maynard, mus dir; Brian Davis, news dir; Jack Mullen II, chief engr. ■ Rates: $13; 12; 13; 12.

WQZK-FM—Co-owned with WKLP(AM). Sept 15, 1973: 94.1 mhz; 15 kw. Ant 801 ft. TL: N39 25 08 W78 57 13. Stereo. Hrs opn: 24. Prog sep from AM. Format: AOR. Target aud: 18-49. Spec prog: Jazz 2 hrs wkly. ■ Jay Maynard, progmg dir. ■ Rates: $18.25; 17.25; 18.25; 17.25.

WKZG(FM)—January 1990: 107.1 mhz; 530 w. Ant 783 ft. TL: N39 31 26 W78 51 44. Stereo. Box 1290, Cumberland, MD (21502). (301) 786-4335. Licensee: Prosperitas Broadcasting System (acq 9-7-89; $300,000; FTR 9-25-89). Format: Oldies. ■ David Aydlotte, gen mgr; Jim Robey, progmg dir & news dir; Marty White, chief engr.

WQZK-FM—Listing follows WKLP(AM).

Kingwood

WFSP(AM)—Aug 25, 1967: 1560 khz; 1 kw-D, 250 w-CH. TL: N39 20 01 W79 43 10. Box 567 (26537). (304) 329-1780. FAX: (304) 329-1781. Licensee: WFSP Inc. (acq 8-24-79). Net: AP. Rep: Dome. Format: Adult contemp, oldies. Target aud: 45 plus. ■ Arthur W. George, pres; Dave Price, gen mgr & gen sls mgr; Mike Barnett, prom mgr; Bob Dewitt, progmg dir & mus dir; Kathy Casseday, news dir; Sam St. Clair, chief engr.

WFSP-FM—June 10, 1991: 107.7 mhz; 1.6 kw. Ant 449 ft. TL: N39 28 50 W79 43 11. Stereo. Hrs opn: 24. Net: AP; W.V. Metronews. Format: Adult contemp. Target aud: 18-45.

WKMM(FM)—Dec 1, 1986: 96.7 mhz; 3 kw. Ant 798 ft. TL: N39 27 29 W79 35 18. Stereo. Hrs opn: 24. Box 28, 420 Morgantown St. (26537). (304) 329-0967. FAX: (304) 329-2131. Licensee: MarPat Corp. (acq 8-1-93; $190,000; FTR 8-23-93). Net: CNN. Format: Country. Target aud: 25-55. ■ P.J. Crogan, pres; Curtis Durst, vp. ■ Rates: $14; 11; 12; 11.

Lewisburg

WKCJ(FM)—October 1981: 105.5 mhz; 540 kw. Ant 781 ft. TL: N37 42 43 W80 30 20. Stereo. Hrs opn: 5:30 AM-midnight. Box 306, 200 W. Washington St. (24901). (304) 536-1310. Licensee: Seneca Broadcasting Inc. (acq 8-8-85; grpsl; FTR 6-10-85). Net: ABC/E. Rep: Rgnl Reps. Format: Modern country. News progmg 12 hrs wkly. Target aud: 25-55. ■ Richard L. Bryant, pres; Jean Bryant, gen mgr; Ken Bryant, opns dir, sls dir & prom mgr; James Fisher, progmg dir, mus dir & news dir; Randy Kerbawy, chief engr. ■ Rates: $6.50; 6.50; 6.50; 6.50.

WRON-FM—See Ronceverte.

Lindside

***WHFI(FM)**—September 1990: 106.7 mhz; 3 kw. Ant 303 ft. TL: N37 28 56 W80 39 40. Stn currently dark. Rt. 1, Box 97 (24951). (304) 832-6724. Licensee: Monroe County Board of Education (acq 5-1-89). Format: MOR. ■ James W. Higginbotham, gen mgr; Dixie West, stn mgr, progmg dir & news dir.

Logan

WLOG(AM)—May 27, 1940: 1230 khz; 1 kw-U. TL: N37 51 32 W81 58 39. Hrs opn: 24. Box 1800, Corner of Chestnut & Kanada (25601). (304) 752-6280. FAX: (304) 752-6243. Licensee: CD Entertainment Inc. (acq 4-16-93; $40,000; FTR 5-3-93). Format: Classic rock, adult contemp. News staff one; news progmg 5 hrs wkly. Target aud: 25 plus. ■ Albert R. Spencer, pres, gen mgr & chief engr; Denise Nally Spencer, stn mgr, opns mgr, gen sls mgr, prom dir & progmg dir; Deloris Landrum, mktg mgr; Chip Spencer, mus dir; Kim Nash, news dir & pub affrs dir. ■ Rates: $6; 6; 6; 6.

WVOW(AM)—May 1954: 1290 khz; 5 kw-D, 1 kw-N, DA-N. TL: N37 51 28 W81 58 16. Hrs opn: 24. Box 1776 (25601). (304) 752-5080. FAX: (304) 752-5081. Licensee: Logan Broadcasting Corp. Net: ABC/I. Format: Adult contemp. News staff 2. Target aud: General. ■ William P. Becker, pres; Larry Bevins, gen mgr & stn mgr; Martha Jane Becker, gen sls mgr & prom mgr; Bill Sheridan, progmg dir; Bill France, mus dir; Bob Weisner, news dir; Terry Bucklew, chief engr.

WVOW-FM—August 1969: 101.9 mhz; 15 kw. Ant 830 ft. TL: N37 51 28 W81 58 16. Hrs opn: 24. Dups AM 100%.

Lost Creek

WOTR(FM)—Dec 9, 1991: 96.3 mhz; 3 kw-H. Ant 302 ft. TL: N39 08 43 W80 19 40. Box 505 (26385). (304) 745-4243. Licensee: Allman Electronics Lab. Allman Electronics Lab. Format: Mixed music, local sports, old time radio, local calendar events. ■ Bill Allman, Patricia S. Allman, gen mgrs.

Madison

WZAC(AM)—Oct 27, 1978: 1450 khz; 1 kw-U. TL: N38 03 24 W81 49 08. Number One Broadcast Place (25130); Box 87, Danville (25053). (304) 369-5201. Licensee: Price Broadcasting Co. (acq 6-30-89). Net: W.V. Metronews. Format: Country. News progmg 7 hrs wkly. Target aud: General. ■ Wayne Price, gen mgr, gen sls mgr & chief engr; Steve Green, progmg dir & mus dir.

Mannington

WTUS(FM)—December 1992: 102.7 mhz; 3.21 kw. Ant 453 ft. TL: N39 32 18 W80 20 16. Suite C, 1489 Kingwood (26537). (304) 363-8888. FAX: (304) 367-1885. Licensee: Joseph Donald Powers (acq 11-15-91; $23,000 for CP; FTR 12-2-91). Format: Country. ■ Aaron Justice, gen mgr.

Martinsburg

WEPM(AM)—Oct 13, 1946: 1340 khz; 1 kw-U. TL: N39 27 48 W77 59 11. Box 767, 1606 W. King St. (25401). (304) 263-8868. FAX: (304) 263-8906. Licensee: Prettyman Broadcasting Co. (group owner; acq 1-1-87; $2 million; FTR 11-10-86). Net: CBS. Rep: Torbet/Select. Format: Country. Spec prog: Relg 6 hrs wkly. ■ Bill Prettyman, pres; Yogi Yoder, gen mgr; John Grissinger, progmg dir; Ken Bethany, mus dir; Richard Strader, news dir; Fran Little, chief engr.

WKMZ(FM)—Co-owned with WEPM(AM). 1949: 97.5 mhz; 12.5 kw. Ant 1,010 ft. TL: N39 27 35 W78 03 49. Stereo. Hrs opn: 24. Prog sep from AM. (304) 263-8869. Net: CNN. Format: CHR. ■ Gary Michaels, progmg dir; Rob Mario, mus dir.

WRNR(AM)—Apr 16, 1976: 740 khz; 500 w-D, 21 w-N, DA-2. TL: N39 28 25 W77 55 57. Hrs opn: 18. Box 709, 2076 Eagle School Rd. (25401). (304) 263-6586. FAX: (304) 263-3082. Licensee: Shenandoah Communications Inc. Net: MBS, NBC Talknet. Rep: Rgnl Reps. Wash atty: James K. Edmundson. Format: News/talk. News staff 2; news progmg 28 hrs wkly. Target aud: 25-54; middle to upper age & income. Spec prog: Relg 2 hrs wkly. ■ Richard S. Wachtel, pres, gen mgr & gen sls mgr; Paddy Alters, progmg dir; Bill Hutton, mus dir; Jon McVey, news dir; Fran Little, chief engr. ■ Rates: $13.75; 13.30; 13.75; 13.30.

***WVEP(FM)**—Feb 11, 1987: 88.9 mhz; 3.6 kw. Ant 1,591 ft. TL: N39 08 38 W78 26 09. Stereo. Hrs opn: 24. 600 Capitol St., Charleston (25301). (304) 558-3000. FAX: (304) 558-4034. Licensee: West Virginia Educational Broadcasting Authority. Net: NPR, APR. Format: News, jazz, classical. News staff 2. Spec prog: Mountain stage 2 hrs wkly. ■ Barbara Herrick, gen mgr; Marilyn DiVita, dev mgr; Nancy Buckingham, prom mgr; Jeanne Fisher, progmg dir; Jim Wallace, news dir; Francis P. Fisher, chief engr.

Matewan

WHJC(AM)—Dec 2, 1951: 1360 khz; 1 kw-D. TL: N37 37 02 W82 10 04. Box 68 (25678). (606) 427-7261. FAX: (606) 427-7260. Licensee: Three States Broadcasting Co. Inc. Net: NBC. Format: Country, Country Gospel. ■ George D. Warren, pres; Harold Cremeans, gen mgr, prom mgr, mus dir & chief engr; Tonda Gannon, gen sls mgr. ■ Rates: $4; 4; 4; 4.

WVKM(FM)—Co-owned with WHJC(AM). Aug 30, 1989: 106.7 mhz; 3 kw. Ant 105 ft. TL: N37 37 54 W82 09 32. Stereo. Prog sep from AM. Format: AOR. News progmg 6 hrs wkly. Target aud: General. ■ Corenia Branham, progmg dir & mus dir. ■ Rates: $7; 7; 7; 7.

Miami

WKAZ(FM)—November 1985: 107.3 mhz; 50 kw. Ant 600 ft. TL: N38 16 25 W81 31 27. Stereo. Hrs opn: 24. 136 High St., Charleston (25311). (304) 342-1490. FAX: (304) 342-4646. Licensee: Empire Broadcasting System (acq 4-8-88). Rep: D & R Radio. Format: Oldies. Target aud: 25-54.

Milton

WNST(AM)—June 26, 1973: 1600 khz; 6 kw-D, 26 w-N. TL: N38 25 46 W82 06 21. Box 266, 1381 Rt. 60 East (25541). (304) 743-9056. FAX: (304) 743-9991. Licensee: Peters Broadcasting Inc. (acq 6-29-84; $225,000; FTR 7-9-84). Net: MBS, ABC TalkRadio. Format: Oldies. Target aud: Adults 25-44; upscale baby boomers. ■ Roscoe Peters, pres; Richard Findley, gen mgr; Bryan Adkins, prom mgr & progmg dir; Mick Halleron, mus dir & chief engr. ■ Rates: $10; 10; 10; 10.

WZZW(FM)—Licensed to Milton. See Huntington.

Montgomery

WMON(AM)—July 14, 1946: 1340 khz; 1 kw-U. TL: N38 10 48 W81 20 06. 1028 First Ave. (25136). (304) 442-5200. FAX: (304) 442-5293. Licensee: R-S Broadcasting Inc. (acq 10-1-86; $35,000; FTR 7-28-86). Net: Unistar. Rep: Keystone (unwired net). Format: Country. Spec prog: Class 2 hrs wkly. ■ Vivian J. Brown, pres & gen mgr; Greg Ring, progmg dir; Michael Brown, chief engr.

WZKM(FM)—Not on air, target date unknown: 93.3 mhz; 400 w. Ant 715 ft. TL: N38 13 14 W81 24 52. 1028 1st Ave. (25136). Licensee: Upper Kanawha Valley Broadcasters Inc.

Morgantown

WAJR(AM)—Dec 7, 1940: 1440 khz; 5 kw-D, 500 w-N, DA-2. TL: N39 40 34 W80 00 12. Hrs opn: 24. 1251 Earl Core Rd. (26505). (304) 296-0029. FAX: (304) 296-3876. Licensee: West Virginia Radio Corp. Net: ABC/E. Wash atty: Putbrese & Hunsaker. Format: Country. News staff 7; news progmg 15 hrs wkly. ■ Dale B. Miller, pres & gen mgr; Harvey Kercheval, vp opns; Jay Redmond, gen sls mgr; Mike Tokash, prom mgr; Dave Harman, progmg dir & mus dir; Jeff Jenkins, news dir; Kay Murray, pub affrs dir; Jim Murphy, engrg dir.

WVAQ(FM)—Co-owned with WAJR(AM). 1948: 101.9 mhz; 50 kw. Ant 500 ft. TL: N39 36 30 W79 59 07. Stereo. Hrs opn: 24. Prog sep from AM. Net: ABC/C, Unistar. Format: CHR. News staff 2; news progmg one hr wkly. ■ John Devincent, progmg dir; Lacy Neff, mus dir. ■ Rates: $30; 30; 30; 25.

WCLG(AM)—December 1954: 1300 khz; 2.5 kw-D, 44 w-N. TL: N39 37 40 W79 58 11. Stereo. Box 885 (26507). (304) 292-2222. FAX: (304) 292-2224. Licensee: Freed Broadcasting Corp. (acq 12-19-59). Net: SMN, NBC Talknet. Rep: Dome. Format: Pure gold. ■ Garry Bowers, pres & gen mgr; Rebecca Hunn, gen sls mgr; Tim Satterfield, progmg dir; Marshall Sears, mus dir; Robert Ice, chief engr.

WCLG-FM—Sept 28, 1974: 100.1 mhz; 6 kw. Ant 300 ft. TL: N39 37 40 W79 58 11. Stereo. Net: NBC the Source. Format: Classic rock. ■ John Delaney, mus dir.

WMQC(FM)—See Westover.

WVAQ(FM)—Listing follows WAJR(AM).

***WVPM(FM)**—May 27, 1981: 90.9 mhz; 5.2 kw. Ant 1,440 ft. TL: N39 41 45 W79 45 45. Stereo. 600 Capitol St., Charleston (25301). (304) 558-3000. FAX: (304) 558-4034. Licensee: West Virginia Educational Broadcasting Authority. Net: NPR, APR. Format: News, classical, jazz. News staff 2. ■ Barbara Herrick, gen mgr; Marilyn DiVita, dev mgr; Nancy Buckingham, prom mgr; Jeanne Fisher, progmg mgr; Jim Wallace, news dir; Francis Fisher, chief engr.

***WWVU-FM**—Aug 20, 1982: 91.7 mhz; 2.6 kw. Ant 180 ft. TL: N39 38 09 W79 56 38. Stereo. Hrs opn: 24. Box 6446, Mountainlair, West Virginia Univ. (26506-6446). (304) 293-3329. FAX: (304) 293-7363. Licensee: University of West Virginia Board of Trustees. Net: ABC/FM. Wash atty: Blair, Joyce & Silva. Format: Div, progsv. News progmg 2 hrs wkly. Target aud: 18-35; mostly high school & college students. Spec prog: Black 9 hrs, classical 4 hrs, jazz 9 hrs, new age 6 hrs, reggae 5 hrs, metal 3 hrs, bluegrass one hr, oldies 8 hrs, big band 2 hrs wkly. ■ Alex Gavula, gen mgr; Brian T. Gessner, prom dir; Andrew Stahl, progmg dir; Tina Lutz, mus dir; Christy Stevenson, asst mus dir; Jennifer Corcoran, Christa Henson, news dirs; Billy Kaiser, pub affrs dir; John Mathews, chief engr.

Moundsville

WRKP(FM)—Jan 15, 1990: 96.5 mhz; 1.45 kw. Ant 594 ft. TL: N39 50 51 W80 45 22. Stereo. Hrs opn: 6 AM-midnight. 2002 First St. (26041). (304) 845-1092; (412) 225-2030. Licensee: RKP International Corp. Net: CBN. Format: Contemp Christian mus, talk. News staff one; news progmg 5 hrs wkly. Target aud: 18-54; young & middle aged adults. ■ Ronald W. King, pres, gen mgr, sls dir & adv dir; Christopher Kitchen, rgnl sls mgr, mktg mgr & adv mgr; LuAnn Jerin, progmg dir & mus dir; Allen Fox, chief engr. ■ Rates: $9.40; 8.70; 9.40; 8.70.

WZAO(AM)—Oct 1, 1950: 1370 khz; 5 kw-D, 20 w-N. TL: N39 54 20 W80 46 42. Hrs opn: 6 AM-7 PM. Box 27, Glendale (26038). (304) 843-1210. FAX: (304) 845-4047. Licensee: Praise Family Worship Center (acq 4-17-91; $1; FTR 5-6-91). Net: USA. Format: Christian MOR. Target aud: 18-36; Christian households. Spec prog: Talk, news, relg. ■ Michael Dunn, gen mgr; Tom Schlosser, gen sls mgr; Heather Cox, progmg dir & mus dir. ■ Rates: $5; 5; 5; na.

Mount Hope

WTNJ(FM)—June 1, 1980: 105.9 mhz; 50 kw. Ant 500 ft. TL: N37 53 12 W81 11 40. Stereo. Hrs opn: 24. Box 1127, Beckley (25802); 609 Main St. (25880). (304) 877-5592. FAX: (304) 877-5289. Licensee: West Virginia Broadcasting Inc. Net: ABC/E. Rep: Roslin. Wash atty: Arent, Fox, Kintner, Plotkin & Kahn. Format: Country. News staff one; news progmg 12 hrs wkly. Target aud: 25-54. ■ Nick Rahall II, pres; Tony Gonzalez, gen mgr; Paul Gonzalez, gen sls mgr; Betsy Gonzalez, prom mgr; Fred Persinger, progmg dir & mus dir; Lori Vecillio, news dir; Randy Kirkaway, chief engr.

Mullens

WPMW(FM)—Sept 30, 1981: 92.7 mhz; 1.65 kw. Ant 443 ft. TL: N37 35 39 W81 23 49. Stereo. Box 488, 14 Moran Ave. (25882). (304) 294-8600; (304) 294-4405. FAX: (304) 294-0520. Licensee: Slab Fork Broadcasting. Net: MBS, SMN. Format: Country. ■ Ranny Parks, gen mgr; Sandra Davis, gen sls mgr; Larry Mullens, progmg dir, mus dir & news dir; Nathan Lane, chief engr.

New Martinsville

WETZ(AM)—May 25, 1953: 1330 khz; 1 kw-D, 60 w-N. TL: N39 39 27 W80 51 34. Rebroadcasts WVVW(AM) St. Marys 100%. Box 249, 325 Main St. (26155). (304) 455-1111. FAX: (304) 455-6170. Licensee: HBN Communications Inc. (acq 1-1-93; $400,000 with co-located FM; FTR 3-9-92). Rep: Dome. Format: Gospel, talk. Target aud: 25 plus. ■ Nelson Hachem, pres & CFO; Bob Eddy, gen mgr, stn mgr, gen sls mgr, mktg dir & chief engr; Dave Hoyt, vp opns, prom dir, progmg dir & mus dir; Tom Tabbert, engrg dir. ■ Rates: $8.25; 8.25; 8.25; 8.25.

WNMR(FM)—Co-owned with WETZ(AM). December 1977: 103.9 mhz; 3 kw. Ant 298 ft. TL: N39 40 40 W80 52 42. Stereo. Hrs opn: 24. Rebroadcasts WRRR-FM St. Marys 97%. (304) 455-1440. Net: NBC. Format: Adult contemp. News progmg 14 hrs wkly. Target aud: 25-54. ■ Rates: $11; 11; 11; 11.

Oak Hill

WAXS(FM)—1948: 94.1 mhz; 25.5 kw. Ant 650 ft. TL: N37 57 30 W81 09 03. Stereo. Hrs opn: 24. Box 1127, Beckley (25802). (304) 877-5592. FAX: (304) 877-5289. Licensee: Plateau Broadcasting Inc. (acq 11-19-92; $500,000; FTR 12-14-92). Net: SMN. Format: Classic rock, oldies. News staff one; news progmg 2 hrs wkly. Target aud: General; baby boomers. ■ Paul Gonzales, pres & gen sls mgr; Tony Gonzales, gen mgr; Fred Persinger, prom dir & mus dir. ■ Rates: $24; 24; 24; 24.

WOAY(AM)—Feb 22, 1947: 860 khz; 10 kw-D, 11 W-N, 5 kw-CH. TL: N37 57 30 W81 09 03. Hrs opn: 6 AM-10 PM. Box 140, 240 Central Ave. (25901). (304) 465-0534. FAX: (304) 465-1486. Licensee: Commissioned Communications Corp. (acq 8-90; $100,000; FTR 8-6-90). Net: Moody. Format: Relg. News progmg 10 hrs wkly. Target aud: General. ■ Eugene Ellison, CEO, pres, gen mgr & news dir; Judy Ellison, vp; Steve Bush, progmg dir; Mark Smith, chief engr. ■ Rates: $9; 9; 9; 9.

WTNJ(FM)—See Mount Hope.

Parkersburg

WADC(AM)—Apr 9, 1954: 1050 khz; 5 kw-D. TL: N39 15 29 W81 33 49. Hrs opn: 24. 703 Market St. (26101). (304) 485-6158. Licensee: Valley Communications Corp. (acq 1993; $1.4 million with co-located FM; FTR 9-13-93). Net: CBS. Rep: Rgnl Reps. Format: Oldies. Target aud: 35-64; buyers. ■ Calvin Dailey, pres & gen mgr; Mark Mayhugh, opns mgr & chief engr; Donn West, gen sls mgr; Dex Gage, progmg dir & news dir.

WHCM(FM)—Co-owned with WADC(AM). Sept 1, 1965: 99.1 mhz; 11.5 kw. Ant 485 ft. TL: N39 15 29 W81 33 49. Stereo. Prog sep from AM. 703 Market St. (26101). Net: CBS. Format: Country. News staff one. Target aud: 25-54; loyal modern country listeners. ■ Randy Dailey, exec vp; Randy Jay, vp opns, vp dev & vp sls; Mark Eveland, progmg dir.

WKYG(AM)—September 1947: 1230 khz; 1 kw-U. TL: N39 16 56 W81 33 17. Hrs opn: 24. Box 368 (26102); 1715 St. Mary's Ave. (26101). (304) 485-4565. Licensee: Fritz Communications Inc. (acq 11-87). Net: ABC/E, NBC Talknet. Rep: McGavren Guild. Format: Country. Target aud: 35 plus. ■ Jack Fritz, gen mgr; Tom McGuire, opns mgr; Kirk McCall, gen sls mgr; Steve McCoy, progmg dir; Chase Conley, news dir; Larry Smith, chief engr.

WXKX(FM)—Co-owned with WKYG(AM). March 1967: 103.1 mhz; 730 w. Ant 551 ft. TL: N39 21 00 W81 33 57. Stereo. Hrs opn: 24. Prog sep from AM. Net: ABC/E. Target aud: 25-54. ■ Tom McGuire, progmg dir.

WLTP(AM)—July 12, 1935: 1450 khz; 1 kw-U. TL: N39 17 23 W81 31 36. Hrs opn: 24. Box 428, 1719 Washington Blvd., Belpre, OH (45714). (614) 423-8213. Licensee: WNUS Inc. (acq 5-24-93; $575,000 with WNUS[FM] Belpre, OH; FTR 6-14-93). Net: Unistar, CNN. Rep: Dome. Format: Country, talk. News staff one; news progmg 2-3 hrs wkly. Target aud: 25-54; middle-aged, middle to upper income. ■ Joel Thrope, CEO & chmn; Jay Reynolds, pres & gen mgr; Penny Lipscomb, gen sls mgr; Jane Reynolds, prom mgr; Brian Knost, progmg dir & mus dir; John Chalfant, news dir; Ralph Matheny, chief engr.

***WVPG(FM)**—July 4, 1985: 90.3 mhz; 9 kw. Ant 321 ft. TL: N39 12 44 W81 35 30. Stereo. Hrs opn: 24. 600 Capitol St., Charleston (25301). (304) 558-3000. FAX: (304) 558-4034. Licensee: West Virginia Educational Broadcasting Authority. Net: NPR, APR. Format: News, classical, jazz. News staff 2. ■ Barbara Herrick, gen mgr; Marilyn DiVita, dev mgr; Nancy Buckingham, prom mgr; Jeanne Fisher, progmg dir; Jim Wallace, news dir; Francis Fisher, chief engr.

WXIL(FM)—Sept 1, 1975: 95.1 mhz; 50 kw. Ant 500 ft. TL: N39 14 47 W81 28 19. Stereo. Hrs opn: 24. Box 1228, 1715 St. Mary's Ave. (26101). (304) 485-7425. Licensee: PBBC Inc. Group owner: Burbach Broadcasting Group (acq 9-1-80; $1 million; FTR 7-7-80). Rep: Katz. Format: CHR. News progmg 2 hrs wkly. Target aud: 25-49; women. ■ Jack Laubach, CEO & chmn; Nick Galli, pres; Kirk McCall, gen mgr & vp sls; Larry Hughes, progmg dir & mus dir; Rob Backstrom, chief engr.

WXKX(FM)—Listing follows WKYG(AM).

Petersburg

WELD-FM—Feb 6, 1987: 101.7 mhz; 1.25 kw. Ant 515 ft. TL: N38 58 34 W79 01 13. Hrs opn: 18. HC 85, Box 1 A, Fisher (26818). (304) 538-6062. FAX: (304) 538-7032. Licensee: South Branch Communications Inc. Net: AP. Format: Country, relg, farm. News progmg 3 hrs wkly. Target aud: General. Spec prog: Gospel 3 hrs wkly. ■ Willard L. Earle, pres & gen mgr; Larry Kuykendall, chief engr. ■ Rates: $9.90; 9; 9.90; 8.

Philippi

***WQAB(FM)**—October 1975: 91.3 mhz; 7.2 kw. Ant 180 ft. TL: N39 09 28 W80 02 52 (CP: TL: N39 09 52 W80 02 57). Box 1428, Withers-Branddon Hall, Alderson-Broaddus College (26416). (304) 457-1700; (304) 457-2916. Licensee: Alderson-Broaddus College. Net: AP. Format: Div, CHR, urban contemp. News progmg 5 hrs wkly. Target aud: 15-40; college students. Spec prog: Jazz 4 hrs, Black 2 hrs, radio drama 2 hrs, children's 2 hrs wkly. ■ W. C. Sizemure, pres; Robert Powell, gen mgr; Jim Greco, opns mgr; Brice Hawk, dev mgr; Linda Walls, progmg dir; Wayne Smith, mus dir; Amy Colan, news dir; George Sommer, chief engr.

Pineville

WWYO(AM)—1949: 970 khz; 1 kw-D. TL: N37 35 20 W81 32 25. Stereo. Box 1475, Rt. 10 (24874). (304) 732-8552. FAX: (304) 732-8063. Licensee: MRJ Inc. (acq 9-23-92; $10,000; FTR 11-9-92). Wash atty: Peter Gutman. Format: Nostalgia. Target aud: 25-40; 30-yr-old housewives. Spec prog: Folk 15 hrs, gospel 20 hrs, relg 20 hrs, sports 20 hrs, educ 20 hrs, community 20 hrs wkly. ■ Rudolph D. Jennings, pres & gen mgr; Deborah Williamson, gen sls mgr; Charlie Alt, news dir. ■ Rates: $5; 5; 5; na.

Pocatalico

WTUN(FM)—Not on air, target date unknown: 98.7 mhz; 1.2 kw. Ant 515 ft. TL: N38 27 42 W81 35 24. 8117 Counselor Rd., Manassas, VA (22111). Licensee: Weigle Broadcasting Corp.

Point Pleasant

WBGS(AM)—Not on air, target date 1994: 1030 khz; 10 kw-D, DA. TL: N38 48 42 W82 05 59. Box 889, Blacksburg, VA (24060). Licensee: Big River Radio Inc. Group owner: Baker Family Stations. Format: Relg. ■ Vernon H. Baker, pres.

WBYG(FM)—Co-owned with WBGS(AM). Not on air, target date 1994: 99.5 mhz; 4.7 kw. Ant 328 ft. TL: N38 47 52 W82 10 07. (703) 552-4252. (Acq 1-28-92.)

Princeton

WAEY(AM)—December 1947: 1490 khz; 1 kw-U. TL: N37 23 23 W81 05 58. Box 5588 (24740). (304) 425-2151. FAX: (304) 487-2016. Licensee: Betap Corp. (acq 1-1-73). Net: ABC/E. Format: Country. News staff one; news progmg 14 hrs wkly. Target aud: 25 plus; blue collar. ■ Henry G. Beam, pres, gen mgr & gen sls mgr; Lee Daugherty, progmg dir; Buddy Andrews, mus dir; Ranny Parks, news dir.

WAEY-FM—Apr 1, 1973: 95.9 mhz; 6 kw. Ant 285 ft. TL: N37 23 23 W81 05 58 (CP: 480 w, ant 1,141 ft, TL: N37 15 30 W81 10 37). Stereo. Dups AM 100%. Format: Country.

WKMY(FM)—April 1983: 100.9 mhz; 630 w. Ant 641 ft. TL: N37 18 20 W81 07 30. Stereo. Hrs opn: 24. Tar Box 7204, Mercer Mall, Bluefield (24701). (304) 327-6124; (304) 425-0001. FAX: (304) 327-6125. Licensee: Mountain Broadcasting Corp. Group owner: Tschudy Communications Corp. (acq 5-8-89); grpsl; FTR 5-29-89). Net: Unistar. Format: Adult Contemp. News staff one. Target aud: 25 plus. ■ Earl Judy Jr., pres; Tina Etter, opns mgr; Linda Slater, gen sls mgr & adv mgr; Steve Stout, prom mgr, progmg dir & progmg dir; Jeff Sparks, mus dir & news dir; Jay Belt, chief engr. ■ Rates: $4.20; 4.20; 4.20; 4.20.

Rainelle

WRRL(AM)—1973: 1130 khz; 1 kw-D. TL: N37 57 28 W80 45 45. 507 Main St. (25962). (304) 438-7811. FAX: (304) 438-9242. Licensee: R.B. Company. Net: Unistar, Metronews Radio Net. Format: Gospel. ■ Darrel K. Cales, pres; Karl McClung, gen mgr; Carolyn Hunter, gen sls mgr; Julie Osborne, prom mgr; Mr. Stacy Sparks, progmg dir; Shawna Allen, mus dir.

WRRL-FM—Feb 1977: 95.3 mhz; 3.1 kw. Ant 460 ft. TL: N37 57 28 W80 45 45. Stereo. Prog sep from AM. (304) 438-8537. Format: C&W. Target aud: 25-54. Spec prog: Gospel.

Ravenswood

WFYZ(FM)—Not on air, target date unknown: 93.1 mhz; 3.3 kw. Ant 446 ft. Box 667, Gibbs & Gallatin St. (26164). Licensee: Osborne Enterprises Inc.

WMOV(AM)—1953: 1360 khz; 1 kw-U. TL: N38 57 52 W81 46 09. Stereo. Hrs opn: 6 AM-midnight. Box 261, Gibbs & Gallatin Sts. (26164). (304) 273-2544. FAX: (304) 273-3020. Licensee: Good Neighbor Broadcasters Inc. (acq 1957; $150,000). Net: ABC. Wash atty: Roy Perkins. Format: Country, oldies, big band. News staff one; news progmg 14 hrs wkly. Target aud: 16 plus, emphasis on 25 plus. Spec prog: Talk 1 hr wkly, folk 2 hrs, jazz 2 hrs, bluegrass 10 hrs wkly. ■ Rex Osborne, CEO, pres, gen mgr & vp engrg; Gerry Gillespie, vp opns; Kathy Gillespie, opns dir & vp prom; Alfred Weekly, dev dir; Dave Karr, dev mgr; P. Bibbee, gen sls mgr; Al Weekly, natl sls mgr; Beth Loomey, rgnl sls mgr; String Sparkman, mktg dir; Robie Harts, prom dir; William Trowbridge, vp adv; Rona Barrett, adv dir; Jack O'Brien, progmg dir; Frank Matthews, asst mus dir; Ray Adams, news dir; Larry Koenig, chief engr. ■ Rates: $8; 8; 8; 8.

WRZZ(FM)—1986: 106.1 mhz; 1.85 kw. Ant 604 ft. TL: N39 02 07 W81 40 04. Stereo. Box 1346, Old Blennerhassett School, Rt. 4, Jewell Rd., Parkersburg (26102). (304) 273-2959; (304) 863-3319. FAX: (304) 863-3310. Licensee: Media Com Inc. (acq 1-90; $305,000). Net: Unistar. Rep: Rgnl Reps. Wash atty: Robert Olender. Format: Classic rock. Target aud: 25-44; baby boomer adult rock listeners. ■ Sam Yoho, pres & progmg dir; Don Staats, gen mgr, gen sls mgr & mus dir; Randy Kensolving, Harry Stephens, chiefs engr. ■ Rates: $10; 8; 10; 8.

Richwood

WVAR(AM)—1956: 600 khz; 1 kw-D. TL: N38 13 50 W80 32 49. Hrs opn: 6 AM-sunset. Box 349 (26651); 713 Main St., Summersville (26651). (304) 846-2514; (304) 872-5202. FAX: (304) 872-6904. Licensee: R&S Broadcasting Co. (acq 1958). Net: ABC/R. Rep: Dome. Format: Country. News staff one; news progmg 13 hrs wkly. Target aud: 25 plus; general. Spec prog: Gospel 11 hrs wkly. ■ C. Farrell Johnson, CEO & chief engr; Vivian Jean Brown, pres & gen sls mgr; Michael D. Brown, gen mgr; Marilyn Hinkle, progmg dir & mus dir; Roy Henderson, news dir. ■ Rates: $7.50; 7.50; 7.50; na.

Ripley

WCEF(FM)—Feb 24, 1981: 98.3 mhz; 3 kw. Ant 300 ft. TL: N38 46 04 W81 41 09. Stereo. Box 798 (25271). (304) 372-9800. FAX: (304) 372-9811. Licensee: McWhorter Communications Corp. (acq 7-90; $420,000; FTR 7-23-90). Net: ABC/C. Format: Country. Target aud: 25-54. ■ Ronald W. Hill, CEO & exec vp; Robert McWhorter, pres; Ric Shannon, gen mgr; Lois Casto, gen sls mgr; Rich Lacey, prom dir, progmg dir & mus dir; Larry Koenig, chief engr.

WVRP(FM)—Not on air, target date unknown: 90.7 mhz; 3 kw. Ant 328 ft. Box 473, 1928 Washington Blvd., Belpre, OH (45714). Licensee: Lower Ohio Valley Educational Corp.

Romney

***WJGF-FM**—Mar 30, 1973: 89.7 mhz; 109 w. Ant 42 ft. TL: N39 20 25 W78 45 04. E. Main St. (26757). (304) 822-4838; (304) 822-3521. FAX: (304) 822-3370. Licensee: West Virginia Schools for the Deaf and Blind. Net: ABC, MBS. Format: Var. ■ George E. Keady, gen mgr; George Parks, stn mgr.

WJJB(FM)—Aug 29, 1988: 100.1 mhz; 480 w. Ant 823 ft. TL: N39 25 20 W78 47 25. Stereo. Hrs opn: 24. Box 477, Cumberland, MD (21501-0477). (301) 724-6000. FAX: (301) 724-0000. Licensee: Charter Equities Inc. Net: Unistar. Wash atty: Baraff, Koerner, Olender & Hochberg. Format: Mellow adult contemp. News staff one; news progmg 15 hrs wkly. Target aud: 25-54; adult decision makers. Spec prog: Christian one hr wkly. ■ Warren Gregory, pres, gen mgr & sls dir; Diane Bean, news dir; David Groth, chief engr. ■ Rates: $22; 18; 18; 18.

Ronceverte

WRON(AM)—1947: 1400 khz; 1 kw-U. TL: N37 45 36 W80 27 18. 276 Seneca Trail N. (24970). (304) 645-1400; (304) 645-1327. FAX: (304) 647-4802. Licensee: Radio Greenbrier (acq 12-86). Net: Westwood One, Moody. Rep: Dome, Rgnl Reps. Format: Adult contemp, talk. News progmg 14 hrs wkly. Target aud: 35 and under. Spec prog: Relg 5 hrs wkly. ■ Elaine B. Pugh, gen mgr & gen sls mgr; Michael J. Kidd, stn mgr & progmg dir; Danny Hutchens, mus dir; Anita Howard, news dir; Larry Carver, chief engr. ■ Rates: $5.30; 5.30; 5.30; 5.30.

WRON-FM—Dec 6, 1983: 97.7 mhz; 1 kw. Ant 800 ft. TL: N37 47 54 W80 30 55. Stereo. Hrs opn: 6 AM-midnight. Dups AM 5%. Format: Oldies. Target aud: 25-60. ■ Anita Howard, asst mus dir. ■ Rates: $6.75; 6.75; 6.75; 6.75.

Rupert

WYKM(AM)—Dec 9, 1981: 1250 khz; 5 kw-D. TL: N37 59 35 W80 41 03. Hrs opn: 6 AM-dusk. Box 627 (25984). (304) 392-6003. FAX: (304) 392-6033. Licensee: Mountain State Broadcasting Co. Net: CBS; Rgnl Reps. Format: Country, gospel. News progmg 7 hrs wkly. ■ Betty D. Crookshanks, pres & gen sls mgr; Linda O'Dell, mus dir; Diane O'Dell, news dir.

St. Albans

WCOZ(AM)—Jan 14, 1956: 1300 khz; 1 kw-D, 49 w-N. TL: N38 23 43 W81 51 00. Hrs opn: 24. 100 Kanawha Terr. (25177). (304) 722-2308. Licensee: WKLC Inc. Group owner: L.M. Communications Inc. (acq 2-23-80). Net: ABC/R, NBC the Source. Rep: D & R Radio. Format: Adult rock. ■ Lynn Martin, pres; Chris Johnson, gen mgr; Brian Rayment, progmg dir & mus dir.

WKLC-FM—Co-owned with WCOZ(AM). Jan 1, 1966: 105.1 mhz; 50 kw. Ant 1,663 ft. TL: N38 25 15 W81 55 27. Stereo. Dups AM 100%.

St. Marys

WVVW(AM)—October 1984: 630 khz; 1 kw-D. TL: N39 23 42 W81 13 49. Box 374 (26170); Green Runs Rd. (26170). (304) 684-3400. Licensee: Seven Ranges Radio Co. Wash atty: Haley, Bader & Potts. Format: Relg. ■ Robert Eddy, pres, gen mgr, gen sls mgr & chief engr; Dave Hoyt, progmg dir. ■ Rates: $4; 4; 4; na.

WRRR-FM—Co-owned with WVVW(AM). Nov 16, 1983: 93.9 mhz; 17 kw. Ant 390 ft. TL: N39 22 49 W81 11 36. Stereo. Prog sep from AM. Net: NBC. Format: Adult contemp. News progmg 14 hrs wkly. Target aud: 25-49. ■ Robert Eddy, stn mgr; Dave Hoyt, opns mgr & prom mgr.

Salem

WOBG-FM—Nov 1, 1990: 105.7 mhz; 6 kw. Ant 581 ft. TL: N39 19 06 W80 26 18. Stereo. Hrs opn: 24. Rebroadcasts WOBG(AM) Clarksburg 100%. Box 3190, Old Weatherservice Bldg., Old Rt. 50 E., Clarksburg (26301). (304) 782-3257. Licensee: Hilber Corp. (acq 8-22-91; $72,000). Net: ABC/E. Rep: Katz & Powell; Commercial Media Sales. Wash atty: Shinis & Peltman. Format: Oldies. Target aud: 25-54; male & female. Spec prog: Health talk one hr wkly. ■ Bob Hilber, pres; Sally Hilber, vp; Bob Hiller, gen mgr; Mike King, gen sls mgr; Dan Terango, progmg dir; Don Niles, mus dir; Barbara Scott, pub affrs dir; Asa Gawthrop, chief engr. ■ Rates: $24; 24; 24; 24.

Shepherdstown

***WSHC(FM)**—1974: 89.7 mhz; 950 w. Ant -10 ft. TL: N39 25 53 W77 48 18. Box 277, Shepherd College, King St. (25443). (304) 876-2521. Licensee: University of West Virginia Board of Directors (acq 10-5-90; grpsl; FTR 10-29-90). Format: Progsv, top-40, div. ■ Doug Shaw, gen mgr; Grant Erie, pub affrs dir.

South Charleston

WSCW(AM)—Dec 13, 1963: 1410 khz; 5 kw-D. TL: N38 22 34 W81 42 13. Box 8600, 605 D St. (25303). (304) 744-5388. Licensee: CLW Communications Group Inc. (group owner; acq 11-75). Net: CBN. Format: Religious. ■ Dr. Spiros Zodhiates, pres; Alice Sypolt, gen mgr; David Johnston, gen sls mgr; B.G. Hamrick, progmg dir & news dir; Scott Argento, mus dir; Lester Lovejoy, chief engr.

WJYP(FM)—Co-owned with WSCW(AM). July 29, 1985: 100.9 mhz; 3 kw. Ant 285 ft. TL: N38 22 34 W81 42 13. Stereo. Hrs opn: 24. Prog sep from AM. Net: Moody. Format: Inspirational, relg. ■ B.G. Hamrick, mus dir.

Spencer

WVRC(AM)—Sept 12, 1961: 1400 khz; 1 kw-U. TL: N38 48 23 W81 21 40. 106 Radio St. (25276). (304) 927-3760. Licensee: Star Communications Inc. (acq 9-22-82; $40,000; FTR 10-11-82). Rep: Rgnl Reps. Format: Country. ■ Gordon Rogers, pres & gen sls mgr; Bob Edwards, gen mgr & progmg dir; Toby Wagoner, news dir; Larry Koenig, chief engr.

WVRC-FM—October 1992: 104.7 mhz; 3 kw. Ant 328 ft. TL: N38 47 40 W81 17 36. 106 Radio St. (25276). (304) 927-3760. FAX: (304) 927-2877. Licensee: Star Communications Inc. (acq 3-1-91; FTR 3-25-91). Format: Country. ■ Bob Edwards, vp & gen mgr.

Summersville

WCWV(FM)—Mar 13, 1983: 92.9 mhz; 11 kw. Ant 900 ft. TL: N38 21 37 W80 38 49. Stereo. 713 Main St. (26651). (304) 872-5203; (304) 872-5204. FAX: (304) 872-6904. Licensee: R&S Broadcasting Inc. Net: ABC/R. Rep: Dome. Format: Adult contemp. News staff one; news progmg 23 hrs wkly. Target aud: 18-45. Spec prog: Gospel 15 hrs wkly. ■ C. Farrell Johnson, chmn & chief engr; Vivian Jean Brown, pres & gen sls mgr; Michael D. Brown, vp, gen mgr, stn mgr & engrg dir; Jeffrey Van Kirk, progmg dir; Roy Henderson, news dir.

***WMLJ(FM)**—Not on air, target date unknown: 90.5 mhz; 11 kw. Ant 948 ft. TL: N38 06 41 W80 35 55. Box 7 (26651). Licensee: Grace Missionary Baptist Church (acq 5-3-93; FTR 5-24-93).

Sutton

WSGB(AM)—Jan 22, 1964: 1490 khz; 1 kw-U. TL: N38 39 11 W80 43 10. Hrs opn: 24. 189A Main St. (26601). (304) 765-7373. Licensee: Mid-State Broadcasting Corp. Group owner: Milliken Investment Corp. (acq 1-1-

Wisconsin   Directory of Radio

87). Format: Country, relg. Target aud: 25 plus. ■ Jim Milliken, pres, gen mgr, stn mgr, gen sls mgr & progmg dir; Lisa Mace, opns mgr & asst mus dir; Cortney Milliken, pub affrs dir.

WCKA(FM)—Co-owned with WSGB(AM). Apr 25, 1987: 97.1 mhz; 25 kw. Ant 193 ft. TL: N38 39 11 W80 43 10. Stereo. Hrs opn: 24. Prog sep from AM. Format: Country, adult contemp. Spec prog: Relg 15 hrs wkly.

Vienna

WDMX(FM)—May 22, 1989: 100.1 mhz; 1.65 kw. Ant 440 ft. TL: N39 20 18 W81 30 01. Stereo. Hrs opn: 24. Box 5559, 6006 Grand Central Ave. (26105). (304) 295-6070; (304) 375-6558. FAX: (304) 295-4389. Licensee: Bennco Inc. Net: SMN. Rep: Katz & Powell, Rgnl Reps. Wash atty: Lauren Colby. Format: Oldies. News staff one; news progmg 2 hrs wkly. Target aud: 25-54. ■ William Benns, pres; Ron Bishop, gen mgr & gen sls mgr; Jim Grywalsky, opns mgr & progmg dir; Melissa Martin, prom dir; Doug Hess, news dir; Brian Kirken, chief engr. ■ Rates: $26.50; 23.50; 26.50; 17.50.

Weirton

WEIR(AM)—Sept 15, 1950: 1430 khz; 1 kw-U, DA-2. TL: N40 26 45 W80 37 36. Stereo. Hrs opn: 24. B-7, 116 Banton Ridge Dr., Wintersville, OH (43952). (304) 723-1430. FAX: (304) 723-1249. Licensee: McGraw Broadcast Corp. Group owner: McGraw Group Stns. (acq 12-89; grpsl; FTR 12-11-89). Net: CBS. Rep: Dome. Wash atty: Fisher, Wayland, Cooper & Leader. Format: Oldies. News staff 2; news progmg 25 hrs wkly. Target aud: General. Spec prog: Ger one hr, cultural one hr, It 2 hrs, Pol one hr wkly. ■ Richard McGraw, pres; Karen McGraw, vp; Todd Elliot, gen mgr; Dave Himmelrick, opns mgr, prom mgr & chief engr; Cindy Smooke, rgnl sls mgr; Alan Davidson, progmg dir. ■ Rates: $60; 40; 50; 25.

Welch

WELC(AM)—Aug 19, 1950: 1150 khz; 5 kw-D. TL: N37 25 01 W81 36 58. Box 949 (24801). (304) 436-2131. FAX: (304) 436-2132. Licensee: Pocahontas Broadcasting Co. Net: CNN. Format: Adult contemp. News staff 2. Target aud: 21-54. ■ Sam Sidote, pres, gen mgr & gen sls mgr; Mary Sidote, prom mgr & progmg dir; John Sidote, mus dir, news dir & chief engr.

WELC-FM—Feb 1, 1990: 102.9 mhz; 1.8 kw. Ant 423 ft. TL: N37 25 01 W81 36 58. Stereo. Hrs opn: 6 AM-11 PM. Dups AM 90%. Target aud: 18-49.

WXEE(FM)—Dec 1, 1955: 1340 khz; 1 kw-U. TL: N37 25 50 W81 35 33. Hrs opn: 18. Box 1340, Rt. 52N at Jr. Poca (24801). (304) 436-4191. FAX: (304) 436-4192. Licensee: Mountaineer Broadcasting (acq 6-1-78). Net: ABC/E, Unistar. Format: Country. Target aud: 24-65. ■ Tommy L. Kuhn, pres; W. Dale Ellis, vp & gen mgr; James A. Sassak, progmg dir & news dir; Deanna L. Hale, mus dir; Jesse Foust, chief engr. ■ Rates: $6; 6; 6; 6.

West Liberty

*****WGLZ(FM)**—Sept 4, 1990: 91.5 mhz; 150 w. Ant 213 ft. TL: N40 09 49 W80 36 06. Box 13, West Liberty State College (26074). (304) 336-8286; (304) 336-8037. FAX: (304) 336-8285. Licensee: West Liberty State College. Format: Alternative. ■ Steve Novotey, stn mgr; Darcey Kennedy, prom dir; Thomas Griffiths, progmg dir; Christian H. Lee, chief engr.

Weston

WHAW(AM)—Feb 14, 1948: 980 khz; 1 kw-D, 50 w-N. TL: N39 02 23 W80 27 20. Hrs opn: 24. Box 980, 300 Harrison Ave. (26452). (304) 269-5555. FAX: (304) 269-5522. Licensee: Stonewall Broadcasting Corp. (acq 10-23-87). Rep: Dome, Rgnl Reps, Katz & Powell. Format: Country. News progmg 5 hrs wkly. Target aud: 25-54. ■ Bruce Beam Jr., pres & gen mgr; Patrick Scott Beam, exec vp; Bryan Todd Beam, sr vp; Louise Bleigh, news dir; Kenneth Smith, chief engr. ■ Rates: $15.88; 14.12; 15.88; 12.35.

WSSN(FM)—Co-owned with WHAW(AM). Aug 29, 1972: 102.3 mhz; 940 w. Ant 489 ft. TL: N39 04 15 W80 31 13 (CP: 25 kw, ant 18 ft., TL: N39 02 25 W80 27 16). Hrs opn: 24. Prog sep from AM. Net: SMN. Format: Adult contemp. Target aud: 18-49. ■ Rates: Same as AM.

Westover

WMQC(FM)—Jan 5, 1983: 100.9 mhz; 3 kw. Ant 198 ft. TL: N39 32 44 W79 55 58. Stereo. 15 Campbell St., Luray, VA (22835). (304) 292-1101. Licensee: Tschudy Communications Corp. (group owner; acq 5-88). Net: MBS. Format: Adult contemp. Spec prog: Relg mus 2 hrs wkly. ■ Earl Judy, pres; Janel Bolam, opns mgr; Ann Tomabene, gen sls mgr; Kevin Arnold, progmg dir & news dir; Rick Williams, chief engr.

Wheeling

WBBD(AM)—Apr 7, 1963: 1600 khz; 5 kw-D, 30 w-N. TL: N40 05 26 W80 42 11. Hrs opn: 24. 98 16th St. (26003). (304) 233-7560. FAX: (304) 233-7563. Licensee: Wheeling Broadcasting Co. Group owner: Burbach Broadcasting Group (acq 4-16-87). Net: Unistar; W.V. Metronews. Rep: Christal. Format: Easy listening. News staff one. Target aud: 45 plus. ■ Nicholas Galli, pres; Steve Peskin, vp; Lily Goddard, gen mgr; Rick Swan, progmg dir; Keith Mack, news dir; Rob Backstrom, chief engr.

WEGW(FM)—Co-owned with WBBD(AM). October 1966: 107.5 mhz; 12.5 kw. Ant 870 ft. TL: N40 03 41 W80 45 08 (CP: 10.5 kw, ant 882 ft.). Stereo. Hrs opn: 24. Prog sep from AM. Format: Rock (AOR). Target aud: 25-54. ■ Carrie Martin, prom dir; Ken Kirby, mus dir.

WKWK(AM)—May 2, 1941: 1400 khz; 1 kw-U. TL: N40 05 49 W80 42 06. Hrs opn: 24. 88 Waddles Run Rd. (26003). (304) 232-2250. Licensee: WKWK Radio Inc. Group owner: MetroCities (acq 5-1-92; grpsl, including co-located FM; FTR 5-25-92). Net: Unistar, ABC/I. Rep: Christal. Rgnl Reps.Format: Sports/information. Target aud: 35 plus. Spec prog: Pol 2 hrs wkly. ■ James Glassman, pres; Michael Allodi, vp, gen mgr & gen sls mgr; Debbie Mills, news dir; Jim Janos, chief engr.

WKWK-FM—March 17, 1948: 97.3 mhz; 50 kw. Ant 470 ft. TL: N40 05 49 W80 42 06. Stereo. Hrs opn: 24. Prog sep from AM. Net: ABC/I. Format: Adult contemp. News staff one. Target aud: 25-54. ■ Doug Daniels, progmg dir & mus dir.

WOVK(FM)—Listing follows WWVA(AM).

*****WPHP(FM)**—Apr 4, 1977: 91.9 mhz; 1 kw. Ant 259 ft. TL: N40 04 07 W80 39 04. Box 1976 (26003). (304) 243-0414. FAX: (304) 243-0449. Licensee: Ohio County Board of Education. Format: Top-40. Spec prog: Black 4 hrs, jazz one hr wkly. ■ Patrick A. Clutter, gen mgr.

*****WVNP(FM)**—Oct 7, 1981: 89.9 mhz; 25 kw. Ant 500 ft. TL: N40 12 58 W80 33 31. Stereo. 600 Capitol St., Charleston (25301). (304) 558-3000. FAX: (304) 558-4034. Licensee: West Virginia Educational Broadcasting Authority. Net: NPR, APR. Format: News, classical, jazz. News staff 2. Spec prog: Mountain stage 2 hrs wkly. ■ Barbara Herrick, gen mgr; Marilyn DiVita, dev mgr; Nancy Buckingham, prom mgr; Jeanne Fisher, progmg dir; Jim Wallace, news dir; Francis Fisher, chief engr.

WWVA(AM)—December 1926: 1170 khz; 50 kw-U, DA-2. TL: N40 06 07 W80 52 02. 1015 Main St. (26003). (304) 232-1170. Licensee: Osborn Communications Corp. (group owner; acq 3-87). Net: NBC. Rep: McGavren Guild. Format: Country. News staff 3; news progmg 12 hrs wkly. Target aud: 25-54. Spec prog: Farm 2 hrs wkly. ■ Larry Anderson, gen mgr; Rob Vandine, stn mgr & gen sls mgr; Tom Miller, opns mgr; Terri Phillips, prom mgr; Bill Berg, progmg dir & mus dir; David Demarest, news dir; John Lane, chief engr.

WOVK(FM)—Co-owned with WWVA(AM). September 1947: 98.7 mhz; 50 kw. Ant 390 ft. TL: N40 04 58 W80 46 18 (CP: 15 kw, ant 906 ft., TL: N40 04 48 W80 46 06).

White Sulphur Springs

WSLW(AM)—1971: 1310 khz; 5 kw-D. TL: N37 48 17 W80 21 03. Hrs opn: 6 AM-sundown. Box 610, 73 E. Main St. (24986). (304) 536-1310. Licensee: Seneca Broadcasting Inc. (acq 8-8-85; grpsl; FTR 6-10-85). Net: ABC/I; Agri-Net. Rep: Rgnl Reps. Format: Adult contemp. News progmg 8 hrs wkly. Target aud: 25-60; secondary 16-25 & 60 plus. ■ Ken Bryant, CEO, prom mgr & news dir; Richard L. Bryant, pres; Jean Bryant, gen mgr, stn mgr, progmg dir & mus dir; K.L. Bryant, gen sls mgr; Randy Kerbway, chief engr. ■ Rates: $5.50; 5.50; 5.50; 5.50.

Williamson

WBTH(AM)—April 19, 1939: 1400 khz; 1 kw-U. TL: N37 40 09 W82 16 09. Box 261 (25661); 5 1/2 E. Second Ave. (25661). (304) 235-3600. FAX: (304) 235-8118. Licensee: Harvit Broadcasting Corp. (acq 6-8-66). Net: MBS. Format: Adult contemp. ■ Denny Frost, gen mgr & opns mgr; David Miller, news dir.

WXCC(FM)—Co-owned with WBTH(AM). Oct 27, 1978: 96.5 mhz; 50 kw. Ant 500 ft. TL: N37 40 09 W82 16 09. Prog sep from AM. Format: Mod country.

Wisconsin

Adams

WDKM(FM)—Oct 8, 1993: 106.1 mhz; 6 kw. Ant 328 ft. TL: N43 57 29 W89 49 43. 408 Hillwood Ln., Friendship (53934). (608) 339-3221. Licensee: Roche-A-Cri Broadcasting. Format: Country. ■ Steve Roekle, gen mgr.

Algoma

WBDK(FM)—Nov 12, 1986: 96.7 mhz; 25 kw. Ant 283 ft. TL: N44 39 26 W87 33 45. Stereo. Box 123, 1500 Mueller St. (54201). (414) 487-5246. FAX: (414) 487-3044. Licensee: Nicolet Broadcasting Inc. (group owner; acq 9-3-93; FTR 9-27-93). Net: SMN. Format: Country. News progmg 5 hrs wkly. Target aud: 24-54. ■ Roger Utnehmer, pres; John Utnehmer, gen mgr; Kelly Kralicek, vp progmg; Michael Krein, chief engr.

Altoona

WEIO(AM)—See Eau Claire.

WISM-FM—Nov 15, 1991: 98.1 mhz; 25 kw. Ant 279 ft. TL: N44 46 36 W91 28 30. 1819 Mitchell Ave., Eau Claire (54701). (715) 826-9476. Licensee: Altoona FM Radio. Rep: Katz & Powell. Format: Classic rock. News staff one; news progmg 15 hrs wkly. Target aud: 25-49. Spec prog: Blues 2 hrs wkly. ■ Cliff Somers, pres; David Barrett, gen mgr; Jeff Stevens, vp opns & progmg dir; Dewey Brott, rgnl sls mgr; Stephanie Rundquist, mktg dir; Martin Meldahl, vp progmg; Phil Conrad, mus dir; Jeff King, asst mus dir; Dean Muldoon, news dir; Jon Zecherle, chief engr. ■ Rates: $25; 25; 25; 15.

Amery

WXCE(AM)—Jan 23, 1978: 1260 khz; 5 kw-U, DA-2. TL: N45 15 25 W92 22 00. Hrs opn: 5 AM-midnight. R.R. 4, Box 1260, 328 S. 100th St. (54001). (715) 268-7185. FAX: (715) 268-7187. Licensee: Murray O. Ritland (acq 8-16-91; $167,000; FTR 9-18-89). Net: CNN. Format: Contemp country. News staff one; news progmg 20 hrs wkly. Target aud: 35-65. Spec prog: Farm 12 hrs wkly. ■ Murray Ritland, pres & gen mgr; Nora Schaefer, prom dir; Lisa Castellano, adv dir; Dave Reid, progmg dir; Greg Mars, mus dir; Jeff McAndrew, news dir. ■ Rates: $9.60; 8; 9.60; 8.

Antigo

WATK(AM)—Mar 15, 1948: 900 khz; 250 w-D, 196 w-N. TL: N45 06 50 W89 08 20. Hrs opn: 24. Box 509, Hwy. 45 S. (54409). (715) 623-4124. FAX: (715) 627-4497. Licensee: Ad-Mark Communications (acq 5-1-88). Net: Unistar. Format: C&W. News staff 2; news progmg 12 hrs wkly. Target aud: 25-59; two-income families. ■ Jeff Wagner, gen mgr; Tim Unsinn, opns mgr; Shaughn Novy, sls dir & mktg mgr; Bill Berg, gen sls mgr; Al Higgins, progmg dir; Jim Greve, news dir; Andy Screder, pub affrs dir; Jim Zastrow, chief engr. ■ Rates: $16.80; 16.80; 16.80; 16.80.

WRLO-FM—Co-owned with WATK(AM). Nov 11, 1973: 105.3 mhz; 100 kw. Ant 541 ft. TL: N45 22 04 W89 08 20. Stereo. Hrs opn: 24. Prog sep from AM. Net: SMN. Format: Adult contemp. Target aud: 21-54. ■ Tim Unsinn, opns dir; Shaughn Novy, gen sls mgr. ■ Rates: $11.20; 11.20; 11.20; 11.20.

Appleton

*****WAAU(FM)**—Not on air, target date unknown: 91.9 mhz; 3.3 kw. Ant 308 ft. 1909 W. Second St. (54914). Licensee: Evangel Ministries Inc.

WAPL-FM—Dec 24, 1965: 105.7 mhz; 100 kw. Ant 1,175 ft. TL: N44 21 32 W87 59 07. Stereo. Hrs opn: 24. Box 1519 (54913). (414) 734-9226. Licensee: Woodward Communications Inc. (group owner; acq 3-75). Format: AOR. News staff one; news progmg 2 hrs wkly. Target aud: Professional & semi-professional adults, mostly male. Spec prog: Jazz 4 hrs wkly. ■ Greg Bell, stn mgr; Garrett Hart, gen mgr & progmg dir; Kevin Streetar, sls dir; Jackie MacLaren, mktg dir; Bob Barron, mus dir.

*****WLFM(FM)**—Mar 10, 1956: 91.1 mhz; 10.5 kw. Ant 120 ft. TL: N44 15 42 W88 23 47. Stereo. Hrs opn: 5 AM-1 AM. 420 E. College Ave. (54911). (414) 832-6566; (414) 832-6568. Licensee: Lawrence Univ. Net: NPR, APR. Wis. Pub. Format: Talk. News progmg 15 hrs wkly. Target aud: 45 plus; socially active, educated. Spec prog: Class 10 hrs wkly. ■ Glen Slaats, stn mgr; Quinn Klinefelter, news dir; Al Rieland, chief engr.

Stations in the U.S.   Wisconsin

WRJQ(AM)—1952: 1570 khz; 1 kw-D, 331 w-N. TL: N44 13 04 W88 24 33. Hrs opn: 24. Box 4056, 2110 S. Memorial Dr. (54915). (414) 749-1570; (414) 749-1575. FAX: (414) 735-4027. Licensee: Winnebago Broadcasting Inc. (acq 4-16-91; $110,000; FTR 4-29-91). Format: Big band. Target aud: 40 plus. Spec prog: Farm 6 hrs, Ger 5 hrs, Slavanian 2 hrs wkly. ■ Robert Artabasy, CEO, chmn, gen mgr, stn mgr & sls dir; Wesley Koeffler, pres; Gerald Luedtke, rgnl sls mgr; Tom Daily, mktg mgr; Jane Koehler, pub affrs dir; Rex King, chief engr. ■ Rates: $13; 9; 13; 9.

Ashland

WATW(AM)—May 1, 1940: 1400 khz; 1 kw-U. TL: N46 34 23 W90 51 56 (CP: 480 w-U, TL: N46 34 25 W90 51 56). Stereo. Hrs opn: 24. Rt. 2, Box 63, 2320 Ellis Ave. (54806). (715) 682-2727; (715) 682-2728. FAX: (715) 682-9338. Licensee: Bay Broadcasting (acq 1-6-85; $320,000; FTR 9-24-84). Net: ABC/E. Wash atty: Smithwich & Bellendink. Format: Classic country. News staff one; news progmg 17 hrs wkly. Target aud: 20-60 plus; middle to upper income adults. Spec prog: Polka one hr, relg 5 hrs wkly. ■ Jerry Hackman, pres & gen mgr; Dave Morris, stn mgr & chief engr; Raymond Nye, Ann Hackman, gen sls mgrs; , Dave Morris, prom dirs; Skip Hunter, progmg dir.

WJJH(FM)—Co-owned with WATW(AM). Aug 1, 1972: 96.7 mhz; 50 kw. Ant 259 ft. TL: N46 34 23 W90 51 56. Stereo. Hrs opn: 24. Prog sep from AM. Net: ABC/FM. Format: Classic rock, oldies. News staff one. Target aud: 25-45. ■ Ann Hackman, vp; Skip Hunter, mus dir; Jim Casey, vp engrg.

WBSZ(FM)—Not on air, target date unknown: 93.3 mhz; 100 kw. Ant 299 ft. 222 11th St. W. (54806). Licensee: Gerald J. Hackman.

WEGZ(FM)—See Washburn.

WJJH(FM)—Listing follows WATW(AM).

Auburndale

*WLBL(AM)—1922: 930 khz; 5 kw-D. TL: N44 36 52 W90 02 08. 3319 W. Beltline Hwy., Madison (53713). (715) 263-3970. Licensee: State of Wis., Education Communications Board. Format: Educ, talk. ■ Vern Alpine, chief engr.

Baraboo

WOLX-FM—Licensed to Baraboo. See Madison.

WRPQ(AM)—June 1967: 740 khz; 250 w-D, 6.4 w-N. TL: N43 27 19 W89 45 13. Stereo. Hrs opn: 24. Box 456, 407 Oak St. (53913). (608) 356-3974. FAX: (608) 356-3974. Licensee: Baraboo Broadcasting Co. (acq 7-1-91; $125,000; FTR 7-13-81). Net: Jones Satellite Audio, USA; Wisconsin Radio Net. Format: Adult contemp. News staff one; news progmg 8 hrs wkly. Target aud: 25-54. Spec prog: Relg 4 hrs wkly. ■ Jeff Smith, pres, gen mgr, sls dir, prom dir & progmg dir; Carol Scott, news dir; Greg Buchwald, vp engrg. ■ Rates: $8.50; 8; 8.50; 6.75.

Beaver Dam

WBEV(AM)—Mar 21, 1951: 1430 khz; 1 kw-U, DA-N. TL: N43 25 43 W88 53 33. Hrs opn: 5 AM-midnight. Box 902, 100 Stoddart St. (53916). (414) 885-4442. FAX: (414) 885-2152. Licensee: Beaver Dam Broadcasting Co. Inc. Group owner: McNaughton Stns. (acq 2-1-73). Net: ABC/I. Wash atty: Leonard S. Joyce. Format: Adult contemp, oldies, news/talk. News staff 3; news progmg 20 hrs wkly. Target aud: General; 30 plus. Spec prog: Farm 8 hrs wkly. ■ W. John Klinger, pres & gen mgr; John A. Moser, gen sls mgr; Frank Beres, progmg dir; Steve Sabatke, news dir; Jim Stowell, pub affrs dir; Warren Jorgensen, chief engr.

WXRO(FM)—Co-owned with WBEV(AM). July 15, 1968: 95.3 mhz; 6 kw. Ant 328 ft. TL: N43 28 09 W88 49 32. Stereo. Hrs opn: 5 AM-midnight. Prog sep from AM. Net: ABC/E. Format: Modern country. News staff 3; news progmg 10 hrs wkly. Target aud: General; 25-54. Spec prog: Farm 6 hrs wkly. ■ John A. Moser, sls dir.

Beloit

*WBCR-FM—Nov 30, 1965: 90.3 mhz; 100 w. Ant 44 ft. TL: N42 30 13 W89 01 55 (CP: 130 w). Beloit College (53511). (608) 363-2409. Licensee: Beloit College. Format: Educ, div. ■ Ali Cohen, gen mgr; Andrew Kaiser, mus dir & news dir.

WBEL(AM)—(South Beloit, Ill.) May 18, 1948: 1380 khz; 5 kw-U, DA-N. TL: N42 27 34 W89 01 43. Stereo. Hrs opn: 24. Box 27, Beloit, WI (53511); 4570 Rockton Rd., Roscoe, IL (61073). (608) 365-6641. FAX: (608) 365-6160. Licensee: WBEL Inc. Group owner: Salter Broadcasting Co. of Delaware (acq 5-18-48). Net: CNN. Rep: Katz & Powell. Format: Adult contemp. News progmg 40 hrs wkly. Target aud: 25 plus. ■ John G. Weitzel, pres & gen mgr; Patty Rinehart, gen sls mgr; Rick West, progmg dir; Tom Tinker, mus dir; Steve Benton, news dir; Chuck Ingle, chief engr. ■ Rates: $25; 22; 25; 19.

WGEZ(AM)—Sept 26, 1948: 1490 khz; 1 kw-U. TL: N42 29 45 W89 01 03. Box 416, 622 Public Ave. (53511). (608) 365-8865. Licensee: Great Radio Broadcasting Inc. (acq 2-1-91; $300,000; FTR 9-17-91). Net: CBS. Format: Oldies. News staff one. Target aud: 25-54; baby boomers. ■ Steve Walrath, pres & gen mgr; Lois Keitch, stn mgr; Chuck Riley, progmg dir & mus dir; Jean Whitcomb, news dir. ■ Rates: $18; 15; 18; 15.

Berlin

WISS(AM)—June 28, 1971: 1090 khz; 500 w-D. TL: N43 56 55 W88 59 09. Box 5, 112 N. Pearl St. (54923). (414) 361-3551; (414) 294-3200. FAX: (414) 361-3737. Licensee: Kingsley H. Murphy Jr. Net: UPI. Format: C&W, farm. News staff one; news progmg 10 hrs wkly. Target aud: 25-54. Spec prog: Oldies 2 hrs wkly. ■ Kingsley H. Murphy Jr., pres; Steven W. Handrich, gen mgr & gen sls mgr; Martin Jury, progmg dir & mus dir; Bob Kilday, news dir; Arthur Lund, chief engr. ■ Rates: $12.50; 10.35; 12.50; 10.35.

WISS-FM—July 31, 1972: 102.3 mhz; 4.5 kw. Ant 155 ft. TL: N43 56 55 W88 59 09. Hrs opn: 24. Dups AM 100%. ■ Martin Jury, news dir. ■ Rates: Same as AM.

Birnamwood

WHET(FM)—Not on air, target date unknown: 92.9 mhz; 6 kw. Ant 100 ft. 1296 Marian Ln., Green Bay (54304). Licensee: Pacer Radio of Mid-Wisconsin.

Black River Falls

WWIS(AM)—Aug 23, 1958: 1260 khz; 1 kw-D. TL: N44 16 39 W90 50 29. Hrs opn: 6 AM- sunset. R.R. 1, Box 279A, Towne Creek Rd. (54615). (715) 284-4391. FAX: (715) 284-9740. Licensee: WWIS Radio Inc. Group owner: Bob Smith Stns. (acq 5-1-68). Net: CBS. Wash atty: Miller & Fields. Format: Adult contemp, country. News staff one. Target aud: General. ■ Robert E. Smith, pres; Nelson Lent, vp & gen mgr; Dick Deno, gen sls mgr; Brian Brauner, mus dir. ■ Rates: $10.50; 10.50; 10.50; na.

WWIS-FM—Jan 21, 1991: 99.7 mhz; 25 kw. Ant 328 ft. TL: N44 19 11 W90 53 31. Stereo. Hrs opn: 5 AM-11 PM. Dups AM 80%. News staff one; news progmg 12 hrs wkly. ■ Lori Wyss, gen sls mgr. ■ Rates: $10.50; 10.50; 10.50; 8.50.

Bloomer

WQRB(FM)—Not on air, target date unknown: 95.1 mhz; 14.7 kw. Ant 430 ft. TL: N45 01 59 W91 21 09. 5001 W. 80th St., Bloomington MN (55437). (715) 235-2112. Licensee: Bloomer Broadcasting Co. Inc. (group owner; acq 4-8-92; $81,311 for CP; FTR 4-27-92). Format: Hot Country. ■ Linda Kuster (asst), gen mgr.

Brillion

WEZR(FM)—March 1993: 107.5 mhz; 6 kw. Ant 328 ft. TL: N44 15 28 W88 11 43 (CP: 25 kw). Hrs opn: 24. Box 1075, Green Bay (54305-1075). (414) 687-1075. FAX: (414) 687-0710. Licensee: Brillion Radio Co. Group owner: Pacer Radio Packerland Inc. Rep: Katz & Powell. Format: Soft adult contemp. Target aud: 25-64. ■ Lyle R. Evans, pres & chief engr; Philip J. Robbins, gen mgr; Mark Mueller, progmg dir & mus dir.

Brookfield

WLJU(FM)—Not on air, target date unknown: 106.9 mhz; 3 kw. Ant 154 ft. TL: N43 07 41 W88 05 36. Licensee: Tran Broadcasting Corp. Inc.

Brule

*WHSA(FM)—Sept 14, 1952: 89.9 mhz; 38 kw. Ant 550 ft. TL: N46 27 59 W91 33 56. 1800 Grand Ave., Superior (54880). (715) 394-8531. FAX: (715) 394-8404. Licensee: State of Wis. Educational Communications Board. Format: Class, talk. ■ John Munson, stn mgr; Jill Schore, dev mgr; Mike Simonson, news dir; Jim Wardman, chief engr.

Burlington

*WBSD(FM)—Apr 7, 1975: 89.1 mhz; 300 w. Ant 107 ft. TL: N42 40 14 W88 16 18. Stereo. 225 Robert St. (53105). (414) 763-0195. FAX: (414) 763-0195. Licensee: Burlington Area School District. Format: Alternative/progsv rock. News progmg one hr wkly. Target aud: 16-34. Spec prog: Jazz 6 hrs, reggae 3 hrs, punk 2 hrs, metal 3 hrs, blues 3 hrs, country 4 hrs wkly. ■ Terry Havel, gen mgr & mus dir; Jeremy Kuzniar, opns dir; Vince Caracci, prom dir; Bill Greeter, progmg dir; Dale Marson, chief engr.

Chetek

*WVXD(FM)—Not on air, target date unknown: 106.7 mhz; 50 kw. TL: N45 13 12 W91 40 56. Box 366 (54728). Licensee: Lakeshore Communications.

Chilton

WMBE(AM)—May 25, 1984: 1530 khz; 250 w-D. TL: N44 01 10 W88 09 32. Hrs opn: Sunrise-sunset. Box 30, 205 E. Grand, (53014). (414) 849-7186. FAX: (414) 849-8454. Licensee: Maszka-Pacer Radio Inc. (acq 12-28-90; $4,469; FTR 1-14-91). Net: USA. Format: Polka, oldies, classic rock. News progmg 11 hrs wkly. Target aud: 35 plus. ■ Lyle Evans, gen mgr & engrg dir; James Choudoir, stn mgr, gen sls mgr & progmg mgr. ■ Rates: $8.60; 7.65; 8.00; na.

Chippewa Falls

WAXX(FM)—See Eau Claire.

WAYY(AM)—Sept 7, 1958: 1150 khz; 5 kw-D. TL: N45 53 05 W91 23 25. Box 6000, 944 Harlem Ave., Altoona (54720). (715) 832-1530. FAX: (715) 832-5329. Licensee: Central Communications (acq 8-1-84). Net: ABC/I. Rep: Torbet, Hyett/Ramsland. Format: News/talk. News staff 6. Target aud: 25-54; general. ■ David L. Nelson, pres; Keith Jones, gen mgr; Marty Green, stn mgr, natl sls mgr, rgnl sls mgr & prom mgr; Brian Ketz, opns dir; Keith Edwards, news dir; Dick Lasiuk, chief engr.

WCFW(FM)—Oct 20, 1968: 105.5 mhz; 3 kw. Ant 300 ft. TL: N44 52 18 W91 17 11. Stereo. Hrs opn: 5:30 AM-midnight. 1034 1/2 Warren St. (54729). (715) 723-2257. FAX: (715) 723-8276. Licensee: Roland L. Bushland dba Bushland Radio/WCFW. Net: AP. Format: MOR, polka. News progmg 8 hrs wkly. Target aud: 35 plus; upscale. Spec prog: Relg 2 hrs wkly. ■ Roland L. Bushland, gen mgr; Patricia Bushland, gen sls mgr & progmg dir. ■ Rates: $15; 10; 15; 10.

Cleveland

WKTT(FM)—Apr 25, 1985: 103.1 mhz; 3 kw. Ant 327 ft. TL: N43 59 11 W87 45 53. Stereo. Hrs opn: 24. Box 26, One Washington Sq. (53015). (414) 693-3103; (414) 726-4477. FAX: (414) 693-3104. Licensee: Tri-County Radio Inc. (acq 3-5-93; $431,000; FTR 3-15-93). Net: SMN; Wis. Radio Net. Wash atty: James Oyster. Format: C&W. News progmg 7 hrs wkly. Target aud: General. Spec prog: Farm 6 hrs wkly. ■ Charles P. Mills, pres; Don Sabatke, gen mgr, gen sls mgr & prom mgr; Kim Hansen, sls dir; Neal Allen, progmg dir; Ken Sweet, chief engr. ■ Rates: $19; 19; 19; 8.

Clintonville

WFCL(AM)—Feb 28, 1983: 1380 khz; 5 kw-D, 2.5 kw-N, DA-2. TL: N44 34 00 W88 44 36. Box 269, 33 E. 3rd St. (54929). (715) 823-5128. FAX: (715) 823-1367. Licensee: Sail Communication Corp. (acq 5-1-86). Net: SMN. Wash atty: Miller & Miller P.L. Format: Adult contemp. News staff one; news progmg 15 hrs wkly. Target aud: 25-54. Spec prog: Farm 8 hrs wkly. ■ E. James Verkest, pres & gen mgr; Mary E. Verkest, opns mgr; Tammy Paul, gen sls mgr; Doug Rogers, prom mgr, progmg dir & mus dir; Stevie West, asst mus dir; Grace Kirchner, news dir; Bob Gorjance, chief engr. ■ Rates: $12; 9; 9; 6.

WJMQ(FM)—Co-owned with WFCL(AM). Oct 27, 1986: 92.3 mhz; 6 kw. Ant 328 ft. TL: N44 34 00 W88 44 36. Stereo. Hrs opn: 24. Prog sep from AM. Format: Country. ■ Rates: Same as AM.

Columbus

WYKY(FM)—July 16, 1990: 100.5 mhz; 6 kw. Ant 328 ft. TL: N43 24 19 W89 06 24. Stereo. Hrs opn: 5 AM-midnight. Box 297 (53925). (414) 885-4949. FAX: (414) 885-2152. Licensee: Beaver Dam Broadcasting Co. Inc. Group owner: McNaughton Stns. (acq 9-28-90; $5,000; FTR 10-15-90). Net: SMN. Wash atty: Leonard S. Joyce. Format: Adult contemp. News staff one; news progmg 8 hrs wkly. Target aud: 25-50. ■ W. John Klinger, pres &

Wisconsin Directory of Radio

gen mgr; John A. Moser, gen sls mgr; Frank Beres, progmg dir; Steve Sabatke, news dir; Jim Stowell, pub affrs dir; Warren Jorgensen, chief engr.

De Pere

WJLW(FM)—Licensed to De Pere. See Green Bay.

Delafield

***WHAD(FM)**—May 30, 1948: 90.7 mhz; 79 kw. Ant 700 ft. TL: N43 01 56 W88 23 31. Suite 1060, 111 E. Kilbourn Ave., Milwaukee (53202). (414) 271-8686. FAX: (414) 271-4170. Licensee: State of Wis. Educational Communications Board. Format: Public radio. ■ Bill Estes, stn mgr; Shavonn Montgomery, gen sls mgr; Chuck Quirmbach, news dir.

Dodgeville

WDMP(AM)—Nov 1, 1968: 810 khz; 250 w-D. TL: N42 55 10 W90 08 06. Box 58, Hwy. 151 S. (53533). (608) 935-2302. FAX: (608) 935-3464. Licensee: Dodge-Point Broadcasting Co. Net: ABC/D. Format: Country. News staff one; news progmg 10 hrs wkly. Target aud: General. ■ Louise E. Hamlin, pres; Kurt Reinicke, gen mgr, gen sls mgr & progmg dir; Brent Sims, mus dir; Robert Brainerd, news dir. ■ Rates: $11.05; 11.05; 11.05; na.

WDMP-FM—Nov 1, 1968: 99.3 mhz; 1.1 kw. Ant 460 ft. TL: N42 55 10 W90 08 06. Stereo. Net: ABC/D. Format: Country. News staff one; news progmg 10 hrs wkly. ■ Rates: Same as AM.

Durand

WRDN(AM)—Nov 21, 1968: 1430 khz; 2 kw-D, 107 w-N. TL: N44 38 28 W91 55 22. Hrs opn: 18. Box 208, 200 3rd Ave. W. (54736). (715) 672-8989. FAX: (715) 672-4622. Licensee: The FM Radio Net. Inc. (acq 3-9-87). Net: MBS. Format: Country, farm. News staff one: news progmg 16 hrs wkly. Target aud: 25-54; people with families. Spec prog: Polka & old time music 9 hrs wkly. ■ Gene Kirchner, pres & gen mgr; Ellen Kirchner, exec vp; Bill Kuehne, gen sls mgr; Emily Kirchner, prom mgr; Kevin Allar, progmg dir, mus dir & news dir; Jon Zecherle, chief engr. ■ Rates: $12; 12; 12; 12.

WRDN-FM—Oct 24, 1973: 95.9 mhz; 9.3 kw. Ant 600 ft. TL: N44 35 07 W91 54 44. Stereo. Prog sep from AM. Net: Goetz Group. Format: News/talk, sports, country. ■ Gene Kirchner, CEO; Ellen Kirchner, stn mgr; Kevin Aller, opns mgr; Mary Trettin, prom mgr. ■ Rates: Same as AM.

Eagle River

WERL(AM)—May 23, 1961: 950 khz; 1 kw-D, 51 w-N. TL: N45 58 38 W89 14 52. Stereo. Box 309, 2477 Hwy. 45 N. (54521). (715) 479-4451. FAX: (715) 479-6511. Licensee: Nicolet Broadcasting Inc. (group owner; acq 9-3-93; with co-located FM; FTR 9-27-93). Net: SMN. Format: Adult contemp, big band, MOR. News staff one; news progmg 7 hrs wkly. Target aud: General. ■ Mary Jo Berner, pres & gen mgr; Michael Krein, opns mgr & chief engr. ■ Rates: $13.50; 13.50; 13.50; 13.50.

WRJO(FM)—Co-owned with WERL(AM). July 31, 1971: 94.5 mhz; 50 kw. Ant 492 ft. TL: N45 58 38 W89 14 52. Stereo. Hrs opn: 24. Prog sep from AM. Format: C&W. Target aud: 20 plus. ■ Rates: $15; 15; 15; 15.

Eau Claire

WAXX(FM)—February 1965: 104.5 mhz; 100 kw. Ant 1,830 ft. TL: N44 39 51 W90 57 41. Stereo. Hrs opn: 24. Box 6000 (54702); 944 Harlem, Altoona (54720). (715) 832-1530. FAX: (715) 832-5329. Licensee: Central Communications Inc. (acq 8-1-84). Net: ABC/I. Rep: Torbet, Hyett/Ramsland. Format: Country. News staff 3. Target aud: 25-54; metro & rgnl adults. Spec prog: Farm 15 hrs wkly. ■ David Nelson, pres; Keith Jones, exec vp & gen mgr; George Roberts, stn mgr & sls dir; George House, opns mgr & progmg dir; Marty Green, natl sls mgr & rgnl sls mgr; John Murphy, prom mgr; Tim Wilson, mus dir; Keith Edwards, news dir; Dick Lasiuk, chief engr.

WBIZ(AM)—Nov 11, 1947: 1400 khz; 1 kw-U. TL: N44 48 48 W91 31 15. Box 24, 619 Cameron St. (54702). (715) 835-1007. FAX: (715) 835-9680. Licensee: Americus Communications Corp. (group owner; acq 4-22-88). Rep: Katz. Wash atty: Kaye, Scholer, Fierman, Hays & Handler. Format: Sports talk. Target aud: 25-54. ■ Richard L. Muzzy, pres & gen mgr; Al Leitl, gen sls mgr; Karen Peterson, prom mgr; Darren Lee, progmg mgr; Mike Sullivan, news dir; Jim Zastrow, chief engr.

WBIZ-FM—December 1967: 100.7 mhz; 100 kw. Ant 740 ft. TL: N44 47 58 W91 27 59. Stereo. Prog sep from AM. Format: Adult CHR. News staff one. ■ Jackie Johnson, mus dir.

WEAQ(AM)—May 1937: 790 khz; 5 kw-U, DA-N. TL: N44 49 51 W91 26 58. Hrs opn: 24. Box 1 (54702-0001). (715) 832-3463. Licensee: Broadcaster Services Inc. (acq 11-1-59). Net: CNN, Unistar. Format: MOR. ■ Steve Dickoff, pres & gen mgr; Rick Roberts, opns mgr, progmg dir & mus dir; Steve Potter, gen sls mgr; Dan Ropa, news dir; Bill Holden, chief engr.

WIAL(FM)—Co-owned with WEAQ(AM). 1948: 94.1 mhz; 85 kw. Ant 350 ft. TL: N44 49 48 W91 26 48. Stereo. Prog sep from AM. Net: CNN, Unistar. Format: Adult contemp.

WEIO(AM)—Apr 1948: 1050 khz; 1 kw-D, 500 w-N. TL: N44 46 36 W91 28 30. Stereo. 1819 Mitchell St. (54701). (715) 836-9476. Licensee: Alpen Glow Communications Inc. (acq 9-1-91; $395,000; FTR 10-28-85). Net: SMN. Rep: Katz & Powell. Format: Children. Target aud: 2-9; children. ■ Cliff Somers, pres; Dave Barrett, CFO, vp & gen mgr; Judi Balter, opns mgr; Dewey Brott, gen sls mgr; Martin Meldahl, prom dir; Jeff Stevens, progmg dir; Phil Conrad, asst mus dir; Jon Zecherle, chief engr. ■ Rates: $15; 15; 15; 15.

***WHEM(FM)**—Not on air, target date unknown: 91.3 mhz; 550 w. Ant 217 ft. TL: N44 47 38 W91 31 22. 3319 W. Beltline Pkwy., Madison (53713). Licensee: Fourth Dimension Inc. (acq 7-2-93; $2,810; FTR 8-2-93).

WIAL(FM)—Listing follows WEAQ(AM).

***WUEC(FM)**—Oct 27, 1975: 89.7 mhz; 740 w. Ant 630 ft. TL: N44 47 58 W91 27 59. Stereo. Fine Arts Ctr., Univ. of Wisconsin-Eau Claire (54701). (715) 836-4170; (715) 836-2300. Licensee: Board of Regents, Univ. of Wisconsin. Net: NPR; Wis. Pub. Format: Class, progsv, news. News progmg 24 hrs wkly. Target aud: General. ■ Dr. Robert L. Bailey, gen mgr; Pat Cleary, prom dir; Richard Gengenbach, progmg dir; Joe Jachimiec, mus dir; Millie Matlock, asst mus dir; Jeff Margrett, news dir; Jonathon Webb, pub affrs dir; Ron Viste, chief engr.

Elk Mound

WECL(FM)—Jan 24, 1991: 92.9 mhz; 3.3 kw. Ant 446 ft. TL: N44 53 40 W91 35 40. Stereo. Hrs opn: 24. 5149-D Old Mill Plaza, Eau Claire (54703). (715) 876-6464. FAX: (715) 876-6465. Licensee: Super Star Communications Inc. Net: Unistar. Wash atty: McFadden, Evans & Sill. Format: Lite adult contemp. Target aud: 31-51. ■ Emalee C. Payne, pres & gen mgr; C. Reed Macknick, gen sls mgr; Jim Zons, prom mgr, progmg dir & mus dir; Jim Zastrow, chief engr.

Evansville

WMJB(FM)—Aug 17, 1989: 105.9 mhz; 1.4 kw. Ant 493 ft. TL: N42 43 38 W89 15 02. Stereo. Hrs opn: 24. One Parker Pl., Janesville (53545); 430 E. Grand, Beloit (53511). (608) 757-1059. FAX: (608) 757-2838. Licensee: Capital Radio Services Inc. Group owner: Capital Radio Holdings Inc. (acq 10-13-89; $77,000; FTR 10-30-89). Rep: Katz & Powell. Wash atty: Verner, Lipfert, Bernhard, McPherson & Hand. Format: Classic rock. News staff one; news progmg 3 hrs wkly. Target aud: 25-54. ■ Carl Hurlebaus, pres; Gary Probst, gen mgr.

Fond du Lac

KFIZ(AM)—July 6, 1922: 1450 khz; 1 kw-U. TL: N43 47 28 W88 28 16. Stereo. Box 1450 (54936-1450); 107 W. Scott (54935). (414) 921-1071. FAX: (414) 921-0757. Licensee: Lakeside Cablevision L.P. (acq 1993; $3.5 million with co-located FM; FTR 9-13-93). Net: MBS, AP. Rep: Banner. Wash atty: Latham & Watkins. Format: MOR, sports/information. News staff 2. Target aud: 35-64. Spec prog: Farm 10 hrs wkly. ■ Donald Jones, CEO; Wally Ranck, gen mgr; Thomas Biolo, gen sls mgr; Scott Bonn, prom mgr; Terry Davis, progmg dir; Greg Stensland, news dir; Ray Yorton, chief engr. ■ Rates: $45; 35; 45; 25.

KFIZ-FM—Oct 5, 1967: 107.1 mhz; 3 kw. Ant 312 ft. TL: N43 50 22 W88 22 06. Stereo. Prog sep from AM. Rep: Banner. Format: Oldies. Target aud: 30-50. ■ Rates: Same as AM.

WYUR-FM—(Ripon). Feb 1, 1965: 96.1 mhz; 3 kw. Ant 403 ft. TL: N43 49 10 W88 43 20. Stereo. Hrs opn: 24. 30 S. Portland, Fond du Lac (54935). FAX: (414) 929-9600. Format: Adult contemp. News staff one; news progmg 3 hrs wkly. Target aud: 25-54; women. ■ Art Beaulieu, opns dir & engrg dir; Jack McDevitt, sls dir; Stan Stricker, mus dir. ■ Rates: $18; 13; 15; 10.

Fort Atkinson

WFAW(AM)—Jan 24, 1963: 940 khz; 500 w-D, 550 w-N, DA-2. TL: N42 54 24 W88 45 06. Box 94 (53538); W. 6355 Eastern Ave. (53538). (414) 563-6351. FAX: (414) 563-0315. Licensee: Goetz Broadcasting Corp. (group owner). Net: ABC/I. Wash atty: Miller & Miller. Format: Oldies. ■ Nathan L. Goetz, pres; Scott M. Trentadue, vp, gen mgr, vp sls & vp mktg; Gary Moen, stn mgr & progmg dir; Jim V. Riezen, rgnl sls mgr; Casey James, mus dir; Tom Pattison, news dir; Clif Groth, vp engrg & chief engr. ■ Rates: $12.40; 12.40; 12.40; 12.40.

WSJY(FM)—Co-owned with WFAW(AM). Sept 4, 1959: 107.3 mhz; 50 kw. Ant 499 ft. TL: N42 50 48 W88 51 16. Stereo. Prog sep from AM. Format: Easy listing/lite. ■ Rates: $23.50; 23.50; 23.50; 23.50.

Goodman

***WGAZ(FM)**—Not on air, target date unknown: 91.3 mhz; 422 w-V. Ant 118 ft. Box 160 (54125). Licensee: School District of Goodman-Armstrong Creek.

Green Bay

WAPL-FM—See Appleton.

WDUZ(AM)—June 19, 1947: 1400 khz; 1 kw-U. TL: N44 29 36 W87 59 13. Stereo. Hrs opn: 24. Box 310, 810 Victoria St. (54305). (414) 468-4100. FAX: (414) 468-0250. Licensee: Green Bay Broadcasting Co. (group owner). Net: ABC/E, CBS, MBS. Rep: McGavren Guild. Format: Adult contemp, news. News staff 3. Target aud: 35-64. ■ William C. Laird, pres; Michael D. Watts, stn mgr; Mike Peot, gen sls mgr; Jon Stubb, prom dir; Gary Evans, progmg dir & mus dir; Rick Cohler, news dir; Doug Moore, chief engr.

WQLH(FM)—Co-owned with WDUZ(AM). July 1, 1967: 98.5 mhz; 100 kw. Ant 1,254 ft. TL: N44 38 41 W88 08 13. Stereo. Prog sep from AM. Net: ABC/E. Format: AC/light hits. ■ Michael Watts, stn mgr; Mike Peot, sls dir; Kathy Larkin, prom dir; Andy Nelson, progmg dir; Jim Taylor, mus dir; Rick Cohler, news dir.

***WGBW(FM)**—Aug 26, 1974: 91.5 mhz; 710 w. Ant 741 ft. TL: N44 21 32 W87 59 07. Stereo. Hrs opn: 5 AM-midnight. 2420 Nicolet Dr. (54311-7001). (414) 465-2444. FAX: (414) 465-2576. Licensee: Univ. of Wisconsin System. Net: NPR, APR; Wis. Pub. Wash atty: Dow, Lohnes & Albertson. Format: Talk. News staff 2; news progmg 18 hrs wkly. Target aud: 40 plus; educated, socially active. Spec prog: Sp one hr, Hmong one hr wkly. ■ Glen Slaats, gen mgr; Ellen Clark, Rick Reyer, dev mgrs; Perry Irwin, news dir; Quinn Klinefelter, pub affrs dir; Al Rieland, Bruce Herzog, chiefs engr.

WGEE(AM)—Apr 6, 1925: 1360 khz; 5 kw-U, DA-N. TL: N44 25 51 W88 04 51. Stereo. Box 23333, 115 S. Jefferson St. (54301). (414) 435-3771. FAX: (414) 455-1155. Licensee: Midwest Communications Inc. (group owner; acq 1975). Net: ABC/D. Rep: Banner. Wash atty: Miller & Miller. Format: Country. Spec prog: Farm 5 hrs wkly. ■ D.E. Wright, pres & gen mgr; Jeff McCarthy, vp; Dennis Quinn, gen sls mgr; Randy Allen, prom mgr & mus dir; Mike Austin, progmg dir; Mark Daniels, news dir; Tim Laes, chief engr.

WIXX(FM)—Co-owned with WGEE(AM). Nov 1, 1960: 101.1 mhz; 100 kw. Ant 1,080 ft. TL: N44 24 35 W88 00 05. Stereo. Format: CHR. ■ Marlynn Krinsky, gen sls mgr; David Burns, prom mgr; Jeff McCarthy, vp progmg; Dan Stone, progmg dir; Kevin Ross, mus dir; Kathi Hall, news dir.

WJLW(FM)—(De Pere). Oct 1, 1984: 95.9 mhz; 25 kw. Ant 308 ft. TL: N44 29 03 W87 56 12 (CP: Ant 272 ft., TL: N44 23 20 W88 01 54). Stereo. Hrs opn: 24. 133 N. Superior St., De Pere-Green Bay (54115). (414) 336-3696. FAX: (414) 336-9685. Licensee: American Communications Co. Net: MBS. Rep: Katz & Powell. Wash atty: Smithwick & Belendiuk. Format: Contemp country. News staff one; news progmg 18 hrs wkly. Target aud: 25-64; mix between 18-49 & 25-64. Spec prog: Early AM farm, pub affrs talk show one hr wkly. ■ Jack Le Duc, pres, gen mgr & gen sls mgr; Bruce Herzog, chief engr. ■ Rates: $35; 35; 35; 15.

WNFL(AM)—Dec 12, 1947: 1440 khz; 5 kw-D, 1 kw-N, DA-2. TL: N44 28 40 W88 00 00. Hrs opn: 24. Box 11907, 1440 Bellevue St. (54307). (414) 468-5445. FAX: (414) 468-7911. Licensee: Green Bay Radio Inc. (acq 11-1-93). Net: NBC Talknet, ABC, CBS, Daynet, MBS. Rep: Christal. Wash atty: Cohn & Marks. Format: News/talk. News staff 3; news progmg 100 hrs wkly. Target aud: 35-64; people in upper-income level with above average education. Spec prog: Sports 15 hrs wkly. ■ Jim Gregori, pres; Hank Zegers, gen mgr; Terry Dugan, opns mgr &

prom mgr; Buck Hein, gen sls mgr; Jay Davis, progmg dir; Terry Charles, news dir; Pat Berger, chief engr.

***WORQ(FM)**—Jan 20, 1993: 90.1 mhz; 6 kw. Ant 289 ft. TL: N44 29 03 W87 56 12. 1075 Brookwood (54304). (414) 494-9010. Licensee: Lakeshore Communications Inc. Format: Christian rock. ■ Rick Sewell, gen mgr; Jim Raider, progmg dir.

***WPNE-FM**—Jan 15, 1973: 89.3 mhz; 100 kw. Ant 940 ft. TL: N44 24 35 W88 00 05. 2420 Nickolt Dr. (54311). (414) 465-2664. FAX: (414) 465-2576. Licensee: State of Wisconsin Educational Communications Board. Format: Class. ■ Glenn Slaats, gen mgr; Ellen Clark, dev dir; Perry Irwin, news dir.

WQLH(FM)—Listing follows WDUZ(AM).

Greenfield

WMCS(AM)—Licensed to Greenfield. See Milwaukee.

Hallie

WOGO(AM)—June 1985: 680 khz; 2.5 kw-D, 500 w-N, DA-2. TL: N44 53 22 W91 23 03. Stereo. Hrs opn: 19. 5558 Hallie Rd., Chippewa Falls (54729). (715) 723-4626. FAX: (715) 723-1348. Licensee: Stewards of Sound Inc. (acq 10-29-93; with WWIB-FM Ladysmith; FTR 11-15-93). Net: BRN, AP. Wash atty: Peter Tannenwald. Format: Southern gospel. News staff one; news progmg 16 hrs wkly. Target aud: 25-54. Spec prog: Sports. ■ Mabel Louise Steward, pres; Terry Steward, gen mgr; Greg Smith, gen sls mgr; Greg Steward, progmg dir; Mark Halverson, news dir; Patrick Wahl, chief engr.

Hartford

WTKM(AM)—1951: 1540 khz: 500 w-D. TL: N43 16 48 W88 23 02. Box 216, 27 N. Main St. (53027). (414) 673-3550; (414) 252-4567. FAX: (414) 673-5472. Licensee: The Kettle Moraine Broadcasting Co. (acq 3-12-90; grpsl; FTR 4-2-90). Net: Central Ag. News Net. Rep: Farmakis. Format: Polka, country. News staff one; news progmg 20 hrs wkly. Target aud: 35 plus. Spec prog: Farm 15 hrs, Ger 15 hrs, Pol one hr, talk 15 hrs, relg 6 hrs wkly. ■ Scott Lopas, pres, gen mgr & stn mgr; Dick Feutz, opns mgr & chief engr; Ron Krauss, gen sls mgr; Michelle Baertlein, prom mgr; Carl Hulbert Jr., progmg dir, mus dir & news dir. ■ Rates: $16; 16; 16; 16.

WTKM-FM—Oct 1, 1973: 104.9 mhz; 5.8 kw. Ant 300 ft. TL: N43 16 48 W88 23 02. Stereo. Hrs opn: 24. Dups AM 100%. Spec prog: Ger 3 hrs wkly. ■ Rates: Same as AM.

Hayward

WHSM(AM)—Dec 21, 1957: 910 khz; 5 kw-D, 75 w-N. TL: N45 59 07 W91 32 21. Stereo. Rt. 8, Box 8277 (54843). (715) 634-4836; (800) 200-WHSM. FAX: (715) 634-8256. Licensee: Arlie L. Davison & Associates Inc. (acq 4-24-91; $20,000; FTR 5-13-91). Format: Adult contemp. Target aud: General. Spec prog: Big band 2 hrs wkly. ■ Arlie L. Davison, pres & gen mgr; Bobi Hopp, stn mgr; Laura Rusk, sls dir; Arlie Davison, progmg dir; Darcy Haime, mus dir; Brent Christenson, chief engr.

WHSM-FM—June 21, 1980: 101.7 mhz; 1.45 kw. Ant 466 ft. TL: N45 59 07 W91 32 21. Stereo. Dups AM 100%.

WRLS-FM—Apr 16, 1968: 92.3 mhz; 6 kw. Ant 321 ft. TL: N46 01 17 W91 30 41. Stereo. Box 1008 (54843). (715) 634-4871. Licensee: Vacationland Broadcasting Inc. (acq 12-9-92; FTR 1-4-93). Net: AP. Format: Adult contemp. News staff one; news progmg 26 hrs wkly. Target aud: 25 plus; general. ■ Tom Koser, pres; Robert Koser, vp; Charles Kowalski, gen mgr; Robert Hague, opns dir & news dir; Gary Hessel, progmg dir. ■ Rates: $10; 8; 10; 8.

Highland

***WHHI(FM)**—Sept 14, 1952: 91.3 mhz; 100 kw. Ant 560 ft. TL: N43 02 58 W90 22 00. 821 Univ. Ave., Madison (53706-1496). (608) 264-9600. FAX: (608) 273-9763. Licensee: State of Wis. Educational Communications Board. Format: Educ, classical, talk. ■ Jack Mitchell, gen mgr; Greg Schnirring, progmg dir; Norman Gilliand, mus dir; Joy Cardin, news dir.

Holmen

WKBH(AM)—July 28, 1984: 1570 khz; 1 kw-D, 500 w-N. TL: N43 55 32 W91 16 02. Hrs opn: 24. Box 1624, 510 Holmen Sq., La Crosse (54602-1624). (608) 784-9524. FAX: (608) 526-6813. Licensee: Riverview Communications Inc. (acq 8-20-91; FTR 6-12-89). Net: SMN, CNN. Wash atty: Smithwick & Belendiuk. Format: Traditional country. News staff one; news progmg 35 hrs wkly. Target aud: 40 plus. ■ Joe Roskos, pres; Tim Scott, stn mgr, progmg dir & mus dir; Madelyn Grabowenski, opns mgr; Jim Timm, gen sls mgr; Pat Delaney, chief engr.

Hudson

WMIN(AM)—Dec 14, 1983: 740 khz; 500 w-D, 8 w-N, DA-2. TL: N44 58 05 W92 40 01. Hrs opn: 6 AM-7 PM. 615 1/2 Second St. (54016). (612) 739-4433. Licensee: Borgen Broadcasting Corp. (acq 12-11-89; $300,000; FTR 1-1-90). Format: Original hits. Target aud: 25-54. ■ Greg Borgen, pres.

Hurley

WHRY(AM)—Mar 1, 1985: 1450 khz; 1 kw-U. TL: N46 24 56 W90 09 34. Box 1450 (54534); 813 E. Cloverland Dr., Ironwood (49938). (906) 932-5234. Licensee: Big G Little O Inc. Format: Oldies 50s, 60s & 70s. ■ Charles H. Gervasio, pres & gen mgr; Jane Waitanek, stn mgr; Greg Daniels, progmg dir.

Jackson

WYLO(AM)—May 1, 1964: 540 khz; 400 w-U, DA-2. TL: N43 20 00 W88 09 11. Stereo. Hrs opn: 24. 3540 D. N. 126th St., Brookfield (53005). (414) 783-2650; (414) 783-2655. FAX: (414) 783-2640. Licensee: Jim Runsdorf, liquidating agent. Group owner: Children's Broadcasting Corp. Wash atty: Lance Riley. Format: Adult contemp Christian, ethnic. News progmg 6 hrs wkly. Target aud: 25-54; adult Christians. Spec prog: Black 8 hrs, Ger 6 hrs, Pol 2 hrs, Serbian one hr, Croatian 2 hrs wkly. ■ Christopher T. Dahl, CEO; Marion Luther, gen mgr & gen sls mgr; Frank Colbourn, progmg dir & mus dir; Bob Bradley, news dir; Jack McLeland, chief engr. ■ Rates: $24; 24; 24; 24.

Janesville

WCLO(AM)—July 1930: 1230 khz; 1 kw-U. TL: N42 39 35 W89 02 32. One S. Parker Dr. (53545). (608) 752-7895. FAX: (608) 752-4438. Licensee: Southern Wis. Radio Inc. Group owner: Gazette Broadcast Co. Net: AP, NBC Talknet. Wash atty: Dow, Lohnes & Albertson. Format: MOR, news/talk. News staff 3; news progmg 15 hrs wkly. Target aud: General. ■ Marshall W. Johnston, chmn; Sidney H. Bliss, pres; Robert Dailey, vp & gen mgr; Mike O'Brien, gen sls mgr; Robert Scheid, news dir; Chuck Flynn, chief engr. ■ Rates: $30; 27; 30; 10.

WJVL(FM)—Co-owned with WCLO(AM). October 1947: 99.9 mhz; 11 kw. Ant 502 ft. TL: N42 43 47 W89 10 10. Stereo. Prog sep from AM. Format: C&W.

WSJY(FM)—See Fort Atkinson.

Kaukauna

WKFX(FM)—Sept 1, 1969: 104.9 mhz; 3 kw. Ant 480 ft. TL: N44 15 28 W88 11 43. Stereo. Hrs opn: 24. Box 11907, 1440 Bellevue St., Green Bay (54307). (414) 468-5445. Licensee: Green Bay Radio Inc. (acq 11/1/93). Rep: Christal. Wash atty: Cohn & Marks. Format: Oldies. News staff 2; news progmg 15 hrs wkly. Target aud: 25-54; adults. ■ Jim Gregori, pres; Hank Zegers, stn mgr; Terry Dugan, opns mgr & prom dir; Buck Hein, gen sls mgr; Jay Davis, progmg dir; Terry Charles, news dir; Pat Burger, chief engr. ■ Rates: $25; 25; 25; 15.

WSGC(AM)—Sept 25, 1965: 1050 khz; 1 kw-D, 500 w-N, DA-2. TL: N44 14 51 W88 18 00. Hrs opn: 24. 1909 W. Second St. (54914). (414) 731-6309. FAX: (414) 749-0474. Licensee: Evangel Ministries Inc. (acq 7-28-93; $380,000; FTR 7-5-93). Wash atty: Leventhal, Senter & Lerman. Format: Country. Target aud: 35-54. ■ Reid Ribble, chmn; Ken Ellis, pres & gen mgr; Chuck Towns, gen sls mgr; Paul Cameron, progmg mgr; Bill Moede, chief engr. ■ Rates: $10; 10; 10; 10.

Kenosha

***WGTD(FM)**—Dec 23, 1975: 91.1 mhz; 5 kw. Ant 135 ft. TL: N42 36 28 W87 50 55. Stereo. 3520 30th Ave. (53144). (414) 656-6973; (800) 321-9483. Licensee: Gateway Vocational, Technical & Adult Educ District. Net: APR, NPR. Format: News/info, class, new age. News staff one; news progmg 64 hrs wkly. Target aud: General. Spec prog: Ger one hr wkly. ■ Frank Falduto, gen mgr; Bonnie Orr, progmg dir; Greg Berg, mus dir; Bill Guy, news dir; Terry Baun, chief engr.

WIIL(FM)—Listing follows WLIP(AM).

WLIP(AM)—May 11, 1947: 1050 khz; 250 w-U. TL: N42 33 10 W87 53 38. Hrs opn: 24. Box 659, 8500 Green Bay Rd. (53142). (414) 694-7800. Licensee: Independence Broadcasting Corp. (group owner; acq 11-87; $11,475,000; FTR 11-16-87). Net: AP, MBS; Wisconsin Radio Net. Rep: Banner. Format: Talk, news & information. News staff 4. Target aud: 35 plus. Spec prog: Milwaukee Brewers, Chicago Blackhawks, high school sports. ■ John Goodwill, pres; Edwin M. Doody, gen mgr; John O'Hearn, gen sls mgr; Kare Vernezze, prom mgr; Paul Kern, progmg dir; David Cole, news dir; Ken Keating, chief engr. ■ Rates: $32; 29; 33; 25.

WIIL(FM)—Co-owned with WLIP(AM). 1961: 95.1 mhz; 50 kw. Ant 384 ft. TL: N42 33 10 W87 53 38. Stereo. Prog sep from AM. Rep: Banner. Format: Adult classic rock. Target aud: 18-54. ■ Randy McCarten, progmg dir; Joanie Meyers, news dir; Karyn Haney, pub affrs dir; Ken Keating, engrg mgr. ■ Rates: $76; 59; 70; 34.

WNIZ-FM—See Zion, Ill.

Kewaunee

WAUN(FM)—1973: 92.7 mhz; 3 kw. Ant 300 ft. TL: N44 29 50 W87 35 12 (CP: 6 kw, ant 293 ft.). Box 219 (54216). (414) 388-4852. FAX: (414) 388-4857. Licensee: Harbor Cities Broadcasting Inc. Net: MBS. Format: Polka. News staff one; news progmg 22 hrs wkly. Target aud: 35 plus; farmers, agri-businessmen, sr citizens, rural folk. Spec prog: Ger 2 hr, Czech one hr, farm 20 hrs, relg 3 hrs wkly. ■ Steve Rugg, gen mgr; Andrew Brusda, opns mgr & chief engr; Cletus J. Bellin, progmg dir, news dir & pub affrs dir; Cletus J. Bellin, Mike Kristoff, mus dirs.

Kimberly

WHBY(AM)—Aug 21, 1970: 1150 khz; 5 kw-U, DA-2. TL: N44 08 48 W88 28 54. Stereo. Hrs opn: 24. Box 1519, 2727 E. Radio Rd. (54913). (414) 733-6639. FAX: (414) 739-0494. Licensee: Woodward Communications Inc. (group owner; acq 3-75). Net: CBS, MBS; Wis. Radio Net. Rep: Eastman. Wash atty: Bryan, Cave, McPheeters & McRoberts. Format: AC, news/talk, sports. News staff 4; news progmg 25 hrs wkly. Target aud: 35 plus; upper middle class, educated. ■ William Skemp, CEO; Susan F. Knaack, vp & gen mgr; Garrett Hart, opns mgr; Greg Bell, gen sls mgr; Sandra Schmidt, natl sls mgr; Jackie McLaren, prom dir; Bob Salm, mus dir; Ray Waiter, news dir; Steve Brown, chief engr.

La Crosse

KQEG(FM)—(La Crescent, Minn). Apr 5, 1989: 102.7 mhz; 1.85 kw. Ant 600 ft. TL: N43 48 23 W91 22 04 (CP: 3.1 kw, ant 863 ft.). Stereo. Hrs opn: 24. Suite 221, 505 King St., La Crosse, WI (54601). (608) 784-1027. Licensee: White Eagle Broadcasting Inc. Net: SMN. Rep: Katz & Powell. Wash atty: Richard Carr. Format: Oldies. News progmg 4 hrs wkly. Target aud: 25-54. ■ Eleanor St. John, pres & gen mgr; Perry J. St. John, vp opns, opns mgr, pub affrs dir & engrg dir; Richard T. Wilson, vp sls, natl sls mgr & rgnl sls mgr. ■ Rates: $35; 25; 28; 20.

***WHLA(FM)**—Nov 21, 1950: 90.3 mhz; 100 kw. Ant 1,010 ft. TL: N43 48 17 W91 22 06. 821 Univ. Ave., Madison (53705-1496). (608) 264-9600. FAX: (608) 263-9763. Licensee: State of Wis. Educational Communications Board. Format: Educ, classical, talk. ■ Greg Schnirring, progmg dir.

WIZM(AM)—Jan 2, 1923: 1410 khz; 5 kw-U, DA-N. TL: N43 50 48 W91 13 03. Hrs opn: 24. Box 99, 432 Cass St. (54602). (608) 782-1230. FAX: (608) 782-1170. Licensee: Family Radio Inc. Group owner: Mid-West Family Stations (acq 7-12-71). Net: ABC/C, NBC, Daynet, NBC Talknet, ABC TalkRadio, MBS. Rep: Christal. Wash atty: Fisher, Wayland, Southmayd & Cooper. Format: News/talk. News staff 4; news progmg 18 hrs wkly. Target aud: 35 plus. ■ Dick Record, pres, gen mgr & news dir; James R. Timm, gen sls mgr; Howard Gloede, rgnl sls mgr; Mike Hayes, prom mgr; Ron Albright, progmg dir; Skylar Thomas, pub affrs dir; Rich Egan, chief engr. ■ Rates: $28; 25; 27; 18.

WIZM-FM—1966: 93.3 mhz; 100 kw. Ant 1,000 ft. TL: N43 44 23 W91 22 04. Stereo. Hrs opn: 24. Prog sep from AM. (Acq 6-15-76). Net: ABC/C. Format: Top-40. News staff 4; news progmg 2 hrs wkly. Target aud: 18-49. ■ Tom Stryker, prom mgr; Samantha Strong, progmg dir; Kelly Wilde, mus dir. ■ Rates: $45; 41; 43; 31.

WKTY(AM)—May 1948: 580 khz; 5 kw-D, 1 kw-N, DA-2. TL: N43 44 25 W91 12 21. Hrs opn: 24. 704 La Crosse St. (54601). (608) 782-6430. FAX: (608) 782-6443. Licensee: LaCrosse May Broadcasting L.P. Group owner: May Broadcasting (acq 7-1-84; $1,675,000; FTR 4-30-84). Net: ABC/I. Rep: Katz. Format: C&W, news. News staff 2. Target aud: 25-54. Spec prog: Farm 10 hrs wkly. ■ Ed May, pres; Bryce Pringle, CFO; Steven Stach, gen mgr; Ellen Finch, gen sls mgr; Ken Koeller, progmg dir; Emil McAndrew, chief engr.

WSPL(FM)—Co-owned with WKTY(AM). January 1972: 95.7 mhz; 50 kw. Ant 410 ft. TL: N43 44 30 W91 18 14. Stereo. Hrs opn: 24. Prog sep from AM. Net: Unistar, ABC/D. Format: Adult contemp. News staff 2; news progmg 20 hrs wkly. Target aud: General. Spec prog: Gospel, farm 15 hrs, relg 4 hrs wkly.

WLFN(AM)—May 1947: 1490 khz; 1 kw-U. TL: N43 49 42 W91 14 27. Stereo. Hrs opn: 24. Box 2017 (54602-2017). Suite 400, 201 Main St. (54601). (608) 782-8335. Licensee: Broadcast Properties of Lacrosse Inc. (acq 6-90; grpsl; FTR 6-18-90). Net: CNN. Rep: Torbet. Format: Adult Standard. News staff one; news progmg 5 hrs wkly. Target aud: 35 plus. ■ Phillip T. Kelly, pres; Bob Clark, gen mgr; Tom Martens, opns mgr & progmg dir; Pat Smith, sls dir. ■ Rates: $25; 20; 22; 15.

WLXR-FM—Co-owned with WLFN(AM). March 1975: 104.9 mhz; 1.35 kw. Ant 430 ft. TL: N43 45 28 W91 17 26. Stereo. Target aud: 18-49. ■ Rick Steele, prom dir. ■ Rates: $35; 30; 30; 20.

WLJO(FM)—Not on air, target date unknown: 106.3 mhz; 12 kw. Ant 476 ft. Suite 507, 625 19th St. NW, Rochester MN (55901). (507) 288-1971. Licensee: Mississippi Valley Broadcasters Inc. Group owner: Howard G. Bill Stations.

***WLSU(FM)**—Jan 4, 1971: 88.9 mhz; 8.3 kw. Ant 540 ft. TL: N43 48 42 W91 11 15. Stereo. Hrs opn: 5 AM-1 AM. U. of Wis.-La Crosse, 1725 State St. (54601). (608) 785-8380. FAX: (608) 782-5575. Licensee: University of Wisconsin System. Net: NPR. Wash atty: Dow, Lohnes & Albertson. Format: Jazz, news. News staff 2; news progmg 40 hrs wkly. Target aud: General. ■ Robert Seaquist, gen mgr; Gene Purcell, opns dir, progmg dir & mus dir; Jackie Jensen-Utz, dev dir & prom mgr; Sandra Harris, news dir; Doug Anderson, pub affrs dir; Sam Sokolik, chief engr.

WLXR-FM—Listing follows WLFN(AM).

WQJY(FM)—(West Salem). Mar 15, 1982: 100.1 mhz; 1.8 kw. Ant 426 ft. TL: N43 51 02 W91 12 08. Stereo. Hrs opn: 24. Box 1624, La Crosse (54602). (608) 784-9524. FAX: (608) 526-6813. Licensee: DN Communications Inc. (acq 6-1-93; $48,000; FTR 6-21-93). Format: Classic rock. News staff one. Target aud: 25-54. ■ Pat Delaney, pres & chief engr; Tim Scott, stn mgr, opns dir & progmg dir; Jim Timm, gen sls mgr; Jim Dixon, prom dir.

WSPL(FM)—Listing follows WKTY(AM).

Ladysmith

WJBL(FM)—Listing follows WLDY(AM).

WLDY(AM)—September 1948: 1340 khz; 1 kw-U. TL: N45 27 52 W91 07 26. Hrs opn: 5:30 AM-11:30 PM. Box 351, W8745 Hwy. 8 (54848-0351). (715) 532-5588. Licensee: Flambeau Broadcasting Co. (acq 7-91). Net: ABC/E. Rep: Courtney. Wash atty: McCabe & Allen. Format: Country, MOR, lite AC. News staff one; news progmg 15 hrs wkly. Target aud: 35 plus; mature audience. Spec prog: Farm 2 hrs, gospel 2 hrs, big band 4 hrs, talk 16 hrs wkly. ■ Gary R. Johnson, CEO, pres, gen mgr & chief engr; Bernice Beyer, sr vp; Pat Alden, opns dir; Kyle Gibbs, sls dir; Sandy Zajec, prom dir & pub affrs dir; Gary Johnson, progmg dir; Larry Lee, news dir. ■ Rates: $7.80; 6.80; 7.80; 6.80.

WJBL(FM)—Co-owned with WLDY(AM). October 1984: 93.1 mhz; 4.9 kw. Ant 358 ft. TL: N45 27 59 W91 07 23. Hrs opn: 5 AM-midnight. Dups AM 90%. Net: ABC, MBS. Format: All stereo oldies. News 10 hrs wkly. Target aud: 25-54. ■ Rates: Same as AM.

WWIB(FM)—Dec 30, 1972: 103.7 mhz; 100 kw. Ant 706 ft. TL: N45 06 35 W91 09 43. Stereo. Hrs opn: 24. 5558 Hallie Rd., Chippewa Falls (54729). (715) 723-1037. FAX: (715) 723-3219. Licensee: Stewards of Sound Inc. (acq 10-29-93; with WOGO[AM] Hallie; FTR 11-15-93). Net: AP, USA. Wash atty: Peter Tannenwald. Format: Relg contemp. News progmg 16 hrs wkly. Target aud: 25-54. Spec prog: Farm 12 hrs wkly. ■ Terry Steward, stn mgr; Greg Steward, progmg dir; Paul Anthony, mus dir; Mark Halverson, news dir; Patrick Wahl, chief engr. ■ Rates: $27; 18; 18.50; 10.

Lake Geneva

WMIR(AM)—May 15, 1964: 1550 khz; 1 kw-D, DA. TL: N42 35 40 W88 23 19. Box 700, Hwy. 50 E. (53147). (414) 249-1555. FAX: (414) 248-2023. Licensee: Southern Wisconsin Co. Inc. Net: CNN; Wis. Net, Ill. News Net. Wash atty: Donald E. Martin. Format: News/talk. News staff one; news progmg 9 hrs wkly. Target aud: 25 plus. Spec prog: Farm. ■ John F. Monroe Jr., pres; Ed Mallonen, gen mgr & gen sls mgr; Sharon Powell, opns mgr; Bill Lawrence, mus dir; Tammy Freund, news dir; Keith Warner, chief engr. ■ Rates: $14; 12; 12; 12.

Lancaster

WGLR(AM)—Sept 9, 1977: 1280 khz; 500 w-D. TL: N42 50 22 W90 40 19. Box 587, 206 S. Sheridan St. (53813). (608) 723-7671. FAX: (608) 723-7674. Licensee: K to Z Ltd. (group owner; acq 9-1-88). Format: C&W. Spec prog: Farm 10 hrs wkly. ■ James Zimmermann, pres & gen mgr; Rick Sanson, gen sls mgr; John Simmons, progmg dir; Doug Wagon, news dir.

WGLR-FM—Sept 9, 1982: 97.7 mhz; 3 kw. Ant 235 ft. TL: N42 50 18 W90 40 14. Stereo.

***WJTY(FM)**—Mar 12, 1983: 88.1 mhz; 12 kw. Ant 476 ft. TL: N42 57 08 W90 25 47. Stereo. 341 S. Washington (53813). (608) 723-7888. Licensee: Joy Public Broadcasting Corp. Net: Moody, USA. Wash atty: Tim Welch. Format: Relg, country, MOR. News staff one; news progmg 11 hrs wkly. Target aud: 30-90; families. ■ Lowell M. Bush, pres & gen mgr; Joyce Bush, progmg dir & mus dir; Gerry Carus, news dir; Dennis Baldridge, chief engr.

Lomira

WFDL(FM)—April 1993: 97.7 mhz. Ant 328 ft. TL: N43 36 06 W88 32 27. Box 977, Fond du Lac (54935). (414) 929-7497. Licensee: Value Radio Corp. Group owner: Mid-West Family Stations. Format: Adult contemp. ■ Rob Cutter, gen mgr.

Madison

***WERN(FM)**—Mar 30, 1947: 88.7 mhz; 25 kw. Ant 990 ft. TL: N43 03 18 W89 28 42. Stereo. 821 University Ave. (53706-1496). (608) 264-9600. FAX: (608) 263-9763. Licensee: State of Wisconsin Educational Communications Bd. Net: NPR, APR; Wis. Pub. Format: News, classical. News progmg 29 hrs wkly. Target aud: General; persons seeking quality music & intellectual stimualtion. ■ Jack Mitchell, gen mgr; Greg Schnirring, progmg dir; Norman Gilliland, mus dir; Joy Cardin, news dir; Don Moran, chief engr.

***WHA(AM)**—1922: 970 khz; 5 kw-D, 51 w-N. TL: N43 02 30 W89 24 31. Hrs opn: 5 AM-midnight. 821 University Ave. (53706). (608) 264-9600. FAX: (608) 263-9763. Licensee: Regents of Univ. of Wisconsin System. Net: NPR, APR; Wis. Pub. Format: Educ, talk/news. Target aud: General. ■ Luke F. Lamb, gen mgr; Jack Mitchell, stn mgr; Peter Wallace, dev mgr & prom mgr; Monika Petkus, mktg mgr; Greg Schnirring, progmg dir; Joy Cardin, news dir; Tom Clark, pub affrs dir; Al Rieland, chief engr. ■ WHA-TV affil.

WHIT(AM)—Aug 14, 1964: 1550 khz; 5 kw-D, DA. TL: N43 00 08 W89 23 08. Box 44408 (53744); 5024 E. Lacy Rd. (53711). (608) 271-6611. FAX: (608) 271-0400. Licensee: Madison Communication Properties L.P. (acq 5-24-88). Net: ABC/E. Rep: Eastman. Format: Country. News staff one. Target aud: 25-54. ■ John Sandvig, gen mgr; Ed Schulz, gen sls mgr; Mark Grantin, prom mgr; Tom Oakes, progmg mgr; Ken Bessel, chief engr.

WIBA(AM)—Apr 2, 1925: 1310 khz; 5 kw-U, DA-N. TL: N42 59 53 W89 25 42. Stereo. Box 99, 2651 S. Fish Hatchery Rd. (53701). (608) 274-5450. FAX: (608) 274-5521. Licensee: Double L Broadcasting (group owner; acq 8-5-87; grpsl; FTR 6-29-87). Net: CBS, Wall Street. Rep: Katz. Wash atty: Dow, Lohnes & Albertson. Format: Adult contemp, news/talk. News staff 5; news progmg 27 hrs wkly. Target aud: 25-64. Spec prog: Farm 3 hrs wkly. ■ Lee Leicinger, pres & gen mgr; Jeff Tyler, opns mgr, prom mgr & progmg dir; Kurt Peterson, gen sls mgr; Bob King, news dir; Ken Sweet, chief engr.

WIBA-FM—Mar 1947: 101.5 mhz; 50 kw. Ant 450 ft. TL: N43 03 22 W89 32 07. Stereo. Prog sep from AM. Format: AOR, classic rock. ■ Jack Mitchell, progmg dir & mus dir.

WMAD(AM)—See Sun Prairie.

WMAD-FM—See Sun Prairie.

WMGN(FM)—Listing follows WTDY(AM).

WMLI(FM)—(Sauk City). Sept 18, 1964: 96.3 mhz; 5.1 kw. Ant 672 ft. TL: N43 12 37 W89 35 57. Stereo. Hrs opn: 24. Suite 300, 4610 University Ave., Madison (53705). (608) 233-9634; (608) 281-0096. FAX: (608) 233-6561. Licensee: Odon Madison L.P. (acq 9-15-87; $1.6 million; FTR 6-29-87). Net: CNN. Rep: McGavren Guild. Wash atty: Leventhal, Senter & Lerman. Format: Alt adult contemp. News staff one; news progmg 2 hrs wkly. Target aud: 25-54. Spec prog: Jazz 2 hrs wkly. ■ William C. O'Donnell, pres; Brian Kelly, opns mgr & engrg dir; Robert Lewin, gen sls mgr; Tom Cook, mktg dir & prom dir; John Anderson, progmg dir; Chris Ryan, mus dir; Tom Patrick, news dir & pub affrs dir. ■ Rates: $26; 28; 25; 19.

***WNWC(FM)**—Apr 30, 1959: 102.5 mhz; 50 kw. Ant 460 ft. TL: N43 02 07 W89 30 25. Stereo. 5606 Medical Cir. (53719). (608) 271-1025. Licensee: Northwestern College. Group owner: Northwestern College Radio Network (acq 1-19-73). Net: UPI. Format: Relg, news. Spec prog: Farm 2 hrs wkly. ■ Greg Walters, gen mgr, prom mgr & progmg dir; Gordon Govier, news dir; Mark Croom, chief engr.

WOLX-FM—(Baraboo). Mar 3, 1946: 94.9 mhz; 37 kw. Ant 1,299 ft. TL: N43 25 40 W89 39 14. Stereo. Hrs opn: 24. 2306 W. Badger Rd., Madison (53713). (608) 273-0077. FAX: (608) 273-2507. Licensee: Shockley Communications Corp. (group owner; acq 5-1-85; $1,900,000; FTR 3-25-85). Rep: Christal. Wash atty: Rosenman & Colin, Howard Braun. Format: Oldies. News staff 2; news progmg 2 hrs wkly. Target aud: 25-54. ■ Terry K. Shockley, chmn & pres; Sandra Shockley, vp & gen sls mgr; Anjie Harris, prom mgr; Dave Dunkin, progmg dir; Bill Phillips, mus dir; Randy Lucas, pub affrs dir. ■ Rates: $80; 70; 80; 50.

***WORT(FM)**—Dec 1, 1975: 89.9 mhz; 2 kw. Ant 900 ft. TL: N43 03 01 W89 29 15. Stereo. Hrs opn: 24. 118 S. Bedford St. (53703). (608) 256-2695. Licensee: Back Porch Radio Broadcasting Inc. Format: Div. News staff one. Target aud: 25-34. Spec prog: Black 3 hrs, class 7 hrs, jazz 15 hrs wkly. ■ Bonnie Kalmbach, pres; Antonette Goroch, dev dir; Randy Ballwahn, mus dir; Mike Wassenaar, news dir; Dave Ritche, chief engr.

WTDY(AM)—September 1948: 1480 khz; 5 kw-U, DA-N. TL: N43 01 30 W89 23 48. Stereo. Hrs opn: 24. Box 2058 (53701); 3220 Syene Rd. (53713). (608) 271-1484. FAX: (608) 281-1329. Licensee: Mid-West Management Inc. Group owner: Mid-West Family Stations. Net: NBC, NBC Talknet, Daynet. Rep: McGavren Guild. Wash atty: Fisher & Wayland. Format: News/talk. News staff 6; news progmg 17 hrs wkly. Target aud: 35-64. ■ William R. Walker, pres; William D. Vancil, exec vp & gen mgr; Robert Lewin, vp sls; Craig Foster, progmg dir; Tim Morrissey, news dir; John Bauer, chief engr.

WMGN(FM)—Co-owned with WTDY(AM). September 1948: 98.1 mhz; 38 kw. Ant 581 ft. TL: N42 57 46 W89 22 46. Stereo. Hrs opn: 24. Prog sep from AM. Format: Adult contemp. Target aud: 25-54. ■ Pat O'Neill, progmg dir.

WTSO(AM)—January 1948: 1070 khz; 10 kw-D, 5 kw-N, DA-2. TL: N42 59 45 W89 18 50. 5721 Tokay Blvd. (53719). (608) 274-1070. FAX: (608) 275-7125. Licensee: Mid-Continent Broadcasting Co. of Wisconsin Inc. Group owner: Midcontinent Media Inc. (acq 9-1-60). Net: ABC/I, MBS, AP; Wis. Radio Net. Rep: Banner. Wash atty: Dow, Lohnes & Albertson. Format: News/talk. News staff 6. Target aud: 35-64. Spec prog: Farm 20 hrs wkly. ■ N.L. Bentson, pres; David Graupner, vp & gen mgr; Marsh Walzer, gen sls mgr; Jim Casale, progmg dir; Jeff Zigler, engrg dir.

WZEE(FM)—Co-owned with WTSO(AM). 1948: 104.1 mhz; 9.4 kw. Ant 1,119 ft. TL: N43 03 09 W89 28 42. Stereo. Hrs opn: 24. Prog sep from AM. (Acq 11-1-74). Format: Adult contemp,contemp hit. News staff 2; news progmg one hr wkly. Target aud: 25-54. ■ Ed Lambert, progmg dir; Don Brooks, mus dir.

WWQM-FM—See Middleton.

WZEE(FM)—Listing follows WTSO(AM).

Manitowoc

WCUB(AM)—(Two Rivers). Nov 1952: 980 khz; 5 kw-U, DA-2. TL: N44 03 50 W87 41 49. Hrs opn: 24. Box 1990, Manitowoc (54221-1990); 1915 Mirro Dr., Manitowoc (54220). (414) 683-6800. FAX: (414) 683-6807. Licensee: Cub Radio Inc. (acq 1-1-61). Net: Unistar. Rep: Katz. Wash atty: Arent, Fox, Kintner, Plotkin & Kahn. Format: C&W, farm. News staff 2; news progmg 16 hrs wkly. Target aud: 25 plus. ■ Lee Davis, pres & gen mgr; Kent Reeves, gen sls mgr; Bob Irish, progmg dir; Mike Kinzel, news dir; Lee Barry, chief engr. ■ Rates: $50; 45; 50; 45.

WLTU(FM)—Co-owned with WCUB(AM). Sept 1, 1966: 92.1 mhz; 1.69 kw. Ant 500 ft. TL: N44 07 31 W87 37 41. Stereo. Prog sep from AM. Net: Jones Satellite Audio. Format: Oldies. Target aud: 25-54. ■ Rates: Same as AM.

WOMT(AM)—Nov 8, 1926: 1240 khz; 1 kw-U. TL: N44 07 31 W87 37 41. Hrs opn: 24. Box 1385, 3730 Mangin St. (54221-1385). (414) 682-0351. FAX: (414) 682-1008. Licensee: Seehafer Broadcasting Corp. (group owner; acq 1-1-70). Net: CBS. Rep: Katz & Powell. Wash atty: Miller & Miller, P.C. Format: Adult contemp, MOR, news. News staff 2; news progmg 45 hrs wkly.

Target aud: 25-54; business executives & mass. Spec prog: Farm one hr, relg 2 hrs wkly. ■ Don Seehafer, pres & gen mgr; Ben Jakel, stn mgr; Russ Matar, gen sls mgr & prom mgr; Jay Thomas, progmg dir; Lee Douglas, mus dir; Fred Barry, news dir; Ed Duellman, chief engr. ■ Rates: $60; 50; 50; 40.

WQTC-FM—Co-owned with WOMT(AM). Nov 19, 1965: 102.3 mhz; 3 kw. Ant 328 ft. TL: N44 07 31 W87 37 41. Stereo. Prog sep from AM. Format: Adult contemp, contemp hit. News progmg 7 hrs wkly. Target aud: 25-34. ■ Rates: $40; 30; 30; 20.

WTRW(AM)—See Two Rivers.

Marinette

WAGN(AM)—See Menominee, Mich.

WHYB(FM)—See Menominee, Mich.

WMAM(AM)—Oct 8, 1939: 570 khz; 250 w-D, 100 w-N. TL: N45 06 02 W87 37 30. Hrs opn: 24. Box 609, N. 2880 Roosevelt Rd. (54143). (715) 735-6631. FAX: (715) 732-0123. Licensee: Near North Broadcasting (acq 10-78). Net: AP, NBC. Rep: Michigan. Format: Country. News staff one; news progmg 4 hrs wkly. Target aud: 25 plus. Spec prog: Farm 3 hrs wkly. ■ Frank J. Lauerman III, pres & gen mgr; Dane Scott, opns mgr, progmg dir & pub affrs dir; David G. Nesbitt, gen sls mgr; Mike Wolf, prom dir; David Dragoo, chief engr. ■ Rates: $15; 15; 15; 15.

WLST(FM)—Co-owned with WMAM. Sept 1, 1976: 95.1 mhz; 100 kw. Ant 500 ft. TL: N45 03 48 W87 39 26 (CP: 133 kw). Stereo. Hrs opn: 24. Prog sep from AM. Net: Unistar. Format: Adult contemp. News progmg 2 hrs wkly. Target aud: 25-49; females. Spec prog: Jazz 4 hrs wkly. ■ Dane Scott, opns dir. ■ Rates: $20; 20; 20; 20.

Marshfield

WDLB(AM)—Feb 2, 1947: 1450 khz; 1 kw-U. TL: N44 41 49 W90 09 20. Hrs opn: 24. Box 630, 1710 N. Central Ave. (54449). (715) 384-2191. Licensee: Goetz Broadcasting Corp. (group owner; acq 7-65). Net: ABC/I; Goetz Group. Wash atty: Miller & Fields. Format: Oldies, news/talk. News staff 3; news progmg 13 hrs wkly. Target aud: General; 25-49. Spec prog: Farm 14 hrs wkly. ■ Nathan Goetz, pres; Jack Hackman, sr vp & gen mgr; William Allen, stn mgr; Arnie Peck, gen sls mgr; Ric Armon, prom dir; Scott Trentadue, vp adv; John Simonson, progmg dir; Thom Gerretsen, news dir; Clif Groth, vp engrg; Jay Latsch, chief engr.

WLJY(FM)—Co-owned with WDLB(AM). Dec 1, 1965: 106.5 mhz; 100 kw. Ant 800 ft. TL: N44 38 41 W89 51 11. Stereo. Prog sep from AM. Format: Easy lstng. News staff 3. Target aud: 25-54. Spec prog: Relg 2 hrs wkly. ■ Scott M. Trentadue, vp sls; Arnie Peck, rgnl sls mgr.

Mauston

WRJC(AM)—Jan 4, 1962: 1270 khz; 500 w-D. TL: N43 49 52 W90 04 51. Hrs opn: 6 AM-midnight. Box 200, Fairway Ln. (53948). (608) 847-6565. FAX: (608) 847-7000. Licensee: WRJC Inc. (acq 2-15-86; $125,000; FTR 12-23-85). Net: ABC/E, CBS, NBC Talknet, Daynet, NBC. Wash atty: Bechtel & Cole. Format: News/talk. News staff one; news progmg 8 hrs wkly. Target aud: General; 25 plus. Spec prog: Rush Limbaugh 15 hrs wkly. ■ Rick Charles, pres, gen mgr & gen sls mgr; Kathy Bakalars, sls dir; Randy McNight, mus dir; Jackie O'Brien, news dir; Ken Ebneter, chief engr. ■ Rates: $17.80; 17.80; 17.80; 17.80.

WRJC-FM—1976: 92.1 mhz; 1.8 kw. Ant 600 ft. TL: N43 47 16 W90 11 52. Stereo. Dups AM 65%. Format: Adult contemp. ■ Rates: $12.45; 12.45; 12.45; 12.45.

Medford

WIGM(AM)—Oct 26, 1941: 1490 khz; 1 kw-U, DA-1. TL: N45 07 55 W90 19 54. Box 59, 630 S. Eighth (54451). (715) 748-2566. Licensee: WIGM Inc. (acq 6-55). Net: ABC/I. Rep: Keystone (unwired net). Format: Adult contemp, oldies, news/talk. News staff 2; news progmg 14 hrs wkly. Target aud: 25 plus; young families, mature adults. Spec prog: Farm 10 hrs wkly. ■ Brad Dahlvig, pres, gen mgr & mus dir; Karen Dahlvig, vp opns & prom mgr; Rita Clark, gen sls mgr; Russ Gowey, progmg dir; Rhonda Koester, news dir; Allen Brace, chief engr. ■ Rates: $10; 9.75; 14; 8.

WIGM-FM—September 1991: 99.3 mhz; 23 kw. Ant 342 ft. TL: N45 07 55 W90 19 54. Stereo. Hrs opn: 24. Dups AM 80%. Format: Adult contemp, oldies. Target aud: 25-54; young to middle-aged adults. ■ Brad Dahlvig, CEO; Karen Dahlvig, sr vp, dev dir & mktg dir; Judy Winter, opns dir; Rita Clark, vp sls; Russ Gowey, vp progmg; B.J. Crocker, mus dir. ■ Rates: $12.75; 11; 16; 9.

Menomonee Falls

WFMR(FM)—July 30, 1966: 98.3 mhz; 6 kw. Ant 328 ft. TL: N43 09 00 W88 07 25. Stereo. West 172 N., 7348 Shady Ln. (53051). (414) 250-0983. Licensee: Harris Classical Broadcasting Co. (acq 6-5-92; FTR 6-29-92). Rep: CMBS. Wash atty: Reed, Smith, Shaw & McClay. Format: Class. News progmg 4 hrs wkly. Target aud: 25 plus. ■ Randy Harris, pres & gen mgr; David Bishop, gen sls mgr; Craig Hebaler, progmg dir & mus dir. ■ Rates: $65; 65; 65; 65.

Menomonie

***WHWC(FM)**—June 28, 1950: 88.3 mhz; 10 kw. Ant 1,050 ft. TL: N45 02 47 W91 51 42 (CP: 20 kw). 821 University Ave., Madison (53706-1496). (608) 264-9600. FAX: (608) 263-9763. Licensee: State of Wisconsin Educational Communications Bd. Format: Educ, class, talk. ■ Greg Schnirring, progmg dir.

WMEQ(AM)—May 1951: 880 khz; 10 kw-D, 210 w-N. TL: N44 48 48 W91 55 34. Stereo. Hrs opn: 5 AM-midnight. Box 880, 430 Crescent St. (54751). (715) 235-2112. FAX: (715) 235-8466. Licensee: Michael A. Phillips (acq 1-27-89; $637,500; FTR 2-13-89). Net: AP. Format: News info. Target aud: 35 plus. Spec prog: Farm 15 hrs wkly. ■ Michael Phillips, Linda Kiester (asst), stn mgrs.

WMEQ-FM—July 19, 1967: 92.1 mhz; 1.3 kw. Ant 490 ft. TL: N44 51 43 W91 52 36 (CP: 9 kw, ant 436 ft.). Stereo. Hrs opn: 24. Prog sep from AM. Net: NBC, CNN; Wis. Radio Net. Format: Oldies. Target aud: 25 plus.

***WVSS(FM)**—Apr 22, 1969: 90.7 mhz; 1.06 kw. Ant 75 ft. TL: N44 52 17 W91 55 34. Stereo. 820 S. Broadway St. (54751); N221 W. Clairemont St. Eau-Claire (54701). (715) 839-3868; (715) 263-5544. FAX: (715) 839-2939. Licensee: Board of Regents, Univ. of Wisconsin Systems. Format: Classical. ■ Dean Kallenbach, gen mgr.

Merrill

WJMT(AM)—May 10, 1960: 730 khz; 1 kw-D, 127 w-N. TL: N45 10 45 W89 38 20. Hrs opn: 24. 1018A E. Main St. (54452). (715) 536-6262. FAX: (715) 536-6208. Licensee: Roberts Broadcasting Inc. (group owner; acq 11-14-75). Net: NBC, NBC Talknet. Rep: D & R Radio. Format: Adult contemp. News staff one. Target aud: 35-59. Spec prog: Relg 3 hrs, farm 7 hrs, Pol 3 hrs wkly. ■ W. Donald Roberts Jr., pres; Wayne H. Smith, gen mgr; John Roberts, gen sls mgr; Steve Resnick, progmg dir & mus dir; Tim Seidler, news dir; Chuck Genarro, chief engr.

WMZK(FM)—Co-owned with WJMT(AM). Aug 25, 1968: 104.1 mhz; 13 kw. Ant 446 ft. TL: N45 06 14 W89 43 05. Stereo. Hrs opn: 24. Prog sep from AM. Net: MBS. Format: Classic rock. News staff one; news progmg 3 hrs wkly. Target aud: 18-49.

Middleton

WHIT(AM)—See Madison.

WWQM-FM—Oct 20, 1970: 106.3 mhz; 4.5 kw. Ant 381 ft. TL: N43 03 01 W89 29 15. Stereo. Hrs opn: 24. 5024 E. Lacy Rd., Madison (53711); Box 44408, Madison (53744-4408). (608) 271-6611. FAX: (608) 271-0400. Licensee: Madison Communication Properties L.P. (acq 5-24-88). Net: ABC/E. Rep: Christal. Format: Country. Target aud: 25-54; general. ■ John Sandvig, gen mgr; Ed Schulz, gen sls mgr; Mark Grantin, prom mgr; Tom Oakes, progmg mgr; Jake Preston, (asst) mus dir; Ken Bessel, chief engr.

Milladore

***WGNV(FM)**—Feb 13, 1986: 88.5 mhz; 25 kw. Ant 330 ft. TL: N44 38 33 W89 50 50. Stereo. Hrs opn: 24. Box 88 (54454). (715) 457-2988. FAX: (715) 457-2987. Licensee: Evangel Ministries Inc. Net: USA. Format: Christian adult contemp. ■ Ken Ellis, pres; Steve Bracco, gen mgr; Bill Moede, chief engr.

Milwaukee

WEMP(AM)—Oct 14, 1935: 1250 khz; 5 kw-U, DA-2. TL: N42 56 44 W88 03 39. Stereo. 11800 W. Grange Ave., Hales Corners (53130). (414) 529-1250. FAX: (414) 529-2122. Licensee: Heritage Wisconsin Broadcasting Corp. Group owner: Heritage Media Corp. (acq 12-31-86; grpsl; FTR 11-17-86). Net: CBS Spectrum, NBC, Unistar. Rep: Eastman. Wash atty: Akin, Gump. Format: Oldies. News staff one; news progmg 4 hrs wkly. Target aud: 25-49. Spec prog: Relg 3 hrs wkly. ■ Craig Hodgson, pres & gen mgr; Kim Guthrie, gen sls mgr; Eric Schuppert, prom mgr; Dan Markus, progmg dir; Jim Stoll, news dir; Leroy Wolniakowski, chief engr.

WMYX(FM)—Co-owned with WEMP(AM). Nov 1, 1962: 99.1 mhz; 50 kw. Ant 450 ft. TL: N42 56 44 W88 03 39. Stereo. Prog sep from AM. Net: CBS Spectrum. Format: Adult contemp. Spec prog: Relg one hr wkly. ■ Eric Schuppert, prom dir.

WEZW(FM)—See Wauwatosa-Milwaukee.

WISN(AM)—1922: 1130 khz; 50 kw-D, 10 kw-N, DA-2. TL: N42 45 18 W88 04 53. Hrs opn: 24. Box 402 (53201); 759 N. 19th St. (53233). (414) 342-1111. FAX: (414) 344-1870. Licensee: The Hearst Corp. Group owner: Hearst Broadcasting Group (acq 1924). Net: ABC/I, ABC Talk-Radio, MBS. Rep: Katz. Format: Talk. News staff 4. Target aud: 25-54. ■ Charles L. DuCoty, vp; Charles L. Ducoty, gen mgr; Bill Hurwitz, gen sls mgr; Jane Werth, prom mgr; Gary Jensen, progmg dir; Jerry Bott, news dir; Bob Johnson, chief engr.

WLTQ(FM)—Co-owned with WISN(AM). January 1961: 97.3 mhz; 15.5 kw. Ant 980 ft. TL: N43 06 41 W87 55 38. Stereo. Hrs opn: 24. Prog sep from AM. Net: ABC/D. Format: Adult contemp. ■ Jack Smith, mus dir. ■ WISN-TV affil.

WKKV-FM—See Racine.

WKLH(FM)—1958: 96.5 mhz; 20 kw. Ant 810 ft. TL: N43 05 48 W87 54 19. Stereo. Hrs opn: 24. Suite 700, 735 W. Wisconsin Ave. (53233). (414) 271-5511. FAX: (414) 273-5477. Licensee: Saga Communications Inc. (group owner; acq 7-18-90). Rep: McGavren Guild. Format: Classic rock. News staff one. Target aud: 25-44; baby boomers. ■ Tom Joerres, gen mgr; Jeff Jean Pierre, gen sls mgr; Brad Wallace, prom mgr; Bob Bellini, progmg dir; Carole Caine, news dir; Dave Janzer, chief engr.

WKTI(FM)—Listing follows WTMJ(AM).

WLTQ(FM)—Listing follows WISN(AM).

WLUM-FM—Listing follows WMCS(AM).

WLZR(AM)—1955: 1340 khz; 1 kw-U. TL: N43 02 49 W87 58 52. Hrs opn: 24. 5407 W. McKinley Ave. (53208). (414) 453-4130. FAX: (414) 453-5708. Licensee: Great American TV & Radio Co. Inc. Group owner: Great American Broadcasting. Net: ABC/FM, CBS. Rep: Eastman. Format: AOR. Target aud: 18-34. ■ David Pugh, pres & gen mgr; Bob Benes, gen sls mgr; John Duncan, progmg dir; Neil Robbins, mus dir; Gary Armstrong, chief engr.

WLZR-FM—October 1960: 102.9 mhz; 50 kw. Ant 440 ft. TL: N43 02 49 W87 58 52. Stereo. Hrs opn: 24. Dups AM 100%.

WMCS(AM)—(Greenfield). Apr 27, 1947: 1290 khz; 5 kw-U, DA-2. TL: N42 55 11 W87 59 17. 4222 W. Capitol Dr., Milwaukee (53216). (414) 444-1290. FAX: (414) 444-1409. Licensee: Suburbanaire. Group owner: All Pro Broadcasting Inc. (acq 5-23-88; 4,400,000; FTR 8-3-87). Net: SMN. Rep: Katz & Powell. Format: Adult contemp, Black. News staff 2; news progmg 6 hrs wkly. Target aud: 25-54; upwardly mobile Blacks. ■ William D. Davis, pres; Don Rosette, gen mgr; Roger Williams, gen sls mgr; Darryn De Walt, prom mgr; Billy Young, progmg dir; Kathy Brown, mus dir; Eric Von, news dir; Ella Smith, pub affrs dir; John Church, chief engr.

WLUM-FM—Co-owned with WMCS(AM). Sept. 1960: 102.1 mhz; 20 kw. Ant 761 ft. TL: N43 05 48 W87 54 19. Stereo. Suite 390, 2500 N. Mayfair Rd. (53226). (414) 785-1021. Net: CBS Spectrum. Format: CHR. News staff one. Target aud: 18-49; teens & adults. ■ Steve Sinicropi, vp & gen mgr; Bill McNulty, gen sls mgr; Tim Dunbar, prom mgr; Dan Kiley, progmg dir.

WMIL(FM)—See Waukesha.

***WMSE(FM)**—Mar 14, 1981: 91.7 mhz; 1 kw. Ant 125 ft. TL: N43 02 43 W87 54 57. Stereo. Hrs opn: 24. 324 E. Juneau Ave. (53202). (414) 277-7247. Licensee: Milwaukee School of Engineering. Format: Alternative. Target aud: 18-35; young adults. Spec prog: Black 13 hrs, jazz 15 hrs, lt 3 hrs, Sp 3 hrs, class 3 hrs wkly. ■ Bob Betts, gen mgr; Paul Host, mus dir; Marc Kellom, chief engr.

***WMWK(FM)**—Dec 7, 1990: 88.1 mhz; 170 w-H. Ant 955 ft. TL: N43 05 24 W87 53 47. Stereo. Hrs opn: 24. 290 Hegenberger Rd., Oakland, CA (94621); Box 11552, 1100 E. Capital Dr. Shorewood, WI (53211). (414) 964-9794. Licensee: Family Stations Inc. (group owner). Net: UPI. Format: Relg.

WMYX(FM)—Listing follows WEMP(AM).

Wisconsin

WNOV(AM)—Aug 15, 1946: 860 khz; 250 w-D, 5 w-N. TL: N43 02 20 W87 54 17 (CP: TL: N43 04 20 W87 57 07). 3815 N. Teutonia Ave. (53206). (414) 449-9668. FAX: (414) 449-9945. Licensee: Courier Communications Corp. (acq 1-2-73). Net: Natl Black. Format: Urban contemp. ■ Jerrel W. Jones, pres; Sandra Robinson, gen mgr, gen sls mgr & prom mgr; Ernie G. Mitchell, progmg dir & mus dir; Benjamin Nabors, news dir.

WOKY(AM)—1947: 920 khz; 5 kw-D, 1 kw-N, DA-2. TL: N42 58 32 W88 03 56. Stereo. Hrs opn: 24. Box 20920 (53220); 12100 W. Howard Ave., Greenfield (53228). (414) 545-5920. FAX: (414) 545-4069. Licensee: Sundance Broadcasting, Inc. Group owner: Sundance Broadcasting, Inc. (acq 6-1-83; grpsl; FTR 5-23-83). Net: MBS, CNN. Rep: CBS. Wash atty: Dow, Lohnes & Albertson. Format: Classic MOR. News staff 2. Target aud: 35-64. ■ Michael D. Jorgenson, pres; Brian Ongaro, gen mgr; Terry Peters, gen sls mgr; Jerry Arndt, natl sls mgr & mktg dir; Bob Piekenbrook, prom mgr; Dan Willis, progmg dir; Margaret Odya, mus dir; Michael O'Shea, news dir; Phil Klingler, chief engr.

WQFM(FM)—June 1958: 93.3 mhz; 12.6 kw. Ant 992 ft. TL: N43 05 15 W87 54 12. Stereo. 633 W. Wisconsin Ave. (53203). (414) 276-2040. FAX: (414) 276-8406. Licensee: Shamrock Communications Inc. (group owner; acq 5-10-73). Net: AP/R. Rep: Torbet. Format: AOR. ■ William R. Lynett, pres; Al Brady Law, gen mgr; Anne Marie King, gen sls mgr; Terry Spilde, prom mgr; Chris Payne, mus dir; Barb Fleming, news dir; Al Hajny, chief engr.

WTMJ(AM)—July 25, 1927: 620 khz; 5 kw-U, DA-N. TL: N43 01 56 W88 07 54. Stereo. 720 E. Capitol Dr. (53212); Box 693 (53201). (414) 332-9611. FAX: (414) 223-5298. Licensee: WTMJ Inc. (group owner). Net: NBC, CBS, NBC Talknet. Rep: Christal. Wash atty: Hogan & Hartson. Format: News/talk, sports. News staff 10; news progmg 27 hrs wkly. Target aud: General. Spec prog: Relg 2 hrs wkly ■ Douglas Kiel, pres & exec vp; Carl Gardner, vp & gen mgr; Jeff Kuether, gen sls mgr; Jim McDonald, mktg dir; Pam Brickman, prom dir; Steve Wexler, progmg dir; Mary Alice Tierney, pub affrs dir; Randy Price, vp engrg; John Schweitzer, chief engr. ■ Rates: $250; 125; 165; 80.

WKTI(FM)—Co-owned with WTMJ(AM). June 1959: 94.5 mhz; 15.5 kw. Ant 911 ft. TL: N43 05 29 W87 54 07. Stereo. Hrs opn: 24. Prog sep from AM. (414) 223-5339. (414) 223-5266. Net: ABC/R. Format: Adult contemp. News staff one. Target aud: 25-54. ■ Danny Clayton, opns dir & progmg dir; Kris Foate, gen sls mgr; Michelle Logan, natl sls mgr; John Reynolds, prom dir; John Harrison, mus dir; Randy Price, engrg dir. ■ WTMJ-TV affil.

***WUWM(FM)**—Sept 24, 1964: 89.7 mhz; 15 kw. Ant 871 ft. TL: N43 05 24 W87 53 47. Hrs opn: 24. Box 413, Univ. of Wisconsin (53201). (414) 229-4664. Licensee: Board of Regents of Univ. of Wisconsin. Net: APR, AP, NPR. Format: All news. News staff 4. Target aud: General. Spec prog: Jazz 13 hrs wkly. ■ Dave Edwards, gen mgr; Ron Kotecki, dev mgr; Bruce Winter, progmg dir & news dir; John Groff, chief engr.

WVCY(FM)—1961: 107.7 mhz; 24 kw. Ant 538 ft. TL: N42 57 57 W88 04 30. Hrs opn: 24. 3434 W. Kilbourn Ave. (53208). (414) 935-3000. FAX: (414) 935-3015. Licensee: Wisconsin Voice of Christian Youth Inc. (group owner; acq 1-70). Format: Relg. ■ Dr. Randall Melchert, pres; Victor Eliason, vp & gen mgr; Jim Schneider, progmg dir; Gordon Morris, news dir; Andy Eliason, chief engr.

WYLO(AM)—See Jackson.

***WYMS(FM)**—Mar 5, 1973: 88.9 mhz; 1.5 kw. Ant 870 ft. TL: N43 05 21 W87 53 47. Stereo. Hrs opn: 24. Drawer 10K, 5225 W. Vilet St. (53201). (414) 475-8890. FAX: (414) 475-8413. Licensee: Milwaukee Board of School Directors. Net: APR, AP. Format: Jazz. News staff one; news progmg 10 hrs wkly. Target aud: General. Spec prog: Folk 3 hrs, Ger 2 hrs, It one hr, Pol 3 hrs, Sp 3 hrs, children's 4 hrs, New Age 14 hrs, polka 4 hrs, Blues 3 hrs wkly. ■ Roger Dobrick, gen mgr & stn mgr; Aenome Rosario, dev mgr; Bill Bruckner, mus dir; Peter Zehren, news dir; Russ Rapczyk, chief engr.

WZTR(FM)—May 10, 1961: 95.7 mhz; 34 kw. Ant 610 ft. TL: N43 05 25 W87 54 54. Stereo. 520 W. Capitol Dr. (53212-1124). (414) 964-8300. FAX: (414) 964-2855. Licensee: Shockley Communications Corp. (group owner; acq 11-91; $5.05 million; FTR 9-23-91). Rep: D & R Radio. Format: Oldies. News staff one; news progmg 23 hrs wkly. Target aud: 25-54; baby boomers. ■ Terry Shockley, pres; Fred Nagle, prom mgr; Fred Brennan, progmg dir; Jill St. John, news dir. ■ Rates: $150; 120; 150; 50.

Minocqua

WMQA(AM)—Aug 1, 1978: 1570 khz; 5 kw-D, 250 kw-N. TL: N45 49 13 W89 43 27 Hrs opn: 24. Box 96, 7380 Hwy. 51 S. (54548). (715) 356-9696; (715) 356-1570. FAX: (715) 356-1977. Licensee: Raven Broadcasting Corp. (acq 11-4-91; $400,000 with co-located FM). Net: ABC/E. Wash atty: Leventhal, Sentner & Lerman. Format: Soft adult-contemporary. News staff one; news progmg 18 hrs wkly. Target aud: 25-54. Spec prog: Relg 3 hrs wkly. ■ Dave Raven, pres & gen mgr; Mark Hartzheim, rgnl sls mgr; Chris Wooldridge, progmg dir; Dave Imlah, news dir; Chris Wooldridge, pub affrs dir; Jim Zastrow, chief engr. ■ Rates: $15; 12; 15; 10.

WMQA-FM—Apr 3, 1975: 95.9 mhz; 25 kw. Ant 289 ft. TL: N45 49 13 W89 43 27. Stereo. Hrs opn: 24. Dups AM 100%. ■ Rates: Same as AM.

Mishicot

WEGV(FM)—Not on air, target date unknown: 94.7 mhz; 6 kw. TL: N44 21 46 W87 45 40. Box 1490, Oshkosh (54903). Licensee: Value Radio Corp.

Monroe

WEKZ(AM)—July 27, 1951: 1260 khz; 1 kw-D. TL: N42 35 40 W89 35 34. Box 460 (53566). (608) 325-2161. FAX: (608) 325-2164. Licensee: Green County Broadcasting Corp. Net: ABC/C, AP. Format: Div, country, news. News staff 4; news progmg 16 hrs wkly. Target aud: 30 plus. Spec prog: Ger 3 hrs, Swiss 3 hrs wkly. ■ Kenneth W. Stuart, pres; Stanley J. Neuberger, gen mgr & gen sls mgr; Don Jacobson, mus dir & news dir; Van Steiner, chief engr.

WEKZ-FM—June 1959: 93.7 mhz; 36 kw. Ant 581 ft. TL: N42 34 35 W89 41 35. Stereo. Prog sep from AM. (608) 325-4869. Net: ABC/D. Format: Easy lstng. News progmg 10 hrs wkly. ■ Stanley J. Neuberger, vp sls.

Mosinee

WOFM(FM)—Oct 7, 1991: 94.7 mhz; 50 kw. Ant 492 ft. TL: N44 59 18 W89 59 42. Stereo. Hrs opn: 24. Box 1206, Wausau (54455-1206). Suite 100, 101 Grand, Wausau (54402). (715) 848-9470. FAX: (715) 848-2238. Licensee: Mosinee Communications Inc. Format: Oldies. News staff one; news progmg 3 hrs wkly. Target aud: 25-54; upscale baby boomers. ■ Peggie Post-Mallery, pres; Dan Zie, CFO; Douglas A. Wilk, gen mgr; Roger Watson, vp opns & vp engrg; Rick Pfieffer, gen sls mgr; Tom King, prom dir, news dir & pub affrs dir; Mike McClain, progmg dir; Steve Stone, mus dir. ■ Rates: $28; 28; 28; 20.

Neenah-Menasha

WEMI(FM)—Sept 9, 1977: 100.1 mhz; 3 kw. Ant 328 ft. TL: N44 15 17 W88 26 13. Stereo. 1909 W. Second St., Appleton (54914). (414) 749-9456. FAX: (414) 749-0474. Licensee: Evangel Ministries Inc. Net: UPI, Moody, Skylight. Wash atty: Leventhal, Senter & Lerman. Format: Relg. News progmg 10 hrs wkly. Target aud: 25-54. ■ Reid Ribble, chmn; Ken Ellis, pres; Chuck Towns, gen sls mgr; Paul Cameron, progmg dir & mus dir; Duane Matz, news dir; Bill Moede, chief engr. ■ Rates: $15; 15; 15; 15.

WNAM(AM)—May 23, 1947: 1280 khz; 5 kw-D, 1 kw-N, DA-2. TL: N44 09 36 W88 27 57 (CP: 5 kw-N). Stereo. Hrs opn: 24. Box 707, 1413 S. Commercial St., Neenah (54957). (414) 727-2040. FAX: (414) 722-0211. Licensee: Odon Communications Group I (acq 10-18-88). Net: ABC/I, Unistar. Rep: Katz & Powell. Format: Nostalgia. News staff 3; news progmg 13 hrs wkly. Target aud: 35 plus. ■ William C. O'Donnell, pres; Dan Zuleger, gen mgr; Robert C. Weber, gen sls mgr; Paul Heling, prom mgr; Ron Ross, progmg dir.

WROE(FM)—November 1971: 94.3 mhz; 5.6 kw. Ant 338 ft. TL: N44 07 10 W88 28 24. Stereo. Box 1035 (54957); 134 S. Fieldcrest Dr., Neenah (54956). (414) 725-4447. FAX: (414) 725-0463. Licensee: Fox Valley Broadcasting Inc. (acq 10-89). Net: AP. Format: Soft hits. ■ Thomas L. Bookey, pres; James Gregori, gen mgr; Bette Running, gen sls mgr; J. Davis, progmg dir; Pat Berger, chief engr.

WUSW(FM)—See Oshkosh.

Neillsville

WCCN(AM)—Sept 22, 1957: 1370 khz; 5 kw-D. TL: N44 34 18 W90 35 15. Box 387, WCCN's Wisconsin Pavillion, 1201 Division St. (54456). (715) 743-2222; (715) 743-3333. FAX: (715) 743-2288. Licensee: Central Wisconsin Broadcasting, Inc. (acq 12-87; FTR 3-25-91). Net: SMN, AP; Tribune. Wash atty: Miller & Fields. Format: MOR, big band. News staff one; news progmg 20 hrs wkly. Target aud: 45 plus. Spec prog: Farm 19 hrs, polka 10 hrs wkly. ■ J. Kevin Grap, pres; Margaret L. Grap, vp; Lonnie Hoff, news dir; John Zecherle, chief engr. ■ Rates: $8.05; 7.60; 7.30; 7.30.

WCCN-FM—July 1964: 107.5 mhz; 100 kw-H. Ant 326 ft. TL: N44 34 18 W90 35 15 (CP: 100 kw, ant 587 ft., TL: N44 35 31 W90 37 13). Stereo. Hrs opn: 24. Prog sep from AM. Format: Classic rock. Target aud: 25-40. ■ Rates: Same as AM.

Nekoosa

WCAE(AM)—Not on air, target date unknown: 1590 khz; 500 w-D. TL: N44 16 05 W89 57 35. R.R. 2, Box 26, Luxemburg (54217). (414) 468-8302. Licensee: Nekoosa Broadcasting Co.

WXEC(FM)—Not on air, target date unknown: 93.7 mhz; 3 kw. Ant 164 ft. TL: N44 16 05 W89 57 35. 1360 Chicago St., Green Bay (54301). Licensee: Berry Radio Co.

New Holstein

KFKQ(FM)—Not on air, target date unknown: 93.1 mhz; 6 kw. Ant 328 ft. TL: N44 02 18 W88 09 06 (CP: 99.5 mhz). W-238, S-6825 Hwy. F, Waukesha (53186). Licensee: F.W.K. Broadcasting Inc. Group owner: Pacer Radio Packerland Inc.

New London

WOZZ(FM)—Oct 6, 1967: 93.5 mhz; 50 kw. Ant 528 ft. TL: N44 21 35 W88 42 46 (CP: Ant 492 ft.). Stereo. Hrs opn: 24. Suite 307, 1500 N. Casaloma Dr., Appleton (54915-8220). (414) 733-4990; (414) 391-0935. FAX: (414) 733-5507. Licensee: Midwest Communications of Iowa Inc. Group owner: Midwest Communications Inc. (acq 6-30-93; $1.85 million with WGEE-FM Sturgeon Bay; FTR 7-26-93). Rep: Banner. Format: Classic rock. News staff 2; news progmg 8 hrs wkly. Target aud: 25-44. ■ Dave Wright, pres & gen mgr; Jeff McCarthy, exec vp; Andrew Ashwood, opns mgr, prom mgr & progmg dir; David Fries, gen sls mgr; Ken O'Brien, mus dir; Michael Meyers, news dir; Randy Bella, pub affrs dir; Jim Rammer, chief engr.

New Richmond

WIXK(AM)—Sept 29, 1960: 1590 khz; 5 kw-D. TL: N45 05 10 W92 34 19. Hrs opn: Sunrise-sunset. 125 E. Third St. (54017). (715) 246-2254; (715) 246-5050. FAX: (715) 246-7090. Licensee: Smith Broadcasting Company Inc. Group owner: Bob Smith Stations (acq 1-1-64). Net: AP, Westwood One, Unistar. Wash atty: Miller & Fields. Format: C&W. News staff one; news progmg 9 hrs wkly. Target aud: 25-54. Spec prog: Farm. ■ Robert E. Smith, CEO & pres; Daniel Smith, vp, gen mgr, gen sls mgr, prom mgr & progmg dir; Bryan Lee, news dir & pub affrs dir; Ken Cummings, chief engr. ■ Rates: $27.50; 25; 27.50; 22.50.

WIXK-FM—Sept 1, 1968: 107.1 mhz; 18 kw. Ant 272 ft. TL: N45 05 10 W92 34 19. Stereo. Hrs opn: 5 AM-1 AM. Dups AM 100%. ■ Rates: Same as AM.

Oconto

WOCO(AM)—Mar 11, 1966: 1260 khz; 1 kw-D. TL: N45 53 31 W87 57 18. Box 197 (54153). (414) 834-3540. Licensee: Lamardo Inc. (acq 8-27-71). Format: C&W, var. ■ Walter P. Kaszynski, pres, gen mgr & chief engr; Larry Kaszynski, gen sls mgr & mus dir; Dorothy Kaszynski, progmg dir; Karen Koenings, news dir.

WOCO-FM—Aug 1, 1968: 107.1 mhz; 3 kw. Ant 210 ft. TL: N44 53 31 W87 57 18. Dups AM 40%. Format: Sounds of now & then.

Omro

WPKR(FM)—Licensed to Omro. See Oshkosh.

Oshkosh

WMGV(FM)—Listing follows WOSH(AM).

WOSH(AM)—Dec 31, 1941: 1490 khz; 1 kw-U. TL: N44 02 46 W88 31 44. Box 1490, 2333 Bowen St. (54902-1490). Licensee: Value Radio Corp. Group owner: Mid West Family Stns. (acq 9-1-59). Net: NBC, NBC Talknet, Unistar. Format: News & talk. News staff 3. ■ Bill Mann, pres & gen mgr; Rick McCoy, gen sls mgr; Ross Holland, prom mgr; Cheryl Logan, news dir; Joe Roskos, chief engr.

WMGV(FM)—Co-owned with WOSH(AM). Sept 1, 1966: 103.9 mhz; 6 kw. Ant 318 ft. TL: N44 02 47 W88 31 44. Stereo. Prog sep from AM. Net: NBC the Source. Format: CHR. ■ Tom Walker, CFO; Rick McCoy, vp sls; Ross Holland, progmg dir; Kelly Stone, mus dir.

WPKR(FM)—(Omro). July 12, 1990: 99.5 mhz; 50 kw. Ant 420 ft. TL: N43 50 51 W88 51 31. Stereo. Hrs opn: 24. Box 3450, 3891 Waukau Ave., Oshkosh, (54903). (414) 236-4242. FAX: (414) 236-4240. Licensee: Midwest Dimensions Inc. Net: NBC. Rep: Hyett/Ramsland. Wash atty: Eugene T. Smith. Format: Country. News staff one; news progmg 15 hrs wkly. Target aud: 25-54. Spec prog: Farm 5 hrs wkly. ■ Jim Coursolle, pres; Paul Vidmar, vp; Don J. Weir, gen mgr; Jim Peronto, gen sls mgr; Kelly Vidmar, prom mgr; Alan Dean, progmg dir & mus dir; Wayne Mausser, news dir; Bruce Herzog, chief engr. ■ Rates: $24; 21; 21; 18.

***WRST-FM**—April 20, 1966: 90.3 mhz; 960 w. Ant 125 ft. TL: N44 01 45 W88 33 08. Stereo. 800 Algoma Blvd. (54901). (414) 424-3113. Licensee: Board of Regents, Univ. of Wisconsin System. Format: Div, jazz, news/talk. Target aud: General. ■ Ben Jarman, gen mgr; Dwight Poppy, chief engr.

WUSW(FM)—Jan 30, 1967: 96.9 mhz; 3 kw. Ant 328 ft. TL: N44 03 51 W88 31 44. Box 707, Neenah (54957); 1413 S. Commercial St., Neenah (54956). (414) 727-2040. FAX: (414) 722-0211. Licensee: ODON Communications Group I, Limited Partnership (acq 10-18-88). Rep: Katz & Powell. Format: Modem country. News staff 3; news progmg 3 hrs wkly. Target aud: 25-54. ■ William C. O'Donnell, pres; Dan Zuleger, gen mgr; Robert C. Weber, gen sls mgr; Paul Heling, prom mgr; Mark Lewis, progmg dir; Kelly Mercer, mus dir.

WXOL(AM)—July 1, 1969: 690 khz; 250 w-D, 77 w-N, DA-2. TL: N44 04 51 W88 33 53. 889 W. County Y Rd. (54904). (414) 426-6220. FAX: (414) 426-6224. Licensee: Sunbright Broadcasting Inc. (acq 6-90; $325,000; FTR 6-11-90). Format: Oldies. News staff one; news progmg 2 hrs wkly. Target aud: 35-45. Spec prog: Farm 7 hrs, Ger 3 hrs, Pol 2 hrs, relg 5 hrs wkly. ■ Steve Rose, pres, gen mgr, progmg dir & mus dir; Bob Hansen, gen sls mgr; Dave Mays, news dir. ■ Rates: $19; 17; 19; 17.

Park Falls

WCQM(FM)—Listing follows WNBI(AM).

***WHBM-FM**—Nov 11, 1988: 90.3 mhz; 17.7 kw. Ant 727 ft. TL: N45 56 43 W90 16 28. 821 Univ. Ave., Madison (53706-1496). (608) 264-9600. FAX: (608) 263-9763. Licensee: State of Wis. Educational Communications Board. Net: Wis. Pub. Format: Talk, drama. ■ Jack Mitchell, gen mgr; Greg Schniring, progmg dir; Joy Cavdin, pub affrs dir.

WNBI(AM)—1953: 980 khz; 1 kw-D, 105 w-N. TL: N45 55 04 W90 26 58. Hrs opn: 5 AM-midnight. Box 309, Hwy. 13 S. (54552). (715) 762-3221. FAX: (715) 762-2358. Licensee: Nicolet Broadcasting Inc. (group owner; acq 9-3-93; with co-located FM; FTR 9-27-93). Net: CNN. Rep: Keystone (unwired net). Format: Adult contemp. News staff one; news progmg 8 hrs wkly. Target aud: 25-54; adults with disposable income. Spec prog: Jazz, big band one hr, polka 2 hrs wkly. ■ Roger Utnehmer, pres & gen mgr; Sandy Durel, stn mgr & gen sls mgr; Paul Eck, progmg dir, mus dir & news dir; Arthur Dunham, chief engr.

WCQM(FM)—Co-owned with WNBI(AM). Apr 13, 1968: 98.3 mhz; 3 kw. Ant 275 ft. TL: N45 55 04 W90 26 58. Hrs opn: 5 AM-midnight. Dups AM 100%.

Peshtigo

WJMR(FM)—Not on air, target date unknown: 96.1 mhz. 3 kw. Ant 230 ft. TL: N45 05 58 W87 40 35. 217 Henes Park Dr., Menominee (49858). (906) 863-6448. Licensee: Janet M. Callow (acq 1992; $30,000).

Platteville

WKPL(FM)—Listing follows WTOQ(AM).

***WSUP(FM)**—Feb 25, 1964: 90.5 mhz; 1 kw. Ant 146 ft. TL: N42 43 57 W90 29 09. Stereo. Hrs opn: 20. One University Plaza, Rm. 42, Pioneer Tower (53818). (608) 342-1165. Licensee: Board of Regents, Univ. of Wisconsin System. Wash atty: Dow, Lohnes & Albertson. Format: AOR. News progmg 10 hrs wkly. Target aud: 18-24; college-age. Spec prog: Class 4 hrs, jazz 3 hrs, alternative 6 hrs, metal 6 hrs wkly. ■ George E. Smith, gen mgr; Tim Trendt, chief engr.

WTOQ(AM)—Feb 22, 1955: 1590 khz; 1 kw-D, 500 w-N, DA-N. TL: N42 44 46 W90 28 28. Hrs opn: 5 AM-midnight. Box One, 1245 N. Fourth St. (53818). (608) 348-2775. Licensee: Kramer Broadcasting of Platteville Inc. Group owner: Kramer Broadcasting Inc. (acq 1-1-83; $710,000). Net: NBC. Rep: Katz & Powell. Wash atty: Robert Olender. Format: News, talk. News staff 2; news progmg 24 hrs wkly. Target aud: 35 plus. Spec prog: Farm 12 hrs, sports 15 hrs wkly. ■ Ed Kramer, pres & gen mgr; Jim Munson, stn mgr; Tom Engels, opns mgr & news dir; Brooke Kramer, gen sls mgr; Kevin Kellogg, progmg dir; Ken Ebneter, chief engr. ■ Rates: $11; 10; 10; 8.

WKPL(FM)—Co-owned with WTOQ(AM). Sept 1, 1966: 107.1 mhz; 3 kw. Ant 235 ft. TL: N42 44 45 W90 38 27. Stereo. Prog sep from AM. Format: New country. News staff 2; news progmg 6 hrs wkly. Target aud: 25-54; general adults. ■ Brooke Kramer, sls dir. ■ Rates: Same as AM.

Plymouth

WJUB(AM)—April 1954: 1420 khz; 500 w-D. TL: N43 44 33 W87 56 21. 5569 N. State Hwy. 57 (53073). (414) 893-2661. FAX: (414) 892-2706. Licensee: Jubilation Ministries Inc. (acq 12-17-90; $185,000; FTR 1-7-91). Net: CNN. Format: Inspirational. Spec prog: Farm 5 hrs wkly.

WXER(FM)—June 1, 1991: 104.5 mhz; 6 kw. Ant 328 ft. TL: N43 43 32 W88 03 07. Stereo. Hrs opn: 24. N. 5569 State Hwy. 57 (53073). (414) 893-1045; (414) 467-0200. Licensee: Sheboygan Broadcasting Corp. Format: Adult contemp. Target aud: 29-54. Spec prog: Ger 3 hrs wkly. ■ Julian Jetzer, pres.

Port Washington

WGLB(AM)—Dec 6, 1963: 1560 khz; 250 w-D, DA. TL: N45 23 11 W87 55 10. Box 347 (53074); 900 E. Green Bay Rd., Saukville (53080). (414) 284-2666. Licensee: WGLB Inc. (acq 3-6-93; $300,000 with co-located FM). Format: Btfl mus. News progmg 3 hrs wkly. Target aud: 35 plus. ■ Mark Heller, pres & gen mgr; Rayford Styles, stn mgr; Sally Martin-Egge, pub affrs dir. ■ Rates: $18; 18; 18; 18.

WGLB-FM—Oct 1969: 100.1 mhz; 3 kw. Ant 180 ft. TL: N43 23 10 W87 55 10. Stereo. Dups AM 100%. ■ Rates: Same as AM.

Portage

WDDC(FM)—Listing follows WPDR(AM).

WPDR(AM)—July 31, 1952: 1350 khz; 1 kw-D, 41 w-N. TL: N43 31 40 W89 25 52. Box 300, Hwy. 51 S. (53901). (608) 742-8833. FAX: (608) 742-1688. Licensee: Kramer Broadcasting Inc. (group owner; acq 7-1-74). Net: ABC/E. Rep: Katz & Powell. Wash atty: Robert Olender. Format: Country. News staff 2; news progmg 14 hrs wkly. Target aud: 35 plus. Spec prog: Talk 12 hrs, farm 9 hrs wkly. ■ Edward Kramer, pres; Robert Hoffman, stn mgr; John Green, opns mgr; Robert Hoffer, sls dir; Susann Gamble, news dir; Kenneth Ebneter, chief engr. ■ Rates: $12; 11; 11; 5.

WDDC(FM)—Co-owned with WPDR(AM). Nov 8, 1966: 100.1 mhz; 3 kw. Ant 300 ft. TL: N43 31 40 W89 25 52 (CP: 1.84 kw, TL: N43 31 42 W89 26 01). Stereo. Hrs opn: 24. Net: ABC/E. Format: New country News staff 2. Target aud: 25-45; office workers, young adults. ■ John Green, progmg dir. ■ Rates: $11; 11; 11; 6.

WZST(FM)—Not on air, target date unknown: 95.9 mhz; 6 kw. Ant 328 ft. 401 Glendale Ave., Tomah (54660). (608) 372-9600. FAX: (608) 372-7566. Licensee: Magnum Communications Inc. Wash atty: Fisher, Wayland, Cooper & Leader. ■ Dave Magnum, gen mgr.

Poynette

WIBU(AM)—July 1925: 1240 khz; 1 kw-U. TL: N43 21 38 W89 24 08. Hrs opn: 24. WIBU Rd. (53955). (608) 635-7341; (800) 666-1240. FAX: (608) 635-7343. Licensee: WIBU Inc. (acq 3-14-88). Net: SMN; Tribune, Wis. Radio Net. Wash atty: James Oyster. Format: Classic MOR. Target aud: 35-64. Spec prog: Farm 20 hrs, polka 9 hrs, Ger one hr wkly. ■ Harry D. Jacobs Jr., pres; Mike Perrine, gen mgr; Bridget Gifford, opns mgr; Robert Trunecek, gen sls mgr; Steve Burczyk, mus dir & news dir; Van Steiner, chief engr. ■ Rates: $24; 21; 24; 18.

Prairie du Chien

WPRE(AM)—Dec 11, 1952: 980 khz; 1 kw-D. TL: N43 03 39 W91 09 26. Hrs opn: 6 AM-sunset. Box 90 (53821). (608) 326-2411. FAX: (608) 326-2412. Licensee: Prairie Broadcasting Co. Format: MOR. ■ W.C. Schlaugat Jr., pres, gen mgr & chief engr; Stella Lipke, gen sls mgr; Norbert Aschom Jr., progmg dir & news dir; Dave Storkson, mus dir.

WPRE-FM—1968: 94.3 mhz; 36 kw. Ant 525 ft. TL: N43 03 35 W91 06 02. Dups AM 100%.

Racine

WBJX(AM)—June 4, 1950: 1460 khz; 500 w-D, 65 w-N. TL: N42 45 06 W87 49 55. 2400 S. 102nd St., West Allis (53227). (414) 321-1007. FAX: (414) 321-2231. Licensee: UNC Media of Milwaukee Inc. (acq 11-11-91; $3,175,000 with co-located FM; FTR 11-4-91). Net: Unistar. Rep: Torbet. Format: Sp. News staff one. Target aud: 25-54; upscale adults, professionals, upper income executives, college grads. Spec prog: Gospel 8 hrs wkly. ■ Edward Dugger III, CEO; Constance W. Balthrop, pres & gen mgr; Bob Jeffers, opns mgr; Herman A. Mosley, gen sls mgr; Peggy Austin, natl sls mgr; Jack McLelland, chief engr.

WKKV-FM—Co-owned with WBJX(AM). August 1948: 100.7 mhz; 50 kw. Ant 500 ft. TL: N42 48 18 W88 02 54. Stereo. Net: Unistar, NBC. Format: Hot urban contemp. ■ Bailey Coleman, prom dir; Tony Fields, progmg mgr; David Michaels, mus dir; Jaci White, news dir.

WHKQ(FM)—Listing follows WRJN(AM).

WKKV-FM—Listing follows WBJX(AM).

WRJN(AM)—December 1926: 1400 khz; 1 kw-U. TL: N42 42 39 W87 49 48. 4201 Victory Ave. (53405). (414) 634-3311. FAX: (414) 634-6515. Licensee: Vision Broadcasting Inc. (acq 2-16-89; $3,665,000; FTR 1-23-89). Net: ABC/I. Rep: Christal. Format: Adult contemp, news/talk. News staff 3; news progmg 40 hrs wkly. Target aud: 35 plus. Spec prog: Sp one hr, class 2 hrs, It one hr wkly. ■ Anthony J. Gazzana, pres & gen mgr; Walter Kofchnitzke, gen sls mgr; Ron Richards, progmg dir; Gary Suhr, news dir; Terry Baun, chief engr.

WHKQ(FM)—Co-owned with WRJN(AM). Aug 6, 1962: 92.1 mhz; 6 kw. Ant 275 ft. TL: N42 40 55 W87 50 59 (CP: 2.7 kw, ant 495 ft.). Stereo. Prog sep from AM. Format: Btfl mus. News progmg 4 hrs wkly. ■ Don Rosen, vp progmg.

Reedsburg

WRDB(AM)—Feb 6, 1953: 1400 khz; 1 kw-U. TL: N43 32 30 W90 02 05. Hrs opn: 24. Box 349, E. 5680A Hwy. 33 (53959). (608) 524-1400. FAX: (608) 524-2474. Licensee: Sauk Broadcasting. Group owner: Goetz Broadcasting Corp. (acq 3-1-71). Net: ABC/I. Wash atty: Miller & Fields. Format: Oldies, farm, news. News staff one; news progmg 14 hrs wkly. Target aud: 25-54. ■ Nathan Goetz, pres; Jack Hackman, exec vp; Tommy Lee Bychinski, vp & gen mgr; Bob Zirngible, gen sls mgr; Scott Trentadue, prom mgr; Bill Watts, mus dir; Curtis Lewis, news dir; Clif Groth, chief engr. ■ Rates: $13.50; 10.50; 10.50; 10.50.

WNFM(FM)—Co-owned with WRDB(AM). July 16, 1967: 104.9 mhz; 1.6 kw. Ant 449 ft. TL: N43 32 30 W90 02 05. Stereo. Hrs opn: 24. Prog sep from AM. (608) 524-1049. Format: C&W. News staff one; news progmg 10 hrs wkly. Target aud: 25 plus. Spec prog: Farm 18 hrs wkly. ■ Jack Hackman, sr vp; Scott Trentadue, vp sls; Bob Zirngible, sls dir; Clif Groth, vp engrg.

Reserve

***WOJB(FM)**—Apr 1, 1982: 88.9 mhz; 100 kw. Ant 604 ft. TL: N45 52 16 W91 20 56. Stereo. Rt. 2, Box 2788, Hayward (54843). (715) 634-2100. Licensee: Lac Courte Oreilles Ojibwa Public Broadcasting Corp. Net: NPR, APR. Format: Div. News staff 8; news progmg 40 hrs wkly. Spec prog: Indian 15 hrs, country 15 hrs, jazz 10 hrs, bluegrass 2 hrs wkly. ■ Camile Lacapa-Morrison, gen mgr; James Bailey, gen sls mgr; David Kellar, progmg dir; Mike Dukin, mus dir; Eric Schubring, news dir; Brent Christensen, chief engr.

Rhinelander

WOBT(AM)—Mar 9, 1947: 1240 khz; 1 kw-U. TL: N45 38 07 W89 22 21. Hrs opn: 24. Box 738 (54501). (715) 362-6140. FAX: (715) 362-4200. Licensee: Northwoods Broadcasting Inc. (acq 10-15-91; $850,000 with co-located FM; FTR 11-4-91). Net: ABC/I, AP, CNN. Wash atty: Fisher, Wayland, Cooper & Leader. Format: Adult contemp. Target aud: 25-55. ■ Thomas Koser, pres; Dane Jensen, gen mgr & gen sls mgr; Mark Winter, progmg dir; Jim Richard, news dir; Rick Kiefer, chief engr.

WRHN(FM)—Co-owned with WOBT(AM). Jan 26, 1966: 100.3 mhz; 25 kw. Ant 385 ft. TL: N45 38 08 W89 22 42 (CP: 100 kw, ant 981 ft., TL: N45 24 03 W89 28 54). Stereo. Hrs opn: 24. Prog sep from AM. Net: ABC/I. Target aud: 30-55.

Wisconsin

*WXPR(FM)—April 24, 1983: 91.7 mhz; 100 kw. Ant 403 ft. TL: N45 46 28 W89 14 54. Stereo. Hrs opn: 5 AM-midnight. 303 W. Prospect St. (54501). (715) 362-6000. FAX: (715) 362-6007. Licensee: White Pine Community Broadcasting Inc. Net: NPR. Format: Div, class, folk. Spec prog: Jazz 8 hrs wkly. ■ Mick Fiocchi, pres & gen mgr; Ken Krall, opns mgr; Walt Gander, pub affrs dir; Elmer Goetsch, chief engr.

WZTT(FM)—Not on air, target date unknown: 97.5 mhz; 100 kw. Ant 771 ft. TL: N45 22 43 W89 11 38. 5314 Valley Rd., Chippewa Falls (54729). (715) 723-2913. Licensee: Raven Broadcasting Corp. (acq 10-29-93; $28,000; FTR 11-15-93).

Rice Lake

WAQE(AM)—Aug 6, 1979: 1090 khz; 5 kw-D. TL: N45 32 16 W91 45 50. Box 703, 2293 19th St. (54868). (715) 234-9059. FAX: (715) 234-1955. Licensee: Red Cedar Broadcasters Inc. FTR (FTR 6-3-85). Net: CNN. Format: True country. News staff one; news progmg 2 hrs wkly. Target aud: 24-59; traditional country music listeners. Spec prog: Farm 2 hrs wkly. ■ Tom Beschta, pres & gen mgr; Pat Brewer, gen sls mgr; Don Tobias, news dir; Allan Brace, chief engr. ■ Rates: $10.80; 10.80; 10.80; 8.80.

WAQE-FM—Nov 20, 1980: 97.7 mhz; 3 kw. Ant 299 ft. TL: N45 32 16 W91 45 50 (CP: 50 kw, ant 492 ft., TL: N45 40 00 W91 40 06). Stereo. Hrs opn: 5 AM-midnight. Dups AM 100%. Format: Adult contemp. News staff one; news progmg 3 hrs wkly. Target aud: 18-49; young, upscale adults. ■ Rates: Same as AM.

WJMC(AM)—1938: 1240 khz; 1 kw-U. TL: N45 30 27 W91 46 28. Box 352 (54868); 1859 21st Ave. (54868). (715) 234-2131. FAX: (715) 234-6942. Licensee: TKC Inc. (acq 1-1-89). Net: MBS; Wis. Radio Net. Wash atty: Fisher, Wayland, Cooper & Leader. Format: Adult contemp. News staff 2; news progmg 18 hrs wkly. Target aud: 25-54. ■ Thomas A. Koser, pres, gen mgr & gen sls mgr; Rick Keefer, opns mgr, progmg dir, mus dir & chief engr; Ron Pierson, rgnl sls mgr.

WJMC-FM—1947: 96.3 mhz; 100 kw. Ant 540 ft. TL: N45 30 27 W91 46 28. Stereo. Hrs opn: 19. Prog sep from AM. Format: Contemp country.

Richland Center

WRCO(AM)—Oct 18, 1949: 1450 khz; 1 kw-U. TL: N43 18 58 W90 22 31. Hrs opn: 5 AM-midnight. Box 529, 2111 Bohmann Dr. (53581-0529). (608) 647-2111. FAX: (608) 647-8025. Licensee: Richland Broadcasting Corp. (acq 1-28-67). Net: CBS. Format: Adult contemp, country. News staff one; news progmg 20 hrs wkly. Target aud: 25-54; general. Spec prog: Farm 8 hrs, Gospel 3 hrs wkly. ■ Peter Athanas, pres & gen mgr; Ron Fruit, stn mgr, opns mgr, sls dir & progmg dir; Phil Nee, mus dir; Brian Kennedy, news dir. ■ Rates: $11; 10; 9.50; 4.50.

WRCO-FM—August 1965: 100.9 mhz; 6 kw. Ant 240 ft. TL: N43 20 14 W90 22 44. Stereo. Hrs opn: 5 AM-midnight. Dups AM 90%. ■ Rates: Same as AM.

Ripon

WCWC(AM)—Sept 15, 1957: 1600 khz; 5 kw-U, DA-2. TL: N43 49 01 W88 50 49. Hrs opn: 19. Box 156, 3 Radio Rd. (54971); 30 S. Portland, Fond du Lac (54935). (414) 748-5111; (414) 688-2380. FAX: (414) 688-2881; (414) 748-5530. Licensee: Radio Broadcasting Ltd. Net: CBS, ABC. Rep: Farmakis. Wash atty: Fisher Wayland. Format: News/talk, MOR. News staff 4; news progmg 25 hrs wkly. Target aud: 25 plus; Fond du lac, Green Lake counties. Spec prog: Chicago cubs-Tribune network, Pol 2 hrs, sports 15 hrs wkly. ■ Joe Goeser, pres; Jack McDevitt, gen mgr & gen sls mgr; Art Beaulieu, opns mgr & chief engr; Lind Krause, mus dir; Aaron Krammer, news dir. ■ Rates: $15; 11; 13; 5.

*WRPN-FM—1961: 90.1 mhz; 231 w. Ant 110 ft. TL: N43 50 37 W88 50 31. Stereo. Box 248, Ripon College, 300 Seward St. (54971). (414) 748-8147. Licensee: Bd of Trustees of Ripon College. Net: AP. Format: Adult contemp, AOR, top-40. Spec prog: Class 4 hrs, jazz 10 hrs, C&W 5 hrs wkly. ■ John Parrish, gen mgr.

WYVR-FM—Licensed to Ripon. See Fond du Lac.

River Falls

WEVR(AM)—Sept 14, 1969: 1550 khz; 1 kw-D. TL: N44 53 19 W92 39 04. Hrs opn: 6 AM-sunset. 178 Radio Rd. (54022). (715) 425-1111; (612) 439-1111. Licensee: Hanten Broadcasting Co. Inc. (acq 6-1-74). Format: Lite adult contemp, sports. Spec prog: Farm 18 hrs, C&W 18 hrs wkly. ■ Carol Hanten, pres & gen mgr; T.J. Campbell, gen sls mgr.

WEVR-FM—Sept 30, 1970: 106.3 mhz; 3 kw. Ant 300 ft. TL: N44 53 19 W92 39 04. Stereo. Hrs opn: 6 AM-11 PM. Dups AM 90%.

*WRFW(FM)—Nov 2, 1968: 88.7 mhz; 3 kw. Ant 82 ft. TL: N44 53 08 W92 39 20. Stereo. Hrs opn: 6 AM-1 AM. Univ. of Wisconsin River Falls, 306 North Hall (54022). (715) 425-3886. Licensee: Univ. of Wisconsin System. Format: Div. Spec prog: CHR, educ, jazz, new age, oldies, AOR, talk, country, farm 10 hrs wkly. ■ Ray Niekamp, gen mgr; Alan E. Murray, chief engr.

Rudolph

WIZD(FM)—Sept 30, 1990: 99.9 mhz; 6 kw. Ant 328 ft. TL: N44 28 55 W89 40 34 Stereo. Hrs opn: 24. Box 850, Plover (54467). (715) 344-6050; (715) 421-4040. FAX: (715) 341-8070. Licensee: Wizard Communications Inc. Net: ABC Format: Oldies. News staff 2; news progmg 3 hrs wkly. Target aud: 25-54; upper income. ■ James P. Schuh, pres & opns mgr; Walt Bergman, exec vp & gen mgr; Dick Raatz, sls dir; Pat Shanahan, progmg dir & mus dir; Bob Holsman, news dir; Rick Westenberger, chief engr. ■ Rates: $17; 13; 14; 11.

Sauk City

WMLI(FM)—Licensed to Sauk City. See Madison.

Schofield

WRIG(AM)—Aug 1, 1958: 1390 khz; 5 kw-U, DA-2. TL: N44 52 42 W89 38 29. Stereo. Hrs opn: 24. Box 2048, Wausau (54402-2048); 920 Grand Ave. (54476). (715) 355-1614. FAX: (715) 359-0520. Licensee: WRIG Inc. Group owner: Midwest Communications Inc. Net: ABC/D. Rep: Banner. Format: Oldies. News staff one; news progmg 4 hrs wkly. Target aud: 25-54. ■ D. E. Wright, pres; Beverly J. Rice, gen mgr; Dave Arrowood, progmg dir; Gene Lewis, news dir; Jim Zastrow, chief engr.

Seymour

WECB(FM)—Not on air, target date 1994: 104.3 mhz; 2.55 kw. Ant 358 ft. Box 1573, Appleton (54913). Licensee: Brooker Broadcasting. Wash atty: Miller & Miller. ■ Earl J. Brooker, CEO, pres & gen mgr.

Shawano

WTCH(AM)—Sept 3, 1948: 960 khz; 1 kw-U, DA-N. TL: N49 46 47 W88 37 53. Hrs opn: 24. 1456 E. Green Bay St. (54166). (715) 524-2194. FAX: (715) 524-2196. Licensee: Wheeler Broadcasting Inc. (group owner; acq 9-81; $950,000; FTR 9-7-81). Net: CBS. Wash atty: James Cooke. Format: Country. News staff one. Target aud: 25-54; northeast Wisconsin adults. Spec prog: Farm 18 hrs wkly. ■ Ray Wheeler, chmn; Bruce Grassman, pres & gen mgr & gen sls mgr; Doug Erdman, prom mgr, mus dir & news dir; Kristen Murphy, progmg dir; Gary Mach, chief engr. ■ Rates: $12; 12; 12; 12.

WOWN(FM)—Co-owned with WTCH(AM). December 1966: 99.3 mhz; 14 kw. Ant 440 ft. TL: N44 45 14 W88 20 01. Stereo. Hrs opn: 24. Dups AM 10%. Format: Lite hits. News staff 2. Target aud: 20-45. Spec prog: Farm 15 hrs wkly. ■ Doug Erdman, prom dir & progmg dir. ■ Rates: Same as AM.

Sheboygan

WCNZ(AM)—January 1956: 950 khz; 500 w-D, DA. TL: N43 44 33 W87 49 00. Hrs opn: 24. Box 1045, 1156 Union Ave. (53082). (414) 457-5561. FAX: (414) 457-0950. Licensee: Star Cablevision Group (acq 3-31-93; $100,000; FTR 4-19-93). Net: ABC/I, CBS, NBC Talknet, Motor Racing Net. Wash atty: Holland & Knight. Format: News/talk, oldies. News staff 2; news progmg 8 hrs wkly. Target aud: 35-64; upscale adults & business decision-makers. Spec prog: Slovenian one hr wkly, farm, business news 4 hrs, auto racing 5 hrs wkly. ■ Tristan Richards, chmn & CFO; Crista McCulloch, vp sls & vp mktg; Guy Hobbs, prom dir; Dan Randall, news dir & pub affrs dir; Jon Zecherle, chief engr. ■ Rates: $19; 14; 14; 12.

WHBL(AM)—Jan 1, 1926: 1330 khz; 5 kw-D, 1 kw-N, DA-2. TL: N43 43 14 W87 44 04. Box 27 (53082); 2100 Washington Ave. (53081). (414) 458-2107. FAX: (414) 458-9775. Licensee: Sheboygan County Broadcasting. Group owner: Walton Co. (acq 7-72). Net: ABC/E. Format: Full Svc. Target aud: General. Spec prog: Farm 10 hrs, Ger one hr wkly. ■ Michael Walton Sr., pres; Howard R. Stieber, gen mgr; Char Pachniak, gen sls mgr.

WWJR(FM)—Co-owned with WHBL(AM). Mar 1, 1977: 93.7 mhz; 6 kw. Ant 296 ft. TL: N43 43 12 W87 44 04 (CP: ant 254 ft.). Stereo. Prog sep from AM. Net: SMN. Format: Adult contemp. Target aud: 25-49; adults in Sheboygan county/Northern Milwaukee metro area.

*WSHS(FM)—Nov 19, 1971: 91.7 mhz; 180 w-vert. Ant 82 ft. TL: N43 46 37 W87 43 08. Stereo. 1042 School Ave. (53083). (414) 459-3610. FAX: (414) 459-3601. Licensee: Sheboygan Area School District. Format: Adult contemp, AOR. News progmg one hr wkly. Target aud: 18-45; young adults & teens. Spec prog: Hmong 3 hrs wkly. ■ George Longo, pres; William Horsch, gen mgr; T.J. Mlada, prom mgr; Meghan Wurtz, progmg dir; Paul Thielhelm, mus dir; Chris Krenz, news dir; Tom Lang, chief engr.

WWJR(FM)—Listing follows WHBL(AM).

Shell Lake

WCSW(AM)—Dec 30, 1967: 940 khz; 1 kw-D. TL: N45 41 36 W91 57 57. Box 190, Hwy. 63 S. (54871). (715) 468-2123; (715) 468-2146. FAX: (715) 468-2811. Licensee: Charles R. Lutz. Net: ABC/E. Format: Country, MOR. News staff one; news progmg 11 hrs wkly. Target aud: General. Spec prog: Farm 3 hrs wkly. ■ Charles R. Lutz, gen mgr & gen sls mgr; Loren Miller, prom mgr; Steve Lutz, progmg dir & mus dir; Randy McKibben, news dir; Del Dayton, chief engr. ■ Rates: $12.80; 8.80; 12.80; 8.80.

WGMO(FM)—Co-owned with WCSW(AM). December 1974: 95.3 mhz; 3 kw. Ant 168 ft. TL: N45 40 26 W91 58 43. Stereo. Dups AM 20%. (715) 468-2811; (715) 822-8707. Format: Relg.

Sparta

WKLJ(AM)—June 1951: 1290 khz; 5 kw-D, 59 w-N. TL: N43 58 06 W90 51 35. 113 W. Oak St. (54656). (608) 269-3307. Licensee: Sparta-Tomah Broadcasting Company, Inc. (acq 1-19-89). Net: MBS. Rep: Roslin. Format: Classic Country. ■ Zel Rice, pres; Jim Michaels, gen mgr & gen sls mgr; Steve Peterson, prom dir & progmg dir; Mike Burns-Gilbert, mus dir; Robin Colbert, news dir. ■ Rates: $11.50; 11.50; 11.50; 10.50.

WCOW-FM—Co-owned with WKLJ(AM). Mar 1, 1960: 97.1 mhz; 100 kw. Ant 587 ft. TL: N43 58 06 W90 51 35. Stereo. Hrs opn: 24. Prog sep from AM. Net: MBS. Format: Contemp country. News staff 2; news progmg 15 hrs wkly. Target aud: General; 25 plus, rural and city residents. ■ Steve Peterson, opns dir. ■ Rates: $22; 22; 22; 19.50.

Spencer

WOSX(FM)—Sept 20, 1984: 92.3 mhz; 6 kw. Ant 300 ft. TL: N44 48 35 W89 22 01 51. Stereo. Hrs opn: 24. Box 921, Hwy. 13 N., Marshfield (54449). (715) 387-3921. FAX: (715) 389-2210. Licensee: Goetz Broadcasting Corp. (group owner; acq 6-4-93; FTR 7-5-93). Net: SMN. Wash atty: Miller & Miller. Format: Pure gold, oldies. News staff one. Target aud: 25-54. ■ Nathan L. Goetz, pres; Jack Hackman, sr vp & gen mgr; Kevin J. O'Brien, opns mgr; Scott Trentadue, vp sls; Ron Eckes, gen sls mgr; Kevin J. O'Brian, news dir; Clif Groth, vp engrg.

Stevens Point

WMGU(FM)—1988: 104.9 mhz; 3 kw. Ant 328 ft. TL: N44 31 37 W89 37 31. Box 588, Eagle Communications, Lufkin, TX (75902). Licensee: Eagle of Wisconsin Inc. Group owner: Eagle Communications. ■ Tom Love, pres.

WSPO(AM)—1949: 1010 khz; 1 kw-D. TL: N44 32 17 W89 35 43. Box 247, 500 Division St. (54481). (715) 341-9800. FAX: (715) 341-0000. Licensee: Americus Communications Corp. (group owner). Net: NBC, SMN. Rep: Katz. Format: News/talk. Target aud: 25-54. Spec prog: Pol one hr wkly. ■ Rick Muzzy, gen mgr; Gary Wescott, stn mgr & news dir; Darren Lee, progmg dir; Jim Zastrow, chief engr.

WSPT(FM)—Co-owned with WSPO(AM). May 1, 1961: 97.9 mhz; 51 kw. Ant 340 ft. TL: N44 32 17 W89 35 43. Stereo. Prog sep from AM. Format: AC ■ Rick Muzzy, pres; Steve Marten, rgnl sls mgr.

*WWSP(FM)—Sept 28, 1968: 89.9 mhz; 11.5 kw. Ant 233 ft. TL: N44 32 17 W89 35 43. Stereo. Hrs opn: 8 AM-2 AM. Rm. 101, 1101 Reserve St., CAC (54481). (715) 346-3755. Licensee: Board of Regents, Univ. of Wisconsin System. Net: AP. Format: Progsv rock, div. College students. Spec prog: Black 3 hrs, jazz 15 hrs, pub affrs 5 hrs, sports 3 hrs wkly. ■ Mark Tolstedt, gen mgr; Rick Westenberger, chief engr.

Sturgeon Bay

WDOR(AM)—Sept 8, 1951: 910 khz; 1 kw-D. TL: N44 49 38 W87 21 27. Box 549, 800 S. 15th Ave. (54235). (414) 743-4411; (414) 487-2822. FAX: (414) 743-2334. Licensee: Door County Broadcasting Inc. Net: ABC/I. Wash atty: Fisher, Wayland, Cooper & Leader. Format: Adult contemp, news. News staff one; news progmg 23 hrs wkly. Target aud: 21-50. ■ Edward Allen III, pres, gen mgr & progmg dir; Frank Flick, gen sls mgr; Roger Levendusky, news dir; Bill Everson, engrg dir. ■ Rates: $12; 9.50; 9.50; 7.

WDOR-FM—Dec 12, 1966: 93.9 mhz; 77 kw. Ant 640 ft. TL: N44 54 23 W87 22 15. Stereo. Hrs opn: 5 AM-midnight. Dups AM 25%. Format: Adult contemp, sports. News progmg 25 hrs wkly. Target aud: 20-40. Spec prog: Farm 5 hrs wkly. ■ Rates: Same as AM.

WFNL(FM)—Apr 18, 1988: 97.7 mhz; 2 kw. Ant 400 ft. TL: N44 54 21 W87 22 15 (CP: Ant 554 ft.). Stereo. Box 555, 949 Egg Harbor Rd. (54235); 11 N. Third Ave. (54235). (414) 743-6677. FAX: (414) 743-9183. Licensee: Fleet Broadcasting Inc. Group owner: Martz Communications Group (acq 3-12-90; $235,000; FTR 4-2-90). Format: Soft AC. Target aud: 25-54. ■ Timothy D. Martz, pres; Mary Ann Moore, stn mgr; Timothy Midgette, opns mgr; Veronica Roberts, gen sls mgr.

WGEE-FM—Mar 4, 1982: 99.7 mhz; 31 kw. Ant 610 ft. TL: N44 54 21 W87 22 15 (CP: 46 kw, ant 512 ft., TL: N44 38 08 W87 37 37). Stereo. Hrs opn: 24. W2221 Block Rd., Kaukana, (54130). (414) 435-6650; (800) 236-9438. FAX: (414) 766-0452. Licensee: Midwest Communications Inc. (group owner; acq 6-18-93; $3.5 million; FTR 7-5-93). Net: Wheeler News Service. Rep: D & R Radio. Wash atty: Wiley, Rein & Fielding. Format: Contemp hit radio. News staff one; news progmg 2.5 hrs wkly. Target aud: 12-34. ■ Quinn W. Martin, pres; John Nehmer, gen mgr; David Fries, gen sls mgr; Ron Ross, prom mgr, progmg dir & mus dir; Kevin Bessler, news dir; Jim Rammer, chief engr.

***WPFF(FM)**—August 1991: 90.5 mhz; 50 kw. Ant 617 ft. TL: N44 54 23 W87 22 15. Stereo. Hrs opn: 24. Box 444, 1715 Michigan St. (54235). (414) 743-7443. FAX: (414) 743-7543. Licensee: Family Educational Broadcasting Corp. Net: USA. Wash atty: Fischer, Wayland, Cooper & Leader. Format: Adult contemp Christian. News progmg 12 hrs wkly. Target aud: 25-49; baby boomers & boomlets. ■ Mark Schwarzbauer, CEO & gen mgr; John Crean, pres; Arnie Clawson, stn mgr & engrg dir; Jeff Clawson, sls dir; Cathy Gossen, prom dir & pub affrs dir.

Sturtevant

WZXA(FM)—June 18, 1993: 104.7 mhz; 3 kw. Ant 328 ft. TL: N42 46 09 W87 53 31. Hrs opn: 24. Box 081047, Racine (53408); 8609 Industrial Rd., Franksville (53126). (414) 637-2801; (414) 884-1047. FAX: (414) 637-3471. Licensee: Pride Communications of Wisconsin (acq 4-22-91; $70,000; FTR 5-20-91). Net: Unistar, AP. Wash atty: Reddy, Begley & Martin. Format: Adult contemp. News staff one. Target aud: 25-54; adult families with school-age children. ■ James Hooker, pres; Patti J. Kuczen, gen mgr; Jesse Garcia, opns mgr, progmg mgr & mus dir; Steve Ludwig, gen sls mgr; Bradley Scott, prom mgr; Brad Stern, news dir & pub affrs dir; Frank McCoy, chief engr. ■ Rates: $35; 30; 32; 25.

Sun Prairie

WMAD(AM)—Jan 12, 1982: 1190 khz; 1 kw-D, DA. TL: N43 09 36 W89 12 41. 3392 Brooks Dr. (53590). (608) 837-9581. FAX: (608) 825-6707. Licensee: WMAD Inc. (acq 3-22-93; $650,000 with co-located FM; FTR 4-12-93). ■ Lee Leicinger, pres & gen mgr; Kurt Peterson, gen sls mgr; Jeff Tyler, progmg dir; Ken Sweet, chief engr.

WMAD-FM—Apr 12, 1972: 92.1 mhz; 1.75 kw. Ant 400 ft. TL: N43 10 25 W89 15 26. Stereo. Prog sep from AM. ■ John Duncan, progmg dir.

Superior

***KUWS(FM)**—Jan 31, 1966: 91.3 mhz; 940 w-H. Ant -72 ft. TL: N46 43 03 W92 05 26 (CP: 83 kw, ant 646 ft., TL: N46 47 21 W92 06 51). Stereo. 1800 Grand Ave., Univ. of Wisconsin-Superior (54880). (715) 394-8530. Licensee: Board of Regents, Univ. of Wisconsin System. Format: Progsv rock, talk, adult urban contemp. Spec prog: Jazz 10 hrs, class 15 hrs, C&W 6 hrs wkly. ■ John Munson, stn mgr; Jeff Larkin, mus dir; Mike Simonson, news dir; Paul Guello, chief engr.

KXTP(AM)—June 18, 1959: 970 khz; 1 kw-D, 27 w-N. TL: N46 43 28 W92 07 11. Hrs opn: 24. Northland Bldg., 419 W. Michigan St., Duluth, MN (55802). (218) 727-7108. FAX: (218) 727-7108. Licensee: Stereo Broadcasting Inc. Group owner: Lew Latto Group of Northland Radio Stns. (acq 12-1-74). Net: ABC/D. Rep: Katz & Powell; O'Malley Communications. Wash atty: John McVeigh. Format: Music of your life. Target aud: 35 plus. ■ Lewis M. Latto, pres & gen mgr; Herb Manthey, chief opns, progmg dir & news dir; Wilfred A. Meys, chief engr. ■ Rates: $14; 14; 14; 14.

KZIO(FM)—Listing follows WDSM(AM).

WAKX(FM)—See Duluth, Minn.

WAVC(FM)—See Duluth, Minn.

WDSM(AM)—October 1939: 710 khz; 10 kw-D, 5 kw-N, DA-N. TL: N46 39 14 W92 08 51. Hrs opn: 24. 1105 E. Superior St., Duluth (55802). (218) 728-6406. FAX: (218) 728-4317. Licensee: WDSM/KZIO Inc. (acq 8-13-84; $1,300,000; FTR 7-2-84). Net: NBC. Rep: Torbet. Format: Modern C&W. News staff 3; news progmg 20 hrs wkly. Target aud: 25-54. Spec prog: Polka one hr, relg 2 hrs wkly. ■ Patricia NcNulty, pres & gen sls mgr; Kenneth Buehler, gen mgr; Mark Edwards, progmg dir; Jennifer Simonson, news dir; Phil Maki, chief engr.

KZIO(FM)—Co-owned with WDSM(AM). Sept 9, 1979: 102.5 mhz; 100 kw. Ant 600 ft. TL: N46 47 21 W92 07 09. Stereo. Hrs opn: 24. Prog sep from AM. Net: ABC/C. Format: CHR. News progmg 3 hrs wkly. Target aud: 18-34. ■ John Michaels, progmg dir; Tom Bishop, mus dir.

Suring

WRVM(FM)—Sept 17, 1967: 102.7 mhz; 100 kw. Ant 499 ft. TL: N44 59 30 W88 23 55. Stereo. Hrs opn: 24. Box 212, Hwy. 32 N. (54174). (414) 842-2839. Licensee: WRVM Inc. (acq 5-15-68). Net: Moody. Wash atty: John Kenkel. Format: Relg. Spec prog: Farm 5 hrs, classical one hr wkly. ■ Ray Dow, pres; Wendell Baxter, gen mgr; Brian Hay, gen sls mgr; Dennis Jones, progmg dir; Howard Lundgren, news dir; Alan Krans, chief engr.

Sussex

WKSH(AM)—October 1979: 1370 khz; 500 w-U, DA-2. TL: N43 04 40 W88 11 32. W223 N3251 Shady Ln., Pewaukee (53072). (414) 691-1036. Licensee: L&L Pewaukee Ventures Inc. Net: Moody. Format: Relg. Target aud: 25-45; Christians. ■ Jim Corbett, pres; Mark Sergeant, gen mgr; Albert Hajny, chief engr.

Tomah

WBOG(FM)—Mar 11, 1992: 96.1 mhz; 6 kw. Ant 1,075 ft. TL: N43 53 56 W90 29 23. Stereo. Hrs opn: 24. Suite 5, 1021 N. Superior Ave. (54660). (608) 372-9600. FAX: (608) 372-7566. Licensee: Magnum Radio Inc. (acq 9-27-91; FTR 10-14-91). Net: Wisconsin Radio Net. Wash atty: Fisher, Wayland, Cooper & Leader. Format: Oldies, classic rock. Target aud: 25-54. ■ Dave Magnum, pres & gen mgr; Paul Chasteen, natl sls mgr; Len DeSomer, mktg dir; Mark Burg, chief engr. ■ Rates: $15; 15; 15; 15.

WTMB(AM)—Apr 19, 1959: 1460 khz; 1 kw-D. TL: N43 58 07 W90 30 50. Hrs opn: 6 AM-6 PM. Box 588 1008 1/2 Superior Ave., (54660). (608) 372-7188. FAX: (608) 372-9480. Licensee: Phyllis J. Rice (acq 11-1-84). Net: AP, Sun. Format: Farm, talk. News staff 2; news progmg 24 hrs wkly. Target aud: 35 plus, 50 plus retirees; mature. ■ Phyllis Rice, pres & gen mgr; Phyllis Ryan, progmg dir; Jamie Westpfahl, news dir; Darrel Sanders, chief engr.

WVCX(FM)—Jan 29, 1965: 98.9 mhz; 100 kw. Ant 991 ft. TL: N43 51 13 W90 27 28. Stereo. Hrs opn: 24. Box 187 (54660). (608) 372-2323. Licensee: Wisconsin Voice of Christian Youth Inc. (group owner). Format: Relg. ■ Dr. Randall Melchert, pres; Vic Eliason, gen mgr; Helmut Fritz, opns mgr; Jim Schneider, progmg dir; Gordon Morris, news dir; Andy Eliason, chief engr.

WZFR(FM)—July 11, 1990: 94.5 mhz; 2.4 kw. Ant 361 ft. TL: N43 53 49 W90 34 57. Stereo. Hrs opn: 24. Box 588, 1008 1/2 Superior Ave. (54660). (608) 372-9400. FAX: (608) 372-9480. Licensee: Jamie Lee Westpfahl. Format: New adult contemp. Target aud: 25-54. ■ Jamie Westpfahl, pres & gen mgr; John Ryan, gen sls mgr & progmg dir; Steve Erickson, news dir; Jim Zastrow, chief engr.

Tomahawk

WJJQ(AM)—August 1968: 810 khz; 10 kw-D, DA. TL: N45 29 29 W89 43 34 (CP: TL: N45 29 27 W89 43 36). Box 10, 81 E. Mohawk Dr. (54487). (715) 453-4481; (715) 457-4482. FAX: (715) 453-7169. Licensee: Albert Broadcasting Inc. (acq 6-11-84). Net: CBS. Rep: Keystone (unwired net). Wash atty: Fisher, Wayland, Cooper & Leader. Format: Adult contemp, oldies, country. News staff 3; news progmg 15 hrs wkly. Target aud: 25 plus. ■ Gregg Albert, pres, gen mgr, sls dir & news dir; Marguarite Albert, vp; Jan Thomas, Mary Lu Voermans, gen sls mgrs; Phil Richards, prom mgr; Mark Everett, progmg dir & mus dir; Ann Beckman, pub affrs dir; Jim Zastrow, chief engr. ■ Rates: $9.95; 9.95; 9.95; 9.

WJJQ-FM—Oct 15, 1984: 92.5 mhz; 25 kw. Ant 259 ft. TL: N45 29 27 W89 43 36. Stereo. Dups AM 90%. ■ Mark Everett, prom dir & (asst) mus dir; Gregg Albert, mus dir.

Trempealeau

WKBH-FM—Nov 24, 1984: 105.5 mhz; 3 kw. Ant 531 ft. TL: N43 56 33 W91 26 03. Stereo. Hrs opn: 24. Box 1624, La Crosse (54602-1624). (608) 784-9524. FAX: (608) 526-6813. Licensee: Riverview Communications Inc. Net: SMN, CNN. Format: Classic rock/AOR. News staff one; news progmg 24 hrs wkly. Target aud: 25-54. ■ Joe Roskos, pres; Tim Scott, stn mgr, prom dir & progmg dir; Madelyn Grabowenski, opns mgr; Jim Timm, gen sls mgr; Pat Delaney, mus dir & chief engr.

Two Rivers

WCUB(AM)—Licensed to Two Rivers. See Manitowoc.

WLTU(FM)—See Manitowoc.

WTRW(AM)—Oct 29, 1951: 1590 khz; 1 kw-D, 33 w-N. TL: N44 10 23 W87 35 37. Hrs opn: 24. 1414 16th St. (54241-3031). (414) 794-1800. Licensee: Wisconsin Great Lakes Broadcasting Inc. (acq 11-5-92; $145,000; FTR 11-23-92). Net: NBC, NBC Talknet. Wash atty: McCabe & Allen. Format: Oldies, talk. News staff one; news progmg 10 hrs wkly. Target aud: 25-54; baby boomers & professionals. ■ Mark Heller, pres, gen mgr, gen sls mgr, news dir & chief engr. ■ Rates: $10; 10; 10; 8.

Verona

WMMM-FM—July 4, 1991: 105.5 mhz; 4.4 kw. Ant 384 ft. TL: N42 57 42 W89 29 32. 6313 Odana Rd., Madison (53719). (608) 273-9774. FAX: (608) 273-8852. Licensee: Woodward Communications. Format: Alternative. ■ Ralph Cohen, gen mgr; Pat Gallaher, progmg dir.

Viroqua

WVRQ(AM)—Feb 25, 1958: 1360 khz; 1 kw-D, 23 w-N. TL: N43 32 04 W90 52 23. Hrs opn: 6 AM-midnight. Rt. 4 (54665). (608) 637-7200. FAX: (608) 637-7299. Licensee: Robinson Corp. Format: Oldies. News staff one; news progmg 14 hrs wkly. Target aud: 25 plus. Spec prog: Farm 3 hrs, relg 6 hrs, polka 12 hrs wkly. ■ David Robinson, pres & gen mgr; James Graham, gen sls mgr; Jeff Robinson, prom mgr & mus dir; Ernest Betts, progmg dir; Julie Day, news dir. ■ Rates: $12; 12; 12; 10.

WVRQ-FM—Oct 6, 1967: 102.3 mhz; 2.25 kw. Ant 300 ft. TL: N43 31 27 W90 51 51. Stereo. Hrs opn: 5 AM-midnight. Prog sep from AM. Net: Central Ag News Net. Format: Country. News progmg 20 hrs wkly. Target aud: 25-54. Spec prog: Bluegrass 2 hrs, farm 8 hrs wkly. ■ Rates: Same as AM.

Washburn

WEGZ(FM)—Oct 5, 1981: 105.9 mhz; 100 kw. Ant 735 ft. TL: N46 41 31 W90 59 27. Stereo. Hrs opn: 24. Box 207, 101 W. Omaha (54891). (715) 373-5151. FAX: (715) 373-5805. Licensee: DDS Communications Ltd. (acq 4-11-90; $98,000; FTR 5-7-90). Net: ABC/D. Format: Country. News staff one; news progmg 4 hrs wkly. Target aud: 25-45; baby boomers. Spec prog: Relg one hr, polka 3 hrs wkly. ■ Howard Moe, pres; John Warren, gen mgr, gen sls mgr, mktg dir & adv mgr; Steve Williams, chief opns, prom dir, progmg dir & mus dir; Rudy Alin, (asst) mus dir, news dir & pub affrs dir; Alan Brace, chief engr. ■ Rates: $15; 12; 15; 10.

Watertown

WJJO(FM)—Aug 1, 1961: 94.1 mhz; 50 kw. Ant 492 ft. TL: N43 11 43 W88 45 17. Stereo. Hrs opn: 24. 2122 Louann Ln., Madison (53713). (608) 273-1000. FAX: (608) 273-2410. Licensee: WJJO Limited Partnership. Group owner: Mid-West Family Stations (acq 6-18-93; $1.6 million; FTR 7-5-93). Rep: D & R Radio. Format: Classic rock. Target aud: 25-49. ■ Ted Waldbillig, gen sls mgr; Mike Thomas, prom mgr; Pat O'Neil, progmg dir; Sarah Freeman, mus dir; Tim Morrissey, news dir; Roy Simmons, chief engr.

WTTN(AM)—Apr 2, 1950: 1580 khz; 1 kw-D, 7.8 w-N. TL: N43 11 43 W88 45 17. Hrs opn: 6 AM-9 PM. Box 509, 100 E. Main St. (53094). (414) 261-1580; (800) 281-1580. FAX: (414) 261-0624. Licensee: Watertown Radio Inc. (acq 3-18-92; $315,719; FTR 4-6-92). Net: Wis. Radio Net. Rep: Roslin. Format: Country. News staff one;

news progmg 15 hrs wkly. Target aud: 25-54. Spec prog: Relg 4 hrs, farm 20 hrs wkly. ■ Donald D. Sabatke, gen mgr & adv mgr; Donald D. Sabatke, Joe Dagvanno, gen sls mgrs; Matt Nelson, progmg dir & mus dir; Kirk Allen, news dir; Ken Sweet, chief engr. ■ Rates: $13; 13; 13; na.

Waukesha

WAUK(AM)—Mar 27, 1947: 1510 khz; 10 kw-D, DA. TL: N43 01 00 W88 11 42. Stereo. Hrs opn: 6 AM-8:30 PM. 1801 Coral Dr. (53186). (414) 544-6800. FAX: (414) 544-1705. Licensee: Walt-West Wisconsin Inc. (acq 2-10-78). Net: SMN. Wash atty: Hough, & Cook. Format: C&W. News staff one. Target aud: 25 plus. Spec prog: Nascar racing. ■ Ed Walters, pres & gen mgr; Mike Walters, vp; Michael S. Saxton, stn mgr; Jeanne Hauck, prom dir; Scott Aebly, Jeanne Hauck, progmg dirs; Mark Anderson, mus dir; Bob Beringer, news dir; Scott Aebly, pub affrs dir; Don Hunjadi, chief engr. ■ Rates: $25; 25; 25; na.

*WCCX(FM)—Sept 1, 1978: 104.5 mhz; 10 w. Ant 50 ft. TL: N43 00 16 W88 13 39. Hrs opn: 12. 100 N. East Ave. (53186); 221 N. East Ave. (53186). (414) 524-7355; (414) 524-7391. FAX: (414) 524-7139. Licensee: Carroll College Broadcast Bureau. Format: Div. High school & college students. Spec prog: Sp 8 hrs, metal 3 hrs, rap 3 hrs wkly. ■ Chris Watermolen, stn mgr & mus dir; Bonnie Benzschawel, progmg dir; Karen Kabowski, news dir; Andy Pforr, pub affrs dir; LeRoy Wolinkowski, chief engr.

WMIL(FM)—Jan 1, 1962: 106.1 mhz; 50 kw. Ant 976 ft. TL: N43 05 18 W87 54 12. Stereo. Hrs opn: 24. Box 20920, Milwaukee (53220); 12100 W. Howard Ave., Greenfield (53228). (414) 545-8900. FAX: (414) 545-4069. Licensee: Sundance Broadcasting Inc. (group owner; acq 6-1-83; $4.75 million; FTR 5-23-83). Rep: Major Mkt. Wash atty: Dow, Lohnes & Albertson. Format: Country. News staff 2. Target aud: 25-54; middle America. ■ Michael D. Jorgenson, pres; Brian Ongaro, gen mgr; Terry Peters, gen sls mgr; Jerry Amdt, natl sls mgr & mktg dir; Susie Austin, prom mgr; Kerry Wolfe, progmg dir; Mitch Morgan, mus dir; Debbie Young, news dir; Phil Klingler, chief engr.

Waunakee

WYZM(FM)—Apr 20, 1992: 105.1 mhz; 6 kw. Ant 328 ft. TL: N43 13 20 W89 18 01. Stereo. 6313 Odana Rd., Madison (53719). (608) 273-9774; (608) 244-2989. FAX: (608) 273-8852. Licensee: Janice and Ronald Fedler (acq 7-9-92; $246,500; FTR 8-3-92). Net: SMN. Format: Country. Target aud: 18-49. ■ Ron Fedler, CEO; Jan Fedler, pres; Ted Waldbillig, gen mgr & natl sls mgr; Ralph Cohen, gen sls mgr; Dave Murphy, progmg dir & mus dir; Pat Ryan, chief engr.

Waupaca

WDUX(AM)—Apr 29, 1956: 800 khz; 5 kw-D, 500 w-N, DA-1. TL: N44 21 15 W89 03 29. Hrs opn: 5 AM-midnight. Box 247 (54981). (715) 258-5528. Licensee: Laird Broadcasting Co. Net: ABC/E; Tribune, Goetz Group. Format: Country. News staff one; news progmg 20 hrs wkly. Target aud: General. Spec prog: Farm 20 hrs wkly. ■ Dorothy J. Laird, pres; Gary Douglas, stn mgr & progmg dir; Amy Welch, gen sls mgr & prom mgr; Jeff Thelen, news dir; Douglas Moore, chief engr.

WDUX-FM—Jan 29, 1967: 92.7 mhz; 6 kw. Ant 255 ft. TL: N44 21 14 W89 03 44. Stereo. Hrs opn: 5 AM-midnight. Dups AM 10%. Format: Adult contemp. Spec prog: Oldies 6 hrs wkly. ■ Terry Logan, progmg dir & mus dir.

Waupun

WMRH(AM)—May 26, 1966: 1170 khz; 1 kw-D. TL: N43 38 30 W88 43 22. 609 Home Ave. (53963). (414) 324-4441. FAX: (414) 324-3139. Licensee: BBK Broadcasting Inc. (acq 7-90; $170,000; FTR 7-2-90). Net: SMN. Format: MOR, nostalgia. News staff one. Target aud: 35 plus; mature adults. Spec prog: Farm 5 hrs wkly. ■ Chris Bernier, pres; Mark Kastein, vp & gen mgr; Kent Waush, news dir. ■ Rates: $14; 12; 14; na.

Wausau

*WCLQ(FM)—May 23, 1988: 89.5 mhz; 3 kw. Ant 328 ft. TL: 44 58 58 W89 36 06 (CP: 8.5kw, ant 328 ft.). Stereo. Hrs opn: 18. 536 Grand Ave., Schofield (54476). (715) 355-5151. FAX: (715) 355-5246. Licensee: Christian Life Communications Inc. Net: USA. Format: Christian CHR/rock. News progmg 9 hrs wkly. Target aud: 18-35; Christian and secular, unchurched audience that relates to pop/rock format. ■ Charles Sepp, pres, gen mgr & adv dir; Deb Lingford, progmg dir; Jeffrey Kaye, mus dir; Jim Zastrow, chief engr.

WDEZ(FM)—Mar 27, 1964: 101.9 mhz; 100 kw. Ant 489 ft. TL: N44 58 58 W89 36 06 (CP: 98 kw, ant 1,076 ft., TL: N44 55 14 W89 41 31). Stereo. Hrs opn: 24. Box 2048 (54402-2048); 920 Grand Ave. (54476). (715) 355-1614. FAX: (715) 359-0520. Licensee: WRIG Inc. Group owner: Midwest Communications Inc. Net: ABC/D. Rep: Banner. Format: Country. News staff one; news progmg 4 hrs wkly. Target aud: 25-54. Spec prog: Farm 4 hrs wkly. ■ D.E. Wright, pres; Beverly Rice, gen mgr; Janelle Meverdan, sls mgr; Shane Finch, prom dir & progmg dir; Lou Stewart, mus dir; Gene Lewis, news dir; Jim Zastrow, chief engr.

*WHRM(FM)—June 10, 1049: 90.9 mhz; 77 kw. Ant 1,120 ft. TL: N44 55 14 W89 41 31. 821 Univ. Ave., Madison (53706-1496). (608) 264-9600. FAX: (608) 263-9763. Licensee: State of Wis. Educational Communications Bd. Format: Classical, talk, educ. ■ Greg Schnirring, progmg dir.

WIFC(FM)—Listing follows WSAU(AM).

WRIG(AM)—See Schofield.

WSAU(AM)—Jan 30, 1937: 550 khz; 5 kw-U, DA-2. TL: N44 51 26 W89 35 13. Hrs opn: 24. Box 5595 (54402-5595); 602 Jefferson St. (54403). (715) 842-1672. FAX: (715) 848-3158. Licensee: WTMJ Inc. (group owner; acq 12-89). Net: ABC/I. Rep: Christal. Format: Adult contemp. News staff 2. Target aud: 35-64. ■ David J. Armstrong, vp & gen mgr; Patrick Dineer, gen sls mgr; Ken Clark, progmg dir; Al Lippert, news dir; Jim Zastrow, chief engr.

WIFC(FM)—Co-owned with WSAU(AM). 1947: 95.5 mhz; 98 kw. Ant 1,150 ft. TL: N44 55 14 W89 41 31. Stereo. Hrs opn: 24. Prog sep from AM. Net: ABC/FM. Format: CHR. Target aud: 18-49. ■ Jimmy Clark, prom mgr; Duff Damos, progmg dir.

WXCO(AM)—Aug 1, 1953: 1230 khz; 1 kw-U. TL: N44 58 10 W89 36 25. Box 778 (54402). (715) 845-8218. FAX: (715) 845-6582. Licensee: Seehafer Broadcasting Corp. (group owner; acq 9-26-73). Net: CBS. Rep: Katz & Powell, RepCom. Format: Country. News progmg 4 hrs wkly. Target aud: 35 plus. ■ Don Seehafer, pres; Tom Chapman, gen sls mgr; Brad Jeffries, progmg dir & mus dir; Jeff Cannon, news dir; Bob Starr, chief engr.

WYCO(FM)—Co-owned with WXCO(AM). Feb 1, 1985: 107.9 mhz; 100 kw. Ant 1,019 ft. TL: N45 03 33 W89 26 10. Stereo. Prog sep from AM. Net: Unistar. Format: Adult contemp. News progmg 2 hrs wkly. Target aud: 25-49; upscale adults.

Wauwatosa-Milwaukee

WEZW(FM)—Jan 1, 1961: 103.7 mhz; 19.5 kw. Ant 840 ft. TL: N43 05 48 W87 54 19. Stereo. 735 W. Wisconsin Ave., Milwaukee (53233). (414) 272-1040. FAX: (414) 272-0908. Licensee: Multimedia Radio Inc. Group owner: Multimedia Broadcasting Co. (acq 5-1-78). Rep: Major Mkt. Format: Adult contemp. ■ William Bolster, pres; Jack M. Sablla, vp & gen mgr; William Moss, stn mgr; Brian Baumann, gen sls mgr; Thomas McCarthy, progmg dir; Phil Cianciola, news dir; Terrence Baun, chief engr.

West Bend

WBKV(AM)—November 1950: 1470 khz; 2.5 kw-U, DA-2. TL: N43 22 14 W88 09 58. Hrs opn: 5 AM-midnight. Box 933, Suite A, 2410 S. Main St. (53095); 2410 S. Main St. (53095). (414) 334-2344. FAX: (414) 334-1512. Licensee: West Bend Broadcasting Co. Group owner: Gazette Broadcast Co. (acq 10-18-70). Net: AP; Wis. Radio Net. Wash atty: Dow, Lohnes & Albertson. Format: Adult contemp, news/talk. News staff 2; news progmg 20 hrs wkly. Target aud: 25 plus; info-hungry adults interested in loc events. ■ Skip Bliss, pres; James N. Hodges, gen mgr & gen sls mgr; Steve Siegel, progmg dir; Bernadette Parr, news dir; Charles Flynn, chief engr. ■ Rates: $11.45; 11.45; 11.45; 9.35.

WBWI-FM—Co-owned with WBKV(AM). September 1958: 92.5 mhz; 20 kw. Ant 530 ft. TL: N43 25 45 W88 17 53. Stereo. Hrs opn: 5 AM-midnight. Prog sep from AM. Net: AP. Format: Country. News staff 2; news progmg 7 hrs wkly. Target aud: 25-54; female country mus listeners with disposable income. ■ Rates: $11.90; 11.90; 11.90; 9.90.

West Salem

WQJY(FM)—Licensed to West Salem. See La Crosse.

Whitehall

WHTL-FM—Sept 10, 1981: 102.3 mhz; 3 kw. Ant 450 ft. TL: N44 24 47 W91 17 03. Stereo. Hrs opn: 24. Box 66 (54773). (715) 538-4341. FAX: (715) 538-4360. Licensee: Coulee Communications Corp. (acq 1-21-93; $196,000; FTR 2-8-93). Net: AP. Format: Country. News staff one; news progmg 24 hrs wkly. Target aud: 25 plus; adult fans of real country mus who make household buying decisions. Spec prog: Nostalgia 2 hrs wkly. ■ Richard Hencley, pres; Kevin Severson, gen mgr, prom mgr & progmg dir; Dennis Johnson, gen sls mgr; Andy King, mus dir; Eric Haas, news dir; Jim Casey, chief engr.

Whitewater

WISQ(FM)—Not on air, target date unknown: 106.5 mhz; 3 kw. Ant 328 ft. 1231 Orchard Ln., Fort Atkinson (53538). Licensee: Scott M. Trentadue.

WSLD(FM)—Nov 16, 1992: 104.5 mhz; 6 kw. Ant 328 ft. TL: N42 45 47 W88 43 16. Stereo. Hrs opn: 24. N 6534 Hwy. 89 Elkhorn (53190); Box 709 (53190). (414) 473-6680; (608) 883-2054. Licensee: State Long Distance Tel. Co. Net: CNN, AP. Wash atty: Hopkins & Sutter. Format: Country. News staff one; news progmg 10 hrs wkly. Target aud: General. ■ William Pappa, exec vp; Benjamin D. Rosenthal, gen mgr; Steve Kelly, progmg dir; Kyle Bender, news dir.

*WSUW(FM)—Jan 10, 1965: 91.7 mhz; 1.3 kw. Ant 185 ft. TL: N42 50 10 W88 44 36. Stereo. Hrs opn: 6 AM-2 AM. 301 Hyer Hall, Univ. of Wisconsin, 800 W. Main St. (53190). (414) 472-2313; (414) 472-1314. FAX: (414) 472-5029. Licensee: Board of Regents, Univ. of Wisconsin System. Format: Alternative rock, adult alternative. Target aud: General. Spec prog: Class 10 hrs, jazz 15 hrs, world beat 15 hrs wkly. ■ Wilfred Tremblay, gen mgr; Carl Searing III, chief engr.

Whiting

WYTE(FM)—Oct 21, 1985: 96.7 mhz; 50 kw. Ant 492 ft. TL: N44 29 24 W89 32 54. Stereo. Hrs opn: 24. Box 1030, Stevens Point (54481); 3012 Post Rd., Whiting (54481). (715) 341-8838. FAX: (715) 341-9744. Licensee: Sharon Broadcasting Corp. Rep: Katz & Powell. Wash atty: Miller & Miller. Format: Country. News staff one; news progmg 7 hrs wkly. Target aud: 25-49. ■ F. Bary Nienow, pres & gen mgr; Sharon A. Nienow, vp; Kevin J. Weber, gen sls mgr; Ken Steckbaver, progmg dir; Lisa Malaak, news dir.

Wisconsin Dells

WNNO-FM—May 1974: 106.9 mhz; 3 kw. Ant 320 ft. TL: N43 38 23 W89 43 14. Stereo. Hrs opn: 5:30 AM-midnight. 721 Superior St. (53965). (608) 254-2546. FAX: (608) 254-7583. Licensee: Armada Broadcasting Co. (acq 1-85; $375,000; FTR 10-29-84). Format: Top-40. Target aud: 18-40. ■ Bob Van Genderen, gen mgr & gen sls mgr; Danny Heier, progmg dir; Teri Van Genderen, news dir; Ken Ebnetter, chief engr.

WNNO(AM)—May 1969: 900 khz; 1 kw-D, 229 w-N. TL: N43 38 23 W89 43 14. Hrs opn: 5:30 AM-midnight. Dups FM 100%.

Wisconsin Rapids

WFHR(AM)—Nov 5, 1940: 1320 khz; 5 kw-D, 500 w-N, DA-N. TL: N44 24 56 W89 50 07. Box 8022, 645 25th Ave. N. (54495). (715) 424-1300. Licensee: Wisconsin Rapids Broadcast Co. Inc. Group owner: Gazette Broadcast Co. (acq 1-7-82; $1,145,000; FTR 12-7-81). Net: CBS, NBC Talknet. Format: MOR, news/talk, info. News staff 2; news progmg 19 hrs wkly. ■ Sydney Bliss Jr., pres; Miles G. Knuteson, gen mgr & gen sls mgr; Greg Gack, progmg dir; Carl Hilke, news dir.

WWRW(FM)—Co-owned with WFHR(AM). Aug 1, 1946: 103.3 mhz; 73 kw. Ant 331 ft. TL: N44 24 56 W89 50 10. Stereo. Prog sep from AM. Format: Adult contemp/Gold. Target aud: 25-49. ■ Ed Paulson, progmg dir.

Wyoming

Afton

KRSV(AM)—Aug 13, 1985: 1210 khz; 5 kw-D, 250 w-N. TL: N42 43 22 W110 57 39. Box 1210 (83110). (307) 886-9832. FAX: (307) 886-9009. Licensee: Western Wyoming Radio (acq 4-85; $1,000,000; FTR 5-20-85). Format: Modern country, loc news-sports. ■ David Horsley, pres & gen mgr; Dick Howe, gen sls mgr & news dir; Jim Allred, chief engr.

KRSV-FM—Nov 13, 1985: 98.3 mhz; 3 kw. Ant 288 ft. TL: N42 51 02 W110 58 46. Dups AM 100%.

Stations in the U.S.   Wyoming

Basin

KZMQ(AM)—See Greybull.

Buffalo

KBBS(AM)—Apr 17, 1956: 1450 khz; 1 kw-U. TL: N44 20 33 W106 40 54. 90 S. Main St. (82834). (307) 684-7070. FAX: (307) 684-7171. Licensee: KBBS Inc. (acq 5-1-64). Net: ABC/I. Format: C&W, oldies. Spec prog: Basque one hr wkly. ■ Taura Ramsey, gen sls mgr; Kate Fraker, mus dir; Jeanette Maxwell, news dir; Glenn Swiderski, chief engr.

KLGT(FM)—Mar 7, 1983: 92.7 mhz; 3 kw. Ant 26 ft. TL: N44 19 44 W106 41 33 (CP: 92.9 mhz, 12 kw-H, 3 kw-V, ant 1,115 ft., TL: N44 36 08 W106 55 52). Stereo. Hrs opn: 20. 1221 Fort St. (82834). (307) 684-5126; (307) 684-2584. FAX: (307) 684-7676. Licensee: Communications Systems III (acq 7-85; $325,000; FTR 3-27-89). Net: NBC. Format: Country. News progmg 9 hrs wkly. Target aud: 24-54; those with spendable income. Spec prog: Relg one hr wkly. ■ Albert Wildeman, pres, CFO, gen mgr & stn mgr; Albert Wildeman, Gay Higley (asst), gen sls mgrs; Rich Sims, news dir; Rich Sims, Penny Loughan, pub affrs dirs; Randy Rocks, Rich Sims, chiefs engr. ■ Rates: $6; 6; 6; 4.75.

Burns

KMUS-FM—Sept 26, 1990: 101.9 mhz; 50 kw. Ant 492 ft. TL: N41 07 01 W104 40 07. Stereo. Hrs opn: 24. 1513 Carey Ave., Cheyenne (82001). (307) 637-8844. FAX: (307) 632-4845. Licensee: KMUS, Inc. (acq 6-13-91; $44,000; FTR 7-8-91). Rep: Christal, Target.Wash atty: Ed Hummers. Format: Country. News staff one; news progmg 3 hrs wkly. Target aud: 25-54. ■ Keith Jones, gen mgr, stn mgr & natl sls mgr; Pam Middleton, opns mgr; Dave Spencer, gen sls mgr; Jim Wilkinson, progmg dir; Rob Black, news dir; Bryan Christopher, pub affrs dir; Ron Krob, chief engr. ■ Rates: $36; 30; 30; 22.

Casper

*****KATI(AM)**—May 5, 1956: 1400 khz; 1 kw-U. TL: N42 51 22 W106 21 41. Stn currently dark. Box 3984, Univ. Station, Univ. of Wyoming, Laramie (82071). (307) 766-4240. Licensee: Univ. of Wyoming (acq 3-89; $350,000; FTR 3-27-89). ■ Jon Schwartz, gen mgr; Dave Worley, chief engr.

*****KCSP(FM)**—1992: 90.3 mhz; 100 kw. Ant 1,922 ft. TL: N42 44 24 W106 18 23. Stereo. Hrs opn: 24. 1400 Kati Ln. (82601). (307) 265-5414. Licensee: Western Inspirational Broadcasters Inc. (acq 10-3-90). Net: USA, AP. Format: Contemp Christian, educ. News progmg 16 hrs wkly. Target aud: General. ■ Tom Hesse, gen mgr; Tim Allen, stn mgr; Paul Lierman, opns dir, news dir & chief engr; Sue Laduke, pub affrs dir.

KMGW(FM)—Listing follows KTWO(AM).

*****KPGM(FM)**—Oct 15, 1990: 106.9 mhz; 100 kw. Ant 1,824 ft. TL: N42 44 24 W106 18 23. Stereo. Hrs opn: 24. 601 W. Collins Dr. (82601). Licensee: Mongo Broadcast Group Inc. Format: Relg, educ.

KQLT(FM)—Oct 7, 1983: 103.7 mhz; 59.3 kw. Ant 1,909 ft. TL: N42 44 37 W106 18 26. Stereo. Hrs opn: 24. Box 4937 (82604); 251 W. First St. (82601). (307) 265-1984; (307) 266-1037. FAX: (307) 237-5836. Licensee: Natrona Broadcasting Co. Inc. Net: SMN. Rep: McGavren Guild. Wash atty: John Fiorini. Format: Country. News staff 3. Target aud: 25-54. ■ Dan Roberts, chmn, pres, gen mgr & chief engr; Lynn Roberts, sr vp & stn mgr; Gene Cole, opns mgr. ■ Rates: $44; 49; 33; 29.

KTRS(FM)—Nov 30, 1981: 95.5 mhz; 100 kw. Ant 1,920 ft. TL: N42 44 37 W106 18 26. Stereo. 251 W. 1st St. (82601). (307) 235-7000. FAX: (307) 237-5836. Licensee: U.S. Media Wyoming Limited Partnership (acq 1-87). Net: ABC/FM, NBC. Rep: Torbet, Interep. Format: Adult contemp, CHR. News staff one; news progmg 2 hrs wkly. Target aud: 25-44; upscale males & females. ■ Bill Hart, gen mgr; Stan Icenogle, opns dir & chief engr; Melody Hart, gen sls mgr; Martha Steele, prom mgr & progmg dir; Dave Collins, mus dir.

KTWO(AM)—Jan 2, 1930: 1030 khz; 50 kw-U, DA-N. TL: N42 50 34 W106 13 07. 150 N. Nichols (82601). (307) 266-5252. FAX: (307) 235-9143. Licensee: Clear Channel Radio Inc. Net: CBS. Rep: Katz. Wash atty: Cohn & Marks. Format: Country. News staff 12; news progmg 24 hrs wkly. Target aud: 25-54. ■ Jack Rosenthal, pres; Bob Price, vp & gen mgr; John Leader, opns mgr; Connie Ashba, gen sls mgr; Rich Bircumshaw, news dir; Randy Evans, chief engr. ■ Rates: $65; 45; 50; 12.

KMGW(FM)—Co-owned with KTWO(AM). Oct 1, 1967: 94.5 mhz; 63 kw. Ant 230 ft. TL: N42 44 03 W106 20 00. Stereo. Prog sep from AM. Format: Adult contemp.

KVOC(AM)—Oct 1, 1946: 1230 khz; 1 kw-U. TL: N42 50 05 W106 17 44. Box 2090 (82602); 2323 E. 15th St. (82609). (307) 265-2727. FAX: (307) 265-1641. Licensee: KVOC Inc. (acq 6-19-64). Net: Intermountain. Format: Modern country. ■ Alice Bubeck, pres; Ray Ebert, gen mgr; Stan Icenogle, chief engr.

Cheyenne

KFBC(AM)—1940: 1240 khz; 1 kw-U. TL: N41 07 17 W014 48 07. Hrs opn: 5 AM-midnight. 1806 Capitol Ave. (82001). (307) 634-4461. FAX: (307) 634-8586. Licensee: Montgomery Broadcasting L.L.C. (acq 7-1-93; $250,000). Net: ABC/I. Rep: Eastman; Art Moore.Format: Oldies, news/talk. News staff 3; news progmg 25 hrs wkly. Target aud: 35-54. Spec prog: Sp 2 hrs wkly. ■ Dave Montgomery, pres & gen mgr; Larry Procitti, opns dir; Pat Turner, news dir. ■ Rates: $12; 8; 8; 6.

KFBQ(FM)—Sept 1, 1968: 97.9 mhz; 100 kw. Ant 541 ft. TL: N41 06 01 W105 00 23. Stereo. Hrs opn: 24. Prog sep from AM. 1806 Capitol Ave. (82001). (307) 637-7771. Licensee: Buck Broadcasting Corp. Rep: Art Moore, Eastman. Format: CHR. Target aud: 18-34. ■ Harold F. Buck, pres; Jill Buck, stn mgr; Allen Fee, opns mgr; Woody Harrelson, mus dir. ■ Rates: $10; 8; 8; 6.

KKAZ(FM)—Listing follows KUUY(AM).

KLEN(FM)—Sept 26, 1983: 106.3 mhz; 3 kw. Ant -3 ft. TL: N41 08 08 W104 48 12. Stereo. Hrs opn: 24. 1416 Bradley Ave. (82001). (307) 637-5555; (307) 637-6051. FAX: (307) 634-8031. Licensee: Blue Sky Broadcasting Inc. Rep: Banner; Target.Wash atty: Barry Skidelsky. Format: Adult contemp. News progmg one hr wkly. Target aud: 25-54; upscale women. ■ Phil Noble, pres, gen mgr & gen sls mgr; Kevin Mee, opns mgr; Ann Peterson, dev dir; Brenda Mee, natl sls mgr, rgnl sls mgr & prom dir; Deborah Hodge-Jennings, mktg dir; Gregg Dobbin, adv dir; Ron Krob, chief engr. ■ Rates: $14; 12; 12; 10.

KMUS-FM—See Burns.

KRAE(AM)—Apr 29, 1961: 1480 khz; 1 kw-D, 67 w-N. TL: N41 07 26 W104 49 10. Stereo. Box 189, 2109 E. 10th St. (82003). (307) 634-5723. FAX: (307) 638-8922. Licensee: KRAE Inc. (acq 1972). Net: AP, CBS. Rep: PRO Radio, Mountain. Format: Solid gold. Spec prog: Sp 2 hrs wkly. ■ Tom Bauman, pres, gen mgr, prom mgr & progmg dir; Gwynn Holloway, gen sls mgr; Brenda Burt, mus dir.

KSHY(AM)—1952: 1370 khz; 1 kw-D, 66 w-N. TL: N41 07 17 W104 50 22 (CP: COL Fox Farm; 1530 khz; 10 kw-D, 1 kw-N, DA-N). 1616 Warren Ave. (82001). (307) 635-8787. Licensee: BDG Enterprises Inc. Group owner: Mid-America Gospel Radio (acq 9-15-86; grpsl; FTR 8-18-86). Format: Christian music and prog. ■ Frank Treblood, gen mgr; Philip W. French, gen sls mgr; Diane Luna, progmg dir & mus dir; Barry Meyer, news dir.

KUUY(AM)—(Orchard Valley). 1952: 650 khz; 8.5 kw-D, 500 w-N, DA-N. TL: N41 03 09 W104 49 53. Stn currently dark. Box 926, Cheyenne (82003-0926). 1370 Southwest Dr., Cheyenne (82007). Licensee: Windsor Communications Inc. of Wyoming ($1 million with co-located FM; FTR 7-5-93). ■ Merry Lowrey, stn mgr.

KKAZ(FM)—Co-owned with KUUY(AM). August 1961: 100.7 mhz; 100 kw. Ant 490 ft. TL: N41 06 01 W105 00 23. Stereo. Stn currently dark.

Cody

KODI(AM)—March 1947: 1400 khz; 1 kw-U. TL: N44 30 30 W109 04 05. Hrs opn: 6 AM-midnight. Box 1210, 2001 Mountain View Dr. (82414). (307) 587-4100. FAX: (307) 527-5045. Licensee: Yellowstone Ventures Inc. (acq 12-26-91; $286,000 with co-located FM; FTR 1-13-92). Net: AP, MBS, SMN. Format: Golden oldies, news. News staff one; news progmg 20 hrs wkly. Target aud: 35 plus. Spec prog: Big band 6 hrs, Rush Limbaugh 15 hrs, talk 3 hrs wkly. ■ Roger Sedam, gen mgr & gen sls mgr; Rob Hamilton, progmg dir & mus dir; Buzzy Hasrick, news dir; Tom Morrison, pub affrs dir; Stan Icenaugle, chief engr.

KTAG(FM)—Co-owned with KODI(AM). Nov 30, 1981: 97.9 mhz; 100 kw. Ant 1,901 ft. TL: N44 29 44 W109 09 13. Stereo. Hrs opn: 6 AM-midnight. Prog sep from AM. Net: SMN. Rep: Torbet. Format: Adult contemp. News progmg 6 hrs wkly. Target aud: 25-39; upper middle class, young families, sub w/some college. 60% female.

*****KYDZ(FM)**—Aug 1976: 90.1 mhz; 10 kw. Ant 459 ft. TL: N44 31 29 W109 04 06. 919 Cody Ave. (82414). (307) 587-5266. Licensee: Park County School District No. 6, State of Wyoming. Format: CHR. ■ Brendan O'Connor, gen mgr.

Diamondville

KBCK(FM)—Not on air, target date unknown: 105.3 mhz; 16.5 kw. Ant 869 ft. TL: N41 47 19 W110 30 29. Box 8085, c/o Radio Property Ventures, Mitchell, IL (62040). Licensee: Radio Property Ventures-Cheyenne Inc. (acq 7-20-89).

Douglas

KKTY(AM)—June 22, 1957: 1470 khz; 1 kw-D, 500 w-N. TL: N42 45 48 W105 23 32. Hrs opn: 6 AM-10 PM. 255 N. Russell Ave. (82633). (307) 358-3636. FAX: (307) 358-3656. Licensee: Douglas Broadcasting (acq 2-11-93; $120,000 with co-located FM; FTR 3-8-93). Format: Country, classic rock. News staff one; news progmg 3 hrs wkly. Target aud: General; miners, railroaders, ranchers, citizens of Converse County. ■ Sherry Fields, pres; Craig Goodrich, vp; Greg Robbins, stn mgr & progmg mgr. ■ Rates: $12; 12; 12; 12.

KKTY-FM—Dec 6, 1982: 99.3 mhz; 813 w. Ant 530 ft. TL: N42 43 42 W105 31 46. Stereo. Hrs opn: 6 AM-10 PM. News staff one; news progmg 2 hrs wkly. ■ Rates: Same as AM.

Evanston

KEVA(AM)—June 27, 1953: 1240 khz; 1000 w-U. TL: N41 15 29 W111 00 51. Box 190, 568 Airport Rd. (82931). (307) 789-9101. FAX: (307) 789-8521. Licensee: Evanston Broadcasting Co. Inc. Group owner: Radio Managemnet Associates Inc. (acq 1979). Rep: Eastman, Art Moore. Format: Adult contemp. News progmg 15 hrs wkly. Target aud: 25-54. ■ David B. Smith, gen mgr & gen sls mgr; Debbie Minear, prom dir; Michael Richard, progmg dir, mus dir & news dir; Dennis Silver, chief engr.

KOTB(FM)—Co-owned with KEVA(AM). June 1982: 106.3 mhz; 110 w. Ant 1,523 ft. TL: N41 21 11 W110 54 28. Stereo. Prog sep from AM. (307) 789-8255. Format: Country.

Evansville

KUYO(AM)—Aug 23, 1985: 830 khz; 10 kw-D. TL: N42 52 13 W106 12 12. Box 90395, Casper (82609); 740 Luker Ln. (82636). (307) 577-5896. Licensee: North Valley Enterprises Inc. Group owner: Enterprise Network. Format: Christian country. ■ Steve Stumbo, gen mgr & gen sls mgr.

Fort Bridger

KBVZ(FM)—Not on air, target date unknown: 99.3 mhz; 6 kw. Ant 154 ft. TL: N41 15 44 W110 20 27. Box 34 (82933). Licensee: James R. Dunker. Format: Adult contemp. ■ James R. Dunker, pres; Leanna Salgowski, gen mgr.

Gillette

KAML-FM—Listing follows KIML(AM).

KGWY(FM)—Jan 5, 1983: 100.7 mhz; 100 kw. Ant 635 ft. TL: N44 14 35 W105 32 19. Stereo. Box 1179 (82717); 2810 Southern Dr. (82716). (307) 686-2242. Licensee: Quality Communications Inc. Group owner: Video Communications & Radio Inc. Net: ABC/C. Format: Adult classic rock. News staff one. Target aud: 20-45. ■ Richard Batenburg Jr., pres; Michael Berry, gen mgr, prom dir & progmg dir; Mat O'Brien, mus dir; Misty Barber, news dir; Art Bendix, chief engr. ■ Rates: $13.15; 13.15; 13.15; 5.50.

KIML(AM)—Sept 13, 1957: 1270 khz; 5 kw-D, 1 kw-N, DA-N. TL: N44 18 12 W015 59 52. Stereo. Box 1009 (82717); 400 E. Third Ave. (82716). (307) 682-4747. FAX: (307) 687-0568. Licensee: Gillette Broadcasting Co. Net: AP. Format: Country. Target aud: 25 plus. ■ Roy Mapel, CEO; Bob Ostlund, pres; Ray Mapel, gen mgr & gen sls mgr; David King, stn mgr & news dir; Joe Lusk, mus dir. ■ Rates: $14.50; 14.50; 14.50; 14.50.

KAML-FM—Co-owned with KIML(AM). May 1976: 96.9 mhz; 100 kw. Ant 456 ft. TL: N44 18 10 W105 27 00. Stereo. Prog sep from AM. (Acq 12-23-88). Format: Oldies. Target aud: 25-54. ■ Rates: Same as AM.

Green River

KSIT(FM)—See Rock Springs.

KUGR(AM)—June 18, 1976: 1490 khz; 1 kw-U. TL: N41 30 56 W109 26 11. Hrs opn: 24. Box 970, 167 E. Railroad (82935). (307) 875-6666. FAX: (307) 875-5847. Licen-

Wyoming Directory of Radio

see: Wagon Wheel Communications Corp. (acq 1-1-79). Net: MBS. Format: Adult contemp. News staff one. Target aud: 30 plus. Spec prog: Sp 4 hrs wkly. ■ Al Harris, pres, gen mgr & chief engr; Sarina Simmons, mus dir; Steve Core, news dir. ■ Rates: $10; 10; 10; 6.

Greybull

KZMQ(AM)—May 20, 1979: 1140 khz; 10 kw-D. TL: N44 27 01 W108 02 56. Box 352 (82426). (307) 765-9422. FAX: (307) 765-9422. Licensee: Big Horn Communications Inc. (group owner; acq 3-87). Net: SMN. Format: Adult contemp. News staff one. Target aud: 25-49. ■ Ray Moser, gen mgr; Jeff Keith, stn mgr; Elaine Morud, opns mgr.

KZMQ-FM—Feb 21, 1986: 100.3 mhz; 56 kw. Ant 2,443 ft. TL: N44 48 41 W107 55 06. Stereo. Prog sep from AM. Format: Country.

Jackson

KMTN(FM)—Listing follows KSGT(AM).

KSGT(AM)—July 20, 1962: 1340 khz; 1 kw-U. TL: N43 30 22 W110 45 16. Box 100, 645 S. Cache (83001). (307) 733-2120. FAX: (307) 733-7773. Licensee: Crecelius-Lundquist Communications Corp. Group owner: Chaparral Communications (acq 11-30-92; $215,000 with KMER[AM] Kemmerer; FTR 12-21-92). Net: ABC/I. Wash atty: Keck, Mahin & Cate. Format: Country. News staff one; news progmg 6 hrs wkly. Target aud: 25 plus. ■ Jerrold Lundquist, pres; Scott Anderson, gen mgr & vp opns; Eric Rosen, gen sls mgr; Del Ray John, progmg dir & mus dir; Thomas G. Ninnemann, news dir. ■ Rates: $16.25; 16.25; 16.25; 15.

KMTN(FM)—Co-owned with KSGT(AM). Dec 16, 1974: 96.9 mhz; 48 kw. Ant 940 ft. TL: N43 27 42 W110 45 10. Stereo. Prog sep from AM. Box 927 (83001). (307) 733-4500. Net: ABC. Format: Adult classic rock. Target aud: 18-54. Spec prog: Class, jazz, new age. ■ Russ Graham, progmg dir & mus dir. ■ Rates: Same as AM.

***KUWJ(FM)**—Nov 1992: 90.3 mhz; 3 kw. Ant 1,105 ft. TL: N43 27 40 W110 45 09. Stereo. Hrs opn: 5 AM-midnight. Rebroadcasts KUWR(FM) Laramie 100%. Box 3984, Laramie (82071). (307) 766-4240. Licensee: University of Wyoming. Net: NPR, APR. Format: News, classical, progsv. News progmg 42 hrs wkly. Target aud: General. Spec prog: Folk 4 hrs, state news 3 hrs wkly. ■ Jon B. Schwartz, gen mgr; Don Woods, opns dir & progmg dir; Kelly Collini, dev dir & sls dir; Nancy Wood, mktg dir & prom dir; Bob Beck, news dir; Chris Heck, engrg dir. ■ Rates: $12; 8; 12; 8.

KZJH(FM)—July 13, 1989: 95.3 mhz; 100 kw. Ant 1,056 ft. TL: N43 27 40 W110 45 09. Hrs opn: 24. Box 2620, 475 N. Cache St., (83001). (307) 733-1770. FAX: (307) 733-4760. Licensee: Teton Broadcasting L.P. Net: SMN. Format: Adult contemp. Target aud: 18-55. ■ Sandy McManus, stn mgr; Silver Jacobson, gen sls mgr; Sean Lowman, progmg dir; John Anthony, mus dir; Amy Richards, news dir; Bill McManus, chief engr.

Kemmerer

KMER(AM)—Dec 7, 1962: 950 khz; 5 kw-D, 500 w-N. TL: N41 47 57 W110 32 44. Box 432, 436 Fossil Butte Dr. (83101). (307) 877-4422. FAX: (307) 877-5537. Licensee: Chaparral Broadcasting Inc. Group owner: Chaparral Communications (acq 11-30-92; $215,000 with KSGT[AM]-KMTN[FM] Jackson; FTR 12-21-92). Net: ABC/I. Format: Country. News staff 2; news progmg 7 hrs wkly. Target aud: 25-54. Spec prog: Farm 3 hrs, news/talk 7 hrs wkly. ■ Jim Carroll, pres & gen mgr; J. C. Jewitt, prom mgr & news dir; Jim Thoeny, progmg dir; Bill Smith, mus dir; William McManus, chief engr. ■ Rates: $13.20; 13.20; 13.20; 13.20.

Lander

KOVE(AM)—1947: 1330 khz; 5 kw-D, 1 kw-N, DA-N. TL: N42 50 35 W108 44 38. Box 430, 7000 N. Hwy. 287 (82520). (307) 332-5683. FAX: (307) 332-5548. Licensee: Fremont Broadcasting Inc. Net: CBS. Format: C&W. News staff one; news progmg 10 hrs wkly. Target aud: 25 plus. Spec prog: Farm 4 hrs wkly. ■ Dan Breece, pres; Joe Kenney, gen mgr & gen sls mgr; Ken Lewis, progmg dir; Kevin Kilmer, news dir; Jim Hime, chief engr. ■ Rates: $12; 11; 11; 9.

KDLY(FM)—Co-owned with KOVE(AM). 1975: 97.5 mhz; 62 kw. Ant 420 ft. TL: N42 49 20 W108 45 48. Stereo. Prog sep from AM. Format: Top-40. News progmg 5 hrs wkly. Target aud: 18-49; general. ■ Joe Kenney, progmg dir. ■ Rates: Same as AM.

Laramie

KCGY-FM—Listing follows KOWB(AM).

KIMX(FM)—Apr 10, 1989: 105.5 mhz; 6 kw. Ant 328 ft. TL: N41 17 15 W105 26 38. Stereo. Hrs opn: 24. Suite 202, 302 S. 2nd (82070). (307) 745-5208. FAX: (307) 745-3315. Licensee: Laramie Women's Hispanic Network Inc. Rep: Target, Art Moore, IMN. Format: Contemp easy lstng. News staff one; news progmg 7 hrs wkly. Target aud: 24-59; upscale, well-to-do adults. ■ Constance S. Lucas, pres; Ronald Lillestol, gen mgr; Timothy A. Branson, gen sls mgr; Tina Bowen, progmg dir; Ronald Krob, chief engr. ■ Rates: $9.50; 9.50; 9.50; 7.50.

KKNG(FM)—Not on air, target date unknown: 104.5 mhz; 3 kw. Ant 951 ft. TL: N41 17 08 W105 26 41. Box 90357, Atlanta, GA (30364). Licensee: dba Centennial Broadcasters.

KLDI(AM)—Feb 27, 1962: 1210 khz; 10 kw-D, 1 kw-N, DA-N. TL: N41 15 19 W105 33 01. Stereo. 409 S. 4th St. (82070). (307) 745-7396. FAX: (307) 745-7397. Licensee: Chaparral Broadcasting Inc. Group owner: Chaparral Communications (acq 11-30-92; $274,000 with co-located FM; FTR 12-21-92). Net: CBS. Rep: Art Moore. Format: Country. Target aud: 25-49. Spec prog: Farm one hr, nostalgia 6 hrs, new age 3 hrs wkly. ■ K.W. Gray-Bow, gen mgr; Kelly Ryan, opns mgr; Susie Sherron, gen sls mgr.

KRQU(FM)—Co-owned with KLDI(AM). Sept 23, 1974: 102.9 mhz; 100 kw. Ant 1,220 ft. TL: N41 18 39 W105 27 12. Stereo. Prog sep from AM.

KOWB(AM)—Feb 20, 1948: 1290 khz; 5 kw-D, 1 kw-N, DA-2. TL: N41 17 02 W105 34 51. Hrs opn: 22. Box 1290, 3525 Soldier Springs Rd. (82070). (307) 745-4888. FAX: (307) 742-4576. Licensee: Gowdy Family Ltd. Partnership (group owner; acq 12-1-66). Net: ABC/I, MBS. Rep: Keystone (unwired net), Art Moore. Format: Adult contemp. News staff one; news progmg 7 hrs wkly. Target aud: 25-54; women. Spec prog: Farm one hr wkly. ■ Curt Gowdy, pres; Andrew W. Hoefer, gen mgr & gen sls mgr; Jim Michaels, prom mgr & mus dir; Ray Hageman, news dir; Rhett Downing, chief engr. ■ Rates: $9.50; 9.50; 9.50; 7.

KCGY-FM—Co-owned with KOWB(AM). Nov 7, 1983: 95.1 mhz; 100 kw. Ant 1,070 ft. TL: N41 18 34 W105 27 11. Stereo. Prog sep from AM. Net: Unistar, CNN. Format: Country. Target aud: 25-54.

KRQU(FM)—Listing follows KLDI(AM).

***KUWR(FM)**—Sept 10, 1966: 91.9 mhz; 100 kw. Ant 1,128 ft. TL: N41 18 39 W105 27 12. Stereo. Hrs opn: 5 AM-midnight. Box 3984, Univ. Stn. (82071). (307) 766-4240. Licensee: Univ. of Wyoming. Net: NPR, APR. Format: News, progsv, class. News staff 3; news progmg 42 hrs wkly. Target aud: 25-54; educated, college graduates, professionals, upper income. Spec prog: Folk 4 hrs, state news 3 hrs wkly. ■ Jon Schwartz, gen mgr; Kelly Collini, dev dir & sls dir; Nancy Wood, mktg dir & prom mgr; Don Woods, progmg dir; Bob Beck, news dir; Chris Heck, chief engr. ■ Rates: $12; 8; 12; 8.

Newcastle

KASL(AM)—July 10, 1953: 1240 khz; 1 kw-U. TL: N43 50 47 W104 12 45. Hrs opn: 24. 227 S. Seneca Ave. (82701-2820). (307) 746-4433. FAX: (307) 746-4435. Licensee: Castle Radio (acq 11-18-91; $50,000; FTR 12-9-91). Net: ABC/I, ABC/C, SMN. Rep: Eastman, Art Moore. Format: Adult contemp, country. News staff one; news progmg 35 hrs wkly. Target aud: 25 plus; farm/ranch & urban adults, county residents. Spec prog: Farm 5 hrs, class 2 hrs wkly. ■ Steve Holloway, pres, gen mgr, opns dir & chief engr; Jerry Baird, gen sls mgr & prom mgr. ■ Rates: $6.55; 5.57; 5.16; na.

Orchard Valley

KUUY(AM)—Licensed to Orchard Valley. See Cheyenne.

Powell

KPOW(AM)—Mar 30, 1941: 1260 khz; 5 kw-D, 1 kw-N, DA-N. TL: N44 42 00 W108 46 00. Hrs opn: 6 AM-1 AM. Box 968, 912 Lane 11 1/2 (82435). (307) 754-5183. FAX: (307) 754-9667. Licensee: Chaparral Broadcasting Inc. Group owner: Chaparral Communications (acq 11-30-92; $215,000 with co-located FM; FTR 12-21-92). Net: ABC/I. Wash atty: Keck, Mahin, Cate. Format: C&W. News staff one; news progmg 38 hrs wkly. Spec prog: Farm 20 hrs wkly. ■ David Merkel, gen mgr; Donna Merkel, sls dir; Scott Mangold, progmg dir; Steve Kramer, mus dir; David James, news dir; David Bateham, chief engr. ■ Rates: $15; 12.20; 13.45; 12.20.

KLZY(FM)—Co-owned with KPOW(AM). May 15, 1982: 92.5 mhz; 100 kw. Ant 1,857 ft. TL: N44 29 49 W109 09 19. Stereo. Hrs opn: 6 AM-midnight. Prog sep from AM. (307) 754-5186. Net: ABC/D. Format: Adult contemp. News progmg 4 hrs wkly. ■ David Merkel, progmg dir; John Kinsella, mus dir. ■ Rates: Same as AM.

Rawlins

KRAL(AM)—February 1947: 1240 khz; 1 kw-U. TL: N41 46 55 W107 15 40. 2346 W. Spruce (82301). (307) 324-3315. FAX: (307) 324-3509. Licensee: Mt. Rushmore Broadcasting Inc. (acq 8-6-93; $80,000 with co-located FM; FTR 8-23-93). ■ Rich Moore, pres.

KIQZ(FM)—Co-owned with KRAL(AM). Nov 12, 1981: 92.7 mhz; 3 kw. Ant 298 ft. TL: N41 46 16 W107 14 15. Stereo.

Riverton

***KCWC-FM**—March 1974: 88.1 mhz; 3 kw. Ant 1,449 ft. TL: N42 34 59 W108 42 36. Stereo. 2660 Peck Ave., Riverton (82501). (307) 856-9291. Licensee: Board of Trustees, Central Wyoming College. Format: Class, jazz, new age. ■ JoAnne McFarland, pres; Greg Ray, gen mgr; Dale Smith, stn mgr; Roger Hicks, chief engr.

KTAK(FM)—Listing follows KVOW(AM).

KTRZ(FM)—Dec 4, 1984: 93.1 mhz; 100 kw. Ant 884 ft. TL: N42 43 10 W108 08 41. Stereo. Hrs opn: 24. Box 808, 1002 N. 8th West (82501). (307) 856-2922. FAX: (307) 856-7552. Licensee: Wind River Communications Inc. Net: Moody, MBS, Westwood One. Rep: Tacher, O'Malley, Interep. Format: Adult contemp, classic rock. News staff 2; news progmg 20 hrs wkly. Target aud: 25-54; Regional/local tourists, agribusiness, core population. Spec prog: Farm 5 hrs, oldies 6 hrs wkly. ■ Kurt Browall, pres, gen mgr & gen sls mgr; Larry Heron, opns mgr & news dir; Wade Werth, prom mgr; Wave Werth, progmg dir; Bob Connelly, chief engr.

KVOW(AM)—July 2, 1948: 1450 khz; 1 kw-U. TL: N43 01 35 W108 20 45. 603 E. Pershing Ave. (82501). (307) 856-2251. FAX: (307) 856-0252. Licensee: Riverton Broadcasting Co. (acq 4-1-61). Net: ABC/I. Rep: Eastman. Format: Country. Spec prog: Farm 5 hrs wkly. ■ Steve Kehl, gen mgr; Brenda Allen, progmg dir; Mike Stevens, news dir; Lonnie Fairfield, chief engr.

KTAK(FM)—Co-owned with KVOW(AM). Dec 15, 1976: 93.9 mhz; 50 kw. Ant 951 ft. TL: N42 43 10 W108 08 45. Stereo. Net: ABC/E. Format: Adult contemp. ■ Ron Twist, progmg dir.

Rock Springs

KQSW(FM)—Listing follows KRKK(AM).

KRKK(AM)—1938: 1360 khz; 5 kw-D, 1 kw-N, DA-N. TL: N41 37 12 W109 14 20. Box 2128 (82901); 2717 Yellowstone Rd. (82901). (307) 362-3793. FAX: (307) 362-8727. Licensee: Southwest Wyoming Broadcast Group Inc. Group owner: Heritage Broadcast Group Inc. (acq 9-1-89). Net: SMN. Format: Oldies. ■ Steven Humphries, pres; Jon Collins, gen mgr & chief engr; Tom Ellis, gen sls mgr; Diane Reynolds, prom mgr; Tim Murphy, progmg dir & mus dir.

KQSW(FM)—Co-owned with KRKK(AM). January 1977: 96.5 mhz; 100 kw. Ant 1,680 ft. TL: N41 25 54 W109 07 01. Prog sep from AM. Format: Country.

KSIT(FM)—October 1981: 104.5 mhz; 100 kw. Ant 1,630 ft. TL: N41 26 00 W109 07 02. Stereo. Hrs opn: 24. Box 1058, Suite B, 1750 Sunset Blvd. (82902). (307) 362-7034; (307) 362-7039. FAX: (307) 875-4545. Licensee: Sunset Broadcasting (acq 12-1-84). Net: ABC/C, ABC/R. Rep: Eastman, Art Moore. Wash atty: Arent, Fox, Kinter, Plotkin & Kahn. Format: CHR, rock/AOR. News staff one; news progmg 10 hrs wkly. Target aud: 18-45; general. ■ Barbara Mathis, pres; Charles Reeves, vp, gen mgr, stn mgr & gen sls mgr; John Beach, opns mgr & progmg dir; Scott August, mus dir & news dir; Charlie Radman, asst mus dir; Dennis Silver, chief engr. ■ Rates: $15; 15; 15; 11.

***KUWZ(FM)**—Not on air, target date Summer 1994: 90.5 mhz; 100 kw. Ant 1,135 ft. Stereo. Hrs opn: Sunrise-sunset. Dups KUWR (FM) Laramie 100%. Box 3984, Laramie (82071). Licensee: Univ. of Wyoming (group owner). Net: NPR, APR. Format: News, classics, AAA. News staff 3; news progmg 52 hrs wkly. Target aud: General. Spec prog: Folk. ■ Jon Schwartz, gen mgr; Kelly Collins, dev dir & sls dir; Nancy Wood, prom dir; Don

Woods, progmg dir; Chris Hock, engrg dir. ■ Rates: $12; 8; 12; 8.

KYCS(FM)—Oct 1, 1986: 95.1 mhz; 100 kw. Ant 1,635 ft. TL: N41 29 50 W109 20 36. Stereo. Box 2046 (82902). (307) 362-6746. FAX: (307) 875-5847. Licensee: Allen Harris. Net: SMN. Format: Top-40. ■ Faith Harris, pres; Hal Hardy, gen mgr & gen sls mgr; Al Harris, mus dir & chief engr; Steve Core, news dir; Bobby Diamond, pub affrs dir.

Sheridan

KROE(AM)—March 18, 1961: 930 khz; 5 kw-D, 117 w-N. TL: N44 47 54 W106 55 51. Hrs opn: 24. Box 5086 (82801); 1716 KROE Ln. (82801). (307) 672-7421. FAX: (307) 672-2933. Licensee: Lovcom Inc. Net: CBS. Rep: Target. Format: Country, div, news/talk. News staff one; news progmg 20 hrs wkly. Target aud: 25-54; general. Spec prog: Pol 2 hrs, big band 5 hrs, oldies 6 hrs wkly. ■ Kim Love, pres & gen mgr; Judy Taylor, gen sls mgr; Bob Grammens, progmg dir; Angela Gorman, news dir; Bruce Faulkner, chief engr. ■ Rates: $9.50; 8.75; 8.75; 8.

KROE-FM—December 1977: 94.9 mhz; 58 kw. Ant 44 ft. TL: N44 47 54 W106 55 51. Stereo. Hrs opn: 24. Prog sep from AM. Format: Contemp hit. Target aud: 18-49; general.

KWYO(AM)—July 9, 1934: 1410 khz; 5 kw-D, 500 w-N. TL: N44 46 15 W106 55 37. Hrs opn: 24. Suite 207, 2 N. Main St. (82801). (307) 672-0701. FAX: (307) 672-8028. Licensee: Community Media Inc. (acq 1-8-81; $937,500 with co-located FM; FTR 1-26-81). Net: ABC/I. Rep: Eastman, Intermountain Net, Art Moore. Wash atty: Leventhal, Senter & Lerman. Format: C&W. News staff one; news progmg 20 hrs wkly. Target aud: 25-54. ■ Jerry Walker, gen mgr & gen sls mgr; Laurel Rogers, opns mgr; prom mgr & progmg dir; Peggy Browning-Hepp, adv mgr; Joel McGinnis, mus dir; Glen Swiderski, chief engr. ■ Rates: $8; 6; 8; 5.

KWYO-FM—September 1978: 96.5 mhz; 25 kw. Ant -13 ft. TL: N44 46 15 W106 55 37. Stereo. Hrs opn: 24. Prog sep from AM. Net: ABC. Format: Oldies. News progmg 4 hrs wkly. Target aud: 20-50. ■ Peggy Browning-Hepp, rgnl sls mgr. ■ Rates: $6; 4; 5; 3.

Thermopolis

KTHE(AM)—April 1957: 1240 khz; 1 kw-U. TL: N43 38 42 W108 12 15. Box 591, 320 Senior Ave. (82443). (307) 864-2119. Licensee: D. Mark Inc. (acq 5-27-93; $76,741; FTR 6-14-93). Net: MBS. Format: Adult contemp, country. News progmg 15 hrs wkly. Target aud: 25-54; varied. ■ D. Mark Jackson, pres & gen mgr.

Torrington

KGOS(AM)—May 15, 1950: 1490 khz; 1 kw-U. TL: N42 04 20 W104 13 40. Hrs opn: 5:30 AM-10:05 PM. Box 40, Rt. 2 (82240). (307) 532-2158. FAX: (307) 532-2641. Licensee: Kath Broadcasting (acq 3-1-56). Net: ABC/I. Rep: IMN/Eastman; Art Moore. Format: Country, oldies, talk. News staff one; news progmg 20 hrs wkly. Target aud: 20 plus; general. Spec prog: Sp one hr, farm 20 hrs wkly. ■ Dee Kath, pres; Jess Pilkington, gen mgr; R.L. Grasmick, stn mgr & progmg dir; Tix Estrada, gen sls mgr; Dona Anderson, news dir; Jim Wellman, chief engr. ■ Rates: $9.25; 6.95; 6.95; 4.50.

KERM(FM)—Co-owned with KGOS(AM). Dec 15, 1976: 98.3 mhz; 3 kw. Ant 300 ft. TL: N41 59 41 W104 12 05. Stereo. Prog sep from AM. ■ Rates: Same as AM.

Wheatland

KYCN(AM)—Nov 16, 1960: 1340 khz; 250 w-U. TL: N42 02 44 W104 56 47. Hrs opn: 5:30 AM-10 PM. Box 248, 450 E. Cole (82201). (307) 322-5926. FAX: (307) 322-9300. Licensee: Smith Broadcasting Inc. (acq 12-6-91; with co-located FM). Net: SMN. Rep: Target, IMN. Wash atty: Bryan, Cave, McPheeters & McRoberts. Format: Adult contemp, country. News staff one; news progmg 14 hrs wkly. Target aud: General. Spec prog: Farm 7 hrs wkly. ■ Kent G. Smith, pres & gen mgr; Sue Hanks, gen sls mgr; Catherine Smith, mktg mgr & adv mgr; Jeff Zamora, mus dir; Suzy Hanks, news dir; Ronald K. Krob, chief engr. ■ Rates: $7.20; 6.60; 6.10; 6.10.

KYCN-FM—February 1985: 101.7 mhz; 3 kw. Ant 156 ft. TL: N42 02 44 W104 56 47. Stereo. Hrs opn: 5:30 AM-10 PM. Dups AM 100%. ■ Rates: Same as AM.

Worland

KWOR(AM)—Mar 7, 1946: 1340 khz; 1 kw-U. TL: N44 01 01 W107 58 14. 1340 Radio Dr., Rt. 2 (82401). (307) 347-3231. FAX: (307) 347-4880. Licensee: KWOR Inc. (acq 9-11-89; $197,515; with co-located FM; FTR 10-2-89). Net: ABC/I, MBS. Rep: Eastman/Intermountain. Wash atty: Eugene Smith. Format: Country. News progmg 21 hrs wkly. Target aud: General. ■ Bruce Long, pres, gen mgr, progmg dir & mus dir; Karen Long, gen sls mgr & prom mgr; Marvin Daugherty, news dir; Al Shorte, chief engr.

KKLX(FM)—Co-owned with KWOR(AM). Dec 1, 1980: 96.1 mhz; 50 kw. Ant 400 ft. TL: N44 04 06 W107 51 57. Stereo. Prog sep from AM. Net: ABC/E, MBS. Format: Adult contemp. News staff 2.

American Samoa

Fagaitua

KPRI(FM)—Not on air, target date unknown: 103.1 mhz; 30 kw. Ant 203 ft. 4929 Pago Pago (96799). Licensee: Aleki Sene.

Leone

WVUV(AM)—Apr 16, 1975: 648 khz; 10 kw-U. TL: S14 21 28 W170 46 36. Box 2567, Pago Pago (96799). (684) 688-7397. Licensee: Radio Samoa Ltd. Group owner: L.S. Berger Stations. Net: MBS, NBC. Rep: ISL. Format: Div, English, Samoan. Spec prog: Class 2 hrs, farm one hr, jazz 15 hrs, C&W 12 hrs wkly. ■ William Faulkerson, gen mgr & chief engr; Malaki Timu, progmg dir.

Pago Pago

KBQN(AM)—January 1987: 585 khz; 50 kw-U. TL: S14 20 52 W170 46 10. Licensee: Ocean Broadcasting Network Ltd. (acq 7-9-91; $25,000 (CP); FTR 7-29-91). Format: Relg. ■ John Gregory, gen sls mgr.

KSBS-FM—Apr 14, 1988: 92.1 mhz; 3 kw. Ant -135 ft. TL: S14 17 41 W170 39 44 (CP: 15 kw, ant -92 ft.). Stereo. Box 793 (96799). (684) 622-7114; (684) 633-7000. FAX: (684) 622-7839. Licensee: Samoa Technologies Inc. Net: AP. Format: Adult contemp, btfl mus. News staff one; news progmg 9 hrs wkly. Target aud: Working adults. ■ Barney Sene, pres; Esther Sene, gen mgr, gen sls mgr & progmg dir; Andrew Thompson, prom mgr; David Katina, mus dir; Bill McFall, news dir; Alex Sene Jr., chief engr.

Federated States of Micronesia

Pohnpei

WSZD(AM)—1964: 1449 khz; 10 kw-U. Hrs opn: 18. Box 1086, Broadcast Bldg., Dolonier, Nett (96941). (691) 320-2296. FAX: (691) 320-5212. Licensee: Santiago Joad. Net: Micronesian Bcstg Net. Format: Div. News progmg 20 hrs wkly. Target aud: General. Spec prog: Farm 30 hrs, folk 21 hrs, gospel 2 hrs, relg 2 hrs wkly. ■ Santiago Joad, pres; Frances Zarred, gen mgr. ■ Rates: $60; 60; 60; na.

Truk

WSZC(AM)—1962: 1593 khz; 5 kw-U, DA-1. Moen, E.C. Is (96942). 011 (691) 330-2593; 011 (691) 330-2596. Format: Div. News staff one; news progmg 21 hrs wkly. Target aud: General. ■ Johnny Esa, gen mgr.

Yap

V6AI—June 9, 1965: 1494 khz; 10 kw-U. Stereo. Box 117, Colonia YAP State Western Caroline Is (96943). (691) 350-2174, (691) 350-2160. FAX: (691) 350-4113. Licensee: Yap State Government. Format: CHR, country, news. Spec prog: Yapese 10 hrs, Micronesian 10 hrs, Filipino 5 hrs, Japanese 5 hrs, relg 4 hrs wkly. News staff 2. ■ Peter Gramafell, gen mgr; Bernie Tiningmow, progmg dir; John Gilmatam, mus dir; John Tamngig, news dir; John Hasamai, news dir; Charles W. Hudson, chief engr.

Guam

Agana

KGUM(AM)—February 1975: 567 khz; 5 kw-U, DA-1. TL: N13 23 21 E144 45 34. Box GM (96910). (671) 477-5700. FAX: (671) 477-3982. Licensee: Sorenson Pacific. Net: CBS. Format: Variety, news/talk. News staff 3; news progmg 20 hrs wkly. Target aud: 35 plus. Spec prog: Filipino 11 hrs, Chamorro 14 hrs, farm one hr wkly. ■ Jon A. Anderson, pres; Rex Sorenson, gen mgr; Micalani Foo, gen sls mgr; Chuck Masty, progmg dir; Kai Maxwell, news dir; Marvin Palmer, chief engr.

KZGZ(FM)—Co-owned with KGUM(AM). Oct 15, 1986: 97.5 mhz; 3.1 kw. Ant 485 ft. TL: N13 29 17 E144 49 30 (CP: 40 kw, ant 538 ft.). Stereo. Prog sep from AM. Format: CHR/AOR. News staff 3; news progmg 15 hrs wkly. Target aud: 18-35; active, upwardly mobile.

KOKU(FM)—Apr 28, 1984: 100.3 mhz; 5 kw. Ant 190 ft. TL: N13 26 28 E144 42 40. Stereo. 530 W. O'Brien Dr. (96910). (671) 477-5658. Licensee: Guam Radio Services Inc. Wash atty: Brown & Neitert. Format: CHR, news. News staff 2; news progmg 36 hrs wkly. Target aud: General. ■ Lee M. Holmes, pres; Ernie A. Galito, gen mgr & prom mgr; Glenn Gibbs, gen sls mgr; Ray Gibson, progmg dir; Roel Bejerana, mus dir; J.T. Thompson, news dir; Richard Garman, chief engr. ■ Rates: $65; 55; 65; 35.

***KPRG(FM)**—Not on air, target date unknown: 89.3 mhz; 2.8 kw. Ant 485 ft. TL: N13 29 17 W144 49 30. Licensee: New Guam Educational Radio Foundation.

KSTO(AM)—Sept 1973: 95.5 mhz; 25 kw. Ant 530 ft. TL: N13 29 17 E144 49 53. Stereo. Hrs opn: 24. Box 20249, Main Facility (96921). (671) 477-7108. Licensee: Inter-Island Communications Inc. (acq 11-77). Format: Adult contemp. News staff one; news progmg 14 hrs wkly. Target aud: 25-54. Spec prog: Country 12 hrs, gospel 6 hrs wkly. ■ Edward Poppe, pres & gen mgr; J.R. Rapp, gen sls mgr; Peter Bie, progmg dir; Dean Reed, chief engr. ■ Rates: $60; 60; 60; 50.

KTWG(AM)—August 1975: 801 khz; 10 kw-U. TL: N13 27 07 W144 42 32. Box ED (96910); 1868 Halsey Dr., Asan (96925-1505). (671) 477-9701. FAX: TELEX: 721-6485. Licensee: Trans World Radio Pacific. Format: Relg. News staff one. Target aud: 19-40. Spec prog: Classical 6 hrs wkly. ■ Harry Bettig, stn mgr; Jim Elliott, progmg dir; Maggie Strickland, mus dir; Glenn Scheyhing, pub affrs dir; Bob Chick, chief engr.

KUAM(AM)—Mar 14, 1954: 610 khz; 10 kw-U. TL: N13 26 53 E144 45 22. Box 368 (96910). Licensee: Pacific Telestations Inc. Group owner: L.S. Berger Stations (acq 9-27-77). Net: CBS. Format: MOR, adult contemp. Spec prog: Chamorro 5 hrs, Tagalog 5 hrs, Japanese 3 hrs wkly. ■ Lawrence Berger, pres; John E. Crawford, gen mgr; Dave Hoebing, progmg dir; Mason Altiery, news dir; David Obenauf, chief engr.

KUAM-FM—Sept 1, 1966: 93.9 mhz; 2 kw. Ant 950 ft. TL: N13 25 53 E144 42 36 (CP: 5.2 kw, ant 948 ft.). Prog sep from AM. Format: Btfl mus. ■ KUAM-TV affil.

KZGZ(FM)—Listing follows KGUM(AM).

Agat

***KSDA-FM**—Nov 22, 1990: 91.9 mhz; 7.59 kw. Ant 981 ft. TL: N13 25 53 E144 42 36 (CP: 3.8 kw, ant 1,000 ft.). Stereo. Hrs opn: 24. Box 7500, (96928). (671) 565-2000; (671) 565-2289. FAX: (671) 565-2983. Licensee: Adventist Broadcasting Service Inc. Format: Relg, class. News progmg 6 hrs wkly. ■ David Barasoain, gen mgr; Charity Espina, progmg dir; Brook Powers, Andrew Hummel, chiefs engr.

Northern Mariana Islands

Garapan-Saipan

KPXP(FM)—Nov 5, 1992: 99.5 mhz; 6.5 kw. Ant 1,492 ft. TL: N15 11 10 E145 44 25. Stereo. Hrs opn: 24. PPP Box 10,000 Saipan MP (96950). (670) 235-7996; (670) 235-7997. FAX: (670) 235-7998. Licensee: K-Z Radio Inc. (acq 10-28-91; $15,000; FTR 11-25-91). Net: CBS. Wash atty: Kaye, Scholer, Fierman, Hays & Handler. Format: Contemp hit. News progmg 14 hrs wkly. Target aud: 18-34. ■ Rex W. Sorensen, CEO; Jon A. Anderson, pres; Kathleen A. Sorensen, vp; Evan Montvel-Cohen, vp opns; Jeannie Karkin, gen sls mgr; David Angell, prom mgr; Charles Zimmerman, progmg dir; Albert Juan, mus dir. ■ Rates: $35; 28; 35; 23.

KRSI(FM)—Not on air, target date unknown: 97.9 mhz; 4.5 kw. Ant 1,519 ft. TL: N15 11 09 E145 44 29. Box 49, Saipan (96950). Licensee: Radio Saipan International Inc.

Puerto Rico | Directory of Radio

Saipan

KSAI(AM)—April 1978: 936 khz; 5 kw-U. TL: N15 07 52 E145 42 26. Hrs opn: 5:30 AM-10 PM. Box 209 (96950). (670) 234-6521. FAX: (670) 234-3428. Licensee: Far East Broadcasting Co. Inc. Net: AP. Format: Relg, loc ethnic. News staff 2; news progmg 10 hrs wkly. Target aud: General. Spec prog: Chamorro 15 hrs, Tagalog 15 hrs wkly. ■ Jim Bowman, chmn; William Tarter, pres; Chris Slabaugh, gen mgr; Andrew A. Mazzella, stn mgr; Douglas L. Campbell, vp opns; David Creel, chief opns; Timothy C. Anderson, progmg dir; Patrick Murphy, news dir; Robert Springer, chief engr. ■ Rates: $15; 10; 15; 10.

San Jose

KCNM(AM)—October 1984: 1053 khz; 1 kw-U, DA-1. TL: N15 13 00 E145 45 00. Box 914, Saipan (96950). Licensee: Inter-Island Communications Inc. (acq 8-6-84). Net: AP. Format: Div. News staff one. Target aud: General. Spec prog: Black, jazz, Chamorro, Philipino. ■ Hans Mickelson, gen mgr; Mark J. Grizzard, gen sls mgr; Marilyn Iakapo, prom mgr; Jun Gases, progmg dir; Rony Lago, news dir; Butch McBride, chief engr.

KZMI(FM)—Co-owned with KCNM(AM). 93.9 mhz; Ant 300 ft. (CP: 103.9 mhz, 3.2 kw). Stereo. Prog sep from AM. Format: Div.

Puerto Rico

Adjuntas

WPJC(AM)—Not on air, target date unknown: 1020 khz; 1 kw-U, DA-N. TL: N18 09 04 W66 42 48. Box 1507, Cuepo No. 80, Utuado (00761). Licensee: Tanama Communications Inc.

Aguada

WNNV(FM)—1975: 105.5 mhz; 3 kw. Ant 1,200 ft. TL: N18 19 31 W67 10 13. Stereo. Hrs opn: 19. Box 847, Mayaguez (00681-0847). (809) 833-2495. FAX: (809) 833-7940. Licensee: Aurio Matos. Format: Relg, Sp. News staff 4. Target aud: 25-49; middle class. ■ Aureo Matos Chaparro, pres & chief engr; Dominga Barreto, gen mgr & sls dir; Juan Carlos Matos, opns mgr; Aurio Matos Jr., gen sls mgr & progmg dir. ■ Rates: $15; 12; 15; 12.

Aguadilla

WABA(AM)—Nov 15, 1951: 850 khz; 5 kw-D, 1 kw-N. TL: N18 24 18 W67 09 44. Box 188, No. 6, Calle Munoz Rivera (00605). (809) 891-1230. FAX: (809) 882-2882. Licensee: Aguadilla Radio & TV Corp. Inc. (acq 1973). Net: AP; Cadena QBS. Rep: Inter-American Pubs, Promociones Max Muniz. Format: Adult contemp. ■ Hector Richard Carbona, pres; Rosipa Pellot, gen mgr; Santos Niavis, news dir; Juan Rivara, chief engr.

WIVA-FM—Apr 16, 1964: 100.3 mhz; 50 kw. Ant 1,000 ft. TL: N18 18 49 W67 11 25. Stereo. Hrs opn: 24. Box 1331 (00726). (809) 744-3131. FAX: (809) 743-0252. Licensee: Arso Radio Corp. (group owner; acq 3-85). Net: UPI. Rep: Lotus. Wash atty: John P. Bankson Jr. Format: Salsa. News staff one; news progmg 5 hrs wkly. Target aud: 12 plus. ■ Anthony Soto, pres & progmg dir; Carmen Pagan, gen mgr; Jose Enrique Alvira, news dir; Luis A. Soto, chief engr. ■ Rates: $25; 20; 25; 20.

WNOZ(AM)—1956: 1340 khz; 1 kw-U. TL: N18 24 25 W67 10 03. Box 1, Munoz Rivera 51 Altos (00605). (809) 268-4200. FAX: (809) 268-3660. Licensee: Nos Inc. (acq 2-88). Net: Notiuno. Format: Sp adult contemp, news. News progmg 19 hrs wkly. Target aud: 20-55. Spec prog: Jazz 3 hrs wkly. ■ David Ortiz-Anglero, pres & progmg dir; Luis O. Ortiz-Gonzalez, gen mgr; Omar Ortiz-Anglero, gen sls mgr; Joselyn Grafals, mus dir; Maximino Perez, chief engr. ■ Rates: $30; 24; 20; 20.

WTPM(FM)—May 27, 1971: 92.9 mhz; 50 kw. Ant 1,223 ft. TL: N18 18 52 W67 10 58. Stereo. Hrs opn: 18. Box 1629, Mayaguez (00681); Bo. Algarrobo, Sector Cuba #1060, Mayaguez (00680). (809) 831-9200; (809) 834-6340. FAX: (809) 265-4044. Licensee: Corp. of the 7th Day Adventists of West Puerto Rico (acq 2-80; $125,000). Net: AP. Wash atty: Mitchell. Format: Btfl mus, relg, Sp. News progmg 11 hrs wkly. Target aud: General; traditional Christian groups. Spec prog: English one hr, class 7 hrs wkly. ■ Fred Hernandez, pres; Julio C. Javier, gen mgr, opns dir, progmg dir & mus dir; Ana M. Baez, sls dir; Juan Rodriguez, prom dir; Antonio Sanchez, adv dir; Marcelina Pena, news dir; Ricardo Vega, chief engr. ■ Rates: 10; 10; 10; 8.

Arecibo

WCMN(AM)—June 24, 1947: 1280 khz; 5 kw-D, 1 kw-N. TL: N18 28 52 W66 41 16. Box 436 (00613). (809) 878-0070. Licensee: Caribbean Broadcasting Corp. Format: Sp news/talk. News staff 3; news progmg 50 hrs wkly. Target aud: 30 plus. ■ Carlos Esteva, pres; Bryon Mitchell, vp; Byron Mitchell, gen mgr; Luis A. Davila, progmg dir; Rafael Gonzalez, pub affrs dir; Carlos Arroyo, chief engr. ■ Rates: $32; 32; 32; 32.

WCMN-FM—Jan 1, 1967: 107.3 mhz; 50 kw. Ant 1,027 ft. TL: N18 14 52 W66 48 43. Stereo. Hrs opn: 24. Prog sep from AM. (809) 781-6303. FAX: (809) 880-1112. Format: Top-40. Target aud: 18-42. ■ Archie Velez, gen mgr & progmg dir; Ivan Soto, sls dir. ■ Rates: $40; 40; 40; 40.

WMIA(AM)—Feb 21, 1957: 1070 khz; 500 w-D, 2.5 kw-N. TL: N18 27 33 W66 45 20. Hrs opn: 19. Box 1055 (00613). (809) 878-1275; (809) 878-2727. FAX: (809) 880-3026. Licensee: Abacoa Radio Corp. Group owner: Pirallo Lopez Stns. Net: Red Alerta. Wash atty: Imlay & Freret. Format: Adult contemp, Sp, news/talk. News staff 7; news progmg 10 hrs wkly. Target aud: 25 plus; the buying power in the area. Spec prog: Farm 2 hrs, relg 10 hrs wkly. ■ Lirio Pirallo, pres; Epifanio Rodriguez-Velez, gen mgr & chief engr; Joe Mercado, progmg dir & news dir; Miguel Melendez, mus dir. ■ Rates: $8; 8; 8; 8.

WNIK(AM)—1957: 1230 khz; 1 kw-U. TL: N18 27 20 W66 44 24. 462 Morell Tocampos Ave., San Luis (00612). (809) 880-2607; (809) 880-2613. FAX: (809) 879-1011. Licensee: Kelly Broadcasting System Corp. (acq 4-87). Format: Div, Sp. News staff one. Target aud: General. ■ Raul Santiago, gen mgr; Frank Velaquez, gen sls mgr & prom mgr; James Santiago, progmg dir; Ronald T. Cushing, chief engr. ■ Rates: $4; 8; 12; 4.

WNIK-FM—July 17, 1965: 106.5 mhz; 19.5 kw. Ant -270 ft. TL: N18 28 28 W66 43 40. Stereo. Prog sep from AM. Box 556 (00613). Format: Sp.

Barceloneta

WBQN(AM)—Mar 1, 1975: 1160 khz; 5 kw-D, 2.5 kw-N, DA-D. TL: N18 26 23 W66 33 07. Box 993, Calle 16 H-6 Urbanizacion, Manati (00674). (809) 854-2450. Licensee: Radio Borinquen Inc. Format: Top-40. Target aud: General. ■ Angel M. Rivera, pres; Luis R. Rivera, gen mgr, prom mgr & progmg dir; Angel M. Rivera Jr., gen sls mgr; Sammy Rivera, mus dir; Francisco Martinez, news dir; Tuto Gomez, chief engr.

Barranquitas

WOLA(AM)—March 1986: 1380 khz; 1 kw-U. TL: N18 11 01 W66 18 24. Box 669-A, Carr 719 KM1 Bo Helechal (00974). (809) 857-1380. FAX: (809) 857-1381. Licensee: N.P. Broadcasting Corp. Format: Top-40. News progmg 14 hrs wkly. Target aud: General. Spec prog: Jazz 5 hrs wkly. ■ Nadine Delgado, gen mgr; Jose R. Delgado, gen sls mgr; Alfredo Miranda, news dir; Jesus R. Gomez, chief engr.

Bayamon

WLDI(FM)—Dec 3, 1959: 94.7 mhz; 32 kw. Ant 1,778 ft. TL: N18 16 44 W65 51 12. Stereo. Hrs opn: 24. 74 Mayaguez St., San Juan (00917). (809) 763-0020. FAX: (809) 250-8005. Licensee: Radio Aeropuerto Inc. Group owner: Pirallo Lopez Stns. (acq 12-31-66). Wash atty: Booth, Freret & Imlay. Format: Oldies Target aud: 12-24; males and females, middle/upper socio-economic. ■ Rates: $50; 48; 50; 46.

WLUZ(AM)—1966: 1600 khz; 5 kw-U, DA-2. TL: N18 21 38 W66 09 30. Box 9394, Santurce (00908). (809) 785-1600. Licensee: Lucas Tomas Muniz. Format: MOR. Lucas Tomas Muniz, pres; Rafo Muniz, gen mgr; William Padilla, gen sls mgr; Tomas G. Muniz, progmg dir; Rodolfo Rivas, chief engr.

WRSJ(AM)—1947: 1560 khz; 5 kw-D, 750 w-N. TL: N18 24 05 W66 07 14. Box 193419, San Juan (00919-3419). (809) 782-6388. FAX: (809) 781-7416. Licensee: A.B.G. Realty and Investment Corp. (acq 6-87; $622,000; FTR 6-22-87). Format: Btfl mus, relg. ■ Abdiel Colberg, gen mgr.

WXYX(FM)—Feb 1, 1979: 100.7 mhz; 50 kw. Ant 781 ft. TL: N18 17 29 W66 11 03. Stereo. HC-67, Box 15390 (00956-9535). (809) 785-9390; (809) 785-9100. FAX: (809) 785-9377. Licensee: RAAD Broadcasting Corp. Format: Top-40. Target aud: 12-34; young teens, adults. ■ Roberto Davila, pres & gen mgr; Hector Moyano, gen sls mgr; Angel Rivera, news dir. ■ Rates: $77; 69; 77; 69.

Cabo Rojo

***NEW FM**—Not on air, target date unknown: 90.9 mhz; 25 kw. Ant 633 ft. TL: N18 04 12 W67 08 03. Licensee: Family Broadcast Aid Center.

WEKO(AM)—Jan 9, 1970: 930 khz; 2.5 kw-U. TL: N18 06 05 W67 09 17. Hrs opn: 21. Box 681, Lolita Cintron Bldg., Rd. 311 KM1 Las Delicias Ward (00623); WEKO Bldg., Rt. 311 KM 1 (00623). (809) 851-1236. FAX: (809) 851-2159. Licensee: David Ortiz Radio Corp. Net: UPI; Notiuno. Rep: Notiuno. Wash atty: Robert DePont. Format: News, top-40. News staff 4. Target aud: General; Mayaguez County residents. ■ David Ortiz, pres & gen mgr; Wilkins Thomas Ortiz, stn mgr & mus dir; Max Perez, chief opns & chief engr; Vanessa Flores, mktg dir, adv mgr & pub affrs dir; Jean Ortiz, prom mgr & progmg dir. ■ Rates: $16; 12; 7; 7.

WMIO(FM)—Jan 10, 1988: 102.3 mhz; 3 kw. Ant 680 ft. TL: N17 59 37 W67 10 27. Stereo. Hrs opn: 6 AM- midnight. Box 1220, Rt. 311, Km. 1.1, Las Delicias Ward (00623). (809) 851-7500. Licensee: Maria I. Ortiz-Aviles. Wash atty: Reddy, Begley & Martin. Format: Adult comtemp. Target aud: General; 18-45. ■ Maria I. Ortiz, pres & gen mgr; Joseph Cow, gen sls mgr; Hector Marrero, mus dir. ■ Rates: $14; 14; 14; 14.

Caguas

WBRQ(FM)—See Cidra.

WNEL(AM)—July 21, 1947: 1430 khz; 5 kw-U. TL: N18 14 53 W66 01 25. Box 487 (00726). (809) 744-3131. FAX: (809) 743-0252. Licensee: Turabo Radio Corp. (acq 4-1-73). Net: UPI. Wash atty: John P. Bankson Jr. Format: Sp adult contemp. News staff one; news progmg 25 hrs wkly. Target aud: 24 plus. ■ Jesus M. Soto, pres; Carmen Pagan, gen mgr; Jose Enrique Alvira, progmg dir; Jacinto Ruiz, news dir; Luis A. Soto, chief engr. ■ Rates: $8; 6; 8; 6.

WPRM-FM—See San Juan.

WVJP(AM)—Nov 24, 1947: 1110 khz; 2.5 kw-D, 500 w-N. TL: N18 13 25 W66 01 11. Box 207 (00726). (809) 743-0103. Licensee: Jorge L. Arzuaga, Frederico Virella, Berta Elisa (acq 9-28-90). Format: Adult contemp, btfl mus, Sp. ■ Jorge L. Arzuaga, gen mgr; Francisco Resto Torres, gen sls mgr; Norma Rodriquez Trinidad, progmg dir; Jesus R. Gomez, chief engr.

WVJP-FM—October 1968: 103.3 mhz; 28 kw. Ant 1,906 ft. TL: N18 16 41 W65 51 09. Stereo. Prog sep from AM.

Camuy

WCHQ(AM)—Oct 23, 1971: 1360 khz; 1 kw-U, DA-D. TL: N18 28 18 W66 51 42. Carretera 119, Bo. Puentes (00627). (809) 898-1360. Licensee: Del Pueblo Radio Corp. Format: Adult contemp, top-40. ■ Joe Cordero, gen mgr.

WCHQ-FM—Aug 15, 1968: 102.9 mhz; 50 kw. Ant 303 ft. TL: N18 28 49 W66 51 14. Box 2780 (00627). (809) 898-2510. Licensee: HQ 103 Inc. (acq 5-28-86). Format: Variety. ■ Reynardo Moreira, gen mgr.

Carolina

WIDA(AM)—March 16, 1964: 1400 khz; 1 kw-U. TL: N18 23 49 W65 56 06. Box 188 (00986). (809) 757-1414; (809) 769-0132. Licensee: Primera Iglesia Bautista de Carolina (acq 7-80; $750,000; FTR 7-28-80). Net: UPI, CRC. Format: Sp. ■ William Lebron, gen mgr; Edwin Carraquillo, progmg dir; Alberto Perereo, chief engr.

***WIDA-FM**—August 1983: 90.5 mhz; 25 kw. Ant 1,900 ft. TL: N18 06 48 W66 03 07. Licensee: Christian Broadcasting Corp.

WVOZ-FM—Mar 3, 1967: 107.7 mhz; 50 kw. Ant 1,636 ft. TL: N18 24 10 W66 03 21. Stereo. Penthouse Darlington Bldg., Munoz Rivera Ave., Rio Piedras (00925). (809) 764-1077; (809) 756-8888. Licensee: International Broadcasting Corporation. Net: CRC. Format: Big band. ■ Pedro Roman Collazo, pres & progmg dir; Margarita Nazario, gen mgr; Jorge G. Blanco, chief engr. ■WVOZ-TV affil.

Cayey

WLEY(AM)—Dec 3, 1965: 1080 khz; 250 w-U. TL: N18 06 55 W66 08 28. Hrs opn: 19. Box 1186 (00737); Box 7213, WLEO/WZAR Bldg. Sector Puerto Viejo, Paseo Sauri, Playa De Ponce, Ponce (00732). (809) 738-2276; (809) 840-1170. FAX: (809) 738-7744. Licensee: Ponce Broadcasting Corp. (group owner). Net: Notiuno. Rep: Carlos Bethel. Wash atty: Borsari & Paxson. Format: Latin, oldies, news/talk. News staff one; news progmg

Broadcasting & Cable Yearbook 1994
B-422

22 hrs wkly. Target aud: 25 plus; 51% women, 49% men. Spec prog: Local sports. ■ J. H. Conesa, pres & vp; J. H. Conesa Jr., gen mgr & mktg mgr; Jesus Ruben, opns mgr; Carmen Quinones, rgnl sls mgr; Marilyn Santiago, prom mgr; Junior Irizarry Palermo, progmg mgr & mus dir; Rafael Acosta, Rafael Pagan, chiefs engr. ■ Rates: $16; 12; 14; 8.

Ceiba

WFAB(AM)—Not on air, target date unknown: 890 khz; 250 w-U. TL: N18 12 16 W65 42 40. Box 1748, Juncos (00666). (809) 752-4495. Licensee: Aerco Broadcasting Corp. ■ Angel E. Roman, pres.

Cidra

WBRQ(FM)—March 1, 1972: 97.7 mhz; 3 kw. Ant 866 ft. TL: N18 13 40 W66 06 05. Stereo. Box 9297, Caguas (00726-9297); Consolidated Mall, Suite 6, Caguas (00725). (809) 720-7797; (809) 743-8260. FAX: (809) 746-6162. Licensee: American National Broadcasting Corp. Group owner: American National Broadcasting (acq 5-27-93; $1.9 million; FTR 6-14-93). Wash atty: Roy Perkins. Format: Sp ballads. Target aud: 25-49; women. ■ Fernand Vigil, chmn & pres; Luiz Leon, opns mgr; Victor Falcon, vp sls & gen sls mgr. ■ Rates: $23; 23; 23; 23.

Coamo

WCPR(AM)—1967: 1450 khz; 1 kw-U. TL: N18 05 29 W66 22 15. Hrs opn: 16. Box 316 (00769). (809) 825-1905. Licensee: Coamo Broadcasting Corp. Format: Top-40, oldies. News progmg 9 hrs wkly. ■ Jose David Soler, pres, gen mgr & chief engr; Otoniel Ollvieri, news dir.

Corozal

WORO(FM)—July 1968: 92.5 mhz; 50 kw. Ant 1,197 ft. TL: N18 15 09 W66 19 58. 415 Carbonell St., Hato Rey (00918). (809) 751-1380. Licensee: Catholic Apostolic & Roman Church, San Juan Archdiocese (acq 1981; $1 million; FTR 3-2-81). Format: Btfl mus. ■ Cardinal H.E. Luis Aponte, pres; Anna Melendez, gen mgr; Carlos Rodriguez, mus dir; Jesus Gomez, chief engr.

Fajardo

WMDD(AM)—May 31, 1947: 1480 khz; 5 kw-U. TL: N18 21 46 W65 38 24. Box 948 (00738). (809) 863-0202. Licensee: Pan Caribbean Broadcasting Corp. (acq 6-15-65). Format: Adult contemp, news, talk. News staff 10; news progmg 126 hrs wkly. Target aud: 25-49. ■ Richard Friedman, pres & gen mgr; Ansel Luis Vozquez, opns mgr; Jimi Reveron, progmg dir; Alejandro Luciano, chief engr.

WDOY(FM)—Co-owned with WMDD(AM). Feb 15, 1969: 96.5 mhz; 11.5 kw. Ant 2,795 ft. TL: N18 18 36 W65 47 41. Hrs opn: 24. Prog sep from AM. Box 948, Yale Bldg., Puerta de Tierra-San Juan (00906). Format: Top 40/tropical. ■ Rita Friedman, gen mgr.

WSAN(FM)—See Vieques.

Guayama

WBJA(AM)—Mar 1, 1981: 1540 khz; 1 kw-D. TL: N17 59 44 W66 04 39. Box 1540 (00785). (809) 866-1540. Licensee: Wigberto Baez Santiago (acq 6-87). Format: Sp. ■ Wingberto Santiago, CEO.

***WCRP(FM)**—1991: 88.1 mhz; 27 kw. Ant 1,889 ft. TL: N18 06 47 W66 03 08. Box 344 (00654). Licensee: Ministerio Radial Cristo Viene Pronto Inc. Format: Educ, relg. ■ Rev. Eugenio Rodriquez Lopez, pres.

WMEG(FM)—Listing follows WXRF(AM).

WXRF(AM)—July 1948: 1590 khz; 1 kw-U. TL: N17 57 40 W66 08 20. Box 1590 (00784). (809) 864-3435. Licensee: Guayama Broadcasting Co. Inc. Format: Sp. ■ Jose Raul Fuster, pres; Mercy Tadilla, gen mgr & gen sls mgr; Victor Colon Fuentes, progmg dir & mus dir; Alberto Pereira, chief engr.

WMEG(FM)—Co-owned with WXRF(AM). November 1966: 106.9 mhz; 25 kw. Ant 1,994 ft. TL: N18 06 48 W66 03 07. Stereo. Prog sep from AM. ■ Jose Raul Fuster, gen mgr & gen sls mgr; David Gleason, prom dir; progmg dir & mus dir; Juan Ramon Rivera, chief engr.

Guayanilla

WOIZ(AM)—Oct 1, 1986: 1130 khz; 200 w-D, 700 w-N. TL: N18 01 03 W66 46 22. Box 8072, Calle Jobos 7, Ponce (00732). (809) 835-1130. Licensee: Gamaliel Bermudez Ruiz (acq 11-6-89; $125,000; FTR 11-6-89). Format: Adult contemp, btfl mus. Target aud: Adults; those who like music from 60s-80s. ■ Juan C. Rodriguez, pres; Mata Mael Bermudez, gen mgr; Ralphael Acosta, chief engr.

Hatillo

WMSW(AM)—Not on air, target date unknown: 1120 khz; 5 kw-U. TL: N18 28 15 W66 50 24. 537 Miramar Ave., Arecibo (00612). Licensee: Aurora Broadcasting Corp.

Hormigueros

WEGM(FM)—Oct 12, 1980: 92.1 mhz; 3 kw. Ant 581 ft. TL: N18 11 15 W67 07 04 (CP: 2 kw, ant 1,105). Stereo. Cobia's Plaza Bldg., Suite 102, 1607 Ponce DeLeon Ave., San Turce (00904). (802) 723-9210. Licensee: Southwestern Broadcasting Corp. Net: CRC. Format: Sp. ■ Jose Fuster, pres; Margarita Nazario, gen sls mgr; Pedro Roman-Collazo, prom mgr; Jose A. Marti, chief engr.

Humacao

WALO(AM)—Feb 11, 1958: 1240 khz; 1 kw-U. TL: N18 08 49 W65 48 49. Hrs opn: 19. Box 1240, State Rd., KM 79-5 (00792). (809) 852-1240; (809) 725-8265. FAX: (809) 852-1280. Licensee: Ochoa Broadcasting Corp. Wash atty: Hopkins & Sutter. Format: Sp, news/talk. News staff 2; news progmg 60 hrs wkly. Target aud: 25 plus. ■ Efrain Archilla-Roig, pres; Efrain Archilla-Diez, gen mgr, gen sls mgr, prom dir & progmg dir; Luis A. Gandara-Gomez, mus dir; Angelo Pena-Perez, news dir; Rudy Rivas, chief engr. ■ Rates: $18; 18; 18; 18.

Isabela

WISA(AM)—Oct 19, 1961: 1390 khz; 1 kw-U. TL: N18 30 08 W67 01 38. Box 750 (00662). (809) 872-0100; (809) 872-2030. FAX: (809) 721-0733. Licensee: Isabela Broadcasting Co. (acq 4-87). Format: MOR. ■ Luis A. Mejia, pres, gen mgr, progmg dir & mus dir; Helen Sampedro, gen sls mgr; Rafael Ortiz, prom mgr; Francisco Cancel, news dir; Juan Rivera, chief engr.

WKSA-FM—Co-owned with WISA(AM). 101.5 mhz; 42 kw. Ant -26 ft. TL: N18 26 36 W67 08 50. (809) 798-7878. Format: Sp.

Juana Diaz

WCGB(AM)—Nov 23, 1967: 1060 khz; 5 kw-D, 500 w-N. TL: N17 59 35 W66 28 33. Box 248, KM 112, Bo. Pastillo, Carretera (Highway #1) (00795). (809) 837-2440. FAX: (809) 837-4225. Licensee: Grace Broadcasters Inc. Format: Relg, MOR, Sp. News staff one. ■ Jose A. Rodriguez, gen mgr; Lawrence Trumbower, chief engr.

Juncos

WRRE(AM)—1971: 1460 khz; 500 w-U, DA-2. TL: N18 12 54 W65 54 33. Box 1231 (00777). (809) 734-8060. Licensee: Aerco Broadcasting Corp. (acq 8-76). ■ Angel E. Roman, pres; Angel O. Roman, gen mgr & gen sls mgr; Adelino Flores, chief engr.

Lajas

WAVB(AM)—1986: 1510 khz; 1 kw-U, DA-1. TL: N18 02 11 W67 04 58. Hrs opn: 16. Box 593, PR Rd. No. 101 306 km 0.7 (00667); Cond. Las Torres Sur 10E, Bayamon (00961). (809) 899-1320; (809) 722-2102. FAX: (809) 899-1320. Licensee: Professional Radio Broadcasting Corp. Format: Sp, news, dir. News, women progmg 34 hrs wkly. Target aud: General. ■ Aurea B. Velez, pres; Nilse LaCourz, gen mgr; Javier Figueroa, progmg dir; German Velez, mus dir.

WCFI(FM)—Not on air, target date unknown: 103.7 mhz; 50 kw. Ant 456 ft. TL: N17 59 37 W67 11 09. Marina D-21 Levittown Lakes, Catano (00632). Licensee: Ramon Rodriguez & Associates.

Lares

WGDL(AM)—February 1983: 1200 khz; 250 w-D. TL: N18 17 40 W66 53 50. Hrs opn: 12. Box 872 (00669). (809) 897-3889. FAX: (809) 897-7821. Licensee: Lares Broadcasting Corp. Net: UPI. Wash atty: John P. Bankson Jr. Format: Top 40. News staff one; news progmg 20 hrs wkly. Target aud: General. ■ Pedro Aernandez, gen & gen mgr. ■ Rates: $6; 4; 6; 4.

Levittown

***WKVN-FM**—Oct 1, 1986: 88.5 mhz; 35 w. Ant 121 ft. TL: N18 26 55 W66 10 26. Box 4000, South Bayamon (00958). (809) 784-8851; (809) 784-8850. Licensee: Clamor Broadcasting Network Inc. (acq 5-20-92; $800,000; FTR 6-8-92). Format: Relg. ■ Jose Raschke, gen mgr.

Manati

WMNT(AM)—May 1961: 1500 khz; 1 kw-D, 250 w-N. TL: N18 26 06 W66 29 54. Box 6 (00674). (809) 854-2223. Licensee: Manati Radio Corp. (acq 7-29-86). Format: Sp, top-40. ■ Jose A. Ribas, pres & mus dir; Pedro Collazo Barbosa, gen mgr, gen sls mgr & news dir; Freddy Ribas, prom mgr; Wilton Collazo, progmg dir; Arcadio Rodriguez, chief engr.

WMTI Exp Stn—unknown: 1580 khz; 250 w-D, 500 w-N. TL: N18 25 37 W66 29 06. Rebroadcasts WMTI (AM) Morovis 100%. Box 995 (00674). (809) 754-0324; (809) 763-1066. Licensee: Wilfredo G. Bianco Pl. Format: Pop Latin music 90%, pop American music, news, oldies. ■ Carmen Galdo, gen mgr.

WNRT(FM)—1973: 96.9 mhz; 50 kw. Ant 882 ft. TL: N18 15 41 W66 32 19. Box 13324 (00701). (809) 758-8562. Licensee: Arecibo Broadcasting Corp. Inc. Format: Christian. ■ Antonio Pauneto, gen mgr.

Maricao

WAEL(AM)—See Mayaguez.

WAEL-FM—July 1970: 96.1 mhz; 24.2 kw. Ant 2,011 ft. TL: N18 09 07 W66 49 15. Stereo. Hrs opn: 18 (24 wknds). Box 1370, Mayaguez (00681-1370). (809) 832-4560; (809) 834-4696. FAX: (809) 792-3140. Licensee: WAEL Inc. Group owner: Pirallo Lopez Stns. Wash atty: Booth, Freret & Imlay. Format: Contemp hit. Target aud: 12-24. ■ Maria del Pilar Pirallo, pres; Luis Pirallo, opns mgr; Guillermo Bonet, chief engr. ■ Rates: $26; 24; 26; 22.

Mayaguez

WAEL(AM)—1949: 600 khz; 1 kw-U, DA-1. TL: N18 10 46 W67 10 14. Box 1370 (00681-1370). Ramirez Pabon Final, Guanatibo Homes (00680). (809) 832-0600; (809) 833-0600. FAX: (809) 792-3140. Licensee: WAEL Inc. Group owner: Pirallo Lopez Stns. (acq 1957). Wash atty: Booth, Freret & Imlay. Format: Sp, oldies, sports. Target aud: 25 plus. ■ Maria del Pilar Pirallo, pres; Luis Pirallo, opns mgr; Pedro Ojeda, gen sls mgr; Eulogio Rodriguez, mus dir; Guillermo Bonet, engrg dir. ■ Rates: $12; 11; 12; 10.

WAEL-FM—See Maricao.

WIOB(FM)—Listing follows WORA(AM).

WIVA-FM—See Aguadilla.

WKJB(AM)—Dec 6, 1946: 710 khz; 10 kw-D, 750 w-N. TL: N18 10 08 W67 09 03. Box 1293 (00708). (809) 834-6666. FAX: (809) 834-8380. Licensee: Radio Stn WKJB AM-FM Inc. Format: Top-40. ■ Jose A. Bechara Jr., gen sls mgr; Allen Corales, progmg dir & mus dir; Rafy Aviles, news dir; Junior Velez, chief engr.

WKJB-FM—Jan 15, 1963: 99.1 mhz; 50 kw. Ant 1,963 ft. TL: N18 09 05 W66 59 19. Stereo. Prog sep from AM. Format: Soft music. Spec prog: Jazz 6 hrs wkly.

WORA(AM)—May 12, 1947: 760 khz; 5 kw-U, DA-1. TL: N18 11 30 W67 09 28. Box 3822 (00681). (809) 832-1150. Licensee: Radio Americas Corp. Group owner Radio Americas/Estereotempo Group (acq 10-18-90; grpsl; FTR 11-5-90). Net: CRC. Format: News. ■ Renardo Royo, pres; Joe Diaz, gen mgr; Nelson Nin, chief engr.

WIOB(FM)—Co-owned with WORA(AM). Oct 12, 1947: 97.5 mhz; 25 kw. Ant 990 ft. TL: N18 19 33 W67 10 13. Prog sep from AM. (Acq 10-17-90; grpsl; FTR 11-12-90). Format: Ballads.

WOYE-FM—1960: 94.1 mhz; 25 kw. Ant 2,967 ft. TL: N18 09 05 W66 59 20. Stereo. Hrs opn: 24. Box 1718, Radio Center, Suite 801, Bosque St. (00681-1718). (809) 834-1094; (809) 265-9494. FAX: (809) 265-4090. Licensee: Prime Time Corp. (acq 1-22-90; $2,660,000; FTR 2-19-90). Net: AP. Wash atty: Fletcher, Heald & Hildreth. Format: CHR (Latin hits). News staff one; news progmg 10 hrs wkly. Target aud: 18-49; middle class. ■ Rafael Oller, pres; Felix A. Bonnet, exec vp, gen mgr, vp progmg & news dir; Raymond Totti, natl sls mgr; Laura Rosas, rgnl sls mgr; Manuel Colon, mktg dir; Oneyda Pacheco, prom dir & pub affrs dir; William Jasalle, mus dir; Nelson Sanchez, asst mus dir; Guillermo Bonet, chief engr. ■ Rates: $55; 50; 45; 43.

Puerto Rico

WPRA(AM)—Oct 16, 1937: 990 khz; 1 kw-U. TL: N18 10 52 W67 10 07. Hrs opn: 18. Box 3250 (00681); Penthouse 3-L, Guanajibo Shopping Ctr., Guanajibo Homes (00680). (809) 834-9500; (809) 834-0990. FAX: (809) 834-9504. Licensee: American National Broadcasting Corp. Group owner: American National Broadcasting (acq 1-17-92; $1.7 million; with WRPC[FM] San German; FTR 2-17-92). Net: AP. Wash atty: Reddy, Begley & Martin. Format: Top-40, Spanish. Target aud: General. ■ Fernando Vigil, pres; Amadeo Nazario, vp & gen mgr; Luisin Mercado, progmg dir; Guillermo Bonet, chief engr.

WRPC(FM)—See San German.

WSOL(AM)—1955: 1090 khz; 250 w-D, 730 w-N. TL: N18 04 44 W67 01 18 (CP: TL: N18 08 18 W67 07 43). Stereo. Box 1373, Hato Rey (00919). (809) 780-4943, (809) 780-4944. Licensee: Frederick Gauthier de Castro dba Radio Sol Broadcasting Co. (acq 5-29-92). Net: Radsol Island Network. Rep: Producciones Panamericana. Wash atty: Roy F. Perkins Jr. Format: Div. News staff 2; news progmg 10 hrs wkly. Target aud: Adults. Spec prog: Farm 2 hrs wkly. ■ Frederick Gauthier DeCastro, pres; Carmen B. Rodriguez, news dir.

WTIL(AM)—November 1950: 1300 khz; 1 kw-U. TL: N18 11 00 W67 10 04. Box 1360 (00709); Post & Bosque Sts. (00708). (809) 834-7272. FAX: (809) 834-9845. Licensee: Mayaguez Radio Corp. (acq 6-52). Format: Adult contemp, oldies, Sp. News staff 3; news progmg 28 hrs. Target aud: 35 plus. ■ Gilbert Mamery, pres & gen mgr; Gricel Mamery, gen sls mgr; Lidia Basora, progmg dir; Jose Ramirez, mus dir; Ismael Segarra, news dir; Guillermo Bonet, chief engr.

WTPM(FM)—See Aguadilla.

Moca

WCXQ(AM)—December 1983: 1040 khz; 250 w-D. TL: N18 24 09 W67 08 47. Box 7, 189 Baldoriety (00676). (809) 877-9525. Licensee: Dominga Bareto Santiago (acq 3-3-93; $110,000; FTR 3-22-93). Format: Div. ■ Dominga Bareto Santiago, pres; Aurio Matos Jr., gen mgr; Aurio Matos III, chief engr.

Morovis

WMTI(AM)—December 1981: 1580 khz; 5 kw-D, 2.5 kw-N, DA-D. TL: N18 20 32 W66 25 08. Box 995, Manati (00674); 155 San Antonio St., Hato Rey (00917). (809) 754-0324; (809) 763-1066. FAX: (809) 763-4195. Licensee: Wifredo G. Bianco Pi. Rep: WAPA. Wash atty: Fletcher, Heald & Hildreth. Format: Pop Latin music, 90%; pop American music, news, oldies. News progmg 30 hrs wkly. Target aud: 30 plus. ■ Wilfredo G. Blanco Pi, pres & chief engr; Carmen Galdo, gen mgr & gen sls mgr; Jorge Blanco, progmg dir, mus dir & news dir. ■ Rates: $5; 5; 5; 3.

Patillas

WEXS(AM)—Not on air, target date unknown: 610 khz; 250 w-D, 1 kw-N, DA-D. TL: N18 00 36 W66 01 28. Box 902, Arroyo (00615). Licensee: Community Broadcasting Inc.

Penuelas

WENA(AM)—See Yauco.

WPPC(AM)—May 25, 1976: 1570 khz; 1 kw-D, 126 w-N. TL: N18 03 47 W66 43 04. Box 9064, Pompanos Station, Ponce (00732-9064). (809) 836-1570; (809) 848-4670. Licensee: Radio Felicidad Inc. (acq 6-18-81; $125,000; FTR 7-13-81). Wash atty: Mitchell & Bizulca. Format: MOR, relig, Sp. News progmg 3 hrs wkly. Target aud: General. ■ Carlos Morrales, pres; Jose L. Torres, chief opns, engrg dir & chief engr; Carlos R. Soto, adv mgr; Luis Fuentes, Roberto Ferris (P.M. progmg dir), progmg dirs.

Ponce

WEUC(AM)—May 1, 1957: 1420 khz; 1 kw-U. TL: N17 59 23 W66 37 21. Stn 6, Ponce Bypass (00732). (809) 842-8046; (809) 841-1027. Licensee: Catholic Univ. of PR Service Assn. Wash atty: Koteen & Naftalin. Format: News, talk, Sp. News staff 5; news progmg 70 hrs wkly. Target aud: 25-55 plus; young professionals, retirees, middle class and up. ■ Fr. Tossello Giangiacomo, CEO; Mons. Juan F. Torres-Oliver, pres; Juan L.R. Ricart, stn mgr, sls dir & vp progmg. ■ Rates: $13; 13; 10; 7.

*WEUC-FM—May 17, 1984: 88.9 mhz; 10.8 kw. Ant 2,912 ft. TL: N18 10 27 W66 35 32. Stereo. (809) 848-8809; (809) 844-8809. FAX: (809) 841-1028. Format: News/talk, btfl mus, educ. News staff 3; news progmg 30 hrs wkly. Target aud: general; professionals, young adults, retirees, mid & upper middle class. ■ Nestor Figueroa, stn mgr.

WIOC(FM)—January 1970: 105.1 mhz; 9 kw. Ant -150 ft. TL: N17 59 49 W66 37 31 (CP: 50 kw, ant -179 ft.). Box 7302 (00732). (809) 842-0166. FAX: (809) 841-6121. Licensee: Cadena Esterotempo Inc. Format: Ballads. ■ Jose J. Santiago, gen mgr.

WISO(AM)—Sept 15, 1953: 1260 khz; 1 kw-U. TL: N17 59 22 W66 37 11. Box 7251 (00732). (809) 842-4124; (809) 842-5189. FAX: (809) 844-1595. Licensee: South P. R. Broadcasting Corp. Group owner: Pirallo Lopez Stns. Format: Talk, news, MOR. News progmg 26 hrs wkly. ■ Luis Pirallo, pres; Nilda P. Freyre, gen mgr & gen sls mgr; Nilda Cardona, prom mgr & progmg dir; Wito Velez, mus dir; Yari Pagan, news dir; Modesto Delgado, chief engr. ■ Rates: $144; 144; 144; na.

WLEO(AM)—Nov 3, 1956: 1170 khz; 250 w-U. TL: N17 58 52 W66 36 51. Stereo. Box no: 24. Box 7213 (00732); WLEO/WZAR Bldg., Sector Puerto Viejo, Paseo Sauri, Playa de Ponce (00731). (809) 842-3038; (809) 840-3160. FAX: (809) 840-0049. Licensee: Ponce Broadcasting Corp. (group owner). Net: Notiuno. Wash atty: Borsari & Paxton. Format: Sp, news/talk, oldies. News staff 4; news progmg 50 hrs wkly. Target aud: 25 plus; mature men & women, blue-collar & professionals. Spec prog: Sports. ■ J.H. Conesa Sr., pres; J.H. Conesa Jr., vp & gen mgr; Eric Gil Sanchez, rgnl sls mgr; Jose Maldonado, progmg mgr; Eduardo Cruz, news dir; Rafael Acosta, chief engr. ■ Rates: $16; 14; 15; 10.

WZAR(FM)—Co-owned with WLEO(AM). Mar 17, 1966: 101.9 mhz; 14 kw. Ant 2,580 ft. TL: N18 01 40 W66 39 14. Stereo. Hrs opn: 24. Prog sep from AM. Format: Adult Contemp, Sp, news. News progmg 15 hrs wkly. Target aud: 18-49; children & adults, professionals. Spec prog: Talk 15 hrs wkly. ■ Carlos Conasa, rgnl sls mgr; Guillermo Droing, progmg mgr; Jose Garcia, mus dir; Teresita Conasa, pub affrs dir; Rafael Acosta, engrg mgr & chief engr. ■ Rates: $35; 33; 32; 28.

WOQI(FM)—Listing follows WPAB(AM).

WPAB(AM)—Aug 14, 1940: 550 khz; 5 kw-U. TL: N17 59 27 W66 37 46. Hrs opn: 20. Box 7243 (00732-7243); Bo. Pampanos, Km 27.2, Playa Ponce (00731). (809) 840-5550. FAX: (809) 840-3530. Licensee: Portorican American Broadcasting Co. Rep: William Fernandez Mascaro & Assoc. Format: Sp news/talk. News staff 16; news progmg 40 hrs wkly. Target aud: 35 plus; concerned adults. ■ Alfonso Gimenez Porrata, CEO & pres; Angie Santiago, opns mgr; Angie Santiago, mktg mgr; Maria-Luisa Gimenez, prom mgr; Jorge Almodovar, news dir; William Batista, chief engr. ■ Rates: $25; 20; 25; 20.

WOQI(FM)—Co-owned with WPAB(AM). May 1969: 93.3 mhz; 16 kw. Ant -225 ft. TL: N17 59 26 W66 37 43. Stereo. Hrs opn: 20. Prog sep from AM. (809) 840-5395. Format: Classic Salsa. News staff one; news progmg 6 hrs wkly. Target aud: 18-49; affluent young adults. ■ Edwin Berrios, progmg dir. ■ Rates: Same as AM.

WPRP(AM)—1936: 910 khz; 5 kw-U. TL: N17 59 49 W66 37 31. Box 7771 (00732). (809) 844-0910. Licensee: Radio Americsa Corp. Group owner: Radio Americas/Estereotempo Group (acq 10-18-90; grpsl; FTR 11-5-90). Net: CRC. Format: Sp pop Salsa music. ■ Reinaldo Royo, pres; Carlos Morales, gen sls mgr. ■ WORA-TV affil.

WRIO(AM)—Not on air, target date unknown: 101.1 mhz; 34 kw. Ant 1,768 ft. TL: N18 09 15 W66 33 15. c/o Box 9297, Caguas (00626). Licensee: Family Broadcasting Group.

WZAR(FM)—Listing follows WLEO(AM).

WZBS(AM)—Feb 1, 1973: 1490 khz; 5 kw-D, 1 kw-N, DA-1. TL: N18 02 41 W66 36 13. Stereo. Hrs opn: 24. Box 7612 (00732). (809) 844-1490; (809) 840-1490. FAX: (809) 840-2460. Licensee: Zaba Radio Corp. (acq 1973). Format: Top-40, Sp. Target aud: 18 plus. Spec prog: Relg 6 hrs wkly. ■ Rene Bartolomei, pres; Pedro J. Soldevila, vp; Inne Rodriguez, gen mgr; Jose Luis Torres, chief engr. ■ Rates: $7; 7; 7; 7.

Quebradillas

WKVN(AM)—Not on air, target date unknown: 960 khz; 500 w-D, 1 kw-N, DA-2. TL: N18 26 38 W66 57 43. Box 3295, Bayamon (00960). Licensee: Clamor Broadcasting Network Inc. (acq 3-2-92; $110,000; FTR 3-23-92). Format: Sp. ■ Idalia Arrieta, gen mgr; Gloria Perez, gen sls mgr; Juan Espinal, prom mgr; Joel Feliciano, progmg dir; Jose Enrique Mendez, mus dir; Juan Feliciano, news dir.

WQQZ(FM)—Nov 17, 1974: 98.3 mhz; 3 kw. Ant 1,000 ft. TL: N18 29 16 W66 56 37. Stereo. Hrs opn: 24. Box 980, Rd. 2 KM 102.5 (00678-0980). (809) 895-2725; (809) 896-0980. FAX: (809) 895-4198. Licensee: Jose J. Arzuaga (acq 7-10-79). Format: Top-40, Sp. News progmg 2 hrs wkly. Target aud: General. ■ Jose J. Arzuaga, pres, gen mgr & chief engr; Idalia Arrieta, opns mgr; Gloria Perez, gen sls mgr; Rosidalia Villafane, vp prom; Giovanny Villafane, progmg dir; Nitza Mercado, mus dir; Rafael Brito, news dir.

Rio Piedras

WFID(FM)—Nov 17, 1958: 95.7 mhz; 50 kw. Ant 941 ft. TL: N18 16 00 W66 05 05. Stereo. Box 363222, San Juan (00936). (809) 758-6096. Licensee: WIN Communications Inc. (group owner; acq 1-11-89; grpsl; FTR 1-30-89). Format: Easy lstng. ■ Carola A. Carnero, vp; Jose Pagan, gen mgr; Ana Velezm, gen sls mgr.

WRAI(AM)—See San Juan.

WUNO(AM)—See San Juan.

Sabana

WJIT(AM)—Not on air, target date 1994: 1250 khz; 1 kw-N, 250 w-D. TL: N18 25 28 W66 20 17. Box 316, Coamo (00769). (809) 825-1905. Licensee: Olga Iris Fernandez.

Sabana Grande

WYKO(AM)—Not on air, target date unknown: 880 khz; 1 kw-D, 500 w-N. TL: N18 04 21 W66 57 06. Box 1373, Hato Rey (00919). (809) 780-4944. Licensee: Juan Galiano Rivera (acq 7-19-90; $450,000; FTR 8-6-90). Format: Btfl mus, Sp. Spec prog: Class 6 hrs, farm 3 hrs, lt 2 hrs, jazz 2 hrs wkly. ■ Juan Galiano Rivera, pres; Juan B. Rodriguez, vp; Frederick Gauthier-DeCastro, gen mgr; Freddie Gauthier, progmg dir; Carmen B. Rodriguez, mus dir; Jaime A. Rodriguez-Alicea, news dir; Rudy Rivas, chief engr.

Salinas

WHOY(AM)—Apr 6, 1967: 1210 khz; 5 kw-U, DA-2. TL: N17 58 38 W66 18 14. Box 1148 (00751). (809) 824-2755; (809) 864-0122. FAX: (809) 824-3420. Licensee: Island Broadcasting Corp. Net: AP. Wash atty: Fletcher, Heald & Hildreath. Format: Sp. ■ Johnny Ortiz, pres, gen mgr, gen sls mgr & chief engr; Zulma Rodriguez, prom mgr & progmg dir; Martin Colon, mus dir & news dir.

San German

WPRA(AM)—See Mayaguez.

WRPC(FM)—Feb 1, 1969: 95.1 mhz; 25 kw. Ant 1,970 ft. TL: N18 08 55 W66 58 54. Hrs opn: 24. Box 3250, Mayaguez (00681). (809) 834-9500; FAX: (809) 834-9504. Licensee: American National Broadcasting Corp. Group owner: American National Broadcasting (acq 1-17-92; $1.7 million with WPRA[AM] Mayaguez; FTR 2-17-92). Format: Btfl mus. ■ Fernando Vigil, pres; Amadeo Nazario, vp & gen mgr.

San Juan

WAPA(AM)—Jan 15, 1947: 680 khz; 10 kw-U. TL: N18 22 18 W66 12 21. 134 Domenech Ave., Hato Rey (00918-3502). (809) 763-1066. FAX: (809) 763-4195. Licensee: Carlos C. Ventura and Wifredo G. Blanco Pi (acq 1-2-91; $1.82 million; FTR 1-28-91). Format: Sp, talk & news. ■ Wifredo G. Blanco Pi, gen mgr; Carmen Galdo, opns mgr; Jorge Blanco, progmg mgr & news dir; Wilfredo Blanco, chief engr.

WBMJ(AM)—1968: 1190 khz; 10 kw-D, 5 kw-N, DA-1. TL: N18 21 00 W66 06 50 (CP: 10 kw-N). Hrs opn: 18. Box 367000 (00936-7000); 4th Fl., 1409 Ponce de Leon, Santurce (00907-4010). (809) 724-1190; (809) 724-2727. FAX: (809) 722-5395. Licensee: Calvary Evangelistic Mission Inc. (acq 11-86). Net: Moody, USA. Wash atty: Steve Lerman. Format: Relg. News progmg 7 hrs wkly. Target aud: General. Spec prog: Sp relg 13 hrs, news 7 hrs wkly. ■ Ruth Luttrell, pres; Janet Luttrell, gen mgr, gen sls mgr & progmg dir; Chad D. Schneider, opns mgr & rgnl sls mgr; Les T. Sowiak, progmg mgr & mus dir; William Heffley, Jose' L. Escobar, chiefs engr.

WCAD(FM)—Mar 5, 1968: 105.7 mhz; 50 kw. Ant 1,100 ft. TL: N18 16 54 W66 06 46. Stereo. Box 4189 (00902-4189). 1667 San Turte (00910). (809) 726-6144. Licensee: Broadcasting & Programming Systems of Puerto Rico Inc. Format: Rock, current & oldies. ■ Ralph Perez, gen mgr.

WDOY(FM)—See Fajardo.

WFID(FM)—See Rio Piedras.

WIAC(AM)—1947: 740 khz; 10 kw-U, DA-1. TL: N18 25 25 W66 08 20. Hrs opn: 24. Box 4504 (00902). (809) 798-7878. FAX: (809) 798-9613. Licensee: Bestov Broadcasting Inc. of Puerto Rico (acq 1954). Net: AP. Wash atty: John P. Bankson. Format: MOR, Sp. Target aud: General. ■ Luis A. Mejia, pres & gen mgr; Ramiro Obrador, stn mgr; Helen Sampedro, gen sls mgr; Francisco Cancel, news dir; Juan Rivera, chief engr.

WIAC-FM—Mar 1, 1961: 102.5 mhz; 50 kw. Ant 1,139 ft. TL: N18 25 25 W66 08 20. Stereo. Prog sep from AM. Format: MOR. ■ Rafael Ortiz, progmg dir.

WIOA(FM)—Mar 1, 1961: 99.9 mhz; 30 kw. Ant 977 ft. TL: N18 26 51 W66 03 59. Stereo. Box 13427 (00908). (809) 721-4020. FAX: (809) 722-6740. Licensee: Cadena Estereotempo Inc. Format: Adult contemp. ■ Alfredo R. De Arellano, pres; Sebastian Robiou, vp & gen mgr.

***WIPR(AM)**—Jan 26, 1948: 940 khz; 10 kw-U, DA-1. TL: N18 25 36 W66 08 29. Box 909, Hato Rey (00919). (809) 766-0505. Licensee: Puerto Rico Corp. for Public Broadcasting. Net: AP, NPR. Format: Educ. ■ Edgaro Gierbolini, gen mgr; Freddy Percy, progmg dir; Luisita Rodriquez, mus dir; Jesus Latimer, news dir; Manuel Collazo, chief engr.

***WIPR-FM**—June 3, 1960: 91.3 mhz; 125 kw. Ant 2,719 ft. TL: N18 06 42 W66 03 05 (CP: 105 kw, ant 2,706 ft.). Dups AM 100%.

WKAQ(AM)—Dec 3, 1922: 580 khz; 10 kw-U, DA-1. TL: N18 25 55 W66 08 07. Box 364668, 383 F.D. Roosevelt Ave. (00936). (809) 758-5800. FAX: (809) 763-1854. Licensee: El Mundo Broadcasting Corp. (acq 10-31-49). Format: All news. Target aud: General. ■ Argentina S. Hills, pres; Hubert E. Biagi, vp & gen mgr; Raul Muxo, gen sls mgr; Amarylis Ortiz, news dir; Carlos Valladares, chief engr.

WKAQ-FM—Oct 8, 1958: 104.7 mhz; 50 kw. Ant 1,120 ft. TL: N18 16 51 W66 06 38. Stereo. Prog sep from AM. Format: Top-40. ■ Hector Marcano, progmg dir.

WKVM(AM)—1951: 810 khz; 50 kw-U, DA-1. TL: N18 21 47 W66 08 13. c/o Arquidiocesis de San Juan, Apartado 1967 (00903). (809) 751-1380. Licensee: Catholic, Apostolic & Roman Church, San Juan Archdiocese (acq 3-4-82; $1,019,000; FTR 1-18-82). Format: Div. ■ H.E. Luis Cardinal Aponte, pres; Anna Melendez, gen mgr; Bitty Pichardo, gen sls mgr; F. Efrain Rodriguez, progmg dir; Silvio Iglesias, mus dir; H. McClure, chief engr. nc

WLDI(FM)—See Bayamon.

WNEL(AM)—See Caguas.

WORO(FM)—See Corozal.

WOSO(AM)—Nov 21, 1977: 1030 khz; 10 kw-U, DA-1. TL: N18 22 07 W66 15 17. Box 4349 (00902). (809) 724-4242. FAX: (809) 724-4245. Licensee: Cavallaro Broadcasting Corp. Net: Wall Street, CBS, NBC Talknet, NBC, MBS. Format: All news/talk. ■ Augustine L. Cavallaro, pres & gen mgr; Sergio Fernandez, stn mgr; Rodolfo Rivas, chief engr.

WPRM-FM—April 1959: 98.5 mhz; 25 kw. Ant 1,910 ft. TL: N18 06 45 W66 03 07. Stereo. Hrs opn: 24. Box 5725 (00926); Box 487, Caguas (00726). (809) 744-3131. FAX: (809) 743-0252. Licensee: Arso Radio Corp. (group owner; acq 4-1-73). Net: CRC. Rep: Lotus. Wash atty: Hammel & Pack. Format: Salsa. News staff one; news progmg 3 hrs wkly. Target aud: 12 plus. ■ Jesus M. Soto, pres; Carmen Pagan, gen mgr; Vicente Belgodere, gen sls mgr; Luis A. Soto, natl sls mgr & chief engr; Anthony Soto, progmg dir; Manuel Rivera, news dir. ■ Rates: $60; 50; 60; 50.

WQBS(AM)—Nov 1, 1954: 870 khz; 10 kw-U, DA-1. TL: N18 22 17 W66 12 17. 218 Almirante Tinzon, El Vedado (00919); Box 1748, Juncos (00777). (809) 756-8700 FAX: (809) 265-0241. Licensee: Aerco Broadcasting Corp. (acq 9-24-90; $800,000; FTR 10-8-90). Net: CRC. Format: Div, Sp. ■ Angel Romandez, pres.

WQII(AM)—1947: 1140 khz; 10 kw-U, DA-1. TL: N18 21 30 W66 08 05. Box 3779, Comm. Council Group Inc., Hato Rey (00919). (809) 723-4848. FAX: (809) 723-4035. Licensee: Huella Broadcasting (acq 1-83). Rep: Bernard Howard. Format: MOR, Sp. ■ Nieves Gonzalez-Avreu, pres & gen mgr; Raymond Hernandez, chief engr.

WRAI(AM)—July 4, 1949: 1520 khz; 10 kw-U, DA-1. TL: N18 21 00 W66 09 25. Hrs opn: 16. 74 Mayaquez St. (00917). (809) 763-0020. FAX: (809) 250-8005. Licensee: Radio Aeropuerto Inc. Group owner: Pirallo Lopez Stns. (acq 12-3-59). Net: WMIA(AM), WAEL(AM). Rep: Contemporary Media, William Fernandez.Wash atty: Freret & Imlay. Format: Sp contemp, talk. Target aud: 35 plus; medium and low income individuals. Spec prog: Puerto Rican and Latin hits played when talk program not aired. ■ Lirio M. Pirallo, pres, gen mgr & progmg dir; Ramon Carlos Ruiz Corraliza, opns dir; Carlos D. Pirallo, gen sls mgr; William Fernandez, rgnl sls mgr; Carmen Parrilla, pub affrs dir; Rudy Rivas, chief engr. ■ Rates: $30; 25; 25; 15.

WRSJ(AM)—See Bayamon.

***WRTU(FM)**—Feb 8, 1980: 89.7 mhz; 50 kw. Ant 796 ft. TL: N18 16 00 W66 05 05. Stereo. Hrs opn: 18. Box 21305, University Station (00931); Monserrate Bldg., P. de Leon Ave. & Cnr Pastrana St., Rio Piedras (00931). (809) 763-4699. FAX: (809) 764-1290. Licensee: University of Puerto Rico. Format: Class, jazz, Sp. News staff 3; news progmg 8 hrs wkly. Target aud: General; young, professional & highly educated. Spec prog: News 7 hrs, talk 2 hrs wkly. ■ Rafael Gracia, gen mgr; Francisco A. Baez, chief opns; Luis Luna, dev mgr; Julio Torresoto, progmg mgr; Nora Soto, news dir; Juan Rivera, chief engr.

WSKN(AM)—Jan 11, 1960: 630 khz; 5 kw-U, DA-2. TL: N18 26 00 W66 07 29. 117 Elenor Roosevelt, Hato Rey (00918). (809) 764-1090. FAX: (809) 764-3460. Licensee: Radio Americas Corp. Group owner: Radio Americas/Estereotempo Group (acq 10-18-90; grpsl; FTR 11-5-90). Rep: Blair. Format: Sp pop Salsa music. ■ Reinaldo Royo, pres & gen mgr; Ivan Vasquez, gen sls mgr; Jesus Gomez, chief engr.

WUNO(AM)—Oct 15, 1949: 1320 khz; 5 kw-D, 1 kw-N. TL: N18 23 00 W66 04 05 (CP: 5 kw-N). Box 3222 (00936). (809) 758-6363. FAX: (809) 756-8545. Licensee: WIN Communications Inc. (group owner; acq 1-11-89; grpsl; FTR 1-30-89). Format: All news. ■ Jose J. Acosta, pres; Carola A. Camero, vp; Joe Batan, gen mgr.

WZNT(FM)—1959: 93.7 mhz; 50 kw. Ant 280 ft. TL: N18 22 42 W66 07 04. Stereo. Hrs opn: 24. Box 949, Rd. 833 Bo Lo Filtros, Guaynabo (00970). (809) 720-5001; (809) 720-8716. FAX: (809) 720-2126. Licensee: Zeta Communications Inc. (acq 10-2-89; $1.2 million; FTR 10-23-89). Wash atty: Fletcher, Heald & Hildreth. Format: Tropical (salsa & merengue). Target aud: 18-34. ■ Rafael Oller, CEO; Raymond Totti, vp, stn mgr & vp sls; Alberto Rivera, prom mgr; Pedro Arroyo, progmg dir & mus dir; Ray Moreira, chief engr. ■ Rates: $115; 105; 105; 100.

San Sebastian

WLRP(AM)—Feb 15, 1965: 1460 khz; 500 w-U. TL: N18 20 50 W66 59 56 (CP: 2.5 kw). Box 1660 (00685). (809) 896-1005; (809) 896-1460. Licensee: Las Raices Pepinianas Inc. Format: Adult contemp. ■ Angel V. Maury, pres; Alfredo Perez, gen mgr; Ramon E. Pratts, prom mgr; Alejandro Aviles, mus dir; Guillermo Bonet, chief engr.

WOYE-FM—See Mayaguez.

WRSS(AM)—April 1984: 1410 khz; 1 kw-U, DA-1. TL: N18 19 14 W66 58 45. Box 1410, Rd. 125 Ave. Emerito Estrada (00685). (809) 896-2121. FAX: (809) 896-5753. Licensee: Occidental Communications Group. Net: Radio Reloj. Format: Adult contemp, CHR, oldies, div. News staff 2; news progmg 14 hrs wkly. ■ Hector Acevedo, pres; Eurogio Cardona, gen sls mgr & vp progmg; Ivan A. Feliu, chief engr.

Utuado

WERR(FM)—Feb 1, 1970: 104.1 mhz; 50 kw. Ant 710 ft. TL: N18 17 31 W66 39 28. Stereo. Hrs opn: 18. Box 29404, San Juan (00929). Licensee: Radio Redentor Inc. (acq 6-75). Wash atty: Stuart B. Michell. Format: Relg, Sp, news. News staff 2; news progmg 10 hrs wkly. Target aud: General; family. ■ Rev. Miguel Cintron, pres; Rev. Lemuel Rivera, gen mgr, stn mgr, adv dir, progmg mgr & news dir; Sr. Gamaiel Rivera, mktg dir; Sr. Jesus Rivera, engrg dir; Carlos Davila, chief engr.

WUPR(AM)—Apr 18, 1964: 1530 khz; 1 kw-D, 250 w-N. TL: N18 16 02 W66 42 38. Hrs opn: 17. Box 868 (00641). (809) 894-2460; (809) 894-1530. FAX: (809) 894-4955. Licensee: Central Broadcasting Corp. Net: Island Radio Net. Format: Sp, MOR, news/talk. News staff 2; news progmg 11 hrs wkly. Target aud: 18-49; middle income adults. ■ Benito Martinez, pres; Jose A. Martinez, gen mgr, gen sls mgr & progmg dir; Manuel E. Andujar, mus dir; Manuel B. Martinez, news dir; Epifanio Rodriguez Velez, chief engr. ■ Rates: $16; 16; 16; 16.

Vega Baja

WEGA(AM)—1972: 1350 khz; 2.5 kw-U, DA-2, TL: N18 28 38 W66 23 43. Box 1488 (00694). (809) 858-0386; (809) 858-0049. FAX: (809) 858-0386. Licensee: Vega Baja Broadcasting Corp. Format: Contemporary Hit/Top-40. ■ Carmello Santiago, vp & gen mgr.

Vieques

WIVV(AM)—Dec 8, 1956: 1370 khz; 5 kw-D, 1 kw-N. TL: N18 06 19 W65 28 03. Hrs opn: 18. Box 367000, San Juan (00936-7000); Box 0338, Vieques Island (00765-0338). (809) 724-2727; (809) 741-8717. FAX: (809) 722-5395. Licensee: Calvary Evangelistic Mission Inc. Wash atty: Steve Lerman. Format: Relg, talk, MOR. News progmg 7 hrs wkly. Target aud: General. Spec prog: Sp 14 hrs, news 7 hrs wkly. ■ Ruth Luttrell, pres; Janet L. Luttrell, gen mgr; Chad D. Schneider, opns mgr & regnl sls mgr; Janet Luttrell, gen sls mgr & progmg dir; Les T. Sowiak, progmg mgr & mus dir; William Heffley, Jose' L. Escobar, chief engrs.

WSAN(FM)—Nov 4, 1978: 98.9 mhz; 50 kw. Ant 751 ft. TL: N18 19 39 W65 18 05. Stereo. Box 237, Culebra (00775). (809) 860-6767. FAX: (809) 721-6767. Licensee: Carlos J. Colon-Ventura. Format: Oldies (Spanish), ballads. ■ Carlos J. Colon-Ventura, pres, gen mgr & news dir; Nydia A. Rios Colon, gen sls mgr; Raisaac Rios Colon, mus dir; Carlos Arroyo, chief engr.

Yabucoa

WXEW(AM)—Jan 1, 1978: 840 khz; 5 kw-D, 1 kw-N, DA-N. TL: N18 02 58 W65 52 07. Hrs opn: 19. Box 100 (00767); Ave. Font Martelo #203, Humacao (00971). (809) 893-3065; (809) 850-0840. FAX: (809) 850-4055. Licensee: Radio Victoria Inc. (acq 9-19-83). Net: Noti-Uno. Format: Talk, MOR, Sp. ■ Victoria Vargas, pres; Victor M. Calderon, vp, gen mgr & progmg dir; Caly Burmudez, gen sls mgr; Brenda Calderon, mktg dir; Jose Calderon, prom mgr & mus dir; Caly Bermudez, news dir; Iwminado Medina, chief engr. ■ Rates: $12; 8; 6; 6.

Yauco

WENA(AM)—Nov 11, 1978: 1330 khz; 2 kw-U, DA-1. TL: N18 01 23 W66 52 16. Stereo. Hrs opn: 24. Box 1338, State Rd. 128 (00698). (809) 267-1330; (809) 856-1330. FAX: (809) 267-1340. Licensee: Southern Broadcasting Inc. Wash atty: Roy F. Perkins, Jr. Format: Sp, CHR, news. News staff 5; news progmg 28 hrs wkly. Target aud: 25 plus; women, young adults. ■ Nephtali Rodriguez, pres, gen mgr & news dir; Israel Rodriguez, vp, vp opns & mus dir; Zaida Ortiz, sls dir; Ramon Ramos, gen sls mgr; Michelin Santiago, natl sls mgr & mktg dir; Lucelenia V. Rodriguez, prom mgr; Ines M. Vasquez, progmg dir; Ronald Cushing, chief engr. ■ Rates: $15; 15; 15; 12.

WKFE(AM)—Nov 3, 1961: 1550 khz; 250 w-U. TL: N18 01 24 W66 52 02. Hrs opn: 24. Box 324 (00698); Box 7213, Ponce (00732). (809) 856-4420; (809) 856-1320. FAX: (809) 856-4420. Licensee: Ponce Broadcasting Corp. (group owner). Net: Notiuno. Rep: Carlos Bethel. Wash atty: Borsari & Paxton. Format: Sp contemp, news/talk. News progmg 27 hrs wkly. Target aud: 25 plus; 60% women, 40% men. Spec prog: Rgnl sports, farm 6 hrs wkly. ■ J.H. Conesa, pres; J.H. Conesa Jr., vp, gen mgr & mktg mgr; Jaime Bermudez, stn mgr & gen sls mgr; Guillermo Valls, progmg dir & mus dir; Rafael Acosta, chief engr. ■ Rates: $16; 13; 12; 8.

Virgin Islands

Charlotte Amalie

WGOD(AM)—1992: 1090 khz; 250 w-D. TL: N18 18 57 W64 53 02. Box 5012, St. Thomas (00803). (809) 774-4498. FAX: (809) 776-0877. Licensee: Three Angels Corp. (acq 7-5-89). Format: Gospel. ■ Rafael A. Figueroa, pres, gen sls mgr & news dir; Lucy E. Figueroa, gen mgr; George Arroyo, chief engr.

WGOD-FM—Sept 1, 1980: 97.9 mhz; 50 kw. Ant 295 ft. TL: N18 21 25 W64 58 00. Stereo. (Acq 8-15-85). Format: Relg, educ. ■ Reynald Charles, pres; Charles Saunders, gen mgr; Ronald Rivas, gen sls mgr; Veeda Charles, progmg dir; Carlos Arryo, chief engr.

WIVI(FM)—Not on air, target date unknown: 96.1 mhz; 2.4 kw. Ant 1,500 ft. TL: N18 21 33 W64 58 18. Stereo. Box 4383, St. Thomas (00803). (809) 774-1972; (809) 776-7760. FAX: (809) 774-9788. Licensee: Rox Radio Enterprises Inc. (acq 6-26-92). Format: Album rock/alternative rock. Target aud: General. ■ Tim English, pres; Gordon Ackley, vp & gen mgr.

WIYC(FM)—Nov 2, 1976: 104.3 mhz; 45 kw. Ant 1,607 ft. TL: N18 21 31 W64 58 21. Stereo. Box 5234, 5-A Caret Bay, St. Thomas (00803). (809) 775-2104. FAX: (809)

Virgin Islands

773-9093. Licensee: Macau Traders Inc. Net: SMN. Format: CHR. News progmg 20 hrs wkly. Target aud: 16-60; Puerto Rico & southern Caribbean. Spec prog: Country gospel 2 hrs wkly. ■ Jonathan Cohen, pres. ■ Rates: $13.50; 11; 13.50; 10.

WSTA(AM)—Aug 1, 1950: 1340 khz; 1 kw-U. TL: N18 20 10 W64 57 17. Hrs opn: 24. Box 1340, 121 Subbase St. Thomas (00801). (809) 774-1340; (809) 777-4500. FAX: (809) 776-1316. Licensee: Ottley Communications Corp. (acq 12-1-84). Net: NBC, ABC/C. Rep: Intercontinental; Shellenberg & Kirwan.Wash atty: Bryan, Cave, McPheeters & McRoberts. Format: Adult contemp, Black. News staff 2; news progmg 20 hrs wkly. Target aud: General. Spec prog: Reggae, calypso. ■ Addie Ottley, pres; Len Stein, gen mgr; Irvin Brown, chief opns; Rudy Kelsick, gen sls mgr; Jean Greaux, progmg mgr; Anita Davis, mus dir; Lee Carle, news dir & chief engr. ■ Rates: $27.50; 19; 24; 19.

WTBN(FM)—unknown: 102.1 mhz; 50 kw. Ant 1,404 ft. TL: N18 21 23 W64 56 43 (CP: 33 kw, ant 1,670 ft.). No. 5A Raphunne Hill, Doctor's Park, St. Thomas (00803). (809) 776-2610. FAX: (809) 775-7299. Licensee: Trans Carribean Broadcasting Co. Format: Jazz, contemp, lite rock. ■ Winthrop Maduro, gen mgr.

WVGN(FM)—Mar 15, 1986: 105.3 mhz; 10 kw. Ant 1,679 ft. TL: N18 21 33 W64 58 18. Stereo. Hrs opn: 24. Rebroadcasts WAVI(FM) Christiansted 94%. Box 10772, The Wells Bldg., #1-D Havensight, St. Thomas (00801). (809) 776-1556. FAX: (809) 777-4566. Licensee: St. Croix Wirless Co. Inc. (acq 10-1-91). Wash atty: Smithwick & Belendiuk. Format: Mass appeal. News progmg 3 hrs wkly. Target aud: 22-54. Spec prog: Caribbean 9 hrs wkly. ■ John Galanses, pres; Doug Harris, gen mgr. ■ Rates: $25; 20; 25; 20.

WVNX(FM)—Not on air, target date unknown: 97.1 mhz; 50 kw. Ant 1,283 ft. TL: N18 20 30 W64 43 59. 4433 Wells Pkwy., University Park, MD (20782). Licensee: Calypso Communications.

WVVI(AM)—Nov 19, 1962: 1000 khz; 5 kw-D, 1 kw-N, U. TL: N18 20 11 W64 41 38. Hrs opn: 24. Box 5678, Franklin Bldg., 3rd Fl., Suite 6, 2303 Kronprindsens Gade, St. Thomas (00803). (809) 776-1000; (809) 774-NEWS. FAX: (809) 776-5357. Licensee: Thousand Islands Corp. (acq 5-15-70). Net: CBS, MBS, Wall Street. Wash atty: Tierney & Swift. Format: Div, adult contemp, news. News staff 2; news progmg 20 hrs wkly. Target aud: 25-54; upwardly mobile middle-class. Spec prog: West Indian 14 hrs, East Indian one hr, Haitian one hr, relg 5 hrs wkly. ■ Robert E. Noble, CEO, pres & gen mgr; Nickey Russell, stn mgr & mus dir; Harvey Henne, vp sls & sls dir; Nicky Russell, progmg dir; Dennis Murphy, progmg mgr; Carter Hague, news dir; Herb Schoenbohm, chief engr. ■ Rates: $40; 24; 40; 24.

Christiansted

WAVI(FM)—Feb 26, 1989: 93.5 mhz; 6 kw. Ant 732 ft. TL: N17 43 53 W64 41 19 (CP: 15 kw). Stereo. Hrs opn: 24. Box 25016 (00824); 118 Est. Mt. Welcome (00820). (809) 773-3693. FAX: (809) 773-3435. Licensee: St. Croix Wireless Co., Inc. Wash atty: Robert W. Healey. Format: Mass appeal. News progmg one hr wkly. Target aud: General; affluent young adult permanent residents. Spec prog: Relg 3 hrs wkly. ■ John T. Galanses, pres; Douglas F. Harris, vp & gen mgr. ■ Rates: $25; 20; 25; 20.

*WIVH(FM)—Not on air, target date unknown: 90.1 mhz; 1 kw. Ant 731 ft. TL: N17 44 10 W64 42 04. R.R. 3, Hunlock Creek, PA (18621). Licensee: Gospel Media Institute.

WJKC(FM)—Oct 29, 1983: 95.1 mhz; 50 kw. Ant 886 ft. TL: N17 44 07 W64 40 46 (CP: Ant 791 ft.). Stereo. 52 King St. (00821). (809) 773-0995. FAX: (809) 773-9093. Licensee: Radio 95 Inc. Wash atty: Dow, Lohnes & Albertson. Format: Top-40, CHR. News progmg 2 hrs wkly. Target aud: General. ■ Jonathan K. Cohen, pres & gen mgr; Robert Miller, gen sls mgr & prom mgr; Johnathan Keyes, progmg dir & mus dir; Phil Shuman, chief engr. ■ Rates: $25; 19.50; 19.50; 19.50.

WSTX(AM)—1952: 970 khz; 5 kw-D, 1 kw-N. TL: N17 45 23 W64 41 38. Box 3279 (00822). (809) 773-0390; (809) 773-0490. FAX: (809) 773-8515. Licensee: Family Broadcasting Inc. (acq 6-14-90; $525,000 with co-located FM; FTR 7-9-90). Rep: Pan American. Format: Div. Spec prog: Sp 2 hrs wkly. ■ G. Luv, A. Jame, gen mgrs; Alvin G. Southwell, mus dir & news dir; Dick Falter, chief engr.

WSTX-FM—Sept. 1984: 100.3 mhz; 50 kw. Ant 1,030 ft. TL: N17 45 20 W64 47 55. Stereo. Prog sep from AM. Format: MOR.

WVIQ(FM)—May 17, 1965: 99.5 mhz; 10.5 kw. Ant 1,080 ft. TL: N17 45 20 W64 47 55. Stereo. Box 4409, St. Croix (00822). (809) 773-1180. FAX: (809) 773-9093. Licensee: Caribbean Media Services Inc. (acq 4-28-87). Format: MOR. ■ Jonathan Keith, gen mgr; Trey Parnell, progmg dir & mus dir; Greg Anduze, news dir.

WVIS(FM)—June 10, 1973: 106.1 mhz; 50 kw. Ant 1,190 ft. TL: N17 44 51 W64 50 11. Stereo. Hrs opn: 18. Box 487, Frederiksted, St. Croix (00841); 77 Estate Castle Coakley (00820). (809) 778-5199; (809) 756-5914. FAX: (809) 756-5914. Licensee: Virgin Islands Stereo Communications. Net: CBS, American Urban, Westwood One. Wash atty: James L. Oyster. Format: Urban contemp. Target aud: 24-49; middle class, mass appeal, young professionals who love music. Spec prog: Black, Sp 2 hrs, talk 6 hrs wkly. ■ Joseph Bahr, pres, progmg dir & mus dir; Ines Oritz, gen mgr; Ines Ortiz, gen sls mgr; Julio Bahr, prom mgr; Rafael Serra, chief engr. ■ Rates: $28; 26; 28; 22.

Cruz Bay

WDCM(FM)—Not on air, target date unknown: 92.3 mhz; 48 kw. Ant 1,302 ft. TL: N18 20 17 W64 43 40. 4007 Bayshore Rd., Sarasota, FL (34234). Licensee: Paradise Broadcasting Corp. (acq 10-1-91; $60,000; FTR 10-28-91). Format: Big band, class, news. News staff 3; news progmg 7 hrs wkly. Target aud: General; Black/white, 50% Caribbean. Spec prog: West Indian 8 hrs wkly.

Frederiksted

WRRA(AM)—1976: 1290 khz; 500 w-D, 250 w-N. TL: N17 43 28 W64 53 03. Hrs opn: 24. Box 277, St. Croix, (00841); Studio & Transmitter, #1 Mahogany Rd., Estate Prosperity, Frederiksted (08840). (809) 772-1290. FAX: (809) 772-2178. Licensee: Carlos Lopez Lay. Net: CNN. Wash atty: Roy F. Perkins Jr. Format: Div, Sp, news. News staff 2; news progmg 25 hrs wkly. Target aud: 18-56. Spec prog: Black, jazz 6 hrs, gospel 12 hrs, relg 10 hrs wkly. ■ Carlos Lopez-Lay Esq., pres; Enrique J. Rodriguez, gen mgr; Alwyn Lynch, stn mgr, sls dir & pub affrs dir; Howard Cloud, opns mgr & progmg dir; Richard Nicks, mktg dir; Merv Bear, vp engrg. ■ Rates: $10; 10; 8; 6.50.

St. Thomas

*WIUJ(FM)—Oct 5, 1979: 102.9 mhz; 150 w. Ant 50 ft. TL: N18 21 23 W64 56 43. Dept. Human Services (00801). (809) 776-5270; (809) 774-6012. FAX: (809) 774-3466. Licensee: Virgin Islands Youth Development Radio (acq 8-6-90). Format: Educ, oldies, news/talk. News staff 2; news progmg 2 hrs wkly. Target aud: General. Spec prog: Class 5 hrs, Fr one hr, Sp one hr wkly. ■ Leo Morone, gen mgr; F. Ottley, opns mgr; Lionel George, progmg dir & mus dir; Mike Morone, (asst) mus dir; Albert Cleland, Ron Hall, Meru Baer, chiefs engr.

WSAN(FM)—See Vieques, P.R.

Directory of Radio Stations in Canada

Alberta

Athabasca

CKBA(AM)—Aug 1, 1989: 850 khz; 1 kw-D. Box 1800 (T0G 0B0). FAX: (403) 675-4938. (403) 675-5301. Licensee: Nor-Net Communications Ltd. (group owner). Net: Newsradio, CBC Mono. Format: C&W. ■ Cindy Methurst, stn mgr.

Blairmore

CJPR(AM)—1972: 1490 khz; 1 kw-D, 250 w-N, DA-2. Box 840 (T0K 0E0). (403) 562-2806. FAX: (403) 562-8114. Licensee: Lethbridge Broadcasting Ltd. Format: Full country.

Brooks

CIBQ(AM)—Apr 15, 1973: 1340 khz; 1 kw-U, DA-1. Box 180 (T1R 1B3). (403) 362-3418. Licensee: Q Radio, div of CHUM. Group owner: CHUM Ltd. (acq 3-81). Format: Comtemp Country. News staff one; news progmg 12 hrs wkly. Target aud: 25-54. ■ Allan Waters, pres; Jim Blundell, gen mgr; Wray Betts, rgnl sls mgr; John Petre, prom dir; Stan Taylor, progmg dir; Kirk Fraser, mus dir; Al Kellington, news dir; Gary Umari, chief engr. ■ Rates: C$32; 22; 22; 11.

Calgary

*CBR(AM)—Oct 1, 1964: 1010 khz; 50 kw-U, DA-2. Hrs opn: 20. Box 2640, 1724 Westmount Blvd. (T2P 2M7). (403) 521-6260. TELEX: 038-21604. Licensee: CBC. Format: Class, div, news/talk. ■ Gerarrd Villeux, pres; Val Boser, progmg dir; Ralph Thurn, mus dir; Ken Rogers, news dir.

*CBR-FM—Sept 29, 1975: 102.1 mhz; 100 kw. Ant 788 ft. Stereo. Dups AM 100%.

CFAC(AM)—May 1922: 960 khz; 50 kw-U. Stereo. 3320 17th Ave. S.W. (T3E 6X6). (403) 246-9696. FAX: (403) 246-6660. Licensee: Rogers Broadcasting Ltd. (acq 12-89). Format: C&W.

CHFM-FM—Co-owned with CFAC(AM). Aug 29, 1962: 95.9 mhz; 100 kw. Ant 480 ft. TL: N51 03 37 W114 10 13. Stereo. Hrs opn: 24. Prog sep from AM. Format: Adult contemp. News staff 5. Target aud: 25-49; females. ■ Robin Hildebrand, gen mgr; Gorde Edlund, prom mgr.

CFCN(AM)—May 18, 1922: 1060 khz; 50 kw-U, DA-N. TL: N50 54 02 W26 113 52 Hrs opn: 24. Box 2750, Station M, Broadcast House, 80 Patina Rise S.W. (T2P 4P8). (403) 240-5800. FAX: (403) 240-5801. Licensee: Standard Radio Inc. Group owner: Standard Broadcasting Corp. (acq 6-19-92). Format: Contemp hit radio. News staff 2; Target aud: 18-34; young adults. ■ Allan Slaight, CEO & chmn; Gary Slaight, pres; David Coriat, CFO & exec vp; Gary Russell, vp & gen mgr; Jim Sproul, dev mgr; Bill Herz, sls dir; Tom Peacock, gen sls mgr; Scott Armstrong, prom dir & news dir; Scott Armstrong (asst), progmg dir; Glen Slingerland, mus dir; Dave Simon, engrg dir; Ken Pasolli, chief engr. ■ Rates: C$112; 88; 106; 153.

CJAY-FM—Co-owned with CFCN(AM). June 1, 1977: 92.1 mhz; 100 kw. Ant 525 ft. Stereo. Hrs opn: 24. Prog sep from AM. (403) 240-5850. FAX: (403) 240-5801; (403) 242-6956. Format: Classic rock. News staff 4; news progmg 5 hrs wkly. Target aud: 25-49; special emphasis on 25-34. ■ Bob Mills, stn mgr & progmg dir; Graeme Macfarlane, prom dir; Ben Jeffery, mus dir. ■ Rates: C$153; 135; 135; 88.

CFFR(AM)—Jan 10, 1984: 660 khz; 50 kw-U, DA-2. Stereo. Hrs opn: 24. 2723 37 Ave. N.E. (T1Y 5R8). (403) 291-0000. FAX: (403) 252-6690. Licensee: RAWLCO Communications Ltd. (group owner). Format: Oldies. News staff 5; news progmg 10 hrs wkly. Target aud: 25-49. Spec prog: Sports 15 hrs wkly. ■ Gordon Rawlinson, pres; Doug Rawlinson, exec vp; Ross Tirrell, Don Robb, Don Armstrong, vps; Vince Cownden, gen mgr; Maureen Neuman, opns mgr; Don Armstrong, vp dev; Ross Tirrell, vp sls; Mark Olson, sls dir; Steve Heintz, gen sls mgr; Genevieve Sawchyn, prom dir; Gayle Zarbatany, Rob Alexander (asst), progmg dirs; Rob Alexander, mus dir; Kevin Usselman, news dir; Lenard Dean, engrg mgr.

CFXL(AM)—1927: 1140 khz; 50 kw-U, DA-2. TL: N50 55 25 W113 49 58. Stereo. Hrs opn: 24. Box 1140, 804 16 Ave. S.W. (T2P 3X5). (403) 228-1140. FAX: (403) 244-3343. Licensee: Golden West Broadcasting Ltd. (group owner; acq 9-1-92). Format: Classic rock. News staff 2. Target aud: 25-49; males. Spec prog: Toronto Blue Jays games. ■ Ken Foord, gen sls mgr; Craig Mills, mktg mgr; Jim Jackson, progmg dir; Jacque Hall, pub affrs dir.

CHFM-FM—Listing follows CFAC(AM).

CHQR(AM)—November 1964: 770 khz; 50 kw-U, DA-2. Stereo. Hrs opn: 24. 1900 125 9th Ave. S.E. (T2G 0P6). (403) 233-0770. FAX: (403) 265-7807. Licensee: CHRQ (A division of Westcom Radio Group Ltd.) Group owner: Western International Communications (acq 4-15-70). Net: BN, NBC. Rep: Canadian Broadcasting Sales, Dora-Clayton. Format: Full service news/talk/sports. News staff 11; news progmg 17 hrs wkly. Target aud: 35 plus. ■ Allan L. Anaka, pres, gen mgr, stn mgr & sls dir; Greg Schneider, rgnl sls mgr; Myke Thomas, mktg dir; Gail Nikiforuk, prom dir; Frank Callaghan, progmg dir; Roberto Dorazio, mus dir; Dave Rutherford, news dir; Mel Hoyme, vp engrg. CKKX-TV affil. ■ Rates: C$140; 84; 103; 74.

CJAY-FM—Listing follows CFCN(AM).

*CJSW-FM—Jan 15, 1985: 90.9 mhz; 1.9 kw. Stereo. Hrs opn: 24. Rm. 127- MacEwan Hall, Univ. Calgary, 2500 Univ. Dr. N.W. (T2N 1N4). (403) 220-5110; (403) 220-3902. FAX: (403) 220-5117. Licensee: University of Calgary Student Radio Society. Format: Alternative, jazz, news/talk. News staff one. Target aud: General; young, trendy & well-heeled. ■ Don McSwiney, pres, gen mgr & adv dir; Al Lalani, gen sls mgr; Jordan Kawchuk, prom mgr; Maizun Jayoussi, progmg dir; Rob Miliar, mus dir; Natalie Roberts, news dir; Greg Landgraf, chief engr. ■ Rates: C$30; 30; 30; 30.

CKIK-FM—Apr 15, 1982: 107.3 mhz; 100 kw. Ant 638 ft. TL: N51 03 54 W114 12 47. Stereo. 1107 7th Ave. S.W. (T2P 1B2). (403) 264-0107. FAX: (403) 232-6492. Licensee: CKIK FM Ltd. Format: Rock (AOR). News staff 6; new progmg 3 hrs wkly. Target aud: 25-44. ■ Harvey Glatt, chmn; Chuck Azzarello, pres; Wes Erickson, Gary Waldron, vps; Wes Erickson, gen mgr, stn mgr, opns mgr & progmg mgr; Gary Waldron, vp sls, gen sls mgr & adv mgr; Donna Rapp, mktg dir & prom dir; Chris Gordon, mus dir; Bruce McDonald, asst mus dir; Dave Taylor, news dir; Wade Wensink, chief engr. ■ Rates: C$120; 106; 106; 80.

CKRY-FM—July 9, 1982: 105.1 mhz; 100 kw. Ant 400 ft. Stereo. Hrs opn: 24. Suite 500, 1121 Centre St. N. (T2E 7K6). (403) 276-6105. FAX: (403) 230-4343. Licensee: Redmond Broadcasting Inc. Rep: Canadian Broadcast Sales. Format: Contemp country. News staff 6; news progmg 7 hrs wkly. Target aud: 25-54. ■ Robert Redmond, chmn; Rick Meaney, pres, gen mgr & stn mgr; Cheryl Meaney, vp; Gerry Bader, natl sls mgr & rgnl sls mgr; Cori Horton, prom mgr; Greg Haraldson, progmg dir; Phil Kalsen, mus dir; Robyn Adair, asst mus dir; Hal Gardner, news dir; Wade Wensink, engrg mgr.

*CKUA-FM-1—unknown; 93.7 mhz; 100 kw. Ant 500 ft. Rebroadcasts CKUA-FM Edmonton. c/o Radio Station CKUA-FM, 4th Fl., 10526 Jasper Ave., Edmonton (T5J 1Z7). (403) 428-7595. FAX: (403) 428-7595. Licensee: Alberta Educational Communications Corp. Format: Multi-format, educ. ■ Jackie Rollans, gen mgr & progmg mgr; John Baldock, mktg dir; Wendy McGrath, vp prom; Monika Martin, vp progmg; Sev Sabaurin, mus dir; Ken Regan, news dir; Neil Lutes, engrg dir.

Camrose

CFCW(AM)—Nov 2, 1954: 790 khz; 50 kw-U, DA-2. Stereo. Hrs opn: 24. 4752-99 St., Edmonton (T6E 5H5). (403) 437-7879. FAX: (403) 436-9803. Licensee: CFCW Broadcasting. Group owner: NewCap Broadcasting Ltd. Rep: Canadian Broadcast Sales. Format: Country. News progmg 11 hrs wkly. Target aud: 25-54; country music, sports and hockey listeners in Edmonton region. Spec prog: Edmonton Oilers, sports open line, farm 5 hrs wkly. ■ W.H. Holte, CEO, pres & gen mgr; Al Anderson, gen sls mgr; J.R. Greening, prom mgr; Larry Donahue, progmg dir; Niel Bergen, mus dir; Mike Geotze, news dir; Lyndy Olson, chief engr.

Canmore

CFHC(AM)—September 1983: 1450 khz; 1 kw-U, DA-1. Rebroadcasts on CFHC-1(AM) 1340 khz Banff. Box 1450 (T0L0M0). (403) 678-2222. TWX: (403) 678-6844. Licensee: Calgary Broadcasting Co. Net: Newsradio. Rep: All Canada. Format: C&W, div.

Drumheller

CKDQ(AM)—1958: 910 khz; 50 kw-U, DA-2. Stereo. Box 1480 (T0J 0Y0). (403) 823-3384. FAX: (403) 823-7241. Licensee: Q Radio Div CHUM Ltd. Group owner: CHUM Ltd. (acq 1981). Net: BN. Rep: Major Market Broadcasters. Format: C&W. ■ Jim Blumdell, gen mgr.

CKUA-FM-13—91.3 mhz; 100 kw. Rehroadcasts CKUA-FM Edmonton. c/o Radio Station CKUA-FM, 10526 Jasper Ave., Edmonton (T5J 1Z7). (403) 428-7595. Licensee: Alberta Educational Communications Corp. Format: Educ.

Edmonton

CBX(AM)—1948: 740 khz; 50 kw-U, DA-2. Box 555, 7909 51 Avenue (T5J 2P4). (403) 468-7500. FAX: (403) 468-7471. Net: CBC. Format: Information, news, talk. Target aud: 35 plus; college educated. ■ Ron Smith, gen mgr; Judy Fantham, stn mgr & progmg dir; Glenn Luff, mktg mgr; John Parker, engrg mgr.

CBX-FM—90.9 mhz; 100 kw. Stereo. Format: Btfl music, class, news.

CFBR-FM—Listing follows CFRN(AM).

CFCW(AM)—See Camrose.

CFRN(AM)—1934: 1260 khz; 50 kw-U, DA-N. Suite 100, 18520 Stony Plain Rd. (T5S 2E2). (403) 486-2800. FAX: (403) 489-6927. Licensee: Standard Radio Inc. Group owner: Standard Broadcasting Corp. (acq 6-19-92). Net: SBN. Rep: Radio-TV Reps, Walton. Format: Oldies. ■ Marty Forbs, gen mgr.

CFBR-FM—Co-owned with CFRN(AM). Apr 25, 1951: 100.3 mhz; 100 kw. Ant 482 ft. Stereo. Prog sep from AM. Rep: Radio-TV Reps (Canada), Hugh Wallace, Oakes (US). Spec prog: Jazz 4 hrs wkly.

CHED(AM)—Mar 3, 1954: 630 khz; 50 kw-U, DA-N. Stereo. 5204-84 St. (T6E 5N8). (403) 440-6300. FAX: (403) 468-6739. Licensee: Westcom Radio Group Ltd. (acq 8-20-92). Net: Newsradio. Format: Top-40. News staff 3. ■ Doug Rutherford, pres & gen mgr; Wayne Keen, gen sls mgr; Pat Cardinal, progmg mgr.

CKNG-FM—Co-owned with CHED(AM). Aug 11, 1982: 92.5 mhz; 100 kw. Ant 900 ft. Stereo. Format: Adult contemp.

*CHFA(AM)—Nov 20, 1949: 680 khz; 10 kw-U, DA-1. Hrs opn: 24. Box 555, 7909 51 Ave., (T5J 2P4). (403) 468-7800. FAX: (403) 468-7812. Licensee: CBC (acq 4-1-74). Net: Radio Canada. Format: Diversified, MOR, news/talk. News staff 9; news progmg 8 hrs wkly. Target aud: General; French speaking adults 20-60. ■ Gerard Veilleux, pres; Eric Upton, gen sls mgr; Pierre Noel, prom mgr; Denis Collette, progmg dir; Norman Fontaine, mus dir; Guy Marcotte, news dir & pub affrs dir; John Parker, chief engr.

CHQT(AM)—Listing follows CISN-FM.

CIRK-FM—1949: 97.3 mhz; 100 kw. Stereo. 10250 108th St. (T5J 2X3). (403) 428-8597. Licensee: 602410 Saskatchewan Ltd. Group owner: Forvest Broadcasting Corp. (acq 11-22-93). Format: Rock (AOR). News staff 5; news progmg 10 hrs wkly. Target aud: 18-54; mobile adults. ■ Marc Charlebois, gen sls mgr; Dave Coulter, engrg mgr.

CISN-FM—June 5, 1982: 103.9 mhz; 100 kw. Ant 757 ft. Stereo. 10550-102nd St. (T5H 2T3). (403) 428-1104. FAX: (403) 426-6502. Licensee: CISN Radio Ltd. Group owner: Shaw Radio. Net: BN. Rep: Radio Sls Group. Format: Contemp country. ■ Bob Lang, stn mgr.

CHQT(AM)—Co-owned with CISN-FM. Aug 19, 1965: 880 khz; 50 kw-U, DA-N. (403) 424-8800. Licensee: CHQT Broadcasting Ltd. (acq 1-22-93). Net: BN. Rep: Standard Brcst Sls. Format: MOR. Spec prog: Class 12 hrs wkly.

CJSR-FM—1984: 88.5 mhz; 900 w. Students' Union Bldg, Rm 224, University of Alberta (T6G 2J7). (403) 492-5244. FAX: (403) 492-4643. Licensee: The First Alberta Campus Radio Association. Format: Alternative progmg. ■ Christine Chomiak, gen mgr.

CKER(AM)—Nov 1, 1980: 1480 khz; 10 kw-U, DA-1. Hrs opn: 24. No. 200, 6005-103rd St. (T6H 2H3). (403) 438-1480. Licensee: CKER Radio Ltd. Net: BN. Rep: Target.

Alberta

Format: Ethnic, relg. News staff one; news progmg 14 hrs wkly. Target aud: General; ethnic audience (24 languages). Spec prog: Ger 10 hrs, It 13 hrs, Sp 13 hrs, Portuguese 2 hrs, Chinese 15 hrs, Ukrainian 7 hrs, Dutch 3 hrs, Pol 6 hrs, E. Indian 12 hrs, Pol 3 hrs wkly. ■ Roger Charest Sr., pres; Diana Parker, gen mgr; Roger Charest Jr., opns mgr; Marg Charest, gen sls mgr. ■ Rates: $34; 31; 28; 25.

CKNG-FM—Listing follows CHED(AM).

CKRA-FM—Nov 15, 1979: 96.3 mhz; 100 kw. Ant 757 ft. Stereo. Hrs opn: 24. 4752-99 St. (T6E 5H5). (403) 437-4996. FAX: (403) 428-7168. Licensee: CFCW Broadcasting. Group owner: NewCap Broadcasting Ltd. Net: BN. Rep: Canadian Broadcast Sales, Eastman, Katz. Format: Adult contemp. News staff 6; news progmg 5 hrs wkly. Target aud: 18-49; urban young adults. ■ W.H. Holte, pres; Al Anderson, gen sls mgr; Candace Hogan, prom mgr; Len Thuesen, progmg dir; Gerry Janzen, mus dir; Mike Goetze, news dir; Lyle Aumueller, chief engr.

*CKUA-FM—June 28, 1948: 94.9 mhz; 100 kw. Ant 400 ft. Stereo. 10526 Jasper Ave. (T5J 1Z7). (403) 428-7595. FAX: (403) 428-7628. Licensee: Alberta Educational Communications Corp. (acq 4-1-74). Net: Newsradio. Format: Div (block progmg), classical, jazz. News staff 7; news progmg 8 hrs wkly. Target aud: General; Alberta population. Spec prog: Ethnic, educ. ■ Don Thomas, CEO; Jackie Rollans, gen mgr; John Baldock, mktg mgr; Wendy McGrath, prom mgr; Ken Regan, news dir; Neil Lutes, engrg mgr.

*CKUA(AM)—Nov 21, 1927: 580 khz; 10 kw-U, DA-2. Dups FM 100%.

Edson

CJYR(AM)—Apr 4, 1968: 970 khz; 10 kw-U, DA-1. Box 6600 (T7E 1T9). (403) 723-4461. FAX: (403) 723-3765. Licensee: Yellowhead Broadcasting Ltd. (group owner). Format: MOR, C&W, top-40. Spec prog: Farm 2 hrs wkly. ■ Mel LazeRenko, pres & gen mgr.

Fort McMurray

CJOK(AM)—Jan 1, 1973: 1230 khz; 1 kw-U. 9912 Franklin Ave. (T9H 2K5). (403) 743-2246. Licensee: OK Radio Group Ltd. Net: SBN. Format: Contemp country. News staff 2. ■ Stu Morton, pres; Brian Blackburn, vp; Kelly Boyd, gen mgr; Rod Deviller, prom dir & progmg dir; Barry Britto, mus dir; Rod McDonald, news dir; larry Howell, chief engr.

CKYX-FM—Co-owned with CJOK(AM). March 1985: 97.9 mhz. Stereo. Prog sep from AM. Format: Rock. ■ Andy Carlson, progmg dir; Bruce Daniels, mus dir.

Grand Centre

CJCM(AM)—Dec 1, 1979: 1340 khz; 1 kw-U, DA-1. Hrs opn: 24. Box 433 (T0A 1T0). (403) 594-2459; (403) 594-6151. FAX: (403) 594-3001. Licensee: Nor-Net Communications Ltd. (group owner; acq 1988). Format: Adult Contemp. News staff 2; news progmg 12 hrs wkly. Target aud: General. ■ Roger Thorpe, gen mgr; Owen Martin, chief engr.

Grande Cache

CKYR-1(AM)—1230 khz; 50 w-U. Box 6600, Edson (T7E 1T9). (403) 723-4461. FAX: (403) 723-3765. Licensee: Yellowhead Broadcasting. Format: Adult contemp, country. ■ Mel Lazarenko, gen mgr.

Grande Prairie

CFGP(AM)—Nov 2, 1937: 1050 khz; 10 kw-U, DA-1. TL: N55 07 10 W118 56 45. Stereo. Hrs opn: 24. 200 Windsor Ct., 9835 - 101 Ave. (T8V 5V4). (403) 532-1050. FAX: (403) 532-1600. Licensee: Rogers Broadcasting Ltd. Net: Sun. Format: Adult contemp & oldies. News staff 4; news progmg 21 hrs wkly. Target aud: 25-55. ■ Edward S. Rogers, CEO; John W. Graham, chmn; Tony Viner, pres; Gary Miles, exec vp; Tom Bedore, vp, gen mgr, stn mgr, opns mgr & progmg dir; Murray Driver, gen sls mgr; Jill Webb, prom dir; Clint Lalonde, progmg mgr & mus dir; Marie Taylor, news dir; Sam Lowe, engrg dir. ■ Rates: $34; 34; 28; 18.50.

CJXX(AM)—Dec 16, 1979: 840 khz; 10 kw-U, DA-1. TL: N55 03 08 W118 51 59. Stereo. Hrs opn: 24. Suite 202, 9817 101st Ave. (T8V 0X6). (403) 532-0840; (403) 539-5599. FAX: (403) 538-1266; (403) 539-6397. Licensee: Monarch Broadcasting Ltd. (group owner). Rep: WTR. Format: C&W. Target aud: 25-49; adults who love country music. ■ W.H. Yuill, CEO; Dwaine Dietrich, vp; Arlene Miller, gen mgr & gen sls mgr; Ken Norman, prom dir & progmg dir; Bob Martineau, mus dir; Gord Sharpe, news dir; Duane Bonokoski, chief engr.

CKUA-FM-4—100.9 mhz; 100 kw. Ant 500 ft. Rebroadcasts CKUA-FM Edmonton. c/o Radio Station CKUA-FM, 10526 Jasper Ave., Edmonton (T5J 1Z7). (403) 428-7595. Licensee: Alberta Educational Communications Corp. Format: Educ.

High Prairie

CKVH(AM)—1990: 1020 khz; 1 kw-D, 400 w-N. Box 2219 (T0G 1E0). (403) 523-5111. FAX: (403) 523-3360. Licensee: Nor-Net Communications Ltd. (group owner). Format: C&W, rebroadcast of CFOK Westlock 24 hrs/wk local progmg. ■ Ken Johnson, gen mgr.

High River

CHRB(AM)—Dec 5, 1977: 1280 khz; 10 kw, DA-2. Hrs opn: 24. 11 5th Ave. S.E. (TIV 1G2). (403) 652-2472. FAX: (403) 652-7861. Licensee: Golden West Broadcasting Ltd. (group owner). Rep: Canadian Broadcast Sales. Format: C&W, relg. Target aud: General. Spec prog: Farm 5 hrs wkly. ■ Elmer Hildebrand, CEO; Lyndon Friesen, stn mgr; Marilyn Kwashuk, gen sls mgr; Nancy Ford, progmg dir; Paul Hanner, mus dir; Don McCracken, news dir; Vern Moores, chief engr.

Hinton

CIYR(AM)—1230 khz; 100 w-U. Box 3140 (T0E 1C0). (403) 865-8804. Licensee: Yellowhead Broadcasting Ltd. Format: EZ country. ■ Mel Lazerenko, gen mgr.

Jasper

CKYR(AM)—Feb 19, 1970: 1450 khz; 100 w. Dups CJYR(AM) Edson. Box 6600, c/o CJYR, Edson (T7E 1T9). (403) 723-4461 (CJYR). Format: Adult contemp, w/mix of country. ■ Kevin Schole, progmg dir.

Lethbridge

CFRV-FM—Listing follows CJOC(AM).

CJOC(AM)—May 10, 1926: 1220 khz; 10 kw-D, 5 kw-N, DA-N. Stereo. Hrs opn: 24. Box 820, 1015 3rd Ave. S. (T1J 3Z9). (403) 320-1220. FAX: (403) 327-5879. Licensee: Rogers Broadcasting Ltd. Net: Newsradio. Rep: Canadian Broadcast Sales. Format: Div, country. Target aud: 25-54. Spec prog: Farm 2 hrs wkly. ■ A.P. Viner, pres; Gary Miles, exec vp; Brent Seely, vp & gen mgr; Norma Thiessen, gen sls mgr; Dean Audet, prom mgr; Tom Gillespie, progmg dir & mus dir; Jim Richardson, news dir; Kris Rodts, chief engr.

CFRV-FM—Co-owned with CJOC(AM). 1979: 107.7 mhz; 100 kw. Ant 160 ft. Stereo. Hrs opn: 24. Prog sep from AM. (403) 328-1077. Format: Adult contemp, classic rock, CHR. News staff 3; news progmg 6 hrs wkly. Target aud: 18-49.

CKRX(AM)—Aug 28, 1959: 1090 khz; 10 kw-D, DA-1. Stereo. Box 1090, 401 Mayor Magrath Dr. (T1J 4A3). (403) 329-1090. TELEX: 038-49154. Licensee: Monarch Broadcasting Ltd. (group owner; acq 1-22-93). Net: BN. Format: Classic rock. News staff 6; news progmg 6 hrs wkly. Target aud: 35 plus. ■ Clyde Ross, pres & gen mgr; Benny Merell, gen sls mgr; Cliff Stoakley, prom dir; Marv Gunderson, progmg dir; Stephen Platt, news dir; Glenn Prins, chief engr. ■ Rates: C$43; 33; 33; 20.

*CKUA-FM-2—Feb 27, 1976: 99.3 mhz; 100 kw. Ant 500 ft. Rebroadcasts CKUA-FM Edmonton. c/o Radio Station CKUA-FM, 10526 Jasper Ave., Edmonton (T5J 1Z7). (403) 428-7595. Licensee: Alberta Educational Communications Corp. Format: Educ.

Lloydminster

CKSA(AM)—Apr 1, 1957: 1080 khz; 50 kw-D, 10 kw-N, DA-N. 5026 50th St. (T9V 1P3). (403) 875-3321. Licensee: Sask-Alta Broadcasters Ltd. Net: BN. Format: Country. ■ Mary Shortell, pres; Ken Ruptash, gen mgr; Graham Brown, gen sls mgr.

Medicine Hat

CHAT(AM)—Nov 1, 1946: 1270 khz; 10 kw-U, DA-2. Hrs opn: 24. Box 1270, 1111 Kingsway Ave. (T1A 7H5). (403) 529-1270. FAX: (403) 529-1292. Licensee: Monarch Broadcasting Ltd. (group owner). Rep: United. Format: New country. News staff 4; news progmg 14 hrs wkly. Target aud: General. ■ W.H. Yuill, CEO & pres; Dwaine Dietrich, exec vp; Bryan Ellis, gen mgr; Kathy Kopperud, gen sls mgr; John Cartwright, prom mgr; Jay Hitchen, progmg dir; Scott O'Brien, mus dir; Brian Konrad, news dir; Joel Simmons, engrg dir. ■ CBC-TV affil.

Directory of Radio

CJCY(AM)—July 1, 1982: 1390 khz; 10 kw-U, DA-2. 2nd Fl., 457-3rd St., S.E. (T1A 0G8). (403) 529-1390. FAX: (403) 527-5971. Licensee: Medicine Hat Broadcasting Ltd. Format: Adult contemp. Spec prog: Farm 2 hrs wkly. ■ *CKUA-FM-3—June 23, 1976: 97.3 mhz; 100 kw. Ant 500 ft. Rebroadcasts CKUA-FM Edmonton. c/o Radio Station CKUA-FM, 10526 Jasper Ave., Edmonton (T5J 1Z7). (403) 428-7595. Licensee: Alberta Educational Communications Corp. Format: Educ.

Medley

*CHCL(AM)—1956: 1450 khz; 40 watts-U, DA-1. Hrs opn: 6 AM-midnight. Box 1000 (T0A 2M0). (403) 594-1450. Licensee: Base Commander, CFB Cold Lake. Net: CBC. Format: Adult contemp, AOR, country. Target aud: 20-45. Spec prog: French. ■ Col. Ed McGillivray, CEO; Ken Hannon, pres; Susan Thir, stn mgr; Larry Nickerson, prom mgr; Don Richard, progmg mgr; Graham Wood (pop), Gord Dahl (country), Sylvain Boulay (French), mus dirs; Bonnie Collins, news dir & pub affrs dir; Trevor Meikle, chief engr.

Peace River

*CKUA-FM-5—96.9 mhz; 100 kw. Ant 500 ft. Rebroadcasts CKUA-FM Edmonton. c/o Radio Station CKUA-FM, 10526 Jasper Ave., Edmonton (T5J 1Z7). (403) 428-7595. Licensee: Alberta Educational Communications Corp. Format: Educ.

CKYL(AM)—Nov 1, 1954: 610 khz; 10 kw-U, DA-2. Bag Service No. 300 (T8S 1T5). (403) 624-2535. FAX: (403) 624-5424. Licensee: Peace River Broadcasting Ltd. (acq 8-1-66). Rep: Target. Format: MOR. News staff 4. ■ Mary Cambridge, gen mgr.

Red Deer

CIZZ-FM—Listing follows CKGY(AM).

CKGY(AM)—Aug 1, 1973: 1170 khz; 50 kw-D, 10 kw-N. Stereo. Hrs opn: 24. Bag 5339 (T4N 6W1). (403) 343-1170. FAX: (403) 346-1230. Licensee: Shaw Radio (group owner; acq 9-1-87). Rep: Major Mkt. Format: "Thunder Country". News staff 4. Target aud: 25 plus; 50% male and 50% female. ■ Jim Shaw, CEO; Terry Strain, pres; Ron Thompson, gen mgr & gen sls mgr; Elsie Lowe, prom mgr; Ritch Nickell, progmg dir; Alan Redel, news dir; Cliff Wheeler, chief engr. ■ Rates: C$64; 47; 54; 26.

CIZZ-FM—Co-owned with CKGY(AM). 1965: 98.9 mhz; 100 kw. Ant 400 ft. Stereo. Prog sep from AM. (403) 342-7625. Format: AOR. Target aud: 18-49; male 55%, female 45%. ■ Ron Thompson, stn mgr; Rob Robson, progmg dir; Dave Gilmore, mus dir; Cliff Wheeler, engrg mgr. ■ Rates: C$43; 31; 36; 38.

CKRD(AM)—1949: 700 khz; 50 kw-D, 25 kw-N, DA-2. Hrs opn: 24. Box 5700, 2840 Bremner Ave. (T4N 6V5). (403) 343-0700. FAX: (403) 343-2573. Licensee: Monarch Broadcasting Ltd. (group owner; acq 1976). Net: BN. Rep: United, Western; WTR. Format: Adult contemp, gold. Target aud: 25-49. ■ W.H. Yuill, pres; Dwaine Dietrich, vp; Paul Mason, gen mgr & stn mgr; Ken Truhn, gen sls mgr; Jeff Rechner, progmg mgr & mus dir; Casey Cunningham, asst mus dir; Brian Walters, news dir; Joel Simmons, chief engr. ■ Rates: $46; 43; 46; 39.

St. Albert

CHMG(AM)—Dec 23, 1978: 1200 khz; 25 kw-U, DA-2. TL: N53 26 00 W113 37 00. Hrs opn: 24. Suite 602, 22 Sir Winston Churchill Ave. (T8N 1B4). (403) 458-1200. FAX: (403) 460-9671. Licensee: Balsa Broadcasting Corp. Format: Oldies. News staff 4; News progmg 6 hrs wkly. Target aud: 25-49; middle to upper income families. ■ Doug Shillington, gen mgr. ■ Rates: $120; 111; 118; 103.

St. Paul

CHLW(AM)—1975: 1310 khz; 10 kw-U, DA-2. Box 910 (T0A 3A0). (403) 645-4425. (403) 645-2383. Licensee: Radio LW. Group owner: Nor-Net Communications Ltd. Net: SBN. Format: Adult contemp, oldies, country rock. News progmg 4 hrs wkly. Target aud: 25-49. Spec prog: Farm 5 hrs wkly. ■ Gary Lelone, gen mgr.

Slave Lake

CKWA(AM)—Nov 1, 1985: 1210 khz; 1 kw-U, DA-1. Box 2470 (T0G 2A0). (403) 849-2577. FAX: (403) 849-4833. Licensee: Nor-Net Communications Ltd. (group owner). Format: Today's country. News staff one; news progmg 15 hrs wkly. Target aud: 25-54. ■ Hugh McKinnon, pres;

Len Novak, vp; Mark Tamagi, gen sls mgr; Barry Collins, natl sls mgr; Bob Bezpalko, rgnl sls mgr; Paul Larsen, prom dir & progmg mgr; Ida May Mulligan, adv dir; Bruce Andrei, mus dir; Darren Rathwell, news dir; Glenn Prins, engrg dir; Owen Martin, chief engr.

Stettler

CKSQ(AM)—Dec 15, 1976: 1400 khz; 1 kw-U, DA-2. 4703 58th St. (T0C 2L1). (403) 742-2930. FAX: (403) 742-0660. Licensee: CHUM Ltd. (group owner). Net: BN. Rep: Major Mkt, Target. Format: Contemp country. News staff one; news progmg 7 hrs wkly. Target aud: 25-54; 55% female, 45% male. ■ Allan Waters, pres; Jim Blundell, gen mgr; Wray Betts, stn mgr & rgnl sls mgr; Russell Thomas, prom mgr & progmg mgr; Kirk Fraser, mus dir; Dan Chabot, news dir; Gary Umari, engrg mgr. ■ Rates: $31; 19; 19; 10.

Taber

CKTA(AM)—Oct 7, 1974: 1570 khz; 10 kw-U, DA-2. Box 2199 (T0K 2G0); Box 1090, Lethbridge (T1J 4A3). (403) 223-4455; (403) 329-4144. FAX: (403) 329-0195. Licensee: Monarch Broadcasting Ltd. (group owner; acq 1-22-93). Net: BN. Format: Contemp country. News staff 6; news progmg 6 hrs wkly. Target aud: 40 plus. Spec prog: Farm 3 hrs wkly. ■ Clyde Ross, gen mgr; Marv Gunderson, progmg dir; Alan Nilsson, mus dir; Steve Platt, news dir; Glenn Prins, chief engr. ■ Rates: $28; 21; 21; 12.

Wainwright

CKKY(AM)—February 1984: 830 khz; 10 kw-D, 3.5 kw-N. Box 1476 (T0B 4P0). (403) 842-4311. FAX: (403) 842-4636. Licensee: Nor-Net Commununications Ltd. (group owner). Net: BN. Rep: RTV Reps. Format: C&W. News staff 6. Spec prog: Farm 10 hrs wkly. ■ Brian Hepp, gen mgr.

Westlock

CFOK(AM)—Aug 19, 1975: 1370 khz; 10 kw-U, DA-2. Hrs opn: 24. Box 1800, 9701 99th St., (T0G 2L0). (403) 349-4421. FAX: (403) 349-6259. Licensee: Nor-Net Communications Ltd. (group owner). Rep: Target. Format: Today's Country. News staff one; news progmg 15 hrs wkly. Target aud: 25-54. ■ Hugh McKinnon, pres; Len Novak, vp; Elaine Feser, sls dir; Mark Tamagi, gen sls mgr; Barry Collins, natl sls mgr; Bob Bezpalko, rgnl sls mgr; Paul Larsen, mktg dir, prom dir & progmg mgr; Bruce Andrei, mus dir; Danny White, asst mus dir; Dave Linden, news dir & pub affrs dir; Glenn Prins, engrg dir; Owen Martin, chief engr.

Wetaskiwin

CJOI(AM)—1971: 1440 khz; 10 kw-U, DA-2. 5220 51st Ave. (T9A 0V4). (403) 352-0144. FAX: (403) 352-0606. Licensee: Nor-Net Communications Ltd. (group owner; acq 8-24-90). Format: C&W, relg. Spec prog: Greek 2 hrs wkly. ■ Mark Tamagi, gen mgr.

British Columbia

Abbotsford-Matsqui

CFVR(AM)—Aug 20, 1962: 850 khz; 10 kw-U, DA-2. Hrs opn: 24. 2722 Allwood St., Abbotsford (V2T 3R8). (604) 859-5277; (604) 524-1359. FAX: (604) 859-9907. Licensee: Fraser Valley Broadcasters Ltd. (group owner). Net: Telemedia; Western Info Net. Rep: Starcom Broadcast Sls. Format: Adult contemp. News staff 4. Target aud: 25-49; adults in the central Fraser Valley area. Spec prog: Farm one hr, Ger one hr wkly. ■ Bill Coombes, CEO, chmn & pres; Robert Singleton, sr vp; Bruce McArthur, gen mgr & progmg dir; Peter Alpen, vp sls & vp mktg; Steve Hemenway, gen sls mgr; Roy Hafelk, prom dir; Roch Shannon Fraser, mus dir; Richard Dettman, news dir; Arnie Schmidt, pub affrs dir.

CFSR-FM—Co-owned with CFVR(AM). Sept 29, 1986: 104.9 mhz; 50 kw. Ant 475 ft. Stereo. Hrs opn: 24. Prog sep from AM. Box 386, Chilliwack (V2P 6J7). (604) 795-7827. Licensee: Star-FM Inc. Group owner: Fraser Valley Broadcasters Ltd. Format: Adult contemp. News staff 2. Target aud: 35-65; adults in British Columbia's lower mainland & Fraser Valley area. ■ Peter Slack, rgnl sls mgr; Barrie McMaster, progmg dir & news dir; Bill Coombes, mus dir.

Big White Ski Village

CKIQ-FM—Nov 8, 1981: 98.1 mhz; 20 w. Ant 60 ft. 2419 Hwy 97N, Kelowna (V1X 4J2). (604) 860-8600. FAX: (604) 860-8856. Licensee: Four Seasons Radio Ltd. Format: Adult contemp, oldies, news. ■ Walter Gray, gen mgr.

Boston Bar

CKGO-FM-1—July 4, 1980: 106.1 mhz; 91 w. Ant -2,871 ft. Rebroadcasts CKGO(AM) Hope. Box 1600, Hope (V0X 1L0). (604) 869-9313. FAX: (604) 369-2450. Licensee: Fraser Valley Broadcasters Ltd. Format: Adult contemp.

Burns Lake

CFLD(AM)—November 1965: 760 khz; 1 kw-D, 500 w-N. Box 600 (V0J 1E0). (604) 692-3414. FAX: (604) 692-3020. TELEX: 047-7119. Licensee: CFBV. Group owner: Cariboo Central Interior Radio Inc. Net: SBN, Newsradio. Format: MOR. ■ Allan Collison, gen mgr.

Campbell River

CFWB(AM)—Sept 10, 1963: 1490 khz; 1 kw-U. Hrs opn: 24. Rebroadcasts CJGR-FM Gold River 100%. 909 Ironwood Rd. (V9W 3E5). (604) 287-7106. FAX: (604) 287-7170. Licensee: CFCP Radio Ltd. Rep: Target. Format: MOR, oldies, adult contemp. News staff 3. Target aud: 20-45. Spec prog: Country 20 hrs. ■ Norma Browne, CEO; Brian Langston, gen mgr; John Stevenson, mus dir; Steven Dinsdale, news dir; Gary Knodel, chief engr. ■ Rates: C$22; 20; 20; 12.

Castlegar

CKQR(AM)—Sept 22, 1969: 760 khz; 20 kw-D, 5 kw-N. Hrs opn: 6 AM-12 AM. 525 11th Ave. (V1N 1J6). (604) 365-7600; (604) 352-7600. FAX: (604) 365-8480. Licensee: Valley Broadcasters Ltd. (acq 11-27-91; $800,000). Net: BN. Rep: Canadian Broadcasting Sales, Target Radio. Format: MOR. News staff one; news progmg 14 hrs wkly. Target aud: General. ■ J. W. Gillespie, chmn; Wilfred R. Warner, pres, gen mgr, stn mgr & vp engrg; Serge Plotnikoff, gen sls mgr; Kevin Bader, prom dir; Melanie Zelinski, mus dir; David Horth, news dir. ■ Rates: C$23; 23; 23; 19.

Chilliwack

CHWK(AM)—June 1927: 1270 khz; 10 kw-D, DA-1. Hrs opn: 24. Box 386 (V2P 6J7). (604) 795-5711. FAX: (604) 795-6643. Licensee: Fraser Valley Broadcasters Ltd. (group owner; acq 1969). Rep: Target. Format: Adult contemp. News staff 4. Target aud: 18-45. Spec prog: Farm 2 hrs wkly. ■ Bill Coombes, pres; Bob Singleton, sr vp; Barrie McMaster, vp opns & vp progmg; Peter Alpen, vp sls & vp mktg; Arnold Schmidt, chief engr.

CKSR-FM—Co-owned with CHWK(AM). Sept 29, 1986: 107.5 mhz; 670 w. Stereo. Hrs opn: 24. Rebroadcasts CFSR-FM Abbotsford. 2722 Alwood St., Abbotsford (V2T 3R8). (604) 795-7827. Licensee: Star-FM Radio Inc. Group owner: Fraser Valley Broadcasters Ltd. Format: MOR. News progmg 6 hrs wkly. Target aud: 35 plus. ■ Bill Coombes, gen mgr.

Clearwater

CHNL-1(AM)—1400 khz; 1 kw-D, 250 w-N. Rebroadcasts CHNL(AM) Kamloops. c/o CHNL(AM), 611 Lansdowne St., Kamloops (V2C 1Y6). (604) 372-2292. FAX: (604) 372-0682. Licensee: NL Broadcasting Ltd. Format: Adult contemp. ■ Robbie Dunn, pres & gen mgr; Bill Waddington, natl sls mgr; Jim Reynolds, progmg dir.

Courtenay

CFCP(AM)—Sept 1, 1959: 1440 khz; 1 kw-D, DA-N. Hrs opn: 24. 1595 Cliffe Ave. (V9N 2K6). (604) 334-2421. Licensee: CFCP Radio Ltd. Rep: Target, Canadian Broadcast Sales. Format: Oldies. News staff 2; news progmg 16 hrs wkly. Target aud: 25-54; women. ■ Norma Browne, pres & gen mgr; George Cowie, gen sls mgr; Greg Phelps, mktg dir & news dir; Ken Armstrong, prom mgr, progmg dir & mus dir; Larry Baker, chief engr. ■ Rates: C$22; 22; 22; na.

Cranbrook

CKEK(AM)—Oct 19, 1957: 570 khz; 10 kw-D, 1 kw-N. 19-9th Ave. S. (V1C 2L9). (604) 426-2224. FAX: (604) 426-5520. Licensee: Columbia Kootenay Broadcasting Co. Ltd. (acq 9-1-81). Net: BN. Rep: Target, United. Format: Adult contemp. News staff 19; news progmg 11 hrs wkly. Target aud: 25 plus. ■ Chris Sorensen, pres; Gary Cavers, gen mgr & gen sls mgr; Rod Schween, prom dir & progmg dir; Joyce Merrick, mus dir; Darren Theberge, news dir; Cliff Blakey, vp engrg & chief engr. ■ Rates: C$60; 53; 53; 32.

Crawford Bay

CBTE-FM—Not on air, target date unknown: 99.7 mhz; 135 w. Box 8478, Ottawa (K1G 3J5). Licensee: Canadian Broadcasting Corp.

Creston

CFKC(AM)—Sept 21, 1968: 1340 khz; 250 w-U, DA-1. Hrs opn: 24. 1560 Second Ave., Trail (V1R 1M4); 138-10 Ave. N., Creston. (V0B 1G0). (604) 428-5311. FAX: FAX (604) 368-8471. Licensee: Four Seasons Radio Ltd. (acq 9-1-85). Rep: Target Media. Format: MOR. Spec prog: Ehnic music 2 hrs wkly. ■ Dennis Gerein, gen mgr.

Dawson Creek

CJDC(AM)—Dec 15, 1947: 890 khz; 10 kw-U. Hrs opn: 24. 901-102 Ave. (V1G 2B6). (604) 782-3341. FAX: (604) 782-3154. Licensee: Mega Communications Ltd. Format: C&W, pop, adult contemp. News staff 7. Target aud: General. Spec prog: Rock 4 hrs wkly. ■ H.L. Michaud, pres; Mike Michaud, vp & gen mgr; Verna Michaud, stn mgr & prom dir; Neil Miller, vp opns; Kelli Robinson, gen sls mgr; Georgina Blake, mus dir; Morley Fountain, chief engr. ■ Rates: C$46; 41; 36; 29.

CJDC-FM—Apr 10, 1989: 92.7 mhz; 100 w. Ant 60 ft. Hrs opn: 24. Dups AM 100%. News progmg 7 hrs wkly. Target aud: 18-54. ■ CJDC-TV affil.

Duncan

CKAY(AM)—October 1964: 1500 khz; 10 kw-D, 1 kw-N, DA-2. Hrs opn: 24. Suite 102, 435 Trunk Rd. (V9L 2P5). (604) 748-1500. FAX: (604) 748-1517. Licensee: CKAY Radio Ltd. (acq 9-1-79). Rep: Target, United. Format: Adult contemp, div, talk. News staff 2; news progmg 12 hrs wkly. Target aud: 35-54. Spec prog: Oldies 12 hrs wkly. ■ Dick Drew, pres & gen mgr; Cam Drew, gen sls mgr & prom mgr; Evelyn Knight, progmg dir; Jim Williams, mus dir; Annette Falk, news dir; Robin Applewhaite, chief engr. ■ Rates: C$26; 21; 22; 10.

Egmont

CIEG-FM—July 1985: 107.5 mhz; 50 w. Ant 300 ft. Rebroadcasts CISQ(FM) Squamish 100%. Box 1068, Squamish (V0N 3G0). (604) 892-1021. FAX: (604) 892-6383. Rep: Canadian Broadcast Sales. Format: Adult contemp. News progmg 7 hrs wkly. Spec prog: Jazz 7 hrs wkly.

Fernie

CFEK(AM)—May 1971: 1240 khz; 1 kw-U, DA-1. Box 1170 (V0B 1M0). (604) 423-4449. FAX: (604) 423-6009. Licensee: E K Radio Ltd. Format: Adult contemp.

Fort Nelson

CFNL(AM)—Nov 21, 1967: 590 khz; 250 w-U, DA-1. Box 880 (VOC 1R0). (604) 774-2525. FAX: (604) 774-2577. TELEX: 036-73138. Licensee: Western Communication Ventures Ltd. Group owner: Nor-Net Communications Ltd. (acq 1971). Net: BN. Format: C&W. ■ Ed Barr, opns mgr; Chris Anderson, mus dir.

Fort St. John

CKNL(AM)—June 1962: 560 khz; 1 kw-U, DA-1. TL: N56 14 00 W120 53 32. 10532 Alaska Rd. (V1J 1B3). (604) 785-6634. TELEX: 036-75116. Licensee: Western Communication Ventures Ltd. Group owner: Nor-Net Communications Ltd. (acq 1962). Rep: Target, Canadian Broadcast Sales. Format: Country. News staff 2; news progmg 20 hrs wkly. Target aud: 18plus. Spec prog: Farm one hr. ■ Hugh McKinnon, CEO; Len Novak, pres; Randy Wilson, gen mgr & gen sls mgr; Mike Carroll, rgnl sls mgr; Mark Rodnar, prom mgr; Russ Beerling, progmg dir; Stacey Sankey, news dir; Aaron Berquist, pub affrs dir; Owen Martin, engrg mgr. ■ Rates: C$40; 34; 34; 16.

Gibsons

CISC-FM—October 1984: 107.5 mhz; 200 w. Ant 1,000 ft. Rebroadcasts CISQ-FM Squamish. Box 1068, Squamish (V0N 3G0). (604) 892-1021.

Golden

CKGR(AM)—1400 khz; 1 kw-D, DA-1. Box 69, Salmon Arm (V1E 4N2). (604) 344-7177. TELEX: 048-8379. Licensee: Copper Island Broadcasting Ltd. Net: SBN. Rep: Target. Format: MOR, Contemp country. ■ Harvey Davidson, gen mgr.

British Columbia

Grand Forks

CKGF(AM)—June 1969: 1340 khz; 1 kw-U, DA-1. Box 1570 (V0H 1H0). (604) 442-8221. FAX: (604) 442-3340. Licensee: Boundary Broadcasting Ltd. Net: SBN. Format: Adult contemp. ■ Gary Dorosz, stn mgr.

Hope

CKGO(AM)—May 1972: 1240 khz; 1 kw-D, 250 w-N, DA-1. Box 1600 (V0X 1L0). (604) 869-9313. FAX: (604) 869-2454. Licensee: Fraser Valley Broadcasters Ltd. (group owner). Net: SBN. Format: Adult contemp. ■ Tom Desorcy, stn mgr.

Invermere

CKIR(AM)—870 khz; 1 kw-U. Rebroadcasts CKGR(AM) Golden. Box 69, Salmon Arm (V1E 4N2). (604) 344-7177. Licensee: Copper Island Broadcasting Ltd. Format: MOR, contemp country. ■ Harvey Davidson, gen mgr.

Kamloops

CFJC(AM)—1927: 550 khz; 25 kw-D, 5 kw-N, DA-2. 460 Pemberton Terrace (V2C 1T5). (604) 372-3322. FAX: (604) 374-0445; (604) 372-5229. Licensee: Jim Pattison Enterprises Ltd. Group owner: Jim Pattison Communications Group (acq 1987). Rep: Target. Format: All hit country. News staff 4; news progmg 12 hrs wkly. Target aud: 30-50; large, loyal audience with disposable income. ■ Rick Amish, vp, gen mgr & stn mgr; Doug Collins, opns mgr, progmg mgr & news dir; Bryan White, gen sls mgr; Bruce Uptigrove, rgnl sls mgr & prom mgr; Rob Cosar, mus dir; Kris Swamy, chief engr.

CIFM-FM—Co-owned with CFJC(AM). 1961: 98.3 mhz; 4.3 kw. Format: Adult rock. News staff 4; news progmg 4 hrs wkly. Target aud: 30-40; baby boomers with disposable income. ■ Doug Collins, chief opns & mus dir; Bruce Uptigrove, mktg mgr & prom mgr; Bill Dinicol, asst mus dir. CFJC-TV.

CHNL(AM)—May 1, 1970: 610 khz; 25 kw-D, 5 kw-N, DA-N. Box 610, 611 Lansdowne St., (V2C 1Y6). (604) 372-2292. FAX: (604) 372-0682. Licensee: NL Broadcasting Ltd. Rep: Major Mkt. Format: Adult contemp, oldies. Target aud: 25-54. ■ Robbie Dunn, pres & gen mgr; Bill Waddington, gen sls mgr; Jim Reynolds, progmg dir; T. Tyler, mus dir; Jim Harrison, news dir; Dave Coulter, chief engr. ■ Rates: C$44; 37; 37; 25.

CIFM-FM—Listing follows CFJC(AM).

CKRV-FM—Jan 28, 1984: 97.5 mhz; 5 kw. Stereo. Hrs opn: 24. 611 Lansdowne St. (V2C 1Y6). (604) 372-2197; (604) 372-2292. FAX: (604) 372-0682. Licensee: NL Broadcasting Ltd. (acq 6-10-93; $925,000). Rep: Major Mkt. Format: Adult contemp. News staff 3; news progmg 5 hrs wkly. Target aud: 25-54. ■ Robbie Dunn, pres & gen mgr; Len Nakashimada, CFO; Bill Waddington, rgnl sls mgr; Kari Collier, prom mgr; Jim Reynolds, progmg dir; Tim Thompson, mus dir; Jim Harrison, news dir & pub affrs dir; Dave Coulter, chief engr. ■ Rates: C$33; 28; 28; 20.

Kaslo

CKKC-FM-2—October 1981: 95.3 mhz; 100 w. Rebroadcasts CKKC(AM) Nelson. 1560 Second Ave., Trail (V1R 1M4). (604) 368-5510. FAX: (604) 368-8471. Licensee: Four Seasons Radio Ltd. (acq 1-25-87). Format: MOR. ■ Dennis Gerring, gen mgr.

Kelowna

***CBTK-FM**—Nov 1987: 88.9 mhz; 4.7 kw. Ant 1,676 ft. 243 Lawrence Ave. (V1Y 6L2). (604) 861-3781. FAX: (604) 861-6644. Licensee: Canadian Broadcasting Corp. Net: CBC Mono. Format: News, pub affrs, entertainment.

CILK-FM—June 21, 1985: 101.5 mhz; 11 kw. Ant 1,246 ft. (CP: 10.3 kw). Stereo. Hrs opn: 24. 1598 Pandosy St. (V1Y 1P4). (604) 860-1010. FAX: (604) 860-0505. Licensee: Silk FM Broadcasting Ltd. Format: Light, easy listening. News progmg 9 hrs wkly. Target aud: 35-64; women. Spec prog: Class 5 hrs, relg 3 hrs wkly. ■ Nick Frost, gen mgr. ■ Rates: $50; 50; 40.

CKIQ(AM)—Nov 8, 1971: 1150 khz; 10 kw-U, DA-N. 2419 Hwy 97N (V1X 4J2). (604) 860-8600. Licensee: Four Seasons Radio Ltd. Net: Western Info Net. Rep: Telemedia. Format: Adult contemp, favorite hits, news. News staff 7; news progmg 16 hrs wkly. Target aud: 25-54. Spec prog: Intl. house of music 2 hrs, home improvements 2 hrs, top 20 countdown 2 hrs, NHL Hockey play by play 10 hrs, country music block 4 hrs wkly. ■ R.J.

Hall, chmn; Walter Gray, pres, gen mgr & stn mgr; Irv Gorby, gen sls mgr; Dirtman McFarlane, prom dir; Dave Pears, progmg dir & mus dir; Mike Guzzi, news dir; George Young, chief engr. ■ Rates: $63; 43; 43; 24.

CKLZ-FM—Listing follows CKOV(AM).

CKOV(AM)—Nov 4, 1931: 630 khz; 5 kw-D, 1 kw-N. TL: N49 50 51 W119 29 05. Stereo. Hrs opn: 24. 3805 Lakeshore Rd. (V1W 3K6). (604) 762-3331. FAX: (604) 762-2141. Licensee: Seacoast Communications Group Inc. (group owner; acq 9-1-88). Rep: Target Radio. Canadian Broadcasting Sales. Format: News/info, adult music favorites. News staff 5; news progmg 13 hrs wkly. Target aud 29-59. ■ Mel Cooper, pres; Bill Hazell, execvp; Terry Spence, Dean Cooper, vps; Dean Cooper, gen mgr; Gerry Gardner, gen sls mgr; Rick Dyer, rgnl sls mgr; Connie Marples, prom mgr; Bill Barnes, progmg mgr; Grant Scott, mus dir; Bruce Smith, news dir; Lorne Gagnon, chief engr. ■ Rates: C$58; 42; 39; 29.

CKLZ-FM—Co-owned with CKOV(AM). 1964: 104.7 mhz; 3.8 kw. Ant 1,611 ft. TL: N49 46 06 W119 29 59. Stereo. Hrs opn: 24. Prog sep from AM. Format: AOR. News staff 2; news progmg 4 hrs wkly. Target aud: 18-49. ■ Rob Bye, progmg mgr; Jim Scanlon, mus dir. ■ Rates: Same as AM.

Kitimat

CKTK(AM)—Mar 23, 1964: 1230 khz; 1 kw-U, DA-1. 350 City Centre (V8C 1T7). (604) 632-2102. Licensee: Skeena Broadcasters, a div of Okanagan Skeena Group Ltd. Net: BN. Format: MOR. ■ Bryan Edwards, sr vp; Tim MacLean, vp; John Taylor, sls dir. ■ CFTK-TV affil.

Langley

CKST(AM)—Jan 19, 1963: 1040 khz; 50 kw-U, DA-2. Stereo. Hrs opn: 24. Suite 101, 1199 W. Pender St., Vancouver (V6E 2R1). (604) 669-4187. FAX: (604) 684-6949. Licensee: 602411 Saskatchewan Ltd. Group owner: Forvest Broadcasting Corp. (acq 11-22-93). Net: Sun. Rep: All-Canada. Format: Variety/adult. News staff 2; news progmg 4 hrs wkly. Target aud: 18-34; intelligent, socially conscious. ■ Brian C. Brenn, stn mgr; Kathryn Romanow, prom mgr; John Dritmanis, progmg dir; Ed Jurak, chief engr. ■ Rates: C$384; 288; 312; 240.

Mackenzie

CKMK(AM)—1240 khz; 1 kw-D, 250 w-N. Box 1210 (V0J 2C0). (604) 997-3400. FAX: (604) 997-4818; TELEX: 047-8613. Licensee: Q Broadcasting Ltd. Group owner: Monarch Broadcasting Ltd. Format: MOR. ■ J. D. Mackenzie, gen mgr.

Merritt

CFJC-FM—May 1, 1926: 99.5 mhz; 35 w. Rebroadcasts CFJC(AM) Kamloops. 460 Pemberton Terr., Kamloops (V2C 1T5). (604) 372-3322. FAX: (604) 374-0445. Licensee: Jim Pattison Enterprises Ltd. on behalf of a company to be incorporated. Group owner: Jim Pattison Communications Group. Format: Country. ■ Richard Arnish, gen mgr.

CJNL(AM)—1970: 1230 khz; 1 kw-D, 250 w-N. Box 1630 (V0K 2B0); 2196 Quichena (V0K 2B0). (604) 378-4288. FAX: (604) 378-6979. Licensee: N. L. Broadcasting Ltd. Rep: Target. Format: Top-40. ■ Robby Dunn, gen mgr & gen sls mgr; Jim Reynolds, progmg dir.

Nanaimo

CHUB(AM)—May 24, 1949: 1570 khz; 10 kw-U, DA-2. 22 Esplanade (V9R 4Y7). (604) 753-4341. FAX: (604) 753-4819. Licensee: Benchmark Ventures Ltd. (acq 9-1-86). Net: BN. Rep: United, Target. Format: Adult contemp, news/talk. News staff 3; news progmg 15 hrs wkly. Target aud: 35-55; professional, business. ■ Hugh McKinnon, pres; Gene Daniel, gen mgr; Ian Thompson, gen sls mgr; Trish Newton-Segal, prom mgr; Duane Bodeker, mus dir; John Norman, news dir.

CKEG(AM)—July 1, 1981: 1350 khz; 10 kw-U, DA-1. Hrs opn: 24. 4550 Wellington Rd. (V9T 2H3). (604) 758-1131. FAX: (604) 758-4644. Licensee: Central Island Broadcasting Ltd. Rep: Canadian Broadcast Sales. Format: Country. News staff 3; news progmg 10 hrs wkly. Target aud: 25-65. ■ Bob Adshead, pres, gen mgr & stn mgr; Bill Clark, vp; Ian Thompson, gen sls mgr, natl sls mgr & rgnl sls mgr; Mike O'Brien, progmg mgr; Bob Linn, mus dir. ■ Rates: C$41; 33; 33; 25.

Nelson

CKKC(AM)—July 15, 1939: 880 khz; 1 kw-D, 700 w-N, DA-1. 1560 Second Ave., Trail (V1R 1M4); (604) 352-5510. FAX: (604) 368-8471. Licensee: Four Seasons Radio Ltd. (acq 9-1-85). Rep: Target. Format: MOR. News staff one. ■ Dennis Gerein, gen mgr & sls mgr; Doug Ozeroff, progmg mgr; Paige Mac Farlaine, news dir; Darren Fowler, engrg dir.

CKKC-FM—Sept 1, 1989 101.1 mhz; 140 w. Prog dups AM 100%.

New Denver

CKKC-FM-1—October 1981: 93.5 mhz; 100 w. Prog dups CKKC(AM) Nelson 100%. 1560 Second Ave., Trail (V1R 1M4). (604) 368-5510. FAX: (604) 368-8471. Licensee: Four Seasons Radio Ltd. (acq 1-25-87). Format: MOR. ■ Dennis Gerring, gen mgr.

New Westminster

CKNW(AM)—Sept 1, 1944: 980 khz; 50 kw-U, DA-2. Stereo. Hrs opn: 24. 815 McBride Plaza (V3L 2C1). (604) 522-2711. FAX: (604) 522-3413. Licensee: CKNW, Division of Westcom Radio Group Ltd. Group owner: Western International Communications Ltd. (acq 4-1-56). Net: Western Info Net. Rep: Canadian Broadcast Sales. Format: MOR, news/talk, adult contemp. News staff 20. Target aud: General. Spec prog: Sports. ■ Rod Gunn, pres & gen mgr; Art Reitmayer, vp; John Iacobucci, vp sls; John Plul, vp mktg; Tom Plasteras, progmg dir & mus dir; Gord MacDonald, news dir; Shirley Stocker, pub affrs dir; Dave Glasstotton, vp engrg.

CFMI-FM—Co-owned with CKNW(AM). Mar 22, 1970: 101.1 mhz; 100 kw. Ant 3,500 ft. Stereo. Prog sep from AM. (604) 521-4808. FAX: (604) 522-3413. Licensee: CFMI-FM, Division of Westcom Radio Group Ltd. Format: Classic rock. News staff 4; news progmg 4 hrs wkly. Target aud: 25-49; general. ■ Steve Scarrow, prom dir; Ross Winters, progmg dir; Benoit Dufresne, mus dir; Graham Hatch, news dir.

100 Mile House

CKBX(AM)—July 30, 1971: 840 khz; 1 kw-D, 250 w-N, DA-1. Box 939 (V0K 2E0). (604) 395-3848. FAX: (604) 395-4147. Licensee: Cariboo Broadcasters Ltd. Group owner: Cariboo Central Interior Radio Inc. (acq 1981). Net: Western Info Net. Format: Country. Spec prog: Class one hr wkly. ■ Spence Henderson, stn mgr.

Osoyoos

CJOR(AM)—December 1966: 1240 khz; 1 kw-U, DA-1. Box 539 (V0H 1V0). (604) 492-2800. FAX: (604) 495-7228. Licensee: Okanagan Radio Ltd. (acq 1976). Rep: All-Canada. Format: MOR, oldies. Spec prog: Por 3 hrs wkly. ■ Ron Clark, stn mgr.

Parksville-Qualicum

CHPQ(AM)—Dec 7, 1973: 1370 khz; 1 kw, DA-1. Box 1370 (V9P 2R3). (604) 248-4211. FAX: (604) 248-4210. Licensee: Benchmark Ventures Inc. Format: Adult contemp. News staff 2. ■ Gene Daniel, gen mgr; E. Thompson, stn mgr; Keith Hamel, gen sls mgr.

Pemberton

CISP-FM—Oct 5, 1982: 104.5 mhz; 750 w. Ant 1,000 ft. Rebroadcasts CISQ-FM Squamish. Box 1068, c/o CISQ-FM, Squamish (V0N 3G0). (604) 892-1021. Format: Adult contemp. ■ Chuck McCoy, gen mgr.

Pender Harbour

CIPN-FM—October 1984: 104.7 mhz; 750 w. Ant 1,500 ft. Rebroadcasts CISQ-FM Squamish. Box 1068, Squamish (V0N 3G0). (604) 892-1021. Format: Adult contemp.

Penticton

CIGV-FM—Oct 18, 1981: 100.7 mhz; 10.6 kw. Ant 4,297 ft. Stereo. Hrs opn: 24. 125 Nanaimo Ave. W. (V2A 1N2). (604) 493-6767. FAX: (604) 493-0098. Licensee: Great Valleys Radio Ltd. Rep: United, Target. Format: C&W, relg. News staff 3; news progmg 16 hrs wkly. Target aud: 18 plus. Spec prog: Class 2 hrs, farm one hr wkly. ■ Ralph J. Robinson, CEO, pres, gen mgr & gen sls mgr; Carl Harris, chmn & mus dir; Jack Crane, progmg mgr; George Cameron, chief engr. ■ Rates: $36; 32; 30; 25.

CJMG-FM—Listing follows CKOR(AM).

Stations in Canada

British Columbia

CKOR(AM)—September 1948: 800 khz; 10 kw-D, 500 w-N. 33 Carmi Ave. (V2A 3G4). (604) 492-2800. FAX: (604) 493-0370. Licensee: Okanagan Radio Ltd. (acq 4-20-72). Net: Western Info Net. Rep: Paul Mulvihill. Format: Gold. ■ Ron Clark, gen mgr; Ernie Blumke, gen sls mgr; Michaele Olstrom, prom mgr.

CJMG-FM—Co-owned with CKOR(AM). June 1, 1965: 97.1 mhz; 1.8 kw. Ant 755 ft. Stereo. Prog sep from AM. Format: AOR.

Port Alberni

CJAV(AM)—Apr 1, 1946: 1240 khz; 1 kw-U. TL: N49 16 41 W124 46 51. Hrs opn: 24. 2970 3rd Ave. (V9Y 7N4). (604) 723-2455. FAX: (604) 723-0797. Licensee: CJAV Ltd. (acq 4-1-72). Rep: Target, Canadian Broadcast Sales. Format: Adult contemp, C&W, talk. News progmg 14 hrs wkly. Target aud: General. Spec prog: European one hr wkly. ■ Bill Gibson, pres & gen mgr; Ike Patterson, opns mgr & gen sls mgr. ■ Rates: C$28; 24; 24; 18.

Port Hardy

CFNI(AM)—Sept 1, 1979: 1240 khz; 1 kw-U, DA-1. Box 1240, 5050 Beaver Harbour Rd. (V0N 2P0). (604) 949-6500. FAX: (604) 949-6580. Licensee: CFCP Ltd. Rep: Target Radio. Canadian Broadcast Sales. Format: Adult contemp, country, oldies. News staff one; news progmg 15 hrs wkly. Target aud: General. ■ Norma Browne, CEO, chmn & pres; Phil Hicks, stn mgr, progmg mgr & mus dir; George Cowie, gen sls mgr; Greg Phelps, prom dir; Larry Baker, engrg dir. ■ Rates: C$23; 17; 17; 13.

Powell River

CHQB(AM)—Mar 21, 1967: 1280 khz; 1 kw-U, DA-1. Hrs opn: 24. 6816 Courtenay St. (V8A 1X1). (604) 485-4207. FAX: (604) 485-4210. Licensee: Sunshine Coast Broadcasting Ltd. (acq 4-75). Net: CBC. Rep: Target Radio, W.R.B.S. Format: Country, MOR. News staff one. Target aud: General. Spec prog: French one hr, religious one hr wkly. ■ Bob McInnes, gen mgr; Derek Bouchard, progmg dir.

Prince George

CBYG-FM—91.5 mhz; 100 kw. Suite 100, 1268 5th Ave. (V2L 3L2). (604) 562-6701. FAX: (604) 562-4777. Licensee: CBC. Net: CBC Radio. Format: Current Affairs.

CIOI-FM—Listing follows CKPG(AM).

CIRX-FM—Listing follows CJCI(AM).

CJCI(AM)—Aug 5, 1970: 620 khz; 10 kw-D, DA-1. Stereo. 1940 3rd Ave. (V2M 1G7). (604) 564-2524. FAX: (604) 562-6611. Licensee: Cariboo Central Interior Radio Inc. (group owner). Net: SBN. Rep: Target. Format: Adult contemp. ■ Terry Shepherd, gen mgr.

CIRX-FM—Co-owned with CJCI(AM). Oct 1, 1983: 94.3 mhz; 3.5 kw. Ant 1,145 ft. Stereo. Format: MOR.

CKPG(AM)—Feb 8, 1945: 550 khz; 10 kw-U, DA-2. 1220 6th Ave. (V2L 3M8). (604) 564-8861. FAX: (604) 562-8768 (TRAFFIC). (604) 562-8159 (NEWS). Licensee: Radio Station CKPG Ltd. Group owner: Monarch Broadcasting Ltd. Net: Western Info Net. Format: Adult contemp. ■ W.H. Yuill, pres; Dwaine Dietrich, vp; Gordon Leighton, gen mgr; Terry Alix, gen sls mgr; Ken Kilcullen, progmg dir; Mike Benny, mus dir; Mike Woodworth, news dir; Ron Kellington, pub affrs dir.

CIOI-FM—Co-owned with CKPG(AM). Mar 1, 1981: 101.3 mhz; 10 kw. Ant 1,000 ft. Stereo. (604) 562-2101. Format: C&W. ■ Rick Kelly, mus dir; Ron Kellington, chief engr. ■ CKPG-TV affil.

Prince Rupert

*****CFPR(AM)**—1936: 860 khz; 10 kw-D, DA-1. 222 3rd Ave. W. (V8J 1L1). (604) 624-2161. FAX: (604) 627-8594. Licensee: CBC (acq 1953). Net: CBC Radio. Format: CBC info, news/talk. Target aud: General. Spec prog: Current affrs. ■ Karen Tankard, news dir.

CHTK(AM)—1965: 560 khz; 1 kw-D, 250 w-N. 346 Stiles Pl. (V8J 3S5). (604) 624-9111. FAX: (604) 624-3100. Licensee: Skeena Broadcasters. Rep: Paul Mulvihill. Format: Adult contemp. ■ Ron Langridge, gen mgr.

Princeton

CIOR(AM)—June 1972: 1400 khz; 1 kw-U, DA-1. Box 1400 (V0E 1W0); 130 Harold Ave. (V0E 1W0). (604) 295-6991. FAX: (604) 295-6628. Licensee: Lawrence M. Currie. Net: BN, SBN. Format: Adult contemp, top-40. ■ Lawrance Currie, gen sls mgr & gen mgr; George Elliott, progmg dir.

Quesnel

CKCQ(AM)—Aug 28, 1957: 920 khz; 10 kw-D, 1 kw-N, DA-N. 160 Front St. (V2J 2K1). (604) 992-7046. FAX: (604) 992-2354. Licensee: C.C.I. Radio Network. Group owner: Cariboo Central Interior Radio Inc. Net: SRN. Rep: Target, United. Format: Country News staff 4. ■ Brian Miles, gen mgr.

Revelstoke

CKCR(AM)—Nov 21, 1965: 1340 khz; 1 kw-D, 250 w-N. Box 69, Salmon Arm (V1E 4N2). (604) 837-2149. Licensee: Copper Island Broadcasting Ltd. Format: MOR, Contemp country. ■ Harvey Davidson, gen mgr; Steve Bender, gen sls mgr; Jae Susoeff, progmg dir.

Richmond

CISL(AM)—May 1, 1980: 650 khz; 10 kw-U, DA-2. No. 20, 11151 Horseshoe Way (V7E 4S5). (604) 272-6500. FAX: (604) 272-5428. Licensee: South Fraser Broadcasting Ltd. Net: BN. Rep: Telemedia. Format: Oldies. ■ Michael Dickenson, pres; Jim McLaughlin, gen mgr; Glenn Chalmers, gen sls mgr; Brad Phillips, progmg dir; Brad Edwards, mus dir; Barry Johnson, engrg mgr.

Salmon Arm

CKXR(AM)—Nov 18, 1965: 580 khz; 10 kw-D, 1 kw-N, DA-2. Box 69 (V1E 4N2). (604) 832-2161. FAX: (604) 832-2240; TELEX: 048-8379. Licensee: Copper Island Broadcasting Ltd. (acq 1-1-82). Net: SBN. Rep: Target. Format: MOR, contemp country. ■ Harvey Davidson, gen mgr; Jae Susoeff, progmg dir.

Sechelt

CISE-FM—July 1985: 104.7 mhz; 750 w. Ant 2,000 ft. Rebroadcasts CISQ-FM Squamish. Box 1068, Squamish (V0N 3G0). (604) 892-1021; (604) 683-8060. FAX: (604) 892-6383. Licensee: Salkirk Communications (acq 2-89). Net: SBN. Rep: Canadian Broadcast. Format: Adult contemp. News progmg 7 hrs wkly. Spec prog: Jazz 7 hrs wkly.

Smithers

CFBV(AM)—Oct 25, 1963: 870 khz; 1 kw-D, 250 w-N. Box 335 (V0J 2N0). (604) 847-2521. FAX: (604) 847-9411. Licensee: CFBV Ltd. Group owner: Cariboo Central Interior Radio Inc. Net: SBN. ■ Al Collison, gen mgr.

Squamish

CISQ-FM—Nov 30, 1981: 107.1 mhz; 20 kw. Ant 800 ft. Hrs opn: 24. Box 1068 (V0N 3G0). (604) 892-1021; (604) 683-8060. FAX: (604) 892-6383. Licensee: Rogers Broadcasting. Rep: Canadian Broadcast Sales. Format: Adult contemp. News staff 2; news progmg 5 hrs wkly. Target aud: primary 18-54; secondary female 25-40. Spec prog: Jazz 7 hrs wkly. ■ Chuck McCoy, pres mgr; Geoff Poulton, stn mgr, opns mgr & progmg mgr; Gary Milne, sls dir & mktg dir; Fawn Duchaine, rgnl sls mgr; Casey Clarke, mus dir; John French, news dir & pub affrs dir; Jack Wiebe, chief engr. ■ Rates: C$31; 19; 31; 19.

Summerland

CHOR(AM)—1972: 1450 khz; 1 kw-U, DA-1. Box 1170 (V0H 1Z0). (604) 494-0333. FAX: (604) 493-0444. Licensee: Okanagan Radio Ltd. Rep: All-Canada. Format: MOR, oldies. Spec prog: Class 3 hrs, jazz 3 hrs wkly. ■ Bob Duck, gen mgr; Michael Olstrom, progmg dir.

Terrace

CFTK(AM)—1960: 590 khz; 1 kw-D, DA-1. 4625 Lazelle Ave. (V8G 1S4). (604) 635-6316. FAX: (604) 638-6320; TWX: 047-85529. Licensee: Skeena Broadcasters, a div of Okanagan Skeena Grp Ltd. Net: SBN. Format: MOR. ■ Brian Edwards, pres; Tim MacLean, gen mgr; Renita Neys, progmg dir; Chris Holtom, news dir; Harry Nutma, chief engr.

CJFW-FM—Co-owned with CFTK(AM). December 1983: 103.1 mhz. Format: Contemp country. ■ Stephanie Weber, gen sls mgr; Peter Turner, mus dir. ■ CFTK-TV affil.

Trail

CJAT(AM)—Dec 25, 1931: 610 khz; 10 kw-D, 1 kw-N, DA-2. 1560 Second Ave. (V1R 1M4). (604) 368-5510. FAX: (604) 368-8471. Licensee: Four Seasons Radio Ltd. (Trail) (acq 9-1-81). Net: SBN. Rep: Target. Format: MOR. Spec prog: Ethnic music 2 hrs wkly. ■ Dennis Gerein, gen mgr & gen sls mgr; Doug Ozeroff, progmg dir.

Vancouver

*****CBU(AM)**—1925: 690 khz; 50 kw-U, DA-1. Hrs opn: 24. Box 4600 (V6B 4A2). (604) 662-6000. FAX: (604) 662-6088. Licensee: Canadian Broadcasting Corp. Format: Class, jazz, news, talk. ■ Robert Sunter, gen mgr; Joan Athey, vp prom.

CBU-FM—1947: 105.7 mhz; 100 kw. Ant 1,823 ft. Stereo. Prog sep from AM.

CBUF-FM—Dec 1, 1967: 97.7 mhz; 50 kw. Ant 1,823 ft. Stereo. Box 4600, 700 Hamilton (V6B 2R5). (604) 662-6169. FAX: (604) 662-6161. Licensee: C3C. Format: Div. ■ Pauline Sincennes, gen mgr; Robert Groulx, progmg dir.

CFOX-FM—Listing follows CKLG(AM).

*****CFRO-FM**—Apr 22, 1975: 102.7 mhz; 5.5 kw. Ant 1,005 ft. 337 Carrall St. (V6B 2J4). (604) 687-8494. Licensee: Vancouver Co-Op Radio. Format: Community. Spec prog: Jazz 11 hrs, class 4 hrs, C&W one hr, Fr 2 hrs, It one hr, Can Indian 3 hrs, black 7 hrs, Sp one hr wkly. ■ Anne Marie Barrett, gen sls mgr; Ian Pringle, progmg mgr.

CFUN(AM)—Apr 20, 1922: 1410 khz; 50 kw-U, DA-2. 1900 W. 4th Ave. (V6J 1M6). (604) 731-9222. FAX: (604) 731-6143. Licensee: CHUM (Western) Ltd. Group owner: CHUM Ltd. (acq 1-1-73). Net: BN. Format: Adult contemp. News staff 5; news progmg 2 hrs wkly. Target aud: 25-49; upscale, well educated, females. ■ Paul Ski, vp & gen mgr; Neil Gallagher, opns mgr & progmg mgr; Wayne Stafford, gen sls mgr; J. J. Richards, news dir; Dave Youell, chief engr.

CHQM-FM—Co-owned with CFUN(AM). Aug 10, 1960: 103.5 mhz; 100 kw. Ant 1,630 ft. Stereo. Prog sep from AM. (Acq 8-23-69). Format: Easy lstng. Spec prog: Class 14 hrs wkly.

CHQM(AM)—Dec 10, 1959: 1320 khz; 50 kw-U, DA-2. 1134 Burrard St. (V6Z 1Y8). (604) 682-3141. FAX: (604) 682-5564. Licensee: 431881 B.C. Ltd. (acq 12-14-93; C$1.8 million). Rep: Major Mkt. Format: Ethnic. ■ Brian Scharf, gen mgr; David Geddes, progmg dir.

CHQM-FM—Listing follows CFUN(AM).

*****CITR-FM**—Apr 1, 1982: 101.9 mhz; 1.8 kw. Ant 170 ft. Stereo. Hrs opn: 7:30 AM-4 AM. Student Union Bldg, Rm 233, University of B.C. (V6T 1Z1). (604) 822-3017; (604) 822-2487. FAX: (604) 822-9364. Licensee: Student Radio Society of Univ. of B.C. Format: Ind mus, arts, info. News progmg 10 hrs wkly. Target aud: General. Spec prog: American Indian one hr, Black 20 hrs, class 5 hrs, country 4 hrs, folk 7 hrs, gospel one hr, jazz 8 hrs, East Indian one hr, women one hr, blues 2 hrs, news 3 hrs, news/talk 7 hrs, metal 8 hrs wkly. ■ Andrew Pavlov, pres; Linda Scholten, stn mgr; Adam Sloan, progmg dir; Mindy Abramovitz, mus dir; Ian Gunn, news dir; Helen Godolphin, pub affrs dir; Richard Anderson, chief engr.

CJJR-FM—Listing follows CKBD(AM).

CJVB(AM)—June 18, 1972: 1470 khz; 50 kw-U, DA-2. Stereo. Hrs opn: 24. 814 Richards St. (V6B 3A7). (604) 688-9931. FAX: (604) 688-6559. Licensee: Great Pacific Broadcasting Ltd. (acq 9-10-92). Rep: Major Mkt, Target. Format: Ethnic, Chinese. News progmg 12 hrs wkly. Target aud: 40 plus; new Canadians. Spec prog: Class 8 hrs, Ger 8 hrs, Pol one hr, It 14 hrs, Portuguese one hr, Greek 4 hrs, Sp one hr, Dutch 7 hrs, Hindi 8 hrs, Punjabi 6 hrs wkly. ■ John E. Stark, CEO, chmn & pres; Ed Ylanen, gen mgr. ■ Rates: C$70; 56; 39; 70.

CKBD(AM)—July 13, 1926: 600 khz; 10 kw-U, DA-N. Stereo. Hrs opn: 24. 1401 W. 8th Ave. (V6H 1C9). (604) 731-6111. FAX: (604) 731-0493. Licensee: Jim Pattison Enterprises Ltd., on behalf of a company to be incorporated. Group owner: The Jim Pattison Communications Group (acq 1965). Rep: United, Tacher. Format: Contemp Christian. News progmg 6 hrs wkly. Target aud: 18-49. ■ Jim Pattison, CEO & chmn; Jim Mackay, pres & gen mgr; Gary Chomyn, gen sls mgr; Mark Wilson, rgnl sls mgr; Gerry Siemens, progmg dir; Brian Yaremus, mus dir; Tom Mark, news dir.

CJJR-FM—Co-owned with CKBD(AM). July 1, 1986: 93.7 mhz; 75 kw. Ant 2,250 ft. Stereo. Hrs opn: 24. Prog sep form AM. (604) 731-7772. Format: Contemp country. Target aud: 25-54. ■ Mark Wilson, mktg dir; Kat Stewart, prom mgr.

CKKS-FM—Listing follows CKWX(AM).

CKLG(AM)—June 1954: 730 khz; 50 kw-U, DA-2. Stereo. 1006 Richards St. (V6B 1S8). (604) 681-7511. FAX:

Manitoba

(604) 681-9134; TWX: 04-532-78. Licensee: Shaw Radio Ltd. Group owner: Shaw Radio (acq 8-20-92). Net: Newsradio. Rep: Mutuelcom, Radio Market, Radio Sls. Format: Talk, adult pop. ■ Chris Pandoff, gen mgr; Dean Hill, Kate Gorman (asst), progmg dirs.

CFOX-FM—Co-owned with CKLG(AM). October 1964: 99.3 mhz; 100 kw. Ant 2,243 ft. Stereo. Prog sep from AM. (604) 684-7221. Format: AOR. Spec prog: Jazz 2 hrs wkly. ■ Mary Anne McKenzie, progmg dir.

CKST(AM)—See Langley.

CKWX(AM)—Apr 1, 1923; 1130 khz; 50 kw-U, DA-N. TL: N49 09 22 W123 04 00. 2440 Ash St. (V5Z 4J6). (604) 873-2599. FAX: (604) 877-4494. Licensee: CKWX Radio. Net: BN, SBN. Rep: All Canada. Format: Country. Target aud: 35-54; women. ■ Brian DePoe, progmg dir. Rebroadcasts on CKFX(SW): 6080 khz; 10 w. ■ Rates: $124; 124; 124; 124.

CKKS-FM—Co-owned with CKWX(AM). Mar 1, 1980: 96.9 mhz; 100 kw. Ant 2,500 ft. TL: N49 21 29 W122 57 09. Stereo. Hrs opn: 24. (604) 872-2557. Format: Adult contemp. News progmg 4 hrs wkly. Target aud: 25-54; females. Spec prog: Jazz 7 hrs wkly. ■ Tony Viner, pres; Chuck McCoy, gen mgr; Sharon Berry, prom mgr; Dale Buote, progmg dir; Doreen Copeland, mus dir; Jack Marion, news dir. ■ Rates: $164; 164; 164; 164.

CKZZ-FM—May 1991: 95.3 mhz; 75 kw. 11151 Horseshoe Way, No. 20, Richmond (V7A 4S5). (604) 241-0953. Licensee: South Fraser Broadcasting Ltd. Format: Dance. ■ Jim McLaughlin, gen mgr; Glenn Chalmers, gen sls mgr; Brad Phillips, progmg dir.

Vanderhoof

CIVH(AM)—November 1973: 1340 khz; 1 kw-D, 500 w-N, DA-1. TL: N54 01 00 W123 59 00. Hrs opn: 6 AM-9 AM, 3 PM-6 PM. Box 1370, 150 W. Columbia St. (V0J 3A0). (604) 567-4914. FAX: (604) 567-4982. Licensee: Prince George Broadcasting. Group owner: Cariboo Central Interior Radio Inc. Net: SBN. Rep: Target. Format: C&W. Target aud: General. Spec prog: Relg 5 hrs wkly. ■ Ron A. East, CEO; Terry Shepard, gen mgr; Tom Bulher, stn mgr; Mel Brundige, gen sls mgr; Tom Bulmer, rgnl sls mgr & progmg mgr; Mike Monroe, prom mgr & mus dir; Bill Russell, vp progmg; Sandy Ziegler, news dir. ■ Rates: $19; 17; 17; 9.

Vernon

CICF(AM)—Oct 23, 1978: 1050 khz; 10 kw-D, 1 kw-N, DA-2. 2800-31st St. (V1T 5H4). (604) 545-9222. FAX: (604) 549-8375. Licensee: Okanagan Radio Ltd. Okanagan-Skeena Group Ltd. Rep: Telemedia. Format: Adult contemp. News staff 4. Target aud: 25-49; female. ■ Bryan Edwards, pres; Michael Tindall, vp & vp sls; James Stuart Hewson, progmg dir; Al Webster, news dir; Renee Dale, engrg mgr. ■ Rates: C$34; 30; 32; 18.

CJIB(AM)—September 1947: 940 khz; 10 kw-U. 3313 32nd Ave. (V1T 2E1). (604) 545-2141. FAX: (604) 545-9008. Licensee: Rogers Broadcasting Ltd. Rep: All-Canada. Format: MOR. Spec prog: Class one hr, big band 3 hrs wkly. ■ Patrick Nicol, gen mgr.

Victoria

CFAX(AM)—Sept 4, 1959: 1070 khz; 10 kw-U, DA-1. TL: N48 23 50 W123 18 20. Stereo. Hrs opn: 24. Mellor Bldg., 825 Broughton St. (V8W 1E5). (604) 386-1070. FAX: (604) 386-5775. Licensee: Seacost Communications Group Inc. (group owner; acq 1-9-73). Rep: Canadian Broadcast Sales, Western. Format: MOR, talk, big band. News staff 8; news progmg 16 hrs wkly. Target aud: General; adults 35-64. ■ Mel Cooper, CEO, pres & gen mgr; Bill Hazell, exec vp & gen sls mgr; Terry Spence, vp, opns mgr, progmg dir & mus dir; Kathy Baan, Erin Mitchell, prom mgrs; Alan Perry, news dir; Bud Goes, chief engr. ■ Rates: C$86; 59; 59; 46.

CFMS-FM—Listing follows CKDA(AM).

*****CFUV-FM**—Dec 17, 1984: 101.9 mhz; 883 w. Ant 265 ft. (CP: 2.29 kw). Stereo. Hrs opn: 24. Box 3035 (V8W 3P3). (604) 721-8607; (604) 721-8702. FAX: (604) 721-8728. Licensee: University of Victoria Student Radio Society. Format: Alt rock, jazz. News progmg 3 hrs wkly. Target aud: General; people tired of commercial radio. Spec prog: Black 6 hrs, class 15 hrs, lt 2 hrs, Canadian Indian 3 hrs, folk 12 hrs, Fr 3 hrs, Pol one hr, Finnish one hr, Punjabi 2 hrs, Chinese one hr, electronic 3 hrs, Sp 3 hrs wkly. ■ Kate Pasieka, stn mgr & engrg mgr; Brian Pareis, sls dir; Magnus Thyvold, vp progmg; Jeff Kruys, mus dir.

CJVI(AM)—Apr 2, 1923: 900 khz; 10 kw-U, DA-1. Stereo. Box 900 (V8W 1H6). (604) 382-0900. FAX: (604)

382-4358. Licensee: Rogers Broadcasting Limited. Net: CBC Mono. Rep: All-Canada. Format: Oldies. ■ Kim Hesketh, pres & gen mgr; Ken Geiger, progmg dir.

CKDA(AM)—Jan 18, 1950: 1220 khz; 50 kw-U, DA-1. Box 1200 (V8W 2S5). (604) 384-9311. FAX: (604) 384-1213. Licensee: Capital Broadcasting System Ltd. Format: Adult contemp. ■ John Sitter, gen mgr.

CFMS-FM—Co-owned with CKDA(AM). March 18, 1965: 98.5 mhz; 100 kw. Ant 567 ft. Stereo. Prog sep from AM. Format: Easy lstng. Spec prog: Class 5 hrs wkly. ■ Mike Gale, progmg dir.

CKKQ-FM—Dec 12, 1987: 100.3 mhz; 100 kw. Ant 400 ft. Hrs opn: 24. 3795 Carey Rd., 2nd Fl. (V8Z 6T8). (604) 382-0100. FAX: (604) 380-6556. Licensee: Victoria Communications Ltd. Rep: All-Canada. Format: Rock. News staff 2; news progmg 4 hrs wkly. Target aud: 18-49. Spec prog: Jazz 4 hrs wkly. ■ Stu Morton, pres; Dan McAllister, gen mgr & natl sls mgr; Brian Blackburn, gen sls mgr; Jack Little, rgnl sls mgr; Erynn Fischer, prom dir; John Shields, progmg dir; Dave Farough, mus dir; Kirk Mason, news dir; Bob Calder, engrg dir. ■ Rates: C$90; 75; 75; 50.

Whistler

CISW-FM—Feb 25, 1982: 102.1 mhz; 900 w. Ant 2,250 ft. Rebroadcasts CISQ-FM Squamish. Box 1068, Squamish (V0N 3G0). (604) 892-1021.

Williams Lake

CKWL(AM)—Feb 25, 1960: 570 khz; 1 kw-U, DA-2. Partially dups CKCQ(AM) Quesnel. 83 S. First Ave. (V2G 1H4). (604) 392-6551. FAX: (604) 392-4142. Licensee: Cariboo Broadcasters Ltd. Group owner: Cariboo Central Interior Radio Inc. (acq 9-1-71). Rep: Target. Format: Adult contemp, classic rock, oldies. News staff 2. Target aud: General. ■ Karen LeComte, stn mgr, gen sls mgr & adv mgr; Brian Miles, progmg dir; Wayne Leslie, mus dir; Floyd Lust, engrg dir. ■ Rates: $22.75; 19.25; 19.25; 9.75.

CFFM-FM—Co-owned with CKWL(AM). Aug 31, 1987: 97.5 mhz. Stereo. Hrs opn: 24. (604) 398-2336. (Acq 12-23-92). Net: BN. Rep: United, Target. Format: Country. Target aud: General; equal split-male/female, 30-64. Spec prog: Country gospel mus 4 hrs wkly. ■ Jim Pattison, CEO; George Madden, pres; Rick Amish, vp; Terry Shepherd, gen mgr; Karen LeComte, stn mgr & gen sls mgr; Eric Sannes, vp progmg & mus dir; Karl Johnston, news dir; Floyd Lust, vp engrg. ■ Rates: Same as AM.

Manitoba

Altona

CFAM(AM)—Mar 13, 1957: 950 khz; 10 kw-U, DA-2. Hrs opn: 24. Box 950 (R0G 0B0). (204) 324-6464. FAX: (204) 324-8918. Licensee: Golden West Broadcasting Ltd. (group owner). Net: BN. Rep: Canadian Broadcast Sales. Format: Agriculture, MOR. News staff 8. Target aud: General. Spec prog: Class 15 hrs wkly. ■ E. Hildebrand, pres; D. Wiebe, gen mgr; M. Friesen, rgnl sls mgr; A. Friesen, progmg mgr; J. Hoeppner, engrg dir.

Boissevain

CJRB(AM)—1973: 1220 khz; 10 kw-U. Box 1220 (R0K 0E0). (204) 324-6464. FAX: (204) 534-6825. Licensee: Golden West Broadcasting Ltd. (group owner). Format: Easy lstng, relg. ■ David Wiede, gen mgr.

Brandon

CKLQ(AM)—October 1977: 880 khz; 10 kw-U, DA-2. 624 14th St. E. (R7A 7E1). (204) 726-8888. FAX: (204) 726-1270. Licensee: Riding Mountain Broadcasting Ltd. Format: C&W. Spec prog: Farm 18 hrs wkly. ■ Bob MacDonald, gen mgr.

CKX(AM)—Dec 11, 1928: 1150 khz; 50 kw-U, DA-2. 2940 Victoria Ave. (R7B 0N2). (204) 728-1150; (204) 727-1150. FAX: (204) 727-2505. Licensee: Craig Broadcast Systems, Inc. Format: Adult contemp. ■ Stuart Craig, CEO; Boyd Craig, gen mgr; Jacki Maginel, vp prom; Al Cruise, vp adv; Kevin Greyton, vp progmg; Bob Bruce, asst mus dir; Lawrence Dubois, pub affrs dir. ■ CKX-TV affil.

CKX-FM—Dec 16, 1963: 96.1 mhz; 100 kw. Ant 1,042 ft. Stereo. Prog sep from AM. Rep: Canadian Broadcast Sales. Format: Rock.

Churchill

CHFC(AM)—Sept 13, 1959: 1230 khz; 250 w-U, DA-1. Rebroadcasts CBW(AM) Winnipeg. Box 160, c/o CBW(AM), Winnipeg (R3C 2H1). (204) 788-3217. Licensee: CBC. Net: CBC AM. Format: Variety/diverse. ■ John Coutanche, gen mgr.

Dauphin

CKDM(AM)—Jan 6, 1951: 730 khz; 10 kw-D, 5 kw-N, DA-N. 27 3rd Ave. N.E. (R7N 0Y5). (204) 638-3230. FAX: (204) 638-8257. Licensee: Dauphin Broadcasting Co. Ltd. (acq 11-23-93). Net: BN. Rep: Messner Media. Format: C&W. ■ Linus J. Westberg, gen mgr; Alan Trueman, gen sls mgr; Bruce Leperre, progmg dir.

Flin Flon

CFAR(AM)—Nov 14, 1937: 590 khz; 10 kw-D, 1 kw-N, DA-2. Hrs opn: 19. Box 430, 316 Green St. (R8A 1N3). (204) 687-3469. FAX: (204) 687-6786. Licensee: Arctic Radio (1982) Ltd. (acq 9-1-82). Rep: Major Mkt. Format: MOR, C&W. Spec prog: Cree music. ■ Doug O'Brien, pres; Joe McMormick, progmg mgr.

Gillam

CFIL-FM—Apr 22, 1981: 97.1 mhz; 89 w. Ant 73 ft. Rebroadcasts CJOB(AM) Winnipeg. c/o Garry H. Shapera, 11 Woodcrest Dr., Winnipeg (R2V 2T1). (204) 339-5939. Licensee: Gary H. Shapera. ■ Gary Shapera, gen mgr.

Jenpeg

CJEN-FM—Apr 22, 1981: 96.1 mhz; 460 w. Ant 172 ft. Rebroadcasts CJOB(AM) Winnipeg. c/o Garry H. Shapera, 11 Woodcrest Dr., Winnipeg (R2V 2T1). (204) 339-5939. Licensee: Gary H. Shapera. ■ Gary H. Shapera, gen mgr.

Limestone

CHGG-FM—Feb 23, 1978: 96.1 mhz; 15 w. Ant 40 ft. Rebroadcasts CJOB(AM) Winnipeg. c/o Garry H. Shapera, 11 Woodcrest Dr., Winnipeg (R2V 2T1). (204) 339-5939. Licensee: Gary H. Shapera. ■ Gary H. Shapera, gen mgr.

Portage la Prairie

CFRY(AM)—Oct 18, 1956: 920 khz; 25 kw-D, 15 kw-N, DA-2. 1500 Saskatchewan Ave. W. (R1N 0N6). (204) 857-5111. FAX: (204) 857-3456. Licensee: Portage-Delta Broadcasting Ltd. Rep: Paul Mulvihill. Format: C&W. Spec prog: Farm 4 hrs wkly. ■ Red Hughes, gen mgr; Bev Edmondson, progmg dir.

St. Boniface

*****CKSB(AM)**—May 27, 1946: 1050 khz; 10 kw-U. 607 Langevin St. (R2H 2W2). (204) 788-3236. FAX: (204) 788-3245. Licensee: CBC (acq 4-1-73). Format: Div, Fr. Target aud: General. ■ Gerard Veilleux, CEO; Patrick Watson, chmn; Huguette Le Call, mktg mgr; Rene Fontaine, progmg dir; Michel Boucher, news dir; Gilles Frechette, pub affrs dir.

Selkirk

CFQX-FM—Nov 9, 1981: 104.1 mhz; 100 kw. Ant 500 ft. Stereo. Hrs opn: 24. Box 400, 701 Greenwood Ave. (R1A 2B3). (204) 284-8591. FAX: (204) 956-5350. Licensee: Radio QX FM Inc. (acq 11-30-93; $1.65 million). Net: BN Voice. Format: Country. News staff 3. Spec prog: Farm 3 hrs, class 2 hrs, gospel 4 hr, folk 6 hrs wkly. ■ James A. Millican, gen mgr, stn mgr & progmg mgr; Rick Jackiw, gen sls mgr; Dan Kern, mus dir.

Steinbach

CHSM(AM)—Mar 19, 1964: 1250 khz; 10 kw-U, DA-2. Hrs opn: 24. Box 1250 (R0A 2A0). (204) 326-3737. Licensee: Golden West Broadcasting Ltd. (group owner). Rep: Canadian Broadcast Sales. Format: MOR. News staff 2. Target aud: General. Spec prog: Farm. ■ Elmer Hildebrand, pres; David Wiebe, gen mgr; L. Friesen, stn mgr; Menno Friesen, rgnl sls mgr; Al Friesen, prom mgr; Jack Hoeppner, engrg dir.

The Pas

CJAR(AM)—1974: 1240 khz; 1 kw-U, DA-1. Box 2980 (R9A 1R7). (204) 623-5307. FAX: (204) 623-5337. Licensee: Arctic Radio Corp. Ltd. Format: Adult contemp, AOR, C&W. ■ Doug O'Brien, pres; Jim Hamm, gen mgr

& gen sls mgr; Joey Rodswinkel, progmg mgr; Len Podbisky, news dir; Danny Parker, chief engr.

Thompson

*CBWK-FM—1980: 100.9 mhz; 9.4 kw. 7 Selkirk Ave. (R8N 0M4). (204) 677-2307. FAX: (204) 677-9517. Licensee: CBC. Net: CBC AM. Format: Div. ■ Margaret Allen, stn mgr.

CHTM(AM)—Mar 29, 1964: 610 khz; 1 kw-U, DA-1. 201 Hayes Rd. (R8N 1M5). (204) 778-7361. FAX: (204) 778-5252. Licensee: Arctic Radio (1982) Ltd. Format: Adult contemp, classic rock, country. News staff one; news progmg 15 hrs wkly. Spec prog: Relg 12 hrs, Cree (American Indian) 10 hrs wkly. ■ Doug O'Brien, pres; Tom O'Brien, gen mgr, opns mgr & gen sls mgr; Ron Krane, progmg dir; Kay Thompson, mus dir; Rob Henderson, news dir & pub affrs dir; Dan Parker, chief engr. ■ Rates: $31.50; 27; 31.50; 17.50.

Winkler-Morden

CKMW(AM)—Aug 1, 1980: 1570 khz; 10 kw-U, DA-2. Hrs opn: 24. Box 1570, Main Plaza, Main St., Winkler (R6W 4B5). (204) 325-9506; (204) 325-7600. FAX: (204) 324-8918. Licensee: Golden West Broadcasting Ltd. (group owner). Rep: Canadian Broadcast Sales. Format: Country. News staff 2. Target aud: General. ■Elmer Hildebrand, pres; David Wiebe, gen mgr; Menno Friesen, rgnl sls mgr; Deb Kauenhofen, mus dir.

Winnipeg

CBW(AM)—Sept 3, 1948: 990 khz; 50 kw-D, 46 kw-N. Box 160 (R3C 2H1). (204) 788-3217. FAX: (204) 788-3227. Licensee: Canadian Broadcasting Corp. Net: CBC. Format: Div. Spec prog: Farm 6 hrs, class 8 hrs, C&W one hr wkly. ■ John Coutanche, gen mgr.

CBW-FM—Oct 11, 1965: 98.3 mhz; 354 kw. Stereo. Dups AM 16%. Net: CBC FM. Format: Class, div. Spec prog: Jazz 3 hrs, educ 5 hrs wkly. ■ CBWT-TV affil.

CHIQ-FM—Listing follows CIFX(AM).

CIFX(AM)—Nov 1, 1963: 1290 khz; 10 kw-U, DA-2. Stereo. 1445 Pembina Hwy. (R3T 5C2). (204) 477-5120. FAX: (204) 453-0815. Licensee: CHUM Ltd. (group owner; acq 7-74). Rep: Major Market, Chum Group Regional. Format: Adult contemp. ■ Brian Stone, gen mgr; Rick Liewicki, gen sls mgr; Howard Kroeger, progmg mgr.

CHIQ-FM—Co-owned with CIFX(AM). Nov 1, 1963: 94.3 mhz; 100 kw. Ant 450 ft. Stereo. Prog sep from AM. Format: Contemp hit.

CITI-FM—Listing follows CKY(AM).

CJKR-FM—Listing follows CJOB(AM).

CJOB(AM)—1946: 680 khz; 50 kw-U, DA-N. 930 Portage Ave. (R3G 0P8). (204) 786-2471. FAX: (204) 783-4512. Licensee: CJOB/CKIS-FM. Net: Newsradio. Rep: Canadian Broadcast Sales. ■ Ralph Warrington, gen mgr; Garth Buchko, gen sls mgr; Ted Farr, progmg dir.

CJKR-FM—Co-owned with CJOB(AM). March 1948: 97.5 mhz; 310 kw. Ant 228 ft. Stereo. Format: Adult contemp. ■ Carter Brown, progmg dir.

CKJS(AM)—Mar 25, 1975: 810 khz; 10 kw-U, DA-1. 520 Corydon Ave. (R3L 0P1). (204) 477-1221. FAX: (204) 453-8244. Licensee: CKJS Limited. Net: BN. Rep: Target. Format: Ethnic. Spec prog: Ger 15 hrs, It 8 hrs, Pol 7 hrs, Sp one hr, Por 8 hrs, Gr one hr, Filipino 15 hrs wkly. ■ Tony Carta, gen mgr & progmg dir; Rick Mueller, gen sls mgr.

CKLU-FM—Listing follows CKRC(AM).

CKRC(AM)—1928: 630 khz; 10 kw-U, DA-2. Stereo. Box 9700, 1700-155 Carlton St. (R3C 3H8). (204) 942-2231. FAX: (204) 943-7687. Licensee: Western World Communications Corp. Group owner: Forvest Broadcasting Corp. Net: BN. Format: Country. ■ Bill Gorrie, gen mgr; Bryan Zilkey, gen sls mgr; Doug Anderson, progmg dir; Greg Mack, mus dir; Daryl Braun, news dir.

CKLU-FM—Co-owned with CKRC(AM). Feb 14, 1980: 103.1 mhz; 100 kw. Stereo. Prog sep from AM. Format: Adult contemp. ■ John Norris, progmg dir; Sandra Dee, mus dir.

CKY(AM)—1949: 580 khz; 50 kw-U, DA-2. Stereo. Polo Park (R3G 0L7). (204) 788-3400. FAX: (204) 788-3401. Licensee: Rogers Broadcasting Ltd. (acq 8-20-92). Rep: Canadian Broadcast Sales. Format: Oldies. News progmg 4 hrs wkly. Target aud: 25-54. ■ Anthony Viner, CEO; Sandy Sanderson, execvp; Donald E. Kay, vp, gen mgr & stn mgr; Ron Kizney, progmg dir; Rob Farina, progmg dir & mus dir; Courtney Jaymes, pub affrs dir; George Buzunis, engrg dir & chief engr.

CITI-FM—Co-owned with CKY(AM). 1962: 92.1 mhz; 360 kw. Ant 700 ft. (CP: 210 kw). Stereo. Prog sep from AM. Format: Oldies, rock. ■ Ford Gardner, progmg dir; Gord Fry, mus dir.

New Brunswick

Bathurst

CKBC(AM)—Apr 18, 1955: 1360 khz; 10 kw-U, DA-N. Hrs opn: 24. Box 1360 (E2A 4J1). (506) 547-1360. FAX: (506) 547-1367. Licensee: Radio Atlantic (CKBC) Ltd. Rep: Canadian Broadcast Sales. Format: Adult contemp, country. News staff 2; news progmg 12 hrs wkly. Target aud: 25-49. Spec prog: French 7 hrs wkly. ■ John Eddy, CEO & pres; Jim Duncan, vp, gen mgr, opns mgr & gen sls mgr; Mike Skerry, prom mgr; Al Hebert, progmg dir; Mike Dennis, mus dir; Ray Burke, news dir; Paul Cormier, pub affrs dir; Kevin Chamberlain, chief engr. ■ Rates: C$35; 28; 28; 19.60.

CKLE-FM—Mar 29, 1990: 92.9 mhz; 100 kw. Stereo. Hrs opn: 24. 195 Main St., Bathurst (E28 3S1). (506) 546-4600. Licensee: Radio De LaBaie Ltee. Format: Light rock. Spec prog: Jazz 2 hrs wkly. ■ Armand Roussy, gen mgr & progmg dir; Edmonde Gonthier, adv dir; Rejean Hebert, mus dir.

Campbellton

CKNB(AM)—1939: 950 khz; 10 kw-D, 1 kw-N, DA-2. Hrs opn: 24. Box 340, 100 Water St. (E3N 3G7). (506) 753-4415. FAX: (506) 789-9505. Licensee: Maritime Broadcasting System Ltd. Format: Adult contemp, country. News staff 2; news progmg 10 hrs wkly. Target aud: General. Spec prog: Fr 18 hrs wkly. ■ Meru Russell, pres; Jim MacMullin, vp, gen mgr & gen sls mgr; John Kennedy, progmg dir; Vic Negus, news dir; Brian Hooper, chief engr. ■ Rates: C$30; 30; 30; 30.

Caraquet

CJVA(AM)—Sept 15, 1977: 810 khz; 10 kw-U, DA-2. Hrs opn: 18. Box 70, 93 Blvd. St. Pierre Est. (E0B 1K0). (506) 727-4426. Licensee: Radio Acadie Ltee. Net: BN, Sun. Rep: All-Canada. Format: Div, adult contemp, MOR. Target aud: 25 plus. Spec prog: C&W 15 hrs wkly. ■ Rufino Landry, pres; Armand Roussy, gen mgr, gen sls mgr, progmg dir & mus dir; Ghislaine Foulem, news dir; Rene Lanteigne, chief engr. ■ Rates: $34; 31; 31; 19.

Edmundston

CFAI-FM—Jan 15, 1991: 101.1 mhz; 1 kw. Stereo. Hrs opn: 24. Box 2348, Grand Falls (E0J 1M0). (506) 735-5536. FAX: (506) 739-8509. Licensee: La Cooperative des Montagnes Ltee. Rep: Target. Format: Top 40, soft rock. News progmg 6 hrs wkly. Target aud: 12-34. ■ Roland Lavoie, gen mgr; Jean Paul D'Astous, gen sls mgr. ■ Rates: C$20.50; 16.50; 16.50; 12.50.

CJEM(AM)—Dec 4, 1944: 570 khz; 5 kw-D, 1 kw-N, DA-2. TL: N47 21 47 W68 17 21. Box 188, 174 Church St. (E3V 3K8). (506) 735-3351. FAX: (506) 739-5803. Licensee: Edmundston Radio Ltd. Net: NTR, BN. Rep: Canadian Broadcast Sales. Format: Adult contemp. ■ Jean Marc Michaud, pres; Claude Boucher, gen mgr, gen sls mgr & progmg dir; Jean Guy Bernier, mus dir; Donald D'Amour, news dir; Murillo Soucy, chief engr.

Fredericton

*CBZ(AM)—Mar 4, 1964: 970 khz; 10 kw-U, DA-1. Box 2200, 1160 Regent St. (E3B 5G4). (506) 451-4000. FAX: (506) 451-4003. TELEX: 014-46175. Licensee: Canadian Broadcasting Corp. Net: CBC Mono. Format: Div. ■ Mike Daigneault, gen mgr.

*CBZ-FM—January 1978: 101.5 mhz; 100 kw. Stereo. Net: CBC Stereo.

CFNB(AM)—Jan 12, 1923: 550 khz; 50 kw-U, DA-2. Box 217, 125 Hanwell Rd. (E3B 4Z4). (506) 459-5555. FAX: (506) 458-1229. Licensee: Radio Atlantic (CFNB) Ltd. (acq 5-3-93). Net: BN. Rep: All-Canada. Format: Classic hits. News staff 4; news progmg 8 hrs wkly. Target aud: 25-54. ■ John Eddy, CEO, pres, vp & stn mgr; Dan Cormier, sls dir, mktg dir & adv dir; Mike Allard, progmg dir; Cheryl Appleby, mus dir; Roger Snowden, news dir; Gary Stone, chief engr. ■ Rates: C$40; 35; 35; 28.

CHSR-FM—Jan 24, 1961: 97.9 mhz; 50 w. Ant 189 ft. Stereo. Hrs opn: 7 AM-3 AM. Box 4400, Student Union Bldg., Univ. of New Brunswick (E3B 5A3). (506) 453-4985. FAX: (506) 453-4958. Licensee: CHSR Broadcasting Inc. Format: Alternative rock. News progmg 6 hrs wkly. Target aud: General. Spec prog: Black 3 hrs, Fr 2 hrs, ethnic 5 hrs, American Indian one hr, class 6 hrs, jazz 6 hrs, Chinese 3 hrs wkly. ■ Jeff Whipple, stn mgr, opns mgr & gen sls mgr; Shantell Powell, adv dir; Tristis Bhaird, progmg dir; Debbie Ervine, news dir; Miranda Cameron, pub affrs dir; Doug Beairsto, engrg dir. ■ Rates: C$12; 10; 12; 10.

CIHI(AM)—Aug 19, 1977: 1260 khz; 10 kw-U, DA-N. 206 Rookwood Ave. (E3B 2M2). (506) 451-9111. FAX: (506) 453-9024. Licensee: Radio One Ltd. Net: BN. Rep: Major Mkt. Format: Adult contemp, oldies, top-40. Spec prog: Fr one hr wkly. ■ Robert Coy, gen mgr; Pat Brennan, gen sls mgr.

CKHJ-FM—Co-owned with CIHI(AM). July 15, 1983: 105.3 mhz; 45 kw. Ant 800 ft. Stereo. Format: Adult contemp, C&W.

Fredericton-St. John

CBZF-FM—Sept 4, 1975: 102.3 mhz; 100 kw. Ant 1,219 ft. Rebroadcasts CBAF-FM Moncton. Box 950, Moncton (E1C 8N8). (506) 853-6666. FAX: (506) 853-6739. Licensee: Canadian Broadcasting Corp. ■ Cheryl Stairs, gen mgr.

Grand Falls

CKMV(AM)—1944: 1490 khz; 1 kw-U, DA-1. C.P. 188, 174 Church St., Edmundston (E3V 3K8). (506) 735-3351. FAX: (506) 739-5803. Licensee: Edmundston Radio Ltd. Rep: Canadian Broadcast Sales. Format: Adult contemp. Target aud: General. ■ Jean Marc Michaud, pres; Claude Boucher, gen mgr & gen sls mgr; Murillo Soucy, chief engr.

Moncton

CBA(AM)—1939: 1070 khz; 50 kw-U. Box 950, 250 Archibald St. (E1C 8N8). (506) 853-6666. FAX: (506) 853-6886. Licensee: CBC. Net: CBC. Format: Div. ■ Cheryl Stairs, gen mgr.

CBA-FM—March 1982: 95.5 mhz; 100 kw. ■ Cheryl Stairs, gen mgr.

CBAF-FM—1982: 88.5 mhz; 95 kw. Box 950, 250 Archibald (E1C 8N8). (506) 853-6666. Licensee: Radio Canada. Net: CBC. Format: Variety, news/talk. ■ Gerard Veilleax, chmn; Claude Bourque, gen mgr; Jacques Robichaud, opns mgr; Robert Nadeau, mktg mgr; Laetitia Cyr, progmg dir; Brigitte Lavoie, mus dir; Donald Langis, news dir; Michael Leblanc, engrg mgr.

CBAL-FM—1983: 98.3 mhz. Stereo. Box 950, 250 Archibald (E1C 8N8). (506) 853-6666. FAX: (506) 853-6661. Licensee: Societe Radio Canada. Net: CBC French. Format: Var. ■ Claude Bourque, gen mgr.

CFQM-FM—Listing follows CKCW(AM).

CJMO-FM—June 19, 1987: 103.1 mhz; 46.8 kw. Stereo. Hrs opn: 24. 27 Arsenault Ct. (E1E 4J8). (506) 858-5525. FAX: (506) 858-5539. Licensee: Atlantic Stereo Ltd. Net: BN. Rep: All-Canada. Format: Classic rock. News staff 4; news progmg 5 hrs wkly. Target aud: 18-44. Spec prog: Jazz 2 hrs wkly. ■ James MacLeod, pres; David Murray, CFO; Pat Donelan, gen mgr; David Ostler, gen sls mgr; Pat D. Onelan, mktg mgr; Dawn Steeves, prom dir; Eric Stafford, progmg dir; Murray Brewster, news dir; Michael Leaman, engrg dir.

CKCW(AM)—1934: 1220 khz; 25 kw-D, DA-2. 1000 St. George Blvd. (E1E 2E1). (506) 858-1220. FAX: (506) 858-1209. Licensee: Maritime Broadcasting Ltd. Format: Adult contemp. ■ Sandy Gillis, gen mgr; Don Hayes, gen sls mgr.

CFQM-FM—Co-owned with CKCW(AM). 1976: 103.9 mhz; 25 kw. (506) 858-1039. Format: Contemp country.

CKUM-FM—1982: 105.7 mhz. Centre Etudiant (E1A 3E9). (506) 858-4485. FAX: (506) 858-4524. Licensee: Les Medias Acadiens Universitaires Inc. Format: Div, top-40. ■ Michael Godbout, gen mgr; Gille Savoie, gen sls mgr; Irois Leger, progmg dir.

Newcastle

CFAN(AM)—Apr 4, 1949: 790 khz; 5 kw-D, 1 kw-N, DA-2. Hrs opn: 24. Box 338, 245 Pleasant St. (E1V 3M4). (506) 622-3311. FAX: (506) 622-3315. Licensee: CFAN Broadcasting Co. Ltd. (acq 4-70). Net: BN. Rep: Paul Mulvihill. Format: Adult contemp, MOR. News staff 2; news progmg 8 hrs wkly. Target aud: General. Spec prog: C&W 19 hrs, relg 4 hrs wkly. ■ Ian Byers, gen mgr & vp sls; Margaret Byers, opns mgr.

Sackville

*CHMA-FM—1985: 106.9 mhz. 315 University Centre, Mount Allison University (E0A 3C0). (506) 364-2221. Licensee: Attic Broadcasting Ltd. Format: Div. ■ Randy Cadman, gen mgr; Francis Poirier, mus dir.

Saint John

CBD-FM—April 1981: 91.3 mhz; 100 kw. Box 2358 (E2L 3V6). (506) 632-7744. FAX: (506) 632-7761. Licensee: Canadian Broadcasting Corp. Net: CBC Radio. ■ Susan Lambert, progmg mgr.

CFBC(AM)—Nov 21, 1946: 930 khz; 50 kw-U, DA-2. Stereo. Box 930, 68 Carleton St. (E2L 4E2). (506) 658-2330. FAX: (506) 658-2320. Licensee: Fundy Cable Ltd. Rep: Major Mkt. Format: Top-40, adult contemp. ■ Ken Casey, gen sls mgr; Donnie Robertson, progmg dir; Andy Scott, mus dir; Gary MacDonald, news dir; Gord Miller, chief engr.

CJYC-FM—Co-owned with CFBC(AM). Mar 12, 1965: 98.9 mhz; 50 kw. Ant 350 ft. Stereo. Prog sep from AM. Format: Classic rock. ■ Roxanne Kirkpatrick, progmg dir; Steve Mackin, mus dir.

CHSJ(AM)—Apr 18, 1934: 700 khz; 10 kw-D, 5 kw-N, DA-2. (CP: 25 kw-D, 10 kw-N). Box 2000 (E2L 3T4); 335 Union St. (E2L 1B3). (506) 632-2222. FAX: (506) 632-3485. Licensee: New Brunswick Broadcasting Co. Ltd. (acq 1945). Rep: Mulvihill. Format: C&W. News staff 5. ■ L. M. Nichols, pres; Robert Towner, gen sls mgr; Bob Henry, progmg mgr & mus dir. ■ CHSJ-TV affil.

CIOK-FM—Aug 10, 1987: 100.5 mhz; 100 kw. Ant 1,650 ft. Hrs opn: 24. 400 Main St. (E2K 1J4). (506) 658-5100. FAX: (506) 658-5116. Licensee: CIOK Broadcasting Co. Ltd. Group owner: MacLean Hunter. Net: Newsradio. Rep: Paul Mulvihill. Format: Adult contemp. News staff 4; news progmg 7 hrs wkly Target aud: 25-49; housewives, families, professionals. Spec prog: Real radio 4 hrs wkly. ■ Merv Russell, pres; Art Noiles, vp, gen mgr & stn mgr; Dave Clarkson, gen sls mgr; Joe Mulvihill, natl sls mgr; Brian Bulley, rgnl sls mgr; Mark Lee, prom mgr, progmg dir & mus dir; Troy Swinimer, asst mus dir; Jim Goldrich, news dir & pub affrs dir; Brian Hooper, chief engr. ■ Rates: C$58; 46; 52; 32.

CJYC-FM—Listing follows CFBC(AM).

Sussex

CJCW(AM)—June 1975: 590 khz; 1 kw-D, 250 w-N, DA-2. Box 5900 (E0E 1P0). (506) 432-2529. FAX: (506) 433-4900. Licensee: Maritime Broadcasting System Ltd. Group owner: McLean Hunter. Format: Adult contemp, C&W, oldies. Target aud: General. Spec prog: Relg 4 hrs wkly. ■ Merv Russell, pres; David Boone, gen mgr & gen sls mgr; Perry White, progmg dir; Dan Barton, mus dir; Brian Hooper, vp engrg. ■ Rates: C$22; 22; 22; na.

Woodstock

CJCJ(AM)—July 31, 1959: 920 khz; 10 kw-D, 1 kw-N, DA-2. Hrs opn: 24. Box 920, 131 Queen St. (E0J 2B0). (506) 325-3030. FAX: (506) 325-3031. Licensee: Carleton-Victoria Broadcasting Co. Ltd. Group owner: Radio One Ltd. (acq 9-91). Net: CBC, Sun. Rep: Major Mkt. Format: Adult contemp, C&W. Target aud: 25-54. Spec prog: Farm 2 hrs wkly. ■ Bob Coy, pres; Bev Whiteway, gen sls mgr; Rick McGuire, prom dir & progmg dir; Terry Mann, mus dir; Dave Rogers, news dir; Dick Cleveland, engrg dir. ■ Rates: $31.50; na; 23.50; 18.50.

Newfoundland

Argentia

CFOZ-FM—100.5 mhz; 5 kw. Box 2050, c/o CHOZ-FM, St. John's (A1C 5R6). (709) 726-2922. FAX: (709) 726-3300. Licensee: Newfoundland Broadcasting Co. (group owner). Format: AOR. ■ Brian Vallis, gen mgr.

Baie Verte

CKIM(AM)—1240 khz; 1 kw-D, 500 w-N. Box 620, Grenfell Heights (A2A 2K2). (709) 489-2192. FAX: (709) 489-8626. Licensee: The Colonial Broadcasting System Ltd. Format: C&W. ■ Jim Coady, gen mgr.

Bonavista Bay

CBGY(AM)—750 khz; 10 kw-U, DA-2. Rebroadcasts CBG(AM) Gander. Box 369, c/o Radio Station CBG, Gander (A1V 1W7). (709) 256-4311. FAX: (709) 651-2021. Licensee: CBC. Format: News, current affairs. ■ Dennis Budgell, stn mgr.

CJOZ-FM—92.1 mhz; 50 kw. Box 2050, c/o CHOZ-FM, St. John's (A1C 5R6). (709) 726-2922. FAX: (709) 726-3300. Licensee: Newfoundland Broadcasting Co. (group owner). Format: AOR. ■ Brian Vallis, gen mgr.

Carbonear

CHVO(AM)—Oct 7, 1980: 560 khz; 5 kw-U, DA-1. Hrs opn: 24. One CHVO Dr. (A1y 1A2). (709) 596-7144; (709) 786-8626. FAX: (709) 596-8626. Licensee: VOCM Radio Newfoundland Ltd. Format: Country. Spec prog: Irish/Nfld 6 hrs wkly. ■ J.V. Butler, pres; John Harvey, gen mgr & gen sls mgr; Tom Ormsby, prom mgr, progmg dir & mus dir; Denis Mulloy, news dir; Harold Steele, chief engr.

Churchill Falls

CFLC-FM—1974: 97.9 mhz; 8 w. Ant 50 ft. Rebroadcasts CFLW(AM) Wabush. Box 6000, c/o CFLW(AM), Wabush (AOR 1BO). (709) 634-3111. FAX: (709) 634-4081. Licensee: Humber Valley Broadcasting Co. LTD. Format: Adult contemp. ■ Gary Peckham, stn mgr.

Clarenville

CJKK-FM—1988: 105.3 mhz. Box 2050, c/o CHOZ-FM, St. John's (A1C 5R6). (709) 726-2922. FAX: (709) 726-3300. Licensee: Newfoundland Broadcasting Co. Format: AOR. ■ Brian Vallis, gen mgr.

CKVO(AM)—710 khz; 10 kw-U. Rebroadcasts VOCM(AM) St. John's. Box 8-590, Station A, c/o VOCM(AM), St. John's (A1B 3P5). (709) 466-2710. FAX: (709) 726-8626. Licensee: VOCM Radio NF Limited. Format: Contemp country. ■ John Murphy, gen mgr; Michael Leblanc, progmg dir; Tom Ormsby, mus dir; Jerry Phelan, news dir.

Corner Brook

*CBY(AM)—1943: 990 khz; 10 kw-U, DA-1. Box 610 (A2H 6G1). (709) 634-3141. FAX: (709) 634-8506. Licensee: CBC. Net: CBC Radio. Format: News/talk. News staff 2. Target aud: Mature 30 plus. ■ Walter Sheppard, stn mgr.

CFCB(AM)—Oct 3, 1960: 570 khz; 1 kw-D. Box 570 (A2H 6H5). (709) 634-3111. FAX: (709) 634-4081. Licensee: Humber Valley Broadcasting Co. Ltd. Group owner: Humber Valley Broadcasting Co. Net: Newsradio. Rep: Paul Mulvihill, Canadian Broadcast Sales. Format: Adult contemp. ■ Noel F. Murphy, pres; James O'Rourke, gen mgr; Roger Humber, stn mgr; Larry Bourne, rgnl sls mgr; Bill Bartlet, progmg dir; David Bouzanne, mus dir; Ed Hynes, news dir; Joe Parsons, chief engr.

CKOZ-FM—92.3 mhz; 50 kw. Box 2050, c/o CHOZ-FM, St. John's (A1C 5R6). (709) 726-2922. Licensee: Newfoundland Broadcasting Co. (group owner). Format: AOR. ■ Brian Vallis, gen mgr.

CKXX(AM)—Aug 6, 1984: 1340 khz; 10 kw-U, DA-2. TL: N48 58 41 W57 57 51. Hrs opn: 24. Rebroadcasts CKXX (FM) Deer Lake 100%. Box 1340, Timco Mall, 43 Maple Valley Rd. (A2H 7B2). (709) 634-1340. FAX: (709) 634-6397. Licensee: NewCap Broadcasting Limited. (group owner; acq 8-29-90). Net: SRN. Rep: Canadian Broadcast Sales. Format: Country. News staff one. Format: Adult 25-54. Spec prog: Traditional Newfoundland 6 hrs wkly. ■ Harry Steele, pres; Bob Templeton, exec vp; Don Oakley, gen mgr, stn mgr & gen sls mgr; Ron Combden, opns mgr & chief engr; Debbie Raynard, prom mgr; Walt Wicks, progmg dir; Pat Good, mus dir; Rick Lafitte, news dir.

Deer Lake

CFDL-FM—1974: 97.9 mhz. Rebroadcasts CFCB(AM) Corner Brook. Box 570, c/o CFCB(AM), Corner Brook (A2H 6H5). (709) 634-3111. FAX: (709) 634-4081. Licensee: Humber Valley Broadcasting Co. LTD. Format: Adult contemp. ■ James O'Rourke, gen mgr.

Gander

*CBG(AM)—1949: 1400 khz; 4 kw-U. Box 369, 98 Sullivan Ave. (A1V 1W7). (709) 256-4311. FAX: (709) 651-2021. Licensee: CBC. Format: Informational. ■ Dennis Budgell, gen mgr; Marie Thompson, progmg dir.

CKGA(AM)—1969: 650 khz; 5 kw-U, DA-2. Box 650 (A1V 1X2). (709) 651-3650. FAX: (709) 256-8626. Licensee: VOCM Radio Newfoundland Ltd. Format: Easy lstng, adult contemp. ■ Paul Stride, gen mgr.

CKXD(AM)—1977: 1010 khz; 5 kw-D, DA. 310 Elizabeth (A1V 1J8). (709) 651-2700. FAX: (709) 651-2787. Licensee: NewCap Broadcasting Ltd. (group owner; acq 8-89). Net: SBN. Rep: Major Mkt. Format: C&W. Spec prog: Newfoundland & Irish 12 hrs wkly. ■ Dave Hillier, gen mgr; Richard King, progmg dir.

Goose Bay

CFLN(AM)—Aug 1, 1974: 1230 khz; 1 kw-D, 250 w-N, DA-1. Box 1199, Station A (A0P 1S0). (709) 896-2968. FAX: (709) 896-8708. Licensee: Humber Valley Broadcasting Co. Ltd. Group owner: Humber Valley Broadcasting Co. Format: Adult contemp. ■ James O'Rourke, gen mgr; Paul Saunders, stn mgr & gen sls mgr.

Grand Falls-Windsor

CBT(AM)—July 1949: 540 khz; 10 kw-U. Box 218 (A2A 2J7). (709) 489-2102. FAX: (709) 489-1055. Licensee: CBC. Format: Informational. ■ Dennis Budgell, gen mgr.

CKCM(AM)—620 khz; 10 kw-U, DA-1. Box 620, Grenfell Heights (A2A 2K2). (709) 489-2192. FAX: (709) 489-8626. Licensee: Colonial Broadcasting System Ltd. Format: C&W, contemp. ■ Jim Coady, gen mgr.

CKXG(AM)—Oct 10, 1977: 680 khz; 10 kw-U, DA-2. Hrs opn: 24. Grenfell Heigts Ext. (A2A 2M4). (709) 489-9663. FAX: (709) 489-1081. Licensee: NewCap Broadcasting Ltd. (group owner; acq 8-89). Format: KIX Country. News staff 2; news progmg 5 hrs wkly. Target aud: 25-49. Spec prog: Traditional music 12 hrs wkly. ■ Harold Steele, pres; Jim McLeod, vp; Dave Hillier, gen mgr & news dir; Richard King, progmg dir; Ron Combden, chief engr.

Happy Valley

CFGB-FM—Feb 23, 1959: 89.5 mhz; 1 kw-U. Box 3015, Station B (A0P 1E0). (709) 896-2911. FAX: (709) 896-8900. Licensee: CBC. Net: CBC Radio. Format: Informational. ■ John Fleet, gen mgr.

Labrador City

CJRM-FM—Sept. 23, 1992: 97.3 mhz; 500 w. Ant 1,998 ft. TL: N52 57 01 W66 55 01. Stereo. Hrs opn: 24. CP 253, Hudson Dr. (A2V 2K5); Carol Lake Shopping Centre (A2V 2K4). (709) 944-7600; (709) 944-2973. FAX: (709) 944-5125. Licensee: Radio Communautaire du Labrador Inc. (acq 4-92). Net: NTR. Rep: ARC du Canada. Format: Contemp hit, div, news/talk. News staff one; news progmg 30 hrs wkly. Target aud: General; bilingual French audience in Labrador West. ■ Francois Meehan, pres; Alain Roy, vp & vp prom; Pierre-Robert Godin, gen mgr, stn mgr, vp dev, vp progmg & mus dir; Francois Meehan, Pierre-Robert Godin, vps opns; Norman Gillespie, vp sls, vp mktg, vp adv, news dir & vp engrg.

Marystown

CHCM(AM)—1961: 740 khz; 10 kw-U, DA-N. Box 560 (A0E 2M0). (709) 279-2560. FAX: (709) 279-3538. Licensee: VOCM Radio Newfoundland Ltd. Format: Adult contemp, C&W. ■ Russell Murphy, gen mgr.

CIOZ-FM—96.3 mhz; 25 kw. Box 2050, c/o CHOZ-FM, St. John's (A1C 5R6). (709) 726-2233. FAX: (709) 726-3300. Licensee: Newfoundland Broadcasting Co. (group owner). Format: AOR. ■ Brian Vallis, gen mgr.

Mount Pearl

*VOAR(AM)—1930: 1210 khz; 10 kw, DA-1. TL: N47 32 01 W52 49 01. Hrs opn: 6:55 AM- 11:05 PM. Box 2520, 1041 Topsail Rd. (A1N 4M7). (709) 745-VOAR. FAX: (709) 745-1600. Licensee: Seventh-Day Adventist Church in Newfoundland. Net: ARN. Format: Relg, gospel. News progmg 12 hrs wkly. Target aud: 25-34; individuals interested in family life and traditional values. ■ D. S. Crook, chmn; Cameron L. Beierle, stn mgr, opns mgr, dev mgr, adv mgr & mus dir; Cameron L. Beierle, Sherry Griffin, Colleen Beierle, prom mgrs; Cameron L. Beierle, Sherry Griffin, progmg mgrs; Sherry Griffin, asst mus dir; Sherry Griffin, Cameron L. Beierle, news dirs; Cameron L. Beierle, Sherry Griffin, Colleen Beierle, pub affrs dirs; Brian Matthews, chief engr.

Musgravetown

CKXB(AM)—670 khz; 10 kw-U, DA-2. Rebroadcasts CKXD(AM) Gander. c/o CKXD(AM), 78 Elizabeth Dr., Gander (A1V 1J8). (709) 651-2787. FAX: (709) 651-2780. Format: Country. ■ Kenton Dumphy, gen mgr; Jennifer Evans, news dir.

Stations in Canada

Port au Choix

CFNW(AM)—1960: 790 khz; 1 kw-U, DA-1. Rebroadcasts CFCB(AM) Corner Brook. Box 570, c/o CFCB(AM), Corner Brook (A2H 6E6). (709) 634-3111. FAX: (709) 634-4081. Licensee: Humber Valley Broadcasting Co. Ltd. Format: Adult contemp. ■ James O'Rourke, gen mgr.

Port-aux-Basques

CFGN(AM)—Apr 9, 1973: 1230 khz; 250 w-U. Box 1230 (A0M 1C0). (709) 695-2183. FAX: (709) 695-9614. Licensee: Humber Valley Broadcasting Co. (group owner). Net: BN, Newsradio, CBC AM. Rep: Andy McDermitt Sls. Format: Country, MOR, oldies. ■ George Critchell, gen mgr.

Rattling Brook

CHOS-FM—95.9 mhz; 50 kw. Box 2050, c/o CHOZ-FM, St. John's (A1C 5R6). (709) 726-2922. FAX: (709) 726-3300. Licensee: Newfoundland Broadcasting Co. (group owner). Format: AOR. ■ Brian Vallis, gen mgr.

Red Rocks

CKSS-FM—Not on air, target date September 1994: 96.9 mhz; 2.5 kw. Box 2050, c/o CHOZ-FM, St. John's (A1C 5R6). (709) 726-2922. Licensee: Newfoundland Broadcasting Co. (group owner). ■ Brian Vallis, gen mgr; Keith Soper, stn mgr; Charlie Peddle, gen sls mgr; Doug Neal, chief engr.

St. Andrews

CFCV-FM—1974: 97.7 mhz. Rebroadcasts CFGN(AM) Port-aux-Basques. Box 1230, c/o CFGN(AM), Port-aux-Basques (A0M 1C0). (709) 695-2183. FAX: (709) 695-9614. Licensee: Humber Valley Broadcasting Co. (group owner). ■ George Crichill, gen mgr.

St. Anthony

CFNN-FM—1974: 97.9 mhz; 126 w. Rebroadcasts CFCB(AM) Corner Brook. Box 570, c/o CFCB(AM), Conerbrook (A2H 6H5). (709) 634-3111. FAX: (709) 634-4081. Licensee: Humber Valley Broadcasting Co. (group owner). Format: Adult Contemp.

St. John's

*****CBN(AM)**—Apr 1, 1949: 640 khz; 10 kw-U. Hrs opn: 19. Box 12010, Station A, 342-44 Duckworth St. (A1B 3T8). (709) 576-5000. FAX: (709) 576-5205. Licensee: CBC. Net: CBC Radio. Format: Div. News staff 6; news progmg 10 hrs wkly. Target aud: General. Spec prog: Fisheries 3 hrs wkly. ■ K. Diane Humber, gen mgr, stn mgr & progmg dir; Don Reynolds, opns dir; John O'Mara, prom mgr; Art Rockwood, mus dir; Philip Daniel, news dir; Diane Humber, pub affrs dir; Addison Kelland, engrg mgr.

*****CBN-FM**—July 1, 1975: 106.9 mhz; 100 kw. Ant 300 ft. Stereo. Net: CBC Stereo. Format: Class, news/talk. News progmg 5 hrs wkly. ■ CBNT-TV affil.

CHMR-FM—January 1986: 93.5 mhz; 50 w. Ant -10 ft. Stereo. Hrs opn: 24. Box A-119, Thompson Student Centre, Memorial University, (A1C 5S7). (709) 737-4777; (709) 737-4778. FAX: (709) 737-4743. Licensee: Memorial Univ. of Newfoundland Radio Society Inc. Format: Div, alternative. News progmg 7 hrs wkly. Target aud: General. Spec prog: Class 10 hrs, folk 6 hrs, French 2 hrs, jazz 6 hrs, relg 4 hrs, blues 6 hrs, rap 2 hrs, reggae 2 hrs, Indian one hr wkly. ■ Paula Grimes, pres; Kathy Rowe-Earle, gen mgr, opns mgr & adv dir; Jim Murphy, Kathy Rowe-Earle, gen sls mgrs; Bob Earle, mktg dir & progmg dir; Scott Kelly, prom dir; Todd Pardy, prom dir; Bill Gregory, Jim Murphy, adv mgrs; Kent Burt, mus dir; Darryl Vardy, asst mus dir; CeAnne Walsh, news dir; CeAnne Walsh, pub affrs dir; Craig Petterman, chief engr.

CHOZ-FM—June 15, 1977: 94.7 mhz; 100 kw. Ant 821 ft. Stereo. Hrs opn: 24. Box 2050, 446 Logy Bay Rd. (A1C 5R6). (709) 726-2922. FAX: (709) 726-3300. Licensee: Newfoundland Broadcasting Co. Ltd. (group owner). Rep: All-Canada. Format: Rock. News progmg 4 hrs wkly. Target aud: 18-44. ■ G.W. Stirling, CEO & chmn; Scott Stirling, pres; Brian Vallis, gen mgr; Keith Soper, stn mgr & progmg mgr; Charlie Peddle, natl sls mgr; Dave Stamp, rgnl sls mgr; Deborah Birmingham, mus dir; Sam Whiffen, asst mus dir; Larry Jay, news dir; Doug Neal, engrg dir. ■ CJON-TV affil.

CJYQ(AM)—1951: 930 khz; 50 kw-N. Hrs opn: 24. Box 8010, Stn. A, 208 Kenmount Rd. (A1B 3M7). (709) 753-4040. FAX: (709) 753-6984; TWX: 016 3347. Licensee:

Newcap Broadcasting. (group owner; acq 1-17-83). Rep: Canadian Broadcast Sales. Format: Oldies. News staff 5. Target aud: 25-54. ■ Harry Steele, CEO; Bob Templeton, pres; Hilary Montbourquette, stn mgr; Sean Russell, gen sls mgr & adv mgr; Lisa MacGlaggan, rgnl sls mgr; Ken Ash, prom dir; Andy Newman, progmg dir & mus dir; Kathie Hicks, news dir; Randy Strilec, chief engr.

CKIX-FM—Co-owned with CJYQ(AM). Oct 15, 1983: 99.1 mhz; 100 kw. Ant 930 ft. Stereo. Prog sep from AM. Format: Today's country. Target aud: 18-49; adults. ■ Hilary Montbourquette, gen mgr; Ken Ash, mktg dir, prom mgr, progmg dir & mus dir.

VOCM(AM)—Oct 19, 1936: 590 khz; 20 kw-U, DA-2. Stereo. Hrs opn: 24. Box 8590, Station A, 391 Kenmount Rd. (A1B 3P5). (709) 726-5590. FAX: (709) 726-4633. TELEX: 016-4944. Licensee: VOCM Radio Newfoundland Ltd. Net: BN. Rep: Paul Mulvihill. Format: Adult contemp, talk. News staff 16. Target aud: 25 plus. ■ Joseph V. Butler, pres; Elmer Harris, exec vp; John Murphy, gen mgr; Gary J. Butler, vp opns; Joseph L. Butler, vp sls; Tom Ormsby, progmg dir; Paul Raynes, mus dir; Gerry Phalen, news dir; Reg McCausland, engrg dir; Brian Mathews, chief engr.

VOCM-FM—September 1982: 97.5 mhz; 100 kw. Stereo. Prog sep from AM. Format: AOR. ■ Dave Newberry, rgnl sls mgr; Chris Steeves, progmg dir; Mike Campbell, mus dir.

*****VOWR(AM)**—June 20, 1924: 800 khz; 10 kw-D, 2.5 kw-N, DA-1. Box 7430 (A1E 3Y5). (709) 579-9233. Licensee: Wesley United Church Radio Board. Format: Div. Target aud: 40 plus. Spec prog: Relg 10 hrs wkly. ■ Gordon Cousens, chmn; John Tessier, gen mgr, opns mgr, prom mgr & progmg mgr; Reg McCausland, chief engr.

Stephenville

CFSX(AM)—Nov 14, 1964: 870 khz; 500 w-U. Hrs opn: 24. 30 Oregon Dr. (A2N 2X9). (709) 643-2191. FAX: (709) 643-5025. Licensee: Humber Valley Broadcasting Co. Ltd. Group owner: Humber Valley Broadcasting Co. (acq 1957). Format: MOR, country. News staff 2. Target aud: General. Spec prog: Relg one hr wkly. ■ Gerry Murphy, stn mgr & prom mgr; Don Gibbon, rgnl sls mgr & adv mgr; Larry Bennett, mus dir; Jim Goosmey, engrg mgr.

CIOS-FM—98.5 mhz; 10 kw. Box 2050, c/o CHOZ-FM, St. John's (A1C 5R6). (709) 726-2922. FAX: (709) 726-3300. Licensee: Newfoundland Broadcasting Co. (group owner). Format: AOR. ■ Brian Vallis, gen mgr.

Wabush

CBDQ(AM)—Apr 2, 1985: 1490 khz; 1 kw-D, 250 w-N. Rebroadcasts CFGB-FM Happy Valley. Box 3015, Station B, c/o CFGB-FM, Happy Valley (A0P 1E0). Format: Radio/ info news. ■ John Fleet, gen mgr.

CFLW(AM)—1971: 1340 khz; 250 w-U, DA-1. Box 6000, 4 Grenfell Dr. (A0R 1B0). (709) 282-3602. FAX: (709) 282-5543. Licensee: Humber Valley Broadcasting Co. (group owner). Format: Classic rock, CHR, country. ■ June Hoskins, gen sls mgr; Gary Peckham, news dir.

Northwest Territories

Alert

CHAR-FM—1975: 105.9 mhz; 76 w. Rebroadcasts CHFI-FM Toronto (part-time). MPO 310, CFS Alert, Belleville, ON (K0K 3S0). Licensee: Major E.A.C. McLean, Commanding Officer. Format: Div. Target aud: General. ■ E.A.C. McLean, gen mgr.

Baker Lake

CKQN-FM—1973: 99.3 mhz; 60 w. Ant -50 ft. Baker Lake (X0C 0A0). (819) 793-2962. Licensee: Qamani'tuap Naalautaa Society. Net: CBC FM. Format: Eskimo, Inuit. ■ Simon Toukome, gen mgr.

Hay River

CJCD-FM-1—Sept 15, 1986: 100.1 mhz; 300 w. Ant 175 ft. Stereo. Rebroadcasts CJCD(AM) Yellowknife. Box 218, Yellowknife (X1A 2N2). (403) 920-4636. FAX: (403) 920-4033. Licensee: CJCD Radio Ltd. Net: BN. Rep: All-Canada. Format: Hot adult contemp. News staff 5; news prgmg 12 hrs wkly. Target aud: 25-49. ■ Charles Dent, pres; Bryan Edwards, exec vp; Dick Peplow, stn mgr; Rod Matthews, mus dir; Drew Wilson, news dir. ■ Rates: $25; 20.50; 20.50; 16.

CKHR-FM—January 1979: 107.3 mhz; 32 w. Ant 185 ft. Box 949 (X0E 0R0). (403) 874-2547. Licensee: Hay River Broadcasting Society. Format: MOR, variety. ■ Al Erickson, pres; Ray Lawson, stn mgr.

Inuvik

CHAK(AM)—Nov 26, 1960: 860 khz; 1 kw-D, DA-1. Bag 8 (X0E 0T0). (403) 979-4411. FAX: (403) 979-2411. Licensee: CBC. Net: CBC AM. Format: Div. Spec prog: Inuvialukton 9 hrs, Loucheux 9 hrs wkly. ■ Ann Crossman, gen mgr.

Iqaluit

CFFB(AM)—Feb 6, 1961: 1230 khz; 1 kw-D, DA-1. Box 490 (X0A 0H0). (819) 979-6100. FAX: (819) 976-6147. Licensee: CBC. Net: CBC AM. Format: Div. ■ Pat Nagle, gen mgr.

Rankin Inlet

CBQR-FM—1988: 105.1 mhz; 87 w-D. Box 130 (X0C 0G0). (819) 645-2885. FAX: (819) 645-2632. Licensee: CBC. Net: CBC Radio. Format: Adult contemp, talk, div. Spec prog: Inuktitut 10 hrs wkly. ■ Elizabeth Kusugak, gen mgr.

Tuktoyaktuk

CFCT(AM)—1971: 600 khz; 1 kw-U. c/o Radio Station CHAK, Bag 8 (INU VIK). (403) 979-4411. Licensee: Tuktoyaktuk Broadcasting Society. Net: SBN, CBC. Format: Div. Spec prog: Eskimo 5 hrs wkly. ■ Ann Crossman, gen mgr.

Yellowknife

*****CFYK(AM)**—Dec 13, 1958: 1340 khz; 2.5 kw-U. Box 160 (X1A 2N2). (403) 920-5400. FAX: (403) 920-5415 ADMIN; (403) 873-2213 PROG. Licensee: CBC. Net: CBC Radio. Format: Div, news/talk. News staff 4; news progmg 3 hrs wkly. Target aud: General. Spec prog: Slavey 8 hrs, Dogrib 4 hrs, Chipewayan 4 hrs wkly. ■ Craig Mackie, gen mgr; Jim MacVicar, opns mgr; Joan Merrill, progmg mgr; Joclyn Cozac, news dir; Bob Carr, chief engr.

CJCD(AM)—Nov 13, 1979: 1240 khz; 1 kw-D, DA-1. TL: N62 27 00 W114 19 00. Box 218, (X1A 2N2). (403) 920-4636. FAX: (403) 920-4033. Licensee: CJCD Radio Ltd. Rep: All-Canada. Format: Adult contemp. News staff 5; news progmg 12 hrs wkly. Target aud: 25-54. ■ Charles Dent, CEO & pres; Bryan Edwards, vp; Dick Peplow, stn mgr; Rod Matthews, mus dir; Drew Wilson, news dir; Ken Pook, chief engr. ■ Rates: C$25; 20.20; 20.50; 16.

CKNM-FM—Dec 11, 1985: 101.9 mhz; 130 w. Ant 162 ft. Stereo. Hrs opn: 6 AM-9 PM M-F, 8 AM-6 PM Sat. rebroadcasts CFWE news. Box 1919, Communications Centre, 5120-49th St. (X1A 1P8). (403) 920-2277. FAX: (403) 920-4205. Licensee: Native Communications Society of the Western N.W.T. Net: Newsradio. Format: C&W. News staff 3. Spec prog: Black one hr wkly. ■ Pat Burke, chmn; Teresa Drew, gen mgr; Drew Williams, gen sls mgr, mktg mgr & prom dir; Peter Hope, progmg dir; Norbert Poitras, mus dir. ■ NCS-TV affil.

Nova Scotia

Amherst

CKDH(AM)—Oct 25, 1957: 900 khz; 1 kw-U, DA-N. 32 Church St. (B4H 3A8). (902) 667-3875. FAX: (902) 667-4490. Licensee: Maritime Broadcasting System Ltd., Maclean Hunter Broadcast Division (acq 1989). Net: BN. Rep: All-Canada. Format: Adult contemp during the day, oldies at night. Target aud: 25-49 day, 18-34 night. Spec prog: C&W 11 hrs, farm 2 hrs wkly. ■ Gary Crowell, gen mgr; David March, progmg mgr.

Antigonish

CJFX(AM)—Mar 25, 1943: 580 khz; 25 kw-U, DA-1. TL: N45 43 06 W62 03 31. Stereo. Hrs opn: 24. Box 5800, Kirk St. (B2G 2R9). (902) 863-4580. FAX: (902) 863-6300. Licensee: Atlantic Broadcasters Ltd. Net: BN. Rep: Canadian Broadcast Sales. Format: MOR, C&W. News staff 3; news progmg 18 hrs wkly. Target aud: General. Spec prog: Farm one hr wkly. ■ Gerald Gillis, pres; David MacLean, gen mgr; Bill Graham, gen sls mgr; Peter McCully, progmg dir & mus dir; John Hello, news dir; Scott MacLeod, chief engr.

Ontario | Directory of Radio

Bridgewater

CKBW(AM)—Dec 24, 1947: 1000 khz; 10 kw-U, DA-N. TL: N44 22 01 W64 32 01. Hrs opn: 24. Rebroadcasts CKBW-FM-1 Liverpool & CKBW-FM-2 Shelburne, 100%. 215 Dominion St. (B4V 2G8). (902) 543-2401. FAX: (902) 543-1208. Licensee: Acadia Broadcasting Ltd. (acq 8-31-89). Net: BN. Rep: Canadian Broadcast Sales, Katz. Format: MOR, C&W, adult contemp. News staff 5; news progmg 11 hrs wkly. Target aud: General; rural and small town urban. Spec prog: Bluegrass, religious, Newfoundland. ■ Larry Nichols, pres; Bob MacLaren, vp, gen mgr & natl sls mgr; Barry Smith, gen sls mgr; Gary Richards, progmg mgr; G. Lowe, mus dir; R. Weir, asst mus dir; Ed Boylan, news dir & pub affrs dir; Frank Grayney, chief engr. ■ Rates: $40; 38; 36; 36.

Dartmouth

CFDR(AM)—Dec 5, 1962: 780 khz; 50 kw-D, 15 kw-N. Box 1007, 45 Alderney Dr. (B2Y 3Z7). (902) 469-9231. FAX: (902) 464-9263. Licensee: New Cap Broadcasting Ltd. (group owner). Net: BN. Rep: All Canada. Format: Contemp hit. ■ Bruce Tinkham, gen mgr; Eldon Mac Keigan, gen sls mgr; Gary Evong, progmg dir.

CFRQ-FM—Co-owned with CFDR(AM). Nov 28, 1983: 104.3 mhz; 100 kw. Ant 400 ft. Stereo. Format: AOR. Spec prog: Jazz 3 hrs wkly. ■ Barry Horne, progmg dir.

Digby

CJLS-FM-2—93.5 mhz; 3 kw. Rebroadcasts CJLS(AM) Yarmouth. c/o Radio Station CJLS(AM), Suite 201, 328 Main St., Yarmouth (B5A 1E4). (902) 742-7175. FAX: (902) 742-3143. Licensee: L.G. Trask. Format: Adult contemp. ■ G. P. Wyman, gen mgr.

CKDY(AM)—Feb 2, 1970: 1420 khz; 1 kw-U, DA-1. Box 1420, 53 Sydney St. (B0V 1A0). (902) 245-2111. FAX: (902) 678-9720 Licensee: Annapolis Valley Radio Ltd. (group owner; acq 8-79). Format: Contemp country. Spec prog: Farm 7 hrs wkly. ■ Gwen Atkinson, gen mgr.

Halifax

CBH-FM—June 1, 1976: 102.7 mhz; 100 kw. Ant 711 ft. Stereo. Box 3000 (B3J 3E9). (902) 420-8311. FAX: (902) 420-4429. Licensee: CBC. Net: CBC Stereo. Format: Div. ■ Susan Milton, gen mgr; Bill Donavan, rgnl sls mgr.

CBHA-FM—1989: 90.5 mhz; 100 kw. Ant 711 ft. Net: CBC Mono. ■ Susan Milton, gen mgr.

CHFX-FM—Listing follows CHNS(AM).

CHNS(AM)—May 12, 1926: 960 khz; 10 kw-U, DA-2. Box 400, 1313 Barrington St. (B3J2R2). (902) 422-1651. FAX: (902) 422-5330. Licensee: Maritime Broadcasting Co. Ltd. (acq 9-79). Rep: Paul Mulvihill. Format: Oldies. News staff 5; news progmg 7 hrs wkly. Target aud: 25-54. ■ Garry Barker, vp & gen mgr; Don Grose, gen sls mgr; Nancy Hilchie, prom dir; Morrissey Dunn, progmg dir.

CHFX-FM—Co-owned with CHNS(AM). Feb 9, 1970: 101.9 mhz; 100 kw. Ant 546 ft. Stereo. Prog sep from AM. (902) 425-5210. Net: Newsradio. Format: C&W. ■ Kelley Ryder, prom dir; John Gold, progmg dir; Paul Kennedy, mus dir.

CIEZ-FM—August 1990: 96.5 mhz; 100 kw. Hrs opn: 24. Sun Tower, 1550 Bedford Hwy., Suite 220, Bedford (B4A 1E6). (902) 835-6100. FAX: (902) 835-1511. Licensee: Sun Radio Ltd. Rep: Canadian Broadcast Sales. Format: Soft adult contemp. News staff 3; news progmg 3 hrs wkly. Target aud: 35-54. ■ A. J. Hustins Jr., pres & gen mgr; George McLean, gen sls mgr; Kim George, mktg mgr; Jane Hustins, progmg mgr; Bruce Morel, mus dir; Joanne Dawson, news dir; Barb Anderson, pub affrs dir; Derrick Forgeron, chief engr.

CIOO-FM—Listing follows CJCH(AM).

CJCH(AM)—Nov 4, 1944: 920 khz; 25 kw-U, DA-D. TL: N44 38 10 W63 40 22. Stereo. Hrs opn: 24. Box 1653, 2900 Agricola St. (B3J 2Z4). (902) 453-2524. FAX: (902) 453-3120; (902) 453-3132. Licensee: CJCH 920/C100 FM Division of CHUM Ltd. Group owner: CHUM Ltd. Format: Oldies, classic rock. News staff 4. ■ Bill Bodnarchuk, gen mgr & gen sls mgr; Murray Brookshaw, progmg mgr & mus dir; Rick Howe, news dir & pub affrs dir; Walter Labrucci, engrg dir.

CIOO-FM—Co-owned with CJCH(AM). Nov 1977: 100.1 mhz; 100 kw. Ant 770 ft. TL: N44 39 05 W63 39 51. Stereo. Hrs opn: 24. Prog sep from AM. Format: Light rock. ■ Trent McGrath, prom dir; Earle Mader, mus dir.

CKDU-FM—February 1985: 97.5 mhz; 50 kw. Ant 300 ft. Stereo. Dalhousie SUB, 6136 University Ave. (B3H 4J2). (902) 494-6479. FAX: (902) 494-5185. Licensee: CKDU-FM Society Ltd. Format: Div. News staff one; news progmg 4 hrs wkly. Target aud: General. Spec prog: Indian, Chinese, comedy, drama, hardcore, blues, metal, world beat, Black 6 hrs, folk 3 hrs, gospel one hr, class 6 hrs, C&W 2 hrs, Fr one hrs, Gr 2 hrs, jazz 9 hrs wkly. ■ Alison Outbit, CFO; Jo-Ann Citrigno, stn mgr; Greg Ash, gen sls mgr; Chris Trowbridge, progmg mgr; Colin McKenzie, mus dir; Brenda Barnes, pub affrs dir; John Matthews, chief engr. ■ Rates: C$36; 36; 36; 36.

Kentville

CKEN(AM)—1948: 1490 khz; 1 kw-U, DA-1. Box 310, 29 Oakdene Ave. (B4N 1H5). (902) 678-2111. FAX: (902) 678-9894. Licensee: Annapolis Valley Radio Ltd. (acq 6-26-79). Rep: Major Mkt. Format: Gold and country. News staff 5. Target aud: 18-49. Spec prog: Farm 5 hrs wkly. ■ Dianne Best-Redden, gen mgr; Terry Webb, gen sls mgr.

CKWM-FM—Co-owned with CKEN(AM). Mar 14, 1965: 97.7 mhz; 18 kw. Ant 680 ft. Stereo. Net: BN. Format: AOR. ■ Dave Bannerman, prom mgr & progmg mgr; Mike Mitchell, mus dir.

Liverpool

CKBW-FM-1—Sept 15, 1980: 94.5 mhz; 8.7 kw. Ant 250 ft. Stereo. Rebroadcasts CKBW(AM) Bridgewater. c/o CKBW(AM), 215 Dominion St., Bridgewater (B4V 2G8). (902) 543-2401. FAX: (902) 543-1208. Licensee: New Brunswick Broadcasting. Rep: Air-Canada, Katz. Format: MOR, country, CHR. Spec prog: Bluegrass, relg. ■ R. A. MacLaren, vp & gen mgr; Gary Richards, mus dir.

Middleton

CKAD(AM)—1962: 1350 khz; 1 kw-U, DA-1. 29 Oakdene Ave., Kentville (B4N 1H5). (902) 678-2111. FAX: (902) 678-9894. Licensee: Annapolis Valley Radio Ltd. (group owner; acq 6-26-79). Net: BN. Format: Country. Spec prog: Farm 3 hrs wkly. ■ Diane Best-Redden, gen mgr; Terry Webb, gen sls mgr.

New Glasgow

CKEC(AM)—Dec 23, 1953: 1320 khz; 25 kw-U, DA-N. Hrs opn: 24. Box 519 (B2H 5E7). (902) 752-4200. FAX: (902) 755-2468. Licensee: D. Freeman (acq 1964). Net: BN. Rep: All-Canada. Format: Adult contemp, country. News staff 3; news progmg 15 hrs wkly. Target aud: General. ■ D.B. Freeman, CEO; Bill Ormond, gen sls mgr; Rod Mackey, progmg dir; Robert Spanik, news dir; Peter Lann, chief engr.

Port Hawkesbury

CIGO(AM)—Oct 29, 1975: 1410 khz; 10 kw-U, DA-2. TL: N45 41 02 W61 26 09. Hrs opn: 24. Box 1410, Light Industrial Park, MacIntosh Ave. (B0E 2V0). (902) 625-1220; (902) 625-1410. FAX: (902) 625-2664. Licensee: MacEachern Broadcasting Ltd. (acq 11-22-93; $125,000). Rep: Target Radio, Major Mkt. Format: Adult contemp. News staff 2; news progmg 4 hrs wkly. Target aud: 18-49; blue collar, high school education, married. Spec prog: Scottish one hr, Irish one hr wkly. ■ Theodore Van Zutphen, pres; John Van Zutphen, vp; Bob MacEachern, stn mgr, gen sls mgr & progmg mgr; Paul Knott, prom mgr & mus mgr; Jack Bonaparte, pub affrs dir; Paul Williams, chief engr. ■ Rates: C$26; 23; 20; 18.

Shelburne

CJLS-FM-1—96.3 mhz; 5.5 kw. Rebroadcasts CJLS(AM) Yarmouth. c/o CJLS(AM), Suite 201, 328 Main St., Yarmouth (B5A 1E4). (902) 742-7175. FAX: (902) 742-3143. Licensee: L.G Trask. Format: Adult contemp. ■ G. P. Wyman, gen mgr.

CKBW-FM-2—Sept 15, 1980: 93.1 mhz; 8.6 kw. Stereo. Rebroadcasts CKBW(AM) Bridgewater. c/o CKBW(AM), 215 Dominion St., Bridgewater (B4V 2G8). (902) 543-2401. FAX: (902) 543-1208. Licensee: New Brunswick Broadcasting. Rep: All-Canada, Katz. Format: MOR, country, CHR. Spec prog: Bluegrass, relg. ■ R. A. MacLaren, gen mgr; Gary Richards, progmg dir.

Sydney

CBI(AM)—Nov 1, 1948: 1140 khz; 10 kw-U, DA-2. Box 700, 285 Alexandria St. (B1S 2E8). (902) 539-5050. FAX: (902) 562-7547. Licensee: CBC. Net: CBC AM. Rep: All Canada, Group One. Format: Information. ■ Craig Crinkley, gen mgr.

CBI-FM—July 1977: 105.1 mhz; 20 kw. Ant 400 ft. Stereo. Prog sep from AM. Format: Classics and light classics.

CHER(AM)—Dec 21, 1985: 950 khz; 10 kw-U, DA-1. Suite 208, 500 King's Rd. (B1S 1B1). (902) 539-8500. FAX: (902) 562-5720. Licensee: Radio Cape Breton Ltd. (acq 1-9-89). Net: BN. Rep: All-Canada. Format: Adult contemp. ■ Florence Marsh, pres; Stewart Marsh, gen mgr.

CJCB(AM)—Feb 14, 1929: 1270 khz; 10 kw-U, DA-N. Stereo. Box 1270, Radio Bldg., Charlotte St. (B1P 6K2). (902) 564-5596. FAX: (902) 564-1057. Licensee: Fundy Cable Limited (acq 9-19-90). Rep: Major Mkt. Format: Adult contemp, contemp hit. ■ Donald Brown, gen mgr; Alan Peddle, gen sls mgr.

CKPE-FM—Co-owned with CJCB(AM). September 1962: 94.9 mhz; 61 kw. Ant 210 ft. Stereo. Prog sep from AM. Box 318, Charlotte St. (B1P 6K2). Format: C&W.

Truro

CKCL(AM)—Sept 10, 1947: 600 khz; 10 kw-D, 1 kw-N, DA-1. Box 788, 187 Industrial Ave. (B2N 5E8). (902) 893-6060. FAX: (902) 893-7771. Licensee: Radio Atlantic Ltd. Net: Newsradio. Rep: All Canada. Format: Country. Target aud: 19-55. Spec prog: Farm 3 hrs wkly. ■ Roy Publicover, vp & gen mgr; Dave Guy, prom dir & progmg dir; Dale Lyon, mus dir; Barry Mingo, asst mus dir; Mike Trenholm, news dir.

CKTO-FM—Co-owned with CKCL(AM). 1965: 100.9 mhz; 50 kw. Ant 189 ft. Stereo. Hrs opn: 24. Prog sep from AM. Format: Adult contemp. News staff 4; news progmg 6 hrs wkly. Target aud: 25-49. ■ Roy Publicover, stn mgr, gen sls mgr & natl sls mgr; Blair Dagget, sls dir, rgnl sls mgr & adv dir; Peter Marshall, prom dir; Doug Branscombe, progmg dir; R. Reeves, mus dir. ■ Rates: $27; 23; 23; 20.

Windsor

CFAB(AM)—1945: 1450 khz; 500 w-U. Box 278 (B0N 2T0). (902) 678-2111. FAX: (902) 798-8140. Licensee: Annapolis Valley Radio Ltd. (group owner). Net: BN. Format: Adult contemp. ■ Karen Corey, gen sls mgr; Dave Bannerman, progmg dir.

Yarmouth

CIFA-FM—Sept 28, 1990: 104.1 mhz; 39.3 w. Ant 475 ft. Stereo. Box 8, Saulnierville (B0W 2Z0). (902) 769-2432. FAX: (902) 769-3101. Licensee: Radio Clare. Format: Div, community news. News progmg one hr wkly. Target aud: General. ■ Janice Belliveau, gen mgr; Barbara Comeau, gen sls mgr.

CJLS(AM)—1968: 1340 khz; 5 kw-D, 4 kw-N, DA-2. Suite 201, 328 Main St. (B5A 1E4). (902) 742-7175. FAX: (902) 742-3143. Licensee: Radio CJLS Ltd. (acq 11-68). Format: Adult contemp. ■ Grant Wyman, gen mgr.

Ontario

Ajax

CHOO(AM)—Nov 21, 1967: 1390 khz; 10 kw-U, DA-2. 339 Westney Rd. S., Suite 201 (L1S 7J6). (905) 428-1390. FAX: (905) 686-2444. Licensee: Community Communications Inc. Group owner: Golden West Broadcasting Ltd. (acq 4-77). Net: BN Voice Service. Format: C&W. News staff 3. ■ E. Hildebrand, pres; Jim Webb, gen mgr; S. Kassey, progmg mgr; Jack Hoeppner, engrg dir.

Akwesasne

CKON-FM—Oct 1, 1984: 97.3 mhz; 150 w. Ant 150 ft. Box 140, Rooseveltown, NY (13683); Box 1496, Cornwall (K6H 5V5). (613) 575-2100; (518) 358-3426. FAX: (613) 575-2935. Licensee: Mohawk Nation Council Group owner: Akwesasne Communication Society. Format: Div. Target aud: General. Spec prog: Mohawk. ■ Andria Cook, pres; Kallen Martin, gen mgr; Randy Jock, sls dir.

Arnprior

CHVR-2(AM)—Apr 18, 1985: 1490 khz; 250 w-U, DA-1. Box 1490, 490 Didak St. (K7S 3R1). (613) 623-7711; (613) 735-1350. FAX: (613) 623-7481. Licensee: Valley Radio. Group owner: Pelmorex Broadcasting Inc. (acq 10-17-86). Rep: United. Format: Adult contemp. Target aud: 25-49. ■ Pierre Morrisette, pres; Don Shaffer, vp; Al

Stations in Canada

Kennedy, gen mgr; Mike Thurnell, opns mgr; Jamie Branburger, news dir.

Atikokan

CKDR-6(AM)—May 1977: 1240 khz. 50 w. Hrs opn: 24. c/o CKDR, Box 580, Dryden (P8N 2Z3). (807) 223-2355. Licensee: Fawcett Broadcasting. Group owner: Fawcett Broadcasting Ltd. Format: Contemp hits of the 60s, 70s, 80s, & 90s. News staff one. Target aud: 25-54. ■ Bruce Walchuk, gen mgr.

Bancroft

CJNH(AM)—Mar 1, 1975: 1240 khz; 1 kw-U. Hrs opn: 24. Box 1240, Highway 28 E. (K0L 1C0). (613) 332-1423. FAX: (613) 332-0481. Licensee: Quinte Broadcasting Ltd. Format: Country, oldies. News staff one. Target aud: General. Spec prog: Relg one hrs, local talk 5 hrs, sports 2 hrs wkly. ■ Myles Morton, CEO; Nan McGhee, stn mgr & gen sls mgr; Mike Cooper, prom mgr, progmg mgr & mus dir; G. Glenn Creamer, news dir; Mike Beeston, pub affrs dir. ■ Rates: C$19; 15; 15; 15.

Barrie

CFJB-FM—Oct. 7, 1988: 95.7 mhz; 50 kw. Ant 500 ft. (CP: 45.5 kw). 400 Bayfield St. (L4M 5A1). (705) 721-1291. FAX: (705) 721-7842. Licensee: Rock 95 Broadcasting (Barrie-Orillia) Ltd. Rep: Major Mkt. Format: AOR. Spec prog: Jazz. ■ Doug Bingley, pres & gen mgr; Jim Cowden, gen sls mgr.

CHAY-FM—May 21, 1977: 93.1 mhz; 100 kw. Ant 1,000 ft. Stereo. Box 937 (L4M 4Y6). (705) 737-3511. FAX: (705) 722-5631, (705) 737-0603. Licensee: CHAY Ltd. Group owner: Shaw Radio. Net: BN. Format: Easy lstng. ■ Paul Fockler, gen mgr; Tom Aikins, gen sls mgr; Paul Richards, progmg dir.

CKBB(AM)—Aug 31, 1949: 950 khz; 10 kw, DA-2. TL: N44 18 06 W79 40 56. Hrs opn: 24. Box 950, 129 Ferris Lane (L4M 4V1). (705) 726-9500. FAX: (705) 726-0022. Licensee: CKBB AM Div of P.B.I. (acq 12-13-83). Rep: Paul Mulvihill. Format: Adult contemp, oldies. News progmg 11 hrs wkly. Target aud: 25-54. ■ Jeff Walther, opns mgr; Doug Coulson, Scott Snelgrove (retail), rgnl sls mgrs. ■ Rates: C$72; 52; 52; 30.

Belleville

CIGL-FM—Listing follows CJBQ(AM).

CJBQ(AM)—Aug 12, 1946: 800 khz; 10 kw-U, DA-2. 10 S. Front St. (K8N 5B2). (613) 969-5555. FAX: (613) 969-0288. Licensee: Quinte Broadcasting Ltd. Net: BN. Rep: Jones, Hooper, Major Mkt. Format: Adult contemp. Spec prog: Farm 3 hrs wkly. ■ Bill Morton, gen mgr; Bill McGuire, gen sls mgr; Peter Thompson, progmg dir.

CIGL-FM—Co-owned with CJBQ(AM). August 1962: 97.1 mhz; 50 kw. Prog sep from AM. Net: BN. Format: Btfl mus. ■ Bill Conlon, progmg dir.

CJLX-FM—October 1992: 92.3 mhz; 50 w. TL: N44 09 50 W77 23 24. Stereo. Hrs opn: 6 AM-midnight. Box 4200, Loyalist College, Wallbridge-Loyalist Rd. (K8N 5B9). (613) 966-0923. FAX: (613) 962-1376. Licensee: Loyalist College Radio Inc. (acq 11-13-90). Net: BN. Format: Rock, community service. News progmg 6 hrs wkly. Target aud: General; all ages targeted at various levels. Spec prog: Canadian Indian one hr, class 6 hrs, farm one hr, folk one hr, F one hr, jazz one hr, Dutch one hr, seniors one hr wkly. ■ Todd Smith, pres; Jennifer Russell, CFO; Lisette LaBlance, exec vp; Greg Schatzmann, gen mgr, prom dir, progmg dir & mus dir; Dave Soverign, sls dir. ■ Rates: C$9; 9; 9; 9.

CJOJ-FM—Dec 1, 1993: 95.5 mhz; 50 kw. CN Tower, 354 Pinnacle St. (K8N 3B4). (613) 966-0955. FAX: (613) 967-2565. Licensee: Belleville Radio Ltd. (acq 11-13-91). Format: CHR/adult contemp. ■ Tony Zwig, gen mgr; Mike Christos, progmg dir; David Lee, chief engr.

Blind River

CJNR(AM)—1955: 730 khz; 1 kw-D, 500 w-N. c/o 15 Charles Walk, Elliot Lake (P5A 2A2). (705) 356-2209. FAX: (705) 848-1378. Licensee: Mid Canada Communications. Group owner: Pelmorex Bcstg Inc. (acq 1985). Format: Adult contemp. ■ Walter Hulne, gen sls mgr.

Bracebridge

CFBG-FM—May 1988: 101.9 mhz. Box 30 (P1L 1T5). (705) 645-2218. FAX: (705) 645-6957. Licensee: Telemedia Communications Ontario Inc. Group owner: Telemedia Communications Inc. Format: Adult contemp. News progmg 40 hrs wkly. Target aud: 34-45; older adult contemporary. Spec prog: Jazz 2 hrs, big band one hr, local magazine one hr wkly. ■ Doug Ackhurst, vp; Doug Pincoe, stn mgr & gen sls mgr; Rick Steward, progmg dir; Steve Young, pub affrs dir. ■ Rates: C$576; 480; 480; 360.

Brampton

CFNY-FM—Aug 8, 1960: 102.1 mhz; 35 kw. Ant 1,378 ft. TL: N43 38 33 W79 23 15. Stereo. Hrs opn: 24. 83 Kennedy Rd. S. (L6W 3P3). (905) 453-7452. FAX: (905) 453-7711. Licensee: Key Radio Ltd. (acq 10-89). Format: Modern rock, progsv/alternative. News progmg 6 hrs wkly. Target aud: 18-34; self motivated, music loving, active, young at heart people. Spec prog: Class 5 hrs, jazz 3 hrs wkly. ■ Harold E. Blackadar, pres; Vince DiMaggio, gen mgr; Chris Sisam, gen sls mgr; David Haydu, chief engr.

CIAO(AM)—Dec 23, 1953: 530 khz; 1 kw-D, 250 w-N, DA-2. Hrs opn: 24. Unit 20, 50 Kennedy R.S. (L6W 3R7). (905) 453-7111; (905) 798-4888. FAX: (905) 453-4788. Licensee: CKMW Radio Ltd. (acq 9-26-83). Rep: Target. Format: Ethnic, multilingual. ■ Angelo Cremisio, pres; Bill Evanov, exec vp; Rick Sargent, opns dir; Anders Yrfelt, gen sls mgr; James Muccilli, natl sls mgr; Carmela Laurignano, rgnl sls mgr; Patrizia Di Vincenzo, progmg dir; Pino Trecozzi, mus dir.

Brantford

CKPC(AM)—December 1923: 1380 khz; 10 kw-U, DA-2. (CP: 25 kw). Hrs opn: 24. 571 West St. (N3T 5P8). (519) 759-1000. FAX: (519) 753-1470. Licensee: Telephone City Broadcast Ltd. Net: BN. Rep: Telemedia. Format: Adult contemp. News staff 8; news progmg 9 hrs wkly. Target aud: 25-54. ■ Richard D. Buchanan, pres & gen mgr; Dale Parker, opns mgr, prom mgr & mus dir; Bill Dawkins, gen sls mgr; Murray Moffatt, news dir; Stewart Bayley, chief engr. ■ Rates: C$53; 45; 45; 37.

CKPC-FM—May 1949: 92.1 mhz; 50 kw. Ant 750 ft. Stereo. Prog sep from AM. News progmg 7 hrs wkly. Target aud: 35-54. Spec prog: Folk one hr, Ger 5 hr wkly. ■ Rates: C$42; 38; 38; 30.

Brockville

CFJR(AM)—April 1926: 830 khz; 5 kw-D, 1 kw-N, DA-2. Hrs opn: 24. Box 666, 601 Stewart Blvd. (K6V 5V9). (613) 345-1666. FAX: (613) 343-2438. Licensee: St. Lawrence Broadcasting Co. Ltd. (acq 11-87). Format: Adult contemp. News staff 2; news progmg 8 hrs wkly. Target aud: General. ■ James Waters, pres; John P. Wright, vp, gen mgr & gen sls mgr; Greg Hinton, progmg dir; Wayne James, mus dir; Gaetanne Mason, news dir; Terry Kelly, engrg dir. ■ Rates: C$32; 20; 20; 13.

CHXL-FM—Co-owned with CFJR(AM). July 28, 1988: 103.7 mhz; 50 kw. Ant 295 ft. Prog sep from AM. Format: AOR. Spec prog: Jazz 2 hrs wkly. ■ John P. Wright, vp sls; Greg Diamond, progmg dir; Gaetanne Mason, news dir.

Burlington

CING-FM—Sept 23, 1976: 107.9 mhz; 50 kw. Ant 256 ft. Stereo. 4144 S. Service Rd. (L7L 4X5). (416) 681-1079. FAX: (416) 681-1758. Licensee: Burlington Broadcasting Inc. (acq 9-76). Net: BN. Rep: Glen Warren. Format: Oldies, dance music. Spec prog: Jazz 5 hrs, class 5 hrs, Ger 12 hrs, It 2 hrs, Black 5 hrs wkly. ■ Bill Evanov, gen mgr; Murray Hanes, gen sls mgr; Junior Chung, progmg dir.

Cambridge

CIAM(AM)—Sept 17, 1954: 960 khz; 1 kw-U, DA-1. 46 Main St. (N1R 1V4). (519) 621-7510. FAX: (519) 621-0165. Licensee: Div. of Power Broadcasting. (acq 4/87). Net: BN. Rep: Paul Mulvihill. Format: CHR. Spec prog: Por 2 hrs wkly. ■ Guus Hazelaar, gen mgr & gen sls mgr; Ron Fitzpatrick, progmg dir.

Chatham

CFCO(AM)—1926: 630 khz; 10 kw-D, 1 kw-N, DA-2. Hrs opn: 24. Box 630, 21 Kiel Dr. (N7M 5V9). (519) 352-3000. FAX: (519) 352-4801; (519) 352-9690. Licensee: Key Radio Ltd. (acq 5-14-62). Net: BN. Rep: Paul Mulvahill, Hooper Jones. Format: Oldies. News progmg 6 hrs wkly. Target aud: 25-49. Spec prog: Farm 3 hrs wkly. ■ Dave Chamberlain, gen mgr; Mike Murphy, gen sls mgr; Doug Rollins, progmg dir; Ted Cribbie, chief engr. ■ Rates: C$62; 47; 42; 22.

CKSY-FM—July 1, 1986: 95.1 mhz; 42 kw. Ant 495 ft. TL: N42 26 14 W82 06 23. Stereo. Hrs opn: 24. Dups CBE(AM) Windsor 100%. Box 100, 117 Keil Dr S. (N7M 5K1). (519) 354-2200; (519) 354-0311. FAX: (519) 354-2880. Licensee: Bea-Ver Communications Inc. Net: SBN. Rep: Major Mkt. Format: Adult contemp. News staff 4; news progmg 6 hrs wkly. Target aud: 18-54. ■ Carl Veroba, CEO, pres, gen mgr, stn mgr & chief engr; Walter Ploegman, opns mgr, progmg dir & mus dir; Kenneth Swirsky, sls dir; Elizabeth Gilmer, prom dir; Tom Gibson, asst mus dir; Dawn Kelly, news dir & pub affrs dir. ■ Rates: C$64; 53; 44; 33.

Cobourg

CFMX-FM—1978: 103.1 mhz; 86.7 KW. Ant 825 ft. TL: N01 44 04 W01 78 09. Stereo. Hrs opn: 24. Box 1031 (K9A 4W5); Unit #1; 884 Division St. (K9A 4J9). (905) 372-4366; (416) 367-5353. FAX: (905) 372-1625; (416) 367-1742. Licensee: Martin Rosenthal (acq 11-30-83; $50,000). Rep: Telemedia. Wash atty: Robson Broadcast Consultants Inc. Format: Classical. News staff 2; news progmg 4 hrs wkly. Target aud: 35+; Well educated, upscale, owners/managers/professionals. ■ Martin Rosenthal, pres; Truus Rosenthal, vp; Wendy Rolph, stn mgr; Rod Walker, gen sls mgr; Monica Tynan Day, prom dir; John van Driel, progmg dir; Robert Bier, Richard Haskell, Michael Lyons, mus dirs; David Franco, Bill Dulmage, news dirs; John Ton, chief engr. ■ Rates: C$45; 45; 45; 45.

CHUC(AM)—Aug 27, 1957: 1450 khz; 8 kw-D, 1 kw-N, DA-2. TL: N43 57 20 W78 13 09. Hrs opn: 24. Box 520 (K9A 4L3); Telephone Rd. (K9A 4J7). (905) 372-5401. FAX: (905) 372-6280. Licensee: Pineridge Broadcasting (acq 7-31-92). Net: BN, Telemedia. Rep: All-Canada. Format: Soft pop, oldies. News staff 3; news progmg 7 hrs wkly. Target aud: 25-54; predominantly female. ■ Don Conway, pres & gen mgr; Fred Ball, gen sls mgr & adv mgr; Paul Laing, prom mgr & progmg mgr; Jim Guy, news dir; John Ton, engrg dir. ■ Rates: $45; 35; 35; 23.

Collingwood

CKCB(AM)—1965: 1400 khz; 1 kw-D. TL: N44 28 54 W80 14 45. Hrs opn: 24. Dups CKBB(AM) Barrie 100%. 1400, Hwy 26 E. (L9Y 4W2). (705) 444-1400. FAX: (705) 444-6776. Licensee: Collingwood Radio (acq 12-13-83). Rep: Paul Mulvihill. Format: Adult contemp, oldies. News staff 2; news progmg 11 hrs wkly. Target aud: 25-54. ■ Pat St.John, gen mgr; Doug Coulson, gen sls mgr; John Nichols, progmg dir. ■ Rates: $45; 33; 33; 18.

Cornwall

CJSS(AM)—1945: 1220 khz; 1 kw-U, DA-2. Hrs opn: 24. Box 969 (K6H 5V1). (613) 932-5180. FAX: (613) 938-0355. Licensee: Tri-Co Broadcasting Ltd. (acq 8-1-63). Net: Newsradio. Rep: Canadian Broadcasting Sales. Format: Adult contemp. News staff 5; news progmg 5 hrs wkly. Target aud: 18-49. ■ Paul Emard, pres; Keith Clingen, gen mgr & gen sls mgr; Gord Shaver, progmg dir; Gus Gilmour, mus dir; Fred Pletsch, news dir; Owen Mekitarian, engrg dir.

CFLG-FM—Co-owned with CJSS(AM). 1957: 104.5 mhz; 9.5 kw. Ant 300 ft. Stereo. Prog sep from AM. Format: Adult contemp. News staff 4; new progmg 5 hrs wkly. Target aud: 18-49. ■ Keith Clingen, vp; Frank Wood, progmg dir & mus dir; John Bolton, asst mus dir.

Dryden

CKDR(AM)—August 1963: 800 khz; 1 kw-D, 700 w-N. Box 580 (P8N 2Z3). (807) 223-2355. FAX: (807) 223-5090. Licensee: Fawcett Broadcasting Ltd. (group owner). Format: Adult contemp, CHR. ■ Bruce Walchuk, gen mgr & gen sls mgr; Ben Lucas, progmg dir.

Elliot Lake

CKNR(AM)—September 1966: 1340 khz; 1 kw-U. 15 Charles Walk (P5A 2A2); 46 Mead Blvd. (P5A 2A2). (705) 848-3608. FAX: (705) 868-1378. Licensee: Mid Canada Communications Corp. Group owner: Pelmorex Bcstg Inc. (acq 1985). Net: BN. Rep: United. Format: Adult contemp. ■ Walter Hulme, gen mgr.

Espanola

CKNS(AM)—Oct 2, 1976: 930 khz; 10 kw-U, DA-2. Rebroadcasts CKNR(AM) Elliot Lake 100%. Box 1910, 46 Mead St. (P0P 1C0). (705) 869-4930. FAX: (705) 869-3764. Licensee: Mid Canada Communications Corp. Group owner: Pelmorex Bcstg Inc. (acq 5-85). Net: CBC Mono. Rep: Canadian Broadcast Sales. Format: Adult contemp. ■ Walter Hulme, gen mgr. ■ CKCY-TV affil.

Ontario

Fort Erie

CKEY-FM—May 19, 1991: 101.1 mhz; 52 kw. TL: N42 53 52 W78 57 27. Stereo. Hrs opn: 24. Box 710, 4668 St. Clair Ave., Niagara Falls (L2E 6X7). (905) 356-6710; (905) 871-2593. FAX: (905) 356-0696. Licensee: CJRN 710 Inc. Net: Telemedia. Rep: Canadian Broadcast Sales. Format: Adult contemp. News staff 3; news progmg 5 hrs wkly. Target aud: 25-54; upper-income adults. ■ Keith Dancy, pres & gen mgr; David Dancy, gen sls mgr, vp mktg & adv mgr; Robert White, prom dir & asst mus dir; Robert Dancy, progmg dir & mus dir; Phil Lester, news dir; Bill McDougall, chief engr. ■ Rates: C$480; 480; 480; 480.

Fort Frances

CFOB(AM)—Nov 11, 1944: 640 khz; 1 kw-U. Hrs opn: 24. Box 489 (P9A 3M8); 242 Scott St. (P9A 1G7). (807) 274-5341. FAX: (807) 274-2033. Licensee: Fawcett Broadcasting Ltd. (group owner; acq 7-1-69). Rep: Major Mkt. Format: Oldies based adult contemp, CHR. News staff one; Target aud: 25-54. ■ Lois Fawcett, CEO, pres & CFO; Scott Fawcett, vp, gen mgr, stn mgr & vp sls; Howard Fawcett, vp opns; Darcy Byrnes, mus dir; John Loregio, news dir; John Sinclair, chief engr.

Guelph

CFRU-FM—Jan 28, 1980: 93.3 mhz; 250 w. Ant 1,085 ft. TL: N43 32 W80 13. Stereo. Hrs opn: 24. Level 2 Univ. Centre, Univ. of Guelph (N1G 2W1). (519) 824-4120, ext 8431. Licensee: University of Guelph Radio-Radio Gryphon. Format: Post-modern rock, div. News staff 2; news progmg 12 hrs wkly. Target aud: General. Spec prog: Black 6 hrs, class 3 hrs, folk 12 hrs, Fr one hr, jazz 8 hrs, Polish 2 hrs, relg one hr, Sp 2 hrs, Portuguese 2 hrs, women positive 4 hrs, gospel one hr wkly. ■ Alex Prediger, opns mgr; Sue Forrest, sls dir; Bob McCarthy, progmg dir; Kevin Lynn, mus dir; Cindy Duffy, news dir; John Matthews, engrg mgr. ■ Rates: C$10; 12; 10; 15.

CIMJ-FM—Listing follows CJOY(AM).

CJOY(AM)—June 14, 1948: 1460 khz; 10 kw-U. Stereo. Hrs opn: 24. 75 Speedvale Ave. E. (N1E 6M3). (519) 824-7000. Licensee: Guelph Broadcasting, a division of Power Broadcasting Inc. Net: BN. Rep: Paul Mulvihill. Format: Oldies. News staff 5; news progmg 8 hrs wkly. Target aud: 25-54. ■ Peter Kruyt, pres; Yvon Chouinard, exec vp; Pat St. John, gen mgr; Mark Bowden, gen sls mgr & natl sls mgr; Larry Mellott, progmg mgr; Dave Hanna, mus dir; Paul Osborne, news dir; Joe Mignacca, vp engrg. ■ Rates: C$56; 45; 52; 36.

CIMJ-FM—Co-owned with CJOY(AM). 1969: 106.1 mhz; 50 kw. Ant 249 ft. Stereo. Hrs opn: 24. Prog sep from AM. Format: Adult contemp. News progmg 6 hrs wkly. Target aud: 18-49. ■ Rates: C$50; 41; 46; 36.

Hamilton

*CFMU-FM—Jan 13, 1978: 93.3 mhz; 250 w. Ant 300 ft. TL: N47 14 41 W79 54 58. Stereo. Hrs opn: 24. Hamilton Hall, Suite 319, McMaster Univ. (L8S 4K1). (905) 525-9140 EXT. 7208; (905) 525-9140 EXT. 2053. FAX: (905) 529-3208. Licensee: CFMU Radio Inc. (acq 1978). Format: Div. News staff one; news progmg 20 hrs wkly. Target aud: 15-35; urban youth. Spec prog: Pub affrs 10 hrs, doc 10 hrs, class 5 hrs, folk 5 hrs, gospel one hr, Sp one hr, world beat/reggae 5 hrs, jazz 10 hrs, blues 5 hrs, American Indian one hr wkly. ■ Jason Hunt, pres; Victoria Fenner, stn mgr & progmg dir; Lauren Hodgson, sls dir & adv dir; Paul Cormack, mus dir; Thilo Kaufmann, news dir & pub affrs dir; John Matthews, chief engr. ■ Rates: $30; 30; 30; 30.

CHAM(AM)—November 1959: 820 khz; 50 kw-D, DA-2. Stereo. CHAM Center, 151 York Blvd. (L8R 3M2). (905) 526-8200. FAX: (905) 525-1416. Licensee: Golden West Broadcasting Ltd. (group owner; acq 9-15-92). Rep: Canadian Broadcast Sales. Format: Country. Target aud: 25-54. ■ Elmer Hildebrand, pres; Mike Ferguson, stn mgr & opns mgr; Angela Reed, gen sls mgr; Doug Sexton, mktg mgr; Brenda Hazell, prom mgr; Scott Mannen, adv mgr; Mark LaPointe, progmg dir; Joel Christie, mus dir; Brian Fisher, news dir; Jack Hoeppner, chief engr.

CHML(AM)—May 27, 1927: 900 khz; 50 kw-U, DA-1. Stereo. Hrs opn: 24. 875 Main St. W. (L8S 4R1). (416) 521-9900. FAX: (416) 521-2306. Licensee: CHML/CJXY. Group owner: Westcom (acq 1974). Net: Telemedia, BN. Rep: Canadian Broadcast Sales. Format: News/talk, sports, oldies. Target aud: 18 plus. ■ Don Luzzi, pres & gen mgr; Ed Duarte, vp sls; Maureen Bulley, mktg dir & prom mgr; Darryl Hartwick, progmg dir; Paul Morris, mus dir; Bill Kelly, asst mus dir; Paul Tipple, news dir; Ted Townsend, engrg dir.

CJXY-FM—Co-owned with CHML(AM). Sept 14, 1964: 95.3 mhz; 100 kw. Ant 1,000 ft. Stereo. Hrs opn: 24. Prog sep from AM. Format: Classic rock. ■ Maureen Bulley, adv dir. ■ CHCH-TV affil.

CKLH-FM—Listing follows CKOC(AM).

CKOC(AM)—May 20, 1922: 1150 khz; 50 kw-U, DA-2. Stereo. Hrs opn: 24. Box 1150, 883 Upper Wentworth St. (L8N 3P5). (416) 574-1150. FAX: (416) 575-6429. Licensee: London Communications Inc. (acq 9-2-93; $3.5 million). Net: BN. Format: Oldies. ■ Jack W. Schoone, pres; Jim MacLeod, exec vp; Wally Solows, gen sls mgr; Christopher Randall, prom mgr; Nevin Grant, progmg dir & mus dir; Doug Farraway, asst mus dir; Gus Sondermeyer, chief engr.

CKLH-FM—Co-owned with CKOC(AM). Oct 7, 1986: 102.9 mhz; 40.3 kw. Stereo. Prog sep from AM. Format: Adult contemp. ■ Pat Cardinal, asst mus dir & news dir.

Hawkesbury

CHPR-FM—February 1986: 102.1 mhz; 789 w. Ant 70 ft. TL: N45 35 01 N45 35 01. Hrs opn: 24. Suite 101, 150 Principale est (K6A 1A1); 385 Principale, Lachute, PQ (J8H 1Y1). (613) 632-1119. FAX: (514) 562-1902. Licensee: Radio Fusion Inc. Group owner: Radio Nord Inc. (acq 8-22-89). Format: Adult contemp. News staff one. Target aud: 25 plus. ■ Gilles Poulin, pres; Kathleen Silas, gen mgr; Yves Trottier, mus dir; Pierre Laberge, chief engr.

Hearst

CHOH(AM)—Dec 23, 1951: 1340 khz; 1 kw-D, 250 w-N, DA-2. 14 Pine St. S. (P4N 7G8). (705) 267-6070. Licensee: Mid Canada Communications Corp. Group owner: Pelmorex Bcstg Inc. Format: Adult contemp. Spec prog: Sp one hr wkly. ■ Dennis Bouchard, gen mgr.

Huntsville

CFBK-FM—September 1987: 105.5 mhz; 5 kw. Box 1055 (P0A 1K0). (705) 789-4461. FAX: (705) 789-1269. Licensee: Muskoka-Parry Sound Broadcasting Ltd. Format: Adult contemp. ■ Joe Duchesne, pres, gen mgr & gen sls mgr; Craig Martin, prom mgr; Stephanie Topp, mus dir; Brian Thompson, news dir; Charles Tryon, chief engr.

Kapuskasing

CHYK(AM)—Feb 2, 1957: 1230 khz; 100 w. (CP: 1 kw-D, 600 w-N). 52 Riverside Dr. (P5N 1A8). (705) 267-6070; (705) 267-6098. FAX: (705) 267-6095. Licensee: Pelmorex Broadcasting Inc. (group owner; acq 9-1-90). Net: BN. Format: Adult contemp, soft rock. Target aud: 18-40; young adult bilingual audience. ■ Denis Bouchard, gen mgr & gen sls mgr. ■ Rates: $18; 15; 18; 12.

CKAP(AM)—July 1, 1965: 580 khz; 10 kw-D, DA. Hrs opn: 24. 52 Riverside Dr. (P5N 1A8). (705) 335-2379. FAX: (705) 337-6391. Licensee: Pelmorex Communications Inc. (group owner, acq 9-1-90). Net: CRN. Rep: Radio-TV Reps, UBS. Format: CHR. News staff one. Target aud: General. ■ Pierre Morrissette, pres; Denis Bouchard, gen mgr & gen sls mgr; Dave Palmer, prom mgr & progmg dir; Marg Jones, news dir.

Kenora

CBQX-FM—Mar 28, 1978: 98.7 mhz; 38 kw. Rebroadcasts CBW(AM) Winnipeg, Man. & CBQT-FM Thunder Bay. 213 Miles St. E., Thunder Bay (P7C 1J5). (416) 205-3700. Licensee: CBC. Net: CBC. Format: Info radio. ■ Wilder Lewis, stn mgr.

CJRL(AM)—Feb 19, 1938: 1220 khz; 5 kw-D, 1 kw-N, DA-1. (CP: 5 kw-U). 128 Main St. S. (P9N 1S9). (807) 468-3181. FAX: (807) 468-4188. Licensee: Fawcett Broadcasting Ltd. (group owner; acq 4-71). Net: SBN. Rep: Major Mkt. Format: Adult contemp, CHR. News staff 2; news progmg 4 hrs wkly. Target aud: 25-54. Spec prog: Ukrainian one hr wkly. ■ Lois Fawcett, CEO; Hugh Syrja, pres; Scott Fawcett, gen mgr, sls dir, vp mktg & vp prom; Howard Fawcett, vp opns & vp progmg.

Kingston

CBBK-FM—May 21, 1979: 92.9 mhz; 1.6 kw. Ant 395 ft. TL: N44 17 32 W76 28 50. Stereo. Hrs opn: 24. Box 500, Terminal A, Toronto (M5W 1E6). (416) 205-3700. FAX: (416) 205-3311. Licensee: Canadian Broadcasting Corp. Net: CBC. Format: Class, jazz. ■ Harold Redekopp, vp; Marilyn Mercer, progmg dir; Rudolf Lingohr (rgnl), chief engr.

CFFX(AM)—Aug 31, 1942: 960 khz; 10 kw-D, 5 kw-N, DA-2. Stereo. 479 Counter St. (K7M 7J3). (613) 549-1911. FAX: (613) 549-7974. Licensee: Division of Power Broadcasting Inc. Net: BN, Newsradio. Rep: Mulvihill. Format: Adult contemp, oldies. Spec prog: Sports, play by play. ■ John Tucker, pres; Mike Tiernay, gen sls mgr; John Begg, prom mgr; Lorne Mathews, progmg mgr; Larry Cameron, vp engrg.

CFMK-FM—Co-owned with CFFX(AM). Aug 31, 1942: 96.3 mhz; 50 kw. Ant 500 ft. Stereo. Prog sep from AM. Format: Country. ■ CKWS-TV affil.

CFLY-FM—Listing follows CKLC(AM).

CFMK-FM—Listing follows CFFX(AM).

*CFRC-FM—January 1953: 101.9 mhz; 3 kw. Ant 295 ft. TL: N44 17 24 W77 25 55. Stereo. Hrs opn: 3 PM-3 AM Mon-Fri, 8 AM-3 AM Sat-Sun. Carruthers Hall, Queens University (K7L 3N6). (613) 545-2121. Licensee: Radio Queen's University. Format: Div. News staff 7; News progmg 5 hrs wkly. Target aud: General. ■ David Smith, pres; Maureen Plunkett, stn mgr; Paul Tukker, mus dir.

CKLC(AM)—Nov 18, 1953: 1380 khz; 10 kw-U, DA-1. Stereo. Box 1380 (K7L 4Y5). (613) 544-1380. FAX: (613) 546-9751. Licensee: St. Lawrence Broadcasting Co. Ltd. (acq 5-14-76). Net: BN. Rep: Major Mkt. Format: Top-40. News progmg 3 hrs wkly. Target aud: 18-34. ■ James Waters, pres; John Wright, vp & gen mgr; Errol Jesse, rgnl sls mgr; Jane Douglas, prom mgr; Scott O'Brien, mus dir; Tony Orr, news dir; Terry Kelly, chief engr.

CFLY-FM—Co-owned with CKLC(AM). 1963: 98.3 mhz; 100 kw. Ant 400 ft. Stereo. Prog sep from AM. Format: Adult contemp. News staff 6; news progmg 5 hrs wkly. Target aud: 25-54; owner/mgr/professional. ■ Jackie St. Pierre, prom mgr; Rob Wood, progmg dir & progmg mgr.

Kirkland Lake

CJKL(AM)—March 30, 1934: 560 khz; 5 kw-D, DA-2. Hrs opn: 24. Box 430, 5 Kirkland St. (P2N 3J4). (705) 567-3366. FAX: (705) 567-6101. Licensee: Connelly Communications Corp. Net: BN Voice Service, CBC Mono. Net: All-Canada. Format: Adult contemp, country. News staff 3. Spec prog: Black 4 hrs, C&W 6 hrs, Jazz 2 hrs wkly. ■ Rob Connelly, CEO, pres, stn mgr, prom dir & mus dir; Ann Connelly, gen sls mgr; Jeff Wilkinson, news dir; Laura Alaire, pub affrs dir; Bob White, engrg dir.

Kitchener

CFCA-FM—Listing follows CKKW(AM).

CHYM-FM—Listing follows CKGL(AM).

CKGL(AM)—1929: 570 khz; 10 kw-U, DA-1. 305 King St. W. (N2G 4E4). (519) 743-2611. FAX: (519) 743-7510. Licensee: Key Radio Ltd. (acq 3-16-67). Net: Newsradio, CBS. Rep: Standard Bcst. Format: Country. Target aud: 18-49. ■ Wolfgang Von Raesfeld, gen mgr; William Leeson, gen sls mgr; Gavin Tucker, progmg dir.

CHYM-FM—Co-owned with CKGL(AM). 1949: 96.7 mhz; 25 kw. Ant 658 ft. (CP: 100 kw). Stereo. Format: Adult contemp. Target aud: 25-54.

CKKW(AM)—Aug 1, 1959: 1090 khz; 10 kw-U, DA-2. Stereo. 864 King St., W. (N2G 4E9). (519) 579-1090. FAX: (519) 743-0364. Licensee: CHUM Ltd. (group owner; acq 7-30-93; $5 million). Net: BN. Format: Contemp hit. ■ Alan Waters, pres; Linda Benoit, gen mgr; N. Aitchison, gen sls mgr; Paul Cugliari, progmg dir; Kirk Dixon, news dir.

CFCA-FM—Co-owned with CKKW(AM). Apr 3, 1967: 105.3 mhz; 100 kw. Ant 812 ft. Stereo. Dups AM 16%. (519) 576-1053. Net: SBN. Format: Btfl mus. Spec prog: Class 17 hrs wkly. ■ Craig Smith, progmg dir. ■ CKCO-TV affil.

CKWR-FM—Licensed to Kitchener. See Waterloo.

Leamington

CHYR-FM—Aug 23, 1993: 96.7 mhz; 19.32 kw. 100 Talbot St. E. (N8H 1L3). (519) 326-6171; (519) 326-6377. FAX: (519) 322-1110. Licensee: Key Radio Ltd. (acq 1987). Net: SRN. Format: Country. News staff 3; news progmg 8 hrs wkly. Target aud: 25-54. Spec prog: Ital 3 hrs, German one hr, relg one hr wkly. ■ Hal Blackadar, CEO; Ike Erickson, gen sls mgr; Chuck Reynolds, progmg dir; Brian Penstone, Cynthia Colby, news dirs. ■ Rates: C$38; 34; 36; 38.

Stations in Canada   **Ontario**

Lindsay

CKLY(AM)—Dec 8, 1955: 910 khz; 10 kw-D, 5 kw-N, DA-2. Hrs opn: 24. 249 Kent St. W. (K9V 2Z3). (705) 324-9103. FAX: (705) 324-4149. Licensee: 993682 Ontario Ltd. (acq 7-30-93; $700,000). Rep: Canadian Broadcast Sales. Format: Adult contemp, oldies. News staff 4; news progmg 14 hrs wkly. Target aud: 35-54. Spec prog: Big band 6 hrs wkly. ■ Harry E. Reynolds, pres; Mike Lynch, opns mgr & progmg mgr; George Morrison, gen sls mgr; D. Illman, mus dir; P. Smith, news dir; R. McMurray, chief engr. ■ Rates: $29; 29; 29; 24.

London

CBBL-FM—Oct 1, 1978: 100.5 mhz; 22.5 kw. TL: N42 57 20 W81 21 20. Stereo. Hrs opn: 24. Box 500, Station A, Toronto (M5W 1E6). (416) 205-7400. FAX: (416) 205-2729. Licensee: Canadian Broadcasting Corp. Net: CBC. Format: Classical. ■ Gloria Bishop, progmg dir; Rudolf Lingohr (rgnl), chief engr.

CBCL-FM—Co-owned with CBBL-FM. 93.5 mhz; 100 kw.

CFPL(AM)—Sept 1922: 980 khz; 10 kw-D, 5 kw-N, DA-2. TL: N42 53 29 W81 12 02. Stereo. Hrs opn: 24. Box 2580, 369 York St. (N6A 4H3). (519) 438-8391. FAX: (519) 438-2415. Licensee: Blackburn Radio Inc. Format: Great oldies, news. News staff 12; news progmg 10 hrs wkly. Target aud: 35-54. ■ W.J. "Bill" Brady, pres & gen mgr; Keith I. Roberts, gen sls mgr; Graham Murray, mktg mgr & prom mgr; Barry Rutledge, progmg mgr; Vic Sinclair, mus dir; Gary Ennett, news dir; Peter Paczynski, chief engr.

CFPL-FM—1948: 95.9 mhz; 179 kw. Ant 885 ft. TL: N42 57 15 W81 15 58. Stereo. Hrs opn: 24. Prog sep from AM. (519) 433-3696. Format: Classic rock. News progmg 5 hrs wkly. Target aud: 25-49. ■ Rick Moss, progmg dir.

*****CHRW-FM**—94.7 mhz; 3 kw. University Community Centre, Room 250, University of Western Ontario (N6A 3K7). (519) 661-3601. FAX: (519) 661-3816. Licensee: Radio Western Inc. Format: Rock/alternative. ■ Mario Circelli, stn mgr; Rob Sweeney, news dir.

CIQM-FM—Listing follows CKSL(AM).

*****CIXX-FM**—Oct 31, 1978: 106.9 mhz; 3 kw. Ant 150 ft. Stereo. 1460 Oxford St. E. (N5V 1W2). (519) 453-2810. FAX: (519) 452-3570. Licensee: Radio Fanshawe Inc. Format: Adult contemp. Spec prog: Class 5 hrs, jazz 5 hrs wkly. ■ Gary O'Brien, gen mgr; Carolynne Hegge, gen sls mgr; Kevin Scott, progmg dir.

CJBC-FM-20—Not on air, target date unknown: 99.3 mhz; 22.5 kw. Rebroadcasts CJBC(AM) Toronto. 100 Carlton St., 2nd Floor, Toronto (M5B 1M3). (416) 975-3566. Licensee: Canadian Broadcasting Corp. ■ Jean-Francois Dubois, gen mgr.

CJBK(AM)—Jan 25, 1967: 1290 khz; 10 kw-U, DA-2. TL: N42 52 08 W81 13 58. Stereo. Hrs opn: 24. 743 Wellington Rd. S. (N6C 4R5). (519) 686-2525. FAX: (519) 686-9067. Licensee: London Communications Inc. (acq 9-2-93; $3.5 million). Net: SBN. Rep: United. Format: Adult contemp, sports. Target aud: 25-49. ■ Tony Zwig, CEO; Jack Schoone, pres; Don Chamberlain, exec vp; Don Peter, gen sls mgr; Randy Timmins, mktg dir & prom mgr; Michelle Scott, asst mus dir; Jeff Guy, vp engrg & chief engr. ■ Rates: C$36; 36; 36; 36.

CJBX-FM—Co-owned with CJBK(AM). Mar 3, 1980: 92.7 mhz; 50 kw. Ant 400 ft. Stereo. Prog sep from AM. Format: Country. News progmg 7 hrs wkly. Target aud: 35-54. ■ Ian McCallum, progmg dir & mus dir. ■ Rates: C$42; 42; 42; 42.

CKSL(AM)—June 1956: 1410 khz; 10 kw-U, DA-2. Stereo. Hrs opn: 24. Box 1410, 380 Wellington St. (N6A 5J2). (519) 667-1410; (416) 368-7200. FAX: (519) 667-2175. Licensee: Telemedia Communications Ontario Inc. Group owner: Telemedia Communications Inc. Rep: Telemedia. Format: News/talk. News staff 10; news progmg 15 hrs wkly. Target aud: 25-54. ■ Jim McCoubrey, CEO; Don Pagnutti, pres; Braden Doerr, gen mgr & progmg mgr; Barry Smith, opns mgr; Tom Cooke, gen sls mgr; Marc Paris, natl sls mgr; Elaine Sawyer, prom mgr; George Gordon, news dir; Bill Tofflemire, engrg mgr.

CIQM-FM—Co-owned with CKSL(AM). June 1, 1986: 97.5 mhz; 50 kw. Ant 300 ft. Stereo. Prog sep from AM. (519) 661-2000. Format: Adult contemp. News progmg 4 hrs wkly. ■ Trisha Freriks, prom mgr; Dave Collins, progmg dir; Lisa LaFontaine, mus dir.

Marathon

CFNO-FM—July 17, 1982: 93.1 mhz; 50 kw. Ant 879 ft. Stereo. Box 1000, 93 Evergreen Dr. (P0T 2E0). (807) 229-1010. FAX: (807) 229-1686. Licensee: North Superior Broadcasting Ltd. (acq 1982). Format: Adult contemp. Spec prog: C&W 4 hrs wkly. ■ Spencer Bell, gen mgr & gen sls mgr.

Midland

CICZ-FM—September 1993: 104.1 mhz; 129 w. Box 609, 355 Cranston Crescent (L4R 4L3). (705) 526-2268. FAX: (705) 526-3060. Licensee: Telemedia Communications Ontario Inc. Group owner: Telemedia Communications Inc. Format: Hot new country. ■ Doug Ackhurst, gen mgr; Mora Austin, stn mgr.

Mississauga

CFMX-FM-1—Licensed to Mississauga. See Toronto.

CJMR(AM)—June 17, 1974: 1320 khz; 20 kw-U. Broadcasting Centre, 284 Church St., Oakville (L6J 7N2). (905) 845-2821; (905) 271-1320. FAX: (905) 842-1250. Licensee: CHWO Radio Ltd. Rep: Target. Format: Adult contemp & ethnic. ■ Michael Caine, gen mgr & progmg dir; Harry McDonald, sls dir.

Moosonee

CHMO(AM)—Feb 29, 1976: 1450 khz; 50 w. Box 400 (P0L 1Y0). (705) 336-2466. Licensee: James Bay Broadcasting Inc. Format: Div. Spec prog: Cree Indian 10 hrs wkly. ■ Bill Sleaver, gen mgr; Ron Spencer, progmg dir.

New Liskeard

CJTT(AM)—August 1967: 1230 khz; 1 kw-D, 250 w-N. 55 Whitewood Ave. (P0J 1P0). (705) 647-7334. FAX: (705) 647-8660. Licensee: Connelly Communications Corp. (acq 9-79). Net: BN. Rep: Paul Mulvihill. Format: Div. ■ Michael Perras, gen mgr & progmg dir; Gail Moore, sls dir.

Newmarket

CKDX(AM)—Feb 28, 1980: 1480 khz; 10 kw-D, 5 kw-N, DA-D. Stereo. 38 Parkside Dr. (L3Y 4R7). (905) 898-1100. FAX: (905) 853-4433. Licensee: CKAN Radio Ltd. Net: Standard Bcst. Format: Classic hits of the 50s, 60s, & 70s.

Niagara Falls

CJRN(AM)—June 1, 1947: 710 khz; 10 kw-D, 2.5 kw-N, DA-2. Stereo. Hrs opn: 24. Box 710 (L2E 6X7). (905) 356-6710. FAX: (905) 356-0696. Licensee: CJRN 710 Inc. (acq 12-78). Net: BN, CRN. Rep: All-Canada. Format: News, oldies, sports. News staff 5; news progmg 26 hrs wkly. Target aud: 25-54; sports fans. ■ Keith J. Dancy, CEO, adv dir & engrg dir; Elizabeth Lewis, opns mgr; David J. Dancy, gen sls mgr; Rob White, prom mgr; Robert K. Dancy, progmg dir & mus dir. ■ Rates: C$60; 50; 40; 50.

Nipigon-Red Rock

CFJQ-FM—Aug 24, 1990: 96.1 mhz. 100 w. Ant 189.4 ft. TL: N48 58 22 W88 18 28. Hrs opn: 24. 285-A Memorial Ave., Thunder Bay (P7B 6H4). (807) 345-5000. FAX: (807) 345-6814. Licensee: Newcap Broadcasting Ltd. Format: Country. News staff 5; news progmg 5 hrs wkly. Target aud: 25 plus. Spec prog: Finnish 2 hrs, It one hr, relg 4 hrs wkly. ■ Harry R. Steele, CEO; Bob Templeton, pres; David C. Saunders, exec vp; Warren Holte, vp; Remy C. Gagne, gen mgr, stn mgr, natl sls mgr & mktg dir; Bob Preston, opns dir & progmg dir; Mitch Larke, sls dir & adv mgr; Tracie Smith, prom dir; Bill Malcolm, mus dir; Tobin Lambie, news dir; John Visser, chief engr. ■ Rates: $45; 35; 25; 25.

North Bay

CFCH(AM)—Mar 3, 1931: 600 khz; 10 kw-D, 5 kw-N, DA-1. Hrs opn: 24. Box 3000 (P1B 8K8). (705) 474-2000. FAX: (705) 474-7761. Licensee: Telemedia Communications Inc. (group owner). Format: Adult contemp. News staff 7; news progmg 6 hrs wkly. Target aud: 25-54. ■ George Ferguson, gen mgr & progmg mgr; Rick Doughty, gen sls mgr; John Powers, asst mus dir; Clancy MacDonald, news dir; Csaba Senyi, engrg dir. ■ Rates: C$42; 38; 40; 36.

CKAT-FM—Co-owned with CFCH(AM). Jan 19, 1967: 101.9 mhz; 68 kw. Ant 350 ft. Stereo. Hrs opn: 24. (705) 474-3693. Format: C&W. Spec prog: Class 3 hrs, jazz 2 hrs wkly. ■ Jim Hamm, progmg dir.

CHUR(AM)—Sept 30, 1985: 840 khz; 10 kw-U, DA-2. Stereo. 215 Oak St. E. (P1B 8P8). (705) 472-1110. FAX: (705) 476-8400. Licensee: Pelmorex Broadcasting Inc. (group owner). Rep: United. Format: Oldies. News staff 4. Target aud: 25-54. Spec prog: Fr one hr wkly. ■ Pierre Morrissette, CEO; Patty Gysel, gen mgr & stn mgr; Rob Coatsworth, vp dev; Rick Ridgway, sls dir; Scott Jackson, progmg dir; Peter McPherson, news dir; Don Elvidge, engrg dir; Dawn Elvidge, chief engr.

CKAT-FM—Listing follows CFCH(AM).

Oakville

CHWO(AM)—Nov 17, 1956: 1250 khz; 10 kw-D, 5 kw-N, DA-2. Broadcasting Centre, 284 Church St. (L6J 7N2). (905) 845-2821; (905) 271-1320. FAX: (905) 842-1250. Licensee: CHWO Radio Ltd. Format: Nice radio/MOR. Spec prog: Portuguese 11 hrs, It 4 hrs, Pol 2 hrs, Sp 3 hrs, E. Indian 8 hrs wkly. ■ Michael Caine, pres & progmg dir; Harry McDonald, gen sls mgr; Berry Morden, mus dir.

Ohsweken

CKRZ-FM—1991: 100.3 mhz; 250 w. Box 189 (N0A 1M0). (519) 445-4140. Licensee: Amos Keye (on behalf of a not-for-profit native organization). Format: C&W. ■ Tom Morrison, gen mgr.

Orangeville

CIDC-FM—May 1, 1987: 103.5 mhz; 50 kw. Stereo. 287 Broadway Ave. (L9W 1L2). (519) 942-1030. FAX: (519) 942-2550. Licensee: Dufferin Communications Inc. Rep: All-Canada. Format: Adult contemp, oldies. News staff 3. Target aud: 25-49. ■ Douglas G. Cunningham, pres; Catherine Barr, opns mgr; Gail Toews, rgnl sls mgr; Vic Scerrie, mus dir; Brian Hatchell, news dir; Todd Ouellette, chief engr. ■ Rates: C$32; 32; 32; 24.

Orillia

CICX-FM—Sept 7, 1993: 105.9 mhz; 43 kw. Box 550 (L3V 6K2). (705) 326-3511. FAX: (705) 835-6505. Licensee: Telemedia Communications Inc. (group owner). Net: BN, Telemedia. Format: Country. ■ Doug Ackhurst, gen mgr; Barry Norman, gen sls mgr; Jack Latimer, progmg mgr.

Oshawa

CKDO(AM)—1946: 1350 khz; 10 kw-D, 5 kw-N, DA-2. Stereo. Hrs opn: 24. 360 King St. W. (L1J 2K2). (416) 571-1350. FAX: (416) 571-1150. Licensee: Power Broadcasting Inc. (group owner; acq 10-10-90). Rep: Paul Mulvihill. Format: Oldies. News staff 4; news progmg 9 hrs wkly. Target aud: 35-54. Spec prog: Relg one hr wkly. ■ Andre Desmarais, chmn; Peter Kruyt, pres; Yvon Chouinard, exec vp; Dave Lyman, vp & gen mgr; Marilyn Louw, vp sls; Martha McCain, prom dir; Lee Sterry, vp progmg; Bill Wilson, mus dir; Mark Orton, news dir; Frances Helyar, pub affrs dir; Paul Kudla, chief engr. ■ Rates: C$48; 44; 39; 25.

CKGE-FM—Co-owned with CKDO(AM). Sept 12, 1957: 94.9 mhz; 50 kw. Ant 474 ft. TL: N43 57 W78 48. Stereo. Hrs opn: 24. Prog sep from AM. Format: Btfl mus. News staff 4; news progmg 5 hrs wkly. Target aud: 45 plus. Spec prog: Jazz 2 hrs, relg one hr wkly. ■ Rates: C$38; 35; 31; 19.

Osnaburgh

CBQN-FM—January 1977: 104.5 mhz; 81 w. Ant 164 ft. Rebroadcasts CBQT-FM Thunder Bay. 213 Miles St. E., Thunder Bay (P7C 1J5). (807) 625-5000. Licensee: CBC. Net: CBC. Format: Info radio. ■ Wilder Lewis, stn mgr.

Ottawa

*****CBO-FM**—Jan 7, 1991: 91.5 mhz; 20 kw. Box 3220, Station C (K1Y 1E4). (613) 724-1200; (613) 598-3400. FAX: (613) 598-3430; (613) 598-3408. Licensee: CBC. Format: Div, talk. News staff 6. ■ Doug Ward, gen mgr.

CBOF(AM)—Aug 1, 1964: 1250 khz; 50 kw-U, DA-2. Box 3220, Station C (K1Y 1E4). (613) 598-3400. TELEX: 053-4260. Licensee: Societe Radio-Canada. Net: CBC. ■ Sylvain Lafrance, gen mgr.

CBOF-FM—Sept 12, 1974: 102.5 mhz; 70 kw. Ant 1,077 ft. Stereo. Dups AM 100%.

Broadcasting & Cable Yearbook 1994

***CBOQ-FM**—Feb 18, 1947: 103.3 mhz; 70 kw. Stereo. Box 3220, Station C (K1Y 1E4). (613) 724-1200; (613) 598-3400. FAX: (613) 598-3430; (613) 598-3408. Licensee: CBC. Format: Div. ■ Doug Ward, gen mgr.

CFGO(AM)—June 7, 1964: 1200 khz; 50 kw-U, DA-2. Stereo. 1575 Carling Ave. (K1Z 7M3). (613) 729-1200. FAX: (613) 729-9829. Licensee: Rawlco Communications. (group owner; acq 1-9-87). Format: CHR. Target aud: 18-34. ■ Gord Rawlinson, pres; Doug Rawlinson, exec vp; Dianne Wilson, gen mgr; Carol Ham, opns mgr; Ross Tirrell, sls dir; Scott Broderick, rgnl sls mgr; Len Hanes, prom dir; Kim Sumers, progmg dir; Don Kollins, mus dir; Steve Kennedy, asst mus dir; Bill Parker, news dir; Judy Villeneuve, pub affrs dir; Marc Germain, chief engr.

CJMJ-FM—Co-owned with CFGO(AM). Aug 13, 1991: 100.3 mhz; 100 kw. Stereo. Hrs opn: 24. Format: Adult contemp. Target aud: 25-54. ■ Don Robb, CFO; Douglas E. Rawlinson, exec vp; Don Armstrong, vp dev; Ross Tirrel, vp sls; Brad Beckler, rgnl sls mgr; Al MacCartney, prom mgr; Sandy Davis, progmg mgr; Kim Summers, mus dir.

CFRA(AM)—May 3, 1947: 580 khz; 50 kw-D, 10 kw-N, DA-2. Hrs opn: 24. 1900 Walkley Rd. (K1H 8P4). (613) 738-2372. FAX: (613) 523-6423; (613) 738-5024. Licensee: CFRA/CKKL-FM (division of CHUM Ltd.) Group owner: CHUM Ltd. Net: BN. Format: Oldies. News progmg 8 hrs wkly. Target aud: 25-54. ■ Allan Waters, pres; Don Holtby, vp & gen mgr; Larry Kelly, natl sls mgr; Jack DeRouin, rgnl sls mgr; Dave Watts, prom mgr; Mark Maheu, progmg mgr; Steve Winogron, news dir; Harry Jones, engrg mgr.

CKKL-FM—Co-owned with CFRA(AM). 1959: 93.9 mhz; 95 kw. Ant 1,077 ft. Stereo. Hrs opn: 24. Prog sep from AM. Format: Adult contemp, new age.

CHEZ-FM—Mar 25, 1977: 106.1 mhz; 100 kw. Ant 998 ft. Stereo. Suite 509, 126 York St. (K1N 5T5). (613) 562-1061. FAX: (613) 562-1515. Licensee: CHEZ-FM Inc. Rep: Paul Mulvihill. Format: AOR. Spec prog: Jazz 2 hrs, blues 2 hrs wkly. ■ Chuck Azzello, pres & gen mgr; David Schutte, prom dir; Diane Benson, news dir.

***CHUO-FM**—May 31, 1991: 89.1 mhz; 18.2 kw. TL: N45 30 11 W75 51 02. Stereo. Hrs opn: 24. 85 University Ave., Suite 227 (K1N 6N5). (613) 564-2903. FAX: (613) 564-5479. Licensee: Radio Ottawa Inc. Format: Diverse, bilingual Eng-Fr. News staff 2; news progmg 6 hrs wkly. Target aud: General. Spec prog: Black 8 hrs, class 4 hrs, folk 3 hrs, Ger 2 hrs, jazz 5 hrs, relg 2 hrs, Sp 3 hrs, Chinese 2 hrs wkly. ■ Matthieu Brennan, pres; Michael Aucoin, CFO; Guy Caron, vp; Patrick Martin, stn mgr; Carole Breton, sls dir; Serge Desrochers, prom dir; Mireille Messier, progmg dir; Arun Parkayastha, mus dir; Ricardo Van Sertima, asst mus dir; Serge Quinty, news dir; Robert Gougeon, pub affrs dir; Ozcan Sersan, engrg mgr; John Matthews, chief engr. ■ Rates: C$50; 40; 50; 20.

CIWW(AM)—June 1, 1949: 1310 khz; 50 kw-U, DA-2. Suite 1900, 112 Kent St. (K1P 6J1). (613) 238-7482. FAX: (613) 236-5382. Licensee: Key Radio Ltd. Net: Newsradio. Format: Classic hits. ■ Paul Nattall, gen mgr; Doug Chard, gen sls mgr; Dan Harvey, progmg dir.

CKBY-FM—Co-owned with CIWW(AM). Oct 29, 1969: 105.3 mhz; 100 kw. Ant 1,077 ft. Stereo. Prog sep from AM. Format: Country.

CJMJ-FM—Listing follows CFGO(AM).

CJRC(AM)—(Gatineau, Que.). June 3, 1968: 1150 khz; 50 kw-D, 5 kw-N, DA-2. 22 St. Louis St., Gatineau, PQ (J8T2R9). (819) 561-8801. Licensee: CJRC Radio Capitale Limit. Group owner: Radiomutuel Inc. Net: Radiomutuel. Format: News/talk. News staff 5; news progmg 45 hrs wkly. Target aud: 25-54. ■ Jacques Papin, gen mgr & sls dir; Michel St.-Cyr, prom dir, progmg dir & news dir; Marc Delorme, mus dir; Andre Bonneau, engrg dir.

CJSB(AM)—Aug 31, 1982: 540 khz; 50 kw-D, 12.5 kw-N, DA-2. Stereo. Hrs opn: 24. 1504 Merivale Rd., Nepean (K2E 6Z5). (613) 226-5450. FAX: (613) 226-8480 NEWS; (613) 226-3381 OFFICE. Licensee: Standard Radio Inc. Group owner: Standard Broadcasting Corp. Net: Telemedia. Rep: Paul Mulvihill. Format: Classic rock, AOR, div. News staff 3; news progmg one hr wkly. Target aud: 18-34; M/F professionals 18-34 & 20-40 demos. ■ Gary Slaight, CEO & pres; Gary Aube, vp, gen mgr, stn mgr, mktg mgr & progmg dir; Peter Mayhew, gen sls mgr & adv mgr; Gord Taylor, prom mgr & mus dir; Gord Taylor (asst), progmg mgr; Brian Kelly, pub affrs dir; Jeff Ruck, chief engr.

NEW FM—Co-owned with CJSB(AM). Not on air, target date unknown: 106.9 mhz; 84 kw. Stereo. Licensee: Standard Radio Corp. (group owner). ■ Peter Mayhew, natl sls mgr; Darryl MacArthur, rgnl sls mgr; Marisa Golini, news dir.

CKBY-FM—Listing follows CIWW(AM).

CKCU-FM—Nov 15, 1975: 93.1 mhz; 12 kw. Ant 853 ft. TL: N45 30 11 W75 51 02. Stereo. Hrs opn: 24. Carleton Univ., 517 Unicentre (K1S 5B6). (613) 788-2898; (613) 788-3572. FAX: (613) 788-4060. Licensee: Radio Carleton Inc. Rep: Target. Format: Progr, div, community. News staff 2; news progmg 25 hrs wkly. Target aud: General; alternative rock and spoken word as well as ethnic audience. Spec prog: Jazz 15 hrs, Black 12 hrs, Fr 2 hrs, Pol one hr, Vietnamese one hr, Canadian Indian 2 hrs, folk 12 hrs, It one hr, relg 3 hrs wkly. ■ Max Wallace, CEO & stn mgr; Karen McHarg, sls dir & adv dir; Kevin Gibbs, mktg dir & prom dir; Lance Baptisse, progmg dir; Shawn Scallin, mus dir; Alka Sharma, news dir; Fred Fayuk, engrg dir.

CKKL-FM—Listing follows CFRA(AM).

NEW FM—Not on air, target date unknown: 96.5 mhz; 100 kw. Licensee: Arthur J. Hustins Jr. (acq 3-5-90). Format: Easy listng.

NEW FM—Listing follows CJSB(AM).

Owen Sound

CFOS(AM)—Mar 1, 1940: 560 khz; 7.5 kw-D, 1 kw-N, DA-2. TL: N44 32 40 W80 54 08 Hrs opn: 24. 270 Ninth St. E. (N4K 1N7). (519) 376-2030. FAX: (519) 371-9683. Licensee: Bayshore Broadcating Corp. Net: SBN. Rep: Paul Mulvihill. Format: Oldies, news/talk. News staff 5; news progmg 12 hrs wkly. Target aud: 35 plus. ■ Ross Kentner, CEO; Douglas Caldwell, pres; Betty Watson, CFO; Mack Frizzell, vp sls; Lynn Scott, mktg mgr; Madelyn Hamilton, progmg dir; Jamie Hall, mus dir; Owen Smart, news dir; Robert Coyne, engrg dir.

CIXK-FM—Co-owned with CFOS(AM). Jan 3, 1988: 106.5 mhz; 100 kw. Ant 555 ft. TL: N44 44 37 W80 54 16. Stereo. Prog sep from AM. Royal LePage Plaza, 328 First St, 2nd Fl., Collingswood (L9Y 3Z3). Net: BN. Format: New Country, acoustic rock. Target aud: 18-40. ■ Adel Middleton, mus dir.

Parry Sound

CKLP-FM—July 1986: 103.3 mhz; 50 kw. Ant 400 ft. (CP: 46.6 kw). Stereo. Hrs opn: 24. 4 Miller St. (P2A 1S8). (705) 746-2163. FAX: (705) 746-4292. Licensee: Playland Broadcasting Ltd. (acq 3-29-86). Rep: Target. Format: MOR, oldies. News staff 2; news progmg 12 hrs wkly. Target aud: General. ■ Bob Bowland, pres, stn mgr & chief engr; Geoff Osborne, opns dir & progmg dir; Ron Beckett, gen sls mgr; Brian Prokopec, rgnl sls mgr; Jeff Orchard, news dir & pub affrs dir. ■ Rates: C$24; 16; 24; 16.

Pembroke

CHVR(AM)—Aug 25, 1942: 1350 khz; 1 kw-U, DA-1. 595 Pembroke St. E. (K8A 3L7). (613) 735-1350. FAX: (613) 735-7748. Licensee: Ottawa Valley Broadcasting Co Ltd. Group owner: Pelmorex Broadcasting Inc. (acq 4-1-81). Rep: United. Format: Adult contemp. News staff 4. Target aud: 25-49. ■ Pierre Morrisette, pres; Don Shaffer, vp; Al Kennedy, gen mgr; Mike Thurnell, opns mgr; Jamie Branburger, news dir. ■ Rates: C$23; 21; 18; 16.

Peterborough

***CFFF-FM**—1969: 96.3 mhz. Trent University (K9J 7B8). (705) 748-1777. FAX: (705) 748-1795. Licensee: Trent Radio. Format: Div. ■ Rob Phillips, gen mgr.

CKPT(AM)—Dec 1959: 1420 khz; 10 kw-D, 5 kw-N, DA-2. Hrs opn: 24. Box 177, 340 George St. N. (K9J GY8). (705) 742-8844. FAX: (705) 742-1417. Licensee: CKPT/CKQM-FM Division of CHUM Ltd. Group owner: CHUM Ltd. Rep: Major Mkt. Format: Adult contemp. News staff 5. ■ Allan Waters, pres; Taylor Baiden, CFO; Fred Sherratt, exec vp; Bob Laine, John Wood, sr vps; Stan Genno, gen mgr; Vicki Bonicci, gen sls mgr; Dan Gall, progmg dir; Don Errey, news dir; Ed Cromptom, engrg dir. ■ Rates: C$38; 31; 31; 17.

CKQM-FM—Co-owned with CKPT(AM). Sept 16, 1977: 105.1 mhz; 50 kw. Ant 301 ft. Stereo. Hrs opn: 24. Prog sep from AM. Format: Country. ■ Rick Walters, progmg dir. ■ Rates: C$43; 36; 36; 24.

CKRU(AM)—Mar 21, 1942: 980 khz; 10 kw-D, 7.5 kw-D, DA-2. 1925 Television Rd. (K9J 6Z9). (705) 742-7708. FAX: (705) 742-7274. Licensee: Power Broadcasting Inc. Net: BN. Rep: Paul Mulvihill. Format: CHR. ■ Randy Redden, pres; Wally Macht, news dir; Ben Wilke, chief engr.

CKWF-FM—Co-owned with CKRU(AM). July 24, 1968: 101.5 mhz; 31.4 kw. Ant 518 ft. (CP: 48.5 kw). Stereo. Prog sep from AM. (705) 748-6101. Net: Newsradio. Format: Lite rock. Spec prog: Jazz 12 hrs wkly.

Pickle Lake

CBQP-FM—May 1977: 105.1 mhz; 83 w. Rebroadcasts CBQT-FM Thunder Bay. c/o CBQT-FM, 213 Miles St. E., Thunder Bay (P7C 1J5). Licensee: CBC. Net: CBC. Format: Info radio. ■ Wilder Lewis, stn mgr.

Port Elgin

CFPS(AM)—June 21, 1978: 1490 khz; 1 kw-U. TL: N44 24 58 W81 23 31. Hrs opn: 24. Rebroadcasts CFOS(AM) Owen Sound. Maple Square Mall, Goderich St. (N0H 2C0). (519) 389-4911. Licensee: Bayshore Broadcasting Corp. Format: Oldies. ■ Ross Kentner, progmg dir; Adel Middleton, mus dir.

Red Lake

CKDR-5(AM)—Aug 1, 1981: 1340 khz; 250 w-U, DA-1. Box 580, c/o CKDR, Dryden (P8N 2Z3). (807) 223-2355. FAX: (807) 223-5090. Licensee: Fawcett Broadcasting Ltd. (group owner). Rep: Major Mkt. Format: Adult contemp, CHR. ■ Bruce Walchuk, gen mgr & progmg dir.

Renfrew

CHVR-1(AM)—Sept 12, 1974: 1400 khz; 1 kw-U, DA-1. 690 Stewart St. (K7V 1Y6). (613) 432-6428. FAX: (613) 432-8236. Licensee: Ottawa Valley Radio. Group owner: Pelmorex Bcstg Inc. (acq 10-17-86). Rep: United. Format: Adult contemp. News staff one. Target aud: 25-49. ■ Pierre Morisette, pres; Al Kennedy, gen mgr; Scott Jackson, opns mgr; Jamie Branburger, news dir. ■ Rates: C$23; 21; 18; 16.

Richmond Hill

CHOG(AM)—July 1, 1957: 640 khz; 50 kw-U, DA-2. Stereo. Suite 1400, 5255 Yonge St., North York (M2N 6P4). (416) 221-6400. FAX: (416) 883-9785. Licensee: Western Radio Group Ltd. (acq 1985). Net: BN. Rep: United Broadcast Sales. Format: Contemp country. News staff 6. ■ Danny Kingsbury, progmg dir.

St. Catharines

CHRE-FM—Mar 1, 1967: 105.7 mhz; 100 kw. Ant 438 ft. Stereo. Hrs opn: 24. Corblock Bldg., 2nd Floor, 80 King St. (L2R 7G1). (905) 688-1057; NEWS (905) 984-6397. FAX: (905) 688-3377; NEWS (905) 688-3522. Format: Adult contemp. News staff 3. Target aud: 25-54. ■ Robert E. Redmond, pres; Jay R. Jackson, exec vp; Erin Redmond, gen mgr & prom dir; Norma Thiessen, gen sls mgr; Craig James, mus dir & pub affrs dir; Frank Fanstone, news dir; Larry Garrington, chief engr.

CHSC(AM)—Mar 20, 1967: 1220 khz; 10 kw-U, DA-2. 36 Queenston St. (L2R 2Y9). (905) 682-6691. FAX: (905) 682-9434. Licensee: Douglas S.K. Setterington (acq 3-13-90). Rep: Paul Mulvihill. Format: Adult contemp. Target aud: 25-54; female. ■ Doug Setterington, pres; John Larocque, opns mgr; Paul Carfagnini, gen sls mgr; Ted Yates, progmg dir & mus dir; Ed Eldred, news dir; Larry Garrington, chief engr.

CHTZ-FM—Listing follows CKTB(AM).

CKTB(AM)—1930: 610 khz; 10 kw-D, 5 kw-N, DA-1. Box 610 (L2R 6X7). (905) 684-1174. FAX: (905) 684-4800. Licensee: CFRB Ltd. Group owner: Standard Broadcasting Corp. Format: MOR.

CHTZ-FM—Co-owned with CKTB(AM). February 1949: 97.7 mhz; 50 kw. Ant 414 ft. Stereo. (905) 688-0977. Format: Rock (AOR).

St. Thomas

CHLO(AM)—May 14, 1948: 1570 khz; 10 kw-U, DA-2. 133 Curtis St. (N5P 485). (519) 637-1572. FAX: (519) 631-4693. Licensee: CHLO Radio Ltd. (acq 9-25-81). Format: Country. ■ Vern Furber, gen mgr.

Sarnia

CBEG-FM—Nov 27, 1977: 90.3 mhz; 50 kw. Ant 375 ft. Rebroadcasts CBE(AM) Windsor. c/o CBE Radio, 267 Pelissier St., Windsor (N9A 4K5). (519) 255-3411. Licensee: CBC. Format: Info Radio. ■ Bruce Taylor, stn mgr.

CFGX-FM—Listing follows CKTY(AM).

CHOK(AM)—July 26, 1946: 1070 khz; 10 kw-U, DA-2. TL: N42 53 30 W82 19 20. Stereo. Hrs opn: 24. Box 1070,

148 N. Front St. (N7T 7K5). (519) 336-1070. FAX: (519) 336-7523. Licensee: W. Wayne Steele, on behalf of a company to be incorporated (acq 12-1-93; $485,000). Rep: Canadian Broadcast Sales. Format: Oldies. News staff 3; news progmg 11 hrs wkly. Target aud: 25-54. ■ Wayne Steele, vp & gen mgr; Paul Godfrey, progmg dir; Len Smith, mus dir; Larry Gordan, news dir; David Barry, chief engr. ■ Rates: $40; 28; 30; 22.

CKTY(AM)—Aug 3, 1968: 1110 khz; 10 kw-D, 1 kw-N, DA-2. 1415 London Rd. (N7S 1P6). (519) 332-5500. FAX: (519) 542-1520. Licensee: Blue Water Broadcasting Ltd. (acq 9-87). Net: BN. Rep: Paul Mulvihill. Format: Country. ■ John Divinski, gen mgr; Tom Yates, gen sls mgr; Steve Glenn, progmg dir; Mark Cartland, mus dir; Barry Wright, news dir; Brian Hinz, chief engr.

CFGX-FM—Co-owned with CKTY(AM). Sept 14, 1981: 99.9 mhz; 27 kw. Stereo. Format: Adult contemp. Spec prog: Jazz 7 hrs wkly. ■ John Harada, progmg dir; Ron Dann, mus dir.

Sault Ste. Marie

CHAS-FM—May 15, 1964: 100.5 mhz; 13.9 kw. Ant 103 ft. Stereo. 642 Great Northern Rd. (P6B 429). (705) 759-9200. FAX: (705) 942-6549. Licensee: Telemedia Communications (group owner; acq 7-2-85). Net: Telemedia. Format: Adult contemp. Spec prog: Class 5 hrs, jazz 2 hrs, It 2 wkly. ■ Tracy Gard, gen mgr & sls dir; James Warner Smith, prom dir & progmg dir; Ray Rylatt, chief engr.

CJQM-FM—May 13, 1964: 104. 3 mhz; 100 kw. Ant 1,000 ft. Stereo. 642 Great Northern Rd. (P6B 429). (705) 759-9200. Licensee: CJQM-FM Radio Group owner: Pelmorex Communications Inc. (acq 3-1-85). Net: Newsradio. Rep: CBS. Format: Country. Spec prog: It 4 hrs wkly. ■ Pierre Morissette, pres; Tracey Gard, gen mgr; Bruce Krause, progmg dir.

Savant Lake

CBQL-FM—January 1977: 104.9 mhz; 78 w. Ant 287 ft. Rebroadcasts CBQT-FM Thunder Bay. c/o CBQT-FM, 213 Miles St. E., Thunder Bay (P7C 1J5). Licensee: CBC. Net: CBC. Format: Info radio. ■ Wilder Lewis, stn mgr.

Simcoe

CHNR(AM)—June 23, 1956: 1600 khz; 10 kw-U, DA-1. Box 1600 (N3Y 4K8). (519) 426-7700. FAX: (519) 426-8574. Licensee: Redmond Broadcasting Co. Inc. Net: BN. Rep: Paul Mulvihill. Format: Adult contemp, farm. ■ Clarke Drennan, gen mgr.

Sioux Narrows

CBQS-FM—May 1977: 95.7 mhz; 1.3 kw. Ant 134 ft. Rebroadcasts CBQT-FM Thunder Bay 100%. c/o CBC Radio, 1500 Bronson Ave., Ottawa (K1G 3J5); 213 Miles St. E., Thunder Bay (P7C 1J5). (807) 625-5000. FAX: (807) 625-5035. Licensee: CBC. Format: Div. Spec prog: Canadian Indian one hr wkly. ■ Wilder Lewis, stn mgr.

Smiths Falls

CJET(AM)—Oct 22, 1955: 630 khz; 10 kw-U, DA-2. Hrs opn: 24. Box 630, Jasper Rd. (K7A 4T4). (613) 283-4630. FAX: (613) 283-7243. Licensee: Rideau Broadcasting (Div. of CHEZ-FM Inc.). (acq 2-84). Rep: Paul Mulvihill. Format: Classical country. News staff 2; news progmg 5 hrs wkly. Target aud: 25-49; classic country fans, relg listeners. Spec prog: Relg 20 hrs wkly. ■ Chuck Azzarello, pres; Gary Perrin, gen mgr & gen sls mgr; Brian Perkin, opns mgr; Wayne Kerfoot, prom mgr; John Chatwood, mus dir; Lynda Steele, news dir; Wayne Henwood, engrg mgr. ■ Rates: C$26; 24; 17; na.

CFMO-FM—Co-owned with CJET(AM). Jan 29, 1969: 101.1 mhz; 100 kw. Ant 500 ft. Stereo. Hrs opn: 24. Prog sep from AM. Net: Telemedia. Format: Easy lstng. News staff 2; news progmg 6 hrs wkly. Target aud: 40 plus; mainstream, Toronto Blue Jays and Montreal Canadiens fans. ■ Rates: C$44; 37; 37; 16.

Stratford

CJCS(AM)—1928: 1240 khz; 1 kw U, DA-1. Box 904, 178 Ontario St. (N5A 6W3). (519) 271-2450. Licensee: Telemedia Communications Inc. (group owner; acq 3-78). Net: Telemedia. Rep: Telemedia Sales. Format: Oldies. News staff 2. Target aud: 25-54. ■ Don Pugnutti, exec vp; Doug Ackhurst, vp; Steve Rae, stn mgr & sls dir; Tracey Nearing, prom dir; Lynn Riddell, progmg mgr; James Cottle, mus dir; Doug Lester, news dir; Gary Hooper, vp engrg. ■ Rates: C$44; 34; 34; 25.

Sudbury

CBCS-FM—June 19, 1978: 99.9 mhz; 50 kw. Ant 250 ft. 15 Mackenzie St. (P3C 4Y1). (705) 688-3200. FAX: (705) 688-3224. Licensee: Radio-Canada/CBC. Net: CBC Radio. Format: Informational. ■ David Henley, gen mgr.

***CBON-FM**—June 19, 1978: 98.1 mhz; 50 kw. Ant 800 ft. Stereo. 15 Mackenzie St. (P3C 4Y1). (705) 688-3200. FAX: (705) 688-3224. Licensee: Radio-Canada/CBC. Net: CBC, Societe Radio-Canada. Format: Var. ■ Claude Hurtubise, gen mgr.

CHNO(AM)—1946: 550 khz; 50 kw-D, 10 kw-N, DA-2. Stereo. 295 Victoria St. (P3C 1K5). (705) 674-6401. Licensee: Pelmorex Broadcasting Inc. (group owner). Rep: United. Format: Oldies. News progmg 7 hrs wkly. Target aud: 25-44; M/F, middle-income. ■ Pierre Morissette, pres; Don Shafer, vp; Gary Duguay, opns dir; Rob Coatsworth, vp dev; Rick Ridgway, sls dir & natl sls mgr; Therese Douval-Blouin, mktg mgr; Vicky Belfiore, prom mgr; Dave Lindsay, mus dir; Paul Scott, news dir; Don Elvidge, engrg dir.

CJMX-FM—Co-owned with CHNO(AM). 1980: 105.3 mhz; 100 kw. Ant 780 ft. Stereo. Prog sep from AM. Format: Adult contemp. News progmg 7 hrs wkly. Spec prog: Nostalgia 4 hrs wkly. ■ Don Shafer, gen mgr.

CHYC(AM)—Dec 8, 1957: 900 khz; 10 kw-D, 1 kw-N, DA-2. 295 Victoria St. (P3C 1K5). (705) 674-6401. FAX: (705) 674-8334. Licensee: Pelmorex Radio Inc. (group owner; acq 9-1-90). Rep: United. Format: CHR, adult contemp. Target aud: General. Spec prog: French. ■ Robert Perreault, progmg dir.

CIGM(AM)—Aug 23, 1935: 790 khz; 50 kw-U, DA-2. 880 Lasalle Blvd. (P3A 5W7). (705) 566-4480. FAX: (705) 560-7232. Licensee: Telemedia Communications Ontario Inc. Group owner: Telemedia Communications Inc. (acq 10-6-86). Rep: Telemedia. Format: Adult contemp. ■ Bob Templeton, gen mgr; Tom Manton, sls dir; Terry Williams, progmg dir; Brian Band, news dir.

CJRQ-FM—Co-owned with CIGM(AM). September 1965: 92.7 mhz; 100 kw. Ant 889 ft. Stereo. Format: C&W.

CJMX-FM—Listing follows CHNO(AM).

CJRQ-FM—Listing follows CIGM(AM).

Thunder Bay

***CBQ-FM**—July 5, 1984: 101.7 mhz; 23.5 kw. 900 ft. Stereo. Hrs opn: 24. 213 Miles St. E. (P7C 1J5). (807) 625-5000. FAX: (807) 625-5035. Licensee: CBC. Net: CBC. Format: Div. ■ Wilder Lewis, stn mgr; Holly Pyhtila, prom mgr; Lisa Brown, progmg mgr; Jim Symonik, news dir; Randy Creighton, engrg dir.

***CBQT-FM**—August 1990: 88.3 mhz; 23.5 kw. Hrs opn: 19. 213 Miles St. E. (P7C 1J5). (807) 625-5000. FAX: (807) 625-5035. Licensee: CBC. Net: CBC. Format: Div. Northwestern Ontario residents. Spec prog: Canadian Indian one hr wkly. ■ Wilder Lewis, gen mgr; Holly Pyhtila, prom mgr; Lisa Brown, progmg dir; Jim Symonik, news dir; Randy Creighton, engrg dir.

CJLB(AM)—Sept 3, 1944: 1230 khz; 4 kw-D, 1 kw-N, DA-1. TL: N48 24 23 W89 13 53. Stereo. Hrs opn: 24. 285-A Memorial Ave. (P7B 6H4). (807) 345-5000. FAX: (807) 345-6814. Licensee: Newcap Broadcasting Ltd. (group owner; acq 5-4-88). Net: Sun. Rep: CBS. Format: Country. News staff 5; news progmg 4 hrs wkly. Target aud: 25 plus. Spec prog: It, relg, Finnish one hr wkly. ■ Harry R. Steele, CEO; Bob Templeton, pres; David C. Saunders, exec vp; Warren Holte, vp; Remy C. Gagne, gen mgr, stn mgr & natl sls mgr; Bob Preston, opns dir & progmg dir; Mitch Larke, sls dir & adv mgr; Tracie Smith, prom dir; Bill Malcolm, mus dir; Tobin Lambie, news dir; John Visser, chief engr. ■ Rates: C$45; 35; 25; 25.

CJSD-FM—Listing follows CKPR(AM).

CKPR(AM)—Feb 3, 1931: 580 khz; 5 kw-D, 1 kw-N. 87 N. Hill St. (P7A 5V6). (807) 346-2580. FAX: (807) 345-4671. Licensee: C.J.S.D. Inc. (acq 5-25-92). Net: Newsradio. Rep: Major Mkt. Format: Adult contemp, classic hits. Target aud: 30-50; families & office workers. Spec prog: Finnish one hr, relg one hr wkly. ■ H.F. Dougall, pres; Jerry G. Cox, gen mgr, natl sls mgr, rgnl sls mgr & progmg dir; Cher Ames-Arbouw, prom mgr; Julie Mazzafgro, mus dir; Victor Karasowski, news dir; Manfred Volbracht, chief engr. ■ Rates: C$72; 56; 64; 35.

CJSD-FM—Co-owned with CKPR(AM). October 1948: 94.3 mhz; 95 kw-U. Ant 1,009 ft. Stereo. Prog sep from AM. Format: Adult rock. Target aud: 18-44. ■ Jerry G. Cox, gen mgr; Rob Brown, progmg dir. CKPR-TV & CHFD-TV affil. ■ Rates: C$89; 69; 64;44.

Tillsonburg

CKOT(AM)—Apr 30, 1955: 1510 khz; 10 kw-D, DA-D. Box 10, 77 Broadway (N4G 4H3). (519) 842-4281. FAX: (519) 842-4284. Licensee: Tillsonburg Broadcasting Co. Ltd. Rep: Target. Format: MOR, adult contemp, CHR. News staff 5; news progmg 7 hrs wkly. Target aud: General; 18-50. Spec prog: Ger one hr, Hungarian one hr, Belgian one hr, Dutch one hr wkly. ■ John D. Lamers, gen mgr; Doug Coofer, progmg dir; Rick Haylowe, news dir; Robert Lamers, chief engr.

CKOT-FM—Dec 1, 1965: 101.3 mhz; 50 kw. Ant 454 ft. Stereo. Format: Btfl mus. Target aud: General; 30 plus. Spec prog: Gospel one hr wkly.

Timmins

CJQQ-FM—Listing follows CKGB(AM).

CKGB(AM)—Sept 15, 1933: 750 khz; 10 kw-U, 5 kw-N, DA-2. Hrs opn: 24. Box 1046, 155 Pine St. S. (P4N 7H8). (705) 264-2351. FAX: (705) 264-2984. Licensee: Telemedia Communications Ontario Inc. (group owner; acq 3-80). Net: Telemedia, BN. Format: Country. News staff 2. Target aud: 35-55. ■ Phillipe De Gaspe Beaubien, chmn; James McCoubrey, pres; Don Pagnutti, exec vp; Chris Ruscica, gen mgr; Gates Cooney, rgnl sls mgr; Art Pultz, progmg mgr; Dave McLaughlin, mus dir; Dale Tonelli, news dir; Gary Hooper, engrg dir; Scott Sloan, chief engr.

CJQQ-FM—Co-owned with CKGB(AM). Sept 6, 1976: 92.1 mhz; 17.2 kw. Ant 400 ft. Stereo. Hrs opn: 24. Prog sep from AM. Net: BN, Telemedia. Format: AOR. Target aud: 18-44.

CKOY(AM)—Dec 23, 1951: 620 khz; 10 kw-D, 5 kw-N, DA-2. Box 1340, Suite 6, 14 Pine St. S. (P4N 7J8). (705) 267-6070; (705) 267-6098. FAX: (705) 267-6095. Licensee: CKOY Radio. Group owner: Pelmorex Broadcasting Inc. (acq 9-1-90). Net: BN. Format: Soft rock, adult contemp. Target aud: 18-40. Spec prog: Finnish. ■ Perre Morisstte, pres; Dennis Bouchard, gen mgr; Marc Moncion, sls dir. ■ Rates: $18; 12; 15; 12.

Toronto

CBL(AM)—1927: 740 khz; 50 kw-U. Box 500, Station A (M5W 1E6). (416) 205-7400. FAX: (416) 205-6336. Licensee: CBC. Net: CBC Radio. Format: Talk. News staff 10. ■ Gloria Bishop, stn mgr.

CBL-FM—1946: 94.1 mhz; 55.7 kw. Ant 389 ft. Stereo. Prog sep from AM. Format: Class, talk.

CFMX-FM-1—(Mississauga). 1988: 96.3 mhz. 43.1 kw. Ant. 930 ft. TL: N56 43 38 W55 79 22 (CP: 13.3 kw). Stereo. Hrs opn: 24. Rebroadcasts CFMX-FM Coburg 100%. Suite 101, 468 Queen St. East, Toronto (M5A 1T7). (416) 367-5353; (905) 372-4366. FAX: (416) 367-1742; (905) 372-1625. Licensee: Martin Rosenthal (acq 1983). Rep: Telemedia. Wash atty: Robson Broadcast Consultants Inc. Format: Class. News staff 2; news progmg 4 hrs wkly. Target aud: 35+; Well educated, upscale, owners/managers/professionals. ■ Martin Rosenthal, pres; Truus Rosenthal, vp; Jerry Good, stn mgr; Rod Walker, gen sls mgr; Monica Tynan Day, prom dir; John van Driel, progmg dir; Robert Bier, Richard Haskell, Michael Lyons, mus dirs; David Franco, Bill Dulmage, news dirs; John Ton, chief engr. ■ Rates: C$75; 75; 75; 75.

CFNY-FM—See Brampton.

CFRB(AM)—Feb 19, 1927: 1010 khz: 50 kw-U, DA-2. Stereo. 2 St. Clair Ave. W. (M4V 1L6). (416) 924-5711. FAX: (416) 323-6830. Licensee: Standard Broadcasting Corp. Ltd. Group owner: Standard Broadcasting Corp. (acq 1985). Rep: United. Format: News & info. Spec prog: Class 7 hrs, farm 2 hrs wkly. ■ Roy Hennessy, gen mgr. ■ CFRX(SW) affil.

CKFM-FM—Co-owned with CFRB(AM). July 1, 1961: 99.9 mhz; 40 kw. Ant 1,550 ft. Stereo. Prog sep from AM. (416) 922-9999. FAX: (416) 323-6800. Group owner: Standard Broadcasting Corp. Format: Adult contemp. News progmg 5 hrs wkly. Target aud: 25-49. Spec prog: Jazz 3 hrs wkly. ■ Gary Slate, gen mgr.

CFTR(AM)—Aug 8, 1962: 680 khz; 50 kw. Stereo. 25 Adelaide St. E. (M5C 1H3). (416) 864-2000. FAX: (416) 864-2002; (416) 864-2090. Licensee: Rogers Broadcasting Ltd. Rep: Canadian Broadcast Sales. Format: All news. News staff 45; news progmg 168 hrs wkly. Target aud: 35-44. ■ Anthony P. Viner, CEO & pres; Sandy Sanderson, exec vp & gen mgr; John Hinnen, vp opns & news

Prince Edward Island | **Directory of Radio**

dir; Gary Murphy, gen sls mgr; Robb Collis, mktg dir & prom mgr; Kirk Nesbitt, chief engr.

CHFI-FM—Co-owned with CFTR(AM). Feb 8, 1957: 98.1 mhz; 44 kw. Ant 1,815 ft. Stereo. (416) 864-2070. Format: Soft adult contemp. News staff one; news progmg 3 hrs wkly. Target aud: 25-54. ■ Scott Parsons, gen sls mgr; Christopher McDowall, prom mgr; Paul Fisher, vp progmg; Drew Keith, mus dir; John Hinnen, news dir; Arlene Bynon, pub affrs dir.

CHIN(AM)—1966: 1540 khz; 50 kw-D, 30 kw-N, DA-2. TL: N43 35 32 W79 39 22. Stereo. Hrs opn: 24. 622 College St. (M6G 1B6). (416) 531-9991. FAX: (416) 531-5274. Licensee: Radio 1540 Ltd. Rep: Target. Format: Ethnic/multilingual (18 languages). News staff 4; news progmg 9 hrs wkly. Target aud: 30 plus; the one million immigrants in the Toronto census metropolitan area. ■ Johnny Lombardi, CEO & pres; Lenny Lombardi, exec vp; Theresa Lombardi (admin), sr vp; Bob Culliton, gen mgr; Carl Redhead, stn mgr & vp opns; Eddie Lelievre, sls dir; Lorne Simon, prom mgr; Umberto Manca (Italian), vp progmg; Marco Manna (Italian), mus dir; Shahnaz Bhatti, engrg dir.

CHIN-FM—1967: 100.7 mhz; 8.5 kw. Ant 1,700 ft. TL: N48 38 33 W79 23 15. Stereo. Hrs opn: 24. Prog sep from AM. Format: Multilingual (20 languages). News progmg 10 hrs wkly. Spec prog: Black/Caribbean 4 hrs, Ger 7 hrs, Pol 5 hrs, S. Asian 6 hrs, Jewish 5 hrs, Serbian/Crotian 10 hrs wkly.

CHOG(AM)—See Richmond Hill.

CHRY-FM—1987: 105.5 mhz. 50 w. Hrs opn: 24. 258A Vanier College, 4700 Keele St., North York (M3J 1P3). (416) 736-5293. FAX: (416) 736-5700. Licensee: CHRY Community Radio Inc. Format: Black, alt, campus comm, div. News staff 4; news progmg 10 hrs wkly. Target aud: General; campus community. Spec prog: Afghan, African, Black, Chinese, envir, French, gospel, jazz, Sp., Hebrew. ■ Stephen Perry, stn mgr; Rudy Dworzak, adv mgr; Fiona York, vp progmg; Matt Galloway, mus dir; Nadira Baksh, news dir; John Matthews, vp engrg.

CHUM(AM)—1945: 1050 khz; 50 kw-U, DA-2. Stereo. 1331 Yonge St. (M4T 1Y1). (416) 925-6666. Licensee: CHUM Ltd. (group owner). Format: Oldies. ■ Allan Waters, pres; Jim Waters, gen mgr; Ross Davies, opns mgr & progmg dir; C.G. O'Brien, prom mgr; Brad Jones, mus dir; Brian Thomas, news dir; B.J. Carnegie, chief engr.

CHUM-FM—Sept 15, 1963: 104.5 mhz; 40 kw. Ant 1,380 ft. Stereo. Format: Adult rock. ■ Mary-Ellen Sheppard, prom mgr; Barry Stewart, mus dir.

CIAO(AM)—See Brampton.

CILQ-FM—May 22, 1977: 107.1 mhz; 40 kw. Ant 1,380 ft. Stereo. Hrs opn: 24. 5255 Yonge St., Suite 1400 (M2N 6P4). (416) 221-0107. FAX: (416) 512-4810. Licensee: Westcom Radio Group. Format: Rock/AOR. Target aud: 18-44. ■ Don Luzi, gen mgr; Ed Duarre, vp sls; Perry Goldberg, mktg dir; Dan Kingsbury, progmg dir; Brian Fukuda, mus dir; Dave Traferd, news dir; Rob Enders, chief engr.

CIRV-FM—1986: 88.9 mhz; 413 w. Stereo. Hrs opn: 24. 1087 Dundas St. W. (M6J 1W9). (416) 537-1088; (416) 588-2472. FAX: (416) 537-2463. Licensee: CIRC Radio Inc. Format: Multicultural/Ethnic. News staff 5. ■ Frank Alvarez, pres, gen mgr & prom dir; Alberto Elmir, vp, vp opns & vp progmg; Jose Mario Coelho, opns dir, mus dir & news dir; Bill Farsalas, sls dir, mktg mgr & vp adv; Maria Fernanda, asst mus dir; Victor Batista, engrg mgr; Wayne Stacey, chief engr. ■ Rates: $25; 30; 40; 40.

CISS-FM—Jan 26, 1993: 92.5 mhz; 4.7 kw. 49 Ontario St., 4th Floor (M5A 2V1). (416) 603-2000. Licensee: Rawlco Communications Ltd. (group owner). Format: New country. ■ Sandy Davis, gen mgr; Keith James, opns dir.

*****CIUT-FM**—1986: 89.5 mhz; 15 kw. 91 St. George St. (M5S 2E8). (416) 595-0909. Licensee: University of Toronto Community Radio Inc. Format: Div. ■David Ackerman, gen mgr.

CJBC(AM)—1947: 860 khz; 50 kw-U. 100 Carlton St., 2nd Floor (M5B 1M3). (416) 205-3566. TELEX: 022-763. Licensee: CBC. Format: Educ, cultural, variety. ■ Jean-Francois Dubois, gen mgr.

CJCL(AM)—Feb 21, 1951: 1430 khz; 50 kw, DA-2. Stereo. Hrs opn: 24. 40 Holly St., 7th Floor (M4S 3C3). (416) 488-1430. FAX: (416) 488-1845. Licensee: Telemedia Communications Inc. (group owner; acq 2-81). Net: Telemedia. Rep: Telemedia. Format: Sports. Target aud: 35-64. ■ Don Pagnutti, vp & gen mgr; Allan Davis, progmg dir.

CJEZ-FM—May 24, 1987: 97.3 mhz; 4 kw. Ant 1,500 ft. (CP: 28.9 kw). 40 Eglington Ave. E. (M4P 3B6). (416) 480-2099. FAX: (416) 480-0688. Licensee: Redmond Broadcasting Inc. Format: Classic hits. News staff 5; news progmg 5 hrs wkly. Target aud: 35-54. ■ Bob Redmond, pres; Jay Jackson, vp & gen mgr; Gene Stevens, opns dir; Michael Mangialarde, gen sls mgr; Walter Levitt, prom dir; Grant Stein, mus dir; Grant Turnpenny, engrg dir.

*****CJRT-FM**—1949: 91.1 mhz; 100 kw. Ant 1,300 ft. Stereo. 150 Mutual (M5B 2W1). (416) 595-0404. FAX: (416) 595-0404. Licensee: CJRT-FM Inc. (acq 1974). Format: Ed, class, jazz. ■ Cam Finley, pres & gen mgr.

CKFM-FM—Listing follows CFRB(AM).

*****CKLN-FM**—July 1983: 88.1 mhz; 250 w. c/o CKLN Radio Inc., 380 Victoria St. (M5B 1W7). (416) 595-1477. Licensee: CKLN Radio Inc. Format: Div. ■ Lisa Binebaum, gen mgr.

CKYC(AM)—1944: 590 khz; 50 kw-U, DA-1. Suite 2500, One Yonge St. (M5E 1G1). (416) 361-1281. FAX: (416) 361-9329. Licensee: KEY Radio Ltd. (acq 1965). Net: Broadcast News. Rep: Paul Mulvihill. Format: C&W. Target aud: 25-49. ■ Vince Di Maggio, gen mgr.

Trenton

CJTN(AM)—January 1979: 1270 khz; 1 kw, DA-2. Hrs opn: 24. Box 9, 31 Quinte St. (K8V 5R1). (613) 392-1237. FAX: (613) 394-6430. Licensee: Quinte Broadcasting Ltd. (group owner). Rep: Major Mkt. Format: C&W, adult contemp. Spec prog: Scottish one hr wkly. ■ Bob Rowbotham, gen mgr.

Waterloo

*****CKMS-FM**—Oct 16, 1977: 100.3 mhz; 250 w. Ant 110 ft. Stereo. 200 University Ave. W. (N2L 3G1). (519) 886-2567. Licensee: Radio Waterloo Inc. Format: Div. ■ Terry Walters, Eva Rucki, mus dirs; Paul Heap, news dir; Bill Wharrie, vp engrg.

CKWR-FM—(Kitchener). Mar 23, 1974: 98.7 mhz; 2.24 kw. Ant 182 ft. Stereo. Hrs opn: 24. Box 216, 56 Regina St. N., Waterloo (N2J 3A3). (519) 886-9870. Licensee: Wired World Inc. Rep: Target. Format: Div, alternative. News staff 2; news progmg 6 hrs wkly. Target aud: General. Spec prog: Black 4 hrs, class 9 hrs, C&W 5 hrs, Romanian 2 hrs, Fr 2 hrs, Ger 4 hrs, Greek 2 hrs, Serbian 2 hrs, jazz 11 hrs, Polish 3 hrs, Native American 5 hrs, Portuguese 4 hrs, Sp 3 hrs, Chinese 2 hrs, relg 12 hrs wkly. ■ Stuart Munroe, pres; Rebecca Knapnaw, CFO; Lev Gnick, exec vp; Frank Fowlie, stn mgr; Joe Downey, vp sls, vp adv & progmg dir; Amanda Hold, prom mgr; Jen Brown, pub affrs dir; Mike Stevens, engrg dir. ■ Rates: C$25; 20; 25; 15.

Wawa

CJWA(AM)—June 30, 1964: 1240 khz; 1 kw-U. 53 Broadway Ave. (P0S 1K0); 642 Great Northern Rd., Sault Ste. Marie (P6B 4Z9). (705) 856-4555; (705) 759-9200. FAX: (705) 856-1520; (705) 942-6549. Licensee: Pelmorex Broadcasting Inc. (group owner). Net: BN. Rep: United. Format: Adult contemp. News progmg 4 hrs wkly. Target aud: 25-54. ■ Rick Labbe, gen mgr.

Welland

CHOW(AM)—June 4, 1957: 1470 khz; 10 kw-U, DA-2. Stereo. Hrs opn: 24. Regional Rd 23. (L3B 5R6). (416) 732-4433. FAX: (416) 732-4780. Licensee: Wellport Broadcasting Ltd. Rep: Canadian Broadcasting Sales. Format: Country. News staff 2. Target aud: 35 plus; professional-white & blue collar. ■ Gordon W. Burnett, pres & gen mgr; Peter Morena, chief opns; Jim Clark, gen sls mgr; Gordon Burnett, natl sls mgr; Bruce Smith, prom mgr; John Marshall, progmg mgr & mus dir; Peter Marina, news dir; Walt Juchnewitch, chief engr. ■ Rates: C$46; 30; 37; 20.

Windsor

CBE(AM)—July 1, 1950: 1550 khz; 10 kw-U, DA-1. 267 Pelissier (N9A 4K5). (519) 255-3411. FAX: (519) 255-3443. Licensee: CBC. Format: Div. Spec prog: Farm 5 hrs, class 19 hrs, jazz 2 hrs, C&W 3 hrs, current affrs 18 hrs wkly. ■ Bruce Taylor, gen mgr.

CBE-FM—Oct 15, 1978: 89.9 mhz; 100 kw. Ant 538 ft. Stereo. Format: Class, div.

CBEF(AM)—May 1970: 540 khz; 2.5 kw-D, 5 kw-N, DA-1. Security Bldg, 267 Pelissier, 8e Et., (N9A 4K5). (519) 255-3411; (519) 255-3546. FAX: (519) 255-3565. Licen-

see: CBC. Net: CBC/AM. Format: Div. ■ Mina Grossman, gen mgr; Marc Thibeault, news dir.

CIMX-FM—Listing follows CKWW(AM).

*****CJAM-FM**—November 1983: 91.5 mhz; 50 w. 401 Sunset Blvd. (N9B 3P4). (519) 971-3606. Licensee: Student Media, University of Windsor. Format: Alternative mus, info, ethnic. News progmg 5 hrs wkly. Target aud: General; listeners in Windsor/Detroit area. ■ Jon Ricci, pres; Marc Fedak, stn mgr.

CKLW(AM)—June 1, 1932: 800 khz; 50 kw-U, DA-2. Hrs opn: 24. Box 480, 1640 Ouellette Ave. (N9A 6M6). (519) 258-8888; (313) 963-1567. FAX: (519) 258-0182. Licensee: CHUM Ltd. (group owner; acq 1-29-93). Rep: Major Mkt. Format: News/talk. Target aud: 25-54. ■ Allan Walter, pres; Wayne Stafford, gen mgr; Eric Proksch, gen sls mgr; Keith Chinnery, prom dir; Wayne McLean, progmg dir; Rob Shervill, news dir; Jim Valvasori, chief engr.

CKLW-FM—1949: 93.9 mhz; 100 kw. Ant 700 ft. Stereo. Hrs opn: 24. Prog sep from AM. Format: Oldies. Target aud: 35-54. ■ Charlie O'Brien, progmg dir; Wendy Duff, mus dir.

CKWW(AM)—Mar 29, 1964: 580 khz; 500 w-U, DA-1. 300 Cabana Rd. E. (N9G 1A3). (519) 258-8888; (313) 961-9811. FAX: (519) 258-0182; (313) 961-1603. Licensee: Division of CHUM Ltd. Group owner: CHUM Ltd. (acq 9-5-85). Net: BN. Rep: Major Mkt. Format: Music of Your Life. Target aud: 45 plus. ■ Allan Waters, pres; Wayne Stafford, gen mgr; Eric Proksch, gen sls mgr; Keith Chinnery, prom mgr; Charlie O'Brien, progmg dir; Wendy Duff, mus dir; Rob Shervill, news dir; Jim Valvasori, chief engr.

CIMX-FM—Co-owned with CKWW(AM). July 10, 1967: 88.7 mhz; 100 kw. Ant 577 ft. Stereo. Prog sep from AM. 30100 Telegraph Rd., Bingham Farms, MI (48025). (313) 961-9811; (519) 258-8888. FAX: (313) 961-1603; (519) 258-0182. Format: Modem rock. Target aud: 18-34. ■ Keith Chinnery, prom mgr; Michelle Denomme, progmg dir; Vince Cannova, mus dir.

Wingham

CKNX(AM)—Feb 20, 1926: 920 khz; 10 kw-D, 1 kw-N, DA-2. Hrs opn: 24. 215 Carling Terrace (N0G 2W0). (519) 357-1310. FAX: (519) 357-1897. Licensee: Blackburn Radio Inc. Net: Seltech, CRN. Rep: All Canada. Format: Country. News progmg 10 hrs wkly. Target aud: 35-54. Spec prog: Religious 6 hrs wkly. ■ Bob Elsden, pres; Al Skelton, vp; Jack Gillespie, stn mgr; Murray Armstrong, gen sls mgr; Tammy King, prom dir; Matt Miller, progmg dir & mus dir; Julie Zbeetnoff, asst mus dir; Gerry Belanger, engrg mgr. ■ Rates: $66.70; 60.20; 53.60; 39.40.

CKNX-FM—Apr 17, 1977: 101.7 mhz; 100 kw. Ant 650 ft. Stereo. (519) 357-4438. Net: BN. Format: Adult contemp. Target aud: 25-49. ■ Al Skelton, gen mgr; Jack Gillesbie, stn mgr. ■ CKNX-TV affil.

Woodstock

CKDK-FM—July 1, 1987: 103.9 mhz; 52 kw. Ant 400 ft. Stereo. Hrs opn: 24. Box 100 Dundas St. (N4S 7W7). (519) 539-1040. FAX: (416) 539-7479. Licensee: Shaw Radio (group owner; acq 1991). Rep: All-Canada. Format: Adult contemp. News staff 3; news progmg 9 hrs wkly. Target aud: 25-54. ■ Terry Strain, pres; Jim Elliott, gen mgr; Sandra Talbot, prom dir; Ed Saunders, progmg dir; Nikki Davis, mus dir; Brad Janssen, news dir; Rick Roi, engrg dir. ■ Rates: C$76; 58; 39; 39.

Prince Edward Island

Charlottetown

CBCT-FM—96.1 mhz; 93.5 kw. Ant 540 ft. Box 2230, 430 University Ave. (C1A 8B9). (902) 368-9400. FAX: (902) 368-8118. Licensee: CBC. Net: CBC AM. Format: Talk. ■ Barbara Trueman, gen mgr.

CFCY(AM)—Aug 15, 1924: 630 khz; 10 kw-U, DA-2. 141 Kent St. (C1A 7M8); Box 1060 (CIA 7M8). (902) 892-1066. FAX: (902) 566-1338. Licensee: Maritime Broadcasting Ltd. Net: Newsradio. Format: Adult contemp, CHR. ■ Frank Lewis, gen mgr.

CHLQ-FM—Co-owned with CFCY(AM). March 1982: 93.1 mhz; 25 kw. Stereo. Prog sep from AM. Format: C&W.

CHTN(AM)—Dec 25, 1974: 720 khz; 10 kw-D, 7.5 kw-N, DA-D. TL: N46 11 22 W63 09 54. Hrs opn: 24. 590 N.

Stations in Canada

Quebec

River Rd. (C1A 8V7). (902) 892-8591. Licensee: New-Cap Broadcasting Ltd. (group owner; acq 10-7-81). Net: BN. Rep: Canadian Broadcast Sales. Format: Classic rock, oldies. News staff 3; news progmg 17 hrs wkly. Target aud: 25-54. Spec prog: "Juke Box Jive" 4 hrs wkly. ■ Harry Steele, CEO; Bob Templeton, pres; Blair Daggett, gen mgr & progmg dir; Heather Tedford, gen sls mgr; Kathy Maher, prom mgr; Kirk MacKinnon, mus dir; John Wedlake, news dir; Gordon Mills, chief engr. ■ Rates: $45; 34; 34; 22.

Summerside

CJRW(AM)—Nov 17, 1948: 1240 khz; 1 kw-U. Hrs opn: 5:57 AM -12:15 AM. 763 Water St. E. (C1N 4J3). (902) 436-2201. FAX: (902) 436-8573. Licensee: The Gulf Broadcasting Co. Ltd. Rep: All-Canada. Format: All hit country. News staff one. Target aud: General. ■ Lois E. Schurman, chmn; Paul M. Schurman, pres, gen mgr & prom dir; Brent Schurman, vp; Roger Ahern, gen sls mgr & adv dir; John V. Perry, progmg dir; Mike Gallant, mus dir; John Perry, news dir & pub affrs dir; Steve Harvey, chief engr.

Quebec

Alma

CFGT(AM)—October 1953: 1270 khz; 10 kw-D, 5 kw-N, DA-2. 1441 boul. Auger (G8B 6V4). (418) 662-6673. Licensee: Radio Lac St. Jean Ltee. (acq 1981). Net: Radiomutuel. Rep: Target. Format: Country. ■ Gilbert Pednault, gen mgr; Daniel Lapointe, progmg dir.

Amos

CHAD(AM)—Dec 1, 1941: 1340 khz; 1 kw-D, 250 w-N. 751 1st Ave. Ouest (J9T 1V7). (819) 732-3215. FAX: (819) 732-6310. Licensee: Radio-Nord Inc. (group owner). Net: Telemedia. Rep: Opex. Format: Adult contemp. ■ Bernard Gauphier, gen mgr.

Amqui

CFVM(AM)—Mar 31, 1980: 1220 khz; 10 kw-D, 5 kw-N, DA-N. Hrs opn: 24. 111 de l'Hopital (G0J 1B0). (418) 629-2025. FAX: (418) 629-2599. Licensee: CFVM une Division de Diffusion Power Inc. (acq 1981). Net: Radiomutuel. Rep: Mutuelcom. Format: MOR, adult contemp. News staff 2; news progmg 6 hrs wkly. Target aud: 18 plus. ■ Adalbert Levesque, pres, opns dir, dev dir & sls dir; Frederic Bureau, progmg dir, asst mus dir & pub affrs dir; Pierre Plante, mus dir; Michel Jogouin, news dir; Jacques Beaudoin, engrg dir.

Asbestos

CJAN(AM)—1972: 1340 khz; 1 kw-U, DA-D. TL: N45 45 05 W71 56 39. Hrs opn: 24. 185 Du Roi (J1T 1S4). (819) 879-5439; (819) 879-5430. FAX: (819) 879-7922. Licensee: Radio Plus BMD Inc. Group owner: Reseau des Appalaches (acq 1-11-90). Net: BN. Rep: Target. Format: Adult contemp, MOR. ■ Marie-Paule Drouin, chmn, gen mgr & progmg mgr; Luc Brouillard, exec vp & sls dir; Serge Drouin, sr vp & prom dir; Remi-Mario Mayette, vp, news dir & pub affrs dir; Raymond Cusson, mus dir; Renaud Cloutier, chief engr.

Baie Comeau

CBMI-FM—May 28, 1974: 93.7 mhz; 3 kw. 1400 Rene Levesque Blvd. E, Montreal (H2L 2M2). (514) 597-4444. Licensee: Canadian Broadcasting Corp. Net: CBC Mono. Format: Public Affairs, info radio. ■ Judith Bleier, gen mgr.

CHLC(AM)—1962: 580 khz; 10 kw-D, 2.5 kw-N, DA-2. 399 Rue de Puyjalon (G5C 2Z7). (418) 589-9086. FAX: (418) 589-9086. Licensee: Cogeco Radio-Television Inc. Group owner: Cogeco Inc. Net: Newsradio. Format: Adult contemp, MOR. Target aud: General. ■ Louis Audet, pres; Camille St-Pierre, vp & sls dir; Daniel Dionne, progmg dir & mus dir.

Cabano

CFVD-FM-1—Sept 10, 1983: 102.7 mhz; 50 w. Rebroadcasts CJMF-FM Quebec. CP 1370, Ville Degelis (G0L 1H0). (418) 853-3370. Licensee: Radio Degelis Inc. Rep: Canadian Broadcast Sales. Format: CHR. ■ Gilles Caron, gen mgr.

CJAF(AM)—1959: 1240 khz; 1 kw-D, 250 w-N. 64 Hotel DeVille Riviere du Loup (G5R 1L5). (418) 862-8241. TELEX: 051-3915. Licensee: Radio CJFP Ltee. Net: CBC. Format: MOR. ■ Guy Simard, pres. ■ CKRT-TV, CIMT-TV affil.

Causapscal

CJBM(AM)—September 1963: 1450 khz; 1 kw-D, 250 w-N. Box 2000, 155 St. Sacrement St., Matane (G4W 3P7). (418) 562-0290. Licensee: CBC. Format: MOR. ■ Louis Pelletier, gen mgr.

Chapais

CFED(AM)—1969: 1340 khz; 250 w-U. Hrs opn: 24. c/o CHRL, 568 boul. St. Joseph, Roberval (G8H 2K6). (418) 275-1831; (418) 748-3931. FAX: (418) 275-2475. Licensee: Radio Chibougamau Inc. (acq 1-6-93). Net: Telemedia. Format: Adult contemp, contemp hit. News staff one; news progmg 20 hrs wkly. Target aud: General; mainly adults. ■ Marc-Andre Levesque, pres; Germain Gagnon, mus dir; Marcel Bolduc, vp engrg. ■ Rates: $20; 18; 18; na.

Chibougamau

CJMD(AM)—Nov 21, 1969: 1240 khz; 1 kw-D, 250 w-N, DA-1. TL: N49 54 35 W74 22 08. c/o CHRL, 568 boul. St. Joseph, Roberval (G8H 2K6). (418) 275-1831; (418) 748-3931. FAX: (418) 275-2475. Licensee: Radio Chibougamau Inc. (acq 1-6-93). Net: Telemedia. Format: Adult contemp, CHR. News staff one; news progmg 20 hrs wkly. Target aud: General; mainly adults. ■ Marc-Andre Levesque, pres; Germain Gagnon, mus dir; Marcel Bolduc, vp engrg. ■ Rates: $20; 18; 18; na.

Chicoutimi

CBJ(AM)—Sept 20, 1933: 1580 khz; 50 kw-D, DA-1. 500 Rue Des Sagueneens (G7H 5E7). (418) 696-6600. TELEX: 011-36121. Licensee: Canadian Broadcasting Corp. Net: CBN, CBC. Format: Var. ■ Remi Villeneuve, stn mgr.

*CBJ-FM—Sept 20, 1933: 100.9 mhz; 98 kw. Ant 294 ft. Format: Contemp, talk. ■ Jean-Roch Maltais, opns mgr.

CBJE-FM—107.9 mhz; 98 kw. Ant 294 ft. Rebroadcasts CBM(AM) Montreal. Weekdays 6-9 a.m., rebroadcasts CBVE-FM Quebec City. Box 6000, c/o CBM(AM), Montreal (H3C 3A8). (514) 283-6607. Licensee: CBC. ■ Patricia Tleszcynska, gen mgr.

CJAB-FM—May 25, 1979: 94.5 mhz; 44.2 kw. Stereo. 121 Racine Est (G7H 5G4). (418) 545-8888. FAX: (418) 545-8196. Licensee: CJAB-FM Inc. Group owner: Radiomutuel Inc. (acq 8-21-92). Net: Radiomutuel. Format: Adult contemp. ■ Richard Turcotte, gen mgr.

CJMT(AM)—Feb 28, 1954: 1420 khz; 10 kw-D, 2.5 kw-N, DA-1. 267 Racine (G7H 1T1). (418) 696-1420. Licensee: Radio Chicoutimi Inc. Group owner: Telemedia Communications Inc. (acq 9-7-89). Net: Telemedia. Format: Adult contemp. ■ Rene A. Tremblay, pres & gen mgr.

Dolbeau

CHVD(AM)—1967: 1230 khz; 10 kw-D, 250 w-N. 1975 Boul Wallberg (G8L 1J5). (418) 276-3333. Licensee: Radio CHVD Inc. (acq 1-6-93). Net: Radiomutuel. Format: MOR. ■ Rosayre LeClerce, gen mgr.

CHVD-FM—January 1992: 92.1 mhz.

Drummondville

CHRD(AM)—Dec 23, 1954: 1480 khz; 10 kw-D, 5 kw-N, DA-2. Hrs opn: 24. 2070 Rue St. Georges (J2C 5G6). (819) 478-1480; (819) 478-7926. FAX: (819) 478-8361. Licensee: Communications Robert Lauzon Inc. dba Radio Drummond CHRD (1993). (acq 12-1-93; $275,500). Net: BN. Format: Adult contemp, MOR, news. News staff 3; News progmg 15 hrs wkly. Target aud: General;18 plus. Spec prog: Relg one hr wkly. ■ Robert Lauzon, gen mgr. ■ Rates: C$36; 34; 30; 22.

CJDM-FM—Aug 15, 1987: 92.1 mhz; 3 kw. Ant 300 ft. Stereo. Hrs opn: 24. Suite 203, 412 Heriot (J2B 1B5). (819) 474-1892; (819) 474-6606. FAX: (819) 474-6610. Licensee: Diffusion Power Inc. Net: Radiomutuel. Rep: United. Format: Adult contemp, French. News staff 2; news progmg 5 hrs wkly. Target aud: 18-44. ■ Pierre Gaudreau, gen mgr & sls dir; Yves Laramee, progmg dir; Caroline Pratte, news dir; Daniel Pelletier, engrg dir. ■ Rates: C$56; 46; 46; 20.

Fermont

CBMR-FM—1982: 105.1 mhz; 16 w. Box 6000, c/o CBM(AM), Montreal (H3C 3A8). (514) 597-5970; (597) 597-4444. FAX: (514) 597-5551. Licensee: Canadian Broadcasting Corp. ■ Patricia Pleszcynska, opns dir.

CFMF-FM—1980: 103.1 mhz; 50 w. Ant 100 ft. Stereo. (418) 287-5147. Licensee: Radio Communautaire de Fermont Inc. Rep: Telemedia. Format: Div, French. News staff one; news progmg one hr wkly. Target aud: 7-55; Spec prog: Jazz one hr, C&W 3 hrs wkly. ■ Louise Larocque, pres; Guy Laprise, gen mgr, gen sls mgr, mktg dir, prom dir & adv dir; Suzanne Cassista, progmg dir; Julie Bernier, asst mus dir; Gilles Soucis, engrg dir. ■ Rates: C$14.50; 9.50; 9.50; 7.50.

Forestville

CFRP(AM)—1977: 620 khz; 1 kw-U. 399 Rue de Puyjalon, Baie Cameau (G5C 2Z7). (418) 589-3771. Licensee: Cogeco Radio-Television Inc. Group owner: Cogeco Inc. Net: Cogeco, BN, Newsradio. Rep: Communications AC. Format: Adult contemp, MOR. ■ Louis Audet, pres.

Fort Coulonge

CHIP-FM—May 1979: 101.7 mhz; 11.9 kw. Stereo. Box 820, La Radio du Pontiac (J0X 1V0). (819) 683-3155. FAX: (819) 683-3211. Licensee: La Radio du Pontiac Inc. Format: MOR. Spec prog: Class 2 hrs wkly. ■ Jean Rochon, Martin Le Lencette, progmg dirs.

Gaspe

CJRG-FM—December 1978: 94.5 mhz; 4.15 kw. Ant 1,150 ft. Stereo. C.P. 380 (G0C 1R0). (418) 368-3511. FAX: (418) 368-1663. Licensee: Radio Gaspesie Inc. Net: BN. Rep: Radio-Unie Quebec. Format: MOR. Spec prog: Class 2 hrs, jazz 2 hrs wkly. ■ Alain Fournier, gen mgr; Michael Vallee, gen sls mgr.

Gatineau

CJRC(AM)—Licensed to Gatineau. See Ottawa, Ont.

CKTF-FM—1988: 104.1 mhz; 7.6 kw. 105 Bellehumeur, Bur. 200 (J8T 6K5). (819) 243-5555. Licensee: Radiomutuel Inc. (group owner). Format: Dance. ■ Geoffrey O. Brown, gen mgr; Andre Bonneau, chief engr.

Granby

CHEF(AM)—Mar 14, 1946: 1450 khz; 10 kw-D, DA. 76 rue Dufferin (G2G 9L4). (514) 375-1450. FAX: (514) 777-1450. Licensee: Les Journaux Trans-Canada (acq 1958). Format: Adult contemp. Target aud: General. Spec prog: C&W one hr wkly. ■ Pierre Gobeil, pres; Sylvia D'Nault, gen mgr & sls dir.

Harrington Harbour

*CFTH-FM—Oct 30, 1991: 98.5 mhz; 188 w. Stereo. Harrington Harbour, Duplessis (G0G 1N0). (418) 795-3344. Licensee: Radio Communautaire de Harrington Harbour. Format: Variety. News staff one. Target aud: General; five fishing villages. ■ Paul Rowsell, pres; Lorraine Roberts, gen mgr & stn mgr; Rowina Anderson, opns dir; Lois Jones, vp sls; Betty Strickland, news dir.

Hull

CKCH(AM)—June 30, 1933: 970 khz; 10 kw-D, 5 kw-N, DA-1. 150 Rue Edmonton (J8Y 3S6). (819) 777-2771. FAX: (819) 777-7724. Licensee: CKCH Radio Ltee. Group owner: Telemedia Communications Inc. (acq 7-1-70). Format: MOR.

CIMF-FM—Co-owned with CKCH(AM). Jan 1, 1970: 94.9 mhz; 74 kw. Ant 1,077 ft. Stereo. Prog sep from AM. (819) 770-2463. FAX: (819) 770-9338.

Iles-de-la-Madeleine

CBGA-FM-8—93.5 mhz; 3.7 kw. Ant 670 ft. Rebroadcasts CBGA(AM) Matane. Box 2000, 155 St. Sacrement St., Matane (G4W 3P7). (418) 562-0290. Licensee: CBC. Format: French. ■ Louis Pelletier, gen mgr.

CFIM-FM—November 15, 1981: 92.7 mhz; 6.3 kw. Stereo. C.P. 490 Cap-Aux-Meules, (G0B 1B0). (418) 986-5233. FAX: (418) 986-5319. Licensee: Diffusion Communautaire des Iles Inc. Format: Div, news, talk. News staff 2; news progmg 5 hrs wkly. Target aud: General. ■ Real Juteau, gen mgr. ■ Rates: C$23; 20; 16; 10.

Joliette

CJLM(AM)—April 1960: 1350 khz; 10 kw-D, 1 kw-N, DA-2. 854 Rue Papineau (J6E 2L5). (514) 759-0772. FAX: (514) 759-8751. Licensee: Radio de Lanaudiere Inc. Rep: United. Format: MOR. News staff 2. ■ Pierre

Broadcasting & Cable Yearbook 1994
B-443

Quebec   Directory of Radio

Cardin, pres, gen mgr, prom mgr, progmg dir & news dir; Edmond Cote, gen sls mgr; Daniel La Tendresse, mus dir. ■ Rates: C$41; 38; 34; 22.

Jonquiere

CHOC-FM—Apr 11, 1977: 92.5 mhz; 3 kw. Stereo. C.P. 306, 2505 Saint Dubart (G7X 5M4). (418) 542-2265; (418) 547-5356. FAX: (418) 547-5356. Licensee: Radio Communautaire de Jonquiere Inc. Rep: Radio-Unie. Format: Div. ■ Danielle Dube, pres; Francois Munger, gen sls mgr; Remi Nadfau, news dir; Sylvain Allard, chief engr.

CKRS(AM)—June 23, 1947: 590 khz; 25 kw-D, 7.5 kw-N. 121 Racine St., Chicoutimi (G7X 7V8). (418) 695-2577. Licensee: Radiomutuel Inc. (group owner; acq 8-21-92). Net: Radiomutuel. Format: Adult contemp. ■ Richard Turcotte, gen mgr.

Kahnawake

*****CKRK-FM**—Mar 30, 1981: 103.5 mhz; 50 w. Ant 75 ft. Stereo. Hrs opn: 18. Box 1035 (J0L 1B0). (514) 638-1313; (514) 638-1409. FAX: (514) 638-4009. Licensee: Conway Jocks. Format: Adult contemp, C&W, contemp hit. News staff one; news progmg 3 hrs wkly. Target aud: General; young adults in Montreal suburban area. Spec prog: Mohawk. ■ Lori Jacobs, CEO, gen mgr, opns mgr & pub affrs dir; Alvin Delisle, chmn; Lois Williams, rgnl sls mgr; David Bush, progmg mgr; Christine Taylor, mus dir; James Jacobs, news dir; Claude Durand, chief engr.

L'Annonciation

CKLO(AM)—1975: 1490 khz; 1 kw-U. 332 De La Madone (J9L 1R9). (819) 623-6610. FAX: (819) 623-7406. Licensee: Radio Mont Laurier Ltee. (acq 3-27-82). Net: Telemedia. Format: Div. ■ Alain Desgardins, gen mgr.

La Malbaie

CBV-FM-6—99.3 mhz; 820 w. 2505 boul. Laurier, Ste. Foy (G1V 2X2). (418) 654-1341. Licensee: CBC. ■ Bertrand Emond, gen mgr.

La Pocatiere

CHOX-FM—Apr 23, 1992: 97.5 mhz; 25 kw. Stereo. CP 550, 1000 6 avenue LaPocatiere (G0R 1Z0). (418) 856-1310; (418) 856-3510. FAX: (418) 856-3747. Licensee: CHOX-FM, Inc. Rep: Opex. Format: Contemp hit. News staff one. ■ Guy Simard, pres; Lise Beiule, opns mgr; Georgette Charent, vp sls; Maurice LeVesque, vp progmg; Gilles Gosselin, progmg dir; Michel Farvey, mus dir; Jacques Dufouier, news dir.

La Sarre

CKLS(AM)—Sept 1, 1950: 1240 khz; 1 kw-D, 250 w-N. 122 5th Ave. Est (J9Z 2Y1). (819) 333-5505. TELEX: 057-45626. Licensee: Radio Nord Inc. (group owner). Net: SBN, CBC AM. Rep: Glen-Warren. Format: MOR. ■ Silvie Bourassa, gen mgr.

La Tuque

CFLM(AM)—Oct 3, 1959: 1240 khz; 1 kw-U, DA-2. C.P. 850, 529 St-Louis (G9X 3P6). (819) 523-4575. FAX: (819) 676-8000. Licensee: Radio Haute Mauricle Inc. (acq 1982). Net: CBC Radio, Telemedia. Rep: Target. Format: Var. ■ Rejean Leclerc, pres, gen mgr & progmg dir; Guy Ethier, vp opns & sls dir; Nancy Armstrong, mus dir; Sylvain Bourassa, news dir.

Lac Megantic

CKFL(AM)—Mar 6, 1968: 1400 khz; 1 kw-U, DA-1. 5088 rue Frontenac (G6B 1H3). (819) 583-0663. Licensee: Communequipe Inc. (acq 5-14-91). Net: Telemedia. Rep: Radio Unie Quebec. Format: Top-40, MOR. ■ Marie-Paul Drouuim, gen mgr; Michel Brochu, progmg dir.

Lac-Etchemin

*****CFIN-FM**—Mar 27, 1992: 100.5 mhz; 9.6 kw. Ant 2,020 ft. TL: N46 24 41 W70 35 44. Stereo. CP 580, 201 Claude-Bilodeau St. (G0R 1S0). (418) 625-3737; (418) 625-2346. FAX: (418) 625-3730. Licensee: Radio Bellechasse. Rep: Target. Format: MOR, AOR, div. News staff 10; news progmg 8 hrs wkly. Target aud: 25-45. Spec prog: Fr, Sp, jazz 3 hrs, class 2 hrs wkly. ■ Jean Royer, pres; Louis Baby, opns dir; Gilles Pilote, progmg dir & mus dir; Dominique Vien, news dir & pub affrs dir. ■ Rates: C$25; 20; 25; 20.

Lachute

CJLA-FM—Dec 1, 1974: 104.9 mhz; 3 kw. Stereo. Hrs opn: 24. 385 Rue Principale (J8H 1Y1). (514) 562-8862. FAX: (514) 562-1902. Licensee: Radio Fusion Inc. Group owner: Radio Nord Inc. (acq 8-22-89). Rep: Target. Format: Adult contemp. News staff one; news progmg 8 hrs wkly. Target aud: 25-59. ■ Giles Poulin, pres; Kathleen Silas, gen mgr & gen sls mgr; Yves Trottier, progmg dir & mus dir; Brigitte Roussy, news dir; Pierre Laberge, chief engr. ■ Rates: C$26; 23; 26; na.

Laval

CFGL-FM—September 1968: 105.7 mhz; 41 kw. Stereo. 2830 boul. St.-Martin (H7E 5A9). (514) 664-1500; (514) 381-5903. FAX: (514) 664-4138; (514) 664-1651. Licensee: Cogeco Radio Television Inc. Group owner: Cogeco Inc. Rep: Standard Bcst. Format: MOR. News staff 6; news progmg 6 hrs wkly. Target aud: 25-54; those preferring soft & easy listening hits. ■ Yves Saucier, gen mgr; M. Jacques Boiteau, natl sls mgr; M. Denis Brousseau, rgnl sls mgr; Mme Denise Gagnon, prom mgr; M. Jacques-Charles Gilliot, vp progmg; M. Rene Bourdages, progmg dir; M. Carol Roy, mus dir; Richard Cayer, Lilianne Randall, Louise Saucier, asst mus dirs; Mme Esther Morin, news dir; M. Jean-Guy Gibault, engrg mgr.

Levis

CFLS-FM—1992: 102.9 mhz; 10 kw-U. Box 3000, 5637 boul. de la Rive Sud (G6V 4Y5). (418) 833-2151. FAX: (418) 833-4462. Licensee: Entreprises Radio Etchemin Inc. (acq 7-10-90). Format: Country.

Longueuil

CIEL-FM—Apr 9, 1977: 98.5 mhz; 40.8 kw. Ant 623 ft. Stereo. 89 Ouest, rue St Charles (J4H 1C5). (514) 527-8321. Licensee: Radio MF CIEL Inc. (acq 1981). Rep: United. Format: MOR. Target aud: 25-54. ■ Jean Pierre Coallier, pres; Edmond Cote, vp; Rejean Beaulieu, sls dir; Micheline Ricard, progmg dir; Michel Lambert, mus dir. ■ Rates: C$145; 105; 145; na.

Magog

CIMO-FM—1979: 106.1 mhz; 50 kw. Suite 100, 1750 Sherbrooke (J1X 2T3). (819) 843-1414. FAX: (819) 843-7769. Licensee: Diffusion CIMO Inc. Group owner: Radiomutuel Inc. Format: Adult contemp. ■ Danielle Chagmon, gen mgr.

Maniwaki

CBOF-1(AM)—Oct 22, 1973: 990 khz; 40 w, DA-1. Radio Canada, Box 6000, Mount Royal Transmitter Site, Montreal (H3C 3A8). (416) 625-5009. Licensee: CBC Montreal. Net: CBC AM. Format: Info radio. ■ Doug Ward, gen mgr; Denis St. Gelais, engrg mgr.

CHGA-FM—Nov 1980: 97.3 mhz; 2.8 kw. Hrs opn: 24. 163 Laurier Maniwaki (J9E 2K6). (819) 449-3959; (819) 449-5590. FAX: (819) 449-7331. Licensee: Radio Communautaire Type B. Format: Div, adult contemp. News staff one; news progmg 15 hrs wkly. Spec prog: Class one hr, jazz 3 hrs, country 8 hrs, folk 5 hrs wkly. ■ Hubert Tremblay, pres; Daniel Smith, opns dir, dev dir, gen sls mgr, rgnl sls mgr & mktg dir; Jean-Guy Cadieux, mus dir; Daniel Labonte, asst mus dir; Georges Vasiloff, engrg dir.

CKMG(AM)—1975: 1340 khz. Hrs opn: 24. Suite 110, 175 Commerciale (J9E 1P1). (819) 449-1211. Licensee: Radio CKMG Inc. Net: Telemedia. Format: MOR, btfl music, big band, (Fr). News staff 7; news progmg 126 hrs wkly. Target aud: 30 plus. ■ Michel Riel, pres; Jean Lacaille, vp & asst mus dir; Roger Nolan, gen mgr & progmg dir; Michel Riel, Guy Langevin, sls dirs; Jean-Guy Cadieux, mus dir; Mike Mathieu, vp engrg.

Matane

CBGA(AM)—1250 khz; 10 kw-N, 5 kw-N, DA-N. Box 200, 155 St. Sacrement St. (G4W 3P7). (418) 562-0290. Licensee: CBC (acq 9-1-72). Format: MOR. ■ Louis Pelletier, gen mgr.

CHRM(AM)—Apr 13, 1975: 1290 khz; 10 kw-U, DA-2. TL: N48 49 27 W67 34 27. 800 Ave. du Phare Ouest (G4W 1V7). (418) 562-4141. FAX: (418) 562-0778. Licensee: Les Communications Matane Inc. Net: Telemedia. Rep: Target. Format: Contemp hit, country, MOR. News progmg 16 hrs wkly. Target aud: 25-54; general. ■ Kenneth Gagne, news dir. ■ Rates: C$27; 27; 25; 22.

Montmagny

CFEL-FM—1988: 102.1 mhz; 7.8 kw. TL: N46 56 21 W70 30 29. Stereo. Hrs opn: 24. 191 Chemen des Poirier (G5V 4L2). (418) 248-1122. FAX: (418) 248-1951. Licensee: Radio Montminy Inc. Group owner: Power Broadcasting Inc. (acq 7-10-91; $247,669). Format: Adult contemp, new age, oldies. News staff 2. Target aud: 25-49. ■ Michel Montminy, gen mgr & vp opns; Michel Montmagny, vp sls; Gilles Lamarre, vp mktg & vp prom; Rene' Nadeau, vp progmg; Louis Labbe', mus dir; Johanne Dube', asst mus dir; Michel Beausoleil, news dir & pub affrs dir; Jean Fournier, vp engrg.

Montreal

CBF(AM)—1937: 690 khz; 50 kw-U. 1400 boul. Rene Levesque East (H2L 2M2). (514) 597-4151. Licensee: CBC. Format: Talk, div. ■ Marcel Pepin, vp & gen mgr.

CBF-FM—1947: 100.7 mhz; 100 kw. Ant 823 ft. Stereo. Prog sep from AM. ■ CBFT(TV) affil.

CBM(AM)—1933: 940 khz; 50 kw-U. Box 6000 (H3C 3A8). (514) 597-5970. FAX: (514) 597-4511. Licensee: Canadian Broadcasting Corp. ■ Patricia Plezynska, opns dir; Judith Bleyer, opns mgr.

CBM-FM—1947: 93.5 mhz; 24.6 kw. Ant 823 ft. Stereo. Prog sep from AM. ■ CBMT(TV) affil.

CFMB(AM)—Dec 21, 1962: 1410 khz; 10 kw-U, DA-1. TL: N45 24 01 W73 25 01. Hrs opn: 24. 35 York St., Westmount (H3Z 2Z5). (514) 483-2362. FAX: (514) 483-1362. Licensee: CFMB Ltee. Net: SBN. Rep: Target. Format: Ethnic. ■ Andrew Mielewczyk, pres & gen sls mgr; A.M. St. Germain, exec vp; Luigi Valente, stn mgr & chief engr; Ivana Bombardieri, prom mgr; Walter Centa, progmg dir; Tony Ferrara, mus dir; Augusto Tomasisni, news dir; Teddy Colantonio, pub affrs dir. ■ Rates: C$85; 65; 85; 65.

CFQR-FM—Listing follows CIQC(AM).

CFZZ-FM—(St. Jean-sur-Richelieu). 1992: 104.1 mhz; 570 w. 104 Rue Richelieu, St. Jean-Sur-Richelieu (J3B 6X3). (514) 346-0104. FAX: (514) 348-2274. Licensee: Power Broadcasting Inc. (acq 1-84). Format: Adult contemp. ■ Daniel Tremblay, gen mgr.

CHOM-FM—Listing follows CKIS(AM).

*****CIBL-FM**—Apr 26, 1980: 101.5 mhz; 315 w. Stereo. Hrs opn: 6 AM-1 AM. 1691 Boul. Pie IX, 2nd Fl. (H1V 2C3). (514) 526-2581. FAX: (514) 526-3583. Licensee: Station De Radio MF Communautaire. Rep: Target. Format: Div. News staff one; news progmg 14 hrs wkly. Target aud: General. Spec prog: Black 13 hrs, class 4 hrs, jazz 14 hrs, reggae 4 hrs, blues 2 hrs, tango 2 hrs wkly. ■ Jacques Primeau, pres; Guy Marion, Guy Leduc, vps; Mario Toussaint, gen mgr, stn mgr & opns dir; Denis Belanger, sls dir; Bertrand Roux, progmg dir; Sylvain Lafreniere, mus dir; Andre' Lazure, news dir & pub affrs dir. ■ Rates: C$20; 20; 20; 20.

CINQ-FM—Jan 27, 1975: 102.3 mhz; 1.29 kw. Ant 180 ft. Stereo. 5212 Boul. St. Laurent (H2T 1S1). (514) 495-2597. Licensee: Radio Centre-Ville Saint Louis Inc. Rep: Target. Format: Multilingual, French. News staff one; news progmg 7 hrs wkly. Target aud: 25-54; French & multilingual, multicultural, educ. h.s. plus. Spec prog: Sp 14 hrs, Port 14 hrs, Gr 13 hrs, Chinese 5 hrs, Haitian 6 hrs, English 18 hrs wkly. ■ Martine Hebert, gen mgr; Martin J. Tarnowski, gen sls mgr, mktg mgr & adv mgr; Martin J. Tarnowksi, prom mgr; Renee Roy, progmg dir & mus dir; Simon Dumais, news dir; Mark Provencher, chief engr. ■ Rates: C$36; 42; 48; 36.

CIQC(AM)—November 1919: 600 khz; 10 kw-D, 5 kw-N, DA-1. Suite 300, 1200 McGill College Ave. (H3B 4G7). (514) 874-4040. FAX: (514) 393-4659. Licensee: Mt. Royal Broadcasting Inc. (acq 10-88). Net: BN. Rep: Canadian Broadcast Sales. Format: Contemp country. News staff 4. Target aud: 35-54. ■ Pierre Beland, pres; Pierre Arcand, exec vp; Claude Dufault, gen mgr; Claude DuFault, vp sls; Kathie Murphy, prom mgr; Ted Silver, progmg mgr. ■ Rates: C$84; 84; 84; 84.

CFQR-FM—Co-owned with CIQC(AM). November 1966: 92.5 mhz; 41.4 kw. Ant 979 ft. Stereo. Hrs opn: 24. Prog sep from AM. Format: Adult contemp. Target aud: 25-54. ■ Ted Silver, progmg dir. ■ Rates: C$273; 196; 175; 126.

*****CISM-FM**—March 1991: 89.3 mhz; 10 kw. Box 6128, Station A, 2332 Edouard Montpetit (H3C 3J7). (514) 343-7511. FAX: (514) 343-2418. Licensee: Communications du Versant Nord. Format: Popular, alternative. ■ Claude Durand, gen mgr.

Stations in Canada | **Quebec**

CITE-FM—May 20, 1977: 107.3 mhz; 42.9 kw. Ant 700 ft. Stereo. 1411, rue Peel, bureau 602 (H3A 1S5). (514) 845-2483. FAX: (514) 288-1073. Licensee: Telemedia Communications Inc. (group owner). Rep: Opex. Format: Adult contemp. Target aud: 25-49. ■ Claude Beaudoin, pres; Lucie Veillet, natl sls dir; Suzanne Audet, rgnl sls mgr; Roger Laurendeau, progmg dir & mus dir; Robert Latreille, engrg mgr.

CJAD(AM)—Dec 8, 1945: 800 khz; 50 kw-D, 10 kw-N, DA-2. 1411 Rue du Fort (H3H 2R1). (514) 989-2523. FAX: (514) 989-3868. Licensee: Standard Radio Inc. Group owner: Standard Broadcasting Corp. Net: SBN. Rep: United. Format: Talk. Spec prog: Class 3 hrs, C&W 3 hrs. ■ Rob Braide, vp & gen mgr.

CJFM-FM—Co-owned with CJAD(AM). Oct 1, 1962: 95.9 mhz; 41.2 kw. Ant 979 ft. Stereo. Net: BN, SBN. Format: Adult contemp. Spec prog: Jazz 3 hrs wkly.

CJMS(AM)—Apr 23, 1954: 1280 khz; 50 kw-U, DA-2. Stereo. Hrs opn: 24. 1717 Boul. Rene Levesque E. (H2L 4E8). (514) 529-3200. FAX: (514) 529-3215. Licensee: Radiomutuel Inc. (group owner; acq 8-29-85). Net: Radiomutuel. Rep: Mutuelcom, United. Format: News/talk. News staff 16; news progmg 28 hrs wkly. Target aud: 25-54; adults. Spec prog: Rock 'N Roll (1955 to 1975). ■ Normand Beauchamp, pres; Paul-Emile Beaulne, exec vp; Raynald Briere, gen mgr & vp progmg; Bernard Migner, opns dir; Robert Leonard, vp sls; Jean-Luc Meilleur, sls dir & gen sls mgr; Marie Chantale Lang, prom dir; Andre' Lallier, mus dir; Colette Roger, asst mus dir; Phlippe Chatillon, news dir; Claude Bouchard, chief engr. ■ Rates: C$185; 185; 185; 75.

CKMF-FM—Co-owned with CJMS(AM). May 11, 1964: 94.3 mhz; 41.4 kw. Ant 979 ft. Stereo. Prog sep from AM. (514) 529-3229. FAX: (514) 529-9308. Net: Radiomutuel. Format: Dance mus, CHR. News progmg 5 hrs wkly. Target aud: 18-44. Spec prog: New age music 4 hrs wkly. ■ Charles Benoit, gen mgr; Yves Guerard, vp opns; Reneault Poliquin, gen sls mgr; Marcel Savard, prom mgr; Luc Tremblay, progmg dir; Claude Bouchard, engrg mgr.

CKAC(AM)—Sept 22, 1922: 730 khz; 50 kw-U, DA-1. 1411 Peel St., Suite 300 (H3A 3L5). (514) 845-5151. FAX: (514) 845-2224. Licensee: Telemedia Communications Inc. (group owner). Net: UPI. Rep: Opex. Format: MOR. News progmg 20 hrs wkly. Target aud: 35-54. Spec prog: "Souvenirs" format and "Retro." ■ R. James McCoubrey, CEO; Philippe de Gaspe Beaubien, chmn; Claude Beaudoin, pres & gen mgr; Luc Sabbatini, gen sls mgr; Marie Vaellan Court, progmg mgr; Jean-Guy Faucher, mus dir; Robert Latreille, engrg dir. ■ Rates: C$51; 37.80; 30; 16.80

CKIS(AM)—Dec 7, 1959: 990 khz; 50 kw-U. 1310 Greene Ave. (H3Z 2B5). (514) 931-4487. FAX: TWX: 05-24827. Licensee: CHUM Ltd. (group owner; acq 9-5-85). Rep: Major Mkt, Hooper. Format: Oldies. ■ Lee Hambleton, gen mgr; JoAnne Rudy, vp opns; Mark Dickie, gen sls mgr & vp mktg; Jennifer Roman, vp prom; Ian Maclean, progmg dir; Dave Reynolds, mus dir; Andrew Carter, news dir; Denis Dion, vp engrg.

CHOM-FM—Co-owned with CKIS(AM). July 16, 1963: 97.7 mhz; 47.1 kw. Ant 979 ft. TL: N45 30 20 W73 35 32. Stereo. Hrs opn: 24. (514) 937-2466. FAX: (514) 935-8301. Format: AOR. News staff 6; news progmg 4 hrs wkly. Target aud: 18-44. ■ Neil Kushnir, mus dir. ■ Rates: $170; 130; 140; 120.

CKMF-FM—Listing follows CJMS(AM).

CKOI-FM—Listing follows CKVL(AM).

*****CKUT-FM**—November 1987: 90.3 mhz. 3480 McTavish St. (H3A 1X9). (514) 398-6787. Licensee: Radio McGill Inc. Format: Div. ■ Pat Dillon, gen mgr; Louise Burns, vp sls; Genevieve Heistek, Rob Gaurin, mus dirs; Stuart Greer, asst mus dir; Becky Scott, news dir; Sarah Toy, vp engrg; Hani Fabashi, engrg dir; Chris Migone, chief engr.

CKVL(AM)—(Verdun). Nov 3, 1946: 850 khz; 50 kw-D, 10 kw-N, DA-2. 211 Gordon Ave., Verdun (H4G 2R2). (514) 766-2311. FAX: (514) 761-2122. Licensee: Metromedia CMR Inc. (acq 8-25-92). Net: Newsradio, BN. Format: Talk, MOR. ■ Pierre La Arcand, stn mgr; Robert Ashby, progmg dir.

CKOI-FM—(Verdun). Co-owned with CKVL(AM). 1953: 96.9 mhz; 307 kw. Ant 712 ft. Stereo. Prog sep from AM. Format: Progsv/contemp. ■ Andre St. Thomas, progmg dir.

New Carlisle

CHNC(AM)—Dec 23, 1933: 610 khz; 10 kw-D, 5 kw-N, DA-1. Box 610, 153 Route 132 (G0C 1Z0). (418) 752-2215. FAX: (418) 752-6939. Licensee: Radio CHNC Ltee. Net: Telemedia. Rep: All-Canada. Format: MOR. ■ Reginald Poirier, gen mgr.

Noranda

CKRN(AM)—See Rouyn.

Plessisville

CKTL(AM)—Oct 18, 1972: 1420 khz; 1 kw-D, 500 w-N, DA-1. Box 142 (G6L 2Y6). (819) 362-3737. FAX: (819) 362-3414. Licensee: Societe CKTL Radio Media Enr. Group owner: Reseau des Appalaches. Net: Telemedia, BN, SBN. Rep: Radio Unie. Format: MOR.■Jean-Pierre Marted, stn mgr.

Pohenegamook

CFVD-FM-2—Sept 10, 1983: 104.9 mhz; 50 w. Hrs opn: 24. Rebroadcasts CJMF-FM Quebec. CP 670, 654 6ieme Rue, Degelis (G0L 1H0). (418) 853-3370; (418) 853-2370. FAX: (418) 853-3321. Licensee: Radio Degelis Inc. Net: Canadian Broadcast Sales. Format: Div. News staff one. Target aud: General. ■ Rino Caissie, pres; Gilles Caron, gen mgr, dev dir, sls dir, mktg dir & progmg dir; Jacques Goulet, natl sls mgr; Guylain Jean, mus dir; Caroline LaFlamme, asst mus dir; Jocelyn Ouellet, news dir; Jacques Martin, chief engr.

Port-Cartier

CIPC(AM)—Oct 4, 1976: 710 khz; 1 kw-U, DA-1. Suite 230, 8 Boul des Iles (G5B 2J4). (418) 766-6868. FAX: (418) 766-6870. Licensee: Radio Port-Cartier Inc. (acq 12-1-80). Net: NTR. Format: Top-40. News staff one; ■ Yvon Savoie, pres & gen mgr; Daniel Cliche, progmg dir; Patrick Lapointe, mus dir; Nicolas Vigneault, news dir; Jean La Verdiere, chief engr.

Quebec

*****CBV(AM)**—Sept 29, 1938: 980 khz; 50 kw-D, DA-D. TL: N46 41 06 W71 23 55. Hrs opn: 5 AM-1:30 AM. 2505 boul. Laurier, Ste. Foy (G1V 2X2). (418) 654-1341; (418) 654-3035. FAX: (418) 656-8505; TWX: 065-28046. Licensee: Societe Radio Canada. Net: SBN, CBC Mono. Format: Div, news, talk. News progmg 15 hrs wkly. Target aud: General.■Bertrand Emond, gen mgr & progmg dir; Jean Claude Picard, news dir; Andre Cote, chief engr. ■ CBVT(TV) affil.

*****CBV-FM**—1974: 95.3 mhz; 100 kw. Ant 541 ft. TL: N46 51 40 W71 04 46. Stereo. Hrs opn: 24. Prog sep from AM. TELEX: 051-2286. Net: CBC. Format: Classical. News progmg 7 hrs wkly. Target aud: General. Spec prog: Jazz 16 hrs, news 7 hrs wkly.

CBVE-FM—March 1979: 104.7 mhz; 100 kw. Ant 411 ft. Suite 100, 900 Place d'Youville (G1R 3P7). (418) 691-3620. FAX: (418) 691-3335. Licensee: Canadian Broadcasting Corp. Net: CBC Radio. Format: News, talk, div. ■ Claude Saindon, gen mgr.

CHIK-FM—Listing follows CJRP(AM).

CHOI-FM—Listing follows CHRC(AM).

CHRC(AM)—Apr 1, 1926: 800 khz; 50 kw-U, DA-1. 2136, Chemin Ste-Foy, Ste-Foy (G1V 1R8). (418) 688-8080. FAX: (418) 682-8429. Licensee: Les Entreprises de Radiodiffusion de la Capitale Inc. (acq 5-22-85). Format: News, sports, MOR & gold. ■ Michel Cadrin, pres & gen mgr.

CHOI-FM—Co-owned with CHRC(AM). Nov 1, 1949: 98.1 mhz; 81 kw. Ant 250 ft. Stereo. Prog sep from AM. Format: Adult contemp. Spec prog: Jazz 8 hrs wkly.

CITF-FM—July 22, 1982: 107.5 mhz; 37.8 kw. Ant 500 ft. Stereo. Hrs opn: 24. Suite 250, 580 Grande Allee St. (G1R 2K2). (418) 525-4545. FAX: (418) 525-6399. Licensee: Telemedia Communications Inc. (group owner). Format: Adult contemp. News staff one. Target aud: 25-54. ■ Claude Beaudoin, CEO; Liette Champagne, gen mgr; Marc Tanguay, opns dir & progmg dir; Diane BeLanger, sls dir.

CJMF-FM—Sept 15, 1979: 93.3 mhz; 48 kw. Ant 1,275 ft. Stereo. Hrs opn: 24. 600 Belvedere (G1S 3E5). (418) 687-9330; (418) 688-9301. FAX: (418) 687-9718. Licensee: CJMF-FM Ltee. Group owner: Cogeco Inc. (acq 11-87; $8 million). Net: NTR. Format: Light adult contemp. News staff 3; news progmg 3 hrs wkly. Target aud: 25-49; mostly female with upscale income. ■ Henri Audet, chmn; Louis Audet, pres; Michael Carter, CFO; Alain Plante, exec vp; Andre Cote, gen mgr & sls dir; Claude Thibodean, natl sls mgr; Claire Girard, prom mgr; Dan Tremblay, progmg dir & mus dir; Marc Landriault, asst mus dir; Denis Langlois, news dir; Martin Brandl, engrg dir. ■ Rates: C$80; 80; 80; 50.

CJRP(AM)—June 15, 1969; 1060 khz; 50 kw-D, 10 kw-N, DA-2. 1300 Boulevard Laurier, Sillery (G1S 1L8). (418) 688-1060. FAX: (418) 683-7058. Licensee: Radiomutuel Inc. division CJRP. Group owner:Radiomutuel Inc. (acq 6-15-69). Net: Radiomutuel. Rep: Mutuelcom. Format: Oldies, talk, news. News staff 6. Spec prog: Hockey. ■ Andre Gasnon, vp; Marleine Simard, gen mgr & sls dir; Daniel Plante, prom dir; Marc Simoneau, asst mus dir; Michel Duval, engrg dir.

CHIK-FM—Co-owned with CJRP(AM). Aug 1, 1982: 98.9 mhz. Suite 105, 1245 Chemin Ste-Foy (G1S 4P2). (418) 687-9900. Format: Dance mus. ■ Marpyne Riouxx, gen mgr; Real Marcotte, sls dir; Daniel Plante, progmg dir.

CKIA-FM—Oct 31, 1984: 96.1 mhz; 6.8 w. Ant 700 ft. TL: N46 48 28 W71 12 57. 570 Rue du Roi (G1K 2X2). (418) 529-9026. FAX: (418) 529-4156. Licensee: Radio Basse-Ville Inc. Format: MOR. News staff 3; news progmg 87 hrs wkly. Target aud: General; all ages, all incomes, all races, all languages. Spec prog: Class 3 hrs, jazz 4 hrs, Sp 4 hrs, Vietnamese one hr, Haitian 2 hrs, Chinois 2 hrs, African one hr wkly. ■ Normand Lapierre, gen mgr; Andre Domerleau, sls dir; Francine Doucet, progmg dir. ■ Rates: C$50; 25; 50; 25.

*****CKRL-FM**—Feb 15, 1973: 89.1 mhz; 1.4 kw. Ant 700 ft. Stereo. 250 Grande Allee W. (G1R 2H4). (418) 640-2575. FAX: (418) 640-1588. Licensee: Campus Laval FM Inc. Format: Div. Spec prog: Class 6 hrs, jazz 4 hrs, Sp 2 hrs, It 2 hrs, Black 6 hrs, Arab 3 hrs wkly. ■ Sylvaim Panjuay, gen mgr.

Rimouski

CFLP(AM)—May 21, 1978: 1000 khz; 10 kw-U, DA-2. 875 Boul. St. Germain Ouest (G5L3T9). (418) 723-2323. FAX: (418) 722-7508. Licensee: Diffusion Power. Net: Radiomutuel. Format: MOR.■Pierre Harvey, pres & gen mgr.

CIKI-FM—Co-owned with CFLP(AM). Feb 14, 1988: 98.7 mhz; 100 kw. Stereo. Prog sep from AM. Format: AOR, CHR.

CJBR(AM)—Nov 15, 1937: 900 khz; 10 kw-U, DA-2. 273 rue St-Jean Baptiste Ouest (G5L 4J8). (418) 723-2217. FAX: (418) 722-7753. Licensee: CJBR Radio Ltee. (acq 1-8-77). Net: CBC AM, Radio Canada. Format: MOR. ■ Yvan Asselin, gen mgr.

CJBR-FM—Feb 28, 1959: 101.5 mhz; 20 kw. Ant 931 ft. Stereo. Prog sep from AM. Net: CBC Stereo.

Riviere au Renard

CJRE-FM—1979: 97.9 mhz; 56 w. Ant 594 ft. C.P. 380, 162 Jacques Cartier (G0C 1R0). (418) 368-3511. Licensee: Radio Gaspesie Inc. Format: MOR. ■ Alain Fournier, gen mgr.

Riviere du Loup

CIBM-FM—1966: 107.1 mhz; 1 kw. Ant 244 ft. 64 Hotel de Ville (G5R 1L5). (418) 867-1071. FAX: (418) 862-7704. TELEX: 051-3956. Licensee: CIBM Mont-Bleu. Net: Telemedia. Rep: Opex. Format: Pop rock. ■ Guy Simard, gen mgr.

CJFP(AM)—1947: 1400 khz; 10 kw-D, 5 kw-N. TL: N47 47 43 W69 35 27. 64 Hotel-de-Ville (G5R 1L5). (418) 862-8241. FAX: (418) 862-7704. Licensee: Radio CJFP Ltee. Rep: Opex. Format: MOR. ■ Guy Simard, pres & gen mgr; Renee Giard, sls dir, natl sls mgr, rgnl sls mgr, mktg dir & prom dir; Daniel St. Pierre, progmg dir, asst mus dir & news dir.

Roberval

CHRL(AM)—June 1, 1949: 910 khz; 10 kw-U, DA-2. TL: N48 26 25 W72 06 47. Hrs opn: 24. 568 Boulevard St. Joseph (G8H 2K6). (418) 275-1831. FAX: (418) 275-2475. Licensee: Radio Roberval Inc. (acq 1-6-93). Net: Telemedia. Rep: Opex. Format: Adult contemp, contemp hit. News staff one; news progmg 20 hrs wkly. Target aud: General; mainly adults.■Marc-Andre Levesque, pres & gen mgr; Germain Gagnon, mus dir; Marcel Bolduc, vp engrg. ■ Rates: $40; 35; 38; 40.

Rouyn

CKRN(AM)—Oct 2, 1939: 1400 khz; 1 kw-D, 250 w-N. 380 Ave. Murdoch, Noranda (J9X 1G5). (819) 762-0741. FAX: (819) 762-2280. Licensee: Radio Nord Inc. (group owner). Net: Telemedia. Rep: Opex Communications. Format: Adult contemp. ■ Gilles Poulin, pres; Bernard

Quebec

Gauthier, gen mgr & gen sls mgr; Real Robert, progmg dir; Roxanne Paradise, news dir.

CHOA-FM—Co-owned with CKRN(AM). Sept 21, 1990: 96.5 mhz; 55 kw. Ant 600 ft. Stereo. Prog dups AM. Net: NTR. News staff one. Target aud: 25-54. ■ CFEM-CKRN TV affil.

Rouyn-Noranda

CJMM-FM—June 17, 1988: 99.1 mhz; 3.5 kw. Ant 200 ft. Stereo. Hrs opn: 24. 33 B Gamble W. (J9X 2R3). (819) 797-2566. FAX: (819) 797-1664. Licensee: Radiomutuel Inc. (group owner). Net: Radiomutuel. Format: AOR. News staff 3; news progmg 5 hrs wkly. Target aud: 18-49. ■ Jean-Guy Veillette, gen mgr & vp sls; Robert Lariviere, prom dir; Alain Dupuis, progmg dir & news dir; Denis Cossette, engrg dir. ■ Rates: C$90; 90; 90; 90.

Saguenay

CHLC(AM)—See Baie Comeau.

St. Eleuthere

CHRT(AM)—1967: 1450 khz; 1 kw-D, 250 w-N. 64 Hotel De Ville (G5R 1R5). (418) 862-8241. FAX: (418) 862-7704. TELEX: 0513915. Licensee: CIBM Mont-Bleu. Format: MOR. ■ Guy Simard, pres.

St. Gabriel-de-Brandon

CFNJ-FM—Aug 10, 1985: 99.1 mhz; 3 kw. Ant 1,300 ft. C.P. 120, 30 rue des Ecoles (J0K 2N0). (514) 835-3437; (514) 835-3438. Licensee: Radio Nord Joli Inc. Format: MOR. Spec prog: Black one hr, class 2 hrs, C&W 4 hrs, jazz 2 hrs. ■ Claude Buysse, gen mgr.

St. Georges-de-Beauce

CKRB(AM)—1953: 1460 khz; 10 kw-D, 5 kw-N, DA-1. CP 100, 170, 120ieme rue (G5Y 5C4). (418) 228-1460. FAX: (418) 228-0096. Licensee: Radio Beauce Inc. (acq 2-73). Net: SBN. Format: Adult contemp. News staff 2; news progmg 7 hrs wkly. Target aud: 18-54. ■ Nelson Jalbert, pres; Jacques Petit, gen mgr.

CIRO-FM—Co-owned with CKRB(AM). June 22, 1987: 99.7 mhz; 100 kw. Ant 350 ft. Stereo. (418) 227-0997. Format: Country. News progmg 4 hrs wkly. Target aud: 25-64.

St. Hilarion

CIHO-FM—Oct 10, 1986: 96.3 mhz. C.P. 160, 315 Cartier Nord (G0A 3V0). (418) 457-3333. FAX: (418) 457-3518. Licensee: Radio MF Charbroin Inc. Net: NTR. Format: MOR. News staff 4. Spec prog: Class 2 hrs, jazz 2 hrs wkly. ■ Lynn Lavoie, gen mgr; Martine Sauve, progmg dir.

St. Hyacinthe

CFEI-FM—1988: 106.5 mhz. 855 rue Ste. Marie (J2S 4R9). (514) 774-6486. FAX: (514) 774-7785. Licensee: Cogeco Radio-Television Inc. Group owner: Cogeco Inc. Format: MOR. ■ Michel Veilleppe, gen mgr.

St. Jean-sur-Richelieu

CFZZ-FM—Licensed to St. Jean-sur-Richelieu. See Montreal.

Ste. Adele

CIME-FM—Mar 25, 1977: 99.5 mhz; 50 kw. Ant 500 ft. Stereo. Box 1260, 400 Boul. Ste. Adele (J0R 1L0). (514) 229-2995. Licensee: Diffusion Laurentides Inc. (acq 1985.) Format: MOR. ■ Jean-Pierre Coallier, pres; Pierre-Paul Elie, gen mgr; Rejean Beaulieu, sls dir; Julie Belanger, progmg dir.

Ste. Anne des Monts

CBGN(AM)—1340 khz; 1 kw-D, 250 w-N. Box 2000, 155 St. Sacrament, Matane (G4W 3P7). (418) 562-0290. Licensee: CBC (acq 9-1-72). Format: MOR. ■ Louis Pelletier, gen mgr.

CJMC(AM)—Nov 10, 1974: 1490 khz; 1 kw-U, DA-1. C.P. 820, 170 Blvd. Ste. Anne (G0E 2G0). (418) 763-5522. FAX: (418) 763-7211. Licensee: Radio du Golfe Inc. Net: Radiomutuel, Newsradio. Rep: Target. Format: MOR. Spec prog: Class 2 hrs, western 2 hrs wkly. ■ Roger Vallee, pres; Jacques Vallee, opns dir, opns mgr, adv dir & progmg dir; Serge Chretien, sls dir, mktg dir & prom dir; Stephane Cyr, mus dir & news dir; Bruno Dumont, chief engr. ■ Rates: $30; 27; 28; 26.

Ste. Anne des Plaines

*****CFIC-FM**—Sept 25, 1993: 103.1 mhz; 50 w. TL: N45 45 69 W73 49 92 Hrs opn: 6 AM-midnight. Rebroadcasts CISM-FM Montreal. 149 rue Valiquet (J0N 1H0). Licensee: Mario Lacombe. Format: MOR, Fr, classic rock. News progmg 6 hrs wkly. Target aud: General; local and rural. ■ Mario Lacombe, pres, gen mgr, stn mgr & opns dir; Christine Gaudrault, CFO; Pierre Houle, exec vp & progmg dir; Mike Mathieu, engrg dir. ■ Rates: C$10; 7; 7; 7.

Ste. Marie-de-Beauce

CJVL(AM)—Dec 12, 1974: 1360 khz; 10 kw-D, 5 kw-N, DA-2. 1360, Rue Notre Dame Sud (G6E-2W9). (418) 387-1360. FAX: (418) 387-3757. Licensee: Clival Inc. (acq 5-1-92; $200,000). Rep: Canadian Broadcast Sales. Format: MOR, adult contemp, C&W. News staff one; news progmg 8 hrs wkly. Target aud: 18 plus. ■ Nelson Jalbert, pres, gen mgr & opns mgr; Jacques Rancourt, sls dir & adv dir; France Berthiaume, natl sls mgr; Jacques Lessard, France Berthiaume, prom dirs; Jacques Lessard, progmg dir; Eric Vachon, mus dir; Patrice Moore, news dir; Gaston Guay, chief engr. ■ Rates: C$27; 22.25; 23.50; na.

Sept-Iles

*****CBSI-FM**—Nov 1, 1982: 98.1 mhz; 96.7 kw. Ant 350 ft. Suite 30, 350 rue Smith (G4R 3X2). (418) 968-0720. FAX: (418) 968-9219. Licensee: CBC. Net: CBC Stereo. Format: Btfl mus, educ, talk. News progmg 6 hrs wkly. Target aud: General. ■ Pierre Lafreniere, stn mgr; Sylvain Lamarre, chief opns.

CKCN(AM)—Mar 10, 1963: 560 khz; 10 kw-D, 5 kw-N, DA-2. 437 Amavd St. (G4R 4K9). (418) 962-3838. FAX: (418) 968-6662. Licensee: Radio Sept-Iles Inc. Format: MOR. ■ Yvon Bergeron, gen mgr.

Shawinigan

CKSM(AM)—Apr 30, 1951: 1220 khz; 10 kw-D, 2.5 kw-N, DA-2. Box 578 (G9N 6V6). (819) 537-8824; (819) 375-4855. FAX: (819) 537-0465. Licensee: Radiomutuel Inc. (acq 8-18-92). Net: BN. Rep: All-Canada. Format: Adult contemp.

Sherbrooke

CHLT(AM)—June 1937: 630 khz; 10 kw-D, 5 kw-N. 25 Bryant St. (G1G 3Z5). (819) 563-6363. Licensee: CHLT Radio/Telemedia Group owner: Telemedia Communications Inc. (acq 6-17-70). Format: MOR. ■ Michel Fortin, gen mgr.

CITE-FM-1—Co-owned with CHLT(AM). September 1962: 102.7 mhz; 92.8 kw. Ant 1,851 ft. Stereo. (819) 566-6655.

CIMO-FM—See Magog.

CITE-FM-1—Listing follows CHLT(AM).

CKTS(AM)—July 1, 1946: 900 khz; 10 kw-U, DA-2. TL: N45 26 00 W72 01 00. Rebroadcasts CJAD(AM) Montreal. c/o CJAD(AM), 1411 Rue du Fort, Montreal (H3H 2R1). (514) 989-2523. FAX: (514) 989-3868. Licensee: Telemedia Communications Ltee, div CKTS. Group owner: Telemedia Communications Inc. Format: Talk. ■ Michel Fortin, gen mgr.

Sorel

CJSO-FM—Sept 27, 1989: 101.7 mhz; 3.5 kw. Ant 327 ft. 100 boul. Couillard Despres (J3P 5C1). (514) 743-2772. FAX: (514) 743-0293. Licensee: Radio Diffusion Sorel-Tracy (acq 7-25-88). Net: NTR. Format: Adult contemp. News staff 4. Spec prog: Class 2 hrs wkly. ■ Normand Niquet, gen mgr; Louis Letreverse, progmg dir.

Thetford Mines

CKLD(AM)—Feb 12, 1950: 1330 khz; 10 kw-U, DA-1. 327 Ave Labbe (G6G 5S3). (418) 335-7533. FAX: (418) 338-0386. Licensee: Radio Megantic Ltee. Group owner: Reseau des Appalaches (acq 12-1-59). Net: NTR. Rep: Radio Uni Quebec. Format: MOR. ■ Francois Labbe, pres; Jeanne Martin, gen mgr & gen sls mgr; Raymond Cusson, progmg dir & mus dir; Luc Berthold, news dir; Renaud Cloutier, chief engr.

CFJO-FM—Co-owned with CKLD(AM). July 15, 1989: 103.3 mhz; 50 kw. Ant 270 ft. Prog dups AM 25%. (418) 338-1009. Net: BN Voice Service. Format: Rock(AOR). Spec prog: Jazz 8 hrs wkly.

Trois Rivieres

CBF-FM-1—July 21, 1977: 100.7 mhz; 38.4 kw. Ant 132 ft. Stereo. Box 6000 (H3C 3A8). (514) 597-5970. Licensee: CBC French. Net: CBC. Format: Class, cultural, drama. ■ Marcel Pepin, vp & gen mgr.

CHEY-FM—Listing follows CHLN(AM).

CHLN(AM)—Oct 17, 1937: 550 khz; 10 kw-D, 5 kw-N, DA-2. 1500 Rue Royale (G9A 6J4). (819) 374-3556. FAX: (819) 374-3222. Licensee: CHLN/55. Group owner: Radiomutuel Communications Inc. (acq 7-70). Net: CBC, Telemedia. Rep: Opex. Format: MOR, top-40. Spec prog: Pub affrs 8 hrs wkly. ■ John Martin, gen mgr.

CHEY-FM—Co-owned with CHLN(AM). Aug 22, 1990: 94.7 mhz; 100 kw. Format: Soft rock. ■ Marc Tangay, progmg dir.

CIGB-FM—Aug 27, 1979: 102.3 mhz; 11 kw. Stereo. Hrs opn: 24. 1675 Boul des Forges (G8Z 1T7). (819) 378-1023. FAX: (819) 378-1360. Licensee: Radiomutuel Inc. (group owner; acq 8-24-90). Net: Radiomutuel. Format: CHR. News staff 5; news progmg 3 hrs wkly. Target aud: 18-49. ■ Normand Beauchamp, pres; Andre Gagnon, vp; Jean-Paul LeMire, gen mgr, stn mgr & sls dir; Danielle Viens, prom dir; Daniel Beaumont, progmg dir; Francois L'Herbier, mus dir; Maurice Bouchard, engrg dir.

CJTR(AM)—Feb 6, 1954: 1140 khz; 50 kw-D, 10 kw-N, DA-2. Edifice Place Royale, 1350 rue Royale (G9A 4J4). (819) 375-4855. FAX: (819) 375-1223. Licensee: CJTR Radio Trois-Rivieres Ltee. Group owner: Radiomutuel Inc. (acq 4-23-68). Net: Radiomutuel. Rep: Mutuelcom. Format: Talk. ■ Jean Paul Lemrre, gen mgr.

Val d'Or

CJMV-FM—June 17, 1989: 102.7 mhz; 65 kw. Ant 200 ft. 173 Perreault St. (J9P 2H3). (819) 825-2568. FAX: (819) 825-2840. Licensee: Radiomutuel Inc. (group owner). Net: Radiomutuel Inc. Rep: Mutuelcom. Format: Pop music. News staff one; news progmg 44 hrs wkly. Target aud: 18-49. ■ Normand Beauchamp, pres; Gaston Morin, gen mgr, opns dir & gen sls mgr; Louis Kirouac, mktg mgr, prom dir & progmg dir; Genevieve Moreau, mus dir; Frederic Plante, pub affrs dir; Denis Cassette, engrg dir.

CKVD(AM)—1939: 900 khz; 10 kw-D, 2.5 kw-N, DA-1. 1729 3e Ave. (J9P 1W3). (819) 825-0010. FAX: (819) 825-7313. Licensee: Radio-Nord Inc. (group owner). Net: Telemedia. Rep: Opex. Format: MOR. News staff 4. Target aud: 35 plus. ■ Gilles Poulin, pres; Daniel Hamel, gen mgr; Bernard Gauthier, gen sls mgr; Jean Gagnon, progmg dir; Onil Marcotte, news dir. ■ Rates: C$26; 26; 20; 18.

Valleyfield

CKOD(AM)—Nov 10, 1961: 1370 khz; 10 kw-D, 5 kw-N. Hrs opn: 24. 249 Victoria St. (J6T 1A9). (514) 373-1370; (514) 455-8400. FAX: (514) 373-4297. Licensee: Radio Express Inc. (acq 3-91). Net: NTR. Rep: Radio Unie, Target. Format: Adult contemp. News progmg 15 hrs wkly. Target aud: General; 18-54. ■ Jean-Pierre Major, pres, gen mgr, vp progmg & mus dir; Suzanne Turbide, vp & opns dir; Gaston LeGault, sls dir; Darcy Kieran, mktg dir; Jadrino Huot, news dir; Pierre LaBerge, chief engr.

Verdun

CKOI-FM—Licensed to Verdun. See Montreal.

CKVL(AM)—Licensed to Verdun. See Montreal.

Victoriaville

CFDA(AM)—Oct 19, 1951: 1380 khz; 10 kw-U, DA-2. Box 490, 55 St. Jean Baptiste St. (G6P 6T3). (819) 752-5545. FAX: (819) 752-7552. Licensee: Radio Victoriaville Ltee. (acq 1-3-70). Rep: Target, Radio Unie. Format: MOR. News staff one. Target aud: General; 25-59. Spec prog: Farm 6 hrs, country 10 hrs wkly. ■ Francois Labbe, pres; Robert Daneau, gen mgr, vp sls & vp progmg; Raymond Cusson, mus dir; Andre Bellavance, news dir; Andre Bellavance, Yvon Moreau, Myriam LaRouche, pub affrs dirs; Jacques Jachon, Renaud Clautier, vps engrg. ■ Rates: $28; 28; 28; 23.

Ville Degelis

CFVD(AM)—Mar 1, 1978: 1370 khz; 1 kw-U. Hrs opn: 24. CP 670, 654 6ieme rue (G0L 1H0). (418) 853-2370; (418) 853-3370. Licensee: Radio Degelis Inc. Rep: Canadian Broadcast Sales. Format: CHR, country, adult contemp. News staff one. Target aud: General. ■ Rino Caissie, chmn; Regis Roy, vp; Gilles Caron, gen mgr;

Stations in Canada

Saskatchewan

Guylain Jean, mus dir; Caroline LaFlamme, asst mus dir; Jocelyn Ouellet, news dir. ■ Rates: C$15; 14.50; 14; 11.

Ville-Marie

CKVM(AM)—January 1950: 710 khz; 10 kw-D, 1 kw-N, DA-2. C.P. 3000 (J0Z 3W0). (819) 629-2710. FAX: (819) 622-0716. Licensee: Radio Temiscamingue Inc. Net: CBC, Telemedia, SBN. Rep: All-Canada. Format: Adult contemp. Target aud: General. ■ Real Dostie, pres; Bernard Barrette, vp; Yvon Lariviere, stn mgr & progmg dir; Raynald Denommee, sls dir & prom dir; Yves Bertand, mus dir; H.P. Raymond, asst mus dir; Yves Hamel, chief engr. ■ Rates: C$29; 28; 27; na.

Westmount

CKIS(AM)—See Montreal.

Saskatchewan

Estevan

CJSL(AM)—August 1959: 1280 khz; 10 kw-U, DA-N. Box 1280 (S4A 2H8). (306) 634-1280. FAX: (306) 634-6364. Licensee: Soo Line Broadcasting Ltd. Rep: Canadian Broadcast Sales. Format: Contemp country. News staff 2; news progmg 14 hrs wkly. Target aud: General. Spec prog: Farm 4 hrs, relg 10 hrs wkly. ■ Jackie Gray, pres & natl sls mgr; Lee Friesen, gen mgr & gen sls mgr; Dave Kirk, mus dir; Dwayne Kocoy, news dir; Jim Hutchings, chief engr. ■ Rates: C$21; 21; 21; 11.

Gravelbourg

***CBKF-1(AM)**—1952: 540 khz; 5 kw-U, DA-2. 2440 Broad, Regina (S4P 4A1). (306) 347-9540. Licensee: Societe Radio Canada en Saskatchewan. Net: CBC AM. Format: Div. ■ Evan Purchase, progmg dir.

Kindersley

CFYM(AM)—July 29, 1987: 1210 khz; 1 kw-U. Box 490, Rosetown (S0L 2V0). (306) 463-4411. FAX: (306) 882-3037. Licensee: Dace Broadcasting Corp. (acq 4-78). Net: BN. Rep: RTVR. Format: All hit gold. ■ Dennis Dyck, gen mgr; Dave Sutherland, adv dir; Harland Lesyk, adv mgr.

La Ronge

***CBKA-FM**—September 1979: 105.9 mhz; 80 w. Box 959 (S0J 1L0). (306) 425-3324. FAX: (306) 425-2270. Licensee: CBC. Net: CBC. Format: Regional current affairs. Spec prog: Cree & Dene 20 hrs wkly. ■ S.B. Lloyd, stn mgr.

Meadow Lake

CJNS(AM)—Nov 1, 1977: 1240 khz; 1 kw-U, DA-1. Box 1660 (S0M 1V0). (306) 236-6494. FAX: (306) 236-6141. Licensee: Northwestern Radio Partnership (acq 5-19-89). Format: C&W. ■ Ken Schiller, stn mgr.

Melfort

CJVR(AM)—Oct 8, 1966: 1420 khz; 10 kw-U, DA-N. TL: N52 47 57 W104 35 25. Stereo. Hrs opn: 24. Box 1420, 611 Main St. N. (S0E 1A0). (306) 752-2867. FAX: (306) 752-5932. Licensee: Radio CJVR Ltd. (acq 9-27-90). Net: BN, Sun. Rep: Telemedia Sales. Format: Uptown country. News staff 3. Target aud: General. Spec prog: Relg 9 hrs wkly. ■ Eugene Fabro Sr., chmn; Eugene W. Fabro, pres; Gary Fitz, vp, gen mgr, stn mgr, natl sls mgr & rgnl sls mgr; Ray Telford, gen sls mgr; Jim Williamson, prom dir; Bill Wood, progmg dir; Calvin Gratton, mus dir; Fred Peters, news dir; Alice McFarlane, pub affrs dir; Bayne Opseth, chief engr. ■ Rates: C$71.10; 62.10; 53.10; 35.10.

Moose Jaw

CHAB(AM)—Apr 22, 1922: 800 khz; 10 kw-U, DA-N. Stereo. 116 Main St. N. (S6H 3J7). (306) 694-0800. FAX: (306) 692-8880. Licensee: Golden West Broadcasting Ltd. (group owner; acq 8-20-92). Rep: Canadian Broadcast Sales, Messner, Dome. Format: Contemp country. Target aud: 25-54. ■ Elmer Hildebrand, pres; Ed Lundberg, stn mgr & gen sls mgr; Barry Vice, prom mgr & progmg mgr; Desiree Daniels, mus dir; Rob Carnie,

news dir; Randy McLaren, engrg dir. ■ Rates: $72; 66; 66; 36.

North Battleford

CJNB(AM)—Jan 28, 1947: 1050 khz; 10 kw-U, DA-1. Box 1460 (S9A 2Z5). (306) 445-2477. FAX: (306) 445-4599. Licensee: Northwestern Radio Partnership (acq 5-19-89). Rep: Canadian Broadcast Sales. Format: Contemp country. Spec prog: Farm 7 hrs, relg 10 hrs wkly. ■ Gord Rawlinson, pres; H.G. Dekker, gen mgr; David Dekker, gen sls mgr; Harry M. Decker, prom mgr; Doug Harrison, progmg dir & mus dir; Linda Lewis, news dir; Dave Senft, chief engr.

Prince Albert

CKBI(AM)—1934: 900 khz; 10 kw-U, DA-N. Box 900 (S6V 7R4). (306) 763-7421. FAX: (306) 764-1850. Licensee: Central Broadcasting Co. Ltd. (acq 1946). Rep: Canadian Broadcast Sales. Format: Adult contemp, MOR, oldies. News staff 7; news progmg 25 hrs wkly. Target aud: 34 plus; working women. Spec prog: Farm 2 hrs wkly. ■ Jim Scarrow, gen mgr; Dave Hryhor, rgnl sls mgr; Neil Headrick, progmg dir; Dale Zimmerman, engrg mgr.

CFMM-FM—Co-owned with CKBI(AM). Jan 30, 1982: 99.1 mhz; 100 kw. Ant 606 ft. Stereo. Prog sep from AM. Box 99 (S6V 5R4). Format: Classic rock, contemp hit. News staff 10; news progmg 35 hrs wkly. ■ Mark Loshack, progmg mgr.

Regina

***CBK(AM)**—July 29, 1939: 540 khz; 50 kw-D, DA. 2440 Broad St. (S4P 4A1). (306) 347-9540. Licensee: CBC. Net: CBC Mono. Format: Div. Spec prog: Farm 5 hrs wkly. ■ Michael Snook, gen mgr.

***CBK-FM**—May 1, 1977: 96.9 mhz; 100 kw. Ant 501 ft. Stereo. Prog sep from AM. Net: SBN, CBC Stereo. ■ CBKT-TV affil.

CBKF-FM—Sept 1, 1973: 97.7 mhz; 13.7 kw. Ant 501 ft. 2440 Broad St. (S4P 4A1). (306) 347-9540. Licensee: Radio Canada. Net: BN, CBC Mono. ■ Richard Marcotte, gen mgr. ■ CBKF-TV affil.

CHMX-FM—Listing follows CKRM(AM).

CIZL-FM—Listing follows CJME(AM).

CJME(AM)—Nov 24, 1959: 1300 khz; 10 kw-U, DA-1. Hrs opn: 24. Suite 210, 2401 Saskatchewan Dr. (S4P 4H8). (306) 569-1300. FAX: (306) 347-8557. Licensee: RAWLCO Communications Ltd. (group owner; acq 4-67). Rep: Major Mkt. Format: Greatest hits of all time. ■ Michael Zaplitny, gen mgr; Ken McFarlane, rgnl sls mgr; Dan Newton, prom mgr; Tom Newton, progmg mgr; Murray Wood, news dir; Gord Stankey, chief engr.

CIZL-FM—Co-owned with CJME(AM). June 1982: 98.9 mhz; 100 kw. Ant 435 ft. Stereo. Prog sep from AM. Format: AOR, classic hits, adult contemp. Target aud: 18-49. ■ Craig Romanyk, rgnl sls mgr; Deenna Dekker, prom mgr; Terry Voth, progmg dir.

CKCK(AM)—July 29, 1922: 620 khz; 10 kw-U, DA-2. Box 6200 (S4P 3H7). (306) 569-6200. FAX: (306) 352-5105. Licensee: Western World Limited Partnership. Group owner: Forvest Broadcasting Corp. Format: Adult contemp. News staff 8. ■ Vic Dubois, gen mgr.

CKIT-FM—Co-owned with CKCK(AM). Apr 15, 1982: 104.9 mhz; 100 kw. Ant 400 ft. Stereo. Prog sep from AM. Box 1049 (S4P 3B2). (306) 924-1049. Rep: United. Format: EZ lstng.

CKRM(AM)—July 27, 1926: 980 khz; 10 kw-D, 5 kw-N, DA-2. Hrs opn: 24. Box 9800, 2060 Halifax St. (S4P 1T7). (306) 566-9800. FAX: (306) 781-7338. Licensee: Harvard Communications (acq 3-1-81). Format: C&W, farm. ■ John Huschi, gen mgr & gen sls mgr; Les Schuster, rgnl sls mgr; Tom Staseson, prom dir; Willy Cole, progmg dir; Wade Willey, mus dir; Lorne Harasen, news dir; Dave Ellis, engrg dir.

CHMX-FM—Co-owned with CKRM(AM). Feb 4, 1966: 92.1 mhz; 100 kw. Ant 499 ft. Stereo. (306) 525-9195. Format: Adult contemp. ■ David Jones, progmg dir & mus dir; Lorne Harasen, news dir.

Rosetown

CJYM(AM)—Aug 8, 1966: 1330 khz; 10 kw-U, DA-1. Box 490 (S0L 2V0). (306) 882-2686. FAX: (306) 882-

3037. Licensee: Dace Broadcasting Corp. (acq 9-79). Rep: RTVR. Format: All hit gold. Spec prog: Relg 15 hrs wkly. ■ Dennis Dyck, gen mgr; Harland Lesyk, adv mgr. ■ Rates: $30; 28; 27; na.

Saskatoon

CBKF-2(AM)—Nov 6, 1952: 860 khz; 10 kw-U, DA-2. 503 CN Tower Bldg. (S7K 1J5). (306) 956-7400. Licensee: Societe Radio-Canada. Rep: CBC Mono French. Format: Div. ■ Gary Crippen, opns mgr.

***CBKS-FM**—July 1, 1978: 105.5 mhz; 98 kw. Ant 586 ft. Stereo. 503 CN Tower Bldg. (S7K 1J5). (306) 956-7400. Licensee: CBC. Net: CBC FM. Format: Div. ■ Gary Crippen, opns mgr.

CFMC-FM—Listing follows CKOM(AM).

CFQC(AM)—July 18, 1923: 600 khz; 10 kw-U, DA-N. 1414 Eighth St. E. (S7H 0T1). (306) 374-3600. FAX: (306) 343-7011. Licensee: QC Radio L.P. (acq 1991). Rep: Telemedia. Format: Adult contemp, Information. ■ George G. Gallagher, pres & gen mgr; Brooke Gallagher, natl sls mgr; Kelly Gallagher, prom dir; Dave Harrison, progmg dir; Peter Silversides, mus dir; Roy Norris, news dir. ■ Rates: C$70; 50; 40; 25.

CHSN-FM—June 1990: 102.1 mhz; 100 kw. Hrs opn: 24. 219—3501 8th St. E. (S7H 0W5). (306) 668-1021. Licensee: High-Line Broadcasting Inc. Format: Adult contemp. News staff 3; news progmg 4 hrs wkly. Target aud: 25-49; well educated, well paid professionals. Spec prog: Relg 6 hrs wkly. ■ Albert Ethier, pres; Matt Bradley, gen mgr, opns dir, progmg dir & mus dir; Keddy Gamble, gen sls mgr; Guy Ethier, prom dir; Dean Thorpe, news dir.

CJWW(AM)—Jan 12, 1976: 750 khz; 10 kw-U, DA-2. Stereo. 345 Fourth Ave S. (S7K 5S5). (306) 244-1975. FAX: (306) 665-7750. Licensee: 602406 Saskatchewan Ltd. Group owner: Forvest Broadcasting Corp. (acq 11-22-93). Rep: Canadian Broadcast Sales. Format: C&W. Target aud: General. ■ C. Forster, chmn; H. Gold, pres; E. Guanzon, vp; V. Dubois, gen mgr, stn mgr & progmg dir; B. Fisher, gen sls mgr; B. Jones, prom dir; D. Lemke-Woronuk, asst mus dir; G. Weibe, news dir; S. Elliott, pub affrs dir; A. Pippin, engrg dir.

CKOM(AM)—June 8, 1951: 650 khz; 10 kw-U, DA-2. 3333 8th St. E. (S7H 0W3). (306) 955-6595. FAX: (306) 373-7587. Licensee: Rawlco Communications Ltd. (group owner). Net: BN. Format: CHR. News staff 7. ■ Pam Carley, gen mgr.

CFMC-FM—Co-owned with CKOM(AM). Dec 12, 1965: 95.1 mhz; 100 kw. Ant 110 ft. Stereo. (306) 955-9500. Rep: Major Mkt. Format: Rock. Spec prog: Class 2 hrs, jazz 2 hrs wkly.

Shaunavon

CJSN(AM)—Dec 6, 1966: 1490 khz; 1 kw-U. 399 Center St. (S0N 2M0). (306) 297-2671. FAX: (306) 297-3051. Licensee: Frontier City Broadcasting Group owner: Golden West Broadcasting Ltd. (acq 1973). Format: C&W, MOR. ■ Warren Neufeld, gen mgr; Ken Audette, news dir.

Swift Current

CIMG-FM—Oct 20, 1979: 94.1 mhz; 100 kw. Ant 400 ft. Stereo. Hrs opn: 24. Box 1590, 4th Ave., N.W. (S9H 4G5). (306) 773-1505. FAX: (306) 778-3737. Licensee: Grasslands Broadcasting Ltd. Net: BN. Rep: United, Target. Format: Adult contemp. News staff 2. Target aud: 25-54; working class people. ■ Jim Warren, pres; Gerry Maier, opns mgr & gen sls mgr; Al Stevens, progmg mgr.

CKSW(AM)—June 1, 1956: 570 khz; 10 kw-U, DA-2. Hrs opn: 24. 134 Central Ave. (S9H 0L1). (306) 773-4605. FAX: (306) 773-6390. Licensee: Frontier City Broadcasting Ltd. Group owner: Golden West Broadcasting Ltd. Rep: Canadian Broadcast Sales. Format: Country. News staff 3. Target aud: General. Spec prog: Farm one hr, Ger one hr wkly. ■ Elmer Hildebrand, pres; David Wiebe, gen mgr; Bill Hildebrand, stn mgr & gen sls mgr; Richard Cloutier, progmg dir; Richard Cloitier, mus dir; Dave Funk, chief engr.

Weyburn

CFSL(AM)—Aug 16, 1957: 1190 khz; 10 kw-D, 5 kw-N, DA-N. Box 340, 305 Souris Ave. (S4H 2K2). (306) 842-4666. FAX: (306) 842-2720. Licensee: Soo Line Broadcasting Ltd. (acq 1970). Net: BN. Rep: Canadian Broadcast Sales. Format: C&W. News staff 2. Target aud: 25 plus. Spec prog: Farm 3 hrs, relg 13 hrs wkly.

■ Jackie Gray, stn mgr, gen sls mgr, vp mktg, vp prom & vp adv; Greg Lee, progmg mgr & mus dir; Grant Urban, asst mus dir; Wayne Ross, news dir; Jim Hutchings, chief engr. ■ Rates: C$27; 27; 27; 22.

Yorkton

CJGX(AM)—Aug 19, 1927: 940 khz; 50 kw-D, 10 kw-N. 120 Smith St. E. (S3N 3V3). (306) 782-2256. FAX: (306) 783-4994. Licensee: Yorkton Broadcasting Ltd. (acq 2-15-89). Format: Country. ■ George G. Gallagher, pres; Lyle J. Walsh, gen mgr; Brad Bazin, progmg dir; Blaise Mitchell, mus dir; Phil DeVos, news dir.

Yukon Territory

Whitehorse

*CFWH(AM)—1958: 570 khz; 5 kw-U, DA-1. 3103 3rd Ave. (Y1A 1E5). (403) 668-8403. FAX: (403) 668-8408. Licensee: CBC. Net: CBC Radio. Format: Adult contemp, talk, info. Spec prog: Fr one hr wkly. ■ Doug Caldwell, gen mgr.

CHON-FM—Feb 1, 1985: 98.1 mhz; 50 w. Ant 250 ft. (CP: 81.3 w). 4228 A Fourth Ave. (Y1A 1K1). (403) 668-6629. FAX: (403) 668-6612. Licensee: Northern Native Broadcasting. Format: C&W, rock. Spec prog: Yukon native lang 15 hrs wkly. ■ Leonard Linklatter, stn mgr; Brenda Chambers, opns dir; Walter Warvalle, mus dir.

CKRW(AM)—November 1969: 610 khz; 1 kw-U, DA-1. 4103 Fourth Ave. (Y1A 1H6). (403) 668-6100. FAX: (403) 668-4209. Licensee: Klondike Broadcasting Co. Ltd. Net: Newsradio. Rep: All-Canada. Format: Adult contemp, C&W, oldies. ■ Glen Darling, gen mgr.

Miscellaneous Radio Services

Armed Forces Radio and Television Service (AFRTS)

AFRTS operates over 800 radio and television outlets located in 134 foreign countries. AFRTS facilities are located with major concentrations of U.S. forces overseas as well as in remote areas of Alaska, U.S. trusts, territories and possessions, aboard 446 Navy ships and as closed-circuit facilities at 250 isolated locations. Most of the land-based stations are grouped into regional AFRTS networks to serve specific geographical areas, i.e. American Forces Network-Europe in Europe and Far East Network in the Pacific. AFRTS networks and independent stations overseas create their own individual radio and television progam schedules from broadcast materials provided by the AFRTS Broadcast Center in Sun Valley, Calif., and from their own local productions. Some outlets are broadcast opns and some are carried on closed circuit systems of various types. Domestic and Intelsat satellite services are leased on a 24 hour-a-day basis, providing real-time stateside radio and TV to overseas locations.

Headquarters, AFRTS. AFRTS is the broadcast arm of DOD's American Forces info Service located at 601 N. Fairfax St., Alexandria, Va. 22314. (703) 274-4856. Melvin Russell, deputy dir; Colonel Joe Cook, chief of staff; Lieutenant Colonel Glen Brady, plans/opns.

AFRTS broadcast Center. 10888 La Tuna Canyon Rd., Sun Valley, Calif. 91352. (818) 504-1201. Captain Connie Haney, commander; Gerry Fry, dir progmg; Bill Houk, industry liaison.

Radio Free Europe/Radio Liberty

Radio Free Europe/Radio Liberty, RFE/RL Inc. Oettingenstr 67 am Englischen Garten, 8000 Munich 22, Germany. E. Eugene Pell, pres/CEO. 1201 Connecticut Ave. N.W., Washington 20036. Broadcasts to East Europe in Bulgarian, Czech, Slovak, Hungarian, Polish, Romanian, Lithuanian, Estonian and Latvian; broadcasts to the Commonwealth of Independent States in Russian, Ukrainian, Belorussian, Armenian, Azeri, Georgian, Tatar-Bashkir, Kazak, Kirghiz, Tajik, Turkmen, Uzbek. Also broadcasts to Afghanistan in Dari and Pashto.

Board for International Broadcasting: 1201 Connecticut Ave. N.W., Suite 400, Washington 20036. (202) 254-8040. Established by Congress in 1973, the board evaluates and makes grants to Radio Free Europe and Radio Liberty and assures that funds are applied consistently with the broad foreign policy objectives of the U.S. government. Board members are Daniel A. Mica, chmn; Cheryl Feldman Halpern, Barry Zorthian, Lane Kirkland, Michael Novak, Kenneth Tomlinson, Karl C. Rove, E. Eugene Pell (exofficio). Staff: Richard W. McBride, exec dir; Patricia Schlueter, finance mgr; Pat Sowick, pub affrs.

U.S. International Radio

These stations, located in the U.S. but beaming overseas, operate on various frequencies depending on the seasons of the year. The frequencies (in the 6-25 mhz band); 5.900-6.200, 7.100-7.600, 9.400-9.990, 11.600-12.100, 13.570-13.870, 15.100-15.800, 17.480-17.900, 18.900-19.020, 21.450-21.850, 25.600-26.100.

Adventist Broadcasting Service Inc. (Adventist World Radio-Asia), Box 7500, Agat, Guam 96928. (671) 565-2000, 2289. **KSDA Agat, Guam.** Two 100 kw shortwave transmitters broadcasting to Asia in 20 languages. Gordon L. Retzer, gen mgr; Ben O. Sumicad, treas; Elvin Vence, chief engr; Greg Scott, prog dir.

Assemblies of Yahweh. Box C, Bethel, Pa. 19507. (717) 933-4781. **WMLK, Bethel, Pa.** Gary McAvin, stn mgr.

Family Stations Inc., 10400 N.W. 240th St., Okeechobee, Fla. 34972. (813) 763-0281. **WYFR Okeechobee, Fla.** Twelve 100 kw transmitters and two 50 kw transmitters in Florida. Broadcasting on various frequencies, in English to Europe, Africa and the Americas (including Caribbean area), in German to Europe, in Russian to East Europe, in Arabic to West Africa, in French to Europe, North Africa, and the Americas and in Spanish to Southern Europe, Central and South America, in Portuguese to South America and West Africa, in Italian to Europe. Harold Camping, pres; Thomas Schaff, progam mgr; Daniel Elyea, stn mgr. Format: Relg.

Far East Broadcasting Co. Inc., Box 1, La Mirada, Calif. 90637. 15700 E. Imperial Highway, La Mirada, Calif. 90638. (213) 947-4651. FAX: (213) 943-0160. **KFBS Saipan, Northern Mariana Islands.** Broadcasting to China, Indonesia, Indochina and the Commonwealth of Independent States. William Tarter, pres; Robert Stiles, asst to pres. **KGEI Redwood City, Calif.** Broadcasting to the Commonwealth of Independent States, Eastern Europe and Latin America. Format: Relg.

Gulf South Broadcasters Ltd., 4539 I-10 Service Rd., Metairie, La. 70002. (504) 889-2424. FAX: (504) 889-0602. **WRNO New Orleans.** 100 kw transmitter commercial service to North America, Central America, Europe and the Far East. Format: news, talk, sports, 80%; mus shows, adult contemp-CHR, 20%. Joseph M. Costello III, pres and gen mgr.

High Adventure Ministries Inc., Voice of Hope International Network, Box 7466, Van Nuys, Calif. 91409. George Otis, pres. Voice of Hope: **KVOH Los Angeles**, 50 kw, 17.775 mhz. John Tayloe, VP; Mark Gallardo, stn mgr; Don Myers, chief engr. Relg format, Sp and English. King of Hope/Middle East: 6.280 mhz in Lebanon. Wings of Hope: 11.530 mhz in Lebanon. Voice of Hope/Superstation: 50 kw AM on 945 khz. Voice of Hope South Lebanon/Northern Israel: 684 khz. Prince of Peace South Lebanon/Northern Israel: FM on 104.5 mhz/105.1 mhz. Wings of Hope Russia/Europe: 11.530 mhz and 9.960 mhz. Voice of Hope Asia/China on the island of Palu: 100 kw on 9.830 mhz broadcasting in 5 languages. Format: Relg. Richard Horner, engr; John Tayloe, international prog dir. Voice of Hope India/Indonesia: 9.965 mhz, 17.630 mhz, 15.395 mhz with 100 kw. Richard Horner, engr; John Tayloe, international prog dir.

Monitor Radio International, One Norway St., C-20, Boston 02115. (617) 450-2000. Monitor Radio International includes three international stations: **KHBI Saipan, Northern Mariana Islands**, 100 kw, broadcasting multilingual daily news and religious progmg to Japan, Taiwan, Hong Kong and China; **WCSN Scotts Corner, Me.**, broadcasting multilingual progmg to Europe, Africa parts of the Middle East; **WSHB Cypress Creek, S.C.**, 500 kw. David Cook, editor, Monitor Broadcasting.

Our Lady's Youth Center, Star Route Box 300, Mesquite, N.M. 88048. Operates **KJES Vado, N.M.**

Radio Miami International, 8500 S.W. Eighth St., Suite 252, Miami 33144. (305) 267-1728. FAX: (305) 267-9253. **WRMI Miami.** stn sells airtime to organizations wanting to reach any part of Latin America in any language. 9,955 kHz shortwave, 50 kw power. Jeff White, gen mgr; Indalecio Espinosa, chief engr.

Trans World Radio, Box 700, Cary, N.C. 27512-0700. **KTWR Agana, Guam.** Four 100-kw shortwave transmitters to broadcast to the eastern and central part of the Commonwealth of Independent States, Far East, Australia and Africa. Format: Relg (25 languages). Paul E. Freed, founder & chmn; Edward Stortro, field dir; Edmund Spieker, international progmg department; George Zenson, chief engr.

Trinity Broadcasting Network, KTBN/Shortwave. Box 18147, Salt Lake City 84118. "Skinny" Johnny Mitchell, stn supvr (801) 250-4111 (office). **KTBN**, 6475 W. 5400 South, West Valley City, Utah 84118.

Two If By Sea Broadcasting Corp. 22720 S.E. 410th St., Enumclaw, Wash. 98022. (206) 825-1099. FAX: (206) 825-4517. **KCBI Dallas.** Format: 24 hours a day of religious & educ progmg. Mike Parker, pres.

United Nations, Media Division, New York 10017. Coverage of UN meetings and other events on film, video and sound; radio broadcasts in several languages; documentary films-TV programs. Francois Giuliani, dir; Barbara Sue-Ting-Len, off-in-chg, audio-visual prom & distribution.

WEWN-A Catholic Radio Service of the Eternal Word Television Network (EWTN), Box 100234, Birmingham, Ala. 35210. (205) 672-7200. FAX: (205) 672-9988. **WEWN Vandiver, Ala.** Catholic religious progmg worldwide via shortwave radio. R.W. Steltemeier, pres; Frank Phillips, gen mgr; Glen Tapley, dir of opns; Napoleon Cacdac, chief engr.

WJCR World Wide, Box 91, Upton, Ky. 42784. (502) 369-8614. **WJCR Millerstown, Ky.** Don Powell, pres.

WNQM Inc. Group owner: F.W. Robbert Broadcasting Co. 1300 WWCR Ave., Nashville 37218. (615) 255-1300; (800) 238-5576. **WWCR Nashville.** Frequencies: 5.935 mhz, 7.435 mhz, 15.610 mhz, 15.685 mhz. Fred P. Westenberger, pres; George McClintock, gen mgr; Adam Lock, prog dir; Watt Hairston, chief engr; Joe Brashier, natl prog dir.

World Christian Broadcasting Corp., opns Center, 605 Bradley Court, Franklin, Tenn. 37064. (615) 371-8707. Fax: (615) 371-8791. **KNLS Anchor Point, Alaska** (transmission facilities): Box 473, Anchor Point, Alaska 99556. (907) 235-8262. Relg and secular progmg beamed to Asia and the Commonwealth of Independent States on the international shortwave bands. Dr. Robert E. Scott, pres/CEO; Edward J. Bailey, VP/COO; Charles Caudill, VP dev; Dale R. Ward, exec prod; Mike Osborne, prod mgr; F.M. Perry, dir of frequency coordination; Kevin C. Chambers, chief engr.

World Harvest Radio International, Box 12, South Bend, Ind. 46624. (219) 291-8200; (219) 299-4243. FAX:(219) 291-9043. **WHRI Indianapolis.** Two 100 kw transmitters serving Central and South America, Europe, Russia, Middle East and Africa. **KWHR Naalehu, Hawaii.** One 100 kw transmitter serving primarily Asia, and also Oceania and New Zealand. Dr. Lester Sumrall, chmn; Steve Sumrall, pres; Peter Sumrall, gen mgr; Joe Hill, sls/opns mgr; Douglas Garlinger, chief engr.

World International Broadcasters Inc., Box 88, Red Lion, Pa. 17356. **WINB Red Lion, Pa.** Beams programs to Western Europe, the Mediterranean and North Africa. John H. Norris, pres; Dorothy Norris, VP; Patricia Norris Slaughter, sec/dir; John C. Norris, dir; Mary Norris Michel, dir. Format: Relg.

Voice of America

Headquarters: 330 Independence Ave. S.W., Washington 20547. (202) 619-2538. FAX: (202) 619-1241. Joseph B. Bruns, actg dir; Robert T. Coonrod, deputy dir; Sid Davis, dir office of prog; Bob Kamosa, dir office engrg; Joe O'Connell, dir pub affrs; Beth Knisley, dir media rel.

Policy: The Voice of America (VOA), the international broadcasting service of the U.S. Information Agency, is governed by its Charter (Public Law 94-350) which stipulates VOA will: (1) serve as a consistently reliable and authoritative source of news and that its news will be accurate, objective and comprehensive; (2) represent America, not any single segment of American society, and will therefore present a balanced and comprehensive projection of significant American thought and institutions; (3) present policies of the United States clearly and effectively, and will also present responsible discussion and opinion on these policies.

Facilities: VOA has 112 medium wave and shortwave transmitters which collectively have a total power in excess of 26 million watts. The power of individual transmitters in VOA's worldwide network ranges from 35 kw to 1000 kw. The VOA standard is to use three transmitters for each broadcast. The transmitters are located at 18 relay stations in the U.S. and abroad in Antigua, Belize, Botswana, Costa Rica, England, Greece, Liberia, Morocco, the Phillipines, Sri Lanka, Thailand and West Germany. Programs originate in the studio complex at VOA headquarters. A 150-channel master control panel is used to route them onto appropiate satellite circuits for delivery to the relay stations.

Programming: U.S. and world events are reported accurately and fully in VOA newscasts and news programs. Features, backgrounders, interviews, on-the-scene coverage of special events and documentaries provide listeners around the world with an accurate, comprehensive portrayal of American life and opinion. Information on U.S. policies is reflected in editorials.

Program placement: VOA progmg is also made available to, and extensively used by, foreign media in more than 100 countries. Radio stations in some countries simply relay VOA's direct broadcasts or tape progam segments from them for rebroadcast at prime local listening times. Satellite or high frequency feeds, dial-up systems, and airmailed tapes are also used to provide VOA progmg in 20 languages to stations in Africa, the American Republics, East and South Asia, the Middle East and Western Europe.

Program hours and languages: The 1,300 hours of progmg produced at VOA each week include two special services: VOA Europe and Radio Marti. VOA Europe is an around-the-clock radio service in English which is delivered to Western Europe by satellite for broadcast on FM and cable radio stations in 10 countries; 70 hours wkly of the VOA Europe broadcast are originated by the VOA staff and the balance is syndicated music programs. The Radio Marti progam is beamed to Cuba 168 hours each week by a 50 kw medium wave transmitter in Florida. All other progmg (1,129 hours weekly) is trans-

Miscellaneous Radio Services

mitted on shortwave and/or medium wave in the following 43 languages:

Voice of America wkly Language Broadcasts (hours and minutes per week). Albanian 7:00; Amharic 7:00; Arabic (Near East and North Africa) 91:00; Armenian 7:00; Azerbaijani 7:00; Bangla 14:00; Bulgarian 10:30; Burmese 10:30; Cantonese 7:00; Chinese (Mandarin) 77:00; Creole 5:15; Czech-Slovak 21:00; Dari 10:30; English (Africa) 70:00; English (Caribbean/American Republics) 44:30; English (East and Southeast Asia/Pacific) 70:00; English (Middle East/North Africa/Europe) 129:30; English (South Asia) 42:00; English VOA Europe 70:00; Estonian 8:45; Farsi 28:00; French (Africa) 32:30; Georgian 5:15; Greek 3:30; Hausa 6:00; Hindi 10:30; Hungarian 17:30; Indonesian 21:00; Khmer 14:00; Korean 7:00; Lao 7:00; Latvian 8:45; Lithuanian 8:45; Pashto 10:30; Polish 28:00; Portuguese (Africa) 17:30; Portuguese (Brazil) 7:00; Romanian 15:45; Russian 98:00; Serbo-Croatian 8:45; Slovene 3:30; Spanish (Latin America) 47:00; Spanish Radio Marti 168:00; Swahili 5:00; Tibetan 1:45; Turkish 7:00; Ukrainian 28:00; Urdu 14:00; Uzbek 14:00; Vietnamese 14:00; Total broadcasts 1367:00.

U.S. AM Stations by Call Letters

KAAA Kingman AZ
KAAB Batesville AR
KAAM Dallas TX
KAAN Bethany MO
KAAY Little Rock AR
KABC Los Angeles CA
KABI Abilene KS
KABL Oakland CA
KABN Long Island AK
KABQ Albuquerque NM
*KABR Alamo Community NM
KACH Preston ID
KACI The Dalles OR
KACT Andrews TX
KACY Lafayette LA
KADA Ada OK
KADR Elkader IA
KADS Elk City OK
KAFF Flagstaff AZ
KAFX Diboll TX
KAFY Bakersfield CA
KAGC Bryan TX
KAGE Winona MN
KAGH Crossett AR
KAGI Grants Pass OR
KAGO Klamath Falls OR
KAGY Port Sulphur LA
KAHI Auburn CA
KAHU Hilo HI
KAHZ Fort Worth TX
KAIM Honolulu HI
KAIN Vidalia LA
KAJK Fortuna CA
KAJO Grants Pass OR
KAKC Tulsa OK
KAKQ Fairbanks AK
KAKS Canyon TX
KALB Alexandria LA
KALE Richland WA
KALI San Gabriel CA
KALL Salt Lake City UT
KALM Thayer MO
KALN Iola KS
KALO Port Arthur TX
KALT Atlanta TX
KALV Alva OK
KALY Los Ranchos de Albuquerque NM
KAMA El Paso TX
KAMD Camden AR
KAMG Victoria TX
KAMI Cozad NE
KAML Kenedy-Karnes City TX
KAMO Rogers AR
KAMP El Centro CA
KAMQ Carlsbad NM
KAMX Albuquerque NM
KAND Corsicana TX
KANE New Iberia LA
KANI Wharton TX
*KANN Roy UT
KANR Nampa ID
KANS Larned KS
KAOI Kihei HI
KAOK Lake Charles LA
KAOL Carrollton MO
KAPA Raymond WA
KAPB Marksville LA
KAPE Cape Girardeau MO
KAPL Apple Valley CA
KAPR Douglas AZ
KAPS Mount Vernon WA
KAPY Port Angeles WA
KAPZ Bald Knob AR
KAQQ Spokane WA
KARI Blaine WA
KARN Little Rock AR
*KARR Kirkland WA
KARS Belen NM
KART Jerome ID
KARV Russellville AR
KARW Longview TX
KARY Prosser WA
KASA Phoenix AZ
KASI Ames IA
KASL Newcastle WY
KASM Albany MN
KASO Minden LA
KASP St. Louis MO
KASR Perry OK
KAST Astoria OR
KATA Arcata CA
KATD Pittsburg CA
KATE Albert Lea MN
*KATI Casper WY
KATK Carlsbad NM
KATL Miles City MT
KATO Safford AZ
KATQ Plentywood MT
KATZ St. Louis MO
KAUS Austin MN
KAVA Burney CA
KAVL Lancaster CA
KAWA Floydada TX
*KAWC Yuma AZ
KAWL York NE
KAWS Hemphill TX
KAWW Heber Springs AR
KAYC Beaumont TX
KAYL Storm Lake IA

KAYO Aberdeen WA
KAYR Van Buren AR
KAYS Hays KS
KAZA Gilroy CA
KAZM Sedona AZ
KAZN Pasadena CA
KBAI Morro Bay CA
KBAL San Saba TX
KBAM Longview WA
KBAR Burley ID
KBAS Bullhead City AZ
KBBA Abilene TX
*KBBI Homer AK
KBBK Rupert ID
KBBO Yakima WA
KBBR North Bend OR
KBBS Buffalo WY
KBBT Portland OR
KBBV Big Bear Lake CA
KBBW Waco TX
KBBY Ventura CA
KBCH Lincoln City OR
KBCL Shreveport LA
KBCO Boulder CO
KBCR Steamboat Springs CO
KBCW Brooklyn Park MN
KBEA Mission KS
KBEC Waxahachie TX
KBEE Modesto CA
KBEL Idabel OK
KBEN Carrizo Springs TX
KBEQ Blue Springs MO
KBET Canyon Country CA
KBEW Blue Earth MN
KBFI Bonners Ferry ID
KBFS Belle Fourche SD
KBFW Bellingham-Ferndale WA
KBGN Caldwell ID
KBHB Sturgis SD
KBHC Nashville AR
KBHS Hot Springs AR
*KBIB Marion KS
KBID Bakersfield CA
KBIF Fresno CA
KBIL Breckenridge TX
KBIM Roswell NM
KBIS Little Rock AR
KBIX Muskogee OK
KBIZ Ottumwa IA
KBJM Lemmon SD
KBJT Fordyce AR
KBKB Fort Madison IA
KBKR Baker City OR
KBLA Santa Monica CA
KBLE Seattle WA
KBLF Red Bluff CA
KBLG Billings MT
KBLL Helena MT
KBLU Yuma AZ
KBLV Bellevue WA
KBLX Berkeley CA
KBMR Bismarck ND
KBMS Vancouver WA
KBMV Birch Tree MO
KBMW Breckenridge MN
KBNA El Paso TX
KBND Bend OR
KBNO Denver CO
KBNP Portland OR
KBOA Kennett MO
KBOE Oskaloosa IA
KBOI Boise ID
KBOK Malvern AR
KBOL Boulder CO
KBOP Pleasanton TX
KBOQ Soquel CA
KBOR Brownsville TX
KBOV Bishop CA
KBOW Butte MT
KBOZ Bozeman MT
*KBPS Portland OR
KBQN Pago Pago AS
KBRB Ainsworth NE
KBRC Mount Vernon WA
KBRE Cedar City UT
KBRF Fergus Falls MN
KBRH Baton Rouge LA
KBRI Brinkley AR
KBRK Brookings SD
KBRL McCook NE
KBRN Boerne TX
KBRO Bremerton WA
KBRT Avalon CA
KBRV Soda Springs ID
*KBRW Barrow AK
KBRX O'Neill NE
KBRZ Freeport TX
KBSF Springhill LA
KBSG Auburn WA
KBSN Moses Lake WA
KBSR Laurel MT
KBST Big Spring TX
*KBSU Boise ID
KBTA Batesville AR
KBTC Houston MO
KBTM Jonesboro AR
KBTN Neosho MO
KBUF Holcomb KS
KBUN Bemidji MN

KBUR Burlington IA
KBUY Ruidoso NM
KBWD Brownwood TX
KBYE Oklahoma City OK
KBYG Big Spring TX
KBYO Tallulah LA
KBYR Anchorage AK
KBZT Indio CA
KBZY Salem OR
KBZZ La Junta CO
KCAB Dardanelle AR
KCAL Redlands CA
KCAM Glennallen AK
KCAP Helena MT
KCAR Clarksville TX
KCAS Slaton TX
*KCAT Pine Bluff AR
KCBC Riverbank CA
KCBF Fairbanks AK
KCBN Reno NV
KCBQ San Diego CA
KCBR Monument CO
KCBS San Francisco CA
KCCB Corning AR
KCCC Carlsbad NM
KCCF Cave Creek AZ
KCCN Honolulu HI
KCCR Pierre SD
KCCS Salem OR
KCCT Corpus Christi TX
KCCV Overland Park KS
KCEO Vista CA
KCFI Cedar Falls IA
KCFO Tulsa OK
KCGN Sioux Falls SD
KCGQ Cape Girardeau MO
KCGS Marshall AR
KCHA Charles City IA
KCHE Cherokee IA
KCHG Somerset MN
KCHI Chillicothe MO
KCHJ Delano CA
KCHK New Prague MN
KCHL San Antonio TX
KCHR Charleston MO
KCHS Truth or Consequences NM
*KCHU Valdez AK
KCID Caldwell ID
KCII Washington IA
KCIM Carroll IA
KCIN Victorville CA
KCIS Edmonds WA
KCJB Minot ND
KCJJ Iowa City IA
KCKC San Bernardino CA
KCKN Roswell NM
KCKX Stayton OR
KCKY Coolidge AZ
KCLA Pine Bluff AR
KCLB Coachella CA
KCLE Cleburne TX
KCLK Asotin WA
KCLL Lompoc CA
KCLP Amarillo Township TX
KCLR Ralls TX
KCLS Flagstaff AZ
KCLV Clovis NM
KCLW Hamilton TX
KCLX Colfax WA
KCMC Texarkana TX
KCMG Mountain Grove MO
KCMJ Palm Springs CA
KCMN Colorado Springs CO
KCMO Kansas City MO
KCMX Ashland OR
KCNI Broken Bow NE
KCNM San Jose MP
KCNN East Grand Forks MN
KCNO Alturas CA
KCNR Salt Lake City UT
KCNW Fairway KS
KCOB Newton IA
KCOG Centerville IA
KCOH Houston TX
KCOL Fort Collins CO
KCOM Comanche TX
KCON Conway AR
KCOR San Antonio TX
KCOW Alliance NE
KCPL Olympia WA
KCPS Burlington IA
KCPX Centerville UT
KCQL Aztec NM
KCRC Enid OK
KCRG Cedar Rapids IA
KCRN San Angelo TX
KCRO Omaha NE
KCRS Midland TX
KCRT Trinidad CO
KCRV Caruthersville MO
KCRX Roswell NM
KCSJ Pueblo CO
KCSR Chadron NE
KCST Florence OR
KCTA Corpus Christi TX
KCTC Sacramento CA
KCTI Gonzales TX
KCTO Columbia LA
KCTQ Thousand Oaks CA

KCTR Billings MT
KCTX Childress TX
KCTY Salinas CA
KCUB Tucson AZ
KCUE Red Wing MN
KCUL Marshall TX
KCUV Englewood CO
KCUZ Clifton AZ
KCVL Colville WA
KCVR Lodi CA
KCWR Bakersfield CA
KCWW Tempe AZ
KCYL Lampasas TX
KDAC Fort Bragg CA
KDAE Sinton TX
KDAK Carrington ND
KDAL Duluth MN
KDAO Marshalltown IA
KDAP Douglas AZ
KDAZ Albuquerque NM
KDBM Dillon MT
KDBS Eugene OR
KDCC Dodge City KS
KDCE Espanola NM
KDDA Dumas AR
KDDD Dumas TX
KDDR Oakes ND
KDEC Decorah IA
KDEF Albuquerque NM
KDEO Waipahu HI
KDES Palm Springs CA
KDET Center TX
KDEX Dexter MO
KDFC Palo Alto CA
KDFL Lakewood WA
KDFN Doniphan MO
KDFT Ferris TX
KDGO Durango CO
KDHI Twentynine Palms CA
KDHL Faribault MN
KDHN Dimmitt TX
KDIA Oakland CA
KDIF Riverside CA
KDIO Ortonville MN
KDIX Dickinson ND
KDJI Holbrook AZ
KDJS Willmar MN
KDJW Amarillo TX
KDKA Pittsburgh PA
KDKD Clinton MO
KDKO Littleton CO
KDLA De Ridder LA
KDLB Henryetta OK
*KDLG Dillingham AK
KDLM Detroit Lakes MN
KDLP Bayou Vista LA
KDLR Devils Lake ND
KDLS Perry IA
KDMA Montevideo MN
KDMI Des Moines IA
KDMN Buena Vista CO
KDMO Carthage MO
KDMS El Dorado AR
KDNT Denton TX
KDOL Henderson NV
KDOM Windom MN
KDOS Laredo TX
KDOV Phoenix OR
KDQN De Queen AR
KDRG Deer Lodge MT
KDRO Sedalia MO
KDRQ Wishek ND
KDRS Paragould AR
KDRY Alamo Heights TX
KDSI Alice TX
KDSJ Deadwood SD
KDSN Denison IA
KDSX Denison-Sherman TX
KDTA Delta CO
KDTH Dubuque IA
KDUK Eugene OR
KDUN Reedsport OR
KDUZ Hutchinson MN
KDWA Hastings MN
KDWN Las Vegas NV
KDXU St. George UT
KDYL Salt Lake City UT
KDYN Ozark AR

KEAN Abilene TX
KEAS Eastland TX
KEBE Jacksonville TX
KEBR Rocklin CA
KECN Blackfoot ID
KECR El Cajon CA
KEDA San Antonio TX
KEDO Longview WA
KEEE Nacogdoches TX
KEEL Shreveport LA
KEES Gladewater TX
KEGG Daingerfield TX
KEIN Great Falls MT
KELA Centralia-Chehalis WA
KELD El Dorado AR
KELG Elgin TX
KELK Elko NV
KELO Sioux Falls SD
KELP El Paso TX
KELY Ely NV

KENA Mena AR
KENE Toppenish WA
KENI Anchorage AK
KENN Farmington NM
KENO Las Vegas NV
KENS San Antonio TX
*KENT Odessa TX
KENU Enumclaw WA
KEOR Atoka OK
KEPS Eagle Pass TX
KERB Kermit TX
KERE Atchison KS
KERI Wasco CA
KERN Bakersfield CA
KERR Polson MT
KERV Kerrville TX
KESM El Dorado Springs MO
KESS Fort Worth TX
KEST San Francisco CA
KESY Omaha NE
KETX Livingston TX
KEUN Eunice LA
KEVA Evanston WY
KEVT Cortaro AZ
KEWI Benton AR
KEX Portland OR
KEXO Grand Junction CO
KEXS Excelsior Springs MO
KEYE Perryton TX
KEYF Dishman WA
KEYG Grand Coulee WA
KEYH Houston TX
KEYL Long Prairie MN
KEYQ Fresno CA
KEYS Corpus Christi TX
KEYX Visalia CA
*KEYY Provo UT
KEYZ Williston ND
KEZC Yuma AZ
KEZD Windsor CA
KEZF Tigard OR
KEZJ Twin Falls ID
KEZM Sulphur LA
KEZO Omaha NE
KEZW Aurora CO
KEZX Seattle WA
KFAB Omaha NE
KFAL Fulton MO
KFAM North Salt Lake City UT
KFAN Minneapolis MN
KFAR Fairbanks AK
KFAS Casa Grande AZ
KFAX San Francisco CA
KFAY Farmington AR
KFBC Cheyenne WY
KFBK Sacramento CA
KFCA Conway AR
KFCR Custer SD
KFDF Van Buren AR
KFDI Wichita KS
KFEL Pueblo CO
KFEQ St. Joseph MO
KFEZ Kansas City MO
KFFA Helena AR
KFFR Eagle River AK
KFGO Fargo ND
*KFGQ Boone IA
KFH Wichita KS
KFI Los Angeles CA
KFIA Carmichael CA
KFIG Fresno CA
KFIL Preston MN
KFIR Sweet Home OR
KFIT Sunset Valley TX
KFIT San Antonio TX
KFIV Modesto CA
KFIZ Fond du Lac WI
KFJB Marshalltown IA
*KFJM Grand Forks ND
KFJZ Fort Worth TX
KFKA Greeley CO
*KFKU Lawrence KS
KFLA Scott City KS
KFLG Bullhead City AZ
KFLN Baker MT
KFLO Shreveport LA
KFLS Klamath Falls OR
*KFLT Tucson AZ
KFLY Corvallis OR
KFMB San Diego CA
KFMO Flat River MO
KFMS North Las Vegas NV
KFNA El Paso TX
KFNN Mesa AZ
KFNS Wood River IL
KFNV Ferriday LA
*KFNW West Fargo ND
KFON Austin TX
KFOR Lincoln NE
KFPW Fort Smith AR
KFQC Davenport IA
KFQD Anchorage AK
KFRA Franklin LA
KFRC San Francisco CA
KFRD Bellville TX
KFRE Fresno CA
KFRM Salina KS
*KFRN Long Beach CA
KFRO Longview TX

Broadcasting & Cable Yearbook 1994
B-451

U.S. AM Stations by Call Letters

KFRU Columbia MO
KFSA Fort Smith AR
KFSB Joplin MO
KFST Fort Stockton TX
KFTM Fort Morgan CO
KFTW Fredricktown MO
KFUN Las Vegas NM
*KFUO Clayton MO
KFVR Crescent City CA
KFWB Los Angeles CA
KFWJ Lake Havasu City AZ
KFXD Nampa ID
KFXX Oregon City OR
KFYI Phoenix AZ
KFYN Bonham TX
KFYO Lubbock TX
KFYR Bismarck ND

KGA Spokane WA
KGAF Gainesville TX
KGAK Gallup NM
KGAS Carthage TX
KGBC Galveston TX
KGBS Dallas TX
KGBT Harlingen TX
KGDD Paris TX
KGDP Orcutt CA
KGEM Boise ID
KGEN Tulare CA
KGEO Bakersfield CA
KGER Long Beach CA
KGEZ Kalispell MT
KGFF Shawnee OK
KGFJ Los Angeles CA
KGFL Clinton AR
KGFW Kearney NE
KGFX Pierre SD
KGGF Coffeyville KS
KGGN Gladstone MO
KGGR Dallas TX
KGHF Pueblo CO
KGHL Billings MT
KGHO Hoquiam WA
KGHS International Falls MN
KGHT Sheridan AR
KGIM Aberdeen SD
KGIW Alamosa CO
KGKL San Angelo TX
KGKO Benton AR
KGLA Gretna LA
KGLD Tyler TX
KGLE Glendive MT
KGLF Robstown TX
KGLN Glenwood Springs CO
KGLO Mason City IA
KGLW San Luis Obispo CA
KGMG Oceanside CA
KGMI Bellingham WA
KGMT Fairbury NE
KGMY Springfield MO
KGNB New Braunfels TX
KGNC Amarillo TX
KGNM St. Joseph MO
KGNN Cuba MO
KGNO Dodge City KS
KGNW Burien-Seattle WA
KGO San Francisco CA
KGOL Humble TX
KGOS Torrington WY
KGPL Dermott AR
KGRB West Covina CA
KGRE Greeley CO
KGRL Bend OR
KGRN Grinnell IA
KGRO Pampa TX
KGRT Las Cruces NM
KGRV Winston OR
KGRZ Missoula MT
KGST Fresno CA
KGTL Homer AK
KGTO Tulsa OK
KGU Honolulu HI
KGUM Agana GU
KGVL Greenville TX
KGVO Missoula MT
KGVW Belgrade MT
KGVY Green Valley AZ
KGWA Enid OK
KGY Olympia WA
KGYN Guymon OK

KHAC Tse Bonito NM
KHAD De Soto MO
KHAK Cedar Rapids IA
KHAR Anchorage AK
KHAS Hastings NE
KHAT Lincoln NE
KHBM Monticello AR
KHBR Hillsboro TX
*KHCB Galveston TX
KHEP Phoenix AZ
KHEY El Paso TX
KHIL Willcox AZ
KHIS Bakersfield CA
KHIT Sun Valley NV
KHJJ Lancaster CA
KHKR East Helena MT
KHLB Burnet TX
KHLO Hilo HI
KHMO Hannibal MO
KHNC Johnstown CO
KHND Harvey ND
KHNR Honolulu HI
KHOB Hobbs NM
KHOL Beulah ND
KHOS Sonora TX

KHOT Madera CA
KHOW Denver CO
KHOZ Harrison AR
KHPY Moreno Valley CA
KHQN Spanish Fork UT
KHRT Minot ND
KHSJ Hemet CA
KHSL Chico CA
KHSN Coos Bay OR
KHSP Texarkana TX
KHTH Dillon CO
KHTZ Truckee CA
KHUB Fremont NE
KHVH Honolulu HI
KHVN Fort Worth TX
KHYM Gilmer TX

KIAK Fairbanks AK
KIAL Unalaska AK
KIAM Nenana AK
KIBL Beeville TX
KICA Clovis NM
KICD Spencer IA
KICN Idaho Falls ID
KICO Calexico CA
KICR Oakdale LA
KICS Hastings NE
KICY Nome AK
KID Idaho Falls ID
KIDD Monterey CA
KIDH Eagle ID
KIDO Boise ID
KIDR Phoenix AZ
KIDS Springfield MO
KIEV Glendale CA
KIEZ Carmel Valley CA
KIFG Iowa Falls IA
*KIFO Pearl City HI
KIFW Sitka AK
KIGO St. Anthony ID
KIGS Hanford CA
KIHN Hugo OK
KIHR Hood River OR
KIID San Luis Obispo CA
KIIS Los Angeles CA
KIIX Wellington CO
KIJN Farwell TX
KIJV Huron SD
KIKC Forsyth MT
KIKI Honolulu HI
KIKK Pasadena TX
KIKO Miami AZ
KIKZ Seminole TX
KILJ Mount Pleasant IA
KILR Estherville IA
KILT Houston TX
KIMB Kimball NE
KIML Gillette WY
KIMM Rapid City SD
KIMP Mount Pleasant TX
KINA Salina KS
KIND Independence KS
KING Seattle WA
KINK Portland OR
KINN Alamogordo NM
KINO Winslow AZ
KINS Eureka CA
KINY Juneau AK
KIOA Des Moines IA
KIOQ Folsom CA
KIOU Shreveport LA
KIOX Bay City TX
KIPA Hilo HI
KIQI San Francisco CA
KIQQ Barstow CA
KIQS Willows CA
KIRL St. Charles MO
KIRO Seattle WA
KIRT Mission TX
KIRV Fresno CA
KIRX Kirksville MO
KISA Honolulu HI
KISN Salt Lake City UT
KIST Santa Barbara CA
KIT Yakima WA
KITA Little Rock AR
KITI Chehalis-Centralia WA
KITO Vinita OK
KITZ Silverdale WA
KIUL Garden City KS
KIUN Pecos TX
KIUP Durango CO
KIVA Corrales NM
KIVY Crockett TX
KIWA Sheldon IA
KIXI Mercer Island-Seattle WA
KIXL Del Valle TX
KIXZ Amarillo TX
KIYU Galena AK

KJAA Globe AZ
KJAM Madison SD
KJAN Atlantic IA
KJAX Stockton CA
KJAY Sacramento CA
KJBC Midland TX
KJBN Little Rock AR
KJBO Los Ranchos de Albuquerque NM
KJBX Lubbock TX
KJCB Lafayette LA
KJCE Rollingwood TX
KJCF Festus MO
KJCK Junction City KS
KJDJ San Luis Obispo CA
KJDY John Day OR

KJEF Jennings LA
KJEL Lebanon MO
KJEM Bentonville-Bella Vista AR
KJIM Sherman TX
KJIN Houma LA
KJIW West Helena AR
KJJK Fergus Falls MN
KJJO St. Louis Park MN
KJJQ Volga SD
KJJR Whitefish MT
KJLA Independence MO
*KJLT North Platte NE
KJMC Mineola TX
KJME Denver CO
KJNA Jena LA
KJNO Juneau AK
KJNP North Pole AK
KJOC Davenport IA
KJOE Ogden UT
KJOJ Conroe TX
KJOP Lemoore CA
KJPW Waynesville MO
KJQI Beverly Hills CA
KJR Seattle WA
KJRB Spokane WA
KJRG Newton KS
KJSA Mineral Wells TX
KJSK Columbus NE
KJTT Oak Harbor WA
KJUG Tulare CA
KJUN Puyallup WA
KJYK Tucson AZ

KKAA Aberdeen SD
KKAJ Ardmore OK
KKAL Arroyo Grande CA
KKAM Lubbock TX
KKAN Phillipsburg KS
KKAQ Thief River Falls MN
KKAR Omaha NE
KKAS Silsbee TX
KKAY White Castle LA
KKBJ Bemidji MN
KKBQ Houston TX
KKCM Shakopee MN
KKCQ Fosston MN
KKCS Colorado Springs CO
KKDA Grand Prairie TX
KKDS South Salt Lake UT
KKDZ Seattle WA
KKEL Hobbs NM
KKEY Portland OR
KKFO Coalinga CA
KKGD Rifle CO
KKHI San Francisco CA
KKHJ Los Angeles CA
KKIC Boise ID
KKID Sallisaw OK
KKIM Albuquerque NM
KKIN Aitkin MN
KKIP Lowell AR
KKIS Concord CA
KKIT Taos NM
KKLE Winfield KS
KKLL Webb City MO
KKLO Leavenworth KS
KKLQ San Diego CA
KKLS Rapid City SD
KKMC Gonzales CA
KKMO Tacoma WA
KKNC Sun Valley MT
KKNK Carson City NV
KKNO Gretna LA
KKOB Albuquerque NM
KKOJ Jackson MN
KKON Kealakekua HI
KKOW Pittsburg KS
KKOY Chanute KS
KKOZ Ava MO
KKPC Pueblo CO
KKPL Opportunity WA
KKPR Kearney NE
KKRT Wenatchee WA
KKRX Lawton OK
KKSB Santa Barbara CA
KKSD Anchorage AK
KKSJ San Jose CA
KKSN Vancouver WA
KKSO Des Moines IA
*KKSU Manhattan KS
KKTR Fresno CA
KKTX Kilgore TX
KKTY Douglas WY
KKUB Brownfield TX
KKUL Hardin MT
KKVV Las Vegas NV
KKXL Grand Forks ND
KKXO Eugene OR
KKXX Paradise CA
KKYD Denver CO
KKYN Plainview TX
KKYR Texarkana AR
KKYX San Antonio TX
KKZZ Santa Paula CA

KLAC Los Angeles CA
KLAD Klamath Falls OR
KLAM Cordova AK
KLAR Laredo TX
KLAT Houston TX
KLAV Las Vegas NV
KLAY Lakewood WA
KLBA Albia IA
KLBB St. Paul MN
KLBJ Austin TX
KLBM La Grande OR

KLBO Monahans TX
KLBS Los Banos CA
KLCB Libby MT
KLCJ Amarillo TX
KLCK Goldendale WA
KLCL Lake Charles LA
KLCN Blytheville AR
KLCY East Missoula MT
KLDI Laramie WY
KLDY Lacey WA
KLEA Lovington NM
KLEB Golden Meadow LA
KLEE Ottumwa IA
KLEH Anamosa IA
KLEM Le Mars IA
KLER Orofino ID
KLEX Lexington MO
KLEY Wellington KS
KLFB Lubbock TX
KLFD Litchfield MN
KLFE San Bernardino CA
KLFJ Springfield MO
KLGA Algona IA
KLGN Logan UT
KLGR Redwood Falls MN
KLHT Honolulu HI
KLIC Monroe LA
KLID Poplar Bluff MO
KLIF Dallas TX
KLIK Jefferson City MO
KLIN Lincoln NE
KLIV San Jose CA
KLIX Twin Falls ID
KLIZ Brainerd MN
KLKC Parsons KS
KLKE Del Rio TX
KLKI Anacortes WA
KLLA Leesville LA
KLLF Wichita Falls TX
KLLK Willits CA
KLLL Lubbock TX
KLLV Breen CO
KLLZ Walker MN
KLMO Longmont CO
KLMR Lamar CO
KLMX Clayton NM
KLNG Council Bluffs IA
KLNT Clinton IA
KLO Ogden UT
KLOA Ridgecrest CA
KLOC Ceres CA
KLOE Goodland KS
KLOG Kelso WA
KLOH Pipestone MN
KLOK San Jose CA
KLOM Lompoc CA
KLOO Corvallis OR
KLOQ Merced CA
KLOV Loveland CO
KLPL Lake Providence LA
KLPW Union MO
KLPZ Parker AZ
KLRA England AR
KLRG North Little Rock AR
KLSR Memphis TX
KLTC Dickinson ND
KLTF Little Falls MN
KLTI Macon MO
KLTK Southwest City MO
KLTT Brighton CO
KLTZ Glasgow MT
KLUP Terrell Hills TX
KLVI Beaumont TX
KLVJ Mountain Home ID
KLVL Pasadena TX
KLVQ Athens TX
KLVT Leveland TX
KLVU Haynesville LA
KLWJ Umatilla OR
KLWN Lawrence KS
KLWT Lebanon MO
KLXR Redding CA
KLXX Bismarck-Mandan ND
KLYC McMinnville OR
KLYQ Hamilton MT
KLYR Clarksville AR
KLZ Denver CO
KLZX Salt Lake City UT

KMA Shenandoah IA
KMAD Madill OK
KMAJ Topeka KS
KMAM Butler MO
KMAN Manhattan KS
KMAQ Maquoketa IA
KMAR Winnsboro LA
KMAS Shelton WA
KMAV Mayville ND
KMAY Billings MT
KMBD Tillamook OR
*KMBI Spokane WA
KMBL Junction TX
KMBS West Monroe LA
KMBY Capitola CA
KMBZ Kansas City MO
KMCD Fairfield IA
KMCL McCall ID
KMDO Fort Scott KS
KMED Medford OR
KMEM Lincoln NE
KMEN San Bernardino CA
KMER Kemmerer WY
KMET Banning CA
KMGR Murray UT
KMHL Marshall MN

KMHT Marshall TX
KMIL Cameron TX
KMIN Grants NM
KMIS Portageville MO
KMIX Turlock CA
KMJ Fresno CA
KMJY Newport WA
KMLB Monroe LA
KMMJ Grand Island NE
KMMO Marshall MO
KMMS Bozeman MT
KMND Midland TX
KMNS Sioux City IA
KMNY Pomona CA
KMOG Payson AZ
KMOM Monticello MN
KMON Great Falls MT
KMOX St. Louis MO
KMOZ Rolla MO
KMPC Los Angeles CA
KMPG Hollister CA
KMPL Sikeston MO
KMPQ Rosenberg-Richmond TX
KMPS Seattle WA
KMRC Morgan City LA
KMRF Marshfield MO
KMRN Cameron MO
KMRR South Tucson AZ
KMRS Morris MN
KMRT Dallas TX
KMRY Cedar Rapids IA
KMSD Milbank SD
KMSL Great Falls MT
KMTA Kinsey MT
KMTI Manti UT
KMTL Sherwood AR
KMTT Tacoma WA
KMTW Las Vegas NV
KMTX Helena MT
KMUL Muleshoe TX
KMUZ Gresham OR
KMVI Wailuku HI
KMVL Madisonville TX
KMVP Commerce City CO
KMWX Yakima WA
KMXN Santa Rosa CA
KMXO Merkel TX
KMYC Marysville CA
KMYX Taft CA
KMYZ Pryor OK

KNAB Burlington CO
KNAF Fredricksburg TX
KNAK Delta UT
KNBO New Boston TX
KNBR San Francisco CA
KNBY Newport AR
KNCB Vivian LA
KNCK Concordia KS
KNCO Grass Valley CA
KNCY Nebraska City NE
KNDA Odessa TX
KNDC Hettinger ND
KNDI Honolulu HI
KNDK Langdon ND
KNDN Farmington NM
KNDY Marysville KS
KNEA Jonesboro AR
KNEB Scottsbluff NE
KNED McAlester OK
KNEI Waukon IA
KNEK Washington LA
KNEL Brady TX
KNEM Nevada MO
KNET Palestine TX
KNEU Roosevelt UT
KNEW Oakland CA
KNFL Tremonton UT
KNFT Bayard NM
KNGL McPherson KS
*KNGN McCook NE
KNHN Kansas City KS
KNIA Knoxville IA
KNIM Maryville MO
KNIN Wichita Falls TX
KNIR New Iberia LA
KNKQ Virginia City NV
KNLV Ord NE
KNMX Las Vegas NM
KNND Cottage Grove OR
KNNS Glendale AZ
KNNT Kennett MO
KNOB Frazier Park CA
KNOC Natchitoches LA
KNOE Monroe LA
*KNOM Nome AK
KNOR Norman OK
KNOT Prescott AZ
*KNOW Minneapolis MN
KNOX Grand Forks ND
KNPT Newport OR
KNRO Redding CA
KNRY Monterey CA
KNSA Unalakleet AK
KNSE Ontario CA
KNSI St. Cloud MN
KNSP Staples MN
KNSS Wichita KS
KNST Tucson AZ
KNTA Santa Clara CA
KNTR Ferndale WA
KNTS Abilene TX
KNUI Kahului HI
KNUJ New Ulm MN
KNUS Denver CO

Broadcasting & Cable Yearbook 1994

U.S. AM Stations by Call Letters

KNUU Paradise NV
KNUZ Houston TX
KNWA Bellefonte AR
*KNWC Sioux Falls SD
*KNWS Waterloo IA
KNWZ Thousand Palms CA
KNX Los Angeles CA
KNXN Sierra Vista AZ
KNZR Bakersfield CA
KNZS Montecito CA
KNZZ Grand Junction CO

KOA Denver CO
*KOAC Corvallis OR
KOAK Red Oak IA
KOAL Price UT
KOAQ Terrytown NE
KOBE Las Cruces NM
KOBO Yuba City CA
KODI Cody WY
KODL The Dalles OR
KODY North Platte NE
KOEL Oelwein IA
KOFC Fayetteville AR
KOFE St. Maries ID
KOFI Kalispell MT
KOFK Milan NM
KOFO Ottawa KS
KOFY San Mateo CA
KOGA Ogallala NE
KOGT Orange TX
KOH Reno NV
KOHI St. Helens OR
KOHO Honolulu HI
KOHU Hermiston OR
KOIL Bellevue NE
KOIT San Francisco CA
KOJM Havre MT
KOJY Costa Mesa CA
KOKA Shreveport LA
KOKB Blackwell OK
KOKC Guthrie OK
KOKK Huron SD
KOKL Okmulgee OK
KOKO Warrensburg MO
KOKX Keokuk IA
KOLE Port Arthur TX
KOLM Rochester MN
KOLT Scottsbluff NE
KOLY Mobridge SD
KOMA Oklahoma City OK
KOMC Branson MO
KOMO Seattle WA
KOMW Omak WA
KONA Kennewick WA
KONO San Antonio TX
KONP Port Angeles WA
KONY Washington UT
KOOL Phoenix AZ
KOOQ North Platte NE
KOPA Scottsdale AZ
KOPY Georgetown TX
KOQO Clovis CA
KORC Waldport OR
KORD Pasco WA
KORE Springfield-Eugene OR
KORG Anaheim CA
KORK Las Vegas NV
KORN Mitchell SD
KORT Grangeville ID
KORV Oroville CA
KOSE Osceola AR
KOSG Camden LA
KOSZ Vermillion SD
KOTA Rapid City SD
KOTD Plattsmouth NE
KOTN Pine Bluff AR
KOTS Deming NM
*KOTZ Kotzebue AK
KOVC Valley City ND
KOVE Lander WY
KOVO Provo UT
KOWA Laughlin NV
KOWB Laramie WY
KOWL South Lake Tahoe CA
KOWO Waseca MN
KOXR Oxnard CA
KOY Phoenix AZ
KOZA Odessa TX
KOZE Lewiston ID
KOZI Chelan WA
KOZQ Waynesville MO
KOZY Grand Rapids MN
KOZZ Reno NV

KPAG Pagosa Springs CO
KPAN Hereford TX
KPAR Granbury TX
KPAY Chico CA
KPBA Pine Bluff AR
KPBC Garland TX
KPBI Greenwood AR
KPCO Quincy CA
KPCR Bowling Green MO
KPDQ Portland OR
KPEL Lafayette LA
KPET Lamesa TX
KPGE Page AZ
KPHN Pittsburg KS
KPHP Lake Oswego OR
KPHX Phoenix AZ
KPKE Gunnison CO
KPLS Orange CA
KPLT Paris TX
KPLY Sparks NV
KPMO Mendocino CA

KPNW Eugene OR
KPOC Pocahontas AR
KPOD Crescent City CA
*KPOF Denver CO
KPOK Bowman ND
KPOP San Diego CA
KPOS Post TX
KPOW Powell WY
KPPC Pasadena CA
KPQ Wenatchee WA
KPRB Redmond OR
KPRC Houston TX
KPRK Livingston MT
KPRL Paso Robles CA
KPRM Park Rapids MN
KPRO Riverside CA
KPRT Kansas City MO
KPRV Poteau OK
KPRZ San Marcos CA
KPSA Alamogordo NM
KPSI Palm Springs CA
KPSL Thousand Palms CA
KPSO Falfurrias TX
KPTL Carson City NV
KPUA Hilo HI
KPUG Bellingham WA
KPUR Amarillo TX
KPWB Piedmont MO
KPWS Crowley LA
KPXE Liberty TX
KPYK Terrell TX

KQAD Luverne MN
KQAM Wichita KS
KQAQ Austin MN
KQCV Oklahoma City OK
KQDJ Jamestown ND
KQDS Duluth MN
KQEN Roseburg OR
KQEO Albuquerque NM
KQHN Nederland TX
KQIK Lakeview OR
KQIL Grand Junction CO
KQKD Redfield SD
KQLL Tulsa OK
KQLO Reno NV
KQLX Lisbon ND
KQMG Independence IA
KQMQ Honolulu HI
KQMS Redding CA
KQNG Lihue HI
KQNK Norton KS
KQQQ Pullman WA
KQRO Cuero TX
KQRS Golden Valley MN
KQSB Santa Barbara CA
KQTL Sahuarita AZ
KQTY Borger TX
KQV Pittsburgh PA
KQWB Fargo ND
KQWC Webster City IA
KQXI Arvada CO
KQXK Springdale AR
KQYX Joplin MO

KRAE Cheyenne WY
KRAF Holdenville OK
KRAI Craig CO
KRAK Sacramento CA
KRAL Rawlins WY
KRBA Lufkin TX
KRBE Houston TX
KRBI St. Peter MN
KRCD Chubbuck ID
KRCK Burbank CA
KRCO Prineville OR
KRCX Roseville CA
KRDD Roswell NM
KRDG Redding CA
KRDO Colorado Springs CO
KRDS Tolleson AZ
KRDU Dinuba CA
KRDZ Wray CO
KRED Eureka CA
KREI Farmington MO
KREW Sunnyside WA
KRFO Owatonna MN
KRFS Superior NE
KRGE Weslaco TX
KRGI Grand Island NE
KRGO Fowler CA
KRGQ West Valley City UT
KRHD Duncan OK
KRIB Mason City IA
KRIL Odessa TX
KRIO McAllen TX
KRIZ Renton WA
KRJH Hallettsville TX
KRJT Bowie TX
KRKC King City CA
KRKE Aspen CO
KRKI Estes Park CO
KRKK Rock Springs WY
KRKL Yountville CA
KRKO Everett WA
KRKS Denver CO
KRKT Albany OR
KRKY Granby CO
KRLA Pasadena CA
KRLC Lewiston ID
KRLD Dallas TX
KRLL Albuquerque NM
KRLN Canon City CO
KRLW Walnut Ridge AR
KRMD Shreveport LA
KRME Hondo TX

KRMG Tulsa OK
KRMH Leadville CO
KRML Carmel CA
KRMO Monett MO
KRMS Osage Beach MO
KRMX Pueblo CO
KRMY Killeen TX
*KRNI Mason City IA
KRNR Roseburg OR
KRNT Des Moines IA
KROC Rochester MN
KROD El Paso TX
KROE Sheridan WY
KROF Abbeville LA
KROP Brawley CA
KROS Clinton IA
KROW Reno NV
KROX Crookston MN
KRPL Moscow ID
KRPT Anadarko OK
KRPX Price UT
KRQC Salinas CA
KRQX Mexia TX
KRRP Coushatta LA
KRRS Santa Rosa CA
KRRU Pueblo CO
KRRV Alexandria LA
KRRZ Minot ND
KRSA Petersburg AK
KRSC Othello WA
KRSL Russell KS
KRSN Los Alamos NM
KRSO San Bernardino CA
KRSR Coos Bay OR
KRSV Afton WY
KRSY Roswell NM
KRTN Raton NM
KRUI Ruidoso Downs NM
KRUN Ballinger TX
KRUS Ruston LA
KRVA Cockrell Hill TX
KRVC Medford OR
KRVN Lexington NE
KRVZ Springerville-Eager AZ
KRWB Roseau MN
KRWC Buffalo MN
KRXR Gooding ID
KRXX Minneapolis-St. Paul MN
KRYS Corpus Christi TX
KRZE Farmington NM
KRZI Waco TX
KRZY Albuquerque NM

KSAC Sacramento CA
KSAH Universal City TX
KSAI Saipan MP
KSAL Salina KS
KSAM Huntsville TX
KSAZ Tucson AZ
KSBN Spokane WA
KSBQ Santa Maria CA
KSCB Liberal KS
KSCJ Sioux City IA
KSCO Santa Cruz CA
KSCR Benson MN
KSD St. Louis MO
KSDN Aberdeen SD
KSDO San Diego CA
*KSDP Sand Point AK
KSDR Watertown SD
KSEI Pocatello ID
KSEL Portales NM
KSEN Shelby MT
KSEO Durant OK
KSEV Tomball TX
KSEY Seymour TX
KSFA Nacogdoches TX
KSFO San Francisco CA
KSFT St. Joseph MO
KSGI St. George UT
KSGL Wichita KS
KSGM Chester IL
KSGT Jackson WY
KSHO Lebanon OR
KSHY Cheyenne WY
KSIB Creston IA
KSID Sidney NE
KSIG Crowley LA
KSIL Silver City NM
KSIM Sikeston MO
KSIR Brush CO
KSIS Sedalia MO
KSIV Clayton MO
KSIW Woodward OK
KSIX Corpus Christi TX
KSJB Jamestown ND
*KSJK Talent OR
KSJX San Jose CA
KSKE Vail CO
*KSKO McGrath AK
KSKY Balch Springs TX
KSL Salt Lake City UT
KSLD Soldotna AK
KSLM Salem OR
KSLO Opelousas LA
KSLQ Washington MO
KSLR San Antonio TX
KSLV Monte Vista CO
KSMA Santa Maria CA
KSMJ Sacramento CA
KSMO Salem MO
KSMX Walla Walla MO
KSNY Snyder TX
KSOK Arkansas City KS

KSON San Diego CA
KSOO Sioux Falls SD
KSOP South Salt Lake UT
KSOS Brigham City UT
KSPA Escondido CA
KSPD Boise ID
KSPE Santa Barbara CA
KSPI Stillwater OK
KSPT Sandpoint ID
KSRA Salmon ID
KSRB Hardy AR
KSRM Soldotna AK
KSRO Santa Rosa CA
KSRR Provo UT
KSRV Ontario OR
KSRX El Dorado KS
KSSK Honolulu HI
KSSQ Conroe TX
KSSR Santa Rosa NM
KSST Sulphur Springs TX
KSTA Coleman TX
KSTC Sterling CO
KSTE Rancho Cordova CA
KSTL St. Louis MO
KSTN Stockton CA
KSTP St. Paul MN
KSTR Grand Junction CO
KSTV Stephenville TX
KSUB Cedar City UT
KSUD West Memphis AR
KSUE Susanville CA
KSUM Fairmont MN
KSUN Phoenix AZ
KSUR Soledad CA
KSUV McFarland CA
KSVC Richfield UT
KSVE El Paso TX
KSVN Ogden UT
KSVP Artesia NM
KSVY Opportunity WA
KSWA Graham TX
KSWB Seaside OR
KSWD Seward AK
KSWM Aurora MO
KSWO Lawton OK
KSWV Santa Fe NM
KSYC Yreka CA
KSYL Alexandria LA
KSZL Barstow CA

KTAE Taylor TX
KTAM Bryan TX
KTAN Sierra Vista AZ
KTAP Santa Maria CA
KTAR Phoenix AZ
KTAT Frederick OK
KTBA Tuba City AZ
KTBB Tyler TX
KTBI Ephrata WA
KTBR Roseburg OR
KTCB Malden MO
KTCD Cottonwood CA
KTCH Wayne NE
KTCJ Minneapolis MN
KTCR Kennewick WA
KTCS Fort Smith AR
KTEK Alvin TX
KTEL Walla Walla WA
KTEM Temple TX
KTFI Twin Falls ID
KTFJ Dakota City NE
KTGE Salinas CA
*KTGG Spring Arbor MI
KTGO Tioga ND
KTGR Columbia MO
KTHE Thermopolis WY
KTHO South Lake Tahoe CA
KTHS Berryville AR
KTIB Thibodaux LA
KTID San Rafael CA
KTIM Wickenburg AZ
KTIP Porterville CA
KTIX Pendleton OR
KTJS Hobart OK
KTKK Sandy UT
KTKN Ketchikan AK
KTKT Tucson AZ
KTLD Pineville LA
KTLK Thornton CO
KTLO Mountain Home AR
KTLQ Tahlequah OK
KTLU Rusk TX
KTLV Midwest City OK
KTMC McAlester OK
KTME Lompoc CA
KTMG Deer Trail CO
KTMP Heber City UT
KTMR Edna TX
KTMS Santa Barbara CA
KTMT Phoenix OR
KTNC Falls City NE
KTNM Tucumcari NM
KTNN Window Rock AZ
KTNO Fort Worth TX
KTNP Lubbock TX
KTNQ Los Angeles CA
KTNS Oakhurst CA
KTOB Petaluma CA
KTOC Jonesboro LA
KTOE Mankato MN
KTOK Oklahoma City OK
KTOL Lacey WA
KTOM Salinas CA
KTON Belton TX

KTOP Topeka KS
KTOQ Rapid City SD
KTOW Sand Springs OK
KTOX Needles CA
KTOZ Springfield MO
KTPA Prescott AR
KTRB Modesto CA
KTRC Santa Fe NM
KTRF Thief River Falls MN
KTRH Houston TX
KTRO Port Hueneme CA
KTRT Claremore OK
KTRW Spokane WA
KTRY Bastrop LA
KTSA San Antonio TX
KTSJ Pomona CA
KTSM El Paso TX
KTTN Trenton MO
KTTR Rolla MO
KTTS Springfield MO
KTTT Columbus NE
KTUC Tucson AZ
KTUE Tulia TX
KTUI Sullivan MO
KTUR Tooele UT
KTWG Agana GU
KTWK Colorado Springs CO
KTWN Texarkana TX
KTWO Casper WY
KTXJ Jasper TX
KTXZ West Lake Hills TX
KTYM Inglewood CA
KTYN Minot ND
KTZR Tucson AZ

KUAI Eleele HI
KUAM Agana GU
*KUAT Tucson AZ
KUAU Haiku HI
KUBA Yuba City CA
KUBC Montrose CO
KUBR San Juan TX
KUDY Spokane WA
KUGN Eugene OR
KUGR Green River WY
KUGT Jackson MO
KUHD Port Neches TX
KUHL Santa Maria CA
KUIK Hillsboro OR
KUJ Walla Walla WA
KUKI Ukiah CA
KUKQ Tempe AZ
KUKU Willow Springs MO
KULA Honolulu HI
KULE Ephrata WA
KULL Seattle WA
KULP El Campo TX
KULY Ulysses KS
KUMA Pendleton OR
KUMU Honolulu HI
KUNO Corpus Christi TX
KUOA Siloam Springs AR
KUOL San Marcos TX
*KUOM Minneapolis MN
KUPI Idaho Falls ID
KUPL Portland OR
KURB Little Rock AR
KURL Billings MT
KURM Rogers AR
KURS San Diego CA
KURV Edinburg TX
KURY Brookings OR
*KUSD Vermillion SD
KUSH Cushing OK
KUTA Blanding UT
KUTE Desert Hot Springs CA
KUTI Selah WA
KUTY Palmdale CA
KUUY Orchard Valley WY
KUVR Holdrege NE
KUYO Evansville WY

KVAC Forks WA
KVAK Valdez AK
KVAN Vancouver WA
KVAS Astoria OR
KVBR Brainerd MN
KVCK Wolf Point MT
KVCL Winnfield LA
KVDB Sioux Center IA
KVDL Quanah TX
KVEC San Luis Obispo CA
KVEG North Las Vegas NV
KVEL Vernal UT
KVEN Ventura CA
KVET Austin TX
KVFC Cortez CO
KVFD Fort Dodge IA
KVGB Great Bend KS
KVI Seattle WA
KVIL Highland Park TX
*KVIP Redding CA
KVIS Miami OK
KVIV El Paso TX
KVJY Pharr TX
KVLA Vidalia LA
KVLD Valdez AK
KVLF Alpine TX
KVLG La Grange TX
KVLH Pauls Valley OK
KVLI Lake Isabella CA
KVLL Woodville TX
KVLV Fallon NV
KVMA Magnolia AR
KVMC Colorado City TX
KVML Sonora CA

Broadcasting & Cable Yearbook 1994
B-453

U.S. AM Stations by Call Letters

KVNA Flagstaff AZ	KWTO Springfield MO	KZMX Hot Springs SD	WALL Middletown NY	WBBB Burlington NC
KVNI Coeur d'Alene ID	KWTX Waco TX	KZNG Hot Springs AR	WALM Albion MI	WBBD Wheeling WV
KVNU Logan UT	KWVR Enterprise OR	KZOK Seattle WA	WALO Humacao PR	WBBE Georgetown KY
KVOC Casper WY	KWWJ Baytown TX	KZOO Honolulu HI	WALT Meridian MS	WBBF Rochester NY
KVOE Emporia KS	KWWX Wenatchee WA	KZOT Marianna AR	WALZ Machias ME	WBBI Madison AL
KVOI Oro Valley AZ	KWXI Glenwood AR	KZPA Fort Yukon AK	WAMA Tampa FL	WBBK Blakely GA
KVOK Kodiak AK	KWXT Dardanelle AR	KZPM Bakersfield CA	WAMB Donelson TN	WBBM Chicago IL
KVOL Lafayette LA	KWXY Cathedral City CA	KZRC Milwaukie OR	WAMD Aberdeen MD	WBBP Memphis TN
KVOM Morrilton AR	KWYD Colorado Springs CO	KZSN Wichita KS	WAME Statesville NC	WBBQ Augusta GA
KVON Napa CA	KWYN Wynne AR	KZSS Albuquerque NM	WAMI Opp AL	WBBR New York NY
KVOO Tulsa OK	KWYO Sheridan WY	KZTA Yakima WA	WAML Laurel MS	WBBT Lyons GA
KVOP Plainview TX	KWYR Winner SD	KZTU Junction City OR	WAMM Woodstock VA	WBBW Youngstown OH
KVOR Colorado Springs CO	KWYS West Yellowstone MT	KZTW Troutdale OR	WAMN Green Valley WV	WBBX Kingston TN
KVOU Uvalde TX	KWYZ Everett WA	KZTY Winchester NV	WAMR Venice FL	WBBZ Ponca City OK
KVOW Riverton WY		KZUE El Reno OK	WAMT Titusville FL	WBCA Bay Minette AL
KVOX Moorhead MN	KXAM Mesa AZ	KZUS Toledo OR	*WAMV Amherst VA	WBCB Levittown-Fairless Hills PA
KVOY Mojave CA	KXAR Hope AR	KZXS San Antonio TX	WAMW Washington IN	WBCE Wickliffe KY
KVOZ Laredo TX	KXBT Vallejo CA	KZXT Beaumont TX	WAMX Saline MI	WBCF Florence AL
KVPI Ville Platte LA	KXBX Lakeport CA	KZXX Kenai AK	WAMY Amory MS	WBCH Hastings MI
KVRC Arkadelphia AR	KXEB Sherman TX	KZXY Apple Valley CA	WANA Anniston AL	WBCK Battle Creek MI
KVRD Cottonwood AZ	KXED Los Angeles CA	KZZB Beaumont TX	WANB Waynesburg PA	WBCO Bucyrus OH
KVRH Salida CO	KXEG Tolleson AZ	KZZJ Rugby ND	WANL Albany GA	WBCP Urbana IL
KVRP Stamford TX	KXEL Waterloo IA	KZZK Springfield OR	WANM Tallahassee FL	WBCR Alcoa TN
KVSA McGehee AR	KXEN Festus-St. Louis MO	KZZN Littlefield TX	WANN Annapolis MD	WBCU Union SC
KVSF Santa Fe NM	KXEO Mexico MO	KZZR Burns OR	WANO Pineville KY	WBCV Bristol TN
KVSH Valentine NE	KXEQ Reno NV		WANR Warren OH	WBCW Jeannette PA
KVSI Montpelier ID	KXER Templeton CA	NEW AM Madisonville TX	WANS Anderson SC	WBDN Brandon FL
KVSL Show Low AZ	KXEW South Tucson AZ	NEW AM Berlin VT	WANV Waynesboro VA	WBEC Pittsfield MA
KVSN Tumwater WA	KXEX Fresno CA	NEW AM Olviedo FL	WANY Albany KY	WBEE Harvey IL
KVSP Oklahoma City OK	KXGF Great Falls MT		WAOC St. Augustine FL	WBEJ Elizabethton TN
KVSV Beloit KS	KXGN Glendive MT	V6AI Yap FM	WAOK Atlanta GA	WBEL South Beloit IL
KVVA Phoenix AZ	KXIC Iowa City IA		WAOS Austell GA	WBEM Windber PA
KVVQ Hesperia CA	KXIT Dalhart TX	WAAA Winston-Salem NC	WAOV Vincennes IN	WBEN Buffalo NY
KVVS Windsor CO	KXJK Forrest City AR	WAAK Dallas NC	WAPA San Juan PR	WBET Brockton MA
KVWC Vernon TX	KXKL Denver CO	WAAM Ann Arbor MI	WAPF McComb MS	WBEU Beaufort SC
KVWG Pearsall TX	KXKS Albuquerque NM	WAAV Leland NC	WAPI Birmingham AL	WBEV Beaver Dam WI
KVWM Show Low AZ	KXKW Tioga LA	WAAX Gadsden AL	WAPZ Wetumpka AL	WBEX Chillicothe OH
KVYK Giddings TX	KXL Portland OR	WABA Aguadilla PR	WAQE Rice Lake WI	WBFC Stanton KY
	KXLA Rayville LA	WABB Mobile AL	WAQI Miami FL	WBFD Bedford PA
KWAC Bakersfield CA	KXLE Ellensburg WA	WABC New York NY	WAQS Charlotte NC	WBFJ Winston-Salem NC
KWAD Wadena MN	KXLO Lewistown MT	WABD Fort Campbell KY	WAQY East Longmeadow MA	WBFN Quitman MS
KWAI Honolulu HI	KXLY Spokane WA	WABF Fairhope AL	WARA Attleboro MA	WBFX Terre Haute IN
KWAK Stuttgart AR	KXNO North Las Vegas NV	WABG Greenwood MS	WARD Pittston PA	WBGD Mount Dora FL
KWAL Wallace ID	KXO El Centro CA	WABH Bath NY	WARE Ware MA	WBGC Chipley FL
KWAM Memphis TN	KXOA Sacramento CA	WABI Bangor ME	WARF Jasper AL	WBGG Saratoga Springs NY
KWAS Joplin MO	KXOJ Sapulpa OK	WABJ Adrian MI	WARK Hagerstown MD	WBGN Bowling Green KY
KWAT Watertown SD	KXOK St. Louis MO	WABK Gardiner ME	WARM Scranton PA	WBGR Baltimore MD
KWAY Waverly IA	KXOL Clinton OK	WABL Amite LA	WARO Claremont VA	WBGS Point Pleasant WV
KWBC Navasota TX	KXOW Hot Springs AR	WABN Abingdon VA	WARU Peru IN	WBGZ Alton IL
KWBE Beatrice NE	KXOX Sweetwater TX	WABO Waynesboro MS	WARV Warwick RI	WBHB Fitzgerald GA
KWBG Boone IA	KXPO Grafton ND	WABQ Cleveland OH	WASA Havre de Grace MD	WBHC Hampton SC
KWBW Hutchinson KS	KXQZ San Angelo TX	WABS Arlington VA	WASB Brockport NY	WBHF Cartersville GA
KWBY Woodburn OR	KXRA Alexandria MN	WABY Albany NY	WASC Spartanburg SC	WBHN Bryson City NC
KWCK Searcy AR	KXRB Sioux Falls SD	WACB Taylorsville NC	WASG Atmore AL	WBHP Huntsville AL
KWCO Chickasha OK	KXRE Manitou Springs CO	WACE Chicopee MA	WASK Lafayette IN	WBHY Mobile AL
KWDF Ball LA	KXRO Aberdeen WA	WACK Newark NY	WASN Campbell OH	WBIB Centreville AL
KWDS Prescott Valley AZ	KXSS Waite Park MN	WACL Waycross GA	WASO Covington LA	WBIC Royston GA
KWEB Rochester MN	KXTD Wagoner OK	WACM West Springfield MA	WASP Brownsville PA	WBIG Aurora IL
KWED Seguin TX	KXTL Butte MT	WACO Waco TX	WASR Wolfeboro NH	WBIL Tuskegee AL
KWEI Weiser ID	KXTN San Antonio TX	WACQ Tallassee AL	WATA Boone NC	WBIN Benton TN
KWEL Midland TX	KXTO Reno NV	WACR Columbus MS	WATH Athens OH	WBIP Booneville MS
KWEY Weatherford OK	KXTP Superior WI	WACT Tuscaloosa AL	WATJ Chardon OH	WBIT Adel GA
KWFM Tucson AZ	KXTQ Lubbock TX	WACV Montgomery AL	WATK Antigo WI	WBIU Denham Springs LA
KWFT Wichita Falls TX	KXVQ Pawhuska OK	WADA Shelby NC	WATN Watertown NY	WBIV Natick MA
KWG Stockton CA	KXXX Colby KS	WADC Parkersburg WV	WATO Oak Ridge TN	WBIW Bedford IN
KWHI Brenham TX	KXXY Oklahoma City OK	WADE Wadesboro NC	WATR Waterbury CT	WBIZ Eau Claire WI
KWHK Hutchinson KS	KXYL Brownwood TX	WADJ Somerset PA	WATS Sayre PA	WBJA Guayama PR
KWHN Fort Smith AR	KXYZ Houston TX	WADK Newport RI	WATT Cadillac MI	WBJX Racine WI
KWHW Altus OK	KXZZ Lake Charles LA	WADM Decatur IN	WATV Birmingham AL	WBKC Painesville OH
KWIK Pocatello ID		WADN Concord MA	WATW Ashland WI	WBKH Hattiesburg MS
KWIL Albany OR	KYAK Anchorage AK	WADO New York NY	WATX Algood TN	WBKV West Bend WI
KWIP Dallas OR	KYBG Aurora CO	WADR Remsen NY	WATZ Alpena MI	WBKZ Jefferson PA
KWIQ Moses Lake North WA	KYCA Prescott AZ	WADS Ansonia CT	WAUB Auburn NY	WBLA Elizabethtown NC
KWIX Moberly MO	KYCN Wheatland WY	WADU Norco LA	WAUC Wauchula FL	WBLB Pulaski VA
KWIZ Santa Ana CA	KYCR Golden Valley MN	WADV Lebanon PA	WAUD Auburn AL	WBLC Lenoir City TN
KWJJ Portland OR	KYET Williams AZ	WADX Trenton GA	WAUG New Hope NC	WBLF Bellefonte PA
KWKA Clovis NM	*KYFR Shenandoah IA	WAEB Allentown PA	WAUK Waukesha WI	WBLJ Dalton GA
KWKH Shreveport LA	KYGO Denver CO	WAEC Atlanta GA	WAUR Sandwich IL	WBLL Bellefontaine OH
KWKW Los Angeles CA	KYJC Medford OR	WAEL Mayaguez PR	WAVB Lajas PR	WBLR Batesburg SC
KWKY Des Moines IA	KYKK Hobbs NM	WAEW Crossville TN	WAVD Decatur AL	WBLT Bedford VA
KWLA Many LA	KYKN Keizer OR	WAEY Princeton WV	WAVG Louisville KY	WBLU Moneta VA
*KWLC Decorah IA	KYLR Huntsville TX	WAFC Clewiston FL	WAVL Apollo PA	WBLX Fairhope AL
KWLL Casa Grande AZ	KYLT Missoula MT	WAFS Atlanta GA	WAVN Southaven MS	WBLY Springfield OH
KWLM Willmar MN	KYMN Northfield MN	WAGC Centre AL	WAVO Rock Hill SC	WBMA Dedham MA
KWLO Waterloo IA	KYMO East Prairie MO	WAGE Leesburg VA	WAVS Davie FL	WBMB West Branch MI
KWLS Pratt KS	KYND Cypress TX	WAGF Dothan AL	WAVU Albertville AL	WBMC McMinnville TN
KWMB Wabasha MN	KYNO Fresno CA	WAGG Birmingham AL	WAVZ New Haven CT	WBMD Baltimore MD
KWMC Del Rio TX	KYNT Yankton SD	WAGL Lancaster SC	WAWK Kendallville IN	WBMJ San Juan PR
KWMT Fort Dodge IA	KYOK Houston TX	WAGN Menominee MI	WAXE Vero Beach FL	WBML Macon GA
KWMX Lakewood CO	KYOO Bolivar MO	WAGR Lumberton NC	WAXO Lewisburg TN	WBMQ Savannah GA
KWNA Winnemucca NV	KYOS Merced CA	WAGS Bishopville SC	WAYB Waynesboro VA	WBMS Wilmington NC
KWNC Quincy WA	KYOT Phoenix AZ	WAGY Forest City NC	WAYC Bedford PA	WBNC Conway NH
KWNK Simi Valley CA	KYRO Potosi MO	WAIK Galesburg IL	WAYE Birmingham AL	WBND Florence KY
KWNO Winona MN	KYSM Mankato MN	WAIM Anderson SC	WAYN Rockingham NC	WBNL Boonville IN
KWOA Worthington MN	KYST Texas City TX	WAIN Columbia KY	*WAYR Orange Park FL	WBNM Gordon NE
KWOC Poplar Bluff MO	*KYUK Bethel AK	WAIS Buchtel OH	WAYT Wabash IN	WBNN Union City IN
KWON Bartlesville OK	KYUU Liberal KS	WAIT Crystal Lake IL	WAYX Waycross GA	WBNR Beacon NY
KWOR Worland WY	KYVA Gallup NM	WAJA Franklin NC	WAYY Chippewa Falls WI	WBNS Columbus OH
KWOS Jefferson City MO	KYW Philadelphia PA	WAJD Gainesville FL	WAZF Yazoo City MS	WBOB Galax VA
KWPC Muscatine IA	KYXE Selah WA	WAJF Decatur AL	WAZL Hazleton PA	WBOK New Orleans LA
KWPM West Plains MO	KYXZ Cabot AR	WAJL Pine Castle-Sky Lake FL	WAZS Summerville SC	WBOW Terre Haute IN
KWPN West Point NE	KYYD Abilene TX	WAJO Marion AL	WAZX Smyrna GA	WBOX Bogalusa LA
KWRD Henderson TX	KYZS Tyler TX	WAJR Morgantown WV		WBPA Elkhorn City KY
KWRE Warrenton MO		WAKE Valparaiso IN	*WBAA West Lafayette IN	WBPZ Lock Haven PA
KWRF Warren AR	KZBK Brookfield MO	WAKI McMinnville TN	WBAC Cleveland TN	WBQN Barceloneta PR
KWRM Corona CA	KZBQ Pocatello ID	WAKK McComb MS	WBAF Barnesville GA	WBRB Mount Clemens MI
KWRO Coquille OR	KZEE Weatherford TX	WAKM Franklin TN	WBAG Burlington-Graham NC	WBRD Palmetto FL
KWRT Boonville MO	KZEP San Antonio TX	WAKO Lawrenceville IL	WBAJ Blythwood SC	WBRG Lynchburg VA
KWSA West Klamath OR	KZEY Tyler TX	WAKR Akron OH	WBAL Baltimore MD	WBRI Indianapolis IN
KWSD Mount Shasta CA	KZIM Cape Girardeau MO	WAKY Greensburg KY	WBAP Fort Worth TX	WBRJ Marietta OH
KWSH Wewoka OK	KZIP Amarillo TX	WALD Walterboro SC	WBAR Bartow FL	WBRK Pittsfield MA
KWSL Sioux City IA	KZIQ Ridgecrest CA	WALE Providence RI	WBAT Marion IN	WBRM Marion NC
KWSN Sioux Falls SD	KZIZ Sumner WA	WALG Albany GA	WBAW Barnwell SC	WBRN Big Rapids MI
*KWSU Pullman WA	KZLO Bozeman MT	WALH Mountain City GA	WBAX Wilkes-Barre PA	WBRO Waynesboro GA
KWSW Eureka CA	KZMO California MO	WALI Cumberland MD	WBBA Pittsfield IL	WBRT Bardstown KY
	KZMQ Greybull WY	WALK Patchogue NY		

Broadcasting & Cable Yearbook 1994

B-454

U.S. AM Stations by Call Letters

WBRV Boonville NY
WBRW Bridgewater NJ
WBRY Woodbury TN
WBSA Boaz AL
WBSC Bennettsville SC
WBSL Bay St. Louis MS
WBSM New Bedford MA
WBSR Pensacola FL
WBT Charlotte NC
WBTA Batavia NY
WBTB Beaufort NC
WBTC Uhrichsville OH
WBTG Sheffield AL
WBTH Williamson WV
WBTM Danville VA
WBTN Bennington VT
WBTO Linton IN
WBTS Bridgeport AL
WBTX Broadway-Timberville VA
WBUC Buckhannon WV
WBUD Trenton NJ
WBUG Amsterdam NY
WBUL Shepherdsville KY
WBUT Butler PA
WBUX Doylestown PA
WBVP Beaver Falls PA
WBXR Hazel Green AL
WBYE Calera AL
WBYS Canton IL
WBYU New Orleans LA
WBYY Rockford MI
WBZ Boston MA
WBZA Glens Falls NY
WBZB Selma NC
WBZI Xenia OH
WBZK York SC
WBZR Destin FL
WBZT West Palm Beach FL
WBZY New Castle PA

WCAB Rutherfordton NC
WCAE Nekoosa WI
WCAM Camden SC
WCAO Baltimore MD
WCAP Lowell MA
WCAR Livonia MI
WCAT Orange-Athol MA
WCAW Charleston WV
WCAZ Carthage IL
WCBA Corning NY
WCBC Cumberland MD
WCBG Chambersburg PA
WCBL Benton KY
WCBM Baltimore MD
WCBQ Oxford MS
WCBR Richmond KY
WCBS New York NY
WCBT Roanoke Rapids NC
WCBX Bassett VA
WCBY Cheboygan MI
WCCC West Hartford CT
WCCD Parma OH
WCCF Punta Gorda FL
WCCM Lawrence MA
WCCN Neillsville WI
WCCO Minneapolis MN
WCCP Clemson SC
WCCS Homer City PA
WCCW Traverse City MI
WCCY Houghton MI
WCDL Carbondale PA
WCDO Sidney NY
WCDS Glasgow KY
WCDT Winchester TN
WCED DuBois PA
WCEG Middleborough Center MA
WCEH Hawkinsville GA
WCEI Easton MD
WCEM Cambridge MD
WCEN Mount Pleasant MI
WCEO Birmingham AL
WCER Canton OH
WCEV Cicero IL
WCFJ Chicago Heights IL
WCFR Springfield VT
WCFY Lafayette IN
WCGA Woodbine GA
WCGB Juana Diaz PR
WCGC Belmont NC
WCGL Jacksonville FL
WCGM Maryville TN
WCGO Chicago Heights IL
WCGR Canandaigua NY
WCGW Nicholasville KY
WCHA Chambersburg PA
WCHB Taylor MI
WCHE West Chester PA
WCHI Chillicothe OH
WCHJ Brookhaven MS
WCHK Canton GA
WCHL Chapel Hill NC
WCHM Clarkesville GA
WCHN Norwich NY
WCHP Champlain NY
WCHQ Camuy PR
WCHS Charleston WV
WCHT Escanaba MI
WCHV Charlottesville VA
WCHY Savannah GA
WCIE Spring Lake NC
WCIL Carbondale IL
WCIN Cincinnati OH
WCIS Morganton NC
WCIT Lima OH
WCJU Columbia MS

WCJW Warsaw NY
WCKB Dunn NC
WCKI Greer SC
WCKL Catskill NY
WCKN Indianapolis IN
WCKW Garyville LA
WCKY Cincinnati OH
WCLA Claxton GA
WCLC Jamestown TN
WCLD Cleveland MS
WCLE Cleveland TN
WCLG Morgantown WV
WCLI Corning NY
WCLM Highland Springs VA
WCLN Clinton NC
WCLO Janesville WI
WCLT Newark OH
WCLU Glasgow KY
WCLW Eden NC
WCLY Raleigh NC
WCLZ Brunswick ME
WCMA Corinth MS
WCMB Harrisburg PA
WCMC Wildwood NJ
WCMF Rochester NY
WCMI Ashland KY
WCMN Arecibo PR
WCMP Pine City MN
WCMQ Miami Springs FL
WCMS Norfolk VA
WCMT Martin TN
WCMY Ottawa IL
WCNC Elizabeth City NC
WCND Shelbyville KY
WCNN North Atlanta GA
WCNR Bloomsburg PA
WCNS Latrobe PA
WCNU Crestview FL
WCNV Charlotte NC
WCNW Fairfield OH
WCNX Middletown CT
WCNZ Sheboygan WI
WCOA Pensacola FL
WCOH Newnan GA
WCOJ Coatesville PA
WCOK Sparta NC
WCOL Columbus OH
WCON Cornelia GA
WCOP Warner Robins GA
WCOR Lebanon TN
WCOS Columbia SC
WCOX Camden AL
WCOZ St. Albans WV
WCPA Clearfield PA
WCPC Houston MS
WCPH Etowah TN
WCPM Cumberland KY
WCPQ Havelock NC
WCPR Coamo PR
WCPS Tarboro NC
WCPT Alexandria VA
WCQL Portsmouth NH
WCQR Fairlawn IL
WCRA Effingham IL
WCRE Cheraw SC
WCRJ Jacksonville FL
WCRK Morristown TN
WCRL Oneonta AL
WCRM Fort Myers FL
WCRN Cherry Valley MA
WCRO Johnstown PA
WCRR Rural Retreat VA
WCRS Greenwood SC
WCRV Collierville TN
WCRW Chicago IL
WCRY Fuquay-Varina NC
WCSI Columbus IN
WCSJ Morris IL
WCSL Cherryville NC
WCSM Celina OH
WCSR Hillsdale MI
WCSS Amsterdam NY
WCST Berkeley Springs WV
WCSV Crossville TN
WCSW Shell Lake WI
WCSY South Haven MI
WCTA Alamo TN
WCTC New Brunswick NJ
*WCTF Vernon CT
WCTG Columbia SC
WCTM Eaton OH
WCTN Potomac-Cabin John MD
WCTR Chestertown MD
WCTS Maplewood MN
WCTT Corbin KY
WCTZ Clarksville TN
WCUB Two Rivers WI
*WCUE Cuyahoga Falls OH
WCUG Cuthbert GA
WCUM Bridgeport CT
WCUZ Grand Rapids MI
WCVA Culpeper VA
WCVC Tallahassee FL
WCVG Covington KY
WCVI Connellsville PA
WCVL Crawfordsville IN
WCVP Murphy NC
WCWA Toledo OH
WCWC Ripon WI
WCXJ Braddock PA
WCXN Claremont NC
WCXQ Moca PR
WCYK Crozet VA
WCYN Cynthiana KY
WCZN Chester PA

WCZR Charleston WV
WDAB Travelers Rest SC
WDAD Indiana PA
WDAE Tampa FL
WDAF Kansas City MO
WDAN Danville IL
WDAO Dayton OH
WDAR Darlington SC
WDAS Philadelphia PA
WDAY Fargo ND
WDBC Escanaba MI
WDBF Delray Beach FL
WDBL Springfield TN
WDBO Orlando FL
WDBQ Dubuque IA
WDCF Dade City FL
WDCQ Pine Island Center FL
WDCR Hanover NH
WDCT Fairfax VA
WDCW Syracuse NY
WDCY Douglasville GA
WDDD Johnston City IL
WDDO Macon GA
WDDT Greenville MS
WDEA Ellsworth ME
WDEB Jamestown TN
WDEC Americus GA
WDEF Chattanooga TN
WDEH Sweetwater TN
WDEL Wilmington DE
WDEN Macon GA
WDER Derry NH
WDEV Waterbury VT
WDEX Monroe NC
WDFB Junction City KY
WDFL Cross City FL
WDGR Dahlonega GA
WDGY St. Paul MN
WDIA Memphis TN
WDIC Clinchco VA
WDIG Steubenville OH
WDIS Norfolk MA
WDJS Mount Olive NC
WDJX Louisville KY
WDJZ Bridgeport CT
WDKD Kingstree SC
WDKN Dickson TN
WDLA Walton NY
WDLB Marshfield WI
WDLC Port Jervis NY
WDLK Dadeville AL
*WDLM East Moline IL
WDLR Delaware OH
WDMG Douglas GA
WDMJ Marquette MI
WDMP Dodgeville WI
WDMV Pocomoke City MD
WDNC Durham NC
WDNE Elkins WV
WDNG Anniston AL
WDNT Dayton TN
WDNY Dansville NY
WDOC Prestonsburg KY
WDOD Chattanooga TN
WDOE Dunkirk NY
WDOG Allendale SC
WDOR Sturgeon Bay WI
WDOS Oneonta NY
WDOV Dover DE
WDOW Dowagiac MI
WDPN Alliance OH
WDQN DuQuoin IL
WDRC Hartford CT
WDSC Dillon SC
WDSL Mocksville NC
WDSM Superior WI
WDSR Lake City FL
WDTL Cleveland MS
WDTM Selmer TN
WDUF Duffield VA
WDUN Gainesville GA
WDUR Durham NC
WDUX Waupaca WI
WDUZ Green Bay WI
WDVA Danville VA
WDWS Champaign IL
WDXE Lawrenceburg TN
WDXI Jackson TN
WDXL Lexington TN
WDXN Clarksville TN
WDXR Paducah KY
WDXY Sumter SC
WDZ Decatur IL

WEAB Adamsville TN
WEAC Gaffney SC
WEAG Starke FL
WEAM Columbus GA
WEAQ Eau Claire WI
WEAS Savannah GA
WEAT West Palm Beach FL
WEAV Plattsburgh NY
WEBC Duluth MN
WEBJ Brewton AL
WEBO Owego NY
WEBQ Harrisburg IL
WEBS Calhoun GA
WEBY Milton FL
WECC St. Mary's GA
WECK Cheektowaga NY
WECM Milton FL
WECO Wartburg TN
WECY Seaford DE
WECZ Punxsutawney PA
WEDC Chicago IL

WEDO McKeesport PA
WEEB Southern Pines NC
WEED Rocky Mount NC
WEEF Highland Park IL
WEEI Boston MA
WEEN Lafayette TN
WEEP Hampton Township PA
WEEU Reading PA
WEFG Whitehall MI
WEGA Vega Baja PR
WEGG Rose Hill NC
WEGO Concord NC
WEHH Elmira Heights-
    Horseheads NY
WEIC Charleston IL
WEIM Fitchburg MA
WEIO Eau Claire WI
WEIR Weirton WV
WEIS Centre AL
WEJL Scranton PA
WEKC Williamsburg KY
WEKG Jackson KY
WEKO Cabo Rojo PR
WEKR Fayetteville TN
WEKT Elkton KY
WEKY Richmond KY
WEKZ Monroe WI
WELB Elba AL
WELC Welch WV
WELD Fisher WV
WELE Ormond Beach FL
WELI New Haven CT
WELL Battle Creek MI
WELM Elmira NY
WELO Tupelo MS
WELR Roanoke AL
WELS Kinston NC
WELV Ellenville NY
WELV Willoughby-Eastlake OH
WELX Callahan FL
WELY Ely MN
WELZ Belzoni MS
WEMB Erwin TN
WEMG Knoxville TN
WEMJ Laconia NH
WEMP Milwaukee WI
WEMR Tunkhannock PA
WENA Yauco PR
WENC Whiteville NC
WENG Englewood FL
WENK Union City TN
WENO Nashville TN
WENR Englewood TN
WENT Gloversville NY
WENY Elmira NY
WEOK Poughkeepsie NY
WEOL Elyria OH
WEPA Eupora MS
WEPG South Pittsburg TN
WEPM Martinsburg WV
WERA Plainfield NJ
WERC Birmingham AL
WERE Cleveland OH
WERH Hamilton AL
WERI Westerly RI
WERK Muncie IN
WERL Eagle River WI
WERT Van Wert OH
WESA Charleroi PA
WESB Bradford PA
WESC Greenville SC
WESL East St. Louis IL
WESO Southbridge MA
WESR Onley-Onancock VA
WEST Easton PA
WESX Salem MA
WESY Leland MS
WETB Johnson City TN
WETC Wendell-Zebulon NC
WETT Ocean City MD
WETZ New Martinsville WV
WEUC Ponce PR
WEUP Huntsville AL
WEVA Emporia VA
WEVD New York NY
WEVE Eveleth MN
WEVR River Falls WI
WEW St. Louis MO
WEWO Laurinburg NC
WEXL Royal Oak MI
WEXS Patillas PR
WEXY Wilton Manors FL
WEYZ North East PA
WEZE Boston MA
WEZJ Williamsburg KY
WEZK Knoxville TN

WFAB Ceiba PR
WFAD Middlebury VT
WFAI Fayetteville NC
WFAM Augusta GA
WFAN New York NY
WFAS White Plains NY
WFAU Augusta ME
WFAW Fort Atkinson WI
WFAX Falls Church VA
WFBA Miami FL
WFBC Greenville SC
WFBG Altoona PA
WFBL Baldwinsville NY
WFCG Franklinton LA
WFCR Fort Wayne IN
WFDF Flint MI
WFDR Manchester GA

WFEA Manchester NH
WFEB Sylacauga AL
WFFF Columbia MS
WFFG Marathon FL
WFGL Fitchburg MA
WFGN Gaffney SC
WFGW Black Mountain NC
WFHK Pell City AL
WFHR Wisconsin Rapids WI
WFIA Louisville KY
WFIC Collinsville VA
WFIF Milford CT
WFIN Findlay OH
WFIR Roanoke VA
WFIS Fountain Inn SC
WFIV Kissimmee FL
WFIW Fairfield IL
WFKJ Cashtown PA
WFKN Franklin KY
WFKY Frankfort KY
WFLA Tampa FL
WFLB Fayetteville NC
WFLE Flemingsburg KY
WFLI Lookout Mountain TN
WFLO Farmville VA
WFLP Erie PA
WFLR Dundee NY
WFLS Fredericksburg VA
WFLT Flint MI
WFLU Florence SC
WFLW Monticello KY
WFMB Springfield IL
WFMC Goldsboro NC
WFMD Frederick MD
WFMH Cullman AL
WFMO Fairmont NC
WFMW Madisonville KY
WFNC Fayetteville NC
WFNR Blacksburg VA
WFNS Plant City FL
WFNT Flint MI
WFNW Naugatuck CT
WFOB Fostoria OH
WFOM Marietta GA
WFOR Hattiesburg MS
WFOY St. Augustine FL
WFPA Fort Payne AL
WFPG Atlantic City NJ
WFPR Hammond LA
WFRA Franklin PA
WFRB Frostburg MD
WFRK Coleman FL
WFRL Freeport IL
WFRM Coudersport PA
WFRN Elkhart IN
WFRO Fremont OH
WFRX West Frankfort IL
WFSC Franklin NC
WFSH Valparaiso-Niceville FL
WFSP Kingwood WV
WFSR Harlan KY
WFST Caribou ME
WFTD Marietta GA
WFTG London KY
WFTH Richmond VA
WFTK Wake Forest NC
WFTL Fort Lauderdale FL
WFTM Maysville KY
WFTN Franklin NH
WFTO Fulton MS
WFTR Front Royal VA
WFTW Fort Walton Beach FL
WFUN Ashtabula OH
WFUR Grand Rapids MI
WFVA Fredericksburg VA
WFVR Valdosta GA
WFWC Springville NY
WFWL Camden TN
WFXW Geneva IL
WFXX South Williamsport PA
WFXY Middlesboro KY
WFYC Alma MI

WGAA Cedartown GA
WGAB Newburgh IN
WGAC Augusta GA
WGAD Gadsden AL
WGAI Elizabeth City NC
WGAM Greenfield MA
WGAN Portland ME
WGAP Maryville TN
WGAS South Gastonia NC
WGAT Gate City VA
WGAU Athens GA
WGAW Gardner MA
WGBB Freeport NY
WGBI Scranton PA
WGBN New Kensington PA
WGBR Goldsboro NC
WGCB Red Lion PA
WGCH Greenwich CT
WGCI Chicago IL
WGCL Bloomington IN
WGCM Gulfport MS
WGCR Brevard NC
WGCV Petersburg VA
WGDL Lares PR
WGDN Gladwin MI
WGEA Geneva AL
WGEE Green Bay WI
WGEM Quincy IL
WGEN Geneseo IL
WGET Gettysburg PA
WGEZ Beloit WI
WGFA Watseka IL

U.S. AM Stations by Call Letters

WGFC Floyd VA
WGFP Webster MA
WGFS Covington GA
WGFT Youngstown OH
WGGA Gainesville GA
WGGG Gainesville FL
WGGH Marion IL
WGGM Chester VA
WGGO Salamanca NY
WGH Newport News VA
WGHB Farmville NC
WGHC Clayton GA
WGHN Grand Haven MI
WGHQ Kingston NY
WGHT Pompton Lakes NJ
WGIA Blackshear GA
WGIG Brunswick GA
WGIL Galesburg IL
WGIR Manchester NH
WGIV Charlotte NC
WGKA Atlanta GA
WGL Fort Wayne IN
WGLB Port Washington WI
WGLC Mendota IL
WGLD Greensboro NC
WGLR Lancaster WI
WGLX Galion OH
WGMA Spindale NC
WGMF Watkins Glen NY
WGMI Bremen GA
WGML Hinesville GA
WGN Chicago IL
WGNA Albany NY
WGNC Gastonia NC
WGNE Panama City FL
WGNS Murfreesboro TN
WGNU Granite City IL
WGNY Newburgh NY
WGNZ Fairborn OH
WGOC Blountville TN
WGOD Charlotte Amalie VI
WGOG Walhalla SC
WGOH Grayson KY
WGOK Mobile AL
WGOM Marion IN
WGOS High Point NC
WGOV Valdosta GA
WGOW Chattanooga TN
WGPA Bethlehem PA
WGPC Albany GA
WGR Buffalo NY
WGRA Cairo GA
WGRD Grand Rapids MI
WGRM Greenwood MS
WGRO Lake City FL
WGRP Greenville PA
WGRV Greeneville TN
WGRY Grayling MI
*WGSB Mebane NC
WGSF Arlington TN
WGSM Huntington NY
WGSN North Myrtle Beach SC
WGSO New Orleans LA
WGSP Charlotte NC
WGST Atlanta GA
WGSV Guntersville AL
WGTA Summerville GA
WGTM Wilson NC
WGTN Georgetown SC
WGTO Pine Hills FL
WGTT Alabaster AL
WGTX DeFuniak Springs FL
WGUD Moss Point MS
WGUL Dunedin FL
WGUN Atlanta GA
WGUS North Augusta SC
WGVA Geneva NY
WGVM Greenville MS
*WGVU Kentwood MI
WGY Schenectady NY
WGYJ Atmore AL
WGYV Greenville AL
WGZS Dothan AL

*WHA Madison WI
WHAG Halfway MD
WHAI Greenfield MA
WHAK Rogers City MI
WHAL Shelbyville TN
WHAM Rochester NY
WHAP Hopewell VA
WHAR Clarksburg WV
WHAS Louisville KY
WHAT Philadelphia PA
WHAV Haverhill MA
WHAW Weston WV
WHAZ Troy NY
WHB Kansas City MO
WHBB Selma AL
WHBC Canton OH
WHBG Harrisonburg VA
WHBK Marshall NC
WHBL Sheboygan WI
WHBN Harrodsburg KY
WHBQ Memphis TN
WHBS Eatonville FL
WHBT Tallahassee FL
WHBU Anderson IN
WHBY Kimberly WI
WHCC Waynesville NC
WHCO Sparta IL
WHCU Ithaca NY
WHDH Boston MA
WHDL Olean NY
WHDM McKenzie TN

WHEE Martinsville VA
WHEN Syracuse NY
WHEO Stuart VA
WHEP Foley AL
WHEV Garner NC
WHEZ Portage MI
WHFB Benton Harbor-
   St. Joseph MI
WHGH Thomasville GA
WHGL Troy PA
WHGR Houghton Lake MI
WHGS Houlton ME
WHGT Waynesboro PA
WHHO Hornell NY
WHHR Hilton Head Island SC
WHHV Hillsville VA
WHHY Montgomery AL
WHIC Hardinsburg KY
WHIE Griffin GA
WHIM East Providence RI
WHIN Gallatin TN
WHIO Dayton OH
WHIP Mooresville NC
WHIR Danville KY
WHIS Bluefield WV
WHIT Madison WI
WHIY Moulton AL
WHIZ Zanesville OH
WHJB Greensburg PA
WHJC Matewan WV
WHJJ Providence RI
WHJM Knoxville TN
WHK Cleveland OH
WHKP Hendersonville NC
WHKY Hickory NC
WHLB Virginia MN
WHLD Niagara Falls NY
WHLF South Boston VA
WHLI Hempstead NY
WHLN Harlan KY
WHLO Akron OH
WHLS Port Huron MI
WHLV Hattiesburg MS
WHMA Anniston AL
WHMI Howell MI
WHMP Northampton MA
WHMT Humboldt TN
WHNC Henderson NC
WHND Monroe MI
WHNK Madison TN
WHNR Cypress Gardens FL
WHNY McComb MS
WHNZ Pinellas Park FL
WHO Des Moines IA
WHOC Philadelphia MS
WHOD Jackson AL
WHOF Wildwood FL
WHOG Hobson City AL
WHOL Allentown PA
WHON Centerville IN
WHOO Orlando FL
WHOP Hopkinsville KY
WHOS Decatur AL
WHOT Youngstown OH
WHOW Clinton IL
WHOY Salinas PR
WHP Harrisburg PA
WHPB Belton SC
WHRD Huntington WV
WHRF Bel Air MD
WHRS Winchester KY
WHRT Hartselle AL
WHRY Hurley WI
WHSC Hartsville SC
WHSM Hayward WI
WHSY Hattiesburg MS
WHTB Fall River MA
WHTC Holland MI
WHTG Eatontown NJ
WHTH Heath OH
WHTK Rochester NY
WHTT Buffalo NY
WHUB Cookeville TN
WHUC Hudson NY
WHUN Huntingdon PA
WHUT Anderson IN
WHVN Charlotte NC
WHVW Hyde Park NY
WHWB Rutland VT
WHWH Princeton NJ
WHYD Columbus GA
WHYL Carlisle PA
WHYM Portage MI
WHYN Springfield MA
WHYS Bluefield VA
WHYZ Sans Souci SC

WIAC San Juan PR
WIAM Williamston NC
WIAN Ishpeming MI
WIBA Madison WI
WIBC Indianapolis IN
WIBG Ocean City NJ
WIBM Jackson MI
WIBR Baton Rouge LA
WIBU Poynette WI
WIBV Belleville IL
WIBW Topeka KS
WIBX Utica NY
WICC Bridgeport CT
WICE Pawtucket RI
WICH Norwich CT
WICK Scranton PA
WICO Salisbury MD
WICY Malone NY

WIDA Carolina PR
WIDE Biddeford ME
WIDG St. Ignace MI
WIDU Fayetteville NC
WIEL Elizabethtown KY
WIEZ Lewistown PA
WIFE Connersville IN
WIFF Auburn IN
WIFI Florence NJ
WIFN Marine City MI
WIGG Wiggins MS
WIGM Medford WI
WIGO Atlanta GA
WIGS Gouverneur NY
WIJK Evergreen AL
WIKB Iron River MI
WIKC Bogalusa LA
WIKE Newport VT
WILA Danville VA
WILC Laurel MD
WILD Boston MA
WILE Cambridge OH
WILI Willimantic CT
WILK Wilkes-Barre PA
*WILL Urbana IL
WILM Wilmington DE
WILO Frankfort IN
WILS Lansing MI
WILY Centralia IL
WIMA Lima OH
WIMG Ewing NJ
WIMN Stillwater MN
WIMO Winder GA
WIMS Michigan City IN
WINA Charlottesville VA
WINC Westminster VA
WIND Chicago IL
WINE Brookfield CT
WING Dayton OH
WINI Murphysboro IL
WINK Fort Myers FL
WINR Binghamton NY
WINS New York NY
WINU Highland IL
WINV Inverness FL
WINW Canton OH
WINX Rockville MD
WINY Putnam CT
WINZ Miami FL
WIOD Miami FL
WIOI New Boston OH
WION Ionia MI
WIOO Carlisle PA
WIOS Tawas City MI
WIOU Kokomo IN
WIOV Reading PA
WIOZ Pinehurst NC
WIP Philadelphia PA
WIPC Lake Wales FL
*WIPR San Juan PR
WIPS Ticonderoga NY
WIQT Horseheads NY
WIRA Fort Pierce FL
WIRC Hickory NC
WIRD Lake Placid NY
WIRL Peoria IL
WIRO Ironton OH
WIRV Irvine KY
WIRY Plattsburgh NY
WISA Isabela PR
WISE Asheville NC
WISK Americus GA
WISL Shamokin PA
WISN Milwaukee WI
WISO Ponce PR
WISR Butler PA
WISS Berlin WI
WISZ Zeeland MI
WITA Knoxville TN
WITH Baltimore MD
WITL Lansing MI
WITS Sebring FL
WITY Danville IL
WITZ Jasper IN
WIVK Knoxville TN
WIVV Vieques PR
WIWO South Bend IN
WIWS Beckley WV
WIXE Monroe NC
WIXK New Richmond WI
WIXN Dixon IL
WIXZ McKeesport PA
WIYD Palatka FL
WIZA Savannah GA
WIZE Springfield OH
WIZK Bay Springs MS
WIZM La Crosse WI
WIZO Franklin TN
WIZR Johnstown NY
WIZS Henderson NC
WIZZ Streator IL

WJAC Johnstown PA
WJAG Norfolk NE
WJAS Pittsburgh PA
WJAT Swainsboro GA
WJAX Jacksonville FL
WJAY Mullins SC
WJBB Haleyville AL
WJBC Bloomington IL
WJBD Salem IL
WJBI Batesville MS
WJBM Jerseyville IL
WJBO Baton Rouge LA

WJBR Wilmington DE
WJBS Holly Hill SC
WJBY Rainbow City AL
WJCE Memphis TN
WJCM Sebring FL
WJCO Jackson MI
WJCV Jacksonville NC
WJCW Johnson City TN
WJDA Quincy MA
WJDB Thomasville AL
WJDM Elizabeth NJ
WJDS Jackson MS
WJDY Salisbury MD
WJEH Gallipolis OH
WJEJ Hagerstown MD
WJEM Valdosta GA
WJEP Ochlocknee GA
WJER Dover-New Philadelphia OH
WJES Johnston SC
WJFC Jefferson City TN
WJFK Baltimore MD
WJHB Fair Bluff NC
WJHO Opelika AL
WJHR Flemington NJ
WJIB Cambridge MA
WJIC Salem NJ
WJIG Tullahoma TN
WJIL Jacksonville IL
WJIM Lansing MI
WJIT Sabana PR
WJJC Commerce GA
WJJD Chicago IL
WJJF Hope Valley RI
WJJJ Christiansburg VA
WJJL Niagara Falls NY
WJJM Lewisburg TN
WJJQ Tomahawk WI
WJJT Jellico TN
WJJY Baxter MN
WJKI Woodruff SC
WJKM Hartsville TN
WJKY Jamestown KY
WJLD Fairfield AL
WJLE Smithville TN
WJLK Asbury Park NJ
WJLS Beckley WV
WJMA Orange VA
WJMC Rice Lake WI
WJML Petoskey MI
WJMO Cleveland Heights OH
WJMP Kent OH
WJMS Ironwood MI
WJMT Merrill WI
WJMW Bloomsburg PA
WJMX Florence SC
WJNC Jacksonville NC
WJNO West Palm Beach FL
WJNT Pearl MS
WJNX Fort Pierce FL
WJOB Hammond IN
WJOC Chattanooga TN
WJOE Port St. Joe FL
WJOL Joliet IL
WJON St. Cloud MN
WJOS Elkin NC
WJOX Birmingham AL
WJOY Burlington VT
WJPA Washington PA
WJPC Chicago IL
WJPF Herrin IL
WJPJ Huntington TN
WJPS Evansville IN
WJQI Chesapeake VA
WJR Detroit MI
WJRA Priceville AL
WJRD Russellville AL
WJRI Lenoir NC
WJRM Troy NY
WJRO Glen Burnie MD
WJRV Loretto TN
WJRZ Toms River NJ
WJSA Jersey Shore PA
WJSB Crestview FL
WJSH Terre Haute IN
WJSM Martinsburg PA
WJTB North Ridgeville OH
WJTH Calhoun GA
WJTN Jamestown NY
WJTO Bath ME
WJTP Newland NC
WJUB Plymouth WI
WJUN Mexico PA
WJWF Columbus MS
WJWS South Hill VA
WJXN Jackson MS
WJXY Conway SC
WJYM Bowling Green OH
WJYZ Albany GA
WJZM Clarksville TN
WJZS Orangeburg SC

WKAC Athens AL
*WKAL Kalkaska MI
WKAM Goshen IN
WKAN Kankakee IL
WKAP Allentown PA
WKAQ San Juan PR
*WKAR East Lansing MI
WKAT North Miami FL
WKAX Charlottesville VA
WKAX Russellville AL
WKBA Vinton VA
WKBC North Wilkesboro NC
WKBF Rock Island IL
WKBH Holmen WI

WKBI St. Marys PA
WKBJ Milan TN
WKBK Keene NH
WKBL Covington TN
WKBN Youngstown OH
WKBO Harrisburg PA
WKBV Richmond IN
WKBY Chatham VA
WKBZ Muskegon MI
WKCB Hindman KY
WKCM Hawesville KY
WKCT Bowling Green KY
WKCU Corinth MS
WKCV Kingsport TN
WKCW Warrenton VA
WKCY Harrisonburg VA
WKDA Nashville TN
WKDB Towson MD
WKDC Elmhurst IL
WKDE Altavista VA
WKDI Denton MD
WKDK Newberry SC
WKDL Silver Spring MD
WKDM New York NY
WKDO Liberty KY
WKDP Corbin KY
WKDR Burlington VT
WKDV Manassas VA
WKDW Staunton VA
WKDZ Cadiz KY
WKED Frankfort KY
WKEE Huntington WV
WKEI Kewanee IL
WKEN Dover DE
WKEQ Burnside KY
WKEU Griffin GA
WKEW Greensboro NC
WKEX Blacksburg VA
WKEY Covington VA
WKFE Yauco PR
WKFI Wilmington OH
WKGA Zion IL
*WKGC Panama City Beach FL
WKGF Arcadia FL
WKGM Smithfield VA
WKGN Knoxville TN
WKGQ Milledgeville GA
WKGT Cantonment FL
WKGX Lenoir NC
WKHF Avon Park FL
WKHM Jackson MI
WKHX Atlanta GA
WKIC Hazard KY
WKIG Glennville GA
WKII Port Charlotte FL
WKIN Kingsport TN
WKIP Poughkeepsie NY
WKIQ Eustis FL
WKIZ Key West FL
WKJB Mayaguez PR
WKJF Cadillac MI
WKJQ Parsons TN
WKJV Asheville NC
WKKD Aurora IL
WKKE St. Pauls NC
WKKP McDonough GA
WKKQ Nashwauk MN
WKKS Vanceburg KY
WKLA Ludington MI
WKLB Manchester KY
WKLF Clanton AL
WKLJ Sparta WI
WKLK Cloquet MN
WKLN St. Augustine Beach FL
WKLP Keyser WV
WKLV Blackstone VA
WKLW Paintsville KY
WKLY Hartwell GA
WKMB Stirling NJ
WKMC Roaring Spring PA
WKMG Newberry SC
WKMI Kalamazoo MI
WKMT Kings Mountain NC
WKND Windsor CT
WKNE Keene NH
WKNG Tallapoosa GA
WKNI Lexington AL
WKNL Knoxville TN
WKNR Cleveland OH
WKNV Dublin VA
WKNW Sault Ste. Marie MI
WKNX Frankenmuth MI
WKNY Kingston NY
WKOK Sunbury PA
WKOP Binghamton NY
WKOR Starkville MS
WKOX Framingham MA
WKOY Bluefield WV
WKOZ Kosciusko MS
WKPA Lynchburg VA
WKPE Orleans MA
WKPR Kalamazoo MI
WKPT Kingsport TN
WKQW Oil City PA
WKRA Holly Springs MS
WKRG Mobile AL
WKRI West Warwick RI
WKRK Murphy NC
WKRL North Syracuse NY
WKRM Columbia TN
WKRO Cairo IL
WKRP North Vernon IN
WKRS Waukegan IL
WKRT Cortland NY
WKSC Kershaw SC

U.S. AM Stations by Call Letters

WKSH Sussex WI
WKSJ Prichard AL
WKSK West Jefferson NC
WKSN Jamestown NY
WKSR Pulaski TN
WKST New Castle PA
WKTA Evanston IL
WKTE King NC
WKTP Jonesborough TN
WKTQ South Paris ME
WKTR Earlysville VA
WKTX Cortland OH
WKTY La Crosse WI
WKUN Monroe GA
WKVA Lewistown PA
WKVG Jenkins KY
WKVI Knox IN
WKVM San Juan PR
WKVN Quebradillas PR
WKVQ Eatonton GA
WKVT Brattleboro VT
WKVX Wooster OH
WKWF Key West FL
WKWK Wheeling WV
WKWL Florala AL
WKWM Kentwood MI
WKXF Eminence KY
WKXG Greenwood MS
WKXI Jackson MS
WKXK Macon GA
WKXL Concord NH
WKXM Winfield AL
WKXO Berea KY
WKXR Asheboro NC
WKXV Knoxville TN
WKXY Sarasota FL
WKY Oklahoma City OK
WKYD Hemingway SC
WKYD Andalusia AL
WKYG Parkersburg WV
WKYK Burnsville NC
WKYO Caro MI
WKYR Burkesville KY
WKYX Paducah KY
WKYY Lancaster KY
WKYZ Gray KY
WKZD Murrayville GA
WKZE Sharon CT
WKZI Casey IL
WKZK North Augusta SC
WKZO Kalamazoo MI
WKZQ Myrtle Beach SC
WKZT Fulton KY
WKZV Washington PA

WLAC Nashville TN
WLAD Danbury CT
WLAF La Follette TN
WLAG La Grange GA
WLAM Gorham ME
WLAN Lancaster PA
WLAP Lexington KY
WLAQ Rome GA
WLAR Athens TN
WLAS Jacksonville NC
WLAT Manchester CT
WLAU Laurel MS
WLAV Grand Rapids MI
WLAW Fairhaven MA
WLAY Muscle Shoals AL
WLBA Gainesville GA
WLBB Carrollton GA
WLBC Muncie IN
WLBE Leesburg FL
WLBG Laurens SC
WLBH Mattoon IL
WLBJ Bowling Green KY
WLBK De Kalb IL
*WLBL Auburndale WI
WLBN Lebanon KY
WLBQ Morgantown KY
WLBR Lebanon PA
WLCK Scottsville KY
WLCM Charlotte MI
WLDS Jacksonville IL
WLDX Fayette AL
WLDY Ladysmith WI
WLEA Hornell NY
WLEC Sandusky OH
WLEE Richmond VA
WLEM Emporium PA
WLEO Ponce PR
WLES Lawrenceville VA
WLET Toccoa GA
WLEW Bad Axe MI
WLEY Cayey PR
WLFH Little Falls NY
WLFN La Crosse WI
WLGC Greenup KY
WLGN Logan OH
WLGO Lexington SC
WLGW Lancaster NH
WLIB New York NY
WLIJ Shelbyville TN
WLIK Newport TN
WLIL Lenoir City TN
WLIM Patchogue NY
WLIP Kenosha WI
WLIR Spring Valley NY
WLIS Old Saybrook CT
WLIV Livingston TN
WLIX Islip NY
WLJA Ellijay GA
WLJN Elmwood Township MI
WLKF Lakeland FL

WLKK Erie PA
WLKM Three Rivers MI
WLKS West Liberty KY
WLKW Providence RI
WLLE Raleigh NC
WLLH Lowell MA
WLLJ Cassopolis MI
WLLL Lynchburg VA
WLLN Lillington NC
WLLR Moline IL
WLLS Hartford KY
WLLV Louisville KY
WLLY Wilson NC
WLMA Greenwood SC
WLMJ Jackson OH
WLMX Rossville GA
WLNA Peekskill NY
WLNC Laurinburg NC
WLNG Sag Harbor NY
WLNH Laconia NH
WLNL Horseheads NY
WLOB Portland ME
WLOC Munfordville KY
WLOD Loudon TN
WLOE Eden NC
WLOG Logan WV
WLOH Lancaster OH
WLOI La Porte IN
WLOJ New Bern NC
WLOK Memphis TN
WLON Lincolnton NC
WLOP Jesup GA
WLOR Huntsville AL
WLOU Louisville KY
WLOV Washington GA
WLPA Lancaster PA
WLPH Irondale AL
WLPM Suffolk VA
WLPO La Salle IL
WLPR Prichard AL
WLPY Purcellville VA
WLPZ Westbrook ME
WLQH Chiefland FL
WLQM Franklin VA
WLQV Detroit MI
WLQY Hollywood FL
WLRB Macomb IL
WLRC Walnut MS
WLRM Ridgeland MS
WLRP San Sebastian PR
WLRV Lebanon VA
WLS Chicago IL
WLSB Copperhill TN
WLSC Loris SC
WLSD Big Stone Gap VA
WLSE Wallace NC
WLSH Lansford PA
WLSI Pikeville KY
WLSM Louisville MS
WLSQ Dalton GA
WLSV Wellsville NY
WLTC Gastonia NC
WLTG Panama City FL
WLTH Gary IN
WLTN Littleton NH
WLTP Parkersburg WV
WLUS Gainesville FL
WLUV Loves Park IL
WLUX Port Allen LA
WLUZ Bayamon PR
WLVA Lynchburg VA
WLVC Fort Kent ME
WLVF Haines City FL
WLVJ Royal Palm Beach FL
WLVL Lockport NY
WLVS Lake Worth FL
WLVU Dunedin FL
WLVV Mobile AL
WLW Cincinnati OH
WLWA Cincinnati OH
WLWI Montgomery AL
WLWL Rockingham NC
WLWZ Easley SC
WLXG Lexington KY
WLXN Lexington NC
WLYC Williamsport PA
WLYN Lynn MA
WLYV Fort Wayne IN
WLZR Milwaukee WI

WMAC Metter GA
WMAD Sun Prairie WI
WMAF Madison FL
WMAJ State College PA
WMAK London KY
WMAL Washington DC
WMAM Marinette WI
WMAN Mansfield OH
WMAP Monroe NC
WMAQ Chicago IL
WMAS Springfield MA
WMAX Bay City MI
WMAY Springfield IL
WMAZ Macon GA
WMBA Ambridge PA
WMBD Peoria IL
WMBE Chilton WI
WMBG Williamsburg VA
WMBH Joplin MO
*WMBI Chicago IL
WMBL Morehead City NC
WMBN Petoskey MI
WMBO Auburn NY
WMBS Uniontown PA
WMBT Shenandoah PA

WMC Memphis TN
WMCA New York NY
WMCB Martinsville IN
WMCH Church Hill TN
WMCJ Moncks Corner SC
WMCL McLeansboro IL
WMCP Columbia TN
WMCR Oneida NY
WMCS Greenfield WI
WMCT Mountain City TN
WMCW Harvard IL
WMDB Nashville TN
WMDC Hazelhurst MS
WMDD Fajardo PR
WMDH New Castle IN
WMDJ Martin KY
WMDO Wheaton MD
WMEK Chase City VA
WMEL Melbourne FL
WMEQ Menomonie WI
WMER Meridian MS
WMET Gaithersburg MD
WMEV Marion VA
WMEX Boston MA
WMFA Raeford NC
WMFC Monroeville AL
WMFD Wilmington NC
WMFG Hibbing MN
WMFJ Daytona Beach FL
WMFL Monticello FL
WMFR High Point NC
WMGA Moultrie GA
WMGJ Gadsden AL
WMGO Canton MS
WMGP Meridian MS
WMGR Bainbridge GA
WMGW Meadville PA
WMGY Montgomery AL
WMIA Arecibo PR
WMIC Sandusky MI
WMID Atlantic City NJ
WMIK Middlesboro KY
WMIN Hudson WI
WMIQ Iron Mountain MI
WMIR Lake Geneva WI
WMIS Natchez MS
WMIW Atlantic Beach SC
WMIX Mt. Vernon IL
WMIY Fairview NC
WMIZ Vineland NJ
WMJK Kissimmee FL
WMJL Marion KY
WMKM Inkster MI
WMKT Charlevoix MI
WMLB Cumming GA
WMLC Monticello MS
WMLD East Point GA
WMLM St. Louis MI
WMLP Milton PA
WMLR Hohenwald TN
WMLT Dublin GA
WMLZ Jupiter FL
WMMB Melbourne FL
WMME Augusta ME
WMMG Brandenburg KY
WMMI Shepherd MI
WMMM Westport CT
WMMN Fairmont WV
WMMW Meriden CT
WMNA Gretna VA
WMNC Morganton NC
WMNI Columbus OH
WMNS Olean NY
WMNT Manati PR
WMNY Elloree-Santee SC
WMNZ Montezuma GA
WMOA Marietta OH
WMOB Mobile AL
WMOC Chattanooga TN
WMOG Brunswick GA
WMOH Hamilton OH
WMOK Metropolis IL
WMOM La Plata MD
WMON Montgomery WV
WMOP Ocala FL
WMOR Morehead KY
WMOU Berlin NH
WMOV Ravenswood WV
WMOX Meridian MS
*WMPC Lapeer MI
WMPL Hancock MI
WMPM Smithfield NC
WMPO Middleport-Pomeroy OH
WMPS Millington TN
WMPX Midland MI
WMQA Minocqua WI
WMQX Winston-Salem NC
WMRB Columbia TN
WMRC Milford MA
WMRE Hughesville PA
WMRH Waupun WI
WMRK Selma AL
WMRN Marion OH
WMRO Nashville TN
WMRV Endicott NY
WMRZ South Miami FL
WMSA Massena NY
WMSG Oakland MD
WMSH Sturgis MI
WMSK Morganfield KY
WMSR Manchester TN
WMST Mt. Sterling KY
WMSW Hatillo PR
WMSX Brockton MA
WMT Cedar Rapids IA

WMTC Vancleve KY
WMTD Hinton WV
WMTE Manistee MI
WMTG Dearborn MI
WMTI Morovis PR
WMTL Leitchfield KY
WMTM Moultrie GA
WMTN Morristown TN
WMTR Morristown NJ
WMTS Murfreesboro TN
WMTX Pinellas Park FL
WMTY Greenwood SC
WMUF Paris TN
WMUS Muskegon MI
WMUU Greenville SC
WMVA Martinsville VA
WMVG Milledgeville GA
WMVI Mechanicsville NY
WMVN Ishpeming MI
WMVO Mount Vernon OH
WMVP Chicago IL
WMVR Sidney OH
WMXH Olyphant PA
WMXY Hogansville GA
WMYF Exeter NH
WMYN Mayodan NC
WMYR Fort Myers FL
WMYT Carolina Beach NC
WMZQ Arlington VA

WNAE Warren PA
WNAH Nashville TN
WNAK Nanticoke PA
WNAM Neenah-Menasha WI
WNAP Norristown PA
WNAT Natchez MS
WNAU New Albany MS
WNAV Annapolis MD
WNAW North Adams MA
WNAX Yankton SD
WNBF Binghamton NY
WNBH New Bedford MA
WNBI Park Falls WI
WNBN Meridian MS
WNBP Newburyport MA
WNBS Murray KY
WNBT Wellsboro PA
WNBY Newberry MI
WNBZ Saranac Lake NY
WNCA Siler City NC
WNCC Barnesboro PA
WNCM Atlantic Beach FL
WNCO Ashland OH
WNCQ Watertown NY
WNCT Greenville NC
WNDB Daytona Beach FL
WNDC Baton Rouge LA
WNDE Indianapolis IN
WNDI Sullivan IN
WNDR Syracuse NY
WNDU South Bend IN
WNDZ Portage IN
WNEA Newnan GA
WNEB Worcester MA
WNED Buffalo NY
WNEG Toccoa GA
WNEL Caguas PR
WNES Central City KY
WNEX Macon GA
WNEZ New Britain CT
WNFL Green Bay WI
WNFO Ridgeland SC
WNGA Nashville GA
WNGO Mayfield KY
WNHA Concord NH
WNHC New Haven CT
WNHV White River Junction VT
WNIK Arecibo PR
WNIS Norfolk VA
WNIV Atlanta GA
WNIX Greenville MS
WNJC Washington Township NJ
WNJR Newark NJ
WNKX Centerville TN
WNKY Neon KY
WNLA Indianola MS
WNLB Rocky Mount VA
WNLC New London CT
WNLK Norwalk CT
WNLR Churchville VA
WNLS Tallahassee FL
WNMT Garden City GA
WNNC Newton NC
WNNJ Newton NJ
WNNO Wisconsin Dells WI
WNNQ Ashburn GA
WNNT Warsaw VA
WNNW Salem NH
WNNZ Westfield MA
WNOE New Orleans LA
WNOG Naples FL
WNOO Chattanooga TN
WNOP Newport KY
WNOR Norfolk VA
WNOS New Bern NC
WNOV Milwaukee WI
WNOW Mint Hill NC
WNOZ Aguadilla PR
WNPC Newport TN
WNPV Lansdale PA
WNQM Nashville TN
WNRB Niles OH
WNRG Grundy VA
WNRI Woonsocket RI

WNRJ Circleville OH
WNRK Newark DE
WNRV Narrows VA
WNSH Beverly MA
WNST Milton WV
WNSW Brewer ME
WNTA Rockford IL
WNTJ Johnstown PA
WNTK Newport NH
WNTL Indian Head MD
WNTN Newton MA
WNTS Beech Grove IN
WNTT Tazewell TN
WNTW Winchester VA
WNTY Southington CT
WNUE Fort Walton Beach FL
WNUZ Talladega AL
WNVA Norton VA
WNVL Nicholasville KY
WNVR Vernon Hills IL
WNWI Valparaiso IN
WNWS Brownsville TN
WNWX Plattsburgh NY
WNWZ Germantown TN
WNXT Portsmouth OH
*WNYC New York NY
WNYG Babylon NY
WNYS Canton NY
WNZK Westland MI
WNZS Jacksonville FL
WNZT Columbia PA

WOAD Jackson MS
WOAI San Antonio TX
WOAP Owosso MI
WOAY Oak Hill WV
WOBG Clarksburg WV
WOBL Oberlin OH
WOBM Lakewood NJ
WOBR Wanchese NC
WOBT Rhinelander WI
WOC Davenport IA
WOCA Ocala FL
WOCC Corydon IN
WOCN Miami FL
WOCO Oconto WI
WOCV Oneida TN
WODX Marco Island FL
WODY Fieldale VA
WODZ Rome NY
WOEQ Royal Palm Beach FL
WOFE Rockwood TN
WOFR Washington Court House OH
WOGL Philadelphia PA
WOGO Hallie WI
WOGR Charlotte NC
WOHI East Liverpool OH
WOHS Shelby NC
*WOI Ames IA
WOIC Columbia SC
WOIR Homestead FL
WOIZ Guayanilla PR
WOJY Hampton VA
WOKA Douglas GA
WOKC Okeechobee FL
WOKE Charleston SC
WOKS Columbus GA
WOKT Cannonsburg KY
WOKV Jacksonville FL
WOKX High Point NC
WOKY Milwaukee WI
WOL Washington DC
WOLA Barranquitas PR
WOLB Baltimore MD
WOLD Marion VA
WOLF Syracuse NY
WOLS Florence SC
WOLY Battle Creek MI
WOMG Columbia SC
WOMI Owensboro KY
WOMP Bellaire OH
WOMT Manitowoc WI
WOMX Orlando FL
WONA Winona MS
WOND Pleasantville NJ
WONE Dayton OH
WONG Canton MS
WONN Lakeland FL
WONQ Oviedo FL
WONW Defiance OH
WONX Evanston IL
WONZ Hammonton NJ
WOOD Grand Rapids MI
WOOF Dothan AL
WOON Woonsocket RI
WOOO Shelbyville IN
WOOW Greenville NC
WOPA Chicago IL
WOPI Bristol VA
WOPP Opp AL
WOR New York NY
WORA Mayaguez PR
WORC Worcester MA
WORD Spartanburg SC
WORL Christmas FL
WORM Savannah TN
WORV Hattiesburg MS
WORX Madison IN
WOSH Oshkosh WI
WOSO San Juan PR
*WOSU Columbus OH
WOW Omaha NE
WOWO Fort Wayne IN

Broadcasting & Cable Yearbook 1994
B-457

U.S. AM Stations by Call Letters

WOXR Oxford AL
WOYK York PA
WOYL Oil City PA
WOZK Ozark AL

WPAB Ponce PR
WPAD Paducah KY
WPAK Farmville VA
WPAL Charleston SC
WPAM Pottsville PA
WPAQ Mount Airy NC
WPAS Zephyrhills FL
WPAT Paterson NJ
WPAX Thomasville GA
WPAY Portsmouth OH
WPAZ Pottstown PA
WPBQ Flowood MS
WPBR Palm Beach FL
WPBS Conyers GA
WPCC Clinton SC
WPCE Portsmouth VA
WPCF Panama City Beach FL
WPCI Greenville SC
WPCO Mt. Vernon IN
WPDC Elizabethtown PA
WPDJ Huntington IN
WPDM Potsdam NY
WPDQ Jacksonville FL
WPDR Portage WI
WPDX Clarksburg WV
WPEH Louisville GA
*WPEL Montrose PA
WPEN Philadelphia PA
WPEO Peoria IL
WPEP Taunton MA
WPES Ashland VA
WPET Greensboro NC
WPFB Middletown OH
WPFD Fairview TN
WPGA Perry GA
WPGC Morningside MD
*WPGM Danville PA
WPGR Philadelphia PA
WPGS Mims FL
WPGW Portland IN
WPHB Philipsburg PA
WPHC Waverly TN
WPHE Phoenixville PA
WPHM Port Huron MI
WPHY Philadelphia PA
WPIC Sharon PA
WPID Piedmont AL
WPIE Trumansburg NY
WPIP Winston-Salem NC
WPIQ Brunswick GA
WPIT Pittsburgh PA
WPJC Adjuntas PR
WPJK Orangeburg SC
WPJL Raleigh NC
WPJM Greer SC
WPJS Conway SC
WPKE Pikeville KY
WPKY Princeton KY
WPLB Greenville MI
WPLK Palatka FL
WPLM Plymouth MA
WPLO Grayson GA
WPLV West Point GA
WPLW Carnegie PA
WPLX Collierville TN
WPMB Vandalia IL
WPMH Portsmouth VA
WPMR Mount Pocono PA
WPMX Tupelo MS
WPNA Oak Park IL
WPNC Plymouth NC
WPNH Plymouth NH
WPNX Phenix City AL
WPOK Pontiac IL
WPOM Riviera Beach FL
WPON Walled Lake MI
WPOP Hartford CT
WPOR Portland ME
WPPA Pottsville PA
WPPC Penuelas PR
WPPI Carrollton GA
WPRA Mayaguez PR
WPRC Lincoln IL
WPRE Prairie du Chien WI
WPRN Butler AL
WPRO Providence RI
WPRP Ponce PR
WPRS Paris IL
WPRT Prestonsburg KY
WPRX Bristol CT
WPRY Perry FL
WPRZ Warrenton VA
WPSE Erie PA
WPSL Port St. Lucie FL
WPSO New Port Richey FL
WPTB Statesboro GA
WPTF Raleigh NC
WPTL Canton NC
WPTN Cookeville TN
WPTR Albany NY
WPTW Piqua OH
WPTX Lexington Park MD
WPUL South Daytona FL
WPUT Brewster NY
WPUV Pulaski VA
WPVG Funksburg MD
WPWC Dumfries-Triangle VA
WPYB Benson NC
WPYK Dora AL

WQAI Fernandina Beach FL
WQAM Miami FL
WQBA Miami FL
WQBB Powell TN
WQBC Vicksburg MS
WQBE Charleston WV
WQBH Detroit MI
WQBK Rensselaer NY
WQBN Temple Terrace FL
WQBQ Leesburg FL
WQBS San Juan PR
WQCH La Fayette GA
WQCR Jackson TN
WQCT Bryan OH
WQDQ Lebanon TN
WQDW Kinston NC
WQDY Calais ME
WQEW New York NY
WQFX Gulfport MS
WQHK Fort Wayne IN
WQHL Live Oak FL
WQII San Juan PR
WQIK Jacksonville FL
WQIS Laurel MS
WQIZ St. George SC
WQKI St. Matthews SC
WQKR Portland TN
WQKS Hopkinsville KY
WQLA La Follette TN
WQLE Kane PA
WQLS Ozark AL
WQMA Marks MS
WQMC Sumter SC
WQMG Greensboro NC
WQNX Aberdeen NC
WQPM Princeton MN
WQRX Valley Head AL
WQSA Sarasota FL
WQSE White Bluff TN
WQSI Frederick MD
WQSN Kalamazoo MI
WQST Forest MS
WQSV Ashland City TN
WQTW Latrobe PA
WQUE New Orleans LA
WQWQ Muskegon Heights MI
WQXA York PA
WQXC Otsego MI
WQXI Atlanta GA
WQXL Columbia SC
WQXO Munising MI
WQXY Hazard KY
WQYK Seffner FL

WRAA Luray VA
WRAB Arab AL
WRAD Radford VA
WRAG Carrollton AL
WRAI San Juan PR
WRAJ Anna IL
WRAK Williamsport PA
WRAM Monmouth IL
WRAQ Brevard NC
WRAR Tappahannock VA
WRAW Reading PA
WRAY Princeton IN
WRBD Pompano Beach FL
WRBE Lucedale MS
WRBQ St. Petersburg FL
WRBR Richland MS
WRCA Waltham MA
WRCC Warner Robins GA
WRCG Columbus GA
WRCO Richland Center WI
WRCP Providence RI
WRCS Ahoskie NC
WRCW Canton OH
WRDB Reedsburg WI
WRDD Ebensburg PA
WRDM Bloomfield CT
WRDN Durand WI
WRDW Augusta GA
WRDZ Cleveland OH
WREA Dayton TN
WREC Memphis TN
WREF Ridgefield CT
WREJ Richmond VA
WREL Lexington VA
WREV Reidsville NC
WREY Millville NJ
WRFA Largo FL
WRFB Cocoa FL
WRFC Athens GA
WRFD Columbus-Worthington OH
WRFM Hialeah FL
WRGA Rome GA
WRGC Sylva NC
WRGM Ontario OH
WRGS Rogersville TN
WRHC Coral Gables FL
WRHD Riverhead NY
WRHI Rock Hill SC
WRHL Rochelle IL
WRIB Providence RI
WRIC Richlands VA
WRIE Erie PA
WRIG Schofield WI
WRIK Brookport IL
WRIN Rensselaer IN
WRIP Lake City SC
WRIS Roanoke VA
WRIT Bamberg-Denmark SC
WRIV Riverhead NY
WRIX Homeland Park SC
WRJC Mauston WI

WRJL Hanceville AL
WRJN Racine WI
WRJQ Appleton WI
WRJW Picayune MS
WRJZ Knoxville TN
WRKB Kannapolis NC
WRKD Rockland ME
WRKG Lorain OH
WRKL New City NY
WRKM Carthage TN
WRKN Brandon MS
WRKO Boston MA
WRKQ Madisonville TN
WRLD Lanett AL
WRLV Salyersville KY
WRMD St. Petersburg FL
WRMG Red Bay AL
WRMN Elgin IL
WRMQ Orlando FL
WRMR Cleveland OH
WRMS Beardstown IL
WRMT Rocky Mount NC
WRNA China Grove NC
WRNE Pensacola FL
WRNJ Hackettstown NJ
WRNR Martinsburg WV
WRNS Kinston NC
WRNY Rome NY
WROA Gulfport MS
WROB West Point MS
WROD Daytona Beach FL
WROK Rockford IL
WROL Boston MA
WROM Rome GA
WRON Ronceverte WV
WROS Jacksonville FL
WROV Roanoke VA
WROW Albany NY
WROX Clarksdale MS
WROY Carmi IL
WRPM Poplarville MS
WRPQ Baraboo WI
WRQQ Farrell PA
WRRA Fredriksted VI
WRRD Blennerhassett WV
WRRE Juncos PR
WRRF Washington NC
WRRL Rainelle WV
WRRO Warren OH
WRRR Rockford IL
WRRZ Clinton NC
WRSC State College PA
WRSJ Bayamon PR
WRSL Stanford KY
WRSM Sumiton AL
WRSS San Sebastian PR
WRSW Warsaw IN
WRTA Altoona PA
WRTH St. Louis MO
WRTP Chapel Hill NC
WRUF Gainesville FL
WRUM Rumford ME
WRUN Utica NY
WRUS Russellville KY
WRVA Richmond VA
WRVC Huntington WV
WRVH Richmond VA
WRVK Mt. Vernon KY
WRVX Mt. Carmel TN
WRWD Cornwall NY
WRWH Cleveland GA
WRXB St. Petersburg Beach FL
WRXO Roxboro NC
WRYM New Britain CT
WRYT Edwardsville IL
WRZN Hernando FL

WSAI Cincinnati OH
*WSAJ Grove City PA
WSAL Logansport IN
WSAM Saginaw MI
WSAO Senatobia MS
WSAR Fall River MA
WSAT Salisbury NC
WSAU Wausau WI
WSB Atlanta GA
WSBA York PA
WSBB New Smyrna Beach FL
WSBC Chicago IL
WSBH Miami Beach FL
WSBI Static TN
WSBM Florence AL
WSBR Boca Raton FL
WSBS Great Barrington MA
WSBT South Bend IN
WSBV South Boston VA
WSCM Cobleskill NY
WSCP Sandy Creek-Pulaski NY
WSCR Chicago IL
WSCW South Charleston WV
WSDM Brazil IN
WSDQ Dunlap TN
WSDR Sterling IL
WSDS Salem Township MI
WSDT Soddy-Daisy TN
WSEL Pontotoc MS
WSEM Donalsonville GA
WSER Elkton MD
WSEV Sevierville TN
WSEZ Paoli IN
WSFB Quitman GA
WSFC Somerset KY
WSFL New Bern NC
WSFN Muskegon MI
WSFT Thomaston GA

WSFW Seneca Falls NY
WSGA Savannah GA
WSGB Sutton WV
WSGC Kaukauna WI
WSGH Lewisville NC
WSGI Springfield TN
WSGO Oswego NY
WSGW Saginaw MI
WSHF Hahira GA
WSHN Fremont MI
WSHO New Orleans LA
WSHP Shippensburg PA
WSHY Shelbyville KY
WSIC Statesville NC
WSIP Paintsville KY
WSIR Winter Haven FL
WSIV East Syracuse NY
WSIZ Ocilla GA
WSJM St. Joseph MI
WSJP Murray KY
WSJR Madawaska ME
WSJS Winston-Salem NC
WSKE Everett PA
WSKI Montpelier VT
WSKN San Juan PR
WSKQ Newark NJ
WSKW Skowhegan ME
WSKY Asheville NC
WSLA Slidell LA
WSLB Ogdensburg NY
WSLC Roanoke VA
WSLI Jackson MS
WSLM Salem IN
WSLR Akron OH
WSLV Ardmore TN
WSLW White Sulphur Springs WV
WSM Nashville TN
WSMB New Orleans LA
WSME Sanford ME
WSMG Greeneville TN
WSMI Litchfield IL
WSML Graham NC
WSMN Nashua NH
WSMQ Bessemer AL
WSMT Sparta TN
WSMX Winston-Salem NC
WSMY Weldon NC
WSNG Torrington CT
WSNJ Bridgeton NJ
WSNO Barre VT
WSNQ Gaylord MI
WSNT Sandersville GA
WSNW Seneca SC
WSOK Savannah GA
WSOL Mayaguez PR
WSOM Salem OH
WSON Henderson KY
WSOO Sault Ste. Marie MI
WSOY Decatur IL
WSPA Spartanburg SC
WSPB Sarasota FL
WSPD Toledo OH
WSPO Stevens Point WI
WSPR Springfield MA
WSPZ Tuscaloosa AL
WSQR Sycamore IL
WSQV Berwick PA
WSRC Durham NC
WSRF Fort Lauderdale FL
WSRO Marlboro MA
WSRW Hillsboro OH
WSSA Morrow GA
WSSC Sumter SC
WSSG Goldsboro NC
WSSH Boston MA
WSSI Carthage MS
WSSJ Camden NJ
WSSL Greenville SC
WSSO Starkville MS
WSSR Georgetown DE
WSTA Charlotte Amalie VI
WSTC Stamford CT
WSTH Columbus GA
WSTJ St. Johnsbury VT
WSTK Colonial Heights VA
WSTL South Glens Falls NY
WSTP Salisbury NC
WSTT Thomasville GA
WSTU Stuart FL
WSTV Steubenville OH
WSTX Christiansted VI
WSUA Miami FL
WSUB Groton CT
WSUH Oxford MS
*WSUI Iowa City IA
WSUN St. Petersburg FL
WSVA Harrisonburg VA
WSVG Mount Jackson VA
WSVM Valdese NC
WSVQ Harrogate TN
WSVS Crewe VA
WSVY Portsmouth VA
*WSWI Evansville IN
WSWL Pensacola FL
WSWN Belle Glade FL
WSWV Pennington Gap VA
WSYA Montgomery AL
WSYB Rutland VT
WSYD Mount Airy NC
WSYL Sylvania GA
WSYR Syracuse NY
WSYW Indianapolis IN
WSYY Millinocket ME
WSZC Truk FM
WSZD Pohnpei FM

WTAB Tabor City NC
WTAC Flint MI
WTAD Quincy IL
WTAE Pittsburgh PA
WTAG Worcester MA
WTAI Melbourne FL
WTAK Huntsville AL
WTAL Tallahassee FL
WTAN Clearwater FL
WTAQ La Grange IL
WTAR Norfolk VA
WTAW College Station TX
WTAX Springfield IL
WTAY Robinson IL
WTBF Troy AL
WTBI Pickens SC
WTBO Cumberland MD
WTBQ Warwick NY
WTBZ Grafton WV
WTCA Plymouth IN
WTCH Shawano WI
WTCJ Tell City IN
WTCL Chattahoochee FL
WTCM Traverse City MI
WTCO Campbellsville KY
WTCR Kenova WV
WTCS Fairmont WV
WTCW Whitesburg KY
WTCY Harrisburg PA
WTDY Madison WI
WTEL Philadelphia PA
WTEM Bethesda MD
WTGA Thomaston GA
WTGC Lewisburg PA
WTGH Cayce SC
WTGM Salisbury MD
WTHB Augusta GA
WTHE Mineola NY
WTHI Terre Haute IN
WTHU Thurmont MD
WTIC Hartford CT
WTIF Tifton GA
WTIG Massillon OH
WTIK Durham NC
WTIL Mayaguez PR
WTIM Taylorville IL
WTIQ Manistique MI
WTIS Tampa FL
WTIV Titusville PA
WTIX New Orleans LA
WTJH East Point GA
WTJS Jackson TN
WTJZ Newport News VA
WTKA Ann Arbor MI
WTKI Huntsville AL
WTKM Hartford WI
WTKN Daleville AL
WTKO Ithaca NY
WTKX Pensacola FL
WTKY Tompkinsville KY
WTLB Utica NY
WTLC Indianapolis IN
WTLK Taylorsville NC
WTLM Alexander City AL
WTLN Apopka FL
WTLO Somerset KY
WTLS Tallassee AL
WTMA Charleston SC
WTMB Tomah WI
WTMC Ocala FL
WTME Lewiston ME
WTMJ Milwaukee WI
WTMM Richmond VA
WTMP Temple Terrace FL
WTMR Camden NJ
WTMS Presque Isle ME
WTMT Louisville KY
WTMY Sarasota FL
WTMZ Dorchester Terrace-Brentwood SC
WTNC Thomasville NC
WTNE Trenton TN
WTNI Hartsville SC
WTNL Reidsville GA
WTNN Farragut TN
WTNR Waynesboro TN
WTNS Coshocton OH
WTNW Tuscaloosa AL
WTNY Watertown NY
WTOB Winston-Salem NC
WTOD Toledo OH
WTOE Spruce Pine NC
WTON Staunton VA
WTOP Washington DC
WTOQ Platteville WI
WTOT Marianna FL
WTOW Washington NC
WTOX Lincoln ME
WTOY Salem VA
WTPR Paris TN
WTQX Selma AL
WTRB Ripley TN
WTRC Elkhart IN
WTRE Greensburg IN
WTRI Brunswick MD
WTRN Tyrone PA
WTRO Dyersburg TN
WTRP La Grange GA
WTRR Sanford FL
WTRS Dunellon FL
WTRW Two Rivers WI
WTRY Troy NY
WTSA Brattleboro VT
WTSB Lumberton NC
WTSH Rome GA

Broadcasting & Cable Yearbook 1994

B-458

U.S. AM Stations by Call Letters

WTSJ Cincinnati OH
WTSK Tuscaloosa AL
WTSL Hanover NH
WTSN Dover NH
WTSO Madison WI
WTSV Claremont NH
WTTB Vero Beach FL
WTTC Towanda PA
WTTF Tiffin OH
WTTI Dalton GA
WTTL Madisonville KY
WTTM Trenton NJ
WTTN Watertown WI
WTTR Westminster MD
WTTT Amherst MA
WTTX Appomattox VA
WTUP Tupelo MS
WTVB Coldwater MI
WTVL Waterville ME
WTVN Columbus OH
WTVR Richmond VA
WTWA Thomson GA
WTWB Auburndale FL
WTWZ Clinton MS
WTXY Whiteville NC
WTYL Tylertown MS
WTYM Kittanning PA
WTYN Tryon NC
WTYR Soddy-Daisy TN
WTYS Marianna FL
WTZE Tazewell VA
WTZQ Hendersonville NC
WTZX Sparta TN

WUAT Pikeville TN
WUBE Cincinnati OH
WUCO Marysville OH
WUFE Baxley GA
WUFF Eastman GA
WUFI Rantoul IL
*WUFL Sterling Heights MI
WUFO Amherst NY
WUHN Pittsfield MA
WUIV Icard Township NC
WUJM Goose Creek SC
WULA Eufaula AL
WULF Alma GA
WUNA Ocoee FL
*WUNN Mason MI
WUNO San Juan PR
WUNR Brookline MA
WUOK West Yarmouth MA
WUPR Utuado PR
WURD Philadelphia PA
WURL Moody AL
WUSS Atlantic City NJ
WUST Washington DC
WUTK Knoxville TN
WUTQ Utica NY
WUWU Cordele GA

WVAA Burnettown SC
WVAC Norwalk OH
WVAL Sauk Rapids MN
WVAM Altoona PA
WVAR Richwood WV
WVBS Burgaw NC
WVCB Shallotte NC
WVCG Coral Gables FL
WVCH Chester PA
WVCQ Brockway PA
WVEI Worcester MA
WVEL Pekin IL

WVFC McConnellsburg PA
WVFN East Lansing MI
WVGB Beaufort SC
WVHI Evansville IN
WVIO Blowing Rock NC
WVIP Mount Kisco NY
WVIX Vicksburg MS
WVJP Caguas PR
WVJS Owensboro KY
WVKO Columbus OH
WVKV Hurricane WV
WVKY Louisa KY
WVKZ Schenectady NY
WVLD Valdosta GA
WVLK Lexington KY
WVLN Olney IL
WVLR Lynchburg VA
WVMG Cochran GA
WVMI Biloxi MS
*WVMR Frost WV
WVMT Burlington VT
WVNA Tuscumbia AL
WVNE Leicester MA
WVNF Alpharetta GA
WVNJ Oakland NJ
WVNN Athens AL
WVNR Poultney VT
WVOC Columbia SC
WVOE Chadbourn NC
WVOG New Orleans LA
WVOH Hazlehurst GA
WVOI Toledo OH
WVOJ Jacksonville FL
WVOL Berry Hill TN
WVOM Iuka MS
WVON Cicero IL
WVOP Vidalia GA
WVOS Liberty NY
WVOT Wilson NC
WVOV Danville VA
WVOW Logan WV
WVOX New Rochelle NY
WVPO Stroudsburg PA
WVRC Spencer WV
WVRQ Viroqua WI
WVSA Vernon AL
WVSC Somerset PA
WVSM Rainsville AL
WVSR Charleston WV
WVTJ Pensacola FL
WVUV Leone AS
WVVW St. Marys WV
WVVI Charlotte Amalie VI

WWAB Lakeland FL
WWAM Jasper TN
WWBC Cocoa FL
WWBF Bartow FL
WWBG Greensboro NC
WWBH New Smyrna Beach FL
WWCA Gary IN
WWCB Corry PA
WWCC Honesdale PA
WWCH Clarion PA
WWCK Flint MI
WWCL Lehigh Acres FL
WWCM Ypsilanti MI
WWCN North Fort Myers FL
WWCO Waterbury CT
WWCS Canonsburg PA
WWDC Washington DC
WWDJ Hackensack NJ
WWES Hot Springs VA

WWEV Decatur GA
WWFE Miami FL
WWFQ Paw Creek NC
WWGP Sanford NC
WWGS Tifton GA
WWGZ Lapeer MI
WWHL Cocoa FL
WWHN Joliet IL
WWIC Scottsboro AL
WWII Shiremanstown PA
WWIL Wilmington NC
WWIN Baltimore MD
WWIS Black River Falls WI
WWIT Canton NC
WWJ Detroit MI
WWJB Brooksville FL
WWJC Duluth MN
WWJQ Holland MI
WWJZ Mount Holly NJ
WWKB Buffalo NY
WWKY Louisville KY
WWL New Orleans LA
WWLG Baltimore MD
WWLK Eddyville KY
WWLO Gainesville FL
WWLS Moore OK
WWLT Manchester KY
WWLX Lawrenceburg TN
WWMO Eden NC
WWNC Asheville NC
WWNH Madbury NH
WWNN Pompano Beach FL
WWNR Beckley WV
WWNS Statesboro GA
WWNT Dothan AL
WWNZ Orlando FL
WWOD Lynchburg VA
WWOF Camp Lejeune NC
WWOK Evansville IN
WWOL Forest City NC
WWON Fenton MI
WWOW Conneaut OH
WWPA Williamsport PA
WWPG Tuscaloosa AL
WWRC Washington DC
WWRK Elberton GA
WWRL New York NY
*WWRV New York NY
WWSC Glens Falls NY
WWSD Quincy FL
WWSJ St. Johns MI
WWSM Annville-Cleona PA
WWSR St. Albans VT
WWSW Pittsburgh PA
WWTC Minneapolis MN
WWTK Lake Placid FL
WWVA Wheeling WV
WWWC Wilkesboro NC
WWWE Cleveland OH
WWWG Rochester NY
WWWM Toledo OH
WWWN Vienna GA
WWWR Roanoke VA
WWWS Buffalo NY
WWWT Randolph VT
WWWW Detroit MI
WWYO Pineville WV
WWZN Winter Park FL
WWZQ Aberdeen MS

WXAL Demopolis AL
WXAM Buffalo KY
WXBD Biloxi MS

WXBQ Bristol VA
WXCE Amery WI
WXCF Clifton Forge VA
WXCL Peoria IL
WXCO Wausau WI
WXCT Hamden CT
WXEE Welch WV
WXEM Buford GA
WXEW Yabucoa PR
WXGI Richmond VA
WXGM Gloucester VA
WXIC Waverly OH
WXKL Sanford NC
WXKN Newburg KY
WXKO Fort Valley GA
WXKS Medford MA
WXKW Allentown PA
WXLA Dimondale MI
WXLI Dublin GA
WXLL Decatur GA
WXLW Indianapolis IN
WXLX Albemarle NC
WXLZ St. Paul VA
WXMC Parsippany-Troy Hills NJ
WXMY Saltville VA
WXOK Baton Rouge LA
WXOL Oshkosh WI
WXPX West Hazleton PA
WXQK Spring City TN
WXRF Guayama PR
WXRL Lancaster NY
WXRQ Mt. Pleasant TN
WXRS Swainsboro GA
WXSS Memphis TN
WXTC Charleston SC
WXTL Jacksonville Beach FL
WXTN Lexington MS
WXTO Winter Garden FL
WXVA Charles Town WV
WXVI Montgomery AL
WXVQ De Land FL
WXVW Jeffersonville IN
WXVX Monroeville PA
WXWY Robertsdale AL
*WXXI Rochester NY
WXXR Cullman AL
WXXU Cocoa Beach FL
*WXYB Indian Rocks Beach FL
WXYT Detroit MI

WYAK Surfside Beach-Garden City SC
WYAL Scotland Neck NC
WYBG Massena NY
WYBT Blountstown FL
WYCB Washington DC
WYCK Wilkes-Barre PA
WYCM Murfreesboro NC
WYCV Granite Falls NC
WYDE Birmingham AL
WYEA Sylacauga AL
WYER Mt. Carmel IL
WYFN Nashville TN
WYFQ Charlotte NC
WYFX Boynton Beach FL
WYGH Paris KY
WYGL Selinsgrove PA
WYGR Wyoming MI
WYIS McRae GA
WYJZ Pittsburgh PA
WYKC Grenada MS
WYKM Rupert WV
WYKO Sabana Grande PR

WYKR Wells River VT
WYLD New Orleans LA
WYLF Penn Yan NY
WYLO Jackson WI
WYLS York AL
WYLT Raleigh NC
WYMB Manning SC
WYMC Mayfield KY
WYNC Yanceyville NC
WYND De Land FL
WYNI Monroeville AL
WYNK Baton Rouge LA
WYNN Florence SC
WYNS Lehighton PA
WYOR Brentwood TN
WYPC Wellston OH
WYRE Annapolis MD
WYRN Louisburg NC
WYRU Red Springs NC
WYRV Cedar Bluff VA
WYSH Clinton TN
WYSL Avon NY
WYTH Madison GA
WYTI Rocky Mount VA
WYUS Milford DE
WYUT Herkimer NY
WYVE Wytheville VA
WYWY Barbourville KY
WYXC Cartersville GA
WYXI Athens TN
WYYR Spartanburg SC
WYZD Dobson NC
WYZE Atlanta GA

WZAC Madison WV
WZAM Norfolk VA
WZAN Portland ME
WZAO Moundsville WV
WZAP Bristol VA
WZAZ Jacksonville FL
WZBO Edenton NC
WZBS Ponce PR
WZCC New Albany IN
WZCM Young Harris GA
WZCT Scottsboro AL
WZEP DeFuniak Springs FL
WZFL Centreville MS
WZJY Mt. Pleasant SC
WZKY Albemarle NC
*WZMC Colonial Heights TN
WZMG Opelika AL
WZNN Rochester NH
WZNZ Jacksonville FL
WZOB Fort Payne AL
WZOE Princeton IL
WZON Bangor ME
WZOO Asheboro NC
WZOR Immokalee FL
WZOT Rockmart GA
WZOU Lewiston ME
WZPQ Jasper AL
WZQR Black Mountain NC
WZRC New York NY
WZRS Smyrna TN
WZRX Jackson MS
WZYX Cowan TN
WZZA Tuscumbia AL
WZZB Seymour IN
WZZD Philadelphia PA
WZZI Pascagoula-Moss Point MS
WZZK Birmingham AL
WZZX Lineville AL
WZZZ Fulton NY

U.S. FM Stations by Call Letters

KAAK(FM) Great Falls MT
KAAN-FM Bethany MO
KAAQ(FM) Alliance NE
KAAR(FM) Butte MT
KAAT(FM) Oakhurst CA
KAAX(FM) Avenal CA
KABD(FM) Brainerd MN
KABE(FM) Lake Ozark MO
*KABF(FM) Little Rock AR
KABH(FM) Shawnee OK
KABK-FM Augusta AR
KABL-FM San Francisco CA
KABX-FM Merced CA
*KACC(FM) Alvin TX
KACE(FM) Inglewood CA
KACH-FM Preston ID
KACI-FM The Dalles OR
KACJ(FM) Boonville MO
KACP(FM) Custer SD
*KACS(FM) Chehalis WA
KACT-FM Andrews TX
KACU(FM) Abilene TX
*KACV-FM Amarillo TX
KACW(FM) North Bend OR
KADA-FM Ada OK
KADF(FM) Horton KS
KADI(FM) Republic MO
KADM(FM) Odessa TX
KADQ(FM) Rexburg ID
*KADV(FM) Modesto CA
KADX(FM) Houston MO
*KAEN(FM) Little Eagle SD
*KAEP(FM) Fort Belknap Agency MT
KAEV(FM) Lake Arrowhead CA
KAEZ(FM) Amarillo TX
KAFE(FM) Bellingham WA
KAFF(FM) Flagstaff AZ
KAFN(FM) Hanford CA
KAFR(FM) Angel Fire NM
KAFW(FM) Osceola AR
KAFX-FM Diboll TX
KAGE-FM Winona MN
KAGF(FM) Columbia CA
KAGG(FM) Marksville LA
KAGH-FM Crossett AR
*KAGJ(FM) Ephraim UT
KAGM(FM) Strasburg CO
*KAGN(FM) Abilene TX
KAGO-FM Klamath Falls OR
KAGP(FM) Grants NM
*KAGU(FM) Spokane WA
KAGV(FM) Arnold CA
KAGZ(FM) Fresno CA
KAHM(FM) Prescott AZ
KAHR(FM) Poplar Bluff MO
KAIM-FM Honolulu HI
KAIR(FM) Crane TX
KAJA(FM) San Antonio TX
KAJK-FM Ferndale CA
KAJN-FM Crowley LA
*KAJX(FM) Aspen CO
KAJZ(FM) Santa Monica CA
KAKJ(FM) Marianna AR
KAKN(FM) Naknek AK
KAKQ-FM Fairbanks AK
KAKS-FM Canyon TX
*KALA(FM) Davenport IA
KALF(FM) Red Bluff CA
KALK(FM) Winfield TX
KALP(FM) Alpine TX
KALQ-FM Alamosa CO
*KALR(FM) Hot Springs AR
KALS(FM) Kalispell MT
KALU(FM) Langston OK
KALW(FM) San Francisco CA
KALX(FM) Berkeley CA
*KAMB(FM) Merced CA
KAMI-FM Cozad NE
KAML-FM Gillette WY
KAMO-FM Rogers AR
KAMS(FM) Mammoth Spring AR
*KAMU-FM College Station TX
KAMX-FM Albuquerque NM
KAMZ(FM) El Paso TX
KAND-FM Corsicana TX
*KANH(FM) Anchorage AK
KANU(FM) Lawrence KS
KANW(FM) Albuquerque NM
*KANZ(FM) Garden City KS
KAOE(FM) Hilo HI
KAOI-FM Wailuku HI
*KAOR(FM) Vermillion SD
*KAOS(FM) Olympia WA
KAOY(FM) Kealakekua HI
KAPB-FM Marksville LA
KAQU(FM) Huntington TX
KARA(FM) Santa Clara CA
KARB(FM) Price UT
KARL(FM) Tracy MN
*KARM(FM) Visalia CA
KARO(FM) Columbia MO
KARP(FM) Glencoe MN
KARQ(FM) Ashdown AR
KARS-FM Belen NM
KARU(FM) Raymondville TX
KARX(FM) Claude TX
KARY-FM Grandview WA
KARZ(FM) Burney CA
*KASB(FM) Bellevue WA

KASE(FM) Austin TX
*KASF(FM) Alamosa CO
KASH-FM Anchorage AK
KASK(FM) Las Cruces NM
KASM-FM Albany MN
KASO-FM Minden LA
KASR-FM Perry OK
KAST-FM Astoria OR
*KASU(FM) Jonesboro AR
KASY(FM) Albuquerque NM
KATB(FM) Anchorage AK
KATF(FM) Dubuque IA
KATG(FM) Comfort TX
KATH(FM) Bozeman MT
KATJ(FM) George CA
KATK-FM Carlsbad NM
KATM(FM) Modesto CA
KATP(FM) Amarillo TX
KATQ-FM Plentywood MT
KATR-FM Wray CO
KATS(FM) Yakima WA
KATT-FM Oklahoma City OK
KATW(FM) Lewiston ID
KATX(FM) Plainview TX
KATY-FM Idyllwild CA
KATZ-FM Alton IL
KAUI(FM) Kekaha HI
KAUM(FM) Colorado City TX
*KAUR(FM) Sioux Falls SD
KAUS-FM Austin MN
KAVC(FM) Rosamond CA
*KAVE(FM) Oakridge OR
KAVS(FM) Mojave CA
KAVV(FM) Benson AZ
*KAWC-FM Yuma AZ
KAWW-FM Heber Springs AR
*KAWZ(FM) Twin Falls ID
*KAXE(FM) Grand Rapids MN
KAXL(FM) Green Acres CA
KAXX(FM) Ventura CA
KAYD(FM) Beaumont TX
*KAYE-FM Tonkawa OK
KAYL-FM Storm Lake IA
KAYO-FM Aberdeen WA
KAYQ(FM) Warsaw MO
KAYX(FM) Richmond MO
*KAZI(FM) Austin TX
KAZO(FM) Soldotna AK
KAZR(FM) Coolidge AZ
*KAZU(FM) Pacific Grove CA
KAZY(FM) Denver CO
KAZZ(FM) Deer Park WA

KBAC(FM) Las Vegas NM
KBAQ(FM) Phoenix AZ
KBAT(FM) Midland TX
KBAX(FM) Fallbrook CA
KBAY(FM) San Jose CA
KBAZ(FM) Basile LA
KBBC(FM) Lake Havasu City AZ
KBBE(FM) McPherson KS
KBBF(FM) Santa Rosa CA
*KBBG(FM) Waterloo IA
KBBM(FM) Winterset IA
KBBN-FM Broken Bow NE
KBBQ-FM Fort Smith AR
KBBY-FM Ventura CA
KBBZ(FM) Kalispell MT
KBCE(FM) Boyce LA
KBCK(FM) Diamondville WY
KBCN-FM Marshall AR
KBCO-FM Boulder CO
KBCQ(FM) Roswell NM
*KBCS(FM) Bellevue WA
*KBCU(FM) North Newton KS
KBCY(FM) Tye TX
KBDR(FM) Mirando City TX
KBDZ(FM) Perryville MO
KBEK(FM) Mora MN
KBEL-FM Idabel OK
*KBEM-FM Minneapolis MN
KBEQ-FM Kansas City MO
KBER(FM) Ogden UT
*KBES(FM) Ceres CA
KBEV(FM) Springdale AR
KBEW-FM Blue Earth MN
KBEY(FM) Garberville CA
KBEZ(FM) Tulsa OK
KBFC(FM) Forrest City AR
KBFL(FM) Buffalo MO
KBFM(FM) Edinburg TX
KBFX(FM) Anchorage AK
*KBHE-FM Rapid City SD
*KBHG(FM) Fayetteville AR
KBHL(FM) Osakis MN
KBHP(FM) Bemidji MN
KBHR(FM) Big Bear City CA
KBHT(FM) Crockett TX
*KBHU-FM Spearfish SD
KBHW(FM) International Falls MN
KBIA(FM) Columbia MO
KBIC(FM) Alice TX
KBIG(FM) Los Angeles CA
KBIM-FM Roswell NM
KBIQ(FM) Fountain CO
KBIU(FM) Lake Charles LA
KBJJ(FM) Marshall MN
*KBJS(FM) Jacksonville TX
KBJZ(FM) Newport Beach CA
KBKB-FM Fort Madison IA

KBKG(FM) Corning AR
KBKL(FM) Grand Junction CO
KBLJ(FM) La Junta CO
KBLK(FM) Burnet TX
KBLL-FM Helena MT
KBLP(FM) Lindsay OK
KBLS(FM) North Fort Riley KS
KBLX(FM) Berkeley CA
KBLZ(FM) Kaneohe HI
KBMA(FM) Bryan TX
*KBMC(FM) Bozeman MT
KBMG(FM) Hamilton MT
*KBMI(FM) Roma TX
*KBMK(FM) Bismarck ND
KBMV-FM Birch Tree MO
KBMX(FM) Eldon MO
*KBNA-FM El Paso TX
*KBNJ(FM) Corpus Christi TX
*KBNL(FM) Laredo TX
KBNN(FM) Julian CA
*KBNR(FM) Brownsville TX
KBOC(FM) Bridgeport TX
KBOE-FM Oskaloosa IA
KBOK-FM Malvern AR
KBOM(FM) Los Alamos NM
*KBOO(FM) Portland OR
KBOQ-FM Marina CA
KBOS-FM Tulare CA
KBOT(FM) Pelican Rapids MN
KBOX(FM) Lompoc CA
KBOY-FM Medford OR
KBOZ-FM Livingston MT
KBPI-FM Denver CO
*KBPK(FM) Buena Park CA
*KBPR(FM) Brainerd MN
*KBPS-FM Portland OR
KBQB(FM) Princeville HI
KBQQ(FM) Minot ND
KBRB-FM Ainsworth NE
KBRE-FM Cedar City UT
KBRG(FM) Fremont CA
KBRJ(FM) Anchorage AK
KBRK-FM Brookings SD
KBRU(FM) Fort Morgan CO
KBRX-FM O'Neill NE
*KBSA(FM) El Dorado AR
*KBSB(FM) Bemidji MN
KBSG-FM Tacoma WA
*KBSM(FM) McCall ID
KBSO(FM) Corpus Christi TX
*KBST-FM Big Spring TX
*KBSU-FM Boise ID
*KBSW(FM) Twin Falls ID
KBSY(FM) Poteau OK
*KBTC-FM Tacoma WA
KBTO(FM) Bottineau ND
KBTS(FM) Big Spring TX
*KBTT(FM) Bridgeport TX
KBUC(FM) Pleasanton TX
KBUG(FM) Osceola MO
KBUK(FM) La Grange TX
KBUL(FM) Carson City NV
KBUS(FM) Paris TX
*KBUT(FM) Crested Butte CO
KBUX(FM) Quartzsite AZ
KBUY-FM Amarillo TX
KBVA(FM) Bella Vista AR
*KBVM(FM) Portland OR
*KBVR(FM) Corvallis OR
*KBVV(FM) Enid OK
KBVZ(FM) Fort Bridger WY
*KBWC(FM) Marshall TX
KBWS-FM Sisseton SD
KBXD(FM) Lawton OK
KBXL(FM) Caldwell ID
KBXR(FM) Ashland MO
KBXT(FM) Bixby OK
KBXX(FM) Houston TX
KBXY(FM) Baker CA
KBYB(FM) El Dorado AR
KBYG-FM Coahoma TX
KBYO-FM Tallulah LA
*KBYU-FM Provo UT
KBYZ(FM) Bismarck-Mandan ND
KBZE(FM) Berwick LA
KBZN(FM) Ogden UT
KBZQ(FM) Lawton OK
KBZS(FM) San Diego CA

*KCAC(FM) Camden AR
KCAL-FM Redlands CA
KCAQ(FM) Oxnard CA
KCAW(FM) Sitka AK
KCAY(FM) Russell KS
*KCBI(FM) Dallas TX
KCBQ-FM San Diego CA
KCBS-FM Los Angeles CA
*KCBX(FM) San Luis Obispo CA
KCCA(FM) Colorado City AZ
*KCCD(FM) Moorhead MN
*KCCK-FM Cedar Rapids IA
*KCCM-FM Moorhead MN
KCCN-FM Honolulu HI
KCCQ(FM) Ames IA
*KCCU(FM) Lawton OK
*KCCV-FM Olathe KS
KCCY(FM) Pueblo CO
*KCDA(FM) Coeur d'Alene ID
*KCDC(FM) Longmont CO

KCDD(FM) Hamlin TX
KCDL(FM) Cordell OK
KCDQ(FM) Monahans TX
*KCDS(FM) Angwin CA
KCDX(FM) San Carlos AZ
KCDY(FM) Carlsbad NM
KCDZ(FM) Twentynine Palms CA
*KCEA(FM) Atherton CA
*KCED(FM) Centralia WA
*KCEP(FM) Las Vegas NV
*KCEQ(FM) Walnut Creek CA
KCES(FM) Eufaula OK
KCEY(FM) Huntsville TX
KCEZ(FM) Corning CA
*KCFA(FM) Arnold CA
*KCFB(FM) St. Cloud MN
*KCFE(FM) Eden Prairie MN
*KCFM(FM) Shingletown CA
*KCFN(FM) Wichita KS
*KCFR(FM) Denver CO
*KCFS(FM) Sioux Falls SD
*KCFV(FM) Ferguson MO
*KCFX(FM) Harrisonville MO
*KCFY(FM) Yuma AZ
KCGB(FM) Hood River OR
*KCGN-FM Ortonville MN
KCGQ-FM Gordonville MO
KCGR(FM) Cottage Grove OR
KCGY-FM Laramie WY
KCHA-FM Charles City IA
KCHE-FM Cherokee IA
KCHI-FM Chillicothe MO
KCHK-FM New Prague MN
*KCHO(FM) Chico CA
KCHQ(FM) Altamont OR
KCHT(FM) Bakersfield CA
KCHX(FM) Midland TX
*KCIA(FM) Medford OR
*KCIC(FM) Grand Junction CO
*KCID(FM) Caldwell ID
*KCIE(FM) Dulce NM
KCII(FM) Washington IA
KCIJ(FM) North Fort Polk LA
*KCIL(FM) Houma LA
*KCIR(FM) Twin Falls ID
KCIV(FM) Mount Bullion CA
KCIX(FM) Garden City ID
KCJC(FM) Russellville AR
*KCJH(FM) Stockton CA
KCKI(FM) Henryetta OK
KCKL(FM) Malakoff TX
KCKR(FM) Waco TX
KCKS(FM) Concordia KS
KCLB-FM Coachella CA
*KCLC(FM) St. Charles MO
KCLD-FM St. Cloud MN
KCLI(FM) Clinton WA
KCLK-FM Clarkston WA
KCLM(FM) Newport OR
KCLN-FM Clinton IA
KCLQ(FM) Lebanon MO
KCLR-FM Boonville MO
KCLT(FM) West Helena AR
*KCLU(FM) Thousand Oaks CA
KCLV-FM Clovis NM
KCLX(FM) San Diego CA
KCLY(FM) Clay Center KS
KCMA(FM) Broken Arrow OK
KCMB(FM) Baker City OR
*KCME(FM) Manitou Springs CO
KCMG-FM Mountain Grove MO
*KCMH(FM) Mountain Home AR
*KCMI(FM) Terrytown NE
KCMJ-FM Indio CA
KCMO-FM Kansas City MO
KCMQ(FM) Columbia MO
KCMR(FM) Mason City IA
KCMS(FM) Edmonds WA
KCMT(FM) Chester CA
*KCMU(FM) Seattle WA
*KCMW-FM Warrensburg MO
KCMX-FM Ashland OR
KCNA(FM) Cave Junction OR
*KCND(FM) Bismarck ND
*KCNE-FM Chadron NE
KCNQ(FM) Kernville CA
KCNT(FM) Hastings NE
KCOB(FM) Newton IA
KCOE(FM) Auburn NE
KCOT(FM) San Augustine TX
*KCOU(FM) Columbia MO
*KCOZ(FM) Point Lookout MO
*KCPB(FM) Thousand Oaks CA
KCPI(FM) Albert Lea MN
*KCPR(FM) San Luis Obispo CA
*KCPW(FM) Salt Lake City UT
KCQR(FM) Ellwood CA
KCQV(FM) Arthur ND
*KCRB-FM Bemidji MN
KCRE-FM Crescent City CA
KCRF-FM Lincoln City OR
*KCRH(FM) Hayward CA
KCRI-FM Helena AR
KCRK-FM Colville WA
KCRL(FM) Rayne LA
KCRN(FM) San Angelo TX
KCRS-FM Midland TX
KCRT-FM Trinidad CO
*KCRU(FM) Oxnard CA

*KCRW(FM) Santa Monica CA
*KCRY(FM) Indio CA
KCRZ(FM) Tucson AZ
*KCSB-FM Santa Barbara CA
*KCSC(FM) Edmond OK
*KCSD(FM) Sioux Falls SD
*KCSM(FM) San Mateo CA
*KCSN(FM) Northridge CA
*KCSP(FM) Casper WY
*KCSS(FM) Turlock CA
KCST-FM Florence OR
*KCSU-FM Fort Collins CO
KCTM(FM) Rio Grande City TX
KCTN(FM) Garnavillo IA
KCTO-FM Columbia LA
KCTR-FM Billings MT
KCTT-FM Yellville AR
KCUA(FM) Coalville UT
KCUB-FM Stephenville TX
*KCUI(FM) Pella IA
*KCUK(FM) Chevak AK
KCUL-FM Marshall TX
*KCUR(FM) Kansas City MO
KCVI(FM) Blackfoot ID
*KCVO-FM Camdenton MO
KCVS(FM) Salina KS
*KCWA-FM Arnold MO
*KCWC-FM Riverton WY
KCWD(FM) Harrison AR
KCWN(FM) New Sharon IA
KCWS(FM) Merkel WA
*KCWX(FM) Columbia Falls MT
KCXY(FM) Camden AR
KCYT(FM) Granbury TX
KCYY(FM) San Antonio TX
KCZE(FM) New Hampton IA
KCZO(FM) Carrizo Springs TX
*KCZP(FM) Kenai AK
KCZQ(FM) Cresco IA
KCZY(FM) Osage IA
KDAB(FM) Prairie Grove AR
KDAL-FM Duluth MN
KDAM(FM) Monroe City MO
KDAO-FM Eldora IA
KDAP-FM Douglas AZ
*KDAQ(FM) Shreveport LA
KDAR(FM) Oxnard CA
KDAY(FM) Independence CA
KDB(FM) Santa Barbara CA
KDBB(FM) Bonne Terre MO
KDBH(FM) Natchitoches LA
KDBM-FM Dillon MT
KDBR(FM) Kalispell MT
KDBX(FM) Banks OR
KDCD(FM) San Angelo TX
*KDCR(FM) Sioux Center IA
KDCV-FM Blair NE
KDDB(FM) Paso Robles CA
KDDK(FM) Jacksonville AR
KDDQ(FM) Comanche OK
KDEA(FM) New Iberia LA
KDEL-FM Arkadelphia AR
KDEM(FM) Deming NM
KDEO-FM Waipahu HI
KDES-FM Palm Springs CA
KDET-FM Center TX
KDEX-FM Dexter MO
KDEZ(FM) Jonesboro AR
KDFC-FM San Francisco CA
*KDFR(FM) Des Moines IA
KDGB(FM) Dodge City KS
KDGE(FM) Gainesville TX
*KDHX(FM) St. Louis MO
*KDIC(FM) Grinnell IA
KDIL(FM) Terrell Hills TX
KDIU(FM) Dimmitt TX
KDJK(FM) Oakdale CA
KDJR(FM) De Soto MO
KDJS-FM Willmar MN
KDKB(FM) Mesa-Phoenix AZ
KDKD(FM) Clinton MO
KDKK-FM Park Rapids MN
KDKS-FM Haughton LA
KDLE(FM) Andover KS
KDLK-FM Del Rio TX
KDLO-FM Watertown SD
KDLS-FM Perry IA
KDLX(FM) Makawao HI
KDLY(FM) Lander WY
KDMG(FM) Burlington IA
KDMM(FM) Herington KS
KDMX(FM) Dallas TX
*KDNA(FM) Yakima WA
*KDNE(FM) Crete NE
*KDNI(FM) Duluth MN
*KDNK(FM) Carbondale CO
KDNO(FM) Delano CA
*KDNW(FM) Duluth MN
KDOG(FM) North Mankato MN
KDOK(FM) Tyler TX
KDOM-FM Windom MN
KDON-FM Salinas CA
*KDPR(FM) Dickinson ND
*KDPS(FM) Des Moines IA
KDQN-FM De Queen AR
*KDRH(FM) Glenwood Springs CO
KDRK-FM Spokane WA
KDRM(FM) Moses Lake WA
*KDSD-FM Pierpont SD

Broadcasting & Cable Yearbook 1994
B-460

U.S. FM Stations by Call Letters

KDSN-FM Denison IA
KDSQ(FM) Denison-Sherman TX
KDSR(FM) Williston ND
KDSS(FM) Ely NV
KDST(FM) Dyersville IA
*KDSU(FM) Fargo ND
KDTK(FM) Prescott Valley AZ
KDUC(FM) Barstow CA
KDUK-FM Florence OR
KDUQ(FM) Ludlow CA
*KDUR(FM) Durango CO
*KDUV(FM) Visalia CA
KDUX-FM Aberdeen WA
KDVL(FM) Devils Lake ND
*KDVS(FM) Davis CA
KDVV(FM) Topeka KS
KDWB-FM Richfield MN
KDWG(FM) Hardin MT
KDXI-FM Mansfield LA
*KDXL(FM) St. Louis Park MN
KDXT(FM) Missoula MT
KDXY(FM) Paragould AR
KDYC(FM) Danville AR
KDYN-FM Ozark AR
KDZA-FM Pueblo CO
KDZN(FM) Glendive MT
KDZR(FM) Denton TX

KEAG(FM) Anchorage AK
KEAN-FM Abilene TX
*KEAR(FM) San Francisco CA
KEAS-FM Eastland TX
KEAZ(FM) De Ridder LA
KEBC(FM) Oklahoma City OK
*KEBR-FM North Highlands CA
*KECC(FM) Miles City MT
*KECG(FM) El Cerrito CA
KECH-FM Sun Valley ID
KECO(FM) Elk City OK
KECR-FM El Cajon CA
*KEDB(FM) Las Vegas NV
KEDG(FM) Las Vegas NV
KEDJ(FM) Sun City AZ
*KEDM(FM) Monroe LA
*KEDP(FM) Las Vegas NM
*KEDR(FM) Sacramento CA
*KEDT-FM Corpus Christi TX
KEDY(FM) Mount Shasta CA
KEEH(FM) Spokane WA
KEEP(FM) Bandera TX
KEEY-FM St. Paul MN
KEEZ-FM Mankato MN
KEFE(FM) Los Alamos NM
KEFM(FM) Omaha NE
*KEFR(FM) Le Grand CA
KEGL(FM) Fort Worth TX
KEGS(FM) Emporia KS
KEGT(FM) Lake Village AR
KEGX(FM) Richland WA
KEJO(FM) Corvallis OR
KEJS(FM) Lubbock TX
KEKA-FM Eureka CA
KEKB(FM) Fruita CO
KEKO(FM) Green Valley AZ
KELE(FM) Mount Vernon MO
KELF(FM) Camarillo CA
KELI(FM) San Angelo TX
KELN(FM) North Platte NE
KELO-FM Sioux Falls SD
KELR-FM Chariton IA
KELY-FM Ely NV
KEMB(FM) Emmetsburg IA
*KEMC(FM) Billings MT
KEMM(FM) Commerce TX
KEMX(FM) Locust Grove OK
KENA-FM Mena AR
KEND(FM) Roswell NM
*KENT-FM Odessa TX
*KENW-FM Portales NM
KEOJ(FM) Caney KS
KEOK(FM) Tahlequah OK
*KEOL(FM) La Grande OR
*KEOM(FM) Mesquite TX
*KEPC(FM) Colorado Springs CO
KEPG(FM) Victoria TX
*KEPO(FM) Eagle Point OR
*KEPX(FM) Eagle Pass TX
*KERA(FM) Dallas TX
KERB-FM Kermit TX
KERC(FM) Clovis NM
KERM(FM) Torrington WY
KERN-FM Bakersfield CA
*KERP(FM) Pueblo CO
KERX(FM) Paris AR
*KESD(FM) Brookings SD
KESE(FM) Seligman MO
KESM-FM El Dorado Springs MO
KESY-FM Omaha NE
KESZ(FM) Phoenix AZ
KETB(FM) Coeur d'Alene ID
*KETR(FM) Commerce TX
KETX-FM Livingston TX
KEWB(FM) Anderson CA
KEWE(FM) Oroville CA
*KEWU-FM Cheney WA
KEXL(FM) Norfolk NE
KEXX(FM) Tracy CA
*KEYA(FM) Belcourt ND
KEYB(FM) Altus OK
KEYE-FM Perryton TX
KEYF-FM Cheney WA
KEYG-FM Grand Coulee WA
KEYI-FM San Marcos TX
KEYJ-FM Abilene TX
KEYN-FM Wichita KS

KEYR(FM) Marlin TX
KEYV(FM) Las Vegas NV
KEYW(FM) Pasco WA
KEZA(FM) Fayetteville AR
KEZB(FM) Hempstead TX
KEZE-FM Spokane WA
KEZG(FM) Lincoln NE
KEZH(FM) Hastings NE
KEZJ-FM Twin Falls ID
KEZK-FM St. Louis MO
KEZL(FM) Fowler CA
KEZN(FM) Palm Desert CA
KEZO-FM Omaha NE
KEZP(FM) Canadian TX
KEZQ(FM) Sheridan AR
KEZR(FM) San Jose CA
KEZS-FM Cape Girardeau MO
KEZT(FM) Ames IA
KEZU(FM) Booneville AR
KEZV(FM) Spearfish SD
KEZX-FM Seattle WA
KEZY(FM) Anaheim CA
KEZZ(FM) Aitkin MN

*KFAC(FM) Santa Barbara CA
KFAD(FM) Alexandria LA
*KFAE-FM Richland WA
*KFAI(FM) Minneapolis MN
KFAN-FM Johnson City TX
KFAT(FM) Corvallis OR
KFAV(FM) Warrenton MO
KFBD-FM Waynesville MO
KFBI(FM) Pahrump NV
*KFBN(FM) Lincoln NE
KFBQ(FM) Cheyenne WY
*KFCF(FM) Fresno CA
KFCL-FM Woodlake CA
KFCM(FM) Cherokee Village AR
KFDI-FM Wichita KS
*KFER(FM) Santa Cruz CA
KFFB(FM) Fairfield Bay AR
KFFM(FM) Yakima WA
KFFX(FM) Emporia KS
KFGE(FM) Lincoln NE
*KFGG(FM) Corpus Christi TX
KFGI-FM Luling TX
KFGO-FM Fargo ND
*KFGQ-FM Boone IA
KFIE(FM) Merced CA
KFIL-FM Preston MN
KFIN(FM) Jonesboro AR
KFIS(FM) Soda Springs ID
KFIZ-FM Fond du Lac WI
*KFJC(FM) Los Altos CA
*KFJM-FM Grand Forks ND
KFKF-FM Kansas City KS
KFKQ(FM) New Holstein WI
KFLD(FM) St. Robert MO
KFLG-FM Bullhead City AZ
KFLL(FM) Floydada TX
*KFLQ(FM) Albuquerque NM
*KFLR-FM Phoenix AZ
KFLS-FM Tulelake CA
KFLX(FM) Kachina Village AZ
KFLZ(FM) Bishop TX
KFMB-FM San Diego CA
KFMC(FM) Fairmont MN
KFMD(FM) Delta UT
KFMF(FM) Chico CA
KFMG(FM) Pella IA
KFMH(FM) Muscatine IA
KFMI(FM) Eureka CA
KFMK(FM) Winton CA
KFML(FM) Little Falls MN
KFMM(FM) Thatcher AZ
KFMN(FM) Lihue HI
KFMR(FM) Stockton CA
KFMS-FM Las Vegas NV
KFMT(FM) Fremont NE
KFMU-FM Oak Creek CO
KFMV(FM) Franklin LA
KFMW(FM) Waterloo IA
KFMX-FM Lubbock TX
KFMZ(FM) Columbia MO
KFNF(FM) Oberlin KS
*KFNO(FM) Fresno CA
KFNV-FM Ferriday LA
*KFNW-FM Fargo ND
KFOG(FM) San Francisco CA
KFOX(FM) Redondo Beach CA
*KFPR(FM) Redding CA
KFRC-FM San Francisco CA
KFRG(FM) San Bernardino CA
KFRO-FM Gilmer TX
KFRQ(FM) Harlingen TX
KFRX(FM) Lincoln NE
KFSD-FM San Diego CA
KFSG(FM) Los Angeles CA
KFSH(FM) Hilo HI
*KFSI(FM) Rochester MN
*KFSK(FM) Petersburg AK
KFSL(FM) Hallettsville TX
KFSO-FM Visalia CA
*KFSR(FM) Fresno CA
KFST-FM Fort Stockton TX
KFTE(FM) Breaux Bridge LA
KFTH(FM) Marion AR
KFTZ(FM) Idaho Falls ID
KFUO-FM Clayton MO
KFXD-FM Nampa ID
KFXE(FM) Cuba MO
KFXI(FM) Marlow OK
KFXJ(FM) Abilene TX
KFXT(FM) Sulphur OK
KFXX-FM Hugoton KS

KFXY(FM) Morgan City LA
KFXZ(FM) Maurice LA
KFYZ-FM Bonham TX

*KGAC(FM) St. Peter MN
KGAL-FM Brownsville OR
KGAP(FM) Clarksville TX
KGAS-FM Carthage TX
KGB-FM San Diego CA
KGBA-FM Holtville CA
*KGBI-FM Omaha NE
KGBR(FM) Gold Beach OR
KGBX-FM Nixa MO
KGBY(FM) Sacramento CA
*KGCB(FM) Prescott AZ
KGCI(FM) Grundy Center IA
KGCR(FM) Goodland KS
KGDN(FM) Pasco WA
KGEE(FM) Monahans TX
KGFM(FM) Bakersfield CA
KGFT(FM) Pueblo CO
KGFX-FM Pierre SD
KGFY(FM) Stillwater OK
KGGG-FM Rapid City SD
KGGI(FM) Riverside CA
KGGO-FM Des Moines IA
KGGY(FM) Dubuque IA
KGHO-FM Hoquiam WA
*KGHP(FM) Gig Harbor WA
*KGHR(FM) Tuba City AZ
KGKL-FM San Angelo TX
KGLC(FM) Miami OK
KGLE-FM South Lake Tahoe CA
KGLI(FM) Sioux City IA
KGLL(FM) Greeley CO
KGLM-FM Anaconda MT
KGLP(FM) Gallup NM
KGLS(FM) Pratt KS
*KGLT(FM) Bozeman MT
KGLX(FM) Gallup NM
*KGLY(FM) Tyler TX
KGMN(FM) Kingman AZ
KGMO(FM) Cape Girardeau MO
*KGMR(FM) Clarksville AR
KGMS(FM) Green Valley AZ
KGMX(FM) Lancaster CA
KGMY-FM Aurora MO
KGMZ(FM) Aiea HI
KGNC-FM Amarillo TX
KGND(FM) Ketchum OK
*KGNU(FM) Boulder CO
*KGNV(FM) Washington MO
*KGNZ(FM) Abilene TX
KGOE(FM) Eureka CA
KGOK(FM) Pauls Valley OK
KGON(FM) Portland OR
KGOR(FM) Omaha NE
KGOT(FM) Anchorage AK
*KGOU(FM) Norman OK
KGOZ(FM) Gallatin MO
*KGPR(FM) Great Falls MT
KGPZ(FM) Coleraine MN
KGRC(FM) Hannibal MO
KGRD(FM) Orchard NE
*KGRG(FM) Auburn WA
KGRI-FM Henderson TX
*KGRM(FM) Grambling LA
KGRS(FM) Burlington IA
KGRT-FM Las Cruces NM
KGRW(FM) Friona TX
*KGSP(FM) Parkville MO
KGSR(FM) Bastrop TX
*KGSU-FM Cedar City UT
KGTR(FM) Port Sulphur LA
*KGTS(FM) College Place WA
KGTW(FM) Ketchikan AK
KGVE(FM) Grove OK
KGVM(FM) Gardnerville-Minden NV
KGVW-FM Belgrade MT
KGWB(FM) Wahpeton ND
KGWY(FM) Gillette WY
KGXY(FM) Lenwood CA
KGY-FM McCleary WA
KGYU(FM) Visalia CA
KGZC(FM) Folsom LA
KGZF(FM) Emporia KS
KGZH(FM) Nyssa OR

KHAC-FM Window Rock AZ
KHAK-FM Cedar Rapids IA
*KHAP(FM) Chico CA
KHAY(FM) Ventura CA
KHAZ(FM) Hays KS
KHBM-FM Monticello AR
KHBT(FM) Humboldt IA
KHCA(FM) Wamego KS
*KHCB-FM Houston TX
*KHCC-FM Hutchinson KS
*KHCD(FM) Salina KS
KHCR(FM) Potosi MO
*KHCS(FM) Palm Desert CA
*KHCT(FM) Great Bend KS
*KHDC(FM) Chualar CA
*KHDX(FM) Conway AR
KHEN(FM) Caldwell TX
KHER(FM) Crystal City TX
KHEY-FM El Paso TX
KHEZ(FM) Caldwell ID
KHFI-FM Georgetown TX
KHFM(FM) Albuquerque NM
KHHH(FM) Honolulu HI
KHHT(FM) Killeen TX
*KHIB(FM) Durant OK
*KHID(FM) McAllen TX
KHII(FM) Security CO

KHIP(FM) Felton CA
KHIS-FM Bakersfield CA
KHIT-FM Reno NV
KHJM(FM) Taft OK
KHKC-FM Atoka OK
*KHKE(FM) Cedar Falls IA
KHKI(FM) Des Moines IA
KHKR-FM East Helena MT
KHKS(FM) Denton TX
KHLA(FM) Lake Charles LA
KHLB-FM Burnet TX
KHLL(FM) Richwood LA
KHLR(FM) Cameron TX
KHLS(FM) Blytheville AR
KHLT(FM) Little Rock AR
KHMB(FM) Hamburg AR
KHME(FM) Winona MN
*KHMS(FM) Victorville CA
KHMX(FM) Houston TX
*KHNE-FM Hastings NE
*KHNS(FM) Haines AK
*KHOE(FM) Fairfield IA
KHOK(FM) Hoisington KS
KHOM(FM) Houma LA
KHOP(FM) Modesto CA
KHOS-FM Sonora TX
KHOV(FM) Mariposa CA
KHOW-FM Denver CO
KHOX(FM) Hoxie AR
*KHOY(FM) Laredo TX
KHOZ-FM Harrison AR
KHPA(FM) Hope AR
KHPE(FM) Albany OR
KHPQ(FM) Clinton AR
*KHPR(FM) Honolulu HI
KHQT(FM) Los Altos CA
KHSL-FM Paradise CA
KHSP-FM Ashdown AR
KHSS(FM) Walla Walla WA
KHST(FM) Lamar MO
*KHSU-FM Arcata CA
KHTN(FM) Los Banos CA
KHTR(FM) Pullman WA
KHTT(FM) Muskogee OK
KHTX(FM) Riverside CA
KHTY(FM) Santa Barbara CA
KHUG(FM) Rocky Ford CO
KHUT(FM) Hutchinson KS
KHWI(FM) Hilo HI
KHWK(FM) Tonopah NV
KHWX(FM) Joshua Tree CA
KHWY(FM) Essex CA
KHXS(FM) Abilene TX
KHYE(FM) Hemet CA
KHYI(FM) Howe TX
KHYL(FM) Auburn CA
KHYS(FM) Port Arthur TX
KHYZ(FM) Mountain Pass CA

KIAI(FM) Mason City IA
KIAK-FM Fairbanks AK
KIAQ(FM) Clarion IA
*KIBC(FM) Burney CA
KIBL-FM Beeville TX
*KIBN(FM) Wichita KS
KIBS(FM) Bishop CA
KIBZ(FM) Lincoln NE
KICA-FM Farwell TX
*KICB(FM) Fort Dodge IA
KICD-FM Spencer IA
KICE(FM) Bend OR
KICK-FM Palmyra MO
KICM(FM) Healdton OK
KICR-FM Oakdale LA
KICT-FM Wichita KS
KICX-FM McCook NE
KICY-FM Nome AK
KID-FM Idaho Falls ID
KIDA-FM Ida Grove IA
*KIDE(FM) Hoopa CA
KIDI(FM) Guadalupe CA
KIDN-FM Hayden CO
KIDX(FM) Billings MT
KIDZ(FM) Brigham City UT
KIFG-FM Iowa Falls IA
KIFM(FM) San Diego CA
KIFX(FM) Roosevelt UT
*KIGC(FM) Oskaloosa IA
KIGL(FM) Spencer IA
KIHX-FM Prescott Valley AZ
KIIK-FM Fairfield IA
KIIM-FM Tucson AZ
KIIS-FM Los Angeles CA
KIIZ-FM Killeen TX
KIJK(FM) Prineville OR
KIJN-FM Farwell TX
KIKC-FM Forsyth MT
KIKF(FM) Garden Grove CA
KIKI-FM Honolulu HI
KIKK-FM Houston TX
KIKM-FM Sherman TX
KIKN(FM) Salem SD
KIKO-FM Claypool AZ
KIKR(FM) Asbury IA
KIKS-FM Iola KS
KIKT(FM) Greenville TX
KIKV-FM Alexandria MN
KIKX-FM Manitou Springs CO
*KILA(FM) Las Vegas NV
KILJ-FM Mount Pleasant IA
KILO(FM) Colorado Springs CO
KILR-FM Estherville IA
KILS(FM) Minneapolis KS
KILT-FM Houston TX
KIMN-FM Fort Collins CO

KIMX(FM) Laramie WY
KIMY(FM) Watonga OK
KIND-FM Independence KS
KINE-FM Honolulu HI
KING-FM Seattle WA
*KINI(FM) Crookston NE
KINK-FM Portland OR
KINL(FM) Eagle Pass TX
KINT-FM El Paso TX
KIOA-FM Des Moines IA
KIOC(FM) Orange TX
KIOI(FM) San Francisco CA
KIOK(FM) Richland WA
KIOL-FM Lamesa TX
KIOO(FM) Porterville CA
*KIOS-FM Omaha NE
KIOT(FM) Espanola NM
KIOW(FM) Forest City IA
KIOX-FM El Campo TX
KIOZ(FM) Oceanside CA
*KIPO-FM Honolulu HI
KIPP(FM) Mesquite NV
KIPR(FM) Pine Bluff AR
KIQK(FM) Rapid City SD
KIQO(FM) Atascadero CA
KIQQ-FM Lenwood CA
KIQS-FM Willows CA
KIQX(FM) Durango CO
KIQZ(FM) Rawlins WY
KIRC(FM) Seminole OK
KIRK(FM) Lebanon MO
KIRO-FM Seattle WA
KISC(FM) Spokane WA
KISD(FM) Pipestone MN
KISF(FM) Lexington MO
KISI(FM) Malvern AR
KISK(FM) Lowell AR
*KISL(FM) Avalon CA
KISM(FM) Bellingham WA
KISN-FM Salt Lake City UT
KISP(FM) Blair NE
KISQ(FM) El Dorado AR
KISR(FM) Fort Smith AR
KISS-FM San Antonio TX
KISW(FM) Seattle WA
KISX(FM) Whitehouse TX
KISZ-FM Cortez CO
KITE(FM) Kerrville TX
KITO-FM Vinita OK
KITR(FM) Creston IA
KITS(FM) San Francisco CA
KITT(FM) Shreveport LA
KITX(FM) Hugo OK
KIUS(FM) Hutchinson KS
KIVY-FM Crockett TX
KIWA-FM Sheldon IA
KIWI(FM) Bakersfield CA
*KIWR(FM) Council Bluffs IA
KIWW(FM) Harlingen TX
KIXA(FM) Lucerne Valley CA
KIXB(FM) El Dorado AR
KIXC-FM Quanah TX
KIXF(FM) Baker CA
KIXK(FM) Canton SD
KIXQ(FM) Webb City MO
KIXR(FM) Ponca City OK
KIXS(FM) Victoria TX
KIXT-FM Grover City CA
KIXV(FM) Brady TX
KIXW(FM) Lenwood CA
KIXX(FM) Watertown SD
KIXY-FM San Angelo TX
KIZN(FM) Boise ID
KIZS(FM) Carson City NV
KIZZ(FM) Minot ND

*KJAB-FM Mexico MO
KJAE(FM) Leesville LA
KJAK(FM) Slaton TX
KJAM-FM Madison SD
KJAV(FM) Alamo TX
KJAZ(FM) Alameda CA
KJBR(FM) Jonesboro AR
KJBZ(FM) Laredo TX
KJCK-FM Junction City KS
*KJCR(FM) Keene TX
KJCS(FM) Nacogdoches TX
KJDE(FM) Sandpoint ID
KJDX(FM) Susanville CA
KJEE(FM) Montecito CA
KJEF-FM Jennings LA
KJET(FM) Kingsburg CA
KJEZ(FM) Poplar Bluff MO
KJFA(FM) Grass Valley CA
KJFM(FM) Louisiana MO
KJFX(FM) Fresno CA
*KJHK(FM) Lawrence KS
KJHY(FM) Emmett ID
KJIB(FM) South Padre Island TX
*KJIC(FM) Pasadena TX
*KJIL(FM) Copeland KS
KJIW-FM West Helena AR
KJJB(FM) Eunice LA
KJJC(FM) Osceola IA
KJJJ(FM) Clifton AZ
KJJK-FM Fergus Falls MN
KJJO-FM St. Louis Park MN
KJJY-FM Ankeny IA
KJJZ(FM) Kodiak AK
KJKJ(FM) Grand Forks ND
KJKS(FM) Cameron TX
KJLH-FM Compton CA
KJLO-FM Monroe LA
KJLS(FM) Hays KS
KJLT-FM North Platte NE

U.S. FM Stations by Call Letters

*KJLU(FM) Jefferson City MO
KJLY(FM) Blue Earth MN
KJMB(FM) Blythe CA
KJMO(FM) Jefferson City MO
KJMS(FM) Memphis TN
KJMX(FM) Tulia TX
KJMZ(FM) Dallas TX
KJNA-FM Jena LA
KJNE(FM) Hillsboro TX
KJNP-FM North Pole AK
KJOI(FM) Dinuba CA
KJOJ-FM Freeport TX
KJOK(FM) Yuma AZ
*KJOL(FM) Grand Junction CO
KJOT(FM) Boise ID
KJOY(FM) Stockton CA
KJPW-FM Waynesville MO
KJQY(FM) San Diego CA
*KJRT(FM) Amarillo TX
KJSN(FM) Modesto CA
*KJTA(FM) Flagstaff AZ
KJTX(FM) Jefferson TX
*KJTY(FM) Topeka KS
KJUG-FM Tulare CA
KJUL(FM) North Las Vegas NV
KJUN-FM Eatonville WA
*KJVH(FM) Longview WA
KJYE-FM Grand Junction CO
KJYL(FM) Eagle Grove IA
KJYO(FM) Oklahoma City OK
KJYY(FM) Brush CO
*KJZZ(FM) Phoenix AZ

KKAJ-FM Ardmore OK
KKAT(FM) Ogden UT
KKAY-FM Donaldsonville LA
KKAZ(FM) Cheyenne WY
KKBB(FM) Shafter CA
KKBC-FM Baker City OR
KKBE-FM Ogden UT
KKBG(FM) Hilo HI
KKBI(FM) Broken Bow OK
KKBJ-FM Bemidji MN
KKBK(FM) Lake Oswego OR
KKBL(FM) Monett MO
KKBN(FM) Twain Harte CA
KKBQ-FM Pasadena TX
KKBR(FM) Billings MT
KKBS(FM) Guymon OK
KKBT(FM) Los Angeles CA
KKBZ(FM) Clarinda IA
KKCA(FM) Fulton MO
KKCD(FM) Omaha NE
KKCH-FM Hayden ID
KKCI(FM) Goodland KS
KKCJ(FM) Liberty MO
KKCK(FM) Marshall MN
KKCL(FM) Lorenzo TX
KKCQ-FM Fosston MN
*KKCR(FM) Salina KS
KKCS-FM Colorado Springs CO
KKCT(FM) Bismarck ND
KKCW(FM) Beaverton OR
KKCY(FM) Colusa CA
KKDA-FM Dallas TX
KKDJ(FM) Fresno CA
KKDL(FM) Detroit Lakes MN
KKDM(FM) Des Moines IA
KKDQ(FM) Thief River Falls MN
KKDY(FM) West Plains MO
KKEE(FM) Long Beach WA
KKEG(FM) Fayetteville AR
KKER(FM) Casa Grande AZ
KKEZ(FM) Fort Dodge IA
KKFG(FM) Bloomfield NM
*KKFI(FM) Kansas City MO
KKFM(FM) Colorado Springs CO
KKFR(FM) Glendale AZ
*KKGL(FM) Pinetop AZ
KKGO-FM Los Angeles CA
KKHI-FM San Francisco CA
KKHQ(FM) Odem TX
KKHR(FM) Anson TX
KKHT(FM) Springfield MO
KKIQ(FM) Livermore CA
KKIX(FM) Fayetteville AR
KKJG(FM) San Luis Obispo CA
KKJI(FM) Gallup NM
KKJJ(FM) Campbell MO
KKJM(FM) St. Joseph MN
KKJO(FM) St. Joseph MO
KKJQ(FM) Garden City KS
KKJR(FM) Hutchinson MN
KKJY-FM Albuquerque NM
KKKK(FM) Odessa TX
KKLA(FM) Los Angeles CA
KKLB(FM) Elgin TX
KKLC(FM) Susanville CA
KKLD(FM) Tucson AZ
KKLF(FM) Gonzales CA
KKLI(FM) Widefield CO
KKLL-FM Webb City MO
KKLQ-FM San Diego CA
KKLR(FM) Poplar Bluff MO
KKLS-FM Sioux Falls SD
KKLT(FM) Phoenix AZ
KKLX(FM) Worland WY
KKLY(FM) Delta CO
KKLZ(FM) Las Vegas NV
KKMA(FM) Le Mars IA
KKMG(FM) Pueblo CO
KKMI(FM) Burlington IA
KKMJ-FM Austin TX
KKMK(FM) Rapid City SD
KKMV(FM) Rupert ID
KKMX(FM) Tri City OR
KKMY(FM) Orange TX
KKNB(FM) Crete NE
KKNG(FM) Laramie WY
KKNU(FM) Springfield-Eugene OR
KKOA(FM) Volcano HI
KKOB-FM Albuquerque NM
KKOK-FM Morris MN
KKOL(FM) Hampton AR
KKOO(FM) Caledonia MN
KKOR(FM) Gallup NM
KKOS(FM) Carlsbad CA
KKOT(FM) Columbus NE
KKOW-FM Pittsburg KS
KKOY-FM Chanute KS
KKOZ-FM Ava MO
KKPR-FM Kearney NE
KKPS(FM) Brownsville TX
KKQQ(FM) Volga SD
KKRB(FM) Klamath Falls OR
KKRC(FM) Granite Falls MN
KKRD(FM) Wichita KS
KKRF(FM) Stuart IA
KKRK(FM) Douglas AZ
KKRL(FM) Carroll IA
KKRP(FM) Delhi LA
KKRQ(FM) Iowa City IA
KKRV(FM) Wenatchee WA
KKRW(FM) Houston TX
KKRX-FM Lawton OK
KKRZ(FM) Portland OR
KKSF(FM) San Francisco CA
KKSI(FM) Eddyville IA
KKSN-FM Portland OR
KKSR(FM) Sartell MN
KKSS(FM) Santa Fe NM
KKSY(FM) Bald Knob AR
KKTX-FM Kilgore TX
KKTY-FM Douglas WY
KKTZ(FM) Mountain Home AR
*KKUA(FM) Wailuku HI
*KKUP(FM) Cupertino CA
KKUR(FM) Ojai CA
KKUS(FM) Tyler TX
KKUZ-FM Sallisaw OK
*KKVO(FM) Altus OK
KKWM(FM) Winfield KS
KKWQ(FM) Warroad MN
KKWS(FM) Wadena MN
KKWZ(FM) Richfield UT
KKXK(FM) Montrose CO
KKXL-FM Grand Forks ND
KKXX-FM Delano CA
KKYC(FM) Muleshoe TX
KKYK-FM Little Rock AR
KKYN-FM Plainview TX
KKYR-FM Texarkana TX
KKYS(FM) Bryan TX
KKYY(FM) Gunnison CO
KKYZ(FM) Sierra Vista AZ
KKZR(FM) Conroe TX
KKZX(FM) Spokane WA

KLAA(FM) Tioga LA
KLAD-FM Klamath Falls OR
KLAK(FM) Durant OK
KLAN(FM) Glasgow MT
KLAQ(FM) El Paso TX
KLAW(FM) Lawton OK
KLAX-FM Long Beach CA
KLAZ(FM) Hot Springs AR
KLBA-FM Albia IA
KLBC(FM) Durant OK
KLBJ-FM Austin TX
KLBQ(FM) El Dorado AR
*KLCC(FM) Eugene OR
*KLCD(FM) Decorah IA
KLCE(FM) Blackfoot ID
KLCI(FM) Nampa ID
KLCM(FM) Lewistown MT
*KLCO(FM) Newport OR
KLCR(FM) Nogales AZ
KLCX(FM) Indio CA
KLCY-FM Vernal UT
KLCZ-FM Corcoran CA
KLDE(FM) Houston TX
*KLDN(FM) Lufkin TX
KLDR(FM) Harbeck-Fruitdale OR
KLDZ(FM) Lincoln NE
KLEA-FM Lovington NM
KLEB-FM Galliano LA
KLEF(FM) Anchorage AK
*KLEL(FM) San Jose CA
KLEN(FM) Cheyenne WY
KLEO(FM) Kahaluu HI
KLER-FM Orofino ID
KLFA(FM) King City CA
*KLFC(FM) Branson MO
KLFM(FM) Great Falls MT
KLFX(FM) Harker Heights TX
KLGA-FM Algona IA
KLGR-FM Redwood Falls MN
KLGS(FM) Versailles MO
KLGT(FM) Buffalo WY
KLHI-FM Lahaina HI
*KLHS-FM Lewiston ID
KLIL(FM) Moreauville LA
KLIR(FM) Columbus NE
KLIS(FM) Palestine TX
KLIT(FM) Glendale CA
KLIX-FM Twin Falls ID
KLIZ-FM Brainerd MN
*KLJC(FM) Kansas City MO
KLKC-FM Parsons KS
KLKK(FM) Clear Lake IA
KLKL(FM) Benton LA
KLKM(FM) Llano TX
KLKO(FM) Elko NV
KLKS(FM) Breezy Point MN
KLKX(FM) Rosamond CA
KLKY(FM) Milton-Freewater OR
KLLI(FM) Hooks TX
KLLK-FM Fort Bragg CA
KLLL-FM Lubbock TX
KLLM(FM) Forks WA
*KLLN(FM) Newark AR
KLLS(FM) Augusta KS
KLLY(FM) Oildale CA
KLLZ-FM Walker MN
KLMA(FM) Hobbs NM
KLMJ(FM) Hampton IA
*KLMN(FM) Amarillo TX
KLMP(FM) Rapid City SD
KLMY(FM) Seaside CA
*KLNE-FM Lexington NE
*KLNI(FM) Decorah IA
*KLNR(FM) Panaca NV
KLOA-FM Ridgecrest CA
*KLOD(FM) Shafter CA
KLOH-FM Slayton MN
KLOL(FM) Houston TX
*KLON(FM) Long Beach CA
KLOR-FM Ponca City OK
KLOS(FM) Los Angeles CA
KLOU(FM) St. Louis MO
KLOW(FM) Caruthersville MO
KLOZ(FM) Eldon MO
*KLPI-FM Ruston LA
KLPL-FM Lake Providence LA
KLPQ(FM) Cabot AR
KLPR(FM) Springfield MN
KLPW-FM Union MO
KLPX(FM) Tucson AZ
KLQB(FM) Oracle AZ
KLQL(FM) Luverne MN
KLQP(FM) Madison MN
KLQZ(FM) Paragould AR
KLRA-FM England AR
KLRB(FM) Aurora NE
*KLRC(FM) Siloam Springs AR
*KLRD(FM) Yucaipa CA
*KLRE-FM Little Rock AR
KLRK(FM) Vandalia MO
KLRQ(FM) Clinton MO
KLRR(FM) Redmond OR
KLRZ(FM) Larose LA
*KLSA(FM) Alexandria LA
KLSC(FM) Socorro NM
*KLSE-FM Rochester MN
KLSK(FM) Santa Fe NM
KLSN(FM) Jefferson IA
*KLSP(FM) Angola LA
KLSR-FM Memphis TX
KLSS-FM Mason City IA
*KLSU(FM) Baton Rouge LA
KLSX(FM) Los Angeles CA
KLSY-FM Bellevue WA
KLSZ-FM Van Buren AR
KLTA(FM) Breckenridge MN
KLTB(FM) Boise ID
KLTD(FM) Temple TX
KLTE(FM) Kirksville MO
KLTG(FM) Corpus Christi TX
KLTH(FM) Kansas City MO
KLTN(FM) Port Arthur TX
KLTQ(FM) Sparta MO
KLTR(FM) Franklin TX
KLTX(FM) Seattle WA
KLTY(FM) Fort Worth TX
KLUA(FM) Kailua-Kona HI
KLUB(FM) Bloomington TX
KLUC-FM Las Vegas NV
KLUE(FM) Soledad CA
*KLUH(FM) Poplar Bluff MO
KLUR(FM) Wichita Falls TX
KLUV(FM) Dallas TX
*KLUX(FM) Robstown TX
KLVE(FM) Los Angeles CA
KLVF(FM) Las Vegas NM
KLVJ-FM Mountain Home ID
*KLVM(FM) Prunedale CA
*KLVR(FM) Santa Rosa CA
KLVT-FM Levelland TX
*KLVV(FM) Ponca City OK
KLXK(FM) Duluth MN
KLXQ(FM) Hot Springs AR
KLXS-FM Pierre SD
KLYF(FM) Des Moines IA
KLYK(FM) Longview WA
KLYN(FM) Lynden WA
KLYR-FM Clarksville AR
*KLYT(FM) Albuquerque NM
KLYV(FM) Dubuque IA
KLZE(FM) Owensville MO
KLZK(FM) Brownfield TX
KLZR(FM) Lawrence KS
KLZX-FM Salt Lake City UT
KLZY(FM) Powell WY
KLZZ(FM) Waite Park MN

KMAC(FM) Gainesville MO
KMAD-FM Madill OK
KMAG(FM) Fort Smith AR
KMAJ-FM Topeka KS
KMAK(FM) Orange Cove CA
KMAL(FM) Malden MO
KMAQ-FM Maquoketa IA
KMAR-FM Winnsboro LA
KMAT(FM) Sutter Creek CA
KMAV-FM Mayville ND
KMAX(FM) Arcadia CA
*KMBH-FM Harlingen TX
*KMBI-FM Spokane WA
KMBQ(FM) Wasilla AK
KMBV(FM) Navasota TX
KMBY-FM Seaside CA
KMCH(FM) Manchester IA
KMCK(FM) Siloam Springs AR
KMCL-FM McCall ID
KMCM-FM Miles City MT
KMCO(FM) McAlester OK
KMCQ(FM) The Dalles OR
KMCR(FM) Montgomery City MO
KMCX(FM) Ogallala NE
KMDL(FM) Kaplan LA
KMEL(FM) San Francisco CA
KMEM-FM Memphis MO
KMEO(FM) Wickenburg AZ
KMEZ(FM) Belle Chasse LA
*KMFA(FM) Austin TX
KMFB(FM) Mendocino CA
KMFC(FM) Centralia MO
KMFM(FM) Premont TX
KMFX(FM) Lake City MN
KMFY(FM) Grand Rapids MN
KMGA(FM) Albuquerque NM
KMGE(FM) Eugene OR
KMGG(FM) Monte Rio CA
KMGI(FM) Pocatello ID
KMGK(FM) Glenwood MN
KMGL(FM) Oklahoma City OK
KMGM(FM) Montevideo MN
KMGN(FM) Flagstaff AZ
KMGO(FM) Centerville IA
KMGQ(FM) Goleta CA
KMGW(FM) Casper WY
KMGX(FM) San Fernando CA
*KMHA(FM) Four Bears ND
*KMHD(FM) Gresham OR
KMIA(FM) Jasper TX
*KMIH(FM) Mercer Island WA
KMIQ(FM) Robstown TX
KMIS-FM New Madrid MO
KMIT(FM) Mitchell SD
KMIX-FM Turlock CA
KMJI(FM) Denver CO
KMJJ-FM Shreveport LA
KMJK(FM) Buckeye AZ
KMJM(FM) St. Louis MO
KMJQ(FM) Houston TX
KMJX(FM) Conway AR
KMJY-FM Newport WA
KMKE(FM) Grand Junction CO
KMKF(FM) Manhattan KS
KMKS(FM) Bay City TX
KMKZ(FM) Lahoma OK
KMLE(FM) Chandler AZ
KMMC(FM) Salem MO
KMML-FM Amarillo TX
KMMM(FM) Madera CA
KMMO-FM Marshall MO
KMMR(FM) Malta MT
KMMS-FM Bozeman MT
KMMT(FM) Mammoth Lakes CA
KMMX(FM) Lamesa TX
KMMY(FM) Muskogee OK
*KMNE-FM Bassett NE
*KMNR(FM) Rolla MO
KMNT(FM) Centralia WA
*KMOC(FM) Wichita Falls TX
KMOD-FM Tulsa OK
KMOE(FM) Butler MO
*KMOJ(FM) Minneapolis MN
KMOK(FM) Lewiston ID
KMON-FM Great Falls MT
KMOO-FM Mineola TX
KMOQ(FM) Baxter Springs KS
KMOR(FM) Scottsbluff NE
KMOU(FM) Roswell NM
KMPH-FM Hanford CA
*KMPO(FM) Modesto CA
KMPQ-FM Rosenberg TX
*KMPR(FM) Minot ND
KMPS-FM Seattle WA
KMQA-FM West Covina CA
KMRE(FM) Dumas TX
KMRK-FM Odessa TX
*KMRO(FM) Camarillo CA
*KMSA(FM) Grand Junction CO
*KMSC(FM) Sioux City IA
*KMSI(FM) Moore OK
*KMSK(FM) Austin MN
*KMSM-FM Butte MT
KMSO(FM) Missoula MT
KMSR(FM) Sauk Centre MN
*KMSU(FM) Mankato MN
KMTB(FM) Murfreesboro AR
*KMTC(FM) Russellville AR
*KMTH(FM) Maljamar NM
KMTN(FM) Jackson WY
KMTS(FM) Glenwood Springs CO
KMTT-FM Tacoma WA
KMTX-FM Helena MT
*KMUD(FM) Garberville CA
*KMUN(FM) Astoria OR
KMUS-FM Burns WY
*KMUW(FM) Wichita KS
KMUZ-FM Camas WA
*KMVC(FM) Marshall MO
KMVI-FM Pukalani HI
KMVK(FM) Benton AR
KMVR(FM) Mesilla Park NM
KMVX(FM) Jerome ID
KMXB(FM) Orem UT
KMXD(FM) Ankeny IA
KMXE(FM) Red Lodge MT
KMXG(FM) Clinton IA
KMXK(FM) Cold Spring MN
KMXL(FM) Carthage MO
KMXQ(FM) Socorro NM
KMXR(FM) Corpus Christi TX
*KMXT(FM) Kodiak AK
KMXU(FM) Manti UT
KMXV(FM) Kansas City MO
KMXX(FM) Imperial CA
KMXZ(FM) Hollister CA
KMYI(FM) Kirtland NM
KMYX-FM Taft CA
KMYY(FM) Monroe LA
KMYZ-FM Pryor OK
KMZA(FM) Seneca KS
KMZE(FM) Woodward OK
KMZQ-FM Henderson NV
KMZU(FM) Carrollton MO
KMZX(FM) Lonoke AR

KNAB-FM Burlington CO
KNAC(FM) Long Beach CA
*KNAI(FM) Phoenix AZ
KNAS(FM) Nashville AR
*KNAU(FM) Flagstaff AZ
KNAX(FM) Fresno CA
*KNBJ(FM) Bemidji MN
KNBT(FM) New Braunfels TX
*KNBU(FM) Baldwin City KS
*KNCA(FM) Burney CA
KNCB-FM Vivian LA
*KNCC(FM) Elko NV
KNCD(FM) Columbia MO
KNCI(FM) Sacramento CA
KNCN(FM) Sinton TX
KNCO-FM Grass Valley CA
KNCQ(FM) Redding CA
*KNCT-FM Killeen TX
KNCY-FM Nebraska City NE
KNDD(FM) Seattle WA
KNDE(FM) Sparks NV
KNDK-FM Langdon ND
KNDR(FM) Mandan ND
KNDY-FM Marysville KS
KNEB-FM Scottsbluff NE
KNEI-FM Waukon IA
KNEK-FM Washington LA
KNEN(FM) Norfolk NE
*KNEO(FM) Neosho MO
KNES(FM) Fairfield TX
KNEV(FM) Reno NV
KNFL-FM Tremonton UT
KNFM(FM) Midland TX
KNFR(FM) Opportunity WA
KNFT-FM Bayard NM
KNFX(FM) Spring Valley MN
*KNGA(FM) St. Peter MN
*KNGM(FM) Emporia KS
KNGS(FM) Coalinga CA
KNGT(FM) Jackson CA
KNGV(FM) Kingsville TX
*KNHC(FM) Seattle WA
KNID(FM) Enid OK
KNIK-FM Anchorage AK
KNIM-FM Maryville MO
KNIN-FM Wichita Falls TX
*KNIS(FM) Carson City NV
KNIX-FM Phoenix AZ
KNJM(FM) Lincoln City OR
KNJO(FM) Thousand Oaks CA
KNJP(FM) Sargent NE
KNJS(FM) Belle Plaine IA
*KNJU(FM) Raton NM
KNJY(FM) Spokane WA
KNKD(FM) Earlimart CA
KNKE-FM Jasper TX
KNKN(FM) Pueblo CO
KNLA(FM) White Rock NM
*KNLB(FM) Lake Havasu City AZ
*KNLE-FM Round Rock TX
KNLF(FM) Quincy CA
KNLR(FM) Bend OR
KNLT(FM) Walla Walla WA
*KNLU(FM) Monroe LA
KNLV-FM Ord NE
*KNMC(FM) Havre MT
*KNMI(FM) Farmington NM
KNMO(FM) Nevada MO
*KNNB(FM) Whiteriver AZ
KNNC(FM) Georgetown TX
KNNG-FM Sterling CO
KNNN(FM) Central Valley CA
KNOD(FM) Harlan IA
KNOE-FM Monroe LA
KNOF(FM) St. Paul MN
*KNOM-FM Nome AK
*KNON(FM) Dallas TX
KNOT-FM Prescott AZ
*KNOW-FM Minneapolis-St. Paul MN
KNOX-FM Grand Forks ND
*KNPR(FM) Las Vegas NV
KNSN(FM) Walla Walla WA
KNSP-FM Staples MN
*KNSQ(FM) Mount Shasta CA
*KNSR(FM) Collegeville MN
*KNSU(FM) Thibodaux LA
KNTI(FM) Lakeport CA
KNTL(FM) Bethany OK
*KNTN(FM) Thief River Falls MN
KNTO(FM) Livingston CA
*KNTU(FM) Denton TX
KNUC(FM) Smithfield UT
KNUE(FM) Tyler TX

KNUI-FM Kahului HI
KNUJ-FM Sleepy Eye MN
*KNWC-FM Sioux Falls SD
*KNWD(FM) Natchitoches LA
*KNWO(FM) Cottonwood ID
*KNWR(FM) Ellensburg WA
*KNWS-FM Waterloo IA
*KNWY(FM) Yakima WA
KNXR(FM) Rochester MN
*KNYD(FM) Broken Arrow OK
KNYN(FM) Santa Fe NM
KNZA(FM) Hiawatha KS

*KOAB-FM Bend OR
KOAI(FM) Fort Worth TX
KOAK-FM Red Oak IA
KOAX(FM) Mason TX
*KOBC(FM) Joplin MO
*KOCC(FM) Oklahoma City OK
KOCD(FM) Columbus KS
KOCN(FM) Pacific Grove CA
*KOCV(FM) Odessa TX
KODA(FM) Houston TX
KODJ(FM) Salt Lake City UT
KODM(FM) Odessa TX
KODS(FM) Carnelian Bay CA
KOEA(FM) Doniphan MO
KOEL-FM Oelwein IA
KOEZ(FM) Newton KS
KOFI-FM Kalispell MT
KOFM(FM) Enid OK
KOFX(FM) El Paso TX
KOGA-FM Ogallala NE
KOGM(FM) Opelousas LA
*KOHL(FM) Fremont CA
*KOHM(FM) Lubbock TX
*KOHS(FM) Orem UT
KOHT(FM) Marana AZ
KOHZ(FM) Billings MT
*KOIR(FM) Edinburg TX
KOIT-FM San Francisco CA
KOJJ(FM) East Porterville CA
*KOJO(FM) Lake Charles LA
KOKE(FM) Giddings TX
*KOKF(FM) Edmond OK
KOKN(FM) Hobbs NM
KOKR(FM) Newport AR
*KOKS(FM) Poplar Bluff MO
KOKU(FM) Agana GU
KOKX-FM Keokuk IA
KOKZ(FM) Waterloo IA
KOLA(FM) San Bernardino CA
KOLL(FM) Maumelle AR
KOLS(FM) Dodge City KS
KOLT-FM Santa Fe NM
*KOLU(FM) Pasco WA
KOLV(FM) Olivia MN
KOLX(FM) Barling AR
KOLY-FM Mobridge SD
KOLZ(FM) Bentonville AR
KOMA-FM Oklahoma City OK
KOMB(FM) Fort Scott KS
KOME(FM) San Jose CA
KOMP(FM) Las Vegas NV
KOMW-FM Omak WA
KOMX(FM) Pampa TX
KONA-FM Kennewick WA
KONE(FM) Lubbock TX
KONI(FM) Lanai City HI
KONO-FM Fredricksburg TX
*KONQ(FM) Dodge City KS
KONY-FM Kanab UT
KONZ(FM) Arizona City AZ
KOOC(FM) Belton TX
KOOI-FM Jacksonville TX
KOOJ(FM) Riverside CA
KOOL-FM Phoenix AZ
*KOOP(FM) Hornsby TX
KOOS(FM) North Bend OR
KOOU(FM) Hardy AR
KOOV(FM) Copperas Cove TX
KOOZ(FM) Great Falls MT
*KOPB-FM Portland OR
KOPE(FM) Medford OR
*KOPN(FM) Columbia MO
KOPR(FM) Butte MT
KOQL(FM) Oklahoma City OK
KOQO-FM Fresno CA
KORA-FM Bryan TX
KORD-FM Richland WA
KORL(FM) Honolulu HI
KORQ-FM Abilene TX
KORT-FM Grangeville ID
KOSI(FM) Denver CO
KOSO(FM) Patterson CA
KOSP(FM) Willard MO
KOST(FM) Los Angeles CA
*KOSU-FM Stillwater OK
KOSZ-FM Idaho Falls ID
KOTB(FM) Evanston WY
KOTD-FM Plattsmouth NE
KOTE(FM) Eureka KS
KOTM-FM Ottumwa IA
*KOTO(FM) Telluride CO
KOTR(FM) Cambria CA
KOTT(FM) Otterville MO
KOUA(FM) Mena AR
KOUL(FM) Sinton TX
KOUN(FM) Sherwood AR
KOUT(FM) Rapid City SD
KOUU(FM) American Falls ID
KOUY(FM) Belle Plaine KS
KOVC-FM Valley City ND
KOWF(FM) Escondido CA
KOXE(FM) Brownwood TX
KOYE(FM) Laredo TX
KOYN(FM) Paris TX
KOYT(FM) Los Lunas NM
KOZE-FM Lewiston ID
KOZI-FM Chelan WA
KOZT(FM) Fort Bragg CA
KOZX(FM) Cabool MO
KOZZ-FM Reno NV

*KPAC(FM) San Antonio TX
*KPAE(FM) Erwinville LA
KPAN-FM Hereford TX
KPAS(FM) Fabens TX
KPAT(FM) Sioux Falls SD
KPAY-FM Chico CA
KPBQ-FM Pine Bluff AR
*KPBS-FM San Diego CA
*KPBX-FM Spokane WA
*KPCC(FM) Pasadena CA
KPCH(FM) Dubach LA
KPCL(FM) Farmington NM
KPCR-FM Bowling Green MO
*KPCW(FM) Park City UT
KPDQ-FM Portland OR
*KPDR(FM) Wheeler TX
KPEL-FM Erath LA
KPEN-FM Soldotna AK
KPER(FM) Hobbs NM
KPEZ(FM) Austin TX
*KPFA(FM) Berkeley CA
*KPFB(FM) Berkeley CA
*KPFK(FM) Los Angeles CA
KPFM(FM) Mountain Home AR
*KPFT(FM) Houston TX
KPFX(FM) Fargo ND
*KPGM(FM) Casper WY
*KPGR(FM) Pleasant Grove UT
*KPHF(FM) Phoenix AZ
KPHR(FM) Milbank SD
KPIG(FM) Freedom CA
KPIK(FM) Beebe AR
KPJN(FM) Gonzales TX
KPKY(FM) Pocatello ID
KPLE(FM) Temple TX
KPLM(FM) Palm Springs CA
*KPLN-FM Plains TX
KPLO-FM Reliance SD
KPLT-FM Paris TX
*KPLU-FM Tacoma WA
KPLV(FM) Port Lavaca TX
KPLX(FM) Fort Worth TX
KPLZ(FM) Seattle WA
KPMW(FM) Haliimaile HI
KPMX(FM) Sterling CO
KPNC-FM Ponca City OK
KPND(FM) Sandpoint ID
*KPNE-FM North Platte NE
*KPNO(FM) Norfolk NE
KPNT(FM) Ste. Genevieve MO
KPNW-FM Eugene OR
KPNY(FM) Alliance NE
KPOA(FM) Lahaina HI
KPOC-FM Pocahontas AR
KPOD-FM Crescent North CA
KPOI-FM Honolulu HI
*KPOO(FM) San Francisco CA
KPOS-FM Post TX
KPPL(FM) Colusa CA
*KPPR(FM) Williston ND
KPQ-FM Wenatchee WA
KPQX(FM) Havre MT
*KPRA(FM) Ukiah CA
*KPRG(FM) Agana GU
KPRI(FM) Fagaitua AS
*KPRJ(FM) Jamestown ND
*KPRN(FM) Grand Junction CO
KPRQ(FM) Price UT
KPRR(FM) El Paso TX
KPRS(FM) Kansas City MO
KPRV-FM Heavener OK
*KPRX(FM) Bakersfield CA
KPSA-FM La Luz NM
*KPSC(FM) Palm Springs CA
KPSD(FM) Faith SD
KPSI-FM Palm Springs CA
KPSM(FM) Brownwood TX
KPSN(FM) Phoenix AZ
KPSO-FM Falfurrias TX
*KPSU(FM) Goodwell OK
KPTX(FM) Pecos TX
KPUR-FM Canyon TX
KPVS(FM) Hilo HI
*KPVU(FM) Prairie View TX
KPVV(FM) Dillingham AK
KPVW(FM) Aspen CO
KPVY(FM) Amarillo TX
KPVZ(FM) Beulah ND
KPWB-FM Piedmont MO
KPWR(FM) Los Angeles CA
KPXA(FM) Sisters OR
KPXC(FM) Indian Springs NV
KPXF(FM) Lacombe LA
KPXG(FM) Gainesville TX
KPXH(FM) Garapan-Saipan MP
KPXI(FM) Mount Pleasant TX
KPXP(FM) Garapan-Saipan MP
KPXR(FM) Anchorage AK
KPYN(FM) Atlanta TX

KQAA(FM) Aberdeen SD
KQAC(FM) Amarillo TX
KQAK(FM) Bend OR
*KQAL(FM) Winona MN
KQAY-FM Tucumcari NM
KQAZ(FM) Springerville-Eager AZ
KQBE(FM) Ellensburg WA
KQBR(FM) Davis CA
KQCL(FM) Faribault MN
KQCR(FM) Cedar Rapids IA
KQCS(FM) Bettendorf IA
KQDF-FM Larned KS
KQDI-FM Great Falls MT
KQDS-FM Duluth MN
KQDY(FM) Bismarck ND
*KQED-FM San Francisco CA
KQEG(FM) La Crescent MN
KQEM(FM) Seaside OR
KQEP(FM) Rock Valley IA
KQEW(FM) Fordyce AR
KQEX(FM) Rohnerville CA
KQFC(FM) Boise ID
*KQFE(FM) Springfield OR
KQFM(FM) Hermiston OR
KQFX(FM) Borger TX
KQHT(FM) Crookston MN
KQIC(FM) Willmar MN
KQID(FM) Alexandria LA
KQIK-FM Lakeview OR
KQIP(FM) Odessa TX
KQIX-FM Grand Junction CO
KQIZ-FM Amarillo TX
KQKD-FM Redfield SD
KQKI(FM) Bayou Vista LA
KQKQ-FM Council Bluffs IA
KQKS(FM) Longmont CO
KQKY(FM) Kearney NE
KQLA(FM) Ogden KS
KQLB(FM) Los Banos CA
KQLL-FM Owasso OK
KQLS(FM) Colby KS
KQLT(FM) Casper WY
KQLX-FM Lisbon ND
KQMA-FM Phillipsburg KS
KQMC-FM Brinkley AR
KQMG-FM Independence IA
*KQMN(FM) Thief River Falls MN
KQMQ-FM Honolulu HI
KQMT(FM) Eagle CO
KQMX(FM) Rolla MO
KQNC(FM) Quincy CA
KQNG-FM Lihue HI
KQNM(FM) Gallup NM
KQNN(FM) Alice TX
KQNS-FM Lindsborg KS
KQPM(FM) Ukiah CA
KQPR-FM Albert Lea MN
KQPT(FM) Sacramento CA
KQQK(FM) Galveston TX
KQQL(FM) Anoka MN
KQRC-FM Leavenworth KS
KQRK(FM) Ronan MT
KQRN(FM) Mitchell SD
KQRO-FM Cuero TX
KQRS-FM Golden Valley MN
KQRX(FM) Midland TX
KQSK(FM) Chadron NE
KQSS(FM) Miami AZ
KQST(FM) Sedona AZ
KQSW(FM) Rock Springs WY
KQTX(FM) Portland TX
KQTZ(FM) Hobart OK
KQUA(FM) Lutesville MO
KQUE(FM) Houston TX
KQUS-FM Hot Springs AR
KQUY-FM Butte MT
KQVN(FM) Royal City WA
KQVO(FM) Calexico CA
KQWB-FM Moorhead MN
KQWC-FM Webster City IA
KQXC(FM) Wichita Falls TX
KQXL-FM New Roads LA
KQXT(FM) San Antonio TX
KQXX(FM) McAllen TX
KQXY-FM Beaumont TX
KQYB(FM) Spring Grove MN
KQYN(FM) Twentynine Palms CA
KQZE(FM) St. Johns AZ

KRAB(FM) Green Acres CA
KRAI-FM Craig CO
KRAJ(FM) Johannesburg CA
KRAK-FM Sacramento CA
KRAO(FM) Colfax WA
KRAQ(FM) Jackson MN
KRAV(FM) Tulsa OK
KRAY-FM Salinas CA
KRAZ(FM) Farmington NM
KRBB(FM) Wichita KS
*KRBD(FM) Ketchikan AK
KRBE-FM Houston TX
KRBF(FM) Bonners Ferry ID
KRBG(FM) Bunkie LA
KRBH(FM) Hondo TX
KRBI-FM St. Peter MN
*KRBM(FM) Pendleton OR
KRBO(FM) Las Vegas NV
KRBZ(FM) Reedsport OR
*KRCB-FM Santa Rosa CA
*KRCC(FM) Colorado Springs CO
KRCH(FM) Rochester MN
KRCI(FM) Avalon CA
*KRCL(FM) Salt Lake City UT
KRCS(FM) Sturgis SD
*KRCU(FM) Cape Girardeau MO
KRCY(FM) Kingman AZ
*KRDC-FM St. George UT
KRDF-FM Spearman TX
KRDI-FM Decorah IA
KRDM(FM) Ardmore OK
KRDO-FM Colorado Springs CO
KRDS-FM Wickenburg AZ
KREA(FM) Ontario CA
KREB(FM) Huntsville AR
KREC(FM) Brian Head UT
KRED-FM Eureka CA
KREJ(FM) Medicine Lodge KS
KREK(FM) Bristow OK
KREL(FM) Copperopolis CA
KREP(FM) Belleville KS
KRES(FM) Moberly MO
KREW-FM Sunnyside WA
*KRFA-FM Moscow ID
KRFD-FM Marysville CA
KRFM(FM) Show Low AZ
KRFO-FM Owatonna MN
KRFS-FM Superior NE
KRFX(FM) Denver CO
KRGI-FM Grand Island NE
KRGQ-FM Roy UT
KRGT(FM) Hutto TX
KRHD-FM Duncan OK
*KRHS(FM) Overland MO
KRHT(FM) Carlsbad NM
KRHU(FM) Big Pine CA
*KRIC(FM) Rexburg ID
KRIG(FM) Nowata OK
KRIM(FM) Payson AZ
KRIO-FM Floresville TX
KRJB(FM) Ada MN
KRJC(FM) Elko NV
KRJT-FM Bowie TX
KRJY(FM) St. Louis MO
KRKC-FM King City CA
KRKM(FM) Kremmling CO
KRKN(FM) Oro Valley AZ
KRKS-FM Boulder CO
KRKT-FM Albany OR
KRKX(FM) Billings MT
KRKZ(FM) Altus OK
KRLB-FM Lubbock TX
*KRLF(FM) Pullman WA
KRLI(FM) Malta Bend MO
KRLK(FM) Cassville MO
KRLN-FM Canon City CO
KRLS(FM) Knoxville IA
KRLT(FM) South Lake Tahoe CA
KRLV(FM) Las Vegas NV
KRLW-FM Walnut Ridge AR
*KRLX(FM) Northfield MN
KRMD-FM Shreveport LA
KRMH-FM Leadville CO
KRMR(FM) Ketchum ID
KRNA(FM) Iowa City IA
*KRNC(FM) Reno NV
*KRNE-FM Merriman NE
*KRNL-FM Mount Vernon IA
KRNO-FM Reno NV
KRNQ(FM) Hampton IA
*KRNU(FM) Lincoln NE
*KRNW(FM) Chillicothe MO
KRNY(FM) Kearney NE
*KROA(FM) Grand Island NE
KROC-FM Rochester MN
KROE-FM Sheridan WY
KROF-FM Abbeville LA
KROG(FM) Phoenix OR
KROK(FM) De Ridder LA
KROL(FM) Las Cruces NM
KROM(FM) San Antonio TX
KROO(FM) Breckenridge TX
KROQ-FM Pasadena CA
KROR(FM) Yucca Valley CA
*KROU(FM) Spencer OK
KRPM-FM Tacoma WA
KRPQ(FM) Rohnert Park CA
*KRPR(FM) Rochester MN
*KRPS(FM) Pittsburg KS
KRPT-FM Anadarko OK
KRQA(FM) Amarillo TX
KRQK(FM) Lompoc CA
KRQQ(FM) Tucson AZ
KRQR(FM) San Francisco CA
KRQS(FM) Pagosa Springs CO
KRQU(FM) Laramie WY
KRRB(FM) Dickinson ND
*KRRC(FM) Portland OR
KRRD(FM) Dickinson ND
KRRG(FM) Laredo TX
KRRI(FM) Boulder City NV
KRRK(FM) Bennington NE
KRRM(FM) Rogue River OR
KRRO(FM) Sioux Falls SD
KRRQ(FM) Lafayette LA
KRRR(FM) Canton MO
KRRV-FM Alexandria LA
KRRW(FM) Dallas TX
KRSB-FM Roseburg OR
*KRSC-FM Claremore OK
*KRSD(FM) Sioux Falls SD
KRSE(FM) Yakima WA
KRSH(FM) Middletown CA
KRSI(FM) Garapan-Saipan MP
KRSJ(FM) Durango CO
*KRSM(FM) Dallas TX
KRSP-FM Salt Lake City UT
KRSR-FM Coos Bay OR
KRSS(FM) Chubbuck ID
KRST(FM) Albuquerque NM
*KRSU(FM) Appleton MN
KRSV-FM Afton WY
*KRSW-FM Worthington-Marshall MN
KRTH(FM) Los Angeles CA
KRTI(FM) Grinnell IA
KRTK(FM) Cleveland TX
*KRTM(FM) Temecula CA
KRTN-FM Raton NM
KRTR-FM Kailua HI
KRTS(FM) Seabrook TX
*KRTU(FM) San Antonio TX
KRTX(FM) Galveston TX
KRTY(FM) Los Gatos CA
KRTZ(FM) Cortez CO
*KRUA(FM) Anchorage AK
KRUE(FM) Waseca MN
*KRUI-FM Iowa City IA
KRUN-FM Ballinger TX
KRUU(FM) Boone IA
*KRUX(FM) Las Cruces NM
KRUZ(FM) Santa Barbara CA
KRVA-FM McKinney TX
KRVD(FM) Rio Dell CA
KRVE(FM) Brusly LA
KRVF(FM) Eudora AR
KRVG(FM) Eagle ID
*KRVH(FM) Rio Vista CA
KRVL(FM) Kerrville TX
*KRVM(FM) Eugene OR
KRVN-FM Lexington NE
KRVR(FM) Davenport IA
*KRVS(FM) Lafayette LA
KRVV(FM) Bastrop LA
KRWA-FM Waldron AR
*KRWG(FM) Las Cruces NM
KRWM(FM) Bremerton WA
KRWN(FM) Farmington NM
KRWQ(FM) Gold Hill OR
KRXK-FM Rexburg ID
KRXL(FM) Kirksville MO
KRXO(FM) Oklahoma City OK
KRXQ(FM) Roseville CA
KRXS-FM Globe AZ
KRXT(FM) Rockdale TX
KRXV(FM) Yermo CA
KRXX-FM Minneapolis MN
KRYD(FM) Telluride CO
KRYK(FM) Chinook MT
KRYL(FM) Gatesville TX
KRYS-FM Corpus Christi TX
*KRZA(FM) Alamosa CO
KRZK(FM) Branson MO
KRZQ-FM Tahoe City CA
KRZR(FM) Hanford CA
KRZZ-FM Derby KS

KSAB(FM) Robstown TX
KSAJ-FM Abilene KS
*KSAK(FM) Walnut CA
KSAM-FM Huntsville TX
KSAN-FM San Francisco CA
KSAR(FM) Salem AR
*KSAU(FM) Nacogdoches TX
KSAY(FM) Fort Bragg CA
*KSBA(FM) Coos Bay OR
*KSBC(FM) Hot Springs AR
KSBH(FM) Coushatta LA
*KSBJ(FM) Humble TX
KSBL(FM) Carpinteria CA
*KSBR(FM) Mission Viejo CA
KSBS-FM Pago Pago AS
KSBT(FM) Steamboat Springs CO
KSBZ(FM) Sitka AK
KSCB-FM Liberal KS
*KSCL(FM) Shreveport LA
KSCQ(FM) Silver City NM
KSCR-FM Benson MN
KSCS(FM) Fort Worth TX
*KSCU(FM) Santa Clara CA
*KSCV(FM) Kearney NE
KSD-FM St. Louis MO
*KSDA-FM Agat GU
*KSDB-FM Manhattan KS
*KSDJ(FM) Brookings SD
KSDL(FM) Sedalia MO
KSDM(FM) International Falls MN
KSDN-FM Aberdeen SD
KSDR-FM Watertown SD
*KSDS(FM) San Diego CA
KSDZ(FM) Gordon NE
KSEA(FM) Greenfield CA
KSEC(FM) Lamar CO
KSED(FM) Sedona AZ
KSEG(FM) Sacramento CA
KSEK-FM Girard KS
KSEL-FM Portales NM
KSEM-FM Seminole TX
KSEQ(FM) Visalia CA
*KSER(FM) Everett WA
KSET(FM) El Paso TX
KSEY-FM Seymour TX
KSEZ(FM) Sioux City IA
*KSFC(FM) Spokane WA
*KSFH(FM) Mountain View CA
KSFI(FM) Salt Lake City UT
KSFM(FM) Woodland CA
*KSFR(FM) Santa Fe NM
KSFX(FM) Roswell NM
KSGC(FM) Tusayan AZ
KSGI-FM St. George UT
*KSGN(FM) Riverside CA
KSHA(FM) Redding CA
KSHE(FM) Crestwood MO
*KSHI(FM) Zuni NM
KSHL(FM) Gleneden Beach OR
KSHN-FM Liberty TX
KSHR-FM Coquille OR
*KSHU(FM) Huntsville TX
KSID-FM Sidney NE
KSIQ(FM) Brawley CA
KSIR-FM Brush CO
KSIT(FM) Rock Springs WY

U.S. FM Stations by Call Letters

KSIZ(FM) Jacksonville TX
*KSJC-FM Stockton CA
*KSJD(FM) Cortez CO
*KSJE(FM) Farmington NM
KSJJ(FM) Redmond OR
KSJL-FM San Antonio TX
*KSJN(FM) Minneapolis MN
KSJO(FM) San Jose CA
KSJQ(FM) Savannah MO
*KSJR-FM Collegeville MN
*KSJS(FM) San Jose CA
*KSJV(FM) Fresno CA
*KSJY(FM) Lafayette LA
KSJZ(FM) Jamestown ND
*KSKA(FM) Anchorage AK
KSKB(FM) Brooklyn IA
KSKD(FM) Sweet Home OR
KSKE-FM Vail CO
*KSKF(FM) Klamath Falls OR
KSKG(FM) Salina KS
KSKI-FM Sun Valley ID
KSKK(FM) Staples MN
KSKL(FM) Scott City KS
KSKS(FM) Fresno CA
KSKU(FM) Hutchinson KS
*KSLC(FM) McMinnville OR
KSLK(FM) Auberry CA
KSLQ-FM Washington MO
KSLS(FM) Liberal KS
KSLT(FM) Spearfish SD
*KSLU(FM) Hammond LA
KSLV-FM Monte Vista CO
KSLX(FM) Scottsdale AZ
KSLY-FM San Luis Obispo CA
KSMB(FM) Lafayette LA
*KSMC(FM) Moraga CA
*KSMF(FM) Ashland OR
KSMG(FM) Seguin TX
*KSMR(FM) Winona MN
KSMT(FM) Breckenridge CO
*KSMU(FM) Springfield MO
KSNI-FM Santa Maria CA
KSNM(FM) Truth or
Consequences NM
KSNN(FM) Arlington TX
KSNO-FM Snowmass Village CO
KSNP(FM) Burlington KS
KSNR(FM) Thief River Falls MN
KSNY-FM Snyder TX
*KSOH(FM) Wapato WA
KSOL(FM) San Mateo CA
KSON-FM San Diego CA
KSOP-FM Salt Lake City UT
*KSOR(FM) Ashland OR
KSOS-FM Brigham City UT
KSOX-FM Raymondville TX
*KSPB(FM) Pebble Beach CA
*KSPC(FM) Claremont CA
KSPG(FM) Clearwater KS
KSPI-FM Stillwater OK
KSPK(FM) Walsenburg CO
KSPN-FM Aspen CO
KSPO(FM) Spokane WA
KSPQ(FM) West Plains MO
KSPY(FM) Quincy CA
KSPZ(FM) Colorado Springs CO
KSQA(FM) Wallace ID
*KSQD-FM Lowry SD
KSQQ(FM) Morgan Hill CA
KSQY(FM) Deadwood SD
KSRA-FM Salmon ID
KSRF(FM) Poipu HI
*KSRH(FM) San Rafael CA
KSRI(FM) Santa Cruz CA
KSRN(FM) Sparks NV
*KSRQ(FM) Thief River Falls MN
*KSRS(FM) Roseburg OR
KSRV-FM Ontario OR
KSRW(FM) Childress TX
KSRY(FM) San Francisco CA
KSSD(FM) Cedar City UT
KSSI(FM) China Lake CA
KSSJ(FM) Shingle Springs CA
KSSK-FM Waipahu HI
KSSN(FM) Little Rock AR
KSSZ-FM Oakes ND
KSTA-FM Coleman TX
KSTG(FM) Sikeston MO
*KSTK(FM) Wrangell AK
KSTN-FM Stockton CA
KSTO(FM) Agana GU
KSTP-FM St. Paul MN
KSTQ(FM) Alexandria MN
KSTR-FM Montrose CO
KSTT-FM Los Osos-
Baywood Park CA
KSTV-FM Stephenville TX
*KSTX(FM) San Antonio TX
KSTZ(FM) Des Moines IA
KSUA(FM) College AK
*KSUI(FM) Iowa City IA
KSUP(FM) Juneau AK
KSUR-FM Greenfield CA
*KSUT(FM) Ignacio CO
KSUV-FM McFarland CA
KSUX(FM) Winnebago NE
KSVA(FM) Corrales NM
*KSVR(FM) Mount Vernon WA
*KSWC(FM) Winfield KS
*KSWH(FM) Arkadelphia AR
KSWR(FM) Clinton OK
*KSWS(FM) Sisseton SD
KSWW(FM) Raymond WA
KSXY(FM) Fresno CA
KSYD(FM) Reedsport OR

*KSYE(FM) Frederick OK
*KSYM-FM San Antonio TX
KSYN(FM) Joplin MO
KSYV(FM) Solvang CA
KSYZ-FM Grand Island NE

KTAA(FM) Kerman CA
KTAG(FM) Cody WY
*KTAI(FM) Kingsville TX
KTAK(FM) Riverton WY
KTAL-FM Texarkana TX
KTAO(FM) Taos NM
KTBG(FM) Paso Robles CA
KTBQ(FM) Nacogdoches TX
*KTCC(FM) Colby KS
KTCF(FM) Crosby MN
KTCH-FM Wayne NE
KTCL(FM) Fort Collins CO
KTCM(FM) Kingman KS
KTCN(FM) Eureka Springs AR
KTCS-FM Fort Smith AR
*KTCU-FM Fort Worth TX
*KTCV(FM) Kennewick WA
KTCY(FM) Denison TX
KTCZ-FM Minneapolis MN
*KTDB(FM) Pine Hill NM
KTDI(FM) Huntsville MO
*KTDN(FM) Palestine TX
KTDR(FM) Del Rio TX
KTDY(FM) Lafayette LA
*KTEC(FM) Klamath Falls OR
KTEI(FM) Piggott AR
*KTEO(FM) Wichita Falls TX
*KTEP(FM) El Paso TX
*KTEQ(FM) Rapid City SD
KTEX(FM) Brownsville TX
KTFA(FM) Groves TX
KTFC(FM) Sioux City IA
KTFG(FM) Sioux Rapids IA
KTFM(FM) San Antonio TX
*KTFR(FM) Claremore OK
KTFX(FM) Tulsa OK
KTGL(FM) Beatrice NE
KTHK(FM) Okmulgee OK
KTHS-FM Berryville AR
KTHT(FM) Fresno CA
KTHX(FM) Reno NV
KTID-FM San Rafael CA
KTIE(FM) Bakersfield CA
KTIG(FM) Pequot Lakes MN
KTIJ(FM) Elk City OK
KTIL-FM Tillamook OR
*KTIS-FM Minneapolis MN
KTJC(FM) Rayville LA
KTJJ(FM) Farmington MO
KTJN(FM) Mercedes TX
*KTJO-FM Ottawa KS
KTJX(FM) Mission TX
KTKC(FM) Springhill LA
KTKU(FM) Juneau AK
KTLB(FM) Twin Lakes IA
KTLE-FM Tooele UT
*KTLF(FM) Colorado Springs CO
KTLI(FM) El Dorado KS
KTLO-FM Mountain Home AR
KTLR-FM Terrell TX
KTLS(FM) Ada OK
KTLT(FM) Wichita Falls TX
*KTLX(FM) Columbus NE
KTMC-FM McAlester OK
KTMN(FM) Los Alamos NM
KTMO(FM) Kennett MO
KTMT-FM Medford OR
KTMX(FM) York NE
*KTNA(FM) Talkeetna AK
*KTNE-FM Alliance NE
KTNT-FM Edmond OK
KTNY(FM) Libby MT
KTOC-FM Jonesboro LA
KTOD-FM Conway AR
KTOF(FM) Cedar Rapids IA
KTOM-FM Salinas CA
*KTOO(FM) Juneau AK
KTOT(FM) Big Bear Lake CA
KTOW-FM Sand Springs OK
KTOZ-FM Marshfield MO
*KTPB(FM) Kilgore TX
*KTPH(FM) Tonopah NV
KTPI(FM) Tehachapi CA
KTPK(FM) Topeka KS
*KTPR(FM) Fort Dodge IA
KTQM-FM Clovis NM
KTQQ(FM) Sulphur LA
*KTQX(FM) Bakersfield CA
KTRA(FM) Farmington NM
KTRI-FM Mansfield MO
KTRN(FM) Silverton CO
KTRR(FM) Loveland CO
KTRS(FM) Casper WY
*KTRU(FM) Houston TX
KTRX(FM) Tarkio MO
KTRY-FM Bastrop LA
KTRZ(FM) Riverton WY
KTSB(FM) Sioux Center IA
*KTSC-FM Pueblo CO
*KTSD-FM Reliance SD
KTSH(FM) Tishomingo OK
KTSL(FM) Medical Lake WA
KTSM-FM El Paso TX
KTSR(FM) College Station TX
*KTSU(FM) Houston TX
*KTSW(FM) San Marcos TX
*KTSY(FM) Caldwell ID
KTTI(FM) Yuma AZ
KTTL(FM) Alva OK

KTTN-FM Trenton MO
KTTS-FM Springfield MO
KTTX(FM) Brenham TX
KTTZ(FM) Ajo AZ
KTUF(FM) Kirksville MO
*KTUH(FM) Honolulu HI
KTUI-FM Sullivan MO
*KTUO(FM) Sonora CA
KTUX(FM) Carthage TX
KTWA(FM) Ottumwa IA
KTWB(FM) Sioux Falls SD
KTWC(FM) Glendale AZ
KTWI(FM) Warm Springs OR
KTWM(FM) Laurel MT
KTWN-FM Texarkana AR
KTWS(FM) Bend OR
KTWV(FM) Los Angeles CA
*KTXB(FM) Beaumont TX
*KTXK(FM) Texarkana TX
KTXN-FM Victoria TX
KTXQ(FM) Fort Worth TX
KTXR(FM) Springfield MO
*KTXT-FM Lubbock TX
KTXX(FM) Devine TX
KTXY(FM) Jefferson City MO
KTYD(FM) Santa Barbara CA
KTYL-FM Tyler TX
KTZA(FM) Artesia NM

*KUAC(FM) Fairbanks AK
KUAD-FM Windsor CO
*KUAF(FM) Fayetteville AR
KUAM-FM Agana GU
*KUAP(FM) Pine Bluff AR
*KUAR(FM) Little Rock AR
*KUAT-FM Tucson AZ
*KUAZ(FM) Tucson AZ
KUBB(FM) Mariposa CA
KUBE(FM) Seattle WA
*KUBO(FM) Calexico CA
KUBQ(FM) La Grande OR
*KUBS(FM) Newport WA
*KUCA(FM) Conway AR
*KUCB-FM Des Moines IA
*KUCI(FM) Irvine CA
*KUCR(FM) Riverside CA
KUCU(FM) Armijo NM
*KUCV(FM) Lincoln NE
KUDL(FM) Kansas City KS
KUDO(FM) Tucson AZ
KUEL(FM) Fort Dodge IA
*KUER(FM) Salt Lake City UT
KUEZ(FM) Lufkin TX
*KUFM(FM) Missoula MT
KUFO(FM) Portland OR
*KUFR(FM) Salt Lake City UT
KUFX(FM) Gilroy CA
KUGN-FM Eugene OR
*KUGS(FM) Bellingham WA
*KUHB(FM) St. Paul Island AK
*KUHF(FM) Houston TX
KUHG(FM) Milford NE
KUIC(FM) Vacaville CA
KUKA(FM) San Diego TX
KUKB(FM) Texarkana AR
KUKI-FM Ukiah CA
KUKN(FM) Kelso WA
KUKU-FM Willow Springs MO
KULE-FM Ephrata WA
KULF(FM) Brenham TX
KUMA-FM Pendleton OR
*KUMD-FM Duluth MN
*KUMM(FM) Morris MN
*KUMR(FM) Rolla MO
KUMT(FM) Centerville UT
KUMU-FM Honolulu HI
KUNA(FM) La Quinta CA
*KUNC-FM Greeley CO
*KUNI(FM) Cedar Falls IA
*KUNM(FM) Albuquerque NM
KUNQ(FM) Houston MO
*KUNR(FM) Reno NV
*KUNV(FM) Las Vegas NV
*KUNY(FM) Mason City IA
*KUOI-FM Moscow ID
KUOO(FM) Spirit Lake IA
*KUOP(FM) Stockton CA
*KUOR-FM Redlands CA
*KUOW(FM) Seattle WA
KUPD-FM Tempe AZ
KUPI-FM Idaho Falls ID
KUPL-FM Portland OR
*KUPS(FM) Tacoma WA
KUPU(FM) Pearl City HI
KURA(FM) Ouray CO
KURB-FM Little Rock AR
KURY-FM Brookings OR
*KUSC(FM) Los Angeles CA
*KUSD-FM Vermillion SD
*KUSF(FM) San Francisco CA
KUSN(FM) Coffeyville KS
*KUSP(FM) Santa Cruz CA
*KUSR(FM) Ames IA
*KUSU-FM Logan UT
*KUT(FM) Austin TX
KUTQ(FM) Bountiful UT
KUTT(FM) Fairbury NE
KUTZ(FM) Lampasas TX
KUUL(FM) Davenport IA
KUUZ(FM) Lake Village AR
KUVA(FM) Uvalde TX
*KUVO(FM) Denver CO
KUVR-FM Holdrege NE
*KUWJ(FM) Jackson WY
*KUWL(FM) Fairbanks AK

*KUWR(FM) Laramie WY
*KUWS(FM) Superior WI
*KUWZ(FM) Rock Springs WY
KUZZ-FM Bakersfield CA

KVAY(FM) Lamar CO
*KVAZ(FM) Henryetta OK
*KVCE(FM) Fallon NV
KVCK-FM Wolf Point MT
KVCL-FM Winnfield LA
*KVCM(FM) Helena MT
*KVCO(FM) Concordia KS
*KVCR(FM) San Bernardino CA
KVCX(FM) Gregory SD
*KVCY(FM) Fort Scott KS
*KVDP(FM) Dry Prong LA
*KVER(FM) El Paso TX
KVET-FM Austin TX
KVFM(FM) Logan UT
KVFX(FM) Manteca CA
KVGB-FM Great Bend KS
*KVHS(FM) Concord CA
KVHT(FM) Vermillion SD
KVIC(FM) Victoria TX
KVIL-FM Highland Park-Dallas TX
*KVIP-FM Redding CA
KVKI-FM Shreveport LA
KVLE(FM) Gunnison CO
KVLI-FM Lake Isabella CA
KVLL-FM Woodville TX
KVLR(FM) Twisp WA
KVLT(FM) Victoria TX
*KVLU(FM) Beaumont TX
KVLV-FM Fallon NV
KVLY(FM) Edinburg TX
KVMA-FM Magnolia AR
*KVMR(FM) Nevada City CA
*KVMV(FM) McAllen TX
KVMX(FM) Eastland TX
KVNA-FM Flagstaff AZ
*KVNE-FM Tyler TX
*KVNF(FM) Paonia CO
*KVNO(FM) Omaha NE
KVNR(FM) Alva OK
KVNV(FM) Norton KS
KVOD(FM) Denver CO
KVOL-FM Opelousas LA
KVOM-FM Morrilton AR
KVOO-FM Tulsa OK
KVOQ(FM) Carmel CA
KVOX-FM Moorhead MN
KVPA(FM) Port Isabel TX
KVPI-FM Ville Platte LA
*KVPR(FM) Fresno CA
KVRD-FM Cottonwood AZ
KVRH-FM Salida CO
KVRI(FM) Salt Lake City UT
KVRP-FM Haskell TX
KVRQ(FM) Atwater CA
*KVRS(FM) Lawton OK
KVRW(FM) Lawton OK
*KVRX(FM) Austin TX
KVRY(FM) Mesa AZ
*KVSC(FM) St. Cloud MN
KVST(FM) Huntsville TX
KVSV-FM Beloit KS
KVTF(FM) Williams AZ
*KVTI(FM) Tacoma WA
*KVTT(FM) Dallas TX
KVUU(FM) Pueblo CO
KVVA-FM Apache Junction AZ
KVVP(FM) Leesville LA
KVVQ-FM Victorville CA
KVVV(FM) Healdsburg CA
KVWC-FM Vernon TX
KVWG-FM Pearsall TX
KVWM-FM Show Low AZ
KVYF(FM) Wilson Creek WA
*KVYM(FM) Chester NE
KVYN(FM) St. Helena CA
KVYS(FM) St. George UT
KVYT(FM) Basalt CO
KVYV(FM) Vinton IA
KVYZ(FM) Thousand Palms CA

KWAN(FM) Gualala CA
*KWAR(FM) Waverly IA
KWAV(FM) Monterey CA
*KWAX(FM) Eugene OR
KWAY-FM Waverly IA
KWAZ(FM) Needles CA
*KWBH(FM) Rexburg ID
*KWBI(FM) Morrison CO
KWBR(FM) Pismo Beach CA
*KWBU(FM) Waco TX
*KWCB(FM) Floresville TX
KWCD(FM) Bisbee AZ
KWCK-FM Searcy AR
KWCL-FM Oak Grove LA
*KWCR-FM Ogden UT
*KWCW(FM) Walla Walla WA
KWCX(FM) Willcox AZ
KWDA(FM) White Hall AR
*KWDM(FM) West Des Moines IA
KWDQ(FM) Woodward OK
KWDX(FM) Silsbee TX
KWEH(FM) Camden AR
KWEI-FM Weiser ID
KWEN(FM) Tulsa OK
KWEO(FM) Garberville CA
KWES(FM) Ruidoso NM
KWEY-FM Weatherford OK
KWEZ(FM) Trumann AR
*KWFC(FM) Springfield MO
*KWFH(FM) Parker AZ
*KWFJ(FM) Roy WA

*KWFL(FM) Roswell NM
KWFM-FM Tucson AZ
KWFS(FM) Wichita Falls TX
KWFX(FM) Woodward OK
KWGH-FM Big Lake TX
*KWGS(FM) Tulsa OK
KWHL(FM) Anchorage AK
KWHN-FM Haynesville LA
KWHO(FM) Weed CA
KWHQ-FM Kenai AK
KWHT(FM) Pendleton OR
KWIC(FM) Topeka KS
KWIN(FM) Lodi CA
KWIQ-FM Moses Lake WA
*KWIT(FM) Sioux City IA
KWIZ-FM Santa Ana CA
*KWJC(FM) Liberty MO
KWJJ-FM Portland OR
KWJM(FM) Farmerville LA
KWKH-FM Shreveport LA
KWKK(FM) Dardanelle AR
KWKQ(FM) Graham TX
KWKR(FM) Leoti KS
KWKS(FM) Winfield KS
KWKZ(FM) Charleston MO
*KWLD(FM) Plainview TX
KWLF(FM) Fairbanks AK
KWLT(FM) North Crossett AR
KWLV(FM) Many LA
KWME(FM) Wellington KS
KWMQ(FM) Southwest City MO
*KWMU(FM) St. Louis MO
KWMW(FM) Maljamar NM
KWMX-FM Lakewood CO
KWNA-FM Winnemucca NV
*KWND(FM) Springfield MO
KWNE(FM) Ukiah CA
KWNG(FM) Red Wing MN
KWNO-FM Rushford MN
KWNR(FM) Henderson NV
KWNS(FM) Winnsboro TX
KWNZ(FM) Carson City NV
KWOA-FM Worthington MN
KWOD-FM Sacramento CA
KWOW(FM) Clifton TX
KWOX(FM) Woodward OK
KWOZ(FM) Mountain View AR
KWPN-FM West Point NE
KWQK(FM) Albuquerque NM
KWQL(FM) Dishman WA
KWRF-FM Warren AR
KWRK(FM) Window Rock AZ
KWRL(FM) La Grande OR
KWRP(FM) San Jacinto CA
*KWRS(FM) Spokane WA
*KWRV(FM) Sun Valley ID
KWRW(FM) Rusk TX
*KWSB-FM Gunnison CO
*KWSC(FM) Wayne NE
KWSM(FM) Sherman TX
*KWSO(FM) Warm Springs OR
KWSP(FM) Santa Margarita CA
KWST(FM) Brawley CA
KWTA(FM) Electra TX
*KWTS(FM) Canyon TX
KWTX-FM Waco TX
KWTY(FM) Cartago CA
*KWUR(FM) Clayton MO
*KWVA(FM) Eugene OR
KWVE(FM) San Clemente CA
KWVR-FM Enterprise OR
KWVS(FM) Kingsville TX
KWVV-FM Homer AK
*KWWC-FM Columbia MO
KWWK(FM) Rochester MN
KWWR(FM) Mexico MO
KWWV(FM) Morro Bay CA
KWWW-FM Quincy WA
KWXA(FM) Durango CO
KWXD(FM) Asbury MO
KWXE(FM) Glenwood AR
KWXH(FM) Sun City CA
KWXN(FM) Texico NM
*KWXP(FM) Magalia CA
KWXX-FM Hilo HI
KWXY-FM Cathedral City CA
KWYI(FM) Kawaihae HI
KWYK-FM Aztec NM
KWYN-FM Wynne AR
KWYO-FM Sheridan WY
KWYR-FM Winner SD
KWYX(FM) Jasper TX

KXAA(FM) Rock Island WA
KXAC(FM) St. James MN
KXAL-FM Pittsburg TX
KXAR-FM Hope AR
KXAX(FM) St. James MN
KXAZ(FM) Page AZ
*KXBJ(FM) Victoria TX
KXBS(FM) Santa Paula CA
KXBX-FM Lakeport CA
KXCC(FM) Rockport TX
*KXCI(FM) Tucson AZ
KXCL(FM) Yuba City CA
*KXCR(FM) El Paso TX
*KXCV(FM) Maryville MO
KXDA(FM) Chowchilla CA
KXDC-FM Carmel CA
KXDD(FM) Yakima WA
KXDE(FM) Merced CA
KXDL(FM) Browerville MN
KXDX(FM) Stuttgart AR
KXDZ(FM) Anchorage AK
*KXEI(FM) Havre MT

Broadcasting & Cable Yearbook 1994
B-464

KXEZ(FM) Los Angeles CA
KXFE(FM) Dumas AR
KXFM(FM) Santa Maria CA
KXFX(FM) Santa Rosa CA
KXGJ(FM) Bay City TX
KXGM-FM Muenster TX
KXGO(FM) Arcata CA
*KXGZ(FM) McAllen TX
KXHA(FM) Shafter CA
KXHM(FM) Orland CA
*KXHV(FM) Sacramento CA
KXHW(FM) Marked Tree AR
KXIA(FM) Marshalltown IA
KXIO(FM) Clarksville AR
KXIQ(FM) Bend OR
KXIT-FM Dalhart TX
*KXJZ(FM) Sacramento CA
*KXKB(FM) Kings Beach CA
KXKC(FM) New Iberia LA
KXKL-FM Denver CO
KXKQ(FM) Safford AZ
KXKT(FM) Atlantic IA
KXKX(FM) Knob Noster MO
KXKY(FM) Holdenville OK
KXKZ(FM) Ruston LA
KXL-FM Portland OR
*KXLC(FM) La Crescent MN
KXLE-FM Ellensburg WA
KXLK(FM) Haysville KS
KXLL(FM) Paradise Valley AZ
KXLM(FM) Oxnard CA
KXLP(FM) New Ulm MN
KXLR(FM) Fairbanks AK
KXLS(FM) Alva OK
*KXLU(FM) Los Angeles CA
KXLY-FM Spokane WA
*KXMS(FM) Joplin MO
KXMX(FM) Madera CA
*KXNE-FM Norfolk NE
KXNP(FM) North Platte NE
KXO-FM El Centro CA
KXOA-FM Sacramento CA
KXOF(FM) Bloomfield IA
KXOJ-FM Sapulpa OK
KXOK-FM Florissant MO
KXOR(FM) Thibodaux LA
KXOX-FM Sweetwater TX
KXOZ(FM) Mountain View MO
KXPC(FM) Lebanon OR
KXPO-FM Grafton ND
*KXPR(FM) Sacramento CA
KXPT(FM) Las Vegas NV
*KXPZ(FM) Lytle TX
KXRA-FM Alexandria MN
KXRC(FM) Clarendon AR
*KXRD(FM) Victorville CA
*KXRJ(FM) Russellville AR
KXRK(FM) Provo UT
KXRX(FM) Seattle WA
KXSA-FM Dermott AR
*KXSR(FM) Groveland CA
KXTC(FM) Thoreau NM
KXTJ(FM) Beaumont TX
KXTN-FM San Antonio TX
KXTQ-FM Lubbock TX
KXTR(FM) Kansas City MO
KXTZ(FM) Henderson NV
KXUS(FM) Springfield MO
KXXK(FM) Chickasha OK
KXXO(FM) Olympia WA
KXXS(FM) Toppenish WA
KXXY-FM Oklahoma City OK
KXXZ(FM) Barstow CA
KXYL-FM Brownwood TX
KXYQ(FM) Salem OR

KYA(FM) San Francisco CA
KYAJ(FM) Merced CA
KYAT(FM) Keokuk IA
KYAX(FM) Alturas CA
KYBA(FM) Stewartville MN
KYBD(FM) Copeland KS
KYBE(FM) Frederick OK
KYBG-FM Castle Rock CO
KYCK(FM) Crookston MN
KYCN-FM Wheatland WY
KYCS(FM) Rock Springs WY
KYCX-FM Mexia TX
*KYDS(FM) Sacramento CA
*KYDZ(FM) Cody WY
KYEA(FM) West Monroe LA
KYEE(FM) Alamogordo NM
KYEZ(FM) Salina KS
*KYFA(FM) Amarillo TX
*KYFB(FM) Pine Bluff AR
*KYFE(FM) Alexandria LA
*KYFF(FM) Fort Smith AR
*KYFI(FM) Lafayette LA
*KYFL(FM) Monroe LA
KYFM(FM) Bartlesville OK
*KYFS(FM) San Antonio TX
*KYFT(FM) Lubbock TX
*KYFW(FM) Wichita KS
KYFX(FM) Little Rock AR
KYGO-FM Denver CO
KYHT-FM Yermo CA
KYIS(FM) Oklahoma City OK
KYJC-FM Grants Pass OR
KYKA(FM) Naches WA
KYKC(FM) Byng OK
KYKD(FM) Bethel AK
KYKN-FM Nephi UT
KYKR(FM) Beaumont TX
KYKS(FM) Lufkin TX
KYKX(FM) Longview TX

KYKY(FM) St. Louis MO
KYKZ(FM) Lake Charles LA
KYLC(FM) Osage Beach MO
*KYMC(FM) Ballwin MO
KYMG(FM) Anchorage AK
KYMI(FM) Los Ybanez TX
KYMO-FM East Prairie MO
KYMS(FM) Santa Ana CA
KYMX(FM) Sacramento CA
KYNG(FM) Dallas TX
KYNN(FM) Lincoln NE
KYNU(FM) Jamestown ND
KYNZ(FM) Lone Grove OK
KYOC(FM) Yoakum TX
KYOO-FM Halfway MO
KYOT-FM Phoenix AZ
KYOU(FM) Wendover NV
KYQQ(FM) Arkansas City KS
KYRE(FM) Yreka CA
KYRK(FM) Eunice NM
KYRS(FM) Atwater MN
KYRX(FM) Chaffee MO
*KYSC(FM) Yakima WA
KYSL(FM) Frisco CO
KYSM-FM Mankato MN
KYSN(FM) East Wenatchee WA
KYSR(FM) Los Angeles CA
KYSS-FM Missoula MT
KYTC(FM) Northwood IA
KYTE(FM) Newport OR
KYTN(FM) Wrightsville AR
KYTT-FM Coos Bay OR
KYTX(FM) Beeville TX
KYUC(FM) Roland OK
KYUF(FM) Uvalde TX
KYXI(FM) Yuma AZ
KYXK(FM) Gurdon AR
KYXS-FM Mineral Wells TX
KYXX(FM) Ozona TX
KYXY(FM) San Diego CA
KYYA(FM) Billings MT
KYYI(FM) Burkburnett TX
KYYK(FM) Palestine TX
KYYS(FM) Kansas City MO
KYYT(FM) Goldendale WA
KYYX(FM) Minot ND
KYYY(FM) Bismarck ND
KYYZ(FM) Williston ND
KYZX(FM) Pueblo CO

KZAK(FM) Incline Village NV
KZAL(FM) Desert Center CA
KZAP(FM) Red Bluff CA
*KZAZ(FM) Bellingham WA
KZBB(FM) Poteau OK
KZBK-FM Brookfield MO
KZBL(FM) Natchitoches LA
KZBQ-FM Pocatello ID
KZCD(FM) Lawton OK
KZCR(FM) Fergus Falls MN
KZDG(FM) Greeley CO
KZDX(FM) Burley ID
KZEL-FM Eugene OR
KZEN(FM) Central City NE
KZEP-FM San Antonio TX
KZEY-FM Marshall TX
KZEZ(FM) St. George UT
KZFM(FM) Corpus Christi TX
KZFN(FM) Moscow ID
*KZFR(FM) Chico CA
KZFX(FM) Lake Jackson TX
KZGL(FM) Cottonwood AZ
KZGZ(FM) Agana GU
KZHE(FM) Stamps AR
KZHR(FM) Dayton WA
KZHT(FM) Provo UT
*KZIG(FM) Cave City AR
KZII-FM Lubbock TX
KZIN-FM Shelby MT
KZIO(FM) Superior WI
KZIQ-FM Ridgecrest CA
KZJH(FM) Jackson WY
KZKK(FM) Huron SD
KZKL-FM Rio Rancho NM
KZKS(FM) Rifle CO
KZKX(FM) Seward NE
KZKZ-FM Greenwood AR
KZLA-FM Los Angeles CA
KZLE(FM) Batesville AR
KZLN-FM Othello WA
KZLO-FM Bozeman MT
KZLS(FM) Great Bend KS
KZLT-FM East Grand Forks MN
KZLZ(FM) Kearny AZ
KZMA(FM) Poplar Bluff MO
KZMC-FM McCook NE
KZMG(FM) New Plymouth ID
KZMI(FM) San Jose MP
KZMK(FM) Sierra Vista AZ
KZMM(FM) Troy MO
KZMO-FM California MO
KZMQ-FM Greybull WY
KZMS(FM) Patterson CA
KZMT(FM) Helena MT
*KZMU(FM) Moab UT
KZMX-FM Hot Springs SD
KZMZ(FM) Alexandria LA
*KZNA(FM) Hill City KS
KZNC(FM) Huron SD
KZNM(FM) Grants NM
KZNN(FM) Rolla MO
KZOC(FM) Osage City KS
*KZOE(FM) Longview WA
KZOK-FM Seattle WA
KZON(FM) Phoenix AZ

KZOQ-FM Missoula MT
KZOR(FM) Hobbs NM
KZOZ(FM) San Luis Obispo CA
KZPD(FM) Ash Grove MO
KZPE(FM) Ford City CA
KZPF(FM) Ozark MO
KZPH(FM) Cashmere WA
KZPK(FM) Paynesville MN
*KZPN(FM) Bayside CA
KZPO(FM) Lindsay CA
KZPR(FM) Minot ND
KZPS(FM) Dallas TX
KZPX(FM) Nisswa MN
KZPY(FM) Los Lunas NM
KZQA(FM) North Little Rock AR
KZQB(FM) Davenport WA
KZQD(FM) Liberal KS
KZRB(FM) New Boston TX
KZRQ(FM) Santa Fe NM
KZRR(FM) Albuquerque NM
KZRX(FM) Globe AZ
KZSA(FM) Placerville CA
*KZSC(FM) Santa Cruz CA
*KZSD-FM Martin SD
*KZSE(FM) Rochester MN
KZSN-FM Hutchinson KS
KZSP(FM) South Padre Island TX
KZSQ-FM Sonora CA
KZSR(FM) Reno NV
KZST(FM) Santa Rosa CA
*KZSU(FM) Stanford CA
KZTA-FM Yakima WA
KZTO(FM) Ottawa KS
KZTQ(FM) Laredo TX
KZTX(FM) Refugio TX
KZUA(FM) Holbrook AZ
KZUB(FM) Tahoka TX
KZUD(FM) Wilburton OK
KZUL-FM Lake Havasu City AZ
*KZUM(FM) Lincoln NE
KZUS-FM Toledo OR
*KZUU(FM) Pullman WA
KZWA(FM) Lake Charles LA
KZWC(FM) Walnut Creek CA
KZXA(FM) Santa Fe NM
KZXB(FM) Homer LA
KZXR(FM) Prosser WA
KZXY-FM Apple Valley CA
KZYP(FM) Pine Bluff AR
KZYQ(FM) St. James MO
KZYR(FM) Avon CO
*KZYX(FM) Philo CA
KZZK-FM Creswell OR
KZZL-FM Pullman WA
KZZP(FM) Paradise CA
KZZT(FM) Moberly MO
KZZU-FM Spokane WA
KZZX-FM Alamogordo NM
KZZY-FM Devils Lake ND
KZZZ(FM) Kingman AZ

NEW FM Clovis NM
*NEW FM Cabo Rojo PR
*NEW FM Ivanhoe VA
NEW FM Swanton OH
NEW FM Brundidge AL
*NEW FM Great Falls MT
NEW FM Britt IA
NEW FM Hudson IA
NEW FM Maumelle AR
NEW FM St. Pauls NC
*NEW FM Ottawa FL
NEW FM Bastrop LA
*NEW FM Kalamazoo MI
NEW FM Epworth IA
*NEW FM Winston-Salem NC

WAAC(FM) Valdosta GA
*WAAE(FM) Hickory NC
WAAF(FM) Worcester MA
WAAG(FM) Galesburg IL
WAAH(FM) Houghton MI
WAAI(FM) Hurlock MD
WAAL(FM) Binghamton NY
WAAN(FM) Blackville SC
WAAO-FM Andalusia AL
WAAT(FM) Tiptonville TN
*WAAU(FM) Appleton WI
WAAW(FM) Williston SC
WAAZ-FM Crestview FL
WABB-FM Mobile AL
*WABE(FM) Atlanta GA
WABK-FM Gardiner ME
WABN-FM Abingdon VA
WABO-FM Waynesboro MS
*WABR-FM Tifton GA
WABT(FM) Dundee IL
WABZ-FM Albemarle NC
WACF(FM) Paris IL
*WACG-FM Augusta GA
WACJ(FM) Bowman SC
WACO-FM Waco TX
WACQ-FM Tuskegee AL
WACR-FM Columbus MS
WACT-FM Tuscaloosa AL
WADB(FM) Point Pleasant NJ
WADI(FM) Corinth MS
WADQ(FM) Westport NY
WADU-FM Reserve LA
WADW(FM) Pickford MI
WADY(FM) Jupiter FL
WAEB-FM Allentown PA
WAEE(FM) Plattsburgh NY
*WAEK(FM) Oakland MI
WAEL-FM Maricao PR
*WAEQ(FM) Palatka FL

*WAER(FM) Syracuse NY
WAES(FM) Teutopolis IL
WAEV(FM) Savannah GA
WAEY-FM Princeton WV
WAFC-FM Clewiston FL
*WAFG(FM) Fort Lauderdale FL
WAFH(FM) Northumberland PA
WAFI(FM) Unadilla GA
WAFL(FM) Milford DE
WAFM(FM) Amory MS
WAFN(FM) East Brewton AL
*WAFP(FM) Oxford NC
*WAFR(FM) FM Tupelo MS
WAFT(FM) Valdosta GA
WAFV(FM) Bridgehampton NY
WAFX(FM) Suffolk VA
WAFY(FM) Middletown MD
*WAFZ(FM) Belton SC
*WAGB(FM) Manahawkin NJ
WAGD(FM) Seelyville IN
WAGH(FM) Fort Mitchell AL
WAGI-FM Gaffney SC
*WAGP(FM) Beaufort SC
WAGR-FM Lexington MS
*WAGW(FM) Waynesboro GA
WAGX(FM) Manchester OH
WAHC(FM) Circleville OH
WAHR(FM) Huntsville AL
*WAHS(FM) Auburn Hills MI
WAIA(FM) Callahan FL
*WAIC(FM) Springfield MA
WAID(FM) Clarksdale MS
*WAIJ(FM) Grantsville MD
WAIL(FM) Key West FL
WAIN-FM Columbia KY
WAIR(FM) Atlanta MI
WAIV(FM) Spring Valley IL
WAJI(FM) Fort Wayne IN
WAJK(FM) La Salle IL
WAJY(FM) New Ellenton SC
WAKB(FM) Wrens GA
WAKG(FM) Danville VA
WAKH(FM) McComb MS
WAKO-FM Lawrenceville IL
WAKQ(FM) Paris TN
WAKU(FM) Crawfordville FL
WAKW(FM) Cincinnati OH
WAKX(FM) Duluth MN
*WALF(FM) Alfred NY
WALK-FM Patchogue NY
WALR(FM) Athens GA
WALV(FM) Cleveland TN
WALX(FM) Selma AL
WALY(FM) Bellwood PA
WALZ-FM Machias ME
WAMB-FM Donelson TN
*WAMC(FM) Albany NY
*WAMF(FM) Tallahassee FL
*WAMH(FM) Amherst MA
WAMI-FM Opp AL
*WAMK(FM) Kingston NY
WAMM-FM Bridgewater VA
WAMO-FM Pittsburgh PA
WAMQ(FM) Great Barrington MA
*WAMU(FM) Washington DC
WAMW-FM Washington IN
WAMZ(FM) Louisville KY
WANB-FM Waynesburg PA
*WANC(FM) Ticonderoga NY
WANT(FM) Lebanon TN
WANV-FM Staunton VA
WANY-FM Albany KY
WAOA(FM) Melbourne FL
*WAOI(FM) Corning NY
*WAOJ(FM) Vero Beach FL
WAOL(FM) Ripley OH
WAOR(FM) Niles MI
WAPE-FM Jacksonville FL
WAPI-FM Birmingham AL
WAPL-FM Appleton WI
*WAPN(FM) Holly Hill FL
WAPP(FM) Berryville VA
WAPQ(FM) Crestline OH
*WAPS(FM) Akron OH
*WAPX-FM Clarksville TN
WAQE-FM Rice Lake WI
WAQK(FM) Germantown TN
WAQQ(FM) Charlotte NC
WAQX-FM Manlius NY
WAQY-FM Springfield MA
WAQZ(FM) Milford OH
*WARC(FM) Meadville PA
*WARG(FM) Summit IL
WARM-FM York PA
WARQ(FM) Columbia SC
WARU-FM Peru IN
WARW(FM) Bethesda MD
WARX(FM) Hagerstown MD
*WARY(FM) Valhalla NY
WASE-FM Fort Knox KY
WASH(FM) Washington DC
WASK-FM Lafayette IN
WASL(FM) Dyersburg TN
WASP-FM Oliver PA
*WASU-FM Boone NC
WASZ(FM) Ashland-Lineville AL
WATB(FM) South Yarmouth MA
WATD-FM Marshfield MA
WATG(FM) Trion GA
WATZ-FM Alpena MI
WAUN(FM) Kewaunee WI
*WAUS(FM) Berrien Springs MI
WAVA(FM) Arlington VA
WAVC(FM) Duluth MN
WAVF(FM) Hanahan SC

WAVH(FM) Mobile AL
WAVI(FM) Christiansted VI
WAVK(FM) Marathon FL
*WAVM(FM) Maynard MA
WAVQ(FM) Inglis FL
WAVR(FM) Waverly NY
WAVT-FM Pottsville PA
WAVV(FM) Marco FL
WAVW(FM) Vero Beach FL
WAVX(FM) Thomaston ME
WAWC(FM) Syracuse IN
*WAWL-FM Red Bank TN
WAWV(FM) Sylacauga AL
WAWZ(FM) Zarephath NJ
WAXI(FM) Rockville IN
WAXM(FM) Big Stone Gap VA
WAXQ(FM) New York NY
WAXS(FM) Oak Hill WV
WAXT(FM) Alexandria IN
WAXX(FM) Eau Claire WI
WAXY(FM) Fort Lauderdale FL
WAXZ(FM) Georgetown OH
WAYA(FM) Spring City TN
WAYB-FM Graysville TN
WAYC-FM Bedford PA
*WAYF(FM) West Palm Beach FL
*WAYG(FM) Sarasota FL
*WAYJ(FM) Fort Myers FL
*WAYL(FM) St. Augustine FL
*WAYM(FM) Columbia TN
WAYS(FM) Macon GA
WAYV(FM) Atlantic City NJ
WAYZ-FM Waynesboro PA
WAZK(FM) Trinity AL
WAZR(FM) Woodstock VA
WAZU(FM) Springfield OH
WAZY(FM) Lafayette IN
WAZZ(FM) Laurinburg NC

*WBAA-FM West Lafayette IN
WBAB-FM Babylon NY
WBAD(FM) Leland MS
*WBAI(FM) New York NY
WBAM-FM Montgomery AL
WBAQ(FM) Greenville MS
WBAR-FM Lake Luzerne NY
*WBAU(FM) Garden City NY
WBAW-FM Barnwell SC
WBAZ(FM) Southold NY
WBBA-FM Pittsfield IL
WBBC-FM Blackstone VA
WBBG(FM) Youngstown OH
WBBK-FM Blakely GA
WBBM-FM Chicago IL
WBBN(FM) Taylorsville MS
WBBO-FM Forest City NC
WBBQ-FM Augusta GA
WBBS(FM) Fulton NY
WBBV(FM) Vicksburg MS
WBBY(FM) Cedar Bluff VA
WBCG(FM) Murfreesboro NC
WBCH-FM Hastings MI
*WBCL(FM) Fort Wayne IN
WBCM(FM) Boyne City MI
WBCN(FM) Boston MA
*WBCR-FM Beloit WI
WBCS(FM) Boston MA
WBCT(FM) Grand Rapids MI
*WBCX(FM) Gainesville GA
*WBCY(FM) Archbold OH
WBDC(FM) Huntingburg IN
*WBDG(FM) Indianapolis IN
WBDK(FM) Algoma WI
WBDX(FM) Trenton GA
WBDY-FM Bluefield VA
WBEA(FM) Montauk NY
WBEB(FM) Philadelphia PA
WBEC-FM Pittsfield MA
WBEE-FM Rochester NY
*WBER(FM) Henrietta NY
WBES-FM Dunbar WV
*WBEZ(FM) Chicago IL
WBFG(FM) Effingham IL
*WBFH(FM) Bloomfield Hills MI
*WBFI(FM) McDaniels KY
WBFL(FM) Bellows Falls VT
WBFM(FM) Seneca SC
*WBFO(FM) Buffalo NY
*WBFR(FM) Birmingham AL
WBGA(FM) Waycross GA
WBGE(FM) Peoria IL
WBGF(FM) Belle Glade FL
*WBGL(FM) Champaign IL
WBGM-FM Tallahassee FL
*WBGO(FM) Newark NJ
*WBGU(FM) Bowling Green OH
WBGV(FM) Marlette MI
*WBGW(FM) Fort Branch IN
WBHA(FM) Hot Springs VA
WBHC-FM Hampton SC
*WBHI(FM) Chicago IL
*WBHL(FM) Florence AL
*WBHM(FM) Birmingham AL
WBHQ(FM) Bloomfield IN
WBHT(FM) Mountaintop PA
WBHV(FM) State College PA
*WBHY-FM Mobile AL
WBIG-FM Washington DC
WBIL-FM Tuskegee AL
*WBIM-FM Bridgewater MA
WBIN-FM Benton TN
WBIO(FM) Philpot KY
WBIP-FM Booneville MS
WBIZ-FM Eau Claire WI
*WBJB-FM Lincroft NJ

Broadcasting & Cable Yearbook 1994
B-465

U.S. FM Stations by Call Letters

*WBJC(FM) Baltimore MD
WBJI(FM) Blackduck MN
*WBKE-FM North Manchester IN
WBKJ(FM) Kosciusko MS
WBKN(FM) Brookhaven MS
WBKR(FM) Owensboro KY
*WBLD(FM) Orchard Lake MI
WBLE(FM) Batesville MS
WBLG(FM) Smiths Grove KY
WBLI(FM) Patchogue NY
WBLK(FM) Depew NY
WBLM(FM) Portland ME
WBLN-FM Murray KY
WBLQ(FM) Block Island RI
WBLS(FM) New York NY
*WBLU-FM Grand Rapids MI
*WBLV(FM) Twin Lake MI
WBLX-FM Mobile AL
WBLZ(FM) Mt. Vernon IN
WBMI(FM) West Branch MI
*WBMT(FM) Boxford MA
WBMW(FM) Ledyard CT
WBMX(FM) Boston MA
WBNF(FM) Marianna FL
*WBNH(FM) Pekin IL
*WBNI-FM Fort Wayne IN
WBNJ(FM) Cape May Court House NJ
WBNK(FM) Christiansburg VA
WBNL-FM Boonville IN
WBNO-FM Bryan OH
WBNQ(FM) Bloomington IL
WBNS-FM Columbus OH
WBNT-FM Oneida TN
WBNV(FM) Barnesville OH
*WBNY(FM) Buffalo NY
WBNZ(FM) Frankfort MI
*WBOB-FM Minneapolis MN
WBOG(FM) Tomah WI
WBOP(FM) Churchville VA
WBOQ(FM) Gloucester MA
*WBOR(FM) Brunswick ME
WBOS(FM) Brookline MA
WBOX-FM Varnado LA
WBPK(FM) Flemingsburg KY
WBPM(FM) Kingston NY
WBPP(FM) Strasburg VA
*WBPV(FM) Charlton MA
WBPW(FM) Presque Isle ME
WBQB(FM) Fredericksburg VA
WBQQ(FM) Kennebunk ME
WBQR(FM) Attica IN
WBRF(FM) Galax VA
*WBRH(FM) Baton Rouge LA
WBRN-FM Big Rapids MI
WBRQ(FM) Cidra PR
WBRR(FM) Bradford PA
*WBRS(FM) Waltham MA
WBRU(FM) Providence RI
WBRV-FM Boonville NY
WBRX(FM) Patton PA
WBSB(FM) Dade City FL
*WBSD(FM) Burlington WI
*WBSL-FM Sheffield MA
*WBSN-FM New Orleans LA
WBSS-FM Millville NJ
*WBST(FM) Muncie IN
*WBSU(FM) Brockport NY
WBSY(FM) Rose Hill NC
WBSZ(FM) Ashland WI
WBT-FM Charlotte NC
WBTF(FM) Attica NY
WBTG-FM Sheffield AL
WBTI(FM) Lexington MI
WBTQ(FM) Buckhannon WV
WBTR-FM Carrollton GA
WBTU(FM) Kendallville IN
WBTY(FM) Homerville GA
WBTZ(FM) Pinconning MI
WBUB(FM) North Charleston SC
WBUC-FM Buckhannon WV
WBUF(FM) Buffalo NY
WBUG-FM Fort Plain NY
WBUK(FM) Fort Shawnee OH
*WBUQ(FM) Bloomsburg PA
*WBUR(FM) Boston MA
WBUS(FM) Kankakee IL
WBVI(FM) Fostoria OH
*WBVM(FM) Tampa FL
*WBVN(FM) Carrier Mills IL
WBVR(FM) Russellville KY
WBWB(FM) Bloomington IN
*WBWC(FM) Berea OH
WBWI-FM West Bend WI
WBWN(FM) Le Roy IL
WBWZ(FM) New Paltz NY
WBXB(FM) Edenton NC
WBXE(FM) Baxter TN
*WBXL(FM) Baldwinsville NY
WBXQ(FM) Cresson PA
WBXX(FM) Battle Creek MI
WBYA(FM) Searsport ME
WBYB(FM) Brunswick GA
WBYG(FM) Point Pleasant WV
WBYN(FM) Boyertown PA
*WBYO(FM) Sellersville PA
*WBYQ(FM) Baltimore MD
WBYR(FM) Van Wert OH
WBYS-FM Canton IL
*WBYW(FM) Grand Rapids MI
WBYZ(FM) Baxley GA
*WBZC(FM) Pemberton NJ
WBZK-FM Chester SC
WBZN(FM) Old Town ME
WBZO(FM) Bay Shore NY

WBZW(FM) Loudonville OH
WBZX(FM) Columbus OH
WBZZ(FM) Pittsburgh PA

WCAC(FM) Sebring FL
WCAD(FM) San Juan PR
*WCAL(FM) Northfield MN
*WCAN(FM) Canajoharie NY
WCAT-FM Athol MA
WCAV(FM) Brockton MA
WCAZ-FM Carthage IL
WCBA-FM Corning NY
WCBH(FM) Casey IL
WCBK-FM Martinsville IN
WCBL-FM Benton KY
*WCBN-FM Ann Arbor MI
WCBR-FM Arlington Heights IL
WCBS-FM New York NY
*WCBU(FM) Peoria IL
WCBW(FM) Columbia IL
WCCA(FM) Shallotte NC
WCCC-FM Hartford CT
*WCCE(FM) Buie's Creek NC
WCCG(FM) Hope Mills NC
*WCCH(FM) Holyoke MA
WCCI(FM) Savanna IL
WCCK(FM) Calvert City KY
WCCN-FM Neillsville WI
WCCQ(FM) Crest Hill IL
WCCR(FM) Clarion PA
*WCCT-FM Harwich MA
*WCCV(FM) Cartersville GA
WCCW-FM Traverse City MI
*WCCX(FM) Waukesha WI
WCCZ(FM) Spangler PA
WCDA(FM) Vorheesville NY
*WCDB(FM) Albany NY
*WCDE(FM) Elkins WV
WCDJ(FM) Truro MA
WCDK(FM) Cadiz OH
WCDO-FM Sidney NY
WCDQ(FM) Sanford ME
*WCDR-FM Cedarville OH
WCDV(FM) Covington IN
WCDX(FM) Mechanicsville VA
*WCEB(FM) Corning NY
WCEF(FM) Ripley WV
WCEI-FM Easton MD
WCEM-FM Cambridge MD
WCEN-FM Mount Pleasant MI
WCEZ(FM) Delaware OH
WCFB(FM) Daytona Beach FL
*WCFE-FM Plattsburgh NY
WCFI(FM) Lajas PR
WCFL(FM) Morris IL
WCFR-FM Springfield VT
WCFW(FM) Chippewa Falls WI
WCFX(FM) Clare MI
WCGQ(FM) Columbus GA
WCGX(FM) Cleveland GA
WCGY(FM) Lawrence MA
*WCHC(FM) Worcester MA
WCHO-FM Washington Court House OH
WCHQ-FM Camuy PR
WCHR(FM) Trenton NJ
*WCHW-FM Bay City MI
WCHX(FM) Lewistown PA
WCHY-FM Savannah GA
WCHZ(FM) Harlem GA
WCIB(FM) Falmouth MA
*WCIC(FM) Pekin IL
*WCID(FM) Friendship NY
*WCIE-FM Lakeland FL
WCIF(FM) Melbourne FL
WCIG(FM) Mullins SC
*WCIH(FM) Elmira NY
*WCII(FM) Spencer NY
WCIK(FM) Bath NY
WCIL-FM Carbondale IL
WCIR-FM Beckley WV
*WCIY(FM) Canandaigua NY
WCIZ(FM) Watertown NY
WCJC(FM) Van Buren IN
WCJM(FM) West Point GA
WCJO(FM) Jackson OH
WCJX(FM) Five Points FL
WCKA(FM) Sutton WV
WCKG(FM) Elmwood Park IL
WCKO(FM) Carrollton AL
WCKQ(FM) Campbellsville KY
WCKR(FM) Hornell NY
WCKS(FM) Fruithurst AL
WCKT(FM) Lehigh Acres FL
WCKU(FM) Nicholasville KY
WCKW-FM La Place LA
WCKX(FM) London OH
WCKZ-FM Gastonia NC
WCLA-FM Claxton GA
WCLB-FM Framingham MA
WCLC-FM Jamestown TN
WCLD-FM Cleveland MS
WCLG-FM Morgantown WV
*WCLH(FM) Wilkes-Barre PA
*WCLK(FM) Atlanta GA
*WCLL-FM Wesson MS
WCLN-FM Clinton NC
*WCLQ(FM) Wausau WI
WCLR(FM) Piqua OH
WCLS(FM) Oscoda MI
WCLT-FM Newark OH
WCLV(FM) Cleveland OH
WCLX(FM) Mio MI
WCLZ-FM Brunswick ME
WCME(FM) Boothbay Harbor ME

WCMF-FM Rochester NY
WCMI-FM Catlettsburg KY
WCMJ(FM) Cambridge OH
*WCML-FM Alpena MI
WCMM(FM) Gulliver MI
WCMN-FM Arecibo PR
*WCMO(FM) Marietta OH
WCMP-FM Pine City MN
WCMQ-FM Hialeah FL
WCMS-FM Norfolk VA
WCMT-FM Martin TN
*WCMU-FM Mount Pleasant MI
*WCMW-FM Harbor Springs MI
*WCMZ-FM Sault Ste. Marie MI
WCNB-FM Connersville IN
WCNG(FM) Murphy NC
WCNH(FM) Belmont NH
*WCNI(FM) New London CT
*WCNJ(FM) Hazlet NJ
WCNL(FM) Carlinville IL
*WCNO(FM) Palm City FL
*WCNY-FM Syracuse NY
WCOD-FM Hyannis MA
WCOE(FM) La Porte IN
WCOF(FM) Tampa FL
WCOL-FM Columbus OH
WCON-FM Cornelia GA
WCOS-FM Columbia SC
*WCOT(FM) Jamestown NY
*WCOU(FM) Warsaw NY
WCOW-FM Sparta WI
*WCPE(FM) Raleigh NC
*WCPN(FM) Cleveland OH
WCPZ(FM) Sandusky OH
WCQA(FM) Fredonia NY
WCQL-FM York Center ME
WCQM(FM) Park Falls WI
*WCQS(FM) Asheville NC
WCRB(FM) Waltham MA
WCRC(FM) Effingham IL
*WCRF(FM) Cleveland OH
*WCRH(FM) Williamsport MD
WCRI(FM) Eureka IL
*WCRP(FM) Guayama PR
WCRQ-FM Arab AL
WCRR-FM Rural Retreat VA
*WCRT(FM) Terre Haute IN
*WCRX(FM) Chicago IL
WCRZ(FM) Flint MI
*WCSB(FM) Cleveland OH
WCSD(FM) Livingston TN
WCSE(FM) Bridgman MI
*WCSF(FM) Joliet IL
*WCSG(FM) Grand Rapids MI
*WCSK(FM) Kingsport TN
WCSM-FM Celina OH
WCSO(FM) Portland ME
WCSR-FM Hillsdale MI
WCST-FM Berkeley Springs WV
*WCSU-FM Wilberforce OH
WCSX(FM) Birmingham MI
WCSY-FM South Haven MI
WCTB(FM) Fairfield ME
WCTH(FM) Plantation Key FL
WCTK(FM) New Bedford MA
WCTL(FM) Union City PA
WCTQ(FM) Venice FL
WCTT-FM Corbin KY
WCTU(FM) Tazewell TN
WCTW(FM) Catskill NY
WCTX(FM) Palmyra PA
WCTY(FM) Norwich CT
*WCUC-FM Clarion PA
WCUL(FM) Culpeper VA
*WCUW(FM) Worcester MA
WCUZ-FM Grand Rapids MI
*WCVE(FM) Richmond VA
*WCVF-FM Fredonia NY
*WCVH(FM) Flemington NJ
*WCVJ(FM) Jefferson OH
*WCVK(FM) Bowling Green KY
*WCVM(FM) Bronson MI
*WCVO(FM) Gahanna OH
WCVP-FM Robbinsville NC
WCVQ(FM) Fort Campbell KY
WCVR-FM Randolph VT
WCVS-FM Virden IL
WCVU(FM) Naples FL
*WCVV(FM) Belpre OH
*WCVY(FM) Coventry RI
*WCVZ(FM) Zanesville OH
WCWB-FM Trenton FL
*WCWL(FM) Stockbridge MA
*WCWM(FM) Williamsburg VA
*WCWP(FM) Brookville NY
*WCWS(FM) Wooster OH
*WCWT-FM Centerville OH
WCWV(FM) Summersville WV
WCXL(FM) Kill Devil Hills NC
WCXR-FM Woodbridge VA
WCXT(FM) Hart MI
WCXU(FM) Caribou ME
WCXX(FM) Madawaska ME
*WCYC(FM) Chicago IL
*WCYJ-FM Waynesburg PA
WCYK-FM Crozet VA
WCYN-FM Cynthiana KY
WCYO(FM) Irvine KY
*WCYT(FM) Lafayette Township IN
WCZI(FM) Washington NC
WCZQ(FM) Monticello IL
WCZX(FM) Hyde Park NY
WCZY-FM Mount Pleasant MI

WDAC(FM) Lancaster PA
WDAI(FM) Pawley's Island SC
WDAQ(FM) Danbury CT
WDAR-FM Darlington SC
WDAS-FM Philadelphia PA
*WDAV(FM) Davidson NC
WDAY-FM Fargo ND
WDBA(FM) DuBois PA
*WDBK(FM) Blackwood NJ
WDBL-FM Springfield TN
*WDBM(FM) East Lansing MI
WDBN(FM) Wrightsville GA
WDBR(FM) Springfield IL
WDBS(FM) Bolingbroke GA
*WDCB(FM) Glen Ellyn IL
*WDCC(FM) Sanford NC
*WDCE(FM) Richmond VA
WDCG(FM) Durham NC
WDCI(FM) Bridgeport WV
WDCK(FM) Williamsburg VA
*WDCL-FM Somerset KY
WDCM(FM) Cruz Bay VI
*WDCO-FM Cochran GA
*WDCU(FM) Washington DC
*WDCV-FM Carlisle PA
WDCX(FM) Buffalo NY
WDCZ(FM) Webster NY
WDDC(FM) Portage WI
WDDD-FM Marion IL
WDDJ(FM) Paducah KY
WDDK(FM) Greensboro GA
WDDQ(FM) Adel GA
WDEB-FM Jamestown TN
WDEC-FM Americus GA
WDEF-FM Chattanooga TN
WDEH-FM Sweetwater TN
WDEK(FM) De Kalb IL
WDEN-FM Macon GA
*WDEQ-FM De Graff OH
*WDET-FM Detroit MI
WDEV-FM Warren VT
WDEZ(FM) Wausau WI
*WDFB-FM Danville KY
*WDFH(FM) Ossining NY
WDFL-FM Cross City FL
WDFM(FM) Defiance OH
WDFX(FM) Cleveland MS
*WDGC-FM Downers Grove IL
WDHA-FM Dover NJ
WDHI(FM) Delhi NY
WDHR(FM) Pikeville KY
WDIC-FM Clinchco VA
WDIF(FM) Marion OH
*WDIH(FM) Salisbury MD
*WDIY(FM) Allentown PA
WDIZ(FM) Orlando FL
WDJB(FM) Columbia City IN
WDJC(FM) Birmingham AL
*WDJM-FM Framingham MA
WDJR(FM) Enterprise AL
*WDJW(FM) Somers CT
WDJX-FM Louisville KY
WDKB(FM) De Kalb IL
WDKC(FM) Covington PA
WDKM(FM) Adams WI
WDKX(FM) Rochester NY
WDLA-FM Walton NY
WDLE(FM) Benton PA
WDLF(FM) Old Fort NC
WDLJ(FM) Indianola MS
*WDLM-FM East Moline IL
WDLS(FM) Dallas PA
WDLT(FM) Chickasaw AL
WDLX(FM) Washington NC
WDLY(FM) Gatlinburg TN
WDME-FM Dover-Foxcroft ME
WDMG-FM Douglas GA
WDML(FM) Woodlawn IL
WDMP-FM Dodgeville WI
WDMS(FM) Greenville MS
WDMT(FM) Eufaula AL
WDMX(FM) Vienna WV
*WDNA(FM) Miami FL
WDND(FM) Wilmington IL
WDNE-FM Elkins WV
WDNH-FM Honesdale PA
WDNL(FM) Danville IL
WDNO(FM) Laurel DE
*WDNR(FM) Chester PA
WDNS(FM) Bowling Green KY
WDNT-FM Dayton TN
*WDNX(FM) Olive Hill TN
WDNY-FM Dansville NY
WDOD-FM Chattanooga TN
WDOG-FM Allendale SC
WDOH(FM) Delphos OH
WDOK(FM) Cleveland OH
*WDOM(FM) Providence RI
WDOR-FM Sturgeon Bay WI
WDOT(FM) Essex NY
WDOW-FM Dowagiac MI
WDOX(FM) Wildwood Crest NJ
WDOY(FM) Fajardo PR
*WDPG(FM) Greenville OH
*WDPR(FM) Dayton OH
*WDPS(FM) Dayton OH
WDQN-FM DuQuoin IL
WDRC-FM Hartford CT
WDRE-FM Garden City NY
WDRK(FM) Callaway FL
WDRM(FM) Decatur AL
WDRP(FM) Windsor NC
WDRZ-FM Etowah TN
WDSD(FM) Dover DE
WDSN(FM) Reynoldsville PA

*WDSO(FM) Chesterton IN
WDSP(FM) Arlington NY
WDST(FM) Woodstock NY
WDSY-FM Pittsburgh PA
WDTL-FM Cleveland MS
*WDTR(FM) Detroit MI
*WDUB(FM) Granville OH
WDUK(FM) Havana IL
*WDUQ(FM) Pittsburgh PA
WDUV(FM) Bradenton FL
WDUX-FM Waupaca WI
WDVE(FM) Pittsburgh PA
*WDVI(FM) Dadeville AL
*WDVR(FM) Delaware Township NJ
*WDVX(FM) Clinton TN
*WDWN(FM) Auburn NY
WDXC(FM) Pound VA
WDXE-FM Lawrenceburg TN
WDXR-FM Golconda IL
WDXX(FM) Selma AL
WDYL(FM) Chester VA
*WDYN-FM Chattanooga TN
WDZQ(FM) Decatur IL
WDZR(FM) Mount Clemens MI
WDZZ-FM Flint MI

*WEAA(FM) Baltimore MD
WEAG-FM Starke FL
WEAI(FM) Lynnville IL
WEAS-FM Savannah GA
WEAT-FM West Palm Beach FL
*WEAX(FM) Angola IN
WEBB(FM) Waterville ME
WEBE(FM) Westport CT
WEBK(FM) Killington VT
WEBN(FM) Cincinnati OH
WEBQ-FM Eldorado IL
*WEBT(FM) Langdale AL
WEBZ(FM) Mexico Beach FL
WECB(FM) Seymour WI
*WECE(FM) Due West SC
*WECI(FM) Richmond IN
WECL(FM) Elk Mound WI
WECO-FM Wartburg TN
WECR(FM) Beech Mountain NC
*WECS(FM) Willimantic CT
*WECU(FM) Peoria IL
*WECW(FM) Elmira NY
WECY-FM Seaford DE
WEDG(FM) Edgewater FL
*WEDM(FM) Indianapolis IN
WEDR(FM) Miami FL
*WEDW-FM Stamford CT
*WEEC(FM) Springfield OH
*WEEE(FM) Cherry Hill NJ
WEEJ(FM) Port Charlotte FL
WEEL(FM) Shadyside OH
*WEEM(FM) Pendleton IN
WEEZ(FM) Heidelberg MS
WEFG-FM Whitehall MI
WEFM(FM) Michigan City IN
*WEFR(FM) Erie PA
*WEFT(FM) Champaign IL
WEFX(FM) Norwalk CT
WEGC(FM) Leesburg GA
WEGE(FM) Crossville TN
*WEGL(FM) Auburn AL
WEGM(FM) Hormigueros PR
WEGR(FM) Memphis TN
*WEGS(FM) Milton FL
WEGV(FM) Mishicot WI
WEGW(FM) Wheeling WV
WEGZ(FM) Washburn WI
*WEHC(FM) Emory VA
WEHM(FM) East Hampton NY
WEHR(FM) Shepherdsville KY
WEIB(FM) Northampton MA
WEIF(FM) Utica NY
*WEIU(FM) Charleston IL
WEIZ(FM) Hogansville GA
*WEJF(FM) Palm Bay FL
WEJS(FM) Bar Harbor ME
WEJT(FM) Shelbyville IL
*WEJY(FM) Monroe MI
WEJZ(FM) Jacksonville FL
*WEKH(FM) Hazard KY
*WEKU-FM Richmond KY
WEKX(FM) Jellico TN
WEKZ-FM Monroe WI
WELA(FM) East Liverpool OH
WELC-FM Welch WV
WELD-FM Petersburg WV
*WELH(FM) Providence RI
WELK(FM) Elkins WV
WELL-FM Marshall MI
WELR-FM Roanoke AL
WELY-FM Ely MN
*WEMC(FM) Harrisonburg VA
WEMG-FM Crete IL
WEMI(FM) Neenah-Menasha WI
WEMM(FM) Huntington WV
*WEMU(FM) Ypsilanti MI
WEMX(FM) Ravena NY
WENL(FM) Gladstone MI
WENN-FM Birmingham AL
WENS(FM) Shelbyville IN
WENU(FM) Hudson Falls NY
WENY-FM Elmira NY
WENZ(FM) Cleveland OH
*WEOS(FM) Geneva NY
WEOW(FM) Key West FL
*WEPR(FM) Greenville SC
*WEPS(FM) Elgin IL
WEQR(FM) Goldsboro NC

Broadcasting & Cable Yearbook 1994
B-466

WEQX(FM) Manchester VT
*WERB(FM) Berlin CT
*WERG(FM) Erie PA
WERH-FM Hamilton AL
WERK-FM Muncie IN
*WERN(FM) Madison WI
WERQ-FM Baltimore MD
WERR(FM) Utuado PR
*WERS(FM) Boston MA
WERT-FM Paulding OH
*WERU-FM Blue Hill ME
WERX-FM Edenton NC
WERZ(FM) Exeter NH
WESA-FM Charleroi PA
WESC-FM Greenville SC
WESE(FM) Baldwyn MS
*WESM(FM) Princess Anne MD
*WESN(FM) Bloomington IL
WESP(FM) Dothan AL
*WESQ(FM) Rocky Mount NC
WESR-FM Onley-Onancock VA
*WESS(FM) East Stroudsburg PA
*WESU(FM) Middletown CT
WESV(FM) Richton MS
WESZ(FM) Lincoln IL
*WETA-FM Washington DC
*WETD(FM) Alfred NY
*WETH(FM) Hagerstown MD
*WETL(FM) South Bend IN
*WETN(FM) Wheaton IL
*WETS(FM) Johnson City TN
*WEUC-FM Ponce PR
*WEUL(FM) Kingsford MI
WEVA-FM Emporia VA
WEVE-FM Eveleth MN
*WEVH(FM) Hanover NH
*WEVL(FM) Memphis TN
*WEVN(FM) Keene NH
*WEVO(FM) Concord NH
WEVR-FM River Falls WI
WEVS(FM) Saugatuck MI
WEXC(FM) Greenville PA
WEYE(FM) Surgoinsville TN
WEYQ(FM) Marietta OH
WEYY-FM Talladega AL
WEZB(FM) New Orleans LA
WEZC(FM) Hickory NC
WEZF(FM) Burlington VT
WEZI(FM) New Market VA
WEZJ-FM Williamsburg KY
WEZK-FM Knoxville TN
WEZL(FM) Charleston SC
WEZN(FM) Bridgeport CT
WEZO(FM) Avon NY
WEZQ(FM) Bangor ME
WEZR(FM) Brillion WI
WEZV-FM Brookston IN
WEZW(FM) Wauwatosa-Milwaukee WI
WEZX(FM) Scranton PA
WEZY-FM Lakeland FL
WEZZ(FM) Clanton AL

*WFAE(FM) Charlotte NC
WFAL(FM) Falmouth MA
*WFAR(FM) Danbury CT
WFAS-FM White Plains NY
WFAT(FM) Portage MI
WFAZ(FM) Thomasville NC
WFBC-FM Greenville SC
*WFBE(FM) Flint MI
*WFBF(FM) Buffalo NY
WFBQ(FM) Indianapolis IN
WFBR(FM) Cambridge MD
WFCA(FM) Ackerman MS
WFCB(FM) Chillicothe OH
WFCC-FM Chatham MA
*WFCF(FM) St. Augustine FL
*WFCH(FM) Charleston SC
*WFCI(FM) Franklin IN
WFCJ(FM) Miamisburg OH
*WFCO(FM) Lancaster OH
*WFCR(FM) Amherst MA
*WFCS(FM) New Britain CT
*WFDD-FM Winston-Salem NC
WFDL(FM) Lomira WI
*WFDU(FM) Teaneck NJ
*WFEN(FM) Rockford IL
WFEZ(FM) Williston FL
*WFFC(FM) Ferrum VA
WFFF-FM Columbia MS
WFFM(FM) Ashburn GA
WFFN(FM) Cordova AL
WFFX(FM) Tuscaloosa AL
*WFGB(FM) Kingston NY
WFGE(FM) Mackinaw City MI
*WFGH(FM) Fort Gay WV
WFGI(FM) State College PA
WFGM(FM) Fairmont WV
WFGO(FM) Erie PA
WFGR(FM) Grand Rapids MI
WFGY(FM) Altoona PA
*WFHB(FM) Bloomington IN
*WFHC(FM) Henderson TN
WFHN(FM) Fairhaven MA
*WFHQ(FM) Pennsuco FL
WFID(FM) Rio Piedras PR
*WFIT(FM) Melbourne FL
*WFIU(FM) Bloomington IN
WFIW-FM Fairfield IL
WFIX(FM) Rogersville AL
WFJA(FM) Sanford NC
WFKS(FM) Palatka FL
WFKX(FM) Henderson TN
WFKZ(FM) Plantation Key FL

WFLC(FM) Miami FL
WFLE-FM Flemingsburg KY
WFLK(FM) Geneva NY
WFLN-FM Philadelphia PA
WFLO-FM Farmville VA
WFLQ(FM) French Lick IN
WFLR-FM Dundee NY
WFLS-FM Fredericksburg VA
WFLY(FM) Troy NY
WFLZ-FM Tampa FL
WFMB-FM Springfield IL
*WFME(FM) Newark NJ
WFMF(FM) Baton Rouge LA
WFMG(FM) Richmond IN
WFMH-FM Cullman AL
WFMI(FM) Bay Minette AL
WFMK(FM) East Lansing MI
WFML(FM) Vincennes IN
*WFMQ(FM) Lebanon TN
WFMR(FM) Menomonee Falls WI
WFMS(FM) Indianapolis IN
WFMT(FM) Chicago IL
*WFMU(FM) East Orange NJ
WFMV(FM) South Congaree SC
WFMX(FM) Statesville NC
WFMZ(FM) Allentown PA
WFNL(FM) Sturgeon Bay WI
*WFNM(FM) Lancaster PA
WFNN(FM) Villas NJ
*WFNP(FM) New Paltz NY
WFNX(FM) Lynn MA
*WFOF(FM) Covington IN
WFOG(FM) Suffolk VA
*WFOS(FM) Chesapeake VA
WFOX(FM) Gainesville GA
WFPC(FM) Petersburg IN
WFPG-FM Atlantic City NJ
*WFPK(FM) Louisville KY
*WFPL(FM) Louisville KY
WFPS(FM) Freeport IL
*WFQS(FM) Franklin NC
WFQX(FM) Front Royal VA
WFRA-FM Franklin PA
WFRB-FM Frostburg MD
*WFRC(FM) Columbus GA
WFRD(FM) Hanover NH
WFRE(FM) Frederick MD
WFRG-FM Utica NY
*WFRH(FM) Kingston NY
*WFRJ(FM) Johnstown PA
WFRM-FM Coudersport PA
WFRN-FM Elkhart IN
WFRO-FM Fremont OH
*WFRS(FM) Smithtown NY
*WFRW(FM) Webster NY
WFRX-FM West Frankfort IL
WFRY(FM) Salladasburg PA
*WFSE(FM) Edinboro PA
*WFSI(FM) Annapolis MD
*WFSK(FM) Nashville TN
WFSP-FM Kingwood WV
*WFSQ(FM) Tallahassee FL
*WFSS(FM) Fayetteville NC
*WFSU-FM Tallahassee FL
*WFSW(FM) Panama City FL
WFSY(FM) Panama City FL
WFTA(FM) Fulton MS
*WFTF(FM) Rutland VT
*WFTI-FM St. Petersburg FL
WFTM-FM Maysville KY
WFTN-FM Franklin NH
WFTR-FM Front Royal VA
WFTZ(FM) Manchester TN
WFUB(FM) Orange MA
WFUD(FM) Honeyoye Falls NY
*WFUM-FM Flint MI
WFUN-FM Bethalto IL
WFUR-FM Grand Rapids MI
*WFUV(FM) New York NY
WFWI(FM) Fort Wayne IN
*WFWM(FM) Frostburg MD
WFXA-FM Augusta GA
WFXB(FM) East St. Louis IL
WFXC(FM) Durham NC
WFXD(FM) Marquette MI
WFXE(FM) Columbus GA
WFXH(FM) Hilton Head Island SC
WFXK(FM) Tarboro NC
WFXM-FM Forsyth GA
WFXO(FM) Iuka MS
WFXQ(FM) Chase City VA
WFXR(FM) Harwichport MA
WFXS(FM) Soddy-Daisy TN
WFXZ(FM) Jacksonville NC
WFYC-FM Alma MI
*WFYI-FM Indianapolis IN
WFYR(FM) Elmwood IL
WFYV-FM Atlantic Beach FL
WFYZ(FM) Ravenswood WV

*WGAJ(FM) Deerfield MA
*WGAO(FM) Franklin MA
WGAP-FM Maryville TN
WGAR-FM Cleveland OH
WGAY(FM) Washington DC
*WGAZ(FM) Goodman WI
WGBF-FM Henderson KY
*WGBH(FM) Boston MA
WGBQ(FM) Galesburg IL
*WGBW(FM) Green Bay WI
*WGCA-FM Quincy IL
WGCB-FM Red Lion PA
*WGCC-FM Batavia NY
WGCI-FM Chicago IL
WGCM-FM Gulfport MS

WGCO(FM) Midway GA
*WGCS(FM) Goshen IN
WGCT(FM) Ellettsville IN
WGCX(FM) Atmore AL
WGCY(FM) Gibson City IL
WGDN-FM Gladwin MI
*WGDR(FM) Plainfield VT
WGEE-FM Sturgeon Bay WI
WGEL(FM) Greenville IL
WGEM-FM Quincy IL
WGEN-FM Geneseo IL
WGER-FM Saginaw MI
WGES(FM) Oswego NY
*WGEV(FM) Beaver Falls PA
WGFA-FM Watseka IL
WGFB(FM) Plattsburgh NY
WGFG(FM) Branchville SC
WGFM(FM) Cheboygan MI
WGFN(FM) Glen Arbor MI
*WGFR(FM) Glens Falls NY
WGFX(FM) Gallatin TN
WGGC(FM) Glasgow KY
WGGD-FM Melbourne FL
*WGGL-FM Houghton MI
WGGN(FM) Castalia OH
WGGR(FM) Greenwood IN
WGGY(FM) Scranton PA
WGGZ(FM) Baton Rouge LA
WGH-FM Newport News VA
WGHN-FM Grand Haven MI
*WGHR(FM) Marietta GA
*WGIB(FM) Birmingham AL
WGIR-FM Manchester NH
WGIX-FM Gouverneur NY
WGKS(FM) Paris KY
WGKX(FM) Memphis TN
WGKY(FM) Wickliffe KY
WGL-FM Roanoke IN
WGLB-FM Port Washington WI
WGLC-FM Mendota IL
*WGLE(FM) Lima OH
WGLF(FM) Tallahassee FL
WGLM(FM) West Lafayette IN
WGLO(FM) Pekin IL
WGLQ(FM) Escanaba MI
WGLR-FM Lancaster WI
*WGLS-FM Glassboro NJ
*WGLT(FM) Normal IL
WGLU(FM) Johnstown PA
WGLV(FM) Hartford VT
WGLY-FM Waterbury VT
*WGLZ(FM) West Liberty WV
*WGMC(FM) Greece NY
WGMD(FM) Rehoboth Beach DE
WGMG(FM) Crawford GA
WGMK(FM) Donalsonville GA
WGMM(FM) Big Flats NY
WGMO(FM) Shell Lake WI
WGMR(FM) Tyrone PA
WGMS-FM Washington DC
WGMT(FM) Lyndon VT
WGMX(FM) Marathon FL
WGMZ(FM) Glencoe AL
WGNA-FM Albany NY
*WGNB(FM) Zeeland MI
WGNE-FM Titusville FL
WGNI(FM) Wilmington NC
WGNL(FM) Greenwood MS
WGNN(FM) Dresden TN
*WGNP(FM) Albany GA
*WGNR(FM) Monee IL
*WGNV(FM) Milladore WI
WGNY-FM Newburgh NY
WGOD-FM Charlotte Amalie VI
WGOG-FM Walhalla SC
*WGOJ(FM) Conneaut OH
WGOL(FM) Lynchburg VA
WGOR(FM) Martinez GA
WGPC-FM Albany GA
*WGPH(FM) Vidalia GA
WGPR(FM) Detroit MI
WGQR(FM) Elizabethtown NC
WGR-FM Buffalo NY
*WGRC(FM) Lewisburg PA
WGRD-FM Grand Rapids MI
*WGRE(FM) Greencastle IN
WGRG(FM) Owego NY
WGRK-FM Greensburg KY
WGRL(FM) Indianapolis IN
WGRM-FM Greenwood MS
*WGRN(FM) Greenville IL
WGRQ(FM) Colonial Beach VA
WGRR(FM) Hamilton OH
*WGRS(FM) Guilford CT
WGRX(FM) Westminster MD
WGRY-FM Roscommon MI
*WGSG(FM) Mayo FL
*WGSK(FM) South Kent CT
*WGSL(FM) Loves Park IL
WGSQ(FM) Cookeville TN
WGST-FM Canton GA
*WGSU(FM) Geneseo NY
WGSY(FM) Phenix City AL
WGTB(FM) Auburn IN
WGTC(FM) New Carlisle IN
*WGTD(FM) Kenosha WI
*WGTE-FM Toledo OH
*WGTF(FM) Dothan AL
WGTH(FM) Richlands VA
WGTK(FM) Middlebury VT
WGTN-FM Andrews SC
WGTR(FM) Bucksport SC
*WGTS-FM Takoma Park MD
WGTY(FM) Gettysburg PA
WGTZ(FM) Eaton OH

*WGUC(FM) Cincinnati OH
WGUD-FM Pascagoula MS
WGUF(FM) Marco FL
WGUL-FM New Port Richey FL
WGUY(FM) Dexter ME
*WGVE(FM) Gary IN
*WGVU-FM Allendale MI
WGWD(FM) Gretna FL
*WGWG(FM) Boiling Springs NC
WGXL(FM) Hanover NH
*WGXM(FM) Dayton OH
WGY-FM Schenectady NY
WGYL(FM) Vero Beach FL
WGZB-FM Corydon IN

WHAA(FM) Madison ME
*WHAD(FM) Delafield WI
WHAI-FM Greenfield MA
WHAJ(FM) Bluefield WV
WHAY(FM) Whitley City KY
WHBC-FM Canton OH
*WHBM-FM Park Falls WI
WHBN-FM Harrodsburg KY
WHBX(FM) Tallahassee FL
*WHCB(FM) Bristol TN
*WHCE(FM) Highland Springs VA
*WHCF(FM) Bangor ME
WHCG(FM) Metter GA
WHCH(FM) Munising MI
*WHCJ(FM) Savannah GA
*WHCL-FM Clinton NY
WHCM(FM) Parkersburg WV
WHCN(FM) Hartford CT
*WHCR-FM New York NY
WHCY(FM) Blairstown NJ
WHDQ(FM) Claremont NH
WHEB(FM) Portsmouth NH
*WHEI(FM) Tiffin OH
WHEL(FM) Helen GA
*WHEM(FM) Eau Claire WI
WHEN-FM Syracuse NY
WHER(FM) Hattiesburg MS
WHET(FM) Birnamwood WI
WHEW(FM) Fort Myers FL
WHFB-FM Benton Harbor MI
*WHFC(FM) Bel Air MD
WHFD(FM) Lawrenceville VA
WHFE(FM) Lakeland GA
*WHFH(FM) Flossmoor IL
*WHFI(FM) Lindside WV
WHFM(FM) Southampton NY
*WHFR(FM) Dearborn MI
WHFS(FM) Annapolis MD
WHFX(FM) Waycross GA
WHGC(FM) Bennington VT
WHGL-FM Canton PA
*WHHB(FM) Holliston MA
WHHH(FM) Indianapolis IN
*WHHI(FM) Highland WI
WHHM-FM Henderson TN
*WHHS(FM) Havertown PA
WHHT(FM) Cave City KY
WHHY-FM Montgomery AL
WHIC-FM Hardinsburg KY
*WHIJ(FM) Ocala FL
*WHIL-FM Mobile AL
WHIZ-FM Zanesville OH
*WHJE(FM) Carmel IN
WHJT(FM) Clinton MS
WHJX-FM Brunswick GA
WHJY(FM) Providence RI
WHKO(FM) Dayton OH
WHKQ(FM) Racine WI
WHKR(FM) Rockledge FL
WHKS(FM) Port Allegany PA
WHKW(FM) Louisville KY
WHKX(FM) Lafayette FL
WHKZ(FM) Cayce SC
*WHLA(FM) La Crosse WI
WHLE(FM) Byhalia MS
WHLG(FM) Jensen Beach FL
WHLM(FM) Bloomsburg PA
WHLQ(FM) Louisburg NC
WHLX(FM) Bethlehem WV
WHLZ(FM) Manning SC
WHMA-FM Anniston AL
*WHMC-FM Conway SC
WHMD(FM) Hammond LA
WHME(FM) South Bend IN
WHMH-FM Sauk Rapids MN
WHMI-FM Howell MI
WHMP-FM Northampton MA
WHMQ(FM) North Baltimore OH
WHMS-FM Champaign IL
WHMX(FM) Lincoln ME
WHNN(FM) Bay City MI
WHOB(FM) Nashua NH
WHOD-FM Jackson AL
WHOK(FM) Lancaster OH
WHOM(FM) Mt. Washington NH
WHOP-FM Hopkinsville KY
WHOT-FM Youngstown OH
WHOU-FM Houlton ME
*WHOV(FM) Hampton VA
WHOW-FM Clinton IL
WHOX(FM) Charlestown IN
WHPA(FM) Hollidaysburg PA
*WHPC(FM) Garden City NY
WHPE-FM High Point NC
*WHPK-FM Chicago IL
*WHPL(FM) West Lafayette IN
*WHPN(FM) Harrisburg PA
WHPO(FM) Hoopeston IL
*WHPR(FM) Highland Park MI
WHPT(FM) Sarasota FL

WHQO(FM) Skowhegan ME
WHQQ(FM) Charleston IL
*WHQR(FM) Wilmington NC
WHQT(FM) Coral Gables FL
WHRB(FM) Cambridge MA
WHRK(FM) Memphis TN
WHRL(FM) Albany NY
*WHRM(FM) Wausau WI
*WHRO-FM Norfolk VA
*WHRV(FM) Norfolk VA
*WHRW(FM) Binghamton NY
WHRZ(FM) Providence KY
*WHSA(FM) Brule WI
WHSB(FM) Alpena MI
WHSC-FM Hartsville SC
*WHSD(FM) Hinsdale IL
WHSM-FM Hayward WI
*WHSN(FM) Bangor ME
*WHSS(FM) Hamilton OH
WHST(FM) Tawas City MI
WHSY-FM Hattiesburg MS
WHTE(FM) Williamston NC
WHTF(FM) Starview PA
WHTG-FM Eatontown NJ
WHTL-FM Whitehall WI
WHTO(FM) Muncy PA
WHTQ(FM) Orlando FL
WHTT-FM Buffalo NY
WHTX(FM) Sharpsville PA
WHTZ(FM) Newark NJ
WHUB-FM Cookeville TN
WHUD(FM) Peekskill NY
WHUG(FM) Jamestown NY
WHUR-FM Washington DC
*WHUS(FM) Storrs CT
WHVK(FM) Tullahoma TN
*WHVP(FM) Hudson NY
*WHVT(FM) Clyde OH
*WHWC(FM) Menomonie WI
*WHWE(FM) Howe IN
WHWK(FM) Binghamton NY
*WHWL(FM) Marquette MI
WHXT(FM) Citronelle AL
WHYB(FM) Menominee MI
*WHYC(FM) Swan Quarter NC
WHYI-FM Fort Lauderdale FL
WHYL-FM Carlisle PA
WHYN-FM Springfield MA
WHYR(FM) Saco ME
WHYT(FM) Detroit MI
*WHYY-FM Philadelphia PA
WHZR(FM) Royal Center IN
WHZT(FM) Mahomet IL

*WIAA(FM) Interlochen MI
WIAC-FM San Juan PR
WIAI(FM) Danville IL
WIAL(FM) Eau Claire WI
WIBA-FM Madison WI
WIBF-FM Jenkintown PA
*WIBI(FM) Carlinville IL
WIBM-FM Jackson MI
WIBN(FM) Earl Park IN
WIBW-FM Topeka KS
WIBZ(FM) Wedgefield SC
*WICB(FM) Ithaca NY
WICI(FM) Sumter SC
*WICN(FM) Worcester MA
WICO-FM Salisbury MD
*WICR(FM) Indianapolis IN
*WIDA-FM Carolina PR
WIDL(FM) Caro MI
*WIDR(FM) Kalamazoo MI
WIFC(FM) Wausau WI
WIFM-FM Elkin NC
WIFO-FM Jesup GA
WIFX-FM Jenkins KY
WIGL(FM) Orangeburg SC
WIGM-FM Medford WI
WIHN(FM) Normal IL
*WIHS(FM) Middletown CT
WIIL(FM) Kenosha WI
WIIN(FM) Vicksburg MS
WIIS(FM) Key West FL
WIIZ(FM) Battle Ground IN
WIJY(FM) Hilton Head Island SC
WIKB-FM Iron River MI
WIKI(FM) Carrollton KY
WIKK(FM) Newton IL
WIKQ(FM) Greeneville TN
WIKS(FM) New Bern NC
WIKX(FM) Punta Gorda FL
WIKY-FM Evansville IN
WIKZ(FM) Chambersburg PA
WIL-FM St. Louis MO
WILI-FM Willimantic CT
*WILL-FM Urbana IL
WILN(FM) Panama City FL
WILQ(FM) Williamsport PA
WILS-FM Lansing MI
WIMC(FM) Crawfordsville IN
WIMI(FM) Ironwood MI
WIMJ(FM) Cincinnati OH
WIMK(FM) Iron Mountain MI
WIMT(FM) Lima OH
WIMX-FM Harrisburg PA
WIMZ-FM Knoxville TN
WINC-FM Winchester VA
WINJ(FM) Pulaski TN
WINK-FM Fort Myers FL
WINL(FM) Linden AL
WINN(FM) North Vernon IN
WINQ(FM) Winchendon MA
WIOA(FM) San Juan PR
WIOB(FM) Mayaguez PR

U.S. FM Stations by Call Letters

WIOC(FM) Ponce PR
WIOG(FM) Bay City MI
WIOK(FM) Falmouth KY
WIOQ(FM) Philadelphia PA
WIOT(FM) Toledo OH
WIOV-FM Ephrata PA
WIOZ-FM Southern Pines NC
*WIPA(FM) Pittsfield IL
*WIPR-FM San Juan PR
WIQB-FM Ann Arbor MI
*WIQH(FM) Concord MA
WIQO-FM Covington VA
WIQQ(FM) Leland MS
WIRE(FM) Lebanon IN
WIRK-FM West Palm Beach FL
*WIRQ(FM) Rochester NY
*WIRR(FM) Virginia-Hibbing MN
WIRX(FM) St. Joseph MI
WISK-FM Americus GA
WISL-FM Shamokin PA
WISM-FM Altoona WI
WISP(FM) Holmes Beach FL
WISQ(FM) Whitewater WI
WISS-FM Berlin WI
WIST(FM) Lobelville TN
*WISU(FM) Terre Haute IN
*WITC(FM) Cazenovia NY
*WITF-FM Harrisburg PA
WITL-FM Lansing MI
*WITR(FM) Henrietta NY
*WITX(FM) Beaver Falls PA
WITZ-FM Jasper IN
*WIUJ(FM) St. Thomas VI
*WIUM(FM) Macomb IL
*WIUP-FM Indiana PA
*WIUS(FM) Macomb IL
*WIUV(FM) Castleton VT
WIVA-FM Aguadilla PR
*WIVH(FM) Christiansted VI
WIVI(FM) Charlotte Amalie VI
WIVK-FM Knoxville TN
WIVM(FM) Elwood IN
WIVY-FM Jacksonville FL
*WIWC(FM) Kokomo IN
WIXC(FM) Essexville MI
WIXI(FM) Naples Park FL
WIXK-FM New Richmond WI
WIXN-FM Dixon IL
*WIXQ(FM) Millersville PA
WIXV(FM) Savannah GA
WIXX(FM) Green Bay WI
WIXY(FM) Champaign IL
WIYC(FM) Charlotte Amalie VI
WIYN(FM) Deposit NY
WIYY(FM) Baltimore MD
WIZD(FM) Rudolph WI
WIZF(FM) Erlanger KY
WIZK-FM Bay Springs MS
WIZM-FM La Crosse WI
WIZN(FM) Vergennes VT
*WIZY(FM) East Jordan MI

WJAA(FM) Austin IN
*WJAB(FM) Huntsville AL
WJAD(FM) Bainbridge GA
WJAM-FM Marion AL
WJAN(FM) Sunderland VT
WJAQ(FM) Marianna FL
WJAT-FM Swainsboro GA
WJAW(FM) McConnelsville OH
*WJAZ(FM) Summerdale PA
WJBB-FM Haleyville AL
WJBD-FM Salem IL
WJBI-FM Winslow ME
WJBL(FM) Ladysmith WI
WJBR-FM Wilmington DE
WJBT(FM) Green Cove Springs FL
WJBX(FM) Fort Myers Beach FL
WJBZ(FM) Seymour TN
*WJCH(FM) Joliet IL
*WJCK(FM) Cedartown GA
WJCL-FM Savannah GA
*WJCR-FM Millerstown KY
*WJCT-FM Jacksonville FL
WJDB-FM Thomasville AL
WJDJ(FM) Burnside KY
WJDK(FM) Morris IL
WJDQ(FM) Meridian MS
WJDR(FM) Prentiss MS
WJDT(FM) Rogersville TN
WJDX(FM) Jackson MS
WJEC(FM) Vernon AL
*WJED(FM) Dogwood Lakes Estate FL
*WJEF(FM) Lafayette IN
*WJEL(FM) Indianapolis IN
WJEQ(FM) Macomb IL
WJER-FM Dover OH
WJET(FM) Erie PA
WJEZ(FM) Pontiac IL
WJFD-FM New Bedford MA
*WJFF(FM) Jeffersonville NY
WJFK-FM Manassas VA
WJFL(FM) Tennille GA
*WJFP(FM) Fort Pierce FL
*WJFR(FM) Jacksonville FL
WJFX(FM) New Haven IN
WJGA-FM Jackson GA
*WJGF-FM Romney WV
WJGG(FM) Lexington-Fayette KY
*WJHD(FM) Portsmouth RI
WJHM(FM) Daytona Beach FL
*WJHS(FM) Columbia City IN
*WJHU-FM Baltimore MD
*WJIE(FM) Okolona KY
*WJIF(FM) Opp AL
*WJIK(FM) Binghamton NY
WJIM-FM Lansing MI
*WJIR(FM) Key West FL
*WJIS(FM) Bradenton FL
WJIV(FM) Cherry Valley NY
WJIZ-FM Albany GA
WJJB(FM) Romney WV
WJJH(FM) Ashland WI
WJJM-FM Lewisburg TN
WJJN(FM) Dothan AL
WJJO(FM) Watertown WI
WJJQ-FM Tomahawk WI
WJJR(FM) Rutland VT
WJJS(FM) Lynchburg VA
*WJJW(FM) North Adams MA
WJJY-FM Brainerd MN
WJJZ(FM) Philadelphia PA
WJKC(FM) Christiansted VI
WJKL(FM) Elgin IL
WJKX(FM) Ellisville MS
WJLB(FM) Detroit MI
WJLC(FM) South Boston VA
WJLE-FM Smithville TN
*WJLF(FM) Gainesville FL
WJLK-FM Asbury Park NJ
WJLM(FM) Salem VA
WJLQ(FM) Pensacola FL
WJLR(FM) Austin IN
WJLS-FM Beckley WV
WJLT(FM) Fort Wayne IN
*WJLU(FM) New Smyrna Beach FL
WJLW(FM) De Pere WI
*WJLY(FM) Ramsey IL
WJMA-FM Orange VA
WJMC-FM Rice Lake WI
WJMD(FM) Hazard KY
*WJMF(FM) Smithfield RI
WJMG(FM) Hattiesburg MS
WJMH(FM) Reidsville NC
WJMI(FM) Jackson MS
*WJMJ(FM) Hartford CT
WJMK(FM) Chicago IL
WJMM-FM Versailles KY
WJMN(FM) Boston MA
WJMO-FM Cleveland Heights OH
WJMQ(FM) Clintonville WI
WJMR(FM) Peshtigo WI
*WJMU(FM) Decatur IL
WJMX-FM Cheraw SC
WJMZ-FM Anderson SC
*WJNF(FM) Marianna FL
WJNN(FM) North Cape May NJ
WJNR-FM Iron Mountain MI
WJNS-FM Yazoo City MS
*WJNY(FM) Watertown NY
WJNZ(FM) Greencastle IN
WJOD(FM) Galena IL
WJOI(FM) Detroit MI
WJOR-FM St. Joseph TN
WJPA-FM Washington PA
WJPC-FM Lansing IL
WJPD(FM) Ishpeming MI
WJPH(FM) Monticello FL
WJPS-FM Newburgh IN
*WJPZ-FM Syracuse NY
WJQI-FM Virginia Beach VA
WJQK(FM) Zeeland MI
WJQZ(FM) Wellsville NY
WJRE(FM) Kewanee IL
*WJRH(FM) Easton PA
WJRQ(FM) Saluda SC
WJRR(FM) Cocoa Beach FL
WJRS(FM) Jamestown KY
WJRZ-FM Manahawkin NJ
WJSA-FM Jersey Shore PA
*WJSC-FM Johnson VT
WJSG(FM) Hamlet NC
WJSK(FM) Lumberton NC
*WJSL(FM) Houghton NY
WJSM-FM Martinsburg PA
WJSN-FM Jackson KY
*WJSO(FM) Pikeville KY
*WJSP-FM Warm Springs GA
WJSQ(FM) Athens TN
*WJSR(FM) Birmingham AL
*WJSU(FM) Jackson MS
*WJSV(FM) Morristown NJ
WJSZ(FM) Ashley MI
*WJTA(FM) Kosciusko MS
*WJTF(FM) Panama City FL
*WJTG(FM) Fort Valley GA
WJTK(FM) Gorham NH
*WJTL(FM) Lancaster PA
WJTT(FM) Red Bank TN
WJTW(FM) Joliet IL
*WJTY(FM) Lancaster WI
WJUK(FM) Mt. Pleasant SC
*WJUL(FM) Lowell MA
WJUN-FM Mexico PA
WJUS(FM) Fort Walton Beach FL
*WJUX(FM) Franklin Lakes NJ
WJVL(FM) Janesville WI
WJVO(FM) South Jacksonville IL
*WJVS(FM) Cincinnati OH
*WJWJ-FM Beaufort SC
WJWL(FM) Bartlett TN
*WJWV(FM) Fort Gaines GA
WJXN-FM Utica MS
WJXQ(FM) Jackson MI
WJXR(FM) Macclenny FL
WJXY-FM Conway SC
WJYE(FM) Buffalo NY
WJYF(FM) Nashville GA
*WJYJ(FM) Fredericksburg VA
*WJYL(FM) New Washington IN
*WJYO(FM) Fort Myers FL
WJYP(FM) South Charleston WV
WJYR(FM) Myrtle Beach SC
WJYY(FM) Concord NH
WJZD(FM) Long Beach MS
WJZE(FM) Oak Harbor OH
WJZR(FM) Rochester NY
WJZZ(FM) Detroit MI

WKAA(FM) Ocilla GA
WKAB(FM) Berwick PA
WKAI(FM) Macomb IL
WKAK(FM) Albany GA
WKAQ-FM San Juan PR
*WKAR-FM East Lansing MI
WKAZ(FM) Miami WV
WKBB(FM) West Point MS
WKBC-FM North Wilkesboro NC
WKBE(FM) Warrensburg NY
WKBG(FM) Martinez GA
WKBH-FM Trempealeau WI
WKBI-FM St. Marys PA
WKBL-FM Covington TN
WKBM(FM) Coal City IL
WKBN-FM Youngstown OH
WKBQ(FM) Granite City IL
WKBX(FM) Kingsland GA
WKBZ-FM Muskegon MI
WKCA(FM) Owingsville KY
WKCB-FM Hindman KY
*WKCC(FM) Grayson KY
WKCG(FM) Augusta ME
WKCI(FM) Hamden CT
WKCJ(FM) Lewisburg WV
*WKCL(FM) Ladson SC
WKCM-FM Hawesville KY
WKCN(FM) Lumpkin GA
*WKCO(FM) Gambier OH
WKCQ(FM) Saginaw MI
*WKCR-FM New York NY
*WKCS(FM) Knoxville TN
WKCX(FM) Rome GA
WKCY-FM Harrisonburg VA
WKDD(FM) Akron OH
WKDE-FM Altavista VA
WKDF(FM) Nashville TN
WKDJ(FM) Clarksdale MS
*WKDN-FM Camden NJ
WKDO-FM Liberty KY
WKDP-FM Corbin KY
WKDQ(FM) Henderson KY
*WKDS(FM) Kalamazoo MI
*WKDU(FM) Philadelphia PA
WKDW-FM Staunton VA
WKDY(FM) Rome NY
WKDZ-FM Cadiz KY
WKEA-FM Scottsboro AL
WKED-FM Frankfort KY
WKEE-FM Huntington WV
*WKES(FM) St. Petersburg FL
*WKET(FM) Kettering OH
WKEZ(FM) Holland MI
WKFR-FM Battle Creek MI
WKFX(FM) Kaukauna WI
WKGB-FM Susquehanna PA
*WKGC-FM Panama City FL
WKGF-FM Arcadia FL
WKGG(FM) Cape Vincent NY
WKGH(FM) Allegan MI
WKGK(FM) Kinston NC
WKGO(FM) Cumberland MD
WKGR(FM) Fort Pierce FL
WKGT-FM Century FL
WKHG(FM) Leitchfield KY
WKHI(FM) Bethany Beach DE
WKHJ(FM) Mountain Lake Park MD
WKHK(FM) Colonial Heights VA
WKHL(FM) Stamford CT
WKHQ-FM Charlevoix MI
*WKHR(FM) Bainbridge OH
*WKHS(FM) Worton MD
WKHT(FM) Bishopville SC
WKHX-FM Marietta GA
WKHY(FM) Lafayette IN
WKID(FM) Vevay IN
WKIG-FM Glennville GA
WKIK(FM) Crewe VA
WKIO(FM) Urbana IL
WKIS(FM) Boca Raton FL
WKIT-FM Brewer ME
WKIX-FM Raleigh NC
WKJA(FM) Belhaven NC
WKJB-FM Mayaguez PR
WKJC(FM) Tawas City MI
WKJE(FM) Hertford NC
WKJF-FM Cadillac MI
WKJK(FM) Salem IN
*WKJL(FM) Clarksburg WV
WKJN-FM Hammond LA
WKJQ-FM Parsons TN
WKJR(FM) Sullivan IL
WKJX(FM) Elizabeth City NC
WKJY(FM) Hempstead NY
WKJZ(FM) Hillman MI
WKKB(FM) Key Colony Beach FL
*WKKC(FM) Chicago IL
WKKD-FM Aurora IL
WKKG(FM) Columbus IN
WKKI(FM) Celina OH
WKKJ(FM) Chillicothe OH
*WKKL(FM) West Barnstable MA
WKKM(FM) Harrison MI
WKKN(FM) Cordele GA
WKKO(FM) Toledo OH
WKKR(FM) Auburn AL
WKKS-FM Vanceburg KY
WKKV-FM Racine WI
WKKW-FM Clarksburg WV
WKKX(FM) Jerseyville IL
WKKY(FM) Geneva OH
WKKZ(FM) Dublin GA
WKLA-FM Ludington MI
WKLC-FM St. Albans WV
WKLD(FM) Oneonta AL
WKLG(FM) Rock Harbor FL
WKLH(FM) Milwaukee WI
WKLI(FM) Albany NY
WKLK-FM Cloquet MN
WKLL(FM) Frankfort NY
WKLM(FM) Millersburg OH
*WKLO(FM) Westport IN
WKLQ(FM) Holland MI
WKLR(FM) Indianapolis IN
WKLS-FM Atlanta GA
WKLT(FM) Kalkaska MI
WKLW-FM Paintsville KY
WKLX(FM) Rochester NY
WKLZ(FM) Petoskey MI
WKMF-FM Tuscola MI
WKML(FM) Lumberton NC
WKMM(FM) Kingwood WV
WKMO(FM) Hodgenville KY
WKMQ(FM) Winnebago IL
*WKMS-FM Murray KY
WKMX(FM) Enterprise AL
WKMY(FM) Princeton WV
WKMZ(FM) Martinsburg WV
*WKNA(FM) Senatobia MS
WKNB(FM) Port St. Joe FL
*WKNC-FM Raleigh NC
WKNE-FM Keene NH
WKNF-FM Oak Ridge TN
*WKNH(FM) Keene NH
WKNK(FM) Edmonton KY
WKNN-FM Pascagoula MS
*WKNO-FM Memphis TN
*WKNP(FM) Jackson TN
*WKNQ(FM) Dyersburg TN
WKNU(FM) Brewton AL
WKNZ(FM) Collins MS
WKOC(FM) Elizabeth City NC
WKOE(FM) Ocean City NJ
WKOJ(FM) Middletown NY
WKOL(FM) Amsterdam NY
WKOM(FM) Columbia TN
WKOO(FM) Jacksonville NC
WKOR-FM Columbus MS
WKOS(FM) Kingsport TN
WKOT(FM) Marseilles IL
WKOV-FM Wellston OH
*WKPB(FM) Henderson KY
WKPE-FM Orleans MA
WKPK(FM) Gaylord MI
WKPL(FM) Platteville WI
WKPQ(FM) Hornell NY
*WKPW(FM) Knightstown IN
*WKPX(FM) Sunrise FL
WKQI(FM) Detroit MI
*WKQK(FM) Wilmington NC
WKQL(FM) Jacksonville FL
WKQM(FM) Churubusco IN
WKQQ(FM) Lexington KY
WKQT(FM) Newport NC
WKQV(FM) Olyphant PA
WKQW-FM Oil City PA
WKQX(FM) Chicago IL
WKQZ(FM) Midland MI
WKRA-FM Holly Springs MS
*WKRB(FM) Brooklyn NY
WKRE-FM Exmore VA
WKRG-FM Mobile AL
WKRH(FM) Bath ME
*WKRJ(FM) New Philadelphia OH
WKRL-FM North Syracuse NY
WKRQ(FM) Cincinnati OH
WKRR(FM) Asheboro NC
WKRV(FM) Vandalia IL
*WKRW(FM) Wooster OH
WKRX(FM) Roxboro NC
WKRY(FM) Key West FL
WKRZ-FM Wilkes-Barre PA
WKSA-FM Isabela PR
WKSB(FM) Williamsport PA
WKSE(FM) Niagara Falls NY
WKSF(FM) Asheville NC
*WKSG(FM) Cedar Creek FL
WKSI(FM) Greensboro NC
WKSJ-FM Mobile AL
WKSL(FM) Greencastle PA
WKSM(FM) Fort Walton Beach FL
WKSO(FM) Orangeburg SC
WKSQ(FM) Ellsworth ME
WKSS(FM) Hartford CT
WKST-FM Ellwood City PA
*WKSU-FM Kent OH
WKSW(FM) Urbana OH
WKSX(FM) Johnston SC
WKSY(FM) Marion SC
WKTC(FM) Goldsboro NC
WKTF(FM) Jackson MS
WKTG(FM) Madisonville KY
WKTI(FM) Milwaukee WI
WKTJ-FM Farmington ME
WKTK(FM) Crystal River FL
*WKTL(FM) Struthers OH
WKTM(FM) Soperton GA
WKTN(FM) Kenton OH
WKTT(FM) Cleveland WI
WKTU(FM) Ocean City NJ
*WKTZ-FM Jacksonville FL
WKUB(FM) Blackshear GA
*WKUE(FM) Elizabethtown KY
WKUL(FM) Cullman AL
WKUZ(FM) Wabash IN
WKVI-FM Knox IN
*WKVN-FM Levittown PR
*WKVR-FM Huntingdon PA
WKVS(FM) Lenoir NC
WKVT-FM Brattleboro VT
*WKWC(FM) Owensboro KY
WKWI(FM) Kilmarnock VA
WKWK-FM Wheeling WV
WKWQ(FM) Batesburg SC
WKWS(FM) Charleston WV
WKWT(FM) Union City TN
WKWX-FM Savannah TN
*WKWZ(FM) Syosset NY
WKXA-FM Findlay OH
WKXB(FM) Burgaw NC
WKXC-FM Aiken SC
WKXD(FM) Monterey TN
WKXE-FM White River Junction VT
WKXH-FM Alma GA
WKXI-FM Magee MS
WKXJ(FM) South Pittsburg TN
WKXL-FM Concord NH
WKXM-FM Winfield AL
WKXN(FM) Greenville AL
WKXO-FM Berea KY
WKXQ(FM) Rushville IL
WKXW(FM) Trenton NJ
WKXX(FM) Attalla AL
WKXZ(FM) Norwich NY
WKYE(FM) Johnstown PA
WKYI(FM) Stamping Ground KY
WKYL(FM) Lawrenceburg KY
WKYM(FM) Monticello KY
WKYN(FM) St. Marys PA
WKYQ(FM) Paducah KY
WKYR-FM Burkesville KY
WKYS(FM) Washington DC
*WKYU-FM Bowling Green KY
WKYW(FM) Frankfort KY
WKZA(FM) Stevenson AL
WKZB(FM) Drew MS
WKZC(FM) Scottville MI
WKZE-FM Salisbury CT
WKZF(FM) Bayboro NC
WKZG(FM) Keyser WV
WKZL(FM) Winston-Salem NC
*WKZM(FM) Sarasota FL
WKZQ-FM Myrtle Beach SC
WKZR(FM) Milledgeville GA
WKZS(FM) Auburn ME
WKZU(FM) Ripley MS
WKZW(FM) Peoria IL
WKZY(FM) La Belle FL

*WLAB(FM) Fort Wayne IN
WLAC-FM Nashville TN
WLAK(FM) Huntingdon PA
WLAN-FM Lancaster PA
WLAV-FM Grand Rapids MI
WLAY-FM Muscle Shoals AL
WLBC-FM Muncie IN
*WLBF(FM) Montgomery AL
WLBH-FM Mattoon IL
WLBI(FM) Warrior AL
WLBW(FM) Fenwick Island DE
*WLCA(FM) Godfrey IL
WLCC(FM) Luray VA
*WLCH(FM) Lancaster PA
WLCQ(FM) Clarksville VA
WLCS(FM) North Muskegon MI
*WLCX(FM) Farmville VA
WLCY(FM) Blairsville PA
WLDI(FM) Bayamon PR
WLDJ(FM) Appomattox VA
WLDR(FM) Traverse City MI
WLEN(FM) Adrian MI
WLER-FM Butler PA
WLET-FM Toccoa GA
WLEV(FM) Easton PA
WLEW-FM Bad Axe MI
WLEZ(FM) Terre Haute IN
*WLFA(FM) Asheville NC
*WLFC(FM) Findlay OH
WLFE(FM) St. Albans VT
*WLFJ(FM) Greenville SC
*WLFM(FM) Appleton WI
*WLFR(FM) Pomona NJ
WLGC-FM Greenup KY
WLGG(FM) Woodville MS
WLGH(FM) DeFuniak Springs FL
*WLGI(FM) Hemingway SC
WLGK(FM) South Waverly PA
WLGL(FM) Riverside PA
WLGN-FM Logan OH
WLGQ(FM) Gaston NC
WLGW-FM Lancaster NH
WLGX(FM) Carolina Beach NC
WLHM(FM) Logansport IN
*WLHS(FM) West Chester OH
WLHT(FM) Grand Rapids MI
*WLIC(FM) Frostburg MD
WLIF-FM Baltimore MD
WLIH(FM) Whitneyville PA
WLIL-FM Lenoir City TN
WLIN(FM) Gluckstadt MS
WLIQ(FM) Harriman TN
WLIT-FM Chicago IL
WLJA-FM Ellijay GA
WLJC(FM) Beattyville KY
WLJE(FM) Valparaiso IN

U.S. FM Stations by Call Letters

WLJI(FM) Summerton SC
WLJJ(FM) Union City TN
*WLJK(FM) Aiken SC
*WLJN-FM Traverse City MI
WLJO(FM) La Crosse WI
*WLJP(FM) Monroe NY
*WLJS-FM Jacksonville AL
WLJU(FM) Brookfield WI
WLJY(FM) Marshfield WI
WLKA(FM) Canandaigua NY
WLKC(FM) Henderson NY
WLKE(FM) Bar Harbor ME
WLKI(FM) Angola IN
*WLKL(FM) Mattoon IL
WLKM-FM Three Rivers MI
WLKQ(FM) Buford GA
WLKR-FM Norwalk OH
WLKS-FM West Liberty KY
WLKX-FM Forest Lake MN
WLKZ(FM) Wolfeboro NH
WLLF(FM) Mercer PA
WLLG(FM) Lowville NY
WLLI-FM Joliet IL
WLLK(FM) Somerset KY
WLLR-FM East Moline IL
WLLS-FM Hartford KY
WLLT(FM) Polo IL
WLLX(FM) Lawrenceburg TN
WLLZ(FM) Detroit MI
WLMD(FM) Bushnell IL
WLME(FM) Cannelton IN
WLMG(FM) New Orleans LA
*WLMH(FM) Morrow OH
WLMI(FM) Kane PA
WLML(FM) Montezuma GA
WLMM-FM Woodbury TN
*WLMS(FM) Lecanto FL
*WLMU(FM) Harrogate TN
*WLMW(FM) Manchester NH
WLMX-FM Rossville GA
WLNB(FM) Ligonier IN
WLNE-FM Montgomery AL
WLNG-FM Sag Harbor NY
WLNH-FM Laconia NH
*WLNX(FM) Lincoln IL
*WLNZ(FM) Lansing MI
WLOC-FM Munfordville KY
WLOL(FM) Cambridge MN
WLOQ(FM) Winter Park FL
WLOV-FM Washington GA
WLOW(FM) Bluffton SC
*WLPE(FM) Augusta GA
WLPF(FM) Ocilla GA
*WLPG(FM) Florence SC
*WLPJ-FM New Port Richey FL
*WLPT(FM) Jesup GA
WLPW(FM) Lake Placid NY
WLQH-FM Chiefland FL
WLQI(FM) Rensselaer IN
WLQM-FM Franklin VA
WLQR(FM) Toledo OH
WLQT(FM) Kettering OH
*WLRA(FM) Lockport IL
*WLRH(FM) Huntsville AL
*WLRN-FM Miami FL
WLRQ-FM Cocoa FL
WLRR(FM) Milledgeville GA
WLRS(FM) Louisville KY
WLRT(FM) Kankakee IL
WLRW(FM) Champaign IL
WLRX(FM) Nappanee IN
WLRZ(FM) Peru IL
WLS-FM Chicago IL
WLSA(FM) Louisa VA
WLSK(FM) Lebanon KY
WLSL(FM) Crisfield MD
WLSM-FM Louisville MS
WLSN(FM) Greenville OH
*WLSO(FM) Sault Ste. Marie MI
WLSR(FM) Lima OH
WLST(FM) Marinette WI
*WLSU(FM) La Crosse WI
WLSW(FM) Scottdale PA
WLSY-FM Jeffersontown KY
WLSZ(FM) Humboldt TN
WLTA(FM) Elkhart IN
WLTD(FM) Lexington MS
WLTE(FM) Minneapolis MN
WLTF(FM) Cleveland OH
WLTI(FM) Detroit MI
WLTJ(FM) Pittsburgh PA
WLTK(FM) Broadway VA
*WLTL(FM) La Grange IL
WLTM(FM) Rantoul IL
WLTN-FM Lisbon NH
WLTQ(FM) Milwaukee WI
*WLTR(FM) Columbia SC
WLTS-FM Slidell LA
WLTT(FM) Shallotte NC
WLTU(FM) Manitowoc WI
WLTW(FM) New York NY
WLTY(FM) Norfolk VA
WLUA(FM) Westwood KY
WLUD(FM) Deltaville VA
WLUE(FM) Pearl MS
WLUJ(FM) Petersburg IL
WLUM-FM Milwaukee WI
WLUN(FM) Lumberton MS
WLUP-FM Chicago IL
*WLUR(FM) Lexington VA
WLUV-FM Loves Park IL
*WLUW(FM) Chicago IL
WLVB(FM) Morrisville VT
WLVE(FM) Miami Beach FL
*WLVF-FM Haines City FL

WLVH(FM) Hardeeville SC
WLVK(FM) Radcliff KY
WLVQ(FM) Columbus OH
*WLVR(FM) Bethlehem PA
WLVU-FM Holiday FL
WLVW-FM Salisbury MD
WLVY(FM) Elmira NY
WLWI-FM Montgomery AL
WLWW(FM) Waxhaw NC
WLWZ-FM Easley SC
WLXP(FM) Marion SC
WLXR-FM La Crosse WI
WLXY(FM) Northport AL
WLYF(FM) Miami FL
WLYK(FM) Lynchburg VA
WLYT(FM) Haverhill MA
WLYU(FM) Lyons GA
WLYZ(FM) Greer SC
WLZA(FM) Eupora MS
WLZQ(FM) South Whitley IN
WLZR-FM Milwaukee WI
WLZW(FM) Utica NY
WLZZ(FM) Montpelier OH

*WMAB-FM Mississippi State MS
WMAD-FM Sun Prairie WI
*WMAE-FM Booneville MS
WMAG(FM) High Point NC
*WMAH-FM Biloxi MS
*WMAO-FM Greenwood MS
WMAP-FM Pageland SC
WMAS-FM Springfield MA
*WMAU-FM Bude MS
*WMAV-FM Oxford MS
*WMAW-FM Meridian MS
WMAX-FM Irondequoit NY
WMBC(FM) Columbus MS
WMBH-FM Joplin MO
*WMBI-FM Chicago IL
WMBN-FM Petoskey MI
*WMBP(FM) Belpre OH
*WMBR(FM) Cambridge MA
*WMBU(FM) Forest MS
*WMBV(FM) Dixon's Mills AL
*WMBW(FM) Chattanooga TN
WMC-FM Memphis TN
WMCD(FM) Statesboro GA
*WMCE(FM) Erie PA
WMCG(FM) Milan GA
WMCI(FM) Mattoon IL
WMCM(FM) Rockland ME
*WMCN(FM) St. Paul MN
*WMCO(FM) New Concord OH
WMCQ-FM Richmond KY
WMCR-FM Oneida NY
*WMCU(FM) Miami FL
*WMCX(FM) West Long Branch NJ
WMCZ(FM) Millbrook AL
WMDC-FM Hazelhurst MS
WMDH-FM New Castle IN
WMDJ-FM Allen KY
WMDM-FM Lexington Park MD
*WMEA(FM) Portland ME
*WMEB-FM Orono ME
*WMED(FM) Calais ME
WMEE(FM) Fort Wayne IN
WMEF(FM) Fort Kent ME
WMEG(FM) Guayama PR
*WMEH(FM) Bangor ME
*WMEJ(FM) Proctorville OH
*WMEM(FM) Presque Isle ME
WMEQ-FM Menomonie WI
WMEV-FM Marion VA
*WMEW(FM) Waterville ME
WMEZ(FM) Pensacola FL
WMFC-FM Monroeville AL
*WMFE-FM Orlando FL
WMFG-FM Hibbing MN
WMFM(FM) Petal MS
*WMFO(FM) Medford MA
WMFQ(FM) Ocala FL
WMFX(FM) St. Andrews SC
WMGB(FM) Jeffersonville GA
WMGE(FM) Danville KY
WMGF(FM) Mount Dora FL
WMGG(FM) Gallipolis OH
WMGH-FM Tamaqua PA
WMGI(FM) Terre Haute IN
WMGK(FM) Philadelphia PA
WMGL(FM) Ravenel SC
WMGM(FM) Atlantic City NJ
WMGN(FM) Madison WI
WMGQ(FM) New Brunswick NJ
WMGS(FM) Wilkes-Barre PA
WMGU(FM) Stevens Point WI
WMGV(FM) Oshkosh WI
WMGX(FM) Portland ME
WMGZ(FM) Sparta GA
*WMHB(FM) Waterville ME
*WMHC(FM) South Hadley MA
*WMHD-FM Terre Haute IN
WMHE(FM) Delta OH
WMHG(FM) Whitehall MI
*WMHI(FM) Cape Vincent NY
*WMHK(FM) Columbia SC
*WMHN(FM) Webster NY
*WMHR(FM) Syracuse NY
*WMHT-FM Schenectady NY
WMHU(FM) Renovo PA
*WMHW-FM Mount Pleasant MI
WMID-FM Pleasantville NJ
*WMIE(FM) Cocoa FL
WMIK-FM Middlesboro KY
WMIL(FM) Waukesha WI
WMIO(FM) Cabo Rojo PR

WMIT(FM) Black Mountain NC
WMIX-FM Mt. Vernon IL
WMJB(FM) Evansville WI
WMJC(FM) Smithtown NY
WMJD(FM) Grundy VA
WMJE(FM) Clarkesville GA
WMJI(FM) Cleveland OH
WMJJ(FM) Birmingham AL
WMJL-FM Marion KY
WMJM(FM) Bowling Green KY
WMJQ(FM) Buffalo NY
WMJR(FM) Hudson Falls NY
WMJS(FM) Prince Frederick MD
WMJV-FM Patterson NY
WMJW(FM) Rosedale MS
WMJX(FM) Boston MA
WMJZ-FM Gaylord MI
WMKB(FM) Ridgebury PA
WMKC(FM) St. Ignace MI
WMKJ(FM) Newnan GA
WMKO(FM) Millen GA
WMKS(FM) Macon GA
*WMKV(FM) Reading OH
WMKX(FM) Brookville PA
*WMKY(FM) Morehead KY
WMKZ(FM) Monticello KY
WMLI(FM) Sauk City WI
*WMLJ(FM) Summersville WV
*WMLN-FM Milton MA
WMLO(FM) Havana FL
WMLQ(FM) Rogers City MI
WMLV(FM) Ironton OH
WMMA(FM) Lebanon OH
WMMC(FM) Marshall IL
WMME-FM Augusta ME
WMMG-FM Brandenburg KY
WMMJ(FM) Bethesda MD
WMMK(FM) Destin FL
WMMM-FM Verona WI
WMMN-FM Barrackville WV
WMMO(FM) Orlando FL
WMMQ(FM) Charlotte MI
WMMR(FM) Philadelphia PA
WMMS(FM) Cleveland OH
*WMMT(FM) Whitesburg KY
WMMX(FM) Dayton OH
WMMY(FM) Solana FL
WMMZ(FM) Ocala FL
WMNA-FM Gretna VA
WMNB(FM) North Adams MA
WMNC-FM Morganton NC
*WMNF(FM) Tampa FL
*WMNJ(FM) Madison NJ
WMNM(FM) Port Henry NY
*WMNR(FM) Monroe CT
WMNV(FM) Rupert VT
WMNW(FM) Beulah MI
WMNX(FM) Wilmington NC
WMOD(FM) Bolivar TN
WMOG-FM St. Simons Island GA
WMOI(FM) Monmouth IL
WMOO(FM) Derby Center VT
WMOQ(FM) Bostwick GA
WMOR-FM Morehead KY
*WMOT(FM) Murfreesboro TN
WMPA(FM) Mansfield PA
*WMPG(FM) Gorham ME
*WMPH(FM) Wilmington DE
WMPI(FM) Scottsburg IN
*WMPN-FM Jackson MS
WMPO-FM Middleport-Pomeroy OH
*WMPR(FM) Jackson MS
WMQA-FM Minocqua WI
WMQC(FM) Westover WV
WMQQ(FM) Springfield KY
WMQT(FM) Ishpeming MI
WMQX-FM Winston-Salem NC
*WMRA(FM) Harrisonburg VA
WMRF-FM Lewistown PA
WMRI(FM) Marion IN
*WMRL(FM) Lexington VA
WMRN-FM Marion OH
WMRR(FM) Muskegon Heights MI
WMRS(FM) Monticello IN
*WMRT(FM) Marietta OH
WMRV-FM Endicott NY
WMRW(FM) Westhampton NY
WMRX-FM Beaverton MI
*WMSC(FM) Upper Montclair NJ
*WMSE(FM) Milwaukee WI
WMSH-FM Sturgis MI
WMSI(FM) Jackson MS
*WMSJ(FM) Harpswell ME
WMSK-FM Morganfield KY
*WMSL(FM) Athens GA
WMSQ(FM) Havelock NC
*WMSS(FM) Middletown PA
WMST-FM Mt. Sterling KY
WMSU(FM) Starkville MS
*WMSV(FM) Starkville MS
WMT-FM Cedar Rapids IA
*WMTB-FM Emmittsburg MD
WMTC-FM Vancleve KY
WMTD-FM Hinton WV
WMTE-FM Manistee MI
*WMTH(FM) Park Ridge IL
WMTK(FM) Littleton NH
WMTM-FM Moultrie GA
WMTO(FM) Port St. Joe FL
WMTR-FM Archbold OH
WMTX-FM Clearwater FL
WMTY-FM Greenwood SC
WMTZ(FM) Johnstown PA
*WMUA(FM) Amherst MA

*WMUB(FM) Oxford OH
*WMUC-FM College Park MD
WMUF-FM Paris TN
*WMUH(FM) Allentown PA
*WMUK(FM) Kalamazoo MI
*WMUL(FM) Huntington WV
WMUS-FM Muskegon MI
WMUU-FM Greenville SC
WMUZ(FM) Detroit MI
WMVR-FM Sidney OH
*WMVV(FM) McDonough GA
WMVY(FM) Tisbury MA
*WMWA(FM) Glenview IL
*WMWK(FM) Milwaukee WI
*WMWM(FM) Salem MA
WMWV(FM) Conway NH
WMXA(FM) Opelika AL
WMXB(FM) Richmond VA
WMXC(FM) Charlotte NC
WMXD(FM) Detroit MI
WMXE(FM) Erie PA
WMXJ(FM) Pompano Beach FL
WMXK(FM) Morristown TN
WMXL(FM) Lexington KY
*WMXM(FM) Lake Forest IL
WMXN(FM) Norfolk VA
WMXO(FM) Olean NY
WMXQ(FM) Lynchburg VA
WMXR(FM) Woodstock VT
WMXT(FM) Pamplico SC
WMXU(FM) Starkville MS
WMXV(FM) New York NY
WMXW(FM) Vestal NY
WMXX-FM Jackson TN
WMYB(FM) Socastee SC
WMYI(FM) Hendersonville NC
WMYJ(FM) Pocomoke City MD
WMYK(FM) Moyock NC
WMYU(FM) Sevierville TN
WMYX(FM) Milwaukee WI
WMYY(FM) Schoharie NY
WMZK(FM) Merrill WI
WMZQ-FM Washington DC
WMZX(FM) Owosso MI

*WNAA(FM) Greensboro NC
*WNAS(FM) New Albany IN
WNAX-FM Yankton SD
*WNAZ-FM Nashville TN
WNBR(FM) Oriental NC
WNBT-FM Wellsboro PA
WNBX(FM) Lebanon NH
WNBY-FM Newberry MI
*WNCB(FM) Duluth MN
WNCD(FM) Niles OH
WNCG(FM) Clyde OH
WNCI(FM) Columbus OH
WNCK(FM) Port Royal SC
*WNCM-FM Jacksonville FL
WNCO-FM Ashland OH
WNCQ-FM Morristown NY
WNCS(FM) Montpelier VT
WNCT-FM Greenville NC
*WNCU(FM) Durham NC
WNCV(FM) Niceville FL
*WNCW(FM) Spindale NC
WNCX(FM) Cleveland OH
WNDA(FM) Huntsville AL
WNDD(FM) Jefferson City TN
WNDH(FM) Napoleon OH
WNDI-FM Sullivan IN
*WNDN-FM Salisbury NC
WNDU-FM South Bend IN
WNDY(FM) Crawfordsville IN
*WNEC-FM Henniker NH
WNED-FM Buffalo NY
*WNEK-FM Springfield MA
WNEU(FM) Eden NC
WNEW(FM) New York NY
WNEX-FM Gordon GA
*WNFA(FM) Port Huron MI
WNFB(FM) Lake City FL
WNFK(FM) Perry FL
WNFM(FM) Reedsburg WI
WNFQ(FM) Newberry FL
*WNFR(FM) Sandusky MI
WNGC(FM) Athens GA
WNGN(FM) Hoosick Falls NY
*WNGX(FM) Fort Ann NY
WNGZ(FM) Montour Falls NY
WNHQ(FM) Peterborough NH
*WNHU(FM) West Haven CT
WNHW(FM) Nags Head NC
WNIB(FM) Chicago IL
WNIC(FM) Dearborn MI
*WNIJ(FM) Rockford IL
WNIK-FM Arecibo PR
*WNIN-FM Evansville IN
WNIR(FM) Kent OH
*WNIU(FM) De Kalb IL
WNIZ-FM Zion IL
*WNJA(FM) Jamestown NY
*WNJB(FM) Bridgeton NJ
*WNJN(FM) Atlantic City NJ
*WNJP(FM) Sussex NJ
*WNJS-FM Berlin NJ
*WNJT-FM Trenton NJ
WNJY(FM) Delphi IN
WNKI(FM) Corning NY
*WNKJ(FM) Hopkinsville KY
WNKO(FM) Newark OH
WNKR(FM) Williamstown KY
*WNKU(FM) Highland Heights KY
WNKV(FM) St. Johnsbury VT
WNKX-FM Centerville TN

WNLA-FM Indianola MS
*WNLE(FM) Fernandina Beach FL
WNLT(FM) Harrison OH
WNMB(FM) North Myrtle Beach SC
*WNMC-FM Traverse City MI
*WNMH(FM) Northfield MA
WNMR(FM) New Martinsville WV
*WNMU-FM Marquette MI
WNMX(FM) Newberry SC
WNND(FM) Fuquay-Varina NC
WNNH(FM) Henniker NH
WNNJ-FM Newton NJ
WNNK-FM Harrisburg PA
WNNN(FM) Canton NJ
WNNO-FM Wisconsin Dells WI
WNNR-FM Sodus NY
WNNS(FM) Springfield IL
WNNT-FM Warsaw VA
WNNV(FM) Aguada PR
WNNX(FM) Atlanta GA
WNOE-FM New Orleans LA
WNOG-FM Naples FL
WNOI(FM) Flora IL
WNOK-FM Columbia SC
WNOR-FM Norfolk VA
WNOX(FM) Loudon TN
WNPC-FM Newport TN
WNPQ(FM) New Philadelphia OH
*WNPR(FM) Norwich CT
WNPT-FM Linden AL
*WNRC(FM) Dudley MA
WNRR(FM) Bellevue OH
WNRT(FM) Manati PR
*WNSB(FM) Norfolk VA
*WNSC-FM Rock Hill SC
WNSL(FM) Laurel MS
WNSN(FM) South Bend IN
WNSP(FM) Bay Minette AL
WNSR(FM) Nashville IL
*WNTE(FM) Mansfield PA
*WNTH(FM) Winnetka IL
*WNTI(FM) Hackettstown NJ
WNTK-FM New London NH
WNTQ(FM) Syracuse NY
WNUA(FM) Chicago IL
*WNUB-FM Northfield VT
WNUC(FM) Wethersfield Township NY
*WNUR-FM Evanston IL
WNUS(FM) Belpre OH
WNUU(FM) Garrison KY
WNUY(FM) Bluffton IN
WNVA-FM Norton VA
WNVZ(FM) Norfolk VA
*WNWC(FM) Madison WI
WNWK-FM Newark NJ
WNWN(FM) Coldwater MI
WNWS-FM Jackson TN
WNWV(FM) Elyria OH
WNXT-FM Portsmouth OH
*WNYC-FM New York NY
*WNYE(FM) New York NY
*WNYK(FM) Nyack NY
*WNYO(FM) Oswego NY
WNYR-FM Waterloo NY
*WNYU-FM New York NY
WNYV(FM) Whitehall NY
WNZE(FM) Plymouth IN
*WNZN(FM) Lorain OH
*WNZR(FM) Mount Vernon OH

WOAB(FM) Ozark AL
*WOAK(FM) La Grange GA
*WOAL-FM Pippa Passes KY
*WOAS(FM) Ontonagon MI
*WOBC-FM Oberlin OH
WOBG-FM Salem WV
WOBM-FM Toms River NJ
*WOBN(FM) Westerville OH
*WOBO(FM) Batavia OH
WOBR-FM Wanchese NC
*WOCG(FM) Huntsville AL
WOCL(FM) De Land FL
WOCO-FM Oconto WI
WOCQ(FM) Berlin MD
*WOCR(FM) Olivet MI
WOCW(FM) Parris Island SC
*WODC(FM) Virginia Beach VA
WODE-FM Easton PA
WODJ(FM) Greenville MI
WODL(FM) Birmingham AL
WODQ(FM) Baraga MI
WODS(FM) Boston MA
WODZ-FM Rome NY
*WOEL-FM Elkton MD
*WOES(FM) Ovid-Elsie MI
WOEZ-FM Milton PA
WOFE-FM Rockwood TN
WOFM(FM) Mosinee WI
WOFX(FM) Fairfield OH
WOGL-FM Philadelphia PA
WOGT(FM) East Ridge TN
WOGY-FM Germantown TN
*WOHC(FM) Chillicothe OH
*WOHP(FM) Portsmouth OH
*WOI-FM Ames IA
*WOJB(FM) Reserve WI
WOJO(FM) Evanston IL
WOKA-FM Douglas GA
WOKC-FM Okeechobee FL
WOKF(FM) Folkston GA
WOKH(FM) Bardstown KY
WOKI-FM Oak Ridge TN
WOKK(FM) Meridian MS
WOKN(FM) Southport NY

WOKO(FM) Burlington VT
WOKQ(FM) Dover NH
WOKW(FM) Curwensville PA
WOLC(FM) Princess Anne MD
WOLD-FM Marion VA
WOLF-FM Houghton MI
WOLL(FM) Riviera Beach FL
*WOLN(FM) Olean NY
*WOLR(FM) Lake City FL
*WOLW(FM) Cadillac MI
WOLX-FM Baraboo WI
WOLZ(FM) Fort Myers FL
WOMC(FM) Detroit MI
WOMG-FM Columbia SC
WOMP-FM Bellaire OH
*WOMR(FM) Provincetown MA
WOMX-FM Orlando FL
WONA-FM Winona MS
*WONB(FM) Ada OH
*WONC(FM) Naperville IL
WONE-FM Akron OH
WONO(FM) Walterboro SC
*WONU(FM) Kankakee IL
*WONY(FM) Oneonta NY
WOOD-FM Grand Rapids MI
WOOF-FM Dothan AL
WOOX(FM) Bedford PA
WOOZ-FM Harrisburg IL
WOQI(FM) Ponce PR
*WORB(FM) Farmington Hills MI
WORD-FM Pittsburgh PA
WORG(FM) Elloree SC
WORK(FM) Barre VT
WORM-FM Savannah TN
WORO(FM) Corozal PR
*WORQ(FM) Green Bay WI
*WORT(FM) Madison WI
*WORW(FM) Port Huron MI
WORX-FM Madison IN
WOSM(FM) Ocean Springs MS
*WOSP(FM) Portsmouth OH
*WOSR(FM) Middletown NY
*WOSS(FM) Ossining NY
*WOSU-FM Columbus OH
*WOSV(FM) Mansfield OH
WOSX(FM) Spencer WI
WOTB(FM) Middletown RI
WOTD(FM) Winamac IN
*WOTJ(FM) Morehead City NC
*WOTL(FM) Toledo OH
WOTR(FM) Lost Creek WV
*WOUB-FM Athens OH
*WOUC-FM Cambridge OH
*WOUH(FM) Chillicothe OH
*WOUI(FM) Chicago IL
*WOUL-FM Ironton OH
WOUR(FM) Utica NY
*WOUZ(FM) Zanesville OH
*WOVI(FM) Novi MI
WOVK(FM) Wheeling WV
WOVU(FM) Clarendon PA
WOVV(FM) Fort Pierce FL
WOW-FM Omaha NE
WOWB(FM) Little Falls NY
WOWE(FM) Vassar MI
WOWI(FM) Norfolk VA
WOWN(FM) Shawano WI
WOWO-FM Huntington IN
WOWQ(FM) DuBois PA
WOWW(FM) Pensacola FL
WOXD(FM) Oxford MS
WOXO-FM Norway ME
WOXY(FM) Oxford OH
WOYE-FM Mayaguez PR
WOYS(FM) Apalachicola FL
WOZI(FM) Presque Isle ME
WOZN(FM) Key West FL
*WOZQ(FM) Northampton MA
WOZZ(FM) New London WI

*WPAA(FM) Andover MA
WPAC(FM) Ogdensburg NY
WPAL-FM Walterboro SC
WPAP-FM Panama City FL
*WPAR(FM) Hickory NC
WPAT-FM Paterson NJ
WPAY-FM Portsmouth OH
WPBC(FM) Pittsfield ME
*WPBX(FM) Southampton NY
*WPCD(FM) Champaign IL
WPCF-FM Panama City Beach FL
WPCH(FM) Atlanta GA
*WPCJ(FM) Pittsford MI
WPCM(FM) Burlington NC
*WPCR-FM Plymouth NH
*WPCS(FM) Pensacola FL
WPCV(FM) Winter Haven FL
WPCX(FM) Auburn NY
WPDA(FM) Jeffersonville NY
WPDH(FM) Poughkeepsie NY
WPDX-FM Clarksburg WV
*WPEA(FM) Exeter NH
*WPEB(FM) Philadelphia PA
WPEG(FM) Concord NC
WPEH-FM Louisville GA
*WPEL-FM Montrose PA
*WPER(FM) Union City IN
WPEZ(FM) Macon GA
WPFB-FM Middletown OH
WPFE(FM) Ogdensburg NY
*WPFF(FM) Sturgeon Bay WI
WPFM(FM) Panama City FL
*WPFR(FM) Netcong NJ
*WPFW(FM) Washington DC
WPGA-FM Perry GA

*WPGB(FM) Blountville TN
WPGC-FM Morningside MD
WPGG(FM) Evergreen AL
*WPGL(FM) Pattersonville NY
*WPGM-FM Danville PA
*WPGT(FM) Roanoke Rapids NC
WPGU(FM) Urbana IL
WPGW-FM Portland IN
WPHB-FM Philipsburg PA
WPHD(FM) Tioga PA
WPHG(FM) Exmore VA
WPHK(FM) Blountstown FL
*WPHN(FM) Gaylord MI
*WPHP(FM) Wheeling WV
WPHR(FM) Ashtabula OH
*WPHS(FM) Warren MI
*WPIB(FM) Bluefield WV
WPIG(FM) Olean NY
WPIK(FM) Summerland Key FL
*WPIM(FM) Martinsville VA
*WPIN(FM) Dublin VA
*WPIO(FM) Titusville FL
*WPIR(FM) Salem VA
WPJB(FM) Narragansett Pier RI
WPKE-FM Elkhorn City KY
WPKM(FM) Scarborough ME
*WPKN(FM) Bridgeport CT
WPKO-FM Bellefontaine OH
WPKR(FM) Omro WI
*WPKT(FM) Meriden CT
WPKX(FM) Enfield CT
WPKY-FM Princeton KY
WPKZ(FM) Elkton VA
WPLB-FM Lakeview MI
WPLC(FM) Spotsylvania VA
*WPLH(FM) Tifton GA
WPLJ(FM) New York NY
WPLM-FM Plymouth MA
*WPLN(FM) Nashville TN
WPLR(FM) New Haven CT
*WPLS-FM Greenville SC
*WPLT(FM) Plattsburgh NY
WPLY(FM) Media PA
WPLZ-FM Petersburg VA
WPME(FM) Topsham ME
WPMR-FM Tobyhanna PA
WPMW(FM) Mullens WV
WPNC-FM Plymouth NC
*WPNE-FM Green Bay WI
WPNH-FM Plymouth NH
*WPNR-FM Utica NY
WPNT-FM Chicago IL
*WPOB-FM Plainview NY
WPOC(FM) Baltimore MD
WPOR-FM Portland ME
WPOS-FM Holland OH
WPOW(FM) Miami FL
WPPL(FM) Blue Ridge GA
WPQR-FM Uniontown PA
WPRB(FM) Princeton NJ
WPRE-FM Prairie du Chien WI
*WPRH-FM Galax VA
WPRJ(FM) Coleman MI
*WPRK(FM) Winter Park FL
*WPRL(FM) Lorman MS
WPRM-FM San Juan PR
WPRO-FM Providence RI
WPRR(FM) Altoona PA
*WPSA(FM) Paul Smiths NY
*WPSC-FM Wayne NJ
WPSK-FM Pulaski VA
*WPSM(FM) Fort Walton Beach FL
*WPSR(FM) Evansville IN
WPST(FM) Trenton NJ
*WPSU(FM) State College PA
WPTG(FM) West Point VA
*WPTH(FM) Olney IL
WPTM(FM) Roanoke Rapids NC
*WPTS-FM Pittsburgh PA
WPUB-FM Camden SC
*WPUM(FM) Rensselaer IN
WPUP(FM) Royston GA
*WPVA(FM) Waynesboro VA
*WPVB(FM) Culpeper VA
WPVR(FM) Roanoke VA
*WPWB(FM) Byron GA
WPXC(FM) Hyannis MA
WPXN(FM) Paxton IL
WPXR-FM Rock Island IL
WPXY-FM Rochester NY
WPXZ-FM Punxsutawney PA
WPYX(FM) Albany NY
WPZX(FM) Big Rapids MI
WPZZ(FM) Franklin IN

*WQAB(FM) Philippi WV
*WQAC-FM Alma MI
WQAL(FM) Cleveland OH
*WQAQ(FM) Hamden CT
WQBA-FM Miami FL
WQBB-FM Knoxville TN
WQBE-FM Charleston WV
WQBK-FM Rensselaer NY
WQBR(FM) Avis PA
WQBZ(FM) Fort Valley GA
WQCB(FM) Brewer ME
WQCD(FM) New York NY
WQCK(FM) Clinton LA
WQCM(FM) Halfway MD
*WQCS(FM) Fort Pierce FL
WQCY(FM) Quincy IL
WQDK(FM) Ahoskie NC
WQDR(FM) Raleigh NC
WQDW-FM Kinston NC
WQDY-FM Calais ME

*WQED-FM Pittsburgh PA
WQEL(FM) Bucyrus OH
WQEN(FM) Gadsden AL
WQEQ(FM) Freeland PA
WQEZ(FM) Chillicothe IL
WQFE(FM) Brownsburg IN
WQFL(FM) Rockford IL
WQFM(FM) Milwaukee WI
WQFN(FM) Walker MI
*WQFS(FM) Greensboro NC
WQGL(FM) Butler AL
WQGN-FM Groton CT
WQHG(FM) Huntingdon PA
WQHH(FM) Dewitt MI
WQHK-FM Decatur IN
WQHL-FM Live Oak FL
WQHQ(FM) Ocean City-Salisbury MD
WQHT(FM) New York NY
WQHY(FM) Prestonsburg KY
WQIC(FM) Lebanon PA
WQID(FM) Biloxi MS
WQIK-FM Jacksonville FL
WQIL(FM) Chauncey GA
WQIO(FM) Mount Vernon OH
WQIX(FM) Horseheads NY
*WQJU(FM) Mifflintown PA
WQJY(FM) West Salem WI
WQKB(FM) New Kensington PA
WQKC(FM) Seymour IN
WQKK(FM) Ebensburg PA
WQKL(FM) Ann Arbor MI
*WQKO(FM) Howe IN
WQKT(FM) Wooster OH
WQKX(FM) Sunbury PA
WQKY(FM) Emporium PA
WQLA-FM La Follette TN
WQLC(FM) Watertown FL
WQLH(FM) Green Bay WI
WQLJ(FM) Oxford MS
WQLK(FM) Richmond IN
*WQLN-FM Erie PA
WQLR(FM) Kalamazoo MI
WQLS-FM Ozark AL
WQLT(FM) Florence AL
WQLV(FM) Millersburg PA
WQLW(FM) Eutaw AL
WQLX(FM) Galion OH
WQLZ(FM) Taylorville IL
WQME(FM) Anderson IN
WQMF(FM) Jeffersonville IN
WQMG-FM Greensboro NC
WQMT(FM) Chatsworth GA
WQMU(FM) Indiana PA
WQMX(FM) Medina OH
WQMZ(FM) Charlottesville VA
*WQNA(FM) Springfield IL
WQNF(FM) Valley Station KY
WQNJ(FM) Ocean Acres NJ
WQNN(FM) Artesia MS
WQNS(FM) Waynesville NC
WQNY(FM) Ithaca NY
WQNZ(FM) Natchez MS
WQOK(FM) South Boston VA
WQOL(FM) Vero Beach FL
WQON(FM) Grayling MI
*WQOX(FM) Memphis TN
WQPM-FM Princeton MN
WQPO(FM) Harrisonburg VA
*WQPR(FM) Muscle Shoals AL
WQPW(FM) Valdosta GA
WQQK(FM) Hendersonville TN
WQQL(FM) Springfield IL
WQQQ(FM) Sharon CT
WQQZ(FM) Quebradillas PR
WQRA(FM) Warrenton VA
WQRB(FM) Bloomer WI
WQRC(FM) Barnstable MA
*WQRI(FM) Bristol RI
WQRK(FM) Bedford IN
WQRL(FM) Benton IL
WQRM(FM) Smethport PA
*WQRP(FM) West Carrollton OH
WQRS(FM) Detroit MI
WQRT(FM) Salamanca NY
WQSB(FM) Albertville AL
WQSM(FM) Fayetteville NC
WQSR(FM) Catonsville MD
WQSS(FM) Camden ME
WQST-FM Forest MS
*WQSU(FM) Selinsgrove PA
WQSY(FM) Hawkinsville GA
WQTC-FM Manitowoc WI
WQTE(FM) Adrian MI
WQTL(FM) Ottawa OH
*WQTQ(FM) Hartford CT
WQTU(FM) Rome GA
WQTY(FM) Linton IN
*WQUB(FM) Quincy IL
WQUE-FM New Orleans LA
WQUL(FM) Griffin GA
WQUT(FM) Johnson City TN
WQVA(FM) Semora NC
WQVE(FM) Camilla GA
WQVR(FM) Southbridge MA
WQWK(FM) State College PA
WQXA-FM York PA
WQXB(FM) Grenada MS
WQXC-FM Otsego MI
WQXE(FM) Elizabethtown KY
WQXJ(FM) Clayton GA
WQXK(FM) Salem OH
WQXQ(FM) Central City KY
WQXR-FM New York NY
WQYK-FM St. Petersburg FL

WQYX(FM) Clearfield PA
WQZK-FM Keyser WV
WQZQ(FM) Dickson TN
WQZS(FM) Meyersdale PA
WQZX(FM) Greenville AL
WQZY(FM) Dublin GA

WRAC(FM) West Union OH
*WRAF-FM Toccoa Falls GA
WRAJ-FM Anna IL
WRAK-FM Williamsport PA
WRAL(FM) Raleigh NC
WRAR-FM Tappahannock VA
*WRAS(FM) Atlanta GA
WRAY-FM Princeton IN
WRBA(FM) Springfield FL
*WRBB(FM) Boston MA
*WRBC(FM) Lewiston ME
WRBE-FM Lucedale MS
*WRBH(FM) New Orleans LA
WRBI(FM) Batesville IN
WRBP(FM) Hubbard OH
WRBQ-FM Tampa FL
WRBR-FM South Bend IN
WRBS(FM) Baltimore MD
WRBT(FM) Mt. Carmel IL
WRBX(FM) Reidsville GA
WRCC-FM Warner Robins GA
WRCD(FM) Clyde NY
WRCH(FM) New Britain CT
WRCI(FM) Hillsboro NH
WRCK(FM) Utica NY
*WRCM(FM) Wingate NC
WRCN-FM Riverhead NY
WRCO-FM Richland Center WI
WRCQ(FM) Dunn NC
WRCR(FM) Rushville IN
*WRCT(FM) Pittsburgh PA
*WRCU-FM Hamilton NY
WRCY(FM) Warrenton VA
WRCZ(FM) Pittsfield MA
*WRDJ(FM) Roanoke VA
*WRDL(FM) Ashland OH
WRDN-FM Durand WI
WRDO(FM) Fitzgerald GA
WRDR(FM) Egg Harbor City NJ
WRDU(FM) Wilson NC
*WRDV(FM) Warminster PA
WRDX(FM) Salisbury NC
*WREK(FM) Atlanta GA
WREL-FM Buena Vista VA
WREO-FM Ashtabula OH
WREZ(FM) Metropolis IL
*WRFG(FM) Atlanta GA
*WRFH(FM) Marietta PA
WRFK(FM) California MD
*WRFL(FM) Lexington KY
WRFR(FM) Franklin NC
*WRFT(FM) Indianapolis IN
*WRFW(FM) River Falls WI
WRFX(FM) Kannapolis NC
WRFY-FM Reading PA
WRGG(FM) Endwell NY
*WRGN(FM) Sweet Valley PA
WRGR(FM) Tupper Lake NY
WRHA(FM) Johnsonville SC
WRHF(FM) Farmington NH
WRHL-FM Rochelle IL
WRHM(FM) Lancaster SC
WRHN(FM) Rhinelander WI
*WRHO(FM) Oneonta NY
WRHQ(FM) Richmond Hill GA
WRHT(FM) Morehead City NC
*WRHU(FM) Hempstead NY
*WRHV(FM) Poughkeepsie NY
WRHY(FM) Centre AL
WRIC-FM Richlands VA
WRIF(FM) Detroit MI
*WRIJ(FM) Masontown PA
WRIK-FM Metropolis IL
WRIL(FM) Pineville KY
WRIO(FM) Ponce PR
WRIQ(FM) Radford VA
*WRIU(FM) Kingston RI
WRIX-FM Honea Path SC
*WRJA-FM Sumter SC
WRJB(FM) Camden TN
WRJC-FM Mauston WI
WRJH(FM) Brandon MS
WRJM-FM Geneva AL
WRJO(FM) Eagle River WI
WRJS(FM) Oil City PA
*WRJV(FM) Berne IN
WRKA(FM) St. Matthews KY
*WRKC(FM) Wilkes-Barre PA
WRKE(FM) Ocean View DE
*WRKF(FM) Baton Rouge LA
WRKI(FM) Brookfield CT
WRKP(FM) Moundsville WV
WRKR(FM) Portage MI
WRKS-FM New York NY
WRKT(FM) North East PA
WRKU-FM Grove City PA
WRKX(FM) Ottawa IL
WRKY(FM) Steubenville OH
WRKZ(FM) Hershey PA
*WRLC(FM) Williamsport PA
WRLD(FM) Valley AL
WRLF(FM) Fairmont WV
WRLG(FM) Smyrna TN
*WRLJ(FM) Freehold Township NJ
WRLO-FM Antigo WI
WRLP(FM) Russell PA
WRLQ(FM) Ladson SC
WRLS-FM Hayward WI

WRLT-FM Franklin TN
WRLV-FM Salyersville KY
WRLX(FM) West Palm Beach FL
*WRMB(FM) Boynton Beach FL
*WRMC-FM Middlebury VT
WRMF(FM) Palm Beach FL
WRMJ(FM) Aledo IL
WRMM-FM Rochester NY
WRMS-FM Beardstown IL
*WRMU(FM) Alliance OH
WRMX(FM) Murfreesboro TN
*WRND(FM) Manchester NH
WRNJ-FM Belvidere NJ
WRNN(FM) Murrell's Inlet SC
WRNO-FM New Orleans LA
WRNQ(FM) Poughkeepsie NY
WRNS-FM Kinston NC
WRNX(FM) Amherst MA
WRNZ(FM) Lancaster KY
WROE(FM) Neenah-Menasha WI
WROG(FM) Cumberland MD
WROI(FM) Rochester IN
WRON-FM Ronceverte WV
WROO(FM) Jacksonville FL
WROQ(FM) Anderson SC
WROU(FM) West Carrollton OH
WROV-FM Martinsville VA
WROW-FM Albany NY
WROX-FM Cape Charles VA
WROZ(FM) Lancaster PA
WRPC(FM) San German PR
*WRPI(FM) Troy NY
*WRPJ(FM) Port Jervis NY
WRPL(FM) Wadesboro NC
*WRPN-FM Ripon WI
*WRPR(FM) Mahwah NJ
*WRPS(FM) Rockland MA
WRQI(FM) South Bristol Township NY
WRQK(FM) Canton OH
WRQN(FM) Bowling Green OH
WRQO(FM) Monticello MS
WRQR(FM) Farmville NC
WRQT(FM) Bear Lake MI
WRQX(FM) Washington DC
WRR(FM) Dallas TX
*WRRC(FM) Lawrenceville NJ
*WRRG(FM) River Grove IL
WRRK(FM) Braddock PA
WRRL-FM Rainelle WV
WRRM(FM) Cincinnati OH
WRRN(FM) Warren PA
WRRR-FM St. Marys WV
WRRX(FM) Micanopy FL
WRSA(FM) Decatur AL
*WRSD(FM) Folsom PA
*WRSE-FM Elmhurst IL
WRSF(FM) Columbia NC
*WRSH(FM) Rockingham NC
WRSI(FM) Greenfield MA
*WRSK(FM) Slippery Rock PA
WRSL-FM Stanford KY
WRSR(FM) Two Harbors MN
*WRST-FM Oshkosh WI
*WRSU-FM New Brunswick NJ
WRSV(FM) Rocky Mount NC
WRSW-FM Warsaw IN
*WRTC-FM Hartford CT
*WRTI(FM) Philadelphia PA
*WRTL(FM) Ephrata PA
WRTN(FM) New Rochelle NY
WRTO(FM) Goulds FL
*WRTQ(FM) Ocean City NJ
*WRTU(FM) San Juan PR
*WRTX(FM) Dover DE
*WRTY(FM) Jackson Township PA
*WRUC(FM) Schenectady NY
WRUF-FM Gainesville FL
WRUL(FM) Carmi IL
*WRUR-FM Rochester NY
*WRUV(FM) Burlington VT
*WRUW-FM Cleveland OH
WRVC-FM Ashland KY
WRVF(FM) Upper Arlington OH
*WRVG(FM) Georgetown KY
*WRVJ(FM) Watertown NY
*WRVL(FM) Lynchburg VA
WRVM(FM) Suring WI
*WRVN(FM) Utica NY
*WRVO(FM) Oswego NY
WRVQ(FM) Richmond VA
WRVR-FM Memphis TN
*WRVS-FM Elizabeth City NC
*WRVT(FM) Rutland VT
*WRVU(FM) Nashville TN
WRVV(FM) Harrisburg PA
WRVW(FM) Hudson NY
WRVY-FM Henry IL
*WRWA(FM) Dothan AL
WRWC(FM) Rockton IL
WRWD-FM Highland NY
*WRWJ(FM) Murrysville PA
WRWX(FM) Sanibel FL
*WRXC(FM) Shelton CT
WRXK-FM Bonita Springs FL
WRXL(FM) Richmond VA
WRXQ(FM) Olive Branch MS
WRXR-FM Aiken SC
WRXS(FM) Ocean City MD
WRXX(FM) Centralia IL
WRZE(FM) Nantucket MA
WRZI(FM) Vine Grove KY
WRZK(FM) Tallahassee FL
WRZQ-FM Greensburg IN
WRZR(FM) Johnstown OH

U.S. FM Stations by Call Letters

WRZX(FM) Indianapolis IN
WRZZ(FM) Ravenswood WV

WSAC(FM) Louisa KY
*WSAE(FM) Spring Arbor MI
*WSAJ-FM Grove City PA
WSAN(FM) Vieques PR
WSAQ(FM) Port Huron MI
WSAY-FM Rocky Mount NC
WSB-FM Atlanta GA
*WSBF-FM Clemson SC
WSBG(FM) Stroudsburg PA
WSBL(FM) Selbyville DE
*WSBU(FM) St. Bonaventure NY
WSBY-FM Salisbury MD
WSCA(FM) Georgetown SC
*WSCB(FM) Springfield MA
*WSCD-FM Duluth MN
*WSCF-FM Vero Beach FL
WSCH(FM) Aurora IN
*WSCI(FM) Charleston SC
*WSCL(FM) Salisbury MD
*WSCN(FM) Cloquet MN
WSCP-FM Pulaski NY
WSCQ(FM) West Columbia SC
*WSCT(FM) Springfield IL
WSCY(FM) Moultonborough NH
WSCZ(FM) Greenwood SC
*WSDH(FM) Sandwich MA
WSDM-FM Brazil IN
*WSDP(FM) Plymouth MI
WSEA(FM) Pawley's Island SC
*WSEB(FM) Englewood FL
WSEG(FM) Brunswick GA
WSEH(FM) Cumberland KY
WSEI(FM) Olney IL
WSEK(FM) Somerset KY
WSEL-FM Pontotoc MS
WSEN-FM Baldwinsville NY
WSEO(FM) Nelsonville OH
*WSEW(FM) Sanford ME
WSEY(FM) Mount Morris IL
WSFL-FM New Bern NC
WSFM(FM) Southport NC
*WSFP-FM Fort Myers FL
WSFW-FM Seneca Falls NY
*WSFX(FM) Nanticoke PA
WSGC-FM Ringgold GA
WSGD-FM Carbondale PA
*WSGE(FM) Dallas NC
WSGL(FM) Naples FL
WSGM(FM) Coalmont TN
*WSGN(FM) Gadsden AL
*WSGR-FM Port Huron MI
WSGS(FM) Hazard KY
WSGY(FM) Tifton GA
*WSHA(FM) Raleigh NC
*WSHC(FM) Shepherdstown WV
*WSHD(FM) Eastport ME
WSHE(FM) Fort Lauderdale FL
WSHG(FM) Ridgeland SC
WSHH(FM) Pittsburgh PA
*WSHJ(FM) Southfield MI
WSHK(FM) Russellville AL
*WSHL-FM Easton MA
WSHN-FM Fremont MI
WSHQ(FM) Cobleskill NY
*WSHR(FM) Lake Ronkonkoma NY
*WSHS(FM) Sheboygan WI
*WSHU(FM) Fairfield CT
WSHV(FM) South Hill VA
WSHW(FM) Frankfort IN
WSHX(FM) Danville VT
*WSIA(FM) Staten Island NY
WSIB(FM) Selmer TN
*WSIE(FM) Edwardsville IL
*WSIF(FM) Wilkesboro NC
WSIG(FM) Mount Jackson VA
WSIP-FM Paintsville KY
*WSIU(FM) Carbondale IL
WSIX-FM Nashville TN
*WSJB-FM Standish ME
WSJD(FM) Princeton IN
WSJL(FM) Cape May NJ
WSJY(FM) Fort Atkinson WI
*WSKB(FM) Westfield MA
WSKE-FM Everett PA
*WSKG-FM Binghamton NY
WSKO(FM) Buffalo Gap VA
WSKP(FM) Key West FL
WSKQ-FM New York NY
WSKR(FM) Petersburg NJ
WSKS(FM) Pittston PA
WSKT(FM) Spencer IN
WSKV(FM) Stanton KY
WSKX(FM) Hinesville GA
WSKZ(FM) Chattanooga TN
WSLD(FM) Whitewater WI
WSLE(FM) Cairo GA
*WSLJ(FM) Watertown NY
WSLK(FM) Saranac Lake NY
*WSLL(FM) Saranac Lake NY
WSLM-FM Salem IN
*WSLN(FM) Delaware OH
*WSLO(FM) Malone NY
WSLQ(FM) Roanoke VA
WSLT(FM) Clearwater SC
*WSLU(FM) Canton NY
*WSLX(FM) New Canaan CT
WSLY(FM) York AL
WSM-FM Nashville TN
*WSMC-FM Collegedale TN
WSMD(FM) Mechanicsville MD
WSMI-FM Litchfield IL
WSMK(FM) Buchanan MI

*WSMS(FM) Memphis TN
WSMT-FM Sparta TN
*WSMU-FM North Dartmouth MA
*WSNC(FM) Winston-Salem NC
*WSND-FM Notre Dame IN
WSNE(FM) Taunton MA
WSNI(FM) Thomasville GA
WSNJ-FM Bridgeton NJ
WSNN(FM) Potsdam NY
WSNT-FM Sandersville GA
WSNU(FM) Lock Haven PA
WSNV(FM) Howland ME
WSNX-FM Muskegon MI
WSNY(FM) Columbus OH
WSOC-FM Charlotte NC
*WSOE(FM) Elon College NC
*WSOF-FM Madisonville KY
*WSOR(FM) Naples FL
WSOS(FM) St. Augustine FL
*WSOU(FM) South Orange NJ
WSOY-FM Decatur IL
WSPA-FM Spartanburg SC
WSPI(FM) Mount Carmel PA
WSPK(FM) Poughkeepsie NY
WSPL(FM) La Crosse WI
*WSPN(FM) Saratoga Springs NY
*WSPS(FM) Concord NH
WSPT(FM) Stevens Point WI
WSPY(FM) Plano IL
*WSQC-FM Oneonta NY
*WSQG-FM Ithaca NY
WSQN(FM) Scranton SC
*WSQX-FM Binghamton NY
*WSRB(FM) Walpole MA
WSRD(FM) Johnstown NY
WSRK(FM) Oneonta NY
WSRM(FM) Coosa GA
*WSRN-FM Swarthmore PA
WSRS(FM) Worcester MA
WSRT(FM) Mercersburg PA
WSRW-FM Hillsboro OH
*WSRX(FM) Naples FL
WSRZ-FM Sarasota FL
*WSSB-FM Orangeburg SC
*WSSD(FM) Chicago IL
WSSH-FM Lowell MA
WSSI-FM Carthage MS
WSSL-FM Gray Court SC
WSSN(FM) Weston WV
WSSP(FM) Goose Creek SC
WSSQ(FM) Sterling IL
*WSSU(FM) Springfield IL
WSSV(FM) Stillwater NY
WSSX-FM Charleston SC
WSSY-FM Talladega AL
WSSZ(FM) Greensburg PA
*WSTB(FM) Streetsboro OH
WSTD(FM) Standish MI
WSTF(FM) St. Augustine FL
WSTG(FM) Biddeford ME
WSTH-FM Alexander City AL
WSTI-FM Quitman GA
WSTO(FM) Owensboro KY
WSTQ(FM) Streator IL
WSTR(FM) Smyrna GA
WSTS(FM) Fairmont NC
WSTW(FM) Wilmington DE
WSTX-FM Christiansted VI
WSTZ-FM Vicksburg MS
*WSUC-FM Cortland NY
WSUE(FM) Sault Ste. Marie MI
*WSUF(FM) Noyack NY
WSUL-FM Monticello NY
*WSUP(FM) Platteville WI
WSUS(FM) Franklin NJ
WSUV(FM) Fort Myers Villas FL
*WSUW(FM) Whitewater WI
WSUY(FM) Charleston SC
*WSVH(FM) Savannah GA
WSVV(FM) Petersburg VA
WSVY-FM Windsor VA
WSWO(FM) Wilmington OH
WSWR(FM) Shelby OH
WSWT(FM) Peoria IL
WSWV-FM Pennington Gap VA
WSWZ(FM) Lancaster OH
WSYA-FM Montgomery AL
*WSYC-FM Shippensburg PA
WSYE(FM) Houston MS
WSYN(FM) Georgetown SC
WSYW-FM Danville IN
WSYY-FM Millinocket ME

WTAK-FM Hartselle AL
WTAO(FM) Murphysboro IL
WTAY-FM Robinson IL
WTAZ(FM) Morton IL
WTBB(FM) Bonifay FL
*WTBC-FM Williston VT
WTBG(FM) Brownsville TN
*WTBH(FM) Chiefland FL
*WTBI-FM Greenville SC
WTBK(FM) Manchester KY
WTBM(FM) Mexico ME
WTBN(FM) Charlotte Amalie VI
WTBX(FM) Hibbing MN
WTBZ-FM Grafton WV
WTCB(FM) Orangeburg SC
*WTCC(FM) Springfield MA
WTCF(FM) Carrollton MI
WTCM-FM Traverse City MI
WTCO-FM Russell Springs KY
WTCQ(FM) Vidalia GA
WTCR-FM Huntington WV
WTCX(FM) Lakeville MN

WTDR(FM) Statesville NC
*WTEB(FM) New Bern NC
WTFM(FM) Kingsport TN
WTFX(FM) Louisville KY
WTGA-FM Thomaston GA
WTGE-FM Baton Rouge LA
*WTGF(FM) Milton FL
*WTGN(FM) Lima OH
*WTGP(FM) Greenville PA
WTGR(FM) Union City OH
WTGV-FM Sandusky MI
WTGY(FM) Charleston MS
WTHI-FM Terre Haute IN
*WTHL(FM) Somerset KY
WTHO-FM Thomson GA
WTHQ(FM) Shelbyville KY
*WTHS(FM) Holland MI
WTHT(FM) Lewiston ME
WTIC-FM Hartford CT
WTID(FM) Reform AL
WTIF-FM Omega GA
*WTJB(FM) Columbus GA
*WTJT(FM) Baker FL
*WTJU(FM) Charlottesville VA
WTKB-FM Huntingdon TN
*WTKC(FM) Kankakee IL
WTKF(FM) Atlantic NC
WTKL(FM) New Orleans LA
WTKM-FM Hartford WI
WTKS(FM) Cocoa Beach FL
WTKT-FM Georgetown KY
WTKW(FM) Bridgeport NY
WTKX-FM Pensacola FL
WTKY-FM Tompkinsville KY
WTLC-FM Indianapolis IN
*WTLG(FM) Starke FL
WTLN-FM Apopka FL
*WTLR(FM) State College PA
WTLZ(FM) Saginaw MI
*WTMD(FM) Towson MD
WTMI(FM) Miami FL
WTMS-FM Presque Isle ME
WTMX(FM) Skokie IL
WTND(FM) Grifton NC
WTNJ(FM) Mount Hope WV
WTNR-FM Waynesboro TN
WTNS-FM Coshocton OH
WTNT(FM) Tallahassee FL
WTNV(FM) Jackson TN
WTNY-FM Watertown NY
WTOF-FM Canton OH
*WTOH(FM) Mobile AL
WTOJ(FM) Carthage NY
WTON-FM Staunton VA
WTOS-FM Skowhegan ME
WTPA(FM) Mechanicsburg PA
*WTPC(FM) Elsah IL
WTPI(FM) Indianapolis IN
WTPM(FM) Aguadilla PR
WTPX(FM) Fort Lauderdale FL
WTQR(FM) Winston-Salem NC
WTRB-FM Ripley TN
WTRC-FM Natchez MS
WTRG(FM) Rocky Mount NC
WTRJ(FM) Troy OH
*WTRK(FM) Bay City MI
*WTRM(FM) Winchester VA
WTRS-FM Dunellon FL
WTRU(FM) Jupiter FL
WTRV(FM) Leland MI
WTRY-FM Rotterdam NY
WTRZ-FM McMinnville TN
WTSA-FM Brattleboro VT
*WTSC-FM Potsdam NY
WTSH-FM Rockmart GA
*WTSR(FM) Trenton NJ
*WTSU(FM) Troy AL
WTSX(FM) Port Jervis NY
WTTC-FM Towanda PA
WTTF-FM Tiffin OH
WTTH(FM) Margate City NJ
WTTL-FM Madisonville KY
WTTS(FM) Bloomington IN
*WTTU(FM) Cookeville TN
WTTX-FM Appomattox VA
WTUA(FM) St. Stephen SC
WTUC(FM) Tuckerton NJ
WTUE(FM) Dayton OH
WTUF(FM) Boston GA
WTUG(FM) Tuscaloosa AL
WTUK(FM) Harlan KY
*WTUL(FM) New Orleans LA
WTUN(FM) Pocatalico WV
WTUS(FM) Mannington WV
WTUX(FM) Meridian MS
WTUZ(FM) Uhrichsville OH
WTVR-FM Richmond VA
WTVY-FM Dothan AL
WTWL(FM) McKinnon TN
WTWR-FM Monroe MI
WTWX-FM Guntersville AL
WTXT(FM) Fayette AL
WTYD(FM) New London CT
WTYJ(FM) Fayette MS
WTYL-FM Tylertown MS
WTYX(FM) Jackson MS
WTZE-FM Tazewell VA

WUAE(FM) Wakefield-Peacedale RI
*WUAG(FM) Greensboro NC
*WUAL-FM Tuscaloosa AL
*WUAW(FM) Erwin NC
WUBB(FM) Tuscola IL
WUBE-FM Cincinnati OH

*WUBJ(FM) Jamestown NY
*WUBS(FM) South Bend IN
WUBU(FM) South Bend IN
*WUCF-FM Orlando FL
*WUCX-FM Bay City MI
WUCZ-FM Carthage TN
*WUEC(FM) Eau Claire WI
*WUEV(FM) Evansville IN
WUEZ(FM) Christopher IL
WUFA(FM) Byesville OH
WUFF-FM Eastman GA
WUFK(FM) Fort Kent ME
*WUFN(FM) Albion MI
*WUFT-FM Gainesville FL
WUFX(FM) Buffalo NY
*WUGA(FM) Athens GA
*WUGN(FM) Midland MI
WUGO(FM) Grayson KY
*WUJC(FM) University Heights OH
*WUKY(FM) Lexington KY
WULA-FM Eufaula AL
WULS(FM) Broxton GA
*WUMB-FM Boston MA
WUME-FM Paoli IN
*WUMF-FM Farmington ME
WUMG(FM) Chattahoochee FL
WUMI(FM) State College MS
WUMS(FM) University MS
WUMX(FM) Tallahassee FL
*WUNC(FM) Chapel Hill NC
*WUNH(FM) Durham NH
WUNS(FM) Lewisburg PA
*WUNV(FM) Albany GA
*WUNW(FM) Key West FL
*WUNY(FM) Utica NY
*WUOG(FM) Athens GA
*WUOL(FM) Louisville KY
*WUOM(FM) Ann Arbor MI
*WUOT(FM) Knoxville TN
WUOY(FM) Wilmington NC
*WUOZ(FM) Belvedere SC
WUPE(FM) Pittsfield MA
*WUPI(FM) Presque Isle ME
WUPK(FM) Marquette MI
WUPM(FM) Ironwood MI
WUPQ(FM) Newberry MI
WUPS(FM) Houghton Lake MI
*WUPX(FM) Marquette MI
WUPY(FM) Ontonagon MI
*WURC(FM) Holly Springs MS
WUSA-FM Tampa FL
*WUSB(FM) Stony Brook NY
*WUSC-FM Columbia SC
WUSD(FM) Wiggins MS
*WUSF(FM) Tampa FL
*WUSI(FM) Olney IL
WUSJ-FM Elizabethton TN
WUSL(FM) Philadelphia PA
*WUSM-FM Hattiesburg MS
WUSN(FM) Chicago IL
*WUSO(FM) Springfield OH
WUSQ-FM Winchester VA
WUSR(FM) Scranton PA
WUSW(FM) Oshkosh WI
WUSY(FM) Cleveland TN
WUSZ(FM) Virginia MN
*WUTC(FM) Chattanooga TN
*WUTK-FM Knoxville TN
*WUTM(FM) Martin TN
*WUTS(FM) Sewanee TN
WUUF(FM) Statesboro GA
WUUU(FM) Remsen NY
WUVA(FM) Charlottesville VA
WUVE(FM) Saginaw MI
*WUVT-FM Blacksburg VA
*WUWF(FM) Pensacola FL
*WUWM(FM) Milwaukee WI
WUZR(FM) Bicknell IN

*WVAC-FM Adrian MI
WVAF(FM) Charleston WV
WVAQ(FM) Morgantown WV
*WVAS(FM) Montgomery AL
WVAV(FM) Hatteras NC
WVAY(FM) Wilmington VT
WVAZ(FM) Oak Park IL
*WVBC(FM) Bethany WV
WVBI(FM) Block Island RI
WVBR-FM Ithaca NY
*WVBU-FM Lewisburg PA
WVCA(FM) Selma AL
WVCC(FM) Linesville PA
WVCO(FM) Loris SC
*WVCP(FM) Gallatin TN
*WVCR-FM Loudonville NY
*WVCS(FM) California PA
*WVCT(FM) Keavy KY
WVCV(FM) Boalsburg PA
WVCX(FM) Tomah WI
WVCY(FM) Milwaukee WI
WVEE(FM) Atlanta GA
*WVEP(FM) Martinsburg WV
WVES(FM) Accomac VA
WVEZ-FM Louisville KY
WVFB(FM) Celina TN
WVFE(FM) Coral Cove FL
WVFG(FM) Uniontown AL
WVFJ-FM Manchester GA
WVFM(FM) Campton NH
*WVFS(FM) Tallahassee FL
WVGN(FM) Charlotte Amalie VI
WVGO(FM) Richmond VA
*WVGR(FM) Grand Rapids MI
*WVGS(FM) Statesboro GA
*WVHC(FM) Herkimer NY

WVHF-FM Clarksburg WV
*WVHM(FM) Benton KY
WVHR(FM) Huntingdon TN
*WVIA-FM Scranton PA
WVIC-FM East Lansing MI
*WVIJ(FM) Port Charlotte FL
*WVIK(FM) Rock Island IL
WVIM-FM Coldwater MS
WVIN-FM Bath NY
WVIP-FM Mount Kisco NY
WVIQ(FM) Christiansted VI
WVIS(FM) Christiansted VI
*WVJC(FM) Mt. Carmel IL
WVJP-FM Caguas PR
*WVKC(FM) Galesburg IL
WVKM(FM) Matewan WV
*WVKR-FM Poughkeepsie NY
WVKS(FM) Toledo OH
WVKX(FM) Irwinton GA
WVLC(FM) Campbellsville KY
WVLE(FM) Scottsville KY
WVLK-FM Lexington KY
*WVLS(FM) Monterey VA
WVLT(FM) Vineland NJ
*WVMC(FM) Mansfield OH
WVMG-FM Cochran GA
*WVMH-FM Mars Hill NC
*WVMM(FM) Grantham PA
*WVMS(FM) Sandusky OH
*WVMW-FM Scranton PA
WVMX(FM) Stowe VT
WVNA-FM Tuscumbia AL
WVNC(FM) Canton NY
*WVNH(FM) Concord NH
WVNI(FM) Nashville IN
WVNM(FM) Cedar Key FL
WVNO-FM Mansfield OH
*WVNP(FM) Wheeling WV
WVNU(FM) Greenfield OH
WVNV(FM) Malone NY
WVNW(FM) Burnham PA
WVNX(FM) Charlotte Amalie VI
WVOA(FM) DeRuyter NY
*WVOB(FM) Dothan AL
WVOD(FM) Manteo NC
*WVOF(FM) Fairfield CT
WVOH-FM Hazlehurst GA
WVOK(FM) Oxford AL
WVOR-FM Rochester NY
WVOS-FM Liberty NY
WVOW-FM Logan WV
WVOZ-FM Carolina PR
*WVPB(FM) Beckley WV
*WVPE(FM) Elkhart IN
*WVPG(FM) Parkersburg WV
*WVPH(FM) Piscataway NJ
*WVPM(FM) Morgantown WV
*WVPN(FM) Charleston WV
*WVPR(FM) Windsor VT
*WVPS(FM) Burlington VT
*WVPW(FM) Buckhannon WV
WVRC-FM Spencer WV
WVRD(FM) Belzoni MS
WVRK(FM) Columbus GA
WVRP(FM) Ripley WV
WVRQ-FM Viroqua WI
WVRT(FM) Baltimore MD
*WVRU(FM) Radford VA
WVRY(FM) Waverly TN
WVSC-FM Somerset PA
*WVSD(FM) Itta Bena MS
*WVSH(FM) Huntington IN
WVSR-FM Charleston WV
*WVSS(FM) Menomonie WI
*WVST(FM) Petersburg VA
*WVSU-FM Birmingham AL
WVSY(FM) Ruckersville VA
WVSZ(FM) Chesterfield SC
*WVTC(FM) Randolph Center VT
*WVTF(FM) Roanoke VA
*WVTR(FM) Marion VA
*WVTU(FM) Charlottesville VA
WVTY(FM) Pittsburgh PA
*WVUA-FM Tuscaloosa AL
*WVUB(FM) Vincennes IN
*WVUD(FM) Newark DE
*WVUM(FM) Coral Gables FL
*WVUR-FM Valparaiso IN
WVVE(FM) Stonington CT
*WVVS(FM) Valdosta GA
WVVV(FM) Blacksburg VA
WVVX(FM) Highland Park IL
WVVY(FM) Fort Valley GA
*WVWC(FM) Buckhannon WV
*WVWV(FM) Huntington WV
WVXA(FM) Signal Mountain TN
*WVXC(FM) Chillicothe OH
*WVXD(FM) Chetek WI
*WVXE(FM) Dillwyn VA
*WVXM(FM) West Union OH
*WVXR(FM) Richmond IN
*WVXU(FM) Cincinnati OH
*WVYC(FM) York PA
WVYF(FM) Sylvester GA
WVZA(FM) Herrin IL
WVZC(FM) Montauk NY
WVZD(FM) Dennysville ME
WVZG(FM) White Stone VA

WWAG(FM) McKee KY
*WWAS(FM) Williamsport PA
WWAV(FM) Santa Rosa Beach FL
WWBB(FM) Providence RI
WWBD(FM) Bamberg SC
WWBE(FM) Mifflinburg PA

U.S. FM Stations by Call Letters

WWBK(FM) Fredericktown OH
WWBL(FM) Washington IN
WWBR(FM) Trussville AL
WWBV(FM) Beaver Springs PA
WWBZ(FM) Chicago IL
WWCD(FM) Grove City OH
WWCK-FM Flint MI
WWCP-FM Clifton Park NY
WWCT(FM) Peoria IL
*WWCU(FM) Cullowhee NC
WWDB(FM) Philadelphia PA
WWDC-FM Washington DC
WWDE-FM Hampton VA
WWDL-FM Scranton PA
WWDM(FM) Sumter SC
WWDO(FM) Vero Beach FL
WWDQ(FM) Morehead KY
*WWDS(FM) Muncie IN
WWDX(FM) St. Johns MI
WWDZ(FM) Danville IL
*WWEB(FM) Wallingford CT
*WWEC(FM) Elizabethtown PA
WWEE(FM) Spencer TN
WWEG(FM) Mitchell IN
WWEL(FM) London KY
WWEM(FM) Rochester NH
WWET(FM) Valdosta GA
*WWEV-FM Cumming GA
WWEZ(FM) Trenton TN
WWFG(FM) Ocean City MD
*WWFM(FM) Trenton NJ
WWFN(FM) Lake City SC
WWFO(FM) Vinton VA
*WWFR(FM) Okeechobee FL
WWFS(FM) Kosciusko MS
WWFX(FM) Belfast ME
WWGA(FM) Georgiana AL
*WWGC(FM) Carrollton GA
WWGL(FM) Lexington NC
WWGM(FM) Alamo TN
WWGO(FM) Silver Springs FL
WWGT(FM) Vergennes VT
WWGZ-FM Lapeer MI
WWHB(FM) Hampton Bays NY
*WWHI(FM) Muncie IN
WWHK(FM) Greenville KY
*WWHR(FM) Bowling Green KY
*WWHS-FM Hampden-Sydney VA
WWHT(FM) Marysville OH
WWIA(FM) Palm Bay FL
WWIB(FM) Ladysmith WI
*WWIH(FM) High Point NC
WWIN-FM Glen Burnie MD
*WWIO(FM) Brunswick GA
WWIP(FM) Wabash IN
WWIQ(FM) Gray GA
WWIR(FM) Fair Bluff NC
WWIS-FM Black River Falls WI
WWIZ(FM) Mercer PA
WWJM(FM) New Lexington OH
WWJO(FM) St. Cloud MN
WWJR(FM) Sheboygan WI
WWJY(FM) Crown Point IN
WWKA(FM) Orlando FL
WWKC(FM) Caldwell OH
WWKF(FM) Fulton KY
WWKI(FM) Kokomo IN
WWKL(FM) Harrisburg PA
WWKS(FM) Beaver Falls PA
WWKT-FM Kingstree SC
WWKX(FM) Woonsocket RI
WWKZ(FM) New Albany MS
WWLF-FM Copenhagen NY
WWLI(FM) Providence RI
*WWLR(FM) Lyndonville VT
WWLW(FM) Carlisle KY
WWLZ(FM) Cadillac MI
WWMD(FM) Hagerstown MD
WWMG(FM) Shelby NC
WWMJ(FM) Ellsworth ME
WWMR(FM) Rumford ME
WWMS(FM) Oxford MS
WWMX(FM) Baltimore MD
*WWNJ(FM) Dover Township NJ
WWNK-FM Cincinnati OH
*WWNO(FM) New Orleans LA
*WWNW(FM) New Wilmington PA
WWOC(FM) Avalon NJ
*WWOG(FM) Cookeville TN
WWOJ(FM) Avon Park FL
*WWOZ(FM) New Orleans LA
*WWPH(FM) Princeton Junction NJ
WWPL(FM) Federalsburg MD
WWPN(FM) Westernport MD
*WWPT(FM) Westport CT
*WWPV-FM Colchester VT
WWQM-FM Middleton WI
WWQQ-FM Wilmington NC
WWRK-FM Elberton GA
WWRM(FM) Tampa FL
WWRQ(FM) Valdosta GA
WWRT(FM) Scotland Neck NC

WWRW(FM) Wisconsin Rapids WI
WWRX-FM Westerly RI
WWSE(FM) Jamestown NY
WWSF-FM Andalusia AL
WWSL(FM) Philadelphia MS
*WWSP(FM) Stevens Point WI
WWSS(FM) Meredith NH
*WWSU(FM) Dayton OH
WWSW-FM Pittsburgh PA
WWTA(FM) Marion MA
WWTN(FM) Manchester TN
WWUA(FM) Inverness FL
WWUF(FM) Waycross GA
*WWUH(FM) West Hartford CT
WWUN-FM Clarksdale MS
WWUS(FM) Big Pine Key FL
WWVR(FM) West Terre Haute IN
WWVU-FM Morgantown WV
WWWB(FM) High Point NC
WWWD(FM) Jersey Shore PA
WWWK(FM) Ellenville NY
WWWM-FM Sylvania OH
WWWO(FM) Hartford City IN
WWWQ(FM) Glasgow KY
WWWV(FM) Charlottesville VA
WWWW-FM Detroit MI
WWWY(FM) Columbus IN
WWWZ(FM) Summerville SC
WWXL-FM Manchester KY
WWXM(FM) Georgetown SC
WWXX(FM) Ocean Springs MS
WWYC(FM) Winchester KY
WWYN(FM) McKenzie TN
WWYZ(FM) Waterbury CT
WWZD(FM) New Albany MS
WWZQ-FM Aberdeen MS
WWZZ(FM) Karns TN

WXAB(FM) McLain MS
*WXAC(FM) Reading PA
WXAH(FM) Orange Beach AL
WXAJ(FM) Hillsboro IL
WXAN(FM) Ava IL
*WXBA(FM) Brentwood NY
WXBB(FM) Kittery ME
WXBC(FM) Hardinsburg KY
WXBM-FM Milton FL
WXBQ-FM Bristol TN
WXCC(FM) Williamson WV
WXCF-FM Clifton Forge VA
WXCH(FM) Versailles IN
*WXCI(FM) Danbury CT
WXCL-FM Pekin IL
WXCV(FM) Homosassa Springs FL
WXCY(FM) Havre de Grace MD
WXDJ(FM) Homestead FL
WXDU(FM) Durham NC
WXEC(FM) Nekoosa WI
WXEJ(FM) Conklin NY
WXEL(FM) West Palm Beach FL
WXER(FM) Plymouth WI
WXEZ(FM) Yorktown VA
WXFG(FM) Augusta GA
WXFL(FM) Florence AL
WXFM(FM) Mt. Zion IL
WXFX(FM) Prattville AL
*WXGC(FM) Milledgeville GA
WXGL-FM Lewiston ME
WXGM-FM Gloucester VA
WXHC(FM) Homer NY
WXHD(FM) Mt. Hope NY
*WXHL(FM) Christiana DE
WXID(FM) Mayfield KY
WXIE(FM) Oakland MD
WXIL(FM) Parkersburg WV
WXIR(FM) Plainfield IN
WXIS(FM) Erwin TN
WXIZ(FM) Waverly OH
WXJB-FM Harrogate TN
*WXJC(FM) Crystal River FL
WXJJ(FM) Mt. Vernon KY
*WXJM(FM) Harrisonburg VA
WXJN(FM) Lewes DE
*WXJX(FM) Washington PA
WXKB(FM) Cape Coral FL
WXKC(FM) Erie PA
WXKE(FM) Fort Wayne IN
WXKI(FM) Moulton AL
WXKO-FM Pana IL
WXKQ(FM) Whitesburg KY
WXKR(FM) Port Clinton OH
WXKS-FM Medford MA
WXKX(FM) Parkersburg WV
WXKZ-FM Prestonsburg KY
WXLC(FM) Waukegan IL
WXLE(FM) Mechanicsville NY
*WXLG(FM) North Creek NY
WXLH(FM) Blue Mountain Lake NY
WXLK(FM) Roanoke VA
WXLN-FM Eminence KY
WXLO-FM Fitchburg MA

WXLP(FM) Moline IL
WXLS-FM Gulfport MS
WXLT(FM) Carterville IL
*WXLU(FM) Peru NY
*WXLV(FM) Schnecksville PA
WXLY(FM) North Charleston SC
WXLZ-FM Lebanon VA
WXMJ(FM) Mount Union PA
WXMK(FM) Dock Junction GA
*WXML(FM) Upper Sandusky OH
WXMX(FM) Canaan VT
WXOD(FM) Winchester NH
WXOF(FM) Beverly Hills FL
WXOQ(FM) Selmer TN
WXPC(FM) Horse Cave KY
*WXPL(FM) Fitchburg MA
*WXPN(FM) Philadelphia PA
*WXPR(FM) Rhinelander WI
WXPS(FM) Briarcliff Manor NY
WXPT(FM) Kennebunkport ME
WXPZ(FM) Milford DE
WXQL(FM) Baldwin FL
WXQR(FM) Jacksonville NC
WXQZ(FM) Canton NY
WXRB(FM) Pittsburgh PA
WXRC(FM) Hickory NC
WXRG(FM) Gulfport MS
*WXRI(FM) Winston-Salem NC
WXRK(FM) New York NY
WXRO(FM) Beaver Dam WI
WXRS-FM Swainsboro GA
WXRT(FM) Chicago IL
WXRX(FM) Belvidere IL
WXRZ(FM) Corinth MS
WXSE(FM) Calhoun TN
WXSR(FM) Quincy FL
WXST(FM) Loudon TN
WXTA(FM) Edinboro PA
WXTB(FM) Clearwater FL
WXTC-FM Charleston SC
WXTK(FM) West Yarmouth MA
WXTM(FM) Monticello NY
WXTQ(FM) Athens OH
WXTR-FM Waldorf MD
*WXTS-FM Toledo OH
WXTU(FM) Philadelphia PA
WXTZ(FM) Noblesville IN
WXUS(FM) Fort Rucker AL
*WXUT(FM) Toledo OH
WXVA-FM Charles Town WV
WXVK(FM) Coal Grove OH
WXVL(FM) Crossville TN
WXVO(FM) Oliver Springs TN
*WXVS(FM) Waycross GA
*WXVU(FM) Villanova PA
*WXXI-FM Rochester NY
WXXK-FM Newport NH
WXXL(FM) Leesburg FL
WXXP(FM) Anderson IN
WXXQ(FM) Freeport IL
WXXW(FM) Webster MA
WXXX(FM) South Burlington VT
WXXZ(FM) Port Matilda PA
*WXYC(FM) Chapel Hill NC
WXYQ(FM) Manistee MI
WXYV(FM) Baltimore MD
WXYX(FM) Bayamon PR
WXZL(FM) Grasonville MD
WXZR(FM) East Lyme CT

WYAI(FM) La Grange GA
*WYAJ(FM) Sudbury MA
WYAK-FM Surfside Beach-Garden City SC
WYAV(FM) Conway SC
WYAY(FM) Gainesville GA
WYBB(FM) Folly Beach SC
WYBC-FM New Haven CT
*WYBF(FM) Radnor Township PA
WYBM(FM) Minor Hill TN
WYBZ(FM) Crooksville OH
WYCA(FM) Hammond IN
WYCD(FM) Detroit MI
*WYCE(FM) Wyoming MI
WYCG(FM) Water Valley MS
WYCO(FM) Wausau WI
WYCQ(FM) Shelbyville TN
WYCR(FM) York-Hanover PA
*WYCS(FM) Yorktown VA
WYCT(FM) Kentwood LA
WYCY(FM) Hawley PA
WYDH(FM) Atmore AL
WYDS(FM) Decatur IL
*WYEP-FM Pittsburgh PA
WYEZ(FM) Bremen IN
WYFA(FM) Waynesboro GA
*WYFB(FM) Gainesville FL
WYFC(FM) Clinton TN
*WYFD(FM) Decatur AL
*WYFE(FM) Tarpon Springs FL
*WYFG(FM) Gaffney SC
*WYFH(FM) North Charleston SC

WYFI(FM) Norfolk VA
WYFJ(FM) Ashland VA
*WYFK(FM) Columbus GA
WYFL(FM) Henderson NC
WYFM(FM) Sharon PA
*WYFO(FM) Lakeland FL
*WYFS(FM) Savannah GA
WYFT(FM) Luray VA
*WYFV(FM) Cayce SC
*WYFW(FM) Winder GA
WYFY(FM) Fisher WV
WYFZ(FM) Evans GA
WYGC(FM) Gainesville FL
WYGL-FM Elizabethville PA
WYGO(FM) Madisonville TN
WYGY(FM) Hamilton OH
WYHC(FM) Charlotte NC
WYHH(FM) Smyrna DE
WYHK(FM) Gibsonburg OH
WYHT(FM) Mansfield OH
WYHY(FM) Lebanon TN
WYII(FM) Williamsport MD
WYIQ(FM) Warner Robins GA
*WYJD(FM) Brewton AL
WYKK(FM) Quitman MS
WYKL(FM) Millington TN
WYKR-FM Haverhill NH
WYKS(FM) Gainesville FL
WYKX(FM) Escanaba MI
WYKY(FM) Columbus WI
WYKZ(FM) Beaufort SC
WYLD-FM New Orleans LA
WYLL(FM) Des Plaines IL
WYLR-FM Glens Falls NY
*WYLV(FM) Alcoa TN
WYMG(FM) Jacksonville IL
WYMJ-FM Beavercreek OH
WYMK(FM) Tunkhannock PA
WYMS(FM) Milwaukee WI
WYMX(FM) Greenwood MS
WYMY(FM) Bedford VA
WYNA(FM) Tabor City NC
WYNG-FM Evansville IN
WYNK-FM Baton Rouge LA
WYNN-FM Florence SC
WYNR(FM) Darien GA
WYNT(FM) Upper Sandusky OH
WYNU(FM) Milan TN
WYNY(FM) Lake Success NY
WYNZ(FM) Westbrook ME
WYOC(FM) High Springs FL
WYOO(FM) Springfield FL
WYOS(FM) Nanticoke PA
WYOU-FM Bangor ME
WYOY(FM) Rutland VT
WYPI(FM) Lagrange IN
*WYPL(FM) Memphis TN
WYRK(FM) Buffalo NY
WYRQ(FM) Little Falls MN
WYRX(FM) Lima OH
WYRY(FM) Hinsdale NH
WYSC(FM) McRae GA
WYSN(FM) Central City PA
*WYSO(FM) Yellow Springs OH
WYSP(FM) Philadelphia PA
WYSR(FM) Waterbury CT
WYSS(FM) Sault Ste. Marie MI
*WYSU(FM) Youngstown OH
*WYSY(FM) Aurora IL
*WYSZ(FM) Maumee OH
WYTE(FM) Whiting WI
WYTM-FM Fayetteville TN
*WYTN(FM) Youngstown OH
WYTW(FM) Cadillac MI
WYUL(FM) Chateaugay NY
WYUR-FM Ripon WI
WYUT-FM Herkimer NY
WYUU(FM) Safety Harbor FL
WYVC(FM) Camden AL
WYWY-FM Barbourville KY
WYXL(FM) Ithaca NY
WYXR(FM) Philadelphia PA
WYYB(FM) Dickson TN
WYYD(FM) Amherst VA
WYYS(FM) Cortland NY
WYYY(FM) Syracuse NY
WYZB(FM) Mary Esther FL
WYZK(FM) Valdosta GA
WYZM(FM) Waunakee WI

WZAC-FM Danville WV
WZAD(FM) Wurtsboro NY
WZAK(FM) Cleveland OH
WZAR(FM) Ponce PR
WZAT(FM) Savannah GA
WZBA(FM) Moss Point MS
WZBB(FM) Rocky Mount VA
*WZBC(FM) Newton MA
WZBD(FM) Berne IN
WZBG(FM) Litchfield CT
WZBH(FM) Georgetown DE
WZBQ-FM Jasper AL

WZBR(FM) Ebenezer MS
*WZBT(FM) Gettysburg PA
WZBX(FM) Sylvania GA
WZDM(FM) Vincennes IN
WZDQ(FM) Humboldt TN
WZEA(FM) Hampton NH
WZEE(FM) Madison WI
WZEW(FM) Fairhope AL
WZEZ(FM) Nashville TN
WZFM(FM) Narrows VA
WZFR(FM) Tomah WI
WZFX(FM) Whiteville NC
WZGC(FM) Atlanta GA
WZGO(FM) Portage PA
WZHT(FM) Troy AL
WZID(FM) Manchester NH
*WZIP(FM) Akron OH
WZIQ(FM) Smithville GA
WZJN(FM) Jackson NH
WZJO(FM) Ocean Pines MD
WZJQ(FM) McClellanville SC
WZJS(FM) Banner Elk NC
WZJU(FM) Wauseon OH
*WZJW(FM) Norris City IL
WZJX(FM) Englewood FL
WZKB(FM) Wallace NC
WZKL(FM) Alliance OH
WZKM(FM) Montgomery WV
WZKT(FM) Farmington IL
WZKX(FM) Poplarville MS
WZLA-FM Abbeville SC
WZLC(FM) Oglesby IL
WZLE(FM) Lorain OH
WZLK(FM) Virgie KY
WZLM(FM) Dadeville AL
WZLQ(FM) Tupelo MS
WZLR(FM) Xenia OH
WZLT(FM) Lexington TN
WZLX(FM) Boston MA
*WZLY(FM) Wellesley MA
*WZMB(FM) Greenville NC
WZMP(FM) Marion MS
WZMQ(FM) Key Largo FL
WZMT(FM) Hazleton PA
WZMX(FM) Hartford MS
WZNF(FM) Rantoul IL
WZNJ(FM) Demopolis AL
WZNL(FM) Norway MI
WZNS(FM) Dillon SC
WZNT(FM) San Juan PR
WZNY(FM) Augusta NY
WZOE-FM Princeton IL
WZOK(FM) Rockford IL
WZOM(FM) Defiance OH
WZOO-FM Edgewood OH
WZOQ(FM) Wapakoneta OH
WZOS(FM) Oswego NY
WZOW(FM) Goshen IN
WZOZ(FM) Oneonta NY
WZPK(FM) Berlin NH
WZPL(FM) Greenfield IN
WZPR(FM) Meadville PA
WZQK(FM) Coeburn VA
WZQQ(FM) Hyden KY
*WZRD(FM) Chicago IL
WZRH(FM) Picayune MS
WZRK(FM) Hancock MI
WZRO(FM) Farmer City IL
WZRQ(FM) Ballston Spa NY
WZRR(FM) Birmingham AL
WZRT(FM) Rutland VT
*WZRU(FM) Roanoke Rapids NC
WZSR(FM) Woodstock IL
WZST(FM) Portage WI
WZTA(FM) Miami Beach FL
WZTR(FM) Milwaukee WI
WZTT(FM) Rhinelander WI
WZTZ(FM) Elba AL
WZVN(FM) Lowell IN
WZVU(FM) Long Branch NJ
WZWW(FM) Bellefonte PA
WZWZ(FM) Kokomo IN
WZXA(FM) Sturtevant WI
WZXL(FM) Wildwood NJ
WZXR(FM) South Williamsport PA
WZXS(FM) Topsail Beach NC
WZXV(FM) Palmyra NY
WZYP(FM) Athens AL
WZYQ(FM) Braddock Heights MD
*WZZE(FM) Glen Mills PA
WZZF-FM Hopkinsville KY
WZZK-FM Birmingham AL
WZZL(FM) Reidland KY
WZZO(FM) Bethlehem PA
WZZP(FM) Kankakee IL
WZZQ(FM) Terre Haute IN
WZZR(FM) Stuart FL
WZZS(FM) Zolfo Springs FL
WZZT(FM) Morrison IL
WZZU(FM) Burlington-Graham NC
WZZW(FM) Milton WV
WZZY(FM) Winchester IN

Canadian AM Stations by Call Letters

CBA(AM) Moncton NB
CBDQ(AM) Wabush NF
CBE(AM) Windsor ON
CBEF(AM) Windsor ON
CBF(AM) Montreal PQ
*CBG(AM) Gander NF
CBGA(AM) Matane PQ
CBGN(AM) Ste. Anne des Monts PQ
CBGY(AM) Bonavista Bay NF
CBI(AM) Sydney NS
CBJ(AM) Chicoutimi PQ
*CBK(AM) Regina SK
*CBKF-1(AM) Gravelbourg SK
CBKF-2(AM) Saskatoon SK
CBL(AM) Toronto ON
CBM(AM) Montreal PQ
*CBN(AM) St. John's NF
CBOF(AM) Ottawa ON
CBOF-1(AM) Maniwaki PQ
*CBR(AM) Calgary AB
CBT(AM) Grand Falls-Windsor NF
*CBU(AM) Vancouver BC
*CBV(AM) Quebec PQ
CBW(AM) Winnipeg MB
CBX(AM) Edmonton AB
*CBY(AM) Corner Brook NF
*CBZ(AM) Fredericton NB
CFAB(AM) Windsor NS
CFAC(AM) Calgary AB
CFAM(AM) Altona MB
CFAN(AM) Newcastle NB
CFAR(AM) Flin Flon MB
CFAX(AM) Victoria BC
CFBC(AM) Saint John NB
CFBV(AM) Smithers BC
CFCB(AM) Corner Brook NF
CFCH(AM) North Bay ON
CFCN(AM) Calgary AB
CFCO(AM) Chatham ON
CFCP(AM) Courtenay BC
CFCT(AM) Tuktoyaktuk NT
CFCW(AM) Camrose AB
CFCY(AM) Charlottetown PE
CFDA(AM) Victoriaville PQ
CFDR(AM) Dartmouth NS
CFED(AM) Chapais PQ
CFEK(AM) Fernie PQ
CFFB(AM) Iqaluit NT
CFFR(AM) Calgary AB
CFFX(AM) Kingston ON
CFGN(AM) Port-aux-Basques NF
CFGO(AM) Ottawa ON
CFGP(AM) Grande Prairie AB
CFGT(AM) Alma PQ
CFHC(AM) Canmore AB
CFJC(AM) Kamloops BC
CFJR(AM) Brockville ON
CFKC(AM) Creston BC
CFLD(AM) Burns Lake BC
CFLM(AM) La Tuque PQ
CFLN(AM) Goose Bay NF
CFLP(AM) Rimouski PQ
CFLW(AM) Wabush NF
CFMB(AM) Montreal PQ
CFNB(AM) Fredericton NB
CFNI(AM) Port Hardy BC
CFNL(AM) Fort Nelson BC
CFNW(AM) Port au Choix NF
CFOB(AM) Fort Frances ON
CFOK(AM) Westlock AB
CFOS(AM) Owen Sound ON
CFPL(AM) London ON
*CFPR(AM) Prince Rupert BC
CFPS(AM) Port Elgin ON
CFQC(AM) Saskatoon SK
CFRA(AM) Ottawa ON

CFRB(AM) Toronto ON
CFRN(AM) Edmonton AB
CFRP(AM) Forestville PQ
CFRY(AM) Portage la Prairie MB
CFSL(AM) Weyburn SK
CFSX(AM) Stephenville NF
CFTK(AM) Terrace BC
CFTR(AM) Toronto ON
CFUN(AM) Vancouver BC
CFVD(AM) Ville Degelis PQ
CFVM(AM) Amqui PQ
CFVR(AM) Abbotsford-Matsqui BC
CFWB(AM) Campbell River BC
*CFWH(AM) Whitehorse YT
CFXL(AM) Calgary AB
*CFYK(AM) Yellowknife NT
CFYM(AM) Kindersley SK
CHAB(AM) Moose Jaw SK
CHAD(AM) Amos PQ
CHAK(AM) Inuvik NT
CHAM(AM) Hamilton ON
CHAT(AM) Medicine Hat AB
*CHCL(AM) Medley AB
CHCM(AM) Marystown NF
CHED(AM) Edmonton AB
CHEF(AM) Granby PQ
CHER(AM) Sydney NS
*CHFA(AM) Edmonton AB
CHFC(AM) Churchill MB
CHIN(AM) Toronto ON
CHLC(AM) Baie Comeau PQ
CHLN(AM) Trois Rivieres PQ
CHLO(AM) St. Thomas ON
CHLT(AM) Sherbrooke PQ
CHLW(AM) St. Paul AB
CHMG(AM) St. Albert AB
CHML(AM) Hamilton ON
CHMO(AM) Moosonee ON
CHNC(AM) New Carlisle PQ
CHNL(AM) Kamloops BC
CHNL-1(AM) Clearwater BC
CHNO(AM) Sudbury ON
CHNR(AM) Simcoe ON
CHNS(AM) Halifax NS
CHOG(AM) Richmond Hill ON
CHOH(AM) Hearst ON
CHOK(AM) Sarnia ON
CHOO(AM) Ajax ON
CHOR(AM) Summerland BC
CHOW(AM) Welland ON
CHPQ(AM) Parksville-Qualicum BC
CHQB(AM) Powell River BC
CHQM(AM) Vancouver BC
CHQR(AM) Calgary AB
CHQT(AM) Edmonton AB
CHRB(AM) High River AB
CHRC(AM) Quebec PQ
CHRD(AM) Drummondville PQ
CHRL(AM) Roberval PQ
CHRM(AM) Matane PQ
CHRT(AM) St. Eleuthere PQ
CHSC(AM) St. Catharines ON
CHSJ(AM) Saint John NB
CHSM(AM) Steinbach MB
CHTK(AM) Prince Rupert BC
CHTM(AM) Thompson MB
CHTN(AM) Charlottetown PE
CHUB(AM) Nanaimo BC
CHUC(AM) Cobourg ON
CHUM(AM) Toronto ON
CHUR(AM) North Bay ON
CHVD(AM) Dolbeau PQ
CHVO(AM) Carbonear NF
CHVR(AM) Pembroke ON
CHVR-1(AM) Renfrew ON
CHVR-2(AM) Arnprior ON
CHWK(AM) Chilliwack BC

CHWO(AM) Oakville ON
CHYC(AM) Sudbury ON
CHYK(AM) Kapuskasing ON
CIAM(AM) Cambridge ON
CIAO(AM) Brampton ON
CIBQ(AM) Brooks AB
CICF(AM) Vernon BC
CIFX(AM) Winnipeg MB
CIGM(AM) Sudbury ON
CIGO(AM) Port Hawkesbury NS
CIHI(AM) Fredericton NB
CIOR(AM) Princeton BC
CIPC(AM) Port-Cartier PQ
CIQC(AM) Montreal PQ
CISL(AM) Richmond BC
CIVH(AM) Vanderhoof BC
CIWW(AM) Ottawa ON
CIYR(AM) Hinton AB
CJAD(AM) Montreal PQ
CJAF(AM) Cabano PQ
CJAN(AM) Asbestos PQ
CJAR(AM) The Pas MB
CJAT(AM) Trail BC
CJAV(AM) Port Alberni BC
CJBC(AM) Toronto ON
CJBK(AM) London ON
CJBM(AM) Causapscal PQ
CJBQ(AM) Belleville ON
CJBR(AM) Rimouski PQ
CJCB(AM) Sydney NS
CJCD(AM) Yellowknife NT
CJCH(AM) Halifax NS
CJCI(AM) Prince George BC
CJCJ(AM) Woodstock NB
CJCL(AM) Toronto ON
CJCM(AM) Grand Centre AB
CJCS(AM) Stratford ON
CJCY(AM) Medicine Hat AB
CJDC(AM) Dawson Creek BC
CJEM(AM) Edmundston NB
CJET(AM) Smiths Falls ON
CJFP(AM) Riviere du Loup PQ
CJFX(AM) Antigonish NS
CJGX(AM) Yorkton SK
CJIB(AM) Vernon BC
CJKL(AM) Kirkland Lake ON
CJLB(AM) Thunder Bay ON
CJLM(AM) Joliette PQ
CJLS(AM) Yarmouth NS
CJMC(AM) Ste. Anne des Monts PQ
CJMD(AM) Chibougamau PQ
CJME(AM) Regina SK
CJMR(AM) Mississauga ON
CJMS(AM) Montreal PQ
CJMT(AM) Chicoutimi PQ
CJNB(AM) North Battleford SK
CJNH(AM) Bancroft ON
CJNL(AM) Merritt BC
CJNR(AM) Blind River ON
CJNS(AM) Meadow Lake SK
CJOB(AM) Winnipeg MB
CJOC(AM) Lethbridge AB
CJOI(AM) Wetaskiwin AB
CJOK(AM) Fort McMurray AB
CJOR(AM) Osoyoos BC
CJOY(AM) Guelph ON
CJPR(AM) Blairmore AB
CJRB(AM) Boissevain MB
CJRC(AM) Gatineau PQ
CJRL(AM) Kenora ON
CJRN(AM) Niagara Falls ON
CJRP(AM) Quebec PQ
CJRW(AM) Summerside PE
CJSB(AM) Ottawa ON
CJSL(AM) Estevan SK

CJSN(AM) Shaunavon SK
CJSS(AM) Cornwall ON
CJTN(AM) Trenton ON
CJTR(AM) Trois Rivieres PQ
CJTT(AM) New Liskeard ON
CJVA(AM) Caraquet NB
CJVB(AM) Vancouver BC
CJVI(AM) Victoria BC
CJVL(AM) Ste. Marie-de-Beauce PQ
CJVR(AM) Melfort SK
CJWA(AM) Wawa ON
CJWW(AM) Saskatoon SK
CJXX(AM) Grande Prairie AB
CJYM(AM) Rosetown SK
CJYQ(AM) St. John's NF
CJYR(AM) Edson AB
CKAC(AM) Montreal PQ
CKAD(AM) Middleton NS
CKAP(AM) Kapuskasing ON
CKAY(AM) Duncan BC
CKBA(AM) Athabasca AB
CKBB(AM) Barrie ON
CKBC(AM) Bathurst NB
CKBD(AM) Vancouver BC
CKBI(AM) Prince Albert SK
CKBW(AM) Bridgewater NS
CKBX(AM) 100 Mile House BC
CKCB(AM) Collingwood ON
CKCH(AM) Hull PQ
CKCK(AM) Regina SK
CKCL(AM) Truro NS
CKCM(AM) Grand Falls-Windsor NF
CKCN(AM) Sept-Iles PQ
CKCQ(AM) Quesnel BC
CKCR(AM) Revelstoke BC
CKCW(AM) Moncton NB
CKDA(AM) Victoria BC
CKDH(AM) Amherst NS
CKDM(AM) Dauphin MB
CKDO(AM) Oshawa ON
CKDQ(AM) Drumheller AB
CKDR(AM) Dryden ON
CKDR-5(AM) Red Lake ON
CKDR-6(AM) Atikokan ON
CKDX(AM) Newmarket ON
CKDY(AM) Digby NS
CKEC(AM) New Glasgow NS
CKEG(AM) Nanaimo BC
CKEK(AM) Cranbrook BC
CKEN(AM) Kentville NS
CKER(AM) Edmonton AB
CKFL(AM) Lac Megantic PQ
CKGA(AM) Gander NF
CKGB(AM) Timmins ON
CKGF(AM) Grand Forks BC
CKGL(AM) Kitchener ON
CKGO(AM) Hope BC
CKGR(AM) Golden BC
CKGY(AM) Red Deer AB
CKIM(AM) Baie Verte NF
CKIQ(AM) Big White Ski Village BC
CKIR(AM) Invermere BC
CKIS(AM) Montreal PQ
CKJS(AM) Winnipeg MB
CKKC(AM) Nelson BC
CKKW(AM) Kitchener ON
CKKY(AM) Wainwright AB
CKLC(AM) Kingston ON
CKLD(AM) Thetford Mines PQ
CKLG(AM) Vancouver BC
CKLO(AM) L'Annonciation PQ
CKLQ(AM) Brandon MB
CKLS(AM) La Sarre PQ
CKLW(AM) Windsor ON
CKLY(AM) Lindsay ON

CKMG(AM) Maniwaki PQ
CKMK(AM) Mackenzie BC
CKMV(AM) Grand Falls NB
CKMW(AM) Winkler-Morden MB
CKNB(AM) Campbellton NB
CKNL(AM) Fort St. John BC
CKNR(AM) Elliot Lake ON
CKNS(AM) Espanola ON
CKNW(AM) New Westminster BC
CKNX(AM) Wingham ON
CKOC(AM) Hamilton ON
CKOD(AM) Valleyfield PQ
CKOM(AM) Saskatoon SK
CKOR(AM) Penticton BC
CKOT(AM) Tillsonburg ON
CKOV(AM) Kelowna BC
CKOY(AM) Timmins ON
CKPC(AM) Brantford ON
CKPG(AM) Prince George BC
CKPR(AM) Thunder Bay ON
CKPT(AM) Peterborough ON
CKQR(AM) Castlegar BC
CKRB(AM) St. Georges-de-Beauce PQ
CKRC(AM) Winnipeg MB
CKRD(AM) Red Deer AB
CKRM(AM) Regina SK
CKRN(AM) Rouyn PQ
CKRS(AM) Jonquiere PQ
CKRU(AM) Peterborough ON
CKRW(AM) Whitehorse YT
CKRX(AM) Lethbridge AB
CKSA(AM) Lloydminster AB
*CKSB(AM) St. Boniface MB
CKSL(AM) London ON
CKSM(AM) Shawinigan PQ
CKSQ(AM) Stettler AB
CKST(AM) Langley BC
CKSW(AM) Swift Current SK
CKTA(AM) Taber SK
CKTB(AM) St. Catharines ON
CKTK(AM) Kitimat BC
CKTL(AM) Plessisville PQ
CKTS(AM) Sherbrooke PQ
CKTY(AM) Sarnia ON
*CKUA(AM) Edmonton AB
CKVD(AM) Val d'Or PQ
CKVH(AM) High Prairie AB
CKVL(AM) Verdun PQ
CKVM(AM) Ville-Marie PQ
CKVO(AM) Clarenville NF
CKWA(AM) Slave Lake AB
CKWL(AM) Williams Lake BC
CKWW(AM) Windsor ON
CKWX(AM) Vancouver BC
CKX(AM) Brandon MB
CKXB(AM) Musgravetown NF
CKXD(AM) Gander NF
CKXG(AM) Grand Falls-Windsor NF
CKXR(AM) Salmon Arm BC
CKXX(AM) Corner Brook NF
CKY(AM) Winnipeg MB
CKYC(AM) Toronto ON
CKYL(AM) Peace River AB
CKYR(AM) Jasper AB
CKYR-1(AM) Grande Cache AB
*VOAR(AM) Mount Pearl NF
VOCM(AM) St. John's NF
*VOWR(AM) St. John's NF

Canadian FM Stations by Call Letters

CBA-FM Moncton NB
CBAF-FM Moncton NB
CBAL-FM Moncton NB
CBBK-FM Kingston ON
CBBL-FM London ON
CBCL-FM London ON
CBCS-FM Sudbury ON
CBCT-FM Charlottetown PE
CBD-FM Saint John NB
CBE-FM Windsor ON
CBEG-FM Sarnia ON
CBF-FM Montreal PQ
CBF-FM-1 Trois Rivieres PQ
CBGA-FM-8 Iles-de-la-Madeleine PQ
CBH-FM Halifax NS
CBHA-FM Halifax NS
CBI-FM Sydney NS
*CBJ-FM Chicoutimi PQ
CBJE-FM Chicoutimi PQ
*CBK-FM Regina SK
*CBKA-FM La Ronge SK
CBKF-FM Regina SK
*CBKS-FM Saskatoon SK
CBL-FM Toronto ON
CBM-FM Montreal PQ
CBMI-FM Baie Comeau PQ
CBMR-FM Fermont PQ
*CBN-FM St. John's NF
*CBO-FM Ottawa ON
CBOF-FM Ottawa ON
*CBON-FM Sudbury ON
*CBOQ-FM Ottawa ON
*CBQ-FM Thunder Bay ON
CBQL-FM Savant Lake ON
CBQN-FM Osnaburgh ON
CBQP-FM Pickle Lake ON
CBQS-FM Rankin Inlet NT
CBQS-FM Sioux Narrows ON
*CBQT-FM Thunder Bay ON
CBQX-FM Kenora ON
*CBR-FM Calgary AB
*CBSI-FM Sept-Iles PQ
CBTE-FM Crawford Bay BC
*CBTK-FM Kelowna BC
CBU-FM Vancouver BC
CBUF-FM Vancouver BC
*CBV-FM Quebec PQ
CBV-FM-6 La Malbaie PQ
CBVE-FM Quebec PQ
CBW-FM Winnipeg MB
*CBWK-FM Thompson MB
CBX-FM Edmonton AB
CBYG-FM Prince George BC
*CBZ-FM Fredericton NB
CBZF-FM Fredericton-St. John NB
CFAI-FM Edmundston NB
CFBG-FM Bracebridge ON
CFBK-FM Huntsville ON
CFBR-FM Edmonton AB
CFCA-FM Kitchener ON
CFCV-FM St. Andrews NF
CFDL-FM Deer Lake NF
CFEI-FM St. Hyacinthe PQ
CFEL-FM Montmagny PQ
*CFFF-FM Peterborough ON

CFFM-FM Williams Lake BC
CFGB-FM Happy Valley NF
CFGL-FM Laval PQ
CFGX-FM Sarnia ON
*CFIC-FM Ste. Anne des Plaines PQ
CFIL-FM Gillam MB
CFIM-FM Iles-de-la-Madeleine PQ
*CFIN-FM Lac-Etchemin PQ
CFJB-FM Barrie ON
CFJC-FM Merritt BC
CFJO-FM Thetford Mines PQ
CFJQ-FM Nipigon-Red Rock ON
CFLC-FM Churchill Falls NF
CFLG-FM Cornwall ON
CFLS-FM Levis PQ
CFLY-FM Kingston ON
CFMC-FM Saskatoon SK
CFMF-FM Fermont PQ
CFMI-FM New Westminster BC
CFMK-FM Kingston ON
CFMM-FM Prince Albert SK
CFMO-FM Smiths Falls ON
CFMS-FM Victoria BC
*CFMU-FM Hamilton ON
CFMX-FM Cobourg ON
CFMX-FM-1 Mississauga ON
CFNJ-FM St. Gabriel-de-Brandon PQ
CFNN-FM St. Anthony NF
CFNO-FM Marathon ON
CFNY-FM Brampton ON
CFOX-FM Vancouver BC
CFOZ-FM Argentia NF
CFPL-FM London ON
CFQM-FM Moncton NB
CFQR-FM Montreal PQ
CFQS-FM Selkirk MB
*CFRC-FM Kingston ON
*CFRO-FM Vancouver BC
CFRQ-FM Dartmouth NS
CFRU-FM Guelph ON
CFRV-FM Lethbridge AB
CFSR-FM Abbotsford-Matsqui BC
*CFTH-FM Harrington Harbour PQ
*CFUV-FM Victoria BC
CFVD-FM-1 Cabano PQ
CFVD-FM-2 Pohenegamook PQ
CFZZ-FM St. Jean-sur-Richelieu PQ
CHAR-FM Alert NT
CHAS-FM Sault Ste. Marie ON
CHAY-FM Barrie ON
CHEY-FM Trois Rivieres PQ
CHEZ-FM Ottawa ON
CHFI-FM Toronto ON
CHFM-FM Calgary AB
CHFX-FM Halifax NS
CHGA-FM Maniwaki PQ
CHGG-FM Limestone MB
CHIK-FM Quebec PQ
CHIN-FM Toronto ON
CHIP-FM Fort Coulonge PQ
CHIQ-FM Winnipeg MB
CHLQ-FM Charlottetown PE
*CHMA-FM Sackville NB

CHMR-FM St. John's NF
CHMX-FM Regina SK
CHOA-FM Rouyn PQ
CHOC-FM Jonquiere PQ
CHOI-FM Quebec PQ
CHOM-FM Montreal PQ
CHON-FM Whitehorse YT
CHOS-FM Rattling Brook NF
CHOX-FM La Pocatiere PQ
CHOZ-FM St. John's NF
CHPR-FM Hawkesbury ON
CHQM-FM Vancouver BC
CHRE-FM St. Catharines ON
*CHRW-FM London ON
CHRY-FM Toronto ON
CHSN-FM Saskatoon SK
CHSR-FM Fredericton NB
CHTZ-FM St. Catharines ON
CHUM-FM Toronto ON
*CHUO-FM Ottawa ON
CHVD-FM Dolbeau PQ
CHXL-FM Brockville ON
CHYM-FM Kitchener ON
CHYR-FM Leamington ON
*CIBL-FM Montreal PQ
CIBM-FM Riviere du Loup PQ
CICX-FM Orillia ON
CICZ-FM Midland ON
CIDC-FM Orangeville ON
CIEG-FM Egmont BC
CIEL-FM Longueuil PQ
CIEZ-FM Halifax NS
CIFA-FM Yarmouth NS
CIFM-FM Kamloops BC
CIGB-FM Trois Rivieres PQ
CIGL-FM Belleville ON
CIGV-FM Penticton BC
CIHO-FM St. Hilarion PQ
CIKI-FM Rimouski PQ
CILK-FM Kelowna BC
CILQ-FM Toronto ON
CIME-FM Ste. Adele PQ
CIMF-FM Hull PQ
CIMG-FM Swift Current SK
CIMJ-FM Guelph ON
CIMO-FM Magog PQ
CIMX-FM Windsor ON
CING-FM Burlington ON
CINQ-FM Montreal PQ
CIOI-FM Prince George BC
CIOK-FM Saint John NB
CIOO-FM Halifax NS
CIOS-FM Stephenville NF
CIOZ-FM Marystown NF
CIPN-FM Pender Harbour BC
CIQM-FM London ON
CIRK-FM Edmonton AB
CIRO-FM St. Georges-de-Beauce PQ
CIRV-FM Toronto ON
CIRX-FM Prince George BC
CISC-FM Gibsons BC
CISE-FM Sechelt BC
*CISM-FM Montreal PQ
CISN-FM Edmonton AB
CISP-FM Pemberton BC

CISQ-FM Squamish BC
CISS-FM Toronto ON
CISW-FM Whistler BC
CITE-FM Montreal PQ
CITE-FM-1 Sherbrooke PQ
CITF-FM Quebec PQ
CITI-FM Winnipeg MB
*CITR-FM Vancouver BC
*CIUT-FM Toronto ON
CIXK-FM Owen Sound ON
*CIXX-FM London ON
CIZL-FM Regina SK
CIZZ-FM Red Deer AB
CJAB-FM Chicoutimi PQ
*CJAM-FM Windsor ON
CJAY-FM Calgary AB
CJBC-FM-20 London ON
CJBR-FM Rimouski PQ
CJBX-FM London ON
CJCD-FM-1 Hay River NT
CJDC-FM Dawson Creek BC
CJDM-FM Drummondville PQ
CJEN-FM Jenpeg MB
CJEZ-FM Toronto ON
CJFM-FM Montreal PQ
CJFW-FM Terrace BC
CJJR-FM Vancouver BC
CJKK-FM Clarenville NF
CJKR-FM Winnipeg MB
CJLA-FM Lachute PQ
CJLS-FM-1 Shelburne NS
CJLS-FM-2 Digby NS
CJLX-FM Belleville ON
CJMF-FM Quebec PQ
CJMG-FM Penticton BC
CJMJ-FM Ottawa ON
CJMM-FM Rouyn-Noranda PQ
CJMO-FM Moncton NB
CJMX-FM Sudbury ON
CJOJ-FM Belleville ON
CJOZ-FM Bonavista Bay NF
CJQM-FM Sault Ste. Marie ON
CJQQ-FM Timmins ON
CJRE-FM Riviere au Renard PQ
CJRG-FM Gaspe PQ
CJRM-FM Labrador City NF
CJRQ-FM Sudbury ON
*CJRT-FM Toronto ON
CJSD-FM Thunder Bay ON
CJSO-FM Sorel PQ
CJSR-FM Edmonton AB
*CJSW-FM Calgary AB
CJXY-FM Hamilton ON
CJYC-FM Saint John NB
CKAT-FM North Bay ON
CKBW-FM-1 Liverpool NS
CKBW-FM-2 Shelburne NS
CKBY-FM Ottawa ON
CKCU-FM Ottawa ON
CKDK-FM Woodstock ON
CKDU-FM Halifax NS
CKEY-FM Fort Erie ON
CKFM-FM Toronto ON
CKGE-FM Oshawa ON
CKGO-FM-1 Boston Bar BC

CKHJ-FM Fredericton NB
CKHR-FM Hay River NT
CKIA-FM Quebec PQ
CKIK-FM Calgary AB
CKIQ-FM Kelowna BC
CKIT-FM Regina SK
CKIX-FM St. John's NF
CKKC-FM Nelson BC
CKKC-FM-1 New Denver BC
CKKC-FM-2 Kaslo BC
CKKL-FM Ottawa ON
CKKQ-FM Victoria BC
CKKS-FM Vancouver BC
CKLE-FM Bathurst NB
CKLH-FM Hamilton ON
*CKLN-FM Toronto ON
CKLP-FM Parry Sound ON
CKLU-FM Winnipeg MB
CKLW-FM Windsor ON
CKLZ-FM Kelowna BC
CKMF-FM Montreal PQ
*CKMS-FM Waterloo ON
CKNG-FM Edmonton AB
CKNM-FM Yellowknife NT
CKNX-FM Wingham ON
CKOI-FM Verdun PQ
CKON-FM Akwesasne ON
CKOT-FM Tillsonburg ON
CKOZ-FM Corner Brook NF
CKPC-FM Brantford ON
CKPE-FM Sydney NS
CKQM-FM Peterborough ON
CKQN-FM Baker Lake NT
CKRA-FM Edmonton AB
*CKRK-FM Kahnawake PQ
*CKRL-FM Quebec PQ
CKRV-FM Kamloops BC
CKRY-FM Calgary AB
CKRZ-FM Ohsweken ON
CKSR-FM Chilliwack BC
CKSS-FM Red Rocks NF
CKSY-FM Chatham ON
CKTF-FM Gatineau PQ
CKTO-FM Truro NS
*CKUA-FM Edmonton AB
*CKUA-FM-1 Calgary AB
CKUA-FM-13 Drumheller AB
*CKUA-FM-2 Lethbridge AB
*CKUA-FM-3 Medicine Hat AB
CKUA-FM-4 Grande Prairie AB
*CKUA-FM-5 Peace River AB
CKUM-FM Moncton NB
*CKUT-FM Montreal PQ
CKWF-FM Peterborough ON
CKWM-FM Kentville NS
CKWR-FM Kitchener ON
CKX-FM Brandon MB
CKYX-FM Fort McMurray AB
CKZZ-FM Vancouver BC
NEW FM Ottawa ON
NEW FM Ottawa ON
VOCM-FM St. John's NF

FM Allotments

The following table of allotments contains the channels (other than noncommercial educational Channels 201-220) designated as of November 1993 for use in communities in the United States, its territories and possessions. All listed channels are for class B stations in Zones I and I-A and for class C stations in Zone II unless otherwise specifically designated.

Alabama
Abbeville 232A
Albertville 286
Alexander City 291
Andalusia 251, 279A
Anniston 263
Arab 224A
Ashland 238A
Athens 282
Atmore 281, 290A
Attalla 275A
Auburn 249A
Bay Minette 288A, 293
Birmingham 229, 233, 243, 258, 284, 295, 299
Brewton 292A
Brundidge 234A
Butler 228A
Camden 272A
Carrollton 231
Centre 290A
Chato 291
Chickasaw 252
Citronelle 271
Clanton 249A
Columbia 221A
Cordova 223A
Cullman 221A, 266
Dadeville 247A
Decatur 245, 271
Demopolis 293
Dothan 238, 259, 267A, 273A
East Brenton 239A
Elba 266A
Enterprise 245, 294
Eufaula 224A, 250A
Eutaw 282A
Evergreen 227
Fairhope 221
Fayette 251
Florence 241A, 297
Fort Mitchell 252A
Fort Rucker 263A
Fruithurst 274A
Gadsden 279
Geneva 229
Georgiana 299A
Glencoe 298A
Greenville 232A, 240A
Guntersville 240
Hamilton 221A
Hartselle 291
Hayleyville 224A
Holly Pond 238A
Homewood 247A
Huntsville 236, 256
Jackson 233
Jasper 273
Linden 253, 275
Luverne 282
Meridianville 231A
Millbrook 246A
Mobile 225, 235, 241, 248, 260
Monroeville 257
Montgomery 222, 241A, 255, 270, 277
Mouton 276A
Muscle Shoals 288A
Northport 264A
Oneonta 249A
Opelika 244A
Opp 272A
Orange Beach 289A
Orrville 294
Oxford 250A
Ozark 280, 285A
Pheonix City 261A
Prattville 236
Reform 269A
Roanoke 272
Rogersville 230A
Russellville 249A
Scottsboro 252A
Selma 261, 265, 287
Sheffield 292
Smiths 267A
Stevenson 269A
Sylacauga 252A
Talladega 224A, 248A
Thomasville 238
Trinity 223A
Troy 289
Trussville 290A
Tuscaloosa 225, 239, 288
Tuscumbia 262
Tuskegee 240A, 260A
Union Springs 231A
Uniontown 298A
Valley 237A
Vernon 293A
Warrior 254A
Wetumpka 250A
Winfield 290A
York 285

Alaska
Anchorage 225, 247, 251, 255, 263, 267, 271, 275, 281, 287, 293, 298
Bethel 252, 261A
College 280
Cordova 265A
Delta Junction 228A
Dillingham 256A
Fairbanks 240, 251, 266, 273, 284
Haines 272A
Homer 278
Houston 232A
Juneau 264, 274, 282A, 286A, 292
Kenai 261
Ketchikan 290, 294A
Kodiak 261A, 266
Kotzebue 280A
Naknek 265A
Nome 241A, 262A
North Pole 262
Palmer 238
Petersburg 265A
Seward 276A
Sitka 276, 284A
Soldotna 243, 269, 269A
Wasilla 259
Wrangell 269A
Yakutat 280A

Arizona
Ajo 252A
Apache Junction 296
Arizona City 292A
Benson 249A
Bisbee 222A
Buckeye 295A
Bullhead City 274
Casa Grande 288A
Chandler 300
Chinle 297A
Claypool 288A
Clifton 271
Colorado City 296
Comobabi 276A
Coolidge 280A
Cottonwood 240, 289A
Douglas 237A, 243A
Eagar 223
Flagstaff 225, 230, 248, 261
Glendale 222, 278
Globe 247A, 262
Green Valley 221, 246A
Holbrook 221
Kearny 286A
Kachina Village 286
Kingman 234, 260, 290
Lake Havasu City 224, 266, 283
Marana 252A
Mesa 227, 284
Miami 252A
Nogales 252A
Oracle 276A
Oraibi 252A
Oro Valley 248A
Page 228
Paradise Valley 290A
Parker 257A
Payson 266, 282
Phoenix 233, 238, 245, 254, 260, 268, 273
Pinetop 294
Prescott 256, 271
Prescott Valley 252, 294
Quartzsite 232A
Safford 231
St. Johns 239
San Carlos 279A
Scottsdale 264
Sedona 275, 298
Seligman 277A
Show Low 228, 243
Sierra Vista 265A, 269A
Springerville 269A
Sun City 292
Tempe 250
Thatcher 256
Tuba City 250
Tucson 225, 229, 235, 241, 258, 281A, 298
Tusayan 221A
Wickenburg 287, 229A
Willcox 252A
Williams 244A
Window Rock 241, 276A
Winslow 236
Yuma 226, 236, 265A

Arkansas
Arkadelphia 265A
Ashdown 221A, 280A
Augusta 249
Bald Knob 296A
Barling 233
Batesville 226
Beebe 268A
Bella Vista 293
Benton 294
Bentonville 239A, 252
Blytheville 242
Booneville 284
Brinkley 272A
Bryville 296
Cabot 273A
Camden 237A, 246, 283A
Cherokee Village 265A
Clarendon 281A
Clarksville 295A
Clinton 221
Conway 224A, 286
Corning 228A
Crossett 285A
Danville 288A
Dardanelle 272
DeQueen 224A
De Witt 244A
Dermott 276A, 289A
Dumas 295A
El Dorado 227, 240A, 254, 277
England 243A
Eudora 268A
Eureka Springs 265A
Fairfield Bay 291
Fayetteville 221, 280, 300
Fordyce 272A
Forrest City 228
Fort Smith 229, 256, 260, 264
Glenwood 283A
Gosnell 230A, 297A
Gould 273A
Greenwood 292
Gurdon 224A
Hamburg 258A
Hampton 293
Hardy 284A
Harrison 241, 244A, 275
Heber Springs 264
Helena 233A, 276
Hope 269, 285A
Horseshoe Bend 293A
Hot Springs 244A, 248, 290
Hot Springs Village 225A
Hoxie 287A
Humnoke 269A
Huntsville 258A
Jacksonville 262
Jonesboro 263, 270, 300
Lake City 285
Lake Village 240A, 278A
Little Rock 231, 239, 253, 258A, 279
Lonoke 292
Lowell 270
Magnolia 300
Malvern 227A, 268A
Mammoth Spring 236
Marianna 287A
Marion 296A
Marked Tree 229A
Marshall 282
Maumelle 245A, 235
Mena 242, 271
Monticello 228A, 260A
Morrilton 269A
Mountain Home 228, 250, 298
Mountain Pine 270A
Mountain View 277
Murfreesboro 258
Nashville 288A
Newport 244
North Crossett 274A
North Little Rock 266A
Osceola —
Ozark 244
Paragould 296A
Paris 237A
Piggott 288A
Pine Bluff 222, 257A, 267, 267A
Pocahontas 280A
Prairie Grove 235
Rogers 232
Russellville 265A
Salem 240A
Searcy 260
Sheridan 275
Sherwood 271A
Siloam Springs 266A, 289
Springdale 285
Stamps 263, 238A
Stuttgart 288A
Texarkana 284A, 292, 296A
Trumann 294A
Van Buren 274
Waldo 256A
Waldron 276
Walnut Ridge 292A
Warren 288A
West Helena 285A
White Hall 283A
Wilson 279A
Wrightsville 299
Wynne 223
Yellville 269A

California
Alameda 224A
Alturas 233
Anaheim 240A
Anderson 234
Apple Valley 272A
Arcadia 296A
Arcata 226
Arnold 240A, 255A, 291A
Arvin 223A
Atascadero 283
Atwater 223A
Auberry 286
Auburn 266
Avalon 224A
Avenal 289A
Baker 235, 268
Bakersfield 221A, 231, 243, 257A, 268, 296A, 300
Barstow 232, 240A
Beaumont 265A
Berkeley 231, 275
Big Bear City 227A
Big Bear Lake 269A
Big Pine 227
Bishop 264
Blythe 262
Brawley 233, 241
Burney 291
Calexico 249A
California City 295A
Calipatria 265A
Calistoga 265A
Camarillo 212, 240
Cambria 235
Carlsbad 240A
Carmel 238A, 269A
Carnelian Bay 279
Carpinteria 269A
Cartago 275A
Cathedral City 253
Central Valley 257
Chester 255
Chico 230, 236, 224A
China Lake 274A
Chowchilla 227A
Coachella 229
Coalinga 261
Columbia 240A, 255A
Colusa 276A, 298
Compton 272A
Copperopolis 288A
Corcoran 272
Corning 264
Crescent City 232
Crescent North 250
Davis 282A
Delano 253, 287
Desert Center 288A
Dinuba 255
Dunsmuir 261
Earlimart 228A
East Porterville 263
El Cajon 227
El Centro 298
El Rio 279A
Ellwood 233
Escondido 221A
Essex 255
Eureka 222, 242, 268, 288
Fallbrook 269A
Felton 265
Ferndale 257A
Firebaugh 276A
Ford City 271A
Fort Bragg 228, 237, 253
Fortuna 262
Fowler 244
Freedom 298A
Fremont 285A
Fresno 229, 239, 250, 257A, 266, 270, 274, 290
Garberville 279, 284
Garden Grove 232A
George 264A
Gilroy 233
Glendale 270
Goleta 292A
Gonzales 282A
Grass Valley 232A, 257A
Green Acres 291
Greenfield 258, 300
Gridley 268A
Grover City 297
Guadalupe 288A
Gualala 263
Hanford 233A, 279, 298
Healdsburg 225, 240A
Hemet 289A
Hollister 233
Holtville 261A
Idyllwild 267A
Imperial 257A
Independence 223
Indio 224A, 272A
Inglewood 280A
Jackson 232A
Johannesburg 280
Joshua Tree 221A
Julian 261A
Kerman 232A
Kernville 273A
King City 230, 271
Kings Beach 299
Kingsburg 292A
La Quinta 244A
Lake Arrowhead 280A
Lake Isabella 283A
Lakeport 252A, 258
Lancaster 292A
Lenwood 285A, 297A, 245A
Lindsay 277A
Livermore 269A
Livingston 240A
Lodi 249A
Lompoc 262, 281, 285A, 294
Long Beach 250, 288A
Los Altos 249A
Los Angeles 222, 226, 230, 234, 238, 242, 246, 254, 258, 262, 266, 274, 278, 282, 286, 290, 298
Los Banos 284, 295A
Los Gatos 237A
Los Osos-Baywood Park 267
Lucerne Valley 293A
Ludlow 289A
Madera 221, 297A
Mammoth Lakes 293
Manteca 244A
Marina 224
Mariposa 242, 280A
Marysville 260
McFarland 275
Mecca 249A
Mendocino 224A
Merced 292A, 231A, 248, 299A
Middletown 254A
Modesto 230A, 272A, 277, 281
Mojave 249A
Monte Rio 249
Montecito 225A
Monterey 245
Morgan Hill 241A
Morro Bay 259A
Mount Bullion 260
Mount Shasta 300
Mountain Pass 258
Needles 250
Newport Beach 276A
Oakdale 236
Oakhurst 296A
Oceanside 271
Oildale 237
Ojai 288A
Ontario 228A
Orange Cove 262A
Orcutt 239
Orland 294
Oroville 249
Oxnard 252A, 275A, 284
Pacific Grove 286
Palm Desert 276A
Palm Springs 263, 284, 291
Paradise 244, 278

FM Allotments

Pasadena 294
Paso Robles 223
Patterson 226, 246A
Pismo Beach 237A
Placerville 221A
Porterville 259
Quincy 240A, 262, 271A
Rancho Mirage 258A
Red Bluff 239, 274
Redding 247, 251, 282
Redlands 244A
Redondo Beach 228A
Ridgecrest 224, 285A
Rio Dell 296A
Riverside 224, 248, 256
Rohnert Park 285A
Rohnerville —
Rosamond 228A, 288A
Roseville 229
Sacramento 223, 241, 245, 253, 263, 278A, 286, 293, 300
Salinas 250A, 264, 273, 278A
San Bernardino 236, 260
San Clemente 285A, 300
San Diego 231, 235, 243, 247, 251, 264, 268, 275, 279, 287, 293
San Fernando 232A
San Francisco 227, 235, 239, 243, 247, 251, 255, 259, 267, 271, 279, 283, 287, 291, 295
San Jacinto 241A
San Joaquin 288A
San Jose 222, 253, 262, 293
San Luis Obispo 227, 241, 246, 251
San Mateo 299
San Rafael 264A
Santa Ana 244A, 292A
Santa Barbara 229, 248, 260, 277, 299
Santa Clara 289
Santa Cruz 256
Santa Margarita 291
Santa Maria 256, 273
Santa Paula 244A
Santa Rosa 261A, 269
Santa Ynez 290A
Seaside 280A, 296
Sebastopol 229A
Shafter 249A, 282A
Shingle Springs 270
Singletown 287
Soledad 287A, 292A
Solvang 244A
Sonora 224A
So. Lake Tahoe 230, 275
So. Oroville 285A
St. Helena 257A
Stockton 257A, 261A, 297
Sun City 225A
Susanville 227, 242
Sutter Creek 298A
Taft 280A
Tahoe City 243
Tehachapi 276A
Temecula 233A
Thousand Oaks 224A
Thousand Palms 234A
Tipton 285
Tracy 265A
Tulare 235, 294
Tulelake 243
Turlock 252A
Twentynine Palms 239, 299A
Twin Harte 228A
Ukiah 233, 277, 290
Vacaville 237
Ventura 236, 264, 296A
Victorville 276A
Visalia 225, 241A, 246
Walnut Creek 221A
Weed 272
West Covina 252A
Willows 288A
Windon 254A
Windsor 281A
Woodlake 281
Woodland 281
Yermo 251, 287A
Yreka 280
Yuba City 280
Yucca Valley 295

Colorado
Alamosa 228A
Aspen 249, 296A
Avon 276
Basalt 291A
Boulder 234, 247
Breckenridge 272A
Brush 292A, 296
Buena Vista 281A
Burlington 281
Canon City 280A
Castle Rock 221
Colorado Springs 225, 232, 236, 251, 270

Cortez 250, 254
Craig 229, 273
Delta 236
Denver 239, 253, 258, 262, 266, 278, 286, 290, 294
Durango 259, 263, 267
Eagle 268
Evergreen 243
Fort Collins 227, 300
Fort Morgan 269A
Fountain 241
Frisco 230A
Fruita 260
Glenwood Springs 224A, 256
Grand Junction 222, 226, 282, 300
Greeley 223, 241
Gunnison 252A, 272A
Hayden 240
Holyoke 222
Idalia 231A
Julesburg 243
Kremmling 292
LaJunta 241, 295A
Lakewood 298
Lamar 227, 289
Las Animas 297A
Leadville 228A
Longmont 282
Loveland 273
Manitou Springs 274
Monte Vista 237A
Montrose 231, 241
Oak Creek 281
Ouray 289
Pagosa Springs 292
Pueblo 245, 255, 260, 264, 283, 296, 300
Rifle 287
Rocky Ford 238
Salida 222
Security 288
Silverton 257A, 279, 297
Snowmass Village 280A
Steamboat Springs 245
Sterling 284, 288A
Strasburg 272A
Telluride 285
Trinidad 223
Vail 284
Walsenburg 272
Widefield 292
Windsor 256
Wray 252
Yuma 265

Connecticut
Bridgeport 260
Brookfield 236
Danbury 252A
East Lyme 254A
Enfield 250A
Groton 288A
Hamden 267
Hartford 229, 243, 275, 290, 295
Hartford-Meriden 239
Ledyard 293A
Litchfield 247A
Middletown 285A
New Britain 263
New Haven 232A, 256
New London 265A
Norwalk 240A
Norwich 249A
Pawcatuck 299A
Salisbury 251A
Sharon 277A
Stamford 244A
Stonington 272A
Waterbury 223, 281
Westport 300
Willimantic 252A

Delaware
Bethany Beach 240, 278A
Dover 234
Fenwick Island 221A
Georgetown 228
Laurel 237A
Lewes 290A
Milford 249A, 267A
Ocean View 269A
Rehoboth Beach 224A
Seaford 252A
Selbyville 250A
Smyrna 225A
Wilmington 229, 258

District of Columbia
Washington 230, 242, 246, 254, 258, 262, 266, 278, 297

Florida
Alachua 223A
Apalachicola 265A, 288A
Apopka 237A
Arcadia 252
Atlantic Beach 283
Avon Park 292A

Baldwin 289A
Belle Glade 228A
Beverly Hills 292
Big Pine Key 284
Blountstown 272A
Boca Raton 260
Bonifay 249
Bonita Springs 241
Bradenton 278
Callahan 227
Callaway 278
Cape Coral 280, 292A
Carrabelle 293
Cedar Key 274
Century 286
Chattahoochee 287A
Chiefland 300A
Clearwater 239, 250
Clewiston 292A
Cocoa 257
Cocoa Beach 266, 281
Coral Cove 300A
Coral Gables 286
Crawfordville 231A
Crestview 284
Cross City 295
Crystal City 253
Dade City 241A
Daytona Beach 233, 270
Defuniak Springs 276
DeLand 290
Destin 221
Dunnellon 272
Edgewater 226
Englewood 290A
Fernandina Beach 287A
Five Points 293A
Ft. Lauderdale 264, 278, 290, 294
Ft. Myers 237, 245, 270
Ft. Myers Beach 257
Ft. Myers Villas 292A
Ft. Pierce 238, 245
Ft. Walton Beach 243, 258
Gainesville 265A, 279, 287A
Gifford 234A
Goulds 252
Graceville 269A
Green Cove Springs 224A
Gretna 227A
Gulf Breeze 291A
Havana 285
Hialeah 222
High Springs 285A
Holiday 246
Holly Hill 277A
Holmes Beach 254
Homestead 239
Homosassa Springs 237A
Immokalee 221A
Indiantown 276
Inglis 282A
Jacksonville 236, 241, 245, 256, 275, 297
Jensen Beach 272A
Jupiter 258A, 288A
Key Colony Beach 288
Key Largo 280
Key West 223, 228, 254, 258, 296A, 300
LaBelle 223A
LaCrosse 258A
Lafayette 260
Lake City 232
Lakeland 231
Lehigh Acres 296
Live Oak 251, 291A
MacClenny 221
Madison 274A
Marathon 232, 249A, 292A
Marco 224A, 266
Marianna 231A, 265A
Mary Esther 288
Melbourne 272A, 292A, 296
Mexico Beach 257
Miami 226, 243, 247, 256, 268, 298
Miami Beach 230, 235
Micanopy 247
Milton 274
Miramar Beach 292A
Monticello 270
Mount Dora 299
Naples 228A, 233, 276A
Naples Park 288A
Newberry 263
New Port Richey 288A
Niceville 262A
Ocala 224A, 229
Okeechobee 276A
Orlando 222, 243, 255, 262, 286
Ormond-By-The-Sea 239A
Palatka 260
Palm Beach 250
Panama City 223, 253, 290, 300
Panama City Beach 261, 286
Pensacola 231, 254, 264, 268, 297
Perry 288A

Plantation Key 262, 276A
Pompano Beach 274
Ponte Vedra Beach 227A
Port Charlotte 261
Port St. Joe 228, 233
Port St. Lucie 267A
Punta Gorda 225
Punta Rassa 249A
Quincy 264A, 268
Riviera Beach 232
Rock Harbor 271
Rockledge 274
St. Augustine 250
St. Petersburg 258, 268, 297
Safety Harbor 223
Sanibel 253A
Santa Rosa Beach 271
Sarasota 273, 288A, 293
Sebring 288A
Silver Springs 238A
Solana 287A
Springfield 240, 267A
Starke 292A
Stuart 224
Summerland Key 273
Tallahassee 235, 241, 255, 276, 281, 291A
Tampa 227, 235, 264, 284
Tavares 294
Tavernier 245A
Tice 229A
Titusville 251
Trenton 269A
Venice 221
Vero Beach 229, 259, 269, 279
Watertown 271
West Palm Beach 221, 282, 300
White City 284A
Williston 267A
Winter Haven 248
Winter Park 276
Yankeetown 242A
Zolfo Springs 295A

Georgia
Adel 221A
Albany 242, 269A, 283
Alma 282A
Americus 234, 254
Ashburn 289A
Athens 238, 284
Atlanta 225, 235, 241, 253, 259, 277
Augusta 272A, 276A, 282, 289
Bainbridge 247
Baxley 233
Blackshear 286
Blakely 266
Blue Ridge 280A
Bolingbroke 271A
Boston 292A
Bostwick 222A
Bowdon 288A
Broxton 279A
Brunswick 264, 268, 281A
Buford 272A
Cairo 272A
Camilla 288A
Canton 289
Carrollton 221A
Chatsworth 255A
Chauncey 267
Clarkesville 275
Claxton 297
Clayton 281A
Cleveland 270A
Cochran 244A
Columbus 275, 285A, 297
Coosa 237A
Cordele 252A
Cornelia 257
Crawford 271
Cusseta 279A
Cuthbert 264A
Dahlonega 282A
Dalton 238A
Darien 299
Dawson 221A
Dock Junction 290
Donalsonville 292A
Douglas 258, 294
Dublin 224, 240
Eastman 248A
Eatontown 249
Elberton 221A
Ellijay 228A
Evans 222A
Fayetteville 248
Fitzgerald 245A
Folkston 223A
Forsyth 261A
Ft. Valley 250, 292
Gainesville 246
Gainsville 294
Gibson 232A
Glennville 292A
Gordon 296A

Gray 243A
Greensboro 280A
Greenville 239
Greenwood 278
Harlem 236
Hawkinsville 280A
Hazelhurst 228
Helen 286A
Hinesville 222, 284
Hogansville 251
Homerville 254A
Irwinton 279A
Jackson 221A
Jeffersonville 229A
Jesup 288A
Kingsland 292A
La Grange 281
LaFayette 298A
Lakeland 290
Leesburg 278
Louisville 221A
Lumpkin 257
Lyons 265A
Mableton 273A
Macon 222A, 256, 287, 300
Manchester 227
Marietta 268
Martinez 230, 299
McRae 274A
Metter 279A
Midway 252
Milan 285
Milledgeville 264, 272A
Millen 235
Montezuma 223A
Moultrie 230
Mount Vernon 269A
Nashville 237
Ocilla 249A, 253A
Omega 298A
Peachtree City 244A
Pearson 270A
Perry 265A
Quitman 287A
Reidsville 281A
Richmond Hill 287
Ringgold 229A, 270A
Rockmart 296
Rome 249, 272A
Rossville 288A
Roswell 298A
Royston 279
St. Marys 227
St. Simons Island 224A
Sandersville 260A
Savannah 226, 231, 238, 243, 247, 271
Smithville 295A
Smyrna 231
Soperton 291A
Sparta 274A
Springfield 280A
Statenville 248A
Statesboro 261, 275
Swainsboro 251A, 263A
Sylvania 293A
Sylvester 271A, 291A
Tennille 270A
Thomaston 266A
Thomasville 296
Thomson 269A
Tifton 262
Toccoa 291
Trenton 274A
Trion 239A
Unadilla 260A
Valdosta 235, 239, 244, 266, 299A
Vidalia 249A
Warner Robbins 269A, 273A
Washington 261A
Warrenton 226A
Waycross 249A, 273, 277
Waynesboro 265A, 296
Westpoint 265A
Wrens 245
Wrightsville 298A

Hawaii
Aiea 300
Hali'imaile 288A
Hilo 224, 234, 240, 246, 250, 262
Honolulu 226, 230, 234, 238, 248, 253, 258, 262, 286, 290
Kahalu'u 291A
Kahului 260
Kailua 242
Kailua-Kona 230
Kaneohe 282
Kawaihae 295A
Kealakekua 268
Kekaha 277
Lahaina 228, 266
Lanai City 284
Lihue 228, 245
Makawao 232A
Paauilo 279
Pearl City 270

FM Allotments

Poipu 240A
Pukalani 252
Volcano 299A
Wailuku 236
Waimea 256
Waipahu 222, 274

Idaho
American Falls 281
Blackfoot Falls 247, 268
Boise 222, 250, 282, 286
Bonners Ferry 221A
Burley 260
Caldwell 231, 277, 296A
Chubbuck 253
Coeur d'Alene 272A, 276
Eagle 300
Emmett 270
Fruitland 258
Garden City 290
Goodin 267A
Grangeville 224
Hayden 233
Idaho Falls 241, 256, 277, 288
Jerome 275
Ketchum 284
Lewiston 243, 268, 295
McCall 252A, 266, 294A
Moscow 291
Mountain Home 256
Nampa 235, 245
New Plymouth 226
Orofino 237
Payette 262
Pocatello 229, 235, 273
Preston 244A
Rexburg 232, 251, 263
Rupert 223
Salmon 224A
Sandpoint 237, 273A
Soda Springs 261A
Sun Valley 237, 279
Twin Falls 239, 243
Wallace 248, 264

Illinois
Aledo 272A
Alton 262
Anna 243
Arcola 300A
Arlington Heights 224A
Augusta 253A
Aurora 240A, 300
Ava 280A
Bartonville 260A
Beardstown 232A
Belvidere 285A
Benton 292
Bethalto 238A
Bloomington 268
Breeze 248A
Bushnell 284A
Canton 265A, 300
Carbondale 268
Carlyle 244A
Carmi 247
Carrier Mills 283A
Carterville 236A
Carthage 221
Casey 282
Centralia 237A
Champaign 233, 248, 262
Charleston 221A
Chicago 226, 230, 234, 238, 242, 246, 250, 254, 258, 262, 266, 278, 282, 298
Chillicothe 232A
Christopher 278A
Clinton 240A
Coal City 264A
Columbia 285
Crest Hill 252A
Crete 272A
Danville 235A, 256, 271
Decatur 226A, 236, 275
DeKalb 223, 235A
Des Plaines 294
Dixon 269A
Duquoin 240A
Dundee 280A
Dwight 255A
East Moline 267
East St. Louis 266
Effingham 239, 249A
Eldorado 272A
Elgin 232A
Elmwood 247
Elmwood Park 290
Eureka 253A
Evanston 286
Fairfield 290A
Farmer City 254
Farmington 243A
Flora 280A
Freeport 221A, 253
Galena 298A
Galesburg 224A, 235

Galva 273A
Geneseo 285A
Gibson City 292A
Golconda 232A
Granite City 293
Greenville 269A
Harrisburg 260
Havana 257A
Henry 263A
Herrin 224A
Highland Park 276A
Hillsboro 259
Hoopeston 265A
Jacksonville 263
Jerseyville 281
Joliet 228A, 244A
Kankakee 224A, 236A, 260
Kewanee 221A
Lansing 292A
LaSalle 257
Lawrenceville 276A
LeRoy 281
Lincoln 230
Litchfield 291
Loves Park 244A
Lutesville 281A
Lynnville 296A
Macomb 261A, 274
Mahomet 290A
Marion 297
Maroa 297A
Marseilles 243A
Marshall 290A
Mattoon 245, 267A
Mendota 261A
Metropolis 252A, 288A
Moline 245
Monmouth 249A
Monticello 288A
Morris 276A, 284
Morrison 236A
Morton 272A
Mount Carmel 235
Mount Morris 239A
Mount Olive 287A
Mount Sterling 294
Mount Vernon 231, 271
Mount Zion 257A
Murphysboro 286
Nashville 284A
Neoga 255A
Newton 278
Normal 244A
Oak Park 274
Ogelsby 271A
Olney 225
Oregon 291A
Ottawa 237A
Pana 265A
Paris 253
Paxton 285A
Pekin 238, 285A
Peoria 222A, 227, 289, 295
Peru 265A
Petersburg 249A
Pinckneyville 282A
Pittsfield 248
Plano 296A
Polo 299A
Pontiac 229
Princeton 251A
Quincy 258, 280A, 286
Ramsey 227A
Rantoul 237A, 241A
Robinson 269A
Rochelle 272A
Rock Island 255
Rockford 248, 265A
Rockton 276A
Rushville 244A
Salem 261A
Savanna 262
Seneca 239A
Shelbyville 286
Skokie 270
South Jacksonville 288A
Spring Valley 277A
Springfield 254, 270, 279, 283
Sterling 232A
Streator 249A, 291A
Sullivan 294
Taylorville 224
Tuscola 228A
Urbana 223, 296A
Vandalia 296A
Virden 244A
Virginia 267A
Watseka 231
Waukegan 272A
West Frankfort 249A
Wilmington 288A
Winnebago 237A
Woodlawn 295A
Woodstock 288A
Zion 245

Indiana
Alexandria 224A
Anderson 250, 254A
Angola 262A
Attica 239A
Auburn 272A
Aurora 257A
Austin 224A, 242A
Batesville 280A
Battleground 254A
Bedford 288A
Berne 224A
Bicknell 289A
Bloomfield 266A
Bloomington 222, 224A, 279
Bluffton 261A
Boonville 296A
Brazil 249A
Bremen 245A
Brookston 237A
Brownsburg 270A
Cannelton 275
Chandler 228A
Charlestown 282A
Churubusco 242
Clarksville 226A
Clinton 230A
Columbia City 292A
Columbus 268, 285A
Connersville 262
Corydon 243A, 299
Covington 276A
Crawfordsville 280A, 292A
Crown Point 280A
Danville 296A
Decatur 286
Delphi 275A
Earl Park 251
Elkhart 264, 284
Ellettsville 286A
Elwood 269A
Evansville 281, 287, 298A
Ferdinand 253A
Fort Branch 268A
Fort Wayne 222A, 236, 247, 269A, 280A
Frankfort 259
Franklin 240A
French Lick 261A
Goshen 249A
Greencastle 232A
Greenfield 258
Greensburg 297
Greenwood 294A
Hammond 222
Hartford City 228A
Huntingburg 265
Huntington 275A
Indianapolis 226, 234, 238, 242A, 277, 283, 289, 300
Jasper 284
Jeffersonville 239
Kendallville 227
Kentland 269A
Knox 257A
Kokomo 224A, 263
Lafayette 228A, 243, 287
Lagrange 288A
LaPorte 244A
Lebanon 265A
Ligonier 274A
Linton 227
Logansport 272A
Loogootee 231A
Lowell 296A
Madison 244A
Marion 295
Martinsville 272A
Michigan City 240A
Mitchell 273A
Monticello 299A
Mount Vernon 294A
Muncie 221A, 281, 285A
Nappanee 239A
Nashville 236A
New Albany 234A
New Carlisle 272A
New Castle 273
New Haven 300A
Newburgh 291A
Noblesville 230A
North Vernon 291
Paoli 237A
Peru 252A
Petersburg 272A
Plainfield 252A
Plymouth 232
Portland 265A
Princeton 251, 263A
Rensselaer 249A
Richmond 241, 267
Roanoke 231A
Rochester 221A
Rockville 285A
Royal Center 279A
Rushville 232A

Salem 250A, 255
Santa Claus 277A
Scottsburg 287A
Seelyville 240A
Seymour 229
Shelbyville 246
South Bend 225, 268, 276A, 280A, 292A
South Whitley 266A
Spencer 224A
Sullivan 237A
Tell City 245A
Terre Haute 260, 264, 274, 298
Valparaiso 288A
Van Buren 257A
Veedersburg 225A
Versailles 276A
Vevay 249A
Vincennes 221A, 244A
Wabash 240A, 290A
Walton 229A
Warsaw 297
Washington 293, 300A
West Lafayette 267A, 294A
West Terre Haute 288A
Winamac 261A
Winchester 252A

Iowa
Albia 244
Algona 224
Ames 281, 296A
Ankeny 223, 292A
Asbury 277
Atlantic 279
Audubon 243
Belle Plaine 238A
Bettendorf 228A
Bloomfield 292
Boone 252, 257A
Britt 258A
Brooklyn 256
Burlington 228A, 276, 297
Carroll 229
Cedar Falls 253
Cedar Rapids 243, 251, 275, 283
Centerville 254
Chariton 287
Charles City 240A
Cherokee 221A, 272A
Clarinda 257
Clarion 245
Clear Lake 276A
Clinton 241, 249A
Council Bluffs 253
Cresco 272A
Creston 267
Davenport 279, 293
Decorah 263, 284A
Denison 296A
Des Moines 227, 235, 247, 262, 273, 298
Dubuque 225, 272A, 287
Dyersville 257A
Eddyville 268
Eldon 282
Eldora 258A
Emmetsburg 261A
Epworth 247
Estherville 240
Fairfield 240A
Forest City 297
Fort Dodge 221A, 233
Fort Madison 269
Garnavillo 261A
Grinnell 294
Grundy Center 249
Harlan 287
Hudson 241A
Humboldt 249A
Ida Grove 225
Independence 237A
Iowa City 231, 264
Iowa Falls 237A
Jefferson 255A
Keokuk 237, 242
Knoxville 221
Lamoni 250
Le Mars 258
Manchester 234
Maquoketa 237A
Marshalltown 266
Mason City 230, 250A, 291
Mount Pleasant 288
Muscatine 259
New Hampton 236A
New Sharon 260
Newton 240A
Northwood 274A
Oelwein 222
Onawa 272
Osage 279A
Osceola 295
Oskaloosa 285
Ottumwa 224A, 249A
Parkersburg 255A
Pella 277

Perry 269A
Red Oak 237
Rock Valley 295
Sac City 286A
Sheldon 287
Sibley 262A
Sioux Center 230
Sioux City 238, 250, 277
Sioux Rapids 275
Spencer 285A, 299
Spirit Lake 280
Stansgar 238A
Storm Lake 268
Stuart 300A
Twin Lakes 290
Vinton 296A
Washington 291A
Waterloo 270, 289, 300
Waukon 278
Waverly 257A
Webster City 239
Winterset 258

Kansas
Abilene 253
Andover 230
Arkansas City 273A, 293
Augusta 283
Baxter Springs 296A
Belle Plaine 224
Belleville 221A
Beloit 288
Burlington 237A
Caney 266A
Chanute 228A
Clay Center 265A
Clearwater 254
Coffeyville 255A
Colby 250, 262
Columbus 287
Concordia 237A
Copeland 251, 256
Derby 242
Dodge City 230, 238
Downs 231
El Dorado 256
Emporia 258A, 269, 285A
Eureka 228A
Fort Scott 280A, 284A
Fredonia 281A
Garden City 247
Girard 256A
Goodland 273, 299
Great Bend 282, 300
Hays 258, 277
Haysville 287
Herington 289
Hiawatha 228
Hill City 270
Hoisington 264
Horton 229
Hugoton 294
Hutchinson 246, 264, 271, 275
Independence 269A
Iola 257A
Junction City 233
Kansas City 231, 251
Kingman 232A, 262
Larned 244A, 295
Lawrence 290
Leavenworth 255
Leoti 260
Liberal 268, 274, 298, 286
Lindsborg 240A
Lyon 291
Manhattan 284
Marysville 275
McPherson 244A
Medicine Lodge 269
Minneapolis 224
Ness City 285A
Newton 222
North Fort Riley 273
Norton 294
Oberlin 266
Ogden 278
Olathe 222
Osage City 225
Ottawa 239
Parsons 228A
Phillipsburg 223, 237A
Pittsburg 245
Plainville 244A
Pratt 226
Russell 240A
St. Marys 275
Salina 229, 260, 285A
Scott City 223
Seneca 231
Sterling 239A
Topeka 247, 257A, 262, 295, 299
Wamego 231
Wellington 228A
Wichita 236, 250, 267, 279, 297
Winfield 240, 300

FM Allotments

Kentucky
Albany 292A
Allen 261A
Ashland 229
Barbourville 241
Bardstown 244A
Beattyville 271A
Beaver Dam 264A
Benton 256A
Berea 294A
Bowling Green 227A, 244
Brandenburg 228A
Burkesville 300A
Burnside 230
Cadiz 292A
Calvert 239A
Campbellsville 281
Carlisle 264A
Carrollton 237A
Catlettsburg 224A
Cave City 279
Central City 270
Columbia 228A
Corbin 258, 297
Cumberland 274A
Cynthiana 272A
Danville 296A
Drakesboro 280A
Edmonton 256A
Elizabethtown 252
Elkhorn City 276A
Eminence 289A
Erlanger 265A
Falmouth 298A
Flemingsburg 292A
Fort Campbell 300
Fort Knox 288A
Frankfort 279A, 285A
Fulton 257A
Garrison 252A
Georgetown 277A
Glasgow 236, 287
Grayson 272A
Greensburg 276A
Greenup 289
Greenville 288A
Hardinsburg 232A, 282A
Harlan 286A
Harold 285A
Harrodsburg 257A
Hartford 292A
Hawesville 289A
Hazard 266, 284A
Henderson 258, 276A
Hindman 296A
Hodgenville 292A
Hopkinsville 254, 262
Horse Cave 294A
Hyden 250A
Irvine 291A
Jackson 293A
Jamestown 285A
Jeffersontown 269A
Jenkins 232
Lancaster 286A
Lawrenceburg 271A
Lebanon 265A
Leitchfield 285A
Lexington 225, 233, 251
Lexington-Fayette 283
Liberty 254
London 222, 280A
Louisa 222A
Louisville 248, 259, 263, 272A, 280A, 295
Madisonville 230, 295A
Manchester 276A, 289A
Mannsville 260
Marion 274A
Mayfield 234
Maysville 240A
McKee 300A
Middlesboro 224A
Midway 300A
Monticello 226A, 269A
Morehead 221A, 242A
Morganfield 237A
Mount Sterling 288A
Mount Vernon 275A
Munfordville 272A
Murray 279
Nicholasville 273A
Owensboro 223, 241
Owingsville 296A
Paducah 227, 245
Paintsville 234, 255
Paris 245
Philpot 234A
Pikeville 226
Pineville 292A
Prestonsburg 238, 288A
Princeton 285A
Providence 249A
Radcliff 278A
Reidland 294A
Richmond 269A
Russell Spring 224A
Russellville 266
St. Matthews 276A
Salyersville 247A
Scottsville 257A
Shelbyville 267A
Shepherdsville 286A
Smiths Grove 296
Somerset 246, 272A
Springfield 274A
Stamping Grd 256A
Stanford 240A
Stanton 285A
Tompkinsville 221A
Valley Station 290A
Vanceburg 285A
Vancleve 260A
Versailles 292A
Vine Grove 268A
Virgie 298A
West Liberty 275A
Westwood 259A
Whitesburg 280A
Whitley City 290A
Wickliffe 240A
Williamsburg 282A
Williamstown 293A
Wilmore 290A
Winchester 261

Louisiana
Abbeville 285
Alexandria 226, 230A, 245, 262
Arcadia 223A
Baker 297A
Basile 271
Bastrop 232A, 261, 277A
Baton Rouge 251, 264, 268, 273
Bayou Vista 237
Belle Chasse 275
Benton 221A
Berwick 290A
Boyce 272
Breaux Bridge 243
Brusley 241
Bunkie 282
Clayton 300A
Clinton 224
Columbia 276
Coushatta 235
Crowley 225
Delhi 228A
DeRidder 221, 269A
Donaldsonville 285A
Dubach 249
Erath 299
Eunice 288A
Farmerville 224A
Ferriday 296
Folsom 285
Franklin 288A
Galliano 232
Hammond 277, 296A
Haughton 279A
Haynesville 288A
Homer 272A, 294
Houma 281, 298
Jena 257A
Jennings 225
Jonesboro 285
Jonesville 266A
Kaplin 247
Kentwood 231
Lacombe 234A
Lafayette 233, 238A, 260
Lake Arthur 297
Lake Charles 241, 258, 279, 287
Lake Providence 224A
LaPlace 222
Larose 262
Leesville 224A, 289
Mamou 266A
Mansfield 224A, 284
Many 296
Marksville 249A
Maurice 292A
Minden 237A
Monroe 270, 281, 287, 291
Moreauville 221A
Morgan City 244
Natchitoches 240A, 247
New Iberia 229, 256
New Orleans 227, 239, 246, 253, 258, 266, 270
New Roads 293
North Fort Polk 294A
Oak Grove 244
Oakdale 254
Opelousas 290A, 296A
Port Sulphur 294
Rayne 294A
Rayville 222
Reserve 235A
Richwood 265A
Ruston 258A, 298
Shreveport 229, 233, 243, 259, 266, 275
Slidell 287
South Fort Polk 267A
Springhill 224A
Sulphur 265A
Tallulah 283
Thibodaux 293
Tioga 278
Troy 264A
Varnado 225A
Vidalia 284A
Ville Platte 223A
Vivian 287A
Washington 284
West Monroe 252
Winnfield 221A
Winnsboro 240A

Maine
Auburn 260
Augusta 222, 267
Bangor 225, 246
Bar Harbor 256, 299
Bath 290
Belfast 284
Biddeford 232
Boothbay Harbor 244
Brewer 262, 293
Brunswick 255
Calais 224A
Camden 273
Caribou 249A
Dennysville 275A
Dexter 271A
Dover-Foxcroft 276A
Ellsworth 233, 239
Fairfield 227A
Farmington 257A
Fort Kent 293
Gardiner 282
Houlton 261A
Howland 280
Kennebunk 257A
Kennebunkport 284A
Kittery 287A
Lewiston 230B
Lincoln 289, 298
Machias 237A
Madawaska 272A
Madison 248A
Mexico 264A
Milbridge 229
Millinocket 235
North Windham 294A
Norway 224A
Old Town 297
Pittsfield 258A
Portland 226, 250, 270, 275
Presque Isle 241, 245, 269A, 291
Rockland 277
Rumford 242
Saco 240A
Sanford 221A
Scarborough 292A
Searsport 269A
Skowhegan 286, 300
Thomaston 295
Topsham 238A
Van Buren 251A
Waterville 253
Westbrook 265A
Winslow 237A
York Center 237A

Maryland
Annapolis 256, 300
Baltimore 222, 226, 236, 250, 270, 274, 282, 293
Berlin 280A
Bethesda 234, 272A
Braddock Heights 280A
California 275A
Cambridge 232A, 292A
Catonsville 289
Crisfield 245A
Cumberland 275, 291
Easton 244
Federalsburg 296A
Frederick 260
Frostburg 246A, 287
Glen Burnie 240A
Grasonville 276A
Hagerstown 284, 295
Halfway 244A
Havre de Grace 279
Hurlock 265A
Lexington Park 249A
Mechanicsville 252A
Middletown 276A
Morningside 238
Mountain Lake Park 283A
Oakland 222A
Ocean City 260, 295A
Ocean City-Salisbury 284
Ocean Pines 246A
Pocomoke City 223A, 293A
Prince Frederick 224A
Princess Anne 273
Salisbury 248A, 255A, 288A
Waldorf 281
Westernport 266A
Westminster 264
Williamsport 240A

Massachusetts
Amherst 265A
Athol 260A
Barnstable 260
Boston 233, 245, 253, 264, 277, 281, 294
Brockton 249A
Brookline 225
Cambridge 237A
Chatham 298
Fairhaven 296A
Falmouth 266A, 270
Fitchburg 283
Framingham 289
Gloucester 285A
Great Barrington 286A
Greenfield 237A, 252A
Harwichport 228A
Haverhill 223
Hyannis 275A, 291
Lawrence 229
Lowell 258
Lynn 269A
Marshfield 240A
Medford 300
Nantucket 242
New Bedford 247, 251
North Adams 261A
Northampton 257A, 292A
Orange 247A
Orleans 284
Pittsfield 240A, 269A, 288A
Plymouth 256
Southbridge 261A
South Yarmouth 280A
Springfield 226, 234, 271
Taunton 227
Tisbury 224A
Truro 272A
Turners Falls 230A
Waltham 273
Webster 255A
West Yarmouth 235
Winchendon 249A
Worcester 241, 297

Michigan
Adrian 237A, 280A
Albion 244A
Allegan 222A
Alma 285A
Alpena 257, 299
Ann Arbor 275, 296A
Ashley 223A
Atlanta 223
Bad Axe 271
Baraga 282
Battle Creek 237A, 277
Bay City 241, 273
Bear Lake 261A
Beaverton 249A
Benton Harbor 235A, 260
Big Rapids 248A, 265A
Birmingham 234
Boyne City 228
Bridgman 248A
Bronson 234A
Brooklyn 287A
Buchanan 256A
Cadillac 225, 244, 296A
Caro 221A
Carrollton 263A
Charlevoix 290
Charlotte 224A
Cheboygan 286
Clare 237A
Coldwater 253
Coleman 268A
Crystal Falls 264
Dearborn 262
Detroit 222, 226, 238, 242, 246, 250, 254, 258, 266, 270, 278, 282, 286, 290, 294, 298
Dewitt 243A
Dowagiac 221A
East Jordan 265A
East Lansing 235, 256
Escanaba 246, 284
Essexville 247A
Flint 224A, 236, 288, 288A, 300
Frankfort 257
Fremont 261A
Gaylord 237A, 294
Gladstone 288
Gladwin 276A
Glen Arbor 238, 251A
Grand Haven 221A
Grand Rapids 229, 239, 245, 250, 255A, 267, 275, 281, 289
Grayling 262
Greenville 297
Gulliver 234
Hancock 228A, 254
Harbor Beach 279
Harbor Springs 280
Harrison 221A
Hart 287
Hartford 279A
Hastings 261A
Hillman 235
Hillsdale 221A
Holland 233, 241
Houghton 242, 249A, 272A
Houghton Lake 253
Howell 228A
Hudson 273A
Iron Mountain 226, 268
Iron River 256
Ironwood 259, 295
Ishpeming 222, 298
Jackson 231, 291
Kalamazoo 271, 293, 299
Kalkaska 248
Kingsford 251A
Lake City 285A, 292A
L'Anse 291
Lansing 248, 264, 269A
Lapeer 276A
Leland 232
Lexington 245A
Ludington 292A
Mackinaw City 232A
Manistee 249A, 268A
Marlette 223A
Marquette 231A, 239, 277
Marshall 285A
Menominee 280A
Midland 227, 259
Mio 230
Monroe 252A
Mount Clemens 274
Mount Pleasant 233, 282A
Munising 252
Muskegon 269, 283, 295, 300
Muskegon Heights 269
Newberry 229, 250
Niles 237A
North Muskegon 252A
Norway 232
Ontonagon 266
Oscoda 239, 264
Otsego 265A
Owasso 280A
Pentwater 231, 276A
Petoskey 242, 255
Pickford 288A
Pinconning 265A
Port Huron 272A, 296A
Portage 243A
Rogers City 244, 260
Roscommon 266A
Saginaw 251, 283A, 292A, 296A
St. Ignace 275
St. Johns 221A
St. Joseph 296A
Sandusky 249A
Saugatuck 224A
Sault Ste. Marie 252A, 258, 267
Scottville 235
Sebewaing 267A
South Haven 257
Spring Arbor 295A
Standish 245A
Stephenson 231
Sturgis 257A
Tawas City 284, 297A
Three Rivers 240A
Traverse City 270, 278, 283A, 298
Tuscola 269A
Vassar 255A
Walker 263A
West Branch 288A
Whitehall 272, 273A
Zeeland 257A

Minnesota
Ada 292A
Aitkin 232
Albany 288A
Albert Lea 235, 241A
Alexandria 222, 257A, 264
Anoka 300
Atwater 231A
Austin 260
Babbitt 294A
Bemidji 266, 279
Benson 228A
Blackduck 252
Blooming Prairie 265A
Brainerd 278A, 294, 298
Breckenridge 286
Breezy Point 282
Browerville 259A
Caledonia 234A
Cambridge 287
Cloquet 243, 263
Coleraine 241
Cold Spring 235

FM Allotments

Crookston 241, 246
Crosby 268
Deer River 288
Detroit Lakes 236, 272
Duluth 225, 235, 239, 247, 255, 269A, 277, 286
East Grand Forks 282
Eden Prairie 289A
Ely 221A
Eveleth 250
Fairmont 293
Faribault 240A, 298
Fergus Falls 243, 277
Forest Lake 240A
Fosston 296
Glencoe 241
Glenwood 296A
Golden Valley 223
Grand Marais 237
Grand Rapids 245
Granite Falls 230A
Hibbing 230, 292
Hutchinson 296A
International Falls 258, 281
Jackson 289
La Crescent 274
Lake City 273
Lakeville 286A
LeSueur 241A
Little Falls 221A, 231A
Luverne 266
Madison 221A
Mankato 244, 256, 278
Marshall 259, 298
Minneapolis 229, 246, 253, 258, 262, 275
Montevideo 288A
Moorhead 254, 260
Moose Lake 296
Mora 238
Morris 239
New Prague 238A
New Ulm 226
Nisswa 227
North Mankato 244A
Olivia 269A
Ortonville 268, 292A
Osakis 280A
Owatonna 285A
Park Rapids 248
Paynesville 255
Pelican Rapids 281
Pequot Lakes 274
Perham 258A
Pine City 221A
Pipestone 254
Preston 276
Princeton 291
Proctor 299A
Red Wing 290
Redwood Falls 249
Richfield 267
Rochester 225A, 243, 248, 269, 295
Roseau 271
Rushford 257
St. Charles 299A
St. Cloud 251, 284
St. James 263, 285A
St. Joseph 225
St. Louis Park 281
St. Paul 233, 237A, 271
St. Peter 288A
Sartell 244
Sauk Centre 232A
Sauk Rapids 269A
Slayton 276A
Sleepy Eye 297A
Spring Grove 252
Spring Valley 282A
Springfield 234
Staples 234A
Stewartville 287
Thief River Falls 257, 262, 274
Tracy 286
Two Harbors 282
Virginia 260
Wadena 290
Waite Park 279
Walker 256
Warroad 223
Waseca 221
Willmar 237, 273
Windom 232A
Winona 237, 266A
Worthington 228A, 236

Mississippi
Aberdeen 287
Ackerman 300
Amory 237A
Artesia 260
Baldwin 223A
Batesville 263
Bay Springs 228A
Belzoni 225A, 296A
Biloxi 229
Booneville 257A
Brandon 249A
Brookhaven 221A
Brooksville 255
Bruce 233A
Byhalia 235A
Calhoun City 272A
Canton 269A
Carthage 252A
Centerville 285A
Charleston 239A
Clarksdale 243, 268, 293
Cleveland 224A, 280A, 252
Clinton 228A
Coldwater 237A
Collins 296A
Columbia 244A
Columbus 235, 276, 280
Corinth 232A, 237A
Drew 237A
Ebenezer 280A
Ellisville 273
Eurpora 271
Fayette 249A
Flora 247
Forest 223
Fulton 270
Gluckstadt 269
Greenville 250, 264, 284
Greenwood 230A, 256, 282
Grenada 261
Gulfport 244A, 272, 296A
Hattiesburg 221A, 226A, 279, 283
Hazelhurst 265
Heidelberg 257
Holly Springs 224A
Houston 227
Indianola 245, 288A
Iuka 285
Jackson 234, 238, 242, 259, 275
Kosciusko 277, 286
Laurel 251A, 262
Leland 232, 272A
Lexington 273
Long Beach 233A
Louisville 296
Lucedale 295A
Lumberton 237
Macon 263A
Magee 298
Marion 236
McComb 289
McLain 245A
Meridian 246, 267, 271A
Monticello 271
Moss Point 285
Mound Bayou 271A
Natchez 236, 247A
New Albany 278, 294
Newton 250A
Ocean Springs 223A, 276
Olive Branch 239A
Oxford 238A, 248, 229
Pascagoula 256, 290
Pearl 230A
Petal 292
Philadelphia 272A
Picayune 291
Pickens 290
Pontotoc 244A
Poplarville 300
Port Gibson 263A
Prentiss 252A
Quitman 255
Richton 243A
Ripley 272A
Rosedale 298
Starkville 221A, 291
State College 283
Sumrall 247A
Taylorsville 240
Tupelo 253
Tylertown 249A
Union 281
University 221A
Utica 225A
Vicksburg 254, 266A, 294
Water Valley 288A
Waynesboro 288A
West Point 265A
Wiggins 250
Winona 244A
Woodville 299A
Yazoo City 221, 229A

Missouri
Asbury 278
Ash Grove 281A
Ashland 291
Aurora 263
Ava 222A
Bethany 238
Birch Tree 296
Bonne Terre 282A
Boonville 230A, 257
Bourbon 244A
Bowling Green 231
Branson 292A
Brookfield 245
Buffalo 260A
Butler 221A
Cabool 251A
California 232
Cameron 261
Campbell 298A
Canton 265
Cape Girardeau 264, 275
Carrollton 264
Carthage 236
Caruthersville 276A
Cassville 261A
Centralia 221A
Chaffee 284A
Charleston 291
Chillicothe 280A
Clayton 256
Clinton 237, 241
Columbia 244, 252, 268, 269, 272A
Crestwood 234
Cuba 271A
DeSoto 261A
Dexter 272A
Doniphan 248
Doolittle 283A
East Prairie 287A
Eldon 224, 270A
Eldorado Springs 288A
Ellington 280A
Farmington 253
Florissant 246
Fulton 263A
Gainesville 259
Gallatin 269
Gordonville 257A
Greenfield 299A
Halfway 226A
Hannibal 225
Harrisonville 266
Houston 257
Huntsville 278
Ironton 224A
Jefferson City 261, 295
Joplin 223, 273
Kansas City 227, 235, 243, 259, 271, 277, 282
Kennett 255, 282A
Kirksville 229, 233, 300
Knob Noster 289
Lake Ozark 274A
Lamar 260A
La Monte 246
Lebanon 279, 300
Lexington 297
Liberty 293
Louisiana 271
Lutesville 281A, 286A
Macon 260A
Malden 224A
Malta Bend 248
Mansfield 240A
Marble Hill 247A
Marshall 275
Marshfield 284
Maryville 246
Memphis 263
Mexico 239
Moberly 234, 288A, 288
Monett 240A
Monroe City 292A
Montgomery City 280A
Mount Vernon 294
Mountain Grove 293A
Mountain View 245
Nevada 249A
New London 290
New Madrid 293
Nixa 290
Osage Beach 228
Osceola 222A
Otterville 299A
Owensville 237
Ozark 225A
Palmyra 250
Perryville 226A
Piedmont 285
Pleasant Hope 238
Poplar Bluff 233, 238, 244A, 278
Potosi 249
Republic 258A
Richmond 223A
Rolla 287, 292A
St. Genevieve 289
St. James 259
St. Joseph 286
St. Louis 222, 229, 242, 251, 273, 277, 299
St. Robert 255A
Salem 240A
Savannah 224
Sedalia 221A
Seligman 227
Sikeston 250
Southwest City 262A
Sparta 243
Springfield 234, 247, 254, 267
Steelville 227
Sullivan 265A
Tarkio 251A
Thayer 222A
Trenton 269A
Union 269A
Vandalia 282A
Versailles 236A
Warrenton 260
Warsaw 249A, 253A
Washington 283A
Waynesville 249A, 250A, 272A
Webb City 230, 250A
West Plains 230, 273
Wheeling 290A
Willard 286
Willow Springs 262

Montana
Anaconda 249
Baker 263
Belgrade 244
Billings 227, 231, 246, 253, 275, 279
Bozeman 229, 236, 260, 271
Butte 224A, 231, 238
Chinook 267
Columbia Falls 240A
Conrad 229A
Cut Bank 274
Deer Lodge 244A
Dillon 252
East Helena 281
Ennis 254
Forsyth 267
Glasgow 228A
Glendive 243
Great Falls 225, 233, 255, 262, 291, 297
Hamilton 240
Hardin 238
Havre 223, 236
Helena 258, 266, 276, 287
Kalispell 246, 253, 280, 292A
Laurel 269
Lewiston 240A
Libby 269A
Livingston 248
Malta 261
Miles City 223
Missoula 227, 235, 261, 273
Outlook 289
Plentywood 261A
Red Lodge 257
Ronan 222
Scobey 239
Shelby 242, 250
Sidney 226, 236
West Yellowstone 243A
Wolf Point 224A

Nebraska
Ainsworth 224A
Albion 224A
Alliance 271, 290
Auburn 288A
Aurora 247
Beatrice 225
Bennington 227A
Blair 292A
Bridgeport 267
Broken Bow 252A
Central City 262
Chadron 234, 248
Columbus 228, 266
Cozad 283
Crete 281
Crookston 241
Fairbury 258
Falls City 267A
Fremont 288A
Gering 280
Gordon 238
Grand Island 239, 243, 299
Hastings 268
Holdrege 249A
Imperial 276A
Kearney 255, 272, 290
Kimball 261A
Lexington 226
Lincoln 236, 270, 274, 287A, 292A, 297
McCook 230, 241A, 253, 287
Milford 251
Nebraska City 249
Norfolk 234, 294
North Platte 235, 246, 278
Ogallala 259, 293
Omaha 222, 231, 241, 260, 264, 283, 290
O'Neill 275
Orchard 287
Ord 280
Plattsmouth 295A
Scottsbluff 225, 231
Seward 245
Sidney 254
South Souix City 296A
Superior 280
Terrytown 245
Wayne 285A
West Point 300
Winnebago 289
York 285

Nevada
Boulder City 288
Carson City 234, 247, 251
Elko 229, 237
Ely 224, 269
Fallon 257A, 267A
Gardnerville-Minden 256
Hawthorne 228A
Henderson 231, 238, 263
Incline Village 261
Indian Springs 257A
Las Vegas 222, 226, 242, 246, 253, 270, 278, 286, 293
Laughlin 228, 300
Mesquite 248
North Las Vegas 282
Pahrump 298
Reno 225, 238, 269A, 283, 289, 295
Sparks 221A, 265A
Tonapah 224A
Wendover 272
Winnemucca 224

New Hampshire
Bedford 243A
Belmont 227A
Berlin 279
Campton 289A
Claremont 291
Concord 272A, 288A
Conway 228A, 283A
Dover 248
Exeter 296A
Farmington 293A
Franklin 231A
Gorham 296A
Hampton 271A
Hanover 222A, 257A
Haverhill 267A
Henniker 256A
Hillsborough 299A
Hinsdale 285A
Jackson 258A
Keene 285
Laconia 252A
Lancaster 272A
Lebanon 263A
Lisbon 244A
Littleton 292A
Manchester 239, 266
Meredith 268A
Moultonborough 295A
Mount Washington 235
Nashau 292A
New London 259A
Newport 269A
Peterborough 221A
Plymouth 261A
Portsmouth 262
Rochester 244A
Somersworth 254A
Walpole 242A
Winchester 254A
Wolfeboro 285A

New Jersey
Asbury Park 232A
Atlantic City 236, 245, 279, 297
Avalon 232A
Belvidere 296A
Blairstown 292A
Bridgeton 299
Camden 295
Canton 269A
Cape May 272A
Cape May Court House 288A
Dover 288A
Eatontown 292A
Egg Harbor City 285
Franklin 272A
Long Branch 296A
Manahawkin 261A, 289
Margate City 241A
Millville 247
New Brunswick 252A
Newark 234, 262, 290
Newton 279
North Cape May 294A
Ocean Acres 253A
Ocean City 252A, 292A
Paterson 233A
Petersburg 274A
Pleasantville 225A
Point Pleasant 240A
Princeton 277
Toms River 224A
Trenton 233, 248, 268

FM Allotments

Tuckerton 259A
Villas 254A
Vineland 221A
Wildwood 264
Wildwood Crest 226A
Zarephath 256

New Mexico
Alamagordo 232, 279, 287
Alamos 298
Albuquerque 222, 227, 231, 242, 258, 262, 267A, 277, 300
Angel Fire 256
Armijo 296
Artesia 225
Aztec 235
Bayard 275
Belen 249
Bloomfield 283
Bosque Farms 284
Carlsbad 221A, 281, 291
Central 237
Clayton 228A
Clovis 256, 260, 268, 272, 298
Corrales 236A
Deming 232A
Espanola 272
Eunice 265A
Farmington 225, 239, 245, 271
Gallup 229, 233, 256, 291
Grants 224, 264, 279, 288
Hatch 266
Hobbs 231, 239, 243A, 275
Jal 296A
Kirtland 275
La Luz 224A
Las Cruces 258, 276A, 280A
Las Vegas 251, 264
Lordsburg 250
Los Alamos 253, 294, 298
Los Lunas 273, 292
Lovington 269
Maljamar 254, 286
Mesilla Park 285A
Portales 237A
Raton 229
Rio Rancho 269A
Roswell 235, 246, 258A, 263, 284, 293
Ruidosa 228
Santa Fe 234, 238, 247, 281, 286, 290
Santa Rosa 240A
Silver City 233A
Socorro 284, 225A
Taos 260, 268
Texico 243A
Thoreau 260
Truth or Consequences 254
Tucumcari 224A
White Rock 266

New York
Albany 238, 265A, 276A, 293, 299
Amsterdam 249A
Arlington 245A
Attica 269A
Auburn 295
Avon 227A
Babylon 272A
Baldwinsville 221
Ballston Spa 272A
Bath 252A, 276A
Bay Shore 276A
Big Flats 249A
Binghamton 251, 256
Boonville 267A
Briarcliff Manor 296A
Bridgehampton 273A
Bridgeport 258A
Brighton 231A
Brockport 288A
Buffalo 225, 233, 241, 245, 258, 273, 277, 281, 293
Calverton-Roanoke 287A
Canajoharie 227A
Canandaigua 272A
Canton 244A, 268A
Cape Vincent 234A, 274A
Carthage 276A
Catskill 253A
Center Moriches 241A
Chateaugay 234A
Cherry Valley (Ostego Co.) 270
Clifton Park 244A
Clyde 229A
Cobleskill 278
Conklin 263A
Copenhagen 294
Corinth 228A
Corning 254A, 291
Cortland 260
Dansville 230A
Dehli 262A
Depew 229
Deposit 234A
Deruyter 286

Dundee 240A
East Hampton 244A
Ellenville 257A
Elmira 224A, 232A
Endicott 289
Endwell 298A
Essex 267A
Fort Plain 266A
Frankfort 235
Fredonia 243A
Fulton 284
Garden City 224A
Geneva 269A
Glens Falls 240A
Gouverneur 237A
Hammondsport 252A
Hampton Bays 296A
Hague 229A
Hempstead 252A
Henderson 264A
Herkimer 224A
Highland 297A
Homer 268A
Honeoye Falls 297A
Hoosick Falls 248A
Hornell 221A, 287
Horseheads 265A
Hudson 228A
Hudson Falls 269A, 296A
Hyde Park 249A
Irondequoit 294A
Ithaca 228A, 247, 279
Jamestown 227, 269A
Jeffersonville 291A
Jewett 250A
Johnstown 285A
Kingston 232A
Lake George 253A
Lake Luzerne 234A
Lake Placid 288A
Lake Success 278
Lakewood 295
Liberty 240A
Little Falls 288A
Lowville 257A
Malone 243A
Manlius 239
Mechanicville 283A
Mexico 280A
Middletown 224A
Montauk 235A, 284A
Monticello 252A, 259A
Montour Falls 285A
Morristown 275A
Mount Kisco 292A
New Paltz 277A
New Rochelle 228A
New York 222, 230, 238, 242, 246, 250, 254, 258, 266, 270, 274, 282, 286, 294, 298
Newburgh 276A
Niagara Falls 253
North Syracuse 265A
Norwich 230
Norwood 241A
Ogdensburg 224A, 254A
Old Forge 231A, 259A
Olean 239, 268A
Oneida 292A
Oneonta 276A, 280A
Oswego 244A, 288A
Owego 269A
Palmyra 259A
Patchogue 248, 291
Patterson 288A
Peekskill 264
Phoenix 271A
Plattsburg 260, 286A
Port Henry 221A
Port Jervis 244A
Potsdam 257A
Poughkeepsie 221A, 241A, 268, 284
Pulaski 269A
Queensbury 289
Ravena 233A
Remsen 228A
Rensselaer 280A
Riverhead 280A
Rochester 223, 243, 250, 255, 263, 267, 280A, 290A
Rome 241, 273
Rotterdam 252A
Sag Harbor 221A
Salamanca 252A
Saranac Lake 269A, 292
Saugerties 225A
Schenectady 258
Schoharie 247A
Seneca Falls 257A
Sidney 265A
Smithtown 232A
Sodus 278A
South Bristol Twp. (Ontario Co.) 236
Southampton 225A, 237A

Southhold 269A
Southport 258A
Star Lake 290
Stillwater 267A
Syracuse 226, 233, 275, 290A, 300
Ticonderoga 280A
Troy 222
Tupper Lake 272A
Utica 245, 254, 264A, 282, 297
Vestal 277
Voorheesville 242A
Walton 221A
Warrensburg 263A
Waterloo 253A
Watertown 228A, 248
Waverly 272A
Webster 274A
Wellsville 228A
Westhampton 253A
Westport 273A
Wethersfield Twp. (Wyoming Co.) 299
White Plains 280A
Whitehall 231A
Whitesboro 250A
Woodstock 261A
Wurtsboro 247A

North Carolina
Ahoskie 257A
Albemarle 265A
Asheboro 222
Asheville 260
Atlantic 297, 298A
Banner Elk 264A
Bayboro 250
Belhaven 266
Biltmore Forest 243A
Black Mountain 295
Burgaw 260
Burlington 230, 266
Carolina Beach 294A
Charlotte 236, 279, 284, 300
Clinton 297
Columbia 289
Concord 250
Dunn 278
Durham 286, 296A
Eden 233
Edenton 261, 273
Elizabeth City 229, 244A
Elizabethtown 289A
Elkin 265A
Fairbluff 287A
Fairmont 265
Farmville 232A
Fayetteville 251
Forest City 227
Franklin 244A
Fuquay-Varina 280
Gaston 250A
Gastonia 270
Goldsboro 245, 272A
Greensboro 246, 254
Greenville 300
Grifton 258
Hamlet 282A
Harkers Island 262
Harrisburg 224A
Hatteras 233, 246
Havelock 286
Henderson 223
Hendersonville 273
Hertford 285
Hickory 239, 275
High Point 238, 258, 262
Highlands 283A
Hope Mills 283A
Jacksonville 222, 254, 288
Kannapolis 259
Kill Devil Hills 281
Kinston 236, 249A, 275A
Laurinburg 243
Leland 231A
Lenoir 277A
Lexington 231
Louisburg 273A
Lumberton 239, 272A
Manteo 251, 256
Morehead City 242
Morgantown 221A
Murfreesboro 252A
Murphy 274A
Nags Head 223
New Bern 232A, 270, 293
Newport 277
North Wilkesboro 247
Ocracoke 257A
Old Fort 282A
Plymouth 240A
Pine Knoll Shores 272A
Pinetops 238
Raleigh 234, 241, 268, 275A
Reidsville 271
Roanoke Rapids 272A
Robbinsville 240A
Rocky Mount 221A, 253A, 264

Rose Hill 284A
Roxboro 244A
St. Pauls 299A
Salisbury 293
Sanford 288A
Semora 294A
Shallotte 252, 279, 292A
Shelby 241
Southern Pines 273A, 295
Southport 298
Statesville 245, 289
Tabor City 285A
Tarboro 282
Thomasville 252A
Topsail Beach 280
Wadesboro 228
Wallace 232A
Wanchese 237
Warrenton 297
Washington 227, 252A
Waxhaw 291
Waynesville 285A
Whiteville 256
Williamston 279
Wilmington 247, 267, 274, 283
Wilson 291
Windsor 249A, 255A
Winston-Salem 226, 281, 298
Wrightsville Beach 229A

North Dakota
Arthur 244A
Beulah 250A
Bismarck 225, 233, 243, 254, 268
Bottineau 270
Carrington 252A
Devils Lake 244A, 273, 278
Dickinson 221, 256
Fargo 229, 250, 270, 300
Grafton 265
Grand Forks 225, 234, 298
Hettinger 228A
Jamestown 227, 238
Kindred 224
Langdon 239A
Lisbon 291
Mandan 284
Mayville 288
Minot 229, 246, 260, 287, 295A
Rugby 237A
Sarles 290
Tioga 280A
Valley City 265, 266
Wahpeton 295
Walhalla 294
Williston 241, 253, 266
Wishek 262

Ohio
Ada 235A
Akron 243, 248
Alliance 223
Archbold 241A
Ashland 267
Ashtabula 246, 252A
Athens 288A
Barnesville 228A
Beavercreek 280A
Bellaire 263A
Bellefontaine 252A
Bellevue 221A
Belpre 296A
Bowling Green 228A
Bryan 265A
Bucyrus 224A
Byesville 249A
Cadiz 292A
Caldwell 285A
Cambridge 244A
Canton 231, 251, 295
Castalia 249A
Celina 232A, 244A
Chillicothe 227, 232
Cincinnati 223, 227, 231, 253, 270, 274, 286
Circleville 296A
Cleveland 226, 238, 253, 258, 264, 271, 277, 281, 289, 293, 300
Cleveland Heights 222
Clyde 265A
Coal Grove 246A
Columbus 222, 234, 242, 246, 250, 259, 298A
Conneaut 288A
Coshocton 257A
Crestline 254A
Crooksville 297A
Dayton 256, 284, 299
Defiance 251, 290A
Delaware 300A
Delphos 296A
Delta 293A
Dover 269A
East Liverpool 282
Eaton 225
Edgewood 273A
Elyria 297

Englewood 233A
Fairfield 235
Findlay 263
Fort Shawnee 298A
Fostoria 244A
Fredericktown 252A
Fremont 256
Gahanna 285A
Galion 272A
Gallipolis 268
Geneva 284A
Georgetown 249A
Gibsonburg 239A
Greenfield 248A
Greenville 293
Grove City 266A
Hamilton 243, 278
Harrison 282A
Hillsboro 294
Holland 272A
Hubbard 270A
Huron 241A
Ironton 296A
Jackson 249A
Johnstown 276A
Kent 261A
Kenton 237A
Kettering 260
Lancaster 238, 278A
Lebanon 247A
Lima 226A, 249A, 271, 285A
Logan 252A
London 292A
Lorain 285A
Loudonville 299A
Manchester 267A
Mansfield 287, 291
Marietta 271
Marion 232A, 295
Marysville 289A
McArthur 254A
McConnelsville 265A
Medina 229
Miamisburg 229
Middleport 221A
Middletown 290
Milford 296A
Millersburg 237A
Montpelier 283A
Mount Gilead 236A
Mount Vernon 229
Napoleon 276A
Nelsonville 299A
New Lexington 292A
New Philadelphia 240A
Newark 262, 269A
Niles 291A
North Baltimore 299A
North Madison 229A
Norwalk 237A
Oak Harbor 247A
Ottawa 292A
Oxford 249A
Paulding 259A
Piketon 261A
Piqua 239
Port Clinton 233
Portsmouth 257A, 281
Richwood 282A
Ripley 258
St. Marys 277A
Salem 286
Sandusky 274
Shadyside 239
Shelby 261A
Sidney 288A
South Webster 235A
Springfield 264, 275
Steubenville 278
Swanton 297A
Sylvania 288A
Tiffin 279
Toledo 223, 260, 268, 284
Troy 245A
Uhrichsville 260A
Union City 248A
Upper Arlington 255A
Upper Sandusky 240A
Urbana 269A
Van Wert 265
Wapakoneta 221A
Washington Court House 288A
Wauseon 245A
Waverly 265A
Wellston 244
West Carrollton 221A
West Union 276A
Westerville 280A
Willard 245A
Wilmington 272A
Wooster 283
Xenia 237A
Youngstown 227, 255, 266
Zanesville 224A, 273

Oklahoma
Ada 227, 244A

Broadcasting & Cable Yearbook 1994
B-480

FM Allotments

Altus 228, 300
Alva 259, 284, 289
Anadarko 288A
Antlers 284A
Ardmore 239
Atoka 276
Bartlesville 261A
Bethany 285A
Bixby 287
Bristow 285A
Broken Arrow 221
Broken Bow 291
Byng 261
Chickasha 288A
Claremore 264A
Clinton 238, 295
Comanche 245
Commerce 259A
Cordell 229A, 257A
Duncan 272A
Durant 248, 296
Edmond 250A
El Dorado 246A
Elk City 232A, 243, 253
Enid 245, 276
Eufaula 272A
Frederick 240A
Grove 257A
Guymon 224
Healdton 229
Heavener 223A
Henryetta 258
Hobart 290
Holdenville 293A
Hollis 223A
Hugo 238
Idabel 244
Ketchum 298
Lahoma 239A
Lawton 232A, 237A, 251, 258, 268, 297
Lindsay 286A
Locust Grove 233A
Lone Grove 294A
Madill 272A
Mangum 249A
Marlow 221
McAlester 267, 286A
Miami 265A
Muskogee 246, 295
Norman 292A
Nowata 232A, 268A
Oklahoma City 223, 234, 241, 255, 263, 270, 274, 281, 299
Okmulgee 231
Owasso 291
Pauls Valley 249A
Pawhuska 285A
Perry 286A
Ponca City 257A, 261A, 265A
Poteau 250, 297
Pryor 283
Roland 222A
Sallisaw 240
Sand Springs 272A
Sapulpa 265A
Seminole 288A
Shawnee 236
Snyder 262A
Spencer 289A
Stillwater 229, 288A
Sulphur 265
Taft 262A
Tahlequah 269
Tishomingo 292A
Tulsa 225, 238, 243, 248, 253, 277
Vinita 241
Wagoner 271A
Watonga 228A
Weatherford 247
Wilburton 279A
Woodward 221, 240A, 261, 266, 272A

Oregon
Albany 260, 300
Altamont 267
Ashland 270, 298
Astoria 225
Baker 237, 284
Bandon 243
Banks 298
Beaverton 277
Bend 231, 248, 252, 264, 289
Brookings 237
Brownsville 272
Burns 224A
Canyon City
Cave Junction 274
Coos Bay 228A, 254
Coquille 247
Corvallis 268, 292
Cottage Grove 263A, 288A
Creswell 237
Eagle Point 292
Enterprise 221A
Eugene 233, 241, 250, 256

Florence 284, 295A
Gleneden Beach 248
Gold Beach 224
Gold Hill 262
Grants Pass 245
Harbeck-Fruitdale 252
Hermiston 257A
Hood River 288A
Klamath Falls 223, 258, 295
LaGrande 254, 260
Lake Oswego 294
Lakeview 228
Lebanon 279
Lincoln City 236, 244
Medford 229, 239, 278
Milton-Freewater 250
Myrtle Point 231A
Newport 224, 274
North Bend 235, 297
Nyssa 254
Oakridge 221A
Ontario 241
Pendelton 278, 299
Phoenix 286
Portland 222, 229, 238, 246, 253, 258, 262, 266, 270
Prineville 236
Redmond 275, 298
Reedsport 221A
Rogue River 234
Roseburg 276
Salem 286
Seaside 251A
Sisters 281
Springfield-Eugene 226
Sutherlin 266A
Sweet Home 296
The Dalles 249, 283
Tillamook 281
Toledo 264A
Tri-City 282
Warm Springs 243

Pennsylvania
Allentown 264, 281
Altoona 251, 261
Avis 260A
Barnesboro 223A
Beaver Falls 249
Beaver Springs 291A
Bedford 265A, 298A
Bellefonte 237A
Bellwood 280A
Benton 240A
Berwick 278A
Bethlehem 236
Blairsville 292A
Bloomsburg 293
Boalsburg 229A
Boyertown 298
Braddock 245
Bradford 261A
Brookville 240A
Burnham 244A
Butler 249A
Canton 262
Carbondale 232A
Carlisle 272A
Central City 269A
Chambersburg 236
Charleroi 252A
Clarendon 282A
Clarion 224A
Clearfield 226
Coudersport 244A
Covington 268A
Cresson 232A
Curwensville 275A
Dallas 229A
Danville 244A
Dubois 271, 297
Easton 241, 260
Ebensburg 250
Edinboro 250
Elizabethville 263A
Ellwood City 221A
Emporium 257A
Ephrata 286
Erie 234A, 260, 272A, 279
Everett 282A
Franklin 257
Freeland 276A
Galeton 264
Gettysburg 299
Greencastle 232A
Greensburg 269A
Greenville 296A
Grove City 236
Harrisburg, 235, 247, 257A, 281
Hawley 287A
Hazelton 250
Hershey 294
Hollidaysburg 285A
Honesdale 237A
Huntingdon 278A, 292A
Indiana 276A
Jenkintown 280A

Jersey Shore 242, 249A
Johnsonburg 277A
Johnstown 221A, 238, 243
Kane 280A
La Porte 280A
Lancaster 233, 245, 267
Lebanon 261A
Lewisburg 279A
Lewistown 240A, 288A
Linesville 269A
Lock Haven 221A
Mansfield 222A
Martinsburg 224A
Masontown 295A
McConnellsburg 279A
Meadville 262
Mechanicsburg 228A
Media 262
Mercer 244A, 280A
Mercersburg 221A
Mexico 223A
Meyersdale 227A
Mifflinburg 252A
Mifflintown 296A
Mill Hall 254A
Millersburg 255A
Milton 265A
Montrose 243
Mountaintop 246A
Mount Carmel 259A
Mount Union 258A
Muncy 227
Naticoke 221A
New Kensington 264
North East 265
Northumberland 297A
Oil City 242A, 253
Oliver 235
Olyphant 239A
Palmyra 221A
Patton 234A
Philadelphia 223, 227, 231, 239, 243, 251, 255, 266, 271, 275, 283, 287, 291
Philipsburg 290A
Pittsburgh 225, 229, 233, 241, 259, 268, 273, 284, 290, 300
Pittston 272A
Port Allegany 235A
Port Mitilda 300
Portage 289A
Pottsville 270
Punxsutawney 288A
Reading 273
Red Lion 241
Renovo 295A
Reynoldsville 258A
Ridgebury 245A
Riverside 222A
Russell 276A
Saegertown 232A
St. Mary's 230
Salladsburg 238A
Scottdale 280A
Scranton 258, 267, 285A, 295A
Shamokin 237A
Sharon 275
Sharpsville 240A
Smethport 292A
Somerset 249A
South Waverly 241A
South Williamsport 257A
Spangler 247A
Starview 224A
State College 233A, 276A
Stroudsburg 228A
Sunbury 231
Susquehanna 223A
Tamaqua 288A
Tioga 234A
Tobyhanna 300A
Towanda 237A
Tunkhannock 299A
Tyrone 266
Union City 292A
Uniontown 257A
University Park 246A
Warren 222
Washington 237A
Waynesboro 268
Waynesburg 276A
Wellsboro 283
Whitneyville 296A
Wilkes-Barre 225, 253
Williamsport 274, 286, 300A
York 277, 289
York-Hanover 253

Rhode Island
Block Island 240A, 257A
Middletown 262A
Narrangansett Pier 274A
Providence 222, 231, 238, 268, 286
Wakefield-Peacedale 259A
Westerly 279
Woonsocket 292A

South Carolina
Abbeville 225A
Aiken 242, 258
Allendale 228A
Anderson 266, 297
Andrews 264A
Bamberg 221A
Barnwell 256
Batesburg 226A, 237A
Beaufort 254
Bishopville 229A
Blackville 250A
Bluffton 295
Bowman 223A
Branchville 286A
Bucksport 300
Camden 232A
Cayce 244A
Charleston 236, 245, 263, 278
Cheraw 277
Chester 257
Chesterfield 297A
Clearwater 252A
Clemson 285A
Columbia 228A, 248, 276A, 284
Conway 230A, 281
Darlington 288
Dillon 225
Easley 280A
Elloree 262
Florence 292A
Folly Beach 251
Gaffney 287
Georgetown 229A, 249, 293
Goose Creek 232A
Gray Court 263
Greenville 223, 229, 233
Greenwood 244A, 278A
Greer 277A
Hampton 276A
Hanahan 241
Hardeeville 266
Hartsville 253A
Hilton Head Island 291, 300
Honea Path 276A
Johnsonville 286A
Johnston 224A
Kingstree 231A, 257
Lake City 261A
Lancaster 296A
Landson 292A
Lexington 253A
Loris 235A
Manning 223
Marion 232A, 263
McClellanville 255
Moncks Corner 287
Mount Pleasant 283
Mullins 296A
Murrell's Inlet 233A
Myrtle Beach 221, 269
New Ellenton 274A
Newberry 292
North Charleston 273
North Myrtle Beach 290
Orangeburg 275A, 280, 294
Pageland 272A
Pamplico 271
Parris Island 221A
Pawley's Island 253A, 262A
Port Royal 259
Ravenel 269
Ridgeland 285
St. Andrews 272A
St. George 298
St. Matthews 230A
St. Stephen 291A
Saluda 221A
Scranton 275A
Seneca 251
Socastee 258A
South Congaree 237A
Spartanburg 255
Summerton 252A
Summerville 227
Sumter 234A, 267
Surfside Beach 276
Walhalla 242A
Walterboro 229A, 265A
Wedgefield 238A
West Columbia 261A
Williston 234A

South Dakota
Aberdeen 231, 235, 294
Belle Fourche 240
Brookings 229
Canton 274A
Custer 286
Deadwood 236
Faith 246
Gregory 268
Hot Springs 244
Huron 256, 286A
Lowry 264
Madison 276A
Martin 273

Milbank 282
Mission 264A
Mitchell 290, 297
Mobridge 258
Pierre 224, 224A, 237
Pine Ridge 228A
Rapid City 230, 250, 254, 262, 281
Redfield 249A, 279
Reliance 233
Salem 263
Sioux Falls 223, 233A, 243, 247, 261A, 270, 279, 284
Sisseton 257A, 275
Spearfish 266, 297
Sturgis 226
Vermillion 292
Volga 272
Watertown 225, 241, 245
Winner 229, 253
Yankton 226, 281

Tennessee
Alamo 226
Athens 269
Atwood 229A
Bartlett 225A
Baxter 299
Benton 226A
Bolivar 234A, 253A
Bristol 245
Brownsville 237A
Byrdstown 244A
Calhoun 281A
Camden 240A
Carthage 281A
Caruthersville 286A
Celina 268A
Centerville 244A
Chattanooga 222, 243, 293
Cleveland 237A, 264
Clinton 237A
Coalmont 284A
Colonial Heights 290A
Columbia 269A
Cookeville 234, 253
Covington 228A
Crossville 257A, 273
Dayton 285A
Dickson 229A, 273
Dresden 232A
Dyer 232A
Dyersburg 261
East Ridge 300
Elizabethton 257
Erwin 280A
Etowah 276
Fayetteville 288A
Franklin 261A
Gallatin 283
Gatlinburg 288A
Germantown 231, 298
Goodlettesville 246
Graysville 239A
Greeneville 235
Harriman 224A
Harrogate 243A
Henderson 239A, 299A
Hendersonville 221A
Humboldt 272A, 287A
Huntingdon 265
Jackson 268A, 276, 281
Jamestown 280A, 286A
Jefferson City 257A
Jellico 274A
Johnson City 268
Karns 226A
Kingsport 253, 285A
Knoxville 248, 278, 283A, 299
Lafayette 271A
LaFollette 285A
Lawrenceburg 240A, 248A
Lebanon 255A, 298
Lenoir City 228A
Lewisburg 232A
Lexington 257A
Livingston 240
Lobelville 233
Loudon 256A, 287A
Madisonville 258A
Manchester 259, 268A
Martin 269A
Maryville 239A
McKenzie 295
McKinnon 268A
McMinnville 280A
Memphis 246, 259, 266, 274, 283, 290
Milan 222
Millington 251
Minor Hill 221A
Monterey 295
Morristown 240A
Mount Juliet 294A
Murfreesboro 242
Nashville 225, 238, 250, 277, 290
Newport 225A
Oak Ridge 232A, 262

FM Allotments

Oliver Springs 254A
Oneida 288A
Paris 231, 288A
Parsons 247A
Pulaski 252A
Red Bank 232A
Ripley 235A
Rockwood 289A
Rogersville 293A
Savannah 228A, 269A
Selmer 230A, 288A
Sevierville 271
Seymour 242A
Shelbyville 257
Signal Mountain 251A
Smithville 269A
Smyrna 231A
Soddy-Daisy 272A
South Pittsburg 247
Sparta 288A
Spencer 297A
Spring City 230
Springfield 232A
St. Joseph 268A
Surgoinsville 282A
Sweetwater 252A
Tazewell 231A
Trenton 248
Tullahoma 227
Tusculum 276A
Union City 285A, 289A
Wartburg 267A
Waverly 286
Waynesboro 235
Woodbury 285A

Texas
Abilene 223, 264, 286, 289A, 292, 300
Alamo 285A
Alice 221A, 275
Alpine 224A
Amarillo 226, 231, 245, 250, 254, 265, 270, 275, 289
Andrews 288A
Anson 251
Arlington 235
Atlanta 261
Austin 229, 238, 251, 264, 272
Ballinger 276A
Bandera 252A
Bastrop 296
Bay City 269, 273
Beaumont 231, 236, 248, 273, 300
Beeville 250, 289
Belton 292
Benavides 299
Big Lake 252A, 280A
Big Spring 232, 237A, 240
Bishop 296A
Bloomington 295
Bonham 252
Borger 282
Bowie 264
Brady 237A
Breckenridge 228
Brenham 231A, 291
Bridgeport 244A
Brownfield 282
Brownsville 258, 262
Brownwood 257, 268, 281
Bryan 252A, 258A, 284
Burkburnett 284
Burnet 223A, 295A
Caldwell 236A
Cameron 267A, 280
Campwood 256A
Canadian 235
Canyon 296A, 300
Carrizo Springs 221A, 228A
Carthage 255, 282A
Center 272A
Centerville 276A
Childress 241
Clarksville 253A
Claude 239
Cleveland 246
Clifton 277
Coahoma 288A
Coleman 296A
College Station 297
Colorado City 291A
Columbus 252A
Comanche 232A
Comfort 236
Commerce 221A
Conroe 295
Copperas Cove 276
Corpus Christi 230, 234A, 238, 243, 256
Corsicana 300
Cotulla 249A
Crane 267
Crockett 224, 228
Crystal Beach 268
Crystal City 232A
Cuero 249A
Daingerfield 295A
Dalhart 240
Dallas 223, 250, 254, 262, 266, 275, 283, 287
Decatur 289
Del Rio 232A, 242
Denison 285
Denison-Sherman 269
Denton 256, 291
Denver City 248
Devine 221A
Diboll 238
Dilley 255
Dimmit 240, 263
Dublin 225
Dumas 237
Eagle Pass 224A
Eastland 244A, 249A
Edinburg 281, 300
Edna 241A
El Campo 245
El Paso 222, 226, 230, 234, 238, 242, 248, 260, 271
Electra 235
Elgin 223A
Fabens 276A
Fairfield 221A
Falfurrias 277A, 292A
Farwell 222, 252
Floresville 231
Floydada 237A
Fort Stockton 232A
Fort Worth 231, 242, 258, 298
Fort Worth-Dallas 246, 271
Franklin 270
Fredericksburg 266
Freeport 277
Freer 240A
Friona 234
Gainesville 233, 300
Galveston 285A, 293
Gatesville 252A
George West 281A
Georgetown 244, 299
Giddings 268
Gilmer 237
Goliad 240A
Gonzales 292A
Graham 206
Granbury 294
Greenville 228
Gregory 283A
Groves 223
Hallettsville 260A
Haltom City 227
Hamilton 221A
Hamlin 279
Harker Heights 288
Harlingen 233, 241
Haskell 238
Hearne 230A
Hebbronville 269A
Hempstead 287
Henderson 260
Hereford 278, 292
Highland Park-Dallas 279
Hillsboro 273
Hondo 253A
Hooks 240
Houston 229, 233, 239, 243, 250, 256, 262, 266, 271, 275, 281, 289
Howe 237
Huntington 270
Huntsville 259A, 269A, 279
Idalou 289A
Ingleside 297A
Jacksboro 269A
Jacksonville 272A, 293
Jasper 264, 274
Jefferson 283A
Johnson City 300
Jourdanton 239A
Junction 228A
Kennedy 221A
Kermit 292A
Kerrville 222, 232
Kilgore 241
Killeen 222A, 227
Kingsville 224, 248
La Grange 285A
Lake Jackson 298
Lamesa 262, 284
Lampasas 255
Leakey 282A
Laredo 224A, 235, 251, 291A
Levelland 288A
Liberty 260
Littlefield 238
Livingston 222
Llano 284
Lometa 270A
Longview 247, 289
Lorenzo 251
Los Ybanez 300
Lubbock 229, 233, 242, 258, 266, 273, 293
Lufkin 257, 286
Luling 243
Madisonville 241
Malakoff 240A
Marfa 228A
Markham 223
Marlin 225
Marshall 222A, 280A
Mason 249
McAllen 245, 253
McCamey 237A
McKinney 295A
Memphis 287
Mercedes 292A
Merkel 274
Mexia 285A
Midland 222, 227, 236, 277, 294
Mineola 244A
Mineral Wells 240
Mirando City 263
Mission 288A
Monahans 260, 271
Mount Pleasant 264
Muenster 293A
Muleshoe 276A
Nacogdoches 277, 299
Navasota 223A
New Boston 278A
New Braunfels 221A
New Ulm 222A
Nolanville 297A
Odem 252
Odessa 241, 245, 250, 256, 299
Olney 248
Orange 283, 291
Ozona 232A
Palacios 264A
Palestine 244A, 252
Pampa 262
Paris 230, 270, 299
Pasadena 225
Pearsall 237A, 281A
Pecos 247, 252A
Perryton 240A
Pittsburg 245A, 276A
Plainview 247, 280, 295
Pleasanton 276A
Port Arthur 227, 253
Port Isabel 266A
Port Lavaca 227
Portland 288A
Post 297
Premont 285A
Quanah 265
Raymondville 271, 289A
Refugio 291
Rio Grande City 276A
Robstown 260, 286A
Rockdale 253A
Rockport 272
Roma 249A
Rosenberg 285A
Round Rock 290
Rusk 249
San Angelo 225, 230, 234, 248, 254, 270, 298
San Antonio 225, 241, 247, 258, 262, 270, 274, 283, 298
San Augustine 223A
San Diego 290A
San Marcos 271
San Saba 246A
Seabrook 221
Seguin 287
Seminole 292A
Seymour 230
Shamrock 224A
Sherman 244A, 281A
Silsbee 269A
Sinton 267, 279
Slaton 224
Snyder 269A
Sonora 221A
South Padre Island 224A, 237A
Spearman 252A
Stamford 221A
Stanton 290A
Stephenville 252A
Sterling City 243
Sulphur Springs 240A
Sweetwater 244A
Tahoka 237A
Taylor 221A
Temple 269, 282
Terrell 296A
Terrell Hills 294
Texarkana 251, 273
Three Rivers 233
Tulia 285
Tye 259
Tyler 221A, 226, 268, 281
Uvalde 224A, 272A, 285A
Vernon 272A
Victoria 222A, 236, 254, 265A, 300
Waco 233A, 238, 248, 260, 296A
Whitehouse 297
Wichita Falls 225, 260, 277, 292, 273A
Winfield 249
Winnsboro 285A
Winters 241A
Woodville 234
Yoakum 223A

Utah
Blanding 221A
Bountiful 258
Brian Head 251
Brigham City 264, 295
Cedar City 223, 235
Centerville 289
Coalville 223A
Delta 239
Kenab 266
Logan 225, 233
Manti 286
Midvale 274
Moab 244
Nephi 280
Ogden 238, 250, 266, 270
Orem 298
Payson 222A
Price 252, 265A
Provo 235, 241
Richfield 229, 248
Roosevelt 230A, 253
Roy 300
St. George 228A, 240, 259
Salt Lake City 227, 231, 246, 254, 262, 278, 282
Smithfield 280A
Spanish Fork 293
Tooele 221A
Torrey 253A
Tremonton 286
Vernal 290

Vermont
Barre 296A
Bellows Falls 296A
Bennington 232A
Brandon 268A
Brattleboro 224A, 244A
Burlington 245, 255, 300
Canaan 231
Danville 239A
Derby Center 221
Hartford 282A
Killington 287
Lyndon 252A
Manchester 274
Marlboro 268A
Middlebury 265A
Montpelier 284
Morrisville 230A
Randolph 271
Royalton 276A
Rupert 281A
Rutland 233, 246, 251
St. Albans 272A
St. Johnsbury 288A
South Burlington 238
Springfield 228A
Stowe 269A
Sunderland 236A
Vergennes 244A, 294
Warren 241A
Waterbury 277A
West Rutland 298
White River Junction 237A
Wilmington 264A
Woodstock 230A

Virginia
Abingdon 224A
Accomac 257
Alberta 278A
Alta Vista 288A
Amherst 300
Appomattox 274, 296A
Arlington 286
Ashland 261A
Bedford 295A
Berryville 288A
Big Stone Gap 228
Blacksburg 287
Blackstone 228A
Bluefield 292A
Bowling Green 245A
Bridgewater 286A
Broadway 241
Buena Vista 244
Buffalo Gap 288A
Cape Charles 241
Cedar Bluff 299A
Charlottesville 224A, 236A, 248, 298A
Chase City 260
Chesapeake-Portsmouth-Va. Beach 271A
Chester 226A
Christiansburg 264A
Churchville 292
Clarksville 252
Clifton Forge 280A
Clincho 221A
Coeburn 259
Colonial Beach 240A
Colonial Heights 237
Covington 265A
Crewe 284
Crozet 272A, 278A
Culpeper 276A
Danville 277
Deltaville 222A
Dillwyn 229A
Elkton 253
Emporia 258A
Exmore 291, 298
Farmville 239, 267A
Fort Lee 243B
Franklin 269A
Fredericksburg 227, 268
Front Royal 237A, 257A
Galax 251
Gloucester 256A
Gretna 292A
Grundy 249A
Hampton 267
Harrisonburg 264, 282
Hot Springs 296A
Kilmarnock 269A
Lawrenceville 288A
Lebanon 297A
Louisa 288A
Luray 280A, 289A
Lynchburg 250, 261, 269, 290A
Manassas 294
Marion 230, 278A
Martinsville 242
Mechanicsville 221
Mount Jackson 245
Narrows 267A
New Market 277A
Newport News 247
Norfolk 239, 254, 259, 263, 275, 283, 287
Norton 292A
Olney-Onancock 277
Orange 255A
Pennington Gap 288A
Petersburg 257A, 262A
Pound 272A
Pulaski 296
Radford 269A
Redlands 264A
Richlands 288A
Richmond 233, 251, 266A, 271, 279, 293
Roanoke 222, 235, 256, 285
Rocky Mount 260A
Ruckersville 270A
Rural Retreat 237A
Salem 228A
Saltville 291A
South Boston 237A, 248
South Hill 255A
Spotsylvania 257A
Staunton 226A, 232, 259
Strasburg 285A
Suffolk 225, 295
Tappahannock 288A
Tazewell 261A
Vinton 268A, 291A
Virginia Beach 235
Warrenton 232A, 299
Warsaw 265A
West Point 300A
White Stone 261A
Williamsburg 243
Winchester 223, 273
Windsor 299A
White Stone 285A
Woodbridge 290
Woodstock 229
Yorktown 231

Washington
Aberdeen 257, 284
Bellevue 223
Bellingham 225, 282
Bremerton 295
Camas 234
Cashmere 266A
Castle Rock 296
Centralia 275
Chelan 228A
Cheney 266
Clarkston 231
Colfax 272A
Colville 221A
Davenport 247A
Dayton 223
Deer Park 296
Dishman 293A
East Wenatchee 249A
Eatonville 285A
Edmonds 287
Ellensburg 237, 276

Broadcasting & Cable Yearbook 1994
B-482

FM Allotments

Ephrata 222, 230
Forks 280A
Goldendale 272
Grand Coulee 253
Grandview 265A
Hoquiam 237A
Ilwaco 280
Kelso 233A
Kennewick 287
Leavenworth 249A
Long Beach 232A
Longview 288A
Lynden 293
McCleary 245
Medical Lake 270
Moses Lake 257A, 262
Naches 245A
Newport 285A
Olympia 241
Omak 226
Opportunity 241
Othello 248
Pasco 252A, 267
Prosser 269
Pullman 258, 282
Quincy 244A
Raymond 249
Richland 235, 274, 293
Rock Island 258A
Royal City 242
Seattle 227, 231, 235, 239, 243, 251, 255, 260, 264, 268, 273, 299
South Bend 289
Spokane 225, 229, 245, 251, 255, 260, 280, 284A, 289, 300
Sunnyside 244A
Tacoma 247, 279, 291
Toppenish 225
Vancouver 290
Walla Walla 227, 239, 246, 264
Wilson Creek 277A
Winlock 236A
Wisp 292A
Wenatchee 271, 285
Yakima 233, 252A, 259, 281, 289, 297

West Virginia
Barrackville 226A
Beckley 258, 279
Berkeley Springs 228A
Bethlehem 288
Bluefield 283
Bridgeport 281A
Buckhannon 228, 267
Charles Town 252A
Charleston 241, 248, 260, 274
Clarksburg 221A, 285A, 293
Danville 223A
Dunbar 233
Elkins 234, 257A
Fairmont 232A, 250
Fisher 279A
Grafton 240A
Hinton 272A
Huntington 263, 277, 300
Keyser 231, 296A
Kingwood 244A, 299A
Lewisburg 276A
Lindside 294A
Logan 270
Lost Creek 242A
Mannington 274A
Martinsburg 248
Matewan 294
Miami 297
Milton 292A
Montgomery 227A
Morgantown 261A, 270
Moundsville 243A
Mount Hope 290
Mullens 224A
New Martinsville 280A
Oak Hill 231
Parkersburg 236, 256, 276A
Petersburg 269A
Pocatalico 254A
Point Pleasant 258A
Princeton 240A, 265A
Rainelle 237A
Ravenswood 226A
Ripley 252A
Romney 261A
Ronceverte 249A
St. Albans 286
St. Mary's 230
Salem 289
South Charleston 265A
Spencer 284A
Summersville 225
Sutton 246
Vienna 261A
Webster Springs 262A
Welch 275A
Weston 272
Westover 265A
Wheeling 247, 254, 298
White Sulphur Springs 227A
Williamson 243

Wisconsin
Adams 291A
Algoma 244
Allouez 294
Altoona 251
Antigo 287, 291
Appleton 289
Ashland 227, 244
Baradoo 235
Beaver Dam 237A
Berlin 272A
Birnamwood 225A
Black River Falls 259
Bloomer 236
Brillion 298A
Brookfield 295A
Chetek 294
Chippewa Falls 288A
Cleveland 251A
Clintonville 222
Columbus 263A
Crandon 276A
De Pere 240
Dodgeville 257A
Durand 240A
Eagle River 233
Eau Claire 231, 264, 283
Elk Mound 225A
Evansville 290A
Fond du Lac 296A
Fort Atkinson 297
Green Bay 253, 266
Hartford 285
Hayward 222, 269A
Iron Wood 297
Janesville 260
Kaukauna 285A, 276
Kenosha 236
Kewaunee 224A
LaCrosse 227, 239, 285A, 292
Ladysmith 226, 279
Lake Geneva 241A
Lancaster 249A
Lomira 249A
Madison 251, 268, 273, 281
Manitowoc 221A
Marinette 236
Marshfield 293
Mauston 221A
Mayville 254A
Medford 257
Menomonee Falls 252A
Menomonie 221
Merrill 281
Middleton 292A
Milwaukee 227, 233, 239, 243, 247, 256, 271, 275, 299
Minocqua 240
Michicot 234A
Monroe 229
Mosinee 234
Neenah-Menasha 232, 262
Neillsville 224A, 298
Nekoosa 229A
New␣Holstein 225A
New London 228
New Richmond 296
Oconto 296A
Omro 258
Oshkosh 245A, 280A
Park Falls 254
Peshtigo 241A
Platteville 296A
Plymouth 283A
Port Washington 261A
Portage 240A, 261A
Prairie Du Chien 232
Racine 221A, 264
Reedsburg 275A, 285A
Rhinelander 248, 261
Rice Lake 242, 249
Richland Center 265A
Ripon 241A
River Falls 292A
Rudolph 260
Sauk City 242
Seymour 282A
Shawano 257
Sheboygan 229A
Shell Lake 237A
Sparta 246
Spencer 222A
Spooner 292A
Stevens Point 250, 285A
Sturgeon Bay 230, 249A, 259
Sturtevant 284A
Sun Prairie 221A
Superior 273
Suring 274
Three Lakes 229
Tomah 233, 241, 255
Tomahawk 223
Trempealeau 288A
Two Rivers 272A
Verona 288A
Viroqua 272A
Washburn 290
Watertown 231
Waukesha 291
Waunakee 286A
Waupaca 224A
Wausau 238, 270, 300
Wautoma 226A
Wauwatosa 279
West Bend 223
West Salem 261A
Whitehall 272A
Whitewater 283A, 293A
Whiting 244
Wisconsin Dells 295A
Wisconsin Rapids 277

Wyoming
Afton 252A
Albin 297
Buffalo 225
Burns 270
Casper 233, 238, 279, 295
Cheyenne 250, 264, 285A, 292
Cody 250
Diamondville 287
Douglas 257A
Evanston 292A
Fort Bridger 257A
Gillette 245, 264
Greybull 262
Jackson 237, 245
Kemmerer 297A
Lander 248
Laramie 236, 275, 283, 288A
Lost Cabin 256
New Castle 257A
Pine Bluffs 287
Pinedale 266
Powell 233, 281
Rawlins 224A
Riverton 226, 230
Rock Springs 236, 243, 283
Saratoga 260
Sheridan 235, 243
Sundance 276A
Thermopolis 252A, 269A
Torrington 252
Wheatland 269A
Worland 241

American Samoa
Fagaitua 276
Leone 266
Pago Pago 221

Central Marianas
Saipan-Garapan 250, 258, 280

Guam
Agana 230, 238, 248, 262, 270

Puerto Rico
Aguada 288A
Aguadilla 225, 262
Arecibo 293, 297
Bayamon 234, 264
Cabo Rojo 272A
Caguas 277
Camuy 275
Carolina 299
Cidra 291A
Corozal 223
Culebra 293A
Fajardo 261
Guayama 295
Hormigueros 221A, 291A
Isabella 268
Lajas 279
Luquillo 221A
Manati 245
Maricao 241
Mayaguez 231, 248, 256
Naguabo 225A
Ponce 227, 266, 270, 286
Quebradillas 252A
Rio Grande 247A
Rio Piedras 239
San German 236
San Juan 229, 253, 260, 273, 284, 289
Utuado 281
Vieques 255

Virgin Islands
Charlotte Amalie 241, 246, 250, 271, 282, 287
Christiansted 228, 236, 258, 262, 291
Cruz Bay 222
Frederiksted 278A

College, University and School-Owned Radio Stations

*KRUA(FM) Anchorage AK
*KCUK(FM) Chevak AK
*KDLG(AM) Dillingham AK
*KUAC(FM) Fairbanks AK
*KUHB(FM) St. Paul Island AK
*WEGL(FM) Auburn AL
*WBHM(FM) Birmingham AL
*WGIB(FM) Birmingham AL
*WJSR(FM) Birmingham AL
*WVSU-FM Birmingham AL
*WYJD(FM) Brewton AL
*WRWA(FM) Dothan AL
*WSGN(FM) Gadsden AL
*WJAB(FM) Huntsville AL
*WLRH(FM) Huntsville AL
*WOCG(FM) Huntsville AL
*WLJS-FM Jacksonville AL
*WHIL-FM Mobile AL
*WTOH(FM) Mobile AL
*WVAS(FM) Montgomery AL
*WQPR(FM) Muscle Shoals AL
*WTSU(FM) Troy AL
*WUAL-FM Tuscaloosa AL
*WVUA-FM Tuscaloosa AL
*KSWH(FM) Arkadelphia AR
*KZIG(FM) Cave City AR
*KHDX(FM) Conway AR
*KUCA(FM) Conway AR
*KBSA(FM) El Dorado AR
*KUAF(FM) Fayetteville AR
*KASU(FM) Jonesboro AR
*KLRE-FM Little Rock AR
*KUAR(FM) Little Rock AR
*KLLN(FM) Newark AR
KOTN(AM) Pine Bluff AR
*KUAP(FM) Pine Bluff AR
*KXRJ(FM) Russellville AR
*KLRC(FM) Siloam Springs AR
*KNAU(FM) Flagstaff AZ
*KNLB(FM) Lake Havasu City AZ
KBAQ(FM) Phoenix AZ
*KJZZ(FM) Phoenix AZ
*KGHR(FM) Tuba City AZ
*KUAZ(FM) Tucson AZ
*KAWC(AM) Yuma AZ
*KAWC-FM Yuma AZ
*KHSU-FM Arcata CA
*KCEA(FM) Atherton CA
*KALX(FM) Berkeley CA
*KBPK(FM) Buena Park CA
*KSPC(FM) Claremont CA
*KVHS(FM) Concord CA
*KDVS(FM) Davis CA
*KECG(FM) El Cerrito CA
*KOHL(FM) Fremont CA
*KFCF(FM) Fresno CA
*KFSR(FM) Fresno CA
*KXSR(FM) Groveland CA
*KCRH(FM) Hayward CA
*KCRY(FM) Indio CA
*KUCI(FM) Irvine CA
*KXKB(FM) Kings Beach CA
*KLON(FM) Long Beach CA
*KFJC(FM) Los Altos CA
*KUSC(FM) Los Angeles CA
*KXLU(FM) Los Angeles CA
*KSBR(FM) Mission Viejo CA
*KADV(FM) Modesto CA
*KSMC(FM) Moraga CA
*KSFH(FM) Mountain View CA
*KCSN(FM) Northridge CA
*KCRU(FM) Oxnard CA
*KPSC(FM) Palm Springs CA
*KPCC(FM) Pasadena CA
*KSPB(FM) Pebble Beach CA
*KLVM(FM) Prunedale CA
*KFPR(FM) Redding CA
*KUOR-FM Redlands CA
*KRVH(FM) Rio Vista CA
*KXHV(FM) Sacramento CA
*KXJZ(FM) Sacramento CA
*KXPR(FM) Sacramento CA
*KYDS(FM) Sacramento CA
*KPBS-FM San Diego CA
*KSDS(FM) San Diego CA
*KALW(FM) San Francisco CA
*KUSF(FM) San Francisco CA
*KLEL(FM) San Jose CA
*KSJS(FM) San Jose CA
*KCPR(FM) San Luis Obispo CA
*KCSM(FM) San Mateo CA
*KSRH(FM) San Rafael CA
*KCSB-FM Santa Barbara CA
*KFAC(FM) Santa Barbara CA
*KSCU(FM) Santa Clara CA
*KZSC(FM) Santa Cruz CA
*KCRW(FM) Santa Monica CA
*KTUO(FM) Sonora CA
*KZSU(FM) Stanford CA
*KCJH(FM) Stockton CA
*KSJC-FM Stockton CA
*KUOP(FM) Stockton CA
*KCPB(FM) Thousand Oaks CA
*KCSS(FM) Turlock CA
*KSAK(FM) Walnut CA
*KCEQ(FM) Walnut Creek CA
*KASF(FM) Alamosa CO
*KRCC(FM) Colorado Springs CO
*KTLF(FM) Colorado Springs CO
*KSJD(FM) Cortez CO
*KDUR(FM) Durango CO
*KCSU-FM Fort Collins CO
*KCIC(FM) Grand Junction CO
*KJOL(FM) Grand Junction CO
*KMSA(FM) Grand Junction CO
*KUNC-FM Greeley CO
*KWSB-FM Gunnison CO
*KCDC(FM) Longmont CO
*KWBI(FM) Morrison CO
*KTSC-FM Pueblo CO
*WERB(FM) Berlin CT
*WXCI(FM) Danbury CT
*WSHU(FM) Fairfield CT
*WVOF(FM) Fairfield CT
*WQAQ(FM) Hamden CT
*WQTQ(FM) Hartford CT
*WRTC-FM Hartford CT
*WESU(FM) Middletown CT
*WFCS(FM) New Britain CT
WYBC-FM New Haven CT
*WCNI(FM) New London CT
*WDJW(FM) Somers CT
*WGSK(FM) South Kent CT
*WHUS(FM) Storrs CT
*WWEB(FM) Wallingford CT
*WWUH(FM) West Hartford CT
*WNHU(FM) West Haven CT
*WWPT(FM) Westport CT
*WECS(FM) Willimantic CT
*WAMU(FM) Washington DC
*WDCU(FM) Washington DC
WHUR-FM Washington DC
*WVUD(FM) Newark DE
*WMPH(FM) Wilmington DE
*WVUM(FM) Coral Gables FL
*WJED(FM) Dogwood Lakes Estate FL
*WNLE(FM) Fernandina Beach FL
*WAFG(FM) Fort Lauderdale FL
*WSFP-FM Fort Myers FL
*WQCS(FM) Fort Pierce FL
*WUFT-FM Gainesville FL
*WKTZ-FM Jacksonville FL
*WCIE-FM Lakeland FL
*WFIT(FM) Melbourne FL
*WLRN-FM Miami FL
*WMCU(FM) Miami FL
*WSOR(FM) Naples FL
*WUCF-FM Orlando FL
*WWIA(FM) Palm Bay FL
*WKGC-FM Panama City FL
*WKGC(AM) Panama City Beach FL
*WPCS(FM) Pensacola FL
*WUWF(FM) Pensacola FL
*WFCF(FM) St. Augustine FL
*WKPX(FM) Sunrise FL
*WAMF(FM) Tallahassee FL
*WFSQ(FM) Tallahassee FL
*WFSU-FM Tallahassee FL
*WVFS(FM) Tallahassee FL
*WUSF(FM) Tampa FL
*WPRK(FM) Winter Park FL
*WMSL(FM) Athens GA
*WUOG(FM) Athens GA
*WCLK(FM) Atlanta GA
*WRAS(FM) Atlanta GA
*WREK(FM) Atlanta GA
*WWGC(FM) Carrollton GA
*WTJB(FM) Columbus GA
*WBCX(FM) Gainesville GA
*WOAK(FM) La Grange GA
WFOM(AM) Marietta GA
*WGHR(FM) Marietta GA
*WXGC(FM) Milledgeville GA
*WHCJ(FM) Savannah GA
*WVGS(FM) Statesboro GA
*WABR-FM Tifton GA
*WRAF-FM Toccoa Falls GA
*WVVS(FM) Valdosta GA
KFSH(FM) Hilo HI
*KTUH(FM) Honolulu HI
*KUSR(FM) Ames IA
*WOI(AM) Ames IA
*WOI-FM Ames IA
*KHKE(FM) Cedar Falls IA
*KUNI(FM) Cedar Falls IA
*KCCK-FM Cedar Rapids IA
*KIWR(FM) Council Bluffs IA
*KALA(FM) Davenport IA
*KWLC(AM) Decorah IA
*KDPS(FM) Des Moines IA
*KICB(FM) Fort Dodge IA
*KTPR(FM) Fort Dodge IA
*KDIC(FM) Grinnell IA
*KRUI-FM Iowa City IA
*WSUI(AM) Iowa City IA
*KUNY(FM) Mason City IA
*KRNL-FM Mount Vernon IA
*KIGC(FM) Oskaloosa IA
*KCUI(FM) Pella IA
*KDCR(FM) Sioux Center IA
*KMSC(FM) Sioux City IA
*KWIT(FM) Sioux City IA
*KNWS(AM) Waterloo IA
*KWAR(FM) Waverly IA
*KWDM(FM) West Des Moines IA
*KBSU(AM) Boise ID
*KBSU-FM Boise ID
*KNWO(FM) Cottonwood ID
*KLHS-FM Lewiston ID
*KBSM(FM) McCall ID
*KRFA-FM Moscow ID
*KUOI-FM Moscow ID
*KRIC(FM) Rexburg ID
*KWBH(FM) Rexburg ID
*WESN(FM) Bloomington IL
*WSIU(FM) Carbondale IL
*WIBI(FM) Carlinville IL
*WPCD(FM) Champaign IL
*WEIU(FM) Charleston IL
*WBHI(FM) Chicago IL
*WCRX(FM) Chicago IL
*WHPK-FM Chicago IL
*WKKC(FM) Chicago IL
*WLUW(FM) Chicago IL
*WOUI(FM) Chicago IL
*WZRD(FM) Chicago IL
*WNIU(FM) De Kalb IL
*WJMU(FM) Decatur IL
*WDGC-FM Downers Grove IL
*WSIE(FM) Edwardsville IL
*WEPS(FM) Elgin IL
*WRSE-FM Elmhurst IL
*WTPC(FM) Elsah IL
*WNUR-FM Evanston IL
*WHFH(FM) Flossmoor IL
*WVKC(FM) Galesburg IL
*WDCB(FM) Glen Ellyn IL
*WMWA(FM) Glenview IL
*WLCA(FM) Godfrey IL
*WGRN(FM) Greenville IL
*WHSD(FM) Hinsdale IL
*WONU(FM) Kankakee IL
*WTKC(FM) Kankakee IL
*WLTL(FM) La Grange IL
*WMXM(FM) Lake Forest IL
*WLNX(FM) Lincoln IL
*WLRA(FM) Lockport IL
*WGSL(FM) Loves Park IL
*WIUM(FM) Macomb IL
*WIUS(FM) Macomb IL
*WLKL(FM) Mattoon IL
*WVJC(FM) Mt. Carmel IL
*WONC(FM) Naperville IL
*WGLT(FM) Normal IL
*WUSI(FM) Olney IL
*WMTH(FM) Park Ridge IL
*WCBU(FM) Peoria IL
*WIPA(FM) Pittsfield IL
*WQUB(FM) Quincy IL
*WRRG(FM) River Grove IL
*WVIK(FM) Rock Island IL
*WFEN(FM) Rockford IL
*WNIJ(FM) Rockford IL
*WQNA(FM) Springfield IL
*WSSU(FM) Springfield IL
*WARG(FM) Summit IL
*WILL(AM) Urbana IL
*WETN(FM) Wheaton IL
*WEAX(FM) Angola IN
*WFIU(FM) Bloomington IN
*WHJE(FM) Carmel IN
*WDSO(FM) Chesterton IN
*WJHS(FM) Columbia City IN
WNDY(FM) Crawfordsville IN
*WVPE(FM) Elkhart IN
*WPSR(FM) Evansville IN
*WSWI(AM) Evansville IN
*WUEV(FM) Evansville IN
*WBCL(FM) Fort Wayne IN
*WFCI(FM) Franklin IN
*WGVE(FM) Gary IN
*WGCS(FM) Goshen IN
*WGRE(FM) Greencastle IN
*WHWE(FM) Howe IN
*WVSH(FM) Huntington IN
*WBDG(FM) Indianapolis IN
*WEDM(FM) Indianapolis IN
*WFYI-FM Indianapolis IN
*WICR(FM) Indianapolis IN
*WJEL(FM) Indianapolis IN
*WRFT(FM) Indianapolis IN
*WJEF(FM) Lafayette IN
*WCYT(FM) Lafayette Township IN
*WBST(FM) Muncie IN
*WWDS(FM) Muncie IN
*WWHI(FM) Muncie IN
*WNAS(FM) New Albany IN
*WBKE-FM North Manchester IN
*WSND-FM Notre Dame IN
*WEEM(FM) Pendleton IN
*WPUM(FM) Rensselaer IN
*WECI(FM) Richmond IN
*WVXR(FM) Richmond IN
*WETL(FM) South Bend IN
*WISU(FM) Terre Haute IN
*WMHD-FM Terre Haute IN
*WVUR-FM Valparaiso IN
*WVUB(FM) Vincennes IN
*WBAA(AM) West Lafayette IN
*WBAA-FM West Lafayette IN
*KNBU(FM) Baldwin City KS
*KTCC(FM) Colby KS
*KVCO(FM) Concordia KS
*KONQ(FM) Dodge City KS
*KHCT(FM) Great Bend KS
*KHCC-FM Hutchinson KS
*KJHK(FM) Lawrence KS
*KKSU(AM) Manhattan KS
*KSDB-FM Manhattan KS
*KBCU(FM) North Newton KS
*KTJO-FM Ottawa KS
*KRPS(FM) Pittsburg KS
*KHCD(FM) Salina KS
*KMUW(FM) Wichita KS
*KSWC(FM) Winfield KS
*WKYU-FM Bowling Green KY
*WKUE(FM) Elizabethtown KY
*WRVG(FM) Georgetown KY
*WKCC(FM) Grayson KY
*WEKH(FM) Hazard KY
*WKPB(FM) Henderson KY
*WNKU(FM) Highland Heights KY
*WRFL(FM) Lexington KY
*WUKY(FM) Lexington KY
*WUOL(FM) Louisville KY
*WMKY(FM) Morehead KY
*WKMS-FM Murray KY
*WJIE(FM) Okolona KY
*WKWC(FM) Owensboro KY
*WOAL-FM Pippa Passes KY
*WEKU-FM Richmond KY
*WDCL-FM Somerset KY
*KLSA(FM) Alexandria LA
KBRH(AM) Baton Rouge LA
*KLSU(FM) Baton Rouge LA
*WBRH(FM) Baton Rouge LA
*KGRM(FM) Grambling LA
*KSLU(FM) Hammond LA
*KRVS(FM) Lafayette LA
*KNLU(FM) Monroe LA
*KNWD(FM) Natchitoches LA
*WTUL(FM) New Orleans LA
*WWNO(FM) New Orleans LA
*KLPI-FM Ruston LA
*KDAQ(FM) Shreveport LA
*KSCL(FM) Shreveport LA
*KNSU(FM) Thibodaux LA
*WAMH(FM) Amherst MA
*WFCR(FM) Amherst MA
*WMUA(FM) Amherst MA
*WPAA(FM) Andover MA
*WBUR(FM) Boston MA
*WERS(FM) Boston MA
*WRBB(FM) Boston MA
*WUMB-FM Boston MA
*WBMT(FM) Boxford MA
*WBIM-FM Bridgewater MA
*WMBR(FM) Cambridge MA
*WBPV(FM) Charlton MA
*WIQH(FM) Concord MA
*WNRC(FM) Dudley MA
*WSHL-FM Easton MA
*WXPL(FM) Fitchburg MA
*WDJM-FM Framingham MA
*WGAO(FM) Franklin MA
*WCCT-FM Harwich MA
*WHHB(FM) Holliston MA
*WCCH(FM) Holyoke MA
*WJUL(FM) Lowell MA
*WAVM(FM) Maynard MA
*WMFO(FM) Medford MA
*WMLN-FM Milton MA
*WZBC(FM) Newton MA
*WJJW(FM) North Adams MA
*WSMU-FM North Dartmouth MA
*WOZQ(FM) Northampton MA
*WNMH(FM) Northfield MA
*WRPS(FM) Rockland MA
*WMWM(FM) Salem MA
*WSDH(FM) Sandwich MA
*WBSL-FM Sheffield MA
*WMHC(FM) South Hadley MA
*WAIC(FM) Springfield MA
*WNEK-FM Springfield MA
*WSCB(FM) Springfield MA
*WTCC(FM) Springfield MA
*WSRB(FM) Walpole MA
*WBRS(FM) Waltham MA
*WZLY(FM) Wellesley MA
*WKKL(FM) West Barnstable MA
*WSKB(FM) Westfield MA
*WCHC(FM) Worcester MA
*WBJC(FM) Baltimore MD
*WBYQ(FM) Baltimore MD
*WEAA(FM) Baltimore MD
*WJHU-FM Baltimore MD
*WHFC(FM) Bel Air MD
*WMUC-FM College Park MD
*WOEL-FM Elkton MD
*WMTB-FM Emmittsburg MD
*WFWM(FM) Frostburg MD
*WESM(FM) Princess Anne MD
*WSCL(FM) Salisbury MD
*WGTS-FM Takoma Park MD
*WTMD(FM) Towson MD
*WHSN(FM) Bangor ME
*WMEH(FM) Bangor ME
*WBOR(FM) Brunswick ME
*WMED(FM) Calais ME
*WSHD(FM) Eastport ME
*WUMF-FM Farmington ME
WUFK(FM) Fort Kent ME
*WMPG(FM) Gorham ME
*WRBC(FM) Lewiston ME
*WMEB-FM Orono ME
*WMEA(FM) Portland ME
*WMEM(FM) Presque Isle ME
*WUPI(FM) Presque Isle ME
*WSJB-FM Standish ME
*WMEW(FM) Waterville ME
*WVAC-FM Adrian MI
*WGVU-FM Allendale MI
*WQAC-FM Alma MI
*WCML-FM Alpena MI
*WCBN-FM Ann Arbor MI
*WUOM(FM) Ann Arbor MI
*WAHS(FM) Auburn Hills MI
*WCHW-FM Bay City MI
*WAUS(FM) Berrien Springs MI
*WBFH(FM) Bloomfield Hills MI
*WHFR(FM) Dearborn MI
*WDET-FM Detroit MI
*WDBM(FM) East Lansing MI
*WKAR(AM) East Lansing MI
*WORB(FM) Farmington Hills MI
*WFUM-FM Flint MI
*WCSG(FM) Grand Rapids MI
*WVGR(FM) Grand Rapids MI
*WTHS(FM) Holland MI
*WGGL-FM Houghton MI
*WIAA(FM) Interlochen MI
*NEW FM Kalamazoo MI
*WIDR(FM) Kalamazoo MI
*WMUK(FM) Kalamazoo MI
*WGVU(AM) Kentwood MI
*WLNZ(FM) Lansing MI
*WNMU-FM Marquette MI
*WUPX(FM) Marquette MI
*WEJY(FM) Monroe MI
*WCMU-FM Mount Pleasant MI
*WMHW-FM Mount Pleasant MI
WUPQ(FM) Newberry MI
*WOVI(FM) Novi MI
*WAEK(FM) Oakland MI
*WOCR(FM) Olivet MI
*WOAS(FM) Ontonagon MI
*WBLD(FM) Orchard Lake MI
*WOES(FM) Ovid-Elsie MI
*WSDP(FM) Plymouth MI
*WORW(FM) Port Huron MI
*WSGR-FM Port Huron MI
*WCMZ-FM Sault Ste. Marie MI
*WSHJ(FM) Southfield MI
*KTGG(AM) Spring Arbor MI
*WNMC-FM Traverse City MI
*WPHS(FM) Warren MI
*WYCE(FM) Wyoming MI
*WEMU(FM) Ypsilanti MI
*KMSK(FM) Austin MN
*KBSB(FM) Bemidji MN
*KDNI(FM) Duluth MN
*KUMD-FM Duluth MN
*KMSU(FM) Mankato MN
*KBEM-FM Minneapolis MN
*KTIS(AM) Minneapolis MN
*KTIS-FM Minneapolis MN
*KUOM(AM) Minneapolis MN
*KCCM-FM Moorhead MN
*KUMM(FM) Morris MN
*KRLX(FM) Northfield MN
*WCAL(FM) Northfield MN
*KRPR(FM) Rochester MN
*KVSC(FM) St. Cloud MN
*KDXL(FM) St. Louis Park MN
*WMCN(FM) St. Paul MN
*KGAC(FM) St. Peter MN
*KSRQ(FM) Thief River Falls MN
*KQAL(FM) Winona MN
*KSMR(FM) Winona MN
*KRSW-FM Worthington-Marshall MN
*KRCU(FM) Cape Girardeau MO
*KRNW(FM) Chillicothe MO
*KWUR(FM) Clayton MO
*KBIA(FM) Columbia MO
*KCOU(FM) Columbia MO
*KWWC-FM Columbia MO
*KCFV(FM) Ferguson MO
*KJLU(FM) Jefferson City MO
*KOBC(FM) Joplin MO
*KXMS(FM) Joplin MO
*KCUR-FM Kansas City MO
*KLJC(FM) Kansas City MO
*KWJC(FM) Liberty MO
*KMVC(FM) Marshall MO
*KXCV(FM) Maryville MO
*KRHS(FM) Overland MO
*KGSP(FM) Parkville MO
*KCOZ(FM) Point Lookout MO
*KMNR(FM) Rolla MO
*KUMR(FM) Rolla MO
*KSMU(FM) Springfield MO
*KWFC(FM) Springfield MO
*KCLC(FM) St. Charles MO
*KWMU(FM) St. Louis MO
*KCMW-FM Warrensburg MO
WHJT(FM) Clinton MS
*WUSM-FM Hattiesburg MS
*WURC(FM) Holly Springs MS
*WVSD(FM) Itta Bena MS
*WJSU(FM) Jackson MS
*WPRL(FM) Lorman MS
*WKNA(FM) Senatobia MS
*WMSV(FM) Starkville MS
WUMS(FM) University MS
*WCLL-FM Wesson MS
*KEMC(FM) Billings MT
*KBMC(FM) Bozeman MT

Broadcasting & Cable Yearbook 1994
B-484

College, University and School-Owned Radio Stations

*KGLT(FM) Bozeman MT
*KMSM-FM Butte MT
*KAEP(FM) Fort Belknap Agency MT
*KNMC(FM) Havre MT
*KECC(FM) Miles City MT
*KUFM(FM) Missoula MT
*WGWG(FM) Boiling Springs NC
*WASU-FM Boone NC
*WCCE(FM) Buie's Creek NC
*WUNC(FM) Chapel Hill NC
*WXYC(FM) Chapel Hill NC
*WWCU(FM) Cullowhee NC
*WSGE(FM) Dallas NC
*WDAV(FM) Davidson NC
*WXDU(FM) Durham NC
*WRVS-FM Elizabeth City NC
*WSOE(FM) Elon College NC
*WUAW(FM) Erwin NC
*WFSS(FM) Fayetteville NC
*WNAA(FM) Greensboro NC
*WQFS(FM) Greensboro NC
*WUAG(FM) Greensboro NC
*WZMB(FM) Greenville NC
*WWIH(FM) High Point NC
*WVMH-FM Mars Hill NC
*WOTJ(FM) Morehead City NC
*WTEB(FM) New Bern NC
*WKNC-FM Raleigh NC
*WSHA(FM) Raleigh NC
*WPGT(FM) Roanoke Rapids NC
*WESQ(FM) Rocky Mount NC
*WDCC(FM) Sanford NC
*WNCW(FM) Spindale NC
*WSIF(FM) Wilkesboro NC
*WRCM(FM) Wingate NC
*WFDD-FM Winston-Salem NC
*WSNC(FM) Winston-Salem NC
*KEYA(FM) Belcourt ND
*KDSU(FM) Fargo ND
*KFJM(FM) Grand Forks ND
*KFNW(AM) West Fargo ND
*KDCV-FM Blair NE
*KDNE(FM) Crete NE
*KROA(FM) Grand Island NE
*KCNT(FM) Hastings NE
*KSCV(FM) Kearney NE
*KRNU(FM) Lincoln NE
*KGBI-FM Omaha NE
*KIOS-FM Omaha NE
*KVNO(FM) Omaha NE
*KWSC(FM) Wayne NE
*WSPS(FM) Concord NH
*WUNH(FM) Durham NH
*WPEA(FM) Exeter NH
*WNEC-FM Henniker NH
*WKNH(FM) Keene NH
*WRND(FM) Manchester NH
*WPCR-FM Plymouth NH
*WDBK(FM) Blackwood NJ
*WFMU(FM) East Orange NJ
*WCVH(FM) Flemington NJ
*WGLS-FM Glassboro NJ
*WNTI(FM) Hackettstown NJ
*WRRC(FM) Lawrenceville NJ
*WBJB-FM Lincroft NJ
*WRPR(FM) Mahwah NJ
*WJSV(FM) Morristown NJ
*WRSU-FM New Brunswick NJ
*WRTQ(FM) Ocean City NJ
*WBZC(FM) Pemberton NJ
*WVPH(FM) Piscataway NJ
*WLFR(FM) Pomona NJ
*WWPH(FM) Princeton Junction NJ
*WSOU(FM) South Orange NJ
*WFDU(FM) Teaneck NJ
*WTSR(FM) Trenton NJ
*WWFM(FM) Trenton NJ
*WMSC(FM) Upper Montclair NJ
*WPSC(FM) Wayne NJ
*WMCX(FM) West Long Branch NJ
*KABR(AM) Alamo Community NM
*KUNM(FM) Albuquerque NM
*KSJE(FM) Farmington NM
*KRUX(FM) Las Cruces NM
*KRWG(FM) Las Cruces NM
*KEDP(FM) Las Vegas NM
*KMTH(FM) Maljamar NM
*KTDB(FM) Pine Hill NM
*KENW-FM Portales NM
*KNJU(FM) Raton NM
*KSFR(FM) Santa Fe NM
*KNCC(FM) Elko NV
*KUNV(FM) Las Vegas NV
*KRNC(FM) Reno NV
*KUNR(FM) Reno NV
*WCDB(FM) Albany NY
*WALF(FM) Alfred NY
*WETD(FM) Alfred NY
*WDWN(FM) Auburn NY
*WBXL(FM) Baldwinsville NY

*WGCC-FM Batavia NY
*WHRW(FM) Binghamton NY
*WXLH(FM) Blue Mountain Lake NY
*WXBA(FM) Brentwood NY
*WBSU(FM) Brockport NY
*WKRB(FM) Brooklyn NY
*WCWP(FM) Brookville NY
*WBFO(FM) Buffalo NY
*WBNY(FM) Buffalo NY
*WSLU(FM) Canton NY
*WITC(FM) Cazenovia NY
*WHCL-FM Clinton NY
*WCEB(FM) Corning NY
*WSUC-FM Cortland NY
*WECW(FM) Elmira NY
*WCVF-FM Fredonia NY
*WBAU(FM) Garden City NY
*WHPC(FM) Garden City NY
*WGSU(FM) Geneseo NY
*WEOS(FM) Geneva NY
*WGFR(FM) Glens Falls NY
*WGMC(FM) Greece NY
*WRCU-FM Hamilton NY
*WRHU(FM) Hempstead NY
*WITR(FM) Henrietta NY
*WVHC(FM) Herkimer NY
*WJSL(FM) Houghton NY
*WICB(FM) Ithaca NY
*WUBJ(FM) Jamestown NY
*WSHR(FM) Lake Ronkonkoma NY
*WVCR-FM Loudonville NY
*WSLO(FM) Malone NY
*WFUV(FM) New York NY
*WHCR-FM New York NY
*WKCR-FM New York NY
*WNYU-FM New York NY
*WXLG(FM) North Creek NY
*WSUF(FM) Noyack NY
*WNYK(FM) Nyack NY
*WOLN(FM) Olean NY
*WONY(FM) Oneonta NY
*WRHO(FM) Oneonta NY
*WOSS(FM) Ossining NY
*WNYO(FM) Oswego NY
*WRVO(FM) Oswego NY
*WPSA(FM) Paul Smiths NY
*WXLU(FM) Peru NY
*WPOB-FM Plainview NY
*WPLT(FM) Plattsburgh NY
*WVKR-FM Poughkeepsie NY
*WIRQ(FM) Rochester NY
*WRUR-FM Rochester NY
*WSLL(FM) Saranac Lake NY
*WSPN(FM) Saratoga Springs NY
*WRUC(FM) Schenectady NY
*WPBX(FM) Southampton NY
*WSBU(FM) St. Bonaventure NY
*WSIA(FM) Staten Island NY
*WUSB(FM) Stony Brook NY
*WKWZ(FM) Syosset NY
*WAER(FM) Syracuse NY
*WJPZ-FM Syracuse NY
*WRPI(FM) Troy NY
*WPNR-FM Utica NY
*WARY(FM) Valhalla NY
*WRVJ(FM) Watertown NY
*WSLJ(FM) Watertown NY
*WONB(FM) Ada OH
*WAPS(FM) Akron OH
*WZIP(FM) Akron OH
*WRMU(FM) Alliance OH
*WRDL(FM) Ashland OH
*WOUB(AM) Athens OH
*WKHR(FM) Bainbridge OH
*WBWC(FM) Berea OH
*WBGU(FM) Bowling Green OH
*WOUC-FM Cambridge OH
*WCDR-FM Cedarville OH
*WCWT-FM Centerville OH
*WOHC(FM) Chillicothe OH
*WOUH(FM) Chillicothe OH
*WVXC(FM) Chillicothe OH
*WGUC(FM) Cincinnati OH
*WJVS(FM) Cincinnati OH
*WVXU(FM) Cincinnati OH
*WCSB(FM) Cleveland OH
*WRUW-FM Cleveland OH
*WOSU(AM) Columbus OH
*WDPS(FM) Dayton OH
*WGXM(FM) Dayton OH
*WWSU(FM) Dayton OH
*WDEQ-FM De Graff OH
*WSLN(FM) Delaware OH
*WLFC(FM) Findlay OH
*WKCO(FM) Gambier OH
*WDUB(FM) Granville OH
*WHSS(FM) Hamilton OH
*WOUL-FM Ironton OH
*WKSU-FM Kent OH
*WKET(FM) Kettering OH

*WFCO(FM) Lancaster OH
*WCMO(FM) Marietta OH
*WMRT(FM) Marietta OH
*WNZR(FM) Mount Vernon OH
*WMCO(FM) New Concord OH
*WKRJ(FM) New Philadelphia OH
*WOBC-FM Oberlin OH
*WMUB(FM) Oxford OH
*WOHP(FM) Portsmouth OH
*WOSP(FM) Portsmouth OH
*WUSO(FM) Springfield OH
*WSTB(FM) Streetsboro OH
*WKTL(FM) Struthers OH
*WHEI(FM) Tiffin OH
*WUJC(FM) University Heights OH
*WLHS(FM) West Chester OH
*WVXM(FM) West Union OH
*WOBN(FM) Westerville OH
*WCSU-FM Wilberforce OH
*WCWS(FM) Wooster OH
*WKRW(FM) Wooster OH
*WYSO(FM) Yellow Springs OH
*WYSU(FM) Youngstown OH
*WOUZ(FM) Zanesville OH
*KRSC-FM Claremore OK
*KHIB(FM) Durant OK
*KCSC(FM) Edmond OK
*KPSU(FM) Goodwell OK
*KALU(FM) Langston OK
*KCCU(FM) Lawton OK
*KGOU(FM) Norman OK
*KOCC(FM) Oklahoma City OK
*KROU(FM) Spencer OK
*KOSU-FM Stilwater OK
*KAYE-FM Tonkawa OK
*KWGS(FM) Tulsa OK
*KSMF(FM) Ashland OR
*KSOR(FM) Ashland OR
*KBVR(FM) Corvallis OR
*KEPO(FM) Eagle Point OR
*KLCC(FM) Eugene OR
*KRVM(FM) Eugene OR
*KMHD(FM) Gresham OR
*KSKF(FM) Klamath Falls OR
*KTEC(FM) Klamath Falls OR
*KEOL(FM) La Grande OR
*KSLC(FM) McMinnville OR
*KLCO(FM) Newport OR
*KBPS-FM Portland OR
*KRRC(FM) Portland OR
*WMUH(FM) Allentown PA
*WGEV(FM) Beaver Falls PA
*WLVR(FM) Bethlehem PA
*WBUQ(FM) Bloomsburg PA
*WVCS(FM) California PA
*WDCV-FM Carlisle PA
*WDNR(FM) Chester PA
*WCUC-FM Clarion PA
*WESS(FM) East Stroudsburg PA
*WJRH(FM) Easton PA
*WFSE(FM) Edinboro PA
*WWEC(FM) Elizabethtown PA
*WRTL(FM) Ephrata PA
*WERG(FM) Erie PA
*WMCE(FM) Erie PA
WPSE(AM) Erie PA
*WRSD(FM) Folsom PA
*WZBT(FM) Gettysburg PA
*WZZE(FM) Glen Mills PA
*WTGP(FM) Greenville PA
*WSAJ(AM) Grove City PA
*WHHS(FM) Havertown PA
*WKVR-FM Huntingdon PA
*WIUP-FM Indiana PA
*WRTY(FM) Jackson Township PA
*WFNM(FM) Lancaster PA
*WVBU-FM Lewisburg PA
*WNTE(FM) Mansfield PA
*WARC(FM) Meadville PA
*WMSS(FM) Middletown PA
*WIXQ(FM) Millersville PA
*WSFX(FM) Nanticoke PA
*WWNW(FM) New Wilmington PA
*WKDU(FM) Philadelphia PA
*WRTI(FM) Philadelphia PA
*WXPN(FM) Philadelphia PA
*WDUQ(FM) Pittsburgh PA
*WPTS-FM Pittsburgh PA
*WYBF(FM) Radnor Township PA
*WXAC(FM) Reading PA
*WXLV(FM) Schnecksville PA
*WVMW-FM Scranton PA
*WQSU(FM) Selinsgrove PA
*WSYC-FM Shippensburg PA
*WRSK(FM) Slippery Rock PA
*WPSU(FM) State College PA
*WTLR(FM) State College PA
*WJAZ(FM) Summerdale PA
*WSRN-FM Swarthmore PA
*WXVU(FM) Villanova PA
*WXJX(FM) Washington PA

*WCYJ-FM Waynesburg PA
*WCLH(FM) Wilkes-Barre PA
*WRKC(FM) Wilkes-Barre PA
*WRLC(FM) Williamsport PA
*WWAS(FM) Williamsport PA
*WVYC(FM) York PA
WEUC(AM) Ponce PR
*WRTU(FM) San Juan PR
*WCVY(FM) Coventry RI
*WRIU(FM) Kingston RI
*WDOM(FM) Providence RI
*WELH(FM) Providence RI
*WJMF(FM) Smithfield RI
*WAFZ(FM) Belton SC
*WUOZ(FM) Belvedere SC
*WSBF-FM Clemson SC
*WUSC(FM) Columbia SC
*WECE(FM) Due West SC
*WPLS-FM Greenville SC
*WTBI-FM Greenville SC
*WKCL(FM) Ladson SC
*WSSB-FM Orangeburg SC
*KESD(FM) Brookings SD
*KSDJ(FM) Brookings SD
*KAUR(FM) Sioux Falls SD
*KCFS(FM) Sioux Falls SD
*KCSD(FM) Sioux Falls SD
*KNWC(AM) Sioux Falls SD
*KRSD(FM) Sioux Falls SD
*KBHU-FM Spearfish SD
*KAOR(FM) Vermillion SD
*WDYN-FM Chattanooga TN
*WUTC(FM) Chattanooga TN
*WAPX-FM Clarksville TN
*WSMC-FM Collegedale TN
*WZMC(AM) Colonial Heights TN
*WTTU(FM) Cookeville TN
*WVCP(FM) Gallatin TN
*WLMU(FM) Harrogate TN
*WFHC(FM) Henderson TN
*WETS(FM) Johnson City TN
*WCSK(FM) Kingsport TN
*WKCS(FM) Knoxville TN
*WUOT(FM) Knoxville TN
WUTK(AM) Knoxville TN
*WFMQ(FM) Lebanon TN
*WUTM(FM) Martin TN
*WQOX(FM) Memphis TN
*WSMS(FM) Memphis TN
*WMOT(FM) Murfreesboro TN
WENO(AM) Nashville TN
*WFSK(FM) Nashville TN
*WNAZ-FM Nashville TN
*WRVU(FM) Nashville TN
*WAWL-FM Red Bank TN
*WUTS(FM) Sewanee TN
*KACU(FM) Abilene TX
*KACC(FM) Alvin TX
*KUT(FM) Austin TX
*KVRX(FM) Austin TX
*KVLU(FM) Beaumont TX
*KWTS(FM) Canyon TX
*KAMU-FM College Station TX
*KETR(FM) Commerce TX
*KRSM(FM) Dallas TX
*KNTU(FM) Denton TX
*KTEP(FM) El Paso TX
*KTCU-FM Fort Worth TX
*KTRU(FM) Houston TX
*KTSU(FM) Houston TX
*KUHF(FM) Houston TX
*KSHU(FM) Huntsville TX
*KJCR(FM) Keene TX
*KTPB(FM) Kilgore TX
*KNCT-FM Killeen TX
*KTAI(FM) Kingsville TX
*KOHM(FM) Lubbock TX
*KTXT-FM Lubbock TX
*KBIB(AM) Marion TX
*KBWC(FM) Marshall TX
KMHT(AM) Marshall TX
*KEOM(FM) Mesquite TX
*KSAU(FM) Nacogdoches TX
*KOCV(FM) Odessa TX
*KPLN-FM Plains TX
*KWLD(FM) Plainview TX
*KPVU(FM) Prairie View TX
*KRTU(FM) San Antonio TX
*KSYM-FM San Antonio TX
*KTSW(FM) San Marcos TX
*KTXK(FM) Texarkana TX
*KWBU(FM) Waco TX
*KGSU-FM Cedar City UT
*KAGJ(FM) Ephraim UT
*KUSU-FM Logan UT
*KWCR-FM Ogden UT
*KOHS(FM) Orem UT
*KPGR(FM) Pleasant Grove UT
*KBYU-FM Provo UT
*KUER(FM) Salt Lake City UT
*KRDC(FM) St. George UT

*WAMV(AM) Amherst VA
*WUVT-FM Blacksburg VA
*WTJU(FM) Charlottesville VA
*WEHC(FM) Emory VA
*WFFC(FM) Ferrum VA
*WWHS-FM Hampden-Sydney VA
*WHOV(FM) Hampton VA
*WEMC(FM) Harrisonburg VA
*WXJM(FM) Harrisonburg VA
*WLUR(FM) Lexington VA
*WMRL(FM) Lexington VA
*WRVL(FM) Lynchburg VA
*WNSB(FM) Norfolk VA
*WVST(FM) Petersburg VA
*WVRU(FM) Radford VA
*WDCE(FM) Richmond VA
*WCWM(FM) Williamsburg VA
*WRUV(FM) Burlington VT
*WIUV(FM) Castleton VT
*WWPV-FM Colchester VT
*WJSC-FM Johnson VT
*WWLR(FM) Lyndonville VT
*WRMC-FM Middlebury VT
*WNUB-FM Northfield VT
*WGDR(FM) Plainfield VT
*WVTC(FM) Randolph Center VT
*WTBC-FM Williston VT
*KGRG(FM) Auburn WA
*KASB(FM) Bellevue WA
*KBCS(FM) Bellevue WA
*KUGS(FM) Bellingham WA
*KCED(FM) Centralia WA
*KEWU-FM Cheney WA
*KGTS(FM) College Place WA
*KGHP(FM) Gig Harbor WA
*KTCV(FM) Kennewick WA
*KMIH(FM) Mercer Island WA
*KSVR(FM) Mount Vernon WA
*KUBS(FM) Newport WA
*KAOS(FM) Olympia WA
*KWSU(AM) Pullman WA
*KZUU(FM) Pullman WA
*KFAE-FM Richland WA
*KCMU(FM) Seattle WA
*KNHC(FM) Seattle WA
*KUOW(FM) Seattle WA
*KAGU(FM) Spokane WA
*KSFC(FM) Spokane WA
*KWRS(FM) Spokane WA
*KPLU-FM Tacoma WA
*KUPS(FM) Tacoma WA
*KVTI(FM) Tacoma WA
*KWCW(FM) Walla Walla WA
*KYSC(FM) Yakima WA
*WLFM(FM) Appleton WI
*WBCR-FM Beloit WI
*WBSD(FM) Burlington WI
*WUEC(FM) Eau Claire WI
*WGAZ(FM) Goodman WI
*WGBW(FM) Green Bay WI
*WGTD(FM) Kenosha WI
*WLSU(FM) La Crosse WI
*WHA(AM) Madison WI
*WNWC(FM) Madison WI
*WVSS(FM) Menomonie WI
*WMSE(FM) Milwaukee WI
*WUWM(FM) Milwaukee WI
*WYMS(FM) Milwaukee WI
*WRST-FM Oshkosh WI
*WSUP(FM) Platteville WI
*WRPN-FM Ripon WI
*WRFW(FM) River Falls WI
*WSHS(FM) Sheboygan WI
*WWSP(FM) Stevens Point WI
*KUWS(FM) Superior WI
*WCCX(FM) Waukesha WI
*WSUW(FM) Whitewater WI
*WVBC(FM) Bethany WV
*WVWC(FM) Buckhannon WV
*WCDE(FM) Elkins WV
*WFGH(FM) Fort Gay WV
*WMVL(FM) Huntington WV
*WWVU-FM Morgantown WV
*WQAB(FM) Philippi WV
*WJGF-FM Romney WV
*WSHC(FM) Shepherdstown WV
*WGLZ(FM) West Liberty WV
*WPHP(FM) Wheeling WV
*KYDZ(FM) Cody WY
*KUWJ(FM) Jackson WY
*KUWR(FM) Laramie WY
*KCWC-FM Riverton WY
*KUWZ(FM) Rock Springs WY

U.S. AM Stations by Frequency

Editor's Note: Clear stations appear in boldface type. Refer to the frequency heading to determine if the station is a class I-A or I-B. All other stations operating on these freequencies are class II. For an explanation of AM stations classes, see the FCC Rules and Regulations in Section A.

540 khz (Canadian & Mexican) I-A
KIEZ(AM) Carmel Valley CA 10 kw-D, 500 w-N, DA-2.
KOJY(AM) Costa Mesa CA 25 kw-D, 400 w-N, DA-3.
*KVIP(AM) Redding CA 2.5 kw-D, 17 w-N.
WGTO(AM) Pine Hills FL 50 kw-U, DA-2.
WSTH(AM) Columbus GA 5 kw-D, 500 w-N, DA-N.
KWMT(AM) Fort Dodge IA 5 kw-D, 200 w-N, DA-N.
KNOE(AM) Monroe LA 5 kw-D, 1 kw-N, DA-2.
WDMV(AM) Pocomoke City MD 5 kw-D, 243 w-N.
WETC(AM) Wendell-Zebulon NC 5 kw-D, 500 w-N, DA-2.
KNMX(AM) Las Vegas NM 5 kw-D, DA.
WLIX(AM) Islip NY 250 w-D, 218 w-N.
WWCS(AM) Canonsburg PA 7.5 kw-D, 500 w-N, DA-2.
WYNN(AM) Florence SC 250 w-U.
WDXN(AM) Clarksville TN 1 kw-D, 54.5 w-N.
KDFT(AM) Ferris TX 1 kw-D, 220 w-N, DA-2.
KNAK(AM) Delta UT 1 kw-D.
WRIC(AM) Richlands VA 1 kw-D, 97 w-N.
WYLO(AM) Jackson WI 400 w-D, DA-2.

550 khz Regional III
KENI(AM) Anchorage AK 5 kw-U.
WASG(AM) Atmore AL 25 kw-D, 144 w-N.
KOY(AM) Phoenix AZ 5 kw-D, 1 kw-N.
KCWR(AM) Bakersfield CA 5 kw-D, DA-N.
KLLV(AM) Breen CO 1.8 kw-D, 80 w-N.
KRAI(AM) Craig CO 5 kw-D, 500 w-N, DA-N.
*WAYR(AM) Orange Park FL 5 kw-D, 0.5 kw-N, DA-1.
WDUN(AM) Gainesville GA 5 kw-D, 2.5 kw-N, DA-N.
KMVI(AM) Wailuku HI 5 kw-U.
KFRM(AM) Salina KS 5 kw-D, 110 w-N, DA-2.
KSD(AM) St. Louis MO 5 kw-U, DA-N.
KBOW(AM) Butte MT 5 kw-D, 1 kw-N, DA-N.
WIOZ(AM) Pinehurst NC 1 kw-D, 260 w-N, DA-N.
WAME(AM) Statesville NC 500 w-D.
KFYR(AM) Bismarck ND 5 kw-U, DA-N.
WGR(AM) Buffalo NY 5 kw-U, DA-2.
WLWA(AM) Cincinnati OH 5 kw-D, 1 kw-N, DA-2.
*KOAC(AM) Corvallis OR 5 kw-U, DA-2.
WJMW(AM) Bloomsburg PA 1 kw-D, DA-2.
WPAB(AM) Ponce PR 5 kw-U.
WICE(AM) Pawtucket RI 1 kw-D, 500 w-N, DA-N.
KCRS(AM) Midland TX 5 kw-D, 1 kw-N, DA-2.
KTSA(AM) San Antonio TX 5 kw-U, DA-N.
WSVA(AM) Harrisonburg VA 5 kw-D, 1 kw-N, DA-N.
WDEV(AM) Waterbury VT 5 kw-D, 1 kw-N, DA-N.
KARI(AM) Blaine WA 5 kw-D, 2.5 kw-N, DA-2.
WSAU(AM) Wausau WI 5 kw-U, DA-2.

560 khz Regional III
KVOK(AM) Kodiak AK 1 kw-U.
WOOF(AM) Dothan AL 5 kw-D, 117 w-N.
KBLU(AM) Yuma AZ 1 kw-U, DA-N.
KSFO(AM) San Francisco CA 5 kw-U, DA-2.
KLZ(AM) Denver CO 5 kw-U, DA-1.
WQAM(AM) Miami FL 5 kw-D, 1 kw-N.
WIND(AM) Chicago IL 5 kw-U, DA-2.
WMIK(AM) Middlesboro KY 500 w-D, 88 w-N.
WHYN(AM) Springfield MA 5 kw-U, DA-N.
WFRB(AM) Frostburg MD 5 kw-D.
WGAN(AM) Portland ME 5 kw-U, DA-2.
WHND(AM) Monroe MI 500 w-D, 27 w-N.
WEBC(AM) Duluth MN 5 kw-U, DA-2.
KWTO(AM) Springfield MO 5 kw-U, DA-N.
KMON(AM) Great Falls MT 5 kw-U, DA-N.
WGAI(AM) Elizabeth City NC 5 kw-D, 500 w-N, DA-2.
WCKL(AM) Catskill NY 1 kw-D, DA.
WPHY(AM) Philadelphia PA 5 kw-U, DA-1.
WVOC(AM) Columbia SC 5 kw-U, DA-N.
WYOR(AM) Brentwood TN 500 w-D, DA.
WHBQ(AM) Memphis TN 5 kw-D, 1 kw-N, DA-N.
KLVI(AM) Beaumont TX 5 kw-U, DA-N.
KPQ(AM) Wenatchee WA 5 kw-U, DA-N.
WJLS(AM) Beckley WV 5 kw-D, 500 w-N, DA-N.

567 khz Regional III
KGUM(AM) Agana GU 5 kw-U, DA-1.

570 khz Regional III
WAAX(AM) Gadsden AL 5 kw-D, 500 w-N, DA-N.
KCNO(AM) Alturas CA 5 kw-D, 200 w-N.
KLAC(AM) Los Angeles CA 5 kw-U, DA-N.
WHNZ(AM) Pinellas Park FL 5 kw-U, DA-2.
WACL(AM) Waycross GA 5 kw-D, 1 kw-N, DA-N.
KQNG(AM) Lihue HI 1 kw-U.
WKYX(AM) Paducah KY 5 kw-D, 500 w-N, DA-N.
WTEM(AM) Bethesda MD 5 kw-D, 1 kw-N, DA-2.
WVMI(AM) Biloxi MS 5 kw-D, 1 kw-N, DA-2.
WWNC(AM) Asheville NC 5 kw-U.
WLLE(AM) Raleigh NC 500 w-D, 54 w-N.
KGRT(AM) Las Cruces NM 5 kw-D, 155 w-N.
WMCA(AM) New York NY 5 kw-U, DA-1.
WSYR(AM) Syracuse NY 5 kw-U, DA-N.
WKBN(AM) Youngstown OH 5 kw-U, DA-N.
WNAX(AM) Yankton SD 5 kw-U.
KLIF(AM) Dallas TX 5 kw-U, DA-N.
KISN(AM) Salt Lake City UT 5 kw-U, DA-2.
KVI(AM) Seattle WA 5 kw-U.
WMAM(AM) Marinette WI 250 w-D, 100 w-N.

580 khz Regional III
KRSA(AM) Petersburg AK 5 kw-U, DA-1.
WBIL(AM) Tuskegee AL 500 w-D, 139 w-N.
KSAZ(AM) Tucson AZ 5 kw-D, 500 w-N, DA-N.
KMJ(AM) Fresno CA 5 kw-U.
KUBC(AM) Montrose CO 5 kw-D, 1 kw-N, DA-N.
WDBO(AM) Orlando FL 5 kw-D, DA-N.
WGAC(AM) Augusta GA 5 kw-D, 1 kw-N, DA-N.
WMGA(AM) Moultrie GA 900 w-D, 250 w-N, DA-N.
KFXD(AM) Nampa ID 5 kw-U, DA-N.
*WILL(AM) Urbana IL 5 kw-D, DA-D.
*KKSU(AM) Manhattan KS 5 kw-D. (ST-WIBW).
WIBW(AM) Topeka KS 5 kw-U, DA-N (S-KKSU).
KALB(AM) Alexandria LA 5 kw-D, 1 kw-N, DA-N.
WTAG(AM) Worcester MA 5 kw-U, DA-N.
WELO(AM) Tupelo MS 1 kw-D, 500 w-N, DA-2.
WTSB(AM) Lumberton NC 1 kw-D, 67 w-N.
WKSK(AM) West Jefferson NC 1 kw-D, 34 w-N.
KCMX(AM) Ashland OR 1 kw-D, DA-N.
WHP(AM) Harrisburg PA 5 kw-D, DA-N.
WKAQ(AM) San Juan PR 10 kw-U, DA-1.
KZMX(AM) Hot Springs SD 500 w-D, 310 w-N.
WOFE(AM) Rockwood TN 1 kw-D.
KJBX(AM) Lubbock TX 500 w-D, 290 w-N, DA-2.
WLES(AM) Lawrenceville VA 500 w-D.
WKTY(AM) La Crosse WI 5 kw-D, 1 kw-N, DA-N.
WCHS(AM) Charleston WV 5 kw-U, DA-N.

585 khz Clear II
KBQN(AM) Pago Pago AS 50 kw-U.

590 khz Regional III
KHAR(AM) Anchorage AK 5 kw-U.
WRAG(AM) Carrollton AL 1 kw-D.
KBHS(AM) Hot Springs AR 5 kw-D, 500 w-N, DA-N.
KRSO(AM) San Bernardino CA 1 kw-U, DA-2.
KTHO(AM) South Lake Tahoe CA 2.5 kw-D, 500 w-N, DA-N.
KCSJ(AM) Pueblo CO 1 kw-U, DA-N.
WAFC(AM) Clewiston FL 930 w-D, 470 w-N.
WGNE(AM) Panama City FL 1.7 kw-D, 2.5 kw-N, DA-N.
WKHX(AM) Atlanta GA 5 kw-U, DA-N.
KSSK(AM) Honolulu HI 7.5 kw-U.
KID(AM) Idaho Falls ID 5 kw-D, 1 kw-N, DA-N
KFNS(AM) Wood River IL 1 kw-U, DA-N.
WVLK(AM) Lexington KY 5 kw-D, 1 kw-N, DA-N.
WEEI(AM) Boston MA 5 kw-U.
WJMS(AM) Ironwood MI 5 kw-D, 1 kw-N, DA-N.
WKZO(AM) Kalamazoo MI 5 kw-U, DA-N.
KGLE(AM) Glendive MT 1 kw-U.
WCAB(AM) Rutherfordton NC 500 w-D, 228 w-N.
WGTM(AM) Wilson NC 5 kw-U, DA-2.
WOW(AM) Omaha NE 5 kw-U.
WROW(AM) Albany NY 5 kw-D, 1 kw-N, DA-2.
KUGN(AM) Eugene OR 5 kw-U, 1 kw-N, DA-N.
WARM(AM) Scranton PA 5 kw-U, DA-2.
WMBS(AM) Uniontown PA 1 kw-U, DA-N.
WWLX(AM) Lawrenceburg TN 750 w-D, 133 w-N.
KLBJ(AM) Austin TX 5 kw-D, 1 kw-N, DA-N.
KSUB(AM) Cedar City UT 5 kw-D, 1 kw-N, DA-N.
WLVA(AM) Lynchburg VA 5 kw-D, 1 kw-N, DA-N.
KAQQ(AM) Spokane WA 5 kw-U.

600 khz Regional III
KCLS(AM) Flagstaff AZ 5 kw-D, 500 w-N, DA-N.
KNRO(AM) Redding CA 1 kw-U.
KKLQ(AM) San Diego CA 5 kw-D, DA-1.
KIIX(AM) Wellington CO 5 kw-D, 500 w-N, DA-2.
WICC(AM) Bridgeport CT 1 kw-D, 500 w-N, DA-2.
WOKV(AM) Jacksonville FL 5 kw-D, 5.4 kw-N, DA-2.
WMT(AM) Cedar Rapids IA 5 kw-D, DA-N.
WKLW(AM) Paintsville KY 5 kw-D, 500 w-N.
WVOG(AM) New Orleans LA 1 kw-D.
WCAO(AM) Baltimore MD 5 kw-U, DA-2.
WFST(AM) Caribou ME 5 kw-D, 127 w-N.
WCHT(AM) Escanaba MI 1 kw-D, 191 w-N, DA-2.
WTAC(AM) Flint MI 1 kw-D, 500 w-N, DA-2.
KGEZ(AM) Kalispell MT 5 kw-D, 1 kw-N, DA-N.
WCVP(AM) Murphy NC 1 kw-D, 20 w-N.
WSJS(AM) Winston-Salem NC 5 kw-D, 5 kw-N, DA-2.
KSJB(AM) Jamestown ND 5 kw-U, DA-1.
WSOM(AM) Salem OH 1 kw-D, 45 w-N, DA-2.
WFRM(AM) Coudersport PA 1 kw-D, 46 w-N.
WAEL(AM) Mayaguez PR 1 kw-U, DA-1.
WREC(AM) Memphis TN 5 kw-U, DA-N.
KROD(AM) El Paso TX 5 kw-U, DA-N.
KERB(AM) Kermit TX 1 kw-D, DA.
KTBB(AM) Tyler TX 5 kw-D, 2.5 kw-N, DA-2.
WVAR(AM) Richwood WV 1 kw-D.

610 khz Regional III
WZZK(AM) Birmingham AL 5 kw-D, 1 kw-N, DA-N.
KARV(AM) Russellville AR 1 kw-D, 500 w-N, DA-2.
KAVL(AM) Lancaster CA 1 kw-D, 500 w-N, DA-N.
KFRC(AM) San Francisco CA 5 kw-U.
KSKE(AM) Vail CO 5 kw-D, 217 w-N.
WSNG(AM) Torrington CT 1 kw-D, 500 w-N, DA-N.
WIOD(AM) Miami FL 10 kw-D, DA-N.
WVTJ(AM) Pensacola FL 5 kw-D, 142 w-N.
WPLO(AM) Grayson GA 1.5 kw-D, 225 w-N.
WCEH(AM) Hawkinsville GA 500 w-D, 128 w-N.
KUAM(AM) Agana GU 5 kw-U.
WRUS(AM) Russellville KY 2.5 kw-D, 73 w-N.
KDAL(AM) Duluth MN 5 kw-U, DA-N.
WDAF(AM) Kansas City MO 5 kw-U.

KOJM(AM) Havre MT 1 kw-U, DA-2.
WAQS(AM) Charlotte NC 5 kw-U, DA-N.
KCSR(AM) Chadron NE 1 kw-D, 137 w-N.
WGIR(AM) Manchester NH 5 kw-U, DA-N.
KZSS(AM) Albuquerque NM 5 kw-U, DA-N.
WTVN(AM) Columbus OH 5 kw-U, DA-N.
KYJC(AM) Medford OR 5 kw-U, DA-2.
WIP(AM) Philadelphia PA 5 kw-U, DA-1.
WEXS(AM) Patillas PR 250 w-D, 1 kw-N, DA-D.
KILT(AM) Houston TX 5 kw-U, DA-N.
KVNU(AM) Logan UT 5 kw-D, 1 kw-N, DA-N.
WSLC(AM) Roanoke VA 5 kw-U, 1 kw-N, DA-N.
WNTW(AM) Winchester VA 500 w-D, DA-2.
KONA(AM) Kennewick WA 5 kw-U, DA-2.

620 khz Regional III
KGTL(AM) Homer AK 5 kw-U.
WKNI(AM) Lexington AL 5 kw-D, 99 w-N.
KTAR(AM) Phoenix AZ 5 kw-U, DA-N.
KIGS(AM) Hanford CA 1 kw-U, DA-N.
KWSD(AM) Mount Shasta CA 1 kw-D.
KSTR(AM) Grand Junction CO 5 kw-U.
WSUN(AM) St. Petersburg FL 5 kw-D, 5.4 kw-N, DA-N.
WTRP(AM) La Grange GA 1 kw-D, 127 w-N.
KIPA(AM) Hilo HI 10 kw-U.
KMNS(AM) Sioux City IA 5 kw-U, DA-N.
KWAL(AM) Wallace ID 1 kw-U, DA-N.
WTMT(AM) Louisville KY 500 w-U, DA-N.
WZON(AM) Bangor ME 5 kw-U, DA-N.
WJDS(AM) Jackson MS 5 kw-U, 1 kw-N, DA-N.
WDNC(AM) Durham NC 5 kw-U, DA-N.
WSKQ(AM) Newark NJ 5 kw-U, DA-2.
KZTY(AM) Winchester NV 500 w-D, 450 w-N, DA-2.
WHEN(AM) Syracuse NY 5 kw-D, 1 kw-N, DA-N.
KINK(AM) Portland OR 5 kw-U, DA-N.
WHJB(AM) Greensburg PA 2.5 kw-D, 500 w-N, DA-N.
WTGH(AM) Cayce SC 1 kw-D, 125 w-N.
WRJZ(AM) Knoxville TN 5 kw-U, DA-N.
KWFT(AM) Wichita Falls TX 5 kw-U, DA-N.
WVMT(AM) Burlington VT 5 kw-U, DA-N.
WTMJ(AM) Milwaukee WI 5 kw-U.
WWNR(AM) Beckley WV 1 kw-D, 500 w-N, DA-N.

630 khz Regional III
KJNO(AM) Juneau AK 5 kw-D, 1 kw-N.
KIAM(AM) Nenana AK 5 kw-D, 2.2 kw-N.
WAVU(AM) Albertville AL 1 kw-D, 28 w-N.
WJDB(AM) Thomasville AL 1 kw-D.
KVMA(AM) Magnolia AR 1 kw-D.
KIDD(AM) Monterey CA 1 kw-U, DA-2.
KHOW(AM) Denver CO 5 kw-U, DA-2.
WMAL(AM) Washington DC 5 kw-U, DA-2.
WBMQ(AM) Savannah GA 5 kw-U, DA-N.
WNEG(AM) Toccoa GA 500 w-D.
KIDO(AM) Boise ID 5 kw-U, DA-2.
WLAP(AM) Lexington KY 5 kw-U, 1 kw-N, DA-2.
WDGY(AM) St. Paul MN 5 kw-D, 500 w-N, DA-N.
KXOK(AM) St. Louis MO 5 kw-U, DA-2.
WIRC(AM) Hickory NC 5 kw-U, 57 w-N.
WMFD(AM) Wilmington NC 5 kw-U, DA-N.
KLEA(AM) Lovington NM 500 w-D.
KOH(AM) Reno NV 5 kw-D, 1 kw-N, DA-N.
KWRO(AM) Coquille OR 5 kw-U.
WEJL(AM) Scranton PA 500 w-D, 32 w-N.
WSKN(AM) San Juan PR 5 kw-U, DA-2.
WPRO(AM) Providence RI 5 kw-U, DA-N.
KSLR(AM) San Antonio TX 5 kw-U, DA-N.
KTKK(AM) Sandy UT 1 kw-D, 500 w-N, DA-2.
KCIS(AM) Edmonds WA 5 kw-D, 2.5 kw-N, DA-N.
KKPL(AM) Opportunity WA 1 kw-D, 32 w-N.
WVVW(AM) St. Marys WV 1 kw-D.

640 khz Clear I-A (1-B Canadian)
KFI(AM) Los Angeles CA 50 kw-U.
*KYUK(AM) Bethel AK 10 kw-U.
WLVJ(AM) Royal Palm Beach FL 25 kw-D, 8.2 w-N, DA-2.
WHOF(AM) Wildwood FL 830 w-D, 980 w-N.
WGST(AM) Atlanta GA 50 kw-D, 1 kw-N, DA-2.
*WOI(AM) Ames IA 5 kw-D, 1 kw-N, DA-N.
WBOW(AM) Terre Haute IN 1 kw, DA-N.
KTIB(AM) Thibodaux LA 5 kw-D, 1 kw-N, DA-2.
WNNZ(AM) Westfield MA 50 kw-D, 1 kw-N, DA-2.
WISZ(AM) Zeeland MI 1 kw-D, 250 w-N.
KGVW(AM) Belgrade MT 10 kw-D, 1 kw-N, DA-2.
WFNC(AM) Fayetteville NC 10 kw-D, 1 kw-N.
WWJZ(AM) Mount Holly NJ 50 kw-D, 950 w-N, DA-2.
WHLO(AM) Akron OH 5 kw-D, 500 w-N, DA-N.
WWLS(AM) Moore OK 5 kw-U, DA-N.
WGOC(AM) Blountville TN 10 kw-D, 810 w-N, DA-N.
WCRV(AM) Collierville TN 50 kw-D, 480 w-N, DA-N.

648 khz Clear II
WVUV(AM) Leone AS 10 kw-U.

650 khz Clear I-A
WSM(AM) Nashville TN 50 kw-U.
KYAK(AM) Anchorage AK 50 kw-U.
KSTE(AM) Rancho Cordova CA 25 kw-D, 1 kw-N, DA-2.
WORL(AM) Christmas FL 50 kw-D, DA.
KHNR(AM) Honolulu HI 10 kw-U.
WKKQ(AM) Nashwauk MN 10 kw-D, 500 w-N, DA-N.
KZTU(AM) Junction City OR 10 kw-D, 1 kw-N, DA-2.
KIKK(AM) Pasadena TX 250 w-D.

U.S. AM Stations by Frequency

KMTI(AM) Manti UT 10 kw-D, 1 kw-N, DA-2.
KQQQ(AM) Pullman WA 1 kw-D, 500 w-N, DA-N.
KUUY(AM) Orchard Valley WY 8.5 kw-D, 500 w-N, DA-N.

660 khz Clear I-A
WFAN(AM) New York NY 50 kw-U.
KFAR(AM) Fairbanks AK 10 kw-U.
WBLX(AM) Fairhope AL 22.5 kw-D, 850 w-N, DA-2.
KTNN(AM) Window Rock AZ 50 kw-D, DA-N.
KGDP(AM) Orcutt CA 10 kw-D, 1 kw-N, DA-2.
WMIC(AM) Sandusky MI 1 kw-D, DA.
WVAL(AM) Sauk Rapids MN 10 kw-D, 250 w-N, DA-2.
KEYZ(AM) Williston ND 5 kw-U, DA-2.
KCRO(AM) Omaha NE 1 kw-D.
WXIC(AM) Waverly OH 1 kw-D.
WESC(AM) Greenville SC 50 kw-D, 10 kw-CH.
KSKY(AM) Balch Springs TX 10 kw-D, 500 w-N, DA-2.
WCRR(AM) Rural Retreat VA 550 w-D.
KAPS(AM) Mount Vernon WA 10 kw-D, 1 kw-N.

670 khz Clear I-A
WMAQ(AM) Chicago IL 50 kw-U.
*KDLG(AM) Dillingham AK 10 kw-U.
WYLS(AM) York AL 4.8 kw-D.
KWXI(AM) Glenwood AR 5 kw-D.
KWNK(AM) Simi Valley CA 5 kw-D, 1 kw-N.
KMVP(AM) Commerce City CO 2.5 kw-D, 1 kw-N, DA-N.
WWFE(AM) Miami FL 50 kw-D, 2.5 kw-N, DA-2.
KPUA(AM) Hilo HI 10 kw-D.
KBOI(AM) Boise ID 50 kw-U, DA-N.
WIEZ(AM) Lewistown PA 5.4 kw-D.
WTNN(AM) Farragut TN 500 w-D.
WARO(AM) Claremont VA 20 kw-D.

680 khz Clear I-B
KNBR(AM) San Francisco CA 50 kw-U.
*KBRW(AM) Barrow AK 10 kw-U.
WRMD(AM) St. Petersburg FL 1 kw-D.
WCNN(AM) North Atlanta GA 60 kw-D, 10 kw-N, DA-2.
WCTT(AM) Corbin KY 1 kw-U, DA-N.
WXKN(AM) Newburg KY 1.3 kw-D, 450 w-N, DA-2.
KXKW(AM) Tioga LA 380 w-D, 740 w-N, DA-N.
WRKO(AM) Boston MA 50 kw-U, DA-N.
WCBM(AM) Baltimore MD 10 kw-D, 5 kw-N, DA-2.
WDBC(AM) Escanaba MI 10 kw-D, 1 kw-N, DA-N.
KFEQ(AM) St. Joseph MO 5 kw-U, DA-2.
KHKR(AM) East Helena MT 5 kw-D.
WPTF(AM) Raleigh NC 50 kw-U, DA-N.
WRGC(AM) Sylva NC 1 kw-D, 250 w-N, DA-N.
KWKA(AM) Clovis NM 5 kw-U, DA-1.
WINR(AM) Binghamton NY 1 kw-D, 500 w-N, DA-2.
WISR(AM) Butler PA 250 w-D.
WAPA(AM) San Juan PR 10 kw-U.
WJCE(AM) Memphis TN 10 kw-D, 5 kw-N, DA-N.
KKYX(AM) San Antonio TX 50 kw-D, 10 kw-N, DA-N.
KLDY(AM) Lacey WA 250 w-D.
KOMW(AM) Omak WA 5 kw-D.
WOGO(AM) Hallie WI 2.5 kw-D, 500 w-N, DA-2.
WCAW(AM) Charleston WV 50 kw-D, 250 w-N, DA-2.

690 khz (Canadian & Mexican) I-A
WJOX(AM) Birmingham AL 50 kw-D, 30 w-N.
KEWI(AM) Benton AR 250 w-D, 73 w-N.
KVNA(AM) Flagstaff AZ 1 kw-D, 500 w-N, DA-2.
KVOI(AM) Oro Valley AZ 250 w-D, DA.
KRMX(AM) Pueblo CO 250 w-D, 24 w-N.
WADS(AM) Ansonia CT 1 kw-D, 33 w-N, DA-2.
WPDQ(AM) Jacksonville FL 50 kw-D, 10 kw-N, DA-N.
KQMQ(AM) Honolulu HI 10 kw-U.
KECN(AM) Blackfoot ID 1 kw-D, 43 w-N.
KGGF(AM) Coffeyville KS 10 kw-D, 5 kw-N, DA-N.
WTIX(AM) New Orleans LA 10 kw-D, 5 kw-N, DA-N.
WNZK(AM) Westland MI 2.5 kw.
KTCJ(AM) Minneapolis MN 500 w-D, DA.
KSTL(AM) St. Louis MO 1 kw-D.
KOAQ(AM) Terrytown NE 1 kw-D, 64 w-N, DA-1.
KRCO(AM) Prineville OR 1 kw-D, 77 w-N.
WPHE(AM) Phoenixville PA 1 kw-D, DA.
*KUSD(AM) Vermillion SD 1 kw-D, 21 w-N, DA-2.
KHEY(AM) El Paso TX 10 kw-D, DA-2.
KPET(AM) Lamesa TX 250 w-U.
KZEY(AM) Tyler TX 1 kw-D, 92 w-N, DA-2.
WZAP(AM) Bristol VA 10 kw-D, 14 w-N.
WNNT(AM) Warsaw VA 250 w-D, 10 w-N.
WXOL(AM) Oshkosh WI 250 w-D, 77 w-N, DA-N.
WELD(AM) Fisher WV 2 kw-D.

700 khz Clear I-A
WLW(AM) Cincinnati OH 50 kw-U.
KBYR(AM) Anchorage AK 10 kw-U.
WGZS(AM) Dothan AL 5 kw-D.
KSUR(AM) Soledad CA 2.5 kw-D, 700 w-N.
WCAT(AM) Orange-Athol MA 2.5 kw-D.
KGRV(AM) Winston OR 25 kw-D, 500 w-N.
KSEV(AM) Tomball TX 25 kw-D, 1 kw-N, DA-2.
KFAM(AM) North Salt Lake City UT 50 kw-D, 1 kw-N, DA-2.
KMJY(AM) Newport WA 1 kw-D, 1 kw-N, DA-N.

710 khz Clear I-A
WOR(AM) New York NY 50 kw-U, DA-1.
KIRO(AM) Seattle WA 50 kw-U, DA-N.
WKRG(AM) Mobile AL 1 kw-D, 500 w-N.
KAPZ(AM) Bald Knob AR 250 w-D, DA.
KFIA(AM) Carmichael CA 10 kw-D, 250 w-N, DA-1.
KMPC(AM) Los Angeles CA 50 kw-D, 10 kw-N, DA-N.
KNUS(AM) Denver CO 5 kw-U, DA-1.
WAQI(AM) Miami FL 50 kw-U.
WUFF(AM) Eastman GA 2.5 kw-D.
WROM(AM) Rome GA 5 kw-D.
WEKC(AM) Williamsburg KY 4.2 kw-D.

KEEL(AM) Shreveport LA 50 kw-D, 5 kw-N, DA-2.
WHB(AM) Kansas City MO 10 kw-D, 5 kw-N, DA-2.
WEPA(AM) Eupora MS 2.5 kw-D.
WZOO(AM) Asheboro NC 1 kw-D, DA.
WEGG(AM) Rose Hill NC 250 w-D.
WKJB(AM) Mayaguez PR 10 kw-D, 750 w-N.
WQKI(AM) St. Matthews SC 1 kw-D, DA.
WTPR(AM) Paris TN .75 kw-D.
WZRS(AM) Smyrna TN 250 w-D.
KGNC(AM) Amarillo TX 10 kw-U, DA-N.
KURV(AM) Edinburg TX 1 kw-U, DA-2.
WFNR(AM) Blacksburg VA 10 kw-D.
WDSM(AM) Superior WI 10 kw-D, 5 kw-N, DA-N.

720 khz Clear I-A
WGN(AM) Chicago IL 50 kw-U.
*KOTZ(AM) Kotzebue AK 10 kw-U.
WRZN(AM) Hernando FL 10 kw-D, 250 w-N, DA-N.
WMXY(AM) Hogansville GA 10 kw-D.
KUAI(AM) Eleele HI 5 kw-D.
WRBR(AM) Richland MS 5 kw-D.
WGCR(AM) Brevard NC 10 kw-D.
KDWN(AM) Las Vegas NV 50 kw-U, DA-N.
WWII(AM) Shiremanstown PA 2 kw-D.
KSAH(AM) Universal City TX 10 kw-D, 1 kw-N, DA-2.

730 khz Clear (Mexican) I-A
WBBI(AM) Madison AL 1 kw-D, 123 w-N.
KSUD(AM) West Memphis AR 250 w-U, DA-N.
WWTK(AM) Lake Placid FL 500 w-D, 340 w-N, DA-1.
WSTT(AM) Thomasville GA 5 kw-D, 27 w-N.
*KBSU(AM) Boise ID 15 kw-D, 500 w-N, DA-2.
KLOE(AM) Goodland KS 1 kw-D, 20 w-N.
WFMW(AM) Madisonville KY 500 w-D, 215 w-N.
WMTC(AM) Vancleve KY 5 kw-D, DA.
KTRY(AM) Bastrop LA 250 w-D.
WASO(AM) Covington LA 250 w-D, 25 w-N.
WACE(AM) Chicopee MA 5 kw-D.
WJTO(AM) Bath ME 1 kw-D, 29 w-N.
WVFN(AM) East Lansing MI 500 w-D, 17.5 w-N, DA-2.
KWOA(AM) Worthington MN 1 kw-D, 159 w-N.
KWRE(AM) Warrenton MO 1 kw-D, 120 w-N.
KURL(AM) Billings MT 5 kw-D, 236 w-N.
WFMC(AM) Goldsboro NC 1 kw-D, 98 w-N.
WOHS(AM) Shelby NC 10 kw-D, 168.4 w-N.
KDAZ(AM) Albuquerque NM 1 kw-D, 76 w-N, DA-2.
KKNC(AM) Sun Valley NV 500 w-U.
WDOS(AM) Oneonta NY 1 kw-D.
WJYM(AM) Bowling Green OH 1 kw-D, DA.
KRVC(AM) Medford OR 1 kw-D, 74 w-N.
WNAK(AM) Nanticoke PA 1 kw-D, 38 w-N.
WPIT(AM) Pittsburgh PA 5 kw-D.
WPAL(AM) Charleston SC 1 kw-D, 100 w-N.
WLIL(AM) Lenoir City TN 1 kw-D, 280 w-N.
KKDA(AM) Grand Prairie TX 500 w-U.
KSVN(AM) Ogden UT 1 kw-D, 66 w-N.
WCPT(AM) Alexandria VA 5 kw-D, 20 w-N.
WMNA(AM) Gretna VA 1 kw-D, 28 w-N, DA-1.
KULE(AM) Ephrata WA 1 kw-D.
WJMT(AM) Merrill WI 1 kw-D, 127 w-N.

740 khz Clear (Canadian) I-A
WLWI(AM) Montgomery AL 50 kw-D, 73 w-N, DA-2.
KIDR(AM) Phoenix AZ 1 kw-D, 292 w-N, DA-2.
KBRT(AM) Avalon CA 10 kw-D, DA.
KCBS(AM) San Francisco CA 50 kw, DA-2.
KTWK(AM) Colorado Springs CO 3.3 kw-D, 1.5 kw-N, DA-2.
KVFC(AM) Cortez CO 1 kw-D, 250 w-N, DA-N.
WSBR(AM) Boca Raton FL 2.5 kw-D, 940 w-N, DA-2.
WWNZ(AM) Orlando FL 50 kw-U, DA-1.
KBOE(AM) Oskaloosa IA 250 w-D, 12 w-N.
WVLN(AM) Olney IL 250 w-D, 7 w-N.
WNOP(AM) Newport KY 1 kw-D, DA.
WJIB(AM) Cambridge MA 250 w-D, 5 w-N.
WMBL(AM) Morehead City NC 1 kw-D, 14 w-N.
WPAQ(AM) Mount Airy NC 10 kw-D, 1 kw-CH.
KATK(AM) Carlsbad NM 1 kw-D, 500 w-N.
WGSM(AM) Huntington NY 25 kw-D.
KRMG(AM) Tulsa OK 50 kw-D, 25 kw-N, DA-2.
WVCH(AM) Chester PA 1 kw-D.
WIAC(AM) San Juan PR 10 kw-U, DA-1.
WBAW(AM) Barnwell SC 1 kw-D.
WSVQ(AM) Harrogate TN 1 kw-D.
WJIG(AM) Tullahoma TN 250 w-D, 67 w-N.
KTRH(AM) Houston TX 50 kw-U, DA-2.
KCMC(AM) Texarkana TX 1 kw-U, DA-1.
WMBG(AM) Williamsburg VA 500 w-D, 8 w-N.
WRPQ(AM) Baraboo WI 250 w-D, 6.4 w-N.
WMIN(AM) Hudson WI 500 w-D, 8 w-N, DA-N.
WRNR(AM) Martinsburg WV 500 w-D, 21 w-N, DA-N.

750 khz Clear I-A
WSB(AM) Atlanta GA 50 kw-U.
KFQD(AM) Anchorage AK 10 kw-U.
WRIK(AM) Brookport IL 500 w-D.
WNDZ(AM) Portage IN 2.5 kw-D, DA.
KKNO(AM) Gretna LA 250 w-D.
WBMD(AM) Baltimore MD 1 kw-D.
KJEL(AM) Lebanon MO 5 kw-D.
KERR(AM) Polson MT 50 kw-D, 1 kw-N, DA-N.
WAUG(AM) New Hope NC 500 w-D.
KMMJ(AM) Grand Island NE 10 kw-D, DA-1.
KKNK(AM) Carson City NV 10 kw-U, DA-2.
WNYS(AM) Canton NY 5 kw-D, 1 kw-N, DA-N.
KSEO(AM) Durant OK 250 w-D.
KXL(AM) Portland OR 50 kw-D, 20 kw-N, DA-2.
WMXH(AM) Olyphant PA 1.6 kw-D.
KAMA(AM) El Paso TX 10 kw-D, 1 kw-N, DA-1.
KOAL(AM) Price UT 10 kw-D, 6.8 kw-N, DA-N.
WPDX(AM) Clarksburg WV 1 kw-D.

760 khz Clear I-A
WJR(AM) Detroit MI 50 kw-U.
WURL(AM) Moody AL 1 kw-D.
KMTL(AM) Sherwood AR 10 kw-D.
KFMB(AM) San Diego CA 50 kw-U, DA-N.
KTLK(AM) Thornton CO 5 kw-D, 1 kw-N, DA-N.
WBDN(AM) Brandon FL 10 kw-D, 1 kw-N, DA-2.
KGU(AM) Honolulu HI 10 kw-D.
KCCV(AM) Overland Park KS 6 kw-D, DA.
WVNE(AM) Leicester MA 25 kw-D.
WCIS(AM) Morganton NC 500 w-D.
WCPS(AM) Tarboro NC 1 kw-D.
WCHP(AM) Champlain NY 25 kw-D, DA.
WORA(AM) Mayaguez PR 5 kw-U, DA-1.
WKNL(AM) Knoxville TN 2.5 kw-D.
WENO(AM) Nashville TN 1 kw-D.
KZXS(AM) San Antonio TX 50 kw-D, 1 kw-N, DA-2.

770 khz Clear I-A
WABC(AM) New York NY 50 kw-U.
*KCHU(AM) Valdez AK 9.7 kw-U.
WVNN(AM) Athens AL 10 kw-D, 250 w-N, DA-N.
KCBC(AM) Riverbank CA 50 kw-D, 1 kw-N, DA-2.
WWCN(AM) North Fort Myers FL 10 kw-D, 1 kw-N, DA-N.
WZCM(AM) Young Harris GA 750 w-D.
WCGW(AM) Nicholasville KY 1 kw-D.
KJCB(AM) Lafayette LA 1 kw-D, 500 w-N, DA-N.
*KUOM(AM) Minneapolis MN 5 kw-D.
WEW(AM) St. Louis MO 1 kw-D.
KATL(AM) Miles City MT 10 kw-D, 1 kw-N, DA-2.
WLWL(AM) Rockingham NC 5 kw-D.
KKOB(AM) Albuquerque NM 50 kw-U, DA-N.
WAIS(AM) Buchtel OH 1 kw-D.
KPBC(AM) Garland TX 10 kw-D, 1 kw-N, DA-2.
WYRV(AM) Cedar Bluff VA 5 kw-D.
KULL(AM) Seattle WA 50 kw-D, 5 kw-N, DA-2.

780 khz Clear I-A
WBBM(AM) Chicago IL 50 kw-U.
*KNOM(AM) Nome AK 10 kw-U.
WZZX(AM) Lineville AL 5 kw-D.
KAZM(AM) Sedona AZ 5 kw-D, 250 w-N, DA-N.
WLRM(AM) Ridgeland MS 5 kw-D.
WCKB(AM) Dunn NC 1 kw-D.
WWOL(AM) Forest City NC 1 kw-D.
WJAG(AM) Norfolk NE 1 kw-U (L-WBBM).
KROW(AM) Reno NV 50 kw-U, DA-N.
KSPI(AM) Stillwater OK 250 w-D.
WPTN(AM) Cookeville TN 1 kw-D.
WABS(AM) Arlington VA 5 kw-D.

790 khz Regional III
KCAM(AM) Glennallen AK 5 kw-U.
WTSK(AM) Tuscaloosa AL 5 kw-D, 36 w-N.
KURM(AM) Rogers AR 5 kw-D, 500 w-N, DA-N.
KKYR(AM) Texarkana AR 1 kw-D, 500 w-N, DA-N.
KNST(AM) Tucson AZ 1 kw-D, 250 w-N, DA-2.
KOQO(AM) Clovis CA 5 kw-D, 2.5 kw-N, DA-N.
KWSW(AM) Eureka CA 5 kw-D, 112 w-N.
KABC(AM) Los Angeles CA 5 kw-U, DA-N.
WLBE(AM) Leesburg FL 5 kw-D, 1 kw-N, DA-N.
WSWL(AM) Pensacola FL 1 kw-D.
WMRZ(AM) South Miami FL 25 kw-U, DA-N.
WQXI(AM) Atlanta GA 5 kw-D, 1 kw-N, DA-N.
WPIQ(AM) Brunswick GA 500 w-D, 115 w-N, DA-2.
WGRA(AM) Cairo GA 1 kw-D.
KKON(AM) Kealakekua HI 5 kw-D.
KSPD(AM) Boise ID 1 kw-D.
KBRV(AM) Soda Springs ID 5 kw-D.
WRMS(AM) Beardstown IL 500 w-D, DA.
KXXX(AM) Colby KS 5 kw-D.
WWKY(AM) Louisville KY 5 kw-D, 1 kw-N, DA-N.
WRUM(AM) Rumford ME 1 kw-D, 50 w-N.
WSGW(AM) Saginaw MI 5 kw-D, 1 kw-N, DA-2.
KGHL(AM) Billings MT 5 kw-U, DA-N.
WTNC(AM) Thomasville NC 1 kw-D, 50 w-N.
KFGO(AM) Fargo ND 5 kw-U, DA-N.
WTNY(AM) Watertown NY 1 kw-U, DA-N.
WLSV(AM) Wellsville NY 1 kw-D, 41 w-N.
WHTH(AM) Heath OH 1 kw-D, DA-N.
KWIL(AM) Albany OR 1 kw-D, DA-2.
WAEB(AM) Allentown PA 1 kw-U, DA-2.
WPIC(AM) Sharon PA 1 kw-D, 51 w-N.
WLKW(AM) Providence RI 5 kw-D, DA-N.
WRIT(AM) Bamberg-Denmark SC 1 k -D, 100 w-N.
WQSV(AM) Ashland City TN 500 w-U.
WETB(AM) Johnson City TN 5 kw-D, 72 w-N.
WMC(AM) Memphis TN 5 kw-U, DA-N.
KKBQ(AM) Houston TX 5 kw-D, DA-2.
KFYO(AM) Lubbock TX 5 kw-D, 1 kw-N, DA-3.
KUTA(AM) Blanding UT 1 kw-D, 113 w-N.
WSVG(AM) Mount Jackson VA 1 kw-D, 40 w-N.
WTAR(AM) Norfolk VA 5 kw-U, DA-1.
KGMI(AM) Bellingham WA 5 kw-D, 1 kw-N, DA-N.
KJRB(AM) Spokane WA 5 kw-U, DA-N.
WEAQ(AM) Eau Claire WI 5 kw-U, DA-N.

800 khz Clear (Mexican) I-A
KINY(AM) Juneau AK 10 kw-D, 5 kw-N.
WHOS(AM) Decatur AL 1 kw-D, 215 w-N.
WMGY(AM) Montgomery AL 1 kw-D, 193 w-N.
KAGH(AM) Crossett AR 250 w-D.
KVOM(AM) Morrilton AR 250 w-D, 42 w-N.
KHIS(AM) Bakersfield CA 250 w-D, 21.25 w-N.
KLTT(AM) Brighton CO 1 kw-D, DA.
WLAD(AM) Danbury CT 1 kw-D, 287 w-N.
WPLK(AM) Palatka FL 1 kw-D, 334 w-N.
WJAT(AM) Swainsboro GA 1 kw-D, 500 w-N.
KXIC(AM) Iowa City IA 1 kw-D, 199 w-N, DA-2.
WKZI(AM) Casey IL 250 w-U.

U.S. AM Stations by Frequency

WSHO(AM) New Orleans LA 1 kw-D, 233 w-N, DA-1.
WCCM(AM) Lawrence MA 1 kw-D.
KQAD(AM) Luverne MN 500 w-D, 80 w-N, DA-2.
KREI(AM) Farmington MO 1 kw-D, 150 w-N.
WKBC(AM) North Wilkesboro NC 1 kw-D, 308 w-N.
WTMR(AM) Camden NJ 5 kw-D, 500 w-N.
KQCV(AM) Oklahoma City OK 2.5 kw-D, 500 w-N, DA.
KPDQ(AM) Portland OR 1 kw-D, 500 w-N.
WVCQ(AM) Brockway PA 500 w-D, DA-2.
WCHA(AM) Chambersburg PA 1 kw-D, 196 w-N.
WDSC(AM) Dillon SC 1 kw-D, 382 w-N.
WPJM(AM) Greer SC 1 kw-D, 438 w-N.
WDEH(AM) Sweetwater TN 1 kw-D, 379 w-N.
KDDD(AM) Dumas TX 250 w-D.
KSOS(AM) Brigham City UT 1 kw-D, 32 w-N.
WSVS(AM) Crewe VA 5 kw-D, 275 w-N.
WDUX(AM) Waupaca WI 5 kw-D, 500 w-N, DA-1.
WKEE(AM) Huntington WV 5 kw-D, 185.3 w-N.

801 khz Clear II
KTWG(AM) Agana GU 10 kw-U.

810 khz Clear I-B
KGO(AM) San Francisco CA 50 kw-U, DA-1.
WGY(AM) Schenectady NY 50 kw-U.
KKGD(AM) Rifle CO 1 kw-D.
WSHF(AM) Hahira GA 2.5 kw-D.
WBIC(AM) Royston GA 250 w-D.
WDDD(AM) Johnston City IL 250 w-U, DA-N.
WSYW(AM) Indianapolis IN 250 w-D.
WEKG(AM) Jackson KY 5 kw-D.
WYRE(AM) Annapolis MD 250 w-D.
WBYY(AM) Rockford MI 500 w-D.
KCMO(AM) Kansas City MO 50 kw-D, 5 kw-N, DA-N.
KSWV(AM) Santa Fe NM 5 kw-D.
WEDO(AM) McKeesport PA 1 kw-D.
WKVM(AM) San Juan PR 50 kw-U, DA-1.
WQIZ(AM) St. George SC 5 kw-D.
KBHB(AM) Sturgis SD 21 kw-D.
WCTA(AM) Alamo TN 250 w-D, DA.
WMTS(AM) Murfreesboro TN 5 kw-D.
KCHG(AM) Somerset TX 250 w-D, DA.
WCYK(AM) Crozet VA 1 kw-D.
WKNV(AM) Dublin VA 350 w-D, DA.
KTBI(AM) Ephrata WA 50 kw-D.
WDMP(AM) Dodgeville WI 250 w-D.
WJJQ(AM) Tomahawk WI 10 kw-D, DA.

820 khz Clear I-A
WBAP(AM) Fort Worth TX 50 kw-U.
KCBF(AM) Fairbanks AK 50 kw-U.
WRFA(AM) Largo FL 50 kw-D, 1 kw-N, DA-2.
WSCR(AM) Chicago IL 5 kw-D.
*WSWI(AM) Evansville IN 250 w-D.
WQSI(AM) Frederick MD 4.3 kw-D, 430 w-N, DA-N.
WWFQ(AM) Paw Creek NC 2.5 kw-D, DA-2.
WIQT(AM) Horseheads NY 5 kw-D, 1 kw-N, DA-2.
*WNYC(AM) New York NY 10 kw-D, 1 kw-N, DA.
*WOSU(AM) Columbus OH 5 kw-D, 790 w-N, (L-WBAP Ft. Worth, Tex.)
KORC(AM) Waldport OR 1000 w-D, 15 w-N.
WWAM(AM) Jasper TN 5 kw-D.
WGGM(AM) Chester VA 10 kw-D, 1 kw-N, DA-2.
KGNW(AM) Burien-Seattle WA 50 kw-D, 5 kw-N, DA-2.

830 khz Clear I-A
WCCO(AM) Minneapolis MN 50 kw-U.
KABN(AM) Long Island AK 10 kw-U.
*KFLT(AM) Tucson AZ 50 kw-D, 1 kw-N, DA-N.
KNCO(AM) Grass Valley CA 5 kw-U.
KPLS(AM) Orange CA 2.5 kw-D, 1 kw-N, DA-N.
WRFM(AM) Hialeah FL 1 kw-D, DA-2.
KIKI(AM) Honolulu HI 10 kw-U.
WADU(AM) Norco LA 5 kw-D, 750 w-N, DA-2.
WCRN(AM) Cherry Valley MA 3 kw-D, 1 kw-N, DA-2.
WMMI(AM) Shepherd MI 1 kw-D.
KBOA(AM) Kennett MO 10 kw-D.
WWMO(AM) Eden NC 50 kw-D, 1.9 kw-N, DA-2.
WKTX(AM) Cortland OH 1 kw-D.
KUYO(AM) Evansville WY 10 kw-D.

840 khz Clear I-A
WHAS(AM) Louisville KY 50 kw-U.
*KSDP(AM) Sand Point AK 1 kw-U.
WBHY(AM) Mobile AL 10 kw-D.
KRKL(AM) Yountville CA 2.5 kw-D, 250 w-N, DA-D.
WRYM(AM) New Britain CT 1 kw-D.
WPGS(AM) Mims FL 250 w-D.
WHGH(AM) Thomasville GA 10 kw-D.
KWDF(AM) Ball LA 10 kw-D.
WKDI(AM) Denton MD 1 kw-D, DA.
WKPN(AM) West Point NE 5 kw-D.
KVEG(AM) North Las Vegas NV 50 kw-D, 25 kw-N, DA-2.
KDBS(AM) Eugene OR 1 kw-D, 220 w-N.
KSWB(AM) Seaside OR 1 kw-D, 500 w-N.
WVPO(AM) Stroudsburg PA 250 w-D.
WXEW(AM) Yabucoa PR 5 kw-W, 1 kw-N, DA-N.
WCTG(AM) Columbia SC 50 kw-D, DA.
KVJY(AM) Pharr TX 5 kw-D, 1 kw-N, DA-2.
WKTR(AM) Earlysville VA 8.2 kw-D.
WLPY(AM) Purcellville VA 250 w-D, DA.

850 khz Clear (U.S. & Mexican) I-B
KOA(AM) Denver CO 50 kw-U.
KICY(AM) Nome AK 10 kw-U.
WYDE(AM) Birmingham AL 50 kw-D.
KGKO(AM) Benton AR 1 kw-D.
KCTQ(AM) Thousand Oaks CA 500 w-D, 250 w-N, DA.
WREF(AM) Ridgefield CT 2.5 kw.
WRUF(AM) Gainesville FL 5 kw-U, DA-N.

WEAT(AM) West Palm Beach FL 5 kw-D, 1 kw-N, DA-2.
WCUG(AM) Cuthbert GA 500 w-D.
WPTB(AM) Statesboro GA 1 kw-U, DA-N.
KHLO(AM) Hilo HI 5 kw-U.
WAIT(AM) Crystal Lake IL 2.5 kw-D.
WHDH(AM) Boston MA 50 kw-U, DA-2.
WKBZ(AM) Muskegon MI 1 kw-U, DA-1.
WWJC(AM) Duluth MN 10 kw-D.
*KFUO(AM) Clayton MO 5 kw-D.
WQST(AM) Forest MS 10 kw-D, DA.
WLRC(AM) Walnut MS 963 w-D.
WYLT(AM) Raleigh NC 10 kw-D, 5 kw-N, DA-N.
WYLF(AM) Penn Yan NY 1 kw-D, 500 w-N.
WRMR(AM) Cleveland OH 10 kw-D, 5 kw-N, DA-2.
KRPT(AM) Anadarko OK 500 w-D.
WJAC(AM) Johnstown PA 10 kw-D, DA-1.
WEEU(AM) Reading PA 1 kw-D, DA-N.
WABA(AM) Aguadilla PR 5 kw-D, 1 kw-N.
WPFD(AM) Fairview TN 500 w-D.
WUTK(AM) Knoxville TN 50 kw-D, DA.
KEYH(AM) Houston TX 10 kw-D, DA.
WNIS(AM) Norfolk VA 50 kw-D, 25 kw-N, DA-2.
KMTT(AM) Tacoma WA 10 kw-D, 1 kw-N, DA.

860 khz Clear (Canadian) I-A
WHRT(AM) Hartselle AL 250 w-D, 17 w-N.
WAMI(AM) Opp AL 1 kw-D, 47 w-N.
KOSE(AM) Osceola AR 1 kw-D, 20 w-N.
KWRF(AM) Warren AR 250 w-D, 55 w-N.
KVVA(AM) Phoenix AZ 1 kw-U, DA.
KTRB(AM) Modesto CA 50 kw-D, 10 kw-N, DA-3.
WRFB(AM) Cocoa FL 5 kw-D, 121 w-N.
WGUL(AM) Dunedin FL 2 kw-D, 1.5 kw-N, DA-2.
WAEC(AM) Atlanta GA 5 kw-D.
WDMG(AM) Douglas GA 5 kw-U, DA.
KWPC(AM) Muscatine IA 250 w-D, 8w-N.
WGOM(AM) Marion IN 1 kw-D, 500 w-N, DA-2.
KKOW(AM) Pittsburg KS 10 kw-D, 5 kw-N, DA-N.
WSON(AM) Henderson KY 500 w-U, DA-N.
WSBS(AM) Great Barrington MA 2.7 kw-D.
WBGR(AM) Baltimore MD 2.5 kw-D, 66 w-N, DA-2.
KNUJ(AM) New Ulm MN 1 kw-U.
WFMO(AM) Fairmont NC 1 kw-D.
WACB(AM) Taylorsville NC 250 w-D.
KARS(AM) Belen NM 250 w-D, DA.
KZTW(AM) Troutdale OR 20 kw-D, 500 w-N, DA-2.
WTEL(AM) Philadelphia PA 10 kw-D, DA.
WYJZ(AM) Pittsburgh PA 1 kw-D, DA.
WLBG(AM) Laurens SC 1 kw-U.
WTZX(AM) Sparta TN 1 kw-D, 9.9 w-N.
KFST(AM) Fort Stockton TX 250 w-D.
KPAN(AM) Hereford TX 250 w-D.
KSFA(AM) Nacogdoches TX 1 kw-D, 500 w-N.
KONO(AM) San Antonio TX 5 kw-D, 1 kw-N, DA-N.
KLZX(AM) Salt Lake City UT 10 kw-D, 195.8 w-N, 3 kw-CH.
WEVA(AM) Emporia VA 1 kw-D.
WNOV(AM) Milwaukee WI 250 w-D, 5 w-N.
WOAY(AM) Oak Hill WV 10 kw-D, 11 kw-N, 5 kw-CH.

870 khz Clear I-A
WWL(AM) New Orleans LA 50 kw-U, DA-1.
*KSKO(AM) McGrath AK 5 kw-U.
WQRX(AM) Valley Head AL 10 kw-D.
KIEV(AM) Glendale CA 10 kw-D, 1 kw-N, DA-2.
KAIM(AM) Honolulu HI 50 kw-U, DA-1.
WMTL(AM) Leitchfield KY 500 w-D.
WLAM(AM) Gorham ME 10 kw-D.
*WKAR(AM) East Lansing MI 10 kw-D, DA.
KPRM(AM) Park Rapids MN 25 kw-D, 1 kw-N, DA-N.
KAAN(AM) Bethany MO 1 kw-D.
KOWA(AM) Laughlin NV 10 kw-D, 1 kw-N, DA-2.
WHCU(AM) Ithaca NY 5 kw-U, DA-1.
WQBS(AM) San Juan PR 10 kw-U, DA-1.
*WZMC(AM) Colonial Heights TN 10 kw-D.
KFJZ(AM) Fort Worth TX 500 w-D.
WFLO(AM) Farmville VA 1 kw-D.
NEW AM Berlin VT 5 kw-U, DA-1.
KORD(AM) Pasco WA 10 kw-U.

880 khz Clear I-A
WCBS(AM) New York NY 50 kw-U.
KGHT(AM) Sheridan AR 220 w.
KUTE(AM) Desert Hot Springs CA 3 w-D, 900 w-N, DA-2.
KKMC(AM) Gonzales CA 10 kw-D, 1 kw-N, DA-2.
KNZS(AM) Montecito CA 780 w-D, 220 w-N, DA-2.
NEW AM Olviedo FL
WBKZ(AM) Jefferson GA 5 kw-D.
WINU(AM) Highland IL 1 kw-D, DA.
KJJR(AM) Whitefish MT 10 kw-D, 500 w-N.
WRRZ(AM) Clinton NC 1 kw-D.
WMIY(AM) Fairview NC 1.1 kw-D, DA.
WPIP(AM) Winston-Salem NC 900 w-D.
KRVN(AM) Lexington NE 50 kw-D, DA-N.
KHAC(AM) Tse Bonito NM 10 kw-D, 430 w-N.
WRFD(AM) Columbus-Worthington OH 9 kw-D.
KWIP(AM) Dallas OR 5 kw-D, 1 kw-N.
KTMT(AM) Phoenix OR 1 kw-U.
WYKO(AM) Sabana Grande PR 1 kw-D, 500 w-N.
WBAJ(AM) Blythwood SC 1.6 kw-D, DA.
WMDB(AM) Nashville TN 2.5 kw-D.
KJOJ(AM) Conroe TX 10 kw-D, 1 kw-N, DA-2.
NEW AM Madisonville TX 1 kw-D, 1 kw-N.
WBLU(AM) Moneta NC 1 kw-D.
KIXI(AM) Mercer Island-Seattle WA 50 kw-D, 10 kw-N, DA-2.
WMEQ(AM) Menomonie WI 210 w-D.

890 khz Clear I-A
WLS(AM) Chicago IL 50 kw-U.
*KBBI(AM) Homer AK 10 kw-U.
WBMA(AM) Dedham MA 1 kw-D, 1 kw-N, DA-2.

KGGN(AM) Gladstone MO 1 kw-D, DA.
WQIS(AM) Laurel MS 10 kw-D.
WHNC(AM) Henderson NC 1 kw-D.
KQLX(AM) Lisbon ND 1 kw-D.
KBYE(AM) Oklahoma City OK 1 kw-D.
WFKJ(AM) Cashtown PA 1 kw-D.
WFAB(AM) Ceiba PR 250 w-U.
KVOZ(AM) Laredo TX 10 kw-D, 1 kw-N, DA-N.
KDXU(AM) St. George UT 10 kw-U, DA-N.
WCQR(AM) Fairlawn VA 2.5 kw-D.

900 khz Clear (Mexican) I-A
KZPA(AM) Fort Yukon AK 5 kw-U.
WATV(AM) Birmingham AL 1 kw-U.
WGOK(AM) Mobile AL 1 kw-D, 381 w-N, DA-2.
WOZK(AM) Ozark AL 1 kw-D, 78 w-N.
KHOZ(AM) Harrison AR 1 kw-D.
KBIF(AM) Fresno CA 1 kw-D, 500 w-N, DA-N.
KGRB(AM) West Covina CA 500 w-D, DA.
WSSR(AM) Georgetown DE 10 kw-D, 1 w-N, DA-1.
WSWN(AM) Belle Glade FL 1 kw-D, 26 w-N.
WMOP(AM) Ocala FL 5 kw.
WJTH(AM) Calhoun GA 1 kw-D, 266 w-N.
WBML(AM) Macon GA 2 kw-D, 145 w-N.
WEAS(AM) Savannah GA 5 kw-D, 157 w-N.
KNUI(AM) Kahului HI 5 kw-U.
KSGL(AM) Wichita KS 250 w-D, 28 w-N, DA-2.
WWLK(AM) Eddyville KY 1 kw-D, 250 w-N, DA-2.
WFIA(AM) Louisville KY 1 kw-D.
WLSI(AM) Pikeville KY 5 kw-D.
KICR(AM) Oakdale LA 250 w-D.
WILC(AM) Laurel MD 1.9 kw-D, 500 w-N.
WCLZ(AM) Brunswick ME 1 kw-D, 66 w-N.
WSNQ(AM) Gaylord MI 1 kw-D, 101 w-N.
*KTIS(AM) Minneapolis MN 25 kw-D, 300 w-N, DA-2.
KFAL(AM) Fulton MO 1 kw-D, 121 w-N.
WDDT(AM) Greenville MS 1 kw-D, 109 w-N.
WYCV(AM) Granite Falls NC 500 w-D, 251 w-N.
WAYN(AM) Rockingham NC 1 kw-D, DA-2.
WIAM(AM) Williamston NC 1 kw-D, 258 w-N.
KJSK(AM) Columbus NE 1 kw-D, 66 w-N.
WBRV(AM) Boonville NY 1 kw-D, 52 w-N.
WBGG(AM) Saratoga Springs NY 250 w-U.
WCER(AM) Canton OH 500 w-D, 78 w-N.
WFRO(AM) Fremont OH 500 w-D, 286.9-N, DA-2.
WCPA(AM) Clearfield PA 2.5 kw-D, 500 w-N, DA-1.
WURD(AM) Philadelphia PA 1 kw-D, 42 w-N, DA-2.
WGSN(AM) North Myrtle Beach SC 500 w-D, DA.
WKXV(AM) Knoxville TN 1 kw-D, 258 w-N.
WCOR(AM) Lebanon TN 500 w-D, 136 w-N.
KALT(AM) Atlanta TX 1 kw-D.
KAWA(AM) Floydada TX 250 w-D.
KCLW(AM) Hamilton TX 250 w-D.
WCBX(AM) Bassett VA 500 w-U, DA-2.
WKDW(AM) Staunton VA 2.5 kw-D, 128 w-N.
KKRT(AM) Wenatchee WA 1 kw-D, 78 w-N.
WATK(AM) Antigo WI 250 w-D, 196 w-N.
WNNO(AM) Wisconsin Dells WI 1 kw-D, 229 w-N.

910 khz Regional III
KIYU(AM) Galena AK 5 kw-U.
KLCN(AM) Blytheville AR 5 kw-D, 85 w-N.
KAMD(AM) Camden AR 5 kw-D, 500 w-N, DA-2.
KFYI(AM) Phoenix AZ 5 kw-U, DA-N.
KECR(AM) El Cajon CA 5 kw-U, DA-2.
KVVQ(AM) Hesperia CA 700 w-D, 500 w-N, DA-N.
KNEW(AM) Oakland CA 5 kw-U, DA.
KOXR(AM) Oxnard CA 5 kw-D, 1 kw-N, DA-2.
*KPOF(AM) Denver CO 5 kw-D, 1 kw-N.
WNEZ(AM) New Britain CT 5 kw-U, DA-N.
WFNS(AM) Plant City FL 5 kw-U, DA-1.
WFVR(AM) Valdosta GA 5 kw-U, DA-1.
*WSUI(AM) Iowa City IA 5 kw-D, DA-N.
WAKO(AM) Lawrenceville IL 500 w-D, 59 w-N, DA-2.
KINA(AM) Salina KS 500 w-D, 29 w-N, DA-2.
WKEQ(AM) Burnside KY 500 w-D.
WNDC(AM) Baton Rouge LA 1 kw-D, DA-1.
WABI(AM) Bangor ME 5 kw-U, DA-N.
WLLJ(AM) Cassopolis MI 1 kw-D, 35 w-N, DA-1.
WFDF(AM) Flint MI 5 kw-D, 1 kw-N, DA-2.
WALT(AM) Meridian MS 1 kw-D.
KBLG(AM) Billings MT 5 kw-D, 63 w-N.
KCJB(AM) Minot ND 5 kw-D, 1 kw-N, DA-2.
WLAS(AM) Jacksonville NC 5 kw-U, DA-N.
KBIM(AM) Roswell NM 5 kw-D, 500 w-N, DA-N.
WRKL(AM) New City NY 1 kw-D.
WBRJ(AM) Marietta OH 5 kw-D, 61 w-N, DA-2.
WPFB(AM) Middletown OH 5 kw-D, 100 w-N.
KVIS(AM) Miami OK 1 kw-D, DA-1.
KURY(AM) Brookings OR 1 kw-D.
WAVL(AM) Apollo PA 5 kw-D, DA.
WGBI(AM) Scranton PA 1 kw-D, 500 w-N.
WSBA(AM) York PA 5 kw-D, 1 kw-N, DA-2.
WPRP(AM) Ponce PR 5 kw-U.
WTMZ(AM) Dorchester Terrace-Brentwood SC 500 w-U, DA-N.
WORD(AM) Spartanburg SC 5 kw-D, 1 kw-N, DA-2.
KJJQ(AM) Volga SD 500 w-D, DA.
WMRB(AM) Columbia TN 500 w-D, 88 w-N.
WJCW(AM) Johnson City TN 5 kw-D, 1 kw-N, DA-N.
WEPG(AM) South Pittsburg TN 5 kw-D, 950 w-N.
KNAF(AM) Fredricksburg TX 1 kw-D, 174 w-N.
KRIO(AM) McAllen TX 5 kw-D, DA-4.
KXEB(AM) Sherman TX 1 kw-D.
KALL(AM) Salt Lake City UT 5 kw-D, 1 kw-N, DA-2.
WRVH(AM) Richmond VA 1 kw-D.
WWWR(AM) Roanoke VA 1 kw-D, 84 w-N.
WNHV(AM) White River Junction VT 1 kw-D, 84 w-N.

U.S. AM Stations by Frequency

KKSN(AM) Vancouver WA 5 kw-U, DA-2.
WHSM(AM) Hayward WI 5 kw-D, 75 w-N.
WDOR(AM) Sturgeon Bay WI 1 kw-D.

920 khz Regional III

KSRM(AM) Soldotna AK 5 kw-U.
WKYD(AM) Andalusia AL 5 kw-D, 500 w-N, DA-N.
WJRD(AM) Russellville AL 1 kw-D, 43 w-N.
KARN(AM) Little Rock AR 5 kw-U, DA-N.
KLOC(AM) Ceres CA 2.5 kw-U, DA-2.
KDES(AM) Palm Springs CA 5 kw-D, 1 kw-N, DA-2.
KVEC(AM) San Luis Obispo CA 1 kw-D, 500 w-N.
KLMR(AM) Lamar CO 5 kw-D, 500 w-N, DA-N.
WTRS(AM) Dunellon FL 500 w-D.
WMEL(AM) Melbourne FL 5 kw-D, 1 kw-N, DA-2.
WAFS(AM) Atlanta GA 5 kw-D, 1 kw-N.
WVOH(AM) Hazlehurst GA 500 w-D, 39 w-N.
*KYFR(AM) Shenandoah IA 5 kw-D, 2.5 w-N, DA-2.
WGNU(AM) Granite City IL 500 w-U, DA-2.
WMOK(AM) Metropolis IL 1 kw-D, 73 w-N.
*WBAA(AM) West Lafayette IN 5 kw-D, 1 kw-N, DA-N.
WTCW(AM) Whitesburg KY 5 kw-D, 47 w-N.
WBOX(AM) Bogalusa LA 1 kw, DA-N.
KTOC(AM) Jonesboro LA 1 kw-D.
WPTX(AM) Lexington Park MD 5 kw-D, 1 kw-N, DA-2.
WMPL(AM) Hancock MI 1 kw-D, 206 w-N.
KDHL(AM) Faribault MN 5 kw-U, DA-2.
KWAD(AM) Wadena MN 1 kw-U, DA-N.
KWYS(AM) West Yellowstone MT 1 kw-D.
WBBB(AM) Burlington NC 5 kw-D, DA-D.
WPTL(AM) Canton NC 500 w-D, 38 w-N.
WTTM(AM) Trenton NJ 1 kw-U, DA-1.
KQEO(AM) Albuquerque NM 1 kw-D, 500 w-N, DA-N.
KORK(AM) Las Vegas NV 5 kw-D, 500 w-N, DA-2.
KQLO(AM) Reno NV 5 kw-D, 1 kw-N, DA-N.
WKRT(AM) Cortland NY 1 kw-D, 500 w-N, DA-N.
WGHQ(AM) Kingston NY 5 kw-D, 77 w-N, DA-1.
WIRD(AM) Lake Placid NY 5 kw-D, 250 w-N.
WMNI(AM) Columbus OH 1 kw-D, 500 w-N, DA-2.
KSHO(AM) Lebanon OR 1 kw-U, DA-1.
WKVA(AM) Lewistown PA 1 kw-D, 500 w-N, DA-N.
WHJJ(AM) Providence RI 5 kw-U, DA-N.
KKLS(AM) Rapid City SD 5 kw-D, 100-N. DA-2.
WLIV(AM) Livingston TN 1 kw-D.
KBNA(AM) El Paso TX 1 kw-D, 360 w-N, DA-N.
*KENT(AM) Odessa TX 1 kw-D, 500 w-N, DA-1.
KYST(AM) Texas City TX 5 kw-D, 1 kw-N, DA-2.
KVEL(AM) Vernal UT 4.5 kw-D, 1 kw-N, DA-N.
KCPL(AM) Olympia WA 5 kw-D, 500 w-N, DA-2.
KXLY(AM) Spokane WA 5 kw-U.
WOKY(AM) Milwaukee WI 5 kw-D, 1 kw-N, DA-2.
WMMN(AM) Fairmont WV 5 kw-U, DA-N.

930 khz Regional III

KTKN(AM) Ketchikan AK 5 kw-D, 1 kw-N.
KNSA(AM) Unalakleet AK 2.5 kw-U.
WYNI(AM) Monroeville AL 5 kw-D, 48 w-N.
WJBY(AM) Rainbow City AL 5 kw-D, 500 w-N, DA-2.
KAPR(AM) Douglas AZ 2.5 kw-D.
KAFF(AM) Flagstaff AZ 5 kw-D, 50 w-N.
KKHJ(AM) Los Angeles CA 5 kw-U, DA-N.
KKXX(AM) Paradise CA 1 kw-D, 37 w-N.
KIUP(AM) Durango CO 5 kw-D, 1 kw-N, DA-N.
KRKY(AM) Granby CO 4.5 kw-D.
WYUS(AM) Milford DE 500 w-D, 100 w-N, DA-1.
WLVF(AM) Haines City FL 500 w-D, DA.
WNZS(AM) Jacksonville FL 5 kw-U, DA-N.
WKXY(AM) Sarasota FL 5 kw-D, 2.5 w-N, DA-2.
WMGR(AM) Bainbridge GA 5 kw-D, 500 w-N.
KSEI(AM) Pocatello ID 5 kw-U, DA-N.
WTAD(AM) Quincy IL 5 kw-D, 1 kw-N, DA-N.
WAUR(AM) Sandwich IL 2.5 kw-D, 2.2 kw-N, DA-2.
WHON(AM) Centerville IN 500 w-D, 114 w-N, DA-2.
WKCT(AM) Bowling Green KY 5 kw-D, 500 w-N, DA-N.
WFMD(AM) Frederick MD 5 kw-D, 2.5 kw-N, DA-2.
WBCK(AM) Battle Creek MI 5 kw-D, 1 kw-N, DA-2.
KKIN(AM) Aitkin MN 2.5 kw-D, 400 w-N.
KWOC(AM) Poplar Bluff MO 5 kw-D, 500 w-N, DA-N.
WSLI(AM) Jackson MS 5 kw-U, DA-N.
KLCY(AM) East Missoula MT 5 kw-D, 1 kw-N, DA-N.
WYFQ(AM) Charlotte NC 5 kw-D, 1 kw-N, DA-N.
WRRF(AM) Washington NC 5 kw-D, 1 kw-N, DA-N.
KOGA(AM) Ogallala NE 5 kw-U, DA-2.
WZNN(AM) Rochester NH 5 kw-U, DA-N.
WPAT(AM) Paterson NJ 5 kw-U, DA-2.
KCCC(AM) Carlsbad NM 1 kw-D, 60 w-N.
WBEN(AM) Buffalo NY 5 kw-U, DA-N.
WIZR(AM) Johnstown NY 1 kw-D.
WEOL(AM) Elyria OH 1 kw-U, DA-2.
WKY(AM) Oklahoma City OK 5 kw-U, DA-N.
KAGI(AM) Grants Pass OR 5 kw-D, 1 kw-N, DA-N.
WCNR(AM) Bloomsburg PA 1 kw-D, 23 w-N.
WEKO(AM) Cabo Rojo PR 2.5 kw-U.
KSDN(AM) Aberdeen SD 5 kw-D, 1 kw-N, DA-2.
WSEV(AM) Sevierville TN 5 kw-D, 148 w-N.
WTNR(AM) Waynesboro TN 500 w-D.
KDET(AM) Center TX 1 kw-D, 36 w-N.
KLUP(AM) Terrell Hills TX 5 kw-D, 1 kw-N, DA-N.
WLLL(AM) Lynchburg VA 5 kw-D, 49 w-N.
KBFW(AM) Bellingham-Ferndale WA 1 kw-D, 500 w-N, DA-N.
KZTA(AM) Yakima WA 1 kw-D, 127 w-N.
*WLBL(AM) Auburndale WI 5 kw-D.
WRVC(AM) Huntington WV 5 kw-D, 1 kw-N, DA-N.
KROE(AM) Sheridan WY 5 kw-D, 117 w-N.

936 khz

KSAI(AM) Saipan MP 5 kw-U.

940 khz Clear (Canadian & Mexican) I-B

KWFM(AM) Tucson AZ 5 kw-D, 1 kw-N, DA-2.
KFRE(AM) Fresno CA 50 kw-U, DA-2.
WINE(AM) Brookfield CT 1 kw-D, 4 w-N.
WLQH(AM) Chiefland FL 1 kw-D.
WINZ(AM) Miami FL 50 kw-D, 10 kw-N.
WMAZ(AM) Macon GA 50 kw-D, 10 kw-N, DA-N.
KDEO(AM) Waipahu HI 10 kw-U.
KIOA(AM) Des Moines IA 10 kw-D, 5 kw-N, DA-2.
WMIX(AM) Mt. Vernon IL 5 kw-D, 1.5 kw-N, DA-2.
WCND(AM) Shelbyville KY 250 w-D.
WYLD(AM) New Orleans LA 10 kw-D, 500 w-N, DA-2.
WGFP(AM) Webster MA 1 kw-D.
WCSY(AM) South Haven MI 1 kw-D, 6 w-N, DA-D.
WIDG(AM) St. Ignace MI 5 kw-D.
KSWM(AM) Aurora MO 1 kw-U.
WCPC(AM) Houston MS 50 kw-D, 250 w-N, DA-2.
WKYK(AM) Burnsville NC 5 kw-D, 250 w-N, DA-N.
KVSH(AM) Valentine NE 5 kw-D, 19.6 w-N.
WCIT(AM) Lima OH 250 w-D, DA-2.
KGRL(AM) Bend OR 10 kw-D, 60 w-N, DA-2.
KWBY(AM) Woodburn OR 250 w-D, 200 w-N.
WESA(AM) Charleroi PA 250 w-D, 5 w-N, U.
WGRP(AM) Greenville PA 1 kw-D, DA.
WADV(AM) Lebanon PA 1 kw-D, 5 w-N.
*WIPR(AM) San Juan PR 10 kw-U, DA-1.
WECO(AM) Wartburg TN 5 kw-D.
KIXZ(AM) Amarillo TX 5 kw-D, 1 kw-N, DA-2.
KTON(AM) Belton TX 1 kw-D, DA.
KTWN(AM) Texarkana TX 2.5 kw-D, 11 w-N.
KBRE(AM) Cedar City UT 10 kw-D.
WNRG(AM) Grundy VA 5 kw-D, 14 w-N.
WKGM(AM) Smithfield VA 10 kw-D, 3.21 kw-N, DA-N.
WFAW(AM) Fort Atkinson WI 500 w-D, 550 w-N, DA-2.
WCSW(AM) Shell Lake WI 1 kw-D.
WRRD(AM) Blennerhassett WV 480 w-D, DA.

950 khz Regional III

KSWD(AM) Seward AK 1 kw-U.
WSYA(AM) Montgomery AL 1 kw-U, DA-N.
KXJK(AM) Forrest City AR 5 kw-D, 500 w-N.
KFSA(AM) Fort Smith AR 1 kw-D, 500 w-N, DA-2.
KAHI(AM) Auburn CA 5 kw-D, 4.2 kw-N, DA-2.
KYGO(AM) Denver CO 5 kw-U, DA-1.
WOMX(AM) Orlando FL 5 kw-U, DA-N.
WGTA(AM) Summerville GA 5 kw-D, 140 w-N.
WGOV(AM) Valdosta GA 5 kw-D, 1 kw-N, DA-N.
KOEL(AM) Oelwein IA 5 kw-D, 500 w-N, DA-2.
KKIC(AM) Boise ID 5 kw-D, 35 w-N.
KOZE(AM) Lewiston ID 5 kw-D, 1 kw-N, DA-2.
WJPC(AM) Chicago IL 1 kw-D, 5 kw-N, DA-N.
WXLW(AM) Indianapolis IN 5 kw-D, 117 w-N, DA-2.
KJRG(AM) Newton KS 500 w-D, 147 w-N.
WYWY(AM) Barbourville KY 1 kw-D.
KRRP(AM) Coushatta LA 500 w-D, 209 w-N, DA-2.
WROL(AM) Boston MA 5 kw-D.
WCTN(AM) Potomac-Cabin John MD 2.5 kw-D, 47 w-N, DA-2.
WWJ(AM) Detroit MI 5 kw-U, DA-N.
KJJO(AM) St. Louis Park MN 1 kw-U, DA-2.
KLIK(AM) Jefferson City MO 5 kw-D, 500 w-N, DA-N.
WBKH(AM) Hattiesburg MS 5 kw-D.
KMTX(AM) Helena MT 5 kw-U, DA-N.
WPET(AM) Greensboro NC 500 w-D.
KNFT(AM) Bayard NM 5 kw-D.
KDCE(AM) Espanola NM 4.2 kw-D, 90 w-N.
WHVW(AM) Hyde Park NY 500 w-D, 57 w-N.
WBBF(AM) Rochester NY 1 kw-U, DA-2.
WIBX(AM) Utica NY 5 kw-U, DA-1.
WDIG(AM) Steubenville OH 1 kw-D, DA.
KTBR(AM) Roseburg OR 1 kw-D.
WNCC(AM) Barnesboro PA 500 w-D.
WPEN(AM) Philadelphia PA 5 kw-U, DA-N.
WMCJ(AM) Moncks Corner SC 500 w-D.
WSPA(AM) Spartanburg SC 5 kw-U, DA-N.
KWAT(AM) Watertown SD 1 kw-U, DA-N.
WAKM(AM) Franklin TN 1 kw-D, 80 w-N.
KDSX(AM) Denison-Sherman TX 500 w-U, DA-2.
KPRC(AM) Houston TX 5 kw-U, DA-N.
KXTQ(AM) Lubbock TX 5 kw-D, 500 w-N, DA-2.
WXGI(AM) Richmond VA 5 kw-D, 64 w-N.
KJR(AM) Seattle WA 5 kw-U, DA-N.
WERL(AM) Eagle River WI 1 kw-D, 51 w-N.
WCNZ(AM) Sheboygan WI 500 w-D, DA.
WQBE(AM) Charleston WV 5 kw-D, 1 kw-N, DA-N.
KMER(AM) Kemmerer WY 5 kw-D, 500 w-N.

960 khz Regional III

WERC(AM) Birmingham AL 5 kw-U, DA-N.
WLPR(AM) Prichard AL 5 kw-U, DA-N.
KCGS(AM) Marshall AR 5 kw-D.
KOOL(AM) Phoenix AZ 5 kw-U, DA-N.
KZXY(AM) Apple Valley CA 5 kw-D, 400 w-N, DA-2.
KCLL(AM) Lompoc CA 500 w-U, DA-N.
KABL(AM) Oakland CA 5 kw-U, DA-1.
WELI(AM) New Haven CT 5 kw-U, DA-N.
WGRO(AM) Lake City FL 500 w-D, 1 kw-N, DA-N.
WJCM(AM) Sebring FL 5 kw-D, 1 kw-N, DA-1.
WJYZ(AM) Albany GA 5 kw-D, DA.
WRFC(AM) Athens GA 5 kw-D, 2.5 kw-N, DA-N.
KMA(AM) Shenandoah IA 5 kw-U, DA-N.
KSRA(AM) Salmon ID 1 kw-D.
*WDLM(AM) East Moline IL 1 kw-D, 102 w-N, DA-2.
WSBT(AM) South Bend IN 5 kw-U, DA-2.
WPRT(AM) Prestonsburg KY 5 kw-D.
KROF(AM) Abbeville LA 1 kw-D, 95 w-N.
WFGL(AM) Fitchburg MA 2.5 kw-D, 1 kw-N, DA-2.
WTGM(AM) Salisbury MD 5 kw-U, DA-2.
WHAK(AM) Rogers City MI 5 kw-D.
KLTF(AM) Little Falls MN 5 kw-D, 35 w-N.
KZIM(AM) Cape Girardeau MO 5 kw-D, 500 w-N, DA-N.
WABG(AM) Greenwood MS 1 kw-D, 500 w-N, DA-N.
KFLN(AM) Baker MT 5 kw-D, 91 w-N.
WAAK(AM) Dallas NC 1 kw-D, 500 w-N, DA-N.
WRNS(AM) Kinston NC 5 kw-D, 1 kw-N, DA-N.
KNEB(AM) Scottsbluff NE 1 kw-D, 500 w-N, DA-2.
KNDN(AM) Farmington NM 5 kw-D, 163 w-N.
WEAV(AM) Plattsburgh NY 5 kw-U, DA-2.
WKVX(AM) Wooster OH 1 kw-D, 32 w-N.
KGWA(AM) Enid OK 1 kw-U, DA-1.
KLAD(AM) Klamath Falls OR 5 kw-U.
WHYL(AM) Carlisle PA 5 kw-D, DA.
WQLE(AM) Kane PA 1 kw-D, 48 w-N.
WPMR(AM) Mount Pocono PA 1 kw-D, 24 w-N, DA-2.
WATS(AM) Sayre PA 5 kw-D.
WKVN(AM) Quebradillas PR 500 w-D, 1 kw-N, DA-2.
WBEU(AM) Beaufort SC 1 kw-D.
WEAB(AM) Adamsville TN 500 w-D.
WQLA(AM) La Follette TN 1 kw-D.
WBMC(AM) McMinnville TN 500 w-D.
KIMP(AM) Mount Pleasant TX 1 kw-D, 75 w-N.
KGKL(AM) San Angelo TX 5 kw-D, 1 kw-N, DA-N.
KOVO(AM) Provo UT 5 kw-D, 1080 w-N, DA-N.
WFIR(AM) Roanoke VA 5 kw-U, DA-N.
KALE(AM) Richland WA 5 kw-D, 1 kw-N, DA-N.
WTCH(AM) Shawano WI 1 kw-U, DA-N.

970 khz Regional III

KIAK(AM) Fairbanks AK 5 kw-U.
WERH(AM) Hamilton AL 5 kw-D.
WTBF(AM) Troy AL 5 kw-D, 500 w-N, DA-N.
KNEA(AM) Jonesboro AR 1 kw-D, 41 w-N.
KVWM(AM) Show Low AZ 5 kw-D, 114 w-N.
KAFY(AM) Bakersfield CA 1 kw-D, 5 kw-N, DA-2.
KCLB(AM) Coachella CA 5 kw-D, 1 kw-N, DA-2.
KBEE(AM) Modesto CA 1 kw-U, DA-2.
KFEL(AM) Pueblo CO 3.2 kw-D, 184 w-N.
WVOJ(AM) Jacksonville FL 500 w-U, DA-1.
WFLA(AM) Tampa FL 5 kw-U, DA-2.
WNIV(AM) Atlanta GA 5 kw-D, 39 w-N.
WVOP(AM) Vidalia GA 5 kw-D.
KBBK(AM) Rupert ID 2.5 kw-D.
WMAY(AM) Springfield IL 1 kw-D, 500 w-N, DA-2.
WFSR(AM) Harlan KY 5 kw-D, 94 w-N.
WAVG(AM) Louisville KY 5 kw-U, DA-2.
KSYL(AM) Alexandria LA 1 kw-U, DA-N.
WESO(AM) Southbridge MA 1 kw-D, 21 w-N.
WAMD(AM) Aberdeen MD 500 w-U, DA-2.
WZAN(AM) Portland ME 5 kw-U, DA-N.
WMVN(AM) Ishpeming MI 5 kw-D.
WKHM(AM) Jackson MI 1 kw-U, DA-2.
KQAQ(AM) Austin MN 5 kw-D, 500 w-N, DA-2.
WRKN(AM) Brandon MS 1 kw-D, DA.
KCTR(AM) Billings MT 5 kw-U, DA-N.
WRCS(AM) Ahoskie NC 1 kw-D.
WWIT(AM) Canton NC 5 kw-D.
WDAY(AM) Fargo ND 5 kw-U, DA-N.
*KJLT(AM) North Platte NE 5 kw-D, 55 w-N.
WWDJ(AM) Hackensack NJ 5 kw-U, DA-2.
KNUU(AM) Paradise NV 5 kw-D, 500 w-N, DA-2.
WNED(AM) Buffalo NY 5 kw-U, DA-1.
WCHN(AM) Norwich NY 1 kw-D.
WFUN(AM) Ashtabula OH 5 kw-D, 1 kw-N, DA-2.
WATH(AM) Athens OH 1 kw-D, 160 w-N.
KCFO(AM) Tulsa OK 2.5 kw-D, 1 kw-N, DA-2.
KBBT(AM) Portland OR 5 kw-U, DA-N.
WBLF(AM) Bellefonte PA 1 kw-D, 61 w-N.
WWSW(AM) Pittsburgh PA 5 kw-U, DA-2.
WJMX(AM) Florence SC 5 kw-D, 3 kw-N, DA-N.
WXQK(AM) Spring City TN 500 w-D.
KIXL(AM) Del Valle TX 1 kw-U.
KHVN(AM) Fort Worth TX 1 kw-D, 270 w-N.
WVOV(AM) Danville VA 1 kw-D.
WANV(AM) Waynesboro VA 5 kw-D, 1 kw-N, DA-2.
WSTX(AM) Christiansted VI 5 kw-D, 1 kw-N.
WHWB(AM) Rutland VT 1 kw-D.
KTRW(AM) Spokane WA 5 kw-D, 1 kw-N, DA-N.
*WHA(AM) Madison WI 5 kw-D, 51 w-N.
KXTP(AM) Superior WI 1 kw-D, 27 w-N.
WWYO(AM) Pineville WV 1 kw-D.

980 khz Regional III

KZXX(AM) Kenai AK 1 kw-U.
WKLF(AM) Clanton AL 1 kw-D.
KCAB(AM) Dardanelle AR 5 kw-D.
KFWJ(AM) Lake Havasu City AZ 1 kw-D, 53 w-N.
KINS(AM) Eureka CA 5 kw-D, 500 w-N, DA-N.
KEYQ(AM) Fresno CA 500 w-D, 48 w-N.
KFWB(AM) Los Angeles CA 5 kw-U.
KCTY(AM) Salinas CA 1 kw-D, 247 w-N, DA-2.
KGLN(AM) Glenwood Springs CO 1 kw-D, 225 w-N.
WSUB(AM) Groton CT 1 kw-D.
WWRC(AM) Washington DC 50 kw-D, 5 kw-N, DA-2.
WLUS(AM) Gainesville FL 5 kw-D, 166 w-N.
WTOT(AM) Marianna FL 1 kw-D, 500 w-N.
WRNE(AM) Pensacola FL 2.5 kw-D, 1 kw-N, DA-2.
WWNN(AM) Pompano Beach FL 5 kw-D, 1 kw-N, DA-D.
WKLY(AM) Hartwell GA 1 kw-D, 140 w-N.
WPGA(AM) Perry GA 5 kw-D, 270 w-N.
WLMX(AM) Rossville GA 500 w-D.
KUPI(AM) Idaho Falls ID 5 kw-D, 1 kw-N, DA-2.
KSGM(AM) Chester IL 1 kw-D, 500 w-N, DA-N.
WITY(AM) Danville IL 1 kw-U, DA-2.
WMAK(AM) London KY 900 w-D, U.
KOKA(AM) Shreveport LA 5 kw-D.
WCAP(AM) Lowell MA 5 kw-U, DA-2.
WQXC(AM) Otsego MI 1 kw-D.
KRXX(AM) Minneapolis-St. Paul MN 5 kw-U, DA-1.
KMBZ(AM) Kansas City MO 5 kw-U, DA-N.
WAPF(AM) McComb MS 5 kw-D, 152 w-N.
WKOR(AM) Starkville MS 1 kw-D.

Broadcasting & Cable Yearbook 1994
B-489

U.S. AM Stations by Frequency

WAAV(AM) Leland NC 5 kw-U, DA-N.
WAAA(AM) Winston-Salem NC 1 kw-D, 69.3 w-N.
KICA(AM) Clovis NM 1 kw-U, DA-N.
KMIN(AM) Grants NM 1 kw-U.
KVLV(AM) Fallon NV 5 kw-U.
WTRY(AM) Troy NY 5 kw-U, DA-N.
WONE(AM) Dayton OH 5 kw-U, DA-N.
WILK(AM) Wilkes-Barre PA 5 kw-D, 1 kw-N, DA-N.
WYCK(AM) Wilkes-Barre PA 5 kw-D, 1 kw-N.
WAZS(AM) Summerville SC 1 kw-D, 131 w-N.
WBZK(AM) York SC 3.15 kw-D, 291 w-N, DA-2.
KDSJ(AM) Deadwood SD 5 kw-D, 1 kw-N, DA-N.
WYFN(AM) Nashville TN 5 kw-U, DA-N.
KMPQ(AM) Rosenberg-Richmond TX 1 kw-D.
KHOS(AM) Sonora TX 1 kw-D, 260 w-N.
KSVC(AM) Richfield UT 5 kw-D, 1 kw-N, DA-N.
WXBQ(AM) Bristol VA 5 kw-D, 1 kw-N, DA-N.
WMEK(AM) Chase City VA 500 w-D.
KUTI(AM) Selah WA 5 kw-D, 500 w-N, DA-N.
WNBI(AM) Park Falls WI 1 kw-D, 105 w-N.
WPRE(AM) Prairie du Chien WI 1 kw-D.
WCUB(AM) Two Rivers WI 5 kw-U, DA.
WHAW(AM) Weston WV 1 kw-D, 50 w-N.

990 khz Clear (Canadian) I-A
WEIS(AM) Centre AL 1 kw-D, 30 w-N.
WLDX(AM) Fayette AL 1 kw-D, 42 w-N.
KTKT(AM) Tucson AZ 10 kw-D, 1 kw-N, DA-2.
KATD(AM) Pittsburg CA 5 kw-U, DA.
KQSB(AM) Santa Barbara CA 5 kw-D, 500 w-N, DA-2.
KRKS(AM) Denver CO 5 kw-D, 390 w-N, DA-N.
WNTY(AM) Southington CT 2.5 kw-D, DA.
WFBA(AM) Miami FL 5 kw-D.
WHOO(AM) Orlando FL 50 kw-D, 5 kw-N, DA-2, 10 kw non-DA-CH.
WGML(AM) Hinesville GA 250 w-D, 76 w-N.
KHVH(AM) Honolulu HI 5 kw-U.
KAYL(AM) Storm Lake IA 250 w-D.
WCAZ(AM) Carthage IL 1 kw-D, 9 w-N.
WITZ(AM) Jasper IN 1 kw-D.
WERK(AM) Muncie IN 250 w-D, 2 w-N, DA-1.
KRSL(AM) Russell KS 1 kw-D, 30 w-N.
WGSO(AM) New Orleans LA 1 kw-D, 400 w-N.
KXLA(AM) Rayville LA 1 kw-D, 250 w-N, DA-2.
WWCM(AM) Ypsilanti MI 500 w-D, 250 w-N, DA-2.
KRMO(AM) Monett MO 2.5 kw-D, 47 w-N.
WABO(AM) Waynesboro MS 1 kw-D.
WEEB(AM) Southern Pines NC 10 kw-D, 5 kw-CH, 500 w-N.
KSVP(AM) Artesia NM 1 kw-N, 250 w-N.
WCMF(AM) Rochester NY 5 kw-D, 2.5 kw-N, DA-2.
WJEH(AM) Gallipolis OH 1 kw-D.
WTIG(AM) Massillon OH 250 w-D, 119-N, DA-2.
KRKT(AM) Albany OR 250 w-D.
WZZD(AM) Philadelphia PA 50 kw-D, 10 kw-N, DA-2.
WVSC(AM) Somerset PA 10 kw-D, 75 w-N, DA-2.
WPRA(AM) Mayaguez PR 1 kw-U.
WALE(AM) Providence RI 50 kw-D, 500 w-N, DA-D.
WIVK(AM) Knoxville TN 10 kw-U, DA-N.
KWAM(AM) Memphis TN 10 kw-D, 450 w-N, DA.
KZZB(AM) Beaumont TX 1 kw-U, DA-1.
KAML(AM) Kenedy-Karnes City TX 250 w-D.
KNIN(AM) Wichita Falls TX 10 kw-D, 1 kw-N, DA-2.
WNRV(AM) Narrows VA 5 kw-D.
WTMM(AM) Richmond VA 1 kw-D, 1 w-N.

1000 khz Clear (U.S. & Mexican) I-B
KOMO(AM) Seattle WA 50 kw-U, DA-N.
WTAK(AM) Huntsville AL 10 kw-D, DA.
WXWY(AM) Robertsdale AL 1 kw-D.
KFLG(AM) Bullhead City AZ 5 kw-D.
KCEO(AM) Vista CA 2.5 kw-D, 500 w-N, DA-2.
WYBT(AM) Blountstown FL 1 kw-D.
WMLZ(AM) Jupiter FL
KIDH(AM) Eagle AL 10 kw-D, DA.
WMVP(AM) Chicago IL 50 kw-U, DA-2.
WKVG(AM) Jenkins KY 1 kw-D.
WXTN(AM) Lexington MS 5 kw-D.
WHEV(AM) Garner NC 1 kw-D.
KOTD(AM) Plattsmouth NE 250 w-D, DA.
WRNJ(AM) Hackettstown NJ 2.5 kw-D, DA.
KKIM(AM) Albuquerque NM 10 kw-D.
WLNL(AM) Horseheads NY 5 kw-D.
WCCD(AM) Parma OH 500 w-D, DA.
KTOK(AM) Oklahoma City OK 5 kw-U, DA-2.
WIOO(AM) Carlisle PA 1 kw-D.
WKYB(AM) Hemingway SC 1 kw-D, 5 kw-CH.
WGOG(AM) Walhalla SC 1 kw-D.
KXRB(AM) Sioux Falls SD 10 kw-D, DA.
WMUF(AM) Paris TN 5 kw-D, DA.
KSTA(AM) Coleman TX 250 w-D.
*KBIB(AM) Marion TX 250 w-D, DA.
KNDA(AM) Odessa TX 250 w-D.
WKDE(AM) Altavista VA 1 kw-D.
WRAR(AM) Tappahannock VA 500 w-D.
WVVI(AM) Charlotte Amalie VI 5 kw-D, 1 kw-N, U.

1010 khz Clear (Canadian) I-A
WPYK(AM) Dora AL 5 kw-D.
KBIS(AM) Little Rock AR 10 kw-D, 5 kw-N, DA-N.
KXEG(AM) Tolleson AZ 1 kw-D, 250 w-N.
KCHJ(AM) Delano CA 5 kw-N, 1 kw-N.
KIQI(AM) San Francisco CA 10 kw-D, 500 w-N, DA-2.
KPSL(AM) Thousand Palms CA 3.6 kw-D, 400 w-N, DA-2.
KSIR(AM) Brush CO 1 kw-D, 20 w-N.
WCNU(AM) Crestview FL 10 kw-D, 84 w-N.
WXTL(AM) Jacksonville Beach FL 10 kw-D, DA.
WQYK(AM) Seffner FL 50 kw-D, 5 kw-N, DA-2.
WGUN(AM) Atlanta GA 50 kw-D, 300 w-N.
*KRNI(AM) Mason City IA 1 kw-D, 15.8 w-N.
WCSI(AM) Columbus IN 500 w-D, 19 w-N.

KIND(AM) Independence KS 250 w-D, 32 w-N.
KDLA(AM) De Ridder LA 1 kw-D.
WCKW(AM) Garyville LA 500 w-D, 42 w-N.
WOLB(AM) Baltimore MD 1 kw-D, 27 w-N.
WITL(AM) Lansing MI 500 w-D, 42 w-N.
KCHI(AM) Chillicothe MO 250 w-D, 37 w-N.
KXEN(AM) Festus-St. Louis MO 50 kw-D, DA.
WMOX(AM) Meridian MS 10 kw-D, 1 kw-N, DA-2.
WXLX(AM) Albemarle NC 1 kw-D.
WFGW(AM) Black Mountain NC 50 kw-D (19 kw-CH), DA-2.
WELS(AM) Kinston NC 1 kw-D, 75 w-N.
WINS(AM) New York NY 50 kw-U, DA-1.
WIOI(AM) New Boston OH 1 kw-D, 22 w-N.
KZRC(AM) Milwaukie OR 4.5 kw-D.
WTGC(AM) Lewisburg PA 1 kw-D, 13 w-N.
WHIN(AM) Gallatin TN 5 kw-D.
WORM(AM) Savannah TN 250 w-D, 27 w-N.
KDJW(AM) Amarillo TX 5 kw-D, 500 w-N, DA-2.
KLAT(AM) Houston TX 5 kw-U.
KBBW(AM) Waco TX 10 kw-D, 2.5 kw-N, DA-2.
KTUR(AM) Tooele UT 1 kw-D, 10 w-N.
WMEV(AM) Marion VA 1 kw-D, 30 w-N.
WPMH(AM) Portsmouth VA 5 kw-D, 449 w-N, DA-2.
WSPO(AM) Stevens Point WI 1 kw-D.
WCST(AM) Berkeley Springs WV 250 w-D, 17 w-N.

1020 khz Clear I-A
KDKA(AM) Pittsburgh PA 50 kw-U.
KFFR(AM) Eagle River AK 10 kw-U, DA-N.
KTNQ(AM) Los Angeles CA 50 kw-U, DA-1.
WKZE(AM) Sharon CT 2.5 kw-D.
WJEP(AM) Ochlocknee GA 1 kw-D.
WCIL(AM) Carbondale IL 1 kw-D.
WPEO(AM) Peoria IL 1 kw-D.
WNTK(AM) Newport NH 10 kw-D.
WIBG(AM) Ocean City NJ 500 w-D.
KCKN(AM) Roswell NM 50 kw-U, DA.
KASR(AM) Perry OK 400 w-D, 250-w, DA-2.
WPJC(AM) Adjuntas PR 1 kw-U, DA-N.
WRIX(AM) Homeland Park SC 10 kw-D.
KWIQ(AM) Moses Lake North WA 2.5 kw-D, 500 w-N, DA-2.
KYXE(AM) Selah WA 5 kw-D, 500 w-N, DA-2.

1030 khz Clear I-A
WBZ(AM) Boston MA 50 kw-U, DA-1.
KFAY(AM) Farmington AR 10 kw-D, 1 kw-N, DA-2.
KEVT(AM) Cortaro AZ 10 kw-D, 1 kw-N, DA-2.
KIOQ(AM) Folsom CA 50 kw-D, 1 kw-N.
KJDJ(AM) San Luis Obispo CA 2.5 kw-D, 700 w-N.
WONQ(AM) Oviedo FL 10 kw-D, 500 w-N, DA-2.
WNVR(AM) Vernon Hills IL 500 w-D.
WBNN(AM) Union City IN 330 kw-D, N.
KBUF(AM) Holcomb KS 25 kw-D, 1 kw-N, DA-2.
WNTL(AM) Indian Head MD 50 kw-D, N.
*WUFL(AM) Sterling Heights MI 5 kw-D, DA.
WCTS(AM) Maplewood MN 50 kw-D, 1 kw-N, DA-2.
KBEQ(AM) Blue Springs MO 1 kw-D, 500 w-N, DA-2.
WNOW(AM) Mint Hill NC 10 kw-D, DA.
WFTK(AM) Wake Forest NC 50 kw-D, N.
WYSL(AM) Avon NY 1 kw-D.
KDUN(AM) Reedsport OR 10 kw-D, 63 w-N.
WOSO(AM) San Juan PR 10 kw-D, DA-1.
WXSS(AM) Memphis TN 50 kw-D, 1 kw-N, DA-N.
WQSE(AM) White Bluff TN 1 kw-D, D-N.
KCTA(AM) Corpus Christi TX 50 kw-D.
WGFC(AM) Floyd VA 1 kw-D.
KMAS(AM) Shelton WA 1 kw-D, DA.
WBGS(AM) Point Pleasant WV 10 kw-D, DA.
KTWO(AM) Casper WY 50 kw-D, DA-N.

1040 khz Clear I-A
WHO(AM) Des Moines IA 50 kw-U.
KURS(AM) San Diego CA 9.5 kw-D, 4.5 kw-N, DA-2.
KCBR(AM) Monument CO 4.6 kw-D.
WYFX(AM) Boynton Beach FL 25 kw-D, 1.2 kw-N, DA-2.
WMTX(AM) Pinellas Park FL 5 kw-D, 500 w-N, DA-N.
KLHT(AM) Honolulu HI 5 kw-U.
WOKT(AM) Cannonsburg KY 2.5 kw-D, DA-D.
KAIN(AM) Vidalia LA 1 kw-D.
WSGH(AM) Lewisville NC 10 kw-D.
WJHR(AM) Flemington NJ 4.7 kw-D, 1 kw-N, DA-2.
WJTB(AM) North Ridgeville OH 5 kw-D.
KEZF(AM) Tigard OR 2.2 kw-D, 200 w-N.
WSKE(AM) Everett PA 10 kw-N, 4 kw-CH.
WCXQ(AM) Moca PR 250 w-D.
WQBB(AM) Powell TN 10 kw-D.
KGGR(AM) Dallas TX 1 kw-D.

1050 khz Clear (Mexican) I-A
WTLM(AM) Alexander City AL 1 kw-D.
WWIC(AM) Scottsboro AL 1 kw-D, 101 w-N.
KJBN(AM) Little Rock AR 1 kw-D, 19 w-N.
KTBA(AM) Tuba City AZ 5 kw-D, 5.2 w-N.
KBBV(AM) Big Bear Lake CA 250 w-D, N.
KNOB(AM) Frazier Park CA 10 kw-D, DA.
KOFY(AM) San Mateo CA 50 kw-D, 10 kw-N, DA-2.
WJSB(AM) Crestview FL 5 kw-D.
WROS(AM) Jacksonville FL 5 kw-D, DA.
WFAM(AM) Augusta GA 5 kw.
WPBS(AM) Conyers GA 1 kw-D, 266 w-N.
WMNZ(AM) Montezuma GA 250 w-D, 42 w-N.
WDZ(AM) Decatur IL 1 kw-U.
WTCA(AM) Plymouth IN 250 w-U, DA-2.
WNES(AM) Central City KY 1 kw-D, 172 w-N.
KLPL(AM) Lake Providence LA 250 w-D.
KVPI(AM) Ville Platte LA 1 kw-D.
WMSG(AM) Oakland MD 1 kw-D, 75 w-N.
WKDL(AM) Silver Spring MD 1 kw-D, 43 w-N.
WTKA(AM) Ann Arbor MI 5 kw-D, 500 w-N, DA-2.
KLOH(AM) Pipestone MN 1 kw-D, 238 w-N.

KMIS(AM) Portageville MO 1 kw-D, 87 w-N.
KSIS(AM) Sedalia MO 1 kw-D, 86 w-N.
WACR(AM) Columbus MS 1 kw-D, 48 w-N, DA.
KMTA(AM) Kinsey MT 10 kw-D, 136 w-N.
WFSC(AM) Franklin NC 1 kw-D.
WLON(AM) Lincolnton NC 1 kw-D, 231 w-N.
WWGP(AM) Sanford NC 1 kw-D, 161 w-N.
WBNC(AM) Conway NH 1 kw-D, 63 w-N.
KJBO(AM) Los Ranchos de Albuquerque NM 1 kw-D, 500 w-N, DA-1.
WFBL(AM) Baldwinsville NY 2.5 kw-D, DA.
WYBG(AM) Massena NY 1 kw-D, 500 PSA.
WEVD(AM) New York NY 50 kw-U, DA-1.
WTSJ(AM) Cincinnati OH 1 kw-D, 278 w-N.
KKRX(AM) Lawton OK 250 w-D, DA.
KGTO(AM) Tulsa OK 1 kw-D.
KORE(AM) Springfield-Eugene OR 5 kw-D, 149 w-N.
WBUT(AM) Butler PA 500 w-D, 65 w-N.
WLYC(AM) Williamsport PA 1 kw-D, 36 w-N.
WJXY(AM) Conway SC 5 kw-D, 473 w-N, DA-2.
WSMT(AM) Sparta TN 1 kw-D.
KRMY(AM) Killeen TX 250 w-D.
KPXE(AM) Liberty TX 250 w-D, DA.
KCAS(AM) Slaton TX 250 w-D.
WGAT(AM) Gate City VA 1 kw-D, 266 w-N.
WBRG(AM) Lynchburg VA 1 kw-D, 100 w-N.
WCMS(AM) Norfolk VA 5 kw-D, 358 w-N, DA-2.
KEYF(AM) Dishman WA 5 kw-D, 335 w-N.
KBLE(AM) Seattle WA 5 kw-D, 453.5 w-N.
WEIO(AM) Eau Claire WI 1 kw-D, 500 w-N.
WSGC(AM) Kaukauna WI 1 kw-D, 500 w-N, DA-2.
WLIP(AM) Kenosha WI 250 w-U.
WAMN(AM) Green Valley WV 1.5 kw-D.
WADC(AM) Parkersburg WV 5 kw-D.

1053 khz
KCNM(AM) San Jose MP 1 kw-U, DA-1.

1060 khz Clear (U.S. & Mexican) I-B
KYW(AM) Philadelphia PA 50 kw-U, DA-1.
KAYR(AM) Van Buren AR 500 w-D, N.
KUKQ(AM) Tempe AZ 5 kw-D, 500 w-N, DA-N.
KPAY(AM) Chico CA 1 kw-D, 1 kw-N.
KXER(AM) Templeton CA 1 kw-U.
KLMO(AM) Longmont CO 10 kw-D, 100 w-N (500 w-CH).
WAMT(AM) Titusville FL 10 kw-D, 5 kw-N, DA-2.
WKGQ(AM) Milledgeville GA 1 kw-D.
WKNG(AM) Tallapoosa GA 5 kw-D.
KAHU(AM) Hilo HI 1 kw-U.
KBGN(AM) Caldwell ID 10 kw-D.
WMCL(AM) McLeansboro IL 2.5 kw-D, DA.
WRHL(AM) Rochelle IL 250 w-D, DA.
WFLE(AM) Flemingsburg KY 1 kw-D, N.
WJKY(AM) Jamestown KY 1 kw-D.
WNOE(AM) New Orleans LA 50 kw-D, 5 kw-N, DA-2.
WBIV(AM) Natick MA 25 kw-D, 2.5 kw-N, DA-2.
WHFB(AM) Benton Harbor-St. Joseph MI 5 kw-D, 2.5 kw-CH.
WBMB(AM) West Branch MI 1 kw-D.
KFIL(AM) Preston MN 1 kw-D.
KTOZ(AM) Springfield MO 500 w-D.
WPMX(AM) Tupelo MS 1 kw-D, 33 w-N, DA-1.
*WGSB(AM) Mebane NC 1 kw-D, DA.
WMAP(AM) Monroe NC 1 kw-D.
WCOK(AM) Sparta NC 800 w-D.
KNLV(AM) Ord NE 1 kw-D.
KKVV(AM) Las Vegas NV 5 kw-D, 43 w-N.
WRCW(AM) Canton OH 5 kw-D, DA.
WCGB(AM) Juana Diaz PR 5 kw-D, 500 w-N.
KGFX(AM) Pierre SD 10 kw-D, 1 kw-N, DA-2.
WNPC(AM) Newport TN 1 kw-D.
WPHC(AM) Waverly TN 1 kw-D.
KFNA(AM) El Paso TX 10 kw-D.
KIJN(AM) Farwell TX 5 kw-D.
KHYM(AM) Gilmer TX 10 kw-D.
KFIT San Antonio TX 1 kw-d, DA.
KFIT(AM) Sunset Valley TX 2 kw-D, DA.
KKDS(AM) South Salt Lake UT 10 kw-D, 1 kw-N, DA-N.

1070 khz Clear (U.S. & Canadian) I-B
KNX(AM) Los Angeles CA 50 kw-U.
WAPI(AM) Birmingham AL 50 kw-D, 5 kw-N, DA-N.
WANM(AM) Tallahassee FL 10 kw-D.
KILR(AM) Estherville IA 250 w-D, DA.
WIBC(AM) Indianapolis IN 50 kw-D, 10 kw-N, DA-2.
KFDI(AM) Wichita KS 10 kw-D, 1 kw-N, DA-N.
WEKT(AM) Elkton KY 500 w-D.
KBCL(AM) Shreveport LA 250 w-D.
KMOM(AM) Monticello MN 10 kw-U, 2.5 kw-N, DA-2.
KHMO(AM) Hannibal MO 5 kw-D, 1 kw-N, DA-3.
KATQ(AM) Plentywood MT 5 kw-D.
WNCT(AM) Greenville NC 10 kw-D, DA-N.
WGOS(AM) High Point NC 1 kw-D.
WKMB(AM) Stirling NJ 250 w-D.
WNWX(AM) Plattsburgh NY 5 kw-D.
WSCP(AM) Sandy Creek-Pulaski NY 2.5 kw-D.
KWSA(AM) West Klamath OR 5 kw-D, 1 kw-CH.
WKOK(AM) Sunbury PA 10 kw-D, 1 kw-N, DA-N.
WMIA(AM) Arecibo PR 500 w-D, 2.5 kw-N.
WHYZ(AM) Sans Souci SC 50 kw-D, 1.5 kw-N, DA-2.
WFLI(AM) Lookout Mountain TN 50 kw-D, 2.5 kw-N, DA-2.
WDIA(AM) Memphis TN 50 kw-D, 5 kw-N, DA-2.
KDSI(AM) Alice TX 1 kw-U, DA-N.
KRBE(AM) Houston TX 250 w-D, 5 kw-N, DA-N.
KWEL(AM) Midland TX 2.5 kw-D.
WINA(AM) Charlottesville VA 5 kw-D, N.
WTSO(AM) Madison WI 10 kw-D, 5 kw-N, DA-2.
WIWS(AM) Beckley WV 10 kw-D.

U.S. AM Stations by Frequency

1080 khz Clear I-B
WTIC(AM) Hartford CT 50 kw-U, DA-N.
KRLD(AM) Dallas TX 50 kw-U, DA-N.
KKSD(AM) Anchorage AK 10 kw-U.
WKAC(AM) Athens AL 5 kw-D.
KGVY(AM) Green Valley AZ 1 kw-D.
KSCO(AM) Santa Cruz CA 10 kw-D, 5 kw-N, DA-2.
WVCG(AM) Coral Gables FL 50 kw-D, 20 kw-N, DA-2.
WFIV(AM) Kissimmee FL 10 kw-D, DA.
WJOE(AM) Port St. Joe FL 1 kw-D.
WFTD(AM) Marietta GA 10 kw-D, DA.
KWAI(AM) Honolulu HI 5 kw-U.
KOAK(AM) Red Oak IA 250 w-D.
KVNI(AM) Coeur d'Alene ID 10 kw-D, 1 kw-N, DA-N.
WRYT(AM) Edwardsville IL 250 w-D.
WPOK(AM) Pontiac IL 1 kw-D, DA.
WNWI(AM) Valparaiso IN 250 w-D.
WDJX(AM) Louisville KY 10 kw-D, 1 kw-N, DA-2.
WOAP(AM) Owosso MI 1 kw-D.
KYMN(AM) Northfield MN 1 kw-D.
KYMO(AM) East Prairie MO 500 w-D.
WSSI(AM) Carthage MS 5 kw-D, DA.
WKGX(AM) Lenoir NC 5 kw-D.
WYCM(AM) Murfreesboro NC 1 kw-D.
WKKE(AM) St. Pauls NC 1 kw-D.
KNDK(AM) Langdon ND 1 kw-D.
WUFO(AM) Amherst NY 1 kw-D.
WMVR(AM) Sidney OH 250 w-D, DA.
KWJJ(AM) Portland OR 50 kw-D, 10 kw-N, DA-2.
WEEP(AM) Hampton Township PA 50 kw-D, DA.
WLEY(AM) Cayey PR 250 w-U.
WALD(AM) Walterboro SC 2.5 kw-D.
KRPX(AM) Price UT 10 kw-D.
WKBY(AM) Chatham VA 1 kw-D.
WVKV(AM) Hurricane WV 5 kw-D, DA.

1090 khz Clear (U.S. & Mexican) I-B
KAAY(AM) Little Rock AR 50 kw-U, DA-N.
WBAL(AM) Baltimore MD 50 kw-U, DA-N.
KAJK(AM) Fortuna CA 10 kw-D.
KTNS(AM) Oakhurst CA 500 w-D.
KYBG(AM) Aurora CO 50 kw-D, 500 w-N, DA-2.
WKGT(AM) Cantonment FL 8.6 kw-D.
WMFL(AM) Monticello FL 1 kw-D.
WKII(AM) Port Charlotte FL 4.5 kw-D, 2.5 kw-N.
WBAF(AM) Barnesville GA 1 kw-D.
KVDB(AM) Sioux Center IA 500 w-D, DA.
*KNWS(AM) Waterloo IA 1 kw-D.
WCRA(AM) Effingham IL 1 kw-D.
WGLC(AM) Mendota IL 250 w-D.
WFCV(AM) Fort Wayne IN 1 kw-D, DA.
WILD(AM) Boston MA 5 kw-D.
WCAR(AM) Livonia MI 250 w-D, 500 w-N, DA-2.
WMUS(AM) Muskegon MI 1 kw-D.
KJJK(AM) Fergus Falls MN 1 kw-D.
KEXS(AM) Excelsior Springs MO 1 kw-D.
KBOZ(AM) Bozeman MT 5 kw-D, DA-N.
WKTE(AM) King NC 1 kw-D.
WBZB(AM) Selma NC 1 kw-D.
KTGO(AM) Tioga ND 1 kw-D.
WKFI(AM) Wilmington OH 1 kw-D, DA.
KLWJ(AM) Umatilla OR 2.5 kw-D.
WSOL(AM) Mayaguez PR 250 w-D, 730 w-N.
WMTY(AM) Greenwood SC 780 w-D.
WENR(AM) Englewood TN 1 kw-D.
WJKM(AM) Hartsville TN 1 kw-D.
WKCV(AM) Kingsport TN 10 kw-D.
KFRD(AM) Bellville TX 250 w-D.
KKYN(AM) Plainview TX 5 kw-D, 500 w-N, DA-2.
WGOD(AM) Charlotte Amalie VI 250 w-D.
KING(AM) Seattle WA 50 kw-U, DA-2.
WISS(AM) Berlin WI 500 w-D.
WAQE(AM) Rice Lake WI 5 kw-D.

1100 khz Clear I-A
WWWE(AM) Cleveland OH 50 kw-U.
KCCF(AM) Cave Creek AZ 25 kw-D, 1 kw-N, DA-2.
KZPM(AM) Bakersfield CA 5 kw-D, 1 kw-N.
KFAX(AM) San Francisco CA 50 kw-D, DA-1.
KNZZ(AM) Grand Junction CO 50 kw-D, 10 kw-N, DA-N.
WLBB(AM) Carrollton GA 1 kw-D.
WCGA(AM) Woodbine GA 10 kw-D.
KKLL(AM) Webb City MO 5 kw-D.
WHLI(AM) Hempstead NY 10 kw-D.
WGPA(AM) Bethlehem PA 250 w-D.
WSGI(AM) Springfield TN 1 kw-D.
KDRY(AM) Alamo Heights TX 11 kw-D, 1 kw-N, DA-2.
WYKR(AM) Wells River VT 5 kw-D.

1110 khz Clear I-B
WBT(AM) Charlotte NC 50 kw-U, DA-N.
WBCA(AM) Bay Minette AL 10 kw-D.
WBIB(AM) Centreville AL 1 kw-D.
KGFL(AM) Clinton AR 5 kw-D.
KGPL(AM) Dermott AR 10 kw-D, DA.
KRLA(AM) Pasadena CA 50 kw-D, 20 kw-N, DA-2.
KRCX(AM) Roseville CA 5 kw-D, 500 w-N, DA-2.
WTIS(AM) Tampa FL 10 kw-D, DA.
WEBS(AM) Calhoun GA 5 kw-D.
KAOI(AM) Kihei HI 5 kw-U.
*WMBI(AM) Chicago IL 5 kw-D (L-WBT Charlotte, NC; KFAB Omaha).
WKDZ(AM) Cadiz KY 1 kw-D.
WCBR(AM) Richmond KY 250 w-D.
WFCG(AM) Franklinton LA 1 kw-D.
KTLD(AM) Pineville LA 500 w-D.
WUHN(AM) Pittsfield MA 5 kw-D, DA.
*WUNN(AM) Mason MI 1 kw-D, DA.
WJML(AM) Petoskey MI 10 kw-D.
WKRA(AM) Holly Springs MS 1 kw-D.

KFAB(AM) Omaha NE 50 kw-U, DA-N.
WNNW(AM) Salem NH 5 kw-D, DA-N.
KYKK(AM) Hobbs NM 1 kw-D.
WSFW(AM) Seneca Falls NY 1 kw-D.
WTBQ(AM) Warwick NY 250 w-D.
WGNZ(AM) Fairborn OH 1.65 kw-D, DA.
KEOR(AM) Atoka OK 5 kw-D, DA.
KBND(AM) Bend OR 25 kw-D, 5 kw-N, DA-N.
WJSM(AM) Martinsburg PA 1 kw-D.
WNAP(AM) Norristown PA 4.8 kw-D, DA.
WKZV(AM) Washington PA 1 kw-D, DA.
WVJP(AM) Caguas PR 2.5 kw-D, 500 w-N.
WHIM(AM) East Providence RI 5 kw-D, 250 w-N, DA-N.
WSLV(AM) Ardmore TN 2.5 kw-D.
WUAT(AM) Pikeville TN 250 w-D.
KTEK(AM) Alvin TX 2.5 kw, DA.
WZAM(AM) Norfolk VA 50 kw-D, DA.
KJTT(AM) Oak Harbor WA 500 w-D.

1120 khz Clear I-A
KMOX(AM) St. Louis MO 50 kw-U.
WHOG(AM) Hobson City AL 500 w-D.
WPRX(AM) Bristol CT 1 kw-D, 500 w-N, DA-N.
WUST(AM) Washington DC 20 kw-D, 3 kw-CH.
WBZR(AM) Destin FL 1 kw-D.
WBNM(AM) Gordon GA 10 kw-D, 2.5 kw-CH.
WADN(AM) Concord MA 5 kw-D, 1 kw-N, DA-2.
WTWZ(AM) Clinton MS 5 kw-D, 2.5 kw-CH.
WHTT(AM) Buffalo NY 1 kw-D.
KPNW(AM) Eugene NY 50 kw-U, DA-1.
WKQW(AM) Oil City PA 1 kw-D.
WMSW(AM) Hatillo PR 5 kw-U.
WFLU(AM) Florence SC 1 kw-D, DA.
WCGM(AM) Maryville TN 500 w-D.
KCLE(AM) Cleburne TX 250 w-D.
WDUF(AM) Duffield VA 1 kw-D.

1130 khz Clear (U.S. & Canadian) I-B
KWKH(AM) Shreveport LA 50 kw-U, DA-N.
WBBR(AM) New York NY 50 kw-U, DA-N.
WACQ(AM) Tallassee AL 1 kw-D.
KAAB(AM) Batesville AR 1 kw-D, DA.
KWDS(AM) Prescott Valley AZ 1 kw-D.
KRDU(AM) Dinuba CA 6.2 kw-D, DA.
KSDO(AM) San Diego CA 10 kw-U, DA-2.
KHTH(AM) Dillon CO 5 kw-D.
WWBF(AM) Bartow FL 2.5 kw-D, 500 w-N, DA-N.
WLBA(AM) Gainesville GA 10 kw-D.
KILJ(AM) Mount Pleasant IA 250 w-D.
WSDM(AM) Brazil IN 500 w-D.
KLEY(AM) Wellington KS 250 w-D, DA.
WKED(AM) Frankfort KY 500 w-D, DA.
WSJP(AM) Murray KY 2.5 kw-D, 250 w-N, DA-2.
WWWW(AM) Detroit MI 50 kw-D, 10 kw-N, DA-2.
KFAN(AM) Minneapolis MN 50 kw-D, 25 kw-N, DA-2.
WQFX(AM) Gulfport MS 500 w-D.
WPYB(AM) Benson NC 1 kw-D.
WCLW(AM) Eden NC 1 kw-D, DA-3.
WJTP(AM) Newland NC 1 kw-D.
KBMR(AM) Bismarck ND 50 kw-D, DA.
KOFK(AM) Milan NM 5 kw-D.
WCTM(AM) Eaton OH 250 w-D, DA.
WASP(AM) Brownsville PA 5 kw-D, DA.
WOIZ(AM) Guayanilla PR 200 w-D, 700 w-N.
WHHR(AM) Hilton Head Island SC 1 kw-D, 500 w-N, DA-N.
KTMR(AM) Edna TX 10 kw-D, DA.
KLSR(AM) Memphis TX 1 kw-D, DA.
WISN(AM) Milwaukee WI 50 kw-D, 10 kw-N, DA-2.
WRRL(AM) Rainelle WV 1 kw-D.

1140 khz Clear (U.S. & Mexican) I-B
WRVA(AM) Richmond VA 50 kw-U, DA-1.
KSLD(AM) Soldotna AK 10 kw-U.
WBXR(AM) Hazel Green AL 15 kw-D, DA.
KVLI(AM) Lake Isabella CA 1 kw-D.
KCMJ(AM) Palm Springs CA 10 kw-D, 2.5 kw-N, DA-2.
KRAK(AM) Sacramento CA 50 kw-U, DA-2.
KNAB(AM) Burlington CO 1 kw-D.
WQBA(AM) Miami FL 50 kw-D, 10 kw-N, DA-2.
WRMQ(AM) Orlando FL 4.1 kw-D.
KNEI(AM) Waukon IA 1 kw-D.
KGEM(AM) Boise ID 10 kw-U, DA-N.
WVEL(AM) Pekin IL 5 kw-D, 3.2 kw-CH.
WAWK(AM) Kendallville IN 1 kw-D.
WMMG(AM) Brandenburg KY 250 w-D.
WRLV(AM) Salyersville KY 1 kw-D.
WKWM(AM) Kentwood MI 5 kw-D, DA.
KPWB(AM) Piedmont MO 1 kw-D.
KLTK(AM) Southwest City MO 250 w-D.
WAKK(AM) McComb MS 1 kw-D.
WSAO(AM) Senatobia MS 5 kw-D.
WRNA(AM) China Grove NC 1 kw-D, 250 w-CH, DA-D.
WNHA(AM) Concord NH 1 kw-D.
KXNO(AM) North Las Vegas NV 10 kw-D, 2.5 kw-N, DA-N.
WCJW(AM) Warsaw NY 1 kw-D, DA.
KVSP(AM) Oklahoma City OK 1 kw-D.
KSOO(AM) Sioux Falls SD 10 kw-D, 5 kw-N, DA-2.
WQII(AM) San Juan PR 10 kw-U, DA-1.
WLOD(AM) Loudon TN 1 kw-D.
KSSQ(AM) Conroe TX 5 kw-D, DA.
KJSA(AM) Mineral Wells TX 250 w-D.
WXLZ(AM) St. Paul VA 2.5 kw-D.
KZMQ(AM) Greybull WY 10 kw-D.

1150 khz Regional III
WGEA(AM) Geneva AL 1 kw-D, 50 w-N.
WSPZ(AM) Tuscaloosa AL 5 kw-D, 1 kw-N, DA-N.
KLRG(AM) North Little Rock AR 1 kw-D.
KCKY(AM) Coolidge AZ 5 kw-D, 1 kw-N, DA-2.

KIIS(AM) Los Angeles CA 5 kw-D, DA-N.
KBAI(AM) Morro Bay CA 5 kw-D, DA-N.
KMXN(AM) Santa Rosa CA 5 kw-D, 500 w-N, DA-N.
KCUV(AM) Englewood CO 5 kw-D, 1 kw-N, DA-N.
WCNX(AM) Middletown CT 2.5 kw-D, 46 w-N.
WDEL(AM) Wilmington DE 5 kw-D, DA-N.
WNDB(AM) Daytona Beach FL 1 kw-U, DA-N.
WTMP(AM) Temple Terrace FL 5 kw-D, 2.5 kw-N, DA-N.
WXKO(AM) Fort Valley GA 1 kw-D, 60 w-N.
WJEM(AM) Valdosta GA 5 kw-D.
KCPS(AM) Burlington IA 500 w-D, 100 w-N, DA-1.
KWKY(AM) Des Moines IA 1 kw-D, DA-2.
WGGH(AM) Marion IL 5 kw-D, DA.
WNTA(AM) Rockford IL 1 kw-D, 60 w-N, DA-2.
KSAL(AM) Salina KS 5 kw-D, DA.
WMST(AM) Mt. Sterling KY 500 w-D, 54 w-N.
WLOC(AM) Munfordville KY 1 kw-D, 61 w-N.
WJBO(AM) Baton Rouge LA 5 kw-D, DA-1.
WMEX(AM) Boston MA 5 kw-U, DA-2.
WMET(AM) Gaithersburg MD 5 kw-D, 500 w-N, DA-2.
WCEN(AM) Mount Pleasant MI 1 kw-D, 500 w-N, DA-2.
KASM(AM) Albany MN 2.5 kw-D, 23 w-N.
KRMS(AM) Osage Beach MO 1 kw-D, 55 w-N.
WONG(AM) Canton MS 500 w-D.
KSEN(AM) Shelby MT 5 kw-U, DA-2.
WBAG(AM) Burlington-Graham NC 1 kw-D, 48 w-N.
WGBR(AM) Goldsboro NC 5 kw-D, 1 kw-N, DA-2.
KDEF(AM) Albuquerque NM 5 kw-D, 500 w-N, DA-2.
WRUN(AM) Utica NY 5 kw-D, 1 kw-N, DA-2.
*WCUE(AM) Cuyahoga Falls OH 5 kw-U, DA-N.
WIMA(AM) Lima OH 1 kw-U, DA-N.
KNED(AM) McAlester OK 1 kw-D, 500 w-N, DA-N.
KAGO(AM) Klamath Falls OR 5 kw-D, 1 kw-N, DA-N.
KKEY(AM) Portland OR 5 kw-D, 47 w-N, DA-1.
WHUN(AM) Huntingdon PA 5 kw-D, 36 w-N.
WGBN(AM) New Kensington PA 1 kw-D, 70 w-N, DA-1.
WJZS(AM) Orangeburg SC 5 kw-D, 500 w-N, DA-N.
WAVO(AM) Rock Hill SC 1 kw-D, 2.6 kw-N.
WSNW(AM) Seneca SC 1 kw-D.
KIMM(AM) Rapid City SD 5 kw-D, 500 w-N, DA-N.
WGOW(AM) Chattanooga TN 5 kw-D, 1 kw-N, DA-N.
WCRK(AM) Morristown TN 5 kw-D, 500 w-N, DA-N.
WDTM(AM) Selmer TN 1 kw-D.
WTAW(AM) College Station TX 1 kw-D, DA-N.
KCCT(AM) Corpus Christi TX 1 kw-D, 500 w-N, DA-N.
KSVE(AM) El Paso TX 1 kw-D, 380 w-N.
KVIL(AM) Highland Park TX 1 kw-D, 6 w-N, DA-2.
KJBC(AM) Midland TX 1 kw-D.
KUHD(AM) Port Neches TX 500 w-D, 63 w-N, DA-N.
KVDL(AM) Quanah TX 500 w-D, DA.
WNLR(AM) Churchville VA 2.5 kw-D, 30 w-N.
KEZX(AM) Seattle WA 5 kw-U, DA-2.
WAYY(AM) Chippewa Falls WI 5 kw-D.
WHBY(AM) Kimberly WI 5 kw-D, DA-2.
WELC(AM) Welch WV 5 kw-D.

1160 khz Clear I-A
KSL(AM) Salt Lake City UT 50 kw-U.
WELX(AM) Callahan FL 5 kw-D, 250 w-N, DA-N.
WMLD(AM) East Point GA 10 kw-D, 400 w-N, DA-2.
WJJD(AM) Chicago IL 50 kw-D, 5 kw-N, DA-2.
WBND(AM) Florence KY 1 kw-D, DA.
WKCM(AM) Hawesville KY 2.5 kw-D, 1 kw-N, DA-N.
WPVG(AM) Funkstown MD 1 kw-D, 500 w-N.
WSKW(AM) Skowhegan ME 10 kw-D, 1 kw-N.
WWON(AM) Fenton MI 1 kw-D, DA-1.
WYRU(AM) Red Springs NC 5 kw-D, 250 w-N.
WTYN(AM) Tryon NC 10 kw-D, 500 w-N, DA-N.
WOBM(AM) Lakewood NJ 5 kw-D, 8.9 kw-N, DA.
WVNJ(AM) Oakland NJ 10 kw-D, 2.5 kw-N, DA-2.
KNKQ(AM) Virginia City NV 5 kw-D.
WMVI(AM) Mechanicsville NY 5 kw-D, 570 w-N.
WPIE(AM) Trumansburg NY 990 w-D, 220 w-N, DA-2.
WCCS(AM) Homer City PA 10 kw-D, 1 kw-N, DA-1.
WYNS(AM) Lehighton PA 4.5 kw-D, 1 kw-N, DA-N.
WBQN(AM) Barceloneta PR 5 kw-D, 2.5 kw-N, DA-D.
WAMB(AM) Donelson TN 50 kw-D, 1 kw-N, DA-N.
KENS(AM) San Antonio TX 10 kw-D, 1 kw-N, DA-N.
WODY(AM) Fieldale VA 5 kw-D, 250 w-N, DA-N.

1170 khz Clear I-B
KVOO(AM) Tulsa OK 50 kw-U, DA-N.
WWVA(AM) Wheeling WV 50 kw-U, DA-2.
KJNP(AM) North Pole AK 50 kw-D, 21 kw-N.
WRJL(AM) Hanceville AL 460 w-D.
WACV(AM) Montgomery AL 10 kw-D, 1 kw-N, DA-N.
KCBQ(AM) San Diego CA 50 kw-D, 1.5 kw-N, DA-N.
KLOK(AM) San Jose CA 50 kw-D, 5 kw-N, DA-2.
KVVS(AM) Windsor CO 1 kw-D.
*WCTF(AM) Vernon CT 1 kw-D, DA.
WAVS(AM) Davie FL 5 kw-D, 250 w-N, DA-N.
WKLN(AM) St. Augustine Beach FL 1 kw-D.
WMLB(AM) Cumming GA 5 kw-D.
KOHO(AM) Honolulu HI 5 kw-U.
KJOC(AM) Davenport IA 1 kw-U, DA-2.
WLBH(AM) Mattoon IL 5 kw-D, DA.
WDFB(AM) Junction City KY 1 kw-D, DA.
KDLP(AM) Bayou Vista LA 500 w-D.
WDIS(AM) Norfolk MA 1 kw-D, DA.
WKPE(AM) Orleans MA 1 kw-D, DA.
KOWO(AM) Waseca MN 1 kw-D.
KUGT(AM) Jackson MO 250 w-D.
WCXN(AM) Claremont NC 10 kw-D.
WCLN(AM) Clinton NC 5 kw-D.
WBRW(AM) Bridgewater NJ 500 w-D, DA.
WRWN(AM) Cornwall NY 1 kw-D, DA.
WLEO(AM) Ponce PR 250 w-U.
WLGO(AM) Lexington SC 10 kw-D.
WPLX(AM) Collierville TN 5 kw-D.
WKPA(AM) Lynchburg VA 3.5 kw-D, DA.

U.S. AM Stations by Frequency

KPUG(AM) Bellingham WA 10 kw-D, 5 kw-N, DA-N.
WMRH(AM) Waupun WI 1 kw-D.

1180 khz Clear I-A
WHAM(AM) Rochester NY 50 kw-U.
KYET(AM) Williams AZ 10 kw-U.
KERI(AM) Wasco CA 50 kw-D, 10 kw-N, DA-2.
WLDS(AM) Jacksonville IL 1 kw-D.
WGAB(AM) Newburgh IN 670 w-D.
WXLA(AM) Dimondale MI 1 kw-D, DA.
WJNT(AM) Pearl MS 50 kw-D, 5 kw-N, DA-N.
KOFI(AM) Kalispell MT 50 kw-D, 10 kw-N, DA-N.
WMYT(AM) Carolina Beach NC 10 kw-D, DA.
KOIL(AM) Bellevue NE 5 kw-D, 1 kw-N.
WJJF(AM) Hope Valley RI 1.8 kw-D.
WFGN(AM) Gaffney SC 2.5 kw-D.
WHJM(AM) Knoxville TN 10 kw-D, 2.6 kw-CH.
KCLP(AM) Amarillo Township TX 1 kw-D, 240 w-N, DA-2.
KGOL(AM) Humble TX 50 kw-D, 1 kw-N, DA-3.
KLAY(AM) Lakewood WA

1190 khz Clear (U.S. & Mexican) I-B
WOWO(AM) Fort Wayne IN 50 kw-U, DA-N.
KEX(AM) Portland OR 50 kw-U, DA-N.
WHIY(AM) Moulton AL 2.5 kw-D.
KJEM(AM) Bentonville-Bella Vista AR 2.5 kw-D.
KRDS(AM) Tolleson AZ 5 kw-D, 250 w-N, DA-2.
KORG(AM) Anaheim CA 10 kw-D, 1.3 kw-N, DA-2.
KXBT(AM) Vallejo CA 1 kw-D.
KBCO(AM) Boulder CO 5 kw-D.
WAJL(AM) Pine Castle-Sky Lake FL 5 kw-D.
WOEQ(AM) Royal Palm Beach FL 1 kw-U, DA-D.
WGKA(AM) Atlanta GA 10 kw-D.
WECC(AM) St. Mary's GA 2.5 kw-D.
KDAO(AM) Marshalltown IA 250 w-D.
KVSV(AM) Beloit KS 2.5 kw-D, DA.
KNEK(AM) Washington LA 250 w-D.
WANN(AM) Annapolis MD 10 kw-D, DA.
KKOJ(AM) Jackson MN 5 kw-D, DA.
KWMB(AM) Wabasha MN 1 kw-D.
KHAD(AM) De Soto MO 5 kw-D, DA.
KFEZ(AM) Kansas City MO 5 kw-D, 250 w-N, DA-N.
WBSL(AM) Bay St. Louis MS 5 kw-D.
WIXE(AM) Monroe NC 1 kw-D.
KXKS(AM) Albuquerque NM 1 kw-D.
WSCM(AM) Cobleskill NY 1 kw-D.
WLIB(AM) New York NY 10 kw-D, DA.
WMRE(AM) Hughesville PA 1 kw-D, 17 w-N.
WBMJ(AM) San Juan PR 10 kw-D, 5 kw-N, DA-1.
WMIW(AM) Atlantic Beach SC 690 w-D.
WJES(AM) Johnston SC 1 kw-D.
WSDQ(AM) Dunlap TN 5 kw-D.
WHMT(AM) Humboldt TN 420 w-D.
KGBS(AM) Dallas TX 50 kw-D, 5 kw-N, DA-2.
WHYS(AM) Bluefield VA 1 kw-D.
WMAD(AM) Sun Prairie WI 1 kw-D, DA.

1200 khz Clear I-A
WOAI(AM) San Antonio TX 50 kw-U.
WQLS(AM) Ozark AL 10 kw-D.
KTCD(AM) Cottonwood CA 10 kw-D, 2.5 kw-N, DA-2.
KBOQ(AM) Soquel CA 25 kw-D, 1 kw-N, DA-N.
WDCQ(AM) Pine Island Center FL 10 kw-D, 2.5 kw-N.
WOPA(AM) Chicago IL 10 kw-D, 1 kw-N, DA-2.
WBCE(AM) Wickliffe KY 1 kw-D.
WKOX(AM) Framingham MA 10 kw-D, 1 kw-N, DA-N.
WNSW(AM) Brewer ME 10 kw-D, DA-1.
WCHB(AM) Taylor MI 25 kw-D, 700 w-N, DA-2.
KYOO(AM) Bolivar MO 1 kw-D, ND.
WSML(AM) Graham NC 10 kw-D, 1 kw-N, DA-N.
*KFNW(AM) West Fargo ND 10 kw-D, 1 kw-N, DA-N.
WGNY(AM) Newburgh NY 10 kw-D, DA.
WKRL(AM) North Syracuse NY 1 kw-D, DA-N.
WBZY(AM) New Castle PA 5 kw-D, 1 kw-N, DA-N.
WGDL(AM) Lares PR 250 w-D.
WQDQ(AM) Lebanon TN 10 kw-D, 500 w-N, DA-N.
WRVX(AM) Mt. Carmel TN 10 kw-D, 250 w-N, DA-N.
WAGE(AM) Leesburg VA 5 kw-D.

1210 khz Clear I-A
WOGL(AM) Philadelphia PA 50 kw-U.
KQTL(AM) Sahuarita AZ 10 kw-D, 1 kw-N, DA-N.
KEBR(AM) Rocklin CA 5 kw-D, 500 w-N, DA-D.
KPRZ(AM) San Marcos CA 20 kw-D, 5 kw-N, DA-2.
WCMQ(AM) Miami Springs FL 25 kw-D, 2.5 kw-N, DA-2.
WDGR(AM) Dahlonega GA 10 kw-D.
KZOO(AM) Honolulu HI 1 kw-U.
WILY(AM) Centralia IL 1 kw-D.
WBIU(AM) Denham Springs LA 10 kw-D, 1 kw-N, DA-N.
WKNX(AM) Frankenmuth MI 10 kw-D, DA-D.
KGYN(AM) Guymon OK 10 kw-U, DA-N.
WDAO(AM) Dayton OH 1 kw-D.
WHOY(AM) Salinas PR 5 kw-D, DA-2.
KOKK(AM) Huron SD 5 kw-D, 1 kw-N, DA-N.
WGSF(AM) Arlington TN 10 kw-U, DA-N.
WSBI(AM) Static TN 1 kw-D.
KUBR(AM) San Juan TX 10 kw-D, 1 kw-N, DA-2.
KONY(AM) Washington UT 10 kw-D, 250 w-N.
KBSG(AM) Auburn WA 27kw-D, 10kw-N.
KREW(AM) Sunnyside WA 10 kw-D, 1 kw-N, DA-N.
KRSV(AM) Afton WY 5 kw-D, 250 w-N.
KLDI(AM) Laramie WY 10 kw-D, 1 kw-N, DA-N.

1220 khz Clear (Mexican) I-A
WAYE(AM) Birmingham AL 1 kw-D, 75 w-N.
WABF(AM) Fairhope AL 1 kw-D, 64 w-N, DA-D.
KVSA(AM) McGehee AR 1 kw-D, 40 w-N.
KBET(AM) Canyon Country CA 1 kw-D, 500 w-N, DA-2.
KRGO(AM) Fowler CA 250 w-D.
KDFC(AM) Palo Alto CA 5 kw-D, 147 w-N.

KTSJ(AM) Pomona CA 250 w-U, DA-2, 1000 w.
KBNO(AM) Denver CO 1 kw-D, 17 w-N.
WXCT(AM) Hamden CT 1 kw-D, 320-N, DA-1.
WJAX(AM) Jacksonville FL 1 kw-D, 37 w-N.
WMJK(AM) Kissimmee FL 1 kw-D.
WQSA(AM) Sarasota FL 1 kw-D, 600 w-N, DA.
WZOT(AM) Rockmart GA 500 w-D, 150 w-N.
WSFT(AM) Thomaston GA 1 kw-D.
KJAN(AM) Atlantic IA 250 w-D, 86 w-N.
KQMG(AM) Independence IA 250 w-D, 166 w-N.
WLPO(AM) La Salle IL 1 kw-D, 500 w-N, DA-2.
WKRS(AM) Waukegan IL 1 kw-D, DA.
WSLM(AM) Salem IN 5 kw-D, 384 w-N, DA-2.
KOFO(AM) Ottawa KS 250 w-D, 40 w-N.
WFKN(AM) Franklin KY 1 kw-D, 90 w-N.
WSME(AM) Sanford ME 1 kw-D, 234 w-N.
WBCH(AM) Hastings MI 250 w-D, 48 w-N.
WIMN(AM) Stillwater MN 5 kw-D, 254 w-N.
KOMC(AM) Branson MO 1 kw-D, 53 w-N.
KCGQ(AM) Cape Girardeau MO 250 w-D, 140 w-N.
KLPW(AM) Union MO 1 kw-D, 151 w-N.
WMDC(AM) Hazelhurst MS 250 w-D, 46 w-N.
WKMT(AM) Kings Mountain NC 1 kw-D.
WREV(AM) Reidsville NC 1 kw-D, 67 w-N.
WENC(AM) Whiteville NC 5 kw-D, 152 w-N.
KDDR(AM) Oakes ND 1 kw-D, 327 w-N.
WKBK(AM) Keene NH 1 kw-U.
WKNR(AM) Cleveland OH 50 kw-D, DA-1.
WERT(AM) Van Wert OH 250 w-U.
KTLV(AM) Midwest City OK 250 w-D, DA.
KCCS(AM) Salem OR 1 kw-D, 171 w-N.
WJUN(AM) Mexico PA 1 kw-D, 40 w-N.
WRIB(AM) Providence RI 1 kw-D, 166 w-N.
WFWL(AM) Camden TN 250 w-D, 140 w-N.
WCPH(AM) Etowah TN 1 kw-D, 108 w-N.
WAXO(AM) Lewisburg TN 1 kw-D.
KMVL(AM) Madisonville TX 500 w-D, 12 w-N.
KZEE(AM) Weatherford TX 500 w-D, 8 w-N.
WLSD(AM) Big Stone Gap VA 1 kw-D, 45 w-N.
WFAX(AM) Falls Church VA 5 kw-D, 100 w-N.

1230 khz Local IV
KIFW(AM) Sitka AK 1 kw-U.
KVAK(AM) Valdez AK 1 kw-U.
WAUD(AM) Auburn AL 1 kw-U.
WKWL(AM) Florala AL 1 kw-U.
WJBB(AM) Haleyville AL 1 kw-U, DA-1.
WBHP(AM) Huntsville AL 1 kw-U.
WHOD(AM) Jackson AL 1 kw-U.
WNUZ(AM) Talladega AL 1 kw-U.
WTNW(AM) Tuscaloosa AL 1 kw-U.
KCON(AM) Conway AR 1 kw-U.
KFPW(AM) Fort Smith AR 1 kw-U, DA-1.
KBTM(AM) Jonesboro AR 1 kw-U.
KAAA(AM) Kingman AZ 1 kw-U.
KYOT(AM) Phoenix AZ 1 kw-U.
KATO(AM) Safford AZ 1 kw-U.
KINO(AM) Winslow AZ 1 kw-U.
KGEO(AM) Bakersfield CA 1 kw-U.
KSZL(AM) Barstow CA 1 kw-U.
KBOV(AM) Bishop CA 1 kw-U.
KXO(AM) El Centro CA 1 kw-U.
KDAC(AM) Fort Bragg CA 1 kw-U.
KGFJ(AM) Los Angeles CA 1 kw-U.
KPRL(AM) Paso Robles CA 1 kw-U.
KLXR(AM) Redding CA 1 kw-U.
KWG(AM) Stockton CA 900 w-U.
KEXO(AM) Grand Junction CO 1 kw-U.
KRMH(AM) Leadville CO 1 kw-U.
KKPC(AM) Pueblo CO 1 kw-U.
KBCR(AM) Steamboat Springs CO 1 kw-U.
KSTC(AM) Sterling CO 1 kw-U.
WLAT(AM) Manchester CT 1 kw-U.
WGGG(AM) Gainesville FL 1 kw-U.
WONN(AM) Lakeland FL 1 kw-U.
WMAF(AM) Madison FL 1 kw-U.
WSBB(AM) New Smyrna Beach FL 1 kw-U.
WTKX(AM) Pensacola FL 1 kw-U.
WWSD(AM) Quincy FL 1 kw-U.
WJNO(AM) West Palm Beach FL 1 kw-U.
WBLJ(AM) Dalton GA 1 kw-U.
WXLI(AM) Dublin GA 1 kw-U.
WFOM(AM) Marietta GA 1 kw-U.
WSOK(AM) Savannah GA 1 kw-U.
WAYX(AM) Waycross GA 1 kw-U.
KFJB(AM) Marshalltown IA 1 kw-U.
KBAR(AM) Burley ID 1 kw-U.
KORT(AM) Grangeville ID 1 kw-U.
KRXK(AM) Rexburg ID 1 kw-U.
WJBC(AM) Bloomington IL 1 kw-U.
WLLR(AM) Moline IL 1 kw-U.
WHCO(AM) Sparta IL 1 kw-U.
WJOB(AM) Hammond IN 1 kw-U.
WSAL(AM) Logansport IN 1 kw-U.
WTCJ(AM) Tell City IN 1 kw-U.
WBFX(AM) Terre Haute IN 250 w-U, DA-2.
WHIR(AM) Danville KY 1 kw-U.
WHOP(AM) Hopkinsville KY 830 w-U.
WANO(AM) Pineville KY 1 kw-U.
KLIC(AM) Monroe LA 1 kw-U.
WBOK(AM) New Orleans LA 1 kw-U.
KSLO(AM) Opelousas LA 1 kw-U.
WNAW(AM) North Adams MA 1 kw-U.
WESX(AM) Salem MA 1 kw-U.
WNEB(AM) Worcester MA 1 kw-U.
WITH(AM) Baltimore MD 1 kw-U.
WALI(AM) Cumberland MD 1 kw-U.
WQDY(AM) Calais ME 1 kw-U.
WSJR(AM) Madawaska ME 1 kw-U.
WCUZ(AM) Grand Rapids MI 1 kw-U.
WGRY(AM) Grayling MI 750 w-U.

WIKB(AM) Iron River MI 1 kw-U.
*WMPC(AM) Lapeer MI 1 kw-U.
WSOO(AM) Sault Ste. Marie MI 1 kw-U.
WMSH(AM) Sturgis MI 1 kw-U, DA-1.
WKLK(AM) Cloquet MN 1 kw-U.
KGHS(AM) International Falls MN 500 w-D, 250 w-N.
KYSM(AM) Mankato MN 1 kw-U.
KMRS(AM) Morris MN 1 kw-U.
KTRF(AM) Thief River Falls MN 1 kw-U.
KWNO(AM) Winona MN 1 kw-U.
KWAS(AM) Joplin MO 1 kw-U.
KLWT(AM) Lebanon MO 1 kw-U.
KWIX(AM) Moberly MO 1 kw-U.
WCMA(AM) Corinth MS 1 kw-U.
WHSY(AM) Hattiesburg MS 1 kw-U.
WSSO(AM) Starkville MS 1 kw-U.
WAZF(AM) Yazoo City MS 1 kw-U.
KZLO(AM) Bozeman MT 1 kw-U, DA-2.
KKUL(AM) Hardin MT 1 kw-U.
KXLO(AM) Lewistown MT 1 kw-U.
KLCB(AM) Libby MT 1 kw-U.
WSKY(AM) Asheville NC 1 kw-U.
WFAI(AM) Fayetteville NC 1 kw-U.
WMFR(AM) High Point NC 1 kw-U.
WQDW(AM) Kinston NC 1 kw-U.
WNNC(AM) Newton NC 1 kw-U.
WCBT(AM) Roanoke Rapids NC 1 kw-U.
KDIX(AM) Dickinson ND 1 kw-U.
KTNC(AM) Falls City NE 500 w-D, 1 kw-N.
KHAS(AM) Hastings NE 1 kw-U.
WMOU(AM) Berlin NH 1 kw-U.
WTSV(AM) Claremont NH 1 kw-U.
WCMC(AM) Wildwood NJ 1 kw-U.
KPSA(AM) Alamogordo NM 1 kw-U.
KOTS(AM) Deming NM 1 kw-U.
KYVA(AM) Gallup NM 1 kw-U.
KFUN(AM) Las Vegas NM 1 kw-U.
KRSY(AM) Roswell NM 1 kw-U.
KELY(AM) Ely NV 250 w-SH.
KLAV(AM) Las Vegas NV 1 kw-U.
KCBN(AM) Reno NV 1 kw-U.
WECK(AM) Cheektowaga NY 1 kw-U.
WENY(AM) Elmira NY 1 kw-U.
WBZA(AM) Glens Falls NY 1 kw-U.
WIGS(AM) Gouverneur NY 1 kw-U.
WHUC(AM) Hudson NY 1 kw-U.
WLFH(AM) Little Falls NY 1 kw-U.
WFAS(AM) White Plains NY 1 kw-U.
WUBE(AM) Cincinnati OH 1 kw-U.
WCOL(AM) Columbus OH 1 kw-U.
WIRO(AM) Ironton OH 1 kw-U.
WCWA(AM) Toledo OH 1 kw-U.
KADA(AM) Ada OK 1 kw-U.
WBBZ(AM) Ponca City OK 1 kw-U.
KVAS(AM) Astoria OR 1 kw-U.
KZZR(AM) Burns OR 1 kw-U.
KHSN(AM) Coos Bay OR 1 kw-U.
KMUZ(AM) Gresham OR 1 kw-U.
KQIK(AM) Lakeview OR 1 kw-U.
*KSJK(AM) Talent OR 1 kw-U.
KZUS(AM) Toledo OR 1 kw-U.
WBVP(AM) Beaver Falls PA 1 kw-U.
WIPI(AM) Easton PA 1 kw-U, DA-2.
WKBO(AM) Harrisburg PA 1 kw-U.
WCRO(AM) Johnstown PA 1 kw-U.
WBPZ(AM) Lock Haven PA 1 kw-U.
WTIV(AM) Titusville PA 1 kw-U.
WNIK(AM) Arecibo PR 1 kw-U.
WERI(AM) Westerly RI 1 kw-U.
WAIM(AM) Anderson SC 1 kw-U.
WOIC(AM) Columbia SC 1 kw-U, DA-N.
WOLS(AM) Florence SC 1 kw-U.
KWSN(AM) Sioux Falls SD 1 kw-U.
WMLR(AM) Hohenwald TN 1 kw-U.
WAKI(AM) McMinnville TN 1 kw-U.
KSIX(AM) Corpus Christi TX 1 kw-U.
KLKE(AM) Del Rio TX 1 kw-U.
KNUZ(AM) Houston TX 1 kw-U.
KERV(AM) Kerrville TX 990 w-U.
KLVT(AM) Levelland TX 1 kw-U.
KEEE(AM) Nacogdoches TX 1 kw-U.
KOZA(AM) Odessa TX 1 kw-U.
KGRO(AM) Pampa TX 1 kw-U.
KSEY(AM) Seymour TX 1 kw-U.
KSST(AM) Sulphur Springs TX 1 kw-U.
KWTX(AM) Waco TX 5 kw-D, 250 w-N, DA-2.
KMGR(AM) Murray UT 1 kw-U.
WABN(AM) Abingdon VA 1 kw-U.
WXCF(AM) Clifton Forge VA 1 kw-U, DA-1.
WFVA(AM) Fredericksburg VA 1 kw-U.
WNOR(AM) Norfolk VA 1 kw-U.
WAMM(AM) Woodstock VA 1 kw-U.
WJOY(AM) Burlington VT 1 kw-U.
KOZI(AM) Chelan WA 1 kw-U.
KWYZ(AM) Everett WA 1 kw-U.
KSBN(AM) Spokane WA 1 kw-U.
WCLO(AM) Janesville WI 1 kw-U.
WXCO(AM) Wausau WI 1 kw-U.
WLOG(AM) Logan WV 1 kw-U.
WKYG(AM) Parkersburg WV 1 kw-U.
KVOC(AM) Casper WY 1 kw-U.

1240 khz Local IV
WEBJ(AM) Brewton AL 1 kw-U.
WULA(AM) Eufaula AL 1 kw-U.
WBCF(AM) Florence AL 1 kw-U.
WMGJ(AM) Gadsden AL 1 kw-U.
WARF(AM) Jasper AL 1 kw-U.
KVRC(AM) Arkadelphia AR 1 kw-U.
KTLO(AM) Mountain Home AR 1 kw-U.
KWAK(AM) Stuttgart AR 1 kw-U.

U.S. AM Stations by Frequency

KJAA(AM) Globe AZ 1 kw-U.
KPOD(AM) Crescent City CA 1 kw-U.
KJOP(AM) Lemoore CA 1 kw-U.
KNRY(AM) Monterey CA 1 kw-U.
KPPC(AM) Pasadena CA 250 w-U.
KLOA(AM) Ridgecrest CA 250 w-U.
KSAC(AM) Sacramento CA 1 kw-U.
KLFE(AM) San Bernardino CA 1 kw-U.
KSON(AM) San Diego CA 1 kw-U.
KSMA(AM) Santa Maria CA 1 kw-U.
KSUE(AM) Susanville CA 1 kw-U.
KRDO(AM) Colorado Springs CO 1 kw-U.
KDGO(AM) Durango CO 1 kw-U.
KSLV(AM) Monte Vista CO 1 kw-U.
KCRT(AM) Trinidad CO 250 w-U.
WWCO(AM) Waterbury CT 1 kw-U.
WBGC(AM) Chipley FL 1 kw-U.
WDFL(AM) Cross City FL 1 kw-U.
WKIQ(AM) Eustis FL 1 kw-U.
WINK(AM) Fort Myers FL 1 kw-U.
WMMB(AM) Melbourne FL 1 kw-U.
WFOY(AM) St. Augustine FL 1 kw-U.
WBHB(AM) Fitzgerald GA 1 kw-U.
WGGA(AM) Gainesville GA 1 kw-U.
WLAG(AM) La Grange GA 1 kw-U.
WDDO(AM) Macon GA 1 kw-U.
WWNS(AM) Statesboro GA 1 kw-U.
WPAX(AM) Thomasville GA 1 kw-U.
WTWA(AM) Thomson GA 1 kw-U.
KDEC(AM) Decorah IA 1 kw-U.
*KWLC(AM) Decorah IA 1 kw-U.
KBIZ(AM) Ottumwa IA 1 kw-U.
KICD(AM) Spencer IA 1 kw-U.
KMCL(AM) McCall ID 500 w-D, 1 kw-N.
KLVJ(AM) Mountain Home ID 1 kw-U.
KWIK(AM) Pocatello ID 1 kw-U.
KOFE(AM) St. Maries ID 1 kw-D, 500 w-N.
WCRW(AM) Chicago IL 1 kw-U (ST WEDC & WSBC).
WEDC(AM) Chicago IL 1 kw-U (ST WCRW & WSBC).
WSBC(AM) Chicago IL 1 kw-U (ST WCRW & WEDC).
WEBQ(AM) Harrisburg IL 1 kw-U.
WTAX(AM) Springfield IL 1 kw-U.
WSDR(AM) Sterling IL 500 w-D, 1 kw-N.
WHBU(AM) Anderson IN 1 kw-U.
KIUL(AM) Garden City KS 1 kw-U.
KNSS(AM) Wichita KS 630 kw-U.
WLLV(AM) Louisville KY 1 kw-U.
WFTM(AM) Maysville KY 1 kw-U.
WPKE(AM) Pikeville KY 1 kw-U.
WSFC(AM) Somerset KY 790 w-U.
KASO(AM) Minden LA 1 kw-U.
KANE(AM) New Iberia LA 1 kw-U.
WHAI(AM) Greenfield MA 1 kw-U.
WUOK(AM) West Yarmouth MA 1 kw-U.
WCEM(AM) Cambridge MD 1 kw-U.
WJEJ(AM) Hagerstown MD 1 kw-U.
WTME(AM) Lewiston ME 1 kw-U.
WSYY(AM) Millinocket ME 1 kw-U.
WATT(AM) Cadillac MI 1 kw-U.
WCBY(AM) Cheboygan MI 1 kw-U.
WIAN(AM) Ishpeming MI 1 kw-U.
WJIM(AM) Lansing MI 1 kw-U.
WMFG(AM) Hibbing MN 1 kw-U.
WJON(AM) St. Cloud MN 1 kw-U.
KFMO(AM) Flat River MO 1 kw-U.
KWOS(AM) Jefferson City MO 1 kw-U.
KNEM(AM) Nevada MO 1 kw-U.
WWZQ(AM) Aberdeen MS 1 kw-U.
WPBQ(AM) Flowood MS 1 kw-U.
WGRM(AM) Greenwood MS 1 kw-U.
WGCM(AM) Gulfport MS 1 kw-U.
WMIS(AM) Natchez MS 1 kw-U.
WAVN(AM) Southaven MS 580 w-U.
KMAY(AM) Billings MT 1 kw-U.
KLTZ(AM) Glasgow MT 1 kw-U.
KLYQ(AM) Hamilton MT 1 kw-U.
KBLL(AM) Helena MT 1 kw-U.
WRAQ(AM) Brevard NC 1 kw-U.
WHVN(AM) Charlotte NC 1 kw-U, DA-1.
WCNC(AM) Elizabeth City NC 1 kw-U.
WJNC(AM) Jacksonville NC 1 kw-U.
WPJL(AM) Raleigh NC 1 kw-U.
WWWC(AM) Wilkesboro NC 1 kw-U.
KDLR(AM) Devils Lake ND 1 kw-U.
KFOR(AM) Lincoln NE 1 kw-U.
KODY(AM) North Platte NE 1 kw-U.
WFTN(AM) Franklin NH 1 kw-U.
WSNJ(AM) Bridgeton NJ 1 kw-U.
KAMQ(AM) Carlsbad NM 1 kw-U.
KCLV(AM) Clovis NM 1 kw-U.
KALY(AM) Los Ranchos de Albuquerque NM 1 kw-U.
KELK(AM) Elko NV 1 kw-U.
WGBB(AM) Freeport NY 1 kw-U.
WGVA(AM) Geneva NY 1 kw-U.
WJTN(AM) Jamestown NY 500 w-D, 1 kw-N.
WVOS(AM) Liberty NY 1 kw-U.
WNBZ(AM) Saranac Lake NY 1 kw-U.
WVKZ(AM) Schenectady NY 1 kw-U.
WATN(AM) Watertown NY 1 kw-U.
WBBW(AM) Youngstown OH 1 kw-U.
WHIZ(AM) Zanesville OH 1 kw-U.
KKAJ(AM) Ardmore OK 1 kw-U.
KADS(AM) Elk City OK 1 kw-U.
KBEL(AM) Idabel OK 1 kw-U.
KOKL(AM) Okmulgee OK 1 kw-U.
KFLY(AM) Corvallis OR 1 kw-U.
KTIX(AM) Pendleton OR 1 kw-U.
KPRB(AM) Redmond OR 1 kw-U.
KQEN(AM) Roseburg OR 1 kw-U.
WRTA(AM) Altoona PA 1 kw-U.
WIOV(AM) Reading PA 1 kw-U.

WYGL(AM) Selinsgrove PA 1 kw-U.
WBAX(AM) Wilkes-Barre PA 1 kw-U.
WALO(AM) Humacao PR 1 kw-U.
WOON(AM) Woonsocket RI 1 kw-U.
WLSC(AM) Loris SC 1 kw-U.
WKDK(AM) Newberry SC 1 kw-U.
WDXY(AM) Sumter SC 1 kw-U.
KCCR(AM) Pierre SD 1 kw-U.
WBEJ(AM) Elizabethton TN 1 kw-U.
WEKR(AM) Fayetteville TN 1 kw-U.
WEZK(AM) Knoxville TN 1 kw-U.
WKDA(AM) Nashville TN 1 kw-U.
WSDT(AM) Soddy-Daisy TN 1 kw-U.
WENK(AM) Union City TN 1 kw-U.
KVLF(AM) Alpine TX 1 kw-U.
KXYL(AM) Brownwood TX 1 kw-U.
KTAM(AM) Bryan TX 1 kw-U.
KXIT(AM) Dalhart TX 1 kw-U.
KAWS(AM) Hemphill TX 1 kw-U.
KKTX(AM) Kilgore TX 1 kw-U.
KXOX(AM) Sweetwater TX 1 kw-U.
WGCV(AM) Petersburg VA 1 kw-U.
WROV(AM) Roanoke VA 1 kw-U.
WTON(AM) Staunton VA 1 kw-U.
WSKI(AM) Montpelier VT 1 kw-U.
KCVL(AM) Colville WA 1 kw-U.
KXLE(AM) Ellensburg WA 1 kw-U.
KGY(AM) Olympia WA 1 kw-U.
WOMT(AM) Manitowoc WI 1 kw-U.
WIBU(AM) Poynette WI 1 kw-U.
WOBT(AM) Rhinelander WI 1 kw-U.
WJMC(AM) Rice Lake WI 1 kw-U.
WKOY(AM) Bluefield WV 1 kw-U.
WVSR(AM) Charleston WV 1 kw-U.
WDNE(AM) Elkins WV 1 kw-U.
KFBC(AM) Cheyenne WY 1 kw-U.
KEVA(AM) Evanston WY 1000 w-U.
KASL(AM) Newcastle WY 1 kw-U.
KRAL(AM) Rawlins WY 1 kw-U.
KTHE(AM) Thermopolis WY 1 kw-U.

1250 khz Regional III

WZOB(AM) Fort Payne AL 5 kw-U.
WAPZ(AM) Wetumpka AL 5 kw-D, 80 w-N.
KOFC(AM) Fayetteville AR 1 kw-D, 62 w-N.
KURB(AM) Little Rock AR 2.5 kw-D, 1.2 kw-N, DA-2.
KTIM(AM) Wickenburg AZ 350 w-D, 202 w-N.
KHIL(AM) Willcox AZ 5 kw-D, 196 w-N.
KHOT(AM) Madera CA 1.5 kw-D, 1 kw-N, DA-2.
KTMS(AM) Santa Barbara CA 2.5 kw-D, 1 kw-N, DA-2.
KDHI(AM) Twentynine Palms CA 1 kw-D, 120 w-N.
KLLK(AM) Willits CA 5.4 kw-D, 2.7 kw-N, DA-2.
WQHL(AM) Live Oak FL 1 kw-D, 83 w-N.
WDAE(AM) Tampa FL 5 kw-U, DA-1.
WANL(AM) Albany GA 1 kw-D, 53 w-N.
WYTH(AM) Madison GA 1 kw-D.
KCFI(AM) Cedar Falls IA 500 w-U, DA-2.
WIZZ(AM) Streator IL 500 w-D, 100 w-N, DA-2.
WGL(AM) Fort Wayne IN 2.5 kw-D, 1.4 kw-N, DA-2.
WRAY(AM) Princeton IN 1 kw-D, 59 w-N.
*KFKU(AM) Lawrence KS 5 kw-U, DA-1.
WNVL(AM) Nicholasville KY 500 w-D.
WLCK(AM) Scottsville KY 1 kw-U.
WARE(AM) Ware MA 5 kw-D, 2.5 kw-N, DA-2.
KBRF(AM) Fergus Falls MN 5 kw-D, 1 kw-N, DA-N.
KCUE(AM) Red Wing MN 1 kw-D, 110 w-N.
KBTC(AM) Houston MO 1 kw-D, 51 w-N.
WHNY(AM) McComb MS 5 kw-D, 1 kw-N, DA-N.
KIKC(AM) Forsyth MT 5 kw-D.
WGHB(AM) Farmville NC 5 kw-D, 2.5 kw-N, DA-2.
WBRM(AM) Marion NC 5 kw-D, 62 w-N.
KTFJ(AM) Dakota City NE 500 w-D, 700 w-N, DA-2.
WMTR(AM) Morristown NJ 1 kw-D, 1 kw-N, DA-2.
WIPS(AM) Ticonderoga NY 1 kw-D.
WOFR(AM) Washington Court House OH 500 w-D.
KCST(AM) Florence OR 1 kw-D, 68 w-N.
WLEM(AM) Emporium PA 2.5 kw-D, 30 w-N.
*WPEL(AM) Montrose PA 1 kw-D.
WTAE(AM) Pittsburgh PA 5 kw-U, DA-N.
WQXA(AM) York PA 1 kw-D.
WJIT(AM) Sabana PR 1 kw-N, 250 w-D.
WTMA(AM) Charleston SC 5 kw-D, 1 kw-N, DA-N.
WKBL(AM) Covington TN 1 kw-D, 106 w-N.
WRKQ(AM) Madisonville TN 500 w-D, 86 w-N.
WNTT(AM) Tazewell TN 500 w-D.
KGDD(AM) Paris TX 500 w-D, 95 w-N.
KALO(AM) Port Arthur TX 5 kw-D, 1 kw-N, DA-N.
KZEP(AM) San Antonio TX 1 kw-U, DA-N.
KIKZ(AM) Seminole TX 1 kw-D, 250 w-N.
KNEU(AM) Roosevelt UT 5 kw-D, 129 w-N.
WDVA(AM) Danville VA 5 kw-U, DA-N.
WLQM(AM) Franklin VA 1 kw-D.
WPRZ(AM) Warrenton VA 5 kw-D, 32 w-N, DA-2.
*KWSU(AM) Pullman WA 5 kw-U.
KKDZ(AM) Seattle WA 5 kw-U, DA-N.
WEMP(AM) Milwaukee WI 5 kw-D, DA-2.
WYKM(AM) Rupert WV 5 kw-D.

1260 khz Regional III

WCEO(AM) Birmingham AL 5 kw-D, 44 w-N.
KCCB(AM) Corning AR 1 kw-D.
KBHC(AM) Nashville AR 500 w-D.
KFAS(AM) Casa Grande AZ 1 kw-D.
KJQI(AM) Beverly Hills CA 5 kw-U, DA-2.
KOIT(AM) San Francisco CA 5 kw-D, 1 kw-N, DA-N.
KRKE(AM) Aspen CO 5 kw-D.
WMMM(AM) Westport CT 1 kw-D, DA.
WWDC(AM) Washington DC 5 kw-U, DA-2.
WNRK(AM) Newark DE 1 kw-D, 42 w-N, DA-2.
WFTW(AM) Fort Walton Beach FL 2.5 kw-D.

WSUA(AM) Miami FL 5 kw-U, DA-2.
WIYD(AM) Palatka FL 5 kw-D, 500 w-N, DA-N.
WUFE(AM) Baxley GA 5 kw-D.
WBBK(AM) Blakely GA 1 kw-D.
WTJH(AM) East Point GA 5 kw-D.
*KFGQ(AM) Boone IA 5 kw-D, 33 w-N, DA-2.
KICN(AM) Idaho Falls ID 5 kw-D, 64 w-N.
KWEI(AM) Weiser ID 1 kw-D, 60 w-N.
WIBV(AM) Belleville IL 5 kw-U, DA-2.
WNDE(AM) Indianapolis IN 5 kw-U, DA-N.
KWHK(AM) Hutchinson KS 1 kw-D, 500 w-N, DA-2.
KBRH(AM) Baton Rouge LA 1 kw-D, 127 w-N.
WEZE(AM) Boston MA 5 kw-U, DA-N.
WALM(AM) Albion MI 1 kw-D, 500 w-N, DA-N.
WWJQ(AM) Holland MI 5 kw-D, 1 kw-N, DA-1.
KROX(AM) Crookston MN 1 kw-D, 500 w-N, DA-N.
KDUZ(AM) Hutchinson MN 1 kw-D, 64 w-N.
KTTS(AM) Springfield MO 5 kw-U, DA-N.
WGVM(AM) Greenville MS 5 kw-U.
WKXR(AM) Asheboro NC 5 kw-D, 500 w-N, DA-2.
WZBO(AM) Edenton NC 1 kw-D, 34 w-N.
KIMB(AM) Kimball NE 1 kw-D, 500 w-N.
WBUD(AM) Trenton NJ 5 kw-U.
KVSF(AM) Santa Fe NM 5 kw-D, 1 kw-N.
WBNR(AM) Beacon NY 5 kw-D, 500 w-N, DA-2.
WNDR(AM) Syracuse NY 5 kw-U, DA-2.
WRDZ(AM) Cleveland OH 5 kw-U, DA-2.
WNXT(AM) Portsmouth OH 5 kw-D, 1 kw-N, DA-2.
KWSH(AM) Wewoka OK 1 kw-D.
KLYC(AM) McMinnville OR 1 kw-U, DA-N.
WRIE(AM) Erie PA 5 kw-U, DA-2.
WPHB(AM) Philipsburg PA 5 kw-D, 34 w-N.
WISO(AM) Ponce PR 1 kw-U.
WMUU(AM) Greenville SC 5 kw-D, 29 w-N.
WRIP(AM) Lake City SC 5 kw-D, 55 w-N.
KWYR(AM) Winner SD 5 kw-D, 146 w-N.
WNOO(AM) Chattanooga TN 5 kw-D.
WMCH(AM) Church Hill TN 1 kw-D.
WDKN(AM) Dickson TN 5 kw-D.
WCLC(AM) Jamestown TN 1 kw-D.
KAFX(AM) Diboll TX 1 kw-D, 109 w-N.
KPSO(AM) Falfurrias TX 500 w-D, 330 w-N.
KXQZ(AM) San Angelo TX 1 kw-D, 250 w-N.
KTAE(AM) Taylor TX 1 kw-D.
KTUE(AM) Tulia TX 1 kw-D, 53 w-N.
WCHV(AM) Charlottesville VA 5 kw-D, 2.5 kw-N, DA-2.
WJJJ(AM) Christiansburg VA 2.5 kw-D, 28 w-N.
WXCE(AM) Amery WI 5 kw-D.
WEKZ(AM) Monroe WI 1 kw-D.
WOCO(AM) Oconto WI 1 kw-D.
WTBZ(AM) Grafton WV 500 w-D.
KPOW(AM) Powell WY 5 kw-D, 1 kw-N, DA-N.

1270 khz Regional III

WGSV(AM) Guntersville AL 1 kw-D.
WKSJ(AM) Prichard AL 5 kw-D, 103 w-N.
KPBA(AM) Pine Bluff AR 5 kw-D.
KDJI(AM) Holbrook AZ 5 kw-D, 130 w-N.
KXBX(AM) Lakeport CA 500 w-D, 97 w-N.
KNWZ(AM) Thousand Palms CA 5 kw-D, 750 w-N, DA-2.
KJUG(AM) Tulare CA 5 kw-D, 1 kw-N, DA-N.
WHBS(AM) Eatonville FL 5 kw-U, DA-N.
WNOG(AM) Naples FL 5 kw-D, 1.9 kw-N, DA-2.
WNLS(AM) Tallahassee FL 5 kw-U, DA-N.
WYXC(AM) Cartersville GA 500 w-D.
WHYD(AM) Columbus GA 5 kw-D.
WJJC(AM) Commerce GA 5 kw-D.
KNDI(AM) Honolulu HI 5 kw-U.
KTFI(AM) Twin Falls ID 5 kw-D, 1 kw-N.
WEIC(AM) Charleston IL 1 kw-D, 500 w-N, DA-3.
WKBF(AM) Rock Island IL 5 kw-U, DA-N.
WFRN(AM) Elkhart IN 5 kw-D, 1 kw-N, DA-2.
WWCA(AM) Gary IN 1 kw-U, DA-1.
WORX(AM) Madison IN 1 kw-D, 58 w-N, DA-2.
KSCB(AM) Liberal KS 1 kw-D, 500 w-N, DA-N.
WAIN(AM) Columbia KY 1 kw-D, 68 w-N.
WKZT(AM) Fulton KY 1 kw-D, 54 w-N.
WVKY(AM) Louisa KY 1 kw-D, 100 w-PSSA.
KVCL(AM) Winnfield LA 1 kw-U, 500 w-CH.
WLAW(AM) Fairhaven MA 5 kw-U, DA-2.
WSPR(AM) Springfield MA 5 kw-D, 1 kw-N, DA-2.
WCBC(AM) Cumberland MD 5 kw-D, 1 kw-N, DA-2.
WMKT(AM) Charlevoix MI 5 kw-D, DA-N.
WXYT(AM) Detroit MI 5 kw-U, DA-N.
WJJY(AM) Baxter MN 5 kw-U.
KWEB(AM) Rochester MN 5 kw-D, 1 kw-N, DA-2.
KGNM(AM) St. Joseph MO 1 kw-D, DA.
KOZQ(AM) Waynesville MO 500 w-D.
WVOM(AM) Iuka MS 1 kw-D.
WLSM(AM) Louisville MS 5 kw-D.
WMLC(AM) Monticello MS 1 kw-D.
WCGC(AM) Belmont NC 5 kw-D, 500 w-N, DA-2.
WMPM(AM) Smithfield NC 5 kw-D.
KLXX(AM) Bismarck-Mandan ND 1 kw-D, 250 w-N.
WTSN(AM) Dover NH 5 kw-D.
WMIZ(AM) Vineland NJ 500 w-D, 350 w-N, DA-N.
KINN(AM) Alamogordo NM 1 kw-D, 500 w-N.
KPLY(AM) Sparks NV 5 kw-U, DA-2.
WHLD(AM) Niagara Falls NY 5 kw-D, 147 w-N, DA-2.
WDLA(AM) Walton NY 5 kw-D, 100 w-N.
WILE(AM) Cambridge OH 1 kw-D.
WUCO(AM) Marysville OH 500 w-U, DA-2.
KTRT(AM) Claremore OK 1 kw-U, DA-N.
KAJO(AM) Grants Pass OR 5 kw-D, 48 w-N.
WLBR(AM) Lebanon PA 5 kw-D.
WBHC(AM) Hampton SC 1 kw-D.
WYAK(AM) Surfside Beach-Garden City SC 5 kw-D, 500 w-N, DA-2.
*KNWC(AM) Sioux Falls SD 2.5 kw-U, DA-N.
WLIK(AM) Newport TN 5 kw-D, 500 w-N, DA-N.

U.S. AM Stations by Frequency

WQKR(AM) Portland TN 1 kw-D, 60 w-N.
KIOX(AM) Bay City TX 1 kw-U, DA-N.
KEPS(AM) Eagle Pass TX 1 kw-D.
KESS(AM) Fort Worth TX 5 kw-U.
WWES(AM) Hot Springs VA 1 kw-D.
WTJZ(AM) Newport News VA 1 kw-U, DA-N.
WHEO(AM) Stuart VA 5 kw-D.
KBAM(AM) Longview WA 5 kw-D, 83 w-N.
WRJC(AM) Mauston WI 500 w-D.
KIML(AM) Gillette WY 5 kw-D, 1 kw-N, DA-N.

1280 khz Regional III

WPID(AM) Piedmont AL 1 kw-D, 84 w-N.
WWPG(AM) Tuscaloosa AL 5 kw-D, 500 w-N, DA-N.
KNBY(AM) Newport AR 1 kw-D, 87 w-N.
KHEP(AM) Phoenix AZ 2.5 kw-D, 230 w-N.
KKAL(AM) Arroyo Grande CA 5-kw-D, 2.5 kw-N, DA-2.
*KFRN(AM) Long Beach CA 1 kw-U, DA-D.
KJAX(AM) Stockton CA 1 kw-U, DA-N
KXKL(AM) Denver CO 5 kw-U, DA-2.
WECY(AM) Seaford DE 1 kw-D, 250 w-N.
WGTX(AM) DeFuniak Springs FL 5 kw-D.
WIPC(AM) Lake Wales FL 1 kw-D, 500 w-N, DA-N.
WTMY(AM) Sarasota FL 2.5 kw-D, 340 w-N, DA-2.
WKXK(AM) Macon GA 5 kw-D, 99 w-N.
KCOB(AM) Newton IA 1 kw-D, 500 w-N.
WBIG(AM) Aurora IL 1 kw-D, 500 w-N, DA-2.
WWOK(AM) Evansville IN 5 kw-D, 1 kw-N, DA-N.
KSOK(AM) Arkansas City KS 1 kw-D, 100 w-N.
WCPM(AM) Cumberland KY 1 kw-D.
WKYY(AM) Lancaster KY 1 kw-D.
WQUE(AM) New Orleans LA 5 kw-U, DA-1.
WEIM(AM) Fitchburg MA 5 kw-D, 1 kw-N, DA-2.
WABK(AM) Gardiner ME 5 kw-U, DA-N.
WFYC(AM) Alma MI 1 kw-D, 45 w-N.
WWTC(AM) Minneapolis MN 5 kw-U, DA-N.
KVOX(AM) Moorhead MN 5 kw-D, 1 kw-N, DA-2.
KDKD(AM) Clinton MO 1 kw-D, 58 w-N.
KYRO(AM) Potosi MO 500 w-D.
WSAT(AM) Salisbury NC 1 kw-U, DA-N.
WYAL(AM) Scotland Neck NC 5 kw.
KCNI(AM) Broken Bow NE 1 kw-D.
KRZE(AM) Farmington NM 5 kw-D.
KDOL(AM) Henderson NV 5 kw-D, 28-N.
WADO(AM) New York NY 5 kw-U, DA-1.
WHTK(AM) Rochester NY 5 kw-U, DA-N.
WONW(AM) Defiance OH 1 kw-D, 500 w-N, DA-N.
WLMJ(AM) Jackson OH 1 kw-D.
KPRV(AM) Poteau OK 1 kw-D.
KDUK(AM) Eugene OR 5 kw-D, 1 kw-N, DA-N.
WSQV(AM) Berwick PA 1 kw-D, 175 w-N.
WKST(AM) New Castle PA 5 kw-D, 1 kw-N, DA-N.
WCMN(AM) Arecibo PR 5 kw-D, 1 kw-N.
WANS(AM) Anderson SC 5 kw-D, 1 kw-N, DA-N.
WJAY(AM) Mullins SC 5 kw-D, 270 w-N.
WMCP(AM) Columbia TN 5 kw-D, 500 w-N, DA-N.
WDNT(AM) Dayton TN 1 kw-D, 345 w-N.
KEAN(AM) Abilene TX 500 w-D, 226 w-N.
KWHI(AM) Brenham TX 1 kw-D, 89 w-N.
KARW(AM) Longview TX 1 kw-D, 56 w-N.
KVWG(AM) Pearsall TX 500 w-D.
KDYL(AM) Salt Lake City UT 5 kw-D, 500 w-N, DA-N.
WTTX(AM) Appomattox VA 1 kw-D.
WYVE(AM) Wytheville VA 2.5 kw-D, 164 w-N.
KTOL(AM) Lacey WA 1 kw-D, 500 w-N.
KUDY(AM) Spokane WA 5 kw-D, DA.
KIT(AM) Yakima WA 5 kw-D, 1 kw-N.
WGLR(AM) Lancaster WI 500 w-D.
WNAM(AM) Neenah-Menasha WI 5 kw-D, 1 kw-N, DA-2.

1290 khz Regional III

WOPP(AM) Opp AL 2.5 kw-D, 500 w-N, DA-2.
WBTG(AM) Sheffield AL 1 kw-D, 79 w-N.
WYEA(AM) Sylacauga AL 1 kw-D, 50 w-N.
KDMS(AM) El Dorado AR 5 kw-D, 106 w-N.
KUOA(AM) Siloam Springs AR 5 kw-D.
KCUB(AM) Tucson AZ 1 kw-U.
KHSL(AM) Chico CA 5 kw-U, DA-N.
KAZA(AM) Gilroy CA 5 kw-D, DA.
KMEN(AM) San Bernardino CA 5 kw-U, DA-2.
KKSB(AM) Santa Barbara CA 500 w-D, 122 w-N.
WCCC(AM) West Hartford CT 490 w-D.
WJBR(AM) Wilmington DE 2.5 kw-U.
WTMC(AM) Ocala FL 5 kw-D, 1 kw-N, DA-N.
WPCF(AM) Panama City Beach FL 270 w-D, 1 kw-N.
WBZT(AM) West Palm Beach FL 5 kw-U, DA-N.
WDEC(AM) Americus GA 1 kw-D, 31 w-N.
WCHK(AM) Canton GA 5 kw-D, 500 w-N, DA-N.
WCHY(AM) Savannah GA 5 kw-U, DA-N.
KLEH(AM) Anamosa IA 500 w-D, 22 w-N DA-2.
KZBQ(AM) Pocatello ID 1 kw-D.
WIRL(AM) Peoria IL 5 kw-U, DA-2.
KWLS(AM) Pratt KS 5 kw-D, 500 w-N, DA-2.
WCBL(AM) Benton KY 5 kw-D.
WKLB(AM) Manchester KY 50 kw-U.
KJEF(AM) Jennings LA 1 kw-U.
WHGR(AM) Houghton Lake MI 4.9 kw-D.
WNIL(AM) Niles MI 500 w-D.
WAMX(AM) Saline MI 500 w-D, DA.
KSCR(AM) Benson MN 500 w-D.
KALM(AM) Thayer MO 1 kw-D, 56 w-N.
WJBI(AM) Batesville MS 730 w-D, 91 w-N.
WNBN(AM) Meridian MS 1 kw-D, 90 w-N.
WTYL(AM) Tylertown MS 1 kw-D.
KGVO(AM) Missoula MT 5 kw-U, DA-N.
WHKY(AM) Hickory NC 5 kw-D, 1 kw-N, DA-N.
WJCV(AM) Jacksonville NC 1 kw-D.
WXKL(AM) Sanford NC 1 kw-D, 44 w-N.
KKAR(AM) Omaha NE 5 kw-U, DA-N.
WKNE(AM) Keene NH 5 kw-U, DA-1.
WNBF(AM) Binghamton NY 5 kw-U, DA-2.
WOMP(AM) Bellaire OH 1 kw-D, 33 w-N.
WHIO(AM) Dayton OH 5 kw-U, DA-N.
KPHP(AM) Lake Oswego OR 5 kw-U, DA-N.
KUMA(AM) Pendleton OR 5 kw-U, DA-N.
WFBG(AM) Altoona PA 5 kw-D, 1 kw-N, DA-N.
WRCP(AM) Providence RI 5 kw-U, DA-2.
WQMC(AM) Sumter SC 1 kw-U, DA-N.
WATO(AM) Oak Ridge TN 5 kw-D, 500 w-N, DA-2.
KIVY(AM) Crockett TX 2.5 kw-D, 175 w-N.
KRGE(AM) Weslaco TX 5 kw-U, DA-N.
KLLF(AM) Wichita Falls TX 5 kw-D, 250 w-N.
WSTK(AM) Colonial Heights VA 5 kw-D, 41 w-N.
WNLB(AM) Rocky Mount VA 3.2 kw-D, 55 w-N.
WRRA(AM) Frederiksted VI 500 w-D, 250 w-N.
KAPY(AM) Port Angeles WA 1 kw-D, 149 w-N, DA-2.
WMCS(AM) Greenfield WI 5 kw-U, DA-2.
WKLJ(AM) Sparta WI 5 kw-D, 59 w-N.
WVOW(AM) Logan WV 5 kw-D, 1 kw-N, DA-N.
KOWB(AM) Laramie WY 5 kw-D, 1 kw-N, DA-2.

1300 khz Regional III

KAKQ(AM) Fairbanks AK 5 kw-U.
WBSA(AM) Boaz AL 1 kw-D.
WTLS(AM) Tallassee AL 1 kw-D.
WKXM(AM) Winfield AL 5 kw-D, 30 w-N.
KWCK(AM) Searcy AR 5 kw-D, 30 w-N.
KROP(AM) Brawley CA 1 kw-D, 500 w-N.
KYNO(AM) Fresno CA 5 kw-D, 1 kw-N, DA-N.
KPMO(AM) Mendocino CA 5 kw-D, 77 w-N.
KAZN(AM) Pasadena CA 5 kw-D, 1 kw-N, DA-2.
KVOR(AM) Colorado Springs CO 5 kw-D, 1 kw-N.
WAVZ(AM) New Haven CT 1 kw-U, DA-N.
WXXU(AM) Cocoa Beach FL 5 kw-D, 1 kw-N, DA-2.
WFFG(AM) Marathon FL 2.5 kw-U, DA-1.
WQBN(AM) Temple Terrace FL 5 kw-D, 1 kw-N, DA-2.
WMTM(AM) Moultrie GA 5 kw-D.
WNEA(AM) Newnan GA 1 kw-D.
WIMO(AM) Winder GA 1 kw-D, 59 w-N.
KGLO(AM) Mason City IA 5 kw-U, DA-N.
KLER(AM) Orofino ID 5 kw-D, 1 kw-U, DA-N.
WTAQ(AM) La Grange IL 5 kw-D, 500 w-N, DA-2.
WFRX(AM) West Frankfort IL 1 kw-D.
WPDJ(AM) Huntington IN 500 w-D, DA.
WJSH(AM) Terre Haute IN 500 w-D.
WLXG(AM) Lexington KY 2.5 kw-D, 1 kw-N, DA-N.
WIBR(AM) Baton Rouge LA 5 kw-D, 1 kw-N, DA-2.
KFLO(AM) Shreveport LA 5 kw-D.
WJDA(AM) Quincy MA 1 kw-D.
WJFK(AM) Baltimore MD 5 kw-U, DA-2.
WOOD(AM) Grand Rapids MI 5 kw-U, DA-N.
WQPM(AM) Princeton MN 1 kw-D, 83 w-N.
KMMO(AM) Marshall MO 1 kw-D, 68 w-N.
WKXI(AM) Jackson MS 5 kw-D, 1 kw-N.
WSSG(AM) Goldsboro NC 1 kw-D, 50 w-N.
WLNC(AM) Laurinburg NC 500 w-D.
WSYD(AM) Mount Airy NC 5 kw-D, 1 kw-N, DA-N.
KBRL(AM) McCook NE 5 kw-D, DA.
WPNH(AM) Plymouth NH 5 kw-D.
WIMG(AM) Ewing NJ 5 kw-D, 1 kw-N, DA-2.
KPTL(AM) Carson City NV 5 kw-D, 500 w-N, DA-N.
WZZZ(AM) Fulton NY 1 kw-D.
WXRL(AM) Lancaster NY 2.4 kw-D, 2.5 kw-N, DA-2.
WQBK(AM) Rensselaer NY 5 kw-U, DA-2.
WLIR(AM) Spring Valley NY 500 w-D, 83 w-N, DA-2.
WERE(AM) Cleveland OH 5 kw-U, DA-1.
WMVO(AM) Mount Vernon OH 500 w-D, DA.
KAKC(AM) Tulsa OK 5 kw-D, 1 kw-N, DA-2.
KDOV(AM) Phoenix OR 20 kw-U, DA-N.
KACI(AM) The Dalles OR 1 kw-D, 54 w-N.
WWCH(AM) Clarion PA 1 kw-D.
WXPX(AM) West Hazleton PA 5 kw-D, 500 w-N, DA-2.
WTIL(AM) Mayaguez PR 1 kw-U.
WCKI(AM) Greer SC 1 kw-D.
WKSC(AM) Kershaw SC 500 w-D.
KOLY(AM) Mobridge SD 5 kw-D, 111 w-N.
WMTN(AM) Morristown TN 5 kw-D, 100 w-N.
WNQM(AM) Nashville TN 5 kw-U, DA-N.
KVET(AM) Austin TX 5 kw-D, 1 kw-N, DA-2.
KKUB(AM) Brownfield TX 1 kw-D.
KLAR(AM) Laredo TX 1 kw-D, 500 w-N, DA-N.
KKAS(AM) Silsbee TX 500 w-D.
WKCY(AM) Harrisonburg VA 5 kw-D.
KMPS(AM) Seattle WA 5 kw-U, DA-N.
WCLG(AM) Morgantown WV 2.5 kw-D, 44 w-N.
WCOZ(AM) St. Albans WV 1 kw-D, 49 w-N.

1310 khz Regional III

WHEP(AM) Foley AL 1 kw-D.
WAJO(AM) Marion AL 5 kw-D.
WJRA(AM) Priceville AL 1 kw-D.
KBOK(AM) Malvern AR 1 kw-D.
KXAM(AM) Mesa AZ 5 kw-D, 500 w-N, DA-N.
KIQQ(AM) Barstow CA 5 kw-D, 118 w-N, DA-1.
KFVR(AM) Crescent City CA 1 kw-D.
KDIA(AM) Oakland CA 5 kw-U, DA-1.
KMYX(AM) Taft CA 1 kw-D, 45 w-N.
KFKA(AM) Greeley CO 5 kw-D, 1 kw-N, DA-N.
WICH(AM) Norwich CT 5 kw-U, DA-2.
WYND(AM) De Land FL 5 kw-D, 95 w-N.
WAUC(AM) Wauchula FL 5 kw-D, 500 w-N, DA-2.
WXLL(AM) Decatur GA 500 w-D.
WOKA(AM) Douglas GA 1 kw-D.
WBRO(AM) Waynesboro GA 1 kw-D.
WPLV(AM) West Point GA 1 kw-D.
KOKX(AM) Keokuk IA 1 kw-D, 500 w-N, DA-N.
KDLS(AM) Perry IA 500 w-D, 300 w-N, DA-2.
KLIX(AM) Twin Falls ID 5 kw-D, 2.5 kw-N, DA-N.
WTLC(AM) Indianapolis IN 5 kw-D, 1 kw-N, DA-N.
KFLA(AM) Scott City KS 500 w-D, 147 w-N.
WTTL(AM) Madisonville KY 1.5 kw-D, 500 w-N, DA-N.
WDOC(AM) Prestonsburg KY 5 kw-D.
KEZM(AM) Sulphur LA 500 w-D, 50 w-N, DA-2.
KMBS(AM) West Monroe LA 5 kw-D, 49 w-N.
WORC(AM) Worcester MA 5 kw-D, 1 kw-N, DA-2.
WLOB(AM) Portland ME 5 kw-U, DA-2.
WMTG(AM) Dearborn MI 5 kw-U, DA-2.
WCCW(AM) Traverse City MI 5 kw-D.
KRBI(AM) St. Peter MN 1 kw-D, 343 w-N, DA-1.
KBMV(AM) Birch Tree MO 1 kw-D, 60 w-N.
KFSB(AM) Joplin MO 5 kw-D, 1 kw-N, DA-2.
WHLV(AM) Hattiesburg MS 1 kw-D.
KEIN(AM) Great Falls MT 5 kw-D, 1 kw-N.
WISE(AM) Asheville NC 5 kw-D, 1 kw-N, DA-N.
WGSP(AM) Charlotte NC 1 kw-D, DA.
WTIK(AM) Durham NC 5 kw-D, 1 kw-N, DA-2.
KNOX(AM) Grand Forks ND 5 kw-U, DA-N.
KGMT(AM) Fairbury NE 500 w-D, 97 w-N.
WJLK(AM) Asbury Park NJ 2.5 kw-D, 1 kw-N, DA-2.
WSSJ(AM) Camden NJ 1 kw-D, 250 w-N.
WXMC(AM) Parsippany-Troy Hills NJ 1 kw-D, 100 w-N, DA.
KIVA(AM) Corrales NM 5 kw-D, 500 w-N, DA-N.
WVIP(AM) Mount Kisco NY 5 kw-D, 33 w-N, DA-2.
WTLB(AM) Utica NY 5 kw-D, 500 w-N, DA-2.
WDPN(AM) Alliance OH 1 kw-D, 500 w-N, DA-2.
KNPT(AM) Newport OR 5 kw-D, 1 kw-N, DA-N.
WAYC(AM) Bedford PA 2.5 kw-D, 85 w-N.
WHGL(AM) Troy PA 500 w-D, 72 w-N.
WNAE(AM) Warren PA 5 kw-D, 94 w-N.
WDKD(AM) Kingstree SC 5 kw-D, 67 w-N.
WDOD(AM) Chattanooga TN 5 kw-U, DA-N.
WDXI(AM) Jackson TN 5 kw-D, 1 kw-N, DA-N.
WOCV(AM) Oneida TN 1 kw-D.
KZIP(AM) Amarillo TX 1 kw-D.
KAAM(AM) Dallas TX 5 kw-D, 2 kw-N, DA-2.
KXTN(AM) San Antonio TX 5 kw-D, 280 w-N, DA-2.
WDCT(AM) Fairfax VA 5 kw-D, 500 w-N, DA-2.
WGH(AM) Newport News VA 5 kw-U, DA-N.
KARY(AM) Prosser WA 5 kw-D, 66 w-N.
WIBA(AM) Madison WI 5 kw-U, DA-N.
WSLW(AM) White Sulphur Springs WV 5 kw-D.

1320 khz Regional III

WAGG(AM) Birmingham AL 5 kw-D, 111 w-N.
WAGF(AM) Dothan AL 1 kw-U, DA-N.
KWHN(AM) Fort Smith AR 5 kw-U, DA-N.
KRLW(AM) Walnut Ridge AR 1 kw-D.
*KAWC(AM) Yuma AZ 1 kw-D, 147 w-N.
KHSJ(AM) Hemet CA 500 w-D, 300 w-N, DA-2.
KGMG(AM) Oceanside CA 9.5 kw, DA-1.
KCTC(AM) Sacramento CA 5 kw-U, DA-2.
WATR(AM) Waterbury CT 5 kw-D, 1 kw-N, DA-2.
WFRK(AM) Coleman FL 500 w-D, 60 w-N.
WLQY(AM) Hollywood FL 5 kw-U, DA-2.
WQIK(AM) Jacksonville FL 5 kw-U, DA-N.
WAMR(AM) Venice FL 5 kw-D, 1 kw-N, DA-2.
WHIE(AM) Griffin GA 5 kw-D, 83 w-N.
KNIA(AM) Knoxville IA 500 w-D, 222 w-N.
KMAQ(AM) Maquoketa IA 500 w-U.
WKAN(AM) Kankakee IL 1 kw-D, 500 w-N, DA-N.
KLWN(AM) Lawrence KS 500 w-D, 250 w-N.
WBRT(AM) Bardstown KY 1 kw-D.
WCVG(AM) Covington KY 500 w-D, 430 w-N, DA-2.
WNGO(AM) Mayfield KY 1 kw-D, 97 w-N.
KNCB(AM) Vivian LA 5 kw-D.
WARA(AM) Attleboro MA 5 kw-U, DA-2.
WICO(AM) Salisbury MD 1 kw-D, 36 w-N.
WILS(AM) Lansing MI 5 kw-D, 1 kw-N, DA-2.
WDMJ(AM) Marquette MI 5 kw-D, 1 kw-N, DA-N.
KOZY(AM) Grand Rapids MN 5 kw-U, DA-2.
KSIV(AM) Clayton MO 5 kw-D, 270 w-N, DA-N.
WRJW(AM) Picayune MS 5 kw-D, 75 kw-N.
WAGY(AM) Forest City NC 1 kw-D, 500 w-N, DA-N.
WGLD(AM) Greensboro NC 5 kw-U, DA-2.
WKRK(AM) Murphy NC 5 kw-D, 62 w-N.
WTOW(AM) Washington NC 500 w-D.
KHRT(AM) Minot ND 2.5 kw-D, 310 w-N.
KOLT(AM) Scottsbluff NE 5 kw-D, 1 kw-N, DA-N.
WDER(AM) Derry NH 5 kw-D, 1 kw-N, DA-2.
KRDD(AM) Roswell NM 1 kw-D.
WHHO(AM) Hornell NY 5 kw-D.
WLOH(AM) Lancaster OH 1 kw-D, 28 w-N.
WOBL(AM) Oberlin OH 1 kw-U, DA-2.
KXOL(AM) Clinton OK 1 kw-D, 108 w-N.
KZZK(AM) Springfield OR 1 kw-D, 40 w-N.
WKAP(AM) Allentown PA 5 kw-D, 1 kw-N, DA-2.
WGET(AM) Gettysburg PA 1 kw-D, 500 w-N, DA-2.
WJAS(AM) Pittsburgh PA 5 kw-U, DA-N.
WUNO(AM) San Juan PR 5 kw-D, 1 kw-N.
WOMG(AM) Columbia SC 5 kw-D, 2.5 kw-N, DA-N.
KELO(AM) Sioux Falls SD 5 kw-U, DA-N.
WKIN(AM) Kingsport TN 5 kw-D, 500 w-N, DA-N.
WMSR(AM) Manchester TN 5 kw-D, 79 w-N.
KVMC(AM) Colorado City TX 1 kw-D.
KXYZ(AM) Houston TX 5 kw-U, DA-N.
KCNR(AM) Salt Lake City UT 50 kw-D, 200 w-N.
WVLR(AM) Lynchburg VA 1 kw-U.
WLEE(AM) Richmond VA 5 kw-D, DA.
WWWT(AM) Randolph VT 1 kw-D, 66 w-N.
KXRO(AM) Aberdeen WA 5 kw-D, 1 kw-N, DA-N.
KSMX(AM) Walla Walla WA 1 kw-D.
WFHR(AM) Wisconsin Rapids WI 5 kw-D, 500 w-N, DA-N.

1330 khz Regional III

WPRN(AM) Butler AL 5 kw-D.
WZCT(AM) Scottsboro AL 5 kw-D, 38 w-N.
KFCA(AM) Conway AR 500 w-D, 64 w-N.
KMRR(AM) South Tucson AZ 2 kw-D, 5 kw-N, DA-N.
KLOM(AM) Lompoc CA 1 kw-D, DA.
KWKW(AM) Los Angeles CA 5 kw-U, DA-N.

Broadcasting & Cable Yearbook 1994
B-494

… U.S. AM Stations by Frequency

KLBS(AM) Los Banos CA 500 w-D, 5 kw-N, DA-N.
KRDG(AM) Redding CA 5 kw-D.
WJNX(AM) Fort Pierce FL 5 kw-D, 1 kw-N, DA-2.
WWAB(AM) Lakeland FL 1 kw-D.
WEBY(AM) Milton FL 5 kw-D, 79 w-N.
WCVC(AM) Tallahassee FL 5 kw-D.
WPPI(AM) Carrollton GA 500 w-D.
WMLT(AM) Dublin GA 5 kw-D, 500 w-N, DA-N.
WKZD(AM) Murrayville GA 1 kw-D.
KWLO(AM) Waterloo IA 5 kw-U, DA-2.
WKTA(AM) Evanston IL 5 kw-D, 17 w-N, DA-1.
WRAM(AM) Monmouth IL 1 kw-D, 50 w-N, DA-1.
WRRR(AM) Rockford IL 1 kw-D, 91 w-N, DA-2.
WVHI(AM) Evansville IN 5 kw-D, 1 kw-N, DA-N.
WTRE(AM) Greensburg IN 500 w-D, 41 w-N, DA-2.
KFH(AM) Wichita KS 5 kw-U, DA-N.
WKDP(AM) Corbin KY 5 kw-D, DA.
WMOR(AM) Morehead KY 1 kw-D.
KVOL(AM) Lafayette LA 5 kw-D, 1 kw-N, DA-2.
WRCA(AM) Waltham MA 5 kw-U, DA-2.
WASA(AM) Havre de Grace MD 5 kw-D, 500 w-N, DA-N.
*KNOW(AM) Minneapolis MN 5 kw-U, DA-2.
KUKU(AM) Willow Springs MO 1 kw-D, 52 w-N.
WFTO(AM) Fulton MS 5 kw-D.
WNIX(AM) Greenville MS 1 kw-D, 500 w-N, DA-N.
WCPQ(AM) Havelock NC 1 kw-D.
KDRQ(AM) Wishek ND 500 w-D, 214 w-N.
KGAK(AM) Gallup NM 5 kw-D, 1 kw-N, DA-N.
*WWRV(AM) New York NY 5 kw-U, DA-1.
WEBO(AM) Owego NY 5 kw-D, 50 w-N.
WFWC(AM) Springville NY 1 kw-U, DA-2.
WHAZ(AM) Troy NY 1 kw-U.
WASN(AM) Campbell OH 500 w-D, 1 kw-N, DA-2.
WFIN(AM) Findlay OH 1 kw-D, 79 w-N.
WYPC(AM) Wellston OH 500 w-D, 50 w-N.
WELW(AM) Willoughby-Eastlake OH 500 w-D.
KUPL(AM) Portland OR 5 kw-U, DA-1.
WFLP(AM) Erie PA 5 kw-U, DA-2.
WADJ(AM) Somerset PA 5 kw-D, 35 w-N, DA-1.
WENA(AM) Yauco PR 2 kw-U, DA-1.
WPJS(AM) Conway SC 5 kw-D, 500 w-N, DA-N.
WFBC(AM) Greenville SC 5 kw-U, DA-N.
WAEW(AM) Crossville TN 1 kw-D.
KMIL(AM) Cameron TX 500 w-D, 97 w-N.
KSWA(AM) Graham TX 500 w-D.
KLBO(AM) Monahans TX 5 kw-D, 1 kw-N, DA-N.
KGLD(AM) Tyler TX 1 kw-D, 500 w-N.
WBTM(AM) Danville VA 5 kw-D, 1 kw-N, DA-N.
WRAA(AM) Luray VA 1 kw-D, 40 w-N.
WOLD(AM) Marion VA 5 kw-D, 31 w-N.
WESR(AM) Onley-Onancock VA 5 kw-D, 51 w-N.
KENU(AM) Enumclaw WA 500 w-D, 26 w-N.
*KMBI(AM) Spokane WA 5 kw-D.
WHBL(AM) Sheboygan WI 5 kw-D, 1 kw-N, DA-2.
WETZ(AM) New Martinsville WV 1 kw-D, 60 w-N.
KOVE(AM) Lander WY 5 kw-D, 1 kw-N, DA-N.

1340 khz Local IV
WXXR(AM) Cullman AL 1 kw-U.
WSBM(AM) Florence AL 1 kw-U.
WMRK(AM) Selma AL 1 kw-U.
WFEB(AM) Sylacauga AL 1 kw-U.
KBTA(AM) Batesville AR 1 kw-U.
KZNG(AM) Hot Springs AR 1 kw-U.
*KCAT(AM) Pine Bluff AR 1 kw-U.
KIKO(AM) Miami AZ 1 kw-U.
KPGE(AM) Page AZ 1 kw-U.
KATA(AM) Arcata CA 1 kw-U.
KWXY(AM) Cathedral City CA 1 kw-U.
KKTR(AM) Fresno CA 1 kw-U.
KVOY(AM) Mojave CA 1 kw-U.
KTOX(AM) Needles CA 1 kw-U.
KORV(AM) Oroville CA 1 kw-U.
KGLW(AM) San Luis Obispo CA 1 kw-U.
KIST(AM) Santa Barbara CA 1 kw-U.
KKYD(AM) Denver CO 1 kw-U.
KQIL(AM) Grand Junction CO 1 kw-U.
KVRH(AM) Salida CO 1 kw-U.
WNHC(AM) New Haven CT 1 kw-U.
WYCB(AM) Washington DC 1 kw-U.
WTAN(AM) Clearwater FL 1 kw-U.
WROD(AM) Daytona Beach FL 1 kw-U.
WDSR(AM) Lake City FL 1 kw-U.
WTYS(AM) Marianna FL 1 kw-U.
WPBR(AM) Palm Beach FL 1 kw-U.
WITS(AM) Sebring FL 1 kw-U.
WFSH(AM) Valparaiso-Niceville FL 1 kw-U.
WGAU(AM) Athens GA 1 kw-U.
WIGO(AM) Atlanta GA 1 kw-U.
WBBQ(AM) Augusta GA 1 kw-U.
WGAA(AM) Cedartown GA 1 kw-U.
WOKS(AM) Columbus GA 1 kw-U.
WBBT(AM) Lyons GA 1 kw-U.
WALH(AM) Mountain City GA 1 kw-U.
WTIF(AM) Tifton GA 1 kw-U.
KROS(AM) Clinton IA 1 kw-U.
KANR(AM) Nampa ID 1 kw-U.
KACH(AM) Preston ID 1 kw-U.
WSOY(AM) Decatur IL 1 kw-U.
WJPF(AM) Herrin IL 1 kw-U.
WJOL(AM) Joliet IL 1 kw-U.
WBIW(AM) Bedford IN 1 kw-U.
WTRC(AM) Elkhart IN 1 kw-U.
WLBC(AM) Muncie IN 1 kw-U.
KNHN(AM) Kansas City KS 1 kw-U.
KPHN(AM) Pittsburg KS 1 kw-U.
WCMI(AM) Ashland KY 1 kw-U.
WBGN(AM) Bowling Green KY 1 kw-U.
WKCB(AM) Hindman KY 6 kw-U.
WNBS(AM) Murray KY 1 kw-U.
WEKY(AM) Richmond KY 1 kw-U.

KRMD(AM) Shreveport LA 1 kw-U.
WGAW(AM) Gardner MA 1 kw-U.
WNBH(AM) New Bedford MA 1 kw-U.
WBRK(AM) Pittsfield MA 1 kw-U.
WFAU(AM) Augusta ME 1 kw-U.
WLVC(AM) Fort Kent ME 250 w-D, 1 kw-N.
WHGS(AM) Houlton ME 1 kw-U.
WLEW(AM) Bad Axe MI 1 kw-D, DA-D.
WLAV(AM) Grand Rapids MI 1 kw-U.
WCSR(AM) Hillsdale MI 500 w-D, 1 kw-N.
WMTE(AM) Manistee MI 1 kw-U.
WAGN(AM) Menominee MI 1 kw-U.
WMBN(AM) Petoskey MI 1 kw-U.
WEXL(AM) Royal Oak MI 1 kw-U, DA-D.
KVBR(AM) Brainerd MN 1 kw-U.
KDLM(AM) Detroit Lakes MN 1 kw-U.
WEVE(AM) Eveleth MN 1 kw-U.
KROC(AM) Rochester MN 1 kw-U.
KWLM(AM) Willmar MN 1 kw-U.
KXEO(AM) Mexico MO 1 kw-U.
KSMO(AM) Salem MO 1 kw-U.
KIDS(AM) Springfield MO 1 kw-U.
WKOZ(AM) Kosciusko MS 1 kw-U.
WAML(AM) Laurel MS 1 kw-U.
KCAP(AM) Helena MT 1 kw-U.
KPRK(AM) Livingston MT 1 kw-U.
KYLT(AM) Missoula MT 1 kw-U.
WOOW(AM) Greenville NC 1 kw-U.
WJRI(AM) Lenoir NC 1 kw-U.
WAGR(AM) Lumberton NC 1 kw-U.
WCBQ(AM) Oxford NC 1 kw-U.
WADE(AM) Wadesboro NC 500 w-U.
WBMS(AM) Wilmington NC 1 kw-U.
WMQX(AM) Winston-Salem NC 1 kw-U.
KPOK(AM) Bowman ND 1 kw-U.
KXPO(AM) Grafton ND 1 kw-U.
KHUB(AM) Fremont NE 500 w-D, 1 kw-N.
KGFW(AM) Kearney NE 1 kw-U.
KSID(AM) Sidney NE 1 kw-U.
WDCR(AM) Hanover NH 1 kw-U.
WWNH(AM) Madbury NH 250 w-U.
WMID(AM) Atlantic City NJ 1 kw-U.
KCQL(AM) Aztec NM 1 kw-U.
KSSR(AM) Santa Rosa NM 1 kw-U.
KSIL(AM) Silver City NM 1 kw-U.
KKIT(AM) Taos NM 1 kw-U.
KMTW(AM) Las Vegas NV 1 kw-U.
KXEQ(AM) Reno NV 1 kw-U.
WMBO(AM) Auburn NY 1 kw-U.
WENT(AM) Gloversville NY 1 kw-U.
WKSN(AM) Jamestown NY 500 w-D, 1 kw-N.
WLVL(AM) Lockport NY 1 kw-U, DA-D.
WMSA(AM) Massena NY 1 kw-U.
WALL(AM) Middletown NY 1 kw-U.
WIRY(AM) Plattsburgh NY 1 kw-U.
WNCO(AM) Ashland OH 1 kw-U.
*WOUB(AM) Athens OH 500 w-D, 1 kw-N.
WIZE(AM) Springfield OH 1 kw-U.
WSTV(AM) Steubenville OH 1 kw-U.
KIHN(AM) Hugo OK 1 kw-U.
KXXY(AM) Oklahoma City OK 1 kw-U.
KTOW(AM) Sand Springs OK 500 w-D, 1 kw-N.
KLOO(AM) Corvallis OR 1 kw-U.
KWRI(AM) Enterprise OR 1 kw-U.
KIHR(AM) Hood River OR 1 kw-U.
KBBR(AM) North Bend OR 1 kw-U.
WCVI(AM) Connellsville PA 1 kw-U.
*WSAJ(AM) Grove City PA 100 w-U.
WOYL(AM) Oil City PA 1 kw-U, DA-D.
WHAT(AM) Philadelphia PA 1 kw-U.
WRAW(AM) Reading PA 1 kw-U.
WTRN(AM) Tyrone PA 1 kw-U.
WWPA(AM) Williamsport PA 1 kw-U.
WNOZ(AM) Aguadilla PR 1 kw-U.
WOKE(AM) Charleston SC 1 kw-U.
WRHI(AM) Rock Hill SC 1 kw-U.
WSSC(AM) Sumter SC 1 kw-U.
KIJV(AM) Huron SD 1 kw-U.
KTOQ(AM) Rapid City SD 1 kw-U.
WBAC(AM) Cleveland TN 1 kw-U.
WKRM(AM) Columbia TN 1 kw-U.
WGRV(AM) Greeneville TN 1 kw-U.
WKGN(AM) Knoxville TN 1 kw-U.
WLOK(AM) Memphis TN 1 kw-U.
WCDT(AM) Winchester TN 1 kw-U.
KYYD(AM) Abilene TX 1 kw-U.
KHLB(AM) Burnet TX 1 kw-U.
KAND(AM) Corsicana TX 1 kw-U.
KVIV(AM) El Paso TX 1 kw-U.
KKAM(AM) Lubbock TX 1 kw-U.
KRBA(AM) Lufkin TX 1 kw-U.
KOLE(AM) Port Arthur TX 1 kw-U.
KCRN(AM) San Angelo TX 1 kw-U.
KAMG(AM) Victoria TX 1 kw-U.
KTMP(AM) Heber City UT 1 kw-U.
WKEY(AM) Covington VA 1 kw-U.
WHAP(AM) Hopewell VA 1 kw-U.
WJMA(AM) Orange VA 1 kw-U.
WBLB(AM) Pulaski VA 1 kw-U.
WSTA(AM) Charlotte Amalie VI 1 kw-U.
WVNR(AM) Poultney VT 1 kw-U.
WSTJ(AM) St. Johnsbury VT 1 kw-U.
KLKI(AM) Anacortes WA 1 kw-U.
KTCR(AM) Kennewick WA 1 kw-U.
KAPA(AM) Raymond WA 1 kw-U.
KWWX(AM) Wenatchee WA 1 kw-U.
WLDY(AM) Ladysmith WI 1 kw-U.
WLZR(AM) Milwaukee WI 1 kw-U.
WHAR(AM) Clarksburg WV 1 kw-U.
WEPM(AM) Martinsburg WV 1 kw-U.

WMON(AM) Montgomery WV 1 kw-U.
WXEE(AM) Welch WV 1 kw-U.
KSGT(AM) Jackson WY 1 kw-U.
KYCN(AM) Wheatland WY 250 w-U.
KWOR(AM) Worland WY 1 kw-U.

1350 khz Regional III
WELB(AM) Elba AL 1 kw-U.
WGAD(AM) Gadsden AL 5 kw-D, 1 kw-N, DA-N.
KYXZ(AM) Cabot AR 2.5 kw-D, 73 w-N.
KBID(AM) Bakersfield CA 1 kw-D, 33 w-N.
KCKC(AM) San Bernardino CA 5 kw-D, 500 w-N, DA-2.
KSRO(AM) Santa Rosa CA 5 kw-U, DA-N.
KGHF(AM) Pueblo CO 5 kw-D, 1 kw-N, DA-N.
WNLK(AM) Norwalk CT 1 kw-D, 500 w-N, DA-N.
WINY(AM) Putnam CT 5 kw-D, 70 w-N.
WWHL(AM) Cocoa FL 1 kw-U, DA-N.
WDCF(AM) Dade City FL 1 kw-D, 500 w-N, DA-N.
WCRM(AM) Fort Myers FL 1 kw-D, 150 w-N.
WGIA(AM) Blackshear GA 5 kw-D.
WRWH(AM) Cleveland GA 1 kw-D.
WCOP(AM) Warner Robins GA 5 kw-D, 500 w-N, DA-N.
KRNT(AM) Des Moines IA 5 kw-U, DA-N.
KRLC(AM) Lewiston ID 5 kw-D, 1 kw-N, DA-N.
WXCL(AM) Peoria IL 1 kw-U, DA-2.
WJBD(AM) Salem IL 430 w-D, 60 w-N.
WIOU(AM) Kokomo IN 5 kw-D, 1 kw-N, DA-2.
KMAN(AM) Manhattan KS 500 w-D, 40 w-N.
WLOU(AM) Louisville KY 5 kw-U, DA-N.
WSMB(AM) New Orleans LA 5 kw-U, DA-2.
WGDN(AM) Gladwin MI 1 kw-D, DA.
WHMI(AM) Howell MI 500 w-D, 29 w-N.
KCHK(AM) New Prague MN 500 w-D, 70 w-N, DA-2.
KDIO(AM) Ortonville MN 1 kw-U.
WCMP(AM) Pine City MN 1 kw-D.
KCHR(AM) Charleston MO 1 kw-D, 79 w-N.
KSLQ(AM) Washington MO 500 w-D, 100 w-N, DA-1.
WKCU(AM) Corinth MS 1 kw-D, 68 w-N.
WQNX(AM) Aberdeen NC 2.5 kw-D, 28 w-N, DA-2.
WZQR(AM) Black Mountain NC 1 kw-D.
WHIP(AM) Mooresville NC 1 kw-D, DA-D.
WLLY(AM) Wilson NC 1 kw-D, 79 w-N.
KBRX(AM) O'Neill NE 1 kw-D.
WLNH(AM) Laconia NH 5 kw-D, 1 kw-N.
WHWH(AM) Princeton NJ 5 kw-D, DA-2.
KABQ(AM) Albuquerque NM 5 kw-D, 500 w-N, DA-N.
WCBA(AM) Corning NY 2 kw-D.
WRNY(AM) Rome NY 500 w-D, 60 w-N.
WSLR(AM) Akron OH 5 kw-U, DA-1.
WCSM(AM) Celina OH 500 w-D, 11 w-N, DA-1.
WCHI(AM) Chillicothe OH 1 kw-D, 250-N.
KRHD(AM) Duncan OK 250 w-D, 100 w-N.
KTLQ(AM) Tahlequah OK 1 kw-D, 61 w-N.
WBEM(AM) Windber PA 2.5 kw-D.
WOYK(AM) York PA 5 kw-D, 1 kw-N, DA-N.
WEGA(AM) Vega Baja PR 2.5 kw-U, DA-2,
WDAR(AM) Darlington SC 1 kw-D.
WLMA(AM) Greenwood SC 1 kw-D, 85 w-N, DA-1.
WRKM(AM) Carthage TN 1 kw-D, 91 w-N.
KCAR(AM) Clarksville TX 500 w-D.
KTXJ(AM) Jasper TX 5 kw-D, 37 w-N.
KCOR(AM) San Antonio TX 5 kw-U, DA-N.
WBLT(AM) Bedford VA 1 kw-D.
WFLS(AM) Fredericksburg VA 1 kw-D, 37 w-N.
WNVA(AM) Norton VA 5 kw-D, 37 w-N.
WSVY(AM) Portsmouth VA 5 kw-U, DA-2.
WPDR(AM) Portage WI 1 kw-D, 41 w-N.

1360 khz Regional III
WZPQ(AM) Jasper AL 1 kw-D, 42 w-N.
WMOB(AM) Mobile AL 5 kw-D, 212 w-N, DA-2.
WMFC(AM) Monroeville AL 1 kw-D.
WELR(AM) Roanoke AL 1 kw-D.
KLYR(AM) Clarksville AR 500 w-D, 98 w-N.
KFFA(AM) Helena AR 1 kw-U, DA-N.
KNNS(AM) Glendale AZ 5 kw-D, 1 kw-N, DA-N.
KFIV(AM) Modesto CA 5 kw-D, 1 kw-N, DA-2.
KZIQ(AM) Ridgecrest CA 1 kw-D, 38 w-N.
KPOP(AM) San Diego CA 5 kw-D, 1 kw-N.
KHNC(AM) Johnstown CO 500 w-D, 450 w-N, DA-2.
WDRC(AM) Hartford CT 5 kw-U, DA-N.
WHNR(AM) Cypress Gardens FL 5 kw-D, 2.5 kw-N, DA-2.
WCGL(AM) Jacksonville FL 5 kw-D.
WKAT(AM) North Miami FL 10 kw-D, 1 kw-N.
WMAC(AM) Metter GA 1 kw-D.
WTSH(AM) Rome GA 500 w-D, 150 w-N.
KHAK(AM) Cedar Rapids IA 1 kw-D, 124 w-N, DA-1.
KBKB(AM) Fort Madison IA 1 kw-D, 35 w-N.
KSCJ(AM) Sioux City IA 5 kw-D, 1 kw-N, DA-N.
WLBK(AM) De Kalb IL 1 kw-D.
WYER(AM) Mt. Carmel IL 500 w-D, 20 w-N.
WGFA(AM) Watseka IL 1 kw-D, DA.
KSRX(AM) El Dorado KS 500 w-D.
WFLW(AM) Monticello KY 1 kw-D.
KNIR(AM) New Iberia LA 1 kw-D, 209 w-N.
KBYO(AM) Tallulah LA 500 w-D.
WLYN(AM) Lynn MA 700 w-D, 76 w-N.
WWLG(AM) Baltimore MD 5 kw-D, 1.7 kw-N, DA-2.
WKYO(AM) Caro MI 1 kw-U, DA-2.
WKMI(AM) Kalamazoo MI 5 kw-D, 1 kw-N, DA-2.
KKBJ(AM) Bemidji MN 5 kw-D, 2.5 kw-N, DA-N.
KRWC(AM) Buffalo MN 500 w-D.
KMRN(AM) Cameron MO 1 kw-D, 25 w-N.
KCMG(AM) Mountain Grove MO 1 kw-D.
WFFF(AM) Columbia MS 1 kw-D, 159 w-N.
WCHL(AM) Chapel Hill NC 5 kw-D, 1 kw-N.
*KNGN(AM) McCook NE 1 kw-D.
WNNJ(AM) Newton NJ 1 kw-D, 75 w-PSSA.
WNJC(AM) Washington Township NJ 5 kw-D, 1 kw-N, DA-2.
KBUY(AM) Ruidoso NM 5 kw-D, 199 w-N.

U.S. AM Stations by Frequency

WKOP(AM) Binghamton NY 5 kw-D, 500 w-N, DA-2.
WMNS(AM) Olean NY 1 kw-D, 30 w-N.
WSAI(AM) Cincinnati OH 5 kw-D, DA-N.
WWOW(AM) Conneaut OH 500 w-D.
KOHU(AM) Hermiston OR 4.3 kw-D, 500 w-N, DA-N.
KUIK(AM) Hillsboro OR 5 kw-U, DA-N.
WIXZ(AM) McKeesport PA 5 kw-D, 1 kw-N, DA-N.
WPPA(AM) Pottsville PA 5 kw-D, 500 w-N, DA-2.
WCHQ(AM) Camuy PR 1 kw-U, DA-D.
WLWZ(AM) Easley SC 1 kw-D.
WBLC(AM) Lenoir City TN 1 kw-D.
WNAH(AM) Nashville TN 1 kw-U.
KLCJ(AM) Amarillo TX 500 w-D, 137 w-N.
KACT(AM) Andrews TX 1 kw-D.
KWWJ(AM) Baytown TX 1 kw-U, DA-2.
KRYS(AM) Corpus Christi TX 1 kw-U.
KAHZ(AM) Fort Worth TX 5 kw-D, 1 kw-N, DA-2.
WBOB(AM) Galax VA 5 kw-D.
WHBG(AM) Harrisonburg VA 4.7 kw-D, 20 w -N.
KKMO(AM) Tacoma WA 5 kw-D.
WGEE(AM) Green Bay WI 5 kw-U, DA-N.
WVRQ(AM) Viroqua WI 5 kw-D, 23 w-N.
WHJC(AM) Matewan WV 1 kw-D.
WMOV(AM) Ravenswood WV 1 kw-U.
KRKK(AM) Rock Springs WY 5 kw-D, 1 kw-N, DA-N.

1370 khz Regional III

WBYE(AM) Calera AL 1 kw-D.
KAWW(AM) Heber Springs AR 1 kw-D.
KTPA(AM) Prescott AR 1 kw-D, 49 w-N.
KWRM(AM) Corona CA 5 kw-D, 2.5 kw-N, DA-2..
KPCO(AM) Quincy CA 5 kw-D, 500 w-N, DA-2.
KKSJ(AM) San Jose CA 5 kw-U, DA-2.
KGEN(AM) Tulare CA 1 kw-D, 136 w-N.
KTMG(AM) Deer Trail CO 5 kw-D, 160 w-N, DA-2.
WOCA(AM) Ocala FL 5 kw-D.
WCOA(AM) Pensacola FL 5 kw-U, DA-N.
WAXE(AM) Vero Beach FL 1 kw-D.
WGHC(AM) Clayton GA 2.5 kw-D.
WLOP(AM) Jesup GA 5 kw-D, 36 w-N.
WFDR(AM) Manchester GA 1 kw-D.
WLOV(AM) Washington GA 1 kw-D.
KLBA(AM) Albia IA 500 w-D, 128 w-N, DA-2.
KDTH(AM) Dubuque IA 5 kw-U, DA-N.
WPRC(AM) Lincoln IL 1 kw-D, 35 w-N.
WGCL(AM) Bloomington IN 5 kw-D, 500 w-N, DA-2.
WLTH(AM) Gary IN 1 kw-D, 500 w-N, DA-N.
KGNO(AM) Dodge City KS 5 kw-D, 1 kw-N, DA-N.
KALN(AM) Iola KS 500 w, 62 w-N.
WABD(AM) Fort Campbell KY 1 kw-D, 53 w-N.
WGOH(AM) Grayson KY 5 kw-D, 21 w-N.
WTKY(AM) Tompkinsville KY 2.1 kw-D.
KAPB(AM) Marksville LA 1 kw-D, 40 w-N.
WDEA(AM) Ellsworth ME 5 kw-U, DA-2.
WKJF(AM) Cadillac MI 5 kw-D, 1 kw-N, DA-N.
WGHN(AM) Grand Haven MI 500 w-D.
KSUM(AM) Fairmont MN 1 kw-U, DA-2.
KWRT(AM) Boonville MO 1 kw-D, 84 w-N.
KCRV(AM) Caruthersville MO 1 kw-D, 63 w-N.
WMGO(AM) Canton MS 1 kw-D, 28 w-N.
KXTL(AM) Butte MT 5 kw-D.
WLTC(AM) Gastonia NC 5 kw-D.
WLLN(AM) Lillington NC 5 kw-D, 49 w-N, DA-2.
WTAB(AM) Tabor City NC 5 kw-D, 109 w-N.
*KFJM(AM) Grand Forks ND 1 kw-D, 250 w-N.
KAWL(AM) York NE 500 w-D, 176 w-N.
WFEA(AM) Manchester NH 5 kw-U, DA-2.
WELV(AM) Ellenville NY 5 kw-D.
WALK(AM) Patchogue NY 500 w-D, 102 w-N.
*WXXI(AM) Rochester NY 5 kw-U, DA-N.
WSPD(AM) Toledo OH 5 kw-U, DA-N.
KRAF(AM) Holdenville OK 500 w-D, 77 w-N.
KAST(AM) Astoria OR 1 kw-U, DA-N.
KFIR(AM) Sweet Home OR 1 kw-D, 72 w-N.
WWCB(AM) Corry PA 1 kw-D, 500 w-N, DA-N.
WPAZ(AM) Pottstown PA 1 kw-D.
WKMC(AM) Roaring Spring PA 5 kw-D, 38 w-N, DA-2.
WIVV(AM) Vieques PR 5 kw-D, 1 kw-N.
WMNY(AM) Elloree-Santee SC 5 kw-D, 177 w-N, DA-2.
WDEF(AM) Chattanooga TN 5 kw-U, DA-N.
WDXE(AM) Lawrenceburg TN 1 kw-D, 44 w-N.
WRGS(AM) Rogersville TN 5 kw-D, 40 w-N.
KFRO(AM) Longview TX 1 kw-U.
KPOS(AM) Post TX 5 kw-D, 158 w-N.
KJCE(AM) Rollingwood TX 5 kw-D, 500 w-N.
KSOP(AM) South Salt Lake UT 5 kw-D, 500 w-N, DA-2.
WHEE(AM) Martinsville VA 5 kw-D, 500 w-N.
WJWS(AM) South Hill VA 5 kw-D.
WBTN(AM) Bennington VT 1 kw-D.
KWNC(AM) Quincy WA 1 kw-D, 500 w-PSA, 40 w-N.
WCCN(AM) Neillsville WI 5 kw-U.
WKSH(AM) Sussex WI 500 w-U, DA-2.
*WVMR(AM) Frost WV 5 kw-D.
WZAO(AM) Moundsville WV 5 kw-D, 20 w-N.
KSHY(AM) Cheyenne WY 1 kw-D, 66 w-N.

1380 khz Regional III

WRAB(AM) Arab AL 1 kw-D.
WGYV(AM) Greenville AL 1 kw-D.
WVSA(AM) Vernon AL 5 kw-D, 39 w-N.
KLPZ(AM) Parker AZ 2.5 kw-D, 58 w-N.
KHJJ(AM) Lancaster CA 1 kw-U, DA.
KSMJ(AM) Sacramento CA 5 kw-U.
KTOM(AM) Salinas CA 5 kw-U, DA-2.
WFNW(AM) Naugatuck CT 5 kw-D, 500 w-N, DA-N.
WLVS(AM) Lake Worth FL 1 kw-D, 500 w-N.
WELE(AM) Ormond Beach FL 5 kw-D, 2.5-N, DA-2.
WRBQ(AM) St. Petersburg FL 5 kw-D.
WAOK(AM) Atlanta GA 5 kw-U, DA-N.
WSIZ(AM) Ocilla GA 5 kw-D.

*KIFO(AM) Pearl City HI 6.1 kw-U.
KCIM(AM) Carroll IA 1 kw-D.
KCII(AM) Washington IA 500 w-D.
WBEL(AM) South Beloit IL 5 kw-U, DA-N.
WQHK(AM) Fort Wayne IN 5 kw-U, DA-2.
KCNW(AM) Fairway KS 2.5 kw-D, 29 w-N.
WHRS(AM) Winchester KY 5 kw-D, 40 w-N.
WYNK(AM) Baton Rouge LA 5 kw-U, DA-N.
WPLB(AM) Greenville MI 1 kw-D, 500 w-N, DA-N.
WPHM(AM) Port Huron MI 5 kw-U, DA-N.
KLIZ(AM) Brainerd MN 5 kw-U, DA-N.
KAGE(AM) Winona MN 4 kw-D.
KASP(AM) St. Louis MO 5 kw-D, 1 kw-N, DA-3.
WNLA(AM) Indianola MS 500 w-D, 44 w-N.
WKJV(AM) Asheville NC 5 kw-D, 1 kw-N, DA-N.
WSFL(AM) New Bern NC 5 kw-D.
WTOB(AM) Winston-Salem NC 5 kw-D, 2.5 kw-N, DA-2.
KUVR(AM) Holdrege NE 500 w-D.
WCQL(AM) Portsmouth NH 1 kw-U, DA-N.
WABH(AM) Bath NY 500 w-D.
WKDM(AM) New York NY 5 kw-D, DA.
WRKG(AM) Lorain OH 1 kw-U, 67 w-N.
KSWO(AM) Lawton OK 1 kw-U, DA-2.
KSRV(AM) Ontario OR 5 kw-D, 1 kw-N, DA-N.
WTYM(AM) Kittanning PA 5 kw-D.
WMLP(AM) Milton PA 1 kw-D, 18 w-N.
WHGT(AM) Waynesboro PA 1 kw-D.
WOLA(AM) Barranquitas PR 1 kw-U.
WNRI(AM) Woonsocket RI 2.5 kw-D.
WAGS(AM) Bishopville SC 1 kw-D.
WGUS(AM) North Augusta SC 5 kw-D, 710 w-N, DA-2.
KOTA(AM) Rapid City SD 5 kw-U, DA-N.
KQKD(AM) Redfield SD 500 w-D, 140 w-N, DA-2.
WYSH(AM) Clinton TN 1 kw-D, 500 w-N, DA-N.
WIZO(AM) Franklin TN 5 kw-D, 500 w-N, DA-N.
WMPS(AM) Millington TN 2.5 kw-D, 1 kw-N, DA-2.
KZXT(AM) Beaumont TX 1 kw-D, 127 w-N.
KBWD(AM) Brownwood TX 1 kw-D, 500 w-N.
KTSM(AM) El Paso TX 5 kw-D, 500 w-N.
KMUL(AM) Muleshoe TX 1 kw-D.
KBOP(AM) Pleasanton TX 4 kw-D, 160 w-N, DA-D.
WLRV(AM) Lebanon VA 1 kw-D, 63 w-N.
WTVR(AM) Richmond VA 5 kw-D, DA-2.
WSYB(AM) Rutland VT 5 kw-D, 1 kw-N, DA-D.
KRKO(AM) Everett WA 5 kw-U, DA-N.
WFCL(AM) Clintonville WI 5 kw-D, 2.5 kw-N, DA-2.
WMTD(AM) Hinton WV 1 kw-D.

1390 khz Regional III

WHMA(AM) Anniston AL 5 kw-D, 1 kw-N, DA-N.
KDQN(AM) De Queen AR 500 w-D.
KAMO(AM) Rogers AR 1 kw-D, DA.
KGER(AM) Long Beach CA 5 kw-D, 3.6 kw-N, DA-2.
KMIX(AM) Turlock CA 5 kw-U, DA-2.
KJME(AM) Denver CO 5 kw-D, DA.
WKHF(AM) Avon Park FL 1 kw-D, 770 w-N.
WAJD(AM) Gainesville FL 5 kw-D, 51 w-N.
WISK(AM) Americus GA 5 kw-N.
WTNL(AM) Reidsville GA 500 w-D.
KLNT(AM) Clinton IA 1 kw-D, 91 w-N, DA-2.
KKSO(AM) Des Moines IA 1 kw-U, DA-1.
WGCI(AM) Chicago IL 5 kw-U, DA-2.
WFIW(AM) Fairfield IL 1 kw-D, 87 w-N.
WZZB(AM) Seymour IN 1 kw-D, 74 w-N.
KNCK(AM) Concordia KS 500 w-D, 54 w-N.
WANY(AM) Albany KY 1 kw-D.
WKIC(AM) Hazard KY 5 kw-D.
KFRA(AM) Franklin LA 500 w-D.
WPLM(AM) Plymouth MA 5 kw-U, DA-2.
WTMS(AM) Presque Isle ME 5 kw-U, DA-N.
WLCM(AM) Charlotte MI 5 kw-D, DA-1.
KRFO(AM) Owatonna MN 500 w-D, 100 w-N.
KXSS(AM) Waite Park MN 2.5 kw-D, 1 kw-N, DA-2.
KJPW(AM) Waynesville MO 5 kw-D, 67 w-N.
WROA(AM) Gulfport MS 5 kw-U, DA-2.
WMER(AM) Meridian MS 5 kw-D, 250 w-N.
WEED(AM) Rocky Mount NC 5 kw-D, 2.5 kw-N, DA-2.
WADA(AM) Shelby NC 1 kw-D, 500 w-N, DA-N.
WJRM(AM) Troy NC 1 kw-D.
KRRZ(AM) Minot ND 5 kw-U, 1 kw-N.
KENN(AM) Farmington NM 5 kw-D, 1.3 kw-N, DA-N.
KHOB(AM) Hobbs NM 5 kw-D, 500 w-N, DA-N.
WEOK(AM) Poughkeepsie NY 5 kw-D, DA.
WRIV(AM) Riverhead NY 1 kw-D, 64 w-N.
WDCW(AM) Syracuse NY 5 kw-U, DA-N.
WBLL(AM) Bellefontaine OH 500 w-D, 81 w-N.
WMPO(AM) Middleport-Pomeroy OH 5 kw-D, 120 w-N.
WHOT(AM) Youngstown OH 9.5 kw-U, DA-N.
KCRC(AM) Enid OK 1 kw-U, DA-1.
KSLM(AM) Salem OR 5 kw-U, 1 kw-N.
WLAN(AM) Lancaster PA 5 kw-U, DA-N.
WRSC(AM) State College PA 2.0 kw-D, 1 kw-N, DA-N.
WISA(AM) Isabela PR 1 kw-U.
WHPB(AM) Belton SC 1 kw-D.
WXTC(AM) Charleston SC 5 kw-U, DA-N.
KJAM(AM) Madison SD 500 w-D, 62 w-N.
WYXI(AM) Athens TN 2.5 kw-D, 62 w-N.
WTJS(AM) Jackson TN 5 kw-U, 1 kw-N, DA-N.
WMCT(AM) Mountain City TN 1 kw-D.
KULP(AM) El Campo TX 500 w-D, 180 w-N.
KBEC(AM) Waxahachie TX 500 w-D, 65 w-N, DA-N.
KLGN(AM) Logan UT 5 kw-D, 500 w-N, DA-N.
WMZQ(AM) Arlington VA 5 kw-U.
WWOD(AM) Lynchburg VA 5 kw-D, 1 kw-N, DA-N.
WKDR(AM) Burlington VT 5 kw-U, DA-N.
KBBO(AM) Yakima WA 5 kw-D, 500 w-N, DA-N.
WRIG(AM) Schofield WI 5 kw-D, DA-2.
WKLP(AM) Keyser WV 1 kw-D, 74 w-N.

1400 khz Local IV

KVLD(AM) Valdez AK 1 kw-D, 250 w-N.
WAVD(AM) Decatur AL 1 kw-U.
WXAL(AM) Demopolis AL 1 kw-U.
WJLD(AM) Fairfield AL 1 kw-U.
WFPA(AM) Fort Payne AL 1 kw-U.
WJHO(AM) Opelika AL 1 kw-U.
KELD(AM) El Dorado AR 1 kw-U.
KCLA(AM) Pine Bluff AR 1 kw-U.
KWYN(AM) Wynne AR 1 kw-U.
KSUN(AM) Phoenix AZ 1 kw-U.
KRVZ(AM) Springerville-Eager AZ 1 kw-U.
KTUC(AM) Tucson AZ 1 kw-U.
KEZC(AM) Yuma AZ 1 kw-U.
KBLX(AM) Berkeley CA 1 kw-U.
KBZT(AM) Indio CA 1 kw-U.
KQMS(AM) Redding CA 1 kw-U.
KIID(AM) San Luis Obispo CA 1 kw-U.
KKZZ(AM) Santa Paula CA 1 kw-U.
KHTZ(AM) Truckee CA 1 kw-U.
KUKI(AM) Ukiah CA 1 kw-U.
KEYX(AM) Visalia CA 1 kw-U.
KRLN(AM) Canon City CO 1 kw-U.
KDTA(AM) Delta CO 1 kw-U.
KFTM(AM) Fort Morgan CO 1 kw-U.
KBZZ(AM) La Junta CO 1 kw-U.
KPAG(AM) Pagosa Springs CO 1 kw-U.
WSTC(AM) Stamford CT 1 kw-U.
WILI(AM) Willimantic CT 1 kw-U.
WFTL(AM) Fort Lauderdale FL 1 kw-U.
WIRA(AM) Fort Pierce FL 1 kw-U.
WNUE(AM) Fort Walton Beach FL 1 kw-U.
WZAZ(AM) Jacksonville FL 1 kw-U.
WPRY(AM) Perry FL 1 kw-U.
WTRR(AM) Sanford FL 1 kw-U.
WPAS(AM) Zephyrhills FL 1 kw-U.
WULF(AM) Alma GA 1 kw-U.
WVNF(AM) Alpharetta GA 1 kw-U.
WWRK(AM) Elberton GA 1 kw-U.
WNEX(AM) Macon GA 1 kw-U.
WCOH(AM) Newnan GA 1 kw-U.
WSGA(AM) Savannah GA 1 kw-U.
KCOG(AM) Centerville IA 500 w-D, 1 kw-N.
KADR(AM) Elkader IA 1 kw-U.
KVFD(AM) Fort Dodge IA 1 kw-U.
KART(AM) Jerome ID 1 kw-U.
KRPL(AM) Moscow ID 1 kw-U.
KSPT(AM) Sandpoint ID 1 kw-U.
KIGO(AM) St. Anthony ID 1 kw-U.
WDWS(AM) Champaign IL 1 kw-U.
WGIL(AM) Galesburg IL 1 kw-U.
WJPS(AM) Evansville IN 1 kw-U.
WBAT(AM) Marion IN 1 kw-U.
KVOE(AM) Emporia KS 1 kw-U.
KAYS(AM) Hays KS 1 kw-U.
WCYN(AM) Cynthiana KY 500 w-D, 1 kw-N.
WIEL(AM) Elizabethtown KY 1 kw-U.
WFTG(AM) London KY 1 kw-U.
WFPR(AM) Hammond LA 1 kw-U.
KAOK(AM) Lake Charles LA 1 kw-U.
KWLA(AM) Many LA 1 kw-U.
KVLA(AM) Vidalia LA 1 kw-U.
WHTB(AM) Fall River MA 1 kw-U.
WLLH(AM) Lowell MA 1 kw-U.
WHMP(AM) Northampton MA 1 kw-U.
WWIN(AM) Baltimore MD 1 kw-U.
WMME(AM) Augusta ME 1 kw-U.
WIDE(AM) Biddeford ME 1 kw-U.
WALZ(AM) Machias ME 1 kw-U.
WQBH(AM) Detroit MI 1 kw-U.
WLJN(AM) Elmwood Township MI 1 kw-U.
WCCY(AM) Houghton MI 1 kw-U.
WQXO(AM) Munising MI 1 kw-U.
WSAM(AM) Saginaw MI 1 kw-U.
WKNW(AM) Sault Ste. Marie MI 250 w-U.
WSJM(AM) St. Joseph MI 880 w-U.
KEYL(AM) Long Prairie MN 1 kw-U.
KMHL(AM) Marshall MN 1 kw-U.
KLBB(AM) St. Paul MN 1 kw-U.
WHLB(AM) Virginia MN 1 kw-U.
KFRU(AM) Columbia MO 1 kw-U.
KJCF(AM) Festus MO 1 kw-U.
KSIM(AM) Sikeston MO 1 kw-U.
KGMY(AM) Springfield MO 1 kw-U.
WBIP(AM) Booneville MS 1 kw-U.
WJWF(AM) Columbus MS 1 kw-U.
WYKC(AM) Grenada MS 1 kw-U.
WFOR(AM) Hattiesburg MS 1 kw-U.
WOAD(AM) Jackson MS 1 kw-U.
KDRG(AM) Deer Lodge MT 1 kw-U.
KXGN(AM) Glendive MT 1 kw-U.
KXGF(AM) Great Falls MT 1 kw-U.
WBTB(AM) Beaufort NC 1 kw-U.
WKEW(AM) Greensboro NC 1 kw-U.
WMFA(AM) Raeford NC 1 kw-U.
WSIC(AM) Statesville NC 1 kw-U.
WLSE(AM) Wallace NC 1 kw-U.
WHCC(AM) Waynesville NC 1 kw-U.
WSMY(AM) Weldon NC 1 kw-U.
KQDJ(AM) Jamestown ND 1 kw-U.
KBRB(AM) Ainsworth NE 1 kw-U.
KCOW(AM) Alliance NE 1 kw-U.
KLIN(AM) Lincoln NE 1 kw-U.
WTSL(AM) Hanover NH 1 kw-U.
WLTN(AM) Littleton NH 1 kw-U.
WOND(AM) Pleasantville NJ 1 kw-U.
KTRC(AM) Santa Fe NM 1 kw-U.
KCHS(AM) Truth or Consequences NM 1 kw-U.
KTNM(AM) Tucumcari NM 1 kw-U.
KWNA(AM) Winnemucca NV 1 kw-U.

U.S. AM Stations by Frequency

WABY(AM) Albany NY 1 kw-U.
WWWS(AM) Buffalo NY 1 kw-U.
WDNY(AM) Dansville NY 1 kw-U.
WSLB(AM) Ogdensburg NY 1 kw-U.
WMAN(AM) Mansfield OH 1 kw-U.
WPAY(AM) Portsmouth OH 1 kw-U.
WKON(AM) Bartlesville OK 1 kw-U.
KTMC(AM) McAlester OK 1 kw-U.
KNOR(AM) Norman OK 1 kw-U.
KNND(AM) Cottage Grove OR 1 kw-U.
KJDY(AM) John Day OR 1 kw-U.
KBCH(AM) Lincoln City OR 1 kw-U.
WEST(AM) Easton PA 1 kw-U.
WLKK(AM) Erie PA 1 kw.
WTCY(AM) Harrisburg PA 1 kw-U.
WJRV(AM) Loretto PA 1 kw-U.
WICK(AM) Scranton PA 1 kw-U.
WKBI(AM) St. Marys PA 1 kw-U.
WRAK(AM) Williamsport PA 1 kw-U.
WIDA(AM) Carolina PR 1 kw-U.
WCOS(AM) Columbia SC 1 kw-U.
WGTN(AM) Georgetown SC 1 kw-U.
WYYR(AM) Spartanburg SC 1 kw-U.
KBJM(AM) Lemmon SD 1 kw-U.
WJZM(AM) Clarksville TN 1 kw-U.
WHUB(AM) Cookeville TN 1 kw-U.
WLSB(AM) Copperhill TN 1 kw-U.
WKPT(AM) Kingsport TN 1 kw-U.
WGAP(AM) Maryville TN 1 kw-U.
WHAL(AM) Shelbyville TN 1 kw-U.
KRUN(AM) Ballinger TX 1 kw-U.
KBYG(AM) Big Spring TX 1 kw-U.
KUNO(AM) Corpus Christi TX 1 kw-U.
*KHCB(AM) Galveston TX 1 kw-U.
KGVL(AM) Greenville TX 1 kw-U.
KYLR(AM) Huntsville TX 250 w-D, 1 kw-N.
KEBE(AM) Jacksonville TX 1 kw-U.
KIUN(AM) Pecos TX 1 kw-U.
KEYE(AM) Perryton TX 1 kw-U.
KVOP(AM) Plainview TX 1 kw-U.
KVRP(AM) Stamford TX 1 kw-U.
KTEM(AM) Temple TX 1 kw-U.
KHSP(AM) Texarkana TX 1 kw-U.
KVOU(AM) Uvalde TX 1 kw-U.
KSRR(AM) Provo UT 1 kw-U.
WKAV(AM) Charlottesville VA 1 kw-U.
WHHV(AM) Hillsville VA 1 kw-U.
WPCE(AM) Portsmouth VA 1 kw-U.
WHLF(AM) South Boston VA 1 kw-U.
WINC(AM) Winchester VA 1 kw-U.
KLCK(AM) Goldendale WA 1 kw-U.
KEDO(AM) Longview WA 1 kw-U.
KRSC(AM) Othello WA 1 kw-U.
KITZ(AM) Silverdale WA 1 kw-D, 890 w-N.
WATW(AM) Ashland WI 1 kw-U.
WBIZ(AM) Eau Claire WI 1 kw-U.
WDUZ(AM) Green Bay WI 1 kw-U.
WRJN(AM) Racine WI 1 kw-U.
WRDB(AM) Reedsburg WI 1 kw-U.
WOBG(AM) Clarksburg WV 1 kw-U.
WRON(AM) Ronceverte WV 1 kw-U.
WVRC(AM) Spencer WV 1 kw-U.
WKWK(AM) Wheeling WV 1 kw-U.
WBTH(AM) Williamson WV 1 kw-U.
*KATI(AM) Casper WY 1 kw-U.
KODI(AM) Cody WY 1 kw-U.

1410 khz Regional III

WLVV(AM) Mobile AL 5 kw-U, DA-N.
WZZA(AM) Tuscumbia AL 500 w-D, 51 w-N.
KTCS(AM) Fort Smith AR 1 kw-D.
KERN(AM) Bakersfield CA 1 kw-U.
KRML(AM) Carmel CA 500 w-D, 16 w-N.
KTME(AM) Lompoc CA 500 w-D, 77 w-N, DA-2.
KMYC(AM) Marysville CA 5 kw-D, 1 kw-N, DA-2.
KCAL(AM) Redlands CA 5 kw-D, 4 kw-N, DA-N.
KCOL(AM) Fort Collins CO 1 kw-U, DA-N.
WPOP(AM) Hartford CT 5 kw-U, DA-2.
WDOV(AM) Dover DE 5.4 kw, DA-2.
WMYR(AM) Fort Myers FL 5 kw-U, DA-N.
WQBQ(AM) Leesburg FL 5 kw-D, 90 w-N.
WHBT(AM) Tallahassee FL 5 kw-D, 39 w-N.
WKKP(AM) McDonough GA 2.5 kw-D.
WYIS(AM) McRae GA 1 kw-D.
WLAQ(AM) Rome GA 1 kw-U.
KGRN(AM) Grinnell IA 500 w-D, 47 w-N.
KLEM(AM) Le Mars IA 1 kw-D, 63 w-N.
WRMN(AM) Elgin IL 1 kw-D, 500 w-N, DA-N.
WTIM(AM) Taylorville IL 1 kw-D, 63 w-N, DA-1.
WCFY(AM) Lafayette IN 1 kw-D, 65 w-N, DA-1.
KKLO(AM) Leavenworth KS 5 kw-D, 500 w-N, DA-N.
KQAM(AM) Wichita KS 5 kw-U, DA-2.
WLBJ(AM) Bowling Green KY 5 kw-D, 1 kw-N, DA-N.
WHLN(AM) Harlan KY 5 kw-D, 94 w-N.
KRRV(AM) Alexandria LA 1 kw-U, 49.5 w-N, ND-1.
WMSX(AM) Brockton MA 1 kw-D, DA-N.
WHAG(AM) Halfway MD 1 kw-D, 99 w-N, DA-2.
WGRD(AM) Grand Rapids MI 1 kw-D.
KLFD(AM) Litchfield MN 500 w-D, 47 w-N.
KRWB(AM) Roseau MN 1 kw-U.
KGNN(AM) Cuba MO 5 kw-D, DA.
WDTL(AM) Cleveland MS 1 kw-D.
WEGO(AM) Concord NC 1 kw-D.
WSRC(AM) Durham NC 5 kw-D, 290 w-N, DA-2.
WVCB(AM) Shallotte NC 500 w-D.
KHOL(AM) Beulah ND 1 kw-D, 180 w-N.
KOOQ(AM) North Platte NE 5 kw-D, 1 kw-N, DA-N.
WHTG(AM) Eatontown NJ 500 w-D.
KFMS(AM) North Las Vegas NV 5 kw-D, DA-N.
WDOE(AM) Dunkirk NY 1 kw-D, 500 w-N, DA-N.
WELM(AM) Elmira NY 5 kw-D, 1 kw-N, DA-N.
WSTL(AM) South Glens Falls NY 1 kw-D, 126 w-N.
WNCQ(AM) Watertown NY 5 kw-D, 1 kw-N, DA-N.
WING(AM) Dayton OH 5 kw-U, DA-N.
KBNP(AM) Portland OR 5 kw-D, 250 w-N.
WLSH(AM) Lansford PA 1 kw-D.
KQV(AM) Pittsburgh PA 5 kw-U, DA-2.
WRSS(AM) San Sebastian PR 1 kw-U, DA-1.
WPCC(AM) Clinton SC 1 kw-D, 100 w-N.
WYMB(AM) Manning SC 1 kw-D, 128 w-N.
WBBX(AM) Kingston TN 500 w-D.
WCMT(AM) Martin TN 700 w-D, 58 w-N.
KLVQ(AM) Athens TX 1 kw-D.
KRJT(AM) Bowie TX 500 w-D, DA.
KCUL(AM) Marshall TX 500 w-D, 90 w-N, DA-2.
KRIL(AM) Odessa TX 1 kw-U, DA-N.
KBAL(AM) San Saba TX 800 w-D, 203 w-N.
WRIS(AM) Roanoke VA 5 kw-D, 72 w-N.
WIZM(AM) La Crosse WI 5 kw-U, DA-N.
WSCW(AM) South Charleston WV 5 kw-D.
KWYO(AM) Sheridan WY 5 kw-D, 500 w-N.

1420 khz Regional III

WACT(AM) Tuscaloosa AL 5 kw-D, 108 w-N.
KXOW(AM) Hot Springs AR 5 kw-D, 87 w-N.
KPOC(AM) Pocahontas AR 1 kw-D.
KMOG(AM) Payson AZ 2.5 kw-D, 500 w-N, DA-N.
KTAN(AM) Sierra Vista AZ 1.5 kw-D, 500 w-N, DA-N.
KSTN(AM) Stockton CA 5 kw-D, 1 kw-N, DA-2.
WLIS(AM) Old Saybrook CT 5 kw-D, 500 w-N, DA-N.
WDBF(AM) Delray Beach FL 5 kw-D, 500 w-N, DA-N.
WBRD(AM) Palmetto FL 2.5 kw-D, 1 kw-N, DA-2.
WAOC(AM) St. Augustine FL 4 kw-D, 460 w-N.
WRCG(AM) Columbus GA 5 kw-U, DA
WWEV(AM) Decatur GA 1 kw-U, DA.
WPEH(AM) Louisville GA 1 kw-D, 159 w-N.
WLET(AM) Toccoa GA 5 kw-D.
WADX(AM) Trenton GA 2.5 kw-D, 112 w-N.
KCCN(AM) Honolulu HI 5 kw-U.
WOC(AM) Davenport IA 5 kw-U.
WINI(AM) Murphysboro IL 420 w-D, 500 w-N, DA-N.
WIMS(AM) Michigan City IN 5 kw-U, DA-2.
KJCK(AM) Junction City KS 1 kw-D, 500 w-N, DA-N.
KULY(AM) Ulysses KS 1 kw-D, 500 w-N, DA-N.
WHBN(AM) Harrodsburg KY 1 kw-D, 46 w-N.
WVJS(AM) Owensboro KY 5 kw-D, 1 kw-N, DA-2.
KPEL(AM) Lafayette LA 1 kw-D, 750 w-N, DA-N.
WBSM(AM) New Bedford MA 5 kw-D, 1 kw-N, DA-N.
WBEC(AM) Pittsfield MA 1 kw-U, DA-N.
WFLT(AM) Flint MI 500 w-D, 142 w-N, DA-2.
WKPR(AM) Kalamazoo MI 1 kw-D, DA.
*WKAL(AM) Kalkaska MI 500 w-D, DA.
KTOE(AM) Mankato MN 1 kw-U.
KZMO(AM) California MO 500 w-D, 225 w-N.
KBTN(AM) Neosho MO 1 kw-D, 500 w-N, DA-N.
WSUH(AM) Oxford MS 1 kw-D, 80 w-N.
WQBC(AM) Vicksburg MS 5 kw-D, 500 w-N.
WIGG(AM) Wiggins MS 5 kw-D.
WMYN(AM) Mayodan NC 1 kw-D, 70 w-N, DA-2.
WGAS(AM) South Gastonia NC 500 w-D.
WVOT(AM) Wilson NC 1 kw-D, 500 w-N, DA-N.
KESY(AM) Omaha NE 1 kw-D, 330 w-N, DA-2.
WASR(AM) Wolfeboro NH 5 kw-D.
WYUT(AM) Herkimer NY 1 kw-D.
WACK(AM) Newark NY 5 kw-D, 500 w-N, DA-N.
WLNA(AM) Peekskill NY 5 kw-D, 1 kw-N, DA-2.
WHK(AM) Cleveland OH 5 kw-U, DA-N.
KTJS(AM) Hobart OK 1 kw-D, 360 w-N.
KRSR(AM) Coos Bay OR 1 kw-D.
WCOJ(AM) Coatesville PA 5 kw-U, DA-N.
WCED(AM) DuBois PA 5 kw-D, 500 w-N, DA-N.
WEUC(AM) Ponce PR 1 kw-D.
WCRE(AM) Cheraw SC 1 kw-D, 97 w-N.
KGIM(AM) Aberdeen SD 1 kw-D, 232 w-N.
WEMB(AM) Erwin TN 5 kw-D.
WKSR(AM) Pulaski TN 1 kw-U, DA-N.
KFYN(AM) Bonham TX 250 w-D, 148 w-N.
KPAR(AM) Granbury TX 500 w-U, DA-N.
KLFB(AM) Lubbock TX 500 w-U, DA-N.
KGNB(AM) New Braunfels TX 1 kw-D, 196-N.
*WAMV(AM) Amherst VA 1 kw-D, 47 w-N.
WXGM(AM) Gloucester VA 740 w-D.
WKCW(AM) Warrenton VA 5 kw-D.
WWSR(AM) St. Albans VT 1 kw-D, 110 w-N.
KITI(AM) Chehalis-Centralia WA 5 kw-D, 1 kw-N, DA-2.
KRIZ(AM) Renton WA 1 kw-D, 500 w-N, DA-2.
KUJ(AM) Walla Walla WA 1 kw-U.
WJUB(AM) Plymouth WI 500 w-D.
WTCR(AM) Kenova WV 5 kw-D, 500 w-N, DA-N.

1430 khz Regional III

WFHK(AM) Pell City AL 5 kw-D.
WRMG(AM) Red Bay AL 1 kw-D.
KHBM(AM) Monticello AR 1 kw-D, 30 w-N, 500 w-PSSA.
KAMP(AM) El Centro CA 1 kw-D.
KFIG(AM) Fresno CA 5 kw-U, DA-1.
KJAY(AM) Sacramento CA 500 w-D, DA.
KALI(AM) San Gabriel CA 5 kw-D, DA-2.
KNTA(AM) Santa Clara CA 1 kw-U, DA-1.
KEZW(AM) Aurora CO 5 kw-D, DA-N.
WWLO(AM) Gainesville FL 2.5 kw-D.
WOIR(AM) Homestead FL 5 kw-D, DA-N.
WLKF(AM) Lakeland FL 5 kw-D, 1 kw-N.
WLTG(AM) Panama City FL 5 kw-U, DA-D.
WGFS(AM) Covington GA 5 kw-D, 250 w-N.
WLSQ(AM) Dalton GA 2.5 kw-D, 72 w-N.
WWGS(AM) Tifton GA 5 kw-U, DA-N.
KASI(AM) Ames IA 1 kw-D, 32 w-N.
WEEF(AM) Highland Park IL 1 kw-D, 29 w-N, DA.
WCMY(AM) Ottawa IL 500 w-D, 38 w-N.
WCKN(AM) Indianapolis IN 5 kw-U, DA-N.
WHHY(AM) Montgomery AL 5 kw-D, 1 kw-N, DA-N.
KITA(AM) Little Rock AR 5 kw-D, 240 w-N.
KKIP(AM) Lowell AR 1 kw-D, 79 w-N.
KOPA(AM) Scottsdale AZ 5 kw-D.
KVON(AM) Napa CA 5 kw-D, 1 kw-N, DA-2.
KDIF(AM) Riverside CA 1 kw-U.
KUHL(AM) Santa Maria CA 5 kw-D, 1 kw-N, DA-N.
KRDZ(AM) Wray CO 5 kw-D, 200 w-N.
WWCL(AM) Lehigh Acres FL 5 kw-D, 1 kw-N, DA-2.
WWZN(AM) Winter Park FL 5 kw-D, 1 kw-N, DA-N.
WGMI(AM) Bremen GA 2.5 kw-D.
WGIG(AM) Brunswick GA 5 kw-D, 1 kw-N, DA-N.
WVMG(AM) Cochran GA 1 kw-D.
KCHE(AM) Cherokee IA 500 w-D.
WRAJ(AM) Anna IL 500 w-D, 109 w-N.
WPRS(AM) Paris IL 1 kw-D, 250 w-N.
WGEM(AM) Quincy IL 5 kw-D, 1 kw-N, DA-2.
WROK(AM) Rockford IL 5 kw-D, 270 w-N, DA-2.
WPGW(AM) Portland IN 500 w-D, 35 w-N, DA-1.
KMAJ(AM) Topeka KS 5 kw-D, 1 kw-N, DA-1.
WCDS(AM) Glasgow KY 5 kw-D.
WMDJ(AM) Martin KY 2.5 kw-D.
WYGH(AM) Paris KY 1 kw-D.
WEZJ(AM) Williamsburg KY 2.5 kw-D, 500 w-N, DA-1.
KMLB(AM) Monroe LA 5 kw-D, 1 kw-N, DA-N.
WVEI(AM) Worcester MA 5 kw-U.
WLPZ(AM) Westbrook ME 5 kw-D, 1 kw-N, DA-1.
WMAX(AM) Bay City MI 5 kw-D, 2.5 kw-N, DA-N.
WDOW(AM) Dowagiac MI 1 kw-D, 89 w-N.
WMKM(AM) Inkster MI 1 kw-U.
KQRS(AM) Golden Valley MN 5 kw-D, 500 w-N, DA-N.
WRBE(AM) Lucedale MS 1 kw-D.
WSEL(AM) Pontotoc MS 890 w-D, DA.
WBLA(AM) Elizabethtown NC 5 kw-D, 189 w-N.
WLXN(AM) Lexington NC 5 kw-D, 1 kw-N, DA-N.
KKXL(AM) Grand Forks ND 1 kw-D, 500 w-N.
WREY(AM) Millville NJ 1 kw-D, 65 w-N, DA-2.
WNYG(AM) Babylon NY 1 kw-D, 38 w-N.
WJJL(AM) Niagara Falls NY 1 kw-D, 55 w-N.
WSGO(AM) Oswego NY 1 kw-D, 42 w-N.
WRGM(AM) Ontario OH 1 kw-D.
WRRO(AM) Warren OH 5 kw-D, DA.
KMED(AM) Medford OR 5 kw-D, 1 kw-N.
KODL(AM) The Dalles OR 5 kw-D, DA-N.
WCDL(AM) Carbondale PA 5 kw-D.
WNPV(AM) Lansdale PA 2.5 kw-D, 500 w-N, DA-N.
WGCB(AM) Red Lion PA 1 kw-D.
WSSL(AM) Greenville SC 5 kw-U, DA-N.
WJBS(AM) Holly Hill SC 1 kw-D, 98 w-N.
WZYX(AM) Cowan TN 5 kw-D, 100 w-N.
WHDM(AM) McKenzie TN 500 w-D.
KPUR(AM) Amarillo TX 5 kw-D, 1 kw-N, DA-N.
KEYS(AM) Corpus Christi TX 1 kw-U, DA-N.
KDNT(AM) Denton TX 5 kw-D, 500 w-N, DA-N.
KELG(AM) Elgin TX 5 kw-D, DA-2.
KETX(AM) Livingston TX 5 kw-D.
WKLV(AM) Blackstone VA 5 kw-D.
WNFL(AM) Green Bay WI 5 kw-D, 1 kw-N, DA-N.
WHIS(AM) Bluefield WV 5 kw-D, 500 w-N.
WAJR(AM) Morgantown WV 5 kw-D, 500 w-N, DA-2.

1440 khz Regional III

WXAM(AM) Buffalo KY 1 kw-D.
WYMC(AM) Mayfield KY 1 kw-D.
KMRC(AM) Morgan City LA 5 kw-D, 100 w-N.
WTTT(AM) Amherst MA 5 kw-D, DA.
WXKS(AM) Medford MA 5 kw-D, 1 kw-N, DA-N.
WNAV(AM) Annapolis MD 5 kw-D, 1 kw-N, DA-N.
WION(AM) Ionia MI 5 kw-D, 330 w-N, DA-2.
WBRB(AM) Mount Clemens MI 500 w-N, 1 kw-N.
KNSP(AM) Staples MN 1 kw-D, 199 w-N.
KKOZ(AM) Ava MO 500 w-U.
KAOL(AM) Carrollton MO 500 w-D, 27 w-N.
WRTH(AM) St. Louis MO 5 kw-U, DA-2.
WLAU(AM) Laurel MS 5 kw-D.
WDEX(AM) Monroe NC 2.5 kw-U, DA-2.
WMNC(AM) Morganton NC 1 kw-D, 1 kw-N, DA-N.
WDJS(AM) Mount Olive NC 1 kw-D.
WRXO(AM) Roxboro NC 1 kw-D, 65 w-N.
KTYN(AM) Minot ND 5 kw-D, 210 w-N.
KRGI(AM) Grand Island NE 5 kw-D, 1 kw-N, DA-N.
WNJR(AM) Newark NJ 5 kw-U, DA-N.
KCRX(AM) Roswell NM 5 kw-D, 1 kw-N, DA-N.
WMRV(AM) Endicott NY 5 kw-U, DA.
WFOB(AM) Fostoria OH 1 kw-D, DA-2.
WCLT(AM) Newark OH 500 w-D, 48 w-N.
KALV(AM) Alva OK 500 w-U, DA-N.
KQLL(AM) Tulsa OK 5 kw-D, DA-N.
KYKN(AM) Keizer OR 5 kw-U.
WVAM(AM) Altoona PA 5 kw-D, 1 kw-N, DA-N.
WNEL(AM) Caguas PR 5 kw-U.
WBLR(AM) Batesburg SC 5 kw-D, 142 w-N.
WNFO(AM) Ridgeland SC 1 kw-D, 880 w-N.
KBRK(AM) Brookings SD 1 kw-D, 100 w-N.
WNWZ(AM) Germantown TN 2.5 kw-D, DA-N.
WEMG(AM) Knoxville TN 5 kw-D.
WHNK(AM) Madison TN 5 kw-D, 1 kw-N, DA.
KBIL(AM) Breckenridge TX 1 kw-D.
KEES(AM) Gladewater TX 5 kw-D, 1 kw-N, DA-N.
KCOH(AM) Houston TX 1 kw-D.
KLO(AM) Ogden UT 5 kw-D, DA-N.
WPES(AM) Ashland VA 1 kw-U.
WKEX(AM) Blacksburg VA 1 kw-D, 62 w-N.
WDIC(AM) Clinchco VA 1 kw-D, DA-1.
KCLK(AM) Asotin WA 5 kw-D, 1 kw-N, DA-2.
KBRC(AM) Mount Vernon WA 5 kw-D, 1 kw-N, DA-N.
WBEV(AM) Beaver Dam WI 1 kw-U.
WRDN(AM) Durand WI 2 kw-D, 107 w-N.
WEIR(AM) Weirton WV 1 kw-D, DA-2.

U.S. AM Stations by Frequency

1449 khz
WSZD(AM) Pohnpei FM 10 kw-U.

1450 khz Local IV
KLAM(AM) Cordova AK 250 w-U.
KIAL(AM) Unalaska AK 50 w-U, DA-1.
WDNG(AM) Anniston AL 1 kw-U.
WSMQ(AM) Bessemer AL 1 kw-U.
WCOX(AM) Camden AL 1 kw-U.
WDLK(AM) Dadeville AL 1 kw-U.
WWNT(AM) Dothan AL 1 kw-U.
WTKI(AM) Huntsville AL 1 kw-U.
WLAY(AM) Muscle Shoals AL 1 kw-U.
KOSG(AM) Camden AR 1 kw-U.
KENA(AM) Mena AR 1 kw-U.
KDAP(AM) Douglas AZ 1 kw-U.
KNOT(AM) Prescott AZ 1 kw-U.
KVSL(AM) Show Low AZ 1 kw-U.
KTZR(AM) Tucson AZ 1 kw-U.
KAVA(AM) Burney CA 1 kw-U, DA-1.
KSPA(AM) Escondido CA 1 kw-U.
KPSI(AM) Palm Springs CA 1 kw-U.
KTIP(AM) Porterville CA 1 kw-U.
KEST(AM) San Francisco CA 1 kw-U.
KVML(AM) Sonora CA 1 kw-U.
KVEN(AM) Ventura CA 1 kw-U.
KOBO(AM) Yuba City CA 500 w-U.
KGIW(AM) Alamosa CO 1 kw-U.
KDMN(AM) Buena Vista CO 1 kw-U.
KGRE(AM) Greeley CO 1 kw-U.
WCUM(AM) Bridgeport CT 1 kw-U.
WOL(AM) Washington DC 1 kw-U.
WILM(AM) Wilmington DE 1 kw-U.
WWJB(AM) Brooksville FL 1 kw-U.
WMFJ(AM) Daytona Beach FL 1 kw-U.
WOCN(AM) Miami FL 1 kw-U.
WBSR(AM) Pensacola FL 1 kw-U.
WSPB(AM) Sarasota FL 1 kw-D.
WSTU(AM) Stuart FL 1 kw-U.
WTAL(AM) Tallahassee FL 1 kw-U.
WGPC(AM) Albany GA 1 kw-U.
WBHF(AM) Cartersville GA 1 kw-U.
WCON(AM) Cornelia GA 1 kw-U.
WKEU(AM) Griffin GA 1 kw-U.
WMVG(AM) Milledgeville GA 1 kw-U.
WIZA(AM) Savannah GA 1 kw-U.
WVLD(AM) Valdosta GA 1 kw-U.
KMRY(AM) Cedar Rapids IA 1 kw-U.
KBFI(AM) Bonners Ferry ID 1 kw-U.
KVSI(AM) Montpelier ID 1 kw-U.
KEZJ(AM) Twin Falls ID 1 kw-U.
WCEV(AM) Cicero IL 1 kw-U (ST WVON).
WVON(AM) Cicero IL 1 kw-U (ST WCEV).
WKEI(AM) Kewanee IL 500 w-D, 1 kw-N.
WFMB(AM) Springfield IL 1 kw-U.
WLYV(AM) Fort Wayne IN 1 kw-U.
WXVW(AM) Jeffersonville IN 1 kw-U.
WASK(AM) Lafayette IN 1 kw-U.
WAOV(AM) Vincennes IN 1 kw-U.
KWBW(AM) Hutchinson KS 1 kw-U.
WTCO(AM) Campbellsville KY 1 kw-U.
WWLT(AM) Manchester KY 1 kw-U.
WDXR(AM) Paducah KY 1 kw-U.
WLKS(AM) West Liberty KY 1 kw-U.
KSIG(AM) Crowley LA 1 kw-U.
KNOC(AM) Natchitoches LA 1 kw-U.
WBYU(AM) New Orleans LA 1 kw-U.
WNBP(AM) Newburyport MA 1 kw-U.
WMAS(AM) Springfield MA 1 kw-U.
WTBO(AM) Cumberland MD 1 kw-U.
WTHU(AM) Thurmont MD 500 w-D, 400 w-N.
WTOX(AM) Lincoln ME 1 kw-U.
WRKD(AM) Rockland ME 1 kw-U.
WKTQ(AM) South Paris ME 1 kw-U, DA-1.
WATZ(AM) Alpena MI 1 kw-U.
WHTC(AM) Holland MI 1 kw-U.
WMIQ(AM) Iron Mountain MI 1 kw-U.
WIBM(AM) Jackson MI 1 kw-U.
WKLA(AM) Ludington MI 1 kw-U.
WNBY(AM) Newberry MI 1 kw-U.
WHLS(AM) Port Huron MI 1 kw-U.
KATE(AM) Albert Lea MN 1 kw-U.
KBUN(AM) Bemidji MN 1 kw-U, DA-1.
KBMW(AM) Breckenridge MN 1 kw-U.
WELY(AM) Ely MN 1 kw-U, DA-N.
KNSI(AM) St. Cloud MN 1 kw-U.
KFTW(AM) Fredricktown MO 1 kw-U.
WMBH(AM) Joplin MO 1 kw-U.
KIRX(AM) Kirksville MO 1 kw-U.
KOKO(AM) Warrensburg MO 1 kw-U.
KWPM(AM) West Plains MO 1 kw-U.
WROX(AM) Clarksdale MS 1 kw-U.
WCJU(AM) Columbia MS 1 kw-U.
WJXN(AM) Jackson MS 1 kw-U.
WMGP(AM) Meridian MS 1 kw-U.
WNAT(AM) Natchez MS 1 kw-U.
WROB(AM) West Point MS 1 kw-U.
KMMS(AM) Bozeman MT 1 kw-U.
KMSL(AM) Great Falls MT 1 kw-U.
KGRZ(AM) Missoula MT 1 kw-U.
KVCK(AM) Wolf Point MT 1 kw-U.
WATA(AM) Boone NC 1 kw-U.
WGNC(AM) Gastonia NC 1 kw-U.
WIZS(AM) Henderson NC 1 kw-U.
WHKP(AM) Hendersonville NC 1 kw-U.
WNOS(AM) New Bern NC 1 kw-U.
WCIE(AM) Spring Lake NC 1 kw-U.
KZZJ(AM) Rugby ND 1 kw-U.
KWBE(AM) Beatrice NE 1 kw-U.
WKXL(AM) Concord NH 1 kw-U.

WFPG(AM) Atlantic City NJ 1 kw-U.
WCTC(AM) New Brunswick NJ 1 kw-U.
KRZY(AM) Albuquerque NM 1 kw-U.
KLMX(AM) Clayton NM 1 kw-U.
KOBE(AM) Las Cruces NM 1 kw-U.
KSEL(AM) Portales NM 1 kw-U.
KOZZ(AM) Reno NV 1 kw-U.
WCLI(AM) Corning NY 1 kw-U.
WWSC(AM) Glens Falls NY 1 kw-U.
WHDL(AM) Olean NY 1 kw-U.
WKIP(AM) Poughkeepsie NY 1 kw-U, DA-D.
WODZ(AM) Rome NY 1 kw-U.
WJER(AM) Dover-New Philadelphia OH 1 kw-U.
WMOH(AM) Hamilton OH 1 kw-U.
WLEC(AM) Sandusky OH 1 kw-U.
KWHW(AM) Altus OK 1 kw-U.
KGFF(AM) Shawnee OK 1 kw-U.
KSIW(AM) Woodward OK 1 kw-U.
KKXO(AM) Eugene OR 1 kw-U.
KFLS(AM) Klamath Falls OR 1 kw-U.
KLBM(AM) La Grande OR 1 kw-U.
*KBPS(AM) Portland OR 1 kw-U.
WPSE(AM) Erie PA 1 kw-U.
WFRA(AM) Franklin PA 1 kw-U.
WDAD(AM) Indiana PA 1 kw-U.
WPAM(AM) Pottsville PA 1 kw-U.
WFXX(AM) South Williamsport PA 1 kw-U.
WMAJ(AM) State College PA 1 kw-U.
WJPA(AM) Washington PA 1 kw-U.
WCPR(AM) Coamo PR 1 kw-U.
WKRI(AM) West Warwick RI 1 kw-U.
WUJM(AM) Goose Creek SC 1 kw-U.
WCRS(AM) Greenwood SC 1 kw-U.
WHSC(AM) Hartsville SC 1 kw-U.
KBFS(AM) Belle Fourche SD 1 kw-U.
KYNT(AM) Yankton SD 1 kw-U.
WLAR(AM) Athens TN 1 kw-U.
WMOC(AM) Chattanooga TN 1 kw-U.
WTRO(AM) Dyersburg TN 1 k-U.
WSMG(AM) Greeneville TN 1 kw-U.
WLAF(AM) La Follette TN 1 kw-U.
WGNS(AM) Murfreesboro TN 1 kw-U.
KAYC(AM) Beaumont TX 1 kw-U.
KBEN(AM) Carrizo Springs TX 1 kw-U.
KCTI(AM) Gonzales TX 1 kw-U.
KMBL(AM) Junction TX 1 kw-U.
KCYL(AM) Lampasas TX 1 kw-U.
KMHT(AM) Marshall TX 1 kw-U.
KNET(AM) Palestine TX 1 kw-U.
KSNY(AM) Snyder TX 1 kw-U.
*KEYY(AM) Provo UT 1 kw-U.
KSGI(AM) St. George UT 1 kw-U.
WFTR(AM) Front Royal VA 1 kw-U.
WCLM(AM) Highland Springs VA 960 kw-U.
WREL(AM) Lexington VA 1 kw-U.
WMVA(AM) Martinsville VA 1 kw-U.
WLPM(AM) Suffolk VA 1 kw-U.
WSNO(AM) Barre VT 1 kw-U.
WTSA(AM) Brattleboro VT 1 kw-U.
KAYO(AM) Aberdeen WA 1 kw-U.
KCLX(AM) Colfax WA 1 kw-U.
KONP(AM) Port Angeles WA 1 kw-U.
KJUN(AM) Puyallup WA 1 kw-U.
KFIZ(FM) Fond du Lac WI 1 kw-U.
WHRY(AM) Hurley WI 1 kw-U.
WDLB(AM) Marshfield WI 1 kw-U.
WRCO(AM) Richland Center WI 1 kw-U.
WZAC(AM) Madison WI 1 kw-U.
WLTP(AM) Parkersburg WV 1 kw-U.
KBBS(AM) Buffalo WY 1 kw-U.
KVOW(AM) Riverton WY 1 kw-U.

1460 khz Regional III
WFMH(AM) Cullman AL 5 kw-D, 500 w-N, DA-N.
WPNX(AM) Phenix City AL 5 kw-D, 1 kw-N, DA-N.
KZOT(AM) Marianna AR 500 w-D, DA.
KWLL(AM) Casa Grande AZ 2.5 kw-D, 1 kw-N.
KTYM(AM) Inglewood CA 5 kw-D, 500 w-N, DA-2.
KRQC(AM) Salinas CA 5 kw-U, DA-1.
KRRS(AM) Santa Rosa CA 1 kw-D, 33 w-N, DA-2.
KKCS(AM) Colorado Springs CO 5 kw-D, 500 w-N, DA-N.
WBAR(AM) Bartow FL 1 kw-D, 155 w-N.
WZEP(AM) DeFuniak Springs FL 5 kw-D, 186 w-N.
WZNZ(AM) Jacksonville FL 5 kw-D, DA-N.
WXEM(AM) Buford GA 5 kw-D.
KULA(AM) Honolulu HI 5 kw-D.
KDMI(AM) Des Moines IA 5 kw-U, DA-N.
WROY(AM) Carmi IL 1 kw-D, 56 w-N.
WIXN(AM) Dixon IL 1 kw-D, DA.
WUFI(AM) Rantoul IL 500 w-D, DA.
WKAM(AM) Goshen IN 2.5 kw-D, 500 w-N, DA-N.
WKRP(AM) North Vernon IN 1 kw-D, 92 w-N.
KKOY(AM) Chanute KS 1 kw-D, 57 w-N.
WBPA(AM) Elkhorn City KY 5 kw-D.
WRVK(AM) Mt. Vernon KY 500 w-D.
WXOK(AM) Baton Rouge LA 5 kw-D, 1 kw-N, DA-3.
KBSF(AM) Springhill LA 1 kw-D, 220 w-N.
WBET(AM) Brockton MA 5 kw-D, 1 kw-N, DA-N.
WCEI(AM) Easton MD 1 kw-D, 500 w-N, DA-2.
WBRN(AM) Big Rapids MI 5 kw-D, 25 w-N, DA-N.
WPON(AM) Walled Lake MI 1 kw-D, 760 w-N, DA-N.
KDWA(AM) Hastings MN 1 kw-D, 45 w-N.
KDMA(AM) Montevideo MN 1 kw-U, DA-N.
KKAQ(AM) Thief River Falls MN 2.5 kw-D.
KIRL(AM) St. Charles MO 5 kw-D, 500 w-N, DA-N.
WELZ(AM) Belzoni MS 1 kw-U.
WGUD(AM) Moss Point MS 1 kw-D, 370 w-N.
WCRY(AM) Fuquay-Varina NC 5 kw-D, 122 w-N, DA-2.
WRKB(AM) Kannapolis NC 500 w-D, 194 w-N.
WEWO(AM) Laurinburg NC 5 kw-D, DA-2.
WHBK(AM) Marshall NC 500 w-D, 139 w-N.

KLTC(AM) Dickinson ND 5 kw-U, DA-N.
KKPR(AM) Kearney NE 5 kw-D, 56 w-N.
WIFI(AM) Florence NJ 5 kw-D, DA.
KENO(AM) Las Vegas NV 5 kw-D, 1 kw-N, DA-N.
WGNA(AM) Albany NY 5 kw-U, DA.
WVOX(AM) New Rochelle NY 500 w-D.
WWWG(AM) Rochester NY 5 kw-U, DA.
WBNS(AM) Columbus OH 5 kw-D, DA-N.
WBKC(AM) Painesville OH 1 kw-D, 500 w-N, DA-2.
KZUE(AM) El Reno OK 500 w-D.
KCKX(AM) Stayton OR 1 kw-D, 15 w-N.
WMBA(AM) Ambridge PA 500 w-U, DA-D.
WCMB(AM) Harrisburg PA 5 kw-D, DA-N.
WEMR(AM) Tunkhannock PA 5 kw-D, 1.25 kw-N, DA-2.
WRRE(AM) Juncos PR 500 w-U, DA-2.
WLRP(AM) San Sebastian PR 500 w-U.
WDOG(AM) Allendale SC 1 kw-D.
WBCU(AM) Union SC 1 kw-U, DA-N.
WQCR(AM) Jackson TN 1 kw-D, 128 w-N.
WEEN(AM) Lafayette TN 1 kw-D, 138 w-N.
WXRQ(AM) Mt. Pleasant TN 1 kw-D, 170 w-N.
KBRZ(AM) Freeport TX 500 w-D, 214 w-N.
KRME(AM) Hondo TX 500 w-D, 226 w-N.
KTNP(AM) Lubbock TX 1 kw-D, 250 w-N.
WACO(AM) Waco TX 1 kw-U, DA-N.
WKDV(AM) Manassas VA 5 kw-U, DA-2.
WRAD(AM) Radford VA 5 kw-D, 500 w-N, DA-N.
*KARR(AM) Kirkland WA 5 kw-D, 2.5 kw-N, DA-2.
KMWX(AM) Yakima WA 5 kw-U, 3.7 kw-N, DA-N.
WBJX(AM) Racine WI 500 w-D, 65 w-N.
WTMB(AM) Tomah WI 1 kw-D.
WBUC(AM) Buckhannon WV 5 kw-D, 87 w-N.

1470 khz Regional III
WIJK(AM) Evergreen AL 1 kw-D.
KNXN(AM) Sierra Vista AZ 2.5 kw-D, 39 w-N.
KKFO(AM) Coalinga CA 5 kw-D, 30 w-N.
KUTY(AM) Palmdale CA 5 kw-D, DA-2.
KXOA(AM) Sacramento CA 5 kw-D, 1 kw-N, DA-2.
KRKI(AM) Estes Park CO 1 kw-U.
WMMW(AM) Meriden CT 2.5 kw-U, DA-N.
WLVU(AM) Dunedin FL 5 kw-D, 500 w-N.
WRBD(AM) Pompano Beach FL 5 kw-D, 2.5 kw-N, DA-2.
WBIT(AM) Adel GA 1 kw-D, 350 w-N.
WCLA(AM) Claxton GA 1 kw-D, 260 w-N.
WRGA(AM) Rome GA 5 kw-U, DA-N.
KWSL(AM) Sioux City IA 5 kw-U, DA-2.
KWAY(AM) Waverly IA 1 kw-D, 61 w-N, DA-N.
WCFJ(AM) Chicago Heights IL 1 kw-U, DA-2.
WMBD(AM) Peoria IL 5 kw-U, DA-2.
WHUT(AM) Anderson IN 1 kw-D, 35 w-N.
KERE(AM) Atchison KS 1 kw-U, DA-1.
KYUU(AM) Liberal KS 1 kw-D, 125 w-N.
WBUL(AM) Shepherdsville KY 1 kw-D, 54 w-N.
WBFC(AM) Stanton KY 1 kw-D.
KLCL(AM) Lake Charles LA 5 kw-U, 500 w-N.
WSRO(AM) Marlboro MA 5 kw-D, DA-N.
WJDY(AM) Salisbury MD 5 kw-D, DA.
WTTR(AM) Westminster MD 1 kw-D, DA-N.
WZOU(AM) Lewiston ME 5 kw-D, DA-1.
WFNT(AM) Flint MI 5 kw-D, 1 kw-N, DA-N.
WQSN(AM) Kalamazoo MI 800 w-D, 1 kw-N.
KBCW(AM) Brooklyn Park MN 5 kw-U, DA-2.
KZBK(AM) Brookfield MO 500 w-D, DA.
KTCB(AM) Malden MO 1 kw-D.
WCHJ(AM) Brookhaven MS 1 kw-D.
WNAU(AM) New Albany MS 500 w-U, DA-N.
WVBS(AM) Burgaw NC 1 kw-D.
WWBG(AM) Greensboro NC 3.5 kw-D, 5 kw-N, DA-2.
WPNC(AM) Plymouth NC 5 kw-D.
WTOE(AM) Spruce Pine NC 5 kw-D, 100 w-N.
KHND(AM) Harvey ND 5 kw-D, 160 w-N.
WTKO(AM) Ithaca NY 5 kw-D, 1 kw-N, DA-N.
WPDM(AM) Potsdam NY 1 kw-D.
WWWM(AM) Toledo OH 1 kw-U, DA-2.
KVLH(AM) Pauls Valley OK 1 kw-D, DA.
KITO(AM) Vinita OK 500 w-D, 88 w-N.
WXKW(AM) Allentown PA 5 kw-U, DA-N.
WRQQ(AM) Farrell PA 1 kw-D, 500 w-N, DA-N.
WHYM(AM) Portage PA 466 w-D, 88 w-N.
WQXL(AM) Columbia SC 5 kw-D, 138 w-N.
WBCR(AM) Alcoa TN 1 kw-D.
WVOL(AM) Berry Hill TN 5 kw-D, 1 kw-N, DA-N.
KNTS(AM) Abilene TX 5 kw-D, 1 kw-N, DA-N.
KDHN(AM) Dimmitt TX 500 w-D, 149 w-N.
KWRD(AM) Henderson TX 5 kw-D.
KUOL(AM) San Marcos TX 250 w-U, DA-N.
KNFL(AM) Tremonton UT 5 kw-D, 109 w-N.
WBTX(AM) Broadway-Timberville VA 5 kw-D.
WTZE(AM) Tazewell VA 5 kw-D.
KELA(AM) Centralia-Chehalis WA 5 kw-D, 1 kw-N, DA-N.
KBSN(AM) Moses Lake WA 1 kw-D, 1 kw-N, DA-2.
WBKV(AM) West Bend WI 2.5 kw-D, DA.
WHRD(AM) Huntington WV 5 kw-D.
KKTY(AM) Douglas WY 1 kw-D, 500 w-N.

1480 khz Regional III
WBTS(AM) Bridgeport AL 1 kw-D.
WLPH(AM) Irondale AL 5 kw-D.
WABB(AM) Mobile AL 5 kw-U, DA-N.
KTHS(AM) Berryville AR 5 kw-D, 64 w-N.
KPHX(AM) Phoenix AZ 1 kw-D, 500 w-N, DA-2.
KKIS(AM) Concord CA 500 w-U.
KRED(AM) Eureka CA 5 kw-D, 1 kw-N.
KYOS(AM) Merced CA 5 kw-D, DA-N.
KWIZ(AM) Santa Ana CA 5 kw-U, DA-N.
KSBQ(AM) Santa Maria CA 1 kw-D, 61 w-N.
KRRU(AM) Pueblo CO 1 kw-U.
WKND(AM) Windsor CT 500 w-D, DA.
WKGF(AM) Arcadia FL 1 kw-D.

Broadcasting & Cable Yearbook 1994
B-498

U.S. AM Stations by Frequency

WODX(AM) Marco Island FL 1 kw-U, DA-2.
WUNA(AM) Ocoee FL 1 kw-D, 71 w-N.
*WKGC(AM) Panama City Beach FL 500 w-D, 87 w-N.
WYZE(AM) Atlanta GA 5 kw-D, 44 w-N.
WRDW(AM) Augusta GA 5 kw-U, DA-N.
KLEE(AM) Ottumwa IA 500 w-D, 33 w-N.
KRXR(AM) Gooding ID 1 kw-D.
WFXW(AM) Geneva IL 1 kw-D, 500 w-N, DA-2.
WJBM(AM) Jerseyville IL 500 w-D, 32 w-N, DA-2.
WTHI(AM) Terre Haute IN 5 kw-D, 1 kw-N, DA-2.
WRSW(AM) Warsaw IN 1 kw-D, 500 w-N.
KBEA(AM) Mission KS 1 kw-D, 500 w-N, DA-2.
KZSN(AM) Wichita KS 5 kw-D, 1 kw-N, DA-2.
WQKS(AM) Hopkinsville KY 1 kw-D, 24 w-N.
WNKY(AM) Neon KY 5 kw-D.
WTLO(AM) Somerset KY 1 kw-U.
KJNA(AM) Jena LA 500 w-D, 155 w-N.
KIOU(AM) Shreveport LA 1 kw-D.
WSAR(AM) Fall River MA 5 kw-U, DA-1.
*WGVU(AM) Kentwood MI 5 kw-U, DA-N.
WSDS(AM) Salem Township MI 750 w-D, DA-2, 5 kw-N.
WIOS(AM) Tawas City MI 1 kw-D, DA-N.
KAUS(AM) Austin MN 1 kw-U, DA-2.
KKCQ(AM) Fosston MN 5 kw-D, 2.5 kw-N, DA-N.
WCNV(AM) Charlotte NC 5 kw-D, DA-2.
WJHB(AM) Fair Bluff NC 1 kw-D.
WAJA(AM) Franklin NC 5 kw-D.
WYRN(AM) Louisburg NC 500 w-D.
KMEM(AM) Lincoln NE 5 kw-D, 1 kw-N, DA-2.
KKEL(AM) Hobbs NM 5 kw-D, 1 kw-N, DA-N.
WLEA(AM) Hornell NY 2.5 kw-D.
WZRC(AM) New York NY 5 kw-U, DA-2.
WADR(AM) Remsen NY 5 kw-D, 50 w-N.
WHBC(AM) Canton OH 5 kw-U.
WCIN(AM) Cincinnati OH 5 kw-D, 500 w-N, DA-1.
WCNS(AM) Latrobe PA 500 w-D, 1 kw-N, DA-N.
WDAS(AM) Philadelphia PA 5 kw-D, 1 kw-N, DA-2.
WISL(AM) Shamokin PA 1 kw-D, 250 w-N, DA-2.
WSHP(AM) Shippensburg PA 500 w-D, 20 w-N.
WMDD(AM) Fajardo PR 5 kw-D.
WZJY(AM) Mt. Pleasant SC 1 kw-D, 44 w-N.
KSDR(AM) Watertown SD 1 kw-D, 53 w-N.
WJFC(AM) Jefferson City TN 500 w-D.
WBBP(AM) Memphis TN 5 kw-D, 100 w-N.
WJLE(AM) Smithville TN 1 kw-D, 34 w-N.
KMRT(AM) Dallas TX 5 kw-D, 1.9 kw-N, DA-2.
KLVL(AM) Pasadena TX 1 kw-D, 500 w-N, DA-N.
KCHL(AM) San Antonio TX 2.5 kw-D, 90 w-N, DA-2.
KHQN(AM) Spanish Fork UT 1 kw-D.
WPWC(AM) Dumfries-Triangle VA 1 kw-D, 500 w-N, DA-2.
WTOY(AM) Salem VA 5 kw-D.
WCFR(AM) Springfield VT 5 kw-D.
KDFL(AM) Lakewood WA 5 kw-D, 1 kw-N, DA-N.
KBMS(AM) Vancouver WA 1 kw-D, 2.5 kw-N, DA-N).
WTDY(AM) Madison WI 5 kw-U, DA-N.
KRAE(AM) Cheyenne WY 1 kw-D, 67 w-N.

1490 khz Local IV
WANA(AM) Anniston AL 1 kw-U.
WAJF(AM) Decatur AL 1 kw-U.
WRLD(AM) Lanett AL 1 kw-U.
WHBB(AM) Selma AL 1 kw-U.
KWXT(AM) Dardanelle AR 1 kw-U.
KXAR(AM) Hope AR 700 w-U.
KDRS(AM) Paragould AR 1 kw-U.
KOTN(AM) Pine Bluff AR 1 kw-U.
KBAS(AM) Bullhead City AZ 1 kw-U.
KCUZ(AM) Clifton AZ 1 kw-U.
KYCA(AM) Prescott AZ 1 kw-U.
KJYK(AM) Tucson AZ 1 kw-U.
KWAC(AM) Bakersfield CA 1 kw-U.
KMET(AM) Banning CA 1 kw-U.
KICO(AM) Calexico CA 1 kw-U.
KRKC(AM) King City CA 1 kw-U.
KTOB(AM) Petaluma CA 1 kw-U.
KBLF(AM) Red Bluff CA 1 kw-U.
KSPE(AM) Santa Barbara CA 1 kw-U.
KOWL(AM) South Lake Tahoe CA 1 kw-U.
KSYC(AM) Yreka CA 1 kw-U.
KBOL(AM) Boulder CO 1 kw-U.
KPKE(AM) Gunnison CO 1 kw-U.
KXRE(AM) Manitou Springs CO 500 kw-U.
WGCH(AM) Greenwich CT 1 kw-U.
WXVQ(AM) De Land FL 1 kw-U.
WZOR(AM) Immokalee FL 1 kw-U.
WSBH(AM) Miami Beach FL 1 kw-U.
WECM(AM) Milton FL 1 kw-U.
WEAG(AM) Starke FL .65 kw-U.
WTTB(AM) Vero Beach FL 1 kw-U.
WSIR(AM) Winter Haven FL 1 kw-U.
WMOG(AM) Brunswick GA 1 kw-U.
WCHM(AM) Clarkesville GA 1 kw-U.
WUWU(AM) Cordele GA 1 kw-U.
WSFB(AM) Quitman GA 1 kw-U.
WSNT(AM) Sandersville GA 1 kw-U.
WSYL(AM) Sylvania GA 1 kw-U.
KBUR(AM) Burlington IA 1 kw-U.
WDBQ(AM) Dubuque IA 1 kw-U.
KRIB(AM) Mason City IA 1 kw-U.
KCID(AM) Caldwell ID 1 kw-U.
KRCD(AM) Chubbuck ID 1 kw-U.
WKRO(AM) Cairo IL 1 kw-U.
WDAN(AM) Danville IL 1 kw-U.
WESL(AM) East St. Louis IL 1 kw-U, DA-2.
WPNA(AM) Oak Park IL 1 kw-U.
WZOE(AM) Princeton IL 1 kw-U.
WKBV(AM) Richmond IN 1 kw-U.
WNDU(AM) South Bend IN 1 kw-U.
KKAN(AM) Phillipsburg KS 1 kw-U.
KTOP(AM) Topeka KS 1 kw-U.
WFKY(AM) Frankfort KY 1 kw-U.

WCLU(AM) Glasgow KY 1 kw-D, DA-1.
WFXY(AM) Middlesboro KY 1 kw-U.
WOMI(AM) Owensboro KY 830 w-U.
WSIP(AM) Paintsville KY 1 kw-U.
WIKC(AM) Bogalusa LA 1 kw-U.
KEUN(AM) Eunice LA 1 kw-U.
KJIN(AM) Houma LA 1 kw-U.
KRUS(AM) Ruston LA 1 kw-U.
WHAV(AM) Haverhill MA 1 kw-U.
WMRC(AM) Milford MA 1 kw-U.
WACM(AM) West Springfield MA 1 kw-U.
WARK(AM) Hagerstown MD 1 kw-U.
WPOR(AM) Portland ME 1 kw-U.
WTVL(AM) Waterville ME 1 kw-U.
WABJ(AM) Adrian MI 1 kw-U.
WTIQ(AM) Manistique MI 1 kw-U.
WMPX(AM) Midland MI 1 kw-U, DA-2.
WEFG(AM) Whitehall MI 1 kw-U.
KXRA(AM) Alexandria MN 1 kw-U.
KQDS(AM) Duluth MN 1 kw-U.
KLGR(AM) Redwood Falls MN 1 kw-U.
KDMO(AM) Carthage MO 1 kw-U.
KTTR(AM) Rolla MO 1 kw-U.
KDRO(AM) Sedalia MO 1 kw-U.
WXBD(AM) Biloxi MS 1 kw-U.
WCLD(AM) Cleveland MS 1 kw-U.
WHOC(AM) Philadelphia MS 1 kw-U.
WTUP(AM) Tupelo MS 1 kw-U.
WVIX(AM) Vicksburg MS 1 kw-U.
KDBM(AM) Dillon MT 1 kw-U.
KBSR(AM) Laurel MT 1 kw-U.
WDUR(AM) Durham NC 1 kw-U.
WLOE(AM) Eden NC 1 kw-U.
WFLB(AM) Fayetteville NC 1 kw-U.
WLOJ(AM) New Bern NC 1 kw-U.
WRMT(AM) Rocky Mount NC 1 kw-U.
WSTP(AM) Salisbury NC 1 kw-U.
WSVM(AM) Valdese NC 1 kw-U.
WWIL(AM) Wilmington NC 1 kw-U.
KNDC(AM) Hettinger ND 1 kw-U.
KOVC(AM) Valley City ND 1 kw-U.
KEZO(AM) Omaha NE 1 kw-U.
WEMJ(AM) Laconia NH 1 kw-U.
WLGW(AM) Lancaster NH 1 kw-U.
WUSS(AM) Atlantic City NJ 1 kw-U.
KRSN(AM) Los Alamos NM 1 kw-U.
KRTN(AM) Raton NM 1 kw-U.
KRUI(AM) Ruidoso Downs NM 1 kw-U.
WCSS(AM) Amsterdam NY 1 kw-U.
WBTA(AM) Batavia NY 500 w-D, 1 kw-N.
WKNY(AM) Kingston NY 1 kw-U.
WICY(AM) Malone NY 1 kw-U.
WDLC(AM) Port Jervis NY 1 kw-U.
WCDO(AM) Sidney NY 1 kw-U.
WOLF(AM) Syracuse NY 1 kw-U, DA-D.
WGMF(AM) Watkins Glen NY 400 w-U.
WBEX(AM) Chillicothe OH 1 kw-U.
WJMO(AM) Cleveland Heights OH 1 kw-U.
WOHI(AM) East Liverpool OH 1 kw-U.
WMOA(AM) Marietta OH 1 kw-U.
WMRN(AM) Marion OH 1 kw-U.
KOKC(AM) Guthrie OK 1 kw-U.
KBIX(AM) Muskogee OK 1 kw-U.
KBKR(AM) Baker City OR 1 kw-U.
KRNR(AM) Roseburg OR 1 kw-U.
KBZY(AM) Salem OR 1 kw-U.
WESB(AM) Bradford PA 1 kw-U.
WAZL(AM) Hazleton PA 1 kw-U.
WNTJ(AM) Johnstown PA 1 kw-U.
WLPA(AM) Lancaster PA 600 w-U.
WBCB(AM) Levittown-Fairless Hills PA 1 kw-U.
WMGW(AM) Meadville PA 1 kw-U.
WNBT(AM) Wellsboro PA 1 kw-U.
WZBS(AM) Ponce PR 5 kw-D, 1 kw-N, DA-1.
WVGB(AM) Beaufort SC 1 kw-U.
WPCI(AM) Greenville SC 1 kw-U.
WTNI(AM) Hartsville SC 1 kw-U.
KFCR(AM) Custer SD 830 w.
KORN(AM) Mitchell SD 1 kw-U.
WJOC(AM) Chattanooga TN 1 kw-U.
WCSV(AM) Crossville TN 1 kw-U.
WITA(AM) Knoxville TN 1 kw-U.
WJJM(AM) Lewisburg TN 1 kw-U.
WDXL(AM) Lexington TN 1 kw-U.
KFON(AM) Austin TX 1 kw-U.
KIBL(AM) Beeville TX 1 kw-U.
KBST(AM) Big Spring TX 1 kw-U.
KQTY(AM) Borger TX 1 kw-U.
KNEL(AM) Brady TX 1 kw-U.
KWMC(AM) Del Rio TX 1 kw-U.
KSAM(AM) Huntsville TX 1 kw-U.
KDOS(AM) Laredo TX 1 kw-U.
KZZN(AM) Littlefield TX 1 kw-U.
KPLT(AM) Paris TX 1 kw-U.
KYZS(AM) Tyler TX 1 kw-U.
KVWC(AM) Vernon TX 1 kw-U.
KVLL(AM) Woodville TX 1 kw-U, DA-1.
KJOE(AM) Ogden UT 1 kw-U.
WOPI(AM) Bristol VA 1 kw-U.
WCVA(AM) Culpeper VA 1 kw-U.
WPAK(AM) Farmville VA 1 kw-U.
WOJY(AM) Hampton VA 1 kw-U.
WAYB(AM) Waynesboro VA 1 kw-U.
WKVT(AM) Brattleboro VT 1 kw-U.
WFAD(AM) Middlebury VT 1 kw-U.
WIKE(AM) Newport VT 1 kw-U.
KBRO(AM) Bremerton WA 1 kw-U.
KVAC(AM) Forks WA 1 kw-U.
KEYG(AM) Grand Coulee WA 1 kw-U.
KGHO(AM) Hoquiam WA 1 kw-U.
KLOG(AM) Kelso WA 1 kw-U.

KENE(AM) Toppenish WA 1 kw-U.
KTEL(AM) Walla Walla WA 1 kw-U.
WGEZ(AM) Beloit WI 1 kw-U.
WLFN(AM) La Crosse WI 1 kw-U.
WIGM(AM) Medford WI 1 kw-U, DA-1.
WOSH(AM) Oshkosh WI 1 kw-U.
WCZR(AM) Charleston WV 1 kw-U.
WTCS(AM) Fairmont WV 1 kw-U.
WAEY(AM) Princeton WV 1 kw-U.
WSGB(AM) Sutton WV 1 kw-U.
KUGR(AM) Green River WY 1 kw-U.
KGOS(AM) Torrington WY 1 kw-U.

1494 khz
V6AI(AM) Yap FM 10 kw. DA-1

1500 khz Clear I-B
WTOP(AM) Washington DC 50 kw-U, DA-2.
KSTP(AM) St. Paul MN 50 kw-U, DA-N.
WGTT(AM) Alabaster AL 1 kw-D.
WVSM(AM) Rainsville AL 1 kw-D.
WKAX(AM) Russellville AL 1 kw-D.
KRCK(AM) Burbank CA 50 kw-D, 14 kw-N, DA-2.
KSJX(AM) San Jose CA 10 kw-D, 5 kw-N, DA-2.
WFIF(AM) Milford CT 5 kw-D, DA.
WKIZ(AM) Key West FL 250 w-U, DA-1.
WPSO(AM) New Port Richey FL 250 w-D.
WSEM(AM) Donalsonville GA 1 kw-D.
WDEN(AM) Macon GA 1 kw-D.
KUMU(AM) Honolulu HI 10 kw-D.
WGEN(AM) Geneseo IL 250 w-D.
WPMB(AM) Vandalia IL 250 w-D.
WKGA(AM) Zion IL 250 w-D, DA.
WBRI(AM) Indianapolis IN 5 kw-D, DA.
WAKE(AM) Valparaiso IN 1 kw-D, DA.
WKXO(AM) Berea KY 250 w-D.
WMJL(AM) Marion KY 250 w-D.
WOLY(AM) Battle Creek MI 1 kw-D, DA.
WLQV(AM) Detroit MI 50 kw-D, 5 kw-N, DA-2.
KDFN(AM) Doniphan MO 2.5 kw-D, DA.
WBFN(AM) Quitman MS 1 kw-D.
WSMX(AM) Winston-Salem NC 10 kw-D (1-kw-CH), DA.
WGHT(AM) Pompton Lakes NJ 1 kw-D, DA.
*KABR(AM) Alamo Community NM 1 kw-D.
WBZI(AM) Xenia OH 500 w-D.
WGFT(AM) Youngstown OH 500 w-D, 250 w-CH, DA.
KXVQ(AM) Pawhuska OK 5 kw-D, 500 w-CH, DA-D.
WMNT(AM) Manati PR 1 kw-D, 250 w-N.
WEAC(AM) Gaffney SC 1 kw-D, 500 w-CH.
WDEB(AM) Jamestown TN 1 kw-D, 500 w-CH.
WTNE(AM) Trenton TN 250 w-D.
KBRN(AM) Boerne TX 250 w-D.
KMXO(AM) Merkel TX 250 w-D.
KJIM(AM) Sherman TX 1 kw-D, DA.
KANI(AM) Wharton TX 500 w-U, DA-N.
KVSN(AM) Tumwater WA 1 kw-D.

1510 khz Clear I-B
WLAC(AM) Nashville TN 50 kw-U, DA-N.
KGA(AM) Spokane WA 50 kw-U, DA-N.
KPBI(AM) Greenwood AR 2.5 kw-D.
KFNN(AM) Mesa AZ 10 kw-D.
KIRV(AM) Fresno CA 10 kw-D.
KNSE(AM) Ontario CA 10 kw-D, 1 kw-N, DA-2.
KTID(AM) San Rafael CA 1 kw-D.
KDKO(AM) Littleton CO 10 kw-D, 1.3 kw-N, DA-2.
WNLC(AM) New London CT 10 kw-D, 5 kw-N, DA-2.
WWBC(AM) Cocoa FL 1 kw-D.
KIFG(AM) Iowa Falls IA 1 kw-D, 500 w CH.
WWHN(AM) Joliet IL 1 kw-D.
WLRB(AM) Macomb IL 1 kw-D.
WAYT(AM) Wabash IN 250 w-D.
KANS(AM) Larned KS 1 kw-D (500 w-CH).
KAGY(AM) Port Sulphur LA 1 kw-D.
WSSH(AM) Boston MA 50 kw-U, DA-2.
WJCO(AM) Jackson MI 5.4 kw-D, DA.
WLKM(AM) Three Rivers MI 500 w-D.
KJLA(AM) Independence MO 10 kw-D, DA.
KMRF(AM) Marshfield MO 250 w-D.
WVIO(AM) Blowing Rock NC 1 kw-D.
WQMG(AM) Greensboro NC 1 kw-D, 250 w-CH.
KTTT(AM) Columbus NE 500 w-D.
WJIC(AM) Salem NJ 2.5 kw-D, DA.
WPUT(AM) Brewster NY 1 kw-D.
WLGN(AM) Logan OH 1 kw-D, 250 w-CH.
WVAC(AM) Norwalk OH 500 w-D, DA.
WWSM(AM) Annville-Cleona PA 5 kw-D, DA.
WXVX(AM) Monroeville PA 1 kw-D, DA.
WAVB(AM) Lajas PR 1 kw-U, DA-1.
WVAA(AM) Burnettown SC 1 kw-D, 250 W-CH.
WJKI(AM) Woodruff SC 1 kw-D, 250 w-N.
KMSD(AM) Milbank SD 5 kw-D.
KAGC(AM) Bryan TX 500 w-D.
KCTX(AM) Childress TX 250 w-D.
KMND(AM) Midland TX 500 w-D.
KJMC(AM) Mineola TX 500 w-D.
KQHN(AM) Nederland TX 5 kw-D, DA-D.
KGLF(AM) Robstown TX 500 w-D.
KSTV(AM) Stephenville TX 500 w-D.
WAUK(AM) Waukesha WI 10 kw-D, DA.

1520 khz Clear I-B
WWKB(AM) Buffalo NY 50 kw-U, DA-1.
KOMA(AM) Oklahoma City OK 50 kw-U, DA-N.
WZMG(AM) Opelika AL 5 kw-D, DA.
KMPG(AM) Hollister CA 5 kw-D, DA-2.
KTRO(AM) Port Hueneme CA 10 kw-D, 1 kw-N, DA-2.
WTLN(AM) Apopka FL 5 kw-D, DA.
*WXYB(AM) Indian Rocks Beach FL 1 kw-D, DA.
WEXY(AM) Wilton Manors FL 3.5 kw-D, 250 w-N, DA-N.

U.S. AM Stations by Frequency

WDCY(AM) Douglasville GA 2.5 kw-D.
WKVQ(AM) Eatonton GA 1 kw-D.
WNMT(AM) Garden City GA 1 kw-D.
KSIB(AM) Creston IA 1 kw-D.
WHOW(AM) Clinton IL 5 kw-D, 1 kw-CH.
WLUV(AM) Loves Park IL 500 w-D
WKVI(AM) Knox IN 250 w-D.
WOOO(AM) Shelbyville IN 1 kw-D, 250 w-N, DA-2.
WLGC(AM) Greenup KY 5 kw-D.
WHIC(AM) Hardinsburg KY 1 kw-D.
WRSL(AM) Stanford KY 1 kw-D.
KACY(AM) Lafayette LA 10 kw-D, 500 w-N, DA-N.
WGAM(AM) Greenfield MA 10 kw-D, DA.
WHRF(AM) Bel Air MD 250 w-D, DA.
WTRI(AM) Brunswick MD 500 w-D, 250 w-CH.
WQWQ(AM) Muskegon Heights MI 10 kw-D, 1 kw, DA-2.
WMLM(AM) St. Louis MI 1 kw-D, DA-2.
KOLM(AM) Rochester MN 10 kw-D.
KMPL(AM) Sikeston MO 5 kw-D, 500 w-N, DA-3.
WQMA(AM) Marks MS 250 w-D.
WDSL(AM) Mocksville NC 5 kw-D, 1 kw-CH.
WGMA(AM) Spindale NC 500 w-D.
KMAV(AM) Mayville ND 2.5 kw-D.
KAMX(AM) Albuquerque NM 1 kw-D.
WTHE(AM) Mineola NY 1 kw-D, 250 w-CH.
WQCT(AM) Bryan OH 500 w-D, 250 w-CH.
WINW(AM) Canton OH 1 kw-D, DA.
WJMP(AM) Kent OH 1 kw-D, DA.
WVOI(AM) Toledo OH 1 kw-U, DA-2.
KFXX(AM) Oregon City OR 50 kw-D, 10 kw-N, DA-2.
WCHE(AM) West Chester PA 250 w-D.
WRAI(AM) San Juan PR 10 kw-U, DA-1.
WKZQ(AM) Myrtle Beach SC 5 kw-D, DA.
WKMG(AM) Newberry SC 1 kw-D.
KCGN(AM) Sioux Falls SD 500 w-D.
WNWS(AM) Brownsville TN 250 w-D.
WREA(AM) Dayton TN 5 kw-D.
KYND(AM) Cypress TX 3 kw-D, DA.
KRJH(AM) Hallettsville TX 250 w-D.

1530 khz Clear I-B
KFBK(AM) Sacramento CA 50 kw-U, DA-2.
WCKY(AM) Cincinnati OH 50 kw-U, DA-N,
(LSS-Sacramento, CA).
KLRA(AM) England AR 250 w-D.
KHPY(AM) Moreno Valley CA 10 kw-D, DA-3.
KCMN(AM) Colorado Springs CO 1 kw-D.
WDJZ(AM) Bridgeport CT 5 kw-D, DA.
WENG(AM) Englewood FL 1 kw-D.
WCRJ(AM) Jacksonville FL 50 kw-D, DA.
WTTI(AM) Dalton GA 10 kw-D, DA (CH).
KDSN(AM) Denison IA 500 w-D.
WKDC(AM) Elmhurst IL 500 w-D, DA.
KQNK(AM) Norton KS 1 kw-D.
WCEG(AM) Middleborough Center MA 1 kw-D.
WCTR(AM) Chestertown MD 250 w-D.
WWGZ(AM) Lapeer MI 5 kw-D, DA-D.
WYGR(AM) Wyoming MI 500 w-D.
KKCM(AM) Shakopee MN 8.6 kw-D, DA-D.
KPCR(AM) Bowling Green MO 1 kw-D, 250 w-CH.
KMAM(AM) Butler MO 500 w-D.
WRPM(AM) Poplarville MS 10 kw-D, 1 kw-CH.
WRTP(AM) Chapel Hill NC 10 kw-D, DA.
WOBR(AM) Wanchese NC 1 kw-D, DA.
KHAT(AM) Lincoln NE 5 kw-D, DA.
WJDM(AM) Elizabeth NJ 500 w-D.
KXTD(AM) Wagoner OK 5 kw-D.
WBCW(AM) Jeannette PA 1 kw-D, 250 w-CH.
WVFC(AM) McConnellsburg PA 1 kw-D, 250 w-CH.
WEYZ(AM) North East PA 1 kw-D, 250 w-CH, DA-1.
WMBT(AM) Shenandoah PA 2.5 kw-D, 500 W-CH.
WUPR(AM) Utuado PR 1 kw-D, 250 w-N.
WASC(AM) Spartanburg SC 1 kw-D, 250 w-CH.
WJPJ(AM) Huntingdon TN 1 kw-D.
KOPY(AM) Georgetown TX 10 kw-D, 900 w-CH.
KGBT(AM) Harlingen TX 50 kw-D, 10 kw-N, DA-N.
KNBO(AM) New Boston TX 2.5 kw-D.
KCLR(AM) Ralls TX 5 kw-D, 1 kw-CH.
WFIC(AM) Collinsville VA 1 kw-D, 250 w-CH.
WMBE(AM) Chilton WI 250 w-D.

1540 khz Clear I-B
KXEL(AM) Waterloo IA 50 kw-U, DA-N.
WRSM(AM) Sumiton AL 1 kw-D.
KDYN(AM) Ozark AR 500 w-D.
KASA(AM) Phoenix AZ 10 kw-D, DA.
KMBY(AM) Capitola CA 10 kw-D, DA-2.
KXED(AM) Los Angeles CA 50 kw-D, 10 kw-N, DA-2.
KISA(AM) Honolulu HI 5 kw-D.
WSMI(AM) Litchfield IL 1 kw-D.
WBNL(AM) Boonville IN 250 w-D.
WADM(AM) Decatur IN 250 w-D.
WLOI(AM) La Porte IN 250 w-D.
WMCB(AM) Martinsville IN 500 w-D.
KNGL(AM) McPherson KS 250 w-D.
KLKC(AM) Parsons KS 250 w-D.
WAKY(AM) Greensburg KY 1 kw-D.
KCTO(AM) Columbia LA 1 kw-D.
KGLA(AM) Gretna LA 1 kw-D.
WMDO(AM) Wheaton MD 5 kw-D.
*KTGG(AM) Spring Arbor MI 450 w-D, 200 w-CH.
KNNT(AM) Kennett MO 1 kw-D.
WKXG(AM) Greenwood MS 1 kw-D.
WOGR(AM) Charlotte NC 2.5 kw-D, DA.
WJOS(AM) Elkin NC 1 kw-D, 500 w-CH.
WTXY(AM) Whiteville NC 1 kw-D.
WYNC(AM) Yanceyville NC 2.5 kw-D.
WMYF(AM) Exeter NH 5 kw-D.
WPTR(AM) Albany NY 50 kw-U, DA-1.
WSIV(AM) East Syracuse NY 1 kw-D.

WBCO(AM) Bucyrus OH 500 w-D, DA.
WNRJ(AM) Circleville OH 1 kw-D.
WABQ(AM) Cleveland OH 1 kw-D.
WNRB(AM) Niles OH 500 w-D, DA.
WBTC(AM) Uhrichsville OH 250 w-D.
WPGR(AM) Philadelphia PA 50 kw-D, DA.
WECZ(AM) Punxsutawney PA 5 kw-D, 1 kw-CH.
WBJA(AM) Guayama PR 1 kw-D.
WADK(AM) Newport RI 1 kw-D.
WTBI(AM) Pickens SC 10 kw-D.
WBIN(AM) Benton TN 1 kw-D.
WJJT(AM) Jellico TN 1 kw-D, 500 w-CH.
WBRY(AM) Woodbury TN 500 w-D.
KTNO(AM) Fort Worth TX 50 kw-D, 1 kw-N, DA-2.
KGBC(AM) Galveston TX 1 kw-D, 250 w-N, DA-N.
KEDA(AM) San Antonio TX 5 kw-D, 1 kw-N, DA-2.
WREJ(AM) Richmond VA 1 kw-D, DA-D.
KBLV(AM) Bellevue WA 5 kw-D, DA-N.
WTKM(AM) Hartford WI 500 w-D.

1550 khz Clear (Canadian & Mexican) I-B
WLOR(AM) Huntsville AL 50 kw-D, 500 w-N, DA-2.
*KUAT(AM) Tucson AZ 50 kw-D.
KAPL(AM) Apple Valley CA 5 kw-D, 500 w-N, DA-2.
KXEX(AM) Fresno CA 5 kw-D, 2.5 kw-N, DA-2.
KKHI(AM) San Francisco CA 10 kw-U, DA-2.
KQXI(AM) Arvada CO 10 kw-D, 166 w-N.
WRDM(AM) Bloomfield CT 5 kw-D, 2.4 kw-N, DA-2.
WRHC(AM) Coral Gables FL 10 kw-D, 500 w-N, DA-2.
WWBH(AM) New Smyrna Beach FL 1 kw-D, 84 w-N.
WAMA(AM) Tampa FL 10 kw-D, 222 w-N.
WTHB(AM) Augusta GA 5 kw-D.
WAZX(AM) Smyrna GA 50 kw-D, 500 w-N, DA-2.
WWWN(AM) Vienna GA 1 kw-D, 23 w-N.
KIWA(AM) Sheldon IA 500 w-D, 11 w-N.
WJIL(AM) Jacksonville IL 1 kw-D, 10 w-N, DA-2.
WCSJ(AM) Morris IL 250 w-D, 6 w-N.
WOCC(AM) Corydon IN 250 w-D.
WCVL(AM) Crawfordsville IN 250 w-D, DA.
WMDH(AM) New Castle IN 250 w-U, DA-2.
WNDI(AM) Sullivan IN 250 w-D.
KDCC(AM) Dodge City KS 1 kw-D, 90 w-N.
KKLE(AM) Winfield KS 250 w-D, 52 w-N.
WIRV(AM) Irvine KY 1 kw-N.
WMSK(AM) Morganfield KY 250 w-D.
WLUX(AM) Port Allen LA 1 kw-D.
WNTN(AM) Newton MA 10 kw-D.
WSHN(AM) Fremont MI 1 kw-D.
WSER(AM) Elkton MD 1 kw-D, 10 w-N, DA-2.
KAPE(AM) Cape Girardeau MO 5 kw-D, 50 w-N, DA-2.
KLFJ(AM) Springfield MO 5 kw-D, 1 kw-N, DA-2.
KSFT(AM) St. Joseph MO 5 kw-D, DA-N.
WCLY(AM) Raleigh NC 1 kw-D, 7 w-N.
WBFJ(AM) Winston-Salem NC 1 kw-D.
KQWB(AM) Fargo ND 10 kw-D, 5 kw-N, DA-N.
KICS(AM) Hastings NE 500 w-D.
WJRZ(AM) Toms River NJ 6 kw-D, 3 kw-N, DA-2.
KXTO(AM) Reno NV 2.5 kw-D, 94 w-N.
WCGR(AM) Canandaigua NY 250 w-D.
WUTQ(AM) Utica NY 1 kw-D.
WDLR(AM) Delaware OH 500 w-D, 29 w-N, DA-2.
KMAD(AM) Madill OK 250 w-D.
KXOJ(AM) Sapulpa OK 2.5 kw-D, 47 w-N, DA-1.
WCXJ(AM) Braddock PA 1 kw-D, 4 w-N.
WARD(AM) Pittston PA 10 kw-D, 500 w-N, DA-2.
WTTC(AM) Towanda PA 1 kw-D.
WKFE(AM) Yauco PR 250 w-U.
WBSC(AM) Bennettsville SC 10 kw-D, 1 kw-N, DA-N.
WBCV(AM) Bristol TN 5 kw-D.
WCTZ(AM) Clarksville TN 2.5 kw-D, 250 w-N, DA-N.
WKJQ(AM) Parsons TN 1 kw-D.
WTYR(AM) Soddy-Daisy TN 1 kw-D.
KAKS(AM) Canyon TX 1 kw-D, 219 w-N.
KCOM(AM) Comanche TX 250 w-D.
KWBC(AM) Navasota TX 250 w-D.
KRGO(AM) West Valley City UT 10 kw-D, 500 w-N.
WKBA(AM) Vinton VA 10 kw-D, DA.
KNTR(AM) Ferndale WA 50 kw-D, 10 kw-N, DA-2.
KSVY(AM) Opportunity WA 10 kw-D, 2.5 kw-N, DA-N.
KVAN(AM) Vancouver WA 10 kw-U, 500 w-N, DA-N.
WMIR(AM) Lake Geneva WI 1 kw-D.
WHIT(AM) Madison WI 5 kw-D, DA.
WEVR(AM) River Falls WI 1 kw-D.
WXVA(AM) Charles Town WV 5 kw-D.

1560 khz Clear (U.S. & Cuban) I-B
KNZR(AM) Bakersfield CA 10 kw-U, DA-1.
WQEW(AM) New York NY 50 kw-U, DA-2.
WAGC(AM) Centre AL 1 kw-D.
WTKN(AM) Daleville AL 5 kw-D, 2.5 kw CH.
KDDA(AM) Dumas AR 500 w-D.
KIQS(AM) Willows CA 250 w-D.
WINV(AM) Inverness FL 5 kw-D, 500 w-N.
WTAI(AM) Melbourne FL 5 kw-D.
WLJA(AM) Ellijay GA 1 kw-D.
WLNG(AM) Council Bluffs IA 1 kw-D.
KCJJ(AM) Iowa City IA 840 w-U, DA-1.
WBYS(AM) Canton IL 250 w-D.
WSHY(AM) Shelbyville IL 500 w-D, 2.1 kw-N, DA.
WSQR(AM) Sycamore IL 250 w-D.
WSEZ(AM) Paoli IN 250 w-D.
WRIN(AM) Rensselaer IN 1 kw-D, (500 w-CH).
KABI(AM) Abilene KS 250 w-D.
WQXY(AM) Hazard KY 1 kw-D, 500 w-CH, DA.
WKDO(AM) Liberty KY 1 kw-D.
WPAD(AM) Paducah KY 10 kw-D, 5 kw-N, DA-3.
KPWS(AM) Crowley LA 1 kw-D, DA.
WSLA(AM) Slidell LA 1 kw-D.
WMOM(AM) La Plata MD 1 kw-D.
WHEZ(AM) Portage MI 4.1 kw-D, DA.

KBEW(AM) Blue Earth MN 1 kw-D.
KQYX(AM) Joplin MO 10 kw-D, DA.
KLTI(AM) Macon MO 1 kw-D.
KTUI(AM) Sullivan MO 1 kw-D.
WYZD(AM) Dobson NC 1 kw-D.
WATJ(AM) Chardon OH 1 kw-D, DA.
WTNS(AM) Coshocton OH 1 kw-D.
WCNW(AM) Fairfield OH 5 kw-D, DA.
WTOD(AM) Toledo OH 5 kw-D, DA.
KWCO(AM) Chickasha OK 1 kw-D, 250 w-N, DA-N.
KKID(AM) Sallisaw OK 250 w-D.
WRSJ(AM) Bayamon PR 1 kw-D, 750 w-N.
WCCP(AM) Clemson SC 1 kw-D, 500 w-CH.
WAGL(AM) Lancaster SC 50 kw-D, DA.
KKAA(AM) Aberdeen SD 10 kw-D, 5 kw-N, DA-2.
WMRO(AM) Nashville TN 10 kw-D, DA.
KBBA(AM) Abilene TX 250 w-D.
KEGG(AM) Daingerfield TX 1 kw-D.
KHBR(AM) Hillsboro TX 250 w-D.
KTXZ(AM) West Lake Hills TX 2.5 kw-D, DA-2.
WSBV(AM) South Boston VA 2.5 kw-D, DA-1.
KZIZ(AM) Sumner WA 5 kw-D.
WGLB(AM) Port Washington WI 250 w-D, DA.
WFSP(AM) Kingwood WV 1 kw-D, 250 w-CH.

1570 khz Clear (Mexican) I-A
WCRL(AM) Oneonta AL 2.5 kw-D.
WTQX(AM) Selma AL 5 kw-D, 43 w-N.
KBRI(AM) Brinkley AR 250 w-D, 44 w-N.
KBJT(AM) Fordyce AR 1 kw-D, 11 w-N.
KSRB(AM) Hardy AR 1 kw-D.
KCVR(AM) Lodi CA 5 kw-D, 34 w-N, DA-2.
KPRO(AM) Riverside CA 5 kw-D, 194 w-N, DA-2.
KTGE(AM) Salinas CA 500 w-D.
KLOV(AM) Loveland CO 1 kw-D.
WTWB(AM) Auburndale FL 5 kw-D.
WQAI(AM) Fernandina Beach FL 5 kw-D.
WOKC(AM) Okeechobee FL 1 kw-D, 14 w-N.
WNNQ(AM) Ashburn GA 1 kw-D, 4 w-N.
WSSA(AM) Morrow GA 5 kw-D, 58 w-N.
KUAU(AM) Haiku HI 1 kw-D, 500 w-N.
KMCD(AM) Fairfield IA 250 w-D, 108 w-N.
KQWC(AM) Webster City IA 250 w-D, 132 w-N.
WBGZ(AM) Alton IL 1 kw-D, 74 w-N.
WFRL(AM) Freeport IL 5 kw-D, 500 w-N, DA-2.
WBEE(AM) Harvey IL 1 kw-D, 500 w-N, DA-2.
WTAY(AM) Robinson IL 250 w-D.
WIFF(AM) Auburn IN 500 w-D, 151 w-N, DA-2.
WILO(AM) Frankfort IN 250 w-U.
WZCC(AM) New Albany IN 1 kw-D, 412 w-N.
KNDY(AM) Marysville KS 250 w-D.
WKYR(AM) Burkesville KY 1 kw-D.
WLBQ(AM) Morgantown KY 1 kw-D, 150 w-N.
WKKS(AM) Vanceburg KY 1 kw-D.
WABL(AM) Amite LA 500 w-D.
KLLA(AM) Leesville LA 1 kw-D.
KMAR(AM) Winnsboro LA 1 kw-D.
WNSH(AM) Beverly MA 1 kw-U, DA-2.
WPEP(AM) Taunton MA 1 kw-D, 227 w-N.
WKDB(AM) Towson MD 5 kw-D, 236 w-N.
WWCK(AM) Flint MI 1 kw-D, 238 w-N.
WFUR(AM) Grand Rapids MI 1 kw-D, 306 w-N.
KYCR(AM) Golden Valley MN 2.5 kw-U, 300 w-N, 500 w-CH.
KLEX(AM) Lexington MO 250 w-D, 58 w-N.
WIZK(AM) Bay Springs MS 5 kw-D.
WONA(AM) Winona MS 1 kw-D.
WNCA(AM) Siler City NC 1 kw-D, 290 w-N.
WTLK(AM) Taylorsville NC 1 kw-D, 248 w-N.
WBUG(AM) Amsterdam NY 1 kw-D, 207 w-N.
WFLR(AM) Dundee NY 5 kw-D, 442 w-N.
WRHD(AM) Riverhead NY 1 kw-D, 500 w-N, DA-2.
WGLX(AM) Galion OH 250 w-U, DA-2.
WPTW(AM) Piqua OH 250 w-U.
WANR(AM) Warren OH 500 w-D, 116 w-N, DA-1.
KTAT(AM) Frederick OK 250 w-D.
KMYZ(AM) Pryor OK 1 kw-D.
*WPGM(AM) Danville PA 2.5 kw-D.
WBUX(AM) Doylestown PA 5 kw-D, 500 w-N, DA-2.
WQTW(AM) Latrobe PA 1 kw-D, 220 w-N.
WPPC(AM) Penuelas PR 1 kw-D, 126 w-N.
KOSZ(AM) Vermillion SD 500 w-D.
WNKX(AM) Centerville TN 5 kw-D.
WCLE(AM) Cleveland TN 5 kw-D, 84 w-N.
WTRB(AM) Ripley TN 1 kw-D, 50 w-N.
KVLG(AM) La Grange TX 250 w-D, DA.
KPYK(AM) Terrell TX 250 w-U.
WSWV(AM) Pennington Gap VA 2.3 kw-D, 191 w-N.
WYTI(AM) Rocky Mount VA 2.5 kw-D, 440 w-N.
WRJQ(AM) Appleton WI 1 kw-D, 331 w-N.
WKBH(AM) Holmen WI 1 kw-D, 500 w-N.
WMQA(AM) Minocqua WI 5 kw-D, 250 w-N.

1580 khz Clear (Canadian) I-A
WOXR(AM) Oxford AL 2.5 kw-D, 22 w-N.
KFDF(AM) Van Buren AR 1 kw-D, 45 w-N.
KCWW(AM) Tempe AZ 50 kw-U, DA-N.
KLOQ(AM) Merced CA 1 kw-D, 297 w-N.
KBLA(AM) Santa Monica CA 50 kw-U, DA-2.
KEZD(AM) Windsor CA 700 w-D, DA.
KWYD(AM) Colorado Springs CO 10 kw-D.
WTCL(AM) Chattahoochee FL 5 kw-D.
WSRF(AM) Fort Lauderdale FL 10 kw-D, 5 kw-N, DA-2.
WBGB(AM) Mount Dora FL 5 kw-D.
WCCF(AM) Punta Gorda FL 1 kw-D, 122 w-N, DA-2.
WEAM(AM) Columbus GA 2.3 kw-D, 1 kw-N, DA-N.
WKIG(AM) Glennville GA 1 kw-D.
WKUN(AM) Monroe GA 1 kw-D.
KCHA(AM) Charles City IA 500 w-D, 10 w-N.
KFQC(AM) Davenport IA 500 w-D, 7 w-N.

WKKD(AM) Aurora IL 250 w-D, 200 w-N, DA-2.
WDQN(AM) DuQuoin IL 250 w-D.
WBBA(AM) Pittsfield IL 250 w-D, 15 w-N.
WBCP(AM) Urbana IL 250 w-D, 10 w-N.
WIFE(AM) Connersville IN 250 w-ND.
WIWO(AM) South Bend IN 1 kw-D, 500 w-N, DA-N.
WAMW(AM) Washington IN 500 w-D, DA-D.
WBBE(AM) Georgetown KY 10 kw-D, 45 w-N, DA-2.
WPKY(AM) Princeton KY 250 w-D.
KLVU(AM) Haynesville LA 1 kw-D, 86 w-N.
KXZZ(AM) Lake Charles LA 1 kw-U, DA-N.
WPGC(AM) Morningside MD 50 kw-D, 250 w-N, DA.
WWSJ(AM) St. Johns MI 1 kw-D, DA.
KDOM(AM) Windom MN 1 kw-D, 2 w-N, DA-2.
KTGR(AM) Columbia MO 250 w-D, 19 w-N.
KESM(AM) El Dorado Springs MO 500 w-D.
KNIM(AM) Maryville MO 250 w-D, 11 w-N.
WAMY(AM) Amory MS 1 kw-D.
WZFL(AM) Centreville MS 250 w-D.
WORV(AM) Hattiesburg MS 1 kw-D, 88 w-N.
WESY(AM) Leland MS 1 kw-D, 48 w-N.
WZZJ(AM) Pascagoula-Moss Point MS 5 kw-D, 50 w-N, DA-2.
WZKY(AM) Albemarle NC 1 kw-D, 167 w-N.
WWOF(AM) Camp Lejeune NC 10 kw-D.
WUIV(AM) Icard Township NC 5 kw-D, DA.
KAMI(AM) Cozad NE 1 kw-D.
WONZ(AM) Hammonton NJ 1 kw-D, 7 w-N.
KRLL(AM) Albuquerque NM 10 kw-D, 47 w-N.
WLIM(AM) Patchogue NY 10 kw-D, 37 w-N, DA-N.
WVKO(AM) Columbus OH 1 kw-D, 250 w-N, DA-2.
KOKB(AM) Blackwell OK 1 kw-D, 49 w-N.
WNZT(AM) Columbia PA 500 w-D, 15 w-N.
WRDD(AM) Ebensburg PA 1 kw-D.
WANB(AM) Waynesburg PA 1 kw-D.
WMTI Exp Stn Manati PR 250 w-D, 500 w-N.
WMTI(AM) Morovis PR 5 kw-D, 2.5 kw-N, DA-D.
WPJK(AM) Orangeburg SC 1 kw-D.
WDAB(AM) Travelers Rest SC 5 kw-D.
WLIJ(AM) Shelbyville TN 1 kw-D, 12 w-N.
KGAF(AM) Gainesville TX 250 w-U, 5 w-N.
KIRT(AM) Mission TX 1 kw-D, 302 w-N.
KTLU(AM) Rusk TX 840 w-D, 250 w-N.
KWED(AM) Seguin TX 1 kw-D, 249 w-N.
KRZI(AM) Waco TX 1 kw-D, 500 w-N, DA-2.
WILA(AM) Danville VA 1 kw-D.
WPUV(AM) Pulaski VA 5 kw-D, 1 kw-CH.
WTTN(AM) Watertown WI 1 kw-D, 7.8 w-N.

1590 khz Regional III
WGYJ(AM) Atmore AL 5 kw-D, 1 kw-N, DA-N.
WVNA(AM) Tuscumbia AL 5 kw-D, 1 kw-N, DA-N.
KQXK(AM) Springdale AR 2.5 kw-D, 58 w-N.
KSUV(AM) McFarland CA 500 w-D, 490 w-N, DA-2.
KLIV(AM) San Jose CA 5 kw-D, DA.
KBBY(AM) Ventura CA 5 kw-D, DA.
KCIN(AM) Victorville CA 500 w-D, 135 w-N.
WPSL(AM) Port St. Lucie FL 5 kw-D, 64 w-N.
WPUL(AM) South Daytona FL 1 kw-D.
WRXB(AM) St. Petersburg Beach FL 5 kw-D, 1 kw-N, DA-2.
WALG(AM) Albany GA 5 kw-D, 1 kw-N, DA-N.
WQCH(AM) La Fayette GA 5 kw-D.
WXRS(AM) Swainsboro GA 2.5 kw-D, 25 w-N.
WTGA(AM) Thomaston GA 500 w-D, 25 w-N.
KWBG(AM) Boone IA 1 kw-D, 500 w-N, DA-N.
WONX(AM) Evanston IL 1 kw-D, 2.5 kw-N, DA-N.
WAIK(AM) Galesburg IL 5 kw-D, 50 w-N, DA-2.
WNTS(AM) Beech Grove IN 5 kw-D, 500 w-N, DA-3.

WPCO(AM) Mt. Vernon IN 500 w-D, 35 w-N.
KVGB(AM) Great Bend KS 5 kw-D, 1 kw-N, DA-N.
WKYZ(AM) Gray KY 500 w-D, 26 w-N.
WLBN(AM) Lebanon KY 1 kw-D, 74 w-N, DA-1.
KKAY(AM) White Castle LA 1 kw-D.
WJRO(AM) Glen Burnie MD 1 kw-D.
WETT(AM) Ocean City MD 1 kw-D, 500 w-N, DA-2.
WTVB(AM) Coldwater MI 5 kw-D, 1 kw-N, DA-N.
WIFN(AM) Marine City MI 1 kw-D, 102 w-N, DA-1.
KCNN(AM) East Grand Forks MN 5 kw-D, 1 kw-N, DA-2.
KDJS(AM) Willmar MN 1 kw-D, 89 w-N, DA-2.
KDEX(AM) Dexter MO 1 kw-D, 78 w-N.
KPRT(AM) Kansas City MO 1 kw-U.
KMOZ(AM) Rolla MO 1 kw-D, 1 kw-N.
WZRX(AM) Jackson MS 5 kw-D, 1 kw-N, DA-N.
WBHN(AM) Bryson City NC 500 w-D.
WVOE(AM) Chadbourn NC 1 kw-D.
WCSL(AM) Cherryville NC 1 kw-D, 42 w-N.
WOKX(AM) High Point NC 1 kw-D, 26 w-N.
KTCH(AM) Wayne NE 2.5 kw-D, 33.4 w-N, DA-2.
WSMN(AM) Nashua NH 5 kw-U, DA-1.
WERA(AM) Plainfield NJ 500 w-U, DA-2.
KHIT(AM) Sun Valley NV 5 kw-D.
WAUB(AM) Auburn NY 500 w-D, 1 kw-N, DA-2.
WASB(AM) Brockport NY 1.8 kw-U, DA-2.
WEHH(AM) Elmira Heights-Horseheads NY 500 w-D, 480 w-N, DA-N.
WGGO(AM) Salamanca NY 5 kw-D.
WAKR(AM) Akron OH 5 kw-U, DA-1.
WSRW(AM) Hillsboro OH 500 w-D.
KDLB(AM) Henryetta OK 500 w-D.
KWEY(AM) Weatherford OK 1 kw-D, DA.
KMBD(AM) Tillamook OR 5 kw-D, 1 kw-N, DA-N.
WPLW(AM) Carnegie PA 1 kw-D, DA.
WCBG(AM) Chambersburg PA 5 kw-D, 1 kw-N, DA-N.
WCZN(AM) Chester PA 3.2 kw-D, 1 kw-N, DA-N.
WWCC(AM) Honesdale PA 2.5 kw-D.
WXRF(AM) Guayama PR 1 kw-U.
WARV(AM) Warwick RI 5 kw-U, DA-2.
WCAM(AM) Camden SC 1 kw-D, 27 w-N.
WATX(AM) Algood TN 1 kw-D, 500 w-N.
WKTP(AM) Jonesborough TN 1.6 kw-D, 5 kw-N, DA-2.
WDBL(AM) Springfield TN 1 kw-D, 30 w-N.
KGAS(AM) Carthage TX 2.5 kw-D, 130 w-N.
KEAS(AM) Eastland TX 500 w-D.
KELP(AM) El Paso TX 5 kw-D, 800 w-N.
KYOK(AM) Houston TX 5 kw-U, DA-N.
KLLL(AM) Lubbock TX 1 kw-U, DA-N.
KRQX(AM) Mexia TX 500 w-D, 128 w-N.
KDAE(AM) Sinton TX 1 kw-D, 500 w-N, DA-2.
WFTH(AM) Richmond VA 1 kw-D, 19 w-N.
KZOK(AM) Seattle WA 5 kw-D, DA-N.
WCAE(AM) Nekoosa WI 500 w-D.
WIXK(AM) New Richmond WI 5 kw-D.
WTOQ(AM) Platteville WI 1 kw-D, 500 w-N, DA-N.
WTRW(AM) Two Rivers WI 1 kw-D, 33 w-N.

1593 khz
WSZC(AM) Truk FM 5 kw-U, DA-1.

1600 khz Regional III
WEUP(AM) Huntsville AL 5 kw-D, 500 w-N, DA-D.
WXVI(AM) Montgomery AL 5 kw-D, 1 kw-N, DA-2.
KNWA(AM) Bellefonte AR 5 kw-D, 50 w-N.
KJIW(AM) West Helena AR 1 kw.
KVRD(AM) Cottonwood AZ 1 kw-D.
KXEW(AM) South Tucson AZ 1 kw-U, DA-N.
KGST(AM) Fresno CA 5 kw-D, DA-N.

KMNY(AM) Pomona CA 5 kw-U, DA-N.
KTAP(AM) Santa Maria CA 470 w-D.
KUBA(AM) Yuba City CA 5 kw-D, 2.5 kw-N, DA-N.
KWMX(AM) Lakewood CO 5 kw-U, DA-N.
WKEN(AM) Dover DE 5 kw-D, 1 kw-N, DA-2.
WNCM(AM) Atlantic Beach FL 5 kw-D, 90 w-N.
WKWF(AM) Key West FL 500 w-U.
WPOM(AM) Riviera Beach FL 5 kw-D, 4.7 kw-N, DA-2.
WXTO(AM) Winter Garden FL 5 kw-U, DA-2.
WAOS(AM) Austell GA 5 kw-D.
WNGA(AM) Nashville GA 1 kw-D.
WRCC(AM) Warner Robins GA 2.5 kw-D, 500 w-N, DA-N.
KLGA(AM) Algona IA 5 kw-D, 500 w-N, DA-2.
KCRG(AM) Cedar Rapids IA 5 kw-U, DA-N.
WCGO(AM) Chicago Heights IL 1 kw-D, 23 w-N, DA-2.
WMCW(AM) Harvard IL 500 w-D, 19 w-N.
WBTO(AM) Linton IN 500 w-D, 32 w-N.
WARU(AM) Peru IN 1 kw-D.
KMDO(AM) Fort Scott KS 1 kw-D, 50 w-N.
WKXF(AM) Eminence KY 500 w-D, 48 w-N.
WLLS(AM) Hartford KY 1 kw-D, DA.
KFNV(AM) Ferriday LA 1 kw-D.
KLEB(AM) Golden Meadow LA 5 kw-D, 250 w-N.
WUNR(AM) Brookline MA 5 kw-U, DA-1.
WAQY(AM) East Longmeadow MA 5 kw-D, 2.5 kw-N, DA-2.
WINX(AM) Rockville MD 1 kw-D, 500 w-N, DA-N.
WAAM(AM) Ann Arbor MI 5 kw-U, DA-2.
WELL(AM) Battle Creek MI 1 kw-U.
WSFN(AM) Muskegon MI 5 kw-U, DA-N.
KLLZ(AM) Walker MN 1 kw-D, 47 w-N.
KATZ(AM) St. Louis MO 5 kw-U, DA-N.
KTTN(AM) Trenton MO 500 w-D.
WGIV(AM) Charlotte NC 1 kw-D, 500 w-N, DA-2.
WIDU(AM) Fayetteville NC 1 kw-D, 25 w-N.
WTZQ(AM) Hendersonville NC 5 kw-D, 500 w-N, DA-2.
KDAK(AM) Carrington ND 500 w-D, 90 w-N.
KNCY(AM) Nebraska City NE 5 kw-D, 31 w-N, DA-2.
KRFS(AM) Superior NE 500 w-D.
WWRL(AM) New York NY 5 kw-U, DA-2.
WMCR(AM) Oneida NY 1 kw-D, 20 w-N.
WLNG(AM) Sag Harbor NY 500 w-D.
WBLY(AM) Springfield OH 1 kw-D, 34 w-N.
WTTF(AM) Tiffin OH 500 w-D, 20 w-N, DA-1.
KUSH(AM) Cushing OK 1 kw-D, 70 w-N.
KOHI(AM) St. Helens OR 1 kw-D, 500 w-CH.
WHOL(AM) Allentown PA 500 w-D, 100 w-N, DA-2.
WBFD(AM) Bedford PA 5 kw-D, 28 w-N.
WPDC(AM) Elizabethtown PA 500 w-D, 79 w-N.
WJSA(AM) Jersey Shore PA 1 kw-D, 20 w-N.
WLUZ(AM) Bayamon PR 5 kw-U, DA-2.
WFIS(AM) Fountain Inn SC 1 kw-D, 25 w-N.
WKZK(AM) North Augusta SC 500 w-D.
WKBJ(AM) Milan TN 2.5 kw-D, 71 w-N.
KBOR(AM) Brownsville TX 1 kw-U, DA-1.
KRVA(AM) Cockrell Hill TX 5 kw-D, 1 kw-N, DA-N.
KQRO(AM) Cuero TX 500 w-U.
KVYK(AM) Giddings TX 500 w-D, 250 w-N, DA-2.
KOGT(AM) Orange TX 1 kw-U, DA-N.
KCPX(AM) Centerville UT 5 kw-D, 1 kw-N, DA-N.
WJQI(AM) Chesapeake VA 5 kw-D.
WXMY(AM) Saltville VA 5 kw-D, 500 w-PSA.
WCWC(AM) Ripon WI 5 kw-U, DA-N.
WNST(AM) Milton WV 6 kw-D, 26 w-N.
WBBD(AM) Wheeling WV 5 kw-D, 30 w-N.

U.S. FM Stations by Frequency

Note: Asterisks (*) denote noncommercial stations or channels. Noncommercial stations can use frequencies allotted for commercial use.

88.1 mhz (ch 201)

*KRUA(FM) Anchorage AK 155 w, 292 ft.
*KCUK(FM) Chevak AK 150 w, 75 ft.
*KNNB(FM) Whiteriver AZ 630 w, 600 ft.
*KCFY(FM) Yuma AZ 3 kw, 239 ft.
*KECG(FM) El Cerrito CA 10 w, 130 ft.
*KFCF(FM) Fresno CA 2.4 kw, 1,900 ft.
*KLON(FM) Long Beach CA 8 kw, 430 ft.
*KNSQ(FM) Mount Shasta CA 2.28 kw, 2,385 ft.
*KSRH(FM) San Rafael CA 10 w, 66 ft.
*KZSC(FM) Santa Cruz CA 1.36 kw, 350 ft.
*WESU(FM) Middletown CT 1.5 kw, 38 ft.
*WMNR(FM) Monroe CT 5.0 kw, 403 ft.
*WJIS(FM) Bradenton FL 100 kw, 397 ft.
*WNCM-FM Jacksonville FL 1 kw, 500 ft.
*WHIJ(FM) Ocala FL 1.25 kw, 394 ft.
*WUWF(FM) Pensacola FL 100 kw, 617 ft.
*WAYF(FM) West Palm Beach FL 50 kw, 417 ft.
*WJSP-FM Warm Springs GA 100 kw, 975 ft.
*KHPR(FM) Honolulu HI 27 kw, 2,000 ft.
*KDPS(FM) Des Moines IA 5.2 kw, 285 ft.
*KICB(FM) Fort Dodge IA 200 w, 130 ft.
*KBBG(FM) Waterloo IA 9.5 kw, 150 ft.
*WESN(FM) Bloomington IL 120 w, 98 ft.
*WCRX(FM) Chicago IL 100 w, 150 ft.
*WSSD(FM) Chicago IL 10 w, 100 ft.
*WLTL(FM) La Grange IL 180 w, 138 ft.
*WLRA(FM) Lockport IL 250 w, 95 ft.
*WPTH(FM) Olney IL 133 w, 203 ft.
*WETN(FM) Wheaton IL 250 w, 140 ft.
*WNTH(FM) Winnetka IL 100 w, 105 ft.
*WVPE(FM) Elkhart IN 10 kw, 400 ft.
*WNAS(FM) New Albany IN 2.85 kw, 3 ft.
*KBCU(FM) North Newton KS 149 w, 56 ft.
*KJTY(FM) Topeka KS 50 kw, 350 ft.
*WDFB-FM Danville KY 170 w, 328 ft.
*WRFL(FM) Lexington KY 250 w, 288.6 ft.
*WMBR(FM) Cambridge MA 360 w, 285 ft.
*WYAJ(FM) Sudbury MA 4 w, 220 ft.
*WCHC(FM) Worcester MA 100 w, 6.56 ft.
*WJHU-FM Baltimore MD 10 kw, 360 ft.
*WMUC-FM College Park MD 8.5 w, 3 ft.
*WBFH(FM) Bloomfield Hills MI 360 w, 180 ft.
*WHPR(FM) Highland Park MI 11 w-horiz, 105 ft.
*WSDP(FM) Plymouth MI 200 w, 793 ft.
*WYCE(FM) Wyoming MI 1 kw, 62 ft.
*KRLX(FM) Northfield MN 100 w, 16 ft.
*KVSC(FM) St. Cloud MN 16.5 kw, 446 ft.
*KLFC(FM) Branson MO 100 w, 328 ft.
*KCOU(FM) Columbia MO 435 w, 110 ft.
*KDHX(FM) St. Louis MO 42.4 kw, 1,314 ft.
*WURC(FM) Holly Springs MS 3 kw, 328 ft.
*WMAW-FM Meridian MS 100 kw, 1,050 ft.
*KAEP(FM) Fort Belknap Agency MT 90 kw, 340 ft.
*WCQS(FM) Asheville NC 260 w, 1,132 ft.
*WPAR(FM) Hickory NC 10 kw, 300 ft.
*WKNC-FM Raleigh NC 3 kw, 260 ft.
*KCNT(FM) Hastings NE 2 kw, 182 ft.
*WNJS-FM Berlin NJ 1 w-H, 120 w-V, 328 ft.
*WPFR(FM) Netcong NJ 2.2 kw-V, 134 ft.
*WNJT-FM Trenton NJ 30 w, 787 ft.
*KCEP(FM) Las Vegas NV 100 w-H, -39 ft.
*WXBA(FM) Brentwood NY 180 w, 90 ft.
*WCWP(FM) Brookville NY 100 w, 190 ft.
*WUBJ(FM) Jamestown NY 265 w, 558 ft.
*WARY(FM) Valhalla NY 171 w, 403 ft.
*WFRW(FM) Webster NY 11.5 kw, 337 ft.
*WZIP(FM) Akron OH 3.3 kw, 810 ft.
*WBGU(FM) Bowling Green OH 450 w, 178 ft.
*WQRP(FM) West Carrollton OH 4 kw, 295 ft.
*KMSI(FM) Moore OK 30 kw-V, 597 ft.
*KWVA(FM) Eugene OR 500 w, 56 ft.
*WEFR(FM) Erie PA 3 kw, 236 ft.
*WTGP(FM) Greenville PA 1.1 kw, 6 ft.
*WHPN(FM) Harrisburg PA 260 w, 217 ft.
*WRWJ(FM) Murrysville PA 100 w, 220 ft.
*WPEB(FM) Philadelphia PA 100 w, 100 ft.
*WRSK(FM) Slippery Rock PA 100 w, 79 ft.
*WRGN(FM) Sweet Valley PA 500 w, 239 ft.
*WWAS(FM) Williamsport PA 100 w, minus 58 ft.
*WVYC(FM) York PA 370 w, 97 ft.
*WCRP(FM) Guayama PR 27 kw, 1,889 ft.
*WELH(FM) Providence RI 25 w-H, 150 w-V, 98 ft.
*WSBF-FM Clemson SC 3 kw, 200 ft.
*WRJA-FM Sumter SC 98 kw, 1,000 ft.
*KRSD(FM) Sioux Falls SD 2 kw, 183 ft.
*WUTC(FM) Chattanooga TN 50 kw-H, 750 ft.
*WFSK(FM) Nashville TN 700 w, 6 ft.
*KGNZ(FM) Abilene TX 75 kw, 710 ft.
*KNTU(FM) Denton TX 100 kw, 442 ft.
*KHOY(FM) Laredo TX 1.8 kw, 348 ft.
*KTXT-FM Lubbock TX 35 kw, 423 ft.
*KHID(FM) McAllen TX 2.1 kw, 253 ft.
*KXGZ(FM) McAllen TX 2.1 kw, 253 ft.
*KJIC(FM) Pasadena TX 440 w, 110 ft.
*KNLE-FM Round Rock TX 700 w, 53 ft.
*KWCR-FM Ogden UT 2 kw, -470 ft.
*KPGR(FM) Pleasant Grove UT 115 w, minus 1,128 ft.
*WHOV(FM) Hampton VA 2 kw-horiz, 8 kw-vert, 200 ft.
*KTCV(FM) Kennewick WA 320 w, 92 ft.
*WJTY(FM) Lancaster WI 12 kw, 476 ft.
*WMWK(FM) Milwaukee WI 170 w-H, 955 ft.
*WVBC(FM) Bethany WV 1.1 kw, 410 ft.
*WKJL(FM) Clarksburg WV
*WMUL(FM) Huntington WV 1.15 kw, -56 ft.
*KCWC-FM Riverton WY 3 kw, 1,449 ft.

88.3 mhz (ch 202)

*KABF(FM) Little Rock AR 91 kw, 777 ft.
*KNAI(FM) Phoenix AZ 22.5 kw, 997 ft.
*KPHF(FM) Phoenix AZ 22.5 kw, 997 ft.
*KHAP(FM) Chico CA 12 kw, 285 ft.
*KAXL(FM) Green Acres CA 360 w, 133 ft.
*KWXP(FM) Magalia CA 1.45 kw, 1,184 ft.
*KUCR(FM) Riverside CA 750 w, 291 ft.
*KEDR(FM) Sacramento CA 50 kw-V, 472 ft.
*KSDS(FM) San Diego CA 830 w, 170 ft.
*KCLU(FM) Thousand Oaks CA 1.2 kw, 535 ft.
*WQAQ(FM) Hamden CT 16 w, minus 82 ft.
*WLMS(FM) Lecanto FL 3.8 kw, 259 ft.
*WFHQ(FM) Pennsuco FL 3 kw, 167 ft.
*WTLG(FM) Starke FL 7 kw, 285 ft.
*WJCK(FM) Cedartown GA 6 kw, 328 ft.
*WLPT(FM) Jesup GA 30 kw, 239 ft.
*KCCK-FM Cedar Rapids IA 10 kw, 420 ft.
*KMSC(FM) Sioux City IA 10 w, 105 ft.
*WZRD(FM) Chicago IL 100 w, 76 ft.
*WDGC-FM Downers Grove IL 250 w, 130 ft.
*WIUS(FM) Macomb IL 120 w, 83 ft.
*WFEN(FM) Rockford IL 5.4 kw, 325 ft.
*WQNA(FM) Springfield IL 3 kw, 80 ft.
*WEAX(FM) Angola IN 920 w, 151 ft.
*WDSO(FM) Chesterton IN 413 w, 180 ft.
*WNIN-FM Evansville IN 45 kw, 510 ft.
*WLAB(FM) Fort Wayne IN 1.45 kw, 100 ft.
*WJYL(FM) New Washington IN 1 kw, 272 ft.
*KVCO(FM) Concordia KS 126.5 w, 77 ft.
*KYFW(FM) Wichita KS 17 kw, 141 ft.
*WRBH(FM) New Orleans LA 54 kw, 600 ft.
*WBMT(FM) Boxford MA 710 w, 17 ft.
*WIQH(FM) Concord MA 10 w, 30 ft.
*WGAO(FM) Franklin MA 125 w, 174 ft.
*WRPS(FM) Rockland MA 100 w, 120 ft.
*WCBN-FM Ann Arbor MI 200 w-vert, 177 ft.
*NEW FM Kalamazoo MI 100 w, 121 ft.
*WAEK(FM) Oakland MI 126 w-V, 316 ft.
*WNFA(FM) Port Huron MI 1.3 kw, 227 ft.
*WSHJ(FM) Southfield MI 125 w, 43 ft.
*KWND(FM) Springfield MO 12 kw, 328 ft.
*WAFR(FM) Tupelo MS 50 kw, 492 ft.
*WGWG(FM) Boiling Springs NC 4.7 kw, 220 ft.
*WUAW(FM) Erwin NC 3 kw, 207 ft.
*WBGO(FM) Newark NJ 10 kw, 431 ft.
*KLYT(FM) Albuquerque NM 1.8 kw, 4,000 ft.
*WVCR-FM Loudonville NY 360 w, 860 ft.
*WXLU(FM) Peru NY 200 w, 1,109 ft.
*WSBU(FM) St. Bonaventure NY 165 w, 90 ft.
*WAER(FM) Syracuse NY 6 kw, 300 ft.
*WCOU(FM) Warsaw NY 7 kw, 492 ft.
*WKHR(FM) Bainbridge OH 125 w, 144 ft.
*WBWC(FM) Berea OH 100 w, 40 ft.
*WJVS(FM) Cincinnati OH 175 w, 105 ft.
*WLFC(FM) Findlay OH 155 w, 66 ft.
*WMRT(FM) Marietta OH 9.2 kw, 205 ft.
*WOHP(FM) Portsmouth OH 1 kw, 643 ft.
*WXTS-FM Toledo OH 1 kw, 125 ft.
*WXUT(FM) Toledo OH 100 w-H, 190 ft.
*KBVM(FM) Portland OR 1.85 kw, 1,434 ft.
*WGEV(FM) Beaver Falls PA 400 w, 240 ft.
*WDCV-FM Carlisle PA 450 w, 150 ft.
*WWEC(FM) Elizabethtown PA 100 w, 373 ft.
*WRCT(FM) Pittsburgh PA 100 w, 53 ft.
*WQRI(FM) Bristol RI 100 w, 75 ft.
*WUOZ(FM) Belvedere SC 4.5 kw, 1,387 ft.
*KESD(FM) Brookings SD 50 kw, 623 ft.
*WPGB(FM) Blountville TN 1 kw, 1,811 ft.
*KJRT(FM) Amarillo TX 6 kw-V, 289 ft.
*KBNR(FM) Brownsville TX 3 kw, 289 ft.
*KJCR(FM) Keene TX 23 kw, 180 ft.
*KPAC(FM) San Antonio TX 100 kw, 820 ft.
*KCPW(FM) Salt Lake City UT 750 w, minus 587 ft.
*WRVL(FM) Lynchburg VA 50 kw, 1,082 ft.
*WNUB-FM Northfield VT 285 w, -387 ft.
*WHWC(FM) Menomonie WI 10 kw, 1,050 ft.

88.5 mhz (ch 203)

*KTNA(FM) Talkeetna AK 1.9 kw, 62 ft.
*WBHY-FM Mobile AL 50 kw, 624 ft.
*KSBR(FM) Mission Viejo CA 620 w, 600 ft.
*KCSN(FM) Northridge CA 52 w, 2,128 ft.
*KPSC(FM) Palm Springs CA 3 kw, 266 ft.
*KQED-FM San Francisco CA 110 w, 1,270 ft.
*KHMS(FM) Victorville CA 55 w, 2,994 ft.
*KGNU(FM) Boulder CO 1.3 kw, 215 ft.
*KCIC(FM) Grand Junction CO 450 w, -431 ft.
*WVOF(FM) Fairfield CT 100 w, 35 ft.
*WEDW-FM Stamford CT 2 kw-H, 1.8 kw-V, 302 ft.
*WAMU(FM) Washington DC 50 kw, 500 ft.
*WWIA(FM) Palm Bay FL 1 kw-V, 98 ft.
*WFCF(FM) St. Augustine FL 6 kw, 141 ft.
*WKPX(FM) Sunrise FL 3 kw, 100 ft.
*WMNF(FM) Tampa FL 70 kw, 520 ft.
*WRAS(FM) Atlanta GA 100 kw, 436 ft.
*KALA(FM) Davenport IA 400 w, 110 ft.
*KDIC(FM) Grinnell IA 100 w, 124 ft.
*KDCR(FM) Sioux Center IA 100 kw, 320 ft.
*WHPK-FM Chicago IL 100 w, 121 ft.
*WHFH(FM) Flossmoor IL 100 w, 92 ft.
*WMWA(FM) Glenview IL 100 w, 100 ft.
*WHSD(FM) Hinsdale IL 200 w, 131 ft.
*WBNH(FM) Pekin IL 4.3 kw, 524 ft.
*WECU(FM) Peoria IL 4.3 kw, 495 ft.
*WGCA-FM Quincy IL 40 kw, 449 ft.
*WCRT(FM) Terre Haute IN 550 w, 308 ft.
*WJIE(FM) Okolona KY 24.5 kw, 623 ft.
*WFCR(FM) Amherst MA 35 kw, 718 ft.
*WWTA(FM) Marion MA 19 w-H, 100 w-V, 53 ft.
*WHCF(FM) Bangor ME 100 kw, 1,604 ft.
*WSEW(FM) Sanford ME 100 w, 387 ft.
*WGVU-FM Allendale MI 3 kw, 311 ft.
*WOAS(FM) Ontonagon MI 10 w, 124 ft.
*KCRB-FM Bemidji MN 95 kw, 994 ft.
*KBEM-FM Minneapolis MN 2.15 kw, 370 ft.
*KFSI(FM) Rochester MN 7 kw, 320 ft.
*KLJC(FM) Kansas City MO 50 kw, 738 ft.
*KUMR(FM) Rolla MO 100 kw, 480 ft.
*WUSM-FM Hattiesburg MS 3 kw, 282 ft.
*WJSU(FM) Jackson MS 3 kw-V, 203 ft.
*WZRU(FM) Roanoke Rapids NC 28.2 kw, 162 ft.
*WHYC(FM) Swan Quarter NC 3 kw, 293 ft.
*WFDD-FM Winston-Salem NC 22 kw, 345 ft.
*KEYA(FM) Belcourt ND 19 kw, 263 ft.
*KFBN(FM) Lincoln NE 4.7 kw-V, 390 ft.
*WNJP(FM) Sussex NJ 500 w, 600 ft.
*WPOB-FM Plainview NY 125 w, 150 ft.
*WRUR-FM Rochester NY 970 w, 120 ft.
*WCII(FM) Spencer NY 6 kw, 485 ft.
*WKWZ(FM) Syosset NY 125 w, 90 ft.
*WMUB(FM) Oxford OH 30 kw, 475 ft.
*WYSU(FM) Youngstown OH 50 kw, 499 ft.
*KSBA(FM) Coos Bay OR 2.2 kw, 532 ft.
*WMCE(FM) Erie PA 250 w, 367 ft.
*WXPN(FM) Philadelphia PA 2.8 kw, 918 ft.
*WYBF(FM) Radnor Township PA 700 w-V, 223 ft.
*WRKC(FM) Wilkes-Barre PA 440 w, -470 ft.
*WKVN-FM Levittown PR 35 w, 121 ft.
*WAFZ(FM) Belton SC 50 kw, 100 ft.
*WFCH(FM) Charleston SC 29.6 kw, 305 ft.
*WECE(FM) Due West SC 20 kw, 518 ft.
*WTTU(FM) Cookeville TN 2.25 kw, 168 ft.
*WVCP(FM) Gallatin TN 1 kw, 390 ft.
*WQOX(FM) Memphis TN 30 kw, 430 ft.
*KOIR(FM) Edinburg TX 3 kw, 285 ft.
*KTEP(FM) El Paso TX 100 kw, 730 ft.
*KEOM(FM) Mesquite TX 61 kw, 514 ft.
*WODC(FM) Virginia Beach VA 300 w, 150 ft.
*KRLF(FM) Pullman WA 420 w-vert, 794 ft.
*KPLU-FM Tacoma WA 58 kw, 2,356 ft.
*KYSC(FM) Yakima WA 3 kw, -254 ft.
*WGNV(FM) Milladore WI 25 kw, 330 ft.
*WVPN(FM) Charleston WV 50 kw, 299 ft.

88.7 mhz (ch 204)

*WDVI(FM) Dadeville AL 9 kw, 328 ft.
*WRWA(FM) Dothan AL 50 kw, 500 ft.
*WQPR(FM) Muscle Shoals AL 20 kw, 430 ft.
*KNAU(FM) Flagstaff AZ 100 kw, 1,549 ft.
*KISL(FM) Avalon CA 100 w, minus 732 ft.
*KUBO(FM) Calexico CA 3 kw, 272 ft.
*KSPC(FM) Claremont CA 3 kw, -265 ft.
*KMPO(FM) Modesto CA 2 kw, 1,500 ft.
*KFAC(FM) Santa Barbara CA 12 kw, 866 ft.
*KRZA(FM) Alamosa CO 5 kw, 2,393 ft.
*KCME(FM) Manitou Springs CO 16 kw, 2,070 ft.
*WNHU(FM) West Haven CT 1.7 kw, 150 ft.
*WAYJ(FM) Fort Myers FL 50 kw, 400 ft.
*WJFR(FM) Jacksonville FL 8 kw, 380 ft.
*KLNI(FM) Decorah IA 100 w, -36 ft.
*KIGC(FM) Oskaloosa IA 230 w, 93 ft.
*KWDM(FM) West Des Moines IA 100 w, 170 ft.
*WPCD(FM) Champaign IL 3.3 kw, 290 ft.
*WLUW(FM) Chicago IL 100 w, 230 ft.
*WSIE(FM) Edwardsville IL 50 kw, 500 ft.
*WRSE-FM Elmhurst IL 100 w, 95 ft.
*WCSF(FM) Joliet IL 100 w, 108 ft.
*WGVE(FM) Gary IN 2.1 kw, 91 ft.
*WICR(FM) Indianapolis IN 2.5 kw, 1,000 ft.
*WMMT(FM) Whitesburg KY 1.4 kw, 1,411 ft.
*KRVS(FM) Lafayette LA 100 kw, 449 ft.
*WIAA(FM) Interlochen MI 100 kw, 1,225 ft.
*KXMS(FM) Joplin MO 10 kw, 185 ft.
*WXDU(FM) Durham NC 1.18 kw, 103 ft.
*WNCW(FM) Spindale NC 17 kw, 3,054 ft.
*KLNE-FM Lexington NE 43.8 kw, 938 ft.
*WRSU-FM New Brunswick NJ 1.365 kw, 150 ft.
*WPSC-FM Wayne NJ 200 w, 299 ft.
*KEDB(FM) Las Vegas NV 112 w, 1,469 ft.
*KUNR(FM) Reno NV 20 kw, 2,169 ft.
*WBFO(FM) Buffalo NY 24 kw, 240 ft.
*WHCL-FM Clinton NY 270 w, 97 ft.
*WRHU(FM) Hempstead NY 470 w, 200 ft.
*WFNP(FM) New Paltz NY 230 w, 1,289 ft.
*WNYK(FM) Nyack NY 14 w, 55 ft.
*WRHV(FM) Poughkeepsie NY 230 w, 1,289 ft.
*WOBO(FM) Batavia OH 15.5 kw, 428 ft.
*WUJC(FM) University Heights OH 850 w, 321 ft.
*KLVV(FM) Ponca City OK 11.5 kw, 479 ft.
*KBVR(FM) Corvallis OR 340 w, -80.6 ft.
*WRFH(FM) Marietta PA 4.1 kw, 679 ft.
*WSYC-FM Shippensburg PA 100 w, 155 ft.
*WCYJ-FM Waynesburg PA 18 w, minus 33 ft.

U.S. FM Stations by Frequency

*WJMF(FM) Smithfield RI 225 w, 130 ft.
*WAGP(FM) Beaufort SC 6 kw, 297 ft.
*WYFV(FM) Cayce SC 150 w, 141 ft.
*WAYM(FM) Columbia TN 3.5 kw, 508 ft.
*KAZI(FM) Austin TX 1.6 kw, 351 ft.
*KFGG(FM) Corpus Christi TX 5 kw, 856 ft.
*KTCU-FM Fort Worth TX 3 kw, 320 ft.
*KUHF(FM) Houston TX 100 kw, 1,800 ft.
*KTPB(FM) Kilgore TX 10 kw-V, 400 ft.
*WFOS(FM) Chesapeake VA 15 kw, 172 ft.
*WXJM(FM) Harrisonburg VA 390 w, 62 ft.
*WWPV-FM Colchester VT 100 w, 82 ft.
*WRVT(FM) Rutland VT 2.77 kw, 1,328 ft.
*KAGU(FM) Spokane WA 100 w, minus 141 ft.
*WERN(FM) Madison WI 25 kw, 990 ft.
*WRFW(FM) River Falls WI 3 kw, 82 ft.

88.9 mhz (ch 205)
*KAWC-FM Yuma AZ 3 kw, 75 ft.
*KUCI(FM) Irvine CA 25 w, 100 ft.
*KXLU(FM) Los Angeles CA 3 kw, 12 ft.
*KFPR(FM) Redding CA 1.3 kw, 1,499 ft.
*KXJZ(FM) Sacramento CA 50 kw, 500 ft.
*KUSP(FM) Santa Cruz CA 860 w, 3,750 ft.
*KRTM(FM) Temecula CA 3 kw, -151 ft.
*KDUV(FM) Visalia CA 1 kw, 2,647 ft.
*WJMJ(FM) Hartford CT 7.2 kw, 580 ft.
*WQCS(FM) Fort Pierce FL 100 kw, 436 ft.
*WDNA(FM) Miami FL 2.3 kw, 710 ft.
*NEW FM Ottawa FL 3 kw, 459 ft.
*WFSU-FM Tallahassee FL 95 kw, 1,243 ft.
*WYFE(FM) Tarpon Springs FL 50 kw, 500 ft.
*WMSL(FM) Athens GA 1.35 kw, 328 ft.
*WXGC(FM) Milledgeville GA 38 w, 110 ft.
*KLHS-FM Lewiston ID 155 w, 810 ft.
*WEIU(FM) Charleston IL 4 kw, 166 ft.
*WOUI(FM) Chicago IL 10 w, 90 ft.
*WEPS(FM) Elgin IL 740 w, 100 ft.
*WMXM(FM) Lake Forest IL 300 w, 100 ft.
*WLNX(FM) Lincoln IL 225 w, 68 ft.
*WRRG(FM) River Grove IL 100 w, 128 ft.
*WARG(FM) Summit IL 500 w, 98 ft.
*WSND-FM Notre Dame IN 3.4 kw, 361 ft.
*WPER(FM) Union City IN 4.1 kw
*KTJO-FM Ottawa KS 150 w, 98 ft.
*WKYU-FM Bowling Green KY 100 kw, 721 ft.
*WEKU-FM Richmond KY 50 kw, 720 ft.
*WERS(FM) Boston MA 4 kw, 614 ft.
*WEAA(FM) Baltimore MD 12.5 kw, 220 ft.
*WDBM(FM) East Lansing MI 2 kw, 279 ft.
*WBLU-FM Grand Rapids MI 650 w, 400 ft.
*KNSR(FM) Collegeville MN 100 kw, 728 ft.
*KRNW(FM) Chillicothe MO 38 kw, 525 ft.
*KJLU(FM) Jefferson City MO 40 kw, 510 ft.
*WMAU-FM Bude MS 100 kw, 960 ft.
*WKNA(FM) Senatobia MS 20 kw, 405 ft.
*WSHA(FM) Raleigh NC 25.5 kw, 115 ft.
*KMPR(FM) Minot ND 100 kw, 930 ft.
*WMNJ(FM) Madison NJ 8 w, 75 ft.
*WBZC(FM) Pemberton NJ 120 w-H, 2.5 kw-V, 171 ft.
*WMCX(FM) West Long Branch NJ 1 kw, 85 ft.
*KNMI(FM) Farmington NM 6.22 kw, 360 ft.
*WDWN(FM) Auburn NY 250 w, 102 ft.
*WCIY(FM) Canandaigua NY 70 w, 1,059 ft.
*WITC(FM) Cazenovia NY 129 w, 33 ft.
*WCVF-FM Fredonia NY 130 w, 125 ft.
*WNYO(FM) Oswego NY 100 w, 10 ft.
*WRPJ(FM) Port Jervis NY 500 w, 590 ft.
*WFRS(FM) Smithtown NY 1.5 kw H, 1.45 kw V, 433 ft.
*WSIA(FM) Staten Island NY 10 w, 650 ft.
*WSLJ(FM) Watertown NY 200 w, 454 ft.
*WRDL(FM) Ashland OH 3 kw, 171 ft.
*WCSU-FM Wilberforce OH 1 kw, 150 ft.
*KOCC(FM) Oklahoma City OK 4.3 kw, 502 ft.
*KQFE(FM) Springfield OR 2 kw, 418 ft.
*WFSE(FM) Edinboro PA 3 kw, 312 ft.
*WFRJ(FM) Johnstown PA 900 w, 1,063 ft.
*WWNW(FM) New Wilmington PA 110 w, minus 39 ft.
*WQSU(FM) Selinsgrove PA 12 kw, 620 ft.
*WBYO(FM) Sellersville PA 100 w, 436 ft.
*WEUC-FM Ponce PR 10.8 kw, 2,912 ft.
*WNSC-FM Rock Hill SC 100 kw, 600 ft.
*WMBW(FM) Chattanooga TN 100 kw, 1,505 ft.
*KETR(FM) Commerce TX 100 kw, 400 ft.
*KMBH-FM Harlingen TX 3 kw, 298 ft.
*KLDN(FM) Lufkin TX 50 kw, 649 ft.
*WCVE(FM) Richmond VA 8.3 kw, 840 ft.
*WLSU(FM) La Crosse WI 8.3 kw, 540 ft.
*WYMS(FM) Milwaukee WI 1.5 kw, 870 ft.
*WOJB(FM) Reserve WI 100 kw, 604 ft.
*WVPW(FM) Buckhannon WV 14 kw, 840 ft.
*WVEP(FM) Martinsburg WV 3.6 kw, 1,591 ft.
*WGNR(FM) Monee IL

89.1 mhz (ch 206)
*WLBF(FM) Montgomery AL 100 kw, 537 ft.
*KUAR(FM) Little Rock AR 100 kw, 882 ft.
*KUAZ(FM) Tucson AZ 3 kw, 10 ft.
*KCEA(FM) Atherton CA 100 w, -216 ft.
*KPRX(FM) Bakersfield CA 12 kw, 500 ft.
*KCRU(FM) Oxnard CA 200 w, 853 ft.
*KUOR-FM Redlands CA 35 w, 2,781 ft.
*KBBF(FM) Santa Rosa CA 1 kw, 2,770 ft.
*WNPR(FM) Norwich CT 5.1 kw, 590 ft.
*WXHL(FM) Christiana DE 1 w-H, 1.2 kw-V, 67 ft.
*WUFT-FM Gainesville FL 100 kw, 771 ft.
*WFSW(FM) Panama City FL 100 kw, 403 ft.
*WAYG(FM) Sarasota FL 50 kw, 462 ft.
*WWIO(FM) Brunswick GA 7 kw, 135 ft.
*WBCX(FM) Gainesville GA 835 w, 544 ft.
*KCUI(FM) Pella IA 10 w, 20 ft.
*KWAR(FM) Waverly IA 40 w, 125 ft.
*WVJC(FM) Mt. Carmel IL 50 kw, 330 ft.
*WONC(FM) Naperville IL 3.9 kw, 98 ft.
*WGLT(FM) Normal IL 2.3 kw, 141 ft.
*WBNI-FM Fort Wayne IN 34 kw, 604 ft.
*KMUW(FM) Wichita KS 100 kw, 450 ft.
*KVDP(FM) Dry Prong LA 3 kw, 207 ft.
*WBSN-FM New Orleans LA 10 kw, 525 ft.
*KLPI-FM Ruston LA 4 kw, 285 ft.
*WETH(FM) Hagerstown MD 900 w, 1,338 ft.
*WTRK(FM) Bay City MI 2 kw, 328 ft.
*WIDR(FM) Kalamazoo MI 100 w, 158 ft.
*WPHS(FM) Warren MI 110 w, 150 ft.
*WEMU(FM) Ypsilanti MI 15.5 kw, 289 ft.
*KWFC(FM) Springfield MO 100 kw, 250 ft.
*KCLC(FM) St. Charles MO 25.5 kw, 257 ft.
*WMBU(FM) Forest MS 100 kw, 640 ft.
*KUFM(FM) Missoula MT 17 kw, 2,510 ft.
*KHNE-FM Hastings NE 64.3 kw, 328 ft.
*WEVO(FM) Concord NH 50 kw, 385 ft.
*WFDU(FM) Teaneck NJ 550 w, 550 ft.
*WWFM(FM) Trenton NJ 3 kw, 180 ft.
*KANW(FM) Albuquerque NM 20 kw, 4,152 ft.
*WBSU(FM) Brockport NY 7.338 kw, 160 ft.
*WCID(FM) Friendship NY 7 kw, 492 ft.
*WNYU-FM New York NY 8.3 kw, 256 ft.
*WPSA(FM) Paul Smiths NY 10 w, 1,679 ft.
*WMHT-FM Schenectady NY 11 kw, 930 ft.
*WJPZ-FM Syracuse NY 100 w, 120 ft.
*WAPS(FM) Akron OH 1.7 kw, 71 ft.
*WOUC-FM Cambridge OH 5 kw, 500 ft.
*WOUL-FM Ironton OH 50 kw, 400 ft.
*WNZN(FM) Lorain OH 2.2 kw, 374 ft.
*WLMH(FM) Morrow OH 100 w, 200 ft.
*WUSO(FM) Springfield OH 10 w-H, 1,109 ft.
*KSMF(FM) Ashland OR 2.3 kw, 1,340 ft.
*KMHD(FM) Gresham OR 7.08 kw, 986 ft.
*WFNM(FM) Lancaster PA 100 w, 150 ft.
*WSFX(FM) Nanticoke PA 100 w, 50 ft.
*WXVU(FM) Villanova PA 710 w-V, 223 ft.
*WLJK(FM) Aiken SC 10 kw, 1,374 ft.
*KAUR(FM) Sioux Falls SD 680 w, 184 ft.
*KBHU-FM Spearfish SD 100 w, 55 ft.
*WYLV(FM) Alcoa TN 80 w-horiz, 3 kw-vert, 102 ft.
*WNAZ-FM Nashville TN 1.4 kw, 120 ft.
*WDNX(FM) Olive Hill TN 100 kw, 150 ft.
*KLMN(FM) Amarillo TX 620 w, 413 ft.
*KOHM(FM) Lubbock TX 50 kw, 525 ft.
*KSTX(FM) San Antonio TX 100 kw, 656 ft.
*KBYU-FM Provo UT 32 kw, 2,913 ft.
*WVTF(FM) Roanoke VA 100 kw, 1,970 ft.
*KFAE-FM Richland WA 100 kw, 1,148 ft.
*WBSD(FM) Burlington WI 300 w, 107 ft.

89.3 mhz (ch 207)
*KATB(FM) Anchorage AK 4.9 kw, 643 ft.
*WLRH(FM) Huntsville AL 100 kw, 810 ft.
*KBHG(FM) Fayetteville AR 5 kw, 1,155 ft.
*KPFB(FM) Berkeley CA 460 w-H, minus 98 ft.
*KOHL(FM) Fremont CA 145 w, 407 ft.
*KVPR(FM) Fresno CA 2.45 kw, 1,890 ft.
*KCRY(FM) Indio CA 775 w, 590 ft.
*KEBR-FM North Highlands CA 3.1 kw-vert, 354 ft.
*KPCC(FM) Pasadena CA 680 w, 2,922 ft.
*KLEL(FM) San Jose CA 100 w, minus 539 ft.
*KUVO(FM) Denver CO 26 kw, 910 ft.
*WRTC-FM Hartford CT 350 w-H, 62 ft.
*WPFW(FM) Washington DC 50 kw, 410 ft.
*WRMB(FM) Boynton Beach FL 100 kw, 500 ft.
*WPIO(FM) Titusville FL 10 kw, 300 ft.
*WRFG(FM) Atlanta GA 24.5 kw, 150 ft.
*KPRG(FM) Agana GU 2.8 kw, 485 ft.
*KIPO-FM Honolulu HI 3.3 kw, 1,968 ft.
*KUCB-FM Des Moines IA 10 kw, 100 ft.
*KUOI-FM Moscow ID 50 w, minus 92 ft.
*WKKC(FM) Chicago IL 250 w, 112 ft.
*WDLM-FM East Moline IL 100 kw, 500 ft.
*WNUR-FM Evanston IL 7.2 kw, 100 ft.
*WIPA(FM) Pittsfield IL 50 kw, 492 ft.
*WJEL(FM) Indianapolis IN 125 w, 180 ft.
*WVXR(FM) Richmond IN 4.2 kw, 187 ft.
*WNKJ(FM) Hopkinsville KY 12 kw, 330 ft.
*WFPL(FM) Louisville KY 100 kw, 310 ft.
*WRKF(FM) Baton Rouge LA 28 kw, 935 ft.
*WAMH(FM) Amherst MA 1.5 kw, 720 ft.
*WHSN(FM) Bangor ME 140 w, 69 ft.
*WHFR(FM) Dearborn MI 270 w, 98 ft.
*WBLD(FM) Orchard Lake MI 10 w, 110 ft.
*WGNB(FM) Zeeland MI 30 kw, 500 ft.
*WNCB(FM) Duluth MN 2.4 kw, 430 ft.
*WCAL(FM) Northfield MN 98 kw, 768 ft.
*KCUR-FM Kansas City MO 100 kw, 820 ft.
*WXYC(FM) Chapel Hill NC 400 w, 280 ft.
*WSOE(FM) Elon College NC 500 w, 104 ft.
*WTEB(FM) New Bern NC 100 kw, 522 ft.
*NEW FM Winston-Salem NC 2.5 kw
*KFJM-FM Grand Forks ND 38 kw, 215 ft.
*KZUM(FM) Lincoln NE 1.5 kw, 174 ft.
*KXNE-FM Norfolk NE 42.3 kw, 984 ft.
*WNJB(FM) Bridgeton NJ 1 w-H, 3 kw-V, 203 ft.
*WCNJ(FM) Hazlet NJ 100 w, 260 ft.
*WSKG-FM Binghamton NY 10.2 kw, 942 ft.
*WGSU(FM) Geneseo NY 1.8 kw, 11 ft.
*WLJP(FM) Monroe NY 200 w, 1,023 ft.
*WMHN(FM) Webster NY 1 kw, 75 ft.
*WVXC(FM) Chillicothe OH 2.5 kw, 115 ft.
*WCSB(FM) Cleveland OH 1 kw, 190 ft.
*WYSZ(FM) Maumee OH 6.3 kw, 321 ft.
*WMKV(FM) Reading OH 340 w, 239 ft.
*WKRW(FM) Wooster OH 2.1 kw, 318 ft.
*KCCU(FM) Lawton OK 2 kw, 463 ft.
*WDIY(FM) Allentown PA 120 w-V, 245 ft.
*WQED-FM Pittsburgh PA 43 kw, 500 ft.
*WRDV(FM) Warminster PA 200 w, 88 ft.
*WSCI(FM) Charleston SC 97 kw, 540 ft.
*WLFJ(FM) Greenville SC 41 kw, 1,100 ft.
*KBHE-FM Rapid City SD 9.8 kw, 410 ft.
*KSWS(FM) Sisseton SD 3 kw, 374 ft.
*WYPL(FM) Memphis TN 2.75 kw, 194 ft.
*KNON(FM) Dallas TX 55 kw, 850 ft.
*KSBJ(FM) Humble TX 100 kw, 840 ft.
*KXBJ(FM) Victoria TX 18.5 kw, 302 ft.
*WVTU(FM) Charlottesville VA 195 w-H, 160 w-V, 1,696 ft.
*KASB(FM) Bellevue WA 10 w, 289 ft.
*KUGS(FM) Bellingham WA 100 w, 384 ft.
*KAOS(FM) Olympia WA 1.5 kw, -19 ft.
*WPNE-FM Green Bay WI 100 kw, 940 ft.

89.5 mhz (ch 208)
*WBFR(FM) Birmingham AL 100 w, 672 ft.
*WGTF(FM) Dothan AL 5.5 kw, 213 ft.
*KCAC(FM) Camden AR 250 w, 161 ft.
KBAQ(FM) Phoenix AZ
*KBES(FM) Ceres CA 30 w-H, 135 ft.
*KSMC(FM) Moraga CA 800 w, 95 ft.
*KVMR(FM) Nevada City CA 1.96 kw, 980 ft.
*KPBS-FM San Diego CA 1.77 kw, 1,902 ft.
*KPOO(FM) San Francisco CA 270 w, 540 ft.
*KSJC-FM Stockton CA 18.6 w, 106 ft.
*KPRA(FM) Ukiah CA 710 w, 1,135 ft.
*KXRD(FM) Victorville CA 1.25 kw, 1,410 ft.
*KPRN(FM) Grand Junction CO 10 kw, 1,191 ft.
*KTSC-FM Pueblo CO 9.8 kw, 165 ft.
*WPKN(FM) Bridgeport CT 10 kw, 550 ft.
*WKSG(FM) Cedar Creek FL 3 kw, 91 ft.
*WGSG(FM) Mayo FL 2.5 kw-H, 20 kw-V, 249 ft.
*WFIT(FM) Melbourne FL 2.35 kw, 112 ft.
*WSRX(FM) Naples FL 550 w, 249 ft.
*WPCS(FM) Pensacola FL 100 kw, 1,328 ft.
*WYFK(FM) Columbus GA 50 kw, 439 ft.
*WYFS(FM) Savannah GA 100 kw, 630 ft.
*WYFW(FM) Winder GA 530 w, 130 ft.
*KHKE(FM) Cedar Falls IA 10 kw, 410 ft.
*KLCD(FM) Decorah IA 100 w, 140 ft.
*KTSY(FM) Caldwell ID 8.3 kw, 2,601 ft.
*KAWZ(FM) Twin Falls ID 3 kw, 328 ft.
*WNIU(FM) De Kalb IL 50 kw, 421 ft.
*WJMU(FM) Decatur IL 1 kw, 95 ft.
*WGRN(FM) Greenville IL 300 w, 206 ft.
*WFCI(FM) Franklin IN 1 kw, 140 ft.
*WBKE-FM North Manchester IN 3 kw, 80 ft.
*KHCD(FM) Salina KS 100 kw, 925 ft.
*WKPB(FM) Henderson KY 23 kw, 1,502 ft.
*KYFL(FM) Monroe LA 1 kw, 397 ft.
*WSKB(FM) Westfield MA 100 w, 130 ft.
*WSCL(FM) Salisbury MD 27 kw, 600 ft.
*WAHS(FM) Auburn Hills MI 100 w, 141 ft.
*WCMU-FM Mount Pleasant MI 100 kw, 423 ft.
*WOVI(FM) Novi MI 100 w, 67 ft.
*KQAL(FM) Winona MN 1.8 kw, 628 ft.
*KOPN(FM) Columbia MO 36 kw-H, 236 ft.
*KCFV(FM) Ferguson MO 100 w, 159 ft.
*KOKS(FM) Poplar Bluff MO 100 kw, 423 ft.
*WMAE-FM Booneville MS 85 kw, 660 ft.
*KPPR(FM) Williston ND 10.5 kw, 492 ft.
*WEEE(FM) Cherry Hill NJ 100 w, 171 ft.
*WSOU(FM) South Orange NJ 2 kw, 370 ft.
*KENW-FM Portales NM 100 kw, 185 ft.
*KVCE(FM) Fallon NV 378 w, 116 ft.
*KNPR(FM) Las Vegas NV 100 kw, 1,532 ft.
*KRNC(FM) Reno NV 5 kw, -3 ft.
*WSLU(FM) Canton NY 40.3 kw, 299 ft.
*WUNY(FM) Utica NY 6.3 kw, 777 ft.
*WBCY(FM) Archbold OH 3 kw, 180 ft.
*WCVV(FM) Belpre OH 3 kw, 199 ft.
*WDPR(FM) Dayton OH 6 kw, 270 ft. (ST *WDPS(FM) Dayton)
*WDPS(FM) Dayton OH 200 w, 198 ft
*WHSS(FM) Hamilton OH 190 w, 282 ft.
*WVMS(FM) Sandusky OH 2.12 kw-H, 5.36 kw-V, 69 ft.
*WVXM(FM) West Union OH 4 kw, 330 ft.
*KWGS(FM) Tulsa OK 50 kw, 1,067 ft.
*KTEC(FM) Klamath Falls OR 250 w, 184 ft.
*WDNR(FM) Chester PA 10 w, 117 ft.
*WITF-FM Harrisburg PA 5.9 kw, 1,361 ft.
*WNTE(FM) Mansfield PA 115 w, minus 320.4 ft.
*KAEN(FM) Little Eagle SD 90 kw, 324 ft.
*WETS(FM) Johnson City TN 66 kw, 2,273 ft.
*WMOT(FM) Murfreesboro TN 50 kw, 210 ft.
*KMFA(FM) Austin TX 65 kw, 853 ft.
*KEPX(FM) Eagle Pass TX 100 kw, 187 ft.
*KXCR(FM) El Paso TX 3 kw, 1,189 ft.
*KLUX(FM) Robstown TX 60 kw, 954 ft.
*KVNE-FM Tyler TX 100 kw, 899 ft.
*KMOC(FM) Wichita Falls TX 3 kw, 672 ft.
*KAGJ(FM) Ephraim UT 100 w, -354 ft.
*WHRV(FM) Norfolk VA 23 kw, 730 ft.
*WVPR(FM) Windsor VT 1.78 kw, 2,160 ft.
*KEWU-FM Cheney WA 10 kw, 1,407 ft.
*KJVH(FM) Longview WA 100 w, 780 ft.
*KNHC(FM) Seattle WA 30 kw, 322 ft.
*KSOH(FM) Wapato WA 9.5 kw, 974 ft.
*WCLQ(FM) Wausau WI 3 kw, 328 ft.

89.7 mhz (ch 209)
*KYFF(FM) Fort Smith AR 1 kw, 387 ft.
*KNCA(FM) Burney CA 2.28 kw, 1,465 ft.
*KFJC(FM) Los Altos CA 250 w, 1,845 ft.
*KLVM(FM) Prunedale CA 54 w, 1,907 ft.
*KSGN(FM) Riverside CA 3 kw, 300 ft.

U.S. FM Stations by Frequency

*KXHV(FM) Sacramento CA 300 w-V, 89 ft.
*KARM(FM) Visalia CA 1 kw, 810 ft.
*KEPC(FM) Colorado Springs CO 7.88 kw, -273 ft.
*WMCU(FM) Miami FL 100 kw, 981 ft.
*WJLU(FM) New Smyrna Beach FL 5 kw, 328 ft.
*WVFS(FM) Tallahassee FL 272 w, 170 ft.
*WUSF(FM) Tampa FL 100 kw, 820 ft.
*WDCO-FM Cochran GA 100 kw, 1,010 ft.
*KIWR(FM) Council Bluffs IA 100 kw, 1,100 ft.
*KRUI-FM Iowa City IA 100 w, 90 ft.
*KRNL-FM Mount Vernon IA 10 w, 984 ft.
*WONU(FM) Kankakee IL 35 kw, 431 ft.
*WHWE(FM) Howe IN 100 w, 68 ft.
*WUBS(FM) South Bend IN 1.5 kw
*WISU(FM) Terre Haute IN 13.5 kw, 512 ft.
*KNBU(FM) Baldwin City KS 100 w, 118 ft.
*WNKU(FM) Highland Heights KY 12 kw, 318 ft.
*WDCL-FM Somerset KY 100 kw, 570 ft.
*WGBH(FM) Boston MA 98 kw, 650 ft.
*WTMD(FM) Towson MD 10.16 kw, 236 ft.
*WMED(FM) Calais ME 30 kw, 525 ft.
*WLNZ(FM) Lansing MI 100 w, 98 ft.
*WOCR(FM) Olivet MI 10 w, 70 ft.
*KBSB(FM) Bemidji MN 115 w, 126 ft.
*KMSU(FM) Mankato MN 20 kw, 400 ft.
*KUMM(FM) Morris MN 223 w, 120 ft.
*KYMC(FM) Ballwin MO 120 w-H, 154 ft.
*KMNR(FM) Rolla MO 450 w, 230 ft.
*WCPE(FM) Raleigh NC 100 kw, 679 ft.
*WNJN(FM) Atlantic City NJ 25 w-H, 6 kw-V, 272 ft-H, 276 ft-V.
*WDVR(FM) Delaware Township NJ 3 kw, 301 ft.
*WRLJ(FM) Freehold Township NJ 1.26 kw-V, 151 ft.
*WGLS-FM Glassboro NJ 120 w, 150 ft.
*KTDB(FM) Pine Hill NM 15 kw, 300 ft.
*WALF(FM) Alfred NY 200 w, 73 ft.
*WEOS(FM) Geneva NY 1.5 kw, minus 7 ft.
*WITR(FM) Henrietta NY 910 w, 154 ft.
*WNJA(FM) Jamestown NY 6 kw, 754 ft.
*WFGB(FM) Kingston NY 3.1 kw, 1,486 ft.
*WRHO(FM) Oneonta NY 150 w, 150 ft.
*WRUC(FM) Schenectady NY 100 w, minus 88 ft.
*WOSU-FM Columbus OH 13.3 kw, 938 ft.
*WKSU-FM Kent OH 50 kw, 390 ft.
*KLCC(FM) Eugene OR 81 kw-h, 54 kw-v, 1,161 ft.
*WRTU(FM) San Juan PR 50 kw, 796 ft.
*WMHK(FM) Columbia SC 100 kw, 420 ft.
*KUSD-FM Vermillion SD 50 kw-H, 21.5 kw-V, 518 ft.
*WDYN-FM Chattanooga TN 100 kw, 205 ft.
*KACU(FM) Abilene TX 33 kw, 215 ft.
*KACC(FM) Alvin TX 5.6 kw, 338 ft.
*KTXB(FM) Beaumont TX 9 kw, 567 ft.
*KWCB(FM) Floresville TX 9 kw, 138 ft.
*KZMU(FM) Moab UT 100 w, minus 581 ft.
*KWFJ(FM) Roy WA 1 kw, 30 ft.
*WUEC(FM) Eau Claire WI 740 w, 630 ft.
*WUWM(FM) Milwaukee WI 15 kw, 871 ft.
*WJGF-FM Romney WV 109 w, 42 ft.
*WSHC(FM) Shepherdstown WV 950 w, minus 10 ft.
*KUAP(FM) Pine Bluff AR 6 kw, 285 ft.

89.9 mhz (ch 210)

*WTSU(FM) Troy AL 100 kw, 560 ft.
*KZIG(FM) Cave City AR 3.3 kw, 351 ft.
*KCDS(FM) Angwin CA 794 w, 3,010.
*KCRH(FM) Hayward CA 19 w, -135 ft.
*KXKB(FM) Kings Beach CA 2.7 kw-H, 715 ft.
*KEFR(FM) Le Grand CA 1.8 kw, 2,142 ft.
*KFER(FM) Santa Cruz CA 200 w, 26 ft.
*KCRW(FM) Santa Monica CA 6.9 kw, 1,110 ft.
*WQTQ(FM) Hartford CT 63 w, 86 ft.
*WWEB(FM) Wallingford CT 10 w, 230 ft.
*WJCT-FM Jacksonville FL 100 kw, 835 ft.
*WUCF-FM Orlando FL 7.9 kw, 160 ft.
*WCNO(FM) Palm City FL 100 kw, 613 ft.
*WJTF(FM) Panama City FL 100 kw, 105 ft.
*WLCA(FM) Godfrey IL 1.4 kw, 112 ft.
*WLKL(FM) Mattoon IL 1.3 kw, 203 ft.
*WCBU(FM) Peoria IL 50 kw, 650 ft.
*WHPL(FM) West Lafayette IN 100 w, 328 ft.
*KRPS(FM) Pittsburg KS 100 kw, 1,000 ft.
*WRVG(FM) Georgetown KY 140 w, 33 ft.
*WSOF-FM Madisonville KY 39.4 kw, 282 ft.
*WWNO(FM) New Orleans LA 50 kw, 640 ft.
*KDAQ(FM) Shreveport LA 100 kw, 932 ft.
*WSCB(FM) Springfield MA 100 w, 35 ft.
*WOEL-FM Elkton MD 3 kw, 259 ft.
*WMTB-FM Emmittsburg MD 100 w, 144 ft.
*WERU-FM Blue Hill ME 15 kw, 899 ft.
*WBYW(FM) Grand Rapids MI 390 w, 144 ft.
*WTHS(FM) Holland MI 1 kw, 154 ft.
*WKDS(FM) Kalamazoo MI 100 w, 150 ft.
*WLJN-FM Traverse City MI 10 kw, 443 ft.
*KMOJ(FM) Minneapolis MN 1 kw, 600 ft.
*KRPR(FM) Rochester MN 1.2 kw, 500 ft.
*KCWA-FM Arnold MO 150 w-H, 84 w-V, 105 ft.
*KGNV(FM) Washington MO 1 kw, 213 ft.
*WMAB-FM Mississippi State MS 63 kw, 1,080 ft.
*KGPR(FM) Great Falls MT 9 kw, 368 ft.
*WDAV(FM) Davidson NC 100 kw, 807 ft.
*WRVS-FM Elizabeth City NC 41 kw, 280 ft.
*KDPR(FM) Dickinson ND 12.5 kw, 488 ft.
*KVYM(FM) Chester NE 50 kw, 492 ft.
*KUNM(FM) Albuquerque NM 13.6 kw, 4,070 ft.
*WFBF(FM) Buffalo NY 20 kw, 59 ft.
*WKCR-FM New York NY 1 kw, 849 ft.
*WXLG(FM) North Creek NY 200 w, 1,994 ft.
*WSUF(FM) Noyack NY 3 kw, 165 ft.
*WRVO(FM) Oswego NY 24 kw, 430 ft.
*WDPG(FM) Greenville OH 50 kw, 403 ft.
*WHEI(FM) Tiffin OH 15.1 w, 52 ft.
*WLHS(FM) West Chester OH 100 w, 338 ft.
*KBPS-FM Portland OR 8.7 kw, 964 ft.
*WERG(FM) Erie PA 3 kw, minus 125 ft.
*WVIA-FM Scranton PA 5 kw, 1,250 ft.
*WTLR(FM) State College PA 25 kw, 584 ft.
*WJWJ-FM Beaufort SC 47 kw, 1,100 ft.
*WDVX(FM) Clinton TN 200 w, 1,960 ft.
*WEVL(FM) Memphis TN 13 kw, 300 ft.
*KACV-FM Amarillo TX 100 kw, 1,041 ft.
*KBNL(FM) Laredo TX 100 kw, 575 ft.
*KTSW(FM) San Marcos TX 10.5 kw, 299 ft.
*WPVB(FM) Culpeper VA 12 kw, 255 ft.
*WFFC(FM) Ferrum VA 100 w, minus 40 ft.
*WMRL(FM) Lexington VA 100 w, 196 ft.
*WVRU(FM) Radford VA 500 w, 15 ft.
*KGRG(FM) Auburn WA 100 w, 570 ft.
*KGHP(FM) Gig Harbor WA 1.5 kw, 190 ft.
*WHSA(FM) Brule WI 38 kw, 550 ft.
*WORT(FM) Madison WI 2 kw, 900 ft.
*WWSP(FM) Stevens Point WI 11.5 kw, 233 ft.
*WVWV(FM) Huntington WV 8.1 kw, 1,200 ft.
*WVNP(FM) Wheeling WV 25 kw, 500 ft.
*KJTA(FM) Flagstaff AZ

90.1 mhz (ch 211)

*WOCG(FM) Huntsville AL 25 kw, 230 ft.
*KSBC(FM) Hot Springs AR 5 kw, 785 ft.
*KWFH(FM) Parker AZ .180 kw, 1,010 ft.
*KTQX(FM) Bakersfield CA 3 kw, 128 ft.
*KBPK(FM) Buena Park CA 20 w, 130 ft.
*KZFR(FM) Chico CA 6.3 kw, 587 ft.
*KCBX(FM) San Luis Obispo CA 5.3 kw, 1,420 ft.
*KZSU(FM) Stanford CA 500 w, -10 ft.
*KCJH(FM) Stockton CA 26 kw, 230 ft.
*KSAK(FM) Walnut CA 3.5 w, 460 ft.
*KLRD(FM) Yucaipa CA 300 w, 1,024 ft.
*KCFR(FM) Denver CO 50 kw, 910 ft.
*WRXC(FM) Shelton CT 100 w, 343 ft.
*WGSK(FM) South Kent CT 150 w, minus 124 ft.
*WECS(FM) Willimantic CT 421 w, 380 ft.
*WDCU(FM) Washington DC 6.8 kw, 450 ft.
*WTJT(FM) Baker FL 5 kw, 253 ft.
*WSFP-FM Fort Myers FL 100 kw, 813 ft.
*WWUA(FM) Inverness FL 4.5 kw, 354 ft.
*WUNW(FM) Key West FL 6.1 kw
*WABE(FM) Atlanta GA 100 kw, 955 ft.
*WXVS(FM) Waycross GA 79 kw-H, 71 kw-V, 918 ft.
*WOI-FM Ames IA 100 kw, 1,490 ft.
*KNWO(FM) Cottonwood ID 250 w, 612 ft.
*WEFT(FM) Champaign IL 10 kw, 135 ft.
*WMBI-FM Chicago IL 100 kw, 440 ft.
*WZJW(FM) Norris City IL 19 kw-V, 295 ft.
*WFYI-FM Indianapolis IN 10 kw, 560 ft.
*KHCC-FM Hutchinson KS 100 kw, 1,080 ft.
*WJCR-FM Millerstown KY 100 kw, 383 ft.
*WJSO(FM) Pikeville KY 3.8 kw, 455 ft.
*WBPV(FM) Charlton MA 100 w, 390 ft.
*WMEA(FM) Portland ME 49 kw, 1,919 ft.
*WUCX-FM Bay City MI 30 kw, 479 ft.
*WNMU-FM Marquette MI 100 kw, 930 ft.
*WLSO(FM) Sault Ste. Marie MI 100 w, 98 ft.
*KSJR-FM Collegeville MN 100 kw, 700 ft.
*KSRQ(FM) Thief River Falls MN 24 kw, 338 ft.
*KKFI(FM) Kansas City MO 100 kw, 503 ft.
*KJAB-FM Mexico MO 380 w, 128 ft.
*KRHS(FM) Overland MO 10 w, 60 ft.
*WMPR(FM) Jackson MS 100 kw, 500 ft.
*KNMC(FM) Havre MT 10 w, 56 ft.
*WCCE(FM) Buie's Creek NC 3 kw, 105 ft.
*WNAA(FM) Greensboro NC 10 kw, 467 ft.
*WPGT(FM) Roanoke Rapids NC 1 kw, 175 ft.
*WGMC(FM) Greece NY 2.05 kw, 46 ft.
*WRCU-FM Hamilton NY 1.9 kw, 155 ft.
*WXHD(FM) Mt. Hope NY 1.1 kw, 680 ft.
*WUSB(FM) Stony Brook NY 4 kw, 223 ft.
*WOHC(FM) Chillicothe OH 2 kw-V, 393 ft.
*WXML(FM) Upper Sandusky OH 3 kw-V, 328 ft.
*WOUZ(FM) Zanesville OH 3 kw, 279 ft.
*KCSC(FM) Edmond OK 100 kw, 430 ft.
*KSOR(FM) Ashland OR 38 kw, 2,657 ft.
*WIUP-FM Indiana PA 1.6 kw, 88 ft.
*WRTI(FM) Philadelphia PA 12.5 kw, 1,010 ft.
*WHMC-FM Conway SC 30 kw, 706 ft.
*WEPR(FM) Greenville SC 85 kw, 1,184 ft.
*WKNP(FM) Jackson TN 17 kw, 528 ft.
*KERA(FM) Dallas TX 95 kw, 1,260 ft.
*KPFT(FM) Houston TX 100 kw, 433 ft.
*KSAU(FM) Nacogdoches TX 3.5 kw, 450 ft.
*KSYM-FM San Antonio TX 3 kw, 128 ft.
*KUER(FM) Salt Lake City UT 38 kw, 2,900 ft.
*WLCX(FM) Farmville VA 10 w, 26 ft.
*NEW FM Ivanhoe VA 250 w
*WDCE(FM) Richmond VA 100 w, 118 ft.
*WPVA(FM) Waynesboro VA 2.5 kw, 984 ft.
*WIVH(FM) Christiansted VI 1 kw, 731 ft.
*WRUV(FM) Burlington VT 460 w, 145 ft.
*KSVR(FM) Mount Vernon WA 100 w, 75 ft.
*KOLU(FM) Pasco WA 3.99 kw, 93 ft.
*KUPS(FM) Tacoma WA 100 w, 65 ft.
*WORQ(FM) Green Bay WI 6 kw, 289 ft.
*WRPN-FM Ripon WI 231 w, 110 ft.
*KYDZ(FM) Cody WY 10 kw, 459 ft.

90.3 mhz (ch 212)

*KANH(FM) Anchorage AK 100 kw, 195 ft.
*WBHM(FM) Birmingham AL 32 kw, 1214 ft.
*KFLR-FM Phoenix AZ 2.2 kw, 354 ft.
*KMRO(FM) Camarillo CA 4.43 kw, 1,250 ft.
*KDVS(FM) Davis CA 5 kw, 150 ft.
*KFNO(FM) Fresno CA 1.35 kw, 1,971 ft.
*KAZU(FM) Pacific Grove CA 4.2 kw, 341 ft.
*KUSF(FM) San Francisco CA 3 kw, 300 ft.
*KBUT(FM) Crested Butte CO 250 w, -667 ft.
*KJOL(FM) Grand Junction CO 1.5 kw, 1,296 ft.
*WWPT(FM) Westport CT 330 w, 110 ft.
*WAFG(FM) Fort Lauderdale FL 3 kw, 280 ft.
*WLVF-FM Haines City FL 800 w, 265 ft.
*WEJF(FM) Palm Bay FL 2 kw, 295 ft.
*WHCJ(FM) Savannah GA 6 kw, 100 ft.
*KTUH(FM) Honolulu HI 100 w, minus 62 ft.
*KWIT(FM) Sioux City IA 100 kw, 910 ft.
*KBSU-FM Boise ID 19 kw, 2,637 ft.
*WUSI(FM) Olney IL 25 kw, 472 ft.
*WQUB(FM) Quincy IL 10 kw, 417 ft.
*WVIK(FM) Rock Island IL 31 kw, 1,096 ft.
*WFOF(FM) Covington IN 19 kw, 265 ft.
*WBCL(FM) Fort Wayne IN 50 kw, 499 ft.
*WMKY(FM) Morehead KY 37 kw, 895 ft.
*WKWC(FM) Owensboro KY 5 kw, 100 ft.
*WBRH(FM) Baton Rouge LA 7 kw, 154 ft.
*KEDM(FM) Monroe LA 87.1 kw, 863 ft.
*WCCT-FM Harwich MA 160 w-H, 640 w-V, 125 ft.
*WZBC(FM) Newton MA 1 kw, 220 ft.
*WAIJ(FM) Grantsville MD 1 kw-H, 880 w-V, 561 ft.
*WDIH(FM) Salisbury MD 378 w, 180 ft.
*WORB(FM) Farmington Hills MI 12 w, 138 ft.
*WBLV(FM) Twin Lake MI 100 kw, 649 ft.
*KFAI(FM) Minneapolis MN 125 w, 440 ft.
*KCCD(FM) Moorhead MN 100 kw, 495 ft.
*KWUR(FM) Clayton MO 10 w, 136 ft.
*WMAH-FM Biloxi MS 100 kw, 1,410 ft.
*WMAV-FM Oxford MS 100 kw, 1,240 ft.
*WAAE(FM) Hickory NC 150 w, 245 ft.
*WWIH(FM) High Point NC 10 w, 150 ft.
*KMNE-FM Bassett NE 92.3 kw, 1,292 ft.
*KRNU(FM) Lincoln NE 100 w, 180 ft.
*WRPR(FM) Mahwah NJ 100 w, 30 ft.
*WVPH(FM) Piscataway NJ 200 w, 7 ft.
*WAMC(FM) Albany NY 10 kw, 1,970 ft.
*WCIH(FM) Elmira NY 7 kw, 400 ft.
*WBAU(FM) Garden City NY 1.1 kw, 157 ft.
*WHPC(FM) Garden City NY 500 w, 213 ft.
*WJSL(FM) Houghton NY 6 kw, 217 ft.
*WHCR-FM New York NY 8 w, 266 ft.
*WDFH(FM) Ossining NY .2 kw, minus 7 ft.
*WCDR-FM Cedarville OH 30 kw, 354 ft.
*WCPN(FM) Cleveland OH 50 kw, 500 ft.
*WOTL(FM) Toledo OH 700 w, 377 ft.
*KVRS(FM) Lawton OK 1 kw-V, 151 ft.
*KSLC(FM) McMinnville OR 320 w, -46 ft.
*WESS(FM) East Stroudsburg PA 1.37 kw, -165 ft.
*WJTL(FM) Lancaster PA 4.7 kw, 198 ft.
*WARC(FM) Meadville PA 150 w, 86 ft.
*WXLV(FM) Schnecksville PA 670 w, 177 ft.
*WRIU(FM) Kingston RI 3.44 kw, 415 ft.
*WSSB-FM Orangeburg SC 90 kw, 225 ft.
*WCSK(FM) Kingsport TN 195 w, 23 ft.
*WUTK-FM Knoxville TN 800 w, 23 ft.
*WUTM(FM) Martin TN 185 w, 250 ft.
*WPLN(FM) Nashville TN 80 kw, 1,132 ft.
*KEDT-FM Corpus Christi TX 100 kw, 802 ft.
*KBJS(FM) Jacksonville TX 3 kw, 266 ft.
*KPLN-FM Plains TX 220 w, 135 ft.
*WHRO-FM Norfolk VA 23 kw, 630 ft.
*WRDJ(FM) Roanoke VA 2.4 kw, 1,345 ft.
*KZOE(FM) Longview WA 860 w, minus 3 ft.
*KCMU(FM) Seattle WA 400 w, 535 ft.
*KWRS(FM) Spokane WA 100 w, 61 ft.
*KNWY(FM) Yakima WA 5 kw, 895 ft.
*WBCR-FM Beloit WI 100 w, 44 ft.
*WHLA(FM) La Crosse WI 100 kw, 1,010 ft.
*WRST-FM Oshkosh WI 960 w, 125 ft.
*WHBM-FM Park Falls WI 17.7 kw, 727 ft.
*WCDE(FM) Elkins WV 100 w, 90 ft.
*WVPG(FM) Parkersburg WV 9 kw, 321 ft.
*KCSP(FM) Casper WY 100 kw, 1,922 ft.
*KUWJ(FM) Jackson WY 3 kw, 1,105 ft.

90.5 mhz (ch 213)

*KLRE-FM Little Rock AR 40 kw, 265 ft.
*KUAT-FM Tucson AZ 12.5 kw, 3,580 ft.
*KHSU-FM Arcata CA 9 kw, 1,490 ft.
*KIBC(FM) Burney CA 412 w, 1,321 ft.
*KVHS(FM) Concord CA 410 w, 450 ft.
*KADV(FM) Modesto CA 1.5 kw, 141 ft.
*KSFH(FM) Mountain View CA 10 w, 100 ft.
*KDNK(FM) Carbondale CO 215 w, 2,798 ft.
*KTLF(FM) Colorado Springs CO 1.2 kw, 2,050 ft.
*KCSU-FM Fort Collins CO 10 kw, -355 ft.
*WPKT(FM) Meriden CT 18.5 kw-H, 13.5 kw-V, 823 ft-H, 817 ft-V.
*WVUM(FM) Coral Gables FL 365 w, 175 ft.
*WYFB(FM) Gainesville FL 100 kw, 679 ft.
*WAMF(FM) Tallahassee FL 1.6 w-V, 167 ft.
*WBVM(FM) Tampa FL 100 kw, 958 ft.
*WAOJ(FM) Vero Beach FL 3 kw, 90 ft.
*WUOG(FM) Athens GA 9.5 kw, 180 ft.
*WPWB(FM) Byron GA 16.5 kw, 453 ft.
*WFRC(FM) Columbus GA 8.5 kw, 248 ft.
*KHOE(FM) Fairfield IA 100 w, 98 ft.
*WCYC(FM) Chicago IL 8 w, 56 ft.
*WMTH(FM) Park Ridge IL 100 w, 103 ft.
*WNIJ(FM) Rockford IL 50 kw, 367 ft.
*WSCT(FM) Springfield IL 850 w, 617 ft.
*WWDS(FM) Muncie IN 10 w, 169 ft.
*WPUM(FM) Rensselaer IN 10 w, 190 ft.
*WMHD-FM Terre Haute IN 160 w-H, 79 ft.
*KZNA(FM) Hill City KS 100 kw, 600 ft.
*WVHM(FM) Benton KY 8 kw-V, 351 ft.
*WUOL(FM) Louisville KY 35 kw, 580 ft.
*WTHL(FM) Somerset KY 20 kw, 590 ft.
*WICN(FM) Worcester MA 8.1 kw, 368 ft.

U.S. FM Stations by Frequency

*WCRH(FM) Williamsport MD 10 kw, 884 ft.
*WKHS(FM) Worton MD 17.5 kw, 215 ft.
*WMHB(FM) Waterville ME 110 w, 98 ft.
*WKAR-FM East Lansing MI 86 kw-V, 57 hw-V, 895 ft.
*WPHN(FM) Gaylord MI 100 kw, 1,000 ft.
*KDNI(FM) Duluth MN 1.3 kw, 804 ft.
*KGAC(FM) St. Peter MN 75 kw, 708 ft.
*KWWC-FM Columbia MO 1.25 kw, 131 ft.
*KXCV(FM) Maryville MO 100 kw, 500 ft.
*KLUH(FM) Poplar Bluff MO 100 w, 80 ft.
*WASU-FM Boone NC 340 w, -120 ft.
*WWCU(FM) Cullowhee NC 330 w, minus 827 ft.
*WVMH-FM Mars Hill NC 250 w, 230 ft.
*WDCC(FM) Sanford NC 3 kw, 148 ft.
*WKQK(FM) Wilmington NC 1 kw, 328 ft.
*WSNC(FM) Winston-Salem NC 125 w, 92 ft.
*KCND(FM) Bismarck ND 100 kw, 1,250 ft.
*WSPS(FM) Concord NH 200 w, 110 ft.
*WPEA(FM) Exeter NH 115 w, 170 ft.
*WCVH(FM) Flemington NJ 78 w, 449 ft.
*WBJB-FM Lincroft NJ 11 kw, 135 ft.
*WJSV(FM) Morristown NJ 124 w, 17 ft.
*KCIE(FM) Dulce NM 100 kw, 1,535 ft.
*KILA(FM) Las Vegas NV 100 kw, 1,269 ft.
*WBXL(FM) Baldwinsville NY 195 w, 195 ft.
*WHRW(FM) Binghamton NY 1.45 kw, minus 47 ft.
*WSUC-FM Cortland NY 241 w, minus 110 ft.
*WBER(FM) Henrietta NY 2.5 kw, 417 ft.
*WJFF(FM) Jeffersonville NY 3.7 kw, 629 ft.
*WSLL(FM) Saranac Lake NY 200 w, 355 ft.
*WHVT(FM) Clyde OH 370 w, 170 ft.
*KNYD(FM) Broken Arrow OK 100 kw, 1,638 ft.
*KLCO(FM) Newport OR 3.2 kw, 256 m.
*WVBU-FM Lewisburg PA 500 w, minus 120 ft.
*WDUQ(FM) Pittsburgh PA 25 kw, 480 ft.
*WIDA-FM Carolina PR 25 kw, 1,900 ft.
*WUSC-FM Columbia SC 2.5 kw, 233 ft.
*WSMC-FM Collegedale TN 100 kw, 554 ft.
*KUT(FM) Austin TX 100 kw, 680 ft.
*KBTT(FM) Bridgeport TX 1 kw, 98 ft.
*KSHU(FM) Huntsville TX 3 kw, 255 ft.
*KENT-FM Odessa TX 6.5 kw, 453 ft.
*KPDR(FM) Wheeler TX 10 kw, 482 ft.
*KTEO(FM) Wichita Falls TX 6.5 kw, 782 ft.
*WJYJ(FM) Fredericksburg VA 18.5 kw, 560 ft.
*WPIM(FM) Martinsville VA 5.9 kw, 326 ft.
*WFTF(FM) Rutland VT 720 w, minus 560 ft.
*KACS(FM) Chehalis WA 3 kw, 98 ft.
*KWCW(FM) Walla Walla WA 160 w, 96 ft.
*WSUP(FM) Platteville WI 1 kw, 146 ft.
*WPFF(FM) Sturgeon Bay WI 50 kw, 617 ft.
*WMLJ(FM) Summersville WV 11 kw, 948 ft.
*KUWZ(FM) Rock Springs WY 100 kw, 1,135 ft.
*WTGF(FM) Milton FL

90.7 mhz (ch 214)
*WVAS(FM) Montgomery AL 25 kw, 308 ft.
*WVUA-FM Tuscaloosa AL 160 w, 142 ft.
*KALX(FM) Berkeley CA 500 w, 778 ft.
*KFSR(FM) Fresno CA 2.55 kw, 66 ft.
*KPFK(FM) Los Angeles CA 112 kw, 2,830 ft.
*KZYX(FM) Philo CA 3.41 kw, 1,686 ft.
*KSJS(FM) San Jose CA 1 kw, -186 ft.
*KCDC(FM) Longmont CO 100 w, 270 ft.
*WMFE-FM Orlando FL 100 kw, 731 ft.
*WKGC-FM Panama City FL 100 kw, 336 ft.
*WXEL(FM) West Palm Beach FL 25 kw, 350 ft.
*WGNP(FM) Albany GA 3 kw, 328 ft.
*WACG-FM Augusta GA 25 kw, 400 ft.
*WWGC(FM) Carrollton GA 500 w, 494 ft.
*WMVV(FM) McDonough GA 11 kw, 300 ft.
*KKUA(FM) Wailuku HI 7 kw, 5,533 ft.
*KCIR(FM) Twin Falls ID 20 kw, 2,519 ft.
*WBHI(FM) Chicago IL 7 w, 55 ft.
*WVKC(FM) Galesburg IL 1 kw, 98 ft.
*WPSR(FM) Evansville IN 14 kw, 130 ft.
*WKPW(FM) Knightstown IN 400 w
*KJHK(FM) Lawrence KS 100 w, 163 ft.
*KKCR(FM) Salina KS 1 kw, 253 ft.
*KIBN(FM) Wichita KS 25 kw-H, 23 kw-V, 335 ft.
*WCVK(FM) Bowling Green KY 14 kw, 448 ft.
*KLSA(FM) Alexandria LA 100 kw, 1,243 ft.
*WWOZ(FM) New Orleans LA 19 w, 279 ft.
*WTCC(FM) Springfield MA 4 kw, 92 ft.
*WKKL(FM) West Barnstable MA 205 w, 71 ft.
*WAUS(FM) Berrien Springs MI 50 kw, 492 ft.
*KBPR(FM) Brainerd MN 34.2 kw, 679 ft.
*KZSE(FM) Rochester MN 1.38 kw, 259 ft.
*KOBC(FM) Joplin MO 30 kw, 230 ft.
*KWMU(FM) St. Louis MO 97 kw, 981 ft.
*WCLL-FM Wesson MS 100 w, 177 ft.
*KECC(FM) Miles City MT 500 w, 502 ft.
*WFAE(FM) Charlotte NC 100 kw, 760 ft.
*WNCU(FM) Durham NC 50 kw, 433 ft.
*WOTJ(FM) Morehead City NC 60 kw, 405 ft.
*KVNO(FM) Omaha NE 3 kw, 640 ft.
*WEVN(FM) Keene NH 1.5 kw, 938 ft.
*WLMW(FM) Manchester NH 15 w, 886 ft.
*WAGB(FM) Manahawkin NJ 1 w-H, 950 w-V, 50 ft.
*KRWG(FM) Las Cruces NM 100 kw, 350 ft.
*KSFR(FM) Santa Fe NM 3 kw, 199 ft.
*WGCC-FM Batavia NY 880 w, 164 ft.
*WFUV(FM) New York NY 50 kw, 215 ft.
*WPGL(FM) Pattersonville NY 30 w, 653 ft.
*WGLE(FM) Lima OH 50 kw, 420 ft.
*WVMC(FM) Mansfield OH 10 w, 235 ft.
*WMCO(FM) New Concord OH 1.3 kw, 84 ft.
*WKTL(FM) Struthers OH 15 kw, 23 ft.
*KALU(FM) Langston OK 10 w, 77 ft.
*KAYE-FM Tonkawa OK 1.2 kw, 67 ft.
*KBOO(FM) Portland OR 25.5 kw, 1,266 ft.
*WRTL(FM) Ephrata PA 650 w, 848 ft.
*WVMM(FM) Grantham PA 100 w, 300 ft.
*WCLH(FM) Wilkes-Barre PA 175 w, 1,020 ft.
*WJHD(FM) Portsmouth RI 360 w, plus 80 ft.
*WYFH(FM) North Charleston SC 50 kw, 492 ft.
*WKNQ(FM) Dyersburg TN 100 kw, 373 ft.
*WUVT-FM Blacksburg VA 3 kw, 156 ft.
*WEHC(FM) Emory VA 100 w, 95 ft.
*WMRA(FM) Harrisonburg VA 24.5 kw, 710 ft.
*WCWM(FM) Williamsburg VA 1.6 kw, 350 ft.
*WJSC-FM Johnson VT 155 w, minus 485 ft.
*WVTC(FM) Randolph Center VT 300 w-H, 203 ft.
*KNWR(FM) Ellensburg WA 5 kw, 2,552 ft.
*KSER(FM) Everett WA 1 kw, 548 ft.
*KZUU(FM) Pullman WA 800 w, 105 ft.
*WHAD(FM) Delafield WI 79 kw, 700 ft.
*WVSS(FM) Menomonie WI 1.06 kw, 75 ft.
*WFGH(FM) Fort Gay WV 7.8 kw, 205 ft.
WVRP(FM) Ripley WV 3 kw, 328 ft.
*WNFR(FM) Sandusky MI 328 ft.
*WPNR-FM Utica NY 450 w, 30 ft.
*KSDJ(FM) Brookings SD 1 kw, 148 ft.

90.9 mhz (ch 215)
*WYJD(FM) Brewton AL 6 kw, 479 ft.
*WJAB(FM) Huntsville AL 100 kw, 334 ft.
*KBSA(FM) El Dorado AR 3 kw, 581 ft.
*KLLN(FM) Newark AR 4 kw, 456 ft.
*KGCB(FM) Prescott AZ 55 kw, 2,486 ft.
*KHDC(FM) Chualar CA 3 kw, 195 ft.
*KXPR(FM) Sacramento CA 50 kw, 500 ft.
*KLOD(FM) Shafter CA 50 kw, 86 ft.
*KASF(FM) Alamosa CO 1 kw, 105 ft.
*KVNF(FM) Paonia CO 3 kw, -171 ft.
*WETA-FM Washington DC 75 kw, 448 ft.
*WKTZ-FM Jacksonville FL 50 kw, 500 ft.
*WJIR(FM) Key West FL 390 w, 121 ft.
*WSOR(FM) Naples FL 36 kw, 909 ft.
*WJWV(FM) Fort Gaines GA 85 kw, 267 ft.
*WOAK(FM) La Grange GA 3.4 kw, 299 ft.
*WRAF-FM Toccoa Falls GA 100 kw, 564 ft.
*WVVS(FM) Valdosta GA 5.3 kw, 68 ft.
*KUNI(FM) Cedar Falls IA 100 kw, 1,782 ft.
*WDCB(FM) Glen Ellyn IL 5 kw, 300 ft.
*WILL-FM Urbana IL 105 kw, 850 ft.
*WBDG(FM) Indianapolis IN 400 w, 78 ft.
*KHCT(FM) Great Bend KS 50 kw, 781 ft.
*WKUE(FM) Elizabethtown KY 5.2 kw, 633 ft.
*WEKH(FM) Hazard KY 33 kw, 1,005 ft.
*KSLU(FM) Hammond LA 3 kw, 143 ft.
*KSJY(FM) Lafayette LA 510 w, 207 ft.
*WBUR(FM) Boston MA 7.2 kw, 1,046 ft.
*WMEH(FM) Bangor ME 13.5 kw, 850 ft.
*WMPG(FM) Gorham ME 110 w-H, 1 kw-V, 233 ft.
*WQAC-FM Alma MI 100 w, 66 ft.
*WDTR(FM) Detroit MI 42 kw-H, 38 kw-V, 437 ft.
*WNMC-FM Traverse City MI 150 w, -88 ft.
*WIRR(FM) Virginia-Hibbing MN 21 kw, 552 ft.
*KRCU(FM) Cape Girardeau MO 6 kw, 259 ft.
*KCMW-FM Warrensburg MO 100 kw, 400 ft.
*WMAO-FM Greenwood MS 100 kw, 880 ft.
*NEW FM Great Falls MT 100 kw, 476 ft.
*WQFS(FM) Greensboro NC 1.9 kw, 200 ft.
*WESQ(FM) Rocky Mount NC 6 kw, 627 ft.
*KUCV(FM) Lincoln NE 16 kw, 600 ft.
*KPNO(FM) Norfolk NE 50 kw, 351 ft.
*KSJE(FM) Farmington NM 15 kw, 390 ft.
*KNJU(FM) Raton NM 100 w, -581 ft.
*KSHI(FM) Zuni NM 100 w, 100 ft.
*WCDB(FM) Albany NY 100 w, 222 ft.
*WETD(FM) Alfred NY 360 w, 282 ft.
*WKRB(FM) Brooklyn NY 10 w, 136 ft.
*WSQG-FM Ithaca NY 5 kw, 294 ft.
*WCOT(FM) Jamestown NY 10 kw, 492 ft.
*WAMK(FM) Kingston NY 940 w, 1,486 ft.
*WSLO(FM) Malone NY 200 w, 354 ft.
*WONY(FM) Oneonta NY 177 w, minus 72 ft.
*WJNY(FM) Watertown NY 7.09 kw, 449 ft.
*WGUC(FM) Cincinnati OH 15 kw, 960 ft.
*WCVJ(FM) Jefferson OH 5.5 kw, 372 ft.
*WFCO(FM) Lancaster OH 200 w, 223 ft.
*WNZR(FM) Mount Vernon OH 100 w, 193 ft.
*WCWS(FM) Wooster OH 1.05 kw, 230 ft.
*KKVO(FM) Altus OK 400 w, 121 ft.
*KOKF(FM) Edmond OK 100 kw, 480 ft.
*KSKF(FM) Klamath Falls OR 2 kw, 2,260 ft.
*KRBM(FM) Pendleton OR 25 kw, 587 ft.
*WITX(FM) Beaver Falls PA 100 w, 167 ft.
*WHYY-FM Philadelphia PA 13.5 kw, 920 ft.
*NEW FM Cabo Rojo PR 25 kw, 633 ft.
*WLGI(FM) Hemingway SC 50 kw, 505 ft.
*KDSD-FM Pierpont SD 70 kw, 1,057 ft.
*KCSD(FM) Sioux Falls SD 2.35 kw, 190 ft.
*WWOG(FM) Cookeville TN 3 kw, 697 ft.
*KAMU-FM College Station TX 32 kw, 340 ft.
*KCBI-FM Dallas TX 100 kw, 1,509 ft.
*KTSU(FM) Houston TX 18.5 kw, 285 ft.
*KYFT(FM) Lubbock TX 5 kw, 236 ft.
*KYFS(FM) San Antonio TX 3 kw, 299 ft.
*KRCL(FM) Salt Lake City UT 16.5 kw, 3,770 ft.
*WTBC-FM Williston VT 1.5 kw, 49 ft.
*KVTI(FM) Tacoma WA 51 kw, 422 ft.
*WHRM(FM) Wausau WI 77 kw, 1,120 ft.
*WPIB(FM) Bluefield WV 740 w-H, 700 w-V, 1,102 ft.
*WVPM(FM) Morgantown WV 5.2 kw, 1,440 ft.

91.1 mhz (ch 216)
*KSKA(FM) Anchorage AK 36 kw, 126 ft.
*WEGL(FM) Auburn AL 3 kw, 190 ft.
*WJSR(FM) Birmingham AL 100 w, 195 ft.
*WVSU-FM Birmingham AL 125 w, 216 ft.
*KSWH(FM) Arkadelphia AR 10 w, 70 ft.
*KYFB(FM) Pine Bluff AR 1 kw, 200 ft.
*KMTC(FM) Russellville AR 360 w, -62 ft.
*KNLB(FM) Lake Havasu City AZ 1.15 kw, 452 ft.
*KMUD(FM) Garberville CA 200 w, 2,483 ft.
*KCSM(FM) San Mateo CA 14 kw, 330 ft.
*KRCB-FM Santa Rosa CA 180 w, 2150 ft.
*KCPB(FM) Thousand Oaks CA 4.9 kw, 1,280 ft.
*KWSB-FM Gunnison CO 135 w, 304 ft.
*KWBI(FM) Morrison CO 100 kw, 1,184 ft.
*WSHU(FM) Fairfield CT 12.5 kw, 595 ft.
*WCNI(FM) New London CT 490 w, 169 ft.
*WJED(FM) Dogwood Lakes Estate FL 700 w, 180 ft.
*WJFP(FM) Fort Pierce FL 6 kw, 157 ft.
*WPSM(FM) Fort Walton Beach FL 383 w, 120 ft.
*WCIE-FM Lakeland FL 100 kw, 500 ft.
*WJNF(FM) Marianna FL 383 w, 154 ft.
*WREK(FM) Atlanta GA 40 kw, 340 ft.
*WSVH(FM) Savannah GA 100 kw, 1,068 ft.
*WABR-FM Tifton GA 30 kw, 249 ft.
*KTPR(FM) Fort Dodge IA 100 kw, 1,052 ft.
*WIBI(FM) Carlinville IL 43 kw, 370 ft.
*WTKC(FM) Kankakee IL 1.75 kw, 305 ft.
*WGSL(FM) Loves Park IL 4 kw, 400 ft.
*WRJV(FM) Berne IN 25 kw, 100 ft.
*WGCS(FM) Goshen IN 7.4 kw, 65 ft.
*WEDM(FM) Indianapolis IN 180 w, 180 ft.
*WCYT(FM) Lafayette Township IN 1 kw, 541 ft.
*WVUB(FM) Vincennes IN 50 kw, 500 ft.
*KANZ(FM) Garden City KS 100 kw, 650 ft.
*KCFN(FM) Wichita KS 100 kw, 345 ft.
*KLSU(FM) Baton Rouge LA 5 kw, 159 ft.
*KNLU(FM) Monroe LA 8.5 kw, 716 ft.
*WMUA(FM) Amherst MA 1 kw, 26 ft.
*WJJW(FM) North Adams MA 423 w, minus 830 ft.
*WSMU-FM North Dartmouth MA 1.2 kw, 300 ft.
*WHFC(FM) Bel Air MD 1.1 kw, 226 ft.
*WBOR(FM) Brunswick ME 300 w-H, 154 ft.
*WOLW(FM) Cadillac MI 50 kw-H, 28 kw-V, 700 ft.
*WFUM-FM Flint MI 18 kw, 489 ft.
*WGGL-FM Houghton MI 100 kw, 809 ft.
*WPCJ(FM) Pittsford MI 100 w, 125 ft.
*KXLC(FM) La Crescent MN 230 w, 843 ft.
*KNOW-FM Minneapolis-St. Paul MN 100 kw, 1,310 ft.
*KCCM-FM Moorhead MN 67 kw, 656 ft.
*KSMU(FM) Springfield MO 40 kw, 403 ft.
*WMSV(FM) Starkville MS 14.1 kw, 449 ft.
XETRA-FM Tijuana MX 100 kw, 1,000 ft.
*WAFP(FM) Oxford NC 5 kw, 272 ft.
*WRSH(FM) Rockingham NC 10 w, 60 ft.
*WNDN-FM Salisbury NC 10 w-H, 754 ft.
*KTNE-FM Alliance NE 92.3 kw, 1,325 ft.
*KDCV-FM Blair NE 10 w, 60 ft.
*WVNH(FM) Concord NH 1 kw, 98 ft.
*WWNJ(FM) Dover Township NJ 10 kw, 165 ft.
*WFMU(FM) East Orange NJ 1.44 kw, 360 ft.
*KEDP(FM) Las Vegas NM 72 w, minus 215 ft.
*WAOI(FM) Corning NY 12.6 kw, 177 ft.
*WOSS(FM) Ossining NY 10 w, 100 ft.
*WTSC-FM Potsdam NY 700 w, 155 ft.
*WSPN(FM) Saratoga Springs NY 253 w, 98 ft.
*WRMU(FM) Alliance OH 2.8 kw, 190 ft.
*WRUW-FM Cleveland OH 1 kw, 270 ft.
*WDUB(FM) Granville OH 100 w, 171 ft.
*KBVV(FM) Enid OK 300 w, 297 ft.
*KWAX(FM) Eugene OR 20 kw, 1,013 ft.
*WBUQ(FM) Bloomsburg PA 1 kw, 500 ft.
*WZBT(FM) Gettysburg PA 180 w, 380 ft.
*WSAJ-FM Grove City PA 200 w, 450 ft.
*WRTY(FM) Jackson Township PA 3.5 kw, 862 ft.
*WMSS(FM) Middletown PA 1.35 w, -69 ft.
*WPSU(FM) State College PA 870 w-H, 850 w-V, minus 78 ft-H, minus 83 ft-V.
*WYFG(FM) Gaffney SC 100 kw, 574 ft.
*KTSD-FM Reliance SD 100 kw, 1,480 ft.
*KAOR(FM) Vermillion SD 120 w, 107 ft.
*WKCS(FM) Knoxville TN 250 w, 73 ft.
*WKNO-FM Memphis TN 100 kw, 580 ft.
*WRVU(FM) Nashville TN 14.5 kw, 457 ft.
*KWTS(FM) Canyon TX 100 w, minus 9 ft.
*KVER(FM) El Paso TX 140 w, 1,118 ft.
*KTAI(FM) Kingsville TX 100 w, 75 ft.
*KBWC(FM) Marshall TX 100 w, 110 ft.
*KGSU-FM Cedar City UT 10 kw, minus 462 ft.
*WTJU(FM) Charlottesville VA 1.5 kw, 305 ft.
*WPRH-FM Galax VA 1 kw-H, 940 w-V, 495 ft.
*WHCE(FM) Highland Springs VA 3 kw, 103 ft.
*WNSB(FM) Norfolk VA 920 w-H, 154 ft.
*WGDR(FM) Plainfield VT 800 w, minus 350 ft.
*KPBX-FM Spokane WA 56 kw, 2,380 ft.
*WLFM(FM) Appleton WI 10.5 kw, 120 ft.
*WGTD(FM) Kenosha WI 5 kw, 135 ft.
*WHVP(FM) Hudson NY

91.3 mhz (ch 217)
*WVOB(FM) Dothan AL 2.5 kw, 328 ft.
*WBHL(FM) Florence AL 30 kw, 600 ft.
*WHIL-FM Mobile AL 100 kw, 245 ft.
*KUCA(FM) Conway AR 5 kw, 346 ft.
*KUAF(FM) Fayetteville AR 60 kw, 1,105 ft.
*KXCI(FM) Tucson AZ 335 w, 3,641 ft.
*KIDE(FM) Hoopa CA 195 w, -1,560 ft.
*KCPR(FM) San Luis Obispo CA 2 kw, minus 350 ft.
*KUOP(FM) Stockton CA 7 kw, 1,220 ft.
*KMSA(FM) Grand Junction CO 500 w, minus 382 ft.
*KSUT(FM) Ignacio CO 425 w, 18 ft.
*WWUH(FM) West Hartford CT 1 kw, 520 ft.
*WVUD(FM) Newark DE 1 kw, 135 ft.
*WSEB(FM) Englewood FL 62 kw-H, 60 kw-V, 282 ft.
*WOLR(FM) Lake City FL 18 kw-V, 285 ft.

U.S. FM Stations by Frequency

*WLRN-FM Miami FL 100 kw, 652 ft.
*WJTG(FM) Fort Valley GA 100 kw, 459 ft.
*KDFR(FM) Des Moines IA 4 kw, 446 ft.
*WIUM(FM) Macomb IL 50 kw, 485 ft.
*WFHB(FM) Bloomington IN 2.5 kw, 266 ft.
*WHJE(FM) Carmel IN 400 w, 100 ft.
*WUKY(FM) Lexington KY 95 kw, 1,004 ft.
*WKMS-FM Murray KY 100 kw, 602 ft.
*KSCL(FM) Shreveport LA 150 w, 79 ft.
*WSHL-FM Easton MA 100 w, 66 ft.
*WXPL(FM) Fitchburg MA 100 w, 134 ft.
*WDJM-FM Framingham MA 100 w, 89 ft.
*WCWL(FM) Stockbridge MA 250 w, 40 ft.
*WCUW(FM) Worcester MA 630 w, 145 ft.
*WESM(FM) Princess Anne MD 50 kw, 347 ft.
*WMEW(FM) Waterville ME 3 kw, 299 ft.
*WCHW-FM Bay City MI 110 w-H, 125 ft.
*WCSG(FM) Grand Rapids MI 37 kw, 570 ft.
*WOES(FM) Ovid-Elsie MI 535 w, 140 ft.
*WSGR-FM Port Huron MI 100 w, 87 ft.
*KRSU(FM) Appleton MN 75 kw, 1,158 ft.
*KMSK(FM) Austin MN 135 w, 221 ft.
*KNBJ(FM) Bemidji MN 60 kw, 974 ft.
*KBIA(FM) Columbia MO 100 kw, 610 ft.
*WMPN-FM Jackson MS 100 kw, 760 ft.
*WLFA(FM) Asheville NC 440 w, 3,340 ft.
*WFQS(FM) Franklin NC 265 w, 2,304 ft.
*WZMB(FM) Greenville NC 282 w, 134 ft.
*WHQR(FM) Wilmington NC 10 kw, 1,142 ft.
*KMHA(FM) Four Bears ND 100 kw, 380 ft.
*KSCV(FM) Kearney NE 1 kw, 100 ft.
*WUNH(FM) Durham NH 17.5 kw, 250 ft.
*WEVH(FM) Hanover NH 150 w, 1,240 ft.
*WKNH(FM) Keene NH 274 w, 79 ft.
*WRTQ(FM) Ocean City NJ .82 kw-H, 10.5 kw-V, 384 ft.
*WTSR(FM) Trenton NJ 1.5 kw, 35 ft.
*KNIS(FM) Carson City NV 67 kw, 2,165 ft.
*WXLH(FM) Blue Mountain Lake NY 78 w, 1,729 ft.
*WBNY(FM) Buffalo NY 100 w, 115 ft.
*WOLN(FM) Olean NY 115 w, 656 ft.
*WVKR-FM Poughkeepsie NY 1 kw, 85 ft.
*WPBX(FM) Southampton NY 1 kw, 165 ft.
*WCNY-FM Syracuse NY 18.6 kw, 740 ft.
*WOUB-FM Athens OH 50 kw, 500 ft.
*WGTE-FM Toledo OH 13.5 kw, 949 ft.
*WYSO(FM) Yellow Springs OH 10 kw, 410 ft.
*KRSC-FM Claremore OK 2.2 kw, 364 ft.
*KOAB-FM Bend OR 25 kw, 604 ft.
*WLVR(FM) Bethlehem PA 185 w, 60 ft.
*WQLN-FM Erie PA 35 kw, 500 ft.
*WLCH(FM) Lancaster PA 160 w, 135 ft.
*WGRC(FM) Lewisburg PA 5 kw, 89 ft.
*WYEP-FM Pittsburgh PA 18.2 kw, 265 ft.
*WXAC(FM) Reading PA 219 w, minus 23 ft.
*WIPR-FM San Juan PR 125 kw, 2,719 ft.
*WDOM(FM) Providence RI 125 w, 130 ft.
*WLTR(FM) Columbia SC 96 kw, 761 ft.
*KTEQ(FM) Rapid City SD 750 w, 300 ft.
*WLMU(FM) Harrogate TN 190 w, 284 ft.
*WUTS(FM) Sewanee TN 200 w, 658 ft.
*KAGN(FM) Abilene TX 300 w, 592 ft.
*KVLU(FM) Beaumont TX 40 kw, 450 ft.
*KNCT-FM Killeen TX 50 kw, 1,170 ft.
*KXPZ(FM) Lytle TX 3 kw, 302 ft.
*KOCV(FM) Odessa TX 5 kw, 300 ft.
*KPVU(FM) Prairie View TX 98.3 kw, 410 ft.
*KGLY(FM) Tyler TX 12 kw, 462 ft.
*WVST(FM) Petersburg VA 100 w, 120 ft.
*WPIR(FM) Salem VA 3.3 kw-H, 3 kw-V, 902 ft.
*WTRM(FM) Winchester VA 6.1 kw, 1,348 ft.
*WIUV(FM) Castleton VT 227 w, minus 235 ft.
*KBCS(FM) Bellevue WA 1.2 kw, 100 ft.
*KCED(FM) Centralia WA 1 kw, -72 ft.
*KGTS(FM) College Place WA 4.6 kw, 1,297 ft.
*WHEM(FM) Eau Claire WI 550 w, 217 ft.
*WGAZ(FM) Goodman WI 422 w-V, 118 ft.
*WHHI(FM) Highland WI 100 kw, 560 ft.
*KUWS(FM) Superior WI 940 w-H, minus 72 ft.
*WQAB(FM) Philippi WV 7.2 kw, 180 ft.

91.5 mhz (ch 218)

*KUWL(FM) Fairbanks AK 380 w, 48 ft.
*WSGN(FM) Gadsden AL 6.3 kw, 520 ft.
*WEBT(FM) Langdale AL 380 w, 85 ft.
*WUAL-FM Tuscaloosa AL 100 kw, 523 ft.
*KALR(FM) Hot Springs AR 1 kw, 282 ft.
*KCMH(FM) Mountain Home AR 400 w, 420 ft.
*KJZZ(FM) Phoenix AZ 96 kw, 1,607 ft.
*KGHR(FM) Tuba City AZ 100 w, minus 82 ft.
*KZPN(FM) Bayside CA 125 w, 823 ft.
*KKUP(FM) Cupertino CA 200 w, 2,294 ft.
*KSJV(FM) Fresno CA 16 kw, 870 ft.
*KUSC(FM) Los Angeles CA 17 kw, 2922 ft.
*KYDS(FM) Sacramento CA 410 w, 108 ft.
*KAJX(FM) Aspen CO 380 w-H, 370 w-V, minus 987 ft.
*KRCC(FM) Colorado Springs CO 1 kw, 2,103 ft.
*KSJD(FM) Cortez CO 145 w, minus 417 ft.
*KUNC-FM Greeley CO 100 kw, 570 ft.
*WGRS(FM) Guilford CT 2 kw, 82 ft.
*WTBH(FM) Chiefland FL 3 kw, 233 ft.
*WMIE(FM) Cocoa FL 20 kw-H, 19 kw-V, 98 ft.
*WJYO(FM) Fort Myers FL 3 kw, 285 ft.
*WAPN(FM) Holly Hill FL 1.8 kw, 300 ft.
*WLPJ-FM New Port Richey FL 2.7 kw, 185 ft.
*WFSQ(FM) Tallahassee FL 100 kw, 662 ft.
*WPRK(FM) Winter Park FL 1.32 kw, 89 ft.
*WWEV-FM Cumming GA 8.9 kw, 960 ft.
*WGPH(FM) Vidalia GA 50 kw, 387 ft.
*KUSR(FM) Ames IA 200 w, 100 ft.
*KUNY(FM) Mason City IA 8 kw-V, 371 ft.
*KWBH(FM) Rexburg ID 100 w-H, -39 ft.
*WBEZ(FM) Chicago IL 8.3 kw, 1,180 ft.
*WCIC(FM) Pekin IL 35 kw, 338 ft.
*WJHS(FM) Columbia City IN 2.65 kw, 219 ft.
*WUEV(FM) Evansville IN 6.1 kw, 150 ft.
*WGRE(FM) Greencastle IN 115 w, 160 ft.
*WRFT(FM) Indianapolis IN 130 w, 180 ft.
*WWHI(FM) Muncie IN 310 w, 79 ft.
*WECI(FM) Richmond IN 400 w, 106 ft.
*WKLO(FM) Westport IN 14.55 kw, 305 ft.
*KANU(FM) Lawrence KS 100 kw, 698 ft.
*WVCT(FM) Keavy KY 113 w, 88 ft.
*WBFI(FM) McDaniels KY 5 kw, 190 ft.
*KPAE(FM) Erwinville LA 5 kw, 167 ft.
*KGRM(FM) Grambling LA 50 kw, 492 ft.
*WTUL(FM) New Orleans LA 1.5 kw, 161 ft.
*KNSU(FM) Thibodaux LA 10 w-horiz, 292 ft.
*WBIM-FM Bridgewater MA 180 w, 71 ft.
*WHHB(FM) Holliston MA 10 w, 52 ft.
*WJUL(FM) Lowell MA 1.7 kw, 39 ft.
*WMFO(FM) Medford MA 125 w, 135 ft.
*WMLN-FM Milton MA 170 w, 98 ft.
*WNMH(FM) Northfield MA 235 w, 308 ft.
*WSDH(FM) Sandwich MA 310 w, 150 ft.
*WMHC(FM) South Hadley MA 100 w, minus 18 ft.
*WSRB(FM) Walpole MA 14 w, 83 ft.
*WZLY(FM) Wellesley MA 10 w, 164 ft.
*WBJC(FM) Baltimore MD 50 kw, 500 ft.
*WRBC(FM) Lewiston ME 150 w, 16 ft.
*WSJB-FM Standish ME 360 w, 85 ft.
*WUPX(FM) Marquette MI 200 w, 138 ft.
*WMHW-FM Mount Pleasant MI 307 w, 112 ft.
*KCFB(FM) St. Cloud MN 800 w, 119 ft.
*KNGA(FM) St. Peter MN 8.5 kw, 600 ft.
*KQMN(FM) Thief River Falls MN 100 kw, 449 ft.
*KNEO(FM) Neosho MO 348 w, 80 ft.
*KMSM-FM Butte MT 50 w, 93 ft.
*WUNC(FM) Chapel Hill NC 100 kw, 810 ft.
*WXRI(FM) Winston-Salem NC 20 kw, 69 ft.
*KPRJ(FM) Jamestown ND 18.6 kw, 354 ft.
*KRNE-FM Merriman NE 92 kw, 964 ft.
*KIOS-FM Omaha NE 55 kw, 408 ft.
*WDBK(FM) Blackwood NJ 100 w, 87 ft.
*KFLQ(FM) Albuquerque NM 22.5 kw, 4,060 ft.
*KRUX(FM) Las Cruces NM 1 kw, minus 194 ft.
*KNCC(FM) Elko NV 50 w, 741 ft.
*KUNV(FM) Las Vegas NV 15 kw, 1,100 ft.
*WJIK(FM) Binghamton NY 1.5 kw, 328 ft.
*WSQX-FM Binghamton NY 560 w, 843 ft.
*WVHC(FM) Herkimer NY 350 w-V, -115 ft.
*WNYE(FM) New York NY 20 kw, 430 ft.
*WXXI-FM Rochester NY 45 kw, 400 ft.
*WRPI(FM) Troy NY 10 kw, 450 ft.
*WKRJ(FM) New Philadelphia OH 3 kw, 217 ft.
*WOBC-FM Oberlin OH 440 w, 124 ft.
*WOSP(FM) Portsmouth OH 110 w, 1,207 ft.
*WSTB(FM) Streetsboro OH 300 w, 125 ft.
*KSYE(FM) Frederick OK 100 kw, 390 ft.
*KVAZ(FM) Henryetta OK 250 w, 178 ft.
*KOPB-FM Portland OR 70 kw-H, 21 kw-V, 1,558 ft.
*KSRS(FM) Roseburg OR 2 kw, 305 ft.
*WVMW-FM Scranton PA 100 w, minus 185 ft.
*WSRN-FM Swarthmore PA 110 w, 140 ft.
*WCVY(FM) Coventry RI 200 w, 36 ft.
*WKCL(FM) Ladson SC 100 kw, 305 ft.
*WHCB(FM) Bristol TN 1.5 kw, 2,326 ft.
*WFHC(FM) Henderson TN 3 kw, 300 ft.
*WFMQ(FM) Lebanon TN 500 w, 100 ft.
*WAWL-FM Red Bank TN 6 kw, 951 ft.
*KTDN(FM) Palestine TX 550 w, 519 ft.
*KWLD(FM) Plainview TX 370 w, 150 ft.
*KTXK(FM) Texarkana TX 5.2 kw, 335 ft.
*KUSU-FM Logan UT 90 kw, 1,140 ft.
*WPIN(FM) Dublin VA 100 w-H, 90 w-V, 1,204 ft.
*WLUR(FM) Lexington VA 225 w, -75 ft.
*WYCS(FM) Yorktown VA 1.3 kw-H, 20 kw-V, 371 ft-H, 331 ft-V.
*WWLR(FM) Lyndonville VT 3 kw, minus 75 ft.
*KUBS(FM) Newport WA 150 w, minus 538 ft.
*WGBW(FM) Green Bay WI 710 w, 741 ft.
*WGLZ(FM) West Liberty WV 150 w, 213 ft.

91.7 mhz (ch 219)

*WYFD(FM) Decatur AL 3 kw, 300 ft.
*KGMR(FM) Clarksville AR 380 w, minus 39 ft.
*KCHO(FM) Chico CA 7.71 kw, 1,219 ft.
*KXSR(FM) Groveland CA 6.9 kw, 1,027 ft.
*KHCS(FM) Palm Desert CA 2.5 kw, 328 ft.
*KALW(FM) San Francisco CA 1.9 kw, 920 ft.
*KOTO(FM) Telluride CO 2.35 kw, -187 ft.
*WXCI(FM) Danbury CT 1.2 kw, 205 ft.
*WHUS(FM) Storrs CT 3.16 kw, 360 ft.
*WRTX(FM) Dover DE 708 w-H, 279 ft.
*WMPH(FM) Wilmington DE 100 w, 143 ft.
*WNLE(FM) Fernandina Beach FL 38 kw, 167 ft.
*WJLF(FM) Gainesville FL 2 kw, 400 ft.
*WEGS(FM) Milton FL 2 kw, 300 ft.
*WWFR(FM) Okeechobee FL 20 kw, 299 ft.
*WVIJ(FM) Port Charlotte FL 380 w, 130 ft.
*WFTI-FM St. Petersburg FL 3 kw, 282 ft.
*WUNV(FM) Albany GA 3 kw, 328 ft.
*WUGA(FM) Athens GA 3 kw, 328 ft.
*WLPE(FM) Augusta GA 1.35 kw, 479 ft.
*WCCV(FM) Cartersville GA 910 w, 537 ft.
*WTJB(FM) Columbus GA 30 kw, 300 ft.
*WWET(FM) Valdosta GA 185 w, 236 ft.
*KSUI(FM) Iowa City IA 100 kw, 1,310 ft.
*KBSM(FM) McCall ID 220 w, 1,912 ft.
*KRFA-FM Moscow ID 1.45 kw, 1,009 ft.
*KBSW(FM) Twin Falls ID 1.95 kw, 492 ft.
*WBGL(FM) Champaign IL 20 kw, 500 ft.
*WIWC(FM) Kokomo IN 2.1 kw, 299 ft.
*WEEM(FM) Pendleton IN 1.2 kw, 154 ft.
*WETL(FM) South Bend IN 3 kw, 200 ft.
*WWHR(FM) Bowling Green KY 100 w, 10 ft.
*WOAL-FM Pippa Passes KY 3 kw, 100 ft.
*KYFE(FM) Alexandria LA 1 kw, 249 ft.
*KLSP(FM) Angola LA 100 w, 90 ft.
*KOJO(FM) Lake Charles LA 3 kw, 328 ft.
*KNWD(FM) Natchitoches LA 255 w-H, 164 ft.
*WPAA(FM) Andover MA 25 w, 209 ft.
*WGAJ(FM) Deerfield MA 100 w, 314 ft.
*WAVM(FM) Maynard MA 16 w, minus 7 ft.
*WMWM(FM) Salem MA 130 w, 132 ft.
*WBSL-FM Sheffield MA 250 w, 50 ft.
*WFWM(FM) Frostburg MD 150 w, 1,242 ft.
*WSHD(FM) Eastport ME 10 w, 98 ft.
*WCML-FM Alpena MI 100 kw, 1,171 ft.
*WUOM(FM) Ann Arbor MI 93 kw, 780 ft.
*KAXE(FM) Grand Rapids MN 100 kw, 460 ft.
*KLSE-FM Rochester MN 100 kw, 953 ft.
*WMCN(FM) St. Paul MN 10 w, 1,004 ft.
*KRSW-FM Worthington-Marshall MN 99 kw, 800 ft.
*KCVO-FM Camdenton MO 10 kw, 435 ft.
*KMVC(FM) Marshall MO 10 w, 51 ft.
*KCOZ(FM) Point Lookout MO 200 w, 151 ft.
*WVSD(FM) Itta Bena MS 3 kw, 292 ft.
*WJTA(FM) Kosciusko MS 383 w, 171 ft.
*WPRL(FM) Lorman MS 3 kw, 300 ft.
*KEMC(FM) Billings MT 100 kw, 520 ft.
*WSGE(FM) Dallas NC 3 kw, 140 ft.
*KPNE-FM North Platte NE 16.5 kw-H, 81 kw-V, 59 ft-H, 289 ft-V.
*WNEC-FM Henniker NH 120 w, minus 210 ft.
*WRND(FM) Manchester NH 1 w-H, 100 w-V, 13 ft.
*WPCR-FM Plymouth NH 215 w, 95 ft.
*WLFR(FM) Pomona NJ 1.35 kw, 135 ft.
KGLP(FM) Gallup NM 100 w, 1,145 ft.
*KLNR(FM) Panaca NV 100 w, 3,424 ft.
*KTPH(FM) Tonopah NV 100 w, 1,433 ft.
*WNGX(FM) Fort Ann NY 1 kw, 1,194 ft.
*WICB(FM) Ithaca NY 5.5 kw, 105 ft.
*WFRH(FM) Kingston NY 950 w, 272 ft.
*WOSR(FM) Middletown NY 1.8 kw, 630 ft.
*WSQC-FM Oneonta NY 570 w-H, 2.3 kw-V, 528 ft.
*WRVJ(FM) Watertown NY 3 kw, 328 ft.
*WMBP(FM) Belpre OH 170 w, 344 ft.
*WVXU(FM) Cincinnati OH 26.1 kw, 683 ft.
*WOSV(FM) Mansfield OH 750 w, 450 ft.
*WYTN(FM) Youngstown OH 3 kw, 299 ft.
*KPSU(FM) Goodwell OK 380 w, 121 ft.
*KOSU-FM Stillwater OK 100 kw, 1,010 ft.
*KEOL(FM) La Grande OR 310 w, minus 750 ft.
*KCIA(FM) Medford OR 1.25 kw, minus 508 ft.
*WMUH(FM) Allentown PA 500 w, minus 3 ft.
*WCUC-FM Clarion PA 2.3 kw, 323 ft.
*WIXQ(FM) Millersville PA 129 w, 69 ft.
*WKDU(FM) Philadelphia PA 110 w, 155 ft.
*WJAZ(FM) Summerdale PA 140 w, 683 ft.
*WRLC(FM) Williamsport PA 740 w-H, minus 298 ft.
*WLPG(FM) Florence SC 10-kw-H, 9.2 kw-V, 492 ft.
*WTBI-FM Greenville SC 3 kw, 328 ft.
*WAPX-FM Clarksville TN 3 kw, 160 ft.
*WSMS(FM) Memphis TN 25 kw, 394 ft.
*KVRX(FM) Austin TX 2 kw, 85 ft.
*KBNJ(FM) Corpus Christi TX 5 kw, 500 ft.
*KVTT(FM) Dallas TX 100 kw, 786 ft.
*KOOP(FM) Hornsby TX 3.13 kw, 27 ft.
*KTRU(FM) Houston TX 50 kw, 492 ft.
*KRTU(FM) San Antonio TX 3 kw, 120 ft.
*KOHS(FM) Orem UT 1.75 kw, -831 ft.
*KUFR(FM) Salt Lake City UT 250 w, minus 354 ft.
*KRDC-FM St. George UT 105 w, -312 ft.
*WEMC(FM) Harrisonburg VA 100 w, 205 ft.
*WRMC-FM Middlebury VT 100 w, 90 ft.
*KZAZ(FM) Bellingham WA 120 w, 334 ft.
*KBTC-FM Tacoma WA 7.9 kw, 553 ft.
*WMSE(FM) Milwaukee WI 1 kw, 125 ft.
*WXPR(FM) Rhinelander WI 100 kw, 403 ft.
*WSHS(FM) Sheboygan WI 180 w-vert, 82 ft.
*WSUW(FM) Whitewater WI 1.3 kw, 185 ft.
*WVPB(FM) Beckley WV 10.5 kw, 920 ft.
*WWVU-FM Morgantown WV 2.6 kw, 180 ft.

91.9 mhz (ch 220)

*KCZP(FM) Kenai AK 4.9 kw, 72 ft.
*KUHB(FM) St. Paul Island AK 3 kw, 56 ft.
*WGIB(FM) Birmingham AL 600 w, 679 ft.
*WMBV(FM) Dixon's Mills AL 62 kw, 613 ft.
*WLJS-FM Jacksonville AL 3 kw, 246 ft.
*WJIF(FM) Opp AL 380 w, 164 ft.
*KASU(FM) Jonesboro AR 100 kw, 692 ft.
*KXRJ(FM) Russellville AR 100 w, minus 92 ft.
*KSPB(FM) Pebble Beach CA 1 kw, 485 ft.
*KVCR(FM) San Bernardino CA 900 w, 1,605 ft.
*KCSB-FM Santa Barbara CA 620 w, 2,910 ft.
*KLVR(FM) Santa Rosa CA 1.25 kw, 2,988 ft.
*KCSS(FM) Turlock CA 151 w, 112 ft.
*KDUR(FM) Durango CO 225 w, minus 447 ft.
*KDRH(FM) Glenwood Springs CO 220 w, 788 ft.
*KERP(FM) Pueblo CO 600 w, 472 ft.
*WSLX(FM) New Canaan CT 10 w-H, 518 ft.
*WXJC(FM) Crystal River FL 3 kw
*WYFO(FM) Lakeland FL 25 kw-H, 23 kw-V, 328 ft.
*WAEQ(FM) Palatka FL 3 kw, 151 ft.
*WAYL(FM) St. Augustine FL 3 kw, 328 ft.
*WSCF-FM Vero Beach FL 15.5 kw, 305 ft.
*WCLK(FM) Atlanta GA 2.5 kw, 300 ft.
*WVGS(FM) Statesboro GA 1 kw, 161 ft.
*KSDA-FM Agat GU 7.59 kw, 981 ft.
*KWRV(FM) Sun Valley ID 100 w, -512 ft.
*WSIU(FM) Carbondale IL 50 kw, 299 ft.
*WJCH(FM) Joliet IL 50 kw, 460 ft.

Broadcasting & Cable Yearbook 1994
B-506

U.S. FM Stations by Frequency

*WSSU(FM) Springfield IL 50 kw, 524 ft.
*WQKO(FM) Howe IN 3 kw, 298 ft.
*WVSH(FM) Huntington IN 920 w, 110 ft.
*WJEF(FM) Lafayette IN 250 w, 100 ft.
*KTCC(FM) Colby KS 3 kw, 199 ft.
*KONQ(FM) Dodge City KS 2.6 kw, 123 ft.
*KNGM(FM) Emporia KS 3 kw, 263 ft.
*KSDB-FM Manhattan KS 1.4 kw, 290 ft.
*WFPK(FM) Louisville KY 100 kw, 350 ft.
*KYFI(FM) Lafayette LA 1.5 kw, 536 ft.
*WUMB-FM Boston MA 660 w, 207 ft.
*WOZQ(FM) Northampton MA 200 w, 115 ft.
*WOMR(FM) Provincetown MA 810 w, 155 ft.
*WAIC(FM) Springfield MA 230 w, 66 ft.
*WGTS-FM Takoma Park MD 29.5 kw, 165 ft.
*WMSJ(FM) Harpswell ME 6 kw, 148 ft.
*WMEB-FM Orono ME 380 w-H, 66 ft.
*WORW(FM) Port Huron MI 188 w, 78 ft.
*KWJC(FM) Liberty MO 182 w, 166 ft.
*KGLT(FM) Bozeman MT 2 kw, 365 ft.
*WFSS(FM) Fayetteville NC 100 kw, 440 ft.
*WRCM(FM) Wingate NC 17.7 kw, 515 ft.
*KDSU(FM) Fargo ND 100 kw, 991 ft.
*KCNE-FM Chadron NE 8.4 kw, 338 ft.
*KTLX(FM) Columbus NE 100 w, 78 ft.
*KDNE(FM) Crete NE 200 w, 66 ft.
*KWSC(FM) Wayne NE 350 w, 96 ft.
*WNTI(FM) Hackettstown NJ 5.6 kw, 510 ft.
*WCEB(FM) Corning NY 10 w-H, 1,784 ft.
*WSHR(FM) Lake Ronkonkoma NY 2.8 kw-H, 141 ft.
*WCFE-FM Plattsburgh NY 380 w, 852 ft.
*WRVN(FM) Utica NY 212 w, minus 82 ft.
*WOUH(FM) Chillicothe OH 750 w, 649 ft.
*WKCO(FM) Gambier OH 266 w, 190 ft.
*WMEJ(FM) Proctorville OH 3.5 kw, 220 ft.
*KHIB(FM) Durant OK 323 w, 135 ft.
*KMUN(FM) Astoria OR 3 kw, 1,060 ft.
*KRVM(FM) Eugene OR 1.9 kw, -36 ft.
*KWSO(FM) Warm Springs OR 3.3 kw, 203 ft.
*WVCS(FM) California PA 3 kw, 160 ft.
*KSQD-FM Lowry SD 100 kw, 725 ft.
*WUOT(FM) Knoxville TN 100 kw, 1,580 ft.
*KYFA(FM) Amarillo TX 2.25 kw, 292 ft.
*KPCW(FM) Park City UT 105 w, minus 23 ft.
*WVTR(FM) Marion VA 4.5 kw, 1,489 ft.
*WVLS(FM) Monterey VA 200 w, 426 ft.
*KSFC(FM) Spokane WA 100 w, 92 ft.
*KDNA(FM) Yakima WA 18.5 kw, 920 ft.
*WAAU(FM) Appleton WI 3.3 kw, 308 ft.
*WPHP(FM) Wheeling WV 1 kw, 259 ft.
*KUWR(FM) Laramie WY 100 kw, 1,128 ft.

92.1 mhz (ch 221)

WKUL(FM) Cullman AL 3 kw, 155 ft.
WZEW(FM) Fairhope AL 13.5 kw, 449 ft.
WERH-FM Hamilton AL 3 kw, 120 ft.
KARQ(FM) Ashdown AR 2.8 kw, 305 ft.
KHPQ(FM) Clinton AR 3 kw, 571 ft.
KKEG(FM) Fayetteville AR 1.15 kw, 459 ft.
KSBS-FM Pago Pago AS 3 kw, minus 135 ft.
KEKO(FM) Green Valley AZ 50 kw, 600 ft.
KZUA(FM) Holbrook AZ 3 kw, 328 ft.
KSGC(FM) Tusayan AZ 1.6 kw, 335 ft.
KIWI(FM) Bakersfield CA 6 kw, 269 ft.
KOWF(FM) Escondido CA 3 kw, 1,024 ft.
KHWX(FM) Joshua Tree CA 6 kw, 328 ft.
KXMX(FM) Madera CA 25 kw, 312 ft.
KZSA(FM) Placerville CA 1.41 kw, 446 ft.
KZWC(FM) Walnut Creek CA 3 kw, 89 ft.
KYBG-FM Castle Rock CO 820 w, 613 ft.
KYSL(FM) Frisco CO 290 w, 1,050 ft.
KBLJ(FM) La Junta CO 3 kw, 300 ft.
KVRH-FM Salida CO 5.8 kw, -655 ft.
WLBW(FM) Fenwick Island DE 3 kw, 328 ft.
WMMK(FM) Destin FL 25 kw, 279 ft.
WKZY(FM) La Belle FL 3 kw, 299 ft.
WJXR(FM) Macclenny FL 25 kw, 328 ft.
WCTQ(FM) Venice FL 6 kw, 300 ft.
WRLX(FM) West Palm Beach FL 3 kw, 365 ft.
WDDQ(FM) Adel GA 3 kw, 300 ft.
WBTR-FM Carrollton GA 580 w, 635 ft.
WWRK-FM Elberton GA 3 kw, 299 ft.
WJGA-FM Jackson GA 2.15 kw, 374 ft.
WPEH-FM Louisville GA 3 kw, 296 ft.
KCHE-FM Cherokee IA 3 kw, 302 ft.
KUEL(FM) Fort Dodge IA 3 kw, 300 ft.
KRLS(FM) Knoxville IA 3 kw, 300 ft.
KRBF(FM) Bonners Ferry ID 3 kw, 63 ft.
WCAZ-FM Carthage IL 25 kw, 328 ft.
WHQQ(FM) Charleston IL 2.2 kw, 140 ft.
WFPS(FM) Freeport IL 3 kw, 300 ft.
WJRE(FM) Kewanee IL 3 kw, 300 ft.
*WBST(FM) Muncie IN 3 kw, 300 ft.
WROI(FM) Rochester IN 4.3 kw, 240 ft.
WZDM(FM) Vincennes IN 2 kw, 400 ft.
KREP(FM) Belleville KS 6 kw, 300 ft.
KMZA(FM) Seneca KS 4.5 kw, 377 ft.
WMOR-FM Morehead KY 3 kw, 288 ft.
WDHR(FM) Pikeville KY 3 kw, 500 ft.
WTKY-FM Tompkinsville KY 6 kw, 328 ft.
KLKL(FM) Benton LA 3 kw, 299 ft.
KROK(FM) De Ridder LA 3 kw, 470 ft.
KLIL(FM) Moreauville LA 3 kw, 300 ft.
KVCL-FM Winnfield LA 6 kw, 284 ft.
WUFK(FM) Fort Kent ME 13.85 w, - 321 ft.
*WUPI(FM) Presque Isle ME 17 w-H, -39 ft.
WCDQ(FM) Sanford ME 1.2 kw, 525 ft.
WMNW(FM) Beulah MI 1.65 kw, 443 ft.
WIDL(FM) Caro MI 6 kw, 318 ft.
WDOW-FM Dowagiac MI 3.3 kw, 299 ft.
WGHN-FM Grand Haven MI 3 kw, 246 ft.
WKKM(FM) Harrison MI 6 kw, 300 ft.
WCSR-FM Hillsdale MI 6 kw, 243 ft.
WWDX(FM) St. Johns MI 6 kw, 400 ft.
WELY-FM Ely MN 6 kw, 328 ft.
WYRQ(FM) Little Falls MN 3 kw, 299 ft.
KLQP(FM) Madison MN 3 kw, 300 ft.
WCMP-FM Pine City MN 3 kw, 300 ft.
KRUE(FM) Waseca MN 25 kw, 286 ft.
KMOE(FM) Butler MO 4.7 kw, 200 ft.
KMFC(FM) Centralia MO 1.85 kw, 418 ft.
KSDL(FM) Sedalia MO 3 kw, 280 ft.
KTTN-FM Trenton MO 2.1 kw, 374 ft.
WBKN(FM) Brookhaven MS 2.5 kw, 351 ft.
WJMG(FM) Hattiesburg MS 3 kw, 300 ft.
WMSU(FM) Starkville MS 1.1 kw, 500 ft.
WUMS(FM) University MS 6 kw, 328 ft.
WJNS-FM Yazoo City MS 20 kw, 300 ft.
WKJA(FM) Belhaven NC 31 kw, 613 ft.
WMNC-FM Morganton NC 6 kw, 327 ft.
WMYK(FM) Moyock NC 18 kw, 384 ft.
WRSV(FM) Rocky Mount NC 1.7 kw, 380 ft.
KRRB(FM) Dickinson ND 630 w, 571 ft.
KNJP(FM) Sargent NE 100 kw, 761 ft.
WNHQ(FM) Peterborough NH 250 w, 1,120 ft.
WVLT(FM) Vineland NJ 3 kw, 328 ft.
KATK-FM Carlsbad NM 3 kw, 190 ft.
KSRN(FM) Sparks NV 440 w, 804 ft.
WSEN-FM Baldwinsville NY 25 kw, 300 ft.
*WGFR(FM) Glens Falls NY 10 w, 62 ft.
WCKR(FM) Hornell NY 1.25 kw, 512 ft.
WMNM(FM) Port Henry NY 18 kw, 10 ft.
WRNQ(FM) Poughkeepsie NY 2.15 kw, 384 ft.
WLNG-FM Sag Harbor NY 5.3 kw, 350 ft.
WDLA-FM Walton NY 690 w, 656 ft.
WNRR(FM) Bellevue OH 3 kw, 161 ft.
WMPO-FM Middleport-Pomeroy OH 4.7 kw, 113 ft.
WZOQ(FM) Wapakoneta OH 3 kw, 320 ft.
WROU(FM) West Carrollton OH 890 w, 597 ft.
KCMA(FM) Broken Arrow OK 27 kw, 656 ft.
KFXI(FM) Marlow OK 100 kw, 718 ft.
KMZE(FM) Woodward OK 2.15 kw, 1,099 ft.
*KEPO(FM) Eagle Point OR 10 w, 50 ft.
KWVR-FM Enterprise OR 3 kw, minus 626 ft.
*KAVE(FM) Oakridge OR 580 w-H, -817 ft.
KSYD(FM) Reedsport OR 2.78 kw-H, 335 ft.
WKST-FM Ellwood City PA 6 kw, 299 ft.
WGLU(FM) Johnstown PA 300 w, 1,043 ft.
WSNU(FM) Lock Haven PA 3 kw, 255 ft.
WSRT(FM) Mercersburg PA 3.3 kw, 295 ft.
WYOS(FM) Nanticoke PA 760 w, 663 ft.
WCTX(FM) Palmyra PA 3 kw, 300 ft.
*WXJX(FM) Washington PA 10 w, 59 ft.
WEGM(FM) Hormigueros PR 3 kw, 581 ft.
WWBD(FM) Bamberg SC 3 kw, 300 ft.
WJYR(FM) Myrtle Beach SC 50 kw, 325 ft.
WOCW(FM) Parris Island SC 3 kw, 284 ft.
WJRQ(FM) Saluda SC 3 kw, 328 ft.
KZNC(FM) Huron SD 3 kw, 184 ft.
WQQK(FM) Hendersonville TN 3 kw, 462 ft.
WYBM(FM) Minor Hill TN 1.2 kw, 460 ft.
KQNN(FM) Alice TX 3 kw, 300 ft.
KCZO(FM) Carrizo Springs TX 3 kw, 296 ft.
KTSR(FM) College Station TX 3 kw, 275 ft.
KEMM(FM) Commerce TX 3 kw, 300 ft.
KTXX(FM) Devine TX 3 kw, 299 ft.
KNES(FM) Fairfield TX 940 w, 500 ft.
KRGT(FM) Hutto TX 3 kw, 300 ft.
KNBT(FM) New Braunfels TX 3 kw, 300 ft.
KRTS(FM) Seabrook TX 33 kw, 630 ft.
KHOS-FM Sonora TX 3 kw, 300 ft.
KDOK(FM) Tyler TX 3 kw, 280 ft.
KTLE-FM Tooele UT 1.4 kw, minus 35 ft.
WDYL(FM) Chester VA 3 kw, 356 ft.
*WWHS-FM Hampden-Sydney VA 10 w, 140 ft.
WMOO(FM) Derby Center VT 2.25 kw, 619 ft.
KCRK-FM Colville WA 3 kw, minus 780 ft.
WLTU(FM) Manitowoc WI 1.69 kw, 500 ft.
WRJC-FM Mauston WI 1.8 kw, 600 ft.
WMEQ-FM Menomonie WI 1.3 kw, 490 ft.
WHKQ(FM) Racine WI 6 kw, 275 ft.
WMAD-FM Sun Prairie WI 1.75 kw, 400 ft.
*WVWC(FM) Buckhannon WV 10 w, 85 ft.

92.3 mhz (ch 222)

WLWI-FM Montgomery AL 100 kw, 1,095 ft.
KIPR(FM) Pine Bluff AR 100 kw, 938 ft.
KWCD(FM) Bisbee AZ 51 w, 2,217 ft.
KKFR(FM) Glendale AZ 100 kw, 1,646 ft.
KRED-FM Eureka CA 25 kw, 1,544 ft.
KKBT(FM) Los Angeles CA 43 kw, 2,910 ft.
KSJO(FM) San Jose CA 50 kw, 464 ft.
KJYE-FM Grand Junction CO 100 kw, 1,378 ft.
WCMQ-FM Hialeah FL 31 kw, 617 ft.
WWKA(FM) Orlando FL 100 kw, 1,380 ft.
WMOQ(FM) Bostwick GA 3 kw, 328 ft.
WYFZ(FM) Evans GA 3 kw, 328 ft.
WSKX(FM) Hinesville GA 50 kw, 482 ft.
WMKS(FM) Macon GA 3 kw, 328 ft.
KSSK-FM Waipahu HI 100 kw, 1,630 ft.
KOEL-FM Oelwein IA 100 kw, 1,000 ft.
KIZN(FM) Boise ID 44 kw, 2,500 ft.
WBGE(FM) Peoria IL 6 kw, 148 ft.
WTTS(FM) Bloomington IN 37 kw, 1,090 ft.
WFWI(FM) Fort Wayne IN 1.9 kw, 400 ft.
WYCA(FM) Hammond IN 50 kw H, 44 kw V, 492 ft.
KOEZ(FM) Newton KS 100 kw, 650 ft.
KCCV-FM Olathe KS 3 kw, 328 ft.
WSAC(FM) Louisa KY 4.48 kw, 377 ft.
WCKW-FM La Place LA 100 kw, 2,000 ft.
KTJC(FM) Rayville LA 26 kw, 492 ft.
WERQ-FM Baltimore MD 37 kw, 571 ft.
WXIE(FM) Oakland MD 1.4 w, 689 ft.
WMME-FM Augusta ME 50 kw, 500 ft.
WKGH(FM) Allegan MI 860 w, 600 ft.
WMXD(FM) Detroit MI 21.5 kw-H, 16.5 kw-V, 699 ft.
WJPD(FM) Ishpeming MI 100 kw, 469 ft.
KXRA-FM Alexandria MN 13.5 kw, 446 ft.
KKOZ-FM Ava MO 6 kw, 381 ft.
KBUG(FM) Osceola MO 3.2 kw, 259 ft.
*KGSP(FM) Parkville MO 10 w, 100 ft.
WIL-FM St. Louis MO 99 kw, 984 ft.
KQRK(FM) Ronan MT 60 kw, 3,500 ft.
WKRR(FM) Asheboro NC 100 kw, 1,275 ft.
WFXZ(FM) Jacksonville NC 35 kw, 236 ft.
KEZO-FM Omaha NE 100 kw, 1,250 ft.
WGXL(FM) Hanover NH 3 kw, 326 ft.
KRST(FM) Albuquerque NM 22.5 kw, 4.110 ft.
KOMP(FM) Las Vegas NV 100 kw, 1,520 ft.
WXRK(FM) New York NY 7.6 kw h, 5.4 kw v, 1,220 ft.
WFLY(FM) Troy NY 17 kw, 850 ft.
WJMO-FM Cleveland Heights OH 40 kw, 548 ft.
WCOL-FM Columbus OH 22 kw, 754 ft.
KYUC(FM) Roland OK 930 w, 571 ft.
KGON(FM) Portland OR 100 kw, 920 ft.
*WKVR-FM Huntingdon PA 10 w, minus 376 ft.
WMPA(FM) Mansfield PA 540 w, 764 ft.
WLGL(FM) Riverside PA 440 w, 833 ft.
WRRN(FM) Warren PA 50 kw, 410 ft.
WPRO-FM Providence RI 39 kw, 550 ft.
WDEF-FM Chattanooga TN 100 kw, 1,180 ft.
WYNU(FM) Milan TN 100 kw, 991 ft.
KOFX(FM) El Paso TX 100 kw, 1,860 ft.
KIJN-FM Farwell TX 100 kw, 433 ft.
KITE(FM) Kerrville TX 3 kw, 299 ft.
KIIZ-FM Killeen TX 3 kw, 259 ft.
KETX-FM Livingston TX 50 kw, 699 ft.
KCUL-FM Marshall TX 3 kw, 328 ft.
KNFM(FM) Midland TX 100 kw, 985 ft.
KVLT(FM) Victoria TX 3 kw, 298 ft.
WLUD(FM) Deltaville VA 3 kw, 328 ft.
WXLK(FM) Roanoke VA 93 kw, 2,050 ft.
WDCM(FM) Cruz Bay VI 48 kw, 1,302 ft.
WJMQ(FM) Clintonville WI 6 kw, 328 ft.
WRLS-FM Hayward WI 6 kw, 321 ft.
WOSX(FM) Spencer WI 6 kw, 300 ft.

92.5 mhz (ch 223)

WAZK(FM) Trinity AL 3.1 kw, 423 ft.
KWYN-FM Wynne AR 25 kw, 328 ft.
KVRQ(FM) Atwater CA 6 kw, 328 ft.
KDDB(FM) Paso Robles CA 17 kw, 760 ft.
KGBY(FM) Sacramento CA 50 kw, 499 ft.
KZDG(FM) Greeley CO 57 kw, 1,237 ft.
WWYZ(FM) Waterbury CT 17.8 kw, 879 ft.
WEOW(FM) Key West FL 100 kw, 600 ft.
WPAP-FM Panama City FL 100 kw, 930 ft.
WYUU(FM) Safety Harbor FL 50 kw, 489 ft.
WOKF(FM) Folkston GA 6 kw, 324 ft.
KJJY-FM Ankeny IA 41 kw, 541 ft.
KKMV(FM) Rupert ID 53 kw, 2,466 ft.
WDEK(FM) De Kalb IL 20 kw, 495 ft.
WKIO(FM) Urbana IL 3 kw, 145 ft.
KQMA-FM Phillipsburg KS 100 kw, 510 ft.
KWIC(FM) Topeka KS 6 kw, 292 ft.
WBKR(FM) Owensboro KY 91 kw, 1,049 ft.
KVPI-FM Ville Platte LA 3 kw-H, 220 ft.
WLYT(FM) Haverhill MA 25 kw, 710 ft.
WJSZ(FM) Ashley MI 3 kw, 328 ft.
WAIR(FM) Atlanta MI 100 kw, 868 ft.
WBGV(FM) Marlette MI 3 kw, 328 ft.
KQRS-FM Golden Valley MN 100 kw, 900 ft.
KKWQ(FM) Warroad MN 100 kw, 472 ft.
*KSMR(FM) Winona MN 4 w, -141 ft.
KTDI(FM) Huntsville MO 6 kw, 328 ft.
KSYN(FM) Joplin MO 100 kw, 430 ft.
KAYX(FM) Richmond MO 6 kw, 500 ft.
WQST-FM Forest MS 100 kw, 1,040 ft.
WWXX(FM) Ocean Springs MS
KPQX(FM) Havre MT 100 kw, 1,485 ft.
KMCM-FM Miles City MT 100 kw, 628 ft.
XHRM-FM Tijuana MX 50 kw, 650 ft.
WYFL(FM) Henderson NC 100 kw, 1,020 ft.
WNHW(FM) Nags Head NC 18.5 kw, 203 ft.
WBEE-FM Rochester NY 50 kw, 500 ft.
WZKL(FM) Alliance OH 50 kw, 500 ft.
WIMJ(FM) Cincinnati OH 16 kw, 910 ft.
WVKS(FM) Toledo OH 50 kw, 480 ft.
KPRV-FM Heavener OK 790 w, 640 ft.
KOMA-FM Oklahoma City OK 98 kw, 984 ft.
KLAD-FM Klamath Falls OR 63 kw, 2,188 ft.
WJUN-FM Mexico PA 3 kw, 1,302 ft.
WXTU(FM) Philadelphia PA 15.5 kw, 900 ft.
WKGB-FM Susquehanna PA 6 kw, 709 ft.
WORO(FM) Corozal PR 50 kw, 1,197 ft.
WESC-FM Greenville SC 100 kw, 2,000 ft.
WHLZ(FM) Manning SC 100 kw, 1,207 ft.
KELO-FM Sioux Falls SD 100 kw, 1,900 ft.
KFXJ(FM) Abilene TX 50 kw, 492 ft.
KBLK(FM) Burnet TX 3 kw, 299 ft.
KZPS(FM) Dallas TX 100 kw, 1,590 ft.
KKLB(FM) Elgin TX 1.6 kw, 449 ft.
KTFA(FM) Groves TX 50 kw, 440 ft.
KMBV(FM) Navasota TX 6 kw, 263 ft.
KCOT(FM) San Augustine TX 150 w, 139 ft.
KYOC(FM) Yoakum TX 3 kw, 300 ft.
KSSD(FM) Cedar City UT 41.6 kw, 1,690 ft.
KCUA(FM) Coalville UT 110 w, minus 1,059 ft.
WINC-FM Winchester VA 22 kw, 1,424 ft.
KLSY-FM Bellevue WA 58 kw, 2,342 ft.
KZHR(FM) Dayton WA 54 kw, 1,243 ft.
WJJQ-FM Tomahawk WI 25 kw, 259 ft.
WBWI-FM West Bend WI 20 kw, 530 ft.

Broadcasting & Cable Yearbook 1994
B-507

U.S. FM Stations by Frequency

WZAC-FM Danville WV 610 w, 697 ft.
KLZY(FM) Powell WY 100 kw, 1,857 ft.

92.7 mhz (ch 224)
WCRQ-FM Arab AL 700 w, 670 ft.
WULA-FM Eufaula AL 3 kw, 328 ft.
WJBB-FM Haleyville AL 3.9 kw, 240 ft.
WEYY-FM Talladega AL 250 w, 870 ft.
KLYR-FM Clarksville AR 3 kw, 292 ft.
KTOD-FM Conway AR 3 kw, 282 ft.
KDQN-FM De Queen AR 3 kw, 220 ft.
KYXK(FM) Gurdon AR 3 kw, 298 ft.
KJAZ(FM) Alameda CA 1.8 kw, 370 ft.
KRCI(FM) Avalon CA 3 kw, 161 ft.
KCMJ(FM) Indio CA 3 kw, 298 ft.
KBOQ(FM) Marina CA 6.9 kw, 567 ft.
KMFB(FM) Mendocino CA 3 kw, 165 ft.
KZIQ(FM) Ridgecrest CA 1.5 kw, 1,296 ft.
KOOJ(FM) Riverside CA 3 kw, 298 ft.
KZSQ(FM) Sonora CA 380 w, 1,289 ft.
KNJO(FM) Thousand Oaks CA 560 w, 630 ft.
KMTS(FM) Glenwood Springs CO 3 kw, minus 301 ft.
KCRT-FM Trinidad CO 3 kw, 150 ft.
WGMD(FM) Rehoboth Beach DE 3 kw, 300 ft.
WJBT(FM) Green Cove Springs FL 6 kw, 300 ft.
WGUF(FM) Marco FL 4.1 kw, 328 ft.
WZZR(FM) Stuart FL 50 kw, 571 ft.
WKKZ(FM) Dublin GA 50 kw, 417 ft.
WMOG-FM St. Simons Island GA 6 kw, 340 ft.
KAOE(FM) Hilo HI 16 kw, -157 ft.
KLGA(FM) Algona IA 50 kw, 226 ft.
KTWA(FM) Ottumwa IA 3 kw, 328 ft.
KORT-FM Grangeville ID 362 w, 2,352 ft.
KSRA(FM) Salmon ID 1.5 kw, minus 880 ft.
WRAJ-FM Anna IL 3 kw, 290 ft.
WCBR-FM Arlington Heights IL 3 kw, 299 ft.
WGBQ(FM) Galesburg IL 3 kw, 355 ft.
WVZA(FM) Herrin IL 6 kw, 325 ft.
WLRT(FM) Kankakee IL 3 kw, 300 ft.
WQLZ(FM) Taylorville IL 2.7 kw, 300 ft.
WJLR(FM) Austin IN 3.9 kw, 400 ft.
WZBD(FM) Berne IN 2.05 kw, 394 ft.
WZWZ(FM) Kokomo IN 3 kw, 298 ft.
WSKT(FM) Spencer IN 1 kw, 480 ft.
KOUY(FM) Belle Plaine KS 4.6 kw, 754 ft.
KILS(FM) Minneapolis KS 50 kw, 492 ft.
WCMI-FM Catlettsburg KY 3 kw, 298 ft.
WMIK-FM Middlesboro KY 130 w, 1,438 ft.
WTCO-FM Russell Springs KY 6 kw, 328 ft.
WQCK(FM) Clinton LA 32 kw, 604 ft.
KWJM(FM) Farmerville LA 6 kw, 328 ft.
KLPL-FM Lake Providence LA 2 kw, 144 ft.
KJAE(FM) Leesville LA 3 kw, 164 ft.
KDXI(FM) Mansfield LA 3 kw, 299 ft.
KTKC(FM) Springhill LA 3 kw, 174 ft.
WMVY(FM) Tisbury MA 3 kw, 300 ft.
WMJS(FM) Prince Frederick MD 2.1 kw, 565 ft.
WQDY(FM) Calais ME 3 kw, 299 ft.
WOXO(FM) Norway ME 2 kw, 360 ft.
WMMQ(FM) Charlotte MI 1.5 kw, 466 ft.
WDZZ-FM Flint MI 3 kw, 260 ft.
WEVS(FM) Saugatuck MI 2.15 kw, 387 ft.
KLOZ(FM) Eldon MO 50 kw, 590 ft.
KMAL(FM) Malden MO 3 kw, 193 ft.
KSJQ(FM) Savannah MO 50 kw, 492 ft.
WDTL-FM Cleveland MS 3 kw, 262 ft.
WKRA-FM Holly Springs MS 3 kw, 299 ft.
KAAR(FM) Butte MT 3 kw, 24 ft.
KVCK-FM Wolf Point MT 860 w, 508 ft.
KSSZ-FM Oakes ND 4 kw, 151 ft.
KBRB-FM Ainsworth NE 4.5 kw, 331 ft.
WOBM-FM Toms River NJ 1.4 kw, 485 ft.
KPSA-FM La Luz NM 3 kw, 192 ft.
KMXQ(FM) Socorro NM 3 kw, -234 ft.
KQAY-FM Tucumcari NM 3 kw, 64 ft.
KDSS(FM) Ely NV 320 w, 941 ft.
KHWK(FM) Tonopah NV 1 kw, 970 ft.
KWNA-FM Winnemucca NV 60 w, 2,120 ft.
WENY-FM Elmira NY 700 w, 561 ft.
WDRE-FM Garden City NY 1 kw, 521 ft.
WYUT-FM Herkimer NY 3 kw, 299 ft.
WKOJ(FM) Middletown NY 3 kw, 300 ft.
WPAC(FM) Ogdensburg NY 3 kw, 310 ft.
WQEL(FM) Bucyrus OH 3 kw, 300 ft.
*WCVZ(FM) Zanesville OH 3 kw, 304 ft.
KKBS(FM) Guymon OK 11.5 kw, 485 ft.
KGBR(FM) Gold Beach OR 265 w, 1,030 ft.
KCLM(FM) Newport OR 12 kw, 472 ft.
WCCR(FM) Clarion PA 3 kw, 400 ft.
WJSM-FM Martinsburg PA 330 w, 984 ft.
WHTF(FM) Starview PA 1.42 kw, 199 ft.
WKSX(FM) Johnston SC 3 kw, 268 ft.
KGFX-FM Pierre SD 3 kw, 245 ft.
WLIQ(FM) Harriman TN 1.25 kw, 440 ft.
KALP(FM) Alpine TX 2.37 kw, 328 ft.
KIVY-FM Crockett TX 50 kw, 497 ft.
KINL(FM) Eagle Pass TX 3 kw, 255 ft.
KNGV(FM) Kingsville TX 3 kw, 210 ft.
KJBZ(FM) Laredo TX 3 kw, 289 ft.
KJAK(FM) Slaton TX 100 kw, 584 ft.
KJIB(FM) South Padre Island TX 3 kw, 279 ft.
WABN(FM) Abingdon VA 1.8 kw, 371 ft.
WUVA(FM) Charlottesville VA 220 w, 3,000 ft.
WCDX(FM) Mechanicsville VA 2.35 kw, 367 ft.
WKVT-FM Brattleboro VT 6 kw, 610 ft.
KOMW-FM Omak WA 3 kw, -836 ft.
WAUN(FM) Kewaunee WI 3 kw, 300 ft.
WDUX-FM Waupaca WI 6 kw, 255 ft.
WVHF-FM Clarksburg WV 660 w, 600 ft.

WPMW(FM) Mullens WV 1.65 kw, 443 ft.
WLGT(FM) Buffalo WY 3 kw, 26 ft.
KIQZ(FM) Rawlins WY 3 kw, 298 ft.

92.9 mhz (ch 225)
WBLX-FM Mobile AL 98 kw, 1,555 ft.
WTUG-FM Tuscaloosa AL 6 kw, 328 ft.
KAFF-FM Flagstaff AZ 100 kw, 1,512 ft.
KRQQ(FM) Tucson AZ 90 kw, 2,037 ft.
KVVV(FM) Healdsburg CA 2.3 kw, 1,800 ft.
KJEE(FM) Montecito CA 363 w, 827 ft.
KWXH(FM) Sun City CA 370 w
KFSO-FM Visalia CA 18.5 kw-H, 17 kw-V, 820 ft.
KSPZ(FM) Colorado Springs CO 53 kw, 2,130 ft.
WYHH(FM) Smyrna DE 1.7 kw, 377 ft.
WMFQ(FM) Ocala FL 50 kw, 476 ft.
WIKX(FM) Punta Gorda FL 50 kw, 361 ft.
WZGC(FM) Atlanta GA 100 kw, 910 ft.
WAAC(FM) Valdosta GA 100 kw, 509 ft.
KATF(FM) Dubuque IA 100 kw, 999 ft.
KIDA-FM Ida Grove IA 16 kw, 295 ft.
WSEI(FM) Olney IL 50 kw, 552 ft.
WNDU-FM South Bend IN 12.5 kw, 800 ft.
KZOC(FM) Osage City KS 50 kw, 480 ft.
WVLK-FM Lexington KY 100 kw, 854 ft.
KJEF-FM Jennings LA 33 kw, 600 ft.
WBOX-FM Varnado LA 3 kw, 321 ft.
WBOS(FM) Brookline MA 8.8 kw, 1,100 ft.
WEZQ(FM) Bangor ME 20 kw, 787 ft.
WKJF-FM Cadillac MI 100 kw-H, 895 ft.
*WSCD-FM Duluth MN 70 kw, 614 ft.
KKJM(FM) St. Joseph MN 25 kw, 328 ft.
KGRC(FM) Hannibal MO 100 kw, 490 ft.
KZPF(FM) Ozark MO 3 kw, 328 ft.
WJXN-FM Utica MS 6 kw, 465 ft.
KLFM(FM) Great Falls MT 100 kw, 450 ft.
KYYY(FM) Bismarck ND 100 kw, 1,180 ft.
KKXL(FM) Grand Forks ND 63 kw, 385 ft.
KTGL(FM) Beatrice NE 100 kw, 809 ft.
KMOR(FM) Scottsbluff NE 100 kw, 1,023 ft.
KTZA(FM) Artesia NM 100 kw, 1,089 ft.
KRWN(FM) Farmington NM 30 kw, 430 ft.
KLSC(FM) Socorro NM 6 kw, minus 177 ft.
KZSR(FM) Reno NV 45 kw, 2,653 ft.
WBUF(FM) Buffalo NY 93 kw, 580 ft.
WGTZ(FM) Eaton OH 31.6 kw, 600 ft.
KBEZ(FM) Tulsa OK 100 kw, 1,319 ft.
KAST-FM Astoria OR 99 kw, 541 ft.
WVCV(FM) Boalsburg PA 265 w, 1,102 ft.
WLTJ(FM) Pittsburgh PA 47 kw, 890 ft.
WMGS(FM) Wilkes-Barre PA 5.3 kw, 1,384 ft.
WTPM(FM) Aguadilla PR 50 kw, 1,223 ft.
WZLA-FM Abbeville SC 6 kw, 243 ft.
WZNS(FM) Dillon SC 100 kw, 1,801 ft.
KSDR-FM Watertown SD 97 kw, 977 ft.
WJWL(FM) Bartlett TN 6 kw, 328 ft.
WZEZ(FM) Nashville TN 100 kw, 1,086 ft.
WNPC-FM Newport TN 3.1 kw, 459 ft.
KEYR(FM) Marlin TX 3 kw, 300 ft.
KKBQ(FM) Pasadena TX 100 kw, 1,919 ft.
KDCD(FM) San Angelo TX 100 kw, 729 ft.
KROM(FM) San Antonio TX 100 kw, 1,016 ft.
KNIN-FM Wichita Falls TX 100 kw, 930 ft.
KBLQ-FM Logan UT 50 kw, 154 ft.
WFOG(FM) Suffolk VA 50 kw, 480 ft.
WEZF(FM) Burlington VT 46 kw, 2,703 ft.
KISM(FM) Bellingham WA 50 kw, 2,440 ft.
KZZU-FM Spokane WA 81 kw, 2,080 ft.
KXXS(FM) Toppenish WA 17 kw, 843 ft.
WHET(FM) Birnamwood WI 6 kw, 100 ft.
WECL(FM) Elk Mound WI 3.3 kw, 446 ft.
WCWV(FM) Summersville WV 11 kw, 900 ft.

93.1 mhz (ch 226)
WGMZ(FM) Glencoe AL 1.55 kw, 636 ft.
KZLE(FM) Batesville AR 100 kw, 984 ft.
*KHDX(FM) Conway AR 8 w, 59 ft.
KJOK(FM) Yuma AZ 100 kw, 80 ft.
KXGO(FM) Arcata CA 93 kw, 1,640 ft.
KCBS-FM Los Angeles CA 54 kw, 5,000 ft.
KOSO(FM) Patterson CA 2.95 kw, 1,791 ft.
KQIX-FM Grand Junction CO 100 kw, minus 95 ft.
WEDG(FM) Edgewater FL 3 kw, 328 ft.
WTMI(FM) Miami FL 96 kw, 1,040 ft.
WEAS-FM Savannah GA 100 kw, 310 ft.
KQMQ-FM Honolulu HI 54 kw, minus 119 ft.
KZMG(FM) New Plymouth ID 50 kw, 2,630 ft.
WXRT(FM) Chicago IL 6.7 kw, 1,310 ft.
WYDS(FM) Decatur IL 6 kw, 328 ft.
WKLR(FM) Indianapolis IN 12.5 kw, 1,023 ft.
KGLS(FM) Pratt KS 100 kw, 1,007 ft.
WMKZ(FM) Monticello KY 2.15 kw, 558 ft.
KQID(FM) Alexandria LA 100 kw, 1,700 ft.
WHYN-FM Springfield MA 8.9 kw, 1,000 ft.
WPOC(FM) Baltimore MD 16 kw, 860 ft.
WMGX(FM) Portland ME 50 kw, 443 ft.
WLTI(FM) Detroit MI 26.5 kw, 669 ft.
WIMK(FM) Iron Mountain MI 100 kw, 590 ft.
KXLP(FM) New Ulm MN 100 kw, 489 ft.
KYOO-FM Halfway MO 2.36 kw, 367 ft.
KBDZ(FM) Perryville MO 1.6 kw, 623 ft.
WMQX-FM Winston-Salem NC 100 kw, 1,050 ft.
KRVN-FM Lexington NE 100 kw, 320 ft.
WPAT-FM Paterson NJ 5.3 kw, 1,210 ft.
WDOX(FM) Wildwood Crest NJ 3.3 kw, 291 ft.
KEYV(FM) Las Vegas NV 24.5 w, 3,724 ft.
WNTQ(FM) Syracuse NY 97 kw, 659 ft.
WZAK(FM) Cleveland OH 27.5 kw, 620 ft.
WYRX(FM) Lima OH 3 kw, 328 ft.

KKNU(FM) Springfield-Eugene OR 100 kw-horiz, 33.3 kw-vert, 985 ft.
WMHU(FM) Renovo PA 3 kw, 328 ft.
WKWQ(FM) Batesburg SC 6 kw, 400 ft.
KRCS(FM) Sturgis SD 100 kw, 1,059 ft.
WWGM(FM) Alamo TN 25 kw, 328 ft.
WBIN-FM Benton TN 6 kw, 307 ft.
WWZZ(FM) Karns TN 1.2 kw, 515 ft.
KQIZ-FM Amarillo TX 100 kw, 700 ft.
KAMZ(FM) El Paso TX 100 kw, 1,422 ft.
KTYL-FM Tyler TX 100 kw, 459 ft.
WDIC-FM Clinchco VA 2.5 kw, 505 ft.
WKDW-FM Staunton VA 2.8 kw, 338 ft.
WJBL(FM) Ladysmith WI 4.9 kw, 358 ft.
KFKQ(FM) New Holstein WI 6 kw, 328 ft.
WMMN-FM Barrackville WV 6 kw, 497 ft.
WFYZ(FM) Ravenswood WV 3.3 kw, 446 ft.
KTRZ(FM) Riverton WY 100 kw, 884 ft.

93.3 mhz (ch 227)
WPGG(FM) Evergreen AL 50 kw, 406 ft.
KISQ(FM) El Dorado AR 8.5 kw, 426 ft.
KBOK(FM) Malvern AR 5.8 kw, 215 ft.
KDKB(FM) Mesa-Phoenix AZ 100 kw, 1,538 ft.
KBHR(FM) Big Bear City CA 3 kw, 299 ft.
KRHU(FM) Big Pine CA
KXDA(FM) Chowchilla CA 2.95 kw, 335 ft.
KECR-FM El Cajon CA 2 kw, 1,850 ft.
KYA(FM) San Francisco CA 50 kw, 492 ft.
KZOZ(FM) San Luis Obispo CA 29.5 kw, 1,470 ft.
KJDX(FM) Susanville CA 100 kw, 1,155 ft.
KTCL(FM) Fort Collins CO 100 kw, 1,328 ft.
KSEC(FM) Lamar CO 100 kw, 498 ft.
*WFAR(FM) Danbury CT 18 w, 210 ft.
WAIA(FM) Callahan FL 50 kw, 462 ft.
WGWD(FM) Gretna FL 3 kw, 328 ft.
WBNF(FM) Marianna FL 3 kw, 328 ft.
WFLZ-FM Tampa FL 99 kw, 1,358 ft.
WVFJ-FM Manchester GA 100 kw, 1,250 ft.
KIOA-FM Des Moines IA 100 kw, 1,063 ft.
WKZW(FM) Peoria IL 41 kw, 548 ft.
*WJLY(FM) Ramsey IL 3 kw, 328 ft.
WBTU(FM) Kendallville IN 50 kw, 450 ft.
WQTY(FM) Linton IN 12 kw, 475 ft.
WKYQ(FM) Paducah KY 89 kw, 440 ft.
WQUE-FM New Orleans LA 93 kw, 459 ft.
WSNE(FM) Taunton MA 50 kw, 620 ft.
WKQZ(FM) Midland MI 39.2 kw, 554 ft.
KZPX(FM) Nisswa MN 100 kw, 768 ft.
KMXV(FM) Kansas City MO 100 kw, 1,066 ft.
KESE(FM) Seligman MO 100 kw, 492 ft.
WSYE(FM) Houston MS 100 kw, 1,804 ft.
KYYA(FM) Billings MT 100 kw, 700 ft.
KDXT(FM) Missoula MT 43 kw, 2,440 ft.
WBBO-FM Forest City NC 87.2 kw, 2,030 ft.
WDLN(FM) Washington NC 100 kw, 1,940 ft.
KSJZ(FM) Jamestown ND 57 kw, 256 ft.
KRRK(FM) Bennington NE 6 kw, 350 ft.
WCNH(FM) Belmont NH 300 w, 1020 ft.
KKOB-FM Albuquerque NM 21.5 kw, 4,150 ft.
WEZO(FM) Avon NY 2.1 kw, 381 ft.
*WCAN(FM) Canajoharie NY 6 kw, 268 ft.
WWSE(FM) Jamestown NY 26.5 kw, 643 ft.
WBWZ(FM) New Paltz NY 350 w, 1328 ft.
WKKJ(FM) Chillicothe OH 50 kw, 335 ft.
WAKW(FM) Cincinnati OH 50 kw, 500 ft.
WBBG(FM) Youngstown OH 50 kw, 280 ft.
KTLS(FM) Ada OK 100 kw, 630 ft.
WQZS(FM) Meyersdale PA 630 w, 964 ft.
WMMR(FM) Philadelphia PA 18 kw, 827 ft.
WOQI(FM) Ponce PR 14.5 kw, minus 225 ft.
WHVK(FM) Tullahoma TN 100 kw, 981 ft.
*KRSM(FM) Dallas TX 33 w-H, 148 ft.
KHHT(FM) Killeen TX 100 kw, 1,948 ft.
KBAT(FM) Midland TX 100 kw, 500 ft.
KLTN(FM) Port Arthur TX 100 kw, 420 ft.
KPLV(FM) Port Lavaca TX 100 kw, 450 ft.
KLZX-FM Salt Lake City UT 26 kw, 3,740 ft.
WFLS-FM Fredericksburg VA 50 kw, 492 ft.
KUBE(FM) Seattle WA 100 kw, 1,291 ft.
WBSZ(FM) Ashland WI 100 kw, 299 ft.
WIZM-FM La Crosse WI 100 kw, 1,000 ft.
WQFM(FM) Milwaukee WI 12.6 kw, 992 ft.
WZKM(FM) Montgomery WV 400 w, 715 ft.

93.5 mhz (ch 228)
WQGL(FM) Butler AL 3 kw, 299 ft.
WRJM-FM Geneva AL 3 kw, 225 ft.
KBKG(FM) Corning AR 3 kw, 138 ft.
KBFC(FM) Forrest City AR 25 kw, 340 ft.
KHBM-FM Monticello AR 3.2 kw, 341 ft.
KXAZ(FM) Page AZ 1.15 kw, 480 ft.
KVWM-FM Show Low AZ 3 kw, 150 ft.
KNKD(FM) Earlimart CA 3 kw, 328 ft.
KMXZ(FM) Hollister CA 116 w, 1,519 ft.
KREA(FM) Ontario CA 3 kw, minus 165 ft.
KFOX(FM) Redondo Beach CA 3 kw, 175 ft.
KLKX(FM) Rosamond CA 3 kw, 207 ft.
KKBN(FM) Twain Harte CA 258 w, 1,630 ft.
KALQ-FM Alamosa CO 2.8 kw, 130 ft.
KRMH(FM) Leadville CO 3 kw, 300 ft.
WZBH(FM) Georgetown DE 11.5 kw, 550 ft.
WBGF(FM) Belle Glade FL 3 kw, 285 ft.
WKRY(FM) Key West FL 31.5 kw, 1,148 ft.
WNOG-FM Naples FL 3 kw, 299 ft.
WMTO(FM) Port St. Joe FL 1.3 kw, 659 ft.
WBBK(FM) Blakely GA 3 kw, 328 ft.
WLJA-FM Ellijay GA 5.2 kw, 272 ft.
WVOH-FM Hazlehurst GA 3 kw, 320 ft.
KPOA(FM) Lahaina HI 1.4 kw, 1,305 ft.

U.S. FM Stations by Frequency

KQNG-FM Lihue HI 100 kw, 226 ft.
KQCS(FM) Bettendorf IA 3.3 kw, 300 ft.
KKMI(FM) Burlington IA 3.0 kw, 300 ft.
WJTW(FM) Joliet IL 3 kw, 259 ft.
WUBB(FM) Tuscola IL 3 kw, 148 ft.
WWWO(FM) Hartford City IN 3.04 kw, 456 ft.
WKHY(FM) Lafayette IN 6 kw, 282 ft.
KOTE(FM) Eureka KS 3 kw, 321 ft.
KLKC-FM Parsons KS 3 kw, 267 ft.
KWME(FM) Wellington KS 3 kw, 200 ft.
WMMG-FM Brandenburg KY 3.4 kw, 290 ft.
WAIN-FM Columbia KY 4.7 kw, 220 ft.
KKRP(FM) Delhi LA 3 kw, 328 ft.
WFXR(FM) Harwichport MA 3 kw, 328 ft.
WCTB(FM) Fairfield ME 13.5 kw, 440 ft.
WBCM(FM) Boyne City MI 14.1 kw, 928 ft.
WZRK(FM) Hancock MI 3 kw-H, 249 ft.
WHMI-FM Howell MI 3 kw, 300 ft.
KSCR-FM Benson MN 3 kw, 200 ft.
KYLC(FM) Osage Beach MO 3 kw, 300 ft.
KTRX(FM) Tarkio MO 6 kw, 235 ft.
WIZK-FM Bay Springs MS 3 kw, 328 ft.
WHJT(FM) Clinton MS 3 kw, 300 ft.
KLAN(FM) Glasgow MT 3 kw, 300 ft.
WRPL(FM) Wadesboro NC 3 kw, 328 ft.
KKOT(FM) Columbus NE 1 kw, 981 ft.
WMWV(FM) Conway NH 3 kw, 420 ft.
KWES(FM) Ruidoso NM 25 kw, 58 ft.
KLKO(FM) Elko NV 3 kw, minus 314 ft.
WRVW(FM) Hudson NY 3 kw, minus 15 ft.
WVBR-FM Ithaca NY 3 kw, 250 ft.
WRTN(FM) New Rochelle NY 3 kw, 325 ft.
WUUU(FM) Remsen NY 6 kw, 300 ft.
WTNY(FM) Watertown NY 4 kw, 330 ft.
WJQZ(FM) Wellsville NY 3 kw, 466 ft.
WBNV(FM) Barnesville OH 6 kw, 489 ft.
WRQN(FM) Bowling Green OH 4.1 kw, 397 ft.
KRKZ(FM) Altus OK 45 kw, 528 ft.
KIMY(FM) Watonga OK 3 kw, 190 ft.
KWFX(FM) Woodward OK 3 kw, 150 ft.
KQIK-FM Lakeview OR 284 w, 1,000 ft.
WQYX(FM) Clearfield PA 3 kw, 98 ft.
WJSA-FM Jersey Shore PA 3 kw, 144 ft.
WTPA(FM) Mechanicsburg PA 1.75 kw, 620 ft.
WSBG(FM) Stroudsburg PA 550 w, 764 ft.
WDOG-FM Allendale SC 3 kw, 300 ft.
WARQ(FM) Columbia SC 3 kw, 443 ft.
WWWZ(FM) Summerville SC 1.1 kw, 459 ft.
WKBL-FM Covington TN 6 kw, 328 ft.
WLIL-FM Lenoir City TN 6 kw, 165 ft.
WKWX-FM Savannah TN 6 kw, 300 ft.
KROO(FM) Breckenridge TX 3 kw, 268 ft.
KBHT(FM) Crockett TX 50 kw, 479 ft.
KIKT(FM) Greenville TX 3 kw, 300 ft.
KZEZ(FM) St. George UT 3 kw, -125 ft.
WAXM(FM) Big Stone Gap VA 2.45 kw, 1,883 ft.
WBBC-FM Blackstone VA 1.8 kw, 370 ft.
WJLM(FM) Salem VA 5.8 kw, 98 ft.
WAVI(FM) Christiansted VI 6 kw, 732 ft.
WCFR-FM Springfield VT 3 kw, 300 ft.
KOZI-FM Chelan WA 590 w, 1,040 ft.
WOZZ(FM) New London WI 50 kw, 528 ft.
WCST-FM Berkeley Springs WV 3 kw, 70 ft.
WBTQ(FM) Buckhannon WV 2.75 kw, 538 ft.

93.7 mhz (ch 229)

WDJC(FM) Birmingham AL 100 kw, 1,007 ft.
KISR(FM) Fort Smith AR 100 kw, 1,250 ft.
KXHW(FM) Marked Tree AR 3 kw, 288 ft.
KWFM-FM Tucson AZ 91 kw, 2,030 ft.
KMEO(FM) Wickenburg AZ 1.4 kw, 659 ft.
KCLB-FM Coachella CA 26.5 kw, 640 ft.
KHIP(FM) Felton CA 656 w, 492 ft.
KSKS(FM) Fresno CA 68 kw, 1,912 ft.
KRXQ(FM) Roseville CA 25 kw, 324 ft.
KDB(FM) Santa Barbara CA 12.5 kw, 870 ft.
KRAI-FM Craig CO 100 kw, 980 ft.
WZMX(FM) Hartford CT 16 kw, 869 ft.
WSTW(FM) Wilmington DE 50 kw, 490 ft.
WMMZ(FM) Ocala FL 100 kw, 1,348 ft.
WGYL(FM) Vero Beach FL 50 kw, 475 ft.
WMGB(FM) Jeffersonville GA 50 kw, 490 ft.
KKRL(FM) Carroll IA 100 kw, 300 ft.
KZBQ-FM Pocatello ID 100 kw, 984 ft.
WQKC(FM) Seymour IN 25 kw, 699 ft.
KADF(FM) Horton KS 25 kw, 328 ft.
KYEZ(FM) Salina KS 100 kw, 510 ft.
WRVC-FM Ashland KY 100 kw, 741 ft.
KDEA(FM) New Iberia LA 34 kw, 590 ft.
KITT(FM) Shreveport LA 95 kw, 1,010 ft.
WCGY(FM) Lawrence MA 50 kw, 430 ft.
WBCT(FM) Grand Rapids MI 320 kw, 781 ft.
WNBY-FM Newberry MI 3.5 kw, 262 ft.
KRXX-FM Minneapolis MN 100 kw, 1,033 ft.
KTUF(FM) Kirksville MO 50 kw, 492 ft.
KSD-FM St. Louis MO 100 kw, 859 ft.
WQID(FM) Biloxi MS 100 kw, 300 ft.
WQLJ(FM) Oxford MS 25 kw, 328 ft.
KATH(FM) Bozeman MT 100 kw, 245 ft.
WKOC(FM) Elizabeth City NC 100 kw, 997 ft.
WDAY-FM Fargo ND 100 kw, 1,040 ft.
KIZZ(FM) Minot ND 98 kw, 571 ft.
KQNM(FM) Gallup NM 62 kw, 161 ft.
WRCD(FM) Clyde NY 2.3 kw, 364 ft.
WBLK(FM) Depew NY 50 kw, 400 ft.
WFCJ(FM) Miamisburg OH 50 kw, 492 ft.
WQIO(FM) Mount Vernon OH 37 kw, 565 ft.
KSPI-FM Stillwater OK 16 kw, 886 ft.
KTMT-FM Medford OR 31 kw, 7,580 ft.
KPDQ-FM Portland OR 97 kw, 1,269 ft.
WDLS(FM) Dallas PA 750 w, 679 ft.
WBZZ(FM) Pittsburgh PA 41 kw, 550 ft.
WZNT(FM) San Juan PR 50 kw, 280 ft.
WKHT(FM) Bishopville SC 3 kw, 328 ft.
WSCA(FM) Georgetown SC 3 kw, 328 ft.
WFBC-FM Greenville SC 100 kw, 1,850 ft.
WONO(FM) Walterboro SC 6 kw, 345 ft.
KBRK-FM Brookings SD 36 kw, 571 ft.
KWYR-FM Winner SD 100 kw, 560 ft.
WBXE(FM) Baxter TN 25 kw, 328 ft.
WYYB(FM) Dickson TN 6 kw, 215 ft.
WTKB-FM Huntingdon TN 6 kw, 328 ft.
KLBJ-FM Austin TX 100 kw, 1,050 ft.
KKRW(FM) Houston TX 100 kw, 1,779 ft.
KXTQ-FM Lubbock TX 100 kw, 740 ft.
KKWZ(FM) Richfield UT 35.7 kw, 3,014 ft.
WVXE(FM) Dillwyn VA 6 kw, 1,656 ft.
WAZR(FM) Woodstock VA 10 kw, -49 ft.
KDRK(FM) Spokane WA 56 kw, 2,380 ft.
WEKZ-FM Monroe WI 36 kw, 581 ft.
WXEC(FM) Nekoosa WI 3 kw, 164 ft.
WWJR(FM) Sheboygan WI 6 kw, 296 ft.

93.9 mhz (ch 230)

WFIX(FM) Rogersville AL 2.25 kw, 531 ft.
KMGN(FM) Flagstaff AZ 100 kw, 1,509 ft.
KFMF(FM) Chico CA 2 kw, 1,128 ft.
KLFA(FM) King City CA 5.4 kw, 719 ft.
KZLA-FM Los Angeles CA 18.5 kw horz, 16 kw vert, 3136 ft.
KRLT(FM) South Lake Tahoe CA 6 kw, minus 190 ft.
KILO(FM) Colorado Springs CO 83 kw, 2,110 ft.
WKYS(FM) Washington DC 24 kw, 707 ft.
WLVE(FM) Miami Beach FL 96 kw, 1,006 ft.
WGOR(FM) Martinez GA 25 kw, 328 ft.
WMTM-FM Moultrie GA 100 kw, 555 ft.
KUAM-FM Agana GU 2 kw, 950 ft.
KIKI(FM) Honolulu HI 100 kw, minus 144 ft.
KLUA(FM) Kailua-Kona HI 5.3 kw, 2,831 ft.
KIAI(FM) Mason City IA 100 kw, 790 ft.
WLIT-FM Chicago IL 4 kw, 1,581 ft.
WXTZ(FM) Noblesville IN
KDLE(FM) Andover KS 25 kw, 328 ft.
KDGB(FM) Dodge City KS 100 kw, 511 ft.
WJDJ(FM) Burnside KY 6 kw, 492 ft.
WKTG(FM) Madisonville KY 27.1 kw, 295 ft.
KFAD(FM) Alexandria LA 6 kw, 328 ft.
WXGL-FM Lewiston ME 27.5 kw, 633 ft.
WCLX(FM) Mio MI 50 kw, 433 ft.
KKRC(FM) Granite Falls MN 6 kw, 262 ft.
WTBX(FM) Hibbing MN 100 kw, 548 ft.
KACJ(FM) Boonville MO 6 kw, 328 ft.
KNCD(FM) Columbia MO 3 kw, 328 ft.
KIXQ(FM) Webb City MO 48 kw, 505 ft.
KSPQ(FM) West Plains MO 100 kw, 650 ft.
KZMI(FM) San Jose MP 300 ft.
WGRM-FM Greenwood MS 3 kw, 328 ft.
WLUE(FM) Pearl MS 6 kw, 328 ft.
WZZU(FM) Burlington-Graham NC 100 kw, 1,269 ft.
WDNY-FM Dansville NY 570 w, 741 ft.
*WNYC-FM New York NY 5.4 kw, 1,418 ft.
WKXZ(FM) Norwich NY 26 kw, 680 ft.
*WPLT(FM) Plattsburgh NY 10 w, 156 ft.
WJXY-FM Conway SC 6 kw, 328 ft.
KKMK(FM) Rapid City SD 100 kw, 650 ft.
WSIB(FM) Selmer TN 3 kw, 328 ft.
WAYA(FM) Spring City TN 2 kw, 344 ft.
KMXR(FM) Corpus Christi TX 100 kw, 840 ft.
KINT-FM El Paso TX 96.2 kw, 1,207 ft.
KOYN(FM) Paris TX 50 kw, 492 ft.
KCRN-FM San Angelo TX 100 kw, 710 ft.
WMEV-FM Marion VA 100 kw, 1,480 ft.
WLVB(FM) Morrisville VT 5.4 kw
WMXR(FM) Woodstock VT 670 w, 682 ft.
WDOR-FM Sturgeon Bay WI 77 kw, 640 ft.
WRRR-FM St. Marys WV 17 kw, 390 ft.
KTAK(FM) Riverton WY 50 kw, 951 ft.

94.1 mhz (ch 231)

WCKO(FM) Carrollton AL 99 kw, 1,007 ft.
KHLT(FM) Little Rock AR 100 kw, 1,601 ft.
KXKQ(FM) Safford AZ 100 kw, minus 320 ft.
KERN-FM Bakersfield CA 4.5 kw, 1,312 ft.
*KPFA(FM) Berkeley CA 59 kw, 1,330 ft.
KYAJ(FM) Merced CA 3 kw, 328 ft.
KFSD-FM San Diego CA 100 kw, 640 ft.
KKXK(FM) Montrose CO 31.5 kw, 1,748 ft.
WAKU(FM) Crawfordville FL 6 kw, 328 ft.
WEZY-FM Lakeland FL 100 kw, 430 ft.
WMEZ(FM) Pensacola FL 100 kw, 1,328 ft.
WSOS(FM) St. Augustine FL 19 kw, 377 ft.
WCHY-FM Savannah GA 100 kw, 1,320 ft.
WSTR(FM) Smyrna GA 100 kw, 910 ft.
KRNA(FM) Iowa City IA 100 kw, 981 ft.
KBXL(FM) Caldwell ID 40 kw, 2,574 ft.
WMIX-FM Mt. Vernon IL 50 kw, 550 ft.
WGFA-FM Watseka IL 26 kw, 405 ft.
WGL-FM Roanoke IN 6 kw, 340 ft.
KFKF-FM Kansas City KS 100 kw, 994 ft.
WYCT(FM) Kentwood LA 100 kw, 981 ft.
WIBM-FM Jackson MI 40 kw, 551 ft.
WUPK(FM) Marquette MI 4.5 kw, 377 ft.
KYRS(FM) Atwater MN 3 kw, 328 ft.
KFML(FM) Little Falls MN 3 kw, 275 ft.
KPCR-FM Bowling Green MO 25 kw, 270 ft.
KRKX(FM) Billings MT 100 kw, 1,023 ft.
KOPR(FM) Butte MT 100 kw, 1,840 ft.
WWGL(FM) Lexington NC 100 kw, 485 ft.
WNBR(FM) Oriental NC 11 kw, 485 kw.
WOW-FM Omaha NE 100 kw, 508 ft.
KNEB-FM Scottsbluff NE 100 kw, 680 ft.
WFTN-FM Franklin NH 6 kw, 328 ft.
KZRR(FM) Albuquerque NM 100 kw, 4,130 ft.
KXTZ(FM) Henderson NV 100 kw, 1,210 ft.
WNYV(FM) Whitehall NY 3 kw, 328 ft.
WHBC-FM Canton OH 50 kw, 500 ft.
WWNK-FM Cincinnati OH 32 kw, 600 ft.
KXIQ(FM) Bend OR 100 kw, 1,028 ft.
WYSP(FM) Philadelphia PA 16 kw, 900 ft.
WQKX(FM) Sunbury PA 16 kw, 879 ft.
WOYE-FM Mayaguez PR 25 kw, 2,967 ft.
WHJY(FM) Providence RI 50 kw, 540 ft.
KSDN-FM Aberdeen SD 100 kw, 440 ft.
WMUF-FM Paris TN 3 kw, 328 ft.
WRLG(FM) Smyrna TN 4.3 kw, 200 ft.
WCTU(FM) Tazewell TN 1.3 kw, 492 ft.
KBUY-FM Amarillo TX 100 kw, 1,082 ft.
KQXY-FM Beaumont TX 100 kw, 1,099 ft.
KULF(FM) Brenham TX 6 kw, 328 ft.
KRIO-FM Floresville TX 22 kw, 695 ft.
KLTY-FM Fort Worth TX 100 kw, 1,585 ft.
KODJ(FM) Salt Lake City UT 40 kw, 3,030 ft.
WXEZ(FM) Yorktown VA 50 kw, 500 ft.
WXMX(FM) Canaan VT 16 kw, 387 ft.
KCLK-FM Clarkston WA 100 kw, 1,233 ft.
KMPS-FM Seattle WA 57 kw, 2,342 ft.
WIAL(FM) Eau Claire WI 85 kw, 350 ft.
WJJO(FM) Watertown WI 50 kw, 492 ft.
WQZK-FM Keyser WV 15 kw, 801 ft.
WAXS(FM) Oak Hill WV 25.5 kw, 650 ft.

94.3 mhz (ch 232)

KADX(FM) Houston AK 6 kw, 262 ft.
WQZX(FM) Greenville AL 1.75 kw, 410 ft.
KAMO-FM Rogers AR 5.2 kw, 709 ft.
KBUX(FM) Quartzsite AZ 205 w, -161 ft.
KDUC(FM) Barstow CA 4.6 kw, 783 ft.
KCRE-FM Crescent City CA 3 kw, -275 ft.
KIKF(FM) Garden Grove CA 3 kw, 245 ft.
KNCO-FM Grass Valley CA 290 w, 980 ft.
KNGT(FM) Jackson CA 230 w, 1,100 ft.
KTAA(FM) Kerman CA 25 kw, 328 ft.
KMGX(FM) San Fernando CA 3 kw, 95 ft.
WYBC-FM New Haven CT 1.2 kw, 122 ft.
WNFB(FM) Lake City FL 50 kw, 492 ft.
WGMM(FM) Marathon FL 3 kw, 160 ft.
WOLL(FM) Riviera Beach FL 1.26 kw, 480 ft.
WDEC-FM Americus GA 3 kw, 180 ft.
KDLX(FM) Makawao HI 3 kw, minus 22 ft.
KTSB(FM) Sioux Center IA 3 kw, 300 ft.
KADQ(FM) Rexburg ID 3 kw, 315 ft.
WRMS-FM Beardstown IL 3 kw, 300 ft.
WJKL(FM) Elgin IL 6 kw, 350 ft.
WDXR-FM Golconda IL 3.1 kw, 449 ft.
WSSQ(FM) Sterling IL 6 kw, 309 ft.
WJNZ(FM) Greencastle IN 3 kw, 165 ft.
WNZE(FM) Plymouth IN 3 kw, 240 ft.
WRCR(FM) Rushville IN 740 w, 550 ft.
WHIC-FM Hardinsburg KY 3.4 kw, 290 ft.
WIFX-FM Jenkins KY 2.8 kw, 1,492 ft.
KTRY-FM Bastrop LA 3 kw-H, 289 ft.
KLEB(FM) Galliano LA 25 kw, 308 ft.
WFBR(FM) Cambridge MD 6 kw, 328 ft.
WICO-FM Salisbury MD 3 kw, 299 ft.
WSTG(FM) Biddeford ME 13 kw, 449 ft.
WTRV(FM) Leland MI 3.6 kw, 426 ft.
WFGE(FM) Mackinaw City MI 3 kw, 300 ft.
WZNL(FM) Norway MI 1.3 kw, 502 ft.
KEZZ(FM) Aitkin MN 3 kw, 328 ft.
KMSR(FM) Sauk Centre MN 3 kw, 286 ft.
KDOM-FM Windom MN 5.7 kw, 335 ft.
KZMO-FM California MO 1.75 kw, 423 ft.
KQMX(FM) Rolla MO 3 kw, 114 ft.
WXRZ(FM) Corinth MS 3.3 kw, 328 ft.
WBAD(FM) Leland MS 3 kw, 300 ft.
WRQR(FM) Farmville NC 1.95 kw, 407 ft.
WVAV(FM) Hatteras NC 6 kw, 197 ft.
WZKB(FM) Wallace NC 3 kw, 300 ft.
WJLK-FM Asbury Park NJ 900 w, 98 ft.
WWOC(FM) Avalon NJ 3 kw, 300 ft.
KYEE(FM) Alamogordo NM 3 kw, minus 492 ft.
KDEM(FM) Deming NM 3 kw, 195 ft.
KRTN-FM Raton NM 3 kw, -531 ft.
WLVY(FM) Elmira NY 3 kw, 497 ft.
WBPM(FM) Kingston NY 1.1 kw, 554 ft.
*WIRQ(FM) Rochester NY 10 w-H, 485 ft.
WMJC(FM) Smithtown NY 3 kw, 300 ft.
WKKI(FM) Celina OH 2.2 kw, 448 ft.
WFCB(FM) Chillicothe OH 25 kw, 266 ft.
WDIF(FM) Marion OH 3 kw, 300 ft.
KTTL(FM) Alva OK 50 kw, 492 ft.
KZCD(FM) Lawton OK 3 kw, 328 ft.
KRIG(FM) Nowata OK 3.5 kw, 429 ft.
KTHK(FM) Okmulgee OK 3 kw, 300 ft.
WSGD-FM Carbondale PA 1.1 kw, 770 ft.
WBXQ(FM) Cresson PA 350 w, 958 ft.
WKSL(FM) Greencastle PA 2.5 kw, 469 ft.
WKBI-FM St. Marys PA 2.9 kw, 339 ft.
WPUB-FM Camden SC 3.3 kw, 299 ft.
WSSP(FM) Goose Creek SC 6 kw, 479 ft.
WLXP(FM) Marion SC 3 kw, 499 ft.
WOGY-FM Germantown TN 3 kw, 300 ft.
WJJM-FM Lewisburg TN 3 kw, 115 ft.
WIST(FM) Lobelville TN 21 kw, 758 ft.
WKNF(FM) Oak Ridge TN 2.5 kw, 515 ft.
WJTT(FM) Red Bank TN 2.8 kw, 331 ft.
WDBL-FM Springfield TN 3 kw, 215 ft.
KBTS(FM) Big Spring TX 20 kw, 374 ft.
KHER(FM) Crystal City TX 3 kw, 135 ft.
KDLK(FM) Del Rio TX 2.65 kw, 200 ft.

U.S. FM Stations by Frequency

KFST-FM Fort Stockton TX 3 kw, 235 ft.
KRVL(FM) Kerrville TX 50 kw, 492 ft.
KYXX(FM) Ozona TX 3 kw, 300 ft.
KSEY-FM Seymour TX 3 kw, 112 ft.
WTON-FM Staunton VA 330 w, 2,263 ft.
WQRA(FM) Warrenton VA 2.1 kw, 397 ft.
WHGC(FM) Bennington VT 3 kw, 110 ft.
KKEE(FM) Long Beach WA 3 kw, 233 ft.
WROE(FM) Neenah-Menasha WI 5.6 kw, 338 ft.
WPRE-FM Prairie du Chien WI 36 kw, 525 ft.
WRLF(FM) Fairmont WV 3 kw, 328 ft.

94.5 mhz (ch 233)

WAPI-FM Birmingham AL 100 kw, 1,214 ft.
WHOD-FM Jackson AL 19 kw, 448 ft.
KOLX(FM) Barling AR 3 kw, 193.52 ft.
KJIW-FM West Helena AR 6 kw, 250 ft.
KOOL-FM Phoenix AZ 100 kw, 1,655 ft.
KYAX(FM) Alturas CA 100 kw, 106 ft.
KWST(FM) Brawley CA 50 kw, 254 ft.
KCQR(FM) Ellwood CA 1 kw, 3,000 ft.
KUFX(FM) Gilroy CA 1.23 kw, 2,535 ft.
KAFN(FM) Hanford CA 3 kw, 100 ft.
KWNE(FM) Ukiah CA 2.15 kw, 2,053 ft.
WCFB(FM) Daytona Beach FL 100 kw, 1,500 ft.
WCVU(FM) Naples FL 100 kw, 1,049 ft.
WKNB(FM) Port St. Joe FL 100 kw, 991 ft.
WBYZ(FM) Baxley GA 100 kw, 1,014 ft.
KKEZ(FM) Fort Dodge IA 100 kw, 640 ft.
KKCH-FM Hayden ID 100 kw, 1,883 ft.
WLRW(FM) Champaign IL 50 kw, 400 ft.
KJCK-FM Junction City KS 100 kw, 630 ft.
KSKL(FM) Scott City KS 100 kw, 345 ft.
WMXL(FM) Lexington KY 100 kw, 640 ft.
KSMB(FM) Lafayette LA 100 kw, 1,079 ft.
KWKH-FM Shreveport LA 99 kw, 1,096 ft.
WJMN(FM) Boston MA 11.5 kw, 1,053 ft.
WKSQ(FM) Ellsworth ME 11.5 kw, 1,027 ft.
WKLQ(FM) Holland MI 50 kw, 499 ft.
WCEN-FM Mount Pleasant MI 100 kw, 994 ft.
KSTP-FM St. Paul MN 100 kw, 1,225 ft.
KRXL(FM) Kirksville MO 100 kw, 1,010 ft.
KKLR(FM) Poplar Bluff MO 100 kw, 807 ft.
WJZD(FM) Long Beach MS 3 kw, 328 ft.
KMON-FM Great Falls MT 36 kw, 470 ft.
WNEU(FM) Eden NC 100 kw, 981 ft.
KQDY(FM) Bismarck ND 100 kw, 1,117 ft.
WCHR(FM) Trenton NJ 50 kw, 492 ft.
KKOR(FM) Gallup NM 100 kw, 1,388 ft.
KSCQ(FM) Silver City NM 6 kw, 1,840 ft.
WNED-FM Buffalo NY 105 kw, 710 ft.
WEMX(FM) Ravena NY 3 kw, 328 ft.
WYYY(FM) Syracuse NY 100 kw, 650 ft.
WZJX(FM) Englewood OH 6 kw, 328 ft.
WXKR(FM) Port Clinton OH 30 kw, 640 ft.
KEMX(FM) Locust Grove OK 2.3 kw, 367 ft.
KMGE(FM) Eugene OR 100 kw-H, 43 kw-V, 1,299 ft.
WDAC(FM) Lancaster PA 19 kw, 810 ft.
WWSW-FM Pittsburgh PA 50 kw, 810 ft.
WFGI(FM) State College PA .94 kw, 581 ft.
WACJ(FM) Bowman SC 3 kw, 328 ft.
WMUU-FM Greenville SC 100 kw, 1,200 ft.
WRNN(FM) Murrell's Inlet SC 6 kw, 420 ft.
KPLO-FM Reliance SD 95 kw, 1,000 ft.
*KCFS(FM) Sioux Falls SD 2.35 kw, 190 ft.
KDGE(FM) Gainesville TX 100 kw, 1,896 ft.
KFRQ(FM) Harlingen TX 100 kw, 1,158 ft.
KLDE(FM) Houston TX 100 kw, 2,000 ft.
KFMX-FM Lubbock TX 100 kw, 817 ft.
KVFM(FM) Logan UT 15.6 kw, 1,148 ft.
WRVQ(FM) Richmond VA 200 kw, 455 ft.
WYOY(FM) Rutland VT 6 kw, 389 ft.
KUKN(FM) Kelso WA 3 kw, 100 ft.
KATS(FM) Yakima WA 100 kw, 850 ft.
WRJO(FM) Eagle River WI 50 kw, 492 ft.
WKTI(FM) Milwaukee WI 15.5 kw, 911 ft.
WZFR(FM) Tomah WI 2.4 kw, 361 ft.
WBES-FM Dunbar WV 3 kw, 328 ft.
KMGW(FM) Casper WY 63 kw, 230 ft.

94.7 mhz (ch 234)

NEW FM Brundidge AL 1.26 kw, 495 ft.
KZZZ(FM) Kingman AZ 46 kw, 2,492 ft.
KEWB(FM) Anderson CA 4.2 kw, 1,565 ft.
KTWV(FM) Los Angeles CA 58 kw, 2,835 ft.
KVYZ(FM) Thousand Palms CA 630 w, 581 ft.
KRKS-FM Boulder CO 100 kw, 984 ft.
WDSD(FM) Dover DE 50 kw, 377 ft.
KWXX-FM Hilo HI 100 kw, minus 330 ft.
KUMU-FM Honolulu HI 100 kw, 78 ft.
KMCH(FM) Manchester IA 6 kw, 328 ft.
WLS-FM Chicago IL 4.4 kw, 1,535 ft.
WFBQ(FM) Indianapolis IN 52 kw, 850 ft.
WXID(FM) Mayfield KY 32 kw, 442 ft.
WKLW-FM Paintsville KY 4.9 kw
WBIO(FM) Philpot KY 3 kw, 328 ft.
KPXF(FM) Lacombe LA 3 kw
WMAS-FM Springfield MA 50 kw, 194 ft.
WARW(FM) Bethesda MD 22.5 kw, 780 ft.
WCSX(FM) Birmingham MI 13.5 kw, 945 ft.
*WCVM(FM) Bronson MI 4.8 kw, 364 ft.
WCMM(FM) Gulliver MI 100 kw, 659 ft.
KKOO(FM) Caledonia MN 3 kw, 328 ft.
KNSP-FM Staples MN 3 kw, 121 ft.
KSKK(FM) Staples MN 6 kw, 125 ft.
KSHE(FM) Crestwood MO 100 kw, 1,019 ft.
KTTS-FM Springfield MO 100 kw, 1,125 ft.
WTYX(FM) Jackson MS 100 kw, 1,168 ft.
WQDR(FM) Raleigh NC 96 kw, 1,679 ft.
*WSIF(FM) Wilkesboro NC 10 w, minus 151 ft.
KNOX-FM Grand Forks ND 100 kw, 325 ft.
KNEN(FM) Norfolk NE 100 kw, 531 ft.
*WFME(FM) Newark NJ 38 kw, 570 ft.
KZXA(FM) Santa Fe NM 35 kw, 2,916 ft.
KIZS(FM) Carson City NV 86.6 kw, 2,072 ft.
*WMHI(FM) Cape Vincent NY 3 kw, 284 ft.
WYUL(FM) Chateaugay NY 1.7 kw, 610 ft.
WIYN(FM) Deposit NY 770 w, 642 ft.
WBAR-FM Lake Luzerne NY 300 w, 892 ft.
WSNY(FM) Columbus OH 22 kw, 753 ft.
KEBC(FM) Oklahoma City OK 98 kw, 1,387 ft.
KRRM(FM) Rogue River OR 130 w, 2,043 ft.
KQEM(FM) Seaside OR 3 kw, 213 ft.
WFGO(FM) Erie PA 1.1 kw, 538 ft.
WBRX(FM) Patton PA 1 kw, 551 ft.
WPHD(FM) Tioga PA 820 w, 895 ft.
WLDI(FM) Bayamon PR 32 kw, 1,778 ft.
WICI(FM) Sumter SC 3 kw, 328 ft.
WAAW(FM) Williston SC 2.11 kw, 561 ft.
WGSQ(FM) Cookeville TN 100 kw, 1,319 ft.
KBSO(FM) Corpus Christi TX 3 kw, 285 ft.
KSET(FM) El Paso TX 61 kw, 1,080 ft.
KFGI-FM Luling TX 100 kw, 1,154 ft.
KIXY-FM San Angelo TX 100 kw, 446 ft.
KVLL-FM Woodville TX 50 kw, 492 ft.
KMUZ-FM Camas WA 3 kw, 223 ft.
WEGV(FM) Mishicot WI 6 kw
WOFM(FM) Mosinee WI 50 kw, 492 ft.
WELK(FM) Elkins WV 5 kw, 728 ft.

94.9 mhz (ch 235)

WKSJ-FM Mobile AL 100 kw, 410 ft.
KOLL(FM) Maumelle AR 96 kw, 1,843 ft.
KDAB(FM) Prairie Grove AR 21 kw, 761 ft.
KKLD(FM) Tucson AZ 97 kw, 1,952 ft.
KBXY(FM) Baker CA 15.5 kw, 417 ft.
KOTR(FM) Cambria CA 25 kw, 328 ft.
KBZS(FM) San Diego CA 21.8 kw, 710 ft.
KSAN-FM San Francisco CA 35 kw, 1,290 ft.
KBOS-FM Tulare CA 16.4 kw, 847 ft.
WZTA(FM) Miami Beach FL 100 kw, 1,007 ft.
WTNT(FM) Tallahassee FL 100 kw, 840 ft.
WWRM(FM) Tampa FL 100 kw, 649 ft.
WPCH(FM) Atlanta GA 100 kw, 984 ft.
WMKO(FM) Millen GA 14.5 kw, 400 ft.
KGGO-FM Des Moines IA 100 kw, 1,059 ft.
KFXD-FM Nampa ID 49 kw, 2,692 ft.
KPKY(FM) Pocatello ID 100 kw, 1,004 ft.
WWDZ(FM) Danville IL 6 kw, 328 ft.
WDKB(FM) De Kalb IL 3 kw, 328 ft.
WAAG(FM) Galesburg IL 50 kw, 350 ft.
WRBT(FM) Mt. Carmel IL 50 kw, 425 ft.
KSBH(FM) Coushatta LA 25 kw, 328 ft.
WADU-FM Reserve LA 1.9 kw, 407 ft.
WXTK(FM) West Yarmouth MA 50 kw, 246 ft.
WSYY-FM Millinocket ME 23.5 kw, 692 ft.
WVIC-FM East Lansing MI 49 kw, 499 ft.
WKJZ(FM) Hillman MI 50 kw, 492 ft.
WKZC(FM) Scottville MI 17 kw, 400 ft.
KMXK(FM) Cold Spring MN 50 kw, 492 ft.
KQDS-FM Duluth MN 100 kw, 730 ft.
KCMO-FM Kansas City MO 100 kw, 1,057 ft.
WHLE(FM) Byhalia MS 6 kw, 328 ft.
WKOR-FM Columbus MS 29.5 kw, 492 ft.
KYSS-FM Missoula MT 15 kw, 2,509 ft.
KJLT-FM North Platte NE 63 kw, 200 ft.
WHOM(FM) Mt. Washington NH 48 kw, 3,760 ft.
KWYK-FM Aztec NM 100 kw, 433 ft.
KBIM-FM Roswell NM 100 kw, 1,880 ft.
WKLL(FM) Frankfort NY 50 kw, 276 ft.
WVZC(FM) Montauk NY 3 kw, 125 ft.
*WONB(FM) Ada OH 3 kw, 328 ft.
WOFX(FM) Fairfield OH 10.5 kw, 1,056 ft.
WQMX(FM) Medina OH 16.2 kw, 880 ft.
KOOS(FM) North Bend OR 56 kw, 502 ft.
*WRSD(FM) Folsom PA 1.4 kw, 20 ft.
WWKL(FM) Harrisburg PA 25 kw, 699 ft.
WASP-FM Oliver PA 205 w, 1,240 ft.
WHKS(FM) Port Allegany PA 530 w, 1090 ft.
KQAA(FM) Aberdeen SD 100 kw, 1,383 ft.
WIKQ(FM) Greeneville TN 100 kw, 1,090 ft.
WTRB-FM Ripley TN 6 kw, 328 ft.
WTNR-FM Waynesboro TN 6 kw, 328 ft.
KSNN(FM) Arlington TX 100 kw, 1,699 ft.
KWTA(FM) Electra TX 50 kw, 397 ft.
KOYE(FM) Laredo TX 100 kw, 1,000 ft.
KBRE-FM Cedar City UT 25.5 kw, 1,681 ft.
KZHT(FM) Provo UT 47 kw, 2,798 ft.
WPVR(FM) Roanoke VA 100 kw, 1,979 ft.
WJQI-FM Virginia Beach VA 50 kw, 499 ft.
KIOK(FM) Richland WA 100 kw, 1,250 ft.
*KUOW(FM) Seattle WA 100 kw, 730 ft.
WOLX-FM Baraboo WI 37 kw, 1,299 ft.
KROE-FM Sheridan WY 58 kw, 44 ft.

95.1 mhz (ch 236)

WNDA(FM) Huntsville AL 50 kw, 110 ft.
WXFX(FM) Prattville AL 50 kw, 492 ft.
KAMS(FM) Mammoth Spring AR 100 kw, 650 ft.
KTTI(FM) Yuma AZ 25 kw, 96.5 ft.
KPAY-FM Chico CA 8.7 kw, 1,171 ft.
KDJK(FM) Oakdale CA 29.5 kw, 633 ft.
KFRG(FM) San Bernardino CA 50 kw, 489 ft.
KBBY-FM Ventura CA 10.8 kw, 925 ft.
KRDO-FM Colorado Springs CO 96 kw, 2,010 ft.
KKLY(FM) Delta CO 100 kw, 969 ft.
WRKI(FM) Brookfield CT 50 kw, 500 ft.
WAPE-FM Jacksonville FL 100 kw, 460 ft.
WCHZ(FM) Harlem GA 6 kw, 328 ft.
WLML(FM) Montezuma GA 6 kw, 157 ft.
KAOI-FM Wailuku HI 100 kw, 1,227 ft.
KCZE(FM) New Hampton IA 5.5 kw, 328 ft.
WXLT(FM) Carterville IL 6 kw, 279 ft.
WDZQ(FM) Decatur IL 50 kw, 500 ft.
WZZP(FM) Kankakee IL 3 kw, 328 ft.
WZZT(FM) Morrison IL 3 kw, 328 ft.
WAJI(FM) Fort Wayne IN 39 kw, 680 ft.
WVNI(FM) Nashville IN 1.6 kw, 636 ft.
*WVUR-FM Valparaiso IN 36 w, 125 ft.
KICT-FM Wichita KS 100 kw, 1,026 ft.
WGGC(FM) Glasgow KY 100 kw, 988 ft.
*WNRC(FM) Dudley MA 14.7 w, 125 ft.
WRBS(FM) Baltimore MD 50 kw, 499 ft.
*WFBE(FM) Flint MI 50 kw, 243 ft.
KKDL(FM) Detroit Lakes MN 100 kw, 970 ft.
KWOA-FM Worthington MN 100 kw, 660 ft.
KMXL(FM) Carthage MO 50 kw, 472 ft.
KLGS(FM) Versailles MO 6 kw, 328 ft.
WZMP(FM) Marion MS 50 kw, 606 ft.
WQNZ(FM) Natchez MS 98 kw, 1,056 ft.
KMMS-FM Bozeman MT 94 kw, 781 ft.
*KXEI(FM) Havre MT 98 kw, 1,699 ft.
WAQQ(FM) Charlotte NC 100 kw, 1,542 ft.
WRNS-FM Kinston NC 95 kw, 1,499 ft.
KLDZ(FM) Lincoln NE 50 kw, 287 ft.
WAYV(FM) Atlantic City NJ 50 kw, 331 ft.
KSVA(FM) Corrales NM 3 kw, minus 531 ft.
WRQI(FM) South Bristol Township NY 9.5 kw, 994 ft.
KABH(FM) Shawnee OK 100 kw, 1,417 ft.
KNJM(FM) Lincoln City OR 24.5 kw, 709 ft.
KIJK(FM) Prineville OR 100 kw, 472 ft.
WZZO(FM) Bethlehem PA 30 kw, 631 ft.
WIKZ(FM) Chambersburg PA 50 kw-H, 42 kw-V, 449 ft.
WRKU-FM Grove City PA 19 kw, 805 ft.
WRPC(FM) San German PR 25 kw, 1,970 ft.
WSSX-FM Charleston SC 100 kw, 361 ft.
KSQY(FM) Deadwood SD 100 kw, 1,707 ft.
WGNN(FM) Dresden TN 6 kw, 328 ft.
KYKR(FM) Beaumont TX 100 kw, 500 ft.
KHEN(FM) Caldwell TX 3 kw, 328 ft.
KATG(FM) Comfort TX 50 kw, 492 ft.
KGRW(FM) Friona TX 3 kw, 285 ft.
KQRX(FM) Midland TX 10.35 kw, 505 ft.
KVIC(FM) Victoria TX 100 kw, 500 ft.
WQMZ(FM) Charlottesville VA 6 kw, 145 ft.
WJKC(FM) Christiansted VI 50 kw, 886 ft.
WJAN(FM) Sunderland VT 48 w, 2,398 ft.
WQRB(FM) Bloomer WI 14.7 kw, 430 ft.
WIIL(FM) Kenosha WI 50 kw, 384 ft.
WLST(FM) Marinette WI 100 kw, 500 ft.
WXIL(FM) Parkersburg WV 50 kw, 500 ft.
KCGY-FM Laramie WY 100 kw, 1,070 ft.
KYCS(FM) Rock Springs WY 100 kw, 1,635 ft.

95.3 mhz (ch 237)

WASZ(FM) Ashland-Lineville AL 1 kw, 541 ft.
WFFN(FM) Cordova AL 2.2 kw, 544 ft.
KCXY(FM) Camden AR 1 kw, 500 ft.
KMTB(FM) Murfreesboro AR 3 kw, 298 ft.
KERX(FM) Paris AR 6 kw, 571 ft.
KKRK(FM) Douglas AZ 3 kw, 210 ft.
KOZT(FM) Fort Bragg CA 3.1 kw, 468 ft.
KRTY(FM) Los Gatos CA 880 w, 860 ft.
KEDY(FM) Mount Shasta CA 3 kw, -1,300 ft.
KLLY(FM) Oildale CA 12.5 kw, 394 ft.
KWBR(FM) Pismo Beach CA 4.2 kw, 390 ft.
KUIC(FM) Vacaville CA 4.3 kw, 280 ft.
KSLV-FM Monte Vista CO 3 kw, 89 ft.
WDNO(FM) Laurel DE 6 kw, 328 ft.
WTLN-FM Apopka FL 6 kw, 315 ft.
WOLZ(FM) Fort Myers FL 97 kw, 453 ft.
WXCV(FM) Homosassa Springs FL 3 kw, 410 ft.
WSRM(FM) Coosa GA 3 kw, 328 ft.
WYSC(FM) McRae GA 3 kw, 289 ft.
WJYF(FM) Nashville GA 1.2 kw, 500 ft.
WTGA-FM Thomaston GA 3 kw, 290 ft.
KQMG-FM Independence IA 3 kw, 200 ft.
KIFG-FM Iowa Falls IA 4.7 kw, 237 ft.
KOKX-FM Keokuk IA 3 kw, 175 ft.
KMAQ-FM Maquoketa IA 3 kw, 328 ft.
KOAK-FM Red Oak IA 20.4 kw, 364 ft.
KCII-FM Washington IA 3 kw, 300 ft.
KLER-FM Orofino ID 100 w, 750 ft.
KPND(FM) Sandpoint ID 1 kw, minus 430 ft.
KECH-FM Sun Valley ID 435 w, 2,168 ft.
WRXX(FM) Centralia IL 3 kw, 217 ft.
WRKX(FM) Ottawa IL 3 kw, 200 ft.
WZNF(FM) Rantoul IL 3 kw, 425 ft.
WKMQ(FM) Winnebago IL 1.25 kw, 512 ft.
WEZV-FM Brookston IN 1.15 kw, 520 ft.
WUME-FM Paoli IN 3 kw, 300 ft.
WNDI-FM Sullivan IN 3 kw, 150 ft.
KSNP(FM) Burlington KS 6 kw, 349 ft.
KCKS(FM) Concordia KS 2.5 kw, 329 ft.
KHCA(FM) Wamego KS 6 kw, 328 ft.
WIKI(FM) Carrollton KY 3 kw, 423 ft.
WMSK-FM Morganfield KY 3 kw, 300 ft.
KQKI(FM) Bayou Vista LA 3 kw, 299 ft.
KASO-FM Minden LA 3 kw, 144 ft.
WHRB(FM) Cambridge MA 3 kw, 110 ft.
WRSI(FM) Greenfield MA 320 w, 780 ft.
WALZ-FM Machias ME 3 kw, 220 ft.
WJBI-FM Winslow ME 5.3 kw, 348 ft.
WCQL-FM York Center ME 1.40 kw hor., 1.35 kw ver, 682 ft.
WQTE(FM) Adrian MI 3 kw, 299 ft.
WBXX(FM) Battle Creek MI 3 kw, 269 ft.
WCFX(FM) Clare MI 6 kw, 328 ft.
WMJZ-FM Gaylord MI 3 kw, 325 ft.
WAOR(FM) Niles MI 3.3 kw, 298 ft.
WMHG(FM) Whitehall MI 2 kw, 360 ft.

Broadcasting & Cable Yearbook 1994
B-510

U.S. FM Stations by Frequency

KCPI(FM) Albert Lea MN 3 kw, 299 ft.
KNOF(FM) St. Paul MN 3 kw, 200 ft.
KDJS-FM Willmar MN 50 kw, 436 ft.
KAGE-FM Winona MN 11 kw, 495 ft.
KDKD-FM Clinton MO 3 kw, 174 ft.
KLZE(FM) Owensville MO 50 kw, 328 ft.
WAFM(FM) Amory MS 3 kw, 255 ft.
WVIM-FM Coldwater MS 1 kw, 299 ft.
WADI(FM) Corinth MS 4.2 kw, 210 ft.
WKZB(FM) Drew MS 3 kw, 344 ft.
WLUN(FM) Lumberton MS 3 kw, 289 ft.
WOBR-FM Wanchese NC 25 kw, 324 ft.
KSEL-FM Portales NM 6 kw, 300 ft.
KRJC(FM) Elko NV 450 w, 761 ft.
WGIX-FM Gouverneur NY 3 kw, 220 ft.
WHFM(FM) Southampton NY 5 kw, 354 ft.
WKTN(FM) Kenton OH 3 kw, 270 ft.
WKLM(FM) Millersburg OH 3 kw, 328 ft.
WLKR-FM Norwalk OH 3 kw, 300 ft.
WZLR(FM) Xenia OH 3 kw, 300 ft.
KBXD(FM) Lawton OK 6 kw, 302 ft.
KKBC(FM) Baker City OR 3 kw, -200 ft.
KURY-FM Brookings OR 3 kw, 90 ft.
KZZK-FM Creswell OR 625 kw, 1,207 ft.
WZWW(FM) Bellefonte PA 933 w, 577 ft.
WDNH(FM) Honesdale PA 3 kw, 256 ft.
WISL-FM Shamokin PA 1.25 w, 505 ft.
WTTC-FM Towanda PA 3 kw, 125 ft.
WJPA-FM Washington PA 2.15 kw, 390 ft.
WFMV(FM) South Congaree SC 3 kw, 328 ft.
KLXS-FM Pierre SD 3 kw, 299 ft.
WTBG(FM) Brownsville TN 5 kw, 150 ft.
WALV(FM) Cleveland TN 3.5 kw, 436 ft.
*WYFC(FM) Clinton TN 540 w, 669 ft.
KBST-FM Big Spring TX 8 kw, 482 ft.
KIXV(FM) Brady TX 3 kw, 299 ft.
KMRE(FM) Dumas TX 3 kw, 260 ft.
KFLL(FM) Floydada TX 3 kw, 240 ft.
KFRO-FM Gilmer TX 2 kw, 572 ft.
KHYI(FM) Howe TX 3.9 kw, 413 ft.
KVWG-FM Pearsall TX 3 kw, 203 ft.
KZSP(FM) South Padre Island TX 3 kw, 353 ft.
KZUB(FM) Tahoka TX 3 kw, 328 ft.
WKHK(FM) Colonial Heights VA 13 kw, 449 ft.
WFTR-FM Front Royal VA 4 kw, 300 ft.
WCRR(FM) Rural Retreat VA 6 kw, 400 ft.
WJLC(FM) South Boston VA 6 kw, 246 ft.
WXXX(FM) South Burlington VT 6 kw, 225 ft.
WKXE-FM White River Junction VT 3 kw, 225 ft.
KXLE-FM Ellensburg WA 1.92 kw-H, 1,345 ft.
KGHO-FM Hoquiam WA 1.15 kw, 750 ft.
WXRO(FM) Beaver Dam WI 6 kw, 328 ft.
WGMO(FM) Shell Lake WI 3 kw, 168 ft.
WRRL-FM Rainelle WV 3.1 kw, 460 ft.
KZJH(FM) Jackson WY 100 kw, 1,056 ft.

95.5 mhz (ch 238)

WTVY-FM Dothan AL 100 kw, 1,078 ft.
WJDB-FM Thomasville AL 3 kw, 300 ft.
KYOT-FM Phoenix AZ 96 kw, 1,570 ft.
KVOQ(FM) Carmel CA 1.05 kw
KLOS(FM) Los Angeles CA 68 kw, 2,920 ft.
WOVV(FM) Fort Pierce FL 100 kw, 981 ft.
WWGO(FM) Silver Springs FL 3 kw, 340 ft.
WNGC(FM) Athens GA 100 kw, 1,268 ft.
WIXV(FM) Savannah GA 100 kw, 900 ft.
KSTO(FM) Agana GU 25 kw, 530 ft.
KAIM-FM Honolulu HI 100 kw, -23 ft.
KNJS(FM) Belle Plaine IA 6 kw, 328 ft.
KGLI(FM) Sioux City IA 100 kw, 900 ft.
WFUN-FM Bethalto IL 6 kw, 328 ft.
WNUA(FM) Chicago IL 8.3 kw, 1,174 ft.
WGLO(FM) Pekin IL 25 kw, 620 ft.
WFMS(FM) Indianapolis IN 13 kw, 1,000 ft.
KOLS(FM) Dodge City KS 100 kw, 570 ft.
WQHY(FM) Prestonsburg KY 100 kw, 1,000 ft.
KRRQ(FM) Lafayette LA 6 kw, 328 ft.
WPGC-FM Morningside MD 50 kw, 500 ft.
WPME(FM) Topsham ME 3 kw, 456 ft.
WKQI(FM) Detroit MI 100 kw, 437 ft.
KBEK(FM) Mora MN 25 kw, 328 ft.
KCHK-FM New Prague MN 3 kw, 328 ft.
KAAN-FM Bethany MO 50 kw, 360 ft.
KJEZ(FM) Poplar Bluff MO 100 kw, 860 ft.
WKTF-FM Jackson MS 100 kw, 1,060 ft.
WOXD(FM) Oxford MS 3 kw, 328 ft.
KQUY-FM Butte MT 50 kw, 1,820 ft.
KDWG(FM) Hardin MT 100 kw, 984 ft.
WHPE-FM High Point NC 100 kw, 440 ft.
WWRT(FM) Scotland Neck NC 3 kw, 328 ft.
KYNU(FM) Jamestown ND 100 kw, 398 ft.
KSDZ(FM) Gordon NE 30 kw, 310 ft.
KNYN(FM) Santa Fe NM 19 kw, 1,850 ft.
KWNR(FM) Henderson NV 100 kw h, 61 kw v, 1,120 ft.
KNEV(FM) Reno NV 60 kw, 2,270 ft.
WROW-FM Albany NY 12 kw, 1,020 ft.
WPLJ(FM) New York NY 6.7 kw, 1,335 ft.
WCLV(FM) Cleveland OH 31 kw, 610 ft.
WHOK(FM) Lancaster OH 50 kw, 492 ft.
KCLI(FM) Clinton OK 50 kw, 492 ft.
KITX(FM) Hugo OK 50 kw, 492 ft.
KWEN(FM) Tulsa OK 96 kw, 1,328 ft.
KXL-FM Portland OR 100 kw, 990 ft.
WKYE(FM) Johnstown PA 57 kw, 1,060 ft.
WFRY(FM) Salladasburg PA 3.9 kw, 239 ft.
WBRU(FM) Providence RI 20 kw, 546 ft.
WLJI(FM) Summerton SC 6 kw, 328 ft.
WIBZ(FM) Wedgefield SC 3 kw, 300 ft.
WSM-FM Nashville TN 100 kw, 1,280 ft.
KKMJ(FM) Austin TX 100 kw-H, 87 kw-V, 1,000 ft.
KZFM(FM) Corpus Christi TX 100 kw, 994 ft.

KAFX-FM Diboll TX 100 kw, 567 ft.
KLAQ(FM) El Paso TX 88 kw, 1,390 ft.
KVRP-FM Haskell TX 100 kw, 531 ft.
KCKR(FM) Waco TX 100 kw, 1,100 ft.
KKBE(FM) Ogden UT 64 kw, 2,368 ft.
WIFC(FM) Wausau WI 98 kw, 1,150 ft.
KTRS(FM) Casper WY 100 kw, 1,920 ft.

95.7 mhz (ch 239)

WAFN(FM) East Brewton AL 6 kw, 328 ft.
WFFX(FM) Tuscaloosa AL 100 kw, 410 ft.
KSSN(FM) Little Rock AR 92 kw, 1,663 ft.
KQZE(FM) St. Johns AZ 91 kw, 1,161 ft.
KJFX(FM) Fresno CA 17.5 kw, 850 ft.
KALF(FM) Red Bluff CA 7 kw, 1,265 ft.
KKHI(FM) San Francisco CA 6.9 kw, 1,500 ft.
KQYN(FM) Twentynine Palms CA 19 kw, 200 ft.
KHOW-FM Denver CO 100 kw, 725 ft.
WKSS(FM) Hartford CT 16.5 kw, 880 ft.
WMTX-FM Clearwater FL 100 kw, 607 ft.
WXDJ(FM) Homestead FL 100 kw, 982 ft.
WATG(FM) Trion GA 600 w, 699 ft.
WQPW(FM) Valdosta GA 35.9 kw, 606 ft.
KQWC-FM Webster City IA 25 kw, 328 ft.
KBBM(FM) Winterset IA 6 kw, 328 ft.
KEZJ-FM Twin Falls ID 50 kw, 670 ft.
WCRC(FM) Effingham IL 50 kw, 480 ft.
WSEY(FM) Mount Morris IL 2.7 kw, 495 ft.
WBQR(FM) Attica IN 4.1 kw, 387 ft.
WQMF(FM) Jeffersonville IN 34 kw, 580 ft.
WLRX(FM) Nappanee IN 1.4 kw, 500 ft.
KZTO(FM) Ottawa KS 100 kw, 987 ft.
WCCK(FM) Calvert City KY 3 kw, 328 ft.
WTKL(FM) New Orleans LA 100 kw, 984 ft.
KNCB-FM Vivian LA 3 kw, 285 ft.
KDAL-FM Duluth MN 100 kw, 830 ft.
KKOK-FM Morris MN 100 kw, 474 ft.
KWWR(FM) Mexico MO 100 kw, 1,027 ft.
WTGY(FM) Charleston MS 3.8 kw, 300 ft.
WRXQ(FM) Olive Branch MS 6 kw, 328 ft.
KCGM(FM) Scobey MT 52 kw, 660 ft.
WXRC(FM) Hickory NC 100 kw, 1,276 ft.
WKML(FM) Lumberton NC 100 kw, 1,064 ft.
KNDK-FM Langdon ND 6 kw, 328 ft.
*KROA(FM) Grand Island NE 100 kw, 460 ft.
WZID(FM) Manchester NH 14.5 kw, 930 ft.
KPCL(FM) Farmington NM 100 kw, 394 ft.
KPER(FM) Hobbs NM 36 kw, 255 ft.
WAQX-FM Manlius NY 25 kw, 300 ft.
WPIG(FM) Olean NY 43 kw, 740 ft.
WYHK(FM) Gibsonburg OH 3.5 kw, 433 ft.
WCLR(FM) Piqua OH 50 kw, 476 ft.
WEEL(FM) Shadyside OH 850 w, minus 626 ft.
KKAJ-FM Ardmore OK 100 kw, 449 ft.
KMKZ(FM) Lahoma OK 5.6 kw, 338 ft.
KBOY-FM Medford OR 100 kw, 935 ft.
WKQV(FM) Olyphant PA 300 w, 1,010 ft.
WFLN-FM Philadelphia PA 50 kw, 500 ft.
WFID(FM) Rio Piedras PR 50 kw, 941 ft.
WAYB-FM Graysville TN 55 kw, 721 ft.
WGAP-FM Maryville TN 3 kw, 328 ft.
KARX(FM) Claude TX 100 kw, 391 ft.
KIKK-FM Houston TX 100 kw, 1,971 ft.
KFMD(FM) Delta UT 100 kw, 7 ft.
WFLO-FM Farmville VA 40 kw, 340 ft.
WLTY(FM) Norfolk VA 40 kw, 881 ft.
WSHX(FM) Danville VT 230 w, 1,174 ft.
KLTX(FM) Seattle WA 100 kw, 1,150 ft.
KNLT(FM) Walla Walla WA 100 kw, 1,401 ft.
WSPL(FM) La Crosse WI 50 kw, 410 ft.
WZTR(FM) Milwaukee WI 34 kw, 610 ft.

95.9 mhz (ch 240)

KXLR(FM) Fairbanks AK 3 kw, 7 ft.
WKXN(FM) Greenville AL 3 kw, 225 ft.
WTWX-FM Guntersville AL 3 kw, 300 ft.
WBIL-FM Tuskegee AL 3 kw, 320 ft.
KREB(FM) Huntsville AR 3 kw, 295 ft.
KUUZ(FM) Lake Village AR 6 kw, 328 ft.
KSAR(FM) Salem AR 2.5 kw, 325 ft.
KZGL(FM) Cottonwood AZ 3 kw, 203 ft.
KEZY(FM) Anaheim CA 2.4 kw, 328 ft.
KAGV(FM) Arnold CA 500 w, 334 ft.
KXXZ(FM) Barstow CA 4.4 kw, 781 ft.
KELF(FM) Camarillo CA 5 kw, 813 ft.
KKOS(FM) Carlsbad CA 3.3 kw, 305 ft.
KNTO(FM) Livingston CA 3 kw, 305 ft.
KIDN-FM Hayden CO 1.8 kw, 1181 ft.
KHUG(FM) Rocky Ford CO 2.6 kw, 85 ft.
WEFX(FM) Norwalk CT 3 kw, 299 ft.
WKHI(FM) Bethany Beach DE 6 kw, 299 ft.
WRBA(FM) Springfield FL 50 kw, 300 ft.
WQZY(FM) Dublin GA 3 kw, 298 ft.
KPVS(FM) Hilo HI 50 kw, 230 ft.
KSRF(FM) Poipu HI 1.13. kw, 738 ft.
KCHA-FM Charles City IA 3 kw, 300 ft.
KILR-FM Estherville IA 6 kw, 300 ft.
KIIK-FM Fairfield IA 2.05 kw, 400 ft.
KCOB-FM Newton IA 2.5 kw, 354 ft.
WKKD-FM Aurora IL 3 kw, 338 ft.
WCNL-FM Carlinville IA 6 kw, 325 ft.
WHOW-FM Clinton IL 3 kw, 300 ft.
WDQN-FM DuQuoin IL 3 kw, 320 ft.
WPZZ(FM) Franklin IN 3 kw, 300 ft.
WEFM(FM) Michigan City IN 3 kw, 230 ft.
WAGD-FM Seelyville IN 6 kw, 100 ft.
WKID(FM) Vevay IN 2.7 kw, 480 ft.

WKUZ(FM) Wabash IN 3 kw, 150 ft.
KQNS-FM Lindsborg KS 1.3 kw, 455 ft.
KCAY(FM) Russell KS 1.35 kw, 487 ft.
KKWM(FM) Winfield KS 50 kw, 492 ft.
WFTM-FM Maysville KY 3 kw, 207 ft.
WRSL-FM Stanford KY 3 kw, 85 ft.
WGKY(FM) Wickliffe KY 3 kw, 759 ft.
KZBL(FM) Natchitoches LA 3 kw, 299 ft.
KMAR-FM Winnsboro LA 3 kw, 171 ft.
WATD-FM Marshfield MA 2.8 kw, 350 ft.
WUPE(FM) Pittsfield MA 1 kw, 560 ft.
WWIN-FM Glen Burnie MD 3 kw-H, 2.55 kw-V, 299 ft.
WYII(FM) Williamsport MD 3 kw, 300 ft.
WHYR(FM) Saco ME 3.3 kw, 300 ft.
WLKM-FM Three Rivers MI 3 kw, 289 ft.
KQCL(FM) Faribault MN 3 kw, 328 ft.
WLKX-FM Forest Lake MN 3 kw, 300 ft.
KTRI-FM Mansfield MO 3 kw, 312 ft.
KKBL(FM) Monett MO 6 kw, 269 ft.
KMMC(FM) Salem MO 4.8 kw, 165 ft.
WESE(FM) Baldwyn MS 5.4 kw, 328 ft.
WBBN(FM) Taylorsville MS 31 kw, 625 ft.
WLGG(FM) Woodville MS 3 kw, 328 ft.
KCWX(FM) Columbia Falls MT 6 kw, 285 ft.
KBMG(FM) Hamilton MT 16 kw, 393 ft.
KLCM(FM) Lewistown MT 3 kw, 205 ft.
WPNC-FM Plymouth NC 2.6 kw, 350 ft.
WCVP-FM Robbinsville NC 60 kw, 2,008 ft.
WADB(FM) Point Pleasant NJ 4 kw, 240 ft.
WFLR-FM Dundee NY 780 w, 600 ft.
WYLR-FM Glens Falls NY 240 w, 918 ft.
WVOS-FM Liberty NY 6 kw, 328 ft.
WNPQ(FM) New Philadelphia OH 3 kw, 400 ft.
WYNT(FM) Upper Sandusky OH 3 kw, 299 ft.
KYBE(FM) Frederick OK 3 kw, 207 ft.
KKUZ-FM Sallisaw OK 30 kw, 600 ft.
WDLE(FM) Benton PA 3 kw, 328 ft.
WMKX(FM) Brookville PA 2 kw, 418 ft.
WMRF-FM Lewistown PA 3.9 kw, 407 ft.
WHTX-FM Sharpsville PA 3 kw, 328 ft.
WVBI(FM) Block Island RI 6 kw, 174 ft.
WFKX(FM) Henderson TN 3 kw, 300 ft.
WDXE-FM Lawrenceburg TN 3 kw, 290 ft.
WCSD(FM) Livingston TN 2.85 kw, 472 ft.
WMXK(FM) Morristown TN 1.1 kw, 771 ft.
KXIT-FM Dalhart TX 3 kw-H, 171 ft.
KDIU(FM) Dimmitt TX 3 kw, 152 ft.
KLLI(FM) Hooks TX 1.4 kw, 449 ft.
KCKL(FM) Malakoff TX 6 kw, 306 ft.
KYXS-FM Mineral Wells TX 25 kw, 295 ft.
KEYE-FM Perryton TX 3 kw, 300 ft.
KVYS(FM) St. George UT 96.6 kw, 1,965 ft.
WGRQ(FM) Colonial Beach VA 6 kw, 524 ft.
KULE-FM Ephrata WA 1.5 kw, 460 ft.
WJLW(FM) De Pere WI 25 kw, 308 ft.
WRDN-FM Durand WI 9.3 kw, 600 ft.
WMQA-FM Minocqua WI 25 kw, 289 ft.
WZST(FM) Portage WI 6 kw, 328 ft.
WTBZ-FM Grafton WV 3 kw, 150 ft.
WAEY-FM Princeton WV 6 kw, 285 ft.

96.1 mhz (ch 241)

*KNOM-FM Nome AK 88 w, -138 ft.
WXFL(FM) Florence AL 2.45 kw, 518 ft.
WAVH(FM) Mobile AL 100 kw, 1,342 ft.
WLNE-FM Montgomery AL 4.5 kw, 820 ft.
KBYB(FM) El Dorado AR 100 kw, 288 ft.
KCWD(FM) Harrison AR 3 kw, 295 ft.
KLPX(FM) Tucson AZ 93 kw, 90 ft.
KWRK(FM) Window Rock AZ 94 kw, 328 ft.
KSIQ(FM) Brawley CA 50 kw, 270 ft.
KSQQ(FM) Morgan Hill CA 530 w, 781 ft.
KYMX(FM) Sacramento CA 50 kw, 476 ft.
KWRP(FM) San Jacinto CA 60 kw, 1,502 ft.
KSLY-FM San Luis Obispo CA 5.6 kw, 1,410 ft.
KGYU(FM) Visalia CA 4.8 kw, 358 ft.
KBIQ(FM) Fountain CO 140 w, 1,978 ft.
KGLL(FM) Greeley CO 100 kw, 660 ft.
KSTR-FM Montrose CO 100 kw, 1,099 ft.
WRXK-FM Bonita Springs FL 100 kw, 1,122 ft.
WBSB(FM) Dade City FL 3.8 kw, 413 ft.
WEJZ(FM) Jacksonville FL 100 kw, 984 ft.
WHBX(FM) Tallahassee FL 3 kw, 300 ft.
WKLS-FM Atlanta GA 99 kw, 984 ft.
KMXG(FM) Clinton IA 100 kw, 980 ft.
NEW FM Hudson IA 3 kw, 312 ft.
KID-FM Idaho Falls ID 100 kw, 1,500 ft.
WLTM(FM) Rantoul IL 3.8 kw, 403 ft.
WQLK(FM) Richmond IN 50 kw, 350 ft.
WYWY-FM Barbourville KY 25 kw, 300 ft.
WSTO(FM) Owensboro KY 100 kw, 1,000 ft.
KRVE(FM) Brusly LA 43 kw, 449 ft.
KYKZ(FM) Lake Charles LA 97 kw, 1,204 ft.
WSRS(FM) Worcester MA 14 kw, 863 ft.
WTMS-FM Presque Isle ME 95 kw, 1,309 ft.
WHNN(FM) Bay City MI 100 kw-H, 90 kw-V, 1,020 ft.
WKEZ(FM) Holland MI 50 kw-H, 45 kw-V, 492 ft.
KQPR-FM Albert Lea MN 6 kw, 328 ft.
KGPZ(FM) Coleraine MN 100 kw, 577 ft.
KQHT(FM) Crookston MN 100 kw, 413 ft.
KARP(FM) Glencoe MN 13.5 kw, 449 ft.
KLRQ(FM) Clinton MO 100 kw, 987 ft.
WLZA(FM) Eupora MS 50 kw, 500 ft.
WKIX-FM Raleigh NC 100 kw, 985 ft.
WWMG(FM) Shelby NC 100 kw, 1,738 ft.
KYYZ(FM) Williston ND 100 kw, 873 ft.
*KINI(FM) Crookston NE 57 kw, 500 ft.
KICX-FM McCook NE 6 kw, 380 ft.
KEFM(FM) Omaha NE 100 kw, 1,458 ft.
WTTH(FM) Margate City NJ 2.3 kw, 371 ft.
WJYE(FM) Buffalo NY 50 kw, 480 ft.

U.S. FM Stations by Frequency

WODZ-FM Rome NY 7.4 kw, 600 ft.
WMTR-FM Archbold OH 3.8 kw, 400 ft.
KXXY-FM Oklahoma City OK 100 kw, 1,167 ft.
KITO-FM Vinita OK 50 kw, 492 ft.
KZEL-FM Eugene OR 100 kw, 1,093 ft.
KSRV-FM Ontario OR 100 kw, 450 ft.
WLEV(FM) Easton PA 50 kw, 500 ft.
WVTY(FM) Pittsburgh PA 50 kw, 500 ft.
WGCB-FM Red Lion PA 50 kw, 500 ft.
WLGK(FM) South Waverly PA 940 w, 590 ft.
WAEL-FM Maricao PR 24.2 kw, 2,011 ft.
WAVF(FM) Hanahan SC 538 w, 1,443 ft.
KIXX(FM) Watertown SD 97 kw, 977 ft.
KXGJ(FM) Bay City TX 50 kw, 492 ft.
KSRW(FM) Childress TX 50 kw, 520 ft.
KIWW(FM) Harlingen TX 100 kw, 449 ft.
KKTX-FM Kilgore TX 32 kw, 620 ft.
KAGG(FM) Madisonville TX 50 kw, 500 ft.
KMRK-FM Odessa TX 50 kw, 440 ft.
KSJL-FM San Antonio TX 100 kw, 479 ft.
KXRK(FM) Provo UT 55 kw, 2,620 ft.
WLTK(FM) Broadway VA 2.6 kw, 1,000 ft.
WROX-FM Cape Charles VA 50 kw, 499 ft.
WIVI(FM) Charlotte Amalie VI 2.4 kw, 1,500 ft.
WDEV-FM Warren VT 3 kw, 4,000 ft.
KXXO(FM) Olympia WA 85 kw, 2100 ft.
KNFR(FM) Opportunity WA 56 kw, 2,378 ft.
WYUR-FM Ripon WI 3 kw, 403 ft.
WBOG(FM) Tomah WI 6 kw, 1,075 ft.
WKWS(FM) Charleston WV 50 kw, 360 ft.
KKLX(FM) Worland WY 50 kw, 400 ft.
WJMR(FM) Peshtigo WI 3 kw, 230 ft.

96.3 mhz (ch 242)

KHLS(FM) Blytheville AR 100 kw, 450 ft.
KOUA(FM) Mena AR 47.18 kw, 1,314 ft.
KFMI(FM) Eureka CA 30 kw, 1,580 ft.
KFSG(FM) Los Angeles CA 54 kw, 479 ft.
KUBB(FM) Mariposa CA 1.9 kw, 2,112 ft.
KKLC(FM) Susanville CA 25 kw, 328 ft.
WHUR-FM Washington DC 24 kw, 669 ft.
WJIZ-FM Albany GA 100 kw, 469 ft.
KRTR-FM Kailua HI 75 kw, 2,120 ft.
WBBM-FM Chicago IL 6.2 kw, 1,174 ft.
WJAA(FM) Austin IN 3 kw, 328 ft.
WKQM(FM) Churubusco IN 3 kw
WHHH(FM) Indianapolis IN 770 w, 656 ft.
KRZZ-FM Derby KS 50 kw, 492 ft.
WWDQ(FM) Morehead KY 6 kw, 328 ft.
WRZE(FM) Nantucket MA 50 kw, 405 ft.
WWMR(FM) Rumford ME 100 kw, 1,433 ft.
WHYT(FM) Detroit MI 20 kw, 787 ft.
WMBN-FM Petoskey MI 100 kw, 981 ft.
KRJY(FM) St. Louis MO 100 kw, 650 ft.
WJDX(FM) Jackson MS 100 kw, 1,450 ft.
KZIN-FM Shelby MT 100 kw, 570 ft.
WRHT(FM) Morehead City NC 100 kw, 492 ft.
KHFM(FM) Albuquerque NM 20 kw, 4,110 ft.
KKLZ(FM) Las Vegas NV 100 kw, 1,170 ft.
WQXR-FM New York NY 7.8 kw h, 5.5 kw v, 1,220 ft.
WCDA(FM) Vorheesville NY 200 w, 1,118 ft.
WLVQ(FM) Columbus OH 40 kw, 550 ft.
WUNS(FM) Lewisburg PA 3 kw, 418 ft.
WKQW-FM Oil City PA 6 kw, 328 ft.
WRXR-FM Aiken SC 15 kw, 889 ft.
WGOG-FM Walhalla SC 6 kw, 328 ft.
WRMX(FM) Murfreesboro TN 100 kw, 827 ft.
WJBZ(FM) Seymour TN 3 kw, 328 ft.
KTDR(FM) Del Rio TX 100 kw, 490 ft.
KHEY-FM El Paso TX 100 kw, 1,390 ft.
KSCS(FM) Fort Worth TX 99 kw, 1,610 ft.
KLLL-FM Lubbock TX 100 kw, 817 ft.
WROV-FM Martinsville VA 13.8 kw, 2,076 ft.
KQVN(FM) Royal City WA 800 w, 1,656 ft.
WJMC-FM Rice Lake WI 100 kw, 540 ft.
WMLI(FM) Sauk City WI 5.1 kw, 672 ft.
WOTR(FM) Lost Creek WV 3 kw-H, 302 ft.
KDBX(FM) Banks OR 2 kw, 397 ft.

96.5 mhz (ch 243)

KAZO(FM) Soldotna AK 10 kw, 259 ft.
WMJJ(FM) Birmingham AL 100 kw, 1,027 ft.
KLRA-FM England AR 3 kw, 148 ft.
KDAP-FM Douglas AZ 3 kw, 30 ft.
KRFM(FM) Show Low AZ 100 kw, 994 ft.
KHIS-FM Bakersfield CA 50 kw, 550 ft.
KYXY(FM) San Diego CA 41 kw, 540 ft.
KOIT-FM San Francisco CA 33 kw, 1,410 ft.
KRZQ-FM Tahoe City CA 4 kw, 2,965 ft.
KFLS-FM Tulelake CA 1.78 kw, 2,132 ft.
WTIC-FM Hartford CT 20 kw, 810 ft.
WJUS(FM) Fort Walton Beach FL 98 kw, 984 ft.
WPOW(FM) Miami FL 100 kw, 1,007 ft.
WHTQ(FM) Orlando FL 100 kw, 1,600 ft.
WWIQ(FM) Gray GA 1.99 kw, 414 ft.
WJCL-FM Savannah GA 100 kw, 1,232 ft.
WMT-FM Cedar Rapids IA 100 kw, 540 ft.
KOZE-FM Lewiston ID 25 kw, 741 ft.
KLIX-FM Twin Falls ID 100 kw, 130 ft.
WZKT(FM) Farmington IL 4.1 kw, 381 ft.
WKOT(FM) Marseilles IL 3 kw, 328 ft.
WGZB-FM Corydon IN 3 kw, 200 ft.
WAZY(FM) Lafayette IN 50 kw, 500 ft.
KFTE(FM) Breaux Bridge LA 22.5 kw, 328 ft.
KVKI-FM Shreveport LA 95 kw, 797 ft.
WQHH(FM) Dewitt MI 3 kw, 328 ft.
WFAT(FM) Portage MI 3 kw, 321 ft.
WKLK-FM Cloquet MN 6 kw, 315 ft.
KJJK-FM Fergus Falls MN 100 kw, 480 ft.
KWWK(FM) Rochester MN 43 kw, 528 ft.
KXTR(FM) Kansas City MO 99 kw, 984 ft.
KLTQ(FM) Sparta MO 3.2 kw, 453 ft.
KFLD(FM) St. Robert MO 6 kw, 328 ft.
WKDJ(FM) Clarksdale MS 6 kw, 184 ft.
WESV(FM) Richton MS 6 kw, 328 ft.
KDZN(FM) Glendive MT 100 kw, 400 ft.
WAZZ-FM Laurinburg NC 100 kw, 650 ft.
KBYZ(FM) Bismarck-Mandan ND 100 kw, 1,000 ft.
KRGI-FM Grand Island NE 100 kw, 416 ft.
KLMA(FM) Hobbs NM 3 kw, 91 ft.
KWXN(FM) Texico NM 4 kw, 390 ft.
WCQA(FM) Fredonia NY 660 w, 686 ft.
WVNV(FM) Malone NY 2.4 kw, 361 ft.
WCMF-FM Rochester NY 50 kw, 457 ft.
WKDD(FM) Akron OH 50 kw, 475 ft.
WYGY(FM) Hamilton OH 19.5 kw, 810 ft.
KRDM(FM) Ardmore OK 3 kw, 328 ft.
KECO(FM) Elk City OK 100 kw, 500 ft.
KRAV(FM) Tulsa OK 100 kw, 137 ft.
KTWI(FM) Warm Springs OR 100 kw, 1,092 ft.
WMTZ(FM) Johnstown PA 50 kw, 489 ft.
*WPEL-FM Montrose PA 57 kw, 459 ft.
WWDB(FM) Philadelphia PA 19 kw, 866 ft.
WDOY(FM) Fajardo PR 11.5 kw, 2,795 ft.
*WPLS-FM Greenville SC 4 w, 66 ft.
*KNWC-FM Sioux Falls SD 100 kw, 1,600 ft.
WDOD-FM Chattanooga TN 100 kw, 1,080 ft.
WXJB-FM Harrogate TN 6 kw, 325 ft.
KLTG(FM) Corpus Christi TX 97 kw, 869 ft.
KHMX(FM) Houston TX 100 kw, 1,952 ft.
WDCK(FM) Williamsburg VA 50 kw, 492 ft.
KXRX(FM) Seattle WA 100 kw, 1,223 ft.
WKLH(FM) Milwaukee WI 20 kw, 810 ft.
WRKP(FM) Moundsville WV 1.45 kw, 594 ft.
WXCC(FM) Williamson WV 50 kw, 500 ft.
KQSW(FM) Rock Springs WY 100 kw, 1,680 ft.
KWYO-FM Sheridan WY 25 kw, minus 13 ft.

96.7 mhz (ch 244)

WMXA(FM) Opelika AL 730 w, 682 ft.
KAWW-FM Heber Springs AR 3 kw, 328 ft.
KLXQ(FM) Hot Springs AR 2.6 kw, 320 ft.
KDYN-FM Ozark AR 1.6 kw, 400 ft.
KVTF(FM) Williams AZ 1 kw, 804 ft.
KLLK-FM Fort Bragg CA 3.7 kw, 420 ft.
KEZL(FM) Fowler CA 22 kw, 348 ft.
KUNA(FM) La Quinta CA 650 w, 578 ft.
KVFX(FM) Manteca CA 3 kw, 328 ft.
KZZP(FM) Paradise CA 3 kw, 328 ft.
KCAL-FM Redlands CA 1.75 kw, 377 ft.
KWIZ-FM Santa Ana CA 3 kw, 200 ft.
KXBS(FM) Santa Paula CA 87 w, 1,500 ft.
KSYV(FM) Solvang CA 3 kw, minus 51 ft.
KSBT(FM) Steamboat Springs CO 870 w, 510 ft.
WKHL(FM) Stamford CT 3 kw, 328 ft.
WVMG-FM Cochran GA 3 kw, 319 ft.
WMKJ(FM) Newnan GA 1 kw, 545 ft.
WYZK(FM) Valdosta GA 3 kw, 300 ft.
KLBA-FM Albia IA 25 kw, 328 ft.
KACH-FM Preston ID 105 w, 226 ft.
WLLI-FM Joliet IL 3 kw, 300 ft.
WLUV-FM Loves Park IL 3 kw, 300 ft.
WIHN(FM) Normal IL 6 kw, 410 ft.
WKXQ(FM) Rushville IL 3 kw, 328 ft.
WCVS-FM Virden IL 6 kw, 328 ft.
WAXT(FM) Alexandria IN 2.3 kw, 367 ft.
WBWB(FM) Bloomington IN 1.65 kw, 439 ft.
WCOE(FM) La Porte IN 3 kw, 265 ft.
WORX-FM Madison IN 3 kw, 320 ft.
WFML(FM) Vincennes IN 3 kw, 377 ft.
KQDF-FM Larned KS 3 kw, 290 ft.
KBBE(FM) McPherson KS 6 kw, 245 ft.
WOKH(FM) Bardstown KY 3 kw, 160 ft.
WMJM(FM) Bowling Green KY 13.5 kw, 521 ft.
*WKCC(FM) Grayson KY 10 w, 55 ft.
KFXY(FM) Morgan City LA 6 kw, 390 ft.
KWCL-FM Oak Grove LA 3 kw, 289 ft.
*WBYQ(FM) Baltimore MD 19 w, 75 ft.
WCEI-FM Easton MD 25 kw, 245 ft.
WQCM(FM) Halfway MD 4.8 kw, 164 ft.
WCME(FM) Boothbay Harbor ME 25 kw, 449 ft.
*WUFN(FM) Albion MI 1.5 kw, 469 ft.
WWLZ(FM) Cadillac MI 1.7 kw, 443 ft.
WMLQ(FM) Rogers City MI 26 kw, 383 ft.
KDOG(FM) North Mankato MN 18 kw, 390 ft.
KKSR(FM) Sartell MN 50 kw, 453 ft.
KCMQ(FM) Columbia MO 18 kw, 344 ft.
KMEM-FM Memphis MO 25 kw, 300 ft.
KAHR(FM) Poplar Bluff MO 3 kw, 328 ft.
WFFF-FM Columbia MS 3 kw, 400 ft.
WXRG(FM) Gulfport MS 3 kw, 245 ft.
WSEL-FM Pontotoc MS 3 kw, 299 ft.
WONA-FM Winona MS 3 kw, 328 ft.
KGVW-FM Belgrade MT 6 kw, 150 ft.
WKJX(FM) Elizabeth City NC 3 kw, 286 ft.
WRFR(FM) Franklin NC 6 kw, minus 200 ft.
WKRX(FM) Roxboro NC 3 kw, 300 ft.
KCQV(FM) Arthur ND 5 kw, 361 ft.
WLTN-FM Lisbon NH 6 kw, 295 ft.
WWEM(FM) Rochester NH 3 kw, 328 ft.
WVNC(FM) Canton NY 2.6 kw, 310 ft.
WWCP-FM Clifton Park NY 3 kw, 328 ft.
WEHM(FM) East Hampton NY 4.3 kw, 383 ft.
WZOS(FM) Oswego NY 3 kw, 328 ft.
WTSX(FM) Port Jervis NY 3 kw, 300 ft.
WCMJ(FM) Cambridge OH 1.3 kw, 420 ft.
WCSM-FM Celina OH 3 kw, 328 ft.
WBVI(FM) Fostoria OH 3 kw, 330 ft.
WKOV-FM Wellston OH 16.5 kw, 430 ft.
KADA-FM Ada OK 3 kw, 299 ft.
KDDQ(FM) Comanche OK 3 kw, 300 ft.
KBEL-FM Idabel OK 3 kw, 300 ft.
KCRF-FM Lincoln City OR 610 w, 670 ft.
WVNW(FM) Burnham PA 450 w, 850 ft.
WFRM-FM Coudersport PA 1.45 kw, 666 ft.
*WPGM-FM Danville PA 340 w, 760 ft.
WLLF(FM) Mercer PA 1.4 kw, 485 ft.
WHKZ(FM) Cayce SC 3.3 kw, 443 ft.
WSCZ(FM) Greenwood SC 4.1 kw, 390 ft.
KZMX-FM Hot Springs SD 3.4 kw, 440 ft.
WMOD(FM) Bolivar TN 3 kw, 300 ft.
WNKX-FM Centerville TN 3 kw, 300 ft.
KBOC(FM) Bridgeport TX 3 kw, 246 ft.
KVMX(FM) Eastland TX 2.85 kw, 306 ft.
KHFI-FM Georgetown TX 100 kw, 951 ft.
KMOO-FM Mineola TX 3 kw, 300 ft.
KLIS(FM) Palestine TX 3 kw, 300 ft.
KIKM-FM Sherman TX 3 kw, 299 ft.
KXOX-FM Sweetwater TX 2.9 kw, 154 ft.
WREL-FM Buena Vista VA 3 kw, 154 ft.
WJMA-FM Orange VA 2.7 kw, 343 ft.
WTSA-FM Brattleboro VT 5.2 kw, 167 ft.
WWGT(FM) Vergennes VT 3.4 kw, 430 ft.
KWWW-FM Quincy WA 440 w, 1,079 ft.
KREW-FM Sunnyside WA 3 kw, minus 1 ft.
WBDK(FM) Algoma WI 25 kw, 283 ft.
WJJH(FM) Ashland WI 50 kw, 259 ft.
WYTE(FM) Whiting WI 50 kw, 492 ft.
WKMM(FM) Kingwood WV 3 kw, 798 ft.

96.9 mhz (ch 245)

WRSA(FM) Decatur AL 100 kw, 1,010 ft.
WDJR(FM) Enterprise AL 100 kw, 1,515 ft.
NEW FM Maumelle AR 3 kw, 328 ft.
KPSN(FM) Phoenix AZ 100 kw, 1,560 ft.
KGXY(FM) Lenwood CA 1 kw, 810 ft.
KWAV(FM) Monterey CA 18 kw, 2,450 ft.
KSEG(FM) Sacramento CA 50 kw, 500 ft.
KCCY(FM) Pueblo CO 100 kw, 320 ft.
WINK-FM Fort Myers FL 100 kw, 1,322 ft.
WKQL(FM) Jacksonville FL 98 kw, 1,014 ft.
WRDO(FM) Fitzgerald GA 6 kw, 328 ft.
WAKB(FM) Wrens GA 1 kw, 489 ft.
KFMN(FM) Lihue HI 100 kw, 400 ft.
KIAQ(FM) Clarion IA 100 kw, 578 ft.
KLCI(FM) Nampa ID 44 kw, 2,520 ft.
WLBH-FM Mattoon IL 50 kw, 500 ft.
WXLP(FM) Moline IL 50 kw, 499 ft.
WNIZ-FM Zion IL 50 kw, 500 ft.
WYEZ(FM) Bremen IN 2.99 kw, 462 ft.
KKOW-FM Pittsburg KS 100 kw, 278 ft.
WDDJ(FM) Paducah KY 100 kw, 340 ft.
WGKS(FM) Paris KY 50 kw, 492 ft.
KZMZ(FM) Alexandria LA 95 kw, 1,450 ft.
WBCS(FM) Boston MA 12.5 kw, 1,010 ft.
WLSL(FM) Crisfield MD 3 kw, 328 ft.
WBPW(FM) Presque Isle ME 100 kw, 440 ft.
WLAV-FM Grand Rapids MI 50 kw, 499 ft.
WBTI(FM) Lexington MI 3 kw, 328 ft.
WSTD(FM) Standish MI 3 kw, 328 ft.
KMFY(FM) Grand Rapids MN 100 kw, 450 ft.
KXOZ(FM) Mountain View MO 50 kw, 420 ft.
WDLJ(FM) Indianola MS 6 kw, 230 ft.
WXAB(FM) McLain MS 6 kw, 328 ft.
WKTC(FM) Goldsboro NC 100 kw, 1,056 ft.
WTDR(FM) Statesville NC 100 kw, 1,550 ft.
KZKX(FM) Seward NE 100 kw, 610 ft.
KCMI(FM) Terrytown NE 100 kw, 692 ft.
WFPG-FM Atlantic City NJ 50 kw, 400 ft.
KRAZ(FM) Farmington NM 100 kw, 1,010 ft.
WDSP(FM) Arlington NY 3 kw, 1,010 ft.
WGR-FM Buffalo NY 12.5 kw, 790 ft.
WOUR(FM) Utica NY 16 kw, 790 ft.
WTRJ(FM) Troy OH 3 kw, 315 ft.
WZJU(FM) Wauseon OH 3 kw, 328 ft.
KNID(FM) Enid OK 100 kw, 550 ft.
KYJC-FM Grants Pass OR 32 kw, 2,058 ft.
WRRK(FM) Braddock PA 44.7 kw, 530 ft.
WLAN-FM Lancaster PA 50 kw, 500 ft.
WMKB(FM) Ridgebury PA 1.55 kw, 430 ft.
WNRT(FM) Manati PR 50 kw, 882 ft.
WXTC-FM Charleston SC 100 kw, 1,750 ft.
KDLO-FM Watertown SD 100 kw, 1,571 ft.
WXBQ-FM Bristol TN 67 kw, 2,200 ft.
KMML-FM Amarillo TX 100 kw, 550 ft.
KIOX-FM El Campo TX 50 kw, 420 ft.
*KVMV(FM) McAllen TX 100 kw, 1,160 ft.
KQIP(FM) Odessa TX 100 kw, 500 ft.
WSIG(FM) Mount Jackson VA 3 kw, minus 28.7 ft.
KGY-FM McCleary WA 2.33 kw, 1,056 ft.
KYKA(FM) Naches WA 5.8 kw, 36 ft.
KSPO(FM) Spokane WA 6 kw, 535 ft.
WUSW(FM) Oshkosh WI 3 kw, 328 ft.
KAML-FM Gillette WY 100 kw, 456 ft.
KMTN(FM) Jackson WY 48 kw, 940 ft.

97.1 mhz (ch 246)

WMCZ(FM) Millbrook AL 3 kw, 328 ft.
KWEH(FM) Camden AR 39 kw, 190 ft.
KGMS(FM) Green Valley AZ 1.65 kw, 500 ft.
KLSX(FM) Los Angeles CA 29.5 kw, 2,998 ft.
KZMS(FM) Patterson CA 145 w, 164 ft.
KSEQ(FM) Visalia CA 17 kw, 777 ft.
WASH(FM) Washington DC 26 kw, 690 ft.
WXOF(FM) Beverly Hills FL 2.5 kw, 354 ft.
WFOX(FM) Gainesville GA 97 kw, 1,571 ft.
KFSH(FM) Hilo HI 40 kw, minus 124 ft.
WNIB(FM) Chicago IL 8.4 kw, 1,196 ft.
WENS(FM) Shelbyville IN 23 kw, 739 ft.
KIUS(FM) Hutchinson KS 25 kw, 500 ft.
WSEK(FM) Somerset KY 27.5 kw, 659 ft.

Broadcasting & Cable Yearbook 1994
B-512

U.S. FM Stations by Frequency

WEZB(FM) New Orleans LA 100 kw, 984 ft.
*WLIC(FM) Frostburg MD 145 w, 1,401 ft.
WZJO(FM) Ocean Pines MD 2.10 kw, 394 ft.
WYOU-FM Bangor ME 5 kw, 1,230 ft.
WJOI(FM) Detroit MI 12 kw, 890 ft.
WGLQ(FM) Escanaba MI 100 kw, 1,070 ft.
KYCK(FM) Crookston MN 100 kw, 360 ft.
KTCZ-FM Minneapolis MN 100 kw, 1,033 ft.
KXOK-FM Florissant MO 100 kw, 560 ft.
KNIM-FM Maryville MO 25 kw, 328 ft.
WOKK(FM) Meridian MS 100 kw, 600 ft.
KKBR(FM) Billings MT 28 kw, 325 ft.
KALS(FM) Kalispell MT 26 kw, 2,488 ft.
WQMG-FM Greensboro NC 100 kw, 1,289 ft.
KYYX(FM) Minot ND 100 kw, 984 ft.
KELN(FM) North Platte NE 100 kw, 458 ft.
KBCQ(FM) Roswell NM 100 kw, 300 ft.
KXPT(FM) Las Vegas NV 50 kw, 1,950 ft.
WQHT(FM) New York NY 6.7 kw, 1,338 ft.
WREO-FM Ashtabula OH 50 kw, 500 ft.
WXVK(FM) Coal Grove OH 3 kw, 472 ft.
WBNS-FM Columbus OH 24 kw, 660 ft.
KMMY(FM) Muskogee OK 100 kw, 1,274 ft.
KKSN-FM Portland OR 100 kw, 1,266 ft.
WBHT(FM) Mountaintop PA 250 w, 1,102 ft.
WQWK(FM) State College PA 3 kw, 403 ft.
KPSD(FM) Faith SD 100 kw, 1,525 ft.
WHRK(FM) Memphis TN 100 kw, 530 ft.
KRTK(FM) Cleveland TX 100 kw, 981 ft.
KEGL(FM) Fort Worth TX 99 kw, 1,460 ft.
KISN-FM Salt Lake City UT 26 kw, 3,650 ft.
WVNX(FM) Charlotte Amalie VI 50 kw, 1,283 ft.
WZRT(FM) Rutland VT 1.15 kw, 2,591 ft.
KNSN(FM) Walla Walla WA 50 kw, 1,360 ft.
WCOW-FM Sparta WI 100 kw, 587 ft.
WCKA(FM) Sutton WV 25 kw, 193 ft.

97.3 mhz (ch 247)
KEAG(FM) Anchorage AK 100 kw, 593 ft.
WZLM(FM) Dadeville AL 3 kw, 328 ft.
WJAM-FM Marion AL 3.71 kw, 419 ft.
KRXS-FM Globe AZ 490 w, 3,418 ft.
KNCQ(FM) Redding CA 28 kw, 3,569 ft.
KSON-FM San Diego CA 50 kw, 442 ft.
KRQR(FM) San Francisco CA 82 kw, 1,100 ft.
KBCO-FM Boulder CO 100 kw, 1,541 ft.
*WERB(FM) Berlin CT 27.5 w, 95 ft.
WZBG(FM) Litchfield CT 3 kw, 328 ft.
WLQH-FM Chiefland FL 6 kw, 328 ft.
WFLC(FM) Miami FL 100 kw, 800 ft.
WJAD(FM) Bainbridge GA 100 kw, 1,200 ft.
WAEV(FM) Savannah GA 100 kw, 1,000 ft.
KHKI(FM) Des Moines IA 115 kw, 500 ft.
NEW FM Epworth IA 20 kw, 367 ft.
KLCE(FM) Blackfoot ID 100 kw, 1,512 ft.
WRUL(FM) Carmi IL 50 kw, 496 ft.
WFYR(FM) Elmwood IL 23.5 kw, 338 ft.
WJEZ(FM) Pontiac IL 3 kw, 500 ft.
WMEE(FM) Fort Wayne IN 50 kw, 689 ft.
KKJQ(FM) Garden City KS 100 kw, 850 ft.
WIBW-FM Topeka KS 100 kw, 1,220 ft.
WRLV-FM Salyersville KY 5.2 kw, 350 ft.
KMDL(FM) Kaplan LA 42 kw, 535 ft.
WJFD-FM New Bedford MA 50 kw, 500 ft.
WFUB(FM) Orange MA 3 kw, 328 ft.
WIXC(FM) Essexville MI 3 kw, 328 ft.
*KDNW(FM) Duluth MN 40 kw, 548 ft.
KXUS(FM) Springfield MO 100 kw, 479 ft.
WTRC(FM) Natchez MS 3 kw, 328 ft.
WKBC-FM North Wilkesboro NC 100 kw, 1,350 ft.
WMNX(FM) Wilmington NC 100 kw, 602 ft.
KLRB(FM) Aurora NE 50 kw, 354 ft.
WBSS-FM Millville NJ 50 kw, 203 ft.
KKSS-FM Santa Fe NM 94 kw, 1,876 ft.
KWNZ(FM) Carson City NV 87.1 kw, 2,126 ft.
WYXL(FM) Ithaca NY 26 kw, 879 ft.
WMYY(FM) Schoharie NY 885 w, 885 ft.
WZAD(FM) Wurtsboro NY 620 w, 718 ft.
*WGXM(FM) Dayton OH 129 w, 100 ft.
WMMA(FM) Lebanon OH 3 kw, 328 ft.
WJZE(FM) Oak Harbor OH 1.15 kw
KWEY-FM Weatherford OK 70 kw, 385 ft.
KSHR-FM Coquille OR 61 kw, 856 ft.
*WZZE(FM) Glen Mills PA 18 w, 180 ft.
WRVV(FM) Harrisburg PA 17 kw, 840 ft.
WCCZ(FM) Spangler PA 2.15 kw, 393 ft.
KPAT(FM) Sioux Falls SD 60 kw, 221 ft.
WKJQ(FM) Parsons TN 6 kw, 256 ft.
WKXJ(FM) South Pittsburg TN 16 kw, 856 ft.
KATX(FM) Plainview TX 100 kw, 500 ft.
KAJA(FM) San Antonio TX 100 kw, 984 ft.
WGH-FM Newport News VA 74 kw, 415 ft.
KZQB(FM) Davenport WA 3 kw, 72 ft.
KBSG-FM Tacoma WA 52 kw, 2,391 ft.
WLTQ(FM) Milwaukee WI 15.5 kw, 980 ft.
WKWK-FM Wheeling WV 50 kw, 470 ft.

97.5 mhz (ch 248)
WABB-FM Mobile AL 100 kw, 1,644 ft.
WSSY-FM Talladega AL 910 w, 574 ft.
KQUS-FM Hot Springs AR 100 kw, 860 ft.
KVNA-FM Flagstaff AZ 100 kw, 1,509 ft.
KRKN(FM) Oro Valley AZ 3 kw, 299 ft.
KABX-FM Merced CA 50 kw, 490 ft.
KHTX(FM) Riverside CA 68 kw, 1,571 ft.
KHTY(FM) Santa Barbara CA 17.5 kw, 2,920 ft.
WPCV(FM) Winter Haven FL 100 kw, 1,017 ft.
WUFF-FM Eastman GA 4 kw, 371 ft.
WEIZ(FM) Hogansville GA 6 kw, 394 ft.
KZGZ(FM) Agana GU 3.1 kw, 485 ft.

KPOI-FM Honolulu HI 83 kw, 46 ft.
WHMS-FM Champaign IL 50 kw, 358 ft.
WBBA-FM Pittsfield IL 10 kw, 300 ft.
WZOK(FM) Rockford IL 50 kw, 235 ft.
WAMZ(FM) Louisville KY 100 kw, 500 ft.
WHAA(FM) Madison ME 6 kw, 328 ft.
WCSE(FM) Bridgman MI 1.9 kw, 413 ft.
WKLT(FM) Kalkaska MI 32 kw, 670 ft.
WJIM-FM Lansing MI 28 kw-H, 440 ft.
*WEJY(FM) Monroe MI 8 w, 135 ft.
WEFG-FM Whitehall MI 3 kw, 430 ft.
KDKK-FM Park Rapids MN 100 kw, 440 ft.
KNXR(FM) Rochester MN 100 kw, 1,055 ft.
KOEA(FM) Doniphan MO 50 kw, 577 ft.
KRLI(FM) Malta Bend MO 3.42 kw, 879 ft.
WWMS(FM) Oxford MS 100 kw, 1,000 ft.
KBOZ-FM Livingston MT 100 kw, 265 ft.
KKCT(FM) Bismarck ND 100 kw, 324 ft.
KQSK(FM) Chadron NE 100 kw, 840 ft.
WOKQ(FM) Dover NH 50 kw, 500 ft.
WPST(FM) Trenton NJ 50 kw, 470 ft.
KIPP(FM) Mesquite NM 100 kw, 981 ft.
WNGN(FM) Hoosick Falls NY 450 w, 1,115 ft.
WALK-FM Patchogue NY 39 kw, 544 ft.
WCIZ(FM) Watertown NY 41 kw, 285 ft.
WONE-FM Akron OH 12 kw, 900 ft.
WVNU(FM) Greenfield OH 2.75 kw, 305 ft.
WTGR(FM) Union City OH 6 kw, 328 ft.
KLAK(FM) Durant OK 45 kw, 513 ft.
KMOD-FM Tulsa OK 100 kw, 1,800 ft.
KNLR(FM) Bend OR 97 kw, 536 ft.
KSHL(FM) Gleneden Beach OR 17 kw, 843 ft.
WKYN(FM) St. Marys PA 32 kw, 617 ft.
WIOB(FM) Mayaguez PR 25 kw, 990 ft.
WCOS-FM Columbia SC 100 kw, 981 ft.
WEZK-FM Knoxville TN 96 kw, 1,296 ft.
WLLX(FM) Lawrenceburg TN 2.3 kw, 535 ft.
WWEZ(FM) Trenton TN 25 kw, 299 ft.
KAYD(FM) Beaumont TX 100 kw, 1,099 ft.
KBNA-FM El Paso TX 100 kw h, 48 kw v, 1,088 ft.
KWVS(FM) Kingsville TX 100 kw, 1,000 ft.
KGKL-FM San Angelo TX 100 kw, 500 ft.
KWTX-FM Waco TX 97 kw, 1,568 ft.
WWWV(FM) Charlottesville VA 50 kw, 450 ft.
WQOK(FM) South Boston VA 100 kw, 981 ft.
KZLN-FM Othello WA 4.6 kw, 656 ft.
WZTT(FM) Rhinelander WI 100 kw, 771 ft.
WQBE-FM Charleston WV 50 kw, 500 ft.
WKMZ(FM) Martinsburg WV 12.5 kw, 1,010 ft.
KDLY(FM) Lander WY 62 kw, 420 ft.

97.7 mhz (ch 249)
WKKR(FM) Auburn AL 1.35 kw, 476 ft.
WEZZ(FM) Clanton AL 3 kw, 245 ft.
WKLD(FM) Oneonta AL 4 kw, 480 ft.
WSHK(FM) Russellville AL 4.5 kw, 321 ft.
KABK-FM Augusta AR 3 kw, 298 ft.
KCTT-FM Yellville AR 2.45 kw, 331 ft.
KAVV(FM) Benson AZ 630 w, 590 ft.
KQVO(FM) Calexico CA 3 kw, 305 ft.
KWIN(FM) Lodi CA 3 kw, 300 ft.
KHQT(FM) Los Altos CA 1.65 kw, 433 ft.
KAVS(FM) Mojave CA 3 kw, 145 ft.
KMGG(FM) Monte Rio CA 250 w, 1,122 ft.
KEWE(FM) Oroville CA 6 kw, 160 ft.
KKBB(FM) Shafter CA 3 kw, 300 ft.
KYRE(FM) Yreka CA 1.4 kw, 2,364 ft.
KSPN(FM) Aspen CO 3 kw, 54 ft.
WCTY(FM) Norwich CT 1.9 kw, 410 ft.
WAFL(FM) Milford DE 6 kw, 328 ft.
WTBB(FM) Bonifay FL 3 kw, 298 ft.
WRRX(FM) Micanopy FL 3.2 kw, 305 ft.
WQUL(FM) Griffin GA 4.4 kw, 380 ft.
WKAA(FM) Ocilla GA 1.8 kw, 400 ft.
WKCX(FM) Rome GA 3.3 kw, 790 ft.
WMGZ(FM) Sparta GA 3 kw, 328 ft.
WTCQ(FM) Vidalia GA 6 kw, 300 ft.
WWUF(FM) Waycross GA 3 kw, 310 ft.
KCLN-FM Clinton IA 3 kw, 300 ft.
KGCI(FM) Grundy Center IA 16 kw, 407 ft.
KHBT(FM) Humboldt IA 3 kw, 275 ft.
KOTM-FM Ottumwa IA 6 kw, 200 ft.
WBFG(FM) Effingham IL 3 kw, 300 ft.
WMOI(FM) Monmouth IL 3.36 kw, 439 ft.
WLUJ(FM) Petersburg IL 6 kw, 328 ft.
WSTQ(FM) Streator IL 3 kw, 328 ft.
WFRX-FM West Frankfort IL 3 kw, 205 ft.
WSDM-FM Brazil IN 6 kw, 300 ft.
WZOW(FM) Goshen IN 2.9 kw, 482 ft.
WLQI(FM) Rensselaer IN 3.3 kw, 300 ft.
WJSN-FM Jackson KY 638 w, 610 ft.
WHRZ(FM) Providence KY 6 kw, 328 ft.
KPCH(FM) Dubach LA 3 kw, 299 ft.
KAPB(FM) Marksville LA 3 kw, 328 ft.
KDBH(FM) Natchitoches LA 3 kw, 328 ft.
WCAV(FM) Brockton MA 3 kw, 300 ft.
WINQ(FM) Winchendon MA 1.85 kw, 417 ft.
WMDM-FM Lexington Park MD 3 kw, 273 ft.
WCXU(FM) Caribou ME 6 kw, 328 ft.
WMRX-FM Beaverton MI 2.03 kw, 400 ft.
WOLF-FM Houghton MI 875 w, 508 ft.
WMTE-FM Manistee MI 3 kw, 200 ft.
WTGV-FM Sandusky MI 3 kw, 325 ft.
KLGR-FM Redwood Falls MN 3 kw, 305 ft.
KZBK-FM Brookfield MO 3 kw, 203 ft.
KNMO-FM Nevada MO 3 kw, 300 ft.
KHCR(FM) Potosi MO 9.4 kw, 528 ft.
KFBD-FM Waynesville MO 3 kw, 192.3 ft.
WRJH(FM) Brandon MS 3.4 kw, 290 ft.
WTYJ(FM) Fayette MS 3 kw, 300 ft.

WTYL-FM Tylertown MS 3 kw, 145 ft.
KGLM-FM Anaconda MT 2.5 kw, 940 ft.
WQDW-FM Kinston NC 3 kw, 248 ft.
KUVR-FM Holdrege NE 3 kw, 240 ft.
KNCY-FM Nebraska City NE 26 kw, 300 ft.
KARS-FM Belen NM 1.8 kw, 381 ft.
WKOL(FM) Amsterdam NY 790 w, 623 ft.
WGMM(FM) Big Flats NY 1.30 kw, 482 ft.
WCZX(FM) Hyde Park NY 300 w, 1,030 ft.
WUFA(FM) Byesville OH 3 kw
WGGN(FM) Castalia OH 1.25 kw, 725 ft.
WAXZ(FM) Georgetown OH 1.6 kw, 390 ft.
WCJO(FM) Jackson OH 3 kw, 300 ft.
*WTGN(FM) Lima OH 6 kw, 300 ft.
WOXY(FM) Oxford OH 3 kw, 255 ft.
KGOK(FM) Pauls Valley OK 3 kw, 303 ft.
KACI-FM The Dalles OR 5 kw, 890 ft.
WLER-FM Butler PA 2.3 kw, 374 ft.
WWWD(FM) Jersey Shore PA 3 kw, 300 ft.
WVSC-FM Somerset PA 3 kw, 265 ft.
WBRQ(FM) Cidra PR 3 kw, 866 ft.
WWXM(FM) Georgetown SC 50 kw, 492 ft.
KQRO(FM) Cuero TX 3 kw, 297 ft.
KEAS-FM Eastland TX 3 kw, 156 ft.
*KBMI(FM) Roma TX 3 kw, 298 ft.
KWRW(FM) Rusk TX 1.4 kw, 185 ft.
KALK(FM) Winfield TX 22.5 kw, 328 ft.
WMJD(FM) Grundy VA 1.4 kw, 490 ft.
KYSN(FM) East Wenatchee WA 3 kw, minus 150 ft.
KSWW(FM) Raymond WA 230 w, 920 ft.
WGLR-FM Lancaster WI 3 kw, 235 ft.
WAQE-FM Rice Lake WI 3 kw, 299 ft.
WFNL(FM) Sturgeon Bay WI 2 kw, 400 ft.
WRON-FM Ronceverte WV 1 kw, 800 ft.
WFDL(FM) Lomira WI 328 ft.

97.9 mhz (ch 250)
WDMT(FM) Eufaula AL 3 kw, 328 ft.
WVOK(FM) Oxford AL 280 kw, 1,082 ft.
KUPD-FM Tempe AZ 100 kw, 1,620 ft.
KPOD-FM Crescent North CA 6 kw, 310 ft.
KNAX(FM) Fresno CA 2.07 kw, 1,987 ft.
KLAX-FM Long Beach CA 50 kw, 390 ft.
KWAZ(FM) Needles CA 2.8 kw, 1,571 ft.
KISZ-FM Cortez CO 100 kw, 1,360 ft.
WPKX(FM) Enfield CT 2.22 kw, 528 ft.
*WFCS(FM) New Britain CT 50 w, 160 ft.
WSBL(FM) Selbyville DE 3 kw, 328 ft.
WXTB(FM) Clearwater FL 100 kw, 649 ft.
WRMF(FM) Palm Beach FL 100 kw, 1,350 ft.
WSTF(FM) St. Augustine FL 50 kw, 482 ft.
WVVY(FM) Fort Valley GA 10.5 kw, 499 ft.
KKBG(FM) Hilo HI 35 kw-H, 29.5 kw-V, minus 240 ft.
*KCMR(FM) Mason City IA 6 kw, 300 ft.
KSEZ(FM) Sioux City IA 100 kw, 643 ft.
KQFC(FM) Boise ID 47 kw, 2,499 ft.
WLUP-FM Chicago IL 6 kw, 1,710 ft.
WXXP(FM) Anderson IN 50 kw, 489 ft.
WSLM-FM Salem IN 3 kw, 220 ft.
KRBB(FM) Wichita KS 100 kw, 993 ft.
WZQQ(FM) Hyden KY 5.7 kw, 335 ft.
WIYY(FM) Baltimore MD 13.5 kw, 945 ft.
WCSO(FM) Portland ME 16 kw, 889 ft.
WJLB(FM) Detroit MI 50 kw, 489 ft.
WGRD-FM Grand Rapids MI 13 kw, 590 ft.
WUPQ(FM) Newberry MI 50 kw, 352 ft.
WEVE-FM Eveleth MN 71 kw, 555 ft.
KICK-FM Palmyra MO 30 kw, 341 ft.
KSTG(FM) Sikeston MO 12.5 kw, 469 ft.
KKLL-FM Webb City MO 6 kw, 400 ft.
KRSI(FM) Garapan-Saipan MP 6 kw, 1,519 ft.
WBAQ(FM) Greenville MS 24.5 kw-horiz, 495 ft.
WUSD(FM) Wiggins MS 3 kw
WKZF(FM) Bayboro NC 2.75 kw, 341 ft.
WPEG(FM) Concord NC 95 kw, 1,608 ft.
WLGQ(FM) Gaston NC 1.35 kw, 488 ft.
KPVZ(FM) Beulah ND 6 kw, 328 ft.
*KFNW-FM Fargo ND 100 kw, 350 ft.
WSKQ-FM New York NY 7.6 kw H, 5.4 kw V, 1,220 ft.
WPXY-FM Rochester NY 50 kw, 456 ft.
WNCI(FM) Columbus OH 175 kw, 560 ft.
KTNT-FM Edmond OK 6 kw, 300 ft.
KZBB(FM) Poteau OK 100 kw, 2,000 ft.
KUGN-FM Eugene OR 100 kw, 1,230 ft.
KLKY(FM) Milton-Freewater OR 50,000 kw, 705 ft.
WXTA(FM) Edinboro PA 10 kw, 505 ft.
WZMT(FM) Hazleton PA 19.5 kw, 722 ft.
WAAN(FM) Blackville SC 6 kw, 328 ft.
KLMP(FM) Rapid City SD 100 kw-H, 390 ft.
WSIX-FM Nashville TN 100 kw, 1,140 ft.
KGNC-FM Amarillo TX 100 kw, 1,285 ft.
KYTX(FM) Beeville TX 50 kw, 492 ft.
KRRW(FM) Dallas TX 99 kw, 1,611 ft.
KBXX(FM) Houston TX 100 kw, 1,920 ft.
KOAX(FM) Mason TX 50 kw, 492 ft.
KODM(FM) Odessa TX 100 kw, 361 ft.
KBZN(FM) Ogden UT 26 kw, 3,770 ft.
WGOL(FM) Lynchburg VA 3 kw, 240 ft.
WGOD-FM Charlotte Amalie VI 50 kw, 295 ft.
WSPT(FM) Stevens Point WI 51 kw, 340 ft.
WFGM(FM) Fairmont WV 32 kw, 500 ft.
KTAG(FM) Cody WY 100 kw, 1,901 ft.
KFBQ(FM) Cheyenne WY 100 kw, 541 ft.

98.1 mhz (ch 251)
KLEF(FM) Anchorage AK 25 kw, minus 85 ft.
KWLF(FM) Fairbanks AK 25 kw, minus 7 ft.
WWSF-FM Andalusia AL 89 kw, 1,090 ft.
WXTT(FM) Fayette AL 100 kw, 984 ft.
WUAF(FM) Valley AL 3 kw, 328 ft.

Broadcasting & Cable Yearbook 1994
B-513

U.S. FM Stations by Frequency

*KVIP-FM Redding CA 30 kw, 1,710 ft.
KIFM(FM) San Diego CA 28 kw, 640 ft.
KABL-FM San Francisco CA 100 kw, 940 ft.
KKJG(FM) San Luis Obispo CA 3.6 kw, 1,624 ft.
KRXV(FM) Yermo CA 1.1 kw, 2,280 ft.
KKFM(FM) Colorado Springs CO 72 kw, 2,300 ft.
WKZE-FM Salisbury CT 1.8 kw, 604 ft.
WQHL-FM Live Oak FL 50 kw, 367 ft.
WGNE-FM Titusville FL 50 kw, 462 ft.
WJAT-FM Swainsboro GA 3 kw, 285 ft-H, 280 ft-V.
KHAK-FM Cedar Rapids IA 100 kw, 485 ft.
KRXK-FM Rexburg ID 3 kw, 299 ft.
WZOE-FM Princeton IL 6 kw, 300 ft.
WIBN(FM) Earl Park IN 25 kw, 328 ft.
WRAY-FM Princeton IN 50 kw, 420 ft.
KYBD(FM) Copeland KS 100 kw, 666 ft.
KUDL(FM) Kansas City KS 100 kw, 994 ft.
WKQQ(FM) Lexington KY 100 kw, 561 ft.
WGGZ(FM) Baton Rouge LA 100 kw, 1,550 ft.
WCTK(FM) New Bedford MA 47.3 kw, 508 ft.
WGFN(FM) Glen Arbor MI 7.9 kw, 590 ft.
*WEUL(FM) Kingsford MI 240 w, 482 ft.
WKCQ(FM) Saginaw MI 50 kw, 500 ft.
KBEW-FM Blue Earth MN 25 kw, 328 ft.
WWJO(FM) St. Cloud MN 97 kw, 1,000 ft.
KOZX(FM) Cabool MO 3 kw, 220 ft.
KYKY(FM) St. Louis MO 90 kw, 1,027 ft.
WQSM(FM) Fayetteville NC 100 kw, 850 ft.
KBAC(FM) Las Vegas NM 97 kw, 1,037 ft.
KBUL(FM) Carson City NV 75.9 kw, 2,273 ft.
WHWK(FM) Binghamton NY 10 kw, 960 ft.
WTOF-FM Canton OH 36 kw, 570 ft.
WDFM(FM) Defiance OH 50 kw, 500 ft.
KKRX-FM Lawton OK 100 kw, 202 ft.
WFGY(FM) Altoona PA 30 kw, 1,020 ft.
WOGL-FM Philadelphia PA 12.5 kw, 1,000 ft.
WYBB(FM) Folly Beach SC 50 kw, 500 ft.
WBFM(FM) Seneca SC 100 kw, 905 ft.
WYKL(FM) Millington TN 100 kw, 1,240 ft.
WVXA(FM) Signal Mountain TN 1 kw, 794 ft.
KKHR(FM) Anson TX 50 kw, 292 ft.
KVET-FM Austin TX 100 kw, 686 ft.
KRRG(FM) Laredo TX 100 kw, 737 ft.
KKCL(FM) Lorenzo TX 50 kw, 431 ft.
KTAL-FM Texarkana TX 100 kw h, 61 kw v, 1,360 ft.
KREC(FM) Brian Head UT 56 kw, 2,526 ft.
WBRF(FM) Galax VA 100 kw, 1,756 ft.
WTVR-FM Richmond VA 50 kw, 1,004 ft.
WJJR(FM) Rutland VT 1.15 kw, 2,953 ft.
KING-FM Seattle WA 58 kw-H, 2,342 ft.
KISC(FM) Spokane WA 94 kw, 2,030 ft.
WISM-FM Altoona WI 25 kw, 279 ft.
WMGN(FM) Madison WI 38 kw, 581 ft.
KUHG(FM) Milford NE 981 ft.

98.3 mhz (ch 252)

WDLT(FM) Chickasaw AL 6 kw, 300 ft.
WAGH(FM) Fort Mitchell AL 3 kw, 328 ft.
WKEA-FM Scottsboro AL 6 kw, 531 ft.
WAWV(FM) Sylacauga AL 2.7 kw, 502 ft.
KOLZ(FM) Bentonville AR 10.5 kw, 339 ft.
KTLO-FM Mountain Home AR 1.4 kw, 420 ft.
KTTZ(FM) Ajo AZ 3 kw, 69 ft.
KOHT(FM) Marana AZ 3 kw, 200 ft.
KQSS(FM) Miami AZ 3 kw, minus 380 ft.
KLCR(FM) Nogales AZ 215 w, 228 ft.
KDTK(FM) Prescott Valley AZ 875 w, 2,526 ft.
KWCX(FM) Willcox AZ 3 kw, 57 ft.
KXBX-FM Lakeport CA 3 kw, 300 ft.
KDAR(FM) Oxnard CA 3 kw, 240 ft.
KMIX-FM Turlock CA 1.6 kw, 390 ft.
KMQA-FM West Covina CA 2.3 w, 328 ft.
KKYY(FM) Gunnison CO 3 kw, 304 ft.
KATR-FM Wray CO 3 kw, 331 ft.
WDAQ(FM) Danbury CT 1.3 kw, 460 ft.
WILI-FM Willimantic CT 1.05 kw, 525 ft.
WECY-FM Seaford DE 3 kw, 328 ft.
WKGF-FM Arcadia FL 2 kw, 400 ft.
WRTO(FM) Goulds FL 1.1 kw, 462 ft.
WKKN(FM) Cordele GA 3 kw, 300 ft.
WGCO(FM) Midway GA 100 kw, 1,047 ft.
KMVI-FM Pukalani HI 3 kw, -546 ft.
KRUU(FM) Boone IA 3 kw, 210 ft.
WBYS-FM Canton IL 3 kw, 265 ft.
WCCQ(FM) Crest Hill IL 3 kw, 300 ft.
WZRO(FM) Farmer City IL 3 kw, 300 ft.
WRIK-FM Metropolis IL 1.3 kw, 456 ft.
WARU-FM Peru IN 3 kw, 43 ft.
WXIR(FM) Plainfield IN 3 kw, 300 ft.
WZZY(FM) Winchester IN 3 kw, 300 ft.
WDNS(FM) Bowling Green KY 6 kw, 300 ft.
WNUU(FM) Garrison KY 2.6 kw, 492 ft.
KYEA(FM) West Monroe LA 50 kw, 492 ft.
WHAI-FM Greenfield MA 2 kw, 403 ft.
WSMD(FM) Mechanicsville MD 3 kw, 328 ft.
WTWR-FM Monroe MI 1.4 kw, 465 ft.
WHCH(FM) Munising MI 32 kw, 357 ft.
WLCS(FM) North Muskegon MI 2.6 kw, 321 ft.
*WCMZ-FM Sault Ste. Marie MI 25 kw, 328 ft.
WCSY-FM South Haven MI 2 kw, 400 ft.
WBJI(FM) Blackduck MN 50 kw, 456 ft.
KQYB(FM) Spring Grove MN 33 kw, 607 ft.
KFMZ(FM) Columbia MO 23.5 kw, 711 ft.
WSSI-FM Carthage MS 3 kw, 300 ft.
WDFX(FM) Cleveland MS 25 kw
WJDR(FM) Prentiss MS 6 kw, 325 ft.
KDBM-FM Dillon MT 10.5 kw, 495 ft.
WBCG(FM) Murfreesboro NC 3 kw, 302 ft.
WFAZ(FM) Thomasville NC 1.68 kw, 429 ft.
WCZI(FM) Washington NC 1.3 kw, 490 ft.
KBBN-FM Broken Bow NE 3.4 kw, 332 ft.
WLNH-FM Laconia NH 1.9 kw, 413 ft.
WMGQ(FM) New Brunswick NJ 1 kw, 525 ft.
WKTU(FM) Ocean City NJ 3 kw, 300 ft.
WVIN-FM Bath NY 3 kw, 351 ft.
WKJY(FM) Hempstead NY 3 kw, 328 ft.
WSUL-FM Monticello NY 3.0 kw, 360 ft.
WTRY-FM Rotterdam NY 3 kw, 328 ft.
WQRT(FM) Salamanca NY 1.6 kw, 430 ft.
WPHR(FM) Ashtabula OH 2 kw, 403 ft.
WPKO-FM Bellefontaine OH 1.3 kw, 430 ft.
WWBK(FM) Fredericktown OH 3 kw, 300 ft.
*WKET(FM) Kettering OH 10 w, 150 ft.
WLGN-FM Logan OH 3 kw, 240 ft.
KTWS(FM) Bend OR 7 kw, 706 ft.
KLDR(FM) Harbeck-Fruitdale OR 185 w, 2,096 ft.
WESA-FM Charleroi PA 6 kw, 300 ft.
WWBE(FM) Mifflinburg PA 3 kw, 403 ft.
WQQZ(FM) Quebradillas PR 3 kw, 1,000 ft.
WSLT(FM) Clearwater SC 2.8 kw, 484 ft.
WRJB(FM) Camden TN 3 kw, 300 ft.
WINJ(FM) Pulaski TN 3 kw, 453 ft.
WDEH-FM Sweetwater TN 2.78 kw, 135 ft.
KEEP(FM) Bandera TX 1.43 kw
KFYZ-FM Bonham TX 3 kw, 300 ft.
KORA-FM Bryan TX 900 w, 528 ft.
KICA-FM Farwell TX 6 kw, 256 ft.
KRYL(FM) Gatesville TX 3 kw, 299 ft.
KKHQ(FM) Odem TX 3 kw, 303 ft.
KYYK(FM) Palestine TX 50 kw, 492 ft.
KPTX(FM) Pecos TX 3 kw, 160 ft.
KBUC(FM) Pleasanton TX 3 kw, 300 ft.
KRDF-FM Spearman TX 3 kw, 220 ft.
KCUB-FM Stephenville TX 3 kw, 328 ft.
KARB(FM) Price UT 3 kw, minus 145 ft.
WLCQ(FM) Clarksville VA 17.5 kw, 394 ft.
WGMT(FM) Lyndon VT 190 w, 1,990 ft.
KEYW(FM) Pasco WA 3 kw, 197 ft.
WFMR(FM) Menomonee Falls WI 6 kw, 328 ft.
WCQM(FM) Park Falls WI 3 kw, 275 ft.
WXVA-FM Charles Town WV 3 kw, 300 ft.
WCEF(FM) Ripley WV 3 kw, 300 ft.
KRSV-FM Afton WY 3 kw, 288 ft.
KERM(FM) Torrington WY 3 kw, 300 ft.

98.5 mhz (ch 253)

WINL(FM) Linden AL 100 kw, 817 ft.
KURB-FM Little Rock AR 99 kw, 1,286 ft.
KWXY-FM Cathedral City CA 50 kw, 499 ft.
KDNO(FM) Delano CA 50 kw, 499 ft.
KSAY(FM) Fort Bragg CA 3.4 kw, 448 ft.
KNCI(FM) Sacramento CA 50 kw, 500 ft.
KOME(FM) San Jose CA 12.5 kw, 880 ft.
KYGO-FM Denver CO 100 kw, 1,820 ft.
WKTK(FM) Crystal River FL 100 kw, 1,332 ft.
WFSY(FM) Panama City FL 100 kw, 1,090 ft.
WRWX(FM) Sanibel FL 2.6 kw, 490 ft.
WSB-FM Atlanta GA 100 kw, 919 ft.
WLPF(FM) Ocilla GA 4.3 kw, 361 ft.
KHHH(FM) Honolulu HI 100 kw, minus 968 ft.
KQKQ-FM Council Bluffs IA 100 kw, 1,074 ft.
KRSS(FM) Chubbuck ID 150 w, 1,350 ft.
WCRI(FM) Eureka IL 3 kw, 328 ft.
WXXQ(FM) Freeport IL 50 kw, 450 ft.
WACF(FM) Paris IL 50 kw, 500 ft.
KSAJ-FM Abilene KS 100 kw, 443 ft.
WQXE(FM) Elizabethtown KY 1.9 kw, 385 ft.
WYLD-FM New Orleans LA 100 kw, 984 ft.
WBMX(FM) Boston MA 9 kw, 1,145 ft.
WEBB(FM) Waterville ME 50 kw, 305 ft.
WNWN(FM) Coldwater MI 50 kw, 500 ft.
WUPS(FM) Houghton Lake MI 100 kw, 981 ft.
*KTIS-FM Minneapolis MN 100 kw, 1,033 ft.
KTJJ(FM) Farmington MO 100 kw, 1,040 ft.
WZLQ(FM) Tupelo MS 100 kw-H, 381 ft.
KIDX(FM) Billings MT 85 kw, 370 ft.
KBBZ(FM) Kalispell MT 58 kw, 2,378 ft.
WSAY-FM Rocky Mount NC 3 kw, 328 ft.
WQNJ(FM) Ocean Acres NJ 6 kw, 328 ft.
KTMN(FM) Los Alamos NM 100 kw, 1,781 ft.
KLUC-FM Las Vegas NV 97 kw, 1,181 ft.
WCTW(FM) Catskill NY 2.1 kw, 393 ft.
WKSE(FM) Niagara Falls NY 46 kw, 420 ft.
WNYR-FM Waterloo NY 3 kw, 328 ft.
WMRW(FM) Westhampton NY 6 kw, 282 ft.
WRRM(FM) Cincinnati OH 17.5 kw, 807 ft.
WNCX(FM) Cleveland OH 16 kw, 960 ft.
*WCMO(FM) Marietta OH 40 w, 105 ft.
KTIJ(FM) Elk City OK 100 kw, 1,089 ft.
KVOO-FM Tulsa OK 100 kw, 1,229 ft.
KUPL-FM Portland OR 100 kw, 1,104 ft.
WRJS(FM) Oil City PA 20 kw, 299 ft.
*WPTS-FM Pittsburgh PA 10 w, 550 ft.
WKRZ-FM Wilkes-Barre PA 8.7 kw, 1,171 ft.
WYCR(FM) York-Hanover PA 10.5 kw, 928 ft.
WPRM-FM San Juan PR 25 kw, 1,910 ft.
WHSC-FM Hartsville SC 3 kw, 328 ft.
WDAI(FM) Pawley's Island SC 6 kw, 328 ft.
WHUB-FM Cookeville TN 50 kw, 492 ft.
WTFM(FM) Kingsport TN 100 kw, 1,260 ft.
KGAP(FM) Clarksville TX 6 kw, 328 ft.
KRBH(FM) Hondo TX 3 kw, 272 ft.
KQXX(FM) McAllen TX 100 kw, 1,400 ft.
KHYS(FM) Port Arthur TX 98 kw, 1,952 ft.
KRXT(FM) Rockdale TX 6 kw, 328 ft.
KIFX(FM) Roosevelt UT 2.65 kw, 1,853 ft.
WPKZ(FM) Elkton VA 900 w, 1,607 ft.
KEYG-FM Grand Coulee WA 25 kw-H, 463 ft.
WQLH(FM) Green Bay WI 100 kw, 1,254 ft.

98.7 mhz (ch 254)

WLBI(FM) Warrior AL 6 kw, 328 ft.
KKLT(FM) Phoenix AZ 100 kw, 1,680 ft.
KYSR(FM) Los Angeles CA 75 kw, 1,180 ft.
KRSH(FM) Middletown CA 3 kw, 213 ft.
KFMK(FM) Winton CA 4.4 kw, 384 ft.
KRTZ(FM) Cortez CO 27 kw, 2,900 ft.
WMZQ-FM Washington DC 50 kw, 490 ft.
WKGR(FM) Fort Pierce FL 100 kw, 1,381 ft.
WISP(FM) Holmes Beach FL 3 kw, 328 ft.
WOZN(FM) Key West FL 100 kw, 300 ft.
WISK-FM Americus GA 25 kw, 302 ft.
KMGO(FM) Centerville IA 100 kw, 500 ft.
WFMT(FM) Chicago IL 16 kw, 1,170 ft.
WNNS(FM) Springfield IL 50 kw, 500 ft.
WQME(FM) Anderson IN 6 kw, 328 ft.
WIIZ(FM) Battle Ground IN 4.4 kw, 384 ft.
KSPG(FM) Clearwater KS 50 kw, 492 ft.
WHOP-FM Hopkinsville KY 100 kw, 304 ft.
WKDO-FM Liberty KY 25 kw, 239 ft.
KICR-FM Oakdale LA 10 kw, 1,053 ft.
WLLZ(FM) Detroit MI 50 kw, 462 ft.
WFGR(FM) Grand Rapids MI 2.75 kw, 492 ft.
KQWB-FM Moorhead MN 100 kw, 460 ft.
KISD(FM) Pipestone MN 100 kw, 700 ft.
KWTO-FM Springfield MO 100 kw, 600 ft.
WIIN(FM) Vicksburg MS 100 kw, 950 ft.
WKSI(FM) Greensboro NC 100 kw, 1,000 ft.
WKOO(FM) Jacksonville NC 100 kw, 1,015 ft.
KSID-FM Sidney NE 62 kw, 368 ft.
WXOD(FM) Winchester NH 6 kw, 328 ft.
WFNN(FM) Villas NJ 3 kw, 292 ft.
*KMTH(FM) Maljamar NM 100 kw, 710 ft.
KSNM(FM) Truth or Consequences NM 100 kw, 2,643 ft.
WCBA-FM Corning NY 2 kw, 393 ft.
WRKS-FM New York NY 7.8 kw-H, 5.5 kw-V, 1,220 ft.
WPFE(FM) Ogdensburg NY 3 kw, 328 ft.
WLZW(FM) Utica NY 25 kw, 660 ft.
WAPQ(FM) Crestline OH 1.8 kw, 418 ft.
*WSLN(FM) Delaware OH 100 w, 105 ft.
KYTT-FM Coos Bay OR 31 kw, 551 ft.
KUBQ(FM) La Grande OR 2.25 kw, 1,942 ft.
KGZH(FM) Nyssa OR 100 kw, 354 ft.
WYKZ(FM) Beaufort SC 100 kw, 1,001 ft.
KOUT(FM) Rapid City SD 100 kw, 515 ft.
WXVO(FM) Oliver Springs TN 6 kw, 328 ft.
WWEE(FM) Spencer TN 1.1 kw, 548 ft.
KQAC(FM) Amarillo TX 100 kw, 480 ft.
KLUV(FM) Dallas TX 98 kw, 1,584 ft.
KELI(FM) San Angelo TX 100 kw, 1,290 ft.
KTXN-FM Victoria TX 100 kw, 253 ft.
KVRI(FM) Salt Lake City UT 40 kw, 2,932 ft.
WNOR-FM Norfolk VA 46 kw, 520 ft.
WTUN(FM) Pocatalico WV 1.2 kw, 515 ft.
WOVK(FM) Wheeling WV 50 kw, 390 ft.
WXZR(FM) East Lyme CT 3.8 kw, 236 ft.

98.9 mhz (ch 255)

KYMG(FM) Anchorage AK 100 kw, 499 ft.
WBAM-FM Montgomery AL 100 kw, 1095 ft.
KCMT(FM) Chester CA 25 kw, 2,417 ft.
KAGF(FM) Columbia CA 300 w, 440 ft.
KJOI(FM) Dinuba CA 19 kw, 820 ft.
KHWY(FM) Essex CA 7.4 kw, 1,073 ft.
KSRY(FM) San Francisco CA 6 kw, 1,143 ft.
KKMG(FM) Pueblo CO 100 kw, 1,715 ft.
WMMO(FM) Orlando FL 38 kw, 439 ft.
WBGM-FM Tallahassee FL 100 kw, 390 ft.
WQMT(FM) Chatsworth GA 3 kw, 299 ft.
KBQB(FM) Princeville HI 100 kw, minus 53 ft.
KRNQ(FM) Hampton IA 6 kw, 325 ft.
KLSN(FM) Jefferson IA 3 kw, 101 ft.
WPXR-FM Rock Island IL 39 kw, 900 ft.
WKJK(FM) Salem IN 50 kw, 300 ft.
KUSN(FM) Coffeyville KS 6 kw, 300 ft.
KQRC-FM Leavenworth KS 100 kw, 990 ft.
WSIP-FM Paintsville KY 94 kw, 600 ft.
WXXW(FM) Webster MA 3 kw, 328 ft.
WKHJ(FM) Mountain Lake Park MD 490 w, 662 ft.
WSBY-FM Salisbury MD 6 kw, 328 ft.
WCLZ-FM Brunswick ME 48 kw, 400 ft.
WKLZ(FM) Petoskey MI 50 kw, 800 ft.
WOWE(FM) Vassar MI 3 kw, 328 ft.
WAKX(FM) Duluth MN 100 kw, 600 ft.
KZPK(FM) Paynesville MN 50 kw, 492 ft.
KTMO(FM) Kennett MO 100 kw, 994 ft.
WYKK(FM) Quitman MS 3 kw, 295 ft.
KAAK(FM) Great Falls MT 100 kw, 500 ft.
WYHC(FM) Charlotte NC 84 w-V, 135 ft.
WDRP(FM) Windsor NC 6 kw, 350 ft.
KKPR-FM Kearney NE 100 kw, 700 ft.
WKLX(FM) Rochester NY 50 kw, 560 ft.
WRVF(FM) Upper Arlington OH 3 kw, 328 ft.
WBYR(FM) Van Wert OH 50 kw, 450 ft.
WKBN-FM Youngstown OH 4.5 kw, 1,370 ft.
KYIS(FM) Oklahoma City OK 100 kw, 1,108 ft.
WQLV(FM) Millersburg PA 780 w, 895 ft.
WUSL(FM) Philadelphia PA 18 kw, 830 ft.
WSAN(FM) Vieques PR 50 kw, 751 ft.
WZJQ(FM) McClellanville SC 50 kw, 492 ft.
WSPA-FM Spartanburg SC 100 kw, 1,910 ft.
WANT(FM) Lebanon TN 5 kw, 320 ft.
KTUX(FM) Carthage TX 100 kw, 1,049 ft.
KLTR(FM) Franklin TX 3 kw, 328 ft.
KUTZ(FM) Lampasas TX 18.5 kw, 1,860 ft.
WHFD(FM) Lawrenceville VA 3 kw, 154 ft.
WOKO(FM) Burlington VT 100 kw, 307 ft.
KEZX-FM Seattle WA 100 kw, 1,110 ft.
KKZX(FM) Spokane WA 100 kw, 1,614 ft.
WVCX(FM) Tomah WI 100 kw, 991 ft.

Broadcasting & Cable Yearbook 1994
B-514

U.S. FM Stations by Frequency

99.1 mhz (ch 256)
KPVV(FM) Dillingham AK 6 kw, 167 ft.
WAHR(FM) Huntsville AL 100 kw, 984 ft.
KMAG(FM) Fort Smith AR 100 kw, 1,968 ft.
KNOT-FM Prescott AZ 6 kw, 200 ft.
KFMM(FM) Thatcher AZ 50 kw, 2,280 ft.
KGGI(FM) Riverside CA 2.55 kw, 1,843 ft.
KSRI(FM) Santa Cruz CA 1.1 kw, 2,487 ft.
KXFM(FM) Santa Maria CA 1.8 kw, 1,905 ft.
*KTUO(FM) Sonora CA 35 w, -150 ft.
KUAD-FM Windsor CO 100 kw, 657 ft.
WPLR(FM) New Haven CT 14.1 kw, 950 ft.
WQIK-FM Jacksonville FL 100 kw, 1,050 ft.
WEDR(FM) Miami FL 100 kw, 926 ft.
WAYS(FM) Macon GA 100 kw, 648 ft.
KSKB(FM) Brooklyn IA 50 kw, 175 ft.
KUPI-FM Idaho Falls ID 100 kw, 1,513 ft.
KLVJ-FM Mountain Home ID 100 kw, minus 1,400 ft.
WIAI(FM) Danville IL 50 kw, 500 ft.
*KJIL(FM) Copeland KS 100 kw, 935 ft.
KTLI(FM) El Dorado KS 45 kw, 492 ft.
KSEK-FM Girard KS 3 kw, 325 ft.
WKNK(FM) Edmonton KY 3 kw, 328 ft.
WKYI(FM) Stamping Ground KY 1.5 kw, 200 ft.
KXKC(FM) New Iberia LA 100 kw, 1,039 ft.
WPLM-FM Plymouth MA 50 kw, 430 ft.
WHFS(FM) Annapolis MD 50 kw, 459 ft.
WLKE(FM) Bar Harbor ME 16.7 kw, 403 ft.
WSMK(FM) Buchanan MI 3 kw, 328 ft.
WFMK(FM) East Lansing MI 28 kw, 600 ft.
WIKB-FM Iron River MI 50 kw, 492 ft.
KEEZ-FM Mankato MN 100 kw, 864 ft.
KLLZ-FM Walker MN 50 kw, 492 ft.
KFUO-FM Clayton MO 100 kw, 1,026 ft.
WYMX(FM) Greenwood MS 100 kw, 1,029 ft.
WKNN-FM Pascagoula MS 100 kw, 1,012 ft.
WVOD(FM) Manteo NC 50 kw, 491 ft.
WZFX(FM) Whiteville NC 100 kw, 1,000 ft.
KRRD(FM) Dickinson ND 100 kw, 712 ft.
WNNH(FM) Henniker NH 6 kw, 712 ft.
WAWZ(FM) Zarephath NJ 37 kw, 570 ft.
KAFR(FM) Angel Fire NM 5.743 kw, 1,377 ft.
KCLV-FM Clovis NM 74.2 kw, 230 ft.
KGLX(FM) Gallup NM 100 kw, 500 ft.
WAAL(FM) Binghamton NY 7.1 kw, 1,089 ft.
WHKO(FM) Dayton OH 50 kw, 1,060 ft.
WFRO-FM Fremont OH 20 kw, 195 ft.
KPNW-FM Eugene OR 100 kw, 1,945 ft.
WQKK(FM) Ebensburg PA 50 kw, 500 ft.
WKJB-FM Mayaguez PR 50 kw, 1,963 ft.
WBAW-FM Barnwell SC 25 kw, 328 ft.
WNOX(FM) Loudon TN 3 kw, 300 ft.
KRYS-FM Corpus Christi TX 100 kw, 1,049 ft.
KDZR(FM) Denton TX 97 kw, 1,168 ft.
KODA(FM) Houston TX 95 kw, 1,920 ft.
KKKK(FM) Odessa TX 100 kw, 500 ft.
WXGM-FM Gloucester VA 6 kw, 328 ft.
WSLQ(FM) Roanoke VA 200 kw, 1,985 ft.
WMYX(FM) Milwaukee WI 50 kw, 450 ft.
WHCM(FM) Parkersburg WV 11.5 kw, 485 ft.

99.3 mhz (ch 257)
WMFC-FM Monroeville AL 3 kw, 328 ft.
KLBQ(FM) El Dorado AR 2.95 kw, 298 ft.
KZYP(FM) Pine Bluff AR 3 kw, 200 ft.
KCHT(FM) Bakersfield CA 6 kw, 154 ft.
KNNN(FM) Central Valley CA 5.3 kw, 328 ft.
KAJK-FM Ferndale CA 3.6 kw, 407 ft.
KAGZ(FM) Fresno CA 3 kw, 328 ft.
KJFA(FM) Grass Valley CA 3 kw, 325 ft.
KMXX(FM) Imperial CA 3 kw, 200 ft.
KVYN(FM) St. Helena CA 3 kw, 1,200 ft.
KJOY(FM) Stockton CA 2.35 kw, 330 ft.
WLRQ-FM Cocoa FL 1.2 kw, 500 ft.
WJBX(FM) Fort Myers Beach FL 50 kw, 476 ft.
WKSM(FM) Fort Walton Beach FL 3 kw, 171 ft.
WEBZ(FM) Mexico Beach FL 50 kw, 519 ft.
WCON-FM Cornelia GA 50 kw, 808 ft.
WKCN(FM) Lumpkin GA 50 kw, 492 ft.
*KFGQ-FM Boone IA 2.55 kw, 351 ft.
KDST(FM) Dyersville IA 3 kw, 298 ft.
KWAY-FM Waverly IA 3 kw, 180 ft.
KWEI-FM Weiser ID 3 kw, minus 185 ft.
WDUK(FM) Havana IL 3 kw, 300 ft.
WAJK(FM) La Salle IL 11 kw, 500 ft.
WXFM(FM) Mt. Zion IL 1.15 kw, 495 ft.
WSCH(FM) Aurora IN 1.15 kw, 525 ft.
WKVI-FM Knox IN 3 kw, 303 ft.
WCJC(FM) Van Buren IN 3 kw, 328 ft.
KIKS-FM Iola KS 3 kw, 300 ft.
WWKF(FM) Fulton KY 3.3 kw, 337 ft.
WHBN-FM Harrodsburg KY 3 kw, 265 ft.
WVLE(FM) Scottsville KY 3 kw, 328 ft.
KJNA-FM Jena LA 3 kw, 299 ft.
WHMP-FM Northampton MA 3 kw, 321 ft.
WKTJ-FM Farmington ME 1.5 kw, 400 ft.
WBQQ(FM) Kennebunk ME 3 kw, 324 ft.
WATZ-FM Alpena MI 17 kw, 843 ft.
WBNZ(FM) Frankfort MI 50 kw, 410 ft.
WMSH-FM Sturgis MI 1.4 kw, 390 ft.
WJQK(FM) Zeeland MI 5.1 kw, 354 ft.
KSTQ(FM) Alexandria MN 6 kw, 285 ft.
KWNO-FM Rushford MN 2.56 kw, 499 ft.
KKDQ(FM) Thief River Falls MN 6 kw, 170 ft.
KCLR-FM Boonville MO 33.2 kw, 590 ft.
KCGQ-FM Gordonville MO 4.2 kw, 390 ft.
KUNQ(FM) Houston MO 3 kw-H, 300 ft.
WBIP-FM Booneville MS 6 kw, 300 ft.
WEEZ(FM) Heidelberg MS 3 kw, 299 ft.
KMXE(FM) Red Lodge MT 45 kw, minus 359 ft.
WQDK(FM) Ahoskie NC 3 kw, 300 ft.
KUTT(FM) Fairbury NE 3 kw, 310 ft.
WFRD(FM) Hanover NH 3.4 kw, 285 ft.
WMID-FM Pleasantville NJ 3.4 kw, 289 ft.
KVLV-FM Fallon NV 2.9 kw, 250 ft.
KGVM(FM) Gardnerville-Minden NV 3 kw, minus 816 ft.
KPXC(FM) Indian Springs NV 6 kw, minus 167 ft.
WWWK(FM) Ellenville NY 100 w, 1,627 ft.
WLLG(FM) Lowville NY 1 kw, 520 ft.
WSNN(FM) Potsdam NY 3 kw, 155 ft.
WSFW-FM Seneca Falls NY 3 kw, 303 ft.
WTNS-FM Coshocton OH 1.2 kw, 440 ft.
WNXT-FM Portsmouth OH 2.25 kw, 536 ft.
KCDL(FM) Cordell OK 3 kw, 200 ft.
KGVE(FM) Grove OK 6 kw, 325 ft.
KLOR-FM Ponca City OK 3 kw, 300 ft.
KQFM(FM) Hermiston OR 3 kw, 300 ft.
WQKY(FM) Emporium PA 3 kw, 492 ft.
WFRA-FM Franklin PA 7.3 kw, 600 ft.
WIMX-FM Harrisburg PA 3 kw, 328 ft.
WZXR(FM) South Williamsport PA 210 w, 1,230 ft.
WPQR-FM Uniontown PA 3 kw, 300 ft.
WBLQ(FM) Block Island RI 4.6 kw, 177 ft.
WBZK-FM Chester SC 7.6 kw, 603 ft.
WWKT-FM Kingstree SC 3 kw, 289 ft.
WXVL(FM) Crossville TN 6 kw, 259 ft.
WUSJ-FM Elizabethton TN 420 w, 2,148 ft.
WNDD(FM) Jefferson City TN 3 kw, 654 ft.
WZLT(FM) Lexington TN 5 kw, 150 ft.
KPYN(FM) Atlanta TX 3 kw, 235 ft.
KPSM(FM) Brownwood TX 800 w, 489 ft.
KUEZ(FM) Lufkin TX 25 kw, 699 ft.
WVES(FM) Accomac VA 16.5 kw, 400 ft.
WFQX(FM) Front Royal VA 3 kw, 295 ft.
WPLZ-FM Petersburg VA 3 kw, 328 ft.
WPLC(FM) Spotsylvania VA 3 kw, 291 ft.
KAYO-FM Aberdeen WA 3 kw, -17 ft.
KDRM(FM) Moses Lake WA 3 kw, 275 ft.
KZTA-FM Yakima WA 630 w, 590 ft.
WDMP-FM Dodgeville WI 1.1 kw, 460 ft.
WIGM-FM Medford WI 23 kw, 342 ft.
WOWN(FM) Shawano WI 14 kw, 440 ft.
WDNE-FM Elkins WV 3 kw, 328 ft.
KKTY-FM Douglas WY 813 w, 530 ft.
KBVZ(FM) Fort Bridger WY 6 kw, 154 ft.

99.5 mhz (ch 258)
WZRR(FM) Birmingham AL 100 kw, 870 ft.
KHMB(FM) Hamburg AR 3 kw, 328 ft.
KYFX(FM) Little Rock AR 3 kw, 312 ft.
KIIM-FM Tucson AZ 90 kw, 2,037 ft.
KSUR-FM Greenfield CA 50 kw, 492 ft.
KNTI(FM) Lakeport CA 2.5 kw, 1,920 ft.
KKLA(FM) Los Angeles CA 30 kw, 669 ft.
KHYZ(FM) Mountain Pass CA 10 kw, 1,710 ft.
KVOD(FM) Denver CO 100 kw, 279 ft.
WGAY(FM) Washington DC 21 kw, 780 ft.
WJBR-FM Wilmington DE 50 kw, 499 ft.
WTRU(FM) Jupiter FL 3 kw, 315 ft.
WAIL(FM) Key West FL 100 kw, 991 ft.
WQYK-FM St. Petersburg FL 100 kw, 984 ft.
WDMG-FM Douglas GA 51 kw, 200 ft.
KORL(FM) Honolulu HI 100 kw, minus 386 ft.
NEW FM Britt IA 6 kw, 124 ft.
KDAO-FM Eldora IA 3 kw, 328 ft.
KKMA(FM) Le Mars IA 100 kw, 790 ft.
WUSN(FM) Chicago IL 8.3 kw, 1,174 ft.
WQCY(FM) Quincy IL 27 kw, 750 ft.
WZPL(FM) Greenfield IN 12.5 kw, 991 ft.
KGZF(FM) Emporia KS 3 kw, 328 ft.
KHAZ(FM) Hays KS 100 kw, 515 ft.
WKDP-FM Corbin KY 25 kw, 709 ft.
WKDQ(FM) Henderson KY 100 kw, 944 ft.
KHLA(FM) Lake Charles LA 100 kw, 371 ft.
WRNO-FM New Orleans LA 100 kw, 1,004 ft.
WSSH-FM Lowell MA 32 kw, 600 ft.
WPBC(FM) Pittsfield ME 3 kw, 243 ft.
WYCD(FM) Detroit MI 21 kw-H, 19-V, 755 ft.
WYSS(FM) Sault Ste. Marie MI 26.5 kw, 275 ft.
KBHW(FM) International Falls MN 100 kw, 580 ft.
*KSJN(FM) Minneapolis MN 100 kw, 1,033 ft.
KADI(FM) Republic MO 6 kw, 328 ft.
KPXP(FM) Garapan-Saipan MP 6.5 kw, 1,492 ft.
KBLL-FM Helena MT 30 kw, 790 ft.
WTND(FM) Grifton NC 16.5 kw, 830 ft.
WMAG(FM) High Point NC 100 kw, 1,500 ft.
WZJN(FM) Jackson NH 465 w, 833 ft.
KMGA(FM) Albuquerque NM 19.5 kw, 4,134 ft.
KROL(FM) Las Cruces NM 100 kw, 1,023 ft.
*KWFL(FM) Roswell NM 3 kw, 73 ft.
WTKW(FM) Bridgeport NY 3 kw, 318 ft.
WDCX(FM) Buffalo NY 110 kw, 640 ft.
*WBAI(FM) New York NY 5.4 kw-H, 3.9 kw-V, 1,220 ft.
WGY-FM Schenectady NY 14.5 kw, 925 ft.
WOKN(FM) Southport NY 1.27 kw, 485 ft.
WGAR-FM Cleveland OH 50 kw, 500 ft.
WAOL(FM) Ripley OH 3 kw, 328 ft.
KCKI(FM) Henryetta OK 100 kw, 984 ft.
KBZQ(FM) Lawton OK 3.428 kw, 276 ft.
KAGO-FM Klamath Falls OR 26.5 kw, 360 ft.
KWJJ-FM Portland OR 50 kw, 1,266 ft.
KRBZ(FM) Reedsport OR 6 kw, 236 ft.
WXMJ(FM) Mount Union PA 300 w, 1,440 ft.
WDSN(FM) Reynoldsville PA 3 kw, 328 ft.
WUSR(FM) Scranton PA 302 w, 1,014 ft.
WKXC-FM Aiken SC 22.5 kw, 728 ft.
WMYB(FM) Socastee SC 14.5 kw, 430 ft.
KOLY-FM Mobridge SD 56 kw, 560 ft.
WYGO(FM) Madisonville TN 2.51 kw, 515 ft.
KKPS(FM) Brownsville TX 100 kw, 1,034 ft.
KBMA(FM) Bryan TX 3 kw, 328 ft.
KPLX(FM) Fort Worth TX 100 kw, 1,680 ft.
KRLB-FM Lubbock TX 100 kw, 817 ft.
KISS-FM San Antonio TX 100 kw, 1,112 ft.
KUTQ(FM) Bountiful UT 39 kw, 2,953 ft.
WEVA-FM Emporia VA 2 kw, 403 ft.
WVIQ(FM) Christiansted VI 10.5 kw, 1,080 ft.
KZZL-FM Pullman WA 81.4 kw, 1,059 ft.
KXAA(FM) Rock Island WA 450 w, 167 ft.
WPKR(FM) Omro WI 50 kw, 420 ft.
WJLS-FM Beckley WV 34 kw, 1,050 ft.
WBYG(FM) Point Pleasant WV 4.7 kw, 328 ft.

99.7 mhz (ch 259)
KMBQ(FM) Wasilla AK 51 kw, minus 187 ft.
WOOF-FM Dothan AL 100 kw, 1,021 ft.
KWWV(FM) Morro Bay CA 220 w-H, 210 w-V, 1,633 ft.
KIOO(FM) Porterville CA 24 kw, 690 ft.
KFRC-FM San Francisco CA 45 kw, 1,299 ft.
KWXA(FM) Durango CO 16 kw, 879 ft.
WWDO(FM) Vero Beach FL 50 kw, 321 ft.
WNNX(FM) Atlanta GA 100 kw, 1,032 ft.
KFMH(FM) Muscatine IA 100 kw, 895 ft.
WXAJ(FM) Hillsboro IL 50 kw, 492 ft.
WSHW(FM) Frankfort IN 50 kw, 460 ft.
WDJX-FM Louisville KY 24 kw, 720 ft.
WLUA(FM) Westwood KY 3 kw, 328 ft.
WIMI(FM) Ironwood MI 100 kw, 561 ft.
*WUGN(FM) Midland MI 100 kw, 712 ft.
KXDL(FM) Browerville MN 6 kw, 328 ft.
KKCK(FM) Marshall MN 100 kw, 925 ft.
KMAC(FM) Gainesville MO 50 kw, 492 ft.
KLTH(FM) Kansas City MO 100 kw, 1,010 ft.
KZYQ(FM) St. James MO 25 kw, 328 ft.
WJMI(FM) Jackson MS 100 kw, 1,060 ft.
WRFX(FM) Kannapolis NC 100 kw, 1,044 ft.
KOGA-FM Ogallala NE 100 kw, 805 ft.
WNTK-FM New London NH 840 w, 613 ft.
WTUC(FM) Tuckerton NJ
WXTM(FM) Monticello NY 6 kw, 328 ft.
WZXV(FM) Palmyra NY 3 kw, 328 ft.
WBZX(FM) Columbus OH 20 kw, 784 ft.
WERT-FM Paulding OH 3 kw, 328 ft.
KXLS(FM) Alva OK 100 kw, 850 ft.
WSPI(FM) Mount Carmel PA 790 w, 646 ft.
WSHH(FM) Pittsburgh PA 10.5 kw, 928 ft.
WUAE(FM) Wakefield-Peacedale RI 3 kw, 328 ft.
WNCK(FM) Port Royal SC 100 kw, 1,250 ft.
WWTN(FM) Manchester TN 100 kw, 2,033 ft.
WMC-FM Memphis TN 300 w, 970 ft.
KRQA(FM) Amarillo TX 6 kw, 328 ft.
KCEY(FM) Huntsville TX 3 kw, 328 ft.
KBCY(FM) Tye TX 100 kw, 744 ft.
KSGI-FM St. George UT 100 kw, 2,033 ft.
WZQK(FM) Coeburn VA 3 kw, 2,850 ft.
WYFI(FM) Norfolk VA 50 kw, 456 ft.
WANV-FM Staunton VA 3.25 kw, 1,692 ft.
WWIS-FM Black River Falls WI 25 kw, 328 ft.
WGEE-FM Sturgeon Bay WI 31 kw, 610 ft.

99.9 mhz (ch 260)
WKRG-FM Mobile AL 100 kw, 1,755 ft.
WACQ-FM Tuskegee AL 2.95 kw, 466 ft.
KTCS-FM Fort Smith AR 100 kw, 1,919 ft.
KWCK-FM Searcy AR 50 kw, 492 ft.
KGMN(FM) Kingman AZ 360 w, 761 ft.
KESZ(FM) Phoenix AZ 100 kw, 1,670 ft.
KRFD-FM Marysville CA 1.74 kw, 2,181 ft.
KCIV(FM) Mount Bullion CA 1.85 kw, 2,099 ft.
KOLA(FM) San Bernardino CA 29.5 kw, 1,663 ft.
KTYD(FM) Santa Barbara CA 34 kw, 1,278 ft.
KEKB(FM) Fruita CO 79 kw, 1,380 ft.
KVUU(FM) Pueblo CO 87.4 kw, 2,200 ft.
WEZN(FM) Bridgeport CT 27.6 kw, 669 ft.
WKIS(FM) Boca Raton FL 100 kw, 986 ft.
WHKX(FM) Lafayette FL 3 kw, 328 ft.
WFKS(FM) Palatka FL 100 kw, 1,201 ft.
WSNT-FM Sandersville GA 3 kw, 184 ft.
WJFL(FM) Tennille GA 6 kw, 328 ft.
KNUI-FM Kahului HI 100 kw, minus 540 ft.
KZDX(FM) Burley ID 25 kw, 2,460 ft.
WOOZ-FM Harrisburg IL 32 kw, 650 ft.
WBUS(FM) Kankakee IL 50 kw, 500 ft.
WTHI-FM Terre Haute IN 50 kw, 494 ft.
KCWN(FM) New Sharon IA 25 kw, 297 ft.
KWKR(FM) Leoti KS 100 kw, 395 ft.
KSKG(FM) Salina KS 100 kw, 570 ft.
WVLC(FM) Campbellsville KY 3 kw, 328 ft.
WMTC-FM Vancleve KY 3 kw, 328 ft.
KTDY(FM) Lafayette LA 100 kw, 984 ft.
WCAT-FM Athol MA 1.85 kw, 407 ft.
WQRC(FM) Barnstable MA 50 kw, 378 ft.
WFRE(FM) Frederick MD 9 kw, 1,100 ft.
WWFG(FM) Ocean City MD 50 kw, 319 ft.
WKZS(FM) Auburn ME 50 kw, 492 ft.
WHFB-FM Benton Harbor MI 50 kw, 497 ft.
KAUS-FM Austin MN 100 kw, 900 ft.
KVOX-FM Moorhead MN 100 kw, 444 ft.
WUSZ(FM) Virginia MN 100 kw, 567 ft.
KBFL(FM) Buffalo MO 4.1 kw, 328 ft.
KHST(FM) Lamar MO 3 kw, 328 ft.
KFAV(FM) Warrenton MO 2.5 kw, 512 ft.
WQNN(FM) Artesia MS 6 kw, 328 ft.
KZLO-FM Bozeman MT 100 kw
WKSF(FM) Asheville NC 53 kw, 2,672 ft.
WKXB(FM) Burgaw NC 100 kw, 520 ft.
KBQQ(FM) Minot ND 100 kw, 500 ft.
KGOR(FM) Omaha NE 115 kw, 1,230 ft.
KTQM-FM Clovis NM 100 kw, 360 ft.
KXTC(FM) Thoreau NM 100 kw, 1,210 ft.
WYYS(FM) Cortland NY 24 kw, 710 ft.

U.S. FM Stations by Frequency

WGFB(FM) Plattsburgh NY 100 kw, 984 ft.
WLQT(FM) Kettering OH 50 kw, 500 ft.
WKKO(FM) Toledo OH 50 kw, 50 ft.
WTUZ(FM) Uhrichsville OH 6 kw, 328 ft.
KRKT-FM Albany OR 100 kw, 1,069 ft.
WQBR(FM) Avis PA 450 w, 823 ft.
WODE-FM Easton PA 50 kw, 449 ft.
WXKC(FM) Erie PA 50 kw, 492 ft.
WIOA(FM) San Juan PR 30 kw, 977 ft.
KTSM-FM El Paso TX 87 kw, 1,820 ft.
KFSL(FM) Hallettsville TX 3 kw, 328 ft.
KGRI-FM Henderson TX 1.35 kw, 420 ft.
KSHN-FM Liberty TX 26 kw, 679 ft.
KGEE(FM) Monahans TX 98 kw, 574 ft.
KSAB(FM) Robstown TX 96 kw, 955 ft.
WACO-FM Waco TX 90 kw, 1,660 ft.
KLUR(FM) Wichita Falls TX 100 kw, 820 ft.
WFXQ(FM) Chase City VA 12 kw, 469 ft.
WZBB(FM) Rocky Mount VA 3 kw, 328 ft.
KISW(FM) Seattle WA 100 kw, 1,150 ft.
KXLY-FM Spokane WA 37 kw, 2,998 ft.
WJVL(FM) Janesville WI 11 kw, 502 ft.
WIZD(FM) Rudolph WI 6 kw, 328 ft.
WVAF(FM) Charleston WV 50 kw, 490 ft.

100.1 mhz (ch 261)

KYKD(FM) Bethel AK 3 kw, 76 ft.
KWHQ-FM Kenai AK 3 kw, 260 ft.
*KMXT(FM) Kodiak AK 3 kw, 3 ft.
WGSY(FM) Phenix City AL 6 kw, 328 ft.
WDXX(FM) Selma AL 50 kw, 288 ft.
KQST(FM) Sedona AZ 500 w, 751 ft.
KNGS(FM) Coalinga CA 3 kw, minus 312 ft.
KGBA-FM Holtville CA 3 kw, 298 ft.
KBNN(FM) Julian CA 48 w, 1,857 ft.
KZST(FM) Santa Rosa CA 6 kw, 240 ft.
KFMR(FM) Stockton CA 6 kw, 285 ft.
WPCF-FM Panama City Beach FL 1.7 kw, 413 ft.
WEEJ(FM) Port Charlotte FL 100 kw, 450 ft.
WFXM-FM Forsyth GA 3 kw, 209 ft.
WMCD(FM) Statesboro GA 50 kw, 300 ft.
WLOV-FM Washington GA 2.4 kw, 321 ft.
KEMB(FM) Emmetsburg IA 3 kw, 300 ft.
KCTN(FM) Garnavillo IA 3 kw, 300 ft.
KFIS(FM) Soda Springs ID 3 kw, minus 174 ft.
WESZ(FM) Lincoln IL 3 kw, 200 ft.
WKAI(FM) Macomb IL 3.08 kw, 463 ft.
WGLC-FM Mendota IL 6 kw, 328 ft.
WJBD-FM Salem IL 1.5 kw, 450 ft.
WNUY(FM) Bluffton IN 2.6 kw, 351 ft.
WFLQ(FM) French Lick IN 6 kw, 300 ft.
WOTD(FM) Winamac IN 3 kw, 300 ft.
WMDJ-FM Allen KY 1.3 kw, 492 ft.
WWYC(FM) Winchester KY 32 kw, 490 ft.
KRVV(FM) Bastrop LA 50 kw, 490 ft.
KMJJ-FM Shreveport LA 50 kw, 462 ft.
WMNB(FM) North Adams MA 3 kw, 501 ft.
WQVR(FM) Southbridge MA 3 kw, 295 ft.
*WBRS(FM) Waltham MA 25 w, 151 ft.
WHOU-FM Houlton ME 3 kw, 298 ft.
WRQT(FM) Bear Lake MI 3 kw, 328 ft.
WSHN-FM Fremont MI 2.75 kw, 295 ft.
WBCH-FM Hastings MI 3 kw, 295 ft.
KTIG(FM) Pequot Lakes MN 6 kw, 300 ft.
KRLK(FM) Cassville MO 2.72 kw, 489 ft.
KDJR(FM) De Soto MO 2 kw, 400 ft.
KJMO(FM) Jefferson City MO 33 kw, 600 ft.
KLRK(FM) Vandalia MO 3 kw, 316 ft.
WQXB(FM) Grenada MS 3 kw, 300 ft.
KMMR(FM) Malta MT 2.25 kw, 370 ft.
KZOQ-FM Missoula MT 3 kw, minus 300 ft.
KATQ-FM Plentywood MT 3 kw, 34 ft.
WBXB(FM) Edenton NC 50 kw, 302 ft.
WPNH-FM Plymouth NH 2.35 kw, 364 ft.
WJRZ-FM Manahawkin NJ 3 kw, 499 ft.
KZAK(FM) Incline Village NV 760 w, 2,955 ft.
WDST(FM) Woodstock NY 2.9 kw, 308 ft.
WNIR(FM) Kent OH 1.95 kw, 390 ft.
WSWR(FM) Shelby OH 3 kw, 300 ft.
KYFM(FM) Bartlesville OK 950 w, 492 ft.
KYKC(FM) Byng OK 50 kw, 492 ft.
KIXR(FM) Ponca City OK 3 kw, 299 ft.
KWRL(FM) La Grande OR 3 kw, 90 ft.
WPRR(FM) Altoona PA 3 kw, 30 ft.
WBRR(FM) Bradford PA 970 w, 535 ft.
WQIC(FM) Lebanon PA 3 kw, 270 ft-H, 265 ft-V.
WWFN(FM) Lake City SC 1.3 kw, 482 ft.
WSCQ(FM) West Columbia SC 5.9 kw, 331 ft.
WASL(FM) Dyersburg TN 26 kw, 676 ft.
WRLT-FM Franklin TN 3 kw, 1,134 ft.
WYFJ(FM) Ashland VA 3.3 kw, 300 ft.
WLYK(FM) Lynchburg VA 730 w, 646 ft.
WTZE-FM Tazewell VA 4.2 kw, 395 ft.
WVZG(FM) White Stone VA 3 kw, 328 ft.
WEMI(FM) Neenah-Menasha WI 3 kw, 328 ft.
WGLB-FM Port Washington WI 3 kw, 180 ft.
WDDC(FM) Portage WI 3 kw, 300 ft.
WQJY(FM) West Salem WI 1.8 kw, 426 ft.
WCLG-FM Morgantown WV 6 kw, 300 ft.
WJJB(FM) Romney WV 480 w, 823 ft.
WDMX(FM) Vienna WV 1.65 kw, 440 ft.

100.3 mhz (ch 262)

KICY-FM Nome AK 84 w, 40 ft.
KJNP-FM North Pole AK 25 kw, 1,570 ft.
WVNA-FM Tuscumbia AL 100 kw, 245 ft.
KDDK(FM) Jacksonville AR 44.2 kw, 1,369 ft.
KDEZ(FM) Jonesboro AR 3 kw, 230 ft.
KZRX(FM) Globe AZ 15 kw, 2,047 ft.
KJMB(FM) Blythe CA 36.4 kw, 57 ft.
KRQK(FM) Lompoc CA 3.65 kw, 863 ft.
KXEZ(FM) Los Angeles CA 5.3 kw, 3,005 ft.
KMAK(FM) Orange Cove CA 72 w, 2,073 ft.
KSPY(FM) Quincy CA 3 kw, minus 495 ft.
KBAY(FM) San Jose CA 14.5 kw, 2,580 ft.
KMJI(FM) Denver CO 100 kw, 331 ft.
WBIG-FM Washington DC 40 kw-H, 38 kw-V, 323 ft.
WNCV(FM) Niceville FL 3 kw, 328 ft.
WDIZ(FM) Orlando FL 100 kw, 1,597 ft.
WCTH(FM) Plantation Key FL 100 kw, 440 ft.
WSGY(FM) Tifton GA 100 kw, 1,100 ft.
KOKU(FM) Agana GU 5 kw, 190 ft.
KHWI(FM) Hilo HI 74 kw, -515 ft.
KCCN-FM Honolulu HI 100 kw-H, 81 kw-V, 1,965 ft.
KLYF(FM) Des Moines IA 100 kw, 1,700 ft.
KATZ-FM Alton IL 50 kw, 482 ft.
WIXY(FM) Champaign IL 12.9 kw, 453 ft.
WPNT-FM Chicago IL 8.3 kw, 1,174 ft.
WCCI(FM) Savanna IL 25 kw, 450 ft.
WLKI(FM) Angola IN 2.05 kw, 393 ft.
WCNB-FM Connersville IN 28 kw, 275 ft.
KQLS(FM) Colby KS 100 kw, 610 ft.
KTCM(FM) Kingman KS 48 kw, 505 ft.
KDVV(FM) Topeka KS 100 kw, 984 ft.
*KSWC(FM) Winfield KS 10 w, 70 ft.
WZZF-FM Hopkinsville KY 100 kw, 602 ft.
KRRV-FM Alexandria LA 100 kw, 1,055 ft.
KLRZ(FM) Larose LA 50 kw, 328 ft.
WKIT-FM Brewer ME 50 kw, 850 ft.
WNIC(FM) Dearborn MI 32 kw, 600 ft.
WQON(FM) Grayling MI 50 kw, 436 ft.
*WBOB-FM Minneapolis MN 97 kw, 905 ft.
KSNR(FM) Thief River Falls MN 100 kw, 620 ft.
KWMQ(FM) Southwest City MO 3 kw, 328 ft.
KUKU-FM Willow Springs MO 50 kw, 492 ft.
KPXH(FM) Garapan-Saipan MP 1.3 kw, 1,489 ft.
WNSL(FM) Laurel MS 100 kw, 1,050 ft.
KOOZ(FM) Great Falls MT 100 kw, 987 ft.
WWWB(FM) High Point NC 100 kw, 1,049 ft.
KZEN(FM) Central City NE 100 kw, 1,854 ft.
WHEB(FM) Portsmouth NH 31 kw, 161 ft.
WHTZ(FM) Newark NJ 7.8 kw, 1,220 ft.
KKJY-FM Albuquerque NM 22.5 kw, 4,110 ft.
WDHI(FM) Delhi NY 770 w, 643 ft.
WCLT-FM Newark OH 50 kw, 390 ft.
KHJM(FM) Taft OK 6 kw, 380 ft.
KRWQ(FM) Gold Hill OR 30 kw, 970 ft.
KKRZ(FM) Portland OR 95 kw, 1,433 ft.
WHGL-FM Canton PA 3.9 kw, 846 ft.
WZPR(FM) Meadville PA 20 kw, 587 ft.
WPLY(FM) Media PA 35 kw, 600 ft.
WIVA-FM Aguadilla PR 50 kw, 1,000 ft.
WOTB(FM) Middletown RI 3.35 kw, 295 ft.
WORG(FM) Elloree SC 25 kw, 328 ft.
WSEA(FM) Pawley's Island SC 3 kw, 328 ft.
KGGG-FM Rapid City SD 100 kw, 450 ft.
WOKI-FM Oak Ridge TN 100 kw, 2,001 ft.
KTEX(FM) Brownsville TX 100 kw, 1,125 ft.
KJMZ(FM) Dallas TX 100 kw, 1,280 ft.
KILT-FM Houston TX 100 kw, 1,920 ft.
KIOL-FM Lamesa TX 100 kw, 800 ft.
KOMX(FM) Pampa TX 32 kw, 300 ft.
KCYY(FM) San Antonio TX 100 kw, 985 ft.
KSFI(FM) Salt Lake City UT 26 kw, 3,740 ft.
WSVV(FM) Petersburg VA 4.7 kw, 328 ft.
WSTX-FM Christiansted VI 50 kw, 1,030 ft.
KWIQ-FM Moses Lake WA 100 kw, 194 ft.
WRHN(FM) Rhinelander WI 25 kw, 385 ft.
KZMQ-FM Greybull WY 56 kw, 2,443 ft.

100.5 mhz (ch 263)

KBFX(FM) Anchorage AK 25 kw, 178 ft.
WHMA-FM Anniston AL 100 kw, 1,141 ft.
WXUS(FM) Fort Rucker AL 3 kw, 328 ft.
KZHE(FM) Stamps AR 50 kw, 500 ft.
KOJJ(FM) East Porterville CA 1.5 kw, 465 ft.
KWAN(FM) Gualala CA 6 kw, 669 ft.
KPSI-FM Palm Springs CA 25 kw, 121 ft.
KQEX(FM) Rohnerville CA 200 w, 1,722 ft.
KQPT(FM) Sacramento CA 115 w-H, 105 w-V, 380 ft.
*KCEQ(FM) Walnut Creek CA 10 w, minus 250 ft.
KRSJ(FM) Durango CO 100 kw, 200 ft.
WRCH(FM) New Britain CT 7.5 kw, 1,250 ft.
WNFQ(FM) Newberry FL 11 kw, 492 ft.
WXRS-FM Swainsboro GA 3 kw, 300 ft.
KRDI-FM Decorah IA 30 kw, 420 ft.
*KRIC(FM) Rexburg ID 75 kw, 403 ft.
WRVY-FM Henry IL 3 kw, 328 ft.
WYMG(FM) Jacksonville IL 50 kw, 500 ft.
WWKI(FM) Kokomo IN 50 kw, 480 ft.
WSJD(FM) Princeton IN 3 kw, 328 ft.
WTFX(FM) Louisville KY 37.6 kw, 567 ft.
*WUMF-FM Farmington ME 13 w-H, -190 ft.
WTCF(FM) Carrollton MI 3 kw, 328 ft.
WQFN(FM) Walker MI 3 kw, 328 ft.
*WSCN(FM) Cloquet MN 100 kw, 875 ft.
KXAC(FM) St. James MN 50 kw, 433 ft.
KGMY-FM Aurora MO 33 kw, 600 ft.
KKCA(FM) Fulton MO 6 kw, 300 ft.
WBLE(FM) Batesville MS 50 kw, 492 ft.
WNBX(FM) Lebanon NH 6 kw, 689 ft.
KSFX(FM) Roswell NM 100 kw, 122 ft.
KMZQ-FM Henderson NV 98 kw, 1,180 ft.
WXEJ(FM) Conklin NY 3.5 kw, 433 ft.
WVOR-FM Rochester NY 50 kw, 480 ft.
WKBE(FM) Warrensburg NY 185 w-H, 1,312 ft.
WOMP-FM Bellaire OH 48 kw, 518 ft.
WKXA-FM Findlay OH 20 kw, 440 ft.
KATT-FM Oklahoma City OK 97 kw, 1,191 ft.
KCGR(FM) Cottage Grove OR 6 kw, 115 ft.
WYGL-FM Elizabethville PA 1.2 kw, 515 ft.
WSSL-FM Gray Court SC 100 kw, 1,240 ft.
WKSY(FM) Marion SC 21.5 kw, 354 ft.
KIKN(FM) Salem SD 100 kw, 981 ft.
KBDR(FM) Mirando City TX 42 kw, 551 ft.
WCMS-FM Norfolk VA 50 kw, 500 ft.
WYKY(FM) Columbus WI 6 kw, 328 ft.
WKEE-FM Huntington WV 53 kw, 560 ft.

100.7 mhz (ch 264)

WLXY(FM) Northport AL 6 kw, 328 ft.
KBBQ-FM Fort Smith AR 50 kw, 459 ft.
KOKR(FM) Newport AR 4.1 kw, 220 ft.
KSLX(FM) Scottsdale AZ 100 kw, 1,847 ft.
KIBS(FM) Bishop CA 1 kw, 2,960 ft.
KCEZ(FM) Corning CA 50 kw, 272 ft.
KATJ(FM) George CA 260 w, 1,548 ft.
KTOM-FM Salinas CA 910 w, 2,575 ft.
KFMB-FM San Diego CA 30 kw-H, 26.5 kw-V, 620 ft.
KHAY(FM) Ventura CA 13.1 kw, 1,210 ft.
KGFT(FM) Pueblo CO 13.5 kw, 2,086 ft.
WHYI-FM Fort Lauderdale FL 100 kw, 928 ft.
WJLQ(FM) Pensacola FL 100 kw, 1,555 ft.
WUSA-FM Tampa FL 100 kw, 600 ft.
WBYB(FM) Brunswick GA 36 kw, 1,463 ft.
WLRR(FM) Milledgeville GA 3 kw, 328 ft.
KJYL(FM) Eagle Grove IA 25 kw, 328 ft.
KKRQ(FM) Iowa City IA 100 kw, 1,350 ft.
KSQA(FM) Wallace ID 75 kw, 2,240 ft.
WKBM(FM) Coal City IL 1.4 kw, 482 ft.
WLTA(FM) Elkhart IN 15 kw, 910 ft.
WMGI(FM) Terre Haute IN 50 kw, 500 ft.
KHOK(FM) Hoisington KS 100 kw, 430 ft.
WWLW(FM) Carlisle KY 6 kw, 269 ft.
WXPC(FM) Horse Cave KY 3 kw, 328 ft.
WTGE-FM Baton Rouge LA 97 kw, 1,499 ft.
WZLX(FM) Boston MA 21.5 kw, 777 ft.
WGRX(FM) Westminster MD 16 kw, 858 ft.
WTBM(FM) Mexico ME 180 w, 1,289 ft.
WITL-FM Lansing MI 26.5 kw, 640 ft.
WCLS(FM) Oscoda MI 20.5 kw, 360 ft.
KIKV-FM Alexandria MN 100 kw, 1,023 ft.
KGMO(FM) Cape Girardeau MO 100 kw, 699 ft.
KMZU(FM) Carrollton MO 98.6 kw, 990 ft.
KZMM(FM) Troy MO 6 kw
WDMS(FM) Greenville MS 52 kw-H, 449 ft.
WZJS(FM) Banner Elk NC 550 w, 758 ft.
WTRG(FM) Rocky Mount NC 100 kw, 1,968 ft.
*KGBI-FM Omaha NE 100 kw, 1,161 ft.
WZXL(FM) Wildwood NJ 38 kw, 350 ft.
KLVF(FM) Las Vegas NM 10 kw, minus 77 ft.
WLKC(FM) Henderson NY 3 kw, 328 ft.
WHUD(FM) Peekskill NY 50 kw, 500 ft.
WEIF(FM) Utica NY 1.16 w, 551 ft.
WMMS(FM) Cleveland OH 34 kw, 600 ft.
*WEEC(FM) Springfield OH 50 kw, 469 ft.
*KTFR(FM) Claremore OK 3 kw, 328 ft.
KICE(FM) Bend OR 50 kw, 598 ft.
KZUS-FM Toledo OR 3 kw, 430 ft.
WFMZ(FM) Allentown PA 11 kw, 1,073 ft.
WQKB(FM) New Kensington PA 17 kw, 850 ft.
WXYX(FM) Bayamon PR 50 kw, 781 ft.
WSUY(FM) Charleston SC 2 kw, 400 ft.
WUSY(FM) Cleveland TN 100 kw, 1,191 ft.
KORQ-FM Abilene TX 100 kw, 1,260 ft.
KASE(FM) Austin TX 100 kw, 1,100 ft.
KRJT-FM Bowie TX 3.1 kw, 459 ft.
KMIA(FM) Jasper TX 5.1 kw, 299 ft.
KPXI(FM) Mount Pleasant TX 100 kw, 984 ft.
KIDZ(FM) Brigham City UT 100 kw, 1,328 ft.
WBNK(FM) Christiansburg VA 3 kw, 328 ft.
WQPO(FM) Harrisonburg VA 50 kw, 492 ft.
WRIC-FM Richlands VA 1.3 kw, 705 ft.
WVAY(FM) Wilmington VT 135 w, 1,460 ft.
KIRO-FM Seattle WA 100 kw, 736 ft.
WBIZ-FM Eau Claire WI 100 kw, 740 ft.
WKKV-FM Racine WI 50 kw, 500 ft.
KKAZ(FM) Cheyenne WY 100 kw, 490 ft.
KGWY(FM) Gillette WY 100 kw, 635 ft.

100.9 mhz (ch 265)

KAKN(FM) Naknek AK 3 kw, 338 ft.
*KFSK(FM) Petersburg AK 2 kw, -482 ft.
WALX(FM) Selma AL 50 kw, 492 ft.
KDEL-FM Arkadelphia AR 3 kw, 95 ft.
KFCM(FM) Cherokee Village AR 3 kw, 298 ft.
KTCN(FM) Eureka Springs AR 1.1 kw, 531 ft.
KCJC(FM) Russellville AR 6 kw, 295 ft.
KZMK(FM) Sierra Vista AZ 3 kw, minus 46 ft.
KYXI(FM) Yuma AZ 3 kw, 274 ft.
KTID-FM San Rafael CA 480 w, 798 ft.
KEXX(FM) Tracy CA 6 kw, 328 ft.
WTYD(FM) New London CT 3 kw, 328 ft.
WOYS(FM) Apalachicola FL 5.4 kw, 344 ft.
WYGC(FM) Gainesville FL 3 kw, 300 ft.
WJAQ(FM) Marianna FL 2.5 kw-H, 331 ft.
WLYU(FM) Lyons GA 3 kw, 328 ft.
WPGA-FM Perry GA 3 kw, 345 ft.
*WAGW(FM) Waynesboro GA 6 kw, 279 ft.
WCJM(FM) West Point GA 1.85 kw, 235 ft.
WHPO(FM) Hoopeston IL 3 kw, 280 ft.
WXKO-FM Pana IL 6 kw, 290 ft.
WLRZ(FM) Peru IL 1.15 kw, 518 ft.
WQFL(FM) Rockford IL 3 kw, 300 ft.
WBDC(FM) Huntingburg IN 3.3 kw, 300 ft.
WIRE(FM) Lebanon IN 3 kw, 300 ft.
WPGW-FM Portland IN 3 kw, 180 ft.
WMPI(FM) Scottsburg IN 3 kw, 300 ft.
KCLY(FM) Clay Center KS 2.8 kw, 255 ft.
WIZF(FM) Erlanger KY 1.25 kw, 508 ft.
WLSK(FM) Lebanon KY 3 kw, 200 ft.

U.S. FM Stations by Frequency

KHLL(FM) Richwood LA 6 kw, 328 ft.
KTQQ(FM) Sulphur LA 3 kw, 328 ft.
WRNX(FM) Amherst MA 1.35 kw, 692 ft.
WAAI(FM) Hurlock MD 1.3 kw, 502 ft.
WYNZ(FM) Westbrook ME 3 kw, 225 ft.
WBRN-FM Big Rapids MI 6 kw, 318 ft.
*WIZY(FM) East Jordan MI 2.8 kw, 489 ft.
WQXC-FM Otsego MI 3 kw, 299 ft.
WBTZ(FM) Pinconning MI 1.3 kw, 495 ft.
KTUI-FM Sullivan MO 3 kw, 276 ft.
WMDC-FM Hazelhurst MS 3 kw, 295 ft.
WKBB(FM) West Point MS 3 kw, 170 ft.
WABZ-FM Albemarle NC 1.8 kw, 541 ft.
WIFM-FM Elkin NC 600 w, 709 ft.
WSTS(FM) Fairmont NC 3 kw, 300 ft.
KXPO-FM Grafton ND 3 kw, 125 ft.
KYRK(FM) Eunice NM 3 kw, 295 ft.
KZNM(FM) Grants NM 10 kw, 223 ft.
KNDE(FM) Sparks NV 2.9 kw, 203 ft.
WKLI(FM) Albany NY 3 kw, 300 ft.
WQIX(FM) Horseheads NY 3 kw, 245 ft.
WKRL-FM North Syracuse NY 6 kw, 164 ft.
WCDO-FM Sidney NY 970 w, 577 ft.
WBNO-FM Bryan OH 6 kw, 299 ft.
WNCG(FM) Clyde OH 3 kw, 300 ft.
WJAW(FM) McConnelsville OH 928 w, 577 ft.
WXIZ(FM) Waverly OH 920 w, 500 ft.
KGLC(FM) Miami OK 3.6 kw, 273 ft.
KPNC-FM Ponca City OK 3 kw, 285 ft.
KXOJ-FM Sapulpa OK 2 kw, 360 ft.
KFXT(FM) Sulphur OK 3 kw, 300 ft.
WOOX(FM) Bedford PA 19 kw, 1,279 ft.
WOEZ-FM Milton PA 640 w, 690 ft.
WRKT(FM) North East PA 6 kw, 252 ft.
WGTN-FM Andrews SC 3 kw, 328 ft.
WPAL-FM Walterboro SC 3 kw, 300 ft.
WVHR(FM) Huntingdon TN 6 kw, 300 ft.
KPVY(FM) Amarillo TX 100 kw
KIXC-FM Quanah TX 3 kw, 192 ft.
KEPG(FM) Victoria TX 2.7 kw, 312 ft.
KPRQ(FM) Price UT 3 kw, 111 ft.
WIQO-FM Covington VA 3 kw, minus 255 ft.
WNNT-FM Warsaw VA 3 kw, 305 ft.
WGTK(FM) Middlebury VT 3 kw, 300 ft.
KARY-FM Grandview WA 6 kw, minus 91 ft.
KHSS(FM) Walla Walla WA 1.3 kw, 1,374 ft.
WRCO-FM Richland Center WI 6 kw, 240 ft.
WKMY(FM) Princeton WV 630 w, 641 ft.
WJYP(FM) South Charleston WV 3 kw, 285 ft.
WMQC(FM) Westover WV 3 kw, 198 ft.
KRRR(FM) Canton MO 12.5 kw, 308 ft.

101.1 mhz (ch 266)

KAKQ-FM Fairbanks AK 25 kw, 131 ft.
KJJZ(FM) Kodiak AK 3.1 kw, 46 ft.
WFMH-FM Cullman AL 87 kw, 330 ft.
WZTZ(FM) Elba AL 640 w, 682 ft.
KZQA(FM) North Little Rock AR 3 kw, 328 ft.
*KLRC(FM) Siloam Springs AR 3.1 kw, 459 ft.
KBBC(FM) Lake Havasu City AZ 100 kw, 988 ft.
KHYL(FM) Auburn CA 36.3 kw, 577 ft.
KSXY(FM) Fresno CA 50 kw, 310 ft.
KRTH(FM) Los Angeles CA 51 kw, 3,130 ft.
KOSI(FM) Denver CO 100 kw, 1,624 ft.
WWDC-FM Washington DC 22.5 kw, 760 ft.
WJRR(FM) Cocoa Beach FL 100 kw, 1,598 ft.
WAVV(FM) Marco FL 100 kw, 981 ft.
WAFT(FM) Valdosta GA 100 kw, 558 ft.
KLHI-FM Lahaina HI 100 kw, 745 ft.
KXIA(FM) Marshalltown IA 75 kw, 300 ft.
KMCL-FM McCall ID 3.9 kw, 1,873 ft.
WKQX(FM) Chicago IL 6 kw, 1,710 ft.
WFXB(FM) East St. Louis IL 44 kw, 525 ft.
WBHQ(FM) Bloomfield IN 3 kw, 300 ft.
WLZQ(FM) South Whitley IN 6 kw, 328 ft.
KEOJ(FM) Caney KS 3 kw, 328 ft.
KFNF(FM) Oberlin KS 100 kw, 420 ft.
WSGS(FM) Hazard KY 100 kw, 1,463 ft.
WBVR(FM) Russellville KY 100 kw, 1,047 ft.
WNOE-FM New Orleans LA 100 kw, 1,004 ft.
KRMD-FM Shreveport LA 98 kw, 1,119 ft.
WFAL(FM) Falmouth MA 3.7 kw, 253 ft.
WWPN(FM) Westernport MD 3 kw, minus 541 ft.
WRIF(FM) Detroit MI 27.2 kw, 879 ft.
WUPY(FM) Ontonagon MI 30 kw, 620 ft.
WGRY-FM Roscommon MI 3.4 kw, 444 ft.
KBHP(FM) Bemidji MN 100 kw, 331 ft.
KLQL(FM) Luverne MN 100 kw, 530 ft.
KHME(FM) Winona MN 6 kw, 350 ft.
KCFX(FM) Harrisonville MO 97.3 kw-H, 79.6 kw-V, 994 ft.
WBBV(FM) Vicksburg MS 1.35 kw, 259 ft.
KZMT(FM) Helena MT 95 kw, 1,899 ft.
WPCM(FM) Burlington NC 100 kw, 910 ft.
KOVC-FM Valley City ND 3 kw, 319 ft.
KDSR(FM) Williston ND 98 kw, 800 ft.
KLIR(FM) Columbus NE 100 kw, 760 ft.
WGIR-FM Manchester NH 11.5 kw, 1,027 ft.
KNLA(FM) White Rock NM 3 kw, 53 ft.
WBUG-FM Fort Plain NY 1.25 kw, 718 ft.
WCBS-FM New York NY 6.8 kw, 1,353 ft.
WWCD(FM) Grove City OH 6 kw, 328 ft.
WHOT-FM Youngstown OH 24 kw, 711 ft.
KWOX(FM) Woodward OK 100 kw, 1,204 ft.
KUFO(FM) Portland OR 100 kw, 1,640 ft.
WBEB-FM Philadelphia PA 12.5 kw, 1,010 ft.
WGMR(FM) Tyrone PA 8.5 kw, 1,171 ft.
WRIO(FM) Ponce PR 34 kw, 1,768 ft.
WROQ(FM) Anderson SC 100 kw, 994 ft.
WLVH(FM) Hardeeville SC 50 kw, 476 ft.
KEZV(FM) Spearfish SD 100 kw, 1,604 ft.
KJMS(FM) Memphis TN 100 kw, 347 ft.
WRR(FM) Dallas TX 100 kw, 1,510 ft.
KONO-FM Fredricksburg TX 98 kw, 1,371 ft.
KLOL(FM) Houston TX 100 kw, 1,920 ft.
KONE(FM) Lubbock TX 100 kw, 750 ft.
KVPA(FM) Port Isabel TX 3 kw, 300 ft.
KONY-FM Kanab UT 99 kw, 786 ft.
KBER(FM) Ogden UT 25 kw, 3,740 ft.
KEYF-FM Cheney WA 100 kw, 1,965 ft.
WIXX(FM) Green Bay WI 100 kw, 1,080 ft.

101.3 mhz (ch 267)

KGOT(FM) Anchorage AK 26 kw, minus 66 ft.
WJJN(FM) Dothan AL 3 kw, 328 ft.
KPBQ-FM Pine Bluff AR 25 kw, 328 ft.
KATY-FM Idyllwild CA 1.15 kw, 731 ft.
KSTT-FM Los Osos-Baywood Park CA 4.86 kw, 1,506 ft.
KIOI(FM) San Francisco CA 125 kw, 1,160 ft.
KIQX(FM) Durango CO 100 kw, 439 ft.
WKCI(FM) Hamden CT 10 kw, 1,070 ft.
WXPZ(FM) Milford DE 3 kw, 328 ft.
WYOO(FM) Springfield FL 5.2 kw, 267 ft.
WFEZ(FM) Williston FL 3.5 kw, 433 ft.
WQIL(FM) Chauncey GA 50 kw, 492 ft.
KITR(FM) Creston IA 3 kw, 255 ft.
WLLR-FM East Moline IL 50 kw, 500 ft.
WMCI(FM) Mattoon IL 3 kw, 318 ft.
WFMG(FM) Richmond IN 50 kw, 280 ft.
*WBAA-FM West Lafayette IN 5 kw, 358 ft.
KFDI-FM Wichita KS 100 kw, 1,139 ft.
WTHQ(FM) Shelbyville KY 3 kw, 328 ft.
WKCG(FM) Augusta ME 50 kw, 321 ft.
WCUZ-FM Grand Rapids MI 50 kw, 420 ft.
WSUE(FM) Sault Ste. Marie MI 100 kw, 978 ft.
KDWB-FM Richfield MN 100 kw, 1,033 ft.
KTXR(FM) Springfield MO 100 kw, 1,181 ft.
WJDQ(FM) Meridian MS 99 kw, 581 ft.
KRYK(FM) Chinook MT 100 kw, 688 ft.
KIKC-FM Forsyth MT 100 kw, 1,010 ft.
WWQQ-FM Wilmington NC 50 kw, 525 ft.
WYKR-FM Haverhill NH 3 kw, 39 ft.
KWQK(FM) Albuquerque NM 4.1 kw, 403 ft.
WBRV-FM Boonville NY 720 w, 348 ft.
WDOT(FM) Essex NY 487 w, 804 ft.
WRMM-FM Rochester NY 27 kw, 640 ft.
WSSV(FM) Stillwater NY 3.66 kw, 413 ft.
WNCO-FM Ashland OH 50 kw, 500 ft.
WAGX(FM) Manchester OH 3 kw, 299 ft.
KMCO(FM) McAlester OK 100 kw, 494 ft.
KCHQ(FM) Altamont OR 60 kw, 882 ft.
WROZ(FM) Lancaster PA 50 kw, 1,289 ft.
WGGY(FM) Scranton PA 7 kw, 1,110 ft.
WWDM(FM) Sumter SC 100 kw, 1,322 ft.
WAAT(FM) Tiptonville TN 25 kw, 328 ft.
WECO-FM Wartburg TN 500 w, 770 ft.
KJKS(FM) Cameron TX 3 kw, 328 ft.
KAIR(FM) Crane TX 50 kw, 328 ft.
KNCN(FM) Sinton TX 100 kw, 401 ft.
WWDE-FM Hampton VA 50 kw, 499 ft.
WZFM(FM) Narrows VA 5.7 kw, minus 403 ft.
KGDN(FM) Pasco WA 6 kw
WBUC-FM Buckhannon WV 50 kw, 497 ft.

101.5 mhz (ch 268)

KPIK(FM) Beebe AR 6 kw, 328 ft.
KRVF(FM) Eudora AR 3 kw, 328 ft.
KISI(FM) Malvern AR 6 kw, 318 ft.
KZON(FM) Phoenix AZ 100 kw, 1,740 ft.
KIXF(FM) Baker CA 4.6 kw, 1,289 ft.
KGFM(FM) Bakersfield CA 4.8 kw, 1,280 ft.
KEKA-FM Eureka CA 100 kw, 3,200 ft.
*KAMB(FM) Merced CA 50 kw, 390 ft.
*KRVH(FM) Rio Vista CA 10 w, 60 ft.
KGB-FM San Diego CA 50 kw, 500 ft.
KQMT(FM) Eagle CO 36 kw, 2,210 ft.
WLYF(FM) Miami FL 100 kw, 810 ft.
WTKX-FM Pensacola FL 100 kw, 633 ft.
WXSR(FM) Quincy FL 50 kw, 476 ft.
*WKES(FM) St. Petersburg FL 100 kw, 1,358 ft.
WHJX-FM Brunswick GA 100 kw, 239 ft.
WKHX-FM Marietta GA 99 kw, 968 ft.
KAOY(FM) Kealakekua HI 6 kw, 2,052 ft.
KKSI(FM) Eddyville IA 49 kw, 498 ft.
KAYL-FM Storm Lake IA 100 kw, 331 ft.
*KCVI(FM) Blackfoot ID 100 kw, 1512 ft.
KATW(FM) Lewiston ID 100 kw, 848 ft.
WBNQ(FM) Bloomington IL 50 kw, 460 ft.
WCIL-FM Carbondale IL 50 kw, 430 ft.
WKKG(FM) Columbus IN 50 kw, 492 ft.
*WBGW(FM) Fort Branch IN 1 kw, 561 ft.
WNSN(FM) South Bend IN 13 kw, 970 ft.
KSLS(FM) Liberal KS 100 kw, 550 ft.
KMKF(FM) Manhattan KS 39 kw, 577 ft.
WRZI(FM) Vine Grove KY 6 kw, 328 ft.
WYNK-FM Baton Rouge LA 100 kw, 1,500 ft.
WPRJ(FM) Coleman MI 2.2 kw, 400 ft.
WJNR-FM Iron Mountain MI 47 kw, 620 ft.
KTCF(FM) Crosby MN 25 kw, 328 ft.
KCGN-FM Ortonville MN 100 kw, 1,001 ft.
KARO(FM) Columbia MO 20 kw, 604 ft.
WRAL(FM) Raleigh NC 96 kw, 1,820 ft.
*KBMK(FM) Bismarck ND 100 kw, 1,151 ft.
KEZH(FM) Hastings NE 50 kw, 265 ft.
WWSS(FM) Meredith NH 3 kw, 302 ft.
WKXW(FM) Trenton NJ 18 kw, 810 ft.
*WMSC(FM) Upper Montclair NJ 10 w, 623 ft.
KTAO(FM) Taos NM 3 kw, -416 ft.
WXQZ(FM) Canton NY 2.4 kw, 364 ft.
WXHC(FM) Homer NY 1.3 kw, 489 ft.
WMXO(FM) Olean NY 1.55 kw, 405 ft.
WPDH(FM) Poughkeepsie NY 4.5 kw, 1,540 ft.
*WCWT-FM Centerville OH 10 w, 110 ft.
WMGG(FM) Gallipolis OH 50 kw, 500 ft.
WLQR(FM) Toledo OH 19.1 kw, 810 ft.
*WOBN(FM) Westerville OH 28 w, 40 ft.
KLAW(FM) Lawton OK 100 kw, 600 ft.
KEJO(FM) Corvallis OR 28 kw, 98 ft.
WDKC(FM) Covington PA 1.45 kw
WORD-FM Pittsburgh PA 48 kw, 505 ft.
WAYZ-FM Waynesboro PA 50 kw-H, 48 kw-V, 230 ft.
WKSA-FM Isabela PR 42 kw, minus 26 ft.
WWBB(FM) Providence RI 13.5 kw, 951 ft.
KVCX(FM) Gregory SD 100 kw, 640 ft.
WVFB(FM) Celina TN 6 kw, 328 ft.
WNWS-FM Jackson TN 3 kw, 300 ft.
WQUT(FM) Johnson City TN 100 kw, 1,500 ft.
WFTZ(FM) Manchester TN 3 kw, 345 ft.
WTWL(FM) McKinnon TN 790 w, 607 ft.
WJOR-FM St. Joseph TN 3 kw, 328 ft.
KOXE(FM) Brownwood TX 100 kw, 727 ft.
KNUE(FM) Tyler TX 100 kw, 1,074 ft.
WBQB(FM) Fredericksburg VA 50 kw, 492 ft.
KPLZ(FM) Seattle WA 100 kw, 1,150 ft.
WIBA-FM Madison WI 50 kw, 450 ft.
WXYQ(FM) Manistee MI 3 kw, 105 ft.

101.7 mhz (ch 269)

KPEN-FM Soldotna AK 25 kw, 239.5 ft.
*KSTK(FM) Wrangell AK 3 kw, minus 294 ft.
WTID(FM) Reform AL 23.37 kw, 727 ft.
WVSV(FM) Stevenson AL 940 w, 490 ft.
KQEW(FM) Fordyce AR 3 kw, 289 ft.
KXAR-FM Hope AR 3 kw, 295 ft.
KENA-FM Mena AR 3 kw, 298 ft.
KVOM-FM Morrilton AR 3 kw, 226 ft.
KKYZ(FM) Sierra Vista AZ 3 kw, 299 ft.
KQAZ(FM) Springerville-Eager AZ 3 kw, -97 ft.
KTOT(FM) Big Bear Lake CA 90 w, 1,500 ft.
KXDC-FM Carmel CA 800 w, 590 ft.
KSBL(FM) Carpinteria CA 310 w, 810 ft.
KKIQ(FM) Livermore CA 4.5 kw, 382 ft.
KXFX(FM) Santa Rosa CA 2.2 kw, 1,056 ft.
KMAT(FM) Sutter Creek CA 1.25 kw, 515 ft.
KBRU(FM) Fort Morgan CO 3 kw, 135 ft.
WRKE(FM) Ocean View DE 3 kw, 328 ft.
WCWB-FM Trenton FL 3 kw, 328 ft.
WAVW(FM) Vero Beach FL 1.48 kw, 471 ft.
WKAK(FM) Albany GA 3 kw, 300 ft.
WKTM(FM) Soperton GA 3 kw, 300 ft.
WTHO-FM Thomson GA 3 kw, 300 ft.
WRCC-FM Warner Robins GA 2.5 kw, 350 ft.
KBKB-FM Fort Madison IA 50 kw, 466 ft.
KDLS-FM Perry IA 3 kw, 300 ft.
WIXN-FM Dixon IL 6 kw, 300 ft.
WGEL(FM) Greenville IL 3 kw, 300 ft.
WTAY-FM Robinson IL 1.45 kw, 449 ft.
WIVM(FM) Elwood IN 3 kw, 328 ft.
WJLT(FM) Fort Wayne IN 3 kw, 328 ft.
KEGS(FM) Emporia KS 3.3 kw, 300 ft.
*KVCY(FM) Fort Scott KS 3 kw, 250 ft.
KIND-FM Independence KS 1.6 kw, 155 ft.
KREJ(FM) Medicine Lodge KS 50 kw, 492 ft.
WLSY-FM Jeffersontown KY 1.4 kw, 413 ft.
WKYM(FM) Monticello KY 1.75 kw, 617 ft.
WMCQ-FM Richmond KY 6 kw, 300 ft.
KEAZ(FM) De Ridder LA 3 kw, 299 ft.
WFNX(FM) Lynn MA 1.65 kw, 440 ft.
WRCZ(FM) Pittsfield MA 3 kw, 145 ft.
WOZI(FM) Presque Isle ME 1.35 kw-H, 420 ft.
WBYA(FM) Searsport ME 6 kw, 236 ft.
WILS-FM Lansing MI 2.1 kw, 377 ft.
WMRR(FM) Muskegon Heights MI 15 kw, 305 ft.
WKMF-FM Tuscola MI 3 kw, 328 ft.
KLXK(FM) Duluth MN 1.5 kw, 466 ft.
KOLV(FM) Olivia MN 6 kw, 285 ft.
KRCH(FM) Rochester MN 39.1 kw, 554 ft.
WHMH-FM Sauk Rapids MN 3 kw, 297 ft.
KGOZ(FM) Gallatin MO 15 kw, 423 ft.
KLPW-FM Union MO 2.1 kw-H, 341 ft.
WWUN-FM Clarksdale MS 3 kw, 198 ft.
WKNZ(FM) Collins MS 1 kw, 541 ft.
WLIN(FM) Gluckstadt MS 3 kw, 300 ft.
KTWM(FM) Laurel MT 100 kw, 420 ft.
KTNY(FM) Libby MT 3 kw, minus 1,029 ft.
WXXK-FM Newport NH 3 kw, 2,006 ft.
WNNN(FM) Canton NJ 3 kw, 263 ft.
KLEA-FM Lovington NM 3 kw, 280 ft.
KZKL-FM Rio Rancho NM 3.2 kw, 99 ft.
KELY-FM Ely NV 480 w, 804 ft.
KTHX(FM) Reno NV 1.3 kw, 426 ft.
WBTF(FM) Attica NY 3 kw, 295 ft.
WFLK(FM) Geneva NY 3 kw, 125 ft.
WENU(FM) Hudson Falls NY 4.6 kw, 180 ft.
WHUG(FM) Jamestown NY 3.3 kw, 300 ft.
WGRG(FM) Owego NY 1.15 kw, 450 ft.
WSCP-FM Pulaski NY 2.5 kw, 364.1 ft.
WSLK(FM) Saranac Lake NY 2.2 kw, 388 ft.
WBAZ(FM) Southold NY 5.5 kw, 341 ft.
WJER-FM Dover OH 3 kw, 280 ft.
WNKO(FM) Newark OH 3 kw, 280 ft.
WKSW(FM) Urbana OH 2.2 kw, 397 ft.
KEOK(FM) Tahlequah OK 3 kw, 300 ft.
WYSN(FM) Central City PA 725 w, 643 ft.
WVCC(FM) Linesville PA 3 kw, 300 ft.
WKZQ-FM Myrtle Beach SC 50 kw, 601 ft.
WMGL(FM) Ravenel SC 3 kw, 482 ft.
WJSQ(FM) Athens TN 7.5 kw, 528 ft.
WKOM(FM) Columbia TN 3 kw, 300 ft.
WCMT-FM Martin TN 6 kw, 328 ft.
WORM-FM Savannah TN 3 kw, 175 ft.
WJLE-FM Smithville TN 3 kw, 195 ft.
KDSQ(FM) Denison-Sherman TX 3 kw, 276 ft.

Broadcasting & Cable Yearbook 1994
B-517

U.S. FM Stations by Frequency

KOKE(FM) Giddings TX 3 kw, 328 ft.
KSAM-FM Huntsville TX 3.8 kw, 420 ft.
KWDX(FM) Silsbee TX 3 kw, 200 ft.
KSNY-FM Snyder TX 3 kw, 295 ft.
KLTD(FM) Temple TX 3 kw, 282 ft.
WLQM-FM Franklin VA 6 kw, 469 ft.
WKWI(FM) Kilmarnock VA 3 kw, 328 ft.
WJJS(FM) Lynchburg VA 3.4 kw, 300 ft.
WRIQ(FM) Radford VA 3 kw, 66 ft.
WVMX(FM) Stowe VT 43 w, 2,653 ft.
KZXR(FM) Prosser WA 3.5 kw, 865 ft.
WHSM-FM Hayward WI 1.45 kw, 466 ft.
WELD-FM Petersburg WV 1.25 kw, 515 ft.
KYCN-FM Wheatland WY 3 kw, 156 ft.

101.9 mhz (ch 270)
WHXT(FM) Citronelle AL 2.07 kw, 436 ft.
WHHY-FM Montgomery AL 100 kw, 1,200 ft.
KJBR(FM) Jonesboro AR 100 kw, 1,059 ft.
KISK(FM) Lowell AR 50 kw, 708 ft.
KOQO-FM Fresno CA 2.25 w, 1,948 ft.
KLIT(FM) Glendale CA 2.4 kw, 2,848 ft.
KQNC(FM) Quincy CA 1.85 kw, 2,115 ft.
KSSJ(FM) Shingle Springs CA 4.1 w, 827 ft.
KKCS-FM Colorado Springs CO 79 kw, 2,178 ft.
WJHM(FM) Daytona Beach FL 28 kw, 1,584 ft.
WHEW(FM) Fort Myers FL 100 kw, 1,020 ft.
WJPH(FM) Monticello FL 6 kw, 249 ft.
WCGX(FM) Cleveland GA 6 kw, 410 ft.
WSGC-FM Ringgold GA 650 w, 702 ft.
KUPU(FM) Pearl City HI 100 kw, 1,948 ft.
*KNWS-FM Waterloo IA 100 kw, 1,010 ft.
KJHY(FM) Emmett ID 57 kw, 2,532 ft.
WTMX(FM) Skokie IL 4.2 kw, 1,561 ft.
WQQL(FM) Springfield IL 50 kw, 300 ft.
WQFE(FM) Brownsburg IN 2.5 kw, 252 ft.
WQXQ(FM) Central City KY 100 kw, 215 ft.
KNOE-FM Monroe LA 97 kw-H, 96 kw-V, 1,670 ft.
WLMG(FM) New Orleans LA 100 kw, 984 ft.
WCIB(FM) Falmouth MA 50 kw, 479 ft.
WLIF-FM Baltimore MD 13.5 kw, 960 ft.
WPOR-FM Portland ME 32.5 kw, 606 ft.
*WDET-FM Detroit MI 79 kw, 450 ft.
WLDR(FM) Traverse City MI 100 kw, 538 ft.
KBMX(FM) Eldon MO 2.25 kw, 545 ft.
WFTA(FM) Fulton MS 100 kw, 560 ft.
WCKZ-FM Gastonia NC 99 kw, 987 ft.
WIKS(FM) New Bern NC 100 kw, 1,020 ft.
KBTO(FM) Bottineau ND 52 kw, 492 ft.
KFGO-FM Fargo ND 100 kw, 866 ft.
KYNN(FM) Lincoln NE 100 kw, 1,132 ft.
KFMS-FM Las Vegas NV 100 kw, 1,181 ft.
WJIV(FM) Cherry Valley NY 8.9 kw, 1,027 ft.
WQCD(FM) New York NY 5.3 kw, 1,420 ft.
WKRQ(FM) Cincinnati OH 16 kw, 876 ft.
WRBP(FM) Hubbard OH 3 kw, 328 ft.
KOQL(FM) Oklahoma City OK 100 kw, 1,390 ft.
KCMX-FM Ashland OR 31.5 kw, 1,457 ft.
KINK-FM Portland OR 100 kw, 1,673 ft.
WAVT-FM Pottsville PA 50 kw, 540 ft.
WZAR(FM) Ponce PR 14 kw, 2,580 ft.
KTWB(FM) Sioux Falls SD 34 kw, 580 ft.
KATP(FM) Amarillo TX 100 kw, 935 ft.
KAQU(FM) Huntington TX 6 kw, 328 ft.
KBUS(FM) Paris TX 50 kw, 500 ft.
KQXT(FM) San Antonio TX 100 kw, 700 ft.
KKAT(FM) Ogden UT 26 kw, 3,740 ft.
WVSY(FM) Ruckersville VA 6 kw, 223 ft.
WDEZ(FM) Wausau WI 100 kw, 489 ft.
WVOW-FM Logan WV 15 kw, 830 ft.
WVAQ(FM) Morgantown WV 50 kw, 500 ft.
KMUS-FM Burns WY 50 kw, 492 ft.
KTSL(FM) Medical Lake WA 12 kw, 495 ft.

102.1 mhz (ch 273)
KPXR(FM) Anchorage AK 25 kw, 174 ft.
WDRM(FM) Decatur AL 100 kw, 981 ft.
KOUN(FM) Sherwood AR 2 kw, 571 ft.
KJJJ(FM) Clifton AZ 2.8 kw, 2221 ft.
KAHM(FM) Prescott AZ 45 kw, 2,551.8 ft.
KZPE(FM) Ford City CA 3 kw, 33 ft.
KRKC-FM King City CA 2.6 kw, 1,820 ft.
KIOZ(FM) Oceanside CA 10 kw, 980 ft.
KDFC-FM San Francisco CA 33 kw, 1,050 ft.
WKLG(FM) Rock Harbor FL 50 kw, 250 ft.
WQLC(FM) Watertown FL 9.0 kw, 531 ft.
WDBS(FM) Bolingbroke GA 3 kw, 328 ft.
WGMG(FM) Crawford GA 6 kw, 328 ft.
WZAT(FM) Savannah GA 100 kw, 1,328 ft.
WDNL(FM) Danville IL 50 kw, 380 ft.
WZLC(FM) Oglesby IL 1.35 kw
KZSN-FM Hutchinson KS 100 kw, 1,032 ft.
WLJC(FM) Beattyville KY 1.2 kw, 520 ft.
WKYL(FM) Lawrenceburg KY 3 kw, 328 ft.
KBAZ(FM) Basile LA 3 kw, 328 ft.
WAQY-FM Springfield MA 50 kw, 780 ft.
WGUY(FM) Dexter ME 26.5 kw, 672 ft.
WLEW-FM Bad Axe MI 50 kw, 492 ft.
*WMUK(FM) Kalamazoo MI 50 kw, 490 ft.
KEEY-FM St. Paul MN 100 kw, 1,033 ft.
KFXE(FM) Cuba MO 3 kw, 236 ft.
KYYS(FM) Kansas City MO 100 kw, 1,000 ft.
KJFM(FM) Louisiana MO 1.85 kw, 387 ft.
WTUX(FM) Meridian MS 800 w, 610 ft.
WRQO(FM) Monticello MS 50 kw, 500 ft.
*KBMC(FM) Bozeman MT 20.5 kw, 768 ft.
WJMH(FM) Reidsville NC 66 kw, 1,065 ft.
KPNY(FM) Alliance NE 100 kw, 521 ft.
WZEA(FM) Hampton NH 3 kw, 328 ft.
KTRA(FM) Farmington NM 100 kw, 1,033 ft.
WDOK(FM) Cleveland OH 12 kw, 1,004 ft.
WIMT(FM) Lima OH 11 kw, 1,060 ft.
WEYQ(FM) Marietta OH 25 kw, 400 ft.
WOWQ(FM) DuBois PA 28.2 kw, 664 ft.
WIOQ(FM) Philadelphia PA 27 kw, 650 ft.
WMXT(FM) Pamplico SC 50 kw, 500 ft.
WMYU(FM) Sevierville TN 100 kw, 1,979 ft.
KPRR(FM) El Paso TX 100 kw, 1,190 ft.
KTXQ(FM) Fort Worth TX 100 kw, 1,447 ft.
KMJQ(FM) Houston TX 100 kw, 1,719 ft.
KCDQ(FM) Monahans TX 100 kw, 977 ft.
KSOX-FM Raymondville TX 17.9 kw, 758 ft.
WRXL(FM) Richmond VA 140 kw, 320 ft.
WTBN(FM) Charlotte Amalie VI 50 kw, 1,404 ft.
KPQ-FM Wenatchee WA 35 kw, 2,655 ft.
WLUM-FM Milwaukee WI 20 kw, 761 ft.

102.3 mhz (ch 272)
*KHNS(FM) Haines AK 3 kw, -1,220 ft.
WYVC(FM) Camden AL 6 kw, 328 ft.
WAMI-FM Opp AL 3.4 kw, 230 ft.
WELR-FM Roanoke AL 3 kw H, 1.25 kw V, 436 ft.
KQMC-FM Brinkley AR 3 kw, 190 ft.
KWKK(FM) Dardanelle AR 200 w, 1,227 ft.
KZXY-FM Apple Valley CA 3 kw, 53 ft.
KJLH-FM Compton CA 3 kw, 300 ft.
KLCZ-FM Corcoran CA 17.5 kw, 380 ft.
KLCX(FM) Indio CA 600 w, 587 ft.
KJSN(FM) Modesto CA 6 kw, 300 ft.
KWHO(FM) Weed CA 5.5 kw, 1,437 ft.
KSMT(FM) Breckenridge CO 3 kw, minus 230 ft.
KVLE(FM) Gunnison CO 3 kw, 200 ft.
KAGM(FM) Strasburg CO 6 kw, 328 ft.
KSPK(FM) Walsenburg CO 17 kw, 377 ft.
WVVE(FM) Stonington CT 3 kw, 298 ft.
WPHK(FM) Blountstown FL 3 kw, 185 ft.
WTRS-FM Dunellon FL 3 kw, 300 ft.
WHLG(FM) Jensen Beach FL 3 kw, 300 ft.
WGGD-FM Melbourne FL 3 kw, 250 ft.
WWAV(FM) Santa Rosa Beach FL 3 kw, 328 ft.
WXFG(FM) Augusta GA 1.5 kw, 666 ft.
WLKQ(FM) Buford GA 3.3 kw, 400 ft.
WSLE(FM) Cairo GA 3 kw, 300 ft.
WKZR(FM) Milledgeville GA 3.3 kw, 300 ft.
WQTU(FM) Rome GA 6 kw, 804 ft.
KCZQ(FM) Cresco IA 3 kw, 328 ft.
KGGY(FM) Dubuque IA 2.4 kw, 410 ft.
KETB(FM) Coeur d'Alene ID 340 w, 764 ft.
WRMJ(FM) Aledo IL 3 kw, 300 ft.
WEMG-FM Crete IL 3 kw, 299 ft h, 295 ft v.
WEBQ-FM Eldorado IL 3 kw, 296 ft.
WTAZ(FM) Morton IL 6 kw, 300 ft.
WRHL-FM Rochelle IL 3 kw, 180 ft.
WAES(FM) Teutopolis IL 6 kw, 100 ft.
WXLC(FM) Waukegan IL 3 kw, 322 ft.
WGTB(FM) Auburn IN 3 kw, 300 ft.
WLHM(FM) Logansport IN 3 kw, 300 ft.
WCBK-FM Martinsville IN 3 kw, 300 ft.
WGTC(FM) New Carlisle IN 2 kw, 397 ft.
WFPC(FM) Petersburg IN 3 kw, 321 ft.
WCBL-FM Benton KY 3 kw, 298 ft.
WCYN-FM Cynthiana KY 1.9 kw, 400 ft.
WUGO(FM) Grayson KY 4.8 kw, 360 ft.
WLRS(FM) Louisville KY 3 kw, 300 ft.
WLOC-FM Munfordville KY 3 kw, 99 ft.
WLLK(FM) Somerset KY 3 kw, 328 ft.
KBCE(FM) Boyce LA 6 kw, 289 ft.
WCDJ(FM) Truro MA 3 kw, 190 ft.
WMMJ(FM) Bethesda MD 2.9 kw, 480 ft.
WCXX(FM) Madawaska ME 1.75 kw, 384 ft.
WPZX(FM) Big Rapids MI 10.5 kw, 436 ft.
WAAH(FM) Houghton MI 1.05 kw, 554 ft.
KDEX-FM Dexter MO 6 kw, 53 ft.
KJPW-FM Waynesville MO 1 kw, 480 ft.
WGCM-FM Gulfport MS 25 kw, 299 ft.
WIQQ(FM) Leland MS 3 kw, 440 ft.
WWSL(FM) Philadelphia MS 3 kw, 200 ft.
WKZU(FM) Ripley MS 3 kw, 300 ft.
WECR(FM) Beech Mountain NC 730 w, 279 ft.
WEQR(FM) Goldsboro NC 6 kw, 292 ft.
WJSK(FM) Lumberton NC 3 kw, 270 ft.
WPTM(FM) Roanoke Rapids NC 6 kw, 300 ft.
KRNY(FM) Kearney NE 25 kw, 328 ft.
WKXL-FM Concord NH 3 kw, 285 ft.
WLGW-FM Lancaster NH 6 kw, minus 66 ft.
WSJL(FM) Cape May NJ 3.2 kw, 292 ft.
WSUS(FM) Franklin NJ 590 w, 745 ft.
*WRRH(FM) Franklin Lakes NJ 10 w, 253 ft.
NEW FM Clovis NM 25 kw, 328 ft.
KIOT(FM) Espanola NM 1.1 kw, 636 ft.
KYOU(FM) Wendover NV 93.8 kw, 1,292 ft.
WBAB-FM Babylon NY 3 kw, 268 ft.
WZRQ(FM) Ballston Spa NY 4.1 kw, 386 ft.
WLKA(FM) Canandaigua NY 3.4 kw, 282 ft.
WRGR(FM) Tupper Lake NY 150 w, 1,446 ft.
WAVR(FM) Waverly NY 1.5 kw, 400 ft.
WQLX(FM) Galion OH 3 kw, 300 ft.
WPOS-FM Holland OH 6 kw, 312 ft.
WSWO(FM) Wilmington OH 3 kw, 300 ft.
KRHD-FM Duncan OK 3 kw, 207 ft.
KCES(FM) Eufaula OK 3 kw, 150 ft.
KMAD-FM Madill OK 3 kw, 233 ft.
KTOW-FM Sand Springs OK 1.7 kw, 436 ft.
KWDQ(FM) Woodward OK 2.35 kw, 355 ft.
KGAL-FM Brownsville OR 6 kw, 961 ft.
WHYL-FM Carlisle PA 3 kw, 328 ft.
WJET(FM) Erie PA 6 kw, 670 ft.
WSKS(FM) Pittston PA 3 kw, 71 ft.
WMIO(FM) Cabo Rojo PR 3 kw, 680 ft.
WMAP-FM Pageland SC 3 kw, 280 ft.
WMFX(FM) St. Andrews SC 3 kw, 322 ft.
KKQQ(FM) Volga SD 25 kw, 234 ft.
WZDQ(FM) Humboldt TN 6 kw, 305 ft.
WFXS(FM) Soddy-Daisy TN 3 kw, 287 ft.
KBIC(FM) Alice TX 3 kw, 300 ft.
KPEZ(FM) Austin TX 20 kw, 685 ft.
KDET-FM Center TX 3 kw, 300 ft.
KSIZ(FM) Jacksonville TX 3 kw, 328 ft.
KWYX(FM) Jasper TX 3 kw, 299 ft.
KXCC(FM) Rockport TX 2.5 kw, 328 ft.
KUVA(FM) Uvalde TX 3 kw, 280 ft.
KVWC-FM Vernon TX 3 kw, 138 ft.
WCYK-FM Crozet VA 4.9 kw, 360 ft.
WOLD-FM Marion VA 6 kw, 1,312 ft.
WDXC(FM) Pound VA 280 w, 992 ft.
WCVR-FM Randolph VT 3 kw, 300 ft.
WLFE(FM) St. Albans VT 440 w, 800 ft.
KRAO(FM) Colfax WA 1.6 kw, 433 ft.
KYYT(FM) Goldendale WA 1.8 kw, 574 ft.
WISS-FM Berlin WI 4.5 kw, 155 ft.
WQTC-FM Manitowoc WI 3 kw, 328 ft.
WVRQ-FM Viroqua WI 2.25 kw, 300 ft.
WHTL-FM Whitehall WI 3 kw, 450 ft.
WMTD-FM Hinton WV 160 w, 1,007 ft.
WSSN(FM) Weston WV 940 w, 489 ft.

102.5 mhz (ch 273)
KIAK-FM Fairbanks AK 26.3 kw, 1,626 ft.
WESP(FM) Dothan AL 6 kw, 328 ft.
WZBQ-FM Jasper AL 13 kw, 2,028 ft.
KLPQ(FM) Cabot AR 3 kw, 328 ft.
KNIX-FM Phoenix AZ 98 kw, 1,620 ft.
KCNQ(FM) Kernville CA 130 w, 1,230 ft.
KDON-FM Salinas CA 18.5 kw, 2,270 ft.
KSNI-FM Santa Maria CA 17.5 kw, 774 ft.
KSFM(FM) Woodland CA 50 kw, 500 ft.
KTRR(FM) Loveland CO 50 kw, 410 ft.
WHPT(FM) Sarasota FL 100 kw, 1,776 ft.
WPIK(FM) Summerland Key FL 50 kw, 413 ft.
*WGHR(FM) Marietta GA 16.5 w, 250 ft.
WYIQ(FM) Warner Robins GA 6 kw, 328 ft.
WBGA(FM) Waycross GA 100 kw, 980 ft.
KSTZ(FM) Des Moines IA 100 kw, 1,248 ft.
KMGI(FM) Pocatello ID 100 kw, 1,023 ft.
KJDE(FM) Sandpoint ID 3 kw, 177 ft.
WWEG(FM) Mitchell IN 6 kw, 282 ft.
WMDH-FM New Castle IN 50 kw, 500 ft.
KKCI(FM) Goodland KS 100 kw, 712 ft.
KBLS(FM) North Fort Riley KS 100 kw, 492 ft.
WCKU(FM) Nicholasville KY 3 kw, 300 ft.
WFMF(FM) Baton Rouge LA 85 kw, 1,260 ft.
WCRB(FM) Waltham MA 15 kw, 918 ft.
WOLC(FM) Princess Anne MD 50 kw, 500 ft.
WQSS(FM) Camden ME 7.9 kw, 1,201 ft.
WIOG(FM) Bay City MI 86 kw, 860 ft.
KMFX(FM) Lake City MN 9.4 kw, 528 ft.
KQIC(FM) Willmar MN 100 kw, 830 ft.
WMBH-FM Joplin MO 100 kw, 410 ft.
KEZK-FM St. Louis MO 100 kw, 1,026 ft.
KKDY(FM) West Plains MO 50 kw, 485 ft.
WJKX(FM) Ellisville MS 50 kw, 492 ft.
WAGR-FM Lexington MS 6 kw, 328 ft.
KMSO(FM) Missoula MT 25 kw, 874 ft.
WERX-FM Edenton NC 26 kw, 689 ft.
WMYI(FM) Hendersonville NC 20 kw, 1,778 ft.
WHLQ(FM) Louisburg NC 6 kw, 328 ft.
KDVL(FM) Devils Lake ND 100 kw, 471 ft.
KOYT(FM) Los Lunas NM 50 kw, 492 ft.
WAFV(FM) Bridgehampton NY 4.5 kw, 112 ft.
WMJQ(FM) Buffalo NY 110 kw, 1,340 ft.
WKDY(FM) Rome NY 27 kw, 649 ft.
WADQ(FM) Westport NY 6 kw, -33 ft.
WZOO-FM Edgewood OH 5.8 kw, 328 ft.
WHIZ-FM Zanesville OH 50 kw, 490 ft.
WDVE(FM) Pittsburgh PA 55 kw, 820 ft.
WRFY-FM Reading PA 19 kw, 807 ft.
WIAC-FM San Juan PR 50 kw, 1,139 ft.
WXLY(FM) North Charleston SC 100 kw, 1,000 ft.
KIXK(FM) Canton SD 3 kw, 243 ft.
*KZSD-FM Martin SD 100 kw, 754 ft.
WEGE(FM) Crossville TN 6 kw, 984 ft.
WQZQ(FM) Dickson TN 50 kw, 500 ft.
KMKS(FM) Bay City TX 50 kw, 492 ft.
KJNE(FM) Hillsboro TX 100 kw, 450 ft.
KZII-FM Lubbock TX 100 kw, 850 ft.
KKYR-FM Texarkana TX 100 kw, 445 ft.
WUSQ-FM Winchester VA 31 kw, 630 ft.
KZOK-FM Seattle WA 100 kw, 1,170 ft.
*WNWC(FM) Madison WI 50 kw, 460 ft.
KZIO(FM) Superior WI 100 kw, 600 ft.

102.7 mhz (ch 274)
WCKS(FM) Fruithurst AL 1.65 kw, 630 ft.
KWLT(FM) North Crossett AR 25 kw, 328 ft.
KLSZ-FM Van Buren AR 3 kw, 295 ft.
KFLG-FM Bullhead City AZ 53 kw, 2,408 ft.
KSSI(FM) China Lake CA 3 kw, minus 22 ft.
KTHT(FM) Fresno CA 50 kw, 500 ft.
KIIS-FM Los Angeles CA 8 kw, 2,960 ft.
KZAP(FM) Red Bluff CA 12 kw, 1,017 ft.
KIKX-FM Manitou Springs CO 100 kw, 2,000 ft.
WVNM(FM) Cedar Key FL 25 kw, 328 ft.
WXBM-FM Milton FL 100 kw, 1,328 ft.
WMXJ(FM) Pompano Beach FL 100 kw, 1,007 ft.
WHKR(FM) Rockledge FL 50 kw, 492 ft.
WBDX(FM) Trenton GA 500 w, 817 ft.
KDEO-FM Waipahu HI 61 kw, 1,893 ft.
KYTC(FM) Northwood IA 6 kw, 318 ft.
WJEQ(FM) Macomb IL 25 kw, 269 ft.
WVAZ(FM) Oak Park IL 6 kw, 1,170 ft.
WLNB(FM) Ligonier IN 3 kw, 328 ft.

WLEZ(FM) Terre Haute IN 50 kw, 500 ft.
WSEH(FM) Cumberland KY 165 w, 1,847 ft.
WMJL-FM Marion KY 3 kw, 328 ft.
WMQQ(FM) Springfield KY 1.9 kw, 417 ft.
WXYV(FM) Baltimore MD 50 kw, 436 ft.
WDZR(FM) Mount Clemens MI 50 kw, 499 ft.
KQEG(FM) La Crescent MN 1.85 kw, 600 ft.
*KNTN(FM) Thief River Falls MN 100 kw, 538 ft.
KABE(FM) Lake Ozark MO 6 kw, 328 ft.
WCNG(FM) Murphy NC 3 kw, 426 ft.
WGNI(FM) Wilmington NC 100 kw, 981 ft.
KFRX(FM) Lincoln NE 100 kw, 500 ft.
WSKR(FM) Petersburg NJ 3.3 kw, 295 ft.
WKGG(FM) Cape Vincent NY 3 kw, 328 ft.
WNEW(FM) New York NY 7.8 kw, 1,220 ft.
WDCZ(FM) Webster NY 1.5 kw, 456 ft.
WEBN(FM) Cincinnati OH 16.6 kw, 876 ft.
WCPZ(FM) Sandusky OH 50 kw, 141 ft.
KJYO(FM) Oklahoma City OK 98 kw, 900 ft.
KCNA(FM) Cave Junction OR 100 kw, 1,976 ft.
KYTE(FM) Newport OR 66 kw, 881 ft.
WKSB(FM) Williamsport PA 53 kw, 1,270 ft.
WPJB(FM) Narragansett Pier RI 5 kw, 148 ft.
WAJY(FM) New Ellenton SC 3 kw, 328 ft.
WEKX(FM) Jellico TN 630 w, 1,008 ft.
WEGR(FM) Memphis TN 100 kw, 970 ft.
KCWS(FM) Merkel TX 100 kw, 1,486 ft.
KTFM(FM) San Antonio TX 100 kw-h, 70 kw-v, 670 ft.
WLDJ(FM) Appomattox VA 22 kw, 745 ft.
WEQX(FM) Manchester VT 1.35 kw, 2,490 ft.
KORD-FM Richland WA 100 kw, 1,100 ft.
WRVM(FM) Suring WI 100 kw, 499 ft.
WVSR-FM Charleston WV 50 kw, 403 ft.
WTUS(FM) Mannington WV 3.21 kw, 453 ft.

102.9 mhz (ch 275)

WKXX(FM) Attalla AL 1.1 kw, 702 ft.
WNPT-FM Linden AL 40 kw, 551 ft.
KHOZ-FM Harrison AR 100 kw, 981 ft.
KEZQ(FM) Sheridan AR 50 kw, 488 ft.
KBLX(FM) Berkeley CA 50 kw, 1,290 ft.
KWTY(FM) Cartago CA 2 kw, minus 1,787 ft.
KSUV-FM McFarland CA 21 kw, 383 ft.
KXLM(FM) Oxnard CA 5.5 kw, 112 ft.
KCLX-FM San Diego CA 32 kw, 616 ft.
KGLE-FM South Lake Tahoe CA 1 kw, 2,794 ft.
WDRC-FM Hartford CT 19.5 kw, 810 ft.
WIVY-FM Jacksonville FL 100 kw, 984 ft.
WMJE(FM) Clarkesville GA 16 kw, 413 ft.
WVRK(FM) Columbus GA 100 kw, 1,521 ft.
WUUF(FM) Statesboro GA 25 kw, 328 ft.
KQCR(FM) Cedar Rapids IA 100 kw, 390 ft.
KTFG(FM) Sioux Rapids IA 50 kw, 479 ft.
KMVX(FM) Jerome ID 100 kw, 760 ft.
WSOY-FM Decatur IL 54 kw, 495 ft.
WNJY(FM) Delphi IN 1.2 kw, 515 ft.
KHUT(FM) Hutchinson KS 28.5 kw, 496 ft.
WKCM-FM Hawesville KY 2.6 kw, 505 ft.
WXJJ(FM) Mt. Vernon KY 2.5 kw, 328 ft.
WLKS-FM West Liberty KY 6 kw, 328 ft.
KMEZ(FM) Belle Chasse LA 5.2 kw, 604 ft.
KAJN-FM Crowley LA 95 kw, 1,499 ft.
WPXC(FM) Hyannis MA 6 kw, 325 ft.
WRFK(FM) California MD 3.7 kw, 407 ft.
WROG(FM) Cumberland MD 32 kw, 1,440 ft.
WVZD(FM) Dennysville ME 3 kw, 328 ft.
WBLM(FM) Portland ME 100 kw, 1,460 ft.
WIQB-FM Ann Arbor MI 49 kw-H, 42 kw-V, 499 ft.
WFUR-FM Grand Rapids MI 50 kw, 492 ft.
WMKC(FM) St. Ignace MI 100 kw, 374 ft.
WLTE(FM) Minneapolis MN 100 kw, 1,033 ft.
KEZS-FM Cape Girardeau MO 100 kw, 947 ft.
KMMO-FM Marshall MO 56 kw, 380 ft.
WMSI(FM) Jackson MS 100 kw, 1,800 ft.
KCTR-FM Billings MT 100 kw, 500 ft.
WEZC(FM) Hickory NC 31 kw, 1,545 ft.
WKGK(FM) Kinston NC 3 kw, 295 ft.
KBRX-FM O'Neill NE 100 kw, 500 ft.
KNFT-FM Bayard NM 3 kw, 135 ft.
KOKN(FM) Hobbs NM 100 kw, 518 ft.
KMYI(FM) Kirtland NM 96 kw, 1,020 ft.
WNCQ-FM Morristown NY 2.4 kw, 367 ft.
*WMHR(FM) Syracuse NY 20 kw, 780 ft.
WAZU(FM) Springfield OH 50 kw, 160 ft.
KSJJ(FM) Redmond OR 100 kw, 400 ft.
WOKW(FM) Curwensville PA 350 w, 959 ft.
WMGK(FM) Philadelphia PA 8.5 kw, 1,140 ft.
WYFM(FM) Sharon PA 44 kw, 455 ft.
WCHQ-FM Camuy PR 50 kw, 303 ft.
WIGL(FM) Orangeburg SC 3 kw, 300 ft.
WSQN(FM) Scranton SC 2.9 kw, 466 ft.
KBWS-FM Sisseton SD 100 kw, 496 ft.
WYCQ(FM) Shelbyville TN 100 kw, 820 ft.
KDMX(FM) Dallas TX 99 kw, 1,348 ft.
KQUE(FM) Houston TX 100 kw, 1,049 ft.
WOWI(FM) Norfolk VA 50 kw, 500 ft.
*WIUJ(FM) St. Thomas VI 150 w, 50 ft.
KMNT(FM) Centralia WA 100 kw, 1,057 ft.
WLZR-FM Milwaukee WI 50 kw, 440 ft.
WELC-FM Welch WV 1.8 kw, 423 ft.
KRQU(FM) Laramie WY 100 kw, 1,220 ft.

103.1 mhz (ch 276)

KXDZ(FM) Anchorage AK 6 kw, 328 ft.
KSBZ(FM) Sitka AK 3 kw, 144 ft.
WXKI(FM) Moulton AL 6 kw, 328 ft.
KXSA-FM Dermott AR 5.5 kw, 328 ft.
KIXB(FM) El Dorado AR 100 kw, 571 ft.
KCRI-FM Helena AR 6 kw, 328 ft.
KRWA-FM Waldron AR 3 kw, 298 ft.
KPRI(FM) Fagaitua AS 30 kw, 203 ft.
KLQB(FM) Oracle AZ 900 w, 502 ft.
KHAC-FM Window Rock AZ 3 kw
KKCY(FM) Colusa CA 135 w, 1,964 ft.
KBJZ(FM) Newport Beach CA 2.57 kw, 322 ft.
KEZN(FM) Palm Desert CA 640 w, 590 ft.
KTBG(FM) Paso Robles CA 1.2 kw, 722 ft.
KNLF(FM) Quincy CA 3 kw, minus 499 ft.
KAJZ(FM) Santa Monica CA 3 kw, 265 ft.
KTPI(FM) Tehachapi CA 3 kw, 580 ft.
KVVQ-FM Victorville CA 95 w, 1,424 ft.
KZYR(FM) Avon CO 1.5 kw, 459 ft.
WLGH(FM) DeFuniak Springs FL 2.6 kw, 350 ft.
WSGL(FM) Naples FL 2 kw, 384 ft.
WOKC-FM Okeechobee FL 3 kw, 321 ft.
WFKZ(FM) Plantation Key FL 6 kw, 250 ft.
WUMX(FM) Tallahassee FL 3 kw, 300 ft.
WLOQ(FM) Winter Park FL 2.65 kw, 351 ft.
WFXA-FM Augusta GA 3 kw, 299 ft.
*WPLH(FM) Tifton GA 29 w-H, 177 ft.
KDMG(FM) Burlington IA 12 kw, 445 ft.
KLKK(FM) Clear Lake IA 6 kw, 300 ft.
KCDA(FM) Coeur d'Alene ID 2.35 kw, 4,400 ft.
WVVX(FM) Highland Park IL 3 kw, 241 ft.
WAKO-FM Lawrenceville IL 6 kw, 328 ft.
WJDK(FM) Morris IL 3 kw, 328 ft.
WRWC(FM) Rockton IL 1.5 kw, 525 ft.
WCDV(FM) Covington IN 3 kw, 300 ft.
WOWO-FM Huntington IN 3 kw, 298 ft.
WHME(FM) South Bend IN 3 kw, 300 ft.
WXCH(FM) Versailles IN 3 kw, 328 ft.
KNDY-FM Marysville KS 9 kw, 389 ft.
WPKE-FM Elkhorn City KY 120 w, 1,371 ft.
WGRK-FM Greensburg KY 2.2 kw, 375 ft.
WGBF-FM Henderson KY 3 kw, 460 ft.
WWXL-FM Manchester KY 3 kw, 328 ft.
WRKA(FM) St. Matthews KY 6 kw, 312 ft.
KCTO-FM Columbia LA 25 kw, 348 ft.
WXZL(FM) Grasonville MD 3 kw, 328 ft.
WAFY(FM) Middletown MD 3 kw, 328 ft.
WDME-FM Dover-Foxcroft ME 3 kw, 285 ft.
WGDN-FM Gladwin MI 11.5 kw, 453 ft.
WWGZ-FM Lapeer MI 3 kw, 299 ft.
KFIL-FM Preston MN 6 kw, 270 ft.
KLOH-FM Slayton MN 3 kw
KLOW(FM) Caruthersville MO 3 kw, 200 ft.
WMBC(FM) Columbus MS 22 kw, 754 ft.
WOSM(FM) Ocean Springs MS 50 kw, 459 ft.
*KVCM(FM) Helena MT 100 kw, 1,916 ft.
*WUAG(FM) Greensboro NC 18.1 w, 230 ft.
KASK(FM) Las Cruces NM 3 kw, minus 111 ft.
WHRL(FM) Albany NY 3 kw, 328 ft.
WCIK(FM) Bath NY 790 w, 532 ft.
WBZO(FM) Bay Shore NY 3 kw, 285 ft.
WTOJ(FM) Carthage NY 3 kw, 500 ft.
WGNY-FM Newburgh NY 6 kw, 275 ft.
WZOZ(FM) Oneonta NY 2 kw, 360 ft.
WRZR(FM) Johnstown OH 3 kw, 444 ft.
WNDH(FM) Napoleon OH 3 kw, 300 ft.
WRAC(FM) West Union OH 3.3 kw, 417 ft.
KHKC-FM Atoka OK 3 kw, 454 ft.
KOFM(FM) Enid OK 25 kw, 298 ft.
KRSB-FM Roseburg OR 2.75 kw, 308 ft.
WQEQ(FM) Freeland PA 730 w, 679 ft.
WQMU(FM) Indiana PA 3 kw, 170 ft.
WRLP(FM) Russell PA 2.1 kw, 351 ft.
WBHV(FM) State College PA 3 kw, -55 ft.
WANB-FM Waynesburg PA 550 w, 620 ft.
WOMG-FM Columbia SC 3 kw, 300 ft.
WBHC-FM Hampton SC 3 kw, 328 ft.
WRIX-FM Honea Path SC 6 kw, 392 ft.
WYAK-FM Surfside Beach-Garden City SC 6 kw, 325 ft.
KJAM-FM Madison SD 6 kw, 321 ft.
WDRZ-FM Etowah TN 50 kw, 492 ft.
WMXX-FM Jackson TN 35 kw, 577 ft.
KRUN-FM Ballinger TX 3 kw, 300 ft.
KEZP(FM) Canadian TX 830 w, 574 ft.
KOOV(FM) Copperas Cove TX 760 w, 630 ft.
KPAS(FM) Fabens TX 3 kw, 300 ft.
KKYC(FM) Muleshoe TX 2.9 kw-H, 75 ft.
KXAL-FM Pittsburg TX 3.824 kw, 328 ft.
KCTM(FM) Rio Grande City TX 1.41 kw, 420 ft.
WCUL(FM) Culpeper VA 3 kw, 300 ft.
KQBE(FM) Ellensburg WA 2 kw, 1,273 ft.
WKTT(FM) Cleveland WI 3 kw, 327 ft.
WXKX(FM) Parkersburg WV 730 w, 551 ft.

103.3 mhz (ch 277)

WSYA-FM Montgomery AL 100 kw, 1,007 ft.
KWOZ(FM) Mountain View AR 100 kw, 987 ft.
KZPO(FM) Lindsay CA 528 w, 751 ft.
KATM(FM) Modesto CA 50 kw, 500 ft.
KRUZ(FM) Santa Barbara CA 105 kw, 2,980 ft.
*KSCU(FM) Santa Clara CA 30 w, 179 ft.
KUKI-FM Ukiah CA 2.7 kw, 1,840 ft.
WQQQ(FM) Sharon CT 1.5 kw, 640 ft.
WDUV(FM) Bradenton FL 100 kw, 649 ft.
WVEE(FM) Atlanta GA 100 kw, 1,022 ft.
WHFX(FM) Waycross GA 100 kw, 1,100 ft.
KAUI(FM) Kekaha HI 85 kw, 810 ft.
KIKR(FM) Asbury IA 25 kw, 328 ft.
KFMG(FM) Pella IA 100 kw, 745 ft.
KTFC(FM) Sioux City IA 100 kw, 271 ft.
KHEZ(FM) Caldwell ID 54 kw, 2,525 ft.
KFTZ(FM) Idaho Falls ID 50 kw, 581 ft.
WAIV(FM) Spring Valley IL 2.5 kw, 118 ft.
WRZX(FM) Indianapolis IN 18 kw, 850 ft.
KJLS(FM) Hays KS 100 kw, 463 ft.
WTKT-FM Georgetown KY 6 kw, 300 ft.
NEW FM Bastrop LA 3 kw, 100 ft.
WKJN-FM Hammond LA 100 kw, 1,004 ft.
WODS(FM) Boston MA 16.5 kw, 938 ft.
WMCM(FM) Rockland ME 31.2 kw, 587 ft.
WKFR-FM Battle Creek MI 50 kw, 500 ft.
WFXD(FM) Marquette MI 100 kw, 544 ft.
*KUMD-FM Duluth MN 95 kw, 820 ft.
KZCR(FM) Fergus Falls MN 100 kw, 620 ft.
KPRS(FM) Kansas City MO 100 kw, 994 ft.
KLOU(FM) St. Louis MO 100 kw, 920 ft.
WWFS(FM) Kosciusko MS 25 kw, 328 ft.
WKVS(FM) Lenoir NC 550 w
WKQT(FM) Newport NC 100 kw, 600 ft.
WPRB(FM) Princeton NJ 14 kw, 731 ft.
KASY(FM) Albuquerque NM 22 kw, 4,069 ft.
WUFX(FM) Buffalo NY 49 kw, 340 ft.
WMXW(FM) Vestal NY 6 kw, 1,014 ft.
*WCRF(FM) Cleveland OH 25.5 kw, 660 ft.
*WDEQ-FM De Graff OH 10 w, 23 ft.
KTFX(FM) Tulsa OK 100 kw, 1,278 ft.
KKCW(FM) Beaverton OR 100 kw, 1,654 ft.
WARM-FM York PA 6.4 kw, 1,305 ft.
WVJP-FM Caguas PR 28 kw, 1,906 ft.
WJMX-FM Cheraw SC 44 kw, 525 ft.
WLYZ(FM) Greer SC 2.7 kw, 495 ft.
WKDF(FM) Nashville TN 100 kw, 1,233 ft.
KWOW(FM) Clifton TX 8.37 kw, 574 ft.
KJOJ-FM Freeport TX 100 kw, 453 ft.
KCRS-FM Midland TX 100 kw, 920 ft.
KJCS(FM) Nacogdoches TX 100 kw, 476 ft.
KWFS(FM) Wichita Falls TX 100 kw, 449 ft.
WAKG(FM) Danville VA 100 kw, 630 ft.
WEZI(FM) New Market VA 2.1 kw, 544 ft.
WESR-FM Onley-Onancock VA 50 kw, 320 ft.
WGLY-FM Waterbury VT 920 w, 891 ft.
KVYF(FM) Wilson Creek WA 6 kw, 328 ft.
WWRW(FM) Wisconsin Rapids WI 73 kw, 331 ft.
WTCR-FM Huntington WV 50 kw, 490 ft.

103.5 mhz (ch 278)

KWVV-FM Homer AK 100 kw, 1,150 ft.
KEGT(FM) Lake Village AR 6 kw, 328 ft.
KTWC(FM) Glendale AZ 52 kw, 2,428 ft.
KOST(FM) Los Angeles CA 12.5 kw, 3,100 ft.
KHSL-FM Paradise CA 1.61 kw, 1250 ft.
KRAY-FM Salinas CA 3 kw, minus 134 ft.
KLMY(FM) Seaside CA 3 kw, 328 ft.
KRFX(FM) Denver CO 100 kw, 1,045 ft.
WGMS-FM Washington DC 44 kw, 518 ft.
WDRK(FM) Callaway FL 100 kw, 475 ft.
WSHE(FM) Fort Lauderdale FL 100 kw, 1,007 ft.
WEGC(FM) Leesburg GA 12.5 kw, 460 ft.
WAFI(FM) Unadilla GA 6 kw, 328 ft.
WWBZ(FM) Chicago IL 4.3 kw, 1,548 ft.
WUEZ(FM) Christopher IL 6 kw, 328 ft.
WIKK(FM) Newton IL 25 kw, 328 ft.
WAWC(FM) Syracuse IN 3 kw, 328 ft.
WLVK(FM) Radcliff KY 6 kw, 321 ft.
KLAA(FM) Tioga LA 50 kw, 476 ft.
*WCCH(FM) Holyoke MA 10 w, 258 ft.
WMUZ(FM) Detroit MI 50 kw, 500 ft.
WTCM-FM Traverse City MI 100 kw, 989 ft.
KABD(FM) Brainerd MN 6 kw, 328 ft.
KYSM-FM Mankato MN 81 kw, 530 ft.
KWXD(FM) Asbury MO 3.8 kw, 413 ft.
KZMA(FM) Poplar Bluff MO 50 kw, 492 ft.
WWKZ(FM) New Albany MS 100 kw, 1,004 ft.
WRCQ(FM) Dunn NC 48 kw, 502 ft.
WCCG(FM) Hope Mills NC 3 kw, 328 ft.
KZZY-FM Devils Lake ND 100 kw, 433 ft.
KXNP(FM) North Platte NE 100 kw, 479 ft.
KEDG(FM) Las Vegas NV 100 kw, 1,158 ft.
WSHQ(FM) Cobleskill NY 50 kw, 492 ft.
WYNY(FM) Lake Success NY 5.4 kw, 1,417 ft.
WAEE(FM) Plattsburgh NY 3 kw, 328 ft.
WNNR-FM Sodus NY 3 kw, 243 ft.
WGRR(FM) Hamilton OH 19.3 kw, 790 ft.
WSWZ(FM) Lancaster OH 6 kw, 328 ft.
WRKY(FM) Steubenville OH 16 kw, 879 ft.
KOPE(FM) Medford OR 100 kw, 1,023 ft.
KWHT(FM) Pendleton OR 100 kw, 720 ft.
WKAB(FM) Berwick PA 2 kw, 387 ft.
WLAK(FM) Huntingdon PA 160 w, 1,427 ft.
WEZL(FM) Charleston SC 100 kw, 659 ft.
WMTY-FM Greenwood SC 25 kw, 328 ft.
WIMZ-FM Knoxville TN 100 kw, 1,723 ft.
KVST(FM) Huntsville TX 3.6 kw, 426 ft.
KZRB(FM) New Boston TX 3 kw, 328 ft.
KEYI-FM San Marcos TX 95.5 kw, 1,256 ft.
KRSP-FM Salt Lake City UT 27.5 kw, 3,630 ft.

103.7 mhz (ch 279)

WAAO-FM Andalusia AL 3 kw, 328 ft.
WQEN(FM) Gadsden AL 100 kw, 1,080 ft.
KKYK-FM Little Rock AR 100 kw, 1,510 ft.
KCDX(FM) San Carlos AZ 3 kw, 298 ft.
KODS(FM) Carnelian Bay CA 6.3 kw, 2,985 ft.
KWEO(FM) Garberville CA 7.64 kw, 2,647 ft.
KRZR(FM) Hanford CA 50 kw, 499 ft.
KJQY(FM) San Diego CA 36 kw, 580 ft.
KKSF(FM) San Francisco CA 7.8 kw, 1,470 ft.
KTRN(FM) Silverton CO 26 kw-H, -582 ft.
WXKB(FM) Cape Coral FL 50 kw, 273 ft.
WRUF-FM Gainesville FL 100 kw, 768 ft.
WQOL(FM) Vero Beach FL 50 kw, 476 ft.
WULS(FM) Broxton GA 6 kw, 328 ft.
WVKX(FM) Irwinton GA 3 kw, 328 ft.
WHCG(FM) Metter GA 3 kw, 299 ft.
WPUP(FM) Royston GA 25 kw, 328 ft.
KXKT(FM) Atlantic IA 100 kw, 1,246 ft.
KUUL(FM) Davenport IA 100 kw, 1,191 ft.
KCZY(FM) Osage IA 6 kw, 154 ft.

U.S. FM Stations by Frequency

KSKI-FM Sun Valley ID 51.8 w, 1,905 ft.
WDBR(FM) Springfield IL 50 kw, 320 ft.
*WFIU(FM) Bloomington IN 34 kw, 590 ft.
WHZR(FM) Royal Center IN 6 kw, 328 ft.
KEYN-FM Wichita KS 95 kw, 859 ft.
WHHT(FM) Cave City KY 13.5 kw, 449 ft.
WKED-FM Frankfort KY 2.5 kw, 350 ft.
WBLN-FM Murray KY 100 kw, 661 ft.
KDKS-FM Haughton LA 6 kw, 328 ft.
KBIU(FM) Lake Charles LA 100 kw, 425 ft.
WXCY(FM) Havre de Grace MD 50 kw, 341 ft.
KKBJ-FM Bemidji MN 100 kw, 460 ft.
KLZZ(FM) Waite Park MN 3 kw, 328 ft.
KIRK(FM) Lebanon MO 100 kw, 984 ft.
WHER(FM) Hattiesburg MS 100 kw, 1,056 ft.
KOHZ(FM) Billings MT 100 kw, 480 ft.
WSOC-FM Charlotte NC 100 kw, 1,040 ft.
WHTE(FM) Williamston NC 50 kw, 331 ft.
WZPK(FM) Berlin NH 22.5 kw, 3,870 ft.
WKNE-FM Keene NH 12.2 kw, 991 ft.
WMGM(FM) Atlantic City NJ 50 kw, 400 ft.
WNNJ-FM Newton NJ 3.5 kw, 757 ft.
WQNY(FM) Ithaca NY 5 kw, 876 ft.
WTTF-FM Tiffin OH 50 kw, 492 ft.
KRPT-FM Anadarko OK 86 kw, 987 ft.
KZUD(FM) Wilburton OK 6 kw, 272 ft.
KXPC(FM) Lebanon OR 100 kw, 1099 ft.
WMXE(FM) Erie PA 50 kw, 499 ft.
WCFI(FM) Lajas PR 50 kw, 456 ft.
WWRX-FM Westerly RI 37 kw, 570 ft.
KQKD-FM Redfield SD 50 kw, 324 ft.
KRRO(FM) Sioux Falls SD 50 kw, 187 ft.
KCDD(FM) Hamlin TX 100 kw, 985 ft.
KVIL-FM Highland Park-Dallas TX 100 kw, 1,571 ft.
KOUL(FM) Sinton TX 100 kw, 941 ft.
WMXB(FM) Richmond VA 18.5 kw, 750 ft.
KMTT-FM Tacoma WA 58 kw, 2,343 ft.
WWIB(FM) Ladysmith WI 100 kw, 706 ft.
WEZW(FM) Wauwatosa-Milwaukee WI 19.5 kw, 840 ft.
WCIR-FM Beckley WV 5 kw, 1,485 ft.
WYFY(FM) Fisher WV 6 kw, 328 ft.
KQLT(FM) Casper WY 59.3 kw, 1,909 ft.
WLTT(FM) Shallotte NC 25 kw, 328 ft.

103.9 mhz (ch 280)

KSUA(FM) College AK 3 kw, 120 ft.
WQLS-FM Ozark AL 3 kw, 328 ft.
KHSP-FM Ashdown AR 2.65 kw, 354 ft.
KKIX(FM) Fayetteville AR 100 kw, 510 ft.
KPOC-FM Pocahontas AR 3 kw, 145 ft.
KAZR(FM) Coolidge AZ 3 kw, 300 ft.
KACE(FM) Inglewood CA 1.65 kw, 390 ft.
KRAJ(FM) Johannesburg CA 1.5 kw, 1,322 ft.
KAEV(FM) Lake Arrowhead CA 38 w, 2,538 ft.
KHOV(FM) Mariposa CA 71 w, 2,047 ft.
KMYX-FM Taft CA 3 kw, 300 ft.
KXCL(FM) Yuba City CA 510 w, 2,024 ft.
KRLN-FM Canon City CO 3 kw, minus 520 ft.
KSNO-FM Snowmass Village CO 3 kw, 328 ft.
WZMQ(FM) Key Largo FL 6 kw, 150 ft.
WPPL(FM) Blue Ridge GA 3 kw, 300 ft.
WDDK(FM) Greensboro GA 3 kw, 299 ft.
WQSY(FM) Hawkinsville GA 25 kw, 255 ft.
KUOO(FM) Spirit Lake IA 50 kw, 492 ft.
KNEI-FM Waukon IA 3 kw, 200 ft.
WXAN(FM) Ava IL 3 kw, 675 ft.
WABT(FM) Dundee IL 3 kw, 299 ft.
WNOI(FM) Flora IL 3.3 kw, 300 ft.
WRBI(FM) Batesville IN 1.95 kw, 360 ft.
WIMC(FM) Crawfordsville IN 1.35 kw, 500 ft.
WWJY(FM) Crown Point IN 3 kw, 330 ft.
WXKE(FM) Fort Wayne IN 3 kw, 380 ft.
WRBR-FM South Bend IN 3 kw, 328 ft.
KOMB(FM) Fort Scott KS 2 kw, 400 ft.
KNZA(FM) Hiawatha KS 3 kw, 300 ft.
KQLA(FM) Ogden KS 3 kw, 315 ft.
WWEL(FM) London KY 3 kw, 190 ft.
WHKW(FM) Louisville KY 1.35 kw, 490 ft.
WXKQ(FM) Whitesburg KY 210 w, 940 ft.
WATB(FM) South Yarmouth MA 3 kw, 315 ft.
WOCQ(FM) Berlin MD 3 kw, 328 ft.
WZYQ(FM) Braddock Heights MD 380 w, 910 ft.
WSNV(FM) Howland ME 54 kw, 1,535 ft.
WLEN(FM) Adrian MI 3 kw, 299 ft.
*WCMW-FM Harbor Springs MI 28 kw, 663 ft.
WHYB(FM) Menominee MI 3 kw, 300 ft.
WMZX(FM) Owosso MI 6 kw, 255 ft.
KBHL(FM) Osakis MN 3 kw, 341 ft.
KCHI-FM Chillicothe MO 1.55 kw, 400 ft.
KMCR(FM) Montgomery City MO 3 kw, 300 ft.
WCLD-FM Cleveland MS 6 kw, 300 ft.
WACR-FM Columbus MS 3 kw, 204 ft.
WZBR(FM) Ebenezer MS 6 kw, 328 ft.
KOFI-FM Kalispell MT 100 kw-H, 55 kw-V, 571 ft.
WNND(FM) Fuquay-Varina NC 1.2 kw, 493 ft.
WZXS(FM) Topsail Beach NC 21.5 kw, 328 ft.
KNLV-FM Ord NE 3.85 kw, 379 ft.
KRFS-FM Superior NE 2 kw, 59 ft.
KGRT-FM Las Cruces NM 3 kw, 150 ft.
WSRK(FM) Oneonta NY 850 w, 520 ft.
WQBK-FM Rensselaer NY 3 kw, 300 ft.
WRCN-FM Riverhead NY 1.5 kw, 466 ft.
WDKX(FM) Rochester NY 800 w, 540 ft.
*WANC(FM) Ticonderoga NY 1.55 kw, 380 ft.
WFAS-FM White Plains NY 600 w, 669 ft.
WYMJ-FM Beavercreek OH 1.15 kw, 522 ft.
WALY(FM) Bellwood PA 3 kw, 984 ft.
WIBF-FM Jenkintown PA 340 w, 1,000 ft.
WLMI(FM) Kane PA 3 kw, 300 ft.
WWIZ(FM) Mercer PA 3 kw, 300 ft.
WHTO(FM) Muncy PA 1.3 kw, 460 ft.
WLSW(FM) Scottdale PA 325 w, 780 ft.
WLWZ-FM Easley SC 3 kw, 328 ft.
WKSO(FM) Orangeburg SC 3 kw, 299 ft.
WXIS(FM) Erwin TN 2.5 kw, 2,600 ft.
WDEB-FM Jamestown TN 1.6 kw, 450 ft.
WTRZ-FM McMinnville TN 5.3 kw, 130 ft.
KWGH-FM Big Lake TX
KLZK(FM) Brownfield TX 3 kw, 320 ft.
KHLR(FM) Cameron TX 25 kw, 695 ft.
KZEY-FM Marshall TX 3 kw, 300 ft.
KKYN-FM Plainview TX 3 kw, 300 ft.
KYKN-FM Nephi UT 6 kw, minus 656 ft.
KNUC(FM) Smithfield UT 3 kw, minus 116 ft.
WXCF-FM Clifton Forge VA 150 w, 1,909 ft.
WYFT(FM) Luray VA 3 kw, 299 ft.
KLLM(FM) Forks WA 3 kw, minus 75 ft.
KNJY(FM) Spokane WA 3 kw, 299 ft.
WMGV(FM) Oshkosh WI 6 kw, 318 ft.
WNMR(FM) New Martinsville WV 3 kw, 298 ft.

104.1 mhz (ch 281)

KBRJ(FM) Anchorage AK 55 kw, 61 ft.
WGCX(FM) Atmore AL 100 kw, 1,555 ft.
KUDO(FM) Tucson AZ 3 kw, 46 ft.
KBOX(FM) Lompoc CA 5.7 kw, 710 ft.
KHOP(FM) Modesto CA 50 kw, 500 ft.
KFCL-FM Woodlake CA 17 kw, 853 ft.
KNAB-FM Burlington CO 50.7 kw, 358 ft.
KFMU-FM Oak Creek CO 1.4 kw, 1,073 ft.
WYSR(FM) Waterbury CT 50 kw, 859 ft.
WTKS(FM) Cocoa Beach FL 100 kw, 1,609 ft.
WGLF(FM) Tallahassee FL 100 kw, 1,359 ft.
WSEG(FM) Brunswick GA 6 kw, 328 ft.
WQXJ(FM) Clayton GA 480 w, 817 ft.
WYAI(FM) La Grange GA 60 kw, 1,217 ft.
WRBX(FM) Reidsville GA 3 kw, 187 ft.
KEZT(FM) Ames IA 100 kw, 1,026 ft.
KOUU(FM) American Falls ID 3 kw, 328 ft.
WKKX(FM) Jerseyville IL 50 kw, 500 ft.
WIKY-FM Evansville IN 39 kw, 580 ft.
WLBC-FM Muncie IN 50 kw, 420 ft.
WCKQ(FM) Campbellsville KY 2.25 kw, 374 ft.
KHOM(FM) Houma LA 100 kw, 1,945 ft.
KJLO-FM Monroe LA 100 kw, 1,017 ft.
WBCN(FM) Boston MA 20.9 kw, 771 ft.
WXTR-FM Waldorf MD 22 kw, 764 ft.
*WVGR(FM) Grand Rapids MI 108 kw, 600 ft.
KSDM(FM) International Falls MN 8.5 kw, 200 ft.
KBOT(FM) Pelican Rapids MN
KJJO-FM St. Louis Park MN 100 kw, 1,040 ft.
KZPD(FM) Ash Grove MO 3 kw, 194 ft.
KHKR-FM East Helena MT 100 kw, 1,896 ft.
WCXL(FM) Kill Devil Hills NC 100 kw, 463 ft.
WTQR(FM) Winston-Salem NC 100 kw, 1,420 ft.
KKNB(FM) Crete NE 50 kw, 613 ft.
KCDY(FM) Carlsbad NM 100 kw, 676 ft.
KLSK(FM) Santa Fe NM 100 kw, 1,876 ft.
WHTT-FM Buffalo NY 50 kw, 500 ft.
WQAL(FM) Cleveland OH 11 kw, 1,060 ft.
WPAY-FM Portsmouth OH 100 kw, 1,000 ft.
KMGL(FM) Oklahoma City OK 100 kw, 1,425 ft.
KPXA(FM) Sisters OR 1.3 kw, 709 ft.
KTIL-FM Tillamook OR 6.5 kw, 150 ft.
WAEB-FM Allentown PA 50 kw, 500 ft.
WNNK-FM Harrisburg PA 22.5 kw, 725 ft.
WERR(FM) Utuado PR 50 kw, 710 ft.
WYAV(FM) Conway SC 100 kw, 600 ft.
KIQK(FM) Rapid City SD 100 kw, 515 ft.
WNAX-FM Yankton SD 97 kw, 981 ft.
WXSE(FM) Calhoun TN 3 kw, 325 ft.
WUCZ-FM Carthage TN 6 kw, 300 ft.
WTNV(FM) Jackson TN 100 kw, 655 ft.
KXYL-FM Brownwood TX 74 kw-H, 321 ft.
KBFM(FM) Edinburg TX 100 kw, 990 ft.
KRBE-FM Houston TX 100 kw, 1,920 ft.
KWSM(FM) Sherman TX 3 kw, 328 ft.
KKUS(FM) Tyler TX 50 kw, 492 ft.
WMNV(FM) Rupert VT 1.5 kw, 249 ft.
KXDD(FM) Yakima WA 61 kw, 781 ft.
WZEE(FM) Madison WI 9.4 kw, 1,119 ft.
WMZK(FM) Merrill WI 13 kw, 446 ft.
WDCI(FM) Bridgeport WV 3 kw, 328 ft.
WBWN(FM) Le Roy IL 25 kw, 299 ft.

104.3 mhz (ch 282)

*KTOO(FM) Juneau AK 1.4 kw, minus 1,016 ft.
WZYP(FM) Athens AL 100 kw, 1,115 ft.
WQLW(FM) Eutaw AL 2.3 kw, 370 ft.
KBCN-FM Marshall AR 100 kw, 820 ft.
KRIM(FM) Payson AZ 100 kw, 1,023 ft.
KKLF(FM) Gonzales CA 6 kw, 328 ft.
KBIG(FM) Los Angeles CA 105 kw, 2,950 ft.
KSHA(FM) Redding CA 100 kw, 1,560 ft.
KXHA(FM) Shafter CA 3 kw, 308 ft.
KMKE(FM) Grand Junction CO 100 kw, 1,296 ft.
KQKS(FM) Longmont CO 5.4 kw, 1,433 ft.
WEAT-FM West Palm Beach FL 100 kw, 1,273 ft.
WKXH-FM Alma GA 1.9 kw, 397 ft.
WBBQ-FM Augusta GA 100 kw, 1,003 ft.
KBLZ(FM) Kaneohe HI 69.4 kw-H, 68.8 kw-V, 209 ft.
KLTB(FM) Boise ID 52 kw, 2,574 ft.
WCBH(FM) Casey IL 11.2 kw, 495 ft.
WJMK(FM) Chicago IL 4.1 kw, 1,575 ft.
WHOX(FM) Charlestown IN 3 kw, 328 ft.
KVGB-FM Great Bend KS 96 kw, 810 ft.
WXBC(FM) Hardinsburg KY 3 kw, 328 ft.
WEZJ-FM Williamsburg KY 1.4 kw, 656 ft.
KRBG(FM) Bunkie LA 18 kw, 384 ft.
WVRT(FM) Baltimore MD 50 kw, 420 ft.
WABK-FM Gardiner ME 50 kw, 492 ft.
WODQ(FM) Baraga MI 100 kw, 997 ft.
WOMC(FM) Detroit MI 190 kw, 361 ft.
WCZY-FM Mount Pleasant MI 3 kw, 328 ft.
KLKS(FM) Breezy Point MN 50 kw, 492 ft.
KZLT-FM East Grand Forks MN 100 kw, 550 ft.
KNFX(FM) Spring Valley MN 2.8 kw, 472 ft.
WRSR(FM) Two Harbors MN 3 kw, 328 ft.
KDBB(FM) Bonne Terre MO 3 kw, 328 ft.
KBEQ-FM Kansas City MO 100 kw, 987 ft.
WGNL(FM) Greenwood MS 3 kw, 312 ft.
WUMI(FM) State College MS 3 kw, 328 ft.
WJSG(FM) Hamlet NC 2.5 kw, 489 ft.
WDLF(FM) Old Fort NC 2.55 kw, 348 ft.
WFXK(FM) Tarboro NC 100 kw, 987 ft.
KJUL(FM) North Las Vegas NV 100 kw, 1,181 ft.
WAXQ(FM) New York NY 7.8 kw h, 5.6 kw v, 1,220 ft.
WFRG-FM Utica NY 100 kw, 500 ft.
WELA(FM) East Liverpool OH 50 kw, 330 ft.
WNLT(FM) Harrison OH 3 kw, 328 ft.
KKMX(FM) Tri City OR 5.6 kw, 1,384 ft.
WSKE-FM Everett PA 6 kw, 968 ft.
KPHR(FM) Milbank SD 100 kw, 981 ft.
WEYE(FM) Surgoinsville TN 6 kw, 300 ft.
KQFX(FM) Borger TX 100 kw, 590 ft.
KGAS-FM Carthage TX 6 kw, 328 ft.
KPLE(FM) Temple TX 34 kw, 597 ft.
KSOP-FM Salt Lake City UT 25 kw, 3,650 ft.
WKCY-FM Harrisonburg VA 50 kw, 409 ft.
WIYC(FM) Charlotte Amalie VI 45 kw, 1,607 ft.
WGLV(FM) Hartford VT 2.7 kw, 489 ft.
KAFE(FM) Bellingham WA 60 kw, 2,310 ft.
KHTR(FM) Pullman WA 24 kw, 1,669 ft.
WECB(FM) Seymour WI 2.55 kw, 358 ft.
WAVQ(FM) Inglis FL 6 kw, 329 ft.

104.5 mhz (ch 283)

KWXE(FM) Glenwood AR 3 kw, 328 ft.
KWDA(FM) White Hall AR 3 kw, 328 ft.
KIQO(FM) Atascadero CA 5.6 kw, 1,410 ft.
KVLI-FM Lake Isabella CA 200 w, 1,260 ft.
KFOG(FM) San Francisco CA 7.9 kw, 1,454 ft.
KYZX(FM) Pueblo CO 50 kw, 344 ft.
WFYV-FM Atlantic Beach FL 100 kw, 984 ft.
WGPC-FM Albany GA 100 kw, 981 ft.
KTOF(FM) Cedar Rapids IA 100 kw, 500 ft.
*WBVN(FM) Carrier Mills IL 3 kw, 328 ft.
WFMB-FM Springfield IL 43 kw, 465 ft.
WGRL(FM) Indianapolis IN 40 kw, 492 ft.
KLLS(FM) Augusta KS 46 kw, 512 ft.
WXLO-FM Fitchburg MA 37 kw, 563 ft.
WSNX-FM Muskegon MI 50 kw, 361 ft.
WUVE(FM) Saginaw MI 2.45 kw, 469 ft.
KJLY(FM) Blue Earth MN 50 kw, 495 ft.
KSLQ-FM Washington MO 3 kw, 328 ft.
WHSY-FM Hattiesburg MS 100 kw, 984 ft.
WUOY(FM) Wilmington NC 4.5 kw, 377 ft.
KAMI-FM Cozad NE 100 kw, 360 ft.
KESY-FM Omaha NE 100 kw, 1,040 ft.
KKFG(FM) Bloomfield NM 100 kw, 1,086 ft.
KHIT-FM Reno NV 25 kw, 2,930 ft.
WXLE(FM) Mechanicsville NY 5 kw
WLZZ(FM) Montpelier OH 3 kw, 328 ft.
WQKT(FM) Wooster OH 52 kw, 330 ft.
KMYZ-FM Pryor OK 78 kw, 1,250 ft.
KMCQ(FM) The Dalles OR 100 kw, 2,001 ft.
WYXR(FM) Philadelphia PA 12.5 kw, 1,008 ft.
WNBT-FM Wellsboro PA 50 kw, 380 ft.
WJUK(FM) Mt. Pleasant SC 28 kw, 656 ft.
WGFX(FM) Gallatin TN 49 kw, 1,312 ft.
WQBB-FM Knoxville TN 6 kw, 394 ft.
WRVR-FM Memphis TN 100 kw, 751 ft.
KKDA-FM Dallas TX 100 kw, 1,585 ft.
KJTX(FM) Jefferson TX 1.75 kw, 423 ft.
KKMY(FM) Orange TX 100 kw, 440 ft.
KZEP-FM San Antonio TX 100 kw, 735 ft.
WNVZ(FM) Norfolk VA 50 kw, 480 ft.
*KMIH(FM) Mercer Island WA 14 w-H, 233 ft.
WAXX(FM) Eau Claire WI 100 kw, 1,830 ft.
WXER(FM) Plymouth WI 6 kw, 328 ft.
*WCCX(FM) Waukesha WI 10 w, 50 ft.
WSLD(FM) Whitewater WI 6 kw, 328 ft.
WHAJ(FM) Bluefield WV 100 kw, 1,200 ft.
KKNG(FM) Laramie WY 3 kw, 951 ft.
KSIT(FM) Rock Springs WY 100 kw, 1,630 ft.
WJGG(FM) Lexington-Fayette KY

104.7 mhz (ch 284)

*KUAC(FM) Fairbanks AK 10.5 kw, 440 ft.
*KCAW(FM) Sitka AK 5 kw, -612 ft.
WZZK-FM Birmingham AL 100 kw, 1,300 ft.
KEZU(FM) Booneville AR 50 kw, 492 ft.
KOOU(FM) Hardy AR 6 kw, 199 ft.
KVRY(FM) Mesa AZ 100 kw, 1,550 ft.
KBEY(FM) Garberville CA 50 kw, 2,650 ft.
KHTN(FM) Los Banos CA 50 kw, 495 ft.
KCAQ(FM) Oxnard CA 2.85 kw, 1,580 ft.
KDES-FM Palm Springs CA 42 kw, 540 ft.
KNNG-FM Sterling CO 100 kw, 500 ft.
KSKE-FM Vail CO 100 kw, 451 ft.
WWUS(FM) Big Pine Key FL 100 kw, 443 ft.
WRBQ-FM Tampa FL 100 kw, 555 ft.
WALR(FM) Athens GA 100 kw, 981 ft.
KONI(FM) Lanai City HI 50 kw, 2,447 ft.
KRMR(FM) Ketchum ID 155 w, 1,922 ft.
WLMD(FM) Bushnell IL 3 kw, 328 ft.
WCFL(FM) Morris IL 50 kw, 496 ft.
WNSR(FM) Nashville IL 3 kw, 328 ft.
WFRN-FM Elkhart IN 50 kw, 488 ft.
WITZ-FM Jasper IN 50 kw, 490 ft.
WJMD(FM) Hazard KY 2.5 kw, 1,135 ft.

KNEK-FM Washington LA 3 kw, 223 ft.
WKPE-FM Orleans MA 50 kw, 504 ft.
WWMD(FM) Hagerstown MD 8.3 kw, 1,379 ft.
WQHQ(FM) Ocean City-Salisbury MD 33 kw, 610 ft.
WWFX(FM) Belfast ME 10 kw, 1,099 ft.
WXPT(FM) Kennebunkport ME 3 kw, 292 ft.
WYKX(FM) Escanaba MI 100 kw, 351 ft.
WKJC(FM) Tawas City MI 50 kw, 492 ft.
KCLD-FM St. Cloud MN 100 kw, 984 ft.
KYRX(FM) Chaffee MO 6 kw, 328 ft.
KTOZ-FM Marshfield MO 3 kw, 299 ft.
KRES(FM) Moberly MO 100 kw, 1025 ft.
WMXC(FM) Charlotte NC 96 kw, 1,210 ft.
WBSY(FM) Rose Hill NC 2.8 kw, 256 ft.
KNDR(FM) Mandan ND 100 kw, 852 ft.
KMOU(FM) Roswell NM 50 kw, 409 ft.
WBBS(FM) Fulton NY 50 kw, 310 ft.
WBEA(FM) Montauk NY 6 kw, 328 ft.
WSPK(FM) Poughkeepsie NY 7.4 kw, 1,250 ft.
WTUE(FM) Dayton OH 50 kw, 499 ft.
WIOT(FM) Toledo OH 50 kw, 540 ft.
KVNR(FM) Alva OK 100 kw, 981 ft.
KCMB(FM) Baker City OR 100 kw, 1,747 ft.
KDUK-FM Florence OR 63 kw, 2,326 ft.
WXRB(FM) Pittsburgh PA 50 kw, 500 ft.
WKAQ-FM San Juan PR 50 kw, 1,120 ft.
WNOK-FM Columbia SC 100 kw, 1,014 ft.
KKLS-FM Sioux Falls SD 100 kw, 705 ft.
WSGM(FM) Coalmont TN 1 kw, 548 ft.
KKYS(FM) Bryan TX 50 kw, 350 ft.
KYYI(FM) Burkburnett TX 100 kw, 1,017
KMMX(FM) Lamesa TX 100 kw, 920 ft.
KLKM(FM) Llano TX 11 kw, 459 ft.
WKIK(FM) Crewe VA 100 kw-H, 84 kw-V, 981 ft.
WNCS(FM) Montpelier VT 1.9 kw, 2,093 ft.
KDUX-FM Aberdeen WA 48 kw, 360 ft.
WZXA(FM) Sturtevant WI 3 kw, 328 ft.
WVRC-FM Spencer WV 3 kw, 328 ft.
KEEH(FM) Spokane WA 317 w, 1,378 ft.

104.9 mhz (ch 285)
WOAB(FM) Ozark AL 2.5 kw, 275 ft.
WSLY(FM) York AL 50 kw, 492 ft.
KAGH-FM Crossett AR 3 kw, 275 ft.
KHPA(FM) Hope AR 3 kw, 298 ft.
KDXY(FM) Paragould AR 3 kw, 277 ft.
KBEV(FM) Springdale AR 1 kw, 479 ft.
KCLT-FM West Helena AR 3 kw, 328 ft.
KBRG(FM) Fremont CA 3 kw, 300 ft.
KIQQ-FM Lenwood CA 1.078 kw, 466 ft.
KOCN(FM) Pacific Grove CA 1.8 kw, 593 ft.
KLOA-FM Ridgecrest CA 750 w, 1 ft.
KRPQ(FM) Rohnert Park CA 340 w, 915 ft.
KRYD(FM) Telluride CO 100 kw, minus 75 ft.
*WIHS(FM) Middletown CT 3 kw, 300 ft.
WAAZ-FM Crestview FL 3 kw, 275 ft.
WMLO(FM) Havana FL 47 kw, 494 ft.
WYOC(FM) High Springs FL 1.6 kw, 450 ft.
WFXE(FM) Columbus GA 6 kw, 289 ft.
WMCG(FM) Milan GA 3 kw, 600 ft.
KLMJ(FM) Hampton IA 4.5 kw, 255 ft.
KBOE-FM Oskaloosa IA 50 kw, 492 ft.
KIGL(FM) Spencer IA 3 kw, 298 ft.
WXRX(FM) Belvidere IL 4 kw, 333 ft.
WCBW(FM) Columbia IL 11.5 kw, 480 ft.
WFIW-FM Fairfield IL 3.4 kw, 273 ft.
WGEN-FM Geneseo IL 3.3 kw, 280 ft.
WPXN(FM) Paxton IL 3 kw, 298 ft.
WXCL-FM Pekin IL 3 kw, 328 ft.
WWWY(FM) Columbus IN 6 kw, 300 ft.
WERK-FM Muncie IN 3 kw, 328 ft.
WAXI(FM) Rockville IN 1.5 kw, 400 ft.
KFFX(FM) Emporia KS 3 kw, 279 ft.
KCVS(FM) Salina KS 3 kw, 269 ft.
WKYW(FM) Frankfort KY 3 kw, 300 ft.
WJRS(FM) Jamestown KY 2 kw, 360 ft.
WKHG(FM) Leitchfield KY 3.5 kw, 250 ft.
WPKY-FM Princeton KY 3 kw, 187 ft.
WSKV(FM) Stanton KY 440 w, 680 ft.
WKKS-FM Vanceburg KY 3 kw, 298 ft.
KKAY-FM Donaldsonville LA 3 kw, 299 ft.
KGZC(FM) Folsom LA 3 kw, 328 ft.
KTOC-FM Jonesboro LA 3 kw, 246 ft.
KBYO-FM Tallulah LA 3 kw, 320 ft.
*WRBB(FM) Boston MA 10.9 w, 89 ft.
WBOQ(FM) Gloucester MA 1.5 kw, 446 ft.
WFYC-FM Alma MI 3 kw-H, 430 w-V, 299 ft.
WELL-FM Marshall MI 3 kw, 300 ft.
KRFO-FM Owatonna MN 4.7 kw, 200 ft.
KXAX(FM) St. James MN 3 kw, 289 ft.
KPWB-FM Piedmont MO 3 kw, 300 ft.
WFXO(FM) Iuka MS 50 kw, 443 ft.
WZBA(FM) Moss Point MS 33 kw, 600 ft.
WMSQ(FM) Havelock NC 3 kw, 186 ft.
WKJE(FM) Hertford NC 3 kw, 281 ft.
WYNA(FM) Tabor City NC 1.5 kw, 400 ft.
WQNS(FM) Waynesville NC 100 w, 1,640 ft.
KTCH-FM Wayne NE 3 kw, 300 ft.
KTMX(FM) York NE 25 kw, 328 ft.
WYRY(FM) Hinsdale NH 1.55 kw, 456 ft.
WLKZ(FM) Wolfeboro NH 3 kw, 300 ft.
WRDR(FM) Egg Harbor City NJ 10 kw, 508 ft.
KMVR(FM) Mesilla Park NM 3 kw, minus 32 ft.
WSRD(FM) Johnstown NY 6 kw, 300 ft.
WNGZ(FM) Montour Falls NY 1 kw, 480 ft.
WWKC(FM) Caldwell OH 3 kw, 300 ft.
*WCVO(FM) Gahanna OH 3 kw, 320 ft.
WKKY(FM) Geneva OH 3 kw, 380 ft.
WLSR(FM) Lima OH 3 kw, 260 ft.
WZLE(FM) Lorain OH 1.3 kw, 499 ft.
KNTL(FM) Bethany OK 3 kw, 299 ft.

KREK(FM) Bristow OK 2.6 kw, 351 ft.
KTMC-FM McAlester OK 1.5 kw, 454 ft.
*WJRH(FM) Easton PA 10 w, 23 ft.
WHPA(FM) Hollidaysburg PA 280 w, 1,417 ft.
WWDL-FM Scranton PA 270 w, 1,092 ft.
WSHG(FM) Ridgeland SC 3 kw, 300 ft.
WDNT-FM Dayton TN 420 w, 699 ft.
WKOS(FM) Kingsport TN 1 kw, 475 ft.
WQLA-FM La Follette TN 1.1 kw, 499 ft.
WKWT(FM) Union City TN 3 kw, 298 ft.
WLMM-FM Woodbury TN 3 kw, 328 ft.
KJAV(FM) Alamo TX 3 kw, 260 ft.
KIBL-FM Beeville TX 3 kw, 300 ft.
KTCY(FM) Denison TX 50 kw, 492 ft.
KRTX(FM) Galveston TX 1.9 kw, 403 ft.
KBUK(FM) La Grange TX 3 kw, 203 ft.
KYCX-FM Mexia TX 3 kw, 301 ft.
KMFM(FM) Premont TX 3 kw, 299 ft.
KMPQ-FM Rosenberg TX 7.4 kw, 230 ft.
KJMX(FM) Tulia TX 7.2 kw, 187 ft.
KYUF(FM) Uvalde TX 3 kw, 263 ft.
KWNS(FM) Winnsboro TX 3 kw, 282 ft.
KNFL-FM Tremonton UT 3 kw, -112 ft.
WVVV(FM) Blacksburg VA 3 kw, 310 ft.
WBPP(FM) Strasburg VA 3 kw, 219 ft.
KJUN-FM Eatonville WA 6 kw, 90 ft.
KMJY-FM Newport WA 3 kw, -33 ft.
KKRV(FM) Wenatchee WA 6.3 kw, 1,312 ft.
WTKM-FM Hartford WI 5.8 kw, 300 ft.
WKFX(FM) Kaukauna WI 3 kw, 480 ft.
WLXR-FM La Crosse WI 1.35 kw, 430 ft.
WNFM(FM) Reedsburg WI 1.6 kw, 449 ft.
WMGU(FM) Stevens Point WI 3 kw, 328 ft.
WPDX-FM Clarksburg WV 2.5 kw, 321 ft.

105.1 mhz (ch 286)
KTKU(FM) Juneau AK 3.84 kw, minus 1,057 ft.
WQSB(FM) Albertville AL 100 kw, 1,000 ft.
KMJX(FM) Conway AR 79 kw, 1,053 ft.
KFLX(FM) Kachina Village AZ 1.0 kw, 1,968 ft.
KZUL-FM Lake Havasu City AZ 280 kw, 426 ft.
KSLK(FM) Auberry CA 590 w, 1,902 ft.
KKGO-FM Los Angeles CA 18 kw, 2,900 ft.
KRAK-FM Sacramento CA 50 kw, 500 ft.
KXXL-FM Denver CO 100 kw, 1,200 ft.
WKGT-FM Century FL 6 kw, 298 ft.
WHQT(FM) Coral Gables FL 100 kw, 1,049 ft.
WOMX-FM Orlando FL 95 kw, 1,309 ft.
WKUB(FM) Blackshear GA 25 kw, 308 ft.
WHEL(FM) Helen GA 1.68 kw, 613 ft.
KINE-FM Honolulu HI 100 kw, 1,948 ft.
KJOT(FM) Boise ID 43 kw, 2,570 ft.
WOJO(FM) Evanston IL 6.2 kw, 1,174 ft.
WTAO(FM) Murphysboro IL 25 kw, 308 ft.
WGEM-FM Quincy IL 27.5 kw, 500 ft.
WEJT(FM) Shelbyville IL 13 kw, 459 ft.
WQHK-FM Decatur IN 2 kw, 397 ft.
WGCT(FM) Ellettsville IN 6 kw, 328 ft.
KZQD(FM) Liberal KS 50 kw, 492 ft.
WTUK(FM) Harlan KY 270 w, 1,037 ft.
WRNZ(FM) Lancaster KY 3 kw, 325 ft.
WEHR(FM) Shepherdsville KY 1.55 kw, 446 ft.
KROF-FM Abbeville LA 25 kw, 300 ft.
WAMQ(FM) Great Barrington MA 1.1 kw, 1,708 ft.
*WNEK-FM Springfield MA 13 w, minus 23 ft.
WTOS-FM Skowhegan ME 50 kw, 2,431 ft.
WGFM(FM) Cheboygan MI 100 kw, 610 ft.
WQRS(FM) Detroit MI 21.7 kw, 726 ft.
WAVC(FM) Duluth MN 100 kw, 789 ft.
WTCX(FM) Lakeville MN 2.6 kw, 499 ft.
KARL(FM) Tracy MN 3 kw, 342 ft.
KQUA(FM) Lutesville MO 1.75 kw, 430 ft.
KKJO(FM) St. Joseph MO 100 kw, 581 ft.
KOSP(FM) Willard MO 50 kw, 492 ft.
WBKJ(FM) Kosciusko MS 100 kw, 355 ft.
WDCG(FM) Durham NC 100 kw, 1,141 ft.
KWMW(FM) Maljamar NM 100 kw, 917 ft.
KZRQ(FM) Santa Fe NM 100 kw, 1,937 ft.
KRBO(FM) Las Vegas NV 50 kw, 1,614 ft.
WVOA(FM) DeRuyter NY 42 kw, 540 ft.
WMXV(FM) New York NY 7.8 kw-H, 5.5 kw-V, 1,220 ft.
WUBE-FM Cincinnati OH 14 kw, 920 ft.
WQXK(FM) Salem OH 88 kw, 430 ft.
KBLP(FM) Lindsay OK 850 w, 564 ft.
KASR-FM Perry OK 6 kw, 297 ft.
KROG(FM) Phoenix OR 52 kw, 545 ft.
KXYQ(FM) Salem OR 100 kw, 1,840 ft.
WIOV-FM Ephrata PA 25 kw, 700 ft.
WILQ(FM) Williamsport PA 9.2 kw, 1,135 ft.
WIOC(FM) Ponce PR 9 kw, minus 154 ft.
WWLI(FM) Providence RI 50 kw, 500 ft.
WGFG(FM) Branchville SC 6 kw, 100 ft.
WRHA(FM) Johnsonville SC 3 kw, 321 ft.
KACP(FM) Custer SD 6.5 kw, 1,312 ft.
KZKK(FM) Huron SD 6 kw, 154 ft.
WCLC-FM Jamestown TN 1.1 kw, 605 ft.
WVRY(FM) Waverly TN 50 kw, 492 ft.
KEAN-FM Abilene TX 100 kw, 810 ft.
KYKS(FM) Lufkin TX 100 kw, 1,066 ft.
KMIQ(FM) Robstown TX 3 kw, 900 ft.
KMXU(FM) Manti UT 63 kw, 2,360 ft.
WAVA(FM) Arlington VA 50 kw, 500 ft.
WAMM-FM Bridgewater VA 6 kw, 328 ft.
WYZM(FM) Waunakee WI 6 kw, 328 ft.
WKLC-FM St. Albans WV 50 kw, 1,663 ft.

105.3 mhz (ch 287)
KNIK-FM Anchorage AK 25 kw, 265 ft.
WVCA(FM) Selma AL 50 kw, 485 ft.
KHOX(FM) Hoxie AR 6 kw, 156 ft.

KAKJ(FM) Marianna AR 6 kw, 100 ft.
KZLZ(FM) Kearny AZ 50 kw, 492 ft.
KRDS-FM Wickenburg AZ 6 kw, minus 1,364 ft.
KKXX-FM Delano CA 50 kw, 547 ft.
KCBQ-FM San Diego CA 29 kw, 620 ft.
KITS(FM) San Francisco CA 15 kw, 1,200 ft.
KCFM(FM) Shingletown CA 10 kw, 1,056 ft.
KYHT-FM Yermo CA 560 w, 1,037 ft.
KZKS(FM) Rifle CO 1.8 kw, 1,275 ft.
*WDJW(FM) Somers CT 9.2 w, -58 ft.
WUMG(FM) Chattahoochee FL 6 kw, 328 ft.
WMMY(FM) Solana FL 3 kw, 328 ft.
WDEN-FM Macon GA 100 kw, 777 ft.
WSTI-FM Quitman GA 3 kw, 300 ft.
WRHQ(FM) Richmond Hill GA 11 kw, 485 ft.
KLYV(FM) Dubuque IA 50 kw, 330 ft.
KNOD(FM) Harlan IA 25 kw, 300 ft.
KIWA-FM Sheldon IA 50 kw, 292 ft.
*WTPC(FM) Elsah IL 17 w, 210 ft.
WYNG-FM Evansville IN 50 kw, 480 ft.
WASK-FM Lafayette IN 50 kw, 375 ft.
KOCD(FM) Columbus KS 6.1 kw, 308 ft.
KXLK(FM) Haysville KS 100 kw, 1,000 ft.
WWWQ(FM) Glasgow KY 25 kw, 318 ft.
KZWA(FM) Lake Charles LA 50 kw, 492 ft.
WLTS-FM Slidell LA 100 kw, 902 ft.
WFRB-FM Frostburg MD 16.5 kw, 960 ft.
WXBB(FM) Kittery ME 2.2 kw, 371 ft.
WCXT(FM) Hart MI 100 kw, 649 ft.
WLOL(FM) Cambridge MN 25 kw, 298 ft.
KYBA(FM) Stewartville MN 50 kw, 492 ft.
KYMO-FM East Prairie MO 3 kw, 207 ft.
KZNN(FM) Rolla MO 100 kw, 631 ft.
WWZQ(FM) Aberdeen MS 25 kw, 299 ft.
KMTX(FM) Helena MT 86.9 kw, 1,878 ft.
WWIR(FM) Fair Bluff NC 1.3 kw, 479 ft.
KZPR(FM) Minot ND 100 kw, 579 ft.
KFGE(FM) Lincoln NE 3 kw, 308 ft.
KZMC(FM) McCook NE 100 kw, 622 ft.
KGRD(FM) Orchard NE 100 kw, 495 ft.
WKPQ(FM) Hornell NY 43 kw, 530 ft.
WYHT(FM) Mansfield OH 50 kw, 370 ft.
KBXT(FM) Bixby OK 25 kw, 328 ft.
WYCY(FM) Hawley PA 2.9 kw, 479 ft.
WDAS-FM Philadelphia PA 3.3 kw, 870 ft.
WAGI-FM Gaffney SC 100 kw, 1,190 ft.
WLSZ(FM) Humboldt TN 3 kw, 328 ft.
WXST(FM) Loudon TN 6 kw, 328 ft.
KYNG(FM) Dallas TX 100 kw, 1,558 ft.
KEZB(FM) Hempstead TX 6 kw, 328 ft.
KLSR-FM Memphis TX 61 kw, 180 ft.
KSMG(FM) Seguin TX 100 kw, 1,240 ft.
WMXN(FM) Norfolk VA 50 kw, 499 ft.
WVGN(FM) Charlotte Amalie VI 10 kw, 1,679 ft.
WEBK(FM) Killington VT 1.15 kw, 2,578 ft.
KCMS(FM) Edmonds WA 115 kw, 722 ft.
KONA-FM Kennewick WA 100 kw, 1,180 ft.
WRLO-FM Antigo WI 100 kw, 541 ft.
KBCK(FM) Diamondville WY 16.5 kw, 869 ft.

105.5 mhz (ch 288)
WNSP(FM) Bay Minette AL 2.6 kw, 348 ft.
WLAY-FM Muscle Shoals AL 530 w, 743 ft.
WACT-FM Tuscaloosa AL 1.5 kw, 400 ft.
KDYC(FM) Danville AR 1.9 kw, 581 ft.
KPFM(FM) Mountain Home AR 33.4, 590 ft.
KNAS(FM) Nashville AR 3 kw, 85 ft.
KTEI(FM) Piggott AR 6 kw, 298 ft.
KXDX(FM) Stuttgart AR 3 kw, 325 ft.
KWRF-FM Warren AR 2.6 kw, 250 ft.
KKER(FM) Casa Grande AZ 1.9 kw, 362 ft.
KREL(FM) Copperopolis CA 1 kw, 781 ft.
KQBR(FM) Davis CA 2.96 kw, 492 ft.
KZAL(FM) Desert Center CA 58 w, 1,965 ft.
KGOE(FM) Eureka CA 28 kw, 1,588 ft.
KIDI(FM) Guadalupe CA 160 w, 1,342 ft.
KNAC(FM) Long Beach CA 1.5 kw, 403 ft.
KKUR(FM) Ojai CA 100 w, 1,358 ft.
KAVC(FM) Rosamond CA 3 kw, 328 ft.
KIQS-FM Willows CA 5.4 kw, 140 ft.
KHII(FM) Security CO 409 w, 2,230 ft.
KPMX(FM) Sterling CO 3 kw, 300 ft.
WQGN-FM Groton CT 3 kw, 275 ft.
WYKS(FM) Gainesville FL 3 kw, 266 ft.
WKKB(FM) Key Colony Beach FL 50 kw, 276 ft.
WYZB(FM) Mary Esther FL 6 kw, 328 ft.
WIXI(FM) Naples Park FL 950 w, 584 ft.
WGUL-FM New Port Richey FL 3 kw, 255 ft.
WNFK(FM) Perry FL 2.45 kw, 345 ft.
*WKZM(FM) Sarasota FL 3 kw, 180 ft.
WCAC(FM) Sebring FL 3 kw, 178 ft.
WQVE(FM) Camilla GA 6 kw, 300 ft.
WBTY(FM) Homerville GA 3 kw, 312 ft.
WIFO-FM Jesup GA 3 kw, 300 ft.
WLMX-FM Rossville GA 3 kw, 270 ft.
KPMW(FM) Haliimaile HI 6 kw, 295 ft.
KELR-FM Chariton IA 1.7 kw, 390 ft.
KILJ-FM Mount Pleasant IA 24 kw, 338 ft.
WREZ(FM) Metropolis IL 6 kw, 328 ft.
WCZQ(FM) Monticello IL 3 kw, 300 ft.
WJVO(FM) South Jacksonville IL 6 kw, 340 ft.
WDND(FM) Wilmington IL 3 kw, 275 ft.
WZSR(FM) Woodstock IL 3 kw, 429 ft.
WQRK(FM) Bedford IN 2 kw, 400 ft.
WYPI(FM) Lagrange IN 3 kw, 328 ft.
WLJE(FM) Valparaiso IN 1.25 kw, 513 ft.
WWVR(FM) West Terre Haute IN 3.3 kw, 314 ft.
KVSV-FM Beloit KS 50 kw, 443 ft.
KKOY-FM Chanute KS 3 kw, 170 ft.
WASE-FM Fort Knox KY 3 kw, 299 ft.
WWHK(FM) Greenville KY 3 kw, 300 ft.

U.S. FM Stations by Frequency

WMST-FM Mt. Sterling KY 3 kw, 300 ft.
WXKZ-FM Prestonsburg KY 3.5 kw, 390 ft.
KJJB(FM) Eunice LA 3 kw, 300 ft.
KFMV(FM) Franklin LA 3 kw, 300 ft.
KWHN-FM Haynesville LA 3 kw, 203 ft.
KVVP(FM) Leesville LA 9 kw, 328 ft.
WBEC-FM Pittsfield MA 975 w, 590 ft.
WLVW-FM Salisbury MD 2.1 kw, 384 ft.
WWCK-FM Flint MI 25 kw, 328 ft.
WENL(FM) Gladstone MI 6 kw, 256 ft.
WADW(FM) Pickford MI 6 kw, 328 ft.
WBMI(FM) West Branch MI 3 kw, 312 ft.
KASM-FM Albany MN 3 kw, 328 ft.
KMGM(FM) Montevideo MN 3 kw, 300 ft.
KRBI-FM St. Peter MN 3 kw, 130 ft.
KESM-FM El Dorado Springs MO 6.0 kw, 187 ft.
KZZT(FM) Moberly MO 25 kw, 328 ft.
WNLA-FM Indianola MS 4.4 kw, 200 ft.
WYCG(FM) Water Valley MS 6 kw, 247 ft.
WABO-FM Waynesboro MS 3 kw, 145 ft.
WXQR(FM) Jacksonville NC 3 kw, 315 ft.
WFJA(FM) Sanford NC 2.25 kw, 377 ft.
KMAV-FM Mayville ND 3 kw, 121 ft.
KCOE(FM) Auburn NE 3 kw, 154 ft.
KFMT(FM) Fremont NE 1.2 kw, 450 ft.
WJYY(FM) Concord NH 1.55 kw, 456 ft.
WBNJ(FM) Cape May Court House NJ 3.3 kw, 295 ft.
WDHA-FM Dover NJ 3 kw, 564 ft.
KZZX-FM Alamogordo NM 6 kw, 157 ft.
KAGP(FM) Grants NM 100 kw, 1,489 ft.
KRRI(FM) Boulder City NV 3.7 kw, 1,588 ft.
WLPW(FM) Lake Placid NY 3 kw, minus 236 ft.
WOWB(FM) Little Falls NY 3 kw, 466 ft.
WGES(FM) Oswego NY 3 kw, 450 ft.
WMJV-FM Patterson NY 1.5 kw, 460 ft.
WXTQ(FM) Athens OH 6 kw, 305 ft.
*WGOJ(FM) Conneaut OH 3 kw, 295 ft.
WMVR-FM Sidney OH 3 kw, 155 ft.
WWWM-FM Sylvania OH 2.15 kw, 390 ft.
WCHO-FM Washington Court House OH 3 kw, 300 ft.
KXXK(FM) Chickasha OK 3 kw, 195 ft.
KIRC(FM) Seminole OK 2.35 kw, 367 ft.
KGFY(FM) Stillwater OK 4.9 kw, 400 ft.
KCGB(FM) Hood River OR 3 kw, minus 460 ft.
WCHX(FM) Lewistown PA 3 kw, 817 ft.
WPXZ-FM Punxsutawney PA 3 kw, 300 ft.
WMGH-FM Tamaqua PA 1.3 kw, 485 ft.
WNNV(FM) Aguada PR 3 kw, 1,200 ft.
WDAR-FM Darlington SC 4 kw, 400 ft.
WNMB(FM) North Myrtle Beach SC 3 kw, 355 ft.
WYTM-FM Fayetteville TN 3 kw, 295 ft.
WDLY(FM) Gatlinburg TN 650 w, 964 ft.
WBNT-FM Oneida TN 3 kw, 280 ft.
WAKQ(FM) Paris TN 6 kw, 419 ft.
WXOQ(FM) Selmer TN 3 kw, 300 ft.
WSMT-FM Sparta TN 3 kw, 35 ft.
KACT-FM Andrews TX 3 kw, 210 ft.
KBYG-FM Coahoma TX 6 kw, 91 ft.
KLFX(FM) Harker Heights TX 930 w, 587 ft.
KLVT-FM Levelland TX 3 kw, 300 ft.
KTJN(FM) Mercedes TX 3 kw, 285 ft.
KTJX(FM) Mission TX 3 kw, 300 ft.
KQTX(FM) Portland TX 1.9 kw, 354 ft.
KQXC(FM) Wichita Falls TX 3 kw, 328 ft.
WKDE-FM Altavista VA 3 kw, 328 ft.
WAPP(FM) Berryville VA 3 kw, 300 ft.
WSKO(FM) Buffalo Gap VA 3 kw, 308 ft.
WLSA(FM) Louisa VA 3.3 kw, 325 ft.
WSWV-FM Pennington Gap VA 3.5 kw, 276 ft.
WGTH(FM) Richlands VA 450 w, 800 ft.
WSHV(FM) South Hill VA 15 kw, 328 ft.
WRAR-FM Tappahannock VA 6 kw, 328 ft.
WNKV(FM) St. Johnsbury VT 400 w, 712 ft.
KLYK(FM) Longview WA 315 w, 859 ft.
WCFW(FM) Chippewa Falls WI 3 kw, 300 ft.
WKBH-FM Trempealeau WI 3 kw, 531 ft.
WMMM-FM Verona WI 4.4 kw, 384 ft.
WHLX(FM) Bethlehem WV 2.7 kw, 313 ft.
WKCJ(FM) Lewisburg WV 540 kw, 781 ft.
KIMX(FM) Laramie WY 6 kw, 328 ft.
KOSZ-FM Idaho Falls ID

105.7 mhz (ch 289)

WXAH(FM) Orange Beach AL 6 kw, 328 ft.
WZHT(FM) Troy AL 100 kw, 1,847 ft.
KMCK(FM) Siloam Springs AR 100 kw, 410 ft.
KVRD-FM Cottonwood AZ 3 kw, 672 ft.
KAAX(FM) Avenal CA 915 w, 597 ft.
KHYE(FM) Hemet CA 170 w, 1,023 ft.
KDUQ(FM) Ludlow CA 1.8 kw, 590 ft.
KARA(FM) Santa Clara CA 50 kw, 500 ft.
KVAY(FM) Lamar CO 100 kw, 545 ft.
KURA(FM) Ouray CO 3.1 kw, -20 ft.
WFFM(FM) Ashburn GA 6 kw, 328 ft.
WZNY(FM) Augusta GA 100 kw, 1,168 ft.
WGST-FM Canton GA 50 kw, 492 ft.
KOKZ(FM) Waterloo IA 100 kw, 1,403 ft.
WWCT(FM) Peoria IL 38 kw, 581 ft.
WUZR(FM) Bicknell IN 3 kw, 292 ft.
WLME(FM) Cannelton IN 2.2 kw, 371 ft.
WTLC-FM Indianapolis IN 50 kw, 445 ft.
KDMM(FM) Herington KS 12.5 kw, 500 ft.
WXLN-FM Eminence KY 3 kw, 325 ft.
WLGC-FM Greenup KY 25 kw, 479 ft.
WTBK(FM) Manchester KY 7.5 kw, 462 ft.
WCLB-FM Framingham MA 8.5 kw, 1,144 ft.
WQSR(FM) Catonsville MD 50 kw, 492 ft.
WHMX(FM) Lincoln ME 50 kw, 413 ft.
WOOD-FM Grand Rapids MI 265 kw, 810 ft.
KCFE(FM) Eden Prairie MN 3 kw, 328 ft.
KRAQ(FM) Jackson MN 25 kw, 328 ft.
KLPR(FM) Springfield MN 3 kw, 328 ft.
KXKX(FM) Knob Noster MO 3 kw, 300 ft.
KPNT(FM) Ste. Genevieve MO 100 kw, 285 ft.
WAKH(FM) McComb MS 100 kw, 489 ft.
WRSF(FM) Columbia NC 100 kw, 613 ft.
WGQR(FM) Elizabethtown NC 6 kw, 387 ft.
WFMX(FM) Statesville NC 100 kw, 1,517 ft.
KSUX(FM) Winnebago NE 50 kw, 463 ft.
WVFM(FM) Campton NH 125 w, 2,001 ft.
KOZZ-FM Reno NV 75 kw, 2,120 ft.
WMRV-FM Endicott NY 35 kw, 570 ft.
WMJI(FM) Cleveland OH 27 kw, 900 ft.
WWHT(FM) Marysville OH 6 kw, 100 ft.
KICM(FM) Healdton OK 50 kw, 632 ft.
*KROU(FM) Spencer OK 4 kw, 328 ft.
KQAK(FM) Bend OR 35 kw, 592 ft.
WZGO(FM) Portage PA 3 kw, 321 ft.
WQXA-FM York PA 25 kw, 705 ft.
WCAD(FM) San Juan PR 50 kw, 1,100 ft.
WOFE-FM Rockwood TN 600 w, 728 ft.
WLJJ(FM) Union City TN 6 kw, 328 ft.
KAEZ(FM) Amarillo TX 6 kw, 236 ft.
*KHCB-FM Houston TX 100 kw, 1,614 ft.
KYKX(FM) Longview TX 100 kw, 1,005 ft.
KARU(FM) Raymondville TX 1.35 kw, 420 ft.
KSTV-FM Stephenville TX 100 kw, 492 ft.
KUMT(FM) Centerville UT 7.3 kw, 3,661 ft.
WLCC(FM) Luray VA 440 w, 1,079 ft.
KEZE-FM Spokane WA 100 kw, 1,910 ft.
KRSE(FM) Yakima WA 100 kw, 584 ft.
WAPL-FM Appleton WI 100 kw, 1,175 ft.
WOBG-FM Salem WV 6 kw, 581 ft.
WXQL(FM) Baldwin FL

105.9 mhz (ch 290)

*KRBD(FM) Ketchikan AK 15 kw, minus 105 ft.
WYDH(FM) Atmore AL 3.7 kw, 446 ft.
WRHY(FM) Centre AL 6 kw, 150 ft.
*WTOH(FM) Mobile AL 10 w, 290 ft.
WWBR(FM) Trussville AL 1 kw, 561 ft.
WKXM-FM Winfield AL 2.5 kw, 410 ft.
KLAZ(FM) Hot Springs AR 95 kw, 994 ft.
KRCY(FM) Kingman AZ 17 kw, 3,060 ft.
KXLL(FM) Paradise Valley AZ 1 kw
KKDJ(FM) Fresno CA 2.4 kw, 1,960 ft.
KPWR(FM) Los Angeles CA 72 kw, 770 ft.
KQPM(FM) Ukiah CA 2.9 kw, 2,017 ft.
KBPI-FM Denver CO 100 kw, 900 ft.
WHCN(FM) Hartford CT 16 kw, 867 ft.
WXJN(FM) Lewes DE 6 kw, 341 ft.
WOCL(FM) De Land FL 100 kw, 1,650 ft.
WAXY(FM) Fort Lauderdale FL 100 kw, 1,048 ft.
WILN(FM) Panama City FL 50 kw, 406 ft.
WXMK(FM) Dock Junction GA 6.2 kw, 489 ft.
WHFE(FM) Lakeland GA 6 kw, 328 ft.
KYAT(FM) Keokuk IA 50 kw, 492 ft.
KTLB(FM) Twin Lakes IA 25 kw, 328 ft.
KCIX(FM) Garden City ID 50 kw, 2,700 ft.
WCKG(FM) Elmwood Park IL 4.2 kw, 1,575 ft.
WHZT(FM) Mahomet IL 1.25 kw, 512 ft.
WMMC(FM) Marshall IL 2.8 kw, 338 ft.
WWIP(FM) Wabash IN 3 kw, 318 ft.
KLZR(FM) Lawrence KS 100 kw, 771 ft.
WQNF(FM) Valley Station KY 3 kw, 328 ft.
WHAY(FM) Whitley City KY 3 kw, 328 ft.
KBZE(FM) Berwick LA 1.8 kw, 403 ft.
KVOL-FM Opelousas LA 3.4 kw, 433 ft.
WKRH(FM) Bath ME 50 kw, 499 ft.
WKHQ-FM Charlevoix MI 100 kw, 899 ft.
WJZZ(FM) Detroit MI 20 kw, 725 ft.
KWNG(FM) Red Wing MN 20 kw, 300 ft.
KKWS(FM) Wadena MN 100 kw, 564 ft.
KGBX-FM Nixa MO 38 kw, 558 ft.
WGUD-FM Pascagoula MS 25 kw, 312 ft.
KAAQ(FM) Alliance NE 100 kw, 700 ft.
KQKY(FM) Kearney NE 96.6 kw, 1,010 ft.
KKCD(FM) Omaha NE 5.2 kw, 346 ft.
WNWK-FM Newark NJ 2.4 kw, 722 ft.
KOLT-FM Santa Fe NM 100 kw, 1,936 ft.
WJZR(FM) Rochester NY 3 kw, 180 ft.
WZOM(FM) Defiance OH 3 kw, 347 ft.
WPFB-FM Middletown OH 34 kw, 590 ft.
KQTZ(FM) Hobart OK 100 kw, 1,020 ft.
WPHB-FM Philipsburg PA 4.8 kw, 216 ft.
WAMO-FM Pittsburgh PA 72 kw, 440 ft.
WVCO(FM) Loris SC 2.65 kw, 495 ft.
KMIT(FM) Mitchell SD 100 kw, 449 ft.
WGKX(FM) Memphis TN 100 kw, 994 ft.
WLAC-FM Nashville TN 100 kw, 1,226 ft.
KUKA(FM) San Diego TX 6 kw, 328 ft.
KLCY-FM Vernal UT 3 kw, 430 ft.
WMXQ(FM) Lynchburg VA 6 kw, 266 ft.
WCXR-FM Woodbridge VA 28 kw, 648 ft.
WMJB(FM) Evansville WI 1.4 kw, 493 ft.
WEGZ(FM) Washburn WI 100 kw, 735 ft.
WTNJ(FM) Mount Hope WV 50 kw, 500 ft.

106.1 mhz (ch 291)

WSTH-FM Alexander City AL 100 kw, 981 ft.
WTAK-FM Hartselle AL 6 kw, 328 ft.
KFFB(FM) Fairfield Bay AR 50 kw, 500 ft.
KIKO-FM Claypool AZ 6 kw, 297 ft.
KARZ(FM) Burney CA 100 kw, 2,000 ft.
KPLM(FM) Palm Springs CA 50 kw, 391 ft.
KMEL(FM) San Francisco CA 69 kw, 1,290 ft.
KWSP(FM) Santa Margarita CA 950 w, 1,467 ft.
KVYT(FM) Basalt CO 1.4 kw-H, 1.35 kw-V, 338 ft.
WRZK(FM) Tallahassee FL 3 kw, 328 ft.
WVYF(FM) Sylvester GA 3 kw, 328 ft.
WLET-FM Toccoa GA 100 kw, 1,132 ft.
KLEO(FM) Kahaluu HI 3 kw, minus 2,585 ft.
KKBZ(FM) Clarinda IA 50 kw, 492 ft.
KLSS-FM Mason City IA 100 kw, 315 ft.
KZFN(FM) Moscow ID 62.1 kw, 921 ft.
WSMI-FM Litchfield IL 50 kw, 500 ft.
WGGR(FM) Greenwood IN 3 kw, 328 ft.
WJPS-FM Newburgh IN 6 kw, 328 ft.
WINN(FM) North Vernon IN 50 kw, 486 ft.
KSKU(FM) Hutchinson KS 100 kw, 659 ft.
WCYO(FM) Irvine KY 1.2 kw, 653 ft.
KMYY(FM) Monroe LA 97 kw, 1,017 ft.
WCOD-FM Hyannis MA 50 kw, 450 ft.
WKGO(FM) Cumberland MD 4 kw, 1,400 ft.
*WMEM(FM) Presque Isle ME 99 kw, 1,079 ft.
WJXQ(FM) Jackson MI 50 kw, 489 ft.
WQPM-FM Princeton MN 35 kw, 620 ft.
KBXR(FM) Ashland MO 50 kw, 492 ft.
KWKZ(FM) Charleston MO 3 kw, 328 ft.
WZRH(FM) Picayune MS 50 kw, 492 ft.
WMXU(FM) Starkville MS 3 kw, 220 ft.
KQDI-FM Great Falls MT 100 kw, 276 ft.
WLWW(FM) Waxhaw NC 3 kw, 111 ft.
WRDU(FM) Wilson NC 100 kw, 1,348 ft.
KQLX-FM Lisbon ND 50 kw, 249 ft.
WHDQ(FM) Claremont NH 9.51 kw, 1,068 ft.
KRHT(FM) Carlsbad NM 50 kw, 492 ft.
KKJI(FM) Gallup NM 26 kw, 185 ft.
WNKI(FM) Corning NY 40 kw, 532 ft.
WPDA(FM) Jeffersonville NY 1.6 kw, 627 ft.
WBLI(FM) Patchogue NY 25 kw, 492 ft.
WVNO-FM Mansfield OH 40 kw, 545 ft.
WNCD(FM) Niles OH 3 kw, 328 ft.
KKBI(FM) Broken Bow OK 50 kw, 1621 ft.
KQLL-FM Owasso OK 100 kw, 1,315 ft.
KFAT(FM) Corvallis OR 100 kw, 1,140 ft.
WWBV(FM) Beaver Springs PA 175 w, 1,312 ft.
WJJZ(FM) Philadelphia PA 22 kw, 740 ft.
WFXH(FM) Hilton Head Island SC 10.5 kw, 794 ft.
WTUA(FM) St. Stephen SC 3 kw, 328 ft.
KTTX(FM) Brenham TX 50 kw, 492 ft.
KHKS(FM) Denton TX 100 kw, 1,584 ft.
KZTQ(FM) Laredo TX 3 kw, 213 ft.
KIOC(FM) Orange TX 100 kw, 1,225 ft.
KZTX(FM) Refugio TX 25 kw, 299 ft.
WPHG(FM) Exmore VA 25 kw, 328 ft.
WWFO(FM) Vinton VA 3 kw, 92 ft.
WVIS(FM) Christiansted VI 50 kw, 1,190 ft.
KRPM-FM Tacoma WA 55 kw, 699 ft.
WDKM(FM) Adams WI 6 kw, 328 ft.
WMIL(FM) Waukesha WI 50 kw, 976 ft.
WRZZ(FM) Ravenswood WV 1.85 kw, 604 ft.
KCFA(FM) Arnold CA 910 w, 840 ft.

106.3 mhz (ch 292)

KSUP(FM) Juneau AK 10 kw, -1,007 ft.
WKNU(FM) Brewton AL 3 kw, 300 ft.
WZNJ(FM) Demopolis AL 3 kw, 300 ft.
WBTG-FM Sheffield AL 6 kw, 682 ft.
KZKZ-FM Greenwood AR 1.7 kw, 433 ft.
KMZX(FM) Lonoke AR 2.5 kw, 354 ft.
KUKB(FM) Texarkana AR 3 kw, 328 ft.
KRLW-FM Walnut Ridge AR 3 kw, 328 ft.
KONZ(FM) Arizona City AZ 3 kw, 298 ft.
KEDJ(FM) Sun City AZ 3.5 kw, 882 ft.
KMGQ(FM) Goleta CA 365 w, 879 ft.
KRAB(FM) Green Acres CA 3.9 kw, 410 ft.
KDAY(FM) Independence CA 3 kw, minus 1,617 ft.
KJET(FM) Kingsburg CA 6 kw, 436 ft.
KGMX(FM) Lancaster CA 3 kw, 210 ft.
KMMT(FM) Mammoth Lakes CA 55 w, 2,158 ft.
KFIE(FM) Merced CA 2.95 kw, 476 ft.
KYMS(FM) Santa Ana CA 3 kw, 130 ft.
KLUE(FM) Soledad CA 6 kw, 1,720 ft.
KJYY(FM) Brush CO 3 kw, 75 ft.
KRKM(FM) Kremmling CO 300 w, 1,096 ft.
KRQS(FM) Pagosa Springs CO 160 w, 1,280 ft.
KKLI(FM) Widefield CO 1.6 kw, 2,224 ft.
WWOJ(FM) Avon Park FL 2.25 kw, 370 ft.
WAFC-FM Clewiston FL 1.5 kw, 460 ft.
WDFL-FM Cross City FL 4.5 kw, 184 ft.
WSUV(FM) Fort Myers Villas FL 6 kw, 266 ft.
WLVU-FM Holiday FL 3 kw, 300 ft.
WAVK(FM) Marathon FL 3 kw-H, 112 ft.
WCIF(FM) Melbourne FL 3 kw, 230 ft.
WSRZ-FM Sarasota FL 3 kw, 280 ft.
WEAG-FM Starke FL 1.35 kw, 495 ft.
WTUF(FM) Boston GA 3 kw, 328 ft.
WGMK(FM) Donalsonville GA 3 kw, 350 ft.
WQBZ(FM) Fort Valley GA 50 kw, 426 ft.
WKIG-FM Glennville GA 3 kw, 300 ft.
WKBX(FM) Kingsland GA 3 kw, 330 ft.
KMXD(FM) Ankeny IA 3 kw, 328 ft.
KXOF(FM) Bloomfield IA 3 kw, 300 ft.
WQRL(FM) Benton IL 12.5 kw, 328 ft.
WGCY(FM) Gibson City IL 3 kw, 292 ft.
WJPC-FM Lansing IL 2 kw, 397 ft.
WKJR(FM) Sullivan IL 7.3 kw, 312 ft.
WDJB(FM) Columbia City IN 1.55 kw, 400 ft.
WNDY(FM) Crawfordsville IN 3 kw, 77 ft.
WUBU(FM) South Bend IN 3 kw, 292 ft.
WANY-FM Albany KY 2.7 kw, 155 ft.
WKDZ-FM Cadiz KY 3 kw, 317 ft.
WBPK(FM) Flemingsburg KY 1.8 kw, 400 ft.
WFLE-FM Flemingsburg KY 1.61 kw, 449 ft.
WLLS-FM Hartford KY 3 kw, 280 ft.
WKMO(FM) Hodgenville KY 3 kw, 400 ft.
WRIL(FM) Pineville KY 350 w, 750 ft.
WJMM-FM Versailles KY 3 kw, 316 ft.
KFXZ(FM) Maurice LA 1.3 kw, 495 ft.
KXOR(FM) Thibodaux LA 6 kw, 302 ft.
WEIB(FM) Northampton MA 3 kw, 289 ft.

WCEM-FM Cambridge MD 3 kw, 298 ft.
WPKM(FM) Scarborough ME 3 kw, 299 ft.
WPLB-FM Lakeview MI 3 kw, 328 ft.
WKLA-FM Ludington MI 4.1 kw, 400 ft.
WGER-FM Saginaw MI 3 kw, 300 ft.
KRJB(FM) Ada MN 3 kw, 276 ft.
WMFG-FM Hibbing MN 600 w-H, 269 ft.
KRZK(FM) Branson MO 5.7 kw, 672 ft.
KDAM(FM) Monroe City MO 3 kw, 302 ft.
WAID(FM) Clarksdale MS 3 kw, 299 ft.
WLTD(FM) Lexington MS 3 kw, 314 ft.
WMFM(FM) Petal MS 3 kw, 400 ft.
KDBR(FM) Kalispell MT 3.9 kw, 403 ft.
WCCA(FM) Shallotte NC 6 kw, 328 ft.
KISP(FM) Blair NE 3 kw, 469 ft.
KIBZ(FM) Lincoln NE 3 kw, 213 ft.
WMTK(FM) Littleton NH 390 w, 1,256 ft.
WHOB(FM) Nashua NH 3 kw, 100 ft.
WHCY(FM) Blairstown NJ 340 w, 859 ft.
WHTG-FM Eatontown NJ 3.9 kw, 328 ft.
WKOE(FM) Ocean City NJ 3 kw, 308 ft.
KZPY(FM) Los Lunas NM 100 kw, 656 ft.
WVIP-FM Mount Kisco NY 3 kw, 440 ft.
WMCR-FM Oneida NY 390 w, 718 ft.
WCDK(FM) Cadiz OH 6 kw, 360 ft.
WCKX(FM) London OH 6 kw, 328 ft.
WWJM(FM) New Lexington OH 1.7 kw, 627 ft.
WQTL(FM) Ottawa OH 3 kw, 297 ft.
*KGOU(FM) Norman OK 3 kw, 300 ft.
KTSH(FM) Tishomingo OK 25 kw, 328 ft.
WLCY(FM) Blairsville PA 2.4 kw, 363 ft.
WQHG(FM) Huntingdon PA 6 kw, 154 ft.
WQRM(FM) Smethport PA 1.2 kw, 731 ft.
WCTL(FM) Union City PA 3.4 kw, 430 ft.
WWKX(FM) Woonsocket RI 1.5 kw, 518 ft.
WYNN-FM Florence SC 1.1 kw, 507 ft.
WRLQ(FM) Ladson SC 3 kw, 100 ft.
WNMX(FM) Newberry SC 25 kw, 328 ft.
KVHT(FM) Vermillion SD 3 kw, 255 ft.
KHXS(FM) Abilene TX 4.6 kw, 201 ft.
KOOC(FM) Belton TX 1.35 kw, 489 ft.
KAUM(FM) Colorado City TX 3 kw, 157 ft.
KPSO-FM Falfurrias TX 180 w, 188 ft.
KPJN(FM) Gonzales TX 3 kw, 167 ft.
KPAN-FM Hereford TX 7 kw, 259 ft.
KERB-FM Kermit TX 3 kw, 276 ft.
KSEM-FM Seminole TX 3 kw, 174 ft.
KTLT(FM) Wichita Falls TX 2.4 kw, 423 ft.
WBDY-FM Bluefield VA 3 kw, 1,122 ft.
WBOP(FM) Churchville VA 10 kw, 328 ft.
WMNA-FM Gretna VA 3 kw, 260 ft.
WNVA-FM Norton VA 1.65 kw, 613 ft.
KVLR(FM) Twisp WA 220 w, 1,633 ft.
WLJO(FM) La Crosse WI 12 kw, 476 ft.
WWQM-FM Middleton WI 4.5 kw, 381 ft.
WEVR-FM River Falls WI 3 kw, 300 ft.
WZZW(FM) Milton WV 560 w, 1,092 ft.
KLEN(FM) Cheyenne WY 3 kw, minus 3 ft.
KOTB(FM) Evanston WY 110 w, 1,523 ft.

106.5 mhz (ch 293)

KWHL(FM) Anchorage AK 100 kw, minus 89 ft.
WFMI(FM) Bay Minette AL 7.3 kw, 607 ft.
WJEC(FM) Vernon AL 6 kw, 328 ft.
KBVA(FM) Bella Vista AR 37 kw, 567 ft.
KIXA(FM) Lucerne Valley CA 150 w
KWOD-FM Sacramento CA 50 kw, 410 ft.
KKLQ-FM San Diego CA 7.4 kw, 1,074 ft.
KEZR(FM) San Jose CA 50 kw, 430 ft.
WBMW(FM) Ledyard CT 6 kw, 514 ft.
WCJX(FM) Five Points FL 3 kw, 328 ft.
WZBX(FM) Sylvania GA 6 kw, 328 ft.
KRVR(FM) Davenport IA 60 kw, 210 ft.
WKBQ(FM) Granite City IL 90 kw, 1,027 ft.
WWBL(FM) Washington IN 50 kw, 340 ft.
KYQQ(FM) Arkansas City KS 100 kw, 1,278 ft.
WNKR(FM) Williamstown KY 1.41 kw, 476 ft.
KQXL-FM New Roads LA 50 kw, 485 ft.
WWMX(FM) Baltimore MD 7.4 kw, 1,217 ft.
WMYJ(FM) Pocomoke City MD 1.8 kw, 341 ft.
WQCB(FM) Brewer ME 98 kw, 1,079 ft.
WMEF(FM) Fort Kent ME 25 kw, 302 ft.
WQLR(FM) Kalamazoo MI 33 kw, 600 ft.
KFMC(FM) Fairmont MN 100 kw, 400 ft.
KKCJ(FM) Liberty MO 100 kw, 981 ft.
KCMG-FM Mountain Grove MO 3 kw, 299 ft.
KMIS-FM New Madrid MO 50 kw, 462 ft.
WSFL-FM New Bern NC 100 kw, 915 ft.
WRDX(FM) Salisbury NC 100 kw, 1,003 ft.
KMCX(FM) Ogallala NE 100 kw, 300 ft.
WRHF(FM) Farmington NH 376 w, 935 ft.
KEND(FM) Roswell NM 52 kw, 135 ft.
KRLV(FM) Las Vegas NV 100 kw, 1,155 ft.
WPYX(FM) Albany NY 15.3 kw, 902 ft.
WYRK(FM) Buffalo NY 50 kw, 390 ft.
WLTF(FM) Cleveland OH 11.3 kw, 1,036 ft.
WMHE(FM) Delta OH 3 kw, 328 ft.
WLSN(FM) Greenville OH 50 kw, 482 ft.
KXKY(FM) Holdenville OK 4.5 kw, 203 ft.
KRSR-FM Coos Bay OR 3 kw, 400 ft.
WHLM(FM) Bloomsburg PA 36.5 kw, 570 ft.
WNIK-FM Arecibo PR 19.5 kw, minus 270 ft.
WSYN(FM) Georgetown SC 50 kw, 530 ft.
WSKZ(FM) Chattanooga TN 100 kw, 1,080 ft.
WJDT(FM) Rogersville TN 6 kw, 1,378 ft.
KQQK(FM) Galveston TX 100 kw, 1,322 ft.
KOOI-FM Jacksonville TX 100 kw, 1,468 ft.
KEJS(FM) Lubbock TX 34 kw, 587 ft.
KXGM-FM Muenster TX 6 kw, 328 ft.
WVGO(FM) Richmond VA 7.6 kw, 1,233 ft.
KWQL(FM) Dishman WA 3 kw, 328 ft.
KLYN(FM) Lynden WA 100 kw, 718 ft.
KEGX(FM) Richland WA 100 kw, 1,082 ft.
WLJY(FM) Marshfield WI 100 kw, 800 ft.
WISQ(FM) Whitewater WI 3 kw, 328 ft.
WKKW-FM Clarksburg WV 50 kw, 500 ft.

106.7 mhz (ch 294)

KGTW(FM) Ketchikan AK 4 kw, minus 308 ft.
WKMX(FM) Enterprise AL 100 kw, 1,068 ft.
KMVK(FM) Benton AR 16 kw, 866 ft.
KWEZ(FM) Trumann AR 6 kw, 328 ft.
*KKGL(FM) Pinetop AZ 100 kw, 1,023 ft.
KIHX-FM Prescott Valley AZ 3.7 kw, 1,627 ft.
KXHM(FM) Orland CA 25 kw, 56 ft.
KROQ-FM Pasadena CA 5.6 kw, 2,000 ft.
KJUG-FM Tulare CA 1.2 kw, 6,100 ft.
KAZY(FM) Denver CO 100 kw, 987 ft.
WTPX(FM) Fort Lauderdale FL 100 kw, 984 ft.
WXXL(FM) Leesburg FL 100 kw, 800 ft.
WOKA-FM Douglas GA 100 kw, 295 ft.
WYAY(FM) Gainesville GA 99 kw, 1,400 ft.
KRTI(FM) Grinnell IA 50 kw, 492 ft.
WYLL(FM) Des Plaines IL 50 kw, 299 ft.
WBLZ(FM) Mt. Vernon IN 3 kw, 295 ft.
WGLM(FM) West Lafayette IN 6 kw, 328 ft.
KFXX-FM Hugoton KS 35 kw, 259 ft.
KVNV(FM) Norton KS 51 kw, 92 ft.
WKXO-FM Berea KY 1.95 kw, 584 ft.
WZZL(FM) Reidland KY 1.35 kw, 492 ft.
KZXB(FM) Homer LA 50 kw, 492 ft.
KCIJ(FM) North Fort Polk LA 6 kw, 328 ft.
KGTR(FM) Port Sulphur LA 100 kw, 981 ft.
KCRL(FM) Rayne LA 3 kw, 328 ft.
WMJX(FM) Boston MA 21.5 kw, 750 ft.
WWWW-FM Detroit MI 61 kw, 510 ft.
WKPK(FM) Gaylord MI 100 kw, 580 ft.
WJJY-FM Brainerd MN 100 kw, 448 ft.
*KDXL(FM) St. Louis Park MN 10 w, 974 ft.
KELE(FM) Mount Vernon MO 25 kw, 328 ft.
WWZD(FM) New Albany MS 50 kw, 499 ft.
WSTZ-FM Vicksburg MS 100 kw, 1,365 ft.
WLGX(FM) Carolina Beach NC 1.8 kw, 253 ft.
WQVA(FM) Semora NC 6 kw, 328 ft.
KEXL(FM) Norfolk NE 100 kw, 1,027 ft.
WJNN(FM) North Cape May NJ 3 kw
KBOM(FM) Los Alamos NM 15.5 kw, 1,948 ft.
WWLF-FM Copenhagen NY 200 w, 1,227 ft.
WMAX-FM Irondequoit NY 3.5 kw, 627 ft.
WLTW(FM) New York NY 7.8 kw v, 5.4 kw h, 1,220 ft.
WSRW-FM Hillsboro OH 50 kw, 300 ft.
KYNZ(FM) Lone Grove OK 5.5 kw, 335 ft.
KKBK(FM) Lake Oswego OR 94 kw, 879 ft.
WWKS(FM) Beaver Falls PA 47 kw, 520 ft.
WRKZ(FM) Hershey PA 14 kw, 499 ft.
WTCB(FM) Orangeburg SC 100 kw, 787 ft.
WAMB-FM Donelson TN 75 w, 250 ft.
KCYT(FM) Granbury TX 100 kw, 991 ft.
KCHX(FM) Midland TX 100 kw, 613 ft.
KDIL(FM) Terrell Hills TX 100 kw, 1,030 ft.
WJFK-FM Manassas VA 22.5 kw-H, 18.5 kw-V, 731 ft.
WIZN(FM) Vergennes VT 50 kw, 373 ft.
KZPH(FM) Cashmere WA 2.45 kw, 513 ft.
*WVXD(FM) Chetek WI 50 kw
*WHFI(FM) Lindside WV 3 kw, 302.5 ft.
WVKM(FM) Matewan WV 3 kw, 105 ft.

106.9 mhz (ch 295)

WODL(FM) Birmingham AL 100 kw, 1,150 ft.
KXIO(FM) Clarksville AR 5.9 kw, 112 ft.
KMJK(FM) Buckeye AZ 6 kw, 305 ft.
KQLB(FM) Los Banos CA 6 kw, 328 ft.
*KEAR(FM) San Francisco CA 80 kw, 1,120 ft.
KROR(FM) Yucca Valley CA 4 kw, 1,371 ft.
WCCC-FM Hartford CT 23 kw, 730 ft.
WZZS(FM) Zolfo Springs FL 6 kw, 328 ft.
WZIQ(FM) Smithville GA 6 kw, 328 ft.
KWYI(FM) Kawaihae HI 5.5 kw, 341 ft.
KJJC(FM) Osceola IA 50 kw, 650 ft.
KQEP(FM) Rock Valley IA 3 kw, 328 ft.
KMOK(FM) Lewiston ID 99 kw, 1,230 ft.
WSWT(FM) Peoria IL 50 kw, 480 ft.
WDML(FM) Woodlawn IL 3 kw, 328 ft.
WMRI(FM) Marion IN 50 kw, 499 ft.
KTPK(FM) Topeka KS 100 kw, 1,210 ft.
WVEZ-FM Louisville KY 24.5 kw, 670 ft.
WTTL-FM Madisonville KY 2 kw, 528 ft.
WARX(FM) Hagerstown MD 15.5 kw, 855 ft.
WRXS(FM) Ocean City MD 3 kw, 328 ft.
WAVX(FM) Thomaston ME 29.5 kw, 633 ft.
WUPM(FM) Ironwood MI 53 kw, 495 ft.
WMUS-FM Muskegon MI 50 kw, 480 ft.
*WSAE(FM) Spring Arbor MI 2.88 kw, 349 ft.
KROC-FM Rochester MN 100 kw, 1,110 ft.
KTXY(FM) Jefferson City MO 100 kw, 1,250 ft.
WRBE-FM Lucedale MS 6 kw, 258 ft.
WMIT(FM) Black Mountain NC 36 kw, 3,090 ft.
NEW FM St. Pauls NC 3 kw, 328 ft.
KOTD-FM Plattsmouth NE 6 kw, 328 ft.
WSCY(FM) Moultonborough NH 150 w, 1,961 ft.
*WKDN-FM Camden NJ 38 kw, 600 ft.
KRNO-FM Reno NV 37 kw, 2,956 ft.
WPCX(FM) Auburn NY 14 kw, 941 ft.
WRQK(FM) Canton OH 27.5 kw, 340 ft.
*WWSU(FM) Dayton OH 10 w, 150 ft.
WMRN-FM Marion OH 25 kw, 340 ft.
KSWR(FM) Clinton OK 100 kw, 285 ft.
KHTT(FM) Muskogee OK 100 kw, 1,005 ft.
KCST-FM Florence OR 2.3 kw, 508 ft.
KKRB(FM) Klamath Falls OR 100 kw, 1,200 ft.
WOVU(FM) Clarendon PA 4.7 kw, 371 ft.
*WRIJ(FM) Masontown PA 3 kw, 328 ft.
WEZX(FM) Scranton PA 190 w, 1,266 ft.
WMEG(FM) Guayama PR 25 kw, 1,994 ft.
WLOW(FM) Bluffton SC 50 kw, 492 ft.
WWYN(FM) McKenzie TN 100 kw, 892 ft.
WKXD(FM) Monterey TN 25 kw, 731 ft.
KLUB(FM) Bloomington TX 6 w, 295 ft.
KHLB-FM Burnet TX 2 kw, 367 ft.
KKZR(FM) Conroe TX 95 kw, 1,128 ft.
KRVA-FM McKinney TX 2.5 kw, 351 ft.
KSOS-FM Brigham City UT 68 kw, 2,369 ft.
WYMY(FM) Bedford VA 180 w, 1,276 ft.
WAFX(FM) Suffolk VA 100 kw, 984 ft.
KRWM(FM) Bremerton WA 100 kw, 819 ft.
WLJU(FM) Brookfield WI 3 kw, 154 ft.
WNNO-FM Wisconsin Dells WI 3 kw, 320 ft.
*KPGM(FM) Casper WY 100 kw, 1,824 ft.

107.1 mhz (ch 296)

KKSY(FM) Bald Knob AR 3 kw, 298 ft.
KTHS-FM Berryville AR 3.6 kw, 627 ft.
KXFE(FM) Dumas AR 2.75 kw, 160 ft.
KKOL(FM) Hampton AR 3 kw, 298 ft.
KFTH(FM) Marion AR 3 kw, 328 ft.
KLQZ(FM) Paragould AR 1.9 kw, 410 ft.
KTWN-FM Texarkana AR 2.9 kw, 479 ft.
KVVA-FM Apache Junction AZ 2.5 kw, 405 ft.
KCCA(FM) Colorado City AZ 6.1 kw, minus 327 ft.
KMAX(FM) Arcadia CA 3 kw, 240 ft.
KTIE(FM) Bakersfield CA 6 kw, 164 ft.
KBAX(FM) Fallbrook CA 3 kw, 300 ft.
KAAT(FM) Oakhurst CA 280 w, 1,070 ft.
KRVD(FM) Rio Dell CA 3 kw, 535 ft.
KMBY-FM Seaside CA 1.85 kw, 587 ft.
KAXX(FM) Ventura CA 280 w, 872 ft.
KPVW(FM) Aspen CO 470 w, 804 ft.
KSIR-FM Brush CO 100 kw, 935 ft.
KNKN(FM) Pueblo CO 50 kw, 338 ft.
WIIS(FM) Key West FL 3 kw, 200 ft.
WCKT(FM) Lehigh Acres FL 15.5 kw, 732 ft.
WAOA(FM) Melbourne FL 100 kw, 500 ft.
WCLA-FM Claxton GA 3 kw, 195 ft.
WNEX-FM Gordon GA 2.25 kw, 541 ft.
WTSH-FM Rockmart GA 3 kw, 300 ft.
WSNI(FM) Thomasville GA 100 kw, 981 ft.
WYFA(FM) Waynesboro GA 6 kw, 328 ft.
KCCQ(FM) Ames IA 3 kw, 300 ft.
KDSN-FM Denison IA 3.3 kw, 300 ft.
KVYV(FM) Vinton IA 6 kw, 328 ft.
KCID-FM Caldwell ID 3 kw, 365 ft.
WEAI(FM) Lynnville IL 6 kw, 328 ft.
WSPY(FM) Plano IL 1.5 kw, 466 ft.
WPGU(FM) Urbana IL 3 kw, 235 ft.
WKRV(FM) Vandalia IL 3 kw, 165 ft.
WBNL-FM Boonville IN 3 kw, 185 ft.
WSYW-FM Danville IN 883 w, 604 ft.
WZVN(FM) Lowell IN 1.29 kw, 499 ft.
KMOQ(FM) Baxter Springs KS 3 kw, 300 ft.
WMGE(FM) Danville KY 3 kw, 185 ft.
WKCB-FM Hindman KY 770 w, 650 ft.
WKCA(FM) Owingsville KY 3 kw, 370 ft.
WBLG(FM) Smiths Grove KY 50 kw, 393 ft.
KFNV-FM Ferriday LA 18.5 kw, 233 ft.
WHMD(FM) Hammond LA 3 kw, 328 ft.
KWLV(FM) Many LA 25 kw, 253 ft.
KOGM(FM) Opelousas LA 3 kw-H, 203 ft.
WFHN(FM) Fairhaven MA 3 kw, 370 ft.
WWPL(FM) Federalsburg MD 3.9 kw, 408 ft.
WQKL(FM) Ann Arbor MI 3 kw, 289 ft.
WYTW(FM) Cadillac MI 1.25 kw, 499 ft.
WSAQ(FM) Port Huron MI 6 kw, 298 ft.
WTLZ(FM) Saginaw MI 4.9 kw, 400 ft.
WIRX(FM) St. Joseph MI 1.2 kw, 498 ft.
KKCQ-FM Fosston MN 50 kw, 482 ft.
KMGK(FM) Glenwood MN 3 kw, 300 ft.
KKJR(FM) Hutchinson MN 4.4 kw, 195 ft.
KBMV-FM Birch Tree MO 3 kw, 299 ft.
WVRD(FM) Belzoni MS 3 kw, 174 ft.
WXLS-FM Gulfport MS 1.85 kw, 394 ft.
WLSM-FM Louisville MS 3 kw, 200 ft.
WCLN-FM Clinton NC 3 kw, 299 ft.
WFXC(FM) Durham NC 1.2 kw, 490 ft.
WIOZ-FM Southern Pines NC 3 kw, 300 ft.
KGWB(FM) Wahpeton ND 3 kw, 302 ft.
WERZ(FM) Exeter NH 5.2 kw, 351 ft.
WJTK(FM) Gorham NH 6 kw, 157 ft.
WRNJ-FM Belvidere NJ 3.9 kw, 395 ft.
WZVU(FM) Long Branch NJ 2.3 kw, 371 ft.
KUCU(FM) Armijo NM 50 kw, 304 ft.
WXPS(FM) Briarcliff Manor NY 3 kw, 325 ft.
WWHB(FM) Hampton Bays NY 3 kw, 280 ft.
WMJR(FM) Hudson Falls NY 280 w, 844 ft.
WNUS(FM) Belpre OH 2.3 kw, 370 ft.
WAHC(FM) Circleville OH 3 kw, 328 ft.
WDOH(FM) Delphos OH 3 kw, 300 ft.
WMLV(FM) Ironton OH 3 kw, 125 ft.
WAQZ(FM) Milford OH 3 kw, 299 ft.
KLBC(FM) Durant OK 6 kw, 365 ft.
KSKD(FM) Sweet Home OR 9 kw, 2,476 ft.
WSSZ(FM) Greensburg PA 1.6 kw, 450 ft.
WEXC(FM) Greenville PA 3 kw, 240 ft.
*WQJU(FM) Mifflintown PA .500 kw, 1,117 ft.
WLIH(FM) Whitneyville PA 3.3 kw, 299 ft.
WRHM(FM) Lancaster SC 3 kw, 500 ft.
WCIG(FM) Mullins SC 3 kw, 328 ft.
KGSR(FM) Bastrop TX 46 kw, 518 ft.
KFLZ(FM) Bishop TX 3 kw, 324 ft.
KPUR-FM Canyon TX 5 kw, 300 ft.
KSTA-FM Coleman TX 3 kw, 180 ft.
KWKQ(FM) Graham TX 3 kw, 100 ft.
KTLR-FM Terrell TX 3.1 kw, 440 ft.

Broadcasting & Cable Yearbook 1994
B-523

U.S. FM Stations by Frequency

*KWBU(FM) Waco TX 3 kw, 190 ft.
WTTX-FM Appomattox VA 300 w
WBHA(FM) Hot Springs VA 160 w, 1,407 ft.
WPSK-FM Pulaski VA 25 kw, 1,207 ft.
WORK(FM) Barre VT 1.5 kw, 410 ft.
WBFL(FM) Bellows Falls VT 1 kw, 530 ft.
KAZZ(FM) Deer Park WA 9 kw, 253 ft.
KFIZ-FM Fond du Lac WI 3 kw, 312 ft.
WIXK-FM New Richmond WI 18 kw, 272 ft.
WOCO-FM Oconto WI 3 kw, 210 ft.
WKPL(FM) Platteville WI 3 kw, 235 ft.
WKZG(FM) Keyser WV 530 w, 783 ft.

107.3 mhz (ch 297)

WQLT(FM) Florence AL 100 kw, 1,000 ft.
KXRC(FM) Clarendon AR 3 kw, 321 ft.
KAFW(FM) Osceola AR 3 kw, 223 ft.
KIXT-FM Grover City CA 4.2 kw, 807 ft.
KIXW(FM) Lenwood CA 440 w, 771 ft.
KMMM(FM) Madera CA 3 kw, 328 ft.
KSTN-FM Stockton CA 8.1 kw, 1,610 ft.
WRQX(FM) Washington DC 34 kw, 602 ft.
WROO(FM) Jacksonville FL 100 kw, 705 ft.
WOWW(FM) Pensacola FL 100 kw, 1,407 ft.
WCOF(FM) Tampa FL 100 kw, 649 ft.
WCGQ(FM) Columbus GA 100 kw, 1,011 ft.
KGRS(FM) Burlington IA 100 kw, 429 ft.
KIOW(FM) Forest City IA 25 kw, 328 ft.
WDDD-FM Marion IL 50 kw, 500 ft.
WRZQ-FM Greensburg IN 41.8 kw, 531 ft.
WRSW-FM Warsaw IN 50 kw, 293 ft.
KKRD(FM) Wichita KS 100 kw, 884 ft.
WCTT-FM Corbin KY 50 kw, 492 ft.
WAAF(FM) Worcester MA 18.6 kw, 820 ft.
WBZN(FM) Old Town ME 50 kw, 308 ft.
WODJ(FM) Greenville MI 50 kw, 493 ft.
WHST(FM) Tawas City MI 6 kw, 280 ft.
KNUJ-FM Sleepy Eye MN 1.13 kw, 528 ft.
KISF(FM) Lexington MO 100 kw, 1,184 ft.
WTKF(FM) Atlantic NC 6 kw, 328 ft.
KEZG(FM) Lincoln NE 100 kw, 551 ft.
WRWD-FM Highland NY 330 w, 968 ft.
WFUD(FM) Honeyoye Falls NY 3 kw, 328 ft.
WRCK(FM) Utica NY 50 kw, 499 ft.
WYBZ(FM) Crooksville OH 3 kw, 328 ft.
WNWV(FM) Elyria OH 50 kw, 466 ft.
NEW FM Swanton OH 3 kw, 328 ft.
KVRW(FM) Lawton OK 50 kw, 492 ft.
KBSY(FM) Poteau OK 100 kw, 1,810 ft.
KACW(FM) North Bend OR 100 kw, 521 ft.
WDBA(FM) DuBois PA 50 kw, 499 ft.
WAFH(FM) Northumberland PA 2 kw, 377 ft.
WCMN-FM Arecibo PR 50 kw, 1,027 ft.
WJMZ-FM Anderson SC 100 kw, 1,008 ft.
WVSZ(FM) Chesterfield SC 3 kw, 328 ft.
KQRN(FM) Mitchell SD 50 kw, 450 ft.
KSLT(FM) Spearfish SD 100 kw, 1,702 ft.
KNKE-FM Jasper TX 3 kw, 298 ft.
KPOS-FM Post TX 50 kw, 334 ft.
KISX(FM) Whitehouse TX 50 kw, 500 ft.
WXLZ-FM Lebanon VA 530 w, 774 ft.
KFFM(FM) Yakima WA 100 kw, 1,500 ft.
WSJY(FM) Fort Atkinson WI 50 kw, 499 ft.
WKAZ(FM) Miami WV 50 kw, 600 ft.

107.5 mhz (ch 298)

KASH-FM Anchorage AK 100 kw, 1,014 ft.
WVFG(FM) Uniontown AL 6 kw, 469 ft.
KKTZ(FM) Mountain Home AR 100 kw, 656 ft.
KSED(FM) Sedona AZ 98.4 kw, 1,463 ft.
KCRZ(FM) Tucson AZ 14.5 kw, 3,526 ft.
KPPL(FM) Colusa CA 28 kw, 600 ft.
KXO-FM El Centro CA 25.5 kw, 115 ft.
KPIG(FM) Freedom CA 2.85 kw, 336 ft.
KMPH-FM Hanford CA 20.3 kw, 784 ft.
KLVE(FM) Los Angeles CA 29.5 kw, 3,100 ft.
KWMX-FM Lakewood CO 100 kw, 670 ft.
WQBA-FM Miami FL 95 kw-H, 80 kw-V, 1,007 ft.
WTIF-FM Omega GA 1.8 kw, 400 ft.
WDBN(FM) Wrightsville GA 3 kw, 295 ft.
KKDM(FM) Des Moines IA 50 kw, 492 ft.
WGCI-FM Chicago IL 33 kw, 600 ft.
WJOD(FM) Galena IL 6 kw, 328 ft.
WZZQ(FM) Terre Haute IN 27.5 kw, 670 ft.
KSCB-FM Liberal KS 100 kw, 511 ft.

WIOK(FM) Falmouth KY 610 w, 695 ft.
WZLK(FM) Virgie KY 580 w
KCIL(FM) Houma LA 100 kw, 649 ft.
KXKZ(FM) Ruston LA 98 kw, 1,066 ft.
WFCC-FM Chatham MA 50 kw, 341 ft.
WTHT(FM) Lewiston ME 35 kw, 610 ft.
WGPR(FM) Detroit MI 50 kw, 360 ft.
WMQT(FM) Ishpeming MI 98 kw, 528 ft.
WCCW-FM Traverse City MI 840 w, 518 ft.
KLIZ-FM Brainerd MN 100 kw, 350 ft.
KBJJ(FM) Marshall MN 25 kw, 213 ft.
KKJJ(FM) Campbell MO 20 kw, 367 ft.
WKXI-FM Magee MS 98 kw, 952 ft.
WMJW(FM) Rosedale MS 25 kw, 328 ft.
WSFM(FM) Southport NC 32 kw, 594 ft.
WKZL(FM) Winston-Salem NC 100 kw, 500 ft.
KJKJ(FM) Grand Forks ND 100 kw, 500 ft.
KERC(FM) Clovis NM 100 kw, 550 ft.
KEFE(FM) Los Alamos NM 100 kw, 300 ft.
KFBI(FM) Pahrump NV 24.5 kw, 3,715 ft.
WRGG(FM) Endwell NY 3 kw, 328 ft.
WBLS(FM) New York NY 5.4 kw-H, 3.8 kw-V, 1,220 ft.
WBUK(FM) Fort Shawnee OH 3 kw, 328 ft.
KGND(FM) Ketchum OK 50 kw, 492 ft.
*KRRC(FM) Portland OR 8 w, minus 49 ft.
KLRR(FM) Redmond OR 100 kw, 985 ft.
WAYC-FM Bedford PA 370 w, 1,309 ft.
WBYN(FM) Boyertown PA 29.9 kw, 611 ft.
WBUB(FM) North Charleston SC 100 kw, 984 ft.
WAQK(FM) Germantown TN 3 kw, 328 ft.
WYHY(FM) Lebanon TN 58 kw, 1,234 ft.
KOAI(FM) Fort Worth TX 25 kw, 1,647 ft.
KZFX(FM) Lake Jackson TX 100 kw, 2,000 ft.
KXTN-FM San Antonio TX 100 kw, 1,514 ft.
KMXB(FM) Orem UT 45 kw, 2,850 ft.
WKRE-FM Exmore VA 50 kw, 259 ft.
WEZR(FM) Brillion WI 6 kw, 328 ft.
WCCN-FM Neillsville WI 100 kw-H, 326 ft.
WEGW(FM) Wheeling WV 12.5 kw, 870 ft.

107.7 mhz (ch 299)

WENN-FM Birmingham AL 100 kw, 1,237 ft.
WWGA(FM) Georgiana AL 6 kw, 328 ft.
KYTN(FM) Wrightsville AR 3 kw, 328 ft.
KXDE(FM) Merced CA 3 kw, 328 ft.
KSOL(FM) San Mateo CA 8.9 kw, 1,162 ft.
KCDZ(FM) Twentynine Palms CA 3 kw, 328 ft.
WMGF(FM) Mount Dora FL 100 kw, 1,584 ft.
WYNR(FM) Darien GA 50 kw, 403 ft.
WKBG(FM) Martinez GA 50 kw, 492 ft.
WWRQ(FM) Valdosta GA 3 kw, 243 ft.
KKOA(FM) Volcano HI 3 kw, 207 ft.
KICD-FM Spencer IA 100 kw, 310 ft.
WLLT(FM) Polo IL 1.35 kw, 476 ft.
WMRS(FM) Monticello IN 4.4 kw, 131 ft.
KGCR(FM) Goodland KS 100 kw, 446 ft.
KMAJ-FM Topeka KS 100 kw, 1,214 ft.
KPEL-FM Erath LA 25 kw, 328 ft.
WEJS(FM) Bar Harbor ME 6.3 kw, 39 ft.
WHSB(FM) Alpena MI 99 kw, 760 ft.
WRKR(FM) Portage MI 50 kw, 500 ft.
KOTT(FM) Otterville MO 6 kw, 328 ft.
KMJM(FM) St. Louis MO 100 kw, 1,027 ft.
KSYZ-FM Grand Island NE 100 kw, 899 ft.
WRCI(FM) Hillsboro NH 3 kw, minus 276 ft.
WSNJ-FM Bridgeton NJ 15.2 kw, 486 ft.
*WRRC(FM) Lawrenceville NJ 17 w, 36 ft.
WGNA-FM Albany NY 12.45 kw, 984 ft.
*WECW(FM) Elmira NY 6 w, minus 312 ft.
WNUC(FM) Wethersfield Township NY 11.5 kw, 800 ft.
WMMX(FM) Dayton OH 50 kw, 420 ft.
WBZO(FM) Loudonville OH 6 kw, 328 ft.
WSEO(FM) Nelsonville OH 3 kw, 1,027 ft.
WHMQ(FM) North Baltimore OH 3 kw, 328 ft.
KRXO(FM) Oklahoma City OK 99 kw, 991 ft.
KUMA-FM Pendleton OR 27.5 kw, 610 ft.
WGTY(FM) Gettysburg PA 16 kw, 829 ft.
WYMK(FM) Tunkhannock PA 235 w, 1,161 ft.
WVOZ-FM Carolina PR 50 kw, 1,636 ft.
WHHM-FM Henderson TN 6 kw, 328 ft.
WIVK-FM Knoxville TN 91 kw, 2,053 ft.
KNNC(FM) Georgetown TX 25 kw, 328 ft.
KTBQ(FM) Nacogdoches TX 50 kw, 492 ft.
KADM(FM) Odessa TX 49 kw, 502 ft.
KPLT-FM Paris TX 35 kw, 300 ft.

WBBY(FM) Cedar Bluff VA 550 w, 751 ft.
WRCY(FM) Warrenton VA 33 kw, 1199 ft.
WSVY-FM Windsor VA 3 kw, 328 ft.
KNDD(FM) Seattle WA 100 kw, 1,194 ft.
WVCY(FM) Milwaukee WI 24 kw, 538 ft.
WFSP-FM Kingwood WV 1.6 kw, 449 ft.

107.9 mhz (ch 300)

KEZA(FM) Fayetteville AR 99 kw, 1,259 ft.
KFIN(FM) Jonesboro AR 100 kw, 600 ft.
KVMA-FM Magnolia AR 100 kw, 351 ft.
KMLE(FM) Chandler AZ 100 kw, 1,735 ft.
KUZZ-FM Bakersfield CA 5.8 kw, 1,358 ft.
KSEA(FM) Greenfield CA 50 kw, 492 ft.
KXOA-FM Sacramento CA 50 kw, 403 ft.
KWVE(FM) San Clemente CA 50 kw, 500 ft.
KIMN-FM Fort Collins CO 100 kw, 470 ft.
KBKL(FM) Grand Junction CO 100 kw, 1,305 ft.
KDZA-FM Pueblo CO 100 kw, 239 ft.
WEBE(FM) Westport CT 50 kw, 383 ft.
WVFE(FM) Coral Cove FL 3 kw, 328 ft.
WSKP(FM) Key West FL 100 kw, 472 ft.
WPFM(FM) Panama City FL 100 kw, 781 ft.
WIRK-FM West Palm Beach FL 100 kw, 340 ft.
WPEZ(FM) Macon GA 100 kw, 690 ft.
KGMZ(FM) Aiea HI 100 kw-H, 79 kw-V, 1,965 ft.
KKRF(FM) Stuart IA 2.75 kw, 472 ft.
KFMW(FM) Waterloo IA 100 kw, 1,850 ft.
KRVG(FM) Eagle ID 1.1 kw, 2,585 ft.
WYSY-FM Aurora IL 22.5 kw, 734 ft.
WTPI(FM) Indianapolis IN 22 kw, 762 ft.
WJFX(FM) New Haven IN 3 kw, 57 ft.
WAMW-FM Washington IN 3 kw, 328 ft.
KZLS(FM) Great Bend KS 100 kw, 886 ft.
KWKS(FM) Winfield KS 50 kw, 397 ft.
WKYR-FM Burkesville KY 6 kw, 312 ft.
WCVQ(FM) Fort Campbell KY 100 kw, 950 ft.
WWAG(FM) McKee KY 2 kw, 400 ft.
WXKS-FM Medford MA 20.5 kw, 771 ft.
*WFSI(FM) Annapolis MD 50 kw, 500 ft.
WHQO(FM) Skowhegan ME 6.50 kw, 676 ft.
*WVAC-FM Adrian MI 13 w-H, 79 ft.
WCRZ(FM) Flint MI 50 kw, 331 ft.
WKBZ-FM Muskegon MI 2.6 kw, 348 ft.
KQQL(FM) Anoka MN 100 kw, 1,080 ft.
KLTA(FM) Breckenridge MN 100 kw, 713 ft.
KLTE(FM) Kirksville MO 100 kw, 715 ft.
KCLQ(FM) Lebanon MO 50 kw, 365 ft.
WFCA(FM) Ackerman MS 100 kw, 614 ft.
WZKX(FM) Poplarville MS 92 kw, 1,460 ft.
WBT-FM Charlotte NC 97 kw, 1,692 ft.
WNCT-FM Greenville NC 100 kw, 1,800 ft.
KPFX(FM) Fargo ND 100 kw, 713 ft.
KWPN-FM West Point NE 6 kw, 328 ft.
*WWPH(FM) Princeton Junction NJ 17 w, 36 ft.
KAMX-FM Albuquerque NM 22.5 kw, 4,130 ft.
WHEN-FM Syracuse NY 50 kw, 490 ft.
WENZ(FM) Cleveland OH 70 kw, 750 ft.
WCEZ(FM) Delaware OH 6 kw, 285 ft.
KEYB(FM) Altus OK 6 kw, 190 ft.
KHPE(FM) Albany OR 100 kw, 1,160 ft.
*WHHS(FM) Havertown PA 14 w, 161 ft.
WDSY-FM Pittsburgh PA 50 kw, 500 ft.
WXXZ(FM) Port Matilda PA 350 w, 469 ft.
WPMR-FM Tobyhanna PA 5.7 kw, 564 ft.
WRAK-FM Williamsport PA 180 w, 1,292 ft.
WGTR(FM) Bucksport SC 36 kw, 571 ft.
WIJY(FM) Hilton Head Island SC 50 kw, 485 ft.
WOGT-FM East Ridge TN 3 kw, 328 ft.
KEYJ-FM Abilene TX 100 kw, 670 ft.
KXTJ(FM) Beaumont TX 100 kw, 1,000 ft.
KAKS-FM Canyon TX 96 kw, 1,322 ft.
KAND-FM Corsicana TX 100 kw, 842 ft.
KVLY(FM) Edinburg TX 100 kw, 765 ft.
KPXG(FM) Gainesville TX 50 kw
KFAN-FM Johnson City TX 37.2 kw, 492 ft.
KYMI(FM) Los Ybanez TX 50 kw, 459 ft.
KIXS(FM) Victoria TX 100 kw, 362 ft.
KRGQ-FM Roy UT 67 kw, 2,383 ft.
WYYD(FM) Amherst VA 20.5 kw, 1,768 ft.
WPTG(FM) West Point VA 6 kw, 328 ft.
*WVPS(FM) Burlington VT 36 kw, 2,640 ft.
*KMBI-FM Spokane WA 56 kw, 2,380 ft.
WYCO(FM) Wausau WI 100 kw, 1,019 ft.
WEMM(FM) Huntington WV 50 kw, 500 ft.

Canadian AM Stations by Frequency

Editor's Note: Clear stations appear in boldface type. For more information on North American clear station regulations, see FCC Rules and Regulations in Section A.

530 khz
CIAO(AM) Brampton ON

540 khz
*CBK(AM) Regina SK
CBT(AM) Grand Falls-Windsor NF
CJSB(AM) Ottawa ON
CBEF(AM) Windsor ON
*CBKF-1(AM) Gravelbourg SK

550 khz
CFJC(AM) Kamloops BC
CKPG(AM) Prince George BC
CFNB(AM) Fredericton NB
CHNO(AM) Sudbury ON
CHLN(AM) Trois Rivieres PQ

560 khz
CKNL(AM) Fort St. John BC
CHTK(AM) Prince Rupert BC
CHVO(AM) Carbonear NF
CJKL(AM) Kirkland Lake ON
CFOS(AM) Owen Sound ON
CKCN(AM) Sept-Iles PQ

570 khz
CKEK(AM) Cranbrook BC
CKWL(AM) Williams Lake BC
CJEM(AM) Edmundston NB
CFCB(AM) Corner Brook NF
CKGL(AM) Kitchener ON
CKSW(AM) Swift Current SK
*CFWH(AM) Whitehorse YT

580 khz
*CKUA(AM) Edmonton AB
CKXR(AM) Salmon Arm BC
CKY(AM) Winnipeg MB
CJFX(AM) Antigonish NS
CKAP(AM) Kapuskasing ON
CFRA(AM) Ottawa ON
CKPR(AM) Thunder Bay ON
CKWW(AM) Windsor ON
CHLC(AM) Baie Comeau PQ

590 khz
CFNL(AM) Fort Nelson BC
CFTK(AM) Terrace BC
CFAR(AM) Flin Flon MB
CJCW(AM) Sussex NB
VOCM(AM) St. John's NF
CKYC(AM) Toronto ON
CKRS(AM) Jonquiere PQ

600 khz
CKBD(AM) Vancouver BC
CKCL(AM) Truro NS
CFCT(AM) Tuktoyaktuk NT
CFCH(AM) North Bay ON
CIQC(AM) Montreal PQ
CFQC(AM) Saskatoon SK

610 khz
CKYL(AM) Peace River AB
CHNL(AM) Kamloops BC
CJAT(AM) Trail BC
CHTM(AM) Thompson MB
CKTB(AM) St. Catharines ON
CHNC(AM) New Carlisle PQ
CKRW(AM) Whitehorse YT

620 khz
CJCI(AM) Prince George BC
CKCM(AM) Grand Falls-Windsor NF
CKOY(AM) Timmins ON
CFRP(AM) Forestville PQ
CKCK(AM) Regina SK

630 khz
CHED(AM) Edmonton AB
CKOV(AM) Kelowna BC
CKRC(AM) Winnipeg MB
CFCO(AM) Chatham ON
CJET(AM) Smiths Falls ON
CFCY(AM) Charlottetown PE
CHLT(AM) Sherbrooke PQ

640 khz
*CBN(AM) St. John's NF
CFOB(AM) Fort Frances ON
CHOG(AM) Richmond Hill ON

650 khz
CISL(AM) Richmond BC
CKGA(AM) Gander NF
CKOM(AM) Saskatoon SK

660 khz
CFFR(AM) Calgary AB

670 khz
CKXB(AM) Musgravetown NF

680 khz
*CHFA(AM) Edmonton AB
CJOB(AM) Winnipeg MB
CKXG(AM) Grand Falls-Windsor NF
CFTR(AM) Toronto ON

690 khz
CBF(AM) Montreal PQ
*CBU(AM) Vancouver BC

700 khz
CKRD(AM) Red Deer AB
CHSJ(AM) Saint John NB

710 khz
CKVO(AM) Clarenville NF
CJRN(AM) Niagara Falls ON
CIPC(AM) Port-Cartier PQ
CKVM(AM) Ville-Marie PQ

720 khz
CHTN(AM) Charlottetown PE

730 khz
CKLG(AM) Vancouver BC
CKDM(AM) Dauphin MB
CJNR(AM) Blind River ON
CKAC(AM) Montreal PQ

740 khz
CBX(AM) Edmonton AB
CHCM(AM) Marystown NF
CBL(AM) Toronto ON

750 khz
CBGY(AM) Bonavista Bay NF
CKGB(AM) Timmins ON
CJWW(AM) Saskatoon SK

760 khz
CFLD(AM) Burns Lake BC
CKQR(AM) Castlegar BC

770 khz
CHQR(AM) Calgary AB

780 khz
CFDR(AM) Dartmouth NS

790 khz
CFCW(AM) Camrose AB
CFAN(AM) Newcastle NB
CFNW(AM) Port au Choix NF
CIGM(AM) Sudbury ON

800 khz
CKOR(AM) Penticton BC
*VOWR(AM) St. John's NF
CJBQ(AM) Belleville ON
CKDR(AM) Dryden ON
CKLW(AM) Windsor ON
CJAD(AM) Montreal PQ
CHRC(AM) Quebec PQ
CHAB(AM) Moose Jaw SK

810 khz
CKJS(AM) Winnipeg MB
CJVA(AM) Caraquet NB

820 khz
CHAM(AM) Hamilton ON

830 khz
CKKY(AM) Wainwright AB
CFJR(AM) Brockville ON

840 khz
CJXX(AM) Grande Prairie AB
CKBX(AM) 100 Mile House BC
CHUR(AM) North Bay ON

850 khz
CKBA(AM) Athabasca AB
CFVR(AM) Abbotsford-Matsqui BC
CKVL(AM) Verdun PQ

860 khz
CJBC(AM) Toronto ON
*CFPR(AM) Prince Rupert BC
CHAK(AM) Inuvik NT
CBKF-2(AM) Saskatoon SK

870 khz
CKIR(AM) Invermere BC
CFBV(AM) Smithers BC
CFSX(AM) Stephenville NF

880 khz
CHQT(AM) Edmonton AB
CKKC(AM) Nelson BC
CKLQ(AM) Brandon MB

890 khz
CJDC(AM) Dawson Creek BC

900 khz
CJVI(AM) Victoria BC
CKDH(AM) Amherst NS
CHML(AM) Hamilton ON
CHYC(AM) Sudbury ON
CJBR(AM) Rimouski PQ
CKTS(AM) Sherbrooke PQ
CKVD(AM) Val d'Or PQ
CKBI(AM) Prince Albert SK

910 khz
CKDQ(AM) Drumheller AB
CKLY(AM) Lindsay ON
CHRL(AM) Roberval PQ

920 khz
CKCQ(AM) Quesnel BC
CFRY(AM) Portage la Prairie MB
CJCJ(AM) Woodstock NB
CJCH(AM) Halifax NS
CKNX(AM) Wingham ON

930 khz
CFBC(AM) Saint John NB
CJYQ(AM) St. John's NF
CKNS(AM) Espanola ON

940 khz
CBM(AM) Montreal PQ
CJIB(AM) Vernon BC
CJGX(AM) Yorkton SK

950 khz
CFAM(AM) Altona MB
CKNB(AM) Campbellton NB
CHER(AM) Sydney NS
CKBB(AM) Barrie ON

960 khz
CFAC(AM) Calgary AB
CHNS(AM) Halifax NS
CIAM(AM) Cambridge ON
CFFX(AM) Kingston ON

970 khz
CJYR(AM) Edson AB
*CBZ(AM) Fredericton NB
CKCH(AM) Hull PQ

980 khz
CKNW(AM) New Westminster BC
CFPL(AM) London ON
CKRU(AM) Peterborough ON
*CBV(AM) Quebec PQ
CKRM(AM) Regina SK

990 khz
CBW(AM) Winnipeg MB
*CBY(AM) Corner Brook NF
CBOF-1(AM) Maniwaki PQ
CKIS(AM) Montreal PQ

1000 khz
CKBW(AM) Bridgewater NS
CFLP(AM) Rimouski PQ

1010 khz
*CBR(AM) Calgary AB
CKXD(AM) Gander NF

1020 khz
CFRB(AM) Toronto ON

1030 khz
CKVH(AM) High Prairie AB

1040 khz
CKST(AM) Langley BC

1050 khz
CFGP(AM) Grande Prairie AB
CICF(AM) Vernon BC
*CKSB(AM) St. Boniface MB
CHUM(AM) Toronto ON
CJNB(AM) North Battleford SK

1060 khz
CFCN(AM) Calgary AB
CJRP(AM) Quebec PQ

1070 khz
CBA(AM) Moncton NB
CFAX(AM) Victoria BC
CHOK(AM) Sarnia ON

1080 khz
CKSA(AM) Lloydminster AB

1090 khz
CKRX(AM) Lethbridge AB
CKKW(AM) Kitchener ON

1110 khz
CKTY(AM) Sarnia ON

1130 khz
CKWX(AM) Vancouver BC

1140 khz
CFXL(AM) Calgary AB
CBI(AM) Sydney NS
CJTR(AM) Trois Rivieres PQ

1150 khz
CKIQ(AM) Kelowna BC
CKX(AM) Brandon MB
CKOC(AM) Hamilton ON
CJRC(AM) Gatineau PQ

1170 khz
CKGY(AM) Red Deer AB

1190 khz
CFSL(AM) Weyburn SK

1200 khz
CHMG(AM) St. Albert AB
CFGO(AM) Ottawa ON

1210 khz
CKWA(AM) Slave Lake AB
*VOAR(AM) Mount Pearl NF
CFYM(AM) Kindersley SK

1220 khz
CJOC(AM) Lethbridge AB
CKDA(AM) Victoria BC
CJRB(AM) Boissevain MB
CKCW(AM) Moncton NB
CJSS(AM) Cornwall ON
CJRL(AM) Kenora ON
CHSC(AM) St. Catharines ON
CFVM(AM) Amqui PQ
CKSM(AM) Shawinigan PQ

1230 khz
CJOK(AM) Fort McMurray AB
CKYR-1(AM) Grande Cache AB
CIYR(AM) Hinton AB
CKTK(AM) Kitimat BC
CJNL(AM) Merritt BC
CHFC(AM) Churchill MB
CFLN(AM) Goose Bay NF
CFGN(AM) Port-aux-Basques NF
CFFB(AM) Iqaluit NT
CHYK(AM) Kapuskasing ON
CJTT(AM) New Liskeard ON
CJLB(AM) Thunder Bay ON
CHVD(AM) Dolbeau PQ

1240 khz
CFEK(AM) Fernie BC
CKGO(AM) Hope BC
CKMK(AM) Mackenzie BC
CJOR(AM) Osoyoos BC
CJAV(AM) Port Alberni BC
CFNI(AM) Port Hardy BC
CJAR(AM) The Pas MB
CKIM(AM) Baie Verte NF

1250 khz
CHSM(AM) Steinbach MB
CHWO(AM) Oakville ON
CBOF(AM) Ottawa ON
CBGA(AM) Matane PQ

1260 khz
CFRN(AM) Edmonton AB
CIHI(AM) Fredericton NB

1270 khz
CHAT(AM) Medicine Hat AB
CHWK(AM) Chilliwack BC
CJCB(AM) Sydney NS
CJTN(AM) Trenton ON
CFGT(AM) Alma PQ

1280 khz
CHRB(AM) High River AB
CHQB(AM) Powell River BC
CJMS(AM) Montreal PQ
CJSL(AM) Estevan SK

1290 khz
CIFX(AM) Winnipeg MB
CJBK(AM) London ON
CHRM(AM) Matane PQ

1300 khz
CJME(AM) Regina SK

1310 khz
CHLW(AM) St. Paul AB
CIWW(AM) Ottawa ON

1320 khz
CHQM(AM) Vancouver BC
CKEC(AM) New Glasgow NS
CJMR(AM) Mississauga ON

1330 khz
CKLD(AM) Thetford Mines PQ
CJYM(AM) Rosetown SK

1340 khz
CIBQ(AM) Brooks AB
CJCM(AM) Grand Centre AB
CFKC(AM) Creston BC
CKGF(AM) Grand Forks BC
CKCR(AM) Revelstoke BC
CIVH(AM) Vanderhoof BC
CKXX(AM) Corner Brook NF
CFLW(AM) Wabush NF
CJLS(AM) Yarmouth NS
*CFYK(AM) Yellowknife NT
CKNR(AM) Elliot Lake ON
CHOH(AM) Hearst ON
CKDR-5(AM) Red Lake ON
CHAD(AM) Amos PQ
CJAN(AM) Asbestos PQ
CFED(AM) Chapais PQ
CKMG(AM) Maniwaki PQ
CBGN(AM) Ste. Anne des Monts PQ

1350 khz
CKEG(AM) Nanaimo BC
CKAD(AM) Middleton NS
CKDO(AM) Oshawa ON
CHVR(AM) Pembroke ON
CJLM(AM) Joliette PQ

1360 khz
CKBC(AM) Bathurst NB
CJVL(AM) Ste. Marie-de-Beauce PQ

1370 khz
CFOK(AM) Westlock AB
CHPQ(AM) Parksville-Qualicum BC
CKOD(AM) Valleyfield PQ
CFVD(AM) Ville Degelis PQ

1380 khz
CKPC(AM) Brantford ON
CKLC(AM) Kingston ON
CFDA(AM) Victoriaville PQ

Canadian AM Stations by Frequency

1390 khz
CJCY(AM) Medicine Hat AB
CHOO(AM) Ajax ON

1400 khz
CKSQ(AM) Stettler AB
CHNL-1(AM) Clearwater BC
CKGR(AM) Golden BC
CIOR(AM) Princeton BC
*CBG(AM) Gander NF
CKCB(AM) Collingwood ON
CHVR-1(AM) Renfrew ON
CKFL(AM) Lac Megantic PQ
CJFP(AM) Riviere du Loup PQ
CKRN(AM) Rouyn PQ

1410 khz
CFUN(AM) Vancouver BC
CIGO(AM) Port Hawkesbury NS
CKSL(AM) London ON
CFMB(AM) Montreal PQ

1420 khz
CKDY(AM) Digby NS
CKPT(AM) Peterborough ON
CJMT(AM) Chicoutimi PQ
CKTL(AM) Plessisville PQ
CJVR(AM) Melfort SK

1430 khz
CJCL(AM) Toronto ON

1440 khz
CJOI(AM) Wetaskiwin AB
CFCP(AM) Courtenay BC

1450 khz
CFHC(AM) Canmore AB
CKYR(AM) Jasper AB
*CHCL(AM) Medley AB
CHOR(AM) Summerland BC
CFAB(AM) Windsor NS

CHUC(AM) Cobourg ON
CHMO(AM) Moosonee ON
CJBM(AM) Causapscal PQ
CHEF(AM) Granby PQ
CHRT(AM) St. Eleuthere PQ

1460 khz
CJOY(AM) Guelph ON
CKRB(AM) St. Georges-de-Beauce PQ

1470 khz
CJVB(AM) Vancouver BC
CHOW(AM) Welland ON

1480 khz
CKER(AM) Edmonton AB
CKDX(AM) Newmarket ON
CHRD(AM) Drummondville PQ

1490 khz
CJPR(AM) Blairmore AB
CFWB(AM) Campbell River BC
CKMV(AM) Grand Falls NB
CBDQ(AM) Wabush NF
CKEN(AM) Kentville NS
CHVR-2(AM) Arnprior ON
CFPS(AM) Port Elgin ON
CKLO(AM) L'Annonciation PQ
CJMC(AM) Ste. Anne des Monts PQ
CJSN(AM) Shaunavon SK

1500 khz
CKAY(AM) Duncan BC

1510 khz
CKOT(AM) Tillsonburg ON

1540 khz
CHIN(AM) Toronto ON

1550 khz
CBE(AM) Windsor ON

1570 khz
CKTA(AM) Taber AB
CHUB(AM) Nanaimo BC
CKMW(AM) Winkler-Morden MB
CHLO(AM) St. Thomas ON

1580 khz
CBJ(AM) Chicoutimi PQ

1600 khz
CHNR(AM) Simcoe ON

Canadian FM Stations by Frequency

Note: Asterisks (*) denote noncommercial stations.

88.1 mhz
*CKLN-FM Toronto ON

88.3 mhz
*CBQT-FM Thunder Bay ON

88.5 mhz
CJSR-FM Edmonton AB
CBAF-FM Moncton NB

88.7 mhz
CIMX-FM Windsor ON

88.9 mhz
*CBTK-FM Kelowna BC
CIRV-FM Toronto ON

89.1 mhz
*CHUO-FM Ottawa ON
*CKRL-FM Quebec PQ

89.3 mhz
*CISM-FM Montreal PQ

89.5 mhz
CFGB-FM Happy Valley NF
*CIUT-FM Toronto ON

89.9 mhz
CBE-FM Windsor ON

90.3 mhz
*CKUT-FM Montreal PQ
CBEG-FM Sarnia ON

90.5 mhz
CBHA-FM Halifax NS

90.9 mhz
*CJSW-FM Calgary AB
CBX-FM Edmonton AB

91.1 mhz
*CJRT-FM Toronto ON

91.3 mhz
CKUA-FM-13 Drumheller AB
CBD-FM Saint John NB

91.5 mhz
CBYG-FM Prince George BC
*CBO-FM Ottawa ON
*CJAM-FM Windsor ON

92.1 mhz
CHVD-FM Dolbeau PQ
CJAY-FM Calgary AB
CITI-FM Winnipeg MB
CJOZ-FM Bonavista Bay NF
CKPC-FM Brantford ON
CJQQ-FM Timmins ON
CJDM-FM Drummondville PQ
CHMX-FM Regina SK

92.3 mhz
CKOZ-FM Corner Brook NF
CJLX-FM Belleville ON

92.5 mhz
CKNG-FM Edmonton AB
CISS-FM Toronto ON
CHOC-FM Jonquiere PQ
CFQR-FM Montreal PQ

92.7 mhz
CJDC-FM Dawson Creek BC
CJBX-FM London ON
CJRQ-FM Sudbury ON
CFIM-FM Iles-de-la-Madeleine PQ

92.9 mhz
CKLE-FM Bathurst NB
CBBK-FM Kingston ON

93.1 mhz
CKBW-FM-2 Shelburne NS
CHAY-FM Barrie ON
CFNO-FM Marathon ON
CKCU-FM Ottawa ON

CHLQ-FM Charlottetown PE

93.3 mhz
CFRU-FM Guelph ON
*CFMU-FM Hamilton ON
CJMF-FM Quebec PQ

93.5 mhz
CKKC-FM-1 New Denver BC
CHMR-FM St. John's NF
CJLS-FM-2 Digby NS
CBCL-FM London ON
CBGA-FM-8 Iles-de-la-Madeleine PQ
CBM-FM Montreal PQ

93.7 mhz
*CKUA-FM-1 Calgary AB
CJJR-FM Vancouver BC
CBMI-FM Baie Comeau PQ

93.9 mhz
CKKL-FM Ottawa ON
CKLW-FM Windsor ON

94.1 mhz
CBL-FM Toronto ON
CIMG-FM Swift Current SK

94.3 mhz
CIRX-FM Prince George BC
CHIQ-FM Winnipeg MB
CJSD-FM Thunder Bay ON
CKMF-FM Montreal PQ

94.5 mhz
CKBW-FM-1 Liverpool NS
CJAB-FM Chicoutimi PQ
CJRG-FM Gaspe PQ

94.7 mhz
CHOZ-FM St. John's NF
*CHRW-FM London ON
CHEY-FM Trois Rivieres PQ

94.9 mhz
*CKUA-FM Edmonton AB
CKPE-FM Sydney NS
CKGE-FM Oshawa ON
CIMF-FM Hull PQ

95.1 mhz
CKSY-FM Chatham ON
CFMC-FM Saskatoon SK

95.3 mhz
CKKC-FM-2 Kaslo BC
CKZZ-FM Vancouver BC
CJXY-FM Hamilton ON
*CBV-FM Quebec PQ

95.5 mhz
CBA-FM Moncton NB
CJOJ-FM Belleville ON

95.7 mhz
CFJB-FM Barrie ON
CBQS-FM Sioux Narrows ON

95.9 mhz
CHFM-FM Calgary AB
CHOS-FM Rattling Brook NF
CFPL-FM London ON
CJFM-FM Montreal PQ

96.1 mhz
CFJQ-FM Nipigon-Red Rock ON
CKX-FM Brandon MB
CJEN-FM Jenpreg MB
CHGG-FM Limestone MB
CBCT-FM Charlottetown PE
CKIA-FM Quebec PQ

96.3 mhz
CFMX-FM-1 Mississauga ON
*CFFF-FM Peterborough ON
CIHO-FM St. Hilarion PQ
CKRA-FM Edmonton AB
CIOZ-FM Marystown NF
CJLS-FM-1 Shelburne NS
CFMK-FM Kingston ON

96.5 mhz
CIEZ-FM Halifax NS
NEW FM Ottawa ON
CHOA-FM Rouyn PQ

96.7 mhz
CHYM-FM Kitchener ON
CHYR-FM Leamington ON

96.9 mhz
*CKUA-FM-5 Peace River AB
CKKS-FM Vancouver BC
CKSS-FM Red Rocks NF
CKOI-FM Verdun PQ
*CBK-FM Regina SK

97.1 mhz
CJMG-FM Penticton BC
CFIL-FM Gillam MB
CIGL-FM Belleville ON

97.3 mhz
CIRK-FM Edmonton AB
*CKUA-FM-3 Medicine Hat AB
CJRM-FM Labrador City NF
CKON-FM Akwesasne ON
CJEZ-FM Toronto ON
CHGA-FM Maniwaki PQ

97.5 mhz
CIQM-FM London ON

97.5 mhz
CFFM-FM Williams Lake BC
CKRV-FM Kamloops BC
CJKR-FM Winnipeg MB
CKDU-FM Halifax NS
CHOX-FM La Pocatiere PQ

97.7 mhz
CFCV-FM St. Andrews NF
CBUF-FM Vancouver BC
CKWM-FM Kentville NS
CHTZ-FM St. Catharines ON
CHOM-FM Montreal PQ
CBKF-FM Regina SK

97.9 mhz
CKYX-FM Fort McMurray AB
CFDL-FM Deer Lake NF
CHSR-FM Fredericton NB
CFLC-FM Churchill Falls NF
CFNN-FM St. Anthony NF
CJRE-FM Riviere au Renard PQ

98.1 mhz
CKIQ-FM Big White Ski Village BC
*CBON-FM Sudbury ON
CHFI-FM Toronto ON
CHOI-FM Quebec PQ
*CBSI-FM Sept-Iles PQ
CHON-FM Whitehorse YT

98.3 mhz
CBAL-FM Moncton NB
CIFM-FM Kamloops BC
CBW-FM Winnipeg MB
CFLY-FM Kingston ON

98.5 mhz
CFMS-FM Victoria BC
CIOS-FM Stephenville NF
*CFTH-FM Harrington Harbour PQ
CIEL-FM Longueuil PQ

98.7 mhz
CBQX-FM Kenora ON
CKWR-FM Kitchener ON
CIKI-FM Rimouski PQ

98.9 mhz
CHIK-FM Quebec PQ
CIZZ-FM Red Deer AB
CJYC-FM Saint John NB
CIZL-FM Regina SK

99.1 mhz
CKIX-FM St. John's NF
CJMM-FM Rouyn-Noranda PQ
CFNJ-FM St. Gabriel-de-Brandon PQ
CFMM-FM Prince Albert SK

99.3 mhz
*CKUA-FM-2 Lethbridge AB
CFOX-FM Vancouver BC
CKQN-FM Baker Lake NT
CJBC-FM-20 London ON
CBV-FM-6 La Malbaie PQ

99.5 mhz
CFJC-FM Merritt BC
CIME-FM Ste. Adele PQ

99.7 mhz
CBTE-FM Crawford Bay BC
CIRO-FM St. Georges-de-Beauce PQ

99.9 mhz
CFGX-FM Sarnia ON
CBCS-FM Sudbury ON
CKFM-FM Toronto ON

100.1 mhz
CIOO-FM Halifax NS
CJCD-FM-1 Hay River NT

100.3 mhz
CFBR-FM Edmonton AB
CKKQ-FM Victoria BC
CKRZ-FM Ohsweken ON
CJMJ-FM Ottawa ON
*CKMS-FM Waterloo ON

100.5 mhz
CIOK-FM Saint John NB
CFOZ-FM Argentia NF
CBBL-FM London ON
CHAS-FM Sault Ste. Marie ON
*CFIN-FM Lac-Etchemin PQ

100.7 mhz
CIGV-FM Penticton BC
CHIN-FM Toronto ON
CBF-FM Montreal PQ
CBF-FM-1 Trois Rivieres PQ

100.9 mhz
CKUA-FM-4 Grande Prairie AB
*CBWK-FM Thompson MB
CKTO-FM Truro NS
*CBJ-FM Chicoutimi PQ

101.1 mhz
CKKC-FM Nelson BC
CFMI-FM New Westminster BC
CFAI-FM Edmundston NB
CKEY-FM Fort Erie ON
CFMO-FM Smiths Falls ON

101.3 mhz
CIOI-FM Prince George BC
CKOT-FM Tillsonburg ON

101.5 mhz
CILK-FM Kelowna BC
*CBZ-FM Fredericton NB
CKWF-FM Peterborough ON
*CIBL-FM Montreal PQ
CJBR-FM Rimouski PQ

101.7 mhz
*CBQ-FM Thunder Bay ON
CKNX-FM Wingham ON
CHIP-FM Fort Coulonge PQ
CJSO-FM Sorel PQ

101.9 mhz
CFBG-FM Bracebridge ON
*CITR-FM Vancouver BC
*CFUV-FM Victoria BC
CHFX-FM Halifax NS
CKNM-FM Yellowknife NT
*CFRC-FM Kingston ON
CKAT-FM North Bay ON

102.1 mhz
*CBR-FM Calgary AB
CISW-FM Whistler BC
CFNY-FM Brampton ON
CHPR-FM Hawkesbury ON
CFEL-FM Montmagny PQ
CHSN-FM Saskatoon SK

102.3 mhz
CBZF-FM Fredericton-St. John NB
CINQ-FM Montreal PQ
CIGB-FM Trois Rivieres PQ

102.5 mhz
CBOF-FM Ottawa ON

102.7 mhz
*CFRO-FM Vancouver BC
CBH-FM Halifax NS

102.9 mhz
CKLH-FM Hamilton ON
CFLS-FM Levis PQ

103.1 mhz
CJFW-FM Terrace BC
CKLU-FM Winnipeg MB
CJMO-FM Moncton NB
CFMX-FM Cobourg ON
CFMF-FM Fermont PQ
*CFIC-FM Ste. Anne des Plaines PQ

103.3 mhz
*CBOQ-FM Ottawa ON
CKLP-FM Parry Sound ON
CFJO-FM Thetford Mines PQ

103.5 mhz
CHQM-FM Vancouver BC
CIDC-FM Orangeville ON
*CKRK-FM Kahnawake PQ

103.7 mhz
CHXL-FM Brockville ON

103.9 mhz
CISN-FM Edmonton AB
CFQM-FM Moncton NB
CKDK-FM Woodstock ON

104.1 mhz
CFQX-FM Selkirk MB
CIFA-FM Yarmouth NS
CICZ-FM Midland ON
CKTF-FM Gatineau PQ
CFZZ-FM St. Jean-sur-Richelieu PQ

104.3 mhz
CFRQ-FM Dartmouth NS
CJQM-FM Sault Ste. Marie ON

104.5 mhz
CISP-FM Pemberton BC
CFLG-FM Cornwall ON
CBQN-FM Osnaburgh ON
CHUM-FM Toronto ON

104.7 mhz
CKLZ-FM Kelowna BC
CIPN-FM Pender Harbour BC
CISE-FM Sechelt BC
CBVE-FM Quebec PQ

104.9 mhz
CFSR-FM Abbotsford-Matsqui BC
CBQL-FM Savant Lake ON
CJLA-FM Lachute PQ
CFVD-FM-2 Pohenegamook PQ
CKIT-FM Regina SK

105.1 mhz
CKRY-FM Calgary AB
CBI-FM Sydney NS
CBQR-FM Rankin Inlet NT
CKQM-FM Peterborough ON
CBQP-FM Pickle Lake ON
CBMR-FM Fermont PQ

105.3 mhz
CJKK-FM Clarenville NF
CKHJ-FM Fredericton NB
CFCA-FM Kitchener ON
CKBY-FM Ottawa ON
CJMX-FM Sudbury ON

105.5 mhz
CHRY-FM Toronto ON
CFBK-FM Huntsville ON
*CBKS-FM Saskatoon SK

CFVD-FM-1 Cabano PQ
CITE-FM-1 Sherbrooke PQ
CJMV-FM Val d'Or PQ

Canadian FM Stations by Frequency

105.7 mhz
CKUM-FM Moncton NB
CBU-FM Vancouver BC
CHRE-FM St. Catharines ON
CFGL-FM Laval PQ

105.9 mhz
CHAR-FM Alert NT
CICX-FM Orillia ON

*CBKA-FM La Ronge SK

106.1 mhz
CKGO-FM-1 Boston Bar BC
CIMJ-FM Guelph ON
CHEZ-FM Ottawa ON
CIMO-FM Magog PQ

106.5 mhz
CFEI-FM St. Hyacinthe PQ

CIXK-FM Owen Sound ON

106.9 mhz
*CHMA-FM Sackville NB
*CBN-FM St. John's NF
*CIXX-FM London ON
NEW FM Ottawa ON

107.1 mhz
CISQ-FM Squamish BC

CILQ-FM Toronto ON
CIBM-FM Riviere du Loup PQ

107.3 mhz
CKIK-FM Calgary AB
CKHR-FM Hay River NT
CITE-FM Montreal PQ

107.5 mhz
CKSR-FM Chilliwack BC

CIEG-FM Egmont BC
CISC-FM Gibsons BC
CITF-FM Quebec PQ

107.7 mhz
CFRV-FM Lethbridge AB

107.9 mhz
CING-FM Burlington ON
CBJE-FM Chicoutimi PQ

Radio Formats Defined

Broadcasting & Cable Yearbook defines a radio format as programming broadcast over 20 hours weekly. Programming broadcast from one to 20 hours weekly is defined as special programming. This is not a hard and fast rule, however. Some stations may report programming unique to their main programming format(s) as "special" programming regardless of the number of broadcast hours.

Most stations broadcast one format, though some stations report having two or more formats. A station that lists four or more formats is categorized as "Variety/Diverse." Formats which did not fit into a specific category (such as beach music) are listed as "Other."

At present, *Broadcasting & Cable Yearbook* recognizes 70 different formats. These formats are listed below, with appropriate definitions.

This listing is followed by a breakdown of formats by state and by province. The chart on page B-542 gives a breakdown of radio programming by AM/FM and commercial/noncommercial stations in the U.S. and Canada.

Adult Contemporary—Recent popular songs, with a few oldies. The songs tend to be upbeat and soft. News and talk segments are prominent during rush hour "drive times." Also known as "Lite."

Agriculture & Farm—News, weather and features of interest to farmers and others involved in agriculture.

Albanian.

American Indian—Programming for North American Indians, includes native language (ie: Navajo) broadcasts.

Arabic.

Armenian.

Beautiful Music—Uninterrupted, instrumental soft music. There is usually very little talk, and few commercials. Also known as "Easy Listening."

Big Band—Popular music from the thirties and forties. Primarily instrumental works by bands such as Glen Miller's Orchestra and Tommy Dorsey. Also see **Nostalgia**.

Black—Music, talk and news targeted at Black listeners. Music at these stations is similar to Urban Contemporary stations, but this format caters more directly to the interests and tastes of Black audiences.

Bluegrass—Related formats are Country and Folk.

Blues—Some Jazz and Progressive stations also program blues music.

Children—Programming for children, usually for educational purposes. Includes music, informational programming, and news presented for young people.

Chinese.

Classic Rock—Popular rock music of the seventies and eighties. Also see **Rock/AOR**.

Classical—Classical music, often long pieces played without interruption. Announcers provide extended commentary and criticism on the pieces. Special features, such as live concerts, are common. Primarily a noncommercial FM format.

Comedy—Recorded stand-up comics and/or old radio comedy series. A rare format.

Contemporary Hit/Top-40—Current hot selling records. Usually a playlist of 20 to 40 songs continuously played throughout the day. DJs are often upbeat "personalities." News and information are given light coverage.

Country—Country music, ranging from older traditional country and western to today's "Hit Country" sounds. The amount of news and talk on country stations varies widely from station to station.

Croation.

Czech.

Disco—High-energy dance music first popular in the seventies. Also see **Black** and **Urban Contemporary**.

Drama/Literature—Dramatic readings, poetry, and broadcasts of live dramatic performances. A rare format in the U.S. and Canada.

Educational—Informative and instructional programming, such as over-the-air college courses. Primarily a noncommercial format.

Farsi.

Filipino.

Finnish.

Folk—Played full-time on very few stations, American folk music is also heard on noncommercial Variety stations. Also see **Bluegrass**.

Foreign Language/Ethnic—In addition to the specific language categories (i.e. French, German), this format denotes multilingual stations and others catering to ethnic minorities.

French.

German.

Gospel—Especially popular in the South, evangelical music is programmed on many Religious format stations.

Greek.

Hebrew.

Hindi.

Hungarian.

Irish.

Italian.

Japanese.

Jazz—Primarily a noncommercial FM format. Some Classical stations program jazz music features.

Jewish.

Korean.

Lithuanian.

MOR (Middle-of-the-Road)—Traditional AM format featuring a balanced mix of music, news and talk. Songs are usually popular standards. Announcers are often personalities who try to keep the listener interested and informed. News, both local and national, plays an important role at most MOR stations; coverage of sporting events and other features of interest to the community is common.

New Age—Soft "fusion" (a form mixing elements of jazz and rock), often played as background entertainment. As the name implies, this format is a recent development.

News—Continous coverage of local, national and international news, including sports, weather forecasts and features.

News/Talk—Combination of news and talk formats. One of these elements may receive more emphasis. Also see **News** and **Talk**.

Nostalgia—Popular tunes from the thirties, forties and fifties. Nostalgia stations often feature on-air personalities, and usually have heavy news and information coverage.

Oldies—Hit songs from the fifties, sixties and seventies. Usually played by upbeat DJs, with news, talk and special features (chart countdowns, trivia contests, etc.) playing an important role.

Other—Programming which falls outside the categories listed here.

Polish.

Polka—Music for the traditional dance. Most polka format stations are located in Wisconsin.

Portuguese.

Progressive—Progressive stations play many types of music, often including avant-garde music not played on conventional stations. Primarily a noncommercial format, common among college radio stations. Also known as "alternative."

Public Affairs—Community interest programming (ie: broadcasts of city council meetings.) Many noncommercial, News, and Talk stations cover local issues on news features or talk shows.

Reggae—Jamaican music. Often played on Progressive stations.

Religious—Inspirational/spiritual talk and music. Most religious stations air Christian sermons or songs. Also see **Gospel**.

Rock/AOR—Rock music from the sixties to the present. Album-oriented-rock features music "sweeps," or uninterrupted sets. News plays a secondary role. Also see **Classic Rock**.

Russian.

Scottish.

Serbian.

Slovak.

Slovenian.

Spanish.

Sports - Play by play and taped coverage, sports news, interviews, discussion.

Talk - Topical programs on various subjects. Includes health, finance, and community issues. Listener call-in and interview shows are common, and the host's personality tends to be an important element. Many talk stations air national satellite-delivered talk programs. News, sports and weather are usually emphasized during "drive times." Also see **News** and **News/Talk**.

Ukranian.

Top 40/Contemporary Hit—See **Contemporary Hit/Top 40**.

Urban Contemporary—Dance music, often from a variety of genres (i.e., rhythm & blues, Rap). Most Urban Contemporary stations emphasize music by black artists. Also see **Black** and **Disco**.

Variety/Diverse—A station listing four or more formats. Typical of noncommerical stations.

Vietnamese.

Women—Programming for women. Emphasis on news and information, pertaining to women's issues.

U.S. Radio Formats by State and Possession

Figures included here reflect only those stations that have provided format information.

United States

Format	Count
AM Stations	4724
FM Stations	6490
Commercial Stations	9494
Non-commercial Stations	1720
Country	2727
Adult Contemp.	2135
Religious	1178
Oldies	1004
News/Talk	820
Contemporary Hit/Top-40	657
News	636
Rock/AOR	624
Variety/Diverse	498
Talk	461
Classical	448
Middle-of-the-Road (MOR)	446
Classic Rock	378
Jazz	377
Spanish	373
Gospel	361
Progressive	288
Sports	284
Urban Contemporary	260
Beautiful Music	243
Educational	242
Black	162
Big Band	157
Agriculture & Farm	95
Nostalgia	93
Foreign Language/Ethnic	60
Public Affairs	59
Other	58
New Age	49
Blues	38
Bluegrass	18
Children	12
Folk	11
Portuguese	8
Polka	6
Greek	5
Korean	5
American Indian	4
Polish	3
Reggae	3
French	2
German	1
Filipino	1
Drama/Literature	1
Arabic	1
Disco	1
Jewish	1

Alabama

Format	Count
AM Stations	151
FM Stations	133
Commercial Stations	256
Non-commercial Stations	28
Country	91
Adult Contemp.	45
Religious	38
Gospel	28
Oldies	21
Urban Contemporary	20
Classic Rock	15
Contemporary Hit/Top-40	13
News/Talk	13
Middle-of-the-Road (MOR)	12
Black	11
Talk	11
Beautiful Music	11
Classical	8
Jazz	8
Rock/AOR	7
Sports	7
Blues	5
Educational	5
News	5
Big Band	3
Progressive	3
Agriculture & Farm	2
Variety/Diverse	2
Public Affairs	1
Nostalgia	1

Alaska

Format	Count
AM Stations	41
FM Stations	45
Commercial Stations	62
Non-commercial Stations	24
Variety/Diverse	20
Adult Contemp.	19
Country	15
News	10
Religious	10
Oldies	9
News/Talk	7
Classic Rock	7
Contemporary Hit/Top-40	7
Rock/AOR	7
Middle-of-the-Road (MOR)	5
Classical	4
Talk	3
Beautiful Music	3
Progressive	2
Jazz	2
Sports	2
Public Affairs	2
Foreign Language/Ethnic	1
New Age	1

Arizona

Format	Count
AM Stations	70
FM Stations	83
Commercial Stations	136
Non-commercial Stations	17
Country	36
Adult Contemp.	30
Oldies	14
Religious	13
Spanish	11
Contemporary Hit/Top-40	10
News	8
News/Talk	8
Rock/AOR	8
Talk	6
Middle-of-the-Road (MOR)	6
Sports	6
Variety/Diverse	6
Jazz	5
Classic Rock	5
Beautiful Music	4
Big Band	3
Educational	3
Classical	3
Public Affairs	2
Nostalgia	2
Other	1
Reggae	1

Arkansas

Format	Count
AM Stations	90
FM Stations	138
Commercial Stations	207
Non-commercial Stations	21
Country	100
Adult Contemp.	33
Religious	30
Contemporary Hit/Top-40	15
News	14
Gospel	12
Oldies	12
News/Talk	11
Variety/Diverse	9
Talk	6
Classical	6
Urban Contemporary	6
Beautiful Music	5
Middle-of-the-Road (MOR)	5
Black	5
Educational	4
Sports	4
Jazz	4
Classic Rock	3
Progressive	2
Rock/AOR	2
Nostalgia	2
Big Band	2
Blues	1
Agriculture & Farm	1
Children	1

U.S. Radio Formats by State and Possession

California

AM Stations	247
FM Stations	421
Commercial Stations	560
Non-commercial Stations	108
Adult Contemp	143
Country	80
Spanish	75
Religious	61
Rock/AOR	46
Oldies	44
News/Talk	40
Talk	38
Contemporary Hit/Top-40	37
News	37
Variety/Diverse	33
Jazz	26
Classical	26
Progressive	19
Classic Rock	19
Educational	18
Beautiful Music	18
Middle-of-the-Road (MOR)	17
Sports	13
Big Band	12
Foreign Language/Ethnic	10
Nostalgia	7
Gospel	7
New Age	6
Black	5
Urban Contemporary	5
Public Affairs	4
Other	4
Korean	3
Portuguese	2
Blues	2
Arabic	1
Children	1
Agriculture & Farm	1

Colorado

AM Stations	76
FM Stations	106
Commercial Stations	154
Non-commercial Stations	28
Country	51
Adult Contemp	41
Rock/AOR	20
Religious	15
Oldies	14
News/Talk	13
Variety/Diverse	13
News	12
Sports	8
Contemporary Hit/Top-40	8
Talk	7
Spanish	6
Progressive	6
Classical	5
Agriculture & Farm	5
Jazz	5
Middle-of-the-Road (MOR)	4
Classic Rock	3
Big Band	3
Educational	3
Beautiful Music	2
Black	2
New Age	1
Urban Contemporary	1
Children	1
Foreign Language/Ethnic	1
Nostalgia	1

Connecticut

AM Stations	41
FM Stations	55
Commercial Stations	68
Non-commercial Stations	28
Adult Contemp	21
News/Talk	11
Rock/AOR	11
Variety/Diverse	10
Classical	8
Spanish	7
Middle-of-the-Road (MOR)	7
Contemporary Hit/Top-40	7
News	6
Oldies	5
Progressive	5
Country	5
Jazz	4
Talk	4
Portuguese	4
Urban Contemporary	4
Educational	3
Religious	3
Big Band	2
Black	2
Classic Rock	1
Other	1
Folk	1
Foreign Language/Ethnic	1
New Age	1
Beautiful Music	1

Delaware

AM Stations	9
FM Stations	17
Commercial Stations	23
Non-commercial Stations	3
Adult Contemp	9
News/Talk	6
Country	3
Rock/AOR	2
Contemporary Hit/Top-40	2
News	1
Jazz	1
Big Band	1
Variety/Diverse	1
Middle-of-the-Road (MOR)	1
Talk	1
Educational	1
Religious	1
Oldies	1
Progressive	1

District of Columbia

AM Stations	7
FM Stations	13
Commercial Stations	16
Non-commercial Stations	4
News/Talk	3
Jazz	3
Adult Contemp	3
Classical	2
Urban Contemporary	2
News	2
Foreign Language/Ethnic	2
Talk	2
Contemporary Hit/Top-40	1
Bluegrass	1
Oldies	1
Gospel	1
Rock/AOR	1
Big Band	1
Country	1
Beautiful Music	1
Sports	1

Florida

AM Stations	210
FM Stations	240
Commercial Stations	383
Non-commercial Stations	67
Adult Contemp	76
Religious	75
Country	62
News/Talk	45
Spanish	37
Talk	31
Oldies	30
News	22
Contemporary Hit/Top-40	19
Middle-of-the-Road (MOR)	19
Rock/AOR	18
Beautiful Music	18
Jazz	16
Classical	15
Gospel	15
Sports	14
Urban Contemporary	14
Big Band	10
Variety/Diverse	9
Educational	9
Classic Rock	9
Black	7
Progressive	5
Other	5
Foreign Language/Ethnic	5
Public Affairs	4
Blues	3
Greek	3
Nostalgia	3
Disco	1

Georgia

AM Stations	183
FM Stations	191

U.S. Radio Formats by State and Possession

Commercial Stations	331
Non-commercial Stations	43
Country	109
Adult Contemp	65
Religious	59
Gospel	36
News/Talk	34
Oldies	34
News	23
Middle-of-the-Road (MOR)	17
Urban Contemporary	17
Sports	16
Black	14
Contemporary Hit/Top-40	14
Classical	12
Talk	10
Progressive	9
Variety/Diverse	7
Rock/AOR	7
Jazz	7
Classic Rock	6
Educational	4
Spanish	4
Other	2
Big Band	2
Bluegrass	2
Public Affairs	2
Beautiful Music	1
Reggae	1
Blues	1

Hawaii

AM Stations	27
FM Stations	33
Commercial Stations	55
Non-commercial Stations	5
Adult Contemp	16
News/Talk	9
Foreign Language/Ethnic	9
Contemporary Hit/Top-40	6
Oldies	5
Religious	5
Rock/AOR	5
Talk	4
Country	4
Beautiful Music	3
Sports	3
Middle-of-the-Road (MOR)	2
Classical	2
Other	2
Jazz	2
Variety/Diverse	2
Classic Rock	1
News	1
Filipino	1

Idaho

AM Stations	42
FM Stations	54
Commercial Stations	84
Non-commercial Stations	12
Country	29
Adult Contemp	20

Religious	8
Contemporary Hit/Top-40	8
Oldies	7
News	6
Classical	6
News/Talk	6
Classic Rock	5
Variety/Diverse	4
Rock/AOR	4
Middle-of-the-Road (MOR)	3
Beautiful Music	2
Spanish	2
Educational	2
Jazz	2
New Age	1
Sports	1
Other	1
Talk	1

Illinois

AM Stations	134
FM Stations	247
Commercial Stations	308
Non-commercial Stations	73
Adult Contemp	79
Country	72
Oldies	33
News/Talk	31
Religious	29
News	29
Rock/AOR	28
Variety/Diverse	25
Middle-of-the-Road (MOR)	24
Contemporary Hit/Top-40	24
Jazz	17
Sports	16
Classical	15
Classic Rock	15
Educational	14
Talk	13
Progressive	12
Spanish	10
Urban Contemporary	9
Agriculture & Farm	7
Public Affairs	6
Foreign Language/Ethnic	6
Big Band	5
Gospel	5
Beautiful Music	5
Black	4
Blues	3
Other	2
Polish	2
Greek	1
Korean	1
German	1

Indiana

AM Stations	87
FM Stations	190
Commercial Stations	227
Non-commercial Stations	50
Adult Contemp	68

Country	56
Oldies	29
Religious	28
Contemporary Hit/Top-40	19
News	18
News/Talk	17
Rock/AOR	17
Variety/Diverse	14
Middle-of-the-Road (MOR)	13
Talk	12
Classic Rock	11
Classical	11
Educational	10
Jazz	10
Sports	9
Beautiful Music	6
Big Band	6
Urban Contemporary	4
New Age	4
Progressive	3
Agriculture & Farm	3
Gospel	3
Public Affairs	3
Nostalgia	1
Other	1
Polish	1
Black	1

Iowa

AM Stations	83
FM Stations	133
Commercial Stations	179
Non-commercial Stations	37
Adult Contemp	64
Country	51
Oldies	32
Middle-of-the-Road (MOR)	23
Religious	15
News/Talk	15
Variety/Diverse	13
Contemporary Hit/Top-40	13
News	12
Classical	10
Jazz	9
Rock/AOR	8
Progressive	7
Classic Rock	6
Educational	5
Gospel	4
Agriculture & Farm	4
Talk	4
Beautiful Music	4
Nostalgia	3
Sports	3
Urban Contemporary	2
Big Band	2
Other	1
Black	1
New Age	1

Kansas

AM Stations	60
FM Stations	103

U.S. Radio Formats by State and Possession

Commercial Stations	138
Non-commercial Stations	25
Country	49
Adult Contemp	37
Religious	20
Oldies	14
News/Talk	14
Variety/Diverse	11
Contemporary Hit/Top-40	10
Rock/AOR	9
News	9
Agriculture & Farm	7
Classical	7
Classic Rock	6
Middle-of-the-Road (MOR)	5
Beautiful Music	4
Progressive	4
Educational	3
Jazz	3
New Age	3
Big Band	2
Urban Contemporary	2
Nostalgia	2
Sports	2
Talk	2

Kentucky

AM Stations	132
FM Stations	164
Commercial Stations	266
Non-commercial Stations	30
Country	122
Adult Contemp	53
Religious	35
Oldies	28
Contemporary Hit/Top-40	23
Gospel	17
News/Talk	13
News	12
Classic Rock	12
Rock/AOR	11
Classical	11
Middle-of-the-Road (MOR)	10
Talk	9
Variety/Diverse	8
Beautiful Music	5
Urban Contemporary	5
Educational	4
Jazz	4
Black	3
Sports	3
Big Band	3
Agriculture & Farm	2
Progressive	2
Nostalgia	2
Folk	1
Bluegrass	1

Louisiana

AM Stations	93
FM Stations	123
Commercial Stations	192
Non-commercial Stations	24

Country	62
Oldies	24
Religious	23
Adult Contemp	22
News/Talk	16
Contemporary Hit/Top-40	14
Urban Contemporary	14
Gospel	12
Jazz	11
Black	11
News	8
Talk	8
Classical	8
Sports	8
Rock/AOR	6
Variety/Diverse	6
Middle-of-the-Road (MOR)	5
Progressive	5
Blues	5
Classic Rock	4
Beautiful Music	4
Other	3
Big Band	3
Spanish	2
Educational	2
French	2
Agriculture & Farm	1
Nostalgia	1
Foreign Language/Ethnic	1

Maine

AM Stations	31
FM Stations	70
Commercial Stations	84
Non-commercial Stations	17
Adult Contemp	26
Country	18
Rock/AOR	11
Oldies	9
Contemporary Hit/Top-40	9
Variety/Diverse	9
Classical	8
News/Talk	7
Public Affairs	5
News	5
Talk	5
Sports	4
Classic Rock	4
Religious	4
Big Band	3
Middle-of-the-Road (MOR)	3
Beautiful Music	2
Progressive	2
Nostalgia	2
Educational	1

Maryland

AM Stations	52
FM Stations	65
Commercial Stations	97
Non-commercial Stations	20
Adult Contemp	25
Country	17

Religious	17
Oldies	14
News/Talk	10
Gospel	7
Contemporary Hit/Top-40	7
Classical	6
News	5
Rock/AOR	5
Classic Rock	5
Jazz	5
Talk	4
Black	3
Nostalgia	3
Sports	3
Beautiful Music	3
Big Band	3
Progressive	3
Urban Contemporary	3
Spanish	2
Educational	2
Middle-of-the-Road (MOR)	1
Folk	1
Other	1
Children	1
New Age	1

Massachusetts

AM Stations	67
FM Stations	104
Commercial Stations	120
Non-commercial Stations	51
Adult Contemp	38
Variety/Diverse	26
Rock/AOR	20
News/Talk	18
Progressive	17
Talk	15
Classical	10
Country	10
Oldies	10
Classic Rock	9
Jazz	9
Contemporary Hit/Top-40	8
Educational	7
News	6
Religious	6
Spanish	5
Foreign Language/Ethnic	5
Sports	5
Urban Contemporary	4
Middle-of-the-Road (MOR)	4
Big Band	4
Folk	3
Other	3
Black	3
Nostalgia	2
Blues	2
Beautiful Music	2
Public Affairs	1
Portuguese	1

U.S. Radio Formats by State and Possession

Michigan

AM Stations	138
FM Stations	225
Commercial Stations	295
Non-commercial Stations	68
Adult Contemp	82
Country	65
Oldies	35
Contemporary Hit/Top-40	30
Religious	30
Rock/AOR	28
News	23
News/Talk	23
Classical	19
Middle-of-the-Road (MOR)	18
Jazz	15
Beautiful Music	13
Variety/Diverse	13
Talk	12
Urban Contemporary	11
Classic Rock	11
Progressive	9
Educational	8
Sports	6
Big Band	5
Foreign Language/Ethnic	4
Gospel	4
Other	3
Nostalgia	3
Black	3
Public Affairs	2
New Age	2
Blues	1
Children	1

Minnesota

AM Stations	100
FM Stations	161
Commercial Stations	212
Non-commercial Stations	49
Country	81
Adult Contemp	54
Oldies	43
News	21
Religious	19
News/Talk	18
Classical	14
Rock/AOR	13
Contemporary Hit/Top-40	13
Variety/Diverse	12
Agriculture & Farm	11
Middle-of-the-Road (MOR)	11
Classic Rock	9
Progressive	7
Talk	6
Sports	5
Educational	4
Beautiful Music	3
Public Affairs	3
Big Band	3
Nostalgia	3
Jazz	3
Other	2
Urban Contemporary	1
Children	1
Polka	1
Black	1

Mississippi

AM Stations	98
FM Stations	123
Commercial Stations	202
Non-commercial Stations	19
Country	72
Religious	30
Adult Contemp	30
Gospel	27
Urban Contemporary	21
Black	16
Oldies	16
Contemporary Hit/Top-40	15
News/Talk	12
News	11
Classical	10
Rock/AOR	9
Blues	7
Agriculture & Farm	6
Talk	6
Classic Rock	5
Jazz	5
Educational	4
Sports	3
Beautiful Music	3
Progressive	2
Big Band	2
Middle-of-the-Road (MOR)	2
New Age	1
Nostalgia	1

Missouri

AM Stations	113
FM Stations	165
Commercial Stations	239
Non-commercial Stations	39
Country	101
Adult Contemp	42
Religious	31
News/Talk	29
Oldies	22
Contemporary Hit/Top-40	22
News	12
Classical	11
Classic Rock	10
Jazz	10
Variety/Diverse	9
Rock/AOR	9
Gospel	9
Beautiful Music	8
Middle-of-the-Road (MOR)	8
Agriculture & Farm	7
Educational	6
Big Band	6
Progressive	6
Talk	5
Sports	5
Urban Contemporary	4
Black	2
Nostalgia	2
Children	2
Other	1
Public Affairs	1
Foreign Language/Ethnic	1
New Age	1
Blues	1

Montana

AM Stations	47
FM Stations	59
Commercial Stations	96
Non-commercial Stations	10
Country	37
Adult Contemp	24
Oldies	10
Middle-of-the-Road (MOR)	8
News/Talk	6
Variety/Diverse	5
Talk	5
Religious	5
Rock/AOR	5
Classic Rock	4
Educational	4
News	3
Classical	3
Jazz	1
Sports	1
Agriculture & Farm	1
Contemporary Hit/Top-40	1
Beautiful Music	1
Foreign Language/Ethnic	1

Nebraska

AM Stations	52
FM Stations	84
Commercial Stations	111
Non-commercial Stations	25
Country	39
Adult Contemp	30
Oldies	13
News/Talk	12
Middle-of-the-Road (MOR)	12
Classical	11
Religious	10
Rock/AOR	8
News	7
Educational	7
Agriculture & Farm	5
Contemporary Hit/Top-40	5
Classic Rock	5
Progressive	4
Jazz	4
Talk	3
Variety/Diverse	2
Gospel	1
Urban Contemporary	1
New Age	1
Big Band	1

Nevada

AM Stations	25
FM Stations	42
Commercial Stations	57
Non-commercial Stations	10
Adult Contemp	13
Country	13
Rock/AOR	7
News/Talk	7
News	6
Classical	5
Classic Rock	5
Talk	5
Religious	5
Sports	3
Nostalgia	3
Contemporary Hit/Top-40	3
Jazz	2
Progressive	2
Beautiful Music	2
Educational	2
Spanish	2
Variety/Diverse	1
Big Band	1
Black	1
Middle-of-the-Road (MOR)	1
New Age	1
Other	1
Oldies	1
Agriculture & Farm	1

New Hampshire

AM Stations	26
FM Stations	40
Commercial Stations	59
Non-commercial Stations	7
Adult Contemp	15
Oldies	7
Rock/AOR	7
News/Talk	6
Talk	5
Classic Rock	5
Country	5
Middle-of-the-Road (MOR)	4
Variety/Diverse	4
Contemporary Hit/Top-40	4
Progressive	4
Sports	4
News	3
Nostalgia	3
Beautiful Music	1
Spanish	1
Public Affairs	1
Black	1
Religious	1
Classical	1

New Jersey

AM Stations	37
FM Stations	76
Commercial Stations	76
Non-commercial Stations	37
Adult Contemp	24
Variety/Diverse	14
News/Talk	14
Progressive	11
Oldies	11
Religious	11
Contemporary Hit/Top-40	7
Rock/AOR	7
Talk	6
Country	6
Jazz	5
Middle-of-the-Road (MOR)	4
Classical	4
Spanish	4
Educational	4
Beautiful Music	4
Nostalgia	4
Foreign Language/Ethnic	3
Big Band	3
Urban Contemporary	2
Classic Rock	2
News	2
Gospel	1
Other	1
Folk	1
Sports	1

New Mexico

AM Stations	62
FM Stations	81
Commercial Stations	127
Non-commercial Stations	16
Country	48
Adult Contemp	24
Spanish	16
Oldies	14
Rock/AOR	13
Religious	11
Variety/Diverse	8
Classical	6
Classic Rock	6
Talk	5
News	5
Contemporary Hit/Top-40	4
Educational	4
News/Talk	4
Nostalgia	3
American Indian	3
Jazz	3
Beautiful Music	2
Sports	1
New Age	1
Public Affairs	1
Big Band	1
Middle-of-the-Road (MOR)	1
Urban Contemporary	1
Progressive	1

New York

AM Stations	165
FM Stations	293
Commercial Stations	347
Non-commercial Stations	111
Adult Contemp	110
Country	53
Oldies	47
Rock/AOR	45
News/Talk	42
Religious	40
News	35
Jazz	29
Variety/Diverse	29
Middle-of-the-Road (MOR)	27
Contemporary Hit/Top-40	25
Classical	24
Progressive	23
Talk	17
Classic Rock	14
Educational	13
Urban Contemporary	11
Sports	11
Big Band	10
Spanish	7
Black	6
Beautiful Music	4
Gospel	4
Public Affairs	3
Nostalgia	3
Other	2
Jewish	1
Foreign Language/Ethnic	1
New Age	1

North Carolina

AM Stations	214
FM Stations	153
Commercial Stations	324
Non-commercial Stations	43
Country	80
Religious	66
Oldies	52
Gospel	47
Adult Contemp	44
News/Talk	38
Talk	19
News	19
Middle-of-the-Road (MOR)	18
Urban Contemporary	18
Contemporary Hit/Top-40	18
Black	14
Sports	13
Variety/Diverse	12
Jazz	12
Classical	11
Rock/AOR	11
Classic Rock	9
Educational	9
Beautiful Music	9
Progressive	6
Big Band	5
Other	3
Nostalgia	2
New Age	2
Bluegrass	1
Blues	1

Broadcasting & Cable Yearbook 1994

U.S. Radio Formats by State and Possession

North Dakota

AM Stations	33
FM Stations	37
Commercial Stations	59
Non-commercial Stations	11
Country	33
Adult Contemp	11
News	8
Jazz	6
Oldies	6
Classical	5
News/Talk	4
Religious	4
Contemporary Hit/Top-40	4
Classic Rock	3
Middle-of-the-Road (MOR)	2
Talk	2
Agriculture & Farm	2
Rock/AOR	2
Variety/Diverse	1
Progressive	1
Big Band	1
Public Affairs	1

Ohio

AM Stations	129
FM Stations	241
Commercial Stations	287
Non-commercial Stations	83
Adult Contemp	72
Country	66
Religious	40
Oldies	38
News/Talk	28
Rock/AOR	28
News	23
Contemporary Hit/Top-40	22
Jazz	21
Talk	20
Classical	16
Classic Rock	16
Variety/Diverse	14
Educational	14
Progressive	13
Middle-of-the-Road (MOR)	12
Urban Contemporary	11
Beautiful Music	9
Sports	9
Nostalgia	8
Gospel	7
Black	5
Public Affairs	4
Big Band	4
Agriculture & Farm	3
New Age	2
Greek	1
Foreign Language/Ethnic	1
Blues	1

Oklahoma

AM Stations	65
FM Stations	116
Commercial Stations	160
Non-commercial Stations	21
Country	74
Adult Contemp	32
Religious	22
Oldies	10
Contemporary Hit/Top-40	10
Talk	9
News/Talk	9
Classic Rock	9
News	8
Sports	7
Rock/AOR	6
Variety/Diverse	5
Gospel	5
Classical	5
Beautiful Music	4
Jazz	4
Educational	3
Big Band	3
Agriculture & Farm	3
Progressive	2
Urban Contemporary	2
Spanish	2
Bluegrass	1
New Age	1

Oregon

AM Stations	89
FM Stations	104
Commercial Stations	164
Non-commercial Stations	29
Country	50
Adult Contemp	35
News/Talk	24
Rock/AOR	16
Oldies	16
Religious	15
News	14
Jazz	14
Middle-of-the-Road (MOR)	12
Classical	10
Contemporary Hit/Top-40	9
Variety/Diverse	8
Talk	7
Classic Rock	6
New Age	5
Sports	5
Progressive	4
Beautiful Music	3
Urban Contemporary	2
Blues	1
Black	1
Spanish	1
Big Band	1
Educational	1
Nostalgia	1
American Indian	1

Pennsylvania

AM Stations	185
FM Stations	259
Commercial Stations	361
Non-commercial Stations	83
Adult Contemp	105
Country	70
Oldies	51
Religious	48
Contemporary Hit/Top-40	35
Rock/AOR	31
Variety/Diverse	29
News/Talk	28
Middle-of-the-Road (MOR)	26
Talk	25
Progressive	25
Classic Rock	20
News	18
Jazz	13
Beautiful Music	10
Classical	9
Sports	9
Gospel	8
Big Band	7
Nostalgia	6
Black	6
Educational	6
Urban Contemporary	5
Spanish	3
New Age	2
Public Affairs	1
Other	1
Foreign Language/Ethnic	1

Rhode Island

AM Stations	15
FM Stations	18
Commercial Stations	26
Non-commercial Stations	7
Adult Contemp	6
News/Talk	4
Oldies	4
Rock/AOR	4
News	4
Variety/Diverse	4
Progressive	4
Spanish	3
Classical	3
Contemporary Hit/Top-40	3
Jazz	3
Religious	2
Sports	2
Country	2
Classic Rock	2
Big Band	1
Reggae	1
Middle-of-the-Road (MOR)	1
Talk	1
Portuguese	1

South Carolina

AM Stations	100
FM Stations	113
Commercial Stations	191
Non-commercial Stations	22
Country	41
Adult Contemp	38

U.S. Radio Formats by State and Possession

Format	Count
Religious	28
Gospel	23
Urban Contemporary	21
Oldies	20
Talk	12
Black	9
News/Talk	9
News	9
Classic Rock	8
Other	6
Contemporary Hit/Top-40	6
Beautiful Music	6
Sports	6
Classical	5
Middle-of-the-Road (MOR)	4
Progressive	3
Variety/Diverse	3
Rock/AOR	3
Big Band	3
Jazz	3
Educational	2
Blues	2
Nostalgia	1

South Dakota

Format	Count
AM Stations	37
FM Stations	53
Commercial Stations	73
Non-commercial Stations	17
Country	28
Adult Contemp	16
Oldies	14
News	9
Middle-of-the-Road (MOR)	8
Rock/AOR	6
Religious	6
News/Talk	6
Jazz	5
Classic Rock	5
Variety/Diverse	5
Classical	5
Agriculture & Farm	4
Progressive	4
Contemporary Hit/Top-40	4
Public Affairs	3
Folk	2
Gospel	1
Sports	1
Talk	1
Big Band	1

Tennessee

Format	Count
AM Stations	176
FM Stations	165
Commercial Stations	305
Non-commercial Stations	36
Country	137
Adult Contemp	48
Religious	40
Gospel	34
News/Talk	24
Oldies	18
News	17

Format	Count
Contemporary Hit/Top-40	14
Talk	12
Jazz	10
Rock/AOR	10
Classical	10
Middle-of-the-Road (MOR)	10
Sports	9
Variety/Diverse	8
Beautiful Music	8
Urban Contemporary	7
Educational	7
Black	6
Classic Rock	6
Progressive	6
Big Band	5
Bluegrass	3
Blues	2
Nostalgia	2
Agriculture & Farm	2
Other	1
New Age	1
Public Affairs	1

Texas

Format	Count
AM Stations	287
FM Stations	420
Commercial Stations	624
Non-commercial Stations	83
Country	257
Spanish	104
Religious	88
Adult Contemp	75
Oldies	50
Contemporary Hit/Top-40	36
News	34
News/Talk	30
Classical	25
Rock/AOR	25
Classic Rock	24
Talk	21
Jazz	21
Variety/Diverse	21
Gospel	18
Educational	16
Sports	15
Middle-of-the-Road (MOR)	14
Beautiful Music	12
Urban Contemporary	12
Progressive	10
Black	9
Agriculture & Farm	8
Big Band	7
Nostalgia	5
Other	3
New Age	3
Children	2
Foreign Language/Ethnic	2
Public Affairs	2

Utah

Format	Count
AM Stations	40
FM Stations	48
Commercial Stations	74

Format	Count
Non-commercial Stations	14
Country	22
Adult Contemp	19
Contemporary Hit/Top-40	7
Rock/AOR	6
Sports	5
News	5
Middle-of-the-Road (MOR)	4
Classical	4
News/Talk	4
Religious	4
Spanish	3
Talk	3
Progressive	2
Variety/Diverse	2
Jazz	2
Oldies	2
Classic Rock	2
Educational	2
New Age	2
Beautiful Music	2
Gospel	1
Nostalgia	1
Urban Contemporary	1
Big Band	1
Children	1

Vermont

Format	Count
AM Stations	20
FM Stations	44
Commercial Stations	51
Non-commercial Stations	13
Country	15
Adult Contemp	14
Rock/AOR	12
News	7
Oldies	6
Variety/Diverse	6
Classic Rock	6
News/Talk	5
Classical	4
Jazz	4
Middle-of-the-Road (MOR)	4
Progressive	4
Religious	4
Contemporary Hit/Top-40	3
Sports	3
Educational	2
Big Band	2
Talk	1
Nostalgia	1

Virginia

Format	Count
AM Stations	144
FM Stations	155
Commercial Stations	267
Non-commercial Stations	32
Country	89
Adult Contemp	56
Religious	44
Oldies	22
News/Talk	22
Gospel	19

U.S. Radio Formats by State and Possession

Talk	15
Rock/AOR	14
News	14
Classical	11
Contemporary Hit/Top-40	11
Variety/Diverse	10
Urban Contemporary	10
Sports	10
Jazz	9
Bluegrass	9
Classic Rock	8
Middle-of-the-Road (MOR)	7
Black	7
Big Band	6
Beautiful Music	6
Progressive	5
Educational	4
Nostalgia	3
Agriculture & Farm	2
Public Affairs	2
Other	1
New Age	1
Folk	1

Washington

AM Stations	105
FM Stations	125
Commercial Stations	189
Non-commercial Stations	41
Country	48
Adult Contemp	44
Religious	26
News	21
News/Talk	19
Oldies	17
Rock/AOR	16
Talk	14
Contemporary Hit/Top-40	11
Spanish	10
Classic Rock	10
Variety/Diverse	9
Progressive	8
Sports	8
Classical	7
Jazz	6
Middle-of-the-Road (MOR)	5
Beautiful Music	4
Educational	4
Big Band	2
Urban Contemporary	2
Black	1
Nostalgia	1
Korean	1
Public Affairs	1
New Age	1
Other	1

West Virginia

AM Stations	69
FM Stations	93
Commercial Stations	140
Non-commercial Stations	22
Country	55

Adult Contemp	29
Religious	18
Oldies	17
Contemporary Hit/Top-40	11
News	9
Rock/AOR	9
Classical	8
Jazz	8
News/Talk	7
Variety/Diverse	7
Classic Rock	6
Talk	5
Progressive	5
Sports	4
Beautiful Music	4
Middle-of-the-Road (MOR)	3
Gospel	3
Other	2
Public Affairs	1
Nostalgia	1
Big Band	1
Urban Contemporary	1
Educational	1
Agriculture & Farm	1

Wisconsin

AM Stations	110
FM Stations	167
Commercial Stations	236
Non-commercial Stations	41
Adult Contemp	72
Country	67
Oldies	33
News/Talk	25
Middle-of-the-Road (MOR)	18
News	15
Religious	15
Talk	15
Contemporary Hit/Top-40	15
Classic Rock	13
Rock/AOR	13
Classical	12
Variety/Diverse	10
Beautiful Music	8
Sports	7
Educational	7
Progressive	6
Agriculture & Farm	6
Polka	5
Nostalgia	4
Big Band	3
Urban Contemporary	3
Jazz	3
Public Affairs	2
Folk	1
Other	1
Drama/Literature	1
New Age	1
Black	1
Children	1

Foreign Language/Ethnic	1
Gospel	1
Spanish	1

Wyoming

AM Stations	29
FM Stations	39
Commercial Stations	61
Non-commercial Stations	7
Country	30
Adult Contemp	18
Oldies	8
Contemporary Hit/Top-40	7
News	5
Religious	4
Classical	4
Classic Rock	3
Progressive	3
Rock/AOR	3
Educational	2
News/Talk	2
New Age	1
Sports	1
Talk	1
Jazz	1
Variety/Diverse	1
Beautiful Music	1

American Samoa

AM Stations	2
FM Stations	1
Commercial Stations	3
Variety/Diverse	1
Adult Contemp	1
Religious	1
Foreign Language/Ethnic	1
Beautiful Music	1

Guam

AM Stations	3
FM Stations	5
Commercial Stations	7
Non-commercial Stations	1
Religious	2
Adult Contemp	2
Contemporary Hit/Top-40	2
Rock/AOR	1
Variety/Diverse	1
News	1
Beautiful Music	1
Talk	1
Middle-of-the-Road (MOR)	1
Classical	1

Federated State of Micronesia

AM Stations	3
Commercial Stations	3
Variety/Diverse	3

Northern Mariana Islands

AM Stations	2
FM Stations	2
Commercial Stations	4
Variety/Diverse	2

U.S. Radio Formats by State and Possession

Contemporary Hit/Top-40 1
Foreign Language/Ethnic 1
Religious 1

Puerto Rico

AM Stations 65
FM Stations 41
Commercial Stations 99
Non-commercial Stations 7
Spanish 54
Contemporary Hit/Top-40 22
News 14
Adult Contemp 14
Middle-of-the-Road (MOR) 11
Religious 11
News/Talk 11
Beautiful Music 10
Oldies 10

Variety/Diverse 8
Talk 6
Educational 4
Other 2
Foreign Language/Ethnic 2
Jazz 1
Sports 1
Big Band 1
Classical 1
Rock/AOR 1

Virgin Islands

AM Stations 5
FM Stations 12
Commercial Stations 16
Non-commercial Stations 1
Middle-of-the-Road (MOR) 4
News 3

Variety/Diverse 3
Contemporary Hit/Top-40 3
Adult Contemp 2
Rock/AOR 2
Educational 2
Progressive 1
Jazz 1
Big Band 1
Spanish 1
Gospel 1
Religious 1
News/Talk 1
Oldies 1
Urban Contemporary 1
Classical 1
Black 1

Canadian Radio Formats by Province

Figures included here reflect only those stations that have provided format information.

Canada

AM Stations	367
FM Stations	296
Commercial Stations	601
Non-commercial Stations	62
Adult Contemp	204
Country	147
Middle-of-the-Road (MOR)	95
Variety/Diverse	85
Oldies	68
Contemporary Hit/Top-40	59
Rock/AOR	48
Talk	23
News/Talk	22
Classic Rock	22
News	19
Classical	16
Foreign Language/Ethnic	14
Beautiful Music	14
Educational	14
Public Affairs	13
Progressive	13
French	7
Sports	7
Jazz	6
Religious	6
Other	4
Big Band	3
Agriculture & Farm	3
New Age	2
Drama/Literature	2
Chinese	1
Gospel	1
Black	1
Disco	1
Nostalgia	1

Alberta

AM Stations	44
FM Stations	23
Commercial Stations	57
Non-commercial Stations	10
Country	28
Adult Contemp	13
Variety/Diverse	7
Educational	6
Oldies	6
Contemporary Hit/Top-40	5
Rock/AOR	5
News/Talk	5
Classical	4
Classic Rock	4
Middle-of-the-Road (MOR)	4
Religious	3
Jazz	2
News	2
Progressive	2
Foreign Language/Ethnic	1
Talk	1
Beautiful Music	1
Sports	1

British Columbia

AM Stations	63
FM Stations	37
Commercial Stations	94
Non-commercial Stations	6
Adult Contemp	36
Country	25
Middle-of-the-Road (MOR)	25
Oldies	10
Contemporary Hit/Top-40	6
Rock/AOR	5
News/Talk	5
News	4
Variety/Diverse	4
Public Affairs	3
Beautiful Music	3
Classic Rock	3
Big Band	2
Jazz	2
Progressive	2
Talk	2
Foreign Language/Ethnic	2
Religious	1
Drama/Literature	1
Classical	1
Chinese	1

Manitoba

AM Stations	18
FM Stations	9
Commercial Stations	25
Non-commercial Stations	2
Country	9
Variety/Diverse	6
Adult Contemp	6
Rock/AOR	3
Middle-of-the-Road (MOR)	3
Oldies	2
Foreign Language/Ethnic	1
Religious	1
Beautiful Music	1
Classic Rock	1
Contemporary Hit/Top-40	1
Classical	1
French	1
Agriculture & Farm	1

New Brunswick

AM Stations	15
FM Stations	13
Commercial Stations	25
Non-commercial Stations	3
Adult Contemp	14
Variety/Diverse	8
Country	7
Contemporary Hit/Top-40	5
Classic Rock	3
Middle-of-the-Road (MOR)	2
Oldies	2
News/Talk	1
Progressive	1

Newfoundland

AM Stations	26
FM Stations	17
Commercial Stations	37
Non-commercial Stations	6
Country	13
Adult Contemp	9
Rock/AOR	9
Variety/Diverse	4
Educational	4
Contemporary Hit/Top-40	3
News/Talk	3
Oldies	2
Middle-of-the-Road (MOR)	2
News	2
Progressive	1
Talk	1
Gospel	1
Classic Rock	1
Classical	1
French	1
Religious	1
Public Affairs	1

Northwest Territories

AM Stations	5
FM Stations	6
Commercial Stations	10
Non-commercial Stations	1
Variety/Diverse	7
Adult Contemp	3
Talk	1
News/Talk	1
Country	1
Middle-of-the-Road (MOR)	1
Foreign Language/Ethnic	1

Nova Scotia

AM Stations	17
FM Stations	15
Commercial Stations	32
Adult Contemp	14
Country	11
Oldies	5
Middle-of-the-Road (MOR)	4
Contemporary Hit/Top-40	4
Variety/Diverse	3
Rock/AOR	2
News	1

Canadian Radio Formats by Province

Public Affairs ... 1
Classic Rock ... 1

Ontario

AM Stations ... 89
FM Stations ... 100
Commercial Stations ... 173
Non-commercial Stations ... 16
Adult Contemp ... 62
Oldies ... 30
Country ... 29
Variety/Diverse ... 25
Contemporary Hit/Top-40 ... 14
Rock/AOR ... 14
Classical ... 7
Foreign Language/Ethnic ... 6
Progressive ... 6
Beautiful Music ... 6
Middle-of-the-Road (MOR) ... 5
Public Affairs ... 5
Classic Rock ... 5
Talk ... 5
Sports ... 4
News/Talk ... 4
Educational ... 3
News ... 3
Other ... 3
Jazz ... 2
Nostalgia ... 1
French ... 1
Black ... 1
New Age ... 1
Agriculture & Farm ... 1

Prince Edward Island

AM Stations ... 3
FM Stations ... 2
Commercial Stations ... 5
Country ... 2
Contemporary Hit/Top-40 ... 1
Oldies ... 1
Classic Rock ... 1
Adult Contemp ... 1
Talk ... 1

Quebec

AM Stations ... 63
FM Stations ... 61
Commercial Stations ... 112
Non-commercial Stations ... 12
Middle-of-the-Road (MOR) ... 47
Adult Contemp ... 36
Contemporary Hit/Top-40 ... 18
Variety/Diverse ... 16
Talk ... 11
Country ... 9
News ... 6
Rock/AOR ... 6
Oldies ... 5
French ... 4
Foreign Language/Ethnic ... 3
News/Talk ... 3
Public Affairs ... 2
Beautiful Music ... 2
Classical ... 2
Progressive ... 1
Big Band ... 1
Classic Rock ... 1
Disco ... 1
Other ... 1
Drama/Literature ... 1
New Age ... 1
Sports ... 1
Educational ... 1

Saskatchewan

AM Stations ... 21
FM Stations ... 10
Commercial Stations ... 26
Non-commercial Stations ... 5
Country ... 11
Adult Contemp ... 7
Variety/Diverse ... 5
Oldies ... 4
Classic Rock ... 2
Contemporary Hit/Top-40 ... 2
Middle-of-the-Road (MOR) ... 2
Rock/AOR ... 2
Public Affairs ... 1
Beautiful Music ... 1
Agriculture & Farm ... 1
News ... 1

Yukon Territory

AM Stations ... 2
FM Stations ... 1
Commercial Stations ... 2
Non-commercial Stations ... 1
Adult Contemp ... 2
Country ... 2
Talk ... 1
Rock/AOR ... 1
Oldies ... 1

U.S. and Canada Radio Programming Formats

	United States					Canada				
Format	Total	AM	FM	Com	Non	Tot	AM	FM	Com	Non
Adult Contemp	2134	661	1473	2065	69	203	123	80	198	5
Agriculture & Farm	95	64	31	95	0	3	3	0	3	0
American Indian	4	3	1	3	1	0	0	0	0	0
Arabic	1	1	0	1	0	0	0	0	0	0
Beautiful Music	329	243	86	157	204	39	14	2 12	13	1
Big Band	157	124	33	146	11	3	3	0	3	0
Black	162	107	55	132	30	1	0	1	1	0
Bluegrass	18	15	3	17	1	0	0	0	0	0
Blues	38	22	16	28	10	0	0	0	0	0
Children	12	10	2	11	1	0	0	0	0	0
Chinese	0	0	0	0	0	1	1	0	1	0
Classic Rock	378	48	330	339	39	22	12	10	21	1
Classical	448	17	431	52	396	16	2	14	9	7
Contemporary Hit/Top-40	657	2	575	571	86	59	38	21	57	2
Country	2727	1279	1448	2703	24	147	109	38	144	3
Disco	1	1	0	1	0	1	0	1	1	0
Drama/Literature	1	0	1	0	1	2	0	2	1	1
Educational	242	20	222	11	231	14	3	11	7	7
Filipino	1	1	0	1	0	0	0	0	0	0
Folk	11	1	10	2	9	0	0	0	0	0
Foreign Language/Ethnic	60	38	22	48	12	14	8	6	12	2
French	2	1	1	2	0	7	1	6	5	2
German	1	0	1	1	0	0	0	0	0	0
Gospel	361	283	78	325	36	1	1	0	0	1
Greek	5	5	0	4	1	0	0	0	0	0
Italian	1	1	0	1	0	0	0	0	0	0
Japanese	2	2	0	2	0	0	0	0	0	0
Jazz	377	27	350	74	303	6	1	5	1	5
Jewish	1	1	0	1	0	0	0	0	0	0
Korean	5	3	2	5	0	0	0	0	0	0
Middle-of-the-Road (MOR)	446	366	80	427	19	95	71	24	92	3
New Age	49	7	42	26	23	2	0	2	2	0
News	636	305	331	347	289	19	13	6	16	3
News/Talk	820	712	108	738	82	22	16	6	12	10
Nostalgia	93	82	11	92	1	1	1	0	1	0
Oldies	1004	525	479	991	13	68	58	10	67	1
Other	58	35	23	41	17	4	0	4	4	0
Polish	3	3	0	3	0	0	0	0	0	0
Polka	6	3	3	6	0	0	0	0	0	0
Portuguese	8	7	1	7	1	0	0	0	0	0
Progressive	288	14	274	40	248	13	0	13	9	4
Public Affairs	59	16	43	16	43	13	3	10	10	3
Reggae	3	0	3	1	2	0	0	0	0	0
Religious	1178	591	587	777	401	6	5	1	5	1
Rock/AOR	623	59	564	456	167	47	3	44	44	3
Spanish	373	268	105	343	30	0	0	0	0	0
Sports	283	250	33	281	2	6	6	0	6	0
Talk	461	380	81	421	40	23	14	9	17	6
Urban Contemporary	260	88	172	220	40	0	0	0	0	0
Variety/Diverse	498	109	389	135	363	85	33	52	50	35

Broadcasting & Cable Yearbook 1994

Programming on Radio Stations in the U.S.

Adult Contemporary
Includes station formats Adult Rock and Light Rock.

KFQD(AM) Anchorage AK
KXDZ(FM) Anchorage AK
KYMG(FM) Anchorage AK
KLAM(AM) Cordova AK
*KDLG(AM) Dillingham AK
KAKQ-FM Fairbanks AK
*KHNS(FM) Haines AK
KGTL(AM) Homer AK
KWVV-FM Homer AK
KINY(AM) Juneau AK
KJNO(AM) Juneau AK
KJJZ(FM) Kodiak AK
KVOK(AM) Kodiak AK
KABN(AM) Long Island AK
KICY(AM) Nome AK
KICY-FM Nome AK
KSRM(AM) Soldotna AK
KVAK(AM) Valdez AK
KMBQ(FM) Wasilla AK
WCRQ-FM Arab AL
WYDH(FM) Atmore AL
WFMI(FM) Bay Minette AL
WDJC(FM) Birmingham AL
*WJSR(FM) Birmingham AL
WMJJ(FM) Birmingham AL
WRHY(FM) Centre AL
WDLT(FM) Chickasaw AL
WFMH(AM) Cullman AL
*WDVI(FM) Dadeville AL
WZLM(FM) Dadeville AL
WOOF-FM Dothan AL
WKMX(FM) Enterprise AL
WDMT(FM) Eufaula AL
WULA-FM Eufaula AL
WQLT(FM) Florence AL
WXFL(FM) Florence AL
WGAD(AM) Gadsden AL
WKXN(FM) Greenville AL
WGSV(AM) Guntersville AL
WHRT(AM) Hartselle AL
WAHR(FM) Huntsville AL
WZBQ-FM Jasper AL
WZPQ(FM) Jasper AL
*WBHY-FM Mobile AL
WKRG-FM Mobile AL
WYNI(AM) Monroeville AL
WLNE-FM Montgomery AL
WSYA(AM) Montgomery AL
WSYA-FM Montgomery AL
WCRL(AM) Oneonta AL
WMXA(FM) Opelika AL
WVOK(FM) Oxford AL
WOZK(FM) Ozark AL
WGSY(FM) Phenix City AL
WPID(AM) Piedmont AL
WALX(FM) Selma AL
WMRK(FM) Selma AL
WAWV(FM) Sylacauga AL
WSSY-FM Talladega AL
WACQ(AM) Tallassee AL
WFFX(FM) Tuscaloosa AL
WVNA-FM Tuscumbia AL
WQRX(AM) Valley Head AL
WJEC(FM) Vernon AL
KDEL-FM Arkadelphia AR
KHSP-FM Ashdown AR
KPIK(FM) Beebe AR
KBRI(AM) Brinkley AR
KXIO(FM) Clarksville AR
KCON(AM) Conway AR
KBKG(FM) Corning AR
KLBQ(FM) El Dorado AR
KEZA(FM) Fayetteville AR
KXJK(AM) Forrest City AR
KCRI-FM Helena AR
KLAZ(FM) Hot Springs AR
KLXQ(FM) Hot Springs AR
KHLT(FM) Little Rock AR
KURB(AM) Little Rock AR
KURB-FM Little Rock AR
KYFX(FM) Little Rock AR
KVMA-FM Magnolia AR
KHBM(AM) Monticello AR
KHBM-FM Monticello AR
KKTZ(FM) Mountain Home AR
KNAS(FM) Nashville AR
KWLT(FM) North Crossett AR
KDXY(FM) Paragould AR
KOTN(AM) Pine Bluff AR
KPOC(AM) Pocahontas AR
KPOC-FM Pocahontas AR
KEZQ(AM) Sheridan AR
KXDX(FM) Stuttgart AR
KTWN-FM Texarkana AR
KLSZ-FM Van Buren AR
KSUD(AM) West Memphis AR
KWYN-FM Wynne AR
KSBS-FM Pago Pago AS
KCUZ(AM) Clifton AZ
KJJJ(FM) Clifton AZ
KZGL(FM) Cottonwood AZ
KKRK(FM) Douglas AZ
KCLS(AM) Flagstaff AZ
KMGN(FM) Flagstaff AZ
KRXS-FM Globe AZ
KEKO(FM) Green Valley AZ

KZZZ(FM) Kingman AZ
KZUL-FM Lake Havasu City AZ
KVRY(FM) Mesa AZ
KIKO(AM) Miami AZ
KLCR(FM) Nogales AZ
KXAZ(FM) Page AZ
KESZ(FM) Phoenix AZ
KKLT(FM) Phoenix AZ
KSUN(AM) Phoenix AZ
KYOT(AM) Phoenix AZ
KIHX-FM Prescott Valley AZ
KWDS(AM) Prescott Valley AZ
KQST(AM) Sedona AZ
KRFM(FM) Show Low AZ
KVWM(AM) Show Low AZ
KVWM-FM Show Low AZ
KZMK(FM) Sierra Vista AZ
KFMM(FM) Thatcher AZ
KKLD(FM) Tucson AZ
KRDS-FM Wickenburg AZ
KEZC(AM) Yuma AZ
KYXI(FM) Yuma AZ
KZXY-FM Apple Valley CA
KCHT(FM) Bakersfield CA
KHIS(AM) Bakersfield CA
KDUC(FM) Barstow CA
KIQQ(AM) Barstow CA
KBLX(AM) Berkeley CA
KBLX(FM) Berkeley CA
KJMB(FM) Blythe CA
*KBPK(FM) Buena Park CA
KARZ(FM) Burney CA
KQVO(FM) Calexico CA
KKOS(FM) Carlsbad CA
KXDC-FM Carmel CA
KSBL(FM) Carpinteria CA
KNNN(FM) Central Valley CA
KCMT(FM) Chester CA
KPAY(AM) Chico CA
KPPL(FM) Colusa CA
KCRE-FM Crescent City CA
KFVR(FM) Crescent City CA
KQBR(FM) Davis CA
KAMP(AM) El Centro CA
KXO(AM) El Centro CA
KXO-FM El Centro CA
KSPA(AM) Escondido CA
KHWY(FM) Essex CA
KFMI(FM) Eureka CA
KRED-FM Eureka CA
KWSW(AM) Eureka CA
KAJK-FM Ferndale CA
KSAY(FM) Fort Bragg CA
KAJK(FM) Fortuna CA
KEZL(FM) Fowler CA
KBRG(FM) Fremont CA
KSXY(FM) Fresno CA
KTHT(FM) Fresno CA
KLIT(FM) Glendale CA
KMGQ(FM) Goleta CA
KATY-FM Idyllwild CA
KMXX(FM) Imperial CA
KCMJ(FM) Indio CA
KACE(FM) Inglewood CA
KNGT(FM) Jackson CA
KRAJ(FM) Johannesburg CA
KBNN(FM) Julian CA
KRKC-FM King City CA
KNTI(FM) Lakeport CA
KXBX-FM Lakeport CA
KGMX(FM) Lancaster CA
KIQQ-FM Lenwood CA
KKIQ(FM) Livermore CA
KNTO(FM) Livingston CA
KBOX-FM Lompoc CA
KTME(AM) Lompoc CA
KBIG(FM) Los Angeles CA
KOST(FM) Los Angeles CA
KTWV(FM) Los Angeles CA
KXEZ(FM) Los Angeles CA
KYSR(FM) Los Angeles CA
KHTN(FM) Los Banos CA
KSTT-FM Los Osos-Baywood Park CA
KXMX(FM) Madera CA
KMMT(FM) Mammoth Lakes CA
KMFB(FM) Mendocino CA
KJSN(FM) Modesto CA
KWAV(FM) Monterey CA
KWWV(FM) Morro Bay CA
KEDY(FM) Mount Shasta CA
KWSD(AM) Mount Shasta CA
KHYZ(FM) Mountain Pass CA
KWAZ(FM) Needles CA
KAAT(FM) Oakhurst CA
KTNS(AM) Oakhurst CA
KLLY(FM) Oildale CA
KKUR(FM) Ojai CA
KORV(AM) Oroville CA
KOCN(FM) Pacific Grove CA
KEZN(FM) Palm Desert CA
KPLM(FM) Palm Springs CA
KZZP(FM) Paradise CA
KOSO(FM) Patterson CA
KTOB(AM) Petaluma CA
KATD(FM) Pittsburg CA
KIOO(FM) Porterville CA
KTIP(AM) Porterville CA
KQNC(FM) Quincy CA
KZAP(FM) Red Bluff CA

KSHA(FM) Redding CA
*KUOR-FM Redlands CA
KZIQ-FM Ridgecrest CA
KQEX(FM) Rohnerville CA
KGBY(FM) Sacramento CA
KXOA-FM Sacramento CA
KYMX(FM) Sacramento CA
KMEN(AM) San Bernardino CA
KBZS(FM) San Diego CA
KFMB(AM) San Diego CA
KFMB-FM San Diego CA
KIFM(FM) San Diego CA
KJQY(FM) San Diego CA
KYXY(FM) San Diego CA
KMGX(FM) San Fernando CA
KIOI(FM) San Francisco CA
KKSF(FM) San Francisco CA
KOIT(AM) San Francisco CA
KOIT-FM San Francisco CA
KSRY(FM) San Francisco CA
KBAY(FM) San Jose CA
KEZR(FM) San Jose CA
KKJG(FM) San Luis Obispo CA
KTID(AM) San Rafael CA
KTID-FM San Rafael CA
KARA(FM) Santa Clara CA
KSRI(FM) Santa Cruz CA
KTAP(AM) Santa Maria CA
KXFM(FM) Santa Maria CA
KAJZ(FM) Santa Monica CA
KZST(FM) Santa Rosa CA
KSSJ(FM) Shingle Springs CA
KCFM(FM) Shingletown CA
KSYV(FM) Solvang CA
KZSQ-FM Sonora CA
KOWL(AM) South Lake Tahoe CA
KRLT(FM) South Lake Tahoe CA
KTHO(AM) South Lake Tahoe CA
KVYN(FM) St. Helena CA
KJOY(FM) Stockton CA
*KRTM(FM) Temecula CA
KNJO(FM) Thousand Oaks CA
KKBN(FM) Twain Harte CA
KCDZ(FM) Twentynine Palms CA
KWNE(FM) Ukiah CA
KUIC(FM) Vacaville CA
KAXX(FM) Ventura CA
KBBY(AM) Ventura CA
KBBY-FM Ventura CA
KCIN(AM) Victorville CA
KVVQ-FM Victorville CA
KSEQ(FM) Visalia CA
KMQA-FM West Covina CA
KRXV(FM) Yermo CA
KYRE(FM) Yreka CA
KXCL(FM) Yuba City CA
KALQ-FM Alamosa CO
KBOL(AM) Boulder CO
KNAB-FM Burlington CO
KRDO-FM Colorado Springs CO
KRAI-FM Craig CO
KKLY(FM) Delta CO
KHOW(AM) Denver CO
KHOW-FM Denver CO
KLZ(AM) Denver CO
KMJI(FM) Denver CO
KOSI(FM) Denver CO
KIQX(FM) Durango CO
KQMT(FM) Eagle CO
KRKI(AM) Estes Park CO
*KCSU-FM Fort Collins CO
KBIQ(FM) Fountain CO
KYSL(FM) Frisco CO
KQIX-FM Grand Junction CO
KRKM(FM) Kremmling CO
KBZZ(AM) La Junta CO
KRMH-FM Leadville CO
*KCDC(FM) Longmont CO
KLOV(AM) Loveland CO
KTRR(FM) Loveland CO
KSLV-FM Monte Vista CO
KFMU-FM Oak Creek CO
KURA(FM) Ouray CO
KFEL(AM) Pueblo CO
KVUU(FM) Pueblo CO
KYZX(FM) Pueblo CO
KVRH(FM) Salida CO
KVRH-FM Salida CO
KBCR-FM Steamboat Springs CO
KSBT(FM) Steamboat Springs CO
KNNG-FM Sterling CO
KPMX(FM) Sterling CO
KSKE(AM) Vail CO
KSKE-FM Vail CO
KKLI(FM) Widefield CO
KATR(AM) Wray CO
KRDZ(AM) Wray CO
WADS(AM) Ansonia CT
WEZN(FM) Bridgeport CT
WICC(AM) Bridgeport CT
WDAQ(FM) Danbury CT
WLAD(AM) Danbury CT
WGCH(AM) Greenwich CT
WZMX(FM) Hartford CT
WBMW(FM) Ledyard CT
WZBG(FM) Litchfield CT
WNTY(AM) New Britain CT
WELI(AM) New Haven CT
WTYD(AM) New London CT
WLIS(AM) Old Saybrook CT

WINY(AM) Putnam CT
WQQQ(FM) Sharon CT
WNTY(AM) Southington CT
WSTC(AM) Stamford CT
WSNG(AM) Torrington CT
WYSR(FM) Waterbury CT
WEBE(FM) Westport CT
WILI(AM) Willimantic CT
WASH(FM) Washington DC
WRQX(FM) Washington DC
WYCB(AM) Washington DC
WDNO(FM) Laurel DE
WAFL(FM) Milford DE
WXPZ(FM) Milford DE
WGMD(FM) Rehoboth Beach DE
WECY(AM) Seaford DE
WECY-FM Seaford DE
WJBR(AM) Wilmington DE
WJBR-FM Wilmington DE
WSTW(FM) Wilmington DE
WOYS(FM) Apalachicola FL
WWUS(FM) Big Pine Key FL
WPHK(FM) Blountstown FL
WTBB(FM) Bonifay FL
WMTX-FM Clearwater FL
WWHL(FM) Cocoa FL
WKTK(FM) Crystal River FL
WBSB(FM) Dade City FL
WCFB(FM) Daytona Beach FL
WLGH(FM) DeFuniak Springs FL
WTPX(FM) Fort Lauderdale FL
WINK-FM Fort Myers FL
WSUV(FM) Fort Myers Villas FL
WIRA(AM) Fort Pierce FL
*WPSM(FM) Fort Walton Beach FL
WMLO(FM) Havana FL
WCMQ-FM Hialeah FL
WLVU-FM Holiday FL
*WAPN(FM) Holly Hill FL
WISP(FM) Holmes Beach FL
WXCV(FM) Homosassa Springs FL
WEJZ(FM) Jacksonville FL
WIVY-FM Jacksonville FL
WZMQ(FM) Key Largo FL
WIIS(FM) Key West FL
*WJIR(FM) Key West FL
WKRY(FM) Key West FL
WHKX(FM) Lafayette FL
WNFB(FM) Lake City FL
*WCIE-FM Lakeland FL
WAVK(FM) Marathon FL
WGMX(FM) Marathon FL
WAVV(FM) Marco FL
WEBZ(FM) Mexico Beach FL
WFLC(FM) Miami FL
WLYF(FM) Miami FL
WQBA-FM Miami FL
WLVE(FM) Miami Beach FL
WCMQ(FM) Miami Springs FL
WMGF(FM) Mount Dora FL
WCVU(FM) Naples FL
WSGL(FM) Naples FL
*WLPJ-FM New Port Richey FL
WMMZ(FM) Ocala FL
WDBO(AM) Orlando FL
WMMO(FM) Orlando FL
WOMX(AM) Orlando FL
WOMX-FM Orlando FL
WRMF(FM) Palm Beach FL
*WCNO(FM) Palm City FL
WCOA(AM) Pensacola FL
WMEZ(FM) Pensacola FL
WFKZ(FM) Plantation Key FL
WMTO(FM) Port St. Joe FL
WIKX(FM) Punta Gorda FL
WOLL(FM) Riviera Beach FL
WWAV(FM) Santa Rosa Beach FL
WHPT(FM) Sarasota FL
WJCM(AM) Sebring FL
WRBA(FM) Springfield FL
WFOY(AM) St. Augustine FL
WSOS(FM) St. Augustine FL
WSTF(FM) St. Augustine FL
WRBQ(AM) St. Petersburg FL
WRMD(FM) St. Petersburg FL
WRXB(AM) St. Petersburg Beach FL
WEAG(AM) Starke FL
WSTU(AM) Stuart FL
WBGM-FM Tallahassee FL
WHBT(FM) Tallahassee FL
WUMX(FM) Tallahassee FL
WAMA(AM) Tampa FL
WDAE(FM) Tampa FL
WUSA-FM Tampa FL
WWRM(FM) Tampa FL
WEAT-FM West Palm Beach FL
WGPC(AM) Albany GA
WGPC-FM Albany GA
WULF(AM) Alma GA
WFFM(AM) Ashburn GA
WRFC(AM) Athens GA
WPCH(FM) Atlanta GA
WQXI(AM) Atlanta GA
WSB-FM Atlanta GA
WZNY(FM) Augusta GA
WJAD(FM) Bainbridge GA
WSLE(FM) Cairo GA
WEBS(AM) Calhoun GA
WMJE(FM) Clarkesville GA

WQXI(FM) Clayton GA
WCGX(FM) Cleveland GA
WGMG(FM) Crawford GA
WBLJ(AM) Dalton GA
WXMK(FM) Dock Junction GA
WGMK(FM) Donalsonville GA
WDMG(AM) Douglas GA
WOKA(AM) Douglas GA
WKKZ(FM) Dublin GA
WMLT(AM) Dublin GA
WBHB(AM) Fitzgerald GA
WVVY(FM) Fort Valley GA
WGGA(AM) Gainesville GA
WKIG-FM Glennville GA
WDDK(FM) Greensboro GA
WKEU(AM) Griffin GA
WSHF(AM) Hahira GA
WQSY(FM) Hawkinsville GA
WEIZ(FM) Hogansville GA
WJGA-FM Jackson GA
WIFO-FM Jesup GA
WPEZ(FM) Macon GA
WFOM(AM) Marietta GA
WHCG(FM) Metter GA
WMAC(AM) Metter GA
WMVG(FM) Milledgeville GA
WMGA(AM) Moultrie GA
WKZD(AM) Murrayville GA
WJYF(FM) Nashville GA
WMKJ(FM) Newnan GA
WJEP(AM) Ochlocknee GA
WPGA-FM Perry GA
WSTI-FM Quitman GA
WRHQ(FM) Richmond Hill GA
WKCX(FM) Rome GA
WQTU(FM) Rome GA
WLMX-FM Rossville GA
WAEV(FM) Savannah GA
WIZA(AM) Savannah GA
WSTR(FM) Smyrna GA
WMOG-FM St. Simons Island GA
WMCD(FM) Statesboro GA
WVYF(FM) Sylvester GA
WTWA(AM) Thomson GA
WLET-FM Toccoa GA
WBDX(FM) Trenton GA
WATG(FM) Trion GA
WQPW(FM) Valdosta GA
WTCQ(FM) Vidalia GA
WRCC-FM Warner Robins GA
WHFX(FM) Waycross GA
WDBN(FM) Wrightsville GA
KSTO(FM) Agana GU
KUAM(AM) Agana GU
KUAI(AM) Eleele HI
KFSH(FM) Hilo HI
KKBG(FM) Hilo HI
KPVS(FM) Hilo HI
KWXX-FM Hilo HI
KISA(AM) Honolulu HI
KSSK(AM) Honolulu HI
KNUI(FM) Kahului HI
KRTR-FM Kailua HI
KKON(AM) Kealakekua HI
KLHI-FM Lahaina HI
KONI(FM) Lanai City HI
KFMN(FM) Lihue HI
KMVI-FM Pukalani HI
KMVI(AM) Wailuku HI
KSSK-FM Waipahu HI
KLGA(AM) Algona IA
KEZT(FM) Ames IA
KSKB(FM) Brooklyn IA
KBUR(AM) Burlington IA
KGRS(FM) Burlington IA
KKMI(FM) Burlington IA
KCIM(AM) Carroll IA
WMT-FM Cedar Rapids IA
KCHA(AM) Charles City IA
KCHA-FM Charles City IA
KLKK(FM) Clear Lake IA
KCLN-FM Clinton IA
KMXG(FM) Clinton IA
KROS(AM) Clinton IA
KCZQ(FM) Cresco IA
KRVR(FM) Davenport IA
KRDI-FM Decorah IA
KDSN(AM) Denison IA
KDSN-FM Denison IA
KLYF(FM) Des Moines IA
KATF(FM) Dubuque IA
WDBQ(AM) Dubuque IA
KKSI(FM) Eddyville IA
KDAO-FM Eldora IA
KADR(AM) Elkader IA
KILR(AM) Estherville IA
KILR-FM Estherville IA
KIOW(FM) Forest City IA
KKEZ(FM) Fort Dodge IA
KBKB(AM) Fort Madison IA
KBKB-FM Fort Madison IA
KLMJ(FM) Hampton IA
KNOD(FM) Harlan IA
KQMG(AM) Independence IA
KCJJ(AM) Iowa City IA
KIFG(FM) Iowa Falls IA
KIFG-FM Iowa Falls IA
KLSN(FM) Jefferson IA
KOKX(FM) Keokuk IA
KNIA(AM) Knoxville IA

Broadcasting & Cable Yearbook 1994
B-543

Programming on Radio Stations in the U.S.

KRLS(FM) Knoxville IA
KKMA(FM) Le Mars IA
KLEM(AM) Le Mars IA
KMCH(FM) Manchester IA
KDAO(AM) Marshalltown IA
KLSS-FM Mason City IA
KWPC(AM) Muscatine IA
KCZE(FM) New Hampton IA
KOEL(AM) Oelwein IA
KCZY(FM) Osage IA
*KIGC(FM) Oskaloosa IA
KTWA(FM) Ottumwa IA
KTSB(FM) Sioux Center IA
KGLI(FM) Sioux City IA
KSCJ(AM) Sioux City IA
KIGL(FM) Spencer IA
KUOO(FM) Spirit Lake IA
KAYL-FM Storm Lake IA
KTLB(FM) Twin Lakes IA
KCII(AM) Washington IA
KCII-FM Washington IA
KWAY-FM Waverly IA
KQWC(AM) Webster City IA
KQWC-FM Webster City IA
KLCE(FM) Blackfoot ID
KBOI(AM) Boise ID
KBFI(AM) Bonners Ferry ID
KCID(AM) Caldwell ID
KVNI(AM) Coeur d'Alene ID
KCIX(FM) Garden City ID
KKCH-FM Hayden ID
KID-FM Idaho Falls ID
KATW(FM) Lewiston ID
KMCL-FM McCall ID
KFXD-FM Nampa ID
KLER(AM) Orofino ID
KSEI(AM) Pocatello ID
KADQ(FM) Rexburg ID
KSRA-FM Salmon ID
KPND(FM) Sandpoint ID
KBRV(AM) Soda Springs ID
KFIS(FM) Soda Springs ID
KSKI-FM Sun Valley ID
KTFI(AM) Twin Falls ID
KATZ-FM Alton IL
WCBR-FM Arlington Heights IL
WBIG(AM) Aurora IL
WYSY-FM Aurora IL
WRMS(AM) Beardstown IL
WCBH(FM) Casey IL
WHQQ(FM) Charleston IL
WKQX(FM) Chicago IL
WLIT-FM Chicago IL
WNUA(FM) Chicago IL
WPNT-FM Chicago IL
WCFJ(AM) Chicago Heights IL
WCGO(AM) Chicago Heights IL
WDNL(FM) Danville IL
WDKB(FM) De Kalb IL
WDZ(AM) Decatur IL
WSOY-FM Decatur IL
WIXN(AM) Dixon IL
WDQN(AM) DuQuoin IL
WEBQ-FM Eldorado IL
WJKL(FM) Elgin IL
WFIW-FM Fairfield IL
WNOI(FM) Flora IL
WFPS(FM) Freeport IL
WFRL(AM) Freeport IL
WGBQ(FM) Galesburg IL
WGEN(AM) Geneseo IL
WGEN-FM Geneseo IL
WFXW(AM) Geneva IL
WMCW(AM) Harvard IL
WINU(AM) Highland IL
WLDS(AM) Jacksonville IL
WJOL(AM) Joliet IL
WJTW(FM) Joliet IL
WKAN(AM) Kankakee IL
WJRE(FM) Kewanee IL
WKEI(AM) Kewanee IL
WAJK(FM) La Salle IL
WAKO(AM) Lawrenceville IL
WAKO-FM Lawrenceville IL
WESZ(FM) Lincoln IL
WSMI-FM Litchfield IL
*WLKL(FM) Mattoon IL
WREZ(FM) Metropolis IL
WMOI(FM) Monmouth IL
WCSJ(AM) Morris IL
WZZT(FM) Morrison IL
WMIX(AM) Mt. Vernon IL
WXFM(FM) Mt. Zion IL
WIKK(FM) Newton IL
WVAZ(FM) Oak Park IL
WSEI(FM) Olney IL
WCMY(AM) Ottawa IL
WRKX(FM) Ottawa IL
WGLO(FM) Pekin IL
WIRL(AM) Peoria IL
WMBD(AM) Peoria IL
WSWT(FM) Peoria IL
WSPY(FM) Plano IL
WLLT(FM) Polo IL
WJEZ(FM) Pontiac IL
WZOE-FM Princeton IL
*WGCA-FM Quincy IL
WTAD(AM) Quincy IL
WLTM(FM) Rantoul IL
WTAY(AM) Robinson IL
WTAY-FM Robinson IL
WRWC(FM) Rockton IL
WJBD(AM) Salem IL
WJBD-FM Salem IL
WEJT(FM) Shelbyville IL
WTMX(FM) Skokie IL
WBEL(AM) South Beloit IL
WHCO(AM) Sparta IL
WNNS(FM) Springfield IL
WSSQ(FM) Sterling IL
WGFA(AM) Watseka IL
WGFA-FM Watseka IL
WDND(FM) Wilmington IL
WXXP(FM) Anderson IN
*WEAX(FM) Angola IN
WLKI(FM) Angola IN
WBQR(FM) Attica IN
WBWB(FM) Bloomington IN
WNUY(FM) Bluffton IN
WBNL-FM Boonville IN
WCDV(FM) Covington IN
WIMC(FM) Crawfordsville IN
WWJY(FM) Crown Point IN
WIBN(FM) Earl Park IN
WLTA(FM) Elkhart IN
WTRC(AM) Elkhart IN
WIKY-FM Evansville IN
WVHI(AM) Evansville IN
WAJI(FM) Fort Wayne IN
WFWI(FM) Fort Wayne IN
WMEE(FM) Fort Wayne IN
WOWO(AM) Fort Wayne IN
WSHW(FM) Frankfort IN
WKAM(AM) Goshen IN
WJNZ(FM) Greencastle IN
WZPL(FM) Greenfield IN
WRZQ-FM Greensburg IN
WWWO(FM) Hartford City IN
WTPI(FM) Indianapolis IN
WITZ(AM) Jasper IN
WITZ-FM Jasper IN
WZWZ(FM) Kokomo IN
WASK(AM) Lafayette IN
WCFY(AM) Lafayette IN
WLNB(FM) Ligonier IN
WLHM(FM) Logansport IN
WZVN(FM) Lowell IN
WORX(AM) Madison IN
WORX-FM Madison IN
WBAT(AM) Marion IN
WGOM(AM) Marion IN
WIMS(AM) Michigan City IN
WLBC(AM) Muncie IN
WLBC-FM Muncie IN
*WWDS(FM) Muncie IN
WLRX(FM) Nappanee IN
WMDH(AM) New Castle IN
WUME-FM Paoli IN
WPGW(AM) Portland IN
WRAY(AM) Princeton IN
WRAY-FM Princeton IN
WLQI(FM) Rensselaer IN
WFMG(FM) Richmond IN
WROI(FM) Rochester IN
WRCR(FM) Rushville IN
WENS(FM) Shelbyville IN
WNSN(FM) South Bend IN
WLZQ(FM) South Whitley IN
WAWC(FM) Syracuse IN
WTCJ(AM) Tell City IN
WJSH(AM) Terre Haute IN
WMGI(FM) Terre Haute IN
WNWI(AM) Valparaiso IN
WZDM(FM) Vincennes IN
WAYT(AM) Wabash IN
WKUZ(FM) Wabash IN
WWIP(FM) Wabash IN
WRSW-FM Warsaw IN
WAMW-FM Washington IN
WGLM(FM) West Lafayette IN
WZZY(FM) Winchester IN
KERE(AM) Atchison KS
KLLS(FM) Augusta KS
KVSV(AM) Beloit KS
KSNP(FM) Burlington KS
KKOY(AM) Chanute KS
KUSN(FM) Coffeyville KS
KQLS(FM) Colby KS
KRZZ-FM Derby KS
KOLS(FM) Dodge City KS
KTLI(FM) El Dorado KS
KVOE(AM) Emporia KS
KKJQ(FM) Garden City KS
KLOE(AM) Goodland KS
KZLS(FM) Great Bend KS
KJLS(FM) Hays KS
KXLK(FM) Haysville KS
KSKU(FM) Hutchinson KS
KIKS-FM Iola KS
KUDL(FM) Kansas City KS
KANS(AM) Larned KS
KLWN(AM) Lawrence KS
KSCB-FM Liberal KS
KMAN(AM) Manhattan KS
KBBE(FM) McPherson KS
KNGL(AM) McPherson KS
KBLS(FM) North Fort Riley KS
KQLA(FM) Ogden KS
KZTO(FM) Ottawa KS
KLKC(AM) Parsons KS
KLKC-FM Parsons KS
KCAY(FM) Russell KS
KRSL(AM) Russell KS
KSAL(AM) Salina KS
KMAJ-FM Topeka KS
KEYN-FM Wichita KS
KRBB(FM) Wichita KS
KKLE(AM) Winfield KS
WOKH(FM) Bardstown KY
WMJM(FM) Bowling Green KY
WKDZ-FM Cadiz KY
WCKQ(FM) Campbellsville KY
WCMI-FM Catlettsburg KY
WHHT(FM) Cave City KY
WCTT-FM Corbin KY
WHIR(AM) Danville KY
WQXE(FM) Elizabethtown KY
WPKE-FM Elkhorn City KY
WCVQ(FM) Fort Campbell KY
WFKY(AM) Frankfort KY
WKED-FM Frankfort KY
WKYW(FM) Frankfort KY
WWWQ(FM) Glasgow KY
WUGO(FM) Grayson KY
WXBC(FM) Hardinsburg KY
WHLN(AM) Harlan KY
WKCB(AM) Hindman KY
WKCB-FM Hindman KY
WJSN-FM Jackson KY
WKYL(FM) Lawrenceburg KY
WLBN(AM) Lebanon KY
WKHG(FM) Leitchfield KY
WMXL(FM) Lexington KY
WVLK(AM) Lexington KY
WFTG(AM) London KY
WSAC(FM) Louisa KY
WAVG(AM) Louisville KY
WHAS(AM) Louisville KY
WHKW(FM) Louisville KY
WLRS(FM) Louisville KY
WVEZ-FM Louisville KY
WTTL-FM Madisonville KY
WFXY(AM) Middlesboro KY
WKYM(FM) Monticello KY
WLBQ(AM) Morgantown KY
WMST(AM) Mt. Sterling KY
WBLN-FM Murray KY
WKYX(AM) Paducah KY
WKLW(AM) Paintsville KY
WKLW-FM Paintsville KY
WGKS(FM) Paris KY
WPKE(AM) Pikeville KY
*WOAL-FM Pippa Passes KY
WQHY(FM) Prestonsburg KY
WPKY(AM) Princeton KY
WPKY-FM Princeton KY
WEKY(AM) Richmond KY
WRUS(AM) Russellville KY
WBLG(FM) Smiths Grove KY
WLLK(FM) Somerset KY
WRZI(FM) Vine Grove KY
KSYL(AM) Alexandria LA
KMEZ(FM) Belle Chasse LA
KRVE(FM) Brusly LA
KDLA(AM) De Ridder LA
KWJM(FM) Farmerville LA
KFNV-FM Ferriday LA
KFMV(FM) Franklin LA
KFRA(AM) Franklin LA
KLEB-FM Galliano LA
KTDY(FM) Lafayette LA
KHLA(FM) Lake Charles LA
KASO-FM Minden LA
KMYY(FM) Monroe LA
KMRC(AM) Morgan City LA
KZBL(FM) Natchitoches LA
KANE(AM) New Iberia LA
WLMG(FM) New Orleans LA
KOGM(FM) Opelousas LA
KITT(FM) Shreveport LA
KVKI-FM Shreveport LA
WLTS-FM Slidell LA
KVPI-FM Ville Platte LA
WCAT-FM Athol MA
WQRC(FM) Barnstable MA
WNSH(AM) Beverly MA
WBMX(FM) Boston MA
WMEX(AM) Boston MA
WMJX(FM) Boston MA
WBET(AM) Brockton MA
WFHN(FM) Fairhaven MA
WEIM(AM) Fitchburg MA
WXLO-FM Fitchburg MA
WGAW(AM) Gardner MA
WAMQ(FM) Great Barrington MA
WSBS(AM) Great Barrington MA
WGAM(AM) Greenfield MA
WHAI(AM) Greenfield MA
WHAI-FM Greenfield MA
WHAV(AM) Haverhill MA
WLYT(FM) Haverhill MA
WCOD-FM Hyannis MA
WSSH-FM Lowell MA
WATD-FM Marshfield MA
WMRC(AM) Milford MA
WRZE(FM) Nantucket MA
WNBP(AM) Newburyport MA
WNAW(AM) North Adams MA
WHMP(AM) Northampton MA
WBRK(AM) Pittsfield MA
WUPE(FM) Pittsfield MA
WESX(AM) Salem MA
*WBSL-FM Sheffield MA
WESO(AM) Southbridge MA
WHYN(AM) Springfield MA
WHYN-FM Springfield MA
WMAS-FM Springfield MA
WSNE(FM) Taunton MA
WINQ(FM) Winchendon MA
WSRS(FM) Worcester MA
WTAG(AM) Worcester MA
WAMD(AM) Aberdeen MD
WNAV(AM) Annapolis MD
WYRE(AM) Annapolis MD
WJFK(AM) Baltimore MD
WLIF-FM Baltimore MD
WVRT(FM) Baltimore MD
WWMX(FM) Baltimore MD
WMMJ(FM) Bethesda MD
WCEM-FM Cambridge MD
WCBC(AM) Cumberland MD
WCEI-FM Easton MD
WSER(AM) Elkton MD
WWIN-FM Glen Burnie MD
WJEJ(AM) Hagerstown MD
WMOM(AM) La Plata MD
WSMD(FM) Mechanicsville MD
WAFY(FM) Middletown MD
WKHJ(FM) Mountain Lake Park MD
WQHQ(FM) Ocean City-Salisbury MD
WMYJ(FM) Pocomoke City MD
WCTN(AM) Potomac-Cabin John MD
WJDY(AM) Salisbury MD
*WTMD(FM) Towson MD
WTTR(AM) Westminster MD
*WKHS(FM) Worton MD
WKZS(FM) Auburn ME
WEZQ(FM) Bangor ME
WCLZ-FM Brunswick ME
WQDY(AM) Calais ME
WQDY-FM Calais ME
WQSS(FM) Camden ME
WCXU(FM) Caribou ME
WDME-FM Dover-Foxcroft ME
WKSQ(FM) Ellsworth ME
WKTJ-FM Farmington ME
WLVC(AM) Fort Kent ME
WABK(AM) Gardiner ME
WABK-FM Gardiner ME
WHGS(AM) Houlton ME
WHOU-FM Houlton ME
WZOU(AM) Lewiston ME
WCXX(FM) Madawaska ME
WSJR(AM) Madawaska ME
WSYY(AM) Millinocket ME
WSYY-FM Millinocket ME
WPBC(FM) Pittsfield ME
WCSO(FM) Portland ME
WGAN(AM) Portland ME
WMGX(FM) Portland ME
WEBB(FM) Waterville ME
WTVL(AM) Waterville ME
WLEN(FM) Adrian MI
WALM(AM) Albion MI
WHSB(FM) Alpena MI
WTKA(AM) Ann Arbor MI
WLEW-FM Bad Axe MI
WMRX-FM Beaverton MI
WHFB-FM Benton Harbor MI
WBRN-FM Big Rapids MI
WKJF(AM) Cadillac MI
WKJF-FM Cadillac MI
WWLZ(FM) Cadillac MI
WIDL(FM) Caro MI
WCFX(FM) Clare MI
WTVB(AM) Coldwater MI
WNIC(FM) Dearborn MI
WKQI(FM) Detroit MI
WLTI(FM) Detroit MI
WXLA(AM) Dimondale MI
WFMK(FM) East Lansing MI
WDBC(AM) Escanaba MI
WGLQ(FM) Escanaba MI
WCRZ(FM) Flint MI
WBNZ(FM) Frankfort MI
WSHN-FM Fremont MI
WMJZ-FM Gaylord MI
WGDN(AM) Gladwin MI
WGHN(AM) Grand Haven MI
WGHN-FM Grand Haven Mi
WLHT(FM) Grand Rapids MI
WOOD(AM) Grand Rapids MI
WQON(FM) Grayling MI
WCXT(FM) Hart MI
WCSR(AM) Hillsdale MI
WCSR-FM Hillsdale MI
WAAH(FM) Houghton MI
WOLF-FM Houghton MI
WUPS(FM) Houghton Lake MI
WHMI(AM) Howell MI
WHMI-FM Howell MI
WJNR-FM Iron Mountain MI
WIMI(FM) Ironwood MI
WUPM(FM) Ironwood MI
WMQT(FM) Ishpeming MI
WKHM(AM) Jackson MI
WQLR(FM) Kalamazoo MI
WJIM-FM Lansing MI
WKLA-FM Ludington MI
WXYQ(FM) Manistee MI
WTIQ(AM) Manistique MI
WMPX(AM) Midland MI
WCLX(FM) Mio MI
WTWR-FM Monroe MI
WKBZ(AM) Muskegon MI
WUPQ(FM) Newberry MI
WZNL(FM) Norway MI
WCLS(FM) Oscoda MI
WQXC(AM) Otsego MI
WQXC-FM Otsego MI
*WOES(FM) Ovid-Elsie MI
WMZX(FM) Owosso MI
WBTZ(FM) Pinconning MI
WPHM(AM) Port Huron MI
WBYY(AM) Rockford MI
WMLQ(FM) Rogers City MI
WGER-FM Saginaw MI
WEVS(FM) Saugatuck MI
WSOO(AM) Sault Ste. Marie MI
WCSY(AM) South Haven MI
WCSY-FM South Haven MI
WSTD(FM) Standish MI
WMSH(AM) Sturgis MI
WMSH-FM Sturgis MI
WHST(FM) Tawas City MI
WLKM(AM) Three Rivers MI
WLKM-FM Three Rivers MI
WLDR(FM) Traverse City MI
WPON(AM) Walled Lake MI
WBMB(AM) West Branch MI
WBMI(FM) West Branch MI
WMHG(FM) Whitehall MI
*WYCE(FM) Wyoming MI
WWCM(AM) Ypsilanti MI
KEZZ(FM) Aitkin MN
KCPI(FM) Albert Lea MN
KQPR-FM Albert Lea MN
KSTQ(FM) Alexandria MN
KAUS(AM) Austin MN
KSCR-FM Benson MN
WJJY-FM Brainerd MN
KLTA(FM) Breckenridge MN
WLOL(FM) Cambridge MN
KROX(AM) Crookston MN
KDLM(AM) Detroit Lakes MN
KDAL-FM Duluth MN
*KUMD-FM Duluth MN
*WNCB(FM) Duluth MN
KZLT-FM East Grand Forks MN
WELY-FM Ely MN
WEVE(AM) Eveleth MN
WEVE-FM Eveleth MN
KFMC(FM) Fairmont MN
KQCL(FM) Faribault MN
KMGK(FM) Glenwood MN
KMFY(FM) Grand Rapids MN
KOZY(AM) Grand Rapids MN
KKRC(FM) Granite Falls MN
KGHS(AM) International Falls MN
KFML(FM) Little Falls MN
KLTF(AM) Little Falls MN
KQAD(AM) Luverne MN
KEEZ-FM Mankato MN
KTOE(AM) Mankato MN
KBJJ(FM) Marshall MN
KKCK(FM) Marshall MN
WLTE(FM) Minneapolis MN
KMOM(AM) Monticello MN
KXLP(FM) New Ulm MN
KYMN(AM) Northfield MN
KCGN-FM Ortonville MN
KDIO(AM) Ortonville MN
KRFO(AM) Owatonna MN
KISD(FM) Pipestone MN
KNXR(FM) Rochester MN
KKSR(FM) Sartell MN
KEEY-FM St. Paul MN
KSTP-FM St. Paul MN
KRBI(AM) St. Peter MN
KRBI-FM St. Peter MN
*KSRQ(FM) Thief River Falls MN
KLLZ(AM) Walker MN
KOWO(AM) Waseca MN
KRUE(FM) Waseca MN
KQIC(FM) Willmar MN
KAGE-FM Winona MN
KHME(FM) Winona MN
KWOA-FM Worthington MN
KDBB(FM) Bonne Terre MO
KBFL(FM) Buffalo MO
KCGQ(AM) Cape Girardeau MO
KMXL(FM) Carthage MO
KLOW(FM) Caruthersville MO
KYRX(FM) Chaffee MO
KLRQ(FM) Clinton MO
KARO(FM) Columbia MO
KESM-FM El Dorado Springs MO
KBMX(FM) Eldon MO
KLOZ(FM) Eldon MO
KJCF(AM) Festus MO
KFMO(AM) Flat River MO
KCGQ-FM Gordonville MO
KGRC(FM) Hannibal MO
KFSB(AM) Joplin MO
KFEZ(AM) Kansas City MO
KLTH(FM) Kansas City MO
KMXV(FM) Kansas City MO
KBOA(AM) Kennett MO
KTUF(FM) Kirksville MO
KMAL(FM) Malden MO
KNIM(AM) Maryville MO
KZZT(FM) Moberly MO
KKBL(FM) Monett MO
KMCR(FM) Montgomery City MO
KXOZ(FM) Mountain View MO
KGBX-FM Nixa MO
KBDZ(FM) Perryville MO
KPWB-FM Piedmont MO
KJEZ(FM) Poplar Bluff MO
KADI(FM) Republic MO
KSDL(FM) Sedalia MO
KKJO(FM) St. Joseph MO
KSFT(AM) St. Joseph MO
KEZK-FM St. Louis MO
KYKY(FM) St. Louis MO
KLPW(AM) Union MO
KOKO(AM) Warrensburg MO
KSLQ(AM) Washington MO
KSLQ-FM Washington MO
KUKU(AM) Willow Springs MO
WWZQ(AM) Aberdeen MS
WWZQ-FM Aberdeen MS
WXBD(AM) Biloxi MS

Broadcasting & Cable Yearbook 1994
B-544

Programming on Radio Stations in the U.S.

WMGO(AM) Canton MS
WAID(FM) Clarksdale MS
WROX(AM) Clarksdale MS
WFFF-FM Columbia MS
WXRZ(FM) Corinth MS
WLZA(FM) Eupora MS
WFTA(FM) Fulton MS
WLIN(FM) Gluckstadt MS
WDMS(FM) Greenville MS
WGRM(AM) Greenwood MS
WGRM-FM Greenwood MS
WYMX(FM) Greenwood MS
WQXB(FM) Grenada MS
WXLS-FM Gulfport MS
WHSY-FM Hattiesburg MS
WJMG(FM) Hattiesburg MS
WSYE(FM) Houston MS
WNLA-FM Indianola MS
WJDS(AM) Jackson MS
WJDX(FM) Jackson MS
WNSL(FM) Laurel MS
WKXI-FM Magee MS
WQLJ(FM) Oxford MS
WMFM(FM) Petal MS
WSSO(AM) Starkville MS
*WCLL-FM Wesson MS
WONA-FM Winona MS
KIDX(FM) Billings MT
KOHZ(FM) Billings MT
KOPR(FM) Butte MT
KQUY-FM Butte MT
KRYK(FM) Chinook MT
KLCY(AM) East Missoula MT
KLAN(FM) Glasgow MT
KDZN(FM) Glendive MT
KAAK(FM) Great Falls MT
KLFM(FM) Great Falls MT
KBMG(FM) Hamilton MT
KOJM(AM) Havre MT
KMTX-FM Helena MT
KZMT(FM) Helena MT
KALS(FM) Kalispell MT
KOFI(AM) Kalispell MT
KLCM(FM) Lewistown MT
KATL(AM) Miles City MT
KMCM-FM Miles City MT
KDXT(FM) Missoula MT
KMSO(FM) Missoula MT
KQRK(FM) Ronan MT
KZIN-FM Shelby MT
KVCK-FM Wolf Point MT
XHRM-FM Tijuana MX
WKSF(FM) Asheville NC
WSKY(AM) Asheville NC
WBT(AM) Charlotte NC
WBT-FM Charlotte NC
WMXC(FM) Charlotte NC
WCLN-FM Clinton NC
WGAI(AM) Elizabeth City NC
WQSM(FM) Fayetteville NC
WRFR(FM) Franklin NC
WLGQ(FM) Gaston NC
WGNC(AM) Gastonia NC
WEQR(FM) Goldsboro NC
WCPQ(AM) Havelock NC
WMSQ(FM) Havelock NC
WMYI(FM) Hendersonville NC
WEZC(FM) Hickory NC
WMAG(FM) High Point NC
WWWB(FM) High Point NC
WLNC(AM) Laurinburg NC
WJRI(AM) Lenoir NC
WLON(AM) Lincolnton NC
WHLQ(FM) Louisburg NC
WVOD(FM) Manteo NC
WMAP(AM) Monroe NC
WMNC-FM Morganton NC
WSYD(AM) Mount Airy NC
WCNG(FM) Murphy NC
WKQT(FM) Newport NC
WNNC(AM) Newton NC
WKBC-FM North Wilkesboro NC
WDLF(FM) Old Fort NC
WRAL(FM) Raleigh NC
WAYN(AM) Rockingham NC
WEED(AM) Rocky Mount NC
WLTT(FM) Shallotte NC
WOHS(AM) Shelby NC
WNCA(AM) Siler City NC
WFXK(FM) Tarboro NC
WZKB(FM) Wallace NC
WOBR-FM Wanchese NC
WDLX(FM) Washington NC
WENC(AM) Whiteville NC
WGNI(FM) Wilmington NC
WVOT(AM) Wilson NC
KFYR(AM) Bismarck ND
KBYZ(FM) Bismarck-Mandan ND
KDVL(FM) Devils Lake ND
KDIX(AM) Dickinson ND
KRRB(FM) Dickinson ND
WDAY(AM) Fargo ND
WDAY-FM Fargo ND
KQDJ(AM) Jamestown ND
KSJZ(FM) Jamestown ND
KIZZ(FM) Minot ND
KGWB(FM) Wahpeton ND
KBRB-FM Ainsworth NE
KCOW(AM) Alliance NE
KPNY(FM) Alliance NE
KWBE(AM) Beatrice NE
KLIR(FM) Columbus NE
KTTT(AM) Columbus NE
*KINI(FM) Crookston NE
KGMT(AM) Fairbury NE

KRGI(AM) Grand Island NE
KSYZ-FM Grand Island NE
KHAS(AM) Hastings NE
KUVR(AM) Holdrege NE
KUVR-FM Holdrege NE
KGFW(AM) Kearney NE
KRVN-FM Lexington NE
KEZG(FM) Lincoln NE
KFOR(AM) Lincoln NE
KICX-FM McCook NE
KEXL(FM) Norfolk NE
KNEN(FM) Norfolk NE
KELN(FM) North Platte NE
KJLT-FM North Platte NE
KBRX(AM) O'Neill NE
KBRX-FM O'Neill NE
KOGA-FM Ogallala NE
KEFM(FM) Omaha NE
KESY(AM) Omaha NE
KESY-FM Omaha NE
KSID-FM Sidney NE
KTMX(FM) York NE
WZPK(FM) Berlin NH
WBNC(AM) Conway NH
WMWV(FM) Conway NH
WOKQ(FM) Dover NH
WFTN-FM Franklin NH
WGXL(FM) Hanover NH
WTSL(AM) Hanover NH
WRCI(FM) Hillsboro NH
WLNH(AM) Laconia NH
WLNH-FM Laconia NH
WLGW(AM) Lancaster NH
WZID(FM) Manchester NH
WHOB(FM) Nashua NH
WNHQ(FM) Peterborough NH
WWEM(FM) Rochester NH
WAYV(FM) Atlantic City NJ
WFPG-FM Atlantic City NJ
WMGM(FM) Atlantic City NJ
*WNJN(FM) Atlantic City NJ
*WNJS-FM Berlin NJ
*WNJB(FM) Bridgeton NJ
WSSJ(AM) Camden NJ
WSUS(FM) Franklin NJ
*WRLJ(FM) Freehold Township NJ
WRNJ(AM) Hackettstown NJ
WJRZ-FM Manahawkin NJ
WTTH(FM) Margate City NJ
WMGQ(FM) New Brunswick NJ
WQNJ(FM) Ocean Acres NJ
WKOE(FM) Ocean City NJ
WXMC(AM) Parsippany-Troy Hills NJ
WADB(FM) Point Pleasant NJ
WGHT(AM) Pompton Lakes NJ
WHWH(AM) Princeton NJ
*WNJP(FM) Sussex NJ
WOBM-FM Toms River NJ
*WNJT-FM Trenton NJ
WFNN(FM) Villas NJ
WVLT(FM) Vineland NJ
KINN(AM) Alamogordo NM
KAMX(FM) Albuquerque NM
KAMX-FM Albuquerque NM
KKOB-FM Albuquerque NM
KMGA(FM) Albuquerque NM
KWYK-FM Aztec NM
KCDY(FM) Carlsbad NM
KTQM-FM Clovis NM
KENN(AM) Farmington NM
KKOR(FM) Gallup NM
KZNM(FM) Grants NM
KZOR(FM) Hobbs NM
KPSA-FM La Luz NM
KASK(FM) Las Cruces NM
KLVF(FM) Las Vegas NM
KRSN(AM) Los Alamos NM
KMVR(FM) Mesilla Park NM
KSEL(AM) Portales NM
KSEL-FM Portales NM
KBCQ(FM) Roswell NM
KBIM-FM Roswell NM
KSSR(AM) Santa Rosa NM
KSCQ(FM) Silver City NM
KQAY-FM Tucumcari NM
KPTL(AM) Carson City NV
KWNZ(FM) Carson City NV
KELK(AM) Elko NV
KDSS(FM) Ely NV
KVLV-FM Fallon NV
KGVM(FM) Gardnerville-Minden NV
KMZQ-FM Henderson NV
KXTZ(FM) Henderson NV
*KILA(FM) Las Vegas NV
KRLV(FM) Las Vegas NV
KRNO-FM Reno NV
KHWK(FM) Tonopah NV
KWNA(AM) Winnemucca NV
WKLI(FM) Albany NY
WROW-FM Albany NY
WKOL(FM) Amsterdam NY
WAUB(AM) Auburn NY
WABH(AM) Bath NY
WVIN-FM Bath NY
WXPS(FM) Briarcliff Manor NY
WBUF(FM) Buffalo NY
WJYE(FM) Buffalo NY
WMJQ(FM) Buffalo NY
WLKA(FM) Canandaigua NY
WVNC(FM) Canton NY
WTOJ(FM) Carthage NY
WCTW(FM) Catskill NY
WWCP-FM Clifton Park NY

WSCM(AM) Cobleskill NY
WSHQ(FM) Cobleskill NY
WCBA-FM Corning NY
WNKI(FM) Corning NY
WRWD(AM) Cornwall NY
WDNY(AM) Dansville NY
WDNY-FM Dansville NY
WDHI(FM) Delhi NY
WIYN(FM) Deposit NY
WFLR-FM Dundee NY
WDOE(AM) Dunkirk NY
WEHM(FM) East Hampton NY
WWWK(FM) Ellenville NY
WENY-FM Elmira NY
WMRV-FM Endicott NY
WCQA(FM) Fredonia NY
WGBB(AM) Freeport NY
WWSC(AM) Glens Falls NY
WENT(AM) Gloversville NY
WGIX-FM Gouverneur NY
WIGS(AM) Gouverneur NY
WKJY(FM) Hempstead NY
WXHC(FM) Homer NY
WKPQ(FM) Hornell NY
WLNL(AM) Horseheads NY
*WJSL(FM) Houghton NY
WHUC(AM) Hudson NY
WENU(FM) Hudson Falls NY
WMJR(FM) Hudson Falls NY
WYXL(FM) Ithaca NY
WJTN(AM) Jamestown NY
WWSE(FM) Jamestown NY
WKNY(AM) Kingston NY
WIRD(AM) Lake Placid NY
WLPW(FM) Lake Placid NY
WOWB(FM) Little Falls NY
WLLG(FM) Lowville NY
WICY(AM) Malone NY
WMSA(AM) Massena NY
WYBG(AM) Massena NY
WBEA(FM) Montauk NY
WSUL-FM Monticello NY
WVIP-FM Mount Kisco NY
WLTW(FM) New York NY
WMXV(FM) New York NY
WACK(AM) Newark NY
WGNY-FM Newburgh NY
WKRL-FM North Syracuse NY
WKXZ(FM) Norwich NY
WSLB(AM) Ogdensburg NY
WMXO(FM) Olean NY
WSRK(FM) Oneonta NY
WGES(FM) Oswego NY
WZOS(FM) Oswego NY
WALK(AM) Patchogue NY
WALK-FM Patchogue NY
WBLI(FM) Patchogue NY
WMJV-FM Patterson NY
WHUD(FM) Peekskill NY
WLNA(AM) Peekskill NY
WEAV(AM) Plattsburgh NY
WGFB(FM) Plattsburgh NY
WIRY(AM) Plattsburgh NY
WTSX(FM) Port Jervis NY
WSNN(FM) Potsdam NY
WRNQ(FM) Poughkeepsie NY
WADR(AM) Remsen NY
WHAM(AM) Rochester NY
WJZR(FM) Rochester NY
WRMM-FM Rochester NY
WVOR-FM Rochester NY
WRNY(AM) Rome NY
WGGO(AM) Salamanca NY
WNBZ(AM) Saranac Lake NY
WGY(AM) Schenectady NY
WSFW(AM) Seneca Falls NY
WSFW-FM Seneca Falls NY
WCDO(AM) Sidney NY
WCDO-FM Sidney NY
WMJC(FM) Smithtown NY
WHFM(FM) Southampton NY
WBAZ(FM) Southold NY
WSSV(FM) Stillwater NY
WYYY(FM) Syracuse NY
WIPS(AM) Ticonderoga NY
WRGR(FM) Tupper Lake NY
WFRG-FM Utica NY
WLZW(FM) Utica NY
WMXW(FM) Vestal NY
WNYR-FM Waterloo NY
WAVR(FM) Waverly NY
WJQZ(FM) Wellsville NY
WFAS-FM White Plains NY
WNYV(FM) Whitehall NY
WDST(FM) Woodstock NY
WAKR(AM) Akron OH
WFUN(AM) Ashtabula OH
WREO-FM Ashtabula OH
WPKO-FM Bellefontaine OH
WBNO-FM Bryan OH
WQCT(AM) Bryan OH
WBCO(AM) Bucyrus OH
WCMJ(FM) Cambridge OH
WHBC-FM Canton OH
WINW(AM) Canton OH
WRCW(AM) Canton OH
WGGN(FM) Castalia OH
WCSM(AM) Celina OH
WCSM-FM Celina OH
WKKI(FM) Celina OH
WFCB(FM) Chillicothe OH
WIMJ(FM) Cincinnati OH
*WJVS(FM) Cincinnati OH
WLW(AM) Cincinnati OH
WRRM(FM) Cincinnati OH

WWNK-FM Cincinnati OH
WDOK(FM) Cleveland OH
WLTF(FM) Cleveland OH
WQAL(FM) Cleveland OH
WBNS(AM) Columbus OH
WNCI(FM) Columbus OH
WSNY(FM) Columbus OH
WTVN(AM) Columbus OH
WTNS-FM Coshocton OH
*WGXM(FM) Dayton OH
WMMX(FM) Dayton OH
WDFM(FM) Defiance OH
WJER-FM Dover OH
WZOO-FM Edgewood OH
WBVI(FM) Fostoria OH
WFOB(AM) Fostoria OH
WFRO(AM) Fremont OH
WFRO-FM Fremont OH
WQLX(FM) Galion OH
WNLT(FM) Harrison OH
WKTN(FM) Kenton OH
WLQT(FM) Kettering OH
WIMA(AM) Lima OH
WLGN(AM) Logan OH
WAGX(FM) Manchester OH
WVNO-FM Mansfield OH
WDIF(FM) Marion OH
WMRN(AM) Marion OH
WWHT(FM) Marysville OH
WJAW(FM) McConnelsville OH
WKLM(FM) Millersburg OH
*WNZR(FM) Mount Vernon OH
WNDH(FM) Napoleon OH
WNKO(FM) Newark OH
WLKR-FM Norwalk OH
WBKC(AM) Painesville OH
WERT-FM Paulding OH
WCLR(FM) Piqua OH
WMVR(AM) Sidney OH
WMVR-FM Sidney OH
WIZE(AM) Springfield OH
WWWM-FM Sylvania OH
WTTF(AM) Tiffin OH
WTTF-FM Tiffin OH
WLQR(FM) Toledo OH
WTRJ(FM) Troy OH
WYNT(FM) Upper Sandusky OH
WKOV-FM Wellston OH
WRAC(FM) West Union OH
WSWO(FM) Wilmington OH
WKBN-FM Youngstown OH
WHIZ(AM) Zanesville OH
KADA-FM Ada OK
KTLS(FM) Ada OK
KXLS(FM) Alva OK
KYFM(FM) Bartlesville OK
KNTL(FM) Bethany OK
KWCO(AM) Chickasha OK
KXXK(FM) Chickasha OK
*KRSC-FM Claremore OK
KCLI(FM) Clinton OK
KLAK(FM) Durant OK
KSEO(AM) Durant OK
KYBE(FM) Frederick OK
KGYN(AM) Guymon OK
KQTZ(FM) Hobart OK
KGND(FM) Ketchum OK
KBZQ(FM) Lawton OK
KYNZ(FM) Lone Grove OK
KTMC-FM McAlester OK
KMGL(FM) Oklahoma City OK
*KOCC(FM) Oklahoma City OK
KYIS(FM) Oklahoma City OK
KASR-FM Perry OK
*KLVV(FM) Ponca City OK
WBBZ(AM) Ponca City OK
KBSY(FM) Poteau OK
KZBB(FM) Poteau OK
KGFF(AM) Shawnee OK
KBEZ(FM) Tulsa OK
KRAV(FM) Tulsa OK
KRMG(AM) Tulsa OK
KMZE(FM) Woodward OK
KWFX(FM) Woodward OK
KCMX-FM Ashland OR
KKCW(FM) Beaverton OR
KSHR-FM Coquille OR
KEJO(FM) Corvallis OR
KWIP(AM) Dallas OR
KMGE(FM) Eugene OR
KUGN(AM) Eugene OR
KCST(AM) Florence OR
KGBR(FM) Gold Beach OR
KMUZ(AM) Gresham OR
KQFM(FM) Hermiston OR
KAGO-FM Klamath Falls OR
KKRB(FM) Klamath Falls OR
KUBQ(FM) La Grande OR
KWRL(FM) La Grande OR
KCRF-FM Lincoln City OR
KLYC(AM) McMinnville OR
KLKY(FM) Milton-Freewater OR
KNPT(AM) Newport OR
KYTE(FM) Newport OR
KACW(FM) North Bend OR
KTIX(AM) Pendleton OR
KEX(AM) Portland OR
KXL-FM Portland OR
KIJK(FM) Prineville OR
KLRR(FM) Redmond OR
KRBZ(FM) Reedsport OR
KSYD(FM) Reedsport OR
KBZY(AM) Salem OR
KSKD(FM) Sweet Home OR
KACI(AM) The Dalles OR

KACI-FM The Dalles OR
KMCQ(FM) The Dalles OR
KMBD(AM) Tillamook OR
KKMX(FM) Tri City OR
WFBG(AM) Altoona PA
WWBV(FM) Beaver Springs PA
WZWW(FM) Bellefonte PA
WALY(FM) Bellwood PA
WKAB(FM) Berwick PA
WGPA(AM) Bethlehem PA
WLCY(FM) Blairsville PA
WESB(AM) Bradford PA
WMKX(FM) Brookville PA
WBUT(AM) Butler PA
WISR(AM) Butler PA
WLER-FM Butler PA
WIOO(AM) Carlisle PA
WCBG(AM) Chambersburg PA
WIKZ(FM) Chambersburg PA
WESA(AM) Charleroi PA
WESA-FM Charleroi PA
WCOJ(AM) Coatesville PA
WCVI(AM) Connellsville PA
WOKW(FM) Curwensville PA
WLEV(FM) Easton PA
WKST-FM Ellwood City PA
WLEM(AM) Emporium PA
WQKY(FM) Emporium PA
WJET(FM) Erie PA
WMXE(FM) Erie PA
WXKC(FM) Erie PA
*WRSD(FM) Folsom PA
WFRA-FM Franklin PA
WGET(AM) Gettysburg PA
WHJB(AM) Greensburg PA
WGRP(AM) Greenville PA
WIMX-FM Harrisburg PA
WRVV(FM) Harrisburg PA
WAZL(AM) Hazleton PA
WZMT(FM) Hazleton PA
WHPA(FM) Hollidaysburg PA
WCCS(AM) Homer City PA
WDNH-FM Honesdale PA
WQHG(FM) Huntingdon PA
WDAD(AM) Indiana PA
WKYE(FM) Johnstown PA
*WFNM(FM) Lancaster PA
WLAN-FM Lancaster PA
WROZ(FM) Lancaster PA
WLSH(AM) Lansford PA
WCNS(AM) Latrobe PA
WBCB(AM) Levittown-Fairless Hills PA
*WGRC(FM) Lewisburg PA
WUNS(FM) Lewisburg PA
WCHX(FM) Lewistown PA
WMRF-FM Lewistown PA
WSNU(FM) Lock Haven PA
WJRV(AM) Loretto PA
*WRIJ(FM) Masontown PA
WMGW(AM) Meadville PA
WSRT(FM) Mercersburg PA
WJUN(AM) Mexico PA
WQLV(FM) Millersburg PA
WOEZ-FM Milton PA
WSPI(FM) Mount Carmel PA
WXMJ(FM) Mount Union PA
WHTO(FM) Muncy PA
WBZY(AM) New Castle PA
WKQW(AM) Oil City PA
WOYL(AM) Oil City PA
WBEB-FM Philadelphia PA
WDAS-FM Philadelphia PA
WMGK(FM) Philadelphia PA
WPEN(AM) Philadelphia PA
*WXPN(FM) Philadelphia PA
WYXR(FM) Philadelphia PA
KDKA(AM) Pittsburgh PA
WLTJ(FM) Pittsburgh PA
WSHH(FM) Pittsburgh PA
WVTY(FM) Pittsburgh PA
WHKS(FM) Port Allegany PA
WPAZ(AM) Pottstown PA
WPXZ-FM Punxsutawney PA
WEEU(AM) Reading PA
WDSN(FM) Reynoldsville PA
WATS(AM) Sayre PA
WLSW(FM) Scottdale PA
WARM(AM) Scranton PA
WGBI(AM) Scranton PA
WWDL-FM Scranton PA
*WBYO(FM) Sellersville PA
WYFM(FM) Sharon PA
WVSC-FM Somerset PA
WKBI-FM St. Marys PA
WRSC(AM) State College PA
WVPO(AM) Stroudsburg PA
WKOK(AM) Sunbury PA
WMGH-FM Tamaqua PA
WTIV(AM) Titusville PA
WTTC(AM) Towanda PA
WTTC-FM Towanda PA
WMBS(AM) Uniontown PA
WPQR-FM Uniontown PA
WNAE(AM) Warren PA
WKRZ-FM Wilkes-Barre PA
WMGS(FM) Wilkes-Barre PA
WKSB(FM) Williamsport PA
WARM-FM York PA
WQXA-FM York PA
WABA(AM) Aguadilla PR
WNOZ(AM) Aguadilla PR
WMIA(AM) Arecibo PR
WMIO(FM) Cabo Rojo PR
WNEL(AM) Caguas PR

Broadcasting & Cable Yearbook 1994
B-545

Programming on Radio Stations in the U.S.

WVJP(AM) Caguas PR
WCHQ(AM) Camuy PR
WMDD(AM) Fajardo PR
WOIZ(AM) Guayanilla PR
WTIL(AM) Mayaguez PR
WZAR(FM) Ponce PR
WIOA(FM) San Juan PR
WLRP(AM) San Sebastian PR
WRSS(AM) San Sebastian PR
WBLQ(FM) Block Island RI
WPJB(FM) Narragansett Pier RI
WPRO(AM) Providence RI
WWLI(FM) Providence RI
WKRI(AM) West Warwick RI
WNRI(AM) Woonsocket RI
WANS(AM) Anderson SC
WGTN-FM Andrews SC
WRIT(AM) Bamberg-Denmark SC
WBAW(AM) Barnwell SC
WBAW-FM Barnwell SC
WVGB(AM) Beaufort SC
WYKZ(FM) Beaufort SC
WPUB-FM Camden SC
WSSX-FM Charleston SC
WSUY(FM) Charleston SC
WXTC(AM) Charleston SC
WXTC-FM Charleston SC
WCRE(AM) Cheraw SC
WBZK-FM Chester SC
WARQ(FM) Columbia SC
WQXL(AM) Columbia SC
WGTN(AM) Georgetown SC
WWXM(FM) Georgetown SC
WIJY(FM) Hilton Head Island SC
WJES(AM) Johnston SC
WKSX(FM) Johnston SC
WYMB(AM) Manning SC
WKDK(AM) Newberry SC
WKMG(AM) Newberry SC
WGSN(AM) North Myrtle Beach SC
WNMB(FM) North Myrtle Beach SC
WTCB(FM) Orangeburg SC
WMXT(FM) Pamplico SC
WDAI(FM) Pawley's Island SC
WMGL(FM) Ravenel SC
WSHG(FM) Ridgeland SC
WRHI(AM) Rock Hill SC
WSQN(FM) Scranton SC
WBFM(FM) Seneca SC
WSPA-FM Spartanburg SC
WGOG-FM Walhalla SC
WIBZ(FM) Wedgefield SC
WSCQ(FM) West Columbia SC
KSDN(AM) Aberdeen SD
KBRK-FM Brookings SD
KZMX(AM) Hot Springs SD
KQRN(FM) Mitchell SD
KOLY-FM Mobridge SD
KCCR(AM) Pierre SD
KKMK(FM) Rapid City SD
KOTA(AM) Rapid City SD
KELO(AM) Sioux Falls SD
KELO-FM Sioux Falls SD
KKLS-FM Sioux Falls SD
KPAT(FM) Sioux Falls SD
*KBHU-FM Spearfish SD
KEZV(FM) Spearfish SD
KIXX(FM) Watertown SD
KWYR-FM Winner SD
WCTA(AM) Alamo TN
WBCR(AM) Alcoa TN
WRJB(FM) Camden TN
WALV(FM) Cleveland TN
WMRB(AM) Columbia TN
WHUB-FM Cookeville TN
WZYX(AM) Cowan TN
WXVL(FM) Crossville TN
WYYB(FM) Dickson TN
WASL(FM) Dyersburg TN
WNWZ(AM) Germantown TN
WIKQ(FM) Greeneville TN
*WLMU(FM) Harrogate TN
WLSZ(FM) Humboldt TN
WZDQ(FM) Humboldt TN
WMXX-FM Jackson TN
WTFM(FM) Kingsport TN
WEZK-FM Knoxville TN
*WKCS(FM) Knoxville TN
WQBB-FM Knoxville TN
WDXE-FM Lawrenceburg TN
WYGO(FM) Madisonville TN
WFTZ(FM) Manchester TN
WCMT-FM Martin TN
WAKI(AM) McMinnville TN
WDIA(AM) Memphis TN
WMC-FM Memphis TN
*WQOX(FM) Memphis TN
WRVR-FM Memphis TN
WYNU(FM) Milan TN
WKXD(FM) Monterey TN
WCRK(AM) Morristown TN
WMXK(FM) Morristown TN
WLAC-FM Nashville TN
WZEZ(FM) Nashville TN
WBNT-FM Oneida TN
WMUF-FM Paris TN
WQBB(AM) Powell TN
WINJ(FM) Pulaski TN
WTRB-FM Ripley TN
WKWX-FM Savannah TN
WSIB(FM) Selmer TN
WMYU(FM) Sevierville TN
WKXJ(FM) South Pittsburg TN
WXQK(AM) Spring City TN
WTNE(AM) Trenton TN
WWEZ(FM) Trenton TN
WENK(AM) Union City TN
*KACU(FM) Abilene TX
KORQ-FM Abilene TX
KAEZ(FM) Amarillo TX
KMML-FM Amarillo TX
KKMJ-FM Austin TX
KRUN(AM) Ballinger TX
KRUN-FM Ballinger TX
KMKS(FM) Bay City TX
KQXY-FM Beaumont TX
KIXV(FM) Brady TX
KXYL(AM) Brownwood TX
KHLB(AM) Burnet TX
KGAP(FM) Clarksville TX
KAUM(FM) Colorado City TX
KMXR(FM) Corpus Christi TX
KBHT(FM) Crockett TX
KDMX(FM) Dallas TX
KMRT(AM) Dallas TX
KDLK(FM) Del Rio TX
KVMX(FM) Eastland TX
KVLY(FM) Edinburg TX
KOFX(FM) El Paso TX
KTSM-FM El Paso TX
KIJN-FM Farwell TX
KLTY(FM) Fort Worth TX
KOAI(FM) Fort Worth TX
KGAF(AM) Gainesville TX
KRTX(FM) Galveston TX
KVIL(AM) Highland Park TX
KVIL-FM Highland Park-Dallas TX
KBXX(FM) Houston TX
KHMX(FM) Houston TX
KKRW(FM) Houston TX
KODA(FM) Houston TX
KEBE(AM) Jacksonville TX
KITE(FM) Kerrville TX
KMMX(FM) Lamesa TX
KRRG(FM) Laredo TX
KSHN-FM Liberty TX
KLKM(FM) Llano TX
KYMI(FM) Los Ybanez TX
KJBX(AM) Lubbock TX
KRLB-FM Lubbock TX
KUEZ(FM) Lufkin TX
*KXPZ(FM) Lytle TX
KEYR(FM) Marlin TX
KLSR(AM) Memphis TX
KLSR-FM Memphis TX
*KEOM(FM) Mesquite TX
KLBO(AM) Monahans TX
KXGM-FM Muenster TX
KTBQ(FM) Nacogdoches TX
KODM(FM) Odessa TX
KKMY(FM) Orange TX
KGRO(AM) Pampa TX
KBUS(FM) Paris TX
KPLT-FM Paris TX
KATX(FM) Plainview TX
KZTX(FM) Refugio TX
KELI(FM) San Angelo TX
KGKL(AM) San Angelo TX
KIXY-FM San Angelo TX
KQXT(FM) San Antonio TX
KROM(FM) San Antonio TX
KSJL-FM San Antonio TX
KEYI-FM San Marcos TX
KSMG(FM) Seguin TX
KCUB-FM Stephenville TX
KJMX(FM) Tulia TX
KTYL-FM Tyler TX
KVWC-FM Vernon TX
KVLT(FM) Victoria TX
KWTX(AM) Waco TX
KTLT(FM) Wichita Falls TX
KALK(FM) Winfield TX
KREC(FM) Brian Head UT
KSOS-FM Brigham City UT
KCPX(AM) Centerville UT
KBLQ-FM Logan UT
KVNU(AM) Logan UT
KMGR(AM) Murray UT
KLO(AM) Ogden UT
KMXB(FM) Orem UT
*KPCW(FM) Park City UT
KPRQ(FM) Price UT
KRPX(AM) Price UT
KSRR(AM) Provo UT
KKWZ(FM) Richfield UT
KIFX(FM) Roosevelt UT
KCNR(AM) Salt Lake City UT
KISN-FM Salt Lake City UT
KSFI(FM) Salt Lake City UT
KSGI(AM) St. George UT
KZEZ(FM) St. George UT
WABN(AM) Abingdon VA
WREL-FM Buena Vista VA
WSKO(FM) Buffalo Gap VA
WQMZ(FM) Charlottesville VA
WJQI(AM) Chesapeake VA
WBOP(FM) Churchville VA
WNLR(AM) Churchville VA
WLCQ(FM) Clarksville VA
WGRQ(FM) Colonial Beach VA
WIQO-FM Covington VA
WCVA(AM) Culpeper VA
WBTM(AM) Danville VA
WEVA(AM) Emporia VA
WEVA-FM Emporia VA
WKRE-FM Exmore VA
WFLO-FM Farmville VA
WBQB(FM) Fredericksburg VA
WFQX(FM) Front Royal VA
WFTR-FM Front Royal VA
WBOB(AM) Galax VA
WXGM(AM) Gloucester VA
WXGM-FM Gloucester VA
WWDE-FM Hampton VA
WKWI(FM) Kilmarnock VA
WAGE(AM) Leesburg VA
WLCC(FM) Luray VA
WLYK(FM) Lynchburg VA
WOLD-FM Marion VA
WMVA(AM) Martinsville VA
WNVA-FM Norton VA
WESR-FM Onley-Onancock VA
WJMA(AM) Orange VA
WJMA-FM Orange VA
WSWV(AM) Pennington Gap VA
WSWV-FM Pennington Gap VA
WSVV(FM) Petersburg VA
*WVST(FM) Petersburg VA
WSVY(AM) Portsmouth VA
WRIC(AM) Richlands VA
WMXB(FM) Richmond VA
WRVA(AM) Richmond VA
WSLQ(FM) Roanoke VA
WWWR(AM) Roanoke VA
WZBB(FM) Rocky Mount VA
WVSY(FM) Ruckersville VA
WHLF(AM) South Boston VA
WJLC(FM) South Boston VA
WTON(AM) Staunton VA
WFOG(FM) Suffolk VA
WRAR-FM Tappahannock VA
WJQI-FM Virginia Beach VA
WQRA(FM) Warrenton VA
WAYB(AM) Waynesboro VA
WINC(AM) Winchester VA
WINC-FM Winchester VA
*WYCS(FM) Yorktown VA
WSTA(AM) Charlotte Amalie VI
WVWI(AM) Charlotte Amalie VI
WORK(FM) Barre VT
WHGC(FM) Bennington VT
WTSA-FM Brattleboro VT
WEZF(FM) Burlington VT
WGMT(FM) Lyndon VT
WSKI(AM) Montpelier VT
WVNR(AM) Poultney VT
WJJR(FM) Rutland VT
WSYB(AM) Rutland VT
WZRT(FM) Rutland VT
WCFR-FM Springfield VT
WSTJ(AM) St. Johnsbury VT
WVMX(FM) Stowe VT
WKXE-FM White River Junction VT
KXRO(AM) Aberdeen WA
KLKI(AM) Anacortes WA
KLSY-FM Bellevue WA
KAFE(FM) Bellingham WA
KRWM(FM) Bremerton WA
KMUZ-FM Camas WA
KELA(AM) Centralia-Chehalis WA
KITI(AM) Chehalis-Centralia WA
KOZI(AM) Chelan WA
KOZI-FM Chelan WA
KCRK-FM Colville WA
KCMS(FM) Edmonds WA
KQBE(FM) Ellensburg WA
KEYG-FM Grand Coulee WA
KLOG(AM) Kelso WA
KONA(AM) Kennewick WA
KONA-FM Kennewick WA
KEDO(AM) Longview WA
KDRM(FM) Moses Lake WA
KBRC(AM) Mount Vernon WA
KGY(AM) Olympia WA
KXXO(FM) Olympia WA
KOMW(AM) Omak WA
KNFR(FM) Opportunity WA
KEYW(FM) Pasco WA
KAPY(AM) Port Angeles WA
KONP(AM) Port Angeles WA
KZXR(FM) Prosser WA
KWNC(AM) Quincy WA
KSWW(FM) Raymond WA
KEZX-FM Seattle WA
KLTX(FM) Seattle WA
KOMO(AM) Seattle WA
KYXE(AM) Selah WA
KMAS(AM) Shelton WA
*KAGU(FM) Spokane WA
KISC(FM) Spokane WA
*KBTC-FM Tacoma WA
KMTT(AM) Tacoma WA
KNLT(FM) Walla Walla WA
KTEL(AM) Walla Walla WA
KPQ-FM Wenatchee WA
KRSE(FM) Yakima WA
WRLO-FM Antigo WI
WRPQ(AM) Baraboo WI
WBEV(AM) Beaver Dam WI
WWIS(AM) Black River Falls WI
WWIS-FM Black River Falls WI
WEZR(FM) Brillion WI
WFCL(AM) Clintonville WI
WYKY(FM) Columbus WI
WERL(AM) Eagle River WI
WIAL(FM) Eau Claire WI
WECL(FM) Elk Mound WI
WYUR-FM Ripon WI
WDUZ(AM) Green Bay WI
WQLH(FM) Green Bay WI
WMCS(AM) Greenfield WI
WHSM(AM) Hayward WI
WHSM-FM Hayward WI
WRLS-FM Hayward WI
WYLO(AM) Jackson WI
WHBY(AM) Kimberly WI
WLFN(AM) La Crosse WI
WLXR-FM La Crosse WI
WSPL(FM) La Crosse WI
WLDY(AM) Ladysmith WI
WFDL(FM) Lomira WI
WIBA(AM) Madison WI
WMGN(FM) Madison WI
WZEE(FM) Madison WI
WOMT(AM) Manitowoc WI
WQTC-FM Manitowoc WI
WLST(FM) Marinette WI
WRJC-FM Mauston WI
WIGM(AM) Medford WI
WIGM-FM Medford WI
WJMT(AM) Merrill WI
*WGNV(FM) Milladore WI
WKTI(FM) Milwaukee WI
WLTQ(FM) Milwaukee WI
WMYX(FM) Milwaukee WI
WROE(FM) Neenah-Menasha WI
WOCO-FM Oconto WI
WCQM(FM) Park Falls WI
WNBI(AM) Park Falls WI
WXER(FM) Plymouth WI
WRJN(AM) Racine WI
WOBT(AM) Rhinelander WI
WRHN(FM) Rhinelander WI
WAQE-FM Rice Lake WI
WJMC(AM) Rice Lake WI
WRCO(AM) Richland Center WI
WRCO-FM Richland Center WI
*WRPN-FM Ripon WI
WEVR(AM) River Falls WI
WEVR-FM River Falls WI
WMLI(FM) Sauk City WI
WOWN(FM) Shawano WI
*WSHS(FM) Sheboygan WI
WWJR(FM) Sheboygan WI
WSPT(FM) Stevens Point WI
WDOR(AM) Sturgeon Bay WI
WDOR-FM Sturgeon Bay WI
WFNL(FM) Sturgeon Bay WI
WZXA(FM) Sturtevant WI
WZFR(FM) Tomah WI
WJJQ(AM) Tomahawk WI
WJJQ-FM Tomahawk WI
WDUX-FM Waupaca WI
WSAU(AM) Wausau WI
WYCO(FM) Wausau WI
WEZW(FM) Wauwatosa-Milwaukee WI
WBKV(AM) West Bend WI
WWRW(FM) Wisconsin Rapids WI
WCIR-FM Beckley WV
WHAJ(FM) Bluefield WV
*WPIB(FM) Bluefield WV
WDCI(FM) Bridgeport WV
WXVA-FM Charles Town WV
WVAF(FM) Charleston WV
WVHF-FM Clarksburg WV
WELK(FM) Elkins WV
*WFGH(FM) Fort Gay WV
WKEE-FM Huntington WV
WFSP(AM) Kingwood WV
WFSP-FM Kingwood WV
WLOG(AM) Logan WV
WVOW(AM) Logan WV
WVOW-FM Logan WV
WNMR(FM) New Martinsville WV
WKMY(FM) Princeton WV
WJJB(FM) Romney WV
WRON(AM) Ronceverte WV
WRRR-FM St. Marys WV
WCWV(FM) Summersville WV
WCKA(FM) Sutton WV
WELC(AM) Welch WV
WELC-FM Welch WV
WSSN(FM) Weston WV
WMQC(FM) Westover WV
WKWK-FM Wheeling WV
WSLW(AM) White Sulphur Springs WV
WBTH(AM) Williamson WV
KTAG(FM) Cody WY
KMGW(FM) Casper WY
KTRS(FM) Casper WY
KLEN(FM) Cheyenne WY
KEVA(AM) Evanston WY
KBVZ(FM) Fort Bridger WY
KUGR(AM) Green River WY
KZMQ(AM) Greybull WY
KZJH(FM) Jackson WY
KOWB(AM) Laramie WY
KASL(AM) Newcastle WY
KLZY(FM) Powell WY
KTAK(FM) Riverton WY
KTRZ(FM) Riverton WY
KTHE(AM) Thermopolis WY
KYCN(AM) Wheatland WY
KYCN-FM Wheatland WY
KKLX(FM) Worland WY

Agriculture & Farm

WASG(AM) Atmore AL
WKLF(AM) Clanton AL
KWCK(AM) Searcy AR
KNZR(AM) Bakersfield CA
KNAB(AM) Burlington CO
KNAB-FM Burlington CO
KTMG(AM) Deer Trail CO
KATR-FM Wray CO
KRDZ(AM) Wray CO
KCIM(AM) Carroll IA
KDLS(AM) Perry IA
KICD(AM) Spencer IA
KICD-FM Spencer IA
WCAZ(AM) Carthage IL
WGIL(AM) Galesburg IL
WGEN-FM Geneseo IL
WSMI(AM) Litchfield IL
WLBH(AM) Mattoon IL
WGEM-FM Quincy IL
WHCO(AM) Sparta IL
WNJY(FM) Delphi IN
WSLM(AM) Salem IN
WSLM-FM Salem IN
KLOE(AM) Goodland KS
KVGB(AM) Great Bend KS
KNDY(AM) Marysville KS
KKOW(AM) Pittsburg KS
KGLS(FM) Pratt KS
KWLS(AM) Pratt KS
WIBW(AM) Topeka KS
WGGC(FM) Glasgow KY
WRUS(AM) Russellville KY
KLIL(FM) Moreauville LA
KYCK(FM) Crookston MN
WYRQ(FM) Little Falls MN
KQAD(AM) Luverne MN
KMHL(AM) Marshall MN
KMRS(AM) Morris MN
KNUJ(AM) New Ulm MN
KOLV(FM) Olivia MN
KLOH(AM) Pipestone MN
KCUE(AM) Red Wing MN
KLGR(AM) Redwood Falls MN
KWMB(AM) Wabasha MN
KKOZ(AM) Ava MO
KAOL(AM) Carrollton MO
KMZU(FM) Carrollton MO
KCRV(AM) Caruthersville MO
KRES(FM) Moberly MO
KTRX(FM) Tarkio MO
KTTN-FM Trenton MO
WBLE(FM) Batesville MS
WJBI(AM) Batesville MS
WTGY(FM) Charleston MS
WWUN-FM Clarksdale MS
WNIX(AM) Greenville MS
WCPC(AM) Houston MS
KGLE(AM) Glendive MT
WDAY(AM) Fargo ND
KNOX(AM) Grand Forks ND
KZEN(FM) Central City NE
KMMJ(AM) Grand Island NE
KRVN(AM) Lexington NE
KNEB-FM Scottsbluff NE
KRFS-FM Superior NE
KVLV(AM) Fallon NV
WRFD(AM) Columbus-Worthington OH
WCTM(AM) Eaton OH
WKFI(AM) Wilmington OH
KWHW(AM) Altus OK
KRAF(AM) Holdenville OK
KXKY(FM) Holdenville OK
KXRB(AM) Sioux Falls SD
KBHB(AM) Sturgis SD
KOSZ(AM) Vermillion SD
KWAT(AM) Watertown SD
WMCP(AM) Columbia TN
WMSR(AM) Manchester TN
KRUN(AM) Ballinger TX
KRUN-FM Ballinger TX
KXIT(AM) Dalhart TX
KXIT-FM Dalhart TX
KDIU(FM) Dimmitt TX
KVWG(AM) Pearsall TX
KVWG-FM Pearsall TX
KVWC(AM) Vernon TX
WLQM(AM) Franklin VA
WLQM-FM Franklin VA
WISS(AM) Berlin WI
WISS-FM Berlin WI
WRDN(AM) Durand WI
WRDB(AM) Reedsburg WI
WTMB(AM) Tomah WI
WCUB(AM) Two Rivers WI
WELD-FM Petersburg WV

American Indian

KNDN(AM) Farmington NM
KGAK(AM) Gallup NM
KHAC(AM) Tse Bonito NM
*KWSO(FM) Warm Springs OR

Arabic

KORG(AM) Anaheim CA

Beautiful Music

Includes station format Easy Listening.

KHAR(AM) Anchorage AK
KGTL(AM) Homer AK
KAKN(FM) Naknek AK
WKYD(AM) Andalusia AL
WAUD(AM) Auburn AL
WRSA(FM) Decatur AL
*WRWA(FM) Dothan AL
*WBHL(FM) Florence AL
WRJM-FM Geneva AL
WERH-FM Hamilton AL
WOXR(AM) Oxford AL
WMRK(AM) Selma AL
*WTSU(FM) Troy AL

Programming on Radio Stations in the U.S.

WTNW(AM) Tuscaloosa AL
KEZU(FM) Booneville AR
KFPW(AM) Fort Smith AR
KXOW(AM) Hot Springs AR
KISI(FM) Malvern AR
KAYR(AM) Van Buren AR
KSBS-FM Pago Pago AS
KIDR(AM) Phoenix AZ
KAHM(FM) Prescott AZ
KBUX(FM) Quartzsite AZ
KQST(FM) Sedona AZ
KSLK(FM) Auberry CA
KGFM(FM) Bakersfield CA
KMET(AM) Banning CA
KWXY(AM) Cathedral City CA
KWXY-FM Cathedral City CA
KPAY-FM Chico CA
KOJY(AM) Costa Mesa CA
KVLI(AM) Lake Isabella CA
KVLI-FM Lake Isabella CA
KABL(AM) Oakland CA
KEWE(FM) Oroville CA
KTIP(AM) Porterville CA
KABL-FM San Francisco CA
KWRP(FM) San Jacinto CA
KRUZ(FM) Santa Barbara CA
KWSP(FM) Santa Margarita CA
KKZZ(AM) Santa Paula CA
KGLE-FM South Lake Tahoe CA
KRDO-FM Colorado Springs CO
KJYE-FM Grand Junction CO
*WJMJ(FM) Hartford CT
WGAY(FM) Washington DC
WBGF(FM) Belle Glade FL
WDUV(FM) Bradenton FL
WYND(AM) De Land FL
WKIQ(AM) Eustis FL
*WAFG(FM) Fort Lauderdale FL
WAVQ(FM) Inglis FL
WJAX(AM) Jacksonville FL
*WKTZ-FM Jacksonville FL
WHLG(FM) Jensen Beach FL
WEZY-FM Lakeland FL
WGUF(FM) Marco FL
WGNE(AM) Panama City FL
WBSR(AM) Pensacola FL
WCTH(FM) Plantation Key FL
*WBVM(FM) Tampa FL
WGYL(FM) Vero Beach FL
WEAT(AM) West Palm Beach FL
WRLX(FM) West Palm Beach FL
*WBCX(FM) Gainesville GA
KUAM-FM Agana GU
KINE-FM Honolulu HI
KUMU(AM) Honolulu HI
KUMU-FM Honolulu HI
KHBT(FM) Humboldt IA
*KCMR(FM) Mason City IA
*KBBG(FM) Waterloo IA
*KNWS-FM Waterloo IA
KHEZ(FM) Caldwell ID
KJHY(FM) Emmett ID
WUEZ(FM) Christopher IL
WHOW-FM Clinton IL
WGCY(FM) Gibson City IL
WLBH-FM Mattoon IL
WGFA(AM) Watseka IL
WYEZ(FM) Bremen IN
WQFE(FM) Brownsburg IN
WHON(AM) Centerville IN
WMRI(FM) Marion IN
WSEZ(AM) Paoli IN
*WVUB(FM) Vincennes IN
KVSV-FM Beloit KS
KBEA(AM) Mission KS
KOEZ(FM) Newton KS
KWME(FM) Wellington KS
WNES(AM) Central City KY
WLOC-FM Munfordville KY
*WOAL-FM Pippa Passes KY
WCBR(AM) Richmond KY
*WTHL(FM) Somerset KY
KFTE(FM) Breaux Bridge LA
WBYU(AM) New Orleans LA
WADU-FM Reserve LA
KVLA(AM) Vidalia LA
WJIB(AM) Cambridge MA
WMNB(FM) North Adams MA
WWPL(FM) Federalsburg MD
WFRE(FM) Frederick MD
WWMD(FM) Hagerstown MD
WEZQ(FM) Bangor ME
WRKD(AM) Rockland ME
WJOI(FM) Detroit MI
WDOW(AM) Dowagiac MI
WDOW-FM Dowagiac MI
WGDN-FM Gladwin MI
WFUR-FM Grand Rapids MI
WOOD-FM Grand Rapids MI
WKEZ(FM) Holland MI
WHGR(AM) Houghton Lake MI
WKLA(AM) Ludington MI
WCZY-FM Mount Pleasant MI
WMRR(FM) Muskegon Heights MI
WMBN-FM Petoskey MI
WIOS(AM) Tawas City MI
KXAC(FM) St. James MN
KDOM(AM) Windom MN
KDOM-FM Windom MN
KGNN(AM) Cuba MO
KHMO(AM) Hannibal MO
KFEZ(AM) Kansas City MO
*KLJC(FM) Kansas City MO
KESE(FM) Seligman MO
KTXR(FM) Springfield MO
KSFT(AM) St. Joseph MO
*KGNV(FM) Washington MO
WBAQ(FM) Greenville MS
WROA(AM) Gulfport MS
WKBB(FM) West Point MS
KMTX(AM) Helena MT
*WGWG(FM) Boiling Springs NC
*WCCE(FM) Buie's Creek NC
*WSGE(FM) Dallas NC
WNND(FM) Fuquay-Varina NC
WNCT-FM Greenville NC
WIOZ(AM) Pinehurst NC
*WZRU(FM) Roanoke Rapids NC
WIOZ-FM Southern Pines NC
WMFD(AM) Wilmington NC
WHOM(FM) Mt. Washington NH
WPAT(AM) Paterson NJ
WPAT-FM Paterson NJ
WCHR(FM) Trenton NJ
WDOX(FM) Wildwood Crest NJ
*KMTH(FM) Maljamar NM
*KENW-FM Portales NM
*KVCE(FM) Fallon NV
KNEV(FM) Reno NV
WROW(AM) Albany NY
WCBA(AM) Corning NY
*WHPC(FM) Garden City NY
WADO(AM) New York NY
WCEZ(FM) Delaware OH
WCTM(AM) Eaton OH
WLSN(FM) Greenville OH
WMLV(FM) Ironton OH
WMOA(AM) Marietta OH
WIOI(AM) New Boston OH
WRGM(AM) Ontario OH
WELW(AM) Willoughby-Eastlake OH
WHIZ-FM Zanesville OH
*KBVV(FM) Enid OK
*KCCU(FM) Lawton OK
WKY(AM) Oklahoma City OK
KSPI(AM) Stillwater OK
*KBVM(FM) Portland OR
KEZF(AM) Tigard OR
KORC(AM) Waldport OR
WFMZ(FM) Allentown PA
*WPGM(AM) Danville PA
*WPGM-FM Danville PA
*WPEL(AM) Montrose PA
*WPEL-FM Montrose PA
WNAK(AM) Nanticoke PA
WCTX(FM) Palmyra PA
WICK(AM) Scranton PA
WSHP(AM) Shippensburg PA
WRRN(FM) Warren PA
WTPM(FM) Aguadilla PR
WRSJ(AM) Bayamon PR
WVJP(AM) Caguas PR
WORO(FM) Corozal PR
WOIZ(AM) Guayanilla PR
WKJB-FM Mayaguez PR
*WEUC-FM Ponce PR
WFID(FM) Rio Piedras PR
WYKO(AM) Sabana Grande PR
WRPC(FM) San German PR
WOKE(AM) Charleston SC
WSLT(FM) Clearwater SC
WMUU-FM Greenville SC
WFXH(FM) Hilton Head Island SC
WJYR(FM) Myrtle Beach SC
WSNW(AM) Seneca SC
WDEF(AM) Chattanooga TN
WDEF-FM Chattanooga TN
WQZQ(FM) Dickson TN
WOGY-FM Germantown TN
WKTP(AM) Jonesborough TN
WKPT(AM) Kingsport TN
WCSD(FM) Livingston TN
*WDNX(FM) Olive Hill TN
KHXS(FM) Abilene TX
KWOW(FM) Clifton TX
KSIX(AM) Corpus Christi TX
KOOI-FM Jacksonville TX
*KNCT-FM Killeen TX
*KHOY(FM) Laredo TX
*KHID(FM) McAllen TX
*KLUX(FM) Robstown TX
KDAE(AM) Sinton TX
KPYK(AM) Terrell TX
*KTXK(FM) Texarkana TX
KVWC-FM Vernon TX
KMXU(FM) Manti UT
KFAM(AM) North Salt Lake City UT
WOPI(AM) Bristol VA
WKAV(AM) Charlottesville VA
WTVR-FM Richmond VA
WPVR(FM) Roanoke VA
WTON-FM Staunton VA
WXEZ(FM) Yorktown VA
KULE-FM Ephrata WA
KCPL(AM) Olympia WA
KXLY-FM Spokane WA
*KSOH(FM) Wapato WA
WSJY(FM) Fort Atkinson WI
WLJY(FM) Marshfield WI
WMQA(AM) Minocqua WI
WMQA-FM Minocqua WI
WEKZ-FM Monroe WI
WGLB(AM) Port Washington WI
WGLB-FM Port Washington WI
WHKQ(FM) Racine WI
WHLX(FM) Bethlehem WV
WBES-FM Dunbar WV
WKEE(AM) Huntington WV
WBBD(AM) Wheeling WV
KIMX(FM) Laramie WY

Big Band

Also see Nostalgia.

WAUD(AM) Auburn AL
WABF(AM) Fairhope AL
WLPR(AM) Prichard AL
KJEM(AM) Bentonville-Bella Vista AR
KFPW(AM) Fort Smith AR
KVRD(AM) Cottonwood AZ
KGVY(AM) Green Valley AZ
KMRR(AM) South Tucson AZ
*KCEA(FM) Atherton CA
KSPA(AM) Escondido CA
KIDD(AM) Monterey CA
KBAI(AM) Morro Bay CA
KTNS(AM) Oakhurst CA
KEWE(FM) Oroville CA
KPRL(AM) Paso Robles CA
*KCSM(FM) San Mateo CA
KKZZ(AM) Santa Paula CA
KMYX(AM) Taft CA
KMYX-FM Taft CA
KGRB(AM) West Covina CA
KEZW(AM) Aurora CO
KCMN(AM) Colorado Springs CO
KIIX(AM) Wellington CO
*WGSK(FM) South Kent CT
*WNHU(FM) West Haven CT
WWDC(AM) Washington DC
WSSR(AM) Georgetown DE
WHNR(AM) Cypress Gardens FL
WROD(AM) Daytona Beach FL
WDBF(AM) Delray Beach FL
WRZN(AM) Hernando FL
WLBE(AM) Leesburg FL
WIXI(FM) Naples Park FL
WGUL-FM New Port Richey FL
WITS(AM) Sebring FL
WFSH(AM) Valparaiso-Niceville FL
WAXE(AM) Vero Beach FL
WRCG(AM) Columbus GA
WNEX-FM Gordon GA
KLNT(AM) Clinton IA
KWSL(AM) Sioux City IA
WRYT(AM) Edwardsville IL
WKDC(AM) Elmhurst IL
WAIK(AM) Galesburg IL
WFXW(AM) Geneva IL
WLBH-FM Mattoon IL
WQFE(FM) Brownsburg IN
WLOI(AM) La Porte IN
WBTO(AM) Linton IN
WQTY(FM) Linton IN
WAXI(FM) Rockville IN
WJSH(AM) Terre Haute IN
KTOP(AM) Topeka KS
KQAM(AM) Wichita KS
WSON(AM) Henderson KY
WPAD(AM) Paducah KY
WCBR(AM) Richmond KY
KAOK(AM) Lake Charles LA
WTIX(AM) New Orleans LA
KVLA(AM) Vidalia LA
WXKS(AM) Medford MA
WPLM(AM) Plymouth MA
WPLM-FM Plymouth MA
WESX(AM) Salem MA
WITH(AM) Baltimore MD
WWLG(AM) Baltimore MD
WCEI(AM) Easton MD
WJTO(AM) Bath ME
WDEA(AM) Ellsworth ME
WRUM(AM) Rumford ME
WFDF(AM) Flint MI
WKNX(AM) Frankenmuth MI
WQXO(AM) Munising MI
WQWQ(AM) Muskegon Heights MI
WYGR(AM) Wyoming MI
KKCQ(AM) Fosston MN
KLBB(AM) St. Paul MN
WHLB(AM) Virginia MN
KWRT(AM) Boonville MO
KDFN(AM) Doniphan MO
KFEZ(AM) Kansas City MO
KTOZ(AM) Springfield MO
KSFT(AM) St. Joseph MO
WEW(AM) St. Louis MO
WGCM(AM) Gulfport MS
WTUP(AM) Tupelo MS
*WSGE(FM) Dallas NC
WZBO(AM) Edenton NC
WMBL(AM) Morehead City NC
WNOS(AM) New Bern NC
WSAT(AM) Salisbury NC
KTYN(AM) Minot ND
KMEM(AM) Lincoln NE
WHTG(AM) Eatontown NJ
WRDR(FM) Egg Harbor City NJ
WMTR(AM) Morristown NJ
KIVA(AM) Corrales NM
KORK(AM) Las Vegas NV
WCBA(AM) Corning NY
WEHH(AM) Elmira Heights-Horseheads NY
WHLI(AM) Hempstead NY
WGSM(AM) Huntington NY
WIZR(AM) Johnstown NY
WRTN(FM) New Rochelle NY
WHLD(AM) Niagara Falls NY
WSGO(AM) Oswego NY
WLIM(AM) Patchogue NY
WYLF(AM) Penn Yan NY
WNCO(AM) Ashland OH
*WKHR(FM) Bainbridge OH
WCTM(AM) Eaton OH
*WMUB(FM) Oxford OH
*KRSC-FM Claremore OK
KSPI(AM) Stillwater OK
KGTO(AM) Tulsa OK
KORC(AM) Waldport OR
WCDL(AM) Carbondale PA
*WSAJ-FM Grove City PA
WPEN(AM) Philadelphia PA
WJAS(AM) Pittsburgh PA
WKMC(AM) Roaring Spring PA
*WRDV(FM) Warminster PA
WBAX(AM) Wilkes-Barre PA
WVOZ-FM Carolina PR
WKRI(AM) West Warwick RI
WLOW(FM) Bluffton SC
WNCK(FM) Port Royal SC
WSNW(AM) Seneca SC
KBRK(AM) Brookings SD
WDOD(AM) Chattanooga TN
WAMB(AM) Donelson TN
WAMB-FM Donelson TN
WTJS(AM) Jackson TN
WHJM(AM) Knoxville TN
KHXS(FM) Abilene TX
KAAM(AM) Dallas TX
KCYT(FM) Granbury TX
KQUE(FM) Houston TX
KOLE(AM) Port Arthur TX
KTWN(AM) Texarkana TX
KTXN-FM Victoria TX
KOVO(AM) Provo UT
WKEX(AM) Blacksburg VA
WOPI(AM) Bristol VA
*WFOS(FM) Chesapeake VA
WTVR(AM) Richmond VA
WMBG(AM) Williamsburg VA
WAZR(FM) Woodstock VA
WDCM(FM) Cruz Bay VI
WFAD(AM) Middlebury VT
WCFR(AM) Springfield VT
KBRO(AM) Bremerton WA
KKMO(AM) Tacoma WA
WRJQ(AM) Appleton WI
WERL(AM) Eagle River WI
WCCN(AM) Neillsville WI
WMOV(AM) Ravenswood WV

Black

Includes station formats Rhythm & Blues and Soul. Also see Urban Contemporary.

WHMA(AM) Anniston AL
WATV(AM) Birmingham AL
WCOX(AM) Camden AL
WRAG(AM) Carrollton AL
WXAL(AM) Demopolis AL
WQLW(FM) Eutaw AL
WMGJ(AM) Gadsden AL
WXVI(AM) Montgomery AL
WZMG(AM) Opelika AL
WTQX(AM) Selma AL
WZZA(AM) Tuscumbia AL
*KABF(FM) Little Rock AR
KAKJ(FM) Marianna AR
KLRG(AM) North Little Rock AR
KPBA(AM) Pine Bluff AR
KCLT(FM) West Helena AR
KMAX(FM) Arcadia CA
*KDVS(FM) Davis CA
KJAY(AM) Sacramento CA
*KSRH(FM) San Rafael CA
*KCEQ(FM) Walnut Creek CA
KDKO(AM) Littleton CO
KKMG(FM) Pueblo CO
*WRTC-FM Hartford CT
*WNHU(FM) West Haven CT
WSWN(AM) Belle Glade FL
WWLO(AM) Gainesville FL
*WAPN(FM) Holly Hill FL
WZAZ(AM) Jacksonville FL
WTOT(AM) Marianna FL
WRBD(AM) Pompano Beach FL
*WAMF(FM) Tallahassee FL
WDEC(AM) Americus GA
WIGO(AM) Atlanta GA
WYZE(AM) Atlanta GA
WEAM(AM) Columbus GA
WOKS(AM) Columbus GA
WPBS(AM) Conyers GA
WXLL(AM) Decatur GA
WXKO(AM) Fort Valley GA
WMXY(AM) Hogansville GA
WJGA-FM Jackson GA
WFDR(AM) Manchester GA
WSOK(AM) Savannah GA
WXRS(AM) Swainsboro GA
WBRO(AM) Waynesboro GA
*KBBG(FM) Waterloo IA
*WOUI(FM) Chicago IL
WVON(AM) Cicero IL
WLUV-FM Loves Park IL
WVEL(AM) Pekin IL
WTLC(AM) Indianapolis IN
WABD(AM) Fort Campbell KY
WVLK(AM) Lexington KY
WLOU(AM) Louisville KY
KTRY(AM) Bastrop LA
KTRY-FM Bastrop LA
WXOK(AM) Baton Rouge LA
KLPL(AM) Lake Providence LA
*KNWD(FM) Natchitoches LA
KQXL-FM New Roads LA
KSLO(AM) Opelousas LA
KVOL-FM Opelousas LA
KXLA(AM) Rayville LA
KOKA(AM) Shreveport LA
KBSF(AM) Springhill LA
*WMUA(FM) Amherst MA
*WTCC(FM) Springfield MA
*WCUW(FM) Worcester MA
WWIN-FM Glen Burnie MD
*WESM(FM) Princess Anne MD
WJDY(AM) Salisbury MD
WMTG(AM) Dearborn MI
WJLB(FM) Detroit MI
WQBH(AM) Detroit MI
*WMCN(FM) St. Paul MN
KATZ(AM) St. Louis MO
KXOK(AM) St. Louis MO
WMGO(AM) Canton MS
WONG(AM) Canton MS
WROX(AM) Clarksdale MS
WWUN-FM Clarksdale MS
WTYJ(FM) Fayette MS
WYKC(AM) Grenada MS
WKRA-FM Holly Springs MS
WCPC(AM) Houston MS
WBAD(FM) Leland MS
WESY(AM) Leland MS
WXTN(AM) Lexington MS
WAKK(AM) McComb MS
WMIS(AM) Natchez MS
WSAO(AM) Senatobia MS
WROB(AM) West Point MS
WAZF(AM) Yazoo City MS
WRCS(AM) Ahoskie NC
WVOE(AM) Chadbourn NC
WCKB(AM) Dunn NC
WIDU(AM) Fayetteville NC
*WNAA(FM) Greensboro NC
WOOW(AM) Greenville NC
WLOJ(AM) New Bern NC
WAUG(AM) New Hope NC
WLLE(AM) Raleigh NC
WRSV(FM) Rocky Mount NC
WEGG(AM) Rose Hill NC
WXKL(AM) Sanford NC
WTAB(AM) Tabor City NC
WAAA(AM) Winston-Salem NC
WDCR(AM) Hanover NH
*KCEP(FM) Las Vegas NV
WBLS(FM) New York NY
*WHCR-FM New York NY
WLIB(AM) New York NY
WWRL(AM) New York NY
*WVKR-FM Poughkeepsie NY
WOLF(AM) Syracuse NY
*WBGU(FM) Bowling Green OH
WCIN(AM) Cincinnati OH
*WSLN(FM) Delaware OH
WCKX(FM) London OH
WWWM(AM) Toledo OH
KSYD(FM) Reedsport OR
*WDNR(FM) Chester PA
*WERG(FM) Erie PA
*WIXQ(FM) Millersville PA
WDAS(AM) Philadelphia PA
WDAS-FM Philadelphia PA
WHAT(AM) Philadelphia PA
WDOG(AM) Allendale SC
WDOG-FM Allendale SC
WPAL(AM) Charleston SC
WOIC(AM) Columbia SC
WPJS(AM) Conway SC
WEAC(AM) Gaffney SC
WMCJ(AM) Moncks Corner SC
*WSSB-FM Orangeburg SC
WASC(AM) Spartanburg SC
WVOL(AM) Berry Hill TN
WNOO(AM) Chattanooga TN
WFKX(FM) Henderson TN
KJMS(FM) Memphis TN
WDIA(AM) Memphis TN
WLOK(AM) Memphis TN
*KAZI(FM) Austin TX
KSKY(AM) Balch Springs TX
KGBC(AM) Galveston TX
KCOH(AM) Houston TX
KYOK(AM) Houston TX
*KBWC(FM) Marshall TX
KALO(AM) Port Arthur TX
*KPVU(FM) Prairie View TX
KFIT(AM) Sunset Valley TX
WBBC-FM Blackstone VA
WKBY(AM) Chatham VA
WILA(AM) Danville VA
*WHOV(FM) Hampton VA
WSVY(AM) Portsmouth VA
WTMM(AM) Richmond VA
WJWS(AM) South Hill VA
WSTA(AM) Charlotte Amalie VI
KRIZ(AM) Renton WA
WMCS(AM) Greenfield WI

Bluegrass

*WAMU(FM) Washington DC
WDGR(AM) Dahlonega GA
WALH(AM) Mountain City GA
WSKV(FM) Stanton KY
WPAQ(AM) Mount Airy NC
KXVQ(AM) Pawhuska OK
WJKM(AM) Hartsville TN
WLOD(AM) Loudon TN

Broadcasting & Cable Yearbook 1994
B-547

Programming on Radio Stations in the U.S.

WLIJ(AM) Shelbyville TN
WFIC(AM) Collinsville VA
WDUF(AM) Duffield VA
WGAT(AM) Gate City VA
WHFD(FM) Lawrenceville VA
WNRV(AM) Narrows VA
WPUV(AM) Pulaski VA
WXGI(AM) Richmond VA
WYTI(AM) Rocky Mount VA
WKCW(AM) Warrenton VA

Blues

WBLX(AM) Fairhope AL
*WJAB(FM) Huntsville AL
WNPT-FM Linden AL
WTSK(AM) Tuscaloosa AL
WWPG(AM) Tuscaloosa AL
KFFA(AM) Helena AR
KDIA(AM) Oakland CA
*KAZU(FM) Pacific Grove CA
WTOT(AM) Marianna FL
WEDR(FM) Miami FL
WPUL(AM) South Daytona FL
WDEC(AM) Americus GA
WCBR-FM Arlington Heights IL
WBEE(AM) Harvey IL
*WGLT(FM) Normal IL
KVOL(AM) Lafayette LA
*WWOZ(FM) New Orleans LA
KVOL-FM Opelousas LA
KRUS(AM) Ruston LA
*KDAQ(FM) Shreveport LA
*WUMB-FM Boston MA
WATD-FM Marshfield MA
WCHB(AM) Taylor MI
KATZ(AM) St. Louis MO
WONG(AM) Canton MS
*WMPR(FM) Jackson MS
WZRX(AM) Jackson MS
*WPRL(FM) Lorman MS
WQMA(AM) Marks MS
WABO(AM) Waynesboro MS
WRDX(FM) Salisbury NC
*KRVM(FM) Eugene OR
WVGB(AM) Beaufort SC
WYNN(AM) Florence SC
WYOR(AM) Brentwood TN
WMDB(AM) Nashville TN

Children

*KUCA(FM) Conway AR
KCTQ(AM) Thousand Oaks CA
KKYD(AM) Denver CO
WKDB(AM) Towson MD
WISZ(AM) Zeeland MI
WWTC(AM) Minneapolis MN
KLZE(FM) Owensville MO
KIDS(AM) Springfield MO
KYYD(AM) Abilene TX
KAHZ(AM) Fort Worth TX
KKDS(AM) South Salt Lake UT
WEIO(AM) Eau Claire WI

Classic Rock

Also see Oldies.
KBFX(FM) Anchorage AK
KXLR(FM) Fairbanks AK
KSUP(FM) Juneau AK
KZXX(AM) Kenai AK
KGTW(FM) Ketchikan AK
KSBZ(FM) Sitka AK
KIAL(AM) Unalaska AK
WZRR(FM) Birmingham AL
*WSGN(FM) Gadsden AL
WTAK-FM Hartselle AL
WTAK(AM) Huntsville AL
WHOD(AM) Jackson AL
WHOD-FM Jackson AL
*WLJS-FM Jacksonville AL
WHIY(AM) Moulton AL
WXKI(FM) Moulton AL
WMXA(FM) Opelika AL
WXFX(FM) Prattville AL
WTID(FM) Reform AL
WHBB(AM) Selma AL
WSSY-FM Talladega AL
WAZK(FM) Trinity AL
KLPQ(FM) Cabot AR
KKEG(FM) Fayetteville AR
KHOX(FM) Hoxie AR
KRXS-FM Globe AZ
KRKN(FM) Oro Valley AZ
KOPA(AM) Scottsdale AZ
KSLX(FM) Scottsdale AZ
KUKQ(AM) Tempe AZ
KXGO(FM) Arcata CA
KCQR(FM) Ellwood CA
KOZT(FM) Fort Bragg CA
KJFX(FM) Fresno CA
KUFX(FM) Gilroy CA
KLCX(FM) Indio CA
KLSX(FM) Los Angeles CA
KVFX(FM) Manteca CA
KLKX(FM) Rosamond CA
KSEG(FM) Sacramento CA
KCLX-FM San Diego CA
KGB-FM San Diego CA
KRQR(FM) San Francisco CA
KZOZ(FM) San Luis Obispo CA
KSRI(FM) Santa Cruz CA
KXBS(FM) Santa Paula CA
KXFX(FM) Santa Rosa CA
KLUE(FM) Soledad CA
*KCEQ(FM) Walnut Creek CA
KKFM(FM) Colorado Springs CO
KRFX(FM) Denver CO
KSTR-FM Montrose CO
WEFX(FM) Norwalk CT
WAIA(FM) Callahan FL
WJBX(FM) Fort Myers Beach FL
WKGR(FM) Fort Pierce FL
WRUF-FM Gainesville FL
WBNF(FM) Marianna FL
WZTA(FM) Miami Beach FL
WRRX(FM) Micanopy FL
WHOO(AM) Orlando FL
WFSY(FM) Panama City FL
WZGC(FM) Atlanta GA
WWIQ(FM) Gray GA
WZIQ(FM) Smithville GA
WMCD(FM) Statesboro GA
WWRQ(FM) Valdosta GA
WWUF(FM) Waycross GA
KHWI(FM) Hilo HI
KGGY(FM) Dubuque IA
KKSI(FM) Eddyville IA
*KDIC(FM) Grinnell IA
*KCUI(FM) Pella IA
KFMW(FM) Waterloo IA
*KWDM(FM) West Des Moines IA
KLVJ(AM) Mountain Home ID
KLVJ-FM Mountain Home ID
KLCI(FM) Nampa ID
KMGI(FM) Pocatello ID
KECH-FM Sun Valley ID
WXRX(FM) Belvidere IL
WRXX(FM) Centralia IL
WFXB(FM) East St. Louis IL
WCKG(FM) Elmwood Park IL
WZZP(FM) Kankakee IL
*WLTL(FM) La Grange IL
*WMXM(FM) Lake Forest IL
WEAI(FM) Lynnville IL
WJEQ(FM) Macomb IL
WRBT(FM) Mt. Carmel IL
WLRZ(FM) Peru IL
WZNF(FM) Rantoul IL
WJVO(FM) South Jacksonville IL
WGFA(AM) Watseka IL
WGFA-FM Watseka IL
*WEAX(FM) Angola IN
WQRK(FM) Bedford IN
WWWY(FM) Columbus IN
WZOW(FM) Goshen IN
WRZX(FM) Indianapolis IN
WKVI(AM) Knox IN
WKHY(FM) Lafayette IN
WMDH(AM) New Castle IN
WARU-FM Peru IN
*WECI(FM) Richmond IN
WQLK(FM) Richmond IN
*KNBU(FM) Baldwin City KS
KOCD(FM) Columbus KS
KFFX(FM) Emporia KS
KSEK-FM Girard KS
KWKR(FM) Leoti KS
KYUU(AM) Liberal KS
WOKH(FM) Bardstown KY
WDNS(FM) Bowling Green KY
WKEQ(AM) Burnside KY
WUGO(FM) Grayson KY
WKQQ(FM) Lexington KY
WKDO-FM Liberty KY
WKTG(FM) Madisonville KY
WTBK(FM) Manchester KY
WDDJ(FM) Paducah KY
WKLW(AM) Paintsville KY
WPKE(AM) Pikeville KY
WGKY(FM) Wickliffe KY
WCKW(AM) Garyville LA
KTOC(AM) Jonesboro LA
WCKW-FM La Place LA
*KNSU(FM) Thibodaux LA
WRNX(FM) Amherst MA
WZLX(FM) Boston MA
*WGAO(FM) Franklin MA
WRSI(FM) Greenfield MA
WPXC(FM) Hyannis MA
WCGY(FM) Lawrence MA
WRCZ(FM) Pittsfield MA
*WSDH(FM) Sandwich MA
WAQY-FM Springfield MA
WARW(FM) Bethesda MD
*WMTB-FM Emmittsburg MD
WQCM(FM) Halfway MD
WXIE(FM) Oakland MD
WTHU(AM) Thurmont MD
WKRH(FM) Bath ME
WQDY(AM) Calais ME
WQDY-FM Calais ME
WCDQ(FM) Sanford ME
WCSX(FM) Birmingham MI
WMMQ(FM) Charlotte MI
WGFM(FM) Cheboygan MI
WMIQ(AM) Iron Mountain MI
WMTE(AM) Manistee MI
WDMJ(AM) Marquette MI
WMBN(AM) Petoskey MI
WRKR(FM) Portage MI
WEVS(FM) Saugatuck MI
WSUE(FM) Sault Ste. Marie MI
WCCW-FM Traverse City MI
KLIZ-FM Brainerd MN
WAKX(FM) Duluth MN
KZCR(FM) Fergus Falls MN
KQWB-FM Moorhead MN
KXLP(FM) New Ulm MN
KWNG(FM) Red Wing MN
KRCH(FM) Rochester MN
*KDXL(FM) St. Louis Park MN
KLLZ-FM Walker MN
KRRR(FM) Canton MO
KCHI(AM) Chillicothe MO
KCHI-FM Chillicothe MO
KSHE(FM) Crestwood MO
KCFX(FM) Harrisonville MO
KRXL(FM) Kirksville MO
KYLC(FM) Osage Beach MO
KQMX(FM) Rolla MO
KSD-FM St. Louis MO
KTTN-FM Trenton MO
WQID(FM) Biloxi MS
WXRG(FM) Gulfport MS
WOXD(FM) Oxford MS
WMXU(FM) Starkville MS
WZLQ(FM) Tupelo MS
KRKX(FM) Billings MT
KQDI-FM Great Falls MT
KBBZ(FM) Kalispell MT
KBSR(AM) Laurel MT
WKRR(FM) Asheboro NC
*WASU-FM Boone NC
WZZU(FM) Burlington-Graham NC
WSTS(FM) Fairmont NC
WRFX(FM) Kannapolis NC
WSFL-FM New Bern NC
WFJA(FM) Sanford NC
WSFM(FM) Southport NC
WTOE(AM) Spruce Pine NC
KPFX(FM) Fargo ND
KBQQ(FM) Minot ND
KYYZ(FM) Williston ND
KLRB(FM) Aurora NE
KTGL(FM) Beatrice NE
KBBN-FM Broken Bow NE
KEZO(AM) Omaha NE
KKCD(FM) Omaha NE
*WPEA(FM) Exeter NH
WLTN-FM Lisbon NH
WMTK(FM) Littleton NH
WPNH(AM) Plymouth NH
WPNH-FM Plymouth NH
*WMNJ(FM) Madison NJ
WMID-FM Pleasantville NJ
KAFR(FM) Angel Fire NM
KUCU(FM) Armijo NM
*KEDP(FM) Las Vegas NM
KSFX(FM) Roswell NM
KLSK(FM) Santa Fe NM
KSNM(FM) Truth or Consequences NM
KLKO(FM) Elko NV
KKLZ(FM) Las Vegas NV
KFBI(FM) Pahrump NV
KOZZ(AM) Reno NV
KOZZ-FM Reno NV
WTKW(FM) Bridgeport NY
WUFX(FM) Buffalo NY
*WECW(FM) Elmira NY
WYLR-FM Glens Falls NY
WQNY(FM) Ithaca NY
WXTM(FM) Monticello NY
WNGZ(FM) Montour Falls NY
WXRK(FM) New York NY
WJJL(AM) Niagara Falls NY
*WRHO(FM) Oneonta NY
WQBK-FM Rensselaer NY
*WSPN(FM) Saratoga Springs NY
WNNR-FM Sodus NY
WRQI(FM) South Bristol Township NY
WONE-FM Akron OH
WQEL(FM) Bucyrus OH
*WCWT-FM Centerville OH
WNCX(FM) Cleveland OH
WOFX(FM) Fairfield OH
WMGG(FM) Gallipolis OH
*WDUB(FM) Granville OH
*WKET(FM) Kettering OH
*WLMH(FM) Morrow OH
WWJM(FM) New Lexington OH
WQTL(FM) Ottawa OH
WXKR(FM) Port Clinton OH
WNXT-FM Portsmouth OH
WAZU(FM) Springfield OH
WBYR(FM) Van Wert OH
*WOBN(FM) Westerville OH
*KRSC-FM Claremore OK
*KRSC-FM Claremore OK
KKRX(AM) Lawton OK
KKRX-FM Lawton OK
KRXO(FM) Oklahoma City OK
KGOK(FM) Pauls Valley OK
KLOR-FM Ponca City OK
KSPI-FM Stillwater OK
KWDQ(FM) Woodward OK
KQAK(FM) Bend OR
KTWS(FM) Bend OR
KZEL-FM Eugene OR
KLDR(FM) Harbeck-Fruitdale OR
KTBR(AM) Roseburg OR
KTWI(FM) Warm Springs OR
WWKS(FM) Beaver Falls PA
*WBUQ(FM) Bloomsburg PA
WRRK(FM) Braddock PA
WCCR(FM) Clarion PA
WFRM-FM Coudersport PA
*WJRH(FM) Easton PA
*WMCE(FM) Erie PA
*WKVR-FM Huntingdon PA
WQMU(FM) Indiana PA
WLLF(FM) Mercer PA
WKQV(FM) Olyphant PA
WYSP(FM) Philadelphia PA
WISL-FM Shamokin PA
WHTX(FM) Sharpsville PA
*WRSK(FM) Slippery Rock PA
WQWK(FM) State College PA
WKGB-FM Susquehanna PA
WYMK(FM) Tunkhannock PA
WNBT(AM) Wellsboro PA
*WWAS(FM) Williamsport PA
WWLI(FM) Providence RI
WWRX-FM Westerly RI
WRXR-FM Aiken SC
WROQ(FM) Anderson SC
WJMX-FM Cheraw SC
WDAR(AM) Darlington SC
WDAR-FM Darlington SC
WZNS(FM) Dillon SC
WSCA(FM) Georgetown SC
WMFX(FM) St. Andrews SC
KPHR(FM) Milbank SD
KGFX-FM Pierre SD
KRRO(FM) Sioux Falls SD
*KAOR(FM) Vermillion SD
KKQQ(FM) Volga SD
*WAPX-FM Clarksville TN
WIZO(AM) Franklin TN
WGFX(FM) Gallatin TN
WEGR(FM) Memphis TN
WFXS(FM) Soddy-Daisy TN
WSMT-FM Sparta TN
KEYJ-FM Abilene TX
KATP(FM) Amarillo TX
KKHR(FM) Anson TX
KPEZ(FM) Austin TX
KARX(FM) Claude TX
KTSR(FM) College Station TX
KKZR(FM) Conroe TX
KZPS(FM) Dallas TX
KAMZ(FM) El Paso TX
KICA-FM Farwell TX
KLFX(FM) Harker Heights TX
KKTX(AM) Kilgore TX
KKTX-FM Kilgore TX
KWVS(FM) Kingsville TX
KZFX(FM) Lake Jackson TX
KRBA(AM) Lufkin TX
KCDQ(FM) Monahans TX
KOLE(AM) Port Arthur TX
KXCC(FM) Rockport TX
KZEP-FM San Antonio TX
KWSM(FM) Sherman TX
KSNY-FM Snyder TX
KCUB-FM Stephenville TX
KALK(FM) Winfield TX
KBRE-FM Cedar City UT
KLZX-FM Salt Lake City UT
WVVV(FM) Blacksburg VA
WNOR(AM) Norfolk VA
WNOR-FM Norfolk VA
WRIC-FM Richlands VA
WRVH(AM) Richmond VA
WRXL(FM) Richmond VA
WAFX(FM) Suffolk VA
WCXR-FM Woodbridge VA
WBFL(FM) Bellows Falls VT
WKVT-FM Brattleboro VT
WEBK(FM) Killington VT
WGTK(FM) Middlebury VT
WVAY(FM) Wilmington VT
WMXR(FM) Woodstock VT
KISM(FM) Bellingham WA
KGY-FM McCleary WA
KAPY(AM) Port Angeles WA
KZOK(AM) Seattle WA
KZOK-FM Seattle WA
KKZX(FM) Spokane WA
KHSS(FM) Walla Walla WA
KKRT(AM) Wenatchee WA
KKRV(FM) Wenatchee WA
KATS(FM) Yakima WA
WISM-FM Altoona WI
WJJH(FM) Ashland WI
WMBE(AM) Chilton WI
WMJB(FM) Evansville WI
WIBA-FM Madison WI
WMZK(FM) Merrill WI
WKLH(FM) Milwaukee WI
WCCN-FM Neillsville WI
WOZZ(FM) New London WI
WBOG(FM) Tomah WI
WKBH-FM Trempealeau WI
WJJO(FM) Watertown WI
WQJY(FM) West Salem WI
*WVWC(FM) Buckhannon WV
WLOG(AM) Logan WV
WZZW(FM) Milton WV
WCLG-FM Morgantown WV
WAXS(FM) Oak Hill WV
WRZZ(FM) Ravenswood WV
KKTY(AM) Douglas WY
KKTY-FM Douglas WY
KTRZ(FM) Riverton WY

Classical

KLEF(FM) Anchorage AK
*KSKA(FM) Anchorage AK
*KUAC(FM) Fairbanks AK
*KTOO(FM) Juneau AK
*WBHM(FM) Birmingham AL
*WRWA(FM) Dothan AL
*WLRH(FM) Huntsville AL
WNPT-FM Linden AL
*WHIL-FM Mobile AL
*WQPR(FM) Muscle Shoals AL
*WTSU(FM) Troy AL
*WUAL-FM Tuscaloosa AL
*KBSA(FM) El Dorado AR
*KUAF(FM) Fayetteville AR
*KASU(FM) Jonesboro AR
*KLRE-FM Little Rock AR
*KUAR(FM) Little Rock AR
*KXRJ(FM) Russellville AR
*KNAU(FM) Flagstaff AZ
*KUAT-FM Tucson AZ
*KAWC-FM Yuma AZ
*KPRX(FM) Bakersfield CA
*KZPN(FM) Bayside CA
KVOQ(FM) Carmel CA
*KCHO(FM) Chico CA
*KVPR(FM) Fresno CA
*KXSR(FM) Groveland CA
KKGO-FM Los Angeles CA
*KUSC(FM) Los Angeles CA
*KADV(FM) Modesto CA
*KSMC(FM) Moraga CA
*KCSN(FM) Northridge CA
*KPSC(FM) Palm Springs CA
KDFC(AM) Palo Alto CA
*KXPR(FM) Sacramento CA
KFSD-FM San Diego CA
KDFC-FM San Francisco CA
KKHI(AM) San Francisco CA
KKHI-FM San Francisco CA
*KCBX(FM) San Luis Obispo CA
KDB(FM) Santa Barbara CA
*KFAC(FM) Santa Barbara CA
*KUSP(FM) Santa Cruz CA
*KRCB-FM Santa Rosa CA
KSUR(AM) Soledad CA
*KUOP(FM) Stockton CA
*KCPB(FM) Thousand Oaks CA
*KRZA(FM) Alamosa CO
*KAJX(FM) Aspen CO
*KCFR(FM) Denver CO
KVOD(FM) Denver CO
*KPRN(FM) Grand Junction CO
*WSHU(FM) Fairfield CT
*WGRS(FM) Guilford CT
*WJMJ(FM) Hartford CT
*WPKT(FM) Meriden CT
*WMNR(FM) Monroe CT
*WSLX(FM) New Canaan CT
*WNPR(FM) Norwich CT
*WRXC(FM) Shelton CT
*WETA-FM Washington DC
WGMS-FM Washington DC
*WSFP-FM Fort Myers FL
*WQCS(FM) Fort Pierce FL
*WUFT-FM Gainesville FL
*WJCT-FM Jacksonville FL
WTMI(FM) Miami FL
*WMFE-FM Orlando FL
*WUCF-FM Orlando FL
*WKGC-FM Panama City FL
*WUWF(FM) Pensacola FL
WSPB(AM) Sarasota FL
WSTF(FM) St. Augustine FL
*WFSQ(FM) Tallahassee FL
*WUSF(FM) Tampa FL
*WXEL(FM) West Palm Beach FL
*WPRK(FM) Winter Park FL
*WUNV(FM) Albany GA
*WUGA(FM) Athens GA
*WABE(FM) Atlanta GA
WGKA(AM) Atlanta GA
*WACG-FM Augusta GA
*WDCO-FM Cochran GA
*WTJB(FM) Columbus GA
*WJWV(FM) Fort Gaines GA
*WSVH(FM) Savannah GA
*WABR-FM Tifton GA
*WWET(FM) Valdosta GA
*WJSP-FM Warm Springs GA
*KSDA-FM Agat GU
*KHPR(FM) Honolulu HI
*KKUA(FM) Wailuku HI
*WOI-FM Ames IA
*KHKE(FM) Cedar Falls IA
*KUNI(FM) Cedar Falls IA
*KIWR(FM) Council Bluffs IA
*KLCD(FM) Decorah IA
*KTPR(FM) Fort Dodge IA
*KSUI(FM) Iowa City IA
*KRNI(AM) Mason City IA
*KDCR(FM) Sioux Center IA
*KWIT(FM) Sioux City IA
*KBSU-FM Boise ID
*KBSM(FM) McCall ID
*KRFA-FM Moscow ID
*KRIC(FM) Rexburg ID
*KWRV(FM) Sun Valley ID
*KBSW(FM) Twin Falls ID
*WSIU(FM) Carbondale IL
*WEIU(FM) Charleston IL
WFMT(FM) Chicago IL
WNIB(FM) Chicago IL
*WNIU(FM) De Kalb IL
*WMWA(FM) Glenview IL
*WIUM(FM) Macomb IL
*WUSI(FM) Olney IL
*WCBU(FM) Peoria IL
*WIPA(FM) Pittsfield IL
*WQUB(FM) Quincy IL
*WVIK(FM) Rock Island IL
*WSSU(FM) Springfield IL
*WILL-FM Urbana IL
WNIZ-FM Zion IL
*WFIU(FM) Bloomington IN

Broadcasting & Cable Yearbook 1994
B-548

Programming on Radio Stations in the U.S.

WSYW-FM Danville IN
*WNIN-FM Evansville IN
*WBNI-FM Fort Wayne IN
*WGCS(FM) Goshen IN
*WFYI-FM Indianapolis IN
WSYW(AM) Indianapolis IN
*WBST(FM) Muncie IN
*WSND-FM Notre Dame IN
*WECI(FM) Richmond IN
*WBAA(AM) West Lafayette IN
*KANZ(FM) Garden City KS
*KHCT(FM) Great Bend KS
*KHCC-FM Hutchinson KS
*KANU(FM) Lawrence KS
*KRPS(FM) Pittsburg KS
*KHCD(FM) Salina KS
*KMUW(FM) Wichita KS
*WKYU-FM Bowling Green KY
*WKUE(FM) Elizabethtown KY
*WEKH(FM) Hazard KY
*WKPB(FM) Henderson KY
*WUKY(FM) Lexington KY
*WFPK(FM) Louisville KY
*WUOL(FM) Louisville KY
*WKMS-FM Murray KY
*WKWC(FM) Owensboro KY
*WEKU-FM Richmond KY
*WDCL-FM Somerset KY
*KLSA(FM) Alexandria LA
*WRKF(FM) Baton Rouge LA
*KSLU(FM) Hammond LA
*KRVS(FM) Lafayette LA
*KEDM(FM) Monroe LA
*WTUL(FM) New Orleans LA
*WWNO(FM) New Orleans LA
*KDAQ(FM) Shreveport LA
*WFCR(FM) Amherst MA
*WBUR(FM) Boston MA
*WGBH(FM) Boston MA
*WUMB-FM Boston MA
WHRB(FM) Cambridge MA
WFCC-FM Chatham MA
WBOQ(FM) Gloucester MA
*WOMR(FM) Provincetown MA
WCRB(FM) Waltham MA
*WICN(FM) Worcester MA
*WBJC(FM) Baltimore MD
*WJHU-FM Baltimore MD
*WHFC(FM) Bel Air MD
*WFWM(FM) Frostburg MD
*WSCL(FM) Salisbury MD
*WGTS-FM Takoma Park MD
*WMEH(FM) Bangor ME
*WMED(FM) Calais ME
WBQQ(FM) Kennebunk ME
*WMEA(FM) Portland ME
*WMEM(FM) Presque Isle ME
WPKM(FM) Scarborough ME
WAVX(FM) Thomaston ME
*WMEW(FM) Waterville ME
*WCML-FM Alpena MI
*WUOM(FM) Ann Arbor MI
*WUCX-FM Bay City MI
*WAUS(FM) Berrien Springs MI
WQRS(FM) Detroit MI
*WIZY(FM) East Jordan MI
*WKAR-FM East Lansing MI
*WFBE(FM) Flint MI
*WFUM-FM Flint MI
*WBLU-FM Grand Rapids MI
*WVGR(FM) Grand Rapids MI
*WGGL-FM Houghton MI
*WIAA(FM) Interlochen MI
*WMUK(FM) Kalamazoo MI
*WKAL(AM) Kalkaska MI
*WNMU-FM Marquette MI
*WCMU-FM Mount Pleasant MI
*WCMZ-FM Sault Ste. Marie MI
*WBLV(FM) Twin Lake MI
*KRSU(FM) Appleton MN
*KCRB-FM Bemidji MN
*KBPR(FM) Brainerd MN
*KSJR-FM Collegeville MN
*WSCD-FM Duluth MN
*KMSU(FM) Mankato MN
*KSJN(FM) Minneapolis MN
*KCCM-FM Moorhead MN
*WCAL(FM) Northfield MN
*KLSE-FM Rochester MN
*KGAC(FM) St. Peter MN
*KQMN(FM) Thief River Falls MN
*WIRR(FM) Virginia-Hibbing MN
*KRSW-FM Worthington-Marshall MN
*KRCU(FM) Cape Girardeau MO
*KRNW(FM) Chillicothe MO
KFUO-FM Clayton MO
*KBIA(FM) Columbia MO
*KXMS(FM) Joplin MO
KXTR(FM) Kansas City MO
*KXCV(FM) Maryville MO
*KCOZ(FM) Point Lookout MO
*KUMR(FM) Rolla MO
*KSMU(FM) Springfield MO
*KWMU(FM) St. Louis MO
*WMAH-FM Biloxi MS
*WMAE-FM Booneville MS
*WMAU-FM Bude MS
*WMAO-FM Greenwood MS
*WUSM-FM Hattiesburg MS
*WMPN-FM Jackson MS
*WMAW-FM Meridian MS
*WMAB-FM Mississippi State MS
*WMAV-FM Oxford MS
*WKNA(FM) Senatobia MS
*KEMC(FM) Billings MT
*KBMC(FM) Bozeman MT
*KGPR(FM) Great Falls MT
*WCQS(FM) Asheville NC
*WGWG(FM) Boiling Springs NC
*WUNC(FM) Chapel Hill NC
*WSGE(FM) Dallas NC
*WDAV(FM) Davidson NC
*WFQS(FM) Franklin NC
*WTEB(FM) New Bern NC
*WCPE(FM) Raleigh NC
*WZRU(FM) Roanoke Rapids NC
*WHQR(FM) Wilmington NC
*WFDD-FM Winston-Salem NC
*KCND(FM) Bismarck ND
*KDPR(FM) Dickinson ND
*KFJM-FM Grand Forks ND
*KMPR(FM) Minot ND
*KPPR(FM) Williston ND
*KTNE-FM Alliance NE
*KMNE-FM Bassett NE
*KCNE-FM Chadron NE
*KHNE-FM Hastings NE
*KLNE-FM Lexington NE
*KUCV(FM) Lincoln NE
*KRNE-FM Merriman NE
*KXNE-FM Norfolk NE
*KPNE-FM North Platte NE
*KIOS-FM Omaha NE
*KVNO(FM) Omaha NE
*WEVO(FM) Concord NH
WWOC(FM) Avalon NJ
*WWNJ(FM) Dover Township NJ
WPRB(FM) Princeton NJ
*WWFM(FM) Trenton NJ
KHFM(FM) Albuquerque NM
*KSJE(FM) Farmington NM
*KRWG(FM) Las Cruces NM
*KMTH(FM) Maljamar NM
*KENW-FM Portales NM
*KSFR(FM) Santa Fe NM
*KNCC(FM) Elko NV
*KNPR(FM) Las Vegas NV
*KLNR(FM) Panaca NV
*KUNR(FM) Reno NV
*KTPH(FM) Tonopah NV
*WAMC(FM) Albany NY
*WSKG-FM Binghamton NY
WNED-FM Buffalo NY
*WCAN(FM) Canajoharie NY
*WRHU(FM) Hempstead NY
*WSQG-FM Ithaca NY
*WJFF(FM) Jeffersonville NY
*WAMK(FM) Kingston NY
*WOSR(FM) Middletown NY
*WKCR-FM New York NY
*WNYC-FM New York NY
WQXR-FM New York NY
*WSQC-FM Oneonta NY
*WCFE-FM Plattsburgh NY
*WRHV(FM) Poughkeepsie NY
*WRUR-FM Rochester NY
*WXXI-FM Rochester NY
*WMHT-FM Schenectady NY
*WPBX(FM) Southampton NY
*WUSB(FM) Stony Brook NY
*WCNY-FM Syracuse NY
*WANC(FM) Ticonderoga NY
*WUNY(FM) Utica NY
*WJNY(FM) Watertown NY
*WRMU(FM) Alliance OH
*WOUB-FM Athens OH
*WOUC-FM Cambridge OH
*WOUH(FM) Chillicothe OH
*WGUC(FM) Cincinnati OH
WCLV(FM) Cleveland OH
*WOSU-FM Columbus OH
*WDPR(FM) Dayton OH
*WOUL-FM Ironton OH
*WKSU-FM Kent OH
*WGLE(FM) Lima OH
*WOSV(FM) Mansfield OH
*WMRT(FM) Marietta OH
*WOSP(FM) Portsmouth OH
*WGTE-FM Toledo OH
*WYSU(FM) Youngstown OH
KCMA(FM) Broken Arrow OK
*KCSC(FM) Edmond OK
*KGOU(FM) Norman OK
*KROU(FM) Spencer OK
*KOSU-FM Stillwater OK
*KSOR(FM) Ashland OR
*KMUN(FM) Astoria OR
*KOAC(AM) Corvallis OR
*KWAX(FM) Eugene OR
KKBK(FM) Lake Oswego OR
*KRBM(FM) Pendleton OR
*KBPS(AM) Portland OR
*KBPS-FM Portland OR
*KOPB-FM Portland OR
*KSRS(FM) Roseburg OR
*WMCE(FM) Erie PA
*WQLN-FM Erie PA
*WSAJ-FM Grove City PA
*WITF-FM Harrisburg PA
*WIXQ(FM) Millersville PA
WFLN-FM Philadelphia PA
*WQED-FM Pittsburgh PA
*WVIA-FM Scranton PA
*WPSU(FM) State College PA
*WRTU(FM) San Juan PR
WVBI(FM) Block Island RI
*WDOM(FM) Providence RI
WLKW(AM) Providence RI
*WJWJ-FM Beaufort SC
*WSCI(FM) Charleston SC
*WHMC-FM Conway SC
*WNSC-FM Rock Hill SC
*WRJA-FM Sumter SC
*KESD(FM) Brookings SD
*KCSD(FM) Sioux Falls SD
*KRSD(FM) Sioux Falls SD
*KUSD(AM) Vermillion SD
*KUSD-FM Vermillion SD
*WSMC-FM Collegedale TN
*WKNQ(FM) Dyersburg TN
*WKNP(FM) Jackson TN
*WETS(FM) Johnson City TN
*WCSK(FM) Kingsport TN
*WUOT(FM) Knoxville TN
*WFMQ(FM) Lebanon TN
*WUTM(FM) Martin TN
*WKNO-FM Memphis TN
*WPLN(FM) Nashville TN
*KACU(FM) Abilene TX
*KMFA(FM) Austin TX
*KVLU(FM) Beaumont TX
KRTK(FM) Cleveland TX
*KAMU-FM College Station TX
*KEDT-FM Corpus Christi TX
WRR(FM) Dallas TX
*KNTU(FM) Denton TX
*KTEP(FM) El Paso TX
*KTCU-FM Fort Worth TX
*KMBH-FM Harlingen TX
*KUHF(FM) Houston TX
*KSHU(FM) Huntsville TX
*KTPB(FM) Kilgore TX
*KOHM(FM) Lubbock TX
*KLDN(FM) Lufkin TX
*KHID(FM) McAllen TX
*KXGZ(FM) McAllen TX
*KOCV(FM) Odessa TX
KRIL(AM) Odessa TX
*KPAC(FM) San Antonio TX
*KRTU(FM) San Antonio TX
KRTS(FM) Seabrook TX
*KTXK(FM) Texarkana TX
*KWBU(FM) Waco TX
*KUSU-FM Logan UT
*KPCW(FM) Park City UT
*KBYU-FM Provo UT
*KUER(FM) Salt Lake City UT
*WTJU(FM) Charlottesville VA
*WFOS(FM) Chesapeake VA
*WFFC(FM) Ferrum VA
*WEMC(FM) Harrisonburg VA
*WMRA(FM) Harrisonburg VA
*WMRL(FM) Lexington VA
*WVTR(FM) Marion VA
*WHRO-FM Norfolk VA
*WVRU(FM) Radford VA
*WCVE(FM) Richmond VA
*WVTF(FM) Roanoke VA
WDCM(FM) Cruz Bay VI
*WVPS(FM) Burlington VT
WFAD(AM) Middlebury VT
*WRVT(FM) Rutland VT
*WVPR(FM) Windsor VT
*KZAZ(FM) Bellingham WA
*KNWR(FM) Ellensburg WA
KSVY(AM) Opportunity WA
*KWSU(AM) Pullman WA
*KFAE-FM Richland WA
KING-FM Seattle WA
*KPBX-FM Spokane WA
*WHSA(FM) Brule WI
*WUEC(FM) Eau Claire WI
*WPNE-FM Green Bay WI
*WHHI(FM) Highland WI
*WGTD(FM) Kenosha WI
*WHLA(FM) La Crosse WI
*WERN(FM) Madison WI
WFMR(FM) Menomonee Falls WI
*WHWC(FM) Menomonie WI
*WVSS(FM) Menomonie WI
*WXPR(FM) Rhinelander WI
*WHRM(FM) Wausau WI
*WVPB(FM) Beckley WV
*WVPW(FM) Buckhannon WV
*WVPN(FM) Charleston WV
*WVWV(FM) Huntington WV
*WVEP(FM) Martinsburg WV
*WVPM(FM) Morgantown WV
*WVPG(FM) Parkersburg WV
*WVNP(FM) Wheeling WV
*KUWJ(FM) Jackson WY
*KUWR(FM) Laramie WY
*KCWC-FM Riverton WY
*KUWZ(FM) Rock Springs WY

Contemporary Hit/Top-40

Includes station formats Contemporary and Contemporary Hit Radio (CHR).

KGOT(FM) Anchorage AK
KPXR(FM) Anchorage AK
KWLF(FM) Fairbanks AK
*KHNS(FM) Haines AK
KTKU(FM) Juneau AK
KWHQ-FM Kenai AK
KSBZ(FM) Sitka AK
WWSF-FM Andalusia AL
WZYP(FM) Athens AL
WAPI-FM Birmingham AL
WQEN(FM) Gadsden AL
*WLJS-FM Jacksonville AL
WABB-FM Mobile AL
WHHY(AM) Montgomery AL
WHHY-FM Montgomery AL
WSHK(FM) Russellville AL
WALX(FM) Selma AL
WNUZ(AM) Talladega AL
WSPZ(AM) Tuscaloosa AL
WVNA-FM Tuscumbia AL
*KSWH(FM) Arkadelphia AR
*KCAC(FM) Camden AR
KMJX(FM) Conway AR
KISQ(FM) El Dorado AR
KLBQ(FM) El Dorado AR
KISR(FM) Fort Smith AR
KHOX(FM) Hoxie AR
KDEZ(FM) Jonesboro AR
KJBR(FM) Jonesboro AR
KKYK-FM Little Rock AR
KISK(FM) Lowell AR
KOKR(FM) Newport AR
KMCK(FM) Siloam Springs AR
KBEV(FM) Springdale AR
KTWN-FM Texarkana AR
KVNA-FM Flagstaff AZ
KKFR(FM) Glendale AZ
KGMS(FM) Green Valley AZ
KBBC(FM) Lake Havasu City AZ
KAZM(AM) Sedona AZ
KNXN(AM) Sierra Vista AZ
KJYK(AM) Tucson AZ
KWCX(FM) Willcox AZ
KWFM(FM) Tucson AZ
KJOK(FM) Yuma AZ
KEZY(FM) Anaheim CA
KXGO(FM) Arcata CA
KDUC(FM) Barstow CA
KSIQ(FM) Brawley CA
*KBPK(FM) Buena Park CA
KCLB(AM) Coachella CA
KKXX-FM Delano CA
*KOHL(FM) Fremont CA
KJFX(FM) Fresno CA
*KCRH(FM) Hayward CA
KVVV(FM) Healdsburg CA
KWIN(FM) Lodi CA
KHQT(FM) Los Altos CA
KIIS(AM) Los Angeles CA
KIIS-FM Los Angeles CA
KPWR(FM) Los Angeles CA
KAVS(FM) Mojave CA
KCAQ(FM) Oxnard CA
KPSI-FM Palm Springs CA
*KRVH(FM) Rio Vista CA
KGGI(FM) Riverside CA
*KXHV(FM) Sacramento CA
KDON-FM Salinas CA
KRAY-FM Salinas CA
KKLQ(AM) San Diego CA
KKLQ-FM San Diego CA
KMEL(FM) San Francisco CA
KSLY-FM San Luis Obispo CA
KSOL(FM) San Mateo CA
KHTY(FM) Santa Barbara CA
*KTUO(FM) Sonora CA
KSTN(AM) Stockton CA
KNJO(FM) Thousand Oaks CA
KBOS-FM Tulare CA
KWNE(FM) Ukiah CA
*KDUV(FM) Visalia CA
KSFM(FM) Woodland CA
KVFC(AM) Cortez CO
KIMN-FM Fort Collins CO
KQIX-FM Grand Junction CO
KWMX(AM) Lakewood CO
KWMX-FM Lakewood CO
KQKS(FM) Longmont CO
KKMG(FM) Pueblo CO
KKPC(AM) Pueblo CO
WQGN-FM Groton CT
WKCI(FM) Hamden CT
*WQAQ(FM) Hamden CT
WKSS(FM) Hartford CT
WTIC-FM Hartford CT
*WDJW(FM) Somers CT
WILI-FM Willimantic CT
WOL(AM) Washington DC
WKHI(FM) Bethany Beach DE
WRKE(FM) Ocean View DE
WXKB(FM) Cape Coral FL
WOVV(FM) Fort Pierce FL
WAJD(AM) Gainesville FL
WYKS(FM) Gainesville FL
WAPE-FM Jacksonville FL
WEOW(FM) Key West FL
WIIS(FM) Key West FL
WXXL(FM) Leesburg FL
WAVV(FM) Marco FL
WAOA(FM) Melbourne FL
WPOW(FM) Miami FL
WMMZ(FM) Ocala FL
WFKS(FM) Palatka FL
WILN(FM) Panama City FL
WPFM(FM) Panama City FL
WJLQ(FM) Pensacola FL
WNFK(FM) Perry FL
WFLZ-FM Tampa FL
WSIR(AM) Winter Haven FL
WBBQ(AM) Augusta GA
WBBQ-FM Augusta GA
WXFG(FM) Augusta GA
WBHF(AM) Cartersville GA
WCGQ(FM) Columbus GA
WXMK(FM) Dock Junction GA
WQZY(FM) Dublin GA
WMGB(FM) Jeffersonville GA
WYSC(FM) McRae GA
*WXGC(FM) Milledgeville GA
WPUP(FM) Royston GA
WZAT(FM) Savannah GA
WMGZ(FM) Sparta GA
WJAT-FM Swainsboro GA
KOKU(FM) Agana GU
KZGZ(FM) Agana GU
KGMZ(FM) Aiea HI
KIKI-FM Honolulu HI
KISA(AM) Honolulu HI
KQMQ(AM) Honolulu HI
KQMQ-FM Honolulu HI
KQNG-FM Lihue HI
KCCQ(FM) Ames IA
KKRL(FM) Carroll IA
KQCR(FM) Cedar Rapids IA
KIAQ(FM) Clarion IA
KQKQ-FM Council Bluffs IA
KSTZ(FM) Des Moines IA
KLYV(FM) Dubuque IA
KIIK-FM Fairfield IA
KOTM-FM Ottumwa IA
*KCUI(FM) Pella IA
*KMSC(FM) Sioux City IA
KFMW(FM) Waterloo IA
KOKZ(FM) Waterloo IA
KZDX(FM) Burley ID
KFTZ(FM) Idaho Falls ID
KMVX(FM) Jerome ID
KMOK(FM) Lewiston ID
KZFN(FM) Moscow ID
KZMG(FM) New Plymouth ID
KPKY(FM) Pocatello ID
KKMV(FM) Rupert ID
WBNQ(FM) Bloomington IL
WCIL-FM Carbondale IL
WCAZ-FM Carthage IL
WLRW(FM) Champaign IL
WBBM-FM Chicago IL
*WLUW(FM) Chicago IL
WDEK(FM) De Kalb IL
WXXQ(FM) Freeport IL
WKBQ(FM) Granite City IL
*WCSF(FM) Joliet IL
WBUS(FM) Kankakee IL
*WLNX(FM) Lincoln IL
WKAI(FM) Macomb IL
WHZT(FM) Mahomet IL
WRIK-FM Metropolis IL
WKZW(FM) Peoria IL
*WGCA-FM Quincy IL
WQCY(FM) Quincy IL
*WRRG(FM) River Grove IL
WPXR-FM Rock Island IL
WZOK(FM) Rockford IL
WDBR(FM) Springfield IL
WKRV(FM) Vandalia IL
WZSR(FM) Woodstock IL
*WHJE(FM) Carmel IN
WDJB(FM) Columbia City IN
WNDY(FM) Crawfordsville IN
WQHK-FM Decatur IN
WMEE(FM) Fort Wayne IN
*WVSH(FM) Huntington IN
*WEDM(FM) Indianapolis IN
WHHH(FM) Indianapolis IN
*WJEL(FM) Indianapolis IN
*WKPW(FM) Knightstown IN
WAZY(FM) Lafayette IN
WBLZ(FM) Mt. Vernon IN
*WNAS(FM) New Albany IN
WINN(FM) North Vernon IN
WHZR(FM) Royal Center IN
WNDU-FM South Bend IN
WLEZ(FM) Terre Haute IN
WWIP(FM) Wabash IN
WZZY(FM) Winchester IN
*KTCC(FM) Colby KS
KOMB(FM) Fort Scott KS
KHOK(FM) Hoisington KS
KSKU(FM) Hutchinson KS
KJCK-FM Junction City KS
KKLO(AM) Leavenworth KS
KQLA(FM) Ogden KS
*KTJO-FM Ottawa KS
KSKG(FM) Salina KS
KKRD(FM) Wichita KS
WANY(AM) Albany KY
WANY-FM Albany KY
WJDJ(FM) Burnside KY
WHHT(FM) Cave City KY
WCVG(AM) Covington KY
WWKF(FM) Fulton KY
*WRVG(FM) Georgetown KY
WWWQ(FM) Glasgow KY
WWHK(FM) Greenville KY
WKIC(AM) Hazard KY
WZZF-FM Hopkinsville KY
WZQQ(FM) Hyden KY
WJSN-FM Jackson KY
WIFX-FM Jenkins KY
WDJX(AM) Louisville KY
WDJX-FM Louisville KY
WTTL(AM) Madisonville KY
WMIK-FM Middlesboro KY
WMOR-FM Morehead KY
WSTO(FM) Owensboro KY
WDDJ(FM) Paducah KY
WXKZ-FM Prestonsburg KY
KQID(FM) Alexandria LA
KZMZ(FM) Alexandria LA
WFMF(FM) Baton Rouge LA
KSMB(FM) Lafayette LA
KBIU(FM) Lake Charles LA
KLRZ(FM) Larose LA

Broadcasting & Cable Yearbook 1994
B-549

Programming on Radio Stations in the U.S.

KMYY(FM) Monroe LA
KNOE-FM Monroe LA
KLIL(FM) Moreauville LA
KFXY(FM) Morgan City LA
WEZB(FM) New Orleans LA
WQUE(AM) New Orleans LA
WQUE-FM New Orleans LA
KXOR(FM) Thibodaux LA
WJMN(FM) Boston MA
*WGAO(FM) Franklin MA
WXKS-FM Medford MA
WRZE(FM) Nantucket MA
WHMP-FM Northampton MA
WBEC-FM Pittsfield MA
*WSDH(FM) Sandwich MA
WINQ(FM) Winchendon MA
WERQ-FM Baltimore MD
WOLB(AM) Baltimore MD
WOCQ(FM) Berlin MD
WZYQ(FM) Braddock Heights MD
WKGO(FM) Cumberland MD
WMDM-FM Lexington Park MD
WPGC-FM Morningside MD
WMME(AM) Augusta ME
WMME-FM Augusta ME
*WHSN(FM) Bangor ME
WWFX(FM) Belfast ME
WBZN(FM) Old Town ME
WPBC(FM) Pittsfield ME
WTMS-FM Presque Isle ME
WHYR(FM) Saco ME
WHQO(FM) Skowhegan ME
WHSB(FM) Alpena MI
WBXX(FM) Battle Creek MI
WKFR-FM Battle Creek MI
WIOG(FM) Bay City MI
WPZX(FM) Big Rapids MI
*WBFH(FM) Bloomfield Hills MI
WTCF(FM) Carrollton MI
WKHQ-FM Charlevoix MI
WCFX(FM) Clare MI
WHYT(FM) Detroit MI
WKQI(FM) Detroit MI
WVFN(AM) East Lansing MI
WVIC-FM East Lansing MI
WLJN(AM) Elmwood Township MI
WWCK(AM) Flint MI
WWCK-FM Flint MI
WKPK(FM) Gaylord MI
WGRD-FM Grand Rapids MI
WUPM(FM) Ironwood MI
WBTI(FM) Lexington MI
WSNX-FM Muskegon MI
WNIL(AM) Niles MI
*WOCR(FM) Olivet MI
*WOES(FM) Ovid-Elsie MI
*WORW(FM) Port Huron MI
WYSS(FM) Sault Ste. Marie MI
*WSHJ(FM) Southfield MI
WIRX(FM) St. Joseph MI
WOWE(FM) Vassar MI
*WPHS(FM) Warren MI
KXRA-FM Alexandria MN
*KBSB(FM) Bemidji MN
KKBJ-FM Bemidji MN
KQHT(FM) Crookston MN
*WNCB(FM) Duluth MN
WTBX(FM) Hibbing MN
KRXX-FM Minneapolis MN
KDOG(FM) North Mankato MN
KISD(FM) Pipestone MN
KDWB-FM Richfield MN
KROC-FM Rochester MN
KCLD-FM St. Cloud MN
KXSS(AM) Waite Park MN
KZBK-FM Brookfield MO
KBFL(FM) Buffalo MO
KCMQ(FM) Columbia MO
*KOPN(FM) Columbia MO
KYMO(AM) East Prairie MO
KXOK-FM Florissant MO
KJLA(AM) Independence MO
KTXY(FM) Jefferson City MO
KSYN(FM) Joplin MO
WMBH(AM) Joplin MO
WMBH-FM Joplin MO
KISF(FM) Lexington MO
KYLC(FM) Osage Beach MO
*KGSP(FM) Parkville MO
KQMX(FM) Rolla MO
KSTG(FM) Sikeston MO
KWTO-FM Springfield MO
KKJO(FM) St. Joseph MO
KTUI-FM Sullivan MO
KFBD-FM Waynesville MO
KOZQ(AM) Waynesville MO
KKDY(FM) West Plains MO
KPXP(FM) Garapan-Saipan MP
WAFM(FM) Amory MS
WQNN(FM) Artesia MS
WVRD(FM) Belzoni MS
WQID(FM) Biloxi MS
WFXO(FM) Iuka MS
WKTF(FM) Jackson MS
WIQQ(FM) Leland MS
WJDQ(FM) Meridian MS
WWKZ(FM) New Albany MS
WZRH(FM) Picayune MS
WZKX(FM) Poplarville MS
WMJW(FM) Rosedale MS
WKOR(AM) Starkville MS
WROB(AM) West Point MS
WONA(AM) Winona MS
KYYA(FM) Billings MT
WKXB(FM) Burgaw NC

WAQQ(FM) Charlotte NC
WBT-FM Charlotte NC
WDCG(FM) Durham NC
WCLW(AM) Eden NC
*WUAW(FM) Erwin NC
WKSI(FM) Greensboro NC
WAZZ(FM) Laurinburg NC
WMAP(AM) Monroe NC
WRHT(FM) Morehead City NC
WLOJ(AM) New Bern NC
WYRU(AM) Red Springs NC
WJMH(FM) Reidsville NC
*WDCC(FM) Sanford NC
WCOK(AM) Sparta NC
WHTE(FM) Williamston NC
WKZL(FM) Winston-Salem NC
KYYY(FM) Bismarck ND
KKXL-FM Grand Forks ND
KSSZ-FM Oakes ND
KYYZ(FM) Williston ND
*KCNT(FM) Hastings NE
KKPR-FM Kearney NE
KQKY(FM) Kearney NE
KFRX(FM) Lincoln NE
KMOR(FM) Scottsbluff NE
WVFM(FM) Campton NH
WERZ(FM) Exeter NH
WKNE-FM Keene NH
WHOB(FM) Nashua NH
WJLK-FM Asbury Park NJ
*WDBK(FM) Blackwood NJ
WBSS-FM Millville NJ
WHTZ(FM) Newark NJ
WNNJ-FM Newton NJ
WPST(FM) Trenton NJ
*WPSC-FM Wayne NJ
KYEE(FM) Alamogordo NM
KQNM(FM) Gallup NM
KKSS(FM) Santa Fe NM
*KSHI(FM) Zuni NM
KELY-FM Ely NV
KLUC-FM Las Vegas NV
KXPT(FM) Las Vegas NV
WABH(AM) Bath NY
WVIN-FM Bath NY
WAAL(FM) Binghamton NY
WMJQ(FM) Buffalo NY
WNKI(FM) Corning NY
WYYS(FM) Cortland NY
*WECW(FM) Elmira NY
WLVY(FM) Elmira NY
WWHB(FM) Hampton Bays NY
WKPQ(FM) Hornell NY
WBPM(FM) Kingston NY
WPLJ(FM) New York NY
WQHT(FM) New York NY
WKSE(FM) Niagara Falls NY
WPAC(FM) Ogdensburg NY
WGRG(FM) Owego NY
WSPK(FM) Poughkeepsie NY
WPXY-FM Rochester NY
WLNG(AM) Sag Harbor NY
WLNG-FM Sag Harbor NY
*WJPZ-FM Syracuse NY
WNTQ(FM) Syracuse NY
WFLY(FM) Troy NY
WRCK(FM) Utica NY
WTNY-FM Watertown NY
WKDD(FM) Akron OH
WXTQ(FM) Athens OH
WOMP-FM Bellaire OH
WNRR(FM) Bellevue OH
WKRQ(FM) Cincinnati OH
WAHC(FM) Circleville OH
WJMO-FM Cleveland Heights OH
WJER(AM) Dover-New Philadelphia OH
WGTZ(FM) Eaton OH
WNWV(FM) Elyria OH
WKXA-FM Findlay OH
WFRO(AM) Fremont OH
WYHT(FM) Mansfield OH
WEYQ(FM) Marietta OH
WQIO(FM) Mount Vernon OH
WWJM(FM) New Lexington OH
WCPZ(FM) Sandusky OH
WRKY(FM) Steubenville OH
WVKS(FM) Toledo OH
WZOQ(FM) Wapakoneta OH
*WCWS(FM) Wooster OH
WHOT-FM Youngstown OH
KRKZ(FM) Altus OK
KRHD(AM) Duncan OK
*KHIB(FM) Durant OK
*KOKF(FM) Edmond OK
KQTZ(FM) Hobart OK
KBXD(FM) Lawton OK
KHTT(FM) Muskogee OK
KJYO(FM) Oklahoma City OK
KIXR(FM) Ponca City OK
KZBB(FM) Poteau OK
*KEPO(FM) Eagle Point OR
KLDR(FM) Harbeck-Fruitdale OR
KCGB(FM) Hood River OR
*KEOL(FM) La Grande OR
KTMT-FM Medford OR
*KAVE(FM) Oakridge OR
KKRZ(FM) Portland OR
KRBZ(FM) Reedsport OR
KXYQ(FM) Salem OR
WAEB-FM Allentown PA
WPRR(FM) Altoona PA
WHLM(FM) Bloomsburg PA
*WVCS(FM) California PA
WQYX(FM) Clearfield PA

WODE-FM Easton PA
WPDC(AM) Elizabethtown PA
*WZZE(FM) Glen Mills PA
WEXC(FM) Greenville PA
WNNK-FM Harrisburg PA
WLAK(FM) Huntingdon PA
WBCW(AM) Jeannette PA
WGLU(FM) Johnstown PA
WLAN-FM Lancaster PA
WQIC(FM) Lebanon PA
WMRF-FM Lewistown PA
*WNTE(FM) Mansfield PA
WPLY(FM) Media PA
*WMSS(FM) Middletown PA
WHTO(FM) Muncy PA
*WWNW(FM) New Wilmington PA
WIOQ(FM) Philadelphia PA
WBZZ(FM) Pittsburgh PA
WSKS(FM) Pittston PA
WAVT-FM Pottsville PA
WRFY-FM Reading PA
WGGY(FM) Scranton PA
*WVMW-FM Scranton PA
WBHV(FM) State College PA
WSBG(FM) Stroudsburg PA
WQKX(FM) Sunbury PA
WTRN(AM) Tyrone PA
WNBT(AM) Wellsboro PA
WNBT-FM Wellsboro PA
WYCR(FM) York-Hanover PA
WCMN-FM Arecibo PR
WBQN(AM) Barceloneta PR
WOLA(AM) Barranquitas PR
WXYX(FM) Bayamon PR
WEKO(AM) Cabo Rojo PR
WCHQ(AM) Camuy PR
WCPR(AM) Coamo PR
WDOY(FM) Fajardo PR
WGDL(AM) Lares PR
WMNT(AM) Manati PR
WAEL-FM Maricao PR
WKJB(AM) Mayaguez PR
WOYE-FM Mayaguez PR
WPRA(AM) Mayaguez PR
WMTI(AM) Morovis PR
WZBS(AM) Ponce PR
WQQZ(FM) Quebradillas PR
WKAQ-FM San Juan PR
WRSS(AM) San Sebastian PR
WEGA(AM) Vega Baja PR
WENA(AM) Yauco PR
*WCVY(FM) Coventry RI
WPRO-FM Providence RI
WWKX(FM) Woonsocket RI
WSSX-FM Charleston SC
WJMX-FM Cheraw SC
WNOK-FM Columbia SC
WYAV(FM) Conway SC
WWXM(FM) Georgetown SC
WMAP-FM Pageland SC
KDSJ(AM) Deadwood SD
KGGG-FM Rapid City SD
*KCFS(FM) Sioux Falls SD
KVHT(FM) Vermillion SD
WSKZ(FM) Chattanooga TN
WSDQ(AM) Dunlap TN
*WVCP(FM) Gallatin TN
WQUT(FM) Johnson City TN
WWZZ(FM) Karns TN
WKOS(FM) Kingsport TN
WYHY(FM) Lebanon TN
WBMC(AM) McMinnville TN
WTRZ-FM McMinnville TN
WYKL(FM) Millington TN
WAKQ(FM) Paris TN
WTRB-FM Ripley TN
WXOQ(FM) Selmer TN
WXQK(AM) Spring City TN
*KACC(FM) Alvin TX
KQIZ-FM Amarillo TX
KXYL(AM) Brownwood TX
KKYS(FM) Bryan TX
KAKS-FM Canyon TX
*KWTS(FM) Canyon TX
KTUX(FM) Carthage TX
KZFM(FM) Corpus Christi TX
KTDR(FM) Del Rio TX
KAFX(AM) Diboll TX
KAFX-FM Diboll TX
KBFM(FM) Edinburg TX
KINT-FM El Paso TX
KPRR(FM) El Paso TX
KQQK(FM) Galveston TX
KHFI-FM Georgetown TX
KCDD(FM) Hamlin TX
KKBQ(AM) Houston TX
KRBE-FM Houston TX
KSAM-FM Huntsville TX
KRRG(FM) Laredo TX
KXTQ(AM) Lubbock TX
KZII-FM Lubbock TX
*KXPZ(FM) Lytle TX
KCHX(FM) Midland TX
KLIS(FM) Palestine TX
*KWLD(FM) Plainview TX
KQTX(FM) Portland TX
KDCD(FM) San Angelo TX
KIXY-FM San Angelo TX
KENS(AM) San Antonio TX
KTFM(FM) San Antonio TX
KEPG(FM) Victoria TX
KWTX-FM Waco TX
KISX(FM) Whitehouse TX
KNIN-FM Wichita Falls TX
KUTQ(FM) Bountiful UT

*KGSU-FM Cedar City UT
KVFM(FM) Logan UT
*KPGR(FM) Pleasant Grove UT
KZHT(FM) Provo UT
KVRI(FM) Salt Lake City UT
*KRDC-FM St. George UT
WABN-FM Abingdon VA
WLDJ(FM) Appomattox VA
WUVA(FM) Charlottesville VA
WZQK(FM) Coeburn VA
WMJD(FM) Grundy VA
WQPO(FM) Harrisonburg VA
*WHCE(FM) Highland Springs VA
WOLD-FM Marion VA
WNVZ(FM) Norfolk VA
WRVQ(FM) Richmond VA
WXLK(FM) Roanoke VA
WIYC(FM) Charlotte Amalie VI
WTBN(FM) Charlotte Amalie VI
WJKC(FM) Christiansted VI
*WNUB-FM Northfield VT
WXXX(FM) South Burlington VT
WVMX(FM) Stowe VT
*KCED(FM) Centralia WA
KLYK(FM) Longview WA
KHTR(FM) Pullman WA
KWWW-FM Quincy WA
KIOK(FM) Richland WA
*KNHC(FM) Seattle WA
KPLZ(FM) Seattle WA
KUBE(FM) Seattle WA
KZZU-FM Spokane WA
*KVTI(FM) Tacoma WA
KFFM(FM) Yakima WA
WBIZ-FM Eau Claire WI
WIXX(FM) Green Bay WI
WIZM-FM La Crosse WI
WZEE(FM) Madison WI
WQTC-FM Manitowoc WI
WLUM-FM Milwaukee WI
WMGV(FM) Oshkosh WI
*WRPN-FM Ripon WI
WGEE-FM Sturgeon Bay WI
*WPFF(FM) Sturgeon Bay WI
KZIO(FM) Superior WI
*WCLQ(FM) Wausau WI
WIFC(FM) Wausau WI
WNNO(AM) Wisconsin Dells WI
WNNO-FM Wisconsin Dells WI
WVSR(AM) Charleston WV
WVSR-FM Charleston WV
WELK(FM) Elkins WV
WFGM(FM) Fairmont WV
WKEE-FM Huntington WV
WKMZ(FM) Martinsburg WV
WVAQ(FM) Morgantown WV
WXIL(FM) Parkersburg WV
*WQAB(FM) Philippi WV
*WSHC(FM) Shepherdstown WV
*WPHP(FM) Wheeling WV
KTRS(FM) Casper WY
KFBQ(FM) Cheyenne WY
*KYDZ(FM) Cody WY
KDLY(FM) Lander WY
KSIT(FM) Rock Springs WY
KYCS(FM) Rock Springs WY
KROE-FM Sheridan WY

Country

Includes station formats Country & Western (C&W), Contemporary Country and Modern Country.

KASH-FM Anchorage AK
KBRJ(FM) Anchorage AK
KYAK(AM) Anchorage AK
*KCUK(FM) Chevak AK
KLAM(AM) Cordova AK
*KDLG(AM) Dillingham AK
KIAK-FM Fairbanks AK
KIYU(AM) Galena AK
*KSKO(AM) McGrath AK
KAKN(FM) Naknek AK
KJNP(AM) North Pole AK
KJNP-FM North Pole AK
KRSA(AM) Petersburg AK
KPEN-FM Soldotna AK
*KUHB(FM) St. Paul Island AK
WQSB(FM) Albertville AL
WSTH-FM Alexander City AL
WTLM(AM) Alexander City AL
WAAO-FM Andalusia AL
WHMA(AM) Anniston AL
WHMA-FM Anniston AL
WRAB(AM) Arab AL
WASZ(FM) Ashland-Lineville AL
WKAC(AM) Athens AL
WASG(AM) Atmore AL
WKXX(FM) Attalla AL
WKKR(FM) Auburn AL
WBCA(AM) Bay Minette AL
WSMQ(AM) Bessemer AL
WJOX(AM) Birmingham AL
WZZK(AM) Birmingham AL
WZZK-FM Birmingham AL
WEBJ(AM) Brewton AL
WKNU(FM) Brewton AL
WBTS(AM) Bridgeport AL
WPRN(AM) Butler AL
WQGL(FM) Butler AL
WBYE(AM) Calera AL
WAGC(AM) Centre AL
WEIS(AM) Centre AL
WRHY(FM) Centre AL
WBIB(AM) Centreville AL

WHXT(FM) Citronelle AL
WEZZ(FM) Clanton AL
WFFN(FM) Cordova AL
WFMH(AM) Cullman AL
WKUL(FM) Cullman AL
WDLK(AM) Dadeville AL
WDRM(FM) Decatur AL
WHOS(AM) Decatur AL
WXAL(AM) Demopolis AL
WPYK(AM) Dora AL
WTVY-FM Dothan AL
WZTZ(FM) Elba AL
WDJR(FM) Enterprise AL
WULA(AM) Eufaula AL
WPGG(FM) Evergreen AL
WLDX(AM) Fayette AL
WTXT(FM) Fayette AL
WFPA(AM) Fort Payne AL
WZOB(AM) Fort Payne AL
WXUS(FM) Fort Rucker AL
WAAX(AM) Gadsden AL
WGYV(AM) Greenville AL
WQZX(FM) Greenville AL
WTWX-FM Guntersville AL
WJBB(AM) Haleyville AL
WJBB-FM Haleyville AL
WERH(AM) Hamilton AL
WERH-FM Hamilton AL
WBXR(AM) Hazel Green AL
WBHP(AM) Huntsville AL
WARF(AM) Jasper AL
WZZX(AM) Lineville AL
WKSJ-FM Mobile AL
WMFC(AM) Monroeville AL
WMFC-FM Monroeville AL
WLWI-FM Montgomery AL
WHIY(AM) Moulton AL
WXKI(FM) Moulton AL
WLAY(AM) Muscle Shoals AL
WLAY-FM Muscle Shoals AL
WAMI(AM) Opp AL
WAMI-FM Opp AL
WOPP(AM) Opp AL
WOAB(FM) Ozark AL
WFHK(AM) Pell City AL
WKSJ(AM) Prichard AL
WVSM(AM) Rainsville AL
WRMG(AM) Red Bay AL
WELR-FM Roanoke AL
WXWY(AM) Robertsdale AL
WJRD(AM) Russellville AL
WKEA-FM Scottsboro AL
WWIC(AM) Scottsboro AL
WDXX(FM) Selma AL
WVSV(FM) Stevenson AL
WRSM(AM) Sumiton AL
WEYY-FM Talladega AL
WTLS(AM) Tallassee AL
WJDB(AM) Thomasville AL
WJDB-FM Thomasville AL
WTBF(AM) Troy AL
WACT-FM Tuscaloosa AL
WVSA(AM) Vernon AL
WKXM(AM) Winfield AL
KVRC(AM) Arkadelphia AR
KARQ(FM) Ashdown AR
KABK-FM Augusta AR
KAPZ(AM) Bald Knob AR
KKSY(FM) Bald Knob AR
KBTA(AM) Batesville AR
KZLE(FM) Batesville AR
KMVK(FM) Benton AR
KTHS(AM) Berryville AR
KTHS-FM Berryville AR
KHLS(FM) Blytheville AR
KQMC-FM Brinkley AR
KAMD(AM) Camden AR
KCXY(FM) Camden AR
KWEH(FM) Camden AR
KLYR(AM) Clarksville AR
KLYR-FM Clarksville AR
KHPQ(FM) Clinton AR
KFCA(AM) Conway AR
KTOD-FM Conway AR
KBKG(FM) Corning AR
KCCB(AM) Corning AR
KAGH(AM) Crossett AR
KWXT(AM) Dardanelle AR
KDQN(AM) De Queen AR
KDQN-FM De Queen AR
KGPL(AM) Dermott AR
KXSA-FM Dermott AR
KDDA(AM) Dumas AR
KXFE(FM) Dumas AR
KBYB(FM) El Dorado AR
KIXB(FM) El Dorado AR
KLRA(AM) England AR
KLRA-FM England AR
KKIX(FM) Fayetteville AR
KBJT(AM) Fordyce AR
KQEW(FM) Fordyce AR
KBFC(FM) Forrest City AR
KMAG(FM) Fort Smith AR
KTCS(AM) Fort Smith AR
KTCS-FM Fort Smith AR
KWXE(FM) Glenwood AR
KWXI(AM) Glenwood AR
KYXK(FM) Gurdon AR
KCWD(FM) Harrison AR
KHOZ-FM Harrison AR
KAWW(AM) Heber Springs AR
KAWW-FM Heber Springs AR
KFFA(AM) Helena AR
KHPA(FM) Hope AR
KXAR(AM) Hope AR

Broadcasting & Cable Yearbook 1994
B-550

Programming on Radio Stations in the U.S.

KBHS(AM) Hot Springs AR
KQUS-FM Hot Springs AR
KHOX(FM) Hoxie AR
KDDK(FM) Jacksonville AR
KFIN(FM) Jonesboro AR
KSSN(FM) Little Rock AR
KVMA(AM) Magnolia AR
KBOK(AM) Malvern AR
KBOK-FM Malvern AR
KAMS(FM) Mammoth Spring AR
KBCN-FM Marshall AR
KENA(AM) Mena AR
KENA-FM Mena AR
KVOM(AM) Morrilton AR
KVOM-FM Morrilton AR
KPFM(FM) Mountain Home AR
KTLO(AM) Mountain Home AR
KWOZ(FM) Mountain View AR
KMTB(FM) Murfreesboro AR
KBHC(AM) Nashville AR
KNBY(AM) Newport AR
KDYN(AM) Ozark AR
KDYN-FM Ozark AR
KDRS(AM) Paragould AR
KLQZ(FM) Paragould AR
KERX(FM) Paris AR
KTEI(FM) Piggott AR
KCLA(AM) Pine Bluff AR
KPBQ-FM Pine Bluff AR
KPOC(AM) Pocahontas AR
KPOC-FM Pocahontas AR
KTPA(AM) Prescott AR
KAMO(AM) Rogers AR
KAMO-FM Rogers AR
KSAR(FM) Salem AR
KWCK(AM) Searcy AR
KWCK-FM Searcy AR
KUOA(AM) Siloam Springs AR
KZHE(FM) Stamps AR
KWAK(AM) Stuttgart AR
KKYR(AM) Texarkana AR
KWEZ(FM) Trumann AR
KRWA-FM Waldron AR
KRLW(AM) Walnut Ridge AR
KRLW-FM Walnut Ridge AR
KWRF(AM) Warren AR
KWRF-FM Warren AR
KWYN(AM) Wynne AR
KCTT-FM Yellville AR
KAVV(FM) Benson AZ
KWCD(FM) Bisbee AZ
KBAS(AM) Bullhead City AZ
KFLG(AM) Bullhead City AZ
KFLG-FM Bullhead City AZ
KKER(FM) Casa Grande AZ
KMLE(FM) Chandler AZ
KVRD-FM Cottonwood AZ
KDAP-FM Douglas AZ
KAFF(AM) Flagstaff AZ
KAFF-FM Flagstaff AZ
KJAA(AM) Globe AZ
KZUA(FM) Holbrook AZ
KGMN(FM) Kingman AZ
KQSS(FM) Miami AZ
KPGE(AM) Page AZ
KLPZ(AM) Parker AZ
KMOG(AM) Payson AZ
KRIM(FM) Payson AZ
KNIX-FM Phoenix AZ
KNOT(AM) Prescott AZ
KNOT-FM Prescott AZ
KBUX(FM) Quartzsite AZ
KXKQ(FM) Safford AZ
KVSL(AM) Show Low AZ
KTAN(AM) Sierra Vista AZ
KRVZ(AM) Springerville-Eager AZ
KCWW(AM) Tempe AZ
*KGHR(FM) Tuba City AZ
KCUB(AM) Tucson AZ
KIIM-FM Tucson AZ
KTIM(AM) Wickenburg AZ
KHIL(AM) Willcox AZ
KTNN(AM) Window Rock AZ
KINO(AM) Winslow AZ
KTTI(FM) Yuma AZ
KYAX(FM) Alturas CA
KEWB(FM) Anderson CA
KZXY(AM) Apple Valley CA
KAHI(AM) Auburn CA
KIXF(FM) Baker CA
KCWR(AM) Bakersfield CA
KTIE(FM) Bakersfield CA
KUZZ-FM Bakersfield CA
KSZL(AM) Barstow CA
KTOT(FM) Big Bear Lake CA
KIBS(FM) Bishop CA
KROP(AM) Brawley CA
KWST(FM) Brawley CA
KAVA(AM) Burney CA
KHSL(AM) Chico CA
KKFO(AM) Coalinga CA
KKCY(FM) Colusa CA
KPOD(AM) Crescent City CA
KPOD-FM Crescent North CA
KOWF(FM) Escondido CA
KEKA-FM Eureka CA
KRED(AM) Eureka CA
KDAC(AM) Fort Bragg CA
KPIG(FM) Freedom CA
KFRE(AM) Fresno CA
KNAX(FM) Fresno CA
KSKS(FM) Fresno CA
KIKF(FM) Garden Grove CA
KATJ(FM) George CA
KNCO-FM Grass Valley CA
KSUR-FM Greenfield CA
KIXT-FM Grover City CA
KHYE(FM) Hemet CA
KCNQ(FM) Kernville CA
KRKC(AM) King City CA
KLAC(AM) Los Angeles CA
KZLA-FM Los Angeles CA
KQLB(FM) Los Banos CA
KRTY(FM) Los Gatos CA
KUBB(FM) Mariposa CA
KATM(FM) Modesto CA
KTRB(AM) Modesto CA
KNEW(AM) Oakland CA
KCMJ(AM) Palm Springs CA
KHSL-FM Paradise CA
KDDB(FM) Paso Robles CA
KALF(FM) Red Bluff CA
KNCQ(FM) Redding CA
KLOA-FM Ridgecrest CA
KHTX(FM) Riverside CA
KOOJ(FM) Riverside CA
KRPQ(FM) Rohnert Park CA
KNCI(FM) Sacramento CA
KRAK(AM) Sacramento CA
KRAK-FM Sacramento CA
KTOM(AM) Salinas CA
KTOM-FM Salinas CA
KFRG(FM) San Bernardino CA
KSON(AM) San Diego CA
KSON-FM San Diego CA
KSAN-FM San Francisco CA
KIID(AM) San Luis Obispo CA
KKSB(AM) Santa Barbara CA
KSNI-FM Santa Maria CA
KVML(AM) Sonora CA
KFMR(FM) Stockton CA
KJDX(FM) Susanville CA
KTPI(FM) Tehachapi CA
KJUG(AM) Tulare CA
KJUG-FM Tulare CA
KMIX(AM) Turlock CA
KMIX-FM Turlock CA
KQPM(FM) Ukiah CA
KUKI-FM Ukiah CA
KHAY(FM) Ventura CA
KWHO(FM) Weed CA
KIQS-FM Willows CA
KSYC(AM) Yreka CA
KUBA(AM) Yuba City CA
KROR(FM) Yucca Valley CA
KGIW(AM) Alamosa CO
KLTT(AM) Brighton CO
KSIR(AM) Brush CO
KSIR-FM Brush CO
KDMN(AM) Buena Vista CO
KNAB(AM) Burlington CO
KRLN-FM Canon City CO
KKCS(AM) Colorado Springs CO
KKCS-FM Colorado Springs CO
KRDO(AM) Colorado Springs CO
KRTZ(FM) Cortez CO
KRAI(AM) Craig CO
KTMG(AM) Deer Trail CO
KDTA(AM) Delta CO
KYGO(AM) Denver CO
KYGO-FM Denver CO
KRSJ(FM) Durango CO
KBRU(FM) Fort Morgan CO
KFTM(AM) Fort Morgan CO
KEKB(FM) Fruita CO
KMTS(FM) Glenwood Springs CO
KRKY(AM) Granby CO
KQIL(AM) Grand Junction CO
KGLL(FM) Greeley CO
KGRE(AM) Greeley CO
KZDG(FM) Greeley CO
KVLE(FM) Gunnison CO
KBLJ(FM) La Junta CO
KLMR(AM) Lamar CO
KSEC(FM) Lamar CO
KVAY(FM) Lamar CO
KRMH(AM) Leadville CO
KDKO(AM) Littleton CO
KLMO(AM) Longmont CO
KIKX-FM Manitou Springs CO
KSLV(AM) Monte Vista CO
KKXK(FM) Montrose CO
KPAG(AM) Pagosa Springs CO
KRQS(FM) Pagosa Springs CO
KCCY(FM) Pueblo CO
KNKN(FM) Pueblo CO
KVRH(AM) Salida CO
KVRH-FM Salida CO
KHII(FM) Security CO
KSTC(AM) Sterling CO
KCRT(AM) Trinidad CO
KCRT-FM Trinidad CO
KSKE(AM) Vail CO
KUAD-FM Windsor CO
KATR-FM Wray CO
KRDZ(AM) Wray CO
WPKX(FM) Enfield CT
WCTY(FM) Norwich CT
WKZE(AM) Sharon CT
*WGSK(FM) South Kent CT
WWYZ(FM) Waterbury CT
WMZQ-FM Washington DC
WDSD(FM) Dover DE
WXJN(FM) Lewes DE
WSBL(FM) Selbyville DE
WKGF-FM Arcadia FL
WWOJ(FM) Avon Park FL
WBAR(AM) Bartow FL
WYBT(AM) Blountstown FL
WKIS(FM) Boca Raton FL
WLQH(AM) Chiefland FL
WAFC-FM Clewiston FL
WAAZ-FM Crestview FL
WJSB(AM) Crestview FL
WDFL(AM) Cross City FL
WDFL-FM Cross City FL
WDCF(AM) Dade City FL
WZEP(AM) DeFuniak Springs FL
WMMK(FM) Destin FL
WTRS(AM) Dunellon FL
WTRS-FM Dunellon FL
WQAI(AM) Fernandina Beach FL
WHEW(FM) Fort Myers FL
WMYR(AM) Fort Myers FL
WYGC(FM) Gainesville FL
WGWD(FM) Gretna FL
WCRJ(AM) Jacksonville FL
WQIK(AM) Jacksonville FL
WQIK-FM Jacksonville FL
WROO(FM) Jacksonville FL
WFIV(AM) Kissimmee FL
WKZY(FM) La Belle FL
WIPC(AM) Lake Wales FL
WQBQ(AM) Leesburg FL
WCKT(FM) Lehigh Acres FL
WQHL-FM Live Oak FL
WJXR(FM) Macclenny FL
WFFG(AM) Marathon FL
WJAQ(FM) Marianna FL
WXBM-FM Milton FL
WMFL(AM) Monticello FL
WMOP(AM) Ocala FL
WOKC-FM Okeechobee FL
WWKA(FM) Orlando FL
WIYD(AM) Palatka FL
WPLK(AM) Palatka FL
WPAP-FM Panama City FL
WOWW(FM) Pensacola FL
WPRY(AM) Perry FL
WKNB(FM) Port St. Joe FL
WKLG(FM) Rock Harbor FL
WHKR(FM) Rockledge FL
WQYK(AM) Seffner FL
WAOC(AM) St. Augustine FL
WQYK-FM St. Petersburg FL
WSUN(AM) St. Petersburg FL
WEAG-FM Starke FL
WPIK(FM) Summerland Key FL
WTNT(FM) Tallahassee FL
WRBQ-FM Tampa FL
WGNE-FM Titusville FL
WCWB-FM Trenton FL
WCTQ(FM) Venice FL
WAVW(FM) Vero Beach FL
WQLC(FM) Watertown FL
WIRK-FM West Palm Beach FL
WPCV(FM) Winter Haven FL
WKAK(FM) Albany GA
WKXH-FM Alma GA
WULF(AM) Alma GA
WDEC-FM Americus GA
WISK(AM) Americus GA
WISK-FM Americus GA
WNGC(FM) Athens GA
WKHX(AM) Atlanta GA
WBAF(AM) Barnesville GA
WBYZ(FM) Baxley GA
WKUB(FM) Blackshear GA
WPPL(FM) Blue Ridge GA
WTUF(FM) Boston GA
WGRA(AM) Cairo GA
WJTH(AM) Calhoun GA
WGST-FM Canton GA
WBTR-FM Carrollton GA
WLBB(AM) Carrollton GA
WPPI(AM) Carrollton GA
WYXC(AM) Cartersville GA
WGAA(AM) Cedartown GA
WQMT(FM) Chatsworth GA
WCLA(AM) Claxton GA
WCLA-FM Claxton GA
WRWH(AM) Cleveland GA
WVMG(AM) Cochran GA
WVMG-FM Cochran GA
WJJC(AM) Commerce GA
WKKN(FM) Cordele GA
WCON(AM) Cornelia GA
WCON-FM Cornelia GA
WMLB(AM) Cumming GA
WCUG(AM) Cuthbert GA
WDGR(AM) Dahlonega GA
WYNR(FM) Darien GA
WDMG-FM Douglas GA
WOKA(AM) Douglas GA
WOKA-FM Douglas GA
WMLT(AM) Dublin GA
WXLI(AM) Dublin GA
WUFF(AM) Eastman GA
WUFF-FM Eastman GA
WKVQ(AM) Eatonton GA
WWRK-FM Elberton GA
WOKF(FM) Folkston GA
WYAY(FM) Gainesville GA
WPLO(AM) Grayson GA
WHIE(AM) Griffin GA
WKLY(AM) Hartwell GA
WVOH(AM) Hazlehurst GA
WVOH-FM Hazlehurst GA
WLOP(AM) Jesup GA
WKBX(FM) Kingsland GA
WQCH(AM) La Fayette GA
WLAG(AM) La Grange GA
WYAI(FM) La Grange GA
WPEH(AM) Louisville GA
WPEH-FM Louisville GA
WKCN(FM) Lumpkin GA
WLYU(FM) Lyons GA
WDEN-FM Macon GA
WMKS(FM) Macon GA
WYTH(AM) Madison GA
WYIS(AM) McRae GA
WMCG(FM) Milan GA
WKZR(FM) Milledgeville GA
WMKO(FM) Millen GA
WKUN(AM) Monroe GA
WLML(FM) Montezuma GA
WMNZ(AM) Montezuma GA
WMTM(AM) Moultrie GA
WMTM-FM Moultrie GA
WALH(AM) Mountain City GA
WNGA(AM) Nashville GA
WCOH(AM) Newnan GA
WNEA(AM) Newnan GA
WKAA(FM) Ocilla GA
WTIF-FM Omega GA
WSFB(AM) Quitman GA
WTSH-FM Rockmart GA
WRGA(AM) Rome GA
WTSH(AM) Rome GA
WSNT(AM) Sandersville GA
WSNT-FM Sandersville GA
WCHY(AM) Savannah GA
WCHY-FM Savannah GA
WJCL-FM Savannah GA
WGTA(AM) Summerville GA
WJAT(AM) Swainsboro GA
WXRS-FM Swainsboro GA
WSYL(AM) Sylvania GA
WZBX(FM) Sylvania GA
WKNG(AM) Tallapoosa GA
WSFT(AM) Thomaston GA
WTGA(AM) Thomaston GA
WTGA-FM Thomaston GA
WTHO-FM Thomson GA
WSGY(FM) Tifton GA
WTIF(AM) Tifton GA
WADX(AM) Trenton GA
WAAC(FM) Valdosta GA
WYZK(FM) Valdosta GA
WWWN(AM) Vienna GA
WRCC(AM) Warner Robins GA
WBGA(FM) Waycross GA
WCJM(FM) West Point GA
WPLV(AM) West Point GA
WIMO(AM) Winder GA
WZCM(AM) Young Harris GA
KHLO(AM) Hilo HI
KDLX(FM) Makawao HI
KDEO(AM) Waipahu HI
KDEO-FM Waipahu HI
KLEH(AM) Anamosa IA
KJJY-FM Ankeny IA
KXKT(FM) Atlantic IA
KXOF(FM) Bloomfield IA
KDMG(FM) Burlington IA
KCRG(AM) Cedar Rapids IA
KHAK(AM) Cedar Rapids IA
KHAK-FM Cedar Rapids IA
KMGO(FM) Centerville IA
KITR(FM) Creston IA
KSIB(AM) Creston IA
KJOC(AM) Davenport IA
KDSN(AM) Denison IA
KKSO(AM) Des Moines IA
KDST(FM) Dyersville IA
KMCD(AM) Fairfield IA
KIOW(FM) Forest City IA
KWMT(AM) Fort Dodge IA
KCTN(FM) Garnavillo IA
KGCI(FM) Grundy Center IA
KLMJ(FM) Hampton IA
KRNQ(FM) Hampton IA
KNOD(FM) Harlan IA
KIDA-FM Ida Grove IA
KQMG-FM Independence IA
KOKX-FM Keokuk IA
KMCH(FM) Manchester IA
KMAQ(AM) Maquoketa IA
KXIA(FM) Marshalltown IA
KIAI(FM) Mason City IA
KILJ-FM Mount Pleasant IA
KCOB(AM) Newton IA
KCOB-FM Newton IA
KOEL-FM Oelwein IA
KJJC(FM) Osceola IA
KBOE(AM) Oskaloosa IA
KBOE-FM Oskaloosa IA
KLEE(AM) Ottumwa IA
KDLS(AM) Perry IA
KDLS-FM Perry IA
KIWA(AM) Sheldon IA
KIWA-FM Sheldon IA
KMA(AM) Shenandoah IA
KVDB(AM) Sioux Center IA
KMNS(AM) Sioux City IA
KICD-FM Spencer IA
KKRF(FM) Stuart IA
KTLB(FM) Twin Lakes IA
KXEL(AM) Waterloo IA
KNEI(AM) Waukon IA
KNEI-FM Waukon IA
KIZN(FM) Boise ID
KKIC(AM) Boise ID
KQFC(FM) Boise ID
KBFI(AM) Bonners Ferry ID
KCID-FM Caldwell ID
KCDA(FM) Coeur d'Alene ID
KRXR(AM) Gooding ID
KORT(AM) Grangeville ID
KORT-FM Grangeville ID
KUPI-FM Idaho Falls ID
KART(AM) Jerome ID
KRLC(AM) Lewiston ID
KMCL-FM McCall ID
KVSI(AM) Montpelier ID
KLER-FM Orofino ID
KWIK(AM) Pocatello ID
KZBQ(AM) Pocatello ID
KACH(AM) Preston ID
KACH-FM Preston ID
KRXK(AM) Rexburg ID
KRXK-FM Rexburg ID
KBBK(AM) Rupert ID
KSRA(AM) Salmon ID
KSRA-FM Salmon ID
KSPT(AM) Sandpoint ID
KOFE(AM) St. Maries ID
KEZJ-FM Twin Falls ID
KWAL(AM) Wallace ID
KWEI-FM Weiser ID
WRMJ(FM) Aledo IL
WRAJ-FM Anna IL
WRMS-FM Beardstown IL
WQRL(FM) Benton IL
WLMD(FM) Bushnell IL
WKRO(AM) Cairo IL
WCNL(FM) Carlinville IL
WRUL(FM) Carmi IL
WCAZ(AM) Carthage IL
WEIC(AM) Charleston IL
KSGM(AM) Chester IL
WUSN(FM) Chicago IL
WHOW(AM) Clinton IL
WCCQ(FM) Crest Hill IL
WIAI(FM) Danville IL
WDZQ(FM) Decatur IL
WIXN-FM Dixon IL
WLLR-FM East Moline IL
WCRC(FM) Effingham IL
WFYR(FM) Elmwood IL
WFIW(AM) Fairfield IL
WZRO(FM) Farmer City IL
WJOD(FM) Galena IL
WAAG(FM) Galesburg IL
WGEN(AM) Geneseo IL
WDXR-FM Golconda IL
WGEL(FM) Greenville IL
WEBQ(AM) Harrisburg IL
WOOZ-FM Harrisburg IL
WDUK(FM) Havana IL
WHPO(FM) Hoopeston IL
WJIL(AM) Jacksonville IL
WJBM(AM) Jerseyville IL
WKKX(FM) Jerseyville IL
WDDD(AM) Johnston City IL
WLRT(FM) Kankakee IL
WBWN(FM) Le Roy IL
WPRC(AM) Lincoln IL
WSMI(AM) Litchfield IL
WLUV(AM) Loves Park IL
WLUV-FM Loves Park IL
WLRB(AM) Macomb IL
WDDD-FM Marion IL
WLBH(AM) Mattoon IL
WMCI(FM) Mattoon IL
WMCL(AM) McLeansboro IL
WGLC(AM) Mendota IL
WGLC-FM Mendota IL
WMOK(AM) Metropolis IL
WLLR(AM) Moline IL
WRAM(AM) Monmouth IL
WCZQ(FM) Monticello IL
WYER(AM) Mt. Carmel IL
WMIX-FM Mt. Vernon IL
WIKK(FM) Newton IL
WZLC(FM) Oglesby IL
WVLN(AM) Olney IL
WXKO-FM Pana IL
WACF(FM) Paris IL
WXCL-FM Pekin IL
WXCL(AM) Peoria IL
WBBA-FM Pittsfield IL
WGEM-FM Quincy IL
WRHL(AM) Rochelle IL
WRHL-FM Rochelle IL
WKBF(AM) Rock Island IL
WCCI(FM) Savanna IL
WFMB(AM) Springfield IL
WFMB-FM Springfield IL
WSTQ(FM) Streator IL
WKJR(FM) Sullivan IL
WUBB(FM) Tuscola IL
WAXT(FM) Alexandria IN
WSCH(FM) Aurora IN
WRBI(FM) Batesville IN
WBIW(AM) Bedford IN
WBHQ(FM) Bloomfield IN
WBNL(AM) Boonville IN
WLME(FM) Cannelton IN
WKKG(FM) Columbus IN
WCNB-FM Connersville IN
WIFE(AM) Connersville IN
WOCC(AM) Corydon IN
WCVL(AM) Crawfordsville IN
WQHK-FM Decatur IN
WGCT(FM) Ellettsville IN
WYNG-FM Evansville IN
WLYV(AM) Fort Wayne IN
WQHK(AM) Fort Wayne IN
WILO(AM) Frankfort IN
WFLQ(FM) French Lick IN
WTRE(AM) Greensburg IN
WBDC(FM) Huntingburg IN
WCKN(AM) Indianapolis IN
WFMS(FM) Indianapolis IN

Programming on Radio Stations in the U.S.

WGRL(FM) Indianapolis IN
WBTU(FM) Kendallville IN
*WKPW(FM) Knightstown IN
WKVI-FM Knox IN
WWKI(FM) Kokomo IN
WCOE(FM) La Porte IN
WASK-FM Lafayette IN
WIRE(FM) Lebanon IN
WSAL(AM) Logansport IN
WCBK-FM Martinsville IN
WMCB(AM) Martinsville IN
WPCO(AM) Mt. Vernon IN
WGTC(FM) New Carlisle IN
WMDH-FM New Castle IN
WFPC(FM) Petersburg IN
WNZE(FM) Plymouth IN
WPGW-FM Portland IN
WRIN(AM) Rensselaer IN
WSLM(AM) Salem IN
WMPI(FM) Scottsburg IN
WQKC(FM) Seymour IN
WOOO(AM) Shelbyville IN
WSKT(FM) Spencer IN
WNDI(AM) Sullivan IN
WNDI-FM Sullivan IN
WTHI-FM Terre Haute IN
WLJE(FM) Valparaiso IN
WCJC(FM) Van Buren IN
WXCH(FM) Versailles IN
WKID(FM) Vevay IN
WFML(FM) Vincennes IN
WAYT(AM) Wabash IN
WWBL(FM) Washington IN
KABI(AM) Abilene KS
KSOK(AM) Arkansas City KS
KYQQ(FM) Arkansas City KS
*KNBU(FM) Baldwin City KS
KREP(FM) Belleville KS
KCLY(FM) Clay Center KS
KSPG(FM) Clearwater KS
KXXX(AM) Colby KS
KNCK(AM) Concordia KS
KGNO(AM) Dodge City KS
KSRX(AM) El Dorado KS
KEGS(FM) Emporia KS
KOTE(FM) Eureka KS
KMDO(AM) Fort Scott KS
KKJQ(FM) Garden City KS
KVGB(AM) Great Bend KS
KHAZ(FM) Hays KS
KDMM(FM) Herington KS
KNZA(FM) Hiawatha KS
KBUF(AM) Holcomb KS
KFXX-FM Hugoton KS
KHUT(FM) Hutchinson KS
KZSN-FM Hutchinson KS
KALN(AM) Iola KS
KJCK(AM) Junction City KS
KFKF-FM Kansas City KS
KSCB(AM) Liberal KS
KSLS(FM) Liberal KS
KNDY(AM) Marysville KS
KNDY-FM Marysville KS
KBBE(FM) McPherson KS
KFNF(FM) Oberlin KS
KZOC(FM) Osage City KS
KOFO(AM) Ottawa KS
KKOW(AM) Pittsburg KS
KKOW-FM Pittsburg KS
KGLS(FM) Pratt KS
KWLS(AM) Pratt KS
KFRM(AM) Salina KS
KYEZ(FM) Salina KS
KMZA(FM) Seneca KS
KTPK(FM) Topeka KS
WIBW(AM) Topeka KS
WIBW-FM Topeka KS
KULY(AM) Ulysses KS
KLEY(AM) Wellington KS
KFDI(AM) Wichita KS
KFDI-FM Wichita KS
KZSN(AM) Wichita KS
WANY(AM) Albany KY
WANY-FM Albany KY
WMDJ-FM Allen KY
WYWY-FM Barbourville KY
WBRT(AM) Bardstown KY
WCBL(AM) Benton KY
WKXO(AM) Berea KY
WKXO-FM Berea KY
WMMG(AM) Brandenburg KY
WMMG-FM Brandenburg KY
WXAM(AM) Buffalo KY
WKYR(AM) Burkesville KY
WKYR-FM Burkesville KY
WKDZ(AM) Cadiz KY
WTCO(AM) Campbellsville KY
WIKI(FM) Carrollton KY
WQXQ(FM) Central City KY
WAIN(AM) Columbia KY
WAIN-FM Columbia KY
WCTT(AM) Corbin KY
WKDP-FM Corbin KY
WCPM(AM) Cumberland KY
WCYN(AM) Cynthiana KY
WCYN-FM Cynthiana KY
WMGE(FM) Danville KY
WKNK(FM) Edmonton KY
WBPA(AM) Elkhorn City KY
WEKT(AM) Elkton KY
WKXF(AM) Eminence KY
WIOK(FM) Falmouth KY
WFLE(AM) Flemingsburg KY
WFLE-FM Flemingsburg KY
WKED(AM) Frankfort KY

WFKN(AM) Franklin KY
WKZT(AM) Fulton KY
WBBE(AM) Georgetown KY
WGGC(FM) Glasgow KY
WGOH(AM) Grayson KY
WGRK-FM Greensburg KY
WLGC-FM Greenup KY
WHIC(AM) Hardinsburg KY
WHIC-FM Hardinsburg KY
WXBC(FM) Hardinsburg KY
WFSR(AM) Harlan KY
WHBN(AM) Harrodsburg KY
WHBN-FM Harrodsburg KY
WLLS(AM) Hartford KY
WLLS-FM Hartford KY
WSGS(FM) Hazard KY
WKDQ(FM) Henderson KY
WKCB(AM) Hindman KY
WKCB-FM Hindman KY
WKMO(FM) Hodgenville KY
WHOP-FM Hopkinsville KY
WCYO(FM) Irvine KY
WIRV(AM) Irvine KY
WEKG(AM) Jackson KY
WJKY(AM) Jamestown KY
WJRS(FM) Jamestown KY
WKYY(AM) Lancaster KY
WLSK(FM) Lebanon KY
WMTL(AM) Leitchfield KY
WVLK-FM Lexington KY
WKDO(AM) Liberty KY
WKDO-FM Liberty KY
WWEL(FM) London KY
WVKY(AM) Louisa KY
WAMZ(FM) Louisville KY
WTMT(AM) Louisville KY
WFMW(AM) Madisonville KY
WKLB(AM) Manchester KY
WMJL(AM) Marion KY
WMJL-FM Marion KY
WMDJ(AM) Martin KY
WNGO(AM) Mayfield KY
WXID(FM) Mayfield KY
WFTM(AM) Maysville KY
WFTM-FM Maysville KY
WMIK(AM) Middlesboro KY
WFLW(AM) Monticello KY
WMKZ(FM) Monticello KY
WMSK(AM) Morganfield KY
WMSK-FM Morganfield KY
WLBQ(AM) Morgantown KY
WMST-FM Mt. Sterling KY
WRVK(AM) Mt. Vernon KY
WLOC(AM) Munfordville KY
WLOC-FM Munfordville KY
WNVL(AM) Nicholasville KY
WBKR(FM) Owensboro KY
WKCA(FM) Owingsville KY
WKYQ(FM) Paducah KY
WSIP(AM) Paintsville KY
WSIP-FM Paintsville KY
WDHR(FM) Pikeville KY
WLSI(AM) Pikeville KY
WANO(AM) Pineville KY
WRIL(FM) Pineville KY
WPRT(AM) Prestonsburg KY
WHRZ(FM) Providence KY
WBVR(FM) Russellville KY
WRLV-FM Salyersville KY
WVLE(FM) Scottsville KY
WCND(AM) Shelbyville KY
WTHQ(FM) Shelbyville KY
WSEK(FM) Somerset KY
WRSL-FM Stanford KY
WSKV(FM) Stanton KY
WTKY(AM) Tompkinsville KY
WTKY-FM Tompkinsville KY
WKKS(AM) Vanceburg KY
WKKS-FM Vanceburg KY
WLKS(AM) West Liberty KY
WLKS-FM West Liberty KY
WTCW(AM) Whitesburg KY
WXKQ(FM) Whitesburg KY
WHAY(FM) Whitley City KY
WEKC(AM) Williamsburg KY
WEZJ(AM) Williamsburg KY
WNKR(FM) Williamstown KY
WHRS(AM) Winchester KY
WWYC(FM) Winchester KY
KRRV(AM) Alexandria LA
KRRV-FM Alexandria LA
WABL(AM) Amite LA
KBAZ(FM) Basile LA
WYNK(AM) Baton Rouge LA
WYNK-FM Baton Rouge LA
KDLP(AM) Bayou Vista LA
KQKI(FM) Bayou Vista LA
WBOX(AM) Bogalusa LA
KSBH(FM) Coushatta LA
KSIG(AM) Crowley LA
KKAY-FM Donaldsonville LA
KEUN(AM) Eunice LA
WFCG(AM) Franklinton LA
KLEB(AM) Golden Meadow LA
WFPR(AM) Hammond LA
WHMD(FM) Hammond LA
WKJN-FM Hammond LA
KCIL(FM) Houma LA
KJIN(AM) Houma LA
KJNA(AM) Jena LA
KJNA-FM Jena LA
KJEF(AM) Jennings LA
KJEF-FM Jennings LA
KTOC(AM) Jonesboro LA
KTOC-FM Jonesboro LA

KMDL(FM) Kaplan LA
WYCT(FM) Kentwood LA
KYKZ(FM) Lake Charles LA
KLPL(AM) Lake Providence LA
KLPL-FM Lake Providence LA
KJAE(FM) Leesville LA
KVVP(FM) Leesville LA
KWLV(FM) Many LA
KAPB(AM) Marksville LA
KAPB-FM Marksville LA
KASO(AM) Minden LA
KJLO-FM Monroe LA
KDBH(FM) Natchitoches LA
KXKC(FM) New Iberia LA
WNOE(AM) New Orleans LA
WNOE-FM New Orleans LA
KWCL-FM Oak Grove LA
KICR-FM Oakdale LA
KSLO(AM) Opelousas LA
KXKZ(FM) Ruston LA
KRMD(AM) Shreveport LA
KRMD-FM Shreveport LA
KWKH(AM) Shreveport LA
KWKH-FM Shreveport LA
KTQQ(FM) Sulphur LA
KBYO-FM Tallulah LA
KLAA(FM) Tioga LA
WBOX-FM Varnado LA
KVPI(AM) Ville Platte LA
KNCB(AM) Vivian LA
KNEK(AM) Washington LA
KNEK-FM Washington LA
KVCL(AM) Winnfield LA
KVCL-FM Winnfield LA
KMAR(AM) Winnsboro LA
KMAR-FM Winnsboro LA
WBCS(FM) Boston MA
WCAV(FM) Brockton MA
WCIB(FM) Falmouth MA
WFAL(FM) Falmouth MA
WCLB-FM Framingham MA
WHAI(AM) Greenfield MA
WHAI-FM Greenfield MA
WFXR(FM) Harwichport MA
WCTK(FM) New Bedford MA
WQVR(FM) Southbridge MA
WANN(AM) Annapolis MD
WPOC(FM) Baltimore MD
WCEM(AM) Cambridge MD
WROG(FM) Cumberland MD
WQSI(AM) Frederick MD
WFRB(AM) Frostburg MD
WFRB-FM Frostburg MD
WPVG(AM) Funkstown MD
WASA(AM) Havre de Grace MD
WXCY(FM) Havre de Grace MD
WAAI(FM) Hurlock MD
WNTL(AM) Indian Head MD
WPTX(AM) Lexington Park MD
WMSG(AM) Oakland MD
WWFG(FM) Ocean City MD
WICO-FM Salisbury MD
WYII(FM) Williamsport MD
WKCG(FM) Augusta ME
WYOU-FM Bangor ME
WCME(FM) Boothbay Harbor ME
WQCB(FM) Brewer ME
WQDY(AM) Calais ME
WQDY-FM Calais ME
WKTJ-FM Farmington ME
WXBB(FM) Kittery ME
WTHT(FM) Lewiston ME
WHMX(FM) Lincoln ME
WTBM(FM) Mexico ME
WOXO-FM Norway ME
WPOR(AM) Portland ME
WPOR-FM Portland ME
WBPW(FM) Presque Isle ME
WOZI(FM) Presque Isle ME
WMCM(FM) Rockland ME
WPME(FM) Topsham ME
WLEN(FM) Adrian MI
WQTE(FM) Adrian MI
WFYC(AM) Alma MI
WFYC-FM Alma MI
WATZ(AM) Alpena MI
WATZ-FM Alpena MI
WLEW(AM) Bad Axe MI
WELL(AM) Battle Creek MI
WBRN(AM) Big Rapids MI
WBCM(FM) Boyne City MI
WYTW(FM) Cadillac MI
WNWN(FM) Coldwater MI
WWWW(AM) Detroit MI
WWWW-FM Detroit MI
WYCD(FM) Detroit MI
WYKX(FM) Escanaba MI
WIXC(FM) Essexville MI
WWON(AM) Fenton MI
WSHN(AM) Fremont MI
WSHN-FM Fremont MI
WBCT(FM) Grand Rapids MI
WCUZ(AM) Grand Rapids MI
WCUZ-FM Grand Rapids MI
WGRY(AM) Grayling MI
WCMM(FM) Gulliver MI
WKKM(FM) Harrison MI
WBCH(AM) Hastings MI
WBCH-FM Hastings MI
WCCY(AM) Houghton MI
WION(AM) Ionia MI
WJMS(AM) Ironwood MI
WIAN(AM) Ishpeming MI
WJPD(FM) Ishpeming MI
WJCO(AM) Jackson MI

WPLB-FM Lakeview MI
WILS(AM) Lansing MI
WILS-FM Lansing MI
WITL(AM) Lansing MI
WITL-FM Lansing MI
WWGZ(AM) Lapeer MI
WIFN(AM) Marine City MI
WELL-FM Marshall MI
WHYB(FM) Menominee MI
WCEN-FM Mount Pleasant MI
WHCH(FM) Munising MI
WMUS(AM) Muskegon MI
WMUS-FM Muskegon MI
WUPY(FM) Ontonagon MI
WSAQ(FM) Port Huron MI
WHAK(AM) Rogers City MI
WGRY-FM Roscommon MI
WKCQ(FM) Saginaw MI
WSDS(AM) Salem Township MI
WMIC(AM) Sandusky MI
WKZC(FM) Scottville MI
WIDG(AM) St. Ignace MI
WMKC(FM) St. Ignace MI
WWSJ(AM) St. Johns MI
WMLM(AM) St. Louis MI
WKJC(FM) Tawas City MI
WTCM-FM Traverse City MI
WKMF-FM Tuscola MI
*WPHS(FM) Warren MI
WEFG(AM) Whitehall MI
WEFG-FM Whitehall MI
KRJB(FM) Ada MN
KKIN(AM) Aitkin MN
KASM(AM) Albany MN
KATE(AM) Albert Lea MN
KIKV-FM Alexandria MN
KYRS(FM) Atwater MN
KAUS-FM Austin MN
KBHP(FM) Bemidji MN
KKBJ(AM) Bemidji MN
KBEW(AM) Blue Earth MN
KLIZ(AM) Brainerd MN
KVBR(AM) Brainerd MN
KBMW(AM) Breckenridge MN
KRWC(AM) Buffalo MN
KYCK(FM) Crookston MN
KTCF(FM) Crosby MN
WAVC(FM) Duluth MN
KSUM(AM) Fairmont MN
KDHL(AM) Faribault MN
KBRF(AM) Fergus Falls MN
KJJK-FM Fergus Falls MN
WLKX-FM Forest Lake MN
KARP(FM) Glencoe MN
KDWA(AM) Hastings MN
KDUZ(AM) Hutchinson MN
KKJR(FM) Hutchinson MN
KSDM(FM) International Falls MN
KKOJ(AM) Jackson MN
KMFX(FM) Lake City MN
KLFD(AM) Litchfield MN
KLTF(AM) Little Falls MN
WYRQ(FM) Little Falls MN
KEYL(AM) Long Prairie MN
KLQL(FM) Luverne MN
KLQP(FM) Madison MN
KYSM-FM Mankato MN
KMHL(AM) Marshall MN
*WBOB-FM Minneapolis MN
KDMA(AM) Montevideo MN
KVOX-FM Moorhead MN
KKOK-FM Morris MN
KMRS(AM) Morris MN
WKKQ(AM) Nashwauk MN
KNUJ(AM) New Ulm MN
KOLV(FM) Olivia MN
KRFO-FM Owatonna MN
KPRM(AM) Park Rapids MN
WCMP-FM Pine City MN
KLOH(AM) Pipestone MN
KFIL(AM) Preston MN
KFIL-FM Preston MN
WQPM(AM) Princeton MN
WQPM-FM Princeton MN
KLGR(AM) Redwood Falls MN
KLGR-FM Redwood Falls MN
KWWK(FM) Rochester MN
KRWB(AM) Roseau MN
KLOH-FM Slayton MN
KNUJ-FM Sleepy Eye MN
KQYB(FM) Spring Grove MN
WWJO(FM) St. Cloud MN
KXAX(FM) St. James MN
KJJO(AM) St. Louis Park MN
KJJO-FM St. Louis Park MN
KEEY-FM St. Paul MN
WDGY(AM) St. Paul MN
KRBI(AM) St. Peter MN
KRBI-FM St. Peter MN
KKAQ(AM) Thief River Falls MN
KKDQ(FM) Thief River Falls MN
*KSRQ(FM) Thief River Falls MN
KARL(FM) Tracy MN
WUSZ(FM) Virginia MN
KWMB(AM) Wabasha MN
KKWS(FM) Wadena MN
KWAD(AM) Wadena MN
KKWQ(FM) Warroad MN
KDJS-FM Willmar MN
KDOM(AM) Windom MN
KDOM-FM Windom MN
KAGE(AM) Winona MN
KGMY-FM Aurora MO
KSWM(AM) Aurora MO
KAAN(AM) Bethany MO

KAAN-FM Bethany MO
KBMV(AM) Birch Tree MO
KBMV-FM Birch Tree MO
KBEQ(AM) Blue Springs MO
KYOO(AM) Bolivar MO
KCLR-FM Boonville MO
KWRT(AM) Boonville MO
KPCR(AM) Bowling Green MO
KPCR-FM Bowling Green MO
KRZK(FM) Branson MO
KBFL(FM) Buffalo MO
KMAM(AM) Butler MO
KMOE(FM) Butler MO
KOZX(FM) Cabool MO
KZMO(AM) California MO
KZMO-FM California MO
KMRN(AM) Cameron MO
KEZS-FM Cape Girardeau MO
KAOL(AM) Carrollton MO
KMZU(FM) Carrollton MO
KDMO(AM) Carthage MO
KCRV(AM) Caruthersville MO
KCHR(AM) Charleston MO
KDKD-FM Clinton MO
KDEX(AM) Dexter MO
KDEX-FM Dexter MO
KOEA(FM) Doniphan MO
KESM(AM) El Dorado Springs MO
KESM-FM El Dorado Springs MO
KEXS(AM) Excelsior Springs MO
KTJJ(FM) Farmington MO
KFTW(AM) Fredricktown MO
KFAL(AM) Fulton MO
KBTC(AM) Houston MO
KUNQ(FM) Houston MO
KLIK(AM) Jefferson City MO
WMBH(AM) Joplin MO
KBEQ-FM Kansas City MO
WDAF(AM) Kansas City MO
WHB(AM) Kansas City MO
KTMO(FM) Kennett MO
KIRX(AM) Kirksville MO
KXKX(FM) Knob Noster MO
KHST(FM) Lamar MO
KIRK(FM) Lebanon MO
KJEL(AM) Lebanon MO
KLWT(AM) Lebanon MO
KKCJ(FM) Liberty MO
KJFM(FM) Louisiana MO
KTRI-FM Mansfield MO
KMMO(AM) Marshall MO
KMMO-FM Marshall MO
KMRF(AM) Marshfield MO
KMEM-FM Memphis MO
KWWR(FM) Mexico MO
KRES(FM) Moberly MO
KRMO(AM) Monett MO
KCMG(AM) Mountain Grove MO
KCMG-FM Mountain Grove MO
KBTN(AM) Neosho MO
KNEM(AM) Nevada MO
KNMO(FM) Nevada MO
KMIS-FM New Madrid MO
KRMS(AM) Osage Beach MO
KBUG(FM) Osceola MO
KICK-FM Palmyra MO
KPWB(AM) Piedmont MO
KPWB-FM Piedmont MO
KKLR(FM) Poplar Bluff MO
KWOC(AM) Poplar Bluff MO
KMIS(AM) Portageville MO
KYRO(AM) Potosi MO
KZNN(FM) Rolla MO
KSMO(AM) Salem MO
KSJQ(FM) Savannah MO
KDRO(AM) Sedalia MO
KLTK(AM) Southwest City MO
KWMQ(FM) Southwest City MO
KLTQ(FM) Sparta MO
KGMY(AM) Springfield MO
KTTS(AM) Springfield MO
KTTS-FM Springfield MO
KFEQ(AM) St. Joseph MO
KSD(AM) St. Louis MO
WIL-FM St. Louis MO
KTUI-FM Sullivan MO
KTRX(FM) Tarkio MO
KALM(AM) Thayer MO
KTTN(AM) Trenton MO
KLPW-FM Union MO
KLGS(FM) Versailles MO
KWRE(AM) Warrenton MO
KAYQ(FM) Warsaw MO
KJPW(AM) Waynesville MO
KJPW-FM Waynesville MO
KIXQ(FM) Webb City MO
KUKU(AM) Willow Springs MO
KUKU-FM Willow Springs MO
WAMY(AM) Amory MS
WBLE(FM) Batesville MS
WIZK(AM) Bay Springs MS
WELZ(AM) Belzoni MS
WBIP(AM) Booneville MS
WBIP-FM Booneville MS
WBKN(FM) Brookhaven MS
WSSI(AM) Carthage MS
WSSI-FM Carthage MS
WTGY(FM) Charleston MS
WKDJ(FM) Clarksdale MS
WDTL-FM Cleveland MS
WVIM-FM Coldwater MS
WKNZ(FM) Collins MS
WFFF(AM) Columbia MS
WKOR-FM Columbus MS
WMBC(FM) Columbus MS

Programming on Radio Stations in the U.S.

WCMA(AM) Corinth MS
WEPA(AM) Eupora MS
WQST(AM) Forest MS
WQST-FM Forest MS
WFTO(AM) Fulton MS
WDDT(AM) Greenville MS
WGVM(AM) Greenville MS
WABG(AM) Greenwood MS
WYKC(AM) Grenada MS
WHER(FM) Hattiesburg MS
WMDC(AM) Hazelhurst MS
WMDC-FM Hazelhurst MS
WKRA(AM) Holly Springs MS
WCPC(AM) Houston MS
WDLJ(FM) Indianola MS
WVOM(AM) Iuka MS
WMSI(FM) Jackson MS
WBKJ(FM) Kosciusko MS
WAGR-FM Lexington MS
WLSM(AM) Louisville MS
WLSM-FM Louisville MS
WRBE(AM) Lucedale MS
WLUN(FM) Lumberton MS
WZMP(FM) Marion MS
WAKH(FM) McComb MS
WMOX(AM) Meridian MS
WOKK(FM) Meridian MS
WMLC(AM) Monticello MS
WRQO(FM) Monticello MS
WZBA(FM) Moss Point MS
WQNZ(FM) Natchez MS
WWZD(FM) New Albany MS
WWMS(FM) Oxford MS
WGUD-FM Pascagoula MS
WKNN-FM Pascagoula MS
WHOC(AM) Philadelphia MS
WRJW(AM) Picayune MS
WRPM(AM) Poplarville MS
WJDR(FM) Prentiss MS
WBFN(AM) Quitman MS
WYKK(FM) Quitman MS
WKZU(FM) Ripley MS
WSAO(AM) Senatobia MS
WMSU(FM) Starkville MS
WBBN(FM) Taylorsville MS
WTYL(AM) Tylertown MS
WTYL-FM Tylertown MS
WBBV(FM) Vicksburg MS
WIIN(FM) Vicksburg MS
WVIX(AM) Vicksburg MS
WABO(AM) Waynesboro MS
WABO-FM Waynesboro MS
WIGG(AM) Wiggins MS
WONA(AM) Winona MS
WONA-FM Winona MS
KGLM-FM Anaconda MT
KFLN(AM) Baker MT
KCTR(AM) Billings MT
KCTR-FM Billings MT
KGHL(AM) Billings MT
KATH(FM) Bozeman MT
KBOZ(AM) Bozeman MT
KZLO-FM Bozeman MT
KAAR(FM) Butte MT
KBOW(AM) Butte MT
KDBM(AM) Dillon MT
KHKR-FM East Helena MT
KIKC(AM) Forsyth MT
KIKC-FM Forsyth MT
KLTZ(AM) Glasgow MT
KEIN(AM) Great Falls MT
KMON(AM) Great Falls MT
KMON-FM Great Falls MT
KOOZ(FM) Great Falls MT
KLYQ(AM) Hamilton MT
KDWG(FM) Hardin MT
KPQX(FM) Havre MT
KBLL-FM Helena MT
KDBR(FM) Kalispell MT
KOFI-FM Kalispell MT
KMTA(AM) Kinsey MT
KXLO(AM) Lewistown MT
KLCB(AM) Libby MT
KBOZ-FM Livingston MT
KPRK(AM) Livingston MT
KYSS-FM Missoula MT
KATQ(AM) Plentywood MT
KATQ-FM Plentywood MT
KERR(AM) Polson MT
KCGM(FM) Scobey MT
KWYS(AM) West Yellowstone MT
KVCK(AM) Wolf Point MT
WQDK(FM) Ahoskie NC
WKXR(AM) Asheboro NC
WWNC(AM) Asheville NC
WZJS(FM) Banner Elk NC
WPYB(AM) Benson NC
WZQR(AM) Black Mountain NC
WBHN(AM) Bryson City NC
WVBS(AM) Burgaw NC
WPCM(FM) Burlington NC
WKYK(AM) Burnsville NC
WPTL(AM) Canton NC
WSOC-FM Charlotte NC
WRRZ(AM) Clinton NC
WRSF(FM) Columbia NC
WTIK(AM) Durham NC
WNEU(FM) Eden NC
WKJX(FM) Elizabeth City NC
*WUAW(FM) Erwin NC
WAGY(AM) Forest City NC
WAJA(AM) Franklin NC
WFSC(AM) Franklin NC
WHEV(AM) Garner NC
WFMC(AM) Goldsboro NC
WTND(FM) Grifton NC
WJSG(FM) Hamlet NC
WHNC(AM) Henderson NC
WIZS(AM) Henderson NC
WIRC(AM) Hickory NC
WGOS(AM) High Point NC
WKTE(AM) King NC
WKMT(AM) Kings Mountain NC
WRNS(AM) Kinston NC
WRNS-FM Kinston NC
WJRI(AM) Lenoir NC
WKGX(AM) Lenoir NC
WKVS(FM) Lenoir NC
WYRN(AM) Louisburg NC
WAGR(AM) Lumberton NC
WKML(FM) Lumberton NC
WBRM(AM) Marion NC
WDSL(AM) Mocksville NC
WIXE(AM) Monroe NC
WMNC(AM) Morganton NC
WPAQ(AM) Mount Airy NC
WKRK(AM) Murphy NC
WNHW(FM) Nags Head NC
WJTP(AM) Newland NC
WKBC(AM) North Wilkesboro NC
WPNC-FM Plymouth NC
WQDR(FM) Raleigh NC
WREV(AM) Reidsville NC
WPTM(FM) Roanoke Rapids NC
WCVP-FM Robbinsville NC
WSAY-FM Rocky Mount NC
WBSY(FM) Rose Hill NC
WKRX(FM) Roxboro NC
WCAB(AM) Rutherfordton NC
*WDCC(FM) Sanford NC
WWGP(AM) Sanford NC
WBZB(AM) Selma NC
WADA(AM) Shelby NC
WMPM(AM) Smithfield NC
WCOK(AM) Sparta NC
WFMX(FM) Statesville NC
WTDR(FM) Statesville NC
WRGC(AM) Sylva NC
WTAB(AM) Tabor City NC
WYNA(FM) Tabor City NC
WACB(AM) Taylorsville NC
WTLK(AM) Taylorsville NC
WJRM(AM) Troy NC
WSVM(AM) Valdese NC
WADE(AM) Wadesboro NC
WLSE(AM) Wallace NC
WTOW(AM) Washington NC
WQNS(FM) Waynesville NC
WETC(AM) Wendell-Zebulon NC
WKSK(AM) West Jefferson NC
WWQQ-FM Wilmington NC
WTQR(FM) Winston-Salem NC
*KEYA(FM) Belcourt ND
KHOL(AM) Beulah ND
KBMR(AM) Bismarck ND
KQDY(FM) Bismarck ND
KBTO(FM) Bottineau ND
KPOK(AM) Bowman ND
KDAK(AM) Carrington ND
KDLR(AM) Devils Lake ND
KZZY-FM Devils Lake ND
KLTC(AM) Dickinson ND
KFGO(AM) Fargo ND
KFGO-FM Fargo ND
KXPO(AM) Grafton ND
KXPO-FM Grafton ND
KKXL(AM) Grand Forks ND
KHND(AM) Harvey ND
KNDC(AM) Hettinger ND
KSJB(AM) Jamestown ND
KYNU(FM) Jamestown ND
KNDK(AM) Langdon ND
KQLX(AM) Lisbon ND
KQLX-FM Lisbon ND
KMAV(AM) Mayville ND
KMAV-FM Mayville ND
KCJB(AM) Minot ND
KYYX(FM) Minot ND
KZPR(FM) Minot ND
KDDR(AM) Oakes ND
KZZJ(AM) Rugby ND
KTGO(AM) Tioga ND
KOVC(AM) Valley City ND
KDSR(FM) Williston ND
KEYZ(AM) Williston ND
KBRB(AM) Ainsworth NE
KAAQ(FM) Alliance NE
KCOE(FM) Auburn NE
KCNI(AM) Broken Bow NE
KZEN(FM) Central City NE
KCSR(AM) Chadron NE
KQSK(FM) Chadron NE
KAMI-FM Cozad NE
*KINI(FM) Crookston NE
KUTT(FM) Fairbury NE
KFMT(FM) Fremont NE
KSDZ(FM) Gordon NE
KMMJ(AM) Grand Island NE
KRGI-FM Grand Island NE
KEZH(FM) Hastings NE
KRNY(FM) Kearney NE
KIMB(AM) Kimball NE
KRVN(AM) Lexington NE
KYNN(FM) Lincoln NE
KBRL(AM) McCook NE
WJAG(AM) Norfolk NE
KXNP(FM) North Platte NE
KBRX(AM) O'Neill NE
KBRX-FM O'Neill NE
KMCX(FM) Ogallala NE
WOW(AM) Omaha NE
WOW-FM Omaha NE
KNLV(AM) Ord NE
KNLV-FM Ord NE
KNEB(AM) Scottsbluff NE
KNEB-FM Scottsbluff NE
KZKX(FM) Seward NE
KSID(AM) Sidney NE
KRFS(AM) Superior NE
KRFS-FM Superior NE
KTCH(AM) Wayne NE
KTCH-FM Wayne NE
KSUX(FM) Winnebago NE
KAWL(AM) York NE
WOKQ(FM) Dover NH
WYKR-FM Haverhill NH
WYRY(FM) Hinsdale NH
WSCY(FM) Moultonborough NH
WXXK-FM Newport NH
WRNJ-FM Belvidere NJ
WHCY(FM) Blairstown NJ
WBNJ(FM) Cape May Court House NJ
WJIC(AM) Salem NJ
WKMB(AM) Stirling NJ
*WFDU(FM) Teaneck NJ
*KABR(AM) Alamo Community NM
KPSA(AM) Alamogordo NM
KZZX-FM Alamogordo NM
KASY(FM) Albuquerque NM
KKIM(AM) Albuquerque NM
KRST(FM) Albuquerque NM
KRZY(AM) Albuquerque NM
KAFR(FM) Angel Fire NM
KUCU(FM) Armijo NM
KTZA(FM) Artesia NM
KNFT-FM Bayard NM
KARS(AM) Belen NM
KARS-FM Belen NM
KKFG(FM) Bloomfield NM
KATK-FM Carlsbad NM
KCCC(AM) Carlsbad NM
KLMX(AM) Clayton NM
KCLV(AM) Clovis NM
KCLV-FM Clovis NM
KOTS(AM) Deming NM
KTRA(FM) Farmington NM
KGAK(AM) Gallup NM
KGLX(FM) Gallup NM
KMIN(AM) Grants NM
KPER(FM) Hobbs NM
KYKK(AM) Hobbs NM
KGRT(AM) Las Cruces NM
KGRT-FM Las Cruces NM
KFUN(AM) Las Vegas NM
KLEA(AM) Lovington NM
KLEA-FM Lovington NM
KWMW(FM) Maljamar NM
*KTDB(FM) Pine Hill NM
KSEL(AM) Portales NM
KCKN(AM) Roswell NM
KEND(FM) Roswell NM
KMOU(FM) Roswell NM
KRSY(AM) Roswell NM
KBUY(AM) Ruidoso NM
KWES(FM) Ruidoso NM
KRUI(AM) Ruidoso Downs NM
KNYN(FM) Santa Fe NM
KOLT-FM Santa Fe NM
KSSR(AM) Santa Rosa NM
KMXQ(FM) Socorro NM
KXTC(FM) Thoreau NM
KCHS(AM) Truth or Consequences NM
KTNM(AM) Tucumcari NM
KBUL(FM) Carson City NV
KIZS(FM) Carson City NV
KRJC(FM) Elko NV
KELY(AM) Ely NV
KVLV(AM) Fallon NV
KWNR(FM) Henderson NV
KFMS-FM Las Vegas NV
KOWA(AM) Laughlin NV
KFMS(AM) North Las Vegas NV
KHIT-FM Reno NV
KROW(AM) Reno NV
KHIT(AM) Sun Valley NV
KWNA-FM Winnemucca NV
WGNA(AM) Albany NY
WGNA-FM Albany NY
WBUG(AM) Amsterdam NY
WBTF(FM) Attica NY
WPCX(FM) Auburn NY
WHWK(FM) Binghamton NY
WBRV(AM) Boonville NY
WBRV-FM Boonville NY
WPUT(AM) Brewster NY
WYRK(FM) Buffalo NY
WFLR(AM) Dundee NY
WBUG-FM Fort Plain NY
WBBS(FM) Fulton NY
WFLK(FM) Geneva NY
WLKC(FM) Henderson NY
WRWD-FM Highland NY
WCKR(FM) Hornell NY
WIQT(AM) Horseheads NY
WQIX(FM) Horseheads NY
WHVW(AM) Hyde Park NY
WHUG(FM) Jamestown NY
WYNY(FM) Lake Success NY
WXRL(AM) Lancaster NY
WVOS(AM) Liberty NY
WVOS-FM Liberty NY
WLFH(AM) Little Falls NY
WVNV(FM) Malone NY
WPIG(FM) Olean NY
WDOS(AM) Oneonta NY
WEBO(AM) Owego NY
WDLC(AM) Port Jervis NY
WPDM(AM) Potsdam NY
WSCP-FM Pulaski NY
WRHD(AM) Riverhead NY
WBEE-FM Rochester NY
WKDY(FM) Rome NY
WQRT(FM) Salamanca NY
WSCP(AM) Sandy Creek-Pulaski NY
WBGG(AM) Saratoga Springs NY
WSTL(AM) South Glens Falls NY
WOKN(FM) Southport NY
WFWC(AM) Springville NY
WHEN-FM Syracuse NY
WNDR(AM) Syracuse NY
WPIE(AM) Trumansburg NY
WCDA(FM) Vorheesville NY
WDLA(AM) Walton NY
WDLA-FM Walton NY
WCJW(AM) Warsaw NY
WNCQ(AM) Watertown NY
WLSV(AM) Wellsville NY
WNUC(FM) Wethersfield Township NY
WNYV(FM) Whitehall NY
WSLR(AM) Akron OH
WNCO-FM Ashland OH
WBLL(AM) Bellefontaine OH
WNUS(FM) Belpre OH
WAIS(AM) Buchtel OH
WCDK(FM) Cadiz OH
WWKC(FM) Caldwell OH
WTOF-FM Canton OH
WKKJ(FM) Chillicothe OH
WTSJ(AM) Cincinnati OH
WUBE(AM) Cincinnati OH
WUBE-FM Cincinnati OH
WGAR-FM Cleveland OH
WXVK(FM) Coal Grove OH
WMNI(AM) Columbus OH
WWOW(AM) Conneaut OH
WTNS(AM) Coshocton OH
*WGXM(FM) Dayton OH
WHKO(FM) Dayton OH
WONW(AM) Defiance OH
WDOH(FM) Delphos OH
WELA(FM) East Liverpool OH
WWBK(FM) Fredericktown OH
WGLX(AM) Galion OH
WJEH(AM) Gallipolis OH
WKKY(FM) Geneva OH
WAXZ(FM) Georgetown OH
WYHK(FM) Gibsonburg OH
WYGY(FM) Hamilton OH
WHTH(AM) Heath OH
WSRW(AM) Hillsboro OH
WSRW-FM Hillsboro OH
WCJO(FM) Jackson OH
WHOK(FM) Lancaster OH
WIMT(FM) Lima OH
WLGN-FM Logan OH
WRKG(AM) Lorain OH
WMRN-FM Marion OH
WUCO(AM) Marysville OH
WQMX(FM) Medina OH
WMPO(AM) Middleport-Pomeroy OH
WPFB-FM Middletown OH
WLZZ(FM) Montpelier OH
WSEO(FM) Nelsonville OH
WCLT-FM Newark OH
WHMQ(FM) North Baltimore OH
WOBL(AM) Oberlin OH
WNXT(AM) Portsmouth OH
WPAY-FM Portsmouth OH
WQXK(FM) Salem OH
WKKO(FM) Toledo OH
WTOD(AM) Toledo OH
WWWM(AM) Toledo OH
WTUZ(FM) Uhrichsville OH
WRVF(FM) Upper Arlington OH
WYNT(FM) Upper Sandusky OH
WKSW(FM) Urbana OH
WCHO-FM Washington Court House OH
WOFR(AM) Washington Court House OH
WXIZ(FM) Waverly OH
WYPC(AM) Wellston OH
WRAC(FM) West Union OH
WKFI(AM) Wilmington OH
WQKT(FM) Wooster OH
WBZI(AM) Xenia OH
WZLR(FM) Xenia OH
KADA(AM) Ada OK
KEYB(FM) Altus OK
KWHW(AM) Altus OK
KALV(AM) Alva OK
KRPT(AM) Anadarko OK
KRPT-FM Anadarko OK
KKAJ(AM) Ardmore OK
KKAJ-FM Ardmore OK
KHKC-FM Atoka OK
KWON(AM) Bartlesville OK
KREK(FM) Bristow OK
KKBI(FM) Broken Bow OK
KSWR(FM) Clinton OK
KDDQ(FM) Comanche OK
KCDL(FM) Cordell OK
KUSH(AM) Cushing OK
KRHD(AM) Duncan OK
KLBC(FM) Durant OK
KECO(FM) Elk City OK
KNID(FM) Enid OK
KOFM(FM) Enid OK
KCES(FM) Eufaula OK
KTAT(AM) Frederick OK
KGVE(FM) Grove OK
KOKC(AM) Guthrie OK
KGYN(AM) Guymon OK
KKBS(FM) Guymon OK
KICM(FM) Healdton OK
KPRV-FM Heavener OK
KCKI(FM) Henryetta OK
KTJS(AM) Hobart OK
KRAF(AM) Holdenville OK
KXKY(FM) Holdenville OK
KITX(FM) Hugo OK
KBEL-FM Idabel OK
KLAW(FM) Lawton OK
KZCD(FM) Lawton OK
KBLP(FM) Lindsay OK
KMAD(AM) Madill OK
KFXI(FM) Marlow OK
KMCO(FM) McAlester OK
KNED(AM) McAlester OK
KTMC(AM) McAlester OK
KMMY(FM) Muskogee OK
KRIG(FM) Nowata OK
KEBC(FM) Oklahoma City OK
KXXY(AM) Oklahoma City OK
KXXY-FM Oklahoma City OK
KOKL(AM) Okmulgee OK
KTHK(FM) Okmulgee OK
KVLH(AM) Pauls Valley OK
KXVQ(AM) Pawhuska OK
KPNC-FM Ponca City OK
KPRV(AM) Poteau OK
KKID(AM) Sallisaw OK
KKUZ-FM Sallisaw OK
KIRC(FM) Seminole OK
KGFY(FM) Stillwater OK
KFXT(FM) Sulphur OK
KHJM(FM) Taft OK
KEOK(FM) Tahlequah OK
KTLQ(AM) Tahlequah OK
KTFX(FM) Tulsa OK
KVOO(AM) Tulsa OK
KVOO-FM Tulsa OK
KWEN(FM) Tulsa OK
KITO(AM) Vinita OK
KITO-FM Vinita OK
KIMY(FM) Watonga OK
KWEY(AM) Weatherford OK
KWEY-FM Weatherford OK
KWSH(AM) Wewoka OK
KSIW(AM) Woodward OK
KWOX(FM) Woodward OK
KRKT(AM) Albany OR
KRKT-FM Albany OR
KVAS(AM) Astoria OR
KCMB(FM) Baker City OR
KKBC-FM Baker City OR
KICE(FM) Bend OR
KZZR(AM) Burns OR
KFAT(FM) Corvallis OR
KKND(AM) Cottage Grove OR
KWVR(AM) Enterprise OR
KWVR-FM Enterprise OR
KUGN-FM Eugene OR
KSHL(FM) Gleneden Beach OR
KGBR(FM) Gold Beach OR
KRWQ(FM) Gold Hill OR
KYJC-FM Grants Pass OR
KOHU(AM) Hermiston OR
KIHR(AM) Hood River OR
KJDY(AM) John Day OR
KLAD(AM) Klamath Falls OR
KLAD-FM Klamath Falls OR
KQIK(AM) Lakeview OR
KQIK-FM Lakeview OR
KXPC(FM) Lebanon OR
KYJC(AM) Medford OR
KBBR(AM) North Bend OR
KOOS(FM) North Bend OR
*KAVE(FM) Oakridge OR
KSRV(AM) Ontario OR
KSRV-FM Ontario OR
KWHT(FM) Pendleton OR
KUPL(AM) Portland OR
KUPL-FM Portland OR
KWJJ(AM) Portland OR
KWJJ-FM Portland OR
KRCO(AM) Prineville OR
KPRB(AM) Redmond OR
KSJJ(FM) Redmond OR
KDUN(AM) Reedsport OR
KRNR(AM) Roseburg OR
KRSB-FM Roseburg OR
KKNU(FM) Springfield-Eugene OR
KOHI(AM) St. Helens OR
KCKX(AM) Stayton OR
KFIR(AM) Sweet Home OR
KODL(AM) The Dalles OR
KMBD(AM) Tillamook OR
KZUS(AM) Toledo OR
KZUS-FM Toledo OR
KWBY(AM) Woodburn OR
WXKW(AM) Allentown PA
WFGY(FM) Altoona PA
WVAM(AM) Altoona PA
WQBR(FM) Avis PA
WBLF(AM) Bellefonte PA
WDLE(FM) Benton PA
WGPA(AM) Bethlehem PA
WCNR(AM) Bloomsburg PA
WJMW(AM) Bloomsburg PA

Broadcasting & Cable Yearbook 1994
B-553

Programming on Radio Stations in the U.S.

WHGL-FM Canton PA
WHYL(AM) Carlisle PA
WHYL-FM Carlisle PA
WCHA(AM) Chambersburg PA
WWCH(AM) Clarion PA
WDLS(FM) Dallas PA
WOWQ(FM) DuBois PA
WXTA(FM) Edinboro PA
WYGL-FM Elizabethville PA
WLEM(AM) Emporium PA
WQKY(FM) Emporium PA
WIOV-FM Ephrata PA
WSKE(AM) Everett PA
WSKE-FM Everett PA
WGTY(FM) Gettysburg PA
WKSL(FM) Greencastle PA
WEEP(AM) Hampton Township PA
WRKZ(FM) Hershey PA
WWCC(AM) Honesdale PA
WHUN(AM) Huntingdon PA
WJAC(AM) Johnstown PA
WMTZ(FM) Johnstown PA
WLMI(FM) Kane PA
WTGC(AM) Lewisburg PA
WKVA(AM) Lewistown PA
WVFC(AM) McConnellsburg PA
WIXZ(AM) McKeesport PA
WZPR(FM) Meadville PA
WWIZ(FM) Mercer PA
WJUN-FM Mexico PA
WWBE(FM) Mifflinburg PA
WQKB(FM) New Kensington PA
WRJS(FM) Oil City PA
WASP-FM Oliver PA
WXTU(FM) Philadelphia PA
WPHB(AM) Philipsburg PA
WPHB-FM Philipsburg PA
WDSY-FM Pittsburgh PA
WXRB(FM) Pittsburgh PA
WZGO(FM) Portage PA
WIOV(AM) Reading PA
WLGL(FM) Riverside PA
WFRY(FM) Salladasburg PA
WYGL(AM) Selinsgrove PA
WHTX(FM) Sharpsville PA
WSHP(AM) Shippensburg PA
WVSC(AM) Somerset PA
WTTC(AM) Towanda PA
WTTC-FM Towanda PA
WHGL(AM) Troy PA
WEMR(AM) Tunkhannock PA
WGMR(FM) Tyrone PA
WMBS(AM) Uniontown PA
WKZV(AM) Washington PA
WAYZ-FM Waynesboro PA
WHGT(AM) Waynesboro PA
WANB(AM) Waynesburg PA
WANB-FM Waynesburg PA
WXPX(AM) West Hazleton PA
WILQ(FM) Williamsport PA
WOYK(AM) York PA
WHIM(AM) East Providence RI
WJJF(AM) Hope Valley RI
WKXC-FM Aiken SC
WDOG(AM) Allendale SC
WDOG-FM Allendale SC
WWBD(FM) Bamberg SC
WBLR(AM) Batesburg SC
WAGS(AM) Bishopville SC
WHKZ(FM) Cayce SC
WEZL(FM) Charleston SC
WCOS(AM) Columbia SC
WCOS-FM Columbia SC
WJXY-FM Conway SC
WFIS(AM) Fountain Inn SC
WAGI-FM Gaffney SC
WSSL-FM Gray Court SC
WESC(AM) Greenville SC
WESC-FM Greenville SC
WSSL(AM) Greenville SC
WSCZ(FM) Greenwood SC
WBHC-FM Hampton SC
WHSC(AM) Hartsville SC
WHSC-FM Hartsville SC
WJBS(AM) Holly Hill SC
WRIX-FM Honea Path SC
WDKD(AM) Kingstree SC
WAGL(AM) Lancaster SC
WRHM(FM) Lancaster SC
WLSC(AM) Loris SC
WHLZ(FM) Manning SC
WKSY(FM) Marion SC
WLXP(FM) Marion SC
WJUK(FM) Mt. Pleasant SC
WJAY(AM) Mullins SC
WGUS(AM) North Augusta SC
WBUB(FM) North Charleston SC
WIGL(FM) Orangeburg SC
WJRQ(FM) Saluda SC
WAZS(AM) Summerville SC
WYAK(AM) Surfside Beach-Garden City SC
WYAK-FM Surfside Beach-Garden City SC
WBCU(AM) Union SC
WONO(FM) Walterboro SC
KGIM(AM) Aberdeen SD
KKAA(AM) Aberdeen SD
KBFS(AM) Belle Fourche SD
KFCR(AM) Custer SD
KOKK(AM) Huron SD
KZNC(FM) Huron SD
KBJM(AM) Lemmon SD
KJAM(AM) Madison SD
KJAM-FM Madison SD

KMIT(FM) Mitchell SD
KOLY-FM Mobridge SD
KGFX(AM) Pierre SD
KIQK(FM) Rapid City SD
KQKD(AM) Redfield SD
KQKD-FM Redfield SD
KPLO-FM Reliance SD
KTWB(FM) Sioux Falls SD
KXRB(AM) Sioux Falls SD
KBWS-FM Sisseton SD
KBHB(AM) Sturgis SD
KRCS(FM) Sturgis SD
KOSZ(AM) Vermillion SD
KJJQ(AM) Volga SD
KDLO-FM Watertown SD
KSDR-FM Watertown SD
KWYR(AM) Winner SD
WNAX(AM) Yankton SD
WQSV(AM) Ashland City TN
WJSQ(FM) Athens TN
WLAR(AM) Athens TN
WGOC(AM) Blountville TN
WMOD(FM) Bolivar TN
WXBQ-FM Bristol TN
WTBG(FM) Brownsville TN
WFWL(AM) Camden TN
WUCZ-FM Carthage TN
WNKX(AM) Centerville TN
WNKX-FM Centerville TN
WDOD(AM) Chattanooga TN
WDOD-FM Chattanooga TN
WCTZ(AM) Clarksville TN
WDXN(AM) Clarksville TN
WCLE(AM) Cleveland TN
WUSY(FM) Cleveland TN
WYSH(AM) Clinton TN
WPLX(AM) Collierville TN
WKRM(AM) Columbia TN
WMCP(AM) Columbia TN
WGSQ(FM) Cookeville TN
WHUB(AM) Cookeville TN
WLSB(AM) Copperhill TN
WKBL-FM Covington TN
WZYX(AM) Cowan TN
WCSV(AM) Crossville TN
WEGE(FM) Crossville TN
WDNT(AM) Dayton TN
WDNT-FM Dayton TN
WDKN(AM) Dickson TN
WYYB(FM) Dickson TN
WSDQ(AM) Dunlap TN
WTRO(AM) Dyersburg TN
WBEJ(AM) Elizabethton TN
WUSJ-FM Elizabethton TN
WENR(AM) Englewood TN
WEMB(AM) Erwin TN
WPFD(AM) Fairview TN
WEKR(AM) Fayetteville TN
WYTM-FM Fayetteville TN
WAKM(AM) Franklin TN
WHIN(AM) Gallatin TN
WDLY(FM) Gatlinburg TN
WGRV(AM) Greeneville TN
WSMG(AM) Greeneville TN
WLIQ(FM) Harriman TN
WXJB-FM Harrogate TN
WJKM(AM) Hartsville TN
WHHM-FM Henderson TN
WMLR(AM) Hohenwald TN
WVHR(FM) Huntingdon TN
WDXI(AM) Jackson TN
WTNV(FM) Jackson TN
WCLC(AM) Jamestown TN
WCLC-FM Jamestown TN
WDEB(AM) Jamestown TN
WDEB-FM Jamestown TN
WJFC(AM) Jefferson City TN
WKTP(AM) Jonesborough TN
WKIN(AM) Kingsport TN
WIVK-FM Knoxville TN
WLAF(AM) La Follette TN
WQLA-FM La Follette TN
WEEN(AM) Lafayette TN
WDXE(AM) Lawrenceburg TN
WLLX(FM) Lawrenceburg TN
WWLX(AM) Lawrenceburg TN
WANT(FM) Lebanon TN
WCOR(AM) Lebanon TN
WLIL(AM) Lenoir City TN
WLIL-FM Lenoir City TN
WAXO(AM) Lewisburg TN
WJJM(AM) Lewisburg TN
WJJM-FM Lewisburg TN
WDXL(AM) Lexington TN
WZLT(FM) Lexington TN
WLIV(AM) Livingston TN
WIST(FM) Lobelville TN
WRKQ(AM) Madisonville TN
WMSR(AM) Manchester TN
WCMT(AM) Martin TN
WGAP(AM) Maryville TN
WGAP-FM Maryville TN
WHDM(AM) McKenzie TN
WWYN(FM) McKenzie TN
WAKI(AM) McMinnville TN
WBMC(AM) McMinnville TN
WGKX(FM) Memphis TN
WMTN(AM) Morristown TN
WMCT(AM) Mountain City TN
WMTS(AM) Murfreesboro TN
WSIX-FM Nashville TN
WSM(AM) Nashville TN
WSM-FM Nashville TN
WLIK(AM) Newport TN
WNPC(AM) Newport TN

WNPC-FM Newport TN
WKNF-FM Oak Ridge TN
WOKI-FM Oak Ridge TN
WXVO(FM) Oliver Springs TN
WMUF(AM) Paris TN
WKJQ-FM Parsons TN
WUAT(AM) Pikeville TN
WKSR(AM) Pulaski TN
WTRB(AM) Ripley TN
WOFE(AM) Rockwood TN
WOFE-FM Rockwood TN
WJDT(FM) Rogersville TN
WRGS(AM) Rogersville TN
WKWX-FM Savannah TN
WORM-FM Savannah TN
WDTM(AM) Selmer TN
WSEV(AM) Sevierville TN
WLIJ(AM) Shelbyville TN
WYCQ(FM) Shelbyville TN
WJLE(AM) Smithville TN
WJLE-FM Smithville TN
WEPG(AM) South Pittsburg TN
WSMT(AM) Sparta TN
WTZX(AM) Sparta TN
WDBL(AM) Springfield TN
WDBL-FM Springfield TN
WSGI(AM) Springfield TN
WJOP-FM St. Joseph TN
WSBI(AM) Static TN
WDEH-FM Sweetwater TN
WCTU(FM) Tazewell TN
WNTT(AM) Tazewell TN
WHVK(FM) Tullahoma TN
WKWT(FM) Union City TN
WECO(AM) Wartburg TN
WPHC(AM) Waverly TN
WTNR(AM) Waynesboro TN
WTNR-FM Waynesboro TN
WCDT(AM) Winchester TN
WBRY(AM) Woodbury TN
KEAN(AM) Abilene TX
KEAN-FM Abilene TX
KQNN(FM) Alice TX
KALP(FM) Alpine TX
KBUY-FM Amarillo TX
KDJW(AM) Amarillo TX
KGNC-FM Amarillo TX
KQAC(FM) Amarillo TX
KACT(AM) Andrews TX
KACT-FM Andrews TX
KSNN(FM) Arlington TX
KALT(AM) Atlanta TX
KPYN(FM) Atlanta TX
KASE(FM) Austin TX
KVET(AM) Austin TX
KVET-FM Austin TX
KRUN(AM) Ballinger TX
KRUN-FM Ballinger TX
KIOX(AM) Bay City TX
KAYC(AM) Beaumont TX
KAYD(FM) Beaumont TX
KYKR(FM) Beaumont TX
KIBL(AM) Beeville TX
KIBL-FM Beeville TX
KOOC(FM) Belton TX
KBYG(AM) Big Spring TX
KFYN(AM) Bonham TX
KQFX(FM) Borger TX
KQTY(AM) Borger TX
KRJT(AM) Bowie TX
KRJT-FM Bowie TX
KNEL(AM) Brady TX
KBIL(AM) Breckenridge TX
KROO(FM) Breckenridge TX
KTTX(FM) Brenham TX
KULF(FM) Brenham TX
KWHI(AM) Brenham TX
KBOC(FM) Bridgeport TX
KLZK(FM) Brownfield TX
KTEX(FM) Brownsville TX
KOXE(FM) Brownwood TX
KXYL-FM Brownwood TX
KORA-FM Bryan TX
KYYI(FM) Burkburnett TX
KHLB-FM Burnet TX
KMIL(AM) Cameron TX
KBEN(AM) Carrizo Springs TX
KGAS(AM) Carthage TX
KGAS-FM Carthage TX
KDET-FM Center TX
KSRW(FM) Childress TX
KCAR(AM) Clarksville TX
KCLE(AM) Cleburne TX
KSTA(AM) Coleman TX
KSTA-FM Coleman TX
KVMC(AM) Colorado City TX
KCOM(AM) Comanche TX
KEMM(FM) Commerce TX
KOOV(FM) Copperas Cove TX
KRYS(AM) Corpus Christi TX
KRYS-FM Corpus Christi TX
KAND(AM) Corsicana TX
KAND-FM Corsicana TX
KIVY-FM Crockett TX
KQRO(AM) Cuero TX
KQRO-FM Cuero TX
KEGG(AM) Daingerfield TX
KXIT(AM) Dalhart TX
KXIT-FM Dalhart TX
KYNG(FM) Dallas TX
KLKE(AM) Del Rio TX
KWMC(AM) Del Rio TX
KDSQ(FM) Denison-Sherman TX
KDSX(AM) Denison-Sherman TX
KTXX(FM) Devine TX

KDHN(AM) Dimmitt TX
KDIU(FM) Dimmitt TX
KDDD(AM) Dumas TX
KMRE(FM) Dumas TX
KINL(FM) Eagle Pass TX
KEAS(AM) Eastland TX
KEAS-FM Eastland TX
KIOX-FM El Campo TX
KHEY(AM) El Paso TX
KHEY-FM El Paso TX
KSET(FM) El Paso TX
KNES(FM) Fairfield TX
KPSO(AM) Falfurrias TX
KPSO-FM Falfurrias TX
KAWA(AM) Floydada TX
KFLL(FM) Floydada TX
KFST(AM) Fort Stockton TX
KFST-FM Fort Stockton TX
KPLX(FM) Fort Worth TX
KSCS(FM) Fort Worth TX
KNAF(AM) Fredricksburg TX
KBRZ(AM) Freeport TX
KJOJ-FM Freeport TX
KGAF(AM) Gainesville TX
KPBC(AM) Garland TX
KRYL(FM) Gatesville TX
KCTI(AM) Gonzales TX
KPJN(FM) Gonzales TX
KSWA(AM) Graham TX
KWKQ(FM) Graham TX
KPAR(AM) Granbury TX
KIKT(FM) Greenville TX
KRJH(AM) Hallettsville TX
KCLW(AM) Hamilton TX
KFRQ(FM) Harlingen TX
KVRP-FM Haskell TX
KAWS(AM) Hemphill TX
KGRI-FM Henderson TX
KWRD(AM) Henderson TX
KPAN(AM) Hereford TX
KPAN-FM Hereford TX
KHBR(AM) Hillsboro TX
KJNE(FM) Hillsboro TX
KRBH(FM) Hondo TX
KRME(AM) Hondo TX
KLLI(FM) Hooks TX
KIKK-FM Houston TX
KILT(AM) Houston TX
KILT-FM Houston TX
KHYI(FM) Howe TX
KSAM(AM) Huntsville TX
KMIA(FM) Jasper TX
KWYX(FM) Jasper TX
KMBL(AM) Junction TX
KAML(AM) Kenedy-Karnes City TX
KRVL(FM) Kerrville TX
KHHT(FM) Killeen TX
KBUK(FM) La Grange TX
KVLG(AM) La Grange TX
KPET(AM) Lamesa TX
KCYL(AM) Lampasas TX
KOYE(FM) Laredo TX
KLVT(AM) Levelland TX
KLVT-FM Levelland TX
KSHN-FM Liberty TX
KZZN(AM) Littlefield TX
KETX(AM) Livingston TX
KETX-FM Livingston TX
KYKX(FM) Longview TX
KFYO(AM) Lubbock TX
KLLL(AM) Lubbock TX
KONE(FM) Lubbock TX
KXTQ-FM Lubbock TX
KRBA(AM) Lufkin TX
KYKS(FM) Lufkin TX
KAGG(FM) Madisonville TX
KCKL(FM) Malakoff TX
KLSR(AM) Memphis TX
KLSR-FM Memphis TX
KCWS(FM) Merkel TX
KRQX(AM) Mexia TX
KYCX-FM Mexia TX
KCRS(AM) Midland TX
KCRS-FM Midland TX
KJBC(AM) Midland TX
KNFM(FM) Midland TX
KMOO-FM Mineola TX
KJSA(AM) Mineral Wells TX
KYXS-FM Mineral Wells TX
KTJX(FM) Mission TX
KCDQ(FM) Monahans TX
KGEE(FM) Monahans TX
KLBO(AM) Monahans TX
KIMP(AM) Mount Pleasant TX
KPXI(FM) Mount Pleasant TX
KKYC(FM) Muleshoe TX
KMUL(AM) Muleshoe TX
KJCS(FM) Nacogdoches TX
KNBT(FM) New Braunfels TX
KOGT(AM) Orange TX
KYXX(FM) Ozona TX
KYYK(FM) Palestine TX
KOMX(FM) Pampa TX
KOYN(FM) Paris TX
KPLT(AM) Paris TX
KPLT-FM Paris TX
KIKK(AM) Pasadena TX
KKBQ-FM Pasadena TX
KVWG(AM) Pearsall TX
KVWG-FM Pearsall TX
KIUN(AM) Pecos TX
KPTX(FM) Pecos TX
KEYE(AM) Perryton TX
KEYE-FM Perryton TX
KXAL-FM Pittsburg TX

KKYN(AM) Plainview TX
KKYN-FM Plainview TX
KVOP(AM) Plainview TX
KBOP(AM) Pleasanton TX
KBUC(FM) Pleasanton TX
KPLV(FM) Port Lavaca TX
KPOS(AM) Post TX
KPOS-FM Post TX
KIXC-FM Quanah TX
KVDL(AM) Quanah TX
KSOX-FM Raymondville TX
KGLF(AM) Robstown TX
KRXT(FM) Rockdale TX
KGKL-FM San Angelo TX
KAJA(FM) San Antonio TX
KCYY(FM) San Antonio TX
KKYX(AM) San Antonio TX
KBAL(AM) San Saba TX
KWED(AM) Seguin TX
KIKZ(AM) Seminole TX
KSEM-FM Seminole TX
KSEY(AM) Seymour TX
KSEY-FM Seymour TX
KIKM-FM Sherman TX
KKAS(AM) Silsbee TX
KWDX(FM) Silsbee TX
KOUL(FM) Sinton TX
KSNY(AM) Snyder TX
KHOS(AM) Sonora TX
KHOS-FM Sonora TX
KRDF-FM Spearman TX
KVRP(AM) Stamford TX
KSTV(AM) Stephenville TX
KSTV-FM Stephenville TX
KSST(AM) Sulphur Springs TX
KXOX(AM) Sweetwater TX
KTAE(AM) Taylor TX
KPLE(FM) Temple TX
KPYK(AM) Terrell TX
KTLR-FM Terrell TX
KDIL(FM) Terrell Hills TX
KCMC(AM) Texarkana TX
KKYR-FM Texarkana TX
KTUE(AM) Tulia TX
KBCY(FM) Tye TX
KNUE(FM) Tyler TX
KVOU(AM) Uvalde TX
KYUF(FM) Uvalde TX
KVWC(AM) Vernon TX
KAMG(AM) Victoria TX
KEPG(FM) Victoria TX
KIXS(FM) Victoria TX
KVIC(FM) Victoria TX
KCKR(FM) Waco TX
WACO(AM) Waco TX
WACO-FM Waco TX
KBEC(AM) Waxahachie TX
KZEE(AM) Weatherford TX
KLUR(FM) Wichita Falls TX
KNIN(AM) Wichita Falls TX
KWFS(FM) Wichita Falls TX
KWNS(FM) Winnsboro TX
KVLL(AM) Woodville TX
KYOC(FM) Yoakum TX
KSOS(AM) Brigham City UT
KSSD(FM) Cedar City UT
KSUB(AM) Cedar City UT
KUMT(FM) Centerville UT
KNAK(AM) Delta UT
KTMP(AM) Heber City UT
KONY-FM Kanab UT
KLGN(AM) Logan UT
KMTI(AM) Manti UT
KYKN-FM Nephi UT
KKAT(FM) Ogden UT
KARB(FM) Price UT
KOAL(AM) Price UT
KSVC(AM) Richfield UT
KNEU(AM) Roosevelt UT
KRGQ-FM Roy UT
KSOP-FM Salt Lake City UT
KSOP(AM) South Salt Lake UT
KTLE-FM Tooele UT
KNFL-FM Tremonton UT
KLCY-FM Vernal UT
KONY(AM) Washington UT
WVES(FM) Accomac VA
WKDE-FM Altavista VA
WYYD(FM) Amherst VA
WMZQ(AM) Arlington VA
WYMY(FM) Bedford VA
WAXM(FM) Big Stone Gap VA
WBDY-FM Bluefield VA
WHYS(AM) Bluefield VA
WAMM-FM Bridgewater VA
WOPI(AM) Bristol VA
WBBY(FM) Cedar Bluff VA
WFXQ(FM) Chase City VA
WMEK(AM) Chase City VA
WBNK(FM) Christiansburg VA
WXCF(AM) Clifton Forge VA
WXCF-FM Clifton Forge VA
WDIC(AM) Clinchco VA
WKHK(FM) Colonial Heights VA
WKEY(AM) Covington VA
WKIK(FM) Crewe VA
WSVS(AM) Crewe VA
WCYK(AM) Crozet VA
WCYK-FM Crozet VA
WCUL(FM) Culpeper VA
WAKG(FM) Danville VA
WPWC(AM) Dumfries-Triangle VA
WPKZ(FM) Elkton VA
WFLO(AM) Farmville VA
WGFC(AM) Floyd VA

WLQM(AM) Franklin VA
WLQM-FM Franklin VA
WFLS(AM) Fredericksburg VA
WFLS-FM Fredericksburg VA
WBRF(FM) Galax VA
WMNA(AM) Gretna VA
WMNA-FM Gretna VA
WNRG(AM) Grundy VA
WHBG(AM) Harrisonburg VA
WKCY(AM) Harrisonburg VA
WKCY-FM Harrisonburg VA
WHHV(AM) Hillsville VA
WHAP(AM) Hopewell VA
WHFD(FM) Lawrenceville VA
WLES(AM) Lawrenceville VA
WLRV(AM) Lebanon VA
WXLZ-FM Lebanon VA
WREL(AM) Lexington VA
WLSA(FM) Louisa VA
WRAA(AM) Luray VA
WJJS(FM) Lynchburg VA
WKDV(AM) Manassas VA
WMEV(AM) Marion VA
WMEV-FM Marion VA
WOLD(AM) Marion VA
WHEE(AM) Martinsville VA
WSIG(FM) Mount Jackson VA
WGH-FM Newport News VA
WCMS(AM) Norfolk VA
WCMS-FM Norfolk VA
WNVA(AM) Norton VA
WNVA-FM Norton VA
WDXC(FM) Pound VA
WPSK-FM Pulaski VA
WPUV(AM) Pulaski VA
WLPY(AM) Purcellville VA
WRAD(AM) Radford VA
WRIQ(FM) Radford VA
WXGI(AM) Richmond VA
WSLC(AM) Roanoke VA
WNLB(AM) Rocky Mount VA
WYTI(AM) Rocky Mount VA
WCRR(AM) Rural Retreat VA
WJLM(FM) Salem VA
WXMY(AM) Saltville VA
WSHV(FM) South Hill VA
WXLZ(AM) St. Paul VA
WKDW(AM) Staunton VA
WHEO(AM) Stuart VA
WTZE(AM) Tazewell VA
WTZE-FM Tazewell VA
WKCW(AM) Warrenton VA
WRCY(FM) Warrenton VA
WNNT(AM) Warsaw VA
WNNT-FM Warsaw VA
WANV(AM) Waynesboro VA
WPTG(FM) West Point VA
WUSQ-FM Winchester VA
WAMM(AM) Woodstock VA
WYVE(AM) Wytheville VA
WSNO(AM) Barre VT
WTSA(AM) Brattleboro VT
WOKO(FM) Burlington VT
WFAD(AM) Middlebury VT
WLVB(FM) Morrisville VT
WIKE(AM) Newport VT
WVNR(AM) Poultney VT
WCVR-FM Randolph VT
WWWT(AM) Randolph VT
*WVTC(FM) Randolph Center VT
WHWB(AM) Rutland VT
WLFE(FM) St. Albans VT
WNKV(FM) St. Johnsbury VT
WJAN(FM) Sunderland VT
WYKR(AM) Wells River VT
KAYO(AM) Aberdeen WA
KAYO-FM Aberdeen WA
KCLK(AM) Asotin WA
KBLV(AM) Bellevue WA
KBFW(AM) Bellingham-Ferndale WA
KMNT(FM) Centralia WA
KCLK-FM Clarkston WA
KCLX(AM) Colfax WA
KCVL(AM) Colville WA
KAZZ(FM) Deer Park WA
KYSN(FM) East Wenatchee WA
KXLE-FM Ellensburg WA
KENU(AM) Enumclaw WA
KULE(AM) Ephrata WA
KWYZ(AM) Everett WA
KLLM(FM) Forks WA
KVAC(AM) Forks WA
KLCK(AM) Goldendale WA
KYYT(FM) Goldendale WA
KEYG(AM) Grand Coulee WA
KARY-FM Grandview WA
KUKN(FM) Kelso WA
KTOL(AM) Lacey WA
KBAM(AM) Longview WA
KWIQ-FM Moses Lake WA
KWIQ(AM) Moses Lake North WA
KAPS(AM) Mount Vernon WA
KMJY(AM) Newport WA
KMJY-FM Newport WA
KOMW-FM Omak WA
KORD(AM) Pasco WA
KARY(AM) Prosser WA
KZZL-FM Pullman WA
KJUN(AM) Puyallup WA
KORD-FM Richland WA
KMPS(AM) Seattle WA
KMPS-FM Seattle WA
KUTI(AM) Selah WA
KDRK-FM Spokane WA
KGA(AM) Spokane WA
KREW-FM Sunnyside WA
KRPM-FM Tacoma WA
KENE(AM) Toppenish WA
KXXS(FM) Toppenish WA
KNSN(FM) Walla Walla WA
KTEL(AM) Walla Walla WA
KXDD(FM) Yakima WA
WDKM(FM) Adams WI
WBDK(FM) Algoma WI
WXCE(AM) Amery WI
WATK(AM) Antigo WI
WATW(AM) Ashland WI
WXRO(FM) Beaver Dam WI
WISS(AM) Berlin WI
WISS-FM Berlin WI
WWIS(AM) Black River Falls WI
WQRB(FM) Bloomer WI
WKTT(FM) Cleveland WI
WJMQ(FM) Clintonville WI
WJLW(FM) De Pere WI
WDMP(AM) Dodgeville WI
WDMP-FM Dodgeville WI
WRDN(AM) Durand WI
WRDN-FM Durand WI
WRJO(FM) Eagle River WI
WAXX(FM) Eau Claire WI
WGEE(AM) Green Bay WI
WTKM(AM) Hartford WI
WTKM-FM Hartford WI
WKBH(AM) Holmen WI
WJVL(FM) Janesville WI
WSGC(AM) Kaukauna WI
WKTY(AM) La Crosse WI
WLDY(AM) Ladysmith WI
WGLR(AM) Lancaster WI
*WJTY(FM) Lancaster WI
WHIT(AM) Madison WI
WMAM(AM) Marinette WI
WWQM-FM Middleton WI
WEKZ(AM) Monroe WI
WIXK(AM) New Richmond WI
WIXK-FM New Richmond WI
WOCO(AM) Oconto WI
WPKR(FM) Omro WI
WUSW(FM) Oshkosh WI
WKPL(FM) Platteville WI
WDDC(FM) Portage WI
WPDR(AM) Portage WI
WNFM(FM) Reedsburg WI
WAQE(AM) Rice Lake WI
WJMC-FM Rice Lake WI
WRCO(AM) Richland Center WI
WRCO-FM Richland Center WI
WTCH(AM) Shawano WI
WCSW(AM) Shell Lake WI
WCOW-FM Sparta WI
WKLJ(AM) Sparta WI
WDSM(AM) Superior WI
WJJQ(AM) Tomahawk WI
WJJQ-FM Tomahawk WI
WCUB(AM) Two Rivers WI
WVRQ-FM Viroqua WI
WEGZ(FM) Washburn WI
WTTN(AM) Watertown WI
WAUK(AM) Waukesha WI
WMIL(FM) Waukesha WI
WYZM(FM) Waunakee WI
WDUX(AM) Waupaca WI
WDEZ(FM) Wausau WI
WXCO(AM) Wausau WI
WBWI-FM West Bend WI
WHTL-FM Whitehall WI
WSLD(FM) Whitewater WI
WYTE(FM) Whiting WI
WJLS-FM Beckley WV
WCST(AM) Berkeley Springs WV
WCST-FM Berkeley Springs WV
WBUC(AM) Buckhannon WV
WBUC-FM Buckhannon WV
WCAW(AM) Charleston WV
WKWS(FM) Charleston WV
WQBE(AM) Charleston WV
WQBE-FM Charleston WV
WKKW-FM Clarksburg WV
WPDX(AM) Clarksburg WV
WPDX-FM Clarksburg WV
WZAC-FM Danville WV
WDNE(AM) Elkins WV
WDNE-FM Elkins WV
WELD(AM) Fisher WV
*WFGH(FM) Fort Gay WV
*WVMR(AM) Frost WV
WTBZ(AM) Grafton WV
WTBZ-FM Grafton WV
WMTD(AM) Hinton WV
WMTD-FM Hinton WV
WTCR-FM Huntington WV
WTCR(AM) Kenova WV
WKMM(FM) Kingwood WV
WKCJ(FM) Lewisburg WV
WZAC(AM) Madison WV
WTUS(FM) Mannington WV
WEPM(AM) Martinsburg WV
WHJC(AM) Matewan WV
WMON(AM) Montgomery WV
WAJR(AM) Morgantown WV
WTNJ(FM) Mount Hope WV
WPMW(FM) Mullens WV
WHCM(FM) Parkersburg WV
WKYG(AM) Parkersburg WV
WLTP(AM) Parkersburg WV
WXKX(FM) Parkersburg WV
WELD-FM Petersburg WV
WAEY(AM) Princeton WV
WAEY-FM Princeton WV
WRRL-FM Rainelle WV
WMOV(AM) Ravenswood WV
WVAR(AM) Richwood WV
WCEF(FM) Ripley WV
WYKM(AM) Rupert WV
WVRC(AM) Spencer WV
WVRC-FM Spencer WV
WCKA(FM) Sutton WV
WSGB(AM) Sutton WV
WXEE(AM) Welch WV
WHAW(AM) Weston WV
WOVK(FM) Wheeling WV
WWVA(AM) Wheeling WV
WXCC(FM) Williamson WV
KRSV(AM) Afton WY
KBBS(AM) Buffalo WY
KLGT(FM) Buffalo WY
KMUS-FM Burns WY
KQLT(FM) Casper WY
KTWO(AM) Casper WY
KVOC(AM) Casper WY
KKTY(AM) Douglas WY
KKTY-FM Douglas WY
KOTB(FM) Evanston WY
KIML(AM) Gillette WY
KZMQ-FM Greybull WY
KSGT(AM) Jackson WY
KMER(AM) Kemmerer WY
KOVE(AM) Lander WY
KCGY-FM Laramie WY
KLDI(AM) Laramie WY
KRQU(FM) Laramie WY
KASL(AM) Newcastle WY
KPOW(AM) Powell WY
KVOW(AM) Riverton WY
KQSW(FM) Rock Springs WY
KROE(AM) Sheridan WY
KWYO(AM) Sheridan WY
KTHE(AM) Thermopolis WY
KERM(FM) Torrington WY
KGOS(AM) Torrington WY
KYCN(AM) Wheatland WY
KYCN-FM Wheatland WY
KWOR(AM) Worland WY

Disco

WOKC(AM) Okeechobee FL

Drama/Literature

*WHBM-FM Park Falls WI

Educational

*WGIB(FM) Birmingham AL
*WYFD(FM) Decatur AL
*WVOB(FM) Dothan AL
*WEBT(FM) Langdale AL
*WLBF(FM) Montgomery AL
*KZIG(FM) Cave City AR
*KSBC(FM) Hot Springs AR
*KCMH(FM) Mountain Home AR
*KUAP(FM) Pine Bluff AR
KVOI(AM) Oro Valley AZ
*KNAI(FM) Phoenix AZ
*KNNB(FM) Whiteriver AZ
*KZPN(FM) Bayside CA
*KALX(FM) Berkeley CA
*KPFB(FM) Berkeley CA
*KBPK(FM) Buena Park CA
*KIBC(FM) Burney CA
*KVHS(FM) Concord CA
*KEFR(FM) Le Grand CA
*KADV(FM) Modesto CA
*KSMC(FM) Moraga CA
*KRVH(FM) Rio Vista CA
*KSGN(FM) Riverside CA
*KVCR(FM) San Bernardino CA
*KALW(FM) San Francisco CA
*KUSF(FM) San Francisco CA
*KBBF(FM) Santa Rosa CA
*KZSU(FM) Stanford CA
*KSJC-FM Stockton CA
*KCLU(FM) Thousand Oaks CA
*KDNK(FM) Carbondale CO
*KCIC(FM) Grand Junction CO
*KERP(FM) Pueblo CO
*WFAR(FM) Danbury CT
*WJMJ(FM) Hartford CT
*WQTQ(FM) Hartford CT
*WVUD(FM) Newark DE
*WRMB(FM) Boynton Beach FL
*WJED(FM) Dogwood Lakes Estate FL
*WSEB(FM) Englewood FL
*WJIR(FM) Key West FL
*WMCU(FM) Miami FL
*WPCS(FM) Pensacola FL
*WVIJ(FM) Port Charlotte FL
*WKZM(FM) Sarasota FL
*WKES(FM) St. Petersburg FL
WWEV(AM) Decatur GA
*WOAK(FM) La Grange GA
*WHCJ(FM) Savannah GA
*WYFS(FM) Savannah GA
*KDPS(FM) Des Moines IA
*KUCB-FM Des Moines IA
*KRUI-FM Iowa City IA
*KBBG(FM) Waterloo IA
*KWAR(FM) Waverly IA
*KBSU(AM) Boise ID
*KCIR(FM) Twin Falls ID
WFUN-FM Bethalto IL
*WIBI(FM) Carlinville IL
*WBGL(FM) Champaign IL
*WPCD(FM) Champaign IL
*WBHI(FM) Chicago IL
*WHPK-FM Chicago IL
*WMBI(AM) Chicago IL
*WMBI-FM Chicago IL
*WZRD(FM) Chicago IL
*WMWA(FM) Glenview IL
*WTKC(FM) Kankakee IL
*WLRA(FM) Lockport IL
*WVJC(FM) Mt. Carmel IL
*WCIC(FM) Pekin IL
*WPSR(FM) Evansville IN
*WGVE(FM) Gary IN
*WGCS(FM) Goshen IN
*WHWE(FM) Howe IN
*WRFT(FM) Indianapolis IN
*WWHI(FM) Muncie IN
*WNAS(FM) New Albany IN
*WEEM(FM) Pendleton IN
*WETL(FM) South Bend IN
*WMHD-FM Terre Haute IN
*KANZ(FM) Garden City KS
*KZNA(FM) Hill City KS
*KKSU(AM) Manhattan KS
*WVCT(FM) Keavy KY
*WSOF-FM Madisonville KY
*WBFI(FM) McDaniels KY
*WTHL(FM) Somerset KY
*KVDP(FM) Dry Prong LA
*KPAE(FM) Erwinville LA
*WBPV(FM) Charlton MA
*WOZQ(FM) Northampton MA
*WMWM(FM) Salem MA
*WSDH(FM) Sandwich MA
*WYAJ(FM) Sudbury MA
*WSRB(FM) Walpole MA
*WKKL(FM) West Barnstable MA
*WBYQ(FM) Baltimore MD
WKDL(AM) Silver Spring MD
*WERU-FM Blue Hill ME
*WOLW(FM) Cadillac MI
*WDTR(FM) Detroit MI
*WPHN(FM) Gaylord MI
*WKDS(FM) Kalamazoo MI
*WKAL(AM) Kalkaska MI
*WOAS(FM) Ontonagon MI
*WPCJ(FM) Pittsford MI
*WSHJ(FM) Southfield MI
*KMSK(FM) Austin MN
*KDNI(FM) Duluth MN
*WCAL(FM) Northfield MN
*KRPR(FM) Rochester MN
*KCVO-FM Camdenton MO
*KLJC(FM) Kansas City MO
*KRHS(FM) Overland MO
*KGSP(FM) Parkville MO
*KMNR(FM) Rolla MO
*KSMU(FM) Springfield MO
WZFL(AM) Centreville MS
*WUSM-FM Hattiesburg MS
*WJTA(FM) Kosciusko MS
*WCLL-FM Wesson MS
*KGLT(FM) Bozeman MT
*KMSM-FM Butte MT
*KGPR(FM) Great Falls MT
*KNMC(FM) Havre MT
*WRVS-FM Elizabeth City NC
*WUAW(FM) Erwin NC
*WPAR(FM) Hickory NC
*WRSH(FM) Rockingham NC
*WESQ(FM) Rocky Mount NC
*WHYC(FM) Swan Quarter NC
WOBR(AM) Wanchese NC
*WSIF(FM) Wilkesboro NC
*WSNC(FM) Winston-Salem NC
*KMNE-FM Bassett NE
*KCNE-FM Chadron NE
*KTLX(FM) Columbus NE
*KCNT(FM) Hastings NE
*KRNE-FM Merriman NE
*KPNE-FM North Platte NE
*KIOS-FM Omaha NE
*WEEE(FM) Cherry Hill NJ
*WGLS-FM Glassboro NJ
*WVPH(FM) Piscataway NJ
*KABR(AM) Alamo Community NM
*KANW(FM) Albuquerque NM
*KSFR(FM) Santa Fe NM
*KSHI(FM) Zuni NM
*KNIS(FM) Carson City NV
*KVCE(FM) Fallon NV
*WXBA(FM) Brentwood NY
*WBSU(FM) Brockport NY
*WCIY(FM) Canandaigua NY
*WGSU(FM) Geneseo NY
*WCOT(FM) Jamestown NY
*WBAI(FM) New York NY
*WNYE(FM) New York NY
*WNYU-FM New York NY
*WONY(FM) Oneonta NY
*WPSA(FM) Paul Smiths NY
*WPOB-FM Plainview NY
*WFRS(FM) Smithtown NY
*WUSB(FM) Stony Brook NY
*WRDL(FM) Ashland OH
*WOHC(FM) Chillicothe OH
*WVXC(FM) Chillicothe OH
*WHVT(FM) Clyde OH
*WDPS(FM) Dayton OH
*WGXM(FM) Dayton OH
*WDEQ-FM De Graff OH
*WHSS(FM) Hamilton OH
*WKET(FM) Kettering OH
*WLMH(FM) Morrow OH
*WMCO(FM) New Concord OH
*WOBC-FM Oberlin OH
*WXUT(FM) Toledo OH
*WLHS(FM) West Chester OH
*KSYE(FM) Frederick OK
*KVAZ(FM) Henryetta OK
*KOSU-FM Stillwater OK
*KBPS(AM) Portland OR
*WLCH(FM) Lancaster PA
*WMSS(FM) Middletown PA
*WRCT(FM) Pittsburgh PA
*WQSU(FM) Selinsgrove PA
*WCLH(FM) Wilkes-Barre PA
*WVYC(FM) York PA
*WCRP(FM) Guayama PR
*WEUC-FM Ponce PR
*WIPR(AM) San Juan PR
*WIPR-FM San Juan PR
*WYFV(FM) Cayce SC
*WTBI-FM Greenville SC
*WHCB(FM) Bristol TN
*WMBW(FM) Chattanooga TN
*WCSK(FM) Kingsport TN
*WEVL(FM) Memphis TN
*WQOX(FM) Memphis TN
*WPLN(FM) Nashville TN
*WDNX(FM) Olive Hill TN
*KACC(FM) Alvin TX
*KLMN(FM) Amarillo TX
*KBNR(FM) Brownsville TX
*KBNJ(FM) Corpus Christi TX
*KRSM(FM) Dallas TX
*KVTT(FM) Dallas TX
*KOIR(FM) Edinburg TX
*KVER(FM) El Paso TX
*KTSU(FM) Houston TX
*KHOY(FM) Laredo TX
KRIO(AM) McAllen TX
*KEOM(FM) Mesquite TX
KCRN(AM) San Angelo TX
*KPDR(FM) Wheeler TX
*KGSU-FM Cedar City UT
*KRCL(FM) Salt Lake City UT
*WVTU(FM) Charlottesville VA
*WJYJ(FM) Fredericksburg VA
*WEMC(FM) Harrisonburg VA
*WRVL(FM) Lynchburg VA
WGOD-FM Charlotte Amalie VI
*WIUJ(FM) St. Thomas VI
*WRUV(FM) Burlington VT
*WVPR(FM) Windsor VT
*KCED(FM) Centralia WA
*KMIH(FM) Mercer Island WA
KKDZ(AM) Seattle WA
*KNHC(FM) Seattle WA
*WLBL(AM) Auburndale WI
*WBCR-FM Beloit WI
*WHHI(FM) Highland WI
*WHLA(FM) La Crosse WI
*WHA(AM) Madison WI
*WHWC(FM) Menomonie WI
*WHRM(FM) Wausau WI
*WVBC(FM) Bethany WV
*KCSP(FM) Casper WY
*KPGM(FM) Casper WY

Filipino

KISA(AM) Honolulu HI

Folk

*WWUH(FM) West Hartford CT
*WNKU(FM) Highland Heights KY
*WUMB-FM Boston MA
WADN(AM) Concord MA
*WOMR(FM) Provincetown MA
*WETH(FM) Hagerstown MD
*WTSR(FM) Trenton NJ
KPSD(FM) Faith SD
*KZSD-FM Martin SD
*WMRL(FM) Lexington VA
*WXPR(FM) Rhinelander WI

Foreign Language/Ethnic

Includes stations with multiple language programing or foreign language programing not covered by a separate heading.

*KYUK(AM) Bethel AK
WVUV(AM) Leone AS
*KUBO(FM) Calexico CA
*KHDC(FM) Chualar CA
*KSJV(FM) Fresno CA
KACE(FM) Inglewood CA
KSQQ(FM) Morgan Hill CA
KAZN(AM) Pasadena CA
KPPC(AM) Pasadena CA
KEST(AM) San Francisco CA
KSJX(AM) San Jose CA
KWIZ-FM Santa Ana CA
*KUVO(FM) Denver CO
WRDM(AM) Bloomfield CT
*WPFW(FM) Washington DC
WUST(AM) Washington DC
WAVS(AM) Davie FL
WLVU(AM) Dunedin FL
WRTO(FM) Goulds FL
*WXYB(AM) Indian Rocks Beach FL
WTIS(AM) Tampa FL
KAHU(AM) Hilo HI

Programming on Radio Stations in the U.S.

KCCN(AM) Honolulu HI
KCCN-FM Honolulu HI
*KIPO-FM Honolulu HI
KNDI(AM) Honolulu HI
KZOO(AM) Honolulu HI
KLHI-FM Lahaina HI
KPOA(FM) Lahaina HI
KMVI(AM) Wailuku HI
WCRW(AM) Chicago IL
WEDC(AM) Chicago IL
WSBC(AM) Chicago IL
WCEV(AM) Cicero IL
WONX(AM) Evanston IL
WPNA(AM) Oak Park IL
*KRVS(FM) Lafayette LA
WUNR(AM) Brookline MA
WLYN(AM) Lynn MA
WJFD-FM New Bedford MA
WNTN(AM) Newton MA
WRCA(AM) Waltham MA
*WBYW(FM) Grand Rapids MI
WCAR(AM) Livonia MI
WPON(AM) Walled Lake MI
WNZK(AM) Westland MI
KSTL(AM) St. Louis MO
KSAI(AM) Saipan MP
KALS(FM) Kalispell MT
WNJR(AM) Newark NJ
WVNJ(AM) Oakland NJ
*WFDU(FM) Teaneck NJ
WHLD(AM) Niagara Falls NY
*WAPS(FM) Akron OH
WWCS(AM) Canonsburg PA
WOQI(FM) Ponce PR
WPRM-FM San Juan PR
KRMY(AM) Killeen TX
KXTN-FM San Antonio TX
WYLO(AM) Jackson WI

French

KEUN(AM) Eunice LA
KCIL(FM) Houma LA

German

WVVX(FM) Highland Park IL

Gospel

Also see Religious.
WGTT(AM) Alabaster AL
WAVU(AM) Albertville AL
WANA(AM) Anniston AL
WGYJ(AM) Atmore AL
WAGG(AM) Birmingham AL
WAYE(AM) Birmingham AL
WDJC(FM) Birmingham AL
WBSA(AM) Boaz AL
WBTS(AM) Bridgeport AL
WYVC(FM) Camden AL
WRAG(AM) Carrollton AL
WEIS(AM) Centre AL
WFMH(AM) Cullman AL
WXAL(AM) Demopolis AL
WIJK(AM) Evergreen AL
WGEA(AM) Geneva AL
WLOR(AM) Huntsville AL
WZZX(AM) Lineville AL
WMGY(AM) Montgomery AL
WURL(AM) Moody AL
WJRA(AM) Priceville AL
WVSM(AM) Rainsville AL
WELR(AM) Roanoke AL
WXWY(AM) Robertsdale AL
WKAX(AM) Russellville AL
WBTG-FM Sheffield AL
WWPG(AM) Tuscaloosa AL
WVSA(AM) Vernon AL
KHSP-FM Ashdown AR
KOLX(FM) Barling AR
KFSA(AM) Fort Smith AR
KWHN(AM) Fort Smith AR
KPBI(AM) Greenwood AR
KNEA(AM) Jonesboro AR
KAAY(AM) Little Rock AR
KZOT(AM) Marianna AR
*KLLN(FM) Newark AR
KLRG(AM) North Little Rock AR
KDAB(FM) Prairie Grove AR
KGHT(AM) Sheridan AR
*KKUP(FM) Cupertino CA
KKLF(FM) Gonzales CA
*KXLU(FM) Los Angeles CA
*KUOR-FM Redlands CA
KZIQ(AM) Ridgecrest CA
*KTUO(FM) Sonora CA
*KCJH(FM) Stockton CA
WYCB(AM) Washington DC
WTLN(AM) Apopka FL
WTWB(AM) Auburndale FL
WBAR(AM) Bartow FL
WYFX(AM) Boynton Beach FL
*WTBH(FM) Chiefland FL
*WJED(FM) Dogwood Lakes Estate FL
*WNLE(FM) Fernandina Beach FL
WLVF(AM) Haines City FL
WLVS(AM) Lake Worth FL
*WYFO(FM) Lakeland FL
WMAF(AM) Madison FL
WRNE(AM) Pensacola FL
WVTJ(AM) Pensacola FL
WPOM(AM) Riviera Beach FL
*WTLG(FM) Starke FL
WBIT(AM) Adel GA
WAOK(AM) Atlanta GA
WYZE(AM) Atlanta GA
WFAM(AM) Augusta GA
WGMI(AM) Bremen GA
WPIQ(AM) Brunswick GA
WGRA(AM) Cairo GA
WCHK(AM) Canton GA
WGHC(AM) Clayton GA
WRWH(AM) Cleveland GA
WSTH(AM) Columbus GA
WCON(AM) Cornelia GA
WDGR(AM) Dahlonega GA
WSEM(AM) Donalsonville GA
WDCY(AM) Douglasville GA
*WJTG(FM) Fort Valley GA
WXKO(AM) Fort Valley GA
WKIG(AM) Glennville GA
WKLY(AM) Hartwell GA
WVOH(AM) Hazlehurst GA
WGML(AM) Hinesville GA
WBKZ(AM) Jefferson GA
WDDO(AM) Macon GA
WDEN(AM) Macon GA
WMNZ(AM) Montezuma GA
WMTM(AM) Moultrie GA
WALH(AM) Mountain City GA
WRBX(FM) Reidsville GA
WTNL(AM) Reidsville GA
WZOT(AM) Rockmart GA
WROM(AM) Rome GA
WBIC(AM) Royston GA
WPTB(AM) Statesboro GA
WJEM(AM) Valdosta GA
WACL(AM) Waycross GA
WIMO(AM) Winder GA
KXOF(FM) Bloomfield IA
KVDB(AM) Sioux Center IA
KTFC(FM) Sioux City IA
KTFG(FM) Sioux Rapids IA
WRAJ(AM) Anna IL
*WKKC(FM) Chicago IL
WEMG-FM Crete IL
WESL(AM) East St. Louis IL
WWHN(AM) Joliet IL
WLYV(AM) Fort Wayne IN
WZCC(AM) New Albany IN
WSLM(AM) Salem IN
WCMI(AM) Ashland KY
*WVHM(FM) Benton KY
WIOK(FM) Falmouth KY
WKZT(AM) Fulton KY
WLGC(AM) Greenup KY
WKVG(AM) Jenkins KY
WMAK(AM) London KY
WLLV(AM) Louisville KY
WWLT(AM) Manchester KY
WWXL-FM Manchester KY
WWAG(FM) McKee KY
*WJCR-FM Millerstown KY
WRVK(AM) Mt. Vernon KY
WNBS(AM) Murray KY
WCGW(AM) Nicholasville KY
WANO(AM) Pineville KY
WRIL(FM) Pineville KY
KWDF(AM) Ball LA
WNDC(AM) Baton Rouge LA
KCTO(AM) Columbia LA
KRRP(AM) Coushatta LA
KPWS(AM) Crowley LA
KKNO(AM) Gretna LA
KWHN-FM Haynesville LA
KTOC-FM Jonesboro LA
WYLD(AM) New Orleans LA
KAGY(AM) Port Sulphur LA
KTJC(FM) Rayville LA
KXLA(AM) Rayville LA
WBGR(AM) Baltimore MD
WCAO(AM) Baltimore MD
WWIN(AM) Baltimore MD
*WLIC(FM) Frostburg MD
WJRO(AM) Glen Burnie MD
*WAIJ(FM) Grantsville MD
WJDY(AM) Salisbury MD
WFLT(AM) Flint MI
WMKM(AM) Inkster MI
*KTGG(AM) Spring Arbor MI
WCHB(AM) Taylor MI
KCRV(AM) Caruthersville MO
KESM(AM) El Dorado Springs MO
KXEN(AM) Festus-St. Louis MO
KPRT(AM) Kansas City MO
KTCB(AM) Malden MO
*KNEO(FM) Neosho MO
KPWB(AM) Piedmont MO
*KOKS(FM) Poplar Bluff MO
KMMC(FM) Salem MO
WELZ(AM) Belzoni MS
WBIP(AM) Booneville MS
WRKN(AM) Brandon MS
WONG(AM) Canton MS
WWUN-FM Clarksdale MS
WVIM-FM Coldwater MS
WQFX(AM) Gulfport MS
WBKH(AM) Hattiesburg MS
WORV(AM) Hattiesburg MS
WKRA-FM Holly Springs MS
WCPC(AM) Houston MS
WNLA(AM) Indianola MS
*WVSD(FM) Itta Bena MS
*WMPR(FM) Jackson MS
WOAD(AM) Jackson MS
WAML(AM) Laurel MS
WESY(AM) Leland MS
WXTN(AM) Lexington MS
WLSM(AM) Louisville MS
WRBE(AM) Lucedale MS
WMGP(AM) Meridian MS
WNBN(AM) Meridian MS
WMLC(AM) Monticello MS
WSAO(AM) Senatobia MS
WAVN(AM) Southaven MS
WJXN-FM Utica MS
WRCS(AM) Ahoskie NC
WZOO(AM) Asheboro NC
WKJV(AM) Asheville NC
WPYB(AM) Benson NC
WVOE(AM) Chadbourn NC
WGIV(AM) Charlotte NC
WGSP(AM) Charlotte NC
WHVN(AM) Charlotte NC
WAAK(AM) Dallas NC
WYZD(AM) Dobson NC
WCKB(AM) Dunn NC
WBXB(FM) Edenton NC
WJOS(AM) Elkin NC
WFMO(AM) Fairmont NC
WGHB(AM) Farmville NC
WIDU(AM) Fayetteville NC
WWOL(AM) Forest City NC
WSSG(AM) Goldsboro NC
*WNAA(FM) Greensboro NC
WQMG(AM) Greensboro NC
*WPAR(FM) Hickory NC
WGOS(AM) High Point NC
WJCV(AM) Jacksonville NC
WRKB(AM) Kannapolis NC
WELS(AM) Kinston NC
WSGH(AM) Lewisville NC
WHBK(AM) Marshall NC
*WGSB(AM) Mebane NC
WIXE(AM) Monroe NC
WCIS(AM) Morganton NC
WCBQ(AM) Oxford NC
WMFA(AM) Raeford NC
WYRU(AM) Red Springs NC
WBSY(FM) Rose Hill NC
WEGG(AM) Rose Hill NC
WBZB(AM) Selma NC
WMPM(AM) Smithfield NC
WGMA(AM) Spindale NC
WKKE(AM) St. Pauls NC
WAME(AM) Statesville NC
WTAB(AM) Tabor City NC
WTNC(AM) Thomasville NC
WETC(AM) Wendell-Zebulon NC
WIAM(AM) Williamston NC
WGTM(AM) Wilson NC
WDRP(FM) Windsor NC
WSMX(AM) Winston-Salem NC
KTFJ(AM) Dakota City NE
WIMG(AM) Ewing NJ
WNGN(FM) Hoosick Falls NY
WTHE(AM) Mineola NY
*WKCR-FM New York NY
WWRL(AM) New York NY
WRDZ(AM) Cleveland OH
WSRW(AM) Hillsboro OH
WLMJ(AM) Jackson OH
WRKG(AM) Lorain OH
WVOI(AM) Toledo OH
WXIC(AM) Waverly OH
WRAC(FM) West Union OH
*KNYD(FM) Broken Arrow OK
*KBVV(FM) Enid OK
KBEL(AM) Idabel OK
KOKL(AM) Okmulgee OK
KHJM(FM) Taft OK
WBFD(AM) Bedford PA
WBYN(FM) Boyertown PA
WPLW(AM) Carnegie PA
WADV(AM) Lebanon PA
*WRIJ(FM) Masontown PA
WGBN(AM) New Kensington PA
WNAP(AM) Norristown PA
WURD(AM) Philadelphia PA
WBSC(AM) Bennettsville SC
WVAA(AM) Burnettown SC
WPAL(AM) Charleston SC
WCTG(AM) Columbia SC
WOIC(AM) Columbia SC
WJXY(AM) Conway SC
WOLS(AM) Florence SC
WYNN(AM) Florence SC
WAGI-FM Gaffney SC
*WTBI-FM Greenville SC
WCKI(AM) Greer SC
WTNI(AM) Hartsville SC
*WLGI(FM) Hemingway SC
WKSC(AM) Kershaw SC
WLGO(AM) Lexington SC
WKZK(AM) North Augusta SC
*WSSB-FM Orangeburg SC
WYYR(AM) Spartanburg SC
WQIZ(AM) St. George SC
WTUA(FM) St. Stephen SC
WQMC(AM) Sumter SC
WGOG(AM) Walhalla SC
WALD(AM) Walterboro SC
KLMP(FM) Rapid City SD
WWGM(FM) Alamo TN
*WYLV(FM) Alcoa TN
WSLV(AM) Ardmore TN
WBIN(AM) Benton TN
WRKM(AM) Carthage TN
WJOC(AM) Chattanooga TN
WMOC(AM) Chattanooga TN
WMCH(AM) Church Hill TN
WLSB(AM) Copperhill TN
WKBL(AM) Covington TN
WGNN(FM) Dresden TN
WSVQ(AM) Harrogate TN
WJPJ(AM) Huntingdon TN
WWAM(AM) Jasper TN
WJJT(AM) Jellico TN
WETB(AM) Johnson City TN
WBBX(AM) Kingston TN
WKXV(AM) Knoxville TN
WQLA(AM) La Follette TN
WIST(FM) Lobelville TN
WRKQ(AM) Madisonville TN
WBMC(AM) McMinnville TN
KWAM(AM) Memphis TN
WBBP(AM) Memphis TN
WXSS(AM) Memphis TN
WMDB(AM) Nashville TN
WNAH(AM) Nashville TN
*WDNX(FM) Olive Hill TN
WJBZ(FM) Seymour TN
WZRS(AM) Smyrna TN
WSDT(AM) Soddy-Daisy TN
WSMT(AM) Sparta TN
WJOR-FM St. Joseph TN
WDEH(AM) Sweetwater TN
KZZB(AM) Beaumont TX
KTON(AM) Belton TX
KDET(AM) Center TX
KSSQ(AM) Conroe TX
KPAS(FM) Fabens TX
KHVN(AM) Fort Worth TX
KOKE(FM) Giddings TX
KAWS(AM) Hemphill TX
KJTX(FM) Jefferson TX
*KYFT(FM) Lubbock TX
KALO(AM) Port Arthur TX
KUHD(AM) Port Neches TX
KCHL(AM) San Antonio TX
KJIM(AM) Sherman TX
KFIT(AM) Sunset Valley TX
KANI(AM) Wharton TX
KNIN(AM) Wichita Falls TX
KWNS(FM) Winnsboro TX
WKDE(AM) Altavista VA
WCBX(AM) Bassett VA
WKLV(AM) Blackstone VA
WBTX(AM) Broadway-Timberville VA
WYRV(AM) Cedar Bluff VA
WDVA(AM) Danville VA
WVOV(AM) Danville VA
WDUF(AM) Duffield VA
WPWC(AM) Dumfries-Triangle VA
WOJY(AM) Hampton VA
WHFD(FM) Lawrenceville VA
WTJZ(AM) Newport News VA
WGCV(AM) Petersburg VA
WBLB(AM) Pulaski VA
WFTH(AM) Richmond VA
WYTI(AM) Rocky Mount VA
WSBV(AM) South Boston VA
WLPM(AM) Suffolk VA
*WTRM(FM) Winchester VA
WGOD(AM) Charlotte Amalie VI
WOGO(AM) Hallie WI
WVKV(AM) Hurricane WV
WHJC(AM) Matewan WV
WETZ(AM) New Martinsville WV

Greek

WTAN(AM) Clearwater FL
*WXYB(AM) Indian Rocks Beach FL
WPSO(AM) New Port Richey FL
WEEF(AM) Highland Park IL
WKTX(AM) Cortland OH

Italian

WEEF(AM) Highland Park IL

Japanese

KOHO(AM) Honolulu HI
KZOO(AM) Honolulu HI

Jazz

KNIK-FM Anchorage AK
*KSKA(FM) Anchorage AK
WAUD(AM) Auburn AL
WFMI(FM) Bay Minette AL
*WVSU-FM Birmingham AL
*WJAB(FM) Huntsville AL
*WLRH(FM) Huntsville AL
*WVAS(FM) Montgomery AL
*WQPR(FM) Muscle Shoals AL
*WUAL-FM Tuscaloosa AL
*KHDX(FM) Conway AR
*KBSA(FM) El Dorado AR
*KUAF(FM) Fayetteville AR
*KABF(FM) Little Rock AR
*KJZZ(FM) Phoenix AZ
*KUAT(AM) Tucson AZ
*KUAZ(FM) Tucson AZ
*KXCI(FM) Tucson AZ
*KAWC-FM Yuma AZ
KJAZ(FM) Alameda CA
*KNCA(FM) Burney CA
KRML(AM) Carmel CA
*KCHO(FM) Chico CA
*KDVS(FM) Davis CA
KEZL(FM) Fowler CA
*KFSR(FM) Fresno CA
*KVPR(FM) Fresno CA
*KXKB(FM) Kings Beach CA
*KLON(FM) Long Beach CA
*KSBR(FM) Mission Viejo CA
KBJZ(FM) Newport Beach CA
KEWE(FM) Oroville CA
*KUOR-FM Redlands CA
*KXJZ(FM) Sacramento CA
KIFM(FM) San Diego CA
*KSDS(FM) San Diego CA
KKSF(FM) San Francisco CA
*KSJS(FM) San Jose CA
*KCBX(FM) San Luis Obispo CA
*KCSM(FM) San Mateo CA
*KUSP(FM) Santa Cruz CA
KSSJ(FM) Shingle Springs CA
*KZSU(FM) Stanford CA
*KUOP(FM) Stockton CA
*KCSS(FM) Turlock CA
*KRZA(FM) Alamosa CO
*KAJX(FM) Aspen CO
*KRCC(FM) Colorado Springs CO
*KUVO(FM) Denver CO
*KTSC-FM Pueblo CO
*WJMJ(FM) Hartford CT
*WESU(FM) Middletown CT
WREF(AM) Ridgefield CT
*WWUH(FM) West Hartford CT
*WDCU(FM) Washington DC
WOL(AM) Washington DC
*WPFW(FM) Washington DC
*WRTX(FM) Dover DE
*WSFP-FM Fort Myers FL
*WUFT-FM Gainesville FL
*WJCT-FM Jacksonville FL
WKRY(FM) Key West FL
*WFIT(FM) Melbourne FL
*WDNA(FM) Miami FL
*WLRN-FM Miami FL
WTMI(FM) Miami FL
WLVE(FM) Miami Beach FL
*WUCF-FM Orlando FL
*WKGC-FM Panama City FL
*WUWF(FM) Pensacola FL
WPUL(AM) South Daytona FL
*WAMF(FM) Tallahassee FL
*WUSF(FM) Tampa FL
WLOQ(FM) Winter Park FL
*WUNV(FM) Albany GA
*WUGA(FM) Athens GA
*WCLK(FM) Atlanta GA
*WDCO-FM Cochran GA
*WTJB(FM) Columbus GA
WNEX-FM Gordon GA
*WHCJ(FM) Savannah GA
*KIPO-FM Honolulu HI
KPOA(FM) Lahaina HI
*WOI(AM) Ames IA
*KHKE(FM) Cedar Falls IA
*KCCK-FM Cedar Rapids IA
*KIWR(FM) Council Bluffs IA
*KALA(FM) Davenport IA
*KTPR(FM) Fort Dodge IA
*KRNI(AM) Mason City IA
*KWIT(FM) Sioux City IA
*KBBG(FM) Waterloo IA
KJHY(FM) Emmett ID
*KBSM(FM) McCall ID
KATZ-FM Alton IL
*WSIU(FM) Carbondale IL
*WEFT(FM) Champaign IL
*WEIU(FM) Charleston IL
*WBEZ(FM) Chicago IL
*WHPK-FM Chicago IL
WNUA(FM) Chicago IL
*WSIE(FM) Edwardsville IL
WKDC(AM) Elmhurst IL
*WDCB(FM) Glen Ellyn IL
WBEE(AM) Harvey IL
*WGLT(FM) Normal IL
*WUSI(FM) Olney IL
*WCBU(FM) Peoria IL
*WIPA(FM) Pittsfield IL
*WNIJ(FM) Rockford IL
*WSSU(FM) Springfield IL
WGTB(FM) Auburn IN
WIFF(AM) Auburn IN
*WFIU(FM) Bloomington IN
WEZV-FM Brookston IN
*WVPE(FM) Elkhart IN
*WBNI-FM Fort Wayne IN
*WBST(FM) Muncie IN
*WVXR(FM) Richmond IN
*WISU(FM) Terre Haute IN
*WBAA(AM) West Lafayette IN
*KANU(FM) Lawrence KS
*KJHK(FM) Lawrence KS
*KMUW(FM) Wichita KS
*WUKY(FM) Lexington KY
*WFPL(FM) Louisville KY
*WKMS-FM Murray KY
*WKWC(FM) Owensboro KY
*KLSA(FM) Alexandria LA
*KLSU(FM) Baton Rouge LA
*WBRH(FM) Baton Rouge LA
*KSLU(FM) Hammond LA
*KRVS(FM) Lafayette LA
*KEDM(FM) Monroe LA
*KNLU(FM) Monroe LA
WTIX(AM) New Orleans LA
*WTUL(FM) New Orleans LA
*WWOZ(FM) New Orleans LA
*KDAQ(FM) Shreveport LA
*WMUA(FM) Amherst MA
WQRC(FM) Barnstable MA
*WBUR(FM) Boston MA

Broadcasting & Cable Yearbook 1994
B-556

Programming on Radio Stations in the U.S.

*WGBH(FM) Boston MA
WHRB(FM) Cambridge MA
*WMLN-FM Milton MA
*WOMR(FM) Provincetown MA
*WBSL-FM Sheffield MA
*WICN(FM) Worcester MA
*WEAA(FM) Baltimore MD
*WJHU-FM Baltimore MD
*WHFC(FM) Bel Air MD
*WFWM(FM) Frostburg MD
*WESM(FM) Princess Anne MD
*WGVU-FM Allendale MI
*WCML-FM Alpena MI
WQKL(FM) Ann Arbor MI
*WUCX-FM Bay City MI
WJZZ(FM) Detroit MI
*WFBE(FM) Flint MI
*WBLU-FM Grand Rapids MI
*WCMW-FM Harbor Springs MI
WMTE-FM Manistee MI
*WNMU-FM Marquette MI
*WCMU-FM Mount Pleasant MI
*WCMZ-FM Sault Ste. Marie MI
*WNMC-FM Traverse City MI
*WBLV(FM) Twin Lake MI
*WEMU(FM) Ypsilanti MI
*KMSU(FM) Mankato MN
*KBEM-FM Minneapolis MN
*KRSW-FM Worthington-Marshall MN
*KRCU(FM) Cape Girardeau MO
*KRNW(FM) Chillicothe MO
*KBIA(FM) Columbia MO
*KJLU(FM) Jefferson City MO
*KCUR-FM Kansas City MO
*KKFI(FM) Kansas City MO
*KXCV(FM) Maryville MO
*KCOZ(FM) Point Lookout MO
*KCLC(FM) St. Charles MO
KIRL(AM) St. Charles MO
*WUSM-FM Hattiesburg MS
*WURC(FM) Holly Springs MS
*WVSD(FM) Itta Bena MS
*WJSU(FM) Jackson MS
*WPRL(FM) Lorman MS
*KBMC(FM) Bozeman MT
*WCQS(FM) Asheville NC
*WGWG(FM) Boiling Springs NC
*WASU-FM Boone NC
*WUNC(FM) Chapel Hill NC
*WFAE(FM) Charlotte NC
*WFSS(FM) Fayetteville NC
WBBO-FM Forest City NC
*WFQS(FM) Franklin NC
*WNAA(FM) Greensboro NC
*WTEB(FM) New Bern NC
*WSHA(FM) Raleigh NC
*WSNC(FM) Winston-Salem NC
*KCND(FM) Bismarck ND
*KDPR(FM) Dickinson ND
*KDSU(FM) Fargo ND
*KFJM(AM) Grand Forks ND
*KMPR(FM) Minot ND
*KPPR(FM) Williston ND
*KSCV(FM) Kearney NE
*KZUM(FM) Lincoln NE
*KIOS-FM Omaha NE
*KVNO(FM) Omaha NE
*WBJB-FM Lincroft NJ
*WBGO(FM) Newark NJ
*WRTQ(FM) Ocean City NJ
*WFDU(FM) Teaneck NJ
*WTSR(FM) Trenton NJ
KKJY-FM Albuquerque NM
*KRWG(FM) Las Cruces NM
*KSFR(FM) Santa Fe NM
*KUNV(FM) Las Vegas NV
*KUNR(FM) Reno NV
*WCDB(FM) Albany NY
WHRL(FM) Albany NY
*WBSU(FM) Brockport NY
*WBFO(FM) Buffalo NY
WNED(AM) Buffalo NY
WEHM(FM) East Hampton NY
WEHH(AM) Elmira Heights-Horseheads NY
*WCVF-FM Fredonia NY
*WEOS(FM) Geneva NY
*WGMC(FM) Greece NY
*WRHU(FM) Hempstead NY
*WNJA(FM) Jamestown NY
*WSHR(FM) Lake Ronkonkoma NY
WRTN(FM) New Rochelle NY
*WHCR-FM New York NY
*WKCR-FM New York NY
WQCD(FM) New York NY
*WOLN(FM) Olean NY
*WCFE-FM Plattsburgh NY
WMNM(FM) Port Henry NY
*WVKR-FM Poughkeepsie NY
WJZR(FM) Rochester NY
*WRUR-FM Rochester NY
*WXXI(AM) Rochester NY
*WSPN(FM) Saratoga Springs NY
*WPBX(FM) Southampton NY
*WSIA(FM) Staten Island NY
*WAER(FM) Syracuse NY
*WANC(FM) Ticonderoga NY
*WONB(FM) Ada OH
*WAPS(FM) Akron OH
*WRMU(FM) Alliance OH
*WOUB-FM Athens OH
*WKHR(FM) Bainbridge OH
*WBGU(FM) Bowling Green OH
*WOUC-FM Cambridge OH
*WOUH(FM) Chillicothe OH
*WVXU(FM) Cincinnati OH
*WCPN(FM) Cleveland OH
*WDPR(FM) Dayton OH
*WDPS(FM) Dayton OH
*WSLN(FM) Delaware OH
WNWV(FM) Elyria OH
*WOUL-FM Ironton OH
*WMRT(FM) Marietta OH
WJZE(FM) Oak Harbor OH
*WMUB(FM) Oxford OH
*WXTS-FM Toledo OH
*WVXM(FM) West Union OH
*WCSU-FM Wilberforce OH
*WYSU(FM) Youngstown OH
KTNT-FM Edmond OK
*KCCU(FM) Lawton OK
*KGOU(FM) Norman OK
*KROU(FM) Spencer OK
*KSMF(FM) Ashland OR
*KMUN(FM) Astoria OR
*KSBA(FM) Coos Bay OR
*KBVR(FM) Corvallis OR
*KLCC(FM) Eugene OR
KAGI(AM) Grants Pass OR
*KMHD(FM) Gresham OR
*KSKF(FM) Klamath Falls OR
*KLCO(FM) Newport OR
*KRBM(FM) Pendleton OR
KINK(AM) Portland OR
KINK-FM Portland OR
*KOPB-FM Portland OR
KLRR(FM) Redmond OR
*WRTL(FM) Ephrata PA
*WQLN-FM Erie PA
*WSAJ(AM) Grove City PA
*WSAJ-FM Grove City PA
*WRTY(FM) Jackson Township PA
WHAT(AM) Philadelphia PA
WJJZ(FM) Philadelphia PA
*WRTI(FM) Philadelphia PA
*WDUQ(FM) Pittsburgh PA
*WVIA-FM Scranton PA
*WPSU(FM) State College PA
*WJAZ(FM) Summerdale PA
*WRKC(FM) Wilkes-Barre PA
*WRTU(FM) San Juan PR
*WRIU(FM) Kingston RI
WOTB(FM) Middletown RI
WBRU(FM) Providence RI
WLOW(FM) Bluffton SC
WYNN(AM) Florence SC
*WLGI(FM) Hemingway SC
KPSD(FM) Faith SD
*KZSD-FM Martin SD
*KAUR(FM) Sioux Falls SD
*KUSD(AM) Vermillion SD
*KUSD-FM Vermillion SD
*WUTC(FM) Chattanooga TN
WTNN(AM) Farragut TN
*WFHC(FM) Henderson TN
WNDD(FM) Jefferson City TN
*WETS(FM) Johnson City TN
*WUOT(FM) Knoxville TN
WNOX(FM) Loudon TN
*WUTM(FM) Martin TN
*WSMS(FM) Memphis TN
*WMOT(FM) Murfreesboro TN
*KAZI(FM) Austin TX
*KVLU(FM) Beaumont TX
*KETR(FM) Commerce TX
*KEDT-FM Corpus Christi TX
KMRT(AM) Dallas TX
KHKS(FM) Denton TX
*KNTU(FM) Denton TX
*KTEP(FM) El Paso TX
*KXCR(FM) El Paso TX
KOAI(FM) Fort Worth TX
*KTCU-FM Fort Worth TX
KCYT(FM) Granbury TX
*KMBH-FM Harlingen TX
*KSHU(FM) Huntsville TX
*KLDN(FM) Lufkin TX
*KXGZ(FM) McAllen TX
*KSAU(FM) Nacogdoches TX
*KPVU(FM) Prairie View TX
*KRTU(FM) San Antonio TX
*KSYM-FM San Antonio TX
*KTXK(FM) Texarkana TX
KBZN(FM) Ogden UT
*KUER(FM) Salt Lake City UT
*WHOV(FM) Hampton VA
WCLM(AM) Highland Springs VA
WJFK-FM Manassas VA
*WHRV(FM) Norfolk VA
*WNSB(FM) Norfolk VA
*WVST(FM) Petersburg VA
*WCVE(FM) Richmond VA
*WVTF(FM) Roanoke VA
WPLC(FM) Spotsylvania VA
WTBN(FM) Charlotte Amalie VI
*WVPS(FM) Burlington VT
*WRVT(FM) Rutland VT
WVAY(FM) Wilmington VT
*WVPR(FM) Windsor VT
*KZAZ(FM) Bellingham WA
*KEWU-FM Cheney WA
KEZX-FM Seattle WA
*KPLU-FM Tacoma WA
KKRV(FM) Wenatchee WA
*KYSC(FM) Yakima WA
*WLSU(FM) La Crosse WI
*WYMS(FM) Milwaukee WI
*WRST-FM Oshkosh WI
*WVPB(FM) Beckley WV
*WVPW(FM) Buckhannon WV
*WVPN(FM) Charleston WV
*WVWV(FM) Huntington WV
*WVEP(FM) Martinsburg WV
*WVPM(FM) Morgantown WV
*WVPG(FM) Parkersburg WV
*WVNP(FM) Wheeling WV
*KCWC-FM Riverton WY

Jewish

WLIR(AM) Spring Valley NY

Korean

KORG(AM) Anaheim CA
KREA(FM) Ontario CA
KBLA(AM) Santa Monica CA
WVVX(FM) Highland Park IL
KKMO(AM) Tacoma WA

Middle-of-the-Road (MOR)

Includes station format Full Service.

KHAR(AM) Anchorage AK
KADX(FM) Houston AK
KTKN(AM) Ketchikan AK
*KFSK(FM) Petersburg AK
KIFW(AM) Sitka AK
WAPI(AM) Birmingham AL
WEBJ(AM) Brewton AL
WOOF(AM) Dothan AL
WABF(AM) Fairhope AL
WBCF(AM) Florence AL
WHEP(AM) Foley AL
*WOCG(FM) Huntsville AL
WLVV(AM) Mobile AL
*WLBF(FM) Montgomery AL
WLWI(AM) Montgomery AL
WQLS-FM Ozark AL
WYLS(AM) York AL
KGKO(AM) Benton AR
KFFB(FM) Fairfield Bay AR
KHOZ(AM) Harrison AR
KARV(AM) Russellville AR
KSUD(AM) West Memphis AR
KGVY(AM) Green Valley AZ
KFWJ(AM) Lake Havasu City AZ
KXAM(AM) Mesa AZ
KOY(AM) Phoenix AZ
KAZM(AM) Sedona AZ
KQAZ(FM) Springerville-Eager AZ
KHIS(AM) Bakersfield CA
KHIS-FM Bakersfield CA
KBOV(AM) Bishop CA
KIEZ(AM) Carmel Valley CA
KSPA(AM) Escondido CA
*KFCF(FM) Fresno CA
KHSJ(AM) Hemet CA
KVVQ(AM) Hesperia CA
KXBX(AM) Lakeport CA
KTME(AM) Lompoc CA
KBEE(AM) Modesto CA
KGMG(AM) Oceanside CA
KLXR(AM) Redding CA
KRSO(AM) San Bernardino CA
KPOP(AM) San Diego CA
*KCJH(FM) Stockton CA
KSUE(AM) Susanville CA
KEZW(AM) Aurora CO
KIUP(AM) Durango CO
*KJOL(FM) Grand Junction CO
*KSUT(FM) Ignacio CO
WDRC(AM) Hartford CT
WMMW(AM) Meriden CT
WNLK(AM) Norwalk CT
WICH(AM) Norwich CT
WREF(AM) Ridgefield CT
WQQQ(FM) Sharon CT
WATR(AM) Waterbury CT
WNRK(AM) Newark DE
WTLN-FM Apopka FL
WWJB(AM) Brooksville FL
WJSB(AM) Crestview FL
WZEP(AM) DeFuniak Springs FL
WLUS(AM) Gainesville FL
WRZN(AM) Hernando FL
WGRO(AM) Lake City FL
WONN(AM) Lakeland FL
*WYFO(FM) Lakeland FL
WLBE(AM) Leesburg FL
WMMB(AM) Melbourne FL
WCMQ(AM) Miami Springs FL
WJPH(FM) Monticello FL
*WSOR(FM) Naples FL
WSBB(AM) New Smyrna Beach FL
WMFQ(FM) Ocala FL
WKII(AM) Port Charlotte FL
WTRR(AM) Sanford FL
WPAS(AM) Zephyrhills FL
WBIT(AM) Adel GA
WMOG(AM) Brunswick GA
WRCG(AM) Columbus GA
WPBS(AM) Conyers GA
WCON(AM) Cornelia GA
WGFS(AM) Covington GA
WDMG-FM Douglas GA
WLJA(AM) Ellijay GA
WLJA-FM Ellijay GA
WQSY(FM) Hawkinsville GA
WBBT(AM) Lyons GA
WKKP(AM) McDonough GA
WMNZ(AM) Montezuma GA
WJEP(AM) Ochlocknee GA
WPAX(AM) Thomasville GA
WNEG(AM) Toccoa GA
*WYFW(FM) Winder GA
KUAM(AM) Agana GU
KIPA(AM) Hilo HI
KPUA(AM) Hilo HI
KJAN(AM) Atlantic IA
KRUU(FM) Boone IA
KWBG(AM) Boone IA
KBUR(AM) Burlington IA
WMT(AM) Cedar Rapids IA
KCOG(AM) Centerville IA
KELR-FM Chariton IA
KCHE(AM) Cherokee IA
KCHE-FM Cherokee IA
KROS(AM) Clinton IA
KDEC(AM) Decorah IA
KRNT(AM) Des Moines IA
KDTH(AM) Dubuque IA
KGRN(AM) Grinnell IA
KMAQ-FM Maquoketa IA
KGLO(AM) Mason City IA
KOEL(AM) Oelwein IA
KOAK(AM) Red Oak IA
KOAK-FM Red Oak IA
KIWA(AM) Sheldon IA
KWSL(AM) Sioux City IA
KICD(AM) Spencer IA
KAYL(AM) Storm Lake IA
KBAR(AM) Burley ID
KSRA(AM) Salmon ID
KTFI(AM) Twin Falls ID
WJBC(AM) Bloomington IL
WCIL(AM) Carbondale IL
WGN(AM) Chicago IL
WJJD(AM) Chicago IL
WAIT(AM) Crystal Lake IL
WDAN(AM) Danville IL
WITY(AM) Danville IL
WLBK(AM) De Kalb IL
WSOY(AM) Decatur IL
WDQN-FM DuQuoin IL
WKDC(AM) Elmhurst IL
WCRI(FM) Eureka IL
WGIL(AM) Galesburg IL
WDUK(FM) Havana IL
WKEI(AM) Kewanee IL
WLPO(AM) La Salle IL
WPRS(AM) Paris IL
WMBD(AM) Peoria IL
WRHL(AM) Rochelle IL
WRHL-FM Rochelle IL
WAUR(AM) Sandwich IL
WPMB(AM) Vandalia IL
WFRX(AM) West Frankfort IL
WFRX-FM West Frankfort IL
WHUT(AM) Anderson IN
WEZV-FM Brookston IN
WWOK(AM) Evansville IN
WJOB(AM) Hammond IN
WIBC(AM) Indianapolis IN
*WRFT(FM) Indianapolis IN
WLOI(AM) La Porte IN
WBTO(AM) Linton IN
WQTY(FM) Linton IN
WKRP(AM) North Vernon IN
WKBV(AM) Richmond IN
WAXI(FM) Rockville IN
WRSW(AM) Warsaw IN
KIUL(AM) Garden City KS
KWBW(AM) Hutchinson KS
KIND(AM) Independence KS
KQNK(AM) Norton KS
KKLE(AM) Winfield KS
*WCVK(FM) Bowling Green KY
WKCT(AM) Bowling Green KY
WKDZ-FM Cadiz KY
WKYZ(AM) Gray KY
WHOP(AM) Hopkinsville KY
WHAS(AM) Louisville KY
WTTL(AM) Madisonville KY
WYMC(AM) Mayfield KY
WPAD(AM) Paducah KY
WCBR(AM) Richmond KY
KLCL(AM) Lake Charles LA
KLLA(AM) Leesville LA
KLIC(AM) Monroe LA
KEEL(AM) Shreveport LA
KTIB(AM) Thibodaux LA
WSRO(AM) Marlboro MA
WHMP(AM) Northampton MA
WJDA(AM) Quincy MA
WMAS(AM) Springfield MA
WCTR(AM) Chestertown MD
WFAU(AM) Augusta ME
WDEA(AM) Ellsworth ME
WRKD(AM) Rockland ME
WAAM(AM) Ann Arbor MI
WBCK(AM) Battle Creek MI
WKYO(AM) Caro MI
WCBY(AM) Cheboygan MI
WJR(AM) Detroit MI
WDOW(AM) Dowagiac MI
WDOW-FM Dowagiac MI
WDBC(AM) Escanaba MI
WPLB(AM) Greenville MI
WCSR(AM) Hillsdale MI
WCSR-FM Hillsdale MI
WHTC(AM) Holland MI
WAGN(AM) Menominee MI
WNBY(AM) Newberry MI
WNIL(AM) Niles MI
WSAM(AM) Saginaw MI
WTGV-FM Sandusky MI
WCCW(AM) Traverse City MI
KATE(AM) Albert Lea MN
*KMSK(FM) Austin MN
KLKS(FM) Breezy Point MN
WELY(AM) Ely MN
KVOX(AM) Moorhead MN
KROC(AM) Rochester MN
WJON(AM) St. Cloud MN
KLBB(AM) St. Paul MN
KTRF(AM) Thief River Falls MN
WHLB(AM) Virginia MN
KWLM(AM) Willmar MN
KZBK-FM Brookfield MO
KREI(AM) Farmington MO
KWAS(AM) Joplin MO
*KNEO(FM) Neosho MO
KMOZ(AM) Rolla MO
KMPL(AM) Sikeston MO
WRTH(AM) St. Louis MO
KPNT(FM) Ste. Genevieve MO
WJBI(AM) Batesville MS
WFOR(AM) Hattiesburg MS
KXTL(AM) Butte MT
KXGN(AM) Glendive MT
KXGF(AM) Great Falls MT
KOFI(AM) Kalispell MT
KTNY(FM) Libby MT
KMMR(FM) Malta MT
KGRZ(AM) Missoula MT
KMXE(FM) Red Lodge MT
WISE(AM) Asheville NC
WFGW(AM) Black Mountain NC
WMIT(FM) Black Mountain NC
WATA(AM) Boone NC
WWOF(AM) Camp Lejeune NC
WDNC(AM) Durham NC
WZBO(AM) Edenton NC
WGLD(AM) Greensboro NC
WHKP(AM) Hendersonville NC
WTZQ(AM) Hendersonville NC
WPAQ(AM) Mount Airy NC
WCVP(AM) Murphy NC
WLOJ(AM) New Bern NC
WYLT(AM) Raleigh NC
WGAS(AM) South Gastonia NC
WSIC(AM) Statesville NC
WCPS(AM) Tarboro NC
WFAZ(FM) Thomasville NC
KNOX(AM) Grand Forks ND
KTYN(AM) Minot ND
KBRB(AM) Ainsworth NE
KTNC(AM) Falls City NE
KHUB(AM) Fremont NE
KRVN-FM Lexington NE
KMEM(AM) Lincoln NE
KNCY(AM) Nebraska City NE
KNCY-FM Nebraska City NE
KOTD(AM) Plattsmouth NE
KOTD-FM Plattsmouth NE
KVSH(AM) Valentine NE
KWPN(AM) West Point NE
KWPN-FM West Point NE
WKNE(AM) Keene NH
WWNH(AM) Madbury NH
WFEA(AM) Manchester NH
WASR(AM) Wolfeboro NH
WHTG(AM) Eatontown NJ
WRNJ(AM) Hackettstown NJ
WBUD(AM) Trenton NJ
WCMC(AM) Wildwood NJ
KKOB(AM) Albuquerque NM
KCBN(AM) Reno NV
WABY(AM) Albany NY
WCSS(AM) Amsterdam NY
WINR(AM) Binghamton NY
WCKL(AM) Catskill NY
WECK(AM) Cheektowaga NY
WCBA(AM) Corning NY
WDOE(AM) Dunkirk NY
WEHH(AM) Elmira Heights-Horseheads NY
WZZZ(AM) Fulton NY
WBZA(AM) Glens Falls NY
WHLI(AM) Hempstead NY
WHHO(AM) Hornell NY
WGHQ(AM) Kingston NY
WLLG(FM) Lowville NY
WVIP(AM) Mount Kisco NY
WRTN(FM) New Rochelle NY
WVOX(AM) New Rochelle NY
WQEW(AM) New York NY
WGNY(AM) Newburgh NY
WDOS(AM) Oneonta NY
*WPSA(FM) Paul Smiths NY
WDLC(AM) Port Jervis NY
WEOK(AM) Poughkeepsie NY
WRIV(AM) Riverhead NY
WUTQ(AM) Utica NY
WATN(AM) Watertown NY
WTNY(AM) Watertown NY
WNCO(AM) Ashland OH
WATH(AM) Athens OH
WILE(AM) Cambridge OH
WCER(AM) Canton OH
WHBC(AM) Canton OH
WINW(AM) Canton OH
WBNS(AM) Columbus OH
WEOL(AM) Elyria OH
WMVO(AM) Mount Vernon OH
WLKR-FM Norwalk OH
WPTW(AM) Piqua OH
WLEC(AM) Sandusky OH
KURY(AM) Brookings OR
KURY-FM Brookings OR
KHSN(AM) Coos Bay OR
KKXO(AM) Eugene OR

Programming on Radio Stations in the U.S.

KCST-FM Florence OR
KAJO(AM) Grants Pass OR
KBCH(AM) Lincoln City OR
KMED(AM) Medford OR
KUMA(AM) Pendleton OR
KEX(AM) Portland OR
KDUN(AM) Reedsport OR
KQEN(AM) Roseburg OR
WKAP(AM) Allentown PA
WCDL(AM) Carbondale PA
WYSN(FM) Central City PA
WCZN(AM) Chester PA
WFRM(AM) Coudersport PA
WEST(AM) Easton PA
WRDD(AM) Ebensburg PA
WFRA(AM) Franklin PA
WHJB(AM) Greensburg PA
WNPV(AM) Lansdale PA
WQTW(AM) Latrobe PA
WLBR(AM) Lebanon PA
WVCC(FM) Linesville PA
WNAK(AM) Nanticoke PA
WKST(AM) New Castle PA
WMXH(AM) Olyphant PA
WJAS(AM) Pittsburgh PA
WYJZ(AM) Pittsburgh PA
WPPA(AM) Pottsville PA
WECZ(AM) Punxsutawney PA
WRAW(AM) Reading PA
WARM(AM) Scranton PA
WBAX(AM) Wilkes-Barre PA
WLYC(AM) Williamsport PA
WBEM(AM) Windber PA
WLUZ(AM) Bayamon PR
WISA(AM) Isabela PR
WCGB(AM) Juana Diaz PR
WPPC(AM) Penuelas PR
WISO(AM) Ponce PR
WIAC(AM) San Juan PR
WIAC-FM San Juan PR
WQII(AM) San Juan PR
WUPR(AM) Utuado PR
WIVV(AM) Vieques PR
WXEW(AM) Yabucoa PR
WERI(AM) Westerly RI
WCAM(AM) Camden SC
WCRS(AM) Greenwood SC
*WKCL(FM) Ladson SC
WDXY(AM) Sumter SC
KBRK(AM) Brookings SD
KZMX-FM Hot Springs SD
KIJV(AM) Huron SD
KCCR(AM) Pierre SD
KTOQ(AM) Rapid City SD
KSOO(AM) Sioux Falls SD
KWSN(AM) Sioux Falls SD
KWAT(AM) Watertown SD
WYXI(AM) Athens TN
WBIN-FM Benton TN
WBAC(AM) Cleveland TN
WAMB(AM) Donelson TN
WAMB-FM Donelson TN
WJCW(AM) Johnson City TN
WQDQ(AM) Lebanon TN
WREC(AM) Memphis TN
WCRK(AM) Morristown TN
WHAL(AM) Shelbyville TN
WBAP(AM) Fort Worth TX
KGBC(AM) Galveston TX
KQUE(FM) Houston TX
KERV(AM) Kerrville TX
KFYO(AM) Lubbock TX
KNBO(AM) New Boston TX
*KENT(AM) Odessa TX
KVJY(AM) Pharr TX
KCAS(AM) Slaton TX
KLUP(AM) Terrell Hills TX
KGLD(AM) Tyler TX
KVWC(AM) Vernon TX
KVWC-FM Vernon TX
KWFT(AM) Wichita Falls TX
KLO(AM) Ogden UT
KDYL(AM) Salt Lake City UT
KSGI(AM) St. George UT
KVEL(AM) Vernal UT
WBLT(AM) Bedford VA
WINA(AM) Charlottesville VA
WFVA(AM) Fredericksburg VA
WMJD(FM) Grundy VA
WNRG(AM) Grundy VA
WPRZ(AM) Warrenton VA
WAZR(FM) Woodstock VA
WVGN(FM) Charlotte Amalie VI
WAVI(FM) Christiansted VI
WSTX-FM Christiansted VI
WVIQ(FM) Christiansted VI
WBTN(AM) Bennington VT
WKVT(AM) Brattleboro VT
WJOY(AM) Burlington VT
WCFR(AM) Springfield VT
KGHO(AM) Hoquiam WA
KIXI(AM) Mercer Island-Seattle WA
KRSC(AM) Othello WA
KAQQ(AM) Spokane WA
KREW(AM) Sunnyside WA
WCFW(FM) Chippewa Falls WI
WERL(AM) Eagle River WI
WEAQ(AM) Eau Claire WI
KFIZ(AM) Fond du Lac WI
WCLO(AM) Janesville WI
WLDY(AM) Ladysmith WI
*WJTY(FM) Lancaster WI
WOMT(AM) Manitowoc WI
WOKY(AM) Milwaukee WI
WCCN(AM) Neillsville WI
WIBU(AM) Poynette WI
WPRE(AM) Prairie du Chien WI
WPRE-FM Prairie du Chien WI
WCWC(AM) Ripon WI
WHBL(AM) Sheboygan WI
WCSW(AM) Shell Lake WI
WMRH(AM) Waupun WI
WFHR(AM) Wisconsin Rapids WI
WKLP(AM) Keyser WV
*WHFI(FM) Lindside WV
WZAO(AM) Moundsville WV

New Age

KNIK-FM Anchorage AK
*KNCA(FM) Burney CA
KXDC-FM Carmel CA
KIFM(FM) San Diego CA
KEST(AM) San Francisco CA
KKSF(FM) San Francisco CA
*KCSS(FM) Turlock CA
KRKS-FM Boulder CO
WVVE(FM) Stonington CT
KWPC(AM) Muscatine IA
*KBSU-FM Boise ID
WGTB(FM) Auburn IN
WIFF(AM) Auburn IN
WIIZ(FM) Battle Ground IN
WEZV-FM Brookston IN
*KHCT(FM) Great Bend KS
*KHCC-FM Hutchinson KS
*KHCD(FM) Salina KS
*WMTB-FM Emmittsburg MD
*WFBE(FM) Flint MI
*WMHW-FM Mount Pleasant MI
*KJLU(FM) Jefferson City MO
WZRH(FM) Picayune MS
WBBO-FM Forest City NC
WKIX-FM Raleigh NC
*KSCV(FM) Kearney NE
KKJY-FM Albuquerque NM
KEYV(FM) Las Vegas NV
WHRL(FM) Albany NY
*WONB(FM) Ada OH
*WVXU(FM) Cincinnati OH
KTNT-FM Edmond OK
*KSMF(FM) Ashland OR
*KSBA(FM) Coos Bay OR
*KOAC(AM) Corvallis OR
KAGI(AM) Grants Pass OR
*KSKF(FM) Klamath Falls OR
*WBUQ(FM) Bloomsburg PA
WXVX(AM) Monroeville PA
*WFHC(FM) Henderson TN
KHKS(FM) Denton TX
KWVS(FM) Kingsville TX
*KSAU(FM) Nacogdoches TX
KBZN(FM) Ogden UT
KHQN(AM) Spanish Fork UT
WPLC(FM) Spotsylvania VA
*KAGU(FM) Spokane WA
*WGTD(FM) Kenosha WI
*KCWC-FM Riverton WY

News

Also see News/Talk.

KKSD(AM) Anchorage AK
*KSKA(FM) Anchorage AK
*KBRW(AM) Barrow AK
KIAK(AM) Fairbanks AK
*KBBI(AM) Homer AK
*KTOO(FM) Juneau AK
KTKN(AM) Ketchikan AK
*KMXT(FM) Kodiak AK
*KFSK(FM) Petersburg AK
*KCAW(FM) Sitka AK
*WBHM(FM) Birmingham AL
*WRWA(FM) Dothan AL
WBBI(AM) Madison AL
*WQPR(FM) Muscle Shoals AL
*WTSU(FM) Troy AL
KEWI(AM) Benton AR
KFCM(FM) Cherokee Village AR
*KGMR(FM) Clarksville AR
*KUCA(FM) Conway AR
*KBSA(FM) El Dorado AR
*KUAF(FM) Fayetteville AR
KBJT(AM) Fordyce AR
KXJK(AM) Forrest City AR
*KASU(FM) Jonesboro AR
*KCAT(AM) Pine Bluff AR
KARV(AM) Russellville AR
KSAR(FM) Salem AR
KWCK(AM) Searcy AR
KWAK(AM) Stuttgart AR
*KNAU(FM) Flagstaff AZ
KRXS-FM Globe AZ
KDJI(AM) Holbrook AZ
*KJZZ(FM) Phoenix AZ
KTKT(AM) Tucson AZ
*KUAT(AM) Tucson AZ
*KAWC-FM Yuma AZ
KEZC(AM) Yuma AZ
*KHSU-FM Arcata CA
KNZR(AM) Bakersfield CA
*KPRX(FM) Bakersfield CA
*KZPN(FM) Bayside CA
*KNCA(FM) Burney CA
*KCHO(FM) Chico CA
*KFCF(FM) Fresno CA
*KVPR(FM) Fresno CA
KMPH-FM Hanford CA
KBNN(FM) Julian CA
*KXKB(FM) Kings Beach CA
*KLON(FM) Long Beach CA
KFWB(AM) Los Angeles CA
KNX(AM) Los Angeles CA
KYOS(AM) Merced CA
KCMJ(AM) Palm Springs CA
KPRL(AM) Paso Robles CA
KMNY(AM) Pomona CA
KQMS(AM) Redding CA
KLKX(FM) Rosamond CA
*KXJZ(FM) Sacramento CA
KSDO(AM) San Diego CA
KCBS(AM) San Francisco CA
KGO(AM) San Francisco CA
*KQED-FM San Francisco CA
KLIV(AM) San Jose CA
KVEC(AM) San Luis Obispo CA
*KCSM(FM) San Mateo CA
*KUSP(FM) Santa Cruz CA
KSMA(AM) Santa Maria CA
KUHL(AM) Santa Maria CA
*KCRW(FM) Santa Monica CA
KSUE(AM) Susanville CA
KKBN(FM) Twain Harte CA
KXBT(AM) Vallejo CA
KOBO(AM) Yuba City CA
KUBA(AM) Yuba City CA
*KRZA(FM) Alamosa CO
*KAJX(FM) Aspen CO
KRLN(AM) Canon City CO
*KDNK(FM) Carbondale CO
*KRCC(FM) Colorado Springs CO
*KCFR(FM) Denver CO
*KCSU-FM Fort Collins CO
*KPRN(FM) Grand Junction CO
KSTR(AM) Grand Junction CO
*KUNC-FM Greeley CO
*KSUT(FM) Ignacio CO
KCBR(AM) Monument CO
*WPKT(FM) Meriden CT
WNEZ(AM) New Britain CT
WNHC(AM) New Haven CT
WNLC(AM) New London CT
*WNPR(FM) Norwich CT
WREF(AM) Ridgefield CT
*WETA-FM Washington DC
WTOP(AM) Washington DC
WILM(AM) Wilmington DE
WLRQ-FM Cocoa FL
WHNR(AM) Cypress Gardens FL
WDCF(AM) Dade City FL
WINK(AM) Fort Myers FL
*WSFP-FM Fort Myers FL
*WJCT-FM Jacksonville FL
WZNZ(AM) Jacksonville FL
WDSR(AM) Lake City FL
WINZ(AM) Miami FL
WOCN(AM) Miami FL
WTMC(AM) Ocala FL
*WMFE-FM Orlando FL
WWNZ(AM) Orlando FL
*WKGC-FM Panama City FL
*WKGC(AM) Panama City Beach FL
WCOA(AM) Pensacola FL
WSOS(FM) St. Augustine FL
WKLN(AM) St. Augustine Beach FL
WANM(AM) Tallahassee FL
*WFSU-FM Tallahassee FL
*WUSF(FM) Tampa FL
*WXEL(FM) West Palm Beach FL
*WUGA(FM) Athens GA
*WABE(FM) Atlanta GA
WBBQ(AM) Augusta GA
WBBQ-FM Augusta GA
WCHM(AM) Clarkesville GA
*WTJB(FM) Columbus GA
WJJC(AM) Commerce GA
WBLJ(AM) Dalton GA
WWEV(AM) Decatur GA
WSEM(AM) Donalsonville GA
*WJWV(FM) Fort Gaines GA
WBNM(AM) Gordon GA
WCEH(AM) Hawkinsville GA
WCNN(AM) North Atlanta GA
WLAQ(AM) Rome GA
WLMX(AM) Rossville GA
*WSVH(FM) Savannah GA
WPAX(AM) Thomasville GA
*WABR-FM Tifton GA
WADX(AM) Trenton GA
*WWET(FM) Valdosta GA
WVOP(AM) Vidalia GA
*WJSP-FM Warm Springs GA
KOKU(FM) Agana GU
KHNR(AM) Honolulu HI
KCFI(AM) Cedar Falls IA
*KCCK-FM Cedar Rapids IA
*KLCD(FM) Decorah IA
*KLNI(FM) Decorah IA
KIOW(FM) Forest City IA
*KTPR(FM) Fort Dodge IA
KNOD(FM) Harlan IA
KXIC(AM) Iowa City IA
*WSUI(AM) Iowa City IA
KWSL(AM) Sioux City IA
KAYL-FM Storm Lake IA
*KNWS(AM) Waterloo IA
KECN(AM) Blackfoot ID
KICN(AM) Idaho Falls ID
*KBSM(FM) McCall ID
*KRFA-FM Moscow ID
KANR(AM) Nampa ID
*KBSW(FM) Twin Falls ID
WKKD(AM) Aurora IL
*WSIU(FM) Carbondale IL
WILY(AM) Centralia IL
WBBM(AM) Chicago IL
*WBHI(FM) Chicago IL
WMAQ(AM) Chicago IL
WIXN(AM) Dixon IL
WMCW(AM) Harvard IL
WINU(AM) Highland IL
WJBM(AM) Jerseyville IL
WSMI(AM) Litchfield IL
WSMI-FM Litchfield IL
*WIUM(FM) Macomb IL
WLBH-FM Mattoon IL
*WUSI(FM) Olney IL
WBBA(AM) Pittsfield IL
WBBA-FM Pittsfield IL
*WIPA(FM) Pittsfield IL
*WQUB(FM) Quincy IL
*WVIK(FM) Rock Island IL
*WNIJ(FM) Rockford IL
WJBD(AM) Salem IL
WJBD-FM Salem IL
WHCO(AM) Sparta IL
WMAY(AM) Springfield IL
*WSSU(FM) Springfield IL
*WILL(AM) Urbana IL
WFRX(AM) West Frankfort IL
WFRX-FM West Frankfort IL
WBIW(AM) Bedford IN
*WFHB(FM) Bloomington IN
*WFIU(FM) Bloomington IN
WSDM(AM) Brazil IN
*WNIN-FM Evansville IN
*WBNI-FM Fort Wayne IN
WJNZ(FM) Greencastle IN
*WFYI-FM Indianapolis IN
WXLW(AM) Indianapolis IN
WLOI(AM) La Porte IN
WORX(AM) Madison IN
WORX-FM Madison IN
WIMS(AM) Michigan City IN
*WBST(FM) Muncie IN
WSLM-FM Salem IN
WZZB(AM) Seymour IN
WBOW(AM) Terre Haute IN
WAOV(AM) Vincennes IN
KVOE(AM) Emporia KS
*KHCT(FM) Great Bend KS
*KHCC-FM Hutchinson KS
KNHN(AM) Kansas City KS
*KANU(FM) Lawrence KS
KKAN(AM) Phillipsburg KS
*KHCD(FM) Salina KS
KMZA(FM) Seneca KS
*KMUW(FM) Wichita KS
WKXO(AM) Berea KY
WKXO-FM Berea KY
*WEKH(FM) Hazard KY
WQXY(AM) Hazard KY
*WNKU(FM) Highland Heights KY
*WUKY(FM) Lexington KY
*WKMS-FM Murray KY
WNOP(AM) Newport KY
WDXR(AM) Paducah KY
*WEKU-FM Richmond KY
*WDCL-FM Somerset KY
WMQQ(FM) Springfield KY
*KLSA(FM) Alexandria LA
WXOK(AM) Baton Rouge LA
KPEL-FM Erath LA
KEUN(AM) Eunice LA
*KEDM(FM) Monroe LA
*WWNO(FM) New Orleans LA
WYLD-FM New Orleans LA
*KDAQ(FM) Shreveport LA
WTTT(AM) Amherst MA
WQRC(FM) Barnstable MA
*WBUR(FM) Boston MA
*WGBH(FM) Boston MA
WESX(AM) Salem MA
WUOK(AM) West Yarmouth MA
*WEAA(FM) Baltimore MD
WMET(AM) Gaithersburg MD
WILC(AM) Laurel MD
WETT(AM) Ocean City MD
*WSCL(FM) Salisbury MD
WCLZ(AM) Brunswick ME
WCXU(FM) Caribou ME
WABK(AM) Gardiner ME
WCXX(FM) Madawaska ME
WSKW(AM) Skowhegan ME
*WGVU-FM Allendale MI
*WCML-FM Alpena MI
*WUOM(FM) Ann Arbor MI
*WUCX-FM Bay City MI
*WAUS(FM) Berrien Springs MI
WKYO(AM) Caro MI
WMKT(AM) Charlevoix MI
*WDET-FM Detroit MI
WWJ(AM) Detroit MI
*WIZY(FM) East Jordan MI
*WBLU-FM Grand Rapids MI
*WVGR(FM) Grand Rapids MI
*WCMW-FM Harbor Springs MI
WHTC(AM) Holland MI
*WGGL-FM Houghton MI
WJCO(AM) Jackson MI
*WNMU-FM Marquette MI
*WCMU-FM Mount Pleasant MI
WSDS(AM) Salem Township MI
*WCMZ-FM Sault Ste. Marie MI
WLKM(AM) Three Rivers MI
*WBLV(FM) Twin Lake MI
*WEMU(FM) Ypsilanti MI
KASM(AM) Albany MN
*KRSU(FM) Appleton MN
*KCRB-FM Bemidji MN
*KNBJ(FM) Bemidji MN
*WSCN(FM) Cloquet MN
*KNSR(FM) Collegeville MN
*KUMD-FM Duluth MN
*KXLC(FM) La Crescent MN
*KMSU(FM) Mankato MN
KMOM(AM) Monticello MN
*KCCD(FM) Moorhead MN
KNUJ(AM) New Ulm MN
WCMP(AM) Pine City MN
WCMP-FM Pine City MN
*KLSE-FM Rochester MN
*KZSE(FM) Rochester MN
*KNGA(FM) St. Peter MN
*KNTN(FM) Thief River Falls MN
KTRF(AM) Thief River Falls MN
*WIRR(FM) Virginia-Hibbing MN
*KRSW-FM Worthington-Marshall MN
KYOO(AM) Bolivar MO
*KRCU(FM) Cape Girardeau MO
*KRNW(FM) Chillicothe MO
*KBIA(FM) Columbia MO
*KCUR-FM Kansas City MO
*KXCV(FM) Maryville MO
KRMO(AM) Monett MO
*KUMR(FM) Rolla MO
*KSMU(FM) Springfield MO
*KWMU(FM) St. Louis MO
KTTN(AM) Trenton MO
KTTN-FM Trenton MO
*WMAH-FM Biloxi MS
*WMAE-FM Booneville MS
*WMAU-FM Bude MS
*WMAO-FM Greenwood MS
*WMPN-FM Jackson MS
WAML(AM) Laurel MS
*WMAW-FM Meridian MS
*WMAB-FM Mississippi State MS
WGUD(AM) Moss Point MS
*WMAV-FM Oxford MS
*WKNA(FM) Senatobia MS
*KEMC(FM) Billings MT
*KGPR(FM) Great Falls MT
KLYQ(AM) Hamilton MT
*WCQS(FM) Asheville NC
WMIT(FM) Black Mountain NC
WGCR(AM) Brevard NC
*WUNC(FM) Chapel Hill NC
WCNV(AM) Charlotte NC
*WFAE(FM) Charlotte NC
*WFQS(FM) Franklin NC
WSML(AM) Graham NC
WNCT(AM) Greenville NC
WCNG(FM) Murphy NC
WCVP(AM) Murphy NC
*WTEB(FM) New Bern NC
WDLF(FM) Old Fort NC
WAYN(AM) Rockingham NC
WCAB(AM) Rutherfordton NC
WSTP(AM) Salisbury NC
*WNCW(FM) Spindale NC
*WFDD-FM Winston-Salem NC
WTOB(AM) Winston-Salem NC
*KCND(FM) Bismarck ND
KDLR(AM) Devils Lake ND
*KDPR(FM) Dickinson ND
*KFJM(AM) Grand Forks ND
*KFJM-FM Grand Forks ND
*KMPR(FM) Minot ND
KDDR(AM) Oakes ND
*KPPR(FM) Williston ND
*KTNE-FM Alliance NE
KCSR(AM) Chadron NE
KMMJ(AM) Grand Island NE
*KHNE-FM Hastings NE
KIMB(AM) Kimball NE
*KLNE-FM Lexington NE
*KUCV(FM) Lincoln NE
*WEVO(FM) Concord NH
WNNW(AM) Salem NH
WASR(AM) Wolfeboro NH
WJLK(AM) Asbury Park NJ
*WNJN(FM) Atlantic City NJ
KARS(AM) Belen NM
KARS-FM Belen NM
*KRWG(FM) Las Cruces NM
*KMTH(FM) Maljamar NM
*KENW-FM Portales NM
KENO(AM) Las Vegas NV
KMTW(AM) Las Vegas NV
*KNPR(FM) Las Vegas NV
*KLNR(FM) Panaca NV
KPLY(AM) Sparks NV
*KTPH(FM) Tonopah NV
*WAMC(FM) Albany NY
WPTR(AM) Albany NY
WBTA(AM) Batavia NY
WKOP(AM) Binghamton NY
*WSKG-FM Binghamton NY
*WBFO(FM) Buffalo NY
WNED(AM) Buffalo NY
*WCAN(FM) Canajoharie NY
*WCIY(FM) Canandaigua NY
WDOE(AM) Dunkirk NY
WCQA(FM) Fredonia NY
WLEA(AM) Hornell NY
*WSQG-FM Ithaca NY
*WCOT(FM) Jamestown NY
*WNJA(FM) Jamestown NY
*WJFF(FM) Jeffersonville NY
*WAMK(FM) Kingston NY
WVIP(AM) Mount Kisco NY
WVIP-FM Mount Kisco NY

Programming on Radio Stations in the U.S.

*WXHD(FM) Mt. Hope NY
WBBR(AM) New York NY
WCBS(AM) New York NY
WINS(AM) New York NY
*WNYC-FM New York NY
WKRL(AM) North Syracuse NY
*WOLN(FM) Olean NY
*WSQC-FM Oneonta NY
*WDFH(FM) Ossining NY
*WRVO(FM) Oswego NY
WNWX(AM) Plattsburgh NY
WNBZ(AM) Saranac Lake NY
WVKZ(AM) Schenectady NY
*WAER(FM) Syracuse NY
*WANC(FM) Ticonderoga NY
WIBX(AM) Utica NY
WFUN(AM) Ashtabula OH
*WCVV(FM) Belpre OH
*WOUC-FM Cambridge OH
*WOHC(FM) Chillicothe OH
*WOUH(FM) Chillicothe OH
WLWA(AM) Cincinnati OH
*WCPN(FM) Cleveland OH
WHK(AM) Cleveland OH
*WOSU(AM) Columbus OH
WING(AM) Dayton OH
WDLR(AM) Delaware OH
WEOL(AM) Elyria OH
WMOH(AM) Hamilton OH
*WOUL-FM Ironton OH
*WKSU-FM Kent OH
WMOA(AM) Marietta OH
*WMUB(FM) Oxford OH
WBLY(AM) Springfield OH
WTRJ(FM) Troy OH
*WVXM(FM) West Union OH
*WYSO(FM) Yellow Springs OH
WKBN(AM) Youngstown OH
*WYSU(FM) Youngstown OH
KITX(FM) Hugo OK
*KCCU(FM) Lawton OK
KKRX(AM) Lawton OK
*KGOU(FM) Norman OK
WBBZ(AM) Ponca City OK
*KROU(FM) Spencer OK
KAKC(AM) Tulsa OK
*KWGS(FM) Tulsa OK
*KSMF(FM) Ashland OR
*KSOR(FM) Ashland OR
KGRL(AM) Bend OR
KZZR(AM) Burns OR
*KSBA(FM) Coos Bay OR
*KLCC(FM) Eugene OR
KAGI(AM) Grants Pass OR
*KSKF(FM) Klamath Falls OR
*KLCO(FM) Newport OR
KUMA(AM) Pendleton OR
KBNP(AM) Portland OR
*KOPB-FM Portland OR
*KSRS(FM) Roseburg OR
*KSJK(AM) Talent OR
WRTA(AM) Altoona PA
WAVL(AM) Apollo PA
WWCS(AM) Canonsburg PA
*WFSE(FM) Edinboro PA
*WQLN-FM Erie PA
WFRA(AM) Franklin PA
WKBO(AM) Harrisburg PA
WLPA(AM) Lancaster PA
WNPV(AM) Lansdale PA
WMXH(AM) Olyphant PA
KYW(AM) Philadelphia PA
*WHYY-FM Philadelphia PA
KQV(AM) Pittsburgh PA
*WDUQ(FM) Pittsburgh PA
*WVIA-FM Scranton PA
WRSC(AM) State College PA
WVPO(AM) Stroudsburg PA
WYCK(AM) Wilkes-Barre PA
WNOZ(AM) Aguadilla PR
WEKO(AM) Cabo Rojo PR
WMDD(AM) Fajardo PR
WAVB(AM) Lajas PR
WORA(AM) Mayaguez PR
WMTI(AM) Morovis PR
WEUC(AM) Ponce PR
WZAR(FM) Ponce PR
WAPA(AM) San Juan PR
WKAQ(AM) San Juan PR
WUNO(AM) San Juan PR
WERR(FM) Utuado PR
WENA(AM) Yauco PR
WBLQ(FM) Block Island RI
WJJF(AM) Hope Valley RI
WICE(AM) Pawtucket RI
WOON(AM) Woonsocket RI
WAIM(AM) Anderson SC
*WJWJ-FM Beaufort SC
WTMA(AM) Charleston SC
WCCP(AM) Clemson SC
WPCC(AM) Clinton SC
WPCI(AM) Greenville SC
WRHM(FM) Lancaster SC
WJZS(AM) Orangeburg SC
WDAB(AM) Travelers Rest SC
KGIM(AM) Aberdeen SD
KBFS(AM) Belle Fourche SD
*KESD(FM) Brookings SD
KMSD(AM) Milbank SD
*KRSD(FM) Sioux Falls SD
*KUSD(AM) Vermillion SD
*KUSD-FM Vermillion SD
KWAT(AM) Watertown SD
WNAX(AM) Yankton SD
WNWS(AM) Brownsville TN
WJZM(AM) Clarksville TN
*WSMC-FM Collegedale TN
*WZMC(AM) Colonial Heights TN
*WKNQ(FM) Dyersburg TN
*WKNP(FM) Jackson TN
WKGN(AM) Knoxville TN
WUTK(AM) Knoxville TN
WHDM(AM) McKenzie TN
*WKNO-FM Memphis TN
WREC(AM) Memphis TN
*WYPL(FM) Memphis TN
WKDA(AM) Nashville TN
WSMT(AM) Sparta TN
WSGI(AM) Springfield TN
WWEZ(FM) Trenton TN
WBRY(AM) Woodbury TN
*KACU(FM) Abilene TX
KNTS(AM) Abilene TX
*KVLU(FM) Beaumont TX
KHLB(AM) Burnet TX
KAKS(AM) Canyon TX
*KAMU-FM College Station TX
*KETR(FM) Commerce TX
*KEDT-FM Corpus Christi TX
KSIX(AM) Corpus Christi TX
KRLD(AM) Dallas TX
*KTEP(FM) El Paso TX
KTSM(AM) El Paso TX
KGVL(AM) Greenville TX
*KMBH-FM Harlingen TX
KRBH(FM) Hondo TX
*KPFT(FM) Houston TX
KTRH(AM) Houston TX
*KUHF(FM) Houston TX
*KLDN(FM) Lufkin TX
KCUL-FM Marshall TX
*KHID(FM) McAllen TX
*KXGZ(FM) McAllen TX
KXGM-FM Muenster TX
KNBO(AM) New Boston TX
KGNB(AM) New Braunfels TX
KRIL(AM) Odessa TX
KNET(AM) Palestine TX
*KSTX(FM) San Antonio TX
KCUB-FM Stephenville TX
KSTV(AM) Stephenville TX
KSTV-FM Stephenville TX
KSST(AM) Sulphur Springs TX
KTBB(AM) Tyler TX
KWFT(AM) Wichita Falls TX
*KPCW(FM) Park City UT
KLZX(AM) Salt Lake City UT
*KUER(FM) Salt Lake City UT
KTLE-FM Tooele UT
KNFL(AM) Tremonton UT
WCPT(AM) Alexandria VA
WBLT(AM) Bedford VA
WDUF(AM) Duffield VA
*WMRA(FM) Harrisonburg VA
WHAP(AM) Hopewell VA
*WMRL(FM) Lexington VA
*WVTR(FM) Marion VA
*WHRV(FM) Norfolk VA
WLPY(AM) Purcellville VA
*WCVE(FM) Richmond VA
WHLF(AM) South Boston VA
WJLC(FM) South Boston VA
WHEO(AM) Stuart VA
WYVE(AM) Wytheville VA
WVWI(AM) Charlotte Amalie VI
WDCM(FM) Cruz Bay VI
WRRA(AM) Frederiksted VI
WJOY(AM) Burlington VT
*WVPS(FM) Burlington VT
*WRVT(FM) Rutland VT
WCFR(AM) Springfield VT
WDEV-FM Warren VT
WDEV(AM) Waterbury VT
*WVPR(FM) Windsor VT
KLKI(AM) Anacortes WA
*KASB(FM) Bellevue WA
KPUG(AM) Bellingham WA
*KZAZ(FM) Bellingham WA
*KCED(FM) Centralia WA
KELA(AM) Centralia-Chehalis WA
KOZI(AM) Chelan WA
KOZI-FM Chelan WA
KONA(AM) Kennewick WA
KLDY(AM) Lacey WA
KEDO(AM) Longview WA
KKPL(AM) Opportunity WA
*KWSU(AM) Pullman WA
KEZX(AM) Seattle WA
*KUOW(FM) Seattle WA
*KPBX-FM Spokane WA
KXLY(AM) Spokane WA
KREW(AM) Sunnyside WA
KREW-FM Sunnyside WA
*KPLU-FM Tacoma WA
KVAN(AM) Vancouver WA
*WHAD(FM) Delafield WI
*WUEC(FM) Eau Claire WI
WDUZ(AM) Green Bay WI
*WGTD(FM) Kenosha WI
WKTY(AM) La Crosse WI
*WLSU(FM) La Crosse WI
*WERN(FM) Madison WI
*WNWC(FM) Madison WI
WOMT(AM) Manitowoc WI
WMEQ(AM) Menomonie WI
*WUWM(FM) Milwaukee WI
WEKZ(AM) Monroe WI
WTOQ(AM) Platteville WI
WRDB(AM) Reedsburg WI
WDOR(AM) Sturgeon Bay WI
WIWS(AM) Beckley WV
*WVPB(FM) Beckley WV
*WVPW(FM) Buckhannon WV
*WVPN(FM) Charleston WV
*WVWV(FM) Huntington WV
*WVEP(FM) Martinsburg WV
*WVPM(FM) Morgantown WV
*WVPG(FM) Parkersburg WV
*WVNP(FM) Wheeling WV
KRSV(AM) Afton WY
KODI(AM) Cody WY
*KUWJ(FM) Jackson WY
*KUWR(FM) Laramie WY
*KUWZ(FM) Rock Springs WY

News/Talk

Also see News; Talk

KBYR(AM) Anchorage AK
KFAR(AM) Fairbanks AK
*KUAC(FM) Fairbanks AK
KABN(AM) Long Island AK
KIFW(AM) Sitka AK
KSRM(AM) Soldotna AK
*KTNA(FM) Talkeetna AK
WKYD(AM) Andalusia AL
WDNG(AM) Anniston AL
WVNN(AM) Athens AL
WERC(AM) Birmingham AL
WEBJ(AM) Brewton AL
WTKN(AM) Daleville AL
WGAD(AM) Gadsden AL
WKRG(AM) Mobile AL
WACV(AM) Montgomery AL
WJHO(AM) Opelika AL
WQLS(AM) Ozark AL
*WUAL-FM Tuscaloosa AL
WVNA(AM) Tuscumbia AL
KGFL(AM) Clinton AR
KELD(AM) El Dorado AR
KFAY(AM) Farmington AR
KAWW(AM) Heber Springs AR
KARN(AM) Little Rock AR
KJBN(AM) Little Rock AR
*KUAR(FM) Little Rock AR
KHBM-FM Monticello AR
KRLW(AM) Walnut Ridge AR
KRLW-FM Walnut Ridge AR
KWYN(AM) Wynne AR
KAAA(AM) Kingman AZ
KFNN(AM) Mesa AZ
KFYI(AM) Phoenix AZ
KTAR(AM) Phoenix AZ
KYCA(AM) Prescott AZ
KAZM(AM) Sedona AZ
KNST(AM) Tucson AZ
KTUC(AM) Tucson AZ
KCNO(AM) Alturas CA
KERN(AM) Bakersfield CA
KIQQ(AM) Barstow CA
KJQI(AM) Beverly Hills CA
KGOE(FM) Eureka CA
KINS(AM) Eureka CA
KIOQ(AM) Folsom CA
KMJ(AM) Fresno CA
KIEV(AM) Glendale CA
KNCO(AM) Grass Valley CA
KHSJ(AM) Hemet CA
KVVQ(AM) Hesperia CA
KAVL(AM) Lancaster CA
KHJJ(AM) Lancaster CA
KPMO(AM) Mendocino CA
KFIV(AM) Modesto CA
KVON(AM) Napa CA
KTOX(AM) Needles CA
KORV(AM) Oroville CA
KPSI(AM) Palm Springs CA
KBLF(AM) Red Bluff CA
KNRO(AM) Redding CA
KLOA(AM) Ridgecrest CA
KCBC(AM) Riverbank CA
KFBK(AM) Sacramento CA
KCKC(AM) San Bernardino CA
*KPBS-FM San Diego CA
*KALW(FM) San Francisco CA
KGLW(AM) San Luis Obispo CA
KTMS(AM) Santa Barbara CA
KSCO(AM) Santa Cruz CA
*KRCB-FM Santa Rosa CA
KSRO(AM) Santa Rosa CA
KTHO(AM) South Lake Tahoe CA
KJAX(AM) Stockton CA
*KUOP(FM) Stockton CA
KNWZ(AM) Thousand Palms CA
KUKI(AM) Ukiah CA
KVEN(AM) Ventura CA
KCEO(AM) Vista CA
KGIW(AM) Alamosa CO
KBOL(AM) Boulder CO
KYBG-FM Castle Rock CO
KVOR(AM) Colorado Springs CO
KNUS(AM) Denver CO
KOA(AM) Denver CO
KIUP(AM) Durango CO
KCOL(AM) Fort Collins CO
KNZZ(AM) Grand Junction CO
KFKA(AM) Greeley CO
KHNC(AM) Johnstown CO
KCSJ(AM) Pueblo CO
KIIX(AM) Wellington CO
WCUM(AM) Bridgeport CT
WPRX(AM) Bristol CT
WINE(AM) Brookfield CT
WSUB(AM) Groton CT
*WQAQ(FM) Hamden CT
WPOP(AM) Hartford CT
WTIC(AM) Hartford CT
WZBG(FM) Litchfield CT
WCNX(AM) Middletown CT
WSTC(AM) Stamford CT
WILI(AM) Willimantic CT
*WAMU(FM) Washington DC
WMAL(AM) Washington DC
*WPFW(FM) Washington DC
WDOV(AM) Dover DE
WGMD(FM) Rehoboth Beach DE
WYHH(FM) Smyrna DE
WDEL(AM) Wilmington DE
WILM(AM) Wilmington DE
*WMPH(FM) Wilmington DE
WSBR(AM) Boca Raton FL
WBDN(AM) Brandon FL
WRFB(AM) Cocoa FL
WRHC(AM) Coral Gables FL
WNDB(AM) Daytona Beach FL
WXVQ(AM) De Land FL
WZEP(AM) DeFuniak Springs FL
WHBS(AM) Eatonville FL
WENG(AM) Englewood FL
*WSEB(FM) Englewood FL
WJNX(AM) Fort Pierce FL
WFTW(AM) Fort Walton Beach FL
WRUF(AM) Gainesville FL
WINV(AM) Inverness FL
WOKV(AM) Jacksonville FL
WVOJ(AM) Jacksonville FL
WWTK(AM) Lake Placid FL
WLKF(AM) Lakeland FL
WTYS(AM) Marianna FL
WTAI(AM) Melbourne FL
WAQI(AM) Miami FL
WIOD(AM) Miami FL
WQBA(AM) Miami FL
WWFE(AM) Miami FL
WEBY(AM) Milton FL
WNOG(AM) Naples FL
WNOG-FM Naples FL
WWBH(AM) New Smyrna Beach FL
WOCA(AM) Ocala FL
WDBO(AM) Orlando FL
WPBR(AM) Palm Beach FL
WLTG(AM) Panama City FL
WHNZ(AM) Pinellas Park FL
WPSL(AM) Port St. Lucie FL
WCCF(AM) Punta Gorda FL
WKXY(AM) Sarasota FL
WYOO(FM) Springfield FL
WFOY(AM) St. Augustine FL
WNLS(AM) Tallahassee FL
WTAL(AM) Tallahassee FL
WFLA(AM) Tampa FL
WAMR(AM) Venice FL
WTTB(AM) Vero Beach FL
WBZT(AM) West Palm Beach FL
WJNO(AM) West Palm Beach FL
WALG(AM) Albany GA
WGAU(AM) Athens GA
WRFC(AM) Athens GA
WGST(AM) Atlanta GA
WGUN(AM) Atlanta GA
WIGO(AM) Atlanta GA
WSB(AM) Atlanta GA
WGAC(AM) Augusta GA
WTHB(AM) Augusta GA
WMGR(AM) Bainbridge GA
WGIG(AM) Brunswick GA
WMOG(AM) Brunswick GA
WJTH(AM) Calhoun GA
WCHK(AM) Canton GA
WCHM(AM) Clarkesville GA
*WDCO-FM Cochran GA
WRCG(AM) Columbus GA
WLSQ(AM) Dalton GA
WDUN(AM) Gainesville GA
WGGA(AM) Gainesville GA
WTRP(AM) La Grange GA
WMAZ(AM) Macon GA
WKGQ(AM) Milledgeville GA
WMVG(AM) Milledgeville GA
WRGA(AM) Rome GA
WBMQ(AM) Savannah GA
WSGA(AM) Savannah GA
WWNS(AM) Statesboro GA
WSTT(AM) Thomasville GA
WWGS(AM) Tifton GA
WLET(AM) Toccoa GA
WVLD(AM) Valdosta GA
WLOV(AM) Washington GA
WCGA(AM) Woodbine GA
KPUA(AM) Hilo HI
KGU(AM) Honolulu HI
KHHH(FM) Honolulu HI
*KHPR(FM) Honolulu HI
KHVH(AM) Honolulu HI
*KIPO-FM Honolulu HI
KWAI(AM) Honolulu HI
*KIFO(AM) Pearl City HI
*KKUA(FM) Wailuku HI
*WOI(AM) Ames IA
KBUR(AM) Burlington IA
KCPS(AM) Burlington IA
KCRG(AM) Cedar Rapids IA
KROS(AM) Clinton IA
*KIWR(FM) Council Bluffs IA
WOC(AM) Davenport IA
WHO(AM) Des Moines IA
KILR(AM) Estherville IA
KLEE(AM) Ottumwa IA
KMA(AM) Shenandoah IA
KSCJ(AM) Sioux City IA
*KWIT(FM) Sioux City IA
KQWC(AM) Webster City IA
KQWC-FM Webster City IA
KIDO(AM) Boise ID
KRCD(AM) Chubbuck ID
KVNI(AM) Coeur d'Alene ID
KID(AM) Idaho Falls ID
KFXD(AM) Nampa ID
KLIX(AM) Twin Falls ID
WBGZ(AM) Alton IL
WIBV(AM) Belleville IL
WDWS(AM) Champaign IL
KSGM(AM) Chester IL
WEDC(AM) Chicago IL
WGN(AM) Chicago IL
WDAN(AM) Danville IL
WRMN(AM) Elgin IL
WKTA(AM) Evanston IL
WFIW(AM) Fairfield IL
WJPF(AM) Herrin IL
WLDS(AM) Jacksonville IL
WJOL(AM) Joliet IL
WKEI(AM) Kewanee IL
WLPO(AM) La Salle IL
WLBH(AM) Mattoon IL
WCSJ(AM) Morris IL
WTAZ(FM) Morton IL
WINI(AM) Murphysboro IL
WCMY(AM) Ottawa IL
WIRL(AM) Peoria IL
WZOE(AM) Princeton IL
WGEM(AM) Quincy IL
WTAD(AM) Quincy IL
WUFI(AM) Rantoul IL
WNTA(AM) Rockford IL
WROK(AM) Rockford IL
WTAX(AM) Springfield IL
WSDR(AM) Sterling IL
WTIM(AM) Taylorville IL
WKRS(AM) Waukegan IL
WGCL(AM) Bloomington IN
WHON(AM) Centerville IN
WCSI(AM) Columbus IN
WTRC(AM) Elkhart IN
WFCV(AM) Fort Wayne IN
WGL(AM) Fort Wayne IN
WLTH(AM) Gary IN
WTRE(AM) Greensburg IN
WJOB(AM) Hammond IN
WKBV(AM) Richmond IN
*WVXR(FM) Richmond IN
WGL-FM Roanoke IN
WRCR(FM) Rushville IN
WSBT(AM) South Bend IN
WTHI(AM) Terre Haute IN
WAKE(AM) Valparaiso IN
*WBAA(AM) West Lafayette IN
KSOK(AM) Arkansas City KS
KKOY(AM) Chanute KS
KGGF(AM) Coffeyville KS
KSRX(AM) El Dorado KS
KFXX-FM Hugoton KS
KLWN(AM) Lawrence KS
*KKSU(AM) Manhattan KS
KMAN(AM) Manhattan KS
KCCV(AM) Overland Park KS
KQMA-FM Phillipsburg KS
KPHN(AM) Pittsburg KS
KFH(AM) Wichita KS
KNSS(AM) Wichita KS
KQAM(AM) Wichita KS
WCMI(AM) Ashland KY
WBGN(AM) Bowling Green KY
*WKUE(FM) Elizabethtown KY
WFKY(AM) Frankfort KY
WCLU(AM) Glasgow KY
*WKCC(FM) Grayson KY
*WKPB(FM) Henderson KY
WHOP(AM) Hopkinsville KY
WLXG(AM) Lexington KY
*WFPL(FM) Louisville KY
WHAS(AM) Louisville KY
WSJP(AM) Murray KY
WOMI(AM) Owensboro KY
WABL(AM) Amite LA
KBRH(AM) Baton Rouge LA
WJBO(AM) Baton Rouge LA
WASO(AM) Covington LA
KKRP(FM) Delhi LA
*KSLU(FM) Hammond LA
KPEL(AM) Lafayette LA
KAOK(AM) Lake Charles LA
KMLB(AM) Monroe LA
WSMB(AM) New Orleans LA
WWL(AM) New Orleans LA
KSLO(AM) Opelousas LA
KEEL(AM) Shreveport LA
WSLA(AM) Slidell LA
KAIN(AM) Vidalia LA
KMBS(AM) West Monroe LA
*WFCR(FM) Amherst MA
WARA(AM) Attleboro MA
WBZ(AM) Boston MA
WHTB(AM) Fall River MA
WEIM(AM) Fitchburg MA
WKOX(AM) Framingham MA
WHAV(AM) Haverhill MA
WCCM(AM) Lawrence MA
WCAP(AM) Lowell MA
WLLH(AM) Lowell MA
WMRC(AM) Milford MA
WBSM(AM) New Bedford MA
WDIS(AM) Norfolk MA
WCAT(AM) Orange-Athol MA

Broadcasting & Cable Yearbook 1994
B-559

Programming on Radio Stations in the U.S.

WBEC(AM) Pittsfield MA
WPEP(AM) Taunton MA
WGFP(AM) Webster MA
WXTK(FM) West Yarmouth MA
WBAL(AM) Baltimore MD
WERQ-FM Baltimore MD
*WJHU-FM Baltimore MD
WOLB(AM) Baltimore MD
WHRF(AM) Bel Air MD
WCTR(AM) Chestertown MD
WFMD(AM) Frederick MD
WFRB(AM) Frostburg MD
WHAG(AM) Halfway MD
WPGC(AM) Morningside MD
WZON(AM) Bangor ME
WIDE(AM) Biddeford ME
WNSW(AM) Brewer ME
WTME(AM) Lewiston ME
WGAN(AM) Portland ME
WSME(AM) Sanford ME
WKTQ(AM) South Paris ME
WABJ(AM) Adrian MI
WAAM(AM) Ann Arbor MI
WJR(AM) Detroit MI
WXYT(AM) Detroit MI
*WKAR(AM) East Lansing MI
WCHT(AM) Escanaba MI
WFNT(AM) Flint MI
WSNQ(AM) Gaylord MI
WGRD(AM) Grand Rapids MI
WMPL(AM) Hancock MI
WHTC(AM) Holland MI
WKMI(AM) Kalamazoo MI
WKZO(AM) Kalamazoo MI
*WMUK(FM) Kalamazoo MI
WJIM(AM) Lansing MI
WOAP(AM) Owosso MI
WJML(AM) Petoskey MI
WHLS(AM) Port Huron MI
WPHM(AM) Port Huron MI
WSGW(AM) Saginaw MI
WKNW(AM) Sault Ste. Marie MI
WSJM(AM) St. Joseph MI
WTCM(AM) Traverse City MI
KSTQ(FM) Alexandria MN
KXRA(AM) Alexandria MN
KAUS(AM) Austin MN
KLIZ(AM) Brainerd MN
WEBC(AM) Duluth MN
KCNN(AM) East Grand Forks MN
KLTF(AM) Little Falls MN
KMHL(AM) Marshall MN
KFAN(AM) Minneapolis MN
*KNOW(AM) Minneapolis MN
*KNOW-FM Minneapolis-
St. Paul MN
KCUE(AM) Red Wing MN
KKCM(AM) Shakopee MN
KNUJ-FM Sleepy Eye MN
KNSI(AM) St. Cloud MN
WJON(AM) St. Cloud MN
*KNGA(FM) St. Peter MN
KWOA(AM) Worthington MN
KKOZ(AM) Ava MO
KOMC(AM) Branson MO
*KCVO-FM Camdenton MO
KMRN(AM) Cameron MO
KAPE(AM) Cape Girardeau MO
KZIM(AM) Cape Girardeau MO
KDKD(AM) Clinton MO
KFRU(AM) Columbia MO
KGNN(AM) Cuba MO
KREI(AM) Farmington MO
KJCF(AM) Festus MO
KHMO(AM) Hannibal MO
KWOS(AM) Jefferson City MO
KQYX(AM) Joplin MO
KCMO(AM) Kansas City MO
KMBZ(AM) Kansas City MO
KNNT(AM) Kennett MO
KLWT(AM) Lebanon MO
*KJAB-FM Mexico MO
*KCOZ(FM) Point Lookout MO
KTTR(AM) Rolla MO
KSIM(AM) Sikeston MO
KFEQ(AM) St. Joseph MO
KMOX(AM) St. Louis MO
KTUI(AM) Sullivan MO
KLPW(AM) Union MO
KOKO(AM) Warrensburg MO
*KGNV(FM) Washington MO
KWPM(AM) West Plains MO
WVMI(AM) Biloxi MS
WCHJ(AM) Brookhaven MS
WSSI(AM) Carthage MS
WPBQ(AM) Flowood MS
WHSY(AM) Hattiesburg MS
WJXN(AM) Jackson MS
WHNY(AM) McComb MS
WMOX(AM) Meridian MS
WSUH(AM) Oxford MS
WJNT(AM) Pearl MS
WKOR(AM) Starkville MS
WQBC(AM) Vicksburg MS
KBLG(AM) Billings MT
KMMS(AM) Bozeman MT
KHKR(AM) East Helena MT
KCAP(AM) Helena MT
KMTA(AM) Kinsey MT
KGVO(AM) Missoula MT
WQNX(AM) Aberdeen NC
WZKY(AM) Albemarle NC
WKJV(AM) Asheville NC
WCGC(AM) Belmont NC
WBBB(AM) Burlington NC
WBAG(AM) Burlington-Graham NC
WCHL(AM) Chapel Hill NC
WDNC(AM) Durham NC
WLOE(AM) Eden NC
*WRVS-FM Elizabeth City NC
WFAI(AM) Fayetteville NC
WFNC(AM) Fayetteville NC
WCRY(AM) Fuquay-Varina NC
WGBR(AM) Goldsboro NC
WKEW(AM) Greensboro NC
WHKY(AM) Hickory NC
WMFR(AM) High Point NC
WJNC(AM) Jacksonville NC
WLAS(AM) Jacksonville NC
WAAV(AM) Leland NC
WLXN(AM) Lexington NC
WTSB(AM) Lumberton NC
WMYN(AM) Mayodan NC
WKRK(AM) Murphy NC
WPTF(AM) Raleigh NC
WREV(AM) Reidsville NC
WNCA(AM) Siler City NC
WEEB(AM) Southern Pines NC
WAME(AM) Statesville NC
*WHYC(FM) Swan Quarter NC
WCPS(AM) Tarboro NC
WOBR(AM) Wanchese NC
WCZI(FM) Washington NC
WHCC(AM) Waynesville NC
WETC(AM) Wendell-Zebulon NC
WTXY(AM) Whiteville NC
WSJS(AM) Winston-Salem NC
WYNC(AM) Yanceyville NC
WDAY(AM) Fargo ND
KNOX(AM) Grand Forks ND
KNDK(AM) Langdon ND
KEYZ(AM) Williston ND
KCOW(AM) Alliance NE
*KMNE-FM Bassett NE
KWBE(AM) Beatrice NE
*KCNE-FM Chadron NE
KLIN(AM) Lincoln NE
*KRNE-FM Merriman NE
KNCY(AM) Nebraska City NE
KNCY-FM Nebraska City NE
KODY(AM) North Platte NE
*KPNE-FM North Platte NE
KFAB(AM) Omaha NE
KKAR(AM) Omaha NE
WTSN(AM) Dover NH
WTSL(AM) Hanover NH
WNBX(FM) Lebanon NH
WLTN(AM) Littleton NH
WGIR(AM) Manchester NH
WZNN(AM) Rochester NH
*WNJS-FM Berlin NJ
*WNJB(FM) Bridgeton NJ
WIFI(AM) Florence NJ
WONZ(AM) Hammonton NJ
WCTC(AM) New Brunswick NJ
WERA(AM) Plainfield NJ
WOND(AM) Pleasantville NJ
WHWH(AM) Princeton NJ
WJIC(AM) Salem NJ
*WNJP(FM) Sussex NJ
WJRZ(AM) Toms River NJ
WBUD(AM) Trenton NJ
*WNJT-FM Trenton NJ
WTTM(AM) Trenton NJ
KCCC(AM) Carlsbad NM
KOBE(AM) Las Cruces NM
KCKN(AM) Roswell NM
KVSF(AM) Santa Fe NM
KPTL(AM) Carson City NV
KDWN(AM) Las Vegas NV
KLAV(AM) Las Vegas NV
KNUU(AM) Paradise NV
KOH(AM) Reno NV
KQLO(AM) Reno NV
*KUNR(FM) Reno NV
WYSL(AM) Avon NY
WINR(AM) Binghamton NY
WNBF(AM) Binghamton NY
*WXBA(FM) Brentwood NY
WBEN(AM) Buffalo NY
WGR(AM) Buffalo NY
WCLI(AM) Corning NY
WFLR(AM) Dundee NY
WFLR-FM Dundee NY
WEHM(FM) East Hampton NY
WELV(AM) Ellenville NY
WENY(AM) Elmira NY
*WHPC(FM) Garden City NY
*WEOS(FM) Geneva NY
WWSC(AM) Glens Falls NY
WLNL(AM) Horseheads NY
WHCU(AM) Ithaca NY
WTKO(AM) Ithaca NY
WGHQ(AM) Kingston NY
WLVL(AM) Lockport NY
WALL(AM) Middletown NY
*WOSR(FM) Middletown NY
WRKL(AM) New City NY
WVOX(AM) New Rochelle NY
WADO(AM) New York NY
*WBAI(FM) New York NY
WEVD(AM) New York NY
*WKCR-FM New York NY
WLIB(AM) New York NY
*WNYC(AM) New York NY
WOR(AM) New York NY
WGNY(AM) Newburgh NY
WMNS(AM) Olean NY
WDOS(AM) Oneonta NY
WLNA(AM) Peekskill NY
*WCFE-FM Plattsburgh NY
WKIP(AM) Poughkeepsie NY
WQBK(AM) Rensselaer NY
*WXXI(AM) Rochester NY
WSYR(AM) Syracuse NY
WRUN(AM) Utica NY
WFAS(AM) White Plains NY
WDPN(AM) Alliance OH
*WOUB(AM) Athens OH
WOMP(AM) Bellaire OH
WBCO(AM) Bucyrus OH
WBEX(AM) Chillicothe OH
WCHI(AM) Chillicothe OH
WCKY(AM) Cincinnati OH
WLW(AM) Cincinnati OH
*WVXU(FM) Cincinnati OH
WNRJ(AM) Circleville OH
WERE(AM) Cleveland OH
WWWE(AM) Cleveland OH
WHIO(AM) Dayton OH
WFIN(AM) Findlay OH
WLOH(AM) Lancaster OH
WCIT(AM) Lima OH
WMAN(AM) Mansfield OH
WBRJ(AM) Marietta OH
*WMRT(FM) Marietta OH
WMVO(AM) Mount Vernon OH
WCLT(AM) Newark OH
WBKC(AM) Painesville OH
WSTV(AM) Steubenville OH
WSPD(AM) Toledo OH
WBTC(AM) Uhrichsville OH
WANR(AM) Warren OH
WBBW(AM) Youngstown OH
WHIZ(AM) Zanesville OH
KWON(AM) Bartlesville OK
KOKB(AM) Blackwell OK
KGWA(AM) Enid OK
KSWO(AM) Lawton OK
KTMC(AM) McAlester OK
KBIX(AM) Muskogee OK
KNOR(AM) Norman OK
KQCV(AM) Oklahoma City OK
KTOK(AM) Oklahoma City OK
KCMX(AM) Ashland OR
KAST(AM) Astoria OR
*KMUN(FM) Astoria OR
KBKR(AM) Baker City OR
KBND(AM) Bend OR
KRSR(AM) Coos Bay OR
KLOO(AM) Corvallis OR
*KOAC(AM) Corvallis OR
KPNW(AM) Eugene OR
KUGN(AM) Eugene OR
KMUZ(AM) Gresham OR
KUIK(AM) Hillsboro OR
KYKN(AM) Keizer OR
KAGO(AM) Klamath Falls OR
KLBM(AM) La Grande OR
KOPE(FM) Medford OR
KTIX(AM) Pendleton OR
KDOV(AM) Phoenix OR
KTMT(AM) Phoenix OR
*KBPS(AM) Portland OR
KXL(AM) Portland OR
KQEN(AM) Roseburg OR
KRNR(AM) Roseburg OR
KLWJ(AM) Umatilla OR
WAEB(AM) Allentown PA
WBVP(AM) Beaver Falls PA
WAYC(AM) Bedford PA
WASP(AM) Brownsville PA
WISR(AM) Butler PA
WCPA(AM) Clearfield PA
WCOJ(AM) Coatesville PA
WNZT(AM) Columbia PA
*WWEC(FM) Elizabethtown PA
WLKK(AM) Erie PA
WPSE(AM) Erie PA
WGET(AM) Gettysburg PA
WCMB(AM) Harrisburg PA
WHP(AM) Harrisburg PA
*WITF-FM Harrisburg PA
WWCC(AM) Honesdale PA
WNTJ(AM) Johnstown PA
WEYZ(AM) North East PA
KDKA(AM) Pittsburgh PA
WTAE(AM) Pittsburgh PA
WARD(AM) Pittston PA
WARM(AM) Scranton PA
WPIC(AM) Sharon PA
WMAJ(AM) State College PA
WILK(AM) Wilkes-Barre PA
WRAK(AM) Williamsport PA
WRAK-FM Williamsport PA
WSBA(AM) York PA
WCMN(AM) Arecibo PR
WMIA(AM) Arecibo PR
WLEY(AM) Cayey PR
WALO(AM) Humacao PR
*WEUC-FM Ponce PR
WISO(AM) Ponce PR
WLEO(AM) Ponce PR
WPAB(AM) Ponce PR
WOSO(AM) San Juan PR
WUPR(AM) Utuado PR
WKFE(AM) Yauco PR
WADK(AM) Newport RI
WHJJ(AM) Providence RI
WPRO(AM) Providence RI
WERI(AM) Westerly RI
WOKE(AM) Charleston SC
WVOC(AM) Columbia SC
WORG(FM) Elloree SC
WJMX(AM) Florence SC
WEAC(AM) Gaffney SC
WFBC(AM) Greenville SC
WRNN(FM) Murrell's Inlet SC
WORD(AM) Spartanburg SC
WSPA(AM) Spartanburg SC
KJAM(AM) Madison SD
KIMM(AM) Rapid City SD
KOTA(AM) Rapid City SD
KQKD(AM) Redfield SD
KWSN(AM) Sioux Falls SD
KYNT(AM) Yankton SD
WBCR(AM) Alcoa TN
WATX(AM) Algood TN
WYXI(AM) Athens TN
WTBG(FM) Brownsville TN
WGOW(AM) Chattanooga TN
WCRV(AM) Collierville TN
WPTN(AM) Cookeville TN
WYYB(FM) Dickson TN
WNWS-FM Jackson TN
WWAM(AM) Jasper TN
*WETS(FM) Johnson City TN
WJCW(AM) Johnson City TN
WIVK(AM) Knoxville TN
WWTN(FM) Manchester TN
WCMT(AM) Martin TN
WDIA(AM) Memphis TN
WMC(AM) Memphis TN
WMTN(AM) Morristown TN
WGNS(AM) Murfreesboro TN
WLAC(AM) Nashville TN
WATO(AM) Oak Ridge TN
WQKR(AM) Portland TN
WSEV(AM) Sevierville TN
WPHC(AM) Waverly TN
KGNC(AM) Amarillo TX
*KLMN(FM) Amarillo TX
KLVQ(AM) Athens TX
KLBJ(AM) Austin TX
KLVI(AM) Beaumont TX
WTAW(AM) College Station TX
KHER(FM) Crystal City TX
*KERA(FM) Dallas TX
KDNT(AM) Denton TX
KURV(AM) Edinburg TX
KEES(AM) Gladewater TX
KPRC(AM) Houston TX
KERV(AM) Kerrville TX
KLAR(AM) Laredo TX
KMVL(AM) Madisonville TX
KCUL(AM) Marshall TX
KMHT(AM) Marshall TX
KEEE(AM) Nacogdoches TX
KRIL(AM) Odessa TX
KXQZ(AM) San Angelo TX
KTSA(AM) San Antonio TX
WOAI(AM) San Antonio TX
*KTSW(FM) San Marcos TX
KWED(AM) Seguin TX
KTEM(AM) Temple TX
KHSP(AM) Texarkana TX
KRZI(AM) Waco TX
KLLF(AM) Wichita Falls TX
KSUB(AM) Cedar City UT
KALL(AM) Salt Lake City UT
KSL(AM) Salt Lake City UT
KDXU(AM) St. George UT
WPES(AM) Ashland VA
WFNR(AM) Blacksburg VA
WXBQ(AM) Bristol VA
WDCT(AM) Fairfax VA
WFLO(AM) Farmville VA
*WJYJ(FM) Fredericksburg VA
WFTR(AM) Front Royal VA
WGAT(AM) Gate City VA
WSVA(AM) Harrisonburg VA
WLRV(AM) Lebanon VA
WAGE(AM) Leesburg VA
WLLL(AM) Lynchburg VA
WMVA(AM) Martinsville VA
WLTY(FM) Norfolk VA
WNIS(AM) Norfolk VA
WTAR(AM) Norfolk VA
*WVST(FM) Petersburg VA
WLEE(AM) Richmond VA
WRVA(AM) Richmond VA
WFIR(AM) Roanoke VA
WTON(AM) Staunton VA
WNTW(AM) Winchester VA
*WIUJ(FM) St. Thomas VI
WKVT(AM) Brattleboro VT
WKDR(AM) Burlington VT
WSYB(AM) Rutland VT
WWSR(AM) St. Albans VT
WSTJ(AM) St. Johnsbury VT
KGMI(AM) Bellingham WA
KARI(AM) Blaine WA
*KNWR(FM) Ellensburg WA
KXLE(AM) Ellensburg WA
KTCR(AM) Kennewick WA
KBSN(AM) Moses Lake WA
KONP(AM) Port Angeles WA
KQQQ(AM) Pullman WA
*KFAE-FM Richland WA
KING(AM) Seattle WA
KIRO(AM) Seattle WA
KIRO-FM Seattle WA
KKDZ(AM) Seattle WA
KITZ(AM) Silverdale WA
KNJY(FM) Spokane WA
KUJ(AM) Walla Walla WA
*KSOH(FM) Wapato WA
KPQ(AM) Wenatchee WA
KIT(AM) Yakima WA
WBEV(AM) Beaver Dam WI
WAYY(AM) Chippewa Falls WI
WRDN-FM Durand WI
WNFL(AM) Green Bay WI
WCLO(AM) Janesville WI
WLIP(AM) Kenosha WI
WHBY(AM) Kimberly WI
WIZM(AM) La Crosse WI
WMIR(AM) Lake Geneva WI
*WHA(AM) Madison WI
WIBA(AM) Madison WI
WTDY(AM) Madison WI
WTSO(AM) Madison WI
WDLB(AM) Marshfield WI
WRJC(AM) Mauston WI
WIGM(AM) Medford WI
WTMJ(AM) Milwaukee WI
WOSH(AM) Oshkosh WI
*WRST-FM Oshkosh WI
WRJN(AM) Racine WI
WCWC(AM) Ripon WI
WCNZ(AM) Sheboygan WI
WSPO(AM) Stevens Point WI
WBKV(AM) West Bend WI
WFHR(AM) Wisconsin Rapids WI
WWNR(AM) Beckley WV
WHIS(AM) Bluefield WV
WKOY(AM) Bluefield WV
WCHS(AM) Charleston WV
WHAR(AM) Clarksburg WV
WMMN(AM) Fairmont WV
WRNR(AM) Martinsburg WV
KFBC(AM) Cheyenne WY
KROE(AM) Sheridan WY

Nostalgia

Also see Big Band.

WAPI(AM) Birmingham AL
KFCM(FM) Cherokee Village AR
KTLO-FM Mountain Home AR
KFWJ(AM) Lake Havasu City AZ
KOY(AM) Phoenix AZ
KEYQ(AM) Fresno CA
KXBX(AM) Lakeport CA
KTME(AM) Lompoc CA
KBAI(AM) Morro Bay CA
KPCO(AM) Quincy CA
KCTC(AM) Sacramento CA
KKSJ(AM) San Jose CA
KEZW(AM) Aurora CO
WGUL(AM) Dunedin FL
WPGS(AM) Mims FL
WGUL-FM New Port Richey FL
KMRY(AM) Cedar Rapids IA
KFQC(AM) Davenport IA
KVFD(AM) Fort Dodge IA
WTCA(AM) Plymouth IN
KBEA(AM) Mission KS
KQAM(AM) Wichita KS
WSON(AM) Henderson KY
WAVG(AM) Louisville KY
WBYU(AM) New Orleans LA
WXKS(AM) Medford MA
WHMP(AM) Northampton MA
WITH(AM) Baltimore MD
WWLG(AM) Baltimore MD
WTBO(AM) Cumberland MD
WLAM(AM) Gorham ME
WZAN(AM) Portland ME
WHFB(AM) Benton Harbor-
St. Joseph MI
WHGR(AM) Houghton Lake MI
WQWQ(AM) Muskegon Heights MI
KJJK(AM) Fergus Falls MN
KLBB(AM) St. Paul MN
WIMN(AM) Stillwater MN
KOMC(AM) Branson MO
KTOZ(AM) Springfield MO
WGCM(AM) Gulfport MS
WHNC(AM) Henderson NC
WMBL(AM) Morehead City NC
WTSV(AM) Claremont NH
WMYF(AM) Exeter NH
WFEA(AM) Manchester NH
WMID(AM) Atlantic City NJ
WRDR(FM) Egg Harbor City NJ
WMTR(AM) Morristown NJ
WBUD(AM) Trenton NJ
KNFT(AM) Bayard NM
KIVA(AM) Corrales NM
KTRC(AM) Santa Fe NM
KORK(AM) Las Vegas NV
KJUL(FM) North Las Vegas NV
KCBN(AM) Reno NV
WSGO(AM) Oswego NY
WYLF(AM) Penn Yan NY
WBBF(AM) Rochester NY
WNCO(AM) Ashland OH
WRMR(AM) Cleveland OH
WKTX(AM) Cortland OH
WPFB(AM) Middletown OH
WVAC(AM) Norwalk OH
WSOM(AM) Salem OH
*WVXM(FM) West Union OH
WHOT(AM) Youngstown OH
KFLY(AM) Corvallis OR
WFLP(AM) Erie PA
WQTW(AM) Latrobe PA
WPEN(AM) Philadelphia PA
WJAS(AM) Pittsburgh PA
WKMC(AM) Roaring Spring PA
WLYC(AM) Williamsport PA
WSSP(FM) Goose Creek SC
WAMB(AM) Donelson TN
WAMB-FM Donelson TN

Programming on Radio Stations in the U.S.

KIXZ(AM) Amarillo TX
KIVY(AM) Crockett TX
KCYT(FM) Granbury TX
KKAM(AM) Lubbock TX
KTXN-FM Victoria TX
KOVO(AM) Provo UT
WKEX(AM) Blacksburg VA
WSTK(AM) Colonial Heights VA
WBLU(AM) Moneta VA
WNHV(AM) White River Junction VT
KKSN(AM) Vancouver WA
WNAM(AM) Neenah-Menasha WI
WOCO-FM Oconto WI
KXTP(AM) Superior WI
WMRH(AM) Waupun WI
WWYO(AM) Pineville WV

Oldies

Includes station formats Golden Oldies, Old Gold and Solid Gold. Also see Classic Rock.

KEAG(FM) Anchorage AK
KLAM(AM) Cordova AK
KCBF(AM) Fairbanks AK
KXLR(FM) Fairbanks AK
KIYU(AM) Galena AK
KSWD(AM) Seward AK
KIFW(AM) Sitka AK
KSLD(AM) Soldotna AK
*KUHB(FM) St. Paul Island AK
WODL(FM) Birmingham AL
WCKO(FM) Carrollton AL
WXXR(AM) Cullman AL
WAVD(AM) Decatur AL
WZNJ(FM) Demopolis AL
WESP(FM) Dothan AL
WELB(AM) Elba AL
WDMT(FM) Eufaula AL
WFPA(AM) Fort Payne AL
WZPQ(AM) Jasper AL
WRLD(AM) Lanett AL
WAVH(FM) Mobile AL
WBAM-FM Montgomery AL
WOPP(AM) Opp AL
WPNX(AM) Phenix City AL
WPID(AM) Piedmont AL
WZCT(AM) Scottsboro AL
WHBB(AM) Selma AL
WAWV(FM) Sylacauga AL
WFEB(AM) Sylacauga AL
WTLS(AM) Tallassee AL
KOLZ(FM) Bentonville AR
KDMS(AM) El Dorado AR
KXJK(AM) Forrest City AR
KBBQ-FM Fort Smith AR
KFPW(AM) Fort Smith AR
KOOU(FM) Hardy AR
KSRB(AM) Hardy AR
KZNG(AM) Hot Springs AR
KOLL(FM) Maumelle AR
KOSE(AM) Osceola AR
KDXY(FM) Paragould AR
KQXK(AM) Springdale AR
KVNA(AM) Flagstaff AZ
KDJI(AM) Holbrook AZ
KRCY(FM) Kingman AZ
KFWJ(AM) Lake Havasu City AZ
KOOL(AM) Phoenix AZ
KOOL-FM Phoenix AZ
KPSN(FM) Phoenix AZ
KIHX-FM Prescott Valley AZ
KBUX(FM) Quartzsite AZ
KATO(AM) Safford AZ
KRQQ-FM Tucson AZ
KWFM(AM) Tucson AZ
KYET(AM) Williams AZ
KBLU(AM) Yuma AZ
KAPL(AM) Apple Valley CA
KATA(AM) Arcata CA
KIQO(FM) Atascadero CA
KHYL(FM) Auburn CA
KERN-FM Bakersfield CA
KGEO(AM) Bakersfield CA
KBET(AM) Canyon Country CA
KIEZ(AM) Carmel Valley CA
KODS(FM) Carnelian Bay CA
KCEZ(FM) Corning CA
KAMP(AM) El Centro CA
KXO(AM) El Centro CA
KFIG(AM) Fresno CA
KYNO(AM) Fresno CA
KAVL(AM) Lancaster CA
KCLL(AM) Lompoc CA
KCBS-FM Los Angeles CA
KGFJ(AM) Los Angeles CA
KRTH(FM) Los Angeles CA
KABX-FM Merced CA
KVOY(AM) Mojave CA
KMGG(FM) Monte Rio CA
KBAI(AM) Morro Bay CA
KEDY(FM) Mount Shasta CA
KDES(AM) Palm Springs CA
KDES-FM Palm Springs CA
KRLA(AM) Pasadena CA
KBLF(AM) Red Bluff CA
KSMJ(AM) Sacramento CA
KXOA(AM) Sacramento CA
KOLA(FM) San Bernardino CA
KCBQ(AM) San Diego CA
KCBQ-FM San Diego CA
KFRC(AM) San Francisco CA
KFRC-FM San Francisco CA
KYA(FM) San Francisco CA
KIST(AM) Santa Barbara CA
KWG(AM) Stockton CA
KSUE(AM) Susanville CA
KEXX(FM) Tracy CA
KXBT(AM) Vallejo CA
KBBY(AM) Ventura CA
KEYX(AM) Visalia CA
KFSO-FM Visalia CA
KRLN(AM) Canon City CO
KSPZ(FM) Colorado Springs CO
KXKL(AM) Denver CO
KXKL-FM Denver CO
KDGO(AM) Durango CO
KRKI(AM) Estes Park CO
KGLN(AM) Glenwood Springs CO
KEXO(AM) Grand Junction CO
KLOV(AM) Loveland CO
KUBC(AM) Montrose CO
KURA(FM) Ouray CO
KDZA-FM Pueblo CO
KGHF(AM) Pueblo CO
KIIX(AM) Wellington CO
WDRC-FM Hartford CT
WKHL(FM) Stamford CT
WVVE(FM) Stonington CT
WWCO(AM) Waterbury CT
WMMM(AM) Westport CT
WBIG-FM Washington DC
WKEN(AM) Dover DE
WWBF(AM) Bartow FL
WTCL(AM) Chattahoochee FL
WFRK(AM) Coleman FL
WROD(AM) Daytona Beach FL
WOCL(FM) De Land FL
WDBF(AM) Delray Beach FL
WAXY(FM) Fort Lauderdale FL
WOLZ(FM) Fort Myers FL
WYOC(FM) High Springs FL
WKQL(FM) Jacksonville FL
WKIZ(AM) Key West FL
WGRO(AM) Lake City FL
WQHL(AM) Live Oak FL
WODX(AM) Marco Island FL
WYZB(FM) Mary Esther FL
WGGD-FM Melbourne FL
WQAM(AM) Miami FL
WSGL(FM) Naples FL
WTKX(AM) Pensacola FL
WMTX(AM) Pinellas Park FL
WMXJ(FM) Pompano Beach FL
WEEJ(FM) Port Charlotte FL
WYUU(FM) Safety Harbor FL
WSRZ-FM Sarasota FL
WCAC(FM) Sebring FL
WWGO(FM) Silver Springs FL
WSTF(FM) St. Augustine FL
WAMT(AM) Titusville FL
WFSH(AM) Valparaiso-Niceville FL
WQOL(FM) Vero Beach FL
WJYZ(AM) Albany GA
WMGR(AM) Bainbridge GA
WLKQ(FM) Buford GA
WEBS(AM) Calhoun GA
WCGX(FM) Cleveland GA
WBLJ(AM) Dalton GA
WWRK(AM) Elberton GA
WRDO(FM) Fitzgerald GA
WFOX(FM) Gainesville GA
WGGA(AM) Gainesville GA
WDDK(FM) Greensboro GA
WQUL(FM) Griffin GA
WQSY(FM) Hawkinsville GA
WHEL(FM) Helen GA
WEIZ(FM) Hogansville GA
WBTY(FM) Homerville GA
WBKZ(AM) Jefferson GA
WEGC(FM) Leesburg GA
WBBT(AM) Lyons GA
WAYS(FM) Macon GA
WGOR(FM) Martinez GA
WHCG(FM) Metter GA
WMAC(AM) Metter GA
WGCO(FM) Midway GA
WPGA(AM) Perry GA
WSGC-FM Ringgold GA
WBIC(AM) Royston GA
WSNI(FM) Thomasville GA
WLET(AM) Toccoa GA
WATG(FM) Trion GA
WVLD(AM) Valdosta GA
WVOP(AM) Vidalia GA
WLOV-FM Washington GA
WAYX(AM) Waycross GA
KAHU(AM) Hilo HI
KHWI(FM) Hilo HI
KIKI(AM) Honolulu HI
KNUI(AM) Kahului HI
KQNG(AM) Lihue HI
KLBA(AM) Albia IA
KASI(AM) Ames IA
KKMI(FM) Burlington IA
KKBZ(FM) Clarinda IA
KLKK(FM) Clear Lake IA
KLNT(AM) Clinton IA
KFQC(AM) Davenport IA
KUUL(FM) Davenport IA
KIOA(AM) Des Moines IA
KIOA-FM Des Moines IA
KGGY(FM) Dubuque IA
WDBQ(AM) Dubuque IA
KKSI(FM) Eddyville IA
KEMB(FM) Emmetsburg IA
KILR(AM) Estherville IA
KILR-FM Estherville IA
*KICB(FM) Fort Dodge IA
KUEL(FM) Fort Dodge IA
KLMJ(FM) Hampton IA
KQMG(AM) Independence IA
KCJJ(AM) Iowa City IA
KKRQ(FM) Iowa City IA
KLSN(FM) Jefferson IA
KFJB(AM) Marshalltown IA
KRIB(AM) Mason City IA
KILJ(AM) Mount Pleasant IA
KYTC(FM) Northwood IA
KBIZ(AM) Ottumwa IA
KCII(AM) Washington IA
KCII-FM Washington IA
KWLO(AM) Waterloo IA
KWAY(AM) Waverly IA
KGEM(AM) Boise ID
KLTB(FM) Boise ID
KUPI(AM) Idaho Falls ID
KATW(FM) Lewiston ID
KOZE(AM) Lewiston ID
KRPL(AM) Moscow ID
KLIX-FM Twin Falls ID
WKKD(AM) Aurora IL
WKKD-FM Aurora IL
WKRO(AM) Cairo IL
WROY(AM) Carmi IL
WCAZ-FM Carthage IL
*WPCD(FM) Champaign IL
WGCI(AM) Chicago IL
WJMK(FM) Chicago IL
WKBM(FM) Coal City IL
WFIW-FM Fairfield IL
WFXW(AM) Geneva IL
WJBM(AM) Jerseyville IL
WJPC-FM Lansing IL
WKOT(FM) Marseilles IL
WCFL(FM) Morris IL
WIKK(FM) Newton IL
WIHN(FM) Normal IL
WPXN(FM) Paxton IL
WGLO(FM) Pekin IL
WIRL(AM) Peoria IL
WBBA(AM) Pittsfield IL
WPOK(AM) Pontiac IL
WRRR(AM) Rockford IL
WKXQ(FM) Rushville IL
WAUR(AM) Sandwich IL
WEJT(FM) Shelbyville IL
WSHY(AM) Shelbyville IL
WMAY(AM) Springfield IL
WQQL(FM) Springfield IL
WIZZ(AM) Streator IL
WKIO(FM) Urbana IL
WCVS-FM Virden IL
WKMQ(FM) Winnebago IL
WUZR(FM) Bicknell IN
WSDM-FM Brazil IN
WWWY(FM) Columbus IN
WCDV(FM) Covington IN
WNJY(FM) Delphi IN
WJPS(AM) Evansville IN
WJLT(FM) Fort Wayne IN
WOWO-FM Huntington IN
WKLR(FM) Indianapolis IN
WXVW(AM) Jeffersonville IN
WAWK(AM) Kendallville IN
*WKPW(FM) Knightstown IN
WIOU(AM) Kokomo IN
*WJEF(FM) Lafayette IN
WEFM(FM) Michigan City IN
WMRS(FM) Monticello IN
WERK(AM) Muncie IN
WERK-FM Muncie IN
WLBC-FM Muncie IN
WMDH(AM) New Castle IN
WJPS-FM Newburgh IN
*WEEM(FM) Pendleton IN
WARU(AM) Peru IN
WTCA(AM) Plymouth IN
WRCR(FM) Rushville IN
WZZB(AM) Seymour IN
WNDU(AM) South Bend IN
WRBR-FM South Bend IN
WJSH(AM) Terre Haute IN
KSAJ-FM Abilene KS
KMOQ(FM) Baxter Springs KS
KKOY-FM Chanute KS
KCKS(FM) Concordia KS
KDCC(AM) Dodge City KS
KVOE(AM) Emporia KS
KAYS(AM) Hays KS
KQDF-FM Larned KS
KYUU(AM) Liberal KS
KNGL(AM) McPherson KS
KINA(AM) Salina KS
KSKL(FM) Scott City KS
KEYN-FM Wichita KS
KWKS(FM) Winfield KS
WMDJ-FM Allen KY
WRVC-FM Ashland KY
WCBL-FM Benton KY
WIEL(AM) Elizabethtown KY
WPKE-FM Elkhorn City KY
WEKT(AM) Elkton KY
WBND(AM) Florence KY
WASE-FM Fort Knox KY
WKYW(FM) Frankfort KY
WTKT-FM Georgetown KY
WCLU(AM) Glasgow KY
WKYZ(AM) Gray KY
WUGO(FM) Grayson KY
WAKY(AM) Greensburg KY
WKCM(AM) Hawesville KY
WQXY(AM) Hazard KY
WRNZ(FM) Lancaster KY
WLAP(AM) Lexington KY
WMDJ(AM) Martin KY
WFTM(AM) Maysville KY
WFTM-FM Maysville KY
WVJS(AM) Owensboro KY
WDOC(AM) Prestonsburg KY
WLVK(FM) Radcliff KY
WMCQ-FM Richmond KY
WTLO(AM) Somerset KY
WMQQ(FM) Springfield KY
WRKA(FM) St. Matthews KY
KROF(AM) Abbeville LA
KROF-FM Abbeville LA
KALB(AM) Alexandria LA
WGGZ(FM) Baton Rouge LA
KLKL(FM) Benton LA
KCTO-FM Columbia LA
KEAZ(FM) De Ridder LA
KPCH(FM) Dubach LA
KJJB(FM) Eunice LA
KHOM(FM) Houma LA
KTOC-FM Jonesboro LA
KWLA(AM) Many LA
KNOE(AM) Monroe LA
KLIL(FM) Moreauville LA
KNOC(AM) Natchitoches LA
KNIR(AM) New Iberia LA
WGSO(AM) New Orleans LA
WTKL(FM) New Orleans LA
KGTR(FM) Port Sulphur LA
KBSF(AM) Springhill LA
KTKC(FM) Springhill LA
KEZM(AM) Sulphur LA
KVPI-FM Ville Platte LA
KNCB(AM) Vivian LA
WODS(FM) Boston MA
WHTB(AM) Fall River MA
WKOX(AM) Framingham MA
WATD-FM Marshfield MA
WNBH(AM) New Bedford MA
WKPE(AM) Orleans MA
WKPE-FM Orleans MA
WUHN(AM) Pittsfield MA
WARE(AM) Ware MA
WORC(AM) Worcester MA
WITH(AM) Baltimore MD
WARW(FM) Bethesda MD
WQSR(FM) Catonsville MD
WALI(AM) Cumberland MD
WCEI-FM Easton MD
WARK(AM) Hagerstown MD
WARX(FM) Hagerstown MD
WMYJ(FM) Pocomoke City MD
WMJS(FM) Prince Frederick MD
WINX(AM) Rockville MD
WLVW-FM Salisbury MD
WSBY-FM Salisbury MD
WXTR-FM Waldorf MD
WGRX(FM) Westminster MD
WABI(AM) Bangor ME
WGUY(FM) Dexter ME
WWMJ(FM) Ellsworth ME
WXGL-FM Lewiston ME
WHMX(FM) Lincoln ME
WRKD(AM) Rockland ME
WHQO(FM) Skowhegan ME
WYNZ(FM) Westbrook ME
WCQL-FM York Center ME
WKGH(FM) Allegan MI
WAIR(FM) Atlanta MI
WHNN(FM) Bay City MI
WATT(AM) Cadillac MI
WLLJ(AM) Cassopolis MI
WOMC(FM) Detroit MI
WCHT(AM) Escanaba MI
WFDF(AM) Flint MI
WSHN-FM Fremont MI
WODJ(FM) Greenville MI
WZRK(FM) Hancock MI
WIKB(AM) Iron River MI
WIKB-FM Iron River MI
WIBM(AM) Jackson MI
WIBM-FM Jackson MI
WTRV(FM) Leland MI
WFXD(FM) Marquette MI
WAGN(AM) Menominee MI
WHND(AM) Monroe MI
WCEN(AM) Mount Pleasant MI
WQXO(AM) Munising MI
WQWQ(AM) Muskegon Heights MI
WNBY-FM Newberry MI
WLCS(FM) North Muskegon MI
WHLS(AM) Port Huron MI
WFAT(FM) Portage MI
WBYY(AM) Rockford MI
WAMX(AM) Saline MI
WEVS(FM) Saugatuck MI
WMMI(AM) Shepherd MI
*WSHJ(FM) Southfield MI
WMSH(AM) Sturgis MI
WMSH-FM Sturgis MI
WCCW-FM Traverse City MI
WBMB(AM) West Branch MI
KCPI(FM) Albert Lea MN
KQQL(FM) Anoka MN
KAUS(AM) Austin MN
WJJY(AM) Baxter MN
KSCR(AM) Benson MN
KLKS(FM) Breezy Point MN
KXDL(FM) Browerville MN
WKLK(AM) Cloquet MN
WKLK-FM Cloquet MN
KMXK(FM) Cold Spring MN
KKDL(FM) Detroit Lakes MN
KDAL-FM Duluth MN
KFMC(FM) Fairmont MN
KDHL(AM) Faribault MN
KARP(FM) Glencoe MN
WMFG(AM) Hibbing MN
WMFG-FM Hibbing MN
KGHS(AM) International Falls MN
KQEG(FM) La Crescent MN
KLFD(AM) Litchfield MN
KFML(FM) Little Falls MN
KYSM(AM) Mankato MN
KMGM(FM) Montevideo MN
KCHK(AM) New Prague MN
KCHK-FM New Prague MN
KYMN(AM) Northfield MN
KDIO(AM) Ortonville MN
KDKK-FM Park Rapids MN
WCMP(AM) Pine City MN
KISD(FM) Pipestone MN
KWNG(FM) Red Wing MN
KOLM(AM) Rochester MN
KROC(AM) Rochester MN
KMSR(FM) Sauk Centre MN
WVAL(AM) Sauk Rapids MN
KRBI(AM) St. Peter MN
KRBI-FM St. Peter MN
KNSP(AM) Staples MN
KSNR(FM) Thief River Falls MN
KDJS(AM) Willmar MN
KDOM(AM) Windom MN
KDOM-FM Windom MN
KWNO(AM) Winona MN
KDBB(FM) Bonne Terre MO
KGMO(FM) Cape Girardeau MO
KCHI(AM) Chillicothe MO
KCHI-FM Chillicothe MO
KKCA(FM) Fulton MO
KMAC(FM) Gainesville MO
KJMO(FM) Jefferson City MO
WMBH-FM Joplin MO
KCMO-FM Kansas City MO
KBOA(AM) Kennett MO
KCLQ(FM) Lebanon MO
KNIM-FM Maryville MO
KXEO(AM) Mexico MO
KDAM(FM) Monroe City MO
KAHR(FM) Poplar Bluff MO
KLID(AM) Poplar Bluff MO
KQMX(FM) Rolla MO
KSIS(AM) Sedalia MO
KASP(AM) St. Louis MO
KLOU(FM) St. Louis MO
KRJY(FM) St. Louis MO
KOSP(FM) Willard MO
WIZK-FM Bay Springs MS
WCLD(AM) Cleveland MS
WNIX(AM) Greenville MS
WGCM-FM Gulfport MS
WFOR(AM) Hattiesburg MS
WJDS(AM) Jackson MS
WTYX(FM) Jackson MS
WKOZ(AM) Kosciusko MS
WAGR-FM Lexington MS
WAKK(AM) McComb MS
WNAT(AM) Natchez MS
WOXD(FM) Oxford MS
WWSL(FM) Philadelphia MS
WELO(AM) Tupelo MS
WAZF(AM) Yazoo City MS
KKBR(FM) Billings MT
KZLO(AM) Bozeman MT
KRYK(FM) Chinook MT
KDRG(AM) Deer Lodge MT
KMSL(AM) Great Falls MT
KBMG(FM) Hamilton MT
KKUL(AM) Hardin MT
KBLL(AM) Helena MT
KGEZ(AM) Kalispell MT
KYLT(AM) Missoula MT
WZKY(AM) Albemarle NC
WKJA(FM) Belhaven NC
WFGW(AM) Black Mountain NC
WWIT(AM) Canton NC
WAQQ(FM) Charlotte NC
WAQS(AM) Charlotte NC
WCSL(AM) Cherryville NC
WEGO(AM) Concord NC
WCLW(AM) Eden NC
WLOE(AM) Eden NC
WCNC(AM) Elizabeth City NC
WBLA(AM) Elizabethtown NC
WGQR(FM) Elizabethtown NC
WIFM-FM Elkin NC
WRQR(FM) Farmville NC
WGNC(AM) Gastonia NC
WGOS(AM) High Point NC
WJNC(AM) Jacksonville NC
WKOO(FM) Jacksonville NC
WCXL(FM) Kill Devil Hills NC
WEWO(AM) Laurinburg NC
WJRI(AM) Lenoir NC
WKGX(AM) Lenoir NC
WLON(AM) Lincolnton NC
WHLQ(FM) Louisburg NC
WYRN(AM) Louisburg NC
WJSK(FM) Lumberton NC
WMYN(AM) Mayodan NC
WDSL(AM) Mocksville NC
WDEX(AM) Monroe NC
WHIP(AM) Mooresville NC
WMNC-FM Morganton NC
WDLF(FM) Old Fort NC
WYRU(AM) Red Springs NC
WCBT(AM) Roanoke Rapids NC
WLWL(AM) Rockingham NC
WRMT(AM) Rocky Mount NC

Broadcasting & Cable Yearbook 1994
B-561

WTRG(FM) Rocky Mount NC
WRXO(AM) Roxboro NC
WSAT(AM) Salisbury NC
WXKL(AM) Sanford NC
WCCA(FM) Shallotte NC
WOHS(AM) Shelby NC
WWMG(FM) Shelby NC
WNCA(AM) Siler City NC
WFAZ(FM) Thomasville NC
WZKB(FM) Wallace NC
WTXY(AM) Whiteville NC
WMFD(AM) Wilmington NC
WVOT(AM) Wilson NC
WMQX(AM) Winston-Salem NC
WMQX-FM Winston-Salem NC
KLXX(AM) Bismarck-Mandan ND
KQWB(AM) Fargo ND
KNOX-FM Grand Forks ND
KBQQ(FM) Minot ND
KRRZ(AM) Minot ND
KOVC-FM Valley City ND
KOIL(AM) Bellevue NE
KGMT(AM) Fairbury NE
KTNC(AM) Falls City NE
KSDZ(FM) Gordon NE
KICS(AM) Hastings NE
KKPR(AM) Kearney NE
KLDZ(FM) Lincoln NE
KNCY(AM) Nebraska City NE
KNCY-FM Nebraska City NE
KOOQ(AM) North Platte NE
KOGA(AM) Ogallala NE
KGOR(FM) Omaha NE
KOAQ(AM) Terrytown NE
WMOU(AM) Berlin NH
WFTN(AM) Franklin NH
WNNH(FM) Henniker NH
WLTN-FM Lisbon NH
WSMN(AM) Nashua NH
WXOD(FM) Winchester NH
WLKZ(FM) Wolfeboro NH
WJLK(AM) Asbury Park NJ
WMID(AM) Atlantic City NJ
WSSJ(AM) Camden NJ
WJDM(AM) Elizabeth NJ
WOBM(AM) Lakewood NJ
WZVU(FM) Long Branch NJ
WNNJ(AM) Newton NJ
WIBG(AM) Ocean City NJ
WKTU(FM) Ocean City NJ
WERA(AM) Plainfield NJ
WKXW(FM) Trenton NJ
KQEO(AM) Albuquerque NM
KRLL(AM) Albuquerque NM
KCQL(AM) Aztec NM
KAMQ(AM) Carlsbad NM
KWKA(AM) Clovis NM
KYVA(AM) Gallup NM
KKEL(AM) Hobbs NM
KPSA-FM La Luz NM
KBOM(FM) Los Alamos NM
KJBO(AM) Los Ranchos de Albuquerque NM
KSEL(AM) Portales NM
KZKL-FM Rio Rancho NM
KBIM(AM) Roswell NM
KNLA(FM) White Rock NM
KRRI(FM) Boulder City NV
WMBO(AM) Auburn NY
WNYG(AM) Babylon NY
WFBL(AM) Baldwinsville NY
WSEN-FM Baldwinsville NY
WABH(AM) Bath NY
WVIN-FM Bath NY
WBZO(FM) Bay Shore NY
WBNR(AM) Beacon NY
WGMM(FM) Big Flats NY
WHTT(AM) Buffalo NY
WHTT-FM Buffalo NY
WWWS(AM) Buffalo NY
WCGR(AM) Canandaigua NY
WRWD(AM) Cornwall NY
WKRT(AM) Cortland NY
WELM(AM) Elmira NY
WMRV(AM) Endicott NY
WGVA(AM) Geneva NY
WLEA(AM) Hornell NY
WIQT(AM) Horseheads NY
WRVW(FM) Hudson NY
WCZX(FM) Hyde Park NY
WKSN(AM) Jamestown NY
WSRD(FM) Johnstown NY
WLVL(AM) Lockport NY
WLLG(FM) Lowville NY
WYBG(AM) Massena NY
WXTM(FM) Monticello NY
WCBS-FM New York NY
WCHN(AM) Norwich NY
WHDL(AM) Olean NY
WUUU(FM) Remsen NY
WKLX(FM) Rochester NY
WODZ(AM) Rome NY
WODZ-FM Rome NY
WTRY-FM Rotterdam NY
WLNG(AM) Sag Harbor NY
WLNG-FM Sag Harbor NY
WGGO(AM) Salamanca NY
WSLK(FM) Saranac Lake NY
WGY-FM Schenectady NY
WCDO-FM Sidney NY
WTRY(AM) Troy NY
WTLB(AM) Utica NY
WGMF(AM) Watkins Glen NY
WNYV(FM) Whitehall NY
WZAD(FM) Wurtsboro NY

WZKL(FM) Alliance OH
WMTR-FM Archbold OH
WFUN(AM) Ashtabula OH
WBNV(FM) Barnesville OH
WYMJ-FM Beavercreek OH
WRQN(FM) Bowling Green OH
WBEX(AM) Chillicothe OH
WCIN(AM) Cincinnati OH
WMJI(FM) Cleveland OH
WNCG(FM) Clyde OH
WBNS-FM Columbus OH
WCOL(AM) Columbus OH
WCOL-FM Columbus OH
WKTX(AM) Cortland OH
WZOM(FM) Defiance OH
WOHI(AM) East Liverpool OH
WGRR(FM) Hamilton OH
WIRO(AM) Ironton OH
WJMP(AM) Kent OH
WSWZ(FM) Lancaster OH
WBZW(FM) Loudonville OH
WAGX(FM) Manchester OH
WTIG(AM) Massillon OH
*WLMH(FM) Morrow OH
WVAC(AM) Norwalk OH
WPAY(AM) Portsmouth OH
WSWR(FM) Shelby OH
WDIG(AM) Steubenville OH
WWWM-FM Sylvania OH
WTTF(AM) Tiffin OH
WTTF-FM Tiffin OH
WCWA(AM) Toledo OH
WBTC(AM) Uhrichsville OH
WERT(AM) Van Wert OH
WRRO(AM) Warren OH
WELW(AM) Willoughby-Eastlake OH
WKVX(AM) Wooster OH
WBBG(FM) Youngstown OH
KADA-FM Ada OK
KRHD-FM Duncan OK
KSEO(AM) Durant OK
KVRW(FM) Lawton OK
KNOR(AM) Norman OK
KOMA(AM) Oklahoma City OK
KOMA-FM Oklahoma City OK
KOQL(FM) Oklahoma City OK
KQLL-FM Owasso OK
KGOK(FM) Pauls Valley OK
KBKR(AM) Baker City OR
KGAL-FM Brownsville OR
KCNA(FM) Cave Junction OR
KWRO(AM) Coquille OR
KLOO(AM) Corvallis OR
KDUK(AM) Eugene OR
KPNW-FM Eugene OR
KFLS(AM) Klamath Falls OR
KLBM(AM) La Grande OR
KSHO(AM) Lebanon OR
KLYC(AM) McMinnville OR
KUMA-FM Pendleton OR
KKSN-FM Portland OR
KTBR(AM) Roseburg OR
KSLM(AM) Salem OR
KWSA(AM) West Klamath OR
WOOX(FM) Bedford PA
WKAB(FM) Berwick PA
WSQV(AM) Berwick PA
WGPA(AM) Bethlehem PA
WBRR(FM) Bradford PA
WSGD-FM Carbondale PA
WCBG(AM) Chambersburg PA
WBUX(AM) Doylestown PA
WCED(AM) DuBois PA
WIPI(AM) Easton PA
WQKK(FM) Ebensburg PA
WLEM(AM) Emporium PA
WQKY(FM) Emporium PA
WRIE(AM) Erie PA
WRQQ(AM) Farrell PA
WQEQ(FM) Freeland PA
WHJB(AM) Greensburg PA
WSSZ(FM) Greensburg PA
WWKL(FM) Harrisburg PA
WAZL(AM) Hazleton PA
WZMT(FM) Hazleton PA
WHPA(FM) Hollidaysburg PA
WWWD(FM) Jersey Shore PA
WTYM(AM) Kittanning PA
WYNS(AM) Lehighton PA
WIEZ(AM) Lewistown PA
WBPZ(AM) Lock Haven PA
WMLP(AM) Milton PA
WYOS(FM) Nanticoke PA
WBZY(AM) New Castle PA
WKQW-FM Oil City PA
WOGL(AM) Philadelphia PA
WOGL-FM Philadelphia PA
WPGR(AM) Philadelphia PA
WWSW(AM) Pittsburgh PA
WWSW-FM Pittsburgh PA
WHYM(AM) Portage PA
WPAM(AM) Pottsville PA
WEJL(AM) Scranton PA
WISL(AM) Shamokin PA
WMBT(AM) Shenandoah PA
WSHP(AM) Shippensburg PA
WADJ(AM) Somerset PA
WCCZ(FM) Spangler PA
WKBI(AM) St. Marys PA
WTTC(AM) Towanda PA
WTTC-FM Towanda PA
*WRDV(FM) Warminster PA
WJPA(AM) Washington PA
WJPA-FM Washington PA

WQXA(AM) York PA
WLDI(FM) Bayamon PR
WLEY(AM) Cayey PR
WCPR(AM) Coamo PR
WAEL(AM) Mayaguez PR
WTIL(AM) Mayaguez PR
WMTI(AM) Morovis PR
WLEO(AM) Ponce PR
WZAR(FM) Ponce PR
WCAD(FM) San Juan PR
WRSS(AM) San Sebastian PR
WICE(AM) Pawtucket RI
WWBB(FM) Providence RI
WWLI(FM) Providence RI
WOON(AM) Woonsocket RI
WZLA-FM Abbeville SC
WBSC(AM) Bennettsville SC
WOKE(AM) Charleston SC
WBZK-FM Chester SC
WOMG(AM) Columbia SC
WOMG-FM Columbia SC
WYBB(FM) Folly Beach SC
WEAC(AM) Gaffney SC
WSYN(FM) Georgetown SC
WSSP(FM) Goose Creek SC
WUJM(AM) Goose Creek SC
WFBC-FM Greenville SC
WPJM(AM) Greer SC
WKDK(AM) Newberry SC
WXLY(FM) North Charleston SC
WOCW(FM) Parris Island SC
WBFM(FM) Seneca SC
WSSC(AM) Sumter SC
WGOG-FM Walhalla SC
WBZK(AM) York SC
KQAA(FM) Aberdeen SD
KBRK(AM) Brookings SD
KDSJ(AM) Deadwood SD
KBJM(AM) Lemmon SD
KMSD(AM) Milbank SD
KMIT(FM) Mitchell SD
KORN(AM) Mitchell SD
KOLY(AM) Mobridge SD
KLXS-FM Pierre SD
KKLS(AM) Rapid City SD
KKLS-FM Sioux Falls SD
KSDR(AM) Watertown SD
KYNT(AM) Yankton SD
WNAX-FM Yankton SD
WKOM(FM) Columbia TN
WZYX(AM) Cowan TN
WREA(AM) Dayton TN
WOGT(FM) East Ridge TN
WIZO(AM) Franklin TN
*WLMU(FM) Harrogate TN
WHMT(AM) Humboldt TN
WLOD(AM) Loudon TN
WXST(FM) Loudon TN
WJCE(AM) Memphis TN
WKBJ(AM) Milan TN
WYBM(FM) Minor Hill TN
WRMX(FM) Murfreesboro TN
WTPR(AM) Paris TN
WORM(AM) Savannah TN
WTYR(AM) Soddy-Daisy TN
WEYE(FM) Surgoinsville TN
WVRY(FM) Waverly TN
KKHR(FM) Anson TX
KYTX(FM) Beeville TX
KBOC(FM) Bridgeport TX
KBWD(AM) Brownwood TX
KTAM(AM) Bryan TX
KEZP(FM) Canadian TX
KPUR-FM Canyon TX
KCTX(AM) Childress TX
*KETR(FM) Commerce TX
KEYS(AM) Corpus Christi TX
KLTG(FM) Corpus Christi TX
KBHT(FM) Crockett TX
KIVY(AM) Crockett TX
KLUV(FM) Dallas TX
KRRW(FM) Dallas TX
KOFX(FM) El Paso TX
KONO-FM Fredricksburg TX
KJOJ-FM Freeport TX
KFRO-FM Gilmer TX
KKDA(AM) Grand Prairie TX
KCLW(AM) Hamilton TX
KLDE(FM) Houston TX
KNUZ(AM) Houston TX
KQUE(FM) Houston TX
KYOK(AM) Houston TX
KYLR(AM) Huntsville TX
KTXJ(AM) Jasper TX
KNGV(FM) Kingsville TX
KSHN-FM Liberty TX
KFRO(AM) Longview TX
KKCL(FM) Lorenzo TX
KFGI-FM Luling TX
KMVL(AM) Madisonville TX
KCUL-FM Marshall TX
KMND(AM) Midland TX
KTJX(FM) Mission TX
KMBV(FM) Navasota TX
KWBC(AM) Navasota TX
KGNB(AM) New Braunfels TX
KQIP(FM) Odessa TX
KGDD(AM) Paris TX
KOLE(AM) Port Arthur TX
KJCE(AM) Rollingwood TX
KTLU(AM) Rusk TX
KWRW(FM) Rusk TX
KONO(AM) San Antonio TX
KSMG(FM) Seguin TX
KZSP(FM) South Padre Island TX

KXOX-FM Sweetwater TX
KDOK(FM) Tyler TX
KBRE(AM) Cedar City UT
KODJ(FM) Salt Lake City UT
WBLT(AM) Bedford VA
WAPP(FM) Berryville VA
WBBC-FM Blackstone VA
WKLV(AM) Blackstone VA
WCHV(AM) Charlottesville VA
WJJJ(AM) Christiansburg VA
WBOP(FM) Churchville VA
WLCQ(FM) Clarksville VA
WDIC-FM Clinchco VA
WSTK(AM) Colonial Heights VA
WKRE-FM Exmore VA
WGOL(FM) Lynchburg VA
WOLD-FM Marion VA
WSVG(AM) Mount Jackson VA
WMXN(FM) Norfolk VA
WSWV(AM) Pennington Gap VA
WSWV-FM Pennington Gap VA
WROV(AM) Roanoke VA
WANV-FM Staunton VA
WBPP(FM) Strasburg VA
WDCK(FM) Williamsburg VA
WMBG(AM) Williamsburg VA
*WIUJ(FM) St. Thomas VI
WVMT(AM) Burlington VT
WMOO(FM) Derby Center VT
WVNR(AM) Poultney VT
WSYB(AM) Rutland VT
WWSR(AM) St. Albans VT
WMXR(FM) Woodstock VT
KBSG(AM) Auburn WA
KEYF-FM Cheney WA
KEYF(AM) Dishman WA
KRKO(AM) Everett WA
KEYG-FM Grand Coulee WA
KKEE(FM) Long Beach WA
KYKA(FM) Naches WA
*KUBS(FM) Newport WA
KJTT(AM) Oak Harbor WA
KZLN-FM Othello WA
KEYW(FM) Pasco WA
KALE(AM) Richland WA
KXAA(FM) Rock Island WA
KULL(AM) Seattle WA
KBSG-FM Tacoma WA
KMWX(AM) Yakima WA
WJJH(FM) Ashland WI
WOLX-FM Baraboo WI
WBEV(AM) Beaver Dam WI
WGEZ(AM) Beloit WI
WWIS-FM Black River Falls WI
WMBE(AM) Chilton WI
KFIZ-FM Fond du Lac WI
WFAW(AM) Fort Atkinson WI
WMIN(AM) Hudson WI
WHRY(AM) Hurley WI
WKFX(FM) Kaukauna WI
WJBL(FM) Ladysmith WI
WLTU(FM) Manitowoc WI
WDLB(AM) Marshfield WI
WIGM(AM) Medford WI
WIGM-FM Medford WI
WMEQ-FM Menomonie WI
WEMP(AM) Milwaukee WI
WZTR(FM) Milwaukee WI
WOFM(FM) Mosinee WI
WOCO-FM Oconto WI
WOXL(AM) Oshkosh WI
WRDB(AM) Reedsburg WI
WIZD(FM) Rudolph WI
WRIG(AM) Schofield WI
WCNZ(AM) Sheboygan WI
WOSX(FM) Spencer WI
WBOG(FM) Tomah WI
WJJQ(AM) Tomahawk WI
WJJQ-FM Tomahawk WI
WTRW(AM) Two Rivers WI
WVRQ(AM) Viroqua WI
WWRW(FM) Wisconsin Rapids WI
WBTQ(FM) Buckhannon WV
WBUC(AM) Buckhannon WV
WXVA(AM) Charles Town WV
WOBG(AM) Clarksburg WV
WRVC(AM) Huntington WV
WKZG(FM) Keyser WV
WFSP(AM) Kingwood WV
WKAZ(FM) Miami WV
WNST(AM) Milton WV
WCLG(AM) Morgantown WV
WAXS(FM) Oak Hill WV
WADC(AM) Parkersburg WV
WMOV(AM) Ravenswood WV
WRON-FM Ronceverte WV
WOBG-FM Salem WV
WDMX(FM) Vienna WV
WEIR(AM) Weirton WV
KBBS(AM) Buffalo WY
KFBC(AM) Cheyenne WY
KRAE(AM) Cheyenne WY
KODI(AM) Cody WY
KAML-FM Gillette WY
KRKK(AM) Rock Springs WY
KWYO-FM Sheridan WY
KGOS(AM) Torrington WY

Other

See individual station listings for description of programing.

KIKO-FM Claypool AZ
KPLS(AM) Orange CA
*KXPR(FM) Sacramento CA
KVEC(AM) San Luis Obispo CA
KWNK(AM) Simi Valley CA
WPRX(AM) Bristol CT
WHBS(AM) Eatonville FL
WCRM(AM) Fort Myers FL
WCRJ(AM) Jacksonville FL
WVOJ(AM) Jacksonville FL
WMJK(AM) Kissimmee FL
WDDQ(FM) Adel GA
WFVR(AM) Valdosta GA
KSSK(AM) Honolulu HI
KWAI(AM) Honolulu HI
*KSUI(FM) Iowa City IA
KFXD(AM) Nampa ID
WGEN(AM) Geneseo IL
*WTKC(FM) Kankakee IL
*WGVE(FM) Gary IN
KEUN(AM) Eunice LA
KAOK(AM) Lake Charles LA
*WRBH(FM) New Orleans LA
*WMFO(FM) Medford MA
WJDA(AM) Quincy MA
WUOK(AM) West Yarmouth MA
WTRI(AM) Brunswick MD
WGRD(AM) Grand Rapids MI
WKBZ(AM) Muskegon MI
*WNFA(FM) Port Huron MI
*KCCM-FM Moorhead MN
*KGAC(FM) St. Peter MN
KKOZ(AM) Ava MO
WVIO(AM) Blowing Rock NC
WGIV(AM) Charlotte NC
WRDX(FM) Salisbury NC
WERA(AM) Plainfield NJ
KLAV(AM) Las Vegas NV
WACK(AM) Newark NY
WVKZ(AM) Schenectady NY
*WRKC(FM) Wilkes-Barre PA
WIOB(FM) Mayaguez PR
WIOC(FM) Ponce PR
*WLJK(FM) Aiken SC
*WYFV(FM) Cayce SC
*WLTR(FM) Columbia SC
*WEPR(FM) Greenville SC
WJBS(AM) Holly Hill SC
WNFO(AM) Ridgeland SC
*WPLN(FM) Nashville TN
KNTS(AM) Abilene TX
KMIQ(FM) Robstown TX
KEDA(AM) San Antonio TX
*WHRO-FM Norfolk VA
KSBN(AM) Spokane WA
*WHAD(FM) Delafield WI
WIWS(AM) Beckley WV
WKWK(AM) Wheeling WV

Polish

WPNA(AM) Oak Park IL
WNVR(AM) Vernon Hills IL
WNDZ(AM) Portage IN

Polka

KASM(AM) Albany MN
WMBE(AM) Chilton WI
WCFW(FM) Chippewa Falls WI
WTKM(AM) Hartford WI
WTKM-FM Hartford WI
WAUN(FM) Kewaunee WI

Portuguese

KIGS(AM) Hanford CA
KLBS(AM) Los Banos CA
WADS(AM) Ansonia CT
WDJZ(AM) Bridgeport CT
*WFAR(FM) Danbury CT
WFNW(AM) Naugatuck CT
WSPR(AM) Springfield MA
WRCP(AM) Providence RI

Progressive

Includes station formats Alternative, Underground, Hardcore, New Wave and Free Form.

*KRUA(FM) Anchorage AK
KSUA(FM) College AK
*WEGL(FM) Auburn AL
*WTOH(FM) Mobile AL
*WVUA-FM Tuscaloosa AL
*KHDX(FM) Conway AR
*KXRJ(FM) Russellville AR
*KALX(FM) Berkeley CA
KMBY(AM) Capitola CA
*KSPC(FM) Claremont CA
KLLK-FM Fort Bragg CA
*KFSR(FM) Fresno CA
*KPFK(FM) Los Angeles CA
KRFD-FM Marysville CA
*KSFH(FM) Mountain View CA
*KSPB(FM) Pebble Beach CA
*KUCR(FM) Riverside CA
KQPT(FM) Sacramento CA
KFOG(FM) San Francisco CA
*KUSF(FM) San Francisco CA
*KSJS(FM) San Jose CA
*KCPR(FM) San Luis Obispo CA
*KCSB-FM Santa Barbara CA
*KSCU(FM) Santa Clara CA
*KCRW(FM) Santa Monica CA
*KRCB-FM Santa Rosa CA
*KASF(FM) Alamosa CO
*KSJD(FM) Cortez CO

Programming on Radio Stations in the U.S.

KTCL(FM) Fort Collins CO
*KMSA(FM) Grand Junction CO
KISZ-FM Cortez CO
KFMU-FM Oak Creek CO
*WXCI(FM) Danbury CT
*WFCS(FM) New Britain CT
WYBC-FM New Haven CT
*WWUH(FM) West Hartford CT
*WNHU(FM) West Haven CT
*WVUD(FM) Newark DE
*WVUM(FM) Coral Gables FL
*WUCF-FM Orlando FL
*WKGC(AM) Panama City Beach FL
*WKPX(FM) Sunrise FL
*WPRK(FM) Winter Park FL
*WUOG(FM) Athens GA
WNNX(FM) Atlanta GA
*WRAS(FM) Atlanta GA
*WREK(FM) Atlanta GA
WCHZ(FM) Harlem GA
*WGHR(FM) Marietta GA
WPUP(FM) Royston GA
*WVGS(FM) Statesboro GA
*WVVS(FM) Valdosta GA
*KALA(FM) Davenport IA
*KWLC(AM) Decorah IA
*KICB(FM) Fort Dodge IA
*KDIC(FM) Grinnell IA
*KRUI-FM Iowa City IA
*KCUI(FM) Pella IA
*KMSC(FM) Sioux City IA
*WEFT(FM) Champaign IL
*WOUI(FM) Chicago IL
*WRSE-FM Elmhurst IL
*WNUR-FM Evanston IL
*WLCA(FM) Godfrey IL
*WHSD(FM) Hinsdale IL
*WLTL(FM) La Grange IL
*WMXM(FM) Lake Forest IL
*WLNX(FM) Lincoln IL
*WIUS(FM) Macomb IL
*WARG(FM) Summit IL
WSQR(AM) Sycamore IL
WIIZ(FM) Battle Ground IN
*WFCI(FM) Franklin IN
*WGRE(FM) Greencastle IN
KOCD(FM) Columbus KS
KLZR(FM) Lawrence KS
*KSDB-FM Manhattan KS
*KSWC(FM) Winfield KS
*WWHR(FM) Bowling Green KY
*WRFL(FM) Lexington KY
*KLSU(FM) Baton Rouge LA
*KNWD(FM) Natchitoches LA
*WTUL(FM) New Orleans LA
*KSCL(FM) Shreveport LA
*KNSU(FM) Thibodaux LA
*WAMH(FM) Amherst MA
*WBIM-FM Bridgewater MA
*WMBR(FM) Cambridge MA
*WIQH(FM) Concord MA
*WXPL(FM) Fitchburg MA
*WDJM-FM Framingham MA
*WJUL(FM) Lowell MA
WFNX(FM) Lynn MA
*WZBC(FM) Newton MA
*WJJW(FM) North Adams MA
*WSMU-FM North Dartmouth MA
*WMWM(FM) Salem MA
*WBSL-FM Sheffield MA
*WZLY(FM) Wellesley MA
*WKKL(FM) West Barnstable MA
*WSKB(FM) Westfield MA
*WCHC(FM) Worcester MA
*WHFC(FM) Bel Air MD
*WMUC-FM College Park MD
*WKHS(FM) Worton MD
*WUMF-FM Farmington ME
WUFK(FM) Fort Kent ME
*WDET-FM Detroit MI
*WDBM(FM) East Lansing MI
*WTHS(FM) Holland MI
*WIDR(FM) Kalamazoo MI
*WMHW-FM Mount Pleasant MI
*WOVI(FM) Novi MI
*WSDP(FM) Plymouth MI
*WSGR-FM Port Huron MI
*WYCE(FM) Wyoming MI
KTCJ(AM) Minneapolis MN
KTCZ-FM Minneapolis MN
*KUOM(AM) Minneapolis MN
*KUMM(FM) Morris MN
*KVSC(FM) St. Cloud MN
*KDXL(FM) St. Louis Park MN
*WMCN(FM) St. Paul MN
*KYMC(FM) Ballwin MO
*KWUR(FM) Clayton MO
*KCOU(FM) Columbia MO
*KCFV(FM) Ferguson MO
WMBH(AM) Joplin MO
*KKFI(FM) Kansas City MO
WZRH(FM) Picayune MS
WUMS(FM) University MS
*WXYC(FM) Chapel Hill NC
*WSOE(FM) Elon College NC
*WQFS(FM) Greensboro NC
*WUAG(FM) Greensboro NC
*WZMB(FM) Greenville NC
*WWIH(FM) High Point NC
*KFJM(AM) Grand Forks ND
*KDCV-FM Blair NE
*KDNE(FM) Crete NE
KKNB(FM) Crete NE
*KRNU(FM) Lincoln NE
*WUNH(FM) Durham NH
WDCR(AM) Hanover NH
*WNEC-FM Henniker NH
*WKNH(FM) Keene NH
*WNTI(FM) Hackettstown NJ
*WRRC(FM) Lawrenceville NJ
*WMNJ(FM) Madison NJ
*WRPR(FM) Mahwah NJ
*WVPH(FM) Piscataway NJ
*WLFR(FM) Pomona NJ
WPRB(FM) Princeton NJ
*WFDU(FM) Teaneck NJ
*WTSR(FM) Trenton NJ
*WMSC(FM) Upper Montclair NJ
*KEDP(FM) Las Vegas NM
*KUNV(FM) Las Vegas NV
KTHX(FM) Reno NV
*WCDB(FM) Albany NY
WDSP(FM) Arlington NY
*WHRW(FM) Binghamton NY
*WBNY(FM) Buffalo NY
*WHCL-FM Clinton NY
*WCVF-FM Fredonia NY
*WEOS(FM) Geneva NY
*WRCU-FM Hamilton NY
*WRHU(FM) Hempstead NY
*WBER(FM) Henrietta NY
*WITR(FM) Henrietta NY
*WFNP(FM) New Paltz NY
*WNYU-FM New York NY
*WRHO(FM) Oneonta NY
*WDFH(FM) Ossining NY
*WPLT(FM) Plattsburgh NY
*WVKR-FM Poughkeepsie NY
*WIRQ(FM) Rochester NY
*WRUR-FM Rochester NY
*WSPN(FM) Saratoga Springs NY
*WRUC(FM) Schenectady NY
*WPBX(FM) Southampton NY
*WPNR-FM Utica NY
*WONB(FM) Ada OH
*WOUB(AM) Athens OH
*WKHR(FM) Bainbridge OH
*WBWC(FM) Berea OH
*WCSB(FM) Cleveland OH
*WKCO(FM) Gambier OH
*WDUB(FM) Granville OH
WWCD(FM) Grove City OH
*WUSO(FM) Springfield OH
*WHEI(FM) Tiffin OH
*WXUT(FM) Toledo OH
*WUJC(FM) University Heights OH
*WOBN(FM) Westerville OH
*KHIB(FM) Durant OK
KCFO(AM) Tulsa OK
*KBVR(FM) Corvallis OR
*KWVA(FM) Eugene OR
*KTEC(FM) Klamath Falls OR
*KSLC(FM) McMinnville OR
*WBUQ(FM) Bloomsburg PA
*WDNR(FM) Chester PA
*WJRH(FM) Easton PA
*WFSE(FM) Edinboro PA
*WWEC(FM) Elizabethtown PA
*WERG(FM) Erie PA
*WZBT(FM) Gettysburg PA
*WTGP(FM) Greenville PA
*WKVR-FM Huntingdon PA
*WVBU-FM Lewisburg PA
*WARC(FM) Meadville PA
*WMSS(FM) Middletown PA
*WIXQ(FM) Millersville PA
WXVX(AM) Monroeville PA
*WKDU(FM) Philadelphia PA
*WPTS-FM Pittsburgh PA
*WYEP-FM Pittsburgh PA
*WYBF(FM) Radnor Township PA
*WXAC(FM) Reading PA
*WRSK(FM) Slippery Rock PA
*WXVU(FM) Villanova PA
*WXJX(FM) Washington PA
*WCLH(FM) Wilkes-Barre PA
*WRLC(FM) Williamsport PA
*WVYC(FM) York PA
*WRIU(FM) Kingston RI
*WDOM(FM) Providence RI
*WELH(FM) Providence RI
*WJMF(FM) Smithfield RI
*WSBF-FM Clemson SC
*WUSC-FM Columbia SC
*WPLS-FM Greenville SC
*KSDJ(FM) Brookings SD
*KTEQ(FM) Rapid City SD
*KBHU-FM Spearfish SD
*KAOR(FM) Vermillion SD
*WTTU(FM) Cookeville TN
WRLT-FM Franklin TN
*WSMS(FM) Memphis TN
*WRVU(FM) Nashville TN
*WAWL-FM Red Bank TN
*WUTS(FM) Sewanee TN
KGSR(FM) Bastrop TX
*KERA(FM) Dallas TX
*KNON(FM) Dallas TX
*KTCU-FM Fort Worth TX
KDGE(FM) Gainesville TX
KNNC(FM) Georgetown TX
KFAN-FM Johnson City TX
*KSAU(FM) Nacogdoches TX
*KSYM-FM San Antonio TX
*KTSW(FM) San Marcos TX
*KOHS(FM) Orem UT
KHQN(AM) Spanish Fork UT
*WTJU(FM) Charlottesville VA
*WFFC(FM) Ferrum VA
*WWHS-FM Hampden-Sydney VA
*WDCE(FM) Richmond VA
*WCWM(FM) Williamsburg VA
WIVI(FM) Charlotte Amalie VI
*WIUV(FM) Castleton VT
*WJSC-FM Johnson VT
WEQX(FM) Manchester VT
*WRMC-FM Middlebury VT
*KASB(FM) Bellevue WA
*KTCV(FM) Kennewick WA
*KMIH(FM) Mercer Island WA
*KSVR(FM) Mount Vernon WA
*KZUU(FM) Pullman WA
*KCMU(FM) Seattle WA
*KWRS(FM) Spokane WA
*KUPS(FM) Tacoma WA
*WBSD(FM) Burlington WI
*WUEC(FM) Eau Claire WI
*WMSE(FM) Milwaukee WI
*WWSP(FM) Stevens Point WI
*KUWS(FM) Superior WI
*WSUW(FM) Whitewater WI
*WVBC(FM) Bethany WV
*WVWC(FM) Buckhannon WV
*WWVU-FM Morgantown WV
*WSHC(FM) Shepherdstown WV
*WGLZ(FM) West Liberty WV
*KUWJ(FM) Jackson WY
*KUWR(FM) Laramie WY
*KUWZ(FM) Rock Springs WY

Public Affairs

*KYUK(AM) Bethel AK
*KFSK(FM) Petersburg AK
*WSGN(FM) Gadsden AL
KFNN(AM) Mesa AZ
*KUAZ(FM) Tucson AZ
*KPFA(FM) Berkeley CA
*KFCF(FM) Fresno CA
KGER(AM) Long Beach CA
*KSJC-FM Stockton CA
WXVQ(AM) De Land FL
*WUFT-FM Gainesville FL
*WUWF(FM) Pensacola FL
*WPIO(FM) Titusville FL
*WRFG(FM) Atlanta GA
*WWET(FM) Valdosta GA
*WBEZ(FM) Chicago IL
*WSSD(FM) Chicago IL
*WLTL(FM) La Grange IL
*WGLT(FM) Normal IL
*WNIJ(FM) Rockford IL
WAIV(FM) Spring Valley IL
*WFHB(FM) Bloomington IN
WRIN(AM) Rensselaer IN
WOTD(FM) Winamac IN
*WRPS(FM) Rockland MA
*WMEH(FM) Bangor ME
*WMED(FM) Calais ME
*WMEA(FM) Portland ME
*WMEM(FM) Presque Isle ME
*WMEW(FM) Waterville ME
WMPL(AM) Hancock MI
*WMUK(FM) Kalamazoo MI
*KMSK(FM) Austin MN
*KCRB-FM Bemidji MN
*WIRR(FM) Virginia-Hibbing MN
*KCUR-FM Kansas City MO
*KEYA(FM) Belcourt ND
WNBX(FM) Lebanon NH
KSWV(AM) Santa Fe NM
*WNYC(AM) New York NY
WOR(AM) New York NY
*WPSA(FM) Paul Smiths NY
WATJ(AM) Chardon OH
*WOSU(AM) Columbus OH
*WGLE(FM) Lima OH
*WGTE-FM Toledo OH
*WDUQ(FM) Pittsburgh PA
KCCR(AM) Pierre SD
*KUSD(AM) Vermillion SD
*KUSD-FM Vermillion SD
*WQOX(FM) Memphis TN
*KNON(FM) Dallas TX
KULP(AM) El Campo TX
*WTJU(FM) Charlottesville VA
*WHRV(FM) Norfolk VA
*KPBX-FM Spokane WA
WLIP(AM) Kenosha WI
WFHR(AM) Wisconsin Rapids WI
WOTR(FM) Lost Creek WV

Reggae

*KGHR(FM) Tuba City AZ
*WVGS(FM) Statesboro GA
WBRU(FM) Providence RI

Religious

Includes station formats Sacred, Christian and Inspirational.
Also see Gospel.

*KATB(FM) Anchorage AK
KFFR(AM) Eagle River AK
KCAM(AM) Glennallen AK
KAKN(FM) Naknek AK
KIAM(AM) Nenana AK
KICY(AM) Nome AK
KICY-FM Nome AK
KJNP(AM) North Pole AK
KJNP-FM North Pole AK
KRSA(AM) Petersburg AK
WRAB(AM) Arab AL
*WBFR(FM) Birmingham AL
WDJC(FM) Birmingham AL
*WGIB(FM) Birmingham AL
*WVSU-FM Birmingham AL
WYDE(AM) Birmingham AL
WCOX(AM) Camden AL
WYVC(FM) Camden AL
WRAG(AM) Carrollton AL
WKLF(AM) Clanton AL
*WDVI(FM) Dadeville AL
*WYFD(FM) Decatur AL
*WMBV(FM) Dixon's Mills AL
WPYK(AM) Dora AL
*WGTF(FM) Dothan AL
*WVOB(FM) Dothan AL
WWNT(AM) Dothan AL
WKWL(AM) Florala AL
*WBHL(FM) Florence AL
WGEA(AM) Geneva AL
WRJL(AM) Hanceville AL
WEUP(AM) Huntsville AL
WNDA(FM) Huntsville AL
*WOCG(FM) Huntsville AL
WLPH(AM) Irondale AL
*WEBT(FM) Langdale AL
WBHY(AM) Mobile AL
*WBHY-FM Mobile AL
WMOB(AM) Mobile AL
*WLBF(FM) Montgomery AL
WJBY(AM) Rainbow City AL
WXWY(AM) Robertsdale AL
WBTG(AM) Sheffield AL
WBTG-FM Sheffield AL
WYEA(AM) Sylacauga AL
WACT(AM) Tuscaloosa AL
WZZA(AM) Tuscumbia AL
WAPZ(AM) Wetumpka AL
KAAB(AM) Batesville AR
KJEM(AM) Bentonville-Bella Vista AR
KYXZ(AM) Cabot AR
*KZIG(FM) Cave City AR
*KGMR(FM) Clarksville AR
KTCN(FM) Eureka Springs AR
KOFC(AM) Fayetteville AR
KZKZ-FM Greenwood AR
KKOL(FM) Hampton AR
*KALR(FM) Hot Springs AR
KNEA(AM) Jonesboro AR
KAAY(AM) Little Rock AR
KITA(AM) Little Rock AR
KAKJ(FM) Marianna AR
KFTH(FM) Marion AR
KCGS(AM) Marshall AR
*KCMH(FM) Mountain Home AR
KBHC(AM) Nashville AR
KLRG(AM) North Little Rock AR
*KCAT(AM) Pine Bluff AR
KPBA(AM) Pine Bluff AR
KCJC(FM) Russellville AR
*KMTC(FM) Russellville AR
KMTL(AM) Sherwood AR
*KLRC(FM) Siloam Springs AR
KFDF(AM) Van Buren AR
KRWA-FM Waldron AR
KJIW(AM) West Helena AR
KSUD(AM) West Memphis AR
KYTN(FM) Wrightsville AR
KBQN(AM) Pago Pago AS
KGMS(FM) Green Valley AZ
*KNLB(FM) Lake Havasu City AZ
*KWFH(FM) Parker AZ
KASA(AM) Phoenix AZ
*KFLR-FM Phoenix AZ
KHEP(AM) Phoenix AZ
*KPHF(FM) Phoenix AZ
KRDS(AM) Tolleson AZ
KXEG(AM) Tolleson AZ
KTBA(AM) Tuba City AZ
*KFLT(AM) Tucson AZ
KRDS-FM Wickenburg AZ
*KCFY(FM) Yuma AZ
KCNO(AM) Alturas CA
*KCDS(FM) Angwin CA
KBRT(AM) Avalon CA
KHIS(AM) Bakersfield CA
KHIS-FM Bakersfield CA
*KMRO(FM) Camarillo CA
KFIA(AM) Carmichael CA
*KHAP(FM) Chico CA
KDNO(FM) Delano CA
KRDU(AM) Dinuba CA
KECR(AM) El Cajon CA
KECR-FM El Cajon CA
KBAX(FM) Fallbrook CA
KBIF(AM) Fresno CA
*KFNO(FM) Fresno CA
KIRV(AM) Fresno CA
KKLF(FM) Gonzales CA
KKMC(AM) Gonzales CA
KGBA-FM Holtville CA
KTYM(AM) Inglewood CA
KJET(FM) Kingsburg CA
*KEFR(FM) Le Grand CA
*KFRN(AM) Long Beach CA
KGER(AM) Long Beach CA
KFSG(FM) Los Angeles CA
KKLA(FM) Los Angeles CA
*KWXP(FM) Magalia CA
*KAMB(FM) Merced CA
*KADV(FM) Modesto CA
KCIV(FM) Mount Bullion CA
*KEBR-FM North Highlands CA
KMAK(FM) Orange Cove CA
KGDP(AM) Orcutt CA
KDAR(FM) Oxnard CA
KKXX(AM) Paradise CA
KPPC(AM) Pasadena CA
KTSJ(AM) Pomona CA
*KLVM(FM) Prunedale CA
KNLF(FM) Quincy CA
KRDG(AM) Redding CA
*KVIP(AM) Redding CA
*KVIP-FM Redding CA
KCBC(AM) Riverbank CA
KPRO(AM) Riverside CA
*KSGN(FM) Riverside CA
KEBR(AM) Rocklin CA
KAVC(FM) Rosamond CA
*KEDR(FM) Sacramento CA
KJAY(AM) Sacramento CA
KLFE(AM) San Bernardino CA
KWVE(FM) San Clemente CA
*KEAR(FM) San Francisco CA
KFAX(AM) San Francisco CA
KYMS(FM) Santa Ana CA
*KLVR(FM) Santa Rosa CA
KMXN(AM) Santa Rosa CA
*KPRA(FM) Ukiah CA
*KXRD(FM) Victorville CA
*KARM(FM) Visalia CA
KERI(AM) Wasco CA
*KLRD(FM) Yucaipa CA
KQXI(AM) Arvada CO
KLLV(AM) Breen CO
KLTT(AM) Brighton CO
*KTLF(FM) Colorado Springs CO
KWYD(AM) Colorado Springs CO
*KPOF(AM) Denver CO
KRKS(AM) Denver CO
KBIQ(FM) Fountain CO
*KCIC(FM) Grand Junction CO
*KJOL(FM) Grand Junction CO
*KWBI(FM) Morrison CO
KURA(FM) Ouray CO
*KERP(FM) Pueblo CO
KFEL(AM) Pueblo CO
KGFT(FM) Pueblo CO
*WIHS(FM) Middletown CT
WFIF(AM) Milford CT
*WCTF(AM) Vernon CT
WXPZ(FM) Milford DE
WTLN(AM) Apopka FL
WTLN-FM Apopka FL
WKGF(AM) Arcadia FL
WKHF(AM) Avon Park FL
*WTJT(FM) Baker FL
WSWN(AM) Belle Glade FL
*WRMB(FM) Boynton Beach FL
*WJIS(FM) Bradenton FL
WTCL(AM) Chattahoochee FL
*WTBH(FM) Chiefland FL
WTAN(AM) Clearwater FL
*WMIE(FM) Cocoa FL
WWBC(AM) Cocoa FL
WVCG(AM) Coral Gables FL
WMFJ(AM) Daytona Beach FL
WYND(AM) De Land FL
*WJED(FM) Dogwood Lakes Estate FL
*WSEB(FM) Englewood FL
*WNLE(FM) Fernandina Beach FL
*WAFG(FM) Fort Lauderdale FL
WHYI-FM Fort Lauderdale FL
WSRF(AM) Fort Lauderdale FL
*WAYJ(FM) Fort Myers FL
*WJYO(FM) Fort Myers FL
*WPSM(FM) Fort Walton Beach FL
*WJLF(FM) Gainesville FL
*WYFB(FM) Gainesville FL
*WLVF-FM Haines City FL
*WAPN(FM) Holly Hill FL
WLQY(AM) Hollywood FL
WCGL(AM) Jacksonville FL
*WJFR(FM) Jacksonville FL
*WNCM-FM Jacksonville FL
WROS(AM) Jacksonville FL
WVOJ(AM) Jacksonville FL
WXTL(AM) Jacksonville Beach FL
*WJIR(FM) Key West FL
*WOLR(FM) Lake City FL
WLVS(AM) Lake Worth FL
*WCIE-FM Lakeland FL
*WYFO(FM) Lakeland FL
WRFA(AM) Largo FL
*WLMS(FM) Lecanto FL
*WJNF(FM) Marianna FL
WCIF(FM) Melbourne FL
*WMCU(FM) Miami FL
WECM(AM) Milton FL
*WEGS(FM) Milton FL
*WSOR(FM) Naples FL
*WSRX(FM) Naples FL
*WLPJ-FM New Port Richey FL
*WJLU(FM) New Smyrna Beach FL
*WHIJ(FM) Ocala FL
*WWFR(FM) Okeechobee FL
*WAYR(AM) Orange Park FL
WELE(AM) Ormond Beach FL
*WCNO(FM) Palm City FL
WPCF(AM) Panama City Beach FL
WPCF-FM Panama City Beach FL
*WPCS(FM) Pensacola FL
WVTJ(AM) Pensacola FL
WAJL(AM) Pine Castle-Sky Lake FL
*WVIJ(FM) Port Charlotte FL
WLVJ(AM) Royal Palm Beach FL
*WKZM(FM) Sarasota FL
*WFTI-FM St. Petersburg FL

Programming on Radio Stations in the U.S.

*WKES(FM) St. Petersburg FL
WCVC(AM) Tallahassee FL
*WBVM(FM) Tampa FL
WTIS(AM) Tampa FL
*WYFE(FM) Tarpon Springs FL
*WPIO(FM) Titusville FL
*WSCF-FM Vero Beach FL
WHOF(AM) Wildwood FL
WEXY(AM) Wilton Manors FL
WANL(AM) Albany GA
*WGNP(FM) Albany GA
*WMSL(FM) Athens GA
WAEC(AM) Atlanta GA
WAFS(AM) Atlanta GA
WNIV(AM) Atlanta GA
WFAM(AM) Augusta GA
*WLPE(FM) Augusta GA
WBAF(AM) Barnesville GA
WUFE(AM) Baxley GA
WGIA(AM) Blackshear GA
WGMI(AM) Bremen GA
WBYB(FM) Brunswick GA
WPIQ(AM) Brunswick GA
*WPWB(FM) Byron GA
*WCCV(FM) Cartersville GA
*WJCK(FM) Cedartown GA
WVMG-FM Cochran GA
WEAM(AM) Columbus GA
*WFRC(FM) Columbus GA
*WYFK(FM) Columbus GA
WJJC(AM) Commerce GA
WPBS(AM) Conyers GA
WUWU(AM) Cordele GA
WMLB(AM) Cumming GA
*WWEV-FM Cumming GA
WTTI(AM) Dalton GA
WWEV(AM) Decatur GA
WXLL(AM) Decatur GA
WSEM(AM) Donalsonville GA
WOKA(AM) Douglas GA
WTJH(AM) East Point GA
WKLY(AM) Hartwell GA
WGML(AM) Hinesville GA
*WLPT(FM) Jesup GA
*WOAK(FM) La Grange GA
WBML(AM) Macon GA
WFDR(AM) Manchester GA
WVFJ-FM Manchester GA
WFOM(AM) Marietta GA
WFTD(AM) Marietta GA
*WMVV(FM) McDonough GA
WSSA(AM) Morrow GA
WJEP(AM) Ochlocknee GA
WSNT(AM) Sandersville GA
WSNT-FM Sandersville GA
*WHCJ(FM) Savannah GA
*WYFS(FM) Savannah GA
WECC(AM) St. Mary's GA
*WRAF-FM Toccoa Falls GA
WAFT(FM) Valdosta GA
*WGPH(FM) Vidalia GA
WCOP(AM) Warner Robins GA
WRCC(AM) Warner Robins GA
*WAGW(FM) Waynesboro GA
WBRO(AM) Waynesboro GA
WYFA(FM) Waynesboro GA
*WYFW(FM) Winder GA
WZCM(AM) Young Harris GA
KTWG(AM) Agana GU
*KSDA-FM Agat GU
KFSH(FM) Hilo HI
KAIM(AM) Honolulu HI
KAIM-FM Honolulu HI
KLHT(AM) Honolulu HI
KNDI(AM) Honolulu HI
KQCS(FM) Bettendorf IA
*KFGQ(AM) Boone IA
*KFGQ-FM Boone IA
KSKB(FM) Brooklyn IA
KTOF(FM) Cedar Rapids IA
KELR-FM Chariton IA
KLNG(AM) Council Bluffs IA
*KDFR(FM) Des Moines IA
KHKI(FM) Des Moines IA
KWKY(AM) Des Moines IA
*KCMR(FM) Mason City IA
*KYFR(AM) Shenandoah IA
*KDCR(FM) Sioux Center IA
*KNWS(AM) Waterloo IA
*KNWS-FM Waterloo IA
KSPD(AM) Boise ID
KBGN(AM) Caldwell ID
KBXL(FM) Caldwell ID
*KTSY(FM) Caldwell ID
KRSS(FM) Chubbuck ID
KIDH(AM) Eagle ID
*KAWZ(FM) Twin Falls ID
*KCIR(FM) Twin Falls ID
WXAN(FM) Ava IL
*WIBI(FM) Carlinville IL
*WBVN(FM) Carrier Mills IL
WKZI(AM) Casey IL
*WBGL(FM) Champaign IL
*WMBI(AM) Chicago IL
*WMBI-FM Chicago IL
WCFJ(AM) Chicago Heights IL
WCBW(FM) Columbia IL
WYLL(FM) Des Plaines IL
*WDLM(AM) East Moline IL
*WDLM-FM East Moline IL
WBFG(FM) Effingham IL
*WGRN(FM) Greenville IL
WRVY-FM Henry IL
*WJCH(FM) Joliet IL
*WONU(FM) Kankakee IL
*WGSL(FM) Loves Park IL
WGGH(AM) Marion IL
*WPTH(FM) Olney IL
*WBNH(FM) Pekin IL
*WCIC(FM) Pekin IL
WVEL(AM) Pekin IL
WPEO(AM) Peoria IL
WLUJ(FM) Petersburg IL
*WGCA-FM Quincy IL
*WJLY(FM) Ramsey IL
*WFEN(FM) Rockford IL
WQFL(FM) Rockford IL
WQME(FM) Anderson IN
WJLR(FM) Austin IN
WNTS(AM) Beech Grove IN
*WFOF(FM) Covington IN
WFRN(AM) Elkhart IN
WFRN-FM Elkhart IN
WVHI(AM) Evansville IN
*WBGW(FM) Fort Branch IN
*WBCL(FM) Fort Wayne IN
WFCV(AM) Fort Wayne IN
*WLAB(FM) Fort Wayne IN
WPZZ(FM) Franklin IN
WWCA(AM) Gary IN
WYCA(FM) Hammond IN
*WBRI(AM) Indianapolis IN
WXLW(AM) Indianapolis IN
WCFY(AM) Lafayette IN
WWEG(FM) Mitchell IN
WERK(AM) Muncie IN
*WJYL(FM) New Washington IN
WXIR(FM) Plainfield IN
WNDZ(AM) Portage IN
WHME(FM) South Bend IN
*WCRT(FM) Terre Haute IN
WAMW(AM) Washington IN
*WHPL(FM) West Lafayette IN
WWVR(FM) West Terre Haute IN
*WKLO(FM) Westport IN
KEOJ(FM) Caney KS
*KJIL(FM) Copeland KS
KTLI(FM) El Dorado KS
*KNGM(FM) Emporia KS
KCNW(AM) Fairway KS
*KVCY(FM) Fort Scott KS
KGCR(FM) Goodland KS
KKLO(AM) Leavenworth KS
KREJ(FM) Medicine Lodge KS
KJRG(AM) Newton KS
*KTJO-FM Ottawa KS
KCCV(AM) Overland Park KS
KCVS(FM) Salina KS
KFLA(AM) Scott City KS
*KJTY(FM) Topeka KS
KHCA(FM) Wamego KS
*KCFN(FM) Wichita KS
*KIBN(FM) Wichita KS
KSGL(AM) Wichita KS
*KYFW(FM) Wichita KS
WYWY(AM) Barbourville KY
WLJC(FM) Beattyville KY
*WCVK(FM) Bowling Green KY
WOKT(AM) Cannonsburg KY
WKDP(AM) Corbin KY
WWLK(AM) Eddyville KY
WEKT(AM) Elkton KY
WXLN-FM Eminence KY
WIOK(FM) Falmouth KY
*WKCC(FM) Grayson KY
WJMD(FM) Hazard KY
*WNKJ(FM) Hopkinsville KY
WKVG(AM) Jenkins KY
WDFB(AM) Junction City KY
*WVCT(FM) Keavy KY
WKDO(AM) Liberty KY
WFIA(AM) Louisville KY
WHKW(FM) Louisville KY
*WSOF-FM Madisonville KY
WFTM-FM Maysville KY
*WBFI(FM) McDaniels KY
WMOR(AM) Morehead KY
*WJIE(FM) Okolona KY
WYGH(AM) Paris KY
*WJSO(FM) Pikeville KY
WRLV(AM) Salyersville KY
WLCK(AM) Scottsville KY
*WTHL(FM) Somerset KY
WRSL(AM) Stanford KY
WBFC(AM) Stanton KY
WMTC(AM) Vancleve KY
WMTC-FM Vancleve KY
WJMM-FM Versailles KY
WTCW(AM) Whitesburg KY
WBCE(AM) Wickliffe KY
KWDF(AM) Ball LA
WQCK(FM) Clinton LA
KAJN-FM Crowley LA
WBIU(AM) Denham Springs LA
*KVDP(FM) Dry Prong LA
*KPAE(FM) Erwinville LA
KFNV(AM) Ferriday LA
KTOC(AM) Jonesboro LA
*KSJY(FM) Lafayette LA
KLIC(AM) Monroe LA
*KYFL(FM) Monroe LA
WBOK(AM) New Orleans LA
*WBSN-FM New Orleans LA
WSHO(AM) New Orleans LA
WVOG(AM) New Orleans LA
KCIJ(FM) North Fort Polk LA
WLUX(AM) Port Allen LA
KBCL(AM) Shreveport LA
KFLO(AM) Shreveport LA
KIOU(AM) Shreveport LA
KOKA(AM) Shreveport LA
KNCB(AM) Vivian LA
KKAY(AM) White Castle LA
WEZE(AM) Boston MA
WROL(AM) Boston MA
WACE(AM) Chicopee MA
WBMA(AM) Dedham MA
WVNE(AM) Leicester MA
WBIV(AM) Natick MA
*WFSI(FM) Annapolis MD
WBGR(AM) Baltimore MD
WBMD(AM) Baltimore MD
WRBS(FM) Baltimore MD
WWIN(AM) Baltimore MD
WKDI(AM) Denton MD
*WOEL-FM Elkton MD
WFRB(AM) Frostburg MD
*WLIC(FM) Frostburg MD
WJRO(AM) Glen Burnie MD
*WAIJ(FM) Grantsville MD
WCTN(AM) Potomac-Cabin John MD
*WESM(FM) Princess Anne MD
WOLC(FM) Princess Anne MD
*WDIH(FM) Salisbury MD
*WGTS-FM Takoma Park MD
*WCRH(FM) Williamsport MD
*WHCF(FM) Bangor ME
WTME(AM) Lewiston ME
WLOB(AM) Portland ME
WKTQ(AM) South Paris ME
*WUFN(FM) Albion MI
WOLY(AM) Battle Creek MI
*WOLW(FM) Cadillac MI
WLCM(AM) Charlotte MI
WPRJ(FM) Coleman MI
WLQV(AM) Detroit MI
WMUZ(FM) Detroit MI
WLJN(AM) Elmwood Township MI
WTAC(AM) Flint MI
*WPHN(FM) Gaylord MI
*WCSG(FM) Grand Rapids MI
WFUR(AM) Grand Rapids MI
WFUR-FM Grand Rapids MI
WWJQ(AM) Holland MI
WMVN(AM) Ishpeming MI
WKPR(AM) Kalamazoo MI
*WEUL(FM) Kingsford MI
*WMPC(AM) Lapeer MI
*WHWL(FM) Marquette MI
*WUNN(AM) Mason MI
*WUGN(FM) Midland MI
*WPCJ(FM) Pittsford MI
*WNFA(FM) Port Huron MI
WEXL(AM) Royal Oak MI
*WSAE(FM) Spring Arbor MI
*WUFL(AM) Sterling Heights MI
*WLJN-FM Traverse City MI
WWCM(AM) Ypsilanti MI
*WGNB(FM) Zeeland MI
WJQK(FM) Zeeland MI
KJLY(FM) Blue Earth MN
*KDNI(FM) Duluth MN
*KDNW(FM) Duluth MN
*WNCB(FM) Duluth MN
WWJC(AM) Duluth MN
KKCQ-FM Fosston MN
KYCR(AM) Golden Valley MN
KBHW(FM) International Falls MN
WCTS(AM) Maplewood MN
*KTIS(AM) Minneapolis MN
*KTIS-FM Minneapolis MN
KCGN-FM Ortonville MN
KBHL(FM) Osakis MN
KTIG(FM) Pequot Lakes MN
KCUE(AM) Red Wing MN
*KFSI(FM) Rochester MN
KKCM(AM) Shakopee MN
*KCFB(FM) St. Cloud MN
KNOF(FM) St. Paul MN
*KCWA-FM Arnold MO
*KLFC(FM) Branson MO
KZBK(AM) Brookfield MO
*KCVO-FM Camdenton MO
KMFC(FM) Centralia MO
*KFUO(AM) Clayton MO
KSIV(AM) Clayton MO
KGNN(AM) Cuba MO
KEXS(AM) Excelsior Springs MO
KXEN(AM) Festus-St. Louis MO
KFMO(AM) Flat River MO
KUGT(AM) Jackson MO
*KOBC(FM) Joplin MO
*KLJC(FM) Kansas City MO
KLTE(FM) Kirksville MO
*KWJC(FM) Liberty MO
*KJAB-FM Mexico MO
*KLUH(FM) Poplar Bluff MO
*KOKS(FM) Poplar Bluff MO
KADI(FM) Republic MO
KMMC(FM) Salem MO
KLFJ(AM) Springfield MO
*KWFC(FM) Springfield MO
*KWND(FM) Springfield MO
KIRL(AM) St. Charles MO
KGNM(AM) St. Joseph MO
KSTL(AM) St. Louis MO
KALM(AM) Thayer MO
*KGNV(FM) Washington MO
KKLL(AM) Webb City MO
KKLL-FM Webb City MO
KSAI(AM) Saipan MP
WFCA(FM) Ackerman MS
WJBI(AM) Batesville MS
WRJH(FM) Brandon MS
WZFL(AM) Centreville MS
WHJT(FM) Clinton MS
WTWZ(AM) Clinton MS
WFFF(AM) Columbia MS
WACR(AM) Columbus MS
WKCU(AM) Corinth MS
WJKX(FM) Ellisville MS
WEPA(AM) Eupora MS
WHLV(AM) Hattiesburg MS
WORV(AM) Hattiesburg MS
WEEZ(FM) Heidelberg MS
*WURC(FM) Holly Springs MS
WDLJ(FM) Indianola MS
WJXN(AM) Jackson MS
*WJTA(FM) Kosciusko MS
WAML(AM) Laurel MS
WESY(AM) Leland MS
WAPF(AM) McComb MS
WMER(AM) Meridian MS
WNBN(AM) Meridian MS
WNAU(AM) New Albany MS
WOSM(FM) Ocean Springs MS
WZZJ(AM) Pascagoula-Moss Point MS
WSAO(AM) Senatobia MS
*WAFR(FM) Tupelo MS
WLRC(AM) Walnut MS
WJNS-FM Yazoo City MS
KGVW(AM) Belgrade MT
KURL(AM) Billings MT
KGLE(AM) Glendive MT
*NEW FM Great Falls MT
*KXEI(FM) Havre MT
WABZ-FM Albemarle NC
*WLFA(FM) Asheville NC
WBTB(AM) Beaufort NC
WFGW(AM) Black Mountain NC
WMIT(FM) Black Mountain NC
WVIO(AM) Blowing Rock NC
WGCR(AM) Brevard NC
*WCCE(FM) Buie's Creek NC
WVBS(AM) Burgaw NC
WWOF(AM) Camp Lejeune NC
WPTL(AM) Canton NC
WMYT(AM) Carolina Beach NC
WRTP(AM) Chapel Hill NC
WOGR(AM) Charlotte NC
WYFQ(AM) Charlotte NC
WRNA(AM) China Grove NC
WCXN(AM) Claremont NC
WCLN(AM) Clinton NC
WSRC(AM) Durham NC
WTIK(AM) Durham NC
WWMO(AM) Eden NC
WBXB(FM) Edenton NC
WGHB(AM) Farmville NC
WFLB(AM) Fayetteville NC
WAJA(AM) Franklin NC
WLTC(AM) Gastonia NC
WSML(AM) Graham NC
WYCV(AM) Granite Falls NC
WPET(AM) Greensboro NC
WJSG(FM) Hamlet NC
WYFL(FM) Henderson NC
WHPE-FM High Point NC
WOKX(AM) High Point NC
WKMT(AM) Kings Mountain NC
WSGH(AM) Lewisville NC
WWGL(FM) Lexington NC
WLLN(AM) Lillington NC
WNOW(AM) Mint Hill NC
*WOTJ(FM) Morehead City NC
WDJS(AM) Mount Olive NC
WYCM(AM) Murfreesboro NC
WLOJ(AM) New Bern NC
WKBC(AM) North Wilkesboro NC
WCLY(AM) Raleigh NC
WPJL(AM) Raleigh NC
*WPGT(FM) Roanoke Rapids NC
WEGG(AM) Rose Hill NC
WXKL(AM) Sanford NC
WYAL(AM) Scotland Neck NC
WVCB(AM) Shallotte NC
WGAS(AM) South Gastonia NC
WCOK(AM) Sparta NC
WCIE(AM) Spring Lake NC
WCPS(AM) Tarboro NC
WTNC(AM) Thomasville NC
WTYN(AM) Tryon NC
WADE(AM) Wadesboro NC
WFTK(AM) Wake Forest NC
WTOW(AM) Washington NC
WSMY(AM) Weldon NC
WIAM(AM) Williamston NC
WWIL(AM) Wilmington NC
WLLY(AM) Wilson NC
*WRCM(FM) Wingate NC
WBFJ(AM) Winston-Salem NC
WSMX(AM) Winston-Salem NC
*KFNW-FM Fargo ND
KNDR(FM) Mandan ND
KHRT(AM) Minot ND
*KFNW(AM) West Fargo ND
KJSK(AM) Columbus NE
*KTLX(FM) Columbus NE
*KROA(FM) Grand Island NE
*KNGN(AM) McCook NE
*KPNO(FM) Norfolk NE
*KJLT(AM) North Platte NE
KCRO(AM) Omaha NE
*KGBI-FM Omaha NE
KGRD(FM) Orchard NE
KCMI(FM) Terrytown NE
WDER(AM) Derry NH
*WKDN-FM Camden NJ
WTMR(AM) Camden NJ
WNNN(FM) Canton NJ
WSJL(FM) Cape May NJ
*WEEE(FM) Cherry Hill NJ
*WRLJ(FM) Freehold Township NJ
WWDJ(AM) Hackensack NJ
*WCNJ(FM) Hazlet NJ
*WFME(FM) Newark NJ
WCHR(FM) Trenton NJ
WAWZ(FM) Zarephath NJ
KDAZ(AM) Albuquerque NM
*KFLQ(FM) Albuquerque NM
KKIM(AM) Albuquerque NM
*KLYT(FM) Albuquerque NM
*KNMI(FM) Farmington NM
KPCL(FM) Farmington NM
KOBE(AM) Las Cruces NM
KROL(FM) Las Cruces NM
KCKN(AM) Roswell NM
*KWFL(FM) Roswell NM
KHAC(AM) Tse Bonito NM
*KNIS(FM) Carson City NV
*KVCE(FM) Fallon NV
*KILA(FM) Las Vegas NV
KKVV(AM) Las Vegas NV
KXEQ(AM) Reno NV
WUFO(AM) Amherst NY
WCIK(FM) Bath NY
WASB(AM) Brockport NY
WDCX(FM) Buffalo NY
*WFBF(FM) Buffalo NY
*WCIY(FM) Canandaigua NY
*WMHI(FM) Cape Vincent NY
WCHP(AM) Champlain NY
WJIV(FM) Cherry Valley NY
WVOA(FM) DeRuyter NY
WSIV(AM) East Syracuse NY
*WCIH(FM) Elmira NY
*WCID(FM) Friendship NY
WIGS(AM) Gouverneur NY
WNGN(FM) Hoosick Falls NY
WLNL(AM) Horseheads NY
*WJSL(FM) Houghton NY
*WHVP(FM) Hudson NY
WLIX(AM) Islip NY
*WCOT(FM) Jamestown NY
*WFGB(FM) Kingston NY
*WFRH(FM) Kingston NY
WTHE(AM) Mineola NY
*WLJP(FM) Monroe NY
WMCA(AM) New York NY
*WWRV(AM) New York NY
WHLD(AM) Niagara Falls NY
*WNYK(FM) Nyack NY
WZXV(FM) Palmyra NY
*WRPJ(FM) Port Jervis NY
WWWG(AM) Rochester NY
WMYY(FM) Schoharie NY
*WFRS(FM) Smithtown NY
*WCII(FM) Spencer NY
WDCW(AM) Syracuse NY
*WMHR(FM) Syracuse NY
WHAZ(AM) Troy NY
WDCZ(FM) Webster NY
*WFRW(FM) Webster NY
*WMHN(FM) Webster NY
WHLO(AM) Akron OH
*WBCY(FM) Archbold OH
*WCVV(FM) Belpre OH
*WMBP(FM) Belpre OH
WJYM(AM) Bowling Green OH
WTOF-FM Canton OH
WGGN(FM) Castalia OH
*WCDR-FM Cedarville OH
*WOHC(FM) Chillicothe OH
WAKW(FM) Cincinnati OH
WABQ(AM) Cleveland OH
*WCRF(FM) Cleveland OH
*WHVT(FM) Clyde OH
WRFD(AM) Columbus-Worthington OH
*WGOJ(FM) Conneaut OH
*WCUE(AM) Cuyahoga Falls OH
WGNZ(AM) Fairborn OH
WCNW(AM) Fairfield OH
*WCVO(FM) Gahanna OH
WNLT(FM) Harrison OH
WPOS-FM Holland OH
*WCVJ(FM) Jefferson OH
*WFCO(FM) Lancaster OH
*WTGN(FM) Lima OH
WZLE(FM) Lorain OH
*WVMC(FM) Mansfield OH
WFCJ(FM) Miamisburg OH
*WNZR(FM) Mount Vernon OH
WCCD(AM) Parma OH
*WOHP(FM) Portsmouth OH
*WMEJ(FM) Proctorville OH
*WEEC(FM) Springfield OH
*WOTL(FM) Toledo OH
WVOI(AM) Toledo OH
*WXML(FM) Upper Sandusky OH
*WQRP(FM) West Carrollton OH
WBZI(AM) Xenia OH
WGFT(AM) Youngstown OH
*WYTN(FM) Youngstown OH
*WCVZ(FM) Zanesville OH
*KKVO(FM) Altus OK
KEOR(AM) Atoka OK
KNTL(FM) Bethany OK
*KOKF(FM) Edmond OK
*KBVV(FM) Enid OK
*KSYE(FM) Frederick OK
*KVAZ(FM) Henryetta OK
*KVRS(FM) Lawton OK

Programming on Radio Stations in the U.S.

KEMX(FM) Locust Grove OK
KTMC(AM) McAlester OK
KGLC(FM) Miami OK
KVIS(AM) Miami OK
KTLV(AM) Midwest City OK
*KMSI(FM) Moore OK
KBYE(AM) Oklahoma City OK
KQCV(AM) Oklahoma City OK
*KLVV(FM) Ponca City OK
KTOW(AM) Sand Springs OK
KXOJ(AM) Sapulpa OK
KXOJ-FM Sapulpa OK
KHJM(FM) Taft OK
KCFO(AM) Tulsa OK
KHPE(FM) Albany OR
KWIL(AM) Albany OR
KDBX(FM) Banks OR
KNLR(FM) Bend OR
KYTT-FM Coos Bay OR
KPHP(AM) Lake Oswego OR
KDOV(AM) Phoenix OR
*KBVM(FM) Portland OR
KPDQ(AM) Portland OR
KCCS(AM) Salem OR
*KQFE(FM) Springfield OR
KORE(AM) Springfield-Eugene OR
KSKD(FM) Sweet Home OR
KLWJ(AM) Umatilla OR
KGRV(AM) Winston OR
WHOL(AM) Allentown PA
WAVL(AM) Apollo PA
WNCC(AM) Barnesboro PA
*WGEV(FM) Beaver Falls PA
*WITX(FM) Beaver Falls PA
WBFD(AM) Bedford PA
WBYN(FM) Boyertown PA
WCXJ(AM) Braddock PA
WPLW(AM) Carnegie PA
WFKJ(AM) Cashtown PA
WVCH(AM) Chester PA
*WPGM(AM) Danville PA
*WPGM-FM Danville PA
WDBA(FM) DuBois PA
WRDD(AM) Ebensburg PA
*WEFR(FM) Erie PA
*WVMM(FM) Grantham PA
WMRE(AM) Hughesville PA
WJSA(AM) Jersey Shore PA
WJSA-FM Jersey Shore PA
WCRO(AM) Johnstown PA
*WFRJ(FM) Johnstown PA
WDAC(FM) Lancaster PA
*WJTL(FM) Lancaster PA
WLAN(AM) Lancaster PA
*WGRC(FM) Lewisburg PA
WJSM(AM) Martinsburg PA
WJSM-FM Martinsburg PA
WLLF(FM) Mercer PA
*WQJU(FM) Mifflintown PA
*WPEL(AM) Montrose PA
*WPEL-FM Montrose PA
*WRWJ(FM) Murrysville PA
WDAS(AM) Philadelphia PA
WPHY(AM) Philadelphia PA
WZZD(AM) Philadelphia PA
WPHB(AM) Philipsburg PA
WPHE(AM) Phoenixville PA
WORD-FM Pittsburgh PA
WPIT(AM) Pittsburgh PA
WGCB(AM) Red Lion PA
WGCB-FM Red Lion PA
*WBYO(FM) Sellersville PA
WWII(AM) Shiremanstown PA
*WTLR(FM) State College PA
*WRGN(FM) Sweet Valley PA
WCTL(FM) Union City PA
WLIH(FM) Whitneyville PA
WNNV(FM) Aguada PR
WTPM(FM) Aguadilla PR
WRSJ(AM) Bayamon PR
*WCRP(FM) Guayama PR
WCGB(AM) Juana Diaz PR
*WKVN-FM Levittown PR
WNRT(FM) Manati PR
WPPC(AM) Penuelas PR
WBMJ(AM) San Juan PR
WERR(FM) Utuado PR
WIVV(AM) Vieques PR
WRIB(AM) Providence RI
WARV(AM) Warwick RI
*WAGP(FM) Beaufort SC
WVGB(AM) Beaufort SC
WHPB(AM) Belton SC
WTGH(AM) Cayce SC
*WYFV(FM) Cayce SC
*WFCH(FM) Charleston SC
WCTG(AM) Columbia SC
*WMHK(FM) Columbia SC
WQXL(AM) Columbia SC
WFGN(AM) Gaffney SC
*WYFG(FM) Gaffney SC
*WLFJ(FM) Greenville SC
WMUU(AM) Greenville SC
*WTBI-FM Greenville SC
WBHC(AM) Hampton SC
WRIX(AM) Homeland Park SC
WRIP(AM) Lake City SC
WLXP(FM) Marion SC
WMCJ(AM) Moncks Corner SC
WZJY(AM) Mt. Pleasant SC
WCIG(FM) Mullins SC
WKZK(AM) North Augusta SC
*WYFH(FM) North Charleston SC
WPJK(AM) Orangeburg SC
WTBI(AM) Pickens SC
WAVO(AM) Rock Hill SC
WGOG(AM) Walhalla SC
WJKI(AM) Woodruff SC
KVCX(FM) Gregory SD
*KCFS(FM) Sioux Falls SD
KCGN(AM) Sioux Falls SD
*KNWC(AM) Sioux Falls SD
*KNWC-FM Sioux Falls SD
KSLT(FM) Spearfish SD
WATX(AM) Algood TN
WGSF(AM) Arlington TN
WQSV(AM) Ashland City TN
*WPGB(FM) Blountville TN
WBCV(AM) Bristol TN
*WHCB(FM) Bristol TN
*WDYN-FM Chattanooga TN
*WMBW(FM) Chattanooga TN
*WYFC(FM) Clinton TN
WSGM(FM) Coalmont TN
WCRV(AM) Collierville TN
WKBL(AM) Covington TN
WREA(AM) Dayton TN
WENR(AM) Englewood TN
WDRZ-FM Etowah TN
WJKM(AM) Hartsville TN
WJPJ(AM) Huntingdon TN
WQCR(AM) Jackson TN
WDEB(AM) Jamestown TN
WEMG(AM) Knoxville TN
WITA(AM) Knoxville TN
WKXV(AM) Knoxville TN
WRJZ(AM) Knoxville TN
WLAF(AM) La Follette TN
WBLC(AM) Lenoir City TN
WFLI(AM) Lookout Mountain TN
WMSR(AM) Manchester TN
WHDM(AM) McKenzie TN
WMPS(AM) Millington TN
WXRQ(AM) Mt. Pleasant TN
WENO(AM) Nashville TN
WLAC(AM) Nashville TN
*WNAZ-FM Nashville TN
WNQM(AM) Nashville TN
WYFN(AM) Nashville TN
*WDNX(FM) Olive Hill TN
WOCV(AM) Oneida TN
WKJQ(AM) Parsons TN
WSGI(AM) Springfield TN
WJIG(AM) Tullahoma TN
*KAGN(FM) Abilene TX
*KGNZ(FM) Abilene TX
KJAV(FM) Alamo TX
KDRY(AM) Alamo Heights TX
KBIC(FM) Alice TX
KTEK(AM) Alvin TX
KLCJ(AM) Amarillo TX
*KLMN(FM) Amarillo TX
KACT(AM) Andrews TX
KACT-FM Andrews TX
KSKY(AM) Balch Springs TX
KEEP(FM) Bandera TX
KWWJ(AM) Baytown TX
*KTXB(FM) Beaumont TX
KTON(AM) Belton TX
*KBNR(FM) Brownsville TX
KPSM(FM) Brownwood TX
KAGC(AM) Bryan TX
KHLR(FM) Cameron TX
KCZO(FM) Carrizo Springs TX
KJOJ(AM) Conroe TX
*KBNJ(FM) Corpus Christi TX
KCTA(AM) Corpus Christi TX
*KFGG(FM) Corpus Christi TX
KYND(AM) Cypress TX
*KCBI-FM Dallas TX
KGGR(AM) Dallas TX
*KVTT(FM) Dallas TX
KIXL(AM) Del Valle TX
*KOIR(FM) Edinburg TX
KELP(AM) El Paso TX
*KVER(FM) El Paso TX
KVIV(AM) El Paso TX
KPAS(FM) Fabens TX
KIJN(AM) Farwell TX
KIJN-FM Farwell TX
KDFT(AM) Ferris TX
*KHCB(AM) Galveston TX
KPBC(AM) Garland TX
KOKE(FM) Giddings TX
KHYM(AM) Gilmer TX
KTFA(FM) Groves TX
KAWS(AM) Hemphill TX
*KHCB-FM Houston TX
KGOL(AM) Humble TX
*KSBJ(FM) Humble TX
*KBJS(FM) Jacksonville TX
*KJCR(FM) Keene TX
*KBNL(FM) Laredo TX
KVOZ(AM) Laredo TX
KRBA(AM) Lufkin TX
KMVL(AM) Madisonville TX
*KBIB(AM) Marion TX
KCUL(AM) Marshall TX
KRIO(AM) McAllen TX
*KVMV(FM) McAllen TX
KMXO(AM) Merkel TX
KNBO(AM) New Boston TX
*KENT(AM) Odessa TX
*KENT-FM Odessa TX
KKKK(FM) Odessa TX
*KTDN(FM) Palestine TX
*KJIC(FM) Pasadena TX
KUHD(AM) Port Neches TX
KMFM(FM) Premont TX
*KLUX(FM) Robstown TX
*KBMI(FM) Roma TX
*KNLE-FM Round Rock TX
KCRN(AM) San Angelo TX
KCRN-FM San Angelo TX
KSLR(AM) San Antonio TX
*KYFS(FM) San Antonio TX
KCAS(AM) Slaton TX
KJAK(FM) Slaton TX
KCHG(AM) Somerset TX
KPYK(AM) Terrell TX
*KGLY(FM) Tyler TX
*KVNE-FM Tyler TX
*KXBJ(FM) Victoria TX
KBBW(AM) Waco TX
KRGE(AM) Weslaco TX
*KPDR(FM) Wheeler TX
KLLF(AM) Wichita Falls TX
*KMOC(FM) Wichita Falls TX
*KEYY(AM) Provo UT
*KANN(AM) Roy UT
*KUFR(FM) Salt Lake City UT
KHQN(AM) Spanish Fork UT
WTTX(AM) Appomattox VA
WTTX-FM Appomattox VA
WABS(AM) Arlington VA
WAVA(FM) Arlington VA
WPES(AM) Ashland VA
WYFJ(FM) Ashland VA
WLSD(AM) Big Stone Gap VA
WZAP(AM) Bristol VA
WLTK(FM) Broadway VA
WDYL(FM) Chester VA
WGGM(AM) Chester VA
WNLR(AM) Churchville VA
WVOV(AM) Danville VA
WKTR(AM) Earlysville VA
WDCT(AM) Fairfax VA
WFAX(AM) Falls Church VA
WODY(AM) Fieldale VA
*WJYJ(FM) Fredericksburg VA
WGAT(AM) Gate City VA
*WEMC(FM) Harrisonburg VA
WYFT(FM) Luray VA
WBRG(AM) Lynchburg VA
WKPA(AM) Lynchburg VA
*WRVL(FM) Lynchburg VA
WOLD(AM) Marion VA
WTJZ(AM) Newport News VA
WYFI(FM) Norfolk VA
WNVA(AM) Norton VA
WSWV(AM) Pennington Gap VA
WSWV-FM Pennington Gap VA
WPCE(AM) Portsmouth VA
WPMH(AM) Portsmouth VA
WGTH(FM) Richlands VA
WREJ(AM) Richmond VA
WRIS(AM) Roanoke VA
WWWR(AM) Roanoke VA
WCRR(AM) Rural Retreat VA
*WPIR(FM) Salem VA
WKGM(AM) Smithfield VA
WXLZ(AM) St. Paul VA
WKBA(AM) Vinton VA
*WODC(FM) Virginia Beach VA
WPRZ(AM) Warrenton VA
*WPVA(FM) Waynesboro VA
WGOD-FM Charlotte Amalie VI
WGLV(FM) Hartford VT
WMNV(FM) Rupert VT
*WFTF(FM) Rutland VT
WGLY-FM Waterbury VT
KARI(AM) Blaine WA
KGNW(AM) Burien-Seattle WA
*KGTS(FM) College Place WA
KCIS(AM) Edmonds WA
KCMS(FM) Edmonds WA
KTBI(AM) Ephrata WA
KNTR(AM) Ferndale WA
KGHO(AM) Hoquiam WA
KGHO-FM Hoquiam WA
*KARR(AM) Kirkland WA
KDFL(AM) Lakewood WA
*KJVH(FM) Longview WA
*KZOE(FM) Longview WA
KLYN(FM) Lynden WA
KTSL(FM) Medical Lake WA
*KOLU(FM) Pasco WA
*KRLF(FM) Pullman WA
KBLE(AM) Seattle WA
KEEH(FM) Spokane WA
*KMBI(AM) Spokane WA
*KMBI-FM Spokane WA
KSPO(FM) Spokane WA
KUDY(AM) Spokane WA
KVSN(AM) Tumwater WA
*KSOH(FM) Wapato WA
KBBO(AM) Yakima WA
*WORQ(FM) Green Bay WI
WYLO(AM) Jackson WI
WWIB(FM) Ladysmith WI
*WJTY(FM) Lancaster WI
*WNWC(FM) Madison WI
*WGNV(FM) Milladore WI
*WMWK(FM) Milwaukee WI
WVCY(FM) Milwaukee WI
WEMI(FM) Neenah-Menasha WI
WJUB(AM) Plymouth WI
WGMO(FM) Shell Lake WI
*WPFF(FM) Sturgeon Bay WI
WRVM(FM) Suring WI
WKSH(AM) Sussex WI
WVCX(FM) Tomah WI
WJLS(AM) Beckley WV
WRRD(AM) Blennerhassett WV
*WPIB(FM) Bluefield WV
*WFGH(FM) Fort Gay WV
WAMN(AM) Green Valley WV
WEMM(FM) Huntington WV
WVKV(AM) Hurricane WV
WRKP(FM) Moundsville WV
WZAO(AM) Moundsville WV
WOAY(AM) Oak Hill WV
WELD-FM Petersburg WV
WBGS(AM) Point Pleasant WV
WRRL(AM) Rainelle WV
WYKM(AM) Rupert WV
WJYP(FM) South Charleston WV
WSCW(AM) South Charleston WV
WVVW(AM) St. Marys WV
WSGB(AM) Sutton WV
*KCSP(FM) Casper WY
*KPGM(FM) Casper WY
KSHY(AM) Cheyenne WY
KUYO(AM) Evansville WY

Rock/AOR

Includes station formats Rock, Album-Oriented Rock (AOR) and Hard Rock.

KWHL(FM) Anchorage AK
*KCUK(FM) Chevak AK
KSUA(FM) College AK
*KDLG(AM) Dillingham AK
KIYU(AM) Galena AK
KSUP(FM) Juneau AK
*KUHB(FM) St. Paul Island AK
WGCX(FM) Atmore AL
*WEGL(FM) Auburn AL
WZEW(FM) Fairhope AL
WTAK-FM Hartselle AL
WTAK(AM) Huntsville AL
WMXA(FM) Opelika AL
WVNA-FM Tuscumbia AL
KNWA(AM) Bellefonte AR
KKEG(FM) Fayetteville AR
KONZ(FM) Arizona City AZ
KZRX(FM) Globe AZ
KDKB(FM) Mesa-Phoenix AZ
KYOT-FM Phoenix AZ
KEDJ(FM) Sun City AZ
KUKQ(AM) Tempe AZ
KUPD-FM Tempe AZ
KLPX(FM) Tucson AZ
KXXZ(FM) Barstow CA
KRCK(AM) Burbank CA
KOTR(FM) Cambria CA
KFMF(FM) Chico CA
KCLB-FM Coachella CA
*KVHS(FM) Concord CA
KCQR(FM) Ellwood CA
KPIG(FM) Freedom CA
KKDJ(FM) Fresno CA
KRAB(FM) Green Acres CA
KRZR(FM) Hanford CA
KRQK(FM) Lompoc CA
KNAC(FM) Long Beach CA
KCBS-FM Los Angeles CA
KLOS(FM) Los Angeles CA
KBOQ-FM Marina CA
KRFD-FM Marysville CA
KMFB(FM) Mendocino CA
KHOP(FM) Modesto CA
*KSFH(FM) Mountain View CA
*KVMR(FM) Nevada City CA
KDJK(FM) Oakdale CA
KIOZ(FM) Oceanside CA
*KAZU(FM) Pacific Grove CA
KROQ-FM Pasadena CA
KWBR(FM) Pismo Beach CA
KCAL-FM Redlands CA
KRXQ(FM) Roseville CA
KWOD-FM Sacramento CA
KRQC(AM) Salinas CA
KGB-FM San Diego CA
KITS(FM) San Francisco CA
*KLEL(FM) San Jose CA
KOME(FM) San Jose CA
KSJO(FM) San Jose CA
KZOZ(FM) San Luis Obispo CA
KTYD(FM) Santa Barbara CA
*KSCU(FM) Santa Clara CA
KXFX(FM) Santa Rosa CA
KMBY-FM Seaside CA
KKBB(FM) Shafter CA
KRZQ-FM Tahoe City CA
KQYN(FM) Twentynine Palms CA
*KSAK(FM) Walnut CA
*KCEQ(FM) Walnut Creek CA
KLLK(AM) Willits CA
*KASF(FM) Alamosa CO
KSPN-FM Aspen CO
KZYR(FM) Avon CO
KBCO(AM) Boulder CO
KBCO-FM Boulder CO
KSMT(FM) Breckenridge CO
KILO(FM) Colorado Springs CO
*KSJD(FM) Cortez CO
KAZY(FM) Denver CO
KBPI-FM Denver CO
*KCSU-FM Fort Collins CO
KGLN(AM) Glenwood Springs CO
*KMSA(FM) Grand Junction CO
KKYY(FM) Gunnison CO
KPKE(AM) Gunnison CO
*KWSB-FM Gunnison CO
KIDN-FM Hayden CO
KISZ-FM Cortez CO
*KTSC-FM Pueblo CO
KSNO-FM Snowmass Village CO
WRKI(FM) Brookfield CT
*WQAQ(FM) Hamden CT
WCCC-FM Hartford CT
WHCN(FM) Hartford CT
*WESU(FM) Middletown CT
WAVZ(AM) New Haven CT
WPLR(FM) New Haven CT
*WCNI(FM) New London CT
*WDJW(FM) Somers CT
*WWEB(FM) Wallingford CT
WCCC(AM) West Hartford CT
WWDC-FM Washington DC
WZBH(FM) Georgetown DE
*WMPH(FM) Wilmington DE
WFYV-FM Atlantic Beach FL
WRXK-FM Bonita Springs FL
WDRK(FM) Callaway FL
WXTB(FM) Clearwater FL
WJRR(FM) Cocoa Beach FL
WSHE(FM) Fort Lauderdale FL
WKSM(FM) Fort Walton Beach FL
WRUF-FM Gainesville FL
WEOW(FM) Key West FL
WOZN(FM) Key West FL
WWCN(AM) North Fort Myers FL
WDIZ(FM) Orlando FL
WHTQ(FM) Orlando FL
WTKX-FM Pensacola FL
WHPT(FM) Sarasota FL
WZZR(FM) Stuart FL
WGLF(FM) Tallahassee FL
WRZK(FM) Tallahassee FL
WKLS-FM Atlanta GA
WVRK(FM) Columbus GA
WQBZ(FM) Fort Valley GA
WRHQ(FM) Richmond Hill GA
WPUP(FM) Royston GA
WIXV(FM) Savannah GA
*WVVS(FM) Valdosta GA
KZGZ(FM) Agana GU
KAOE(FM) Hilo HI
KPOI-FM Honolulu HI
KAOY(FM) Kealakekua HI
KAUI(FM) Kekaha HI
KAOI-FM Wailuku HI
KDMI(AM) Des Moines IA
KGGO-FM Des Moines IA
*KICB(FM) Fort Dodge IA
KRNA(FM) Iowa City IA
KFMH(FM) Muscatine IA
KFMG(FM) Pella IA
KSEZ(FM) Sioux City IA
KFMW(FM) Waterloo IA
KJOT(FM) Boise ID
*KLHS-FM Lewiston ID
KOZE-FM Lewiston ID
*KAWZ(FM) Twin Falls ID
WHMS-FM Champaign IL
*WPCD(FM) Champaign IL
*WEIU(FM) Charleston IL
WLUP-FM Chicago IL
WWBZ(FM) Chicago IL
WXRT(FM) Chicago IL
WQEZ(FM) Chillicothe IL
WWDZ(FM) Danville IL
WABT(FM) Dundee IL
*WRSE-FM Elmhurst IL
*WTPC(FM) Elsah IL
*WLCA(FM) Godfrey IL
WVVX(FM) Highland Park IL
WYMG(FM) Jacksonville IL
*WCSF(FM) Joliet IL
WLLI-FM Joliet IL
WSMI-FM Litchfield IL
*WLKL(FM) Mattoon IL
WRIK-FM Metropolis IL
WXLP(FM) Moline IL
*WVJC(FM) Mt. Carmel IL
WTAO(FM) Murphysboro IL
*WONC(FM) Naperville IL
WWCT(FM) Peoria IL
WZNF(FM) Rantoul IL
WQLZ(FM) Taylorville IL
*WPGU(FM) Urbana IL
WXLC(FM) Waukegan IL
*WEAX(FM) Angola IN
WIIZ(FM) Battle Ground IN
WTTS(FM) Bloomington IN
*WDSO(FM) Chesterton IN
WIVM(FM) Elwood IN
*WSWI(AM) Evansville IN
WXKE(FM) Fort Wayne IN
*WBDG(FM) Indianapolis IN
WFBQ(FM) Indianapolis IN
WQMF(FM) Jeffersonville IN
WKHY(FM) Lafayette IN
*WPUM(FM) Rensselaer IN
WBFX(AM) Terre Haute IN
*WMHD-FM Terre Haute IN
WZZQ(FM) Terre Haute IN
*WVUR-FM Valparaiso IN
WZZY(FM) Winchester IN
KFFX(FM) Emporia KS
*KJHK(FM) Lawrence KS
KQRC-FM Leavenworth KS
KQNS-FM Lindsborg KS
KMKF(FM) Manhattan KS
*KSDB-FM Manhattan KS
KDVV(FM) Topeka KS
KICT-FM Wichita KS
*KSWC(FM) Winfield KS
WDNS(FM) Bowling Green KY
WAIN(AM) Columbia KY
WCVG(AM) Covington KY
WCPM(AM) Cumberland KY

Programming on Radio Stations in the U.S.

WBPK(FM) Flemingsburg KY
WLLS(AM) Hartford KY
WLLS-FM Hartford KY
WGBF-FM Henderson KY
WKQQ(FM) Lexington KY
WKTG(FM) Madisonville KY
WXKZ-FM Prestonsburg KY
WTGE-FM Baton Rouge LA
KROK(FM) De Ridder LA
WCKW-FM La Place LA
*KNLU(FM) Monroe LA
*KNWD(FM) Natchitoches LA
WRNO-FM New Orleans LA
*WPAA(FM) Andover MA
WBCN(FM) Boston MA
*WRBB(FM) Boston MA
*WBMT(FM) Boxford MA
WBOS(FM) Brookline MA
WHRB(FM) Cambridge MA
*WMBR(FM) Cambridge MA
*WBPV(FM) Charlton MA
*WIQH(FM) Concord MA
*WGAJ(FM) Deerfield MA
WAQY(AM) East Longmeadow MA
*WGAO(FM) Franklin MA
WRSI(FM) Greenfield MA
WPXC(FM) Hyannis MA
WFNX(FM) Lynn MA
*WMLN-FM Milton MA
*WMHC(FM) South Hadley MA
WMVY(FM) Tisbury MA
*WZLY(FM) Wellesley MA
WAAF(FM) Worcester MA
WHFS(FM) Annapolis MD
WIYY(FM) Baltimore MD
*WFWM(FM) Frostburg MD
WXZL(FM) Grasonville MD
WQCM(FM) Halfway MD
*WHSN(FM) Bangor ME
WSTG(FM) Biddeford ME
WKIT-FM Brewer ME
*WUMF-FM Farmington ME
WUFK(FM) Fort Kent ME
WHMX(FM) Lincoln ME
*WMEB-FM Orono ME
WBLM(FM) Portland ME
WTMS-FM Presque Isle ME
*WUPI(FM) Presque Isle ME
WTOS-FM Skowhegan ME
*WQAC-FM Alma MI
WIQB-FM Ann Arbor MI
*WCHW-FM Bay City MI
WRQT(FM) Bear Lake MI
*WBFH(FM) Bloomfield Hills MI
WLLZ(FM) Detroit MI
WRIF(FM) Detroit MI
WGFN(FM) Glen Arbor MI
WLAV(AM) Grand Rapids MI
WLAV-FM Grand Rapids MI
WKLQ(FM) Holland MI
WOLF-FM Houghton MI
WIMK(FM) Iron Mountain MI
WJXQ(FM) Jackson MI
WKLT(FM) Kalkaska MI
WWGZ-FM Lapeer MI
WKQZ(FM) Midland MI
*WEJY(FM) Monroe MI
WDZR(FM) Mount Clemens MI
WAOR(FM) Niles MI
*WBLD(FM) Orchard Lake MI
WKLZ(FM) Petoskey MI
*WSDP(FM) Plymouth MI
*WSGR-FM Port Huron MI
WRKR(FM) Portage MI
WWDX(FM) St. Johns MI
*WNMC-FM Traverse City MI
*WPHS(FM) Warren MI
KQDS(AM) Duluth MN
KQDS-FM Duluth MN
KQRS(AM) Golden Valley MN
KQRS-FM Golden Valley MN
KTCJ(AM) Minneapolis MN
KTCZ-FM Minneapolis MN
KRXX(AM) Minneapolis-St. Paul MN
*KRPR(FM) Rochester MN
WHMH-FM Sauk Rapids MN
*KVSC(FM) St. Cloud MN
*KDXL(FM) St. Louis Park MN
*KSRQ(FM) Thief River Falls MN
*KSMR(FM) Winona MN
KLRQ(FM) Clinton MO
KFMZ(FM) Columbia MO
KSHE(FM) Crestwood MO
KYYS(FM) Kansas City MO
KRXL(FM) Kirksville MO
KTOZ-FM Marshfield MO
*KGSP(FM) Parkville MO
KXUS(FM) Springfield MO
KSPQ(FM) West Plains MO
WWZQ(AM) Aberdeen MS
WWZQ-FM Aberdeen MS
WBSL(AM) Bay St. Louis MS
WXBD(AM) Biloxi MS
WXLS-FM Gulfport MS
WZLQ(FM) Tupelo MS
WUMS(FM) University MS
WSTZ-FM Vicksburg MS
KMMS-FM Bozeman MT
KAAR(FM) Butte MT
KDBM-FM Dillon MT
KQDI-FM Great Falls MT
KZOQ-FM Missoula MT
XETRA-FM Tijuana MX
*WASU-FM Boone NC
*WWCU(FM) Cullowhee NC
WRCQ(FM) Dunn NC
WERX-FM Edenton NC
WKOC(FM) Elizabeth City NC
WXRC(FM) Hickory NC
WXQR(FM) Jacksonville NC
WRFX(FM) Kannapolis NC
WSFL(AM) New Bern NC
*WKNC-FM Raleigh NC
WRDU(FM) Wilson NC
KJKJ(FM) Grand Forks ND
KBQQ(FM) Minot ND
KRRK(FM) Bennington NE
KKOT(FM) Columbus NE
*KINI(FM) Crookston NE
*KSCV(FM) Kearney NE
KIBZ(FM) Lincoln NE
KZMC-FM McCook NE
KEZO-FM Omaha NE
*KWSC(FM) Wayne NE
WHDQ(FM) Claremont NH
WJYY(FM) Concord NH
WFRD(FM) Hanover NH
WGIR-FM Manchester NH
*WPCR-FM Plymouth NH
WHEB(FM) Portsmouth NH
WNNW(AM) Salem NH
WDHA-FM Dover NJ
WHTG-FM Eatontown NJ
*WNTI(FM) Hackettstown NJ
*WJSV(FM) Morristown NJ
*WSOU(FM) South Orange NJ
*WMCX(FM) West Long Branch NJ
WZXL(FM) Wildwood NJ
*KABR(AM) Alamo Community NM
KZRR(FM) Albuquerque NM
KZSS(AM) Albuquerque NM
KDEM(FM) Deming NM
KRWN(FM) Farmington NM
KBAC(FM) Las Vegas NM
*KEDP(FM) Las Vegas NM
KTMN(FM) Los Alamos NM
KSFX(FM) Roswell NM
KZRQ(FM) Santa Fe NM
KSIL(AM) Silver City NM
KTAO(FM) Taos NM
KSNM(FM) Truth or Consequences NM
KEDG(FM) Las Vegas NV
KOMP(FM) Las Vegas NV
KXNO(AM) North Las Vegas NV
KTHX(FM) Reno NV
KZAK(FM) Incline Village NV
KNDE(FM) Sparks NV
KHWK(FM) Tonopah NV
WPYX(FM) Albany NY
*WETD(FM) Alfred NY
*WDWN(FM) Auburn NY
WBAB-FM Babylon NY
WZRQ(FM) Ballston Spa NY
*WGCC-FM Batavia NY
WXPS(FM) Briarcliff Manor NY
*WCWP(FM) Brookville NY
WGR-FM Buffalo NY
*WHCL-FM Clinton NY
*WCEB(FM) Corning NY
*WSUC-FM Cortland NY
WKLL(FM) Frankfort NY
*WBAU(FM) Garden City NY
WDRE-FM Garden City NY
*WGSU(FM) Geneseo NY
*WGFR(FM) Glens Falls NY
WMAX-FM Irondequoit NY
*WICB(FM) Ithaca NY
WVBR-FM Ithaca NY
*WJFF(FM) Jeffersonville NY
*WVCR-FM Loudonville NY
WAQX-FM Manlius NY
WKOJ(FM) Middletown NY
WBWZ(FM) New Paltz NY
WAXQ(FM) New York NY
WNEW(FM) New York NY
WZRC(AM) New York NY
*WRHO(FM) Oneonta NY
WZOZ(FM) Oneonta NY
*WDFH(FM) Ossining NY
*WPOB-FM Plainview NY
WPDH(FM) Poughkeepsie NY
WQBK-FM Rensselaer NY
WRCN-FM Riverhead NY
WCMF(AM) Rochester NY
WCMF-FM Rochester NY
WRQI(FM) South Bristol Township NY
*WSBU(FM) St. Bonaventure NY
*WSIA(FM) Staten Island NY
WOUR(FM) Utica NY
*WARY(FM) Valhalla NY
WCIZ(FM) Watertown NY
WGMF(AM) Watkins Glen NY
WMRW(FM) Westhampton NY
*WAPS(FM) Akron OH
WONE-FM Akron OH
*WZIP(FM) Akron OH
*WRDL(FM) Ashland OH
WRQK(FM) Canton OH
WEBN(FM) Cincinnati OH
WENZ(FM) Cleveland OH
WMMS(FM) Cleveland OH
WBZX(FM) Columbus OH
WLVQ(FM) Columbus OH
WAPQ(FM) Crestline OH
WTUE(FM) Dayton OH
*WWSU(FM) Dayton OH
*WSLN(FM) Delaware OH
*WLFC(FM) Findlay OH
*WHSS(FM) Hamilton OH
WRZR(FM) Johnstown OH
*WKET(FM) Kettering OH
WLSR(FM) Lima OH
*WCMO(FM) Marietta OH
WAQZ(FM) Milford OH
WWJM(FM) New Lexington OH
WNCD(FM) Niles OH
WOXY(FM) Oxford OH
WEEL(FM) Shadyside OH
*WSTB(FM) Streetsboro OH
WIOT(FM) Toledo OH
*WOBN(FM) Westerville OH
KCRC(AM) Enid OK
KATT-FM Oklahoma City OK
KMYZ(AM) Pryor OK
KMYZ-FM Pryor OK
*KAYE-FM Tonkawa OK
KMOD-FM Tulsa OK
KAST-FM Astoria OR
KXIQ(FM) Bend OR
KZZK-FM Creswell OR
KDUK-FM Florence OR
*KEOL(FM) La Grande OR
KBOY-FM Medford OR
KRVC(AM) Medford OR
KZRC(AM) Milwaukie OR
*KRBM(FM) Pendleton OR
KBBT(AM) Portland OR
KGON(FM) Portland OR
KINK(AM) Portland OR
KINK-FM Portland OR
KUFO(FM) Portland OR
KSYD(FM) Reedsport OR
KZZK(AM) Springfield OR
WAYC-FM Bedford PA
WZZO(FM) Bethlehem PA
WBXQ(FM) Cresson PA
*WFSE(FM) Edinboro PA
WRKU-FM Grove City PA
WRVV(FM) Harrisburg PA
*WKVR-FM Huntingdon PA
WIBF-FM Jenkintown PA
*WFNM(FM) Lancaster PA
*WVBU-FM Lewisburg PA
*WNTE(FM) Mansfield PA
WTPA(FM) Mechanicsburg PA
WXVX(AM) Monroeville PA
WPMR(AM) Mount Pocono PA
WRKT(FM) North East PA
WMMR(FM) Philadelphia PA
WDVE(FM) Pittsburgh PA
WRLP(FM) Russell PA
WEZX(FM) Scranton PA
*WQSU(FM) Selinsgrove PA
*WSYC-FM Shippensburg PA
*WRSK(FM) Slippery Rock PA
WZXR(FM) South Williamsport PA
WKYN(FM) St. Marys PA
WHTF(FM) Starview PA
WKGB-FM Susquehanna PA
WPHD(FM) Tioga PA
WPMR-FM Tobyhanna PA
WNBT-FM Wellsboro PA
*WRKC(FM) Wilkes-Barre PA
*WVYC(FM) York PA
WCAD(FM) San Juan PR
*WQRI(FM) Bristol RI
WBRU(FM) Providence RI
WHJY(FM) Providence RI
*WJMF(FM) Smithfield RI
WAVF(FM) Hanahan SC
WKZQ(AM) Myrtle Beach SC
WKZQ-FM Myrtle Beach SC
KSDN-FM Aberdeen SD
*KSDJ(FM) Brookings SD
KSQY(FM) Deadwood SD
KQRN(FM) Mitchell SD
*KAUR(FM) Sioux Falls SD
*KAOR(FM) Vermillion SD
*WAPX-FM Clarksville TN
WXIS(FM) Erwin TN
WRLT-FM Franklin TN
WQUT(FM) Johnson City TN
WEZK(AM) Knoxville TN
WIMZ-FM Knoxville TN
*WUTK-FM Knoxville TN
WKDF(FM) Nashville TN
WRLG(FM) Smyrna TN
WFXS(FM) Soddy-Daisy TN
KEYJ-FM Abilene TX
*KACV-FM Amarillo TX
KATP(FM) Amarillo TX
KLBJ-FM Austin TX
KGSR(FM) Bastrop TX
*KWTS(FM) Canyon TX
*KRSM(FM) Dallas TX
KDZR(FM) Denton TX
KLAQ(FM) El Paso TX
KEGL(FM) Fort Worth TX
KTXQ(FM) Fort Worth TX
KRTX(FM) Galveston TX
KNNC(FM) Georgetown TX
KLOL(FM) Houston TX
KRBE(AM) Houston TX
*KSHU(FM) Huntsville TX
KWVS(FM) Kingsville TX
KUTZ(FM) Lampasas TX
KFMX-FM Lubbock TX
KBAT(FM) Midland TX
KKHQ(FM) Odem TX
KIOC(FM) Orange TX
KISS-FM San Antonio TX
KNCN(FM) Sinton TX
KTAL-FM Texarkana TX
KBER(FM) Ogden UT
KJOE(AM) Ogden UT
KKBE-FM Ogden UT
KXRK(FM) Provo UT
KRSP-FM Salt Lake City UT
KNUC(FM) Smithfield UT
WVVV(FM) Blacksburg VA
WREL-FM Buena Vista VA
WROX-FM Cape Charles VA
WWWV(FM) Charlottesville VA
*WLCX(FM) Farmville VA
*WXJM(FM) Harrisonburg VA
WROV-FM Martinsville VA
WNOR(AM) Norfolk VA
WNOR-FM Norfolk VA
WRVH(AM) Richmond VA
WRXL(FM) Richmond VA
WVGO(FM) Richmond VA
WKDW-FM Staunton VA
WRCY(FM) Warrenton VA
WIVI(FM) Charlotte Amalie VI
WTBN(FM) Charlotte Amalie VI
WBFL(FM) Bellows Falls VT
WKVT-FM Brattleboro VT
WIZN(FM) Vergennes VT
*WWPV-FM Colchester VT
WEBK(FM) Killington VT
*WWLR(FM) Lyndonville VT
WEQX(FM) Manchester VT
WNCS(FM) Montpelier VT
*WNUB-FM Northfield VT
*WVTC(FM) Randolph Center VT
WVMX(FM) Stowe VT
WVAY(FM) Wilmington VT
KDUX-FM Aberdeen WA
*KGRG(FM) Auburn WA
*KASB(FM) Bellevue WA
KISM(FM) Bellingham WA
*KMIH(FM) Mercer Island WA
*KUBS(FM) Newport WA
KEGX(FM) Richland WA
KISW(FM) Seattle WA
KNDD(FM) Seattle WA
KXRX(FM) Seattle WA
KEZE-FM Spokane WA
*KSFC(FM) Spokane WA
KMTT-FM Tacoma WA
KHSS(FM) Walla Walla WA
*KWCW(FM) Walla Walla WA
*KYSC(FM) Yakima WA
WAPL-FM Appleton WI
*WORQ(FM) Green Bay WI
WIIL(FM) Kenosha WI
WIBA-FM Madison WI
WLZR(AM) Milwaukee WI
WLZR-FM Milwaukee WI
WQFM(FM) Milwaukee WI
*WSUP(FM) Platteville WI
*WRPN-FM Ripon WI
*WSHS(FM) Sheboygan WI
WKBH-FM Trempealeau WI
WMMM-FM Verona WI
*WCLQ(FM) Wausau WI
WCZR(AM) Charleston WV
*WCDE(FM) Elkins WV
WRLF(FM) Fairmont WV
WTCS(AM) Fairmont WV
WQZK-FM Keyser WV
WVKM(FM) Matewan WV
WCOZ(AM) St. Albans WV
WKLC-FM St. Albans WV
WEGW(FM) Wheeling WV
KGWY(FM) Gillette WY
KMTN(FM) Jackson WY
KSIT(FM) Rock Springs WY

Spanish

KVVA-FM Apache Junction AZ
KAPR(AM) Douglas AZ
KDAP(AM) Douglas AZ
KZLZ(FM) Kearny AZ
KOHT(FM) Marana AZ
*KNAI(FM) Phoenix AZ
KPHX(AM) Phoenix AZ
KVVA(AM) Phoenix AZ
KQTL(AM) Sahuarita AZ
KXEW(AM) South Tucson AZ
KTZR(AM) Tucson AZ
KMAX(FM) Arcadia CA
KAFY(AM) Bakersfield CA
KIWI(FM) Bakersfield CA
*KTQX(FM) Bakersfield CA
KWAC(AM) Bakersfield CA
KICO(AM) Calexico CA
KQVO(FM) Calexico CA
KELF(FM) Camarillo CA
*KMRO(FM) Camarillo CA
KLOC(AM) Ceres CA
KOQO(AM) Clovis CA
KWRM(AM) Corona CA
KCHJ(AM) Delano CA
KRGO(AM) Fowler CA
KBRG(FM) Fremont CA
KGST(AM) Fresno CA
KOQO-FM Fresno CA
*KSJV(FM) Fresno CA
KXEX(AM) Fresno CA
KAZA(AM) Gilroy CA
KMPG(AM) Hollister CA
KGBA-FM Holtville CA
KMXX(FM) Imperial CA
KBZT(AM) Indio CA
KTAA(FM) Kerman CA
KLFA(FM) King City CA
KRKC-FM King City CA
KUNA(FM) La Quinta CA
KJOP(AM) Lemoore CA
KNTO(FM) Livingston CA
KCVR(AM) Lodi CA
KLAX-FM Long Beach CA
KKHJ(AM) Los Angeles CA
KLVE(FM) Los Angeles CA
KTNQ(AM) Los Angeles CA
KWKW(AM) Los Angeles CA
KXED(AM) Los Angeles CA
KLBS(AM) Los Banos CA
KHOT(AM) Madera CA
KMMM(FM) Madera CA
KSUV(AM) McFarland CA
KSUV-FM McFarland CA
KFIE(FM) Merced CA
KLOQ(AM) Merced CA
*KMPO(FM) Modesto CA
KHPY(AM) Moreno Valley CA
KNSE(AM) Ontario CA
KOXR(AM) Oxnard CA
KUTY(AM) Palmdale CA
KZSA(FM) Placerville CA
KTRO(AM) Port Hueneme CA
KCAL(AM) Redlands CA
KDIF(AM) Riverside CA
KRCX(AM) Roseville CA
KCTY(AM) Salinas CA
KRAY-FM Salinas CA
KTGE(AM) Salinas CA
KURS(AM) San Diego CA
KIQI(AM) San Francisco CA
KALI(AM) San Gabriel CA
KLOK(AM) San Jose CA
KOFY(AM) San Mateo CA
KWIZ(AM) Santa Ana CA
KSPE(AM) Santa Barbara CA
KNTA(AM) Santa Clara CA
KSBQ(AM) Santa Maria CA
KTAP(AM) Santa Maria CA
*KBBF(FM) Santa Rosa CA
KMXN(AM) Santa Rosa CA
KRRS(AM) Santa Rosa CA
KSTN-FM Stockton CA
KGEN(AM) Tulare CA
KZWC(FM) Walnut Creek CA
KMQA-FM West Covina CA
KIQS(AM) Willows CA
KBNO(AM) Denver CO
KJME(AM) Denver CO
KCUV(AM) Englewood CO
KRMX(AM) Pueblo CO
KRRU(AM) Pueblo CO
KVVS(AM) Windsor CO
WADS(AM) Ansonia CT
WCUM(AM) Bridgeport CT
WDJZ(AM) Bridgeport CT
WXCT(AM) Hamden CT
WLAT(AM) Manchester CT
WFNW(AM) Naugatuck CT
WRYM(AM) New Britain CT
WTAN(AM) Clearwater FL
WAFC(AM) Clewiston FL
WXXU(AM) Cocoa Beach FL
WRHC(AM) Coral Gables FL
WHBS(AM) Eatonville FL
WCRM(AM) Fort Myers FL
WRTO(FM) Goulds FL
WCMQ-FM Hialeah FL
WRFM(AM) Hialeah FL
WLQY(AM) Hollywood FL
WOIR(AM) Homestead FL
WXDJ(FM) Homestead FL
WZOR(AM) Immokalee FL
WTRU(FM) Jupiter FL
WZMQ(FM) Key Largo FL
WWCL(AM) Lehigh Acres FL
WAQI(AM) Miami FL
*WDNA(FM) Miami FL
WOCN(AM) Miami FL
WQBA(AM) Miami FL
WQBA-FM Miami FL
WSUA(AM) Miami FL
WWFE(AM) Miami FL
WCMQ(AM) Miami Springs FL
WKAT(AM) North Miami FL
WUNA(AM) Ocoee FL
WOKC(AM) Okeechobee FL
WRMQ(AM) Orlando FL
WONQ(AM) Oviedo FL
WRNE(AM) Pensacola FL
WOEQ(AM) Royal Palm Beach FL
WTMY(AM) Sarasota FL
WRMD(AM) St. Petersburg FL
WAMA(AM) Tampa FL
WQBN(AM) Temple Terrace FL
WAUC(AM) Wauchula FL
WXTO(AM) Winter Garden FL
WAOS(AM) Austell GA
WXEM(AM) Buford GA
WLBA(AM) Gainesville GA
WAZX(AM) Smyrna GA

Broadcasting & Cable Yearbook 1994
B-566

Programming on Radio Stations in the U.S.

*KBSU(AM) Boise ID
KWEI(AM) Weiser ID
WCRW(AM) Chicago IL
WEDC(AM) Chicago IL
WIND(AM) Chicago IL
*WMBI(AM) Chicago IL
WOPA(AM) Chicago IL
WCGO(AM) Chicago Heights IL
WOJO(FM) Evanston IL
WONX(AM) Evanston IL
WTAQ(AM) La Grange IL
WKGA(AM) Zion IL
KGLA(AM) Gretna LA
WADU(AM) Norco LA
WUNR(AM) Brookline MA
WACE(AM) Chicopee MA
WLLH(AM) Lowell MA
WACM(AM) West Springfield MA
*WCUW(FM) Worcester MA
WILC(AM) Laurel MD
WMDO(AM) Wheaton MD
WNNW(AM) Salem NH
*WCNJ(FM) Hazlet NJ
WREY(AM) Millville NJ
WSKQ(AM) Newark NJ
WMIZ(AM) Vineland NJ
KABQ(AM) Albuquerque NM
KXKS(AM) Albuquerque NM
KARS(AM) Belen NM
KATK(AM) Carlsbad NM
KCCC(AM) Carlsbad NM
KICA(AM) Clovis NM
KDCE(AM) Espanola NM
KHOB(AM) Hobbs NM
KOBE(AM) Las Cruces NM
KFUN(AM) Las Vegas NM
KNMX(AM) Las Vegas NM
KALY(AM) Los Ranchos de Albuquerque NM
KCRX(AM) Roswell NM
KRDD(AM) Roswell NM
KSWV(AM) Santa Fe NM
KKIT(AM) Taos NM
KDOL(AM) Henderson NV
KLAV(AM) Las Vegas NV
*WBER(FM) Henrietta NY
WADO(AM) New York NY
*WHCR-FM New York NY
*WKCR-FM New York NY
WKDM(AM) New York NY
WSKQ-FM New York NY
*WWRV(AM) New York NY
KZUE(AM) El Reno OK
KTLV(AM) Midwest City OK
KWBY(AM) Woodburn OR
*WLCH(FM) Lancaster PA
WTEL(AM) Philadelphia PA
WPHE(AM) Phoenixville PA
WNNV(FM) Aguada PR
WIVA-FM Aguadilla PR
WNOZ(AM) Aguadilla PR
WTPM(FM) Aguadilla PR
WCMN(AM) Arecibo PR
WMIA(AM) Arecibo PR
WNIK(AM) Arecibo PR
WNIK-FM Arecibo PR
WNEL(AM) Caguas PR
WVJP(AM) Caguas PR
WIDA(AM) Carolina PR
*WIDA-FM Carolina PR
WLEY(AM) Cayey PR
WBRQ(FM) Cidra PR
WBJA(AM) Guayama PR
WMEG(FM) Guayama PR
WXRF(AM) Guayama PR
WEGM(FM) Hormigueros PR
WALO(AM) Humacao PR
WKSA-FM Isabela PR
WCGB(AM) Juana Diaz PR
WAVB(AM) Lajas PR
WMNT(AM) Manati PR
WAEL(AM) Mayaguez PR
WOYE-FM Mayaguez PR
WPRA(AM) Mayaguez PR
WTIL(AM) Mayaguez PR
WMTI(AM) Morovis PR
WPPC(AM) Penuelas PR
WEUC(AM) Ponce PR
WLEO(AM) Ponce PR
WPAB(AM) Ponce PR
WPRP(AM) Ponce PR
WZAR(FM) Ponce PR
WZBS(AM) Ponce PR
WKVN(AM) Quebradillas PR
WQQZ(FM) Quebradillas PR
WYKO(AM) Sabana Grande PR
WHOY(AM) Salinas PR
WAPA(AM) San Juan PR
WIAC(AM) San Juan PR
WQBS(AM) San Juan PR
WQII(AM) San Juan PR
WRAI(AM) San Juan PR
*WRTU(FM) San Juan PR
WSKN(AM) San Juan PR
WZNT(FM) San Juan PR
WERR(FM) Utuado PR
WUPR(AM) Utuado PR
WSAN(FM) Vieques PR
WXEW(AM) Yabucoa PR
WENA(AM) Yauco PR
WKFE(AM) Yauco PR
WRCP(AM) Providence RI
WRIB(AM) Providence RI
WKRI(AM) West Warwick RI
KBBA(AM) Abilene TX
KDSI(AM) Alice TX
KZIP(AM) Amarillo TX
KIBL(AM) Beeville TX
KFRD(AM) Bellville TX
KFLZ(FM) Bishop TX
*KBNR(FM) Brownsville TX
KBOR(AM) Brownsville TX
KKPS(FM) Brownsville TX
KMIL(AM) Cameron TX
KBEN(AM) Carrizo Springs TX
KRVA(AM) Cockrell Hill TX
KCOM(AM) Comanche TX
*KBNJ(FM) Corpus Christi TX
KCCT(AM) Corpus Christi TX
KUNO(AM) Corpus Christi TX
KHER(FM) Crystal City TX
KTDR(FM) Del Rio TX
KEPS(AM) Eagle Pass TX
*KOIR(FM) Edinburg TX
KTMR(AM) Edna TX
KAMA(AM) El Paso TX
KBNA(AM) El Paso TX
KBNA-FM El Paso TX
KELP(AM) El Paso TX
KFNA(AM) El Paso TX
KSVE(AM) El Paso TX
*KVER(FM) El Paso TX
KVIV(AM) El Paso TX
KELG(AM) Elgin TX
KKLB(FM) Elgin TX
KPAS(FM) Fabens TX
KPSO(AM) Falfurrias TX
KPSO-FM Falfurrias TX
KRIO-FM Floresville TX
KESS(AM) Fort Worth TX
KFJZ(AM) Fort Worth TX
KTNO(AM) Fort Worth TX
*KHCB(AM) Galveston TX
KQQK(FM) Galveston TX
KCLW(AM) Hamilton TX
KGBT(AM) Harlingen TX
KIWW(FM) Harlingen TX
KRME(AM) Hondo TX
KEYH(AM) Houston TX
KLAT(AM) Houston TX
KXYZ(AM) Houston TX
KERB(AM) Kermit TX
KERB-FM Kermit TX
*KBNL(FM) Laredo TX
KDOS(AM) Laredo TX
*KHOY(FM) Laredo TX
KJBZ(FM) Laredo TX
KLVT(AM) Levelland TX
KYMI(FM) Los Ybanez TX
KLFB(AM) Lubbock TX
KTNP(AM) Lubbock TX
KXTQ(AM) Lubbock TX
*KBIB(AM) Marion TX
KQXX(FM) McAllen TX
KRIO(AM) McAllen TX
KRVA-FM McKinney TX
KTJN(FM) Mercedes TX
KMXO(AM) Merkel TX
KJBC(AM) Midland TX
KWEL(AM) Midland TX
KIRT(AM) Mission TX
KTJX(FM) Mission TX
KLBO(AM) Monahans TX
KIMP(AM) Mount Pleasant TX
KKYC(FM) Muleshoe TX
KMUL(AM) Muleshoe TX
KMRK-FM Odessa TX
KOZA(AM) Odessa TX
KLVL(AM) Pasadena TX
KVWG(AM) Pearsall TX
KVWG-FM Pearsall TX
KIUN(AM) Pecos TX
*KWLD(FM) Plainview TX
KLTN(FM) Port Arthur TX
KMFM(FM) Premont TX
KVDL(AM) Quanah TX
KCLR(AM) Ralls TX
KCTM(FM) Rio Grande City TX
KSAB(FM) Robstown TX
*KBMI(FM) Roma TX
KMPQ-FM Rosenberg TX
KMPQ(AM) Rosenberg-Richmond TX
KCOR(AM) San Antonio TX
KENS(AM) San Antonio TX
KXTN(AM) San Antonio TX
KUKA(FM) San Diego TX
KXEB(AM) Sherman TX
KTLR-FM Terrell TX
KYST(AM) Texas City TX
KSAH(AM) Universal City TX
KUVA(FM) Uvalde TX
KVOU(AM) Uvalde TX
KEPG(FM) Victoria TX
KRGE(AM) Weslaco TX
KTXZ(AM) West Lake Hills TX
KSVN(AM) Ogden UT
KTUR(AM) Tooele UT
KRGQ(AM) West Valley City UT
WRRA(AM) Frederiksted VI
KZHR(FM) Dayton WA
*KSVR(FM) Mount Vernon WA
KYXE(AM) Selah WA
KREW(AM) Sunnyside WA
KKMO(AM) Tacoma WA
KSMX(AM) Walla Walla WA
KWWX(AM) Wenatchee WA
*KDNA(FM) Yakima WA
KZTA(AM) Yakima WA
KZTA-FM Yakima WA
WBJX(AM) Racine WI

Sports

KBYR(AM) Anchorage AK
KIAK(AM) Fairbanks AK
WAGF(AM) Dothan AL
WGAD(AM) Gadsden AL
WKNI(AM) Lexington AL
WKRG(AM) Mobile AL
WACV(AM) Montgomery AL
WLWI(AM) Montgomery AL
WVNA(AM) Tuscumbia AL
KEWI(AM) Benton AR
KBIS(AM) Little Rock AR
KKTZ(FM) Mountain Home AR
KARV(AM) Russellville AR
KCKY(AM) Coolidge AZ
KNNS(AM) Glendale AZ
KJAA(AM) Globe AZ
KIKO(AM) Miami AZ
KNST(AM) Tucson AZ
KTUC(AM) Tucson AZ
KKAL(AM) Arroyo Grande CA
KHSJ(AM) Hemet CA
KMPC(AM) Los Angeles CA
KMYC(AM) Marysville CA
KBEE(AM) Modesto CA
KNRY(AM) Monterey CA
KTOX(AM) Needles CA
KORV(AM) Oroville CA
KLOA(AM) Ridgecrest CA
KCTC(AM) Sacramento CA
KSAC(AM) Sacramento CA
KNBR(AM) San Francisco CA
KVEC(AM) San Luis Obispo CA
KQXI(AM) Arvada CO
KYBG(AM) Aurora CO
KBOL(AM) Boulder CO
KVOR(AM) Colorado Springs CO
KOA(AM) Denver CO
KNZZ(AM) Grand Junction CO
KCSJ(AM) Pueblo CO
KSPK(FM) Walsenburg CO
WWDC(AM) Washington DC
WSBR(AM) Boca Raton FL
WXVQ(AM) De Land FL
WNUE(AM) Fort Walton Beach FL
WNZS(AM) Jacksonville FL
WOKV(AM) Jacksonville FL
WDSR(AM) Lake City FL
WINZ(AM) Miami FL
WQAM(AM) Miami FL
WTMC(AM) Ocala FL
WLTG(AM) Panama City FL
WHNZ(AM) Pinellas Park FL
WFNS(AM) Plant City FL
WBZT(AM) West Palm Beach FL
WWZN(AM) Winter Park FL
WALG(AM) Albany GA
WRFC(AM) Athens GA
WGUN(AM) Atlanta GA
WGAC(AM) Augusta GA
WGIG(AM) Brunswick GA
WDUN(AM) Gainesville GA
WCEH(AM) Hawkinsville GA
WTRP(AM) La Grange GA
WKXK(AM) Macon GA
WMAZ(AM) Macon GA
WLML(FM) Montezuma GA
WCNN(AM) North Atlanta GA
WLAQ(AM) Rome GA
WEAS(AM) Savannah GA
WWNS(AM) Statesboro GA
WVOP(AM) Vidalia GA
KPUA(AM) Hilo HI
KGU(AM) Honolulu HI
KAOI(AM) Kihei HI
KCFI(AM) Cedar Falls IA
KWKY(AM) Des Moines IA
KAYL-FM Storm Lake IA
KFXD(AM) Nampa ID
WKKD(AM) Aurora IL
WBYS-FM Canton IL
WMVP(AM) Chicago IL
WSCR(AM) Chicago IL
WDAN(AM) Danville IL
WDZ(AM) Decatur IL
WGEN-FM Geneseo IL
WINU(AM) Highland IL
WLUV(AM) Loves Park IL
WLUV-FM Loves Park IL
WTAZ(FM) Morton IL
WFMB(AM) Springfield IL
WTAX(AM) Springfield IL
WFRX(AM) West Frankfort IL
WFRX-FM West Frankfort IL
KFNS(AM) Wood River IL
WLTH(AM) Gary IN
WJNZ(FM) Greencastle IN
WNDE(AM) Indianapolis IN
WIMS(AM) Michigan City IN
WGL-FM Roanoke IN
WIWO(AM) South Bend IN
WSBT(AM) South Bend IN
WBOW(AM) Terre Haute IN
WAOV(AM) Vincennes IN
KMAN(AM) Manhattan KS
WIBW(AM) Topeka KS
WDXR(AM) Paducah KY
WKYX(AM) Paducah KY
WPAD(AM) Paducah KY
WIBR(AM) Baton Rouge LA
WJBO(AM) Baton Rouge LA
WASO(AM) Covington LA
KPCH(FM) Dubach LA
KWHN-FM Haynesville LA
KACY(AM) Lafayette LA
KEEL(AM) Shreveport LA
KFLO(AM) Shreveport LA
WARA(AM) Attleboro MA
WEEI(AM) Boston MA
WHTB(AM) Fall River MA
WEIM(AM) Fitchburg MA
WVEI(AM) Worcester MA
WTEM(AM) Bethesda MD
WETT(AM) Ocean City MD
WTGM(AM) Salisbury MD
WIDE(AM) Biddeford ME
WNSW(AM) Brewer ME
WOXO-FM Norway ME
WLPZ(AM) Westbrook ME
WMAX(AM) Bay City MI
WPLB(AM) Greenville MI
WKHM(AM) Jackson MI
WQSN(AM) Kalamazoo MI
WSFN(AM) Muskegon MI
WPHM(AM) Port Huron MI
KBUN(AM) Bemidji MN
KLIZ(AM) Brainerd MN
KFAN(AM) Minneapolis MN
WCMP-FM Pine City MN
KMSR(FM) Sauk Centre MN
KHMO(AM) Hannibal MO
KLWT(AM) Lebanon MO
KTTR(AM) Rolla MO
KMOX(AM) St. Louis MO
KTUI-FM Sullivan MO
WCPC(AM) Houston MS
WHNY(AM) McComb MS
WGUD(AM) Moss Point MS
KMAY(AM) Billings MT
XETRA(AM) Tijuana MX
WBAG(AM) Burlington-Graham NC
WAQS(AM) Charlotte NC
WDNC(AM) Durham NC
WTIK(AM) Durham NC
WZBO(AM) Edenton NC
WNCT(AM) Greenville NC
WLXN(AM) Lexington NC
WMYN(AM) Mayodan NC
WYLT(AM) Raleigh NC
WCAB(AM) Rutherfordton NC
WSAT(AM) Salisbury NC
WSTP(AM) Salisbury NC
WBMS(AM) Wilmington NC
WTSN(AM) Dover NH
WLTN(AM) Littleton NH
WGIR(AM) Manchester NH
WCQL(AM) Portsmouth NH
WSKR(FM) Petersburg NJ
KDEF(AM) Albuquerque NM
KENO(AM) Las Vegas NV
KVEG(AM) North Las Vegas NV
KPLY(AM) Sparks NV
WPTR(AM) Albany NY
WWKB(AM) Buffalo NY
WVNC(FM) Canton NY
WIGS(AM) Gouverneur NY
WIQT(AM) Horseheads NY
WHCU(AM) Ithaca NY
WTKO(AM) Ithaca NY
WFAN(AM) New York NY
WADR(AM) Remsen NY
WRNY(AM) Rome NY
*WAER(FM) Syracuse NY
WASN(AM) Campbell OH
WERE(AM) Cleveland OH
WKNR(AM) Cleveland OH
WWWE(AM) Cleveland OH
WONE(AM) Dayton OH
WOHI(AM) East Liverpool OH
WTIG(AM) Massillon OH
WBLY(AM) Springfield OH
WKBN(AM) Youngstown OH
KGND(FM) Ketchum OK
WWLS(AM) Moore OK
WBBZ(AM) Ponca City OK
KAKC(AM) Tulsa OK
KQLL(AM) Tulsa OK
KITO(AM) Vinita OK
KXTD(AM) Wagoner OK
KAST(AM) Astoria OR
KGRL(AM) Bend OR
KDUK(AM) Eugene OR
KFXX(AM) Oregon City OR
KTIL-FM Tillamook OR
WCBG(AM) Chambersburg PA
WCPA(AM) Clearfield PA
WPDC(AM) Elizabethtown PA
WPSE(AM) Erie PA
WTYM(AM) Kittanning PA
WIP(AM) Philadelphia PA
WPIC(AM) Sharon PA
WFXX(AM) South Williamsport PA
WYCK(AM) Wilkes-Barre PA
WAEL(AM) Mayaguez PR
WICE(AM) Pawtucket RI
WOON(AM) Woonsocket RI
WVAA(AM) Burnettown SC
WCCP(AM) Clemson SC
WPCC(AM) Clinton SC
WPCC(AM) Clinton SC
WDSC(AM) Dillon SC
WRHM(FM) Lancaster SC
KBFS(AM) Belle Fourche SD
WJZM(AM) Clarksville TN
WYYB(FM) Dickson TN
WJCW(AM) Johnson City TN
WQLA-FM La Follette TN
WHBQ(AM) Memphis TN
WREC(AM) Memphis TN
WGNS(AM) Murfreesboro TN
WLAC(AM) Nashville TN
WATO(AM) Oak Ridge TN
KPUR(AM) Amarillo TX
KSKY(AM) Balch Springs TX
WTAW(AM) College Station TX
KSIX(AM) Corpus Christi TX
KRLD(AM) Dallas TX
KURV(AM) Edinburg TX
KGVL(AM) Greenville TX
KTRH(AM) Houston TX
KEEE(AM) Nacogdoches TX
KQHN(AM) Nederland TX
KZEP(AM) San Antonio TX
*KTSW(FM) San Marcos TX
KCMC(AM) Texarkana TX
KSEV(AM) Tomball TX
KTBB(AM) Tyler TX
KSUB(AM) Cedar City UT
KALL(AM) Salt Lake City UT
KISN(AM) Salt Lake City UT
KTLE-FM Tooele UT
KNFL(AM) Tremonton UT
WXBQ(AM) Bristol VA
WDCT(AM) Fairfax VA
WHAP(AM) Hopewell VA
WLRV(AM) Lebanon VA
WLLL(AM) Lynchburg VA
WGH(AM) Newport News VA
WRVH(AM) Richmond VA
WHLF(AM) South Boston VA
WJLC(FM) South Boston VA
WYVE(AM) Wytheville VA
WVMT(AM) Burlington VT
WDEV-FM Warren VT
WDEV(AM) Waterbury VT
KLKI(AM) Anacortes WA
KCIS(AM) Edmonds WA
KONP(AM) Port Angeles WA
KIRO(AM) Seattle WA
KJR(AM) Seattle WA
KJRB(AM) Spokane WA
KTRW(AM) Spokane WA
KREW-FM Sunnyside WA
WRDN-FM Durand WI
WBIZ(AM) Eau Claire WI
KFIZ(AM) Fond du Lac WI
WHBY(AM) Kimberly WI
WTMJ(AM) Milwaukee WI
WEVR(AM) River Falls WI
WDOR-FM Sturgeon Bay WI
WCAW(AM) Charleston WV
WCHS(AM) Charleston WV
WOTR(FM) Lost Creek WV
WKWK(AM) Wheeling WV
KRSV(AM) Afton WY

Talk

Includes stations with formats discussion, interview, information. Also see News/Talk.

KENI(AM) Anchorage AK
*KYUK(AM) Bethel AK
KAKQ(AM) Fairbanks AK
WASG(AM) Atmore AL
WCEO(AM) Birmingham AL
WDJC(FM) Birmingham AL
WAJF(AM) Decatur AL
WIJK(AM) Evergreen AL
WHEP(AM) Foley AL
*WLRH(FM) Huntsville AL
WTKI(AM) Huntsville AL
WKNI(AM) Lexington AL
WBHY(AM) Mobile AL
WQLS-FM Ozark AL
KEWI(AM) Benton AR
*KUCA(FM) Conway AR
KBTM(AM) Jonesboro AR
KBIS(AM) Little Rock AR
KWAK(AM) Stuttgart AR
KWYN-FM Wynne AR
KCKY(AM) Coolidge AZ
KJAA(AM) Globe AZ
KVOI(AM) Oro Valley AZ
KHEP(AM) Phoenix AZ
*KNAI(FM) Phoenix AZ
KRDS(AM) Tolleson AZ
KORG(AM) Anaheim CA
KBRT(AM) Avalon CA
KNZR(AM) Bakersfield CA
KTOT(FM) Big Bear Lake CA
*KUBO(FM) Calexico CA
KWTY(FM) Cartago CA
KDNO(FM) Delano CA
KEYQ(AM) Fresno CA
KKTR(AM) Fresno CA
*KXSR(FM) Groveland CA
KABC(AM) Los Angeles CA
KFI(AM) Los Angeles CA
KYOS(AM) Merced CA
KVOY(AM) Mojave CA
KNRY(AM) Monterey CA

Programming on Radio Stations in the U.S.

KDAR(FM) Oxnard CA
KCMJ(AM) Palm Springs CA
KKXX(AM) Paradise CA
KPRL(AM) Paso Robles CA
KMNY(AM) Pomona CA
KSTE(AM) Rancho Cordova CA
KQMS(AM) Redding CA
KFOX(FM) Redondo Beach CA
KAVC(FM) Rosamond CA
KJAY(AM) Sacramento CA
KLFE(AM) San Bernardino CA
KSDO(AM) San Diego CA
KEST(AM) San Francisco CA
KFAX(AM) San Francisco CA
KGO(AM) San Francisco CA
KSFO(AM) San Francisco CA
KVEC(AM) San Luis Obispo CA
KPRZ(AM) San Marcos CA
KQSB(AM) Santa Barbara CA
KSMA(AM) Santa Maria CA
KUHL(AM) Santa Maria CA
KPSL(AM) Thousand Palms CA
KOBO(AM) Yuba City CA
KYBG(AM) Aurora CO
KTWK(AM) Colorado Springs CO
KWYD(AM) Colorado Springs CO
KHTH(AM) Dillon CO
KCUV(AM) Englewood CO
KSTR(AM) Grand Junction CO
KTLK(AM) Thornton CO
WICC(AM) Bridgeport CT
WPRX(AM) Bristol CT
WQQQ(FM) Sharon CT
WATR(AM) Waterbury CT
WUST(AM) Washington DC
WWRC(AM) Washington DC
WYUS(AM) Milford DE
WNCM(AM) Atlantic Beach FL
WTKS(FM) Cocoa Beach FL
WYND(AM) De Land FL
WKIQ(AM) Eustis FL
WFTL(AM) Fort Lauderdale FL
WINK(AM) Fort Myers FL
WGGG(AM) Gainesville FL
WDSR(AM) Lake City FL
WWAB(AM) Lakeland FL
WQHL(AM) Live Oak FL
WFFG(AM) Marathon FL
WMEL(AM) Melbourne FL
WOCN(AM) Miami FL
WQAM(AM) Miami FL
WSBH(AM) Miami Beach FL
WPGS(AM) Mims FL
*WLPJ-FM New Port Richey FL
WPSO(AM) New Port Richey FL
WBRD(AM) Palmetto FL
WCOA(AM) Pensacola FL
WSWL(AM) Pensacola FL
WGTO(AM) Pine Hills FL
WDCQ(AM) Pine Island Center FL
WFNS(AM) Plant City FL
WWNN(AM) Pompano Beach FL
WLVJ(AM) Royal Palm Beach FL
WTRR(AM) Sanford FL
WTMY(AM) Sarasota FL
WMRZ(AM) South Miami FL
WAOC(AM) St. Augustine FL
WHOF(AM) Wildwood FL
WBYB(FM) Brunswick GA
WHIE(AM) Griffin GA
WCEH(AM) Hawkinsville GA
WNEX(AM) Macon GA
WSSA(AM) Morrow GA
WMGA(AM) Moultrie GA
WLAQ(AM) Rome GA
WROM(AM) Rome GA
WEAS(AM) Savannah GA
WADX(AM) Trenton GA
KGUM(AM) Agana GU
KHLO(AM) Hilo HI
KIPA(AM) Hilo HI
KIKI(AM) Honolulu HI
KAOI(AM) Kihei HI
KCFI(AM) Cedar Falls IA
KILR-FM Estherville IA
KIWA-FM Sheldon IA
*KWDM(FM) West Des Moines IA
KSPD(AM) Boise ID
WRIK(AM) Brookport IL
*WBEZ(FM) Chicago IL
WJJD(AM) Chicago IL
WLS(AM) Chicago IL
WLS-FM Chicago IL
WITY(AM) Danville IL
WDZ(AM) Decatur IL
WGIL(AM) Galesburg IL
WGNU(AM) Granite City IL
WJIL(AM) Jacksonville IL
WMIX(AM) Mt. Vernon IL
WJBD(AM) Salem IL
WIZZ(AM) Streator IL
WHBU(AM) Anderson IN
WBQR(FM) Attica IN
WBIW(AM) Bedford IN
WBRI(AM) Indianapolis IN
WBTO(AM) Linton IN
WQTY(FM) Linton IN
WGOM(AM) Marion IN
WMRS(FM) Monticello IN
WERK(AM) Muncie IN
WGAB(AM) Newburgh IN
WIWO(AM) South Bend IN
WAOV(AM) Vincennes IN

KWBW(AM) Hutchinson KS
KMAJ(AM) Topeka KS
WOKT(AM) Cannonsburg KY
WKDP(AM) Corbin KY
WHOP(AM) Hopkinsville KY
WLBN(AM) Lebanon KY
WVLK(AM) Lexington KY
*WUOL(FM) Louisville KY
WWKY(AM) Louisville KY
WKYX(AM) Paducah KY
WSFC(AM) Somerset KY
KKRP(FM) Delhi LA
WBIU(AM) Denham Springs LA
KPEL-FM Erath LA
KACY(AM) Lafayette LA
KNOC(AM) Natchitoches LA
*WRBH(FM) New Orleans LA
WSHO(AM) New Orleans LA
WVOG(AM) New Orleans LA
WEEI(AM) Boston MA
WEZE(AM) Boston MA
WHDH(AM) Boston MA
WRKO(AM) Boston MA
WROL(AM) Boston MA
WSSH(AM) Boston MA
WMSX(AM) Brockton MA
WSAR(AM) Fall River MA
WGAW(AM) Gardner MA
WNTN(AM) Newton MA
WBRK(AM) Pittsfield MA
WMAS(AM) Springfield MA
WUOK(AM) West Yarmouth MA
WNNZ(AM) Westfield MA
WTAG(AM) Worcester MA
WCBM(AM) Baltimore MD
WMET(AM) Gaithersburg MD
WICO(AM) Salisbury MD
WTHU(AM) Thurmont MD
WZON(AM) Bangor ME
WABK(AM) Gardiner ME
WTOX(AM) Lincoln ME
WLOB(AM) Portland ME
WLPZ(AM) Westbrook ME
WATZ(AM) Alpena MI
WKYO(AM) Caro MI
WMKT(AM) Charlevoix MI
WPLB(AM) Greenville MI
WKHM(AM) Jackson MI
*WGVU(AM) Kentwood MI
WCAR(AM) Livonia MI
WIFN(AM) Marine City MI
WSFN(AM) Muskegon MI
WIOS(AM) Tawas City MI
WPON(AM) Walled Lake MI
WYGR(AM) Wyoming MI
KQAQ(AM) Austin MN
KKBJ(AM) Bemidji MN
*KBPR(FM) Brainerd MN
KMOM(AM) Monticello MN
KWEB(AM) Rochester MN
KSTP(AM) St. Paul MN
KYOO(AM) Bolivar MO
*KKFI(FM) Kansas City MO
KWTO(AM) Springfield MO
KGNM(AM) St. Joseph MO
KSLQ-FM Washington MO
WCJU(AM) Columbia MS
WKRA(AM) Holly Springs MS
WSLI(AM) Jackson MS
WAPF(AM) McComb MS
WLRM(AM) Ridgeland MS
WELO(AM) Tupelo MS
KMAY(AM) Billings MT
KURL(AM) Billings MT
KMSL(AM) Great Falls MT
KBSR(AM) Laurel MT
KJJR(AM) Whitefish MT
WXLX(AM) Albemarle NC
*WLFA(FM) Asheville NC
WBTB(AM) Beaufort NC
WRAQ(AM) Brevard NC
WZBO(AM) Edenton NC
WGHB(AM) Farmville NC
WIDU(AM) Fayetteville NC
WGNC(AM) Gastonia NC
WSML(AM) Graham NC
WNCT(AM) Greenville NC
WOOW(AM) Greenville NC
WKTE(AM) King NC
WEWO(AM) Laurinburg NC
WMAP(AM) Monroe NC
WSTP(AM) Salisbury NC
WSIC(AM) Statesville NC
WYNA(FM) Tabor City NC
WRRF(AM) Washington NC
WBMS(AM) Wilmington NC
*KDSU(FM) Fargo ND
KQWB(AM) Fargo ND
KAMI(AM) Cozad NE
*KGBI-FM Omaha NE
KOLT(AM) Scottsbluff NE
WKBK(AM) Keene NH
WEMJ(AM) Laconia NH
WNTK-FM New London NH
WNTK(AM) Newport NH
WCQL(AM) Portsmouth NH
WFPG(AM) Atlantic City NJ
WMID(AM) Atlantic City NJ
*WNJN(FM) Atlantic City NJ
*WVPH(FM) Piscataway NJ
WKXW(FM) Trenton NJ
WNJC(AM) Washington Township NJ

KPSA(AM) Alamogordo NM
KDAZ(AM) Albuquerque NM
KSVP(AM) Artesia NM
KRSN(AM) Los Alamos NM
KTNM(AM) Tucumcari NM
*KNIS(FM) Carson City NV
KKVV(AM) Las Vegas NV
KVEG(AM) North Las Vegas NV
KFBI(FM) Pahrump NV
KPLY(AM) Sparks NV
WWKB(AM) Buffalo NY
WCHP(AM) Champlain NY
WDNY(AM) Dansville NY
WDNY-FM Dansville NY
WZZZ(AM) Fulton NY
WBZA(AM) Glens Falls NY
WHHO(AM) Hornell NY
WLEA(AM) Hornell NY
WJTN(AM) Jamestown NY
WABC(AM) New York NY
WMCA(AM) New York NY
WWRL(AM) New York NY
WKRL(AM) North Syracuse NY
WHTK(AM) Rochester NY
WVKZ(AM) Schenectady NY
WHEN(AM) Syracuse NY
WIBX(AM) Utica NY
*WRMU(FM) Alliance OH
WBNO-FM Bryan OH
WQCT(AM) Bryan OH
WRCW(AM) Canton OH
*WCDR-FM Cedarville OH
WSAI(AM) Cincinnati OH
WONE(AM) Dayton OH
WOHI(AM) East Liverpool OH
WFOB(AM) Fostoria OH
*WCVO(FM) Gahanna OH
WMOH(AM) Hamilton OH
WNIR(FM) Kent OH
WMOA(AM) Marietta OH
*WOHP(FM) Portsmouth OH
WBLY(AM) Springfield OH
WBTC(AM) Uhrichsville OH
WKFI(AM) Wilmington OH
WKBN(AM) Youngstown OH
*WCVZ(FM) Zanesville OH
WHIZ-FM Zanesville OH
KOKB(AM) Blackwell OK
KTRT(AM) Claremore OK
KXOL(AM) Clinton OK
KADS(AM) Elk City OK
KRAF(AM) Holdenville OK
KXKY(FM) Holdenville OK
KKRX(AM) Lawton OK
KCFO(AM) Tulsa OK
KRMG(AM) Tulsa OK
KNND(AM) Cottage Grove OR
KDBS(AM) Eugene OR
KPHP(AM) Lake Oswego OR
KNPT(AM) Newport OR
KFXX(AM) Oregon City OR
KKEY(AM) Portland OR
KOHI(AM) St. Helens OR
WRTA(AM) Altoona PA
WMBA(AM) Ambridge PA
WBYN(FM) Boyertown PA
WCXJ(AM) Braddock PA
WESA(AM) Charleroi PA
WRDD(AM) Ebensburg PA
WHJB(AM) Greensburg PA
WBCW(AM) Jeannette PA
WCRO(AM) Johnstown PA
WNPV(AM) Lansdale PA
WLBR(AM) Lebanon PA
WEDO(AM) McKeesport PA
WMLP(AM) Milton PA
WOYL(AM) Oil City PA
WKQV(FM) Olyphant PA
WDAS(AM) Philadelphia PA
WHAT(AM) Philadelphia PA
WWDB(FM) Philadelphia PA
WHYM(AM) Portage PA
WEEU(AM) Reading PA
WCHE(AM) West Chester PA
WYCK(AM) Wilkes-Barre PA
WWPA(AM) Williamsport PA
WBEM(AM) Windber PA
WQXA(AM) York PA
WMDD(AM) Fajardo PR
WEUC(AM) Ponce PR
WAPA(AM) San Juan PR
WRAI(AM) San Juan PR
WIVV(AM) Vieques PR
WXEW(AM) Yabucoa PR
WALE(AM) Providence RI
WAIM(AM) Anderson SC
WVAA(AM) Burnettown SC
WTMA(AM) Charleston SC
WCCP(AM) Clemson SC
WTMZ(AM) Dorchester Terrace-Brentwood SC
WMNY(AM) Elloree-Santee SC
WFIS(AM) Fountain Inn SC
WHHR(AM) Hilton Head Island SC
WDKD(AM) Kingstree SC
WJAY(AM) Mullins SC
WAJY(FM) New Ellenton SC
WJZS(AM) Orangeburg SC
KMSD(AM) Milbank SD
*WHCB(FM) Bristol TN
WDOD(AM) Chattanooga TN
WJZM(AM) Clarksville TN
WAEW(AM) Crossville TN

WTNN(AM) Farragut TN
WQCR(AM) Jackson TN
WTJS(AM) Jackson TN
WAKI(AM) McMinnville TN
*WSMS(FM) Memphis TN
WWEZ(FM) Trenton TN
WENK(AM) Union City TN
WBRY(AM) Woodbury TN
KNTS(AM) Abilene TX
KPUR(AM) Amarillo TX
KFON(AM) Austin TX
KRYS(AM) Corpus Christi TX
KGBS(AM) Dallas TX
KGGR(AM) Dallas TX
KLIF(AM) Dallas TX
*KVTT(FM) Dallas TX
KROD(AM) El Paso TX
KTSM(AM) El Paso TX
KPSO-FM Falfurrias TX
KGVL(AM) Greenville TX
KXYZ(AM) Houston TX
KGNB(AM) New Braunfels TX
KZXS(AM) San Antonio TX
KSTV(AM) Stephenville TX
KSTV-FM Stephenville TX
KSEV(AM) Tomball TX
KTBB(AM) Tyler TX
KYZS(AM) Tyler TX
KTXZ(AM) West Lake Hills TX
KUTA(AM) Blanding UT
KVNU(AM) Logan UT
KTKK(AM) Sandy UT
WAVA(FM) Arlington VA
WMEK(AM) Chase City VA
WKCY(AM) Harrisonburg VA
WHAP(AM) Hopewell VA
WBRG(AM) Lynchburg VA
WLVA(AM) Lynchburg VA
WMXQ(FM) Lynchburg VA
WJFK-FM Manassas VA
WHEE(AM) Martinsville VA
WGH(AM) Newport News VA
WNVA(AM) Norton VA
WESR(AM) Onley-Onancock VA
*WVTF(FM) Roanoke VA
WRAR(AM) Tappahannock VA
WINC(AM) Winchester VA
WVMT(AM) Burlington VT
KELA(AM) Centralia-Chehalis WA
KOZI(AM) Chelan WA
KOZI-FM Chelan WA
KCIS(AM) Edmonds WA
KTBI(AM) Ephrata WA
KNTR(AM) Ferndale WA
KDFL(AM) Lakewood WA
KLAY(AM) Lakewood WA
*KUBS(FM) Newport WA
KGDN(FM) Pasco WA
KVI(AM) Seattle WA
KJRB(AM) Spokane WA
KSPO(FM) Spokane WA
KTRW(AM) Spokane WA
*WLFM(FM) Appleton WI
*WLBL(AM) Auburndale WI
*WHSA(FM) Brule WI
WBIZ(AM) Eau Claire WI
*WGBW(FM) Green Bay WI
*WHHI(FM) Highland WI
*WHLA(FM) La Crosse WI
*WHWC(FM) Menomonie WI
WISN(AM) Milwaukee WI
*WHBM-FM Park Falls WI
WTOQ(AM) Platteville WI
*KUWS(FM) Superior WI
WTMB(AM) Tomah WI
WTRW(AM) Two Rivers WI
*WHRM(FM) Wausau WI
WAMN(AM) Green Valley WV
WRKP(FM) Moundsville WV
WETZ(AM) New Martinsville WV
WLTP(AM) Parkersburg WV
WRON(AM) Ronceverte WV
KGOS(AM) Torrington WY

Urban Contemporary

WNSP(FM) Bay Minette AL
WATV(AM) Birmingham AL
WENN-FM Birmingham AL
WJJN(FM) Dothan AL
WQLW(FM) Eutaw AL
WJLD(AM) Fairfield AL
WSBM(AM) Florence AL
WAGH(FM) Fort Mitchell AL
WMGJ(AM) Gadsden AL
WHOG(AM) Hobson City AL
WEUP(AM) Huntsville AL
WAJO(AM) Marion AL
WBLX-FM Mobile AL
WGOK(AM) Mobile AL
WZMG(AM) Opelika AL
WZHT(FM) Troy AL
WTUG(FM) Tuscaloosa AL
WZZA(AM) Tuscumbia AL
WBIL(AM) Tuskegee AL
WSLY(FM) York AL
KXAR-FM Hope AR
KAKJ(FM) Marianna AR
*KCAT(AM) Pine Bluff AR
KIPR(FM) Pine Bluff AR
KZYP(FM) Pine Bluff AR
KCLT(FM) West Helena AR
KJLH-FM Compton CA

KOJJ(FM) East Porterville CA
KMXZ(FM) Hollister CA
KAEV(FM) Lake Arrowhead CA
KKBT(FM) Los Angeles CA
KKMG(FM) Pueblo CO
*WQTQ(FM) Hartford CT
WNHC(AM) New Haven CT
WYBC-FM New Haven CT
WKND(AM) Windsor CT
WHUR-FM Washington DC
WKYS(FM) Washington DC
WSWN(AM) Belle Glade FL
WYFX(AM) Boynton Beach FL
WTCL(AM) Chattahoochee FL
WHQT(FM) Coral Gables FL
WJHM(FM) Daytona Beach FL
WJBT(FM) Green Cove Springs FL
WZOR(AM) Immokalee FL
WRNE(AM) Pensacola FL
WXSR(FM) Quincy FL
WRBQ(AM) St. Petersburg FL
WRXB(AM) St. Petersburg Beach FL
WHBX(FM) Tallahassee FL
WTMP(AM) Temple Terrace FL
WFEZ(FM) Williston FL
WJIZ-FM Albany GA
WALR(FM) Athens GA
WVEE(FM) Atlanta GA
WFXA-FM Augusta GA
WRDW(AM) Augusta GA
WHJX-FM Brunswick GA
WQVE(FM) Camilla GA
WFXE(FM) Columbus GA
WFXM-FM Forsyth GA
WSKX(FM) Hinesville GA
WMXY(AM) Hogansville GA
WBKZ(AM) Jefferson GA
WEAS-FM Savannah GA
WHGH(AM) Thomasville GA
WGOV(AM) Valdosta GA
WBRO(AM) Waynesboro GA
WAKB(FM) Wrens GA
*KALA(FM) Davenport IA
*KDIC(FM) Grinnell IA
*WCRX(FM) Chicago IL
*WCYC(FM) Chicago IL
WGCI-FM Chicago IL
WJPC(AM) Chicago IL
*WKKC(FM) Chicago IL
WVON(AM) Cicero IL
*WRRG(FM) River Grove IL
*WARG(FM) Summit IL
WBCP(AM) Urbana IL
WGZB-FM Corydon IN
WTLC-FM Indianapolis IN
WJFX(FM) New Haven IN
*WISU(FM) Terre Haute IN
*KIBN(FM) Wichita KS
*KSWC(FM) Winfield KS
WIZF(FM) Erlanger KY
WQKS(AM) Hopkinsville KY
WLSY-FM Jeffersontown KY
WLOU(AM) Louisville KY
WCKU(FM) Nicholasville KY
KRVV(FM) Bastrop LA
KBZE(FM) Berwick LA
KBCE(FM) Boyce LA
*KGRM(FM) Grambling LA
KJCB(AM) Lafayette LA
KXZZ(AM) Lake Charles LA
KFXZ(FM) Maurice LA
WQUE(AM) New Orleans LA
WYLD-FM New Orleans LA
KQXL-FM New Roads LA
KRUS(AM) Ruston LA
KMJJ-FM Shreveport LA
KBYO(AM) Tallulah LA
KYEA(FM) West Monroe LA
WILD(AM) Boston MA
*WRBB(FM) Boston MA
*WMLN-FM Milton MA
*WMHC(FM) South Hadley MA
WXYV(FM) Baltimore MD
WMMJ(FM) Bethesda MD
WJDY(AM) Salisbury MD
WLLJ(AM) Cassopolis MI
WGPR(FM) Detroit MI
WJLB(FM) Detroit MI
WMXD(FM) Detroit MI
WQHH(FM) Dewitt MI
WXLA(AM) Dimondale MI
WDZZ-FM Flint MI
WKWM(AM) Kentwood MI
WKBZ-FM Muskegon MI
WTLZ(FM) Saginaw MI
WOWE(FM) Vassar MI
*KMOJ(FM) Minneapolis MN
*KJLU(FM) Jefferson City MO
KPRS(FM) Kansas City MO
KMAL(FM) Malden MO
KMJM(FM) St. Louis MO
WESE(FM) Baldwyn MS
WMGO(AM) Canton MS
WCLD-FM Cleveland MS
WACR-FM Columbus MS
WKZB(FM) Drew MS
WGNL(FM) Greenwood MS
WKXG(AM) Greenwood MS
WJMG(FM) Hattiesburg MS
WORV(AM) Hattiesburg MS
*WVSD(FM) Itta Bena MS
WJMI(FM) Jackson MS

WKXI(AM) Jackson MS
*WMPR(FM) Jackson MS
WKOZ(AM) Kosciusko MS
WQIS(AM) Laurel MS
WBAD(FM) Leland MS
*WPRL(FM) Lorman MS
WALT(AM) Meridian MS
WMGP(AM) Meridian MS
WNBN(AM) Meridian MS
WPMX(AM) Tupelo MS
WVOE(AM) Chadbourn NC
WPEG(FM) Concord NC
WDUR(AM) Durham NC
WFXC(FM) Durham NC
*WRVS-FM Elizabeth City NC
WCKZ-FM Gastonia NC
*WNAA(FM) Greensboro NC
WQMG-FM Greensboro NC
WOOW(AM) Greenville NC
WMYK(FM) Moyock NC
WBCG(FM) Murfreesboro NC
WIKS(FM) New Bern NC
*WKNC-FM Raleigh NC
WJMH(FM) Reidsville NC
WADE(AM) Wadesboro NC
WSMY(AM) Weldon NC
WZFX(FM) Whiteville NC
WMNX(FM) Wilmington NC
*KZUM(FM) Lincoln NE
WUSS(AM) Atlantic City NJ
WTTH(FM) Margate City NJ
*KANW(FM) Albuquerque NM
*WCDB(FM) Albany NY
WUFO(AM) Amherst NY
*WKRB(FM) Brooklyn NY
WBLK(FM) Depew NY
*WVCR-FM Loudonville NY
WBLS(FM) New York NY
WRKS-FM New York NY
WDKX(FM) Rochester NY
WJZR(FM) Rochester NY
WOLF(AM) Syracuse NY
*WPNR-FM Utica NY
*WZIP(FM) Akron OH
WPKO-FM Bellefontaine OH
WZAK(FM) Cleveland OH
WJMO(AM) Cleveland Heights OH
WVKO(AM) Columbus OH
WDAO(AM) Dayton OH
WCKX(FM) London OH
WNRB(AM) Niles OH
WJTB(AM) North Ridgeville OH
WANR(AM) Warren OH
*WCSU-FM Wilberforce OH
KVSP(AM) Oklahoma City OK
KTOW-FM Sand Springs OK
*KBVR(FM) Corvallis OR
*KWVA(FM) Eugene OR
WCXJ(AM) Braddock PA
WTCY(AM) Harrisburg PA
WIOQ(FM) Philadelphia PA
WUSL(FM) Philadelphia PA
WAMO-FM Pittsburgh PA
WJMZ-FM Anderson SC
WBAW-FM Barnwell SC
WKWQ(FM) Batesburg SC
WLWZ(AM) Easley SC
WLWZ-FM Easley SC
WYNN-FM Florence SC
WLMA(AM) Greenwood SC
WMTY(AM) Greenwood SC
WMTY-FM Greenwood SC
WLVH(FM) Hardeeville SC
WWKT-FM Kingstree SC
WLBG(AM) Laurens SC
WCIG(FM) Mullins SC
WNMX(FM) Newberry SC
WKSO(FM) Orangeburg SC
WPJK(AM) Orangeburg SC
*WSSB-FM Orangeburg SC
WQKI(AM) St. Matthews SC
WWWZ(FM) Summerville SC
WWDM(FM) Sumter SC
WPAL-FM Walterboro SC
WFKX(FM) Henderson TN
WQQK(FM) Hendersonville TN
WEMG(AM) Knoxville TN
WKGN(AM) Knoxville TN
KJMS(FM) Memphis TN
WHRK(FM) Memphis TN
WJTT(FM) Red Bank TN
KJMZ(FM) Dallas TX
KKDA-FM Dallas TX
KMJQ(FM) Houston TX
KYOK(AM) Houston TX
KIIZ-FM Killeen TX
KARW(AM) Longview TX
KZEY-FM Marshall TX
KZRB(FM) New Boston TX
KHYS(FM) Port Arthur TX
*KPVU(FM) Prairie View TX
KSJL-FM San Antonio TX
KZEY(AM) Tyler TX
*KWCR-FM Ogden UT
WPAK(AM) Farmville VA
*WHOV(FM) Hampton VA
WVLR(AM) Lynchburg VA
WCDX(FM) Mechanicsville VA
WOWI(FM) Norfolk VA
WPLZ-FM Petersburg VA
WREJ(AM) Richmond VA
WTOY(AM) Salem VA
WQOK(FM) South Boston VA
WSVY-FM Windsor VA
WVIS(FM) Christiansted VI
KZIZ(AM) Sumner WA
KBMS(AM) Vancouver WA
WNOV(AM) Milwaukee WI
WKKV-FM Racine WI
*KUWS(FM) Superior WI
*WQAB(FM) Philippi WV

Variety/Diverse

Includes stations self-described as Variety and stations programing four or more formats.

*KBRW(AM) Barrow AK
*KYUK(AM) Bethel AK
*KUAC(FM) Fairbanks AK
KZPA(AM) Fort Yukon AK
*KHNS(FM) Haines AK
*KBBI(AM) Homer AK
*KTOO(FM) Juneau AK
*KRBD(FM) Ketchikan AK
*KMXT(FM) Kodiak AK
*KOTZ(AM) Kotzebue AK
KABN(AM) Long Island AK
*KSKO(AM) McGrath AK
*KNOM(AM) Nome AK
*KNOM-FM Nome AK
*KSDP(AM) Sand Point AK
*KCAW(FM) Sitka AK
*KTNA(FM) Talkeetna AK
KIAL(AM) Unalaska AK
*KCHU(AM) Valdez AK
*KSTK(FM) Wrangell AK
WABB(AM) Mobile AL
WTQX(AM) Selma AL
KBVA(FM) Bella Vista AR
KLCN(AM) Blytheville AR
*KZIG(FM) Cave City AR
*KHDX(FM) Conway AR
KAGH-FM Crossett AR
*KABF(FM) Little Rock AR
KVSA(AM) McGehee AR
KURM(AM) Rogers AR
*KXRJ(FM) Russellville AR
WVUV(AM) Leone AS
KZON(FM) Phoenix AZ
KSED(FM) Sedona AZ
*KGHR(FM) Tuba City AZ
*KXCI(FM) Tucson AZ
*KNNB(FM) Whiteriver AZ
*KAWC(AM) Yuma AZ
*KHSU-FM Arcata CA
*KALX(FM) Berkeley CA
*KPFA(FM) Berkeley CA
*KPFB(FM) Berkeley CA
*KZFR(FM) Chico CA
*KHDC(FM) Chualar CA
*KSPC(FM) Claremont CA
*KKUP(FM) Cupertino CA
*KDVS(FM) Davis CA
*KECG(FM) El Cerrito CA
*KMUD(FM) Garberville CA
*KIDE(FM) Hoopa CA
KTYM(AM) Inglewood CA
*KUCI(FM) Irvine CA
*KFJC(FM) Los Altos CA
*KXLU(FM) Los Angeles CA
*KVMR(FM) Nevada City CA
*KAZU(FM) Pacific Grove CA
*KPCC(FM) Pasadena CA
*KZYX(FM) Philo CA
*KUCR(FM) Riverside CA
*KYDS(FM) Sacramento CA
*KALW(FM) San Francisco CA
*KPOO(FM) San Francisco CA
*KUSF(FM) San Francisco CA
*KSRH(FM) San Rafael CA
*KCSB-FM Santa Barbara CA
*KZSC(FM) Santa Cruz CA
KKZZ(AM) Santa Paula CA
*KZSU(FM) Stanford CA
*KSJC-FM Stockton CA
*KCSS(FM) Turlock CA
*KSAK(FM) Walnut CA
*KASF(FM) Alamosa CO
*KGNU(FM) Boulder CO
*KDNK(FM) Carbondale CO
*KEPC(FM) Colorado Springs CO
*KRCC(FM) Colorado Springs CO
*KBUT(FM) Crested Butte CO
*KDUR(FM) Durango CO
KIUP(AM) Durango CO
KTCL(FM) Fort Collins CO
*KMSA(FM) Grand Junction CO
*KUNC-FM Greeley CO
*KVNF(FM) Paonia CO
*KOTO(FM) Telluride CO
*WPKN(FM) Bridgeport CT
*WVOF(FM) Fairfield CT
*WRTC-FM Hartford CT
*WESU(FM) Middletown CT
*WSLX(FM) New Canaan CT
WKZE-FM Salisbury CT
*WGSK(FM) South Kent CT
*WHUS(FM) Storrs CT
*WWPT(FM) Westport CT
*WECS(FM) Willimantic CT
*WVUD(FM) Newark DE
WBGC(AM) Chipley FL
WLVU(AM) Dunedin FL
WEBZ(FM) Mexico Beach FL
*WLRN-FM Miami FL
WPGS(AM) Mims FL
WHOO(AM) Orlando FL
WQSA(AM) Sarasota FL
*WAMF(FM) Tallahassee FL
*WMNF(FM) Tampa FL
WSZD(AM) Pohnpei FM
WSZC(AM) Truk FM
V6AI(AM) Yap FM
*WREK(FM) Atlanta GA
*WRFG(FM) Atlanta GA
*WWGC(FM) Carrollton GA
WNMT(AM) Garden City GA
WYTH(AM) Madison GA
*WPLH(FM) Tifton GA
*WXVS(FM) Waycross GA
KGUM(AM) Agana GU
KIPA(AM) Hilo HI
*KTUH(FM) Honolulu HI
KLGA-FM Algona IA
*KUSR(FM) Ames IA
*KUNI(FM) Cedar Falls IA
KROS(AM) Clinton IA
*KWLC(AM) Decorah IA
*KDPS(FM) Des Moines IA
*KUCB-FM Des Moines IA
*KRUI-FM Iowa City IA
*KUNY(FM) Mason City IA
*KRNL-FM Mount Vernon IA
*KIGC(FM) Oskaloosa IA
KAYL(AM) Storm Lake IA
*KWAR(FM) Waverly IA
*KBSU(AM) Boise ID
*KUOI-FM Moscow ID
KSRA-FM Salmon ID
*KBSW(FM) Twin Falls ID
*WESN(FM) Bloomington IL
WBYS(AM) Canton IL
WBYS-FM Canton IL
*WEFT(FM) Champaign IL
*WBHI(FM) Chicago IL
WGN(AM) Chicago IL
*WHPK-FM Chicago IL
*WOUI(FM) Chicago IL
*WZRD(FM) Chicago IL
*WJMU(FM) Decatur IL
*WDGC-FM Downers Grove IL
WDQN-FM DuQuoin IL
*WEPS(FM) Elgin IL
*WHFH(FM) Flossmoor IL
*WVKC(FM) Galesburg IL
*WDCB(FM) Glen Ellyn IL
*WMXM(FM) Lake Forest IL
*WLRA(FM) Lockport IL
*WVJC(FM) Mt. Carmel IL
*WMTH(FM) Park Ridge IL
*WQUB(FM) Quincy IL
*WQNA(FM) Springfield IL
WGFA-FM Watseka IL
*WETN(FM) Wheaton IL
*WNTH(FM) Winnetka IL
*WFHB(FM) Bloomington IN
*WJHS(FM) Columbia City IN
*WPSR(FM) Evansville IN
*WUEV(FM) Evansville IN
*WGCS(FM) Goshen IN
WTRE(AM) Greensburg IN
WPDJ(AM) Huntington IN
*WICR(FM) Indianapolis IN
WMRS(FM) Monticello IN
*WBKE-FM North Manchester IN
WNDZ(AM) Portage IN
*WECI(FM) Richmond IN
*WVXR(FM) Richmond IN
WKJK(FM) Salem IN
*KVCO(FM) Concordia KS
KDCC(AM) Dodge City KS
*KONQ(FM) Dodge City KS
*KANZ(FM) Garden City KS
*KZNA(FM) Hill City KS
KIND(AM) Independence KS
*KBCU(FM) North Newton KS
*KTJO-FM Ottawa KS
KKAN(AM) Phillipsburg KS
KQMA-FM Phillipsburg KS
*KIBN(FM) Wichita KS
WWLW(FM) Carlisle KY
WXBC(FM) Hardinsburg KY
WHBN(AM) Harrodsburg KY
WHBN-FM Harrodsburg KY
*WMKY(FM) Morehead KY
WLOC-FM Munfordville KY
WRUS(AM) Russellville KY
*WMMT(FM) Whitesburg KY
*KLSP(FM) Angola LA
*KLSU(FM) Baton Rouge LA
WIKC(AM) Bogalusa LA
*KLPI-FM Ruston LA
*KSCL(FM) Shreveport LA
KVCL(AM) Winnfield LA
*WMUA(FM) Amherst MA
*WERS(FM) Boston MA
*WBIM-FM Bridgewater MA
*WMBR(FM) Cambridge MA
WBMA(AM) Dedham MA
*WSHL-FM Easton MA
WSAR(AM) Fall River MA
WRSI(FM) Greenfield MA
*WCCT-FM Harwich MA
*WHHB(FM) Holliston MA
*WCCH(FM) Holyoke MA
*WJUL(FM) Lowell MA
*WAVM(FM) Maynard MA
*WMLN-FM Milton MA
*WOZQ(FM) Northampton MA
*WNMH(FM) Northfield MA
*WMHC(FM) South Hadley MA
*WAIC(FM) Springfield MA
*WNEK-FM Springfield MA
*WSCB(FM) Springfield MA
*WTCC(FM) Springfield MA
*WSRB(FM) Walpole MA
*WBRS(FM) Waltham MA
*WZLY(FM) Wellesley MA
*WCUW(FM) Worcester MA
*WICN(FM) Worcester MA
*WERU-FM Blue Hill ME
*WBOR(FM) Brunswick ME
*WSHD(FM) Eastport ME
WUFK(FM) Fort Kent ME
*WMPG(FM) Gorham ME
*WRBC(FM) Lewiston ME
WWMR(FM) Rumford ME
*WSJB-FM Standish ME
*WMHB(FM) Waterville ME
*WVAC-FM Adrian MI
*WCBN-FM Ann Arbor MI
*WBFH(FM) Bloomfield Hills MI
*WHFR(FM) Dearborn MI
*WORB(FM) Farmington Hills MI
WMJZ-FM Gaylord MI
*WKDS(FM) Kalamazoo MI
*WKAL(AM) Kalkaska MI
*WEJY(FM) Monroe MI
*WOAS(FM) Ontonagon MI
*WBLD(FM) Orchard Lake MI
*WNMC-FM Traverse City MI
*WPHS(FM) Warren MI
KATE(AM) Albert Lea MN
*KBSB(FM) Bemidji MN
KLKS(FM) Breezy Point MN
KDAL(AM) Duluth MN
*KAXE(FM) Grand Rapids MN
*KFAI(FM) Minneapolis MN
WCCO(AM) Minneapolis MN
*KRLX(FM) Northfield MN
KOLV(FM) Olivia MN
WCMP(AM) Pine City MN
*KVSC(FM) St. Cloud MN
*KQAL(FM) Winona MN
*KWWC-FM Columbia MO
*KMVC(FM) Marshall MO
KWIX(AM) Moberly MO
KRMO(AM) Monett MO
*KRHS(FM) Overland MO
*KMNR(FM) Rolla MO
*KUMR(FM) Rolla MO
*KDHX(FM) St. Louis MO
*KCMW-FM Warrensburg MO
KCNM(AM) San Jose MP
KZMI(FM) San Jose MP
*KGLT(FM) Bozeman MT
*KMSM-FM Butte MT
*KECC(FM) Miles City MT
*KUFM(FM) Missoula MT
KSEN(AM) Shelby MT
WRAQ(AM) Brevard NC
*WCCE(FM) Buie's Creek NC
*WXDU(FM) Durham NC
*WSOE(FM) Elon College NC
WAJA(AM) Franklin NC
WFMC(AM) Goldsboro NC
*WVMH-FM Mars Hill NC
WDJS(AM) Mount Olive NC
WPTF(AM) Raleigh NC
*WZRU(FM) Roanoke Rapids NC
*WHYC(FM) Swan Quarter NC
*WSNC(FM) Winston-Salem NC
*KMHA(FM) Four Bears ND
KICS(AM) Hastings NE
*KZUM(FM) Lincoln NE
WKXL(AM) Concord NH
WKXL-FM Concord NH
*WSPS(FM) Concord NH
WDCR(AM) Hanover NH
*WNJS-FM Berlin NJ
*WNJB(FM) Bridgeton NJ
WSNJ(AM) Bridgeton NJ
WSNJ-FM Bridgeton NJ
*WDVR(FM) Delaware Township NJ
*WFMU(FM) East Orange NJ
*WCVH(FM) Flemington NJ
*WGLS-FM Glassboro NJ
*WNTI(FM) Hackettstown NJ
*WMNJ(FM) Madison NJ
*WRSU-FM New Brunswick NJ
*WWPH(FM) Princeton Junction NJ
*WNJT-FM Trenton NJ
*KUNM(FM) Albuquerque NM
KIOT(FM) Espanola NM
*KSJE(FM) Farmington NM
KASK(FM) Las Cruces NM
*KRUX(FM) Las Cruces NM
KRTN(AM) Raton NM
KRTN-FM Raton NM
KKIT(AM) Taos NM
*KUNV(FM) Las Vegas NV
*WALF(FM) Alfred NY
*WBXL(FM) Baldwinsville NY
*WXLH(FM) Blue Mountain Lake NY
*WXBA(FM) Brentwood NY
*WBSU(FM) Brockport NY
*WCWP(FM) Brookville NY
*WSLU(FM) Canton NY
*WITC(FM) Cazenovia NY
*WHCL-FM Clinton NY
*WSUC-FM Cortland NY
*WCVF-FM Fredonia NY
*WBAU(FM) Garden City NY
WHHO(AM) Hornell NY
*WSQG-FM Ithaca NY
*WSLO(FM) Malone NY
*WBAI(FM) New York NY
*WFUV(FM) New York NY
*WXLG(FM) North Creek NY
*WONY(FM) Oneonta NY
*WOSS(FM) Ossining NY
*WXLU(FM) Peru NY
*WTSC-FM Potsdam NY
*WVKR-FM Poughkeepsie NY
*WSLL(FM) Saranac Lake NY
*WSIA(FM) Staten Island NY
*WUSB(FM) Stony Brook NY
*WKWZ(FM) Syosset NY
*WRPI(FM) Troy NY
*WSLJ(FM) Watertown NY
*WOBO(FM) Batavia OH
*WBGU(FM) Bowling Green OH
*WVXC(FM) Chillicothe OH
*WRUW-FM Cleveland OH
WEOL(AM) Elyria OH
*WKCO(FM) Gambier OH
*WMCO(FM) New Concord OH
*WOBC-FM Oberlin OH
*WKTL(FM) Struthers OH
*WXUT(FM) Toledo OH
*WUJC(FM) University Heights OH
WELW(AM) Willoughby-Eastlake OH
*WCWS(FM) Wooster OH
*WYSO(FM) Yellow Springs OH
*KOKF(FM) Edmond OK
*KPSU(FM) Goodwell OK
KIHN(AM) Hugo OK
*KALU(FM) Langston OK
KRMG(AM) Tulsa OK
KUGN(AM) Eugene OR
*KWVA(FM) Eugene OR
*KEOL(FM) La Grande OR
*KLCO(FM) Newport OR
*KBOO(FM) Portland OR
*KBVM(FM) Portland OR
*KRRC(FM) Portland OR
*KWSO(FM) Warm Springs OR
*WMUH(FM) Allentown PA
*WLVR(FM) Bethlehem PA
*WDCV-FM Carlisle PA
*WDNR(FM) Chester PA
*WCUC-FM Clarion PA
WWCB(AM) Corry PA
*WESS(FM) East Stroudsburg PA
*WWEC(FM) Elizabethtown PA
*WMCE(FM) Erie PA
*WTGP(FM) Greenville PA
*WHHS(FM) Havertown PA
*WIUP-FM Indiana PA
*WFNM(FM) Lancaster PA
*WLCH(FM) Lancaster PA
*WVBU-FM Lewisburg PA
WEDO(AM) McKeesport PA
WIXZ(AM) McKeesport PA
*WARC(FM) Meadville PA
*WSFX(FM) Nanticoke PA
*WPEB(FM) Philadelphia PA
WPHE(AM) Phoenixville PA
*WRCT(FM) Pittsburgh PA
*WXLV(FM) Schnecksville PA
*WPSU(FM) State College PA
*WSRN-FM Swarthmore PA
*WCYJ-FM Waynesburg PA
*WCLH(FM) Wilkes-Barre PA
*WRLC(FM) Williamsport PA
WNIK(AM) Arecibo PR
WCHQ-FM Camuy PR
WAVB(AM) Lajas PR
WSOL(AM) Mayaguez PR
WCXQ(AM) Moca PR
WKVM(AM) San Juan PR
WQBS(AM) San Juan PR
WRSS(AM) San Sebastian PR
*WRIU(FM) Kingston RI
*WJHD(FM) Portsmouth RI
*WDOM(FM) Providence RI
WOON(AM) Woonsocket RI
WBEU(AM) Beaufort SC
*WJWJ-FM Beaufort SC
*WLGI(FM) Hemingway SC
*KSDJ(FM) Brookings SD
*KDSD-FM Pierpont SD
*KBHE-FM Rapid City SD
*KTEQ(FM) Rapid City SD
*KTSD-FM Reliance SD
WSGM(FM) Coalmont TN
WEMB(AM) Erwin TN
WIZO(AM) Franklin TN
*WVCP(FM) Gallatin TN
*WCSK(FM) Kingsport TN
*WEVL(FM) Memphis TN
*WFSK(FM) Nashville TN
*WUTS(FM) Sewanee TN
KVLF(AM) Alpine TX
*KAZI(FM) Austin TX
*KUT(FM) Austin TX
KBST(AM) Big Spring TX
KBST-FM Big Spring TX
KFYZ-FM Bonham TX
KKUB(AM) Brownfield TX
*KPFT(FM) Houston TX

Programming on Radio Stations in the U.S.

*KTRU(FM) Houston TX
*KTSU(FM) Houston TX
*KTAI(FM) Kingsville TX
KIOL-FM Lamesa TX
*KTXT-FM Lubbock TX
KLSR(AM) Memphis TX
KLSR-FM Memphis TX
*KEOM(FM) Mesquite TX
*KPLN-FM Plains TX
KTAE(AM) Taylor TX
KTXN-FM Victoria TX
*KWBU(FM) Waco TX

*KZMU(FM) Moab UT
*KRCL(FM) Salt Lake City UT
*WAMV(AM) Amherst VA
*WUVT-FM Blacksburg VA
*WTJU(FM) Charlottesville VA
*WVTU(FM) Charlottesville VA
WMNA-FM Gretna VA
*WLUR(FM) Lexington VA
*WVRU(FM) Radford VA
*WDCE(FM) Richmond VA
WTMM(AM) Richmond VA
*WCWM(FM) Wiiliamsburg VA

WVVI(AM) Charlotte Amalie VI
WSTX(AM) Christiansted VI
WRRA(AM) Frederiksted VI
*WRUV(FM) Burlington VT
*WJSC-FM Johnson VT
*WRMC-FM Middlebury VT
*WGDR(FM) Plainfield VT
WDEV-FM Warren VT
WDEV(AM) Waterbury VT
*KBCS(FM) Bellevue WA
*KUGS(FM) Bellingham WA
*KSER(FM) Everett WA

*KGHP(FM) Gig Harbor WA
*KSVR(FM) Mount Vernon WA
*KAOS(FM) Olympia WA
*KZUU(FM) Pullman WA
*KCMU(FM) Seattle WA
*KWCW(FM) Walla Walla WA
*WBCR-FM Beloit WI
*WORT(FM) Madison WI
WEKZ(AM) Monroe WI
WOCO(AM) Oconto WI
*WRST-FM Oshkosh WI
*WOJB(FM) Reserve WI

*WXPR(FM) Rhinelander WI
*WRFW(FM) River Falls WI
*WWSP(FM) Stevens Point WI
*WCCX(FM) Waukesha WI
*WVBC(FM) Bethany WV
*WHRD(FM) Huntington WV
WOTR(FM) Lost Creek WV
*WWVU-FM Morgantown WV
*WQAB(FM) Philippi WV
*WJGF-FM Romney WV
*WSHC(FM) Shepherdstown WV
KROE(AM) Sheridan WY

Programming on Radio Stations in Canada

Adult Contemporary

CHFM-FM Calgary AB
CFBR-AM Edmonton AB
CKNG-FM Edmonton AB
CKRA-FM Edmonton AB
CJCM(AM) Grand Centre AB
CKYR-1(AM) Grande Cache AB
CFGP(AM) Grande Prairie AB
CKYR(AM) Jasper AB
CFRV-FM Lethbridge AB
CJCY(AM) Medicine Hat AB
*CHCL(AM) Medley AB
CKRD(AM) Red Deer AB
CHLW(AM) St. Paul AB
CFSR-FM Abbotsford-Matsqui BC
CFVR(AM) Abbotsford-Matsqui BC
CKGO-FM-1 Boston Bar BC
CFWB(AM) Campbell River BC
CHWK(AM) Chilliwack BC
CHNL-1(AM) Clearwater BC
CKEK(AM) Cranbrook BC
CJDC(AM) Dawson Creek BC
CJDC-FM Dawson Creek BC
CKAY(AM) Duncan BC
CIEG-FM Egmont BC
CFEK(AM) Fernie BC
CKGF(AM) Grand Forks BC
CKGO(AM) Hope BC
CHNL(AM) Kamloops BC
CKRV-FM Kamloops BC
CKIQ(AM) Kelowna BC
CKIQ-FM Big White Ski Village BC
CHUB(AM) Nanaimo BC
CKNW(AM) New Westminster BC
CHPQ(AM) Parksville-Qualicum BC
CISP-FM Pemberton BC
CIPN-FM Pender Harbour BC
CJAV(AM) Port Alberni BC
CFNI(AM) Port Hardy BC
CJCI(AM) Prince George BC
CKPG(AM) Prince George BC
CHTK(AM) Prince Rupert BC
CIOR(AM) Princeton BC
CISE-FM Sechelt BC
CISQ-FM Squamish BC
CFUN(AM) Vancouver BC
CKKS-FM Vancouver BC
CICF(AM) Vernon BC
CKDA(AM) Victoria BC
CKWL(AM) Williams Lake BC
CKX(AM) Brandon MB
CJAR(AM) The Pas MB
CHTM(AM) Thompson MB
CIFX(AM) Winnipeg MB
CJKR-FM Winnipeg MB
CKLU-FM Winnipeg MB
CKBC(AM) Bathurst NB
CKNB(AM) Campbellton NB
CJVA(AM) Caraquet NB
CFAI-FM Edmundston NB
CJEM(AM) Edmundston NB
CIHI(AM) Fredericton NB
CKHJ-FM Fredericton NB
CKMV(AM) Grand Falls NB
CKCW(AM) Moncton NB
CFAN(AM) Newcastle NB
CFBC(AM) Saint John NB
CIOK-FM Saint John NB
CJCW(AM) Sussex NB
CJCJ(AM) Woodstock NB
CFLC-FM Churchill Falls NF
CFCB(AM) Corner Brook NF
CFDL-FM Deer Lake NF
CKGA(AM) Gander NF
CFLN(AM) Goose Bay NF
CHCM(AM) Marystown NF
CFNW(AM) Port au Choix NF
CFNN-FM St. Anthony NF
VOCM(AM) St. John's NF
CKDH(AM) Amherst NS
CKBW(AM) Bridgewater NS
CJLS-FM-2 Digby NS
CIEZ-FM Halifax NS
CIOO-FM Halifax NS
CKEC-FM New Glasgow NS
CIGO(AM) Port Hawkesbury NS
CJLS-FM-1 Shelburne NS
CBI-FM Sydney NS
CHER(AM) Sydney NS
CJCB(AM) Sydney NS
CKTO-FM Truro NS
CFAB(AM) Windsor NS
CJLS(AM) Yarmouth NS
CJCD-FM-1 Hay River NT
CBQR-FM Rankin Inlet NT
CJCD(AM) Yellowknife NT
CHVR-2(AM) Arnprior ON
CKBB(AM) Barrie ON
CJBQ(AM) Belleville ON
CJOJ-FM Belleville ON
CJNR(AM) Blind River ON
CFBG-FM Bracebridge ON
CKPC(AM) Brantford ON
CKPC-FM Brantford ON
CFJR(AM) Brockville ON
CKSY-FM Chatham ON
CHUC(AM) Cobourg ON
CKCB(AM) Collingwood ON
CFLG-FM Cornwall ON

CJSS(AM) Cornwall ON
CKDR(AM) Dryden ON
CKNR(AM) Elliot Lake ON
CKNS(AM) Espanola ON
CKEY-FM Fort Erie ON
CFOB(AM) Fort Frances ON
CIMJ-FM Guelph ON
CKLH-FM Hamilton ON
CHPR-FM Hawkesbury ON
CHOH(AM) Hearst ON
CFBK-FM Huntsville ON
CHYK(AM) Kapuskasing ON
CJRL(AM) Kenora ON
CFFX(AM) Kingston ON
CFLY-FM Kingston ON
CJKL(AM) Kirkland Lake ON
CHYM-FM Kitchener ON
CKLY(AM) Lindsay ON
CIQM-FM London ON
*CIXX-FM London ON
CJBK(AM) London ON
CFNO-FM Marathon ON
CJMR(AM) Mississauga ON
CFCH(AM) North Bay ON
CIDC-FM Orangeville ON
CJMJ-FM Ottawa ON
CKKL-FM Ottawa ON
CHVR(AM) Pembroke ON
CKPT(AM) Peterborough ON
CKWF-FM Peterborough ON
CKDR-5(AM) Red Lake ON
CHVR-1(AM) Renfrew ON
CFGX-FM Sarnia ON
CHAS-FM Sault Ste. Marie ON
CHNR(AM) Simcoe ON
CHRE-FM St. Catharines ON
CHSC-FM St. Catharines ON
CHYC(AM) Sudbury ON
CIGM(AM) Sudbury ON
CJMX-FM Sudbury ON
CKPR(AM) Thunder Bay ON
CKOT(AM) Tillsonburg ON
CKOY(AM) Timmins ON
CHFI-FM Toronto ON
CKFM-FM Toronto ON
CJTN(AM) Trenton ON
CJWA(AM) Wawa ON
CKNX-FM Wingham ON
CKDK-FM Woodstock ON
CFCY(AM) Charlottetown PE
CHAD(AM) Amos PQ
CFVM(AM) Amqui PQ
CJAN(AM) Asbestos PQ
CHLC(AM) Baie Comeau PQ
CFED(AM) Chapais PQ
CJMD(AM) Chibougamau PQ
CJAB-FM Chicoutimi PQ
CJMT(AM) Chicoutimi PQ
CHRD(AM) Drummondville PQ
CJDM-FM Drummondville PQ
CFRP(AM) Forestville PQ
CHEF(AM) Granby PQ
*CFTH-FM Harrington Harbour PQ
CKRS(AM) Jonquiere PQ
*CKRK-FM Kahnawake PQ
CJLA-FM Lachute PQ
CIMO-FM Magog PQ
CHGA-FM Maniwaki PQ
CFEL-FM Montmagny PQ
CFQR-FM Montreal PQ
CITE-FM Montreal PQ
CJFM-FM Montreal PQ
CHOI-FM Quebec PQ
CITF-FM Quebec PQ
CJMF-FM Quebec PQ
CHRL(AM) Roberval PQ
CHOA-FM Rouyn PQ
CKRN(AM) Rouyn PQ
CKSM-FM Shawinigan PQ
CJSO-FM Sorel PQ
CKRB(AM) St. Georges-de-Beauce PQ
CFZZ-FM St. Jean-sur-Richelieu PQ
CJVL(AM) Ste. Marie-de-Beauce PQ
CKOD(AM) Valleyfield PQ
CFVD(AM) Ville Degelis PQ
CKVM(AM) Ville-Marie PQ
CKBI(AM) Prince Albert SK
CHMX-FM Regina SK
CIZL-FM Regina SK
CKCK(AM) Regina SK
CFQC(AM) Saskatoon SK
CHSN-FM Saskatoon SK
CIMG-FM Swift Current SK
*CFWH(AM) Whitehorse YT
CKRW(AM) Whitehorse YT

Agriculture & Farm

CFAM(AM) Altona MB
CHNR(AM) Simcoe ON
CKRM(AM) Regina SK

Beautiful Music

CBX-FM Edmonton AB
CILK-FM Kelowna BC
CHQM-FM Vancouver BC

CFMS-FM Victoria BC
CJRB(AM) Boissevain MB
CHAY-FM Barrie ON
CIGL-FM Belleville ON
CFCA-FM Kitchener ON
CKGE-FM Oshawa ON
NEW FM Ottawa ON
CKOT-FM Tillsonburg ON
CKMG(AM) Maniwaki PQ
*CBSI-FM Sept-Iles PQ
CKIT-FM Regina SK

Big Band

CKOV(AM) Kelowna BC
CFAX(AM) Victoria BC
CKMG(AM) Maniwaki PQ

Black

CHRY-FM Toronto ON

Chinese

CJVB(AM) Vancouver BC

Classic Rock

CFXL(AM) Calgary AB
CJAY-FM Calgary AB
CFRV-FM Lethbridge AB
CKRX(AM) Lethbridge AB
CFMI-FM New Westminster BC
CKBD(AM) Vancouver BC
CKWL(AM) Williams Lake BC
CHTM(AM) Thompson MB
CFNB(AM) Fredericton NB
CJMO-FM Moncton NB
CJYC-FM Saint John NB
CFLW(AM) Wabush NF
CJCH(AM) Halifax NS
CJXY-FM Hamilton ON
CFPL-FM London ON
CKDX-FM Newmarket ON
CIWW(AM) Ottawa ON
CJSB(AM) Ottawa ON
CHTN(AM) Charlottetown PE
CFIC-FM Ste. Anne des Plaines PQ
CFMM-FM Prince Albert SK
CIZL-FM Regina SK

Classical

*CBR(AM) Calgary AB
*CBR-FM Calgary AB
CBX-FM Edmonton AB
*CKUA-FM Edmonton AB
*CBU(AM) Vancouver BC
CBW-FM Winnipeg MB
*CBN-FM St. John's NF
CFMX-FM Cobourg ON
CBBK-FM Kingston ON
CBBL-FM London ON
CFMX-FM-1 Mississauga ON
CBL-FM Toronto ON
*CJRT-FM Toronto ON
CBE-FM Windsor ON
*CBV-FM Quebec PQ
CBF-FM-1 Trois Rivieres PQ

Contemporary Hit/Top-40

CIBQ(AM) Brooks AB
CFCN(AM) Calgary AB
CHED(AM) Edmonton AB
CJYR(AM) Edson AB
CFRV-FM Lethbridge AB
CJDC(AM) Dawson Creek BC
CJDC-FM Dawson Creek BC
CKIQ(AM) Kelowna BC
CJNL(AM) Merritt BC
CIOR(AM) Princeton BC
CKLG(AM) Vancouver BC
CHIQ-FM Winnipeg MB
CKLE-FM Bathurst NB
CFAI-FM Edmundston NB
CIHI(AM) Fredericton NB
CKUM-FM Moncton NB
CFBC(AM) Saint John NB
CKCM(AM) Grand Falls-Windsor NF
CJRM-FM Labrador City NF
CFLW(AM) Wabush NF
CFDR-FM Dartmouth NS
CKBW-FM-1 Liverpool NS
CKBW-FM-2 Shelburne NS
CJCB-FM Sydney NS
CKDR-6(AM) Atikokan ON
CJOJ-FM Belleville ON
CIAM(AM) Cambridge ON
CKDR(AM) Dryden ON
CFOB(AM) Fort Frances ON
CKAP(AM) Kapuskasing ON
CJRL(AM) Kenora ON
CKLC(AM) Kingston ON
CKKW(AM) Kitchener ON
CFGO(AM) Ottawa ON

CKRU(AM) Peterborough ON
CKDR-5(AM) Red Lake ON
CHYC(AM) Sudbury ON
CKOT(AM) Tillsonburg ON
CFCY(AM) Charlottetown PE
CFVD-FM-1 Cabano PQ
CFED(AM) Chapais PQ
CJMD(AM) Chibougamau PQ
*CBJ-FM Chicoutimi PQ
CJDM-FM Drummondville PQ
*CKRK-FM Kahnawake PQ
CHOX-FM La Pocatiere PQ
CKFL(AM) Lac Megantic PQ
CHRM(AM) Matane PQ
CKMF-FM Montreal PQ
CIPC(AM) Port-Cartier PQ
CIKI-FM Rimouski PQ
CHRL(AM) Roberval PQ
CHLN(AM) Trois Rivieres PQ
CIGB-FM Trois Rivieres PQ
CJMV-FM Val d'Or PQ
CKOI-FM Verdun PQ
CFVD(AM) Ville Degelis PQ
CFMM-FM Prince Albert SK
CKOM(AM) Saskatoon SK

Country

CKBA(AM) Athabasca AB
CJPR(AM) Blairmore AB
CIBQ(AM) Brooks AB
CFAC(AM) Calgary AB
CKRY-FM Calgary AB
CFCW(AM) Camrose AB
CFHC(AM) Canmore AB
CKDQ(AM) Drumheller AB
CISN-FM Edmonton AB
CJYR(AM) Edson AB
CJOK(AM) Fort McMurray AB
CKYR-1(AM) Grande Cache AB
CJXX(AM) Grande Prairie AB
CHRB(AM) High River AB
CIYR(AM) Hinton AB
CKYR(AM) Jasper AB
CJOC(AM) Lethbridge AB
CKSA(AM) Lloydminster AB
CHAT(AM) Medicine Hat AB
*CHCL(AM) Medley AB
CKGY(AM) Red Deer AB
CKWA(AM) Slave Lake AB
CHLW(AM) St. Paul AB
CKSQ(AM) Stettler AB
CKTA(AM) Taber AB
CKKY(AM) Wainwright AB
CFOK(AM) Westlock AB
CJOI(AM) Wetaskiwin AB
CKBX(AM) 100 Mile House BC
CJDC(AM) Dawson Creek BC
CJDC-FM Dawson Creek BC
CFNL(AM) Fort Nelson BC
CKNL(AM) Fort St. John BC
CKGR(AM) Golden BC
CKGO(AM) Hope BC
CKIR(AM) Invermere BC
CFJC(AM) Kamloops BC
CFJC-FM Merritt BC
CKEG(AM) Nanaimo BC
CJOR(AM) Osoyoos BC
CIGV-FM Penticton BC
CJAV(AM) Port Alberni BC
CFNI(AM) Port Hardy BC
CHQB-FM Powell River BC
CIOI-FM Prince George BC
CKCQ(AM) Quesnel BC
CKCR(AM) Revelstoke BC
CKXR(AM) Salmon Arm BC
CJFW-FM Terrace BC
CJJR-FM Vancouver BC
CKWX(AM) Vancouver BC
CIVH(AM) Vanderhoof BC
CFFM-FM Williams Lake BC
CKLQ(AM) Brandon MB
CKDM(AM) Dauphin MB
CFAR(AM) Flin Flon MB
CFRY(AM) Portage la Prairie MB
CFQX-FM Selkirk MB
CJAR(AM) The Pas MB
CHTM(AM) Thompson MB
CKMW(AM) Winkler-Morden MB
CKRC(AM) Winnipeg MB
CKBC(AM) Bathurst NB
CKNB(AM) Campbellton NB
CKHJ(AM) Fredericton NB
CFQM-FM Moncton NB
CHSJ(AM) Saint John NB
CJCW(AM) Sussex NB
CJCJ(AM) Woodstock NB
CKIM(AM) Baie Verte NF
CHVO(AM) Carbonear NF
CKVO(AM) Clarenville NF
CKXX(AM) Corner Brook NF
CKXD(AM) Gander NF
CKCM(AM) Grand Falls-Windsor NF
CKXG(AM) Grand Falls-Windsor NF
CHCM(AM) Marystown NF
CKXB(AM) Musgravetown NF
CFGN(AM) Port-aux-Basques NF
CKIX-FM St. John's NF

CFSX(AM) Stephenville NF
CFLW(AM) Wabush NF
CJFX(AM) Antigonish NS
CKBW(AM) Bridgewater NS
CKDY(AM) Digby NS
CHFX-FM Halifax NS
CKEN(AM) Kentville NS
CKBW-FM-1 Liverpool NS
CKAD(AM) Middleton NS
CKEC(AM) New Glasgow NS
CKBW-FM-2 Shelburne NS
CKPE-FM Sydney NS
CKCL(AM) Truro NS
CKNM-FM Yellowknife NT
CHOO(AM) Ajax ON
CJNH(AM) Bancroft ON
CHAM(AM) Hamilton ON
CFMK-FM Kingston ON
CJKL(AM) Kirkland Lake ON
CKGL(AM) Kitchener ON
CHYR-FM Leamington ON
CJBX-FM London ON
CICZ-FM Midland ON
CFJQ-FM Nipigon-Red Rock ON
CKAT-FM North Bay ON
CKRZ-FM Ohsweken ON
CICX-FM Orillia ON
CKBY-FM Ottawa ON
CIXK-FM Owen Sound ON
CKQM-FM Peterborough ON
CHOG(AM) Richmond Hill ON
CKTY(AM) Sarnia ON
CJQM-FM Sault Ste. Marie ON
CJET(AM) Smiths Falls ON
CHLO(AM) St. Thomas ON
CJRQ-FM Sudbury ON
CJLB-FM Thunder Bay ON
CKGB(AM) Timmins ON
CISS-FM Toronto ON
CKYC(AM) Toronto ON
CJTN(AM) Trenton ON
CHOW(AM) Welland ON
CKNX(AM) Wingham ON
CHLQ-FM Charlottetown PE
CJRW(AM) Summerside PE
CFGT(AM) Alma PQ
*CFTH-FM Harrington Harbour PQ
*CKRK-FM Kahnawake PQ
CFLS-FM Levis PQ
CHRM(AM) Matane PQ
CIQC(AM) Montreal PQ
CIRO-FM St. Georges-de-Beauce PQ
CJVL(AM) Ste. Marie-de-Beauce PQ
CFVD(AM) Ville Degelis PQ
CJSL(AM) Estevan SK
CJNS(AM) Meadow Lake SK
CJVR(AM) Melfort SK
CHAB(AM) Moose Jaw SK
CJNB(AM) North Battleford SK
CKRM(AM) Regina SK
CJWW(AM) Saskatoon SK
CJSN(AM) Shaunavon SK
CKSW(AM) Swift Current SK
CFSL(AM) Weyburn SK
CJGX(AM) Yorkton SK
CHON-FM Whitehorse YT
CKRW(AM) Whitehorse YT

Disco

CHIK-FM Quebec PQ

Drama/Literature

*CITR-FM Vancouver BC
CBF-FM-1 Trois Rivieres PQ

Educational

*CKUA-FM-1 Calgary AB
CKUA-FM-13 Drumheller AB
CKUA-FM-4 Grande Prairie AB
*CKUA-FM-2 Lethbridge AB
*CKUA-FM-3 Medicine Hat AB
*CKUA-FM-5 Peace River AB
*CBG(AM) Gander NF
CBT(AM) Grand Falls-Windsor NF
CFGB-FM Happy Valley NF
CJRM-FM Labrador City NF
CBCS-FM Sudbury ON
CJBC(AM) Toronto ON
*CJRT-FM Toronto ON
*CBSI-FM Sept-Iles PQ

Foreign Language/Ethnic

CKER(AM) Edmonton AB
CHQM(AM) Vancouver BC
CJVB(AM) Vancouver BC
CKJS(AM) Winnipeg MB
CKQN-FM Baker Lake NT
CIAO(AM) Brampton ON
CJMR(AM) Mississauga ON
CHIN(AM) Toronto ON
CHIN-FM Toronto ON
CIRV-FM Toronto ON

Programming on Radio Stations in Canada

*CJAM-FM Windsor ON
CFMB(AM) Montreal PQ
CINQ-FM Montreal PQ
*CFIC-FM Ste. Anne des Plaines PQ

French

*CKSB(AM) St. Boniface MB
CJRM-FM Labrador City NF
*CHUO-FM Ottawa ON
CJDM-FM Drummondville PQ
CFMF-FM Fermont PQ
CBGA-FM-8 Iles-de-la-Madeleine PQ
CINQ-FM Montreal PQ

Gospel

*VOAR(AM) Mount Pearl NF

Jazz

*CJSW-FM Calgary AB
*CKUA-FM Edmonton AB
*CBU(AM) Vancouver BC
*CFUV-FM Victoria BC
CBBK-FM Kingston ON
*CJRT-FM Toronto ON

Middle-of-the-Road (MOR)

*CHFA(AM) Edmonton AB
CHQT(AM) Edmonton AB
CJYR(AM) Edson AB
CKYL(AM) Peace River AB
CFLD(AM) Burns Lake BC
CFWB(AM) Campbell River BC
CKQR(AM) Castlegar BC
CKSR-FM Chilliwack BC
CFKC(AM) Creston BC
CKGR(AM) Golden BC
CKIR(AM) Invermere BC
CKKC-FM-2 Kaslo BC
CKOV(AM) Kelowna BC
CKTK-FM Kitimat BC
CKMK(AM) Mackenzie BC
CKKC(AM) Nelson BC
CKKC-FM Nelson BC
CKKC-FM-1 New Denver BC
CKNW(AM) New Westminster BC
CJOR(AM) Osoyoos BC
CHQB(AM) Powell River BC
CIRX-FM Prince George BC
CKCR(AM) Revelstoke BC
CKXR(AM) Salmon Arm BC
CHOR(AM) Summerland BC
CFTK(AM) Terrace BC
CJAT(AM) Trail BC
CJIB(AM) Vernon BC
CFAX(AM) Victoria BC
CFAM(AM) Altona MB
CFAR(AM) Flin Flon MB
CHSM(AM) Steinbach MB
CJVA(AM) Caraquet NB
CFAN(AM) Newcastle NB
CFGN(AM) Port-aux-Basques NF
CFSX(AM) Stephenville NF
CJFX(AM) Antigonish NS
CKBW(AM) Bridgewater NS
CKBW-FM-1 Liverpool NS
CKBW-FM-2 Shelburne NS
CKHR-FM Hay River NT
CHWO(AM) Oakville ON
CKLP-FM Parry Sound ON
CFMO-FM Smiths Falls ON
CKTB(AM) St. Catharines ON
CKOT(AM) Tillsonburg ON
CFVM(AM) Amqui PQ
CJAN(AM) Asbestos PQ
CHLC(AM) Baie Comeau PQ
CJAF(AM) Hay Lake PQ
CJBM(AM) Causapscal PQ
CHVD(AM) Dolbeau PQ
CHVD-FM Dolbeau PQ
CHRD(AM) Drummondville PQ
CFRP(AM) Forestville PQ
CHIP-FM Fort Coulonge PQ
CJRG-FM Gaspe PQ
CIMF-FM Hull PQ
CKCH(AM) Hull PQ
CJLM(AM) Joliette PQ
CKLS(AM) La Sarre PQ
CKFL(AM) Lac Megantic PQ
*CFIN-FM Lac-Etchemin PQ
CFGL-FM Laval PQ

CIEL-FM Longueuil PQ
CKMG(AM) Maniwaki PQ
CBGA(AM) Matane PQ
CHRM(AM) Matane PQ
CKAC(AM) Montreal PQ
CHNC(AM) New Carlisle PQ
CKTL(AM) Plessisville PQ
CHRC(AM) Quebec PQ
CKIA-FM Quebec PQ
CFLP(AM) Rimouski PQ
CJBR(AM) Rimouski PQ
CJRE-FM Riviere au Renard PQ
CJFP(AM) Riviere du Loup PQ
CKCN(AM) Sept-Iles PQ
CHLT(AM) Sherbrooke PQ
CHRT(AM) St. Eleuthere PQ
CFNJ-FM St. Gabriel-de-Brandon PQ
CIHO-FM St. Hilarion PQ
CFEI(AM) St. Hyacinthe PQ
CIME-FM Ste. Adele PQ
CBGN(AM) Ste. Anne des Monts PQ
CJMC(AM) Ste. Anne des Monts PQ
*CFIC-FM Ste. Anne des Plaines PQ
CJVL(AM) Ste. Marie-de-Beauce PQ
CKLD(AM) Thetford Mines PQ
CHLN(AM) Trois Rivieres PQ
CKVD(AM) Val d'Or PQ
CKVL(AM) Verdun PQ
CFDA(AM) Victoriaville PQ
CKBI(AM) Prince Albert SK
CJSN(AM) Shaunavon SK

New Age

CKKL-FM Ottawa ON
CFEL-FM Montmagny PQ

News

CBX(AM) Edmonton AB
CBX-FM Edmonton AB
*CBTK-FM Kelowna BC
CKIQ(AM) Kelowna BC
CKIQ-FM Big White Ski Village BC
*CFPR(AM) Prince Rupert BC
CBGY(AM) Bonavista Bay NF
CBDQ(AM) Wabush NF
CIFA-FM Yarmouth NS
CFPL(AM) London ON
CFRB(AM) Toronto ON
CFTR(AM) Toronto ON
CHRD(AM) Drummondville PQ
CFIM-FM Iles-de-la-Madeleine PQ
*CBV(AM) Quebec PQ
CBVE-FM Quebec PQ
CHRC(AM) Quebec PQ
CJRP(AM) Quebec PQ
CFQC(AM) Saskatoon SK

News/Talk

*CBR(AM) Calgary AB
*CBR-FM Calgary AB
CHQR(AM) Calgary AB
*CJSW-FM Calgary AB
*CHFA(AM) Edmonton AB
CKOV(AM) Kelowna BC
CHUB(AM) Nanaimo BC
CKNW(AM) New Westminster BC
*CFPR(AM) Prince Rupert BC
*CBU(AM) Vancouver BC
CBAF-FM Moncton NB
*CBY(AM) Corner Brook NF
CJRM(AM) Labrador City NF
*CBN-FM St. John's NF
*CFYK(AM) Yellowknife NT
CHML(AM) Hamilton ON
CKSL(AM) London ON
CFOS(AM) Owen Sound ON
CKLW(AM) Windsor ON
CJRC(AM) Gatineau PQ
*CFTH-FM Harrington Harbour PQ
CJMS(AM) Montreal PQ

Nostalgia

CKWW(AM) Windsor ON

Oldies

CFFR(AM) Calgary AB
CFRN(AM) Edmonton AB

CFGP(AM) Grande Prairie AB
CKRD(AM) Red Deer AB
CHMG(AM) St. Albert AB
CHLW(AM) St. Paul AB
CFWB(AM) Campbell River BC
CFCP(AM) Courtenay BC
CHNL(AM) Kamloops BC
CKIQ-FM Big White Ski Village BC
CKOR(AM) Penticton BC
CFNI(AM) Port Hardy BC
CISL(AM) Richmond BC
CHOR(AM) Summerland BC
CJVI(AM) Victoria BC
CKWL(AM) Williams Lake BC
CITI-FM Winnipeg MB
CKY(AM) Winnipeg MB
CIHI(AM) Fredericton NB
CJCW(AM) Sussex NB
CFGN(AM) Port-aux-Basques NF
CJYQ(AM) St. John's NF
CKDH(AM) Amherst NS
CHNS(AM) Halifax NS
CJCH(AM) Halifax NS
CKEN(AM) Kentville NS
CBI-FM Sydney NS
CKDR-6(AM) Atikokan ON
CJNH(AM) Bancroft ON
CKBB(AM) Barrie ON
CING-FM Burlington ON
CFCO(AM) Chatham ON
CHUC(AM) Cobourg ON
CKCB(AM) Collingwood ON
CFOB(AM) Fort Frances ON
CJOY(AM) Guelph ON
CHML(AM) Hamilton ON
CKOC(AM) Hamilton ON
CFFX(AM) Kingston ON
CKLY(AM) Lindsay ON
CFPL(AM) London ON
CJRN(AM) Niagara Falls ON
CHUR(AM) North Bay ON
CHWO(AM) Oakville ON
CIDC-FM Orangeville ON
CKDO(AM) Oshawa ON
CFRA(AM) Ottawa ON
CFOS(AM) Owen Sound ON
CKLP-FM Parry Sound ON
CFPS(AM) Port Elgin ON
CHOK(AM) Sarnia ON
CJCS(AM) Stratford ON
CHNO(AM) Sudbury ON
CKPR(AM) Thunder Bay ON
CHUM(AM) Toronto ON
CJEZ-FM Toronto ON
CKLW-FM Windsor ON
CHTN(AM) Charlottetown PE
*CFTH-FM Harrington Harbour PQ
CFEL-FM Montmagny PQ
CKIS(AM) Montreal PQ
CHRC(AM) Quebec PQ
CJRP(AM) Quebec PQ
CFYM(AM) Kindersley SK
CKBI(AM) Prince Albert SK
CJME(AM) Regina SK
CJYM(AM) Rosetown SK
CKRW(AM) Whitehorse YT

Other

CJLX-FM Belleville ON
CING-FM Burlington ON
CBEG-FM Sarnia ON
CBMI-FM Baie Comeau PQ

Progressive

*CJSW-FM Calgary AB
CJSR-FM Edmonton AB
*CITR-FM Vancouver BC
*CFUV-FM Victoria BC
CHSR-FM Fredericton NB
CHMR-FM St. John's NF
CFNY-FM Brampton ON
CFRU-FM Guelph ON
CKWR-FM Kitchener ON
CKCU-FM Ottawa ON
CHRY-FM Toronto ON
*CJAM-FM Windsor ON
CKOI-FM Verdun PQ

Public Affairs

*CBTK-FM Kelowna BC
CBYG-FM Prince George BC
*CFRO-FM Vancouver BC
CBGY-FM Bonavista Bay NF
CBI(AM) Sydney NS

CBQX-FM Kenora ON
CBQN-FM Osnaburgh ON
CKCU-FM Ottawa ON
CBQP-FM Pickle Lake ON
CBQL-FM Savant Lake ON
CBMI-FM Baie Comeau PQ
CBOF-1(AM) Maniwaki PQ
*CBKA-FM La Ronge SK

Religious

CKER(AM) Edmonton AB
CHRB(AM) High River AB
CJOI(AM) Wetaskiwin AB
CIGV-FM Penticton BC
CJRB(AM) Boissevain MB
*VOAR(AM) Mount Pearl NF

Rock/AOR

CKIK-FM Calgary AB
CIRK-FM Edmonton AB
CKYX-FM Fort McMurray AB
*CHCL(AM) Medley AB
CIZZ-FM Red Deer AB
CIFM-FM Kamloops BC
CKLZ-FM Kelowna BC
CJMG-FM Penticton BC
CFOX-FM Vancouver BC
CKKQ-FM Victoria BC
CKX-FM Brandon MB
CJAR(AM) The Pas MB
CITI-FM Winnipeg MB
CFOZ-FM Argentia NF
CJOZ-FM Bonavista Bay NF
CJKK-FM Clarenville NF
CKOZ-FM Corner Brook NF
CIOZ-FM Marystown NF
CHOS-FM Rattling Brook NF
CHOZ-FM St. John's NF
VOCM-FM St. John's NF
CIOS-FM Stephenville NF
CFRQ-FM Dartmouth NS
CKWM-FM Kentville NS
CFJB-FM Barrie ON
CJLX-FM Belleville ON
CFNY-FM Brampton ON
CHXL-FM Brockville ON
*CHRW-FM London ON
CHEZ-FM Ottawa ON
CJSB-FM Ottawa ON
CIXK-FM Owen Sound ON
CHTZ-FM St. Catharines ON
CJSD-FM Thunder Bay ON
CJQQ-FM Timmins ON
CHUM-FM Toronto ON
CILQ-FM Toronto ON
CIMX-FM Windsor ON
*CFIN-FM Lac-Etchemin PQ
CHOM-FM Montreal PQ
CIKI-FM Rimouski PQ
CIBM-FM Riviere du Loup PQ
CJMM-FM Rouyn-Noranda PQ
CFJO-FM Thetford Mines PQ
CIZL-FM Regina SK
CFMC-FM Saskatoon SK
CHON-FM Whitehorse YT

Sports

CHQR(AM) Calgary AB
CHML(AM) Hamilton ON
CJBK(AM) London ON
CJRN(AM) Niagara Falls ON
CJCL(AM) Toronto ON
CHRC(AM) Quebec PQ

Talk

CBX(AM) Edmonton AB
CKAY(AM) Duncan BC
CFAX(AM) Victoria BC
VOCM(AM) St. John's NF
CBQR-FM Rankin Inlet NT
CJRN(AM) Niagara Falls ON
*CBO-FM Ottawa ON
CBL(AM) Toronto ON
CBL-FM Toronto ON
*CJAM-FM Windsor ON
CBCT-FM Charlottetown PE
*CBJ-FM Chicoutimi PQ
CFIM-FM Iles-de-la-Madeleine PQ
CBF(AM) Montreal PQ
CJAD(AM) Montreal PQ
*CBV(AM) Quebec PQ
CBVE-FM Quebec PQ
CJRP(AM) Quebec PQ

*CBSI-FM Sept-Iles PQ
CKTS(AM) Sherbrooke PQ
CJTR(AM) Trois Rivieres PQ
CKVL(AM) Verdun PQ
*CFWH(AM) Whitehorse YT

Variety/Diverse

*CBR(AM) Calgary AB
*CBR-FM Calgary AB
*CKUA-FM-1 Calgary AB
CFHC(AM) Canmore AB
*CHFA(AM) Edmonton AB
*CKUA-FM Edmonton AB
CJOC(AM) Lethbridge AB
CKAY(AM) Duncan BC
CKST(AM) Langley BC
CJAV(AM) Port Alberni BC
CBUF-FM Vancouver BC
CHFC(AM) Churchill MB
*CKSB(AM) St. Boniface MB
*CBWK-FM Thompson MB
CBW(AM) Winnipeg MB
CBW-FM Winnipeg MB
CJVA-FM Caraquet NB
*CBZ(AM) Fredericton NB
*CBZ-FM Fredericton NB
CBA(AM) Moncton NB
CBAF-FM Moncton NB
CBAL-FM Moncton NB
CKUM-FM Moncton NB
*CHMA-FM Sackville NB
CJRM-FM Labrador City NF
*CBN(AM) St. John's NF
CHMR-FM St. John's NF
*VOWR(AM) St. John's NF
CBH-FM Halifax NS
CKDU-FM Halifax NS
CIFA-FM Yarmouth NS
CHAR-FM Alert NT
CKHR-FM Hay River NT
CHAK(AM) Inuvik NT
CFFB(AM) Iqaluit NT
CBQR-FM Rankin Inlet NT
CFCT(AM) Tuktoyaktuk NT
*CFYK-FM Yellowknife NT
CKON-FM Akwesasne NT
CFRU-FM Guelph ON
*CFMU-FM Hamilton ON
*CFRC-FM Kingston ON
CKWR-FM Kitchener ON
CHMO(AM) Moosonee ON
CJTT(AM) New Liskeard ON
*CBO-FM Ottawa ON
*CBOQ-FM Ottawa ON
*CHUO-FM Ottawa ON
CJSB(AM) Ottawa ON
CKCU-FM Ottawa ON
*CFFF-FM Peterborough ON
CBQS-FM Sioux Narrows ON
*CBON-FM Sudbury ON
*CBQ-FM Thunder Bay ON
*CBQT-FM Thunder Bay ON
CHRY-FM Toronto ON
*CIUT-FM Toronto ON
CJBC(AM) Toronto ON
*CKLN-FM Toronto ON
*CKMS-FM Waterloo ON
CBE(AM) Windsor ON
CBE-FM Windsor ON
CBEF(AM) Windsor ON
CBJ(AM) Chicoutimi PQ
CFMF-FM Fermont PQ
CFIM-FM Iles-de-la-Madeleine PQ
CHOC-FM Jonquiere PQ
CKLO(AM) L'Annonciation PQ
CFLM(AM) La Tuque PQ
*CFIN-FM Lac-Etchemin PQ
CHGA-FM Maniwaki PQ
CBF(AM) Montreal PQ
*CIBL-FM Montreal PQ
*CISM-FM Montreal PQ
*CKUT-FM Montreal PQ
CFVD-FM-2 Pohenegamook PQ
*CBV(AM) Quebec PQ
CBVE-FM Quebec PQ
*CKRL-FM Quebec PQ
*CBKF-1(AM) Gravelbourg SK
*CBK(AM) Regina SK
*CBK-FM Regina SK
*CBKF-2(AM) Saskatoon SK
*CBKS-FM Saskatoon SK

Special Programming on Radio Stations in the U.S.

Adult Contemporary

*WLJS-FM Jacksonville AL
KNTI(FM) Lakeport CA 3 hrs
KOLV(FM) Olivia MN
*KSRQ(FM) Thief River Falls MN 6 hrs
*WHYC(FM) Swan Quarter NC 24 hrs
KHRT(AM) Minot ND 1 hr
KITX(FM) Hugo OK 2 hrs
*WWEC(FM) Elizabethtown PA 15 hrs

Agriculture & Farm

WANA(AM) Anniston AL 1 hr
WKAC(AM) Athens AL 5 hrs
WVNN(AM) Athens AL 2 hrs
WYDH(FM) Atmore AL 5 hrs
WAUD(AM) Auburn AL 2 hrs
WEBJ(AM) Brewton AL 1 hr
WKNU(FM) Brewton AL 3 hrs
WRAG(AM) Carrollton AL 2 hrs
WAGC(AM) Centre AL 1 hr
WRHY(FM) Centre AL 1 hr
WKUL(FM) Cullman AL 15 hrs
WXXR(AM) Cullman AL 2 hrs
WTVY-FM Dothan AL 10 hrs
WKMX(FM) Enterprise AL 2 hrs
WULA(AM) Eufaula AL 2 hrs
WULA-FM Eufaula AL
WABF(AM) Fairhope AL 1 hr
WKWL(AM) Florala AL 2 hrs
WHEP(AM) Foley AL 2 hrs
WZOB(AM) Fort Payne AL 2 hrs
WAAX(AM) Gadsden AL 6 hrs
WQZX(FM) Greenville AL
WJBB(AM) Haleyville AL 3 hrs
WERH(AM) Hamilton AL
WRJL(AM) Hanceville AL 1 hr
WBHP(AM) Huntsville AL 6 hrs
WACV(AM) Montgomery AL 5 hrs
WHIY(AM) Moulton AL 6 hrs
WOPP(AM) Opp AL 4 hrs
WKEA-FM Scottsboro AL 1 hr
WHBB(AM) Selma AL 10 hrs
WBTG-FM Sheffield AL 1 hr
WRSM(AM) Sumiton AL 1 hr
WACQ(AM) Tallassee AL
WTLS(AM) Tallassee AL 6 hrs
WTBF(AM) Troy AL 17 hrs
KAPZ(AM) Bald Knob AR 3 hrs
KAAB(AM) Batesville AR 5 hrs
KTHS(AM) Berryville AR 15 hrs
KFCA(AM) Conway AR 6 hrs
KDDA(AM) Dumas AR 6 hrs
KXFE(FM) Dumas AR 6 hrs
KLRA(AM) England AR 5 hrs
KLRA-FM England AR 5 hrs
KXJK(AM) Forrest City AR 16 hrs
KCRI-FM Helena AR 12 hrs
KFFA(AM) Helena AR 12 hrs
KXAR(AM) Hope AR 6 hrs
*KASU(FM) Jonesboro AR 7 hrs
KFIN(FM) Jonesboro AR 13 hrs
KNEA(AM) Jonesboro AR 6 hrs
KVMA(AM) Magnolia AR 2 hrs
KZOT(AM) Marianna AR 7 hrs
KVSA(AM) McGehee AR 5 hrs
KHBM(AM) Monticello AR 5 hrs
KHBM-FM Monticello AR 5 hrs
KOSE(AM) Osceola AR 5 hrs
KDRS(AM) Paragould AR 10 hrs
KTEI(FM) Piggott AR 5 hrs
KOTN(AM) Pine Bluff AR 6 hrs
KPOC(AM) Pocahontas AR 10 hrs
KURM(AM) Rogers AR 10 hrs
KARV(AM) Russellville AR 5 hrs
KSAR(FM) Salem AR 4 hrs
KWCK(AM) Searcy AR 10 hrs
KWCK-FM Searcy AR 3 hrs
KGHT(AM) Sheridan AR 10 hrs
KWAK(AM) Stuttgart AR 6 hrs
KTWN-FM Texarkana AR 2 hrs
KRWA-FM Waldron AR 5 hrs
KWYN(AM) Wynne AR 6 hrs
WVUV(AM) Leone AS 1 hr
KAPR(AM) Douglas AZ 2 hrs
KDJI(AM) Holbrook AZ 8 hrs
KLPZ(AM) Parker AZ 1 hr
KVSL(AM) Show Low AZ 2 hrs
KBLU(AM) Yuma AZ 6 hrs
KEZC(AM) Yuma AZ 1 hr
KCNO(AM) Alturas CA 1 hr
KERN(AM) Bakersfield CA 1 hr
*KZPN(FM) Bayside CA 2 hrs
KROP(AM) Brawley CA 18 hrs
*KZFR(FM) Chico CA 1 hr
KXO(AM) El Centro CA 7 hrs
KMJ(AM) Fresno CA 6 hrs
*KMUD(FM) Garberville CA 1 hr
KRKC(AM) King City CA 10 hrs
KCLL(AM) Lompoc CA 3 hrs
KLBS(AM) Los Banos CA 5 hrs
KUBB(FM) Mariposa CA 2 hrs
KYOS(AM) Merced CA 5 hrs
KBEE(AM) Modesto CA 3 hrs
KVON(AM) Napa CA 3 hrs
KCMJ(AM) Palm Springs CA 5 hrs
KBLF(AM) Red Bluff CA 5 hrs
KRAK(AM) Sacramento CA 4 hrs
KRAK-FM Sacramento CA 5 hrs
KSTN(AM) Stockton CA 3 hrs
KJDX(FM) Susanville CA 3 hrs
KSUE(AM) Susanville CA 2 hrs
KJUG(AM) Tulare CA 5 hrs
KJUG-FM Tulare CA 5 hrs
KWNE(FM) Ukiah CA 1 hr
KIQS(AM) Willows CA 2 hrs
KIQS-FM Willows CA 3 hrs
KSYC(AM) Yreka CA
KUBA(AM) Yuba City CA 4 hrs
KGIW(AM) Alamosa CO 6 hrs
KSIR(AM) Brush CO 16 hrs
KRAI(AM) Craig CO 1 hr
KTMG(AM) Deer Trail CO
KDTA(AM) Delta CO 1 hr
KIDN-FM Hayden CO 1 hr
KLMR(AM) Lamar CO 19 hrs
KLMO(AM) Longmont CO 1 hr
KSLV(AM) Monte Vista CO 2 hrs
KKXK(FM) Montrose CO 2 hrs
KSTC(AM) Sterling CO 10 hrs
KCRT(AM) Trinidad CO 1 hr
KIIX(AM) Wellington CO 5 hrs
WYUS(AM) Milford DE 2 hrs
WGMD(FM) Rehoboth Beach DE 2 hrs
WDEL(AM) Wilmington DE 1 hr
WAFC-FM Clewiston FL 1 hr
WDCF(AM) Dade City FL 2 hrs
WKGR(FM) Fort Pierce FL 1 hr
WFIV(AM) Kissimmee FL 7 hrs
WKZY(FM) La Belle FL 1 hr
WLBE(AM) Leesburg FL 3 hrs
WJXR(FM) Macclenny FL 1 hr
WTYS(AM) Marianna FL 1 hr
WMFL(AM) Monticello FL 2 hrs
WMOP(AM) Ocala FL 1 hr
WTMC(AM) Ocala FL 5 hrs
WCWB-FM Trenton FL 2 hrs
WJYZ(AM) Albany GA 10 hrs
WKXH-FM Alma GA 2 hrs
WULF(AM) Alma GA 2 hrs
WDEC-FM Americus GA 1 hr
WGAC(AM) Augusta GA 4 hrs
WGIA(AM) Blackshear GA 10 hrs
WJTH(AM) Calhoun GA 1 hr
WQVE(FM) Camilla GA 10 hrs
WLBB(AM) Carrollton GA 1 hr
WYXC(AM) Cartersville GA 5 hrs
WGAA(AM) Cedartown GA 2 hrs
WRCG(AM) Columbus GA 3 hrs
WJJC(AM) Commerce GA 2 hrs
WCUG(AM) Cuthbert GA 8 hrs
WDMG(AM) Douglas GA 20 hrs
WMLT(AM) Dublin GA 6 hrs
WBHB(AM) Fitzgerald GA 6 hrs
WCEH(AM) Hawkinsville GA 5 hrs
WVOH(AM) Hazlehurst GA 2 hrs
WIFO-FM Jesup GA 10 hrs
WLOP(AM) Jesup GA 10 hrs
WQCH(AM) La Fayette GA 2 hrs
WBBT(AM) Lyons GA 6 hrs
WYTH(AM) Madison GA 15 hrs
WFDR(AM) Manchester GA 15 hrs
WKKP(AM) McDonough GA 1 hr
WMCG(FM) Milan GA 1 hr
WMKO(FM) Millen GA 10 hrs
WKUN(AM) Monroe GA 10 hrs
WMGA(AM) Moultrie GA 10 hrs
WMTM(AM) Moultrie GA 16 hrs
WALH(AM) Mountain City GA 2 hrs
WPGA(AM) Perry GA 2 hrs
WSTI-FM Quitman GA 5 hrs
WPTB(AM) Statesboro GA 3 hrs
WWNS(AM) Statesboro GA 12 hrs
WJAT(AM) Swainsboro GA 5 hrs
WSYL(AM) Sylvania GA 10 hrs
WSFT(AM) Thomaston GA 2 hrs
WPAX(AM) Thomasville GA 2 hrs
WTHO-FM Thomson GA 2 hrs
WTIF(AM) Tifton GA 5 hrs
WNEG(AM) Toccoa GA 1 hr
WRCC-FM Warner Robins GA 3 hrs
WZCM(AM) Young Harris GA 1 hr
KGUM(AM) Agana GU 1 hr
KLGA(AM) Algona IA
KLEH(AM) Anamosa IA 5 hrs
KJAN(AM) Atlantic IA 12 hrs
KRUU(FM) Boone IA 15 hrs
KWBG(AM) Boone IA 15 hrs
KBUR(AM) Burlington IA 14 hrs
KCPS(AM) Burlington IA 10 hrs
WMT(AM) Cedar Rapids IA 19 hrs
KCHA(AM) Charles City IA 12 hrs
KCHA-FM Charles City IA 12 hrs
KCHE(AM) Cherokee IA 12 hrs
KLNT(AM) Clinton IA 10 hrs
KROS(AM) Clinton IA 5 hrs
KCZQ(FM) Cresco IA 12 hrs
WOC(AM) Davenport IA 10 hrs
KDSN(AM) Denison IA 7 hrs
KDSN-FM Denison IA 7 hrs
WHO(AM) Des Moines IA 15 hrs
KDTH(AM) Dubuque IA 8 hrs
KDST(FM) Dyersville IA
KKSI(FM) Eddyville IA 1 hr
KEMB(FM) Emmetsburg IA 10 hrs
KILR(AM) Estherville IA 4 hrs
KILR-FM Estherville IA 4 hrs
KIIK-FM Fairfield IA 7 hrs
KMCD(AM) Fairfield IA 10 hrs
KIOW(FM) Forest City IA 15 hrs
KWMT(AM) Fort Dodge IA
KCTN(FM) Garnavillo IA
KGRN(AM) Grinnell IA 12 hrs
KGCI(FM) Grundy Center IA 1 hr
KLMJ(FM) Hampton IA 16 hrs
KNOD(FM) Harlan IA 3 hrs
KHBT(FM) Humboldt IA 10 hrs
KIDA-FM Ida Grove IA 10 hrs
KQMG(AM) Independence IA 6 hrs
KQMG-FM Independence IA 10 hrs
KCJJ(AM) Iowa City IA 3 hrs
KIFG(AM) Iowa Falls IA 5 hrs
KIFG-FM Iowa Falls IA 5 hrs
KLSN(FM) Jefferson IA 15 hrs
KOKX(AM) Keokuk IA 6 hrs
KOKX-FM Keokuk IA 5 hrs
KLEM(AM) Le Mars IA 18 hrs
KMCH(FM) Manchester IA 7 hrs
KMAQ(AM) Maquoketa IA 10 hrs
KGLO(AM) Mason City IA 15 hrs
KCZE(FM) New Hampton IA 12 hrs
KCOB(AM) Newton IA 4 hrs
KCOB-FM Newton IA 4 hrs
KOEL(AM) Oelwein IA 16 hrs
KCZY(FM) Osage IA 12 hrs
KJJC(FM) Osceola IA 8 hrs
KBOE(AM) Oskaloosa IA 5 hrs
KBOE-FM Oskaloosa IA 5 hrs
KBIZ(AM) Ottumwa IA 12 hrs
*KCUI(FM) Pella IA
KMA(AM) Shenandoah IA
*KDCR(FM) Sioux Center IA 2 hrs
KMNS(AM) Sioux City IA 20 hrs
KSCJ(AM) Sioux City IA 16 hrs
KTFC(FM) Sioux City IA 5 hrs
KWSL(AM) Sioux City IA 2 hrs
KUOO(FM) Spirit Lake IA 5 hrs
KAYL(AM) Storm Lake IA 20 hrs
KKRF(FM) Stuart IA 5 hrs
KTLB(FM) Twin Lakes IA 15 hrs
KCII(AM) Washington IA
KCII-FM Washington IA
KWLO(AM) Waterloo IA
KXEL(AM) Waterloo IA 18 hrs
KQWC(AM) Webster City IA 8 hrs
KBOI(AM) Boise ID 3 hrs
KKIC(AM) Boise ID 5 hrs
KBFI(AM) Bonners Ferry ID 2 hrs
KCID(AM) Caldwell ID 16 hrs
KCID-FM Caldwell ID 4 hrs
KVNI(AM) Coeur d'Alene ID 1 hr
KORT(AM) Grangeville ID 2 hrs
KKCH-FM Hayden ID 1 hr
KID(AM) Idaho Falls ID 18 hrs
KOZE(AM) Lewiston ID 2 hrs
KRLC(AM) Lewiston ID 5 hrs
KVSI(AM) Montpelier ID 2 hrs
KRPL(AM) Moscow ID 4 hrs
KZFN(FM) Moscow ID 4 hrs
KSEI(AM) Pocatello ID 1 hr
KWIK(AM) Pocatello ID 3 hrs
KACH(AM) Preston ID
KSRA(AM) Salmon ID 4 hrs
KOFE(AM) St. Maries ID 2 hrs
KEZJ-FM Twin Falls ID 5 hrs
KLIX(AM) Twin Falls ID 2 hrs
KTFI(AM) Twin Falls ID 3 hrs
WXAN(FM) Ava IL 2 hrs
WIBV(AM) Belleville IL 3 hrs
WQRL(FM) Benton IL 3 hrs
WBNQ(FM) Bloomington IL 1 hr
WJBC(AM) Bloomington IL 13 hrs
WLMD(FM) Bushnell IL 6 hrs
WCIL(AM) Carbondale IL 1 hr
WCNL(FM) Carlinville IL 6 hrs
WROY(AM) Carmi IL 6 hrs
WDWS(AM) Champaign IL 10 hrs
WEIC(AM) Charleston IL 8 hrs
KSGM(AM) Chester IL 2 hrs
WHOW(AM) Clinton IL 10 hrs
WHOW-FM Clinton IL 6 hrs
WDAN(AM) Danville IL 5 hrs
WIAI(FM) Danville IL 10 hrs
WLBK(AM) De Kalb IL 12 hrs
WDZQ(FM) Decatur IL 8 hrs
WSOY(AM) Decatur IL 17 hrs
WIXN(AM) Dixon IL 11 hrs
WLLR-FM East Moline IL 1 hr
WBFG(FM) Effingham IL 15 hrs
WCRI(FM) Eureka IL 16 hrs
WFIW(AM) Fairfield IL 16 hrs
WFIW-FM Fairfield IL 12 hrs
WZRO(FM) Farmer City IL 5 hrs
WFRL(AM) Freeport IL 15 hrs
WXXQ(FM) Freeport IL 7 hrs
WAAG(FM) Galesburg IL 5 hrs
WGEL(FM) Greenville IL 19 hrs
WEBQ(AM) Harrisburg IL 6 hrs
WMCW(AM) Harvard IL 6 hrs
WDUK(FM) Havana IL 8 hrs
WINU(AM) Highland IL 3 hrs
WJIL(AM) Jacksonville IL 8 hrs
WLDS(AM) Jacksonville IL 20 hrs
WJBM(AM) Jerseyville IL 18 hrs
WKAN(AM) Kankakee IL 10 hrs
WKEI(AM) Kewanee IL 20 hrs
WLPO(AM) La Salle IL 10 hrs
WPRC(AM) Lincoln IL 10 hrs
WSMI(AM) Litchfield IL
WSMI-FM Litchfield IL 18 hrs
WLUV(AM) Loves Park IL 6 hrs
WLRB(AM) Macomb IL 6 hrs
WGGH(AM) Marion IL 2 hrs
WLBH-FM Mattoon IL 9 hrs
WMCI(FM) Mattoon IL 5 hrs
WGLC(AM) Mendota IL 5 hrs
WLLR(AM) Moline IL 1 hr
WMOI(FM) Monmouth IL 8 hrs
WRAM(AM) Monmouth IL 18 hrs
WCZQ(FM) Monticello IL 11 hrs
WCFL(FM) Morris IL 15 hrs
WCSJ(AM) Morris IL 20 hrs
WYER(AM) Mt. Carmel IL 5 hrs
WMIX(AM) Mt. Vernon IL 18 hrs
WMIX-FM Mt. Vernon IL 12 hrs
WVLN(AM) Olney IL 10 hrs
WCMY(AM) Ottawa IL 9 hrs
WPRS(AM) Paris IL 6 hrs
WPXN(FM) Paxton IL 10 hrs
WMBD(AM) Peoria IL 15 hrs
WBBA(AM) Pittsfield IL 10 hrs
WBBA-FM Pittsfield IL 10 hrs
WSPY(FM) Plano IL 18 hrs
WPOK(AM) Pontiac IL 16 hrs
WZOE(AM) Princeton IL 15 hrs
WTAD(AM) Quincy IL
WTAY(AM) Robinson IL 12 hrs
WTAY-FM Robinson IL 12 hrs
WKBF(AM) Rock Island IL 9 hrs
WKXQ(FM) Rushville IL 6 hrs
WJBD(AM) Salem IL 4 hrs
WJBD-FM Salem IL 4 hrs
WAUR(AM) Sandwich IL 15 hrs
WSHY(AM) Shelbyville IL 5 hrs
WTAX(AM) Springfield IL 16 hrs
WSDR(AM) Sterling IL 16 hrs
WSQR(AM) Sycamore IL 3 hrs
WTIM(AM) Taylorville IL 7 hrs
*WILL(AM) Urbana IL 7 hrs
WPMB(AM) Vandalia IL 4 hrs
WGFA-FM Watseka IL 20 hrs
WSCH(FM) Aurora IN 3 hrs
WRBI(FM) Batesville IN 5 hrs
WBIW(AM) Bedford IN 3 hrs
WSDM(AM) Brazil IN 10 hrs
WWWY(FM) Columbus IN 2 hrs
WCNB-FM Connersville IN 6 hrs
WIFE(AM) Connersville IN 6 hrs
WCVL(AM) Crawfordsville IN 5 hrs
WADM(AM) Decatur IN 2 hrs
WFRN(AM) Elkhart IN 5 hrs
WIKY-FM Evansville IN 17 hrs
WILO(AM) Frankfort IN 12 hrs
WSHW(FM) Frankfort IN 8 hrs
WFLQ(FM) French Lick IN 3 hrs
WJNZ(FM) Greencastle IN 3 hrs
WTRE(AM) Greensburg IN 10 hrs
WBDC(FM) Huntingburg IN 5 hrs
WCOE(FM) La Porte IN 8 hrs
WLOI(AM) La Porte IN 8 hrs
WASK(AM) Lafayette IN 2 hrs
WASK-FM Lafayette IN 3 hrs
WIRE(FM) Lebanon IN 12 hrs
WLNB(FM) Ligonier IN 1 hr
WSAL(AM) Logansport IN 10 hrs
WORX(AM) Madison IN 3 hrs
WORX-FM Madison IN 3 hrs
WCBK-FM Martinsville IN 1 hr
WMCB(AM) Martinsville IN 1 hr
WPCO(AM) Mt. Vernon IN 5 hrs
*WNAS(FM) New Albany IN 1 hr
WMDH(AM) New Castle IN 2 hrs
WMDH-FM New Castle IN 1 hr
WKRP(AM) North Vernon IN 5 hrs
WSEZ(AM) Paoli IN 7 hrs
WTCA(AM) Plymouth IN 11 hrs
WLQI(FM) Rensselaer IN 15 hrs
WRIN(AM) Rensselaer IN 12 hrs
WKBV(AM) Richmond IN 4 hrs
WROI(FM) Rochester IN 10 hrs
WAXI(FM) Rockville IN 5 hrs
WRCR(FM) Rushville IN 10 hrs
WZZB(AM) Seymour IN 2 hrs
WSBT(AM) South Bend IN 3 hrs
WNDI(AM) Sullivan IN 6 hrs
WBFX(AM) Terre Haute IN 6 hrs
WKID(FM) Vevay IN 8 hrs
WKUZ(FM) Wabash IN 5 hrs
WRSW(AM) Warsaw IN 11 hrs
WAMW-FM Washington IN 2 hrs
WWBL(FM) Washington IN 15 hrs
WOTD(FM) Winamac IN 10 hrs
WZZY(FM) Winchester IN 10 hrs
KSOK(AM) Arkansas City KS 10 hrs
KERE(AM) Atchison KS 7 hrs
KREP(FM) Belleville KS
KVSV(AM) Beloit KS 7 hrs
KGNO(AM) Dodge City KS 15 hrs
KSRX(AM) El Dorado KS
KIUL(AM) Garden City KS 5 hrs
KGCR(FM) Goodland KS 2 hrs
KHAZ(FM) Hays KS 10 hrs
KNZA(FM) Hiawatha KS 14 hrs
KBUF(AM) Holcomb KS 15 hrs
KFXX-FM Hugoton KS 12 hrs
KANS(AM) Larned KS 10 hrs
KLWN(AM) Lawrence KS 1 hr
KYUU(AM) Liberal KS 12 hrs
KZOC(FM) Osage City KS 18 hrs
KOFO(AM) Ottawa KS 3 hrs
KLKC(AM) Parsons KS 2 hrs
KKAN(AM) Phillipsburg KS 10 hrs
KRSL(AM) Russell KS 2 hrs
KFRM(AM) Salina KS 5 hrs
KINA(AM) Salina KS 4 hrs
KSAL(AM) Salina KS 6 hrs
KSKG(FM) Salina KS 2 hrs
KFLA(AM) Scott City KS 5 hrs
KMZA(FM) Seneca KS 7 hrs
KULY(AM) Ulysses KS 12 hrs
WANY(AM) Albany KY 2 hrs
WBRT(AM) Bardstown KY 10 hrs
WKCT(AM) Bowling Green KY 2 hrs
WKYR(AM) Burkesville KY 5 hrs
WKDZ(AM) Cadiz KY 2 hrs
WWLW(FM) Carlisle KY 5 hrs
WNES(AM) Central City KY 7 hrs
WAIN(AM) Columbia KY 2 hrs
WCPM(AM) Cumberland KY 1 hr
WCYN(AM) Cynthiana KY 15 hrs
WKNK(FM) Edmonton KY 15 hrs
WFKN(AM) Franklin KY 6 hrs
WAKY(AM) Greensburg KY 15 hrs
WXBC(FM) Hardinsburg KY 5 hrs
WKCM(AM) Hawesville KY 3 hrs
WSON(AM) Henderson KY 2 hrs
WKMO(FM) Hodgenville KY 2 hrs
WHOP-FM Hopkinsville KY 17 hrs
WQKS(AM) Hopkinsville KY 1 hr
WVLK(AM) Lexington KY 5 hrs
WHAS(AM) Louisville KY 15 hrs
WKLB(AM) Manchester KY 1 hr
WWLT(AM) Manchester KY 1 hr
WWXL-FM Manchester KY 1 hr
WMJL(AM) Marion KY 3 hrs
WMJL-FM Marion KY 3 hrs
WNGO(AM) Mayfield KY 4 hrs
WYMC(AM) Mayfield KY 8 hrs
WFTM(AM) Maysville KY 6 hrs
WFTM-FM Maysville KY 6 hrs
WMIK(AM) Middlesboro KY 1 hr
WFLW(AM) Monticello KY 5 hrs
WLOC-FM Munfordville KY 2 hrs
WNBS(AM) Murray KY 6 hrs
WBKR(FM) Owensboro KY 2 hrs
WVJS(AM) Owensboro KY 1 hr
WKCA(FM) Owingsville KY 2 hrs
WPKY(AM) Princeton KY 5 hrs
WHRZ(FM) Providence KY 2 hrs
WLCK(AM) Scottsville KY 3 hrs
WVLE(FM) Scottsville KY 3 hrs
WCND(AM) Shelbyville KY 6 hrs
WTHQ(FM) Shelbyville KY 6 hrs
WSEK(FM) Somerset KY 1 hr
WSFC(AM) Somerset KY 2 hrs
WTLO(AM) Somerset KY 1 hr
WMQQ(FM) Springfield KY 10 hrs
WRSL(AM) Stanford KY 4 hrs
WRSL-FM Stanford KY 4 hrs
WBFC(AM) Stanton KY 2 hrs
WMTC(AM) Vancleve KY 2 hrs
WLKS(AM) West Liberty KY 5 hrs
KCTO(AM) Columbia LA 3 hrs
KCTO-FM Columbia LA 3 hrs
KPWS(AM) Crowley LA 4 hrs
KSIG(AM) Crowley LA 5 hrs
KFNV-FM Ferriday LA 2 hrs
KJNA(AM) Jena LA 3 hrs
KLCL(AM) Lake Charles LA 2 hrs
KLPL(AM) Lake Providence LA 8 hrs
KLPL-FM Lake Providence LA 10 hrs
KAPB(AM) Marksville LA 6 hrs
KAPB-FM Marksville LA 6 hrs
KNOC(AM) Natchitoches LA 1 hr
KANE(AM) New Iberia LA 2 hrs
KAIN(AM) Vidalia LA 3 hrs
KVPI(AM) Ville Platte LA 12 hrs
KNEK(AM) Washington LA 4 hrs
WBZ(AM) Boston MA 1 hr
WTRI(AM) Brunswick MD 2 hrs
WCTR(AM) Chestertown MD 5 hrs
WSER(AM) Elkton MD 1 hr
WJEJ(AM) Hagerstown MD 1 hr
WMOM(AM) La Plata MD 2 hrs
WSBY-FM Salisbury MD 2 hrs
WTTR(AM) Westminster MD 4 hrs
WABJ(AM) Adrian MI 7 hrs
WLEN(FM) Adrian MI 6 hrs
WFYC(AM) Alma MI 4 hrs
WFYC-FM Alma MI 4 hrs
WATZ(AM) Alpena MI 2 hrs
WTKA(AM) Ann Arbor MI 9 hrs
WLEW(AM) Bad Axe MI 4 hrs
WHFB(AM) Benton Harbor-St. Joseph MI 4 hrs
WBRN(AM) Big Rapids MI 6 hrs
WBCM(FM) Boyne City MI 1 hr
WYTW(FM) Cadillac MI
WKYO(AM) Caro MI 18 hrs
WTVB(AM) Coldwater MI 6 hrs

Special Programming on Radio Stations in the U.S.

WDOW(AM) Dowagiac MI 7 hrs
WCHT(AM) Escanaba MI 1 hr
WGHN(AM) Grand Haven MI 5 hrs
WOOD(AM) Grand Rapids MI 6 hrs
WCSR(AM) Hillsdale MI 3 hrs
WWJQ(AM) Holland MI 1 hr
WION(AM) Ionia MI 8 hrs
WKZO(AM) Kalamazoo MI 10 hrs
WWGZ(AM) Lapeer MI 5 hrs
WCEN(AM) Mount Pleasant MI 5 hrs
WCEN-FM Mount Pleasant MI 5 hrs
WOAP(AM) Owosso MI 2 hrs
WPHM(AM) Port Huron MI 1 hr
WSGW(AM) Saginaw MI 10 hrs
WMIC(AM) Sandusky MI 12 hrs
WCSY(AM) South Haven MI 3 hrs
WCSY-FM South Haven MI 3 hrs
WMLM(AM) St. Louis MI 5 hrs
WLKM(AM) Three Rivers MI 3 hrs
WTCM(AM) Traverse City MI 5 hrs
WEFG(AM) Whitehall MI 1 hr
KATE(AM) Albert Lea MN 18 hrs
KIKV-FM Alexandria MN 20 hrs
KXRA(AM) Alexandria MN 5 hrs
KSCR(AM) Benson MN 10 hrs
KJLY(FM) Blue Earth MN 5 hrs
WLOL(FM) Cambridge MN 8 hrs
WKLK(AM) Cloquet MN 1 hr
KROX(AM) Crookston MN 10 hrs
KCNN(AM) East Grand Forks MN 6 hrs
KFMC(FM) Fairmont MN 4 hrs
KSUM(AM) Fairmont MN 18 hrs
KBRF(AM) Fergus Falls MN 15 hrs
KKCQ(AM) Fosston MN 5 hrs
*KAXE(FM) Grand Rapids MN 1 hr
KDUZ(AM) Hutchinson MN 18 hrs
KKOJ(AM) Jackson MN 15 hrs
KLFD(AM) Litchfield MN 20 hrs
KLTF(AM) Little Falls MN 8 hrs
KEYL(AM) Long Prairie MN 5 hrs
KLQL(FM) Luverne MN 10 hrs
KLQP(FM) Madison MN 5 hrs
KYSM(AM) Mankato MN 4 hrs
KYSM-FM Mankato MN 4 hrs
KDMA(AM) Montevideo MN 7 hrs
KMGM(FM) Montevideo MN 1 hr
KYMN(AM) Northfield MN 2 hrs
KCGN-FM Ortonville MN 6 hrs
KDIO(AM) Ortonville MN 10 hrs
WCMP(AM) Pine City MN 6 hrs
WQPM(AM) Princeton MN 9 hrs
KOLM(AM) Rochester MN 3 hrs
KROC(AM) Rochester MN 12 hrs
WVAL(AM) Sauk Rapids MN 3 hrs
KNSP(AM) Staples MN 6 hrs
KSNR(FM) Thief River Falls MN 1 hr
KTRF(AM) Thief River Falls MN 12 hrs
KWAD(AM) Wadena MN 10 hrs
KDJS(AM) Willmar MN 5 hrs
KWLM(AM) Willmar MN 8 hrs
KAGE(AM) Winona MN
KWOA(AM) Worthington MN
KAAN(AM) Bethany MO 10 hrs
KPCR(AM) Bowling Green MO 9 hrs
KPCR-FM Bowling Green MO 9 hrs
KZBK-FM Brookfield MO 2 hrs
KMAM(AM) Butler MO 15 hrs
KOZX(FM) Cabool MO 2 hrs
KZMO(AM) California MO 5 hrs
KMRN(AM) Cameron MO 12 hrs
KZIM(AM) Cape Girardeau MO 5 hrs
KDMO(AM) Carthage MO 12 hrs
KDFN(AM) Doniphan MO 5 hrs
KREI(AM) Farmington MO 5 hrs
KTJJ(FM) Farmington MO 6 hrs
KUNQ(FM) Houston MO 2 hrs
KLIK(AM) Jefferson City MO 12 hrs
WMBH(AM) Joplin MO 1 hr
KNNT(AM) Kennett MO 5 hrs
KIRX(AM) Kirksville MO 10 hrs
KJEL(AM) Lebanon MO 8 hrs
KLWT(AM) Lebanon MO 2 hrs
KMMO(AM) Marshall MO 6 hrs
KMMO-FM Marshall MO 6 hrs
KNIM(AM) Maryville MO 5 hrs
KMEM-FM Memphis MO 8 hrs
KWWR(FM) Mexico MO 4 hrs
KXEO(AM) Mexico MO 3 hrs
KZZT(FM) Moberly MO 3 hrs
KRMO(AM) Monett MO 10 hrs
KMCR(FM) Montgomery City MO 2 hrs
KBTN(AM) Neosho MO 6 hrs
KNEM(AM) Nevada MO 7 hrs
KNMO(FM) Nevada MO 5 hrs
KRMS(AM) Osage Beach MO 2 hrs
KBDZ(FM) Perryville MO 2 hrs
KZNN(FM) Rolla MO 3 hrs
KSMO(AM) Salem MO 4 hrs
KDRO(AM) Sedalia MO 6 hrs
KMPL(AM) Sikeston MO 6 hrs
KTTS(AM) Springfield MO 5 hrs
KTTS-FM Springfield MO 5 hrs
KWTO(AM) Springfield MO 20 hrs
KIRL(AM) St. Charles MO 3 hrs
KFEQ(AM) St. Joseph MO 20 hrs
KSTL(AM) St. Louis MO 1 hr
KXOK(AM) St. Louis MO 5 hrs
KTTN(AM) Trenton MO 4 hrs
KTTN-FM Trenton MO 7 hrs
KLGS(FM) Versailles MO 2 hrs
KOKO(AM) Warrensburg MO 4 hrs
KWRE(AM) Warrenton MO 10 hrs
KUKU-FM Willow Springs MO 6 hrs
WAMY(AM) Amory MS 1 hr
WRJH(FM) Brandon MS 1 hr
WRKN(AM) Brandon MS 1 hr
WSSI(AM) Carthage MS 2 hrs
WSSI-FM Carthage MS
WAID(FM) Clarksdale MS 3 hrs
WQST-FM Forest MS 2 hrs
WBAQ(FM) Greenville MS 2 hrs
WDDT(AM) Greenville MS 10 hrs
WGVM(AM) Greenville MS 12 hrs
WABG(AM) Greenwood MS 15 hrs
WROA(AM) Gulfport MS 1 hr
WMDC(AM) Hazelhurst MS 5 hrs
WCPC(AM) Houston MS
WJDS(AM) Jackson MS 2 hrs
WMSI(FM) Jackson MS 1 hr
WIQQ(FM) Leland MS 6 hrs
WQMA(AM) Marks MS 4 hrs
WRQO(FM) Monticello MS 1 hr
WMIS(AM) Natchez MS 6 hrs
WWMS(FM) Oxford MS 2 hrs
WZZJ(AM) Pascagoula-Moss Poin MS 1 hr
WHOC(AM) Philadelphia MS 2 hrs
WRJW(AM) Picayune MS 6 hrs
WBFN(AM) Quitman MS 2 hrs
WKOR(AM) Starkville MS 1 hr
WELO(AM) Tupelo MS 1 hr
WTYL(AM) Tylertown MS 6 hrs
WIGG(AM) Wiggins MS 5 hrs
WJNS-FM Yazoo City MS 16 hrs
KFLN(AM) Baker MT 10 hrs
KBOZ(AM) Bozeman MT 1 hr
KBOW(AM) Butte MT 5 hrs
KRYK(FM) Chinook MT 3 hrs
KDRG(AM) Deer Lodge MT 2 hrs
KMON(AM) Great Falls MT 25 hrs
KXGF(AM) Great Falls MT 2 hrs
KOJM(AM) Havre MT 4 hrs
KPQX(FM) Havre MT 6 hrs
*KXEI(FM) Havre MT 1 hr
KGEZ(AM) Kalispell MT 5 hrs
KMTA(AM) Kinsey MT 6 hrs
KXLO(AM) Lewistown MT
KMCM-FM Miles City MT 1 hr
KGRZ(AM) Missoula MT 2 hrs
KATQ(AM) Plentywood MT 5 hrs
KATQ-FM Plentywood MT 5 hrs
KCGM(FM) Scobey MT 6 hrs
KSEN(AM) Shelby MT 8 hrs
KZIN-FM Shelby MT 4 hrs
KVCK(AM) Wolf Point MT 6 hrs
KVCK-FM Wolf Point MT 1 hr
WQDK(FM) Ahoskie NC 7 hrs
WKXR(AM) Asheboro NC 1 hr
WWNC(AM) Asheville NC 1 hr
*WGWG(FM) Boiling Springs NC 1 hr
WCSL(AM) Cherryville NC 1 hr
WCLN(AM) Clinton NC 3 hrs
WCKB(AM) Dunn NC 3 hrs
WGAI(AM) Elizabeth City NC 3 hrs
WBLA(AM) Elizabethtown NC 5 hrs
WFMO(AM) Fairmont NC 10 hrs
WGBR(AM) Goldsboro NC 6 hrs
WNCT(AM) Greenville NC 10 hrs
WIZS(AM) Henderson NC 2 hrs
WKTE(AM) King NC 2 hrs
WTSB(AM) Lumberton NC 3 hrs
WHBK(AM) Marshall NC 3 hrs
*WOTJ(FM) Morehead City NC 1 hr
WMNC(AM) Morganton NC 2 hrs
WPAQ(AM) Mount Airy NC 2 hrs
WYCM(AM) Murfreesboro NC 10 hrs
WCVP(AM) Murphy NC 3 hrs
WKRK(AM) Murphy NC 2 hrs
WNOS(AM) New Bern NC 3 hrs
WCBQ(AM) Oxford NC
WPTF(AM) Raleigh NC 10 hrs
WYRU(AM) Red Springs NC 5 hrs
WREV(AM) Reidsville NC 10 hrs
WPTM(FM) Roanoke Rapids NC 15 hrs
WEGG(AM) Rose Hill NC 9 hrs
WKRX(FM) Roxboro NC 4 hrs
WRXO(AM) Roxboro NC 8 hrs
WWGP(AM) Sanford NC 7 hrs
WYAL(AM) Scotland Neck NC 2 hrs
WBZB(AM) Selma NC 5 hrs
WNCA(AM) Siler City NC 5 hrs
WMPM(AM) Smithfield NC
*WHYC(FM) Swan Quarter NC 2 hrs
WTAB(AM) Tabor City NC 8 hrs
WADE(AM) Wadesboro NC 1 hr
WLSE(AM) Wallace NC 20 hrs
WETC(AM) Wendell-Zebulon NC 5 hrs
WKSK(AM) West Jefferson NC 3 hrs
WENC(AM) Whiteville NC 5 hrs
WTXY(AM) Whiteville NC 2 hrs
KHOL(AM) Beulah ND 6 hrs
KBMR(AM) Bismarck ND 4 hrs
KPOK(AM) Bowman ND 2 hrs
KFGO(AM) Fargo ND 20 hrs
*KMHA(FM) Four Bears ND 1 hr
KXPO(AM) Grafton ND 18 hrs
KXPO-FM Grafton ND 18 hrs
KKXL(AM) Grand Forks ND 18 hrs
KQDJ(AM) Jamestown ND 6 hrs
KSJB(AM) Jamestown ND 12 hrs
KNDK(AM) Langdon ND 12 hrs
KCJB(AM) Minot ND 4 hrs
KZPR(FM) Minot ND 4 hrs
KDDR(AM) Oakes ND 15 hrs
KSSZ-FM Oakes ND 15 hrs
KZZJ(AM) Rugby ND 20 hrs
KDSR(FM) Williston ND
KAAQ(FM) Alliance NE 4 hrs
KCOW(AM) Alliance NE 8 hrs
KWBE(AM) Beatrice NE 14 hrs
KCNI(AM) Broken Bow NE
KCSR(AM) Chadron NE 25 hrs
KGMT(AM) Fairbury NE 18 hrs
KUTT(FM) Fairbury NE 12 hrs
KHUB(AM) Fremont NE 6 hrs
KHAS(AM) Hastings NE 2 hrs
KUVR(AM) Holdrege NE 5 hrs
KUVR-FM Holdrege NE 5 hrs
KIMB(AM) Kimball NE 7 hrs
KICX-FM McCook NE 6 hrs
KNCY(AM) Nebraska City NE 6 hrs
KNCY-FM Nebraska City NE 6 hrs
KNEN(FM) Norfolk NE 10 hrs
WJAG(AM) Norfolk NE
KOOQ(AM) North Platte NE 4 hrs
KBRX(AM) O'Neill NE 12 hrs
KBRX-FM O'Neill NE 12 hrs
KMCX(FM) Ogallala NE 2 hrs
KOGA(AM) Ogallala NE 10 hrs
KGRD(FM) Orchard NE 1 hr
KNLV(AM) Ord NE 8 hrs
KNLV-FM Ord NE 8 hrs
KOTD(AM) Plattsmouth NE 6 hrs
KNEB(AM) Scottsbluff NE 18 hrs
KNEB-FM Scottsbluff NE 18 hrs
KOLT(AM) Scottsbluff NE 5 hrs
KSID(AM) Sidney NE 5 hrs
KRFS(AM) Superior NE 5 hrs
KOAQ(AM) Terrytown NE 5 hrs
KTCH(AM) Wayne NE 20 hrs
KWPN(AM) West Point NE 14 hrs
KSUX(FM) Winnebago NE
KAWL(AM) York NE 7 hrs
WYKR-FM Haverhill NH 1 hr
WSNJ(AM) Bridgeton NJ 10 hrs
WSNJ-FM Bridgeton NJ 10 hrs
KPSA(AM) Alamogordo NM 1 hr
KSVP(AM) Artesia NM 1 hr
KCLV-FM Clovis NM 6 hrs
KICA(AM) Clovis NM 12 hrs
KWKA(AM) Clovis NM 3 hrs
KOTS(AM) Deming NM 5 hrs
KGRT(AM) Las Cruces NM 1 hr
KSEL(AM) Portales NM 15 hrs
KEND(FM) Roswell NM 1 hr
KMOU(FM) Roswell NM 6 hrs
KRSY(AM) Roswell NM 6 hrs
KWNA(AM) Winnemucca NV 2 hrs
WBTA(AM) Batavia NY 10 hrs
WABH(AM) Bath NY 1 hr
WVIN-FM Bath NY 1 hr
WBRV-FM Boonville NY 3 hrs
WSCM(AM) Cobleskill NY 1 hr
WKRT(AM) Cortland NY 5 hrs
WSIV(AM) East Syracuse NY 1 hr
WZZZ(AM) Fulton NY 1 hr
*WGSU(FM) Geneseo NY 1 hr
WWSC(AM) Glens Falls NY 1 hr
WGIX-FM Gouverneur NY 1 hr
WIGS(AM) Gouverneur NY 1 hr
WRWD-FM Highland NY 1 hr
WHHO(AM) Hornell NY
WLEA(AM) Hornell NY 2 hrs
WJTN(AM) Jamestown NY 1 hr
WLVL(AM) Lockport NY 6 hrs
WICY(AM) Malone NY 1 hr
WALL(AM) Middletown NY 1 hr
WACK(AM) Newark NY 5 hrs
WCHN(AM) Norwich NY 2 hrs
WEOK(AM) Poughkeepsie NY 2 hrs
WRIV(AM) Riverhead NY 8 hrs
WHAM(AM) Rochester NY 5 hrs
WODZ-FM Rome NY
WBGG(AM) Saratoga Springs NY 1 hr
WGY(AM) Schenectady NY 3 hrs
WFWC(AM) Springville NY 5 hrs
WSYR(AM) Syracuse NY 12 hrs
WIPS(AM) Ticonderoga NY 6 hrs
WIBX(AM) Utica NY 14 hrs
WDLA(AM) Walton NY 2 hrs
WCJW(AM) Warsaw NY 6 hrs
WTNY(AM) Watertown NY 3 hrs
WNYV(FM) Whitehall NY 1 hr
WNCO(AM) Ashland OH 3 hrs
WATH(AM) Athens OH 4 hrs
WBCO(AM) Bucyrus OH 8 hrs
WHBC(AM) Canton OH 1 hr
WTOF-FM Canton OH 1 hr
WCSM(AM) Celina OH 5 hrs
WKKI(FM) Celina OH 1 hr
WMNI(AM) Columbus OH 2 hrs
WWOW(AM) Conneaut OH 1 hr
WDOH(FM) Delphos OH 8 hrs
WJER(AM) Dover-New Philadelphia OH 2 hrs
WFIN(AM) Findlay OH 7 hrs
WFRO(AM) Fremont OH 4 hrs
WFRO-FM Fremont OH 4 hrs
WAXZ(FM) Georgetown OH 10 hrs
WKTN(FM) Kenton OH 2 hrs
WLOH(AM) Lancaster OH 1 hr
WIMA(AM) Lima OH 3 hrs
WBRJ(AM) Marietta OH 3 hrs
WMOA(AM) Marietta OH 1 hr
WMRN(AM) Marion OH 5 hrs
WMPO(AM) Middleport-Pomeroy OH 1 hr
WLKR-FM Norwalk OH 3 hrs
WOBL(AM) Oberlin OH 5 hrs
WQTL(FM) Ottawa OH
WSOM(AM) Salem OH 2 hrs
WLEC(AM) Sandusky OH 2 hrs
WSWR(FM) Shelby OH 12 hrs
WMVR(AM) Sidney OH 10 hrs
*WEEC(FM) Springfield OH 1 hr
WTTF(AM) Tiffin OH 3 hrs
WTTF-FM Tiffin OH 3 hrs
WSPD(AM) Toledo OH 3 hrs
WTUZ(FM) Uhrichsville OH 1 hr
WYNT(FM) Upper Sandusky OH 6 hrs
WOFR(AM) Washington Court House OH 5 hrs
WRAC(FM) West Union OH 10 hrs
WQKT(FM) Wooster OH 2 hrs
WHIZ(AM) Zanesville OH 2 hrs
KEYB(FM) Altus OK 2 hrs
KALV(AM) Alva OK 4 hrs
KKAJ(AM) Ardmore OK 2 hrs
KKBI(FM) Broken Bow OK 2 hrs
KZUE(AM) El Reno OK 7 hrs
KADS(AM) Elk City OK 8 hrs
KGWA(AM) Enid OK 3 hrs
KTAT(AM) Frederick OK 2 hrs
KOKC(AM) Guthrie OK 1 hr
KGYN(AM) Guymon OK 8 hrs
KIHN(AM) Hugo OK 3 hrs
KMAD(AM) Madill OK 2 hrs
KFXI(FM) Marlow OK 4 hrs
KMMY(FM) Muskogee OK 5 hrs
KVLH(AM) Pauls Valley OK 6 hrs
KXVQ(AM) Pawhuska OK 5 hrs
KPNC-FM Ponca City OK 5 hrs
KHJM(FM) Taft OK 1 hr
KTFX(FM) Tulsa OK 2 hrs
KVOO(AM) Tulsa OK 5 hrs
KIMY(FM) Watonga OK 1 hr
KSIW(AM) Woodward OK
KWOX(FM) Woodward OK 10 hrs
KCMX(AM) Ashland OR 3 hrs
KBKR(AM) Baker City OR 4 hrs
KZZR(AM) Burns OR 6 hrs
KWVR(AM) Enterprise OR 4 hrs
KAGO(AM) Klamath Falls OR 3 hrs
KLAD(AM) Klamath Falls OR 1 hr
KLBM(AM) La Grande OR 4 hrs
KQIK(AM) Lakeview OR 10 hrs
KQIK-FM Lakeview OR 10 hrs
KSHO(AM) Lebanon OR 1 hr
KBCH(AM) Lincoln City OR 2 hrs
KMED(AM) Medford OR 5 hrs
KSRV(AM) Ontario OR 15 hrs
KSRV-FM Ontario OR 15 hrs
KSLM(AM) Salem OR 2 hrs
KCKX(AM) Stayton OR 15 hrs
KODL(AM) The Dalles OR 4 hrs
KLWJ(AM) Umatilla OR 1 hr
KWBY(AM) Woodburn OR 3 hrs
WCNR(AM) Bloomsburg PA 3 hrs
WISR(AM) Butler PA 10 hrs
WFRM(AM) Coudersport PA 2 hrs
WDLS(FM) Dallas PA 3 hrs
WPDC(AM) Elizabethtown PA 4 hrs
WGET(AM) Gettysburg PA 12 hrs
WKSL(FM) Greencastle PA 6 hrs
WQHG(FM) Huntingdon PA
WBCW(AM) Jeannette PA 1 hr
WDAC(FM) Lancaster PA 16 hrs
WJRV(AM) Loretto PA 1 hr
WJSM(AM) Martinsburg PA 1 hr
WJSM-FM Martinsburg PA 1 hr
WVFC(AM) McConnellsburg PA 1 hr
WJUN-FM Mexico PA 1 hr
*WPEL(AM) Montrose PA 1 hr
WOYL(AM) Oil City PA 1 hr
WEEU(AM) Reading PA 2 hrs
WGCB(AM) Red Lion PA 1 hr
WATS(AM) Sayre PA 1 hr
*WQSU(FM) Selinsgrove PA 3 hrs
WKOK(AM) Sunbury PA
WKGB-FM Susquehanna PA 1 hr
WEMR(AM) Tunkhannock PA 1 hr
WMBS(AM) Uniontown PA 1 hr
WSBA(AM) York PA 4 hrs
WMIA(AM) Arecibo PR 2 hrs
WSOL(AM) Mayaguez PR 2 hrs
WYKO(AM) Sabana Grande PR 3 hrs
WKFE(AM) Yauco PR 6 hrs
WRIT(AM) Bamberg-Denmark SC 1 hr
WCRE(AM) Cheraw SC 2 hrs
WHSC(AM) Hartsville SC 3 hrs
WHSC-FM Hartsville SC 3 hrs
WJBS(AM) Holly Hill SC 2 hrs
WJAY(AM) Mullins SC 10 hrs
WJZS(AM) Orangeburg SC 3 hrs
WJRQ(FM) Saluda SC 2 hrs
WQMC(AM) Sumter SC 2 hrs
WBZK(AM) York SC 1 hr
KGIM(AM) Aberdeen SD 12 hrs
KKAA(AM) Aberdeen SD 13 hrs
KSDN(AM) Aberdeen SD 15 hrs
KBFS(AM) Belle Fourche SD 6 hrs
KBRK(AM) Brookings SD 9 hrs
KZMX(AM) Hot Springs SD 6 hrs
KOKK(AM) Huron SD 5 hrs
KBJM(AM) Lemmon SD 10 hrs
KJAM(AM) Madison SD 11 hrs
KMSD(AM) Milbank SD 6 hrs
KMIT(FM) Mitchell SD 18 hrs
KORN(AM) Mitchell SD 10 hrs
KOLY(AM) Mobridge SD
KGFX(AM) Pierre SD 18 hrs
KIMM(AM) Rapid City SD 1 hr
KOTA(AM) Rapid City SD 15 hrs
KTOQ(AM) Rapid City SD 3 hrs
KPLO-FM Reliance SD 5 hrs
KSDR-FM Watertown SD 8 hrs
KKYA(FM) Yankton SD 5 hrs
KYNT(AM) Yankton SD 5 hrs
WLAR(AM) Athens TN 2 hrs
*WHCB(FM) Bristol TN 1 hr
WNKX(AM) Centerville TN 1 hr
WDXN(AM) Clarksville TN 3 hrs
WHUB(AM) Cookeville TN 3 hrs
WZYX(AM) Cowan TN 2 hrs
WSDQ(AM) Dunlap TN 1 hr
WEKR(AM) Fayetteville TN 1 hr
WHIN(AM) Gallatin TN 5 hrs
WXJB-FM Harrogate TN 2 hrs
WDXI(AM) Jackson TN 12 hrs
WCLC(AM) Jamestown TN 2 hrs
WDEB(AM) Jamestown TN 3 hrs
WJFC(AM) Jefferson City TN 1 hr
WEEN(AM) Lafayette TN 5 hrs
WQDQ(AM) Lebanon TN 2 hrs
WLIL(AM) Lenoir City TN 4 hrs
WLIV(AM) Livingston TN 2 hrs
WIST(FM) Lobelville TN 1 hr
WAKI(AM) McMinnville TN 2 hrs
WBMC(AM) McMinnville TN 5 hrs
WMC(AM) Memphis TN 11 hrs
WREC(AM) Memphis TN 3 hrs
WMTN(AM) Morristown TN 5 hrs
WGNS(AM) Murfreesboro TN 3 hrs
WMTS(AM) Murfreesboro TN 3 hrs
WSM(AM) Nashville TN 6 hrs
*WDNX(FM) Olive Hill TN 1 hr
WMUF(AM) Paris TN 2 hrs
WUAT(AM) Pikeville TN 5 hrs
WLIJ(AM) Shelbyville TN 3 hrs
WYCQ(FM) Shelbyville TN 1 hr
WSDT(AM) Soddy-Daisy TN 1 hr
WDBL(AM) Springfield TN 10 hrs
WDBL-FM Springfield TN 10 hrs
WSGI(AM) Springfield TN 5 hrs
WKWT(FM) Union City TN 2 hrs
WCDT(AM) Winchester TN 15 hrs
WBRY(AM) Woodbury TN 1 hr
KGNC(AM) Amarillo TX 11 hrs
KLVI(AM) Beaumont TX 5 hrs
KIBL-FM Beeville TX 6 hrs
KBYG(AM) Big Spring TX 2 hrs
KFYN(AM) Bonham TX 6 hrs
KRJT(AM) Bowie TX 4 hrs
KNEL(AM) Brady TX 14 hrs
KBOC(FM) Bridgeport TX 8 hrs
KOXE(FM) Brownwood TX 3 hrs
KHLR(FM) Cameron TX 1 hr
KBEN(AM) Carrizo Springs TX 4 hrs
KCAR(AM) Clarksville TX 2 hrs
KCLE(AM) Cleburne TX 2 hrs
KSTA(AM) Coleman TX 14 hrs
KSTA-FM Coleman TX 14 hrs
WTAW(AM) College Station TX 10 hrs
KVMC(AM) Colorado City TX 8 hrs
KULM(FM) Columbus TX 4 hrs
KEGG(AM) Daingerfield TX 1 hr
KDIU(FM) Dimmitt TX 6 hrs
KURV(AM) Edinburg TX 14 hrs
KHEY(AM) El Paso TX 6 hrs
KNES(FM) Fairfield TX 3 hrs
KICA-FM Farwell TX 5 hrs
KIJN(AM) Farwell TX 3 hrs
KAWA(AM) Floydada TX 8 hrs
KFLL(FM) Floydada TX 8 hrs
WBAP(AM) Fort Worth TX 6 hrs
KNAF(AM) Fredricksburg TX 5 hrs
KGAF(AM) Gainesville TX 2 hrs
KRYL(FM) Gatesville TX 5 hrs
KOKE(FM) Giddings TX 1 hr
KCTI(AM) Gonzales TX 5 hrs
KPJN(FM) Gonzales TX 5 hrs
KPAR(AM) Granbury TX 1 hr
KGVL(AM) Greenville TX 2 hrs
KRJH(AM) Hallettsville TX 6 hrs
KCLW(AM) Hamilton TX 12 hrs
KVRP-FM Haskell TX 8 hrs
KAWS(AM) Hemphill TX 2 hrs
KWRD(AM) Henderson TX 5 hrs
KPAN(AM) Hereford TX 18 hrs
KPAN-FM Hereford TX 18 hrs
KYLR(AM) Huntsville TX 1 hr
KEBE(AM) Jacksonville TX 9 hrs
KOOI-FM Jacksonville TX 9 hrs
KTXJ(AM) Jasper TX 5 hrs
KMBL(AM) Junction TX 6 hrs
KAML(AM) Kenedy-Karnes City TX 12 hrs
KVLG(AM) La Grange TX 4 hrs
KCYL(AM) Lampasas TX 5 hrs
KZZN(AM) Littlefield TX 7 hrs
KYMI(FM) Los Ybanez TX 12 hrs
KFYO(AM) Lubbock TX 15 hrs
KCUL(AM) Marshall TX 3 hrs
KCUL-FM Marshall TX 3 hrs

Broadcasting & Cable Yearbook 1994
B-574

Special Programming on Radio Stations in the U.S.

KCRS(AM) Midland TX 5 hrs
KCRS-FM Midland TX 5 hrs
KMUL(AM) Muleshoe TX 3 hrs
KNBO(AM) New Boston TX 7 hrs
KRIL(AM) Odessa TX 2 hrs
KNET(AM) Palestine TX 2 hrs
KOMX(FM) Pampa TX 10 hrs
KGDD(AM) Paris TX 5 hrs
KIUN(AM) Pecos TX 3 hrs
KEYE(AM) Perryton TX 2 hrs
KXAL-FM Pittsburg TX 6 hrs
KATX(FM) Plainview TX 12 hrs
KKYN(AM) Plainview TX 12 hrs
KKYN-FM Plainview TX 12 hrs
KVOP(AM) Plainview TX 20 hrs
KBOP(AM) Pleasanton TX 3 hrs
KBUC(FM) Pleasanton TX 3 hrs
KPLV(FM) Port Lavaca TX 1 hr
KIXC-FM Quanah TX 5 hrs
KGKL(AM) San Angelo TX 6 hrs
KBAL(AM) San Saba TX 2 hrs
KWED(AM) Seguin TX 6 hrs
KIKZ(AM) Seminole TX 5 hrs
KSEM-FM Seminole TX 5 hrs
KJIM(AM) Sherman TX 12 hrs
KDAE(AM) Sinton TX 6 hrs
KHOS(AM) Sonora TX 2 hrs
KRDF-FM Spearman TX 18 hrs
KVRP(AM) Stamford TX 8 hrs
KSTV(AM) Stephenville TX 5 hrs
KSTV-FM Stephenville TX 5 hrs
KXOX(AM) Sweetwater TX 5 hrs
KTAE(AM) Taylor TX 4 hrs
KCMC(AM) Texarkana TX
KTUE(AM) Tulia TX 10 hrs
KVOU(AM) Uvalde TX 12 hrs
KAMG(AM) Victoria TX 1 hr
WACO(AM) Waco TX 5 hrs
KBEC(AM) Waxahachie TX 3 hrs
KZEE(AM) Weatherford TX 1 hr
KWFT(AM) Wichita Falls TX 13 hrs
KVLL(AM) Woodville TX 02 hrs
KSOS(AM) Brigham City UT 8 hrs
KSUB(AM) Cedar City UT 6 hrs
KNAK(AM) Delta UT
KVNU(AM) Logan UT 2 hrs
KMTI(AM) Manti UT 6 hrs
KOAL(AM) Price UT 5 hrs
KSVC(AM) Richfield UT 14 hrs
KHQN(AM) Spanish Fork UT 4 hrs
KVEL(AM) Vernal UT 2 hrs
WABN(AM) Abingdon VA 5 hrs
WBLT(AM) Bedford VA 5 hrs
WREL-FM Buena Vista VA 3 hrs
WINA(AM) Charlottesville VA 4 hrs
WMEK(AM) Chase City VA 3 hrs
WDIC(AM) Clinchco VA 1 hr
WKIK(FM) Crewe VA 10 hrs
WSVS(AM) Crewe VA 10 hrs
WDUF(AM) Duffield VA 5 hrs
WPWC(AM) Dumfries-Triangle VA 3 hrs
WEVA(AM) Emporia VA 1 hr
WEVA-FM Emporia VA 3 hrs
WPAK(AM) Farmville VA 1 hr
WFVA(AM) Fredericksburg VA 1 hr
WBOB(AM) Galax VA 1 hr
WXGM(AM) Gloucester VA 2 hrs
WXGM-FM Gloucester VA 2 hrs
WMNA(AM) Gretna VA 8 hrs
WMNA-FM Gretna VA 8 hrs
WNRG(AM) Grundy VA 5 hrs
WKCY(AM) Harrisonburg VA 1 hr
WKCY-FM Harrisonburg VA 1 hr
WSVA(AM) Harrisonburg VA 8 hrs
WHHV(AM) Hillsville VA 2 hrs
WKWI(FM) Kilmarnock VA 2 hrs
WAGE(AM) Leesburg VA 2 hrs
WREL(AM) Lexington VA 3 hrs
WLSA(FM) Louisa VA 2 hrs
WLCC(FM) Luray VA 1 hr
WSIG(FM) Mount Jackson VA 3 hrs
WRVA(AM) Richmond VA 1 hr
WXGI(AM) Richmond VA 2 hrs
WKGM(AM) Smithfield VA 02 hrs
WSBV(AM) South Boston VA 1 hr
WXLZ(AM) St. Paul VA 2 hrs
WKDW(AM) Staunton VA 1 hr
WHEO(AM) Stuart VA 4 hrs
WRAR(AM) Tappahannock VA 5 hrs
WRAR-FM Tappahannock VA 5 hrs
WKCW(AM) Warrenton VA 1 hr
WNNT(AM) Warsaw VA 5 hrs
WNNT-FM Warsaw VA 5 hrs
WANV(AM) Waynesboro VA 2 hrs
WAMM(AM) Woodstock VA 2 hrs
WBTN(AM) Bennington VT 2 hrs
WKVT(AM) Brattleboro VT 1 hr
WKVT-FM Brattleboro VT 1 hr
WFAD(AM) Middlebury VT 1 hr
*WGDR(FM) Plainfield VT 1 hr
WVNR(AM) Poultney VT 1 hr
WDEV(AM) Waterbury VT 6 hrs
WYKR(AM) Wells River VT 1 hr
KARI(AM) Blaine WA 3 hrs
KMNT(FM) Centralia WA 1 hr
KOZI(AM) Chelan WA 3 hrs
KOZI-FM Chelan WA 3 hrs
KCLX(AM) Colfax WA 5 hrs
KYSN(FM) East Wenatchee WA 1 hr
KTBI(AM) Ephrata WA 15 hrs
KULE-FM Ephrata WA 5 hrs
KONA(AM) Kennewick WA 3 hrs
KLDY(AM) Lacey WA 2 hrs
KLYN(FM) Lynden WA 6 hrs
KBSN(AM) Moses Lake WA 20 hrs
KWIQ-FM Moses Lake WA 20 hrs
KWIQ(AM) Moses Lake North WA 20 hrs
*KUBS(FM) Newport WA 2 hrs
KOMW(AM) Omak WA 2 hrs
KOMW-FM Omak WA 1 hr
KQQQ(AM) Pullman WA 3 hrs
KWNC(AM) Quincy WA 5 hrs
KORD-FM Richland WA 4 hrs
KYXE(AM) Selah WA 2 hrs
KAQQ(AM) Spokane WA 6 hrs
KGA(AM) Spokane WA 1 hr
KXLY(AM) Spokane WA 6 hrs
KENE(AM) Toppenish WA 1 hr
KTEL(AM) Walla Walla WA 2 hrs
KTEL-FM Walla Walla WA 2 hrs
KPQ(AM) Wenatchee WA 3 hrs
KIT(AM) Yakima WA 6 hrs
WXCE(AM) Amery WI 12 hrs
WRJQ(AM) Appleton WI 6 hrs
WBEV(AM) Beaver Dam WI 8 hrs
WXRO(FM) Beaver Dam WI 6 hrs
WKTT(FM) Cleveland WI 6 hrs
WFCL(AM) Clintonville WI 8 hrs
WJLW(FM) De Pere WI
WAXX(FM) Eau Claire WI 15 hrs
KFIZ(AM) Fond du Lac WI 10 hrs
WGEE(AM) Green Bay WI 5 hrs
WTKM(AM) Hartford WI 15 hrs
WAUN(FM) Kewaunee WI 20 hrs
WKTY(AM) La Crosse WI 10 hrs
WSPL(FM) La Crosse WI 15 hrs
WLDY(AM) Ladysmith WI 2 hrs
WWIB(FM) Ladysmith WI 12 hrs
WGLR(AM) Lancaster WI 10 hrs
WIBA(AM) Madison WI 3 hrs
*WNWC(FM) Madison WI 2 hrs
WTSO(AM) Madison WI 20 hrs
WOMT(AM) Manitowoc WI 1 hr
WMAM(AM) Marinette WI 3 hrs
WDLB(AM) Marshfield WI 14 hrs
WIGM(AM) Medford WI 10 hrs
WMEQ(AM) Menomonie WI 15 hrs
WJMT(AM) Merrill WI 7 hrs
WCCN(AM) Neillsville WI 19 hrs
WCCN-FM Neillsville WI 19 hrs
WIXK(AM) New Richmond WI
WPKR(FM) Omro WI 5 hrs
WXOL(AM) Oshkosh WI 7 hrs
WTOQ(AM) Platteville WI 12 hrs
WJUB(AM) Plymouth WI 5 hrs
WPDR(AM) Portage WI 9 hrs
WIBU(AM) Poynette WI 20 hrs
WNFM(FM) Reedsburg WI 18 hrs
WAQE(AM) Rice Lake WI 2 hrs
WRCO(AM) Richland Center WI 8 hrs
WEVR(AM) River Falls WI 18 hrs
*WRFW(FM) River Falls WI 10 hrs
WOWN(FM) Shawano WI 15 hrs
WTCH(AM) Shawano WI 18 hrs
WCNZ(AM) Sheboygan WI
WHBL(AM) Sheboygan WI 10 hrs
WCSW(AM) Shell Lake WI 3 hrs
WDOR-FM Sturgeon Bay WI 05 hrs
WRVM(FM) Suring WI 5 hrs
WVRQ(AM) Viroqua WI 3 hrs
WVRQ-FM Viroqua WI 8 hrs
WTTN(AM) Watertown WI 20 hrs
WDUX(AM) Waupaca WI 20 hrs
WMRH(AM) Waupun WI 5 hrs
WDEZ(FM) Wausau WI 4 hrs
WELD(AM) Fisher WV 3 hrs
*WVMR(AM) Frost WV 5 hrs
WTBZ(AM) Grafton WV 2 hrs
WTBZ-FM Grafton WV 2 hrs
WMOV(AM) Ravenswood WV 2 hrs
WWVA(AM) Wheeling WV 2 hrs
KMER(AM) Kemmerer WY 3 hrs
KOVE(AM) Lander WY 4 hrs
KCGY-FM Laramie WY 1 hr
KLDI(AM) Laramie WY 1 hr
KOWB(AM) Laramie WY 1 hr
KASL(AM) Newcastle WY 5 hrs
KPOW(AM) Powell WY 20 hrs
KTAK(FM) Riverton WY 5 hrs
KTRZ(FM) Riverton WY 5 hrs
KVOW(AM) Riverton WY 5 hrs
KGOS(AM) Torrington WY 20 hrs
KYCN(AM) Wheatland WY 3 hrs
KYCN-FM Wheatland WY 7 hrs

Albanian

*WCUW(FM) Worcester MA 1 hr

American Indian

*KBRW(AM) Barrow AK 15 hrs
*KDLG(AM) Dillingham AK 1 hr
KIYU(AM) Galena AK 2 hrs
KCAM(AM) Glennallen AK 1 hr
*KTOO(FM) Juneau AK 1 hr
*KRBD(FM) Ketchikan AK 1 hr
*KMXT(FM) Kodiak AK 3 hrs
*KSKO(AM) McGrath AK 1 hr
KICY(AM) Nome AK 11 hrs
*KNOM(AM) Nome AK 6 hrs
*KNOM-FM Nome AK 6 hrs
KJNP(AM) North Pole AK 3 hrs
*KTNA(FM) Talkeetna AK 2 hrs
*KSTK(FM) Wrangell AK 4 hrs
WASG(AM) Atmore AL 2 hrs
WYDH(FM) Atmore AL 1 hr
*KABF(FM) Little Rock AR 2 hrs
KJAA(AM) Globe AZ 3 hrs
*KGHR(FM) Tuba City AZ 20 hrs
KTBA(AM) Tuba City AZ 28 hrs
*KUAT(AM) Tucson AZ 1 hr
*KXCI(FM) Tucson AZ 1 hr
*KNNB(FM) Whiteriver AZ 8 hrs
*KKUP(FM) Cupertino CA 3 hrs
*KDVS(FM) Davis CA 2 hrs
*KFCF(FM) Fresno CA 2 hrs
*KMUD(FM) Garberville CA 1 hr
*KIDE(FM) Hoopa CA 20 hrs
*KALW(FM) San Francisco CA 2 hrs
*KZSC(FM) Santa Cruz CA 2 hrs
*KGNU(FM) Boulder CO 1 hr
KRTZ(FM) Cortez CO 1 hr
*KSUT(FM) Ignacio CO
*WWUH(FM) West Hartford CT 2 hrs
*WUCF-FM Orlando FL 1 hr
WRCC-FM Warner Robins GA 2 hrs
*KBSU(AM) Boise ID 1 hr
*KUOI-FM Moscow ID 2 hrs
KWIK(AM) Pocatello ID 1 hr
*WSIU(FM) Carbondale IL 1 hr
*WEFT(FM) Champaign IL 1 hr
*WMFO(FM) Medford MA 6 hrs
*WOZQ(FM) Northampton MA 2 hrs
*WMPG(FM) Gorham ME 2 hrs
*WUPI(FM) Presque Isle ME 2 hrs
*WBYW(FM) Grand Rapids MI 2 hrs
*KAXE(FM) Grand Rapids MN 3 hrs
*KFAI(FM) Minneapolis MN 1 hr
*KOPN(FM) Columbia MO 3 hrs
*KKFI(FM) Kansas City MO 2 hrs
WSSI(AM) Carthage MS 1 hr
KVCK-FM Wolf Point MT 1 hr
WTSB(AM) Lumberton NC 2 hrs
*KEYA(FM) Belcourt ND 4 hrs
*KMHA(FM) Four Bears ND 4 hrs
*KTNE-FM Alliance NE 1 hr
*KINI(FM) Crookston NE 4 hrs
*KHNE-FM Hastings NE 1 hr
*KLNE-FM Lexington NE 1 hr
*WDVR(FM) Delaware Township NJ 2 hrs
*WRSU-FM New Brunswick NJ 2 hrs
*KABR(AM) Alamo Community NM 10 hrs
*KUNM(FM) Albuquerque NM 3 hrs
KPCL(FM) Farmington NM 7 hrs
KYVA(AM) Gallup NM 6 hrs
*KTDB(FM) Pine Hill NM
*KSFR(FM) Santa Fe NM 1 hr
KMXQ(FM) Socorro NM 1 hr
*KSHI(FM) Zuni NM 20 hrs
*KUNV(FM) Las Vegas NV 1 hr
*WBAI(FM) New York NY 1 hr
*WFUV(FM) New York NY 2 hrs
KRPT(AM) Anadarko OK 1 hr
KRPT-FM Anadarko OK 1 hr
KZUE(AM) El Reno OK 1 hr
KXVQ(AM) Pawhuska OK 5 hrs
KIRC(FM) Seminole OK 1 hr
*KOSU-FM Stillwater OK 1 hr
KTLQ(AM) Tahlequah OK 1 hr
KWSH(AM) Wewoka OK 1 hr
*KMUN(FM) Astoria OR 2 hrs
KOLY(AM) Mobridge SD
KOLY-FM Mobridge SD 1 hr
*KBHE-FM Rapid City SD 1 hr
KTOQ(AM) Rapid City SD
*KTSD-FM Reliance SD 1 hr
*KUSD(AM) Vermillion SD 1 hr
KUTA(AM) Blanding UT 5 hrs
*KZMU(FM) Moab UT 5 hrs
*KRCL(FM) Salt Lake City UT 3 hrs
*WGDR(FM) Plainfield VT 1 hr
*KAOS(FM) Olympia WA 3 hrs
*KDNA(FM) Yakima WA 2 hrs
*WOJB(FM) Reserve WI 15 hrs

Arabic

*KPOF(AM) Denver CO 1 hr
*WDNA(FM) Miami FL 2 hrs
WONX(AM) Evanston IL 1 hr
WVVX(FM) Highland Park IL 6 hrs
WPNA(AM) Oak Park IL 2 hrs
WRCA(AM) Waltham MA 2 hrs
WNTL(AM) Indian Head MD
WCAR(AM) Livonia MI 3 hrs
*WSOU(FM) South Orange NJ 2 hrs
WHLD(AM) Niagara Falls NY 15 hrs
*WAPS(FM) Akron OH 2 hrs
*WCSB(FM) Cleveland OH 1 hr

Armenian

KTYM(AM) Inglewood CA 3 hrs
*KUSF(FM) San Francisco CA 1 hr
WVVX(FM) Highland Park IL 1 hr
*WJUL(FM) Lowell MA 2 hrs
*WICN(FM) Worcester MA 2 hrs
*WSOU(FM) South Orange NJ 2 hrs
WRIB(AM) Providence RI 1 hr

Beautiful Music

WABF(AM) Fairhope AL 4 hrs
*WBVM(FM) Tampa FL 4 hrs
*KUSR(FM) Ames IA
*WMHB(FM) Waterville ME 2 hrs
*KUMM(FM) Morris MN 2 hrs
KCHR(AM) Charleston MO 5 hrs
*KWWC-FM Columbia MO 20 hrs
*WHYC(FM) Swan Quarter NC 8 hrs
*KCND(FM) Bismarck ND 8 hrs
*KDPR(FM) Dickinson ND 8 hrs
KHND(AM) Harvey ND 3 hrs
*KMPR(FM) Minot ND 8 hrs
*KPPR(FM) Williston ND 8 hrs

Big Band

WRJM-FM Geneva AL 5 hrs
*KUAF(FM) Fayetteville AR 2 hrs
KWDS(AM) Prescott Valley AZ 5 hrs
KQST(FM) Sedona AZ 4 hrs
KTAN(AM) Sierra Vista AZ 4 hrs
*KOHL(FM) Fremont CA 4 hrs
KGMG(AM) Oceanside CA 4 hrs
*KUOR-FM Redlands CA 5 hrs
KJAY(AM) Sacramento CA 5 hrs
KLOV(AM) Loveland CO 3 hrs
*WGRS(FM) Guilford CT 8 hrs
*WMNR(FM) Monroe CT 8 hrs
*WRXC(FM) Shelton CT 8 hrs
*WVUD(FM) Newark DE 3 hrs
WGMD(FM) Rehoboth Beach DE 8 hrs
WTAN(AM) Clearwater FL 6 hrs
*WMNF(FM) Tampa FL
*WUNV(FM) Albany GA
*WRAS(FM) Atlanta GA 1 hr
KROS(AM) Clinton IA 3 hrs
KIDA-FM Ida Grove IA 3 hrs
KCJJ(AM) Iowa City IA 4 hrs
KTLB(FM) Twin Lakes IA 4 hrs
*WSIU(FM) Carbondale IL 4 hrs
*WEIU(FM) Charleston IL 3 hrs
WCRI(FM) Eureka IL 6 hrs
WGEN(AM) Geneseo IL 5 hrs
*WDCB(FM) Glen Ellyn IL 2 hrs
*WUSI(FM) Olney IL 3 hrs
WSHY(AM) Shelbyville IL 4 hrs
WGFA(AM) Watseka IL 2 hrs
WBQR(FM) Attica IN
WNJY(FM) Delphi IN 3 hrs
*WSWI(AM) Evansville IN 3 hrs
WMRS(FM) Monticello IN 4 hrs
WARU(AM) Peru IN 2 hrs
WROI(FM) Rochester IN 2 hrs
*WVUR-FM Valparaiso IN 3 hrs
WKUZ(FM) Wabash IN 3 hrs
KLKC(AM) Parsons KS 3 hrs
*KCFN(FM) Wichita KS 4 hrs
KLCL(AM) Lake Charles LA 4 hrs
KVCL(AM) Winnfield LA 3 hrs
WGAM(AM) Greenfield MA 2 hrs
*WBYQ(FM) Baltimore MD 6 hrs
*WESM(FM) Princess Anne MD 8 hrs
*WKHS(FM) Worton MD 2 hrs
WALM(AM) Albion MI 12 hrs
*WBFH(FM) Bloomfield Hills MI 5 hrs
*WHFR(FM) Dearborn MI 3 hrs
WBNZ(FM) Frankfort MI 2 hrs
*WBYW(FM) Grand Rapids MI 10 hrs
WMLM(AM) St. Louis MI 4 hrs
WIOS(AM) Tawas City MI 6 hrs
*KBSB(FM) Bemidji MN 2 hrs
KLTF(AM) Little Falls MN 5 hrs
KOLV(FM) Olivia MN
*KQAL(FM) Winona MN 4 hrs
KZBK-FM Brookfield MO 11 hrs
*KWWC-FM Columbia MO 3 hrs
*KXMS(FM) Joplin MO 2 hrs
KIRX(AM) Kirksville MO 3 hrs
KRYK(FM) Chinook MT 2 hrs
KWYS(AM) West Yellowstone MT 4 hrs
*WCCE(FM) Buie's Creek NC 6 hrs
WVOD(FM) Manteo NC 3 hrs
*WHYC(FM) Swan Quarter NC 8 hrs
KUVR(AM) Holdrege NE 5 hrs
KUVR-FM Holdrege NE 5 hrs
WKNE(AM) Keene NH 4 hrs
WPNH(AM) Plymouth NH 6 hrs
WSNJ(AM) Bridgeton NJ
WSNJ-FM Bridgeton NJ
*WNTI(FM) Hackettstown NJ 4 hrs
WGHT(AM) Pompton Lakes NJ 1 hr
*WPSC-FM Wayne NJ 2 hrs
KPSA(AM) Alamogordo NM 6 hrs
KHWK(FM) Tonopah NV
WDNY(AM) Dansville NY 3 hrs
WDNY-FM Dansville NY 3 hrs
WWSC(AM) Glens Falls NY 5 hrs
*WRHU(FM) Hempstead NY 9 hrs
*WFUV(FM) New York NY 2 hrs
WDOS(AM) Oneonta NY 7 hrs
WSFW(AM) Seneca Falls NY 2 hrs
WSFW-FM Seneca Falls NY 2 hrs
WRGR(FM) Tupper Lake NY 2 hrs
WNYV(FM) Whitehall NY 3 hrs
WATH(AM) Athens OH 15 hrs
WOHI(AM) East Liverpool OH 4 hrs
WKFI(AM) Wilmington OH 5 hrs
WBBZ(AM) Ponca City OK 2 hrs
KBEZ(FM) Tulsa OK 5 hrs
WBVP(AM) Beaver Falls PA 4 hrs
WAZL(AM) Hazleton PA 5 hrs
WNPV(AM) Lansdale PA 4 hrs
WLSH(AM) Lansford PA 3 hrs
WRAW(AM) Reading PA 5 hrs
WWII(AM) Shiremanstown PA 2 hrs
WXPX(AM) West Hazleton PA 4 hrs
WVBI(FM) Block Island RI 4 hrs
WPJB(FM) Narragansett Pier RI
WJMX(AM) Florence SC 3 hrs
WHSC(AM) Hartsville SC 3 hrs
WHSC-FM Hartsville SC 3 hrs
WJYR(FM) Myrtle Beach SC
WEMB(AM) Erwin TN 2 hrs
*KNCT-FM Killeen TX 6 hrs
KLKM(FM) Llano TX 10 hrs
*WCVE(FM) Richmond VA 2 hrs
WTON-FM Staunton VA 2 hrs
WVNR(AM) Poultney VT 3 hrs
WSTJ(AM) St. Johnsbury VT 3 hrs
KELA(AM) Centralia-Chehalis WA 3 hrs
KEYG(AM) Grand Coulee WA 4 hrs
WHSM(AM) Hayward WI 2 hrs
WHSM-FM Hayward WI 2 hrs
WLDY(AM) Ladysmith WI 4 hrs
WCQM(FM) Park Falls WI 1 hr
WNBI(AM) Park Falls WI 1 hr
WXVA-FM Charles Town WV 4 hrs
*WVMR(AM) Frost WV 4 hrs
*WWVU-FM Morgantown WV 2 hrs
KODI(AM) Cody WY 6 hrs
KROE(AM) Sheridan WY 5 hrs

Black

*KHNS(FM) Haines AK 4 hrs
KIAL(AM) Unalaska AK 04 hrs
WANA(AM) Anniston AL 12 hrs
WASZ(FM) Ashland-Lineville AL 6 hrs
WASG(AM) Atmore AL
WYDH(FM) Atmore AL 1 hr
WBYE(AM) Calera AL 9 hrs
WEZZ(FM) Clanton AL 5 hrs
WKLF(AM) Clanton AL 3 hrs
WULA(AM) Eufaula AL 3 hrs
WULA-FM Eufaula AL
*WJAB(FM) Huntsville AL 3 hrs
WMGY(AM) Montgomery AL 15 hrs
WOPP(AM) Opp AL 2 hrs
WKAX(AM) Russellville AL 4 hrs
WHBB(AM) Selma AL 18 hrs
WJDB(AM) Thomasville AL 8 hrs
WJDB-FM Thomasville AL 8 hrs
KAMD(AM) Camden AR 5 hrs
KWEH(FM) Camden AR 5 hrs
KDDA(AM) Dumas AR 5 hrs
KXFE(FM) Dumas AR 5 hrs
KFFA(AM) Helena AR 4 hrs
KITA(AM) Little Rock AR 19 hrs
KZOT(AM) Marianna AR 12 hrs
KOSE(AM) Osceola AR 6 hrs
KTKT(AM) Tucson AZ 1 hr
*KXCI(FM) Tucson AZ 10 hrs
*KAWC(AM) Yuma AZ 3 hrs
*KPFA(FM) Berkeley CA 20 hrs
*KZFR(FM) Chico CA 3 hrs
KJLH-FM Compton CA
*KFCF(FM) Fresno CA 20 hrs
*KFSR(FM) Fresno CA 8 hrs
*KSJV(FM) Fresno CA 3 hrs
*KMUD(FM) Garberville CA 3 hrs
*KUCI(FM) Irvine CA 14 hrs
KGER(AM) Long Beach CA 8 hrs
KGFJ(AM) Los Angeles CA 16 hrs
*KPFK(FM) Los Angeles CA 17 hrs
*KXLU(FM) Los Angeles CA 8 hrs
*KMPO(FM) Modesto CA 3 hrs
*KVMR(FM) Nevada City CA 4 hrs
*KPCC(FM) Pasadena CA 1 hr
*KSPB(FM) Pebble Beach CA 18 hrs
*KZYX(FM) Philo CA 6 hrs
*KUCR(FM) Riverside CA 18 hrs
*KALW(FM) San Francisco CA 2 hrs
KFAX(AM) San Francisco CA 8 hrs
*KSJS(FM) San Jose CA 6 hrs
*KCPR(FM) San Luis Obispo CA 8 hrs
*KCSB-FM Santa Barbara CA 20 hrs
*KUSP(FM) Santa Cruz CA 20 hrs
*KZSC(FM) Santa Cruz CA 15 hrs
*KCRW(FM) Santa Monica CA
*KZSU(FM) Stanford CA 18 hrs
*KCJH(FM) Stockton CA 6 hrs
*KCSS(FM) Turlock CA 12 hrs
*KASF(FM) Alamosa CO 20 hrs
*KGNU(FM) Boulder CO 7 hrs
KLTT(AM) Brighton CO 2 hrs
KYGO(AM) Denver CO 1 hr
*KMSA(FM) Grand Junction CO 9 hrs
*WVOF(FM) Fairfield CT 12 hrs
WFIF(AM) Milford CT 15 hrs
*WCNI(FM) New London CT 3 hrs
*WWUH(FM) West Hartford CT 10 hrs
WKEN(AM) Dover DE 1 hr

Broadcasting & Cable Yearbook 1994
B-575

Special Programming on Radio Stations in the U.S.

*WVUD(FM) Newark DE 10 hrs
WKGF(AM) Arcadia FL 7 hrs
WPHK(FM) Blountstown FL 12 hrs
WYFX(AM) Boynton Beach FL
*WVUM(FM) Coral Gables FL 3 hrs
WAVS(AM) Davie FL
WDBF(AM) Delray Beach FL 6 hrs
WKGR(FM) Fort Pierce FL 1 hr
WOVV(FM) Fort Pierce FL 1 hr
WRUF(AM) Gainesville FL 4 hrs
WRUF-FM Gainesville FL 1 hr
WGWD(FM) Gretna FL 20 hrs
WIPC(AM) Lake Wales FL 2 hrs
WLBE(AM) Leesburg FL 3 hrs
WMAF(AM) Madison FL 21 hrs
WTYS(AM) Marianna FL 4 hrs
*WDNA(FM) Miami FL 2 hrs
WIYD(AM) Palatka FL 5 hrs
*WKGC-FM Panama City FL 6 hrs
WPRY(AM) Perry FL 2 hrs
WAOC(AM) St. Augustine FL 3 hrs
*WKPX(FM) Sunrise FL 6 hrs
*WMNF(FM) Tampa FL
WSIR(AM) Winter Haven FL 6 hrs
WBIT(AM) Adel GA 2 hrs
WDEC-FM Americus GA 5 hrs
*WUOG(FM) Athens GA 4 hrs
*WRFG(FM) Atlanta GA 2 hrs
WGIA(AM) Blackshear GA 10 hrs
WMOG(AM) Brunswick GA 8 hrs
WGRA(AM) Cairo GA 6 hrs
WEBS(AM) Calhoun GA 2 hrs
WBTR-FM Carrollton GA 5 hrs
*WWGC(FM) Carrollton GA 6 hrs
WYXC(AM) Cartersville GA 2 hrs
WCUG(AM) Cuthbert GA 4 hrs
WDMG(AM) Douglas GA 3 hrs
WUFF(AM) Eastman GA 5 hrs
WBHB(AM) Fitzgerald GA 4 hrs
WIFO-FM Jesup GA 4 hrs
WLAG(AM) La Grange GA 1 hr
WYTH(AM) Madison GA 13 hrs
WFDR(AM) Manchester GA 13 hrs
WYIS(AM) McRae GA 4 hrs
WMVG(AM) Milledgeville GA 4 hrs
WJEP(AM) Ochlocknee GA 2 hrs
WQTU(FM) Rome GA 3 hrs
WTSH(AM) Rome GA 4 hrs
WECC(AM) St. Mary's GA 4 hrs
WPTB(AM) Statesboro GA 4 hrs
WJAT(AM) Swainsboro GA 5 hrs
WJAT-FM Swainsboro GA 10 hrs
WSFT(AM) Thomaston GA 12 hrs
WTGA(AM) Thomaston GA 4 hrs
WLET(AM) Toccoa GA 1 hr
WNEG(AM) Toccoa GA 3 hrs
*WVVS(FM) Valdosta GA 3 hrs
*KUSR(FM) Ames IA
*KUNI(FM) Cedar Falls IA 15 hrs
*KWLC(AM) Decorah IA
*KTPR(FM) Fort Dodge IA 2 hrs
*KDIC(FM) Grinnell IA 12 hrs
*KRUI-FM Iowa City IA 12 hrs
*KUNY(FM) Mason City IA 12 hrs
*KIGC(FM) Oskaloosa IA 8 hrs
*KUOI-FM Moscow ID 3 hrs
KATZ-FM Alton IL
WIBV(AM) Belleville IL 1 hr
*WESN(FM) Bloomington IL 18 hrs
*WSIU(FM) Carbondale IL 1 hr
*WEFT(FM) Champaign IL 8 hrs
*WEIU(FM) Charleston IL 3 hrs
*WHPK-FM Chicago IL 1 hr
*WRSE-FM Elmhurst IL 1 hr
*WVKC(FM) Galesburg IL 6 hrs
WGNU(AM) Granite City IL 18 hrs
*WCSF(FM) Joliet IL 2 hrs
*WMXM(FM) Lake Forest IL 6 hrs
*WLRA(FM) Lockport IL 15 hrs
*WIUS(FM) Macomb IL 16 hrs
*WEAX(FM) Angola IN 2 hrs
WIIZ(FM) Battle Ground IN 3 hrs
WNDY(FM) Crawfordsville IN 3 hrs
*WSWI(AM) Evansville IN 3 hrs
*WBNI-FM Fort Wayne IN 3 hrs
WYCA(FM) Hammond IN 10 hrs
*WBKE-FM North Manchester IN 2 hrs
*WECI(FM) Richmond IN 4 hrs
WIWO(AM) South Bend IN 2 hrs
*WBAA(AM) West Lafayette IN 1 hr
WWVR(FM) West Terre Haute IN 6 hrs
*KONQ(FM) Dodge City KS 10 hrs
KWBW(AM) Hutchinson KS 2 hrs
*KJTY(FM) Topeka KS
*WCVK(FM) Bowling Green KY 2 hrs
WCPM(AM) Cumberland KY 3 hrs
*WRVG(FM) Georgetown KY 3 hrs
WHBN(AM) Harrodsburg KY 1 hr
*WNKJ(FM) Hopkinsville KY 5 hrs
WTTL(AM) Madisonville KY 20 hrs
WFXY(AM) Middlesboro KY 2 hrs
*WMKY(FM) Morehead KY 5 hrs
*WKWC(FM) Owensboro KY 15 hrs
WEKY(AM) Richmond KY 12 hrs
*KLSP(FM) Angola LA 10 hrs
KAJN-FM Crowley LA 2 hrs
KPWS(AM) Crowley LA 3 hrs
KFNV(AM) Ferriday LA 12 hrs
WFCG(AM) Franklinton LA 12 hrs
WCKW(AM) Garyville LA 6 hrs
*KSLU(FM) Hammond LA
KAOK(AM) Lake Charles LA 16 hrs
*KLPI-FM Ruston LA 3 hrs
*KSCL(FM) Shreveport LA 3 hrs
KAIN(AM) Vidalia LA 2 hrs
KVPI-FM Ville Platte LA 10 hrs
KVCL(AM) Winnfield LA 3 hrs
*WAMH(FM) Amherst MA 12 hrs
WEZE(AM) Boston MA 2 hrs
WRKO(AM) Boston MA 2 hrs
*WBIM-FM Bridgewater MA 3 hrs
WUNR(AM) Brookline MA 20 hrs
WHRB(FM) Cambridge MA 18 hrs
*WMBR(FM) Cambridge MA 15 hrs
WBMA(AM) Dedham MA 4 hrs
*WGAJ(FM) Deerfield MA 5 hrs
*WDJM-FM Framingham MA 3 hrs
*WCCH(FM) Holyoke MA 2 hrs
*WJUL(FM) Lowell MA 2 hrs
WLLH(AM) Lowell MA 1 hr
*WMFO(FM) Medford MA 12 hrs
*WZBC(FM) Newton MA 2 hrs
*WOZQ(FM) Northampton MA 10 hrs
*WNMH(FM) Northfield MA 8 hrs
*WMWM(FM) Salem MA 16 hrs
*WBSL-FM Sheffield MA 2 hrs
*WMHC(FM) South Hadley MA 15 hrs
WMAS(AM) Springfield MA 1 hr
*WNEK-FM Springfield MA 8 hrs
*WYAJ(FM) Sudbury MA 6 hrs
*WBRS(FM) Waltham MA 14 hrs
WASA(AM) Havre de Grace MD
WINX(AM) Rockville MD 1 hr
*WTMD(FM) Towson MD 1 hr
*WMPG(FM) Gorham ME 10 hrs
*WUPI(FM) Presque Isle ME 2 hrs
*WMHB(FM) Waterville ME 12 hrs
WOLY(AM) Battle Creek MI 6 hrs
*WDTR(FM) Detroit MI 8 hrs
WLQV(AM) Detroit MI 10 hrs
*WDBM(FM) East Lansing MI 5 hrs
*WORB(FM) Farmington Hills MI 4 hrs
WKNX(AM) Frankenmuth MI 2 hrs
WSHN-FM Fremont MI 3 hrs
*WBYW(FM) Grand Rapids MI 8 hrs
*WIDR(FM) Kalamazoo MI 8 hrs
WSJM(AM) St. Joseph MI 3 hrs
*WNMC-FM Traverse City MI 20 hrs
*WPHS(FM) Warren MI 4 hrs
WYGR(AM) Wyoming MI 2 hrs
*KAXE(FM) Grand Rapids MN 2 hrs
*KFAI(FM) Minneapolis MN 10 hrs
*WCAL(FM) Northfield MN 2 hrs
*KVSC(FM) St. Cloud MN 5 hrs
KNOF(FM) St. Paul MN 2 hrs
*KWUR(FM) Clayton MO 24 hrs
*KCOU(FM) Columbia MO 4 hrs
*KOPN(FM) Columbia MO 3 hrs
KMAL(FM) Malden MO 6 hrs
*KMVC(FM) Marshall MO 10 hrs
KDRO(AM) Sedalia MO 1 hr
KSTG(FM) Sikeston MO 4 hrs
*KDHX(FM) St. Louis MO 12 hrs
*KCMW-FM Warrensburg MO 3 hrs
WBLE(FM) Batesville MS 3 hrs
WBIP(AM) Booneville MS 7 hrs
WBIP-FM Booneville MS 6 hrs
WSSI(AM) Carthage MS 2 hrs
WTGY(FM) Charleston MS 12 hrs
WKDJ(FM) Clarksdale MS 15 hrs
WGVM(AM) Greenville MS 5 hrs
WABG(AM) Greenwood MS 10 hrs
WGRM(AM) Greenwood MS 2 hrs
WMDC(AM) Hazelhurst MS 18 hrs
WNBN(AM) Meridian MS
WZZJ(AM) Pascagoula-Moss Point MS 4 hrs
WRJW(AM) Picayune MS 8 hrs
WJDR(FM) Prentiss MS 5 hrs
WKOR(AM) Starkville MS 20 hrs
WSSO(AM) Starkville MS 12 hrs
*KGLT(FM) Bozeman MT 1 hr
WFGW(AM) Black Mountain NC 1 hr
WMYT(AM) Carolina Beach NC 15 hrs
WRRZ(AM) Clinton NC 5 hrs
WGAI(AM) Elizabeth City NC 12 hrs
*WRVS-FM Elizabeth City NC 15 hrs
*WUAW(FM) Erwin NC
WFMO(AM) Fairmont NC 5 hrs
WAGY(AM) Forest City NC 1 hr
WSML(AM) Graham NC 18 hrs
WKEW(AM) Greensboro NC 10 hrs
*WQFS(FM) Greensboro NC 4 hrs
*WUAG(FM) Greensboro NC 3 hrs
*WZMB(FM) Greenville NC 14 hrs
WRKB(AM) Kannapolis NC 5 hrs
WYRN(AM) Louisburg NC
WDSL(AM) Mocksville NC 1 hr
WHIP(AM) Mooresville NC 6 hrs
WDJS(AM) Mount Olive NC 3 hrs
WNNC(AM) Newton NC 2 hrs
WREV(AM) Reidsville NC 7 hrs
WRXO(AM) Roxboro NC 4 hrs
WBZB(AM) Selma NC 6 hrs
WGAS(AM) South Gastonia NC 5 hrs
*WHYC(FM) Swan Quarter NC 8 hrs
WLSE(AM) Wallace NC 6 hrs
WTOW(AM) Washington NC 5 hrs
*KZUM(FM) Lincoln NE 13 hrs
*KIOS-FM Omaha NE 1 hr
*KWSC(FM) Wayne NE 4 hrs
*WUNH(FM) Durham NH 3 hrs
WFPG(AM) Atlantic City NJ 2 hrs
WIMG(AM) Ewing NJ 7 hrs
*WRRC(FM) Lawrenceville NJ 10 hrs
*WMNJ(FM) Madison NJ 6 hrs
*WRSU-FM New Brunswick NJ 7 hrs
WERA(AM) Plainfield NJ 3 hrs
*WSOU(FM) South Orange NJ 3 hrs
WTTM(AM) Trenton NJ 6 hrs
*WKNJ-FM Union Township NJ 2 hrs
*WMSC(FM) Upper Montclair NJ 4 hrs
*WPSC-FM Wayne NJ 4 hrs
KKIM(AM) Albuquerque NM 2 hrs
*KUNM(FM) Albuquerque NM 3 hrs
*KRUX(FM) Las Cruces NM 2 hrs
*KEDP(FM) Las Vegas NM 15 hrs
KKVV(AM) Las Vegas NV 2 hrs
KLAV(AM) Las Vegas NV 6 hrs
WHRL(FM) Albany NY 2 hrs
*WXBA(FM) Brentwood NY 5 hrs
*WBSU(FM) Brockport NY 6 hrs
*WBNY(FM) Buffalo NY 12 hrs
WGR(AM) Buffalo NY 1 hr
*WHCL-FM Clinton NY 14 hrs
WVOA(FM) DeRuyter NY 17 hrs
WSIV(AM) East Syracuse NY 4 hrs
*WCVF-FM Fredonia NY 8 hrs
*WEOS(FM) Geneva NY 12 hrs
*WRCU-FM Hamilton NY 10 hrs
WHUC(AM) Hudson NY 1 hr
*WHVP(FM) Hudson NY 1 hr
*WICB(FM) Ithaca NY 20 hrs
WVBR-FM Ithaca NY 4 hrs
*WFGB(FM) Kingston NY 1 hr
*WLJP(FM) Monroe NY 1 hr
WRKL(AM) New City NY 2 hrs
*WFNP(FM) New Paltz NY 10 hrs
WVOX(AM) New Rochelle NY 1 hr
*WBAI(FM) New York NY 10 hrs
*WKCR-FM New York NY 10 hrs
*WNYE(FM) New York NY 20 hrs
*WNYU-FM New York NY 5 hrs
WHLD(AM) Niagara Falls NY 18 hrs
WJJL(AM) Niagara Falls NY 2 hrs
*WONY(FM) Oneonta NY 3 hrs
*WPLT(FM) Plattsburgh NY 9 hrs
*WRPJ(FM) Port Jervis NY 1 hr
WSPK(FM) Poughkeepsie NY 1 hr
*WRUR-FM Rochester NY 13 hrs
WWWG(AM) Rochester NY 18 hrs
WRNY(AM) Rome NY 3 hrs
WVKZ(AM) Schenectady NY 5 hrs
*WUSB(FM) Stony Brook NY 12 hrs
*WJPZ-FM Syracuse NY 12 hrs
WNDR(AM) Syracuse NY 1 hr
WNTQ(FM) Syracuse NY 6 hrs
*WRPI(FM) Troy NY 8 hrs
*WOUB(AM) Athens OH 8 hrs
*WBWC(FM) Berea OH 5 hrs
WTOF-FM Canton OH 3 hrs
*WCSB(FM) Cleveland OH 20 hrs
WERE(AM) Cleveland OH 6 hrs
WNCX(FM) Cleveland OH 2 hrs
*WOSU(AM) Columbus OH 1 hr
*WDPS(FM) Dayton OH 5 hrs
*WWSU(FM) Dayton OH 6 hrs
*WKCO(FM) Gambier OH 10 hrs
*WDUB(FM) Granville OH 5 hrs
WMAN(AM) Mansfield OH 1 hr
*WOBC-FM Oberlin OH 20 hrs
WLEC(AM) Sandusky OH 6 hrs
*WEEC(FM) Springfield OH 1 hr
*WXUT(FM) Toledo OH 4 hrs
*WUJC(FM) University Heights OH 3 hrs
*WQRP(FM) West Carrollton OH 12 hrs
*WVXM(FM) West Union OH 1 hr
*WOBN(FM) Westerville OH 2 hrs
WGFT(AM) Youngstown OH 14 hrs
KOKC(AM) Guthrie OK 2 hrs
KWSH(AM) Wewoka OK 1 hr
*KMUN(FM) Astoria OR 2 hrs
*KLCC(FM) Eugene OR 3 hrs
*KRVM(FM) Eugene OR 2 hrs
*KWVA(FM) Eugene OR 20 hrs
*KEOL(FM) La Grande OR 12 hrs
*KSLC(FM) McMinnville OR 2 hrs
*KLCO(FM) Newport OR 3 hrs
*KBOO(FM) Portland OR 18 hrs
*KRRC(FM) Portland OR 10 hrs
KLWJ(AM) Umatilla OR 1 hr
*KWSO(FM) Warm Springs OR 2 hrs
*WMUH(FM) Allentown PA 4 hrs
WBVP(AM) Beaver Falls PA 2 hrs
*WLVR(FM) Bethlehem PA 12 hrs
*WVCS(FM) California PA 4 hrs
WFKJ(AM) Cashtown PA 2 hrs
WCZN(AM) Chester PA 4 hrs
*WCUC-FM Clarion PA 6 hrs
*WESS(FM) East Stroudsburg PA 3 hrs
*WFSE(FM) Edinboro PA 15 hrs
*WMCE(FM) Erie PA 4 hrs
*WKVR-FM Huntingdon PA 10 hrs
*WIUP-FM Indiana PA 14 hrs
*WFNM(FM) Lancaster PA 6 hrs
*WNTE(FM) Mansfield PA 5 hrs
*WARC(FM) Meadville PA 8 hrs
WKST(AM) New Castle PA 1 hr
*WKDU(FM) Philadelphia PA 8 hrs
*WRCT(FM) Pittsburgh PA 12 hrs
*WXAC(FM) Reading PA 3 hrs
*WVMW-FM Scranton PA 2 hrs
*WPSU(FM) State College PA 11 hrs
WSBA(AM) York PA 3 hrs
*WRIU(FM) Kingston RI 17 hrs
WALE(AM) Providence RI
WBRU(FM) Providence RI 18 hrs
WARV(AM) Warwick RI 2 hrs
WBLR(AM) Batesburg SC 2 hrs
WBSC(AM) Bennettsville SC 15 hrs
*WSCI(FM) Charleston SC 3 hrs
WCRE(AM) Cheraw SC 5 hrs
*WUSC-FM Columbia SC 6 hrs
WFIS(AM) Fountain Inn SC 2 hrs
WGTN(AM) Georgetown SC 2 hrs
WJBS(AM) Holly Hill SC 17 hrs
WRIX(AM) Homeland Park SC 7 hrs
WMAP-FM Pageland SC 2 hrs
WJKI(AM) Woodruff SC 12 hrs
WBZK(AM) York SC 4 hrs
*KTEQ(FM) Rapid City SD 6 hrs
WYXI(AM) Athens TN 1 hr
WMOC(AM) Chattanooga TN 15 hrs
*WAPX-FM Clarksville TN 6 hrs
WBAC(AM) Cleveland TN 1 hr
WKRM(AM) Columbia TN 1 hr
*WTTU(FM) Cookeville TN 3 hrs
WKBL(AM) Covington TN 12 hrs
WHIN(AM) Gallatin TN 2 hrs
*WVCP(FM) Gallatin TN 8 hrs
WTJS(AM) Jackson TN 2 hrs
WITA(AM) Knoxville TN 8 hrs
WLIL(AM) Lenoir City TN 1 hr
WDXL(AM) Lexington TN 4 hrs
*WUTM(FM) Martin TN 15 hrs
*WEVL(FM) Memphis TN 10 hrs
*WQOX(FM) Memphis TN 5 hrs
WXRQ(AM) Mt. Pleasant TN 4 hrs
WGNS(AM) Murfreesboro TN 6 hrs
*WFSK(FM) Nashville TN
WLAC(AM) Nashville TN 20 hrs
*WRVU(FM) Nashville TN 3 hrs
WOFE(AM) Rockwood TN 1 hr
*WUTS(FM) Sewanee TN 2 hrs
WLIJ(AM) Shelbyville TN 1 hr
WDBL(AM) Springfield TN
WDBL-FM Springfield TN
WKWT(FM) Union City TN 5 hrs
KEYJ(AM) Abilene TX 4 hrs
*KACV-FM Amarillo TX 8 hrs
KLVQ(AM) Athens TX 1 hr
KALT(AM) Atlanta TX 5 hrs
KPYN(FM) Atlanta TX 5 hrs
KAGC(AM) Bryan TX 2 hrs
KDET(AM) Center TX 10 hrs
*KAMU-FM College Station TX 3 hrs
*KVTT(FM) Dallas TX 2 hrs
KIXL(AM) Del Valle TX 6 hrs
KTMR(AM) Edna TX 3 hrs
KNES(FM) Fairfield TX 3 hrs
KHYM(AM) Gilmer TX 4 hrs
KGVL(AM) Greenville TX 1 hr
*KPFT(FM) Houston TX 15 hrs
KSAM(AM) Huntsville TX 4 hrs
*KSHU(FM) Huntsville TX 6 hrs
KYLR(AM) Huntsville TX 6 hrs
*KBJS(FM) Jacksonville TX 1 hr
KVLG(AM) La Grange TX 1 hr
KSHN-FM Liberty TX 3 hrs
KFRO(AM) Longview TX 3 hrs
*KTXT-FM Lubbock TX 6 hrs
KEYR(FM) Marlin TX 4 hrs
KWBC(AM) Navasota TX 3 hrs
KKKK(FM) Odessa TX 5 hrs
KLVL(AM) Pasadena TX 4 hrs
*KSYM-FM San Antonio TX 3 hrs
KTAE(AM) Taylor TX 14 hrs
KRZI(AM) Waco TX 4 hrs
*KZMU(FM) Moab UT 3 hrs
*KWCR-FM Ogden UT 12 hrs
*KRCL(FM) Salt Lake City UT 12 hrs
WKDE-FM Altavista VA 5 hrs
WMEK(AM) Chase City VA 3 hrs
WKEY(AM) Covington VA 1 hr
WPWC(AM) Dumfries-Triangle VA 4 hrs
WKRE-FM Exmore VA 6 hrs
WFAX(AM) Falls Church VA 3 hrs
WMNA(AM) Gretna VA 2 hrs
WMNA-FM Gretna VA 2 hrs
WKPA(AM) Lynchburg VA
*WVRU(FM) Radford VA 6 hrs
WKBA(AM) Vinton VA 10 hrs
WNNT(AM) Warsaw VA 10 hrs
WNNT-FM Warsaw VA 10 hrs
WANV(AM) Waynesboro VA 3 hrs
WVIS(FM) Christiansted VI
WRRA(AM) Frederiksted VI
*WGDR(FM) Plainfield VT 8 hrs
*KUGS(FM) Bellingham WA 5 hrs
KGNW(AM) Burien-Seattle WA
*KSVR(FM) Mount Vernon WA 10 hrs
*KZUU(FM) Pullman WA 12 hrs
*KNHC(FM) Seattle WA 4 hrs
KITZ(AM) Silverdale WA 2 hrs
*KUPS(FM) Tacoma WA 12 hrs
KBBO(AM) Yakima WA 2 hrs
WYLO(AM) Jackson WI 8 hrs
*WORT(FM) Madison WI 3 hrs
*WMSE(FM) Milwaukee WI 13 hrs
*WWSP(FM) Stevens Point WI 3 hrs
*WCCX(FM) Waukesha WI 3 hrs
*WVWC(FM) Buckhannon WV 2 hrs
WQBE(AM) Charleston WV 1 hr
*WWVU-FM Morgantown WV 9 hrs
*WQAB(FM) Philippi WV 2 hrs
*WPHP(FM) Wheeling WV 4 hrs

Bluegrass

*WQPR(FM) Muscle Shoals AL
*WUAL-FM Tuscaloosa AL
KXAR(AM) Hope AR 2 hrs
*KABF(FM) Little Rock AR 6 hrs
*KFJC(FM) Los Altos CA 8 hrs
*KCSN(FM) Northridge CA 5 hrs
*KCSM(FM) San Mateo CA 5 hrs
*KUOP(FM) Stockton CA 12 hrs
*KAJX(FM) Aspen CO
*KDNK(FM) Carbondale CO 10 hrs
*WWUH(FM) West Hartford C T 7 hrs
*WVUD(FM) Newark DE 5 hrs
WWOJ(FM) Avon Park FL 2 hrs
WJXR(FM) Macclenny FL 1 hr
*WUCF-FM Orlando FL 3 hrs
WCWB-FM Trenton FL
*WRFG(FM) Atlanta GA 10 hrs
WTHO-FM Thomson GA 2 hrs
*WDCB(FM) Glen Ellyn IL 3 hrs
WBQR(FM) Attica IN 3 hrs
WMRS(FM) Monticello IN 2 hrs
*WECI(FM) Richmond IN 10 hrs
WKJK(FM) Salem IN
*WMHD-FM Terre Haute IN 1 hr
*KANU(FM) Lawrence KS 4 hrs
WGOH(AM) Grayson KY 15 hrs
WFLW(AM) Monticello KY 3 hrs
*WMKY(FM) Morehead KY 2 hrs
*WMMT(FM) Whitesburg KY 10 hrs
WTCW(AM) Whitesburg KY 10 hrs
WNKR(FM) Williamstown KY 4 hrs
KWKH(AM) Shreveport LA 1 hr
KWKH-FM Shreveport LA 1 hr
*WOMR(FM) Provincetown MA 3 hrs
*WZLY(FM) Wellesley MA 2 hrs
*WCUW(FM) Worcester MA 3 hrs
*WICN(FM) Worcester MA 4 hrs
*WDET-FM Detroit MI 3 hrs
WJCO(AM) Jackson MI 2 hrs
*WMUK(FM) Kalamazoo MI 8 hrs
WSDS(AM) Salem Township MI 6 hrs
*KBEM-FM Minneapolis MN 5 hrs
*KOPN(FM) Columbia MO 6 hrs
KTJJ(FM) Farmington MO 2 hrs
KYRO(AM) Potosi MO 1 hr
KMOZ(AM) Rolla MO 6 hrs
*KUMR(FM) Rolla MO 5 hrs
*KCLC(FM) St. Charles MO 12 hrs
*WMAH-FM Biloxi MS 3 hrs
*WMAE-FM Booneville MS 3 hrs
*WMAU-FM Bude MS 3 hrs
*WMAO-FM Greenwood MS 3 hrs
*WMPN-FM Jackson MS 3 hrs
*WMAW-FM Meridian MS 3 hrs
*WMAB-FM Mississippi State MS 3 hrs
*WMAV-FM Oxford MS 3 hrs
*WCCE(FM) Buie's Creek NC 4 hrs
WPCM(FM) Burlington NC 3 hrs
WCXN(AM) Claremont NC
WDSL(AM) Mocksville NC 10 hrs
WKBC(AM) North Wilkesboro NC 2 hrs
WEGG(AM) Rose Hill NC 10 hrs
WKRX(FM) Roxboro NC 6 hrs
WTQR(FM) Winston-Salem NC 2 hrs
*WBJB-FM Lincroft NJ 3 hrs
*KRWG(FM) Las Cruces NM 8 hrs
*WAMC(FM) Albany NY 8 hrs
*WBFO(FM) Buffalo NY 3 hrs
*WCAN(FM) Canajoharie NY 4 hrs
*WBAU(FM) Garden City NY 2 hrs
WXHC(FM) Homer NY 2 hrs
*WSQG-FM Ithaca NY 7 hrs
*WAMK(FM) Kingston NY 4 hrs
*WOSR(FM) Middletown NY 4 hrs
*WVKR-FM Poughkeepsie NY 5 hrs
*WCNY-FM Syracuse NY 3 hrs
*WOSU(AM) Columbus OH 12 hrs
*WYSO(FM) Yellow Springs OH 5 hrs
KRPT(AM) Anadarko OK 2 hrs
KRPT-FM Anadarko OK 2 hrs
KCES(FM) Eufaula OK 3 hrs
*KBOO(FM) Portland OR 8 hrs
WSKE(AM) Everett PA 3 hrs
WSKE-FM Everett PA 3 hrs
WPHB(AM) Philipsburg PA 5 hrs
*WYEP-FM Pittsburgh PA 4 hrs

Special Programming on Radio Stations in the U.S.

WVBI(FM) Block Island RI 4 hrs
WCSV(AM) Crossville TN 2 hrs
WEGE(FM) Crossville TN 1 hr
WEMB(AM) Erwin TN 2 hrs
WSMG(AM) Greeneville TN 2 hrs
WCLC(AM) Jamestown TN 3 hrs
WWAM(AM) Jasper TN 1 hr
WLAF(AM) La Follette TN 7 hrs
*WRVU(FM) Nashville TN 3 hrs
*WUTS(FM) Sewanee TN 2 hrs
WSBI(AM) Static TN 1 hr
*KETR(FM) Commerce TX 5 hrs
WCBX(AM) Bassett VA 4 hrs
WKEX(AM) Blacksburg VA 2 hrs
WOPI(AM) Bristol VA 4 hrs
WGFC(AM) Floyd VA 18 hrs
WMNA(AM) Gretna VA 15 hrs
WMNA-FM Gretna VA 15 hrs
*WEMC(FM) Harrisonburg VA 6 hrs
WHHV(AM) Hillsville VA 17 hrs
WLSA(FM) Louisa VA 8 hrs
WBLU(AM) Moneta VA
*WOJB(FM) Reserve WI 2 hrs
WVRQ-FM Viroqua WI 2 hrs
*WVMR(AM) Frost WV 4 hrs
*WWVU-FM Morgantown WV 1 hr
WMOV(AM) Ravenswood WV 10 hrs

Blues

*KUAC(FM) Fairbanks AK 4 hrs
*KSKO(AM) McGrath AK 3 hrs
*KTNA(FM) Talkeetna AK 5 hrs
*WVSU-FM Birmingham AL 2 hrs
*WQPR(FM) Muscle Shoals AL
*WUAL-FM Tuscaloosa AL
*WVUA-FM Tuscaloosa AL 3 hrs
*KABF(FM) Little Rock AR 20 hrs
*KSPC(FM) Claremont CA 3 hrs
*KKUP(FM) Cupertino CA 19 hrs
KCQR(FM) Ellwood CA 1 hr
*KFSR(FM) Fresno CA 18 hrs
*KFJC(FM) Los Altos CA 4 hrs
*KSBR(FM) Mission Viejo CA 4 hrs
*KVMR(FM) Nevada City CA 5 hrs
KDJK(FM) Oakdale CA 2 hrs
*KZYX(FM) Philo CA 3 hrs
KNCI(FM) Sacramento CA 1 hr
*KCPR(FM) San Luis Obispo CA 3 hrs
*KCSM(FM) San Mateo CA 5 hrs
*KCSB-FM Santa Barbara CA 6 hrs
*KSCU(FM) Santa Clara CA 12 hrs
KKBB(FM) Shafter CA 1 hr
*KUOP(FM) Stockton CA 3 hrs
*KDNK(FM) Carbondale CO 10 hrs
*KDUR(FM) Durango CO 3 hrs
KTCL(FM) Fort Collins CO 2 hrs
*KWSB-FM Gunnison CO 1 hr
*KVNF(FM) Paonia CO 3 hrs
*KOTO(FM) Telluride CO 7 hrs
*WESU(FM) Middletown CT 10 hrs
*WFCS(FM) New Britain CT 2 hrs
*WDCU(FM) Washington DC 2 hrs
*WVUM(FM) Coral Gables FL 3 hrs
WJBX(FM) Fort Myers Beach FL 5 hrs
WIIS(FM) Key West FL 1 hr
*WUCF-FM Orlando FL 2 hrs
WRBD(AM) Pompano Beach FL 6 hrs
*WKPX(FM) Sunrise FL 3 hrs
*WMNF(FM) Tampa FL
*WUOG(FM) Athens GA 2 hrs
*WCLK(FM) Atlanta GA 3 hrs
*WRAS(FM) Atlanta GA 2 hrs
*WVVS(FM) Valdosta GA 3 hrs
*KUNI(FM) Cedar Falls IA 10 hrs
KROS(AM) Clinton IA 1 hr
*KRUI-FM Iowa City IA 3 hrs
*KWIT(FM) Sioux City IA 1 hr
*WEFT(FM) Champaign IL 10 hrs
*WJMU(FM) Decatur IL 3 hrs
*WSIE(FM) Edwardsville IL 1 hr
*WNUR-FM Evanston IL 3 hrs
*WDCB(FM) Glen Ellyn IL 3 hrs
*WIUM(FM) Macomb IL 7 hrs
WPNA(AM) Oak Park IL 8 hrs
*WQUB(FM) Quincy IL 2 hrs
*WNIJ(FM) Rockford IL 4 hrs
WTTS(FM) Bloomington IN 5 hrs
*WVPE(FM) Elkhart IN 5 hrs
*WFYI-FM Indianapolis IN 5 hrs
*WISU(FM) Terre Haute IN 10 hrs
*WMHD-FM Terre Haute IN 1 hr
*WVUR-FM Valparaiso IN 3 hrs
KOCD(FM) Columbus KS 5 hrs
KOTE(FM) Eureka KS 2 hrs
*KANU(FM) Lawrence KS 4 hrs
*KJHK(FM) Lawrence KS 2 hrs
*KRPS(FM) Pittsburg KS 4 hrs
*WRFL(FM) Lexington KY 3 hrs
*WMMT(FM) Whitesburg KY 2 hrs
*KLSU(FM) Baton Rouge LA 3 hrs
KBCE(FM) Boyce LA 1 hr
KROK(FM) De Ridder LA
*KEDM(FM) Monroe LA 4 hrs
*KNLU(FM) Monroe LA 3 hrs
*KNWD(FM) Natchitoches LA 2 hrs
*WTUL(FM) New Orleans LA 2 hrs
*KSCL(FM) Shreveport LA 1 hr
*WMUA(FM) Amherst MA 15 hrs
*WGBH(FM) Boston MA 8 hrs
*WCCH(FM) Holyoke MA 6 hrs
*WMLN-FM Milton MA 3 hrs
*WOMR(FM) Provincetown MA 3 hrs
*WBRS(FM) Waltham MA 14 hrs
*WCUW(FM) Worcester MA 6 hrs
WHFS(FM) Annapolis MD 2 hrs
*WESM(FM) Princess Anne MD 4 hrs
*WTMD(FM) Towson MD 3 hrs
*WKHS(FM) Worton MD 2 hrs
*WERU-FM Blue Hill ME 5 hrs
*WRBC(FM) Lewiston ME 2 hrs
*WMEB-FM Orono ME 7 hrs
WCDQ(FM) Sanford ME 3 hrs
*WMHB(FM) Waterville ME 64 hrs
WLLJ(AM) Cassopolis MI 4 hrs
*WHFR(FM) Dearborn MI 3 hrs
*WDET-FM Detroit MI 8 hrs
*WDTR(FM) Detroit MI 4 hrs
*WDBM(FM) East Lansing MI 4 hrs
*WIDR(FM) Kalamazoo MI 3 hrs
WWGZ-FM Lapeer MI
WRKR(FM) Portage MI 3 hrs
*WPHS(FM) Warren MI 2 hrs
KTCJ(AM) Minneapolis MN 1 hr
KTCZ-FM Minneapolis MN 1 hr
*KUMM(FM) Morris MN 2 hrs
*KVSC(FM) St. Cloud MN
*KWUR(FM) Clayton MO 6 hrs
*KCOU(FM) Columbia MO 2 hrs
*KOPN(FM) Columbia MO 12 hrs
*KJLU(FM) Jefferson City MO
*KKFI(FM) Kansas City MO 9 hrs
KYLC(FM) Osage Beach MO 1 hr
*KCLC(FM) St. Charles MO 7 hrs
*KDHX(FM) St. Louis MO 10 hrs
*WUSM-FM Hattiesburg MS 2 hrs
WKRA-FM Holly Springs MS 12 hrs
*WJSU(FM) Jackson MS 2 hrs
WPMX(AM) Tupelo MS 6 hrs
*WASU-FM Boone NC 2 hrs
*WNAA(FM) Greensboro NC 3 hrs
*WQFS(FM) Greensboro NC 7 hrs
*WUAG(FM) Greensboro NC 3 hrs
*WZMB(FM) Greenville NC 3 hrs
*WKNC-FM Raleigh NC 3 hrs
*WSHA(FM) Raleigh NC 8 hrs
*WNCW(FM) Spindale NC 4 hrs
*KFJM(AM) Grand Forks ND 2 hrs
*KZUM(FM) Lincoln NE 13 hrs
KKCD(FM) Omaha NE 1 hr
*KWSC(FM) Wayne NE 2 hrs
WHDQ(FM) Claremont NH 3 hrs
WFRD(FM) Hanover NH 1 hr
*WNEC-FM Henniker NH 3 hrs
*WKNH(FM) Keene NH 3 hrs
WMTK(FM) Littleton NH
*WNTI(FM) Hackettstown NJ 5 hrs
*WBJB-FM Lincroft NJ 3 hrs
*WMNJ(FM) Madison NJ 4 hrs
*KRUX(FM) Las Cruces NM 2 hrs
*KUNV(FM) Las Vegas NV 2 hrs
*WBFO(FM) Buffalo NY 6 hrs
WELM(AM) Elmira NY 3 hrs
*WEOS(FM) Geneva NY 12 hrs
*WGMC(FM) Greece NY 3 hrs
*WRHU(FM) Hempstead NY 2 hrs
WQNY(FM) Ithaca NY 3 hrs
*WCFE-FM Plattsburgh NY 4 hrs
*WSPN(FM) Saratoga Springs NY 9 hrs
*WAER(FM) Syracuse NY 3 hrs
*WUSO(FM) Springfield OH 3 hrs
*WXTS-FM Toledo OH 5 hrs
*WXUT(FM) Toledo OH 2 hrs
*WYSO(FM) Yellow Springs OH 16 hrs
*KRSC-FM Claremore OK 6 hrs
*KGOU(FM) Norman OK 10 hrs
*KROU(FM) Spencer OK 10 hrs
*KAYE-FM Tonkawa OK 1 hr
*KSMF(FM) Ashland OR 6 hrs
*KSBA(FM) Coos Bay OR 6 hrs
KZZK-FM Creswell OR 2 hrs
*KLCC(FM) Eugene OR 3 hrs
*KWVA(FM) Eugene OR 4 hrs
*KSKF(FM) Klamath Falls OR 6 hrs
*KLCO(FM) Newport OR 4 hrs
KYTE(FM) Newport OR 2 hrs
KMCQ(FM) The Dalles OR 2 hrs
*KWSO(FM) Warm Springs OR 1 hr
*WDCV-FM Carlisle PA 6 hrs
*WDNR(FM) Chester PA 2 hrs
*WKDU(FM) Philadelphia PA 3 hrs
*WPEB(FM) Philadelphia PA 18 hrs
*WYEP-FM Pittsburgh PA 7 hrs
*WPSU(FM) State College PA 3 hrs
*WRDV(FM) Warminster PA 3 hrs
WRAK-FM Williamsport PA 3 hrs
*WRLC(FM) Williamsport PA 2 hrs
*WRIU(FM) Kingston RI 3 hrs
*WUSC-FM Columbia SC 3 hrs
*WSSB-FM Orangeburg SC 2 hrs
*WTTU(FM) Cookeville TN 3 hrs
WRLT-FM Franklin TN 3 hrs
*WFHC(FM) Henderson TN 4 hrs
WQQK(FM) Hendersonville TN 6 hrs
*WETS(FM) Johnson City TN 12 hrs
*WEVL(FM) Memphis TN 22 hrs
*WQOX(FM) Memphis TN 5 hrs
*WRVU(FM) Nashville TN 3 hrs
*WUTS(FM) Sewanee TN 3 hrs
WRLG(FM) Smyrna TN 2 hrs
*KAZI(FM) Austin TX 6 hrs
*KSAU(FM) Nacogdoches TX 2 hrs
*KPVU(FM) Prairie View TX 4 hrs
KNCN(FM) Sinton TX 2 hrs
*KZMU(FM) Moab UT 19 hrs
*KRCL(FM) Salt Lake City UT 5 hrs
*WWHS-FM Hampden-Sydney VA 2 hrs
*WHOV(FM) Hampton VA 3 hrs
*WCWM(FM) Williamsburg VA 3 hrs
WIZN(FM) Vergennes VT 3 hrs
*WIUV(FM) Castleton VT 3 hrs
*KUGS(FM) Bellingham WA 15 hrs
*KSER(FM) Everett WA 8 hrs
*KAOS(FM) Olympia WA 5 hrs
KXRX(FM) Seattle WA
KKZX(FM) Spokane WA 2 hrs
*KBTC-FM Tacoma WA 2 hrs
*KPLU-FM Tacoma WA 9 hrs
KKRT(AM) Wenatchee WA
KKRV(FM) Wenatchee WA
*WBSD(FM) Burlington WI 3 hrs
*WYMS(FM) Milwaukee WI 3 hrs

Children

*KSKO(AM) McGrath AK 1 hr
*KZFR(FM) Chico CA 5 hrs
*KMUD(FM) Garberville CA 3 hrs
*KPFK(FM) Los Angeles CA 2 hrs
*KVMR(FM) Nevada City CA 3 hrs
KWVE(FM) San Clemente CA 3 hrs
*WUGA(FM) Athens GA 4 hrs
KLHI-FM Lahaina HI 2 hrs
*KCIR(FM) Twin Falls ID 2 hrs
*WMBI(AM) Chicago IL 7 hrs
*KJTY(FM) Topeka KS 5 hrs
*WUMB-FM Boston MA 1 hr
WADN(AM) Concord MA 1 hr
*WOMR(FM) Provincetown MA 6 hrs
*WBRS(FM) Waltham MA 2 hrs
WGFP(AM) Webster MA 1 hr
*WKHS(FM) Worton MD 5 hrs
WAVX(FM) Thomaston ME 1 hr
WJCO(AM) Jackson MI 1 hr
*KTGG(AM) Spring Arbor MI 18 hrs
*WSAE(FM) Spring Arbor MI 10 hrs
KJLY(FM) Blue Earth MN 4 hrs
KGNM(AM) St. Joseph MO 8 hrs
*WRHO(FM) Oneonta NY 2 hrs
*KMUN(FM) Astoria OR 6 hrs
WFKJ(AM) Cashtown PA 14 hrs
WDBA(FM) DuBois PA 2 hrs
*WPEB(FM) Philadelphia PA 8 hrs
*WXPN(FM) Philadelphia PA 5 hrs
WCTL(FM) Union City PA 2 hrs
*WRLC(FM) Williamsport PA 2 hrs
*KVNE-FM Tyler TX 4 hrs
*WEMC(FM) Harrisonburg VA 2 hrs
WGLV(FM) Hartford VT 3 hrs
WGLY-FM Waterbury VT 3 hrs
WVAY(FM) Wilmington VT 1 hr
KENE(AM) Toppenish WA 1 hr
*WYMS(FM) Milwaukee WI 4 hrs
*WQAB(FM) Philippi WV 2 hrs

Chinese

KGBA-FM Holtville CA 4 hrs
*KALW(FM) San Francisco CA 3 hrs
KEST(AM) San Francisco CA 5 hrs
*KUSF(FM) San Francisco CA 9 hrs
KNDI(AM) Honolulu HI 6 hrs
*WUMB-FM Boston MA 1 hr
*WZLY(FM) Wellesley MA 1 hr
KLAV(AM) Las Vegas NV 6 hrs
*WUSB(FM) Stony Brook NY 1 hr
*WRPI(FM) Troy NY 2 hrs
*KHCB(AM) Galveston TX 10 hrs
KNTR(AM) Ferndale WA 1 hr

Classic Rock

*KTNA(FM) Talkeetna AK 5 hrs
KMMT(FM) Mammoth Lakes CA 5 hrs
KVFC(AM) Cortez CO 6 hrs
WBGM-FM Tallahassee FL 5 hrs
*KUSR(FM) Ames IA
*KWLC(AM) Decorah IA
*WCSF(FM) Joliet IL 4 hrs
*WBKE-FM North Manchester IN 6 hrs
*WVUR-FM Valparaiso IN 3 hrs
*WRBC(FM) Lewiston ME 11 hrs
*WQAC-FM Alma MI 4 hrs
*KUMM(FM) Morris MN 2 hrs
*KMVC(FM) Marshall MO 4 hrs
WERX-FM Edenton NC
KSCQ(FM) Silver City NM
*WPLT(FM) Plattsburgh NY 12 hrs
*WKHR(FM) Bainbridge OH
*WCWS(FM) Wooster OH 16 hrs
*KAYE-FM Tonkawa OK 2 hrs
WMKX(FM) Brookville PA 6 hrs
WCBG(AM) Chambersburg PA 6 hrs
*WCLH(FM) Wilkes-Barre PA 9 hrs
*WDOM(FM) Providence RI 3 hrs
*WPLS-FM Greenville SC 2 hrs
KNCN(FM) Sinton TX 1 hr
*KUPS(FM) Tacoma WA 8 hrs
*WVBC(FM) Bethany WV 8 hrs

Classical

*KBRW(AM) Barrow AK 2 hrs
*KYUK(AM) Bethel AK 4 hrs
KCAM(AM) Glennallen AK 5 hrs
*KHNS(FM) Haines AK 14 hrs
*KBBI(AM) Homer AK 20 hrs
*KTOO(FM) Juneau AK 17 hrs
*KRBD(FM) Ketchikan AK 11 hrs
*KOTZ(AM) Kotzebue AK 4 hrs
*KSKO(AM) McGrath AK 2 hrs
KICY-FM Nome AK 2 hrs
KRSA(AM) Petersburg AK 5 hrs
*KTNA(FM) Talkeetna AK 10 hrs
*KSTK(FM) Wrangell AK 4 hrs
*WLJS-FM Jacksonville AL
KOLZ(FM) Bentonville AR 2 hrs
*KUCA(FM) Conway AR 4 hrs
KTCN(FM) Eureka Springs AR 5 hrs
WVUV(AM) Leone AS 2 hrs
*KNAU(FM) Flagstaff AZ 3 hrs
KWDS(AM) Prescott Valley AZ 1 hr
*KAWC(AM) Yuma AZ 13 hrs
*KHSU-FM Arcata CA 18 hrs
*KPFA(FM) Berkeley CA 20 hrs
*KSPC(FM) Claremont CA 12 hrs
*KKUP(FM) Cupertino CA 4 hrs
*KDVS(FM) Davis CA 2 hrs
*KFCF(FM) Fresno CA 10 hrs
*KMUD(FM) Garberville CA 4 hrs
*KUCI(FM) Irvine CA 5 hrs
*KPFK(FM) Los Angeles CA 14 hrs
*KVMR(FM) Nevada City CA 8 hrs
*KAZU(FM) Pacific Grove CA 3 hrs
*KPCC(FM) Pasadena CA 3 hrs
*KZYX(FM) Philo CA 14 hrs
KQNC(FM) Quincy CA 5 hrs
*KUCR(FM) Riverside CA 14 hrs
*KALW(FM) San Francisco CA 2 hrs
*KUSF(FM) San Francisco CA 6 hrs
*KCPR(FM) San Luis Obispo CA 3 hrs
*KCSB-FM Santa Barbara CA 4 hrs
*KUSP(FM) Santa Cruz CA 21 hrs
*KZSC(FM) Santa Cruz CA 6 hrs
*KCSS(FM) Turlock CA 6 hrs
*KASF(FM) Alamosa CO 4 hrs
*KGNU(FM) Boulder CO 13 hrs
KSMT(FM) Breckenridge CO 4 hrs
*KDNK(FM) Carbondale CO 10 hrs
*KPOF(AM) Denver CO 16 hrs
*KDUR(FM) Durango CO 9 hrs
KIUP(AM) Durango CO 2 hrs
*KCIC(FM) Grand Junction CO 14 hrs
*KWSB-FM Gunnison CO 3 hrs
*KSUT(FM) Ignacio CO 10 hrs
*KVNF(FM) Paonia CO 15 hrs
KVRH(AM) Salida CO 3 hrs
KVRH-FM Salida CO 3 hrs
*KOTO(FM) Telluride CO 9 hrs
*WPKN(FM) Bridgeport CT 2 hrs
*WVOF(FM) Fairfield CT 8 hrs
*WRTC-FM Hartford CT 4 hrs
*WESU(FM) Middletown CT 2 hrs
*WFCS(FM) New Britain CT 2 hrs
*WCNI(FM) New London CT 6 hrs
WLIS(AM) Old Saybrook CT 2 hrs
*WWEB(FM) Wallingford CT 2 hrs
*WWUH(FM) West Hartford CT 20 hrs
*WNHU(FM) West Haven CT 18 hrs
*WECS(FM) Willimantic CT 15 hrs
*WVUD(FM) Newark DE 10 hrs
WKRY(FM) Key West FL
*WFIT(FM) Melbourne FL 3 hrs
*WLRN-FM Miami FL 16 hrs
*WRAS(FM) Atlanta GA 3 hrs
*WREK(FM) Atlanta GA 8 hrs
*WRFG(FM) Atlanta GA 2 hrs
WMOG(AM) Brunswick GA 1 hr
*WWGC(FM) Carrollton GA 5 hrs
WYTH(AM) Madison GA 1 hr
WFDR(AM) Manchester GA 1 hr
*WXGC(FM) Milledgeville GA 7 hrs
WPAX(AM) Thomasville GA 5 hrs
KTWG(AM) Agana GU 6 hrs
KFSH(FM) Hilo HI 3 hrs
*KTUH(FM) Honolulu HI 18 hrs
*KWLC(AM) Decorah IA
*KDIC(FM) Grinnell IA 12 hrs
*KCMR(FM) Mason City IA 5 hrs
*KWAR(FM) Waverly IA 10 hrs
KBFI(AM) Bonners Ferry ID 3 hrs
KHEZ(FM) Caldwell ID 2 hrs
*KUOI-FM Moscow ID 3 hrs
KSRA(AM) Salmon ID 1 hr
*WESN(FM) Bloomington IL 6 hrs
*WSIU(FM) Carbondale IL 4 hrs
*WEFT(FM) Champaign IL 1 hr
*WHPK-FM Chicago IL 10 hrs
*WJMU(FM) Decatur IL 2 hrs
*WEPS(FM) Elgin IL 3 hrs
*WRSE-FM Elmhurst IL 1 hr
*WTPC(FM) Elsah IL 3 hrs
*WNUR-FM Evanston IL 3 hrs
*WVKC(FM) Galesburg IL 18 hrs
*WDCB(FM) Glen Ellyn IL 6 hrs
*WJCH(FM) Joliet IL 2 hrs
*WMXM(FM) Lake Forest IL 3 hrs
*WLRA(FM) Lockport IL 6 hrs
*WUSI(FM) Olney IL 4 hrs
*WMTH(FM) Park Ridge IL 4 hrs
WLRZ(FM) Peru IL 5 hrs
WGFA(AM) Watseka IL 1 hr
*WEAX(FM) Angola IN 4 hrs
*WDSO(FM) Chesterton IN 1 hr
WNDY(FM) Crawfordsville IN 8 hrs
*WSWI(AM) Evansville IN 10 hrs
*WGVE(FM) Gary IN 16 hrs
WMRS(FM) Monticello IN 1 hr
*WNAS(FM) New Albany IN 1 hr
*WBKE-FM North Manchester IN 10 hrs
*WVXR(FM) Richmond IN 5 hrs
*WMHD-FM Terre Haute IN 2 hrs
WNWI(AM) Valparaiso IN 2 hrs
*WVUR-FM Valparaiso IN 3 hrs
WOTD(FM) Winamac IN 5 hrs
*KONQ(FM) Dodge City KS 10 hrs
*WRVG(FM) Georgetown KY 6 hrs
WMTC(AM) Vancleve KY 15 hrs
*WMMT(FM) Whitesburg KY 2 hrs
*KLSU(FM) Baton Rouge LA 3 hrs
*WTUL(FM) New Orleans LA 15 hrs
*KLPI-FM Ruston LA 3 hrs
KVLA(AM) Vidalia LA 7 hrs
*WAMH(FM) Amherst MA 3 hrs
WTTT(AM) Amherst MA 2 hrs
*WMBR(FM) Cambridge MA 2 hrs
WBMA(AM) Dedham MA 10 hrs
*WXPL(FM) Fitchburg MA 2 hrs
WRSI(FM) Greenfield MA 6 hrs
*WCCH(FM) Holyoke MA 2 hrs
*WJUL(FM) Lowell MA 4 hrs
*WMFO(FM) Medford MA 3 hrs
*WZBC(FM) Newton MA 3 hrs
*WJJW(FM) North Adams MA 3 hrs
*WOZQ(FM) Northampton MA 3 hrs
*WNMH(FM) Northfield MA 2 hrs
*WMHC(FM) South Hadley MA 15 hrs
*WTCC(FM) Springfield MA 3 hrs
*WYAJ(FM) Sudbury MA 3 hrs
WMVY(FM) Tisbury MA 4 hrs
*WBRS(FM) Waltham MA 3 hrs
*WZLY(FM) Wellesley MA 4 hrs
*WSKB(FM) Westfield MA 3 hrs
*WCUW(FM) Worcester MA 5 hrs
*WBYQ(FM) Baltimore MD 3 hrs
*WERU-FM Blue Hill ME 5 hrs
*WBOR(FM) Brunswick ME 10 hrs
*WUPI(FM) Presque Isle ME 4 hrs
*WSJB-FM Standish ME 2 hrs
*WOLW(FM) Cadillac MI 1 hr
*WHFR(FM) Dearborn MI 4 hrs
*WDET-FM Detroit MI 4 hrs
*WPHN(FM) Gaylord MI 5 hrs
*WBYW(FM) Grand Rapids MI 2 hrs
*WOES(FM) Ovid-Elsie MI 1 hr
WMZX(FM) Owosso MI 1 hr
*WSHJ(FM) Southfield MI 3 hrs
WELY(AM) Ely MN 6 hrs
*KAXE(FM) Grand Rapids MN 2 hrs
*KFAI(FM) Minneapolis MN 4 hrs
*KUMM(FM) Morris MN 3 hrs
KYMN(AM) Northfield MN 2 hrs
KNXR(FM) Rochester MN 4 hrs
*KVSC(FM) St. Cloud MN 3 hrs
*KQAL(FM) Winona MN 14 hrs
KZBK-FM Brookfield MO 4 hrs
*KWUR(FM) Clayton MO 4 hrs
*KWWC-FM Columbia MO 6 hrs
WMBH-FM Joplin MO 3 hrs
KFEZ(AM) Kansas City MO 17 hrs
*KDHX(FM) St. Louis MO 4 hrs
WBAQ(FM) Greenville MS 2 hrs
*KGLT(FM) Bozeman MT 11 hrs
*KMSM-FM Butte MT 2 hrs
*KNMC(FM) Havre MT 10 hrs
KALS(FM) Kalispell MT 1 hr
KWYS(AM) West Yellowstone MT 1 hr
WFGW(AM) Black Mountain NC 1 hr
WVIO(AM) Blowing Rock NC 2 hrs
*WQFS(FM) Greensboro NC 2 hrs
*WZMB(FM) Greenville NC 3 hrs
WVOD(FM) Manteo NC 6 hrs
*WHYC(FM) Swan Quarter NC 4 hrs
WTYN(AM) Tryon NC 2 hrs
*WSNC(FM) Winston-Salem NC 4 hrs
*KROA(FM) Grand Island NE 1 hr
KHAS(AM) Hastings NE 2 hrs
*KSCV(FM) Kearney NE 18 hrs
KCMI(FM) Terrytown NE 4 hrs
*WUNH(FM) Durham NH 2 hrs
*WPEA(FM) Exeter NH 2 hrs
WDCR(AM) Hanover NH 8 hrs
*WKNH(FM) Keene NH 4 hrs
WFPG(AM) Atlantic City NJ 2 hrs
*WKDN-FM Camden NJ 2 hrs
WSJL(FM) Cape May NJ 1 hr
*WDR(FM) Delaware Township NJ 4 hrs
*WCVH(FM) Flemington NJ 15 hrs
*WMNJ(FM) Madison NJ 2 hrs
*WRSU-FM New Brunswick NJ 2 hrs
*WLFR(FM) Pomona NJ 4 hrs

Special Programming on Radio Stations in the U.S.

*KANW(FM) Albuquerque NM 6 hrs
*KUNM(FM) Albuquerque NM 12 hrs
KPCL(FM) Farmington NM 1 hr
KTMN(FM) Los Alamos NM 10 hrs
KSSR(AM) Santa Rosa NM 1 hr
*WXLH(FM) Blue Mountain Lake NY
*WBSU(FM) Brockport NY 14 hrs
*WBFO(FM) Buffalo NY 1 hr
*WSLU(FM) Canton NY
*WHCL-FM Clinton NY 9 hrs
*WSUC-FM Cortland NY 4 hrs
WVOA(FM) DeRuyter NY 1 hr
*WGSU(FM) Geneseo NY 3 hrs
*WRCU-FM Hamilton NY 4 hrs
*WJSL(FM) Houghton NY 5 hrs
*WSLO(FM) Malone NY
WVIP(AM) Mount Kisco NY 1 hr
*WBAI(FM) New York NY 5 hrs
*WXLG(FM) North Creek NY
*WONY(FM) Oneonta NY 3 hrs
WSRK(FM) Oneonta NY 2 hrs
*WXLU(FM) Peru NY
*WVKR-FM Poughkeepsie NY 3 hrs
*WSLL(FM) Saranac Lake NY
*WSBU(FM) St. Bonaventure NY 2 hrs
*WUSB(FM) Stony Brook NY 14 hrs
*WKWZ(FM) Syosset NY 6 hrs
*WPNR-FM Utica NY 10 hrs
*WSLJ(FM) Watertown NY
WDST(FM) Woodstock NY 15 hrs
*WBWC(FM) Berea OH 5 hrs
*WBGU(FM) Bowling Green OH 3 hrs
WEBN(FM) Cincinnati OH 4 hrs
*WRUW-FM Cleveland OH 4 hrs
*WCUE(AM) Cuyahoga Falls OH 2 hrs
*WWSU(FM) Dayton OH 3 hrs
*WKCO(FM) Gambier OH 3 hrs
*WDUB(FM) Granville OH 5 hrs
*WVMC(FM) Mansfield OH 1 hr
*WMCO(FM) New Concord OH 6 hrs
*WOBC-FM Oberlin OH 15 hrs
*WUSO(FM) Springfield OH 3 hrs
*WUJC(FM) University Heights OH 4 hrs
*WVXM(FM) West Union OH 5 hrs
*WCWS(FM) Wooster OH 12 hrs
*WYSO(FM) Yellow Springs OH 10 hrs
*WYTN(FM) Youngstown OH 2 hrs
KALV(AM) Alva OK 1 hr
WBBZ(AM) Ponca City OK 5 hrs
*KBVR(FM) Corvallis OR 3 hrs
KIHR(AM) Hood River OR 3 hrs
*KTEC(FM) Klamath Falls OR 2 hrs
*KEOL(FM) La Grande OR 4 hrs
*KBOO(FM) Portland OR 18 hrs
*KRRC(FM) Portland OR 4 hrs
*WMUH(FM) Allentown PA 6 hrs
*WLVR(FM) Bethlehem PA 8 hrs
WDBA(FM) DuBois PA 1 hr
*WESS(FM) East Stroudsburg PA 4 hrs
*WWEC(FM) Elizabethtown PA 3 hrs
*WZBT(FM) Gettysburg PA 3 hrs
*WVMM(FM) Grantham PA 4 hrs
*WSAJ(AM) Grove City PA 2 hrs
*WKVR-FM Huntingdon PA 2 hrs
*WIUP-FM Indiana PA 15 hrs
WJSA(AM) Jersey Shore PA 1 hr
WJSA-FM Jersey Shore PA 1 hr
*WFNM(FM) Lancaster PA 2 hrs
*WARC(FM) Meadville PA 10 hrs
*WMSS(FM) Middletown PA 2 hrs
*WPEL(AM) Montrose PA 1 hr
WKST(AM) New Castle PA 1 hr
*WWNW(FM) New Wilmington PA 6 hrs
*WHYY-FM Philadelphia PA 9 hrs
*WPEB(FM) Philadelphia PA 2 hrs
*WRCT(FM) Pittsburgh PA 3 hrs
WRAW(AM) Reading PA 1 hr
*WXLV(FM) Schnecksville PA 13 hrs
*WVMW-FM Scranton PA 7 hrs
WSHP(AM) Shippensburg PA 5 hrs
WRSC(AM) State College PA 3 hrs
WRAK-FM Williamsport PA 1 hr
*WRLC(FM) Williamsport PA 1 hr
*WVYC(FM) York PA 8 hrs
WTPM(FM) Aguadilla PR 7 hrs
WYKO(AM) Sabana Grande PR 6 hrs
*WRIU(FM) Kingston RI 15 hrs
WPJB(FM) Narragansett Pier RI
WOKE(AM) Charleston SC 4 hrs
*WUSC-FM Columbia SC 3 hrs
WMUU-FM Greenville SC 14 hrs
WJYR(FM) Myrtle Beach SC
WSPA-FM Spartanburg SC 2 hrs
WQMC(AM) Sumter SC 15 hrs
*KTEQ(FM) Rapid City SD 3 hrs
*WHCB(FM) Bristol TN 1 hr
*WVCP(FM) Gallatin TN 15 hrs
WQDQ(AM) Lebanon TN 3 hrs
*WEVL(FM) Memphis TN 1 hr
*WDNX(FM) Olive Hill TN 5 hrs
*WUTS(FM) Sewanee TN 4 hrs
*KACV-FM Amarillo TX 16 hrs
*KNTU(FM) Denton TX 15 hrs
*KTRU(FM) Houston TX 8 hrs
*KJCR(FM) Keene TX 4 hrs
*KHOY(FM) Laredo TX 4 hrs
*KWLD(FM) Plainview TX 5 hrs
KDCD(FM) San Angelo TX 3 hrs
*KGLY(FM) Tyler TX 14 hrs
*KGSU-FM Cedar City UT 3 hrs
*KPCW(FM) Park City UT 17 hrs
*KRDC-FM St. George UT 15 hrs
KRGQ(AM) West Valley City UT 2 hrs
*WAMV(AM) Amherst VA 4 hrs
*WWHS-FM Hampden-Sydney VA 2 hrs
*WDCE(FM) Richmond VA 3 hrs
*WCWM(FM) Williamsburg VA 11 hrs
*WIUJ(FM) St. Thomas VI 5 hrs
WBTN(AM) Bennington VT 1 hr
*WRUV(FM) Burlington VT 6 hrs
*WIUV(FM) Castleton VT 3 hrs
WGLV(FM) Hartford VT 5 hrs
*WJSC-FM Johnson VT 3 hrs
*WWLR(FM) Lyndonville VT 2 hrs
*WRMC-FM Middlebury VT 15 hrs
WNCS(FM) Montpelier VT 4 hrs
*WNUB-FM Northfield VT 6 hrs
*WGDR(FM) Plainfield VT 3 hrs
WDEV(AM) Waterbury VT 1 hr
WYKR(AM) Wells River VT 2 hrs
*KUGS(FM) Bellingham WA 5 hrs
KELA(AM) Centralia-Chehalis WA 2 hrs
KULE-FM Ephrata WA 5 hrs
*KSER(FM) Everett WA 4 hrs
KEYG(AM) Grand Coulee WA 4 hrs
KONA-FM Kennewick WA 2 hrs
*KARR(AM) Kirkland WA
*KAOS(FM) Olympia WA 10 hrs
*KAGU(FM) Spokane WA 2 hrs
*WLFM(FM) Appleton WI 10 hrs
*WORT(FM) Madison WI 7 hrs
*WMSE(FM) Milwaukee WI 3 hrs
*WSUP(FM) Platteville WI 4 hrs
WRJN(AM) Racine WI 2 hrs
*WRPN-FM Ripon WI 4 hrs
*KUWS(FM) Superior WI 15 hrs
WRVM(FM) Suring WI 1 hr
*WSUW(FM) Whitewater WI 10 hrs
*WVBC(FM) Bethany WV 2 hrs
*WVWC(FM) Buckhannon WV 2 hrs
WBES-FM Dunbar WV 2 hrs
WMON(AM) Montgomery WV 2 hrs
*WWVU-FM Morgantown WV 4 hrs
KMTN(FM) Jackson WY
KASL(AM) Newcastle WY 2 hrs

Comedy

KWDS(AM) Prescott Valley AZ 1 hr
KGLW(AM) San Luis Obispo CA
*KSAK(FM) Walnut CA
KVFC(AM) Cortez CO 2 hrs
KTCL(FM) Fort Collins CO 1 hr
*WPFW(FM) Washington DC 3 hrs
WFMT(FM) Chicago IL 1 hr
WGNU(AM) Granite City IL 1 hr
*WAMH(FM) Amherst MA 3 hrs
WCRB(FM) Waltham MA 1 hr
WKLT(FM) Kalkaska MI 2 hrs
*WKRB(FM) Brooklyn NY 1 hr
WVBR-FM Ithaca NY 2 hrs
*WXUT(FM) Toledo OH 2 hrs
WRAK-FM Williamsport PA 1 hr

Contemporary Hit/Top-40

*KNOM(AM) Nome AK 12 hrs
*KNOM-FM Nome AK 12 hrs
KSIQ(FM) Brawley CA
KPSI-FM Palm Springs CA
*KCRW(FM) Santa Monica CA
WADS(AM) Ansonia CT 4 hrs
*WXCI(FM) Danbury CT 3 hrs
WPIK(FM) Summerland Key FL 5 hrs
*WMNF(FM) Tampa FL
WPAS(AM) Zephyrhills FL 10 hrs
KIOW(FM) Forest City IA 19 hrs
*WBKE-FM North Manchester IN 10 hrs
KJLS(FM) Hays KS 3 hrs
WOCQ(FM) Berlin MD 6 hrs
*KUMM(FM) Morris MN 2 hrs
KOLV(FM) Olivia MN
KATQ(AM) Plentywood MT
KATQ-FM Plentywood MT
*WHYC(FM) Swan Quarter NC 8 hrs
*WIRQ(FM) Rochester NY 3 hrs
*WSBU(FM) St. Bonaventure NY 4 hrs
WQIO(FM) Mount Vernon OH 4 hrs
*KAYE-FM Tonkawa OK 2 hrs
WRAI(AM) San Juan PR 15 hrs
*KNTU(FM) Denton TX 2 hrs
KGUL(AM) Port Lavaca TX
WABN(AM) Abingdon VA 3 hrs
WABN-FM Abingdon VA 4 hrs
*KSER(FM) Everett WA 6 hrs
*WRFW(FM) River Falls WI

Country

*KYUK(AM) Bethel AK 4 hrs
*KHNS(FM) Haines AK 17 hrs
*KBBI(AM) Homer AK 4 hrs
*KRBD(FM) Ketchikan AK 14 hrs
KIAL(AM) Unalaska AK 04 hrs
*KSTK(FM) Wrangell AK 16 hrs
*KABF(FM) Little Rock AR 18 hrs
WVUV(AM) Leone AS 12 hrs
*KXCI(FM) Tucson AZ 6 hrs
*KPFA(FM) Berkeley CA 20 hrs
*KKUP(FM) Cupertino CA 11 hrs
*KDVS(FM) Davis CA 3 hrs
*KMUD(FM) Garberville CA 6 hrs
*KFJC(FM) Los Altos CA 8 hrs
*KVMR(FM) Nevada City CA 4 hrs
*KAZU(FM) Pacific Grove CA 6 hrs
*KPCC(FM) Pasadena CA 2 hrs
*KCSB-FM Santa Barbara CA 2 hrs
*KZSC(FM) Santa Cruz CA 4 hrs
*KASF(FM) Alamosa CO 2 hrs
*KGNU(FM) Boulder CO 3 hrs
*KDUR(FM) Durango CO 3 hrs
*KVNF(FM) Paonia CO 5 hrs
*KOTO(FM) Telluride CO 12 hrs
*WVOF(FM) Fairfield CT 3 hrs
*WESU(FM) Middletown CT 2 hrs
WNLC(AM) New London CT 2 hrs
*WWEB(FM) Wallingford CT 2 hrs
*WAMU(FM) Washington DC 4 hrs
*WUOG(FM) Athens GA 2 hrs
*WRFG(FM) Atlanta GA 7 hrs
WLET(AM) Toccoa GA 4 hrs
KSTO(FM) Agana GU 12 hrs
KQNG(AM) Lihue HI 5 hrs
KROS(AM) Clinton IA 6 hrs
KGRN(AM) Grinnell IA 12 hrs
KIFG(AM) Iowa Falls IA 10 hrs
KIFG-FM Iowa Falls IA 10 hrs
*KCUI(FM) Pella IA
*KUOI-FM Moscow ID 1 hr
*WEFT(FM) Champaign IL 5 hrs
*WPCD(FM) Champaign IL 5 hrs
*WEIU(FM) Charleston IL 3 hrs
*WHPK-FM Chicago IL 1 hr
*WNUR-FM Evanston IL 5 hrs
WTAY(AM) Robinson IL 12 hrs
WTAY-FM Robinson IL 12 hrs
WHCO(AM) Sparta IL 10 hrs
WLNB(FM) Ligonier IN 3 hrs
*WNAS(FM) New Albany IN 2 hrs
WSLM-FM Salem IN
WKUZ(FM) Wabash IN 13 hrs
WOTD(FM) Winamac IN 5 hrs
KLEY(AM) Wellington KS 10 hrs
WKKS(AM) Vanceburg KY 4 hrs
*WMMT(FM) Whitesburg KY 6 hrs
*KLSP(FM) Angola LA 6 hrs
*WTUL(FM) New Orleans LA 3 hrs
*WBIM-FM Bridgewater MA 2 hrs
WHRB(FM) Cambridge MA 5 hrs
WRSI(FM) Greenfield MA 6 hrs
*WCCH(FM) Holyoke MA 2 hrs
*WZBC(FM) Newton MA 5 hrs
*WTCC(FM) Springfield MA 4 hrs
*WBRS(FM) Waltham MA 2 hrs
WARE(AM) Ware MA 5 hrs
*WCUW(FM) Worcester MA 2 hrs
*WKHS(FM) Worton MD 2 hrs
*WUPI(FM) Presque Isle ME 2 hrs
*WSJB-FM Standish ME 3 hrs
*WMHB(FM) Waterville ME 10 hrs
*WDBM(FM) East Lansing MI 4 hrs
WNIL(AM) Niles MI 10 hrs
*KBSB(FM) Bemidji MN 3 hrs
WELY(AM) Ely MN 6 hrs
*KAXE(FM) Grand Rapids MN 3 hrs
*WMCN(FM) St. Paul MN 4 hrs
*KQAL(FM) Winona MN 1 hr
*KCOU(FM) Columbia MO 3 hrs
*KOPN(FM) Columbia MO 6 hrs
KTCB(AM) Malden MO 6 hrs
*KDHX(FM) St. Louis MO 10 hrs
*WMUW(FM) Columbus MS 10 hrs
*KXEI(FM) Havre MT 1 hr
WVIO(AM) Blowing Rock NC 3 hrs
*WGWG(FM) Boiling Springs NC 5 hrs
*WASU-FM Boone NC 8 hrs
*WHYC(FM) Swan Quarter NC 8 hrs
WSMX(AM) Winston-Salem NC 3 hrs
*KMHA(FM) Four Bears ND 8 hrs
KCNI(AM) Broken Bow NE
*WNEC-FM Henniker NH 3 hrs
WPNH(AM) Plymouth NH 4 hrs
*WDVR(FM) Delaware Township NJ 15 hrs
*WRSU-FM New Brunswick NJ 8 hrs
WPRB(FM) Princeton NJ 2 hrs
KKIM(AM) Albuquerque NM 1 hr
*KEDP(FM) Las Vegas NM 11 hrs
KTAO(FM) Taos NM 5 hrs
KHWK(FM) Tonopah NV
WNYG(AM) Babylon NY 2 hrs
WSCM(AM) Cobleskill NY 3 hrs
*WBAU(FM) Garden City NY 1 hr
*WRHU(FM) Hempstead NY 3 hrs
WVBR-FM Ithaca NY 4 hrs
WICY(AM) Malone NY 3 hrs
*WFUV(FM) New York NY 3 hrs
*WKCR-FM New York NY 10 hrs
WGGO(AM) Salamanca NY 5 hrs
*WCII(FM) Spencer NY 1 hr
*WKWZ(FM) Syosset NY 6 hrs
*WRPI(FM) Troy NY 2 hrs
WATH(AM) Athens OH 6 hrs
*WBGU(FM) Bowling Green OH 4 hrs
WMVO(AM) Mount Vernon OH 3 hrs
*WMCO(FM) New Concord OH 12 hrs
*WKTL(FM) Struthers OH 4 hrs
*WYSO(FM) Yellow Springs OH 2 hrs
*WYSO(FM) Yellow Springs OH 5 hrs
*KRSC-FM Claremore OK 5 hrs
*KRVM(FM) Eugene OR 1 hr
*KBOO(FM) Portland OR 3 hrs
*KRRC(FM) Portland OR 2 hrs
*KWSO(FM) Warm Springs OR 15 hrs
WISR(AM) Butler PA 1 hr
WFKJ(AM) Cashtown PA 8 hrs
*WCUC-FM Clarion PA 6 hrs
WWCB(AM) Corry PA 10 hrs
WOYL(AM) Oil City PA 3 hrs
*WRCT(FM) Pittsburgh PA 3 hrs
WPAZ(AM) Pottstown PA 1 hr
*WRDV(FM) Warminster PA 4 hrs
*WDOM(FM) Providence RI 2 hrs
*KTEQ(FM) Rapid City SD 6 hrs
WSLV(AM) Ardmore TN 10 hrs
*WEVL(FM) Memphis TN 15 hrs
WQKR(AM) Portland TN 2 hrs
*WUTS(FM) Sewanee TN 2 hrs
*KWLD(FM) Plainview TX 15 hrs
KPOS(AM) Post TX 4 hrs
KPOS-FM Post TX 4 hrs
*KPCW(FM) Park City UT 18 hrs
WKEX(AM) Blacksburg VA 4 hrs
*WVST(FM) Petersburg VA 2 hrs
*WVRU(FM) Radford VA 1 hr
*WIUV(FM) Castleton VT 2 hrs
*WJSC-FM Johnson VT 3 hrs
*WNUB-FM Northfield VT 6 hrs
*KUGS(FM) Bellingham WA 5 hrs
*KUBS(FM) Newport WA 5 hrs
*KAOS(FM) Olympia WA 10 hrs
KJUN(AM) Puyallup WA 6 hrs
*KWRS(FM) Spokane WA 2 hrs
*KUPS(FM) Tacoma WA 3 hrs
*WBSD(FM) Burlington WI 4 hrs
*WOJB(FM) Reserve WI 15 hrs
*WRPN-FM Ripon WI 5 hrs
WEVR(AM) River Falls WI 18 hrs
WEVR-FM River Falls WI 18 hrs
*WRFW(FM) River Falls WI
*KUWS(FM) Superior WI 6 hrs

Croatian

KTYM(AM) Inglewood CA 1 hr
WCEV(AM) Cicero IL 3 hrs
WGNU(AM) Granite City IL 1 hr
*WKTL(FM) Struthers OH 1 hr
WELW(AM) Willoughby-Eastlake OH 4 hrs
WKBN(AM) Youngstown OH 2 hrs
WMBA(AM) Ambridge PA 1 hr
WESA(AM) Charleroi PA 1 hr
WESA-FM Charleroi PA 1 hr
WYLO(AM) Jackson WI 2 hrs

Czech

WCEV(AM) Cicero IL 2 hrs
*WOES(FM) Ovid-Elsie MI 1 hr
WOMP(AM) Bellaire OH 2 hrs
*WCSB(FM) Cleveland OH 1 hr
WERE(AM) Cleveland OH 1 hr
WRMR(AM) Cleveland OH 1 hr
KMIL(AM) Cameron TX 8 hrs
KULP(AM) El Campo TX 5 hrs
KRJH(AM) Hallettsville TX 3 hrs
KHBR(AM) Hillsboro TX 2 hrs
KVLG(AM) La Grange TX 6 hrs
KTEM(AM) Temple TX 3 hrs
WAUN(FM) Kewaunee WI 1 hr

Disco

KSIQ(FM) Brawley CA
*WMHB(FM) Waterville ME 2 hrs
*KRUX(FM) Las Cruces NM 2 hrs
*WBSU(FM) Brockport NY 2 hrs
*WITR(FM) Henrietta NY 3 hrs
*WVBU-FM Lewisburg PA 6 hrs

Drama/Literature

WBCF(AM) Florence AL 7 hrs
*KUCA(FM) Conway AR 6 hrs
*KZPN(FM) Bayside CA 4 hrs
*KZYX(FM) Philo CA 3 hrs
*KSJS(FM) San Jose CA 2 hrs
KGLW(AM) San Luis Obispo CA
*KCRW(FM) Santa Monica CA
*KOTO(FM) Telluride CO 3 hrs
*WGSK(FM) South Kent CT 1 hr
*WPFW(FM) Washington DC 1 hr
*WUNV(FM) Albany GA
*WUGA(FM) Athens GA 6 hrs
*WRFG(FM) Atlanta GA 4 hrs
WFMT(FM) Chicago IL 2 hrs
*WNUR-FM Evanston IL 1 hr
*WSWI(AM) Evansville IN 2 hrs
WAVX(FM) Thomaston ME 1 hr
*WOES(FM) Ovid-Elsie MI 1 hr
*KMSK(FM) Austin MN 3 hrs
KEYL(AM) Long Prairie MN 1 hr
*KMSU(FM) Mankato MN 3 hrs
*WCAL(FM) Northfield MN 2 hrs
*WMCN(FM) St. Paul MN 5 hrs
*WUSM-FM Hattiesburg MS 1 hr
*WNCW(FM) Spindale NC 3 hrs
*WRHU(FM) Hempstead NY 3 hrs
*WNYC-FM New York NY 5 hrs
*WCFE-FM Plattsburgh NY 2 hrs
*WIUP-FM Indiana PA 1 hr
*WXPN(FM) Philadelphia PA 4 hrs
*WQED-FM Pittsburgh PA 1 hr
*WJHD(FM) Portsmouth RI
KIOL-FM Lamesa TX
*KAGU(FM) Spokane WA 2 hrs
*WQAB(FM) Philippi WV 2 hrs

Educational

*KXRJ(FM) Russellville AR
*KZPN(FM) Bayside CA 3 hrs
*KCRH(FM) Hayward CA 1 hr
*KLEL(FM) San Jose CA 5 hrs
WGCH(AM) Greenwich CT 1 hr
*WKGC(AM) Panama City Beach FL 8 hrs
*KWLC(AM) Decorah IA
*WEPS(FM) Elgin IL 13 hrs
*WDCB(FM) Glen Ellyn IL 18 hrs
WWIP(FM) Wabash IN 3 hrs
WADN(AM) Concord MA 1 hr
*WFWM(FM) Frostburg MD 5 hrs
*WNMU-FM Marquette MI
*WSGE(FM) Dallas NC 6 hrs
WYBG(AM) Massena NY 1 hr
WCDK(FM) Cadiz OH
*KWVA(FM) Eugene OR 4 hrs
KSLT(FM) Spearfish SD 12 hrs
*KAZI(FM) Austin TX
WWYO(AM) Pineville WV 20 hrs
WOBG-FM Salem WV 1 hr

Filipino

*KBRW(AM) Barrow AK 2 hrs
*KMXT(FM) Kodiak AK 2 hrs
KCHJ(AM) Delano CA 3 hrs
*KECG(FM) El Cerrito CA 2 hrs
*KSJV(FM) Fresno CA 1 hr
*KMPO(FM) Modesto CA 1 hr
KEST(AM) San Francisco CA 5 hrs
KTAP(AM) Santa Maria CA 3 hrs
KGUM(AM) Agana GU 11 hrs
KIPA(AM) Hilo HI 7 hrs
KNUI(AM) Kahului HI 12 hrs
KQNG(AM) Lihue HI 12 hrs
KMVI(AM) Wailuku HI 11 hrs
*WSOU(FM) South Orange NJ 2 hrs
KITZ(AM) Silverdale WA 1 hr

Finnish

*KUSF(FM) San Francisco CA 1 hr
WLVS(AM) Lake Worth FL 4 hrs
*WOAS(FM) Ontonagon MI 1 hr
WUPY(FM) Ontonagon MI 2 hrs
WEVE(AM) Eveleth MN 1 hr
*KAXE(FM) Grand Rapids MN 2 hrs
*WBXL(FM) Baldwinsville NY 2 hrs

Folk

*KUAC(FM) Fairbanks AK 10 hrs
*KHNS(FM) Haines AK 6 hrs
*KTOO(FM) Juneau AK 6 hrs
*KRBD(FM) Ketchikan AK 10 hrs
WDJC(FM) Birmingham AL
*WQPR(FM) Muscle Shoals AL 5 hrs
*WUAL-FM Tuscaloosa AL 5 hrs
*KUCA(FM) Conway AR 12 hrs
*KUAF(FM) Fayetteville AR 4 hrs
*KABF(FM) Little Rock AR 6 hrs
KCTT-FM Yellville AR 10 hrs
*KHSU-FM Arcata CA 15 hrs
*KPFA(FM) Berkeley CA 10 hrs
*KZFR(FM) Chico CA 8 hrs
*KKUP(FM) Cupertino CA 12 hrs
*KDVS(FM) Davis CA 9 hrs
KCQR(FM) Ellwood CA 2 hrs
*KFCF(FM) Fresno CA 20 hrs
*KSJV(FM) Fresno CA 4 hrs
*KUCI(FM) Irvine CA 6 hrs
*KPFK(FM) Los Angeles CA 10 hrs
*KSBR(FM) Mission Viejo CA 2 hrs
*KMPO(FM) Modesto CA 4 hrs
*KVMR(FM) Nevada City CA 10 hrs
*KAZU(FM) Pacific Grove CA 6 hrs
*KZYX(FM) Philo CA 8 hrs
*KALW(FM) San Francisco CA 3 hrs
*KCBX(FM) San Luis Obispo CA 15 hrs
*KUSP(FM) Santa Cruz CA 10 hrs
*KUOP(FM) Stockton CA 12 hrs
*KAJX(FM) Aspen CO 4 hrs
*KGNU(FM) Boulder CO 20 hrs
*KCSU-FM Fort Collins CO 10 hrs

Special Programming on Radio Stations in the U.S.

*KMSA(FM) Grand Junction CO 3 hrs
*KSUT(FM) Ignacio CO 7 hrs
*KVNF(FM) Paonia CO 6 hrs
*WSHU(FM) Fairfield CT 2 hrs
*WGRS(FM) Guilford CT 2 hrs
*WMNR(FM) Monroe CT 2 hrs
WYBC-FM New Haven CT 3 hrs
*WCNI(FM) New London CT 9 hrs
*WRXC(FM) Shelton CT 2 hrs
*WGSK(FM) South Kent CT 4 hrs
*WNHU(FM) West Haven CT 6 hrs
*WETA-FM Washington DC 7 hrs
*WVUD(FM) Newark DE 15 hrs
*WDNA(FM) Miami FL 5 hrs
*WUCF-FM Orlando FL 2 hrs
*WKGC(AM) Panama City Beach FL 2 hrs
*WUWF(FM) Pensacola FL
*WKPX(FM) Sunrise FL 3 hrs
*WUGA(FM) Athens GA 6 hrs
*WUOG(FM) Athens GA 2 hrs
*WSVH(FM) Savannah GA 3 hrs
*WVVS(FM) Valdosta GA 3 hrs
*WOI(AM) Ames IA 6 hrs
*WOI-FM Ames IA 4 hrs
*KUNI(FM) Cedar Falls IA 12 hrs
KROS(AM) Clinton IA 2 hrs
*KWLC(AM) Decorah IA
*KRUI-FM Iowa City IA 3 hrs
*KCUI(FM) Pella IA
*KRFA-FM Moscow ID
*WSIU(FM) Carbondale IL 3 hrs
*WEFT(FM) Champaign IL 10 hrs
WFMT(FM) Chicago IL 4 hrs
*WHPK-FM Chicago IL 6 hrs
*WOUI(FM) Chicago IL 3 hrs
*WNIU(FM) De Kalb IL 4 hrs
*WNUR-FM Evanston IL 4 hrs
*WDCB(FM) Glen Ellyn IL 2 hrs
*WIUM(FM) Macomb IL 7 hrs
*WQUB(FM) Quincy IL 2 hrs
*WILL-FM Urbana IL 1 hr
WBQR(FM) Attica IN
*WVPE(FM) Elkhart IN 9 hrs
WMRS(FM) Monticello IN 2 hrs
*WECI(FM) Richmond IN 10 hrs
*KRPS(FM) Pittsburg KS 3 hrs
*WKYU-FM Bowling Green KY 5 hrs
*WKUE(FM) Elizabethtown KY 5 hrs
*WKPB(FM) Henderson KY 5 hrs
*WRFL(FM) Lexington KY 3 hrs
*WDCL-FM Somerset KY 5 hrs
*KSLU(FM) Hammond LA
KXZZ(AM) Lake Charles LA 4 hrs
*WTUL(FM) New Orleans LA 2 hrs
*KSCL(FM) Shreveport LA 6 hrs
*WFCR(FM) Amherst MA 4 hrs
*WMUA(FM) Amherst MA 15 hrs
*WGBH(FM) Boston MA 10 hrs
WHRB(FM) Cambridge MA 15 hrs
*WMBR(FM) Cambridge MA 6 hrs
WCOD-FM Hyannis MA 4 hrs
WBIV(AM) Natick MA 2 hrs
*WBSL-FM Sheffield MA 2 hrs
*WBRS(FM) Waltham MA 6 hrs
*WZLY(FM) Wellesley MA 2 hrs
*WSKB(FM) Westfield MA 3 hrs
*WCUW(FM) Worcester MA 15 hrs
*WICN(FM) Worcester MA 12 hrs
*WMTB-FM Emmittsburg MD 1 hr
*WTMD(FM) Towson MD 3 hrs
*WERU-FM Blue Hill ME 15 hrs
*WBOR(FM) Brunswick ME 12 hrs
*WMPG(FM) Gorham ME 10 hrs
*WMEB-FM Orono ME 4 hrs
*WMHB(FM) Waterville ME 12 hrs
*WCBN-FM Ann Arbor MI 3 hrs
*WDET-FM Detroit MI 4 hrs
*WFBE(FM) Flint MI 3 hrs
WBNZ(FM) Frankfort MI 2 hrs
*WBLU-FM Grand Rapids MI 5 hrs
*WCMW-FM Harbor Springs MI 3 hrs
*WIAA(FM) Interlochen MI 1 hr
*WIDR(FM) Kalamazoo MI 2 hrs
*WBLV(FM) Twin Lake MI 5 hrs
*KMSK(FM) Austin MN 5 hrs
*KAXE(FM) Grand Rapids MN 6 hrs
*KMSU(FM) Mankato MN 5 hrs
*KFAI(FM) Minneapolis MN 6 hrs
*KUMM(FM) Morris MN 1 hr
*KGAC(FM) St. Peter MN 9 hrs
*KWUR(FM) Clayton MO 6 hrs
*KKFI(FM) Kansas City MO 4 hrs
*KGSP(FM) Parkville MO 6 hrs
*KCOZ(FM) Point Lookout MO 10 hrs
*KUMR(FM) Rolla MO 5 hrs
*WMAH-FM Biloxi MS 3 hrs
*WMAE-FM Booneville MS 3 hrs
*WMAU-FM Bude MS 3 hrs
*WMAO-FM Greenwood MS 3 hrs
*WMPN-FM Jackson MS 3 hrs
*WMAW-FM Meridian MS 3 hrs
*WMAB-FM Mississippi State MS 3 hrs
*WMAV-FM Oxford MS 3 hrs
*KEMC(FM) Billings MT 5 hrs
*KGLT(FM) Bozeman MT 12 hrs
*WCQS(FM) Asheville NC 11 hrs
*WFQS(FM) Franklin NC 11 hrs
*WTEB(FM) New Bern NC 2 hrs
*WNCW(FM) Spindale NC 12 hrs
*WFDD-FM Winston-Salem NC 6 hrs
*KEYA(FM) Belcourt ND 8 hrs
*KCND(FM) Bismarck ND 5 hrs
*KDPR(FM) Dickinson ND 6 hrs
*KDSU(FM) Fargo ND
*KFJM(AM) Grand Forks ND 4 hrs
*KMPR(FM) Minot ND 6 hrs
*KPPR(FM) Williston ND 6 hrs
*KTNE-FM Alliance NE 2 hrs
*KHNE-FM Hastings NE 2 hrs
*KLNE-FM Lexington NE 2 hrs
*KZUM(FM) Lincoln NE 8 hrs
*WEVO(FM) Concord NH 5 hrs
*WUNH(FM) Durham NH 4 hrs
*WNEC-FM Henniker NH 3 hrs
*WKNH(FM) Keene NH 6 hrs
*WDVR(FM) Delaware Township NJ 6 hrs
*WRSU-FM New Brunswick NJ 1 hr
*KRWG(FM) Las Cruces NM 8 hrs
*KEDP(FM) Las Vegas NM 2 hrs
*KUNV(FM) Las Vegas NV 4 hrs
*KUNR(FM) Reno NV 2 hrs
*WAMC(FM) Albany NY 8 hrs
*WXLH(FM) Blue Mountain Lake NY
*WBNY(FM) Buffalo NY 3 hrs
*WCAN(FM) Canajoharie NY 4 hrs
*WSLU(FM) Canton NY
*WCVF-FM Fredonia NY 3 hrs
*WEOS(FM) Geneva NY 10 hrs
*WGMC(FM) Greece NY 4 hrs
*WICB(FM) Ithaca NY 2 hrs
*WSQG-FM Ithaca NY 7 hrs
WVBR-FM Ithaca NY 7 hrs
*WJFF(FM) Jeffersonville NY 8 hrs
*WAMK(FM) Kingston NY 4 hrs
*WSLO(FM) Malone NY
*WOSR(FM) Middletown NY 4 hrs
*WBAI(FM) New York NY 2 hrs
*WKCR-FM New York NY 5 hrs
*WXLG(FM) North Creek NY
*WRHO(FM) Oneonta NY 5 hrs
*WXLU(FM) Peru NY
*WCFE-FM Plattsburgh NY 7 hrs
*WRUR-FM Rochester NY 15 hrs
*WSLL(FM) Saranac Lake NY
*WSPN(FM) Saratoga Springs NY 6 hrs
WMJC(FM) Smithtown NY 2 hrs
*WSBU(FM) St. Bonaventure NY 1 hr
*WUSB(FM) Stony Brook NY 15 hrs
*WRPI(FM) Troy NY 2 hrs
*WJNY(FM) Watertown NY 3 hrs
*WSLJ(FM) Watertown NY
*WBGU(FM) Bowling Green OH 4 hrs
*WRUW-FM Cleveland OH 12 hrs
*WDPS(FM) Dayton OH 4 hrs
*WKCO(FM) Gambier OH 5 hrs
*WKSU-FM Kent OH 12 hrs
*WOBC-FM Oberlin OH 4 hrs
*WMUB(FM) Oxford OH 5 hrs
*WXUT(FM) Toledo OH 2 hrs
*WYSU(FM) Youngstown OH 3 hrs
*KRSC-FM Claremore OK 5 hrs
*KSMF(FM) Ashland OR 3 hrs
*KMUN(FM) Astoria OR 18 hrs
*KSBA(FM) Coos Bay OR 3 hrs
*KLCC(FM) Eugene OR 12 hrs
*KRVM(FM) Eugene OR 3 hrs
*KWVA(FM) Eugene OR 4 hrs
*KSKF(FM) Klamath Falls OR 3 hrs
*KLCO(FM) Newport OR 12 hrs
*KBOO(FM) Portland OR 8 hrs
*WESS(FM) East Stroudsburg PA 3 hrs
*WMCE(FM) Erie PA 2 hrs
*WZBT(FM) Gettysburg PA 6 hrs
*WKVR-FM Huntingdon PA 2 hrs
*WIUP-FM Indiana PA 4 hrs
*WHYY-FM Philadelphia PA 4 hrs
*WRCT(FM) Pittsburgh PA 3 hrs
*WPSU(FM) State College PA 10 hrs
*WRDV(FM) Warminster PA 3 hrs
*WRIU(FM) Kingston RI 15 hrs
*WUSC-FM Columbia SC 3 hrs
*KCSD(FM) Sioux Falls SD 5 hrs
*WHCB(FM) Bristol TN 1 hr
*WETS(FM) Johnson City TN 14 hrs
*WQOX(FM) Memphis TN 3 hrs
*KAMU-FM College Station TX 3 hrs
*KTRU(FM) Houston TX 3 hrs
*KZMU(FM) Moab UT 6 hrs
*KRCL(FM) Salt Lake City UT 12 hrs
*WMRA(FM) Harrisonburg VA 20 hrs
*WHRV(FM) Norfolk VA 7 hrs
*WCVE(FM) Richmond VA 2 hrs
*WRUV(FM) Burlington VT 9 hrs
*WIUV(FM) Castleton VT 4 hrs
*WRMC-FM Middlebury VT 15 hrs
WNCS(FM) Montpelier VT 2 hrs
*WGDR(FM) Plainfield VT 10 hrs
*WVPR(FM) Windsor VT 6 hrs
*KZAZ(FM) Bellingham WA
*KNWR(FM) Ellensburg WA
*KSER(FM) Everett WA 8 hrs
*KAOS(FM) Olympia WA 20 hrs
*KZUU(FM) Pullman WA 4 hrs
*KFAE-FM Richland WA
*KAGU(FM) Spokane WA 2 hrs
*KPBX-FM Spokane WA
*WYMS(FM) Milwaukee WI 3 hrs
*WVBC(FM) Bethany WV 2 hrs
WWYO(AM) Pineville WV 15 hrs
WMOV(AM) Ravenswood WV 2 hrs
*KUWJ(FM) Jackson WY 4 hrs
*KUWR(FM) Laramie WY 4 hrs
*KUWZ(FM) Rock Springs WY

Foreign Language/Ethnic

KJNP(AM) North Pole AK 1 hr
*KCAW(FM) Sitka AK 3 hrs
*KTNA(FM) Talkeetna AK 5 hrs
*WVSU-FM Birmingham AL 1 hr
*KDVS(FM) Davis CA 20 hrs
*KECG(FM) El Cerrito CA 2 hrs
*KFCF(FM) Fresno CA 1 hr
*KMUD(FM) Garberville CA 1 hr
*KUSC(FM) Los Angeles CA 2 hrs
KMYC(AM) Marysville CA 2 hrs
*KVMR(FM) Nevada City CA 3 hrs
*KAZU(FM) Pacific Grove CA 6 hrs
*KPSC(FM) Palm Springs CA 2 hrs
KJAY(AM) Sacramento CA 2 hrs
*KXJZ(FM) Sacramento CA 10 hrs
KEST(AM) San Francisco CA 1 hr
*KUSF(FM) San Francisco CA 3 hrs
*KFAC(FM) Santa Barbara CA 2 hrs
*KCRW(FM) Santa Monica CA
*KSJC-FM Stockton CA 3 hrs
*KCPB(FM) Thousand Oaks CA 2 hrs
KOBO(AM) Yuba City CA 3 hrs
KUBA(AM) Yuba City CA 4 hrs
*KASF(FM) Alamosa CO 6 hrs
*KRZA(FM) Alamosa CO 3 hrs
*WFAR(FM) Danbury CT 1 hr
*WJMJ(FM) Hartford CT 1 hr
*WWUH(FM) West Hartford CT 2 hrs
*WDCU(FM) Washington DC 2 hrs
WHUR-FM Washington DC 6 hrs
*WRTX(FM) Dover DE 4 hrs
WIRA(AM) Fort Pierce FL 2 hrs
WFIV(AM) Kissimmee FL 5 hrs
WLVS(AM) Lake Worth FL 14 hrs
*WDNA(FM) Miami FL 13 hrs
*WLRN-FM Miami FL 3 hrs
WSBH(AM) Miami Beach FL
WKAT(AM) North Miami FL 20 hrs
WSIR(AM) Winter Haven FL 2 hrs
*WRFG(FM) Atlanta GA 9 hrs
WCOP(AM) Warner Robins GA
KGUM(AM) Agana GU 14 hrs
KUAM(AM) Agana GU 10 hrs
KUAI(AM) Eleele HI 5 hrs
*KHPR(FM) Honolulu HI 2 hrs
KNDI(AM) Honolulu HI 14 hrs
KWAI(AM) Honolulu HI 19 hrs
KAOI(AM) Kihei HI 15 hrs
KDEO(AM) Waipahu HI 1 hr
*KUCB-FM Des Moines IA 20 hrs
*KDCR(FM) Sioux Center IA 1 hr
*WHPK-FM Chicago IL 10 hrs
WCEV(AM) Cicero IL 2 hrs
WONX(AM) Evanston IL 14 hrs
WEEF(AM) Highland Park IL
WVVX(FM) Highland Park IL 5 hrs
*WARG(FM) Summit IL
WGRL(FM) Indianapolis IN 4 hrs
*WICR(FM) Indianapolis IN 1 hr
WNDZ(AM) Portage IN 4 hrs
*WBAA(AM) West Lafayette IN 1 hr
*KANU(FM) Lawrence KS 2 hrs
*WMMT(FM) Whitesburg KY 1 hr
*KLSU(FM) Baton Rouge LA 3 hrs
WKJN-FM Hammond LA 3 hrs
KAOK(AM) Lake Charles LA 20 hrs
KLCL(AM) Lake Charles LA 14 hrs
KAPB(AM) Marksville LA 3 hrs
KAPB-FM Marksville LA 3 hrs
KVOL-FM Opelousas LA
*KSCL(FM) Shreveport LA 3 hrs
*WMUA(FM) Amherst MA 12 hrs
*WRBB(FM) Boston MA 5 hrs
*WMFO(FM) Medford MA 4 hrs
*WZBC(FM) Newton MA 4 hrs
*WCUW(FM) Worcester MA 2 hrs
*WICN(FM) Worcester MA 3 hrs
*WEAA(FM) Baltimore MD
WMET(AM) Gaithersburg MD 1 hr
*WMEB-FM Orono ME 3 hrs
*WUPI(FM) Presque Isle ME 2 hrs
*WHFR(FM) Dearborn MI 3 hrs
*WFBE(FM) Flint MI 1 hr
*WIDR(FM) Kalamazoo MI 2 hrs
*WSHJ(FM) Southfield MI 3 hrs
*WMCN(FM) St. Paul MN 10 hrs
*KKFI(FM) Kansas City MO 7 hrs
KSTL(AM) St. Louis MO 18 hrs
*WKNC-FM Raleigh NC 3 hrs
*WSHA(FM) Raleigh NC 6 hrs
KUVR(AM) Holdrege NE 1 hr
KUVR-FM Holdrege NE 1 hr
KNLV(AM) Ord NE 5 hrs
KNLV-FM Ord NE 5 hrs
*WEVO(FM) Concord NH 2 hrs
*WFMU(FM) East Orange NJ 15 hrs
*WBJB-FM Lincroft NJ 3 hrs
*WRSU-FM New Brunswick NJ 2 hrs
*WRTQ(FM) Ocean City NJ 4 hrs
WPRB(FM) Princeton NJ 2 hrs
*KANW(FM) Albuquerque NM 2 hrs
*KRUX(FM) Las Cruces NM 4 hrs
KLAV(AM) Las Vegas NV 7 hrs
*KUNR(FM) Reno NV 9 hrs
*WICB(FM) Ithaca NY 2 hrs
WJTN(AM) Jamestown NY 1 hr
WTHE(AM) Mineola NY 5 hrs
*WFNP(FM) New Paltz NY 3 hrs
*WFUV(FM) New York NY 2 hrs
*WNYE(FM) New York NY 10 hrs
*WRHO(FM) Oneonta NY 2 hrs
*WRHV(FM) Poughkeepsie NY 1 hr
*WSPN(FM) Saratoga Springs NY 3 hrs
*WAER(FM) Syracuse NY 4 hrs
*WRPI(FM) Troy NY 1 hr
*WBWC(FM) Berea OH 5 hrs
*WCSB(FM) Cleveland OH 3 hrs
*WDPS(FM) Dayton OH 2 hrs
KVAS(AM) Astoria OR 1 hr
*KLCO(FM) Newport OR 3 hrs
*KBOO(FM) Portland OR 4 hrs
KKEY(AM) Portland OR 2 hrs
*WMUH(FM) Allentown PA 3 hrs
WPLW(AM) Carnegie PA 2 hrs
*WRTY(FM) Jackson Township PA 4 hrs
*WKDU(FM) Philadelphia PA 12 hrs
*WRTI(FM) Philadelphia PA 4 hrs
*WYEP-FM Pittsburgh PA 6 hrs
WGCB(AM) Red Lion PA 1 hr
*WJAZ(FM) Summerdale PA 4 hrs
WTPM(FM) Aguadilla PR 1 hr
*WEVL(FM) Memphis TN 1 hr
KLVI(AM) Beaumont TX 5 hrs
*KVTT(FM) Dallas TX 1 hr
KLAR(AM) Laredo TX 8 hrs
KALO(AM) Port Arthur TX 4 hrs
KEDA(AM) San Antonio TX 4 hrs
*KSYM-FM San Antonio TX 5 hrs
*KZMU(FM) Moab UT 1 hr
*KRCL(FM) Salt Lake City UT 10 hrs
WDCT(AM) Fairfax VA 3 hrs
WREJ(AM) Richmond VA 1 hr
WSTA(AM) Charlotte Amalie VI
WVGN(FM) Charlotte Amalie VI 9 hrs
WVWI(AM) Charlotte Amalie VI 16 hrs
*KSER(FM) Everett WA 16 hrs
KBLE(AM) Seattle WA 2 hrs
*KPBX-FM Spokane WA
*KUPS(FM) Tacoma WA 5 hrs
WRJQ(AM) Appleton WI 2 hrs
*WGBW(FM) Green Bay WI 1 hr
WEKZ(AM) Monroe WI 3 hrs
*WSUW(FM) Whitewater WI 15 hrs
WEIR(AM) Weirton WV 1 hr
KBBS(AM) Buffalo WY 1 hr

French

KTYM(AM) Inglewood CA 1 hr
*KUSF(FM) San Francisco CA 2 hrs
*KSRH(FM) San Rafael CA 1 hr
WPRX(AM) Bristol CT 2 hrs
WXXU(AM) Cocoa Beach FL 9 hrs
WZOR(AM) Immokalee FL 3 hrs
*WDNA(FM) Miami FL 2 hrs
WSBH(AM) Miami Beach FL 10 hrs
*WUCF-FM Orlando FL 1 hr
WXTO(AM) Winter Garden FL 9 hrs
*KCUI(FM) Pella IA
*KBSU(AM) Boise ID 2 hrs
*WNAS(FM) New Albany IN 1 hr
KROF(AM) Abbeville LA 10 hrs
KROF-FM Abbeville LA 10 hrs
KBAZ(FM) Basile LA 5 hrs
WYNK(AM) Baton Rouge LA 2 hrs
WYNK-FM Baton Rouge LA 2 hrs
KPWS(AM) Crowley LA 2 hrs
KSIG(AM) Crowley LA 18 hrs
KJJB(FM) Eunice LA 5 hrs
KLEB(AM) Golden Meadow LA 12 hrs
KJIN(AM) Houma LA 2 hrs
KJEF(AM) Jennings LA 12 hrs
KJEF-FM Jennings LA 12 hrs
KMDL(FM) Kaplan LA 3 hrs
KLPL(AM) Lake Providence LA 2 hrs
KLPL-FM Lake Providence LA 2 hrs
KAPB(AM) Marksville LA 3 hrs
KAPB-FM Marksville LA 3 hrs
KLIL(FM) Moreauville LA 2 hrs
KSLO(AM) Opelousas LA 20 hrs
KAGY(AM) Port Sulphur LA 3 hrs
KTIB(AM) Thibodaux LA 3 hrs
KVPI(AM) Ville Platte LA 15 hrs
WROL(AM) Boston MA 15 hrs
*WMBR(FM) Cambridge MA 2 hrs
WHTB(AM) Fall River MA 1 hr
WNTN(AM) Newton MA 3 hrs
*WNMH(FM) Northfield MA 2 hrs
*WBRS(FM) Waltham MA 4 hrs
WRCA(AM) Waltham MA
*WSKB(FM) Westfield MA 1 hr
*WCUW(FM) Worcester MA 2 hrs
WFAU(AM) Augusta ME 2 hrs
*WRBC(FM) Lewiston ME 2 hrs
WZOU(AM) Lewiston ME 2 hrs
*WMEB-FM Orono ME 4 hrs
*WCBN-FM Ann Arbor MI 1 hr
*KFAI(FM) Minneapolis MN 2 hrs
WMOU(AM) Berlin NH 3 hrs
WFEA(AM) Manchester NH 2 hrs
WSMN(AM) Nashua NH 3 hrs
*KUNV(FM) Las Vegas NV 1 hr
WCHP(AM) Champlain NY
*WECW(FM) Elmira NY 6 hrs
*WFUV(FM) New York NY 3 hrs
*KMUN(FM) Astoria OR 2 hrs
*KRRC(FM) Portland OR 2 hrs
WIBF-FM Jenkintown PA 1 hr
WARV(AM) Warwick RI 2 hrs
WKRI(AM) West Warwick RI 1 hr
WNRI(AM) Woonsocket RI 4 hrs
WOON(AM) Woonsocket RI 3 hrs
*WRVU(FM) Nashville TN 1 hr
*WUTS(FM) Sewanee TN 2 hrs
KALO(AM) Port Arthur TX 3 hrs
*WYCS(FM) Yorktown VA 1 hr
*WIUJ(FM) St. Thomas VI 1 hr

German

KNNS(AM) Glendale AZ 2 hrs
*KXCI(FM) Tucson AZ 2 hrs
KTYM(AM) Inglewood CA 2 hrs
*KCSN(FM) Northridge CA 3 hrs
*KPCC(FM) Pasadena CA 5 hrs
*KUOR-FM Redlands CA 1 hr
KEST(AM) San Francisco CA 3 hrs
KMXN(AM) Santa Rosa CA 2 hrs
KDTA(AM) Delta CO 1 hr
*KPOF(AM) Denver CO 1 hr
KFKA(AM) Greeley CO 1 hr
*WVOF(FM) Fairfield CT 2 hrs
WLVU(AM) Dunedin FL 15 hrs
WSRF(AM) Fort Lauderdale FL 2 hrs
WINK(AM) Fort Myers FL 1 hr
WGKA(AM) Atlanta GA 1 hr
KSKB(FM) Brooklyn IA 1 hr
*KCUI(FM) Pella IA
WAIT(AM) Crystal Lake IL 1 hr
WKTA(AM) Evanston IL 4 hrs
WFXW(AM) Geneva IL 4 hrs
WGNU(AM) Granite City IL 3 hrs
WINU(AM) Highland IL 1 hr
WNVR(AM) Vernon Hills IL 4 hrs
WGRL(FM) Indianapolis IN 2 hrs
*WNAS(FM) New Albany IN 1 hr
WNDZ(AM) Portage IN 2 hrs
*WNKU(FM) Highland Heights KY 2 hrs
*WOZQ(FM) Northampton MA 1 hr
*WBRS(FM) Waltham MA 4 hrs
WBMD(AM) Baltimore MD 1 hr
WATZ(AM) Alpena MI 2 hrs
WKNX(AM) Frankenmuth MI 3 hrs
*WBYW(FM) Grand Rapids MI 2 hrs
WKCQ(FM) Saginaw MI 3 hrs
KASM(AM) Albany MN 2 hrs
KSTL(AM) St. Louis MO 1 hr
KBRX(AM) O'Neill NE 6 hrs
KBRX-FM O'Neill NE 6 hrs
*KVNO(FM) Omaha NE 1 hr
KOTD(AM) Plattsmouth NE 2 hrs
WJDM(AM) Elizabeth NJ 2 hrs
WIMG(AM) Ewing NJ 1 hr
WTTM(AM) Trenton NJ 2 hrs
KLAV(AM) Las Vegas NV 1 hr
*KUNV(FM) Las Vegas NV 14 hrs
*WBXL(FM) Baldwinsville NY 3 hrs
WCKL(AM) Catskill NY 1 hr
WRWD(AM) Cornwall NY 1 hr
WHVW(AM) Hyde Park NY 1 hr
WKNY(AM) Kingston NY 1 hr
WXRL(AM) Lancaster NY 2 hrs
WTHE(AM) Mineola NY 1 hr
*WFUV(FM) New York NY 2 hrs
WWWG(AM) Rochester NY 2 hrs
*WAPS(FM) Akron OH 2 hrs
*WCPN(FM) Cleveland OH 1 hr
*WCSB(FM) Cleveland OH 1 hr
WONW(AM) Defiance OH 4 hrs
WCWA(AM) Toledo OH 1 hr
*WQRP(FM) West Carrollton OH 5 hrs
KKRX(AM) Lawton OK 1 hr
WGPA(AM) Bethlehem PA 2 hrs
*WDCV-FM Carlisle PA 1 hr
WBZY(AM) New Castle PA 1 hr
WTEL(AM) Philadelphia PA 5 hrs
WPAZ(AM) Pottstown PA 1 hr
WEEU(AM) Reading PA 2 hrs
WWII(AM) Shiremanstown PA 1 hr
WVPO(AM) Stroudsburg PA 1 hr
WYYR(AM) Spartanburg SC 2 hrs
*WRVU(FM) Nashville TN 1 hr
KHLR(FM) Cameron TX 1 hr
*KTEP(FM) El Paso TX 1 hr
KNAF(AM) Fredericksburg TX 2 hrs
KOKE(FM) Giddings TX 1 hr
KRJH(AM) Hallettsville TX 3 hrs
*KPFT(FM) Houston TX 2 hrs
KVLG(AM) La Grange TX 1 hr
KGNB(AM) New Braunfels TX 1 hr
KIKZ(AM) Seminole TX 1 hr

Special Programming on Radio Stations in the U.S.

KSEM-FM Seminole TX 1 hr
KYOC(FM) Yoakum TX 2 hrs
KRGQ(AM) West Valley City UT 1 hr
WKGM(AM) Smithfield VA 02 hrs
*WYCS(FM) Yorktown VA 1 hr
KARI(AM) Blaine WA 2 hrs
KDFL(AM) Lakewood WA 2 hrs
KBLE(AM) Seattle WA 1 hr
KKMO(AM) Tacoma WA 2 hrs
WRJQ(AM) Appleton WI 5 hrs
WTKM(AM) Hartford WI 15 hrs
WTKM-FM Hartford WI 3 hrs
WYLO(AM) Jackson WI 6 hrs
*WGTD(FM) Kenosha WI 1 hr
WAUN(FM) Kewaunee WI 1 hr
*WYMS(FM) Milwaukee WI 2 hrs
WEKZ(AM) Monroe WI 3 hrs
WXOL(AM) Oshkosh WI 3 hrs
WXER(FM) Plymouth WI 3 hrs
WIBU(AM) Poynette WI 1 hr
WHBL(AM) Sheboygan WI 1 hr

Gospel

KFAR(AM) Fairbanks AK 2 hrs
KIYU(AM) Galena AK 3 hrs
KCAM(AM) Glennallen AK 19 hrs
*KHNS(FM) Haines AK 3 hrs
KRSA(AM) Petersburg AK 2 hrs
KIAL(AM) Unalaska AK 02 hrs
WCRQ-FM Arab AL 5 hrs
WVNN(AM) Athens AL 3 hrs
WYDH(FM) Atmore AL 12 hrs
WAUD(AM) Auburn AL 2 hrs
WEBJ(AM) Brewton AL 1 hr
WAGC(AM) Centre AL 10 hrs
WRHY(FM) Centre AL 5 hrs
WDLK(AM) Dadeville AL 20 hrs
WZLM(FM) Dadeville AL 3 hrs
WOOF(AM) Dothan AL 14 hrs
WELB(AM) Elba AL 12 hrs
WBLX(AM) Fairhope AL
WFPA(AM) Fort Payne AL 18 hrs
WZOB(AM) Fort Payne AL 5 hrs
WGAD(AM) Gadsden AL 5 hrs
WJBB(AM) Haleyville AL 5 hrs
WERH(AM) Hamilton AL
*WJAB(FM) Huntsville AL 5 hrs
WTAK(AM) Huntsville AL 3 hrs
WZPQ(AM) Jasper AL 6 hrs
WRLD(AM) Lanett AL 17 hrs
WAMI(AM) Opp AL 15 hrs
WAMI-FM Opp AL 15 hrs
WOPP(AM) Opp AL 19 hrs
WQLS(AM) Ozark AL 12 hrs
WQLS-FM Ozark AL 8 hrs
WJRD(AM) Russellville AL 4 hrs
WTQX(AM) Selma AL
WFEB(AM) Sylacauga AL 6 hrs
KPIK(FM) Beebe AR
KAMD(AM) Camden AR 19 hrs
KWEH(FM) Camden AR 19 hrs
KBJT(AM) Fordyce AR 11 hrs
KAWW(AM) Heber Springs AR 14 hrs
KAWW-FM Heber Springs AR 10 hrs
KBHS(AM) Hot Springs AR 4 hrs
*KABF(FM) Little Rock AR 20 hrs
KMTB(FM) Murfreesboro AR 4 hrs
KZHE(FM) Stamps AR 8 hrs
KTWN-FM Texarkana AR 2 hrs
KWRF(AM) Warren AR 8 hrs
KWRF-FM Warren AR 8 hrs
KCLT(FM) West Helena AR 15 hrs
KVOI(AM) Oro Valley AZ 3 hrs
*KZFR(FM) Chico CA 3 hrs
KJLH-FM Compton CA 7 hrs
*KKUP(FM) Cupertino CA 2 hrs
*KDVS(FM) Davis CA 3 hrs
*KECG(FM) El Cerrito CA 5 hrs
*KFCF(FM) Fresno CA 3 hrs
KNRY(AM) Monterey CA 6 hrs
*KVMR(FM) Nevada City CA 2 hrs
KDIA(AM) Oakland CA 20 hrs
*KAZU(FM) Pacific Grove CA 5 hrs
*KZYX(FM) Philo CA 2 hrs
KEST(AM) San Francisco CA 5 hrs
KFAX(AM) San Francisco CA 4 hrs
*KUSP(FM) Santa Cruz CA 2 hrs
KUBA(AM) Yuba City CA 2 hrs
*KGNU(FM) Boulder CO 2 hrs
KKCS-FM Colorado Springs CO 3 hrs
*KCSU-FM Fort Collins CO 3 hrs
KSLV(AM) Monte Vista CO 6 hrs
KKXK(FM) Montrose CO 2 hrs
KUBC(AM) Montrose CO 2 hrs
KRQS(FM) Pagosa Springs CO 3 hrs
*KVNF(FM) Paonia CO 3 hrs
KFEL(AM) Pueblo CO 4 hrs
WRDM(AM) Bloomfield CT 2 hrs
*WRTC-FM Hartford CT 6 hrs
*WESU(FM) Middletown CT 6 hrs
WYBC-FM New Haven CT 8 hrs
*WCNI(FM) New London CT 3 hrs
WWCO(AM) Waterbury CT 2 hrs
*WNHU(FM) West Haven CT 5 hrs
*WDCU(FM) Washington DC 11 hrs
WHUR-FM Washington DC 14 hrs
WAFL(FM) Milford DE 2 hrs
*WVUD(FM) Newark DE 2 hrs
WKGF(AM) Arcadia FL 5 hrs
WXXU(AM) Cocoa Beach FL 12 hrs
WDCF(AM) Dade City FL 6 hrs
WZEP(AM) DeFuniak Springs FL 8 hrs
*WLVF-FM Haines City FL 18 hrs
WKZY(FM) La Belle FL 3 hrs
WWTK(AM) Lake Placid FL 5 hrs
WWAB(AM) Lakeland FL 6 hrs
WLBE(AM) Leesburg FL 4 hrs
WQHL(AM) Live Oak FL 7 hrs
WQHL-FM Live Oak FL 2 hrs
WTYS(AM) Marianna FL 11 hrs
WTAI(AM) Melbourne FL 2 hrs
WPGS(AM) Mims FL 4 hrs
WTMC(AM) Ocala FL 4 hrs
WLTG(AM) Panama City FL 6 hrs
WRNE(AM) Pensacola FL
WTMY(AM) Sarasota FL 4 hrs
WRBQ(AM) St. Petersburg FL 2 hrs
*WMNF(FM) Tampa FL
WTMP(AM) Temple Terrace FL 20 hrs
WCWB-FM Trenton FL
WXTO(AM) Winter Garden FL 12 hrs
WSIR(AM) Winter Haven FL 6 hrs
WALR(FM) Athens GA 2 hrs
WNGC(FM) Athens GA 2 hrs
*WCLK(FM) Atlanta GA 17 hrs
WTUF(FM) Boston GA 7 hrs
WJTH(AM) Calhoun GA 2 hrs
WQVE(FM) Camilla GA 8 hrs
WCHM(AM) Clarkesville GA
WCON-FM Cornelia GA 10 hrs
WDCY(AM) Douglasville GA
WBHB(AM) Fitzgerald GA 10 hrs
WRDO(FM) Fitzgerald GA 6 hrs
WOKF(FM) Folkston GA 5 hrs
WPLO(AM) Grayson GA 6 hrs
WLOP(AM) Jesup GA 10 hrs
WLAG(AM) La Grange GA 3 hrs
WTRP(AM) La Grange GA 5 hrs
WYIS(AM) McRae GA 10 hrs
WNEA(AM) Newnan GA 15 hrs
WJEP(AM) Ochlocknee GA 3 hrs
WJAT(AM) Swainsboro GA 10 hrs
WXRS(AM) Swainsboro GA 14 hrs
WPAX(AM) Thomasville GA 6 hrs
WTHO-FM Thomson GA 1 hr
WLET(AM) Toccoa GA 8 hrs
WLET-FM Toccoa GA
WADX(AM) Trenton GA 17 hrs
WAAC(FM) Valdosta GA 4 hrs
WGOV(AM) Valdosta GA 14 hrs
WVLD(AM) Valdosta GA 2 hrs
KSTO(FM) Agana GU 6 hrs
*KALA(FM) Davenport IA 11 hrs
*KUCB-FM Des Moines IA 12 hrs
KKSI(FM) Eddyville IA 1 hr
KYTC(FM) Northwood IA 1 hr
KBOE(AM) Oskaloosa IA 11 hrs
KBOE-FM Oskaloosa IA 11 hrs
KLEE(AM) Ottumwa IA 6 hrs
KTLB(FM) Twin Lakes IA 2 hrs
*KBBG(FM) Waterloo IA
KPKY(FM) Pocatello ID 2 hrs
KWIK(AM) Pocatello ID 2 hrs
WKRO(AM) Cairo IL 12 hrs
*WEFT(FM) Champaign IL 6 hrs
WSBC(AM) Chicago IL 2 hrs
WCEV(AM) Cicero IL 7 hrs
WKBM(FM) Coal City IL 8 hrs
WZRO(FM) Farmer City IL
*WDCB(FM) Glen Ellyn IL 2 hrs
WHPO(FM) Hoopeston IL 7 hrs
WJBM(AM) Jerseyville IL 12 hrs
*WMXM(FM) Lake Forest IL 3 hrs
WLBH(AM) Mattoon IL 5 hrs
WPNA(AM) Oak Park IL 9 hrs
WVAZ(FM) Oak Park IL 4 hrs
WBBA(AM) Pittsfield IL 3 hrs
WBBA-FM Pittsfield IL 3 hrs
WKGA(AM) Zion IL 6 hrs
WNJY(FM) Delphi IN 7 hrs
WTLC(AM) Indianapolis IN 18 hrs
WTLC-FM Indianapolis IN 14 hrs
WXLW(AM) Indianapolis IN 5 hrs
WMRS(FM) Monticello IN 5 hrs
WGTC(FM) New Carlisle IN 2 hrs
*WJYL(FM) New Washington IN
WNDZ(AM) Portage IN 2 hrs
WRIN(AM) Rensselaer IN 2 hrs
WAXI(FM) Rockville IN 2 hrs
WKJK(FM) Salem IN
WIWO(AM) South Bend IN 2 hrs
WTCJ(AM) Tell City IN 6 hrs
WAYT(AM) Wabash IN 6 hrs
KFXX-FM Hugoton KS 7 hrs
KHUT(FM) Hutchinson KS 5 hrs
KWBW(AM) Hutchinson KS 11 hrs
KANS(AM) Larned KS 6 hrs
KFNF(FM) Oberlin KS 6 hrs
KQLA(FM) Ogden KS 2 hrs
KKAN(AM) Phillipsburg KS 12 hrs
KFRM(AM) Salina KS 5 hrs
KULY(AM) Ulysses KS 7 hrs
*KMUW(FM) Wichita KS 6 hrs
WANY(AM) Albany KY 6 hrs
WKXO(AM) Berea KY 6 hrs
WAIN(AM) Columbia KY 18 hrs
WWLK(AM) Eddyville KY 20 hrs
WABD(AM) Fort Campbell KY 10 hrs
WGOH(AM) Grayson KY 8 hrs
WLBN(AM) Lebanon KY 5 hrs
WVKY(AM) Louisa KY
WKLB(AM) Manchester KY 4 hrs
WFTM(AM) Maysville KY 5 hrs
WFTM-FM Maysville KY 5 hrs
WFXY(AM) Middlesboro KY 3 hrs
WMIK(AM) Middlesboro KY 2 hrs
WFLW(AM) Monticello KY 10 hrs
WLOC(AM) Munfordville KY 19 hrs
WCKU(FM) Nicholasville KY 6 hrs
WKYQ(FM) Paducah KY 2 hrs
WKKS(AM) Vanceburg KY 16 hrs
WBCE(AM) Wickliffe KY
KBZE(FM) Berwick LA 10 hrs
KBCE(FM) Boyce LA 19 hrs
KPCH(FM) Dubach LA 5 hrs
WCKW(AM) Garyville LA 12 hrs
*KGRM(FM) Grambling LA 17 hrs
KJEF(AM) Jennings LA 6 hrs
KJCB(AM) Lafayette LA 20 hrs
KAOK(AM) Lake Charles LA 5 hrs
KFXZ(FM) Maurice LA 4 hrs
KJLO-FM Monroe LA 4 hrs
KFXY(FM) Morgan City LA 6 hrs
KMRC(AM) Morgan City LA 10 hrs
KNOC(AM) Natchitoches LA 6 hrs
*KNWD(FM) Natchitoches LA 6 hrs
KRUS(AM) Ruston LA 12 hrs
KBSF(AM) Springhill LA 3 hrs
KYEA(FM) West Monroe LA 20 hrs
KVCL(AM) Winnfield LA 5 hrs
*WMUA(FM) Amherst MA 9 hrs
WBET(AM) Brockton MA 1 hr
WCAV(FM) Brockton MA 2 hrs
WJIB(AM) Cambridge MA 6 hrs
*WMBR(FM) Cambridge MA 2 hrs
*WAIC(FM) Springfield MA
*WEAA(FM) Baltimore MD
*WMTB-FM Emmittsburg MD 1 hr
WAAI(FM) Hurlock MD 3 hrs
*WESM(FM) Princess Anne MD 20 hrs
*WMPG(FM) Gorham ME 3 hrs
WQTE(FM) Adrian MI 2 hrs
*WCBN-FM Ann Arbor MI 1 hr
WLLJ(AM) Cassopolis MI 10 hrs
*WDET-FM Detroit MI 2 hrs
*WDTR(FM) Detroit MI 2 hrs
WXLA(AM) Dimondale MI 5 hrs
WDZZ-FM Flint MI 8 hrs
*WIDR(FM) Kalamazoo MI 2 hrs
WWGZ-FM Lapeer MI
WTLZ(FM) Saginaw MI 6 hrs
WMLM(AM) St. Louis MI 2 hrs
KYCR(AM) Golden Valley MN 3 hrs
KDUZ(AM) Hutchinson MN 3 hrs
KLQL(FM) Luverne MN 5 hrs
*KFAI(FM) Minneapolis MN 3 hrs
WQPM-FM Princeton MN 3 hrs
KBFL(FM) Buffalo MO 2 hrs
KZMO(AM) California MO 3 hrs
KCHR(AM) Charleston MO 10 hrs
*KOPN(FM) Columbia MO 3 hrs
KGNN(AM) Cuba MO 10 hrs
KFTW(AM) Fredricktown MO 8 hrs
*KJLU(FM) Jefferson City MO
KNNT(AM) Kennett MO 5 hrs
KMRF(AM) Marshfield MO 7 hrs
KRMO(AM) Monett MO 10 hrs
KYRO(AM) Potosi MO 14 hrs
*KCLC(FM) St. Charles MO 9 hrs
KSPQ(FM) West Plains MO 5 hrs
KWPM(AM) West Plains MO 5 hrs
WJBI(AM) Batesville MS
WIZK-FM Bay Springs MS 21 hrs
WRKN(AM) Brandon MS
WBKN(FM) Brookhaven MS 12 hrs
WCHJ(AM) Brookhaven MS 12 hrs
WKNZ(FM) Collins MS 2 hrs
WCJU(AM) Columbia MS 4 hrs
WFFF(AM) Columbia MS 10 hrs
WJKX(FM) Ellisville MS 12 hrs
WQST(AM) Forest MS 15 hrs
WQST-FM Forest MS 6 hrs
WHER(FM) Hattiesburg MS 3 hrs
WKRA(AM) Holly Springs MS 12 hrs
*WJSU(FM) Jackson MS 18 hrs
*WPRL(FM) Lorman MS 16 hrs
WNAT(AM) Natchez MS 18 hrs
WNAU(AM) New Albany MS
WAVN(AM) Southaven MS 19 hrs
WKOR(AM) Starkville MS 6 hrs
WROB(AM) West Point MS 2 hrs
WKXR(AM) Asheboro NC 5 hrs
WSKY(AM) Asheville NC 6 hrs
WWNC(AM) Asheville NC 3 hrs
WGCR(AM) Brevard NC
WKYK(AM) Burnsville NC 15 hrs
WCXN(AM) Claremont NC
WPEG(FM) Concord NC 6 hrs
WCNC(AM) Elizabeth City NC 18 hrs
*WRVS-FM Elizabeth City NC 19 hrs
WFSC(AM) Franklin NC 14 hrs
WLTC(AM) Gastonia NC 10 hrs
WYCV(AM) Granite Falls NC
WHNC(AM) Henderson NC 7 hrs
WLNC(AM) Laurinburg NC 4 hrs
WLON(AM) Lincolnton NC 5 hrs
WBRM(AM) Marion NC 5 hrs
WDSL(AM) Mocksville NC 18 hrs
WDJS(AM) Mount Olive NC 10 hrs
WNHW(FM) Nags Head NC 3 hrs
WIKS(FM) New Bern NC 4 hrs
WJTP(AM) Newland NC 10 hrs
WPJL(AM) Raleigh NC
*WSHA(FM) Raleigh NC 20 hrs
WREV(AM) Reidsville NC 7 hrs
WADA(AM) Shelby NC 5 hrs
WNCA(AM) Siler City NC
*WNCW(FM) Spindale NC 2 hrs
WRGC(AM) Sylva NC 10 hrs
WACB(AM) Taylorsville NC 12 hrs
WSVM(AM) Valdese NC 4 hrs
WTOW(AM) Washington NC 13 hrs
WKSK(AM) West Jefferson NC 5 hrs
WYNC(AM) Yanceyville NC
KXPO(AM) Grafton ND 5 hrs
KXPO-FM Grafton ND 4 hrs
KHRT(AM) Minot ND 3 hrs
*KINI(FM) Crookston NE 6 hrs
KTNC(AM) Falls City NE 1 hr
KUVR(AM) Holdrege NE 5 hrs
KUVR-FM Holdrege NE 5 hrs
KRFS(AM) Superior NE 3 hrs
WUSS(AM) Atlantic City NJ 3 hrs
*WDVR(FM) Delaware Township NJ 1 hr
WTTH(FM) Margate City NJ 5 hrs
*WTSR(FM) Trenton NJ 8 hrs
*WMSC(FM) Upper Montclair NJ 2 hrs
KPSA(AM) Alamogordo NM 8 hrs
KLAV(AM) Las Vegas NV 1 hr
WROW(AM) Albany NY 3 hrs
*WXLH(FM) Blue Mountain Lake NY
*WKRB(FM) Brooklyn NY 1 hr
*WSLU(FM) Canton NY
WBLK(FM) Depew NY 20 hrs
*WEOS(FM) Geneva NY 3 hrs
*WSLO(FM) Malone NY
WRKL(AM) New City NY 1 hr
WVOX(AM) New Rochelle NY 1 hr
*WKCR-FM New York NY 2 hrs
*WXLG(FM) North Creek NY
*WXLU(FM) Peru NY
*WSLL(FM) Saranac Lake NY
WGY(AM) Schenectady NY 1 hr
*WAER(FM) Syracuse NY 3 hrs
*WSLJ(FM) Watertown NY
*WONB(FM) Ada OH 6 hrs
*WZIP(FM) Akron OH 3 hrs
WABQ(AM) Cleveland OH
WOHI(AM) East Liverpool OH 1 hr
WMPO(AM) Middleport-Pomeroy OH 18 hrs
*WOBC-FM Oberlin OH 3 hrs
WPAY(AM) Portsmouth OH 6 hrs
WERT(AM) Van Wert OH 3 hrs
WBZI(AM) Xenia OH 6 hrs
KADA(AM) Ada OK
KOKB(AM) Blackwell OK 11 hrs
*KRSC-FM Claremore OK 4 hrs
KDDQ(FM) Comanche OK 2 hrs
KCDL(FM) Cordell OK 2 hrs
KCES(FM) Eufaula OK 3 hrs
KOKC(AM) Guthrie OK 3 hrs
KGYN(AM) Guymon OK 3 hrs
KPRV-FM Heavener OK 12 hrs
KIHN(AM) Hugo OK 5 hrs
KITX(FM) Hugo OK 3 hrs
KFXI(FM) Marlow OK 4 hrs
KTMC(AM) McAlester OK 5 hrs
KTMC-FM McAlester OK 2 hrs
KVLH(AM) Pauls Valley OK 5 hrs
KXVQ(AM) Pawhuska OK 10 hrs
WBBZ(AM) Ponca City OK 2 hrs
KPRV(AM) Poteau OK 12 hrs
KVOO(AM) Tulsa OK 2 hrs
KIMY(FM) Watonga OK 4 hrs
KURY(AM) Brookings OR 1 hr
KURY-FM Brookings OR 1 hr
KYKN(AM) Keizer OR 3 hrs
WCZN(AM) Chester PA 4 hrs
*WERG(FM) Erie PA 3 hrs
WFLP(AM) Erie PA 4 hrs
WCMB(AM) Harrisburg PA 2 hrs
WTCY(AM) Harrisburg PA 4 hrs
*WIUP-FM Indiana PA 1 hr
WJSA(AM) Jersey Shore PA 2 hrs
WJSA-FM Jersey Shore PA 2 hrs
WNPV(AM) Lansdale PA 2 hrs
WTGC(AM) Lewisburg PA 12 hrs
WJUN(AM) Mexico PA 3 hrs
WHAT(AM) Philadelphia PA 12 hrs
*WKDU(FM) Philadelphia PA 4 hrs
*WPEB(FM) Philadelphia PA 10 hrs
WRAW(AM) Reading PA 1 hr
*WXLV(FM) Schnecksville PA 4 hrs
*WBYO(FM) Sellersville PA 10 hrs
WWII(AM) Shiremanstown PA 2 hrs
*WPSU(FM) State College PA 2 hrs
*WRLC(FM) Williamsport PA 2 hrs
WALE(AM) Providence RI
WZLA-FM Abbeville SC 5 hrs
WGTN-FM Andrews SC 5 hrs
WOKE(AM) Charleston SC 2 hrs
WBZK-FM Chester SC 6 hrs
WFIS(AM) Fountain Inn SC 3 hrs
WGTN(AM) Georgetown SC 2 hrs
WMTY(AM) Greenwood SC 7 hrs
WHSC(AM) Hartsville SC 3 hrs
WHSC-FM Hartsville SC 3 hrs
WLBG(AM) Laurens SC 18 hrs
WZJY(AM) Mt. Pleasant SC
WATX(AM) Algood TN
WVOL(AM) Berry Hill TN 19 hrs
WFWL(AM) Camden TN 8 hrs
WRJB(FM) Camden TN 4 hrs
WNKX(AM) Centerville TN 5 hrs
WDXN(AM) Clarksville TN 3 hrs
WZYX(AM) Cowan TN 10 hrs
WSDQ(AM) Dunlap TN 7 hrs
WEMB(AM) Erwin TN 10 hrs
WIZO(AM) Franklin TN 3 hrs
*WLMU(FM) Harrogate TN 4 hrs
WXJB-FM Harrogate TN 2 hrs
*WFHC(FM) Henderson TN 5 hrs
WHHM-FM Henderson TN 10 hrs
WQQK(FM) Hendersonville TN 2 hrs
WDXI(AM) Jackson TN 16 hrs
WDEB-FM Jamestown TN 24 hrs
WJFC(AM) Jefferson City TN 19 hrs
WNDD(FM) Jefferson City TN 4 hrs
WKGN(AM) Knoxville TN 15 hrs
WLIL(AM) Lenoir City TN 18 hrs
WAXO(AM) Lewisburg TN 12 hrs
WDXL(AM) Lexington TN 10 hrs
WLOD(AM) Loudon TN 12 hrs
WRKQ(AM) Madisonville TN 12 hrs
WCMT(AM) Martin TN 8 hrs
WDIA(AM) Memphis TN
WMTN(AM) Morristown TN 5 hrs
WTRB(AM) Ripley TN 6 hrs
WJLE(AM) Smithville TN 15 hrs
WJLE-FM Smithville TN 15 hrs
WTZX(AM) Sparta TN 6 hrs
WDBL(AM) Springfield TN 10 hrs
WDBL-FM Springfield TN 10 hrs
WSGI(AM) Springfield TN 16 hrs
WSBI(AM) Static TN 5 hrs
WNTT(AM) Tazewell TN
WKWT(FM) Union City TN 7 hrs
WTNR(AM) Waynesboro TN
WTNR-FM Waynesboro TN
WBRY(AM) Woodbury TN 16 hrs
KIXZ(AM) Amarillo TX 6 hrs
*KAZI(FM) Austin TX 20 hrs
KIOX(AM) Bay City TX 4 hrs
KIBL-FM Beeville TX 7 hrs
KULF(FM) Brenham TX 10 hrs
KBOC(FM) Bridgeport TX 6 hrs
KHLR(FM) Cameron TX 10 hrs
KMIL(AM) Cameron TX 6 hrs
KCAR(AM) Clarksville TX 6 hrs
KSTA(AM) Coleman TX 7 hrs
KSTA-FM Coleman TX 7 hrs
KCOM(AM) Comanche TX 5 hrs
KBHT(FM) Crockett TX 6 hrs
KQRO(AM) Cuero TX 2 hrs
KQRO-FM Cuero TX 2 hrs
KAFX(AM) Diboll TX 7 hrs
KAFX-FM Diboll TX
KEAS(AM) Eastland TX 6 hrs
*KTEP(FM) El Paso TX 4 hrs
KNES(FM) Fairfield TX 3 hrs
KPSO(AM) Falfurrias TX
KPSO-FM Falfurrias TX
KOKE(FM) Giddings TX 10 hrs
*KJCR(FM) Keene TX 2 hrs
KERV(AM) Kerrville TX 2 hrs
KYMI(FM) Los Ybanez TX 3 hrs
KCRS(AM) Midland TX 4 hrs
KCRS-FM Midland TX 4 hrs
KLBO(AM) Monahans TX 3 hrs
KJCS(FM) Nacogdoches TX 6 hrs
KLIS(FM) Palestine TX 2 hrs
KPLT(AM) Paris TX 4 hrs
KPLT-FM Paris TX 4 hrs
KXAL-FM Pittsburg TX 3 hrs
*KPVU(FM) Prairie View TX 4 hrs
KSJL-FM San Antonio TX 8 hrs
KCAS(AM) Slaton TX 1 hr
KHOS(AM) Sonora TX 5 hrs
KTLR-FM Terrell TX 4 hrs
KCMC(AM) Texarkana TX 15 hrs
KTWN(AM) Texarkana TX 2 hrs
KTBB(AM) Tyler TX 5 hrs
*KVNE-FM Tyler TX 2 hrs
KZEY(AM) Tyler TX 16 hrs
KVWC(AM) Vernon TX 16 hrs
KALK(FM) Winfield TX 5 hrs
KVLL(AM) Woodville TX 02 hrs
KBLQ-FM Logan UT 8 hrs
*KUER(FM) Salt Lake City UT 3 hrs
WKDE-FM Altavista VA 5 hrs
WKEX(AM) Blacksburg VA 6 hrs
WMEK(AM) Chase City VA 5 hrs
WKRE-FM Exmore VA 6 hrs
WPAK(AM) Farmville VA 12 hrs
WGFC(AM) Floyd VA 18 hrs
WLQM(AM) Franklin VA 12 hrs
WLQM-FM Franklin VA 12 hrs
WMNA(AM) Gretna VA 15 hrs
WMNA-FM Gretna VA 15 hrs
*WHOV(FM) Hampton VA 5 hrs
*WEMC(FM) Harrisonburg VA 8 hrs
WHHV(AM) Hillsville VA 15 hrs
WLSA(FM) Louisa VA 3 hrs
WVLR(AM) Lynchburg VA 19 hrs
WMEV(AM) Marion VA 2 hrs
WNVA(AM) Norton VA 15 hrs
WSVY(AM) Portsmouth VA
WREJ(AM) Richmond VA 1 hr
WXMY(AM) Saltville VA 8 hrs
WHLF(AM) South Boston VA 7 hrs
WQOK(FM) South Boston VA 9 hrs
WXLZ(AM) St. Paul VA 15 hrs
WQRA(FM) Warrenton VA 5 hrs
WMBG(AM) Williamsburg VA 5 hrs

Special Programming on Radio Stations in the U.S.

WYVE(AM) Wytheville VA 4 hrs
WIYC(FM) Charlotte Amalie VI 2 hrs
WRRA(AM) Frederiksted VI 12 hrs
KGNW(AM) Burien-Seattle WA
KLLM(FM) Forks WA 4 hrs
KVAC(AM) Forks WA 4 hrs
*KAOS(FM) Olympia WA 2 hrs
*KNHC(FM) Seattle WA 6 hrs
WSPL(FM) La Crosse WI
WLDY(AM) Ladysmith WI 2 hrs
WBJX(AM) Racine WI 8 hrs
WRCO(AM) Richland Center WI 3 hrs
WELD-FM Petersburg WV 3 hrs
WWYO(AM) Pineville WV 20 hrs
WRRL-FM Rainelle WV
WMOV(AM) Ravenswood WV 24 hrs
WVAR(AM) Richwood WV 11 hrs
WYKM(AM) Rupert WV
WCWV(FM) Summersville WV 15 hrs

Greek

*KPCC(FM) Pasadena CA 2 hrs
KJAY(AM) Sacramento CA 1 hr
KEST(AM) San Francisco CA 5 hrs
*KPOF(AM) Denver CO 1 hr
WLVU(AM) Dunedin FL 1 hr
WSRF(AM) Fort Lauderdale FL 10 hrs
*WBVM(FM) Tampa FL 1 hr
WGKA(AM) Atlanta GA 1 hr
WEDC(AM) Chicago IL 1 hr
WCEV(AM) Cicero IL 5 hrs
WKDC(AM) Elmhurst IL 1 hr
WONX(AM) Evanston IL 2 hrs
WVVX(FM) Highland Park IL 5 hrs
WJOB(AM) Hammond IN 1 hr
WCAV(FM) Brockton MA 1 hr
WUNR(AM) Brookline MA 17 hrs
WLLH(AM) Lowell MA 2 hrs
WLYN(AM) Lynn MA 4 hrs
WNTN(AM) Newton MA 17 hrs
WQVR(FM) Southbridge MA 1 hr
*WTCC(FM) Springfield MA 2 hrs
*WBRS(FM) Waltham MA 4 hrs
*WCUW(FM) Worcester MA 2 hrs
WORC(AM) Worcester MA 1 hr
WBMD(AM) Baltimore MD 2 hrs
WINX(AM) Rockville MD 2 hrs
KSTL(AM) St. Louis MO 1 hr
WRKB(AM) Kannapolis NC 1 hr
*WKNH(FM) Keene NH 2 hrs
*WRSU-FM New Brunswick NJ 1 hr
KLAV(AM) Las Vegas NV 1 hr
WKOP(AM) Binghamton NY 1 hr
WHLD(AM) Niagara Falls NY 1 hr
*WUSB(FM) Stony Brook NY 1 hr
*WRPI(FM) Troy NY 2 hrs
WINW(AM) Canton OH 1 hr
WRMR(AM) Cleveland OH 1 hr
WZLE(FM) Lorain OH 1 hr
*WKTL(FM) Struthers OH 1 hr
WIBF-FM Jenkintown PA 6 hrs
WBZY(AM) New Castle PA 1 hr
WRIB(AM) Providence RI 1 hr
WFAX(AM) Falls Church VA 1 hr
WEIR(AM) Weirton WV 1 hr

Hebrew

*WHPK-FM Chicago IL 1 hr
KLAV(AM) Las Vegas NV 1 hr
WLIR(AM) Spring Valley NY 2 hrs
*WKDU(FM) Philadelphia PA 3 hrs

Hindi

KEST(AM) San Francisco CA 8 hrs
WSBC(AM) Chicago IL 6 hrs
WEEF(AM) Highland Park IL
*WCUW(FM) Worcester MA 2 hrs
WYGR(AM) Wyoming MI 1 hr
KLAV(AM) Las Vegas NV 1 hr
*WAPS(FM) Akron OH 1 hr
*WYSO(FM) Yellow Springs OH 1 hr
*KBOO(FM) Portland OR 1 hr
*WEVL(FM) Memphis TN 1 hr
KTEK(AM) Alvin TX 3 hrs
*KPFT(FM) Houston TX 3 hrs

Hungarian

KTYM(AM) Inglewood CA 1 hr
*WVOF(FM) Fairfield CT 2 hrs
WNDU(AM) South Bend IN 1 hr
WSBT(AM) South Bend IN 1 hr
WCTC(AM) New Brunswick NJ 1 hr
*WRSU-FM New Brunswick NJ 1 hr
*WAPS(FM) Akron OH 1 hr
*WCPN(FM) Cleveland OH 1 hr
*WCSB(FM) Cleveland OH 1 hr
*WKTL(FM) Struthers OH 1 hr
*WQRP(FM) West Carrollton OH 3 hrs
WELW(AM) Willoughby-Eastlake OH 1 hr
WIBF-FM Jenkintown PA 1 hr

Irish

KIEV(AM) Glendale CA 1 hr
*KUSF(FM) San Francisco CA 1 hr
WADS(AM) Ansonia CT 1 hr
*WVOF(FM) Fairfield CT 2 hrs
WYBC-FM New Haven CT 2 hrs
*WNHU(FM) West Haven CT 5 hrs
WLVU(AM) Dunedin FL 1 hr
*WUCF-FM Orlando FL 1 hr
*WHPK-FM Chicago IL 1 hr
WSBC(AM) Chicago IL 1 hr
WCEV(AM) Cicero IL 2 hrs
WPNA(AM) Oak Park IL 7 hrs
WGRL(AM) Indianapolis IN 1 hr
*WGBH(FM) Boston MA 2 hrs
WBET(AM) Brockton MA 2 hrs
WUNR(AM) Brookline MA 2 hrs
WACE(AM) Chicopee MA 2 hrs
WHTB(AM) Fall River MA 1 hr
WATD-FM Marshfield MA 6 hrs
WNBP(AM) Newburyport MA 4 hrs
WNTN(AM) Newton MA 8 hrs
WBRK(AM) Pittsfield MA 1 hr
WESX(AM) Salem MA 2 hrs
*WCUW(FM) Worcester MA 2 hrs
*WICN(FM) Worcester MA 2 hrs
WORC(AM) Worcester MA 1 hr
WUFK(FM) Fort Kent ME 3 hrs
*WKNH(FM) Keene NH 2 hrs
WJDM(AM) Elizabeth NJ 2 hrs
*WRSU-FM New Brunswick NJ 1 hr
WXMC(AM) Parsippany-Troy Hills NJ 2 hrs
*WSOU(FM) South Orange NJ 2 hrs
WKOP(AM) Binghamton NY 1 hr
WCKL(AM) Catskill NY 2 hrs
WRWD(AM) Cornwall NY 1 hr
WZZZ(AM) Fulton NY 1 hr
*WBAU(FM) Garden City NY 2 hrs
*WHPC(FM) Garden City NY 1 hr
*WRHU(FM) Hempstead NY 4 hrs
WHVW(AM) Hyde Park NY 1 hr
WKNY(AM) Kingston NY 1 hr
*WFUV(FM) New York NY 7 hrs
*WKCR-FM New York NY 2 hrs
WHLD(AM) Niagara Falls NY 1 hr
WVKZ(AM) Schenectady NY 1 hr
WSFW(AM) Seneca Falls NY 2 hrs
WSFW-FM Seneca Falls NY 2 hrs
*WAPS(FM) Akron OH 2 hrs
WRMR(AM) Cleveland OH 1 hr
WWCD(FM) Grove City OH 1 hr
*WKTL(FM) Struthers OH 1 hr
WELW(AM) Willoughby-Eastlake OH 1 hr
*WMCE(FM) Erie PA 1 hr
WGBN(AM) New Kensington PA 2 hrs
*WYEP-FM Pittsburgh PA 1 hr
WPAM(AM) Pottsville PA 1 hr
*KPFT(FM) Houston TX 1 hr

Italian

KTYM(AM) Inglewood CA 4 hrs
KJAY(AM) Sacramento CA 1 hr
KEST(AM) San Francisco CA 1 hr
*KUSF(FM) San Francisco CA 1 hr
*WFAR(FM) Danbury CT 1 hr
*WVOF(FM) Fairfield CT 1 hr
WNLC(AM) New London CT 1 hr
WREF(AM) Ridgefield CT 3 hrs
WWCO(AM) Waterbury CT 2 hrs
*WWUH(FM) West Hartford CT 3 hrs
WMMM(AM) Westport CT 7 hrs
WGUL(AM) Dunedin FL 1 hr
WLVU(AM) Dunedin FL 15 hrs
WSRF(AM) Fort Lauderdale FL 12 hrs
WGUL-FM New Port Richey FL 1 hr
*WUCF-FM Orlando FL 1 hr
WPSL(AM) Port St. Lucie FL 2 hrs
WGKA(AM) Atlanta GA 1 hr
WEDC(AM) Chicago IL 1 hr
WKDC(AM) Elmhurst IL 6 hrs
WBET(AM) Brockton MA 2 hrs
WUNR(AM) Brookline MA 12 hrs
WKOX(AM) Framingham MA 1 hr
WLYN(AM) Lynn MA 4 hrs
WNTN(AM) Newton MA 2 hrs
*WTCC(FM) Springfield MA 2 hrs
*WBRS(FM) Waltham MA 4 hrs
*WZLY(FM) Wellesley MA 1 hr
WITH(AM) Baltimore MD 2 hrs
*WFBE(FM) Flint MI 1 hr
WKNX(AM) Frankenmuth MI 1 hr
WSSJ(AM) Camden NJ 2 hrs
WIMG(AM) Ewing NJ 1 hr
KLAV(AM) Las Vegas NV 1 hr
WNYG(AM) Babylon NY 4 hrs
WRWD(AM) Cornwall NY 1 hr
WVOA(FM) DeRuyter NY 1 hr
WSIV(AM) East Syracuse NY 1 hr
*WCVF-FM Fredonia NY 3 hrs
*WBAU(FM) Garden City NY 2 hrs
*WRHU(FM) Hempstead NY 4 hrs
WHUC(AM) Hudson NY 1 hr
WHVW(AM) Hyde Park NY 1 hr
WJTN(AM) Jamestown NY 1 hr
WLVL(AM) Lockport NY 2 hrs
*WFUV(FM) New York NY 2 hrs
*WKCR-FM New York NY 2 hrs
WHLD(AM) Niagara Falls NY 8 hrs
WJJL(AM) Niagara Falls NY 4 hrs
WWWG(AM) Rochester NY 4 hrs
*WRUC(FM) Schenectady NY 1 hr
WVKZ(AM) Schenectady NY
WSFW(AM) Seneca Falls NY 2 hrs
WSFW-FM Seneca Falls NY 2 hrs
WUTQ(AM) Utica NY 2 hrs
*WAPS(FM) Akron OH 2 hrs
WASN(AM) Campbell OH 2 hrs
WERE(AM) Cleveland OH 1 hr
WRDZ(AM) Cleveland OH 4 hrs
WDIG(AM) Steubenville OH 3 hrs
*WUJC(FM) University Heights OH 2 hrs
WELW(AM) Willoughby-Eastlake OH 1 hr
WBBW(AM) Youngstown OH 6 hrs
KKEY(AM) Portland OR 1 hr
WMBA(AM) Ambridge PA 1 hr
WCDL(AM) Carbondale PA 3 hrs
*WERG(FM) Erie PA 3 hrs
WIBF-FM Jenkintown PA 6 hrs
WNPV(AM) Lansdale PA 1 hr
WGBN(AM) New Kensington PA 2 hrs
WTEL(AM) Philadelphia PA 5 hrs
WURD(AM) Philadelphia PA 3 hrs
WPIC(AM) Sharon PA 2 hrs
WYKO(AM) Sabana Grande PR 2 hrs
WALE(AM) Providence RI 2 hrs
WRIB(AM) Providence RI 5 hrs
WKRI(AM) West Warwick RI 3 hrs
WFAX(AM) Falls Church VA 1 hr
WREJ(AM) Richmond VA 1 hr
*WMSE(FM) Milwaukee WI 3 hrs
*WYMS(FM) Milwaukee WI 1 hr
WRJN(AM) Racine WI 1 hr
WTCS(AM) Fairmont WV 4 hrs
WEIR(AM) Weirton WV 2 hrs

Japanese

KTYM(AM) Inglewood CA 1 hr
KEST(AM) San Francisco CA 5 hrs
KUAM(AM) Agana GU 3 hrs
KIPA(AM) Hilo HI 8 hrs
KPUA(AM) Hilo HI 6 hrs
KMVI(AM) Wailuku HI 6 hrs
*WAMH(FM) Amherst MA 2 hrs
*WZLY(FM) Wellesley MA 1 hr
WCAR(AM) Livonia MI 1 hr
*WBXL(FM) Baldwinsville NY 1 hr
KKMO(AM) Tacoma WA 10 hrs

Jazz

*KBRW(AM) Barrow AK 6 hrs
*KUAC(FM) Fairbanks AK 15 hrs
KIYU(AM) Galena AK 4 hrs
*KHNS(FM) Haines AK 5 hrs
*KRBD(FM) Ketchikan AK 10 hrs
*KSKO(AM) McGrath AK 3 hrs
KRSA(AM) Petersburg AK 1 hr
*KTNA(FM) Talkeetna AK 5 hrs
*KSTK(FM) Wrangell AK 8 hrs
WNSP(FM) Bay Minette AL 3 hrs
*WBHM(FM) Birmingham AL 13 hrs
WZRR(FM) Birmingham AL 3 hrs
*WRWA(FM) Dothan AL 5 hrs
WZEW(FM) Fairhope AL 6 hrs
*WSGN(FM) Gadsden AL 19 hrs
WRJM-FM Geneva AL 4 hrs
WEUP(AM) Huntsville AL 2 hrs
WQLS-FM Ozark AL 4 hrs
*WTSU(FM) Troy AL 5 hrs
WWPG(AM) Tuscaloosa AL 2 hrs
KEZU(FM) Booneville AR 2 hrs
KEZA(FM) Fayetteville AR
*KASU(FM) Jonesboro AR 4 hrs
*KUAR(FM) Little Rock AR 10 hrs
*KXRJ(FM) Russellville AR 15 hrs
WVUV(AM) Leone AS 15 hrs
KGVY(AM) Green Valley AZ
KLCR(FM) Nogales AZ 4 hrs
KESZ(FM) Phoenix AZ 4 hrs
KIHX-FM Prescott Valley AZ 2 hrs
KQST(FM) Sedona AZ 15 hrs
*KAWC-FM Yuma AZ 15 hrs
*KHSU-FM Arcata CA 15 hrs
*KZPN(FM) Bayside CA 6 hrs
*KPFA(FM) Berkeley CA 20 hrs
KNNN(FM) Central Valley CA 3 hrs
*KZFR(FM) Chico CA 10 hrs
*KSPC(FM) Claremont CA 12 hrs
*KKUP(FM) Cupertino CA 9 hrs
*KECG(FM) El Cerrito CA
KFMI(FM) Eureka CA 3 hrs
*KOHL(FM) Fremont CA 4 hrs
*KCFF(FM) Fresno CA 20 hrs
*KSJV(FM) Fresno CA 19 hrs
*KMUD(FM) Garberville CA 6 hrs
KMGQ(FM) Goleta CA 13 hrs
*KUCI(FM) Irvine CA 20 hrs
*KFJC(FM) Los Altos CA 10 hrs
*KPFK(FM) Los Angeles CA 12 hrs
*KUSC(FM) Los Angeles CA 1 hr
*KXLU(FM) Los Angeles CA 11 hrs
KMMT(FM) Mammoth Lakes CA 3 hrs
*KVMR(FM) Nevada City CA 16 hrs
KDJK(FM) Oakdale CA 2 hrs
*KPSC(FM) Palm Springs CA 1 hr
*KZYX(FM) Philo CA 11 hrs
KIOO(FM) Porterville CA 5 hrs
*KUCR(FM) Riverside CA 6 hrs
KJAY(AM) Sacramento CA 5 hrs
*KVCR(FM) San Bernardino CA
*KALW(FM) San Francisco CA 5 hrs
*KUSF(FM) San Francisco CA 3 hrs
KEZR(FM) San Jose CA 5 hrs
*KCPR(FM) San Luis Obispo CA 3 hrs
KKJG(FM) San Luis Obispo CA 2 hrs
*KCSB-FM Santa Barbara CA 10 hrs
*KUSP(FM) Santa Cruz CA 23 hrs
*KZSC(FM) Santa Cruz CA 19 hrs
*KCRW(FM) Santa Monica CA
KXFX(FM) Santa Rosa CA 5 hrs
KZSQ-FM Sonora CA 13 hrs
*KUOP(FM) Stockton CA 3 hrs
*KCPB(FM) Thousand Oaks CA 1 hr
*KCSS(FM) Turlock CA 3 hrs
KKBN(FM) Twain Harte CA 4 hrs
KWNE(FM) Ukiah CA 1 hr
*KSAK(FM) Walnut CA
*KASF(FM) Alamosa CO 4 hrs
KBCO(AM) Boulder CO 3 hrs
*KGNU(FM) Boulder CO 15 hrs
KSMT(FM) Breckenridge CO 3 hrs
*KDNK(FM) Carbondale CO 17 hrs
*KDUR(FM) Durango CO 6 hrs
KIUP(AM) Durango CO 4 hrs
KTCL(FM) Fort Collins CO 2 hrs
*KMSA(FM) Grand Junction CO 10 hrs
*KPRN(FM) Grand Junction CO
*KWSB-FM Gunnison CO 3 hrs
*KSUT(FM) Ignacio CO 5 hrs
KFMU-FM Oak Creek CO 2 hrs
*KVNF(FM) Paonia CO 17 hrs
*KOTO(FM) Telluride CO 9 hrs
*WXCI(FM) Danbury CT 3 hrs
*WVOF(FM) Fairfield CT 10 hrs
*WPKT(FM) Meriden CT 8 hrs
*WFCS(FM) New Britain CT 4 hrs
WYBC-FM New Haven CT 8 hrs
*WCNI(FM) New London CT 9 hrs
WLIS(AM) Old Saybrook CT 2 hrs
WREF(AM) Ridgefield CT 5 hrs
*WNHU(FM) West Haven CT 12 hrs
*WECS(FM) Willimantic CT 12 hrs
WKND(AM) Windsor CT 3 hrs
*WAMU(FM) Washington DC 5 hrs
*WVUD(FM) Newark DE 15 hrs
WGMD(FM) Rehoboth Beach DE 2 hrs
*WVUM(FM) Coral Gables FL 3 hrs
WDBF(AM) Delray Beach FL 10 hrs
WISP(FM) Holmes Beach FL 3 hrs
WXCV(FM) Homosassa Springs FL 7 hrs
WIVY-FM Jacksonville FL 14 hrs
WAVV(FM) Marco FL 3 hrs
WSBB(AM) New Smyrna Beach FL 1 hr
WRBD(AM) Pompano Beach FL 6 hrs
WRXB(AM) St. Petersburg Beach FL 15 hrs
*WKPX(FM) Sunrise FL 3 hrs
WBGM-FM Tallahassee FL 4 hrs
WHBT(AM) Tallahassee FL 4 hrs
WGYL(FM) Vero Beach FL 4 hrs
WDEC(AM) Americus GA 5 hrs
*WUOG(FM) Athens GA 6 hrs
*WABE(FM) Atlanta GA 11 hrs
*WRAS(FM) Atlanta GA 2 hrs
*WREK(FM) Atlanta GA 15 hrs
*WRFG(FM) Atlanta GA 18 hrs
*WWGC(FM) Carrollton GA 6 hrs
WEAM(AM) Columbus GA 1 hr
*WTJB(FM) Columbus GA 5 hrs
*WXGC(FM) Milledgeville GA 12 hrs
*WVGS(FM) Statesboro GA 5 hrs
*WVVS(FM) Valdosta GA 6 hrs
*WJSP-FM Warm Springs GA
KUAI(AM) Eleele HI 4 hrs
*KTUH(FM) Honolulu HI 21 hrs
KAOI(AM) Kihei HI 10 hrs
*KUSR(FM) Ames IA
*WOI-FM Ames IA 18 hrs
KMXG(FM) Clinton IA 2 hrs
KROS(AM) Clinton IA 2 hrs
*KLCD(FM) Decorah IA 14 hrs
*KWLC(AM) Decorah IA
*KUCB-FM Des Moines IA 10 hrs
*KRUI-FM Iowa City IA 3 hrs
KFMH(FM) Muscatine IA 4 hrs
*KIGC(FM) Oskaloosa IA 2 hrs
*KCUI(FM) Pella IA 3 hrs
KFMG(FM) Pella IA 6 hrs
*KWAR(FM) Waverly IA 10 hrs
KHEZ(FM) Caldwell ID 4 hrs
KATW(FM) Lewiston ID 3 hrs
*KRFA-FM Moscow ID
KECH-FM Sun Valley ID 5 hrs
*KBSW(FM) Twin Falls ID 20 hrs
*WESN(FM) Bloomington IL 6 hrs
*WPCD(FM) Champaign IL 6 hrs
*WOUI(FM) Chicago IL 9 hrs
WITY(AM) Danville IL 2 hrs
*WJMU(FM) Decatur IL 3 hrs
WFXB(FM) East St. Louis IL 6 hrs
*WEPS(FM) Elgin IL 6 hrs
*WRSE-FM Elmhurst IL 1 hr
*WTPC(FM) Elsah IL 3 hrs
*WNUR-FM Evanston IL 1 hr
*WVKC(FM) Galesburg IL 15 hrs
WYMG(FM) Jacksonville IL 2 hrs
*WCSF(FM) Joliet IL 2 hrs
*WMXM(FM) Lake Forest IL 6 hrs
WJPC-FM Lansing IL 15 hrs
*WLRA(FM) Lockport IL 15 hrs
*WIUM(FM) Macomb IL 5 hrs
WLBH(AM) Mattoon IL 1 hr
*WMTH(FM) Park Ridge IL 2 hrs
*WQUB(FM) Quincy IL 7 hrs
*WVIK(FM) Rock Island IL 9 hrs
*WILL-FM Urbana IL 10 hrs
WZSR(FM) Woodstock IL 5 hrs
*WEAX(FM) Angola IN 2 hrs
WBQR(FM) Attica IN
WIIZ(FM) Battle Ground IN 4 hrs
WQRK(FM) Bedford IN 4 hrs
WNDY(FM) Crawfordsville IN 8 hrs
WNJY(FM) Delphi IN 3 hrs
WPZZ(FM) Franklin IN 10 hrs
*WGRE(FM) Greencastle IN 3 hrs
*WBDG(FM) Indianapolis IN 7 hrs
*WFYI-FM Indianapolis IN 4 hrs
WTLC-FM Indianapolis IN 14 hrs
*WNAS(FM) New Albany IN 2 hrs
*WBKE-FM North Manchester IN 5 hrs
*WECI(FM) Richmond IN 16 hrs
*WMHD-FM Terre Haute IN 1 hr
*WVUR-FM Valparaiso IN 3 hrs
*WVUB(FM) Vincennes IN 4 hrs
WWIP(FM) Wabash IN 2 hrs
*KNBU(FM) Baldwin City KS 15 hrs
*KONQ(FM) Dodge City KS 10 hrs
*KANZ(FM) Garden City KS 15 hrs
*KHCT(FM) Great Bend KS 1 hr
*KZNA(FM) Hill City KS 15 hrs
*KHCC-FM Hutchinson KS 1 hr
KIND(AM) Independence KS
*KRPS(FM) Pittsburg KS 21 hrs
*KHCD(FM) Salina KS 1 hr
*KCFN(FM) Wichita KS 4 hrs
KRBB(FM) Wichita KS 6 hrs
*WKYU-FM Bowling Green KY 15 hrs
*WKUE(FM) Elizabethtown KY 20 hrs
WIZF(FM) Erlanger KY
*WRVG(FM) Georgetown KY 3 hrs
WTKT-FM Georgetown KY 6 hrs
*WKPB(FM) Henderson KY 14 hrs
*WRFL(FM) Lexington KY 6 hrs
*WUOL(FM) Louisville KY 1 hr
WCKU(FM) Nicholasville KY 4 hrs
*WDCL-FM Somerset KY 15 hrs
*WMMT(FM) Whitesburg KY 5 hrs
*KLSP(FM) Angola LA 7 hrs
KTRY-FM Bastrop LA 8 hrs
KBCE(FM) Boyce LA 3 hrs
*KGRM(FM) Grambling LA 15 hrs
KJCB(AM) Lafayette LA 2 hrs
*WWNO(FM) New Orleans LA 18 hrs
WYLD-FM New Orleans LA 5 hrs
*KSCL(FM) Shreveport LA 3 hrs
*WAMH(FM) Amherst MA 8 hrs
*WFCR(FM) Amherst MA 9 hrs
*WMBR(FM) Cambridge MA 14 hrs
*WGAJ(FM) Deerfield MA 2 hrs
*WXPL(FM) Fitchburg MA 4 hrs
*WDJM-FM Framingham MA 3 hrs
WRSI(FM) Greenfield MA 6 hrs
*WCCH(FM) Holyoke MA 2 hrs
*WJUL(FM) Lowell MA 8 hrs
WFNX(FM) Lynn MA 8 hrs
*WZBC(FM) Newton MA 6 hrs
*WJJW(FM) North Adams MA 4 hrs
*WNMH(FM) Northfield MA 10 hrs
*WMWM(FM) Salem MA 3 hrs
*WBSL-FM Sheffield MA 15 hrs
*WMHC(FM) South Hadley MA 15 hrs
*WYAJ(FM) Sudbury MA 5 hrs
WMVY(FM) Tisbury MA 4 hrs
WCRB(FM) Waltham MA 2 hrs
*WZLY(FM) Wellesley MA 2 hrs
*WSKB(FM) Westfield MA 6 hrs
*WCUW(FM) Worcester MA 17 hrs
WARX(FM) Hagerstown MD 3 hrs
WTHU(AM) Thurmont MD 4 hrs
*WKHS(FM) Worton MD 2 hrs
*WERU-FM Blue Hill ME 18 hrs
*WBOR(FM) Brunswick ME 20 hrs
*WMPG(FM) Gorham ME 10 hrs
*WRBC(FM) Lewiston ME 4 hrs
*WMEB-FM Orono ME 13 hrs
*WUPI(FM) Presque Isle ME 2 hrs
WPKM(FM) Scarborough ME 5 hrs
*WSJB-FM Standish ME 3 hrs
*WMHB(FM) Waterville ME 8 hrs
*WQAC-FM Alma MI 2 hrs
*WCBN-FM Ann Arbor MI 18 hrs
*WUOM(FM) Ann Arbor MI 6 hrs
*WHFR(FM) Dearborn MI 15 hrs
*WDTR(FM) Detroit MI 2 hrs
WXLA(AM) Dimondale MI 3 hrs
*WDBM(FM) East Lansing MI 5 hrs
*WKAR-FM East Lansing MI 7 hrs
WDZZ-FM Flint MI 11 hrs

Special Programming on Radio Stations in the U.S.

*WFUM-FM Flint MI 10 hrs
WGFN(FM) Glen Arbor MI 4 hrs
*WVGR(FM) Grand Rapids MI 6 hrs
*WTHS(FM) Holland MI 6 hrs
*WIAA(FM) Interlochen MI 2 hrs
*WIDR(FM) Kalamazoo MI 4 hrs
*WMUK(FM) Kalamazoo MI 6 hrs
WKWM(AM) Kentwood MI 6 hrs
*WOAS(FM) Ontonagon MI 8 hrs
*WSGR-FM Port Huron MI 4 hrs
*WPHS(FM) Warren MI 1 hr
KSTQ(FM) Alexandria MN 1 hr
*KAXE(FM) Grand Rapids MN 6 hrs
*KFAI(FM) Minneapolis MN 12 hrs
KTCJ(AM) Minneapolis MN 3 hrs
KTCZ-FM Minneapolis MN 3 hrs
*KUMM(FM) Morris MN 3 hrs
*WCAL(FM) Northfield MN 3 hrs
*KVSC(FM) St. Cloud MN 12 hrs
*KQAL(FM) Winona MN 20 hrs
*KWUR(FM) Clayton MO 6 hrs
*KCOU(FM) Columbia MO 10 hrs
*KOPN(FM) Columbia MO 9 hrs
*KWWC-FM Columbia MO 25 hrs
KGRC(FM) Hannibal MO 4 hrs
KFEZ(AM) Kansas City MO 5 hrs
*KKFI(FM) Kansas City MO 10 hrs
KYLC(FM) Osage Beach MO
*KMNR(FM) Rolla MO 3 hrs
*KUMR(FM) Rolla MO 3 hrs
*KSMU(FM) Springfield MO 10 hrs
*KDHX(FM) St. Louis MO 12 hrs
KMOX(AM) St. Louis MO 4 hrs
KXOK(AM) St. Louis MO 2 hrs
KFBD-FM Waynesville MO 2 hrs
KOZQ(AM) Waynesville MO 2 hrs
*WMAH-FM Biloxi MS 10 hrs
*WMAE-FM Booneville MS 10 hrs
*WMAU-FM Bude MS 10 hrs
*WMUW(FM) Columbus MS 10 hrs
WGNL(FM) Greenwood MS 6 hrs
*WMAO-FM Greenwood MS 10 hrs
*WMPN-FM Jackson MS 10 hrs
WZRX(AM) Jackson MS 2 hrs
WIQQ(FM) Leland MS 2 hrs
*WMAW-FM Meridian MS 10 hrs
*WMAB-FM Mississippi State MS 10 hrs
*WMAV-FM Oxford MS 10 hrs
WUMS(FM) University MS 2 hrs
*KEMC(FM) Billings MT 16 hrs
*KMSM-FM Butte MT 5 hrs
WSKY(AM) Asheville NC 6 hrs
WRAQ(AM) Brevard NC 8 hrs
*WSGE(FM) Dallas NC 5 hrs
*WXDU(FM) Durham NC 18 hrs
*WRVS-FM Elizabeth City NC 19 hrs
*WQFS(FM) Greensboro NC 4 hrs
*WUAG(FM) Greensboro NC 3 hrs
WOOW(AM) Greenville NC 5 hrs
*WZMB(FM) Greenville NC 3 hrs
WVOD(FM) Manteo NC 4 hrs
WIKS(FM) New Bern NC 2 hrs
WAUG(AM) New Hope NC 3 hrs
WNNC(AM) Newton NC 3 hrs
*WKNC-FM Raleigh NC 3 hrs
*WNCW(FM) Spindale NC 5 hrs
*WHYC(FM) Swan Quarter NC 8 hrs
WTYN(AM) Tryon NC 3 hrs
WOBR-FM Wanchese NC 2 hrs
*WHQR(FM) Wilmington NC 20 hrs
WRDU(FM) Wilson NC 5 hrs
*WFDD-FM Winston-Salem NC 16 hrs
*KTNE-FM Alliance NE 2 hrs
*KINI(FM) Crookston NE 4 hrs
*KHNE-FM Hastings NE 2 hrs
*KLNE-FM Lexington NE 2 hrs
*KRNU(FM) Lincoln NE 6 hrs
*KUCV(FM) Lincoln NE 5 hrs
*KXNE-FM Norfolk NE 5 hrs
KEZO-FM Omaha NE 3 hrs
*KIOS-FM Omaha NE 1 hr
KKCD(FM) Omaha NE 4 hrs
*KWSC(FM) Wayne NE 2 hrs
*WEVO(FM) Concord NH 9 hrs
WBNC(AM) Conway NH 5 hrs
WMWV(FM) Conway NH 5 hrs
*WUNH(FM) Durham NH 5 hrs
WDCR(AM) Hanover NH 6 hrs
*WNEC-FM Henniker NH 3 hrs
*WKNH(FM) Keene NH 3 hrs
WUSS(AM) Atlantic City NJ 2 hrs
*WDVR(FM) Delaware Township NJ 11 hrs
*WNTI(FM) Hackettstown NJ 5 hrs
*WMNJ(FM) Madison NJ 2 hrs
*WRSU-FM New Brunswick NJ 2 hrs
WXMC(AM) Parsippany-Troy Hill s NJ 8 hrs
*WLFR(FM) Pomona NJ 10 hrs
WPRB(FM) Princeton NJ 20 hrs
*WSOU(FM) South Orange NJ 1 hr
*WKNJ-FM Union Township NJ 8 hrs
*WMSC(FM) Upper Montclair NJ 2 hrs
*WPSC-FM Wayne NJ 5 hrs
KAFR(FM) Angel Fire NM 4 hrs
KWYK-FM Aztec NM 3 hrs
KBAC(FM) Las Vegas NM 5 hrs
KSFX(FM) Roswell NM 4 hrs
KTAO(FM) Taos NM 5 hrs
KNEV(FM) Reno NV 2 hrs
*WAMC(FM) Albany NY 19 hrs
WYSL(AM) Avon NY 2 hrs
WVIN-FM Bath NY 2 hrs
*WSKG-FM Binghamton NY
*WXLH(FM) Blue Mountain Lake NY
*WKRB(FM) Brooklyn NY 1 hr
*WBNY(FM) Buffalo NY 3 hrs
*WCAN(FM) Canajoharie NY 18 hrs
*WSLU(FM) Canton NY
*WHCL-FM Clinton NY 9 hrs
*WSUC-FM Cortland NY 4 hrs
WELM(AM) Elmira NY 2 hrs
*WBAU(FM) Garden City NY 2 hrs
*WGSU(FM) Geneseo NY 14 hrs
*WGMC(FM) Greece NY 5 hrs
*WRCU-FM Hamilton NY 12 hrs
*WICB(FM) Ithaca NY 16 hrs
WQNY(FM) Ithaca NY 2 hrs
*WSQG-FM Ithaca NY 8 hrs
*WJFF(FM) Jeffersonville NY 15 hrs
*WAMK(FM) Kingston NY 17 hrs
*WSLO(FM) Malone NY
*WOSR(FM) Middletown NY 18 hrs
WRKL(AM) New City NY 2 hrs
*WFNP(FM) New Paltz NY 4 hrs
*WBAI(FM) New York NY 5 hrs
*WNYE(FM) New York NY 5 hrs
WQEW(AM) New York NY 2 hrs
WQXR-FM New York NY 2 hrs
*WXLG(FM) North Creek NY
*WONY(FM) Oneonta NY 6 hrs
*WRHO(FM) Oneonta NY 4 hrs
WZOZ(FM) Oneonta NY 3 hrs
*WRVO(FM) Oswego NY 19 hrs
*WXLU(FM) Peru NY
*WRHV(FM) Poughkeepsie NY 2 hrs
WQBK-FM Rensselaer NY 2 hrs
WDKX(FM) Rochester NY 4 hrs
*WSLL(FM) Saranac Lake NY
WGY(AM) Schenectady NY 6 hrs
*WMHT-FM Schenectady NY 1 hr
*WRUC(FM) Schenectady NY 15 hrs
WMJC(FM) Smithtown NY 2 hrs
*WSBU(FM) St. Bonaventure NY 2 hrs
*WUSB(FM) Stony Brook NY 20 hrs
*WKWZ(FM) Syosset NY 12 hrs
*WCNY-FM Syracuse NY 7 hrs
WOUR(FM) Utica NY 2 hrs
*WPNR-FM Utica NY 14 hrs
*WJNY(FM) Watertown NY 5 hrs
*WSLJ(FM) Watertown NY
WGMF(AM) Watkins Glen NY 3 hrs
WDST(FM) Woodstock NY 15 hrs
*WRDL(FM) Ashland OH 5 hrs
*WBWC(FM) Berea OH 5 hrs
*WGUC(FM) Cincinnati OH 12 hrs
*WCSB(FM) Cleveland OH 12 hrs
WNCX(FM) Cleveland OH 2 hrs
*WRUW-FM Cleveland OH 15 hrs
WCEZ(FM) Delaware OH 3 hrs
WFRO(AM) Fremont OH 10 hrs
WFRO-FM Fremont OH 10 hrs
*WKCO(FM) Gambier OH 3 hrs
*WDUB(FM) Granville OH 10 hrs
WLQT(FM) Kettering OH 4 hrs
WMOA(AM) Marietta OH 6 hrs
WDIF(FM) Marion OH 2 hrs
*WMCO(FM) New Concord OH 20 hrs
*WOBC-FM Oberlin OH 15 hrs
WIZE(AM) Springfield OH 2 hrs
*WUSO(FM) Springfield OH 6 hrs
WIOT(FM) Toledo OH 2 hrs
WLQR(FM) Toledo OH 6 hrs
*WXUT(FM) Toledo OH 4 hrs
*WUJC(FM) University Heights OH 4 hrs
*WOBN(FM) Westerville OH 1 hr
*WCWS(FM) Wooster OH 8 hrs
*WYSO(FM) Yellow Springs OH 18 hrs
KADA-FM Ada OK 7 hrs
KCMA(FM) Broken Arrow OK 7 hrs
*KRSC-FM Claremore OK 5 hrs
*KHIB(FM) Durant OK 1 hr
*KOCC(FM) Oklahoma City OK 6 hrs
KHSN(AM) Coos Bay OR 2 hrs
*KOAC(AM) Corvallis OR 12 hrs
*KWVA(FM) Eugene OR 4 hrs
KAGO-FM Klamath Falls OR 5 hrs
*KEOL(FM) La Grande OR 6 hrs
KRVC(AM) Medford OR 3 hrs
KYTE(FM) Newport OR 4 hrs
*KBPS(AM) Portland OR 8 hrs
KKEY(AM) Portland OR 15 hrs
*KRRC(FM) Portland OR 10 hrs
KMCQ(FM) The Dalles OR 6 hrs
*WMUH(FM) Allentown PA 14 hrs
*WLVR(FM) Bethlehem PA 12 hrs
*WBUQ(FM) Bloomsburg PA 3 hrs
WMKX(FM) Brookville PA 3 hrs
WISR(AM) Butler PA 3 hrs
*WDCV-FM Carlisle PA 6 hrs
*WDNR(FM) Chester PA 2 hrs
*WCUC-FM Clarion PA 3 hrs*WESS(FM) East Stroudsburg PA 6 hrs
*WJRH(FM) Easton PA 9 hrs
*WWEC(FM) Elizabethtown PA 2 hrs
*WZBT(FM) Gettysburg PA 2 hrs
*WVMM(FM) Grantham PA 10 hrs
*WSAJ(AM) Grove City PA 2 hrs
*WKVR-FM Huntingdon PA 3 hrs
*WIUP-FM Indiana PA 15 hrs
*WFNM(FM) Lancaster PA 8 hrs
*WVBU-FM Lewisburg PA 3 hrs
*WNTE(FM) Mansfield PA 2 hrs
*WARC(FM) Meadville PA 4 hrs
*WMSS(FM) Middletown PA 2 hrs
*WIXQ(FM) Millersville PA 2 hrs
*WHYY-FM Philadelphia PA 3 hrs
*WPEB(FM) Philadelphia PA 17 hrs
*WRCT(FM) Pittsburgh PA 18 hrs
*WXLV(FM) Schnecksville PA 6 hrs
*WVMW-FM Scranton PA 10 hrs
*WQSU(FM) Selinsgrove PA 18 hrs
WKGB-FM Susquehanna PA 2 hrs
WPHD(FM) Tioga PA 2 hrs
*WRDV(FM) Warminster PA 3 hrs
*WCLH(FM) Wilkes-Barre PA 3 hrs
WMGS(FM) Wilkes-Barre PA 2 hrs
WLYC(AM) Williamsport PA
WRAK-FM Williamsport PA 1 hr
*WRLC(FM) Williamsport PA 3 hrs
*WWAS(FM) Williamsport PA 2 hrs
*WVYC(FM) York PA 8 hrs
WNOZ(AM) Aguadilla PR 3 hrs
WOLA(AM) Barranquitas PR 5 hrs
WKJB-FM Mayaguez PR 6 hrs
WYKO(AM) Sabana Grande PR 2 hrs
WHKZ(FM) Cayce SC 2 hrs
WPAL(AM) Charleston SC 9 hrs
*WSCI(FM) Charleston SC 15 hrs
WOIC(AM) Columbia SC 6 hrs
*WUSC-FM Columbia SC 3 hrs
WZNS(FM) Dillon SC 1 hr
*WPLS-FM Greenville SC 2 hrs
WIJY(FM) Hilton Head Island SC 4 hrs
*WSSB-FM Orangeburg SC 10 hrs
KSQY(FM) Deadwood SD 2 hrs
*KTEQ(FM) Rapid City SD 15 hrs
*KCSD(FM) Sioux Falls SD 10 hrs
*WAPX-FM Clarksville TN 6 hrs
*WTTU(FM) Cookeville TN 3 hrs
WAMB(AM) Donelson TN 3 hrs
WAMB-FM Donelson TN 3 hrs
WRLT-FM Franklin TN 7 hrs
*WVCP(FM) Gallatin TN 15 hrs
WQQK(FM) Hendersonville TN 6 hrs
*WFMQ(FM) Lebanon TN 4 hrs
WQDQ(AM) Lebanon TN 3 hrs
*WEVL(FM) Memphis TN 15 hrs
*WQOX(FM) Memphis TN 5 hrs
WMXK(FM) Morristown TN 1 hr
*WFSK(FM) Nashville TN
*WRVU(FM) Nashville TN 18 hrs
WJTT(FM) Red Bank TN 2 hrs
*WUTS(FM) Sewanee TN 4 hrs
WRLG(FM) Smyrna TN 7 hrs
*KACU(FM) Abilene TX 3 hrs
*KACV-FM Amarillo TX 12 hrs
KGSR(FM) Bastrop TX 6 hrs
*KAMU-FM College Station TX 10 hrs
*KETR(FM) Commerce TX 10 hrs
KFRO-FM Gilmer TX 5 hrs
KKRW(FM) Houston TX 4 hrs
*KPFT(FM) Houston TX 6 hrs
*KTRU(FM) Houston TX 6 hrs
*KTPB(FM) Kilgore TX 4 hrs
*KNCT-FM Killeen TX 15 hrs
*KHOY(FM) Laredo TX 4 hrs
KMND(AM) Midland TX 1 hr
*KOCV(FM) Odessa TX 10 hrs
KRIL(AM) Odessa TX 4 hrs
KKMY(FM) Orange TX 6 hrs
KSJL-FM San Antonio TX 8 hrs
*KSTX(FM) San Antonio TX 6 hrs
*KSYM-FM San Antonio TX 19 hrs
KDIL(FM) Terrell Hills TX 4 hrs
*KWBU(FM) Waco TX 10 hrs
KBLQ-FM Logan UT 4 hrs
*KPCW(FM) Park City UT 12 hrs
*KRDC-FM St. George UT 10 hrs
WVES(FM) Accomac VA 3 hrs
*WWHS-FM Hampden-Sydney VA 6 hrs
*WEMC(FM) Harrisonburg VA 2 hrs
*WVRU(FM) Radford VA 12 hrs
*WDCE(FM) Richmond VA 9 hrs
WQOK(FM) South Boston VA 2 hrs
WFOG(FM) Suffolk VA 3 hrs
*WCWM(FM) Williamsburg VA 13 hrs
WRRA(AM) Frederiksted VI 6 hrs
WBFL(FM) Bellows Falls VT 3 hrs
*WRUV(FM) Burlington VT 20 hrs
*WIUV(FM) Castleton VT 10 hrs
*WWLR(FM) Lyndonville VT 3 hrs
WEQX(FM) Manchester VT 4 hrs
WNCS(FM) Montpelier VT 5 hrs
*WNUB-FM Northfield VT 10 hrs
*WGDR(FM) Plainfield VT 6 hrs
WVAY(FM) Wilmington VT 2 hrs
*KUGS(FM) Bellingham WA 20 hrs
*KNWR(FM) Ellensburg WA
*KSER(FM) Everett WA 10 hrs
*KUBS(FM) Newport WA 2 hrs
*KAOS(FM) Olympia WA 19 hrs
*KWSU(AM) Pullman WA 14 hrs
*KZUU(FM) Pullman WA 12 hrs
*KFAE-FM Richland WA 15 hrs
*KUOW(FM) Seattle WA 5 hrs
*KAGU(FM) Spokane WA 2 hrs
*KPBX-FM Spokane WA
*KWRS(FM) Spokane WA 9 hrs
*KDNA(FM) Yakima WA 4 hrs
WAPL-FM Appleton WI 4 hrs
*WBSD(FM) Burlington WI 3 hrs
*WORT(FM) Madison WI 15 hrs
WLST(FM) Marinette WI 4 hrs
*WMSE(FM) Milwaukee WI 15 hrs
*WUWM(FM) Milwaukee WI 13 hrs
WCQM(FM) Park Falls WI 1 hr
WNBI(AM) Park Falls WI 1 hr
*WSUP(FM) Platteville WI 3 hrs
*WOJB(FM) Reserve WI 10 hrs
*WXPR(FM) Rhinelander WI 8 hrs
*WRPN-FM Ripon WI 10 hrs
*WRFW(FM) River Falls WI
WMLI(FM) Sauk City WI 2 hrs
*WWSP(FM) Stevens Point WI 15 hrs
*KUWS(FM) Superior WI 10 hrs
*WSUW(FM) Whitewater WI 15 hrs
*WVWC(FM) Buckhannon WV 4 hrs
WKWS(FM) Charleston WV 3 hrs
*WCDE(FM) Elkins WV 3 hrs
WQZK-FM Keyser WV 2 hrs
*WWVU-FM Morgantown WV 9 hrs
*WQAB(FM) Philippi WV 4 hrs
WMOV(AM) Ravenswood WV 2 hrs
*WPHP(FM) Wheeling WV 1 hr
KMTN(FM) Jackson WY

Jewish

KNNS(AM) Glendale AZ 2 hrs
KIEV(AM) Glendale CA 1 hr
*KCSN(FM) Northridge CA 3 hrs
*WVOF(FM) Fairfield CT 2 hrs
*WWUH(FM) West Hartford CT 1 hr
WSBH(AM) Miami Beach FL 2 hrs
WPBR(AM) Palm Beach FL 3 hrs
*WMNF(FM) Tampa FL
WEEF(AM) Highland Park IL
WKOX(AM) Framingham MA 1 hr
*WBRS(FM) Waltham MA 1 hr
*WCUW(FM) Worcester MA 1 hr
WCBM(AM) Baltimore MD 1 hr
WINX(AM) Rockville MD 3 hrs
*WBYW(FM) Grand Rapids MI 2 hrs
WCTC(AM) New Brunswick NJ 1 hr
*WSOU(FM) South Orange NJ 2 hrs
WMCA(AM) New York NY 10 hrs
WRMR(AM) Cleveland OH 2 hrs
*KVAZ(FM) Henryetta OK 1 hr
WIBF-FM Jenkintown PA 14 hrs
*WHCB(FM) Bristol TN 1 hr
WCPT(AM) Alexandria VA 1 hr

Korean

KEST(AM) San Francisco CA 15 hrs
WNCM(AM) Atlantic Beach FL 1 hr
*WNKJ(FM) Hopkinsville KY 1 hr
*WUSB(FM) Stony Brook NY 1 hr
*KVTT(FM) Dallas TX 2 hrs

Lithuanian

KTYM(AM) Inglewood CA 1 hr
*WWUH(FM) West Hartford CT 2 hrs
WCEV(AM) Cicero IL 10 hrs
WPNA(AM) Oak Park IL 4 hrs
WNDZ(AM) Portage IN 4 hrs
*WICN(FM) Worcester MA 1 hr
WBMD(AM) Baltimore MD 1 hr
*WSOU(FM) South Orange NJ 2 hrs
*WGMC(FM) Greece NY 1 hr
*WCPN(FM) Cleveland OH 1 hr
*WKTL(FM) Struthers OH 1 hr

Middle-of-the-Road (MOR)

WSNJ(AM) Bridgeton NJ
WSNJ-FM Bridgeton NJ

New Age

*KUAC(FM) Fairbanks AK 3 hrs
*WBHM(FM) Birmingham AL 12 hrs
*WQPR(FM) Muscle Shoals AL 20 hrs
*WUAL-FM Tuscaloosa AL 20 hrs
KQST(FM) Sedona AZ 10 hrs
KLLK-FM Fort Bragg CA 2 hrs
*KFSR(FM) Fresno CA 6 hrs
*KVCR(FM) San Bernardino CA 15 hrs
KLLK(AM) Willits CA 2 hrs
*KASF(FM) Alamosa CO 4 hrs
*KRCC(FM) Colorado Springs CO 6 hrs
*KDUR(FM) Durango CO 3 hrs
KTCL(FM) Fort Collins CO 3 hrs
*KVNF(FM) Paonia CO 6 hrs
*WXCI(FM) Danbury CT 3 hrs
*WGRS(FM) Guilford CT 1 hr
*WESU(FM) Middletown CT 2 hrs
*WMNR(FM) Monroe CT 1 hr
*WRXC(FM) Shelton CT 1 hr
*WWUH(FM) West Hartford CT 4 hrs
*WMFE-FM Orlando FL 4 hrs
*WUCF-FM Orlando FL 3 hrs
*WUGA(FM) Athens GA 10 hrs
*WRAS(FM) Atlanta GA 3 hrs
*WVVS(FM) Valdosta GA 3 hrs
*KUSR(FM) Ames IA
*KHKE(FM) Cedar Falls IA 7 hrs
*KUNI(FM) Cedar Falls IA 12 hrs
*KCCK-FM Cedar Rapids IA 7 hrs
*KTPR(FM) Fort Dodge IA 7 hrs
*KCUI(FM) Pella IA 2 hrs
*KWIT(FM) Sioux City IA 2 hrs
*WSIU(FM) Carbondale IL 4 hrs
*WEIU(FM) Charleston IL 3 hrs
*WSIE(FM) Edwardsville IL 16 hrs
*WTPC(FM) Elsah IL 3 hrs
*WUSI(FM) Olney IL 4 hrs
*WQUB(FM) Quincy IL 1 hr
*WNIJ(FM) Rockford IL 3 hrs
*WILL-FM Urbana IL 1 hr
WWWY(FM) Columbus IN 3 hrs
*WVPE(FM) Elkhart IN 5 hrs
*WECI(FM) Richmond IN 2 hrs
*WVUR-FM Valparaiso IN 3 hrs
*KRPS(FM) Pittsburg KS 4 hrs
*KEDM(FM) Monroe LA 7 hrs
*WWNO(FM) New Orleans LA 1 hr
*KSCL(FM) Shreveport LA 1 hr
*WBRS(FM) Waltham MA 14 hrs
*WICN(FM) Worcester MA 3 hrs
*WRBC(FM) Lewiston ME 16 hrs
*WMEB-FM Orono ME 3 hrs
*WMHB(FM) Waterville ME 2 hrs
*WSGR-FM Port Huron MI 4 hrs
*KMSK(FM) Austin MN 5 hrs
*KMSU(FM) Mankato MN 5 hrs
KTCJ(AM) Minneapolis MN 2 hrs
KTCZ-FM Minneapolis MN 2 hrs
KIRK(FM) Lebanon MO 6 hrs
*KGSP(FM) Parkville MO 6 hrs
*KCOZ(FM) Point Lookout MO 10 hrs
*KDHX(FM) St. Louis MO 6 hrs
*WMAH-FM Biloxi MS 10 hrs
*WMAE-FM Booneville MS 10 hrs
*WMAU-FM Bude MS 5 hrs
*WMAO-FM Greenwood MS 10 hrs
*WUSM-FM Hattiesburg MS 10 hrs
*WMPN-FM Jackson MS 10 hrs
*WMAW-FM Meridian MS 10 hrs
*WMAB-FM Mississippi State MS 10 hrs
*WMAV-FM Oxford MS 10 hrs
*KFJM-FM Grand Forks ND 4 hrs
*KZUM(FM) Lincoln NE 8 hrs
*WKNH(FM) Keene NH 2 hrs
*WRSU-FM New Brunswick NJ 1 hr
*WKNJ-FM Union Township NJ 8 hrs
*KRUX(FM) Las Cruces NM 2 hrs
WLKA(FM) Canandaigua NY 6 hrs
*WEOS(FM) Geneva NY 5 hrs
*WGMC(FM) Greece NY 3 hrs
*WVKR-FM Poughkeepsie NY 9 hrs
*WAER(FM) Syracuse NY 3 hrs
*WBWC(FM) Berea OH 5 hrs
*KGOU(FM) Norman OK 4 hrs
*KROU(FM) Spencer OK 4 hrs
*WQLN-FM Erie PA 2 hrs
*WIUP-FM Indiana PA 4 hrs
*WVBU-FM Lewisburg PA 1 hr
*WHYY-FM Philadelphia PA 10 hrs
*WKDU(FM) Philadelphia PA 2 hrs
*WPSU(FM) State College PA 3 hrs
WPHD(FM) Tioga PA 2 hrs
*WRDV(FM) Warminster PA 3 hrs
WVBI(FM) Block Island RI 4 hrs
*WPLS-FM Greenville SC 2 hrs
*KTEQ(FM) Rapid City SD 3 hrs
WRLT-FM Franklin TN 2 hrs
*WUTS(FM) Sewanee TN 4 hrs
*KTRU(FM) Houston TX 1 hr
*KTPB(FM) Kilgore TX 6 hrs
KUTQ(FM) Bountiful UT 2 hrs
*KRCL(FM) Salt Lake City UT 5 hrs
WLDJ(FM) Appomattox VA 8 hrs
*KPBX-FM Spokane WA
*WYMS(FM) Milwaukee WI 14 hrs
*WRFW(FM) River Falls WI
*WVWC(FM) Buckhannon WV 4 hrs
*WWVU-FM Morgantown WV 6 hrs
KMTN(FM) Jackson WY
KLDI(AM) Laramie WY 3 hrs

News

KIAL(AM) Unalaska AK 14 hrs
KJBN(AM) Little Rock AR
KWXY(AM) Cathedral City CA 2 hrs
KWXY-FM Cathedral City CA 2 hrs
KZIQ-FM Ridgecrest CA
*KDNK(FM) Carbondale CO 10 hrs
KTMG(AM) Deer Trail CO
WILI-FM Willimantic CT 1 hr
WRZN(AM) Hernando FL 4 hrs
WOZN(FM) Key West FL 1 hr

Broadcasting & Cable Yearbook 1994
B-582

Special Programming on Radio Stations in the U.S.

WMGA(AM) Moultrie GA 4 hrs
WJEM(AM) Valdosta GA
KLGA(AM) Algona IA
*KHKE(FM) Cedar Falls IA 17 hrs
KTFC(FM) Sioux City IA 10 hrs
WCBR-FM Arlington Heights IL 4 hrs
*WPCD(FM) Champaign IL 8 hrs
WUZR(FM) Bicknell IN
WXBC(FM) Hardinsburg KY 15 hrs
WMJL(AM) Marion KY
WMJL-FM Marion KY
WADN(AM) Concord MA 7 hrs
WACM(AM) West Springfield MA
WSMD(FM) Mechanicsville MD 14 hrs
*WPHS(FM) Warren MI 5 hrs
KJJK(AM) Fergus Falls MN
KDWA(AM) Hastings MN
KSIM(AM) Sikeston MO
KMSO(FM) Missoula MT 3 hrs
WHLQ(FM) Louisburg NC
KDSR(FM) Williston ND
*KZUM(FM) Lincoln NE 11 hrs
WMSA(AM) Massena NY
WJZR(FM) Rochester NY 1 hr
WRQI(FM) South Bristol Township NY 1 hr
WNYV(FM) Whitehall NY 1 hr
KVLH(AM) Pauls Valley OK 18 hrs
*WRLC(FM) Williamsport PA 12 hrs
WBMJ(AM) San Juan PR 7 hrs
*WRTU(FM) San Juan PR 7 hrs
WIVV(AM) Vieques PR 7 hrs
WRIP(AM) Lake City SC
WAMB(AM) Donelson TN 6 hrs
WAMB-FM Donelson TN 6 hrs
WTRB-FM Ripley TN
KXYL(AM) Brownwood TX
KCYL(AM) Lampasas TX 14 hrs
KTWN(AM) Texarkana TX
WHLF(AM) South Boston VA
WHEO(AM) Stuart VA 10 hrs
*KASB(FM) Bellevue WA 3 hrs
KBRO(AM) Bremerton WA
*KSER(FM) Everett WA 17 hrs
WCNZ(AM) Sheboygan WI 4 hrs
*KUWJ(FM) Jackson WY 3 hrs
*KUWR(FM) Laramie WY 3 hrs

News/Talk

WCCC-FM Hartford CT 10 hrs
WCCC(AM) West Hartford CT 10 hrs
*WWGC(FM) Carrollton GA 1 hr
KBKB(AM) Fort Madison IA 15 hrs
KWEI(AM) Weiser ID
*WHFH(FM) Flossmoor IL 1 hr
WFXW(AM) Geneva IL 15 hrs
WKKX(FM) Jerseyville IL 3 hrs
*WLTL(FM) La Grange IL 10 hrs
*WLRA(FM) Lockport IL 10 hrs
WITZ-FM Jasper IN 3 hrs
WCBR(AM) Richmond KY
*WUMB-FM Boston MA 17 hrs
WDLF(FM) Old Fort NC 5 hrs
WCBQ(AM) Oxford NC
WSNJ(AM) Bridgeton NJ
WSNJ-FM Bridgeton NJ
*WJSV(FM) Morristown NJ 3 hrs
*WITC(FM) Cazenovia NY 3 hrs
WHUC(AM) Hudson NY 3 hrs
*WFNP(FM) New Paltz NY 5 hrs
WJJL(AM) Niagara Falls NY 5 hrs
KIMY(FM) Watonga OK 7 hrs
*WFSE(FM) Edinboro PA 3 hrs
*WQLN-FM Erie PA 3 hrs
WBCU(AM) Union SC 10 hrs
*KAZI(FM) Austin TX
KTWN(AM) Texarkana TX
WZAO(AM) Moundsville WV
WMOV(AM) Ravenswood WV 2 hrs
KMER(AM) Kemmerer WY 7 hrs

Nostalgia

*KSPC(FM) Claremont CA 3 hrs
KMJ(AM) Fresno CA 7 hrs
*KSAK(FM) Walnut CA
KWHO(FM) Weed CA 2 hrs
*WAMU(FM) Washington DC 4 hrs
*WVUD(FM) Newark DE 1 hr
*KTPR(FM) Fort Dodge IA 4 hrs
KCJJ(AM) Iowa City IA 7 hrs
*KCMR(FM) Mason City IA 10 hrs
WCRI(FM) Eureka IL 5 hrs
KWKS(FM) Winfield KS 3 hrs
KPCH(FM) Dubach LA 7 hrs
*WBYQ(FM) Baltimore MD 6 hrs
KCHK(AM) New Prague MN 18 hrs
KCHK-FM New Prague MN 18 hrs
KBMG(FM) Hamilton MT 3 hrs
WDOS(AM) Oneonta NY 2 hrs
WASN(AM) Campbell OH 5 hrs
*WFSE(FM) Edinboro PA 2 hrs
WLSH(AM) Lansford PA 3 hrs
WWDB(FM) Philadelphia PA 10 hrs
WCSV(AM) Crossville TN 5 hrs
WEGE(FM) Crossville TN 5 hrs
KLSR(AM) Memphis TX 3 hrs
KLSR-FM Memphis TX 3 hrs
WSTK(AM) Colonial Heights VA 2 hrs
WNHV(AM) White River Junction VT
KEYG(AM) Grand Coulee WA 4 hrs
WHTL-FM Whitehall WI 2 hrs
KLDI(AM) Laramie WY 6 hrs
KRQU(FM) Laramie WY 6 hrs

Oldies

*KSKO(AM) McGrath AK 6 hrs
KRSA(AM) Petersburg AK 5 hrs
*WVSU-FM Birmingham AL 4 hrs
WEBJ(AM) Brewton AL 14 hrs
WRJM-FM Geneva AL 11 hrs
*WJAB(FM) Huntsville AL 3 hrs
WQLS-FM Ozark AL 6 hrs
KTCN(FM) Eureka Springs AR 2 hrs
KEZA(FM) Fayetteville AR
*KAZU(FM) Pacific Grove CA 5 hrs
*KSPB(FM) Pebble Beach CA 4 hrs
*KUOP(FM) Stockton CA 3 hrs
*KCEQ(FM) Walnut Creek CA 3 hrs
KRAI-FM Craig CO 9 hrs
*KWSB-FM Gunnison CO 1 hr
KIDN-FM Hayden CO 8 hrs
*WESU(FM) Middletown CT 2 hrs
*WDCU(FM) Washington DC 3 hrs
*WPFW(FM) Washington DC 3 hrs
WKHI(FM) Bethany Beach DE 7 hrs
*WVUD(FM) Newark DE 6 hrs
WECY(AM) Seaford DE 6 hrs
WECY-FM Seaford DE 6 hrs
WXCV(FM) Homosassa Springs FL 6 hrs
WIIS(FM) Key West FL 5 hrs
WKAT(AM) North Miami FL 3 hrs
WHBT(AM) Tallahassee FL 5 hrs
WCWB-FM Trenton FL
WRFC(AM) Athens GA 6 hrs
*WUOG(FM) Athens GA 2 hrs
*WCLK(FM) Atlanta GA 3 hrs
WYTH(AM) Madison GA 10 hrs
WJAT-FM Swainsboro GA 10 hrs
WGOV(AM) Valdosta GA 10 hrs
WBIW(AM) Bedford IN
WLNB(FM) Ligonier IN 6 hrs
*WECI(FM) Richmond IN 3 hrs
KKJQ(FM) Garden City KS 10 hrs
KJLS(FM) Hays KS 5 hrs
KFNF(FM) Oberlin KS 3 hrs
WCKU(FM) Nicholasville KY 5 hrs
WKKS(AM) Vanceburg KY 7 hrs
WLKS(AM) West Liberty KY 19 hrs
*KLPI-FM Ruston LA 12 hrs
WXLO-FM Fitchburg MA 5 hrs
WHAI(AM) Greenfield MA 13 hrs
WHAI-FM Greenfield MA 13 hrs
WRSI(FM) Greenfield MA 5 hrs
*WAVM(FM) Maynard MA 1 hr
*WMLN-FM Milton MA 4 hrs
*WEAA(FM) Baltimore MD 4 hrs
*WTMD(FM) Towson MD 3 hrs
*WKHS(FM) Worton MD 6 hrs
WCFX(FM) Clare MI 3 hrs
WUPY(FM) Ontonagon MI 4 hrs
KASM(AM) Albany MN
KZLT-FM East Grand Forks MN 8 hrs
KEYL(AM) Long Prairie MN 3 hrs
KNUJ(AM) New Ulm MN 8 hrs
KXLP(FM) New Ulm MN 15 hrs
KOLV(FM) Olivia MN
KSTP-FM St. Paul MN 4 hrs
KKAQ(AM) Thief River Falls MN 6 hrs
KGRC(FM) Hannibal MO 3 hrs
*KJLU(FM) Jefferson City MO
KIRK(FM) Lebanon MO 6 hrs
WUMS(FM) University MS 2 hrs
*WNAA(FM) Greensboro NC 2 hrs
WCCA(FM) Shallotte NC 6 hrs
*WHYC(FM) Swan Quarter NC 16 hrs
KXPO(AM) Grafton ND 4 hrs
KXPO-FM Grafton ND 4 hrs
KRFS-FM Superior NE 8 hrs
*WDVR(FM) Delaware Township NJ 13 hrs
*WNTI(FM) Hackettstown NJ 3 hrs
*WTSR(FM) Trenton NJ 3 hrs
KHWK(FM) Tonopah NV
*WCEB(FM) Corning NY 6 hrs
WWSC(AM) Glens Falls NY 2 hrs
WVBR-FM Ithaca NY 10 hrs
*WFUV(FM) New York NY 2 hrs
*WNYU-FM New York NY 3 hrs
WKXZ(FM) Norwich NY 4 hrs
WHUD(FM) Peekskill NY 5 hrs
WPDH(FM) Poughkeepsie NY 2 hrs
WSFW(AM) Seneca Falls NY 3 hrs
WSFW-FM Seneca Falls NY 3 hrs
*WRDL(FM) Ashland OH 4 hrs
KYTE(FM) Newport OR 6 hrs
KMCQ(FM) The Dalles OR 6 hrs
WMKX(FM) Brookville PA 8 hrs
*WDNR(FM) Chester PA 2 hrs
WOKW(FM) Curwensville PA 2 hrs
WCCS(AM) Homer City PA 9 hrs
WIXZ(AM) McKeesport PA 9 hrs
WLSW(FM) Scottdale PA 6 hrs
*WPSU(FM) State College PA 3 hrs
WPJS(AM) Conway SC
WBHC-FM Hampton SC 14 hrs
WHSC-FM Hartsville SC 6 hrs
WSHG(FM) Ridgeland SC 4 hrs
WCSV(AM) Crossville TN 2 hrs
WEGE(FM) Crossville TN 2 hrs
WMXX-FM Jackson TN 15 hrs
WIST(FM) Lobelville TN 18 hrs
*WFSK(FM) Nashville TN 3 hrs
WCDT(AM) Winchester TN 6 hrs
KORQ-FM Abilene TX 2 hrs
KFYN(AM) Bonham TX 6 hrs
KFYZ-FM Bonham TX 6 hrs
*KTRU(FM) Houston TX 3 hrs
KMIA(FM) Jasper TX 6 hrs
KKMY(FM) Orange TX 17 hrs
KBUS(FM) Paris TX 6 hrs
WTSA-FM Brattleboro VT 16 hrs
WIZN(FM) Vergennes VT 3 hrs
WISS(AM) Berlin WI 2 hrs
WISS-FM Berlin WI 2 hrs
WRDN(AM) Durand WI 4 hrs
*WRFW(FM) River Falls WI
WDUX-FM Waupaca WI 6 hrs
*WFGH(FM) Fort Gay WV 19 hrs
*WWVU-FM Morgantown WV 8 hrs
KTRZ(FM) Riverton WY 6 hrs
KROE(AM) Sheridan WY 6 hrs

Other

KADX(FM) Houston AK 2 hrs
KABN(AM) Long Island AK
*KTNA(FM) Talkeetna AK 3 hrs
*WVSU-FM Birmingham AL 3 hrs
*WMBV(FM) Dixon's Mills AL 9 hrs
WABF(AM) Fairhope AL 4 hrs
*WVUA-FM Tuscaloosa AL 3 hrs
KWXI(AM) Glenwood AR
KBHS(AM) Hot Springs AR 1 hr
KIXF(FM) Baker CA
*KKUP(FM) Cupertino CA 13 hrs
KVVQ(AM) Hesperia CA
KNAC(FM) Long Beach CA 2 hrs
*KFJC(FM) Los Altos CA 4 hrs
*KPFK(FM) Los Angeles CA 13 hrs
*KSBR(FM) Mission Viejo CA 10 hrs
*KMPO(FM) Modesto CA 3 hrs
KTRB(AM) Modesto CA 1 hr
*KCSN(FM) Northridge CA 5 hrs
*KZYX(FM) Philo CA 8 hrs
KNBR(AM) San Francisco CA 14 hrs
*KSJS(FM) San Jose CA 2 hrs
KGLW(AM) San Luis Obispo CA
KVEC(AM) San Luis Obispo CA
*KUSP(FM) Santa Cruz CA 20 hrs
*KZSC(FM) Santa Cruz CA 2 hrs
KRZQ-FM Tahoe City CA 2 hrs
*KCEQ(FM) Walnut Creek CA 5 hrs
*KRCC(FM) Colorado Springs CO 5 hrs
KWYD(AM) Colorado Springs CO 1 hr
KKLY(FM) Delta CO 6 hrs
*KDUR(FM) Durango CO 3 hrs
KTCL(FM) Fort Collins CO 2 hrs
KLOV(AM) Loveland CO 18 hrs
KRDZ(AM) Wray CO 3 hrs
*WGRS(FM) Guilford CT 1 hr
WCCC-FM Hartford CT 10 hrs
*WRTC-FM Hartford CT 6 hrs
*WESU(FM) Middletown CT 5 hrs
*WMNR(FM) Monroe CT 1 hr
*WCNI(FM) New London CT 3 hrs
*WRXC(FM) Shelton CT 1 hr
*WGSK(FM) South Kent CT 4 hrs
WSNG(AM) Torrington CT 1 hr
WCCC(AM) West Hartford CT 10 hrs
*WWUH(FM) West Hartford CT 1 hr
*WPFW(FM) Washington DC 2 hrs
WWUS(FM) Big Pine Key FL 4 hrs
WWTK(AM) Lake Placid FL 1 hr
WPBR(AM) Palm Beach FL 17 hrs
*WUWF(FM) Pensacola FL
WDCQ(AM) Pine Island Center FL
WWNN(AM) Pompano Beach FL
WHKR(FM) Rockledge FL 1 hr
WPIK(FM) Summerland Key FL 4 hrs
*WBVM(FM) Tampa FL 8 hrs
*WUOG(FM) Athens GA 3 hrs
*WRAS(FM) Atlanta GA 7 hrs
*WREK(FM) Atlanta GA 14 hrs
WGAC(AM) Augusta GA 3 hrs
*WGHR(FM) Marietta GA
KAHU(AM) Hilo HI
KWXX-FM Hilo HI 20 hrs
*KTUH(FM) Honolulu HI 11 hrs
KWAI(AM) Honolulu HI 12 hrs
KRTR-FM Kailua HI 4 hrs
*KIFO(AM) Pearl City HI 2 hrs
*KKUA(FM) Wailuku HI 2 hrs
KLGA(AM) Algona IA
*KRUI-FM Iowa City IA 8 hrs
KRLC(AM) Lewiston ID 2 hrs
KMCL-FM McCall ID 1 hr
WXAN(FM) Ava IL 5 hrs
*WSIU(FM) Carbondale IL 1 hr
*WLUW(FM) Chicago IL 12 hrs
*WTPC(FM) Elsah IL 9 hrs
*WNUR-FM Evanston IL 2 hrs
*WHFH(FM) Flossmoor IL 4 hrs
WYMG(FM) Jacksonville IL 1 hr
*WLRA(FM) Lockport IL 15 hrs
*WUSI(FM) Olney IL 1 hr
WGFA-FM Watseka IL 2 hrs
WBQR(FM) Attica IN 3 hrs
*WSWI(AM) Evansville IN 1 hr
WBDC(FM) Huntingburg IN 5 hrs
*WBDG(FM) Indianapolis IN 5 hrs
*WVXR(FM) Richmond IN 8 hrs
WAWC(FM) Syracuse IN 5 hrs
KPHN(AM) Pittsburg KS
KULY(AM) Ulysses KS 4 hrs
*KCFN(FM) Wichita KS 2 hrs
KICT-FM Wichita KS 8 hrs
*WKCC(FM) Grayson KY 3 hrs
*WUOL(FM) Louisville KY 7 hrs
WMQQ(FM) Springfield KY 12 hrs
*KLSP(FM) Angola LA 4 hrs
KEUN(AM) Eunice LA 6 hrs
KFXZ(FM) Maurice LA 4 hrs
*KNWD(FM) Natchitoches LA 2 hrs
*WTUL(FM) New Orleans LA 6 hrs
KVLA(AM) Vidalia LA
*WFCR(FM) Amherst MA 4 hrs
*WGBH(FM) Boston MA 3 hrs
*WUMB-FM Boston MA 5 hrs
WUNR(AM) Brookline MA 2 hrs
*WXPL(FM) Fitchburg MA 2 hrs
*WDJM-FM Framingham MA 2 hrs
WLLH(AM) Lowell MA 7 hrs
WFNX(FM) Lynn MA 3 hrs
WBIV(AM) Natick MA 7 hrs
WNTN(AM) Newton MA 1 hr
*WOMR(FM) Provincetown MA 2 hrs
*WYAJ(FM) Sudbury MA 3 hrs
WRCA(AM) Waltham MA
WSMD(FM) Mechanicsville MD 1 hr
*WSCL(FM) Salisbury MD 3 hrs
*WERU-FM Blue Hill ME 4 hrs
WQDY(AM) Calais ME 2 hrs
WQDY-FM Calais ME 2 hrs
*WRBC(FM) Lewiston ME 6 hrs
*WMEB-FM Orono ME 10 hrs
WAAM(AM) Ann Arbor MI 8 hrs
WYTW(FM) Cadillac MI
*WDBM(FM) East Lansing MI 1 hr
WILS(AM) Lansing MI 6 hrs
WMPX(AM) Midland MI
*WOAS(FM) Ontonagon MI 3 hrs
*WSGR-FM Port Huron MI 6 hrs
*WPHS(FM) Warren MI 1 hr
WKLK(AM) Cloquet MN 1 hr
WLKX-FM Forest Lake MN 9 hrs
KTCJ(AM) Minneapolis MN 1 hr
KTCZ-FM Minneapolis MN 1 hr
*WMCN(FM) St. Paul MN 10 hrs
*WMCN(FM) St. Paul MN 4 hrs
*KWUR(FM) Clayton MO 12 hrs
*KCOU(FM) Columbia MO 4 hrs
*KCFV(FM) Ferguson MO 4 hrs
KXOK(AM) St. Louis MO 5 hrs
*WUSM-FM Hattiesburg MS 3 hrs
WJNS-FM Yazoo City MS 16 hrs
*WSGE(FM) Dallas NC 10 hrs
WERX-FM Edenton NC
*WUAG(FM) Greensboro NC 3 hrs
WKGX(AM) Lenoir NC 5 hrs
WVOD(FM) Manteo NC 4 hrs
*WKNC-FM Raleigh NC 9 hrs
WWMG(FM) Shelby NC
WTAB(AM) Tabor City NC
WYNA(FM) Tabor City NC 6 hrs
KHOL(AM) Beulah ND
KHRT(AM) Minot ND 6 hrs
*KWSC(FM) Wayne NE 2 hrs
KAWL(AM) York NE 3 hrs
WMOU(AM) Berlin NH 3 hrs
WDCR(AM) Hanover NH 3 hrs
WFRD(FM) Hanover NH 1 hr
WFRD(FM) Hanover NH 2 hrs
WMTK(FM) Littleton NH
WWNH(AM) Madbury NH 24 hrs
*WMNJ(FM) Madison NJ 6 hrs
*WRSU-FM New Brunswick NJ 2 hrs
WADB(FM) Point Pleasant NJ 1 hr
*WPSC-FM Wayne NJ 12 hrs
*KRUX(FM) Las Cruces NM 2 hrs
KBAC(FM) Las Vegas NM 5 hrs
*KEDP(FM) Las Vegas NM 6 hrs
*KSFR(FM) Santa Fe NM 10 hrs
*KUNV(FM) Las Vegas NV 10 hrs
*WCDB(FM) Albany NY 3 hrs
*WBNY(FM) Buffalo NY 3 hrs
*WSUC-FM Cortland NY 7 hrs
WDNY(AM) Dansville NY 4 hrs
WZZZ(AM) Fulton NY 1 hr
*WGSU(FM) Geneseo NY 11 hrs
*WGMC(FM) Greece NY 1 hr
WHUC(AM) Hudson NY 1 hr
WLVL(AM) Lockport NY 6 hrs
WYBG(AM) Massena NY
WABC(AM) New York NY 29 hrs
*WFUV(FM) New York NY 5 hrs
*WNYU-FM New York NY 13 hrs
*WONY(FM) Oneonta NY 6 hrs
WSGO(AM) Oswego NY 1 hr
WNWX(AM) Plattsburgh NY 17 hrs
*WPLT(FM) Plattsburgh NY 10 hrs
WEOK(AM) Poughkeepsie NY 2 hrs
*WVKR-FM Poughkeepsie NY 8 hrs
WQBK(AM) Rensselaer NY 5 hrs
WNYV(FM) Whitehall NY 3 hrs
WPKO-FM Bellefontaine OH
*WBWC(FM) Berea OH 10 hrs
WCEZ(FM) Delaware OH 1 hr
WPFB(AM) Middletown OH 2 hrs
*WOBC-FM Oberlin OH 8 hrs
*WOBN(FM) Westerville OH 2 hrs
*WYSU(FM) Youngstown OH 1 hr
*KOKF(FM) Edmond OK 7 hrs
KKBS(FM) Guymon OK 5 hrs
KTFX(FM) Tulsa OK 1 hr
*KWGS(FM) Tulsa OK 50 hrs
KZZK-FM Creswell OR 4 hrs
*KLCC(FM) Eugene OR 9 hrs
*KEOL(FM) La Grande OR 20 hrs
KQIK(AM) Lakeview OR 1 hr
KQIK-FM Lakeview OR 1 hr
*KLCO(FM) Newport OR 6 hrs
*KBOO(FM) Portland OR 3 hrs
*WDCV-FM Carlisle PA 1 hr
*WJRH(FM) Easton PA 6 hrs
*WVBU-FM Lewisburg PA 2 hrs
WEDO(AM) McKeesport PA 3 hrs
WXVX(AM) Monroeville PA
*WKDU(FM) Philadelphia PA 4 hrs
WJAS(AM) Pittsburgh PA 2 hrs
*WRCT(FM) Pittsburgh PA 12 hrs
*WXAC(FM) Reading PA 5 hrs
*WXLV(FM) Schnecksville PA 6 hrs
WPIC(AM) Sharon PA 12 hrs
WRAK-FM Williamsport PA 2 hrs
*WRIU(FM) Kingston RI 6 hrs
WALE(AM) Providence RI 1 hr
WVGB(AM) Beaufort SC
*WPLS-FM Greenville SC 4 hrs
WHSC(AM) Hartsville SC 6 hrs
WJBS(AM) Holly Hill SC 2 hrs
WSHG(FM) Ridgeland SC 3 hrs
WQMC(AM) Sumter SC 2 hrs
WNAX(AM) Yankton SD 15 hrs
*WHCB(FM) Bristol TN 2 hrs
WWAM(AM) Jasper TN 1 hr
WKGN(AM) Knoxville TN 1 hr
WEGR(FM) Memphis TN
KHKS(FM) Denton TX
*KNTU(FM) Denton TX 9 hrs
KPRC(AM) Houston TX 16 hrs
KMIA(FM) Jasper TX 2 hrs
*KTPB(FM) Kilgore TX 2 hrs
*KOCV(FM) Odessa TX 4 hrs
KNCN(FM) Sinton TX 1 hr
WNVA(AM) Norton VA
WHLF(AM) South Boston VA
WDCM(FM) Cruz Bay VI 8 hrs
NEW AM Berlin VT 24 hrs
*WVPS(FM) Burlington VT 2 hrs
WMOO(FM) Derby Center VT 3 hrs
WIKE(AM) Newport VT 5 hrs
WVNR(AM) Poultney VT 4 hrs
*WRVT(FM) Rutland VT 2 hrs
*KGRG(FM) Auburn WA 5 hrs
KBLV(AM) Bellevue WA 12 hrs
KGNW(AM) Burien-Seattle WA
KLDY(AM) Lacey WA 9 hrs
KTOL(AM) Lacey WA 6 hrs
*KZUU(FM) Pullman WA 2 hrs
*KWRS(FM) Spokane WA 4 hrs
KMTT(AM) Tacoma WA
*KPLU-FM Tacoma WA 2 hrs
*KVTI(FM) Tacoma WA 3 hrs
*WBSD(FM) Burlington WI 5 hrs
*WSUP(FM) Platteville WI 6 hrs
*WCCX(FM) Waukesha WI 3 hrs
*WVPB(FM) Beckley WV 2 hrs
*WVPN(FM) Charleston WV 2 hrs
*WVWV(FM) Huntington WV 2 hrs
*WVEP(FM) Martinsburg WV 2 hrs
*WVNP(FM) Wheeling WV 2 hrs

Polish

*KXCI(FM) Tucson AZ 2 hrs
*KSPC(FM) Claremont CA 3 hrs
KTYM(AM) Inglewood CA 1 hr
*KPCC(FM) Pasadena CA 1 hr
KEST(AM) San Francisco CA 1 hr
*KUSF(FM) San Francisco CA 1 hr
KDTA(AM) Delta CO 1 hr
WADS(AM) Ansonia CT 14 hrs
WPRX(AM) Bristol CT 8 hrs
*WVOF(FM) Fairfield CT 3 hrs
*WRTC-FM Hartford CT 3 hrs
WMMW(AM) Meriden CT 1 hr
WCNX(AM) Middletown CT 1 hr
WRYM(AM) New Britain CT 5 hrs
*WCNI(FM) New London CT 3 hrs
WICH(AM) Norwich CT 1 hr
WATR(AM) Waterbury CT 2 hrs
WWCO(AM) Waterbury CT 1 hr
*WWUH(FM) West Hartford CT 3 hrs
WILI(AM) Willimantic CT 2 hrs
WLVU(AM) Dunedin FL 1 hr
WLBE(AM) Leesburg FL 2 hrs
WPSO(AM) New Port Richey FL 2 hrs
WSBB(AM) New Smyrna Beach FL 1 hr
WQSA(AM) Sarasota FL 1 hr
*WBVM(FM) Tampa FL 1 hr
KSKB(FM) Brooklyn IA 1 hr
*KCUI(FM) Pella IA
WEDC(AM) Chicago IL 7 hrs
WSBC(AM) Chicago IL 11 hrs
WCEV(AM) Cicero IL 23 hrs
WVVX(FM) Highland Park IL 8 hrs
WJOB(AM) Hammond IN 2 hrs
WIMS(AM) Michigan City IN 3 hrs
WIWO(AM) South Bend IN 7 hrs

Broadcasting & Cable Yearbook 1994
B-583

Special Programming on Radio Stations in the U.S.

*WMUA(FM) Amherst MA 5 hrs
WBET(AM) Brockton MA 2 hrs
WUNR(AM) Brookline MA 2 hrs
WACE(AM) Chicopee MA 2 hrs
WHTB(AM) Fall River MA 2 hrs
WHAV(AM) Haverhill MA 1 hr
WLYN(AM) Lynn MA 2 hrs
WCTK(FM) New Bedford MA 2 hrs
WDIS(AM) Norfolk MA 2 hrs
*WJJW(FM) North Adams MA 3 hrs
WHMP(AM) Northampton MA 3 hrs
*WOZQ(FM) Northampton MA 3 hrs
WBRK(AM) Pittsfield MA 2 hrs
WESX(AM) Salem MA 2 hrs
*WBSL-FM Sheffield MA 1 hr
WESO(AM) Southbridge MA 2 hrs
WQVR(FM) Southbridge MA 2 hrs
*WTCC(FM) Springfield MA 2 hrs
WARE(AM) Ware MA 3 hrs
WGFP(AM) Webster MA 1 hr
*WCUW(FM) Worcester MA 3 hrs
WORC(AM) Worcester MA 1 hr
WBMD(AM) Baltimore MD 2 hrs
*WTMD(FM) Towson MD 2 hrs
WATZ(AM) Alpena MI 2 hrs
WLEW(AM) Bad Axe MI 2 hrs
WRQT(FM) Bear Lake MI 2 hrs
WKNX(AM) Frankenmuth MI 5 hrs
WSNQ(AM) Gaylord MI 2 hrs
WIBM(AM) Jackson MI 2 hrs
WXYQ(FM) Manistee MI 6 hrs
WIFN(AM) Marine City MI 3 hrs
*WOES(FM) Ovid-Elsie MI 1 hr
WMIC(AM) Sandusky MI 4 hrs
*WPHS(FM) Warren MI 2 hrs
WBMB(AM) West Branch MI 6 hrs
WKKQ(AM) Nashwauk MN 2 hrs
KCHK(AM) New Prague MN 18 hrs
KSTL(AM) St. Louis MO 2 hrs
KJSK(AM) Columbus NE 13 hrs
KOTD(AM) Plattsmouth NE 2 hrs
*WUNH(FM) Durham NH 2 hrs
WSMN(AM) Nashua NH 1 hr
WJDM(AM) Elizabeth NJ 3 hrs
WCTC(AM) New Brunswick NJ 2 hrs
*WRSU-FM New Brunswick NJ 1 hr
WERA(AM) Plainfield NJ 2 hrs
*WSOU(FM) South Orange NJ 2 hrs
WTTM(AM) Trenton NJ 2 hrs
WCSS(AM) Amsterdam NY 5 hrs
WAUB(AM) Auburn NY 4 hrs
*WBFO(FM) Buffalo NY 3 hrs
WHTT(AM) Buffalo NY 10 hrs
WHTT-FM Buffalo NY 10 hrs
WWKB(AM) Buffalo NY 1 hr
WVOA(FM) DeRuyter NY 2 hrs
WDOE(AM) Dunkirk NY 6 hrs
WSIV(AM) East Syracuse NY 1 hr
WELM(AM) Elmira NY 3 hrs
*WBAU(FM) Garden City NY 2 hrs
*WHPC(FM) Garden City NY 1 hr
*WGMC(FM) Greece NY 1 hr
*WRHU(FM) Hempstead NY 3 hrs
WHUC(AM) Hudson NY 1 hr
WKNY(AM) Kingston NY 1 hr
WXRL(AM) Lancaster NY 5 hrs
*WVCR-FM Loudonville NY 3 hrs
*WFUV(FM) New York NY 2 hrs
*WNYE(FM) New York NY 5 hrs
WHLD(AM) Niagara Falls NY 19 hrs
WSGO(AM) Oswego NY 1 hr
WEOK(AM) Poughkeepsie NY 1 hr
*WVKR-FM Poughkeepsie NY 5 hrs
WRIV(AM) Riverhead NY 4 hrs
WGGO(AM) Salamanca NY 1 hr
*WSPN(FM) Saratoga Springs NY 3 hrs
WVKZ(AM) Schenectady NY
*WUSB(FM) Stony Brook NY 1 hr
WIBX(AM) Utica NY 3 hrs
WRUN(AM) Utica NY 1 hr
WUTQ(AM) Utica NY 4 hrs
WNYV(FM) Whitehall NY 1 hr
*WAPS(FM) Akron OH 1 hr
WOMP(AM) Bellaire OH 2 hrs
WASN(AM) Campbell OH 1 hr
*WCPN(FM) Cleveland OH 1 hr
*WCSB(FM) Cleveland OH 1 hr
WERE(AM) Cleveland OH 2 hrs
*WRUW-FM Cleveland OH 3 hrs
*WKTL(FM) Struthers OH 14 hrs
WCWA(AM) Toledo OH 1 hr
WTOD(AM) Toledo OH 4 hrs
WELW(AM) Willoughby-Eastlake OH 2 hrs
*WYSO(FM) Yellow Springs OH 2 hrs
*WMUH(FM) Allentown PA 3 hrs
WXKW(AM) Allentown PA 3 hrs
WVAM(AM) Altoona PA 1 hr
WGPA(AM) Bethlehem PA 2 hrs
WCDL(AM) Carbondale PA 8 hrs
WPLW(AM) Carnegie PA 2 hrs
WESA(AM) Charleroi PA 2 hrs
WESA-FM Charleroi PA 2 hrs
WOWQ(FM) DuBois PA 3 hrs
*WERG(FM) Erie PA 3 hrs
WFLP(AM) Erie PA 1 hr
*WMCE(FM) Erie PA 3 hrs
WPSE(AM) Erie PA 3 hrs
WHJB(AM) Greensburg PA 4 hrs
WCCS(AM) Homer City PA 3 hrs
WBCW(AM) Jeannette PA 5 hrs
WIBF-FM Jenkintown PA 2 hrs
WLSH(AM) Lansford PA 3 hrs
WQTW(AM) Latrobe PA 5 hrs
WYOS(FM) Nanticoke PA 3 hrs
WGBN(AM) New Kensington PA 3 hrs
WTEL(AM) Philadelphia PA 7 hrs
*WRCT(FM) Pittsburgh PA 20 hrs
WARD(AM) Pittston PA 6 hrs
WPAZ(AM) Pottstown PA 1 hr
WRAW(AM) Reading PA 2 hrs
*WXLV(FM) Schnecksville PA 6 hrs
WISL(AM) Shamokin PA 2 hrs
WPIC(AM) Sharon PA 6 hrs
WVPO(AM) Stroudsburg PA 1 hr
WMBS(AM) Uniontown PA 2 hrs
WKZV(AM) Washington PA 3 hrs
WICE(AM) Pawtucket RI 1 hr
WRIB(AM) Providence RI 2 hrs
WKRI(AM) West Warwick RI 2 hrs
WNRI(AM) Woonsocket RI 2 hrs
WOON(AM) Woonsocket RI 6 hrs
KYNT(AM) Yankton SD 1 hr
KQRO-FM Cuero TX 3 hrs
KPJN(FM) Gonzales TX 5 hrs
KVLG(AM) La Grange TX 6 hrs
KBEC(AM) Waxahachie TX 2 hrs
KANI(AM) Wharton TX 6 hrs
WVNR(AM) Poultney VT 1 hr
WSYB(AM) Rutland VT 1 hr
WTKM(AM) Hartford WI 1 hr
WYLO(AM) Jackson WI 2 hrs
WJMT(AM) Merrill WI 3 hrs
*WYMS(FM) Milwaukee WI 3 hrs
WXOL(AM) Oshkosh WI 2 hrs
WCWC(AM) Ripon WI 2 hrs
WSPO(AM) Stevens Point WI 1 hr
WMOV(AM) Ravenswood WV 1 hr
WEIR(AM) Weirton WV 1 hr
WKWK(AM) Wheeling WV 2 hrs
KROE(AM) Sheridan WY 2 hrs

Polka

*KUOR-FM Redlands CA 6 hrs
KLOV(AM) Loveland CO 3 hrs
*WQAQ(FM) Hamden CT 4 hrs
*WMNF(FM) Tampa FL
KCRG(AM) Cedar Rapids IA 4 hrs
KDSN(AM) Denison IA 4 hrs
KMAQ(AM) Maquoketa IA 3 hrs
KLEE(AM) Ottumwa IA 1 hr
WCEV(AM) Cicero IL 5 hrs
WAIT(AM) Crystal Lake IL 4 hrs
WLUV(AM) Loves Park IL 6 hrs
WLUV-FM Loves Park IL 6 hrs
WPNA(AM) Oak Park IL 24 hrs
KCAY(FM) Russell KS
KRSL(AM) Russell KS 4 hrs
WNBY(AM) Newberry MI 2 hrs
WUPY(FM) Ontonagon MI 1 hr
WOAP(AM) Owosso MI 3 hrs
WYGR(AM) Wyoming MI 6 hrs
WKLK(AM) Cloquet MN 2 hrs
*KAXE(FM) Grand Rapids MN 2 hrs
WMFG(AM) Hibbing MN 4 hrs
KDUZ(AM) Hutchinson MN 8 hrs
WYRQ(FM) Little Falls MN 2 hrs
WHLB(AM) Virginia MN 8 hrs
KWNO(AM) Winona MN 5 hrs
KHOL(AM) Beulah ND 2 hrs
*KFJM(AM) Grand Forks ND 3 hrs
KHND(AM) Harvey ND 3 hrs
KTNC(AM) Falls City NE 1 hr
KMMJ(AM) Grand Island NE 3 hrs
KOTD(AM) Plattsmouth NE 4 hrs
*WDVR(FM) Delaware Township NJ 2 hrs
WGHT(AM) Pompton Lakes NJ 1 hr
WEHH(AM) Elmira Heights-Horseheads NY 2 hrs
WZZZ(AM) Fulton NY 8 hrs
WTHE(AM) Mineola NY 1 hr
*WAPS(FM) Akron OH 2 hrs
*WZIP(FM) Akron OH 3 hrs
WDPN(AM) Alliance OH 2 hrs
WNDH(FM) Napoleon OH 10 hrs
WKBN(AM) Youngstown OH 2 hrs
KCRC(AM) Enid OK 1 hr
WGPA(AM) Bethlehem PA 5 hrs
WHYL(AM) Carlisle PA 2 hrs
WLSH(AM) Lansford PA 3 hrs
WMXH(AM) Olyphant PA 7 hrs
WHYM(AM) Portage PA 14 hrs
WPAM(AM) Pottsville PA 3 hrs
WWII(AM) Shiremanstown PA 7 hrs
WBAX(AM) Wilkes-Barre PA
KYNT(AM) Yankton SD 1 hr
KWHI(AM) Brenham TX 2 hrs
KQRO(AM) Cuero TX 3 hrs
KCTI(AM) Gonzales TX 5 hrs
KAML(AM) Kenedy-Karnes City TX 1 hr
WATW(AM) Ashland WI 1 hr
WRDN(AM) Durand WI 5 hrs
*WYMS(FM) Milwaukee WI 4 hrs
WCCN(AM) Neillsville WI 10 hrs
WCQM(FM) Park Falls WI 2 hrs
WNBI(AM) Park Falls WI 2 hrs
WIBU(AM) Poynette WI 9 hrs
WDSM(AM) Superior WI 1 hr
WVRQ(AM) Viroqua WI 12 hrs
WEGZ(FM) Washburn WI 3 hrs

Portuguese

KIGS(AM) Hanford CA 12 hrs
*KXLU(FM) Los Angeles CA 1 hr
*KZSC(FM) Santa Cruz CA 2 hrs
KMXN(AM) Santa Rosa CA 2 hrs
KSTN-FM Stockton CA 14 hrs
KXBT(AM) Vallejo CA 1 hr
*WRTC-FM Hartford CT 8 hrs
*WWUH(FM) West Hartford CT 3 hrs
KNDI(AM) Honolulu HI 3 hrs
WEZE(AM) Boston MA 1 hr
WUNR(AM) Brookline MA 2 hrs
WHTB(AM) Fall River MA 6 hrs
WSAR(AM) Fall River MA 3 hrs
*WJUL(FM) Lowell MA 2 hrs
WLLH(AM) Lowell MA 2 hrs
*WMFO(FM) Medford MA 3 hrs
WMRC(AM) Milford MA 2 hrs
*WOZQ(FM) Northampton MA 2 hrs
WPEP(AM) Taunton MA 5 hrs
*WBRS(FM) Waltham MA 2 hrs
WRCA(AM) Waltham MA 1 hr
*WKCR-FM New York NY 2 hrs
WIBF-FM Jenkintown PA 4 hrs
WPHE(AM) Phoenixville PA 3 hrs
WNRI(AM) Woonsocket RI 2 hrs
*WRVU(FM) Nashville TN 1 hr

Progressive

KLCR(FM) Nogales AZ 4 hrs
*KSPC(FM) Claremont CA 3 hrs
KKXX-FM Delano CA 3 hrs
*KUOP(FM) Stockton CA 8 hrs
WRUF-FM Gainesville FL 2 hrs
WXXL(FM) Leesburg FL 6 hrs
*WMNF(FM) Tampa FL
*WRFG(FM) Atlanta GA 6 hrs
*WVVS(FM) Valdosta GA 3 hrs
KQKQ-FM Council Bluffs IA 3 hrs
*WPCD(FM) Champaign IL 12 hrs
WTTS(FM) Bloomington IN 4 hrs
*WDSO(FM) Chesterton IN 8 hrs
*WBDG(FM) Indianapolis IN 5 hrs
*WBKE-FM North Manchester IN 7 hrs
*WECI(FM) Richmond IN 12 hrs
*KLPI-FM Ruston LA 3 hrs
*WHSN(FM) Bangor ME 8 hrs
*WUPI(FM) Presque Isle ME 2 hrs
*WDTR(FM) Detroit MI 1 hr
*WDBM(FM) East Lansing MI 4 hrs
*WFBE(FM) Flint MI 4 hrs
*KWUR(FM) Clayton MO 2 hrs
*KWWC-FM Columbia MO 20 hrs
*KCFV(FM) Ferguson MO 4 hrs
*KMVC(FM) Marshall MO 10 hrs
*KCLC(FM) St. Charles MO 7 hrs
*WKNC-FM Raleigh NC 12 hrs
*KZUM(FM) Lincoln NE 15 hrs
*WPSC-FM Wayne NJ 12 hrs
*KANW(FM) Albuquerque NM 3 hrs
*WITC(FM) Cazenovia NY 10 hrs
WKOJ(FM) Middletown NY 2 hrs
*WONY(FM) Oneonta NY 3 hrs
*WIRQ(FM) Rochester NY 3 hrs
*WSBU(FM) St. Bonaventure NY 10 hrs
*WBGU(FM) Bowling Green OH
*WHSS(FM) Hamilton OH 2 hrs
*KRSC-FM Claremore OK 12 hrs
*WVCS(FM) California PA 6 hrs
*WCUC-FM Clarion PA 9 hrs
WTEL(AM) Philadelphia PA 3 hrs
WPHD(FM) Tioga PA 2 hrs
*WWAS(FM) Williamsport PA 4 hrs
*KTEQ(FM) Rapid City SD 9 hrs
WRLG(FM) Smyrna TN 9 hrs
*WHRV(FM) Norfolk VA 14 hrs
WIZN(FM) Vergennes VT 1 hr
*KZUU(FM) Pullman WA 10 hrs
*WSUP(FM) Platteville WI 6 hrs
*WVWC(FM) Buckhannon WV 4 hrs
*WCDE(FM) Elkins WV 12 hrs

Public Affairs

WEUP(AM) Huntsville AL 1 hr
KMLE(FM) Chandler AZ 1 hr
*KGHR(FM) Tuba City AZ 5 hrs
*KZFR(FM) Chico CA 2 hrs
*KSPC(FM) Claremont CA 3 hrs
*KKUP(FM) Cupertino CA 13 hrs
*KOHL(FM) Fremont CA 4 hrs
*KCRH(FM) Hayward CA 5 hrs
KNAC(FM) Long Beach CA 3 hrs
KYSR(FM) Los Angeles CA 2 hrs
KTRB(AM) Modesto CA 2 hrs
KPSI-FM Palm Springs CA
KDDB(FM) Paso Robles CA
*KCPR(FM) San Luis Obispo CA 9 hrs
KTYD(FM) Santa Barbara CA 1 hr
KMJI(FM) Denver CO 2 hrs
KVVS(AM) Windsor CO
*WWUH(FM) West Hartford CT 20 hrs
WSTW(FM) Wilmington DE 1 hr
WXTB(FM) Clearwater FL 4 hrs
*WVUM(FM) Coral Gables FL 2 hrs
WHOO(AM) Orlando FL
WVOP(AM) Vidalia GA 2 hrs
KKMI(FM) Burlington IA
*KCUI(FM) Pella IA 5 hrs
WCBR-FM Arlington Heights IL 2 hrs
*WEFT(FM) Champaign IL 5 hrs
*WEIU(FM) Charleston IL 5 hrs
*WDGC-FM Downers Grove IL 6 hrs
WLLR-FM East Moline IL 6 hrs
*WEPS(FM) Elgin IL 3 hrs
WLLR(AM) Moline IL 4 hrs
WVAZ(FM) Oak Park IL 2 hrs
WDJB(FM) Columbia City IN
WWLW(FM) Carlisle KY 5 hrs
WVEZ-FM Louisville KY 4 hrs
WWKY(AM) Louisville KY 4 hrs
WMJL(AM) Marion KY 1 hr
WMJL-FM Marion KY 1 hr
*WMMT(FM) Whitesburg KY 3 hrs
WNSH(AM) Beverly MA 2 hrs
*WMLN-FM Milton MA 2 hrs
WBIV(AM) Natick MA 1 hr
*WOMR(FM) Provincetown MA 15 hrs
WSNE(FM) Taunton MA 4 hrs
WMOM(AM) La Plata MD 1 hr
WSMD(FM) Mechanicsville MD 3 hrs
WPGC(AM) Morningside MD
*WERU-FM Blue Hill ME 9 hrs
*WCBN-FM Ann Arbor MI 5 hrs
WJZZ(FM) Detroit MI 2 hrs
*WFBE(FM) Flint MI 10 hrs
WCCY(AM) Houghton MI 1 hr
WOAP(AM) Owosso MI 2 hrs
*KJLU(FM) Jefferson City MO
KCMO-FM Kansas City MO 1 hr
*WUSM-FM Hattiesburg MS 10 hrs
WDUR(AM) Durham NC 4 hrs
WPAQ(AM) Mount Airy NC 1 hr
WKRK(AM) Murphy NC 3 hrs
*KZUM(FM) Lincoln NE 11 hrs
*WRPR(FM) Mahwah NJ 12 hrs
WNNJ(AM) Newton NJ 2 hrs
*WTSR(FM) Trenton NJ 8 hrs
WNJC(AM) Washington Township NJ
*KUNV(FM) Las Vegas NV 10 hrs
WAUB(AM) Auburn NY 10 hrs
*WXLH(FM) Blue Mountain Lake NY
WWHB(FM) Hampton Bays NY
*WRHU(FM) Hempstead NY 4 hrs
*WJFF(FM) Jeffersonville NY 8 hrs
*WSLO(FM) Malone NY
WAQX-FM Manlius NY 1 hr
WKDM(AM) New York NY
*WXLG(FM) North Creek NY
*WDFH(FM) Ossining NY 20 hrs
WZOS(FM) Oswego NY 2 hrs
*WXLU(FM) Peru NY
*WCFE-FM Plattsburgh NY 10 hrs
WRHD(AM) Riverhead NY 3 hrs
WKDY(FM) Rome NY 1 hr
*WSLL(FM) Saranac Lake NY
*WPBX(FM) Southampton NY 1 hr
*WJPZ-FM Syracuse NY 13 hrs
*WARY(FM) Valhalla NY 10 hrs
*WSLJ(FM) Watertown NY
*WAPS(FM) Akron OH 1 hr
*WZIP(FM) Akron OH 2 hrs
WRQN(FM) Bowling Green OH 1 hr
*WRUW-FM Cleveland OH 5 hrs
*WDPS(FM) Dayton OH 6 hrs
WKKY(FM) Geneva OH 2 hrs
*WHSS(FM) Hamilton OH 5 hrs
*KOCC(FM) Oklahoma City OK 4 hrs
*KSMF(FM) Ashland OR 7 hrs
*KSOR(FM) Ashland OR 7 hrs
*KSBA(FM) Coos Bay OR 7 hrs
*KSKF(FM) Klamath Falls OR 7 hrs
WSGD-FM Carbondale PA
*WQLN-FM Erie PA 5 hrs
WCMB(AM) Harrisburg PA 2 hrs
WEYZ(AM) North East PA 1 hr
WRKT(FM) North East PA 1 hr
WIOQ(FM) Philadelphia PA
WSHH(FM) Pittsburgh PA 1 hr
*WRSK(FM) Slippery Rock PA 1 hr
*WRLC(FM) Williamsport PA 2 hrs
WAGS(AM) Bishopville SC 2 hrs
WBIN-FM Benton TN 2 hrs
WQBB-FM Knoxville TN 2 hrs
WGKX(FM) Memphis TN
WQBB(AM) Powell TN 2 hrs
WTRB-FM Ripley TN
KBFM(FM) Edinburg TX
KLDE(FM) Houston TX 1 hr
KHHT(FM) Killeen TX 2 hrs
*KSWP(FM) Lufkin TX 2 hrs
KFGI-FM Luling TX 2 hrs
KKYX(AM) San Antonio TX 2 hrs
KNCN(FM) Sinton TX 1 hr
KVEL(AM) Vernal UT 1 hr
WBRF(FM) Galax VA 1 hr
WVNR(AM) Poultney VT 5 hrs
WJJR(FM) Rutland VT 1 hr
KEDO(AM) Longview WA 2 hrs
*KAOS(FM) Olympia WA 14 hrs
*KWRS(FM) Spokane WA 2 hrs
WJLW(FM) De Pere WI 1 hr
*WWSP(FM) Stevens Point WI 5 hrs
WWYO(AM) Pineville WV 20 hrs

Reggae

*KTNA(FM) Talkeetna AK 2 hrs
*WJAB(FM) Huntsville AL 4 hrs
*WVUA-FM Tuscaloosa AL 3 hrs
*KABF(FM) Little Rock AR 10 hrs
*KSPC(FM) Claremont CA 6 hrs
*KKUP(FM) Cupertino CA 15 hrs
KCQR(FM) Ellwood CA 1 hr
*KFCF(FM) Fresno CA 3 hrs
*KFSR(FM) Fresno CA 3 hrs
*KFJC(FM) Los Altos CA 8 hrs
*KSBR(FM) Mission Viejo CA 4 hrs
*KVMR(FM) Nevada City CA 4 hrs
*KSPB(FM) Pebble Beach CA 2 hrs
*KZYX(FM) Philo CA 5 hrs
*KUOR-FM Redlands CA 4 hrs
*KCPR(FM) San Luis Obispo CA 3 hrs
*KCRW(FM) Santa Monica CA
*KUOP(FM) Stockton CA 6 hrs
*KCSU-FM Fort Collins CO 3 hrs
KTCL(FM) Fort Collins CO 2 hrs
*KWSB-FM Gunnison CO 1 hr
*WXCI(FM) Danbury CT 2 hrs
*WESU(FM) Middletown CT 10 hrs
WKHI(FM) Bethany Beach DE 1 hr
*WDNA(FM) Miami FL 4 hrs
WRBD(AM) Pompano Beach FL 5 hrs
*WKPX(FM) Sunrise FL 5 hrs
*WMNF(FM) Tampa FL
*WCLK(FM) Atlanta GA 3 hrs
*WRAS(FM) Atlanta GA 4 hrs
*WRFG(FM) Atlanta GA 20 hrs
*WVGS(FM) Statesboro GA 3 hrs
KWXX-FM Hilo HI 20 hrs
*KTUH(FM) Honolulu HI 9 hrs
*KUCB-FM Des Moines IA 12 hrs
*KRUI-FM Iowa City IA 3 hrs
*WHPK-FM Chicago IL 8 hrs
*WNUR-FM Evanston IL 4 hrs
*WDCB(FM) Glen Ellyn IL 2 hrs
WGRL(FM) Indianapolis IN 1 hr
*WMHD-FM Terre Haute IN 2 hrs
*KJHK(FM) Lawrence KS 3 hrs
*WRFL(FM) Lexington KY 3 hrs
*KLSU(FM) Baton Rouge LA 3 hrs
*WTUL(FM) New Orleans LA 2 hrs
*KLPI-FM Ruston LA 6 hrs
*KSCL(FM) Shreveport LA 4 hrs
*WBIM-FM Bridgewater MA 2 hrs
WHRB(FM) Cambridge MA 3 hrs
*WJUL(FM) Lowell MA 4 hrs
*WBRS(FM) Waltham MA 7 hrs
*WZLY(FM) Wellesley MA 2 hrs
WHFS(FM) Annapolis MD 2 hrs
*WESM(FM) Princess Anne MD 6 hrs
*WTMD(FM) Towson MD 2 hrs
*WERU-FM Blue Hill ME 4 hrs
*WBOR(FM) Brunswick ME 10 hrs
*WMEB-FM Orono ME 7 hrs
WCDQ(FM) Sanford ME 2 hrs
*WDET-FM Detroit MI 2 hrs
*WDBM(FM) East Lansing MI 4 hrs
*WIDR(FM) Kalamazoo MI 1 hr
*WSGR-FM Port Huron MI 4 hrs
*KUMM(FM) Morris MN 2 hrs
*KVSC(FM) St. Cloud MN
*KCOU(FM) Columbia MO 2 hrs
*KJLU(FM) Jefferson City MO
*WUSM-FM Hattiesburg MS 2 hrs
*WJSU(FM) Jackson MS 2 hrs
WUMS(FM) University MS 1 hr
*WFSS(FM) Fayetteville NC 3 hrs
*WNAA(FM) Greensboro NC 4 hrs
*WQFS(FM) Greensboro NC 9 hrs
*WZMB(FM) Greenville NC 7 hrs
*WKNC-FM Raleigh NC 1 hr
KKCD(FM) Omaha NE 1 hr
*WUNH(FM) Durham NH 2 hrs
WDCR(AM) Hanover NH 9 hrs
*WKNH(FM) Keene NH 4 hrs
*WNTI(FM) Hackettstown NJ 3 hrs
*WCDB(FM) Albany NY 2 hrs
*WBSU(FM) Brockport NY 2 hrs
*WBNY(FM) Buffalo NY 3 hrs
*WHCL-FM Clinton NY 10 hrs
*WCVF-FM Fredonia NY 3 hrs
*WEOS(FM) Geneva NY 20 hrs
*WITR(FM) Henrietta NY 5 hrs
*WICB(FM) Ithaca NY 2 hrs
*WFNP(FM) New Paltz NY 5 hrs
WLIB(AM) New York NY
*WNYU-FM New York NY 2 hrs
*WSBU(FM) St. Bonaventure NY 1 hr
*WPNR-FM Utica NY 5 hrs
*WAPS(FM) Akron OH 2 hrs
*WKHR(FM) Bainbridge OH
*WRUW-FM Cleveland OH 7 hrs
WWCD(FM) Grove City OH 2 hrs
*WOBC-FM Oberlin OH 6 hrs
*WXUT(FM) Toledo OH 4 hrs
*WCWS(FM) Wooster OH 12 hrs
*KEOL(FM) La Grande OR 7 hrs
*KBOO(FM) Portland OR 10 hrs
*WLVR(FM) Bethlehem PA 6 hrs
*WJRH(FM) Easton PA 6 hrs
*WERG(FM) Erie PA 4 hrs
*WKVR-FM Huntingdon PA 3 hrs
*WPEB(FM) Philadelphia PA 12 hrs
*WPSU(FM) State College PA 3 hrs
*WRDV(FM) Warminster PA 3 hrs

Broadcasting & Cable Yearbook 1994
B-584

Special Programming on Radio Stations in the U.S.

*WRIU(FM) Kingston RI 7 hrs
*WUSC-FM Columbia SC 3 hrs
*WSSB-FM Orangeburg SC 4 hrs
*WTTU(FM) Cookeville TN 3 hrs
*WEVL(FM) Memphis TN 4 hrs
*WFSK(FM) Nashville TN 3 hrs
*WRVU(FM) Nashville TN 3 hrs
*WUTS(FM) Sewanee TN 5 hrs
WRLG(FM) Smyrna TN 3 hrs
*KAZI(FM) Austin TX 6 hrs
*KTRU(FM) Houston TX 6 hrs
*KTSU(FM) Houston TX 8 hrs
*KSAU(FM) Nacogdoches TX 2 hrs
KSJL-FM San Antonio TX 2 hrs
*KRCL(FM) Salt Lake City UT 8 hrs
*WWHS-FM Hampden-Sydney VA 4 hrs
*WHOV(FM) Hampton VA 3 hrs
*WCWM(FM) Williamsburg VA 6 hrs
WSTA(AM) Charlotte Amalie VI
WIZN(FM) Vergennes VT 1 hr
*WRUV(FM) Burlington VT 15 hrs
*WIUV(FM) Castleton VT 60 hrs
*KAOS(FM) Olympia WA 5 hrs
*KWRS(FM) Spokane WA 2 hrs
*KUPS(FM) Tacoma WA 11 hrs
*WBSD(FM) Burlington WI 3 hrs
*WCDE(FM) Elkins WV 3 hrs
*WWVU-FM Morgantown WV 5 hrs

Religious

KYMG(FM) Anchorage AK 1 hr
*KBRW(AM) Barrow AK 7 hrs
*KSKO(AM) McGrath AK 3 hrs
*KNOM(AM) Nome AK 15 hrs
*KNOM-FM Nome AK 15 hrs
KSWD(AM) Seward AK 4 hrs
KIFW(AM) Sitka AK 5 hrs
KIAL(AM) Unalaska AK 04 hrs
WCRQ-FM Arab AL 2 hrs
*WVSU-FM Birmingham AL 17 hrs
WEBJ(AM) Brewton AL 9 hrs
WKNU(FM) Brewton AL 4 hrs
WZOB(AM) Fort Payne AL 5 hrs
WJRD(AM) Russellville AL 10 hrs
WKEA-FM Scottsboro AL 4 hrs
WJDB-FM Thomasville AL 13 hrs
WTNW(AM) Tuscaloosa AL 1 hr
*WVUA-FM Tuscaloosa AL 3 hrs
KARQ(FM) Ashdown AR 4 hrs
KEZU(FM) Booneville AR 5 hrs
KLYR(AM) Clarksville AR 8 hrs
KDEZ(FM) Jonesboro AR 1 hr
KHBM(AM) Monticello AR 6 hrs
KHBM-FM Monticello AR 6 hrs
KDRS(AM) Paragould AR 8 hrs
KGHT(AM) Sheridan AR 5 hrs
KRLW(AM) Walnut Ridge AR 9 hrs
KRLW-FM Walnut Ridge AR 9 hrs
KAVV(FM) Benson AZ 3 hrs
KCUZ(AM) Clifton AZ 2 hrs
KNNS(AM) Glendale AZ 1 hr
KRIM(FM) Payson AZ 1 hr
KOY(AM) Phoenix AZ 2 hrs
KQST(FM) Sedona AZ 5 hrs
KTKT(AM) Tucson AZ 2 hrs
KAPL(AM) Apple Valley CA 4 hrs
KERN(AM) Bakersfield CA 1 hr
KSZL(AM) Barstow CA 1 hr
*KZPN(FM) Bayside CA 3 hrs
KCMT(FM) Chester CA 1 hr
KJLH-FM Compton CA 7 hrs
KNCO(AM) Grass Valley CA 8 hrs
KCNQ(FM) Kernville CA 1 hr
KLBS(AM) Los Banos CA 8 hrs
KMFB(FM) Mendocino CA
KPMO(AM) Mendocino CA 2 hrs
*KSMC(FM) Moraga CA 3 hrs
KPCO(AM) Quincy CA 1 hr
KEST(AM) San Francisco CA 24 hrs
*KUSF(FM) San Francisco CA 5 hrs
KKJG(FM) San Luis Obispo CA 3 hrs
KVML(AM) Sonora CA 3 hrs
KSTN(AM) Stockton CA 5 hrs
KSUE(AM) Susanville CA 3 hrs
KPSL(AM) Thousand Palms CA 17 hrs
KXBT(AM) Vallejo CA 5 hrs
KUBA(AM) Yuba City CA 1 hr
*KSJD(FM) Cortez CO 1 hr
KFKA(AM) Greeley CO 4 hrs
KLOV(AM) Loveland CO 6 hrs
KUBC(AM) Montrose CO 2 hrs
KVRH(AM) Salida CO 4 hrs
KVRH-FM Salida CO 4 hrs
KCRT(AM) Trinidad CO 5 hrs
KIIX(AM) Wellington CO 1 hr
KRDZ(AM) Wray CO 4 hrs
WPRX(AM) Bristol CT 3 hrs
*WQAQ(FM) Hamden CT 4 hrs
WMMW(AM) Meriden CT
WNLC(AM) New London CT 3 hrs
WILI(AM) Willimantic CT 2 hrs
*WDCU(FM) Washington DC 3 hrs
WSSR(AM) Georgetown DE 6 hrs
WYUS(AM) Milford DE 10 hrs
WGMD(FM) Rehoboth Beach DE 2 hrs
*WMPH(FM) Wilmington DE 4 hrs
WSTW(FM) Wilmington DE 2 hrs
WWOJ(FM) Avon Park FL 3 hrs
WYBT(AM) Blountstown FL 15 hrs
WLQH(AM) Chiefland FL 9 hrs
WAFC-FM Clewiston FL 5 hrs
*WVUM(FM) Coral Gables FL 6 hrs
WDFL(AM) Cross City FL 5 hrs
WDFL-FM Cross City FL 5 hrs
WHNR(AM) Cypress Gardens FL 5 hrs
WDCF(AM) Dade City FL 6 hrs
WLVU(AM) Dunedin FL 1 hr
WJNX(AM) Fort Pierce FL 7 hrs
WKGR(FM) Fort Pierce FL 1 hr
WKZY(FM) La Belle FL 1 hr
WIPC(AM) Lake Wales FL 5 hrs
WONN(AM) Lakeland FL 2 hrs
WQHL(AM) Live Oak FL 6 hrs
WQHL-FM Live Oak FL 2 hrs
WTAI(AM) Melbourne FL 3 hrs
WQAM(AM) Miami FL 4 hrs
WCVU(FM) Naples FL 4 hrs
WSBB(AM) New Smyrna Beach FL 5 hrs
WKAT(AM) North Miami FL 2 hrs
WTMC(AM) Ocala FL 4 hrs
WHOO(AM) Orlando FL
WCOA(AM) Pensacola FL 6 hrs
WRBD(AM) Pompano Beach FL 6 hrs
WKII(AM) Port Charlotte FL 4 hrs
WKNB(FM) Port St. Joe FL 5 hrs
WTRR(AM) Sanford FL 3 hrs
WQSA(AM) Sarasota FL 5 hrs
WSOS(FM) St. Augustine FL 2 hrs
WPIK(FM) Summerland Key FL 1 hr
WANM(AM) Tallahassee FL 6 hrs
*WPRK(FM) Winter Park FL 1 hr
WJTH(AM) Calhoun GA 16 hrs
WLBB(AM) Carrollton GA 12 hrs
WCHM(AM) Clarkesville GA 5 hrs
WPBS(AM) Conyers GA 6 hrs
WGFS(AM) Covington GA 14 hrs
WBLJ(AM) Dalton GA
WDDK(FM) Greensboro GA 6 hrs
WCEH(AM) Hawkinsville GA 6 hrs
WSKX(FM) Hinesville GA 6 hrs
WLAG(AM) La Grange GA 2 hrs
WMAZ(AM) Macon GA 4 hrs
WKKP(AM) McDonough GA 5 hrs
WMGA(AM) Moultrie GA 5 hrs
WPGA(AM) Perry GA 6 hrs
WGTA(AM) Summerville GA 18 hrs
WPAX(AM) Thomasville GA 3 hrs
WTHO-FM Thomson GA 2 hrs
WWGS(AM) Tifton GA 6 hrs
WADX(AM) Trenton GA 6 hrs
WVOP(AM) Vidalia GA 8 hrs
WRCC(AM) Warner Robins GA 2 hrs
WRCC-FM Warner Robins GA 12 hrs
WIMO(AM) Winder GA 14 hrs
KWAI(AM) Honolulu HI 4 hrs
KCHE-FM Cherokee IA 4 hrs
KLKK(FM) Clear Lake IA 2 hrs
KROS(AM) Clinton IA 4 hrs
*KWLC(AM) Decorah IA
KILR(AM) Estherville IA 11 hrs
KILR-FM Estherville IA 11 hrs
KNOD(FM) Harlan IA 2 hrs
KNIA(AM) Knoxville IA 18 hrs
KRLS(FM) Knoxville IA 18 hrs
KMCH(FM) Manchester IA 4 hrs
KRIB(AM) Mason City IA 5 hrs
KYTC(FM) Northwood IA 2 hrs
KTLB(FM) Twin Lakes IA 2 hrs
KMCL-FM McCall ID 1 hr
KVSI(AM) Montpelier ID 2 hrs
KRPL(AM) Moscow ID 2 hrs
KZFN(FM) Moscow ID 2 hrs
KWIK(AM) Pocatello ID 1 hr
KADQ(FM) Rexburg ID 6 hrs
KSPT(AM) Sandpoint ID 2 hrs
KTFI(AM) Twin Falls ID 5 hrs
WRMJ(FM) Aledo IL 3 hrs
KATZ-FM Alton IL 2 hrs
WBIG(AM) Aurora IL 6 hrs
WKKD(AM) Aurora IL 8 hrs
WKKD-FM Aurora IL 2 hrs
WLMD(FM) Bushnell IL 1 hr
KSGM(AM) Chester IL 6 hrs
WHOW(AM) Clinton IL 15 hrs
WDKB(FM) De Kalb IL 1 hr
WKDC(AM) Elmhurst IL 1 hr
WONX(AM) Evanston IL 2 hrs
WAIK(AM) Galesburg IL 6 hrs
WFXW(AM) Geneva IL 4 hrs
*WMWA(FM) Glenview IL 2 hrs
WDXR-FM Golconda IL 2 hrs
WGNU(AM) Granite City IL 15 hrs
WJBM(AM) Jerseyville IL 3 hrs
WKEI(AM) Kewanee IL 10 hrs
*WLNX(FM) Lincoln IL 4 hrs
WLBH(AM) Mattoon IL 5 hrs
WMOK(AM) Metropolis IL 5 hrs
WTAZ(FM) Morton IL 3 hrs
WINI(AM) Murphysboro IL 6 hrs
*WONC(FM) Naperville IL 4 hrs
WPNA(AM) Oak Park IL 1 hr
WSWT(FM) Peoria IL 3 hrs
WBBA(AM) Pittsfield IL 3 hrs
WBBA-FM Pittsfield IL 3 hrs
WKXQ(FM) Rushville IL 6 hrs
WJBD(AM) Salem IL 6 hrs
WHCO(AM) Sparta IL 20 hrs
WTIM(AM) Taylorville IL 4 hrs
WGFA(AM) Watseka IL 2 hrs
WQME(FM) Anderson IN 15 hrs
WBQR(FM) Attica IN
WIFF(AM) Auburn IN 15 hrs
WNUY(FM) Bluffton IN 4 hrs
WCNB-FM Connersville IN 6 hrs
WIFE(AM) Connersville IN 6 hrs
WLTA(FM) Elkhart IN 2 hrs
WTRE(AM) Greensburg IN 3 hrs
WJOB(AM) Hammond IN 2 hrs
WBDC(FM) Huntingburg IN 5 hrs
WLNB(FM) Ligonier IN 3 hrs
WORX(AM) Madison IN 6 hrs
WORX-FM Madison IN 6 hrs
WGAB(AM) Newburgh IN 5 hrs
*WBKE-FM North Manchester IN 2 hrs
WKRP(AM) North Vernon IN 9 hrs
WARU(AM) Peru IN 10 hrs
WRIN(AM) Rensselaer IN 10 hrs
WFMG(FM) Richmond IN 4 hrs
WROI(FM) Rochester IN 6 hrs
WAXI(FM) Rockville IN 4 hrs
WKJK(FM) Salem IN
WSLM-FM Salem IN
WZZB(AM) Seymour IN 6 hrs
WSKT(FM) Spencer IN 6 hrs
WAWC(FM) Syracuse IN 4 hrs
*WMHD-FM Terre Haute IN 4 hrs
WCJC(FM) Van Buren IN 3 hrs
WAMW-FM Washington IN 7 hrs
WZZY(FM) Winchester IN 5 hrs
KSOK(AM) Arkansas City KS 5 hrs
KYQQ(FM) Arkansas City KS 2 hrs
KDCC(AM) Dodge City KS
KXLK(FM) Haysville KS 2 hrs
KHOK(FM) Hoisington KS 2 hrs
KANS(AM) Larned KS 5 hrs
KLWN(AM) Lawrence KS 6 hrs
KNGL(AM) McPherson KS 5 hrs
KZOC(FM) Osage City KS 5 hrs
KZTO(FM) Ottawa KS 1 hr
KSKG(FM) Salina KS 3 hrs
WIBW(AM) Topeka KS 6 hrs
KLEY(AM) Wellington KS 4 hrs
KRBB(FM) Wichita KS 1 hr
KWKS(FM) Winfield KS 2 hrs
WMMG(AM) Brandenburg KY 8 hrs
WKDZ(AM) Cadiz KY 6 hrs
WAIN-FM Columbia KY 18 hrs
WKDP-FM Corbin KY 5 hrs
WCPM(AM) Cumberland KY 9 hrs
WCYN(AM) Cynthiana KY 10 hrs
WABD(AM) Fort Campbell KY 4 hrs
WFKY(AM) Frankfort KY 6 hrs
WKED(AM) Frankfort KY 2 hrs
WFKN(AM) Franklin KY
*WRVG(FM) Georgetown KY 12 hrs
WKYZ(AM) Gray KY 12 hrs
WXBC(FM) Hardinsburg KY 7 hrs
WHBN(AM) Harrodsburg KY 15 hrs
WQKS(AM) Hopkinsville KY 6 hrs
WKYL(FM) Lawrenceburg KY 5 hrs
*WRFL(FM) Lexington KY 3 hrs
WMAK(AM) London KY 6 hrs
WHAS(AM) Louisville KY 3 hrs
WVEZ-FM Louisville KY 4 hrs
WWKY(AM) Louisville KY 4 hrs
WFTM(AM) Maysville KY 5 hrs
WFXY(AM) Middlesboro KY 3 hrs
WSJP(AM) Murray KY 6 hrs
*WKWC(FM) Owensboro KY 15 hrs
WKYX(AM) Paducah KY 6 hrs
WPAD(AM) Paducah KY 7 hrs
WTLO(AM) Somerset KY 4 hrs
WNKR(FM) Williamstown KY 1 hr
KBAZ(FM) Basile LA 1 hr
KFRA(AM) Franklin LA 3 hrs
KJEF-FM Jennings LA 6 hrs
KAOK(AM) Lake Charles LA 7 hrs
KVVP(FM) Leesville LA 9 hrs
KAPB(AM) Marksville LA 4 hrs
KAPB-FM Marksville LA 4 hrs
KAGY(AM) Port Sulphur LA 3 hrs
KVCL(AM) Winnfield LA 15 hrs
WARA(AM) Attleboro MA 1 hr
WBZ(AM) Boston MA 02 hrs
*WRBB(FM) Boston MA 4 hrs
WRKO(AM) Boston MA 1 hr
*WMBR(FM) Cambridge MA 4 hrs
WBEC(AM) Pittsfield MA 3 hrs
WBRK(AM) Pittsfield MA 2 hrs
WESX(AM) Salem MA 2 hrs
*WMWM(FM) Salem MA 3 hrs
WMAS(AM) Springfield MA 2 hrs
*WZLY(FM) Wellesley MA 2 hrs
WACM(AM) West Springfield MA
WANN(AM) Annapolis MD 8 hrs
WCBM(AM) Baltimore MD 1 hr
WOLB(AM) Baltimore MD 2 hrs
WTRI(AM) Brunswick MD 7 hrs
WSER(AM) Elkton MD 3 hrs
*WMTB-FM Emmittsburg MD 4 hrs
WXCY(FM) Havre de Grace MD 2 hrs
WCTN(AM) Potomac-Cabin John MD
WTHU(AM) Thurmont MD 5 hrs
WQDY(AM) Calais ME 2 hrs
WQDY-FM Calais ME 2 hrs
WSYY(AM) Millinocket ME 2 hrs
WSKW(AM) Skowhegan ME
WABJ(AM) Adrian MI 3 hrs
WALM(AM) Albion MI 3 hrs
*WQAC-FM Alma MI 2 hrs
WAAM(AM) Ann Arbor MI 5 hrs
*WAUS(FM) Berrien Springs MI 10 hrs
WPZX(FM) Big Rapids MI 1 hr
WYTW(FM) Cadillac MI
WCFX(FM) Clare MI 1 hr
WXLA(AM) Dimondale MI 5 hrs
WDBC(AM) Escanaba MI 4 hrs
WSNQ(AM) Gaylord MI 2 hrs
WCSR(AM) Hillsdale MI 10 hrs
*WTHS(FM) Holland MI 14 hrs
WCCY(AM) Houghton MI 1 hr
WKZO(AM) Kalamazoo MI 5 hrs
WKWM(AM) Kentwood MI 12 hrs
WWGZ(AM) Lapeer MI 3 hrs
WMPX(AM) Midland MI 3 hrs
WQWQ(AM) Muskegon Heights MI 5 hrs
WMZX(FM) Owosso MI 1 hr
WOAP(AM) Owosso MI 4 hrs
WJML(AM) Petoskey MI 8 hrs
WEFG(AM) Whitehall MI
WYGR(AM) Wyoming MI 4 hrs
KSTQ(FM) Alexandria MN 3 hrs
KXRA(AM) Alexandria MN 2 hrs
WKLK(AM) Cloquet MN 5 hrs
WELY(AM) Ely MN 6 hrs
WEVE-FM Eveleth MN 5 hrs
KBRF(AM) Fergus Falls MN 7 hrs
WLKX-FM Forest Lake MN 6 hrs
KKCQ(AM) Fosston MN 4 hrs
WMFG(AM) Hibbing MN 4 hrs
KLFD(AM) Litchfield MN 3 hrs
KLTF(AM) Little Falls MN 1 hr
KEYL(AM) Long Prairie MN 4 hrs
KQAD(AM) Luverne MN 5 hrs
KMHL(AM) Marshall MN 7 hrs
KMOM(AM) Monticello MN 4 hrs
KQYB(FM) Spring Grove MN 3 hrs
*KSRQ(FM) Thief River Falls MN 6 hrs
WHLB(AM) Virginia MN 5 hrs
KQIC(FM) Willmar MN 2 hrs
KAGE(AM) Winona MN
KAAN(AM) Bethany MO 1 hr
KCRV(AM) Caruthersville MO 23 hrs
*KWUR(FM) Clayton MO 1 hr
KFAL(AM) Fulton MO 9 hrs
KFEZ(AM) Kansas City MO 5 hrs
*KMVC(FM) Marshall MO 16 hrs
KMEM-FM Memphis MO 4 hrs
KMCR(FM) Montgomery City MO 2 hrs
KNEM(AM) Nevada MO 5 hrs
KNMO(FM) Nevada MO 5 hrs
KMIS-FM New Madrid MO 12 hrs
KBDZ(FM) Perryville MO 5 hrs
KMIS(AM) Portageville MO 12 hrs
*KCLC(FM) St. Charles MO 7 hrs
KMOX(AM) St. Louis MO 1 hr
KTTN(AM) Trenton MO 7 hrs
KLPW(AM) Union MO 7 hrs
KLPW-FM Union MO 6 hrs
KLGS(FM) Versailles MO 3 hrs
KOKO(AM) Warrensburg MO 6 hrs
KJPW(AM) Waynesville MO 3 hrs
KKDY(FM) West Plains MO 7 hrs
KSPQ(FM) West Plains MO 10 hrs
KWPM(AM) West Plains MO 10 hrs
WRKN(AM) Brandon MS
WSSI(AM) Carthage MS 2 hrs
WHJT(FM) Clinton MS 6 hrs
WBAQ(FM) Greenville MS 4 hrs
WNIX(AM) Greenville MS 6 hrs
WFOR(AM) Hattiesburg MS 8 hrs
WHER(FM) Hattiesburg MS 2 hrs
WCPC(AM) Houston MS
WQIS(AM) Laurel MS 11 hrs
WIQQ(FM) Leland MS 6 hrs
WLSM(AM) Louisville MS 2 hrs
WQMA(AM) Marks MS 4 hrs
WMLC(AM) Monticello MS 20 hrs
WRQO(FM) Monticello MS 10 hrs
WQLJ(FM) Oxford MS 9 hrs
WZZJ(AM) Pascagoula-Moss Point MS 2 hrs
WRJW(AM) Picayune MS 16 hrs
WPMX(AM) Tupelo MS 12 hrs
*KMSM-FM Butte MT 3 hrs
KMTA(AM) Kinsey MT 1 hr
KMSO(FM) Missoula MT 1 hr
KATQ(AM) Plentywood MT 6 hrs
KATQ-FM Plentywood MT 6 hrs
WWNC(AM) Asheville NC 3 hrs
*WASU-FM Boone NC 3 hrs
WWIT(AM) Canton NC 7 hrs
WRRZ(AM) Clinton NC 6 hrs
*WWCU(FM) Cullowhee NC 4 hrs
WBLA(AM) Elizabethtown NC 8 hrs
*WZMB(FM) Greenville NC 3 hrs
WIZS(AM) Henderson NC 6 hrs
WIRC(AM) Hickory NC 7 hrs
WJNC(AM) Jacksonville NC 6 hrs
WBRM(AM) Marion NC 7 hrs
WMAP(AM) Monroe NC 10 hrs
WHIP(AM) Mooresville NC 6 hrs
WJTP(AM) Newland NC 5 hrs
WDLF(FM) Old Fort NC 2 hrs
WPTM(FM) Roanoke Rapids NC 3 hrs
WCCA(FM) Shallotte NC 2 hrs
WNCA(AM) Siler City NC 12 hrs
WTOE(AM) Spruce Pine NC 8 hrs
WSIC(AM) Statesville NC 6 hrs
*WHYC(FM) Swan Quarter NC 4 hrs
WHCC(AM) Waynesville NC 3 hrs
WENC(AM) Whiteville NC 4 hrs
WTXY(AM) Whiteville NC 10 hrs
WMQX(AM) Winston-Salem NC 6 hrs
WMQX-FM Winston-Salem NC
KHOL(AM) Beulah ND 7 hrs
KXPO(AM) Grafton ND 3 hrs
KXPO-FM Grafton ND 3 hrs
KNDK(AM) Langdon ND 6 hrs
KHRT(AM) Minot ND 2 hrs
KTYN(AM) Minot ND 1 hr
KEYZ(AM) Williston ND 5 hrs
KZEN(FM) Central City NE 3 hrs
KLIR(FM) Columbus NE 4 hrs
*KINI(FM) Crookston NE 6 hrs
KRVN(AM) Lexington NE 6 hrs
KZMC-FM McCook NE 1 hr
KRFS(AM) Superior NE 3 hrs
*WPEA(FM) Exeter NH 2 hrs
WHCY(FM) Blairstown NJ 1 hr
WSSJ(AM) Camden NJ 8 hrs
*WDVR(FM) Delaware Township NJ 12 hrs
WRDR(FM) Egg Harbor City NJ 4 hrs
*WMNJ(FM) Madison NJ 2 hrs
WTTH(FM) Margate City NJ 1 hr
WNNJ(AM) Newton NJ 2 hrs
WGHT(AM) Pompton Lakes NJ 2 hrs
WNJC(AM) Washington Township NJ 6 hrs
*WPSC-FM Wayne NJ 1 hr
KPSA(AM) Alamogordo NM 4 hrs
KAFR(FM) Angel Fire NM 8 hrs
KCHS(AM) Truth or Consequences NM 11 hrs
KDSS(FM) Ely NV 1 hr
KLAV(AM) Las Vegas NV 1 hr
KNEV(FM) Reno NV 1 hr
WBNR(AM) Beacon NY 1 hr
WBRV-FM Boonville NY 3 hrs
WGR(AM) Buffalo NY 2 hrs
WJYE(FM) Buffalo NY 2 hrs
WWKB(AM) Buffalo NY 5 hrs
WVNC(FM) Canton NY 4 hrs
*WHCL-FM Clinton NY 2 hrs
WSCM(AM) Cobleskill NY 3 hrs
WDNY(AM) Dansville NY 1 hr
WDNY-FM Dansville NY 1 hr
WELV(AM) Ellenville NY 2 hrs
WELM(AM) Elmira NY 1 hr
WLVY(FM) Elmira NY 1 hr
WZZZ(AM) Fulton NY 3 hrs
WBZA(AM) Glens Falls NY 3 hrs
WXHC(FM) Homer NY 1 hr
WHUC(AM) Hudson NY 3 hrs
WTKO(AM) Ithaca NY 1 hr
WGHQ(AM) Kingston NY 3 hrs
WXRL(AM) Lancaster NY 6 hrs
WYBG(AM) Massena NY 2 hrs
WALL(AM) Middletown NY 3 hrs
WSUL-FM Monticello NY 1 hr
WRKL(AM) New City NY 2 hrs
WVOX(AM) New Rochelle NY 3 hrs
WOR(AM) New York NY 10 hrs
WGNY(AM) Newburgh NY
WDOS(AM) Oneonta NY 7 hrs
WZOS(FM) Oswego NY 2 hrs
WEBO(AM) Owego NY 6 hrs
*WPLT(FM) Plattsburgh NY 3 hrs
WEOK(AM) Poughkeepsie NY 2 hrs
WVKZ(AM) Schenectady NY 1 hr
WSFW(AM) Seneca Falls NY 4 hrs
WSFW-FM Seneca Falls NY 4 hrs
WFWC(AM) Springville NY 2 hrs
*WSBU(FM) St. Bonaventure NY 1 hr
WHAZ(AM) Troy NY 3 hrs
WRGR(FM) Tupper Lake NY 1 hr
WRUN(AM) Utica NY 12 hrs
WUTQ(AM) Utica NY 5 hrs
WNYV(FM) Whitehall NY 2 hrs
*WONB(FM) Ada OH 8 hrs
WDPN(AM) Alliance OH 4 hrs
*WRDL(FM) Ashland OH 7 hrs
WBLL(AM) Bellefontaine OH 6 hrs
WNRR(FM) Bellevue OH 3 hrs
WBCO(AM) Bucyrus OH 4 hrs
WQEL(FM) Bucyrus OH 2 hrs
WINW(AM) Canton OH 2 hrs
WKKI(FM) Celina OH 2 hrs
WERE(AM) Cleveland OH 2 hrs
WMNI(AM) Columbus OH 2 hrs
*WWSU(FM) Dayton OH 2 hrs
WZOM(FM) Defiance OH 6 hrs
WIRO(AM) Ironton OH 7 hrs
WMLV(FM) Ironton OH 2 hrs
WBZW(FM) Loudonville OH 5 hrs
WMOA(AM) Marietta OH 1 hr
WMPO(AM) Middleport-Pomeroy OH 6 hrs
WMPO-FM Middleport-Pomeroy OH 6 hrs
WMVO(AM) Mount Vernon OH 7 hrs
WOBL(AM) Oberlin OH 1 hr
WLEC(AM) Sandusky OH 6 hrs

Broadcasting & Cable Yearbook 1994
B-585

Special Programming on Radio Stations in the U.S.

WCWA(AM) Toledo OH 3 hrs
WSPD(AM) Toledo OH 5 hrs
WVOI(AM) Toledo OH
WBTC(AM) Uhrichsville OH 2 hrs
WTUZ(FM) Uhrichsville OH 1 hr
*WUJC(FM) University Heights OH 12 hrs
*WOBN(FM) Westerville OH 4 hrs
WELW(AM) Willoughby-Eastlake OH 4 hrs
WHIZ-FM Zanesville OH 1 hr
KALV(AM) Alva OK 7 hrs
KRPT(AM) Anadarko OK 2 hrs
KRPT-FM Anadarko OK 2 hrs
KYFM(FM) Bartlesville OK 5 hrs
*KHIB(FM) Durant OK 1 hr
KTNT-FM Edmond OK 5 hrs
KCES(FM) Eufaula OK 5 hrs
KOKC(AM) Guthrie OK 2 hrs
KGYN(AM) Guymon OK 10 hrs
KTJS(AM) Hobart OK 15 hrs
KTMC-FM McAlester OK 5 hrs
*KOCC(FM) Oklahoma City OK 8 hrs
WBBZ(AM) Ponca City OK 4 hrs
KGFF(AM) Shawnee OK 2 hrs
KGFY(FM) Stillwater OK 4 hrs
KSIW(AM) Woodward OK
KBKR(AM) Baker City OR 4 hrs
KNND(AM) Cottage Grove OR 3 hrs
KUIK(AM) Hillsboro OR 2 hrs
KLBM(AM) La Grande OR 4 hrs
KNPT(AM) Newport OR 2 hrs
KACI(AM) The Dalles OR 1 hr
KACI-FM The Dalles OR 1 hr
KWBY(AM) Woodburn OR 5 hrs
WBVP(AM) Beaver Falls PA 6 hrs
WAYC(AM) Bedford PA 3 hrs
WCNR(AM) Bloomsburg PA 4 hrs
WHLM(FM) Bloomsburg PA 3 hrs
WJMW(AM) Bloomsburg PA 3 hrs
*WVCS(FM) California PA 6 hrs
WCDL(AM) Carbondale PA 3 hrs
WIOO(AM) Carlisle PA 5 hrs
WYSN(FM) Central City PA 5 hrs
WWCH(AM) Clarion PA 8 hrs
WCOJ(AM) Coatesville PA 8 hrs
*WFSE(FM) Edinboro PA 4 hrs
*WWEC(FM) Elizabethtown PA 4 hrs
WQKY(FM) Emporium PA 2 hrs
*WMCE(FM) Erie PA 2 hrs
*WTGP(FM) Greenville PA 1 hr
*WKVR-FM Huntingdon PA 3 hrs
WQHG(FM) Huntingdon PA
WDAD(AM) Indiana PA 2 hrs
WTYM(AM) Kittanning PA 4 hrs
WLPA(AM) Lancaster PA 2 hrs
WROZ(FM) Lancaster PA 2 hrs
WNPV(AM) Lansdale PA 5 hrs
WCNS(AM) Latrobe PA 2 hrs
WEDO(AM) McKeesport PA 1 hr
WJUN(AM) Mexico PA 6 hrs
*WMSS(FM) Middletown PA 6 hrs
WXMJ(FM) Mount Union PA 2 hrs
WNAK(AM) Nanticoke PA 8 hrs
WGBN(AM) New Kensington PA 2 hrs
WCTX(FM) Palmyra PA 6 hrs
WIOQ(FM) Philadelphia PA
WBZZ(FM) Pittsburgh PA 2 hrs
WHKS(FM) Port Allegany PA 2 hrs
WPAZ(AM) Pottstown PA 12 hrs
WRAW(AM) Reading PA 1 hr
*WQSU(FM) Selinsgrove PA 3 hrs
WPIC(AM) Sharon PA 2 hrs
*WRSK(FM) Slippery Rock PA 1 hr
WPHD(FM) Tioga PA 1 hr
WEMR(AM) Tunkhannock PA 3 hrs
WRAK-FM Williamsport PA 1 hr
*WRLC(FM) Williamsport PA 3 hrs
WMIA(AM) Arecibo PR 10 hrs
WZBS(AM) Ponce PR 6 hrs
WVBI(FM) Block Island RI 2 hrs
WICE(AM) Pawtucket RI 2 hrs
WALE(AM) Providence RI 4 hrs
WGTN-FM Andrews SC 2 hrs
WBLR(AM) Batesburg SC 5 hrs
WAGS(AM) Bishopville SC 5 hrs
WOKE(AM) Charleston SC 9 hrs
WPJS(AM) Conway SC
WGTN(AM) Georgetown SC 1 hr
WMUU-FM Greenville SC 20 hrs
*WPLS-FM Greenville SC 2 hrs
WBHC-FM Hampton SC 6 hrs
WHSC(AM) Hartsville SC 6 hrs
WHSC-FM Hartsville SC 6 hrs
WIGL(FM) Orangeburg SC 6 hrs
WMAP-FM Pageland SC 5 hrs
WSPA-FM Spartanburg SC 3 hrs
*KAUR(FM) Sioux Falls SD 12 hrs
WNAX(AM) Yankton SD 16 hrs
WYXI(AM) Athens TN 8 hrs
WGOC(AM) Blountville TN 16 hrs
WJZM(AM) Clarksville TN
WYSH(AM) Clinton TN 15 hrs
*WZMC(AM) Colonial Heights TN 5 hrs
WKRM(AM) Columbia TN 4 hrs
*WTTU(FM) Cookeville TN 9 hrs
WCSV(AM) Crossville TN 5 hrs
WEGE(FM) Crossville TN 5 hrs
WDKN(AM) Dickson TN 12 hrs
WIZO(AM) Franklin TN 3 hrs
WXJB-FM Harrogate TN 2 hrs
WJFC(AM) Jefferson City TN 4 hrs
WNDD(FM) Jefferson City TN 2 hrs
WJCW(AM) Johnson City TN 4 hrs
WKGN(AM) Knoxville TN 5 hrs
WLIV(AM) Livingston TN 15 hrs
WCMT-FM Martin TN 6 hrs
WKBJ(AM) Milan TN 15 hrs
WMXK(FM) Morristown TN 2 hrs
WGNS(AM) Murfreesboro TN 6 hrs
*WFSK(FM) Nashville TN
WKDA(AM) Nashville TN 2 hrs
WLAC-FM Nashville TN 6 hrs
WLIK(AM) Newport TN 18 hrs
WUAT(AM) Pikeville TN 15 hrs
WJTT(FM) Red Bank TN 4 hrs
WLIJ(AM) Shelbyville TN 11 hrs
WSMT(AM) Sparta TN 10 hrs
WSGI(AM) Springfield TN
KGNC(AM) Amarillo TX 4 hrs
KQIZ-FM Amarillo TX 2 hrs
KLVQ(AM) Athens TX 8 hrs
KLVI(AM) Beaumont TX 2 hrs
KIBL(AM) Beeville TX 6 hrs
KBYG(AM) Big Spring TX 2 hrs
KFYN(AM) Bonham TX 6 hrs
KQTY(AM) Borger TX 12 hrs
KBOC(FM) Bridgeport TX 6 hrs
KGAS(AM) Carthage TX 10 hrs
KGAS-FM Carthage TX 10 hrs
KCTX(AM) Childress TX 10 hrs
KSRW(FM) Childress TX 5 hrs
*KAMU-FM College Station TX 1 hr
KHER(FM) Crystal City TX 2 hrs
KTDR(FM) Del Rio TX 2 hrs
KWMC(AM) Del Rio TX 5 hrs
KTXX(FM) Devine TX 18 hrs
KDIU(FM) Dimmitt TX 10 hrs
KPSO(AM) Falfurrias TX
KPSO-FM Falfurrias TX
KAWA(AM) Floydada TX 10 hrs
KFLL(FM) Floydada TX 10 hrs
KJOJ-FM Freeport TX 4 hrs
KRYL(FM) Gatesville TX 5 hrs
KGVL(AM) Greenville TX 6 hrs
KCLW(AM) Hamilton TX 6 hrs
KHBR(AM) Hillsboro TX 7 hrs
KLDE(FM) Houston TX 1 hr
KERV(AM) Kerrville TX 2 hrs
KRVL(FM) Kerrville TX 2 hrs
KVLG(AM) La Grange TX 5 hrs
KIOL-FM Lamesa TX
KZZN(AM) Littlefield TX 5 hrs
KYMI(FM) Los Ybanez TX 3 hrs
KFYO(AM) Lubbock TX 6 hrs
KCKL(FM) Malakoff TX 7 hrs
KEYR(FM) Marlin TX 2 hrs
KLSR(AM) Memphis TX 5 hrs
KLSR-FM Memphis TX 5 hrs
KCRS(AM) Midland TX 4 hrs
KCRS-FM Midland TX 4 hrs
KCDQ(FM) Monahans TX 3 hrs
KQHN(AM) Nederland TX 4 hrs
KGNB(AM) New Braunfels TX 2 hrs
KNBT(FM) New Braunfels TX 3 hrs
KGDD(AM) Paris TX 4 hrs
KEYE(AM) Perryton TX 3 hrs
KXAL-FM Pittsburg TX 6 hrs
KMIQ(FM) Robstown TX 6 hrs
KELI(FM) San Angelo TX 4 hrs
KIKZ(AM) Seminole TX 6 hrs
KSEM-FM Seminole TX 6 hrs
KJIM(AM) Sherman TX 12 hrs
KOUL(FM) Sinton TX
KCAS(AM) Slaton TX 4 hrs
KHOS(AM) Sonora TX 2 hrs
KVRP(AM) Stamford TX 6 hrs
KSTV(AM) Stephenville TX 6 hrs
KSTV-FM Stephenville TX 6 hrs
KBCY(FM) Tye TX 5 hrs
KWTX(AM) Waco TX 2 hrs
KTXZ(AM) West Lake Hills TX 6 hrs
KWFT(AM) Wichita Falls TX 8 hrs
KVLL(AM) Woodville TX 03 hrs
KSUB(AM) Cedar City UT
KVNU(AM) Logan UT 3 hrs
*KBYU-FM Provo UT 2 hrs
KDXU(AM) St. George UT 4 hrs
KVEL(AM) Vernal UT
KRGQ(AM) West Valley City UT 4 hrs
WABN(AM) Abingdon VA 18 hrs
WBLT(AM) Bedford VA 10 10 hrs
WDIC(AM) Clinchco VA 12 hrs
WPWC(AM) Dumfries-Triangle VA 6 hrs
WFLO(AM) Farmville VA 10 hrs
WFLO-FM Farmville VA 10 hrs
WGFC(AM) Floyd VA 6 hrs
WBQB(FM) Fredericksburg VA 2 hrs
WFTR(AM) Front Royal VA 2 hrs
WXGM(AM) Gloucester VA 2 hrs
WXGM-FM Gloucester VA 2 hrs
WLSA(FM) Louisa VA 3 hrs
WRAA(AM) Luray VA 15 hrs
WMEV(AM) Marion VA 12 hrs
WTAR(AM) Norfolk VA 2 hrs
WPUV(AM) Pulaski VA
*WDCE(FM) Richmond VA 3 hrs
WXGI(AM) Richmond VA 6 hrs
WYTI(AM) Rocky Mount VA 10 hrs
WHEO(AM) Stuart VA 10 hrs
WFOG(FM) Suffolk VA 2 hrs
WKCW(AM) Warrenton VA 3 hrs
WNNT(AM) Warsaw VA 8 hrs
WNNT-FM Warsaw VA 8 hrs
WVWI(AM) Charlotte Amalie VI 5 hrs
WAVI(FM) Christiansted VI 3 hrs
WRRA(AM) Frederiksted VI 10 hrs
*WRMC-FM Middlebury VT 1 hr
WVNR(AM) Poultney VT 2 hrs
WYKR(AM) Wells River VT 2 hrs
KLKI(AM) Anacortes WA 1 hr
KYSN(FM) East Wenatchee WA 1 hr
KARY-FM Grandview WA 8 hrs
KDFL(AM) Lakewood WA 12 hrs
*KSVR(FM) Mount Vernon WA 10 hrs
KRSC(AM) Othello WA 14 hrs
KAPY(AM) Port Angeles WA 5 hrs
KARY(AM) Prosser WA 8 hrs
KIRO-FM Seattle WA 2 hrs
KITZ(AM) Silverdale WA 5 hrs
*KWRS(FM) Spokane WA 6 hrs
KHSS(FM) Walla Walla WA 3 hrs
*KDNA(FM) Yakima WA 6 hrs
*KYSC(FM) Yakima WA 3 hrs
WATW(AM) Ashland WI 5 hrs
WRPQ(AM) Baraboo WI 4 hrs
WCFW(FM) Chippewa Falls WI 2 hrs
WTKM(AM) Hartford WI 6 hrs
WAUN(FM) Kewaunee WI 3 hrs
WSPL(FM) La Crosse WI 4 hrs
WOMT(AM) Manitowoc WI 2 hrs
WLJY(FM) Marshfield WI 2 hrs
WJMT(AM) Merrill WI 3 hrs
WEMP(AM) Milwaukee WI 3 hrs
WMYX(FM) Milwaukee WI 1 hr
WTMJ(AM) Milwaukee WI 2 hrs
WMQA(AM) Minocqua WI 3 hrs
WXOL(AM) Oshkosh WI 5 hrs
*WRFW(FM) River Falls WI
WDSM(AM) Superior WI 2 hrs
WVRQ(AM) Viroqua WI 6 hrs
WEGZ(FM) Washburn WI 1 hr
WTTN(AM) Watertown WI 4 hrs
*WVBC(FM) Bethany WV 4 hrs
WKOY(AM) Bluefield WV 5 hrs
WBTQ(FM) Buckhannon WV 4 hrs
WBUC(AM) Buckhannon WV 7 hrs
*WVWC(FM) Buckhannon WV 4 hrs
WFGM(FM) Fairmont WV 3 hrs
WELD(AM) Fisher WV 10 hrs
*WVMR(AM) Frost WV 10 hrs
WTBZ(AM) Grafton WV 8 hrs
WRVC(AM) Huntington WV 3 hrs
WEPM(AM) Martinsburg WV 6 hrs
WRNR(AM) Martinsburg WV 2 hrs
WZAO(AM) Moundsville WV 15 hrs
WWYO(AM) Pineville WV 20 hrs
WJJB(FM) Romney WV 1 hr
WRON(AM) Ronceverte WV 5 hrs
WCKA(FM) Sutton WV 15 hrs
WMQC(FM) Westover WV
KLGT(FM) Buffalo WY 1 hr

Rock/AOR

*KTNA(FM) Talkeetna AK 5 hrs
KIAL(AM) Unalaska AK 08 hrs
*WVUA-FM Tuscaloosa AL 4 hrs
KLCR(FM) Nogales AZ 9 hrs
KNAC(FM) Long Beach CA 2 hrs
*KPFK(FM) Los Angeles CA 16 hrs
*KSPB(FM) Pebble Beach CA 2 hrs
*KZYX(FM) Philo CA 6 hrs
*KCPR(FM) San Luis Obispo CA 5 hrs
*KSCU(FM) Santa Clara CA 5 hrs
*KCEQ(FM) Walnut Creek CA 1 hr
*WXCI(FM) Danbury CT 3 hrs
*WNHU(FM) West Haven CT 9 hrs
*WVUM(FM) Coral Gables FL 3 hrs
*WVVS(FM) Valdosta GA 6 hrs
*KUSR(FM) Ames IA
*WARG(FM) Summit IL
*WBKE-FM North Manchester IN 6 hrs
*WVUR-FM Valparaiso IN 3 hrs
WWLW(FM) Carlisle KY 1 hr
*WRFL(FM) Lexington KY 6 hrs
*WDJM-FM Framingham MA 8 hrs
*WOMR(FM) Provincetown MA 12 hrs
*WRBC(FM) Lewiston ME 4 hrs
*WUPI(FM) Presque Isle ME 4 hrs
*WMHB(FM) Waterville ME 6 hrs
*WDBM(FM) East Lansing MI 4 hrs
WWGZ-FM Lapeer MI
*WSDP(FM) Plymouth MI 5 hrs
*WSGR-FM Port Huron MI 20 hrs
*KUMM(FM) Morris MN 2 hrs
*KYMC(FM) Ballwin MO 3 hrs
*WUAG(FM) Greensboro NC 3 hrs
*WRRC(FM) Lawrenceville NJ 10 hrs
*KRUX(FM) Las Cruces NM 2 hrs
KHWK(FM) Tonopah NV
*WCDB(FM) Albany NY 2 hrs
*WSUC-FM Cortland NY 3 hrs
*WBER(FM) Henrietta NY 4 hrs
WVBR-FM Ithaca NY 8 hrs
*WONY(FM) Oneonta NY 3 hrs
WPDH(FM) Poughkeepsie NY 2 hrs
WSFW(AM) Seneca Falls NY 4 hrs
WSFW-FM Seneca Falls NY 4 hrs
*WKHR(FM) Bainbridge OH
*WBWC(FM) Berea OH 10 hrs
*WHSS(FM) Hamilton OH 1 hr
*WXUT(FM) Toledo OH 4 hrs
*KSLC(FM) McMinnville OR 7 hrs
*WBUQ(FM) Bloomsburg PA 15 hrs
*WVCS(FM) California PA 5 hrs
WPHD(FM) Tioga PA 3 hrs
*WCLH(FM) Wilkes-Barre PA 18 hrs
*WJHD(FM) Portsmouth RI
*WDOM(FM) Providence RI 6 hrs
*WTTU(FM) Cookeville TN 3 hrs
*WVCP(FM) Gallatin TN 10 hrs
WHHM-FM Henderson TN 6 hrs
WSBI(AM) Static TN 1 hr
KNCN(FM) Sinton TX 2 hrs
*KRCL(FM) Salt Lake City UT 9 hrs
*WIUV(FM) Castleton VT 1 hr
*KUGS(FM) Bellingham WA 15 hrs
*KWRS(FM) Spokane WA 2 hrs
*KUPS(FM) Tacoma WA 13 hrs
*KYSC(FM) Yakima WA 10 hrs
*WRFW(FM) River Falls WI
*WWVU-FM Morgantown WV 3 hrs

Russian

KICY(AM) Nome AK 6 hrs
KJNP(AM) North Pole AK 11 hrs
WEDC(AM) Chicago IL 1 hr
WSBC(AM) Chicago IL 1 hr
WKTA(AM) Evanston IL 1 hr
WEEF(AM) Highland Park IL
WVVX(FM) Highland Park IL 1 hr
WNVR(AM) Vernon Hills IL 1 hr
*WZLY(FM) Wellesley MA 1 hr
*WUPI(FM) Presque Isle ME 2 hrs
KSTL(AM) St. Louis MO 1 hr
*WKRB(FM) Brooklyn NY 2 hrs
*WDCV-FM Carlisle PA 1 hr
*WDCV-FM Carlisle PA 1 hr
WIBF-FM Jenkintown PA 1 hr
*WRVU(FM) Nashville TN 1 hr
KNTR(AM) Ferndale WA 1 hr

Scottish

*WCUW(FM) Worcester MA 2 hrs

Serbian

KTYM(AM) Inglewood CA 1 hr
WAIT(AM) Crystal Lake IL 1 hr
WKTA(AM) Evanston IL 12 hrs
WNDZ(AM) Portage IN 2 hrs
WNWI(AM) Valparaiso IN 1 hr
*WBWC(FM) Berea OH 5 hrs
*WCPN(FM) Cleveland OH 1 hr
*WCSB(FM) Cleveland OH 1 hr
WRDZ(AM) Cleveland OH 1 hr
WYLO(AM) Jackson WI 1 hr

Slovak

*WVOF(FM) Fairfield CT 2 hrs
*WWPT(FM) Westport CT 3 hrs
*WCPN(FM) Cleveland OH 1 hr
WERE(AM) Cleveland OH 1 hr
*WKTL(FM) Struthers OH 2 hrs
WCDL(AM) Carbondale PA 2 hrs

Slovenian

WCEV(AM) Cicero IL 1 hr
*WAPS(FM) Akron OH 2 hrs
*WCPN(FM) Cleveland OH 1 hr
*WCSB(FM) Cleveland OH 1 hr
WELW(AM) Willoughby-Eastlake OH 14 hrs
WBCW(AM) Jeannette PA 4 hrs
WCNZ(AM) Sheboygan WI 1 hr

Spanish

*KSKA(FM) Anchorage AK 3 hrs
KIYU(AM) Galena AK 3 hrs
*KTOO(FM) Juneau AK 1 hr
*KMXT(FM) Kodiak AK 1 hr
*WJAB(FM) Huntsville AL 2 hrs
KFPW(AM) Fort Smith AR 6 hrs
KAAY(AM) Little Rock AR 2 hrs
*KABF(FM) Little Rock AR 2 hrs
KVNA(AM) Flagstaff AZ 4 hrs
KJAA(AM) Globe AZ 10 hrs
KIKO(AM) Miami AZ 6 hrs
*KFLR-FM Phoenix AZ 1 hr
KHEP(AM) Phoenix AZ 5 hrs
*KFLT(AM) Tucson AZ 1 hr
*KUAT(AM) Tucson AZ 5 hrs
*KUAZ(FM) Tucson AZ 6 hrs
*KAWC(AM) Yuma AZ 15 hrs
*KPFA(FM) Berkeley CA 10 hrs
*KZFR(FM) Chico CA 6 hrs
KKCY(FM) Colusa CA 1 hr
KCEZ(FM) Corning CA 1 hr
*KKUP(FM) Cupertino CA 3 hrs
*KDVS(FM) Davis CA 5 hrs
KECR-FM El Cajon CA 7 hrs
*KECG(FM) El Cerrito CA 3 hrs
KWSW(AM) Eureka CA 1 hr
KSAY(FM) Fort Bragg CA 6 hrs
*KFCF(FM) Fresno CA 5 hrs
*KMUD(FM) Garberville CA 2 hrs
KKMC(AM) Gonzales CA 3 hrs
KTYM(AM) Inglewood CA 1 hr
KNTI(FM) Lakeport CA 3 hrs
*KPFK(FM) Los Angeles CA 11 hrs
*KUSC(FM) Los Angeles CA 2 hrs
*KXLU(FM) Los Angeles CA 24 hrs
KVOY(AM) Mojave CA 8 hrs
KVON(AM) Napa CA 5 hrs
*KPSC(FM) Palm Springs CA 2 hrs
*KPCC(FM) Pasadena CA 6 hrs
KTSJ(AM) Pomona CA 15 hrs
KBLF(AM) Red Bluff CA 4 hrs
KEST(AM) San Francisco CA 1 hr
*KSJS(FM) San Jose CA 5 hrs
*KCPR(FM) San Luis Obispo CA 3 hrs
KPRZ(AM) San Marcos CA 13 hrs
*KCSB-FM Santa Barbara CA 12 hrs
*KFAC(FM) Santa Barbara CA 2 hrs
*KUSP(FM) Santa Cruz CA 2 hrs
*KZSC(FM) Santa Cruz CA 6 hrs
KOWL(AM) South Lake Tahoe CA 4 hrs
*KZSU(FM) Stanford CA 6 hrs
*KSJC-FM Stockton CA 10 hrs
*KCPB(FM) Thousand Oaks CA 2 hrs
KERI(AM) Wasco CA 13 hrs
KXCL(FM) Yuba City CA 3 hrs
KGIW(AM) Alamosa CO 6 hrs
*KRZA(FM) Alamosa CO 14 hrs
*KGNU(FM) Boulder CO 3 hrs
KSIR-FM Brush CO 3 hrs
*KDNK(FM) Carbondale CO 2 hrs
KDTA(AM) Delta CO 3 hrs
*KPOF(AM) Denver CO 1 hr
*KUVO(FM) Denver CO 15 hrs
KYGO(AM) Denver CO 1 hr
KIUP(AM) Durango CO 3 hrs
KFTM(AM) Fort Morgan CO 4 hrs
*KJOL(FM) Grand Junction CO 2 hrs
KLMR(AM) Lamar CO 3 hrs
KVAY(FM) Lamar CO 6 hrs
KLMO(AM) Longmont CO 1 hr
KSLV(AM) Monte Vista CO 10 hrs
KURA(FM) Ouray CO 1 hr
*KVNF(FM) Paonia CO 2 hrs
*WPKN(FM) Bridgeport CT 4 hrs
WPRX(AM) Bristol CT 6 hrs
*WVOF(FM) Fairfield CT 12 hrs
*WRTC-FM Hartford CT 6 hrs
WNHC(AM) New Haven CT 1 hr
*WCNI(FM) New London CT 3 hrs
*WHUS(FM) Storrs CT 3 hrs
*WWUH(FM) West Hartford CT 3 hrs
*WNHU(FM) West Haven CT 12 hrs
WMMM(AM) Westport CT 7 hrs
*WDCU(FM) Washington DC 2 hrs
*WRTX(FM) Dover DE 4 hrs
WYUS(AM) Milford DE 6 hrs
*WVUD(FM) Newark DE 2 hrs
WDCF(AM) Dade City FL 3 hrs
WKIQ(AM) Eustis FL
*WAPN(FM) Holly Hill FL 4 hrs
WIIS(FM) Key West FL 3 hrs
WKRY(FM) Key West FL 2 hrs
WFIV(AM) Kissimmee FL 5 hrs
WIPC(AM) Lake Wales FL 6 hrs
*WLRN-FM Miami FL 3 hrs
WSBH(AM) Miami Beach FL 10 hrs
*WUCF-FM Orlando FL 3 hrs
WRNE(AM) Pensacola FL 6 hrs
WPOM(AM) Riviera Beach FL
WSPB(AM) Sarasota FL 1 hr
WTMY(AM) Sarasota FL
WTIS(AM) Tampa FL 1 hr
WSIR(AM) Winter Haven FL 6 hrs
*WRFG(FM) Atlanta GA 5 hrs
WFAM(AM) Augusta GA 1 hr
WBLJ(AM) Dalton GA 2 hrs
WSKX(FM) Hinesville GA 2 hrs
WKZD(AM) Murrayville GA 4 hrs
WCOP(AM) Warner Robins GA
KLNG(AM) Council Bluffs IA 17 hrs
*KALA(FM) Davenport IA 15 hrs
*KRUI-FM Iowa City IA 3 hrs
KWPC(AM) Muscatine IA 6 hrs
*KCUI(FM) Pella IA
*KWIT(FM) Sioux City IA 2 hrs
KBGN(AM) Caldwell ID 5 hrs
KCID(AM) Caldwell ID 4 hrs
KRCD(AM) Chubbuck ID 4 hrs
KRSS(FM) Chubbuck ID 4 hrs
KART(AM) Jerome ID
*KUOI-FM Moscow ID 2 hrs
KLVJ(AM) Mountain Home ID 5 hrs
KLVJ-FM Mountain Home ID 5 hrs
KBBK(AM) Rupert ID
WKKD(AM) Aurora IL 3 hrs
*WEFT(FM) Champaign IL 3 hrs
*WLUW(FM) Chicago IL 4 hrs
WSBC(AM) Chicago IL 18 hrs
WRMN(AM) Elgin IL 10 hrs
WVVX(FM) Highland Park IL 10 hrs
WHPO(FM) Hoopeston IL 1 hr
WWHN(AM) Joliet IL 1 hr
WJPC-FM Lansing IL 12 hrs
WLUV-FM Loves Park IL 1 hr
WPNA(AM) Oak Park IL 10 hrs
WSDR(AM) Sterling IL 2 hrs

Special Programming on Radio Stations in the U.S.

*WGCS(FM) Goshen IN 5 hrs
WGRL(FM) Indianapolis IN 1 hr
WIBC(AM) Indianapolis IN 2 hrs
WTPI(FM) Indianapolis IN 1 hr
WLNB(FM) Ligonier IN 1 hr
*WBKE-FM North Manchester IN 1 hr
*WEEM(FM) Pendleton IN 5 hrs
WNDU(AM) South Bend IN 1 hr
WSBT(AM) South Bend IN 1 hr
WRSW(AM) Warsaw IN 2 hrs
WRSW-FM Warsaw IN 2 hrs
KDCC(AM) Dodge City KS
*KONQ(FM) Dodge City KS 5 hrs
KCNW(AM) Fairway KS 1 hr
*KANZ(FM) Garden City KS 6 hrs
*KZNA(FM) Hill City KS 6 hrs
KWKR(FM) Leoti KS 3 hrs
KYUU(AM) Liberal KS 5 hrs
*KMUW(FM) Wichita KS 2 hrs
*WMMT(FM) Whitesburg KY 1 hr
*WAMH(FM) Amherst MA 2 hrs
*WFCR(FM) Amherst MA 4 hrs
*WMUA(FM) Amherst MA 9 hrs
*WBUR(FM) Boston MA 5 hrs
WEZE(AM) Boston MA 2 hrs
*WRBB(FM) Boston MA 4 hrs
WROL(AM) Boston MA 10 hrs
*WUMB-FM Boston MA 5 hrs
WHRB(FM) Cambridge MA 3 hrs
*WDJM-FM Framingham MA 8 hrs
WKOX(AM) Framingham MA 2 hrs
WHAV(AM) Haverhill MA 3 hrs
*WCCH(FM) Holyoke MA 2 hrs
*WJUL(FM) Lowell MA 15 hrs
*WMFO(FM) Medford MA 3 hrs
*WOZQ(FM) Northampton MA 3 hrs
*WNMH(FM) Northfield MA 4 hrs
*WBSL-FM Sheffield MA 2 hrs
WESO(AM) Southbridge MA 2 hrs
*WTCC(FM) Springfield MA 14 hrs
WPEP(AM) Taunton MA 3 hrs
*WBRS(FM) Waltham MA 2 hrs
WRCA(AM) Waltham MA
*WZLY(FM) Wellesley MA 1 hr
*WCUW(FM) Worcester MA 19 hrs
WORC(AM) Worcester MA 1 hr
WOLB(AM) Baltimore MD 2 hrs
*WMPG(FM) Gorham ME 2 hrs
WLEN(FM) Adrian MI 4 hrs
*WCBN-FM Ann Arbor MI 3 hrs
*WDET-FM Detroit MI 2 hrs
*WDTR(FM) Detroit MI 1 hr
*WKAR(AM) East Lansing MI 3 hrs
WKNX(AM) Frankenmuth MI 9 hrs
*WBYW(FM) Grand Rapids MI 12 hrs
WLAV(AM) Grand Rapids MI 1 hr
WHTC(AM) Holland MI 3 hrs
*WTHS(FM) Holland MI 8 hrs
WWJQ(AM) Holland MI 2 hrs
WIBM(AM) Jackson MI 1 hr
*WMUK(FM) Kalamazoo MI 1 hr
WCAR(AM) Livonia MI 5 hrs
WKCQ(FM) Saginaw MI 3 hrs
*WNMC-FM Traverse City MI 3 hrs
KATE(AM) Albert Lea MN 2 hrs
KYSM-FM Mankato MN 1 hr
*KBEM-FM Minneapolis MN 3 hrs
*KFAI(FM) Minneapolis MN 8 hrs
KRFO(AM) Owatonna MN 2 hrs
KXAX(FM) St. James MN 1 hr
*KWUR(FM) Clayton MO 2 hrs
KCMO(AM) Kansas City MO 1 hr
*KCUR-FM Kansas City MO 2 hrs
*KKFI(FM) Kansas City MO 16 hrs
*KDHX(FM) St. Louis MO 4 hrs
KSTL(AM) St. Louis MO 10 hrs
KBSR(AM) Laurel MT 8 hrs
*WGWG(FM) Boiling Springs NC 1 hr
WCLW(AM) Eden NC 6 hrs
*WFSS(FM) Fayetteville NC 6 hrs
*WQFS(FM) Greensboro NC 2 hrs
WIZS(AM) Henderson NC 6 hrs
*WSHA(FM) Raleigh NC 3 hrs
WNCA(AM) Siler City NC 3 hrs
WKSK(AM) West Jefferson NC 1 hr
WBFJ(AM) Winston-Salem NC 1 hr
*KDSU(FM) Fargo ND
KXPO(AM) Grafton ND 2 hrs
KXPO-FM Grafton ND 2 hrs
*KZUM(FM) Lincoln NE 4 hrs
*KJLT(AM) North Platte NE 1 hr
*KVNO(FM) Omaha NE 2 hrs
KNEB(AM) Scottsbluff NE 5 hrs
WUSS(AM) Atlantic City NJ 6 hrs
WSSJ(AM) Camden NJ 10 hrs
WJDM(AM) Elizabeth NJ 2 hrs
*WBJB-FM Lincroft NJ 4 hrs
*WRSU-FM New Brunswick NJ 2 hrs
*WRTQ(FM) Ocean City NJ 4 hrs
WERA(AM) Plainfield NJ 2 hrs
*WSOU(FM) South Orange NJ 1 hr
WTTM(AM) Trenton NJ 6 hrs
*WMSC(FM) Upper Montclair NJ 2 hrs
*KANW(FM) Albuquerque NM 6 hrs
*KFLQ(FM) Albuquerque NM 3 hrs
*KUNM(FM) Albuquerque NM 9 hrs
KSVP(AM) Artesia NM 15 hrs
KCQL(AM) Aztec NM 6 hrs
KATK-FM Carlsbad NM
KOTS(AM) Deming NM 8 hrs
KYVA(AM) Gallup NM 2 hrs
KROL(FM) Las Cruces NM 15 hrs
*KRWG(FM) Las Cruces NM 15 hrs
*KEDP(FM) Las Vegas NM 5 hrs
KLEA(AM) Lovington NM 6 hrs
KBUY(AM) Ruidoso NM 4 hrs
KWES(FM) Ruidoso NM 4 hrs
KSSR(AM) Santa Rosa NM 15 hrs
KSIL(AM) Silver City NM 13 hrs
KMXQ(FM) Socorro NM 3 hrs
KTAO(FM) Taos NM 3 hrs
KCHS(AM) Truth or Consequences NM 12 hrs
KTNM(AM) Tucumcari NM 18 hrs
KPTL(AM) Carson City NV 4 hrs
*KUNV(FM) Las Vegas NV 9 hrs
KROW(AM) Reno NV 2 hrs
WCSS(AM) Amsterdam NY 3 hrs
*WHRW(FM) Binghamton NY 20 hrs
*WXBA(FM) Brentwood NY 5 hrs
WCHP(AM) Champlain NY
WVOA(FM) DeRuyter NY 1 hr
WDOE(AM) Dunkirk NY 2 hrs
WEHM(FM) East Hampton NY 1 hr
WSIV(AM) East Syracuse NY 1 hr
*WGMC(FM) Greece NY 10 hrs
*WRHU(FM) Hempstead NY 1 hr
*WHVP(FM) Hudson NY 1 hr
WJTN(AM) Jamestown NY 1 hr
*WFGB(FM) Kingston NY 1 hr
WXRL(AM) Lancaster NY 2 hrs
WVOS(AM) Liberty NY 2 hrs
*WVCR-FM Loudonville NY 6 hrs
WTHE(AM) Mineola NY 10 hrs
*WLJP(FM) Monroe NY 1 hr
*WFNP(FM) New Paltz NY 3 hrs
*WBAI(FM) New York NY 3 hrs
*WFUV(FM) New York NY 4 hrs
*WKCR-FM New York NY 15 hrs
WHLD(AM) Niagara Falls NY 15 hrs
*WRHO(FM) Oneonta NY 2 hrs
*WRPJ(FM) Port Jervis NY 1 hr
*WVKR-FM Poughkeepsie NY 3 hrs
*WRUR-FM Rochester NY 3 hrs
WWWG(AM) Rochester NY 3 hrs
*WSPN(FM) Saratoga Springs NY 3 hrs
*WRUC(FM) Schenectady NY 3 hrs
*WUSB(FM) Stony Brook NY 3 hrs
WRUN(AM) Utica NY 1 hr
*WAPS(FM) Akron OH 1 hr
*WBGU(FM) Bowling Green OH 4 hrs
*WCSB(FM) Cleveland OH 12 hrs
WRDZ(AM) Cleveland OH 17 hrs
WEOL(AM) Elyria OH 4 hrs
WFOB(AM) Fostoria OH 3 hrs
WYHK(FM) Gibsonburg OH 8 hrs
*WOBC-FM Oberlin OH 8 hrs
WCCD(AM) Parma OH 1 hr
WXKR(FM) Port Clinton OH 1 hr
*WKTL(FM) Struthers OH 1 hr
WERT(AM) Van Wert OH 1 hr
KWHW(AM) Altus OK 16 hrs
KCLI(FM) Clinton OK 3 hrs
KCFO(AM) Tulsa OK 1 hr
*KMUN(FM) Astoria OR 5 hrs
*KBVR(FM) Corvallis OR 1 hr
*KLCC(FM) Eugene OR 5 hrs
*KWVA(FM) Eugene OR 4 hrs
KOHU(AM) Hermiston OR 4 hrs
KUIK(AM) Hillsboro OR 17 hrs
KIHR(AM) Hood River OR 2 hrs
KAGO(AM) Klamath Falls OR 5 hrs
KLYC(AM) McMinnville OR 3 hrs
KYJC(AM) Medford OR 3 hrs
*KLCO(FM) Newport OR 5 hrs
KUMA(AM) Pendleton OR 1 hr
*KBOO(FM) Portland OR 10 hrs
*KBPS(AM) Portland OR 1 hr
*KBVM(FM) Portland OR 2 hrs
*KRRC(FM) Portland OR 2 hrs
*KSJK(AM) Talent OR 6 hrs
KODL(AM) The Dalles OR 2 hrs
KLWJ(AM) Umatilla OR 1 hr
WHOL(AM) Allentown PA 13 hrs
*WMUH(FM) Allentown PA 4 hrs
WGPA(AM) Bethlehem PA 1 hr
*WDCV-FM Carlisle PA 1 hr
*WJRH(FM) Easton PA 6 hrs
*WERG(FM) Erie PA 3 hrs
*WMCE(FM) Erie PA 3 hrs
*WQLN-FM Erie PA 1 hr
*WZBT(FM) Gettysburg PA 1 hr
*WRTY(FM) Jackson Township PA 4 hrs
WCTX(FM) Palmyra PA 1 hr
*WRTI(FM) Philadelphia PA 4 hrs
WRAW(AM) Reading PA 3 hrs
*WXAC(FM) Reading PA 8 hrs
*WJAZ(FM) Summerdale PA 4 hrs
*WVYC(FM) York PA 1 hr
WBMJ(AM) San Juan PR 13 hrs
WIVV(AM) Vieques PR 14 hrs
*WRIU(FM) Kingston RI 3 hrs
WALE(AM) Providence RI 4 hrs
WARV(AM) Warwick RI 1 hr
*WHCB(FM) Bristol TN 1 hr
WAMB(AM) Donelson TN 6 hrs
*WFMQ(FM) Lebanon TN 3 hrs
*WEVL(FM) Memphis TN 3 hrs
*WRVU(FM) Nashville TN 1 hr
KVLF(AM) Alpine TX 10 hrs
KTEK(AM) Alvin TX 2 hrs
KRUN(AM) Ballinger TX 4 hrs
KRUN-FM Ballinger TX 4 hrs
*KVLU(FM) Beaumont TX 5 hrs
KIXV(FM) Brady TX 12 hrs
KNEL(AM) Brady TX 12 hrs
KBOC(FM) Bridgeport TX 1 hr
KKUB(AM) Brownfield TX 16 hrs
KXYL(AM) Brownwood TX 16 hrs
KSTA(AM) Coleman TX 5 hrs
KSTA-FM Coleman TX 5 hrs
*KAMU-FM College Station TX 2 hrs
KCTA(AM) Corpus Christi TX 6 hrs
*KEDT-FM Corpus Christi TX 4 hrs
KQRO(AM) Cuero TX 5 hrs
KQRO-FM Cuero TX 5 hrs
*KVTT(FM) Dallas TX 2 hrs
*KNTU(FM) Denton TX 6 hrs
KDHN(AM) Dimmitt TX 17 hrs
KDIU(FM) Dimmitt TX 17 hrs
KDDD(AM) Dumas TX 16 hrs
KTMR(AM) Edna TX 12 hrs
KULP(AM) El Campo TX 14 hrs
*KTEP(FM) El Paso TX 7 hrs
KFST(AM) Fort Stockton TX 20 hrs
KFST-FM Fort Stockton TX 20 hrs
KJOJ-FM Freeport TX 10 hrs
KGBC(AM) Galveston TX 5 hrs
KCTI(AM) Gonzales TX 6 hrs
KPJN(FM) Gonzales TX 6 hrs
*KMBH-FM Harlingen TX 3 hrs
KPAN(AM) Hereford TX 15 hrs
KPAN-FM Hereford TX 15 hrs
*KHCB-FM Houston TX 10 hrs
*KPFT(FM) Houston TX 7 hrs
KGOL(AM) Humble TX 9 hrs
*KBJS(FM) Jacksonville TX 1 hr
KERV(AM) Kerrville TX 1 hr
KYMI(FM) Los Ybanez TX
KRBA(AM) Lufkin TX 30 hrs
*KHID(FM) McAllen TX 3 hrs
KLSR(AM) Memphis TX 6 hrs
KLSR-FM Memphis TX 6 hrs
KVOP(AM) Plainview TX 12 hrs
*KLUX(FM) Robstown TX 2 hrs
KRXT(FM) Rockdale TX 4 hrs
KTLU(AM) Rusk TX 4 hrs
KWRW(FM) Rusk TX 4 hrs
*KSYM-FM San Antonio TX 4 hrs
KIKZ(AM) Seminole TX 26 hrs
KSEM-FM Seminole TX 26 hrs
KSNY(AM) Snyder TX 6 hrs
KCHG(AM) Somerset TX
KHOS(AM) Sonora TX 19 hrs
KRDF-FM Spearman TX 7 hrs
KVRP(AM) Stamford TX 20 hrs
KXOX(AM) Sweetwater TX 8 hrs
KXOX-FM Sweetwater TX 8 hrs
KTAE(AM) Taylor TX 14 hrs
KTEM(AM) Temple TX 2 hrs
KPYK(AM) Terrell TX 2 hrs
*KVNE-FM Tyler TX 2 hrs
KUVA(FM) Uvalde TX 19 hrs
KVWC(AM) Vernon TX 4 hrs
KRZI(AM) Waco TX 14 hrs
KBEC(AM) Waxahachie TX 10 hrs
KANI(AM) Wharton TX 3 hrs
*KPDR(FM) Wheeler TX 5 hrs
KLLF(AM) Wichita Falls TX 18 hrs
KSOS(AM) Brigham City UT 2 hrs
*KWCR-FM Ogden UT 12 hrs
*KRCL(FM) Salt Lake City UT 1 hr
KVEL(AM) Vernal UT
WPWC(AM) Dumfries-Triangle VA 1 hr
WFAX(AM) Falls Church VA 1 hr
*WHOV(FM) Hampton VA 9 hrs
WKGM(AM) Smithfield VA 01 hr
*WYCS(FM) Yorktown VA 1 hr
WSTX(AM) Christiansted VI 2 hrs
WVIS(FM) Christiansted VI 1 hr
*WIUJ(FM) St. Thomas VI 1 hr
*WIUV(FM) Castleton VT 1 hr
*WRMC-FM Middlebury VT 1 hr
*KBCS(FM) Bellevue WA 4 hrs
*KUGS(FM) Bellingham WA 3 hrs
KARI(AM) Blaine WA 1 hr
KOZI(AM) Chelan WA 4 hrs
KOZI-FM Chelan WA 4 hrs
KNTR(AM) Ferndale WA 1 hr
KARY-FM Grandview WA
KBSN(AM) Moses Lake WA 9 hrs
KWIQ-FM Moses Lake WA 4 hrs
KWIQ(AM) Moses Lake North WA 4 hrs
KBRC(AM) Mount Vernon WA 3 hrs
*KAOS(FM) Olympia WA 6 hrs
*KAOS(FM) Olympia WA 6 hrs
KOMW(AM) Omak WA 2 hrs
KARY(AM) Prosser WA
*KZUU(FM) Pullman WA 3 hrs
KWNC(AM) Quincy WA 7 hrs
KBLE(AM) Seattle WA 7 hrs
*KUOW(FM) Seattle WA 2 hrs
*KBTC-FM Tacoma WA 2 hrs
KBBO(AM) Yakima WA 2 hrs
*WGBW(FM) Green Bay WI 1 hr
*WMSE(FM) Milwaukee WI 3 hrs
*WYMS(FM) Milwaukee WI 3 hrs
WRJN(AM) Racine WI 1 hr
*WCCX(FM) Waukesha WI 8 hrs
KFBC(AM) Cheyenne WY 2 hrs
KRAE(AM) Cheyenne WY 2 hrs
KUGR(AM) Green River WY 4 hrs
KGOS(AM) Torrington WY 1 hr

Sports

KABN(AM) Long Island AK
WHMA(AM) Anniston AL
WAUD(AM) Auburn AL 10 hrs
*WMBV(FM) Dixon's Mills AL 1 hr
WBLX(AM) Fairhope AL 12 hrs
*WBHL(FM) Florence AL
WMGY(AM) Montgomery AL 6 hrs
WVNA(AM) Tuscumbia AL
WQRX(AM) Valley Head AL
KPIK(FM) Beebe AR
KJBN(AM) Little Rock AR
KKER(FM) Casa Grande AZ 7 hrs
KVNA(AM) Flagstaff AZ 12 hrs
KDJI(AM) Holbrook AZ 10 hrs
KAAA(AM) Kingman AZ
KPGE(AM) Page AZ
KQST(FM) Sedona AZ
KAPL(AM) Apple Valley CA 20 hrs
KATA(AM) Arcata CA
KROP(AM) Brawley CA 7 hrs
KMJ(AM) Fresno CA 8 hrs
KHSJ(AM) Hemet CA
KRKC(AM) King City CA 9 hrs
KAVL(AM) Lancaster CA
KTME(AM) Lompoc CA
KLAC(AM) Los Angeles CA
KKHI(AM) San Francisco CA
*KSCU(FM) Santa Clara CA 2 hrs
KVOR(AM) Colorado Springs CO
KIQX(FM) Durango CO
KIUP(AM) Durango CO 4 hrs
KRSJ(FM) Durango CO 4 hrs
KPKE(AM) Gunnison CO 10 hrs
KIIX(AM) Wellington CO 3 hrs
WGCH(AM) Greenwich CT 6 hrs
WWBF(AM) Bartow FL
*WVUM(FM) Coral Gables FL 5 hrs
WMLO(FM) Havana FL 3 hrs
WRFM(AM) Hialeah FL
WGTO(AM) Pine Hills FL
WKII(AM) Port Charlotte FL
WQYK(AM) Seffner FL 20 hrs
WYOO(FM) Springfield FL 8 hrs
WFOY(AM) St. Augustine FL
WQYK-FM St. Petersburg FL
WNLS(AM) Tallahassee FL
WAMR(AM) Venice FL
WGAU(AM) Athens GA
WRFC(AM) Athens GA 12 hrs
WMGR(AM) Bainbridge GA 15 hrs
WGAA(AM) Cedartown GA
WQSY(FM) Hawkinsville GA 10 hrs
KPUA(AM) Hilo HI
KHVH(AM) Honolulu HI
KWAI(AM) Honolulu HI 3 hrs
KCPS(AM) Burlington IA 10 hrs
*KWLC(AM) Decorah IA 6 hrs
KMCH(FM) Manchester IA 7 hrs
KCII(AM) Washington IA
KWLO(AM) Waterloo IA
*KWDM(FM) West Des Moines IA 3 hrs
KATW(FM) Lewiston ID
KSPT(AM) Sandpoint ID 6 hrs
KOFE(AM) St. Maries ID 3 hrs
KTFI(AM) Twin Falls ID 3 hrs
WCNL(FM) Carlinville IL 3 hrs
WGN(AM) Chicago IL
WMAQ(AM) Chicago IL
WZRO(FM) Farmer City IL 5 hrs
WAIK(AM) Galesburg IL 10 hrs
WGBQ(FM) Galesburg IL 10 hrs
WGEN(AM) Geneseo IL
*WMWA(FM) Glenview IL 8 hrs
WJBM(AM) Jerseyville IL 13 hrs
*WLTL(FM) La Grange IL 5 hrs
WLLR(AM) Moline IL
WBBA(AM) Pittsfield IL 6 hrs
WGFA-FM Watseka IL 20 hrs
WFRX-FM West Frankfort IL
WHBU(AM) Anderson IN
WBQR(FM) Attica IN
WBIW(AM) Bedford IN
WUZR(FM) Bicknell IN
WGCL(AM) Bloomington IN
WQFE(FM) Brownsburg IN
WLME(FM) Cannelton IN 6 hrs
*WJHS(FM) Columbia City IN
WLYV(AM) Fort Wayne IN
WJOB(AM) Hammond IN
WERK(AM) Muncie IN
*WEEM(FM) Pendleton IN 10 hrs
WKJK(FM) Salem IN
WSLM-FM Salem IN
WKID(FM) Vevay IN 12 hrs
WZZY(FM) Winchester IN 10 hrs
KAYS(AM) Hays KS
WWLW(FM) Carlisle KY
WKCM(AM) Hawesville KY 6 hrs
WKYL(FM) Lawrenceburg KY 4 hrs
WLSK(FM) Lebanon KY
WLXG(AM) Lexington KY
WWKY(AM) Louisville KY
WMDJ(AM) Martin KY
WDXR(AM) Paducah KY
WCBR(AM) Richmond KY
KALB(AM) Alexandria LA 15 hrs
KEZM(AM) Sulphur LA
KXOR(FM) Thibodaux LA
WKOX(AM) Framingham MA 15 hrs
WORC(AM) Worcester MA 8 hrs
WVEI(AM) Worcester MA
WBAL(AM) Baltimore MD
WTRI(AM) Brunswick MD 5 hrs
WALI(AM) Cumberland MD
WXCY(FM) Havre de Grace MD 6 hrs
WMOM(AM) La Plata MD 8 hrs
WTHU(AM) Thurmont MD 3 hrs
*WBOR(FM) Brunswick ME 5 hrs
WDEA(AM) Ellsworth ME
WSKW(AM) Skowhegan ME
WAAM(AM) Ann Arbor MI 4 hrs
*WBFH(FM) Bloomfield Hills MI 6 hrs
WJZZ(FM) Detroit MI 2 hrs
WWJ(AM) Detroit MI
WMJZ-FM Gaylord MI 26 hrs
WWGZ(AM) Lapeer MI 4 hrs
WAGN(AM) Menominee MI 12 hrs
WNBY-FM Newberry MI
WUPY(FM) Ontonagon MI 1 hr
WMZX(FM) Owosso MI 4 hrs
*WPHS(FM) Warren MI 3 hrs
WYGR(AM) Wyoming MI 3 hrs
KXDL(FM) Browerville MN 2 hrs
KDWA(AM) Hastings MN
KLFD(AM) Litchfield MN
KEYL(AM) Long Prairie MN 10 hrs
KWEB(AM) Rochester MN
KMSR(FM) Sauk Centre MN 6 hrs
KSTP(AM) St. Paul MN
KZIM(AM) Cape Girardeau MO 10 hrs
KWAS(AM) Joplin MO
KBDZ(FM) Perryville MO 5 hrs
KSIM(AM) Sikeston MO
WMLC(AM) Monticello MS 5 hrs
WMFM(FM) Petal MS 3 hrs
WRJW(AM) Picayune MS 4 hrs
KGVW(AM) Belgrade MT
KBLG(AM) Billings MT 10 hrs
KMON(AM) Great Falls MT 5 hrs
KMSL(AM) Great Falls MT
KMTA(AM) Kinsey MT 3 hrs
KBSR(AM) Laurel MT
KPRK(AM) Livingston MT
WZZU(FM) Burlington-Graham NC
WCSL(AM) Cherryville NC 3 hrs
WLOE(AM) Eden NC 20 hrs
WFAI(AM) Fayetteville NC 20 hrs
WIRC(AM) Hickory NC 5 hrs
WLAS(AM) Jacksonville NC
WHLQ(FM) Louisburg NC
WCBQ(AM) Oxford NC
WNCA(AM) Siler City NC 6 hrs
WAME(AM) Statesville NC
WSVM(AM) Valdese NC 15 hrs
WTQR(FM) Winston-Salem NC
KLXX(AM) Bismarck-Mandan ND 6 hrs
KDLR(AM) Devils Lake ND
KFGO(AM) Fargo ND 20 hrs
KIMB(AM) Kimball NE
KNCY(AM) Nebraska City NE 6 hrs
KNCY-FM Nebraska City NE 6 hrs
*WJSV(FM) Morristown NJ 3 hrs
WOND(AM) Pleasantville NJ
WHWH(AM) Princeton NJ
*WMSC(FM) Upper Montclair NJ 3 hrs
WNJC(AM) Washington Township NJ
KKEL(AM) Hobbs NM
KSNM(FM) Truth or Consequences NM 4 hrs
KROW(AM) Reno NV
WAUB(AM) Auburn NY 4 hrs
WBTA(AM) Batavia NY 9 hrs
*WHCL-FM Clinton NY 4 hrs
WDNY-FM Dansville NY 4 hrs
WVBR-FM Ithaca NY 4 hrs
WMSA(AM) Massena NY
*WNYE(FM) New York NY 10 hrs
*WRUC(FM) Schenectady NY 4 hrs
*WSBU(FM) St. Bonaventure NY 3 hrs
WNYV(FM) Whitehall NY 3 hrs
WAKR(AM) Akron OH 14 hrs
WFUN(AM) Ashtabula OH
WBNO-FM Bryan OH
WQCT(AM) Bryan OH
WCDK(FM) Cadiz OH
WBNS(AM) Columbus OH
WFIN(AM) Findlay OH 12 hrs
WMOH(AM) Hamilton OH
WLOH(AM) Lancaster OH 8 hrs
WMOA(AM) Marietta OH 15 hrs
WTIG(AM) Massillon OH 20 hrs
WKLM(FM) Millersburg OH
WCWA(AM) Toledo OH 15 hrs
WELW(AM) Willoughby-Eastlake OH 10 hrs
WHIZ(AM) Zanesville OH
WHIZ-FM Zanesville OH 3 hrs
KKAJ(AM) Ardmore OK
KCLI(FM) Clinton OK 6 hrs
KXOL(AM) Clinton OK
KBEL(AM) Idabel OK
KBEL-FM Idabel OK
KXXY(AM) Oklahoma City OK

Broadcasting & Cable Yearbook 1994
B-587

Special Programming on Radio Stations in the U.S.

KXXY-FM Oklahoma City OK
KGFF(AM) Shawnee OK
KTWS(FM) Bend OR
KPNW(AM) Eugene OR
KYKN(AM) Keizer OR
KWJJ(AM) Portland OR
KCKX(AM) Stayton OR
WZWW(FM) Bellefonte PA 3 hrs
WCNR(AM) Bloomsburg PA 12 hrs
WCDL(AM) Carbondale PA 8 hrs
WNZT(AM) Columbia PA 4 hrs
*WFSE(FM) Edinboro PA
WRQQ(AM) Farrell PA 12 hrs
WHUN(AM) Huntingdon PA
*WFNM(FM) Lancaster PA 2 hrs
WLAN-FM Lancaster PA
WLPA(AM) Lancaster PA 20 hrs
WBPZ(AM) Lock Haven PA
*WMSS(FM) Middletown PA 5 hrs
WQLV(FM) Millersburg PA
WEYZ(AM) North East PA 4 hrs
WRKT(FM) North East PA 4 hrs
WMMR(FM) Philadelphia PA
WOGL(AM) Philadelphia PA
KQV(AM) Pittsburgh PA
WARM(AM) Scranton PA
*WRSK(FM) Slippery Rock PA 1 hr
WMAJ(AM) State College PA 20 hrs
WXPX(AM) West Hazleton PA
WBAX(AM) Wilkes-Barre PA
*WWAS(FM) Williamsport PA 2 hrs
WWPA(AM) Williamsport PA
WLEY(AM) Cayey PR
WLEO(AM) Ponce PR
WKFE(AM) Yauco PR
*WDOM(FM) Providence RI 2 hrs
WBLR(AM) Batesburg SC 10 hrs
WVGB(AM) Beaufort SC
WAGS(AM) Bishopville SC 6 hrs
WOKE(AM) Charleston SC 20 hrs
WOMG(AM) Columbia SC
WPJS(AM) Conway SC
WAGI-FM Gaffney SC
WFBC(AM) Greenville SC
WDAI(FM) Pawley's Island SC
WORD(AM) Spartanburg SC
WBCU(AM) Union SC 10 hrs
KPHR(FM) Milbank SD 5 hrs
KSDR-FM Watertown SD 8 hrs
WNAX(AM) Yankton SD 10 hrs
WBIN-FM Benton TN
WDEF(AM) Chattanooga TN
WAKF(AM) Franklin TN 4 hrs
WIZO(FM) Franklin TN 6 hrs
WDXI(AM) Jackson TN 16 hrs
WGKX(FM) Memphis TN
WMC(AM) Memphis TN
*WQOX(FM) Memphis TN 6 hrs
*WSMS(FM) Memphis TN
WTRB-FM Ripley TN
WTNE(AM) Trenton TN
WWEZ(FM) Trenton TN 20 hrs
WBRY(AM) Woodbury TN 10 hrs
KSKY(AM) Balch Springs TX 14 hrs
KAKS(AM) Canyon TX
KCAR(AM) Clarksville TX 10 hrs
KRYS(AM) Corpus Christi TX
KDSX(AM) Denison-Sherman TX 10 hrs
KROD(AM) El Paso TX
KAWA(AM) Floydada TX
KFLL(FM) Floydada TX
WBAP(AM) Fort Worth TX
KGAF(AM) Gainesville TX 3 hrs
KCYL(AM) Lampasas TX 8 hrs
KCUL-FM Marshall TX

KPOS(AM) Post TX 8 hrs
KPOS-FM Post TX 8 hrs
KJAK(FM) Slaton TX 5 hrs
KJMX(FM) Tulia TX
KZEE(AM) Weatherford TX 8 hrs
WABN(AM) Abingdon VA 5 hrs
WBBC-FM Blackstone VA 10 hrs
WFTR-FM Front Royal VA
WMEV(AM) Marion VA
WMEV-FM Marion VA
WTAR(AM) Norfolk VA
WYTI(AM) Rocky Mount VA
WLPM(AM) Suffolk VA 8 hrs
WNTW(AM) Winchester VA
WTSA(AM) Brattleboro VT
WFAD(AM) Middlebury VT 10 hrs
WNHV(AM) White River Junction VT
*KASB(FM) Bellevue WA 6 hrs
KCLX(AM) Colfax WA 7 hrs
KLLM(FM) Forks WA 20 hrs
KVAC(AM) Forks WA 20 hrs
KONA(AM) Kennewick WA 8 hrs
KONA-FM Kennewick WA 3 hrs
KTCR(AM) Kennewick WA
KTOL(AM) Lacey WA 6 hrs
KJUN(AM) Puyallup WA 6 hrs
KOMO(AM) Seattle WA
KJRB(AM) Spokane WA
KTRW(AM) Spokane WA
KREW(AM) Sunnyside WA
WNFL(AM) Green Bay WI 15 hrs
WOGO(AM) Hallie WI
WLIP(AM) Kenosha WI
WTOQ(AM) Platteville WI 15 hrs
WCWC(AM) Ripon WI
WCNZ(AM) Sheboygan WI 5 hrs
*WWSP(FM) Stevens Point WI 3 hrs
WAUK(AM) Waukesha WI
WJLS(AM) Beckley WV 10 hrs
WWNR(AM) Beckley WV
WWYO(FM) Pineville WV 20 hrs

Talk

WKYD(AM) Andalusia AL 20 hrs
WAPI(AM) Birmingham AL 17 hrs
WJDB(AM) Thomasville AL 15 hrs
WVNA(AM) Tuscumbia AL
KHOZ(AM) Harrison AR 12 hrs
KCUZ(AM) Clifton AZ 8 hrs
KLPZ(AM) Parker AZ 15 hrs
KFMM(FM) Thatcher AZ 8 hrs
*KMUD(FM) Garberville CA 7 hrs
KKMC(AM) Gonzales CA 10 hrs
KHSJ(AM) Hemet CA
KWBR(FM) Pismo Beach CA 1 hr
KVEC(AM) San Luis Obispo CA
*KSCU(FM) Santa Clara CA 1 hr
KSCO(AM) Santa Cruz CA
KIIX(AM) Wellington CO 4 hrs
KRDZ(AM) Wray CO 15 hrs
WGCH(AM) Greenwich CT 4 hrs
WINY(AM) Putnam CT 10 hrs
WEBE(AM) Westport CT 1 hr
WOL(AM) Washington DC 20 hrs
WTLN-FM Apopka FL 17 hrs
WDCF(AM) Dade City FL 16 hrs
WIIS(AM) Key West FL 5 hrs
WAVK(FM) Marathon FL 1 hr
WPGS(AM) Mims FL 1 hr
WKAT(AM) North Miami FL 3 hrs
WRNE(AM) Pensacola FL
WRFC(AM) Athens GA 12 hrs
*WRFG(FM) Atlanta GA 9 hrs
WBAF(AM) Barnesville GA 5 hrs

*WFRC(FM) Columbus GA 8 hrs
WQSI(AM) Hawkinsville GA 15 hrs
WYTH(AM) Madison GA 15 hrs
*KUCB-FM Des Moines IA 13 hrs
KCJJ(AM) Iowa City IA 1 hr
KLVJ(AM) Mountain Home ID 15 hrs
WFMT(FM) Chicago IL 5 hrs
*WHFH(FM) Flossmoor IL 1 hr
WAIK(AM) Galesburg IL 10 hrs
WGEN(AM) Geneseo IL
WEEF(AM) Highland Park IL 5 hrs
*WCSF(FM) Joliet IL 4 hrs
WGFA(AM) Watseka IL 1 hr
WQFE(AM) Brownsburg IN
WIOU(AM) Kokomo IN 15 hrs
WKJK(FM) Salem IN
WSLM-FM Salem IN
WKID(AM) Vevay IN 2 hrs
WLBN(AM) Lebanon KY 5 hrs
WTBK(FM) Manchester KY 8 hrs
KBCE(FM) Boyce LA 1 hr
KVLA(AM) Vidalia LA 15 hrs
*WAMH(FM) Amherst MA 2 hrs
WFNX(FM) Lynn MA 4 hrs
WACM(AM) West Springfield MA
*WEAA(FM) Baltimore MD 14 hrs
WTRI(AM) Brunswick MD 2 hrs
WJEJ(AM) Hagerstown MD 8 hrs
*WRBC(FM) Lewiston ME 2 hrs
WATZ(AM) Alpena MI 15 hrs
WLTI(FM) Detroit MI 1 hr
WKLK(AM) Cloquet MN 1 hr
WWJC(AM) Duluth MN 8 hrs
*KUMM(FM) Morris MN 3 hrs
KARL(FM) Tracy MN
KRZK(AM) Branson MO 1 hr
KIRX(AM) Kirksville MO 12 hrs
KSIM(AM) Sikeston MO
WRFX(AM) Kannapolis NC 3 hrs
*WKNC-FM Raleigh NC 1 hr
WRGC(AM) Sylva NC 5 hrs
WDAY(AM) Fargo ND
WMOU(AM) Berlin NH 2 hrs
*WCVH(FM) Flemington NJ 2 hrs
WRNJ(AM) Hackettstown NJ 10 hrs
KYKK(AM) Hobbs NM 18 hrs
KMOU(FM) Roswell NM 5 hrs
KRSY(AM) Roswell NM 15 hrs
KLKO(FM) Elko NV 15 hrs
WBTA(AM) Batavia NY 15 hrs
*WKRB(FM) Brooklyn NY 2 hrs
WCGR(AM) Canandaigua NY 6 hrs
WEHM(FM) East Hampton NY 5 hrs
WELV(AM) Ellenville NY 3 hrs
WENT(AM) Gloversville NY 1 hr
WVOS(AM) Liberty NY 2 hrs
WEOK(AM) Poughkeepsie NY 5 hrs
WNDR(AM) Syracuse NY 10 hrs
WONW(AM) Defiance OH 3 hrs
WCIT(AM) Lima OH 5 hrs
WNXT(AM) Portsmouth OH
*KNYD(FM) Broken Arrow OK 5 hrs
*KOKF(FM) Edmond OK 3 hrs
KCRC(AM) Enid OK 5 hrs
*KMSI(FM) Moore OK 5 hrs
KGFF(AM) Shawnee OK
KVOO(AM) Tulsa OK 2 hrs
KAST(AM) Astoria OR
KWIP(AM) Dallas OR 5 hrs
KWVR(AM) Enterprise OR 15 hrs
WBFD(AM) Bedford PA 10 hrs
*WBUQ(FM) Bloomsburg PA 1 hr
*WPEB(FM) Philadelphia PA 16 hrs
WANB(AM) Waynesburg PA 5 hrs

WXPX(AM) West Hazleton PA 2 hrs
WZAR(FM) Ponce PR 15 hrs
*WRTU(FM) San Juan PR 2 hrs
WKRI(AM) West Warwick RI
WAGI-FM Gaffney SC 10 hrs
*WPLS-FM Greenville SC 3 hrs
WRIX-FM Honea Path SC 20 hrs
WBIN-FM Benton TN
WZYX(FM) Cowan TN
KIXZ(AM) Amarillo TX 2 hrs
KBOC(AM) Bridgeport TX 5 hrs
KNES(AM) Fairfield TX 15 hrs
KLDE(AM) Houston TX 2 hrs
KMJQ(AM) Houston TX 3 hrs
KYOK(AM) Houston TX 12 hrs
*KSTX(FM) San Antonio TX 6 hrs
KZEE(AM) Weatherford TX 5 hrs
KSUB(AM) Cedar City UT
WABN(AM) Abingdon VA 2 hrs
WVES(AM) Accomac VA 2 hrs
WSVY-FM Windsor VA 5 hrs
WVIS(FM) Christiansted VI 6 hrs
WKXE-FM White River Junction VT 2 hrs
KGNW(AM) Burien-Seattle WA
*KVTI(FM) Tacoma WA 4 hrs
WTKM(FM) Hartford WI 15 hrs
WLDY(AM) Ladysmith WI 4 hrs
WRJC(AM) Mauston WI 15 hrs
WPDR(AM) Portage WI 12 hrs
*WRFW(FM) River Falls WI
WOBG(AM) Clarksburg WV
KODI(AM) Cody WY 18 hrs

Ukrainian

WILI(AM) Willimantic CT 1 hr
WEDC(AM) Chicago IL 1 hr
WSBC(AM) Chicago IL 1 hr
WCEV(AM) Cicero IL 4 hrs
WPNA(AM) Oak Park IL 4 hrs
*WFUV(FM) New York NY 1 hr
WHLD(AM) Niagara Falls NY 3 hrs
*WCPN(FM) Cleveland OH 1 hr
WRMR(AM) Cleveland OH 1 hr
*WKTL(FM) Struthers OH 1 hr
WIBF-FM Jenkintown PA 1 hr
*WPEL(FM) Montrose PA 1 hr
KARI(AM) Blaine WA 1 hr

Urban Contemporary

*KFJC(FM) Los Altos CA 4 hrs
*KSCU(FM) Santa Clara CA 6 hrs
*KZSC(FM) Santa Cruz CA 10 hrs
*KUOP(FM) Stockton CA 6 hrs
*KCSS(FM) Turlock CA 10 hrs
*WREK(FM) Atlanta GA 2 hrs
*WVVS(FM) Valdosta GA 3 hrs
*KUSR(FM) Ames IA
*KUCB-FM Des Moines IA 20 hrs
*KICB(FM) Fort Dodge IA 2 hrs
*WVUR-FM Valparaiso IN 3 hrs
KQLA(FM) Ogden KS 4 hrs
*WRFL(FM) Lexington KY 3 hrs
*WTUL(FM) New Orleans LA 2 hrs
*WDJM-FM Framingham MA 2 hrs
*WBOR(FM) Brunswick ME 10 hrs
*WMEB-FM Orono ME 5 hrs
*WSGR-FM Port Huron MI 14 hrs
*KCFV(FM) Ferguson MO 4 hrs
*KMVC(FM) Marshall MO 20 hrs
*WASU-FM Boone NC 6 hrs
*WSUC-FM Cortland NY 7 hrs
*WEOS(FM) Geneva NY 18 hrs
*WITR(FM) Henrietta NY 5 hrs

*WIRQ(FM) Rochester NY 3 hrs
*WBGU(FM) Bowling Green OH
*WUSO(FM) Springfield OH 9 hrs
*WCWS(FM) Wooster OH 3 hrs
*WVCS(FM) California PA 12 hrs
*WDCV-FM Carlisle PA 15 hrs
*WWAS(FM) Williamsport PA 2 hrs
*WDOM(FM) Providence RI 16 hrs
*WPLS-FM Greenville SC 2 hrs
WBHC-FM Hampton SC 20 hrs
*KCFS(FM) Sioux Falls SD 6 hrs
*WFSK(FM) Nashville TN
*KSAU(FM) Nacogdoches TX 2 hrs
WJMA(AM) Orange VA 15 hrs
WJMA-FM Orange VA 15 hrs
*WIUV(FM) Castleton VT 5 hrs
*WRMC-FM Middlebury VT 12 hrs
*KAOS(FM) Olympia WA 5 hrs

Variety/Diverse

*WEGL(FM) Auburn AL
*KSPC(FM) Claremont CA 1 hr
KVEC(AM) San Luis Obispo CA
*WQAC-FM Alma MI 13 hrs
*WSDP(FM) Plymouth MI 3 hrs
*KGAC(FM) St. Peter MN 8 hrs
WPEG(FM) Concord NC 8 hrs
*WSHA(FM) Raleigh NC 4 hrs
*WCFE-FM Plattsburgh NY 20 hrs
*WHSS(FM) Hamilton OH 1 hr

Vietnamese

*KSJV(FM) Fresno CA 4 hrs
KEST(AM) San Francisco CA 5 hrs
*KSJS(FM) San Jose CA 1 hr
KWIZ-FM Santa Ana CA
*KSJC-FM Stockton CA 1 hr
*WBRS(FM) Waltham MA 2 hrs
*KVTT(FM) Dallas TX 1 hr
*KHCB(AM) Galveston TX 3 hrs
*WSHS(FM) Sheboygan WI 3 hrs

Women

*KABF(FM) Little Rock AR 3 hrs
*KPFA(FM) Berkeley CA 10 hrs
*KPFK(FM) Los Angeles CA 4 hrs
*KAZU(FM) Pacific Grove CA 6 hrs
*KSJS(FM) San Jose CA 1 hr
*KSJS(FM) San Jose CA 1 hr
*KZSC(FM) Santa Cruz CA 5 hrs
*WCNI(FM) New London CT 3 hrs
*WPFW(FM) Washington DC 3 hrs
*WRFG(FM) Atlanta GA 5 hrs
KROS(AM) Clinton IA 5 hrs
*WEKH(FM) Hazard KY 4 hrs
*WEKU-FM Richmond KY 2 hrs
*WMMT(FM) Whitesburg KY 2 hrs
*WMUA(FM) Amherst MA 12 hrs
*WZLY(FM) Wellesley MA 2 hrs
*WCUW(FM) Worcester MA 3 hrs
*WDBM(FM) East Lansing MI 2 hrs
WNBN(AM) Meridian MS
*WQFS(FM) Greensboro NC 2 hrs
KAWL(AM) York NE 3 hrs
*KUNV(FM) Las Vegas NV 2 hrs
*WRPI(FM) Troy NY 2 hrs
KZZK-FM Creswell OR 2 hrs
*KBOO(FM) Portland OR 4 hrs
*WFSK(FM) Nashville TN 3 hrs
*KTRU(FM) Houston TX 1 hr
*KRCL(FM) Salt Lake City UT 7 hrs
KGNW(AM) Burien-Seattle WA
*KAOS(FM) Olympia WA 2 hrs

Special Programming on Radio Stations in Canada

Agriculture & Farm
CFCW(AM) Camrose AB 5 hrs
CJYR(AM) Edson AB 2 hrs
CHRB(AM) High River AB 5 hrs
CJOC(AM) Lethbridge AB 2 hrs
CJCY(AM) Medicine Hat AB 2 hrs
CHLW(AM) St. Paul AB 5 hrs
CKTA(AM) Taber AB 3 hrs
CKKY(AM) Wainwright AB 10 hrs
CFVR(AM) Abbotsford-Matsqui BC 1 hr
CHWK(AM) Chilliwack BC 2 hrs
CKNL(AM) Fort St. John BC 1 hr
CIGV-FM Penticton BC 1 hr
CKLQ(AM) Brandon MB 18 hrs
CFRY(AM) Portage la Prairie MB 4 hrs
CFQX-FM Selkirk MB 3 hrs
CHSM(AM) Steinbach MB
CBW(AM) Winnipeg MB 6 hrs
CJCJ(AM) Woodstock NB 2 hrs
CKDH(AM) Amherst NS 2 hrs
CJFX(AM) Antigonish NS 1 hr
CKDY(AM) Digby NS 7 hrs
CKEN(AM) Kentville NS 5 hrs
CKAD(AM) Middleton NS 3 hrs
CKCL(AM) Truro NS 3 hrs
CJBQ(AM) Belleville ON 3 hrs
CJLX-FM Belleville ON 1 hr
CFCO(AM) Chatham ON 3 hrs
CFRB(AM) Toronto ON 2 hrs
CBE(AM) Windsor ON 5 hrs
CFDA(AM) Victoriaville PQ 6 hrs
CJSL(AM) Estevan SK 4 hrs
CJNB(AM) North Battleford SK 7 hrs
CKBI(AM) Prince Albert SK 2 hrs
*CBK(AM) Regina SK 5 hrs
CKSW(AM) Swift Current SK 1 hr
CFSL(AM) Weyburn SK 3 hrs

American Indian
*CITR-FM Vancouver BC 1 hr
CFAR(AM) Flin Flon MB
CHTM(AM) Thompson MB 10 hrs
CHSR-FM Fredericton NB 1 hr
CKDU-FM Halifax NS
CKON-FM Akwesasne ON
*CFMU-FM Hamilton ON 1 hr
CKWR-FM Kitchener ON 5 hrs
CHMO(AM) Moosonee ON 10 hrs
CKCU-FM Ottawa ON 2 hrs
CBQS-FM Sioux Narrows ON 1 hr
*CKRK-FM Kahnawake PQ
*CBKA-FM La Ronge SK 20 hrs

Arabic
*CKRL-FM Quebec PQ 3 hrs

Big Band
CJIB(AM) Vernon BC 3 hrs
CFBG-FM Bracebridge ON 1 hr
CKLY(AM) Lindsay ON 6 hrs

Black
*CFRO-FM Vancouver BC 7 hrs
*CITR-FM Vancouver BC 20 hrs
*CFUV-FM Victoria BC 6 hrs
CHSR-FM Fredericton NB 3 hrs
CKDU-FM Halifax NS 4 hrs
CKNM-FM Yellowknife NT 1 hr
CING-FM Burlington ON 5 hrs
CFRU-FM Guelph ON 6 hrs
CJKL(AM) Kirkland Lake ON 4 hrs
CKWR-FM Kitchener ON 5 hrs
*CHUO-FM Ottawa ON 8 hrs
CKCU-FM Ottawa ON 12 hrs
CHIN-FM Toronto ON 4 hrs
CHRY-FM Toronto ON
*CIBL-FM Montreal PQ 13 hrs
*CKRL-FM Quebec PQ 6 hrs
CFNJ-FM St. Gabriel-de-Brandon PQ 1 hr

Bluegrass
CKBW(AM) Bridgewater NS
CKBW-FM-1 Liverpool NS
CKBW-FM-2 Shelburne NS

Blues
*CITR-FM Vancouver BC 2 hrs
CHMR-FM St. John's NF 6 hrs
CKDU-FM Halifax NS
*CFMU-FM Hamilton ON 5 hrs
CHEZ-FM Ottawa ON 2 hrs
*CIBL-FM Montreal PQ 2 hrs

Chinese
CKER(AM) Edmonton AB 15 hrs
*CFUV-FM Victoria BC 1 hr
CHSR-FM Fredericton NB 3 hrs

CKDU-FM Halifax NS
CKWR-FM Kitchener ON 2 hrs
*CHUO-FM Ottawa ON 2 hrs
CHRY-FM Toronto ON
CINQ-FM Montreal PQ 5 hrs

Classic Rock
CJMS(AM) Montreal PQ

Classical
CHQT(AM) Edmonton AB 12 hrs
CKBX(AM) 100 Mile House BC 1 hr
CILK-FM Kelowna BC 2 hrs
CIGV-FM Penticton BC 2 hrs
CHOR(AM) Summerland BC 3 hrs
*CFRO-FM Vancouver BC 4 hrs
CHQM-FM Vancouver BC 14 hrs
*CITR-FM Vancouver BC 5 hrs
CJVB(AM) Vancouver BC 8 hrs
CJIB(AM) Vernon BC 1 hr
CFMS-FM Victoria BC 5 hrs
*CFUV-FM Victoria BC 15 hrs
CFAM(AM) Altona MB 15 hrs
CFQX-FM Selkirk MB 2 hrs
CBW(AM) Winnipeg MB 8 hrs
CHSR-FM Fredericton NB 6 hrs
CHMR-FM St. John's NF 10 hrs
CKDU-FM Halifax NS 6 hrs
CJLX-FM Belleville ON 6 hrs
CFNY-FM Brampton ON 5 hrs
CING-FM Burlington ON 5 hrs
CFRU-FM Guelph ON 3 hrs
*CFMU-FM Hamilton ON 5 hrs
CFCA-FM Kitchener ON 17 hrs
CKWR-FM Kitchener ON 9 hrs
*CIXX-FM London ON 5 hrs
CKAT-FM North Bay ON 3 hrs
*CHUO-FM Ottawa ON 4 hrs
CHAS-FM Sault Ste. Marie ON 5 hrs
CFRB(AM) Toronto ON 7 hrs
CBE(AM) Windsor ON 19 hrs
CHIP-FM Fort Coulonge PQ 2 hrs
CJRG-FM Gaspe PQ 2 hrs
*CFIN-FM Lac-Etchemin PQ 2 hrs
CHGA-FM Maniwaki PQ 1 hr
*CIBL-FM Montreal PQ 4 hrs
CJAD(AM) Montreal PQ 3 hrs
CKIA-FM Quebec PQ 3 hrs
*CKRL-FM Quebec PQ 6 hrs
CJSO-FM Sorel PQ 2 hrs
CFNJ-FM St. Gabriel-de-Brandon PQ 1 hr
CIHO-FM St. Hilarion PQ 2 hrs
CJMC(AM) Ste. Anne des Monts PQ 2 hrs
CFMC-FM Saskatoon SK 2 hrs

Contemporary Hit/Top-40
CKIQ(AM) Kelowna BC 2 hrs

Country
CFWB(AM) Campbell River BC 20 hrs
CKIQ(AM) Kelowna BC 4 hrs
*CFRO-FM Vancouver BC 1 hr
*CITR-FM Vancouver BC 4 hrs
CBW(AM) Winnipeg MB 1 hr
CJVA(AM) Caraquet NB 15 hrs
CFAN(AM) Newcastle NB 19 hrs
CKDH(AM) Amherst NS 11 hrs
CKDU-FM Halifax NS 2 hrs
CJKL(AM) Kirkland Lake ON 6 hrs
CKWR-FM Kitchener ON 5 hrs
CFNO-FM Marathon ON 4 hrs
CBE(AM) Windsor ON 3 hrs
CFMF-FM Fermont PQ 3 hrs
CHEF(AM) Granby PQ 1 hr
CHGA-FM Maniwaki PQ 8 hrs
CJAD(AM) Montreal PQ 3 hrs
CFNJ-FM St. Gabriel-de-Brandon PQ 4 hrs
CJMC(AM) Ste. Anne des Monts PQ 2 hrs
CFDA(AM) Victoriaville PQ 10 hrs

Croatian
CHIN-FM Toronto ON 5 hrs

Drama/Literature
CKDU-FM Halifax NS

Educational
*CKUA-FM Edmonton AB
CBW-FM Winnipeg MB 5 hrs
CHRY-FM Toronto ON

Filipino
CKJS(AM) Winnipeg MB 15 hrs

Finnish
*CFUV-FM Victoria BC 1 hr
CFJQ-FM Nipigon-Red Rock ON 2 hrs
CJLB(AM) Thunder Bay ON 1 hr
CKOY(AM) Timmins ON

Folk
*CITR-FM Vancouver BC 7 hrs
*CFUV-FM Victoria BC 12 hrs
CFQX-FM Selkirk MB 6 hrs
CHMR-FM St. John's NF 6 hrs
CKDU-FM Halifax NS 3 hrs
CJLX-FM Belleville ON 1 hr
CKPC-FM Brantford ON 1 hr
CFRU-FM Guelph ON 12 hrs
*CFMU-FM Hamilton ON 5 hrs
*CHUO-FM Ottawa ON 3 hrs
CKCU-FM Ottawa ON 12 hrs
CHGA-FM Maniwaki PQ 5 hrs

Foreign Language/Ethnic
CKER(AM) Edmonton AB 15 hrs
*CKUA-FM Edmonton AB
CFKC(AM) Creston BC 2 hrs
CJAV(AM) Port Alberni BC 1 hr
CJAT(AM) Trail BC 2 hrs
*CFRO-FM Vancouver BC 3 hrs
*CITR-FM Vancouver BC 1 hr
CJVB(AM) Vancouver BC 6 hrs
*CFUV-FM Victoria BC 5 hrs
CHSR-FM Fredericton NB 5 hrs
CKXX(AM) Corner Brook NF 6 hrs
CHAK(AM) Inuvik NT 18 hrs
CBQR-FM Rankin Inlet NT 10 hrs
CFCT(AM) Tuktoyaktuk NT 5 hrs
CFYK(AM) Yellowknife NT 16 hrs
CJLX-FM Belleville ON 2 hrs
CKWR-FM Kitchener ON 5 hrs
*CBQT-FM Thunder Bay ON 1 hr
CJLB(AM) Thunder Bay ON 1 hr
CKPR(AM) Thunder Bay ON 1 hr
CKOT(AM) Tillsonburg ON 2 hrs
CHRY-FM Toronto ON
CINQ-FM Montreal PQ 24 hrs
CKIA-FM Quebec PQ 5 hrs
CHON-FM Whitehorse YT 15 hrs

French
*CHCL(AM) Medley AB
CHQB(AM) Powell River BC 1 hr
*CFRO-FM Vancouver BC 2 hrs
*CFUV-FM Victoria BC 3 hrs
CKBC(AM) Bathurst NB 2 hrs
CKNB(AM) Campbellton NB 18 hrs
CHSR-FM Fredericton NB 6 hrs
CIHI(AM) Fredericton NB 1 hr
CHMR-FM St. John's NF 6 hrs
CKDU-FM Halifax NS 1 hr
CJLX-FM Belleville ON 1 hr
CFRU-FM Guelph ON 1 hr
CKWR-FM Kitchener ON 2 hrs
CHUR-FM North Bay ON 1 hr
CKCU-FM Ottawa ON 2 hrs
CHYC(AM) Sudbury ON
CHRY-FM Toronto ON
*CFIN-FM Lac-Etchemin PQ
*CFWH(AM) Whitehorse YT 1 hr

German
CKER(AM) Edmonton AB 10 hrs
CFVR(AM) Abbotsford-Matsqui BC 1 hr
CJVB(AM) Vancouver BC 8 hrs
CKJS(AM) Winnipeg MB 15 hrs
CKPC-FM Brantford ON 5 hrs
CING-FM Burlington ON 12 hrs
CKWR-FM Kitchener ON 4 hrs
CHYR-FM Leamington ON 1 hr
*CHUO-FM Ottawa ON 2 hrs
CKOT(AM) Tillsonburg ON 1 hr
CHIN-FM Toronto ON 7 hrs
CKSW(AM) Swift Current SK 1 hr

Gospel
*CITR-FM Vancouver BC 1 hr
CFFM-FM Williams Lake BC 4 hrs
CFQX-FM Selkirk MB 4 hrs
CKDU-FM Halifax NS 1 hr
CFRU-FM Guelph ON 1 hr
*CFMU-FM Hamilton ON 1 hr
CKOT-FM Tillsonburg ON 1 hr
CHRY-FM Toronto ON

Greek
CJOI(AM) Wetaskiwin AB 2 hrs
CJVB(AM) Vancouver BC 4 hrs
CKJS(AM) Winnipeg MB 3 hrs
CKDU-FM Halifax NS 2 hrs
CKWR-FM Kitchener ON 2 hrs
CINQ-FM Montreal PQ 13 hrs

Hebrew
CHRY-FM Toronto ON

Hindi
CJVB(AM) Vancouver BC 8 hrs
CHMR-FM St. John's NF 1 hr
CHWO(AM) Oakville ON 8 hrs

Hungarian
CKOT(AM) Tillsonburg ON 1 hr

Irish
CHVO(AM) Carbonear NF 6 hrs
CKXD(AM) Gander NF 12 hrs
CIGO(AM) Port Hawkesbury NS 1 hr

Italian
CKER(AM) Edmonton AB 13 hrs
*CFRO-FM Vancouver BC 1 hr
CJVB(AM) Vancouver BC 14 hrs
*CFUV-FM Victoria BC 2 hrs
CKJS(AM) Winnipeg MB 8 hrs
CING-FM Burlington ON 2 hrs
CHYR-FM Leamington ON 3 hrs
CFJQ-FM Nipigon-Red Rock ON 1 hr
CHWO(AM) Oakville ON 4 hrs
CKCU-FM Ottawa ON 1 hr
CHAS-FM Sault Ste. Marie ON 2 hrs
CJQM-FM Sault Ste. Marie ON 4 hrs
CJLB(AM) Thunder Bay ON
*CKRL-FM Quebec PQ 2 hrs

Jazz
CFBR-FM Edmonton AB 4 hrs
CIEG-FM Egmont BC 7 hrs
CISE-FM Sechelt BC 2 hrs
CISQ-FM Squamish BC 7 hrs
CHOR(AM) Summerland BC 3 hrs
CFOX-FM Vancouver BC 2 hrs
*CFRO-FM Vancouver BC 11 hrs
*CITR-FM Vancouver BC 8 hrs
CKKS-FM Vancouver BC 7 hrs
CKKQ-FM Victoria BC 4 hrs
CBW-FM Winnipeg MB 3 hrs
CKLE-FM Bathurst NB 2 hrs
CHSR-FM Fredericton NB 6 hrs
CJMO-FM Moncton NB 2 hrs
CFRQ-FM Dartmouth NS 3 hrs
CKDU-FM Halifax NS 9 hrs
CFJB-FM Barrie ON
CJLX-FM Belleville ON 1 hr
CFBG-FM Bracebridge ON 2 hrs
CFNY-FM Brampton ON 3 hrs
CHXL-FM Brockville ON 2 hrs
CING-FM Burlington ON 5 hrs
CFRU-FM Guelph ON 8 hrs
*CFMU-FM Hamilton ON 5 hrs
CJKL-FM Kirkland Lake ON 2 hrs
CKWR-FM Kitchener ON 15 hrs
*CIXX-FM London ON 5 hrs
CKAT-FM North Bay ON 2 hrs
CKGE-FM Oshawa ON 2 hrs
CHEZ-FM Ottawa ON 2 hrs
*CHUO-FM Ottawa ON 5 hrs
CKCU-FM Ottawa ON 15 hrs
CKWF-FM Peterborough ON 12 hrs
CFGX-FM Sarnia ON 7 hrs
CHAS-FM Sault Ste. Marie ON 2 hrs
CHRY-FM Toronto ON
CKFM-FM Toronto ON 3 hrs
CBE(AM) Windsor ON 2 hrs
CFMF-FM Fermont PQ 1 hr
CJRG-FM Gaspe PQ 2 hrs
*CFIN-FM Lac-Etchemin PQ 3 hrs
CHGA-FM Maniwaki PQ 3 hrs
*CIBL-FM Montreal PQ 14 hrs
CJFM-FM Montreal PQ 3 hrs
*CBV-FM Quebec PQ 16 hrs
CHOI-FM Quebec PQ 3 hrs
CKIA-FM Quebec PQ 4 hrs
*CKRL-FM Quebec PQ 4 hrs
CFNJ-FM St. Gabriel-de-Brandon PQ 2 hrs
CIHO-FM St. Hilarion PQ 2 hrs
CFJO-FM Thetford Mines PQ 8 hrs
CFMC-FM Saskatoon SK 2 hrs

Jewish
CHIN-FM Toronto ON 5 hrs

New Age
CKMF-FM Montreal PQ 4 hrs

News
*CFPR(AM) Prince Rupert BC
*CITR-FM Vancouver BC 3 hrs
*CFMU-FM Hamilton ON 10 hrs
*CBV-FM Quebec PQ 7 hrs

News/Talk
*CITR-FM Vancouver BC 7 hrs

Nostalgia
CJMX-FM Sudbury ON 4 hrs

Oldies
CKAY(AM) Duncan BC 12 hrs

Other
CKIQ(AM) Kelowna BC 4 hrs
*CITR-FM Vancouver BC 8 hrs
*CFUV-FM Victoria BC 2 hrs
CIOK-FM Saint John NB 4 hrs
CKXG(AM) Grand Falls-Windsor NF 12 hrs
*CBN(AM) St. John's NF 3 hrs
CKBW(AM) Bridgewater NS
CJLX-FM Belleville ON 1 hr
CFBG-FM Bracebridge ON 1 hr
*CHTN(AM) Charlottetown PE 4 hrs
*CIBL-FM Montreal PQ 2 hrs
CKAC(AM) Montreal PQ

Polish
CKER(AM) Edmonton AB 6 hrs
CJVB(AM) Vancouver BC 1 hr
*CFUV-FM Victoria BC 1 hr
CKJS(AM) Winnipeg MB 7 hrs
CFRU-FM Guelph ON 2 hrs
CKWR-FM Kitchener ON 3 hrs
CHWO(AM) Oakville ON 5 hrs
CKCU-FM Ottawa ON 1 hr
CHIN-FM Toronto ON 5 hrs

Portuguese
CKER(AM) Edmonton AB 2 hrs
CJOR(AM) Osoyoos BC 3 hrs
CJVB(AM) Vancouver BC 1 hr
CKJS(AM) Winnipeg MB 8 hrs
CIAM(AM) Cambridge ON 2 hrs
CFRU-FM Guelph ON 5 hrs
CKWR-FM Kitchener ON 4 hrs
CHWO(AM) Oakville ON 11 hrs
CINQ-FM Montreal PQ 14 hrs

Public Affairs
*CFPR(AM) Prince Rupert BC
*CFMU-FM Hamilton ON 10 hrs
CBE(AM) Windsor ON 18 hrs
CHLN(AM) Trois Rivieres PQ 8 hrs

Reggae
CHMR-FM St. John's NF 2 hrs
*CFMU-FM Hamilton ON 5 hrs
*CIBL-FM Montreal PQ 4 hrs

Religious
CILK-FM Kelowna BC 3 hrs
CHQB(AM) Powell River BC 1 hr
CIVH(AM) Vanderhoof BC 5 hrs
CHTM(AM) Thompson MB 12 hrs
CFAN(AM) Newcastle NB 4 hrs
CJCW(AM) Sussex NB 4 hrs
CHMR-FM St. John's NF 4 hrs
*VOWR(AM) St. John's NF 10 hrs
CFSX(AM) Stephenville NF 1 hr
CKBW(AM) Bridgewater NS
CKBW-FM-1 Liverpool NS
CKBW-FM-2 Shelburne NS
CJNH-FM Bancroft ON 1 hr
CFRU-FM Guelph ON 1 hr
CKWR-FM Kitchener ON 12 hrs
CHYR-FM Leamington ON 1 hr
CFJQ-FM Nipigon-Red Rock ON 4 hrs
CKDO(AM) Oshawa ON 1 hr
CKGE-FM Oshawa ON 1 hr
*CHUO-FM Ottawa ON 2 hrs
CKCU-FM Ottawa ON 3 hrs
CJET(AM) Smiths Falls ON 20 hrs
CJLB(AM) Thunder Bay ON
CKPR(AM) Thunder Bay ON 1 hr
CKNX(AM) Wingham ON 6 hrs
CHRD(AM) Drummondville PQ 1 hr
CJSL(AM) Estevan SK 6 hrs
CJVR(AM) Melfort SK 9 hrs
CJNB(AM) North Battleford SK 10 hrs
CJYM(AM) Rosetown SK 15 hrs
CHSN-FM Saskatoon SK 6 hrs
CFSL(AM) Weyburn SK 13 hrs

Special Programming on Radio Stations in Canada

Rock/AOR
CJDC(AM) Dawson Creek BC 4 hrs
CJDC-FM Dawson Creek BC 4 hrs

Scottish
CIGO(AM) Port Hawkesbury NS 1 hr
CJTN(AM) Trenton ON 1 hr

Serbian
CHIN-FM Toronto ON 5 hrs

Spanish
CKER(AM) Edmonton AB 13 hrs
*CFRO-FM Vancouver BC 1 hr
CJVB(AM) Vancouver BC 1 hr
*CFUV-FM Victoria BC 3 hrs
CKJS(AM) Winnipeg MB 1 hr
CFRU-FM Guelph ON 2 hrs
*CFMU-FM Hamilton ON 1 hr
CHOH(AM) Hearst ON 1 hr
CKWR-FM Kitchener ON 3 hrs
CHWO(AM) Oakville ON 3 hrs
*CHUO-FM Ottawa ON 3 hrs
CHRY-FM Toronto ON
*CFIN-FM Lac-Etchemin PQ
CINQ-FM Montreal PQ 14 hrs
CKIA-FM Quebec PQ 4 hrs
*CKRL-FM Quebec PQ 2 hrs

Sports
CFFR(AM) Calgary AB 15 hrs
CFXL(AM) Calgary AB
CFCW(AM) Camrose AB
CKIQ(AM) Kelowna BC 10 hrs
CKNW(AM) New Westminster BC
CJNH(AM) Bancroft ON 2 hrs
CFFX(AM) Kingston ON
CJRP(AM) Quebec PQ

Talk
CJNH(AM) Bancroft ON 5 hrs

Ukrainian
CKER(AM) Edmonton AB 7 hrs
CJRL(AM) Kenora ON 1 hr

Vietnamese
CKCU-FM Ottawa ON 1 hr
CKIA-FM Quebec PQ 1 hr

Women
*CITR-FM Vancouver BC 1 hr
CFRU-FM Guelph ON 4 hrs

U.S. Radio Markets

The following is the Arbitron population ranking for Fall 1993, based on market definitions at that time. It is based on the 1990 U.S. Bureau of Census estimates updated and projected to January 1, 1994.

The MSA number is the population of all persons aged 12 or older in the Metro Survey Area. The TSA number is the population total of all persons 12 or older in the Total Survey Area. Following that are the call letters of stations that fall within the market as defined by Arbitron.

Certain market population totals are also embedded in larger nearby markets. It is therefore possible for a station to be listed in more than one market.

Abilene, TX: Rank 219
MSA: 118,500; TSA: 212,900
Stations: KBBA, KBCY-FM, KCDD-FM, KCWS-FM, KEAN, KEAN-FM, KEYJ-FM, KHXS-FM, KKHR-FM, KMXO, KNTS, KORQ-FM, KVRP, KVRP-FM, KXOX-FM, KYYD.

Akron, OH: Rank 68
MSA: 560,700; TSA: 1,087,400
Stations: WAKR, WHLO, WJMP, WKDD-FM, WNIR-FM, WONE-FM, WQMX-FM, WSLR.

Albany, GA: Rank 245
MSA: 88,900; TSA: 358,200
Stations: WALG, WANL, WAZE-FM, WEGC-FM, WGPC, WGPC-FM, WJAD-FM, WJIZ-FM, WJYZ, WKAK-FM, WQVE-FM, WSGY-FM.

Albany-Schenectady-Troy, NY: Rank 57
MSA: 739,900; TSA: 1,326,100
Stations: WABY, WBGG, WBUG, WBUG-FM, WCDA-FM, WCKL, WCSS, WCTW-FM, WEQX-FM, WFLY-FM, WGNA, WGNA-FM, WGY, WGY-FM, WHAZ, WHRL-FM, WHUC, WIZR, WKLI-FM, WKOL-FM, WMYY-FM, WNGN-FM, WPTR, WPYX-FM, WQBK, WQBK-FM, WRAV-FM, WROW, WROW-FM, WRVW-FM, WSHQ-FM, WSRD-FM, WSSV-FM, WSTL, WTRY, WTRY-FM, WUHN, WVKZ, WWCP-FM, WXLE-FM, WYLR-FM, WZRQ-FM, WZZM-FM.

Albuquerque: Rank 71
MSA: 522,100; TSA: 838,100
Stations: KABQ, KALY, KAMX, KAMX-FM, KARS, KARS-FM, KASY-FM, KDAZ, KDEF, KHFM-FM, KIVA, KJBO, KKIM, KKJY-FM, KKOB, KKOB-FM, KKSS-FM, KLSK-FM, KMGA-FM, KOLT-FM, KQEO, KRST-FM, KRZY, KTMN-FM, KUCU-FM, KXKS, KZKL, KZKL-FM, KZRQ-FM, KZRR-FM, KZSS.

Alexandria, LA: Rank 194
MSA: 151,900; TSA: 382,600
Stations: KALB, KAPB, KAPB-FM, KBCE-FM, KEZP-FM, KFAD-FM, KICR-FM, KLAA-FM, KLIL-FM, KQID-FM, KRRV, KRRV-FM, KSYL, KTLD, KWDF, KZMZ-FM.

Allentown-Bethlehem, PA: Rank 64
MSA: 598,400; TSA: 937,800
Stations: WAEB, WAEB-FM, WEST, WFMZ-FM, WGPA, WHCY-FM, WHOL, WIPI, WKAP, WLEV-FM, WLSH, WODE-FM, WRNJ, WRNJ-FM, WXKW, WYNS, WZZO-FM.

Altoona, PA: Rank 230
MSA: 109,900; TSA: 539,200
Stations: WALY-FM, WBRX-FM, WFBG, WFGY-FM, WGMR-FM, WHPA-FM, WJSM, WJSM-FM, WKMC, WPRR-FM, WRTA, WTRN, WVAM.

Amarillo, TX: Rank 193
MSA: 157,100; TSA: 298,400
Stations: KAEZ-FM, KAKS, KAKS-FM, KARX-FM, KATP-FM, KBUY-FM, KDJW, KGNC, KGNC-FM, KIXZ, KLCJ, KLSF-FM, KMML-FM, KPUR, KPUR-FM, KQFX-FM, KQIZ-FM, KZIP.

Anaheim-Santa Ana, CA: Rank 16
MSA: 2,148,800; TSA: 2,148,800
Note: Part of Los Angeles Metro.

Anchorage: Rank 165
MSA: 196,900; TSA: 268,000
Stations: KASH-FM, KBFX-FM, KBRJ-FM, KBYR, KEAG-FM, KENI, KFFR, KFQD, KGOT-FM, KHAR, KKSD, KLEF-FM, KMBQ-FM, KNIK-FM, KPXR-FM, KWHL-FM, KYAK, KYMG-FM.

Ann Arbor, MI: Rank 144
MSA: 249,400; TSA: 325,700
Stations: WAAM, WAMX-FM, WIQB-FM, WQKL-FM, WSDS, WTKA, WWCM.

Appleton-Oshkosh, WI: Rank 136
MSA: 267,600; TSA: 733,300
Stations: WAPL-FM, WEMI-FM, WFON-FM, WHBY, WKFX-FM, WMBE, WMGV-FM, WNAM, WOSH, WOZZ-FM, WPKR-FM, WRJQ, WROE-FM, WSGC, WUSW-FM, WXOL.

Asheville, NC: Rank 180
MSA: 169,700; TSA: 375,800
Stations: WFGW, WHBK, WISE, WKSF-FM, WMIT-FM, WQNS-FM, WSKY, WWNC, WZQR.

Atlanta: Rank 12
MSA: 2,681,900; TSA: 3,622,200
Stations: WAEC, WAFS, WALR-FM, WAOK, WAOS, WAZX, WCHK, WCNN, WCOH, WDCY, WDPC, WFOM, WFOX-FM, WFTD, WGFS, WGKA, WGST, WGST-FM, WGUN, WHIE, WIGO, WIMO, WJGA-FM, WKEU, WKHX, WKHX-FM, WKKP, WKLS-FM, WKUN, WLKQ-FM, WMKJ-FM, WMBL, WNEA, WNIV, WNNX-FM, WPBS, WPCH-FM, WPLO, WQUL-FM, WQXI, WSB, WSB-FM, WSSA, WSTR-FM, WTJH, WVEE-FM, WVNF, WXEM, WXLL, WYAI-FM, WYAY-FM, WYZE, WZGC-FM.

Atlantic City-Cape May, NJ: Rank 134
MSA: 278,400; TSA: 392,700
Stations: WAYV-FM, WBNJ-FM, WBSS-FM, WCMC, WDOX-FM, WFNN-FM, WFPG, WFPG-FM, WIBG, WJNN-FM, WKOE-FM, WKTU-FM, WMGM-FM, WMID, WMID-FM, WOND, WONZ, WRDR-FM, WSJL-FM, WSKR-FM, WTTH-FM, WUSS, WWOC-FM, WZXL-FM.

Augusta, GA: Rank 114
MSA: 338,100; TSA: 509,400
Stations: WAGW-FM, WAJY-FM, WAKB-FM, WBBQ, WBBQ-FM, WCHZ-FM, WFAM, WFXA-FM, WGAC, WGOR-FM, WGUS, WJES, WKSX-FM, WKXC-FM, WKZK, WRDW, WRXR-FM, WSLT-FM, WTHB, WTHO-FM, WTWA, WVAA, WXFG-FM, WZNY-FM.

Augusta-Waterville, ME: Rank 238
MSA: 97,800; TSA: 376,300
Stations: WABK, WABK-FM, WFAU, WHQO-FM, WKCG-FM, WMME, WMME-FM, WSKW, WTOS-FM, WTVL, WTVL-FM, WWMR-FM.

Austin, TX: Rank 55
MSA: 759,000; TSA: 1,056,100
Stations: KASE-FM, KELG, KEYI-FM, KFGI-FM, KFIT, KFON, KGSR-FM, KHFI-FM, KHHT-FM, KIXL, KJCE, KKLB-FM, KKMJ-FM, KLBJ, KLBJ-FM, KLKM-FM, KNNC-FM, KPEZ-FM, KRGT-FM, KTAE, KTXZ, KUOL, KUTZ-FM, KVET, KVET-FM.

Bakersfield, CA: Rank 86
MSA: 412,600; TSA: 746,100
Stations: KAFY, KBID, KCHJ, KCHT-FM, KCNQ-FM, KCWR, KDNO-FM, KERI, KERN, KERN-FM, KGEO, KGFM-FM, KHIS, KHIS-FM, KIWI-FM, KKBB-FM, KKXX-FM, KLLY-FM, KMYX, KMYX-FM, KNZR, KRAB-FM, KSUV-FM, KTIE-FM, KUZZ-FM, KVLI, KVLI-FM, KWAC, KXEM.

Baltimore: Rank 19
MSA: 2,036,100; TSA: 2,780,600
Stations: WAMD, WANN, WASA, WBAL, WBGR, WBMD, WBYQ-FM, WCAO, WCBM, WERQ-FM, WGRX-FM, WHRF, WITH, WIYY-FM, WJFK, WJRO, WKDB, WLIF-FM, WNAV, WOLB, WPOC-FM, WQSR-FM, WRBS-FM, WTTR, WVRT-FM, WWIN, WWIN-FM, WWLG-AM, WWMX-FM, WXCY-FM, WXYV-FM, WXZL-FM, WYRE.

Bangor, ME: Rank 252
MSA: 76,600; TSA: 330,900
Stations: WABI, WHMX-FM, WKIT-FM, WKSQ-FM, WNSW, WQCB-FM, WSHZ-FM, WWFX-FM, WWMJ-FM, WYOU-FM, WZON.

Baton Rouge: Rank 82
MSA: 441,100; TSA: 1,260,400
Stations: KBRH, KKAY, KKAY-FM, KQXL-FM, KRVE-FM, WBIU, WFMF-FM, WGGZ-FM, WIBR, WJBO, WKJN-FM, WLUX, WNDC, WQCK-FM, WSLG, WTGE-FM, WXOK, WYCT-FM, WYNK, WYNK-FM.

Battle Creek, MI: Rank 226
MSA: 113,700; TSA: 463,000
Stations: WALM, WBCK, WBXX-FM, WELL, WELL-FM, WOLY.

Beaumont-Port Arthur, TX: Rank 127
MSA: 296,400; TSA: 519,800
Stations: KALO, KAYC, KAYD-FM, KIOC-FM, KKAS, KKFH, KKMY-FM, KLVI, KOGT, KOLE, KQHN, KQXY-FM, KTFA-FM, KUHD-FM, KWDX-FM, KYKR-FM, KZZB.

Beckley, WV: Rank 257
MSA: 63,600; TSA: 348,900
Stations: WAXS-FM, WCIR-FM, WHAJ-FM, WIWS, WJLS, WJLS-FM, WOAY, WTNJ-FM, WWNR.

Billings, MT: Rank 240
MSA: 95,500; TSA: 208,300
Stations: KBLG, KBSR, KCTR, KCTR-FM, KDWG-FM, KGHL, KIDX-FM, KKBR-FM, KMAY, KOHZ-FM, KRKX-FM, KURL, KYYA-FM.

Biloxi-Gulfport, MS: Rank 183
MSA: 167,200; TSA: 305,400
Stations: WBSL, WGCM, WGCM-FM, WKNN-FM, WQFX, WQID-FM, WROA, WUSD-FM, WVMI, WXLS, WXLS-FM, WXRG-FM, WZKX-FM.

Binghamton, NY: Rank 152
MSA: 219,800; TSA: 564,200
Stations: WAAL-FM, WAVR-FM, WEBO, WGRG-FM, WHWK-FM, WINR, WIYN-FM, WKGB-FM, WKOP, WMRV, WMRV-FM, WMXW-FM, WNBF.

Birmingham, AL: Rank 54
MSA: 775,300; TSA: 1,611,800
Stations: WAGG, WAPI, WAPI-FM, WARF, WATV, WAYE, WBYE, WCEO, WCRL, WDJC-FM, WENN-FM, WERC, WFFN-FM, WFHK, WGTT, WJLD, WJOX, WKIJ, WKLD-FM, WLBI-FM, WLPH, WMJJ-FM, WODL-FM, WPYK, WRSM, WSMQ, WURL, WWBR-FM, WYDE, WZPQ, WZRR-FM, WZZK, WZZK-FM.

Bismarck, ND: Rank 255
MSA: 68,600; TSA: 218,900
Stations: KBMR, KBYZ-FM, KFYR, KLXX, KNDR-FM, KQDY-FM, KYYY-FM.

Bloomington, IL: Rank 227
MSA: 113,200; TSA: 212,100
Stations: WBNQ-FM, WBWN-FM, WIHN-FM, WJBC.

Boise, ID: Rank 138
MSA: 262,300; TSA: 475,100
Stations: KANR, KBGN, KBOI, KBXL-FM, KCID, KCID-FM, KCIX-FM, KFXD, KFXD-FM, KGEM, KHEZ-FM, KIDO, KIZN-FM, KJOT-FM, KKIC, KLCI-FM, KLTB-FM, KQFC-FM, KSPD, KWEI, KZMG-FM.

Boston: Rank 9
MSA: 3,191,300; TSA: 6,086,800
Stations: WAAF-FM, WADN, WATD-FM, WBCN-FM, WBCS-FM, WBET, WBIV, WBMX-FM, WBOQ-FM, WBOS-FM, WBZ, WCAP, WCAV-FM, WCCM, WCEG-FM, WCGY-FM, WCLB-FM, WCRB-FM, WDIS, WEEI, WESX, WEZE, WFNX-FM, WHAV, WHDH, WHRB-FM, WILD, WJDA, WJIB, WJMN-FM, WKOX, WLLH, WLYN, WLYT-FM, WMEX, WMJX-FM, WMSX, WNBP, WNSH, WNTN, WODS-FM, WPLM, WPLM-FM, WRCA, WRKO, WROL, WSRO, WSSH, WSSH-FM, WUNR, WXKS, WXKS-FM, WZLX-FM.

Bridgeport, CT: Rank 104
MSA: 262,900; TSA: 362,900
Stations: WADS, WCUM, WDJZ, WEZN-FM, WFIF, WICC.

Broadcasting & Cable Yearbook 1994
B-591

U.S. Radio Markets

Bryan-College Station, TX: Rank 231
MSA: 106,300; TSA: 156,100
Stations: KAGC, KAGG-FM, KBMA-FM, KKYS-FM, KMBV-FM, KORA-FM, KTAM, KTSR-FM, KTTX-FM, WTAW.

Buffalo-Niagara Falls: Rank 40
MSA: 991,900; TSA: 1,392,500
Stations: CJRN, CKEY-FM, WBEN, WBLK-FM, WBUF-FM, WDCX-FM, WECK, WFWC, WGR, WGRF-FM, WHLD, WHTT, WHTT-FM, WJJL, WJYE-FM, WKSE-FM, WLVL, WMJQ-FM, WNUC-FM, WUFO, WUFX-FM, WWKB, WWWS, WXRL, WYRK-FM.

Burlington, VT: Rank 220
MSA: 118,300; TSA: 417,300
Stations: WDEV-FM, WEZF-FM, WGLY-FM, WIZN-FM, WJOY, WKDR, WLFE-FM, WMNM-FM, WNCS-FM, WNWX, WOKO-FM, WVMT, WXXX-FM.

Canton, OH: Rank 115
MSA: 332,300; TSA: 618,700
Stations: WCER, WDPN, WHBC, WHBC-FM, WINW, WNPQ-FM, WRCW, WRQK-FM, WTIG, WTOF-FM, WZKL-FM.

Cape Cod, MA: Rank 185
MSA: 165,300; TSA: 180,900
Stations: WATB-FM, WCIB-FM, WCOD-FM, WFAL-FM, WFCC-FM, WFXR-FM, WKPE, WKPE-FM, WMVY-FM, WPXC-FM, WQRC-FM, WRZE-FM, WUOK, WXTK-FM.

Casper, WY: Rank 260
MSA: 49,300; TSA: 115,000
Stations: KMGW-FM, KQLT-FM, KTRS-FM, KTWO, KUYO, KVOC.

Cedar Rapids, IA: Rank 199
MSA: 144,100; TSA: 464,000
Stations: KCRG, KHAK, KHAK-FM, KKRQ-FM, KMRY, KQCR-FM, KRNA-FM, KTOF-FM, KXIC, WMT, WMT-FM.

Champaign, IL: Rank 197
MSA: 148,500; TSA: 427,000
Stations: WBCP, WDWS, WHMS-FM, WHZT-FM, WIXY-FM, WKIO-FM, WLRW-FM, WLTM-FM, WPGU-FM, WUFI, WZNF-FM.

Charleston, SC: Rank 84
MSA: 432,800; TSA: 741,500
Stations: WAVF-FM, WAZS, WBUB-FM, WEZL-FM, WJUK-FM, WJYQ-FM, WMCJ, WMGL-FM, WOKE, WPAL, WQIZ, WSSP-FM, WSSX-FM, WSUY-FM, WTMA, WTMZ, WTUA-FM, WUJM, WWWZ-FM, WXLY-FM, WXTC, WXTC-FM, WYBB-FM, WZJY.

Charleston, WV: Rank 155
MSA: 214,400; TSA: 551,400
Stations: WBES-FM, WCAW, WCHS, WCOZ, WCZR, WJYP-FM, WKAZ-FM, WKLC-FM, WKWS-FM, WQBE, WQBE-FM, WSCW, WVAF-FM, WVKV, WVSR, WVSR-FM.

Charlotte-Gastonia-Rock Hill, NC-SC: Rank 38
MSA: 1,034,800; TSA: 2,122,000
Stations: WAAK, WAGL, WAQQ-FM, WAQS, WAVO, WBT, WBT-FM, WBZK, WCGC, WCKZ-FM, WCNV, WCSL, WDEX, WEGO, WEZC-FM, WGAS, WGIV, WGNC, WGSP, WGTL, WHVN, WIXE, WLON, WLTC, WMAP, WMAP-FM, WMXC-FM, WNOW, WOGR, WPEG-FM, WRDX-FM, WRFX-FM, WRHI, WRHM-FM, WRKB, WRNA, WSAT, WSOC-FM, WSTP, WTDR-FM, WWMG-FM, WXRC-FM.

Charlottesville, VA: Rank 221
MSA: 117,300; TSA: 175,400
Stations: WANV-FM, WCHV, WCYK, WCYK-FM, WINA, WKAV, WKTR, WLSA-FM, WQMZ-FM, WUVA-FM, WVSY-FM, WWWV-FM.

Chattanooga: Rank 98
MSA: 371,600; TSA: 791,900
Stations: WADX, WBDX-FM, WDEF, WDEF-FM, WDOD, WDOD-FM, WEPG, WFLI, WFXS-FM, WGOW, WJOC, WJTT-FM, WKXJ-FM, WLMX, WLMX-FM, WMOC, WNOO, WOGT-FM, WQCH, WSDQ, WSDT, WSGC-FM, WSKZ-FM, WTYR, WUSY-FM, WWAM.

Cheyenne, WY: Rank 258
MSA: 61,900; TSA: 61,900
Stations: KCGY-FM, KFBC, KFBQ-FM, KKAZ-FM, KLDI, KLEN-FM, KMUS-FM, KRAE, KRQU-FM, KSHY, KUUY.

Chicago: Rank 3
MSA: 6,805,900; TSA: 9,106,600
Stations: WABT-FM, WAIT, WAKE, WAUR, WBBM, WBBM-FM, WBEE, WBIG, WBUS-FM, WCBR-FM, WCCQ-FM, WCEV, WCFJ, WCFL-FM, WCGO, WCKG-FM, WCRW, WCSJ, WDND-FM, WEDC, WEEF, WEMG-FM, WFMT-FM, WFXW, WGCI, WGCI-FM, WGN, WIIL-FM, WIND, WJDK-FM, WJJD, WJKL-FM, WJMK-FM, WJOB, WJOL, WJPC, WJPC-FM, WJTW-FM, WKBM-FM, WKDC, WKGA, WKKD, WKKD-FM, WKQX-FM, WKRS, WKTA, WLIP, WLIT-FM, WLJE-FM, WLLI-FM, WLS, WLS-FM, WLTH, WLUP-FM, WMAQ, WMCW, WMVP, WNDZ, WNIB-FM, WNIZ-FM, WNUA-FM, WNVR, WNWI, WOJO-FM, WONX, WOPA, WPNA, WPNT-FM, WRMN, WSBC, WSCR, WSPY-FM, WTAQ, WTMX-FM, WUSN-FM, WVAZ-FM, WVON, WVVX-FM, WWBZ-FM, WWCA, WWHN, WWJY-FM, WXLC-FM, WXRT-FM, WYCA-FM, WYLL-FM, WYSY-FM, WZSR-FM, WZVN-FM.

Chico, CA: Rank 186
MSA: 164,900; TSA: 301,300
Stations: KALF-FM, KCEZ-FM, KEWE-FM, KFMF-FM, KHSL, KHSL-FM, KKCY-FM, KKXX, KLRS-FM, KORV, KPAY, KPAY-FM, KPPL-FM, KZZP-FM.

Cincinnati: Rank 25
MSA: 1,528,500; TSA: 1,969,100
Stations: WAKW-FM, WAOL-FM, WAQZ-FM, WBND, WCIN, WCKY, WCNW, WCVG, WEBN-FM, WGRR-FM, WIMJ-FM, WIOK-FM, WIZF-FM, WKRQ-FM, WLW, WLWA, WNLT-FM, WNOP, WOFX-FM, WOXY-FM, WRRM-FM, WSAI, WSCH-FM, WTSJ, WUBE, WUBE-FM, WWNK-FM, WYGY-FM.

Cleveland: Rank 23
MSA: 1,758,200; TSA: 3,365,300
Stations: WABQ, WATJ, WBKC, WCCD, WCLV-FM, WDOK-FM, WELW, WENZ-FM, WEOL, WERE, WGAR-FM, WHK, WJMO, WJMO-FM, WJTB, WKNR, WLTF-FM, WMJI-FM, WMMS-FM, WNCX-FM, WNWV-FM, WOBL, WQAL-FM, WRDZ, WRKG, WRMR, WWWE, WZAK-FM, WZLE-FM.

Colorado Springs: Rank 106
MSA: 358,500; TSA: 581,600
Stations: KBIQ-FM, KCBR, KCMN, KGFT-FM, KHII-FM, KIKX-FM, KILO-FM, KKCS, KKCS-FM, KKFM-FM, KKLI-FM, KKMG-FM, KRDO, KRDO-FM, KSPZ-FM, KTWK-AM, KVOR, KVUU-FM, KWYD, KXRE.

Columbia, MO: Rank 235
MSA: 99,400; TSA: 261,200
Stations: KARO-FM, KCLR-FM, KCMQ-FM, KFAL, KFMZ-FM, KFRU, KMFC-FM, KTGR, KTXY-FM, KWWR-FM, KZZT-FM.

Columbia, SC: Rank 91
MSA: 391,100; TSA: 771,000
Stations: WARQ-FM, WBLR, WCOS, WCOS-FM, WFMV-FM, WHKZ-FM, WKWQ-FM, WLGO, WMFX-FM, WNMX-FM, WNOK-FM, WOIC, WOMG, WOMG-FM, WQXL, WSCQ-FM, WTCB-FM, WTGH, WVOC, WWDM-FM.

Columbus, GA: Rank 161
MSA: 207,400; TSA: 487,400
Stations: WAGH-FM, WCGQ-FM, WEAM, WFXE-FM, WGSY-FM, WHYD, WKCN-FM, WOKS, WPNX, WRCG, WSTH, WSTH-FM, WVFJ-FM, WVRK-FM.

Columbus, OH: Rank 34
MSA: 1,197,200; TSA: 1,896,500
Stations: WAHC-FM, WBNS, WBNS-FM, WBZX-FM, WCEZ-FM, WCKX-FM, WCLT, WCLT-FM, WCOL, WCOL-FM, WDLR, WHOK-FM, WHTH, WLOH, WLVQ-FM, WMNI, WNCI-FM, WNKO-FM, WNRJ, WRFD, WRVF-FM, WRZR-FM, WSNY-FM, WSWZ-FM, WTVN, WUCO, WVKO, WWCD-FM, WWHT-FM.

Corpus Christi, TX: Rank 130
MSA: 286,800; TSA: 430,800
Stations: KBSO-FM, KCCT, KCTA, KDAE, KEYS, KFLZ-FM, KGLF, KINE, KKHQ-FM, KLTG-FM, KMIQ-FM, KMXR-FM, KNCN-FM, KOUL-FM, KQTX-FM, KRYS, KRYS-FM, KSAB-FM, KSIX, KUNO, KWVS-FM, KYTX-FM, KZFM-FM.

Dallas-Fort Worth: Rank 7
MSA: 3,458,600; TSA: 4,709,300
Stations: KAAM, KAHZ, KBEC, KBOC-FM, KCLE, KCYT-FM, KDFT, KDGE-FM, KDMX-FM, KDNT, KDZR-FM, KEGL-FM, KESS, KFJZ, KGBS, KGGR, KHKS-FM, KHVN, KJMZ-FM, KJSA, KKDA, KKDA-FM, KLIF, KLTY-FM, KLUV-FM, KMRT, KOAI-FM, KPAR, KPBC, KPLX-FM, KPYK, KRLD, KRRW-FM, KRVA, KRVA-FM, KSCS-FM, KSKY, KSNN-FM, KSTV-FM, KTLR-FM, KTNO-AM, KTXQ-FM, KVIL, KVIL-FM, KYNG-FM, KYXS-FM, KZEE, KZPS-FM, WBAP, WRR-FM.

Danbury, CT: Rank 191
MSA: 157,600; TSA: 157,600
Stations: WDAQ-FM, WINE, WLAD, WREF, WRKI-FM.

Danville, IL: Rank 254
MSA: 72,300; TSA: 157,700
Stations: WCDV-FM, WDAN, WDNL-FM, WHPO-FM, WIAI-FM, WITY, WWDZ-FM.

Dayton, OH: Rank 48
MSA: 838,400; TSA: 1,633,800
Stations: WAZU-FM, WBLY, WBZI, WCLR-FM, WCTM, WDAO, WFCJ-FM, WGNZ, WGTZ-FM, WHIO, WHKO-FM, WING, WIZE, WKSW-FM, WLQT-FM, WMMX, WONE, WPFB, WPFB-FM, WPTW, WQLK-FM, WROU-FM, WTRJ-FM, WTUE-FM, WYMJ-FM, WZLR-FM.

Daytona Beach, FL: Rank 96
MSA: 378,200; TSA: 736,400
Stations: WEDG-FM, WELE, WFKS-FM, WGNE-FM, WMFJ, WNDB, WPUL, WROD, WSBB, WWBH, WXVQ, WYND.

Denver-Boulder: Rank 24
MSA: 1,636,500; TSA: 2,600,900
Stations: KAZY-FM, KBCO, KBCO-FM, KBNO, KBOL, KBPI-FM, KCUV, KDEN, KDKO, KEZW, KHIH-FM, KHOW, KJME, KLMO, KLTT, KLZ, KMJI-FM, KNUS, KOA, KOSI-FM, KQKS-FM, KQXI, KRFX-FM, KRKS, KRKS-FM, KRZN, KTCL-FM, KTMG, KVOD-FM, KWMX, KWMX-FM, KXKL, KXKL-FM, KYBG, KYBG-FM, KYGO, KYGO-FM, KZDG-FM.

Des Moines, IA: Rank 113
MSA: 339,900; TSA: 991,100
Stations: KDLS, KDLS-FM, KDMI-FM, KEZT-FM, KFMG-FM, KGGO, KGGO-FM, KIOA, KIOA-FM, KJJC-FM, KJJY-FM, KKSO, KLYF-FM, KMXD-FM, KRNT, KRUU-FM, KSTZ-FM, KWKY, KXLQ, WHO.

Detroit: Rank 6
MSA: 3,643,100; TSA: 5,327,000
Stations: CIMX-FM, CKLW, CKLW-FM, CKWW, WCAR, WCHB, WCSX-FM, WDZR-FM, WEXL, WGPR-FM, WGRT-FM, WHLS, WHMI, WHMI-FM, WHND, WHYT-FM, WIFN, WJLB-FM, WJOI-FM, WJR, WJZZ-FM, WKQI-FM, WLLZ-FM, WLQV, WLTI-FM, WMKM, WMTG, WMUZ-FM, WMXD-FM, WNIC-FM, WNZK, WOMC-FM, WPHM, WPON, WQBH, WQRS-FM, WRIF-FM, WSAQ-FM, WWJ, WWWW, WWWW-FM, WXYT, WYCD-FM.

Dothan, AL: Rank 175
MSA: 179,100; TSA: 403,300
Stations: WAGF, WDJR-FM, WELB, WESP-FM, WGEA, WJJN-FM, WKMX-FM, WLHQ, WOAB-FM, WOOF, WOOF-FM, WOZK, WQLS, WQLS-FM, WRJM-FM, WTKN, WTVY-FM, WWNT, WXUS-FM, WZTZ-FM.

Dubuque, IA: Rank 210
MSA: 129,800; TSA: 218,100
Stations: KATF-FM, KDST-FM, KDTH, KGGY-FM, KLYV-FM, WDBQ, WGLR, WGLR-FM, WJOD-FM, WKPL-FM, WTOQ.

Duluth-Superior, MN-WI: Rank 211
MSA: 128,100; TSA: 377,300
Stations: KDAL, KDAL-FM, KMFY-FM, KQDS, KQDS-FM, KXTP, KZIO-FM, WAKX-FM, WAVC-FM, WDSM, WEBC, WHLB, WUSZ-FM, WWJC.

Eau Claire, WI: Rank 222
MSA: 116,600; TSA: 436,700
Stations: WAXX-FM, WAYY, WBIZ, WBIZ-FM, WCFW-FM, WEAQ, WECL-FM, WEIO, WIAL-FM, WISM-FM, WMEQ-FM, WOGO, WQRB-FM, WWIB-FM.

El Paso, TX: Rank 77
MSA: 505,500; TSA: 725,900
Stations: KAMA, KAMZ-FM, KBNA, KBNA-FM, KELP, KFNA, KHEY, KHEY-FM, KINT-FM, KLAQ-FM, KOFX-FM, KPAS-FM, KPRR-FM, KROD, KSET-FM, KSVE, KTSM, KTSM-FM, KVIV, XEWG, XHH-FM, XROK.

Erie, PA: Rank 149
MSA: 229,000; TSA: 420,100
Stations: WCTL-FM, WEYZ, WFGO-FM, WFLP, WJET-FM, WLKK, WMXE-FM, WPSE, WRIE, WRKT-FM, WWCB, WXKC-FM, WXTA-FM, WZPR-FM.

Eugene-Springfield, OR: Rank 145
MSA: 245,500; TSA: 553,800
Stations: KCST, KCST-FM, KDBS, KDUK, KDUK-FM, KEED, KGAL-FM, KKNU, KKXO, KMGE-FM, KNND, KORE, KPNW, KPNW-FM, KUGN, KUGN-FM, KZEL-FM, KZZK, KZZK-FM.

Evansville, IN: Rank 148
MSA: 233,600; TSA: 626,500
Stations: WBLZ-FM, WBNL, WBNL-FM, WGAB, WGBF-FM, WIKY-FM, WJPS, WJPS-FM, WKDQ-FM, WPCO, WRBT-FM, WSON, WSTO-FM, WVHI, WWOK, WYNG-FM.

U.S. Radio Markets

Fargo-Moorhead, ND-MN: Rank 209
MSA: 130,900; TSA: 454,200
Stations: KFGO, KFGO-FM, KKDL-FM, KLTA-FM, KPFX-FM, KQWB, KQWB-FM, KSSZ-FM, KVOX, KVOX-FM, WDAY, WDAY-FM.

Fayetteville, NC: Rank 123
MSA: 317,200; TSA: 657,400
Stations: WAGR, WAZZ-FM, WCIE, WFAI, WFLB, WFMO, WFNC, WGQR-FM, WIDU, WJSK-FM, WKKE, WKML-FM, WQSM-FM, WRCQ-FM, WSTS-FM, WTSB, WXKL, WYRU, WZFX-FM, WZNS-FM.

Fayetteville-Springdale, AR: Rank 167
MSA: 191,600; TSA: 297,700
Stations: KAMO, KAMO-FM, KBEV-FM, KBVA-FM, KDAB-FM, KESE-FM, KEZA-FM, KFAY, KISK-FM, KJEM, KKEG-FM, KKIX-FM, KMCK-FM, KOFC, KOLZ-FM, KQXK, KUOA, KURM.

Flint, MI: Rank 110
MSA: 347,700; TSA: 515,000
Stations: WCRZ-FM, WDZZ-FM, WFDF, WFLT, WFNT, WKMF-FM, WOWE-FM, WTAC, WWCK, WWCK-FM, WWGZ, WWGZ-FM, WWON.

Florence, SC: Rank 195
MSA: 149,400; TSA: 239,500
Stations: WDAR, WDAR-FM, WHLZ-FM, WHSC, WHSC-FM, WJMX, WJMX-FM, WKSY-FM, WLXP-FM, WMXT-FM, WOLS, WRIP, WSQN-FM, WTNI, WWFN-FM, WYNN, WYNN-FM.

Fort Myers, FL: Rank 121
MSA: 321,500; TSA: 634,800
Stations: WAVV-FM, WCKT-FM, WCRM, WCVU-FM, WDCQ, WHEW-FM, WINK, WINK-FM, WJBX-FM, WKZY-FM, WMYR, WOLZ-FM, WRXK-FM, WSUV-FM, WWCL, WWCN, WXKB-FM.

Fort Pierce-Stuart-Vero Beach, FL: Rank 120
MSA: 323,000; TSA: 349,700
Stations: WAVW-FM, WAXE, WGYL-FM, WHLG-FM, WIRA, WJNX, WPSL, WQOL-FM, WSTU, WTTB, WZZR-FM.

Fort Smith, AR: Rank 168
MSA: 189,800; TSA: 350,800
Stations: KAYR, KBBQ-FM, KBSY-FM, KERX-FM, KEZU-FM, KFDF, KFPW, KFSA, KISR-FM, KKID, KKUZ-FM, KLSZ-FM, KMAG-FM, KOLX-FM, KPBI, KPRV, KPRV-FM, KTCS, KTCS-FM, KWHN, KZBB-FM, KZKZ-FM.

Fort Walton Beach, FL: Rank 213
MSA: 126,600; TSA: 152,200
Stations: WAAZ-FM, WCNU, WFSH, WFTW, WJSB, WKSM-FM, WKYD, WLGH-FM, WMMK-FM, WNCV-FM, WNUE, WWAV-FM, WWSF-FM, WYZB-FM.

Fort Wayne, IN: Rank 93
MSA: 380,900; TSA: 850,300
Stations: WAJI-FM, WBTU-FM, WBYR-FM, WDJB-FM, WFCV, WFWI-FM, WGL, WGL-FM, WGTB-FM, WIFF, WJFX-FM, WJLT-FM, WLYV, WLZQ-FM, WMEE-FM, WOWO, WOWO-FM, WQHK, WQHK-FM, WXKE-FM.

Frederick, MD: Rank 206
MSA: 132,300; TSA: 132,300
Note: Part of Washington, D.C., Metro.

Fresno, CA: Rank 66
MSA: 580,000; TSA: 1,174,500
Stations: KAAT-FM, KBIF, KBOS-FM, KEYQ, KEZL-FM, KFCL-FM, KFIG, KFRE, KFSO-FM, KGST, KHOT, KIGS, KIRV, KJFX-FM, KJOI-FM, KKDJ-FM, KKFO, KKTR, KMAK-FM, KMJ, KMMM-FM, KMPH-FM, KNAX-FM, KNGS-FM, KOQO, KOQO-FM, KRDU, KRGO, KRZR-FM, KSEQ-FM, KSKS-FM, KSLK-FM, KSXY-FM, KTAA-FM, KTHT-FM, KXEX, KXMX-FM, KYNO.

Gainesville-Ocala, FL: Rank 111
MSA: 346,100; TSA: 659,900
Stations: WAJD, WGGG, WKTK-FM, WLUS, WMFQ-FM, WMMZ-FM, WMOP, WOCA, WRRX-FM, WRUF, WRUF-FM, WTMC, WTRS, WTRS-FM, WWGO-FM, WWLO, WYGC-FM, WYKS-FM, WYOC-FM.

Grand Forks, ND-MN: Rank 246
MSA: 85,400; TSA: 172,500
Stations: KCNN, KJKJ-FM, KKCQ, KKCQ-FM, KKXL, KKXL-FM, KNOX, KNOX-FM, KQHT-FM, KROX, KSNR-FM, KYCK-FM, KZLT-FM.

Grand Junction, CO: Rank 249
MSA: 82,600; TSA: 184,800
Stations: KBKL-FM, KEKB-FM, KEXO, KJYE-FM, KKLY-FM, KNZZ, KQIL, KQIX-FM, KSTR, KSTR-FM.

Grand Rapids, MI: Rank 67
MSA: 577,200; TSA: 1,364,800
Stations: WBCT-FM, WBYY, WCUZ, WCUZ-FM, WFGR-FM, WFUR, WFUR-FM, WGHN, WGHN-FM, WGRD, WGRD-FM, WHTC, WJQK-FM, WKEZ-FM, WKLQ-FM, WKWM, WLAV, WLAV-FM, WLHT-FM, WODJ-FM, WOOD, WOOD-FM, WQFN-FM, WWJQ, WYGR.

Great Falls, MT: Rank 256
MSA: 67,300; TSA: 170,600
Stations: KAAK-FM, KEIN, KLFM-FM, KMON, KMON-FM, KMSL, KQDI-FM, KXGF.

Green Bay, WI: Rank 184
MSA: 165,600; TSA: 686,700
Stations: WDUZ, WEZR-FM, WGEE, WGEE-FM, WIXX-FM, WJLW-FM, WNFL, WQLH-FM.

Greensboro-Winston Salem-High Point, NC: Rank 43
MSA: 925,600; TSA: 1,919,900
Stations: WAAA, WBFJ, WDIX, WDSL, WFAZ-FM, WGLD, WGOS, WHPE-FM, WJMH-FM, WKEW, WKRR-FM, WKSI-FM, WKTE, WKXR, WKZL-FM, WLXN, WMAG-FM, WMFR, WMQX, WMQX-FM, WNEU-FM, WPCM-FM, WPET, WQMG, WQMG-FM, WSGH, WSJS, WSMX, WTNC, WTOB, WTQR-FM, WWGL-FM, WWMO, WWWB-FM, WZOO.

Greenville-New Bern-Jacksonville, NC: Rank 81
MSA: 451,600; TSA: 879,000
Stations: WARR, WBTB, WBZQ, WCPQ, WCZI-FM, WDLX-FM, WELS, WGHB, WHTE-FM, WIKS-FM, WJCV, WJNC, WKGK-FM, WKJA-FM, WKOO-FM, WKQT-FM, WKZF-FM, WLAS, WLOJ, WMBL, WMSQ-FM, WNBR-FM, WNCT, WNCT-FM, WNOS, WOOW, WRHT-FM, WRNS, WRNS-FM, WRQR-FM, WRRF, WSFL, WSFL-FM, WTKF-FM, WTND-FM, WTOW, WWOF, WXQR-FM.

Greenville-Spartanburg, SC: Rank 61
MSA: 681,800; TSA: 1,459,400
Stations: WAGI-FM, WAIM, WANS, WASC, WBBO-FM, WCCP, WCCP-FM, WCKI, WDAB, WESC, WESC-FM, WFBC, WFBC-FM, WFIS, WHPB, WHYZ, WJKI, WJMZ-FM, WLWZ, WLWZ-FM, WLYZ-FM, WMUU, WMUU-FM, WMYI-FM, WORD, WPCI, WPJM, WRIX, WRIX-FM, WROQ-FM, WSPA, WSPA-FM, WSSL, WSSL-FM, WTBI, WYYR.

Hagerstown-Chambersburg-Waynesboro, MD-PA: Rank 159
MSA: 209,600; TSA: 317,600
Stations: WARK, WARX-FM, WAYZ-FM, WCBG, WCHA, WHAG, WHGT, WIKZ-FM, WJEJ, WKMZ-FM, WKSL-FM, WPVG, WQCM-FM, WSRT-FM, WWMD-FM, WYII-FM.

Harrisburg-Lebanon-Carlisle, PA: Rank 74
MSA: 510,900; TSA: 1,457,400
Stations: WADV, WAHT, WCMB, WCTX-FM, WHP, WHYL, WHYL-FM, WIMX-FM, WIOO, WKBO, WLBR, WNNK-FM, WQIC-FM, WQIN, WQLV-FM, WRKZ-FM, WRVV-FM, WSHP, WTCY, WTPA-FM, WWII, WWKL-FM, WYGL-FM.

Harrisonburg, VA: Rank 251
MSA: 77,500; TSA: 265,400
Stations: WAMM-FM, WAZR-FM, WBOP-FM, WBTX, WHBG, WKCY, WKCY-FM, WLTK-FM, WPKZ-FM, WQPO-FM, WSVA.

Hartford-New Britain-Middletown, CT: Rank 42
MSA: 970,200; TSA: 2,625,200
Stations: WBIS, WCCC, WCCC-FM, WCNX, WCTF, WDRC, WDRC-FM, WHCN-FM, WKND, WKSS-FM, WLAT, WLVX, WMMW, WNEZ, WNTY, WPOP, WRCH-FM, WRYM, WTIC, WTIC-FM, WYSR-FM, WZMX-FM.

Honolulu: Rank 59
MSA: 727,800; TSA: 727,800
Stations: KAIM, KAIM-FM, KCCN, KCCN-FM, KDEO, KDEO-FM, KGMZ-FM, KGU, KHHH-FM, KHNR, KHVH, KIKI, KIKI-FM, KINE-FM, KISA, KLHT, KNDI, KOHO, KPOI-FM, KQMQ, KQMQ-FM, KRTR-FM, KSSK, KSSK-FM, KULA, KUMU, KUMU-FM, KWAI, KZOO.

Houston-Galveston: Rank 10
MSA: 3,184,200; TSA: 3,941,000
Stations: KBRZ, KBXX-FM, KCOH, KEYH, KGBC, KGOL, KHMX-FM, KHYS-FM, KIKK, KIKK-FM, KILT, KILT-FM, KJOJ, KJOJ-FM, KKBQ, KKBQ-FM, KKZR-FM, KLAT, KLDE-FM, KLEV, KLOL-FM, KLTN-FM, KLTR-FM, KLVL, KMJQ-FM, KMPQ, KMPQ-FM, KNUZ, KODA, KPRC, KQQK-FM, KQUE-FM, KRBE, KRBE-FM, KRTS-FM, KRTX-FM, KSEV, KSHN-FM, KSSQ, KTEK, KTRH, KWWJ, KXTJ-FM, KXYZ, KYOK, KYST, KZFM-FM.

Huntington-Ashland, WV-KY: Rank 137
MSA: 266,000; TSA: 651,800
Stations: WCMI, WCMI-FM, WEMM-FM, WGOH, WIRO, WKEE, WKEE-FM, WLGC, WLGC-FM, WMGG-FM, WMLV-FM, WNST, WOKT, WRVC-FM, WTCR, WTCR-FM, WTKZ, WUGO-FM, WVKY, WXVK-FM, WZZW-FM.

Huntsville, AL: Rank 108
MSA: 352,900; TSA: 801,500
Stations: WAHR-FM, WAJF, WAVD, WAZK-FM, WBBI, WBHP, WBXR, WDRM-FM, WEUP, WHOS, WHRT, WHVK-FM, WJRA, WKAC, WLOR, WNDA-FM, WQLT-FM, WRSA-FM, WTAK, WTAK-FM, WTKI, WVNN, WZYP-FM.

Indianapolis: Rank 37
MSA: 1,070,700; TSA: 2,242,700
Stations: WBRI, WCBK-FM, WCKN, WENS-FM, WFBQ-FM, WFMS-FM, WGRL-FM, WHHH-FM, WIBC, WIRE-FM, WKLR-FM, WMCB, WNDE, WNTS, WOOO, WPZZ-FM, WQFE-FM, WRZX-FM, WSYW, WSYW-FM, WTLC, WTLC-FM, WTPI-FM, WTTS-FM, WXIR-FM, WXLW, WXTZ-FM, WXXP-FM, WYIC, WZPL-FM.

Ithaca, NY: Rank 247
MSA: 83,200; TSA: 139,700
Stations: WHCU, WKRT, WPIE, WQNY-FM, WTKO, WVBR-FM, WYXL-FM, WYYS-FM.

Jackson, MS: Rank 116
MSA: 331,600; TSA: 894,500
Stations: WBKJ-FM, WHJT-FM, WIIN-FM, WJDS, WJDX-FM, WJMI-FM, WJNT, WJXN, WJXN-FM, WKTF-FM, WKXI, WKXI-FM, WLIN-FM, WLRM, WMGO, WMSI-FM, WOAD, WONG, WRJH-FM, WRKN, WSLI, WSTZ-FM, WTWZ, WTYX-FM, WWDF, WZRX.

Jacksonville, FL: Rank 50
MSA: 817,600; TSA: 1,068,000
Stations: WAIA-FM, WAOC, WAPE-FM, WBYB-FM, WCGL, WCRJ, WEJZ-FM, WFOY, WFYV-FM, WHJX-FM, WIVY-FM, WJBT-FM, WJXR-FM, WKLN, WKQL-FM, WNCM, WNZS, WOKV, WPDQ, WQAI, WQIK, WQIK-FM, WROO-FM, WROS, WSOS-FM, WSTF-FM, WSVE, WVOJ, WXQL-FM, WXTL, WZAZ, WZNZ.

Johnson City-Kingsport-Bristol, TN-VA: Rank 94
MSA: 380,700; TSA: 728,900
Stations: WABN, WABN-FM, WBCV, WBEJ, WDUF, WEMB, WETB, WEYE-FM, WGAT, WGOC, WIKQ-FM, WITM, WJCW, WJDT-FM, WKIN, WKOS-FM, WKPT, WKTP, WMCH, WMEV, WMEV-FM, WOPI, WQUT-FM, WRGS, WTFM-FM, WUSJ-FM, WXBQ, WXBQ-FM, WXIS-FM, WZAP, WZMC.

Johnstown, PA: Rank 164
MSA: 201,200; TSA: 383,100
Stations: WADJ, WBEM, WBXQ-FM, WCCZ-FM, WCRO, WGLU-FM, WHYM, WJAC, WJRV, WKYE-FM, WMTZ-FM, WNCC, WNTJ-FM, WQKK-FM, WQZS-FM, WRDD, WVSC, WVSC-FM, WYSN-FM, WZGO-FM.

Joplin, MO: Rank 225
MSA: 114,100; TSA: 327,300
Stations: KBTN, KDMO, KFSB, KIXQ-FM, KKLL, KKLL-FM, KKOW, KKOW-FM, KMOQ-FM, KMXL-FM, KOCD-FM, KQYX, KSYN-FM, KWAS, KWXB-FM, WMBH, WMBH-FM.

Kalamazoo, MI: Rank 169
MSA: 188,300; TSA: 447,300
Stations: WFAT-FM, WHEZ, WKFR-FM, WKGH-FM, WKMI, WKPR, WKZO, WNWN-FM, WQLR-FM, WQSN, WQXC, WQXC-FM, WRKR-FM.

Kansas City, MO-KS: Rank 30
MSA: 1,338,000; TSA: 2,195,300
Stations: KAYX-FM, KBEA, KBEQ-FM, KCCV, KCFX-FM, KCMO, KCMO-FM, KCNW, KCXL, KEXS, KFEZ, KFKF-FM, KISF-FM, KJLA, KKCJ-FM, KKLO, KLEX, KLTH-FM, KMBZ, KMXV-FM, KNHN, KPHN, KPRS-FM, KPRT, KQRC-FM, KUDL-FM, KXTR-FM, KYYS-FM, WDAF-FM, WHB.

Killeen-Temple, TX: Rank 163
MSA: 201,900; TSA: 280,200
Stations: KIIZ, KLFX-FM, KOOC-FM, KOOV-FM, KPLE-FM, KRMY, KRYL-FM, KTEM, KTON.

Knoxville, TN: Rank 73
MSA: 517,800; TSA: 1,281,000
Stations: WATO, WBCR, WCGM, WDLY-FM, WDMF, WEMG, WEZK, WEZK-FM, WGAP, WGAP-FM, WHJM, WIMZ-FM, WITA, WIVK, WIVK-FM, WJBZ-FM, WJFC, WKGN, WKNF-FM, WKXV-FM, WLIL, WLIL-FM, WLIQ-FM, WMYU-FM, WNDD-FM, WNOX-FM, WOKI-FM, WQBB, WQBB-FM, WRJZ, WSEV, WTNN, WUTK, WWZZ-FM, WXST-FM, WYSH.

U.S. Radio Markets

La Crosse, WI: Rank 248
MSA: 83,000; TSA: 310,000
Stations: KAGE, KAGE-FM, KQEG-FM, WCOW-FM, WIZM, WIZM-FM, WKBH, WKBH-FM, WKLJ, WKTY, WLFN, WLXR-FM, WQJY-FM, WSPL-FM.

Lafayette, IN: Rank 224
MSA: 115,500; TSA: 278,300
Stations: WASK, WASK-FM, WAZY-FM, WCFY, WEZV-FM, WGLM-FM, WIIZ-FM, WKHY-FM, WSHW-FM.

Lafayette, LA: Rank 133
MSA: 278,700; TSA: 441,500
Stations: KACY, KAJN-FM, KDEA-FM, KFTE-FM, KFXZ-FM, KJCB, KMDL-FM, KPEL, KPEL-FM, KROF, KROF-FM, KSMB-FM, KTDY-FM, KVOL, KVOL-FM, KXKC-FM.

Lake Charles, LA: Rank 200
MSA: 138,100; TSA: 279,100
Stations: KAOK, KBIU-FM, KEZM, KHLA-FM, KLCL, KTQQ-FM, KXZZ, KYKZ-FM.

Lakeland-Winter Haven, FL: Rank 107
MSA: 358,300; TSA: 440,100
Stations: WBAR, WEZY-FM, WHNR, WIPC, WLKF, WLVF, WONN, WPCV-FM, WSIR, WTWB, WWAB, WWBF, WXPQ.

Lancaster, PA: Rank 101
MSA: 364,800; TSA: 758,800
Stations: WDAC-FM, WIOV-FM, WLAN, WLAN-FM, WLPA, WNZT, WPDC, WROZ-FM.

Lansing-East Lansing, MI: Rank 103
MSA: 363,800; TSA: 888,000
Stations: WFMK-FM, WIBM-FM, WILS, WILS-FM, WITL, WITL-FM, WJCO, WJIM, WJIM-FM, WJXQ-FM, WLCM, WMMQ-FM, WQHH-FM, WVFN, WVIC-FM, WWDX-FM, WWSJ, WXLA.

Las Vegas: Rank 58
MSA: 731,300; TSA: 888,200
Stations: KDOL, KDWN, KEDG-FM, KENO, KEYV-FM, KFBI-FM, KFMS, KFMS-FM, KJUL-FM, KKLZ-FM, KKVV, KLAV, KLUC-FM, KLUK-FM, KMTW, KMZQ-FM, KNUU, KOMP-FM, KORK, KOWA, KRBO-FM, KRLV-FM, KRRI-FM, KVEG, KWNR-FM, KXNO, KXPT-FM, KXTZ-FM.

Laurel-Hattiesburg, MS: Rank 203
MSA: 134,200; TSA: 246,400
Stations: WAML, WBBN-FM, WBKH, WEEZ-FM, WFOR, WHER-FM, WHLV, WHSY, WHSY-FM, WIZK, WIZK-FM, WJKX-FM, WJMG-FM, WKNZ-FM, WLAU, WLUN-FM, WMFM-FM, WMXI-FM, WNSL-FM, WORV, WQIS.

Lawton, OK: Rank 242
MSA: 93,200; TSA: 143,000
Stations: KBZQ-FM, KKRX, KKRX-FM, KLAW-FM, KMGZ-FM, KQTZ-FM, KRPT, KRPT-FM, KSWO, KVRW-FM, KZCD-FM.

Lexington-Fayette, KY: Rank 124
MSA: 309,900; TSA: 900,300
Stations: WBBE, WCGW, WCKU-FM, WGKS-FM, WHRS, WJMM-FM, WKQQ-FM, WLAP, WLXG, WMXL-FM, WNVL, WRPZ, WTKT-FM, WVLK, WVLK-FM, WWYC-FM, WYGH.

Lima, OH: Rank 213
MSA: 126,600; TSA: 327,600
Stations: WBUK-FM, WCIT, WCSM, WCSM-FM, WDOH-FM, WIMA, WIMT-FM, WKKI-FM, WLSR-FM, WYRX-FM, WZOQ-FM.

Lincoln, NE: Rank 173
MSA: 185,100; TSA: 323,000
Stations: KEZG-FM, KFGE-FM, KFOR, KFRX-FM, KHAT, KIBZ-FM, KKNB-FM, KLDZ-FM, KLIN, KMEM, KTGL-FM, KYNN-FM, KZKX-FM.

Little Rock, AR: Rank 83
MSA: 440,000; TSA: 1,024,200
Stations: KAAY, KARN, KBIS, KCON, KDDK-FM, KEWI, KEZQ-FM, KFCA, KGHT, KGKO, KHLT-FM, KIPR-FM, KITA, KJBN, KKYK-FM, KLPQ-FM, KLRG, KMJX-FM, KMTL, KMVK-FM, KMZX-FM, KOLL-FM, KPAL, KQUS-FM, KSSN-FM, KTOD-FM, KURB, KURB-FM, KYFX-FM, KYTN-FM, KYXZ.

Los Angeles: Rank 2
MSA: 9,705,900; TSA: 13,338,000
Stations: KABC, KACE-FM, KAJZ-FM, KALI, KAVC-FM, KAVL, KAZN, KBET, KBIG-FM, KBJZ-FM, KBLA, KBOB-FM, KBRT, KCBS-FM, KEZY-FM, KFI, KFOX-FM, KFRN, KFSG-FM, KFWB, KGER, KGFJ, KGMX-FM, KGRB, KHJJ, KIEV, KIIS, KIIS-FM, KIKF-FM, KJLH-FM, KJOI, KKBT-FM, KKGO-FM, KKHJ, KKLA-FM, KLAC, KLAX-FM, KLIT-FM, KLOS-FM, KLSX-FM, KLVE-FM, KMAX-FM, KMGX-FM, KMNY, KMPC, KNAC-FM, KNX, KOJY, KORG, KOST-FM, KPPC, KPWR-FM, KRLA, KROQ-FM, KRTH-FM, KTNQ, KTSJ, KTWV-FM, KTYM, KUTY, KWIZ, KWIZ-FM, KWKW, KWNK, KWVE-FM, KXED, KXEZ-FM, KYMS-FM, KYSR-FM, KZLA-FM.

Louisville, KY: Rank 52
MSA: 810,900; TSA: 1,334,000
Stations: WAMZ-FM, WAVG, WBUL, WCND, WDGS, WDJX, WDJX-FM, WEHR-FM, WFIA, WGZB-FM, WHAS, WHKW-FM, WKXF, WLLV, WLOU, WLRS-FM, WLSY-FM, WMPI-FM, WOCC, WQMF-FM, WQNF-FM, WRKA-FM, WTFX-FM, WTHQ-FM, WTMT, WVEZ-FM, WWKY, WXKN, WXLN-FM, WXVW, WZCC.

Lubbock, TX: Rank 172
MSA: 186,500; TSA: 345,800
Stations: KCAS, KEJS, KFMX-FM, KFYO, KJAK-FM, KJBX, KKAM, KKCL-FM, KLFB, KLLL, KLLL-FM, KMMX-FM, KONE-FM, KRLB-FM, KTNP, KXTQ, KXTQ-FM, KZII-FM.

Macon, GA: Rank 147
MSA: 237,700; TSA: 517,000
Stations: WAYS-FM, WBML, WBNM, WCOP, WDDO, WDEN, WDEN-FM, WFXM-FM, WKXK, WMAZ, WMKS-FM, WNEX, WNEX-FM, WPEZ-FM, WPGA, WPGA-FM, WQBZ-FM, WRCC, WRCC-FM, WVVY-FM, WXKO.

Madison, WI: Rank 121
MSA: 321,500; TSA: 766,700
Stations: WHIT, WIBA, WIBA-FM, WIBU, WJJO-FM, WMAD, WMAD-FM, WMGN-FM, WMLI-FM, WMMM-FM, WOLX-FM, WSJY-FM, WTDY, WTSO, WWQM-FM, WYZM-FM, WZEE-FM.

Manchester, NH: Rank 179
MSA: 171,800; TSA: 480,600
Note: A portion of Rockingham County is also included in the Portsmouth-Dover-Rochester, NH, Metro.

Marion-Carbondale (Southern Illinois), IL: Rank 201
MSA: 135,800; TSA: 247,900
Stations: WCIL, WCIL-FM, WDDD, WDDD-FM, WFRX, WFRX-FM, WGGH, WINI, WJPF, WOOZ-FM, WQRL-FM, WTAO-FM, WUEZ-FM, WXAN-FM, WXLT-FM.

McAllen-Brownsville-Harlingen, TX: Rank 70
MSA: 540,200; TSA: 600,100
Stations: KBFM-FM, KBOR, KFRQ-FM, KGBT, KIRT, KIWW-FM, KJAV-FM, KKPS-FM, KQXX-FM, KRGE, KSOX, KSOX-FM, KTEX-FM, KTJN-FM, KTJX-FM, KUBR, KURV, KVJY, KVLY-FM, KVPA-FM, KZSP-FM, XERT.

Medford-Ashland, OR: Rank 208
MSA: 131,000; TSA: 305,200
Stations: KBOY-FM, KCMX, KCMX-FM, KCNA-FM, KDOV, KMED, KOPE-FM, KROG-FM, KRWQ-FM, KTMT, KTMT-FM, KYJC, KYJC-FM.

Melbourne-Titusville-Cocoa, FL: Rank 97
MSA: 372,300; TSA: 720,300
Stations: WAMT, WAOA-FM, WGGD-FM, WHKR-FM, WLRQ-FM, WMEL, WMMB, WPGS, WRFB, WTAI, WWBC, WWHL, WXXU.

Memphis: Rank 44
MSA: 915,300; TSA: 1,675,200
Stations: KFTH-FM, KHLS-FM, KJMS-FM, KLCN, KOSE, KSUD, KWAM, WAVN, WBBP, WCRV, WDIA, WEGR-FM, WGKX-FM, WGSF, WHBQ, WHRK-FM, WJCE, WKBL, WKBL-FM, WKRA, WKRA-FM, WLOK, WMC, WMC-FM, WMPS, WNWZ, WOGY-FM, WPLX, WREC, WRVR-FM, WSTN, WVIM-FM, WXSS, WYKL-FM.

Meridian, MS: Rank 258
MSA: 61,900; TSA: 254,800
Stations: WALT, WJDQ-FM, WMER, WMGP, WMOX, WNBN, WOKK-FM, WTUX-FM, WZMP-FM.

Miami-Fort Lauderdale-Hollywood, FL: Rank 11
MSA: 2,823,900; TSA: 3,747,000
Stations: WAQI, WAVS, WAXY-FM, WCMQ, WCMQ-FM, WEDR, WEXY, WFLC-FM, WFTL, WHQT-FM, WHYI-FM, WINZ, WIOD, WKAT, WKIS-FM, WLQY, WLVE-FM, WLYF-FM, WMRZ, WMXJ-FM, WOCN, WOIR, WPOW-FM, WQAM, WQBA, WQBA-FM, WRBD, WRFM, WRHC, WRTO-FM, WSBH, WSHE-FM, WSRF, WSUA, WTMI-FM, WTPX-FM, WVCG, WWFE, WWNN, WXDJ-FM, WZTA-FM.

Milwaukee-Racine: Rank 28
MSA: 1,342,000; TSA: 1,867,300
Stations: WAUK, WBJX, WBKV, WBWI-FM, WEMP, WEZW-FM, WFMR-FM, WGLB, WGLB-FM, WHKQ-FM, WISN, WKKV-FM, WKLH-FM, WKSH, WKTI-FM, WLTQ-FM, WLUM-FM, WLZR, WLZR-FM, WMCS, WMIL-FM, WMIR, WMYX-FM, WNOV, WOKY, WQFM-FM, WRJN, WTKM, WTKM-FM, WTMJ, WYLO, WZTR-FM, WZXA-FM.

Minneapolis-St. Paul: Rank 17
MSA: 2,120,500; TSA: 3,219,700
Stations: KBCW, KCFE-FM, KCHK, KCHK-FM, KDWA, KDWB-FM, KEEY-FM, KFAN, KJJO, KJJO-FM, KKCM, KLBB, KMAP, KMOM, KNOF-FM, KQQL-FM, KQRS, KQRS-FM, KRWC, KRXX, KRXX-FM, KSTP, KSTP-FM, KTCJ, KTCZ-FM, KYCR, WBOB-FM, WCCO, WCTS, WDGY, WEVR, WEVR-FM, WIMN, WIXK, WIXK-FM, WLKX-FM, WLOL-FM, WLTE-FM, WMIN, WTCX-FM, WWTC.

Minot, ND: Rank 261
MSA: 47,100; TSA: 126,300
Stations: KBQQ-FM, KCJB, KHRT, KHRT-FM, KIZZ-FM, KRRZ, KTYN, KYYX-FM, KZPR-FM.

Mobile, AL: Rank 90
MSA: 405,300; TSA: 931,500
Stations: WABB, WABB-FM, WABF, WASG, WAVH-FM, WBCA, WBHY, WBLX, WBLX-FM, WDLT-FM, WFMI-FM, WGCX-FM, WGOK, WHEP, WKQR-FM, WKRG, WKRG-FM, WKSJ, WKSJ-FM, WLPR, WLVV, WMOB, WNSP-FM, WXWY, WZBA-FM, WZEW-FM.

Modesto, CA: Rank 119
MSA: 325,500; TSA: 974,900
Stations: KABX-FM, KATM-FM, KBEE, KCBC, KDJK-FM, KFIV, KHOP-FM, KHTN-FM, KJSN-FM, KLOC, KMIX, KMIX-FM, KNTO-FM, KOSO-FM, KTRB, KUBB-FM, KVFX-FM.

Monmouth-Ocean, NJ: Rank 47
MSA: 862,300; TSA: 862,300
Note: Monmouth County is also included in the New York Metro.

Monroe, LA: Rank 223
MSA: 116,100; TSA: 381,800
Stations: KJLO-FM, KLIC, KLIP-FM, KMBS, KMGC-FM, KMLB, KNOE, KNOE-FM, KPCH-FM, KRVV-FM, KTJC-FM, KTRY, KTRY-FM, KXKZ-FM, KXLA, KYEA-FM.

Monterey-Salinas-Santa Cruz, CA: Rank 79
MSA: 496,900; TSA: 527,900
Stations: KBOQ-FM, KCTY, KDON-FM, KIDD, KIEZ, KKLF-FM, KKMC, KLAU, KLFA-FM, KLUE-FM, KMBY-FM, KMXZ-FM, KNRY, KOCN-FM, KOMY, KPIG-FM, KQKE, KQKE-FM, KRAY-FM, KRKC, KRKC-FM, KRML, KSCO, KSRI-FM, KTGE, KTOM, KTOM-FM, KWAV-FM, KXDC-FM.

Montgomery, AL: Rank 143
MSA: 250,000; TSA: 548,300
Stations: WACQ, WACV, WAPZ, WBAM-FM, WHHY, WHHY-FM, WLNE-FM, WLWI, WLWI-FM, WMCZ-FM, WMGY, WSKN, WSYA, WSYA-FM, WTLS, WXFX-FM, WXVI, WZHT-FM, WZTN.

Morristown, NJ: Rank 105
MSA: 359,900; TSA: 359,900
Note: Part of New York Metro.

Muskegon, MI: Rank 207
MSA: 131,500; TSA: 406,100
Stations: WCXT-FM, WEFG, WEFG-FM, WKBZ, WKBZ-FM, WLCS-FM, WMHG-FM, WMRR-FM, WMUS, WMUS-FM, WQWQ, WSFN, WSHN, WSHN-FM, WSNX-FM.

Myrtle Beach, SC: Rank 178
MSA: 174,500; TSA: 296,400
Stations: WBPR-FM, WGSN, WGTN, WGTN-FM, WGTR-FM, WJXY, WJXY-FM, WJYR-FM, WKZQ, WKZQ-FM, WLSC, WNMB-FM, WPJS, WRNN-FM, WSCA-FM, WSYN-FM, WVBX, WVCO-FM, WYAK, WYAK-FM, WYAV-FM.

Naples-Marco Island, FL: Rank 195
MSA: 149,400; TSA: 493,700
Stations: WCOO-FM, WGUF-FM, WIXI-FM, WNOG, WNOG-FM, WODX, WSGL-FM, WZOR.

Nashville: Rank 46
MSA: 864,000; TSA: 1,710,900
Stations: WAKM, WAMB, WAMB-FM, WAMG, WANT-FM, WCOR, WDBL, WDBL-FM, WDKN, WENO, WGFX-FM, WGNS, WHIN, WIZO, WKDA, WKDF-FM, WLAC, WLAC-FM, WMDB, WMTS, WNAH, WNKX, WNKX-FM, WNQM, WQKR, WQQK-FM, WQSE, WQSV, WQZQ-FM, WRLG-FM, WRLT-FM, WRMX-FM, WSGI, WSIX-FM, WSM, WSM-FM, WVOL, WVRY-FM, WWTN-FM, WYCQ-FM, WYHY-FM, WYOR, WYYB-FM, WZEZ-FM.

U.S. Radio Markets

Nassau-Suffolk, NY (Long Island): Rank 14
MSA: 2,249,400; TSA: 2,249,400
Note: Part of New York Metro.

New Bedford-Fall River, MA: Rank 85
MSA: 427,000; TSA: 427,000
Note: Part of Providence-Warwick-Pawtucket, RI, Metro.

New Haven, CT: Rank 92
MSA: 385,200; TSA: 1,031,700
Stations: WAVZ, WELI, WKCI-FM, WNHC, WPLR-FM, WXCT, WYBC-FM.

New London, CT: Rank 157
MSA: 211,900; TSA: 393,600
Stations: WBMW-FM, WCTY-FM, WICH, WNLC, WQGN-FM, WSUB, WTYD-FM, WVVE-FM.

New Orleans: Rank 39
MSA: 1,024,400; TSA: 1,761,500
Stations: KAGY, KCIL-FM, KGLA, KGTR-FM, KHOM-FM, KKNO, KMEZ-FM, WADU, WADU-FM, WASO, WBOK, WBYU, WCKW, WCKW-FM, WEZB-FM, WLMG-FM, WLTS-FM, WNOE, WNOE-FM, WQUE, WQUE-FM, WRNO-FM, WSHO, WSLA, WSMB, WTIX, WTKL-FM, WVOG, WWL, WYAT, WYLD, WYLD-FM, WZRH-FM.

New York: Rank 1
MSA: 14,033,500; TSA: 17,110,700
Stations: WABC, WADO, WALK, WALK-FM, WAWZ-FM, WBAB-FM, WBAZ-FM, WBBR, WBEA-FM, WBLI-FM, WBLS-FM, WBRW, WBZO, WCBS, WCBS-FM, WCTC, WDHA-FM, WDRE-FM, WEBE-FM, WEFX-FM, WEHM-FM, WERA, WEVD, WFAN, WFAS, WFAS-FM, WFME-FM, WGBB, WGCH, WGHT, WGSM, WHFM-FM, WHLI, WHTG, WHTG-FM, WHTZ-FM, WHUD-FM, WINS, WJDM, WJLK, WJLK-FM, WKDM, WKHL-FM, WKJY-FM, WKMB, WLIB, WLIM, WLIR, WLIX, WLNA, WLNG, WLNG-FM, WLTW-FM, WMCA, WMGQ-FM, WMJC-FM, WMJU-FM, WMMM, WMRW-FM, WMTR, WMXV-FM, WNCN-FM, WNEW-FM, WNJR, WNLK, WNWK-FM, WNYG, WOR, WPAT, WPAT-FM, WPLJ-FM, WPUT, WQCD-FM, WQEW, WQHT-FM, WQXR-FM, WRCN-FM, WRHD, WRIV, WRKL, WRKS-FM, WRTN-FM, WSKQ, WSKQ-FM, WSTC, WTHE, WVIP, WVOX, WWDJ, WWHB-FM, WWRL, WWRV, WXMC, WXPS-FM, WXRK-FM, WYNY-FM, WZRC, WZVU-FM.

Newburgh-Middletown, NY (Mid-Hudson Valley): Rank 140
MSA: 261,600; TSA: 289,100
Stations: WALL, WDLC, WELV, WGNY, WGNY-FM, WKOJ-FM, WRWD, WTBQ, WTSX-FM, WWWK-FM, WZAD-FM.

Norfolk-Virginia Beach-Newport News, VA: Rank 33
MSA: 1,198,300; TSA: 1,844,400
Stations: WAFX-FM, WCMS, WCMS-FM, WCXL-FM, WFOG-FM, WGH, WGH-FM, WJQI, WJQI-FM, WKGM, WKOC-FM, WLPM, WLTY-FM, WMBG, WMXN-FM, WMYK-FM, WNIS, WNOR, WNOR-FM, WNVZ-FM, WOJY, WOWI-FM, WPCE, WPMH, WROX-FM, WSVY, WSVY-FM, WTAR, WTJZ, WVAB, WWDE-FM, WXEZ-FM, WXGM, WXGM-FM.

Northwest Michigan, MI (Traverse City-Petoskey-Charlevoix): Rank 197
MSA: 148,500; TSA: 349,700
Stations: WAIR-FM, WBCM-FM, WBNZ-FM, WCCW, WCCW-FM, WCMW-FM, WGFN-FM, WJML, WKHQ-FM, WKJF-FM, WKLT-FM, WKLZ-FM, WKPK-FM, WLDR-FM, WMBN, WMBN-FM, WMKC-FM, WMKT, WTCM, WTCM-FM, WTRV-FM.

Odessa-Midland, TX: Rank 174
MSA: 179,400; TSA: 296,500
Stations: KBAT-FM, KCDQ-FM, KCHX-FM, KCRS, KCRS-FM, KERB, KERB-FM, KGEE-FM, KIOL-FM, KJBC, KKKK-FM, KMND, KMRK-FM, KNFM-FM, KODM-FM, KOYL, KOZA, KQIP-FM, KRIL, KWEL.

Oklahoma City: Rank 51
MSA: 811,400; TSA: 1,397,200
Stations: KATT-FM, KBYE, KEBC-FM, KGFF, KIRC-FM, KJYO-FM, KMGL-FM, KNOR, KNTL-FM, KOKC, KOMA, KOMA-FM, KOQL-FM, KQCV, KRXO-FM, KTLV, KTNT-FM, KTOK, KVSP, KWCO, KXXK-FM, KXXY, KXXY-FM, KYIS-FM, KZUE, WKY, WWLS.

Omaha-Council Bluffs, NE-IA: Rank 72
MSA: 518,000; TSA: 1,123,800
Stations: KBWH-FM, KCRO, KEFM-FM, KESY, KESY-FM, KEZO, KEZO-FM, KFAB, KGOR-FM, KKAR, KKCD-FM, KLNG, KOIL, KOTD, KQKQ-FM, KRRK-FM, KXKT-FM, KZEN-FM, WOW, WOW-FM.

Orlando, FL: Rank 41
MSA: 988,800; TSA: 2,455,800
Stations: WAJL, WCFB-FM, WDBO, WDIZ-FM, WFIV, WGTO, WHBS, WHOO, WHTQ-FM, WJHM-FM, WJRR, WLOQ-FM, WMGF-FM, WMJK, WMMO-FM, WOCL-FM, WOMX, WOMX-FM, WONQ, WRMQ-AM, WTKS-FM, WTLN, WTLN-FM, WTRR, WUNA, WWKA-FM, WWNZ, WWZN, WXTO, WXXL-FM.

Owensboro, KY: Rank 253
MSA: 72,400; TSA: 685,800
Stations: WBKR-FM, WOMI, WQXQ-FM, WVJS.

Oxnard-Ventura, CA: Rank 117
MSA: 331,100; TSA: 738,300
Stations: KAXX-FM, KBBY, KBBY-FM, KCAQ-FM, KDAR-FM, KELF-FM, KHAY-FM, KKUR-FM, KKZZ, KOXR, KTRO, KVEN, KXBS-FM, KXLM-FM.

Palm Springs, CA: Rank 151
MSA: 220,800; TSA: 220,800
Stations: KBZT, KCLB, KCLB-FM, KCMJ, KCMJ-FM, KDES, KDES-FM, KEZN-FM, KLCX-FM, KNWZ, KPLM-FM, KPSI, KPSI-FM, KPSL-AM, KROR-FM, KUNA, KWXY, KWXY-FM.

Panama City, FL: Rank 228
MSA: 111,500; TSA: 255,100
Stations: WAKT-FM, WDRK-FM, WEBZ-FM, WFSY-FM, WGNE, WILN-FM, WFNB-FM, WLTG, WMTO-FM, WPAP-FM, WPCF, WPCF-FM, WPFM-FM, WRBA-FM, WYOO-FM.

Parkersburg-Marietta, WV-OH: Rank 216
MSA: 125,200; TSA: 328,200
Stations: WADC, WBRJ, WDMX-FM, WEYQ-FM, WHCM-FM, WKYG, WLTP, WMOA, WNUS-FM, WRZZ-FM, WXIL-FM, WXKX-FM.

Pensacola, FL: Rank 126
MSA: 300,300; TSA: 612,600
Stations: WBSR, WCOA, WEBY, WECM, WGYJ, WJLQ-FM, WKGT, WKGT-FM, WMEZ-FM, WOWW-FM, WRNE, WSWL, WTKX, WTKX-FM, WVTJ, WXBM-FM.

Peoria, IL: Rank 131
MSA: 282,400; TSA: 529,500
Stations: WBGE-FM, WCRI-FM, WFYR-FM, WGLO-FM, WIRL, WKZW-FM, WMBD, WPEO, WQEZ-FM, WSWT-FM, WTAZ-FM, WVEL, WWCT-FM, WXCL, WXCL-FM.

Philadelphia: Rank 5
MSA: 4,101,700; TSA: 7,319,900
Stations: KYW, WBCB, WBEB-FM, WBUX, WCHE, WCOJ, WCZN, WDAS, WDAS-FM, WFLN-FM, WHAT, WIBF-FM, WIOQ-FM, WIP, WJJZ-FM, WMGK-FM, WMMR-FM, WNAP, WNJC, WNPV, WOGL, WOGL-FM, WPAZ, WPEN, WPGR, WPHE, WPHY, WPLY-FM, WSSJ, WTEL, WTMR, WURD, WUSL-FM, WVCH, WWDB-FM, WWJZ, WXTU-FM, WYSP-FM, WYXR-FM, WZZD.

Phoenix: Rank 21
MSA: 1,880,000; TSA: 2,535,600
Stations: KASA, KCKY, KCLV, KDKB-FM, KEDJ-FM, KESZ-FM, KFNN, KFYI, KHEP, KIDR, KKFR-FM, KKLT-FM, KMEO-FM, KMJK-FM, KMLE-FM, KNIX-FM, KNNS, KONZ-FM, KOOL, KOOL-FM, KOPA, KOY, KPHX, KPSN-FM, KRDS, KRDS-FM, KSLX-FM, KSUN, KTAR, KTIM, KUKQ, KUPD-FM, KVRY-FM, KVVA, KVVA-FM, KXAM, KXEG, KYOT, KYOT-FM, KZON-FM, KZRX-FM.

Pittsburgh: Rank 20
MSA: 2,023,800; TSA: 3,206,900
Stations: KDKA, KQV, WAMO-FM, WASP, WASP-FM, WBCW, WBVP, WBZZ-FM, WCNS, WCVI, WCXJ, WDSY-FM, WDVE-FM, WEDO, WEEP, WELA-FM, WESA, WESA-FM, WGBN, WHJB, WIXZ, WJAS, WJPA, WJPA-FM, WKZV, WLSW-FM, WLTJ-FM, WMBA, WMBS, WORD-FM, WPIT, WPLW, WPQR-FM, WQKB-FM, WQTW, WRRK-FM, WSHH-FM, WSSZ-FM, WTAE, WVTY-FM, WWCS, WWKS-FM, WWSW, WWSW-FM, WXRB-FM, WXVX, WYJZ.

Portland, ME: Rank 162
MSA: 205,100; TSA: 750,500
Stations: WBLM, WCLZ, WCLZ-FM, WCSO-FM, WGAN, WHOM-FM, WHYR-FM, WJTO, WKRH-FM, WKZS-FM, WLAM, WLOB, WLPZ, WMGX-FM, WPKM-FM, WPOR, WPOR-FM, WSTG-FM, WTHT-FM, WXGL-FM, WYNZ-FM, WZAN, WZPK-FM.

Portland, OR: Rank 26
MSA: 1,511,600; TSA: 2,020,900
Stations: KBBT, KBMS, KBNP, KBZY, KCCS, KCKX, KDBX-FM, KEX, KFXX, KGON-FM, KINK, KINK-FM, KKBK-FM, KKCW-FM, KKEY, KKRZ-FM, KKSN, KKSN-FM, KLYC, KMUZ, KMUZ-FM, KPDQ, KPDQ-FM, KPHP, KSLM, KUFO-FM, KUIK, KUPL, KUPL-FM, KVAN, KWBY, KWIP, KWJJ, KWJJ-FM, KXL, KXL-FM, KXPC-FM, KXYQ-FM, KYKN, KZRC.

Portsmouth-Dover-Rochester, NH: Rank 112
MSA: 342,100; TSA: 472,500
Stations: WCDQ-FM, WCQL, WCQL-FM, WDER, WERZ-FM, WHEB-FM, WMYF, WNNW, WOKQ-FM, WTSN, WWEM-FM, WWNH, WXBB-FM, WZEA-FM, WZNN.

Poughkeepsie, NY: Rank 150
MSA: 222,600; TSA: 684,800
Stations: WBNR, WBWZ-FM, WCZX-FM, WDSP-FM, WEOK, WHVW, WKIP, WKXE-FM, WMJV-FM, WPDH-FM, WRNQ-FM, WRWD-FM, WSPK-FM.

Providence-Warwick-Pawtucket, RI: Rank 32
MSA: 1,278,400; TSA: 2,113,800
Stations: WADK, WALE, WARA, WARV, WBLQ-FM, WBRU-FM, WBSM, WCTK-FM, WERI, WFHN-FM, WHIM, WHJJ, WHJY-FM, WHTB, WICE, WJFD-FM, WJJF, WKRI, WLKW, WNBH, WNRI, WOON, WOTB-FM, WPEP, WPJB-FM, WPRO, WPRO-FM, WRCP, WRIB, WSAR, WSNE-FM, WWBB-FM, WWKX-FM, WWLI-FM, WWRX-FM.

Pueblo, CO: Rank 232
MSA: 103,600; TSA: 562,900
Stations: KCCY-FM, KCSJ, KDZA-FM, KFEL, KGHF, KKPC, KNKN-FM, KRMX, KRRU, KYZX-FM.

Quad Cities (Davenport-Rock Island-Moline), IA-IL: Rank 129
MSA: 288,000; TSA: 684,200
Stations: KFMH-FM, KFQC, KJOC, KMXG-FM, KQCS-FM, KRVR-FM, KUUL-FM, WGEN, WGEN-FM, WJRE-FM, WKBF, WKEI, WLLR, WLLR-FM, WOC, WPXR-FM, WRMJ-FM, WXLP-FM.

Raleigh-Durham, NC: Rank 53
MSA: 786,000; TSA: 1,708,800
Stations: WAUG, WCHL, WCLY, WCRY, WDCG-FM, WDNC, WDUR, WETC, WFTK, WFXC-FM, WFXK-FM, WGSB, WHEV, WHLQ-FM, WKIX, WKTC-FM, WLLE, WNND-FM, WPJL, WPTF, WQDR-FM, WQOK-FM, WRAL-FM, WRDU-FM, WRTP, WSRC, WTIK, WTRG-FM, WYLT-FM, WYRN, WZZU-FM.

Rapid City, SD: Rank 244
MSA: 89,900; TSA: 162,300
Stations: KBHB, KEZV-FM, KGGG-FM, KIMM, KIQK-FM, KKLS, KKMK-FM, KLMP-FM, KOTA, KRCS-FM, KSLT-FM, KSQY-FM, KTOQ.

Reading, PA: Rank 128
MSA: 292,600; TSA: 292,600
Stations: WBYN-FM, WEEU, WIOV, WRAW, WRFY-FM.

Redding, CA: Rank 202
MSA: 134,700; TSA: 255,900
Stations: KARZ-FM, KAVA, KEWB-FM, KLXR, KNCQ-FM, KNNN-FM, KNRO, KQMS, KRDG, KSHA-FM, KZAP-FM.

Reno, NV: Rank 141
MSA: 261,400; TSA: 458,000
Stations: KBUL-FM, KCBN, KHIT, KHIT-FM, KIZS-FM, KNDE-FM, KNEV-FM, KODS-FM, KOH, KOZZ, KOZZ-FM, KPLY, KPTL, KQLO, KRNO-FM, KROW, KRZQ-FM, KSRN-FM, KTHX-FM, KWNZ-FM, KXEQ, KXTO, KZAK-FM.

Richmond, VA: Rank 56
MSA: 752,800; TSA: 990,500
Stations: WCDX-FM, WCLM, WDCK-FM, WDYL-FM, WFTH, WGCV, WGGM, WHAP, WKHK-FM, WKIK-FM, WLEE, WMXB-FM, WPES, WPLZ-FM, WREJ, WRVA, WRVH, WRVQ-FM, WRXL-FM, WSTK, WSVV-FM, WTVR, WTVR-FM, WVGO-FM, WXGI.

Riverside-San Bernardino, CA: Rank 27
MSA: 1,348,400; TSA: 2,099,500
Stations: KAEV-FM, KATY-FM, KCAL, KCAL-FM, KCKC, KDIF, KFRG-FM, KGGI-FM, KHPY, KHSJ, KHTX-FM, KHYE-FM, KLFE, KMEN, KMET, KOLA-FM, KOOJ-FM, KPRO, KRSO, KTOT-FM, KWRM, KWRP-FM.

Roanoke-Lynchburg, VA: Rank 99
MSA: 371,500; TSA: 1,028,700
Stations: WAMV, WBLT, WBLU, WBRG, WFIR, WGOL-FM, WJJS-FM, WJLM-FM, WKBA, WKDE, WKDE-FM, WKPA, WLLL, WLVA, WLYK-FM, WODI, WPVR-FM, WRIS, WROV, WROV-FM, WSLC-FM, WTOY, WTTX, WTTX-FM, WVLR-FM, WVRV-FM, WWWR, WXLK-FM, WXYU, WYMY-FM, WYYD-FM.

U.S. Radio Markets

Rochester, MN: Rank 243
MSA: 90,400; TSA: 387,300
Stations: KMFX-FM, KNXR-FM, KOLM, KRCH-FM, KROC, KROC-FM, KWEB, KWWK-FM, KYBA-FM.

Rochester, NY: Rank 45
MSA: 888,100; TSA: 1,161,800
Stations: WACK, WASB, WBBF, WBEE-FM, WCGR, WCMF, WCMF-FM, WDCZ-FM, WDKX-FM, WDNY, WDNY-FM, WEZO-FM, WFLK-FM, WGVA, WHAM, WHTK, WJZR-FM, WKLZ-FM, WKPQ-FM, WLKA-FM, WMAX-FM, WNNR-FM, WNYR-FM, WPXY-FM, WRMM-FM, WRQI-FM, WVOR-FM, WWWG, WYSL, WZXV-FM.

Rockford, IL: Rank 146
MSA: 240,400; TSA: 533,000
Stations: WBEL, WKMQ-FM, WLUV, WLUV-FM, WNTA, WQFL-FM, WROK, WRRR, WRWC-FM, WXRX-FM, WXXQ-FM, WZOK-FM.

Sacramento, CA: Rank 29
MSA: 1,340,100; TSA: 2,802,900
Stations: KAHI, KCTC, KFBK, KFIA, KGBY-FM, KGLE-FM, KHYL-FM, KJAY, KNCI-FM, KOWL, KQBR-FM, KQPT-FM, KRAK, KRAK-FM, KRCX, KRFD-FM, KRLT-FM, KRXQ-FM, KSAC, KSEG-FM, KSFM-FM, KSMJ, KSSJ-FM, KSTE, KTHO, KWOD-FM, KXOA, KXOA-FM, KYMX-FM, KZSA-FM.

Saginaw-Bay City-Midland, MI: Rank 118
MSA: 326,700; TSA: 1,123,200
Stations: WBTZ-FM, WCEN-FM, WGER-FM, WHNN-FM, WIOG-FM, WIXC-FM, WKCQ-FM, WKNX, WKQZ-FM, WMAX, WMPX, WSAM, WSGW, WTCF-FM, WTLZ-FM, WUVE-FM.

St. Cloud, MN: Rank 187
MSA: 161,000; TSA: 357,400
Stations: KASM, KCLD-FM, KKSR-FM, KLZZ-FM, KMSR-FM, KMXK-FM, KNSI, KXSS, WHMH-FM, WJON, WQPM-FM, WVAL, WWJO-FM.

St. Louis: Rank 18
MSA: 2,080,300; TSA: 2,713,500
Stations: KASP, KATZ, KATZ-FM, KDJR-FM, KEZK-FM, KFAV-FM, KFNS, KFUO-FM, KHAD, KIRL, KJCF-FM, KLOU-FM, KLPW, KLPW-FM, KMJM-FM, KMOX, KPNT-FM, KRJY-FM, KSD, KSD-FM, KSHE-FM, KSIV, KSLQ, KSLQ-FM, KSTL, KTUI, KTUI-FM, KWRE, KXEN, KXOK-FM, KYKY-FM, WBGZ, WCBW-FM, WESL, WEW, WFUN-FM, WFXB-FM, WGNU, WHCO, WIBV, WIL-FM, WINU, WJBM, WKBQ-FM, WKKX-FM, WRTH, WRYT.

Salisbury-Ocean City, MD: Rank 153
MSA: 219,000; TSA: 415,800
Stations: WAFL-FM, WDMV, WDNO-FM, WDSD-FM, WECY, WECY-FM, WETT, WGMD-FM, WICO, WICO-FM, WJDY, WKHI-FM, WLVW-FM, WMYJ-FM, WOCQ-FM, WOLC-FM, WQHQ-FM, WRKE-FM, WSBL-FM, WSBY-FM, WSSR, WTGM, WWFG-FM, WXJN-FM, WXPZ-FM, WYUS, WZBH-FM.

Salt Lake City-Ogden-Provo: Rank 36
MSA: 1,099,000; TSA: 1,469,900
Stations: KALL, KALL-FM, KANN, KBER-FM, KBZN-FM, KCNR, KCPX-FM, KDYL, KEYY, KFAM, KHQN, KISN, KISN-FM, KJOE, KKAT-FM, KKBE-FM, KKDS, KLLB, KLO, KLZX, KLZX-FM, KMGR, KMXB-FM, KNFL, KNFL-FM, KNUC-FM, KOVO, KQOL-FM, KRGQ, KRGQ-FM, KRSP-FM, KSFI-FM, KSL, KSOP, KSOP-FM, KSOS, KSOS-FM, KSRR, KSVN, KTKK, KTLE-FM, KTUR, KUMT-FM, KUTQ-FM, KVRI-FM, KXRK-FM, KZHT-FM.

San Angelo, TX: Rank 250
MSA: 82,000; TSA: 127,900
Stations: KDCD-FM, KELI-FM, KGKL, KGKL-FM, KIXY-FM, KKLK-FM, KSJT-FM, KXQZ.

San Antonio-Victoria: Rank 35
MSA: 1,135,300; TSA: 1,721,300
Stations: KAJA-FM, KBOP, KBUC, KBUC-FM, KCHG, KCHL, KCOR, KCYY-FM, KDIL-FM, KDRY, KEDA, KENS, KGNB, KISS-FM, KKYX, KLUP, KNBT-FM, KONO, KONO-FM, KQXT-FM, KRIO-FM, KROM-FM, KSAH, KSJL, KSLR, KSMG-FM, KTFM-FM, KTSA, KWED, KXTN, KXTN-FM, KZEP, KZEP-FM, KZXS, WOAI.

San Diego: Rank 15
MSA: 2,213,500; TSA: 2,213,500
Stations: KBAX-FM, KBNN-FM, KBZS-FM, KCBQ, KCBQ-FM, KCEO, KCLX-FM, KFMB, KFMB-FM, KFSD-FM, KGB-FM, KGMG, KIFM-FM, KIOZ-FM, KJQY-FM, KKLQ, KKLQ-FM, KKOS-FM, KOWF-FM, KPOP, KPRZ, KSDO, KSON, KSON-FM, KSPA, KURS, KYXY-FM, XEBG, XEMO, XEXX, XHFG-FM, XHKY-FM, XHRM-FM, XHTZ-FM, XLTN-FM, XTRA, XTRA-FM.

San Diego North County, CA: Rank 60
MSA: 700,300; TSA: 700,300
Note: Part of San Diego Metro.

San Francisco: Rank 4
MSA: 5,304,600; TSA: 8,379,700
Stations: KABL, KABL-FM, KARA-FM, KATD, KAZA, KBAY-FM, KBLX, KBLX-FM, KBRG-FM, KCBS, KDFC, KDFC-FM, KDIA, KEAR-FM, KEEN, KEST, KEZR-FM, KFAX, KFOG-FM, KFRC, KFRC-FM, KGO, KHQT-FM, KIOI-FM, KIQI, KITS-FM, KJAZ-FM, KKHI, KKHI-FM, KKIQ-FM, KKSF-FM, KLIV, KLOK, KMEL-FM, KMGG-FM, KMXN, KNBA, KNBR, KNEW, KNTA, KOFY, KOIT, KOIT-FM, KOME-FM, KRPQ-FM, KRQR-FM, KRRS, KRTY-FM, KSAN-FM, KSFO, KSJO-FM, KSJX, KSOL-FM, KSQQ-FM, KSRO, KSRY-FM, KTID, KTID-FM, KUFX-FM, KUIC-FM, KVON, KVVV-FM, KVYN-FM, KWUN, KXFX-FM, KYA-FM, KZST-FM, KZWC-FM.

San Jose, CA: Rank 31
MSA: 1,282,100; TSA: 3,502,700
Note: Part of San Francisco Metro.

San Luis Obispo, CA: Rank 166
MSA: 191,800; TSA: 344,900
Stations: KBAI, KDDB-FM, KGLW, KIQO-FM, KIXT, KIXT-FM, KDJ, KKAL, KKJG-FM, KOTR-FM, KPRL, KSLY-FM, KSTT-FM, KUHL, KVEC, KWBR-FM, KWSP-FM, KWWV-FM, KZOZ-FM.

Santa Barbara, CA: Rank 182
MSA: 169,400; TSA: 653,600
Stations: KCQR-FM, KDB-FM, KHTY-FM, KIST, KKSB, KMGQ-FM, KQSB, KRUZ-FM, KSBL-FM, KSPE, KTMS, KTYD-FM.

Santa Fe, NM: Rank 233
MSA: 102,800; TSA: 738,600
Stations: KBAC-FM, KBOM-FM, KDCE, KIOT-FM, KNLA-FM, KNYN-FM, KRSN, KSWV, KTRC, KVSF.

Santa Rosa, CA: Rank 109
MSA: 348,300; TSA: 348,300
Note: Part of San Francisco Metro.

Sarasota-Bradenton, FL: Rank 80
MSA: 461,500; TSA: 596,100
Stations: WAMR, WBRD, WCTQ-FM, WDUV-FM, WENG, WISP-FM, WJRB, WKXY, WQSA, WSPB, WSRZ-FM, WTMY.

Savannah, GA: Rank 154
MSA: 218,800; TSA: 619,400
Stations: WAEV-FM, WBMQ, WCHY, WCHY-FM, WEAS, WEAS-FM, WGCO-FM, WHHR, WIXV-FM, WIZA, WJCL-FM, WLOW-FM, WLVH-FM, WNMT, WQQT-FM, WRHQ-FM, WSGA, WSOK, WZAT-FM.

Seattle-Tacoma: Rank 13
MSA: 2,623,500; TSA: 3,152,400
Stations: KARR, KBLE, KBLV, KBRO, KBSG, KBSG-FM, KCIS, KCMS-FM, KDFL, KENU, KEZX, KEZX-FM, KGNW, KING, KING-FM, KIRO, KIRO-FM, KISW-FM, KITZ, KIXI, KJR, KJUN, KKDZ, KKMO, KLAY, KLSY-FM, KLTX-FM, KMPS, KMPS-FM, KMTT, KMTT-FM, KNDD-FM, KOMO, KPLZ-FM, KRIZ, KRKO, KRPM-FM, KRWM-FM, KUBE-FM, KULL, KVI, KWYZ, KXRX-FM, KZIZ, KZOK, KZOK-FM.

Shreveport, LA: Rank 125
MSA: 303,700; TSA: 793,800
Stations: KASO, KASO-FM, KBCL, KBSF, KDKS-FM, KEEL, KFLO, KIOU, KITT-FM, KLKL-FM, KMJJ-FM, KNCB, KOKA, KRMD, KRMD-FM, KTAL-FM, KTKC-FM, KTUX-FM, KVKI-FM, KWHN-FM, KWKH, KWKH-FM.

Sioux City, IA: Rank 241
MSA: 95,000; TSA: 258,100
Stations: KGLI-FM, KKMA-FM, KMNS, KSCJ, KSEZ-FM, KSUX-FM, KTFC-FM, KTFJ, KWSL.

Sioux Falls, SD: Rank 212
MSA: 127,300; TSA: 357,100
Stations: KCGN, KELO, KELO-FM, KKLS-FM, KLQL-FM, KPAT-FM, KQAD, KRRO-FM, KSOO, KTWB-FM, KWSN, KXRB.

South Bend, IN: Rank 160
MSA: 208,600; TSA: 807,700
Stations: WAOR-FM, WFRN-FM, WGTC-FM, WHME-FM, WIWO, WLLJ, WLTA-FM, WNDU, WNDU-FM, WNSN-FM, WRBR-FM, WSBT, WUBU-FM.

Spokane, WA: Rank 95
MSA: 378,800; TSA: 724,100
Stations: KAQQ, KAZZ-FM, KCDA-FM, KDRK-FM, KEYF, KEYF-FM, KEZE-FM, KGA, KISC-FM, KJRB, KKCH-FM, KKPL, KKZX-FM, KNFR-FM, KNJY-FM, KSBN, KSVY, KTRW, KTSL-FM, KUDY, KVNI, KXLY, KXLY-FM, KZZU-FM.

Springfield, IL: Rank 188
MSA: 160,200; TSA: 350,900
Stations: WCVS-FM, WDBR-FM, WFMB, WFMB-FM, WLUJ-FM, WMAY, WNNS-FM, WQLZ-FM, WQQL-FM, WTAX, WYMG-FM.

Springfield, MA: Rank 76
MSA: 506,600; TSA: 564,900
Stations: WACE, WACM, WAQY, WAQY-FM, WARE, WHMP, WHMP-FM, WHYN, WHYN-FM, WMAS, WMAS-FM, WNNZ, WPKX-FM, WRNX-FM, WSPR, WTTT.

Springfield, MO: Rank 156
MSA: 213,600; TSA: 552,200
Stations: KADI-FM, KGBX-FM, KGMY, KGMY-FM, KIDS, KKHT-FM, KLFJ, KLTQ-FM, KOSP-FM, KTOZ, KTOZ-FM, KTTS, KTTS-FM, KTXR-FM, KWTO, KXBR-FM, KXUS-FM, KZBE-FM.

Stamford-Norwalk, CT: Rank 135
MSA: 277,300; TSA: 277,300
Note: Part of New York Metro.

State College, PA: Rank 229
MSA: 111,000; TSA: 175,700
Stations: WBHV-FM, WBLF, WFGI-FM, WMAJ, WPHB, WPHB-FM, WQWK-FM, WRSC, WZWW-FM.

Steubenville-Weirton, OH-WV: Rank 218
MSA: 120,500; TSA: 120,500
Stations: WCDK-FM, WDIG, WEIR, WRKY-FM, WSTV.

Stockton, CA: Rank 89
MSA: 409,600; TSA: 471,600
Stations: KCVR, KEXX-FM, KFMR-FM, KJAX, KJOY-FM, KSTN, KSTN-FM, KWG, KWIN-FM.

Syracuse, NY: Rank 69
MSA: 550,300; TSA: 994,500
Stations: WAQX-FM, WBBS-FM, WDCW, WFBL, WGES-FM, WHEN, WHEN-FM, WKRL, WKRL-FM, WMCR, WMCR-FM, WNDR, WNTQ-FM, WOLF, WPCX-FM, WSCP, WSCP-FM, WSEN-FM, WSGO, WSIV, WSYR, WTKW-FM, WVOA-FM, WYYY-FM, WZOS-FM, WZZZ.

Tallahassee, FL: Rank 170
MSA: 187,500; TSA: 421,000
Stations: WANM, WBGM-FM, WCVC, WFHT-FM, WGLF-FM, WHBT, WHBX-FM, WHKX-FM, WJPH-FM, WMFL, WMLO-FM, WNLS, WRZK-FM, WSNI-FM, WTAL, WTNT-FM, WUMX-FM, WWSD.

Tampa-St. Petersburg-Clearwater: Rank 22
MSA: 1,869,400; TSA: 3,026,900
Stations: WAMA, WBDN, WBSB-FM, WCOF-FM, WDAE, WDCF, WFLA, WFLZ-FM, WFNS, WGUL, WGUL-FM, WHNZ, WHPT-FM, WLVU, WLVU-FM, WMTX, WMTX-FM, WPAS, WPSO, WQBN, WQYK, WQYK-FM, WRBQ, WRBQ-FM, WRFA, WRMD, WRXB, WSUN, WTAN, WTIS, WTMP, WUSA-FM, WWJB, WWRM-FM, WXTB-FM, WYUU-FM.

Terre Haute, IN: Rank 180
MSA: 169,700; TSA: 454,300
Stations: WACF-FM, WAXI-FM, WBFX, WBOW, WCBH-FM, WJSH, WKZI, WLEZ-FM, WMGI-FM, WMMC-FM, WNDI, WNDI-FM, WPRS, WSDM, WSDM-FM, WTHI, WTHI-FM, WWVR-FM, WZZQ-FM.

Texarkana, TX-AR: Rank 235
MSA: 99,400; TSA: 271,500
Stations: KCMC, KHSP, KHSP-FM, KKYR, KKYR-FM, KLLI-FM, KNBO, KPYN-FM, KTOY-FM, KTWN, KTWN-FM, KXAR-FM, KZRB-FM.

Toledo, OH: Rank 74
MSA: 510,900; TSA: 1,083,000
Stations: WCWA, WFOB, WHMQ-FM, WIOT-FM, WJYM, WKKO-FM, WLQR-FM, WMTR-FM, WRQN-FM, WSPD, WTOD, WTWR-FM, WVKS-FM, WVOI, WWWM, WWWM-FM, WXKR-FM, WYHK-FM.

Topeka, KS: Rank 176
MSA: 176,900; TSA: 483,000
Stations: KDVV-FM, KLZR-FM, KMAJ, KMAJ-FM, KMKF-FM, KTOP, KTPK-FM, KWIC-FM, KZOC-FM, KZTO-FM, WIBW, WIBW-FM, WREN.

Trenton, NJ: Rank 132
MSA: 279,500; TSA: 372,900
Stations: WBUD, WCHR-FM, WHWH, WIMG, WKXW-FM, WPRB-FM, WPST-FM, WTTM.

Tri-Cities (Richland-Kennewick-Pasco), WA: Rank 213
MSA: 126,600; TSA: 288,800
Stations: KALE, KARY, KEGX-FM, KEYW-FM, KIOK-FM, KNLT-FM, KONA, KONA-FM, KORD, KORD-FM, KTCR, KZXR-FM.

U.S. Radio Markets

Tucson: Rank 65
MSA: 591,400; TSA: 800,400
Stations: KCRZ-FM, KCUB, KEKO-FM, KGMS-FM, KGVY, KIIM-FM, KJYK, KKLD-FM, KLPX-FM, KLQB-FM, KMRR, KNST, KOHT-FM, KQTL, KRKN-FM, KRQQ-FM, KTKT, KTUC, KTZR, KVOI, KWFM, KWFM-FM, KXEW.

Tulsa, OK: Rank 63
MSA: 633,300; TSA: 1,230,600
Stations: KAKC, KBEZ-FM, KBIX-FM, KCFO, KCKI-FM, KCMA-FM, KEMX-FM, KGND-FM, KGTO, KHJM-FM, KHTT-FM, KMMY-FM, KMOD-FM, KMYB-FM, KMYZ, KMYZ-FM, KQLL, KQLL-FM, KRAV-FM, KREK-FM, KRMG, KTFX-FM, KTHK-FM, KTOW, KTOW-FM, KTRT, KVOO, KVOO-FM, KWEN-FM, KXOJ, KXOJ-FM, KXTD, KXVQ.

Tupelo, MS: Rank 177
MSA: 174,900; TSA: 459,100
Stations: WACR-FM, WAFM-FM, WAMY, WBIP, WBIP-FM, WCPC, WELO, WESE-FM, WFTA-FM, WFTO, WNAU, WPMX, WSEL-FM, WSYE-FM, WTUP, WWKZ-FM, WWMS-FM, WWZD-FM, WWZQ, WWZQ-FM, WZLQ-FM.

Tuscaloosa, AL: Rank 204
MSA: 133,300; TSA: 225,900
Stations: WACT, WACT-FM, WCKO-FM, WFFX-FM, WLXY-FM, WQLW-FM, WSPZ, WTID-FM, WTNW, WTSK, WTUG-FM, WTXT-FM, WWPG, WZBQ-FM.

Tyler-Longview, TX: Rank 142
MSA: 251,700; TSA: 629,800
Stations: KARW, KDOK-FM, KEBE, KEES, KFRO, KFRO-FM, KGLD, KHYM, KISX-FM, KKTX, KKTX-FM, KKUS-FM, KNUE-FM, KOOI-FM, KPXI-FM, KSIZ-FM, KTBB, KTLU, KTYL-FM, KWRW-FM, KYKX-FM, KYYK-FM, KYZS, KZEY.

Utica-Rome, NY: Rank 139
MSA: 262,200; TSA: 482,100
Stations: WADR, WBRV, WBRV-FM, WFRG-FM, WIBX, WKDY-FM, WKLL-FM, WLFH, WLZW-FM, WODZ, WODZ-FM, WOUR-FM, WOWB-FM, WRCK-FM, WRNY, WRUN, WTLB, WUTQ, WUUU-FM.

Waco, TX: Rank 189
MSA: 159,000; TSA: 500,100
Stations: KBBW, KCKR-FM, KEYR-FM, KJNE-FM, KRZI, KWOW-FM, KWTX, KWTX-FM, WACO, WACO-FM.

Washington, DC: Rank 8
MSA: 3,451,000; TSA: 4,949,000
Stations: WABS, WAFY-FM, WAGE, WARW-FM, WASH-FM, WAVA-FM, WBIG-FM, WCPT, WCTN, WCXR-FM, WDCT, WFAX, WFMD, WFRE-FM, WGAY-FM, WGMS-FM, WHFS-FM, WHUR-FM, WILC, WINX, WJFK-FM, WKDL, WKDV, WKYS-FM, WMAL, WMDM-FM, WMDO, WMET, WMJS-FM, WMMJ-FM, WMOM, WMZQ, WMZQ-FM, WNTL, WOL, WPGC, WPGC-FM, WPWC, WQSI, WRCY-FM, WRQX-FM, WSMD-FM, WTEM, WTHU, WTOP, WTRI, WUST, WWDC, WWDC-FM, WWRC, WXTR-FM, WYCB, WZYQ-FM.

Waterbury, CT: Rank 171
MSA: 186,800; TSA: 282,000
Stations: WATR, WFNW, WWCO, WWYZ-FM.

Waterloo-Cedar Falls, IA: Rank 217
MSA: 121,100; TSA: 358,600
Stations: KCFI, KFMW-FM, KGCI-FM, KOEL-FM, KOKZ-FM, KQMG, KQMG-FM, KWAY, KWAY-FM, KWLO, KWOF, KXEL.

Watertown, NY: Rank 239
MSA: 95,600; TSA: 212,100
Stations: WATN, WCIZ-FM, WKGG-FM, WLKC-FM, WMHI-FM, WNCQ, WTNY, WTNY-FM, WTOJ-FM.

Wausau-Stevens Point, WI: Rank 158
MSA: 210,600; TSA: 479,000
Stations: WDEZ-FM, WDLB, WFHR, WIFC-FM, WIZD-FM, WLJY-FM, WMGU-FM, WMZK-FM, WOFM-FM, WOSX-FM, WRIG, WSAU, WSPO, WSPT-FM, WWRW-FM, WXCO, WYCO-FM, WYTE-FM.

West Palm Beach-Boca Raton, FL: Rank 49
MSA: 829,300; TSA: 2,272,300
Stations: WAFC, WAFC-FM, WBGF-FM, WBZT, WDBF, WEAT, WEAT-FM, WIRK-FM, WJNO, WKGR-FM, WLVJ, WLVS, WOEQ, WOLL-FM, WOVV-FM, WPBR, WPOM, WRLX-FM, WRMF-FM, WSBR, WSWN, WTRU-FM, WYFX.

Wheeling, WV: Rank 205
MSA: 132,600; TSA: 335,400
Stations: WBBD, WBNV-FM, WEEL-FM, WEGW-FM, WHLX-FM, WKWK, WKWK-FM, WOMP, WOMP-FM, WOVK-FM, WRKP-FM, WWVA, WZAO.

Wichita, KS: Rank 88
MSA: 410,500; TSA: 707,400
Stations: KDLE-FM, KEYN-FM, KFDI, KFDI-FM, KFH, KICT-FM, KJRG, KKRD-FM, KLLS-FM, KNSS, KOEZ-FM, KQAM, KRBB-FM, KRZZ-FM, KSGL, KSRX, KTLI-FM, KXLK-FM, KYQQ-FM, KZSN, KZSN-FM.

Wichita Falls, TX: Rank 237
MSA: 99,200; TSA: 323,400
Stations: KLLF, KLUR-FM, KNIN, KNIN-FM, KTLT-FM, KWFS-FM, KWFT, KYYI-FM.

Wilkes Barre-Scranton, PA: Rank 62
MSA: 634,700; TSA: 1,064,900
Stations: WARD, WARM, WAZL, WBAX, WBHT-FM, WCDL, WCNR, WDLE-FM, WDLS-FM, WEJL, WEMR, WEZX-FM, WGBI, WGGY-FM, WHLM-FM, WICK, WILK, WJMW, WKAB-FM, WKQV-FM, WKRZ-FM, WMGS-FM, WMXH, WNAK, WPMR, WPMR-FM, WQEQ-FM, WSBG-FM, WSGD-FM, WSQV, WTLQ-FM, WTSS, WVPO, WWDL-FM, WWSH-FM, WXPX, WYCK, WYMK-FM, WYOS-FM.

Williamsport, PA: Rank 234
MSA: 100,900; TSA: 353,200
Stations: WFXX, WHTO-FM, WHUM-FM, WILQ-FM, WJSA, WJSA-FM, WKSB-FM, WLYC, WMRE, WMRE-FM, WRAK, WRAK-FM, WSNU-FM, WWPA, WWWD-FM, WZXR-FM.

Wilmington, DE: Rank 78
MSA: 499,900; TSA: 594,400
Stations: WDEL, WILM, WJBR, WJBR-FM, WJIC, WNNN-FM, WNRK, WSER, WSTW-FM.

Wilmington, NC: Rank 192
MSA: 157,300; TSA: 249,500
Stations: WAAV, WBMS, WCCA-FM, WDZD-FM, WGNI-FM, WKXB-FM, WMFD, WMNX-FM, WMYT, WSFM-FM, WVBS, WVCB, WWIL, WWQQ-FM.

Worcester, MA: Rank 100
MSA: 370,400; TSA: 682,100
Stations: WCAT, WGFP, WMRC, WORC, WQVR-FM, WSRS-FM, WTAG, WVEI, WVNE, WXLO-FM.

Yakima, WA: Rank 189
MSA: 159,000; TSA: 197,200
Stations: KARY-FM, KATS-FM, KBBO, KENE, KFFM-FM, KHYT-FM, KIT, KMWX, KREW, KREW-FM, KRSE-FM, KUTI, KXDD-FM, KYKA-FM, KYXE, KZTA, KZTA-FM.

York, PA: Rank 102
MSA: 364,500; TSA: 1,296,700
Stations: WARM-FM, WFKJ, WGCB, WGCB-FM, WGET, WGTY-FM, WHTF-FM, WHVR, WOYK, WQXA, WQXA-FM, WSBA, WYCR-FM.

Youngstown-Warren, OH: Rank 87
MSA: 411,400; TSA: 684,700
Stations: WANR, WASN, WBBG-FM, WBBW, WGFT, WHOT, WHOT-FM, WHTX-FM, WKBN, WKBN-FM, WKTX, WLLF-FM, WNCD-FM, WNRB, WQXK-FM, WRBP-FM, WRKU-FM, WRQQ, WRRO, WSOM, WWIZ-FM, WYFM-FM.

U.S. Radio Markets: Arbitron Metro Survey Area Ranking

This chart ranks the 261 radio markets by Metro Survey Area population (see also the following chart of rankings by Total Survey Area). Figures include all persons aged 12 or older and are based on 1990 U.S. Bureau of Census estimates updated and projected to January 1, 1994. Data reflects the Fall 1993 Arbitron market definitions.

A single asterisk (*) following a market name indicates that the market is embedded in a larger nearby market. See *U.S. Radio Markets* beginning on pg. B-591 for details. The double asterisk (**) following the Monmouth-Ocean, NJ, market indicates that Monmouth County is included in both the Monmouth-Ocean, NJ, and New York Metro markets. The triple asterisk (***) following the Manchester, NH, market indicates that a portion of Rockingham County is included in both the Manchester, NH, and Portsmouth-Dover-Rochester, NH, markets.

Rank	Market	Population
1.	New York	14,033,500
2.	Los Angeles	9,705,900
3.	Chicago	6,805,900
4.	San Francisco	5,304,600
5.	Philadelphia	4,101,700
6.	Detroit	3,643,100
7.	Dallas-Fort Worth	3,458,600
7.	Washington, D.C.	3,451,000
9.	Boston	3,191,300
10.	Houston-Galveston	3,184,200
11.	Miami-Fort Lauderdale-Hollywood, FL	2,823,900
12.	Atlanta	2,681,900
13.	Seattle-Tacoma	2,623,500
14.	Nassau-Suffolk, NY (Long Island)*	2,249,400
15.	San Diego	2,213,500
16.	Anaheim-Santa Ana, CA (Orange County)*	2,148,800
17.	Minneapolis-St. Paul	2,120,500
18.	St. Louis	2,080,300
19.	Baltimore	2,036,100
20.	Pittsburgh	2,023,800
21.	Phoenix	1,880,000
22.	Tampa-St. Petersburg-Clearwater, FL	1,869,400
23.	Cleveland	1,758,200
24.	Denver-Boulder	1,636,500
25.	Cincinnati	1,528,500
26.	Portland, OR	1,511,600
27.	Riverside-San Bernardino, CA	1,348,400
28.	Milwaukee-Racine	1,342,000
29.	Sacramento, CA	1,340,100
30.	Kansas City, MO-KS	1,338,000
31.	San Jose, CA*	1,282,100
32.	Providence-Warwick-Pawtucket, RI	1,278,400
33.	Norfolk-Virginia Beach-Newport News, VA	1,198,300
34.	Columbus, OH	1,197,200
35.	San Antonio-Victoria, TX	1,135,300
36.	Salt Lake City-Ogden-Provo	1,099,000
37.	Indianapolis	1,070,700
38.	Charlotte-Gastonia-Rock Hill, NC-SC	1,034,800
39.	New Orleans	1,024,400
40.	Buffalo-Niagara Falls, NY	991,900
41.	Orlando, FL	988,800
42.	Hartford-New Britain-Middletown, CT	970,200
43.	Greensboro-Winston Salem-High Point, NC	925,600
44.	Memphis	915,300
45.	Rochester, NY	888,100
46.	Nashville	864,000
47.	Monmouth-Ocean, NJ**	862,300
48.	Dayton, OH	838,400
49.	West Palm Beach-Boca Raton, FL	829,300
50.	Jacksonville, FL	817,600
51.	Oklahoma City	811,400
52.	Louisville, KY	810,900
53.	Raleigh-Durham, NC	786,000
54.	Birmingham, AL	775,300
55.	Austin, TX	759,000
56.	Richmond, VA	752,800
57.	Albany-Schenectady-Troy, NY	739,900
58.	Las Vegas	731,300
59.	Honolulu	727,800
60.	San Diego North County*	700,300
61.	Greenville-Spartanburg, SC	681,600
62.	Wilkes Barre-Scranton, PA	634,700
63.	Tulsa, OK	633,300
64.	Allentown-Bethlehem, PA	598,400
65.	Tucson, AZ	591,400
66.	Fresno, CA	580,000
67.	Grand Rapids, MI	577,200
68.	Akron, OH	560,700
69.	Syracuse, NY	550,300
70.	McAllen-Brownsville-Harlingen, TX	540,200
71.	Albuquerque	522,100
72.	Omaha-Council Bluffs, NE-IA	518,000
73.	Knoxville, TN	517,800
74.	Harrisburg-Lebanon-Carlisle, PA	510,900
74.	Toledo, OH	510,900
76.	Springfield, MA	506,000
77.	El Paso, TX	505,100
78.	Wilmington, DE	499,900
79.	Monterey-Salinas-Santa Cruz, CA	496,900
80.	Sarasota-Bradenton, FL	461,500
81.	Greenville-New Bern-Jacksonville, NC	451,600
82.	Baton Rouge	441,100
83.	Little Rock, AR	440,000
84.	Charleston, SC	432,800
85.	New Bedford-Fall River, MA*	427,000
86.	Bakersfield, CA	412,600
87.	Youngstown-Warren, OH	411,400
88.	Wichita, KS	410,500
89.	Stockton, CA	409,800
90.	Mobile, AL	405,300
91.	Columbia, SC	391,100
92.	New Haven, CT	385,200
93.	Fort Wayne, IN	380,900
94.	Johnson City-Kingsport-Bristol, TN-VA	380,700
95.	Spokane, WA	378,800
96.	Daytona Beach, FL	378,200
97.	Melbourne-Titusville-Cocoa, FL	372,300
98.	Chattanooga	371,600
99.	Roanoke-Lynchburg, VA	371,500
100.	Worcester, MA	370,400
101.	Lancaster, PA	364,800
102.	York, PA	364,500
103.	Lansing-East Lansing, MI	363,800
104.	Bridgeport, CT	362,900
105.	Morristown, NJ*	359,900
106.	Colorado Springs, CO	358,500
107.	Lakeland-Winter Haven, FL	358,300
108.	Huntsville, AL	352,900
109.	Santa Rosa, CA*	348,300
110.	Flint, MI	347,700
111.	Gainesville-Ocala, FL	346,100
112.	Portsmouth-Dover-Rochester, NH	342,100
113.	Des Moines, IA	339,900
114.	Augusta, GA	338,100
115.	Canton, OH	332,300
116.	Jackson, MS	331,600
117.	Oxnard-Ventura, CA	331,100
118.	Saginaw-Bay City-Midland, MI	326,700
119.	Modesto, CA	325,500
120.	Fort Pierce-Stuart-Vero Beach, FL	323,000
121.	Fort Myers, FL	321,500
121.	Madison, WI	321,500
123.	Fayetteville, NC	317,200
124.	Lexington-Fayette, KY	309,900
125.	Shreveport, LA	303,700
126.	Pensacola, FL	300,300
127.	Beaumont-Port Arthur, TX	296,400
128.	Reading, PA	292,600
129.	Quad Cities, IA-IL (Davenport-Rock Island-Moline)	288,000
130.	Corpus Christi, TX	286,800
131.	Peoria, IL	282,400
132.	Trenton, NJ	279,500
133.	Lafayette, LA	278,700
134.	Atlantic City-Cape May, NJ	278,400
135.	Stamford-Norwalk, CT*	277,300
136.	Appleton-Oshkosh, WI	267,600
137.	Huntington-Ashland, WV-KY	266,000
138.	Boise, ID	262,300
139.	Utica-Rome, NY	262,200
140.	Newburgh-Middleton, NY (Mid-Hudson Valley)	261,600

U.S. Radio Markets: Arbitron Metro Survey Area Ranking

141. Reno, NV	261,400
142. Tyler-Longview, TX	251,700
143. Montgomery, AL	250,000
144. Ann Arbor, MI	249,400
145. Eugene-Springfield, OR	245,500
146. Rockford, IL	240,400
147. Macon, GA	237,700
148. Evansville, IN	233,600
149. Erie, PA	229,000
150. Poughkeepsie, NY	222,600
151. Palm Springs, CA	220,800
152. Binghamton, NY	219,800
153. Salisbury-Ocean City, MD	219,000
154. Savannah, GA	218,800
155. Charleston, WV	214,400
156. Springfield, MO	213,600
157. New London, CT	211,900
158. Wausau-Stevens Point, WI (Central Wisconsin)	210,600
159. Hagerstown-Chambersburg-Waynesboro MD-PA	209,600
160. South Bend, IN	208,600
161. Columbus, GA	207,400
162. Portland, ME	205,100
163. Killeen-Temple, TX	201,900
164. Johnstown, PA	201,200
165. Anchorage, AK	196,900
166. San Luis Obispo, CA	191,800
167. Fayetteville-Springdale, AR	191,600
168. Fort Smith, AR	189,800
169. Kalamazoo, MI	188,300
170. Tallahassee, FL	187,500
171. Waterbury, CT	186,800
172. Lubbock, TX	186,500
173. Lincoln, NE	185,100
174. Odessa-Midland, TX	179,400
175. Dothan, AL	179,100
176. Topeka, KS	176,900
177. Tupelo, MS	174,900
178. Myrtle Beach, SC	174,500
179. Manchester, NH***	171,800
180. Asheville, NC	169,700
180. Terre Haute, IN	169,700
182. Santa Barbara, CA	169,400
183. Biloxi-Gulfport, MS	167,200
184. Green Bay, WI	165,600
185. Cape Cod, MA	165,300
186. Chico, CA	164,900
187. St. Cloud, MN	161,000
188. Springfield, IL	160,200
189. Waco, TX	159,000
189. Yakima, WA	159,000
191. Danbury, CT	157,600
192. Wilmington, NC	157,300
193. Amarillo, TX	157,100
194. Alexandria, LA	151,900
195. Florence, SC	149,400
195. Naples-Marco Island, FL	149,400
197. Champaign, IL	148,500
197. Northwest Michigan (Traverse City-Petosky-Charlevoix)	148,500
199. Cedar Rapids, IA	144,100
200. Lake Charles, LA	138,100
201. Marion-Carbondale (Southern Illinois)	135,800
202. Redding, CA	134,700
203. Laurel-Hattiesburg, MS	134,200
204. Tuscaloosa, AL	133,300
205. Wheeling, WV	132,600
206. Frederick, MD*	132,300
207. Muskegon, MI	131,500
208. Medford-Ashland, OR	131,000
209. Fargo-Moorhead, ND-MN	130,900
210. Dubuque, IA	129,800
211. Duluth-Superior, MN-WI	128,100
212. Sioux Falls, SD	127,300
213. Fort Walton Beach, FL	126,600
213. Lima, OH	126,600
213. Tri-Cities, WA (Richland-Kennewick-Pasco)	126,600
216. Parkersburg-Marietta, WV-OH	125,200
217. Waterloo-Cedar Falls, IA	121,100
218. Steubenville-Weirton, OH-WV	120,500
219. Abilene, TX	118,500
220. Burlington, VT	118,300
221. Charlottesville, VA	117,300
222. Eau Claire, WI	116,600
223. Monroe, LA	116,100
224. Lafayette, IN	115,500
225. Joplin, MO	114,100
226. Battle Creek, MI	113,700
227. Bloomington, IL	113,200
228. Panama City, FL	111,500
229. State College, PA	111,000
230. Altoona, PA	109,900
231. Bryan-College Station, TX	106,300
232. Pueblo, CO	103,600
233. Santa Fe, NM	102,800
234. Williamsport, PA	100,900
235. Columbia, MO	99,400
235. Texarkana, TX-AR	99,400
237. Wichita Falls, TX	99,200
238. Augusta-Waterville, ME	97,800
239. Watertown, NY	95,600
240. Billings, MT	95,500
241. Sioux City, IA	95,000
242. Lawton, OK	93,200
243. Rochester, MN	90,400
244. Rapid City, SD	89,900
245. Albany, GA	88,900
246. Grand Forks, ND-MN	85,400
247. Ithaca, NY	83,200
248. La Crosse, WI	83,000
249. Grand Junction, CO	82,600
250. San Angelo, TX	82,000
251. Harrisonburg, VA	77,500
252. Bangor, ME	76,600
253. Owensboro, KY	72,400
254. Danville, IL	72,300
255. Bismarck, ND	68,600
256. Great Falls, MT	67,300
257. Beckley, WV	63,600
258. Cheyenne, WY	61,900
258. Meridian, MS	61,900
260. Casper, WY	49,300
261. Minot, ND	47,100

U.S. Radio Markets: Population Ranking

This chart ranks the 261 radio markets by Total Survey Area population (see also the preceding chart of markets ranked by Metro Survey Area). Population figures include all persons aged 12 or older and are based on 1990 U.S. Bureau of Census estimates updated and projected to January 1, 1994. Data reflects the Fall 1993 Arbitron market definitions.

A single asterisk (*) following a market name indicates that the market is embedded in a larger nearby market. See *U.S. Radio Markets* beginning on pg B-591 for details. The double asterisk (**) following the Monmouth-Ocean, NJ, market indicates that Monmouth County is included in both the Monmouth-Ocean, NJ, and New York Metro markets. The triple asterisk (***) following the Manchester, NH, market indicates that a portion of Rockingham County is included in both the Manchester, NH, and Portsmouth-Dover-Rochester, NH, markets.

1. New York	17,110,700
2. Los Angeles	13,338,000
3. Chicago	9,106,600
4. San Francisco	8,379,700
5. Philadelphia	7,319,900
6. Boston	6,086,600
7. Detroit	5,327,000
8. Washington, DC	4,949,000
9. Dallas-Fort Worth	4,709,300
10. Houston-Galveston	3,941,000
11. Miami-Fort Lauderdale-Hollywood, FL	3,747,000
12. Atlanta	3,622,200
13. San Jose, CA*	3,502,700
14. Cleveland	3,365,300
15. Minneapolis-St. Paul	3,219,700
16. Pittsburgh	3,206,900
17. Seattle-Tacoma	3,152,400
18. Tampa-St. Petersburg-Clearwater, FL	3,026,900
19. Sacramento, CA	2,802,900
20. Baltimore	2,780,600
21. St. Louis	2,713,500
22. Hartford-New Britain-Middletown, CT	2,625,200
23. Denver-Boulder	2,600,900
24. Phoenix	2,535,600
25. Orlando, FL	2,455,800
26. West Palm Beach-Boca Raton, FL	2,272,300
27. Nassau-Suffolk, NY (Long Island)*	2,249,400
28. Indianapolis	2,242,700
29. San Diego	2,213,500
30. Kansas City, KS	2,195,300
31. Anaheim-Santa Ana, CA (Orange County)*	2,148,800
32. Charlotte-Gastonia-Rock Hill, NC-SC	2,122,000
33. Providence-Warwick-Pawtucket, RI	2,113,800
34. Riverside-San Bernardino, CA	2,099,500
35. Portland, OR	2,020,900
36. Cincinnati	1,969,100
37. Greensboro-Winston Salem-High Point, NC	1,919,900
38. Columbus, OH	1,896,500
39. Milwaukee-Racine	1,867,300
40. Norfolk-Virginia Beach-Newport News, VA	1,844,400
41. New Orleans	1,761,500
42. San Antonio-Victoria, TX	1,721,300
43. Nashville	1,710,900
44. Raleigh-Durham, NC	1,708,800
45. Memphis	1,675,200
46. Dayton, OH	1,633,800
47. Birmingham, AL	1,611,800
48. Salt Lake City-Ogden-Provo	1,469,700
49. Greenville-Spartanburg, SC	1,459,400
50. Harrisburg-Lebanon-Carlisle, PA	1,457,400
51. Oklahoma City	1,397,200
52. Buffalo-Niagara Falls, NY	1,392,500
53. Grand Rapids, MI	1,364,800
54. Louisville, KY	1,334,000
55. Albany-Schenectady-Troy, NY	1,326,100
56. York, PA	1,296,700
57. Knoxville, TN	1,281,000
58. Baton Rouge	1,260,400
59. Tulsa, OK	1,230,600
60. Fresno, CA	1,174,500
61. Rochester, NY	1,161,800
62. Omaha-Council Bluffs, NE-IA	1,123,800
63. Saginaw-Bay City-Midland, MI	1,123,200
64. Akron, OH	1,087,400
65. Toledo, OH	1,083,000
66. Jacksonville, FL	1,068,000
67. Wilkes Barre-Scranton, PA	1,064,900
68. Austin, TX	1,056,100
69. New Haven, CT	1,031,700
70. Roanoke-Lynchburg, VA	1,028,700
71. Little Rock, AR	1,024,200
72. Syracuse, NY	994,500
73. Des Moines, IA	991,100
74. Richmond, VA	990,500
75. Modesto, CA	974,900
76. Allentown-Bethlehem, PA	937,800
77. Mobile, AL	931,500
78. Lexington-Fayette, KY	900,300
79. Jackson, MS	894,500
80. Las Vegas	888,200
80. Lansing-East Lansing, MI	888,200
82. Greenville-New Bern-Jacksonville, NC	879,000
83. Monmouth-Ocean, NJ**	862,300
84. Fort Wayne, IN	850,300
85. Albuquerque	838,100
86. South Bend, IN	807,700
87. Huntsville, AL	801,500
88. Tucson, AZ	800,400
89. Shreveport, LA	793,800
90. Chattanooga	791,900
91. Columbia, SC	771,000
92. Madison, WI	766,700
93. Lancaster, PA	758,800
94. Portland, ME	750,500
95. Bakersfield, CA	746,100
96. Charleston, SC	741,500
97. Santa Fe, NM	738,600
98. Oxnard-Ventura, CA	738,300
99. Daytona Beach, FL	736,400
100. Appleton-Oshkosh, WI	733,300
101. Johnson City-Kingsport-Bristol, TN-VA	728,900
102. Honolulu	727,800
103. El Paso, TX	725,900
104. Spokane, WA	724,100
105. Melbourne-Titusville-Cocoa, FL	720,300
106. Wichita, KS	707,400
107. San Diego North County*	700,300
108. Green Bay, WI	686,700
109. Owensboro, KY	685,800
110. Poughkeepsie, NY	684,800
111. Youngstown-Warren, OH	684,700
112. Quad Cities, IA-IL (Davenport-Rock Island-Moline)	684,200
113. Worcester, MA	682,100
114. Gainesville-Ocala, FL	659,900
115. Fayetteville, NC	657,400
116. Santa Barbara, CA	653,600
117. Huntington-Ashland, WV-KY	651,800
118. Fort Myers, FL	634,800
119. Tyler-Longview, TX	629,800
120. Evansville, IN	626,500
121. Savannah, GA	619,400
122. Canton, OH	618,700
123. Pensacola, FL	612,600
124. McAllen-Brownsville Harlingen, TX	600,100
125. Sarasota-Bradenton, FL	596,100
126. Wilmington, DE	594,400
127. Colorado Springs, CO	581,600
128. Springfield, MA	564,900
129. Binghamton, NY	564,200
130. Pueblo, CO	562,900
131. Eugene-Springfield, OR	553,800
132. Springfield, MO	552,200
133. Charleston, WV	551,400
134. Montgomery, AL	548,300
135. Altoona, PA	539,200
136. Rockford, IL	533,000
137. Peoria, IL	529,500
138. Monterey-Salinas-Santa Cruz, CA	527,900
139. Beaumont-Port Arthur, TX	519,800
140. Macon, GA	517,000

U.S. Radio Markets: Population Ranking

141. Flint, MI	515,000
142. Augusta, GA	509,400
143. Waco, TX	500,100
144. Naples-Marco Island, FL	493,700
145. Columbus, GA	487,400
146. Topeka, KS	483,000
147. Utica-Rome, NY	482,100
148. Manchester, NH***	480,600
149. Wausau-Stevens Point, WI (Central Wisconsin)	479,000
150. Boise, ID	475,100
151. Portsmouth-Dover-Rochester, NH	472,500
152. Stockton, CA	471,600
153. Cedar Rapids, IA	464,000
154. Battle Creek, MI	463,000
155. Tupelo, MS	459,100
156. Reno, NV	458,000
157. Terre Haute, IN	454,300
158. Fargo-Moorhead, ND-MN	454,200
159. Kalamazoo, MI	447,300
160. Lafayette, LA	441,500
161. Lakeland-Winter Haven, FL	440,100
162. Eau Claire, WI	436,700
163. Corpus Christi, TX	430,800
164. Champaign, IL	427,000
164. New Bedford-Fall River, MA*	427,000
166. Tallahassee, FL	421,000
167. Erie, PA	420,100
168. Burlington, VT	417,300
169. Salisbury-Ocean City, MD	415,800
170. Muskegon, MI	406,100
171. Dothan, AL	403,300
172. New London, CT	393,600
173. Atlantic City-Cape May, NJ	392,700
174. Rochester, MN	387,300
175. Johnstown, PA	383,100
176. Alexandria, LA	382,600
177. Monroe, LA	381,800
178. Duluth-Superior, MN-WI	377,300
179. Augusta-Waterville, ME	376,300
180. Asheville, NC	375,800
181. Trenton, NJ	372,900
182. Bridgeport, CT	362,900
183. Morristown, NJ*	359,900
184. Waterloo-Cedar Falls, IA	358,600
185. Albany, GA	358,200
186. St. Cloud, MN	357,400
187. Sioux Falls, SD	357,100
188. Williamsport, PA	353,200
189. Springfield, IL	350,900
190. Fort Smith, AR	350,800
191. Fort Pierce-Stuart-Vero Beach, FL	349,700
191. Northwest Michigan (Traverse City-Petosky-Charlevoix)	349,700
193. Beckley, WV	348,900
194. Santa Rosa, CA*	348,300
195. Lubbock, TX	345,800
196. San Luis Obispo, CA	344,900
197. Wheeling, WV	335,400
198. Bangor, ME	330,900
199. Parkersburg-Marietta, WV-OH	328,200
200. Lima, OH	327,600
201. Joplin, MO	327,300
202. Ann Arbor, MI	325,700
203. Wichita Falls, TX	323,400
204. Lincoln, NE	323,000
205. Hagerstown-Chambersburg-Waynesboro MD-PA	317,600
206. La Crosse, WI	310,000
207. Biloxi-Gulfport, MS	305,400
208. Medford-Ashland, OR	305,200
209. Chico, CA	301,300
210. Amarillo, TX	298,400
211. Fayetteville-Springdale, AR	297,700
212. Odessa-Midland, TX	296,500
213. Myrtle Beach, SC	296,400
214. Reading, PA	292,600
215. Newburgh-Middleton, NY (Mid-Hudson Valley)	289,100
216. Tri-Cities, WA (Richland-Kennewick-Pasco)	288,800
217. Waterbury, CT	282,000
218. Killeen-Temple, TX	280,200
219. Lake Charles, LA	279,100
220. Lafayette, IN	278,300
221. Stamford-Norwalk, CT*	277,300
222. Texarkana, TX-AR	271,500
223. Anchorage	268,000
224. Harrisonburg, VA	265,400
225. Columbia, MO	261,200
226. Sioux City, IA	258,100
227. Redding, CA	255,900
228. Panama City, FL	255,100
229. Meridian, MS	254,800
230. Wilmington, NC	249,500
231. Southern Illinois (Marion-Carbondale)	247,900
232. Laurel-Hattiesburg, MS	246,400
233. Florence, SC	239,500
234. Tuscaloosa, AL	225,900
235. Palm Springs, CA	220,800
236. Bismarck, ND	218,900
237. Dubuque, IA	218,100
238. Abilene, TX	212,900
239. Watertown, NY	212,100
239. Bloomington, IL	212,100
241. Billings, MT	208,300
242. Yakima, WA	197,200
243. Grand Junction, CO	184,800
244. Cape Cod, MA	180,900
245. State College, PA	175,700
246. Charlottesville, VA	175,400
247. Grand Forks, ND-MN	172,500
248. Great Falls, MT	170,600
249. Rapid City, SD	162,300
250. Danville, IL	157,700
251. Danbury, CT	157,600
252. Bryan-College Station, TX	156,100
253. Fort Walton Beach, FL	152,200
254. Lawton, OK	143,000
255. Ithaca, NY	139,700
256. Frederick, MD*	132,300
257. San Angelo, TX	127,900
258. Minot, ND	126,300
259. Steubenville-Weirton, OH-WV	120,500
260. Casper, WY	115,000
261. Cheyenne, WY	61,900

Growth of Radio Broadcasting Pre-Television 1922-1945

The following tables represent a record of broadcasting growth in the United States before the advent of television. All information is from the records of the Federal Communications Commission.

AM Authorizations Before Television

Date	Licensed	Under Construction	Total Authorized
Jan. 1, 1922			30
Mar. 1, 1923			556
Oct. 1, 1924			530
June 20, 1925			571
June 30, 1926			528
Feb. 23, 1927			733
July 1, 1928			677
July 1, 1931	603	9	612
Jan. 1, 1932	601	7	608
Jan. 1, 1933	599	11	610
Jan. 1, 1934	583	8	591
Jan. 1, 1935	585	20	605
Jan. 1, 1936	616	39	632
Jan. 1, 1937	646	39	685
Jan. 1, 1938	689	32	721
Jan. 1, 1939	722	42	764
Jan. 1, 1940	765	49	814
June 30, 1941			897
June 30, 1942			925
June 30, 1943			912
June 30, 1944			924
July 20, 1945	933	23	956

FM Authorizations Before Television

Date	Licensed	Under Construction	Total Authorized
June 30, 1940		50	
June 30, 1941		69	
June 30, 1942		74	
June 30, 1943		26	74
June 30, 1944		6	58
June 30, 1945		3	56

U.S. Radio Set Sales 1958-1992

Data was compiled by Electronic Industries Association. All figures are in thousands (add 000).

Year	Domestic Label Units	Domestic Label Dollars	Other Imports Units	Other Imports Dollars	Total Table, Clock, Portable Units	Total Table, Clock, Portable Dollars	Total Auto Radio Units	Total Auto Radio Dollars	Total Units	Total Dollars
1958	8,227	159,000	2,570	....	10,797	....	3,715	96,000	14,512	....
1959	9,947	192,000	5,825	....	15,772	....	5,501	130,000	21,273	....
1960	10,13	190,000	7,518	....	18,031	....	6,432	154,000	24,463	....
1961	11,590	190,000	12,064	....	23,654	....	5,568	134,000	29,222	....
1962	11,811	207,000	12,970	....	24,781	....	7,249	181,000	32,030	....
1963	10,439	179,000	13,163	....	23,602	....	7,946	206,000	31,548	....
1964	10,836	179,000	12,722	88,000	23,558	267,000	8,313	205,000	31,871	472,000
1965	13,812	212,000	17,877	116,000	31,689	328,000	10,037	248,000	41,726	576,000
1966	14,468	231,000	20,311	115,000	34,779	346,000	9,394	267,000	44,173	613,000
1967	12,568	201,000	19,116	132,000	31,684	333,000	9,527	259,000	41,211	592,000
1968	11,660	191,000	22,662	180,000	34,322	371,000	12,510	330,000	46,832	701,000
1969	10,400	166,000	29,014	256,000	39,414	422,000	11,939	316,000	51,353	738,000
1970	7,948	124,000	26,101	256,000	34,049	380,000	10,378	271,000	44,427	651,000
1971	8,224	131,000	25,811	356,000	34,105	487,000	13,505	315,000	47,610	802,000
1972	9,848	157,000	32,301	449,000	42,149	606,000	13,162	377,000	55,311	983,000
1973	....	....	....	....	37,652	572,000	12,546	391,000	50,198	963,000
1974	....	....	....	....	33,076	557,331	10,762	369,998	43,838	927,329
1975	....	....	....	....	25,544	372,970	9,239	355,001	34,783	727,971
1976	....	....	....	....	28,264	355,885	12,445	497,053	40,709	852,938
1977	....	....	....	....	41,463	522,422	12,890	534,033	54,353	1,056,456
1978	....	....	....	....	31,776	435,749	12,668	581,968	44,444	1,017,717
1979	....	....	....	....	27,380	435,896	12,381	623,012	39,761	1,058,908
1980	....	....	....	....	28,062	467,827	11,470	960,957	39,532	1,428,784
1981	....	....	....	....	29,415	501,213	12,883	1,082,945	42,298	1,584,158
1982	....	....	....	....	32,663	529,683	12,306	1,048,963	44,969	1,578,646
1983	....	....	....	....	39,496	565,352	12,081	1,147,937	51,577	1,713,291
1984	....	....	....	....	46,453	661,316	15,630	1,902,336	62,083	2,563,652
1985	....	....	....	....	21,574	379,285	15,497	1,566,456	37,071	1,945,741
1986	....	....	....	....	25,363	407,504	15,783	1,683,033	41,146	2,090,537
1987	....	....	....	....	28,110	409,338	....	....	....	....
1988	....	....	....	....	23,623	377,173	....	....	....	....
1989	....	....	....	....	25,253	378,689	....	....	....	....
1990	....	....	....	....	21,585	359,699	....	....	....	....
1991	....	....	....	....	18,530	310,324	....	....	....	....
1992	....	....	....	....	21,553	324,000	....	....	....	....

Prior to 1971, data reflects factory sales by U.S. manufacturers plus those products imported directly by distributors or dealers for resale. All import statistics are based upon average value as published by the U.S. Department of Commerce, which is F.O.B. and therefore excludes U.S. import duties, freight charged from the foreign country to the United States, and insurance.

Record of Radio Station Growth Since Television Began

Date	AM Authorized	On Air	FM Authorized	On Air
Jan. 1, 1946*	1,004		456	55
June 30, 1946*				
Jan. 1, 1947*	1,517			
June 30, 1947			918	238
Jan. 1 1948*	1,962	1,621	926	458
Jan. 1, 1949	2,127	1,912	966	700
Jan. 1, 1950	2,234	2,086	788	733
Jan. 1, 1951	2,351	2,232	703	676
Jan. 1, 1952	2,408	2,331	650	637
Jan. 1, 1953*	2,524	2,391		
June 30, 1953*			601	580
Jan. 1, 1954	2,636	2,521	580	560
Jan. 1, 1955	2,774	2,669	559	552
Jan. 1, 1956	2,935	2,824	557	540
Jan. 1, 1957	3,125	3,008	554	530
Jan. 1, 1958	3,295	3,196	590	537
Jan. 1, 1959	3,440	3,326	695	578
Jan. 1, 1960	3,527	3,398	838	688
Jan. 1, 1961	3,667	3,539	1,018	815
Jan. 1, 1962	3,911	3,693	1,128	960
Jan. 1, 1963	3,924	3,810	1,128	1,081
Jan. 1, 1964	4,039	3,937	1,249	1,146
Jan. 1, 1965	4,077	4,009	1,468	1,270
Jan. 1, 1966	4,129	4,049	1,657	1,446
Jan. 1, 1967	4,190	4,121	1,865	1,643
Jan. 1, 1968	4,249	4,156	3,005	1,753
Jan. 1, 1969	4,300	4,237	2,114	1,938
Jan. 1, 1970	4,344	4,269	2,651	2,476
Jan. 1, 1971	4,383	4,323	2,795	2,636
Jan. 1, 1972	4,411	4,355	2,971	2,783
Jan. 1, 1973	4,431	4,382	3,162	2,965
Jan. 1, 1974	4,448	4,395	3,360	3,151
Jan. 1, 1975	4,477	4,432	3,617	3,353
Jan. 1, 1976	4,513	4,463	3,752	3,571
Jan. 1, 1977	4,536	4,497	3,969	3,743
Jan. 1, 1978	4,569	4,513	4,130	3,972
Jan. 1, 1979	4,599	4,549	4,310	4,089
Jan. 1, 1980	4,651	4,558	4,463	4,190
Jan. 1, 1981	4,700	4,589	4,588	4,374
Jan. 1, 1982	4,763	4,634	4,736	4,467
Jan. 1, 1983	4,828	4,685	4,970	4,505
Jan. 1, 1984	4,897	4,733	5,240	4,649
Jan. 1, 1985	4,924	4,754	5,479	4,888
Oct. 30, 1985	4,975	4,805	5,657	5,066
Oct. 31, 1986	5,026	4,856	5,781	5,190
Jan. 1, 1988	5,072	4,902	5,933	5,342
Jan. 1, 1989	5,199	4,932	6,434	5,529
Jan. 1, 1990	5,223	4,966	6,705	5,665
Jan. 1, 1991	5,226	4,984	7,037	5,810
Jan. 1, 1992	5,223	4,988	7,356	6,036
Jan. 1, 1993	5,147	4,963	7,538	6,312
Jan. 1, 1994		4,945		6,613

*Comparable figures for all services not available this date.

U.S. Radio Audiences

Radio was in more U.S. homes than ever as 1994 approached. The Radio Advertising Bureau (RAB) estimated that 99% of 96.6 million U.S. homes were radio-equipped as of January 1, 1993. RAB also estimated that the number of working-order radio sets in the United States totaled 576.5 million in 1993: 367.4 million of these were home and personal radio sets; 209.1 million were out-of-home receivers.

Year	Radio Homes (millions)
1949	40.8
1950	42.1
1951	43.6
1952	44.8
1953	45.0
1954	45.4
1955	46.2
1956	47.2
1957	48.2
1958	48.9
1959	49.5
1960	49.5
1961	49.5
1962	51.1
1963	52.3
1964	54.9
1965	55.2
1966	57.0
1967	57.5
1968	58.5
1969	60.6
1970	62.0
1971	62.6
1972	64.1
1973	67.4
1974	68.9
1975	70.4
1976	71.4
1977	72.9
1978	74.6
1979	76.5
1980	78.6
1981	80.5
1982	84.3
1983	84.6
1984	84.6
1985	86.7
1986	87.1
1987	88.1
1988	89.9
1989	91.1
1990	92.8
1991	94.4
1992	94.4
1993	96.6

# Section C
Television

Table of Contents

Table of Contents	C-1
Key to Listings	C-2
Directory of Television Stations in the United States and Canada	
United States	C-3
Canada	C-81
Television Stations by Call Letters	
United States	C-90
Canada	C-93
Low Power Television Stations	C-94
Spanish-Language Television Stations	C-110
Experimental Television Stations	C-111
U.S. Independent Television Stations	C-112
College, University and School-Owned Television Stations	C-113
U.S. Television Stations Broadcasting in Stereo	C-114
Television Stations by Channel	
United States	C-115
Canada	C-119
Television Assignments by State	C-120
Television Market Statistics	
Arbitron ADI Market Atlas	C-123
Multi-City ADI Cross-Reference	C-201
Non-ADI Markets	C-202
Television Markets Ranked by Size	C-203
Television Markets by Nielsen Marketing Research Territory	C-208
The Top 100 Companies	C-210
How Network Delivery Varies by Market	C-213
U.S. Sales of Television Receivers 1983-1992	C-217
Record of Television Station Growth Since Television Began	C-218
U.S. Television Audiences	C-219

Key to Television Listings

Television listings include TV stations in the United States, its territories and Canada. All collected data for these listings include information current to January 1994. To use the television key, see boldface numbers and corresponding explanations.

(1) WOF-TV—(2) ch 17, 2,200 kw vis, 20 kw aur, ant 500t/300g. TL: N36 49 21 W108 47 32. (CP: ant 750t/550g). **(3)** On air date: April 13, 1952. **(4)** Box 100, 71701. (909) 555-1000. FAX: (909) 999-9999. **(5)** Licensee: WOF Bcstg Co. **(6)** Group owner: Acme Stations, see Cross-Ownership (acq 7-20-69; $2 million; **(6a)** FTR 3-6-87). **(7)** CBS, NBC. Sp 2 hrs wkly. **(8)** Rep: Jones, Tri-State. Wash atty: Goltz & Stick. **(9)** Jud Jones, pres & gen mgr; D. Spark, chief engr. **(10)** On 6 CATVs—20,000 subs. On 10 trans. **(11)** Co-owned radio: WOF-AM-FM. **(12)** Rates: $100; 83; 70.

(1) Station call letters as assigned by the Federal Communications Commission (FCC) or Canadian Radio-television and Telecommunications Commission (CRTC).

(2) Channel, power, antenna, location and construction permit. WOF-TV operates with 2,200 kilowatts (effective radiated power) visual and 20 kilowatts aural. Its antenna is 500 feet above average terrain and 300 feet above ground. "N36 49 21 W108 47 32" refers to the geographical coordinates (latitude and longitude) of the transmitter location. WOF-TV holds a construction permit for an antenna height change to 750 feet above average terrain, 550 feet above ground.

(3) Date station first went on the air (regardless of subsequent ownership changes).

(4) Address and zip code, telephone and FAX number. Teletype Writer Exchange may also be included.

(5) Licensee name.

(6) Ownership and date of acquisition (if not original owner). If a station has been sold, any available sale information is listed following the acquisition date. WOF-TV is owned by Acme Stations, which also owns several other broadcast properties. For details on group owners, see *Group Ownership* listings in Section A. WOF-TV also has print media connections, which are detailed in the *Cross-Ownership* listings, also in Section A. Principal stockholders of independently owned stations may also be listed.

(6a) FTR date refers to *Broadcasting & Cable* magazine's weekly "For the Record" column, where station sales are recorded as received from the FCC.

(7) Network and foreign language programming. The primary WOF-TV national network is CBS, the secondary affiliation is with NBC. The station broadcasts two hours of Spanish programming per week.

(8) Representatives and Washington attorney. Sales representatives are listed with the national rep first, then regional.

(9) Key Personnel.

(10) Cable systems, subscribers and translators. WOF-TV is carried on six cable TV systems with a total of 20,000 subscribers, and on 10 rebroadcasting translators.

(11) Co-owned radio. WOF-TV has the same licensee as WOF-AM-FM.

(12) Advertising rates. This data indicates the prices the station charges for a 30-second spot during the following time slots: primetime; early fringe; daytime, respectively. If a time slot is not applicable "na" replaces the rate.

An asterisk (*) preceding station call letters indicates noncommercial stations.

Note: Listed beneath each city heading is the ranked market Area of Dominant Influence (ADI) in which the city falls. ADI details are presented in the ADI Market Atlas on page C-123.

Directory of Television Stations in the U.S.

Alabama

Anniston

ADI No. 195; see Anniston market

WJSU-TV—ch 40, 724 kw vis, 93.3 kw aur, ant 880t/243g. TL: N33 39 30 W85 48 56. On air date: Oct 26, 1969. Box 40, Radio Bldg., 1330 Noble St. (36202). (205) 237-8651. FAX: (205) 236-7336. Licensee: RKZ Television Inc. Group owner: Osborn Communications Corp. (acq 5-1-87; grpsl). ■ Net: CBS. Rep: Katz. Wash atty: Haley, Bader & Potts. News staff 15; news progmg 9 hrs wkly. ■ Dick Wagschal, vp & gen mgr; Boyce Holt, gen sls mgr; Fred Winsor, natl sls mgr; Mark Norman, prom mgr; Lisa Bedford, progmg dir; Phil Cox, news dir; John Murrell, chief engr. ■ On 28 CATVs—73,437 subs. ■ Rates: $350; 150; 40.

Birmingham

ADI No. 50; see Birmingham market

WABM—ch 68, 1,442 kw vis, 144 kw aur, ant 1,029 ft. TL: N33 27 57 W86 47 45. Hrs opn: 24. On air date: January 1986. 517 Beacon Pkwy W. (35209). (205) 290-6800. FAX: (205) 945-8895. Licensee: Krypton Broadcasting Corp. Ownership: C.E. Feltner Jr., 100% Group owner: Kypton Broadcasting Corp. (acq 1-11-91; $3.6 million; 12-17-90). ■ C.E. Feltner Jr., pres; Dave Griffiths, gen mgr; Fred Procise, sls dir; Gary L. Brandt, gen sls mgr; Robert Klenk, natl sls mgr; Mary Stephens, adv mgr & pub affrs mgr; Cliff Curley, progmg dir; Daniel Dayton, film buyer; Ed Murphy, chief engr. ■ On 25 CATVs—160,000. ■ Rates: $100; 75; 50.

*****WBIQ**—ch 10, 316 kw vis, 31.6 kw aur, ant 1,325t/1,042g. TL: N33 29 19 W86 47 58. On air date: April 28, 1955. Suite 400, 2112 11th Ave. S. (35205). (205) 328-8756. FAX: (205) 251-2192. Licensee: Alabama ETV Commission. ■ Net: PBS. ■ Judy Stone, CEO.

WBMG—ch 42, 2,163 kw vis, 216 kw aur, ant 1,382t/1,134g. TL: N33 29 02 W86 48 21. Stereo. On air date: Oct 17, 1965. 2075 Goldencrest Dr. (35209). (205) 322-4200. FAX: (205) 320-2713. Licensee: Birmingham TV Corp. Ownership: Roy H. Park 89.9% Group owner: Park Communications Inc. (acq 7-17-73; $4.75 million; 6-25-73). ■ Net: CBS. Rep: Blair. Wash atty: Wiley, Rein & Fielding. ■ Tom Thomas, pres; Hoyle Broome, vp & gen mgr; Dave Medley, opns mgr; Gary Andrich, gen sls mgr; Wendy Wammack, prom mgr; Eric Smith, progmg mgr; H. Broome Jr., film buyer; John Harrod, news dir; Fred Vinson, chief engr. ■ On 46 CATVs.

WBRC-TV—ch 6, 100 kw vis, 10 kw aur, ant 1,377t/1,010g. TL: N33 29 19 W86 47 58. (CP: Ant 1,086t). Hrs opn: 24. On air date: July 1, 1949. Box 6 (35201), Atop Red Mountain (35209). (205) 322-6666. FAX: (205) 583-4386; TWX: 810-733-3650. Licensee: Great American TV & Radio Co. Inc. (Group owner: Great American Broadcasting acq 5-8-57; grpsl; 5-13-57). ■ Net: ABC. Rep: Telerep. Wash atty: Koteen & Naftalin. News staff 53; news progmg 21 hrs wkly. ■ Craig Millar, pres & gen mgr; Bob Cleary, vp sls; Tommy DeRamus, natl sls mgr; Becky Dan, vp prom; Lynne Songer, progmg dir; Stan Knott, news dir; Sallie Datnoff, pub affrs dir; J.P. Thorn, vp engrg. ■ On 106 CATVs—517,986 subs.

WTTO—ch 21, 1,042 kw vis, 104.2 kw aur, ant 1,342t/1,058g. TL: N33 30 42 W86 48 24. Stereo. On air date: April 21, 1982. Suite 105, 651 Beacon Pkwy W. (35209). (205) 290-2100. FAX: (205) 290-2114. Licensee: BBM L.P. Group owner: ABRY Communications (acq 12-21-90). ■ Net: Fox. Rep: Katz. Wash atty: Arter & Hadden. ■ Royce Yudkoff, CEO; Andrew Banks, chmn; Peni Garber, CFO; Penny Haft, pres; Katy Hodges, gen sls mgr; Pete Hollenstein, natl sls mgr; Guy Chancey, adv dir; Marilyn Greene Clark, progmg dir; Nolan Otts, pub affrs dir; John Batson, chief engr. ■ On 90 CATVs—300,000 subs. On 62 trans.

WVTM-TV—ch 13, 316 kw vis, 47.4 kw aur, ant 1,340t/1,073g. TL: N33 29 26 W86 48 40. Stereo. On air date: May 1949. Box 10502 (35202); 1732 Valley View Dr. (35209). (205) 933-1313. Licensee: WVTM Argyle Television Inc. Group owner: Argyle Alabama Television Inc. (acq 7-93; $45 million; 7-93). ■ Net: NBC. Rep: Harrington, Righter & Parsons. Wash atty: Wilmer, Cutler & Pickering. ■ John Dawson, gen mgr; Phil Hutchings, opns dir & progmg dir; Jeff Davis, prom mgr; Guy Beverlin, chief engr. ■ On 175 CATVs—420,000 subs.

Decatur

WAFF—See Huntsville.

Demopolis

ADI No. 111; see Montgomery-Selma market

*****WIIQ**—ch 41, 447 kw vis, 44.7 kw aur, ant 1,082t/999g. TL: N32 22 01 W87 52 03. On air date: Sept 13, 1971. Suite 400, 2112 11th Ave. S., Birmingham (35256). (205) 328-8756. FAX: (205) 251-2192. Licensee: Alabama ETV Commission. ■ Net: PBS. ■ Judy Stone, CEO.

Dothan

ADI No. 165; see Dothan market

WDHN—ch 18, 1,080.4 kw vis, 108 kw aur, ant 730t/796g. TL: N31 14 30 W85 18 48. On air date: Aug 7, 1970. Box 6237, (36302); 5274 E. Hwy. 52, Webb (36376). (205) 793-1818. FAX: (205) 793-2623. Licensee: Morris Network of Alabama Inc. Group Owner: Morris Network Inc. acq 7-18-86; grpsl; 6-16-86). ■ Net: ABC. Rep: Katz. Wash atty: Fletcher, Heald & Hildreth. News staff 5; news progmg 6 hrs wkly. ■ H. Dean Hinson, pres; Aubrey Wood, gen mgr; Tony Scott, gen sls mgr; Margaret Monprode, prom dir, progmg dir & pub affrs dir; Ken Curtis, news dir; Dan Billings, chief engr. ■ On 26 CATVs—55,000 subs. ■ Rates: $450; 65; 50.

WRKJ—ch 60, 1,510 kw vis, 151 kw aur, ant 1,230t. TL: N31 15 16 W85 15 39. Not on air, target date unknown. 106 Yale Court (36303). (205) 792-3443. Licensee: Marcum Broadcasting Corp. ■ Douglas J. Marcum, pres.

WTVY—ch 4, 100 kw vis, 20 kw aur, ant 1,670t/1,909g. TL: N30 55 10 W85 44 28. Stereo. Hrs opn: 24. On air date: Feb 12, 1955. Box 1089, 227 N. Foster St. (36303). (205) 792-3195. FAX: (205) 793-3947. Licensee: Dothan Holdings II Inc. (acq 3-16-93; 4-5-93). ■ Net: CBS. Rep: Seltel. Wash atty: Kenkel & Barnard. ■ Donald R. Tomlin, vp; Paul Tanton, opns mgr; Carl Blackmon, gen sls mgr; Danny Richards, prom mgr; Jack Quick, progmg dir & film buyer; Jerry Vann, news dir; Doug Dansby, chief engr. ■ On 79 CATVs—180,000 subs. ■ Rates: $600; 300; 120.

Dozier

ADI No.111; see Montgomery-Selma market

*****WDIQ**—ch 2, 100 kw vis, 10 kw aur, ant 695t/566g. TL: N31 33 16 W86 23 32. On air date: Aug 8, 1956. Suite 400, 2112 11th Ave. S., Birmingham (35205). (205) 328-8756. FAX: (205) 251-2192. Licensee: Ala. ETV Commission. ■ Net: PBS. ■ Judy Stone, CEO.

Florence

ADI No. 81; see Huntsville-Decatur-Florence market

*****WFIQ**—ch 36, 589 kw vis, 58.9 kw aur, ant 760t/538g. TL: N34 34 40 W87 46 54. (CP: 1,276 kw vis). On air date: Aug 16, 1967. Suite 400, 2112 11th Ave. S., Birmingham (35205). (205) 328-8756. FAX: (205) 251-2192. Licensee: Alabama ETV Commission. ■ Net: PBS. ■ Judy Stone, CEO.

WOWL-TV—ch 15, 1,410 kw vis, 400 kw aur, ant 730t/562g. TL: N34 35 01 W87 47 14. Hrs opn: 19. On air date: Oct 29, 1957. Box 2220, 840 Cypress Mill Rd. (35630). (205) 767-1515. FAX: (205) 764-7750. Licensee: Television Muscle Shoals Inc. Ownership: Richard B. (Dick) Biddle, 73%; Frederick A. (Rick) Biddle, 16%; Holly Biddle, 11% ■ Net: NBC. Rep: Roslin. News staff 9; news progmg 4 hrs wkly. ■ Rick Biddle, pres & gen mgr; Lincoln Williams, opns mgr, progmg dir & film buyer; Mitch Faulkner, dev dir & mktg dir; Earl Shoborg, natl sls mgr; Beverly Gooch, prom mgr; Bobby Robertson, chief engr. ■ On 29 CATVs—50,000 subs. ■ Rates: $175; 100; 40.

WYLE—ch 26, 690 kw vis, 69 kw aur, ant 756 ft. TL: N34 34 38 W87 46 57. On air date: April 19, 1986. Box 850, 4150 Underwood Mountain Rd., Tuscumbria (35674). (205) 381-2600; (205) 381-2616. FAX: (205) 383-4986. Licensee: Bridgeland Television Inc. Ownership: Les White, 100% (acq 10-88). Wash atty: B. Scott Johnson. News staff 2; news progmg 5 hrs wkly. ■ Les White, CEO, gen mgr, film buyer & pub affrs dir; Diana Gifford, opns mgr; Jack Baldwin, gen sls mgr; Deborah Springer, prom mgr; Karen Snear, progmg dir; Frank Green, news dir; Nick Scott, engrg mgr. ■ On 51 CATVs—193,000 subs. On one trans.

Gadsden

ADI No. 50; see Birmingham market

WNAL-TV—ch 44, 2,750 kw vis, 275 kw aur, ant 1,000t/500g. TL: N33 57 11 W86 13 00. Stereo. Hrs opn: 24. On air date: April 26, 1986. Box 8249, Carden Bldg., 510 Chestnut St. (35901). (205) 547-4444. FAX: (205) 547-1789. Licensee: WNAL-TV Inc. Ownership: Anthony Jay Fant, 80%; Thomas Stanly Fant, 10%; Kyla Beth Fant, 10% ■ Net: Fox. Wash atty: Anne P. Jones. ■ Anthony J. Fant, pres & gen mgr; Robert D. Hill, exec vp; Debra White, opns mgr & progmg dir; Angie Strawn, gen sls mgr & prom mgr; Robert Hill, film buyer; Jimmy Chivers, chief engr. ■ On 30 CATVs—100,000 subs. ■ Rates: $65; 100; 40.

WTJP—ch 60, 5,000 kw vis, 500 kw aur, ant 1,139t. TL: N33 48 53 W86 26 55. On air date: July 22, 1986. 313 Rosedale Ave. (35901-5361). (205) 546-8860. FAX: (205) 543-8623. Licensee: All American TV Inc. Wash atty: Colby M. May. ■ Sonny Arguinzoni, pres; Gary Hodges, gen mgr; Gary Penovich, progmg dir; Curtiss Kemp, chief engr. ■ On 15 CATVs—60,000 subs.

Huntsville

ADI No. 81; see Huntsville-Decatur-Florence market

WAAY-TV—ch 31, 1,255 kw vis, 125 kw aur, ant 1,790t/999g. TL: N34 44 15 W86 32 02. Stereo. On air date: Aug 1, 1959. 1000 Monte Sano Blvd. (35801). (205) 533-3131. FAX: (205) 533-6616. Licensee: Rocket City TV Inc. Ownership: Smith Broadcasting Inc. (acq 1963; $509,775). ■ Net: ABC. Rep: Petry. Wash atty: Cohn & Marks. ■ M.D. Smith IV, pres & gen mgr; Daniel Whitsett, vp & gen sls mgr; Greg Carroll, prom mgr; Debi Benson, progmg dir; Mark McGee, news dir; Robert Gay, chief engr. ■ On 26 CATVs—90,000 subs.

WAFF—ch 48, 1,170 kw vis, 234 kw aur, ant 1,900t/1,526g. TL: N34 42 39 W86 32 07. Stereo. On air date: July 4, 1954. Box 2116 (35804). (205) 533-4848. FAX: (205) 533-1337; TWX: 810-726-2192. Licensee: American Valley Corp. Ownership: American Family Broadcast Group Inc. (acq 6-1-78; $3.35 million). ■ Net: NBC. Rep: Blair. Wash atty: Sidley & Austin. ■ Walt McCroba, pres; Lee Brantley, gen mgr; Dorothy Fees, gen sls mgr; Judy Cornelius, prom mgr & progmg dir; Garry Kelly, news dir; Rod Hughes, chief engr. ■ On 35 CATVs—123,112 subs.

*****WHIQ**—ch 25, 631 kw vis, 126 kw aur, ant 1,170t/342g. TL: N34 44 14 W86 31 46. (CP: 1,225 kw vis, ant 1,155t). On air date: November 1965. Suite 400, 2112 11th Ave. S., Birmingham (35205). (205) 328-8756. FAX: (205) 251-2192. Licensee: Alabama ETV Commission. ■ Net: PBS. ■ Judy Stone, CEO.

WHNT-TV—ch 19, 1,279 kw vis, 254 kw aur, ant 1,750t/944g. TL: N34 44 19 W86 31 56. On air date: Nov 28, 1963. 200 Holmes Ave. (35801); Box 19 (35804). (205) 533-1919. FAX: (205) 533-4503; TWX: 810-726-2221. Licensee: New York Times Bcstg Svcs Inc. Group owner: The New York Times Co. (acq 2-2-80; $12 million; 3-27-80). ■ Net: CBS. Rep: Katz. Wash atty: Koteen &

Naftalin. ■ Linda Spalla, pres & gen mgr; Robert Browning, vp; Bill Ambrose, gen sls mgr; Jack Miller, prom mgr; Richard Wright, progmg dir; Don Roden, chief engr. ■ On CATVs—6,695 subs. ■ Rates: $500; 215; 60.

WZDX—ch 54, 2,223 kw vis, 222 kw aur, 1,692t/1,001g. TL: N34 38 11 W86 30 42. On air date: April 14, 1985. Box 3889 (35810). (205) 859-5454. FAX: (205) 859-2194. Licensee: Huntsville Television Acquisition Corp. Group owner: Media Central Inc. (acq 4-90; $6.1 million). Rep: Seltel. ■ Milton Grant, pres; Randy Stone, gen sls mgr; Frank White, prom mgr; Dennis Packard, chief engr. ■ On 30 CATVs.

Louisville

ADI No. 122; see Columbus, GA market

*****WGIQ**—ch 43, 5,000 kw vis, ant 902t/715g. TL: N31 43 05 W85 26 03. On air date: Sept 9, 1968. 2112 11th Ave. S., Suite 400, Birmingham (35205). (205) 328-8756. FAX: (205) 251-2192. Licensee: Alabama ETV Commission. ■ Net: PBS. ■ Judy Stone, CEO.

Mobile

ADI No. 58; see Mobile-Pensacola, FL market

WALA-TV—ch 10, 316 kw vis, 47 kw aur, ant 1,246t/1,200g. TL: N30 41 17 W87 47 54. On air date: Jan 14, 1953. Box 1548 (36633); 210 Government St. (36602). (205) 434-1010. FAX: (205) 434-1073. Licensee: Burnham Broadcasting Co. (group owner; acq 6-30-89). ■ Net: NBC. Rep: Harrington, Righter & Parsons. Wash atty: Fisher, Wayland, Cooper & Leader. ■ Joseph Cook, pres & gen mgr; Scott Wilson, gen sls mgr; Paula Dupuis, prom mgr; Larry Pate, progmg dir & film buyer; Chuck Bark, news dir; John Reece, chief engr. ■ On 32 CATVs.

WEAR-TV—(Pensacola, FL). ch 3, 100 kw vis, 20 kw aur, ant 1,220t/1,257g. TL: N30 37 38 W87 37 31. On air date: Jan 13, 1954. Box 12278, Pensacola, FL (32581). (904) 456-3333. FAX: (904) 455-0159. Licensee: WEAR-TV Ltd. Group owner: Heritage Media Corp. (acq 8-87). ■ Net: ABC. Rep: Petry. Wash atty: Akin, Gump, Strauss, Hauer & Feld. News staff 30; news progmg 14 hrs wkly. ■ Carl Leahy, pres, gen mgr & film buyer; Joe Smith, dev dir; Rusty Hoyle, gen sls mgr; Marcia Francis, prom mgr; J. Landon Smith, progmg dir; S. Peter Neumann, news dir; Sue Straughn, pub affrs dir; David Brown, chief engr. ■ On 48 CATVs—100,000 subs.

*****WEIQ**—ch 42, 1,170 kw vis, 117 kw aur, ant 600t/545g. TL: N30 39 33 W87 53 33. On air date: Nov 6, 1964. Suite 400, 2112 11th Ave. S., Birmingham (35205). (205) 328-8756. FAX: (205) 251-2192. Licensee: Alabama ETV Commission. ■ Net: PBS. ■ Judy Stone, CEO.

WJTC—See Pensacola, Fla.

WKRG-TV—ch 5, 100 kw vis, 20 kw aur, ant 1,906t/1,879g. TL: N30 41 20 W87 49 49. Stereo. On air date: Sept 5, 1955. 555 Broadcast Dr. (36606). (205) 479-5555. FAX: (205) 473-8100; TWX: 810-741-4263. Licensee: WKRG-TV Inc. Ownership: Ansley G. Green, etal. (acq 7-3-91; 7-22-91). ■ Net: CBS. Rep: Katz. Wash atty: Leventhal, Senter & Lerman. ■ D.H. "Buck" Long Jr., pres, progmg dir & film buyer; T.H. Westley Diamond, vp & stn mgr; Bob Spielmann, natl sls mgr; Robin Delaney, prom mgr; Bill Farris, news dir; Carmen Brown, pub affrs dir; Jim Richardson, chief engr. ■ On 35 CATVs—122,000 subs. Co-owned radio: WKRG-AM-FM.

WMPV-TV—ch 21, 4,336 kw vis, 433.6 kw aur, ant 1,400t. TL: N30 35 18 W87 33 16. Hrs opn: 24. On air date: Dec 19, 1985. Box 81521 (36689); 120 Ziegler Cir. E. (36608). (205) 633-2100. FAX: (205) 633-2174. Licensee: Sonlight Broadcasting System Inc. Ownership: Jay A. Sekulow, Stewart J. Roth (acq 6-11-92; grpsl). Wash atty: Fisher, Wayland, Cooper & Leader. ■ Stuart J. Roth, CEO; Jay A. Sekulow, pres; Stephen B. Box, CFO & opns dir; Joel Bennett, progmg dir; Alaina Box, pub affrs dir; Charles W. Davis, engrg dir. ■ On 5 CATVs—68,000 subs.

WPMI—ch 15, 5,000 kw vis, 500 kw aur, ant 1,706t/1,729g. TL: N30 37 35 W87 38 50. On air date: March 12, 1982. Box 9038 (36691-0038); 661 Azalea Rd. (36609). (205) 602-1500. FAX: (205) 602-1515. Licensee: Clear Channel Television Licenses Inc. (group owner: (acq 8-5-92). ■ Net: Fox. Wash atty: Cohn & Marks. ■ Dan Sullivan, pres; David D'Antuono, vp & gen mgr; Bill Parks, gen sls mgr; Michelle Stroecker, natl sls mgr; Joe Curlette, rgnl sls mgr; Sara Moreland, prom mgr; Mary Zieman, progmg dir; Betty Gurley, pub affrs dir; Harold Johnson, chief engr. ■ On 45 CATVs.

Montgomery

ADI No. 111; see Montgomery-Selma market

*****WAIQ**—ch 26, 1,420 kw vis, 142 kw aur, ant 600t/525g. TL: N32 22 52 W86 17 30. On air date: Dec 18, 1962. 2112 11th Ave. S., Suite 400, Birmingham (35205). (205) 328-8756. FAX: (205) 251-2192. Licensee: Alabama ETV Commission. ■ Net: PBS. Wash atty: Hogan & Hartson. ■ Judy Stone, CEO & gen mgr; Jacob Walker Jr., pres; Phyllis Paramore, CFO; Price Broughton, mktg dir; Mike McKenzie, prom dir; Henry L. Bonner, progmg dir; Joe Terry, pub affrs dir; James Foley, engrg dir. ■ On 80 CATVs—200,000 subs.

WCOV-TV—ch 20, 550 kw vis, 112 kw aur, ant 740t/793g. TL: N32 20 06 W86 17 16. On air date: April 23, 1953. One WCOV Ave. (36111). (205) 288-7020. FAX: (205) 288-5414. Licensee: Woods Communications Corp. Ownership: David D. Woods, 100% (acq 9-26-85; $4 million; 6-10-85). ■ Net: Fox. Rep: Seltel. Wash atty: Kenkel & Barnard. ■ David Woods, pres, gen mgr, progmg dir & film buyer; Sonny Strassburger, gen sls mgr; Tara Carter, prom mgr; Phil Witt, chief engr. ■ On 16 CATVs—90,000 subs.

WHOA-TV—ch 32, 4,600 kw vis, 460 kw aur, ant 2,049t/1,798g. TL: N32 08 30 W86 44 43. Stereo. Hrs opn: 6 AM-1 AM. On air date: March 12, 1964. Box 3236 (36109); 3251 Harrison Rd. (36109). (205) 272-5331. FAX: (205) 271-6348. Licensee: Montgomery Ala. ch. 32 Operating Co. (acq 6-10-85; $10,225,000; 5-6-85). ■ Net: ABC. Rep: Petry. Wash atty: Lowndes, Dostick, Doster, Kastor & Reed (Orlando, Fla). News staff 8; news progmg 4 hrs wkly. ■ Louis Frey Jr., pres; Michael M. Sanders, gen mgr; David Murphy, opns mgr & progmg dir; John Crawford, gen sls mgr; Max Lail, rgnl sls mgr; Chris Johnson, prom mgr & pub affrs dir; Debbie Williams, news dir; Johnnie Wright, chief engr. ■ On 30 CATVs—132,700 subs. ■ Rates: $325; 50; 45.

WMCF-TV—ch 45, 600 kw vis, 60 kw aur, ant 1,010t/1,169g. TL: N32 24 11 W86 11 48. (CP: 619.4 kw vis). On air date: Oct 12, 1985. Box 45 (36101); 6000 Monticello Dr. (36117). (205) 277-4545. FAX: (205) 277-6635. Licensee: Sonlight Broadcasting System Inc. Ownership: Stuart J. Roth, Jay A. Sekulow (acq 6-11-92; grpsl). Wash atty: Baraff, Keorner, Olender & Hochberg. ■ Marcus D. Lamb, pres & gen mgr; Dric Williford, stn mgr; Steve Wilhite, gen sls mgr; Jennifer Clements, progmg dir; Dave Thompson, chief engr. ■ On 3 CATVs—70,000 subs. ■ Rates: $30; 20; 10.

WSFA—ch 12, 316 kw vis, 63.2 kw aur, ant 2,000t/1,935g. TL: N31 58 32 W86 09 46. Hrs opn: 5:30 AM-3:05 AM. On air date: Dec 25, 1954. Box 250251 (36125-0251); 10 E. Delano Ave. (36105). (205) 281-2900. FAX: (205) 281-2512; (205) 281-7509. Licensee: Cosmos Broadcasting Corp. (group owner; acq 9-2-59; $2.22 million; 9-14-59). ■ Net: NBC. Rep: Harrington, Righter & Parsons. Wash atty: Dow, Lohnes & Albertson. ■ James Sefert, pres; J. Harold Culver v, pres & gen mgr; Carl Stephens, opns mgr & progmg dir; James Belton, natl sls mgr; Mark Wilder, prom mgr; Lucy Riley, news dir; Andrew Findley, pub affrs dir; Ken Thayer, chief engr. ■ On 78 CATVs—248,000.

Mount Cheaha State Park

ADI No. 50; see Birmingham market

*****WCIQ**—ch 7, 316 kw vis, 31.6 kw aur, ant 2,000t/537g. TL: N33 29 07 W85 48 33. On air date: Jan 7, 1955. 2112 11th Ave. S., Suite 400, Birmingham (35205). (205) 328-8756. FAX: (205) 251-2192. Licensee: Alabama ETV Commission. ■ Net: PBS. ■ Judy Stone, CEO.

Opelika

ADI No. 122; see Columbus, GA market

WSWS-TV—ch 66, 794.3 kw vis, 79.43 kw aur, ant 679t. TL: N32 38 33 W85 14 13. On air date: May 16, 1982. Box 870, 1800 Pepperell Pkwy. (36801). (205) 749-5766. FAX: (205) 749-5583. Licensee: Christian Television Corp. of Alabama. ■ Robert R. D'Andrea, pres; Walter Dix, gen mgr & progmg dir.

Ozark

ADI No. 165; see Dothan market

WDAU—ch 34, 1,120 kw vis, ant 466t. TL: N31 12 30 W85 36 51. Stereo. Hrs opn: 21. On air date: Feb 23, 1991. Box 759, 318 El Palacio Plaza (36360). (205) 774-8000. FAX: (205) 774-1118. Licensee: Judah Broadcasting Systems Inc. (acq 4-2-92). ■ Net: Fox. Wash atty: Borsari & Kump. ■ Samuel D. Judah, pres & gen mgr; Osbem Henley, vp opns & chief engr; Tim Strickland, vp sls; Buddy Johnson, natl sls mgr & rgnl sls mgr; Gina McGee, vp prom, progmg dir & film buyer. ■ On 12 CATVs.

Selma

ADI No. 111; see Montgomery-Selma market

WAKA—ch 8, 316 kw vis, 63.5 kw aur, ant 1,760t/1,757g. TL: N32 08 58 W86 46 48. Stereo. Hrs opn: 24. On air date: March 17, 1960. Box 230667, Montgomery (36123); 3020 E. Blvd. (36116). (205) 271-8888; (205) 279-8787. FAX: (205) 279-9294. Licensee: Alabama Broadcasting Partners (acq 7-20-92). ■ Net: CBS. Rep: Katz. News staff 22; news progmg 9 hrs wkly. ■ Cy N. Bahakel, pres; Ken Hawkins, gen mgr; Mike Elrod, gen sls mgr; Marty Williams, prom mgr; Mark Smith, progmg dir; Bill Zortman, news dir; Evelyn Babcock, pub affrs dir; Bryan Baker, chief engr. ■ On 59 CATVs—102,000 subs.

Troy

ADI No. 111; see Montgomery-Selma market

WRJM-TV—ch 67, 4,641 kw vis, ant 1,930t/1,840g. TL: N31 59 32 W86 09 46. Stereo. Not on air, target date unknown. 409 E. Broad St., Ozark (36360). (205) 774-9323. Permittee: Shelley Broadcasting Co. Ownership: H. Jack Misell, 100%. Wash atty: John Borsari. ■ Jack Mizell, CEO; Jim Powell, gen mgr, vp opns & vp sls; Osborn Henley, vp engrg. ■ On 5 CATVs—300,000 subs. Co-owned radio: WRJM-FM. ■ Rates: $250; 85; 175.

Tuscaloosa

ADI No. 186; see Tuscaloosa market

WCFT-TV—ch 33, 1,225 kw vis, 203 kw aur, ant 540t/442g. TL: N33 10 27 W87 29 09. On air date: Oct 27, 1965. 4000 37th St. E. (35405). (205) 553-1333. FAX: (205) 556-4814. Licensee: Federal Broadcasting Co. (group owner; acq 2-20-91; $7.5 million; 3-11-91). ■ Net: CBS. Rep: Katz. Wash atty: Hogan & Hartson. ■ W. Tommy Ray, gen mgr & film buyer; Ron Quarles, gen sls mgr; Sharon Wolfe, prom mgr; Orzell Spencer, progmg dir; Kip Tyner, news dir; John Fletcher, chief engr. ■ On 10 CATVs—40,100 subs. ■ Rates: $210; 75; 50.

WDBB—ch 17, 3,720 kw vis, 744 kw aur, ant 2,215t/2,000g. TL: N33 28 51 W87 24 03. Stereo. Hrs opn: 24. On air date: Oct 1, 1984. 5455 Jug Factory Rd. E. (35403); Box 031710 (35403). (205) 345-1117. FAX: (205) 345-1173. Licensee: Channel 17 Associates Ltd. ■ Net: Fox. Rep: Adam Young. Wash atty: Mullin, Rhyne, Emmons & Topel. ■ David R. DuBose, pres, gen mgr & vp progmg; Grey Brennan, vp & stn mgr; Padgett Watkins, opns mgr; David B. Hickman, gen sls mgr & adv dir; Tina Hartman, pub affrs dir; Skip Reynolds, engrg mgr; John Batson, chief engr. ■ On 29 CATVs—108,419 subs. ■ Rates: $100; 75; 50.

Alaska

Anchorage

*****KAKM**—ch 7, 165 kw vis, 16.5 kw aur, ant 750t/808g. TL: N61 25 22 W149 52 20. On air date: May 7, 1975. 3877 University Dr. (99508). (907) 563-7070. FAX: (907) 273-9192. Licensee: Alaska Public Television Inc. ■ Net: PBS. Wash atty: Dow, Lohnes & Albertson. ■ Dean Hoke, gen mgr; James V. Alexander, opns mgr; Dick Enders, progmg mgr; Frank A. Mengel, chief engr. ■ On 4 CATVs—100,000 subs.

KDMD—ch 33, 5,000 kw vis, 500 kw aur, ant 98t. TL: N61 09 57 W149 54 01. Hrs opn: 24. On air date: February 1990. Suite 220, 6921 Brayton Dr. (99507). (907) 344-7817. FAX: (907) 344-7817. Licensee: GREENTV Corp. (acq 1-31-92; $75,000; 2-17-92). ■ Frank Martin, gen mgr, adv mgr, progmg mgr & chief engr; Donnie Webb, prom mgr. ■ On one CATV—52,000 subs.

KIMO—ch 13, 38.1 kw vis, 7.76 kw aur, ant 100t/250g. TL: N61 11 52 W149 52 31. On air date: Oct 31, 1967. 2700 E. Tudor Rd. (99507). (907) 561-1313. FAX: (907) 561-1377. Licensee: The Alaska 13 Corp. (acq 5-28-71; grpsl; 6-21-71). ■ Net: ABC. Rep: Katz. ■ Irwin Starrn, gen mgr; B.G. Randlett, vp opns & vp engrg; Wanda Givens, sls dir & mktg mgr; Larry Hogue, natl sls mgr; Winnifred Lange, prom mgr; David Geesin, progmg dir & film buyer; Dan Grubb, news dir. ■ On 74 trans. ■ Rates: $600; 110; 60.

KTBY—ch 4, 38.9 kw vis, 7.8 kw aur, ant 180t. TL: N61 13 11 W149 53 24. Hrs opn: 24. On air date: Dec 2, 1983. Suite 101, 1840 S. Bragaw St. (99508). (907) 274-0404. FAX: (907) 264-5180. Licensee: KTBY Inc. Ownership: Ronald K. Bradley, 100% (acq 12-31-84; 1,000,000; 1-7-85). ■ Net: Fox. Rep: Seltel. Wash atty: Dow, Lohnes & Albertson. ■ Ronald K. Bradley, CEO, pres & gen mgr; Marguerite F. Bradley, CFO; Sean M. Bradley, stn mgr & gen sls mgr; Terri Bradley, opns mgr & progmg dir; Chris Monroe, prom mgr; Mike Boslet, chief engr. ■ On 4 CATVs—50,000 subs.

KTUU-TV—ch 2, 100 kw vis, 10 kw aur, 721t/715g. TL: N61 25 22 W149 52 20. On air date: December 1953. Box 102880, 630 N. 4th Ave. (99510). (907) 257-0202. FAX: (907) 276-5888; (907) 274-3318. Licensee: Ch 2 Bsctg Co. Ownership: Zaser & Longston Inc. (acq 3-81; grpsl). ■ Net: NBC. Rep: Blair. ■ Jessica L. Longston, pres; Al Bramstedt Jr., gen mgr; Bill Dowd, opns mgr; Al Bramstedt, Jr., gen sls mgr; Nancy Johnson, mktg mgr & film buyer; Greg Lytle, prom mgr; Sandy Moore, progmg dir; John Tracy, news dir; Leland Verschueren, chief engr. ■ On 2 CATVs—48,000 subs. On 4 trans.

KTVA—ch 11, 45.0 kw vis, 5.0 kw aur, 300t/392g. TL: N61 11 33 W149 54 01. Stereo. Hrs opn: 24. On air date: Dec 11, 1953. 1007 W. 32nd Ave. (99503); Box 102200 (99510-5516). (907) 562-3456; (907) 561-4200. FAX: (907) 562-0953. Licensee: Northern TV Inc. (group owner). ■ Net: CBS. Rep: Adam Young; Art Moore. Wash atty: Wilkinson, Barker, Knauer & Quinn. News staff 10; news progmg 4 hrs wkly. ■ A.G. Hiebert, CEO & chmn; Julianna Guy, pres, CFO & gen mgr; Bruce Sloan, vp opns & vp progmg; Steven R. Strait, gen sls mgr; Melissa Addams, prom mgr; Steve MacDonald, news dir; Duane Millsap, chief engr. ■ On 4 CATVs—65,000 subs. On 12 trans. Co-owned radio: KBYR(AM)-KNIK-FM. ■ Rates: $350; 200; 45.

KYES—ch 5, 100 kw vis, 10 kw aur, ant -879t/160g. TL: N61 20 10 W149 30 50. Stereo. (CP: 5.9 kw vis; ant 82 ft). Hrs opn: 24. On air date: November 1989. 3700 Woodland Dr., #600 (99517). (907) 248-5937. FAX: (907) 243-0709. Licensee: Fireweed Communications Corp. Ownership: Jeremy Lansman (51%), Carol Schatz (49%) (acq 12-11-91; $100 & assumption of debt; 1-6-92). Rep: Roslin. Wash atty: Benjamin Perez. News progmg one hr wkly. ■ Jeremy Lansman, pres & chief engr; Carol Schatz, gen mgr & progmg dir; E. Parker, opns dir; R. Fessanden, chief opns; Sandra Jones, vp sls; Janet Taylor, prom mgr. ■ On 2 CATVs—72,000 subs. ■ Rates: $85; 65; 25.

***KZXC**—ch 9, 316 kw vis, ant 781 ft. TL: N61 25 22 W149 52 20. Not on air, target date unknown. 3211 Providence Dr., K-102 (99508). (907) 786-1626. Permittee: University of Alaska.

Bethel

***KYUK-TV**—ch 4, 4.68 kw vis, 933 w aur, ant 206t/253g. TL: N60 47 33 W161 46 22. On air date: August 1973. Pouch 468 (99559). (907) 543-3131. Licensee: Bethel Broadcasting Inc. ■ Net: PBS, ABC, CBS, NBC. Wash atty: Wilkinson, Barker, Knauer & Quinn. Yupik Eskimo 2 hrs wkly. News staff 5; news progmg 3 hrs wkly. ■ Andrew Guy, pres; John A. McDonald, gen mgr; Jennifer Duford, dev dir; Allen Auxier, progmg dir; Rhonda McBride, news dir; Joe Siebert, chief engr. ■ On one CATV—500 subs. Co-owned radio: KYUK(AM).

Fairbanks

KATN—ch 2, 28.2 kw vis, 5.5 kw aur, ant 200t/151g. TL: N64 50 42 W147 42 52. On air date: March 1, 1955. Suite 400, 516 2nd Ave. (99701). (907) 452-2125. Licensee: Fairbanks TV Inc. Ownership: Alaska Television Net (acq 7-1-84; $2 million). ■ Net: ABC, NBC. Rep: Katz. News progmg one hr wkly. ■ Bob Underwood, sr vp & gen mgr; Suzanne Pep, dev dir; Terri Beck, gen sls mgr; Jennifer Twomey, prom mgr; Terry Hotaling, progmg dir; Buck Mahler, news dir; Dan Spliethof, engrg mgr. ■ On 3 CATVs—30,000 subs. On 9 trans.

KTVF—ch 11, 50 kw vis, 5 kw aur, ant 50t/168g. TL: N64 50 36 W147 42 48. On air date: Feb 17, 1955. 3528 International (99701). (907) 452-5121. FAX: (907) 452-5120. Licensee: Northern Television Inc. (group owner). ■ Net: CBS, NBC. Rep: Adam Young, Art Moore. Wash atty: Wilkinson, Barker, Knauer & Quinn. News staff 5; news progmg 5 hrs wkly. ■ Henry H. Hove, pres; Meg Gaydosik, opns mgr & prom mgr; Sally Crawford, gen sls mgr; Melissa Lewis, progmg dir; Chuck Hinde, news dir. ■ On 4 CATVs—6,500 subs. On 4 trans. Co-owned radio: KCBF(AM). ■ Rates: $190; 75; 50.

***KUAC-TV**—ch 9, 46.8 kw vis, 8.33 kw aur, ant 500t/151g. TL: N64 54 42 W147 46 38. On air date: Dec 22, 1971. Box 755620, Univ. of Alaska-Fairbanks (99775-5620). (907) 474-7491. Licensee: U. of Alaska. ■ Net: PBS. ■ Joan K. Wadlow, CEO; Bruce L. Smith, gen mgr; Kara Metty, dev dir; Richard G. Ruff, progmg dir; Mark O. Badger, pub affrs dir; Tom McGrane, engrg dir. ■ On 4 CATVs. On 4 trans. Co-owned radio: *KUAC-FM.

Juneau

KJUD—ch 8, 239 w vis, 47 w aur, ant 1,160t/69g. TL: N58 18 06 W134 26 29. On air date: Feb 19, 1956. 1107 W. 8th St. (99801). (907) 586-3145. FAX: (907) 463-3041. Licensee: Alaska 13 Corp. Ownership: Duane L. Triplett, Richard M. Zook, B.G. Randlett (acq 11-24-82; $275,000). ■ Net: ABC, NBC. Rep: Katz. Wash atty: Haley, Bader & Potts. News staff 2; news progmg 3 hrs wkly. ■ Elizabeth Arnett, gen mgr & gen sls mgr; George Heacock, opns dir & chief engr; Gail Tilson, prom mgr & progmg dir; Gary Essex, news dir. ■ On one CATV—6,000 subs.

***KTOO-TV**—ch 3, 2.45 kw vis, .49 kw aur, ant -1,016t/259g. TL: N58 18 4 W134 25 21. On air date: Oct 1, 1978. 224 Fourth St. (99801-1198). (907) 586-1670. FAX: (907) 586-3612. Licensee: Capital Community Broadcasting Inc. ■ Net: PBS. Wash atty: Schwartz, Woods & Miller. ■ Bill Legere, pres & gen mgr; Lori Brothenton, vp; Ron Clarke, dev dir; Sarah McDaniel, prom dir; Betsy Brenneman, progmg dir; Claire Richardson, pub affrs dir; Jack McKain, engrg dir. ■ On 6 CATVs—18,000 subs. On 8 trans. Co-owned radio: KTOO(FM).

North Pole

KJNP-TV—ch 4, 18.66 kw vis, 2.8 kw aur, ant 1,619t/191g. TL: N64 52 44 W 148 03 10. On air date: Dec 7, 1981. Box O (99705). (907) 488-2216. Licensee: Evangelistic Alaska Missionary Fellowship. Wash atty: Fletcher, Heald & Hildreth. ■ Donald L. Nelson, pres; Roger Skold, gen mgr & news dir; Richard T. Olson, gen sls mgr; Julie K. Arestad, prom mgr; Beverly Olson, progmg dir; Eric Nichols, chief engr. ■ Co-owned radio: KNJP-AM-FM.

Sitka

KTNL—ch 13, 199 w vis, 30 w aur, ant -782t/155g. TL: N57 03 27 W135 20 02 (CP: 2.25 kw vis, ant -843t, TL: N57 03 02 W135 20 03). On air date: Sept 1, 1966. Box 1309, Lloyd's Center, 520 Lake St. (99835-1309). (907) 747-6002. FAX: (907) 747-6003. Licensee: Sitka News Bureau Inc. Ownership: Marty W. Baggen (acq 5-10-83; $250,000; 12-2-91). ■ Net: CBS, ABC. Rep: Tacher. Wash atty: Haley, Bader & Potts. News staff 3; news progmg 5 hrs wkly. ■ Marty Baggen, pres & sls dir; Jeff Seifert, gen mgr, opns mgr & progmg mgr; Carrie Baggen, vp opns & adv dir; Bob Barger, news dir; Dennis Lanham, chief engr. ■ On one CATV—2,800 subs.

Arizona

Flagstaff

ADI No. 204; see Flagstaff market

KKTM—ch 13, 1 kw vis, ant 1,778t. TL: N35 14 29 W111 36 33. Hrs opn: 24. On air date: 1991. Box 3808 2158 N. 4th St. (86003). (602) 527-1300. FAX: (602) 527-1394. Licensee: Michael C. Gelfand M.D. News staff 2; news progmg 2 hrs wkly. ■ Dr. Michael Gelfand, pres; Ernie Durst, vp; Beverly C. Bishop, gen mgr, gen sls mgr, adv dir & progmg dir; Gregg Cooper, news dir; Ray Matzkanir, chief engr. ■ On 5 CATVs. ■ Rates: $50; 20; 15.

KNAZ-TV—ch 2, 100 kw vis, 5 kw aur, ant 1,597t/284g. TL: N34 58 06 W111 30 28. On air date: May 2, 1970. 2201 N. Vickey St. (86004). (602) 526-2232. FAX: (602) 526-8110. Licensee: Grand Canyon Television Co. Group owner: Grand Canyon Television Company Inc. (acq 5-7-92). ■ Net: NBC. Rep: Katz. Wash atty: Dow, Lohnes & Albertson. ■ Dan Robbins, vp & gen mgr; Stan Koplowitz, sls dir; Shawn Harrison, prom mgr; Marge Devine, progmg dir; Nick Matesi, news dir; Gary Kabrick, chief engr. ■ On 12 CATVs—40,000 subs. On 5 trans.

KZJC—ch 4, 100 kw vis, ant 377t. TL: N35 04 24 W111 34 06. Not on air, target date unknown. Box 3434, Fort Pierce, FL (33454). Permittee: WTWV Inc.

Green Valley

ADI No. 79; see Tucson market

KXGR—ch 46, 4,898 kw vis, Ant 2,037t. TL: N32 14 56 W111 06 59. Not on air, target date unknown. 2309 N. Hampton, Tucson (85719). Permittee: Sungilt Corp.

Kingman

ADI No. 21; see Phoenix market

KMOH-TV—ch 6, 100 kw vis, 10 kw aur, ant 1,920t. TL: N35 01 57 W114 21 56. On air date: Feb 22, 1988. Suite 9, 1355 Ramar Rd., Bullhead City (86442). (602) 758-7333. FAX: (602) 758-8139. Licensee: Grand Canyon Television Co. Inc. (group owner; acq 5-7-92; with KNAZ-TV Flagstaff; 6-15-92). Rep: Katz. Wash atty: Dow, Lohnes & Albertson. News staff 19; news progmg 9 hrs wkly. ■ Dan Robbins, vp & gen mgr; Stan Koplowitz, sls dir & gen sls mgr; Bill Thomas, prom mgr; Marge Divine, progmg mgr; Gary Kabrick, engrg dir. ■ On 5 CATVs—23,500 subs. On one trans.

Mesa

KPNX—Licensed to Mesa. See Phoenix.

Phoenix

ADI No. 21; see Phoenix market

***KAET**—ch 8, 316 kw vis, 47.9 kw aur, ant 1,756t/346g. TL: N33 20 00 W112 03 49. Stereo. Hrs opn: 24. On air date: Jan 30, 1961. Stauffer Hall B-wing, Arizona State Univ., Tempe (85287-1405). (602) 965-3506. FAX: (602) 965-1000. Licensee: Arizona Board of Regents. ■ Net: PBS. Wash atty: Schwartz, Woods & Miller. Sp one hr, Japanese one hr wkly. News staff 7; news progmg 3 hrs wkly. ■ Charles R. Allen, gen mgr; Beth Vershure, stn mgr; John Martinez, opns mgr; John Lang, mktg mgr; Patti Anderson, prom mgr; John Wilson, progmg mgr & film buyer; Michael Wong, news dir; Joseph Manning, engrg mgr. ■ On 85 CATVs—559,490 subs. On 16 trans. Co-owned radio: KJZZ-FM, KBAQ-FM.

KNXV-TV—ch 15, 631 kw vis, 63.1 kw aur, ant 1,710t/282g. TL: N33 20 00 W112 03 46. On air date: Sept 9, 1979. 4625 S. 33rd Pl. (85040). (602) 243-4151. FAX: (602) 232-5995. Licensee: Scripps Howard Broadcasting Co. (group owner, see Cross-Ownership; acq 1-9-85; $26.6 million). ■ Net: Fox. Rep: Katz. Wash atty: Baker & Hostetler. ■ Ray Hunt, gen mgr; Jon Keaton, opns mgr; Carolyn McBurney, prom mgr; Bill Franks, progmg dir; Don Thomas, chief engr. ■ Rates: $500; 400; 75.

***KPAZ-TV**—ch 21, 1,282 kw vis, 247 kw aur, ant 2,143t/178g. TL: N33 20 03 W112 03 42. On air date: Sept 16, 1967. 3551 E. McDowell (85008). (602) 273-1477. FAX: (602) 267-9427. Licensee: Trinity Bcstg of Ariz. Inc. Group owner: Trinity Broadcasting Network (acq 1977). Wash atty: May & Dunne. ■ Paul F. Crouch, pres & gen mgr; Mrs. Billie Watts, stn mgr; Virginia Gonzales, progmg dir & pub affrs dir; Gary Nichols, chief engr. ■ On 10 CATVs—30,000 subs. On 3 trans.

KPHO-TV—ch 5, 100 kw vis, 10 kw aur, ant 1,770t/387g. TL: N33 20 02 W112 03 40. Stereo. Hrs opn: 24. On air date: Dec 4, 1949. Box 20100 (85036); 4016 N. Black Canyon (85017). (602) 264-1000. FAX: (602) 263-8818. Licensee: Meredith Corp. Group owner: Meredith Bcstg Group, Meredith Corp. See Cross-Ownership (acq 6-25-52; grpsl; 6-30-52). Rep: MMT. Wash atty: Haley, Bader & Potts. News staff 23; news progmg 11 hrs wkly. ■ Patrick North, vp & gen mgr; Rich Engberg, gen sls mgr; Greg Brannan, progmg mgr; Graham Robertson, news dir; Gene Steinburg, chief engr. ■ On 7 CATVs—573,100 subs. On 23 trans.

KPNX—(Mesa). ch 12, 316 kw vis, 46.8 kw aur, ant 1,780t/350g. TL: N33 20 00 W112 03 48. Stereo. Hrs opn: 24. On air date: April 23, 1953. Box 711, Phoenix (85001); 1101 N. Central Ave., Phoenix (85004). (602) 257-1212. FAX: (602) 258-8186; (602) 257-6619 NEWS. Licensee: KPNX Broadcasting Co. Group owner: Gannett Co. Inc. (acq 6-7-79; grpsl; 6-11-79). ■ Net: NBC. Rep: Blair. Wash atty: Reed, Smith, Shaw & McClay. News staff 70. ■ C.E. "Pep" Cooney, pres & gen mgr; Paul Trelstad, gen sls mgr; Jeff Bumton, natl sls mgr; John Turver, rgnl sls mgr; Donna Vogt, prom dir; Lynn Beall, vp progmg; Bob Sullivan, news dir; Lucia Madrid, pub affrs dir; Chuck Deen, vp engrg. ■ On 15 CATVs—20,000 subs.

KTSP-TV—ch 10, 316 kw vis, 47 kw aur, ant 1,700t/264g. TL: N33 20 03 W112 03 43. (CP: Ant 1,829t). On air date: Oct 24, 1953. 511 W. Adams St.

(85003). (602) 257-1234. FAX: (602) 271-9477; (602) 262-0456 (SALES). Licensee: Great American TV & Radio Co. Inc. Group owner: Great American Broadcasting (acq 10-7-87). ■ Net: CBS. Rep: Harrington, Righter & Parsons. Wash atty: Koteen & Naftalin. ■ Ron Bergamo, pres; Don Locke, vp & gen sls mgr; Jim Girodo, mktg dir; Tom Dolan, news dir; Al Hillstrom, chief engr. ■ On 61 CATVs—190,714 subs. On 27 trans. ■ Rates: $3000; 500; 300.

KTVK—ch 3, 100 kw vis, 15.1 kw aur, ant 1,670t/231g. TL: N33 20 01 W112 03 45. (CP: Ant 1,778t). On air date: Feb 28, 1955. 3435 N. 16th St. (85016); Box 5068 (85010). (602) 263-3333. FAX: (602) 263-3377. Licensee: Media America Corp. Ownership: Delbert R. Lewis, 57% ■ Net: ABC. Rep: Telerep. ■ Jewell M. Lewis, chmn; Delbert R. Lewis, gen mgr; Bill Miller, stn mgr & vp opns; Jim Galvin, gen sls mgr; Lynn Lovick Handley, prom mgr; Sue Schwartz, progmg dir; Phil Alvidrez, news dir; Marlene Klotz, pub affrs dir; William Lawrence, chief engr. ■ On 6 CATVs. On 16 trans. Co-owned radio: KESZ-FM.

KTVW-TV—ch 33, 2,290 kw vis, 229 kw aur, ant 1,710t/282g. TL: N33 20 00 W112 03 46. On air date: Sept 2, 1979. 3019 E. Southern Ave. (85040). (602) 243-3333. FAX: (602) 276-8658. Licensee: KTVW Inc. Group owner: Perenchio Television Inc. (acq 5-17-89; $23 million; 6-5-89). ■ Net: Univision. Sp full-time. ■ Ruben R. Luera, vp & gen mgr; Tom Kloski, opns mgr; Blaine R. Decker, gen sls mgr; Virginia Luna, progmg dir & pub affrs dir; Carlos Jurado, news dir; Bruce Sherman, chief engr. ■ On 7 CATVs—60,000 subs. On one trans.

KUTP—ch 45, 2,750 kw vis, 275 kw aur, ant 1,792t/381g. TL: N33 20 01 W112 03 32. Stereo. Hrs opn: 24. On air date: Dec 23, 1985. 4630 S. 33rd St. (85040). (602) 268-4500. FAX: (602) 276-4082. Licensee: KUTP/United Television Inc. Group owner: United Television Inc. Rep: Petry. Wash atty: Wilmer, Cutler & Pickering. ■ Bob Furlong, vp & gen mgr; Seth Parker, opns dir, progmg dir & pub affrs dir; Mike Durand, gen sls mgr; Curtis Pap, natl sls mgr; Kathlene Riter, prom mgr; Tom Foy, chief engr. ■ On 51 CATVs—493,000 subs. On 7 trans.

Prescott

ADI No. 21; see Phoenix market

KUSK—ch 7, 8.79 kw vis, 1.76 kw aur, ant 2,814t/120g. TL: N34 41 15 W112 07 01. On air date: Sept 5, 1982. 3211 Tower Dr. (86301). (602) 778-6770. FAX: (602) 445-5210. Licensee: KUSK Inc. Ownership: William H. Sauro, 53% Wash atty: Leventhal, Senter & Lerman. News progmg 6 hrs wkly. ■ William H. Sauro, pres; Rich Howe, gen mgr & vp sls; Patricia Gray-Stone, vp opns & progmg dir; Tonya Mock, prom mgr, news dir & pub affrs dir; Wally Macomber, chief engr. ■ On 14 CATVs—231,500 subs. On 6 trans. ■ Rates: $120; 90; 50.

Tucson

ADI No. 79; see Tucson market

KGUN—ch 9, 110 kw vis, 21.94 kw aur, 3,722t/237g. TL: N32 24 54 W110 42 59. Stereo. Hrs opn: 20. On air date: June 3, 1956. Box 17990 (85731-7990); 7280 E. Rosewood St. (85710). (602) 722-5486. FAX: (602) 290-7642; (602) 290-7636. Licensee: KGUN Inc. Group owner: Lee Enterprises Inc. (acq 11-7-86; grpsl; 10-6-86). ■ Net: ABC. Rep: Katz. Wash atty: Pierson, Ball & Dowd. News staff 32; news progmg 13 hrs wkly. ■ Karen Lee Rice, gen mgr; Debra Hastings, opns mgr & progmg dir; Andrew Stewart, gen sls mgr; Martin Camacho, prom mgr; Bill Cummings, news dir; Martin Glos, chief engr. ■ On 18 CATVs—110,000 subs. On 4 trans. ■ Rates: $400; 90; 80.

KHRR—ch 40, 1,534 kw vis, 153.4 kw aur, ant 2,090t/199.5g. TL: N32 14 55 W111 06 57. Stereo. Hrs opn: 6 AM-1:30 AM. On air date: Jan 1, 1985. 2919 E. Broadway, Garden Level (85716). (602) 322-6888. FAX: (602) 881-7926. Licensee: Jay S. Zucker (acq 10-16-91; $45,000; 11-16-91). Rep: Telemundo. News staff 2; news progmg 3 hrs wkly. ■ Jay S. Zucker, CEO, pres & gen mgr; Dale Taylor, opns mgr & chief engr; Patty Ruiz, gen sls mgr; Lupita Celaya, prom dir; Melinda Miranda Zucker, progmg dir; Abelardo Oquita, news dir; Joe Goodale, engrg mgr. ■ On 5 CATVs. On one trans. ■ Rates: $125; 95; 45.

KMSB-TV—ch 11, 316 kw vis, 15 kw aur, ant 1,662t/200g. Hrs opn: 8:30 AM-5:30 PM. On air date: Feb 1, 1967. 1855 N. 6th Ave. (85705-5661). (602) 770-1123. FAX: (602) 629-7185. Licensee: Mountain States Broadcasting Inc. Group owner: Providence Journal Bcstg Group (acq 11-11-84; $13 million). ■ Net: Fox. Rep: Telerep. Wash atty: Covington & Burling. ■ Ken Middleton, pres & gen mgr; Randy Cantrell, vp; Doug Gervais, prom mgr; Allen Trattner, adv mgr; Harry West, progmg dir & film buyer; Sharry Karam, pub affrs dir; Roy Mitchell, chief engr. ■ On 23 CATVs—153,992 subs. ■ Rates: $125; 100; 40.

KOLD-TV—ch 13, 107 kw vis, 15.6 kw aur, ant 3,610t/201g. TL: N32 24 57 W110 42 49. (CP: 302 kw vis, ant 2,040t/187g. TL: N32 14 56 W110 06 58). On air date: Jan 13, 1953. 115 W. Drachman St. (85705). (602) 624-2511. FAX: (602) 629-8553; TWX: 910-952-1122. Licensee: New Vision Television I Inc. Group owner: New Vision Television Inc. (acq 9-7-93; $110 million as part of eight-stn sale; 9-27-93). ■ Net: CBS. Wash atty: Dow, Lohnes & Albertson. Sp progmg. ■ David Joseph, vp & gen mgr; Matt Malyn, news dir; Jimmie A. Stembridge, chief engr. ■ On 29 CATVs—159,983 subs. On 3 trans.

KTTU-TV—ch 18, 2,510 kw vis, 251 kw aur, ant 1,970t/200g. TL: N32 14 55 W111 06 57. Hrs opn: 8:30 AM-5:30 PM. On air date: Dec 31, 1984. 1855 N. 6th Ave. (85705). (602) 624-0180. FAX: (602) 629-7185. Licensee: Clear Channel Television Licenses Inc. (group owner; acq 8-5-92). Rep: ITS. Wash atty: Hogan & Hartson. Sp one hr wkly. ■ Bishop Manuel D. Moreno, pres; Jack Jacobson, gen mgr; Frank C. Idaspe, gen sls mgr; Doug Gervais, prom mgr; Allen Trattner, adv mgr; Harry West, progmg dir; Lynn Sertich, pub affrs dir; Roy Mitchell, chief engr. ■ On 7 CATVs—95,257 subs.

***KUAS-TV**—ch 27, 151 kw vis, 15.1 kw aur, 570t/15g. TL: N32 12 53 W111 00 21. (CP: 30.2 kw vis). On air date: January 1986. U. of Arizona (85721). (602) 621-5828. FAX: (602) 621-9105. Licensee: Arizona Board of Regents/Univ. of Arizona ■ Net: PBS. Wash atty: Dow, Lohnes & Albertson. Sp one hr wkly. ■ Donald Burgess, gen mgr & progmg dir; Michael Serres, prom mgr; Olivia Smith, film buyer; Hector Gonzalez, news dir; Tom Boone, chief engr. Co-owned radio: *KUAT-AM-FM.

***KUAT-TV**—ch 6, 35.5 kw vis, 3.5 kw aur, ant 3,630t/196g. TL: N32 24 55 W110 42 54. On air date: March 8, 1959. Univ. of Arizona (85721). (602) 621-5828. FAX: (602) 621-9105. Licensee: Arizona Board of Regents, Univ. of Arizona. ■ Net: PBS. Wash atty: Dow, Lohnes & Albertson. Sp 7 hrs wkly. ■ Donald Burgess, gen mgr; Michael Serres, prom mgr; Olivia Smith, progmg dir & film buyer; Hector Gonzalez, news dir; Tom Boone, chief engr. ■ On 33 CATVs—29,338 subs. On one trans. Co-owned radio: *KUAT-AM-FM.

KVOA-TV—ch 4, 35 kw vis, 18 kw aur, ant 3,610t/223g. TL: N32 12 53 W111 00 20. Stereo. Hrs opn: 24. On air date: Sept 15, 1953. Box 5188 (85703); 209 W. Elm St. (85705). (602) 792-2270. FAX: (602) 620-1309. Licensee: KVOA Communications Inc. (acq 10-28-93; $13.25 million; 11-15-93). ■ Net: NBC. Rep: Petry. Wash atty: Dow, Lohnes & Albertson. News staff 43; news progmg 18 hrs wkly. ■ Jon F. Ruby, vp; Bob Manown, vp sls; Jodi Thompson, prom mgr; David Hatfield, vp progmg; Mick Jensen, news dir; Ralph Turk, vp engrg. ■ On 32 CATVs—179,928 subs. On 19 trans.

Yuma

ADI No. 178; see El Centro, CA-Yuma market

KSWT—ch 13, 316 kw vis, 31.6 kw aur, ant 1,700t/203g. TL: N33 03 17 W114 49 34. Stereo. Hrs opn: 5:45 AM-3 AM. On air date: Dec 1, 1963. Box 592, 1301 3rd Ave. (85364); Suite 316, 1681 W. Main St., El Centro CA (92243). (602) 782-5113. FAX: (602) 782-0320. Licensee: KB Media Inc. Ownership: John A. Radeck, 33.3%; William H. Sanders, 33.3% Kenneth L. Bazzle, 33.3% ■ Net: Katz, Telemundo. Rep: Katz. Wash atty: Fletcher, Heald & Hildreth. Sp 21 hrs wkly. News staff 12; news progmg 7 hrs wkly. ■ John Radeck, pres; Peter Padilla, gen mgr, gen sls mgr & film buyer; Vern Batterson, rgnl sls mgr; Jerry Rosner, prom mgr; Ashley Webster, news dir; Dick Sampson, chief engr. ■ On 8 CATVs—65,000 subs. On 2 trans.

KYMA—ch 11, 316 kw vis, 31.6 kw aur, 518t/1,617g. TL: N33 03 10 W114 49 40. On air date: January 1988. Box 550 (85366); 1385 S. Pacific Ave. (85365). (602) 782-1111. FAX: (602) 782-5401. Licensee: Sunbelt Broadcasting Co. (acq 6-6-89; $60,000; 6-26-89). ■ Net: ABC. Rep: Blair. ■ Jim Rogers, pres; Bruce Franzen, gen mgr; Jack O'Connor, gen sls mgr; Cathy Dafpe, progmg dir; Ken Booth, news dir; Dick Wellman, chief engr. ■ On 4 CATVs.

Arkansas

Arkadelphia

ADI No. 56; see Little Rock market

***KETG**—ch 9, 316 kw vis, 31.6 kw aur, ant 1,070t/1,110g. TL: N33 54 26 W93 06 46. On air date: Oct 2, 1976. Box 1250, 350 S. Donaghey St., Conway (72032). (501) 450-1727; (501) 682-2386. FAX: (501) 682-4122. Licensee: Arkansas Educational Television Commission. ■ Net: PBS; SECA. Wash atty: Dow, Lohnes & Albertson. ■ Susan J. Howarth, gen mgr; Allen Weatherly, stn mgr; Mike McCullars, dev dir; Ron Johnson, prom mgr & adv dir; Kathy Atkinson, progmg dir; Ray Nielsen, film buyer; Gary Schultz, engrg dir. ■ On one trans.

El Dorado

ADI No. 131; see Monroe, LA-El Dorado market

KNOE-TV—See Monroe, La.

KTVE—ch 10, 316 kw vis, 63.1 kw aur, ant 2,027t/2,001g. TL: N33 04 41 W92 13 31. On air date: Dec 3, 1955. 2909 Kilpatrick Blvd., Monroe, LA (71201); 400 W. Main St., El Dorado (71730). (318) 323-1300; (501) 862-6651. TWX: 510-977-5386. Licensee: KTVE Inc. Group owner: Gray Communications Systems Inc. (acq 12-4-67; $3.25 million; 12-11-67). ■ Net: NBC. Rep: Katz. Wash atty: Sidley & Austin. News staff 26; news progmg 11 hrs wkly. ■ John Williams, pres; Andy Lee, gen mgr & film buyer; David Clark, opns mgr; David Brown, gen sls mgr; Susan Allain, prom mgr; Ginger McMullen, progmg dir; Jerry Mayer, news dir; Mike Caruso, chief engr. ■ On 49 CATVs—85,419 subs. ■ Rates: $300; 125; 50.

Fayetteville

ADI No. 117; see Fort Smith market

***KAFT**—ch 13, 316 kw vis, 31.6 kw aur, ant 1,660t/1,138g. TL: N35 48 53 W94 01 41. On air date: 1976. Box 1250, 350 S. Donaghey St., Conway (72032). (501) 450-1727; (501) 682-2386. FAX: (501) 682-4122. Licensee: Arkansas Educational Television Commission. ■ Net: PBS; SECA. Wash atty: Dow, Lohnes & Albertson. ■ Susan J. Howarth, gen mgr; Allen Weatherly, stn mgr; Mike McCullars, dev dir; Ron Johnson, prom mgr & adv dir; Kathy Atkinson, progmg dir; Ray Nielsen, film buyer; Gary Schultz, engrg dir. ■ On one trans.

KHBS—See Fort Smith.

KHOG-TV—ch 29, 1,410 kw vis, 150 kw aur, ant 890t/556g. TL: N36 00 57 W94 04 59. Hrs opn: 24 Sun-Fri. On air date: December 1977. Box 1029, 15 N. Church St. (72702). (501) 521-1010. FAX: (501) 521-9124. Licensee: Sigma Broadcasting Group owner: Sigma Broadcasting Inc. (acq 2-19-85; grpsl). ■ Net: ABC. Rep: Petry. News staff 18; news progmg 17 hrs wkly. ■ Darrel Cunningham, CEO, pres & gen mgr; Bob Hemreich, chmn; Cliff Walker, vp & stn mgr; Scott Morgan, opns mgr; Ron Evans, gen sls mgr; Tim Bass, progmg dir; Marvin Macedo, chief engr. ■ On 21 CATVs—70,000 subs. ■ Rates: $300; 170; 40.

Fort Smith

ADI No. 117; see Fort Smith market

KFSM-TV—ch 5, 100 kw vis, 12.7 kw aur, ant 1,086t/1,173g. TL: N35 30 43 W94 21 38. Stereo. On air date: Dec 3, 1956. Box 369, 318 N. 13th St. (72902). (501) 783-3131. FAX: (501) 783-3131, ext. 222. Licensee: Times Southwest Broadcasting Co. Group owner: The New York Times Co. (acq 8-6-79; $17.5 million; 8-13-79). ■ Net: CBS. Rep: Katz. Wash atty: Koteen & Naftalin. ■ Robert Eoff, pres & gen mgr; Gene Graham, gen sls mgr; Jim Bell, mktg dir; Mary Lee Frase, prom mgr; Jim Turpin, news dir; Larry Duncan, chief engr.

KHBS—ch 40, 3,160 kw vis, 316 kw aur, ant 2,000t/500g. TL: N35 04 16 W94 40 46. On air date: July 28, 1971. Box 4150 (72904); 2415 N. Albert Pike (72914). (501) 783-4040. FAX: (501) 783-0550. Licensee: Sigma Broadcasting Inc. (group owner; acq 2-19-85; grpsl). ■ Net: ABC. Rep: Petry. Wash atty: Farrow, Schildhause, Wilson & Rains. ■ Robert Hernreich, chmn; Darrel E. Cunningham, pres & gen mgr; Cynthia Hemreich, sr vp; Don Vest, vp opns & vp engrg; Jarrell Wyatt, vp sls; Lori

Evans, prom mgr; Tim Bass, progmg dir; Craig Cannon, news dir. ■ Rates: $400; 240; 70.

KHOG-TV—See Fayetteville.

KPOM-TV—ch 24, 2,510 kw vis, 251 kw aur, ant 1,040t/499g. TL: N35 42 37 W94 08 15. On air date: Nov 12, 1978. Box 4610 (72914). (501) 785-2400. TWX: 910-720-0029. Licensee: JDG Television Inc. Ownership: Griffin Entities. ■ Net: NBC. Rep: Telerep. Wash atty: Fletcher, Heald & Hildreth. ■ Mike Hart, opns mgr; Lori Archer, prom mgr; Verlene Tadlock, progmg dir; Charles Hoing, chief engr. ■ On 50 CATVs—87,656 subs.

Hot Springs

ADI No. 56; see Little Rock market

KRZB-TV—ch 26, 245 kw vis, 24.5 kw aur, ant 941t. TL: N32 22 20 W93 02 47. (CP: 5,000 kw vis, ant 902t, TL: N34 22 17 W93 02 16). On air date: 1991. Box 25616, Little Rock (72221-5616). (501) 525-4726. Licensee: PPD & G Inc.

Jonesboro

ADI No. 177; see Jonesboro market

NEW TV—ch 48, 1,062 kw vis, ant 1,017t. Not on air, target date unknown. 9165 White Dr., Cord (72524). Permittee: Arkansas Rural Television Co.

KAIT-TV—ch 8, 316 kw vis, 47.9 kw aur, ant 1,750t/1,799g. TL: N35 53 17 W90 56 09. Stereo. On air date: July 15, 1963. Box 790 (72403-0790); Hwy. 141 N. (72401). (501) 931-8888. FAX: (501) 933-8058; (501) 933-6503. Licensee: Cosmos Broadcasting Corp. (group owner; acq 11-12-86; grpsl). ■ Net: ABC. Rep: Harrington, Righter & Parsons. Wash atty: Dow, Lohnes & Albertson. News staff 20; news progmg 10 hrs wkly. ■ Clyde Anderson, stn mgr; Linda Rega, prom mgr; Toni Innboden, progmg dir; Will Corporon, news dir; Gerald Erickson, chief engr. ■ On 115 CATVs—192,000 subs. On one trans. ■ Rates: $650; 320; 125.

*KTEJ—ch 19, 1,230 kw vis, 123 kw aur, ant 1,020t/969g. TL: N35 54 14 W90 46 14. On air date: May 1, 1976. Box 1250, 350 S. Donaghey, Conway (72032). (501) 450-1727; (501) 682-2386. FAX: (501) 682-4122. Licensee: Arkansas ETV Commission. ■ Net: PBS; SECA. Wash atty: Dow, Lohnes & Albertson. ■ Susan J. Howarth, gen mgr; Allen Weatherly, stn mgr; Mike McCullars, dev dir; Ron Johnson, prom mgr & adv dir; Kathy Atkinson, progmg dir; Ray Nielsen, film buyer; Gary Schultz, engrg dir. ■ On one trans.

Little Rock

ADI No. 56; see Little Rock market

KARK-TV—ch 4, 100 kw vis, 20 kw aur, ant 1,650t/1,175g. TL: N34 47 57 W92 29 59. Stereo. Hrs opn: 24. On air date: Apr 15, 1954. Box 748 (72203). (501) 376-4444. FAX: (501) 376-1852. Licensee: KARK-TV Inc. Group owner: Morris Network Inc. (2-17-83; $25 million). ■ Net: NBC. Rep: Blair. Wash atty: Fletcher, Heald & Hildreth. News staff 40; news progmg 17 hrs wkly. ■ H. Dean Hinson, pres & gen mgr; Tom Bonner, stn mgr; Bob Denman, gen sls mgr; Susan Newkirk, prom mgr; Mitch Chandler, progmg dir; Al Sandabre, news dir; Bill Addington, chief engr. ■ On 104 CATVs—130,583 subs.

KATV—ch 7, 316 kw vis, 36.5 kw aur, 2,272t/2,000g. TL: N34 28 23 W92 12 11. On air date: Dec 18, 1953. Box 77, 401 Main St. (72203); 401 S. Main St. (72201). (501) 324-7777. Licensee: KATV Television Inc. Group owner: Allbritton Communications Co. (acq 2-14-83; grpsl). ■ Net: ABC. Rep: Petry. Wash atty: Hogan & Hartson. ■ Dale Nicholson, pres & gen mgr; Ron Kelly, gen sls mgr; David Hershey, prom dir; Richard Farrester, progmg dir; Jim Pitcock, news dir; Cindy Watkins, pub affrs dir; James Tidwell, chief engr. ■ On 94 CATVs—150,000 subs.

*KETS—ch 2, 100 kw vis, 10 kw aur, ant 1,780t/2,000g. TL: N34 28 23 W92 12 11. Stereo. On air date: Dec 4, 1966. Box 1250, 350 S. Donaghey, Conway (72033). (501) 450-1727; (501) 682-2386. FAX: (501) 682-4122. Licensee: Arkansas ETV Commission. ■ Net: PBS; SECA. Wash atty: Dow, Lohnes & Albertson. ■ Susan J. Howarth, gen mgr; Allen Weatherly, stn mgr; Mike McCullars, dev dir; Ron Johnson, prom mgr & adv dir; Kathy Atkinson, progmg dir; Ray Nielsen, film buyer; Gary Schultz, engrg dir. ■ On one trans.

Carole Adornetto, pub affrs dir; Gary Schultz, engrg dir. ■ On one trans.

KLRT—ch 16, 5,000 kw vis, 500 kw aur, ant 1,772t/1,266g. TL: N34 47 57 W92 29 52. Stereo. Hrs opn: 20. On air date: June 26, 1983. Box 21616 (72221-1616); 11711 W. Markham (72211). (501) 225-0016. FAX: (501) 225-0428. Licensee: Clear Channel Television of Little Rock. Group owner: Clear Channel Communications Inc. (acq 6-19-91; $6.6 million; 7-8-91). ■ Net: Fox. Rep: MMT. Wash atty: Crowell & Moring. ■ Jerry Whitener, gen mgr & stn mgr; Vicki Tenant, progmg dir; Tom McLeroy, chief engr.

KTHV—ch 11, 316 kw vis, 38 kw aur, ant 1,709t. TL: N34 47 57 W92 29 59. Stereo. On air date: Nov 27, 1955. Box 269 (72203); 720 Izard St. (72202). (501) 376-1111. FAX: (501) 376-3719. Licensee: Arkansas Television Co. Ownership: K.A. Engel Trust, 55%; Robert L. Brown, 6%; C. Stanley Berry, 3.6%; Marcus B. George, 4.6%. ■ Net: CBS. Rep: Seltel. Wash atty: Peper, Martin, Jensen, Maichel & Hetlage. ■ Robert L. Brown, pres & gen mgr; Doug Laughter, vp opns; Lonnie Gibbons, natl sls mgr; Suzanne Ramsel, rgnl sls mgr; Dan McFadden, prom dir; Bob Hicks, progmg dir; John Rehrauer, news dir; Fred Anderson, chief engr. ■ On 140 CATVs. On one trans. ■ Rates: $400; 100; 50.

KVUT—ch 42, TL: N34 52 28 W92 00 35. Not on air, target date unknown. 102 Fairmont Circle, Daphne, AL (36526). Permittee: Leininger-Geddes Partnership.

Mountain View

ADI No. 56; see Little Rock market

*KEMV—ch 6, 100 kw vis, 10 kw aur, ant 1,390t/995g. TL: N35 48 47 W92 17 24. On air date: Nov 11, 1980. Box 1250, 350 S. Donaghey, Conway (72032). (501) 450-1727; (501) 682-2386. FAX: (501) 682-4122. Licensee: Arkansas Educational Television Commission. ■ Net: PBS; SECA. Wash atty: Dow, Lohnes & Albertson. ■ Susan J. Howarth, gen mgr; Allen Weatherly, stn mgr; Mike McCullars, dev dir; Ron Johnson, prom mgr & adv dir; Kathy Atkinson, progmg dir; Ray Nielsen, film buyer; Gary Schultz, engrg dir. ■ On one trans.

Newark

ADI No. 56; see Little Rock market

*KLEP—ch 17, 14.9 kw vis, 1.49 kw aur, ant 530t/499g. TL: N35 43 25 W91 26 40. On air date: Jan 1, 1985. 1502 N. Hill St. (72562). (501) 799-8691, ext. 201. FAX: (501) 799-8647. Licensee: Newark Public School System. ■ Fred Ahlborn, stn mgr. ■Co-owned radio: *KLLN(FM).

Pine Bluff

ADI No. 56; see Little Rock market

KASN—ch 38, 5,000 kw vis, 500 kw aur, ant 2,008t/1,910g. TL: N34 26 31 W92 13 03. On air date: June 17, 1986. Box 21616, 11711 W. Markham, Little Rock (72221). (501) 225-0038. FAX: (501) 225-0428. Licensee: Mercury Broadcasting Co. (group owner; acq 12-24-91; $14,299,652; 2-3-92). Rep: Blair. Wash atty: Kenkel & Barnard. ■ Jerry Whitener, gen mgr; Joanne Canelli, gen sls mgr; Kim DeGraw, progmg dir; Tom McKleroy, chief engr.

KVTN—ch 25, 4,368 kw vis, 43.7 kw aur, ant 624t. TL: N34 31 52 W92 02 42. On air date: Dec 1, 1988. Box 22007, Little Rock (72221); 701 Napa Valley, Little Rock (72211). (501) 223-2525. FAX: (501) 221-3837. Licensee: Agape Church Inc. (acq 6-87; $41,000; 5-1-87). Wash atty: John Fiorini. ■ H. L. Caldwell, pres; Randy Wright, gen mgr; Kim Worden, progmg dir; Bob Porto, chief engr.

Rogers

ADI No. 117; see Fort Smith market

KFAA—ch 51, 79.4 kw vis, 500 kw aur, ant 476t. TL: N36 12 15 W94 06 05 (CP: 104 kw vis, ant 469t). Hrs opn: 6 AM-1:30 AM. On air date: Aug 23, 1989. 114 S. First St. (72756). (501) 631-8851; (501) 442-0051. FAX: (501) 631-1853. Licensee: J.D.G. Television. ■ Net: NBC. Rep: Telerep. ■ John Griffin, CEO; David Needham, gen mgr; Chuck Crossno, stn mgr & gen sls mgr; Tammy Barre, opns mgr & prom mgr; Verlene Tadlock, progmg mgr & film buyer; Lori Archer, pub affrs dir; Charles Hoing, engrg mgr. ■ On 26 CATVs—53,000 subs. ■ Rates: $300; 185; 75.

Springdale

ADI No. 117; see Fort Smith market

KHOG-TV—See Fayetteville.

KSBN-TV—ch 57, 171.68 kw vis, ant 384t. Not on air, target date unknown. Box 1400 (72764). Permittee: Total Life Community Educational Foundation.

California

Anaheim

ADI No. 2; see Los Angeles market

KDOC-TV—ch 56, 3,266 kw vis, 652 kw aur, ant 5,500t/240g. TL: N34 11 14 W117 42 01. Stereo. On air date: Oct 1, 1982. 1730 S. Clementine St. (92802). (714) 999-5000. FAX: (714) 999-1218. Licensee: Golden Orange Broadcasting Co. Inc. Ownership: Pat Boone, 36.43%; Calvin C. Brack, 23.7%; William G. Simon, 23.59% Wash atty: Cohn & Marks. Japanese 10 hrs wkly. ■ Calvin Brack, CEO; Pat Boone, pres; Charles Velona, vp & gen mgr; Shur Lee Thompson, gen sls mgr; Steve Schaub, prom mgr; Lisa Starr, progmg mgr; Michelle Marker, pub affrs dir; Roger Knipp, chief engr. ■ On 64 CATVs—1,362,112 subs.

Arcata

ADI No. 187; see Eureka market

KAEF—ch 23, 141 kw vis, 14 kw aur, ant 1,672t. TL: N40 43 36 W123 58 18. (CP: 195 kw vis, 19 kw aur.) On air date: Aug 1, 1987. 540 E St., Eureka (95501). (707) 444-2323. Licensee: California Oregon Broadcasting Inc. (group owner). ■ Net: Fox. Rep: Adam Young. Wash atty: Arter & Hadden. ■ Patsy Smullin, pres; Doreeta Domke, gen mgr & progmg dir; Dennis Siewert, gen sls mgr; Glenn Marsh, prom mgr; Doug Bash, chief engr. ■ On 11 CATVs—40,000 subs. On one trans. ■ Rates: $45; 35; 25.

Bakersfield

ADI No. 130; see Bakersfield market

KBAK-TV—ch 29, 1,700 kw vis, 340 kw aur, ant 3,730t/230g. TL: N35 27 11 W118 35 25. On air date: Aug 23, 1953. Box 2929 (93303). (805) 327-7955. TWX: 910-327-1109. Licensee: Burnham Broadcasting Co. (group owner; acq 10-2-86; $15 million; 9-1-86). ■ Net: ABC. Rep: Katz Television. Wash atty: Fisher, Wayland, Cooper, & Leander. ■ Philip Nye, pres & gen mgr; Marlene Delano, vp sls; Mary Beth Richmond, prom mgr; Nancy Clarke, progmg dir; Chris Long, news dir; Phil Dunton, engrg dir; Robert Banks, chief engr. ■ On 15 CATVs—145,000 subs. On 4 trans.

KERO-TV—ch 23, 1,760 kw vis, 64.6 kw aur, ant 3,700t/183g. TL: N35 27 14 W118 35 37. On air date: Sept 26, 1953. 321 21st St. (93301); Box 2367 (93303). (805) 327-1441. TWX: 910-327-1103. Licensee: McGraw-Hill Broadcasting Co. Group owner: McGraw-Hill Broadcasting Group (acq 3-8-72; grpsl; 3-13-72). ■ Net: CBS. Rep: Harrington, Righter & Parsons. Wash atty: Koteen & Naftalin. ■ Chris Westerkamp, vp & gen mgr; David W. Carfolite, gen sls mgr; Louis Rapage, prom mgr & progmg dir; Walt Brown, news dir; Lynn Noel, pub affrs dir; Norman E. Hall, chief engr. ■ On 7 CATVs—76,897 subs. On 3 trans.

KGET—ch 17, 5,000 kw vis, 500 kw aur, ant 1,400t/288g. TL: N35 26 20 W118 44 23. On air date: Nov 8, 1959. Box 1700 (93302); 2831 Eye St. (93301). (805) 327-7511. FAX: (805) 327-1994. Licensee: KGET TV Inc. (group owner). ■ Net: NBC. Rep: Blair. Wash atty: Rubin, Winston & Diercks. ■ Raymond A. Watson, vp & gen mgr; Tom Randour, gen sls mgr; Steve Hall, prom mgr; Shirley Sanford, progmg dir; Jack Bowe, news dir; Tom Ballew, chief engr. ■ On 5 CATVs—84,900 subs.

KUZZ-TV—ch 45, 5,000 kw vis, 500 kw aur, 1,325t/144g. TL: N36 26 20 W118 44 24. Stereo. Hrs opn: 24. On air date: Dec 18, 1988. 3223 Sillect Ave. (93308). (805) 326-1011. FAX: (805) 328-7576. Licensee: Buck Owens Productions Inc. (group owner; acq 11-9-90). Rep: Seltel. Wash atty: Mullin, Rhyne, Emmons & Topel. ■ Buck Owens, pres; Dorothy Owens, vp, gen mgr & film buyer; Bill Hickey, opns mgr & chief engr; Kalvin Pike, gen sls mgr & natl sls mgr; Teresa Ford, prom mgr &

California

progmg dir; Sylvia Cariker, pub affrs dir. ■ Co-owned radio: KCWR(AM)-KUZZ-FM. ■ Rates: $145; 125; 25.

Barstow

ADI No. 2; see Los Angeles market

KHIZ—ch 64, 3,134 kw vis, 627 kw aur, ant 1,701t. TL: N34 36 34 W117 17 11. On air date: 1987. Box 6464, Victorville (92393); 15605 Village Dr., Victorville (92392). (619) 241-5888. FAX: (619) 241-0056. Licensee: Sunbelt Television Inc. Ownership: Riley Jackson,Ray Webb,Pat Buttram. Rep: Roslin. Wash atty: Dan J. Alpert. ■ Margaret Jackson, pres; Sam Frew, gen mgr; Steve Sipe, gen sls mgr; Janet Kruse, film buyer; Mark Berryhill, news dir. ■ Rates: $300; 100; 50.

Chico

ADI No. 125; see Chico-Redding market

KCPM—ch 24, 5,000 kw vis, 600 kw aur, ant 1,849/997g. TL: N40 15 31 W122 05 20. Stereo. On air date: Sept 24, 1985. 180 E. 4th St. (95928). (916) 893-2424. FAX: (916) 893-1033; TWX: 910-372-0107. Licensee: KCPM Licensee Co. (group owner; acq 7-29-88). ■ Net: NBC. Rep: Katz. Wash atty: Leventhal, Senter & Lerman. ■ Barbara Goldfarb, pres, gen mgr & prom mgr; John Flores, gen sls mgr; Mark Watson, progmg dir; Betty Anderson, news dir; Monty Cheney, chief engr. ■ On 11 CATVs—38,705 subs. On one trans.

KHSL-TV—ch 12, 316 kw vis, 38 kw aur, ant 1,300t/287g. TL: N39 57 30 W121 42 48. On air date: Aug 29, 1953. Box 489 (95927). (916) 342-0141. Licensee: Golden Empire Broadcasting Co. Ownership: Mrs. Hugh McClung, 95%; Hugh McClung Jr., 5% ■ Net: CBS. Rep: Seltel. Wash atty: Haley, Bader & Potts. ■ Russ Pope, CEO & chief engr; Hugh McClung Jr., pres; W.D. Corbin, gen mgr & progmg dir; Steve Sorenson, opns dir; Bill Meyer, gen sls mgr; Brian Corbitt, mktg dir; Bruce Lang, news dir; Ron Palmen, pub affrs dir. ■ On 76 CATVs—185,974 subs. On 23 trans. Co-owned radio: KHSL(AM).

KRCR-TV—See Redding.

Clovis

ADI No. 57; see Fresno-Visalia market

KGMC—ch 43, 3,160 kw vis, ant 2,415t. TL: N36 44 45 W119 16 52. Not on air, target date unknown. 14830 Valley View Ave., La Mirada (90638); 706 W. Herndon Ave., Fresno (93650). (209) 432-4300. FAX: (209) 435-3201. Permittee: Solid State Components Corp.

Concord

ADI No. 5; see San Francisco-Oakland-San Jose market

KFCB—ch 42, 1,205 kw vis, 241 kw aur, ant 2,773t/90g. TL: N37 53 34 W121 53 53. On air date: June 19, 1983. Box 6498 (94524). (510) 676-8969. Licensee: First Century Broadcasting Wash atty: Gammon & Grange. ■ Ronald C. Haus, pres & gen mgr; Kaye Allen, stn mgr; Debra C. Fraser, gen sls mgr; Rachel Adams, pub affrs dir; Norman Wright, chief engr. ■ On 50 CATVs—600,000 subs. On one trans. ■ Rates: $150; 100; 50.

Corona

KVEA—Licensed to Corona. See Los Angeles.

Cotati

ADI No. 5; see San Francisco-Oakland-San Jose market

***KRCB-TV**—ch 22, 68,823 kw vis, 6.882 kw aur, ant 2,034t. TL: N38 25 07 W122 40 33. Hrs opn: 6 AM-11 PM. On air date: Dec 2, 1984. 5850 Labath Ave., Rohnert Park (94928). (707) 585-8522. Licensee: Rural California Broadcasting Corp. ■ Net: PBS. Sp one hr wkly. ■ Nancy Dobbs, CEO; Gary Lester, chmn; Lucie Alexander, vp; Paul Froug, pres; John Moorhead, gen sls mgr & mktg mgr; Roni Berg, adv mgr & pub affrs dir; Karin Iwata, progmg dir; Larry Stratton, chief engr. ■ On 10 CATVs—400,000 subs. Co-owned radio: KRCB-FM.

El Centro

ADI No. 178; see El Centro-Yuma, AZ market

KECY-TV—ch 9, 316 kw vis, 31.6 kw aur, ant 1,720t/460g. TL: N33 03 19 W114 49 39. On air date: Dec 11, 1968. 646 Main St. (92243). (619) 353-9990. FAX: (619) 352-5471; TWX: 910-322-1109. Licensee: Pacific Media Corp. Ownership: Robinson O. Everett, executor (acq 4-24-92). ■ Net: CBS, Fox. Rep: Seltel. Wash atty: Baraff, Koerner, Olender & Hochberg. Sp one hr wkly. ■ Robinson Everett, pres; Peter C. Sieler, gen mgr; Steve Millspaugh, prom mgr; Steve Shippert, progmg dir; Lisa Hunter, news dir; Steve Easley, chief engr. ■ On 5 CATVs—48,000 subs. ■ Rates: $175; 125; 40.

KLXO—ch 7, 316 kw vis, ant 895t. TL: N33 03 21 W115 49 44. Not on air, target date unknown. 232 W. Sixth St., Ontario (96001). Permittee: La Paz Wireless Ltd., a California L.P.

Eureka

ADI No. 187; see Eureka market

KBVU—ch 29, 1,450 kw vis, 145 kw aur, ant 1,676t. TL: N40 43 36 W123 58 18. Not on air, target date unknown. Box 4159, Modesto (95352). (209) 523-0777. FAX: (209) 523-0898. Permittee: Sainte Sepulveda Inc. Ownership: Sharon D. Sepulveda, 51%; Sainte L.P., 49% Wash atty: Fletcher, Heald & Hildreth. ■ Sharon D. Sepulveda, pres.

***KEET**—ch 13, 64.6 kw vis, 12.9 kw aur, ant 1,690t/337g. TL: N40 43 36 W123 58 19. (CP: 187 kw vis, 28 kw aur). On air date: Apr 14, 1969. Box 13 (95502); 7246 Humboldt Hill Rd. (95503). (707) 445-0813. Licensee: Redwood Empire Pub TV Inc. ■ Net: PBS. Wash atty: Greeley & Bernard. Progmg for the deaf 15 hrs wkly. ■ Sile Bauridel, pres; St. Clair B. Adams, gen mgr; Susan Seamen, prom mgr; Karen Barnes, progmg dir; Joel Householter, chief engr. ■ On 5 CATVs—40,000 subs. On 3 trans.

KIEM-TV—ch 3, 100 kw vis, 10 kw aur, ant 1,650t/249g. TL: N40 43 52 W123 57 06. On air date: Oct 25, 1953. 5650 S. Broadway (95503). (707) 443-3123. FAX: (707) 442-6084. Licensee: Precht Television Assoc Inc. (acq 8-2-85; $4 million). ■ Net: NBC. Rep: Katz. ■ Marcy Levine, vp & gen mgr; Hank Ingham, gen sls mgr; Phil Wright, prom mgr & progmg dir; Kevin Brummond, news dir; Rick Repnak, chief engr. ■ On 16 CATVs—21,000 subs. On 12 trans.

KVIQ—ch 6, 100 kw vis, 10.5 kw aur, ant 1,740t/377g. TL: N40 43 36 W123 28 18. On air date: Apr 1, 1958. 1800 Broadway (95501). (707) 443-3061. FAX: (707) 443-4435; TWX: 510-742-6265. Licensee: Miller Broadcasting Co. Ownership: Ronald W. Miller, 95%; Pattison J. Christensen, 5% (acq 7-17-86; $3.9 million; 5-5-86). ■ Net: CBS. Rep: Seltel. Wash atty: Pierson, Ball & Dowd. ■ Ronald W. Miller, pres; Pattison J. Christensen, vp & gen mgr; Susan Swanson, gen sls mgr; Terry Jensen, progmg dir; Gina D'Amore, news dir; David Shallenberger, chief engr. ■ On 7 CATVs—35,737 subs.

Fort Bragg

ADI No. 5; see San Francisco-Oakland-San Jose market

KFWU—ch 8, 225 kw vis, 22.5 kw aur, ant 2,446t/186g. TL: N39 41 38 W123 34 43. On air date: Feb 1, 1990. c/o KRCR TV 755 Auditorium Dr., (95437); 303B N. Main (95437). (916) 243-7777. FAX: (916) 243-0217. Licensee: California Oregon Broadcasting Inc. (group owner). ■ Net: ABC. Rep: Blair, Art Moore. Wash atty: Pierson, Ball & Dowd. ■ Patsy Smullin, pres; Doreeta Domke, gen mgr, vp opns & progmg dir; Dennis Siewert, gen sls mgr; Glenn Marsh, prom mgr; Cal Hunter, news dir; Doug Bush, chief engr. ■ On 2 CATVs—17,000 subs. ■ Rates: $125; 50; 25.

Fresno

ADI No. 57; see Fresno-Visalia market

KAIL—ch 53, 2,510 kw vis, 251 kw aur, ant 1,906t/140g. TL: N37 04 23 W119 15 52. Hrs opn: 19. On air date: Dec 18, 1961. 1590 Alluvial Ave., Clovis (93612). (209) 299-9753. FAX: (209) 299-1523. Licensee: Trans-America Broadcasting Corp. Ownership: Albert J. Williams, 79.9%; Jack M. Reeder, 20.1% (acq 12-23-66; $236,500; 12-26-66). Wash atty: Miller & Fields. ■ Albert J. Williams, pres; C.B. "Benezra" Reis, gen mgr; Charles Williams, stn mgr & gen sls mgr; Bob Jenkins, opns mgr; Bob Harris, dev mgr & news dir; Robert Jenkins, prom mgr; Clemencia Vargas, progmg dir & film buyer; Craig Reed, pub affrs dir; Michael Messina, chief engr. ■ On 14 CATVs—160,731 subs.

KFSN-TV—ch 30, 316 kw vis, 31.6 kw aur, ant 2,040t/271g. TL: N37 04 38 W119 26 00. Stereo. Hrs opn: 24. On air date: May 10, 1956. 1777 G St. (93706). (209) 442-1170. FAX: (209) 233-5844. Licensee: Capital Cities/ABC Inc. Group owner: Capital Cities/ABC Broadcast Group (acq 4-28-71). ■ Net: ABC. Rep: Capital Cities/ABC Natl Sls. Wash atty: Wilmer, Cutler & Pickering. News staff 50; news progmg 15 hrs wkly. ■ Marc Edwards, vp & gen mgr; Dudley Few, gen sls mgr; Mark Arminio, rgnl sls dir; Wes McKee, prom mgr; Fernando Granado, progmg dir; Douglas Caldwell, news dir; David Converse, chief engr. ■ On 66 CATVs—173,900 subs. On one trans.

KFTV—See Hanford

KJEO—ch 47, 2,624 kw vis, 529 kw aur, ant 1,959t/262g. TL: N37 04 14 W119 25 31. On air date: Oct 1, 1953. Box 5455 (93755); 4880 N. First (93726). (209) 222-2411. FAX: (209) 222-5593; TWX: 910-362-3181. Licensee: Retlaw Enterprises Inc. Group owner: Retlaw Broadcasting Co. (acq 8-17-68; $3.654 million; 4-29-68). ■ Net: CBS. Rep: Katz Continental. Wash atty: Wiley, Rein & Fielding. ■ Benjamin Tucker, pres; Don Drilling, vp & gen mgr; Jeralynn Stout, gen sls mgr; Patti Houlihan, progmg dir; George Faulder, news dir; Mike Barrett, chief engr. ■ On 26 CATVs—180,000 subs.

KMPH—(Visalia). ch 26, 2,950 kw vis, 442 kw aur, ant 2,730t/252g. TL: N36 17 12 W118 50 20. Stereo. (CP: 3,240 kw vis, 324 kw aur, ant 2,571t, TL: N36 40 02 W118 52 42). On air date: Oct 11, 1971. 5111 E. McKinley Ave., Fresno (93727). (209) 255-2600. FAX: (209) 255-0275. Licensee: Pappas Telecasting Inc. Group owner: Pappas Telecasting Companies (acq 6-1-78; $3,105,550). ■ Net: Fox. Rep: Telerep. Wash atty: Fletcher, Heald & Hildreth. News staff 14; news progmg 5 hrs wkly. ■ Harry J. Pappas, CEO; Lise Markham, vp & gen mgr; Will Givens, prom mgr; Debbie Sweeney, progmg dir; Roger Gadley, news dir; Brandy Nikaido, pub affrs dir; Dale Kelly, engrg dir. ■ On 29 CATVs—182,168 subs. On 2 trans.

KMSG-TV—(Sanger). ch 59, 1,350 kw vis, 350 kw aur, ant 1,940t/135g. TL: N37 04 26 W119 25 52. Stereo. Hrs opn: 24. On air date: July 17, 1985. 706 W. Herndon Ave., Fresno (93650); Box 3790, Pinedale (93650). (209) 435-5900. FAX: (209) 435-1448. Licensee: Sanger Telecasters Inc. Ownership: Diane D. Cocola, 90%; James K. Zahn, 10% ■ Net: Telemundo. Rep: Telemundo. Wash atty: Cohn & Marks. Sp 100 hrs wkly. ■ Diane D. Dostinich, pres; Jim Zahn, progmg dir; Al Kinney, chief engr. ■ On 40 CATVs—106,000 subs. ■ Rates: $300; 150; 75.

KSEE—ch 24, 1,600 kw vis, 320 kw aur, ant 2,350t/321g. TL: N36 44 45 W119 16 53. Stereo. On air date: June 1, 1953. Box 2400 (93779); 5035 E. McKinley (93727). (209) 454-2424. FAX: (209) 454-2487. Licensee: Granite Broadcasting Corp. (group owner; acq 12-93; $32 million with WTVH(TV) Syracuse, NY; 8-30-93). ■ Net: NBC. Rep: MMT. Wash atty: Haley, Bader & Potts. Sp one hr wkly. ■ Marty Edelman, gen mgr; Doug Stewart, prom mgr; George Hillis, progmg dir & chief engr; Ralph Green, news dir. ■ On 35 CATVs—228,000 subs. On 2 trans. ■ Rates: $500; 200; 80.

***KVPT**—ch 18, 562 kw vis, 112 kw aur, ant 2,220t/245g. TL: N36 44 45 W119 16 52. Stereo. Hrs opn: 6 AM-11:59 PM. On air date: Apr 10, 1977. 1544 Van Ness Ave. (93721). (209) 266-1800. FAX: (209) 443-5433. Licensee: Valley Public Television Inc. (acq 11-1-87). ■ Net: PBS. Wash atty: Richard Hildreth. ■ Colin Dougherty, gen mgr; Virginia Mikula, dev dir; John White, progmg dir; Rodger Hixon, chief engr. ■ On 19 CATVs.

Hanford

ADI No. 57; see Fresno-Visalia market

KFTV—ch 21, 2,190 kw vis, 21.9 kw aur, ant 1,840t/160g. TL: N37 04 24 W119 25 42. Hrs opn: 18. On air date: July 1972. 3239 W. Ashlan Ave., Fresno (93722); 1626 19th St., Suite 14, Bakersfield (93302). (209) 222-2121; (209) 584-3362. FAX: (209) 222-0917. Licensee: KFTV L.P., G.P. Group owner: Perenchio Television Inc. (acq 8-87). ■ Net: Univision. Rep: Univision. Wash atty: Leventhal, Senter & Lerman. Sp 130 hrs wkly. News staff 12; news progmg 8 hrs wkly. ■ Mario M. Carrera, vp & gen mgr; Bram J. Watkins, gen sls mgr; Jess Gonzalez, prom mgr & progmg dir; Daniel Rodriguez, news dir; Ken Holden, chief engr. ■ On 2 trans.

Huntington Beach

ADI No 2; see Los Angeles market

***KOCE-TV**—ch 50, 5,000 kw vis, 500 kw aur, ant 1,082t/246g. TL: N33 58 19 W117 56 57. Hrs opn: 5:30 AM-12:30 PM. On air date: November 1972. Box 2476, 15751 Gothard St. (92647). (714) 895-5623. FAX: (714) 895-0852. Licensee: Board of Trustees, Coast Community College District. Ownership: Coast Community College District. ■ Net: PBS. Wash atty: John L. Tierney. ■ William A. Furniss, pres; Robert C. Moffett, stn mgr;

Roberta Smith, progmg dir; Don Sinex, chief engr. ■ On 45 CATVs—800,000 subs.

Los Angeles

ADI No. 2; see Los Angeles market

KABC-TV—ch 7, 159 kw vis, 31.7 kw aur, ant 2,970t/234g. TL: N34 13 37 W118 03 58. Stereo. (CP: 141.25 kw vis, 28.9 kw aur, ant 3,213t). On air date: Sept 16, 1949. 4151 Prospect Ave. (90027). (310) 557-7777. FAX: (310) 557-5036. Licensee: Capital Cities/ABC Inc. Group owner: Capital Cities/ABC Broadcast Group (acq 1-6-86); grpsl; 7-15-85). ■ Net: ABC. Wash atty: McKenna, Wilkinson & Kittner. ■ Alan Nesbitt, pres & gen mgr; John Riedl, gen sls mgr; Richard Swanson, prom mgr; Vic Heman, progmg dir & film buyer; Roger Bell, news dir; Steven C. Pair, chief engr. ■ Co-owned radio: KABC(AM)/KLOS(FM).

KCAL—ch 9, 141 kw vis, 28.2 kw aur, ant 3,184t/464g. TL: N34 13 38 W118 04 00. Stereo. Hrs opn: 24. On air date: Oct 6, 1948. 5515 Melrose Ave., Los Angeles (90038). (213) 467-9999. FAX: (213) 460-6265. Licensee: Fidelity Television Inc. Ownership: The Walt Disney Co. Rep: Blair. ■ David J. Woodcock, pres; Chris Winners, vp opns; Janet Schoff, gen sls mgr; Robert Blagman, natl sls mgr; John Smart, rgnl sls mgr; Marshall Hites, prom dir; Barbara Zaneri, progmg mgr; Bob Henry, news dir; Elaine Walker, pub affrs dir; Thomas Mann, chief engr. ■ On 350 CATVs—1,050,000 subs.

KCBS-TV—ch 2, 36.3 kw vis, 7.26 kw aur, ant 3,632t/974g. TL: N34 13 57 W118 04 18. Stereo. Hrs opn: 24. On air date: May 6, 1948. 6121 Sunset Blvd. (90028). (213) 460-3000. FAX: (213) 460-3733. Licensee: CBS Inc. Group owner: CBS Broadcast Group (acq 12-27-50; $3.6 million; 1-1-51). ■ Net: CBS. Rep: CBS TV Stns Natl Sls. News staff 128; news progmg 17 hrs wkly. ■ William Applegate, vp & gen mgr; Cheryl Marlowe, opns dir; D'Artagnan Bebel, gen sls mgr; Michael Sweeney, prom dir; Jay Strong, progmg dir; Bob Jordan, news dir; Joseph Dyer, pub affrs dir; Robert Davis, engrg dir. ■ Co-owned radio: KNX(AM) and KCBS-FM.

*KCET—ch 28, 2,455 kw vis, 245.5 kw aur, ant 3,038t/330g. TL: N34 13 26 W118 03 44. Hrs opn: 19. On air date: Sept 28, 1964. 4401 Sunset Blvd. (90027). (213) 666-6500. FAX: (213) 665-6067. Licensee: Community TV of Southern Calif. ■ Net: PBS; EEN, Pacific Mtn. Wash atty: Arent, Fox, Kintner, Plotkin & Kahn. ■ William H. Kobin, pres; Donald G. Youpa, vp; Stephen Kulczycki, stn mgr; Barbara Goen, prom mgr; Jackie Kain, progmg dir & film buyer; Blain Baggett, news dir; William Landers, chief engr. ■ On 160 CATVs. On 4 trans.

KCOP—ch 13, 162 kw vis, 32.4 kw aur, ant 2,953t/240g. TL: N34 13 42 W118 04 02. On air date: Sept 17, 1948. 915 N. La Brea Ave. (90038). (213) 851-1000. FAX: (213) 850-6197. Licensee: KCOP TV Inc. Group owner: Chris Craft Industries Inc. (acq 1-28-60; $5 million; 2-8-60). Rep: Katz. Wash atty: Wilmer, Cutler & Pickering. ■ Richard Feldman, vp & stn mgr; Jill Kauffman, gen sls mgr; Carol Martz, progmg dir; Jeff Wald, news dir; Bishop Elison, chief engr. ■ On 147 CATVs.

*KEEF-TV—ch 68, 2,198 kw vis, 219.8 kw aur, ant 2,884t/160g. TL: N34 13 36 W118 03 59. Not on air, target date unknown. 4241 Redwood Ave. (90066). Permittee: Black TV Workshop of Los Angeles.

KHSC-TV—(Ontario). ch 46, 2,450 kw vis, 372 kw aur, ant 3,040t/323g. TL: N34 13 37 W118 03 58. Hrs opn: 24. On air date: Apr 21, 1984. 3833 Ebony St., Ontario (91761). (909) 986-4503. FAX: (909) 986-2143. Licensee: HSN Broadcasting of Southern California Inc. Group owner: Silver King Communications Inc. (acq 10-30-86; $35 million; 9-2-86). Wash atty: Dow, Lohnes & Albertson. News staff 3; news progmg one hr wkly. ■ Jeff McGrath, pres; Bart Pearce, vp, gen mgr & gen sls mgr; Vicky Botka, progmg dir; Julio Brito, engrg dir. ■ On 63 CATVs—2,000,000 subs. ■ Rates: $400; 325; 240.

*KLCS—ch 58, 550 kw vis, 110 kw aur, ant 3,050t/180g. TL: N34 13 26 W118 03 45. Hrs opn: 6 AM-midnight. On air date: Nov 5, 1973. 1061 W. Temple St. (90012). (213) 625-6958. Licensee: Los Angeles Unified School District. Ownership: Los Angeles Unified School Dist. ■ Net: PBS. Wash atty: Cohn & Marks. ■ Patricia P. Marshall, gen mgr; Lowell P. Thomas, mktg mgr; Sabrina Fair Thomas, progmg mgr; Hector Viera, pub affrs dir; John Russell, chief engr. ■ On 71 CATVs.

KMEX-TV—ch 34, 1,950 kw vis, 195 kw aur, ant 2,940t/170g. TL: N34 13 35 W118 03 56. On air date: Sept 30, 1962. 15th Fl. 6701 Center Dr. W., (90045). (310) 216-3434. Licensee: Univision Station Groups. Group owner: Perenchio Television Inc. ■ Net: Univision. All Sp. ■ Augustine Martinez, gen mgr; Dick Morse, opns mgr; Martin Dugan, sls dir; Mayra Crespo, natl sls mgr; Gerardo Pallares, prom mgr; Maria E. Beltran, progmg dir; Miguel Banojian, news dir; Maria Gutierrez, pub affrs dir; Richard Morse, chief engr. ■ On 71 CATVs.

KNBC-TV—ch 4, 44.7 kw vis, 7.76 kw aur, ant 3,200t/496g. TL: N34 13 32 W118 03 52. Stereo. On air date: Jan 16, 1949. 3000 W. Alameda Ave., Burbank (91523). (818) 840-4444. FAX: (818) 840-3003. Licensee: NBC Subsidiary Inc. Group Owner: NBC TV Stations; (acq 6-5-86). ■ Net: NBC. Rep: Harrington, Righter & Parsons. ■ Reed Manville, pres & gen mgr; Ray Heacox, sls dir; Tobie Pate, vp prom; Mark Hoffman, news dir.

KTBN-TV—(Santa Ana). ch 40, 631 kw vis, 126 kw aur, ant 2,890t/202g. TL: N34 13 32 W118 03 44. On air date: Jan 5, 1967. Box A, Santa Ana (92711). (714) 832-2950. Licensee: Trinity Broadcasting Network. (group owner; acq 8-2-74); $1,266,400; 8-19-74). Wash atty: May, Dunne & Gay. ■ Paul F. Crouch, pres & gen mgr; Vicki Davenport, prom mgr & progmg dir; Ben Miller, chief engr. ■ On 878 CATVs—12,400,000 subs.

KTLA—ch 5, 44.7 kw vis, 6.7 kw aur, ant 6,176t/473g. TL: N34 13 36 W118 03 56. Stereo. (CP: Ant 3,201t). Hrs opn: 24. On air date: Jan 22, 1947. 5800 Sunset Blvd., (90028). (213) 460-5500. FAX: (213) 460-5952. Licensee: KTLA Inc. Group owner: Tribune Broadcasting Co. (acq 12-23-85; $510 million). Rep: Telerep. Wash atty: Sidley & Austin. Sp 22 hrs wkly. News progmg 17 hrs wkly. ■ Greg Nathanson, gen mgr; John Reardon, stn mgr; Tom Amost, gen sls mgr; Leonidia Gonsalves, prom dir; Virginia Hunt, progmg dir; Warren Cereghino, news dir; Ira Goldstone, chief engr. ■ On 222 CATVs—3,396,925 subs.

KTTV—ch 11, 166 kw vis, 20 kw aur, ant 2,940t/237g. TL: N34 13 29 W118 03 47. Stereo. Hrs opn: 24. On air date: Jan 1, 1949. 5746 Sunset Blvd. (90028). (213) 856-1000. Licensee: Fox Television Stations Inc. (group owner; acq 11-14-86); grpsl). ■ Net: Fox. ■ Mitchell Stern, pres; Tom Capra, vp & gen mgr; Lorraine Velona, opns dir; Greg Dilte, natl sls mgr; Peter Martin, prom dir; John Frenzel, progmg dir; Jose Rios, news dir; Will Dishong, vp engrg. ■ On 196 CATVs—2,800,000 subs.

KVEA—(Corona). ch 52, 2,630 kw vis, 263 kw aur, ant 2,890t/200g. TL: N34 13 27 W118 03 45. On air date: June 29, 1966. 1130A Air Way, Glendale (91201). (818) 502-5700. FAX: (818) 502-0029. Licensee: Estrella Communications Inc. Ownership: Telemundo Group Inc. 100% (group owner; acq 7-17-85; $30 million; 6-10-85). ■ Net: Telemundo. Wash atty: Susan Wing. Sp progmg. ■ Jose A. Ronstadt, vp & gen mgr; Jon Yasuda, gen sls mgr; Fernando Lopez, news dir; Glenn Mcjennett, chief engr. ■ On 20 CATVs—1,123,856 subs. ■ Rates: $2,000; 1,000; 350.

KWHY-TV—ch 22, 2,630 kw vis, 257 kw aur, ant 2,916t/182g. TL: N34 13 36 W118 03 59. Hrs opn: 20. On air date: Mar 25, 1993. 5545 Sunset Blvd. (90028). (213) 466-5441. FAX: (213) 466-3613. Licensee: Harriscope of Los Angeles Inc. Group owner: Harriscope Corp. (acq 11-20-81; $5.3 million; 12-14-81). Wash atty: Cohn & Marks. Sp 87 hrs wkly. News staff 6; news progmg 12 hrs wkly. ■ Buzz Harris Jr., pres; Dick Jolliffe, gen mgr; Eduardo Dominguez, stn mgr; David Bergen, opns mgr; Linda Miller, gen sls mgr; C. Holt, prom mgr; Kevin Apper, news dir. ■ On 75 CATVs—1,700,000 subs.

Merced

ADI No. 57; see Fresno-Visalia market

KNSO—ch 51, 15.85 kw vis, 3.425 kw aur, ant 268t/293g. TL: N37 15 11 W120 22 57. Not on air, target date unknown. Box 4159, c/o Chester Smith, Gen Ptnr, Modesto (95352). (209) 523-0777. Permittee: Sainte Ltd.

Modesto

ADI No. 19; see Sacramento-Stocton-Modesto market

KCSO—Licensed to Modesto. See Sacramento.

KRBK-TV—See Sacramento.

Monterey

KCCN-TV—Licensed to Monterey. See Salinas.

KSBW—See Salinas.

KSMS-TV—Licensed to Monterey. See Salinas.

Oakland

KTVU—Licensed to Oakland. See San Francisco.

Ontario

KHSC-TV—Licensed to Ontario. See Los Angeles.

Oxnard

ADI No. 112; see Santa Barbara-Santa Maria-San Luis Obispo market

KADY-TV—ch 63, 1,782 kw vis, 513 kw aur, ant 1,800t/335g. TL: N34 19 49 W119 01 24. Stereo. Hrs opn: 6 AM-2 AM. On air date: Aug 17, 1985. 663 Maulhardt Ave. (93030). (805) 983-0044. Licensee: Riklis Broadcasting Co. Ownership: MBC Holdings Inc. (acq 1991). Rep: ITS. Wash atty: McFadden, Evans & Sills. Sp one hr wkly. ■ John Huddy, pres & gen mgr; Robert Cowie, opns mgr; Shane Morger, vp sls; Edward C. Branca, gen sls mgr; Juliet Green, prom mgr; Erica Huddy, progmg dir; Dan Green, news dir; Ken Richter, engrg mgr. ■ On 13 CATVs—260,000 subs. On one trans. ■ Rates: $200; 140; 80.

Palm Springs

ADI No. 162; see Palm Springs market

KESQ-TV—ch 42, 10 kw vis, 1.6 kw aur, ant 1,650t/60g. TL: N33 51 58 W116 26 02. Hrs opn: 24. On air date: Oct 5, 1968. 42-650 Melanie Pl., Palm Desert (92211). (619) 773-0342. FAX: (619) 773-5107. Licensee: EGF Broadcast Corp. Ownership: Grant Fitts, 100% (acq 8-23-85; $4.4 million). ■ Net: ABC. Rep: Katz. Wash atty: Arnold & Porter. News staff 15; news progmg 12 hrs wkly. ■ Grant Fitts, CEO; Bill Evans, gen mgr & progmg dir; Kristy West Santiago, natl sls mgr; Bill Kasal, prom mgr; Dana Beards, news dir; David Gray, chief engr. ■ On 8 CATVs—115,000 subs. On one trans.

KMIR-TV—ch 36, 490 kw vis, ant 679t/123g. TL: N33 52 00 W116 25 56. Stereo. Hrs opn: 24. On air date: Oct 26, 1968. Box 1506 (92263); 72920 Parkview Dr., Palm Desert (92260). (619) 568-3636; (619) 340-1623. FAX: (619) 568-1176. Licensee: Desert Empire TV Corp. Ownership: John & Sirpuhe Conte, 100% ■ Net: NBC. Rep: Seltel. Wash atty: Koteen & Naftalin. News staff 10; news progmg 8 hrs wkly. ■ John Conte, pres & gen mgr; Harry Hein, opns mgr, mktg dir & adv dir; Tom Hickey, prom mgr; Pat Vander Hoeven, progmg mgr; John Schubeck, news dir; Jenny Dean, pub affrs dir; Jan Pearce, chief engr. ■ On 5 CATVs—90,000 subs.

Paradise

ADI No. 19; see Sacramento-Stockton-Modesto market

KCVU—ch 30, 2,510 kw vis, 252 kw aur, ant 2,447t/250g. TL: N39 57 45 W121 42 40. Hrs opn: 19. On air date: November 1990. 587 Country Dr., Chico (95928). (916) 893-1234. FAX: (916) 893-1266. Licensee: Sainte Ltd. (group owner; acq 10-15-86). Wash atty: Fletcher, Heald & Hildreth. ■ Chester Smith, pres; Robynn Delgado, progmg dir; Herb Crenshaw, chief engr.

Porterville

ADI No. 57; see Fresno-Visalia market

KKAK—ch 61, 2,510 kw vis, 251 kw aur, ant 1,443t. TL: N36 17 14 W118 50 17. Stereo. Hrs opn: 24. On air date: May 6, 1992. 1077 W. Morton Ave. (93257). (209) 781-6100. FAX: (209) 782-0364. Licensee: Kralowec Children's Family Trust. ■ Art Kralowec, gen mgr.

Rancho Palos Verdes

ADI No. 2; see Los Angeles market

KRPA—ch 44, 5,000 kw vis, 500 kw aur, ant 1,694t/93g. TL: N33 23 12 W118 24 00. Not on air, target date unknown. 2610 Stevart Tower, San Francisco (94105). Permittee: Rancho Palos Verdes Broadcasters Inc. Ownership: Channel 44 Associates, a California L.P. ■ Terence E. Crosby, pres; Adam Kimmell, vp.

Redding

ADI No. 125; see Chico-Redding market

***KIXE-TV**—ch 9, 115 kw vis, 12 kw aur, ant 3,590t/99g. TL: N40 36 09 W122 39 01. Hrs opn: 16. On air date: Oct 5, 1964. Box 9 (96099). (916) 243-5493. FAX: (916) 243-7443. Licensee: Northern California Educational TV Association Inc. ■ Net: PBS. Wash atty: Schwartz, Woods & Miller. ■ Mark LeBlanc, pres; Lyle Mettler, gen mgr & gen sls mgr; Mike Lampella, opns dir; Chris Verrill, dev dir & mktg mgr; Kathy Coulter, prom mgr; Myron A. Tisdel, progmg dir & film buyer; Brantley Hunter, chief engr. ■ On 14 CATVs—98,000. On 12 trans.

KRCR-TV—ch 7, 115 kw vis, 22.4 kw aur, ant 3,620t/126g. TL: N40 36 10 W122 39 00. On air date: Aug 1, 1956. 755 Auditorium Dr. (96001). (916) 243-7777. FAX: (916) 243-0217. Licensee: California Oregon Broadcasting Inc. (group owner; acq 8-12-86). ■ Net: ABC. Rep: Blair, Art Moore & Assoc. Wash atty: Pierson, Ball & Dowd. ■ Patsy Smullin, pres; Doreeta Domke, gen mgr, vp opns & progmg dir; Dennis Siewert, gen sls mgr; Glenn Marsh, prom mgr; Calvin Hunter, news dir; Doug Bush, chief engr. ■ On 36 CATVs—151,000 subs. On 38 trans. ■ Rates: $350; 150; 50.

Riverside

ADI No. 2; see Los Angeles market

KRCA—ch 62, 2,366 kw vis, 237 kw aur, ant 2,258t/150g. TL: N34 11 16 W117 41 55. (CP: 2,340 kw vis. ant 2,332t). On air date: Dec 17, 1988. 1813 Victory Pl., Burbank (91504). (818) 563-5722. FAX: (818) 972-2694. Licensee: Fouce Amusement Enterprises Inc. (acq 6-18-90; $3.575 million). Wash atty: Crowell & Moring. Korean 23 hrs wkly. ■ Stephen J. Fouce, pres; Massoud Salarvand, vp & gen mgr; Kim St. Dennis, opns mgr; Chris Buchanan, chief engr. ■ Rates: $250; 175; 125.

Sacramento

ADI No. 19; see Sacramento-Stockton-Modesto market

KCMY—ch 29, 5,000 kw vis, 500 kw aur, ant 1,296t/1,300g. TL: N38 37 49 W120 51 20. (CP: 5,000 kw vis, ant 1,053t). Hrs opn: 24. On air date: Aug 27, 1990. Suite 23, 1029 K St. (95814-3815). (916) 443-2929. Licensee: Ponce-Nicasio Broadcasting, a Ltd Partnership. Ownership: Carmen Briggs, 54.1%; Mary Ann Alonzo, 15%; Yolanda Nava, 15% Wash atty: Covington & Burling. ■ Mrs. Carmen Briggs, pres & gen mgr; Dan Briggs, pub affrs dir; Rory Boyce, chief engr.

KCRA-TV—ch 3, 100 kw vis, 10 kw aur, ant 1,951t/2,000g. TL: N38 15 52 W121 29 22. Stereo. Hrs opn: 24. On air date: Sept 3, 1955. 3 Television Cir. (95814-0794). (916) 446-3333. FAX: (916) 325-3731. (916) 441-4050, NEWS. Licensee: Kelly Broadcasting Co. (group owner; acq 4-8-62; grpsl; 4-23-62). ■ Net: NBC. Rep: Blair. Wash atty: Koteen & Naftalin. ■ John Serrao, gen mgr; Greg Kelly, stn mgr; Dorothy Lucas, gen sls mgr; Phil Adams, natl sls mgr; Val Nicholas, prom mgr; Linda Bayley, progmg dir; Bill Bauman, news dir; Jerry Agresti, engrg dir. ■ On 114 CATVs—1,076,496 subs. On 5 trans.

KCSO—(Modesto). ch 19, 5,000 kw vis, 560 kw aur, ant 1,877t/250g. TL: N38 14 20 W121 28 52. On air date: Aug 26, 1966. Box 3689, Modesto (95352). (209) 578-1900. FAX: (209) 527-2129. Licensee: Sainte Limited. Group owner: Sainte Limited (acq 10-15-86). ■ Net: Univision. Rep: Univision. Wash atty: Fletcher, Heald & Hildreth. Sp full-time. ■ Sharon Sepulveda, gen mgr; David Castro, natl sls mgr; Dave Brady, rgnl sls mgr; Xochitil Avellano, news dir; Chuck Tifft, chief engr. ■ On 27 CATVs—177,000 subs.

KOVR—(Stockton). ch 13, 316 kw vis, 47.4 kw aur, ant 2,000t/2,000g. TL: N38 14 24 W121 30 03. Stereo. Hrs opn: 24. On air date: Sept 5, 1954. 2713 KOVR Dr., West Sacramento (95605). (916) 374-1313. FAX: (916) 374-1459. Licensee: KOVR-TV Inc. Group owner: Continental Broadcasting Ltd. ■ Net: ABC. Rep: Katz. Wash atty: Hogan & Hartson. News staff 60; news progmg 22 hrs wkly. ■ Michael J. Fiorile, vp & gen mgr; Marty Ross, gen sls mgr; S. Thomas Cochran, natl sls mgr; Dave Ulrickson, rgnl sls mgr; Dennis Marshall, prom mgr; Jim Sanders, news dir; Tina Morrill, pub affrs dir; Don Duncan, chief engr. ■ On 83 CATVs—763,921 subs.

KRBK-TV—ch 31, 5,000 kw vis, 500 kw aur, ant 1,830t/2,000g. TL: N38 15 52 W121 29 22. Stereo. On air date: Oct 5, 1974. 500 Media Place (95815). (916) 929-0300. FAX: (916) 920-1078. Licensee: Koplar Communications of Calif. Inc. Group owner: Koplar Communications Inc. (acq 4-2-81; $7.7 million). Rep: Petry. Wash atty: Cohn & Marks. ■ Edward J. Koplar, pres; Elliott Troshinsky, vp & gen mgr; Andy Crittenden, prom mgr; Brent Baader, news dir; Jack Davis, chief engr. ■ On 100 CATVs—424,118 subs. On one trans.

KSCH-TV—(Stockton). ch 58, 5,000 kw vis, 500 kw aur, ant 1,834t. TL: N38 14 24 W121 30 03. On air date: April 13, 1986. 3033 Gold Canal Dr., Rancho Cordova (95670-6129). (916) 635-5858. FAX: (916) 635-9251. Licensee: Pegasus Broadcasting of Stockton/Sacramento Calif. Inc. Group owner: Pegasus Broadcasting Inc. (acq 9-11-90; grpsl; 10-8-90). Rep: Seltel. Wash atty: Fletcher, Heald & Hildreth. ■ Harry J. Delaney, pres & gen mgr; John Mansker, gen sls mgr; Steve Halliwell, prom mgr; Donna Reith, progmg dir; Jeniffer Sharpe, pub affrs dir; Bob Olson, chief engr. ■ On 44 CATVs—475,000 subs.

KTXL—ch 40, 5,000 kw vis, 1,000 kw aur, ant 1,962t/1,968g. TL: N38 16 18 W121 30 18. Hrs opn: 6 days at 24; one day at 20. On air date: Oct 26, 1968. 4655 Fruitridge Rd. (95820). (916) 454-4422. FAX: (916) 739-1079. Licensee: Channel 40 Licensee Inc. Group owner: Renaissance Communications Group Corp. (acq 1-31-89; $56 million; 2-20-89). ■ Net: Fox. Rep: MMT. Wash atty: Reed, Smith, Shaw & McClay. ■ Michael Fisher, pres & gen mgr; Bill Pulliam, gen sls mgr; Audrey Farrington, prom mgr; Cal Bollwinkel, progmg dir; Michael Burke, news dir; William Kreutzer, chief engr. ■ On 72 CATVs—899,148 subs.

***KVIE**—ch 6, 100 kw vis, 10 kw aur, ant 1,869t. TL: N38 14 18 W121 30 18. On air date: Feb 23, 1959. Box 6 (95812). (916) 929-5843. Licensee: KVIE Inc. ■ Net: PBS. Wash atty: Dow, Lohnes & Albertson. ■ John Hershberger, pres & gen mgr; Susan Prince, progmg dir; Michael Wall, chief engr. ■ On 31 CATVs. On 4 trans.

KXTV—ch 10, 316 kw vis, 5.13 kw aur, ant 1,953t/1,960g. TL: N38 14 24 W121 30 03. Stereo. On air date: March 20, 1955. 400 Broadway (95818). (916) 441-2345. FAX: (916) 441-3054. Licensee: Great Western Broadcasting Corp. (group owner; acq 11-28-83; grpsl 12-19-83). ■ Net: CBS. Wash atty: Dow, Lohnes & Albertson. ■ Jim Saunders, pres & gen mgr; Ron Longinotti, gen sls mgr; Deborah Brown, rgnl sls mgr; Matt Chan, progmg dir; Rod Robinson, chief engr.

Salinas

ADI No. 103; see Salinas-Monterey market

KCBA—ch 35, 2,328 kw vis, 283 kw aur, ant 2,414t/355g. TL: N36 45 19 W121 30 05. Stereo. Hrs opn: 24. On air date: Nov 1, 1981. Box 3560 (93912); 1550 Moffett St. (93905). (408) 422-3500. FAX: (408) 754-1120. Licensee: Cypress Broadcasting Inc. Group owner: Ackerley Communications Inc. (acq 6-4-86; $13.1 million; 4-14-86). ■ Net: Fox. Rep: Blair. Wash atty: Rubin, Winston, Diercks & Harris. News progmg 10 hrs wkly. ■ Steve Comrie, vp & gen mgr; Mark Faylor, gen sls mgr; Mary Moore, prom mgr & progmg dir; Steve Momrie, film buyer; Bill Piggott, news dir; Karl Kauffman, chief engr. ■ On 7 CATVs—150,500 subs.

KCCN-TV—(Monterey). ch 46, 1,350 kw vis, 135 kw aur, ant 2,530t/222g. TL: N36 32 05 W121 37 14. On air date: Feb 2, 1969. Box 1938, 2200 Garden Rd., Monterey (93940). (408) 649-0460. FAX: (408) 646-1973. Licensee: Harron-Smith Television Partnership (acq 3-11-93; $8.2 million; 3-29-93). ■ Net: CBS. Rep: Katz. Wash atty: Wiley, Rein & Fielding. News staff 25; news progmg 8 hrs wkly. ■ Byron H. Elton, vp & gen mgr; Tom Tucker, gen sls mgr; Randy Cobb, prom mgr; Mark Chassman, adv dir; Celeste Ricks, progmg mgr; Doug McKnight, news dir; Alan Richmond, pub affrs dir; Charlie Goode, chief engr. ■ On 12 CATVs—307,000 subs. On 2 trans.

KSBW—ch 8, 158 kw vis, 15.8 kw aur, ant 2,940t/1,552g. TL: N37 03 30 W121 46 33. Stereo. On air date: Sept 11, 1953. Box 81651 (93912); 238 John St. (93901). (408) 758-8888. FAX: (408) 424-3750. Licensee: KSBW Licensee Inc. Group owner: GHTV Inc. (acq 7-27-92; with KSBY-TV San Luis Obispo; 8-17-92). ■ Net: NBC. Rep: Telerep. Wash atty: Pepper & Corazzini. News progmg 18 hrs wkly. ■ Cynthia A. Lindsay-McGillen, pres & gen mgr; Wendy Hillan, gen sls mgr; Bob Stock, prom mgr; Teresa Burgess, progmg dir; Maria Barrs, news dir; Larry Estteam, chief engr. ■ On 22 CATVs—317,785 subs. On 2 trans.

KSMS-TV—(Monterey). ch 67, 1,260 kw vis, ant 2,299t, TL: N36 45 23 W121 30 05. On air date: Sept 1, 1986. 67 Garden Ct., Monterey (93940). (408) 373-6767. FAX: (408) 373-6700. Licensee: KSMS-TV L.P. (acq 9-11-90; $2.6 million; 10-15-90). ■ Net: Univision. Rep: Univision. Wash atty: Leventhal, Senter & Lerman. Sp full-time. ■ Daniel D. Villanueva, pres; Carlos Ramos, vp & gen sls mgr; Fidel Soto, news dir; Jeff Hoffman, chief engr.

San Bernardino

ADI No. 2; see Los Angeles market

KSCI—ch 18, 3,090 kw vis, 618 kw aur, ant 2,393t/203g. TL: N34 11 15 W117 41 54. Hrs opn: 24. On air date: June 30, 1977. 12401 W. Olympic, West Los Angeles (90064). (310) 478-1818. Licensee: KSCI Inc. (acq 6-9-87; $40.5 million; 11-3-86). Rep: Asian TV Sls. Wash atty: Leventhal, Senter & Lerman. Asian, European, Mid Eastern progmg. News staff 12; news progmg 10 hrs wkly. ■ Ray Beindorf, pres; Rosemary Fincher Danon, gen mgr; Leanne Warren, opns mgr; Richard Miller, sls dir; Robin Thornton, prom mgr; Eva McKeown, progmg mgr; Joseph Jinn, news dir; Martie Quan, pub affrs dir; Bill Welty, chief engr. ■ On 83 CATVs—3,500,000 subs. On one trans.

***KVCR-TV**—ch 24, 1,318 kw vis, 131.8 kw aur, ant 3,166t/215g. TL: N30 57 57 W117 17 05. On air date: Sept 11, 1962. 701 S. Mt. Vernon Ave. (92410). (714) 888-6511, ext. 1301; (714) 888-6511, ext. 1602. Licensee: San Bernardino Community College District. ■ Net: PBS; Pacific Mtn. Wash atty: Tierney & Swift. Progmg for the deaf 22 hrs wkly. ■ Thomas Little, gen mgr; Lew Warren, stn mgr; Al Gondos, opns dir; David Hinman, dev dir; Don Leiffer, progmg dir; Patty Littlejohn, pub affrs dir; Thomas Guptill, chief engr. ■ On 40 CATVs—50,000 subs. Co-owned radio: KVCR-FM.

KZKI—ch 30, 3,800 kw vis, 251 kw aur, ant 2,345t. TL: N34 11 15 W117 41 58. Not on air, target date unknown. 1360 N. Sanburg Terr., Chicago IL (60610). Permittee: Jose M. Oti dba Sandino Telecaster.

San Diego

ADI No. 24; see San Diego market

KFMB-TV—ch 8, 316 kw vis, 63.2 kw aur, ant 760t/248g. TL: N32 50 17 W117 14 56. Stereo. On air date: May 16, 1949. 7677 Engineer Rd. (92111); Box 85888 (92186-5888). (619) 571-8888. FAX: (619) 569-4203. Licensee: Midwest Television Inc. (group owner; acq 2-19-64; grpsl). ■ Net: CBS. Rep: Petry. Wash atty: Covington & Burling. News progmg 20 hrs wkly. ■ Arnold J. Kleiner, pres; Weldon Donaldson, gen sls mgr; Tim Hnedak, prom mgr; Jules Moreland, progmg dir; Steve Ramsey, news dir; John Weigand, chief engr. ■ On 24 CATVs—542,000 subs. Co-owned radio: KFMB-AM-FM.

KGTV—ch 10, 316 kw vis, 31.6 kw aur, ant 261t/261g. TL: N32 50 20 W117 14 56. Stereo. Hrs opn: 24. On air date: Sept 13, 1953. Box 85347 (92186). (619) 237-1010. FAX: (619) 262-1302. Licensee: McGraw-Hill Broadcasting Co. Group owner: McGraw-Hill Broadcasting Group (acq 6-1-72; grpsl; 3-13-72). ■ Net: ABC. Rep: MMT. Wash atty: Koteen & Naftalin. ■ Ed Quinn, vp & gen mgr; Darrell Brown, gen sls mgr; Judy Vance, mktg dir; Don Lundy, progmg dir & film buyer; Ron Jennings, chief engr. ■ On 20 CATVs—510,000 subs.

KNSD—ch 39, 5,000 kw vis, 500 kw aur, ant 1,910t/180g. TL: N32 41 48 W116 56 06. Stereo. (CP: 2,500 kw vis). On air date: Nov 14, 1965. 8330 Engineer Rd. (92111). (619) 279-3939. FAX: (619) 279-1076. Licensee: KNSD License Inc. Group owner: SCI Television Inc. (acq 2-19-93; grpsl; 4-26-93). ■ Net: NBC. Wash atty: Pepper & Corazzini. Sp 3 hrs wkly. ■ Neil E. Derrough, pres & gen mgr; Randy Fleury, CFO; Joe Collins, gen sls mgr; Doug Gilmore, prom mgr; Penny Martin, progmg dir & film buyer; Irv Kass, news dir; Tom Wimberly, chief engr. ■ On 9 CATVs—645,470 subs. On one trans.

***KPBS**—ch 15, 3,020 kw vis, 302 kw aur, ant 2,007t/185g. TL: N32 41 47 W116 56 07. Stereo. Hrs opn: 18. On air date: June 25, 1967. San Diego State Univ. (92182-0527). (619) 594-1515. FAX: (619) 265-6417. Licensee: Board of Trustees, The California State Univ. for San Diego State Univ. ■ Net: PBS. Wash atty: Bryan, Cave, McPheeters & McRoberts. ■ Doug Myrland, gen mgr; Patricia Finn, prom dir & adv dir; Michael Flester, progmg dir; John Folson, engrg mgr; William Haught, chief engr. ■ On 17 CATVs—420,000 subs. On one trans. Co-owned radio: *KPBS-FM.

KTTY—ch 69, 4,790 kw vis, 479 kw aur, ant 1,950t/151g. TL: N32 41 47 W116 56 07. On air date: Oct 1, 1984. Box 121569, 1696 Frontage Rd., Chula Vista (92112). (619) 575-6969. FAX: (619) 575-6951. Licensee: San Diego Television Inc. Ownership: Helen Smith, 41.3%; Joseph Alvarez, 21.4% Rep: Seltel. Wash atty: Hopkins, Sutter, Hamel & Park. ■ James M. Harmon, pres & gen mgr; Gayle Garrett, natl sls mgr; Andy Feldman, rgnl sls mgr; Sandi Bannister, prom mgr; Shirley Dixon, progmg dir; Helen Smith, film buyer; Bill Cantrell, chief engr. ■ On 11 CATVs.

KUSI-TV—ch 51, 2,880 kw vis, 288 kw aur, ant 1,902t/205g. TL: N32 41 52 W116 56 02. On air date: Sept 13, 1982. Box 719051 (92171); 4575 Viewridge Ave. (92123). (619) 571-5151. Licensee: Channel 51 of San Diego Inc. (Group owner: McKinnon Broadcasting Co.) (acq 6-29-90; $17 million; 4-30-90.) Rep: Katz. Wash atty: Cohn & Marks. News staff 30; news progmg 7 hrs wkly. ■ Michael D. McKinnon Sr., pres & gen mgr; James A. Gillece, CFO; Michael Dean McKinnon, vp opns; Bruce Stein, gen sls mgr; Judy Ritchey, natl sls mgr; Tom McCarthy, prom mgr; Al Ittleson, vp progmg; Dick Tuininga, news dir; Darla Davis, pub affrs dir; Richard Large, engrg dir. ■ On 21 CATVs—530,000 subs.

XETV—(Tijuana, MX). ch 6, 100 kw vis, 50 kw aur, ant 1,000t/550g. Stereo. Hrs opn: 6 AM-2 AM. On air date: Jan 29, 1953. 8253 Ronson Rd., San Diego CA (92111). (619) 279-6666. FAX: (619) 268-5719. Licensee: Bay City Television. ■ Net: Fox. Rep: Telerep. Wash atty: Haley, Bader & Potts. ■ Martin M. Colby, vp & gen mgr; Joan O'Laughlin, stn mgr & gen sls mgr; Rosemary Ortiz, opns mgr; Chuck Dunning, rgnl sls mgr; Judy Albrecht, prom mgr; Valerie Hoffman, progmg mgr; Raphael Ahlgren, pub affrs dir; Felipe Fernandez, engrg dir. ■ On 11 CATVs—680,000 subs.

XEWT-TV—(Tijuana, MX). ch 12, 325 kw vis, 32.5 kw aur, ant 1,000t/200g. TL: N32 30 49 W117 01 08. Stereo. Hrs opn: 20. On air date: July 12, 1960. Suite 660, 3131 Camino del Rio N., San Diego, CA (92108). (619) 528-1212. FAX: (619) 280-9398. Licensee: Televisora de Calimex, S.A. Ownership: Televisa, S.A. Rep: TeleRep. Wash atty: Haley, Bader & Potts. Sp progmg. ■ Jose Luis Gausch, pres, vp & gen mgr; Juan Urias, opns dir; Kathia Bustillos, gen sls mgr; Ricardo Jimenez, vp prom & progmg mgr; Fernando del Monte, news dir; Nina Romero, pub affrs dir; Salvador Hernandez, engrg dir. ■ On 6 CATVs—400,000 subs. ■ Rates: $600; 500; 400.

Margret Haney
GRAHAM-HANEY
Media Brokers/Consultants
2995 WOODSIDE ROAD, WOODSIDE, CA 94062
TEL: 415/325-5552, FAX: 415/325-5556

San Francisco

ADI No. 5; see San Francisco-Oakland-San Jose market

KBHK-TV—ch 44, 5,000 kw vis, 500 kw aur, ant 1,610t/977g. TL: N37 45 20 W122 27 05. On air date: Jan 2, 1968. 650 California St. (94108). (415) 249-4444. FAX: (415) 397-1924. Licensee: UTV of San Francisco Inc. Group owner: Chris Craft Industries Inc. (acq 5-31-83; 6-13-83). Rep: Katz. Wash atty: Wilmer, Cutler & Pickering. ■ John C. Siegel, pres; Jerry Braet, gen mgr; Larry Burden, opns mgr & engrg mgr; Richard Doutre Jones, gen sls mgr; Suzanne Toner, prom mgr; Tom Spitz, progmg dir; Suzanne Guyette, pub affrs dir. ■ On 107 CATVs—1,415,417 subs.

KCNS—ch 38, 5,000 kw vis, 500 kw aur, ant 1,443t/726g. TL: N37 45 20 W122 27 05. Hrs opn: 24. On air date: Jan 3, 1986. Suite 850, 1550 Bryant St. (94103). (415) 863-3800. Licensee: West Coast United Broadcasting Co. Wash atty: Sidley & Austin. Chinese/Vietnamese 120 hrs wkly. ■ Leo Chen, pres; Brent Scheiner, stn mgr & sls dir; Paul Haines, engrg dir.

***KCSM-TV**—See San Mateo.

KDTV—ch 14, 2,570 kw vis, 257 kw aur, ant 1,250t/228g. TL: N37 41 07 W122 26 01. On air date: Aug 13, 1975. 2200 Palou Ave. (94124). (415) 641-1400. FAX: (415) 641-8677. Licensee: KDTV L.P. Group owner: Perenchio Television Inc. ■ Net: Univision. Rep: Univision. Wash atty: Wiley, Rein & Fielding. Sp full time. ■ August Ruiz, vp & gen mgr; Ed Rivera, gen sls mgr; Francisco Jaramillo, progmg dir; Antonio LaGreca, news dir; Luis Echegoyen, pub affrs dir; Mac McKenzie, chief engr. ■ On 62 CATVs—1,100,000 subs.

KGO-TV—ch 7, 316 kw vis, 63.2 kw aur, ant 1,670t/977g. TL: N37 45 20 W122 27 05. On air date: May 5, 1949. 900 Front St. (94111). (415) 954-7777. FAX: (415) 954-7294. Licensee: KGO-TV Inc. Group owner: Capital Cities/ABC Broadcast Group (acq 6-27-86; grpsl; 7-15-85). ■ Net: ABC. Rep: Capital Cities/ABC Natl TV Sls. Wash atty: McKenna, Wilkinson & Kittner. ■ Jim Topping, pres & gen mgr; Bob Young, gen sls mgr; Greg Saunders, prom dir; John Moczulski, progmg dir; Milt Weiss, news dir; Rose Guilbault, pub affrs dir; Chuck Walker, chief engr. ■ On 94 CATVs—793,521 subs. On one trans. Co-owned radio: KGO(AM).

***KMTP-TV**—ch 32, 1,334 kw vis, 267 kw aur, ant 1,610t/885g. TL: N37 45 20 W122 27 05. Stereo. Hrs opn: 19. On air date: Aug 31, 1991. Suite 200, 1311 Sutter St. (94109). (415) 882-5566. Licensee: Minority Television Project. ■ Net: PBS. ■ Otis McGee Jr., pres; Booker T. Wade Jr., gen mgr; Humberto Cintron, opns dir, dev dir & pub affrs dir; Dulce Zamora, progmg dir; Will Washington, chief engr.

KOFY-TV—ch 20, 3,470 kw vis, 347 kw aur, ant 1,550t. TL: N37 45 20 W122 27 05. Stereo. On air date: April 1, 1968. 2500 Marin St. (94124). (415) 821-2020. Licensee: Pacific FM Inc. Ownership: James Gabbert, 85%; Michael Lincoln, 15% (acq 9-5-80; $9.85 million). Rep: MMT. ■ Jim Gabbert, pres; Mike Lincoln, gen mgr; John Perry, opns dir; David La France, gen sls mgr; Andy Polisky, natl sls mgr; Karen Provenza, prom dir; Michele Ball, progmg dir; Carole Fertick, pub affrs dir; Steve Coulam, engrg dir. ■ On 50 CATVs—550,000 subs. Co-owned radio: KOFY-AM.

KPIX—ch 5, 100 kw vis, 10 kw aur, ant 1,660t/980g. TL: N37 45 20 W122 27 05. Stereo. On air date: Dec 22, 1948. 855 Battery St. (94111). (415) 362-5550. FAX: (415) 765-8844; TWX: 910-372-6564. Licensee: Westinghouse Broadcasting Inc. (group owner; acq 7-2-54; $7.5 million; 7-12-54). ■ Net: CBS. Rep: Group W. Wash atty: Wilkes, Artis, Hedrick & Lane. ■ Rick Blangiardi, vp & gen mgr; Alan Buckman, gen sls mgr; Ron Lorentzen, prom mgr; Rosemary Roach, progmg dir; Harry Fuller, news dir; Dave Phillips, chief engr. ■ On 115 CATVs—1,449,103 subs.

***KQED**—ch 9, 316 kw vis, 37 kw aur, ant 1,670t/980g. TL: N37 45 17 W122 27 06. Stereo. Hrs opn: 24. On air date: June 10, 1954. 2601 Mariposa St. (94110). (415) 864-2000. FAX: (415) 553-2380. Licensee: KQED Inc. ■ Net: PBS. Wash atty: Arent, Fox, Kintner, Plotkin, & Kahn. News staff 8; news progmg one hr wkly. ■ Mary G.F. Bitterman, pres; Robert A. Johnston, Jr., CFO; Patricia Wilson, dev dir; Kevin Harris, progmg dir; Ron Santora, progmg mgr; Larry Reid, engrg mgr. ■ On 173 CATVs—1,350,000 subs. Co-owned radio: *KQED-FM, *KQEC(TV).

KRON-TV—ch 4, 100 kw vis, 15.1 kw aur, ant 1,680t/977g. TL: N37 45 20 W122 27 05. Stereo. On air date: Nov 15, 1949. 1001 Van Ness Ave. (94109). (415) 441-4444. FAX: (415) 561-8136. Licensee: Chronicle Broadcasting of San Francisco Inc. Group owner: Chronicle Broadcasting Co. ■ Net: NBC. Rep: Petry. Wash atty: Fletcher, Heald & Hildreth. ■ Amy S. McCombs, pres & gen mgr; E. Richard Cerussi, gen sls mgr; Gayle Allen, prom mgr; David Salinger, progmg dir; Al Holzer, news dir; Warren Allgyer, chief engr. ■ On 68 CATVs—180,000 subs. On 7 trans.

KTSF—ch 26, 2,510 kw vis, 500 kw aur, ant 1,380t/259g. TL: N37 41 12 W122 26 03. Hrs opn: 24. On air date: Sept 4, 1976. 100 Valley Dr., Brisbane (94005-1350). (415) 468-2626. FAX: (415) 467-7559. Licensee: Lincoln Broadcasting Co., A California LimitedPartnership. Wash atty: Akin, Gump, Strauss, Hauer & Feld. Asian languages 80 hrs, European languages 20 hrs wkly. News staff 12; news progmg 7 hrs wkly. ■ Lillian L. Howell, pres; Brian Holton, gen mgr; Michael Sherman, stn mgr; Victor Marino, opns mgr; Janice Yuen, prom mgr; Martin Diaz, progmg dir; Rose Shirinian, news dir & pub affrs dir; Mike Fusaro, engrg dir. ■ On 55 CATVs—1,821,000 subs.

KTVU—(Oakland). ch 2, 100 kw vis, 20 kw aur, ant 1,811t/980g. TL: N37 45 20 W122 27 05. Hrs opn: 24. On air date: Mar 3, 1958. Box 22222, (94623); #2 Jack London Square, (94607). (510) 834-1212. FAX: (510) 272-9957. Licensee: KTVU Inc. Group owner: Cox Broadcasting (acq 10-16-63; $12.36 million; 10-21-63). ■ Net: Fox. Rep: Telerep. Wash atty: Dow, Lohnes & Albertson. ■ Kevin P. O'Brien, vp & gen mgr; Sterling Davis, opns dir & engrg dir; Jeff Block, gen sls mgr; Cheryl Cox, Scott Sanders, natl sls mgrs; Steve Poitras, mktg dir; Caroline Chang, progmg mgr; Fred Zehnder, news dir; Rosy Chu, pub affrs dir. ■ On 190 CATVs—2,096,975 subs. On 10 trans.

San Jose

ADI No. 5; see San Francisco-Oakland-San Jose market

KICU-TV—ch 36, 4,098 kw vis, 409.8 kw aur, ant 2305t/600g. TL: N37 29 17 W121 51 59. Stereo. Hrs opn: 24. On air date: Oct 3, 1967. Box 36 (95109); 1585 Schallenberger Rd. (95131). (408) 298-3636. FAX: (408) 298-1353. Licensee: KICU Inc. Ownership: Ralph C. Wilson Jr., 75%;James H. Evers, 6.25%;John W. DuBois, 6.25%;William S. Beeman, 2.50% (acq 10-26-90; $34 million). Rep: Blair. Wash atty: Leventhal, Senter & Lerman. News progmg 8 hrs wkly. ■ James H. Evers, pres & gen mgr; William S. Beeman, John DuBois, vps; William S. Beeman, vp opns; John DuBois, vp sls; Bruce Gossett, natl sls mgr; David Wolfe, prom mgr; Melissa Tench-Stevens, progmg dir; Michael Konczal, news dir; Roy Avila, pub affrs dir; Curt Porter, engrg mgr. ■ On 109 CATVs—1,810,323 subs. On 3 trans.

KLXV-TV—ch 65, 3,060 kw vis, 1,179 kw aur, ant 2,667t/223g. TL: N37 06 41 W121 50 30. On air date: Nov 12, 1986. Box 2 B (95109-0002); 2315 Canoas Garden Rd. (95125). (408) 264-6565. FAX: (408) 723-1670. Licensee: Friendly Bible Church Inc. also known as Cathedral of Faith. Ownership: Friendly Bible Church Inc., 100% (acq 3-87; $3,050,000; 3-2-87). Wash atty: May & Dunne. Sp 3 hrs wkly. ■ Roy K. Foreman, pres; Kurt Foreman, gen mgr; Tim Ordaz, sls dir, prom dir, adv dir & progmg dir; Skip Moretti, chief engr. ■ On 25 CATVs—650,000 subs. ■ Rates: $50; 35; 25.

KNTV—ch 11, 80 kw vis, 8 kw aur, ant 2,770t/291g. TL: N37 06 40 W121 50 34. Hrs opn: 20. On air date: Sept 12, 1955. 645 Park Ave. (95110). (408) 286-1111. FAX: (408) 295-5461. Licensee: KNTV Inc. Group owner: Granite Broadcasting Corp. ■ Net: ABC. Rep: Harrington, Righter & Parsons. Wash atty: Akin, Gump, Strauss, Hauer & Feld. News progmg 12 hrs wkly. ■ Stewart Park, pres, gen mgr & progmg dir; Marty Edelman, gen sls mgr; Bob Anderson, prom mgr; Terry McElhatton, news dir; Lou Bell, engrg dir.

KSTS—ch 48, 4,550 kw vis, 455 kw aur, ant 2,070t/322g. TL: N37 29 05 W121 51 51. On air date: May 31, 1981. 2349 Bering Dr. (95131). (408) 435-8848. FAX: (408) 433-5921. Licensee: Telemundo of Northern California Inc. Group owner: Telemundo Group Inc. (acq 8-14-87; $10.9 million; 7-6-87). ■ Net: Telemundo. Wash atty: Hogan & Hartson. Sp 100 hrs wkly. News staff 10; news progmg 3 hrs wkly. ■ Paul Niedermeyer, vp & gen mgr; Ralph Herrera, gen sls mgr; Alicia Vazquez, mktg dir; Maribel Madrigal, prom mgr; Lulu Lopez, progmg dir; Dante Betteo, news dir; Gloria Estrada, pub affrs dir. ■ On 18 CATVs—106,000 subs. ■ Rates: $800; 300; 150.

***KTEH**—ch 54, 661 kw vis, 132 kw aur, ant 1,922t/137g. TL: N37 29 07 W121 51 57. On air date: October 1964. 100 Skyport Dr. (95110-1301). (408) 437-5454. FAX: (408) 437-5454. Licensee: KTEH-TV Foundation (acq 8-10-87). ■ Net: PBS; Pacific Mtn. Wash atty: Schwartz, Woods & Miller. Sp bilingual 3 hrs, closed captioned progmg 5 hrs wkly. ■ Tom Fanella, pres & gen mgr; Jean Zeller, dev dir; Lina Sullivan, prom dir & adv dir; Karen Roberts, progmg dir; George Sampson, pub affrs dir; Michele Muller, chief engr. ■ On 65 CATVs. On 6 trans.

San Luis Obispo

ADI No. 112; see Santa Barbara-Santa Maria-San Luis Obispo market

KADE—ch 33, 60.3 kw vis, ant 1,443t. TL: N35 21 38 W120 39 21. Not on air, target date unknown. 414 Higuersa St. (93401). Permittee: Riklis Broadcasting Corp. (acq 3-23-93; $825,000; 4-12-93). ■ Alene Renee Whitten, pres.

KSBY—ch 6, 100 kw vis, 12 kw aur, ant 2,250t/452g. TL: N35 21 37 W120 39 17. Stereo. On air date: May 1953. 467 Hill St. (93405). (805) 541-6666. FAX: (805) 541-5142. Licensee: KSBY Licensee Inc. Group owner: GHTV Inc. (acq 7-27-92; with KSBW(TV) Salinas; 8-17-92). ■ Net: NBC. Rep: Telerep. Wash atty: Pepper & Corazzini. ■ Cynthia Lindsay McGillen, pres & gen mgr; James Brodsky, opns mgr & chief engr; Mark Libby, gen sls mgr; Madeline Palaszewski, prom mgr; Teresa Burgess, progmg dir; John Wessling, news dir. ■ On 10 CATVs—160,000 subs. On 3 trans. ■ Rates: $1800; 275; 110.

Colorado

Directory of Television

San Mateo

ADI No. 5; see San Francisco-Oakland-San Jose market

*KCSM-TV—ch 60, 1,550 kw vis, 229 kw aur, ant 1,240t/226g. TL: N37 41 07 W122 26 01. Hrs opn: 6 AM-midnight. On air date: Oct 12, 1964. 1700 W. Hillsdale Blvd. (94402). (415) 574-6586. FAX: (415) 574-6675. Licensee: San Mateo County Community College District. ■ Net: PBS. Wash atty: Tierney & Swift. ■ David Hosley, gen mgr; Richard Zanardi, stn mgr; Jeff Byers, dev dir; Darrell Scoggins, progmg mgr. ■ On 44 CATVs—400,000 subs. Co-owned radio: *KCSM-FM.

Sanger

KMSG-TV—Licensed to Sanger. See Fresno.

Santa Ana

KTBN-TV—Licensed to Santa Ana. See Los Angeles.

Santa Barbara

ADI No. 112; see Santa Barabara-Santa Maria-San Luis Obispo market

KEYT-TV—ch 3, 50 kw vis, 5.9 kw aur, ant 3,010t/210g. TL: N34 31 32 W119 57 28. On air date: July 24, 1953. Box 730, Miramonte Dr. (93109); Box 729 (93102). (805) 965-8533. FAX: (805) 962-2342. Licensee: Smith Broadcasting of California Inc. Group owner: Smith Broadcasting Group Inc. (acq 6-16-87). ■ Net: ABC. Rep: HRP. Wash atty: Hogan & Hartson. ■ Sandra Benton, vp & gen mgr; Arnold Witchel, gen sls mgr; Jeff Martin, prom mgr; Renee Foley, progmg dir; King Harris, news dir; Brian Neal, chief engr. ■ On 64 CATVs—256,000 subs. On 3 trans.

Santa Maria

ADI No. 112; see Santa Barbara-Santa Maria-San Luis Obispo market

KCOY-TV—ch 12, 115 kw vis, 22.9 kw aur, ant 1,940t/140g. TL: N34 54 37 W120 11 08. Stereo. On air date: Mar 16, 1964. 1211 W. McCoy Ln. (93455). (805) 925-1200. TWX: 910-351-5875. Licensee: Stauffer Communications Inc. (group owner; acq 8-1-80). ■ Net: CBS. Rep: Petry. Wash atty: Dow, Lohnes & Albertson. ■ Charles S. Stauffer, gen mgr & film buyer; Joe Marcoe, gen sls mgr; Robyn Winch, prom mgr; John Pilios, news dir; Dennis Bornhoft, chief engr. ■ On 20 CATVs—155,300 subs. On one trans. ■ Rates: $1,000; 250; 100.

Santa Rosa

ADI No. 5; see San Francisco-Oakland-San Jose market

KFTY—ch 50, 302 kw vis, 60.4 kw aur, 3,080t/172g. TL: N38 40 10 W122 37 52. On air date: May 1, 1981. Box 1150, 533 Mendocino Ave. (95402). (707) 526-5050. FAX: (707) 526-7929. Licensee: KFTY Broadcasting Inc. Ownership: KFTY Broadcasting Inc. (acq 10-26-90) at $2.25 million; 11-19-90). Rep: Adam Young. Wash atty: Keck, Mahin & Cate. ■ Gary Heck, chmn & pres; John Burgess, stn mgr & news dir; Randy Rogers, natl sls mgr; Melanie Bartlette, prom dir; Jack Hirsch, progmg dir; Charlie Coburn, chief engr. ■ On 32 CATVs—400,000 subs. On 4 trans. ■ Rates: $300; 175; 50.

Stockton

ADI No. 19; see Sacramento-Stockton-Modesto market

KFTL—ch 64, 1,950 kw vis, 195 kw aur, ant 2,980t/90g. TL: N37 53 35 W121 53 58. Stereo. Hrs opn: 24. On air date: July 11, 1988. 403 McCormick St., San Leandro (94577). (510) 632-5385. FAX: (510) 632-8943. Licensee: Family Stations Inc. (group owner). Sp 3 hrs wkly. ■ Harold Camping, pres; Scott Smith, vp; Matt V. Tuter, gen mgr; Bettina Montez, prom mgr & pub affrs mgr; Paul Strieby, chief engr. ■ On 27 CATVs—525,000 subs. On one trans. Co-owned radio: KEBR-AM, KEAR-FM.

KOVR—Licensed to Stockton. See Sacramento.

KRBK-TV—See Sacramento.

KSCH-TV—Licensed to Stockton. See Sacramento.

*KVIE—See Sacramento.

Twentynine Palms

ADI No. 2; see Los Angeles market

KVMD—ch 31, 36.4 kw vis, ant 295t. TL: N34 11 34 W116 06 22. Not on air, target date unknown. No. 12, 270 Ohio St., Pasadena (91106). Permittee: Mike Parker (acq 11-23-92; assumption of debt; 12-14-92).

Vallejo

ADI No. 5; see San Francisco-Oakland-San Jose market

KPST-TV—ch 66, 3,459 kw vis, 346 kw aur, ant 1,529t/977g. TL: N37 45 20 W122 27 05. Stereo. On air date: Nov 25, 1986. Suite 308, 475 El Camino Real, Millbrae (94030). (415) 697-6682. Licensee: Pan Pacific Television Inc. Ownership: Wallace Lee, 30%; Victor Sun, 25%; Shirley Lau, 25%; David Li, 20% Wash atty: Mullin, Rhyne, Emmons & Topel. Chinese 9 hrs wkly. ■ David Li, pres & gen mgr; C. T. Tuan, gen sls mgr; Sammy Yang, prom mgr & progmg dir; Paul Strieby, chief engr. ■ Rates: $100; 85; 70.

Ventura

ADI No. 2; see Los Angeles market

KSTV-TV—ch 57, 1,120 kw vis, ant 833t. TL: N34 18 10 W119 13 41. On air date: October 1990. Suite A, 6020 Nicolle Ave. (93003). (805) 650-8857. FAX: (805) 650-8875. Licensee: Costa de Oro Television Inc. ■ Leopoldo L. Ramos, pres; Walter Ulloa, gen mgr.

Visalia

ADI No. 57; see Fresno-Visalia market

KMPH—Licensed to Visalia. See Fresno.

*KNXT—ch 49, 2,140 kw vis, 214 kw vis, ant 2,739t. TL: N36 17 14 W118 50 17. Hrs opn: 17. On air date: Nov 2, 1986. 1550 N. Fresno St., Fresno (93703). (209) 488-7440. FAX: (209) 488-7444. Licensee: Board of Directors Diocese of Fresno Education Corp. Wash atty: Pierson, Ball & Dowd. Sp, Por, Hmong, Lao, Armenian progmg. ■ Marvin G. Harrison, gen mgr; RosaMaria Gendron, pub affrs dir; Steve Lebel, chief engr. ■ On 3 CATVs—200,000 subs.

Watsonville

ADI No. 103; see Salinas-Monterey market

*KCAH—ch 25, 52.5 kw vis, ant 2,198t. TL: N36 45 23 W121 30 05. On air date: Nov 1989. Box 1541, Salinas (93902). (408) 754-1540. Licensee: California Community Television Network. ■ Arlene Kimata, gen mgr; Felipe Rivar, stn mgr.

Colorado

Boulder

ADI No. 20; see Denver market

KTVJ—ch 14, 5,000 kw vis, 501 kw aur, ant 1,000t/378g. TL: N39 43 51 W105 13 56. On air date: March 1986. 1645 W. Fullerton, Chicago, IL (60614). (312) 975-0400. Licensee: Newsweb Corp. (group owner). Wash atty: Fletcher, Heald & Hildreth. ■ Fred Eychaner, pres; Barbara Richardson, gen mgr; Neal Sabin, progmg dir.

Broomfield

*KBDI-TV—Licensed to Broomfield. See Denver.

Castle Rock

ADI No. 20; see Denver market

KWHD—ch 53, 5,000 kw vis, 1,000 kw aur, ant 713t. TL: N39 25 58 W104 39 18. On air date: July 1, 1990. 5450 S. Syracuse St. Englewood (80111). (303) 773-9953. FAX: (303) 773-9960. Licensee: LeSea Broadcasting (group owner). Rep: Landin. ■ Lester Sumrall, pres; Mark Winslow, gen mgr; Mark Scheribel, gen sls mgr; Paul Des Chenes, chief engr.

Colorado Springs

ADI No. 97; see Colorado Springs-Pueblo market

KJCT—See Grand Junction.

KKTV—ch 11, 234 kw vis, 46.8 kw aur, ant 2,380t/351g. TL: N38 44 41 W104 51 41. On air date: Dec 7, 1952. Box 2110 (80901); 3100 N. Nevada Ave. (80907). (719) 634-2844. FAX: (719) 634-3741. Licensee: KKTV Inc. Group owner: Ackerley Communications Inc. (acq 1-19-83; $15.5 million; 2-21-83). ■ Net: CBS. Wash atty: Rubin, Winston & Diercks. ■ Jim Lucas, vp & gen mgr; Lloyd G. Wright, stn mgr & news dir; Dan Smith, gen sls mgr; Pie Malsom, natl sls mgr; George Sanchez, prom mgr; Lorna Duncan, progmg dir; Rick Craddock, chief engr.

KOAA-TV—(Pueblo). ch 5, 100 kw vis, 10 kw aur, ant 1,310t/977g. TL: N38 22 25 W104 33 27. Stereo. On air date: June 13, 1953. Box 195, 2200 7th Ave., Pueblo (81003); 530 Communications Cir., Colorado Springs (80905). (719) 544-5781; (719) 632-5030. FAX: (719) 544-7733; (719) 473-1675. Licensee: Sangre De Cristo Communications Inc. Group owner: Evening Post Publishing Co. (acq 8-6-76; $4.5 million; 8-30-76). ■ Net: NBC. Rep: Petry. Wash atty: Dow, Lohnes & Albertson. News staff 23; news progmg 7 hrs wkly. ■ John O. Gilbert, pres & gen mgr; Paul Doll, natl sls mgr; Phill Emmert, rgnl sls mgr; Rebecca Tyrrell, prom mgr; Ron Eccher, progmg dir & film buyer; Andy Lyon, news dir; Patricia Vaughan, pub affrs dir; Ken Renfrow, chief engr. ■ On 10 CATVs—38,700 subs. On 35 trans. ■ Rates: $395; 69; 50.

KRDO-TV—ch 13, 282 kw vis, 29 kw aur, ant 2,080t/100g. TL: N38 44 41 W104 51 38. On air date: Sept 21, 1953. Box 1457 (80901); 399 S. 8th St. (80905). (719) 632-1515. TWX: 910-920-4871. Licensee: Pikes Peak Broadcasting Co. Ownership: Harry W. Hoth Jr., 100% (group owner). ■ Net: ABC. Rep: Blair. Wash atty: Fletcher, Heald & Hildreth. ■ Harry W. Hoth Jr., chmn; Patti L. Hoth, pres; Neil O. Klockziem, gen mgr, progmg dir & film buyer; Brenda Sickinger, opns mgr; Hank Colvert, gen sls mgr; Tom Grinewich, prom mgr; Paul Unwin, news dir; Charles Upton, chief engr. ■ On 11 CATVs. On 31 trans. Co-owned radio: KRDO-AM-FM.

*KTSC—See Pueblo.

KXRM-TV—ch 21, 1,054 kw vis, 105.4 kw aur, ant 2,085t/125g. TL: N38 44 40 W104 51 37. Hrs opn: 24. On air date: Dec 24, 1984. Box 15789 (80935); 560 Wooten Rd. (80915). (719) 596-2100. FAX: (719) 591-4180. Licensee: KXRM Partnership. Ownership: Edison Media Inc., 50%; Z/L Media Inc., 50% (acq 1-1-87). ■ Net: Fox. Rep: Seltel; Art Moore. Wash atty: Cohn & Marks. ■ Larry W. Douglas, pres, gen mgr, progmg dir & film buyer; Kim A. Carlson, exec vp; Kim Carlson, gen sls mgr; Cindy Aubrey, prom mgr; Joe Duckett, chief engr. ■ On 24 CATVs—146,000 subs. On 2 trans. ■ Rates: $250; 150; 25.

Denver

ADI No. 20; see Denver market

*KBDI-TV—(Broomfield). ch 12, 229 kw vis, 22.9 kw aur, 2,420t/66g. TL: N39 40 55 W105 29 49. On air date: Feb 22, 1980. Box 1740, Denver (80201); 2246 N. Federal, Denver (80211). (303) 458-1200. FAX: (303) 458-6634. Licensee: Front Range Educational Media Corp. ■ Net: PBS. Wash atty: Mintz, Levin, Cohn, Ferris, Glovsky & Popeo. ■ Ted Krichels, gen mgr; Richard Eversley, vp opns; David Nash, dev mgr; Jane Jacobson, prom mgr; Kirby McClure, progmg dir; Ivy Morgan, pub affrs dir; Saundra Kelly, chief engr. ■ On 60 CATVs—300,000 subs. On 2 trans.

KCEC—ch 50, 2,498 kw vis, ant 764t. TL: N39 43 47 W105 07 16. On air date: Oct 19, 1990. TV Station KCEC, Suite C, 11111 W. 8th Ave., Lakewood (80215). (303) 235-0049. Fax: (303) 235-0259. Licensee: Golden Hills Broadcasting Corp. ■ Net: Univision. Wash atty: Kaye, Scholer, Fierman, Hays & Handler. Sp 168 hrs wkly. ■ Erma Atencio, pres, gen mgr & progmg mgr; Ron Silva, gen sls mgr; Dennis Visser, engrg mgr. ■ On 4 CATVs.

KCNC-TV—ch 4, 100 kw vis, 35.1 kw aur, ant 1,480t/833g. TL: N39 43 48 W105 14 02. Stereo. Hrs opn: 24. On air date: Dec 24, 1953. Box 5012 (80217). (303) 861-4444. FAX: (303) 830-6537. Licensee: NBC Subsidiary (KCNC-TV) Inc. Group owner: NBC TV Sta-

Stations in the U.S.

tions Division (acq 6-5-68; grpsl; 6-1-68). ■ Net: NBC. Rep: Petry. ■ Roger Ogden, pres & gen mgr; James MacDermott, vp & stn mgr; David Layne, opns mgr; Susan McEldoon, gen sls mgr; Brian Sullivan, mktg mgr; Mike Jackson, prom mgr; Wendy Holmes, progmg mgr; Marv Rockford, news dir; John Baich, chief engr. ■ On 43 CATVs—48,000 subs. On 29 trans.

KDVR—ch 31, 5,000 kw vis, 500 kw aur, ant 1,038t/440g. TL: N39 43 45 W105 14 12. Hrs opn: 24. On air date: Aug 10, 1983. 501 Wazee (80204); Box 3100 (80201). (303) 595-3131. FAX: (303) 595-8312; (303) 595-4657. Licensee: 31 Licensee Inc. Group owner: Renaissance Communications (acq 1-11-93); grpsl; 3-18-93). ■ Net: Fox. Rep: Seltel. Wash atty: Koteen & Naftalin. ■ Ed Karlik, pres; Rod Bacon, vp & gen mgr; Mary Carole McDonald, opns mgr, prom dir & progmg dir; Kathryn Bridgman, gen sls mgr; Joan Golden, pub affrs dir; Fred Baumgartner, chief engr. ■ On 45 CATVs—401,000 subs.

KMGH-TV—ch 7, 316 kw vis, 50 kw aur, ant 1,010t/285g. TL: N39 43 46 W105 14 12. Stereo. On air date: Nov 1, 1953. 123 Speer Blvd. (80203); Box 5007 (80217). (303) 832-7777. FAX: (303) 832-0138. Licensee: McGraw Hill Broadcasting Co. Group owner: McGraw-Hill Broadcasting Group (acq 6-1-72; grpsl; 3-13-72). ■ Net: CBS. Rep: MMT. Wash atty: Koteen & Naftalin. News progmg 18 hrs wkly. ■ Edward T. Reilly, pres; John B. Proffitt, vp, gen mgr & vp progmg; Ray Milius, opns dir & engrg mgr; Cathy Leibowitz, natl sls mgr; Carl Stieneker, mktg dir; Arlin Stevens, news dir; Kelli Kindel, pub affrs dir. ■ On 41 CATVs—150,000 subs. On 39 trans. ■ Rates: $2,500; 500; 150.

*__KRMA-TV__—ch 6, 100 kw vis, 15.1 kw aur, ant 880t/213g. TL: N39 43 48 W105 15 00. Stereo. (CP: Ant 1,230t. TL: N39 43 48 W105 15 00). On air date: Jan 30, 1956. 1089 Bannock St. (80204). (303) 892-6666. FAX: (303) 620-5600. Licensee: Council For Public Television, Channel 6 Inc. ■ Net: PBS. Wash atty: Dow, Lohnes & Albertson. ■ James N. Morgese, pres & stn mgr; Donna Sanford, progmg dir; Rudy Norman, chief engr. ■ On 90 CATVs—300,000 subs. On 65 trans.

KTVD—ch 20, 3,148 kw vis, 425 kw aur, ant 2,548t/172g. TL: N39 40 18 W109 13 12. Stereo. Hrs opn: 24. On air date: Dec 1, 1988. Box 6522, 11203 E. Peakview, Englewood (80111). (303) 792-2020. FAX: (303) 790-4633. Licensee: Twenver Inc. Ownership: N. Richard Miller 50% plus. Rep: Katz. Wash atty: Goldberg & Spector. ■ N. Richard Miller, pres; Terence J. Brown, gen mgr & progmg dir; Dennis Christine, gen sls mgr; Kevin Burdge, rgnl sls mgr; Phil Kane, prom mgr. ■ Rates: $250; 200; 50.

KUBD—ch 59, 5,000 kw vis, 500 kw aur, ant 1,109t/87g. TL: N39 40 31 W104 52 22. Hrs opn: 24. On air date: Sept 10, 1987. 9805 E. Iliff (80231). (303) 751-5959. Licensee: UHF Channel 59 Corp. Ownership: Chas Ergen, 80%; David M. Drucker, 20% (acq 6-16-92; 7-6-92). ■ Net: Telemundo. Rep: Telemundo. Wash atty: Cole, Raywid & Braverman. Sp 60 hrs wkly. ■ David M. Drucker, pres; Clara I. Rivas, gen mgr, gen sls mgr, mktg mgr & adv mgr; Cheryl Menke-George, progmg dir; Mike Molins, film buyer; Rodolfo Gardenas, news dir; Rosario Iraola, pub affrs dir; Gunter Auerbach, chief engr. ■ 600 subs. ■ Rates: $140; 50.

KUSA-TV—ch 9, 316 kw vis, 45.3 kw aur, ant 950t/277g. TL: N39 43 46 W105 14 08. Stereo. (CP: 316 kw vis, ant 918t. TL: N39 43 46 W105 14 08). On air date: Oct 12, 1952. 500 Speer Blvd. (80203). (303) 871-9999; FAX: (303) 871-1819; (303) 698-4719 (SALES). Licensee: KUSA Broadcasting Inc. Group owner: Gannett Broadcasting (Division of Gannett Co. Inc.) (acq 6-7-79; grpsl; 6-11-79). ■ Net: ABC. Rep: Blair. Wash atty: Pierson, Ball & Dowd. ■ Joe Franzgrote, pres & gen mgr; Cindy Velasquez, vp; Mark Cometta, gen sls mgr; Jim Seifert, rgnl sls mgr; Steve Thaxton, vp mktg; Dave Lougee, news dir; Myron Oliner, chief engr. ■ On 40 trans.

*__KWBI-TV__—ch 41, 741 kw vis, ant 1,140t/169g. TL: N39 35 59 W105 12 35. Hrs opn: 15. On air date: Aug 20, 1988. 16075 W. Belleview Ave., Morrison (80465). (303) 697-5924. FAX: (303) 697-5944. Licensee: Faith Bible Chapel. (acq 1993). Wash atty: Pepper & Corazzini. ■ George Morrison, pres; Michael K. Brinks, gen mgr; Don Whipple, dev dir; Shelly Frohs, prom mgr & progmg dir; Al Stewart, chief engr.

KWGN-TV—ch 2, 100 kw vis, 20 kw aur, 1,050t/449g. TL: N39 43 59 W105 14 12. Stereo. On air date: July 18, 1952. 6160 S. Wabash Way, Englewood (80111); Box 5222 Englewood (80155). (303) 740-2222. FAX: (303) 740-2847; TWX: 910-935-0877. Licensee: KWGN Inc. Group owner: Tribune Broadcasting Co., see Cross-Ownership (acq 3-3-66; $3.5 million). Rep: Telerep. Wash atty: Sidley & Austin. News staff 29; news progmg 7 hrs wkly. ■ James C. Dowdle, CEO; James C. Dowdle, Dennis Fitzsimons, presdts; John Suder, gen mgr; Dave Dornseif, gen sls mgr; Debbee Coe Baca, mktg mgr; Ken Hoagland, prom mgr; Laura Nelson, progmg dir; Steve Grund, news dir; Greg Guinan, pub affrs dir; Kent Gratteau, chief engr. ■ On 236 CATVs—859,000 subs. On 50 trans.

Durango

ADI No. 188; see Grand Junction-Durango market

KREZ-TV—ch 6, 3.16 kw vis, 500 w aur, ant 460t/186g. TL: N37 15 44 W107 53 58. (CP: 6.2 kw vis, 1.36 kw aur). On air date: Sept 4, 1965. Box 789, Grand Junction (81501); Box 2508 (81301). (303) 259-6666. Licensee: W. Russell Withers, Jr. Group owner: Withers Broadcasting Co. (acq 6-5-85). ■ Net: CBS, NBC. Rep: Katz. ■ Joe Carriere, gen mgr. ■ On 6 CATVs—5,000 subs. On 9 trans. ■ Rates: $95; 35; 25.

Fort Collins

ADI No. 20; see Denver market

KFCT—ch 22, 5,000 kw vis, 500 kw aur, 1,243t/235g. TL: N40 37 23 W105 14 53. Not on air, target date unknown. c/o Television Station KDVR, 501 Wazee, Denver (80204). (303) 595-3131. Permittee: 31 Licensee Inc. Group owner: Renaissance Communications Corp. (acq 8-12-93; 8-30-93). ■ Rod Bacon, gen mgr.

Glenwood Springs

ADI No. 20; see Denver market

KREG-TV—ch 3, 67.6 kw vis, 6.76 kw aur, ant 2,530t/256g. TL: N39 25 05 W107 22 01. On air date: Dec 15, 1983. P.O. Box 789, Grand Junction (81502). (303) 963-3333. Licensee: W. Russell Withers Jr. Group owner: Withers Broadcasting Co. ■ Net: CBS, NBC. Rep: Katz. Wash atty: Gardener, Carton & Douglas. ■ Joe Carrier, gen mgr; Mike Moran, news dir; John Dady, chief engr. ■ On 8 CATVs—25,000 subs. On 43 trans.

Grand Junction

ADI No. 188; see Grand Junction-Durango market

KJCT—ch 8, 120.2 kw vis, 12 kw aur, ant 2,720t/141g. TL: N39 02 55 W108 15 06. On air date: Oct 22, 1979. Box 3788 (81502). (303) 245-8880. FAX: (303) 245-8249. Licensee: Pikes Peak Broadcasting Co. Group owner. ■ Net: ABC. Rep: Blair. Wash atty: Fletcher, Heald & Hildreth. Some Sp progmg. ■ Patti Hoth, pres; Jan Hammer, gen mgr; Layne Montgomery, opns mgr; Hank Colvert, gen sls mgr; Tom Meyer, prom mgr & pub affrs dir; Mona Dyer, news dir; Roger Hightower, chief engr. ■ On 7 CATVs—27,000 subs. On 13 trans.

KJWA—ch 4, 10.6 kw vis. Stereo. Box 10, 800 Gold Creek Rd., Ohio City (81237). Licensee: John Harvey Rees.

KREX-TV—ch 5, 12.9 kw vis, 2.5 kw aur, ant 10t/343g. TL: N39 05 15 W108 33 56. Stereo. On air date: May 22, 1954. Box 789 (81502). (303) 242-5000. FAX: (303) 242-0886. Licensee: W. Russell Withers Jr. Group owner: Withers Broadcasting Co. (acq 6-24-85; grpsl). ■ Net: CBS, NBC. Rep: Katz. ■ Joseph A. Carriere, gen mgr, natl sls mgr & progmg dir; Don Bona, sls dir; Doug Pribble, prom mgr; Mike Moran, news dir; Al Ladage, vp engrg. ■ On 34 CATVs—78,405 subs. On 64 trans.

Longmont

ADI No. 20; see Denver market

KZJG—ch 25, 5,000 kw vis, ant 1,089t. TL: N40 05 48 W104 53 59. Not on air, target date unknown. Box 984, Little Rock, AR (72203). (501) 753-5338. Permittee: Colorado Broadcasters.

Montrose

ADI No. 188; see Grand Junction-Durango market

KREY-TV—ch 10, 6.17 kw vis, 1.36 kw aur, ant 79t/113g. TL: N38 31 02 W107 51 12. On air date: Aug 26, 1956. 614 N. First (81401). (303) 249-9601. FAX: (303) 249-9610. Licensee: W. Russell Withers Jr. Group owner: Withers Broadcasting Co. (acq 6-24-85; grpsl). ■ Net: CBS, NBC. Rep: Katz. ■ Joseph A. Carriere, gen mgr. ■ On 5 CATVs—9,000 subs. On 6 trans. ■ Rates: $80; 30; 20.

Pueblo

ADI No. 97; see Colorado Springs-Pueblo market

KKTV—See Colorado Springs.

KOAA-TV—Licensed to Pueblo. See Colorado Springs.

KRDO-TV—See Colorado Springs.

*__KTSC__—ch 8, 316 kw vis, 63.2 kw aur, ant 1,224t/972g. TL: N38 22 25 104 33 27 (CP: 233 kw vis, ant 2,386t, TL: N38 44 41 W104 51 38). On air date: Feb 3, 1971. 2200 Bonforte Blvd. (81001-4901). (719) 543-8800. FAX: (719) 549-2208. Licensee: University of Southern Colo. Ownership: State Board of Agriculture. ■ Net: PBS. ■ Gregory B. Sinn, gen mgr; Thomas Aube, chief engr. ■ On 32 CATVs—120,000 subs. On 12 trans. Co-owned radio: KTSC-FM.

Steamboat Springs

ADI No. 20; see Denver market

KSBS-TV—ch 24, 5,500 kw vis, 500 kw aur, ant 515t/98g. TL: N40 27 43 W106 51 02. Hrs opn: 24. On air date: May 1988. KBCR Radio, Box 774050, Attn: Tom Palmer, General Manager 1104 Lincoln Ave. (80477). Licensee: F&I T.V. Inc. (acq 1-15-92; $250,000; 2-3-92). Wash atty: Baraff, Koerner, Olender & Hochberg. News staff one; news progmg one hr wkly. ■ Ron Shaffer, pres; Tom Palmer, gen mgr; Tom Whiddon, gen sls mgr; L.D. Shoffner, progmg dir; John Larson, news dir; Tom Pearson, chief engr. ■ On one CATV. On 2 trans. Co-owned radio: KBCR; KSBT. ■ Rates: $18; 12; 8.

Sterling

ADI No. 196; see Cheyenne, WY-Scottsbluff, NE market

KTVS—ch 3, 60.6 kw vis, 6 kw aur, ant 760t/604g. TL: N40 34 57 W103 01 56. Hrs opn: 20. On air date: Jan 1, 1964. Box 868 (80751). (303) 522-5743. FAX: (303) 522-7813. Licensee: Stauffer Communications Inc. (group owner; acq 7-21-86; grpsl). ■ Net: CBS, ABC. Rep: Katz. News staff One; news progmg 3 hrs wkly. ■ Frank Shepherd, CEO; John Stauffer, pres; Carl Occhipinti, gen mgr; Richard E. Holland, stn mgr; Susan Holley, film buyer & news dir; Laura Pinzer, pub affrs dir; Tony Schaeffer, chief engr. ■ On 15 CATVs—14,419 subs. On 2 trans. ■ Rates: $40; 12; 25.

Connecticut

Bridgeport

ADI No. 1; see New York, NY market

*__WEDW__—ch 49, 1,950 kw vis, ant 728t. TL: N41 16 43 W73 11 08. On air date: Dec 17, 1967. 307 Atlantic St. Stamford (06901). (203) 965-0440. FAX: (203) 965-0447. Licensee: Connecticut Public Broadcasting. ■ Net: PBS. ■ Lynn Laitman, gen mgr; Don Lamy, chief engr.

WHAI-TV—ch 43, 2.5 kw vis, 2 kw aur, ant 620t/300g. TL: N41 21 43 W73 06 48. On air date: Sept 28, 1987. 312 Boston Post Rd., Orange (06447). (203) 795-0061. FAX: (203) 789-4833. Licensee: Bridgeways Communications Corp. Ownership: L. Vlock, W. Curran, M. Trachten. Wash atty: Crowell & Moring. ■ Michael K. Vlock, pres.

Hartford

ADI No. 25; see Hartford-New Haven market

*__WEDH__—ch 24, 692 kw vis, 69 kw aur, ant 860t/455g. TL: N41 46 27 W72 48 20. Stereo. On air date: Oct 1, 1962. Box 6240, 240 New Britain Ave. (06106-0240). (203) 278-5310. FAX: (203) 278-2157. Licensee: Connecticut Public Broadcasting Inc. ■ Net: PBS; EEN. Wash atty: Schwartz, Woods & Miller. ■ Jerry Franklin, pres; Larry Rifkin, vp & progmg dir; Jay Whitsett, chief engr. ■ On 29 CATVs. On one trans. Co-owned radio: *WPKT(FM) & *WNPR(FM).

WFSB—ch 3, 100 kw vis, 20 kw aur, ant 904t/518g. TL: N41 46 30 W72 48 20. Stereo. On air date: Sept 23, 1957. Broadcast House, 3 Constitution Plaza (06103-1892). (203) 728-3333. FAX: (203) 247-8940; (203) 728-0263 (News Room). Licensee: Post-Newsweek Stations (group owner; acq 3-8-74; $33.9 million; 2-11-74). ■ Net: CBS. Rep: Blair TV. Wash atty: Covington & Burling. Sp one hr wkly. ■ Christopher J. Rohrs, gen mgr; Kathleen Keefe, gen sls mgr; Matt Mixon, progmg dir; Mark Effron, news dir; Dale Werner, chief engr. ■ On 77 CATVs—1,035,000 subs.

WHCT-TV—ch 18, 3,272 kw vis, 327.2 kw aur, ant 980t. TL: N41 46 30 W72 48 04. Stereo. On air date: Aug 4, 1954. 18 Garden St. (06105). (203) 547-1818. FAX: (203) 727-9891. Licensee: Astroline Communications Co. Ltd Partnership (acq 1-23-85; $5 million). Wash atty: Baker & Hostetler. ■ Terry Planell, gen mgr; Thomas Forst, gen sls mgr; Sandra Doerr, prom mgr; Sheila Havican, progmg dir; Paul Rossi, chief engr. ■ On 28 CATVs—971,000 subs.

WTIC-TV—ch 61, 5,000 kw vis, 1,000 kw aur, ant 1,692t/1,339g. TL: N41 42 13 W72 49 57. Stereo. On air date: Sept 17, 1984. One Corporate Ctr. (06103). (203) 527-6161. Licensee: Renaissance Communications (group owner; acq 1-11-93; grpsl; 2-1-93). ■ Net: Fox. Rep: Seltel. Wash atty: Koteen & Naftalin. News staff 22; news progmg 4 hrs wkly. ■ Edward T. Karlik, pres; Robert Gluck, gen mgr & stn mgr; Jerome Martin, gen sls mgr; Corey Lewis, natl sls mgr; John Mason, prom mgr & progmg mgr; Coleen Marren, news dir; Gemma Joseph, pub affrs dir; Jim Perry, Charlie Allen, chiefs engr. ■ On 44 CATVs—1,150,000 subs. Co-owned radio: WTIC-AM-FM.

WVIT—(New Britain). ch 30, 3,090 kw vis, 309 kw aur, ant 1,479t/1,051g. TL: N41 42 00 W72 49 59. Stereo. Hrs opn: 24. On air date: Feb 13, 1953. 1422 New Britain Ave., West Hartford (06110). (203) 521-3030. FAX: (203) 521-3110. Licensee: Viacom Broadcasting Inc. (group owner; acq 3-13-78; $16 million). ■ Net: NBC. Rep: Telerep. Wash atty: Arent, Fox, Kintner, Plotkin & Kahn. ■ Pat Brady, pres; Al Bova, vp & gen mgr; Ronni Attenello, opns mgr & progmg mgr; Ron Pulena, gen sls mgr; Rob Ewent, natl sls mgr; Nancy Green, mktg mgr; Steve Schwaid, news dir; Fred Badecker, chief engr. ■ On 36 CATVs—1,094,411 subs. On one trans. ■ Rates: $5,000; 900; 200.

New Britain

WVIT—Licensed to New Britain. See Hartford.

New Haven

ADI No. 25; see Hartford-New Haven market

***WEDY**—ch 65, 4.47 kw vis, 500 w aur, ant 270t/102g. TL: N41 19 42 W72 54 25. On air date: November 1974. Box 6240, 240 New Britain Ave., Hartford (06106-0240). (203) 278-5310. FAX: (203) 278-2151. Licensee: Connecticut Public Broadcasting Inc. ■ Net: PBS. ■ Jerry Franklin, gen mgr.

WTNH-TV—ch 8, 115 kw vis, 22.9 kw aur, ant 1,210t/909g. TL: N41 25 23 W72 57 06. (CP: 166 kw vis, 33.1 kw aur). On air date: June 15, 1948. Box 1859 (06508). (203) 784-8888. Licensee: Cook Inlet Communications Corp. Ownership: Whitcom Ptnrs & Assoc L.P., ltd ptnr 51%; Cook Inlet Region Inc., gen ptnr 49% (acq 1-2-86; $170 million; 9-9-85). ■ Net: ABC. Rep: Katz. Wash atty: Wilmer, Cutler & Pickering. ■ Lewis Freifeld, pres & gen mgr; Larry Manne, stn mgr; Lou Verruto, gen sls mgr; Cathy Gugerty, mktg dir; Liz Crane, news dir; Bob Russo, chief engr. ■ On 22 CATVs—902,608 subs.

WTVU—ch 59, 2,570 kw vis, 257 kw aur, ant 1,309t/1,083g. TL: N41 22 12 W75 45 12. Not on air, target date unknown. K-W TV Inc., 4930 W. Oakton St., Skokie, IL (60077). (708) 982-9600. Permittee: K-W TV Inc. (acq 12-30-75; 1-26-76). Wash atty: Leventhal, Senter & Lerman.

New London

ADI No. 25; see Hartford-New Haven market

WTWS—ch 26, 2,792 kw vis, 279 kw aur, ant 1,251t. TL: N41 25 05 W72 11 55. On air date: Sept 15, 1986. 216 Broad St. (06320). (203) 444-2626. Licensee: R&R Media Corp. Ownership: Richard R. Rangoon, 95%; Dale Foshee, 2.5% (acq 8-87). News progmg 3 hrs wkly. ■ Nancy Schoenthal, stn mgr; Bruce Fox, gen sls mgr; Glenn Peltier, progmg dir & film buyer. ■ On 16 CATVs—600,000 subs.

Norwich

ADI No. 25; see Hartford-New Haven market

***WEDN**—ch 53, 801.64 kw vis, 80.16 kw aur, ant 480t/476g. TL: N41 31 11 W72 10 04. On air date: Mar 5, 1967. Box 6240, 240 New Britain Ave., Hartford (06106-0240). (203) 278-5310. FAX: (203) 278-2157. Licensee: Connecticut Public Broadcasting. ■ Net: PBS; EEN. ■ Jerry Franklin, gen mgr. ■ On one CATV.

Waterbury

ADI No. 25; see Hartford-New Haven market

WTXX—ch 20, 2,239 kw vis, 223.9 kw aur, ant 1,200t/1,013g. TL: N41 31 04 W73 01 07. Stereo. On air date: Sept 4, 1953. 15 Peach Orchid Rd., Prospect (06712). (203) 575-2020. FAX: (203) 758-3908. Licensee: Counterpoint Communications Inc. (acq 1-14-93; $3.601 million; 2-8-93). Rep: MMT. Wash atty: Koteen & Naftalin. ■ Edward Taddie, vp & gen mgr; Steve Ruccio, gen sls mgr & film buyer; Nancy McCormick, progmg dir; Charles Allen, chief engr. ■ On 21 CATVs—600,000 subs.

Delaware

Seaford

ADI No. 163; see Salisbury, MD market

***WDPB**—ch 64, 191 kw vis, 19.1 kw aur, ant 640t/657g. TL: N38 39 15 W75 36 42. On air date: December 1982. The Linden Bldg., 625 Orange St., Wilmington (19801). (302) 888-1200. Licensee: WHYY Inc. (acq 2-28-86). ■ Net: PBS. Wash atty: Schwartz, Woods & Miller. News staff 10; news progmg 3 hrs wkly. ■ David A. Othmer, gen mgr; William J. Weber, vp engrg. ■ On 2 CATVs—35,000 subs.

Wilmington

ADI No. 4; see Philadelphia, PA market

***WHYY-TV**—ch 12, 309 kw vis, 30.9 kw aur, ant 960t/1,148g. TL: N40 02 30 W75 14 24. Stereo. On air date: Sept 12, 1963. Independence Mall West, 150 N. 6th St., Philadelphia, PA (19106); 625 Orange St. (19801). (215) 351-1200; (302) 888-1200. FAX: (215) 351-0398. Licensee: WHYY Inc. Ownership: WHYY Inc. ■ Net: PBS. Wash atty: Schwartz, Woods & Miller. News staff 10; news progmg 5 hrs wkly. ■ Frederick Breitenfeld, Jr., CEO & pres; Robert C. Prindible, CFO; David A. Othmer, vp & stn mgr; Robert C. Altman, vp dev & vp mktg; Nessa Forman, vp prom; David Rubinsohn, vp progmg; William J. Weber, vp engrg. ■ On 2 CATVs—35,000 subs.

WTGI-TV—ch 61, 3,000 kw vis, 300 kw aur, ant 958t/950g. TL: N39 41 43 W75 17 55. Stereo. Hrs opn: 24. On air date: July 9, 1986. 520 N. Delaware Ave., Philadelphia, PA (19123). (215) 923-2661. FAX: (215) 923-2677. Licensee: Delaware Valley Broadcasters Ltd Partnership (acq 6-5-87). ■ Net: Telemundo. Wash atty: Gammon & Grange. ■ Daniel G. Slape, pres & gen mgr; Daniel Borowicz, opns mgr & chief engr; Uriel Rendon, gen sls mgr; Pircilla Bower, prom mgr & progmg dir. ■ On 9 CATVs—513,000 subs. ■ Rates: $80; 50; 20.

District of Columbia

Washington

ADI No. 7; see Washington, DC market

WDCA—ch 20, 4,000 kw vis, 400 kw aur, 770t/809g. TL: N38 57 49 W77 06 18. Stereo. On air date: Apr 20, 1966. 5202 River Rd., Bethesda, MD (20816). (301) 986-9322. FAX: (301) 654-3517. Licensee: Paramount Stations Group of Washington Inc. Group owner: Paramount Communications Inc. (acq 2-20-87; grpsl; 12-15-86). Rep: Seltel. Wash atty: Leventhal, Senter & Lerman. ■ Richard H. Williams, gen mgr; Sandra Pastoor, opns dir & progmg dir; Cindi Johnson, dev dir; Helen Feinbloom, gen sls mgr; Carl Miller, natl sls mgr; Mark Feldman, mktg mgr & prom mgr; Lisa Weir, pub affrs dir; Pedro Perez, chief engr. ■ On 104 CATV's—1,582,932 subs. ■ Rates: $840; 650; 200.

***WETA-TV**—ch 26, 2,290 kw vis, ant 771t. TL: N38 57 49 W77 06 18. Stereo. (CP: Ant 764t). On air date: Oct 2, 1961. Box 2626 (20013). (703) 998-2600. FAX: (703) 824-8343; TWX: 710-955-9846. Licensee: Greater Washington Educational Telecommunications Assn Inc. ■ Net: PBS; EEN. Wash atty: Cohn & Marks. ■ Sharon Percy Rockefeller, CEO; Daniel Mayers, chmn; Lynwood Lloyd, CFO; Neil Mahrer, gen mgr; Cheryl Head, vp opns; Michael Sapen, mktg mgr; Elise Adde, vp prom; Richard Hutton, vp progmg; David Mcgowen, news dir; Jerry Butler, chief engr. ■ On 64 CATVs—700,000 subs. On one trans. Co-owned radio: *WETA-FM.

WFTY—ch 50, 2,450 kw vis, 1860 kw aur, 570t/509g. TL: N38 57 44 W77 01 36. (CP: 2,438 kw vis, ant 810t). On air date: November 1981. 12276 Wilkins Ave. Rockville, MD (20852). (301) 230-1550. FAX: (301) 881-3441. Licensee: JASAS Corp. (acq 10-15-93; with WUNI-TV Worcester, MA; 11-8-93). Wash atty: Patton, Boggs & Blow. ■ Nolanda Hill, pres; Michael Jones, vp; Ed Shea, gen mgr; Terri Bornstein, gen sls mgr; Jackie Massay, mktg dir; Andy Zmidzinski, prom mgr; Michelle Dowd, progmg mgr; Curtis Garris, chief engr. ■ On 10 CATVs.

***WHMM**—ch 32, 500 kw vis, 158 kw aur, 700t/809g. TL: N38 57 49 W77 06 18. On air date: Nov 17, 1980. 2222 4th St. N.W. (20059). (202) 636-5600. Licensee: Howard University. ■ Net: PBS. Wash atty: Arnold & Porter. ■ Edward Jones Jr., gen mgr; Leon Haines, dev dir; Milton Clipper, mktg dir & adv dir; Brenda Otis, progmg dir; Elloitt Wiley, pub affrs dir. ■ On 24 CATVs—600,000 subs. Co-owned radio: *WHUR-FM.

WJLA-TV—ch 7, 316 kw vis, 48 kw aur, ant 770t/640g. TL: N38 57 01 W77 04 47. Stereo. On air date: Oct 3, 1947. 3007 Tilden St., N.W. (20008). (202) 364-7777. FAX: (202) 364-1556; TWX: 710-822-9505. Licensee: WJLA Inc. Group owner: Allbritton Communications Co., see also cross-ownership (acq 1-76; grpsl). ■ Net: ABC. Rep: Katz. Wash atty: Hogan & Hartson. News progmg 20 hrs wkly. ■ John D. Sawhill, pres; John Tollefson, vp opns & vp engrg; Donna Weston, vp dev; Judy Williams, sls dir; Cynthia Wold, natl sls mgr; Bryn Burn, mktg mgr; Carol Powell, progmg mgr; Gary Wordlaw, news dir.

WRC-TV—ch 4, 100 kw vis, 15.1 kw aur, ant 778t/662g. TL: N38 56 24 W77 04 54. Stereo. Hrs opn: 24. On air date: June 27, 1947. 4001 Nebraska Ave. N.W. (20016). (202) 885-4000. FAX: (202) 885-4104. Licensee: NBC Subsidiary Inc. 5. Group owner: NBC TV Stations Division. ■ Net: NBC. Rep: Petry. ■ Allan Horlick, pres & gen mgr; Jim Powell, chief opns; Marga McNally, sls dir; Steve Dickler, natl sls mgr; Sandy Yost, adv dir; Kathleen McCampbell, progmg dir; Richard A. Reingold, news dir; Angela Owens, pub affrs dir; Mike Benetato, chief engr.

WTTG—ch 5, 100 kw vis, 15 kw aur, ant 770t/705g. TL: N38 57 21 W77 04 57. On air date: Jan 1, 1947. 5151 Wisconsin Ave. N.W. (20016). (202) 244-5151. FAX: (202) 244-1745. Licensee: Fox Television Stations Inc. (group owner; acq 3-86; grpsl). ■ Net: Fox. Rep: Telerep. Wash atty: Hogan & Hartson. ■ Jim Burke, gen sls mgr; Jan Evans, natl sls mgr; Glenn Dyer, progmg dir; Richard Slenker, chief engr. ■ On 140 CATVs. On 2 trans.

WUSA—ch 9, 316 kw vis, 31.6 kw aur, ant 780t/639g. **TL: N38 57 01 W77 04 47. Hrs opn: 24. On air date: Jan 16, 1949. 4100 Wisconsin Ave., N.W. (20016). (202) 895-5999. FAX: (202) 966-7948. Licensee: The Detroit News Inc. Group owner: Gannett Broadcasting (Division of Gannett Co. Inc.) (acq 2-18-86). ■ Net: CBS. Rep: Blair. Wash atty: Pierson, Ball & Dowd. ■ Henry K. Yaggi III, pres & gen mgr; Sandra B. Butler-Jones, vp opns & progmg dir; Chuck Cowdrey, vp sls; Paul Malkie, vp prom; Dave Pearce, news dir; William Beckner, chief engr. ■ On 90 CATVs—1,400,000 subs. On 6 trans.**

Florida

Boca Raton

ADI No. 46; see West Palm Beach-Ft. Pierce-Vero Beach market

***WPPB-TV**—ch 63, 5,000 kw vis, 500 kw aur, ant 651t/662g. TL: N25 59 34 W80 10 27. (CP: 3,176 kw vis; 1,017t). Not on air, target date unknown. 572 S. Country Club Dr., Lake Worth (33461-1227). Permittee: Palmetto Broadcasters Associated for Communities Inc.

Stations in the U.S.
Florida

Bradenton

ADI No. 16; see Tampa-St. Petersburg market

WTBG-TV—ch 66, 5,000 kw vis, 500 kw aur, ant 1,158t. TL: N27 48 59 W82 16 15. Not on air, target date unknown. 515 First Ave. E. (34208). (813) 747-2879. Permittee: Bradenton Broadcast Television Co. Ltd. Ownership: Anita Rogers, 22%; MFR Inc. Limited Partner, 78%.

Cape Coral

ADI No. 87; see Ft. Myers-Naples market

WFTX—Licensed to Cape Coral. See Fort Myers.

Clearwater

ADI No. 16; see Tampa-St. Petersburg market

WCLF—ch 22, 5,000 kw vis, 500 kw aur, ant 1,410t/1,538g. TL: N28 11 04 W82 45 39. Hrs opn: 24. On air date: October 1979. Box 6922 (34618); 6922 142nd Ave. N., Largo (34641). (813) 535-5622. FAX: Call for FAX #. Licensee: Christian Television Corp. (acq 3-77). Wash atty: James Gammon. Sp 2 hrs wkly. ■ Robert R. D'Andrea, CEO, pres & gen mgr; Neville Chankersingh, CFO; Don MacAllister, vp; Jack Jarvis, opns dir; Cardin Hesselton, sls dir & progmg dir; Burdette Price, pub affrs dir; Carl Berger, engrg dir. ■ On 69 CATVs—1,026,950 subs. ■ Rates: $125; 125; 125.

Clermont

ADI No. 23; see Orlando-Daytona Beach-Melbourne market

WKCF—ch 18, 2,639 kw vis, ant 1,485t. TL: N28 34 51 W81 04 32. On air date: December 1988. Suite 200, 602 Cortlandt St., Orlando (32804). (407) 645-1818. Licensee: Press Broadcasting Co. Ownership: Asbury Park Press Inc., 90%; Channel 68 Inc., 10%, see Cross-Ownership. Rep: ITS. Wash atty: Dow, Lohnes & Albertson. ■ Robert E. McAllan, pres; Nelle Ayers, gen mgr & stn mgr; Wayne Stewart, gen sls mgr; Dave Ward, prom mgr & progmg dir; Joe Addalia, chief engr. ■ Rates: $200-500; 75-150; 25-75.

Cocoa

ADI No. 23; see Orlando-Daytona Beach-Melbourne market

***WBCC**—ch 68, 5,000 kw vis, ant 613t. TL: N28 18 26 W80 54 48. (CP: 2,844 kw vis, 284 kw aur, ant 941t). On air date: Jan 12, 1988. 1519 Clearlake Rd. (32922). (407) 632-1111, ext. 2322. FAX: (407) 631-3138. Licensee: Brevard Community College. Sp 126 hrs wkly. ■ Dr. Maxwell King, pres; Dr. Bert Purga, vp; Joe Williams, gen mgr; Phil Wallace, stn mgr; Lois Shock Broyles, progmg dir; Art Carlson, chief engr. ■ On 2 CATVs—165,000 subs.

WTGL-TV—ch 52, 4,680 kw vis, 468 kw aur, ant 934t/1,005g. TL: N28 18 26 W80 54 48. On air date: Aug 16, 1982. 653 W. Michigan St., Orlando (32805). (407) 423-5200. FAX: (407) 422-0120. Licensee: Good Life Broadcasting Inc. Wash atty: Gammon & Grange. ■ Don L. Collins, chmn; Ken Mikesell, pres & gen mgr; Paul Kuck, vp; Brock Lesperance, opns dir; Kathy Mikesell, dev dir; Cardin Hesselton, natl sls mgr; Tony Scott, prom dir; Annette Smith, progmg dir; Keith Roberts, chief engr. ■ On 34 CATVs—678,000 subs.

Daytona Beach

WAYQ—Licensed to Daytona Beach. See Orlando.

WESH—Licensed to Daytona Beach. See Orlando.

WOFL—See Orlando.

Fort Lauderdale

ADI No. 15; see Miami-Ft. Lauderdale market

WSCV—ch 51, 5,000 kw vis, ant 827t. TL: N25 57 59 W80 12 33. On air date: Dec 6, 1968. 2340 W. 8th Ave., Hialeah (33010). (305) 888-5151. Licensee: Telemundo Group Inc. (group owner; acq 12-24-87). Sp full-time. ■ J. Manuel Calvo, vp & gen mgr; Ramon Pineda, gen sls mgr; Beatrice Montalvo, prom mgr; Maria Christina Barrells, progmg mgr; Myrna Sonora, news dir; Luis Duarte, chief engr.

Fort Myers

ADI No. 87; see Ft. Myers-Naples market

WBBH-TV—ch 20, 5,000 kw vis, 500 kw aur, ant 1,482t/1,500g. TL: N26 49 27 W81 45 51. On air date: Dec 19, 1968. Box 7578 (33911-7578). 3719 Central Ave. (33970). (813) 939-2020. FAX: (813) 936-7771. Licensee: Waterman Broadcasting Corp. of Fla. Group owner: Waterman Broadcasting Corp. ■ Net: NBC. Rep: Katz. Wash atty: Cohn & Marks. ■ Steve Pontius, vp & gen mgr; Diane Gower, gen sls mgr; Kim Dobb, progmg dir; Chere Avery, news dir; Bob Cleveland, chief engr. ■ On 60 CATVs—100,000 subs.

WFTX—(Cape Coral). ch 36, 4,550 kw vis, 450 kw aur, ant 1,503t/1,450g. TL: N26 47 43 W81 48 04. On air date: Oct 14, 1985. 621 S.W. Pine Island Rd. (33991). (813) 574-3636. FAX: (813) 574-4803; TWX: 510-600-4582. Licensee: Hulman & Co. (group owner; acq 7-13-92; grpsl; 11-2-92). ■ Net: Fox. Rep: ITS. Wash atty: Dow, Lohnes & Albertson. ■ Chris Duffy, pres; Chris Andrews, vp & gen mgr; Mark Pierce, stn mgr; Ron Brown, gen sls mgr; Jon Esther, prom mgr; Merrily Carlson, progmg dir; Jerry Blevins, chief engr. ■ On 13 CATVs—198,800 subs.

WINK-TV—ch 11, 316 kw vis, 31.6 kw aur, ant 1,478t/1,519g. TL: N26 48 01 W81 45 48. Stereo. Hrs opn: 24. On air date: Mar 18, 1954. Box 1060 (33902); 2824 Palm Beach Blvd. (33916). (813) 334-1131. FAX: (813) 334-0744. Licensee: Fort Myers Broadcasting Co. Ownership: Arthur B. McBride, 50%; Edward J. McBride, 50%. ■ Net: CBS. Rep: Blair. Wash atty: Leibowitz & Spencer. News progmg 22 hrs wkly. ■ Edward McBride, pres; Joe Schwartzel, vp & gen mgr; Mel Martin, stn mgr & news dir; Gary Gardner, gen sls mgr; Ron Cooke, natl sls mgr; Paul Greeley, prom mgr; Pam Sheffield, progmg mgr; Galen Hassinger, engrg dir. ■ On 30 CATVs—1,000,205 subs. Co-owned radio: WINK-AM-FM.

***WSFP-TV**—ch 30, 1,321 kw vis, 158 kw aur, ant 963t/992g. TL: N26 48 54 W81 45 44. On air date: Aug 15, 1983. Channel 30 Dr., Bonita Springs (33923). (813) 598-9737. FAX: (813) 598-2598. Licensee: State Board of Regents of the State of Florida. ■ Net: PBS. Wash atty: Cohn & Marks. ■ James B. Heck, gen mgr; Kirk Lehtoman, stn mgr; Toby Ann Cook, prom mgr; Terry Dugas, progmg dir; Earl Carron, chief engr. Co-owned radio: WSFP-FM.

Fort Pierce

ADI No. 46; see West Palm Beach-Ft. Pierce-Vero Beach market

***WTCE**—ch 21, 2,285.6 kw vis, 457.12 kw aur, 973t/1,002g. TL: N27 26 05 W80 21 42. On air date: May 1990. 1040 S. 37th St. (34947). (407) 489-2701. FAX: (407) 486-6833. Licensee: Jacksonville Educators Broadcasting Inc. (acq 7-6-90 / $630,089). ■ Bob Constantino, gen mgr.

WTVX—ch 34, 5,000 kw vis, 500 kw aur, ant 1,492t/1,520g. TL: N27 07 20 W80 23 21. On air date: Apr 5, 1966. 3601 N. 25th St. (34946); 23rd Fl., 599 Lexingotn Ave., New York, NY (10022). (407) 464-3434. FAX: (407) 464-0967; TWX: 510-953-7581. Licensee: Krypton Broadcasting Corp. (acq 2-1-91 / $8 million; 2-18-91). Rep: Seltel. Wash atty: Haley, Bader & Potts. ■ Doug Farrell, gen mgr & gen sls mgr; Tom Hatcher, prom mgr; Cliff Curley, progmg dir; Milton Patrick, chief engr. ■ On 18 CATVs—375,000 subs. ■ Rates: $450; 250; 50.

Fort Walton Beach

ADI No. 58; see Mobile, AL-Pensacola market

WAWD—ch 58, 490 kw vis, ant 161t. TL: N30 23 35 W86 29 41. On air date: July 1991. Box 5527, 602 Mountain Dr., Destin (32541). (904) 837-1091. Licensee: Rainbow 58 Broadcasting Inc. Ownership: Wendell M. Rowans Ministries Inc., 49%; Clem Ross, 51%. Wash atty: Baraff, Koerner, Olender & Hochberg. ■ Wendell M. Rowan, pres & gen mgr.

WFGX—ch 35, 635 kw vis, 63.6 kw aur, 280t/250g. TL: N30 26 36 W86 35 56. On air date: Apr 7, 1987. Suite B-1, 105 Beach Dr. (32547). (904) 863-3235. FAX: (904) 862-6247. Licensee: Bowers Network Inc. (acq 1-27-92 / $210,000; 2-17-92). ■ Claude Bowers, pres & prom mgr; Clyd Bowers, gen mgr; Claireence Kibler, gen sls mgr; Clairece Kibler, prom mgr; Arthur Ellington, chief engr. ■ On 6 CATVs—57,706 subs.

WPAN—ch 53, 3,088 kw vis, 309 kw aur, 720t/749g. TL: N30 24 09 W86 59 35. On air date: Feb 14, 1984. 1897 Broyhill Ln., Pensacola (32526-6594). (904) 433-2109. Licensee: John Franklin Ministries Inc. Ownership: John L. Franklin, 20%; Delores A. Franklin, 20%; Joseph C. Denison, 20%; Robert Gatlin, 20%; Glyn Lowery, 20% (acq 5-23-88). Wash atty: Pepper & Corazzini. ■ John Franklin, pres. ■ On 14 CATVs—150,000 subs. On one trans.

Gainesville

ADI No. 166; see Gainesville market

WCJB—ch 20, 2,818 kw vis, 282 kw aur, ant 1,049t/985g. TL: N29 32 11 W82 24 00. On air date: April 7, 1971. Box 147020, 6220 N.W. 43rd St. (32614-7020). (904) 377-2020. Licensee: Diversified Communications (group owner; acq 12-1-76; 11-1-76). ■ Net: ABC. Rep: Blair. News staff 23; news progmg 10 hrs wkly. ■ Carolyn Catlin, pres & gen mgr; Andrew Shenkan, gen sls mgr & rgnl sls mgr; Skip Painton, natl sls mgr; Karen Watts, mktg mgr & progmg dir; Robin Snyder, prom mgr; Bob Williams, news dir; Michael Sherrill, chief engr. ■ On 46 CATVs—90,000 subs. On one trans.

WOGX—See Ocala.

***WUFT**—ch 5, 100 kw vis, 20 kw aur, ant 860t/869g. TL: N29 42 34 W82 23 40. Stereo. Hrs opn: 21. On air date: Nov 10, 1958. 2200 Weimer, U. of Fla. (32611). (904) 392-5551. FAX: (904) 392-5731. Licensee: Florida Board of Regents. ■ Net: PBS. Wash atty: Schwartz, Woods & Miller. News staff 3; news progmg 3 hrs wkly. ■ Richard Lehner, gen mgr; Rick Schneider, stn mgr; Frank Counts, opns mgr; Brent Williams, dev dir; Donna Davis, sls dir; Deb Rossi, mktg dir; Sue Williams, prom dir; Vickie Villines, progmg dir; Merline Durant, film buyer; Catherine Harwood, news dir; Myra Monroe, pub affrs dir; Al Holt, chief engr. ■ On 40 CATVs—350,000 subs.

High Springs

ADI No. 166; see Gainesville market

WGFL—ch 53, 1,493 kw vis, 53 kw aur, ant 859t. TL: N29 43 59 W82 25 16. Not on air, target date unknown. c/o Budd Broadcasting Co., 900 N.W. 8th Ave., Gainesville (32605). (904) 371-7772. Permittee: Harvey and Ilene S. Budd (acq 8-28-90).

Hollywood

ADI No. 15; see Miami-Ft. Lauderdale market

WYHS-TV—ch 69, 5,000 kw vis, 500 kw aur, ant 866t/869g. TL: N25 57 59 W80 12 33. Stereo. Hrs opn: 24. On air date: Aug 10, 1988. 10306 USA Today Way, Miramar (33025). (305) 435-6900. FAX: (305) 435-7406. Licensee: HSN Broadcasting of Hollywood Florida Inc. Group owner: Silver King Communications Inc. (acq 12-21-88). Wash atty: Dow, Lohnes & Albertson. ■ Jeff McGrath, pres; Eddie L. Whitehead, vp, gen mgr & gen sls mgr; Lily Guzman, prom mgr & progmg dir; Michael Kuszewski, chief engr.

Inverness

ADI No. 16; see Tampa-St. Petersburg market

WGOX—ch 64, 3,470 kw vis, 347 kw aur, 1,358t. TL: N28 53 21 W82 22 17. Not on air, target date unknown. Box 1000, Bushnell (33513). Permittee: West Florida Television Ltd. Ownership: Peggy R. Pendergrass; James E. & Roberta Johnson.

Jacksonville

ADI No. 54; see Jacksonville market

WAWS—ch 30, 2,789 kw vis, 278.9 kw aur, ant 991t/1,030g. TL: N30 16 53 W81 36 15. Stereo. (CP: 5,000 kw vis, 508 kw aur, ant 991t/997g). On air date:

Feb 15, 1981. 8675 Hogan Rd. (32216). (904) 642-3030. FAX: (904) 646-0115. Licensee: Clear Channel Television Licenses Inc. (group owner; acq 8-5-92). ■ Net: Fox. Rep: Katz. Wash atty: Cohn & Marks. News progmg 3 hrs wkly. ■ Josh McGraw, vp & gen mgr; Keith True, gen sls mgr; Doreen Morgan, prom mgr; Bob Keele, progmg dir; Martin Layne, chief engr. ■ On 37 CATVs—320,000 subs. ■ Rates: $1,500; 350; 75.

***WJCT**—ch 7, 316 kw vis, 31.6 kw aur, ant 910t/1,030g. TL: N30 16 53 W81 34 15. Hrs opn: 18. On air date: Sept 10, 1958. 100 Festival Park Ave. (32202). (904) 353-7770. FAX: (904) 354-6846. Licensee: WJCT Inc. ■ Net: PBS. Wash atty: Schwartz, Woods & Miller. Progmg for the deaf 49 hrs wkly. ■ Gene Napier, exec vp & gen mgr; Karen Greene, vp dev; Vic DiGenti, vp prom; Dick Brown, vp progmg; Dick Heuer, progmg dir; Jim Bedore, chief engr. ■ On 14 CATVs. Co-owned radio: WJCT-FM.

***WJEB-TV**—ch 59, 3,311 kw vis, ant 948t. TL: N30 16 34 W81 33 53. On air date: May 29, 1991. Box 5219 (32247-5219); 3101 Emerson Expwy. (32247). (904) 399-8413. Licensee: Jacksonville Educators Broadcasting Inc. ■ Net: PBS. ■ H. J. Clarey, stn mgr.

WJKS—ch 17, 4,680 kw vis, 500 kw aur, ant 1,049t. TL: N30 16 36 W81 33 47. Stereo. Hrs opn: 22. On air date: Feb 19, 1966. Box 17000, 9117 Hogan Rd. (32216). (904) 641-1700. Licensee: Jacksonville Television Inc. Group owner: Media General Broadcast Group (acq 12-23-82; $18 million; 11-8-82). ■ Net: ABC. Wash atty: Cohn & Marks. News staff 22; news progmg 7 hrs wkly. ■ Jim Matthews, pres, vp & gen mgr; George Bimbaum, opns mgr & chief engr; John C. Simons, Jr., gen sls mgr; Lee Lopez, prom dir; Debbie Knight, progmg dir; Jay Solomon, news dir; Debbie Moore, pub affrs dir. ■ On 36 CATVs—203,467 subs. ■ Rates: $750; 120; 80.

WJXT—ch 4, 100 kw vis, 20 kw aur, ant 930t/996g. TL: N30 16 23 W81 33 13. (CP: Ant 436t). Hrs opn: 24. On air date: Sept 15, 1949. Box 5270, 4 Broadcast Place (32247). (904) 399-4000. FAX: (904) 399-1828. Licensee: Post-Newsweek Stations, Fla. Inc. Group owner: Post-Newsweek Stations Inc. (acq 1-28-53; grpsl; 2-2-53). ■ Net: CBS. Rep: Telerep. Wash atty: Covington & Burling. News progmg 19 hrs wkly. ■ Steve Wasserman, Ann Pace, vps; Steve Wasserman, gen mgr; Ann Pace, stn mgr & progmg mgr; Tammie McMillan, opns mgr; Tom Bornhauser, gen sls mgr; Steve Danowski, natl sls mgr; Nancy Shafran, news dir; Jim Biggers, chief engr. ■ On 28 CATVs—90,000 subs.

WNFT—ch 47, 5,000 kw vis, 500 kw aur, ant 980t/990g. TL: N30 16 34 W81 33 58. On air date: Aug 1, 1980. Suite 0204, One Independent Dr. (32202). (904) 355-4747. FAX: (904) 353-8400. Licensee: Krypton Broadcasting of Jacksonville Inc. Group owner: Krypton Broadcasting Corp. (acq 6-19). Rep: Seltel. Wash atty: Gammon & Grange. News staff one; news progmg 3 hrs wkly. ■ Elvin Feltner, pres; Ron Gall, gen mgr; Marguerite Turner, opns mgr; Ed Hunt, gen sls mgr; Marty Leonard, rgnl sls mgr; Kent Kirby, prom mgr & progmg dir; Bill Carter, news dir; Martin Kahl, chief engr. ■ On 34 CATVs—267,212 subs.

WTLV—ch 12, 316 kw vis, 31.6 kw aur, ant 1,049t/999g. TL: N30 16 23 W81 33 13. Stereo. Hrs opn: 24. On air date: Sept 1, 1957. Box TV-12 (32231); 1070 E. Adams St. (32202). (904) 354-1212. FAX: (904) 633-8899. Licensee: Television 12 of Jacksonville Inc. Group owner: Gannett Broadcasting (Division of Gannett Co. Inc.) (acq 5-12-75; $11,401,217; 4-14-75). ■ Net: NBC. Rep: Blair. Wash atty: Reed, Smith, Shaw & McClay. News staff 55; news progmg 17 hrs wkly. ■ Ken Tonning, pres & gen mgr; Tom Wait, opns mgr; Jerry Campbell, gen sls mgr; Bonnie Solloway, mktg mgr; Roz Fields, vp prom & vp progmg; Kevin Brennan, news dir; Mary Anne Christensen, pub affrs dir; Jerry Nordsiek, vp engrg. ■ On 8 CATVs—205,000 subs.

Key West

ADI No. 15; see Miami-Ft. Lauderdale market

WEYS—ch 22, 11.2 kw vis, 1.1 kw aur, ant 203t. TL: N24 33 18 W81 48 07. Not on air, target date unknown. Box 255, 5275 Hatch Dr., Evergreen, CO (80439). (303) 526-1039. Permittee: Penny Drucker.

WWFD—ch 8, 316 kw vis, 31.6 kw aur, ant 472t. TL: N24 39 33 W81 32 07. Not on air, target date unknown. 909 Fleming St. (33040). (305) 294-8088. Permittee: Hispanic Keys Broadcasting Corp. ■ Charles P. Curry Jr., pres; C. Michael Curry, vp.

Lake Worth

ADI No. 46; see West Palm Beach-Ft. Pierce-Vero Beach market

WHBI—ch 67, 1,700 kw vis, 170 kw aur, ant 492t. TL: N26 47 59 W80 04 33. Not on air, target date 1994. 2203 N.E. 203 Terr., North Miami Beach (33180). (305) 822-2100. Permittee: Hispanic Broadcasting Inc.

Lakeland

ADI No. 16; see Tampa-St. Pertsburg market

WTMV—ch 32, 3,020 kw vis, 302 kw aur, ant 889t/890g. TL: N27 50 15 W81 56 53. Stereo. (CP: 2,950 kw vis; ant 1,086t/1,087g). On air date: Apr 24, 1986. Box 32, Tampa (33601); 7201 E. Hillsborough Ave., Tampa (33610). (813) 626-3232. FAX: (813) 622-7732. Licensee: Public Interest Corp. (acq 12-24-87). Rep: Hugh Wallace. Wash atty: Benedict P. Cottone, Frank Mullen. ■ Dan L. Johnson, chmn & gen mgr; Betty Jo Johnson, pres; Michael Pachelli, opns mgr; Gary O'Halloran, gen sls mgr; Robert Hughes, prom mgr & film buyer; Jo Johnson, progmg dir; Joe Pauly, progmg mgr; John Norvell, chief engr. ■ On 17 CATVs—448,420 subs. On one trans. ■ Rates: $120; 150; 70.

Leesburg

ADI No. 23; see Orlando-Daytona Beach-Melbourne market

WACX—Licensed to Leesburg. See Orlando.

Live Oak

ADI No. 115; see Tallahassee-Thomasville market

WFXU—ch 57, 1,858 kw vis, ant 476t. TL: N30 03 52 W82 49 04. Not on air, target date unknown. 204 Market St., Marianna (32446). Permittee: Frank A. Baker. Ownership: Frank A. Baker, 100%.

Melbourne

ADI No. 23; see Orlando-Daytona Beach-Melbourne market

WBSF—ch 43, 4,170 kw vis, 854 kw aur, ant 1,049t/1,005g. TL: N28 18 26 W80 54 48. Hrs opn: 24. On air date: July 5, 1982. 4450-L Enterprise Court (32934). (407) 254-4343. FAX: (407) 242-0863. Licensee: Blackstar Communications Inc. (group owner; acq 4-20-88; $5 million; 2-29-88). Wash atty: Dow, Lohnes & Albertson. ■ John Oxendine, pres; Ed Parker, CFO, vp, gen mgr & gen sls mgr; Ron Marshall, chief opns & chief engr; Delores McLaughlin, pub affrs dir. ■ On 30 CATVs—560,000 subs.

WIRB—ch 56, 2,040 kw vis, 204 kw aur, ant 1,028t/1,024g. TL: N27 49 35 W80 42 20. Hrs opn: 24. On air date: June 1986. 6525 Babcock St. S.E., Palm Bay (32909). (407) 725-0056. FAX: (407) 951-2669. Licensee: Treasure Coast Communications Inc. Ownership: Robert J. Rich (acq 4-6-92; $1,250,000; 4-27-92). ■ Robert J. Rich, CEO & pres; Bill Watts, rgnl sls mgr; Wayne Fleenor, prom mgr & progmg dir; Dina Lipari, pub affrs dir; Bob Russ, chief engr. ■ On 22 CATVs—685,000 subs.

Miami

ADI No. 15; see Miami-Ft. Lauderdale market

WBFS-TV—ch 33, 5,000 kw vis, 500 kw aur, ant 924g. TL: N25 57 59 W80 12 33. On air date: Dec 9, 1984. 16550 N.W. 52nd Ave. (33014). (305) 621-3333. Licensee: Combined Broadcasting of Miami Inc. Group owner: Combined Broadcasting Inc. Rep: Katz. Wash atty: Fisher, Wayland, Cooper & Leader. ■ Robert O'Connor, pres; Jerry Carr, vp & gen mgr; Eli Math, gen sls mgr; Lee Rowand, prom mgr; Stan Wasilik, progmg dir; Tim L. Cottrill, chief engr. ■ On 48 CATVs—1,000,000 subs.

WCIX—ch 6, 100 kw vis, 15.9 kw aur, ant 1,842t/1,841.5g. TL: N25 32 24 W80 28 07. Stereo. On air date: Sept 20, 1967. 8900 N.W. 18th Terrace (33172). (305) 593-0606. FAX: (305) 471-6666. Licensee: CBS Inc. Group owner: CBS Broadcast Group (acq 4-1-87; $59 million). ■ Net: CBS. Rep: CTS Spot Sls. ■ Allen Shaklan, vp & gen mgr; Joe Calim, sls dir; Brian Blum, prom dir; Jerry Birdwell, progmg dir; Sue Kawalerski, news dir; Bernie Wimmers, engrg dir. ■ On 25 CATVs. On 4 trans.

WCTD—ch 35, 5,000 kw vis, 500 kw aur, ant 1,174t/1,166g. TL: N24 41 05 W80 18 52. Stereo. Hrs opn: 24. On air date: Oct 15, 1992. One Datran Center, Suite 1804, 9100 S. Dadeland Blvd. (33156). (305) 670-3535. FAX: (305) 670-0135. Permittee: William C. de la Pena (acq 12-7-92; $1.6 million; 1-4-93). ■ William De La Pena, pres; Richard A. Vanhook, gen mgr & chief engr.

WDZL—ch 39, 3,980 kw vis, 398 kw aur, ant 735t/733g. TL: N25 58 48 W80 11 47. Hrs opn: Mon-Sat 24; Sun 6 AM-1 AM. On air date: Oct 16, 1982. 2055 Lee St., Hollywood (33020). (305) 925-3939; (305) 949-3900. FAX: (305) 922-3965. Licensee: Channel 39 Licensee Inc. Group owner: Renaissance Communications Corp. (acq 3-1-89; $29.5 million; 12-26-88). Rep: MMT. Wash atty: Reed, Smith, Shaw & McClay. ■ Harvey E. Cohen, pres & gen mgr; Jeff Eggleston, opns mgr; Marilyn Hansen, gen sls mgr; Alan Rosenfeld, natl sls mgr; Lori Lathrop, mktg mgr; Robert Ramsey, prom mgr & progmg mgr; Jeanette Jordan, pub affrs dir; Robert Castillo, chief engr. ■ On 31 CATVs—846,130 subs.

WHFT—ch 45, 2,400 kw vis, 240 kw aur, ant 1,020t. TL: N25 59 34 W80 10 27. On air date: Mar 17, 1975. 3324 Pembroke Rd., Pembroke Park (33021). (305) 962-1700. FAX: (305) 962-2817. Licensee: Trinity Broadcasting of Florida Inc. Group owner: Trinity Broadcasting Network (acq 5-14-80; $10 million). Wash atty: May, Dunn & Gay. Some Sp progmg. ■ Paul F. Crouch, pres; Michael Everett, gen mgr; Tee Thomas, chief engr. ■ On 10 CATVs.

***WLRN-TV**—ch 17, 2,860 kw vis, 286 kw aur, ant 1,013t/1,039g. TL: N25 57 30 W80 12 44. (CP: 2,825 kw vis, 283 kw aur, ant 1,014t, TL: N25 57 30 W80 12 44). On air date: June 26, 1962. 172 N.E. 15th St. (33132). (305) 995-2204. FAX: (305) 995-2299. Licensee: School Board of Dade County. ■ Net: PBS; SECA. ■ Don MacCullough, gen mgr; Marcia Hope, prom mgr; Steve Weisberg, progmg dir; Clarence Mosley, chief engr. ■ On 11 CATVs—260,000 subs. Co-owned radio: *WLRN-FM.

WLTV—ch 23, 661 kw vis, 66.1 kw aur, ant 1,049t/1,039g. TL: N25 57 30 W80 12 44. Stereo. On air date: Nov 15, 1967. 9405 N.W. 41st St. (33178). (305) 470-2323. Licensee: WLTV L.P. Group owner: Perenchio Television Inc. (acq 8-7-88). ■ Net: Univision. Wash atty: Wiley, Rein & Fielding. Sp full time. ■ Judith Whittaker, vp; Tony Oquendo, gen mgr; Mara Rankin, stn mgr; Zeida Mendez, prom mgr; Rosy Almeida, progmg dir; Alina Falcon, news dir; Efrain Rivera, chief engr. ■ Rates: $1,700; 600; 350.

***WPBT**—ch 2, 100 kw vis, 20 kw aur, 932t/923g. TL: N25 57 30 W80 12 44. Stereo. Hrs opn: 20. On air date: Aug 12, 1955. Box 2 (33161-0002); 14901 N.E. Sesame St. (33181). (305) 949-8321. FAX: (305) 944-4211. Licensee: Community Television Foundation of S. Florida Inc. ■ Net: PBS. Wash atty: Wilmer, Cutler & Pickering. Progmg for the deaf. ■ George Dooley, CEO & pres; William L. Ford Jr., chmn; Craig A. Brush, Barry O. Chase, sr vps; Linda O'Bryon, vp; John Reynolds, vp dev; Craig A. Brush, vp mktg; John Felton, vp progmg; Jack Gibson, progmg dir; Graham Simmons, vp engrg. ■ On 38 CATVs—1,126,410 subs.

WPLG—ch 10, 316 kw vis, 47.9 kw aur, ant 1,042t/1,046g. TL: N25 57 59 W80 12 44. On air date: Nov 20, 1961. 3900 Biscayne Blvd. (33137). (305) 576-1010. FAX: (305) 325-2381. Licensee: Post-Newsweek Stations, Fla. Inc. Group owner: Post-Newsweek Stations Inc. (acq 9-27-69; grpsl; 10-6-69). ■ Net: ABC. Rep: Telerep. Wash atty: Covington & Burling. ■ John G. Garwood, vp & gen mgr; Sharon Harrison, opns mgr; Bill Lamb, gen sls mgr; Jim Hayek, prom mgr; Oscar Welch, progmg dir; Tom Doerr, news dir; Steve Flanagan, chief engr. ■ On 23 CATVs—820,000 subs.

WSVN—ch 7, 316 kw vis, 30.2 kw aur, ant 950t/1,002g. TL: N25 57 49 W80 12 44. Stereo. Hrs opn: 24. On air date: July 29, 1956. 1401 79th St. Causeway (33141). (305) 751-6692. TWX: 810-848-6151. Licensee: Sunbeam TV Corp. Ownership: Edmund N. Ansin. (acq 10-4-67; $185,000; 10-16-67). ■ Net: Fox. Rep: HRP. Wash atty: Koteen & Naftalin. ■ Edmund N. Ansin, pres; Robert W. Leider, exec vp & gen mgr; Joel Cheatwood, sr vp; Michael Draman, gen sls mgr; Beatriz Montalvo, prom mgr; Bert Medina, progmg dir; Brian Greif, news dir; Charlie Folds, pub affrs dir; John Bak, chief engr.

WTVJ—ch 4, 100 kw vis, 10 kw aur, ant 950t/995g. TL: N25 59 10 W80 11 39. Stereo. Hrs opn: 24. On air date: Mar 21, 1949. 316 N. Miami Ave. (33128). (305) 379-4444. FAX: (305) 789-4273. Licensee: NBC Subsidiary (WTVJ) Inc. Group owner: NBC TV Stations Division (acq 9-17-87). ■ Net: NBC. Rep: Petry. News staff 85; news progmg 25 hrs wkly. ■ Donald V. Browne, pres & gen mgr; Bruce Carter, opns dir; Barry Allentuck, sls dir; Steve Brooks, natl sls mgr; Carol DeVane, mktg mgr; Barry Leffler, prom dir; Maritza Kaniewski, progmg dir;

Stations in the U.S. | Florida

Marina Angleton, pub affrs dir; Paul Russell, chief engr. ■ On 17 CATVs—340,700 subs.

Naples

ADI No. 87; see Ft. Myers-Naples market

WEVU—ch 26, 5,000 kw vis; 500 kw aur, ant 1,206t/1,224g. TL: N26 25 22 W81 37 49. On air date: Aug 21, 1974. 3451 Bonita Bay Blvd., Bonita Springs (33923). (813) 495-9388. FAX: (813) 947-1722. Licensee: Elcom of South Carolina Inc. Group owner: Ellis Communications (acq 7-3-92; $15 million with WACH-TV Columbia, SC; 10-25-93). ■ Net: ABC. Rep: Seltel. Wash atty: Cordon & Kelly. ■ Robert White, vp, gen mgr & film buyer; Jesse Daniels, gen sls mgr; Randy Keiser, progmg dir; James Goin, pub affrs dir; David McKelvey, chief engr. ■ On 12 CATVs—75,000 subs.

WNPL-TV—ch 46, 5,000 kw vis, 500 kw aur, ant 1,000t/1,224g. TL: N26 25 22 W81 37 49. (CP: 3,192 kw vis). Hrs opn: 18. On air date: Oct 22, 1990. Suite 800, 2150 Goodlette Rd. N., (33940); Box 7099 (33941). (813) 261-4600. FAX: (813) 261-4603. Licensee: Southwest Florida Telecommunications Inc. Ownership: William T. Darling (acq 9-1-89; $650,250; 9-25-89). Rep: MBS. Wash atty: Latham & Watkins. News progmg 7 hrs wkly. ■ William T. Darling, CEO, pres & vp progmg; Jack L. Spiess, gen mgr; Phil Beckman, chief engr.

New Smyrna Beach

ADI No. 23; see Orlando-Daytona Beach-Melbourne market

***WCEU**—ch 15, 708 kw vis, 201.4 kw aur, ant 576t. TL: N29 10 24 W81 09 24. On air date: Feb 1, 1988. Box 9245, Daytona Beach (32120-9245); 1200 International Speedway Blvd., Daytona Beach (32120). (904) 254-4415. FAX: (904) 254-3008. Licensee: Coastal Educational Broadcasters Inc. ■ Net: PBS. ■ Don A. Thigpen, gen mgr; N. M. Robertson, gen sls mgr; Pete Miniscalko, progmg mgr; Bill Schwartz, chief engr.

Ocala

ADI No. 166; see Gainesville market

WOGX—ch 51, 2,750 kw vis, 275 kw aur, ant 918t/855g. TL: N29 21 32 W82 19 53. Hrs opn: 6 AM-2 AM. On air date: Nov 1, 1983. Box 3985 (34478); 1551 S.W. 37th Ave. (34474). (904) 351-5151. FAX: (904) 237-5423. Licensee: Hulman & Co. (group owner; acq 7-13-92; grpsl; 11-2-92). ■ Net: Fox. Rep: Katz. Wash atty: Dow, Lohnes & Albertson. ■ Mel Grossman, vp & gen mgr; Clay Brinker, gen sls mgr; Darren Morgan, prom mgr; John Jones, chief engr. ■ On 12 CATVs—150,000 subs. ■ Rates: $450; 150; 60.

Orange Park

ADI No. 54; see Jacksonville market

WYDP—ch 25, 2,040 kw vis, ant 495t. TL: N30 04 27 W81 48 23. Not on air, target date unknown. Box 250 (32067). (904) 284-5077. Permittee: Clay Television Inc.

Orlando

ADI No. 23; see Orlando-Daytona Beach-Melbourne market

WACX—(Leesburg). ch 55, 5,000 kw vis, 500 kw aur, ant 1,690t/1,669g. TL: N28 55 16 W81 19 09. Stereo. Hrs opn: 24. On air date: Mar 6, 1982. 4520 Parkbreeze Ct., Orlando (32808); 900 N. Blvd West, Leesburg (34748). (407) 297-0155; (904) 787-2287. Licensee: Sharp Communications Inc. Ownership: Associated Christian Television System Inc., 100% (acq 6-8-83; 7-4-83). Wash atty: James C. Koerner. Some Sp progmg. ■ Claud Bowers, pres & gen mgr; Claireece Kibler, gen sls mgr & adv mgr; Linda Jarrell, progmg dir; John Copeland, news dir; Jackie Benton, pub affrs dir; Gary Hawkins, chief engr. ■ On 88 CATVs—760,000 subs. On one trans. ■ Rates: $75; 29; 40.

WAYQ—(Daytona Beach). ch 26, 2,786 kw vis, 278.6 kw aur, ant 997t. TL: N29 17 10 W81 29 37. On air date: October 1988. c/o George E. Mills Jr., 9334 Bay Vista Estates Blvd., Orlando (32836). (407) 352-0405. Licensee: George E. Mills Jr., trustee.

WCPX-TV—ch 6, 74.1 kw vis, 14.8 kw aur, ant 1,460t/1,484g. TL: N28 36 08 W81 05 37. (CP: 100 kw vis, 20 kw aur, ant 1,840t). Hrs opn: 24. On air date: July 1, 1954. Box 606000 (32860); 4466 John Young Pkwy. (32804). (407) 291-6000. FAX: (407) 578-1321. Licensee: First Media L.P. Ownership: Richard E. Marriott, 61.92%; Nancy P. Marriott, 22.34%; Glenn T. Potter, 1.60% (acq 6-29-86; $200 million). ■ Net: CBS. Rep: Katz. Wash atty: Dow, Lohnes & Albertson.■ Michael J. Schweitzer, pres & gen mgr; James Posey, gen sls mgr; Craig Burick, prom mgr; Judith Broes, progmg dir; Ron Bilek, news dir; Robert Diehl, chief engr.

WESH—(Daytona Beach). ch 2, 100 kw vis, 10 kw aur, ant 1,650t/1,670g. TL: N28 56 17 W81 18 58. Stereo. On air date: June 11, 1956. Box 1551, Daytona Beach (32115); 1021 N. Wymore Rd., Winter Park (32789). (904) 226-2222; (407) 645-2222. FAX: (904) 226-2127. Licensee: WESH-TV Broadcasting. Group owner: Pulitzer Broadcasting Co. (acq 1993). ■ Net: NBC. Rep: Petry. Wash atty: Verner, Liipfert, Bernhard, McPherson & Hand.■ Jeffrey H. Lee, vp & gen mgr; Nick Nicholson, gen sls mgr; James "Jimmy" Cromwell, natl sls mgr; Paul Shemo, mktg mgr & prom mgr; Lynn Stepanian, progmg dir; John Harris, news dir; Kelley Lesperance, pub affrs dir; John Demshock, chief engr.

WFTV—ch 9, 316 kw vis, 31.6 kw aur, ant 1,570t/1,543g. TL: N28 36 08 W81 05 37. Stereo. On air date: Feb 1, 1958. Box 999 (32802); 490 E. South St. (32801-2841). (407) 841-9000. FAX: (407) 244-8302. Licensee: WFTV Inc. Group owner: Cox Broadcasting (acq 8-85; $185 million). ■ Net: ABC. ■ Merritt S. Rose Jr., vp & gen mgr; Skip Skiffington, prom mgr; Lou Supowitz, gen sls mgr; Joe Chaplinski, natl sls mgr; Karen Clark, mktg dir & prom dir; Chris Schmidt, news dir; Paul Warnock, chief engr. ■ On 100 CATVs—480,000 subs. ■ Rates: $4,500; 1,000; 375.

***WMFE-TV**—ch 24, 1,202 kw vis, 240 kw aur, ant 1,254t/1,228g. TL: N28 36 08 W81 05 37. Hrs opn: 18. On air date: March 25, 1965. 11510 E. Colonial Dr. (32817). (407) 273-2300. Licensee: Community Communications Inc. ■ Net: PBS. Wash atty: Schwartz, Woods & Miller. Foreign lang progmg 120 hrs wkly. ■ Stephen M. Steck, CEO, vp progmg & news dir; Leon Handley, chmn; Malcolm Wall, exec vp & gen mgr; Peter Dominowski, vpdev; Mike Hennessy, mktg mgr; Barbara Gibson, prom mgr; Mike Simmons, engrg dir. ■ On 28 CATVs—300,000 subs. Co-owned radio: WMFE-FM.

WOFL—ch 35, 2,570 kw vis, 513 kw aur, ant 1,470t/1,486g. TL: N28 36 17 W81 03 13. Hrs opn: 24. On air date: Oct 15, 1979. 35 Skyline Dr., Lake Mary (32746). (407) 644-3535. Licensee: Meredith Corp. Group owner: Meredith Bcstg Group, Meridith Corp. See Cross-Ownership (acq 6-1-83; $16 million; 5-9-83). ■ Net: Fox. Rep: MMT Sales. Wash atty: Haley, Bader & Potts. ■ Norris Reichel, vp & gen mgr; Tom Meek, opns dir & pub affrs dir; Tom Calato, gen sls mgr; George Wilson, news dir; Jim Doyas, chief engr. ■ On 85 CATVs—750,000 subs.

WRBW—ch 65, 5,000 kw vis, ant 1,525t. TL: N28 34 51 W81 04 32. Not on air, target date unknown. c/o Rainbow Broadcasting Co., 151 Crandon Blvd. #110, Key Biscayne (33149). Permittee: Rainbow Broadcasting Co. Ownership: Joseph Rey.

WZWY—ch 27, 5,000 kw vis, 500 kw aur, ant 1,804t TL: N28 29 21 W81 46 13. 22 E. Pine St. (32801). Licensee: Reese Associates Ltd.

Palm Beach

ADI No. 46; see West Palm Beach-Ft. Pierce-Vero Beach market

WFGC—ch 61., (CP: 5,000 kw vis, 500 kw aur, ant 268t. TL: N26 38 28 W80 05 08.) Hrs opn: 6:30 AM-midnight. On air date: May 21, 1993. Not on air, target date unknown. Bldg. #2, 2406 S. Congress Ave., West Palm Beach (33400). (407) 642-3361; (407) 967-1761. FAX: Call for Fax #. Licensee: Christian TV of Palm Beach County Inc. Wash atty: Gammon & Grange.■ Robert R. D'Andrea, CEO & chmn; Neville Chankersingh, CFO; Don Price, gen mgr, stn mgr & opns mgr; Cardin Hesselton, sls dir & adv dir; Burdette Price, pub affrs dir; Carl Berger, engrg dir. ■ On 17 CATVs—452,760 subs. ■ Rates: $100; 100; 100.

Panama City

ADI No. 164; see Panama City market

***WFSG**—ch 56, 1,147 kw vis, 48.6 kw aur, ant 509t/499g. TL: N30 22 02 W85 55 29. Stereo. On air date: July 11, 1988. 2565 Pottsdamer St., Tallahassee (32310). (904) 487-3170. Licensee: Board of Regents of Florida (acq 2-28-86). ■ Net: PBS. ■ Madison Hodges, gen mgr; Rick Johnson, stn mgr; Kathleen Stafford, opns dir; Denise Hall, progmg dir; Les Dumas, pub affrs dir; David Lauther, chief engr. Simulcast WFSU-TV.

WJHG-TV—ch 7, 316 kw vis, 34 kw aur, ant 870t/887g. TL: N30 26 00 W85 24 51. Hrs opn: 24. On air date: Dec 1, 1953. Box 2349 (32402); 8195 Front Beach Rd., Panama City Beach (32407). (904) 234-2125. FAX: (904) 233-6647. Licensee: WJHG-TV Inc. Group owner: Gray Communications Systems Inc. (acq 6-29-60; $340,000; 7-4-60). ■ Net: NBC. Rep: Katz. Wash atty: Sidley & Austin.■ Jerry Smithwick, vp, gen mgr & film buyer; Jack Crusan, opns dir; Roger Jones, gen sls mgr; Ron Jones, prom mgr; Mike Voznick, adv dir; Marg Sheperd, progmg dir; Joe Moore, news dir; Wade Thomaston, chief engr. ■ On 22 CATVs.

WMBB—ch 13, 316 kw vis, 63 kw aur, ant 1,549t/1,464g. TL: N30 21 09 W85 23 26. On air date: Oct 3, 1973. Box 1340, 613 Harrison Ave. (32402). (904) 769-2313. FAX: (904) 769-8231. Licensee: The Spartan Broadcasting Co. Group owner: Spartan Radiocasting Company Inc. (acq 4-10-90; $10.4 million). ■ Net: ABC. Rep: Blair. Wash atty: Covington & Burling. News staff 16; news progmg 9 hrs wkly. ■ Nick Evans, pres; Hugh V. Roche, gen mgr; Bill Byrd, gen sls mgr; Teri Basford, prom mgr; Patti Clements, progmg dir & film buyer; Larche Hardy, news dir; Wendell Nelson, chief engr. ■ On 40 CATVs—55,000 subs.

WPGX—ch 28, 1,260 kw vis, 126 kw aur, ant 748t. TL: N30 23 42 W85 32 02. Hrs opn: 18. On air date: May 21, 1988. Box 16028, 28 Corporate Park, 700 W. 23rd St. (32405); Box 16028 (32406-6028). (904) 784-0028. FAX: (904) 784-1773. Licensee: Ashling Broadcast Group Inc. Ownership: Edward W. Gibbons, 70%; Elizabeth Wilde Mooney, 30% (acq 4-30-90; $500,000). ■ Net: Fox. Rep: Seltel. Wash atty: Fisher, Wayland, Cooper & Leader. ■ Elizabeth Wilde Mooney, pres; Mike Harding, vp & gen mgr; Sandie Moore, opns mgr & progmg mgr; Chris Hundley, gen sls mgr; Chris Beason, prom mgr & pub affrs dir.

Pensacola

ADI No. 58; see Mobile, AL-Pensacola market

WEAR-TV—Licensed to Pensacola. See Mobile, Ala.

WHBR—ch 33, 5,000 kw vis, 500 kw aur, ant 1,365t/1,330g. TL: N30 37 35 W87 38 50. (CP: 3,500 kw vis). Hrs opn: 17. On air date: Jan 27, 1986. Box 2633 (32532); 3030 Blackshear Ave. (32503). (904) 433-8633. Licensee: Christian Television of Pensacola/Mobile Inc. Wash atty: Gammon & Grange. ■ Robert R. D'Andrea, pres & gen mgr; Cardin A. Hesselton, gen sls mgr & progmg dir; David Mayo, prom mgr; Bill Cobert, chief engr. ■ On 13 CATVs—155,000 subs.

WJTC—ch 44, 3,289 kw vis, 328.9 kw aur, ant 1,493t. TL: N30 35 18 W87 33 16. Hrs opn: 24. On air date: November 1984. 661 Azalea Rd., Mobile, AL (36609). (205) 602-1544. FAX: (205) 602-1547. Licensee: Mercury Broadcasting Co. Inc. (group owner; acq 3-30-92; $2.25 million; 4-13-92). ■ Net: ABC, CBS. Rep: Seltel. Wash atty: John Scot. ■ David L. Herbstreith, gen mgr & progmg dir; Tim Woodard, opns mgr; Michelle Strocker, natl sls mgr; Joe Curlette, rgnl sls mgr; Sara Moreland, prom mgr; Nona Simmons, pub affrs dir; Glenn Davis, chief engr.■ On 40 CATVs—164,065 subs. ■ Rates: $60; 40; 25.

***WSRE**—ch 23, 3,020 kw vis, 610 kw aur, ant 487t/466g. TL: N30 26 36 W87 14 03. Stereo. On air date: Sept 11, 1967. 1000 College Blvd. (32504-8998). (904) 484-1200. FAX: (904) 484-1255. Licensee: Dist Bd of Trustees of Pensacola Jr. College (acq 8-31-71). ■ Net: PBS. ■ Allan Pizzato, gen mgr; Steve Sox, progmg dir; Steve Agerton, chief engr. ■ On 8 CATVs—80,000 subs.

St. Petersburg

WTOG—Licensed to St. Petersburg. See Tampa-St. Petersburg.

WTSP—Licensed to St. Petersburg. See Tampa-St. Petersburg.

WTTA—Licensed to St. Petersburg. See Tampa-St. Petersburg.

Florida

Sarasota

ADI No. 153; see Sarasota market

WWSB—ch 40, 2,871 kw vis, 431 kw aur, ant 771t/814g. TL: N27 33 27 W82 21 59. Hrs opn: 20. On air date: Oct 23, 1971. 5725 Lawton Dr. (34233). (813) 923-8840. FAX: (813) 924-3971. Licensee: Southern Broadcast Corp. of Sarasota. Ownership: Calkins Newspapers Inc, 53%; R.R. Nelson, 28.5%; Southern Broadcast Group, 18.5% (acq 3-26-86; $40,500). ■ Net: ABC. Rep: Seltel. Wash atty: Leibowitz & Spencer. News staff 26; news progmg 10 hrs wkly. ■ Stan Crumley, pres, gen mgr & progmg dir; Glen Eklund, exec vp, vp opns & vp prom; Terry Douma, opns mgr; Kim Urbuteit, natl sls mgr; Dave Collins, news dir; Mike Burnham, chief engr. ■ On 10 CATVs—405,000 subs. ■ Rates: $800; 650; 175.

Tallahassee

ADI No. 115; see Tallahassee-Thomasville market

WCTV—(Thomasville, GA). ch 6, 97.5 kw vis, 19.5 kw aur, ant 2,031t/2,000g. TL: N30 40 13 W83 56 26. On air date: Sept 15, 1955. Box 3048, Tallahassee (32315). (904) 893-6666. FAX: (904) 893-5193; TWX: 910-997-0058. Licensee: John H. Phipps Inc. (acq 5-11-55; 5-23-55). ■ Net: CBS. Rep: Blair. Wash atty: Wiley & Rein. ■ Dennis O. Boyle, pres; David Olmsted, gen mgr; Melvin Blank, opns mgr & progmg dir; Don Wargo, gen sls mgr; Mike Smith, news dir; Bob Morgan, chief engr. ■ On 96 CATVs—152,462 subs. ■ Rates: $775; 440; 195.

***WFSU-TV**—ch 11, 316 kw vis, 31.6 kw aur, ant 777t/774g. TL: N30 21 29 W84 36 39. Stereo. On air date: Sept 20, 1960. 1600 Red Barber Plaza (32310). (904) 487-3170. FAX: (904) 487-3093. Licensee: Florida Board of Regents & Fla. State U. ■ Net: PBS. ■ Madison Hodges, gen mgr; Rick Johnson, stn mgr; Kathleen Stafford, opns dir; Denise Hall, progmg dir; Les Dumas, pub affrs dir; Woodfin O. Walker, chief engr. Co-owned radio: *WFSU-FM/WFSQ-FM.

WTLH—(Bainbridge, GA). ch 49, 1,620 kw vis, 162 kw aur, ant 806t/806g. TL: N30 47 48 W84 19 28. On air date: 1991. 1203 Governors Square Blvd., #501 Tallahassee (32301). (904) 942-4900. FAX: (904) 942-0062. Licensee: WTLH Inc. ■ Net: Fox. Rep: Seltel. ■ Paul Lansat, CEO; Frank Watson, pres, gen mgr & gen sls mgr; Don Abel, opns mgr & progmg dir; Jan Wheeless, prom mgr; Jim Bowman, engrg dir. ■ On 32 CATVs—107,000 subs. On one trans. ■ Rates: $400; 65; 35.

WTWC—ch 40, 3,160 kw vis, 316 kw aur, ant 880t/821g. TL: N30 35 11 84 14 11. Hrs opn: 22. On air date: April 21, 1983. 8440 Deerlake Rd. (32312). (904) 893-4140. FAX: (904) 893-6974. Licensee: Holt-Robinson Television Inc. Group owner: Holt Broadcasting Service (acq 4-13-93). ■ Net: NBC. Rep: Katz. ■ Thomas M. Duddy, CEO; John F. Friedlein, gen mgr; Ed Shaper, opns mgr; Cliff Thompson, gen sls mgr; Gil Daspit, prom dir; Paige Dietz, progmg mgr; Michael Brown, chief engr. ■ On 44 CATVs—102,653 subs. ■ Rates: $350; 75; 45.

WTXL-TV—ch 27, 1,184.7 kw vis, 118.46 kw aur, ant 1,041t/901g. TL: N30 34 27 W84 12 09. On air date: Sept 16, 1976. 8927 Thomasville Rd. (32312). (904) 893-3127. FAX: (904) 668-1460. Licensee: Media Venture Management Inc. Ownership: F. Tracy Lavery and Elio Betty, 50% each (acq 5-26-93; $5 million; 7-14-93). ■ Net: ABC. Rep: Blair. Wash atty: Keck, Mahin & Cate. News staff 21; news progmg 24 hrs. ■ Dan Akens, gen mgr; David Arrington, gen sls mgr; Mike Plummer, prom mgr; Janice Gargus, progmg dir; Chris Huston, news dir; Brad Strommen, chief engr. ■ On 28 CATVs—160,000 subs.

Tampa

WBHS-TV—Licensed to Tampa. See Tampa-St. Petersburg.

***WEDU**—Licensed to Tampa. See Tampa-St. Petersburg.

WFLA-TV—Licensed to Tampa. See Tampa-St. Petersburg.

WFTS—Licensed to Tampa. See Tampa-St. Petersburg.

WTVT—Licensed to Tampa. See Tampa-St. Petersburg.

***WUSF-TV**—Licensed to Tampa. See Tampa-St. Petersburg.

Tampa-St. Petersburg

ADI No. 16; see Tampa-St. Petersburg market

WBHS-TV—(Tampa). ch 50, 4,200 kw vis, 420 kw aur, ant 1,600t/1,580g. TL: N27 50 32 W82 15 46. Hrs opn: 24. On air date: Feb 1, 1988. Suite 301, 12425 28th St. N., St. Petersburg (33716). (813) 573-5550. FAX: (813) 573-2501. Licensee: Silver King Broadcasting of Tampa Inc. Group owner: Silver King Communications Inc. Wash atty: Dow, Lohnes & Albertson. ■ W. James Goodman, gen mgr; Cheryl Barron, progmg dir; J. Allen McCarty, chief engr.

***WEDU**—(Tampa). ch 3, 100 kw vis, 20 kw aur, ant 1551t. TL: N27 49 48 W82 15 59. Stereo. On air date: Oct 27, 1958. Box 4033, Tampa (33677-4033); 1300 N. Blvd., Tampa (33607). (813) 254-9338. FAX: (813) 253-0826. Licensee: Florida West Coast Pub Broadcasting Inc. ■ Net: PBS. Wash atty: Schwartz, Woods & Miller. Closed-captioned progmg 7 hrs wkly. ■ Stephen L. Rogers, CEO & pres; Elsie Garner, sr vp & stn mgr; Gustavo Sagustume, vp opns; Johanna Antes, dev dir; Paul Dietrich, vp mktg; Christine Beyer, prom mgr; Steve Strout, progmg dir; Frank Wolynskt, chief engr. ■ On 46 CATVs.

WFLA-TV—(Tampa). ch 8, 302 kw vis, 30.2 kw aur, ant 1,575t/1,575g. TL: N27 50 32 W82 14 26. (CP: Ant 1,930t). On air date: Feb 14, 1955. 905 E. Jackson St., Tampa (33602). (813) 228-8888. FAX: (813) 221-5787. Licensee: Tampa Television Inc. Group owner: Media General Broadcast Group. See Cross-Ownership (acq 1965; $17.5 million). ■ Net: NBC. Rep: MMT. Wash atty: Cohn & Marks. ■ Jim Zimmerman, vp; Paul Catoe, stn mgr; Jack Lyons, gen sls mgr; Melinda Bacon, mktg mgr; Russ Myerson, progmg dir; Peter Holst, film buyer; Dan Bradley, news dir; Ardell Hill, chief engr. ■ On 22 CATVs.

WFTS—(Tampa). ch 28, 2.63 kw vis, .26 kw aur, ant 1,546t/1,649g. TL: N27 50 32 W82 15 46. Hrs opn: 24. On air date: Dec 14, 1981. 4501 E. Columbus Dr., Tampa (33605-3212). (813) 623-2828. FAX: (813) 744-2828. Licensee: Tampa Bay Television Inc. Group owner: Scripps Howard Broadcasting Co., see Cross-Ownership (acq 1-2-86; grpsl). ■ Net: Fox. Rep: Katz. Wash atty: Baker & Hostetler. ■ Jim Major, vp & gen mgr; Lu Romero, opns mgr; Larry Jopek, gen sls mgr; Chris Raynor, prom mgr; Joseph Logsdon, progmg dir; Joy Petit, pub affrs dir; Lee Melvin, engrg mgr. ■ On 45 CATVs—875,000 subs.

WTOG—(St. Petersburg). ch 44, 5,000 kw vis, 285 kw aur, ant 1,649t/1,507g. TL: N27 49 48 W82 15 59. Hrs opn: 24. On air date: Nov 4, 1968. 365 105th Terrace N.E., St. Petersburg (33716). (813) 576-4444. FAX: (813) 577-1806. Licensee: WTOG-TV Inc. Group owner: Hubbard Broadcasting Inc. Rep: Petry. Wash atty: Fletcher, Heald & Hildreth. News staff 25; news progmg 5 hrs wkly. ■ Stanley S. Hubbard, CEO; Edward G. Aiken, pres & gen mgr; Mike Gehring, gen sls mgr; Dotti McKeehan, natl sls mgr; Jonathan Katz, prom mgr; Robert B. Affe, progmg dir; Jim LaBranche, news dir; Beth Maguire, pub affrs dir; John Kays, chief engr. ■ On 105 CATVs—1,150,000 subs. On 3 trans.

WTSP—(St. Petersburg). ch 10, 316 kw vis, 31.6 kw aur, ant 1,549t/1,538g. TL: N28 11 04 W82 45 39. On air date: July 17, 1965. 11450 Gandy Blvd., St. Petersburg (33702). Box 10000 (33733). (813) 577-1010. FAX: (813) 578-7637. Licensee: Great American Television & Radio Co. Group owner: Great American Broadcasting (acq 10-7-87). ■ Net: ABC. Wash atty: Koteen & Naftalin. ■ Steve Mauldin, pres & gen mgr; Noreen Parker, vp sls; Marty Rolnick, Ron Oldham, natl sls mgrs; Barbara Sobocinski, vp mktg & vp progmg; Mike Cavender, news dir; John Holland, chief engr. ■ On 43 CATVs—242,000 subs. Co-owned radio: WXTB.

WTTA—(St. Petersburg). ch 38, 5,000 kw vis, 500 kw aur, ant 1,867t/1,500g. TL: N27 50 32 W82 15 46. Hrs opn: 24. On air date: June 21, 1991. Suite 38, 5510 W. Gray St., Tampa (33609). (813) 289-3838; (813) 894-3838. FAX: (813) 289-0000. Licensee: Bay Television Inc. Wash atty: Fisher, Wayland, Cooper & Leader. ■ David Smith, pres; Tom Watson, gen mgr; Jenifer Beaver, opns dir; Bruce Stamo, gen sls mgr; Marie Procise, mktg dir; Jenifer Isonhower, prom dir & progmg dir; Debra Cutler Lurie, pub affrs dir; Steve Hess, chief engr. ■ On 35 CATVs—782,000 subs.

WTVT—(Tampa). ch 13, 316 kw vis, 47.4 kw aur, ant 1,416t/1,549g. TL: N27 49 09 W82 14 26. Stereo. Hrs opn: 24. On air date: April 1955. Box 31113, Tampa (33631-3113); 3213 W. Kennedy Blvd., Tampa (33609). (813) 876-1313. FAX: (813) 875-8329. Licensee: TVT License Inc. Group owner: SCI Television Inc. (acq 4-13-93; $163.25 million; 4-26-93). ■ Net: CBS. Rep: Telerep. Wash atty: Pepper & Corazzini. News staff 85; news progmg 23 hrs wkly. ■ C. David Whitaker, pres & gen mgr; Bob Franklin, vp opns; Mark Higgins, vp sls; Bob Linger, natl sls mgr; Mark Demopoulos, mktg dir; Nancy Dudenhoefer, prom mgr; Daniel Webster, news dir; Karen Capp, pub affrs dir; Lowell Otto, engrg mgr. ■ On 60 CATVs—850,717 subs.

***WUSF-TV**—(Tampa). ch 16, 1,620 kw vis, 162 kw aur, ant 1,010t. TL: N27 50 53 W82 15 48. Stereo. Hrs opn: 18. On air date: Sept 12, 1966. Univ. of South Florida, WRB 219, 4202 Fowler Ave., Tampa (33620). (813) 974-4000; (813) 974-2075. FAX: (813) 974-4806. Licensee: State Board of Regents of the State of Florida. ■ Net: PBS. Wash atty: Cohn & Marks. ■ James B. Heck, gen mgr; David B. Rochelle, stn mgr; Gerald Leonard, gen sls mgr; William Buxton, progmg dir; Don Freeman, chief engr. ■ On 42 CATVs—250,000 subs. Co-owned radio: *WUSF-FM.

Tequesta

ADI No. 46; see West Palm Beach-Ft. Pierce-Vero Beach market

WPBF—ch 25, 5,000 kw vis, 500 kw aur, ant 1,529t/1,549g. TL: N26 50 09 W80 05 44. Stereo. Hrs opn: 20. On air date: Jan 1, 1989. Suite 7007, 3970 RCA Blvd., Palm Beach Gardens (33410). (407) 694-2525. FAX: (407) 624-1089. Licensee: Phipps-Potamkin Television Partners. Ownership: John H. Phipps Inc., 50%; Potamkin of Manhattan, 50% (acq 8-5-89; 9-5-89). ■ Net: ABC. Rep: Telerep. Wash atty: Wiley, Rein & Fielding. News staff 42; news progmg 11 hrs wkly. ■ Dennis Boyle, pres; Robert E. Ware, gen mgr; Thomas A. Foos, opns mgr, progmg dir & film buyer; Robert Young, gen sls mgr; Bob Hellinger, news dir; John Falvi, chief engr. ■ On 18 CATVs.

Tice

ADI No. 87; see Ft. Myers-Naples market

WRXY-TV—ch 49, 5,000 kw vis, 500 kw aur, ant 800t/790.5g. TL: N26 47 08 W81 47 41. Not on air, target date unknown. Box 6922, Clearwater (34618). (813) 535-5622. Permittee: Golden Media Inc. (acq 6-15-87). ■ Robert R. D'Andrea, CEO & gen mgr; Don McAllister, vp; Carl Berger, opns mgr & engrg dir; Cardin Hesselton, sls dir, mktg dir & progmg dir; Bob Kennedy, prom dir; Burdette Price, pub affrs dir.

Venice

ADI No. 153; see Sarasota market

WBSV Sarasota's #1 Independent — adam young inc

WBSV-TV—ch 62, 5,000 kw vis, 500 kw aur, ant 572t/570g. TL: N27 06 01 W82 22 18. Hrs opn: Mon-Thurs 5:30 AM-1 AM; Fri-Sat 24; Sun 6 AM-midnight. On air date: May 3, 1991. 2065 Cantu Ct., Sarasota (34232). (813) 379-0062. FAX: (813) 378-9224; (813) 377-9359. Licensee: DeSoto Broadcasting Inc. (acq 5-10-89; 5-29-89). Rep: Adam Young. Wash atty: Pepper & Corazzini. News staff 4; news progmg 3 hrs wkly. ■ Danford L. Sawyer, CEO & gen mgr; James W. O'Neill, vp sls & gen sls mgr; Tom Wilson, prom dir, progmg dir & film buyer; Lee Nolan, news dir & pub affrs dir; Jack Dillon, chief engr. ■ On 13 CATVs—193,400 subs. ■ Rates: $175; 125; 50.

Vero Beach

WTVX—See Fort Pierce.

West Palm Beach

ADI No. 46; see West Palm Beach-Ft. Pierce-Vero Beach market

WFLX—ch 29, 5,000 kw vis, 500 kw aur, 1,540t/1,533g. TL: N26 34 37 W80 14 32. Stereo. Hrs opn: 24. On air date: Aug 14, 1982. 4119 W. Blue Heron Blvd. (33404). (407) 845-2929. FAX: (407) 863-1238. Licensee: Malrite Communications Group Inc. (group owner). ■ Net: Fox. Rep: Petry. Wash atty: Kaye, Scholer, Fierman, Hays & Handler. ■ Murray J. Green, vp & gen mgr; Ken Beedle, stn mgr; David D'Eugenio, natl sls mgr; Lois Kwasman, mktg dir & prom dir; Ralph Capobianco, prom mgr; Barbie Billens, progmg dir; Angelo Figurella, chief engr. ■ On 54 CATVs—664,973 subs. On one trans.

WPBF—See Tequesta.

WPEC—ch 12, 316 kw vis, 56.2 kw aur, ant 980t/1,027g. TL: N26 35 17 W80 12 28. Stereo. On air date: Jan 1, 1955. Box 24612 (33416-4612). (407) 844-1212. FAX: (407) 881-0741; TWX: 510-952-7639. Licensee: Photo Electronics Corp. (acq 10-26-73; $3,535,000; 11-12-73). ■ Net: CBS. Rep: Katz American. Wash atty: Leventhal, Senter & Lerman. ■ Alex Dreyfoos, chmn; Bill Peterson, pres & gen mgr; Donn Colee, stn mgr; John Emmert, opns mgr; Doug Wolfmueller, gen sls mgr; Gerry Marcelo, prom mgr; Donn Colee Jr., progmg dir; Aneta Sewell, pub affrs dir; George Danner, chief engr.

WPTV—ch 5, 100 kw vis, 20 kw aur, ant 990t/1,031g. TL: N26 35 20 W80 12 43. Stereo. Hrs opn: 24. On air date: Aug. 22, 1954. Box 510, Palm Beach (33480); 622 N. Flagler Dr. (33401). (407) 655-5455; (407) 653-5603. FAX: (407) 655-8947; (407) 653-5657. Licensee: Scripps Howard Broadcasting (group owner; acq 12-27-61; $2 million; 12-25-61). ■ Net: NBC. Rep: Blair. Wash atty: Baker & Hostetler. News staff 62; news progmg 22 hrs wkly. ■ Lawrence A. Leser, pres; P. Frank Gardner, exec vp; William J. Brooks, vp & gen mgr; Michael McBryde, opns dir; Roger E. Green, gen sls mgr; Wayne R. Cunningham, mktg mgr; Bernadette O'Grady, progmg dir; J. Patrick Burns, news dir; Edward J. Roos, engrg mgr. ■ On 45 CATVs—739,000 subs.

***WXEL-TV**—ch 42, 2,150 kw vis, 2.15 kw aur, ant 1,440t/1,533g. TL: N26 34 37 W80 14 32. Stereo. On air date: July 7, 1982. 3401 S. Congress Ave., Boynton Beach (33426); Box 6607 (33405). (407) 737-8000. FAX: (407) 369-3067. Licensee: South Florida Public Telecommunications Inc. ■ Net: PBS. Wash atty: Schwartz, Woods & Miller. ■ Mary Souder, pres & gen mgr; Jim Moran, stn mgr; Anita Kirchen, vp dev; Bill Biggert, chief engr. ■ On 40 CATVs—650,000 subs. Co-owned radio: *WXEL-FM.

Georgia

Albany

ADI No. 154; see Albany, GA market

WALB-TV—ch 10, 316 kw vis, 43.6 kw aur, ant 964t/1,000g. TL: N31 19 52 W83 51 44. On air date: Apr 7, 1954. Box 3130, 1709 Stuart Ave. (31708-7601). (912) 883-0154. FAX: (912) 436-3134. Licensee: WALB-TV Inc. Group owner: Gray Communications Systems Inc. ■ Net: NBC. Rep: Katz. Wash atty: Sidley & Austin. News staff 24; news progmg 14 hrs wkly. ■ Jere Pigue, pres, gen mgr & progmg dir; James Wilcox, vp sls & gen sls mgr; Dave Miller, prom mgr; Rick Williams, news dir & pub affrs dir; William N. Williams, chief engr. ■ On 99 CATVs—194,000 subs.

WFXL—ch 31, 1,580 kw vis, 150 kw aur, ant 990t/1,000g. TL: N31 19 52 W83 51 43. On air date: Feb 14, 1982. Box 4050 (31708). (912) 435-3100. FAX: (912) 435-0485. Licensee: NewSouth Broadcasting (acq 10-26-87; $2.25 million; 4-27-87). ■ Net: Fox. Rep: Seltel. Wash atty: Baraff, Koerner, Olender & Hochberg. ■ Manny Cantu, vp & gen mgr; Mary Anne Genus, gen sls mgr; Bettina Smith, prom mgr, progmg dir & film buyer; Dawn Hobby, news dir; Hugh Allegood, chief engr. ■ On 38 CATVs—100,000 subs.

Athens

ADI No. 11; see Atlanta market

***WGTV**—ch 8, 316 kw vis, 56.2 kw aur, ant 1,132t/420g. TL: N33 48 18 W84 08 40. Stereo. Hrs opn: 6 AM-midnight. On air date: May 23, 1960. 1540 Stewart Ave. S.W., Atlanta (30310). (404) 756-4700. FAX: (404) 756-4476. Licensee: Georgia Public Telecommunications Commission. Ownership: Ga. Public TV Net. ■ Net: PBS. Wash atty: Arent, Fox, Kintner, Plotkin & Kahn. ■ Marcia Killingsworth, prom mgr; Kent Steele, progmg dir; Al Korn, chief engr. ■ On 72 CATVs—392,000 subs.

WNGM-TV—ch 34, 1,258 kw vis, 125.8 kw aur, ant 1,351t/1,236g. TL: N34 12 27 W83 47 38. On air date: April 1989. 185 Ben Burton Cir., Bogart (30622). (404) 353-3400. FAX: (404) 549-5844. Licensee: NGM TV Partners. Ownership: GAMTN, 60%; Flowers Partners, 40%. Wash atty: William Barnard. ■ E. Lanierfinch, pres. ■ On 10 CATVs. ■ Rates: $125; 75; 35.

Atlanta

ADI No. 11; see Atlanta market

WAGA-TV—ch 5, 100 kw vis, 10 kw aur, 1,076t/1,103g. TL: N33 47 49 W84 20 00. On air date: April 1949. 1551 Briarcliff Rd. N.E. (30306). (404) 875-5555. FAX: (404) 898-0238. Licensee: WAGA License Inc. Group owner: SCI Television Inc. (acq 2-19-93; grpsl; 4-26-93). ■ Net: CBS. Rep: Harrington, Righter & Parsons. Wash atty: Pepper & Corazzini. Sp one hr wkly. ■ Jack Sander, pres & gen mgr; John Dolive, opns dir & chief engr; Chuck Wing, gen sls mgr; John Kukla, prom mgr; Leslie Glenn, progmg dir; Bud McEntee, news dir; Linda Torrence, pub affrs dir. ■ On 102 CATVs—721,000 subs. On 2 trans.

***WATC**—ch 57, 398 kw vis, 39.8 kw aur, ant 423t. TL: N33 48 40 W84 21 51. Not on air, target date unknown. c/o Carolina Christian Broadcasting Inc., Box 1616, Greenville, SC (29602). (803) 244-1616. Permittee: Action for Communities to Community Television Inc. Group owner: Carolina Christian Broadcasting Inc. (acq 6-3-93; $79,866; 6-28-93).

WATL—ch 36, 2,682 kw vis, 402 kw aur, ant 1,170t/1,174g. TL: N33 48 27 W84 20 26. Stereo. On air date: July 5, 1976. One Monroe Place (30324). (404) 881-3600. FAX: (404) 881-3635. Licensee: FTS Atlanta Inc. Group owner: Fox Television Stations Inc. (acq 4-21-93; $60 million; 5-10-93). ■ Net: Fox. Rep: Seltel. ■ Mitch Stearns, pres; Joanna Hemleb, rgnl sls mgr; Merrilyn Crouch, prom mgr; Don Hess, progmg dir & film buyer; Doris Hines, pub affrs dir. ■ On 66 CATVs—419,173 subs. ■ Rates: $1,000; 300; 40.

WGNX—ch 46, 2,333 kw vis, 233 kw aur, ant 1,170t/1,174g. TL: N33 48 27 W84 20 26. Stereo. Hrs opn: 24. On air date: June 6, 1971. Box 98097 (30359); 1810 Briarcliff Rd. N.E. (30329). (404) 325-4646. FAX: (404) 633-8358; (404) 248-0016. Licensee: WGNX Inc. Group owner: Tribune Broadcasting Co. (acq 12-19-83; $32 million; 12-19-83). Rep: MMT. Wash atty: Sidley & Austin. News staff 33; news progmg 7 hrs wkly. ■ Herman Ramsey, vp & gen mgr; Michael Norten, gen sls mgr; Dustin Lecate, Robyn Greenberg, natl sls mgrs; Barry Stinson, prom mgr; Lorrie Shilling, progmg mgr & film buyer; Jack Frazier, news dir; Daniel Highland, chief engr.

***WGTV**—See Athens.

***WPBA**—ch 30, 1,380 kw vis, ant 1,096t. TL: N33 45 35 W84 20 07. Stereo. 6 AM-midnight. On air date: Feb 17, 1958. 740 Bismarck Rd. N.E. (30324). (404) 827-8900. FAX: (404) 827-8956; TWX: 810-751-8164. Licensee: Board of Education of the City of Atlanta. ■ Net: PBS. Wash atty: Steptoe & Johnson. One hr wkly. News progmg 3 hrs wkly. ■ Lester W. Butts, CEO; John Hughes, chmn; Danny Royal, gen mgr; Mary Armstrong, stn mgr; Bernice Chandler, vp dev & vp sls; Eric Weston, prom dir; Joanne Cox, progmg dir; Duncan Pearson, chief engr. ■ On 58 CATVs—328,000 subs. On one trans. Co-owned radio: *WABE(FM).

WSB-TV—ch 2, 100 kw vis, 20 kw aur, ant 1,037t/1,076g. TL: N33 45 51 W84 21 42. Stereo. On air date: Sept 29, 1948. 1601 W. Peachtree St. N.E. (30309). (404) 897-7000. FAX: (404) 897-7525; TWX: 810-751-3532. Licensee: Georgia Television Co. Group owner: Cox Broadcasting. ■ Net: ABC. Wash atty: Dow, Lohnes & Albertson. ■ James C. Kennedy, CEO & chmn; Gregory J. Stone, gen mgr; Bill Spell, gen sls mgr; Lee Armstrong, mktg dir, prom dir & progmg dir; John Woodin, news dir; Jocelyn Dorsey, pub affrs dir; David M. Lamothe, engrg dir. Co-owned radio: WSB-AM-FM.

WTBS—ch 17, 2,224 kw vis, 224 kw aur, ant 1,093t/1,042g. TL: N33 46 57 W84 23 20. On air date: Sept 1, 1967. 1050 Techwood Dr. N.W. (30318). (404) 827-1717. FAX: (404) 885-4947. Licensee: Superstation Inc., div of Turner Broadcasting System. Ownership: R.E. Turner III, 32.03%; TCI, 24.43%; Time-Warner, 20.34% (acq 1-70). Rep: Turner. Wash atty: Bert Carp. ■ Scott Sassa, pres; Terry Segal, exec vp; Joe Wheeler, vp opns; Joel Westbrook, vp dev; John Barbera, gen sls mgr; Tom Kounelis, mktg dir; Kate McSweeny, Bill Cox, vps progmg; Terri Tingle, pub affrs dir; Jack Verner, chief engr. ■ On 14,992 CATVs—57,325,000 subs. On 8 trans.

WVEU—ch 69, 2,630 kw vis, 263 kw aur, ant 980t/848g. TL: N33 45 34 W84 23 19. Stereo. Hrs opn: 24. On air date: Aug 22, 1981. Phoenix Business Park, Bldg. A, 2700 Northeast Expwy. (30345). (404) 325-6929. FAX: (404) 633-4567. Licensee: Broadcast Corporation of Georgia. Ownership: David J. Harris, 75%. ■ Rep: Roslin. Wash atty: E. William Henry. Japanese & Sp progmg 6 hrs wkly. ■ David J. Harris, pres; Vance L. Eckersley, vp & gen mgr; Mann Reed, stn mgr & gen sls mgr; Peter L. Mandell, prom mgr; Tracy Swann, progmg mgr; Gary Kelly, chief engr. ■ On 49 CATVs—842,628 subs.

WXIA-TV—ch 11, 316 kw vis, 63.2 kw aur, ant 1,048t/1,040g. TL: N33 45 24 W84 19 55. Stereo. On air date: Sept 30, 1951. 1611 W. Peachtree St. N.E. (30309). (404) 892-1611. FAX: (404) 892-0182. Licensee: Pacific & Southern Co. Inc. Group owner: Gannett Broadcasting, division of Gannett Co. Inc. (acq 6-7-79; grpsl; 6-11-79). ■ Net: NBC. Rep: Blair. Wash atty: Reed, Smith, Shaw & McClay. ■ Craig A. Dubow, pres & gen mgr; John Heinen, vp opns & progmg dir; Peter McCampbell, gen sls mgr; Shawn Perez, prom mgr; Mark Pimentel, news dir; Jerry Michel, chief engr. ■ On 96 CATVs—350,000 subs. On one trans.

Augusta

ADI No. 110; see Augusta market

WAGT—ch 26, 65 kw vis, 6.5 kw aur, ant 1,590t/1,478g. TL: N33 25 15 W81 50 19. Stereo. On air date: Dec 24, 1968. Box 1526 (30903-1526); 905 Broad St. (30901). (706) 826-0026. Licensee: WAGT Television Inc. Group owner: Schurz Communications Inc. (acq 7-1-80; $5 million). ■ Net: NBC. Rep: Katz. Wash atty: Hogan & Hartson. News staff 4; news progmg 3 hrs wkly. ■ Hal Edwards, pres & gen mgr; James Halpin, gen sls mgr; Reggie Cofer, prom mgr & progmg dir; Reese LeRoy, news dir; Rick Harper, pub affrs dir; Ronald Davis, chief engr. ■ On 35 CATVs—186,000 subs.

WFXG—ch 54, 4,517 kw vis, 451 kw aur, ant 1,120t/1,506g. TL: N33 25 00 W81 50 60. Stereo. (CP: 2,491 kw vis, ant 1,164t.) Hrs opn: 24. On air date: May 23, 1991. Box 204540 (30917-4540); 3933 Washington Rd. (30907). (706) 650-5400. FAX: (706) 650-8411. Licensee: Augusta Family Broadcasting. Group Owner: Pezold Broadcasting. ■ Net: Fox. Rep: Seltel. Wash atty: Miller & Fields. ■ Steven Friedheim, gen mgr; Jim Ricks, opns dir, progmg dir & film buyer; Paul Brewer, gen sls mgr; Marty Miller, natl sls mgr; Chris Kidd, prom mgr; Barbara Morgan, pub affrs dir; Charlie McCoy, chief engr. ■ On 10 CATVs—100,000 subs. ■ Rates: $550; 90; 80.

WJBF—ch 6, 100 kw vis, 20 kw aur, ant 1,300t/1,292g. TL: N33 24 15 W81 50 15. On air date: Nov 23, 1953. Box 1404 (30903); 1001 Reynolds St. (30901). (706) 722-6664. FAX: (706) 722-0022. Licensee: Hickory Hill Broadcasting Co. Group owner: Spartan Radiocasting Company Inc. (acq 12-15-92). ■ Net: ABC. Rep: Blair. Wash atty: Covington & Burling. News staff 32; news progmg 12 hrs wkly. ■ Walter J. Brown, CEO; Nick Evans, Jr., pres; Boyd Bunting, CFO; Louis Wall, gen mgr; Charles Coleman, gen sls mgr; Glenn Tomlinson, prom mgr; Mary Jones, progmg dir; Pete Michenfelder, news dir; Gerald Levy, pub affrs dir; Bill Doker, chief engr. ■ On 49 CATVs—131,979 subs. ■ Rates: $500; 180; 95.

WRDW-TV—ch 12, 316 kw vis, 30.2 kw aur, ant 1,590t/1,506g. TL: N33 24 29 W81 50 36. On air date: Feb 15, 1955. Drawer 1212 (30913-1212); 1301 Georgia Ave., North Augusta, SC (29841). (803) 278-1212. FAX: (803) 279-8316. Licensee: WRDW Associates. Group owner: Television Station Partners (acq 1-18-83; grpsl; 2-7-83). ■ Net: CBS. Rep: Petry. Wash atty: Wiley, Rein & Fielding. ■ I. Martin Pompadur, CEO; William G. Evans, gen mgr, progmg dir & film buyer; Henry Goldman, opns mgr; Steve Johnston, gen sls mgr; Denny Van Volkenburg, natl sls mgr; Jenny Guthrie, prom mgr; Brian Trauring, news dir; Paul Wolfe, pub affrs dir; James F. Myers, chief engr. ■ On 42 CATVs—179,198 subs.

Bainbridge

ADI No. 115; see Tallahassee-Thomasville market

WTLH—Licensed to Bainbridge. See Tallahassee, Fla.

Georgia

Baxley

ADI No. 101; see Savannah market

WUBI—ch 34, 316 kw vis, ant 482 ft. TL: N31 45 53 W82 13 38. On air date: May 1, 1992. Box 1080, E. Jekyll Rd. (31513). (912) 367-3434. FAX: (912) 367-5299. Licensee: Upchurch Broadcasting Inc. ■ Jimmy Upchurch, gen mgr.

Brunswick

ADI No. 54; see Jacksonville, FL market

WBSG-TV—ch 21, 2,636 kw vis, ant 1,020t. TL: N31 08 22 W81 56 15. Stereo. Hrs opn: 19. On air date: Apr 2, 1990. 7434 Blyth Island Hwy. (31525). (912) 267-0021. FAX: (912) 267-9583. Licensee: WBSG-TV Ltd. (acq 7-17-89; 8-7-89). ■ J.R. Wright, gen mgr; Wayne Crawsall, gen sls mgr; Penelope G. H. Sloan, prom mgr; Andrew B. Sloan, progmg dir; Hector Garcia, news dir; Dave Garvin, chief engr. ■ On 36 CATVs.

Chatsworth

ADI No. 85; see Chattanooga market

*WCLP-TV—ch 18, 5,000 kw vis, ant 1,851t. TL: N34 45 06 W84 42 54. On air date: Feb 1, 1967. Rt. 7, Box 7007 (30705). (706) 695-2422. Licensee: Ga. Public Telecommunications Commission. ■ Net: PBS. Wash atty: Arent, Fox, Kintner, Plotkin & Kahn. ■ Frank Bugg, opns mgr; Kent Steele, progmg dir; Jackie Grizzle, chief engr. ■ On 6 trans.

Cochran

ADI No. 119; see Macon market

*WDCO-TV—ch 29, 5,000 kw vis, 50 kw aur, ant 1,087t/1,168g. TL: N32 28 11 W83 15 17. Stereo. On air date: Jan 1, 1968. Box 269 (31014). (912) 934-2220. Licensee: Ga. Public Telecommunications Commission. ■ Net: PBS. ■ Mell Bland, chief engr.

Columbus

ADI No. 122; see Columbus, GA market

*WJSP-TV—ch 28, 5,000 kw vis, 500 kw aur, ant 1,512t/2,378g. TL: N32 51 08 W84 42 04. Stereo. On air date: Aug 10, 1964. Rt. 1, Box 140, Warm Springs (31830). (706) 655-2145. Licensee: Ga. Public Telecommunications Commission. ■ Net: PBS. ■ Kent Steele, progmg dir; Al Korn, engrg dir; John H. Davis, chief engr. ■ On 2 trans. Co-owned radio: WJSP-FM.

WLTZ—ch 38, 1,070 kw vis, 209 kw aur, ant 1,310t/1,319g. TL: N32 27 29 W84 53 08. Stereo. Hrs opn: 24. On air date: Oct 29, 1970. Box 12289, 6140 Buena Vista Rd. (31907). (706) 561-3838. FAX: (706) 563-8467. Licensee: Lewis Broadcasting Corp. (group owner; acq 7-1-81; $3.25 million). ■ Net: NBC. Rep: Petry. Wash atty: Reed, Smith, Shaw & McClay. News staff 10; news progmg 5 hrs wkly. ■ J. Curtis Lewis Jr., pres; Bob Walton, vp & gen mgr; Tom Breazeale, gen sls mgr; Ron Bartlett, prom mgr & progmg dir; Borden Black, news dir; Cathy Bart, pub affrs dir; Dennis Boswell, chief engr. ■ On 27 CATVs—155,000 subs.

WRBL—ch 3, 100 kw vis, 12 kw aur, ant 1,780t/1,749g. TL: N30 19 25 W84 46 46. On air date: Nov 15, 1953. Box 270 (31902-0270). 1350 13th Ave. (31901). (706) 323-3333. FAX: (706) 327-6655; TWX: 810-758-4335. Licensee: Avant Development Corp. Ownership: TCS Management Corp. (MC Media, 50.005%; Commonwealth, 48.995%; TCB Management, 1%) (acq 3-26-93; grpsl; 4-12-93). ■ Net: CBS. Rep: Katz. Wash atty: Dow, Lohnes & Albertson. ■ Ray J. Chumley, gen mgr; Al Parsons, gen sls mgr; Darlene Hughes, prom mgr; Alice Upshaw, progmg dir & film buyer; Jean O'Riley, news dir; Jack Smith, chief engr. ■ On 50 CATVs—140,000 subs. ■ Rates: $500; 100; 65.

WTVM—ch 9, 284 kw vis, 52.5 kw aur, ant 1,650t/1,749g. TL: N32 19 25 W84 46 46. On air date: Oct 6, 1953. Box 1848 (31994). (706) 324-6471. TWX: 810-768-4326. Licensee: WTVM Television Inc. Group owner: AFLAC Broadcast Division (acq 2-16-89; $45 million; 3-6-89). ■ Net: ABC. Rep: Harrington, Righter & Parsons. Wash atty: Fletcher, Heald & Hildreth. ■ Jim Wareham, vp & gen mgr; Richard Heath, gen sls mgr; Cathy Davis, natl sls mgr; Robert Brines, prom mgr; Carroll Ward, progmg dir & film buyer; Dale Cerbin, news dir; W. David Williams, chief engr. ■ On 56 CATVs—183,901 subs.

WXTX—ch 54, 1,000 kw vis, 100 kw aur, ant 1,140t/1,121g. TL: N32 27 49 W84 52 37. On air date: June 17, 1983. Box 12188, 6524 Buena Vista Rd. (31907). (706) 561-5400. FAX: (706) 561-6505; (706) 561-5965 (Sales). Licensee: Columbus Family Broadcasting Inc. Ownership: John D. Pezold, 100% (acq 7-1-89). ■ Net: Fox. Rep: Seltel. ■ John D. Pezold, CEO; Sharon Moloney, sr vp & gen mgr; Sharon Davlin, opns dir & progmg dir; Steve Thomas, vp sls & gen sls mgr; Celeste Edwards, prom dir; Jackie McDonell, pub affrs dir; Morris Pollock, vp engrg. ■ On 22 CATVs—110,000 subs. ■ Rates: $600; 200; 50.

Cordele

ADI No. 154; see Albany, GA market

WSST-TV—ch 55, 100 kw vis, ant 410t. TL: N31 54 15 W83 48 12. On air date: May 22, 1989. Box 917, 112 S. Seventh St. (31015). (912) 273-0001. FAX: (912) 273-8894. Licensee: Sunbelt-South Telecommunications Ltd. Ownership: William B. Goodson, Phillip A. Streetman. Wash atty: Ward & Mendelsohn. ■ William B. Goodson, pres, gen mgr & chief engr; Sara J. Howell, gen sls mgr; Lee W. Wright, progmg dir & film buyer.

Dalton

ADI No. 85; see Chattanooga market

WELF—ch 23, 3,378 kw vis, ant 1,466t. TL: N34 57 07 85 22 58. Not on air, target date unknown. c/o Sonlight Broadcasting Systems Inc., 120 Zeigler Cir. E., Mobile, AL (36608). (205) 633-2100. Permittee: Sonlight Broadcasting Systems Inc. (group owner; acq 7-27-92; $195,000; 9-21-92). ■ Stuart J. Roth, CEO; Jay A. Sekulow, pres; Stephen B. Box, CFO & opns dir; Joel Bennett, progmg dir; Alaina Box, pub affrs dir; Charles W. Davis, engrg mgr.

Dawson

ADI No. 154; see Albany, GA market

*WACS-TV—ch 25, 363 kw vis, 36.3 kw aur, ant 1,045t/1,096g. TL: N31 56 15 W84 33 15. Stereo. Hrs opn: 19. On air date: March 6, 1967. Rt. 1, Box 75A, Parrott (31777); 1540 Stuart Ave. S.W., Atlanta (30310). (404) 756-4700. Licensee: Ga. Public Telecommunications Commission. ■ Net: PBS. Wash atty: Arent, Fox, Kintner, Plotkin & Kahn. ■ Lewis C. Rickerson, gen mgr & chief engr; Frank Bugg, opns dir; Kent Steele, progmg dir. ■ On 6 CATVs.

Macon

ADI No. 119; see Macon market

WGNM—ch 64, 52 kw vis, 5.2 kw aur, 608t/685g. TL: N32 44 58 W83 33 35. Hrs opn: 17. On air date: Nov 30, 1990. Box 2637 (31203); 2525 Beech Ave. (31204). (912) 746-6464. Licensee: Good News Television Wash atty: Allen, Moline & Harold. ■ Donald R. Wood, gen mgr; Marvin Thompson, stn mgr; Ken Sauer, opns mgr; Dan Jaskula, gen sls mgr & adv mgr; George Foster, pub affrs dir; John Simmons, chief engr. ■ On 5 CATVs—85,000 subs.

WGXA—ch 24, 1,290 kw vis, 252 kw aur, ant 800t/898g. TL: N32 45 08 W83 33 38. On air date: April 21, 1982. Box 340, 599 Broadway (31297). (912) 745-2424. FAX: (912) 750-4347; (912) 745-6057. Licensee: Russell Rowe Communications Inc. Ownership: Herman Russell, 51%; Martin Seretean, 31%; Don Elliot Heald, 8%. ■ Net: ABC. Rep: Blair. Wash atty: Leibowitz & Spencer. ■ Don Elliot Heald, pres; Ken Gerdes, vp & gen mgr; Kim Bene, opns mgr; Frank Shurling, gen sls mgr; Elena Peterman, prom mgr; Ron Wildman, news dir; Richard Blanton, chief engr.

WMAZ-TV—ch 13, 316 kw vis, 62 kw aur, ant 780t/1,209g. TL: N32 45 10 W83 33 32. Stereo. On air date: Sept 27, 1953. Box 5008 (31213); 1314 Gray Hwy. (31211). (912) 752-1313. FAX: (912) 752-1331. Licensee: Multimedia WMAZ Inc. Group owner: Multimedia Broadcasting Co. (acq 1967). ■ Net: CBS. Rep: Katz. Wash atty: Dow, Lohnes & Albertson. News staff 32; news progmg 22 hrs wkly. ■ Pat Servodidio, pres; Don McGouirk, vp & gen mgr; Lacy Worrell, opns mgr & chief engr; Gostin Freeney, gen sls mgr; Faye Butts, prom mgr; Sydney Thum, progmg dir; Dodie Cantrell, news dir; William O. Tribble, pub affrs dir. ■ On 48 CATVs—188,114 subs. Co-owned radio: WMAZ(AM), WAYS(FM).

WMGT—ch 41, 760 kw vis, 154 kw aur, ant 893t/837g. TL: N32 45 12 W83 33 46. Stereo. On air date: Aug 26, 1968. Box 4328 (31213). 6525 Ocmulgee E. Blvd. (31201). (912) 745-4141. FAX: (912) 742-2626. Licensee: Morris Network Inc. (group owner; acq 11-30-78; $2.8 million; 12-18-78). ■ Net: NBC. Rep: Adam Young. Wash atty: McFadden, Evans & Sill. ■ L.A. Sturdivant, gen mgr; David Hickman, gen sls mgr; Leigh Smith, prom mgr; Debbie Green, progmg dir; Paul Vitchkoski, chief engr. ■ On 54 CATVs—208,000 subs.

Marietta

ADI No. 11; see Talnat market

WTLK-TV—ch 14, 4,900 kw vis, 490 kw aur, ant 2021t/787g. TL: N34 18 47 W84 38 55. Stereo. Hrs opn: 24. On air date: Jan 15, 1988. Suite 114, 200 N. Cobb Pkwy., Marietta (30161). (404) 528-1400. FAX: (404) 528-1422. Licensee: TV-14 Inc. Group owner: Sudbrink Broadcasting. (acq 8-13-86; $250,000; 6-30-86). Wash atty: Haley, Bader & Potts. ■ Woody Sudbrink, CEO; Hal Gore, pres & gen mgr; Carla Odom, opns dir; Sue Parks, dev dir; Jack Crumpler, vp sls; Bill McAllister, prom dir; Susan Parks, pub affrs dir; Charles W. McHan Jr., engrg dir; Charles Meeks, chief engr.

Monroe

ADI No. 11; see Atlanta market

WHSG—ch 63, 5,000 kw vis, ant 1,191t. TL: N33 44 22 W84 00 14. On air date: Feb 22, 1991. Box 450189, Atlanta (30345-0189); 1550 Agape Way, Decatur (30035). (404) 288-1156. FAX: (404) 288-5613. Licensee: Trinity Broadcasting Network Inc. (group owner; acq 11-21-89). ■ Gary Smith, gen mgr; Angela Jacobs, pub affrs dir; Ray Vice, chief engr.

Pelham

ADI No. 154; see Albany, GA market

*WABW-TV—ch 14, 5,000 kw vis, 500 kw aur, ant 1,240t/1,224g. TL: N31 08 05 W84 04 06 16. On air date: Jan 1, 1968. Box 249 (31779). (912) 294-8313. Licensee: Ga. Public Telecommunications Commission. ■ Net: PBS. ■ Don Mitchell, chief engr.

Perry

ADI No. 119; see Macon market

WPGA-TV—ch 58, 759 kw vis, 75.9 kw aur, ant 325t. TL: N32 33 20 W83 44 14. Not on air, target date unknown. Box 980 (31069). (912) 987-2980. Permittee: Radio Perry Inc. ■ Lowell L. Register, pres. $1 Co-owned radio: WPGA-AM-FM.

Savannah

ADI No. 101; see Savannah market

WJCL—ch 22, 3,830 kw vis, 383 kw aur, ant 1,430t/1,478g. TL: N32 03 30 W81 20 20. Stereo. Hrs opn: 21. On air date: July 18, 1970. Box 61268, 10001 Abercorn St. (31406). (912) 925-0022. Licensee: Lewis Broadcasting Co. (group owner). ■ Net: ABC. Rep: Petry. Wash atty: Reed, Smith, Shaw & McClay. News staff 14; news progmg 3 hrs wkly. ■ J.C. Lewis, pres; J. Fred Pierce, vp, gen mgr & gen sls mgr; Frank Bryson, vp mktg; Bryan Steele, adv dir; Mary Poytress, progmg dir; Scott Pierce, news dir; Mark Taylor, pub affrs dir; Wallace Tidwell, chief engr. ■ On 50 CATVs. Co-owned radio: WJCL-FM.

WSAV-TV—ch 3, 100 kw vis, 20 kw aur, ant 1,476t/1,532g. TL: N32 03 34 W81 17 57. On air date: Feb. 1, 1956. 1430 E. Victory Dr. (31404). (912) 651-0300. FAX: (912) 651-0300 Licensee: New Vision Television Inc. Group owner: New Vision Television Inc. (acq 9-7-93; $110 million as part of eight-stn sale; 9-27-93). ■ Net: NBC. Rep: Blair. Wash atty: Dow, Lohnes & Albertson. ■ David R. Bradley Jr., pres; Harvey Libow, gen mgr; Dale Kovacostas, Shila Mallard, gen sls mgrs; Dan Kurtz, prom dir; Dave Stagnitto, prom mgr & progmg dir; David Winstrom, news dir. ■ On 55 CATVs—184,000 subs.

WTOC-TV—ch 11, 316 kw vis, 31.6 kw aur, ant 1,470t/1,531g. TL: N32 03 14 W81 21 01. On air date: Feb 14, 1954. Box 8086 (31412); 516 Abercorn (31401). (912) 234-1111. FAX: (912) 238-5133; TWX: 810-784-5619. Licensee: American Savannah Broadcasting Co. Group owner: AFLAC Broadcast Division (acq 10-1-79). ■ Net: CBS. Rep: Katz. Wash atty: Sidley & Austin. ■

Stations in the U.S.

William Cathcart, vp & gen mgr; Randy Peltier, gen sls mgr; Jim Clayton, natl sls mgr; Shey Merritt, prom mgr & pub affrs dir; Douglas Weathers, news dir; Bill Elken, chief engr. ■ On 26 CATVs—72,000 subs.

*WVAN-TV—ch 9, 316 kw vis, 34.7 kw aur, ant 1,050t/1,086g. TL: N32 08 48 W81 37 05. Hrs opn: 18. On air date: Sep 16, 1963. Box 367, 100 Vandiver St., Pembroke (31321-0367). (912) 653-4996. Licensee: Ga. Public Telecommunications Commission. ■ Net: PBS. ■ Richard E. Ottinger (exec dir), CEO; Amy Scully, dev dir & mktg dir; Kent Steele, progmg dir; Carolyn Kowalski, pub affrs dir; Al Korn, engrg dir; W.J. Anderson, chief engr.

Thomasville

WCTV—Licensed to Thomasville. See Tallahassee, Fla.

Toccoa

ADI No. 35; see Greenville, SC-Anderson, SC-Spartanburg, SC-Asheville, NC market

WNEG-TV—ch 32, 647 kw vis, 129 kw aur, ant 835t/600g. TL: N34 36 44 W83 22 05. Hrs opn: 6 AM-1 AM. On air date: Sept 9, 1984. Box 907, 100 Blvd. (30577). (404) 886-0032. Licensee: Stephens County Broadcasting Co. Ownership: Roy E. Gaines, 51%. ■ Rep: Roslin. Wash atty: Bryan, Cave, McPheeters & McRoberts. News staff 5; news progmg 5 hrs wkly. ■ Roy E. Gaines, pres & gen mgr; David Austin, gen sls mgr; Jeff Canupp, prom mgr; Connie Gaines, progmg dir & film buyer; John DeFloor, news dir; Bill Wood, chief engr. ■ On 30 CATVs—95,000 subs. Co-owned radio: WNEG(AM). ■ Rates: $150; 75; 40.

Valdosta

ADI No. 115; see Tallahassee-Thomasville market

WVGA—ch 44, 1,285.3 kw vis, 257 kw aur, ant 920t/950g. TL: N31 10 18 W83 21 57. (CP: 1,365 kw vis, 922t). Hrs opn: 21. On air date: Dec 24, 1980. Box 1588, 275 Norman Dr. (31603). Licensee: Morris Networks Inc. (group owner; acq 7-18-86; $850,000; 6-16-86). ■ Net: ABC. Wash atty: Fletcher, Heald & Hildreth. ■ Dean Hinson, pres; Tony Scott, gen mgr & gen sls mgr; Janet Stump, progmg dir; David Schmidt, news dir; John Young, chief engr. ■ On 14 CATVs—37,917 subs.

Waycross

ADI No. 54; see Jacksonville, Fl market

*WXGA-TV—ch 8, 316 kw vis, 47.9 kw aur, ant 1,030t/1,089g. TL: N31 13 17 W82 34 24. On air date: Dec 4, 1961. Box 842 (31501). (912) 283-4838. Licensee: Ga. Public Telecommunications Commission. ■ Net: PBS. ■ Knox Carreker, chief engr.

Wrens

ADI No. 110; see Augusta market

*WCES-TV—ch 20, 5,000 kw vis, 500 kw aur, ant 1,480t/1,465g. TL: N33 15 33 W82 17 09. Stereo. On air date: Sept 12, 1966. Box 525 (30833). (706) 547-2107. Licensee: Ga. Public Telecommunications Commission. ■ Net: PBS. ■ William A. Newsome, chief engr.

Hawaii

Hilo

KGMD-TV—ch 9, 9.77 kw vis, 1.71 kw aur, ant -290t/285g. TL: N19 43 00 W155 08 13. On air date: May 15, 1955. c/o KGMB, 1534 Kapiolani Blvd., Honolulu, (96814). (808) 973-5462. Licensee: Lee Enterprises Inc. (group owner; acq 9-10-85; $10,000). Partially co-owned satellite of KGMB-TV Honolulu. ■ Net: CBS. ■ Dick Grimm, gen mgr.

KHAW-TV—ch 11, 2.09 kw vis, 275 w aur, ant -620t/139g. TL: N19 43 56 W155 04 04. On air date: Nov 27, 1961. c/o KHON-TV, 1116 Auahi St., Honolulu (96814). Licensee: Burnham Broadcasting Co. (group owner; acq 3-10-86). ■ Net: NBC. Satellite of KHON-TV Honolulu.

KHBC-TV—ch 2, 2,317 kw vis, 1.37 kw aur, ant 90t/130g. TL: N19 43 51 W155 04 11. On air date: Aug 22, 1983. c/o KHNL, 150-B Puuhale Rd., Honolulu (96819). (808) 847-3246. Licensee: King Broadcasting Co. Ownership: King Holding Corp. (acq 8-27-91; $355 million; grpsl; 9-9-91). Wash atty: Robert Olender. ■ Doug Armstrong, pres.

KHVO—ch 13, 4.68 kw vis, 1.59 kw aur, ant -823t/80g. TL: N19 43 57 W155 04 04. On air date: May 15, 1960. 1290 Ala Moana Blvd., Honolulu (96850). (808) 545-4444. FAX: (808) 537-3467. Licensee: Tak Communications Inc. (acq 1-27-87; grpsl; 12-1-86). ■ Net: ABC. Rep: Seltel. Wash atty: Leventhal, Senter & Lerman. ■ Richard F. Schaller, gen mgr. ■ On 2 trans.

KWHH—ch 14, 13.2 kw vis, 1.32 kw aur, ant -557t/145g. TL: N19 43 51 W155 04 11. On air date: Oct 1, 1989. Suite 502, 1188 Bishop St., Honolulu (96813). (808) 538-1414. FAX: (808) 526-0326. Licensee: Le Sea Broadcasting Corp. (group owner; acq 10-1-89; $8,277; 12-26-89). Vandin Media. Wash atty: Heron, Burchette, Rukert & Rothwell. ■ Steve Sumrall, pres; Pete Sumrall, exec vp & film buyer; Tony Boquer, gen mgr; Gerry Kaman, gen sls mgr; Alan Sutterfield, progmg dir; Mike Fister, pub affrs dir; Keith Spencer, chief engr. ■ On 5 CATVs—360,000 subs. On 2 trans. ■ Rates: $100; 50; 75.

Honolulu

KBFD—ch 32, 146 kw vis, 14.6 kw aur, ant 405t/428g. TL: N21 18 49 W157 51 43. Hrs opn: 12. On air date: Mar 7, 1986. Century Sq., Penthouse One, 1188 Bishop St. (96813). (808) 521-8066; (808) 521-8067. FAX: (808) 521-5233. Licensee: Allen Broadcasting Corp. Ownership: Kea Sung Chung, 65%; Ok Soon Chung, 10%; Jaeh Hoon Chung, 15%; June Ho Chung, 10% (acq 1-7-86; $35,000; 12-16-85). Wash atty: Brad Carey. Korean 35 hrs wkly. ■ Kea Sung Chung, pres & gen mgr; June Ho Chung, exec vp; Jeff Chung, stn mgr; Ok Soon Chung, vp opns; Yun Chung, vp sls; Dan Kawakani, vp mktg; Helen Chung, vp adv; Jaeh Hoon Chung, progmg dir; David Moore, chief engr.

KFVE—ch 5, 95.5 kw vis, 19.8 kw aur, ant 161t/2,640g. TL: N21 24 03 W158 06 10. Stereo. Hrs opn: 24. On air date: Feb 7, 1988. 150-B Puuhale Rd. (96819-2282); 530 W. O'Brien Dr., Agana, GU (96910). (808) 842-5555. FAX: (808) 842-4594. Licensee: KFVE Joint Venture. Rep: Blair. Wash atty: Brown, Finn & Nietert. ■ Lee M. Holmes, pres; Donna Kam, gen mgr; John Fink, gen sls mgr; Michael Langley, prom mgr; Dan Schmidt, progmg dir; Keith Adtaki, chief engr. ■ On 10 CATVs.

KGMB—ch 9, 209 kw vis, 29.5 kw aur, ant -50t/436g. TL: N21 17 46 W157 50 36. (CP: Ant 45t/495g). On air date: Dec 1, 1962. 1534 Kapiolani Blvd. (96814). (808) 973-5462. FAX: (808) 941-8153. Licensee: Lee Enterprises Inc. (group owner; acq 1976; grpsl). ■ Net: CBS. Rep: Katz. Wash atty: Pierson, Ball & Dowd. ■ Richard T. Grimm, gen mgr; Tim Diedrich, gen sls mgr; Bob Bowen, rgnl sls mgr; Bob Turner, progmg dir; Bob Jones, news dir; Jim Doney, pub affrs dir; Rod Shimabukuro, chief engr. ■ On 2 CATVs—210,000 subs. On 3 trans.

*KHET—ch 11, 148 kw vis, 29.5 kw aur, ant -75t/431g. TL: N21 17 46 W157 50 36. Hrs opn: 17. On air date: Apr 15, 1966. 2350 Dole St. (96822). (808) 955-7878. Licensee: Hawaii Public Broadcasting Authority. ■ Net: PBS. Wash atty: Wilkes, Artis, Hedrick & Lane. ■ James B. Young, gen mgr; Don Robbs, stn mgr; Jerri Chong, prom mgr; Carlos Molina, progmg dir; Chris Conybeare, news dir; Al Ono, chief engr. ■ On 12 trans.

KHNL—ch 13, 316 kw vis, 46.8 kw aur, ant 20t. TL: N21 17 46 W157 50 19. On air date: July 4, 1962. 150 B. Puuhale Rd. (96819). (808) 847-3246. FAX: (808) 845-3616. Licensee: King Broadcasting Co. Ownership: King Holding Corp. (acq 8-27-91; $355 million; grpsl; 9-9-91). ■ Net: Univision. Rep: Blair. Wash atty: Suzanne Sorknes. Japanese 6 hrs wkly. ■ Douglas L. Armstrong, pres & gen mgr; John L. Fink, gen mgr; Terry Joiner, prom mgr; Dan Schmidt, progmg dir; Keith Aotaki, chief engr. ■ On 3 CATVs—250,000 subs. On one trans.

KHON-TV—ch 2, 100 kw vis, 20 kw aur, ant 59t/498g. TL: N21 17 39 W157 50 18. Stereo. On air date: Dec 15, 1952. 1116 Auahi St. (96814). (808) 531-8585. FAX: (808) 523-1785. Licensee: Burnham Broadcasting Co. (group owner; acq 11-1-85; grpsl). ■ Net: NBC. Rep: Harrington, Righter & Parsons. Wash atty: Fisher, Wayland, Cooper & Leader. News staff 39; news progmg 13 hrs wkly. ■ Steve Hiramoto, gen sls mgr & vp mktg; Phyllis Kihara, rgnl sls mgr; Linda Brock, prom mgr; Al Hoffman, progmg dir & film buyer; Kent Baker, news dir; Greg Johnson, chief engr. ■ On 6 CATVs. On one trans.

KIKU—ch 20, 467 kw vis, 46.7 kw aur, ant 2,040t. TL: N21 23 51 W158 06 01. Hrs opn: Mon-Fri 6:30 AM-midnight; Sat 9 AM-12:30 AM; Sun 8:30 AM-midnight. On air date: Dec 30, 1983. Suite 2021, 197 Sand Island Access Rd. (96819). (808) 847-2021. FAX: (808) 841-3326. Licensee: KHAI Inc. (acq 9-18-89; $1.5 million; 9-11-89). Rep: Asian TV Sls. Wash atty: Leventhal, Senter & Lerman. Asian 60 hrs wkly. ■ Joanne Ninomiya, gen mgr & film buyer; Sharon Kanaley, stn mgr; Bob Furukawa, opns mgr; David Odo, gen sls mgr; Karlton Tomomitsu, prom mgr; Joanne Ninomiyya, Sharon Kanaley, progmg dirs; Karton Tomomitsu, pub affrs dir; Henry A. Kaul, engrg dir. ■ On 3 CATVs—250,000 subs. ■ Rates: $250; 75; 50.

KITV—ch 4, 100 kw vis, 20 kw aur, ant 50t/495g. TL: N21 17 37 W157 50 34. On air date: Apr 16, 1954. 1290 Ala Moana Blvd. (96814). (808) 545-4444. FAX: (808) 537-3467. Licensee: Tak Communications Inc. (group owner; acq 1-27-87; grpsl; 12-1-86). ■ Net: ABC. Wash atty: Leventhal, Senter & Lerman. News staff 35; news progmg 7 hrs wkly. ■ Richard F. Schaller, gen mgr; William D. Gaeth, gen sls mgr; Erik Nolder, prom mgr; Tracy Kelilhoomalu, progmg dir; Walter Zimmermann, news dir; Celeste Fox, pub affrs dir; Dave Moore, engrg dir; Bob Kato, chief engr. ■ On 11 CATVs—28,000 subs. On one trans. ■ Rates: $1,400; 250; 80.

KOBN—ch 26, 75.9 kw vis, 7.59 kw aur, ant 2,118t. TL: N21 19 49 W157 45 24. Hrs opn: 24. On air date: Dec 23, 1982. 970 N. Kalaheo Ave., Kailua-Honolulu (96734). (808) 254-5826. FAX: (808) 254-1313. Licensee: Oceania Broadcasting Network. ■ Chris Racine, pres & gen sls mgr; Lambert Rezentes, chief opns; Susan Simms, progmg mgr; Roland Wongwai, chief engr. ■ On 2 CATVs—155,000 subs. ■ Rates: $80; 60; 20.

KWHE—ch 14, 75.9 kw vis, ant 26t. TL: N21 18 49 W157 51 43. On air date: Mar 7, 1988. Century Sq., 1188 Bishop St., Suite 502 (96813). (808) 538-1414. FAX: (808) 526-0326. Licensee: LeSea Broadcasting Corp. (group owner; acq 8-15-86; $825,000; 6-16-86). Rep: Landin Media. ■ Steve Sumrall, pres; Pete Sumrall, exec vp; Tony Boquer, gen mgr; Jose Yumang, gen sls mgr; M'Lou Watumull, progmg dir; David Whitelaw, film buyer; Mike Fister, pub affrs dir; Keith Spencer, chief engr. ■ On 2 CATVS—250,000 subs. On one trans. ■ Rates: $100; 50; 75.

Kailua-Kona

KLEI—ch 6, 52.5 kw vis, 6.7 kw aur, ant 2,910t. TL: N19 42 56 W155 55 00. On air date: 1988. Suite C134, 970 N. Kaiaheo Ave., Kailua (96734). (808) 254-5826. Licensee: Oceana Broadcasting Network Inc.

Wailuku

KAII-TV—ch 7, 29.8 kw vis, 5.9 kw aur, ant 5,940t/75g. TL: N20 42 41 W156 15 26. On air date: Nov 17, 1958. 1116 Auahi St. (96814). Licensee: Burnham Broadcasting Co. (group owner; acq 10-23-85). ■ Net: NBC. Satellite of KHON-TV Honolulu.

KGMV—ch 3, 14.1 kw vis, 2.69 kw aur, ant 5,950t/60g. TL: N20 42 41 W156 15 35. On air date: April 24, 1955. c/o KGMB, 1534 Kapiolani Blvd., Honolulu (96814). (808) 973-5462. Licensee: Lee Enterprises Inc. (group owner; acq 9-10-85; $10,000). ■ Net: CBS. ■ Tom Yoshida, gen mgr.

KMAU—ch 12, 27.5 kw vis, 4.36 kw aur, ant 5,910t/70g. TL: N20 42 41 W156 15 26. On air date: Nov 28, 1955. 1290 Ala Moana Blvd., Honolulu (96814). (808) 545-4444. FAX: (808) 537-3467. Licensee: Tak Communications Inc. (acq 4-8-87; grpsl; 12-1-86). ■ Net: ABC. Rep: Seltel. Wash atty: Leventhal, Senter & Lerman. ■ Richard F. Schaller, gen mgr; William D. Gaeth, gen sls mgr; Erik Nolder, prom mgr; Tracy Keliihoomalu, progmg dir; Wally Zimmermann, news dir; Celeste Fox, pub affrs dir; Dave Moore, engrg dir; Bob Kato, chief engr.

*KMEB—ch 10, 30.9 kw vis, 6 kw aur, ant 5,940t/47g. TL: N20 42 40 W156 15 34. On air date: Sept 22, 1966. 2350 Dole St., Honolulu (96822). (808) 955-7878. TWX: 723-8553. Licensee: Hawaii Public Broadcasting Authority. ■ Net: PBS. Satellite of *KHET Honolulu.

KOGG—ch 15, 759 kw vis, 75.9 kw aur, ant 5,653t/75g. TL: N20 42 34 W156 15 54. On air date: Aug 22, 1989. c/o KHNL, 150 B. Puuhale Rd., Honolulu (96819). (808) 847-3246. Licensee: King Broadcasting Co. Ownership: King Holding Corp. (acq 8-27-91; $355 million; grpsl; 9-9-91). ■ Doug Armstrong, pres.

KWHM—ch 21, 44.25 kw vis. Ant -371t. TL: N20 53 25 W156 30 22. On air date: 1993. Suite 502, 1188 Bishop St., Honolulu (96813). (808) 538-1414. Licensee: Le Sea Broadcasting Corp. (group owner). Rep: Landin Media. ■ Steve Sumrall, pres; Pete Sumrall, exec vp; Tony Boquer, gen mgr. Satellite of KWHE Honolulu.

Idaho

Blackfoot

KPVI—See Idaho Falls.

Boise

ADI No. 132; see Boise market

*KAID—ch 4, 57.2 kw vis, 5.7 kw aur, ant 2,474t/142g. TL: N43 45 16 W116 05 56. Stereo. On air date: Dec 31, 1971. 1455 N. Orchard (83726). (208) 373-7220. Licensee: Idaho State Bd of Education.■ Net: PBS. News staff 5; news progmg 3 hrs wkly. ■ Jerold A. Garber, gen mgr; Lynn Allen, stn mgr; Robert Pyle, opns mgr; Nancy Viano, dev dir; Allen Parks, prom mgr; Ron Pisaneschi, progmg dir; Roger Fuhrman, news dir; Rick Strack, chief engr. ■ On 8 trans.

KBCI-TV—ch 2, 65 kw vis, 7.0l kw aur, ant 2,550t/100g. TL: N43 45 17 W116 05 53. On air date: Nov 26, 1953. 140 N. 16th St. (83707). (208) 336-5222. FAX: (208) 336-9183; TWX: 910-970-5790. Licensee: Northwest Television Inc. (group owner; acq 10-21-76; $2,087,000; 9-27-76). ■ Net: CBS. Rep: Katz, Art Moore. Wash atty: Dow, Lohnes & Albertson. News progmg 7 hrs wkly. ■ Donald E. Tykeson, pres; Timothy J. Bever, gen mgr, progmg dir & film buyer; Scott Eymer, gen sls mgr; Mary Mcbrize, prom mgr; Mark Montgomery, news dir; Larry Smith, chief engr. ■ On 25 CATVs—16,775 subs. On 36 trans.

KIVI—(Nampa). ch 6, 60.3 kw vis, 12.0 kw aur, ant 2,660t/210g. TL: N43 45 20 W116 05 55. Stereo. On air date: Feb 1, 1974. 1866 E. Chisholm Dr., Nampa (83687). (208) 336-0500. FAX: (208) 465-5417; TWX: 910-970-5945. Licensee: Sawtooth Communications Inc. Group owner: Cordillera Communications Inc. ($11.5 million). ■ Net: ABC. Rep: Seltel, Tacher. Wash atty: Dow, Lohnes & Albertson. News staff 20. ■ Larry J. Chase, pres & gen mgr; Don Jensen, opns mgr; Ken Ritchie, gen sls mgr; Kraig Spille, prom mgr; Brink Chipman, news dir; Shelly Houston, pub affrs dir; Andrew Suk, chief engr. ■ On 35 CATVs—60,000 subs. On 23 trans. ■ Rates: $300; 100; 50.

KTVB—ch 7, 160 kw vis, 26.2 kw aur, ant 2,645t/226g. TL: N43 45 16 W116 05 56. Hrs opn: 24. On air date: July 12, 1953. Box 7 (83707); 5407 Fairview Ave. (83706). (208) 375-7277. FAX: (208) 378-1762. Licensee: KTVB Inc. Group owner: King Broadcasting Co. (acq 8-27-91; $355 million; grpsl; 9-9-91). ■ Net: NBC. Rep: Blair. Wash atty: Covington & Burling. ■ Robert E. Krueger, pres, gen mgr, progmg dir & film buyer; John Souza, opns dir; John Lewis, gen sls mgr; P.J. Laws, prom mgr; Rod Gramer, news dir & pub affrs dir; Peter Hoekzema, chief engr. ■ On 79 CATVs. On 42 trans. ■ Rates: $300; 175; 60.

Caldwell

ADI No. 132; see Boise market

KHDT-TV—ch 9, 155 kw vis, 15.5 kw aur, ant 2,736t. TL: N43 45 18 W116 05 52. Not on air, target date unknown. Suite 402, 816 W. Bannock St., Boise (83702). (208) 343-9990. FAX: (208) 344-0119. Permittee: Schuyler Broadcasting Corp. (acq 5-21-91; $105,000; 6-10-91).

Coeur d'Alene

ADI No. 78; see Spokane, WA market

*KCDT—ch 26, 12.3 kw, ant 1,525t. TL: N47 43 54 W116 43 47. Stereo. Hrs opn: 17. On air date: October 1991. Suite 217-A, 408 Sherman (83814); Radio & Television Ctr., Univ. of Idaho, Moscow (83843). (208) 765-9193. FAX: (208) 385-3442. Permittee: State Board of Education, State of Idaho. ■ Net: PBS. Wash atty: Fletcher, Heald & Hildreth. ■ Jerold A. Garber, gen mgr; Ron Pisaneschi, progmg dir; Vaun J. McArthur, chief engr. ■ On 4 trans.

Filer

*KBGH—ch 19., Not on air, target date unknown. Box 1238, Twin Falls (83303-1238). 315 Falls Ave., Twin Falls (83301). (208) 733-9554. Permittee: College of Southern Idaho. ■ Bon Mauldin, chief engr.

Idaho Falls

ADI No. 158; see Idaho Falls-Pocatello market

KIDK—ch 3, 100 kw vis, 14.4 kw aur, ant 1,600t/200g. TL: N43 29 51 W112 39 50. On air date: Dec 20, 1953. Box 2008 (83403); 4880 N. 1st St., Fresno (93755). (208) 522-5100. FAX: (208) 522-5103; TWX: 910-977-5721. Licensee: Retlaw Enterprises Inc. (group owner; acq 2-1-88; $6.8 million). ■ Net: CBS. Rep: Katz. Wash atty: Wiley, Rein & Fielding. News staff 12; news progmg 12 hrs wkly. ■ Ben Tucker, pres; Gerry Cornwell, vp, gen mgr & gen sls mgr; Kim Southwick, vp opns & film buyer; Jim Kunz, natl sls mgr; Karen Cornwell, mktg dir, progmg dir & pub affrs dir; Denis Dye, prom mgr; Terry Miller, news dir; Gary Smith, chief engr. ■ On 22 CATVs—42,000 subs. On 28 trans. ■ Rates: $160; 100; 40.

KIFI-TV—ch 8, 316 kw vis, 63.1 kw aur, ant 1,520t/180g. TL: N43 30 02 W112 39 36. Stereo. On air date: Jan 21, 1961. Box 2148 (83403); 1915 N. Yellowstone Hwy. (83401). (208) 525-8888. FAX: (208) 522-1930. Licensee: The Post Co. (group owner). ■ Net: NBC. Rep: Tacher, Petry. Wash atty: Reddy, Begley & Martin. ■ Jerry M. Brady, pres; Rickie Orchin Brady, gen mgr; Reed Larsen, gen sls mgr; Kate Salomon, prom mgr; Kathy Walden, progmg dir; Tonia Ellis, news dir; Teresa Wilson, chief engr. ■ On 12 CATVs—63,000 subs. On 25 trans. ■ Rates: $275; 120; 25.

KPVI—(Pocatello). ch 6, 100 kw vis, 17.4 kw aur, ant 1,530t/619g. TL: N42 55 15 W112 20 44. On air date: Apr 26, 1974. Box 667, Pocatello (83204-0667); 425 E. Center, Pocatello (83201). (208) 232-6666. FAX: (208) 233-6678. Licensee: Ambassador Media Corp. (acq 10-26-83; $3.2 million; 11-14-83). ■ Net: ABC. Rep: Seltel; Art Moore. Wash atty: Hamel & Park. ■ William L. Armstrong, pres; Harry Neuhardt, vp, gen mgr & film buyer; Bruce Kamp, news dir; Nick Davidson, chief engr. ■ On 31 CATVs—,966 subs. On 33 trans.

Lewiston

ADI No. 78; see Spokane, WA market

KLEW-TV—ch 3, 56.2 kw vis, 1.38 kw aur, ant 1,260t/303.5g. TL: N46 27 25 W117 05 57. Hrs opn: 19. On air date: December 1956. Box 615, 2626 17th St. (83501). (208) 746-2636. FAX: (208) 746-4819. Licensee: Retlaw Enterprises Inc. (group owner; acq 11-25-86; grpsl; 10-27-86). ■ Net: CBS. Rep: Katz. Wash atty: Wiley, Rein & Fielding. News staff 4; news progmg 5 hrs wkly. ■ Fred Fickenwirth, gen mgr & gen sls mgr; Greg Meyer, opns mgr; Steve Elenich, prom mgr; Stu Seibel, progmg dir & film buyer; Joe Martin, news dir; Julia Sandstrom, pub affrs dir; Marlin Jackson, chief engr. Satellite of KIMA-TV Yakima, Wash. ■ Rates: $80; 70; 15.

Moscow

ADI No. 78; see Spokane, WA market

*KUID-TV—ch 12, 300 kw vis, 57.5 kw aur, ant 2,060t. TL: N46 48 16 W116 50 18. On air date: July 1, 1965. Radio-TV Ctr, Univ. of Idaho (83843). (208) 885-6723. Licensee: Regents of Univ. of Idaho. ■ Net: PBS. ■ Jerold A. Garber, gen mgr; Russell Spain, stn mgr; Ron Pisaneschi, progmg dir; Ken Segota, chief engr. ■ On 18 CATVs—38,000 subs. On 11 trans.

Nampa

ADI No. 132; see Boise market

KIVI—Licensed to Nampa. See Boise.

KTRV—ch 12, 178 kw vis, 18.2 kw aur, ant 2,760t/220g. TL: N43 45 18 W116 05 52. Stereo. On air date: Oct 18, 1981. Box 1212, 679 65th St. N., ext. (83652). (208) 466-1200. FAX: (208) 467-6958. Licensee: Idaho Independent Television Inc. Group owner: Blade Communications Inc. (acq 4-23-85; $4.9 million; 3-25-85). ■ Net: Fox. Rep: Petry. Wash atty: Dow, Lohnes & Albertson. News staff one; news progmg one hr wkly. ■ Allan Block, chmn; Rex L. McArthur, pres & gen mgr; James Barto, CFO; Diane Frisch, vp, stn mgr & progmg dir; Ron Grisham, natl sls mgr; Bill Hatch, news dir; Francis D. Wilson, chief engr. ■ On 29 CATVs—94,000 subs. ■ Rates: $425; 175; 40.

Pocatello

ADI No. 158; see Idaho Falls-Pocatello market

KIDK—See Idaho Falls.

KIFI-TV—See Idaho Falls.

*KISU-TV—ch 10, 122 kw vis, 12.2 kw aur, ant 1,527t/144g. TL: N43 30 02 W112 39 36. Stereo. On air date: July 7, 1971. Box 8111, Idaho State U. (83209-0009). (208) 236-2857. FAX: (208) 236-2848. Licensee: Idaho State Board of Education. ■ Net: PBS. ■ Jerold A. Garber, gen mgr; Marcia J. Hosking, stn mgr & dev dir; Ron Pisaneschi, progmg dir; Pat Grimes, news dir; David Turnmire, chief engr. ■ On 40 CATVs—30,000 subs. On 17 trans.

KPVI—Licensed to Pocatello. See Idaho Falls.

Twin Falls

ADI No. 201; see Twin Falls market

*KIPT—ch 13, 22.4 kw vis, ant 528t/69g. TL: N42 43 48 W114 25 06. On air date: Jan 18, 1992. c/o KAID, 1910 University Dr., Boise (83725). (208) 734-3108. Licensee: State Board of Education, State of Idaho. ■ Net: PBS. ■ George Alvarez, pres; Gary D. Fax, vp; Jerold A. Garber, gen mgr.

KKVI—ch 35, 100 kw vis, ant 538t. TL: N42 43 42 W114 24 43. Hrs opn: 24. On air date: Jan 31, 1989. 1061 Blue Lakes Blvd. N. (83301). (208) 733-0035. FAX: (208) 733-0160. Licensee: Ambassador Media Corp. ■ Net: ABC. Rep: Seltel. Wash atty: Hamel & Park. News progmg 2 hrs wkly. ■ Dick McMahon, gen mgr, mktg mgr, prom mgr & adv mgr; Harry Neuhardt, progmg mgr; Tim Novotny, news dir; Nick Davidson, chief engr. ■ On 7 CATVs—18,000 subs. On 2 trans.

KMVT—ch 11, 316 kw vis, 31.6 kw aur, ant 1,190t/690g. TL: N42 43 48 W114 24 52. Hrs opn: 20. On air date: May 30, 1955. 1100 Blue Lakes Blvd N. (83301). (208) 733-1100. FAX: (208) 733-4649. Licensee: KMVT Broadcasting Inc. Group owner: Root Communications Inc. (acq 1-6-84; $883,000). ■ Net: CBS. Rep: Katz. Wash atty: Dow, Lohnes & Albertson. News staff 15; news progmg 8 hrs wkly. ■ Charles Cohoon, pres; Lee Wagner, gen mgr; Robert Thomas, gen sls mgr; Penne Main, vp prom & pub affrs dir; George Brown, progmg dir; Doug Maughan, news dir; Dennis Lowe, chief engr. ■ On 11 CATVs—20,000 subs. On 5 trans.

Illinois

Aurora

ADI No. 3; see Chicago market

WEHS-TV—ch 60, 5,000 kw vis, 500 kw aur, ant 1,600t/1,621g. TL: N41 52 44 W87 38 10. On air date: Apr 20, 1982. 100 S. Sanagamon, Chicago (60607). (708) 851-5960; (312) 829-8860. FAX: (312) 829-1059. Licensee: Silver King Broadcasting of Illinois Inc. Group owner: Silver King Communications Inc. (acq 12-26-86; $25 million; 11-10-86). Wash atty: Dow, Lohnes & Albertson. ■ Jeff McGrath, pres; Fred Weintraub, vp & gen mgr; Renee Genova, progmg dir; Sally Huffer, news dir; Keith Wilson, chief engr. ■ On 21 CATVs—600,000 subs.

Bloomington

ADI No. 107; see Peoria-Bloomington market

WYZZ-TV—ch 43, 1,200 kw vis, 112 kw aur, ant 979t/1,006g. TL: N40 38 45 W89 10 45. On air date: Oct 18, 1982. 2714 E. Lincoln (61704). (309) 662-4373. FAX: (309) 663-6943. Licensee: Bloomington Comco Inc. Group owner: R Group Communication (acq 6-14-85; $500,000; 5-13-85). ■ Net: Fox. Rep: Seltel. Wash atty: Arnold & Porter. ■ G.J. Robinson, pres; Larry Halcomb,

Stations in the U.S.   Illinois

gen sls mgr; Bill Killian, prom mgr; Larry Entner, chief engr. ■ On 19 CATVs—168,096 subs.

Carbondale

ADI No. 77; see Paducah, KY-Cape Girardeau, MO-Harrisburg-Marion, IL market

*WSIU-TV—ch 8, 316 kw vis, 40.7 kw aur, ant 890t/903g. TL: N38 06 15 W89 14 37. Hrs opn: 17. On air date: November 1961. 1048 Communications Bldg., Southern Ill. Univ. (62901). (618) 453-4343. FAX: (618) 453-6186. Licensee: Board of Trustees of Southern Ill. U. ■ Net: PBS. Wash atty: Cohn & Marks. ■ Lee D. O'Brien, CEO & gen mgr; Jerry Parks, CFO; Robert Gerig, stn mgr; progmg dir & film buyer; Robert Henderson, opns mgr; Renee Dillard, mktg dir; Jay Pearce, pub affrs dir; Jerry Kline, chief engr. Co-owned radio: *WSIU(FM), WUSI-TV.

Champaign

ADI No. 75; see Springfield-Decatur-Champaign market

WCIA—ch 3, 100 kw vis, 20 kw aur, ant 940t/981g. TL: N40 06 23 W88 26 59. On air date: Nov 14, 1953. Box 20, 509 S. Neil (61824-0020). (217) 356-8333. Licensee: Midwest Television Inc. (group owner). ■ Net: CBS. Rep: Petry. Wash atty: Covington & Burling. ■ August C. Meyer Jr., pres; Guy Main, gen mgr; Gerald J. Johnson, gen sls mgr; Sheila Hickman, progmg dir; Dave Shaul, news dir; Dale Fleming, chief engr.

WICD—ch 15, 358 kw vis, 35 kw aur, ant 1,300t/1,338g. TL: N40 04 11 W87 54 45. Hrs opn: 6 AM-1 AM. On air date: Apr 24, 1959. 250 S. County Fair Dr. (61821). (217) 351-8500. FAX: (217) 351-6056. Licensee: Plains TV Partnership. Group owner: Balaban Stns (acq 7-27-60; $75,000; 8-8-60). ■ Net: NBC. Rep: Katz. Wash atty: Wiley, Rein & Fielding. ■ Elmer Balaban, pres; Joe Norris, gen mgr, gen sls mgr & prom dir; Larry Waters, progmg dir; Richard Porter, news dir; David Boyer, chief engr. ■ On 75 CATVs—250,000 subs.

Charleston

ADI No. 75; see Springfield-Decatur-Champaign market

*WEIU-TV—ch 51, 48.5 kw vis, 4.85 kw aur, ant 234t/213g. TL: N39 28 43 W88 10 21. On air date: July 1, 1986. Radio & TV Center, 139 Buzzard, Eastern Ill. Univ. (61920). (217) 581-5956. Licensee: Eastern Illinois University. ■ Net: PBS. Wash atty: Cohn & Marks. News staff 3; news progmg 5 hrs wkly. ■ John L. Beabout, gen mgr; Eric Larson, gen sls mgr; Gaye Harrison, prom mgr; Sue Kaufman, news dir; Ron Amyx, chief engr. ■ On 54 CATVs—72,000 subs.

Chicago

ADI No. 3; see Chicago market

WBBM-TV—ch 2, 35.4 kw vis, 7.08 kw aur, ant 1,350t/1,456g. TL: N41 53 56 W87 37 23. On air date: August 1940. 630 N. McClurg Court (60611). (312) 944-6000. FAX: (312) 440-0591. Licensee: CBS Inc. Group owner: CBS Broadcast Group (acq 2-9-53; $6 million; 2-16-53). ■ Net: CBS. Rep: CBS-TV Natl Sales. ■ Robert McGann, vp & gen mgr; Wayne Weber, opns mgr; Richard Tracy, sls dir; Martha Sweney, mktg mgr; Leslie Lyndon, prom mgr; Marion Meginnis, progmg mgr; Mark Toney, news dir; Monroe Anderson, pub affrs dir; Ken Wilkey, chief engr. Co-owned radio: WBBM-AM-FM.

WCFC-TV—ch 38, 1,260 kw vis, 25.1 kw aur, ant 1,210t/1,453g. TL: N41 53 56 W87 37 23. On air date: May 31, 1976. 38 S. Peoria St. (60607). (312) 433-3838. FAX: (312) 433-3839. Licensee: Christian Communications of Chicagoland (acq 1-16-76; $850,000; 2-2-76). Wash atty: Fisher, Wayland, Cooper & Leader. Foreign lang progmg 3 hrs wkly. ■ Jerry Rose, pres; Philip Mowbray, opns mgr; David Scott, vp dev; Kevin L. San Hamel, gen sls mgr; Eric Au Coin, mktg dir; Alan Bolds, prom mgr; David Oseland, progmg dir; Norman Block, chief engr.

WCIU-TV—ch 26, 2,000 kw vis, 200 kw aur, ant 1,555t/1,552g. TL: N41 52 44 W87 38 10. On air date: Feb 6, 1964. 141 W. Jackson Blvd. (60604). (312) 663-0260. FAX: (312) 663-0585. Licensee: Weigel Broadcasting Co. Ownership: Howard Shapiro, 71.2% (acq 3-22-77; $616,949; 4-18-77). ■ Net: Univision. Wash atty: Cohn & Marks. Sp 70 hrs wkly. ■ Howard Shapiro, pres & gen mgr; Peter Zomaya, gen sls & progmg dir; Norman Shapiro, prom mgr & film buyer; Edward Arruza, news dir; Bernard Hoelting, chief engr. ■ On 55 CATVs. On 3 trans.

WFLD—ch 32, 5,000 kw vis, 500 kw aur, ant 1,415t/1,456g. TL: N41 53 55 W87 37 23. Stereo. On air date: Jan 6, 1966. 205 N. Michigan Ave. (60601). (312) 565-5532. FAX: (312) 565-0420. Licensee: Fox Television Stations Inc. (group owner; acq 11-14-86; grpsl). ■ Net: Fox. Rep: Petry. Wash atty: Thomas R. Herwitz. ■ Stacey Marks-Bronner, vp & gen mgr; Randy Ingram, opns mgr; Mike Turner, vp sls; Scott Wert, natl sls mgr; Phil C. Waterman, rgnl sls mgr; Robert Simone, progmg dir; Debra Juarez-West, news dir; Wanda Wells, pub affrs dir; Dwain Schoonover, vp engrg & chief engr. ■ On 155 CATVs—1,138,394 subs.

WGBO-TV—See Joliet.

WGN-TV—ch 9, 110 kw vis, 22 kw aur, ant 1,360t/1,453g. TL: N41 53 56 W87 37 23. Stereo. On air date: Apr 5, 1948. 2501 Bradley W. Pl. (60618). (312) 528-2311. FAX: (312) 528-6857. Licensee: WGN Continental Broadcasting Co. Group owner: Tribune Broadcasting Co., see Cross-Ownership. Rep: TeleRep. Wash atty: Sidley & Austin. News staff 60; news progmg 12 hrs wkly. ■ Peter Walker, vp & gen mgr; John J. Vitanovec, stn mgr; David Tynan, gen sls mgr; Pam Pearson, prom mgr; Jim Zerwekh, progmg dir; Jennifer Schulze, news dir; Marc Drazen, chief engr. Co-owned radio: WGN(AM).

WLS-TV—ch 7, 55 kw vis, 11.2 kw aur, ant 1,688t/1,710.28g. TL: N41 52 44 W87 38 10. On air date: Sept 17, 1948. 190 N. State St. (60601). (312) 750-7777. Licensee: WLS Television Inc. Group owner: Capital Cities/ABC Inc. Broadcast Group (acq 6-27-86; grpsl; 7-15-85). ■ Net: ABC. Rep: ABC-TV Spot Sales. Wash atty: McKenna, Wilkinson & Kittner. ■ Joseph A. Ahern, pres & gen mgr; Mark Grant, gen sls mgr; Sherry Burns, progmg dir; Jim Owens, engrg dir. Co-owned radio: WLS-AM-FM.

WMAQ-TV—ch 5, 40.1 kw vis, 8.0 kw aur, ant 1,320t/1,456g. TL: N41 53 56 W87 37 23. Stereo. On air date: January 1948. 454 N. Columbus Dr. (60611). (312) 836-5555. FAX: (312) 836-5520. Licensee: NBC Subsidiary Inc. Group owner: NBC TV Stations Division (acq 6-5-86). ■ Net: NBC. Rep: Harrington, Righter & Parsons. ■ Patrick Wallace, pres & gen mgr; Lisa Churchville, sls dir; Joe Saarela, mktg dir; Rich Brace, prom dir & adv dir; Diana Borri, progmg dir; Michael Ward, news dir; Tom Powers, chief engr.

WPWR-TV—(Gary, IN). ch 50, 5,000 kw vis, 600 kw aur, ant 1,620t/1,624g. TL: N41 52 44 W87 38 10. Stereo. Hrs opn: 24. On air date: Jan 18, 1987. 2151 N. Elston Ave., Chicago, IL (60614). (312) 276-5050. FAX: (312) 276-6477; (312) 276-1717. Licensee: Newsweb Corp. (group owner). Rep: MMT. Wash atty: Fletcher, Heald & Hildreth. ■ Fred Eychaner, pres; Al DeVaney, gen mgr; Greg Armstrong, opns mgr; Mat Thornton, natl sls mgr; Debbie Carpenter, rgnl sls mgr; Michael Malone, prom mgr; Neal Sabin, progmg dir; Bob Minor, chief engr. ■ On 136 CATVs—1,600,000 subs.

WSNS—ch 44, 4,260 kw vis, 500 kw aur, ant 1,420t/1,456g. TL: N41 53 56 W87 37 23. On air date: Apr 5, 1970. 430 W. Grant Pl. (60614). (312) 929-1200. FAX: (312) 929-8153. Licensee: Video 44. Group owner: Harriscope Corp. (acq 9-90). ■ Net: Telemundo. Rep: Telemundo. Wash atty: Cohn & Marks. Sp 138 hrs wkly. News staff 12; news progmg 5 hrs wkly. ■ Jose Francisco Lamas, gen mgr; David Cordova, opns dir & news dir; Armando Triana, gen sls mgr; Enrique Fernandez y Martinez, prom mgr; Marissa Quiles, progmg dir; Henry Ruh, engrg dir.

*WTTW—ch 11, 60.3 kw vis, 12 kw aur, ant 1,630t/1,710g. TL: N41 52 44 W87 38 10. Stereo. On air date: Sept 6, 1955. 5400 N. St. Louis Ave. (60625). (312) 583-5000. FAX: (312) 583-3046. Licensee: Chicago EducTV Assn. ■ Net: PBS. Wash atty: Schwartz, Woods & Miller. News progmg 5 hrs wkly. ■ William McCarter, CEO & pres; David Buehrer, vp opns; Richard Bowman, Paul Nebenzahl, vps dev; Bruce Marcus, vp mktg; Larry Ocker, vp engrg. ■ On 300 CATVs.

*WYCC—ch 20, 2,421 kw vis, 242.1 kw aur, ant 1,239t/1,110g. TL: N41 53 56 W87 37 23. On air date: Sept 20, 1965. 7500 S. Pulaski Rd. (60652). (312) 838-4853. Licensee: College Dist. #508, County of Cook (acq 11-3-81). ■ Net: PBS. Wash atty: Dow, Lohnes & Albertson. Sp 5 hrs wkly. ■ Elynne Chaplik Aleskow, gen mgr; Gina Sclafani, progmg dir; Donald Rhodes, chief engr. ■ On 25 CATVs.

Decatur

ADI No. 75; see Springfield-Decatur-Champaign market

WAND—ch 17, 5,000 kw vis, 1,000 kw aur, ant 1,290t/1,314g. TL: N39 37 07 W88 49 55. Stereo. On air date: Aug 16, 1953. 904 Southside Dr. (62525). (217) 424-2500. FAX: (217) 422-8203. Licensee: WAND Television Inc. Group owner: LIN Broadcasting Corp. (acq 12-22-65; $2 million; 1-3-66). ■ Net: ABC. Rep: Blair. Wash atty: Schwartz, Woods & Miller. ■ T. J. Vaughan, pres & gen mgr; Larry Katt, vp sls; Carol Thomas, prom mgr; Pat Peters, progmg dir; Lee Williams, news dir; Larry Oaks, chief engr. ■ On 106 CATVs—233,861 subs. On one trans.

WFHL—ch 23, 1,951 kw vis, 195.1 kw aur, ant 1,289t. TL: N39 57 07 W88 49 55. Hrs opn: 20. On air date: May 14, 1984. 2510 Parkway Ct. (62526). (217) 428-2323. FAX: (217) 428-6455. Licensee: Decatur Foursquare Broadcasting Inc. Wash atty: Farrad, Cooper, Metzler & Bruiniers. News progmg 3 hrs wkly. ■ Mark Dreistadt, CEO & gen mgr; Dale Downs, pres; Matthew Begue, opns mgr & chief engr; Jack Cluney, gen sls mgr; Pam Haycraft, dir & progmg dir; Jennifer Peabody, prom dir; Jim Rossi, adv mgr; Paul Osborne, news dir; Douglas Krassow, pub affrs dir. ■ On 91 CATVs—165,000 subs. ■ Rates: $30; 25; 20.

East St. Louis

ADI No. 18; see St. Louis, MO market

WHSL—ch 46, 5,000 kw vis, 500 kw aur, ant 1,749t/849g. TL: N38 23 18 W90 29 16. On air date: March 1988. Suite 300, 1408 N. King's Hwy. Blvd., St. Louis, MO (63113). (314) 367-4600. FAX: (314) 367-0174. Licensee: Roberts Broadcasting Co. Group owner: Home Shopping Network (acq 3-88). Wash atty: John Feore. ■ Steven C. Roberts, gen mgr; Michael V. Roberts, gen sls mgr; Mark W. Roberts, prom mgr; Monica L. Nettles, progmg dir & news dir; Keith Martin, chief engr.

Freeport

WIFR—Licensed to Freeport. See Rockford.

Harrisburg

ADI No. 77; see Paducah, KY-Cape Girardeau, MO-Harrisburg-Marion, IL market

WSIL-TV—ch 3, 100 kw vis, 20 kw aur, ant 1,120t/1,000g. TL: N37 36 46 W88 52 20. Stereo. On air date: December 1953. Rt. 13, Carterville (62918). (618) 985-2333. Licensee: WSIL TV Inc. Group owner: Mel Wheeler Inc. (acq 5-12-83; grpsl; 6-6-83). ■ Net: ABC. Rep: Adam Young. Wash atty: Vincent Pepper. ■ Steve Wheeler, pres, gen mgr & progmg dir; Don Brown, news dir; Pat Victoria, chief engr.

Jacksonville

ADI No. 75; see Springfield-Decatur-Champaign market

*WSEC—ch 14, 28.25 kw vis, 2.83 kw aur, ant 313t/339g. TL: N39 44 08 W90 10 32. Hrs opn: 18. On air date: Aug 21, 1984. Box 6248, Springfield (62708). (217) 786-6647; (800) 232-3605. FAX: (217) 786-7267. Licensee: West Central Illinois Education Telecommunication Corp. ■ Net: PBS. Wash atty: Dow, Lohnes & Albertson. ■ Jerold Gruebel, pres & gen mgr; Richard Plotkin, opns mgr; Joy Hutchcraft, dev dir; Scott Mulford, progmg dir. ■ On 69 CATVs. On one trans.

Joliet

ADI No. 3; see Chicago market

WGBO-TV—ch 66, 5,000 kw vis, 500 kw aur, ant 1,296t/1,456g. TL: N41 53 56 W87 37 23. On air date: Sept 17, 1991. Suite 1100, 541 N. Fairbanks Ct., Chicago (60611). (312) 751-6666. FAX: (312) 670-1037. Licensee: Combined Broadcasting of Chicago Inc. Group owner: Combined Broadcasting Inc. (acq 7-1-88). Rep: Katz. Wash atty: Fisher, Wayland, Cooper & Leader. ■ Bob O'Connor, pres; Randy Swanson, stn mgr; Jonas Jones, gen sls mgr; Shari Valentine, natl sls mgr; George Leh, prom mgr & progmg dir; Jean Halevi, pub affrs dir; Chuck Jennings, chief engr. ■ On 97 CATVs—1,123,000 subs.

LaSalle

ADI No. 3; see Chicago market

WWTO-TV—ch 35, 117.5 kw vis, 11.7 kw aur, ant 1,900t/1,371g. TL: N41 16 51 W88 56 13. Hrs opn: 24. On air date: Dec 1, 1986. 420 E. Stevenson Rd, Ottawa (61350). (815) 434-2700. Licensee: All American TV Inc. Ownership: Cruz S. Arguinzoni, 25%; Nicky Cruz, 25%;

Illinois

Terry Hickey, 25%; John Castoria Jr., 25%.■ Wash atty: May & Dunne. ■ Cruz S. Arguinzoni, pres; Don Gladden, gen mgr; Gary Penovich, progmg dir; Bob Biggs, chief engr. ■ On 6 CATVs—50,000 subs.

Macomb

ADI No. 159; see Quincy-Hannibal, MO market

*WMEC—ch 22, 24.15 kw vis, 2.42 kw aur, ant 519t/535g. TL: N40 25 40 W90 40 58. Hrs opn: 6:15 AM-midnight. On air date: Oct 1, 1984. Box 6248 (62708). (217) 786-6647; (800) 232-3605. FAX: (217) 786-7267. Licensee: W. Central Ill. Educational Telecommunications Corp. ■ Net: PBS. Wash atty: Dow, Lohnes & Albertson. ■ Jerold Gruebel, pres & gen mgr; Richard Plotkin, opns dir; Joy Hutchcraft, dev dir; Scott Mulford, progmg dir. ■ On 69 CATVs.

Marion

ADI No. 77; see Paducah, KY-Cape Girardeau, MO-Harrisburg-Marion makret

WTCT—ch 27, 2,600 kw vis, 260 kw aur, ant 775t/500g. TL: N37 33 26 W89 01 24. On air date: Aug 16, 1981. Box 1010, Rt. 37 N. (62959). (618) 997-9333. FAX: (618) 997-1859. Licensee: Tri-State Christian TV (group owner; acq 5-29-84; 1.2 million). Wash atty: May & Dunne. ■ Garth Coonce, pres; Christine M. Coonce, vp & news dir; Robert L. Stien, gen mgr; Robert Hills, pub affrs dir; Tim Deterding, chief engr. ■ On 39 CATVs—50,441 subs. On one trans.

Moline

ADI No. 84; see Davenport-Rock Island-Moline market

WQAD-TV—ch 8, 282 kw vis, 23.2 kw aur, ant 1,010t/1,066g. TL: N41 18 44 W90 22 47. On air date: Aug 1, 1963. 3003 Park 16th St. (61265). (309) 764-8888. TWX: 910-225-1481. Licensee: The New York Times Co. (group owner, see Cross-Ownership). ■ Net: ABC. Rep: Katz. ■ Perry Chester, gen mgr; Gene Smith, gen sls mgr; Kristi Peterson, mktg mgr; Rick Serre, chief engr. ■ On 36 CATVs—135,000 subs.

*WQPT-TV—ch 24, 148 kw vis, 14.8 kw aur, ant 320t/355g. TL: N41 28 31 W90 26 50. Hrs opn: 17. On air date: Nov 3, 1983. 6600 34th Ave. (61265). (309) 796-2424. FAX: (309) 796-2484; (309) 792-5976. Licensee: Black Hawk College. ■ Net: PBS. Wash atty: Arter & Hadden. Sp 2 hrs wkly. News staff 3; news progmg 5 hrs wkly. ■ Leo Whalen, chmn; Maurice Bresnahan, pres & gen mgr; Charles Law, exec vp; Rick Best, chief opns; Cindy Adams, dev mgr; Kimberly Merchant, vp sls; Tim Sales, rgnl sls mgr; Jerry Myers, progmg dir; Susan McBride, pub affrs vp; Steve Ellis, chief engr. ■ On 32 CATVs—142,000 subs. On 2 trans.

Mount Vernon

ADI No. 18; see St. Louis market

WCEE—ch 13, 302 kw vis, 30.2 kw aur, ant 991t/441g. TL: N38 32 39 W88 55 26. (CP: 316 kw vis, 31.6 kw aur). Hrs opn: 21. On air date: Mar 1, 1983. 4751 Carter Rd. (62853); 125 N. 11th St. (62864). (618) 242-8813; (618) 822-6900. FAX: (618) 242-8643. Licensee: Sudbrink Broadcasting Corp. of Illinois. Group owner: Sudbrink Broadcasting (acq 1-1-86; $3.6 million; 9-30-85). Wash atty: Haley, Bader & Potts. ■ Dennis Linsin, gen mgr; Dee Rose, natl sls mgr; Michelle Philips, progmg dir; Jason Bruce, engrg mgr. ■ On 97 CATVs—100,000 subs.

Olney

ADI No. 138; see Terre Haute, IN market

*WUSI-TV—ch 16, 977 kw vis, 195 kw aur, ant 930t/976g. TL: N38 50 18 W88 07 46. On air date: Aug 19, 1968. Box 430 (62450). (618) 754-3335; (618) 395-3422. FAX: (618) 754-3336. Licensee: Board of Trustees, Southern Illinois Univ. ■ Net: PBS. Wash atty: Cohn & Marks. ■ Lee D. O'Brien, CFO; Kenneth J. Garry, stn mgr & progmg mgr; Helen Donsbach, opns dir; Kayla Yockey, dev dir; Bryan Piepenburg, pub affrs dir; Bernie Kunze, chief engr. ■ On 23 CATVs—209,000 subs. Co-owned radio: WUSI-FM.

Peoria

ADI No. 107; see Peoria-Bloomington market

WEEK-TV—ch 25, 2,410 kw vis, 239 kw aur, ant 680t/604.9g. TL: N40 37 48 W89 23 51. Hrs opn: 20. On air date: Feb 1, 1953. 2907 Springfield Rd., East Peoria (61611). (309) 698-2525. Licensee: Granite Broadcasting Corp. (group owner; acq 10-31-88; $33 million). ■ Net: NBC. Rep: Katz. Wash atty: Akin, Gump, Strauss, Hauer & Feld. News staff 26; news progmg 15 hrs wkly. ■ Dennis Upah, gen mgr & progmg dir; John Deushane, gen sls mgr; Duane Greer, prom mgr; Phil Supple, news dir; Ken Tofanelli, chief engr. ■ On 83 CATVs—140,800 subs.

WHOI—ch 19, 2,240 kw vis, 224 kw aur, ant 636t/632g. TL: N40 39 11 W89 35 14. On air date: Oct 20, 1953. 500 N. Stewart St. (61611). (309) 698-1919. FAX: (309) 698-0008. Licensee: Brissette TV of Peoria Inc. (group owner; acq 12-24-91; grpsl). ■ Net: ABC. Rep: Blair. Wash atty: Wiley, Rein & Fielding. ■ Mike Lennon, pres & gen mgr; Scott Barnes, chief opns & chief engr; Jo Ferguson, rgnl sls mgr & adv mgr; Devoe Slisher, prom mgr & progmg dir; Mark J. Cummings, film buyer; Sheldon Ripson, news dir. ■ On 87 CATVs—176,229 subs. ■ Rates: $1200; 350; 175.

WMBD-TV—ch 31, 2,050 kw vis, 406 kw aur, ant 635t/548g. TL: N40 38 07 W89 32 19. Stereo. On air date: Jan 1, 1958. 3131 N. University St. (61604). (309) 688-3131. FAX: (309) 686-8650; TWX: 910-652-0139. Licensee: Midwest Television Inc. (group owner; acq 6-15-60; 6-10-60). ■ Net: CBS. Rep: Petry. Wash atty: Covington & Burling. ■ August C. Meyer Jr., pres; Gene Robinson, gen mgr; James Donovan, gen sls mgr; John Birks, prom mgr; Lloyd Peterson, progmg dir; Duane Wallace, news dir; Paul Baumgartner, chief engr. ■ On 82 CATVs—178,993 subs. Co-owned radio: WMBD(AM), WKZW(FM).

*WTVP—ch 47, 1,410 kw vis, 251 kw aur, ant 710t/599g. TL: N40 37 44 W89 34 12. Hrs opn: 17. On air date: June 23, 1971. 1501 W. Bradley Ave. (61625). (309) 677-4747. Licensee: Illinois Valley Public Telecommunication Corp. ■ Net: PBS. Wash atty: Dow, Lohnes & Albertson. ■ Elwin L. Basquin, pres & gen mgr; Jackie Luboke, opns mgr; Andrea Carmen, dev dir; Linda Miller, prom mgr; Shirley Rochman, progmg dir; Keith Turcot, chief engr. ■ On 37 CATVs—175,000 subs.

Quincy

ADI No. 159; see Quincy-Hannibal, MO market

KHQA-TV—(Hannibal, MO). ch 7, 316 kw vis, ant 889t/805g. TL: N39 58 22 W91 19 54. On air date: Sept 23, 1953. 510 Maine St., Quincy, IL (62301); Box 905, Quincy (62306). (217) 222-6200. FAX: (217) 228-3164. Licensee: Benedek Broadcasting Co. (group owner; acq 10-30-86; $13 million; 9-22-86). ■ Net: CBS. Rep: Katz. Wash atty: Crowell & Moring. ■ John Hurley, gen mgr; Ron Heller, stn mgr & news dir; Hank Mayhall, opns mgr & progmg dir; Terry Hurley, gen sls mgr; Lisa Lee, prom dir; Lee Gray, chief engr. ■ On 46 CATVs—96,767 subs.

WGEM-TV—ch 10, 316 kw vis, 31.6 kw aur, ant 780t/673g. TL: N39 57 03 W91 19 54. On air date: Sept 4, 1953. Box 80, 513 Hampshire (62306). (217) 228-6600. Licensee: Quincy Broadcasting Co. Group owner: Quincy Newspapers Inc. ■ Net: NBC. Rep: Petry. Wash atty: Wilkinson, Barker, Knauer & Quinn. ■ T.A. Oakley, pres; Ralph M. Oakley, vp & gen mgr; Leo Henning, opns dir; Jonathon VanNess, gen sls mgr; Don Hale, mktg dir; Jim Lawrence, prom mgr; Brady Dreasler, progmg dir; Les Sachs, news dir; Jim Martens, chief engr. ■ On 61 CATVs. Co-owned radio: WGEM-AM-FM.

*WQEC—ch 27, 14.8 kw vis, 1.48 kw aur, ant 567t/495g. TL: N39 58 44 W91 18 33. Hrs opn: 6:15 AM-midnight. On air date: Mar 11, 1985. Box 6248, Springfield (62708). (217) 786-6647; (800) 232-3605. FAX: (217) 786-7267. Licensee: West Central Illinois Educational Telecommunications Corp. ■ Net: PBS. Wash atty: Dow, Lohnes & Albertson. ■ Jerold Gruebel, pres & gen mgr; Richard Plotkin, opns dir; Joy Hutchcraft, dev dir; Scott Mulford, progmg dir. ■ On 69 CATVs.

WTJR—ch 16, 179.2 kw vis, 31.5 kw aur, ant 1,025t/948g. TL: N39 58 18 W91 19 42. Hrs opn: 24. On air date: Jan 1, 1986. Box 3112, R.R. 8, Old Cannonball Rd. (62305). (217) 228-1275. FAX: (217) 228-1616. Licensee: Believer's Broadcasting Corp. ■ Carl Geisendorfer, pres, gen mgr & gen sls mgr; Kenneth Geisendorfer, exec vp; Patricia Geisendorfer, prom mgr; Anita Geisendorfer, progmg dir & film buyer; Jason Geisendorfer, news dir; Joseph Caproni, chief engr. ■ On 22 CATVs—22,000 subs.

Directory of Television

Rock Island

ADI No. 84; see Davenport-Rock Island-Moline market

WHBF-TV—ch 4, 100 kw vis, 10 kw aur, ant 1,342t/1,383g. TL: N41 32 49 W90 28 35. On air date: July 1, 1950. 231 18th St. (61201). (309) 786-5441. FAX: (309) 788-4975. Licensee: Coronet Communications Co. Group owner: Citadel Communications Co. Ltd. (acq 3-16-87; grpsl; 11-17-86). ■ Net: CBS. Rep: MMT. Wash atty: Latham & Watkins. News staff 15; news progmg 7 hrs wkly. ■ Philip J. Lombardo, pres; Greg O'Conner, gen sls mgr; Jim Sparks, prom mgr; Al Uzzell, progmg dir; Joe Corcoran, news dir; Coy Bullard, chief engr. ■ On 35 CATVs—91,151 subs. ■ Rates: $500; 225; 70.

Rockford

ADI No. 134; see Rockford market

WIFR—(Freeport). ch 23, 676 kw vis, 85.2 kw aur, ant 720t/731g. TL: N42 17 48 W89 10 15. On air date: Sept 12, 1965. Box 123, Rockford (61105); Suite 210, 308 W. State St., Rockford (61101). (815) 987-5300. FAX: (815) 965-0985; TWX: 910-631-0746. Licensee: Benedek Broadcasting of Illinois Inc. Group owner: Benedek Broadcasting Co. (acq 11-5-86). ■ Net: CBS. Rep: Katz TV Continental. Wash atty: Crowell & Moring. ■ Jim Grimes, gen mgr & film buyer; Doug Warkenthien, opns dir; Bob Smith, gen sls mgr; Della Saunders, prom mgr & pub affrs dir; Carol Comella, progmg dir; Arles Hendershott, news dir; Will Shears, chief engr. ■ On 22 CATVs—100,000 subs.

WQRF-TV—ch 39, 525 kw vis, 5.25 kw aur, ant 575t/575g. TL: N42 17 26 W89 09 51. On air date: Nov 27, 1978. 401 S. Main St. (61101). (815) 987-3950. FAX: (815) 964-9974. Licensee: Petracom Inc. (group owner; acq 9-12-89; $2 million; 10-2-89). ■ Net: Fox. Wash atty: Cohn & Marks. ■ Henry A. Ash, pres; Greg Graber, vp & gen mgr; Kemp Nichol, gen sls mgr; Bill Zuckerman, prom mgr & progmg dir; Audra Johnson, pub affrs dir; Dean Turman, chief engr. ■ On 28 CATVs—242,000 subs.

WREX-TV—ch 13, 316 kw vis, 39.8 kw aur, ant 710t/652g. TL: N42 17 50 W89 14 24. On air date: Oct 1, 1953. Box 530, (61105); 10322 W. Auburn Rd. (61103). (815) 335-2213. FAX: (815) 335-2055; TWX: 910-642-0770. Licensee: WREX Associates. Group owner: RP Companies Inc. (acq 9-1-87; $18 million). ■ Net: ABC. Rep: Petry. Wash atty: Wiley, Rein & Fielding. ■ John White, gen mgr; Dave George, gen sls mgr; Jeanne Foster, progmg dir & pub affrs dir; Mike Robinson, news dir; Gerry Meinders, chief engr. ■ On 43 CATVs—57,000 subs.

WTVO—ch 17, 759 vis, 79.4 kw aur, ant 674t/710g. TL: N42 17 14 W89 10 16. On air date: May 3, 1953. Box 470, 1917 N. Meridian Rd. (61105); 1917 N. Meridian Rd. (61102). (815) 963-5413. FAX: (815) 963-0201. Licensee: Young Broadcasting Inc. (group owner; acq 7-27-88; $18 million; 8-15-88). ■ Net: NBC. Wash atty: Wiley, Rein & Fielding. News staff 8; news progmg 7 hrs wkly. ■ Tom Best, gen mgr; Dicky Geyer, gen sls mgr; Wilma Hollis, progmg dir; Paul Freifeld, news dir; Al Petzke, chief engr.

Springfield

ADI No. 75; see Springfield-Decatur-Champaign market

WCFN—ch 49, 200 kw vis, 20 kw aur, ant 620t/655g. TL: N39 47 27 W89 30 53. On air date: 1987. Box 20, 509 S. Neil St., Champaign (61824-0020). (217) 356-8333. Licensee: Midwest Television Inc. (group owner). ■ Net: CBS. ■ Guy F. Main, vp. Satelitte of WCIA-TV Champaign.

WICS—ch 20, 676 kw vis, 67.6 kw aur, ant 1,430t/1,458g. TL: N39 48 15 W89 27 40. Stereo. Hrs opn: 19. On air date: Oct 30, 1953. 2680 E. Cook St. (62703). (217) 753-5620. FAX: (217) 753-8177. Licensee: Gannett Publishing Co. Group owner: Guy Gannett Broadcasting Services Inc. (acq 3-12-85; $18 million). ■ Net: NBC. Rep: Katz. Wash atty: Dow, Lohnes & Albertson. News staff 24; news progmg 13 hrs wkly. ■ Jim Shaffer, pres; Mike Bock, vp; Jack Connors, gen mgr & film buyer; Frank Lilley, opns dir; Don Squires, gen sls mgr; Gary Spears, progmg dir; Les Vann, news dir; Elizabeth Moore, pub affrs dir; Jerry Merritt, chief engr. ■ On 45 CATVs—137,000 subs.

WRSP-TV—ch 55, 2,000 kw vis, 200 kw aur, ant 1,442t/1,449g. TL: N39 47 56 W89 26 45. On air date: June 1, 1979. 3003 Old Rochester Rd. (62703). (217) 523-8855. FAX: (217) 523-4410; TWX: 910-242-0516.

Stations in the U.S.

Licensee: Springfield Broadcasting Partners. Group owner: Bahakel Communications (acq 7-20-92). ■ Net: Fox. Rep: Seltel. ■ Cy N. Bahakel, pres; Beverly Poston, vp; Greg Thomas, gen mgr & film buyer; Tom York, gen sls mgr; Jennifer Best, prom mgr & progmg mgr; Theresa Harvey, pub affrs dir; Matt Begue, chief engr. ■ On 78 CATVs—196,875 subs. ■ Rates: $350; 150; 45.

Urbana

ADI No. 75; see Springfield-Decatur-Champaign market

WCCU—ch 27, 3,360 kw vis, 218 kw aur, ant 442t/829.5g. TL: N40 18 42 W87 54 48. On air date: 1987. 712 Killarney St. (61801). (217) 367-8827. FAX: (217) 367-8839. Licensee: Urbana Broadcasting Partners. Group owner: Bahakel Communications (acq 7-20-92). ■ Net: Fox. Rep: Seltel. ■ Greg Thomas, gen mgr; Tom York, gen sls mgr; Jennifer Best, prom dir & progmg dir; Juli Cornwell, chief engr.

***WILL-TV**—ch 12, 316 kw vis, 63.1 kw aur, ant 990t/1,047g. TL: N40 02 18 W88 40 10. Hrs opn: 19. On air date: Aug 1, 1955. 1110 W. Main St. (61801). (217) 333-1070. FAX: (217) 244-6386. Licensee: Univ of Ill. Board of Trustees. ■ Net: PBS. Wash atty: Dow, Lohnes & Albertson. Foreign lang progmg 3 hrs wkly. ■ Donald P. Mullally, gen mgr; Ellis R. Bromberg, stn mgr; Deborah Day, dev dir; Terry Bush, prom mgr; Elaine Sprenkle, progmg dir; Larry Inman, chief engr. ■ On 129 CATVs—120,000 subs. Co-owned radio: *WILL-AM-FM.

Indiana

Angola

ADI No. 102; see Ft. Wayne market

WINM—ch 63, 5,000 kw vis, 500 kw aur, ant 499g. TL: N41 27 15 W84 48 10. (CP: Ant 473t, 1,374 kw vis). On air date: Mar 10, 1983. R.R. 1 State Line Rd., Edgerton, OH (43517). (419) 298-3703. FAX: (419) 298-3706. Licensee: Tri-State Christian TV (group owner; acq 1-24-91; $400,000; 2-11-91). Wash atty: Lauren J. Colby. ■ Stephen Canniday, gen mgr; Margo France, prom mgr; Roger Rhodes, progmg dir & film buyer; Stephen Buyze, chief engr. ■ On 4 CATVs—60,000 subs. ■ Rates: $15; 30; 35.

Bloomington

ADI No. 26; see Indianapolis market

WCLJ—ch 42, 5,000 kw vis, 500 kw aur, ant 1,039t. TL: N39 24 12 W86 08 50. On air date: August 1987. 2528 U.S. 31 S., Greenwood (46143). (317) 535-5542. FAX: (317) 535-8584. Licensee: Trinity Broadcasting of Indiana Inc. Group owner: Trinity Broadcasting Network. Wash atty: Colby May. ■ Randall Lohr, gen mgr; Diana Lohr, progmg dir; Cynthia Hamilton, pub affrs dir; Don Renollet, chief engr. ■ On 10 CATVs—150,000 subs.

WIIB—ch 63, 2,000 kw vis, 200 kw aur, ant 1,053t/2,300g. TL: N39 24 16 W86 08 37. Hrs opn: 24. On air date: Dec 27, 1988. Rt. 1, Box 516A, Trafalgar, IN (46181). (317) 878-5407. FAX: (317) 878-4458. Licensee: Channel 63 Inc. (acq 9-28-90; grpsl: 10-15-90). Wash atty: Fisher, Wayland, Cooper & Leader. ■ Barbara Kerr, gen mgr; Scott Burgett, chief engr. ■ On 35 CATVs—400,000 subs. ■ Rates: $50; 40; 25; 10.

***WTIU**—ch 30, 200 kw vis, 39.8 kw aur, ant 710t/647g. TL: N39 08 32 W86 29 43. Stereo. (CP: 832 kw, ant 708 ft). Hrs opn: 19. On air date: March 1969. Radio-TV Bldg., Indiana Univ. (47405). (812) 855-5900; (812) 855-8000. FAX: (812) 855-0729. Licensee: Trustees of Indiana Univ. ■ Net: PBS. Wash atty: Crowell & Moring. ■ Don Agostino, gen mgr; Barrie Zimmerman, opns dir; Judith Witt, Marla Keller, dev dirs; Suzann Owen, prom mgr; Keith Klein, progmg dir; Bradley Howard, chief engr. ■ On 27 CATVs—125,000 subs. Co-owned radio: *WFIU(FM).

WTTV—Licensed to Bloomington. See Indianapolis.

Elkhart

***WNIT-TV**—See South Bend.

WSJV—Licensed to Elkhart. See South Bend.

Evansville

ADI No. 94; see Evansville market

WEHT—ch 25, 60 kw vis, 6.2 kw aur, ant 1,030t/988g. TL: N37 51 56 W87 34 04. On air date: Sept 11, 1953. Box 25 (47701); 800 Marywood Dr., Henderson, KY (42420). (812) 424-9215. FAX: (502) 826-6823. Licensee: Gilmore Broadcasting Corp. Group owner: James S. Gilmore Stns (acq 7-20-64; grpsl; 7-27-64). ■ Net: CBS. Rep: Blair. Wash atty: Wiley, Rein & Fielding. ■ Jim Gilmore Jr., pres; Doug Padgett, vp & gen mgr; Jenny Funk, opns mgr; Mike Riley, gen sls mgr & adv mgr; Melisse Marks, mktg mgr; Ginny Powers, progmg dir; Lloyd Winnecke, news dir; Ralph Martinis, chief engr. ■ On 58 CATVs—115,280 subs.

WEVV—ch 44, 1,250 kw vis, 125 kw aur, ant 1,000t/1,000g. TL: N37 53 17 W87 32 37. Hrs opn: 20. On air date: Nov 17, 1983. 44 Main St. (47708-1450). (812) 464-4444. FAX: (812) 465-4559. Licensee: WEVV Inc. (acq 1-1-92). ■ Net: Fox. Rep: Katz. Wash atty: Leventhal, Senter & Lerman. News staff 6; news progmg 5 hrs wkly. ■ Ralph C. Wilson, chmn; J.A. "Skip" Simms, pres & gen mgr; Jeff Littman, CFO; Harry Strader, opns mgr & pub affrs dir; Dick Schappa, gen sls mgr; Alice Lovell, progmg dir; Dale Cox, news dir; Donald W. Hollingsworth, chief engr. ■ On 74 CATVs—165,000 subs.

WFIE-TV—ch 14, 2,208 kw vis, 331 kw aur, ant 1,022t/949g. TL: N37 53 14 W87 31 07. Stereo. Hrs opn: 20. On air date: Nov 9, 1953. Box 1414, 1115 Mt. Auburn Rd. (47712). (812) 426-1414. TWX: 810-353-0507. Licensee: Cosmos Broadcasting Corp. (group owner); acq 7-19-56; $586,937; 7-30-56). ■ Net: NBC. Wash atty: Dow, Lohnes & Albertson. ■ John R. Cottingham, gen mgr; Shirley Kirk, opns mgr & progmg dir; Mike Rickwald, gen sls mgr; Jerry Grimes, prom mgr; Bob Freeman, news dir; Marion B. Paul, chief engr. ■ On 119 CATVs—187,600 subs. ■ Rates: $650; 225; 100.

***WNIN**—ch 9, 282 kw vis, 56.2 kw aur, ant 570t/570g. TL: N38 01 27 W87 21 43. Stereo. On air date: Mar 16, 1970. 405 Carpenter St. (47708). (812) 423-2973. Licensee: Tri-State Public Teleplex Inc. (acq 9-12-73). ■ Net: PBS. Wash atty: Dow, Lohnes & Albertson. ■ David Dial, pres & gen mgr; David Whitaker (prod mgr), opns dir; Carolyn McClintock, vp dev; Libby Currier, mktg mgr; Pamela Filippi, prom mgr; Bonnie Reinhardt, progmg mgr; Jerry Kissinger, chief engr. ■ 44 CATVs-60,000 subs. Co-owned radio: WNIN-FM.

WTVW—ch 7, 316 kw vis, 63.2 kw aur, ant 1,013t/880g. TL: N38 01 27 W87 21 43. On air date: Aug 26, 1956. Box 7 (47701); 477 Carpenter St. (47708). (812) 422-1121. FAX: (812) 421-4040. Licensee: Woods Communications Group Inc. (group owner; acq 3-16-93; grpsl; 4-5-93). ■ Net: ABC. Wash atty: Kenkel & Barnard. News staff 16; news progmg 18 hrs wkly. ■ Charles Woods, pres; Ken Schreiber, gen mgr & gen sls mgr; Dave Castrale, opns mgr; Jim Moore, rgnl sls mgr; Andy Herbertz, mktg mgr, prom mgr & adv mgr; Pam Miller, progmg mgr; Dave Smith, news dir; Ted Klipsch, pub affrs dir; John Schuta, chief engr. ■ On 109 CATVs—190,585 subs. ■ Rates: $400; 75; 40.

Fort Wayne

ADI No. 102; see Ft. Wayne market

WANE-TV—ch 15, 437 kw vis, 43.7 kw aur, ant 830t/839g. TL: N41 05 38 W85 10 48. Hrs opn: 21. On air date: Sept 26, 1954. Box 1515, 2915 W. State Blvd. (46801). (219) 424-1515. FAX: (219) 424-1515. Licensee: Indiana Broadcasting Corp. Group owner: LIN Broadcasting Corp. (acq 3-1-84; 12-19-83). ■ Net: CBS. Rep: Petry. Wash atty: Covington & Burling. ■ Frank N. Moore, pres, gen mgr & film buyer; R. Bruce Cynar, gen sls mgr; Lynn Lawson, natl sls mgr; James Gill, prom mgr; Jim Riecken (prod mgr), progmg mgr; Vince Robinson, news dir; Karen Bartik, pub affrs dir; Thomas Harford, chief engr. ■ On 36 CATVs—160,000 subs.

WFFT-TV—ch 55, 600 kw vis, 60 kw aur, ant 780t/805g. TL: N41 06 33 W85 11 44. On air date: Dec 21, 1977. 3707 Hillegas Rd. (46808); Box 8655 (46898). (219) 471-5555. FAX: (219) 484-4331. Licensee: Great Trails Broadcasting Corp. (group owner; acq 12-27-87; grpsl). ■ Net: Fox. Rep: Katz. Wash atty: Haley, Bader & Potts. News progmg 4 hrs wkly. ■ Alexander Williams, pres; Frank Hawkins, stn mgr & gen sls mgr; Steve Pozezanac, opns mgr, prom mgr & progmg mgr; Steven R. Shine, news dir; Bonnie Presser, pub affrs dir; "Mac" McShane, chief engr. ■ On 126 CATVs—225,000 subs.

***WFWA**—ch 39, 1,380 kw vis, 138 kw aur, ant 820t/744g. TL: N41 06 13 W85 11 28. On air date: Dec 1, 1989. Box

Indiana

39 (46801). (219) 484-8839. FAX: (219) 482-3632. Licensee: Fort Wayne Public Television. ■ Net: PBS. News progmg 2 hrs wkly. ■ Roger Rhodes, pres & gen mgr; Kathleen Nadolny, dev dir & progmg dir; Tracy Brenneman, gen sls mgr; Kristen Rajchel, mktg mgr & pub affrs dir; George Castle, chief engr. ■ On 10 CATVs.

WKJG-TV—ch 33, 594 kw vis, 59 kw aur, ant 770t/793g. TL: N41 05 40 W85 10 36. Stereo. On air date: Nov 21, 1953. 2633 W. State Blvd. (46808). (219) 422-7474. Licensee: Corporation for General Trade. Ownership: Joseph A. Cloutier, trustee, the Joseph R. Cloutier Trust, 100% (acq 3-12-90). ■ Net: NBC. Rep: Seltel. Wash atty: Haley, Bader & Potts. News staff 18; news progmg 12 hrs wkly. ■ Joseph Cloutier, pres; William B. Nichols, gen mgr; Marvin Gottlieb, gen sls mgr; Robert Miller, rgnl sls mgr; Mark Meyer, progmg dir; Karen Frankola, news dir; W. Elly Price, pub affrs dir; Matt Kyle, chief engr. ■ On 50 CATVs—161,193 subs.

WPTA—ch 21, 562 kw vis, 55 kw aur, ant 760t/770g. TL: N41 06 08 W85 11 04. Hrs opn: 20. On air date: Sept 28, 1957. Box 2121 (46801); 3401 Butler Rd. (46808). (219) 483-0584. Licensee: Granite Broadcasting Corp. (group owner; acq 12-11-89; $25.15 million; 10-9-89). ■ Net: ABC. Rep: Blair. Wash atty: Akin, Gump, Strauss, Hauer & Field. ■ Barbara Wigham, pres, gen mgr & film buyer; Bill Ransom, gen sls mgr; Dave Fisher, prom mgr; Jan D'Italia, progmg dir; Don Bradley, news dir; Ray Krueger, chief engr. ■ On 236 CATVs—122,100 subs. ■ Rates: $900; 300; 65.

Gary

ADI No. 3; see Chicago, IL market

WPWR-TV—Licensed to Gary. See Chicago, Ill.

***WYIN**—ch 56, 1,353 kw vis, 1.3 kw aur, ant 1,003t/998g. TL: N41 20 56 W87 24 02. On air date: Nov 15, 1987. 8625 Indiana Pl., Merrillville (46410). (219) 736-5656. FAX: (219) 755-4312. Licensee: Northwest Indiana Public Broadcasting Inc. ■ Net: PBS. Wash atty: Gordon & Healy. ■ Richard Parker, pres & gen mgr; Jason Wille, prom mgr; Patrick Ennis, chief engr. ■ On 15 CATVs.

Hammond

ADI No. 3; see Chicago, IL market

WJYS—ch 62, 5,000 kw vis, 300 kw aur, ant 741.28t. TL: N41 33 10 W87 47 09. (CP: Ant 479t). Hrs opn: 24. On air date: Mar 2, 1991. 18600 S. Oak Park Ave., Tinley Park, IL (60477). (708) 633-0001. Licensee: Jovon Broadcasting Corp. ■ Joseph Stroud, gen mgr.

Indianapolis

ADI No. 26; see Indianapolis market

***WFYI**—ch 20, 1,135 kw vis, 114 kw aur, ant 847t/867g. TL: N39 53 59 W86 12 01. Stereo. Hrs opn: 6 AM-1 AM. On air date: Oct 4, 1970. 1401 N. Meridian (46202). (317) 636-2020; (317) 633-7410. FAX: (317) 633-7418. Licensee: Metro Indianapolis Public Broadcasting. ■ Net: PBS. ■ Lloyd Wright, pres & gen mgr; Jerry Hughes, CFO; Paul Tyler, sr vp; Alan Coe, vp opns; Jeanelle Adamak, vp dev; Daina Chamness, mktg mgr; Vicki Wright, prom mgr; Alan Cloe, vp progmg; Steve Jensen, engrg dir. ■ On 39 CATVs—410,000 subs. Co-owned radio: WFYI-FM.

WHMB-TV—ch 40, 2,090 kw vis, 209 kw aur, ant 991t/1,007g. TL: N39 53 39 W86 12 19. Hrs opn: 24. On air date: Jan 25, 1971. Box 50450 (46250); 10511 Greenfield Ave., Noblesville (46060). (317) 773-5050. Licensee: LeSea Broadcasting Corp. (group owner; acq 8-15-72; $354,618; 9-4-72). Wash atty: Heron, Burchette, Ruckert & Rothwell. ■ Steve Sumrall, pres; Pete Sumrall, vp; Thom Ewing, gen mgr, gen sls mgr & progmg mgr; David Streit, opns mgr; Phil Voorhees, pub affrs dir; Douglas W. Garlinger, engrg dir; Dave Gooding, chief engr. ■ On 209 CATVs—283,000 subs.

WISH-TV—ch 8, 316 kw vis, 42.7 kw aur, ant 990t/997g. TL: N39 45 39 W86 00 21. On air date: July 1, 1954. Box 7088, 1950 N. Meridian St. (46207). (317) 923-8888. FAX: (317) 926-1144. Licensee: Indiana Broadcasting Corp. Group owner: LIN Broadcasting Corp. (acq 2-29-84; grpsl; 12-19-83). ■ Net: CBS. Wash atty: Covington & Burling. ■ Paul Karpowicz, pres & gen mgr; Scott Blumenthal, gen sls mgr; Tim Warner, natl sls mgr; Peter Nikiel, prom mgr; Rick Thedwall, progmg dir; R. Lee Giles, news dir; Terry VanBibber, chief engr. ■ On 40 CATVs—176,000 subs.

Iowa | Directory of Television

WRTV—ch 6, 100 kw vis, 20 kw aur, ant 990t/1,019g. TL: N39 53 59 W86 12 02. On air date: May 30, 1949. 1330 N. Meridian St. (46202). (317) 635-9788. FAX: (317) 269-1400. Licensee: McGraw-Hill Broadcasting Co. Group owner: McGraw-Hill Broadcasting Group (acq 6-1-72). ■ Net: ABC. Rep: MMT. Wash atty: Koteen & Naftalin. News progmg 20 hrs wkly. ■ Edward T. Reilly, pres; David W. Ingraham, CFO; John Long, vp & gen mgr; Deanne Haviland, gen sls mgr; Paul Montgomery, progmg dir; David Baer, news dir; Judith Waugh, pub affrs dir; Richard Pratt, engrg dir. ■ On 60 CATVs—591,000 subs. ■ Rates: $2100; 650; 240.

*** WTBU**—ch 69, 10.5 kw vis, ant 548t. TL: N39 50 25 W86 10 34. On air date: April 1992. 2835 N. Illinois St. (46208). (317) 926-9252. FAX: (317) 927-5971. Licensee: Butler University. ■ Net: PBS. Wash atty: Hadley, Bader, Potts. ■ Kenneth Creech, gen mgr; Jack Tiller, opns mgr; Tami Crabtree, dev dir; Wayne Hepler, prom mgr; Richard Miles, progmg mgr; Scott Bridge, news dir; Peggy Huston, pub affrs dir; David Fort, chief engr. ■ On 5 CATVS—300,000 subs.

WTHR—ch 13, 316 kw vis, 31.6 kw aur, ant 980t/1,039g. TL: N39 55 43 W86 10 55. Stereo. On air date: Oct 30, 1957. 1000 N. Meridian St. (46204); Box 1313 (42606). (317) 636-1313. FAX: (317) 636-3717. Licensee: VideoIndiana Inc. Group owner: Dispatch Printing Co. (acq 10-1-75; $17.65 million; 9-1-75). ■ Net: NBC. Rep: Blair. Wash atty: Crowell & Moring. ■ Eugene D'Angelo, pres; Michael J. Corken, vp & gen mgr; Tom Rose, opns dir; Marlene Campbell, gen sls mgr; Steve Click, natl sls mgr; Rod Porter, prom dir; Bob Campbell, news dir; Linda Kirby, pub affrs dir; Harold Thompson, chief engr. ■ On 114 CATVs—424,452 subs.

WTTV—(Bloomington). ch 4, 55 kw vis, 11 kw aur, ant 1,200t/1,170g. TL: N39 24 26 W86 08 52. Hrs opn: 24. On air date: Nov 11, 1949. 3490 Bluff Rd., Indianapolis (46217). (317) 782-4444 FAX: (317) 780-5464. Licensee: WTTV Inc. Group owner: River City Broadcasting. Rep: Telerep. Wash atty: Dow, Lohnes & Albertson. ■ Ric Gorman, vp & gen mgr; Peter O'Brien, opns dir; Michael Granados, vp sls; Clyde Dutton, natl sls mgr; John O'Laughlin, prom mgr; Susanne McAlister, pub affrs dir; Rick Barber, chief engr. ■ On 200 CATVs—900,000 subs.

WXIN—ch 59, 2,090 kw vis, 209 kw aur, ant 990t/1,030g. TL: N39 53 20 W86 12 07. Stereo. On air date: Feb 1, 1984. 1440 N. Meridian (46202). (317) 632-5900. FAX: (317) 687-6531; (317) 687-6532. Licensee: 59 Licensee Inc. Group owner: Renaissance Communications (acq 3-1-93; grpsl; 2-1-93). ■ Net: Fox. Rep: Seltel. Wash atty: Sidley & Austin. News progmg 4 hrs wkly. ■ Edward Karlik, pres; Joseph Young, vp & gen mgr; George Boggs, stn mgr & progmg dir; Tom Comersford, gen sls mgr; Randa Minkarah, natl sls mgr; Judy Dages, prom mgr; Ron Petrovich, news dir; Mike McKinnon, chief engr. ■ On 93 CATVs—524,086 subs.

Kokomo

ADI No. 26; see Indianaplois market

WLFI-TV—See Lafayette.

WTTK—ch 29, 3,090 kw vis, 309 kw aur, ant 775t/774g. TL: N40 20 20 W85 57 15. Hrs opn: 24. On air date: May 1988. 3490 Bluff Road, Indianapolis (46217). (317) 782-4444. FAX: (317) 780-5464. Licensee: WTTV Inc. Group owner: River City Broadcasting. Rep: Telerep. Wash atty: Fletcher, Heald & Hildreth. ■ Ric Gorman, gen mgr; Mike Granados, gen sls mgr; John O'Laughlin, prom mgr; Ranie Jarboe, progmg dir. Satellite of WTTV Bloomington.

Lafayette

ADI No. 191; see Lafayette, IN market

WLFI-TV—ch 18, 1,490 kw vis, 298 kw aur, ant 778t/755.99g. TL: N40 23 20 W86 36 46. Stereo. Hrs opn: 6 AM-2:30 AM. On air date: June 15, 1953. Box 2618, 2605 Yeager Rd., West Lafayette (47906). (317) 463-1800. FAX: (317) 463-7979. Licensee: WLFI-TV Inc. Ownership: The Block Family, 100%. Group owner: Blade Communications Inc. (acq 9-13-79; $3,153,750). ■ Net: CBS. Rep: Katz. Wash atty: Dow, Lohnes & Albertson. News staff 20; news progmg 13 hrs wkly. ■ Robert A. Ford, pres & gen mgr; Tina Parker, opns mgr & prom mgr; Tom Combs, gen sls mgr; Shirley Ehrman, progmg mgr; Mike Piggott, news dir; Ken Fitzgerald, chief engr. ■ On 58 CATVs—132,455 subs.

Marion

ADI No. 26; see Indianapolis market

WMCC—ch 23, 5,000 kw vis, 600 kw aur, ant 1,082t. TL: N40 08 57 W85 56 15. Hrs opn: 24. On air date: Nov 1, 1987. Box 228, Indianapolis (46206-0228). 13044 E. 246th St., Noblesville (46060). (317) 920-9544; (317) 552-0804. FAX: (317) 920-9632; TWX: 910-250-5554. Licensee: Marion T.V. Inc. Group owner: R Group Communication (acq 5-30-86; $52,168). Wash atty: Arnold & Porter. ■ G.J. Robinson, pres; Kenneth S. Robinson, vp & natl sls mgr; James E. "Jed" Duvall, gen mgr & chief opns; Doug Housemeyer, gen sls mgr, prom dir & adv mgr; Eric Randles, progmg dir; Bob Pinnix, chief engr.

Muncie

ADI No. 26; see Indianapolis market

*** WIPB**—ch 49, 676 kw vis, 67.6 kw aur, ant 510t/548g. TL: N40 09 38 W85 22 42. Stereo. Hrs opn: 6:45 AM-midnight M-F, 9 AM-midnight Sat-Sun. On air date: May 8, 1953. Edmund F. Ball Bldg., Ball State Univ. (47306). (317) 285-1249. FAX: (317) 285-5548. Licensee: Ball State Univ. (acq 10-31-71; $125,000; 12-6-71). ■ Net: PBS, CEN. Wash atty: Schwartz, Woods & Miller. Deaf progmg 4 hrs wkly. ■ John Worthen, pres; Mary Ann Olinger, dev mgr, sls dir & mktg mgr; Bob Smith, prom mgr & progmg dir; Jim Miller, chief engr. ■Co-owned radio: WBST(FM).

Richmond

ADI No. 52; see Dayton, OH market

WKOI—ch 43, 1,410 kw vis, 141 kw aur, ant 990t/1,002g. TL: N39 30 44 W84 38 09. On air date: May 11, 1982. 1702 S. Ninth St. (47374). (317) 935-2390. Licensee: Trinity Broadcasting of Indiana. Group owner: Trinity Broadcasting Network (acq 9-81). Wash atty: Gammon & Grange. ■ Paul Crouch, pres; Mary Blaird, gen mgr; Mary Laird, opns mgr; Joseph Hoyer, progmg dir; Carl Dole, chief engr. ■ On 3 CATVs.

Salem

ADI No. 47; see Louisville, KY market

WFTE—ch 58, 5,000 kw vis, Ant 1,305t. TL: N38 42 29 W86 05 57. Not on air, target date unknown. Rt. 3, Box 157, c/o James T. Ledford (47167). (812) 883-5963. Permittee: Kentuckiana Broadcasting Inc. ■ James T. Ledford, pres.

South Bend

ADI No. 83; see South Bend-Elkhart market

WHME-TV—ch 46, 1,600 kw vis, 160 kw aur, ant 1,000t/982g. TL: N41 35 43 W86 09 38. Hrs opn: 24. On air date: July 27, 1974. Box 12, 61300 S. Ironwood (46614). (219) 291-8200. FAX: (219) 291-9043. Licensee: Lester Sumrall Evangelistic Assoc. Group owner: LeSea Broadcasting (acq 6-10-77; $496,000; 7-27-77). Rep: Landin Media. Wash atty: Gardner Carton. ■ Lester Sumrall, pres; Peter Sumrall, gen mgr; Lois Anderson, rgnl sls mgr; Chris Mars, prom mgr; Dar Monesmith, chief engr. ■ On 200 CATVs—200,000 subs. Co-owned radio: WHME-FM. ■ Rates: $125; 75; 50.

WNDU-TV—ch 16, 3,770 kw vis, 754 kw aur, ant 1,070t/1,046g. TL: N41 36 20 W86 12 45. Stereo. On air date: July 15, 1955. Box 1616 (46634); 54516 Business U.S. 31 N. (46637). (219) 239-1616. FAX: (219) 282-2916. Licensee: Michiana Telecasting Corp. Ownership: Univ. of Notre Dame du Lac, 100%. ■ Net: NBC. Rep: Adam Young Inc. Wash atty: Pepper, Martin, Jensen, Maichel & Hetlage. ■ Bazil O'Hagan, pres & gen mgr; Mike Leyes, gen sls mgr; Melissa Collins, prom mgr; Karen Heisler, progmg dir; Ellen Crooke, news dir; George Molnar, chief engr. ■ On 35 CATVs. Co-owned radio: WNDU-AM-FM.

*** WNIT-TV**—ch 34, 708 kw vis, 77 kw aur, ant 530t/500g. TL: N41 36 52 W86 11 01. Stereo. (CP: 691.8 kw vis, ant 264t). Hrs opn: 16. On air date: Feb 14, 1974. Box 3434, 2300 Charger Blvd., Elkhart (46514). (219) 674-5961. Licensee: Michiana Public Broadcasting Corp. ■ Net: PBS. Wash atty: Dow, Lohnes & Albertson. ■ James Shea Jr., chmn; Jonathon Housand Jr., pres; Kevin R. Gill, stn mgr; Tom Zapiecki, opns dir; Gail Martin, dev dir; Laura Coyne, prom dir; Kevin Gill, progmg dir; Charles R. Pitts, chief engr. ■ On 48 CATVs.

WSBT-TV—ch 22, 4,790 kw vis, 479 kw aur, ant 1,070t/1,047g. TL: N41 37 00 W86 13 01. Stereo. Hrs opn: 24. On air date: Dec 21, 1952. 300 W. Jefferson Blvd. (46601). (219) 233-3141. FAX: (219) 288-6630; (219) 289-0622. Licensee: WSBT Inc. Group owner: Schurz Communications Inc., see Cross-Ownership. ■ Net: CBS. Rep: Katz. Wash atty: Hogan & Hartson. News staff 30; news progmg 17 hrs wkly. ■ James D. Freeman, pres & gen mgr; Roland T. Adeszko, stn mgr & gen sls mgr; Robert Johnson, opns dir & prom mgr; Theresa Butler, mktg dir; Julius DeCocq, progmg dir; Bill Crafton, news dir; Chris Thornton, chief engr. ■ On 22 CATVs. Co-owned radio: WSBT(AM), WNSN(FM). ■ Rates: $350; 100; 65.

WSJV—(Elkhart). ch 28, 5,000 kw vis, 500 kw aur, ant 1,086t/1,045g. TL: N41 36 58 W86 11 38. Stereo. Hrs opn: 24. On air date: Mar 15, 1954. 58096 CR No. 7 S., Elkhart (46517); Box 1646, Elkhart (46515). (219) 293-8616; (219) 674-5106. FAX: (219) 294-1324. Licensee: WSJV Television Inc. Group owner: Quincy Newspapers Inc., see Cross-Ownership (acq 3-31-75; $3.2 million; 4-14-75). ■ Net: ABC. Rep: Petry. Wash atty: Wilkinson, Barker, Knauer & Quinn. News staff 19; news progmg 11 hrs wkly. ■ Thomas A. Oakley, pres; F. Robert Kalthoff, vp & gen mgr; Kevin Sargent, opns mgr & progmg dir; Dick Frid, gen sls mgr; B.J. Whittet, prom mgr; Larry Ford, news dir; Pamela Lamb, pub affrs dir; Ed Schmidt, chief engr. ■ On 80 CATVs.

Terre Haute

ADI No. 138; see Terre Haute market

WBAK-TV—ch 38, 2,140 kw vis, 214 kw aur, ant 976t/1,004g. TL: N39 13 58 W87 23 49. On air date: Apr 3, 1973. Box 719 (47808); 138 Poplar St. (47807). (812) 238-1515. FAX: (812) 235-3854. Licensee: Terre Haute Independent Broadcasters Inc. Group owner: Bahakel Communications (acq 2-28-77; $649,000; 3-21-77). ■ Net: ABC. Rep: Adam Young. ■ Cy N. Bahakel, pres; Lorraine Lancaster, vp; Linda Snyder, gen mgr & gen sls mgr; Dennis Roberts, prom mgr & progmg dir; David Pierce, chief engr. ■ On 18 CATVs—49,000 subs. ■ Rates: $250; 65; 40.

WTHI-TV—ch 10, 316 kw vis, 31.6 kw aur, ant 960t/993g. TL: N39 14 36 W87 23 07. On air date: July 22, 1954. Box 1486, 918 Ohio St. (47808). (812) 232-9481. FAX: (812) 232-8953. Licensee: Hulman & Co. (group owner; 7-13-92; grpsl; 9-21-92). ■ Net: CBS. Wash atty: Dow, Lohnes & Albertson. ■ David Bailey, vp & gen mgr; Rod Garvin, opns dir & progmg dir; Phil Johnson, gen sls mgr; Steve Rifkin, prom mgr; Brian Clark, news dir; Jeff Tucker, chief engr.

WTWO—ch 2, 100 kw vis, 19.5 kw aur, ant 950t/999g. TL: N39 14 33 W87 23 29. 24. On air date: Sept 1, 1965. Box 299 (47808). (812) 696-2121. FAX: (812) 696-2755; TWX: 810-350-2470. Licensee: Fabri Development Corp. Ownership: TCS Management Corp. (MC Media, 50.005%; Commonwealth, 48.995%; TCB Management, 1%) (acq 3-26-93; grpsl; 4-12-93). ■ Net: NBC. Rep: Petry. Wash atty: Cohn & Marks. ■ I. Martin Pompadur, CEO; Christopher W. Jones, gen mgr; John Chadwick, gen sls mgr; Karen Granato, prom mgr; Phylis Martindale, progmg dir; Mark Edwards, news dir; Harold Wesley, chief engr. ■ On 52 CATVs—110,000 subs.

Vincennes

ADI No. 138; see Terre Haute market

*** WVUT**—ch 22, 1,150 kw vis, 115 kw aur, ant 570t/560g. TL: N38 39 06 W87 28 37. On air date: Feb 15, 1968. Davis Hall, 1200 N. Second St. (47591). (812) 885-5326. FAX: (812) 882-2237. Licensee: Vincennes Univ. Trustees (acq 9-16-76; 10-11-76). ■ Net: PBS. Wash atty: Fletcher, Heald & Hildreth. Foreign lang progmg 106 hrs wkly. News staff 4; news progmg 5 hrs wkly. ■ Timothy J. Fisher, gen mgr & pub affrs dir; Jill Ballinger, opns mgr; Julie Sievers, prom mgr; Sharon Keifer, progmg dir; John Szink, news dir; Jim Evans, chief engr. ■ On 12 CATVs—25,000 subs. Co-owned radio: *WVUB(FM).

Iowa

Ames

ADI No. 68; see Des Moines market

WOI-TV—Licensed to Ames. See Des Moines.

Stations in the U.S.

Iowa

Burlington

ADI No. 84; see Davenport-Rock Island-Moline market

KJMH—ch 26, 54.3 kw vis, 5.43 kw aur, ant 315.4t/232.9g. TL: N40 49 25 91 08 22. On air date: Jan 6, 1988. 4th Fl. Suite 200 Jefferson St. (52601). (319) 752-0026. Licensee: Burlington Broadcasting Co. Ltd. Ownership: Steven S. Hoth, 55%. ■ Net: Fox. ■ Steven S. Hoth, pres; George Van Hagen, gen mgr & gen sls mgr; Jerry Johnson, prom mgr; Joi Harris, progmg dir & film buyer; Victoria Lind, news dir; Jim Yard, chief engr. ■ On 15 CATVs—50,000.

Cedar Rapids

ADI No. 82; see Cedar Rapids-Waterloo-Dubuque market

KCRG-TV—ch 9, 316 kw vis, 63.2 kw aur, ant 1,988t/1,926g. TL: N42 18 59 W91 51 31. Stereo. On air date: Oct 15, 1953. Box 816 (52406-0816); 2nd Ave. at 5th St. S.E. (52401). (319) 398-8422. FAX: (319) 398-8378. Licensee: Cedar Rapids TV Co. Group owner: The Gazette Co. (acq 8-12-54; $101,500; 8-23-54). ■ Net: ABC. Rep: Petry. Wash atty: Wiley & Rein. ■ J.F. Hladky Jr., CEO; Joseph F. Hladky III, pres; Bob Allen, vp & gen mgr; John Ganahl, opns dir & progmg dir; Linda Blackburn, gen sls mgr; Dean Bunting, news dir; Karen Ultis, pub affrs dir; Bruce Kruse, chief engr. ■ On 178 CATVs—170,000 subs. Co-owned radio: KCRG(AM).

KGAN—ch 2, 100 kw vis, 20 kw aur, ant 1,450t/1,355g. TL: N42 17 39 W91 53 10. On air date: Sept 30, 1953. Box 3131 (52406). (319) 395-9060. FAX: (319) 395-0987. Licensee: Gannett Publishing Co. Group owner: Guy Gannett Broadcasting Services Inc. (acq 8-14-81; $13 million). ■ Net: CBS. Rep: Katz. Wash atty: Dow, Lohnes & Albertson. ■ Richard Herbst, gen mgr; Dan Kumpel, gen sls mgr; Denise Noonan, natl sls mgr; Bill Anderson, progmg dir; Dennis Camble, news dir; Bob Burns, chief engr. ■ On 55 CATVs—198,693 subs. On 3 trans.

KOCR—ch 28, 1,499.7 kw vis, 149.97 kw aur, ant 436.85t/376.1g. TL: N42 02 46 W91 38 42. (CP: 2,316 kw vis). On air date: February 1988. 605 Boysen Rd., N.E. (52402). (319) 378-1028. FAX: (319) 378-1737. Licensee: Metro Program Network Inc. Ownership: Gerald Fitzgerald, 100%. ■ Net: Fox. Rep: Roslin. ■ Gerald Fitzgerald, pres, gen mgr, gen sls mgr & film buyer; Kelly Fitzgerald, prom mgr; Todd Erickson, progmg dir; Dell Morse, chief engr.

KTVC—ch 48, 5,000 kw vis, 500 kw air, ant 466t. TL: N42 04 51 W91 41 45. On air date: November 1992. 1404 Fifth Ave. S.E., Altoona (50009). (515) 967-6228. Licensee: Jefferson Broadcasting Company Inc. Ownership: Jerry Montgomery, 23.1%; Donna Montgomery, 23%; Denny Workmen, 49.9%; others, 4% ■ Jerry D. Montgomery, gen mgr & vp progmg; Donna Montgomery, pub affrs dir.

KWWL—(Waterloo). ch 7, 316 kw vis, 27 kw aur, ant 1,980t/2,000g. TL: N42 24 04 W91 50 43. Stereo. On air date: November 1953. 500 E. Fourth, Waterloo (50703). (319) 291-1200. FAX: (319) 291-1255. Licensee: AFLAC Broadcast Partners. AFLAC Broadcast Division. ■ Net: NBC. Rep: Blair. Wash atty: Sidley & Austin. News staff 30; news progmg 17 hrs wkly. ■ James B. Waterbury, pres & gen mgr; Mark Mathis, vp opns, gen sls mgr & progmg dir; John Sampson, natl sls mgr; Sherre Sharp, prom mgr; Nevin Gnagey, news dir; Jim Ohmstede, chief engr. ■ On 190 CATVs—187,000 subs.

Council Bluffs

ADI No. 73; see Omaha market

***KBIN**—ch 32, 575 kw vis, 57.5 kw aur, ant 317t/163g. TL: N41 15 15 W95 50 07. On air date: Sept 7, 1975. Box 6450, Johnston (50131). (515) 242-3100. Licensee: Iowa Public Broadcasting Board. ■ Net: PBS. Wash atty: Dow, Lohnes & Albertson.

Davenport

ADI No. 84; Davenport-Rock Island market

KLJB-TV—ch 18, 3,000 kw vis, 300 kw aur, ant 1,010t/993g. TL: N41 19 17 W90 22 47. (CP: Ant 989t/942g). Hrs opn: 6 AM-2 AM. On air date: July 28, 1985. Suite D, 937 E. 53rd St. (52807). (319) 386-1818. FAX: (319) 386-8543. Licensee: Quad Cities Television Acquisition. Ownership: Milton Grant, John H. Markley, William D. Towe, Gregory B. Maffei, & Huntsville Television Holdings Corp. ■ Net: Fox. Rep: Seltel. Wash atty: Wilmer & Schneider. ■ Milton Grant, pres; Drew Pfeiffer, gen mgr & film buyer; Matt Pryor, gen sls mgr; Pat Stiphout, prom mgr; Don Bargmann, chief engr. ■ On 80 CATVs—175,000 subs. ■ Rates: $600; 250; 25.

***KQCT**—ch 36, 6.76 kw vis, 676 w aur, ant 213t. TL: N41 31 58 W90 34 40. On air date: December 1991. 6600 34th Ave., Moline (61265). (309) 796-2424. Licensee: Black Hawk College. ■ Maurice Bresnahan, pres & gen mgr; Steve Ellis, chief engr. Satellite of *WQPT-TV Moline, Ill.

KWQC-TV—ch 6, 100 kw vis, 15.1 kw aur, ant 940t/978g. TL: N41 32 49 W90 28 35. Stereo. On air date: Oct 31, 1949. 805 Brady St. (52803). (319) 383-7000. FAX: (319) 383-7165. Licensee: Broad Street Television Corp. Ownership: Richard L. Geismar, Allen R. Adler, Fred E. Walker (acq 7-19-89; $45.82 million; 8-7-89). ■ Net: NBC. Rep: Blair. Wash atty: Dow, Lohnes & Albertson. ■ D. Russell Hamilton, pres & gen mgr; Bill Yeu, opns mgr; Russ Whitnah, gen sls mgr; Allen Wiese, natl sls mgr; Trish Tague, mktg dir; Duane Mathias, vp prom & vp progmg; Doug Retherford, news dir; John Hegeman, chief engr. ■ On 19 CATVs—105,330 subs.

WHBF-TV—See Rock Island, Ill.

WQAD-TV—See Moline, Ill.

Des Moines

ADI No. 68; see Des Moines market

KCCI-TV—ch 8, 316 kw vis, 31.6 kw aur, ant 1,953t/1,997g. TL: N41 48 35 W93 37 16. Stereo. Hrs opn: 24. On air date: July 31, 1955. Box 10305 (50306); 888 Ninth St. (50309). (515) 247-8888. FAX: (515) 243-4931. Licensee: H & C Communications Inc. (group owner; acq 1993; $22.2 million). ■ Net: CBS. Rep: Petry. Wash atty: Dow, Lohnes & Albertson. News staff 30; news progmg 15 hrs wkly. ■ Paul Fredericksen, pres & gen mgr; John Pascuzzi, vp opns; Dave Porepp, gen sls mgr & adv mgr; Anne Marie Caudron, natl sls mgr; Robert Day, progmg dir & pub affrs dir; Dave Busiek, news dir; Steve Houg, chief engr. ■ On 150 CATVs—225,000. On one trans. ■ Rates: $750; 150; 150.

***KDIN-TV**—ch 11, 316 kw max vis, 31.6 kw max aur, 1,973t/2,000g. TL: N41 48 33 W93 36 53. Stereo. On air date: Apr 27, 1959. Box 6450, Johnston (50131). (515) 281-4500. Licensee: Iowa Public Broadcasting Bd. ■ Net: PBS. Wash atty: Dow, Lohnes & Albertson. ■ Dan Miller, progmg dir; Don Saveraid, chief engr. ■ On 21 CATVs—51,669 subs. On 2 trans.

KDSM-TV—ch 17, 3,020 kw vis, 311 kw aur, ant 1,516t/1,503g. TL: N41 48 01 W93 36 27. 4023 Fleur Dr. (50321). (515) 287-1717. FAX: (515) 287-0064; TWX: 910-520-2704. Licensee: River City L.P. Group owner: River City Broadcasting (acq 1-4-91; $1.36 million; 1-4-91). ■ Net: Fox. Rep: Seltel. Wash atty: Tierney & Swift. ■ Will Davis, gen mgr; Ted Stevens, stn mgr; Ted Stephens, gen sls mgr; Kerry Schwartz, prom mgr; Dave Iound, progmg dir; Bob West, news dir; Martin Mohrefeld, chief engr. ■ On 175 CATVs—200,000 subs. ■ Rates: $300; 200; 60.

WHO-TV—ch 13, 316 kw vis max, 47.9 kw aur max, 1,970t/2,000g. TL: N41 48 33 W93 36 53. Stereo. On air date: Apr 15, 1954. 1801 Grand Ave. (50309). (515) 242-3500. FAX: (515) 242-3797; (515) 242-3796 (News). Licensee: Palmer Communications Inc. (acq 11-91; grpsl; FTR 11-18-91). ■ Net: NBC. Rep: Blair. ■ William J. Ryan, pres; Joe Lentz, vp & gen mgr; Cheryl Semerad, gen sls mgr; Chuck Hensley, rgnl sls mgr; Nanci Elder, mktg dir; Mary Bracken, progmg dir; Ray Carter, news dir; Brad Olk, chief engr. ■ On 94 CATVs—166,304 subs. On one trans. Co-owned radio: WHO(AM)-KLYF(FM) ■ Rates: $2,200; 500; 200.

WOI-TV—(Ames). ch 5, 100 kw vis, 20 kw aur, ant 1,850t/1,503g. TL: N41 48 33 W93 36 53. Stereo. On air date: Feb 21, 1950. WOI Building, Ames (50011). (515) 294-5555. FAX: (515) 294-8503. Licensee: Citadel Communications Co. Group owner: Citadel Communications Company Ltd., Coronet Communications. (acq 1993; $12.7 million). ■ Net: ABC. Rep: Katz. Wash atty: Cohn & Marks. ■ Bob Helmers, pres & gen mgr; Ray Johnson, gen sls mgr; Terry MacFarlane, prom mgr; Leo Runge, chief engr. ■ On 224 CATVs—100,000 subs. On one trans.

Dubuque

ADI No. 82; see Cedar Rapids-Waterloo-Dubuque market

KDUB-TV—ch 40, 646 kw vis, 64.6 kw aur, ant 841.3t/836.6g. TL: N42 31 05 W90 37 16. On air date: Sept 12, 1976. Suite 930, One Cycare Plaza (52001). (319) 556-4040. FAX: (319) 557-7101. Licensee: Dubuque TV L.P. (acq 1985). ■ Net: ABC. Rep: Roslin. Wash atty: Kaye, Scholer, Fierman, Hays & Handler. ■ Thomas Bond, gen mgr & gen sls mgr; Joe Denk, progmg dir; Steve Sarber, news dir; Gary Haverland, chief engr. ■ On 35 CATVs—36,000 subs.

Fort Dodge

ADI No. 68; see Des Moines market

***KTIN**—ch 21, 1,580 kw vis, 158 kw aur, ant 1,160t/1,206g. TL: N42 49 03 W94 24 41. On air date: Apr 8, 1977. Box 6450, Johnston (50131). (515) 242-3100. Licensee: Iowa Public Broadcasting Board. ■ Net: PBS. Wash atty: Dow, Lohnes & Albertson. ■ On 10 CATVs—9,537 subs.

Iowa City

ADI No. 82; see Cedar Rapids-Waterloo-Dubuque market

***KIIN-TV**—ch 12, 316 kw vis, 31.6 kw aur, ant 1,440t/1,449g. TL: N41 43 15 W91 20 30. On air date: Feb 8, 1970. Box 6450, Johnston (50131). (515) 242-3100. Licensee: Iowa Public Broadcasting Bd. ■ Net: PBS. Wash atty: Dow, Lohnes & Albertson. ■ On 19 CATVs-103,547 subs. On 2 trans.

Mason City

ADI No. 148; see Rochester-Mason City-Austin market

KIMT—ch 3, 100 kw vis, 10 kw aur, ant 1,510t/1,525g. TL: N43 22 20 W92 49 59. (CP: 5 kw aur, 97.7 kw vis, 1,550t/1,569g). Hrs opn: 21. On air date: May 15, 1954. Box 620, 112 N. Pennsylvania Ave. (50401). (515) 423-2540. FAX: (515) 423-7960. Licensee: Spartan Radiocasting Co. Group owner: Spartan Radiocasting Company Inc. (acq 6-12-84; grpsl). ■ Net: CBS. Rep: Katz. Wash atty: Covington & Burling. ■ John Shine, gen mgr; Dave Presler, gen sls mgr; Kip Ireland, prom mgr; Jerome Risting, progmg dir; Doug Merback, news dir; Dale Byre, chief engr. ■ On 78 CATVs—95,220 subs.

***KYIN**—ch 24, 1,740 kw vis, 174 kw aur, ant 1,430t/1,565g. TL: N43 22 20 W92 49 59. On air date: May 14, 1977. Box 6450, Johnston (50131). (515) 242-3100. Licensee: Iowa Public Broadcasting Board. ■ Net: PBS. Wash atty: Dow, Lohnes & Albertson.

Ottumwa

ADI No. 200; see Ottumwa-Kirksville market

KTVO—(Kirksville, MO). ch 3, 100 kw vis, 14.3 kw aur, ant 1,971t. TL: N40 31 47 W92 26 29. On air date: Nov 21, 1955. Box 949, Kirksville, MO (63501). (816) 627-3333. Licensee: Federal Broadcasting Co. (group owner; acq 7-87; grpsl). ■ Net: ABC. Rep: Blair. Wash atty: Hogan & Hartson. ■ Peter Kizer, pres; Greg Wittland, gen mgr & gen sls mgr; Pam Small, prom mgr & progmg dir; Roy Clem, news dir; John Wise, chief engr. ■ On 48 CATVs—70,000 subs.

KYOU-TV—ch 15, 166 kw vis, 16.6 kw aur, ant 461t/447g. TL: N40 57 50 W92 23 50. (CP: 2,213 kw vis, ant 1,189t, TL: N41 11 42 W91 57 15). Hrs opn: 21. On air date: June 29, 1987. 820 W. Second St. (52501). (515) 684-5415. FAX: (515) 682-5173. Licensee: Public Interest Broadcast Group Inc. (acq 8-87; $900; 4-13-87). ■ Net: Fox. ■ Dirk Engstrom, pres, gen mgr & vp progmg; Sheri Locke-Ward, gen sls mgr; Jennifer Leitner, prom mgr; Ron Tucker, film buyer; Phil Benjamin, chief engr. ■ On 53 CATVs—48,000 subs. On one trans.

Red Oak

ADI No. 73; see Omaha market

***KHIN**—ch 36, 2,040 kw vis, 204 kw aur, ant 1,560t/1,503g. TL: N41 20 40 W95 15 21. On air date: Sept 7, 1975. Box 6450, Johnston (50131). (515) 242-3100. Licensee: Iowa Public Broadcasting Board. ■ Net: PBS. Wash atty: Dow, Lohnes & Albertson. ■ On 30 CATVs—308,000 subs. On 2 trans.

Sioux City

ADI No. 140; see Sioux City market

KCAU-TV—ch 9, 245 kw vis, 49 kw aur, ant 2,020t/2,000g. TL: N42 35 12 W96 13 57. On air date: March 28, 1953. 7th & Douglas Sts. (51101). (712) 277-2345. FAX: (712) 277-3733. Licensee: Citadel Communications Co. Ltd. Group owner: Citadel

Communications Co. Ltd., Coronet Communications Co. (acq 10-1-85; $15 million). ■ Net: ABC. Rep: Katz. Wash atty: Latham & Watkins. ■ Raymond Cole, gen mgr; Jim Rupert, gen sls mgr; Randy Chapman, prom mgr; J.D. Walls, progmg dir; Jon Barnett, chief engr. ■ On 180 CATVs—124,491 subs. On 4 trans.

KMEG—ch 14, 280 kw vis, 75.9 kw aur, ant 1,152t/1,000g. TL: N42 30 53 W96 18 13. On air date: Sept 5, 1967. Box 657 (51102). (712) 277-3554. FAX: (712) 277-4732. Licensee: KMEG Television Inc. Ownership: Frederic L. Thompson, Nathanial B. Thompson, Julie T. Fralich, Marjorie W. Rines, Anne R. Stanley, Henry M. Rines, David M. Rines, James P. Rines & Leanorna W. Rines. Group owner: Maine Radio and Television Co. (acq 11-86; $4 million; 8-25-86). ■ Net: CBS, Fox. Rep: Blair. Wash atty: Wilkinson, Barker, Knauer & Quinn. ■ Bruce McCorrill, pres; Bruce Lewis, vp & gen mgr; Gary Duffy, gen sls mgr; Fritz Miller, prom mgr; Clayton Koehler, progmg dir; Dick Herr, chief engr. ■ On 129 CATVs—83,000 subs. On 3 trans. ■ Rates: $130; 130; 15.

***KSIN**—ch 27, 4,070 kw vis, 407 kw aur, ant 1,070.2t/875g. TL: N42 30 53 W96 18 13. On air date: Jan 4, 1975. Box 6450, Johnston (50131). (515) 242-3100. Licensee: Iowa Public Broadcasting Board. ■ Net: PBS. Wash atty: Dow, Lohnes & Albertson. ■ On 4 CATVs—8,209 subs.

KTIV—ch 4, 100 kw vis, 20 kw aur, ant 1,920t/2,000g. TL: N42 35 12 W96 13 57. Stereo. Hrs opn: 19. On air date: Oct 9, 1954. 3135 Floyd Blvd. (51105). (712) 239-4100. FAX: (712) 239-2621. Licensee: New Jersey Herald Inc. Group owner: Quincy Newspapers Inc., see Cross-Ownership (acq 11-20-89). ■ Net: NBC. Rep: Petry. Wash atty: Wilkinson, Barker, Knauer & Quinn. News staff 15; news progmg 12 hrs wkly. ■ William F. Turner, vp & gen mgr; Paul O'Bryan, natl sls mgr; Kim Cleaver, rgnl sls mgr; Jerry Johnson, prom mgr; Dave Madsen, progmg dir; Dave Nixon, Jr., news dir; Scot Krayenhagen, chief engr. ■ On 171 CATVs. On 3 trans. ■ Rates: $350; 290; 40.

Waterloo

ADI No. 82; see Cedar Rapids-Waterloo-Dubuque market

KCRG-TV—See Cedar Rapids.

KGAN—See Cedar Rapids.

***KRIN**—ch 32, 5,000 kw vis, 500 kw aur, ant 1,851t/1,759g. TL: N42 18 59 W91 51 31. On air date: Dec 15, 1974. Box 6450, Johnston (50131). (515) 242-3100. Licensee: Iowa Public Broadcasting Board. ■ Net: PBS. Wash atty: Dow, Lohnes & Albertson. ■ On 8 CATVs—6,166 subs.

KWWL—Licensed to Waterloo. See Cedar Rapids.

Kansas

Colby

ADI No. 62; see Wichita-Hutchinson market

KLBY—ch 4, 100 kw vis, 21 kw aur, ant 770t/3,420g. TL: N39 15 25 W101 21 10. Hrs opn: 6 AM-2 AM. On air date: July 4, 1984. 990 S. Range (67701). (913) 462-8644. Licensee: Chronicle Publishing Co. Group owner: Chronicle Broadcasting Co. (acq 10-10-86; $1,382,000; 9-1-86). Rep: Petry. Wash atty: Covington. Ger one hr wkly. News staff 2. ■ Debra Schwanke, stn mgr; Rich Epp, gen sls mgr; Debbie Schwanke, news dir; Jeff Wolf, pub affrs dir; Bernie Schmidt, chief engr. ■ Rates: $40; 35; 20.

Ensign

ADI No. 62; see Wichita-Hutchinson market

KBSD-TV—ch 6, 100 kw vis, 10 kw aur, ant 720t/600g. TL: N37 38 28 W100 20 40. On air date: July 24, 1957. Box 157, Dodge City (67801). (316) 227-3121. FAX: (316) 225-1675. Licensee: KBS Inc. Group owner: Smith Broadcasting Group Inc. ■ Net: CBS. Rep: Telerep. ■ Sandy D. Pasquale, pres; Gayle Kiger, gen mgr & gen sls mgr; Cyd Champlin, news dir; Ben Davis, chief engr. ■ On 28 CATVs—20,000 subs.

Fort Scott

ADI No. 146; see Joplin, MO-Pittsburgh market

KKFT—ch 20, 5,000 kw vis, 500 w aur, ant 765t/804g. TL: N37 26 36 W97 39 31. Stereo. Hrs opn: 24. On air date: October 1992. 1404 5th Ave., S.E., Altoona, IA (50009); 1625 Scott St. (68701). (515) 967-6228. Licensee: Family Broadcasting Company Inc. (group owner). ■ Net: Fox. ■ Jerry D. Montgomery, pres, adv mgr & vp progmg; Donna Montgomery, pub affrs dir; Gary McGlothler, chief engr.

Garden City

ADI No. 62; see Wichita-Hutchinson market

KSNG—ch 11, 200 kw vis, 24.5 kw aur, ant 800t/837g. TL: N37 46 40 W100 52 08. On air date: Nov 5, 1958. 204 Fulton Terrace (67846). (316) 276-2311. FAX: (316) 275-5076. Licensee: Wichita License Subsidiary Corp. Group owner: SJL Broadcast Management Corp. (acq 10-1-88; grpsl; 8-29-88). ■ Net: NBC. Rep: Katz. Wash atty: Latham & Watkins. ■ Sharolyn Mayfield, gen mgr; Jim Bowers, chief engr. ■ On 30 CATVs—34,766 subs.

KUPK-TV—ch 13, 87.1 kw vis, 17.4 kw aur, ant 870t/881g. TL: N37 39 01 W100 40 06. (CP: 225 kw vis, 45 kw aur). On air date: Nov 8, 1964. Box 10, Wichita (67201-0010); Box 2649 (67846). (316) 275-1560. FAX: (316) 275-1572. Licensee: Chronicle Broadcasting Co. (group owner; acq 3-80; grpsl). ■ Net: ABC. Rep: Petry. Wash atty: Fletcher, Heald & Hildreth. ■ Jan McDaniel, pres; Bob Surber, gen mgr; Bryce Baker, gen sls mgr; Curt Hutchinson, news dir; Brad Jones, chief engr. ■ On 6 CATVs. ■ Rates: $55; 42; 36.

Goodland

ADI No. 62; see Wichita-Hutchinson market

KBSL-TV—ch 10, 316 kw vis, 56.2 kw aur, ant 990t/975.9g. TL: N39 28 09 W101 33 20. On air date: Apr 28, 1959. Box 569, Broadcast Plaza (67735). (913) 899-2321. FAX: (913) 899-3138. Licensee: KBS License Corp. Group owner: Smith Broadcasting Group Inc. ■ Net: CBS. ■ Sandy DiPasquale, CEO; Wayne Roberts, gen mgr; Terry Stover, rgnl sls mgr; Kimberly Newell, prom mgr; Don Newell, adv mgr. Satellite of KBSH-TV Hays. ■ Rates: $50; 40; 20.

Great Bend

ADI No. 62; see Wichita-Hutchinson markets

KSNC—ch 2, 100 kw vis, 17.8 kw aur, ant 970t/1,005g. TL: N38 25 54 W98 46 18. On air date: Nov 28, 1954. R.R. 5, Box 262 (67530). (316) 793-7868. FAX: (316) 793-3079. Licensee: SJL Inc. Group owner: SJL Broadcast Management Corp. (acq 6-13-62; grpsl; 6-18-62). ■ Net: NBC. ■ Mark Nichols, gen mgr & gen sls mgr; Terry Weathers, prom mgr; Tim McQuade, news dir; Jim Bowers, chief engr. ■ On 18 CATVs—23,337 subs. On 1 trans.

Hays

ADI No. 62; see Wichita-Hutchinson markets

KBSH-TV—ch 7, 316 kw vis, 33.6 kw aur, ant 710t/812g. TL: N38 53 01 W99 20 15. On air date: Sept 1, 1958. Box 817, 2300 Hall St. (67601). (913) 625-5277. FAX: (913) 625-1161. Licensee: KBS Inc. Group owner: Smith Broadcasting Group Inc. ■ Net: CBS. ■ Sandy DiPasquale, pres; Pat Manning, gen mgr; Dennis Massier, chief engr. ■ On 19 CATVs—25,000 subs. On one trans. ■ Rates: $90; 70; 30.

***KOOD**—ch 9, 316 kw vis, 31.6 kw aur, ant 2,959t/1,119g. TL: N38 46 16 W98 44 17. On air date: Nov 10, 1982. Box 9, Bunker Hill (67626). (913) 483-6990. FAX: (913) 483-4605. Licensee: Smoky Hills Public Television Corp. ■ Net: PBS. Wash atty: Dow, Lohnes & Albertson. Sp one hr wkly. ■ Nick V. Slechta, CEO; Randall Weller, chmn; Dave Wilson, gen mgr; Linda Trowbridge, progmg dir; Les Kinderknecht, news dir; Dawn Mermis, pub affrs dir; Lloyd E. Mintzlmyer, chief engr. ■ On 46 CATVs—31,000 subs. On 3 trans.

Hutchinson

ADI No. 62; see Wichita-Hutchinson market

***KPTS**—ch 8, 229 kw vis, 22.9 kw aur, ant 800t/785g. TL: N38 03 21 W97 46 35. Stereo. On air date: Jan 7, 1970. 320 W. 21st St. N., Wichita (67203). (316) 838-3090. Licensee: Kansas Public Telecommunications Service Inc. (acq 1979). ■ Net: PBS. Wash atty: Dow, Lohnes & Albertson. ■ Zoel Parenteau, pres & gen mgr; Dale Heckel, gen mgr; Sandra Davis, vp dev; Carl Chance, vp mktg; James Lewis, vp progmg; Dale Goter, pub affrs dir. ■ On 85 CATVs—121,970 subs.

KWCH-TV—Licensed to Hutchinson. See Wichita.

Joplin

KOAM-TV—See Pittsburg.

Lakin

ADI No. 62; see Wichita-Hutchinson market

***KSWK**—ch 3, 100 kw vis, 20 kw aur, ant 561t/586g. TL: N37 49 38 W101 06 35. On air date: Mar 15, 1989. 6th & Elm Sts., Bunker Hill (67626). (316) 355-7211. FAX: (316) 483-4605. Licensee: Smoky Hills Public Television Corp. ■ Dave Wilson, CEO & gen mgr; Linda Trowbridge, progmg dir; Les Kinderknecht, news dir; Lloyd Mintzmyer, chief engr.

Lawrence

ADI No. 29; see Kansas City, MO market

KMCI—ch 38, 5,000 kw vis, 1,000 kw aur, ant 1,038g. TL: N38 53 46 W95 10 29. Stereo. (CP: Ant 1,101t). Hrs opn: 24. On air date: February 1988. Box 66, U.S. 56 at 1st St., Baldwin City (66006). (913) 594-3086. FAX: (913) 594-3080. Licensee: Miller Broadcasting Inc. Ownership: Monte M. Miller & Doris J. Miller, 50.1%; Willard W. Garvey, 49.9%. Wash atty: Booth, Freret & Imlay. ■ Monte M. Miller, pres & gen mgr; Christopher D. Miller, gen sls mgr; Doris J. Miller, prom mgr; Gary Krohe, chief engr. ■ On 18 CATVs—176,638 subs.

Pittsburg

ADI No. 146; see Joplin, MO-Pittsburg market

KOAM-TV—ch 7, 316 kw vis, 63.1 kw aur, ant 1,090t/1,159g. TL: N37 13 15 W94 42 25. Stereo. Hrs opn: 5:30 AM-1:30 AM. On air date: Dec 13, 1953. Box 659, Hwy. 69 & Lawton Rd. (66762); 745 Range Line Rd., Joplin, MO (64801). (417) 624-0233; (417) 623-6111. FAX: (417) 624-3158; (417) 624-3115. Licensee: Scarecrow Inc. (acq 5-28-93; 6-28-93). ■ Net: CBS. Rep: Seltel. Wash atty: Latham & Watkins. News progmg 18 hrs wkly. ■ Richard B. Armfield, gen mgr & film buyer; Danny Thomas, gen sls mgr; Cathy Coomer, progmg dir & pub affrs dir; Shirley Beer, news dir; Walter Ward, chief engr. ■ On 64 CATVs—94,540 subs. ■ Rates: $400; 40; 45.

KODE-TV—See Joplin, Mo.

KSNF—See Joplin, Mo.

Salina

ADI No. 62; see Wichita-Hutchinson market

KAAS-TV—ch 18, 238.3 kw vis, 23.83 kw aur, ant 663t/466g. TL: N39 06 16 W97 36 30. Hrs opn: 24. On air date: April 1988. 316 N. West St., Wichita (67203). (316) 942-2424. FAX: (316) 942-8927. Licensee: Clear Channel Television Licenses Inc. (group owner; acq 8-5-92). ■ Net: Fox. ■ Steve Spendlove, gen mgr.

Topeka

ADI No. 139; see Topeka market

KSNT—ch 27, 912 kw vis, 138 kw aur, ant 1,050t/1,149g. TL: N39 05 34 W95 47 04. On air date: Dec 28, 1967. Box 2700 (66601). (913) 582-4000. Licensee: SJL Inc. Group owner: SJL Broadcast Management Corp. (acq 8-5-88; $12 million; 8-29-88). ■ Net: NBC. Rep: Katz. Wash atty: Latham & Watkins. ■ Gary W. Sotir, vp & gen mgr; Shannon Hart, gen sls mgr; John Sheridan, prom dir; Debbie Bush, news dir; Chris Davies, chief engr. ■ On 114 CATVs—229,064 subs. On 6 trans.

KTKA-TV—ch 49, 3,475 kw vis, 347.5 kw aur, ant 1,507t/1,439g. TL: N39 01 34 W95 54 58. On air date: June 19, 1983. 101 S.E. Monroe (66603-3626). (913) 234-4949. FAX: (913) 234-5256. Licensee: Northeast Kansas Broadcast Service Inc. Ownership: Marion Brechner, 100% (acq 5-1-86; $6.5 million; 4-7-86). ■ Net: ABC. Rep: Seltel. Wash atty: Cohn & Marks. News staff 18; news progmg 15 hrs wkly. ■ Berl Brechner, pres; Jack R. Donahue, vp & gen mgr; Robert Fulmen, gen sls mgr; Melissa McPherson, prom mgr; Nancy Weeden, progmg dir & film buyer; Marty Mathews, news dir. ■ On 97 CATVs—115,812 subs.

***KTWU**—ch 11, 316 kw vis, 31.6 kw aur, ant 1,000t/952g. TL: N39 03 51 W95 45 49. On air date: Oct 21, 1965. 301 N. Wanamaker Rd. (66606-9601). (913) 272-8181. FAX: (913) 272-8181. Licensee: Washburn Univ. of Topeka.

Stations in the U.S.

Kentucky

■ Net: PBS. ■ Hugh L. Thompson, pres; Dale N. Anderson, gen mgr; Robert Fidler, opns dir; Cindy Berry, dev dir; David Pomeroy, progmg dir & film buyer; Ernie Hedges, chief engr. ■ On 75 CATVs. On one trans.

WIBW-TV—ch 13, 204 kw vis, 40.7 kw aur, ant 1,380t/1,255.2g. TL: N39 03 00 W96 02 58. Stereo. Hrs opn: 24. On air date: Nov 15, 1953. Box 119 (66601); 5600 W. Sixth St. (66606). (913) 272-3456. FAX: (913) 272-0117. Licensee: Stauffer Communications Inc. (group owner; acq 12-20-56; grpsl; 12-24-56). ■ Net: CBS. Rep: Blair. Wash atty: Dow, Lohnes & Albertson. News staff 22; news progmg 15 hrs wkly. ■ Jerry Holley, gen mgr; Frank Hoogstraten, opns dir; Vince Frye, gen sls mgr; Bobbie Athon, prom mgr; Susan White, progmg mgr; Mary Loftus, news dir; Elmer Gunderson, chief engr. ■ On 112 CATVs—156,000 subs. Co-owned radio: WIBW-AM-FM.

Wichita

ADI No. 62; see Wichita-Hutchinson market

KAKE-TV—ch 10, 316 kw vis, 44.7 kw aur, ant 1,030t/1,079g. TL: N37 46 54 W97 31 10. Stereo. Hrs opn: 24. On air date: Oct 19, 1954. Box 10 (67201); 1500 N. West (67203). (316) 943-4221. FAX: (316) 943-5160. Licensee: The Chronicle Publishing Co. Group owner: Chronicle Broadcasting Co. (acq 1-21-80; grpsl; 2-4-80). ■ Net: ABC. Rep: Petry. Wash atty: Covington & Burling. News staff 40; news progmg 16 hrs wkly. ■ Jan McDaniel, pres & gen mgr; Don Golledge, opns dir & progmg dir; Steve South, gen sls mgr; Mark Chamberlin, mktg dir & pub affrs dir; Kurt Bartolich, prom mgr; Shawn Briggs, news dir; Dale Morrell, chief engr. ■ On 45 CATVs—210,000 subs. On 7 trans. ■ Rates: $800; 125; 75.

*****KPTS**—See Hutchinson.

KSAS-TV—ch 24, 3,300 kw vis, 331 kw aur, ant 1,120t/1,165g. TL: N37 46 40 W97 30 37. Hrs opn: 24. On air date: Aug 24, 1985. 316 N. West St. (67203). (316) 942-2424. Licensee: Clear Channel Television Licenses Inc. (group owner; acq 8-5-92). ■ Net: Fox. Rep: Seltel. Wash atty: Cohn & Marks. ■ W. Ripperton Riordan, vp; Steve Spendlove, gen mgr & gen sls mgr; Stacy Sercus, natl sls mgr; Tom Gdisis, prom mgr; David Herrmann, progmg dir; David Bird, chief engr. ■ On 123 CATVs—207,233 subs.

KSNW—ch 3, 100 kw vis, 20 kw aur, ant 1,000t/1,071g. TL: N37 46 37 W97 31 01. On air date: Sept 1, 1955. Box 333 (67201); 833 N. Main (67203). (316) 265-3333. FAX: (316) 292-1197. Licensee: SJL of Kansas Corp. dba Kansas State Network. Group owner: SJL Broadcast Management (acq 10-1-88; grpsl; 8-29-88). ■ Net: NBC. Rep: Katz. Wash atty: Latham & Watkins. ■ George Lilly, pres; Al Buch, vp & gen mgr; Mike Hanrahan, gen sls mgr; Jim Tellus, progmg dir; Joan Smith, progmg dir; Rob Puglisi, news dir; Bob Locke, chief engr. ■ On 107 CATVs—122,900 subs. On one trans.

KWCH-TV—(Hutchinson). ch 12, 316 kw vis, 63.1 kw aur, ant 1,522t/1,504g. TL: N38 03 40 W97 45 49. Stereo. On air date: July 1, 1953. Box 12, Wichita (67201). 2815 E. 37th St. N., Wichita (67219). (316) 838-1212. FAX: (316) 838-3524; TWX: 910-741-6998. Licensee: KBS L.P. Group owner: Smith Broadcasting Group Inc. (acq 11-24-82; $12 million). ■ Net: CBS; Kan. Net. Rep: Telerep. Wash atty: Hogan & Hartson. News staff 36; news progmg 15 hrs wkly. ■ Mr. Sandy DiPasquale, CEO, pres & gen mgr; Randy Pratt, gen sls mgr; Susan Kimmell, prom mgr & pub affrs dir; Jim Martin, progmg dir & film buyer; Eric Lerner, news dir; Clell Lacy, chief engr. ■ On 118 CATVs—188,000 subs. ■ Rates: $1,600; 300; 200.

KWCV—ch 33, 74.7 kw vis, ant 459t. TL: N37 33 58 W97 19 28. Not on air, target date unknown. R.R. 1, Box 203, Stockton, IA (52769). Permittee: Wichita Communications.

Kentucky

Ashland

ADI No. 55; see Charleston, WV-Huntington, WV market

*****WKAS**—ch 25, 162 kw vis, 16.2 kw aur, ant 500t/400g. TL: N38 27 43 W82 37 12. On air date: Sept 23, 1968. c/o WKLE, 600 Cooper Dr., Lexington (40502). (606) 258-7000. Licensee: Kentucky Authority for Educational TV. ■ Net: PBS. ■ Virginia G. Fox, CEO; Donna Moore, chmn; Sally Hamilton, pres; M. Ferguson, opns dir; S. Martin, dev mgr; William Wilson, vp mktg; E. Mastrean, prom mgr; D. Hoffman, progmg dir; D. Holtzclaw, film buyer; C. Stuart Talbert, engrg dir. ■ On one CATV—2,500 subs.

WTSF—ch 61, 36.3 kw vis, 3.72 kw aur, ant 464t/499g. TL: N38 25 11 W82 24 06. Hrs opn: 24. On air date: Apr 30, 1983. Box 2616, 3100 Bath Ave. (41101). (606) 329-2700. Licensee: Tri-State Family Broadcasting Inc. Wash atty: Southmayd & Powell. ■ Claude H. Messinger, CEO & gen mgr; Anne W. Bledsoe, progmg dir; Greg Payton, chief engr. ■ On 30 CATVs—148,000 subs. Rates: $75; 35; 15.

Beattyville

ADI No. 70; see Lexington market

WLJC-TV—ch 65, 92.75 kw vis, 9.275 kw aur, ant 665.84t/534.96g. TL: N37 36 23 W83 41 16. (CP: 73.45 kw vis, 7.345 kw aur, ant 646.2t). On air date: Oct 16, 1982. Rt. 36, Box 50, 219 Radio Station Loop (41311). (606) 464-3600. FAX: (606) 464-0044. Licensee: Hour of Harvest Inc. Rep: Rgnl Reps. Wash atty: Reddy, Begley & Martin. ■ Forest Drake, pres; Jonathan Drake, gen mgr & chief engr; Bonnie Best, gen sls mgr; Rachel Drake, progmg dir; John Stone, news dir. ■ On 18 CATVs—13,000 subs. Co-owned radio: WLJC-FM ■ Rates: $25; 20; 15.

Bowling Green

ADI No. 181; see Bowling Green market

WBKO—ch 13, 316 kw vis, 30.2 kw aur, ant 740t/603g. TL: N37 03 52 W86 26 07. Hrs opn: 20. On air date: June 3, 1962. Box 13000 (42102-9800); 2727 Russellville Rd. (42101). (502) 781-1313. FAX: (502) 781-1814; TWX: 810-531-3667. Licensee: Bluegrass Television Inc. Group owner: Benedek Broadcasting Group (acq 4-26-83; $4 million; 3-7-83). ■ Net: ABC. Rep: Katz. Wash atty: Covington & Burling. News staff 17; news progmg 14 hrs wkly. ■ A. Richard Benedek, pres; Clyde G. Payne, vp & gen mgr; Rick McCue, gen sls mgr; Chris Allen, prom mgr; Steve Crabtree, progmg dir; Steve Crabtree, Clyde G. Payne, film buyers; Charles Fortney, news dir; Gene Prather, pub affrs dir; Dave Chumley, chief engr. ■ On 49 CATVs.

*****WKGB-TV**—ch 53, 562 kw vis, 112 kw aur, ant 810t/618g. TL: N37 05 22 W86 38 05. On air date: Sept 23, 1968. 600 Cooper Dr., Lexington (40502). (606) 258-7000. Licensee: Kentucky Authority for Educational TV. ■ Net: PBS. ■ Virginia G. Fox, CEO; Donna Moore, chmn; Sally Hamilton, pres; M. Ferguson, opns dir; M. Fazey, rgnl sls mgr; William Wilson, mktg dir; E. Mastrean, prom mgr; L. Hobson, adv dir; D. Hoffman, progmg dir; C. Stuart Talbert, engrg dir. ■ On 3 CATVs—2,500 subs.

WKNT—ch 40, 631 kw vis, 63.1 kw aur, ant 561t. TL: N37 02 10 W86 10 20. 776 kw vis, 77.6 kw aur. Hrs opn: 24. On air date: Dec 15, 1991. Box 51827 (42102-6827); 855 Lover's Lane (42103). (502) 781-2140. FAX: (502) 842-7140. Licensee: Southeastern Communications Inc. (acq 10-91). ■ Net: Roslin. Wash atty: Schwartz, Woods & Miller. ■ Dave Benz, gen mgr; John Scheibel, gen sls mgr; Marty Bagby, progmg dir; Charles Fortney, news dir; Mike Graham, chief engr. ■ On 3 CATVs—25,000 subs. ■ Rates: $125; 75; 50.

*****WKYU-TV**—ch 24, 400 kw vis, 20 kw aur, ant 648t/603g. TL: N37 03 52 W86 26 07. On air date: Jan 17, 1989. Academic Complex 153 (42101). (502) 745-2153. Licensee: Western Kentucky Univ. ■ Net: PBS. Wash atty: Cohn & Marks. News staff One; news progmg one hr wkly. ■ Dr. Thomas C. Meredith, pres; Charles M. Anderson, gen mgr; Michael Lasater, stn mgr; Joseph Fulmer, opns mgr; Melinda Craft, dev mgr; Linda Oldham, progmg dir. ■ On 15 CATVs—35,000 subs. Co-owned radio: WKYU-FM, WDCL-FM, WKVE-FM, WKPB-FM.

Campbellsville

ADI No. 181; see Bowling Green market

WGRB—ch 34, 600 kw vis, 108 kw aur, ant 1,030t/900g. TL: N37 10 05 W85 18 32. Hrs opn: 5 AM-2 AM. On air date: Apr 6, 1983. Box 400 (42719); 1210 Cane Valley Rd., Cane Valley (42720). (502) 465-2223; (502) 384-4738. FAX: (502) 384-6864. Licensee: Green River Broadcasting Inc. Ownership: Billy Speer, 100%. ■ Net: Fox. Rep: Roslin. Wash atty: Schwartz, Woods & Miller. News staff 2; news progmg 3 hrs wkly. ■ Dave Benz, gen mgr; John Scheibel, gen sls mgr; Marty Bagby, progmg dir; Connie Leonard, news dir; Mike Graham, chief engr. ■ On 43 CATVs—45,000 subs. ■ Rates: $125; 75; 45.

Covington

ADI No. 31; see Cincinncati, OH market

*****WCVN**—ch 54, 162 kw vis, 16.2 kw aur, ant 400t/312g. TL: N39 01 50 W84 30 23. On air date: Sept 9, 1969. 600 Cooper Dr., Lexington (40502). (606) 258-7000. Licensee: Kentucky Authority for Educational TV. ■ Net: PBS. ■ Virginia G. Fox, CEO; Donna Moore, chmn; Sally Hamilton, pres; M. Ferguson, opns mgr; S. Martin, dev mgr; M. Fazey, rgnl sls mgr; William Wilson, mktg dir; E. Mastrean, prom mgr; D. Hoffman, progmg dir; C. Stuart Talbert, engrg dir.

Danville

ADI No. 70; see Lexington market

WDKY-TV—ch 56, 3,427 kw vis, 342 kw aur, ant 1,150t/1,099g. TL: N37 47 18 W84 40 49. Stereo. (CP: 3,390 kw vis, 339 kw aur). On air date: Feb 10, 1986. 434 Interstate Ave., Lexington (40505); Box 12650, Lexington (40583). (606) 293-5656. FAX: (606) 293-5691. Licensee: Superior Communications Group Inc. (acq 8-19-92; $10.3 million; 9-21-92). ■ Net: Fox. Rep: Seltel. Wash atty: Hogan & Hartson. ■ Tylin J. Smith, vp & gen mgr; Juri R. Rasums, opns dir & progmg dir; Jim Donnelly, gen sls mgr & rgnl sls mgr; Joy Scarbrough, prom mgr & adv dir; Randy Cookman, chief engr.

Elizabethtown

ADI No. 47; see Luisville market

*****WKZT-TV**—ch 23, 575 kw vis, 115 kw aur, ant 650t/655g. TL: N37 40 55 W85 50 32. On air date: Sept 23, 1968. 600 Cooper Dr., Lexington (40502). (606) 258-7000. Licensee: Kentucky Authority for Educational TV. ■ Net: PBS. ■ Virginia G. Fox, CEO; Donna Moore, chmn; Sally Hamilton, pres; M. Ferguson, opns dir; S. Martin, dev mgr; M. Fazey, rgnl sls mgr; William Wilson, vp mktg; E. Mastrean, prom mgr; D. Hoffman, progmg dir; C. Stuart Talbert, engrg dir. ■ On 10 CATVs—3,500 subs.

Hazard

ADI No. 70; see Lexington market

*****WKHA**—ch 35, 417 kw vis, 83.2 kw aur, ant 1,260t/608g. TL: N37 11 34 W83 11 16. On air date: June 6, 1968. 600 Cooper Dr., Lexington (40502). (606) 258-7000. Licensee: Kentucky Authority for Educational TV. ■ Net: PBS. ■ Virginia G. Fox, CEO; Donna Moore, chmn; Sally Hamilton, pres; M. Ferguson, opns dir; William Wilson, vp mktg; E. Mastrean, prom mgr; D. Hoffman, progmg dir; D. Holtzclaw, film buyer; C. Stuart Talbert, engrg mgr; B. Ball, engrg dir. ■ On 40 CATVs—4,000 subs.

WYMT-TV—ch 57, 2,630 kw vis, 263 kw aur, ant 1,560t/1,029g. TL: N37 11 38 W83 10 52. On air date: Oct 20, 1969. Box 1299, U.S. 15 Bypass (41702). (606) 436-5757. Licensee: Kentucky Central Television Inc. Ownership: Kentucky Central Life Insurance Co. Group owner: Bluegrass Broadcasting Co. Inc. (acq 6-10-85; $1 million; 6-10-85). ■ Net: CBS. Wash atty: Latham & Watkins. ■ Ernestine Cornett, pres & gen mgr; Jim Boggs, gen sls mgr & adv mgr; Sharon Williams, prom mgr & progmg dir; Tony Turner, news dir. ■ On 115 CATVs—173,300 subs. Co-owned radio: WVLK-AM-FM.

Henderson

*****WNIN**—See Evansville, Ind.

Lexington

ADI No. 70; see Lexington market

*****WKLE**—ch 46, 1,050 kw vis, 105 kw aur, ant 870t/850g. TL: N37 52 45 W84 19 33. On air date: Sept 23, 1968. 600 Cooper Dr. (40502). (606) 258-7000. Licensee: Kentucky Authority for Educational TV. ■ Net: PBS; SECA. Wash atty: Kenkel & Barnard. ■ Virgina G. Fox, CEO; S. Martin, gen mgr; M. Fazey, gen sls mgr; Bill Wilson, mktg dir; E Mastrean, prom mgr; Donna Moore, progmg dir; C. Stuart Talbert, engrg dir.

WKYT-TV—ch 27, 1,510 kw vis, 151 kw aur, ant 984t/992g. TL: N38 02 22 W84 24 11. Stereo. On air date: Sept 30, 1957. Box 55037 (40555-5037); 2851 Winchester Rd. (40509). (606) 299-0411. FAX: (606) 299-2494. Licensee: Kentucky Central TV Inc. Group owner: Bluegrass Broadcasting Co. Inc. (acq 1-21-76; 2-9-76). ■

Net: CBS. Rep: Harrington, Righter & Parsons. Wash atty: Latham & Watkins. ■ Ralph W. Gabbard, pres; Wayne Martin, gen mgr; Micheal D. Kanarek, opns mgr; Kathy Plomin, gen sls mgr; Barbara Carden, progmg dir; John Bobel, news dir; Chas Callaway, chief engr. ■ On 117 CATVs—311,641 subs. On one trans. Co-owned radio: WVLK-AM-FM.

WLEX-TV—ch 18, 1,104 kw max vis, 221 kw aur, ant 640t/670g. TL: N37 55 23 W84 09 14. Stereo. Hrs opn: 22. On air date: Mar 15, 1955. Box 1457 (40591); 1065 Russell Cave Rd. (40505). (606) 255-4404. FAX: (606) 255-2418; TWX: 510-476-8896. Licensee: WLEX-TV Inc. ■ Net: NBC. Rep: Blair. Wash atty: Fletcher, Heald, & Hildreth. ■ Jack Atchison, chmn; John A. Duvall, pres & gen mgr; Sim Wilson, CFO; Al Greenfield, stn mgr; Joe Oliver, vp; Larry Neuzel, progmg dir; David Lander, news dir; Bill Crawford, pub affrs dir; David Powell, chief engr. ■ On 231 CATVs—201,124 subs. ■ Rates: $2,500; 400; 250.

WTVQ-TV—ch 36, 1,580 kw vis; 158 kw aur, ant 1,029t/996g. TL: N38 02 03 W84 23 39. On air date: June 2, 1968. Box 5590 (40555); 2940 Bryant Rd. (40509). (606) 233-3600. FAX: (606) 293-5002. Licensee: Park Broadcasting of Kentucky Inc. Group owner: Park Communications Inc. (acq 12-18-91; $11 million; 1-20-92). ■ Net: ABC. Rep: Katz. Wash atty: Wiley, Rein & Fielding. ■ Roy H. Park, CEO & chmn; Wright M. Thomas, pres; Randel Stair, CFO; W. Randall Odil, exec vp; Chris Aldridge, vp & gen mgr; Dick Kelly, gen sls mgr; Michael Castengera, news dir; Jim Brady, engrg dir. ■ On 98 CATVs—201,000 subs. ■ Rates: $600; 150; 60.

Louisville

ADI No. 47; see Louisville market

WAVE—ch 3, 100 kw vis, 10 kw aur, ant 1820t/1690g. TL: N38 27 23 W85 25 28. Stereo. On air date: Nov 24, 1948. 725 S. Floyd St. (40203); Box 789, Greenville, SC (29602). (502) 585-2201. FAX: (502) 561-4115. Licensee: Cosmos Broadcasting Corp. (group owner; acq 10-16-81). ■ Net: NBC. Rep: HRP. Wash atty: Dow, Lohnes & Albertson. ■ Guy Hempel, vp & gen mgr; Jim Brandenburg, opns dir; Steve Langford, gen sls mgr; Ed Godfrey, progmg dir; Kathy Beck, news dir; Bill Eschbach, chief engr. ■ On 73 CATVs—364,453 subs. ■ Rates: $1,595; 330; 220.

WBNA—ch 21, 2,000 kw vis, 200 kw aur, ant 696t. TL: N38 01 59 W85 45 16. On air date: Apr 2, 1986. 3701 Fern Valley Rd. (40219). (502) 964-2121. Licensee: Word Broadcasting Network Inc. (group owner). Wash atty: Pepper & Corazzini. ■ Robert W. Rodgers, pres; John D. Bradshaw, gen mgr & gen sls mgr; Phil Keith, progmg dir; John Bradshaw, chief engr. ■ On 10 CATVs—200,000 subs.

WDRB-TV—ch 41, 5,000 kw vis, 500 kw aur, ant 1,283t/1,003g. TL: N38 21 00 W85 50 57. Stereo. On air date: Feb 28, 1971. Independence Sq. (40203). (502) 584-6441. TWX: 810-535-3328. Licensee: Independence TV Co. Group owner: Blade Communications Inc., see Cross-Ownership (acq 3-84; $10 million; 1-2-84). ■ Net: Fox. Rep: Petry. Wash atty: Dow, Lohnes & Albertson. News progmg 4 hrs wkly. ■ John Dorkin, pres & gen mgr; Jack Ratterman, gen sls mgr; Kim Craven Gram, natl sls mgr; Sherean Malekzedah, mktg dir, prom dir & adv dir; Judy McDonald, progmg dir; Hal Stopfel, news dir; Glen Cook, chief engr. ■ On 61 CATVs—296,000 subs.

WHAS-TV—ch 11, 135 kw vis, 13.5 kw aur, ant 1,290t/973g. TL: N38 21 23 W85 50 52. Stereo. On air date: March 27, 1950. Box 1100 (40201); 520 W. Chestnut St. (40202). (502) 582-7840. Licensee: Journal Broadcasting of Kentucky Inc. Group owner: Providence Journal Bcstg Corp. (acq 12-1-86; 7-21-86). ■ Net: ABC. Wash atty: Covington & Burling. News progmg 24 hrs wkly. ■ Jack C. Ckufferd, pres; Joseph A. Goleniowski, pres & gen mgr; George Hulcher, stn mgr; Eric Bergman, chief opns & chief engr; Charles Gordon, gen sls mgr; Anne Adkins, prom mgr; Dan Miller, progmg dir; Mike Rausch, news dir. ■ On 80 CATVs—402,231 subs.

WKMJ—ch 68, 1,170 kw vis, 230 kw aur, ant 835t/570.6g. TL: N38 22 02 W85 49 53. On air date: Aug 31, 1970. 600 Cooper Dr., Lexington (40502). (606) 258-7000. Licensee: Kentucky Authority for Educational TV. ■ Net: PBS. ■ Virginia G. Fox, CEO; Donna Moore, chmn; Sally Hamilton, pres; M. Ferguson, opns mgr; S. Martin, dev mgr; M. Fazey, rgnl sls mgr; William Wilson, vp mktg; E. Mastrean, prom mgr; D. Hoffman, progmg dir; C. Stuart Talbert, engrg dir.

*****WKPC-TV**—ch 15, 263 kw vis, 46.8 kw aur, ant 860t/549g. TL: N38 22 02 W85 49 53. (CP: 525 kw, 589 kw max, ant 860t). On air date: Sept 5, 1958. Box 37380 (40233); 4309 Bishop Lane (40218). (502) 459-9572. FAX: (502) 459-9572, ext. 25. Licensee: Fifteen Telecommunications Inc. ■ Net: PBS. Wash atty: Schwartz, Woods & Miller. ■ John-Robert Curtin, CEO, pres & gen mgr; V.M. Brucchieri, CFO; Steve Ulrich, sr vp; Carolyn Neustadt, vp dev; Lois Haynie, prom dir; Darrell Garrett, vp progmg. ■ On 16 CATVs.

WLKY-TV—ch 32, 4,300 kw vis, 430 kw aur, ant 1,260t/989g. TL: N38 22 10 W85 50 02. On air date: Sept 18, 1961. Box 6205, 1918 Mellwood Ave. (40206). (502) 893-3671. FAX: (502) 897-2384; TWX: 810-535-3212. Licensee: Pulitzer Broadcasting Co. Group owner: see Cross-Ownership; acq 5-12-83; $15.4 million; 5-23-83). ■ Net: CBS. Rep: Katz. Wash atty: Verner, Liipfert, Bernhard, McPherson & Hand. ■ A. Rabun Matthews, gen mgr; Bill Stanley, gen sls mgr; Michael Bright, mktg mgr; Bruce Burns, prom mgr; Steve Sabato, news dir; Al Grossniklaus, chief engr. ■ On 52 CATVs—197,000 subs.

Madisonville

ADI No. 94; see Evansville, IN

*****WKMA**—ch 35, 513 kw vis, 51.3 kw aur, ant 1,040t/998g. TL: N37 11 25 W87 30 47. On air date: Sept 23, 1968. 600 Cooper Dr., Lexington (40502). (606) 258-7000. FAX: (606) 258-7390. Licensee: Kentucky Authority for Educational TV. ■ Virginia G. Fox, CEO. ■ On 5 CATVs—4500 subs.

WLCN—ch 19, 1,143 kw vis, 114.3 kw aur, ant 1,194t/1,053g. TL: N37 24 46 W87 31 32. (CP: 2,676 kw vis, ant 790t). On air date: September 1983. Box 1087, 27 Grapevine Rd. (42431). (502) 821-5433. Licensee: Life Anew Ministries Inc. Wash atty: Baraff, Koerner & Olender. ■ John Stalls, pres; John Price, vp.

Morehead

ADI No. 70; see Lexington market

WAOM—ch 67, 575 kw vis, 115 aur, ant 812t/722g. TL: N38 17 25 W83 22 56. Not on air, target date unknown. c/o Garcia Communications, 3052 Via Papeete, San Diago, CA (92154). Permittee: Garcia Communications.

*****WKMR**—ch 38, 575 kw vis, 115 kw aur, ant 960t/607g. TL: N38 10 38 W83 24 18. On air date: Sept 23, 1968. c/o WKLE, 600 Cooper Dr., Lexington (40502). (606) 258-7000. Licensee: Kentucky Authority for Educational TV. ■ Net: PBS. ■ Virginia G. Fox, CEO; Donna Moore, chmn; Sally Hamilton, pres; M. Fazey, rgnl sls mgr; William Wilson, vp mktg; D. Hoffman, progmg dir; M. Clark, progmg mgr; D. Holtzclaw, film buyer; C. Stuart Talbert, engrg dir; B. Ball, engrg mgr. ■ On 20 CATVs—2,500 subs.

Murray

ADI No. 77; see Paducah-Cape Girardeau, MO-Harrisburg, IL-Marion, IL market

*****WKMU**—ch 21, 575 kw vis, 115 kw aur, ant 660t/655g. TL: N36 41 33 W88 32 10. On air date: Oct 9, 1968. 600 Cooper Dr., Lexington (40502). (606) 258-7000. Licensee: Kentucky Authority for Educational TV. ■ Net: PBS. ■ Virginia G. Fox, CEO; Donna Moore, chmn; Sally Hamilton, pres; M. Ferguson, opns mgr; S. Martin, dev mgr; M. Fazey, rgnl sls mgr; William Wilson, mktg dir; E. Mastrean, prom mgr; D. Hoffman, progmg dir; C. Stuart Talbert, engrg dir. ■ On 2 CATVs—1,200 subs.

Newport

WXIX-TV—Licensed to Newport. See Cincinnati, Ohio.

Owensboro

ADI No. 94; see Evansville, IN market

*****WKOH**—ch 31, 692 kw vis, 55 kw aur, ant 460t/500g. TL: N37 51 06 W87 19 43. (CP: 617 kw, 708 kw max). On air date: Mar 1, 1979. 600 Cooper Dr., Lexington (40502). (606) 258-7000. Licensee: Kentucky Authority for Educational TV. ■ Net: PBS; SECA. Wash atty: Kenkel & Barnard. ■ Virginia G. Fox, CEO; Donna Moore, chmn; Sally Hamilton, pres; M. Ferguson, opns mgr; S. Martin, dev mgr; M. Fazey, rgnl sls mgr; William Wilson, vp mktg; E. Mastrean, prom mgr; D. Hoffman, progmg dir; C. Stuart Talbert, engrg dir.

*****WNIN**—See Evansville, Ind.

Owenton

ADI No. 31; see Cincinnati, OH market

*****WKON**—ch 52, 562 kw vis, 115 kw aur, ant 710t/602g. TL: N38 31 32 W84 48 40. On air date: Sept 23, 1968. 600 Cooper Dr., Lexington (40502). (606) 258-7000. Licensee: Kentucky Authority for Educational TV. ■ Net: PBS. ■ Virginia G. Fox, CEO; Donna Moore, chmn; Sally Hamilton, pres; M. Ferguson, opns mgr; S. Martin, dev mgr; M. Fazey, rgnl sls mgr; William Wilson, vp mktg; E. Mastrean, prom mgr; D. Hoffman, progmg dir; C. Stuart Talbert, engrg dir. ■ On 3 CATVs—2,500 subs.

Paducah

ADI No. 77; see Paducah-Cape Girardeau, Mo-Harrisburg, IL-Marion, IL market

WDKA—ch 49, 2,610 kw vis, 275 kw aur, ant 1,975t/1,848g. TL: N37 11 56 W88 58 32. Not on air, target date unknown. c/o Sudbrink Broadcasting, Suite 303, 2001 Palm Beach Lakes Blvd., West Palm Beach, FL (33409). (407) 684-7488. Permittee: Robert W. Sudbrink. Group owner: Sudbrink Broadcasting (acq 9-4-92; $200; 10-19-92).

*****WKPD**—ch 29, 676 kw vis, 67.6 kw aur, ant 709t. TL: N36 57 42 W88 41 22. (CP: 145 kw vis, ant 499t, TL: N37 05 38 W88 40 19). On air date: May 31, 1971. 600 Cooper Dr., Lexington (40502). (606) 258-7000. Licensee: Kentucky Authority for Educational TV (acq 2-28-78). ■ Net: PBS; SECA. Wash atty: Kenkel & Barnard. ■ Virginia G. Fox, exec vp; Donna Moore, sr vp; Sally Hamilton, vp; M. Ferguson, opns mgr; S. Martin, dev mgr; M. Fazey, rgnl sls mgr; William Wilson, vp mktg; E. Mastrean, prom mgr; D. Hoffman, progmg dir; C. Stuart Talbert, engrg dir.

WPSD-TV—ch 6, 100 kw vis, 13.8 kw aur, ant 1,600t/1,638g. TL: N37 11 31 W88 58 53. Stereo. On air date: May 28, 1957. Box 1197 (42002-1197); 100 Television Lane (42003-5098). (502) 442-8214. FAX: (502) 442-2096; (502) 442-8214. Licensee: Paducah Newspapers Inc. Ownership: Paxton Family, see Cross-Ownership. ■ Net: NBC. Rep: Blair. Wash atty: Covington & Burling. ■ Fred Paxton, pres; John Williams, vp & gen mgr; Richard Paxton, stn mgr; Dan Steele, opns mgr & progmg dir; Ann Eaves, natl sls mgr; Cathy Crecelius, prom mgr; John Rinkenbaugh, news dir; Don Brown, chief engr. ■ On 117 CATVs. On 88 trans.

Pikeville

ADI No. 55; see Charleston, WV-Huntington, WV market

*****WKPI**—ch 22, 468 kw vis, 93.3 kw aur, ant 1,410t/153g. TL: N37 17 06 W82 31 29. On air date: April 8, 1968. 600 Cooper Dr., Lexington (40502). (606) 233-3000. Licensee: Kentucky Authority for Educational TV. ■ Net: PBS. ■ Virginia G. Fox, CEO; Donna Moore, chmn; Sally Hamilton, pres; M. Ferguson, opns mgr; S. Martin, dev mgr; M. Fazey, rgnl sls mgr; William Wilson, mktg dir; E. Mastrean, prom mgr; D. Hoffman, progmg dir; C. Stuart Talbert, engrg dir. ■ On 50 CATVs—6,000 subs.

Somerset

ADI No. 70; see Lexington market

*****WKSO-TV**—ch 29, 584 kw vis, 117 kw aur, ant 1,460t/1,000g. TL: N37 10 00 W84 49 28. On air date: Sept 23, 1968. 600 Cooper Dr., Lexington (40502). (606) 258-7000. Licensee: Kentucky Authority for Educational TV. ■ Net: PBS. ■ Virginia G. Fox, CEO; Donna Moore, chmn; Sally Hamilton, pres; M. Ferguson, opns mgr; S. Martin, dev mgr; William Wilson, vp mktg; E. Mastrean, prom mgr; D. Hoffman, progmg dir; C. Stuart Talbert, engrg dir; B. Ball, engrg mgr. ■ On 25 CATVs—2,500 subs. On 2 trans.

Louisiana

Alexandria

ADI No. 169; see Alexandria, LA market

KALB-TV—ch 5, 100 kw vis, 20 kw aur, ant 1,590t/1,586g. TL: N31 02 15 W92 29 45. Stereo. On air date: Sept 29, 1954. Box 951, 605-11 Washington St. (71309). (318) 445-2456. FAX: (318) 442-7427. Licensee: Park Broadcasting of Louisiana Inc. Group owner: Park Communications Inc. (acq 9-17-93; $21 million plus non-compete agreement worth up to $5 million; 10-11-93). ■ Net: NBC. Rep: Katz. Wash atty: Wiley, Rein, & Fielding. ■ Ted Kimbell, pres; Les Golmon, vp; Jim Reardon, gen mgr & gen sls mgr; Frances Yeager, prom mgr & progmg dir; Tom Webb, news dir; Roland Phillips, chief engr. ■ On 31 CATVs—40,600 subs.

KLAX-TV—ch 31, 1,309 kw vis, 131 kw aur, ant 1,092t/1,028g. TL: N31 33 54 W92 33 00. Hrs opn: 24. On air date: Mar 3, 1982. Box 8818, 1811 England Dr. (71306). (318) 473-0031. FAX: (318) 442-4646. Licensee: Pollack-Belz Communications Inc. Ownership: William Pollack, 33.3%;David Pollack, 33.3%;Martin S. Belz, 33.3% (acq 6-3-88; $1.1 million). ■ Net: ABC. Rep: Blair. Wash atty: Jones, Waldo, Holbrook & McDonough. News staff 15; news progmg 6 hrs wkly. ■ William H. Pollack, pres & film buyer; Sam McLeod, gen mgr; Keith Smith, gen sls mgr; Lydia Allen, natl sls mgr; Keith Collins, prom mgr; Lori Kelley-Johnson, progmg dir; Bill Thompson, news dir; Charles Flowers, chief engr. ■ On 73 CATVs—76,796 subs. ■ Rates: $270; 75; 60.

***KLPA-TV**—ch 25, 2,040 kw vis, 204 kw aur, ant 1,360t/1,329g. TL: N31 33 56 W92 32 50. Hrs opn: 17. On air date: July 1, 1983. 7860 Anselmo Ln., Baton Rouge (70810). (504) 767-5660; (800) 272-8161. FAX: (504) 767-4299; (504) 767-4277. Licensee: Louisiana Educational Television Authority. ■ Net: PBS. Wash atty: Schwartz, Woods & Miller. ■ Patsy Adams, prom mgr; Jennifer Howze, progmg dir; Coy F. Simmons, engrg dir. ■ On 5 CATVs—43,855 subs.

Baton Rouge

ADI No. 95; see Baton Rouge market

WAFB—ch 9, 316 kw vis, 63 kw aur, ant 1,670t/1,729g. TL: N30 21 58 W91 12 47. On air date: Apr 19, 1953. 844 Government St. (70802). (504) 383-9999. FAX: (504) 379-7891; TWX: 510-993-3406. Licensee: American Family Broadcast Group Inc. (group owner; acq 4-88). ■ Net: CBS. Rep: Katz. Wash atty: Wiley, Rein & Fielding. ■ Ronald Winders, gen mgr. ■ On 58 CATVs—445,550 subs. Co-owned radio: WAFB-FM.

WBRZ—ch 2, 100 kw vis, 10 kw aur, ant 1,676t/1,724g. TL: N30 17 49 W91 11 40. On air date: Apr 14, 1955. Box 2906 (70821); 1650 Highland Rd. (70802). (504) 387-2222. FAX: (504) 336-2246. EASYLINK: 620-44-844. Licensee: Louisiana TV Broadcasting Corp. Group owner: Manship Stations (acq 1958; $548,000). ■ Net: ABC. Rep: Blair. Wash atty: Cohn & Marks. ■ Douglas Manship Sr., chmn; Richard F. Manship, pres; Pat Cheramie, gen mgr; John Spain, stn mgr; Jim Rocky Daboval, sls dir; Denise Akers, mktg dir; Suzanne Sims (supvr), progmg dir; Bill Vance, news dir; Clyde Pierce, chief engr. ■ On 150 CATVs—320,000 subs. ■ Rates: $900; 300; 150.

WGMB—ch 44, 3,871 kw vis, Ant 1,164t. TL: N30 19 35 W91 16 36. Hrs opn: 24. On air date: Aug 11, 1991. 5800 Florida Blvd. (70806). Box 96044 (70896-9044). (504) 926-4444. Licensee: Galloway Media Inc. Ownership: Thomas R. Galloway Sr. (acq 5-24-91). ■ Net: Fox. Wash atty: Fletcher, Heald & Hildreth. ■ Tom R. Galloway Sr., pres; Wayne Elmore, CFO; Clark White, vp; Damian Calato, gen mgr & adv dir; Bret Benge, gen sls mgr; Tammy DuPuy, progmg mgr; Karen Mire, pub affrs dir; Terry Freeman, chief engr. ■ On 56 CATVs—205,000 subs. ■ Rates: $425; 75; 25.

***WLPB-TV**—ch 27, 2,570 kw vis, 257 kw aur, ant 994t/1,030g. TL: N30 22 22 W91 12 16. Stereo. Hrs opn: 17. On air date: Sept 6, 1975. 7860 Anselmo Ln. (70810). (504) 767-5660; (800) 272-8161. FAX: (504) 767-4277; (504) 767-4299. Licensee: Louisiana Educational Television Authority. ■ Net: PBS. Wash atty: Schwartz, Woods & Miller. Fr, Japanese 4 hrs wkly. News staff 3; news progmg one hr wkly. ■ Beth Courtney, CEO; William Arceneaux, chmn; Don Ballard, opns mgr; Quinn Rainwater, dev dir; Sharon Beningfield, prom mgr; Jennifer Howze, progmg dir; Clay Fourrier, news dir; Jeff Duhe, pub affrs dir; Coy F. Simmons, engrg dir. ■ On 120 CATVs—297,516 subs.

WVLA—ch 33, 5,000 kw vis, 1,000 kw aur, ant 1,750t. TL: N30 19 35 W91 16 36. Stereo. Hrs opn: 22. On air date: Oct 16, 1971. 5220 Essen Lane (70809); Box 14685 (70898). (504) 766-3233; (504) 769-2996. FAX: (504) 766-4112; (504) 767-7988. Licensee: Vetter Communications Co. Inc. Ownership: Cyril Vetter, 100% (acq 1-9-79; $742,000; 1-29-79). ■ Net: NBC. Rep: Katz. Wash atty: Dow, Lohnes & Albertson. News staff 5; news progmg 4 hrs wkly. ■ Cyril E. Vetter, chmn; Courtney B. Westbrook, pres & gen mgr; Larry Dietz, vp opns & news dir; Peggy Day, gen sls mgr; Jason Furrate, mktg mgr; Joyce Harvey, progmg dir; Felton Coleman, pub affrs dir; Tom Woodside, chief engr. ■ On 44 CATVs—233,453 subs. Co-owned radio: WTGE-FM. ■ Rates: $500; 145; 90.

Lafayette

ADI No. 120; see Lafayette, LA market

KADN—ch 15, 2,630 kw vis, 231 kw aur, ant 1,181t/1,282g. TL: N30 21 44 W92 12 53. On air date: Feb 28, 1980. 1500 Eraste Landry Rd. (70506). (318) 237-1500. FAX: (318) 237-2237; TWX: 510-975-5031. Licensee: KADN Broadcasting Inc. (acq 6-30-87). ■ Net: Fox, ABC. Rep: Blair. Wash atty: Mullin, Rhyne, Emmons & Topel. Fr one hr wkly. ■ Charles Chatelain, pres; Clark White, gen mgr; Pat Newberg, gen sls mgr; Ed Blanchard, prom mgr, progmg dir & film buyer; Neil Goodlet, chief engr. ■ On 28 CATVs—140,000 subs. ■ Rates: $250; 225; 100.

KATC—ch 3, 100 kw vis, 20 kw aur, ant 1,740t/1,793g. TL: N30 02 19 W92 22 15. On air date: Sept 19, 1962. Box 93133 (70509). (318) 235-3333. FAX: (318) 234-3680. Licensee: KATC Associates Group owner: RP Companies Inc. (acq 2-2-87; $28 million; 10-6-86). ■ Net: ABC. Rep: Katz. Wash atty: Wiley, Rein & Fielding. ■ Richard Harbinson, gen mgr & progmg dir; Bill Bowers, gen sls mgr; Claudia Vincent, prom mgr; Bill Lager, Debrah Puller, news dirs; Bill Rumsey, chief engr. ■ On 28 CATVs—166,265 subs.

KLFY-TV—ch 10, 309 kw vis, 44.7 kw aur, ant 1,738t/1,761g. TL: N30 19 18 W92 22 41. Stereo. (CP: 295 kw vis). On air date: June 3, 1955. Box 90665, 2410 Eraste Landry Rd. (70509). (318) 981-4823. FAX: (318) 984-8323. Licensee: Young Broadcasting of Louisiana Inc. Group owner: Young Broadcasting Inc. (acq 5-28-88; $51 million; 12-14-87). ■ Net: CBS. Rep: Adam Young. Wash atty: Wiley, Rein & Fielding. Fr 3 hrs wkly. News staff 23; news progmg 14 hrs wkly. ■ Ronald J. Kwasnick, pres; Joe Varholy, vp & gen mgr; Mike Barras, gen sls mgr; Mike Harrelson, prom mgr; Terry Dover, progmg dir & film buyer; Maria Placer, news dir; Dave Hebert, chief engr. ■ On 70 CATVs—245,000 subs.

***KLPB-TV**—ch 24, 2,140 kw vis, 214 kw aur, ant 1,190t/1,225g. TL: N30 02 38 W92 22 14. Hrs opn: 17. On air date: May 2, 1981. 7860 Anselmo Ln., Baton Rouge (70810). (504) 767-5660; (800) 272-8161. FAX: (504) 767-4299; (504) 767-4277. Licensee: Louisiana Educational Television Authority. ■ Net: PBS. Wash atty: Schwartz, Woods & Miller. ■ Beth Courtney, CEO; William Arceneaux, chmn; Don Ballard, opns mgr; Quinn Rainwater, dev dir; Sharon Beningfield, prom mgr; Jennifer Howze, progmg dir; Clay Fourrier, news dir; Coy F. Simmons, engrg dir. ■ On 10 CATVs—106,769 subs.

Lake Charles

ADI No. 174; see Lake Charles market

***KLTL-TV**—ch 18, 1,260 kw vis, 126 kw aur, ant 1,030t/1,058g. TL: N30 23 59 W93 00 10. Hrs opn: 17. On air date: May 5, 1981. 7860 Anselmo Ln., Baton Rouge (70810). (504) 767-5660; (800) 272-8161. FAX: (504) 767-4277; (504) 767-4299. Licensee: Louisiana Educational Television Authority. ■ Net: PBS; SECA. Wash atty: Schwartz, Woods & Miller. ■ Jenny Howze, progmg dir; Coy F. Simmons, engrg dir. ■ On 8 CATVs—54,239 subs.

KPLC-TV—ch 7, 295 kw vis, 55 kw aur, ant 1,480t/1,519g. TL: N30 23 43 W93 00 08. Stereo. On air date: September 1954. 320 Division St. (70601); Box 1488 (70602). (318) 439-9071; (318) 437-7568 (NEWS). FAX: (318) 437-7600. Licensee: Cosmos Broadcasting Corp. (group owner; acq 11-13-86; grpsl). ■ Net: NBC. Rep: Harrington, Righter & Parson. Wash atty: Dow, Lohnes & Albertson. ■ Jim Serra, gen mgr; Diana Mayo, opns mgr; Tom Pears, gen sls mgr; Dolores Tutt (local), rgnl sls mgr; Tim Bourgeois, prom dir; Robin Daugereau, progmg dir; James Smith, news dir; Ron Blansett, chief engr. ■ On 42 CATVs—139,671 subs.

KVHP—ch 29, 700 kw vis, 131 kw aur, ant 453t/404g. TL: N30 11 50 W93 13 12. (CP: 2,507 kw vis, ant 1,292t). On air date: Dec 12, 1982. 129 W. Prien Lake Rd. (70602). (318) 474-1316. TWX: 510-971-7500. Licensee: KVHP-TV Partners Ownership: Gary D. Hardesty, Micheal Dillon, Jon Kurtin, Sol Gerber, Donald Muckenthaler (acq 4-30-87). ■ Net: Fox. Rep: ITS. Wash atty: Baraff, Koerner, Olender & Hochberg. ■ Gary D. Hardesty, pres, gen mgr & gen sls mgr; Tom Voinche, prom mgr; Lori Burson, progmg dir; Bill Leger, news dir; Tim Triche, chief engr. ■ On 34 CATVs. ■ Rates: $150; 75; 50.

Monroe

ADI No. 131; see Monroe-El Dorado, AR market

KARD-TV—See West Monroe.

***KLTM-TV**—ch 13, 316 kw vis, 31.6 kw aur, ant 1,777t/1,989g. TL: N32 11 45 W92 04 10. Hrs opn: 17. On air date: Sept 8, 1976. 7860 Anselmo Ln., Baton Rouge (70810). (504) 767-5660; (800) 272-8161. FAX: (504) 767-4277; (504) 767-4299. Licensee: Louisiana Educational Television Authority. Group owner: WLPB-TV. ■ Net: PBS. Wash atty: Schwartz, Woods & Miller. ■ On 17 CATVs—105,130 subs.

KNOE-TV—ch 8, 316 kw vis, 63.2 kw aur, ant 1,930t/1,985g. TL: N32 11 45 W92 04 10. On air date: Sept 27, 1953. Box 4067 (71211); 1400 Oliver Rd. (71201). (318) 388-8888. FAX: (318) 388-0070; TWX: 510-977-5384. Licensee: Noe Enterprises Inc. Ownership: John A. Noe Jr., 100%. ■ Net: CBS. Rep: Blair. Wash atty: Cohn & Marks. ■ James A. Noe Jr., pres; Dick French, gen mgr; Kathleen McLain, gen sls mgr; David Price, prom mgr; Jack McCall, progmg dir; Roy Frostenson, news dir; Jerry Harkins, chief engr. ■ On 34 CATVs—64,000 subs. On 1 trans. Co-owned radio: KNOE-AM-FM ■ Rates: $500; 290; 140.

KTVE—See El Dorado, Ark.

New Orleans

ADI No. 39; see New Orleans market

NEW TV—ch 20, 5,000 kw vis, 500 kw aur, ant 905t. TL: N29 55 11 W90 01 29. Not on air, target date unknown. 11 Richmond Place (70115). Permittee: Delta Broadcasting of Louisiana Ltd.

WCCL—ch 49, 5,000 kw vis, 500 kw aur, ant 1,049t/1,050g. TL: N29 55 11 W90 01 29. Stereo. On air date: Mar 19, 1989. 620 Desire St. (70117). Licensee: George S. Flinn Jr. (acq 4-30-93; $135,000; 5-24-93).

WDSU—ch 6, 100 kw vis, 20 kw aur, ant 930t/973g. TL: N29 57 01 W89 57 28. Stereo. On air date: Dec 18, 1948. 520 Royal St. (70130). (504) 527-0666. FAX: (504) 527-0145. Licensee: WDSU Television Inc. Group owner: Pulitzer Bcstg Co. (acq 12-14-89; $46.8 million; 10-9-89). ■ Net: NBC. Rep: Katz. Wash atty: Verner, Liipfert, Bernhard, McPherson & Hand. News staff 51; news progmg 18 hrs wkly. ■ Wayne Barnett, vp & gen mgr; Fred Steurer, opns dir & engrg dir; John Carpenter, gen sls mgr; Scott Chastain, mktg dir & prom dir; Lenora Cannon, progmg dir; Kurt Davis, news dir. ■ On 33 CATVs—48,000 subs.

WGNO—ch 26, 2,690 kw vis, 269.9 kw aur, ant 1,015t/1,049g. TL: N29 58 55 W89 56 58. (CP: 2,690 kw, ant 1,010 ft). Hrs opn: 24. On air date: Oct 16, 1967. Suite 2800, World Trade Center (70130). (504) 581-2600. FAX: (504) 522-1885; TWX: 810-951-6158. Licensee: WGNO Inc. Group owner: Tribune Broadcasting Co. (acq 9-1-83; $21 million; 8-8-83). Rep: Telerep. Wash atty: Schnader, Harrison, Segal & Lewis. ■ James Dowdle, pres; Robert Gremillion, gen mgr & stn mgr; Michael LaBonia, gen sls mgr; Jeff Clemons, prom mgr; Kathleen Quinn, progmg dir; Randy Davis, chief engr. ■ On 25 CATVs—300,000 subs. ■ Rates: $400; 250; 75.

***WLAE-TV**—ch 32, 55 kw vis, 11 kw aur, ant 1,020t/1,045g. TL: N29 58 57 W89 57 09. (CP: 2,290 kw vis, 229 kw aur). On air date: July 8, 1984. 2929 S. Carrollton Ave. (70118). (504) 866-7411. FAX: (504) 861-5186. Licensee: Educational Broadcasting Foundation Inc. ■ Net: PBS. Wash atty: Marmet & McCombs. Sp 3 hrs, Fr 2 hr wkly. ■ Phillip M. Hannan, pres; John Pela, gen mgr; Joslyn Yeager, progmg dir. ■ On 7 CATVs—271,348 subs.

WNOL-TV—ch 38, 5,000 kw vis, 500 kw aur, ant 1,049t/1,049g. TL: N29 58 41 W89 56 26. Stereo. On air date: Mar 25, 1984. 1661 Canal St. (70112). (504) 525-3838. FAX: (504) 569-0908. Licensee: Quincy Jones Broadcasting Inc. (acq 11-17-89). ■ Net: Fox. Rep: Seltel. ■ Quincy Jones, pres; Madelyn Mix Bonnot, vp & gen mgr; Jenny Zoeller, opns mgr; Steve Scollard, sls dir; Mike Zikmund, natl sls mgr; Dale Foshee, rgnl sls mgr; Dan Spangler, prom mgr; Charles Paige, progmg mgr; Bob Lawrence, chief engr. ■ On 38 CATVs—350,000 subs. ■ Rates: $500; 150; 50.

WVUE—ch 8, 316 kw vis, 31.6 kw aur, ant 990t/1,046g. TL: N29 57 14 W89 56 58. Hrs opn: 24. On air date: Feb 1, 1959. Box 13847 (70185); 1025 S. Jefferson Davis Pkwy. (70125). (504) 486-6161. FAX: (504) 483-1212. Licensee: Burnham Broadcasting Co. (group owner; acq 9-2-87; $60 million). ■ Net: ABC. Wash atty: Fisher, Wayland, Cooper & Leader. ■ Wayne W. Lansche, pres &

gen mgr; John Nagel, CFO; Rick Oster, natl sls mgr; Dan Wanko (local), rgnl sls mgr; Greg Buisson, prom dir; Kathy Kovacevich, progmg dir; Tom Rosenbaum, news dir; Fred Barrett, chief engr. ■ On 35 CATVs—353,280 subs.

WWL-TV—ch 4, 100 kw vis, 10 kw aur, ant 1,000t/1,049g. TL: N29 54 23 W90 02 23. Stereo. Hrs opn: 24. On air date: Sept 7, 1957. 1024 N. Rampart St. (70116). (504) 529-4444. FAX: (504) 592-1949. Licensee: Rampart Operating Partnership (acq 5-23-90; $102.85 million). ■ Net: CBS. Rep: Petry. Wash atty: Holland & Knight. ■ J. Michael Early, pres, gen mgr & progmg dir; Jimmie B. Phillips, gen sls mgr; Dee Joyce, prom mgr; Phil Johnson, film buyer; Joe Duke, news dir; Gary Coullard, chief engr. ■ On 20 CATVs—150,000 subs. On 2 trans.

*WYES-TV—ch 12, 316 kw vis, 31.6 kw aur, ant 1,010t/1,046g. TL: N89 56 58 W29 57 14. Stereo. On air date: Apr 1, 1957. 916 Navarre Ave. (70124); Box 24026 (70184). (504) 486-5511. FAX: (504) 483-8408. Licensee: Greater New Orleans Educational TV Foundation. ■ Net: PBS. Wash atty: Schwartz, Woods & Miller. ■ Randall Feldman, pres & gen mgr; Linda Delaney, opns mgr; Judith Holton, dev dir; Roy Taglialavore, prom dir, adv dir & pub affrs dir; Elizabeth Arroyo Utterback, progmg dir; Randall Davis, engrg dir. ■ On 25 CATVs—78,000 subs.

Shreveport

ADI No. 71; see Shreveport-Texarkana market

*KLTS-TV—ch 24, 1,620 kw vis, 162 kw aur, ant 1,070t/1,080g. TL: N32 40 41 W93 55 35. Hrs opn: 17. On air date: Aug 9, 1978. 7860 Anselmo Ln., Baton Rouge (70810). (504) 767-5660; (800) 272-8161. FAX: (504) 767-4299; (504) 767-4277. Licensee: Louisiana Education Television Authority. ■ Net: PBS. Wash atty: Schwartz, Woods & Miller. ■ Beth Courtney, CEO; William Arceneaux, chmn; Don Ballard, opns mgr; Quinn Rainwater, dev dir; Sharon Beningfield, prom mgr; Clay Fourrier, news dir; Gary Allen, pub affrs dir; Coy F. Simmons, engrg dir. ■ On 10 CATVs—82,527 subs.

KMSS-TV—ch 33, 4,570 kw vis, 457 kw aur, ant 1,813t/1,781g. TL: N32 36 51 W93 48 59. Stereo. Hrs opn: 5 AM-3 AM Sun-Thurs, 24 Fri-Sat. On air date: Oct 6, 1985. Box 30033, 3519 Jewella Ave. (71130). (318) 631-5677. FAX: (318) 631-4195. Licensee: SWMM/Shreveport Corp. Group owner: Southwest Multimedia Corp. (acq 8-21-87; $7 million; 5-25-87). ■ Net: Fox. Rep: Seltel. Wash atty: Semmes, Bowen & Semmes. ■ Art Lanham, pres, gen mgr & film buyer; Susan Newman, stn mgr & vp sls; Phyliss Phillips, vp opns; Karl Cole, prom mgr; Doug Ginn, progmg mgr; Chuck Smith, pub affrs dir; Richard Logan, chief engr. ■ On 95 CATVs—217,000 subs.

KSLA-TV—ch 12, 316 kw vis, 40.7 kw aur, ant 1,800t/1,800g. TL: N32 40 29 W93 55 59. On air date: Jan 1, 1954. Box 41812, 1812 Fairfield Ave. (71134); 1812 Fairfield Ave. (71101). (318) 222-1212. FAX: (318) 677-6703; TWX: 510-973-4013. Licensee: VSC Communications Inc. Group owner: Viacom Broadcasting Inc. (acq 6-3-83; 4-18-83). ■ Net: CBS. Rep: Telerep. ■ Alan Cartwright, vp & gen mgr; Mike Thomas, opns mgr & prom mgr; Marc Stover, sls dir & adv dir; Donna Frank, progmg dir; Walker Campbell, news dir; Jim Womack, chief engr. ■ On 101 CATVs—232,989 subs. ■ Rates: $900; 300; 300.

KTAL-TV—(Texarkana, TX). ch 6, 100 kw vis, 10 kw aur, ant 1,580t/1,552g. TL: N32 54 12 W94 00 23. On air date: Aug 16, 1953. 3150 N. Market St., Shreveport, LA (71107). (318) 425-2422. FAX: (318) 425-2488; TWX: 510-973-4169. Licensee: KTAL-TV Inc. ■ Net: NBC. Rep: Blair. Wash atty: Covington & Burling. ■ Walter E. Hussman, pres; Douglas Yoder, vp, gen mgr & gen sls mgr; Jean Byrd, prom mgr & progmg dir; Gordon Grafton, news dir; George Tracy, chief engr. ■ On 43 CATVs. Co-owned radio: KCMC(AM) Texarkana, TX, KTAL-FM Shreveport, LA.

KTBS-TV—ch 3, 100 kw vis, 20 kw aur, ant 1,780t/1,800g. TL: N32 41 08 W93 46 00. Stereo. Hrs opn: 24. On air date: Sept 3, 1955. Box 44227 (71134-4227); 312 E. Kings Hwy. (71104). (318) 861-5800. FAX: (318) 862-9430; (318) 862-9431 (NEWS). Licensee: KTBS Inc. Ownership: Helen H. Wray, Florence H. Wray. ■ Net: ABC. Rep: Katz. Wash atty: Fletcher, Heald & Hildreth. ■ George D. Wray Jr., chmn; Edwin Wray, pres & gen mgr; Lois W. Rowe, vp; George Sirven, gen sls mgr & mktg dir; Susan Yarbrough, rgnl sls mgr; Marvin Perry, progmg dir; Andrew Pontz, news dir; David Hendricks, chief engr. ■ On 110 CATVs—209,420 subs.

KWLB—ch 45, 786 kw vis, ant 662t. TL: N32 35 38 W93 51 39. Not on air, target date unknown. 4425 Meriwether Rd. (71109). (318) 687-9960. Permittee: Word of Life Ministries Inc.

West Monroe

ADI No. 131; see Monroe-El Dorado, AR market

KARD—ch 14, 5,000 kw vis, 500 kw aur, ant 2,049t/1,929g. TL: N32 05 41 W92 10 39. Stereo. On air date: Oct 6, 1974. Suite 22, 102 Thomas Rd. (71291). (318) 323-1972. FAX: (318) 322-0926; TWX: 510-977-5366. Licensee: BANAM Broadcasting Inc. (group owner; acq 3-16-93; grpsl; 4-5-93). ■ Net: ABC. Rep: Seltel. Wash atty: Jack Kenkel. ■ Paula Garrett, pres; Lydia Sandifer, gen mgr; Joe Currie, gen sls mgr; Lydia Sandifer (local), rgnl sls mgr; Trisa Beavers, prom mgr; Irma Camble, progmg dir & pub affrs dir; Rodney Evans, chief engr.

KMCT-TV—ch 39, 560 kw vis, 56 kw aur, ant 498t/500g. TL: N32 30 21 W92 08 54. On air date: Apr 7, 1986. 701 Parkwood Dr. (71291-5435). (318) 322-1399. Licensee: Carolina Christian Broadcasting Inc. (group owner). Wash atty: Fisher, Wayland, Cooper & Leader. ■ Charles Reed, pres, gen mgr, prom mgr & progmg dir; Matt Romano, gen sls mgr; Ray Summerall, chief engr. ■ On 2 CATVs—5,000 subs.

KNOE-TV—See Monroe, La.

Maine

Augusta

ADI No. 76; see Portland-Poland Spring market

*WCBB—ch 10, 309 kw vis, 30.9 kw aur, ant 1,000t/641g. TL: N44 09 16 W70 00 37. Stereo. On air date: Nov 13, 1961. 1450 Lisbon St., Lewiston (04240); 65 Texas Ave., Bangor (04401). (207) 941-1010; (207) 783-9101. FAX: (207) 783-5193; (207) 942-2867. Licensee: Maine Public Broadcasting Corp. (acq 6-23-92; 7-13-92). ■ Net: PBS; EEN. Wash atty: Tierney & Swift. ■ Robert H. Gardiner, pres & dev dir; Angelo Andrianos, CFO; Russell Peotter, gen mgr & mktg dir; Jennifer Halpern, prom mgr; William McCarthy, adv mgr; Bernie Roscetti, progmg dir; Harry J. Wiest Jr., film buyer; Gil Maxwell, engrg dir. ■ On 53 CATVs—198,851 subs. On 4 trans.

Bangor

ADI No. 155; see Bangor market

WABI-TV—ch 5, 40 kw vis, 6 kw aur, ant 1,316t/490g. TL: N44 42 13 W69 04 47. On air date: Jan 25, 1953. 35 Hildreth St. (04401). (207) 947-8321. FAX: (207) 941-9378. Licensee: Community Broadcasting Service. Group owner: Diversified Communications (acq 10-7-53; $125,000; 10-12-53). ■ Net: CBS. Rep: Blair. Wash atty: Dow, Lohnes & Albertson. ■ George H. Anderson, pres; George Gonyar, vp & gen mgr; Michael Young, gen sls mgr; Paul Saliwanchek, prom mgr; Joe Carr, progmg dir; Don Colson, news dir; Dale Carter, chief engr. ■ On 16 CATVs. On 2 trans. Co-owned radio: WABI(AM)-WYOU(FM).

WLBZ-TV—ch 2, 51.3 kw vis, 10.2 kw aur, ant 640t/99g. TL: N44 44 10 W68 40 17. On air date: Sept 12, 1954. Box 415, Mt. Hope Ave. (04402); 329 Mt. Hope Ave. (04401). (207) 942-4822. FAX: (207) 945-6816; TWX: 710-222-1877. Licensee: Maine Broadcasting Co. Ownership: No stockholder owns more than 11% (acq 5-15-58; $600,000; 5-26-58). ■ Net: NBC. Rep: Katz. Wash atty: Wilkinson, Barker, Knauer & Quinn. ■ Fred L. Thompson, pres; Jeff Marks, gen mgr; James Bartlett, gen sls mgr; Diann Beck, prom mgr; Judy Horan, news dir; Jim Chadwick, chief engr. ■ On 27 CATVs—50,000 subs. On one trans.

WVII-TV—ch 7, 316 kw vis, 31.6 kw aur, ant 819t/137g. TL: N44 45 35 W68 34 01. On air date: Oct 15, 1965. 371 Target Industrial Circle (04401). (207) 945-6457. FAX: (207) 942-0511. Licensee: Bangor Communications Inc. Group owner: Seaway Communications (acq 11-10-82; $3.8 million). ■ Net: ABC. Rep: Seltel. Wash atty: Mullin, Connor, Rhyne, Emmons & Topel. News staff 15; news progmg 6 hrs wkly. ■ Dr. Jamese Buckner, CEO; Dr. James Buckner, chmn; Bernie Chase, CFO & gen mgr; Michael Lawrence Blinder, gen sls mgr; James Parisi, news dir; Mike Staples, chief engr. ■ On 20 CATVs—180,000 subs.

Biddeford

ADI No. 76; see Portland-Poland Spring market

*WMEA-TV—ch 26, 589 kw vis, 117 kw aur, ant 800t/550g. TL: N43 25 00 W70 48 09. On air date: March 1975. 1450 Lisbon St., Lewiston (04240); 65 Texas Ave., Bangor (04401). (207) 941-1010; (207) 783-9101. FAX: (207) 783-5193; (207) 942-2857. Licensee: Maine Public Broadcastig Corp. (acq 6-23-92; 7-13-92). ■ Net: PBS. Wash atty: Dow, Lohnes & Albertson. ■ Robert H. Gardiner, pres; Angelo Andrianos, CFO; Russell Peotter, dev dir & mktg dir; Jennifer Halpern, prom mgr; William McCarthy, adv mgr; Bernie Roscetti, progmg dir; Harry Wiest, film buyer; Gil Maxwell, engrg dir. ■ On 14 CATVs.

Calais

ADI No. 155; see Bangor market

*WMED-TV—ch 13, 31.6 kw vis, 6.2 kw aur, ant 430t/190g. TL: N45 01 44 W67 19 24. (CP: 100 kw vis, ant 439t). On air date: September 1965. 1450 Lisbon St., Lewiston (04240); 65 Texas Ave., Bangor (04401). (207) 941-1010; (207) 783-9101. FAX: (207) 783-5193; (207) 942-2857. Licensee: Maine Public Broadcasting Corp. (acq 6-23-92; 7-13-92). ■ Net: PBS. Wash atty: Dow, Lohnes & Albertson. ■ Robert H. Gardiner, pres; Angelo Andrianos, CFO; Russell Peotter, dev dir & mktg dir; Jennifer Halpern, prom mgr; William McCarthy, adv mgr; Bernie Roscetti, progmg dir; Gil Maxwell, engrg dir. ■ On 2 CATVs.

Lewiston

ADI No. 76; see Portland-Poland Spring market

WWLA—ch 35, 500 kw vis, 100 kw aur, ant 840t. TL: N43 51 06 W70 19 40. Not on air, target date unknown. 10 Common St., Waterville (04901). (207) 873-4546. Permittee: Kennebec Valley Television Inc. Ownership: V. Wilson Hickam, 20%; Elie J. Roy, 20%; Ronald & Joan G. Fournier, 20%; Judith P. Williams, 20%; Clarence Ostlakiewicz, 20%.

Orono

ADI No. 155; see Bangor market

*WMEB-TV—ch 12, 299 kw vis, 30 kw aur, ant 990t/369g. TL: N44 45 36 W68 33 59. On air date: Sept 23, 1963. 65 Texas Ave., Bangor (04401); 1450 Lisbon St., Lewiston (04240). (207) 941-1010; (207) 783-9101. FAX: (207) 942-2857. Licensee: Maine Public Broadcasting Corp. (acq 6-23-92; 7-13-92). ■ Net: PBS; EEN. Wash atty: Dow, Lohnes & Albertson. ■ Robert H. Gardiner, gen mgr; Bernard Roscetti, opns dir; Vicki Hendrickson, gen sls mgr; Russ Peotter, mktg dir; Harry Wiest, progmg dir; Alexander G. Maxwell Jr., engrg dir. ■ On 20 CATVs—10,000 subs. On 4 trans.

Poland Spring

WMTW-TV—Licensed to Poland Spring. See Portland.

Portland

ADI No. 76; see Portland-Poland Spring market

WCSH-TV—ch 6, 100 kw vis, 20 kw aur, ant 2,000t/1,292g. TL: N43 51 32 W70 42 40. Stereo. On air date: Dec 1, 1953. One Congress Sq. (04101). (207) 828-6666. FAX: (207) 828-6630. Licensee: Maine Radio and Television Co. (group owner). ■ Net: NBC. Rep: Katz. Wash atty: Wilkinson, Barker, Knauer & Quinn. ■ Frederic L. Thompson, pres; Bruce S. McGorrill, vp; Lew Colby, gen mgr & stn mgr; Mike Marshall, opns mgr; Mike Cohen, gen sls mgr; Cary Collette, prom mgr; Larry Johnson, news dir; Jim Boutin, chief engr. ■ On 22 CATVs—200,000 subs.

WGME-TV—ch 13, 295 kw vis, 29.5 kw aur, ant 1,609t/1,665g. TL: N43 55 28 W70 29 28. Stereo. On air date: May 16, 1954. Box 1731 (04104); Northport Business Park, 1335 Washington Ave. (04103). (207) 797-9330. FAX: (207) 878-3505. Licensee: Gannett Publishing Co. Group owner: Guy Gannett Broadcasting Services Inc. ■ Net: CBS. Rep: Telerep. Wash atty: Dow, Lohnes & Albertson. News staff 35; news progmg 12 hrs wkly. ■ Bill Stough, vp & gen mgr; Tom Samad, opns mgr; Paul Saltin, gen sls mgr; Mike Colello (local), rgnl sls mgr; Towle Tompkins, mktg dir & progmg dir; Larry Henrichs, news dir; Towle Tompkins, pub affrs dir; Craig Clark, chief engr. ■ On 74 CATVs—350,000 subs.

Stations in the U.S.

WMTW-TV—(Poland Spring). ch 8, 105 kw vis, 21 kw aur, ant 3,850t/120g. TL: N44 16 13 W71 18 13. Hrs opn: 24. On air date: Aug 31, 1954. Box 8, 99 Danville Cor Rd., Auburn (04210). Box 9501 D.T.S., 119 Middle St., Portland (04112-9501). (207) 775-1800; (207) 782-1800. FAX: (207) 783-7371. Licensee: Harron Communications Corp. Ownership: Margaret E. Harron, 50%; Paul F. Harron, 42.5%; and Regina Hanson, 7.5% (acq 11-8-67; grpsl; 11-20-67). ■ Net: ABC. Rep: Petry. Wash atty: Hogan & Hartson. News staff 22; news progmg 12 hrs wkly. ■ Paul Harron, pres; Bob Rice, gen mgr & progmg dir; David Kaufman, gen sls mgr; Doug Albert, natl sls mgr; Joseph Rushing, mktg mgr, adv mgr & pub affrs dir; Miles Resnick, news dir; Charles Goode, engrg dir. ■ On 57 Canadian CATVs—760,072 subs; 110 U.S. CATVs—414,000 subs. ■ Rates: $600; 125; 50.

WPXT—ch 51, 3,035 kw vis, 303 kw aur, ant 1,000t/720g. TL: N43 51 06 W70 19 40. Stereo. Hrs opn: 19. On air date: Sept 14, 1986. 2320 Congress St. (04102). (207) 774-0051. FAX: (207) 774-6849. Licensee: Portland Broadcasting Inc. Ownership: John W. Bride, 100%. ■ Net: Fox. Rep: Seltel. Wash atty: Hamel & Park. News staff 8; news progmg 3 hrs wkly. ■ John W. Bride, pres; Doug Finck, vp & gen mgr; Jenifer Van Der Werf, vp opns; Tony Palminteri, vp sls & gen sls mgr; Roy Ouellette, chief engr. ■ On 42 CATVs—237,547 subs.

Presque Isle

ADI No. 205; see Presque Isle market

WAGM-TV—ch 8, 58.9 kw vis, 5.37 kw aur, ant 350t/290g. TL: N46 43 44 W68 00 07. On air date: Oct 13, 1956. Box 1149 (04769). (207) 764-4461. FAX: (207) 764-5329; TELEX: 629-58-642. Licensee: Peter P. Kosloski (acq 3-8-91; grpsl; 4-1-91). ■ Net: CBS, ABC, NBC. Rep: Katz. Wash atty: Koteen & Naftalin. ■ Norman W. Johnson, vp & gen mgr; Kathleen McLain, gen sls mgr; Sue Bernard, news dir; Ed Dery, chief engr. ■ On 8 CATVs—40,000 subs. On 4 trans. ■ Rates: $130; 80; 70.

*****WMEM-TV**—ch 10, 299 kw vis, 30 kw aur, ant 1,090t/158g. TL: N46 33 05W 67 48 37. On air date: Feb 17, 1964. 1450 Lisbon St., Lewiston (04240); 65 Texas Ave., Bangor (04401). (207) 941-1010; (207) 783-9101. FAX: (207) 783-5193; (207) 942-2857. Licensee: Maine Public Broadcasting Corp. (acq 6-23-92; 7-13-92). ■ Net: PBS. ■ Robert H. Gardiner, pres; Angelo Andrianos, CFO; Russell Peotter, dev dir & mktg dir; Jennifer Halpern, prom mgr; William McCarthy, adv mgr; Bernie Roscetti, progmg dir; Harry Wiest, film buyer; Gil Maxwell, engrg dir. ■ On 16 CATVs.

Maryland

LAUREN A. COLBY
301-663-1086
COMMUNICATIONS ATTORNEY
Special Attention to
Difficult Cases

Annapolis

ADI No. 22; see Baltimore market

*****WMPT**—ch 22, 3,890 kw vis, 389 kw aur, ant 874t/852g. TL: N39 00 36 W76 36 33. Stereo. On air date: July 16, 1975. 11767 Owings Mills Blvd., Owings Mills (21117). (410) 356-5600. FAX: (410) 581-4304. Licensee: Maryland Public Broadcasting Commission. ■ Net: PBS. Wash atty: Schwartz, Woods & Miller.

Baltimore

ADI No. 22; see Baltimore market

WBAL-TV—ch 11, 316 kw vis, 31.6 kw aur, ant 1,000t/998g. TL: N39 20 05 W76 39 03. On air date: Mar 11, 1948. 11 TV Hill (21211). (410) 467-3000. FAX: (410) 338-6460. Licensee: The Hearst Corp. Group owner: Hearst Broadcasting Group, see Cross-Ownership. ■ Net: CBS. Rep: Blair. Wash atty: Tharrington, Smith & Hargrove. News staff 63; news progmg 24 hrs wkly. ■ Phil Stolz, vp; Joseph Heston, gen mgr; Joe Ram, dev mgr; Bill Fine, gen sls mgr; Kerry Richards, prom mgr; Emerson Coleman, progmg mgr; David Roberts, news dir; Wanda Draper, pub affrs dir; Hank Volpe, engrg mgr. ■ On 329 CATVs—537,442 subs. Co-owned radio: WBAL(AM), WIYY(FM).

WBFF—ch 45, 1,292 kw vis, 258 kw aur, ant 1,266t. TL: N39 20 10 W76 38 59. On air date: Apr 11, 1971. 2000 W. 41 St. (21211). (410) 467-4545. Licensee: Chesapeake Television Inc. Group owner: Sinclair Broadcast Group Inc. (acq 9-10-90; grpsl; 10-15-90). ■ Net: Fox. Rep: Telerep. Wash atty: Fisher, Wayland, Cooper & Leader. News progmg 7 hrs wkly. ■ David D. Smith, pres; Steven M. Marks, gen mgr; Del Parks, opns dir; Robert Epstein, gen sls mgr; George Brust, natl sls mgr; Darren Shapiro, rgnl sls mgr; Karen Meekens, mktg dir; Michael Schroeder, prom mgr & progmg dir; Dennis Winters, chief engr.

WHSW-TV—ch 24, 1,170 kw vis, 117 kw aur, ant 1,069t/996g. TL: N39 17 15 W76 45 38. Hrs opn: 24. On air date: December 1985. Suite M-N, 4820 Seton Dr. (21215). (410) 358-2400. FAX: (410) 764-7232. Licensee: HSN Broadcasting of Maryland Inc. Group owner: Silver King Communications Inc. (acq 1-6-86; $15 million). Wash atty: Dow, Lohnes & Albertson. ■ Jeff McGrath, pres; Kenneth Becker, vp & stn mgr; Carole Taylor, prom mgr & progmg dir; John Skelnik, chief engr. ■ On 6 CATVs—515,000 subs.

WJZ-TV—ch 13, 316 kw vis, 31.6 kw aur, ant 1,000t/998g. TL: N39 20 05 W76 39 03. Stereo. (CP: 215 kw vis, ant 876t, TL: N39 20 05 W76 39 03). On air date: Nov 2, 1948. TV Hill (21211). (410) 466-0013. FAX: (410) 578-7502. Licensee: Westinghouse Broadcasting Co. Inc. (group owner; acq 6-28-57; $4.4 million; 7-1-57). ■ Net: ABC. Rep: Group W. Wash atty: Hedrick & Lane. ■ Burt Staniar, CEO; Marcellus W. Alexander Jr., vp & gen mgr; Larry Manogue, opns mgr; Fran Tivald, gen sls mgr; Phil Arrington, prom mgr; Michael Easterling, progmg mgr; Gail Bending, news dir; Phyllis Reese, pub affrs dir; Rick Seaby, chief engr. ■ On 78 CATVs—387,992 subs.

WMAR-TV—ch 2, 100 kw vis, 11 kw aur, ant 1,000t/999g. TL: N39 20 05 W76 39 03. Stereo. Hrs opn: 24. On air date: Oct 27, 1947. 6400 York Rd. (21212). (410) 377-2222. Licensee: Scripps-Howard Broadcasting Co. (group owner; acq 1991; $125 million; 9-3-90). ■ Net: NBC. Rep: Katz. Wash atty: Baker & Hostetler. ■ H. Joseph Lewin, gen mgr; Emily L. Barr, stn mgr; Mark Distler, gen sls mgr & adv dir; George Carlino, natl sls mgr; Marc Robertz, prom dir; Emily Barr, progmg dir; Jack Cahalan, news dir; Darcel Guy, pub affrs dir; Joseph Bruno, engrg dir. ■ On 101 CATVs—1,096,433.

*****WMPB**—ch 67, 646 kw vis, 76.38 kw aur, ant 820t/693g. TL: N39 27 01 W76 46 37. Stereo. On air date: Oct 6, 1969. 11767 Owings Mills Blvd., Owings Mills (21117). (410) 356-5600. FAX: (410) 581-4304. Licensee: Maryland Public Broadcasting Commission. ■ Net: PBS. Wash atty: Schwartz, Woods & Miller. ■ Raymond K.K. Ho, pres; Tom Bohn, vp opns; Joan Frangos, vp dev & vp mktg; Michael Styer, vp progmg; Ann Engleman, film buyer; Everet Marshburn, news dir; Bruce Herget, vp engrg. ■ On one trans.

WNUV-TV—ch 54, 5,000 kw vis, 500 kw aur, ant 1,148t/998g. TL: N39 15 W76 45 38. Stereo. Hrs opn: 24. On air date: July 1, 1982. 3001 Druid Park Dr. (21215-7813). (410) 462-5400. FAX: (410) 523-4319. Licensee: WNUV-TV 54 L.P. Group owner: ABRY Communications Inc. (acq 3-1-89). Rep: Petry. Wash atty: Arter & Hadden. ■ Joseph A. Koff, gen mgr; Michael Kelly, gen sls mgr; Debbie Kramer, natl sls mgr; Maura McCoy, prom mgr; Paul Garnet, chief engr. ■ On 45 CATVs—745,000 subs.

Frederick

ADI No. 7; see Washington, DC market

*****WFPT**—ch 62, 70 kw vis, ant 1,921t/199g. TL: N39 17 53 W77 20 35. Stereo. (CP: 3,366 kw vis, ant 453t). On air date: 1986. 11767 Owings Mills Blvd., Owings Mills (21117). (410) 356-5600. FAX: (410) 581-4304. Licensee: Maryland Public Broadcasting Commission. ■ Net: PBS. Wash atty: Schwartz, Woods & Miller.

Hagerstown

ADI No. 192; see Hagerstown market

WHAG-TV—ch 25, 1,352 kw vis; 135.2 kw aur, ant 1,230t/453g. TL: N39 39 35 W77 57 57. Stereo. Hrs opn: 24. On air date: Jan 3, 1970. 13 E. Washington St. (21740). (301) 797-4400. FAX: (301) 733-1735. Licensee: Williams Communications Inc. Group owner: Great Trails Broadcasting Corp. (acq 12-23-86). ■ Net: NBC.

Massachusetts

Rep: Katz. Wash atty: Haley, Bader & Potts. News staff 12; news progmg 9 hrs wkly. ■ Hugh J. Breslin, vp, gen mgr & gen sls mgr; Chuck Noland, opns dir, prom mgr & progmg dir; Bob Borngesser, news dir; Glenn Presgraves, pub affrs dir; Wayne Younkins, chief engr. ■ On 45 CATVs—197,223 subs. ■ Rates: $550; 170; 50.

WJAL—ch 68, 4,000 kw vis, 400 kw aur, ant 1,335t/275g. TL: N39 53 31 W77 58 02. Hrs opn: 24. On air date: May 5, 1987. Box 229, 262 Swamp Fox Rd., Chambersburg, PA (17201). (719) 375-4000. FAX: (719) 375-4052. Licensee: Channel 68 Broadcasting Corp. Rep: Dome & Associates. Wash atty: McCabe & Allen. ■ Jerold Jacobs, pres; Meredith "Buddy" S. Merrick, sr vp, gen mgr & progmg dir; Ed Klitch, chief opns; Mike Patterson, gen sls mgr & prom dir; Bob Baker, chief engr. ■ On 40 CATVs—155,000. ■ Rates: $100; 40; 30.

*****WWPB**—ch 31, 436 kw vis, 51.65 kw aur, ant 1,230t/415g. TL: N39 39 04 W77 58 15. Stereo. On air date: Oct 5, 1974. 11767 Owings Mills Blvd., Owings Mills (21117). (410) 356-5600. FAX: (410) 581-4306. Licensee: Maryland Public Broadcasting Commission. ■ Net: PBS. Wash atty: Schwartz, Woods & Miller.

Oakland

ADI No. 17; see Pittsburgh, PA market

*****WGPT**—ch 36, 25 kw vis, ant 3,225t/199g. TL: N39 24 14 W79 17 37. Stereo. On air date: 1986. 11767 Owings Mills Blvd., Owings Mills (21117). (410) 356-5600. FAX: (410) 581-4304. Licensee: Maryland Public Broadcasting Commission. ■ Net: PBS. Wash atty: Schwartz, Woods & Miller.

Salisbury

ADI No. 163; see Salisbury market

WBOC-TV—ch 16, 4,070 kw vis, 407 kw aur, ant 980t/1,003g. TL: N38 30 16 W75 38 35. On air date: July 15, 1954. Box 2057, Radio-TV Park (21802). (410) 749-1111. TWX: 710-862-9672. Licensee: Draper Communications Inc. (group owner; $8 million). ■ Net: CBS. Rep: Katz. Wash atty: Arent, Fox, Kintner, Plotkin & Kahn. ■ Thomas Draper, pres; William K. Kenton Jr., gen mgr; Charlie Timmons, gen sls mgr; Denise Adams, progmg dir; Marilyn Buerkle, news dir; Gene Horner, chief engr. ■ On 26 CATVs. ■ Rates: $400; 200; 125.

*****WCPB**—ch 28, 708 kw vis, 82 kw aur, ant 510t/551g. TL: N38 23 09 W75 35 33. Stereo. (CP: 2,179 kw vis, ant 515 ft, TL: N38 23 09 W75 35 32.5). On air date: Mar 21, 1971. 11767 Owings Mills Blvd., Owings Mills (21117). (410) 356-5600. FAX: (410) 581-4338. Licensee: Maryland Public Broadcasting Commission. ■ Net: PBS. Wash atty: Schwartz, Woods & Miller. ■ Artie Buffkins, sr vp; Ann Engleman, film buyer; Everet Marshburn, news dir; Bruce Herget, vp engrg; Bob Hoerr, chief engr.

WMDT—ch 47, 2,190 kw vis, 219 kw aur, ant 997t/1,024g. TL: N38 30 06 W75 44 09. Stereo. Hrs opn: 24. On air date: Apr 11, 1980. 202 Downtown Plaza (21801); Box 4009 (21803-4009). (410) 742-4747. FAX: (410) 742-5767. Licensee: Delmarva Broadcasting Service G.P. Ownership: Marion B. Brechner 80%; Berl M. Brechner 20% (acq 12-13-90; 1-7-91). ■ Net: ABC, NBC. Rep: Blair. Wash atty: Cohn & Marks. ■ Frank Pilgrim, gen mgr, stn mgr & film buyer; Susan Kelly, gen sls mgr; John Cannon, prom mgr & adv mgr; Betty Talkington, progmg mgr; Tedd O'Connell, news dir; Bill Hoctor, chief engr. ■ On 22 CATVs—158,829 subs. On one trans. ■ Rates: $400; 100; 25.

Massachusetts

Adams

ADI No. 53; see Albany-Schenectady-Troy market

WCDC—ch 19, 538 kw vis, 53 kw aur, ant 3,688t/248g. TL: N42 38 14 W73 10 07. Hrs opn: 20. On air date: Feb 5, 1954. 341 Northern Blvd., Albany, NY (12204). (518) 436-4822. FAX: (518) 462-6065. Licensee: Young Broadcasting of Albany Inc. Group owner: Young Broadcasting Inc. (acq 10-11-89; grpsl; 9-11-89). ■ Net: ABC. Wash atty: Wiley, Rein & Fielding. News staff 37; news progmg 15 hrs wkly. ■ Vincent Young, chmn; Ron Kwasnick, pres; Bob Peterson, gen mgr & progmg dir; Mike Funk, gen sls mgr; Lynn Riley, prom mgr; Don Decker, news dir; Harold Lansing, chief engr. ■ On 70 CATVs—300,000 subs. On 3 trans. Satellite of WTEN Albany.

Michigan | Directory of Television

Boston

ADI No. 6; see Boston market

WABU—ch 68, 1,350 kw vis, 135 kw aur, ant 870t/885g. TL: N42 20 50 W71 04 59. Hrs opn: 24. On air date: January 1979. 1660 Soldiers Field Rd. (02135). (617) 787-6868. FAX: (617) 562-4280. Licensee: Boston University. Ownership: Dr. John Silber (acq 9-7-93; $3.8 million; 9-27-93). Sp 10 hrs wkly. News progmg 20 hrs wkly. ■ Robert Gordon, pres; Will Meyl, vp & stn mgr; William F. Spitzer, vp dev; Mike Sobel, gen sls mgr; Bruce Binenfeld, progmg dir; Ted O'Brien, news dir; Joe Sweeny, chief engr.

WBZ-TV—ch 4, 60.3 kw vis, 9.75 kw aur, ant 1,160t/1,199g. TL: N42 18 37 W71 14 14. Stereo. Hrs opn: 24. On air date: June 9, 1948. 1170 Soldiers Field Rd. (02134). (617) 787-7000. FAX: (617) 787-5969. Licensee: Westinghouse Broadcasting Co. Inc. (group owner). ■ Net: NBC. Rep: Katz. Wash atty: Wilkes, Artis, Hedrick & Lane. Sp one hr wkly. News staff 81; news progmg 20 hrs wkly. ■ Burton Staniar, chmn; Bill Korn, pres; Debra Zeyen, vp & gen mgr; Ed Goldman, stn mgr; Pam Bergeron, gen sls mgr; Kim Harbin, mktg mgr; Francine Achbar, progmg mgr; Peter Brown, news dir; Lois Roach, pub affrs dir; Bob Hess, chief engr. ■ On 220 CATVs—1,500,000 subs. Co-owned radio: WBZ(AM).

WCVB-TV—ch 5, 100 kw vis, 10 kw aur, ant 980t/1,194g. TL: N42 18 37 W71 14 14. Stereo. Hrs opn: 24. On air date: Mar 19, 1972. 5 TV Place (02194). (617) 449-0400. FAX: (617) 449-6682. Licensee: The Hearst Corp. Group owner: Hearst Broadcasting Group (acq 3-6-86; $450 million). ■ Net: ABC. Rep: Katz. Wash atty: Tharrington, Smith, & Hargrove. Sp one hr, close captioning news & pub affrs 8 hrs wkly. News staff 111; news progmg 20 hrs wkly. ■ S. James Coppersmith, pres & gen mgr; Thomas J. Bringola, CFO; Paul La Camera, stn mgr; Deborah Sinay, vp sls & gen sls mgr; Therese Mulvey, mktg mgr; Paul LaCamera, vp progmg & progmg dir; Candy Altman, news dir; Ross Kaufman, vp engrg & engrg dir. ■ On 200 CATVs—500,000 subs.

WFXT—ch 25, 1,380 kw vis, 106 kw aur, ant 1,170t/1,101g. TL: N42 18 12 W71 13 08. Stereo. Hrs opn: 21. On air date: Oct 10, 1977. 1000 Providence Hwy., Dedham (02026). (617) 326-8825. FAX: (617) 326-9984; (617) 326-9826. Licensee: Boston Celtics Broadcasting L.P. Ownership: Boston Celtics Broadcasting L.P. (acq 5-11-90; $10 million). ■ Net: Fox. Rep: Petry. News progmg 4 hrs wkly. ■ Gerald R. Walsh, pres & gen mgr; Deborah C. Smith, gen sls mgr; Jim Byrne, prom mgr & progmg dir; Leah Hollenberger, pub affrs dir; Gunnar Rieger, chief engr. ■ On 136 CATVs—1,517,500 subs. Co-owned radio: WEEI-AM.

*****WGBH-TV**—ch 2, 87.1 kw vis, 8.71 kw aur, ant 1,040t/1,199g. TL: N42 13 37 W71 14 14. Stereo. Hrs opn: 6:30 AM-1 AM On air date: May 2, 1955. 125 Western Ave. (02134). (617) 492-2777. FAX: (617) 787-0714. Licensee: WGBH Educational Foundation. ■ Net: PBS; EEN. Wash atty: Covington & Burling. Progmg for the deaf. ■ Henry P. Becton Jr., pres & gen mgr; Andrew S. Griffiths, CFO; David B. Liroff, stn mgr; Vicky Devlin, dev dir; Roberta MacCarthy, mktg dir; Jeanne Hopkins, prom dir; Dan Everett, progmg dir; Ron Bachman, progmg mgr; David MacCarn, engrg dir. ■ On 155 CATVs—1,896,000 subs. On 1 trans. Co-owned radio: *WGBH(FM).

*****WGBX-TV**—ch 44, 977 kw vis, 97.7 kw aur, ant 1,080t/1,119g. TL: N42 18 37 W71 14 14. On air date: Sept 25, 1967. 125 Western Ave. (02134). (617) 492-2777. FAX: (617) 787-0714. Licensee: WGBH Educational Foundation. ■ Net: PBS. Progmg for the deaf 13 hrs wkly. ■ Jim Lewis, gen mgr; Mark Erstling, progmg dir; Ray Miller, chief engr. ■ On 240 CATVs—216,000 subs.

WHDH-TV—ch 7, 316 kw vis, 63.2 kw aur, ant 1,000t/1,069g. TL: N42 18 40 W71 13 00. Stereo. On air date: June 21, 1948. 7 Bulfinch Pl., Boston (02114). (617) 725-0777. TWX: 710-321-0361. Licensee: WHDH-TV Inc. Ownership: Sunbeam Television Corp. (acq 6-3-93; $204 million; 6-21-93). ■ Net: CBS. Rep: Telerep. Wash atty: Koteen & Naftalin. ■ Edmund Ansin, chmn; Mark Mayo, CFO; Michael Carson, vp & gen mgr; Tim Ermish, natl sls mgr; Laura Hale, mktg dir & adv dir; Alison Kelly, progmg mgr; Joel Cheatwood, news dir; Jim Shultis, engrg dir. ■ On 120 CATVs—2,000,000 subs.

WLVI-TV—(Cambridge). ch 56, 2,240 kw vis, 166 kw aur, ant 1,186t/1,201g. TL: N42 18 12 W71 13 08. On air date: Aug 31, 1953. 75 Morrissey Blvd., Boston (02125). (617) 265-5656. FAX: (617) 265-2538. Licensee: Gannett Mass. Broadcasting Inc. Group owner: Gannett Broadcasting (division of Gannett Co. Inc.) (acq 6-23-83; $47 million; 5-23-83). Rep: Blair. Sp one hr wkly. News staff 44; news progmg 7 hrs wkly. ■ Peter Temple, pres & gen mgr; Ron Becker, vp opns & news dir; Gracelyn Brown, prom dir & progmg dir; Natalie Christian, pub affrs dir; Jim Gilbert, engrg dir. ■ On 150 CATVs—1,906,725 subs.

WSBK-TV—ch 38, 3,160 kw vis, 316 kw aur, ant 1,161t/1,013g. TL: N42 18 12 W71 13 08. Hrs opn: 24. On air date: Oct 12, 1964. 83 Leo Birmingham Pkwy., Brighton (02135). (617) 783-3838. FAX: (617) 783-1875. Licensee: WSBK License Inc. Group owner: SCI Television Inc. (acq 2-19-93; grpsl; 4-26-93). Rep: HRP. Wash atty: Pepper & Corazzini. ■ Daniel J. Berkery, pres & gen mgr; Stuart P. Tauber, stn mgr; John S. Viall, opns dir; Francis X. Comerford, gen sls mgr; John Anderson, mktg mgr; Vikki Kendall, prom mgr; Meg LaVigne, progmg dir & pub affrs dir; Jim McCarthy, chief engr. ■ On 350 CATVs—4,100,000 subs. On one trans. ■ Rates: $7,000; 2,500; 600.

Cambridge

WLVI-TV—Licensed to Cambridge. See Boston.

Lawrence

ADI No. 6; see Boston market

WMFP—ch 62, 2,221 kw vis, 222 kw aur, ant 454t/226g. TL: N42 42 25 W71 00 54. (CP: 5,000 kw vis, ant 649t). On air date: Oct 16, 1987. One Parker St. (01843). (508) 975-3053. FAX: (508) 683-6262. Licensee: MFP Inc. Ownership: Avi Nelson, 35%; Peter Fuller, 15%; Totman & Co. 10%. Wash atty: Hopkins & Sutter. ■ Avi Nelson, pres. ■ 700,000 subs. ■ Rates: $100; 100; 100.

Marlborough

ADI No. 6; see Boston market

WHSH-TV—ch 66, 3,160 kw vis, 316 kw aur, ant 1,070t/1,198g. TL: N42 23 01 W71 11 24. Stereo. On air date: Feb 12, 1985. 71 Parmenter Rd., Hudson (01749). (508) 562-0660. FAX: (508) 562-1166. Licensee: HSN Broadcasting of Massachusetts Inc. Group owner: Silver King Communications Inc. (acq 10-3-86; 8-25-86). Wash atty: Dow, Lohnes & Albertson. News staff 2; news progmg 2 hrs wkly. ■ Jeff McGrath, pres; Merril Buchhalter, vp, gen mgr & gen sls mgr; Robin Belle-Isle, opns mgr; Francesca Bryden, progmg dir, film buyer & news dir; Mark Arpino, chief engr. ■ On 38 CATVs—65,748 subs.

Needham

WUNI—ch 27, 1,195 kw vis, 245 kw aur, ant 1,531t/1,349g. TL: N42 20 07 W71 42 54. (CP: 2,301 kw vis, 230 kw aur). On air date: Jan 2, 1970. 33 Fourth Ave. (02194). (617) 433-2727. FAX: (617) 433-2750. Licensee: JASAS Corp. (acq 10-15-93; with WFTY-TV Washington; 11-8-93). ■ Net: Univision. Rep: Univision. Wash atty: Patton, Boggs & Blow. News staff 5; news progmg 5 hrs wkly. ■ Nolanda Hill, pres; Ken White, CFO; Michael Nurse, vp & gen mgr; Gary Marder, gen sls mgr; Frank Litardo, prom mgr & pub affrs dir; Lillian Chan, progmg dir; Wilma Colon, news dir; Fran Vacarri, chief engr. ■ On 53 CATVs—1,200,000 subs. On one trans. ■ Rates: $500; 300; 150.

New Bedford

WFDG—Licensed to New Bedford. See Providence, R.I.

WLNE—Licensed to New Bedford. See Providence, R.I.

Norwell

ADI No. 6; see Boston market

WHRC—ch 46, 2,937.6 kw max vis, 293.76 kw max aur, ant 314t/299g. TL: N42 09 17 W70 51 10. (CP: 706 kw vis, 660 w aur, ant 272t). Not on air, target date unknown. Suite 813, 10573 W. Pico Blvd., Los Angeles, CA (90064). Permittee: Mass. Channel 46 Corp.

Springfield

ADI No. 98; see Springfield, MA market

*****WGBY-TV**—ch 57, 776 kw vis, 155 kw aur, ant 1,000t/141g. TL: N42 14 30 W72 38 56. Hrs opn: 6:45 AM-3 AM. On air date: Sept 26, 1971. 44 Hampden St. (01103). (413) 781-2801. FAX: (413) 731-5093. Licensee: WGBH Educational Foundation. ■ Net: PBS. Wash atty: Covington & Burling. ■ Jim Lewis, gen mgr; Mark Erstling, stn mgr; Jean Boyd Erstling, prom mgr; Elizabeth Carley, progmg dir; Ray Miller, chief engr. ■ On 28 CATVs—402,379 subs.

WGGB-TV—ch 40, 4,250 kw vis, 425 kw aur, ant 1,056t/167g. TL: N42 14 30 W72 38 56. Stereo. Hrs opn: 24. On air date: Apr 14, 1953. Box 40, 1300 Liberty St. (01102-0040). (413) 733-4040. FAX: (413) 781-1363; TWX: 710-350-1369. Licensee: Gannett Publishing Co. Group owner: Guy Gannett Broadcasting Services Inc. (acq 6-7-67; grpsl; 6-19-67). ■ Net: ABC. Rep: Katz. Wash atty: Dow, Lohnes & Albertson. ■ Kevin P. LeRoux, vp & gen mgr; Michael Moran, stn mgr; adv mgr & progmg dir; Mary Deliso, rgnl sls mgr; Dan Salamone, news dir; Theodore Gratkowski, chief engr. ■ On 17 CATVs. ■ Rates: $2,500; 200; 150.

WWLP—ch 22, 4,170 kw vis, 417 kw aur, ant 877t/530g. TL: N42 05 05 W72 42 14. Stereo. On air date: Mar 17, 1953. Box 2210 (01102). (413) 786-2200. Licensee: Brissette TV of Springfield Inc. (group owner: Brissette Broadcasting Corp.; acq 12-24-91; grpsl). ■ Net: NBC. Rep: Blair. Wash atty: Wiley & Rein. ■ William M. Pepin, pres & gen mgr; E. Holland Low, vp & gen sls mgr; Anna Giza, prom mgr; Keith Silver, news dir; Max Marek, chief engr. ■ On 33 CATVs—196,000 subs. ■ Rates: $1,000; 300; 65.

Vineyard Haven

ADI No. 45; see Providence-New Bedford market

WCVX—ch 58, 1,191 kw vis, 119.1 kw aur, ant 470t/350g. TL: N41 41 19 W70 20 49. Stereo. (CP: 1,150 kw vis, ant 492t). On air date: July 19, 1985. 29 Bassett Lane, Hyannis (02601). (617) 787-6868. Permittee: Cape Television Inc. Ownership: Paul P. Flynn (acq 6-18-92; $826,000; 7-6-92). Wash atty: Arter & Hadden. ■ Daniel N. Carney, pres & gen mgr; John Quinlan, gen sls mgr; Robert Kinkead, progmg dir & film buyer; Robert Halloran, news dir; Donald P. Moore, chief engr. ■ On 10 CATVs—115,000 subs.

Worcester

ADI No. 6; see Boston market

*****WYDN**—ch 48, 5 kw vis, 100 kw aur, ant 1,305t. TL: N42 08 32 W72 13 28. Not on air, target date unknown. Box 1975, San Benito, TX (78586). Permittee: Worcester Educational Corp. Inc.

Michigan

Alpena

ADI No. 209; see Alpena market

WBKB-TV—ch 11, 316 kw vis, 32.4 kw aur, ant 665t/500g. TL: N44 42 25 W83 31 23. On air date: Sept 22, 1975. 1390 Bagley St. (49707). (517) 356-3434. FAX: (517) 356-4188. Licensee: Thunder Bay Broadcasting Corp. Ownership: Stephen A. Marks, 88.56%. ■ Net: CBS. Rep: Seltel. Wash atty: Cohn & Marks. ■ Stephen A. Marks, pres; Curt Smith, vp, gen mgr, progmg dir & film buyer; Barbara Bowen, gen sls mgr; Bob Race, prom mgr; Terese Thomas, news dir; Mark Nowak, chief engr. ■ On 10 CATVs—34,397 subs.

*****WCML-TV**—ch 6, 100 kw vis, 15.1 kw aur, ant 1,472t/1,349g. TL: N45 08 17 W84 09 44. Hrs opn: 6:45 AM-midnight. On air date: 1975. Central Michigan Univ., 3965 E. Broomfield Rd., Mt. Pleasant (48859). (517) 774-3105. FAX: (517) 774-4427. Licensee: Central Michigan University. ■ Net: PBS. Wash atty: Dow, Lohnes & Albertson. ■ William J. Grigaliunas, gen mgr; Monte L. Higgins, stn mgr; Randi Richardson, mktg mgr; Linda Hyde, prom mgr; Rick Schudiske, progmg dir; Randy Kapenga, chief engr. ■ On 14 CATVs—72,774 subs. On 2 trans. Satellite of WCMU-TV Mt. Pleasant. Co-owned radio: *WCML-FM.

Ann Arbor

ADI No. 105; see Lansing market

WBSX—ch 31, 1,220 kw vis, 217 kw aur, ant 1,080t/1,044g. TL: N42 22 25 W84 04 10. Hrs opn: 24. On air date: Jan 12, 1981. Box 2267 (48106); 3975 Varsity Dr. (48108). (313) 973-7900. FAX: (313) 973-7906. Licensee: Blackstar Communications of Michigan Inc. Ownership: John E. Oxendine 75%; Wesley S. Williams Jr., 18.75% (acq 7-10-89; $4,350,000; 7-31-89). Wash atty: Verner, Liipfert, Bernhard, McPherson & Hand. ■ John Oxendine, pres; Christopher Webb, vp & gen mgr;

Karen Keys, pub affrs dir; Robert Thompson, chief engr. ■ On 29 CATVs—576,000 subs. ■ Rates: $50; 35; 20.

Bad Axe

ADI No. 60; see Flint-Saginaw-Bay City market

***WUCX-TV**—ch 35, 85.9 kw vis, 8.59 kw aur, ant 510t/489g. TL: N43 41 28 W82 46 26. Stereo. On air date: Dec 12, 1986. University Center, Delta Rd., University Ctr. (48710). (517) 686-9350. FAX: (517) 686-9350. Licensee: Delta College. ■ Net: PBS. Wash atty: Cohn & Marks. ■ Donald J. Carlyon, pres; Presley D. Holmes, gen mgr; Thomas Haskell, progmg dir; Harold J. Conley, chief engr.

Battle Creek

ADI No. 37; see Grand Rapids-Kalamazoo-Battle Creek market

WJUE—ch 43, 5,000 kw vis, 500 kw aur, ant 1,058t. TL: N42 40 45 W85 03 57. Hrs opn: 24. Not on air, target date Spring 1994. Box 907, Jenison (49429-0907). (616) 457-6871. FAX: (616) 457-8203. Permittee: Western Michigan Christian Broadcasting. Ownership: William Popjes, 100% (acq 10-20-92; $55,467; 11-23-92). ■ William B. Popjes, CEO; James Bronkema, CFO; A. David Bos, vp; Curtis N. Render, sls dir; Marvin Van Voorst, pub affrs dir. ■ On 120 CATVs—513,000 subs. ■ Rates: $250; 200; 150.

WOTV—ch 41, 2,000 kw vis, 200 kw aur, ant 1,076t/963g. TL: N42 34 15 W85 28 11. Hrs opn: 6 AM-2AM. On air date: July 24, 1971. Box 1616, 5200 W. Dickman Rd. (49016). (616) 968-9341. FAX: (616) 966-6837. Licensee: Channel 41 Inc. Ownership: John W. Lawrence, 58%;Wm. J. Lawrence Jr., 39%;Jerry P. Colvin, 1%;Dr. Lewis Batts, 2% Group owner: Northstar Television Group Inc. (acq 5-30-74; 6-17-74). ■ Net: ABC. Rep: Blair. Wash atty: Covington & Burling. News staff 10; news progmg 6 hrs wkly. ■ Jerry P. Colvin, pres & gen mgr; Bob Weinstein, gen sls mgr; Molly Kelly, mktg dir & prom dir; Tom Richards, progmg dir & film buyer; Bert Mosley, news dir; Colleen Pierson, pub affrs dir; Mike Laemers, engrg dir. ■ On 30 CATVs—276,331 subs. ■ Rates: $300; 50; 25.

Bay City

WNEM-TV—Licensed to Bay City. See Flint.

Cadillac

ADI No. 121; see Traverse City-Cadillac market

***WCMV**—ch 27, 274.2 kw vis, 27.42 kw aur, ant 587t/303g. TL: N44 08 22 W85 20 28. On air date: Sept 7, 1984. Central Michigan Univ., 3965 E. Broomfield Rd., Mt. Pleasant (48859). (517) 774-3105. FAX: (517) 774-4427. Licensee: Central Michigan University. ■ Net: PBS. Wash atty: Dow, Lohnes & Albertson. ■ William J. Grigaliunas, gen mgr. Satellite of WCMU-TV Mt. Pleasant.

WGKI—ch 33, 61.52 kw vis, 6.152 kw aur, ant 1,023t/650g. TL: N44 08 53 W85 20 45. Stereo. Hrs opn: 24. On air date: Oct 12, 1989. 7400 S. 45 Rd. (49601). (616) 775-9813; (616) 775-0330. FAX: (616) 775-1898. Licensee: GRK Productions Joint Venture. Ownership: GRK Productions Inc., mgng ptnr, 70%;GRK Productions-Joint Ventures, 30%. ■ Net: Fox. Rep: Adam Young. Wash atty: Harry Martin. ■ Gary Knapp, pres & gen mgr; Julie Brinks, opns mgr & prom mgr; Donna Horning, gen sls mgr; Joyce Bassett, progmg dir; Dan Somes, engrg dir; Glen Walker, chief engr. ■ On 45 CATVs—130,000 subs.

WPBN-TV—See Traverse City.

WWTV—ch 9, 316 kw vis, 63.1 kw aur, ant 1,635t/1,295g. TL: N44 08 12 W85 20 33. On air date: Dec 11, 1953. Box 627 (49601). (616) 775-3478. FAX: (616) 775-3671. Licensee: Heritage Broadcasting Co. of Michigan. Ownership: Mario F. Iacobelli (acq 3-3-89; grpsl; 3-20-89). ■ Net: CBS. Wash atty: Hogan & Hartson. ■ Mario F. Iacobelli, pres; William E. Kring, CFO & stn mgr; Laurie Rutkowski, mktg dir; Sherri McKinley, progmg dir; Lowell Shore, chief engr. ■ On 62 CATVs—385,900 subs. ■ Rates: $400; 150; 50.

Cheboygan

ADI No. 121; see Traverse City-Cadillac market

WTOM-TV—ch 4, 100 kw vis, 20 kw aur, ant 620t/590g. TL: N45 39 01 W84 20 37. Stereo. Hrs opn: 24. On air date: May 16, 1959. M-72 W. Box 546, Traverse City (49684). (616) 947-7770; (616) 946-2504. FAX: (616) 947-0354. Licensee: Federal Broadcasting Co. (group owner; acq 9-17-90). ■ Net: NBC. Rep: Katz. Wash atty: Hogan & Hartson. ■ Peter Kizer, pres; Greg Wittland, gen mgr & progmg dir; Linda Kimbel, gen sls mgr & natl sls mgr; Cathy Marsh, rgnl sls mgr; Michele Brown, prom mgr; Mike Conway, news dir; Curt Morgan, chief engr.

Detroit

ADI No. 9; see Detroit market

WDIV—ch 4, 100 kw vis, 10 kw aur, ant 1,004t. TL: N42 28 58 W83 12 19. Stereo. On air date: Mar 4, 1947. 550 W. Lafayette Blvd. (48231). (313) 222-0444. FAX: (313) 222-0471. Licensee: Post-Newsweek Stations, Michigan Inc. Group owner: Post-Newsweek Stns Inc. (acq 6-24-78). ■ Net: NBC. Rep: Blair. Wash atty: Covington & Burling. ■ Alan W. Frank, vp & gen mgr; Sue Ayalla, opns mgr; Ted Pearse, gen sls mgr; Henry Maldonado, vp prom & vp progmg; Terry Turpin-Amato, prom mgr; Carol Rueppel, news dir; Marcus Williams, chief engr.

WGPR-TV—ch 62, 759 kw vis, 75.9 kw aur, ant 970t/1,000g. TL: N42 27 13 W83 09 50. On air date: September 1975. 3146 E. Jefferson Ave. (48207). (313) 259-8862. FAX: (313) 259-6662. Licensee: WGPR Inc. Ownership: International Free and Accepted Modem Masons Inc., principal. Rep: R.A. Lazar. Wash atty: Hogan & Hartson. ■ George Mathews, CEO & pres; Patricia Watson, gen sls mgr; Celestine Harris, prom mgr; Joe Spencer, progmg dir; Lucia Harvin, news dir; Albert Ruedemann, chief engr.

WJBK-TV—ch 2, 100 kw vis, 10 kw aur, ant 1,000t/1,057g. TL: N42 27 38 W83 12 47. Hrs opn: 24. On air date: Oct 24, 1948. Box 2000, 16550 W. Nine Mile Rd., Southfield (48037). (313) 557-2000. FAX: (313) 552-0280. Licensee: WJBK License Inc. Group owner: SCI Television Inc. (acq 2-19-93; grpsl; 4-26-93). ■ Net: CBS. Wash atty: Pepper & Corazzini. News staff 100; news progmg 27 hrs wkly. ■ Steve Antoniotti, pres & gen mgr; Spencer Koch, stn mgr & vp sls; Jeff Forster, opns dir & chief engr; Steve Schram, mktg dir; Carolyn Worford, progmg dir; Mort Meisner, news dir; Katy Baetz-Matthews, pub affrs dir. ■ On 27 CATVs—252,000 subs.

WKBD—ch 50, 2,340 kw vis, 209 kw aur, ant 960t/1,053g. TL: N42 29 01 W83 18 44. Stereo. On air date: Jan 10, 1965. Box 50, 26905 W. 11 Mile Rd., Southfield (48037-0050). (313) 350-5050. FAX: (313) 355-2692. Licensee: WKBD Inc. Group owner: Paramount Stations Group (acq 9-1-93; $105 million; 9-13-93). ■ Net: Fox. Rep: Telerep. ■ Duane G. Kell, vp & gen mgr; Bob Fitzgerald, opns dir; Ellen Bramson, gen sls mgr; Toby Cunningham, prom dir; Paul A. Prange, progmg dir; Helen Pasakarnis, news dir; Amyre Makupson, pub affrs dir; Gene Faukner, chief engr. ■ On 366 CATVs—642,000 subs.

***WTVS**—ch 56, 2,200 kw vis, 200 kw aur, ant 960t/1,049g. TL: N42 29 01 W83 18 44. Stereo. Hrs opn: 24. On air date: Oct 3, 1955. 7441 Second Blvd. (48202). (313) 873-7200. FAX: (313) 876-8118. Licensee: Detroit Educational Television Foundation. ■ Net: PBS; CEN. Wash atty: Schwartz, Woods & Miller. ■ Robert Larson, pres & gen mgr; Daniel Alpert, sr vp & stn mgr; Kamal A. Amenra, opns mgr; Daniel Krichbaum, vp dev; Catherine Anderson, vp mktg; Paula Sulinski, vp prom; Jerome K. Trainor, vp progmg; Clarence Abram, vp engrg. ■ On 81 CATVs—950,000 subs.

WXON—ch 20, 1,200 kw vis, 120 kw aur, ant 961t/1,051g. TL: N42 29 01 W83 18 44. Stereo. (CP: 2,190 kw vis, 219 kw aur, 971t/1,061g). On air date: Sept 15, 1968. Suite 1220, 27777 Franklin Rd., Southfield (48034). (313) 355-2020. FAX: (313) 355-0368. Licensee: WXON-TV Inc. Ownership: Aben E. Johnson Jr., 95%; Johnson Trust, 5% (acq 6-72; $233,952). Rep: TV Rep Inc. Wash atty: Arthur V. Belendiuk. ■ Mike Berman, vp & progmg dir; Doug Johnson, gen mgr; A.J. Schweizer, opns mgr; Jack Dabbah, gen sls mgr; Tracey Menczer, prom mgr; Melanie Johnson, news dir; Sharon McClendon, pub affrs dir; Gary King, chief engr. ■ On 65 CATVs.

WXYZ-TV—ch 7, 316 kw vis, 31.6 kw aur, ant 1,000t/1,073g. TL: N42 28 15 W83 15 00. Stereo. Hrs opn: 24. On air date: Oct 9, 1948. Box 789, 20777 W. 10 Mile Rd., Southfield (48037). (313) 827-7777. FAX: (313) 827-4454. Licensee: Channel 7 Detroit Inc. Group owner: Scripps Howard Broadcasting Co., see Cross-Ownership (acq 1-2-86; grpsl). ■ Net: ABC. Rep: Katz. Wash atty: Baker & Hostetler. ■ Thomas Griesdorn, vp & gen mgr; Grace Gilchrist, stn mgr; Bob Sliva, gen sls mgr; Gary Schlaff, mktg dir; Tom Polk, prom dir; Marla Drutz, progmg dir; Walter Kraft, news dir; Lewis C. Stokes, pub affrs dir; Michael Doback, chief engr. ■ On 128 CATVs—881,800 subs.

East Lansing

ADI No. 105; see Lansing market

***WKAR-TV**—ch 23, 1,100 kw vis, 219 kw aur, ant 975t/1,038g. TL: N42 42 08 W84 24 51. On air date: Jan 15, 1954. 212 Communication Arts Bldg. (48824-1212). (517) 355-2300. FAX: (517) 353-7124. Licensee: Michigan State Univ. ■ Net: PBS. Wash atty: Schwartz, Woods & Miller. ■ Steven K. Meuche, gen mgr; Doug Schrems, opns mgr; Jayne Marsh, dev dir; Eileen Tomber, mktg mgr; Jeanie Croope, prom mgr; Mary Jane Wilson, progmg dir & film buyer; Robert Albers, pub affrs dir; Gary Blievernicht, engrg dir. ■ On 56 CATVs—300,000 subs. Co-owned radio: WKAR-AM-FM.

Escanaba

ADI No. 175; see Marquette market

WJMN-TV—ch 3, 100 kw vis, 20 kw aur, ant 1,192t/1,048g. TL: N48 06 04 W86 56 52. On air date: Oct 7, 1969. Box 19055, 1181 E. Mason St., Green Bay, WI (54307). (906) 786-7767. FAX: (906) 786-9390. Licensee: WFRV TV Inc. Group owner: CBS Inc. ■ Net: CBS. Rep: Telerep. ■ R. Perry Kidder, vp & gen mgr; Alan Eaton, opns dir; Jackie Stewart, gen sls mgr; Gerald Jensen, news dir; Dan Ullmer, chief engr. Satellite of WFRV-TV Green Bay, WI.

Flint

ADI No. 60; see Flint-Saginaw-Bay City market

WEYI-TV—(Saginaw). ch 25, 2,035 kw vis, 203 kw aur, ant 1,320t/1,359g. TL: N43 13 01 W83 43 17. Hrs opn: 24. On air date: Apr 5, 1953. Box 250, 2225 W. Willard Rd., Clio (48420). (517) 755-0525; (313) 687-1000. FAX: (313) 687-4925. Licensee: WEYI Associates. Group owner: Television Station Partners (acq 3-24-83; grpsl; 2-7-83). ■ Net: CBS. Rep: Petry. Wash atty: Wiley, Rein & Fielding. News staff 11; news progmg 4 hrs wkly. ■ Eric S. Land, vp & gen mgr; Michael W. Collins, gen sls mgr; Don Weatherup, prom mgr; Jon Bengtson, progmg dir & film buyer; Terry Stanton, news dir; Jim Barnes, chief engr. ■ On 56 CATVs—232,984 subs. ■ Rates: $600; 300; 100.

***WFUM**—ch 28, 2,400 kw vis, 240 kw aur, ant 967t/929g. TL: N42 53 57 W83 27 42. Stereo. On air date: Aug 23, 1980. The Univ. of Michigan-Flint, 1321 E. Court St. (48503). (313) 762-3028. FAX: (313) 233-6017. Licensee: Board of Regents, Univ. of Michigan. ■ Net: PBS. Wash atty: Dow, Lohnes & Albertson. ■ Gordon A. Lawrence, gen mgr; Jim Gaver, stn mgr, prom mgr & progmg dir; Ray Miller, opns mgr; Carolyn Meldrum, dev dir; Wayne Henderson, chief engr. ■ On 43 CATVs—100,000 subs. Co-owned radio: *WFUM-FM.

WJRT-TV—ch 12, 316 kw vis, 31.6 kw aur, ant 940t/999g. TL: N43 13 48 W84 03 35. Hrs opn: 24. On air date: Oct 12, 1958. 2302 Lapeer Rd. (48503). (313) 233-3130. FAX: (313) 257-2834. Licensee: SJL of Michigan Corp. Group owner: Media-Communications Partners Ltd. (acq 4-28-92; 5-18-92). ■ Net: ABC. Rep: Katz. Wash atty: Latham & Watkins. News staff 30; news progmg 14 hrs wkly. ■ George Lilly, pres; Dave McCurdy, exec vp; Thomas Bryson, vp & gen mgr; Daniel C. Aube, gen sls mgr; Sara Jo Gallock, mktg dir & progmg dir; James Bleicher, news dir; Pam Schlosser, pub affrs dir; Skip Orvis, chief engr. ■ On 75 CATVs—250,000 subs.

WNEM-TV—(Bay City). ch 5, 100 kw vis, 20 kw aur, ant 1,029t/1,049g. TL: N43 28 13 W83 50 35. On air date: Feb 16, 1954. Box 531, 107 N. Franklin St., Saginaw (48606). (517) 755-8191. FAX: (517) 758-2110. Licensee: Meredith Corp. Group owner: Meredith Bcstg Group, Meredith Corp. See Cross-Ownership (acq 4-16-69; $11.5 million; 4-21-69). ■ Net: NBC. Rep: MMT Sales. Wash atty: Haley, Bader & Potts. ■ Paul Virciglio, vp & gen mgr; Peggy Madigan, gen sls mgr; Julie Zoumbaris, natl sls mgr; Michele Keilitz, prom mgr; Bill Avery, progmg mgr; Nelson Burg, news dir; Greg Surma, chief engr. ■ On 62 CATVs—225,319 subs.

WSMH—ch 66, 1,435.5 vis, 143.55 kw aur, ant 1,340t/1,284g. TL: N43 13 18 W84 03 14. Hrs opn: 24. On air date: Dec 15,1984. 2288 S. Ballenger Hwy. (48503). (313) 767-8866. FAX: (313) 767-2314. Licensee: Flint TV Inc. Group owner: R Group Communication (acq 5-1-86). ■ Net: Fox. Rep: Seltel. ■ G. J. Robinson, pres; Roger Baerwolf, gen mgr; Dave Wittkamp, vp opns; Steve Ruby, gen sls mgr; Ken Robinson, vp

Michigan

progmg; Fred Merle, pub affrs dir; John Grover, chief engr. ■ On 30 CATVs—150,000 subs.

Grand Rapids

ADI No. 37; see Grand Rapids-Kalamazoo-Battle Creek market

*WGVU-TV—ch 35, 1,000 kw vis, 100 kw aur, ant 857t/859g. TL: N42 57 35 W85 53 45. Stereo. Hrs opn: 20. On air date: Dec 17, 1972. 301 W. Fulton St. (49504-6492). (616) 771-6666. FAX: (616) 771-6625. Licensee: Board of Control, Grand Valley State Univ. ■ Net: PBS. Wash atty: Cohn & Marks. Foreign lang progmg 5 hrs wkly. News progmg 3 hrs wkly. ■ Paul Johnson, chmn; Ron Van Steeland, CFO; Michael T. Walenta, gen mgr; Gary DeSantis, dev mgr; Jan McKinnon, gen sls mgr; Kevin Frazier, prom mgr & pub affrs dir; Carrie Corbin, progmg mgr; David Moore, news dir; Bob Lumbert, engrg dir. ■ On 59 CATVs—319,052 subs. Co-owned radio: WGVU-FM.

WOOD-TV—ch 8, 316 kw vis, 31.6 kw aur, ant 991t. TL: N42 41 13 W85 30 35. Stereo. Hrs opn: 24. On air date: Aug 15, 1949. Box B (49501). (616) 456-8888. FAX: (616) 456-9169. Licensee: LCH Communications Inc. Group owner: LIN Broadcasting Corp. (acq 2-16-83; $32 million; 2-23-83). ■ Net: NBC. Rep: Blair. Wash atty: Covington & Burling. ■ Steve Caminis, pres & gen mgr; Dick McKay, gen sls mgr; Molly Kelly, prom mgr; Tom Richards, progmg dir; Colleen Pierson, pub affrs dir; Mike Laemers, engrg dir; Don Gallagher, chief engr. ■ On 42 CATVs—431,737 subs.

WXMI—ch 17, 1,300 kw vis, 130 kw aur, ant 802t/1,081g. TL: N42 41 15 W85 31 57. Hrs opn: 21. On air date: March 1982. 3117 Plaza Dr. N.E. (49505). (616) 364-8722. FAX: (616) 364-8506. Licensee: TV 17 Unlimited Inc. Group owner: Dudley Communications Corp. ■ Net: Fox. Rep: Petry. Wash atty: Wiley, Rein & Fielding. ■ John Dudley, pres; Patrick J. Mullen, vp & gen mgr; Pamela Swenk, opns dir; Ed Fernandez, sls dir; Pennie J. Westers, prom mgr; Mark Krause, progmg dir; Sarah Holland, pub affrs dir; Dale Scholten, chief engr. ■ On 56 CATVs—340,000 subs.

WZZM-TV—ch 13, 295 kw vis, 63 kw aur, ant 1,000t/991g. TL: N43 18 34 W85 54 44. Hrs opn: 24. On air date: Nov 1, 1962. Box Z (49501); 645 Three Mile Rd. N.W. (49504). (616) 785-1313. FAX: (616) 785-1301. Licensee: Northstar Television Group Inc. (group owner; acq 11-1-89; grpsl; 9-25-89). ■ Net: ABC. Rep: Katz. Wash atty: Haley, Bader & Potts. ■ Richard Appleton, pres; Al Forist, Robert Tepper, vps; Al Forist, opns dir & film buyer; Robert Tepper, dev dir; Buss Kunst, gen sls mgr; Tim Siegel, natl sls mgr; Ken Kolbe, news dir; Chuck Milkowski, chief engr. ■ On 57 CATVs—303,996 subs.

Iron Mountain

ADI No. 175; see Marquette market

WDHS—ch 8, 2 kw vis, 200 w aur, ant 508t. TL: N45 49 14 W88 02 39. On air date: September 1986. Box 2130, Kingford (49802). (906) 779-5213. Licensee: Danny Hood Evangelistic Association (acq 5-21-92). ■ Danny Hood, pres.

Kalamazoo

ADI No. 37; see Grand Rapids-Kalamazoo-Battle Creek market

*WGVK—ch 52, 44.7 kw vis, 4.47 kw aur, ant 410t/295g. TL: N42 18 24 W85 39 26. Stereo. Hrs opn: 18. On air date: Oct 1, 1984. 301 W. Fulton St., Grand Rapids (49504-6492). (616) 771-6666. FAX: (616) 771-6625. Licensee: Grand Valley State Univ. ■ Net: PBS. Wash atty: Cohn & Marks. News progmg one hr wkly. ■ Michael T. Walenta, Chuck Furman (asst), gen mgrs; Gary DeSantis, dev mgr; Jan McKinnon, gen sls mgr; Kevin Frazier, prom mgr; Carrie Corbin, progmg dir; David Moore, news dir; Robert Lumbert, engrg dir. ■ On 59 CATVs—825,000 subs. Co-owned radio: WGVU-AM-FM.

WLLA—ch 64, 2,510 kw vis, 251 kw aur, ant 1,000t/956g. TL: N42 34 15 W85 28 11. Hrs opn: 5 AM-1 AM. On air date: June 30, 1987. Box 3157 (49003); 7048 E. Kilgore Rd. (49001). (616) 345-6421. Licensee: Christian Faith Broadcasting Inc. (group owner; acq 1-13-86; $35,000; 12-9-85). Wash atty: Colby May. ■ Shelby Gillam, pres; Richard Hawkins, gen mgr & sls dir; Dan Behrmann, progmg dir; Rusty Yost, chief engr. ■ On 60 CATVs—275,000 subs. ■ Rates: $60; 40; 25.

WWMT—ch 3, 100 kw vis, 20 kw aur, ant 1,000t/1,130g. TL: N42 37 56 W85 32 16. On air date: June 1, 1950. 590 W. Maple St. (49008). (616) 388-3333. FAX: (616) 388-8322; (616) 388-6089. Licensee: Busse Broadcasting Corp. (group owner; acq 9-21-87). ■ Net: CBS. Wash atty: Pepper & Corazzini. ■ Lawrence A. Busse, pres & gen mgr; Gil Buettner, stn mgr; Rob Gray, opns mgr; Christopher Cornelius, gen sls mgr; David Comisar, prom mgr & progmg dir; Michael Rindo, news dir; Nancy Bruce, pub affrs dir; James Steffey, chief engr. ■ On 65 CATVs.

Lansing

ADI No. 105; see Lansing market

WILX-TV—See Onondaga.

WLAJ—ch 53, 1,660 kw vis, 166 kw aur, ant 976t/1,009g. TL: N42 25 11 W84 31 26. Stereo. (CP: 3,320 kw vis, 332 kw aur, ant 981t/1,014g) Hrs opn: 24. On air date: Oct 13, 1990. Box 27307, 5815 S. Pennsylvania Ave. (48909-7307). (517) 394-5300. FAX: (517) 887-0077. Licensee: Lansing 53 Inc. ■ Net: ABC. Rep: Katz. ■ Joel Ferguson, pres; Tom Jones, gen mgr; Sheldon Lewis, opns mgr; Jon Harpst, gen sls mgr; Yolanda Gary, prom mgr; John Jones, progmg mgr; Dori Ferguson, pub affrs dir; Larry Estlack, chief engr. ■ On 30 CATVs—181,000 subs.

WLNS-TV—ch 6, 100 kw vis, 20 kw aur, ant 1,000t/1,023g. TL: N42 41 14 W84 22 35. On air date: May 1, 1950. 2820 E. Saginaw (48912). (517) 372-8282. FAX: (517) 374-7610. TWX: 810-241-0805. Licensee: Young Broadcasting Inc. (group owner; acq 9-15-86; $72 million; 4-14-86). ■ Net: CBS. Wash atty: Wiley, Rein & Fielding. ■ Ronald J. Kwasnick, pres; Ross P. Woodstock, vp & gen mgr; Dan Batchelder, gen sls mgr; Kim Westmoreland, natl sls mgr; Marvin Holt, prom mgr; Teresa Morton, progmg dir; Michael Kent, news dir; Robert Harrison, chief engr. ■ On 65 CATVs—240,000 subs. ■ Rates: $1,050; 150; 250.

WSYM-TV—ch 47, 1,350 kw vis, 135 kw aur, ant 1,000t/1,036g. TL: N42 28 03 W84 39 06. Hrs opn: 22. On air date: Dec 1, 1982. Suite 47, 600 W. St. Joseph St. (48933). (517) 484-7747. FAX: (517) 484-3144. Licensee: WTMJ Inc. (group owner; acq 11-9-85; $8.25 million; 12-3-84). ■ Net: Fox. Rep: Petry. Wash atty: Crowell & Moring. ■ Steve Smith, pres; Douglas Kiel, exec vp; Judy Kenney, vp & gen mgr; William Shipley, opns mgr; Thom Lilly, natl sls mgr; Jeff Cartwright (loc), rgnl sls mgr; Bill Shipley, prom mgr, progmg dir, film buyer & pub affrs dir; Bill Tessman, chief engr. ■ On 55 CATVs—180,000 subs.

Manistee

ADI No. 121; see Traverse City-Cadillac market

*WCMW—ch 21, 224.4 kw vis, 22.44 kw aur, ant 340t/298g. TL: N44 03 57 W86 19 58. On air date: Sept 7, 1984. Central Michigan Univ., 3965 E. Broomfield Rd., Mt. Pleasant (48859). (517) 774-3105. FAX: (517) 774-4427. Licensee: Central Michigan University. ■ Net: PBS. Wash atty: Dow, Lohnes & Albertson. ■ William J. Grigaliunas, gen mgr. Satellite of WCMU-TV Mt. Pleasant.

Marquette

ADI No. 175; see Marquette market

WJMY—ch 19, 1,000 kw vis, 100 kw aur, ant 3,414t. TL: N46 21 56 W87 49 34. Not on air, target date unknown. c/o James C. Tomlin, 153 Detrie Dr., Green Bay, WI (54301). (414) 337-9900. Permittee: Upper Peninsula Telecasting Corp. Ownership: James L. Tomlin, 100%. ■ James L. Tomlin, pres.

WLUC-TV—ch 6, 100 kw vis, 20 kw aur, ant 978t/1,018g. TL: N46 20 11 W87 50 55. Hrs opn: 20. On air date: Apr 29, 1956. 177 U.S. Hwy.41, Negaunee (49866). (906) 475-4161; (906) 475-414 (News). FAX: (906) 475-4824; (906) 475-5070 (News). Licensee: Federal Broadcasting Co. (group owner; 9-18-87; grpsl). ■ Net: ABC, NBC. Rep: Katz. Wash atty: Hogan & Hartson. Finnish one hr wkly. News staff 16; news progmg 9 hrs wkly ■ Brad Van Sluyters, vp & gen mgr; Ed Kearney, opns mgr; Dan Diloreto, natl sls dir; Kim Parker, mktg dir & progmg dir; Chris Brooks, adv dir; Steve Asplund, news dir; Grant Guston, pub affrs dir; John Truitt, chief engr. ■ On 34 CATVs—75,000 subs. On 3 trans.

*WNMU-TV—ch 13, 316 kw vis, 63.1 kw aur, ant 1,090t/1,000g. TL: N46 21 09 W87 51 32. Stereo. On air date: Dec 28, 1972. Northern Michigan Univ. (49855). (906) 227-1300. FAX: (906) 227-2905. Licensee: Board of Control of Northern Michigan Univ. ■ Net: PBS. Wash atty: Cohn & Marks. News progmg one hr wkly. ■ Scott K. Seaman, gen mgr; Bruce S. Turner, stn mgr & progmg dir; Eric Smith, opns mgr; Darcia Mattson, dev mgr; April Lindala, prom mgr; Earl Littich, chief engr. ■ On 28 CATVs—170,000 subs. Co-owned radio: WNMU-FM.

Mount Clemens

ADI No. 9; see Detroit market

WADL—ch 38, 1,243 kw vis, 248 kw aur, ant 630t. TL: N42 33 15 W82 53 15. On air date: May 20, 1989. 22590 15 Mile Rd., Clinton Twp. (48035-2841). (313) 790-3838. FAX: (313) 790-3841. Licensee: Adell Broadcasting Corp. ■ Franklin Z. Adell, pres & gen mgr; Jim Panagos, gen sls mgr & progmg dir; John Grover, chief engr.

Mount Pleasant

ADI No. 60; see Flint-Saginaw-Bay City market

*WCMU-TV—ch 14, 200 kw vis, 40 kw aur, ant 520t/547g. TL: N43 34 24 W84 46 21. Hrs opn: 6 AM-midnight. On air date: Mar 29, 1967. Central Michigan Univ., 3965 E. Broomfield Rd. (48859). (517) 774-3105. FAX: (517) 774-4427. Licensee: Central Mich. U. ■ Net: PBS. Wash atty: Dow, Lohnes & Albertson. ■ William J. Grigaliunas, gen mgr; Monte Higgins, stn mgr; Linda Hyde, prom mgr; Rick Schudiske, progmg dir; Randy Kapenga, chief engr. ■ On 6 CATVs—31,975 subs. Co-owned radio: *WCMU-FM.

Muskegon

ADI No. 37; see Grand Rapids-Kalamazoo-Battle Creek market

WTLJ—ch 54, 4,395 kw vis, 440 kw aur, ant 1,000t/989g. TL: N42 57 25 W85 54 07. Hrs opn: 24. On air date: Nov 1, 1986. 10290 48th Ave., Allendale (49401). (616) 895-4154. FAX: (616) 892-4401. Licensee: Tri-State Christian TV Inc. (acq 1-15-92; $1.5 million; 2-10-92). ■ Garth W. Coonce, pres; Herb Smith, stn mgr; Steve Winter, pub affrs dir; Frank Ayre, chief engr. ■ On 14 CATVs—275,000 subs. ■ Rates: $60; 60; 60.

Onondaga

ADI No. 105; see Lansing market

WILX-TV—ch 10, 309 kw vis, 61.7 kw aur, ant 970t/983g. TL: N42 39 W84 34 21. Stereo. On air date: Mar 15, 1959. Box 30380, Lansing (48909); 500 American Rd., Lansing (48911). (517) 783-2621; (517) 393-0110. FAX: (517) 787-9744. Licensee: Brissette TV of Lansing Inc. (group owner; acq 12-24-91; grpsl). ■ Net: NBC. Rep: Blair. ■ Grant Santimore, pres & gen mgr; David Weems, gen sls mgr; Pat Gorsman, prom mgr; Paul Brissette, film buyer; Tim Staudt, news dir; Ray Schiferilli, pub affrs dir; Bill Hineman, chief engr. ■ On 7 CATVs—15,000 subs.

Saginaw

ADI No. 60; see Flint-Saginaw-Bay City market

WAQP—ch 49, 1,000 kw vis, 100 kw aur, ant 1,023t/1,049g. TL: N43 13 18 W84 03 14. Hrs opn: 24. On air date: Mar 26, 1985. Box 2215 (48605); 707 Federal Ave. (48607). (517) 754-1038. FAX: (517) 754-8668. Licensee: Tri-State Christian TV (group owner). Wash atty: May & Dunne. ■ Garth W. Coonce, pres; Michael Socier, stn mgr & rgnl sls mgr; Annette Cames, pub affrs dir; Ronald L. Booth, chief engr. ■ On 39 CATVs—194,020 subs. On 2 trans.

WEYI-TV—Licensed to Saginaw. See Flint.

WNEM-TV—See Flint.

Sault Ste. Marie

ADI No. 121; see Traverse City-Cadillac market

WGTQ—ch 8, 316 kw vis, 163.6 kw aur, ant 978t/864g. TL: N46 03 06 W84 06 40. On air date: Nov 3, 1976. 300 Court St. (49783). (616) 946-2900. FAX: (616) 946-1600. Licensee: Scanlan Communications Inc. (acq 9-25-89). ■ Net: ABC. Rep: Seltel. ■ Thomas Scanlan, pres; Jerry Moore, vp & gen mgr; Linda Garlitz, rgnl sls mgr; Dennis Bernard, chief engr. ■ On 33 CATVs—75,000 subs. Satellite of WGTU(TV) Traverse City. ■ Rates: $500; 150; 75.

WWUP-TV—ch 10, 316 kw vis, 31.6 kw aur, ant 1,214t/1,130g. TL: N46 03 49 W84 06 08. On air date: June 15, 1962. Box 627, Cadillac (49601). (616) 775-3478. FAX: (616) 775-3671. Licensee: Heritage Broadcasting Co. of Michigan. Ownership: Mario F. Iacobelli (acq 3-3-89; grpsl; 3-20-89). ■ Net: CBS. Rep: Seltel.

Wash atty: Leventhal, Senter & Lerman. ■ Mario Iacobelli, pres; Woody Webb, gen mgr & film buyer; Frank Brady, gen sls mgr; Jackie McKinley, progmg dir; Robert Young, news dir; Lowell Shore, chief engr. ■ On 55 CATVs—169,313 subs.

Traverse City

ADI No. 121; see Traverse City-Cadillac market

WGTU—ch 29, 1,000 kw vis, 200 kw aur, ant 1,304t/1,242g. TL: N44 44 54 W85 04 08. (CP: 2,000 kw vis, ant 1,309t/1,252g). Hrs opn: 20. On air date: Aug 23, 1971. 201 E. Front St. (49684). (616) 946-2900. FAX: (616) 946-1600. Licensee: Scanlan Communications Inc. ■ Net: ABC. Rep: Seltel. Wash atty: Koteen & Naftalin. ■ Tom Scanlan, pres & gen sls mgr; Jerry K. Moore, vp, gen mgr & film buyer; Mike Sherman, opns dir; Jan Dickman, rgnl sls mgr; Nancy Sundstrom, prom mgr & progmg dir; Ron Stark, chief engr. ■ On 60 CATVs—95,000 subs. ■ Rates: $500; 200; 60.

WPBN-TV—ch 7, 316 kw vis, 63.2 kw aur, ant 1,348t/1,130g. TL: N44 16 33 W85 42 49. Hrs opn: 24. On air date: Sept 13, 1954. Box 546, M-72 W. (49684). (616) 947-7770; (616) 946-2504. FAX: (616) 947-0354. Licensee: Federal Broadcasting Co. (group owner; acq 1990). ■ Net: NBC. Rep: Katz. Wash atty: Hogan & Hartson. ■ Dale Rands, CEO; Peter Kizer, pres; Jim Kizer, exec vp; Greg Wittland, gen mgr & progmg dir; Linda Kimbel, gen sls mgr; Michele Brown, prom mgr; Mike Conway, news dir; Curt Morgan, chief engr. ■ On 86 CATVs—110,300 subs.

WWTV—See Cadillac.

University Center

ADI No. 60; see Flint-Saginaw-Bay City market

*WUCM-TV—ch 19, 1,290 kw vis, 129 kw aur, ant 459t/493g. TL: N43 33 43 W85 58 54. Stereo. On air date: Oct 12, 1964. Delta Rd. (48710). (517) 686-9350. Licensee: Delta College. ■ Net: PBS. Wash atty: Cohn & Marks. ■ Donald J. Carlyon, pres; Presley D. Holmes, gen mgr; Thomas E. Haskell, progmg dir; Harold J. Conley, chief engr. ■ On 9 CATVs—56,000 subs.

Vanderbilt

ADI No. 121; see Traverse City-Cadillac market

WGKU—ch 45, 76.56 kw vis, ant 951t, 499 g. TL: N45 10 12 W84 45 04. Stereo. Hrs opn: 24. On air date: Sept 24, 1992. 7400 S. 45 Rd., Cadillac (49601). (616) 775-9813; (616) 775-0330. FAX: (616) 775-1898. Licensee: GRK Productions Joint Venture (group owner). ■ Net: Fox. Rep: Roslin. Wash atty: Reddy, Begley & Martin. ■ Gary Knapp, CEO & gen mgr; Julie Brinks, opns dir & mktg dir; Dawna Marie, gen sls mgr & adv mgr; Joyce Bassett, progmg dir; Tammy Knapp, pub affrs dir; Dan Somes, engrg dir; Glen Walker, chief engr. ■ On 47 CATVs—153,000 subs. On one trans. ■ Rates: $300; 100; 35.

Minnesota

Alexandria

ADI No. 14; see Minneapolis-St. Paul market

KCCO-TV—ch 7, 316 kw vis, 63.1 kw aur, ant 1,120t/1,133g. TL: N45 41 03 W95 08 14. On air date: Oct 8, 1958. 720 Hawthorne St. (56308). (612) 763-5166. FAX: (612) 763-4991. Licensee: KCCO Television Inc. Group owner: Midwest Communications Inc. ■ Net: CBS. Rep: Telerep. Wash atty: Rosenman & Colin. ■ Ken Rees, stn mgr; John Ginther, gen sls mgr; Raelin Storey, news dir; Wayne Quernemoen, chief engr. ■ On 101 CATVs—56,800 subs.

KSAX—ch 42, 2,770 kw vis, 277 kw aur, ant 1,176t/1,164g. TL: N45 41 59 W95 10 36. On air date: Sept 15, 1987. Box 189, 415 Fillmore Ave. (56308). (612) 763-5729. FAX: (612) 763-4627. Licensee: KSAX-TV Inc. Group owner: Hubbard Broadcasting Inc. ■ Net: ABC. Rep: Petry. Wash atty: Fletcher, Heald & Hildreth. ■Harold Crump, pres; Robert Hubbard, vp; Michael Burgess, gen mgr; Susan Anderson, stn mgr; Donna Corle, opns mgr; Mark Vanderwerf, news dir; Joe Yarnott, chief engr. ■ On 80 CATVs. On 9 trans.

Appleton

ADI No. 14; see Minneapolis-St. Paul market

*KWCM-TV—ch 10, 316 kw vis, 37.1 kw aur, ant 1,250t/1,274g. TL: N45 10 03 W96 00 02. Hrs opn: 18. On air date: Feb 7, 1966. 120 W. Schlieman (56208). (612) 289-2622. FAX: (612) 289-2634. Licensee: West Central Minnesota Educational TV Co. Ownership: Phil Greseth (acq 1993; 9-20-93). ■ Net: PBS. Wash atty: Reddy, Begley & Martin. ■ Gail Nelson, pres; Ansel Doll, gen mgr; Judith Pfaff, stn mgr & adv dir; Dale Lien, progmg dir; Arlan Raasch, chief engr. ■ On 30 CATVs—48,000 subs. On 2 trans.

Austin

ADI No. 148; see Rochester-Mason City-Austin market

KAAL—ch 6, 100 kw vis, 10 kw aur, ant 1,049t/1,000g. TL: N43 37 42 W93 09 12. On air date: Aug 17, 1953. Box 577 1701 10th Pl. N.E. (55912). (507) 437-6666. TWX: 910-565-2104. Licensee: MDM Corp. Group owner: Dix Communications (acq 12-85). ■ Net: ABC. Rep: Blair. Wash atty: Baker & Hostetler. News staff 18; news progmg 9 hrs wkly. ■ Clark Cipra, pres, gen mgr & progmg dir; John Ginther, gen sls mgr; Angela Kucharski, news dir; Jerald Jones, chief engr. ■ On 42 CATVs—95,000 subs. On one trans.

*KSMQ-TV—ch 15, 1,215.24 kw vis, 121.8 kw aur, ant 380t/448g. TL: N43 40 34 W93 00 09. On air date: Oct 17, 1972. 2000 8th Ave. N. (55912). (507) 433-0678. FAX: (507) 433-0670. Licensee: Independent School District 492. ■ Net: PBS; CEN. Wash atty: Cohn & Marks. ■ Barry G. Baker, gen mgr; Debbie Britton, opns mgr; Mary Banninga, dev dir; Dani Heiny, prom mgr; Mark Goddard, progmg dir; John Wilcox, chief engr. ■ On 30 CATVs—54,500 subs.

Bemidji

ADI No. 14; see Minneapolis-St. Paul market

*KAWE—ch 9, 316 kw vis, 31.6 kw aur, ant 1,080t/1,000g. TL: N47 42 03 W94 29 15. Stereo. Hrs opn: 18. On air date: June 1, 1980. Box 9, BSU, 1400 Birchmont Dr. (56601). (218) 751-3407. FAX: (218) 751-3142. Licensee: Northern Minnesota Public TV Inc. ■ Net: PBS. Wash atty: Dow, Lohnes & Albertson. ■ Randall Burl, pres; Emily Lahti, gen mgr; Mike Smith, opns mgr; Jeanne Sanford, dev dir; Ron Johnson, prom mgr; Mark Brewer, progmg mgr; Bill Sanford, chief engr.

Brainerd

ADI No. 14; see Minneapolis-St. Paul market

*KAWB—ch 22, 214 kw vis, ant 745t. TL: N46 25 21 W94 27 41. Hrs opn: 5:45 AM-12:30 AM. On air date: Mar 1, 1988. Box 9, BSU, 1400 Birchmont Dr., Bemidji (56601). (218) 751-3407. FAX: (218) 751-3142. Licensee: Northern Minnesota Public TV Inc. ■ Net: PBS. Wash atty: Dow, Lohnes & Albertson. ■ Randall Burg, pres; Emily Lahti, stn mgr; Mike Smith, opns mgr; Jeanne Sanford, dev dir; Ron Johnson, prom mgr; Mark Brewer, progmg mgr; Bill Sanford, chief engr.

Duluth

ADI No. 126; Duluth-Superior market

KBJR-TV—(Superior, WI). ch 6, 100 kw vis, 20 kw aur, ant 1,010t/804g. TL: N46 47 21 W92 06 51. On air date: Mar 11, 1954. 230 E. Superior Street, Duluth, MN (55802). (218) 727-8484. FAX: (218) 727-1737; TWX: 910-561-2490. Licensee: RJR Communications Inc. Group owner: Granite Broadcasting Corp. (acq 11-1-88; $12.8 million; 9-23-74). ■ Net: NBC. Rep: Katz. Wash atty: Akin, Gump, Strauss, Hauer & Feld. News staff 21; news progmg 10 hrs wkly. ■ Maria A. Moore, pres & gen mgr; Robert J. Wilmers, stn mgr & engrg dir; Carl Keller, gen sls mgr; Todd Wentworth, rgnl sls mgr; Steve Eberhart, mktg mgr; Barbara Tollefson, progmg dir; David Jensch, news dir; Mary Dippel, pub affrs dir. ■ On 54 CATVs—85,000 subs. On 14 trans. ■ Rates: $500; 50; 37.

KDLH—ch 3, 100 kw vis, 20 kw aur, ant 990t/816g. TL: N46 47 07 W92 07 15. On air date: Mar 14, 1954. 425 W. Superior St. (55802). (218) 727-8911. FAX: (218) 727-7515. Licensee: Blue Grass Television Inc. Group owner: Benedek Broadcasting Co. (acq 7-12-85; $9.5 million; 6-10-85). ■ Net: CBS. Rep: Blair. Wash atty: Crowell & Moring. ■ Bruce R. Miller, vp, progmg dir & film buyer; Craig Spellerberg, opns dir; Walt Ledingham, gen sls mgr; Doug Karsko, prom mgr; Terry Bynum, news dir; John Talcott, chief engr. ■ On 32 CATVs. On 23 trans.

KRBR—ch 21, 955 kw vis, ant 590 ft. TL: N46 47 41 W92 07 05. Not on air, target date unknown. 1012 Third St., Altoona, PA (16601). Permittee: Robin C. Brandt.

WDIO-TV—ch 10, 316 kw vis, 105 kw aur, ant 987t/836g. TL: N46 47 19 W92 07 17. Hrs opn: 21. On air date: Jan 24, 1966. Box 16897 (55811-0897); 10 Observation Rd. (55811). (218) 727-6864. FAX: (218) 727-4415. Licensee: Hubbard Broadcasting Inc. (group owner; acq 12-87; grpsl). ■ Net: ABC. Rep: Petry. Wash atty: Fletcher, Heald & Hildreth. News staff 18; news progmg 9 hrs wkly. ■ George Couture, vp & gen mgr; Joe Golden, gen sls mgr; Jeff Laundergan, prom mgr; David Poirier, progmg dir; Joel Anderson, news dir; George Woody, chief engr. ■ On 20 CATVs—30,000 subs. On 10 trans.

*WDSE-TV—ch 8, 316 kw vis, 31.6 kw, aur, ant 950t/788g. TL: N46 47 31 W92 07 21. Stereo. On air date: Sept 1, 1964. 1202 E. University Cir. (55811). (218) 724-8567. Licensee: Duluth-Superior Area Educ TV Corp. ■ Net: PBS. Wash atty: Arent, Fox, Kintner, Plotkin & Kahn. ■ Mark Johnson, pres; George C. Jauss, gen mgr; Ronald Anderson, prom mgr, progmg dir & film buyer; Rex Greenwell, chief engr. ■ On 20 CATVs. On 3 trans.

Hibbing

ADI No. 126; see Duluth-Superior market

WIRT—ch 13, 125 kw vis, 21.6 kw aur, ant 670t/476g. TL: N47 22 52 W92 57 18. On air date: Sept 1, 1967. 10 Observation Rd., Duluth (55811). (218) 727-6864. FAX: (218) 727-4415. Licensee: WDIO-TV Inc. Group owner: Hubbard Broadcasting Inc. (acq 12-87; grpsl). ■ Net: ABC. ■ George Couture, gen mgr. Satellite of WDIO-TV Duluth.

Mankato

ADI No. 206; see Mankato market

KEYC-TV—ch 12, 316 kw vis, 63 kw aur, ant 1,045t/1,116g. TL: N43 56 14 W94 24 41. Stereo. Hrs opn: 6 AM-1 AM. On air date: Oct 5, 1960. 1570 Lookout Dr., North Mankato (56003); Box 128 (56002). (507) 625-7905. FAX: (507) 625-5745. Licensee: United Communications Corp. (group owner; acq 10-14-77; $5 million). ■ Net: CBS. Rep: Katz. Wash atty: Jones, Waldo, Holbrook & McDonough. News staff 11; news progmg 9 hrs wkly. ■ Dennis M. Wahlstrom, vp, gen mgr & natl sls mgr; Sharon Freitag, opns mgr; Bob Matson, rgnl sls mgr; Elaine Peterson, prom mgr & progmg dir; Dan Lemke, news dir; David Hooge, chief engr. ■ On 150 CATVs—133,800 subs. On one trans. ■ Rates: $600; 100; 90.

Minneapolis

KARE—Licensed to Minneapolis. See Minneapolis-St. Paul.

KITN-TV—Licensed to Minneapolis. See Minneapolis-St. Paul.

KLGT-TV—Licensed to Minneapolis. See Minneapolis-St. Paul.

KMSP-TV—Licensed to Minneapolis. See Minneapolis-St. Paul.

KVBM-TV—Licensed to Minneapolis. See Minneapolis-St. Paul.

WCCO-TV—Licensed to Minneapolis. See Minneapolis-St. Paul.

Minneapolis-St. Paul

ADI No. 14; see Minneapolis-St. Paul market

KARE—(Minneapolis). ch 11, 316 kw vis, 31.6 kw aur, ant 1,440t/1,375g. TL: N45 03 44 W93 08 21. Stereo. On air date: Sept 1, 1953. 8811 Olson Memorial Hwy, Minneapolis (55427). (612) 546-1111; (612) 541-8061. FAX: (612) 546-8590. Licensee: Combined Communications Corp. Group owner: Gannett Broadcasting (division of Gannett Co. Inc.) (acq 4-13-83; $75 million; 5-7-83). ■ Net: NBC. Rep: Blair. Wash atty: Pierson, Ball & Dowd. ■ Henry "Hank" Price, pres & gen mgr; John Remes, vp sls & gen sls mgr; Jerry Ness, natl sls mgr; Nan Diley, rgnl sls mgr; Susan Adams Loyd, mktg dir; Mark DeSantis, vp prom & vp progmg; Janet Mason, news dir; Kathryn Bardins (vp), pub affrs dir; Mike Pamme, chief engr. ■ On 6 trans.

KITN-TV—(Minneapolis). ch 29, 5,000 kw vis, 500 kw aur, ant 1,223t/1,205g. TL: N45 03 30 W93 07 27. Stereo.

Mississippi   Directory of Television

On air date: October 1982. 7325 Aspen Ln. N., Minneapolis (55428). (612) 424-2929. FAX: (612) 424-2649. Licensee: Nationwide Communications Inc. (group owner; acq 10-3-93; $36 million; 10-25-93). ■ Net. Fox. Rep: MMT. Wash atty: Wiley, Rein & Fielding. ■ Rip Riordan, exec vp; Mael Hernandez, dev mgr; Andrew Comegys, gen sls mgr; Mary O'Neill, prom mgr; Julie O'Neil, progmg dir; Ann Latia, pub affrs dir; Don Kirby, chief engr.

KLGT-TV—(Minneapolis). ch 23, 1,740 kw vis, 174 kw aur, ant 1,150t/1,450g. TL: N45 03 30 W93 07 27. Stereo. Hrs opn: 24. On air date: Sept 22, 1982. 1640 Como Ave., St. Paul (55108). (612) 646-2300. FAX: (612) 646-1220. Licensee: Sonlight Television Inc. Ownership: Robert Beale (50%) and Linda R. Brook (acq 3-92; 12-9-91). Rep: Roslin. Wash atty: Fisher, Wayland, Cooper & Leader. ■ Linda Rios Brook, pres, gen mgr & progmg dir; Dave Petersen, gen sls mgr; Larry Brook, vp mktg & vp adv; Wendy Kocon, prom dir; Barb Schultz, pub affrs dir; Steven Lunde, chief engr. ■ On 54 CATVs—634,000 subs. On 2 trans. ■ Rates: $250; 200; 75.

KMSP-TV—(Minneapolis). ch 9, 316 kw vis, 31.6 kw aur, ant 1,427t/1,430g. TL: N44 51 32 W93 25 09. Hrs opn: 24. On air date: Jan 9, 1955. 11358 Viking Dr., Eden Prairie (55344-7258). (612) 944-9999. FAX: (612) 942-0286. Licensee: United TV Inc. (group owner; acq 10-21-59; $4.1 million; 11-9-59). Rep: Katz. Wash atty: Wilmer, Cutler & Pickering. News staff 29; news progmg 7 hrs wkly. ■ Evan C. Thompson, pres; Stuart Z. Swartz, vp, gen mgr & film buyer; Stephanie Peterson, gen sls mgr; Gene Steinberg (creative svs), progmg dir; Penny Parrish, news dir; D. G. Arvidson, chief engr. ■ On 178 CATVs—611,599 subs. On 10 trans.

KSTP-TV—(St. Paul). ch 5, 100 kw vis, 15.1 kw aur, ant 1,430t/1,375g. TL: N45 03 45 W93 08 22. On air date: Apr 23, 1948. 3415 University Ave., St. Paul (55114). (612) 646-5555. FAX: (612) 642-4172. Licensee: Hubbard Broadcasting Inc. (group owner). ■ Net: ABC. Rep: Petry. Wash atty: Fletcher, Heald & Hildreth. ■ Stanley S. Hubbard, chmn; Harold C. Crump, pres; Larry Shrum, vp; Harold C. Crump, Larry Shrum (asst) gen mgrs; Karl Gensheimer, vp sls; Dayna Deutsch, pub affrs dir; Joe Taylor, chief engr. ■ On 205 CATVs—435,240 subs. On 15 trans. Co-owned radio: KSTP-AM-FM.

*****KTCA-TV**—(St. Paul). ch 2, 100 kw vis, 20 kw aur, ant 1,336t/1,372g. TL: N45 03 30 W93 07 27. On air date: Sept 3, 1957. 172 E. 4th St., St. Paul (55101). (612) 222-1717. FAX: (612) 229-1282. Licensee: Twin Cities Public TV Inc. ■ Net: PBS. ■ Richard O. Moore, pres & gen mgr; Jerry Huiting, opns mgr; James Kutzner, chief engr. ■ On 61 CATVs—138,000 subs. On 7 trans.

*****KTCI-TV**—(St. Paul). ch 17, 331 kw vis, 33.1 kw aur, ant 1,298t/1,471g. TL: N45 03 29 W93 07 27. On air date: May 3, 1965. 172 E. 4th St., St. Paul (55101). (612) 222-1717. FAX: (612) 229-1282. Licensee: Twin Cities Public TV Inc. ■ Net: PBS. ■ Richard O. Moore, pres & gen mgr; James Kutzner, chief engr.

KVBM-TV—(Minneapolis). ch 45, 5,000 kw vis, 500 kw aur, ant 627t. TL: N44 59 02 W93 12 13. Not on air, target date April 1994. Box 75100, St. Paul (55175). (612) 723-7625. Licensee: KVBM Television Inc. Ownership: Daniel Peters. ■ Daniel Peters, pres.

WCCO-TV—(Minneapolis). ch 4, 100 kw vis, 10 kw aur, ant 1,430t/1,375g. TL: N45 03 45 W93 08 21. Stereo. On air date: July 1, 1949. 90 S. 11th St., Minneapolis (55403). (612) 339-4444. FAX: (612) 330-2603. Licensee: WCCO Television Inc. Group owner: CBS Inc. (acq 7-12-76; grpsl; 7-26-76). ■ Net: CBS. Rep: CBS Spot Sales. ■ John Culliton, gen mgr; Ken Rees, stn mgr; Greg Keck, opns dir; Bill Bradley, sls dir; Kevin Cuddihy, gen sls mgr; Dave Baker, natl sls mgr; Lori Fink, progmg dir; John Lansing, news dir; Debbie Berg, pub affrs dir; Skip Erickson, engrg dir. ■ On 7 CATVs—289,000 subs. Co-owned radio: WCCO-AM. ■ Rates: $5,000; 1,000; 500.

Moorhead

KVRR—See Fargo, N.D.

Redwood Falls

ADI No. 14; see Minneapolis-St. Paul market

KRWF—ch 43, 1,230 kw vis, 123 kw aur, ant 548t/536g. TL: N44 29 03 W95 29 27. Hrs opn: 24. On air date: Apr 14, 1987. Box 189, 415 Filmore, Alexandria (56308). (612) 763-5729. Licensee: KSAX-TV Inc. Group owner: Hubbard Broadcasting Inc. ■ Net: ABC. Rep: Petry. Wash atty: Fletcher, Heald & Hildreth. ■ Robert Hubbard, pres; Susan Anderson, stn mgr; Donna Corle, chief opns; Mark Vanderwerf, news dir. ■ On 100 CATVs. On 9 trans.

Rochester

ADI No. 148; see Rochester-Mason City-Austin market

KTTC—ch 10, 316 kw vis, 46.8 kw aur, ant 1,260t/1,314g. TL: N43 34 15 W92 25 37. Stereo. On air date: July 16, 1953. 601 First Ave. S.W. (55902). (507) 288-4444. FAX: (507) 288-6324; (507) 288-6278 (News). Licensee: KTTC TV Inc. Ownership: Quincy Newspapers Inc. (acq 7-1-76; $4.25 million; 5-24-76). ■ Net: NBC. Rep: Petry. Wash atty: Wilkinson, Barker, Knauer & Quinn. News staff 15; news progmg 7 hrs wkly. ■ Jerry Watson, gen mgr; Ron Gruber, opns mgr, prom mgr & progmg dir; Elizabeth Dahlen, gen sls mgr; Gene Carlson, news dir; Bonnie Bickel, pub affrs dir; Bud Sanders, chief engr. ■ On 115 CATVs—123,353 subs. On 4 trans. ■ Rates: $1,500; 150; 65.

KXLT-TV—ch 47, 107.2 kw vis, 10.72 kw aur, ant 340t/274g. TL: N44 02 39 W92 23 56. Hrs opn: 24. On air date: March 1985. Box 407, 22727 176th St., Big Lake (55309). (612) 263-8666. FAX: (612) 263-6600. Licensee: KX Acquisition L.P. (group owner; acq 3-90; grpsl). Wash atty: Mullin, Rhyne, Emmons & Topel. ■ Dale W. Lang, pres; Ron Eikens, gen mgr; Mariana Reid, stn mgr; Rebecca Mix, progmg mgr; Tim Morgan, chief engr. ■ On 5 CATVs—36,533 subs. Satellite of KXLI St. Cloud.

St. Cloud

ADI No. 14; see Minneapolis-St. Paul market

KXLI—ch 41, 2,750 kw vis, 275 kw aur, ant 1,469t/1,498g. TL: N45 23 00 W93 42 30. Hrs opn: 24. On air date: Nov 24, 1982. Box 407, 22727 176th Street, Big Lake (55309). (612) 263-8666. FAX: (612) 263-6600. Licensee: KX Acquisition L.P. (group owner; acq 3-90; grpsl). Wash atty: Mullin, Rhyne, Emmons & Topel. ■ Dale W. Lang, pres; Ron Eikens, gen mgr; Mariana Reid, stn mgr; Denton Strohschein, chief opns; Rebecca Mix, progmg mgr; Tim Morgan, chief engr. ■ On 52 CATVS—463,500 subs.

St. Paul

KSTP-TV—Licensed to St. Paul. See Minneapolis-St. Paul.

*****KTCA-TV**—Licensed to St. Paul. See Minneapolis-St. Paul.

*****KTCI-TV**—Licensed to St. Paul. See Minneapolis-St. Paul.

Thief River Falls

ADI No. 109; see Fargo market

KBRR—ch 10, 158 kw vis, 15.8 kw aur, ant 600t/478g. TL: N48 01 19 W96 22 12. Stereo. On air date: July 1985. Box 9115, 4015 9th Ave. S.W., Fargo, ND (58106). (701) 277-1515. FAX: (701) 277-1830. Licensee: Red River Broadcast Corp. Group owner: Red River Broadcast Corp. ■ Net: Fox. Rep: Blair. ■ Ro Grignon, gen mgr; Kathy Law, stn mgr. ■ On 100 CATVs—121,905 subs. On 5 trans.

Walker

ADI No. 14; see Minneapolis-St. Paul market

KCCW-TV—ch 12, 316 kw vis, 63.1 kw aur, ant 930t/999g. TL: N46 56 03 W94 27 25. On air date: Jan 1, 1964. 720 Hawthorne St., Alexandria (56308). (612) 763-5166. FAX: (612) 763-4991; TWX: 910-576-3401. Licensee: CBS Inc. Group owner: CBS Broadcast Group. ■ Net: CBS. Rep: Telerep. Wash atty: Roseman & Colin. ■ Mark Proudfoot, gen sls mgr; Raelin Storey, news dir; Wayne Quememoen, chief engr.

Mississippi

Biloxi

ADI No. 180; see Biloxi-Gulfport-Pascagoula market

WLOX-TV—ch 13, 316 kw vis, 57.5 kw aur, ant 1,340t/1,319g. TL: N30 43 25 W89 05 29. Stereo. On air date: Sept 15, 1962. Box 4596, 208 De Buys Rd. (39535-4596). (601) 896-1313. FAX: (601) 896-0749. Licensee: Love Broadcasting Co. (group owner; acq 5-5-78). ■ Net: ABC. Rep: Blair. Wash atty: Fletcher, Heald & Hildreth. News staff 44; news progmg 16 hrs wkly. ■ John Hash, pres; Aubrey Collum, CFO; Leon Long, gen mgr; Roger Garrett, chief opns; Bobby Edwards, gen sls mgr; Ralph Caudill, natl sls mgr; Darlene Duffano, progmg dir; David Vincent, news dir; Barbara Salloun, pub affrs dir; James Fleming, chief engr. ■ On 43 CATVs—130,225 subs. ■ Rates: $450; 100; 100.

*****WMAH-TV**—ch 19, 1,480 kw vis, 148 kw aur, ant 1,558t/1,537g. TL: N30 45 14 W88 56 44. (CP; 1,620 kw vis, ant 1,568t/1,547g). Hrs opn: 19. On air date: Jan 14, 1972. Box 1101, 3825 Ridgewood Rd., Jackson (39215-1101). (601) 982-6565. FAX: (601) 982-6746. Licensee: Mississippi Authority for Educational TV. ■ Net: PBS. Wash atty: Schwartz, Woods & Miller. ■ Sarah Dutton, gen mgr; Herbert M. Jolly, chief engr. ■ On one trans. Co-owned radio: WMAH-FM.

WXXV-TV—See Gulfport.

Booneville

ADI No. 127; see Columbus-Tupelo market

*****WMAE-TV**—ch 12, 44.7 kw vis, 8.91 kw aur, ant 750t/578g. TL: N34 40 00 W88 45 05. On air date: Aug 11, 1974. Box 1101, 3825 Ridgewood Dr., Jackson (39215-1101). (601) 982-6565. FAX: (601) 982-6746. Licensee: Mississippi Authority for Educational TV. ■ Net: PBS. ■ Sarah Dutton, gen mgr. ■Co-owned radio: WMAE-FM.

Bude

ADI No. 88; see Jackson, MS market

*****WMAU-TV**—ch 17, 550 kw vis, 55 kw aur, ant 1,121t/1,066g. TL: N31 22 19 W90 45 05. Hrs opn: 6 AM-12:30 AM. On air date: Jan 14, 1972. Box 1101, 3825 Ridgewood Rd., Jackson (39215-1101). (601) 982-6565. FAX: (601) 982-6746. Licensee: Mississippi Authority for Educational TV. ■ Net: PBS. Wash atty: Schwartz, Woods & Miller. ■ Sarah Dutton, gen mgr; Herbert M. Jolly, chief engr. ■Co-owned radio: WMAU-FM.

Columbus

ADI No. 127; see Columbus-Tupelo market

WCBI-TV—ch 4, 100 kw vis, 10 kw aur, ant 1,996t/1,800g. TL: N33 45 06 W88 52 40. Stereo. Hrs opn: 24. On air date: July 13, 1956. Box 271, 201 5th St. S. (39703). (601) 327-4444. FAX: (601) 328-5222; EASYLINK: 62522560. Licensee: Columbus TV Inc. Group owner: Imes Communications, see Stockholders. ■ Net: CBS. Rep: Seltel. Wash atty: Latham & Watkins. ■ Birney Imes Jr., pres; Frank Imes, gen mgr; Gary Sotir, gen sls mgr; Elizabeth Orr, mktg mgr & prom mgr; Vallory Williamson, progmg dir; Jeffrey Rupp, news dir; Jarrell Kautz, chief engr. ■ On 47 CATVs—79,800 subs.

WTVA—See Tupelo.

Greenville

ADI No. 179; see Greenwood-Greenville market

WABG-TV—See Greenwood.

*****WMAO-TV**—(Greenwood). ch 23, 537 kw vis, 53.7 kw aur, ant 1,040t/1,061g. TL: N33 22 34 W90 32 32. Hrs opn: 6 AM-12:30 AM. On air date: Sept 15, 1972. Box 1101, 3825 Ridgewood Rd., Jackson (39215-1101). (601) 982-6565. FAX: (601) 982-6746. Licensee: Mississippi Authority for Educational TV. ■ Net: PBS. Wash atty: Schwartz, Woods & Miller. ■ Sarah Dutton, gen mgr; Herbert M. Jolly, chief engr. ■Co-owned radio: WMAO-FM.

WXVT—ch 15, 2,746 kw vis, 549 kw aur, ant 887t/919g. TL: N33 39 26 W90 42 18. On air date: Nov 7, 1980. 3015 E. Reed Rd. (38703). (601) 334-1500. FAX: (601) 378-8122. Licensee: Greenville Television Inc. Ownership: John F. Hash, Aubrey L. Collum, Larry Harris, Leon D. Long, Jo Love Little (acq 8-28-91; $1.43 million; 9-16-91). ■ Net: CBS. Rep: Seltel. Wash atty: Koteen & Naftalin. ■John Hash, pres; Larry Harris, gen mgr; David Jernigan, gen sls mgr; Nat Brown, prom mgr; Gina Smith, progmg dir & film buyer; Mary Collins, news dir; Pete Sparks, chief engr. ■ On 33 CATVs—58,946 subs. ■ Rates: $300; 125; 75.

Greenwood

ADI No. 179; see Greenwood-Greenville market

WABG-TV—ch 6, 100 kw vis, 10 kw aur, ant 2,000t/2,136g. TL: N33 22 23 W90 32 31. Hrs opn: 5:30 AM-1:30 AM. On air date: Oct 20, 1959. Box 1243, 849

Washington Ave., Greenville (38701); Box 720, 2001 Garrand Ave. (38930). (601) 332-0949. FAX: (601) 334-6420. Licensee: Mississippi Broadcasting Partners. Group owner: Bahakel Communications ■ Net: ABC. Rep: Katz. News staff 16; news progmg 6 hrs wkly. ■ Cy N. Bahakel, pres; John Rogers, gen mgr; Randy Swan, stn mgr & news dir; Donnie Reid, opns mgr; Harvey Hutchinson, gen sls mgr; Tad Frank, prom mgr & progmg dir; Linda Rule, pub affrs dir; Brad LeBrun, chief engr. ■ On 58 CATVs—138,000 subs. Co-owned radio: WABG(AM). ■ Rates: $400; 125; 125.

*WMAO-TV—Licensed to Greenwood. See Greenville.

Gulfport

ADI No. 180; see Biloxi-Gulfport-Pascagoula market

WLOX-TV—See Biloxi.

WXXV-TV—ch 25, 2,240 kw vis, 224 kw aur, ant 1,780t/1,540g. TL: N30 44 48 W89 03 30. Hrs opn: 6 AM-12:30 AM. On air date: Jan 15, 1985. Box 2500 (39505); Highway 49 N. (39503). (601) 832-2525. FAX: (601) 832-4442. Licensee: Prime Cities Broadcasters Corp. of Mississippi. Ownership: Richard Shivehy 40%; John Tupper 40% (acq 5-1-91; $3.2 million; 5-20-91). ■ Net: Fox. Rep: Blair. Wash atty: Bryan, Cave, McPheeters & McRoberts. ■ Bill Ritchie, gen mgr; Leon Serruys, gen sls mgr; Curt Mabry, prom mgr; Cathy Hayes, progmg dir; Ray Luke, chief engr. ■ On 15 CATVs—158,670 subs. ■ Rates: $500; 100; 35.

Hattiesburg

ADI No. 167; see Laurel-Hattiesburg market

WDAM-TV—(Laurel). ch 7, 316 kw vis, 47 kw aur, ant 510t/575g. TL: N31 27 12 W89 17 05. On air date: June 8, 1956. Box 16269, Hattiesburg (39402). (601) 544-4730. FAX: (601) 584-9302. Licensee: Federal Broadcasting Co. (group owner; acq 7-31-90). ■ Net: NBC. Rep: Katz. Wash atty: Hogan & Hartson. ■ Jim Cameron, vp & gen mgr; Tim Perry, gen sls mgr; Cindy Smith, natl sls mgr; Louis Young, prom dir & pub affrs dir; Betty Young, progmg dir; Bob Noonan, news dir; Bobby Smith, engrg mgr. ■ On 34 CATVs—74,600 subs. ■ Rates: $700; 400; 200.

WHLT—ch 22, 1,200 kw vis, 120 kw aur, ant 800t/707g. TL: N31 24 20 W89 14 13. Stereo. On air date: Jan 12, 1987. Box 232, 990 Hardy St. (39401). (601) 545-2077. FAX: (601) 582-2245. Licensee: New Vision Television I Inc. Group owner: New Vision Television Inc. (acq 9-7-93; $110 million as part of eight-stn sale; 9-27-93). ■ Net: CBS. Rep: Blair. ■ John MacGregor, pres; Randy Cleland, gen mgr & film buyer; Dave Fergison, prom mgr; Walter Johnson, news dir; Clyde Walker, chief engr. ■ On 32 CATVs—63,000 subs. ■ Rates: $350; 90; 60.

Holly Springs

ADI No. 42; see Memphis market

WBUY—ch 40, 4,680 kw vis, 468 kw aur, ant 466t. TL: N34 59 20 W89 41 13. Not on air, target date unknown. 120 Zeigler Circle E., Mobile, AL (36608-4829); Box 38421, Memphis (38183-0421). (714) 361-3198. Permittee: Sonlight Broadcasting Systems Inc. Ownership: Stuart J. Roth, Jay A. Sekulow (acq 6-11-92; grpsl). ■ Stuart J. Roth, CEO; Jay Sekulow, pres; Stephen B. Box, CFO & opns dir; Ed Goetze, stn mgr; Joel Bennnett, progmg dir; Alaina Box, pub affrs dir; Charles W. Davis, engrg dir.

Jackson

ADI No. 88; see Jackson, MS market

WAPT—ch 16, 1,047 kw vis, 276 kw aur, ant 1,170t/1,072g. TL: N32 16 39 W90 17 41. Hrs opn: 24. On air date: Oct 3, 1970. Box 10297 (39289); One Channel 16 Way (39209). (601) 922-1607. FAX: (601) 922-1663. Licensee: NTG Inc. Group owner: Northstar Television Group Inc. (acq 9-11-89; grpsl; 9-25-89). ■ Net: ABC. Rep: Petry. Wash atty: Haley, Bader & Potts. News staff 16; news progmg 12 hrs wkly. ■ Frank Osborn, chmn; Richard Appleton, pres; Stuart Kellogg, gen mgr; Ted Batson, gen sls mgr; Susan Acklen, prom mgr; Joe Root, progmg dir; Dave Cochran, news dir; Teresia Gray, pub affrs dir; Tom Bondurant, chief engr. ■ On 55 CATVs—100,000 subs.

WDBD—ch 40, 1,492 kw vis, 149 kw aur, ant 1,210t/1,078g. TL: N32 16 53 W90 17 41. On air date: Nov 30, 1984. Box 10888, 7440 Channel 16 Way (39289). (601) 922-1234. FAX: (601) 922-6752. Licensee: Pegasus Broadcast Television L.P. (group owner; acq 2-18-93; $21 million with WDSI-TV Chattanooga, TN; 3-8-93). ■ Net: Fox. Rep: Seltel. Wash atty: Baraff, Koerner, Olender & Hochberg. ■ Doug Donatelli, pres; Al Tankesley, gen mgr; Lee Carpenter, opns dir & engrg dir; Terrill Weiss, gen sls mgr; Johnny Lewis, rgnl sls mgr; Tim Hess, prom mgr; Melinda Downey, progmg dir. ■ On 68 CATVs—142,000 subs.

WJTV—ch 12, 316 kw vis, 63.1 kw aur, ant 1,630t/1,615g. TL: N32 14 26 W90 24 15. On air date: Mar 15, 1954. Box 8887 (39284); 1820 TV Road (39204). (601) 372-6311. FAX: (601) 372-6311. Licensee: New Vision Television I Inc. Group owner: New Vision Television Inc. (acq 9-7-93; $110 million as part of eight-stn sale; 9-27-93). ■ Net: CBS. Rep: Blair. Wash atty: Dow, Lohnes & Albertson. ■ John A. MacGregor, pres; Michael R. Brooks, exec vp & gen mgr; Glenda McKay, prom mgr & progmg dir; Michael Sipes, news dir; Mike Godwin, chief engr. ■ On 83 CATVs—123,454 subs.

WLBT—ch 3, 95.7 kw vis, 19.1 kw aur, ant 2,419t/1,999g. TL: N32 12 46 W90 22 54. Stereo. Hrs opn: 24. On air date: Dec 28, 1953. 715 S. Jefferson St. (39205). (601) 948-3333. FAX: (601) 960-4435; TWX: 810-966-2616. Licensee: TV-3 Inc. Group owner: Civic Communication Corp. (acq 12-12-83; grpsl; 1-2-84). ■ Net: NBC. Rep: Katz. Wash atty: Blair, Joyce & Silva. ■ Frank Melton, CEO; Dan Modisett, pres, gen mgr & progmg dir; Steve Lavin, opns mgr; Frankie Thomas, gen sls mgr; Jackie Ellens, prom mgr; Dennis Smith, news dir; Goldia Revies, pub affrs dir; Curtis McKnight, chief engr. ■ On 55 CATVs—180,000 subs.

*WMPN-TV—ch 29, 457 kw vis, 45.7 aur, ant 1,958t/1,997g. TL: N32 12 46 W90 22 54. (CP: 922.6 kw vis, ant 1,961t). On air date: Feb 1, 1970. Box 1101 (39215-1101). (601) 982-6565. Licensee: Mississippi Authority for Educational TV. ■ Net: PBS. Wash atty: Schwartz, Woods & Miller. ■ Jeannine Fulmer, progmg dir. ■ On 10 CATVs—18,616 subs. Co-owned radio: WMPN-FM.

Laurel

WDAM-TV—Licensed to Laurel. See Hattiesburg.

Meridian

ADI No. 183; see Meridian market

*WGBC—ch 30, 89.1 kw vis, 8.91 kw aur, 610t/405g. TL: N32 19 34 W88 41 12. Stereo. (CP: 1,600 kw vis, ant 613t/408g). Hrs opn: 24. On air date: Sept 15, 1991. 116 Skyland Dr. (39301). (601) 485-3030. TWX: 810-966-2616. Licensee: Global Communications Inc. Ownership: Charles L. Young, 100%. ■ Net: NBC. Rep: Seltel. Wash atty: Wiley, Rein & Fielding. News staff 9; news progmg 8 hrs wkly. ■ Charles L. Young, pres; Larry Nicks, sr vp, gen mgr, gen sls mgr & adv mgr; Ray Denton, opns mgr & engrg dir; Terry Dalton, prom mgr; Kathie Austin, progmg dir; Mike Stafford, news dir. ■ On 14 CATVs—25,000 subs. ■ Rates: $500; 75; 50.

*WMAW-TV—ch 14, 550 kw vis, 55 kw aur, ant 1,210t/1,069g. TL: N32 08 18 W89 05 36. Hrs opn: 6 AM-12:30 AM. On air date: Jan 14, 1972. Box 1101, 3825 Ridgewood Rd., Jackson (39215-1101). (601) 982-6565. FAX: (601) 982-6746. Licensee: Mississippi Authority For Educational TV. ■ Net: PBS. Wash atty: Schwartz, Woods & Miller. ■ Sarah Dutton, gen mgr; Herbert M. Jolly, chief engr. ■Co-owned radio: WMAW-FM.

WTOK-TV—ch 11, 316 kw vis, 47.9 kw aur, ant 536t/315g. TL: N32 19 38 W88 41 28. On air date: Sept 27, 1953. Box 2988 (39302). (601) 693-1441. FAX: (601) 483-3266. Licensee: Benedek Broadcasting Co. (group owner; acq 1988). ■ Net: ABC. Rep: Katz. Wash atty: Covington & Burling. ■ Tom Wall, gen mgr; Bob Holland, stn mgr; Tracey Jones, gen sls mgr; Tim Walker, prom mgr; Cassandra Turney, progmg dir; John Johnson, news dir; Tom Ford, chief engr. ■ On 39 CATVs—72,000 subs.

WTZH—ch 24, 724 kw vis, 72.4 kw aur, ant 662t/388g. TL: N32 19 40 W88 41 31. (CP: 724 kw vis, ant 581 ft, TL: N32 18 43 W88 41 33). Hrs opn: 24. On air date: June 10, 1968. c/o H.A. LeBrun III, 93 Forrest Pl. N.E., Atlanta, GA (30328-4872). FAX: (404) 250-0953. Licensee: Meridian Broadcasting Partnership. Ownership: Meridian Broadcasting Partnership, 60%; Meridian Broadcasting Corp., 25%, H.A. LeBrun III, 15% (acq 2-28-86; $4 million). Wash atty: Reddy, Begley & Martin. ■ H. A. LeBrun III, pres.

Mississippi State

ADI No. 127; see Columbus-Tupelo market

*WMAB-TV—ch 2, 100 kw vis, 10 kw aur, ant 1,250t/1,091g. TL: N33 21 07 W89 08 56. Hrs opn: 6 AM-12:30 AM. On air date: July 4, 1971. Box 1101, 3825 Ridgewood Rd., Jackson (39215-1101). (601) 982-6565. FAX: (601) 982-6746. Licensee: Mississippi Authority for Educational TV. ■ Net: PBS. Wash atty: Schwartz, Woods & Miller. ■ Sarah Dutton, gen mgr; Herbert M. Jolly, chief engr.■Co-owned radio: WMAB-FM.

Natchez

ADI No. 88; see Jackson, MS market

WNTZ—ch 48, 1,170 kw vis, 117 kw aur, ant 843t/848g. TL: N31 30 33 W91 24 19. On air date: Nov 16, 1985. Box 1836 (39121). (601) 442-4800. FAX: (601) 446-7019. Licensee: Delta Management Corp. Ownership: Charles H. Chatelain (group owner; acq 9-25-92; $100,000; 11-9-92). Rep: MBS. Wash atty: Tom Root. ■ Ed Blanchard, gen mgr; Pat Newburg, gen sls mgr; Mark McKay, prom mgr & progmg dir; Donald B. Wilburn, film buyer; Gwen Belton, news dir; Charles Fisher, chief engr. ■ On 10 CATVs—20,000 subs.

Oxford

ADI No. 42; see Memphis market

*WMAV-TV—ch 18, 347 kw vis, 34.7 kw aur, ant 1,390t/1,304g. TL: N34 17 26 W89 42 24. On air date: May 19, 1972. Box 1101, 3825 Ridgewood Rd., Jackson (39215-1101). (601) 982-6565. FAX: (601) 982-6746. Licensee: Mississippi Authority for Educational TV. ■ Net: PBS. ■ Sarah Dulton, gen mgr. ■Co-owned radio: WMAV-FM.

Pascagoula

WLOX-TV—See Biloxi.

Tupelo

ADI No. 127; see Columbus-Tupelo market

WTVA—ch 9, 316 vis, 31.6 kw aur, ant 1,781t/1,585g. TL: N33 47 40 W89 05 16. On air date: Mar 18, 1957. Box 350 (38801). (901) 842-7620. Licensee: WTVA Inc. Ownership: F.K Spain, 60%; Margaret H. Spain, 40%. ■ Net: NBC. Rep: Katz. Wash atty: Haley, Bader & Potts. ■ Frank K. Spain, pres; Mark Ledbetter, gen mgr; Ed Bishop, progmg dir; Terry Smith, news dir; Wendell Robinson, chief engr.

West Point

ADI No. 127; see Columbus-Tupelo market

WLOV-TV—ch 27, 2,000 kw vis, 200 kw aur, ant 1,80t/1,442g. TL: N33 47 40 W89 05 16. On air date: May 29, 1983. Box 350, Beech Springs Rd., Tupelo (38802). (601) 842-7620; (601) 842-2227. FAX: (601) 844-7061. Licensee: Love Communications Co. (acq 6-24-91; $1.65 million; 7-8-91). ■ Net: ABC. Rep: Katz. ■ On 27 CATVs—51,015 subs.

Missouri

Cape Girardeau

ADI No. 77; See Paducah, KY-Cape Girardeau-Harrisburg, IL-Marion, IL market

KBSI—ch 23, 1,860 kw vis, 186 kw aur, ant 1,768t/1,524g. TL: N37 24 23 W89 33 44. Hrs opn: 5 AM-3 AM. On air date: Sept 10, 1983. 806 Enterprise (63701). (314) 334-1223. FAX: (314) 334-1208. Licensee: Engles Communications Inc. Ownership: David Engles, 75%; Steven Engles 25% (acq 2-13-90; $3.35 million). ■ Net: Fox. Rep: Petry. News staff One; news progmg 2 hrs wkly. ■ David Engles, chmn; Steven Engles, pres & gen mgr; Robert Steinberg, CFO; Jim Humphreys, natl sls mgr; Beth Ford, rgnl sls mgr; Bryan Uptain, prom mgr; Mark Culbertson, progmg dir; John Baker, chief engr. ■ On 168 CATVs—185,000 subs. ■ Rates: $1,000; 250; 150.

KFVS-TV—ch 12, 316 kw vis, 63.2 kw aur, ant 2,001t/1,678g. TL: N37 25 46 W89 30 14. On air date: Oct 3, 1954. 310 Broadway (63701). (314) 335-1212.

FAX: (314) 335-6303. Licensee: AFLAC Broadcast Partners. Group owner: AFLAC Broadcast Division (acq 4-25-79; $22,235,984; 4-30-79). ■ Net: CBS. Rep: Harrington, Righter & Parsons. Wash atty: Schnader, Harrison, Segal & Lewis. ■ Howard Meagle, gen mgr; John Blim, opns mgr & progmg dir; Paul Keener, prom mgr; Mike Beecher, news dir; Arnold Killian, chief engr.

Columbia

ADI No. 151; see Columbia-Jefferson City market

KMIZ—ch 17, 1,580 kw vis, 400 kw aur, ant 1,141t/1,113g. TL: N38 46 29 W92 33 22. On air date: Dec 5, 1971. 501 Business Loop 70 E. (65201). (314) 449-0917. FAX: (314) 875-7078. Licensee: Stauffer Communications Inc. (group owner; acq 1-1-85; $5 million). ■ Net: ABC. Rep: Blair. Wash atty: Dow, Lohnes & Albertson. ■ Carlos Fernandez, gen mgr; Tom Chapman, opns mgr, progmg dir & film buyer; Pat Dalbey, gen sls mgr; Jean Viox, natl sls mgr; Tina Gibson, prom mgr; Teresa Snow, news dir; Neil Pedersen, chief engr. ■ On 70 CATVs—97,471 subs.

KOMU-TV—ch 8, 316 kw vis, 31.6 kw aur, ant 790t/774g. TL: N38 53 16 W92 15 48. Stereo. On air date: Dec 21, 1953. Highway 63 S. (65201). (314) 882-8888. FAX: (314) 884-8888; TWX: 910-760-1444. Licensee: The Curators of the Univ. of Missouri (group owner). ■ Net: NBC. Rep: Petry. Wash atty: Fisher, Wayland, Cooper & Leader. News staff 10; news progmg 6 hrs wkly. ■ Thomas R. Gray, gen mgr; John Strecker, gen sls mgr; Susie Sapp, natl sls mgr; Becky Cooper, mktg dir, prom mgr & progmg dir; Stacey Woelfel, news dir; Lee Eggers, chief engr. ■ On 114 CATVs—100,000 subs. On one trans. ■ Rates: $260; 55; 35.

KRCG—See Jefferson City.

Hannibal

KHQA-TV—Licensed to Hannibal. See Quincy, Ill.

Jefferson City

ADI No. 151; see Columbia-Jefferson City market

KNLJ—ch 25, 2,040 kw vis, 204 kw aur, ant 1,028t/945g. TL: N38 42 16 W92 05 20. Hrs opn: 24. On air date: Mar 30, 1986. Box 2525, New Bloomfield (65603); 9810 State Rd. AE, New Bloomfield (65063). (314) 896-5105. FAX: (314) 896-4376. Licensee: New Life Evangelistic Center Inc. Wash atty: John Midlen. ■ Larry Rice, pres; Penny Rice, gen mgr, gen sls mgr & progmg dir; Joe Hoffmann, natl sls mgr; Robert Hickman, chief engr. ■ On 11 CATVs. ■ Rates: $25; 50; 20.

KOMU-TV—See Columbia.

KRCG—ch 13, 316 kw vis, 47.4 kw aur, ant 1,010t/929g. TL: N38 41 28 W92 05 43. Stereo. Hrs opn: 5 AM-2 AM. On air date: Feb 13, 1955. Box 659 (65102); Old Hwy. 54, Holts Summit (65043). (314) 896-5144. TWX: 910-760-2923. Licensee: Mel Wheeler Inc. (group owner; acq 11-88). ■ Net: CBS, Fox. Rep: Katz Continental. Wash atty: Pepper & Corazzini. News staff 14; news progmg 9 hrs wkly. ■ M.J. "Bob" Groothand, vp, gen mgr & film buyer; Betsy Farris, rgnl sls mgr; Laura Reynolds, prom mgr & pub affrs dir; Lee Gordon Jr., progmg dir; Jeff Karnowski, news dir; Steve Metzger, chief engr. ■ On 37 CATVs—57,621 subs. On one trans. ■ Rates: $500; 120; 100.

Joplin

ADI No. 146; see Joplin-Pittsburg, KS market

KODE-TV—ch 12, 316 kw vis, 63.2 kw aur, ant 1,020t/999g. TL: N37 04 36 W94 32 10. On air date: Sept 26, 1954. Box 46, 1928 W. 13th St. (64801). (417) 623-7260. FAX: (417) 623-3736. Licensee: Eastern Broadcasting Corp. ■ Net: ABC. Rep: Blair. Wash atty: Schwartz, Woods & Miller. News staff 15; news progmg 10 hrs wkly. ■ Roger Neuhoff, chmn; Brian Byrnes, pres; Jerry Montgomery, gen mgr, natl sls mgr & film buyer; John Hoffman, gen sls mgr; Mark Current, prom mgr; Julie Rogers, progmg dir; Larry Young, news dir; Don Ross, Kieth Wedel, chief engr. ■ On 60 CATVs—91,048 subs. ■ Rates: $350; 75; 50.

***KOZJ**—ch 26, 51.3 kw vis, 5.13 kw aur, ant 932t/849g. TL: N37 04 36 W94 32 10. Stereo. 832 kw vis, 8.3 kw aur. On air date: June 1, 1986. Box 1226 (64802); Webster Hall #138, MSSC (64801). (417) 782-1226. Licensee: Ozark Public Telecommunications Inc. ■ Net: PBS. ■ Art Luebke, gen mgr; Miff Dikeman, stn mgr; William R. Ellis, engrg dir; Rex Chambers, chief engr. Satellite of *KOZK Springfield.

KSNF—ch 16, 2,570 kw vis, 257 kw aur, ant 1,027t/1,013g. TL: N37 04 33 W94 33 16. On air date: Sept 2, 1967. Box 1393 (64802). (417) 781-2345. TWX: 910-774-4520. Licensee: Tri-State Broadcasting Corp. Group owner: Price Communications Corp. (acq 9-15-87; $11.8 million; 10-6-86). ■ Net: NBC. Rep: Katz. Wash atty: Mullin, Rhyne, Emmons & Topel. ■ Bill Bengtson, gen mgr; Bill Ward, gen sls mgr; Mike Pound, prom mgr; Steve Russell, news dir; Mel Brooks, chief engr. ■ On 100 CATVs—103,067 subs.

Kansas City

ADI No 29; see Kansas City market

***KCPT**—ch 19, 1,150 kw vis, 115 kw aur, ant 1,171t. TL: N39 04 59 W94 28 49. Stereo. On air date: Mar 29, 1961. 125 E. 31st St. (64108). (816) 756-3580. FAX: (816) 931-2500. Licensee: Public TV 19 Inc. (acq 1-1-72; $22,226; 2-14-72). ■ Net: PBS. Wash atty: Dow, Lohnes & Albertson. ■ William T. Reed, pres & gen mgr; Craig Westhoff, opns mgr; Warren Maus, vp dev; Paul Francis, prom dir; Stephen Baker, adv dir; David Welsh, vp progmg; Katherine Soden, progmg mgr; Deborah Holmes, pub affrs dir; John Long, engrg dir. ■ On 45 CATVs.

KCTV—ch 5, 100 kw vis, 15.1 kw aur, ant 1,130t/1,042g. TL: N39 04 15 W94 34 57. Stereo. On air date: Sept 27, 1953. Box 5555 (64109); 4500 Shawnee Mission Pkwy., Fairway (66205). (913) 677-5555. FAX: (913) 677-7284. Licensee: Meredith Corp. Group owner: Meredith Bcstg Group, Meredith Corp. See Cross-Ownership (acq 10-1-53; $2 million; 11-23-53). ■ Net: CBS. Rep: MMT. Wash atty: Haley, Bader & Potts. ■ Philip A. Jones, pres; John C. Rose, vp & gen mgr; Erwin Parthe, stn mgr, progmg dir & film buyer; Bon Frey, gen sls mgr; Mary Rimann, natl sls mgr; Don North, news dir; Joseph Snelson, engrg dir. ■ On 95 CATVs—375,000 subs.

KMBC-TV—ch 9, 316 kw vis, 36.8 kw aur, ant 1,171t/1,124g. TL: N39 05 01 W94 30 57. On air date: Aug 1, 1952. 1049 Central (64105). (816) 221-9999. FAX: (816) 421-4163. Licensee: Hearst Corp., KMBC-TV Division. Group owner: Hearst Broadcasting Group, see Cross-Ownership (acq 5-18-82; $79 million; 4-5-82). ■ Net: ABC. Rep: Katz. Wash atty: Pepper, Martin, Jensen, Maichel & Hetlage. ■ Paul Dinovitz, vp & gen mgr; Tracy Boschert, gen sls mgr; John Calver, prom mgr; Pat Patton, progmg dir; Brian Bracco, news dir; Jerry Dixon, chief engr. ■ On 166 CATVs—463,019 subs. ■ Rates: $1,600; 600; 200.

KSHB-TV—ch 41, 1,320 kw vis, 132 kw aur, ant 1,059t/1,162g. TL: N39 04 20 W94 35 45. Stereo. Hrs opn: 24. On air date: Sept 28, 1970. 4720 Oak St. (64112). (816) 753-4141. FAX: (816) 932-4122. Licensee: Scripps Howard Broadcasting Co. (group owner; acq 10-28-77; $7.5 million; 10-3-77). ■ Net: Fox. Rep: Blair. Wash atty: Baker & Hostetler. News staff 18; news progmg 41 hrs wkly. ■ Charlotte Moore English, vp & gen mgr; Herb Willis, opns mgr; JoAnn Campo, gen sls mgr; Sandy Martin, prom mgr; Dana Boyd, progmg dir; Mark Olinger, news dir; James O'Connor, chief engr. ■ On 225 CATVs—645,000 subs.

KSMO-TV—ch 62, 2,190 kw vis, 219 kw aur, ant 1,115t/1,222g. TL: N39 04 59 W98 28 49. (CP: 2,183 kw vis, ant 1,115t). On air date: Dec 7, 1983. Suite 300, 10 E. Cambridge Cir. Dr. (66103). (913) 621-6262. FAX: (913) 621-4703. Licensee: Kansas City TV 62 L.P. Group owner: ABRY Communications (acq 9-21-90). Wash atty: Howard Liberman. ■ Jim MacDonald, gen mgr; Rich Deutsch, gen sls mgr; Bruce Stone, prom mgr; Byron King, progmg dir; David Pulido, film buyer; Rob Wharton, pub affrs dir; David Birdsong, chief engr. ■ On 69 CATVs—365,000 subs.

KYFC—ch 50, 678 kw vis, 67.8 kw aur, ant 1,119t/1,164g. TL: N39 01 19 W94 30 50. On air date: Dec 1, 1978. 4715 Rainbow Blvd., Shawnee Mission, KS (66205). (913) 262-1700. FAX: (913) 262-1782. Licensee: Kansas City Youth for Christ Inc. Wash atty: Wiley, Rein & Fielding. Sp 2 hrs wkly. ■ Ronnie Metsker, pres; Wayne Antrim, gen mgr & opns mgr; Kathy Burton, sls dir & mktg dir; Christi Evans, prom dir; Sue Copling, progmg dir & film buyer; Tom Talbert, news dir; Ron Rockrohr, engrg dir. ■ On 11 CATVs—275,000 subs.

WDAF-TV—ch 4, 100 kw vis, 10 kw aur, ant 1,130t/1,163g. TL: N39 04 20 W94 35 45. On air date: Oct 16, 1949. Signal Hill (64108). (816) 753-4567. FAX: (816) 932-3984. Licensee: Great American Broadcasting Co. (group owner). ■ Net: NBC. Rep: Telerep. Wash atty: Koteen & Naftalin. News staff 40. ■ Ed Piette, gen mgr; Cheryl Kerns McDonald, vp sls; Lisa Ravere Hickok, prom mgr; Mike MacDonald, news dir; Jim Moore, chief engr. Co-owned radio: WDAF(AM)-KYYS(FM).

Kirksville

KTVO—Licensed to Kirksville. See Ottumwa, Iowa.

Poplar Bluff

ADI No. 77; see Paducah, KY-Cape Girardeau-Harrisburg, IL-Marion, IL markets

KPOB-TV—ch 15, 389 kw vis, 38.9 kw aur, ant 600t/526g. TL: N36 48 02 W90 27 03. On air date: Sept 15, 1967. Rt. 13, Carterville, IL (62918). (618) 985-2333. Licensee: Mel Wheeler Inc. (group owner; acq 5-12-83; $6.6 million; 6-6-83). ■ Net: ABC. Rep: MMT. Wash atty: Pepper & Corazzini. ■ Mel Wheeler, pres; Steve Wheeler, gen mgr; Leonard Wheeler, gen sls mgr; Bonnie Wheeler, news dir; J. W. Davis, chief engr. ■ On 35 CATVs.

St. Joseph

ADI No. 193; see St. Joseph market

KQTV—ch 2, 100 kw vis, 20 kw aur, ant 810t/750g. TL: N39 46 12 W94 47 53. On air date: Sept 27, 1953. Box 6247, 40th & Faraon Sts. (64506). (816) 364-2222. FAX: (816) 364-3787; TWX: 910-777-7872. Licensee: Fabri Development Corp. Ownership: TCS Management Corp. (MC Media 50.005%; Commonwealth, 48.995%; TCB Management, 1%) (acq 3-26-93; grpsl; 4-12-93). ■ Net: ABC. Rep: Katz. Wash atty: Cohn & Marks. News staff 15; news progmg 10 hrs wkly. ■ Jerry Condra, vp & gen mgr; Judy Crawford, gen sls mgr; Dave Ledden, rgnl sls mgr; Rob Boenau, Lisa Robison, prom mgrs; Dru Hadwal, news dir; Larry Gunther, chief engr. ■ On 195 CATVs—318,472 subs.

KTAJ—ch 16, 5,000 kw vis, 500 kw aur, ant 1,071t/1,027g. TL: N39 39 03 W94 40 11. Hrs opn: 24. On air date: Oct 6, 1986. 4410-B S. 40th St. (64503). (816) 364-1616. Licensee: All-American TV. Wash atty: May & Dunn. ■ Sonny Arguinzoni, pres; Gary Penovich, gen mgr; Gene Seibel, stn mgr; Donna Seibel, prom dir; Julie Arquinzoni, progmg dir; Eugene Seibel, chief engr. ■ On 3 CATVs.

St. Louis

ADI No. 18; see St. Louis market

KDNL-TV—ch 30, 2,190 kw vis, 109.5 kw aur, ant 1,100t/1,148g. TL: N38 34 50 W90 19 45. Stereo. On air date: June 8, 1969. 1215 Cole St. (63106). (314) 436-3030. FAX: (314) 259-5763. Licensee: River City L.P. Group owner: River City Broadcasting (acq 8-31-89; $21.5 million; 7-31-89). ■ Net: Fox. Rep: MMT. Wash atty: Dow, Lohnes & Albertson. News staff one. ■ Barry Baker, pres; Larry Marcus, CFO; Gregg Filandrinos, vp & gen mgr; James K. Lowery, opns mgr & chief engr; Tom Ehlmann, gen sls mgr; Tom Rogers, prom mgr; Bob West, progmg dir; Sherry Sissac, pub affrs dir. ■ On 124 CATVs—423,007 subs. ■ Rates: $3,000; 750; 75.

***KETC**—ch 9, 295 kw vis, 29.5 kw aur, ant 1,070t/1,073g. TL: N38 28 56 W90 23 53. Stereo. On air date: Sept 20, 1954. 6996 Millbrook Blvd. (63130). (314) 725-2460. Licensee: St. Louis Regional Educational and Public Television Commission. ■ Net: PBS. Wash atty: Dow, Lohnes & Albertson. ■ Michael Hardgrove, pres & gen mgr; Andrew McMaster, vp; Ted Garcia, opns mgr; Rebecca Goodrum, prom mgr; Douglas Leonard, progmg dir; James Marlow, chief engr. ■ On 23 CATVs—80,000 subs.

KMOV—ch 4, 100 kw vis, 15 kw aur, ant 1,097t/1,201g. TL: N38 31 47 W90 17 58. 24. On air date: July 8, 1954. One Memorial Dr. (63102). (314) 621-4444. FAX: (314) 444-3367; (314) 444-3368. Licensee: Viacom Broadcasting of Missouri. Group owner: Viacom Broadcasting Inc. (acq 5-16-86; $122.5 million; 1-13-86). ■ Net: CBS. Rep: Telerep. News staff 65; news progmg 12 hrs wkly. ■ Allan Cohen, vp & gen mgr; Jim Rothschild, opns dir; Tom Raponi, gen sls mgr; Bob Totsch, natl sls mgr; Genia Weinstein, mktg dir; Dan Dillon, prom mgr; Liz Mullen, progmg mgr; Steve Hammel, news dir; Mary Cannon, pub affrs dir; Walt Nichol, chief engr.

KNLC—ch 24, 3,090 kw vis, 309 kw aur, ant 1,000t. TL: N38 21 40 W90 32 58. On air date: Sept 12, 1982. Box 924 (63188). (314) 436-2424. FAX: (314) 436-2434. Licensee: New Life Evangelistic Center. Wash atty: John Midlen. ■ Larry Rice, pres & gen mgr; Judy Redlich, progmg dir.

KPLR-TV—ch 11, 316 kw vis, 32 kw aur, ant 1,010t/1,214g. TL: N38 31 47 W90 17 58. Stereo. On air date: Apr 28, 1959. 4935 Lindell Blvd. (63108-1587). (314) 367-7211. FAX: (314) 454-6488. Licensee: Koplar

Communications Inc. (group owner; acq 4-28-59). Rep: Petry. Wash atty: Koteen & Naftalin. ■ Edward Kopler, pres; Max Lummis, CFO, sr vp & gen mgr; Dan Neumann, stn mgr; James P. Wright, opns mgr; Paul Wise, sls dir; Suzi Schrappen, prom mgr; Howard Stevens, progmg dir; Bill Rees, news dir. ■ On 162 CATVs—521,042 subs. ■ Rates: $1,500; 1,000; 900.

KSDK—ch 5, 100 kw vis, 20 kw aur, ant 1,090t/1,148g. TL: N38 34 05 W90 19 55. Stereo. Hrs opn: 24. On air date: Feb 8, 1947. Television Plaza, 1000 Market St. (63101). (314) 421-5055; (314) 444-5260. FAX: (314) 444-5289. Licensee: Multimedia KSDK Inc. Group owner: Multimedia Broadcasting Co. (acq 2-17-83; grpsl; 1-9-84). ■ Net: NBC. Rep: Katz. Wash atty: Dow, Lohnes & Albertson. ■ J. William Grimes, CEO & pres; John Kueneke, vp & gen mgr; Steve Smith, chief opns & chief engr; Bob Drewel, gen sls mgr; Marie McGlynn, mktg mgr; Rebecca Rahm, progmg mgr; Tim Larson, news dir. ■ On 55 CATVs—239,530 subs.

KTVI—ch 2, 100 kw vis, 20 kw aur, ant 1,085t/1,049g. TL: N38 32 07 W90 22 23. 24. On air date: Aug 10, 1953. 5915 Berthold Ave. (63110). (314) 647-2222. FAX: (314) 644-7419. Licensee: KTVI Argyle Inc. Group owner: Argyle Television Holding Inc. (acq 5-14-93; $35 million; 5-31-93). ■ Net: ABC. Rep: Blair. Wash atty: Wilmer, Cutler & Pickering. News progmg 18 hrs wkly. ■ Bud Carey, pres; Kenneth MacQueen, gen mgr; Terry Dunning, gen sls mgr; Robert Earl Smith, prom mgr; Susan Matthews, progmg dir; William M. Berra, news dir; Cason W. Capps, chief engr.

Sedalia

ADI No. 29; see Kansas City market

***KMOS-TV**—ch 6, 100 kw vis, 25 kw aur, ant 772t/797g. TL: N38 44 47 W93 16 30. Stereo. Hrs opn: 18. On air date: Dec 22, 1979. Central Missouri State Univ., Wood II, Warrensburg (64093). (816) 543-4155. FAX: (816) 543-8863. Licensee: Central Missouri State Univ. (acq 6-6-78; $1,000). ■ Net: PBS. Wash atty: Fisher, Wayland, Cooper & Leader. ■ Donald W. Peterson, gen mgr; Fred Hunt, opns mgr; Michael O'Keefe, prom mgr & film buyer; Trina Cuggen, news dir; Dan L. Davis, chief engr. ■ On 34 CATVs—67,000 subs. Co-owned radio: KCMW-FM.

Springfield

ADI No. 80; see Springfield, MO market

KDEB-TV—ch 27, 5,000 kw vis, 500 kw aur, ant 1,690t/1,621g. TL: N37 11 40 W92 56 04. Stereo. On air date: Sept 22, 1968. 3000 Cherry St. (65802). (417) 862-2727. FAX: (417) 831-4209. Licensee: BANAM Broadcasting Inc. (group owner; acq 3-16-93; grpsl; 4-5-93). ■ Net: Fox. Rep: Seltel. Wash atty: Kenkel, Barnard & Edmundson. ■ Paula Garrett, pres, CFO & gen mgr; Jack McGee, opns mgr; Keith Abercrombie, gen sls mgr; Hallie Roberts, prom mgr; Nancy Bingaman, progmg dir; Rick Lipps, film buyer; Randy Selvidge, chief engr. ■ On 80 CATVs—123,717 subs. ■ Rates: $250; 100; 40.

KOLR-TV—ch 10, 316 kw vis, 31.6 kw aur, ant 2,070t/1,887g. TL: N37 13 08 W92 56 56. Stereo. Hrs opn: 24. On air date: Mar 14, 1953. Box 1716 (65801); 2650 E. Division (65803). (417) 862-1010. FAX: (417) 862-6439; TWX: 910-775-4718. Licensee: Independent Broadcasting Co. Ownership: J.H. Cooper, 49.62%.; J.O. Cooper, 49.62% ■ Net: CBS. Rep: Katz. News staff 24; news progmg 12 hrs wkly. ■ J. H. Cooper, pres; Ellis Shook, vp & gen mgr; Owen Fliehr, gen sls mgr; Cathy Rippee, natl sls mgr; Dean Wasson, prom mgr & progmg mgr; Steve Snyder, news dir; Tom Trtan, pub affrs dir; Don Miller, chief engr. ■ On 95 CATVs—137,000 subs. ■ Rates: $600; 150; 75.

***KOZK**—ch 21, 1,410 kw vis, 141 kw aur, ant 1,791t/2,001g. TL: N37 13 08 W92 56 56. Stereo. Hrs opn: 6 AM-midnight. On air date: Jan 21, 1975. Box 21 (65801). (417) 865-2100. Licensee: Ozark Public Telecommunications Inc. ■ Net: PBS. Wash atty: Dow, Lohnes & Albertson. ■ Arthur T. Luebke, CEO; Bill Acker, vp dev; Pamela Pyatt, vp mktg; Kim Meyer, vp progmg; William R. Ellis, vp engrg; John Flanders, chief engr.

KSPR—ch 33, 5,010 kw vis, 112 kw aur, ant 1,995t/1,816g. TL: N37 13 08 W92 56 56. Stereo. (CP: 1,000 kw aur). On air date: Mar 9, 1983. 1359 St. Louis St. (65802). (417) 831-1333. FAX: (417) 831-4125. Licensee: Davis-Goldfarb Co. (group owner). ■ Net: ABC. Rep: Petry. Wash atty: Leventhal, Senter & Lerman. News staff 11; news progmg 12 hrs wkly. ■ Clyde L. Helton, gen mgr; David Middleton, opns mgr; Brian Keith, gen sls mgr; Melissa Ward, prom mgr, adv dir & pub affrs dir; Leland Sanders, progmg dir; Pat Madden, news dir; Montey Chaney, chief engr. ■ On 96 CATVs—95,000 subs. ■ Rates: $300; 200; 75.

KYTV—ch 3, 100 kw vis, 20 kw aur, ant 2,040t/2,000g. TL: N37 10 11 W92 56 30. On air date: Oct 1, 1953. Box 3500 (65808); 999 W. Sunshine (65807). (417) 868-3800. FAX: (417) 868-3894. Licensee: KY-3 Inc. Group owner: Schurz Communications Inc. (acq 2-19-87; $50.8 million; 1-19-87). ■ Net: NBC. Rep: Blair. Wash atty: Hogan & Hartson. ■ Gary DeHaven, pres & gen mgr; Dan White, opns mgr; Mike Scott, gen sls mgr; Linda Cleeton, mktg dir; Jim Becker, prom mgr; Cathy Adams, progmg dir & film buyer; Marci Burdick, news dir; Truman Krumholz, chief engr. ■ On 181 CATVs—147,000 subs. On 2 trans.

Montana

Billings

ADI No. 171; see Billings market

KSVI—ch 6, 100 kw vis, 10 kw aur, ant 817t. TL: N45 48 26 W108 20 25. Hrs opn: 24. On air date: 1993. Box 23309, 445 S. 24th St. W. (59104-3309). Licensee: Big Horn Communications Inc. (acq 5-3-91; $200,000; 6-3-91). ■ Net: ABC. Rep: Adam Young. Wash atty: F. Joseph Brinig. ■ Thomas Hendrickson, pres; Ray Moser, vp, gen mgr & stn mgr; Dan Michael , gen sls mgr, natl sls mgr & rgnl sls mgr; Pat Rookhuizen, progmg dir; Steve Lakey, pub affrs dir; Ron Walden, chief engr. ■ On 23 CATVs. On 24 trans.

KTVQ—ch 2, 100 kw vis, 10.2 kw aur, ant 670t/383g. TL: N45 46 00 W108 27 27. Stereo. On air date: Nov 9, 1953. Box 2557 (59103). (406) 252-5611. FAX: (406) 252-9938. Licensee: SJL of Montana Associates L.P. Group owner: SJL Broadcast Management Corp. (acq 12-15-83). ■ Net: CBS. Rep: Blair. Wash atty: Latham & Watkins. ■ Kelly Sugai, gen mgr & film buyer; Monty Wallis, gen sls mgr; Janet Skorupa, prom mgr; Pam Hofferber, progmg dir; Jon Stepanek, news dir; Ron Jacobson, chief engr. ■ On 42 CATVs. On 62 trans.

KULR-TV—ch 8, 316 kw vis, 38.9 kw aur, ant 750t/531g. TL: N45 45 35 W108 27 14. Hrs opn: 24. On air date: March 15, 1958. Box 80810 (59108-0810); 2045 Overland Ave. (59102). (406) 656-8000. (406) 652-8207. Licensee: KULR Corp. Group owner: Dix Communications (acq 12-12-86; grpsl; 11-3-86). ■ Net: NBC. Rep: Katz. Wash atty: Baker & Hostetler. News staff 11; news progmg 9 hrs wkly. ■ Stan Whitman, pres & gen mgr; Bruce Cummings, gen sls mgr & adv dir; Julie Omvig, prom mgr; Linda Shandy, progmg mgr; George Mills, news dir; Pat Shearer, chief engr. ■ On 17 CATVs—49,500 subs. On 48 trans.

Bozeman

ADI No. 189; see Butte market

KCTZ—ch 7, 43.7 kw vis, 4.37 kw aur, ant 816t. TL: N45 40 24 W110 52 02. (CP: Ant 1,122t). On air date: September 1987. Box 6040 (59771); 1128 E. Main St. (59715). (406) 586-3280. FAX: (406) 586-4135. Licensee: Big Horn Broadcasting Inc. Group Owner: Big Horn Communications Inc. ■ Net: ABC. Rep: American TV Sls. ■ Thomas Hendrickson, pres; Tim Gazy, gen mgr; Mike Douglas, gen sls mgr; Patsi Peterson, progmg dir; Jean Brodeur, news dir; J. R. Middleton, chief engr. ■ On 5 CATVs. ■ Rates: $100; 60; 15.

***KUSM**—ch 9, 302 w vis, 30.2 w aur, ant -338t/134g. TL: N45 40 00 W111 03 10. (CP: 3.39 kw vis, ant -341t/131g). On air date: Oct 1, 1984. Visual Comm. Bldg., Room 172, Montana St. Univ. (59717). (406) 994-3437. FAX: (406) 994-6221. Licensee: Montana State Univ. ■ Net: PBS. ■ Jack Hyyppa, gen mgr; Joe Pastori, dev dir; Jackie Whiteman, prom dir; Ronn Gjestson, progmg mgr; Tom Jenkins, chief engr. ■ On 23 CATVs—130,000 subs. On one trans.

Butte

ADI No. 189; see Butte market

KTVM—ch 6, 100 kw vis, 10 kw aur, ant 1,940t/213g. TL: N46 00 29 W112 26 30. Stereo. On air date: May 12, 1970. Box 3118, Suite One, 750 Dewey Blvd (59701). (406) 494-7603. FAX: (406) 494-2572. Licensee: Eagle Communications Inc. (group owner; acq 11-78; grpsl). ■ Net: NBC. Rep: Katz. Wash atty: Leventhal, Senter & Lerman. ■ Robert Precht, pres & gen mgr; Charlie Cannaliato, vp opns; Jim Harmon, dev dir; Jane English, vp sls; Pat Grant, natl sls mgr; Kathy McCleerey, prom mgr; Jean Zosel, progmg dir; Rex Kendall, news dir; Billy Ward, chief engr. ■ On 6 CATVs. On 12 trans. ■ Rates: $250; 80; 35.

KWYB—ch 18, 2,684 kw vis, ant 1,955 ft. TL: N46 00 29 W112 26 30. Stereo. Not on air, target date unknown. 118 Sixth St. S., Great Falls (59405). Permittee: CTN Butte Inc. Group owner: Continental Television Network Inc. ■ Net: ABC. Wash atty: Redy, Begley & Martin. ■ James M. Colla, pres; Penny L. Adkins, exec vp; Cheryl A. Cordeiro, stn mgr.

KXLF-TV—ch 4, 100 kw vis, 20 kw aur, ant 1,890t/202g. TL: N46 00 27 W112 26 30. Stereo. Hrs opn: 6 AM-1:30 AM. On air date: Aug 14, 1953. Box 3500, 1003 S. Montana (59701). (406) 782-0444. FAX: (406) 782-8906. Licensee: KXLF Communications Inc. Group owner: Cordillera Communications Inc. (acq 12-15-86; grpsl; 9-29-86). ■ Net: CBS. Rep: Seltel. Wash atty: Dow, Lohnes & Albertson. News staff 8; news progmg 9 hrs wkly. ■ Ron Cass, pres, gen mgr & natl sls mgr; Pat Cooney, gen sls mgr; Margaret McIntosh, progmg dir; Jay Kohn, news dir; Ron Schlosser, chief engr. ■ On 21 CATVs—56,000 subs. On 21 trans. ■ Rates: $225; 30; 15.

Glendive

ADI No. 152; see Minot, ND-Bismark, ND-Dickinson, ND-Glendive

KXGN-TV—ch 5, 14.8 kw vis, 2.9 kw aur, ant 500t/146g. TL: N47 03 15 W104 40 45. On air date: Nov 1, 1957. 210 S. Douglas (59330). (406) 365-3377. FAX: (406) 365-2181. Licensee: Glendive Broadcasting Corp. Ownership: Stephen A. Marks. ■ Net: CBS, NBC. Rep: Hooper, Jones, & Assoc. Wash atty: Daly, Joyce & Borsari. ■ Stephen A. Marks, pres; Dan Frenzel, gen mgr; Rosemary Bunting, gen sls mgr & progmg dir; Ed Ager, news dir; Bob Brenner, chief engr. ■ On 11 CATVs—6,500 subs. On 7 trans. Co-owned radio: KXGN(AM). ■ Rates: $125; 65; 40.

Great Falls

ADI No. 182; see Great Falls market

KFBB-TV—ch 5, 100 kw vis, 20 kw aur, ant 590t/540g. TL: N47 32 08 W111 17 02. Stereo. Hrs opn: 18. On air date: March 21, 1954. Box 1139, Havre Hwy. (59403). (406) 453-4377. FAX: (406) 727-9703; TWX: 910-975-1917. Licensee: KFBB Corp. Group owner: Dix Communications (acq 7-1-82; $5.2 million; 5-17-82). ■ Net: ABC. Rep: Katz. Wash atty: Baker & Hostetler. News staff 6; news progmg 6 hrs wkly. ■ Stan Whitman, pres; Jack May, gen mgr & gen sls mgr; Deb Murphy, prom mgr; Carol Funston, progmg dir; Dick Pompa, news dir; Mike Warner, chief engr. ■ On 22 CATVs—36,360 subs. On 40 trans. ■ Rates: $125; 70; 25.

KRTV—ch 3, 100 kw vis, 10 kw aur, ant 590t/550g. TL: N47 32 09 W111 17 02. On air date: Oct 5, 1958. Box 2989 (59403). (406) 453-2431. FAX: (406) 453-8041; TWX: 629-48-919. Licensee: KRTV Communications Inc. Group owner: Cordillera Communications Inc. ■ Net: CBS. Rep: Blair. Wash atty: Dow, Lohnes & Albertson. ■ Don Bradley, pres, gen mgr & natl sls mgr; Bill Preston, rgnl sls mgr; Joe Lawson, prom mgr; Joel Lundstad, news dir; Marlowe Rames, chief engr. ■ On 25 CATVs—22,800 subs. On 44 trans.

KTGF—ch 16, 2,040 kw vis, 204 kw aur, ant 1,046t/830g. TL: N47 36 26 W111 21 27. Stereo. Hrs opn: 5 AM-1 AM. On air date: Sept 21, 1986. Box 1219, 118 6th St. S. (59405). (406) 761-8816. FAX: (406) 454-3484. Licensee: Continental Television Network Inc. (group owner). ■ Net: NBC. Rep: Blair. Wash atty: Dennis Begley. News staff 6; news progmg 6 hrs wkly. ■ James M. Colla, pres & gen mgr; Penny L. Adkins, vp; Cheryl A. Cordeiro, stn mgr; Mike DeCock, chief opns; Tim Spinder, natl sls mgr & rgnl sls mgr; Penny Adkins, prom dir, adv dir & progmg dir; Kenneth Rich, chief engr. ■ On 22 CATVs—34,800 subs. On 14 trans.

Hardin

ADI No. 171; see Billings market

KOUS-TV—ch 4, 100 kw vis, 10 kw aur, ant 1,062t/628g. TL: N45 44 29 W108 08 19. Box 23309, Billings (59104-3309). (406) 652-4743. Licensee: Big Horn Communications Inc. (group owner). Wash atty: F. Joseph Brinig. ■ Thomas Hendrickson, pres.

Nebraska

Helena

ADI No.207; see Helena market

KHBB—ch 10, 5.01 kw vis, ant 731t. TL: N46 46 12 W112 42 33. Not on air, target date unknown. Permittee: KFBB Corp.

KTVH—ch 12, 105 kw vis, 10.5 kw aur, ant 2,250t/176g. TL: N46 49 35 W111 42 33. Hrs opn: 24. On air date: Jan 1, 1958. Box 6125 (59604); 2433 N. Montana Ave. (59601). (406) 443-5050. FAX: (406) 442-5106. Licensee: Big Sky Broadcasting. Ownership: John Radeck; Will Sanders (acq 10-7-88). ■ Net: NBC. Rep: Seltel, Tacher. Wash atty: Bryan, Cave, McPheeters & McRoberts. News staff 8; news progmg 7 hrs wkly. ■ John Radeck, pres; Bill Stebbins, gen mgr, gen sls mgr & pub affrs dir; Janice Radeck, progmg dir & film buyer; Mellisa Anderson, news dir; Allen Knuth, chief engr. ■ On 11 CATVs—17,650 subs. On 5 trans.

Kalispell

ADI No. 176; see Missoula market

KCFW-TV—ch 9, 26.5 kw vis, 5.3 kw aur, ant 2,794t/240g. TL: N48 00 48 W114 21 55. Stereo. Hrs opn: 24. On air date: June 10, 1968. Box 857, 401 First Ave. E. (59901). (406) 755-5239. FAX: (406) 752-8002. Licensee: Eagle Communications Inc. (group owner; acq 9-78; grpsl). ■ Net: NBC, ABC. Rep: Katz. Wash atty: Cohn & Marks. News staff 4; news progmg 6 hrs wkly. ■ Robert Precht, pres; Jane English, exec vp; Steve Fetveit, gen mgr & gen sls mgr; Kelly Buechler, news dir; Chris Neuhausen, chief engr. ■ On 3 CATVs—17,680 subs. On 4 trans.

Miles City

ADI No. 171; see Billings market

KYUS-TV—ch 3, 10.4 kw vis, 1 kw aur, ant 102t/42g, ant 102t/42g. TL: N46 24 48 W105 51 04. On air date: Aug 29, 1969. Box 23309, Billings (59104-3301). (406) 232-3540. Licensee: Big Horn Communications Inc. (group owner). ■ Net: ABC. Rep: Adam Young. ■ Daniel W. Coon, pres; Ray Moser, gen mgr; Dan Michael, natl sls mgr & rgnl sls mgr; Steve Lakey, prom mgr & pub affrs dir; Pat Rookhuizen, progmg dir; Ron Walden, chief engr. ■ On 2 CATVs—3,000 subs. On 4 trans. ■ Rates: $75; 50; 30.

Missoula

ADI No. 176; see Missoula market

KECI-TV—ch 13, 302 kw vis, 30.2 kw aur, ant 2,001t/290g. TL: N47 01 04 W114 00 47. Stereo. On air date: July 1, 1954. 340 W. Main (59802). (406) 721-2063. FAX: (406) 549-6507. Licensee: Eagle Communications Inc. (group owner; acq 11-1-78; grpsl). ■ Net: NBC. Rep: Katz. Wash atty: Cohn & Marks. ■ Robert Precht, pres & gen mgr; Pat Grant, natl sls mgr; Jim Harmon, vp mktg; Kathy McCleerey, prom mgr; Jean Zosel, progmg dir; Larry Frost, news dir; Larry Arbaugh, chief engr. ■ On 24 CATVs—23,300 subs. On 19 trans. ■ Rates: $300; 100; 50.

KPAX-TV—ch 8, 275 kw vis, 49 kw aur, ant 2,150/284g. TL: N47 01 06 W114 00 41. Stereo. Hrs opn: 24. On air date: June 5, 1970. Box 4827, 2204 Regent St. (59801). (406) 543-7106. FAX: (406) 543-7111. Licensee: KPAX-TV Communications Inc. Group owner: Cordillera Communications Inc. ■ Net: CBS. Rep: Blair. Wash atty: Dow, Lohnes & Albertson. News progmg 9 hrs wkly. ■ William F. Sullivan, pres & gen mgr; Tammy Engle, opns mgr, progmg dir & film buyer; Bob Hermes, adv mgr; William T. Davey, news dir; Brent Trantum, pub affrs dir; Mark Rapson, chief engr. ■ On 21 CATVs—45,800 subs. On 14 trans. ■ Rates: $400; 200; 80.

KTMF—ch 23, 1,820 kw vis, ant 2,054t. TL: N47 01 10 W114 00 46. Stereo. 6 AM-1 AM. On air date: Nov 16, 1990. 2200 Stephens Ave. (59801). (406) 542-8900. FAX: (406) 728-4800. Licensee: CTN Missoula Inc. Group owner: Continental Television Network Inc. ■ Net: ABC; Blair. Wash atty: Reddy, Begley & Martin. ■ James M. Colla, pres; Penny L. Adkins, exec vp, vp prom & vp progmg; Cheryl A. Cordeiro, stn mgr; John Sherman, chief opns; Tim Spinder, natl sls mgr; Beth Humble, progmg dir; Ken Rich, chief engr.

*KUFM-TV—ch 11, 125 kw vis, ant 2,116t/259g. Not on air, target date unknown. Telecommunications Center, PARTV 180 (59812). Permittee: The University of Montana. Co-owned radio: *KUFM(FM).

Nebraska

Albion

ADI No. 99; see Lincoln-Hastings-Kearney market

KCAN—ch 8, 316 kw vis, 31.6 kw aur, ant 2,001t/1,974g. TL: N41 32 28 W97 40 45. On air date: Dec 3, 1964. c/o KCAU-TV, Sioux City, IA (51101). (712) 277-2345. FAX: (712) 277-3733. Licensee: Citadel Communications Co. Ltd. Group owner: Citadel Communications Co. Ltd., Coronet Communications Co. (acq 11-15-86; $3 million; 7-28-86). ■ Net: ABC. Rep: Katz. Wash atty: Latham & Watkins. ■ Philip J. Lombardo, pres; Raymond Cole, gen mgr; Dan Ackerman, chief engr. ■ On 59 CATVs. On one trans.

Alliance

ADI No. 168; see Rapid City market

KDUH-TV—See Scottsbluff.

*KTNE-TV—ch 13, 316 kw vis, 31.6 kw aur, ant 1,542t/1,499g. TL: N41 50 24 W103 03 18. Stereo. On air date: Sept 7, 1966. Box 83111, 1800 N. 33rd St., Lincoln (68501). (402) 472-3611. FAX: (402) 472-1785. Licensee: Nebraska Educational Telecommunications Commission. ■ Net: PBS. Wash atty: Dow, Lohnes & Albertson. ■ Jack McBride, gen mgr; Ron Hull, stn mgr; Verle Finke, opns mgr; Don Gill, dev dir; Kathryn Stephens, prom dir; Gene Bunge, progmg dir; Bill Ganzel, news dir; William Ramsay, chief engr. ■ On 16 CATVs—39,130 subs. On 3 trans. Satellite of *KUON-TV Lincoln. Co-owned radio: *KTNE-FM.

Bassett

ADI No. 99; see Lincoln-Hastings-Kearney market

*KMNE-TV—ch 7, 316 kw vis, 31.6 kw aur, ant 1,484t/1,524g. TL: N42 20 05 W99 29 01. Stereo. On air date: Sept 1, 1967. Box 83111, 1800 N. 33rd St., Lincoln (68501). (402) 472-3611. FAX: (402) 472-1785. Licensee: Nebraska Educational Telecommunications Commission. ■ Net: PBS. Wash atty: Dow, Lohnes & Albertson. ■ Jack McBride, gen mgr; Ron Hull, stn mgr; Verle Finke, opns dir; Don Gill, dev dir; Steve Lenzen, mktg dir; Kathryn Stephens, prom dir; Eugene Bunge, progmg dir; Bill Ganzel, news dir; William Ramsay, chief engr. ■ On 16 CATVs—10,182 subs. On 1 trans. Satellite of *KUON-TV Lincoln. Co-owned radio: *KMNE-FM.

Gering

KSTF—See Scottsbluff.

Grand Island

ADI No. 99; see Lincoln-Hastings-Kearney market

KGIN—ch 11, 316 kw vis, 55 kw aur, ant 1,010t/1,069g. TL: N40 35 20 W98 48 10. On air date: Oct 1, 1961. Box 1069 (68801). (308) 382-6100. TWX: 910-621-8114. Licensee: Busse Broadcasting Corp. (acq 7-31-87). ■ Net: CBS. Rep: Telerep. Wash atty: Dow, Lohnes & Albertson. ■ Frank Jonas, gen mgr; Richard Nelson, gen sls mgr. ■ On 110 CATVs—273,000 subs. On 19 trans. Satellite of KOLN-TV Lincoln.

KHGI-TV—See Kearney.

KTVG—ch 17, 219 kw vis, 21.9 kw aur, ant 266t/270g. TL: N40 51 01 W98 24 40. Hrs opn: 24. On air date: December 1992. 5324 S. Engleman Rd., (68802). (308) 384-1717. FAX: (308) 384-1986. Licensee: Hill Broadcasting Inc. (group owner). ■ Net: Fox. ■ Robert Hill, pres; Lee McAliley, gen mgr & progmg dir; Marty Godsey, pub affrs dir.

Hastings

ADI No. 99; see Lincoln-Hastings-Kearney market

KHAS-TV—ch 5, 100 kw vis, 20 kw aur, ant 731t/768g. TL: N40 39 06 W98 23 04. Stereo. Hrs opn: 6 AM-12:35 PM. On air date: Jan 1, 1956. Box 578, N. Hwy. 281 (68901). (402) 463-1321. FAX: (402) 463-6551. Licensee: Nebraska Television Corp. Group owner: Seaton Stations, see Cross-Ownership (7-15-74). ■ Net: NBC. Wash atty: Dow, Lohnes & Albertson. ■ Donald R. Seaton, pres; John T. Benson, exec vp, gen mgr, gen sls mgr & film buyer; Deb Dixon, prom mgr; Jackie Ackerman, progmg dir; Chris Hanefeld, news dir; Diana DeCola, pub affrs dir; Dave Block, chief engr. ■ On 75 CATVs—103,000 subs. On 2 trans. ■ Rates: $300; 115; 75.

KHGI-TV—See Kearney.

*KHNE-TV—ch 29, 605 kw vis, 60.5 kw aur, ant 1,220t/1,238g. TL: N40 46 16.5W 98 05 21.9. Stereo. On air date: Nov 17, 1968. Box 83111 1800 N. 33rd St., Lincoln (68501). (402) 472-3611. FAX: (402) 472-1785. Licensee: Nebraska Educational Telecommunications Commission. ■ Net: PBS. Wash atty: Dow, Lohnes & Albertson. ■ Jack McBride, gen mgr; Ron Hull, stn mgr; Verle Finke, opns mgr; Don Gill, dev dir & mktg dir; Kathryn Stephens, prom dir; Gene Bunge, progmg dir; Bill Ganzel, news dir; William Ramsay, chief engr. ■ On 48 CATVs—25,624 subs. Satellite of *KUON-TV Lincoln. Co-owned radio: *KHNE-FM.

Hayes Center

ADI No. 99; see Lincoln-Hastings-Kearney market

KWNB-TV—ch 6, 100 kw vis, 21.6 kw aur, ant 737t/586g. TL: N40 37 29 W101 01 58. Hrs opn: 20. On air date: Feb 9, 1956. Box 220, 13 S. Hwy. 44, Kearney (68848). (308) 743-2494. FAX: (308) 743-2644; TWX: 910-960-3746. Licensee: Fant Broadcasting Co. of Nebraska Inc. (group owner; acq 5-14-93; grpsl; 5-31-93). ■ Net: ABC. Rep: Katz Continental. News staff 26; news progmg 25 hrs wkly. ■ Steve Barry, pres, gen mgr & vp sls; Doug Conrad, rgnl sls mgr; Mitchell Bowles, prom dir, adv dir & pub affrs dir; Teri Dyer, progmg mgr; Al Zobel, news dir; Jerry Fuehrer, chief engr. ■ On 282 CATVs—270,000 subs. On 11 trans. ■ Rates: $950; 175; 75.

Kearney

ADI No. 99; see Lincoln-Hastings-Kearney market

KHGI-TV—ch 13, 316 kw vis, 31.6 kw aur, ant 1,110t/1,163g. TL: N40 39 28 W98 52 04. On air date: Dec 24, 1953. Box 220, 13 S. Hwy. 44 (68848-0220). (308) 743-2494. FAX: (308) 743-2644. Licensee: Fant Broadcasting Co. of Nebraska Inc. (group owner; acq 5-14-93; grpsl; 5-31-93). ■ Net: ABC. Rep: Katz Continental. News staff 26; news progmg 25 hrs wkly. ■ Steve Barry, pres, gen mgr & vp sls; Doug Conrad, rgnl sls mgr; Mitchell Bowles, prom dir, adv dir & pub affrs dir; Teri Dyer, progmg mgr; Al Zobel, news dir; Jerry Fuehrer, chief engr. ■ On 282 CATVs—270,000 subs. On 11 trans. ■ Rates: $950; 175; 75.

Lexington

ADI No. 99; see Lincoln-Hastings-Kearney market

*KLNE-TV—ch 3, 100 kw vis, 10 kw aur, ant 1,062t/1,065g. TL: N40 23 05 W99 27 30. Stereo. On air date: Sept 6, 1965. Box 83111, 1800 N. 33rd St., Lincoln (68501). (402) 472-3611. FAX: (402) 472-1785. Licensee: Nebraska Educational Telecommunications Commission. ■ Net: PBS. Wash atty: Dow, Lohnes & Albertson. ■ Jack McBride, gen mgr; Ron Hull, stn mgr; Don Gill, dev dir; Kathryn Stephens, prom dir; Gene Bunge, progmg dir; Bill Ganzel, news dir; William Ramsay, chief engr. ■ On 24 CATVs—21,383 subs. On one trans. Satellite of *KUON-TV Lincoln. Co-owned radio: *KLNE-FM.

Lincoln

ADI No. 99; see Lincoln-Hastings-Kearney market

KOLN—ch 10, 316 kw vis, 36.3 kw aur, ant 1,530t/1,500g. TL: N40 48 08 W97 10 46. On air date: Feb 18, 1953. Box 30350 (68503). (402) 467-4321. FAX: (402) 467-9210. Licensee: Busse Broadcasting Corp. (group owner; acq 8-21-87). ■ Net: CBS. Rep: TeleRep. Wash atty: Pepper & Corazzini. ■ Frank Jonas, pres & gen mgr; Dick Nelson, gen sls mgr; Kris Ryan, natl sls mgr; Charlie Peterson, prom mgr & progmg mgr; John Denney, news dir; Kim Rogers, pub affrs dir; Carl Iverson, chief engr. ■ On 112 CATVs—275,000 subs. On 19 trans.

*KUON-TV—ch 12, 316 kw vis, 31.6 kw aur, ant 830t/879g. TL: N41 08 18 W96 27 19. Stereo. On air date: Nov 1, 1954. Box 83111 (68501); Neb. Telecommunications Ctr., 1800 N. 33rd St. (68503). (402) 472-3611. FAX: (402) 472-1785. Licensee: Univ. of Nebraska (acq 7-28-54; 8-2-54). ■ Net: PBS. Wash atty: Dow, Lohnes & Albertson. News progmg 2 hrs wkly. ■ Jack McBride, gen mgr; Ron Hull, stn mgr; Don Gill, dev dir; Steve Lenzen, mktg dir; Kathryn Stephens, prom dir; Eugene E. Bunge, progmg dir; Bill Ganzel, news dir; William Ramsay, chief engr. ■ On 72 CATVs—133,237 subs. On 16 trans.

Broadcasting & Cable COVERS THE WORLD

If you're involved in television anywhere in the world, you should be reading the magazine that covers the world like no other, Broadcasting & Cable. Never before has getting the latest news and information been so important to your industry. Subscribe to Broadcasting & Cable and stay on top of the world.

Broadcasting & Cable covers *your* world. Our special reports include vital subjects like Telcos, Satellites, Radio & TV Software, Advertising, Equipment, Movie Packages, Radio Syndication, Cable Marketing, Children's TV, and Journalism. We cover the important conventions including NAPTE, MIP-TV, NAB and MIPCOM. And we cover the news of the industry, as it happens, with a new issue every week.

Why Subscribe?

At last, the global potential of broadcasting is being realized. Whether by radio frequency, wire, fiber optics, satellite or microwave transmission, more radio and television signals are being distributed to more people in more places around the world every day. Digital compression technologies, 500-channel cable systems, telcos in television, booming expansion in Europe–it's an exciting time to be in broadcasting. And a great time to subscribe to Broadcasting & Cable and keep up with it all.

IMMEDIATE ATTENTION!
To Broadcasting & Cable Order Dept.

FAX THIS FORM
1-310-782-7012

Order your subscription to Broadcasting & Cable today and keep up with the fast-changing world of broadcasting and cable.

Fax this form or detach and mail with proper postage. Subscription will commence upon receipt of payment.

☐ **YES!** Enter my one-year subscription to Broadcasting & Cable.

☐ Foreign/Air: $300. ☐ Canada: $129. (includes GST)
☐ Foreign Surface: $149. ☐ Domestic: $99.
☐ Payment enclosed ☐ Bill Me All orders must be paid in U.S. funds.
☐ Charge my: ☐ VISA ☐ MC ☐ AMEX

Card # _____ Exp. Date _____

Signature _____

Name _____

Company _____

Address _____

City _____ State _____

Country _____ Postal Code _____

Broadcasting & Cable, P.O. Box 6399, Torrance, CA 90504, FAX: 1-310-782-7012   **G4ABCY**

McCook

ADI No. 62; see Wichita-Hutchinson market

KSNK—ch 8, 295 kw vis, 60 kw aur, ant 709t/676g. TL: N39 49 48 W100 42 04. Hrs opn: 24. On air date: Nov 28, 1959. Box 238, Oberlin, KS (67749). (913) 475-2248. FAX: (913) 475-3944. Licensee: SJL Inc. Group owner: SJL Broadcast Management Corp. (acq 6-13-62; grpsl; 6-18-62). ■ Net: NBC. Rep: Katz. Wash atty: Latham & Watkins. ■ L. Dwayne Detter, gen mgr & stn mgr; Gary Gore, gen sls mgr; Jim Tellus, prom dir; Joan Smith, progmg dir; Julie Kennedy, news dir; Jack Benton, chief engr. ■ On 36 CATVs—5,698 subs. ■ Rates: $55; 40; 20.

Merriman

ADI No. 108; see Sioux Falls-Mitchell market

***KRNE-TV**—ch 12, 316 kw vis, 31.6 kw aur, ant 1,066t/1,029g. TL: N42 40 38 W101 42 36. Stereo. Hrs opn: 4:45 AM-11 PM. On air date: Dec 9, 1968. Box 83111, 1800 N. 33rd St., Lincoln (68501). (402) 472-3611. FAX: (402) 472-1785. Licensee: Nebraska Educational Telecommunications Commission. ■ Net: PBS. Wash atty: Dow, Lohnes & Albertson. ■ Jack G. McBride, gen mgr; Ron Hull, gen sls mgr; Kathryn Stephens, prom mgr; Gene Bunge, progmg dir; William Ramsay, chief engr. ■ On 2 CATVs—1,640 subs. Satellite of KUON-TV Lincoln. Co-owned radio: *KRNE-FM.

Norfolk

ADI No. 140; see Sioux City market

***KXNE-TV**—ch 19, 1,682.67 kw vis, ant 1,141t. TL: N42 14 15 W97 16 41. (CP: 776 kw vis, ant 1,122t/1,149g). On air date: Nov 10, 1967. Box 83111, 1800 N. 33rd St., Lincoln (68501). (402) 472-3611. FAX: (402) 472-1785. Licensee: Nebraska Educational Telecommunications Commission. ■ Net: PBS. Wash atty: Dow, Lohnes & Albertson. ■ Jack McBride, gen mgr; Ron Hull, stn mgr; Verle Finke, opns mgr; Don Gill, dev dir; Steve Lenzen, mktg dir; Kathryn Stephens, prom mgr; Gene Bunge, progmg dir; Bill Ganzel, news dir; William Ramsay, chief engr. ■ On 30 CATVs—25,280 subs. On one trans. Satellite of *KUON-TV Lincoln. Co-owned radio: *KXNE-FM.

North Platte

ADI No. 208; see North Platte market

KNOP-TV—ch 2, 100 kw vis, 15 kw aur, ant 630t/608g. TL: N41 12 13 W100 43 58. Stereo. On air date: Dec 2, 1958. Box 749 (69103). (308) 532-2222. FAX: (308) 532-9579. Licensee: North Platte Television Inc. Ownership: Shively Communications (acq 10-28-70; 11-16-70). ■ Net: NBC. Rep: Adam Young. Wash atty: Ed O'Neill. ■ Richard F. Shively, pres; Ulysses A. Carlini, vp, gen mgr & gen sls mgr; Lewys Carlini, opns mgr; Rick Nielsen, chief engr. ■ On 2 CATVs—1,500 subs. On 5 trans.

***KPNE-TV**—ch 9, 316 kw vis, 31.6 kw aur, ant 1,020t/1,006g. TL: N41 01 16 W101 09 10. On air date: Sept 12, 1966. Box 83111, Lincoln (68501); Neb. Telecommunications Ctr., 1800 N. 33rd St., Lincoln (68503). (402) 472-3611. FAX: (402) 472-1785. Licensee: Nebraska Educational Telecommunications Commission. ■ Net: PBS. Wash atty: Dow, Lohnes & Albertson. ■ Jack G. McBride, gen mgr; Ron Hull, stn mgr; Verle Finke, opns mgr; Don Gill, dev dir; Steve Lenzen, mktg dir; Kathryn Stephens, prom dir; Gene Bunge, progmg dir; Bill Ganzel, news dir; William Ramsay, chief engr. ■ On 16 CATVs—22,420 subs. On 5 trans. Satellite of *KUON-TV Lincoln.

Omaha

ADI No. 73; see Omaha market

KETV—ch 7, 316 kw vis, 31.6 kw aur, ant 1,356t/1,362g. TL: N41 18 32 W96 01 37. Stereo. Hrs opn: 6 AM-1:30 AM. On air date: Sept 17, 1957. 2665 Douglas St. (68131-2699). (402) 345-7777. FAX: (402) 978-8922 (SALES); (402) 978-8931 (NEWS). Licensee: Pulitzer Broadcasting Co. (group owner; acq 2-26-76; $9,453,000; 3-8-76). ■ Net: ABC. Rep: Blair. Wash atty: Verner, Liipfert, Bernhard, McPherson & Hand. News staff 38; news progmg 14 hrs wkly. ■ Ken Elkins, pres; David Summers, vp & gen mgr; Don Grugaugh, natl sls mgr; Phyllis Ned, rgnl sls mgr; Phil Clark, prom mgr; Bettie Denny, progmg dir; Rose Ann Shannon, news dir; Don Clausen, chief engr. ■ On 39 CATVs—751,140 subs. On one trans. ■ Rates: $665; 125; 85.

KMTV—ch 3, 100 kw vis, 20 kw aur, ant 1,371t/1,409g. TL: N41 18 25 W96 01 37. Stereo. Hrs opn: 19. On air date: Sept 1, 1949. 10714 Mockingbird Dr. (68127). (402) 592-3333. FAX: (402) 592-3658. Licensee: KMTV Inc. Group owner: Lee Enterprises Inc. (acq 11-5-86; grpsl; 9-22-86). ■ Net: CBS. Rep: Katz. ■ Howard Kennedy, gen mgr; David Kuehn, gen sls mgr; John Sullivan, prom mgr; Donald E. Browers, progmg dir & film buyer; Loren Tobia, news dir; Larry Steele, chief engr. ■ On 26 CATVs—150,000 subs. On 4 trans.

KPTM—ch 42, 5,000 kw vis, 500 kw aur, ant 1,558t/1,464g. TL: N41 04 15 W96 13 30. Stereo. (CP: Ant 1,893t/1,799g). On air date: Apr 6, 1986. 4625 Farnam St. (68132). (402) 558-4200. FAX: (402) 554-4290. Licensee: Pappas Telecasting of the Midlands. Group owner: Pappas Telecasting Companies (acq 3-14-86). ■ Net: Fox. Rep: Telerep. Wash atty: Bryan, Cave, McPheeters & McRoberts. News staff 6; news progmg 3 hrs wkly. ■ Harry J. Pappas, pres; Howard Shrier, gen mgr; James F. McKernan, stn mgr & gen sls mgr; Dina Olson, opns mgr; Donna Ridgley, prom mgr; Brad Gonzalez, progmg mgr & news dir; Dale Scherbring, chief engr. ■ On 163 CATVs—263,179 subs.

***KYNE-TV**—ch 26, 525 kw vis, 52.5 kw aur, ant 426t/396g. TL: N41 15 28 W96 00 32. On air date: Oct 19, 1965. 1800 N. 33rd St. Lincoln (68503). (402) 472-3611. FAX: (402) 472-1785. Licensee: Nebraska Educational Telecommunications Commission. ■ Net: PBS. Wash atty: Dow, Lohnes & Albertson. ■ Jack G. McBride, gen mgr; Ron Hull, gen sls mgr; Kathryn Stephens, prom mgr; Gene Bunge, progmg dir; William Ramsay, chief engr. ■ On 10 CATVs—78,000 subs. Satellite of *KUON-TV Lincoln.

WOWT—ch 6, 100 kw vis, 20 kw aur, ant 1,371t/1,344g. TL: N41 18 40 W96 01 37. Stereo. On air date: Aug 29, 1949. 3501 Farnam St. (68131). (402) 346-6666. FAX: (402) 346-9249; (402) 346-6740. TWX: 910-622-0488. Licensee: Chronicle Broadcasting Co. (group owner; acq 7-9-75; $9,158,500; 6-9-75). ■ Net: NBC. Rep: Petry. Wash atty: Fletcher, Heald & Hildreth. ■ D. R. Oswald, vp, gen mgr & film buyer; Karen Bride, opns mgr & adv mgr; Chris Bailey, gen sls mgr; Carl Bauman, mktg dir & prom dir; John Clark, news dir; Jack Davidson, chief engr. ■ On 134 CATVs—225,000 subs. On 2 trans.

Scottsbluff

ADI No. 196; see Cheyenne, WY-Scottsbluff market

KDUH-TV—ch 4, 100 kw vis, 20 kw aur, ant 2,001t/1,966g. TL: N42 10 21 W103 13 57. Hrs opn: 24. On air date: Mar 5, 1958. Box 1529, 1523 1st Ave. (69363-1529). (308) 632-3071. FAX: (308) 632-3596. Licensee: Duhamel Broadcasting Enterprises (group owner). ■ Net: ABC. Rep: Katz. Wash atty: Fisher, Wayland, Cooper & Leader. News staff 6; news progmg 2 hrs wkly. ■ William F. Duhamel, pres; Rex A. Swanson, gen mgr; Monte Loos, opns mgr, progmg dir & film buyer; Wes Haugen, gen sls mgr; Deb Anderson, prom mgr; Mitch Krebs, news dir; Bruce Mues, chief engr. ■ On 31 CATVs—10,000 subs. On 34 trans.

KSTF—ch 10, 240 kw vis, 24 kw aur, ant 840t/674g. TL: N41 59 58 W103 39 55. On air date: Aug 7, 1955. 3385 N. 10th Ave., Gering (69341). (308) 632-6107. FAX: (308) 632-3470. Licensee: Stauffer Communications Inc. (group owner, see Cross-Ownership; acq 7-22-86; grpsl). ■ Net: CBS, Fox. Rep: Katz. Wash atty: Dow, Lohnes & Albertson. News staff 6; news progmg 8 hrs wkly. ■ Ray Blomenkamt, gen mgr & gen sls mgr; Barbara Parenti, progmg dir; Steve Wilson, news dir; Tony Schaefer, chief engr. ■ On 18 CATVs—30,900 subs. On 5 trans.

Superior

ADI No. 99; see Lincoln-Hastings-Kearney market

KSNB-TV—ch 4, 100 kw vis, 12.6 kw aur, ant 1,131t/1,086g. TL: N40 05 13 W97 55 13. On air date: Oct 1, 1965. Box 220, 13 S. Hwy 44, Kearney (68848-0220). (308) 743-2494. FAX: (308) 743-2644; TWX: 910-960-3746. Licensee: Fant Broadcasting Company of Nebraska Inc. (group owner; acq 5-14-93; grpsl; 5-31-93). ■ Net: ABC. Rep: Katz Continental. News staff 26; news progmg 25 hrs wkly. ■ Steve Barry, pres, gen mgr & vp sls; Mitch Bowles, prom dir; Mitchell Bowles, adv dir & pub affrs dir; Teri Dyer, progmg mgr; Al Zobel, news dir; Jerry Fuehrer, chief engr. ■ On 282 CATVs—270,000 subs. On 11 trans. ■ Rates: $950; 175; 75.

Nevada

Henderson

KVVU-TV—Licensed to Henderson. See Las Vegas.

Las Vegas

ADI No. 74; see Las Vegas market

KFBT—ch 33, 1,350 kw vis, 500 kw aur, ant 1,906t/80g. TL: N35 56 44 W115 02 31. Hrs opn: 24. On air date: Aug 1, 1989. 3840 S. Jones Blvd. (89103). (702) 873-0033. FAX: (702) 873-6192. Licensee: Channel 33 Inc. Ownership: Don Koker, 85%, Larry DePaulis, 15% Rep: Adam Young. Wash atty: Fletcher, Heald & Hildreth. ■ Dan Koker, pres, gen mgr, progmg dir & film buyer; Jack Paris, gen sls mgr; Korie Fera, prom mgr; Jeff Gotts, chief engr. ■ Rates: $100; 75; 25.

KLAS-TV—ch 8, 316 kw vis, 57.5 kw, ant 2,001t/272g. TL: N35 56 44 W115 02 33. On air date: July 8, 1953. Box 15047 (89114); 3228 Channel 8 Dr. (89109). (702) 792-8888. FAX: (702) 734-7437. Licensee: KLAS Inc., a Nevada Corp. Group owner: Landmark Communications Inc. (acq 7-1-78; $8 million). ■ Net: CBS. Wash atty: Hogan & Hartson. News progmg 22 hrs wkly. ■ Dick Fraim, gen mgr; Andy Henderson, gen sls mgr; John Dalrymple, natl sls mgr; Julie O'Connor, rgnl sls mgr; Terry McFarlane, mktg dir; Pat Monson, progmg dir; Emily Neilson, news dir; Allison Copening, pub affrs dir; John Nelson, chief engr. ■ On 24 trans.

***KLVX**—ch 10, 295 kw vis, 29.5 kw aur, ant 1,220t/176g. TL: N36 00 27 W115 00 24. On air date: Mar 25, 1968. 4210 Channel 10 Dr. (89119). (702) 737-1010. Licensee: Clark County School District Board of Trustees. ■ Net: PBS. Wash atty: Wiley, Rein & Fielding. ■ Ruth Uhls, prom mgr & progmg dir; Lee Winston, news dir; Marty Vodovoz, chief engr. ■ On 2 CATVs. On 14 trans.

KRLR—ch 21, 400 kw vis, 40 kw aur, ant 1,160t/115g. TL: N36 00 26 W115 00 24. Stereo. Hrs opn: 24. On air date: July 31, 1984. 920 S. Commerce (89106). (702) 382-2121. FAX: (702) 382-1351. Licensee: DRES Media Inc. Ownership: Frank E. Scott Family, 70%; Broadcast West Inc., 10%; Alden Communications Corp., 10%; Channel 21, 10% (acq 6-16-83). Rep: Seltel. Wash atty: Miller & Fields. ■ Frank E. Scott, CEO & chmn; Charlene Scott, pres; Rick Scott, exec vp, gen mgr & gen sls mgr; Wayne Gartley, stn mgr; Rita Wotherspoon, opns mgr; Ron Maestri, progmg dir; Steve Scott, chief engr. ■ On 8 CATVs—172,000 subs. On 7 trans. ■ Rates: $300; 150; 35.

KTNV—ch 13, 316 kw, vis, 15.8 kw aur, ant 2,001t/259g. TL: N35 56 43 W115 02 32. Stereo. On air date: May 4, 1956. 3355 S. Valley View Blvd. (89102). (702) 876-1313. FAX: (702) 876-2237; (702) 871-1961. Licensee: KTNV, a division of WTMJ Inc. Group owner: WTMJ Inc. (acq 6-29-79). ■ Net: ABC. Rep: Petry. Wash atty: Crowell & Moring. News staff 32; news progmg 13 hrs wkly. ■ Peter Bannister, vp, gen mgr & film buyer; Mike Williams, opns mgr; Gary Plumlee, gen sls mgr; Donna Dube, prom mgr; Matthew Zelkind, news dir; Bob Blaskey, pub affrs dir; Roman Hlohowsky, chief engr. ■ On 5 trans.

KVBC—ch 3, 100 kw vis, 10 kw aur, ant 1,269t/252g. TL: N36 00 30 W115 00 20. On air date: Oct 1, 1979. 1500 Foremaster Ln. (89101). (702) 642-3333. FAX: (702) 642-7303 (NEWS); (702) 399-0767; TWX: 910-397-6997. Licensee: Valley Broadcasting Co. Ownership: James Rogers, 49.97%; Louis Wiener Jr., 30%; Janet Rogers, 12.53%. ■ Net: NBC. Rep: Blair. Wash atty: Dow, Lohnes & Albertson. ■ James E. Rogers, pres; Rolla Cleaver, gen mgr; Gene Greenberg, gen sls mgr; Glenn Turner, prom dir; Judith Reich, progmg dir & film buyer; Mike Cutler, news dir; Charlene Herst, pub affrs dir; Frank Haynes, chief engr. ■ On 39 trans. ■ Rates: $2,000; 750; 300.

KVVU-TV—(Henderson). ch 5, 100 kw vis, 20 kw aur, ant 1,191t/140g. TL: N36 00 26 W115 00 23. On air date: October 1967. 25 TV-5 Dr., Henderson (89014). (702) 435-5555. FAX: (702) 451-4220. Licensee: KVVU Broadcasting Corp. Group owner: Meredith Broadcasting Group, Meredith Corp., see Cross-Ownership (acq 5-85; $36 million). ■ Net: Fox. Rep: MMT. Wash atty: Haley, Bader & Potts. ■ Phil Jones, pres; Rusty Durante, gen mgr, progmg dir & film buyer; Jim Utton, opns mgr; William W. Utton, gen sls mgr; Tom Purney, prom mgr; Jack Smith, chief engr. ■ On 9 trans.

Paradise

ADI No. 74; see Las Vegas market

KBLR—ch 39, 1,320 kw vis, 132 kw aur, ant 1,204t/223g. TL: N36 00 31 W115 00 22. On air date: Apr 20, 1989. 5000 W. Oakley, Las Vegas (89102). Licensee: Summit Media Limited-Labilty Co. Ownership: Scott Gentry, Bruce F. Becker, William O'Connell, et al (acq 1993; $1.5 million; 9-20-93). ■ Scott Gentry, pres; Jim Williams, gen mgr; Tony Malone, gen sls mgr; John Romanko, chief engr.

Reno

ADI No. 118; see Reno market

KAME-TV—ch 21, 692 kw vis, 69.2 kw aur, ant 620t/152g. TL: N39 19 07 W119 47 51. Hrs opn: 21. On air date: Oct 12, 1981. 4920 Brookside Ct. (89502). (702) 856-2121. FAX: (702) 856-9146. Licensee: Page Enterprises. Ownership: William Andrews, 21%; Helene Investments, 35%; Manny Gutterman & Sons, 39%; Thomas Letizia, 5%■ Net: Fox. Rep: Seltel. Wash atty: Bryan, Cave, McPheeters & McRoberts. ■ William C. Andrews, pres & gen mgr; B. J. Andrews, stn mgr & film buyer; Mike Andrews, gen sls mgr; Debbie Holder, progmg dir; Walt Butler, chief engr. ■ On 14 CATVs—84,400 subs. On 7 trans.

*****KNPB**—ch 5, 5.01 kw vis, 1 kw aur, ant 459t/93g. TL: N39 35 01 W119 47 52. On air date: October 1983. Box 14730 (89507). (702) 784-4555. FAX: (702) 784-1438. Licensee: Channel 5 Public Broadcasting Inc. ■ Net: PBS. Wash atty: Schwartz, Woods & Miller. ■ James Pagliarini, gen mgr; Linda Tabkin, progmg dir; Tom Werner, chief engr.

KOLO-TV—ch 8, 166 kw vis, 30.2 aur, ant 2,929t/119g. TL: N39 18 49 W119 53 00. Stereo. Hrs opn: 24. On air date: Sept 27, 1953. Box 10000 (89510); 4850 Ampere Dr. (89502). (702) 858-8888; (702) 858-8880. FAX: (702) 858-8855. Licensee: DR Partners. Group owner: Donrey Media Group Stns, see Cross-Ownership. ■ Net: ABC. Rep: Blair. Wash atty: Haley, Bader & Potts. Sp one hr wkly. News staff 31; news progmg 20 hrs wkly. ■ Fred W. Smith, CEO; Ross Pendergraft, exec vp; Charles S. Alvey, gen mgr; Bill Hall, natl sls mgr; David Ward, rgnl sls mgr; Earl Ling, prom mgr; John Csia, progmg dir; Judith Mathews, news dir; Robert Northam, chief engr. ■ On 29 CATVs—138,200 subs. On 36 trans. ■ Rates: $1400; 375; 150.

KREN-TV—ch 27, 1,820 kw vis, 182 kw aur, ant 2,923t/139g. TL: N39 18 47 W119 52 59. On air date: Nov 1, 1985. Suite 130, 961 Matley Lane (89502). (702) 333-2727. FAX: (702) 333-5264. Licensee: Sainte Ltd. (group owner). ■ Net: Univision. Wash atty: Fletcher, Heald & Hildreth. ■ Chester Smith, CEO; Debbie Perez, stn mgr; Paul A. Acosta, opns mgr; Herbert Crenshaw, chief engr.

KRNV—ch 4, 17.4 kw vis, 3.4 kw aur, ant 420t/92g. TL: N39 35 03 W119 48 06. On air date: Sept 30, 1962. Box 7160, 1790 Vassar St. (89510). (702) 322-4444. FAX: (702) 785-1200; (702) 785-1206. Licensee: Sierra Broadcasting Co. Ownership: James E. Rogers, Janet F. Rogers & Louis Wiener. Group owner: Sunbelt Broadcasting Co. (acq 9-13-89).■ Net: NBC. Rep: Petry. Wash atty: Gerald Rourke. News staff 26; news progmg 14 hrs wkly. ■ James E. Rogers, chmn & pres; Joan Zucker, CFO; Ralph Toddre, gen mgr, progmg dir & film buyer; Jack Hartman, natl sls mgr; Craig Brown, rgnl sls mgr; Ted Meairis, mktg dir; Coreen Scott, prom dir; Eric Hulnick, news dir; Richard Wheatley, chief engr. ■ On 22 CATVs—60,000 subs. On 26 trans.

KRXI—ch 11, 178 kw vis, 17.8 kw aur, ant 2,808t/207g. TL: N39 35 25 W119 55 40. Not on air, target date unknown. 3500 Lakeside Ct. (89509). Permittee: Nevada Television Corp. Ownership: Luther Mack, 40%; Ann Bersi, 30%; Jane Manning, 30%

KTVN—ch 2, 89.1 kw vis, 8.9 kw aur, ant 2,152t/150g. TL: N39 15 28 W119 42 36. (CP: 89.1 kw vis, 8.9 kw aur, ant 2,152t, TL: N39 15 28 W119 42 36). Hrs opn: 24. On air date: June 4, 1967. 4925 Energy Way (89502); Box 7220 (89519). (702) 858-2222. FAX: (702) 858-2345. Licensee: Sarkes Tarzian Inc. (group owner; acq 8-13-80; $12.5 million). ■ Net: CBS. Rep: Katz. Wash atty: Leventhal, Senter & Lerman. News staff 26; news progmg 19 hrs wkly. ■ Lawson Fox, pres & gen mgr; John Richardson, gen sls mgr; Cecilia Atkins, prom mgr; Cecilia Atkins, vp adv; Sharon Asher, progmg dir; Nancy Cope, news dir; Al Richards, chief engr. ■ On 12 CATVs—143,900 subs. On 38 trans. ■ Rates: $550; 175; 50.

New Hampshire

Concord

ADI No. 6; see Boston, MA market

WNHT—ch 21, 1,860 kw vis, 186 kw aur, ant 1,128t. TL: N43 11 04 W71 19 12. Stn currently dark. On air date: Apr 16, 1984. 126 Brookline Ave., Boston MA (02215); 21 Media Park (03301). (617) 536-5390; (508) 283-8718. Licensee: New England Television (acq 11-91; $1.5 million; 12-16-91).

Derry

ADI No. 6; see Boston, MA market

WNDS—ch 50, 4,790 kw vis, 479 kw aur, ant 699t. TL: N42 44 07 W71 23 36. On air date: Sept 5, 1983. 50 TV Place (03038). (603) 434-8850. FAX: (603) 434-8627. Licensee: CTV of Derry Inc. Ownership: Nash Family, 51%; James Stellos, 4% Rep: Savalli, Schutz & Peterson. Wash atty: Reddy, Begley & Martin. News progmg one hr wkly. ■ Donna Cole, gen mgr; Mark Lehner, gen sls mgr; Bill Ritchotte, prom mgr; Joe Gaughan, progmg dir & film buyer; Rick Carcenito, news dir; Paul Hunter, chief engr. ■ On 46 CATVs—575,000 subs. ■ Rates: $225; 200; 105.

Durham

ADI No. 6; see Boston, MA market

*****WENH-TV**—ch 11, 316 kw vis, 31.6 kw aur, ant 970t/390g. TL: N43 10 33 W71 12 29. Stereo. Hrs opn: 7 AM-1:30 AM. On air date: July 6, 1959. Box 1100 (03824). (603) 868-1100. FAX: (603) 868-7552. Licensee: U. of N.H. ■ Net: PBS; EEN. Wash atty: Schwartz, Woods & Miller. News progmg 2 hrs wkly. ■ Arthur J. Singer, gen mgr; Kelly Looma, progmg dir; Marilyn Pennell, news dir; Bob Ross, engrg dir. ■ On 117 CATVs.

Keene

ADI No. 6; see Boston, MA market

*****WEKW-TV**—ch 52, 95.5 kw vis, 9.55 kw aur, ant 1,080t/455g. TL: N43 02 00 W72 22 04. Stereo. Hrs opn: 19. On air date: May 21, 1968. Box 1100, Durham (03824). (603) 868-1100. FAX: (603) 868-7552. Licensee: Univ. of New Hampshire. ■ Net: PBS. Wash atty: Schwartz, Woods & Miller. ■ Arthur J. Singer, gen mgr; Kelly Louma, progmg dir; Marilyn Pennell, news dir; Bob Ross, engrg dir. ■ On 7 CATVs—12,537 subs.

Littleton

ADI No. 93; see Burlington-Plattsburgh market

*****WLED-TV**—ch 49, 93.3 kw vis, 9.33 kw aur, ant 1,280t/400g. TL: N44 21 14 W71 44 23. Stereo. Hrs opn: 19. On air date: Feb 7, 1968. Box 1100, Durham (03824). (603) 868-1100. FAX: (603) 868-7552. Licensee: U. of N.H. ■ Net: PBS. Wash atty: Schwartz, Woods & Miller. ■ Arthur J. Singer, gen mgr; Kelly Luoma, progmg dir; Marilyn Pennell, news dir; Bob Ross, engrg dir. ■ On 6 CATVs—9,490 subs.

Manchester

ADI No. 6; see Boston, MA market

WMUR-TV—ch 9, 282 kw vis, 33.5 kw aur, ant 1,030t/227g. TL: N42 58 59 W71 35 19. Hrs opn: 24. On air date: Mar 9, 1954. Box 9, 50 Phillippe Cote St. (03105). (603) 669-9999. FAX: (603) 641-9044; (603) 641-9045. Licensee: WMUR-TV Inc. Group owner: Imes Communications (acq 4-25-86). ■ Net: ABC. Rep: Seltel. Wash atty: Arent, Fox, Kinter, Plotkin & Kahn. ■ Birney Imes Jr., pres; Larry Gilpin, vp & gen mgr; Valerie Bey, gen sls mgr; Betsey Barrett, natl sls mgr; Tom Bonnar, progmg dir; Joe Paciorkowski, film buyer & chief engr; Jack Heath, news dir; Kristi Young, pub affrs dir. ■ On 65 CATVs—150,000 subs.

Merrimack

ADI No. 6; see Boston, MA market

WGOT—ch 60, 1,410 kw vis, 141 kw aur, ant 1,010t/136g. TL: N42 59 02 W71 35 18. Hrs opn: 19. On air date: 1987. Suite 501, One Sundial Ave., Manchester (03103). (603) 647-6060. FAX: (603) 644-0060. Licensee: Paugus Television Inc. (acq 1-6-89; $1.35 million; 1-23-89). Wash atty: Davis, Wright & Tremaine. ■ Lon Mirolli, pres, gen mgr & gen sls mgr; Don Hill, opns mgr; Susan Furey, natl sls mgr; Kathleen Strange, prom mgr & pub affrs dir; Doreen Warchal, progmg dir; Rhonda Mann, news dir; Ed Williams, engrg dir. ■ On 35 CATVs—650,000 subs.■ Rates: $100; 125; 30.

New Jersey

Atlantic City

ADI No. 4; see Philadelphia, PA market

WACI—ch 62, 5,000 kw vis, 500 kw aur, ant 436t. TL: N39 36 48 W74 15 50. On air date: 1990. Suite 503, 400 W. Hortter, Philadelphia, PA (19119). (215) 848-9471. Licensee: Garden State Communications dba WACI-TV Inc. Ownership: Gloria Penn Easton, 51% Wash atty: Baker & Hostetler. ■ Gloria Penn Easton, pres.

WWAC-TV—ch 53, 12.3 kw vis, 1.2 kw aur, ant 279t. TL: N39 22 51 W74 27 03. On air date: Oct 1, 1986. Cellular Phone Centers Inc., 844 N. 4th St., Philadelphia, PA (19123); 1825 Murray Ave. (08001). (215) 574-9240; (609) 344-6800. FAX: (215) 574-9240. Licensee: Cellular Phone Centers Inc. Ownership: David W. Allen; Harry R. Jenny Jr. (acq 5-9-91; $20,000; 5-27-91). Wash atty: Schwartz, Woods & Miller. ■ David W. Allen, Harry Jenny, gen mgrs; David W. Allen, Harry Jenny, stn mgrs.

Burlington

ADI No. 4; see Philadelphia, PA market

WGTW—ch 48, 2,340 kw vis, 234 kw aur, ant 1,099t. TL: N40 02 36 W75 14 33. Hrs opn: 24. On air date: August 1992. 642 N. Broad St., Philadelphia, PA (19130). (215) 765-4800. FAX: (215) 765-1228. Licensee: Brunson Communications Inc. (acq 1989). ■ Dorothy Brunson, gen mgr; John M. Duffin, rgnl sls mgr; Rose M. Johnson, pub affrs dir; Roger DuFault, chief engr. ■ On 18 CATVs—1,249,000 subs.

Camden

ADI No. 4; see Philadelphia, PA market

*****WNJS**—ch 23, 2,323 kw vis, 348 kw aur, ant 890t/937g. TL: N39 43 41 W74 50 39. Stereo. Hrs opn: 8 AM-midnight. On air date: Oct 23, 1972. CN777, Trenton (08625-0777;). 25 S. Stockton St., Trenton (08611). (609) 777-5000. FAX: (609) 633-2920. Licensee: New Jersey Public Broadcasting Authority. ■ Net: PBS. Wash atty: Schwartz, Woods & Miller. Sp one hr wkly. ■ George Hoover, gen mgr. Satellite of *WNJT Trenton.

Linden

WNJU—Licensed to Linden. See Newark.

Montclair

ADI No. 1; see New York, NY market

*****WNJM**—ch 50, 2,094 kw vis, 314 kw aur, ant 800t/656g. TL: N40 51 53 W74 12 03. Stereo. Hrs opn: 8 AM-midnight. On air date: June 5, 1973. CN777, Trenton (08625-0777;). 25 S. Stockton St., Trenton (08611). (609) 777-5000. FAX: (609) 633-2920. Licensee: New Jersey Public Broadcasting Authority. ■ Net: PBS. Wash atty: Schwartz, Woods & Miller. Sp one hr wkly. ■ George Hoover, gen mgr. Satellite of *WNJT Trenton.

New Brunswick

ADI No. 1; see New York, NY market

*****WNJB**—ch 58, 1,321 kw vis, 132 kw aur, ant 726t/401g. TL: N40 37 17 W74 30 15. Hrs opn: Mon-Fri 8 AM-midnight; Sat-Sun 7 AM-midnight. On air date: June 5, 1973. CN 777, Trenton (08625-0777;). 25 S. Stockton St., Trenton (08611). (609) 777-5000. FAX: (609) 633-2920. Licensee: New Jersey Public Broadcasting Authority. ■ Net: PBS. Wash atty: Schwartz, Woods & Miller. Sp one hr wkly. ■ Harvey Fisher, CEO; George Hoover, gen mgr; Karen Spencer, dev dir; Lawrence Holden, progmg dir; William Jobes, news dir. ■ On 107 CATVs—On 2 trans. Satellite of *WNJT Trenton.

Newark

ADI No. 1; see New York, NY market

WHSE-TV—ch 68, 2,190 kw vis, 219 kw aur, ant 1,430t/1,445g. TL: N40 44 54 W73 59 10. Stereo. (CP: 2,630 kw vis, ant 1,440t). On air date: Sept 29, 1974. 390 W. Market St. (07107). (201) 643-6800. FAX: (201) 643-1903. Licensee: HSN Broadcasting of New Jersey Inc. Group owner: Silver King Communications Inc. (acq 9-18-86); grpsl; 8-25-86). Wash atty: Dow, Lohnes & Albertson. ■ Jeff McGrath, pres; Ella Conners, vp, gen mgr & gen sls mgr; William Roller, progmg dir, film buyer & news dir. ■ On 15 CATVs—834,425 subs.

*****WNET**—Licensed to Newark. See New York, N.Y.

WNJU—(Linden). ch 47, 4,570 kw vis, 977 kw aur, ant 1,508t/1,730g. TL: N40 42 43 W74 00 49. On air date: May 16, 1965. 47 Industrial Ave., Teterboro (07608). (201) 288-5550. FAX: (201) 288-5166. Licensee: WNJU-TV Broadcasting Corp. Group owner: Telemundo Group Inc. (acq 1-2-87; $70 million; 11-10-86). ■ Net: Telemundo. Wash atty: Hogan & Hartson. Sp full-time. ■ Manuel Martinez-Lorian, vp & gen mgr; George Kraus, stn mgr & chief engr; Luis Roldan, gen sls mgr; Cristina Espasade, prom mgr; Sylvia Pasqual, progmg mgr; Sandra Lilley, news dir.

Newton

ADI No. 1; see New York, NY market

WMBC-TV—ch 63, 1,510 kw vis, 500 kw aur, ant 731t. TL: N41 00 36 W74 35 39. Not on air, target date unknown. 500 Weldon Rd., Jefferson (07468); 6 Sparrow Circle, Newton (07860). (201) 697-0063. FAX: (201) 579-7440. Permittee: Mountain Broadcasting Corp. Ownership: Sun Young Joo, 50%. ■ Sun Young Joo, pres & gen mgr.

Paterson

ADI No. 1; see New York, NY market

WXTV—ch 41, 2,340 kw vis, 234 kw aur, ant 1,381t. TL: N40 44 54 W73 59 10. On air date: Aug 4, 1968. 24 Meadowland Pkwy., Secaucus (07094). (201) 348-4141. FAX: (201) 348-4104. Licensee: WXTV L.P. Group owner: Perenchio Television Inc. (acq 1986; grpsl). ■ Net: Univision. Wash atty: Fisher, Wayland, Cooper & Leader. Sp full time. ■ Tomas T. Johansen, vp & gen mgr; Leandro Blanco, vp opns; Cristina Schwarz, gen sls mgr; Rosemary Gama, natl sls mgr; Maria Denis, progmg dir; Ricardo Alvarez, news dir; Arlene Torres, pub affrs dir; Alan Cohen, chief engr. ■ On 2 trans.

Secaucus

WWOR-TV—Licensed to Secaucus. See New York, N.Y.

Trenton

ADI No. 4; see Philadelphia, PA market

*****WNJT**—ch 52, 1,950 kw vis, 285 kw aur, ant 1,049t/989g. TL: N40 16 58 W74 41 11. Stereo. Hrs opn: 8AM-midnight. On air date: April 2, 1971. CN777 (08625-0777;). 25 S. Stockton St. (08611). (609) 777-5000. FAX: (609) 633-2920. Licensee: New Jersey Public Broadcasting Authority. ■ Net: PBS; EEN. Wash atty: Schwartz, Woods & Miller. Sp one hr wkly. News progmg 5 hrs wkly. ■ George Hoover, gen mgr; Susan Swords, prom mgr; Larry Holden, progmg dir & film buyer; William Jobes, news dir. ■ On 40 CATVs—1,000,000 subs. On one trans. Co-owned radio: WNJT-FM.

Vineland

ADI No. 4; see Philadelphia, PA market

WHSP-TV—ch 65, 3,800 kw vis, 380 kw aur, ant 918t/928g. TL: N39 44 07 W74 50 29. Stereo. Hrs opn: 24. On air date: July 13, 1981. 4449 N. Delsea Dr., Newfield (08344). (609) 691-6565. FAX: (609) 691-2483. Licensee: HSN Broadcasting of Vineland Inc. Group owner: Silver King Communications Inc. (acq 1-6-87; $23 million; 9-1-86). Wash atty: Dow, Lohnes & Albertson. News staff 3; news progmg 13 hrs wkly. ■ Jeff McGrath, pres; Mary Fama McKee, vp, gen mgr & gen sls mgr; Linda Donovan, progmg dir & news dir; Robert Pritchard, chief engr. ■ On 14 CATVs—649,073 subs.

West Milford

ADI No. 1; see New York, NY market

*****WFME-TV**—ch 66, 24 kw vis, ant 711t. TL: N74 12 03 W41 07 14. Not on air, target date unknown. 290 Hegenberger Rd., Oakland, CA (94621). (510) 568-6200. Permittee: Family Stations of New Jersey.

Wildwood

ADI No. 4; see Philadelphia, PA market

WMGM-TV—ch 40, 741 kw vis, 74.1 kw aur, ant 420t/416g. TL: N39 07 28 W74 45 56. On air date: Jan 25, 1966. 1601 New Rd., Linwood (08221). (609) 927-4440. Licensee: South Jersey Radio Inc. Group owner: The Green Group (acq 12-19-85; $108,000; 10-21-85). ■ Net: NBC. Wash atty: Cordin & Kelly. ■ Howard L. Green, pres & film buyer; Jane B. Stark, gen mgr; Ron Smith, gen sls mgr; Stephanie Finch, prom mgr; Laurie DeWinton, progmg dir; Jeff Whitaker, news dir; Dan Merlo, chief engr. ■ On 18 CATVs—190,000 subs. Co-owned radio: WOND(AM), WMGM-FM ■ Rates: $250; 140; 90.

New Mexico

Albuquerque

ADI No. 48; see Albuquerque market

*****KAZQ**—ch 32, 42.7 kw vis, 4.3 kw aur, ant 4054t. TL: N35 12 51 W106 27 01. Hrs opn: 6 AM-10 PM M-F, 8 AM-10 PM Sat. & Sun. On air date: Oct 12, 1987. 4501 Montgomery N.E. (87109). (505) 884-8355. FAX: (505) 883-1229. Licensee: Alpha-Omega Broadcasting of Albuquerque Inc. Wash atty: John H. Midlen. Sp 2 hrs wkly. ■ Raymond L. Franks, pres; Brenton D. Franks, gen mgr & opns mgr; Ron Romero, prom mgr & progmg dir; Richard Elton, pub affrs dir; Rob Ramseyer, chief engr.

KKIK-TV—ch 50, 1,450 kw, ant 4,153t. TL: N35 12 45 W106 26 56. Not on air, target date unknown. 3800 Carlisle N.E. (87117). (505) 881-2000. Permittee: Mary Moran.

KLUZ-TV—ch 41, 26.5 kw vis, 2.65 kw aur, ant 4,144t/106g. TL: N35 12 41 W106 26 56. On air date: September 1987. 2725 F Broadbent Pkwy. N.E. (87107). (505) 344-5589. FAX: (505) 344-8714. Licensee: Kluz L.P. Group owner: Perenchio Television Inc. ■ Net: Univision. Sp progmg. ■ Marcela Medina, gen mgr; Adrianna Gautreau, progmg dir; Fred Baca, news dir; Kambiz Victory, chief engr.

KNAT—ch 23, 1,200 kw vis, 120 kw aur, ant 4,130t/128g. TL: N35 12 54 W106 27 02. On air date: Oct 17, 1975. 1510 Coors Rd. N.W. (87121). (505) 836-6585. Licensee: All American TV Inc. Ownership: AAT Inc. (acq 11-6-89; $2.4M). Wash atty: May & Dunne. Sp 2 hrs wkly. ■ Linda Hernandez, CEO; Sonny Arguinzoni, pres; Deanna J. Sebastian, gen mgr; Deanna Sebastian, dev dir, sls dir & progmg mgr; Cindy Mansfield, pub affrs dir; Ron Crawford, chief engr. ■ On 12 CATVs—115,000 subs.

*****KNME-TV**—ch 5, 26.9 kw vis, 5.6 kw aur, ant 4,228t/201g. TL: N35 12 44 W106 26 57. On air date: May 5, 1958. 1130 University Blvd N.E. (87102). (505) 277-2121. Licensee: Regents of Univ. of New Mexico and Bd. of Education, Albuquerque. ■ Net: PBS. Wash atty: Dow, Lohnes & Albertson. News staff 4; news progmg one hr wkly. ■ Jon Cooper, gen mgr; Chris Johnson, opns dir; Martha Day, dev dir; Joan Rebecchi, mktg mgr; Shirley Casados, progmg dir; John Morand, engrg dir; John Ramp, chief engr. ■ On 16 CATVs—47,984 subs.

KOAT-TV—ch 7, 87.1 kw vis, 17.4 kw aur, ant 4,240t/233g. TL: N35 12 53 W106 27 01. Stereo. On air date: Sept 28, 1953. Box 25982 (87125); 3801 Carlisle N.E. (87107). (505) 884-7777; (505) 884-6280. (505) 884-6282; TWX: 910-989-1687. Licensee: KOAT-TV Inc. Group owner: Pulitzer Broadcasting Co., see Cross-Ownership (acq 5-7-69; $5 million; 5-19-69). ■ Net: ABC. Rep: Blair. Wash atty: Verner, Liipfert, Bernhard, McPherson & Hand. ■ Ken J. Elkins, pres; C. Wayne Godsey, exec vp; Mary Lynn Roper, vp & gen mgr; Jeffrey N. Sales, gen sls mgr; H. Parker Harms, mktg dir; Roy Leone, progmg dir; Lisa Breeden, news dir; Jennifer Threet, pub affrs dir; Charles Amy, chief engr. ■ On 34 CATVs—92,300 subs. On 84 trans.

KOB-TV—ch 4, 26.9 kw vis, 2.7 kw aur, ant 4,198t/178g. TL: N35 12 42 W106 26 57. Stereo. Hrs opn: 24. On air date: Nov 29, 1948. Box 1351 (87103); 4 Broadcast Plaza S.W. (87104). (505) 243-4411. FAX: (505) 764-2522. Licensee: KOB-TV Inc. Group owner: Hubbard Broadcasting Inc. (acq 3-15-57; grpsl; 3-18-57). ■ Net: NBC. Rep: Petry. Wash atty: Fletcher, Heald, Rowell, Kenehan & Hildreth. News progmg 12 hrs wkly. ■ Jerry Danziger, pres; Mike Burgess, vp & gen mgr; Bob Evans, gen sls mgr; Paula Maes, prom mgr; Joel Anderson, news dir; Sam Tikkanen, chief engr. ■ On 49 CATVs. On 80 trans.

KRQE—ch 13, 89.1 kw vis, 9 kw aur, ant 4,178t/141g. TL: N35 12 40 W106 26 57. Stereo. On air date: Oct 3, 1953. Box 1294 (87103). (505) 243-2285. FAX: (505) 842-8483. Licensee: New Mexico Broadcasting Co. Inc. Group owner: Lee Enterprises Inc. (acq 9-16-91; with KBIM-TV Roswell; 9-30-91). ■ Net: CBS. Rep: Katz. Jim Thompson, pres & gen mgr; Loren Neuharth, gen sls mgr; John Tischerdorf, prom mgr & progmg dir; Jim Loy, news dir; Alan P. Deme, chief engr. ■ On 61 trans.

Carlsbad

ADI No. 48; see Albuquerque market

KOCT—ch 6, 100 kw vis, 10 kw aur, ant 1,201t/1,048g. TL: N32 47 39 W104 12 27. On air date: August 1959. c/o KOAT-TV, Box 25982, Albuquerque (87125). (505) 884-7777. Licensee: Pulitzer Broadcasting Co. (group owner; acq 12-27-92; $1.75 million; 1-18-93). ■ Net: ABC. Rep: Katz. Wash atty: Kirkland & Ellis. ■ Mary Lynn Roper, vp & gen mgr. ■ On 4 CATVs. On 2 trans. Satellite of KOAT-TV Albuquerque. ■ Rates: $125; 110; 45.

Clovis

ADI No. 129; see Amarillo market

KVIH-TV—ch 12, 178 kw vis, 35.3 kw aur, ant 670t/719g. TL: N34 11 34 W103 16 44. Stereo. On air date: December 1957. One Broadcast Ctr., Amarillo, TX (79101). (806) 373-1787. FAX: (806) 371-7329. Licensee: Marsh Media Inc. (group owner, acq 7-28-86; $1.5 million; 10-14-85). ■ Net: ABC. Rep: Katz. Wash atty: Wiley, Rein & Fielding. ■ James R. McCormick, pres, gen mgr & progmg dir; Jackie Smith, opns mgr; John Patrick, gen sls mgr; John Morales, prom mgr; Steve Pritchett, news dir; Bill Canady, chief engr. Satellite to KVII-TV Amarillo, Tex.

Farmington

ADI No. 48; see Albuquerque market

KOBF—ch 12, 316 kw vis, 31.6 kw aur, ant 410t/209g. TL: N36 41 43 W108 13 14. Hrs opn: 24. On air date: 1972. Box 1620 (87499); 825 W. Broadway (87401). (505) 326-1141. FAX: (505) 326-1141, ext. 37. Licensee: KOB-TV Inc. Group owner: Hubbard Broadcasting Inc. (acq 9-19-83; $2.35 million; 8-15-83). ■ Net: NBC. Rep: Petry. Wash atty: Fletcher, Heald & Hildreth. ■ Steve Henderson, gen mgr; Scott Michlin, news dir; Dan Harlin, chief engr. ■ On 7 CATVs—20,000 subs. On 6 trans.

Gallup

ADI No. 48; see Albuquerque market

KOFT—ch 3, 24 kw vis, 2.4 kw aur, ant 102t. TL: N35 32 29 W108 44 31. Not on air, target date unknown. Box 25982, Albuquerque (87125); 3801 Carlisle N.E., Albuquerque (81707). (505) 884-7777. Permittee: KOAT Television Inc.

Stations in the U.S.   New York

Hobbs

ADI No. 48; see Albuquerque market

KHFT—ch 29, 7.94 kw vis, 794 w aur, ant 522t. TL: N32 43 28 W103 05 46. On air date: 1989. Box 96 (88241). (505) 393-6208. Licensee: Warren Electronic Systems Inc. Ownership: Warren Electronic Systems, 74.5%;Lowell Payton, 25.5% (acq 9-25-89; 10-16-89). Wash atty: Jim Oyster. News progmg one hr wkly. ■ Kimberly Brunson, gen mgr & opns mgr; Pete Warren, chief engr. ■ Rates: $10; 8; 7.

Las Cruces

ADI No. 100; see El Paso market

*****KRWG-TV**—ch 22, 1,550 kw vis, 155 kw aur, ant 449t/402g. TL: N32 15 24 W106 58 34. Hrs opn: 6:45 AM-11:30 PM. On air date: June 29, 1973. Box 30001, Dept. 3TV22 (88003). (505) 646-2222. FAX: (505) 646-1924. Licensee: Regents of New Mexico State Univ. ■ Net: PBS. Wash atty: Dow, Lohnes & Albertson. Sp 2 hrs. wkly. News staff one; news progmg 3 hrs wkly. ■ Ronald K. Salak, gen mgr; Edith Treadwell, prom mgr; James Ficklin, progmg dir; Gary Worth, news dir & pub affrs dir; Carl Natone, chief engr. ■ On 49 CATVs—32,000 subs. On 7 trans. Co-owned radio: *KRWG-FM.

KZIA—ch 48, 79.4 kw vis, 7.9 kw aur, ant 113t. TL: N32 02 30 W106 27 41. On air date: Nov 11, 1984. Suite 150, 500 S. Main St. (88001). (505) 524-2103. FAX: (505) 526-0938. Licensee: Lee Enterprises Inc. (group owner; acq 2-26-93; $440,000; 3-15-93). ■ Net: ABC, NBC. Rep: Spot Time. Wash atty: Southmayd & Powell. ■ Jim Thompson, gen mgr; Mike Ferrales, opns mgr; Frank Montoya, gen sls mgr. ■ Rates: $90; 80; 60.

Portales

ADI No. 48; see Albuquerque market

*****KENW**—ch 3, 100 kw vis, 20 kw aur, ant 1,150t/1,085g. TL: N33 33 19 W103 39 03. On air date: Sept 1, 1974. Eastern New Mexico Univ., 52 Broadcast Center (88130). (505) 562-2112. FAX: (505) 562-2590. Licensee: Regents of Eastern New Mexico Univ. ■ Net: PBS; Pacific Mtn. News staff 2; news progmg 3 hrs wkly. ■ Everett L. Frost, pres; Duane R. Wyan, gen mgr; Orlando Ortega, opns dir; Jan Smartnick, Sandi Bergman, dev dirs; Sheryl Borden, mktg dir; Bobby Trujillo, prom dir; Linda Stefanovic, progmg dir; Rick Iler, news dir; Don Criss, pub affrs dir; John Johnson, Doug Lynch, chiefs engr. ■ On 4 trans. Co-owned radio: *KENW-FM, *KMTH(FM)

Roswell

ADI No. 48; see Albuquerque market

KBIM-TV—ch 10, 316 kw vis, 40.7 kw aur, ant 1,999t/1,839g. TL: N33 03 20 W103 49 12. Hrs opn: 24. On air date: Feb 26, 1966. Box 910, 214 N. Main St. (88201). (505) 622-2120. FAX: (505) 623-6606; TWX: 910-986-0072. Licensee: New Mexico Broadcasting Co. (group owner: Lee Enterprises Inc.; acq 9-16-91; with KRQE Albuquerque; 9-30-91). ■ Net: CBS. Rep: Katz. Wash atty: Dow, Lohnes & Albertson. News staff 11; news progmg 6 hrs wkly. ■ Richard Gotlieb, CEO; Gary Schmedding, vp; Jim Thompson, gen mgr; Gary McNair, stn mgr; Julie Harrison, opns mgr; Andrew Wyatt, gen sls mgr; Cindi Lucero, prom mgr; John Tischendorf, progmg mgr; David Gonzalez, news dir; Rick Counts, chief engr. ■ On 21 CATVs—73,000 subs. On 6 trans. ■ Rates: $450; 325; 75.

KOBR—ch 8, 316 kw vis, 52.5 kw aur, ant 1,760t/1,610g. TL: N33 22 32 W103 46 05. On air date: June 24, 1953. 124 E. Fourth St. (88201). (505) 625-8888. FAX: (505) 625-8866. Licensee: Stanley S. Hubbard Trust. Group owner: Hubbard Broadcasting Inc. (acq 8-1-85). ■ Net: NBC. Rep: Petry. Wash atty: Fletcher, Heald & Hildreth. News staff 4.■ Stanley S. Hubbard, pres, Dotrew Paulus, gen mgr; Melodi Salas, rgnl sls mgr; Robert Alarcon, prom mgr & progmg mgr; Mike Anthony, news dir; Wayne Koontz, chief engr. ■ On 15 CATVs.

KRPV—ch 27, 871 kw vis, 67 kw aur, ant 377t/500g. TL: N33 24 58 W104 33 59. Hrs opn: 24. On air date: Sept 15, 1986. Box 967, 2606 S. Main (88201). (505) 622-5778. Licensee: Prime Time Christian Broadcasting. Sp 4 hrs wkly. ■ Al Cooper, pres & gen mgr; Randy Duebler, gen sls mgr & prom mgr; Dave Whitley, progmg dir; Eddie Sills, chief engr. ■ On 11 CATVs. On 7 trans.

Santa Fe

ADI No. 48; see Albuquerque market

KASA-TV—ch 2, 100 kw vis, 10 kw aur, ant 1,968t/178g. TL: N35 46 50 W106 31 35. On air date: Oct 31, 1983. Television Station KASA-TV, 1377 University Blvd. N.E., Albuquerque (87102). (505) 246-2222. FAX: (505) 242-1355. Licensee: Journal Broadcasting of New Mexico. (acq 12-22-92; 1-18-93). ■ Net: Fox. Rep: Telerep. Wash atty: Covington & Burling. ■ Erick B. Steffens, pres, gen mgr & film buyer; Jim Gonsey, opns mgr; John McCormick, gen sls mgr; Michael Maulano, natl sls mgr; Brian Anderson, prom mgr; Stella Lavis, news dir & pub affrs dir; Dudley Bullock, chief engr. ■ On 53 CATVs—230,000 subs. On 12 trans.

KCHF—ch 11, 263 kw vis, 26.3 kw aur, ant 2,027t/272g. TL: N35 47 15 W106 31 35. On air date: Jan 21, 1984. Box 4338, Albuquerque (87106). (505) 883-1111; (505) 473-1111. Licensee: Son Broadcasting Inc. Wash atty: James Gammon. Sp 4 hrs wkly. ■ Belarmino R. Gonzales, pres & gen mgr; Mary Kay Gonzales, prom mgr & progmg mgr; Rob Ramseyer, chief engr. ■ Rates: $200; 70; 20.

Silver City

ADI No. 48; see Albuquerque market

KOVT—ch 10, 8.71 kw vis, 871 w, ant 1,591t/112g. TL: N32 51 46 W108 14 28. Stereo. On air date: Sept 9, 1987. Box 25982, Albuquerque (87125); 3801 Carlisle N.E., Albuquerque (87107). (505) 884-7777; (505) 884-6280. FAX: (505) 884-6282. Licensee: KOAT Television Inc. Group owner: Pulitzer Broadcasting, see Cross-Ownership. ■ Net: ABC. Rep: Blair. Wash atty: Verner, Liipfert, Bernhard, McPherson & Hand. ■ Mary Lyn Roper, gen mgr; Chuck Amy, chief engr. Satellite of KOAT Albuquerque.

New York

Albany

ADI No. 53; see Albany-Schenectady-Troy market

WNYT—ch 13, 178 kw vis, 19.9 kw aur, ant 1,171t/737g. TL: N42 47 08 W73 37 44. On air date: June 15, 1956. Box 4035, 15 N. Pearl St. (12204). (518) 436-4791. FAX: (518) 436-8723. Licensee: Viacom Broadcasting Inc. (group owner; acq 3-25-80). ■ Net: NBC. Rep: Telerep. ■ Donald D. Perry, vp & gen mgr; Steve Baboulis, opns mgr & news dir; Jerry Brehm, natl sls mgr; Noelle Wall, mktg dir; Douglas Jones, progmg dir & pub affrs dir; Richard Klein, chief engr. ■ On 55 CATVs—272,875 subs. On 5 trans.

WRGB—(Schenectady). ch 6, 93.3 kw vis, 11 kw aur, ant 1,020t/314g. TL: N42 38 12 W73 59 45. On air date: Nov 6, 1939. 1400 Balltown Rd., Schenectady (12309). (518) 346-6666. TWX: 710-442-2974. Licensee: WRGB Broadcasting Inc. Group owner: Freedom Newspapers Inc., Broadcast Division (acq 3-4-86; $56 million; 11-25-85). ■ Net: CBS. Rep: Petry. Wash atty: Latham & Watkins. ■ David M. Lynch, vp & gen mgr; Cheryl J. Snell, gen sls mgr; Mary Gregg, natl sls mgr; William Brandt, prom mgr; Terry Walden, progmg dir; Gary S. Whitaker, news dir; Dan Fiorillo, chief engr. ■ On 70 CATVs—260,000 subs.

WTEN—ch 10, 316 kw vis, 31.6 kw aur, ant 1,000t/276g. TL: N42 38 15 W73 59 54. Hrs opn: 20. On air date: Oct 14, 1953. 341 Northern Blvd. (12204). (518) 436-4822. FAX: (518) 462-6065. Licensee: Young Broadcasting of Albany Inc. Group owner: Young Broadcasting Inc. (acq 10-11-89; grpsl). ■ Net: ABC. Wash atty: Wiley, Rein & Fielding. News staff 37; news progmg 15 hrs wkly. ■ Vincent Young, chmn; Ron Kwasnick, pres; Bob Peterson, gen mgr & progmg dir; Harold Lansing, opns mgr & chief engr; Theresa Cusey, dev mgr; Mike Funk, gen sls mgr; Lynn Riley, prom mgr; Don Decker, news dir. ■ On 45 CATVs—370,000 subs.

WXXA-TV—ch 23, 3,020 kw vis, 302 kw aur, ant 1,200t/465g. TL: N42 37 01 W74 00 46. On air date: July 30, 1982. 815 Central Ave. (12206-1502). (518) 438-8700. FAX: (518) 438-8714. Licensee: Heritage Broadcasting Group (group owner; acq 11-4-86; $10.1 million; 8-11-86). ■ Net: Fox. Rep: Blair. Wash atty: Hogan & Hartson. ■ Catherine Cascracane, gen mgr & stn mgr; Gary Deluke, gen sls mgr; Sargent Cathrall, chief engr. ■ On 36 CATVs—244,240 subs.

Amsterdam

ADI No. 53; see Albany-Schenectady-Troy market

WOCD—ch 55, 5,000 kw vis, 500 kw aur, ant 731t. TL: N42 59 05 W74 10 49. Hrs opn: 24. On air date: Dec 14, 1987. 165 Freeman's Bridge Rd., Scotia (12302). (518) 372-8855. FAX: (518) 372-8874. Licensee: Cornerstone Broadcasting Inc. Group owner: R. Russell Bixler (acq 5-8-92; $375,000; 6-1-92). ■ Russ Bixler, pres; Timothy S. Horton, stn mgr; Blake Richert, vp engrg.

Binghamton

ADI No. 135; see Binghamton market

WBNG-TV—ch 12, 166 kw vis, 18.2 kw aur, ant 1,210t/785g. TL: N42 02 33 W75 57 06. Stereo. Hrs opn: 24 Mon-Sat, 6 AM-2 AM Sun. On air date: Dec 1, 1949. Box 12, 12 Gateway Plaza, Columbia Dr., Johnson City (13970). (607) 729-8812. FAX: (607) 797-6211. Licensee: Gateway Communications Inc. (group owner; acq 9-72; grpsl). ■ Net: CBS. Rep: Blair. Wash atty: Bryan, Cave, McPheeters & McRoberts. News staff 16.■ Monty Pinker, pres; John S. Mucha, vp & gen mgr; Alice Lannon, opns mgr; Joseph P. McNamara, gen sls mgr; Mark Prutisto, mktg mgr & progmg dir; Paul Daffinee, news dir; Veronica McQuillan, pub affrs dir; Ronald Shoemaker, engrg mgr. ■ On 110 CATVs—109,000 subs.

WICZ-TV—ch 40, 468 kw vis, 46.8 kw aur, ant 1,230t/934g. TL: N42 03 22 W75 56 39. Stereo. On air date: Nov 1, 1957. Box 40, 4600 Vestal Parkway E., Vestal (13850). (607) 770-4040. FAX: (607) 798-7950. Licensee: Stainless Broadcasting Co. (group owner; acq 4-7-71; $780,000; 3-8-71). ■ Net: NBC. Rep: Petry. Wash atty: Dow, Lohnes & Albertson. News staff 18. ■ Nora L. Guzewicz, pres; Dave Tillery, gen mgr; Alice B. Riehl, gen sls mgr; Vernon Rowlands, prom mgr; Darcy

---

Golden Lamb Productions

- Location Production -

Serving the Northeast from Upstate NY

ENG	SNG
EFP	Lives
News	Sports

Experienced Crews

New Britain Rd., E. Chatham, NY 12060

Phone (518) 766-5950   **Pager (518) 422-6772**

Fauci, news dir; Gino Ricciardelli, vp engrg & chief engr. ■ On 63 CATVs—214,363 subs. ■ Rates: $400; 160; 40.

WMGC-TV—ch 34, 1,480 kw vis, 148 kw aur, ant 922t/567g. TL: N42 03 39 W75 56 36. On air date: Nov 25, 1962. Box 813, Ingraham Hill Rd. (13902). (607) 723-7464. FAX: (607) 723-1034. Licensee: Citadel Communications Co. Ltd. Group owner: Citadel Communications Co. Ltd., Coronet Communications Co. (acq 9-22-86; $5 million; 7-7-86). ■ Net: ABC. Rep: Katz; Wash atty: Latham & Watkins. ■ Philip Lombardo, pres; John Leet, vp & gen mgr; John Birchall, gen sls mgr; Bill Luxford, progmg dir & film buyer; Mike Dotson, news dir; Mike Calkins, chief engr. ■ On 44 CATVs—134,235 subs. ■ Rates: $500; 150; 50.

***WSKG-TV**—ch 46, 603 kw vis, 60.3 kw aur, ant 1,230t/927g. TL: N42 03 22 W75 56 39. On air date: May 12, 1968. Box 3000 (13902); 601 Gates Rd., Vestal (13850). (607) 729-0100. FAX: (607) 729-7328. Licensee: WSKG Public Telecommunications Council. ■ Net: PBS; EEN. Wash atty: Dow, Lohnes & Albertson. ■ Michael J. Ziegler, CEO & pres; Manfred Edwards, June Smith, sr vps; Trudy Noble, progmg mgr; Peter Iglinski, news dir; Mark Polovick, vp engrg. ■ On 37 CATVs—177,520 subs. On 37 trans. Co-owned radio: *WSKG-FM, WSQC-FM, WSQG-FM.

Buffalo

ADI No. 38; see Buffalo market

WGRZ-TV—ch 2, 100 kw vis, 20 kw aur, ant 941t/899g. TL: N42 43 06 W73 22 48. On air date: Aug 14, 1954. 259 Delaware Ave. (14202). (716) 856-1414. FAX: (716) 849-5703; TWX: 710-522-1729. Licensee: Tak Communications Inc. (group owner; acq 7-31-86; $56 million; 4-21-86). ■ Net: NBC. Rep: Katz. Radio-Television Rep (Canada). Wash atty: Dow, Lohnes & Albertson. ■ Stephen Cohen, pres & gen mgr; Robert Connell, opns dir; Jim Graham, Tim Busch, gen sls mgrs; Peggy Penders, prom mgr; Carla Contino, progmg dir & film buyer; Robert Pfeiffer, news dir; Larry Floss, chief engr. ■ On 28 CATVs—150,000 subs. ■ Rates: $850; 275; 110.

WIVB-TV—ch 4, 100 kw vis, 20 kw aur, ant 1,201t/1,060g. TL: N42 39 33 W78 37 33. On air date: May 14, 1948. 2077 Elmwood Ave. (14207). (716) 874-4410. Licensee: Buffalo Management Enterprises Co. Inc. (acq 4-17-92). ■ Net: CBS. Rep: Telerep, Airtime TV Sales Inc. (Canada). Wash atty: Wilmer, Cutler & Pickering. ■ David Hogenkamp, vp sls & vp mktg; Twila Henneberger, progmg dir; Kirk Varner, news dir; Ken Britton, chief engr. ■ On 59 CATVs.

WKBW-TV—ch 7, 100 kw vis, 18.2 kw aur, ant 1,420t/1,076g. TL: N42 38 15 W78 37 12. On air date: Nov 30, 1958. 7 Broadcast Plaza (14202). (716) 845-6100. TWX: 710-522-1846. Licensee: Queen City Broadcasting of New York Inc. Ownership: Queen City Broadcasting Inc. (acq 1-86; $65 million; 9-30-85). ■ Net: ABC. Wash atty: Wilkes, Artis, Hedrick & Lane. ■ Paul Cassidy, pres & gen mgr; Tim Gilbert, vp sls; Timothy Gilbert, vp mktg; John Discuillo, prom mgr; Sarah Norat-Phillips, progmg dir; Chuck Samuels, news dir; Don Holland, chief engr. ■ On 125 CATVs—220,000 subs.

***WNED-TV**—ch 17, 2,510 kw vis, 251 kw aur, ant 1,082t/1,091g. TL: N43 01 48 W78 55 15. Stereo. Hrs opn: 6:45 AM-11 PM. On air date: Mar 30, 1959. Horizon Plaza (14202). (716) 845-7000. FAX: (716) 845-7036. Licensee: Western N.Y. Public Broadcasting Assn. ■ Net: PBS; EEN. Wash atty: Schwartz, Woods & Miller. Progmg for the deaf 10 hrs wkly. News staff 3; news progmg one hr wkly. ■ J. Michael Collins, pres; Michael G. Sutton, CFO; Tony Buttino, vp; Susan W. Hayes, vp dev; Debra Beller, prom dir; Richard Hanratty, progmg dir & film buyer; Jon Herrington, engrg dir. ■ On 35 CATVs—350,000 subs. On 25 trans. Co-owned radio: WNED-AM-FM.

***WNEQ-TV**—ch 23, 955 kw vis, 95.5 kw aur, ant 1,030t/1,039g. TL: N43 01 48 W78 55 15. Hrs opn: 6:45 AM-11 PM. On air date: May 13, 1987. Horizon Plaza (14202). (716) 845-7000. FAX: (716) 845-7036. Licensee: Western New York Public Broadcasting Association. ■ Net: PBS. Wash atty: Schwartz, Woods & Miller. News staff 3; news progmg one hr wkly. ■ J. Michael Collins, pres; Michael G. Sutton, CFO; Tony Buttino, vp; Susan W. Hayes, vp dev; Debra Beller, prom dir; Richard Hanratty, progmg dir & film buyer; Jon Herrington, engrg dir. Satellite of WNED-TV. Co-owned radio: WEBR(AM), WNED-FM, WNJA-FM.

***WNYB-TV**—ch 49, 4,900 kw vis, 414 kw aur, ant 1,233t/1,047g. TL: N42 46 58 W78 27 28. Stereo. On air date: Sept 2, 1987. Suite 100, 699 Hertel Ave. (14207). (716) 875-4919. Licensee: Tri-State Christian TV (group owner; acq 10-19-89). ■ Garth Coonce, pres; Francis Stack, stn mgr; John Bivin, chief engr. ■ On 34 CATVs—447,701 subs. On one trans.

WUTV—ch 29, 1,050 kw vis, 105 kw aur, ant 920t/959g. TL: N43 01 27 W78 55 40. Stereo. Hrs opn: 24. On air date: Dec 21, 1970. 951 Whitehaven Rd., Grand Island (14072). (716) 773-7531. FAX: (716) 773-5753. Licensee: Act III Broadcasting of Buffalo Inc. (group owner; acq 6-28-90). ■ Net: Fox. Rep: Seltel; Airtime TV Sls. Wash atty: Goldberg & Spector. ■ Willard J. Stone, vp & gen mgr; Lois M. Ringle, opns dir, mktg dir & prom dir; Michael Anger, chief opns & chief engr; Donald Moran, gen sls mgr; Dennis Cruz, natl sls mgr; Lois Ringle, progmg dir. ■ On 83 CATVs—2,309,033 subs. ■ Rates: $450; 360; 80.

Carthage

WWNY-TV—Licensed to Carthage. See Watertown.

Corning

ADI No. 171; see Elmira market

WETM-TV—See Elmira.

WYDC—ch 48, 136 kw vis, ant 423t. TL: N42 02 29 W77 15 18. Not on air, target date unknown. c/o Cornerstone TeleVision Inc., Wall, PA (15148-1499). (412) 824-3930. Permittee: Cornerstone TeleVision Inc. (group owner; acq 8-31-92; 9-21-92). ■ R. Russell Bixler, pres.

Elmira

ADI No. 171; see Elmira market

WENY-TV—ch 36, 468 kw vis, 85.4 kw aur, ant 1,050t/840g. TL: N42 06 20 W76 52 17. On air date: Nov 19, 1969. Box 208 (14902). (607) 739-3636. Licensee: WENY Inc. Group owner: The Green Group. ■ Net: ABC. Wash atty: Cordon & Kelly. ■ Howard L. Green, exec vp & film buyer; Patrick M. Parish, gen mgr & progmg dir; Meade Murtland, stn mgr & gen sls mgr; John Herrick, news dir. ■ On 36 CATVs—105,000 subs. On 2 trans. Co-owned radio: WENY(AM), WENY-FM.

WETM-TV—ch 18, 166 kw vis, 22.4 kw aur, ant 1,220t/843g. TL: N42 06 20 W76 52 17. Hrs opn: 5:30 AM-2:30 AM. On air date: Sept 10, 1956. One Broadcast Center (14901). (607) 733-5518. FAX: (607) 734-1176. Licensee: Smith Television of New York Inc. Group owner: Smith Television Investment Co. (acq 4-27-92). ■ Net: NBC. Rep: Katz. Wash atty: Hogan & Hartson. News staff 14; news progmg 8 hrs wkly. ■ Robert N. Smith, pres; Robert D. Grissom, gen mgr; Jack Kelley, rgnl sls mgr; Heather Wingate, progmg dir; Crawford Hurley, news dir; Chris Zell, chief engr. ■ On 44 CATVs—72,000 subs.

Garden City

ADI No. 1; see New York market

***WLIW**—ch 21, 3,160 kw vis, 316 kw aur, ant 400t/429g. TL: N40 47 19 W73 27 09. Hrs opn: 24. On air date: Jan 6, 1969. Box 21, Channel 21 Dr., Plainview (11803). (516) 367-2100. FAX: (516) 454-8924 (Adm. Off); (516) 692-7629 (Studio). Licensee: Long Island ETV Council Inc. Wash atty: Schwartz, Woods & Miller. ■ Terrel L. Cass, pres & gen mgr; Susan Avery Klein, prom mgr; Christopher Funkhouser, progmg dir; Peter Gordon, progmg mgr; Thomas D'Agostino, chief engr. ■ On 45 CATVs—1,150,000 subs.

Jamestown

ADI No. 38; see Buffalo market

WTJA—ch 26, 661 kw vis, 66.1 kw aur, ant 597t. TL: N42 05 06 W79 17 23. (CP: 457 kw vis, 45.7 kw aur). On air date: Sept 24, 1988. 4853 Manor Hill Dr., Syracuse (13215). (315) 468-0904. Licensee: Jamestown TV Asooc. Ownership: Craig Fox, 50% George Kimble, 50% Wash atty: James L. Oyster.

Kingston

ADI No. 1; see New York market

WTZA—ch 62, 5,000 kw vis, 500 kw aur, ant 1,939t/276g. TL: N42 05 06 W74 06 00. On air date: Dec 15, 1985. Box 1609, 721 Broadway (12401). (914) 339-6200. FAX: (914) 339-6264; (914) 339-6210 (News). Licensee: WTZA-TV Associates Ltd. Ownership: Richard French Jr. (acq 10-27-93; $2.5 million; 11-15-93). Wash atty: Wiley & Rein. News staff 9; news progmg 20 hrs wkly. ■ David Earle, vp & gen mgr; Rich Haddard, opns mgr; Art Depasqua, gen sls mgr; Greg Floyd, news dir; Edward Zellefrow, chief engr. ■ On 33 CATVs—274,000 subs. ■ Rates: $150; 200; 50.

New York

ADI No. 1; see New York market

WABC-TV—ch 7, 64.6 kw vis, 6.5 kw aur, ant 1,611t/1,730g. TL: N40 42 43 W74 00 49. On air date: Aug 10, 1948. 7 Lincoln Sq. (10023). (212) 456-7777. FAX: (212) 456-2290. Licensee: WABC Television Inc. Group owner: Capital Cities/ABC Broadcast Group (acq 6-27-86; 7-15-85). ■ Net: ABC. Rep: Cap Cities/ABC. Wash atty: McKenna, Wilkinson & Kittner. ■ Walter C. Liss Jr., pres & gen mgr; Art Moore, progmg dir; Henry Florsheim, news dir; James Baker, chief engr. Co-owned radio: WABC(AM)-WPLJ(FM).

WCBS-TV—ch 2, 21.4 kw vis, 4.07 kw aur, ant 1,581t/1,589g. TL: N40 42 43 W74 00 49. On air date: July 1, 1941. 524 W. 57 St. (10019). (212) 975-4321. FAX: (212) 867-7987. Licensee: CBS Inc. Group owner: CBS Broadcast Group. ■ Net: CBS. Rep: CBS-TV Stns Natl Sls. ■ Bud Carey, gen mgr; Jim Picinich, opns mgr; Peter Schruth, sls dir; Robert Klinger, gen sls mgr; Dan Scher, mktg dir; Lee Minard, prom dir; Dean Daniels, news dir. Co-owned radio: WCBS-AM-FM.

WHSE-TV—See Newark, N.J.

WNBC—ch 4, 17.4 kw vis, 3.47 kw aur, ant 1,689t/1,728g. TL: N40 42 43 W74 00 49. Stereo. On air date: July 1, 1941. 30 Rockefeller Plaza (10112). (212) 664-4444. FAX: (212) 664-6449. Licensee: NBC Subsidiary Inc. Group owner: NBC TV Station Division (acq 6-5-86; grpsl). ■ Net: NBC. ■ William L. Bolster, pres & gen mgr; Adele Rifkin, opns dir & progmg dir; Joe Gangone, sls dir; Randy Pyburn, prom dir; Terry Dell, adv dir; Bruno Cohen, news dir; Carolyn Forrest, pub affrs dir; Rich Cervini, chief engr.

***WNET**—(Newark, NJ). ch 13, 60.3 kw vis, 5 kw aur, ant 1,640t/1,652g. TL: N40 42 43 W74 00 49. Stereo. Hrs opn: 24. On air date: Jan 2, 1948. 356 W. 58th St., New York, NY (10019). (212) 560-2000. FAX: (212) 582-3297. Licensee: Educational Broadcasting Corp. (acq 1970). ■ Net: PBS; EEN. Wash atty: Leventhal, Senter & Lerman. News progmg 5 hrs wkly. ■ Dr. William F. Baker, pres; George L. Miles Jr., gen mgr; H. Melvin Ming, vp opns; Jonathan Olken, sls dir; Harry Chancey Jr., vp progmg; Les Crystal, news dir; Frank Graybill, chief engr.

***WNYC-TV**—ch 31, 55 kw vis, 5.5 kw aur, ant 1,543t/1,569g. TL: N40 42 43 W74 00 49. Stereo. Hrs opn: 7 AM-2 AM. On air date: Nov 1, 1962. One Centre St. (10007). (212) 669-7800. FAX: (212) 669-3585. Licensee: City of N.Y. Ownership: WNYC Communications Group. ■ Net: PBS. Wash atty: Arnold & Porter. Japanese, It, Chin, Pol, Ukrain, Korean 25 hrs wkly. News staff 6; news progmg 3 hrs wkly. ■ Thomas B. Morgan, pres; David C. Sit, gen mgr & vp progmg; Ernie Dachel, vp opns; Polly Runyon, dev dir; John McCrory, vp sls; Todd Chanko, Barbara Mayfield, film buyers; Dick Hinchliffe, news dir; Martin Yoskowitz, chief engr. ■ On 67 CATVs—3,000,000 subs. Co-owned radio: *WNYC-AM-FM.

***WNYE-TV**—ch 25, 646 kw vis, 117 kw aur, ant 581t/601g. TL: N40 41 21 W73 58 37. (CP: 2,450 kw vis, 245 kw aur, ant 1,296t, TL: N40 44 54 W73 59 10). On air date: Apr 3, 1967. 112 Tillary St., Brooklyn (11201). (718) 935-4480. Licensee: Board of Education of the City of New York. ■ Net: PBS. Wash atty: Arnold & Porter. Foreign lang progmg 12 hrs wkly. ■ Terence M. O'Driscoll, gen mgr & progmg dir; Troy Holman, chief engr. ■ On 45 CATVs. Co-owned radio: *WNYE-FM

WNYW—ch 5, 17.4 kw vis, 1.74 kw aur, ant 1,689t/1,729g. TL: N40 42 43 W74 00 49. Hrs opn: 24. On air date: May 2, 1944. 205 E. 67th St. (10021). (212) 452-5555. FAX: (212) 249-1182. Licensee: Fox Television Stations Inc. (group owner; acq 11-14-86; grpsl). ■ Net: Fox. Rep: Petry. ■ Mitchell Stern, exec vp; Hilary Hendler, vp & gen mgr; Lou Abitabilo, gen sls mgr; Phyllis Seifer, vp prom & vp progmg; Ian Rae, news dir; Joe Berini, engrg dir.

WPIX—ch 11, 58.9 kw vis, 11.7 kw aur, ant 1,660t/1,760g. TL: N40 42 43 W74 00 49. Stereo. On air date: June 15, 1948. 220 E. 42nd St. (10017). (212) 949-1100. FAX: (212) 986-1032. Licensee: WPIX Inc. Group owner: Tribune Broadcasting Co. Rep: Telerep. News progmg 15 hrs wkly. ■ Michael Eigner, gen mgr; Paul Bissonette, stn mgr; Liz Goldberg, opns mgr; Betty Ellen Berlamino, gen sls mgr; Vincent Manzi, natl sls mgr; Wendy Kaiser, prom dir; Julie Nunnari, progmg dir; John Corporon, news dir; Kathleen Shepherd, pub affrs dir;

Frank Geraty, vp engrg. ■ On 416 CATVs—4,600,000 subs.

WWOR-TV

WWOR-TV—(Secaucus, NJ). ch 9, 47.9 kw vis, 4.79 kw aur, ant 1,640t/1,729g. TL: N40 42 43 W74 00 49. Stereo. Hrs opn: 24. On air date: Oct 11, 1949. 9 Broadcast Plaza, Secaucus, NJ (07096). (201) 348-0009. FAX: (201) 330-2488. Licensee: BHC Communications. Group owner: Chris Craft Industries Inc. (acq 8-24-92). Rep: Katz. Wash atty: Wilmer, Cutler & Pickering. News staff 76; news progmg 6 hrs wkly. ■ Robert Qudeen, vp & gen mgr; Barbara Landers, vp opns; Bob Woodruff, vp dev; Donna Zapata, vp sls; Ed Aaronson, prom dir & adv dir; Karen Corbin, progmg dir; Will Wright, news dir; Rick Miner, vp engrg. ■ On 1,700 CATVs—13,000,000 subs. On one trans.

WXTV—See Paterson, N.J.

North Pole

WPTZ—Licensed to North Pole. See Plattsburgh.

Norwood

ADI No. 170; see Watertown-Carthage market

*WNPI-TV—ch 18, 661 kw vis, 83.4 kw aur, ant 800t/761g. TL: N44 29 30 W74 51 29. On air date: Aug 30, 1971. 1056 Arsenal St., Watertown (13601). (315) 782-3142. FAX: (315) 782-2491. Licensee: St. Lawrence Valley ETV Council. ■ Net: PBS; EEN. Wash atty: Schwartz, Woods & Miller. ■ William J. Saiff Jr., pres & gen mgr; H. Ross Ney, opns dir; Jeremy Graves, dev dir & mktg dir; Tatia Kennedy, prom dir; Janette Thune, progmg dir & film buyer; James W. Edwards, chief engr. ■ On 14 CATVs.

Plattsburgh

ADI No. 93; see Burlington-Plattsburgh market

*WCFE-TV—ch 57, 794 kw vis, 79.4 kw aur, ant 2,431t/1,226g. TL: N44 41 43 W73 53 00. Hrs opn: 7 AM-1:30 AM. On air date: Mar 6, 1977. One Sesame St. (12901). (518) 563-9770. FAX: (518) 561-1928. Licensee: Northeast N.Y. Public Telecommunications Council Inc. ■ Net: PBS. Wash atty: Dow, Lohnes & Albertson. ■ Lambert Heyniger, chmn; Gerald Bates, pres; John Flanzer, vp & progmg dir; Allison Arnold, opns mgr; Jane Ashley, gen sls mgr; Janice LaFave, prom mgr; Joanne Taylor, pub affrs dir; Charles Zarbo, chief engr. ■ On 11 CATVs—45,000 subs. Co-owned radio: WCFE-FM.

WPTZ—(North Pole). ch 5, 25.1 kw vis, 4.3 kw aur, ant 1,991t/978g. TL: N44 34 26 W73 40 29. Stereo. On air date: Dec 8, 1954. 5 Television Dr., Plattsburgh (12901). (518) 561-5555. FAX: (518) 561-5940. Licensee: Heritage Media Corp. (group owner; acq 3-28-56; $500,000; 4-2-56). ■ Net: NBC. Rep: Petry. Wash atty: Pepper & Corazzini. News staff 19; news progmg 8 hrs wkly. ■ Bob Shields, pres & gen mgr; Sam Dieterich Jr., gen sls mgr; Dick Roberts, prom mgr; Joe Krone, progmg dir; Stewart Ledbetter, news dir; Thomas Bradshaw, chief engr.

Poughkeepsie

ADI No. 1; see New York market

WTBY—ch 54, 5,000 kw vis, 500 kw aur, ant 852t/894g. TL: N41 43 09 W73 59 47. On air date: Apr 19, 1981. Box 534, Merritt Rd. & Rt. 9, Fishkill (12524). (914) 896-4610. FAX: (914) 896-4614. Licensee: Trinity Broadcasting of N.Y. Inc. Ownership: Trinity Broadcasting Network (acq 7-13-82; $2.97 million; 6-21-82). Wash atty: May, Dunne & Gay. ■ Paul Crouch, pres; Campbell Thompson, gen mgr; Rich Bemillo, gen sls mgr; Vicki Davenport, progmg dir; Lou MacDonald, chief engr. ■ On 16 CATVs—96,306 subs.

Riverhead

ADI No. 1; see New York market

WLIG—ch 55, 5,000 kw vis, 474 kw aur, ant 700t/600g. TL: N40 53 50 W72 54 56. Hrs opn: 20. On air date: Apr 28, 1985. Box 1355, 270 S. Service Rd., Melville (11747). (516) 777-8855. FAX: (516) 777-8180. Licensee: WLIG TV Inc. Ownership: Trexar Corp., 100% Wash atty: Arent, Fox, Kintner, Plotkin & Kahn. News staff 4; news progmg 2 hrs wkly. ■ Michael Pascucci, pres; Michael Wach, vp & gen mgr; Gerald Diorio, opns mgr; Tracy Speed, prom mgr; Stan Hopkins, news dir; Ron Scotto, engrg mgr. ■ On 9 CATVs—855,500 subs. On one trans. ■ Rates: $400; 400; 200.

Rochester

ADI No. 69; see Rochester, NY market

WHEC-TV—ch 10, 316 kw vis, 39.8 kw aur, ant 499t/352g. TL: N43 08 07 W77 35 02. Hrs opn: 24. On air date: Nov 1, 1953. 191 East Ave. (14604). (716) 546-5670. FAX: (716) 454-7433; (716) 546-5688. Licensee: Viacom International Inc. Group owner: Viacom Broadcasting Inc. (acq 10-17-83; grpsl; 11-17-83). ■ Net: NBC. Rep: Telerep. Wash atty: Arent, Fox, Kintner, Plotkin & Kahn. ■ Arnold Klinsky, vp & gen mgr; Harvey Lazear, gen sls mgr; John Doyle, prom mgr; Terry Fauth, progmg dir; Rob Elmore, news dir; John Walsh, chief engr. ■ On 42 CATVs—460,970 subs.

WOKR—ch 13, 316 kw vis, 47.9 kw aur, ant 500t/363.5g. TL: N43 08 07 W77 35 03. On air date: Sept 15, 1962. Box 20555, 4225 W. Henrietta Rd. (14602-0555). (716) 334-8700. FAX: (716) 359-1570. Licensee: Hughes Broadcasting Partners. Ownership: VS&A Communications Partners & Smith Barney Investors L.P. ■ Net: ABC. Rep: Harrington, Righter & Parsons Inc. Wash atty: Wilmer, Cutler & Pickering. ■ Gary Nielsen, pres & gen mgr; Don Loy, opns dir & prom mgr; Kent Beckwith, gen sls mgr; Keith Connors, news dir; Fred McWharf, chief engr. ■ On 34 CATVs—397,658 subs.

WROC-TV—ch 8, 316 kw vis, 48.5 kw aur, ant 499t/345g. TL: N43 08 07 W77 35 02. Stereo. On air date: June 14, 1949. 201 Humboldt St. (14610). (716) 288-8400. TWX: 510-253-5407. Licensee: WRPC Associates/Television Station Partners, L.P. (group owner; acq 1-18-83; grpsl; 2-7-83). ■ Net: CBS. Rep: Petry, Canadian Communications (Canadian Rep). Wash atty: Wiley, Rein & Fielding. News staff 32; news progmg 14 hrs wkly. ■ I. Martin Pompadr, chmn; Gary R. Bolton, gen mgr & film buyer; Jeff Ulrich, opns mgr, mktg mgr, prom mgr & progmg dir; Lynda Peterson, gen sls mgr; Scott Benjamin, news dir; Tom Connolly, pub affrs dir; John Coon, chief engr. ■ On 49 CATVs—969,457 subs. ■ Rates: $800; 100; 100.

WUHF—ch 31, 1,200 kw vis, 200 kw aur, ant 497t/345g. TL: N43 08 07 W77 35 03. Stereo. On air date: January 1980. 360 East Ave. (14604). (716) 232-3700. FAX: (716) 546-4774. Licensee: Act III Broadcasting of Rochester. Group owner: Act III Broadcasting Inc. (acq 4-16-89; $12 million; 2-6-89). ■ Net: Fox. Rep: Katz. Wash atty: Goldberg & Spector. ■ Heather Farnsworth, vp & gen mgr; Jeff Guilbert, gen sls mgr; Barbara Browning, prom mgr; Dale Hartnett, progmg dir; Rick Finnie, chief engr. ■ On 29 CATVs—248,879 subs.

*WXXI-TV—ch 21, 906 kw vis, 90.6 kw aur, ant 500t/343g. TL: N43 08 07 W77 35 03. On air date: September 1966. Box 21 (14601). (716) 325-7500. FAX: (716) 325-7514. Licensee: Rochester Area ETV Assn Inc. ■ Net: PBS; EEN. Wash atty: Schwartz, Woods & Miller. Sp, Fr & Ger progmg. ■ William J. Pearce, pres & gen mgr; Deborah Onslow, sr vp; Nancy Brush, dev dir & vp mktg; Adelle McCarthy, prom mgr; Robert Owens, progmg dir. ■ On 13 CATVs. Co-owned radio: WXXI-AM-FM

Schenectady

ADI No. 53; see Albany-Schenectady-Troy market

*WMHT—ch 17, 2,000 kw vis, 200 kw aur, ant 983t/271g. TL: N42 38 13 W74 00 06. Stereo. On air date: May 2, 1962. Box 17 (12301); 17 Fern Ave. (12306). (518) 356-1700. FAX: (518) 356-0173. Licensee: WMHT Educational Telecommunications. ■ Net: PBS; EEN. Wash atty: Schwartz, Woods & Miller. Sp & Fr one hr wkly. ■ Donn Rogosin, gen mgr; Tom Merklinger, opns dir; Glenda Bullock, dev dir & prom dir; Marianne Potter, progmg dir; Derk Van Rijsewijk, chief engr. ■ On 40 CATVs—334,105 subs. On 7 trans. Co-owned radio: *WMHT-FM.

WRGB—Licensed to Schenectady. See Albany.

Smithtown

ADI No. 1; see New York market

WHSI-TV—ch 67, 2,630 kw vis, 263 kw aur, ant 720t/678g. TL: N40 53 23 W72 57 13. Stereo. On air date: November 1973. Box 609, 3200 Expressway Dr. S., Central Islip (11722). (516) 582-6700. FAX: (516) 582-8337. Licensee: Silver King Broadcasting Inc. Group owner: Silver King Communications Inc. (acq 9-18-86; grpsl; 8-25-86). Wash atty: Dow, Lohnes & Albertson. News progmg 4 hrs wkly. ■ David Porrello, progmg mgr & news dir; Alvin Saltzman, chief engr. ■ On 2 CATVs—229,000 subs.

Springville

WNGS—ch 67, 15 kw vis, ant 438t. Not on air, target date unknown. 1536 Logan Ave., Altoona, PA (16602). Permittee: Unicorn Springville.

Syracuse

ADI No. 67; see Syracuse market

*WCNY-TV—ch 24, 2,312 kw vis, 231 kw aur, ant 1,380t/964g. TL: N42 56 42 W76 01 28. Stereo. Hrs opn: 6:45 AM-midnight. On air date: Dec 20, 1965. Box 2400, 506 Old Liverpool Rd. (13220-2400). (315) 453-2424. FAX: (315) 451-8824. Licensee: Public Broadcasting Council of Central New York. ■ Net: PBS; EEN. Wash atty: Haley, Bader & Potts. ■ Richard W. Russell, CEO & pres; Thomas A. Burton, dev dir; Paul Dunn, prom mgr; Jack Neal, progmg dir; Hugh J. Cleland, chief engr. ■ On 60 CATVs—500,000 subs. On 2 trans. Co-owned radio: *WCNY-FM, WJNY-FM, WUNY-FM.

WIXT—ch 9, 79.4 kw vis, 11.8 kw aur, ant 1,515t/959g. TL: N42 56 42 W76 01 28. On air date: Sept 9, 1962. Box 9, East Syracuse (13057). (315) 446-4780. FAX: (315) 446-0045. Licensee: WIXT Television Inc. Group owner: Ackerley Communications Inc. (acq 4-16-82; $13.8 million; 5-10-82). ■ Net: ABC. Rep: Blair. Wash atty: Rubin, Winston & Diercks. ■ Barry Ackerley, pres; A. Stephen Kronquest, vp & gen mgr; Kathleen Vanaktyne, gen sls mgr; Vince Spicola, prom dir; Sherry Potter, progmg dir; Ron Lombard, news dir; John King, chief engr. ■ On 80 CATVs—300,000 subs. On 2 trans. ■ Rates: $720; 180; 120.

WSNR-TV—ch 43, 17.8 kw vis, 1.8 kw aur, ant 115t/125g. TL: N43 03 33 W76 08 10. On air date: Oct 7, 1989. Rt. 1, Box 203A, Castleton, VA (22716). (703) 937-4800. FAX: (703) 937-2148. Licensee: Salt of the Earth Broadcasting Ltd. Ownership: James L. Oyster, 100%. ■ James Oyster, pres.

WSTM-TV—ch 3, 100 kw vis, 20 kw aur, ant 1,000t/594g. TL: N42 56 40 W76 07 08. Stereo. On air date: Feb 15, 1950. 1030 James St. (13203). (315) 474-5000. FAX: (315) 474-5082. Licensee: Federal Broadcasting Co. (group owner; acq 10-1-92; $19.2 million; 8-31-92). ■ Net: NBC. Rep: Katz. Wash atty: Hogan & Hartson. ■ Peter A. Kizer, pres; Edward O. Ruffley, CFO; James A. Kiezer, gen mgr; Samuel J. Curcuru, stn mgr; Toni Rhodes, natl sls mgr; Denise Bradshaw, prom mgr; Charles S. Bivins Jr., progmg dir; Mark Carros, news dir; Laura Hand, pub affrs dir; John Merrill, chief engr. ■ On 60 CATVs—358,397 subs.

WSYT—ch 68, 1,000 kw vis, 100 kw aur, ant 1,469t/527g. TL: N42 52 50 W76 11 59. Stereo. Hrs opn: 24. On air date: Feb 15, 1986. 1000 James St. (13203). (315) 472-6800. FAX: (315) 471-8889. Licensee: Encore Communications Inc. of Syracuse. Ownership: Charles A. McFadden, 100% (acq 8-1-90; $7 million). ■ Net: Fox. Rep: Seltel. Wash atty: Waysdorf & VanBergh. ■ Charles A. McFadden, pres; Linda Cochran, vp & gen mgr; Dan Walding, gen sls mgr; Connie Howard-Banks, natl sls mgr; Stephanie Haring, prom mgr & adv mgr; Jeryl Jonza, progmg dir; Michael J. Maville, chief engr. ■ On 53 CATVs—310,000 subs.

WTVH—ch 5, 100 kw vis, 20 kw aur, ant 950t/556g. TL: N42 57 19 W76 06 34. Stereo. Hrs opn: 24. On air date: Dec 1, 1948. 980 James St. (13203). (315) 425-5555. FAX: (315) 425-5513. Licensee: Granite Broadcasting Corp. (group owner; acq 8-9-93; $32 million with KSEE(TV) Fresno, CA; 8-30-93). ■ Net: CBS. Rep: MMT, Mulvihill (Canada). Wash atty: Haley, Bader & Potts. News staff 31; news progmg 16 hrs wkly. ■ Ed Bradley, gen mgr; Sandra Coyle, gen sls mgr; David Tinsch, mktg dir &

Utica

ADI No. 161; see Utica market

WFXV—ch 33, 42.7 kw vis, 4.27 kw aur, ant 646t/189g. TL: N43 02 14 W75 26 40. Stereo. On air date: Dec 9, 1986. 33 Greenfield Rd., Rome (13440). (315) 337-3300. FAX: (315) 337-1862. Licensee: Mohawk Valley Broadcasting Inc. Ownership: Craig Fox, 37.5%; Kevin O'Kane, 37.5%; John Bunkfeldt, 25%. ■ Net: Fox. Rep: MBS. Wash atty: James L. Oyster. ■ Kevin O'Kane, pres, gen mgr & progmg dir; Russell Reitz, gen sls mgr; Mike Moran, prom mgr; John Bunkfeldt, chief engr. ■ On 5 CATVs—79,500 subs. On one trans. ■ Rates: $100; 50; 25.

WKTV—ch 2, 34.7 kw vis, 6.9 kw aur, ant 1,380t/1,065g. TL: N43 06 09 W74 56 27. On air date: Dec 1, 1949. Box 2 (13503). (315) 733-0404. FAX: (315) 793-3498. Licensee: Smith Television of New York Inc. Group owner: Smith Broadcasting Group Inc. (acq 5-27-92). ■ Net: NBC. Rep: Katz, Continental. Wash atty: Hogan & Hartson. ■ Sheldon Storrier, vp & gen mgr; S. F. Storrier, gen sls mgr; Tom Coyne, prom mgr, progmg dir & film buyer; Kevin Nunn, news dir; Dane Kistner, chief engr. ■ On 35 CATVs—264,625 subs.

WUTR—ch 20, 1,150 kw vis, 173 kw aur, ant 800t/427g. TL: N43 08 43 W75 10 35. On air date: Feb 28, 1970. Box 20 (13503). (315) 797-5220. TWX: 510-242-1994. Licensee: Roy H. Park Broadcasting of Utica-Rome Inc. Group owner: Park Communications Inc. ■ Net: ABC. Rep: Blair. Wash atty: Wiley, Rein & Fielding. ■ Roy H. Park, pres; Paul R. Kennedy, gen mgr; Steven Berry, gen sls mgr; Dave Phoenix, prom mgr; Luke Michaels, news dir; Robert Hajec, chief engr. ■ On 25 CATVs—212,619 subs. On one trans. ■ Rates: $350; 90; 30.

Watertown

ADI No. 170; see Watertown-Carthage market

*WNPE-TV—ch 16, 525 kw vis, 105 kw aur, ant 1,214t/943g. On air date: Aug 5, 1971. 1056 Arsenal St. (13601). (315) 782-3142. FAX: (315) 782-2491. Licensee: St. Lawrence Valley TV Council. ■ Net: PBS; EEN. Wash atty: Schwartz, Woods & Miller. ■ William J. Saiff Jr., pres & gen mgr; H. Ross Ney, opns dir; Jeremy Graves, dev dir & mktg dir; Tatia Kennedy, prom dir; Janette Thune, progmg dir & film buyer; James W. Edwards, chief engr. ■ On 13 CATVs—38,687 subs.

WWNY-TV—(Carthage). ch 7, 316 kw vis, 47 kw aur, ant 718t/572g. TL: N43 57 16 W75 43 45. Stereo. (CP: ant 725t/579g). Hrs opn: 6 AM-2 AM. On air date: Oct 22, 1954. 120 Arcade St., Watertown (13601). (315) 788-3800. FAX: (315) 782-7468. Licensee: United Communications Corp. (group owner; acq 12-5-81; $8.1 million; 6-1-81). ■ Net: CBS, NBC. Rep: Katz. Wash atty: Jones, Waldo, Holbrook & McDonough. News staff 16; news progmg 10 hrs wkly. ■ Howard J. Brown, pres; Kevin T. Mastellon, gen mgr; Nickolas W. Darling, gen sls mgr; Jennifer Goodwin, progmg dir; Cathy Pircsuk, news dir; Donald Rohr, chief engr. ■ On 18 CATVs—65,551 subs.

WWTI—ch 50, 1,200 kw vis, 120 kw aur, ant 1,268t/1,000g. TL: N43 52 47 W75 43 11. Stereo. Hrs opn: 6 AM-1 AM. On air date: January 1988. Box 6250 1222 Arsenal St. (13601). (315) 785-8850. FAX: (315) 785-0127. Licensee: Desert Communications V Inc. Ownership: Don A. Luttenegger (acq 8-18-92; 9-7-92). ■ Net: ABC. Wash atty: Latham, Watkins & Hills. ■ Richard Whelan, gen mgr & natl sls mgr; John Moore, prom mgr & pub affrs dir; Melissa Carty, progmg dir; Robert Kurtz, chief engr. ■ On 22 CATVs—110,400 subs. On one trans. ■ Rates: $500; 150; 50.

North Carolina

Asheville

ADI No. 35; see Greenville, SC-Spartanburg, SC-Asheville, NC-Anderson, SC

WASV-TV—ch 62, 8.51 kw vis, 851 w aur, ant 151t. TL: N35 34 59 W82 32 45. (CP: 11.9 kw vis, ant 1,105t, TL: N35 31 39 W82 29 44). On air date: June 1986. Box 2527, Sarasota, FL (34230). (813) 923-3029. FAX: (813) 923-8227. Licensee: Video Marketing Network Inc. Ownership: Robert J. Murley, 34% (acq 1-1-88). ■ Robert J. Murley, pres; Harvey Budd, progmg dir.

WHNS—Licensed to Asheville. See Greenville, S.C.

WLOS—Licensed to Asheville. See Greenville, S.C.

*WUNF-TV—ch 33, 1,510 kw vis, 302 kw aur, ant 2,620t/339g. TL: N35 25 32 W82 45 25. On air date: Sept 11, 1967. Box 14900, 10 T.W. Alexander Dr., Research Triangle Park (27709). (919) 549-7000. FAX: (919) 549-7201. Licensee: Univ. of North Carolina. ■ Net: PBS. ■ Tom Howe, gen mgr; Bob Royster, opns dir; H. Camille Patterson, dev dir; Diana Hatch, prom dir; Diane Lucas, progmg dir; Richard W. Hatch, pub affrs dir; Willard Campbell, engrg dir; Harvey Arnold, chief engr. ■ On 51 CATVs—84,872 subs. On 2 trans.

Belmont

ADI No. 30; see Charlotte market

WJZY—ch 46, 500 kw vis, 50 kw aur, ant 1,948t/1,949g. TL: N35 21 44 W81 09 19. Stereo. On air date: March 9, 1987. Box 668400, Charlotte (28266-8400); 3501 Performance Rd., Charlotte (28214). (704) 398-0046. FAX: (704) 393-8407. Licensee: WJZY-TV Inc. Group owner: Capitol Broadcasting Co. Inc. (acq 11-87; $1.581 million). Wash atty: Fletcher, Heald & Hildreth. ■ James Goodmon, pres; Mark Conrad, gen mgr; Thomas Schenck, gen sls mgr; Mark Moseley, natl sls mgr; Mark Gray, prom dir; Bill Graff, progmg dir; Jeff Johnson, pub affrs dir; John Bishop, chief engr. ■ On 81 CATVs—510,301 subs.

Burlington

ADI No. 49; see Greensboro-Winston Salem-High Point market

WAAP—ch 16, 1,910 kw vis, 191 kw aur, ant 840t/500g. TL: N35 56 22 W79 25 47. Hrs opn: 24. On air date: Aug 7, 1984. Box 16, 5235 Mountain Trail Rd., Snow Camp (27349-0016). (919) 376-6016. FAX: (919) 376-6018. Licensee: Television Communications Inc. Ownership: Jack Rehburg, 100% (acq 1-7-86; $2.8 million; 10-14-85). Rep: Roslin. Wash atty: Baraff, Koerner, Olender & Hochberg. News staff 14; news progmg 10 hrs wkly. ■ Jack Rehburg, pres; Steve Rehburg, exec vp, gen mgr & gen sls mgr; John Marsh, news dir; Ken Maynard, engrg mgr & chief engr. ■ On 7 CATVs—180,000 subs. ■ Rates: $45; 30; 20.

Chapel Hill

ADI No. 32; see Raleigh-Durham market

*WUNC-TV—ch 4, 100 kw vis, 20 kw aur, ant 1,027t. TL: N35 51 59 W79 10 22. Stereo. On air date: Jan 8, 1955. Box 14900, 10 T.W. Alexander Dr., Research Triangle Park (27709). (919) 549-7000. FAX: (919) 549-7201. Licensee: Univ. of North Carolina. ■ Net: PBS. Wash atty: Schwartz, Woods & Miller. ■ Tom Howe, gen mgr; Bob Royster, opns dir; H. Camille Patterson, dev dir; Diana Hatch, prom dir; Chancy M. Kapp, progmg dir; Diane Lucas, progmg mgr; Richard W. Hatch, pub affrs dir; Willard Campbell, engrg dir; Harvey Arnold, chief engr. ■ On 145 CATVs—291,200 subs.

Charlotte

ADI No. 30; see Charlotte market

WBTV—ch 3, 100 kw vis, 10 kw aur, ant 1,860t/1,987g. TL: N35 21 51 W81 11 13. Stereo. On air date: July 15, 1949. One Julian Price Pl. (28208). (704) 374-3500. TWX: 810-621-0449. Licensee: Jefferson Pilot. Group owner: Jefferson-Pilot Communications Co. ■ Net: CBS. Rep: Petry. Wash atty: Wiley, Rein & Fielding. ■ John H. Hutchinson, pres & gen mgr; Ron Miller, vp & stn mgr; Bill Napier, vp opns & chief engr; Gerald Pelletier, vp sls; Mike Burney, mktg dir & progmg dir; Shannon Reichley, news dir. ■ On 42 CATVs. Co-owned radio: WBT-AM-FM.

WCCB—ch 18, 2,090 kw vis, 230 kw aur, ant 1,276t/1,143g. TL: N35 15 56 W80 44 06. On air date: Dec 7, 1953. One TV Pl. (28205). (704) 372-1800. FAX: (704) 376-3415. Licensee: North Carolina Broadcasting Partners (acq 7-20-92). ■ Net: Fox. Rep: Katz. ■ Cy N. Bahakel, pres; Cullie Tarleton, gen mgr; Gene Doss, gen sls mgr; Jeff Arrowood, prom mgr; Steven Soldinger, progmg dir & film buyer; Doug Bell, news dir; Robert Phillips, chief engr. ■ On 90 CATVs—489,000 subs.

WCNC-TV—ch 36, 5,000 kw vis, 500 kw aur, ant 1,964t/1,954g. TL: N35 20 49 W81 10 15. Stereo. On air date: July 9, 1967. 1001 Wood Ridge Center Dr. (28217-1901). (704) 329-3636. FAX: (704) 357-4980. Licensee: Journal Broadcasting of Charlotte Inc. Group owner: Providence Journal Bcstg Corp. (acq 11-29-88). ■ Net: NBC. Rep: Harrington, Righter & Parsons. Wash atty: Covington & Burling. ■ John Llewellyn, pres & gen mgr; Nicholas Magnini, opns mgr; Eleanor Waller, natl sls mgr; Glenn Nash, prom mgr; Tim Bloodworth, progmg dir & film buyer; Bob Young, news dir; Jean Fuller, pub affrs dir; David Folsom, chief engr. ■ On 45 CATVs—400,000 subs.

WSOC-TV—ch 9, 316 kw vis, 31.6 kw aur, ant 1,179t/1,073g. TL: N35 15 41 W80 43 38. Stereo. On air date: Apr 28, 1957. Box 34665 (28234); 1901 N. Tryon St. (28206). (704) 335-4999. Licensee: WSOC Television Inc. Group owner: Cox Broadcasting (acq 4-13-59; grpsl; 4-13-59). ■ Net: ABC. Rep: Telerep. Wash atty: Dow, Lohnes & Albertson. ■ Nicholas D. Trigony, pres; Bruce R. Baker, gen mgr; Jack Dabney, gen sls mgr; Phil Michael (creative svcs), prom dir; Jack Callaghan, progmg dir; Michael Kronley, news dir; Merle Thomas, engrg dir. ■ On 41 CATVs—430,224 subs.

*WTVI—ch 42, 2,750 kw vis, 550 kw aur, ant 1,247t/1,221g. TL: N35 12 25 W80 47 30. Stereo. On air date: Aug 27, 1965. 3242 Commonwealth Ave. (28205). (704) 372-2442. FAX: (704) 335-1358. Licensee: Charlotte-Mecklenburg Public Broadcasting Authority. ■ Net: PBS. Wash atty: Schwartz, Woods & Miller. ■ Richard K. Wagner, chmn; Hal Bouton, pres & gen mgr; Elliot Sanderson, sr vp; Carol Sasser (personnel), opns mgr; Mary Ciminelli, vp dev; Steve Maag, dev mgr; Charlie Caldwell, vp mktg & prom dir; Shelia Tucker, vp progmg; Jim Luttrell, vp engrg. ■ On 12 CATVs—96,000 subs.

Columbia

ADI No. 104; see Greenville-New Bern-Washington market

*WUND-TV—ch 2, 100 kw vis, 15 kw aur, ant 990t/1,041g. TL: N35 53 59 W76 20 52. On air date: Sept 10, 1965. Box 14900, 10 T.W. Alexander Dr., Research Triangle Park (27709). (919) 549-7000. FAX: (919) 549-7201. Licensee: Univ. of North Carolina. ■ Net: PBS. ■ Tom Howe, gen mgr; Bob Royster, opns dir; H. Camille Patterson, dev dir; Diana Hatch, prom dir; Diane Lucas, progmg mgr; Richard W. Hatch, pub affrs dir; Willard Campbell, engrg dir; Harvey Arnold, chief engr. ■ On 29 CATVs—20,164 subs.

Concord

ADI No. 30; see Charlotte market

*WUNG-TV—ch 58, 1,230 kw vis, 123 kw aur, ant 1,289t/1,304g. TL: N35 15 06 W80 40 12. (CP: 5,000 kw vis, 124 kw aur, ant 1,390t, TL: N35 21 30 W80 36 37). On air date: Sept 11, 1967. Box 14900, 10 T.W. Alexander Dr., Research Triangle Park (27709). (919) 549-7000. FAX: (919) 549-7201. Licensee: Univ. of North Carolina. ■ Net: PBS. ■ Tom Howe, gen mgr; Bob Royster, opns dir; H. Camille Patterson, dev dir; Diana Hatch, prom dir; Diane Lucas, progmg dir; Richard W. Hatch, pub affrs dir; Willard Campbell, engrg dir; Harvey Arnold, chief engr. ■ On 58 CATVs—136,770 subs. On 2 trans.

Durham

ADI No. 32; see Raleigh-Durham market

WRDC—ch 28, 5,000 kw vis, 250 kw aur, ant 2,000t/1,976g. TL: N35 40 35 W78 32 09. Stereo. Hrs opn: 24. On air date: Nov 4, 1968. 3012 Highwoods Blvd. (27604). (919) 876-0674. FAX: (919) 790-6254; TWX: 510-928-1852. Licensee: F.S.F. Acquisition Corp. (acq 6-14-91; grpsl; 7-1-91). ■ Net: NBC. Rep: Blair. Wash atty: Tharrington, Smith & Hargrove. ■ Vicki Street, vp & gen mgr; Greg Adams, gen sls mgr; Phil Valens, prom mgr; David Grirsch, progmg dir & chief engr; Sheila Conlin, news dir. ■ On 73 CATVs—256,950 subs. ■ Rates: $750; 200; 75.

WTVD—ch 11, 316 kw vis, 47.4 kw aur, ant 1,990t/2,000g. TL: N35 40 05 W78 31 58. On air date: Sept 2, 1954. Box 2009 (27702). (919) 683-1111. FAX: (919) 682-7476; TWX: 510-927-1810. Licensee: Capital Cities/ABC Inc. Group owner: Capital Cities/ABC Broadcast Group (acq 5-24-57; $1,417,800; 5-3-57). ■ Net: ABC. Wash atty: Wilmer, Cutler & Pickering. ■ Tim Bennett, pres & gen mgr; Denis J. O'Connor, gen sls mgr; David Rhoades, prom mgr; Jon Myhr, progmg dir & film buyer; Lee Meredith, news dir; Brett Chambers, pub affrs dir; Curtis Meredith, chief engr.

Fayetteville

ADI No. 32; see Raleigh-Durham market

WFAY—ch 62, 337.3 kw vis, 33.7 kw aur, ant 846t/855g. TL: N34 53 05 W79 04 31. On air date: Mar 14, 1985.

Drawer 62, Lumber Bridge (28357). (919) 843-3884. FAX: (919) 843-2873; TWX: 810-621-0037. Licensee: Fayetteville Cumberland Telecasters Inc. Ownership: Robinson O. Everett, executor; Mark Conrad, 5% (acq 4-24-92). Rep: Adam Young. Wash atty: Baraff, Koerner, Olender & Hochberg. ■ James Thrath, gen mgr & film buyer; Carolyn Jordon, gen sls mgr; Liza Babirak, prom mgr; Robbie Brock, progmg dir; David Smith, chief engr. ■ On 7 CATVs—83,000 subs. ■ Rates: $100; 75; 45.

WKFT—ch 40, 5,000 kw vis, 500 kw aur, ant 1,842t/1,749g. TL: N35 30 45 W75 58 40. Stereo. On air date: June 1, 1981. Box 2509, 230 Donaldson St. (28302-2509). (919) 323-4040. FAX: (919) 323-3924. Licensee: Delta Broadcasting Inc. (group owner; acq 4-3-91). Rep: Adam Young. Wash atty: Tharrington, Smith & Hargrove. ■ Elbert Boyd, pres; Mitchell Saieed, vp & natl sls mgr; Ray Sasser, gen mgr; Peter Getzen, stn mgr; Harry L. Thornton, gen sls mgr; Cynthia Johnsong, prom mgr; Carolyn Kleinert, progmg dir; Abby Melvin, pub affrs dir; David Rickels, chief engr.■On 44 CATVs—340,000 subs.

WTVD—See Durham.

Goldsboro

ADI No. 32; see Raleigh-Durham market

WYED—ch 17, 2,570 kw vis, 257 aur, ant 1,610t/1,529g. TL: N35 37 01 W78 28 38. Stereo. Hrs opn: 24. On air date: Apr 11, 1988. Box 1117, 622 S. Barbour St., Clayton (27520). (919) 553-1700. FAX: (919) 553-0984. Licensee: Group H Broadcasting Corp. Group owner: Beasley Broadcast Group. ■ George G. Beasley, pres; Bob Belchir, gen sls mgr; Allan Horowitz, prom mgr & news dir; Bob Peretic, film buyer; Matthew Brandis, chief engr. ■ On 6 CATVs—41,000 subs. Co-owned radio: $250; 150; 50.

Greensboro

ADI No. 49; see Greensboro-Winston Salem-High Point market

WFMY-TV—ch 2, 100 kw vis, 19.5 kw aur, ant 1,842t/1,914g. TL: N35 52 13 W79 50 25. Stereo. Hrs opn: 24. On air date: Sept 22, 1949. Box TV2 (27420); 1615 Phillips Ave. (27405). (919) 379-9369. FAX: (919) 273-3444; TWX: 510-925-1193. Licensee: Gannett Co. Inc. Group owner: Gannett Broadcasting (division of Gannett Co. Inc.) (acq 2-1-88). ■ Net: CBS. Rep: Blair. News staff 50; news progmg 23 hrs wkly. ■ Colleen Brown, pres & gen mgr; Brein Kennidy, gen sls mgr; Martha Brown, prom mgr; Jim Collins, news dir; David Jones, chief engr. ■ On 50 CATVs—195,000 subs.

WGGT—ch 48, 1,100 kw vis, 110 kw aur, ant 1,696t/1,726g. TL: N35 52 13 W79 50 25. Hrs opn: 6 AM-4 AM. On air date: May 9, 1981. 330 S. Greene St. (27401). (919) 274-4848. FAX: (919) 230-1315. Licensee: Guilford Telecasters Inc., debtor in possession. Ownership: Robinson O. Everett, executor (acq 4-24-92). ■ Net: Fox. Wash atty: Baraff, Koerner, Olender & Hochberg. ■ James Thrash, pres & gen mgr; Ginny Brown, opns mgr, progmg mgr & pub affrs dir. ■ On 36 CATVs—286,517 subs.

WGHP-TV—See High Point.

WLXI-TV—ch 61, 501 kw vis, 50 kw aur, ant 573t/499g. TL: N36 08 58 W80 03 21. On air date: Mar 1, 1984. 2109 Patterson St. (27407). (919) 855-5610. FAX: (919) 854-3465. Licensee: Radiant Life Ministries Inc. Ownership: Garth W. Coonce (group owner; acq 10-7-91; $1.9 million; 10-28-91). Wash atty: May & Dunne. ■ Larry Patton, gen mgr; Ed Kasovic, chief engr. ■ On 14 CATVs.

WXII—See Winston-Salem.

Greenville

ADI No. 104; see Greenville-New Bern-Washington market

WCTI—(New Bern). ch 12, 316 kw vis, 31 kw aur, ant 1,923t/1,999g. TL: N35 08 03 W77 03 51. On air date: Sept 1, 1963. Box 12325, 400 Glenburnie Dr., New Bern (28561). (919) 638-1212. FAX: (919) 637-4141; (919) 636-6855. Licensee: Lamco Communications Inc. (group owner; acq 8-2-93; $12.3 million; 8-23-93). ■ Net: ABC. Rep: Katz. Wash atty: Koteen & Naftalin. News staff 7; news progmg 24 hrs wkly. ■ Clay Milstead, vp & gen mgr; Bill Pole, gen sls mgr; Jim Woltjen, rgnl sls mgr; Drew Rhodes, prom mgr; Carolyn Stevens, progmg mgr; Terry Heaton, news dir; Ken Hughes, chief engr. ■ On 18 CATVs—85,000 subs.

WGTJ—ch 38, 5,000 kw vis, 500 kw aur, ant 474t/470g. TL: N35 27 25 W77 12 21. Not on air, target date unknown. 222 New St., New Bern (28650). Permittee: Community Service Telecasters Inc. Ownership: Athene B. Bunn, 10%; Thalius J. Markum, 50%; KeRhe M. Vestal, 40%

WITN-TV—(Washington). ch 7, 316 kw vis, 31.6 kw aur, ant 2,026t/2,000g. TL: N35 21 55 W77 23 38. Stereo. On air date: Sept 28, 1955. Box 468, Hwy. 17 S., Washington (27889). (919) 946-3131. FAX: (919) 946-9265. Licensee: WITN TV Inc. Group owner: AFLAC Broadcast Division (acq 6-26-85; $24,572,377). ■ Net: NBC. Rep: Harrington, Righter & Parsons. Wash atty: Sidley & Austin. ■ Michael D. Weeks, vp & gen mgr; Michael Smythe, gen sls mgr; Al Riggs, natl sls mgr; Dean Leipsner, prom mgr; Mike Riddle, progmg dir; Ron Comings, news dir; Al Manning, chief engr. ■ On 77 CATVs—314,000 subs.

WNCT-TV—ch 9, 316 kw vis, 31.6 kw aur, ant 1,879t/2,000g. TL: N35 21 55 W77 23 38. On air date: Dec 22, 1953. Box 898, 3221 Evans St. (27835-0898). (919) 355-8500. Licensee: Roy H. Park Broadcasting Inc. Group owner: Park Communications Inc. (acq 2-6-62; $2,557,458; 2-12-62). ■ Net: CBS. Rep: Blair. Wash atty: Wiley, Rein & Fielding. ■ Roy H. Park, pres; Edward J. Adams, gen mgr; John Fusco, gen sls mgr; Shirley Dale, progmg dir; Roy Hardee, news dir; Bertie Cartwright, chief engr. ■ On 33 CATVs—206,934 subs. Co-owned radio: WNCT-AM-FM.

*****WUNK-TV**—ch 25, 1,260 kw vis, 126 kw aur, ant 1,151t/1,170g. TL: N35 33 01 W77 36 02. On air date: 1972. Box 14900, 10 T. W. Alexander Dr., Research Triangle Park (27709). (919) 549-7000. FAX: (919) 549-7201. Licensee: Univ. of North Carolina. ■ Net: PBS. Wash atty: Schwartz, Woods & Miller. ■ Tom Howe, gen mgr; Bob Royster, opns dir; H. Camille Patterson, dev dir; Diana Hatch, prom dir; Diane Lucas, progmg dir; Richard W. Hatch, pub affrs dir; Willard Campbell, engrg dir; Harvey Arnold, chief engr. ■ On 80 CATVs—80,746 subs.

WYDO—ch 14, 1,104 kw vis, ant 686 ft. TL: N35 26 44 W77 22 08. Hrs opn: 24. On air date: June 30, 1992. Box 2044 (27836). (919) 746-8014. FAX: (919) 746-2555. Licensee: KS Family Television Inc. Ownership: Frederick J. McCune (acq 8-4-92; $4,000; 11-9-92). Wash atty: Wilkinson, Barker, Knauer & Quinn. ■ Fred McCune, gen mgr & chief engr; Hamp Ferguson, stn mgr, vp opns, vp sls & vp mktg. ■ On 13 CATVs—52,285 subs.

Hickory

ADI No. 30; see Charlotte market

WHKY-TV—ch 14, 656.1 kw vis, 65.6 kw aur, ant 600t/487g. TL: N35 43 57 W81 19 52. Hrs opn: 6 AM-midnight. On air date: Feb 14, 1968. Box 1059 (28603); 526 Main Ave. S.E. (28602). (704) 322-5115. FAX: (704) 322-8256. Licensee: The Long Family Partnership (acq 3-16-87; 10-1-76). Rep: Roslin. News staff 2; news progmg 5 hrs wkly. ■ Thomas E. Long, gen mgr & chief engr; Jeffrey B. Long, stn mgr, prom mgr & progmg dir; Jim Carr, gen sls mgr; Lou Anne Kincaid, news dir; Susie Woods, pub affrs dir. ■ On 10 CATVs—70,000 subs. Co-owned radio: WHKY(AM). ■ Rates: $60; 40; 30.

High Point

ADI No. 49; see Greensboro-Winston Salem-High Point market

WFMY-TV—See Greensboro.

WGHP-TV—ch 8, 316 kw vis, 31.6 kw aur, ant 1,270t/1,256g. TL: N35 48 47 W79 50 36. Hrs opn: 24. On air date: Oct 14, 1963. HP-8 (27261); 2005 Francis St. (27263). (919) 841-8888. FAX: (919) 841-8051; TWX: 510-926-1640. Licensee: Great American Television and Radio Co. Inc. Ownership: Great American Communications (group owner; acq 11-91; $27 million; FTR 11-18-91). ■ Net: ABC. Rep: Telerep. Wash atty: Koteen & Naftalin. ■ David Boylan, pres & gen mgr; Larry Blackerby, vp opns & vp progmg; Dan Brazda, prom dir; Karen Adams, adv dir; Scott Libin, news dir; Ross Mason, engrg dir. ■ On 65 CATVs—364,395 subs. ■ Rates: $1600; 375; 125.

WXII—See Winston-Salem.

Jacksonville

ADI No. 104; see Greenville-New Bern-Washington market

*****WUNM-TV**—ch 19, 3,020 kw vis, 302 kw aur, ant 1,840t/1,761g. TL: N35 06 18 W77 20 15. On air date: March 1982. Box 14900, 10 T. W. Alexander Dr., Research Triangle Park (27709). (919) 549-7000. FAX: (919) 549-7201. Licensee: Univ. of North Carolina. ■ Net: PBS. Wash atty: Schwartz, Woods & Miller. ■ Tom Howe, gen mgr; Bob Royster, opns dir; H. Camille Patterson, dev dir; Diana Hatch, prom dir; Diane Lucas, progmg dir; Richard W. Hatch, pub affrs dir; Willard Campbell, engrg dir; Harvey Arnold, chief engr.

Kannapolis

ADI No. 30; see Charlotte market

WKAY—ch 64, 2,570 kw vis, ant 1,351t. TL: N35 15 05 W80 41 15. Not on air, target date unknown. Box 8186 (28081). Permittee: Community Action Communications Inc.

Lexington

ADI No. 49; see Greensboro-Winston Salem-High Point market

WEJC—ch 20, 4,570 kw vis, 457 kw aur, ant 976t/661g. TL: N35 58 09 W79 49 29. On air date: Oct 30, 1985. 622-G Guilford College Rd., Greensboro (27409). (919) 547-0020. Licensee: Koinonia Inc. Wash atty: Gammon & Grange. ■ William P. Register, pres & gen mgr. ■ On 8 CATVs—210,000 subs.

Linville

ADI No. 30; see Charlotte market

*****WUNE-TV**—ch 17, 2,140 kw vis, 214 kw aur, ant 1,807t/449g. TL: N36 03 47 W81 50 33. On air date: Sept 11, 1967. Box 14900, 10 T. W. Alexander Dr., Research Triangle Park (27709). (919) 549-7000. FAX: (919) 549-7201. Licensee: Univ. of North Carolina. ■ Net: PBS. Wash atty: Schwartz, Woods & Miller. ■ Tom Howe, gen mgr; Bob Royster, opns dir; H. Camille Patterson, dev dir; Diana Hatch, prom dir; Diane Lucas, progmg dir; Richard W. Hatch, pub affrs dir; Willard Campbell, engrg dir; Harvey Arnold, chief engr.

Morehead City

ADI No. 104; see Greenville-New Bern-Washington market

WFXI—ch 8, 316 kw vis, 31.6 kw aur, ant 817t/835g. TL: N34 53 01 W76 30 21. Stereo. Hrs opn: 24. On air date: Nov 1, 1989. Box 2069, One Television Pl., Hwy. 70E (28557). (919) 240-0888. FAX: (919) 240-2028. Licensee: Local Television Associates Inc. Ownership: John W. Gainey, 18.545%; Frederick J. McCune, 17.54%. ■ Net: Fox. Rep: Seltel. Wash atty: Fisher, Wayland, Cooper & Leader. ■ John W. Gainey, pres; LaRhe Vestal, gen mgr, progmg dir & film buyer; Glenn Rose, gen sls mgr & natl sls mgr; Sam Lawson, prom mgr; Dave Gernoske, chief engr. ■ On 28 CATVs—113,145 subs.

New Bern

WCTI—Licensed to New Bern. See Greenville.

Raleigh

ADI No. 32; see Raleigh-Durham market

WACN—ch 50, 5,000 kw vis, 500 kw aur, ant 1,088t/967g. TL: N35 42 55 W78 49 04. Not on air, target date unknown. c/o Cotton Broadcasting Co., 2337 Guess Rd., Durham (27704). Permittee: Cotton Broadcasting Co.

WLFL—ch 22, 5,000 kw vis, 232 kw aur, ant 1,675t/1,150g. TL: N35 42 52 W78 49 01. Stereo. On air date: Dec 18, 1981. 1205 Front St. (27609). (919) 821-2200. FAX: (919) 836-1540; TWX: 510-927-0510. Licensee: Paramount Stations Group of Raleigh/Durham Inc. Group owner: Paramount Communications Inc. (acq 4-9-86; $14.5 million; 7-1-85). ■ Net: Fox. Rep: Seltel. Wash atty: Leventhal, Senter & Lerman. ■ Adam G. Polacek, gen mgr; Kathy Baske, gen sls mgr; Richard Davis, prom mgr; Meliane Gerig, progmg dir; Kevin Kelly, news dir; Don Ingram, chief engr. ■ On 42 CATVs.

WRAL-TV—ch 5, 100 kw vis, 10 kw aur, ant 2,005t/2,000g. TL: N35 40 35 W78 32 09. Stereo. Hrs opn: 24. On air date: Dec 15, 1956. Box 12000 (27605); 2619 Western Blvd. (20606). (919) 821-8555. FAX: (919) 821-8566; TWX: 510-928-1833. Licensee: Capitol Broadcasting Co. Inc. (group owner). ■ Net: CBS. Rep: Telerep. Wash atty: Fletcher, Heald & Hildreth. News staff 60; news progmg 21 hrs wkly. ■ James F. Goodmon, pres; Fred Barber, gen mgr; Thomas G. Allen, stn mgr;

Leah Chauncey, opns mgr; Quinn Koontz, gen sls mgr; Cindy Sink, prom mgr; Jim Griffin, progmg dir; Doug Ballin, newsdir; Waltye Rasulala, pub affrs dir; Al Dunbar, chief engr. ■ On 80 CATVs—331,000 subs. Co-owned radio: WRAL-FM.

Roanoke Rapids

ADI No. 32; see Raleigh-Durham market

*WUNP-TV—ch 36, 1,550 kw vis, 155 kw aur, ant 1,207t/1,172g. TL: N36 17 28 W77 50 10. On air date: 1985. Box 14900, 10 T. W. Alexander Dr., Research Triangle Park (27709). (919) 549-7000. FAX: (919) 549-7201. Licensee: The Univ. of North Carolina. ■ Net: PBS. Wash atty: Schwartz, Woods & Miller. ■ Tom Howe, gen mgr; Bob Royster, opns dir; H. Camille Patterson, dev dir; Diana Hatch, prom dir; Diane Lucas, progmg dir; Richard W. Hatch, pub affrs dir; Willard Campbell, engrg dir; Harvey Arnold, chief engr.

Rocky Mount

ADI No. 32; see Raleigh-Durham market

WRMY—ch 47, 12.3 vis, ant 318t. TL: N35 57 03 W77 55 37. Stereo. Hrs opn: 24. On air date: Aug 31, 1987. Box 4750 (27803-0750); 126 N. Washington St. (27801). (919) 972-4747. FAX: (919) 985-1447. Licensee: Family Broadcasting Enterprises. Ownership: Robert M. Chandler Jr, 50%; V. Bruce Whitehead, 50% (acq 11-25-91; $100,000; 12-16-91). Rep: Roslin. Wash atty: Mitchell & Fielstra. ■ Dr. Robert J. Pelletier, CEO, gen mgr & chief engr; Robert M. Chandler, pres; Dr. Robert J. Pellletier, vp; Lynda Cooke, stn mgr, opns dir, sls dir & progmg dir; Kevin Pelletier, adv mgr. ■ On 4 CATVs—25,350 subs. On one trans. ■ Rates: $56; 45; 32.

Washington

WITN-TV—Licensed to Washington. See Greenville.

Wilmington

ADI No. 142; see Wilmington market

WECT—ch 6, 100 kw vis, 20 kw aur, ant 2,054t/2,000g. TL: N34 34 43 W78 26 13. Stereo. On air date: Apr 9, 1954. Box 4029 (28406). (919) 791-8070. FAX: (919) 392-1509. TWX: 510-937-0314. Licensee: New Vision Television I Inc. Group owner: New Vision Television Inc. (acq 9-7-93; $110 million as part of eight stn sale; 9-27-93). ■ Net: NBC. Rep: Katz. Wash atty: Dow, Lohnes & Albertson. ■ David Bradley Jr., pres; Robert B. Beall, gen mgr & film buyer; Diane Lomax, prom mgr & progmg dir; Tom LaMont, news dir; Wayne Tiner, chief engr. ■ On 29 CATVs—197,000 subs.

WJKA—ch 26, 4,370 kw vis, 437 kw aur, ant 1,640t/1,625g. TL: N34 07 51 W78 11 16. On air date: Sept 24, 1984. 1926 Oleander Dr. (28403). (919) 343-8826. FAX: (919) 251-0978. Licensee: Wilmington Telecasters Inc. Ownership: Robinson O. Everett, executor (acq 4-24-92). ■ Net: CBS. Rep: Seltel. Wash atty: Baraff, Koerner, Olender & Hochberg. ■ Kathrine Everett, pres; Bob Watson, gen mgr & gen sls mgr; Carl Bahner, chief engr. ■ On 40 CATVs—100,000 subs.

*WUNJ-TV—ch 39, 4,470 kw vis, 447 kw aur, ant 1,813t. TL: N34 07 51 W78 11 16. On air date: 1971. Box 14900, 10 T.W. Alexander Dr., Research Triangle Park (27709). (919) 549-7000. FAX: (919) 549-7201. Licensee: Univ. of North Carolina. ■ Net: PBS. ■ Tom Howe, gen mgr; Bob Royster, opns dir; H. Camille Patterson, dev dir; Diana Hatch, prom dir; Diane Lucas, progmg dir; Richard W. Hatch, pub affrs dir; Willard Campbell, engrg dir; Harvey Arnold, chief engr. ■ On 30 CATVs—58,583 subs.

WWAY—ch 3, 100 kw vis, 10 kw aur, ant 1,953t/1,941g. TL: N34 07 51 W78 11 16. On air date: Oct 1, 1964. Box 2068, 615 N. Front St. (28402). (919) 762-8581. FAX: (919) 762-8367; (919) 341-7926. Licensee: CLG Media of Wilmington Inc. (acq 12-27-92; grpsl; 12-14-92). ■ Net: ABC. Rep: Blair. ■ Gina H. Teague, vp & gen mgr; Kelly Newton, gen sls mgr; Diane Fulton, rgnl sls mgr; Ginger Harris, prom mgr; Rhonda Beck, progmg dir; Jon Evans, news dir; Dan Sullivan, chief engr. ■ On 25 CATVs—140,000 subs. ■ Rates: $350; 125; 60.

Winston-Salem

ADI No. 49; see Greensboro-Winston Salem-High Point market

WFMY-TV—See Greensboro.

WGHP-TV—See High Point.

WNRW—ch 45, 5,000 kw vis, 500 kw aur, ant 2,000t/768g. TL: N36 22 37 W80 22 10. Hrs opn: 22. On air date: Sept 24, 1979. 3500 Myer-Lee Dr. (27101). (910) 722-4545. FAX: (910) 723-8217. Licensee: Act III Broadcasting of Greensboro Inc. Group owner: Act III Broadcasting Inc. (acq 12-17-86; $11 million; 11-17-86). ■ Net: Fox. Rep: Seltel. Wash atty: Goldberg & Spector. ■ Donita Todd, vp & gen mgr; F. L. Armstrong III, opns dir; Marsha Woodworth, gen sls mgr; Joel Kaczmarek, natl sls mgr; Vikki Riggs, mktg dir & prom mgr; Frank Armstrong, progmg dir & pub affrs dir; Wendy Bernard, Richard Ballinger, film buyers; Charles G. Couch, engrg dir. ■ On 47 CATVs—265,000 subs. On 1 trans.

*WUNL-TV—ch 26, 759 kw vis, 151 kw aur, ant 1,670t/363g. TL: N36 22 34 W80 22 14. (CP: 5,000 kw vis, 500 kw aur, ant 1,653t/346g). On air date: Feb 22, 1973. Box 14900, 10 T.W. Alexander Dr., Research Triangle Park (27709). (919) 549-7000. FAX: (919) 549-7201. Licensee: Univ. of North Carolina. ■ Net: PBS. ■ Tom Howe, gen mgr; Bob Royster, opns dir; H. Camille Patterson, dev dir; Diana Hatch, prom dir; Diane Lucas, progmg dir; Richard W. Hatch, pub affrs dir; Willard Campbell, engrg dir; Harvey Arnold, chief engr. ■ On 39 CATVs—103,971 subs. On one trans.

WXII—ch 12, 316 kw vis, 63.5 kw aur, ant 1,980t/680g. TL: N36 22 31 W78 08 50. Stereo. Hrs opn: 24. On air date: Sept 30, 1953. Box 11847, 700 Coliseum Dr. (27116). (919) 721-9944. FAX: (919) 722-7685. Licensee: Pulitzer Broadcasting Co. (group owner; see Cross-Ownership; acq 2-28-83; grpsl; 3-14-83). ■ Net: NBC. Rep: Katz. Wash atty: Verner, Liipfert, Bernhard, McPherson & Hand. ■ Ken J. Elkins, pres; Reynard A. Corley, vp & gen mgr; Boots Walker, gen sls mgr; Marge Meyer, natl sls mgr; Michael Pulitzer, rgnl sls mgr; Jim Hart, mktg dir; Bill Sandefur, news dir; Barbara Chew, pub affrs dir; Henry Hunt, chief engr. ■ On 41 CATVs—195,000 subs.

North Dakota

Bismarck

ADI No. 152; see Minot-Bismarck-Dickinson-Glendive, MT market

*KBME—ch 3, 79.4 kw vis, 7.9 kw aur, ant 1,394t/1,044g. TL: N46 35 17 W100 48 30. On air date: June 18, 1979. Box 3240, 207 N. 5th St., Fargo (58108-3240). (701) 241-6900. FAX: (701) 239-7650. Licensee: Prairie Public Broadcasting Inc. ■ Net: PBS. Wash atty: Dow, Lohnes & Albertson. News staff 2; news progmg 2 hrs wkly. ■ Dennis L. Falk, pres; Larry White, gen mgr; Tom Rendon, prom mgr; Robert Dambach, progmg dir; Darrell Dorgan, news dir; Bruce Jacobs, chief engr. Satellite of *KFME Fargo.

KBMY—ch 17, 513 kw vis, 89.1 kw aur, ant 950t/649g. TL: N46 35 11 W100 48 20. On air date: Mar 31, 1985. Box 7277 (58507); 919 S. 7th St. (58504). (701) 223-1700. FAX: (701) 258-0886. Licensee: Forum Communications. Group owner: Forum Publishing Co. ■ Net: ABC. Rep: Katz. Wash atty: Marmet Professional Corp. ■ Marc Prather, gen mgr; Chuck Peterson, gen sls mgr; Kris Goetzfried, prom mgr; Susan J. Eider, progmg dir; Dennis Wilson, chief engr. ■ On 30 CATVs—30,000 subs. ■ Rates: $120; 65; 40.

KFYR-TV—ch 5, 100 kw vis, 13.5 kw aur, ant 1,400t/1,101g. TL: N46 36 17 W100 48 30. Stereo. On air date: Dec 19, 1953. Box 1738 (58502); 200 N. 4th St. (58501). (701) 255-5757. FAX: (701) 255-8220. Licensee: Meyer Broadcasting Co. (group owner). ■ Net: NBC. Rep: Blair. Wash atty: Hogan & Hartson. News staff 15; news progmg 11 hrs wkly. ■ Judith Ekberg Johnson, pres; Thomas G. Barr, vp & gen mgr; Jim Sande, opns dir & progmg dir; Penny Borg, gen sls mgr; Linda Wurtz, prom mgr & pub affrs dir; Dick Heidt, news dir; Rich Beierle, chief engr. ■ On 32 CATVs—240,000 subs. Co-owned radio: KFYR-AM; KYYY-FM.

KXMB-TV—ch 12, 316 kw vis, 31.6 kw aur, ant 1,530t/1,204g. TL: N46 35 17 W100 48 26. On air date: Nov 19, 1955. Box 1617 (58502); 1811 N. 15th St. (58501). (701) 223-9197. FAX: (701) 223-3320. Licensee: Reiten Television Inc. (acq 1-27-71; $1.2 million; 2-8-71). ■ Net: CBS. Rep: Katz. Wash atty: Fisher, Wayland, Cooper & Leader. News staff 15; news progmg 9 hrs wkly. ■ David Reiten, pres; John Von Rueden, gen mgr, gen sls mgr & film buyer; Kathleen Reiten, prom mgr; George McDonald, progmg dir; Tim Reiten, news dir; Rocky Hefty, chief engr. ■ On 51 CATVs. Co-owned radio: KCJB(AM)-KYYX(FM). ■ Rates: $90; 55; 40.

Devils Lake

ADI No. 109; see Fargo market

WDAZ-TV—ch 8, 316 kw vis, 50 kw aur, ant 1,480t/1,461g. TL: N48 08 24 W97 59 38. On air date: Jan 29, 1967. Box 12639, 600 DeMers Ave., Grand Forks (58208). Licensee: WDAY Inc. Group owner: Forum Publishing Co. ■ Net: ABC. Rep: Katz. Wash atty: Holland & Knight. ■ Robert Kerr, gen mgr; Jill McConnell, prom mgr; Jack Eisenzimmer, adv dir; Paul Amundson, news dir; Dennis Clemenson, engrg dir. ■ On 22 CATVs—141,635 subs. On 3 trans. Satellite of WDAY-TV Fargo.

Dickinson

ADI No. 152; see Minot-Bismarck-Dickinson-Glendive, MT market

*KDSE—ch 9, 214 kw vis, 21.4 kw aur, ant 806t/538g. TL: N46 43 34 W102 54 56. On air date: Aug 4, 1982. Box 3240, 207 N. 5th St., Fargo (58108-3240). (701) 241-6900. FAX: (701) 239-7650. Licensee: Prairie Public Broadcasting Inc. ■ Net: PBS. Wash atty: Dow, Lohnes & Albertson. News staff 2; news progmg 2 hrs wkly. ■ Dennis L. Falk, pres; Larry White, gen mgr; Tom Rendon, progmg dir; Darrell Dorgan, news dir; Bruce Jacobs, chief engr. Satellite of *KFME Fargo.

KQCD-TV—ch 7, 316 kw vis, 31.6 kw aur, ant 731t/645g. TL: N46 56 48 W102 59 17. Stereo. Hrs opn: 24. On air date: July 28, 1980. Box 1577 (58601). (701) 225-6843. Licensee: Meyer Broadcasting Co. (group owner). ■ Net: NBC. Rep: Blair. Wash atty: Hogan & Hartson. ■ Judith Ekberg Johnson, pres; Tom Barr, gen mgr; Joe Hetzel, opns dir; Penny Borg, rgnl sls mgr & adv mgr; Jim Sande, progmg dir; Dick Heidt, news dir; Rich Byerly, chief engr. ■ Rates: $54; 34; 18.

KXMA-TV—ch 2, 100 kw vis, 10 kw aur, ant 840t/621g. TL: N46 43 30 W102 54 58. On air date: October 1956. Drawer B, 119 2nd Ave. (58602). (701) 227-1400. FAX: (701) 227-8896. Licensee: Reiten Television Inc. Ownership: Chester Reiten and family, 100% (acq 12-4-84; $362,500). ■ Net: CBS. Rep: Seltel. Wash atty: Fisher, Wayland, Cooper and Leader. ■ Charles Tibor, gen mgr & gen sls mgr; Shawn Beahan, prom mgr & chief engr. ■ On 19 CATVs. On 6 trans.

Ellendale

ADI No. 109; see Fargo market

*KJRE—ch 19, 407 kw vis, 40.7 kw aur, ant 587t. TL: N46 17 55 W98 51 58. On air date: May 12, 1992. Box 3240, Fargo (58108-3240). (701) 241-6900. FAX: (701) 239-7650. Licensee: Prairie Public Broadcasting Inc. ■ Net: PBS. Wash atty: Dow, Lohnes & Albertson. Sp progmg. News staff 2; news progmg 2 hrs wkly. ■ Dennis Falk, CEO & gen mgr; David Borlang, chmn; Larry White, stn mgr; Cheryl Heller, opns mgr; Virginia Dambach, dev dir; Tom Rendon, prom mgr; Robert Dambach, progmg mgr; Darrell Dorgan, news dir; Bruce Jacobs, chief engr. Satellite of *KFME Fargo.

Fargo

ADI No. 109; see Fargo market

*KFME—ch 13, 245 kw vis, 24.6 kw aur, ant 1,138t/1,145g. TL: N47 00 48 W97 11 37. Stereo. On air date: Jan 19, 1964. Box 3240, 207 N. 5th St. (58108-3240). (701) 241-6900. FAX: (701) 239-7650. Licensee: Prairie Public Broadcasting Inc. ■ Net: PBS. Wash atty: Dow, Lohnes & Albertson. News staff 2; news progmg 2 hrs wkly. ■ Dennis L. Falk, pres; Larry White, gen mgr; Tom Rendon, prom mgr; Robert Dambach, progmg dir; Darrell Dorgan, news dir; Bruce Jacobs, chief engr. ■ On 39 CATVs—180,000 subs. On 2 trans.

KTHI-TV—ch 11, 304 kw vis, 45.7 kw aur, ant 2,000t/2,063g. TL: N47 20 36 W97 17 17. Stereo. On air date: Oct 11, 1959. Box 1878 (58107). (701) 237-5211. TWX: 910-673-8302. Licensee: Spokane TV Inc. Group owner: Morgan Murphy Stns. (acq 1-22-69; $1.491 million; 2-3-69). ■ Net: NBC. Rep: HRP. Wash atty: Robert Rini. ■ Elizabeth Murphy Burns, pres; John Hrubesky, vp & gen mgr; Dale Bosch, stn mgr & progmg dir; Pete Anderson, gen sls mgr; Pam Petrik, prom mgr; Charley Johnson, news dir; Roger Johnson, chief engr. ■ On 30 CATVs. On 9 trans.

KVRR—ch 15, 4,150 kw vis, 415 kw aur, ant 1,095t. TL: N46 40 26 W96 13 40. Stereo. On air date: Feb 14, 1983. Box 9115, 4015 9th Ave. S.W. (58106). (701) 277-1515. FAX: (701) 277-1830. Licensee: Red River Broadcast

Stations in the U.S.

Group. Group owner: Red River Broadcast Corp. ■ Net: Fox. Rep: Blair. Wash atty: Crowell & Moring. ■ Ro Grignon, pres & gen mgr; Kent Lien, progmg dir. ■ On 121 CATVs—131,596 subs. On 9 trans.

KXJB-TV—(Valley City). ch 4, 97.7 kw vis, 10 kw aur, ant 2,030t/2,060g. TL: N47 16 45 W97 20 18. Hrs opn: 20. On air date: Sept 11, 1954. Box 10399, 4302 13th Ave. S., Fargo (58106). (701) 282-0444. FAX: (701) 282-9331. Licensee: North American Communication Corp. (acq 2-2-79; $3.2 million; 12-18-78). ■ Net: CBS. Rep: Seltel, Hyett/Ramsland. Wash atty: Reed, Smith, Shaw & McClay. News staff 25; news progmg 10 hrs wkly. ■ Bruce E. Barnes, pres & gen mgr; Paul Wickre, stn mgr & gen sls mgr; Linda Birmingham, prom mgr; Bernie Hendrickson, progmg dir; Dave Hoglin, news dir; Arvid Sonstelie, chief engr. ■ On 38 CATVs—218,358 subs. On 7 trans.

WDAY-TV—ch 6, 100 kw vis, 11.4 kw aur, ant 1,150t/1,206g. TL: N47 00 43 W97 11 58. On air date: June 1, 1953. Box 2466 (58108). (701) 237-6500. FAX: (701) 241-5368. Licensee: Forum Publishing Co. Group owner: Forum Publishing Co. (acq 7-20-60; $900,000; 7-25-60). ■ Net: ABC. Rep: Katz. ■ William Marcil, pres; Mark Prather, gen mgr; Charles Gardner, gen sls mgr; Sue Eider, prom mgr, progmg dir & film buyer; Al Aamodt, news dir; Tom Thompson, chief engr. ■ On 39 CATVs—150,000 subs. On 10 trans. Co-owned radio: WDAY-AM-FM. ■ Rates: $290; 85; 70.

Grand Forks

ADI No. 109; see Fargo market

*****KGFE**—ch 2, 100 kw vis, 10 kw aur, ant 1,382t/1,255g. TL: N48 08 24 W97 59 38. On air date: Sept 9, 1974. Box 3240, 207 N. 5th St., Fargo (58108-3240). (701) 241-6900. FAX: (701) 239-7650. Licensee: Prairie Public Broadcasting Inc. ■ Net: PBS. Wash atty: Dow, Lohnes & Albertson. News staff 2; news progmg 2 hrs wkly. ■ Dennis L. Falk, pres; Larry White, gen mgr; Tom Rendon, prom mgr; Robert Dambach, progmg dir; Darrell Dorgan, news dir; Bruce Jacobs, chief engr. Satellite of *KFME Fargo.

KTHI-TV—See Fargo.

Jamestown

ADI No. 109; see Fargo market

KJRR—ch 7, 316 kw vis, 31.6 kw aur, ant 443t. TL: N46 55 30 W98 46 21. Stereo. On air date: Sept 1, 1988. Box 9115, 4015 9th Ave., S.W., Fargo (58106). (701) 277-1515. FAX: (701) 277-1830. Licensee: Red River Broadcast Corp. (group owner). Rep: Blair. Wash atty: Wilkerson, Barker, Knauer & Quinn. ■ Myron Kunin, pres; Jane Boler, gen mgr; Greg Baldwin, gen sls mgr; Wayne Ramsey, prom mgr; Kent Lien, progmg dir.

Mandan

KXMB-TV—See Bismarck.

Minot

ADI No. 152; see Minot-Bismarck-Dickinson-Glendive, MT market

KMCY—ch 14, 513 kw vis, 89.1 kw aur, ant 2,720t/649g. TL: N48 03 13 W101 23 05. On air date: June 22, 1985. Box 2276 (58702). (701) 838-6614. FAX: (701) 852-9315. Licensee: WDAY Inc. Group owner: Forum Publishing Co. ■ Net: ABC. Rep: Katz. Wash atty: Marmet & McCombs. ■ Marc Prather, vp; Chuck Peterson, gen mgr & gen sls mgr; Kris Goetzfried, prom mgr; Susan J. Eider, progmg dir; Dennis Wilson, chief engr. ■ On 40 CATVs—19,000 subs. ■ Rates: $65; 35; 15.

KMOT—ch 10, 214 kw vis, 42.7 kw aur, ant 680t/690g. TL: N48 12 56 W101 19 05. Stereo. On air date: Jan 21, 1958. Box 1120, 1800 S.W. 16th (58702). (701) 852-4101. FAX: (701) 852-4211. Licensee: Meyer Broadcasting Co. (group owner). ■ Net: NBC. Wash atty: Hogan & Hartson. ■ Judith Ekberg Johnson, pres; Wayne L. Sanders, gen mgr; Rod Wilson, opns mgr; Colleen Anderson, gen sls mgr; Dave Benton, news dir; Ray Roberts, chief engr. ■ On 14 CATVs—16,000 subs. On 3 trans. Satellite of KFYR-TV Bismarck. Co-owned radio: KIZZ(FM).

*****KSRE**—ch 6, 100 kw vis, 10 kw aur, ant 1,059t/983g. TL: N48 03 03 W101 23 24. On air date: January 1980. Box 3240, 207 N. 5th St., Fargo (58108-3240). (701) 241-6900. FAX: (701) 239-7650. Licensee: Prairie Public Broadcasting Inc. ■ Net: PBS. Wash atty: Dow, Lohnes & Albertson. News staff 2; news progmg 2 hrs wkly. ■ Dennis L. Falk, pres; Larry White, gen mgr; Tom Rendon, prom mgr; Robert Dumbach, progmg dir; Darrell Dorgan, news dir; Bruce Jacobs, chief engr. Satellite of *KFME Fargo.

KXMC-TV—ch 13, 316 kw vis, 31.6 kw aur, ant 1,128t/1,061g. TL: N48 03 02 W101 20 29. On air date: Apr 1, 1953. Box 1686 (58702). 3425 S. Broadway (58701). (701) 852-2104. Licensee: Reiten Television Inc. Ownership: Chester Reiten, 55%; and others (acq 7-31-74; 8-19-74). ■ Net: CBS. Rep: Katz. Wash atty: Fisher, Wayland, Cooper & Leader. ■ David Reiten, pres, opns mgr, gen sls mgr & film buyer; Jerry Romine, prom mgr; Mark Narum, news dir; Duane Aase, chief engr. ■ On 10 CATVs—20,000 subs. On 6 trans. Co-owned radio: KCJB(AM), KHHT(FM).

Pembina

ADI No. 109; see Fargo market

KNRR—ch 12, 316 kw vis, 31.6 kw aur, ant 1,394t. TL: N48 59 42 W97 24 26. (CP: 158 kw vis, 15.8 kw aur). On air date: 1985. Box 9115, 4015 9th Ave. S.W. (58106). (701) 277-1515. FAX: (701) 277-1830; TWX: 510-600-6414. Licensee: Red River Broadcast Group. Group owner: Red River Broadcast Corp. ■ Net: Fox. Satellite of KVRR Fargo.

Valley City

KXJB-TV—Licensed to Valley City. See Fargo.

Williston

ADI No. 152; see Minot-Bismarck-Dickinson-Glendive, MT market

KUMV-TV—ch 8, 166 kw vis, 33.1 kw aur, ant 1,060t/874g. TL: N48 08 02 W103 51 36. Stereo. Hrs opn: 24. On air date: Feb 11, 1957. Box 1287, 602 Main St. (58801). (701) 572-4676. Licensee: Meyer Broadcasting Co. (group owner). ■ Net: NBC. News staff 2; news progmg 6 hrs wkly. ■ Judith Ekberg Johnson, pres; Tom Barr, vp; Deborah Murphy, gen mgr, sls dir & adv mgr; Diana Maleckar, prom mgr; Jim Sande, progmg mgr; Barbara Meyer, news dir; Kris Bloom, pub affrs dir; Mikel Huseby, chief engr. ■ On 8 CATVs. On 10 trans. Semi-satellite of KFYR-TV Bismarck. ■ Rates: $58; 46; 30.

KWSE—ch 4, 79.4 kw vis, 7.94 kw aur, ant 912t/785g. TL: N48 08 30 W103 53 34. On air date: March 1983. Box 3240, 207 N. 5th St., Fargo (58108-3240). (701) 241-6900. FAX: (701) 239-7650. Licensee: Prairie Public Broadcasting Inc. ■ Net: PBS. Wash atty: Dow, Lohnes & Albertson. News staff 2; news progmg 2 hrs wkly. ■ Dennis Falk, pres; Larry White, gen mgr; Tom Rendon, prom mgr; Robert Dambach, progmg dir; Darrell Dorgan, news dir; Bruce Jacobs, chief engr. Satellite of *KFME Fargo.

KXMD-TV—ch 11, 174 kw vis, 17.4 kw aur, ant 980t/840g. TL: N48 08 22 W103 53 24. On air date: Oct 25, 1969. Box 790 (58801). (701) 572-2345. FAX: (701) 572-0658. Licensee: Reiten Television Inc. ■ Net: CBS. Rep: Katz. Wash atty: Fisher, Wayland, Cooper & Leader. ■ Chester Reiten, pres; Marilyn Karst, gen mgr & gen sls mgr; Rodney Romine, progmg dir; Wayne Mac-Namara, chief engr.

Ohio

Akron

ADI No. 12; see Cleveland market

WAKC-TV—ch 23, 1,290 kw vis, 175 kw aur, ant 961t/926g. TL: N41 03 51 W81 34 59. Stereo. Hrs opn: 24. On air date: July 19, 1953. 853 Copley Rd. (44320). (216) 535-7831. FAX: (216) 535-5370. Licensee: Group One Broadcasting L.P. ■ Net: ABC. Wash atty: Wiley, Rein & Fielding. ■ Roger Berk Jr., pres; Robert Berk, gen mgr; Chip Fox, gen sls mgr; William O'Neil Jr., progmg dir; Mark Williamson, news dir; Earl Miller, chief engr. ■ On 69 CATVs—560,000 subs.

WBNX-TV—ch 55, 7,000 kw vis, 500 kw aur, ant 2,049t/1,131g. TL: N41 23 02 W81 41 44. Hrs opn: 18. On air date: Dec 1, 1985. Box 91660, Cleveland (44101); 2690 State Rd., Cuyahoga Falls (44223). (216) 843-5555; (216) 928-5711. Licensee: Winston Broadcasting Network Inc. (acq 5-20-87; 1-19-87). Wash atty: Sutherland, Asbill & Brennan. ■ Lou Spangler, pres; Anne Catherine Keith, exec vp, stn mgr & progmg mgr; Colleen Metheney, opns mgr; Ms. Eddie Brown, gen sls mgr; Debbie Stone, prom mgr; Michele Hatch, pub affrs dir; Stephen Nelson, chief engr. ■ 1,000,000 subs.

*****WEAO**—ch 49, 685 kw vis, 68.56 kw aur, ant 1,047t/923g. TL: N40 04 58 W81 38 00. Stereo. Hrs opn: 19. On air date: September 1975. Box 5191, 1750 Campus Center Dr., Kent (44240-5191). (216) 677-4549; (216) 678-1656. FAX: (216) 672-7995. Licensee: Northeastern Educational TV of Ohio Inc. ■ Net: PBS. Wash atty: Dow, Lohnes & Albertson. ■ William E. Glaeser, pres & gen mgr; Dave Day, dev dir; Lisa Martinez, prom mgr; Don Freeman, progmg dir; Allan Creed, engrg dir. ■ On 37 CATVs.

Alliance

ADI No. 92; see Youngstown market

*****WNEO**—ch 45, 1,260 kw vis, 126 kw aur, ant 830t/770g. TL: N40 54 23 W80 54 40. Stereo. Hrs opn: 19. On air date: May 1973. Box 5191, 1750 Campus Center Dr., Kent (44240-5191). (216) 677-4549; (216) 678-1656. FAX: (216) 672-7995. Licensee: Northeastern Educational TV of Ohio Inc. ■ Net: PBS. Wash atty: Dow, Lohnes & Albertson. ■ William E. Glaeser, pres & gen mgr; Dave Day, dev dir; Lisa Martinez, prom mgr; Don Freeman, progmg dir; Allan Creed, engrg dir. ■ On 48 CATVs. On one trans.

Athens

ADI No. 55; see Charleston, WV-Huntington, WV market

*****WOUB-TV**—ch 20, 1,000 kw vis, 100 kw aur, ant 800t/856g. TL: N39 18 50 W82 08 54. On air date: Jan 3, 1963. 9 S. College St. (45701). (614) 593-4555. FAX: (614) 593-0240. Licensee: Ohio Univ. ■ Net: PBS; Ohio Educ Bcstg. Wash atty: Cohn & Marks. ■ Joseph Welling, gen mgr; Jeff Spalding, opns mgr; Mercedes Sabio, progmg dir; Nancy Burton, news dir; Joe Berman, chief engr. ■ On 70 CATVs—70,000 subs. On 2 trans. Co-owned radio: *WOUB-AM-FM.

Bowling Green

ADI No. 64; see Toledo market

*****WBGU-TV**—ch 27, 1,000 kw vis, 100 kw aur, ant 1,060t/1,035g. TL: N41 08 13 W83 54 23. Stereo. Hrs opn: 18. On air date: Feb 10, 1964. 245 Troup St. (43403). (419) 372-2700. FAX: (419) 372-7048. Licensee: Bowling Green State Univ. (acq 11-17-76; 12-13-76). ■ Net: PBS; Ohio Educ Bcstg. Wash atty: Cohn & Marks. ■ Patrick Fitzgerald, gen mgr; Ronald J. Gargasz, stn mgr, progmg dir & film buyer; Patricia Koehler, dev dir & mktg dir; Tim Smith, prom mgr; Judy Paschalis, pub affrs dir; William Leutz, chief engr. ■ On 57 CATV.

Cambridge

ADI No. 144; see Wheeling, WV-Steubenville market

*****WOUC-TV**—ch 44, 550 kw vis, 87.1 kw aur, ant 1,289t/1,213g. TL: N40 05 32 W81 17 19. On air date: July 23, 1973. College St., Athens (45701). (614) 593-4555. FAX: (614) 593-0240. Licensee: Ohio University (acq 12-10-75; 12-22-75). ■ Net: PBS; Ohio Educ Bcstg. Wash atty: Cohn & Marks. ■ N. Joseph Welling, gen mgr; Barbara Krug, prom mgr; Mercedes Sabin, progmg dir; Nancy Burton, news dir; Joe Berman, chief engr. ■ On 25 CATVs. On 2 trans. Co-owned radio: WOUB-AM-FM-TV, WOUC-FM, WOUL-FM, WOUH-FM.

Canton

ADI No. 12; see Cleveland market

WAKC-TV—See Akron.

WDLI—ch 17, 436 kw vis, 42 kw aur, ant 450t/450g. TL: N40 51 04 W81 16 37. Hrs opn: 24. On air date: Jan 3, 1967. 6600 Atlantic Blvd., Louisville (44641). (216) 875-5542. FAX: (216) 875-5547. Licensee: Trinity Broadcasting Network (group owner); acq 4-15-86; $4.5 million; 9-23-85). Wash atty: May, Dunne & Gay. ■ Paul F. Crouch, pres; Dale K. Osborn, stn mgr & chief engr; Rebecca S. Osborn, progmg mgr; Diana Schumacher, pub affrs dir. ■ On 19 CATVs—156,108 subs. ■ Rates: $60; 60; 60.

WOAC—ch 67, 1,429 kw vis, 142.9 kw aur, ant 290t/275g. TL: N40 51 49 W81 26 29. Hrs opn: 7 AM-4 AM. On air date: March 1982. Box 35367 (44735-5367); 4867 Fulton Dr. N.W. (44718-2398). (216) 492-5267. FAX: (216) 492-8487. Licensee: Canton 67. Ownership:

Morton Kent, 100%. Wash atty: Akin, Gump, Strauss, Hauer & Feld. News staff one; news progmg 6 hrs wkly. ■ Morton J. Kent, pres; Mike Larson, gen mgr; Phil Sherck, gen sls mgr; Gary Rockey, prom mgr & pub affrs dir; Kevin Hoffman, progmg dir & film buyer; Scott Davis, news dir; Marc Anderson, chief engr. ■ On 25 CATVs—293,918 subs. On one trans.

Chillicothe

ADI No. 34; see Columbus, OH market

WWAT—ch 53, 3,250 kw vis, 325 kw aur, ant 679t. TL: N39 35 30 W86 06 38. Hrs opn: 24. On air date: Aug 31, 1987. 1281 River Rd. (45601); Suite D, 3855 W. Broad St., Columbus (43235). (614) 775-3578; (614) 272-5353. FAX: (614) 775-3584. Licensee: Triplett & Assocs. Ownership: Wendell A. Triplett, 54%; Marc Triplett, 26%; Robert Triplett, 20%. Wash atty: Roy F. Perkins. ■ Marc S. Triplett, pres & gen mgr; William Scott, vp, opns mgr, gen sls mgr & progmg dir; Betra Johnson, prom mgr; Mike Smith, news dir & pub affrs dir; Craig Stevenson, chief engr.

Cincinnati

ADI No. 31; see Cincinnati market

***WCET**—ch 48, 2,240 kw vis, 224 kw aur, ant 1,069t/899g. TL: N39 07 30 W84 31 18. Stereo. On air date: July 26, 1954. 1223 Central Pkwy. (45214-2890). (513) 381-4033. FAX: (513) 381-7520. Licensee: Greater Cincinnati TV Educational Foundation. ■ Net: PBS. Wash atty: Cohn & Marks. ■ W. Wayne Godwin, pres & gen mgr; John T. Dominic, C. Scott Elliott, W. Dolores Shaffer, sr vps; Phillip Meyer, prom mgr; Grace Hill, progmg dir; Jerry Blankenbeker, chief engr. ■ On 41 CATVs—396,561. On one trans.

WCPO-TV—ch 9, 316 kw vis, 28.2 kw aur, ant 1,000t/890g. TL: N39 07 31 W84 29 57. Stereo. Hrs opn: 24. On air date: July 26, 1949. 500 Central Ave. (45202). (513) 721-9900. TWX: 810-461-2690. Licensee: Scripps Howard Broadcasting Co. (group owner). ■ Net: CBS. Rep: Blair. Wash atty: Baker & Hostetler. News staff 65; news progmg 20 hrs wkly. ■ J. B. Chase, vp & gen mgr; Iris Simpson, gen sls mgr; Craig Allison, natl sls mgr; Paul Harper, prom mgr; Jim Timmerman, progmg dir; Jim Zarchin, news dir; Hasker Nelson, pub affrs dir; Ron Arendall, chief engr. ■ On 60 CATVs—260,000 subs.

WKRC-TV—ch 12, 316 kw vis, 31.6 kw aur, ant 1,000t/974g. TL: N39 06 58 W84 30 05. Stereo. Hrs opn: 24. On air date: April 1949. 1906 Highland Ave. (45219). (513) 763-5500. FAX: (513) 651-0704. Licensee: Great American Television & Radio. Group owner: Great American Broadcasting (acq 9-87). ■ Net: ABC. Rep: Telerep. Wash atty: Koteen & Naftalin. ■ William Moll, pres & gen mgr; Sherry Gunton, gen sls mgr; Peter Barrett, prom mgr; Steve Minium, news dir; Leon F. Brown, vp engrg. Co-owned radio: WKRQ(FM).

WLWT—ch 5, 100 kw vis, 10 kw aur, ant 1,000t/849g. TL: N39 07 28 W84 31 18. Hrs opn: 24. On air date: Feb 9, 1948. 140 W. Ninth St. (45202). (513) 352-5000. FAX: (513) 352-5028. Licensee: Multimedia Entertainment Inc. Group owner: Multimedia Broadcasting Co. (acq 3-2-76; $16.3 million; 2-2-76). ■ Net: NBC. Rep: Katz. Wash atty: Dow, Lohnes & Albertson. ■ James Clayton, vp & gen mgr; Mike Renda, sls dir; Julie Weindel, prom mgr; Tom Storey, progmg dir; Rob Allman, news dir; Al Sakalas, engrg dir. ■ On 77 CATVs—265,945 subs.

WSTR-TV—ch 64, 1,150 kw vis, 20 kw aur, ant 941t/950g. TL: N39 07 28 W84 31 18. Stereo. (CP: 5,000 kw vis, 500 kw aur, ant 1,105t, TL: N39 12 01 W84 31 22). On air date: January 1980. 5177 Fishwick Dr. (45216). (513) 641-4400. FAX: (513) 242-2633; TWX: 810-461-2264. Licensee: ABRY Communications (group owner; acq 9-22-89; $8 million; 10-9-89). Rep: Seltel. Wash atty: Cole, Raywid & Braverman. ■ David Smith, gen mgr; Steve Daniloff, gen sls mgr; Merry Ewing, natl sls mgr; Jill Casagrande, progmg dir; Greg Buzzell, chief engr. ■ Rates: $400; 350; 75.

WXIX-TV—(Newport, KY). ch 19, 4,495 kw vis, 449.5 kw aur, ant 990t/1,022g. TL: N39 07 19 W84 32 52. Stereo. (CP: 4,646 kw vis, 464 kw aur). On air date: Aug 1, 1968. 10490 Taconic Terrace, Cincinnati, OH (45215). (513) 772-1919. TELEX: 21-4364. Licensee: Malrite Comm. Grp Inc. (group owner; acq 11-8-83; $45 million; 12-5-83). ■ Net: Fox. Rep: Petry. Wash atty: Kaye, Scholer, Fierman, Hays & Handler. ■ John Chaffee, pres; Stuart Powell, gen mgr; Bob Bee, gen sls mgr; Jane Peak, prom mgr; Tom Feie, progmg dir; Hugh Dermody, news dir; Bob Thurber, chief engr. ■ On 50 CATVs—95,000 subs.

Cleveland

ADI No. 12; see Cleveland market

WEWS—ch 5, 93.3 kw vis, 10 kw aur, ant 1,020t/851g. TL: N41 22 27 W81 43 06. On air date: Dec 17, 1947. 3001 Euclid Ave. (44115). (216) 431-5555. FAX: (216) 431-3666; TWX: 810-421-8593. Licensee: Scripps Howard Broadcasting Co. (group owner, see Cross-Ownership). ■ Net: ABC. Rep: Blair. Wash atty: Baker & Hostetler. ■ Gary R. Robinson, vp & gen mgr; Jane Sherwin, gen sls mgr; Gary A. Stark, progmg dir; John Ray, news dir; Ed Miller, chief engr.

WJW-TV—ch 8, 316 kw vis, 31.6 kw aur, ant 1,000t/775g. TL: N41 21 47 W81 42 58. On air date: Dec 19, 1949. 5800 S. Marginal Rd. (44103). (216) 431-8888. TWX: 810-421-8406. Licensee: WJW License Inc. Group owner: SCI Television Inc. (acq 2-19-93; grpsl; 4-26-93). ■ Net: CBS. Rep: Telerep. ■ Virgil Dominic, pres & gen mgr; Louis Gattozzi, opns mgr; Bob Sexton, gen sls mgr; Don Alexander, rgnl sls mgr; Kevin Salyer, prom dir; Phyllis Quail, news dir; Ingrid Nelson, pub affrs dir; Tom Miller, chief engr. ■ On 65 CATVs—268,392 subs.

WKYC-TV—ch 3, 100 kw vis, 20 kw aur, ant 1,000t/906g. TL: N41 23 09 W81 41 23. Stereo. On air date: October 1948. 1403 E. 6th St. (44114). (216) 344-3333. FAX: (216) 344-3326. Licensee: Multimedia Inc. Group owner: Multimedia Broadcasting Co. (acq 12-26-90; $130 million; 1-14-91). ■ Net: NBC. Rep: Katz. Wash atty: Dow, Lohnes & Albertson. ■ Bill Scaffide, gen mgr; William C. Fallon, opns dir; Kathy T. McNulty, dev dir; John Tamerlano, gen sls mgr; David Kaye, natl sls mgr; Daniel Klintworth, prom mgr; Richard L. O'Dell, progmg mgr; Tony Ballew, news dir.

WQHS-TV—ch 61, 2,000 kw vis, 200 kw aur, ant 1,160t/1,029g. TL: N41 23 02 W81 42 06. Stereo. Hrs opn: 24. On air date: Mar 3, 1981. 2861 W. Ridgewood Dr., Parma (44134). (216) 888-0061. FAX: (216) 888-6551. Licensee: HSN Broadcasting of Ohio Inc. Group owner: Silver King Communications Inc. (acq 11-5-86; $15 million; 9-8-86). Wash atty: Dow, Lohnes & Albertson. ■ Jeff McGrath, pres; Gerald C. Kerwin, vp, gen mgr & gen sls mgr; Sharon Roman, progmg dir, film buyer & news dir; Dave Smith, chief engr. ■ On 27 CATVs—491,391 subs.

WUAB—(Lorain). ch 43, 4,680 kw vis, 468 kw aur, ant 1,102t/947g. TL: N41 22 45 W81 43 12. Stereo. (CP: 204 kw vis, ant 866 ft). Hrs opn: 22. On air date: Sept 15, 1968. 8443 Day Dr., Cleveland (44129). (216) 845-6043. FAX: (216) 845-6061. Licensee: Cannell Communications L.P. (group owner; acq 6-19-90; $60 million). Wash atty: Dow, Lohnes & Albertson. News staff 31; news progmg 7 hrs wkly. ■ William A. Schwartz, pres; Brooke Spectorsky, gen mgr; Ronald St. Charles, opns mgr & progmg dir; Jim Robinson, gen sls mgr; Micki Byrnes, mktg dir; Dave Howitt, adv dir; Daniel Acklen, news dir; Monica Banks, pub affrs dir; Rex Rickly, chief engr.

***WVIZ-TV**—ch 25, 2,140 kw vis, 214 kw aur, ant 997t/809g. TL: N41 20 28 W81 44 24. Stereo. On air date: Feb 7, 1965. 4300 Brookpark Rd. (44134). (216) 398-2800. FAX: (216) 749-2560; TWX: 810-421-8875. Licensee: Educational TV Association of Metro Cleveland. ■ Net: PBS. ■ Jerry Wareham, pres & gen mgr; Frank E. Strnad, opns mgr; Kent A. Geist, dev dir; Peg Neeson, prom mgr; Mark A. Rosenberger, vp progmg; Robert M. Olive, progmg dir; Gary Bluhm, chief engr. ■ On 22 CATVs.

Columbus

ADI No. 34; see Columbus, OH market

WBNS-TV—ch 10, 316 kw vis, 31.6 kw aur, ant 890t/1,029g. TL: N39 58 16 W83 01 40. Stereo. On air date: Oct 5, 1949. 770 Twin Rivers Dr. (43215). (614) 460-3700. FAX: (614) 460-2812. Licensee: WBNS TV Inc. Group owner: Dispatch Printing Co. ■ Net: CBS. Rep: Blair. Wash atty: Crowell & Moring. News staff 52; news progmg 14 hrs wkly. ■ John F. Wolfe, pres; Tom Stewart, gen mgr; Doug Parker, opns mgr & progmg mgr; Gary Lowell, gen sls mgr; Tim Londergan, mktg mgr; Phil Pikelny, prom mgr; Paul Dughi, news dir; Chuck White, pub affrs dir; Marvin Born, chief engr. ■ On 84 CATVs—387,991 subs. Co-owned radio: WBNS-AM-FM. ■ Rates: $3,000; 1,200; 800.

WCMH—ch 4, 100 kw vis, 15 kw aur, ant 903t/1,029g. TL: N39 58 15 W83 01 39. Stereo. Hrs opn: 24. On air date: April 3, 1949. 3165 Olentangy River Rd. (43202); Box 4 (43216). (614) 263-4444. FAX: (614) 447-9107. Licensee: Outlet Broadcasting Inc. Group owner: Outlet Communications Inc. (acq 7-31-86; grpsl). ■ Net: NBC. Rep: Katz. Wash atty: Koteen & Naftalin. News staff 59; news progmg 25 hrs wkly. ■ James G. Babb, CEO, chmn & pres; Douglas E. Gealy, vp & gen mgr; Larry Pozzi, opns dir & chief engr; Bill Lanesey, gen sls mgr; Bob Shaw, mktg dir; Tom Burke, news dir. ■ On 107 CATVs—589,045 subs.

***WOSU-TV**—ch 34, 1,170 kw vis, 117 kw aur, ant 1,079t/1,124g. TL: N40 09 34 W82 55 22. On air date: Feb 20, 1956. 2400 Olentangy River Rd. (43210). (614) 292-9678. FAX: (614) 292-7625. Licensee: Ohio State Univ. ■ Net: PBS; CEN. Wash atty: Dow, Lohnes & Albertson. ■ Dale K. Ouzts, gen mgr; Edwin Clay, stn mgr; Joyce Schreiber, dev mgr; Don Scott, mktg mgr; Willis Parker, progmg dir; Tom Lahr, chief engr. ■ On 88 CATVs—280,640 subs. On 2 trans. Co-owned radio: *WOSU-AM-FM.

WSYX—ch 6, 100 kw vis, 10 kw aur, ant 535t/672g. TL: N40 01 02 W83 01 11. (CP: Ant 938t., TL: N39 56 16 W83 01 16.) On air date: Aug 30, 1949. Box 718, 1261 Dublin Rd. (43216-0718). (614) 481-6666. FAX: (614) 481-6624; (614) 481-6828. Licensee: Continental Broadcasting Ltd. (group owner; acq 10-6-87). ■ Net: ABC. Rep: Petry. Wash atty: Hogan & Hartson. ■ Benjamin Diesbach, CEO; Patrick Murphy, CFO; Terry Connelly, vp & gen mgr; Robert Wagley, gen sls mgr; Toni McHugh, natl sls mgr; Pat Cramer (local), rgnl sls mgr; Jim Strader, prom mgr; Steve Doerr, news dir; Pete Ford, engrg dir.

WTTE—ch 28, 1,910 kw vis, 191 kw aur, ant 961t/1,116g. TL: N40 09 33 W82 55 21. On air date: June 1, 1984. Box 280 (43216-0280); 6130 Sunbury Rd., Westerville (43081-9312). (614) 895-2800. FAX: (614) 895-3159. Licensee: WTTE Channel 28 Inc. Group owner: Sinclair Broadcast Group Inc. (acq 10-15-90; grpsl; 10-15-90). ■ Net: Fox. Rep: Telerep. Wash atty: Fisher, Wayland, Cooper & Leader. ■ David Smith, pres; John T. Quigley, gen mgr; Oran Gough, opns dir; Robert Heyde, gen sls mgr; Jeff Avon, natl sls mgr; Chuck Williams, mktg dir; Susan Burton, prom mgr; Steve Johnson, pub affrs dir; Joe Subich, chief engr. ■ On 98 CATVs—480,000 subs.

Dayton

ADI No. 52; see Dayton market

WDTN—ch 2, 100 kw vis, 20 kw aur, ant 1,000t/960g. TL: N39 43 07 W84 15 22. On air date: Mar 15, 1949. 4595 S. Dixie Ave. (45439); Box 741 (45401). (513) 293-2101. FAX: (513) 294-6542. Licensee: The Hearst Corp. Group owner: Hearst Broadcasting Group (acq 7-16-81; $49.9 million). ■ Net: ABC. Rep: Blair. Wash atty: Tharrington, Smith & Hargrove. ■ Cheryl A. Craigie, gen mgr; Steven L. Fisher, stn mgr & progmg dir; Larry Ryan, vp sls; Kim Peters, mktg dir & prom dir; Michael Hevel, news dir; Sharon Fair, pub affrs dir; Dave Nortman, chief engr. ■ On 51 CATVs—703,216 subs.

WHIO-TV—ch 7, 200 kw vis, 38 kw aur, ant 1,140t/1,096g. TL: N39 44 02 W84 14 52. Stereo. (CP: 100 kw vis, ant 571t, TL: N39 43 17 W84 08 57). Hrs opn: 24. On air date: Jan 26, 1949. 1414 Wilmington Ave. (45420); Box 1206 (45401). (513) 259-2111. FAX: (513) 259-2024. Licensee: Miami Valley Broadcasting Corp. Group owner: Cox Broadcasting. ■ Net: CBS. Rep: Telerep. Wash atty: Dow, Lohnes & Albertson. ■ David B. Lippoff, vp & gen mgr; Don Kemper, stn mgr, progmg dir & film buyer; Otis "Ted" Lester, opns dir; John Hayes, gen sls mgr; Mark Casey, news dir. ■ On 59 CATVs—300,000 subs. Co-owned radio: WHIO(AM) and WHKO(FM).

WKEF—ch 22, 2,340 kw vis, 234 kw aur, ant 1,152t/1,094g. TL: N39 43 15 W84 15 39. Stereo. Hrs opn: 24. On air date: Sept 27, 1964. 1731 Soldiers Home Rd. (45418). (513) 263-2662. FAX: (513) 268-2332. Licensee: KT Communications L.P. (acq 1-2-89; $71.5 million; 1-23-89). ■ Net: NBC. Rep: Katz. Wash atty: Wiley, Rein & Fielding. News staff 27; news progmg 7 hrs wkly. ■ James Graham, gen mgr, progmg dir & film buyer; Bob Heinzelmann, gen sls mgr & natl sls mgr; Sandy Patton, prom mgr & pub affrs dir; Lori Webster, news dir; Darrell Hunter, chief engr. ■ On 65 CATVs—216,000 subs. ■ Rates: $900; 140; 50.

***WPTD**—ch 16, 1,140 kw vis, 114 kw aur, ant 1,188t/1,170g. TL: N39 43 16 W84 15 00. Stereo. (CP: 1,500 kw vis, ant 1,149t, TL: N39 43 16 W84 15 00). Hrs opn: 6 AM-1 AM. On air date: March 20, 1967. 110 S. Jefferson St., Dayton (45402-2402). (513) 220-1600. FAX: (513) 220-1642. Licensee: Greater Dayton Public TV Inc. ■ Net: PBS; EEN, CEN, Ohio Educ Bcstg. Wash atty: Dow, Lohnes & Albertson. News staff one; news progmg one hr wkly. ■ Dave Fogarty, pres & gen mgr; Mark Stanislawski, gen sls mgr; H. Fred Stone, chief engr. ■ On 30 CATVs—445,764 subs. On 2 trans.

Stations in the U.S.

Ohio

WRGT-TV—ch 45, 5,000 kw vis, 501 kw aur, ant 1,171t/1,158g. TL: N39 43 28 W84 15 18. On air date: Sept 23, 1984. 45 Broadcast Plaza (45408). (513) 263-4500. Licensee: Act III Broadcasting of Dayton Inc. (group owner). ■ Net: Fox. Rep: Seltel. Wash atty: Goldberg & Spector. ■ Richard Ballinger, pres; Dave Miller, vp & gen mgr; Dale Remy, gen sls mgr; Ann Love, prom mgr; Michael Davis, progmg dir & film buyer; Ron Schuetze, chief engr. ■ On 60 CATVs—580,000 subs.

Lima

ADI No. 199; see Lima market

WLIO—ch 35, 661 kw vis, 132 kw aur, ant 540t/549g. TL: N40 44 54 W84 07 55. On air date: March 1953. Box 1689 (45802); 1424 Rice Ave. (48505). (419) 228-8835. FAX: (419) 229-7091. Licensee: Lima Communications Corp. Group owner: Blade Communications Inc. (acq 2-1-72; $1.5 million). ■ Net: NBC. Rep: Katz. Wash atty: Dow, Lohnes & Albertson. News staff 16; news progmg 15 hrs wkly. ■ James C. Dages, pres & gen mgr; Grover K. Blazer, opns mgr; Bruce A. Opperman, vp sls; Antelle Haithcock, mktg mgr; James D. Garling, progmg dir & film buyer; George Dunster, news dir; Vickie A. Smith, pub affrs dir; Fred Vobbe, chief engr. ■ On 44 CATVs—125,000 subs. ■ Rates: $300; 200; 100.

WTLW—ch 44, 912 kw vis, 91.2 kw aur, ant 679t/706g. TL: N40 45 47 W84 10 59. Hrs opn: 24. On air date: June 13, 1982. 1844 Baty Rd. (45807). (419) 339-4444. FAX: (419) 339-6812. Licensee: American Christian Television Services Inc. Wash atty: Wiley, Rein & Fielding. News staff 8; news progmg 5 hrs wkly. ■ Robert Placie, CEO & gen mgr; Robert Blankemeyer, chmn; James Baker, CFO; Tom Stoffel, opns dir; Harry Barnes, gen sls mgr; William Clinger, mktg dir; Michele Wassink, adv dir; Jeffrey Millslagle, progmg dir; Lisa Kroehler, news dir. ■ On 80 CATVs—110,000 subs. ■ Rates: $40; 30; 20.

Lorain

WUAB—Licensed to Lorain. See Cleveland.

Mansfield

ADI No. 12; see Cleveland market

WMFD-TV—ch 68, 294 kw vis, 29.4 kw aur, ant 591t/472g. TL: N40 45 50 W82 37 04. Hrs opn: 24. On air date: Mar 3, 1988. 2900 Park Ave. W. (44906). (419) 529-5900. FAX: (419) 529-2319. Licensee: Mid-State Television Inc. (acq 5-31-92; 6-15-92). Wash atty: Fletcher, Heald & Hildreth. News staff 21; news progmg 36 hrs wkly. ■ Gunther Meisse, pres & gen mgr; James Holmes, opns mgr; Glenn Cheesman, gen sls mgr; Jim Holmes, progmg dir; Steve Nelson, news dir & pub affrs dir; Wayne Fick, chief engr. ■ On 16 CATVs—91,000 subs.

Marietta

WTAP-TV—See Parkersburg, W.Va.

Newark

ADI No. 34; see Columbus, OH market

WSFJ—ch 51, 724 kw vis, 72.4 kw aur, ant 620t/500g. TL: N39 56 53 W82 24 33. Hrs opn: 24. On air date: Mar 1, 1981. Box 770, 10077 Jacksontown Rd. S.E., Thornville (43076); Box C, Newark (43055). (614) 833-0771; (614) 323-0771. FAX: (614) 323-3242. Licensee: Christian Television of Ohio. Wash atty: Baraff, Koerner, Olender & Hochberg. News staff one. ■ Betty J. Stanley, CEO & pres; William S. Jasper, chmn; Teddy W. Ross, gen mgr; James D. Williams, opns mgr; Ed Griffis, gen sls mgr & progmg dir; Joel Riley, news dir; Loriann Mokros, pub affrs dir; Jim Williams, chief engr. ■ On 48 CATVs—347,000 subs. ■ Rates: $65; 45; 35.

Oxford

ADI No. 31; see Cincinnati market

*****WPTO**—ch 14, 204 kw vis, 40.7 kw aur, ant 332t/342g. TL: N39 30 26 W84 44 09. Hrs opn: 19. On air date: Oct 14, 1959. 110 S. Jefferson St., Dayton (45402-2402). (513) 220-1600. FAX: (513) 220-1642. Licensee: Greater Dayton Public Television Inc. ■ Net: PBS; CEN, Ohio Educ Bcstg. Wash atty: Dow, Lohnes & Albertson. News staff one; news progmg one hr wkly. ■ Dave Fogarty, pres & gen mgr; Suzanne O'Brien, stn mgr; Mike Stanislawski, gen sls mgr; H. Fred Stone, chief engr. ■ On 6 CATVs—76,993 subs.

Portsmouth

ADI No. 55; see Charleston, WV-Huntington, WV market

*****WPBO-TV**—ch 42, 525 kw vis, 52.5 kw aur, ant 1,240t/950g. TL: N38 45 42 W83 03 41. (CP: Ant 1,253t). On air date: October 1973. 2400 Olentangy River Rd., Columbus (43210). (614) 292-9678. FAX: (614) 292-7625. Licensee: The Ohio State Univ. ■ Net: PBS; CEN. Wash atty: Dow, Lohnes & Albertson. Deaf progmg 3 hrs wkly. ■ Dale K. Ouzts, gen mgr; Edwin Clay, stn mgr; Joyce Schreiber, dev mgr; Don Scott, mktg mgr & prom mgr; Willis Parker, progmg dir; Tom Lahr, chief engr. ■ On 4 CATVs—22,471 subs. Co-owned radio: WOSU-AM-FM.

WUXA—ch 30, 1,350 kw vis, 135 kw aur, ant 777t/388g. TL: N38 45 42 W83 03 41. Not on air, target date unknown. Box 90307, Knoxville, TN (37990). (615) 694-4079. Permittee: Television Properties Inc.

Sandusky

ADI No. 12; see Cleveland market

WGGN-TV—ch 52, 1,480 kw vis, 148 kw aur, ant 774t/730g. TL: N41 23 48 W82 47 31. Hrs opn: 17. On air date: Dec 5, 1982. Box 247, 3809 Maple Ave., Castalia (44824). (419) 684-5311. FAX: (419) 684-5378. Licensee: Christian Faith Broadcasting Inc. (group owner). Wash atty: May & Dunne. ■ Shelby Gillam, pres; Rusty Yost, gen mgr; Gene Asberry, chief engr. ■ On 11 CATVs.

Shaker Heights

ADI No. 12; see Cleveland market

WOIO—ch 19, 3,720 kw vis, 372 kw aur, ant 1,151t/1,041g. TL: N41 23 15 W81 41 43. Stereo. On air date: May 19, 1985. 2720 Van Aken Blvd., Cleveland (44120). (216) 561-1919. FAX: (216) 991-1932. Licensee: Channel 19 Inc. Group owner: Malrite Communications Group Inc. ■ Net: Fox. Rep: Petry. Wash atty: Kaye, Scholer, Fierman, Hays & Handler. ■ Dennis Thatcher, vp & gen mgr; Richard Sullivan, stn mgr & progmg dir; George Cavender, opns mgr; Tom Humpage, gen sls mgr; Douglas Cross, natl sls mgr; Judy Hackett, mktg mgr; Emily Davis, pub affrs dir; Jim Somich, chief engr. ■ On 67 CATVs—700,000 subs. Co-owned radio: WHK(AM), WMMS-FM. ■ Rates: $1,950; 550; 60.

Springfield

ADI No. 52; see Dayton market

WTJC—ch 26, 1,170 kw vis, 117 kw aur, ant 500t/500g. TL: N39 54 33 W83 51 36. Hrs opn: 24. On air date: September 1980. 2675 Dayton Rd. (45506). (513) 323-0026. Licensee: Video Mall Communications Inc. Ownership: Marvin D. Sparks, 82.3529%; Richard L. Woodby, 17.6471% (acq 1-15-91; grpsl; 2-4-91). Wash atty: Miller & Miller. ■ Marvin D. Sparks, chmn & pres; Richard L. Woodby C.P.A., CFO; Richard Stafford, opns mgr & chief engr; Natalie Rector, rgnl sls mgr & progmg mgr; Josephine Hill, prom mgr, news dir & pub affrs dir. ■ On 18 CATVs—203,000 subs. ■ Rates: $45; 30; 30.

Steubenville

ADI No. 144; see Wheeling, WV-Steubenville market

WTOV-TV—ch 9, 316 kw vis, 31.6 kw aur, ant 951t/885g. TL: N40 20 32 W80 37 14. Stereo. On air date: Dec 10, 1953. Box 9999, Altamont Hill (43952); Riley Bldg., 14th & Chapline St., Wheeling, WV (26003). (614) 282-0911; (304) 232-6933. FAX: (614) 282-0439. Licensee: WTOV Associates. Group owner: Television Station Partners (acq 3-25-83; grpsl; 2-7-83). ■ Net: NBC. Rep: Petry. Wash atty: Wiley, Rein & Fielding. News staff 21; news progmg 10 hrs wkly. ■ I. Martin Pompadur, CEO & pres; Arthur E. Daube, vp & gen mgr; Tim McCoy, opns mgr, prom mgr & progmg dir; James Emmerling, gen sls mgr; Micah Johnson, news dir; Leonard Smith, chief engr. ■ On 88 CATVs.

WTRF-TV—See Wheeling, W.Va.

Toledo

ADI No. 64; see Toledo market

*****WGTE-TV**—ch 30, 1,000 kw vis, 135 kw aur, ant 1,017t/1,034g. TL: N41 39 27 W83 25 55. Stereo. On air date: Oct 10, 1960. Box 30, 136 Huron St. (43697). (419) 243-3091. FAX: (419) 243-9711. Licensee: Public Broadcasting Foundation of N.W. Ohio. ■ Net: PBS; CEN, Ohio Educ Bcstg. Wash atty: Schwartz, Woods & Miller. ■ Shirley E. Timonere, CEO, pres & gen mgr; Thomas E. Fairhurst, chmn; Leslie O'Connell, opns mgr; Joseph Campbell III, progmg dir; Kathleen Kozy, pub affrs dir; Dan Niedzwiecki, chief engr. ■ On 42 CATVs—435,276 subs. Co-owned radio: WGTE-FM, WGLE(FM).

WNWO-TV—ch 24, 4,370 kw vis, 437 kw aur, ant 1,391t/1,437g. TL: N41 40 03 W83 21 22. Stereo. On air date: May 3, 1966. 300 S. Byrne Rd. (43615). (419) 535-0024. FAX: (419) 535-0202. Licensee: WNWO Associates. Group owner: Toledo Television Investors (acq 5-8-86). ■ Net: ABC. Rep: Petry. Wash atty: Wiley, Rein & Fielding. News staff 12; news progmg 3 hrs wkly. ■ Brett D. Cornwell, pres & gen mgr; Ray Jackson, mktg dir; Michael Palmer, prom mgr; Tino Ramos, news dir; Harold W. Thompson, chief engr. ■ On 46 CATVs—227,000 subs.

WTOL-TV—ch 11, 316 kw vis, 38 kw aur, ant 1,000t/1,046g. TL: N41 40 22 W80 22 47. Stereo. On air date: Dec 5, 1958. Box 111 (43699-1111). (419) 248-1111. FAX: (419) 248-1177. Licensee: Cosmos Broadcasting Corp. (group owner; acq 4-15-65; grpsl; 3-15-65). ■ Net: CBS. Rep: Harrington, Righter & Parsons Inc. Wash atty: Dow, Lohnes & Albertson. ■ Melbourne Stebbins, vp & gen mgr; Steve Israel, opns dir; Gary Albers, prom dir; C.J. Beutien, news dir; Milissa Morelli-Barone, pub affrs dir; Stewart Hinze, chief engr. ■ On 71 CATVs. ■ Rates: $1,200; 350; 250.

WTVG—ch 13, 316 kw vis, 18.2 kw aur, ant 1,000t/1,049g. TL: N41 41 00 W83 24 49. Stereo. Hrs opn: 18. On air date: July 21, 1948. 4247 Dorr St. (43607). (419) 531-1313. FAX: (419) 531-1399. Licensee: WTVG Inc. Group owner: Media Communications Ptnrs L.P. (acq 12-3-91; $200.01; 1-6-92). ■ Net: ABC. Rep: Katz. Wash atty: Koteen & Naftalin. News staff 30; news progmg 10 hrs wkly. ■ David Zamichow, pres & gen mgr; Barbara Vaughn, CFO; Marsha Schroeder, prom mgr, progmg dir & film buyer; Alan Audet, news dir; Barry Gries, chief engr. ■ On 73 CATVs—1,457,000 subs. ■ Rates: $1,200; 500; 150.

WUPW—ch 36, 1,950 kw vis, 195 kw aur, ant 1,220t/1,250g. TL: N41 39 21 W83 26 40. Stereo. On air date: Sept 22, 1985. Four SeaGate (43604). (419) 244-3600. FAX: (419) 244-8842. Licensee: Elcom of Ohio Inc. Group owner: Ellis Communications (acq 10-7-93; $24 million; 10-25-93). ■ Net: Fox. Rep: Blair. Wash atty: Shrinsky, Weitzman & Eisen. ■ Larry Blum, pres & gen mgr; Larry Scott, gen sls mgr; Chris Phares, prom mgr; Dennis C. Katell, progmg dir; Steven W. Puntieri, chief engr.

WXAE—ch 40, 2,400 kw vis, 240 kw aur, ant 735t/735g. Not on air, target date unknown. 215 Melody Ln. (43615). Permittee: Dominion Broadcasting Inc.

Youngstown

ADI No. 92; see Youngstown market

WFMJ-TV—ch 21, 3,720 kw vis, 372 kw aur, ant 990t/1,085g. TL: N41 04 46 W80 38 25. Stereo. On air date: Mar 8, 1953. Box 6230 (44501-6230). (216) 744-8611. Licensee: WFMJ Television Inc. Ownership: Mark A. Brown and Betty H. Brown Jagnow (acq 7-14-93; 8-2-93). ■ Net: NBC. Rep: Blair. Wash atty: Fisher, Wayland, Cooper & Leader. News staff 20; news progmg 10 hrs wkly. ■ Betty Brown Jagnow, pres; Mark A. Brown, exec vp; John A. Grdic, gen mgr & mktg mgr; Jack Stevenson, opns mgr; Kathie Brickman, natl sls mgr; Jim Terry, prom mgr; Art Jordan, news dir; Carl Bryant, pub affrs dir; Rudy Recklies, chief engr. ■ On 59 CATVs. ■ Rates: $2,000; 400; 300.

WKBN-TV—ch 27, 871 kw vis, 87.1 kw aur, ant 1,430t/1,432g. TL: N41 03 28 W80 38 42. On air date: Jan 6, 1953. 3930 Sunset Blvd. (44512). (216) 782-1144. FAX: (216) 782-3504. Licensee: WKBN Broadcasting Corp. Ownership: Warren P. Williamson Jr. and Family, 100% (acq 1958). ■ Net: CBS. Rep: Katz. Wash atty: Bryan, Cave, McPheeters & McRoberts. ■ J.D. Williamson II, pres; Mike Seachman, opns mgr; Richard Wade, gen sls mgr & adv mgr; Karen Renner, prom mgr; Michael Seachman, progmg dir; Gary Hanson, news dir; Robert Flis, engrg mgr. ■ On 52 CATVs—277,794 subs. Co-owned radio: WKBN-AM-FM. ■ Rates: $1,000; 400; 125.

WYTV—ch 33, 912 kw vis, 110 kw aur, ant 580t/637g. TL: N41 03 43 W80 38 07. On air date: Oct 30, 1957. 3800 Shady Run Rd. (44502). (216) 783-2930. FAX: (216) 782-6661; TWX: 810-435-2816. Licensee: Youngstown Broadcasting Co. Inc. Group owner: Benedek

Oklahoma

Broadcasting Co. (acq 11-25-85; $9 million; 5-16-83). ■ Net: ABC. Rep: Petry. Wash atty: Crowell & Moring. News staff 19; news progmg 10 hrs wkly. ■ A. Richard Benedek, pres; Raymond Maselli, vp & gen mgr; James C. Vickery Jr., gen sls mgr; Frank Marafiote, prom mgr & progmg dir; Tom Mock, news dir; Arthur W. Taylor, chief engr. ■ On 58 CATVs.

Zanesville

ADI No. 203; see Zanesville market

WHIZ-TV—ch 18, 588 kw vis, 58.8 kw aur, ant 540t/508g. TL: N39 55 42 W81 59 06. Stereo. On air date: May 23, 1953. 629 Downard Rd. (43701). (614) 452-5431. FAX: (614) 452-6553; TWX: 810-238-2641. Licensee: Southeastern Ohio TV System. Ownership: Mrs. W.O. Littick, 63%; Southeastern Ohio Broadcasting System, 20%; Ernest B. Graham, 11%; Ernest B. Graham Jr., 3%.; John C. Graham, 3% ■ Net: NBC. Rep: Katz, Rgnl Reps. News staff 14; news progmg 10 hrs wkly. ■ Norma J. Littick, pres; Allan Land, vp, gen mgr & film buyer; Barbara Mitter, opns mgr & progmg dir; Van Vannelli, gen sls mgr; George Hiotis, news dir & pub affrs dir; C. E. Hartmeyer, chief engr. ■ On 48 CATVs—332,865 subs. Co-owned radio: WHIZ-AM-FM.

Oklahoma

Ada

ADI No. 156; see Sherman-Ada market

KTEN—ch 10, 316 kw vis, 47.5 kw aur, ant 1,458t/1,500g. TL: N34 21 34 W96 33 34. Hrs opn: 24. On air date: June 1, 1954. Box 1450, Suite 300, 101 E. Main, Denison, TX (75020). (903) 465-5836. FAX: (903) 465-5859; TWX: 910-830-6740. Licensee: William E. Rutledge, Trustee. Ownership: Tom L. Johnson. ■ Net: ABC, NBC. Rep: Katz. Wash atty: Haley, Bader & Potts. News staff 15; news progmg 12 hrs wkly. ■ Dirk W. Johnston, vp, gen mgr, stn mgr, prom dir & progmg dir; Gary Carter, gen sls mgr; Rick Fox, news dir; Donna Perry, pub affrs dir; Howell Hill, engrg mgr; Harold Walker, chief engr. ■ On 49 CATVs—105,000 subs. On one trans. ■ Rates: $155; 110; 25.

Bartlesville

ADI No. 59; see Tulsa market

KDOR—ch 17, 3,980 kw vis, 398 kw aur, ant 1,040t/1,089g. TL: N36 30 59 W95 46 10. Hrs opn: 24. On air date: Jan 11, 1987. 2120 N. Yellowood, Broken Arrow (74012). (918) 250-0777. Licensee: All American TV Inc. (acq 1986). Wash atty: Colby M. May. Sp one hr wkly. ■ Sonny Arguinzoni, pres; Linda Hernandez, exec vp; Nicky Cruz, vp; Thomas Harrison, gen mgr. ■ On 29 CATVs—20,000 subs.

Cheyenne

ADI No. 43; see Oklahoma City market

*KWET—ch 12, 316 kw vis, 31.6 kw aur, ant 981t/903g. TL: N35 35 36 W99 40 02. On air date: Aug 6, 1978. Box 14190, 7403 N. Kelley Ave., Oklahoma City (73113). (405) 848-8501. FAX: (405) 841-9282. Licensee: Oklahoma Educational TV Authority. ■ Net: PBS. Wash atty: Cohn & Marks. Robert L. Allen, gen mgr; Bill Thrash, opns dir & progmg dir; Mike Palmer, opns mgr; Pam Henry, news dir; Earle Connors, engrg dir. ■ On 10 CATVs—14,857 subs. On 6 trans.

Claremore

ADI No. 59; see Tulsa market

*KRSC-TV—ch 35, 2,750 kw vis, ant 840t. TL: N36 24 05 W95 36 33. Hrs opn: 16. On air date: July 1, 1987. College Hill (74017). (918) 341-7510, ext. 377. FAX: (918) 342-5966. Licensee: Rogers State College. Wash atty: Schwartz, Woods & Miller. Sp 2 hrs wkly. ■ Virgle L. Smith, exec vp & gen mgr; Eddie Norfleet, opns mgr; Chip Rodgers, dev dir & mktg dir; Dale A. McKinney, prom mgr; Frankye Green, progmg dir; Jean Heck, pub affrs dir; Tom Needham, chief engr. ■ On 60 CATVs—100,000 subs. Co-owned radio: *KRSC-FM.

Enid

KAFU—ch 20, 141 kw vis. TL: N36 28 35 W97 53 52. Not on air, target date unknown. G & D Communications Inc., 1627 Eye St. N.W., Suite 550, Washington, DC (20006). Permittee: G & D Communications Inc.

Eufaula

ADI No. 59; see Tulsa market

*KOET—ch 3, 100 kw vis, 10 kw aur, ant 1,310t/699g. TL: N35 11 01 W95 20 20. On air date: Aug 22, 1978. 7403 N. Kelley Ave., Oklahoma City (73113). Box 14190, Oklahoma City (73113). (405) 848-8501. FAX: (405) 841-9282. Licensee: Oklahoma Educational Television Authority. ■ Net: PBS. Wash atty: Cohn & Marks. Robert L. Allen, gen mgr; Bill Thrash, Steve Staton, opns dirs; Bill Thrash, progmg dir; Pam Henry, news dir; Lisa Mason, pub affrs dir; Earle Connors, engrg dir. ■ On 4 CATVs—6,167 subs. On 2 trans.

Lawton

ADI No. 141; see Wichita Falls-Lawton market

KSWO-TV—ch 7, 316 kw vis, 63.1 kw aur, ant 1,050t/1,059g. TL: N34 12 55 W98 43 13. Stereo. On air date: Mar 8, 1953. Box 708, Hwy. 7 (73502). (405) 355-7000. FAX: (405) 357-3811; TWX: 910-836-3600. Licensee: KSWO TV Inc. Group owner: R.H. Drewry Group. ■ Net: ABC. Rep: Petry. ■ R. H. Drewry, pres; Larry Patton, gen mgr; Mike Taylor, chief opns & progmg dir; Jerry Purseley, gen sls mgr; Jan Stratton, news dir; Derrick McMillan, chief engr. ■ On 40 CATVs—56,140 subs. Co-owned radio: KSWO(AM).

Oklahoma City

ADI No. 43; see Oklahoma City market

*KETA—ch 13, 316 kw vis, 31.6 kw aur, ant 1,525t/1,578g. TL: N35 32 58 W97 29 50. On air date: Apr 13, 1956. Box 14190, 7403 N. Kelley (73113). (405) 848-8501. FAX: (405) 841-9282. Licensee: Oklahoma Educational TV Authority. ■ Net: PBS. Wash atty: Cohn & Marks. News staff 14; news progmg 3 hrs wkly. ■ Robert L. Allen, gen mgr; Bill Thrash, Steve Staton, opns dirs; Bill Thrash, progmg dir; Pam Henry, news dir; Lisa Mason, pub affrs dir; Earle Conners, engrg dir. ■ On 45 CATVs—113,475 subs. On 7 trans.

KFOR-TV—ch 4, 97.7 kw vis, 19.5 kw aur, ant 1,540t/1,602g. TL: N35 34 07 W97 29 20. Stereo. Hrs opn: 24. On air date: June 6, 1949. Box 14068 (73113); 444 E. Britton Rd. (73114). (405) 424-4444. Licensee: Palmer Communications Inc. ■ Net: NBC. Rep: Katz. News staff 73; news progmg 29 hrs wkly. ■ William J. Katsafanas, vp & gen mgr; Robert Brooks, opns mgr & progmg dir; Tom Heston, gen sls mgr; Julie Paulson, natl sls mgr; Wes Millbourn, rgnl sls mgr; Michelle Fink, vp prom; Melissa Klinzing, news dir; Gene Parrish, chief engr. ■ On 206 CATVs.

KMNZ—ch 62, 1,000 kw vis, ant 763t. TL: N35 33 26 W97 28 31. Hrs opn: 24. On air date: December 1992. Box 530777, Harlingen, TX (78553). Licensee: Faith Pleases God Church Corp. Ownership: FPG Television Network. ■ Carlos Ortiz, CEO, vp adv, progmg dir & chief engr; Clark Ortiz, vp opns; Melysa Reyna, vp dev; Kevin Ortiz, vp sls; Carlos Ortiz Jr., natl sls mgr; Alma Rodriguez, vp mktg; Julie Ortiz, vp prom.

KOCB—ch 34, 1,170 kw vis, 117 kw aur, ant 1,210t/1,258g. TL: N35 33 36 W97 29 07. On air date: Oct 28, 1979. 1501 N.E. 85th St. (73131); Box 13034 (73113). (405) 478-3434. FAX: (405) 478-1027. Licensee: Oklahoma City Broadcasting Co. Ownership: Superior Broadcasting Inc. (acq 10-15-93; $11 million; 11-8-93). Wash atty: Fisher, Wayland, Cooper & Leader. ■ Ted Baze, pres, gen mgr & film buyer; T. Dan Loving, gen sls mgr; Brian Hill, prom mgr; Gregory Miller, chief engr. ■ On 150 CATVs—400,000 subs. On 4 trans.

KOCO-TV—ch 5, 100 kw vis, 14.5 kw aur, ant 1,519t/1,562g. TL: N35 33 45 W97 29 24. Stereo. (CP: Ant 1,515t/1,558g). On air date: July 15, 1954. Box 14555 (73113). (405) 478-3000. FAX: (405) 478-6675. Licensee: Combined Communications Corp. of Oklahoma. Group owner: Gannett Broadcasting (division of Gannett Co. Inc.) (acq 4-9-70; $25 million; 7-27-70). ■ Net: ABC. Rep: Blair. Wash atty: Pierson, Ball & Dowd. ■ Lawrence Herbster, vp; Lawrence P. Herbster, gen mgr; Brent Hensley, gen sls mgr; Harold Patterson, natl sls mgr; Jim Williston, rgnl sls mgr; Susan Kelley, news dir; Carol Wilkinson, pub affrs dir; Terry Smith, chief engr. ■ On 41 CATVs—80,510 subs. On 4 trans. ■ Rates: $2,000; 200; 250.

KOKH-TV—ch 25, 1,410 kw vis, 141 kw aur, ant 1,540t/1,619g. TL: N35 32 58 W97 29 18. Hrs opn: 24. On air date: Jan 26, 1959. 1228 E. Wilshire Blvd. (73111); Box 14925 (73113). (405) 843-2525. FAX: (405) 478-4343. Licensee: KOKH Inc. Group Owner: Heritage Media Services Inc. (acq 3-30-92). ■ Net: Fox, NBC. Rep: Petry. Wash atty: Pepper & Corazzini. ■ Jay Holmes, opns mgr; Harlan Reams, gen sls mgr; Dian Johnson, prom mgr & progmg dir; ■ On 131 CATVs—282,500 subs.

KSBI—ch 52, 1,355 kw vis, 135 kw aur, ant 600t/601g. TL: N35 22 54 W97 29 20. Hrs opn: 6 AM-midnight. On air date: Sept 19, 1988. Box 26404, 1350 S.E. 82nd St. (73126). (405) 631-7335. FAX: (405) 631-7351; (405) 631-0585. Licensee: Locke Supply Co. Wash atty: Baraff, Koerner, Olender & Hochberg. ■ Don J. Locke, pres; Kimberly Finley, gen mgr & progmg dir; Jack Kroth, pub affrs dir; Bill Key, chief engr.

KTBO-TV—ch 14, 575 kw vis, 116 kw aur, ant 1,135t/1,185g. TL: N35 34 30 W97 29 04. (CP: 1,216 kw vis, 243 kw aur). Hrs opn: 24. On air date: Mar 6, 1981. 3705 N.W. 63rd St. (73116). (405) 848-1414. Licensee: Trinity Broadcasting of Oklahoma. Group owner: Trinity Broadcasting Network. Wash atty: May, Dunne & Gay. Sp progmg. ■ Paul F. Crouch, pres; John Gordon, gen mgr & chief engr.

KTLC—ch 43, 1,950 kw vis, 195 kw aur, ant 1,560t/1,596g. TL: N35 35 22 W97 29 03. Hrs opn: 24. On air date: Nov 3, 1980. Box 14190, 11901 N. Eastern Ave. (73113). (405) 478-4300. FAX: (405) 478-8716; TWX: 910-831-4072. Licensee: Oklahoma Educational TV Authority Foundation Inc. (acq 6-27-91; $1.5 million; 7-15-91). ■ Net: Fox. Rep: Petry. Wash atty: Pepper & Corazzini. ■ Bob Allen, CEO; Earl Connors, chief engr.

KWTV—ch 9, 316 kw vis, 33.9 kw aur, ant 1,525t/1,537g. TL: N35 32 68 W97 29 50. Stereo. On air date: Dec 20, 1953. Box 14159 (73113); 7401 N. Kelley Ave. (73111). (405) 843-6641. FAX: (405) 841-9135. Licensee: Griffin Television Inc. ■ Net: CBS. Rep: Telerep. Wash atty: Fletcher, Heald & Hildreth. ■ David F. Griffin, pres & gen mgr; Jerry Dalrymple, exec vp; Dick Dutton, opns mgr; Rob Krier, gen sls mgr; Vikki Adams, prom mgr; Angela Jaramillo, progmg dir; , news dir; Julie Cameron, chief engr. ■ On 128 CATVs—315,000 subs. On 8 trans. ■ Rates: $750; 150; 100.

Okmulgee

ADI No. 59; see Tulsa market

KGLB-TV—ch 44, 578.1 kw vis, 559.4 kw aur, ant 538t. TL: N35 43 25 W95 59 20. Not on air, target date unknown. c/o KOKL(AM), Box 756 (74447). (918) 756-3646. Permittee: Broadcasting Systems Inc. ■ James R. Brewer, gen mgr.

Tulsa

ADI No. 59; see Tulsa market

KJRH—ch 2, 100 kw vis, 10 kw aur, ant 1,828t. TL: N36 01 15 W95 40 32. Stereo. On air date: Dec 5, 1954. Box 2, 3701 S. Peoria (74105). (918) 743-2222. FAX: (918) 748-1460. Licensee: Scripps Howard Broadcasting Co. Group owner: Scripps Howard Stns (see Cross-Ownership; acq 1-1-71; $7.8 million). ■ Net: NBC. Rep: Blair. Wash atty: Baker & Hostetler. ■ Lawrence Leser, CEO; William J. Donahue, gen mgr; Michael J. Vrabac, gen sls mgr; Steve Arnett, mktg mgr; Cynthia Scales, pub affrs dir; Vic Turner, chief engr. ■ On 94 CATVs—253,801 subs.

*KOED-TV—ch 11, 316 kw vis, 25 kw aur, ant 1,661t/1,833g. TL: N36 01 15 W95 40 32. On air date: Jan 12, 1959. 811 N. Sheridan (74115). (918) 838-7611; (918) 838-7614. FAX: (918) 838-1807. Licensee: Oklahoma Educational TV Authority. ■ Net: PBS. Wash atty: Cohn & Marks. Sp, Fr 8 hrs wkly. ■ Jack Frank, gen mgr, stn mgr & news dir; Jack Maynard, chief engr.

KOKI-TV—ch 23, 3,310 kw vis, 331 kw aur, ant 1,313t/1,274g. TL: N36 01 36 W95 40 44. On air date: Oct 26, 1980. 5416 S. Yale Ave. (74135). (918) 491-0023. FAX: (918) 491-6650; TWX: 910-845-3036. Licensee: Clear Channel Television Licenses Inc. (group owner; acq 8-5-92). ■ Net: Fox. Rep: Katz. Wash atty: Cohn & Marks. ■ Dan Sullivan, pres; Hal Capron, gen mgr; Dan Lyons, gen sls mgr; Suzanne Meeks, mktg mgr; Charlie Ray, prom mgr; Julie O'Neil, progmg dir; Jack Bunds, news dir; Mike Decluceo, engrg dir; Leon Hall, chief engr. ■ On 100 CATVs—300,000 subs. Co-owned radio: KAKC(AM)-KMOD-FM.

KOTV—ch 6, 100 kw vis, 50 kw aur, ant 1,885t/1,849g. TL: N36 01 15 W95 40 32. Hrs opn: 24. On air date: Nov 30, 1949. Box 6 (74101); 302 S. Frankfort (74120). (918)

Get the entertainment information you need with weekly

Variety is the oldest and most famous publication in the field. Founded in 1905, it has been covering the industry continuously for over 85 years.

Variety covers the world of entertainment business like no one else can. Movies, television, cable, home video, and music are all included in *Variety's* global view of the industry. New features on finance and the international scene make *Variety* the most comprehensive show business publication in the world.

Variety brings breaking stories into perspective, seeking out and analyzing trends and new developments. Entertainment people, throughout the U.S. and around the world, rely on *Variety* each week to keep them informed.

Subscribe to *Variety* today and be prepared for the business deals of tomorrow.

CALL 1-800-323-4345
TO ORDER YOUR SUBSCRIPTION TODAY!

582-6666. FAX: (918) 582-0678. Licensee: KOTV Inc. Group owner: A.H. Belo Corp., Broadcast Division (acq 11-22-83; $41 million; 12-19-83). ■ Net: CBS. Rep: Telerep. Wash atty: Dow, Lohnes & Albertson. News staff 40. ■ Robert Decherd, CEO & chmn; Ward Huey, pres; Mike Perry, CFO & sr vp; Jim Moroney, exec vp, vp & gen mgr; John Quesnel, opns mgr; Don Stafford, chief engr. ■ On 127 CATVs—325,000 subs.

KTFO—ch 41, 1,350 kw vis, 270 kw aur, ant 1,510t/1,368g. TL: N36 01 10 W95 39 24. On air date: May 17, 1981. 5416 S. Yale (74135). (918) 250-4100. Licensee: RDS Broadcasting Inc. (group owner; acq 8-23-89; $500,000; 9-11-89). Rep: Mutual TeleSales. Wash atty: Ward & Mendelsohn. ■ Robert Rosenheim, pres; Hal Capron, gen mgr; Harry Ford, prom mgr. ■ On 26 CATVs—250,000 subs. On one trans. ■ Rates: $125; 125; 100.

KTUL—ch 8, 316 kw vis, 31.6 kw aur, ant 1,900t/1,809g. TL: N35 58 08 W95 36 55. Hrs opn: 24. On air date: Sept 18, 1954. Box 8 (74101); Lookout Mt., 3200 W. 29th St. (74107). (918) 445-8888. FAX: (918) 445-9316. Licensee: KTUL Television Inc. Group owner: Allbritton Communications Co. (acq 4-83; grpsl). ■ Net: ABC. Rep: Petry. Wash atty: Hogan & Hartson. ■ Dan Bates, pres & gen mgr; Roger Herring, opns dir; Garry Porterfield, gen sls mgr; Larry Nitz, prom mgr; Denis King, news dir; Randi Carson, pub affrs dir. ■ On 78 CATVs.

KWHB—ch 47, 1,660 kw vis, 166 kw aur, ant 1,509t/2,084g. TL: N36 01 15 W95 40 32. Hrs opn: 24. On air date: Apr 1, 1985. 11414 E. 58th St. (74146). (918) 250-9402. FAX: (918) 254-5614. Licensee: LeSea Broadcasting (group owner; acq 5-14-86; $3.4 million; 4-14-86). Wash atty: John Fiorini. ■ Peter Sumrall, vp; Steve Morgan, gen mgr & progmg dir; Gary Murphy, gen sls mgr; Sherry Egermeier, pub affrs dir; Jim Hobbs, chief engr. ■ On 130 CATVs—210,000 subs. ■ Rates: $50; 45; 35.

KWMJ—ch 53, 5,000 kw vis, 500 kw aur, ant 1,510t/1,333g. TL: N36 01 10 W95 39 24. Not on air, target date unknown. 3401 First National Tower (74103). Permittee: Native American Broadcasting Co. Ownership: Phillip Ruffin L.P., 75%; Willis Mathews, gen ptnr, 15%; Jay Whitecrow, gen ptnr, 10%.

Oregon

Bend

ADI No. 202; see Bend market

***KOAB-TV**—ch 3, 58.9 kw vis, 5.89 kw aur, ant 746t/299g. TL: N44 04 41 W121 19 57. Stereo. On air date: Feb 24, 1970. Box 509 (97709). (503) 244-9900. Licensee: Oregon Public Broadcasting. Ownership: Charles J. Swindells (acq 1993; grpsl; 9-20-93). ■ Net: PBS. Wash atty: Schwartz, Woods & Miller. ■ Thomas Doggett, vp; Max Culbertson, chief engr. ■ On 48 CATVs—53,000 subs. On 4 trans.

KTVZ—ch 21, 126 kw vis, 12.6 kw aur, ant 646t/269g. TL: N44 04 40 W121 19 49. Stereo. On air date: Nov 6, 1977. Box 149 (97709); 62990 O. B. Riley Rd. (97701). (503) 383-2121; (503) 389-6511. FAX: (503) 382-1616; (503) 389-0208. Licensee: Resort Broadcasting Co. Group owner: Stainless Broadcasting Co. (acq 12-16-86; $3.9 million; 9-29-86). ■ Net: NBC. Rep: Katz. Wash atty: Dow, Lohnes & Albertson. News staff 9; news progmg 9 hrs wkly. ■ John Larkin, gen mgr; Duncan Laing, gen sls mgr; Natalie Forwood, prom dir & progmg dir; Bryan Hazell, news dir; Lee Faria, pub affrs dir; Ernie Pendergraft, chief engr. ■ On 10 CATVs—29,000 subs. On 8 trans.

Coos Bay

ADI No. 116; see Eugene market

KCBY-TV—ch 11, 11.5 kw vis, 1.1 kw aur, ant 680t/200g. TL: N43 23 26 W124 07 47. On air date: Oct 1, 1960. Box 1156, 611 Coalbank Slough Rd. (97420). (503) 269-1111. FAX: (503) 269-7464. Licensee: Northwest Television Inc. (group owner). ■ Net: CBS. Rep: Katz, Art Moore. Wash atty: Dow, Lohnes & Albertson. News staff 4. ■ Donald E. Tykeson, pres; Bruce Bennett, stn mgr, adv mgr & pub affrs dir; Mary C. Walker, prom mgr; Joseph Lowe, chief engr. ■ On 14 CATVs—19,332 subs. On 6 trans.

KMTZ—ch 23, 12.3 kw, ant 623t. TL: N43 23 39 W124 07 56. Stereo. On air date: July 8, 1991. Box 7308, Eugene (97401). (503) 746-1600. FAX: (503) 747-0866. Licensee: KMTR Inc. ■ Net: NBC. Rep: Petry. Wash atty: Haley, Bader & Potts. ■ Robert W. Davis, gen mgr; Robert L. Rector, gen sls mgr; Mardi Martin, prom dir & pub affrs dir; Julie Strandlien, progmg dir; Jim Frandin, news dir; Jerry Madsen, chief engr. ■ On 2 CATVs—13,642 subs. Satellite of KMTR Eugene. ■ Rates: Sold in combination with KMTR.

Corvallis

ADI No. 116; see Eugene market

***KOAC-TV**—ch 7, 245 kw vis, ant 1,500t/279g. TL: N44 38 25 W123 16 25. Hrs opn: 20. On air date: Oct 7, 1957. 7140 S.W. Macadam Ave., Portland (97219); 239 Covell Hall (97331). (503) 244-9900. FAX: (503) 293-1919. Licensee: Oregon Public Broadcasting. Ownership: Charles J. Swindells (acq 1993; grpsl; 9-20-93). ■ Net: PBS. Wash atty: Schwartz, Woods & Miller. ■ Maynard E. Orme, pres; Nevton Dunn, vp; Ellen Bloch, prom mgr; Tom Doggett, progmg dir; Ron Highburger, chief engr. ■ On 70 CATVs—75,000 subs. On 8 trans. Co-owned radio: *KOAC(AM).

Eugene

ADI No. 116; see Eugene market

***KEPB-TV**—ch 28, 389 kw vis, 38.9 kw aur, ant 905t. TL: N44 00 06 W123 06 48. Hrs opn: 17. On air date: Sept 27, 1990. 7140 S.W. Macadam Ave., Portland (97219). (503) 244-9900. FAX: (503) 293-1919. Licensee: Oregon Public Broadcasting. Ownership: Charles J. Swindells (acq 1993; grpsl; 9-20-93). ■ Net: PBS. ■ Maynard E. Orme, pres; Tom Doggett, vp & progmg dir; Jim Brock, chief engr.

KEVU—ch 34, 3,090 kw vis, 309 kw aur, ant 850t/200g. TL: N44 00 04 W123 06 22. On air date: Oct 31, 1991. Box 1526 (97440); 809 Glory Dr. (97404). (503) 461-3436. FAX: (503) 689-2733. Licensee: Telecasters of Eugene Inc. Wash atty: Fletcher, Heald & Hildreth. ■ Raul Palazuelos, CEO, pres & gen mgr; Sandy Keefer, stn mgr, gen sls mgr & progmg mgr. ■ On 4 CATVs—53,000 subs.

KEZI—ch 9, 316 kw vis, 47.4 kw aur, ant 1,768t/495g. TL: N44 06 57 W122 59 57. On air date: Dec 19, 1960. Box 7009, 2225 Coburg Rd. (97401). (503) 485-5611. Licensee: KEZI Inc. Ownership: Carolyn S. Chambers, 100% (acq 8-30-83; $18 million). ■ Net: ABC. Rep: Seltel; Tacher. ■ Carolyn S. Chambers, CEO & pres; Bruce R. Liljegren, gen mgr; Bruce Barrett, gen sls mgr; Lauren McMichaels, prom mgr; David Larson, progmg dir; Rebecca Force, news dir; Dennis Hunt, chief engr. ■ On 53 CATVs—130,000 subs. On 23 trans.

KMTR—ch 16, 1,919 kw vis, 370.99 kw aur, ant 1,685t/478g. TL: N44 06 58 W122 59 55. Stereo. Hrs opn: 18. On air date: Oct 4, 1982. Box 7308 (97401); 3825 International Ct., Springfield (97477). (503) 746-1600. FAX: (503) 747-0866. Licensee: KMTR Inc. Ownership: R.A. Paisley, 17.28%;H.E. Davis, 15.85;L.M. Davis Trust, 14.66%;R.W. Davis, 8.43%;13 others (acq 1-16-84). ■ Net: NBC. Rep: Petry. Wash atty: Haley, Bader & Potts. News staff 18; news progmg 10 hrs wkly. ■ Robert W. Davis, pres & gen mgr; Robert L. Rector, gen sls mgr; Mardi Martin, prom mgr; Julie Strandlien, progmg dir; Jim Frandin, news dir; Jerry Madsen, chief engr. ■ On 58 CATVs—137,958 subs. On 5 trans. ■ Rates: $350; 100; 30.

KVAL-TV—ch 13, 316 kw vis, 63.1 kw aur, ant 1,480t/851g. TL: N44 00 07 W123 06 53. On air date: Apr 16, 1954. Box 1313 (97440). (503) 342-4961. FAX: (503) 342-7252. Licensee: Northwest Television Inc. (group owner). ■ Net: CBS. Rep: Katz. Wash atty: Dow, Lohnes & Albertson. ■ Donald E. Tykeson, pres; James W. Putney, vp & gen mgr; Dave Weinkauf, gen sls mgr; Wade Hughes, prom mgr; Paul Greene, progmg dir; Paul Riess, news dir; Jim Bowen, engrg dir. ■ On 24 CATVs—49,897 subs. On 17 trans.

Klamath Falls

ADI No. 145; see Medford market

KDKF—ch 31, 6.03 kw vis, 603 w aur, ant 2,267t/164g. TL: N42 05 50 W121 37 59. Hrs opn: 5:30 AM-2 AM. On air date: Oct 17, 1989. Suite 308, 4509 S. 6th St. (97603). (503) 883-3131; (503) 882-5648. FAX: (503) 883-8931. Licensee: Soda Mountain Broadcasting Inc. (acq 7-1-93). ■ Net: ABC. Rep: Katz. Wash atty: Fletcher, Heald & Hildreth. ■ Carolyn S. Chambers, pres; Scott D. Chambers, exec vp; Sylvia Sycamore, vp; Keith A. Lollis, gen mgr, natl sls mgr & progmg dir; Jonathon Piff, rgnl sls mgr; Larry Black, prom mgr & pub affrs dir; Renaurd Maiuri, news dir; Rick Carrara, chief engr.

***KFTS**—ch 22, 9.23 kw vis, 923 w aur, ant 2,152t/103g. TL: N42 05 50 W121 37 59. On air date: March 1989. 34 S. Fir St., Medford (97501). (503) 779-0808. Licensee: Southern Oregon Public Television Inc. ■ Net: PBS. ■ Regina Cox, pres; William R. Campbell, gen mgr; Jim Otey, opns mgr; Lisa Vandever, prom mgr & film buyer; Don McKay, chief engr.

KOTI—ch 2, 35.5 kw vis, 3.55 kw aur, ant 2,001t/150g. TL: N42 41 49 W121 37 57. (CP: 85.1 kw vis). Hrs opn: 24. On air date: Aug 12, 1956. Box 2K, 222 S. 7th (97601). (503) 884-8131. Licensee: California Oregon Broadcasting Inc. (group owner). ■ Net: NBC. Rep: Blair, Art Moore. Wash atty: Reed, Smith, Shaw & McClay. ■ Patricia C. Smullin, pres; Ed Zander, gen mgr; Mark Logan, stn mgr; Scott McMahon, chief engr. ■ On 9 CATVs—31,500 subs. On 13 trans.

La Grande

ADI No. 27; see Portland, OR market

***KTVR**—ch 13, 7.24 kw vis, 724 w aur, ant 2,581t. TL: N45 18 35 W117 43 57. Hrs opn: 17. On air date: Dec 6, 1964. 7140 S.W. Macadam Ave., Portland (97219). (503) 244-9900. FAX: (503) 293-1919. Licensee: Oregon Public Broadcasting. Ownership: Charles J. Swindells (acq 1993; grpsl; 9-20-93). ■ Net: PBS. Wash atty: Schwartz, Woods & Miller. ■ Maynard E. Orme, pres; Nevton Dunn, vp; Thomas M. Doggett, progmg dir; Fred Leitch, chief engr. ■ On 8 CATVs. On 5 trans.

Medford

ADI No. 145; see Medford market

KDRV—ch 12, 191 kw vis, 38.1 kw aur, ant 2,701t/168g. TL: N42 41 32 W123 13 46. On air date: Feb 26, 1984. 1090 Knutson Ave. (97504). (503) 773-1212. Licensee: Soda Mountain Broadcasting Inc. Group owner: Chambers Communications Corp. (acq 7-1-93). ■ Net: ABC. Rep: Katz. Wash atty: Fletcher, Heald & Hildreth. ■ Carolyn Chambers, pres; Keith A. Lollis, gen mgr, natl sls mgr & progmg dir; Jonathon Piff, rgnl sls mgr; Larry Black, prom mgr; Renard Maiuri, news dir; Rick Carrara, chief engr. ■ On 20 CATVs—71,731 subs. On 14 trans.

KMVU—ch 26, 28.5 kw vis, ant 1,348t. TL: N42 17 54 W122 44 59. Not on air, target date unknown. 2032 Amsterdam Ave., Modesto, CA (95356). Permittee: Junko K. and Bobby C. Shehan.

KOBI—ch 5, 60.3 kw vis, 8.13 kw aur, ant 2,700t/155g. TL: N42 41 49 W123 13 39. Stereo. Hrs opn: 24. On air date: Aug 1, 1953. Box 5M, 125 S. Fir (97501). (503) 779-5555. FAX: (503) 779-5564. Licensee: California Oregon Broadcasting Inc. (group owner). ■ Net: NBC. Rep: Blair. Wash atty: Reed, Smith, Shaw & McClay. ■ Patricia C. Smullin, pres; Ed Zander, gen mgr; Amy Belkin, news dir; Steve Aase, chief engr.

***KSYS**—ch 8, 60.3 kw vis, 6.03 kw aur, ant 2,670t. TL: N42 41 31 W123 13 46. On air date: Jan 17, 1977. 34 S. Fir (97501). (503) 779-0808. Licensee: Southern Oregon Public Television Inc. (acq 6-20-73; $27 million). ■ Net: PBS; Pacific Mtn. Progmg for the deaf 3 hrs wkly. ■ Regina Cox, pres; William R. Campbell, gen mgr; Jim Otey, opns mgr; Lisa Vandever, prom mgr & progmg mgr; Don McKay, chief engr. ■ On 14 CATVs—61,400 subs. On 12 trans.

KTVL—ch 10, 132 kw vis, 26.3 aur, ant 3,310t/151g. TL: N42 04 55 W122 43 07. On air date: Oct 3, 1961. Box 10, 1440 Rossanley Dr. (97501). (503) 773-7373. FAX: (503) 779-0451. Licensee: Freedom Communications Inc. Group owner: Freedom Newspapers Inc., Broadcast Division (acq 8-28-81; $12.5 million). ■ Net: CBS. Rep: Petry. Wash atty: Latham & Watkins. News staff 16; news progmg 11 hrs wkly. ■ Thomas Long, vp, gen mgr, gen sls mgr & natl sls mgr; Kingsley Kelley, opns mgr, progmg dir & film buyer; Barry Tevis, prom mgr; Gayle Mitchell, news dir; Mel Tynan, chief engr. ■ On 21 CATVs—60,236 subs. On 33 trans. ■ Rates: $400; 150; 40.

North Bend

KCBY-TV—See Coos Bay.

Portland

ADI No. 27; see Portland, OR market

KATU—ch 2, 100 kw vis, 20 kw aur, ant 1,560t/918g. TL: N45 31 14 W122 44 37. Stereo. On air date: Mar 15, 1962. 2153 N.E. Sandy Blvd. (97232); Box 2 (97207). (503) 231-4222. FAX: (503) 231-4233; TWX: 910-464-4700. Licensee: Fisher Broadcasting Inc. (group owner). ■ Net: ABC. Rep: Telerep. Wash atty: Fisher, Wayland,

Stations in the U.S.

Leader & Cooper. News progmg 19 hrs wkly. ■ Patrick Scott, CEO; John Behnke, chmn; James L. Boyer, gen mgr; Terry Deming, opns mgr; Karen Heniger, gen sls mgr; Phelps Fisher, vp mktg; Laurie Dahl, prom mgr; Leland Petrik, progmg dir; Jan Allen, news dir; Rhonda Shelby, pub affrs dir; Don Wilkinson, vp engrg. ■ On 70 CATVs—553,847 subs. On 16 trans.

KGW-TV—ch 8, 316 kw vis, 60.3 kw aur, ant 1,768t/924g. TL: N45 31 21 W122 44 46. Stereo. On air date: Dec 15, 1956. 1501 S.W. Jefferson St. (97201). (503) 226-5000. FAX: (503) 226-4448. Licensee: King Broadcasting Co. Group owner: Providence Journal Broadcasting Corp. (acq 8-27-91; $355 million; grpsl; 9-9-91). ■ Net: NBC. Rep: Blair, Paul Mulvihill (Canada). Wash atty: Fletcher, Heald & Hildreth. ■ Dennis Williamson, vp & gen mgr; Bob Blacher, gen sls mgr; Jeanna Shelley, prom mgr; Brenda Buratti, progmg dir & film buyer; Steve Tuttle, news dir; Eric Dausman, chief engr. ■ On 56 CATVs—67,000 subs. On 21 trans.

KNMT-TV—ch 24, 2,690 kw vis, 269 kw aur, ant 1,519t/2,535g. TL: N45 30 58 W122 43 59. On air date: Nov 17, 1989. 432 N.E. 74th Ave. (97213). (503) 252-0792. FAX: (503) 256-4205. Licensee: National Minority TV Inc. Ownership: Paul F. Crouch, 33.3%.; Jane Duff, 33.3%; David Espinoza, 33.3%. Wash atty: May & Dunne Chartered. ■ Paul F. Crouch, pres; James McClellan, stn mgr; Connie McClellan, pub affrs dir; Mark Fountain, chief engr.

KOIN—ch 6, 100 kw vis, 15.1 kw aur, ant 1,760t/989g. TL: N45 30 58 W122 43 59. Stereo. Hrs opn: 24. On air date: Oct 15, 1953. 222 S.W. Columbia St. (97201). (503) 464-0600. FAX: (503) 464-0717. Licensee: KOIN-TV Inc. Group owner: Lee Enterprises Inc. See Cross-Ownership. ■ Net: CBS. Rep: Harrington, Righter & Parsons, Art Moore. Wash atty: Reed, Smith, Shaw & McClay. News progmg 18 hrs wkly. ■ R. M. Schafbuch, exec vp; Greg Veon, vp & gen mgr; Peter F. Maroney, opns mgr & progmg dir; Charlie Hogetvedt, sls dir; Dave K. Berkeley, natl sls mgr; Jim Hanning, rgnl sls mgr; Dick Vardanega, prom mgr; Lee A. Wood, engrg dir. ■ On 97 CATVs—300,688 subs. On 27 trans.

*KOPB-TV—ch 10, 316 kw vis, 31.6 kw aur, ant 1,740t/1,081g. TL: N45 31 22 W122 45 07. On air date: Feb 6, 1961. 7140 S.W. Macadam Ave. (97219). (503) 244-9900. FAX: (503) 293-1919. Licensee: Oregon Public Broadcasting. Ownership: Charles J. Swindells (acq 1993; grpsl; 9-20-93). Net: PBS. Wash atty: Schwartz, Woods & Miller. ■ Maynard E. Orme, pres; Nevton Dunn, opns mgr; Thomas M. Doggett, progmg dir; Bryce Howard, chief engr. ■ On 5 trans. Co-owned radio: *KOPB-FM.

KPTV—ch 12, 316 kw vis, 31.6 kw aur, ant 1,780t/1,049g. TL: N45 31 19 W122 44 53. On air date: Sept 20, 1952. Box 3401 (97208). (503) 222-9921. TWX: 910-464-6136. Licensee: Oregon Television Inc. Group owner: Chris Craft Industries Inc. (acq 7-22-59; $3.75 million; 7-27-59). Rep: Katz. Wash atty: Hogan & Hartson. ■ Martin Brantley, gen mgr; Connie Martin, gen sls mgr; Barbara Deaton, prom mgr; Marvin Rhodes, progmg dir; John Sears, news dir; Bob Nelson, chief engr. ■ On 126 CATVs—554,517. On 18 trans. ■ Rates: $500; 650; 140.

Roseburg

ADI No. 116; see Eugene market

KLSR-TV—ch 36, 42.7 kw vis, ant 692t. TL: N43 14 09 W123 19 16. Not on air, target date unknown. 888 Goodpaster Island Rd., Eugene (97401). Permittee: Metrocom of Oregon Inc. Group owner: California Oregon Broadcasting Inc.

KMTX-TV—ch 46, 13.63 kw vis, ant 728t. TL: N43 14 08 W123 19 17. Stereo. Hrs opn: 18. On air date: Apr 8, 1992. 3825 International Ct., Springfield (97477); Box 7308, Eugene (97401). (503) 746-1600. FAX: (503) 747-0866. Licensee: KMTR Inc. ■ Net: NBC. Rep: Petry. Wash atty: Haley, Bader & Potts. ■ Robert W. Davis, pres & gen mgr; Robert L. Rector, gen sls mgr; Mardi Martin, prom mgr; Julie Strandlien, progmg dir; Jim Frandin, news dir; Jerry Madsen, chief engr.

KPIC—ch 4, 5.37 kw vis, 550 w aur, ant 1,000t/173g. TL: N43 14 20 W123 18 42. On air date: Apr 1, 1956. Box 1345, 655 W. Umpqua (97470). (503) 672-4481. FAX: (503) 672-4482. Licensee: South West Oregon TV Broadcasting Corp. Group owner: California Oregon Broadcasting Inc. ■ Net: CBS. Rep: Katz, Art Moore. Wash atty: Dow, Lohnes & Albertson. ■ Jim Putney, gen mgr; Don Clithero, stn mgr, opns mgr; Wade Hughes, prom mgr; Paul Greene, progmg dir; Dan Bain, news dir & pub affrs dir; Jim Bowen, engrg dir; Mike Hill, chief engr. ■ On 9 CATVs—18,150 subs. On 6 trans. ■ Rates: $110; 70; 30.

Salem

ADI No. 27; see Portland, OR market

KBSP-TV—ch 22, 1,702 kw vis, 170 kw aur, ant 1,187t/945g. TL: N45 00 00 W122 41 37. Hrs opn: 24. On air date: Nov 21, 1981. 4923 Indian School Rd. N.E. (97305). (503) 390-2202. FAX: (503) 390-6829. Licensee: Blackstar Communications of Oregon Inc. Group owner: Blackstar Communications Inc. (acq 4-20-88; $5.135 million; 2-29-88). Wash atty: Verner, Liipfert, Bernhard, McPherson & Hand. ■ Judith Koenig, vp, gen mgr, gen sls mgr & progmg dir; Tom Craven, prom mgr; Dick Bond, pub affrs dir; Tim Mance, chief engr. ■ On 29 CATVs—416,899 subs. On one trans.

KEBN—ch 32, 3,577 kw vis, 358 kw aur, ant 1,786t. TL: N45 00 28 W122 20 05. On air date: May 1989. 10255 S.W. Arctic Dr., Beaverton (97005). FAX: (503) 644-6300. Licensee: James R. McDonald, Receiver ■ Glen Chambers, pres.

Pennsylvania

Allentown

ADI No. 4; see Philadelphia market

WFMZ-TV—ch 69, 1,078 kw vis, 21.9 kw aur, ant 1,025t/494g. TL: N40 33 54 W75 26 26. (CP: 2,140 kw vis, 214 kw aur, ant 1,079t/674g). On air date: Nov 25, 1976. 300 E. Rock Rd. (18103). (215) 797-4530. Licensee: Maranatha Broadcasting Co. Ownership: Richard C. Dean & others, 55%; Robert Reichard, 25%; Paul Brittin & Richard Dean Sr., 7% each; David Hinson, 5%. Rep: Spot Time, Dome. Sp one hr wkly. ■ Richard Dean, pres; David Hinson, gen mgr & progmg dir; Dean Dallman, gen sls mgr; Eric Reinert, prom mgr; Brad Rinehart, news dir; Barry Fisher, chief engr. ■ On 22 CATVs—305,000 subs. Co-owned radio: WFMZ-FM. ■ Rates: $260; 130; 65.

*WLVT-TV—ch 39, 490 kw vis, 97.7 kw aur, ant 990t/516g. TL: N40 33 58 W75 26 06. Stereo. Hrs opn: 24. On air date: September 1965. S. Mountain Dr., Bethlehem (18015). (215) 867-4677. FAX: (215) 867-3544. Licensee: Lehigh Valley Public Telecommunications Corp. ■ Net: PBS, EEN, Pa. Pub Net. Wash atty: Dow, Lohnes & Albertson. Sp one hr wkly. ■ Sheldon P. Siegel, CEO & pres; David A. Donio, dev dir, mktg dir & adv dir; S. P. Siegel, prom mgr; Donald L. Robert, progmg dir & news dir; Gilbert Aykroyd, engrg dir; Barry Wittchen, engrg mgr. ■ On 55 CATVs—500,000 subs.

Altoona

ADI No. 89; see Johnstown-Altoona market

WATM-TV—ch 23, 182 kw vis, 18.2 kw aur, ant 1,062t/276g. TL: N40 34 05 W78 26 40. Stereo. Hrs opn: 20. On air date: November 1974. 1450 Scalp Ave., Johnstown (15904). (814) 266-8088. FAX: (814) 266-7749; TELEX: 4112-62488950. Licensee: Evergreen Broadcasting Corp. Group owner: Smith Broadcasting Group Inc. (acq 1986). ■ Net: ABC. Rep: Katz. Wash atty: Hogan & Hartson. News staff 10; news progmg 3 hrs wkly. ■ Marty Ostrow, vp, gen mgr & gen sls mgr; Chris Taylor, stn mgr; Jeff Alan, news dir; Jill Fondelier, pub affrs dir; Bob Andrade, chief engr. ■ On 75 CATVS—189,766 subs. On one trans.

WKBS-TV—ch 47, 1,510 kw vis, 151 kw aur, ant 1,010t/184g. TL: N40 34 12 W78 26 26. On air date: 1985. 1813 Valley View Blvd. (16602). (814) 942-3400. Licensee: Altoona Christian Television. Wash atty: Gammon & Grange. ■ R. Russell Bixler, pres; Oleen Eagle, vp & gen mgr; Blake Richert, chief engr. ■ On 17 CATVs—75,000 subs. Satellite of WPCB-TV, Greensburg.

*WTAJ—ch 10, 214 kw vis, 21.9 kw aur, ant 1,110t/277g. TL: N40 34 01 W78 26 31. Stereo. Hrs opn: 24. On air date: March 1, 1953. Box 10, Commerce Park (16603). (814) 944-2031. FAX: (814) 946-8746. Licensee: Gateway Communications Inc. Ownership: Macromedia, 100%. (group owner; acq 10-72; $14.4 million). ■ Net: CBS. Rep: Blair. Wash atty: Bryan, Cave, McPheeters & McRoberts. ■ Lamont T. Pinker, pres; Rick Reeves, vp & gen mgr; Pete James, gen sls mgr; Dan Dillier, prom mgr; Lowell Sollenberger, progmg dir; Dave Hopkins, prom dir; John Blatt, chief engr. ■ On 116 CATVs—290,560 subs.

Bethlehem

ADI No. 4; see Philadelphia market

WBPH-TV—ch 60, 12 kw vis, 1.2 kw aur, ant 758t/250g. TL: N40 37 33 W75 15 19. On air date: 1991. 428 Gaffney Hill Rd., Easton (18042). (215) 250-8860. Licensee: Sonshine Family TV Inc. Ownership: Patricia Huber, 100%. ■ Patricia Huber, pres.

*WLVT-TV—See Allentown.

Clearfield

ADI No. 89; see Johnstown-Altoona market

*WPSX-TV—ch 3, 100 kw vis, 20 kw aur, ant 879t/538g. TL: N41 07 21 W78 26 28. On air date: Mar 1, 1965. Wagner Annex, University Park (16802). (814) 865-3333. FAX: (814) 865-3145. Licensee: The Pennsylvania State Univ. ■ Net: PBS, EEN, CEN, Pa. Pub Net. Wash atty: Bryan, Cave, McPheeters & McRoberts. ■ Mark Erstling, gen mgr; George Thurman, opns dir; Rosa Maria Pavelko, dev dir; Greg Petersen, prom mgr; Kathleen Pavelko, progmg dir; Carl Fisher, chief engr. ■ On 87 CATVs—206,633 subs. On one trans. Co-owned radio: *WPSU(FM) University Park.

Erie

ADI No. 142; see Erie market

WETG—ch 66, 35.5 kw vis, 3.6 kw aur, ant 886t/694g. TL: N42 02 11 W80 03 57. (CP: 562 kw vis, 56.2 kw aur, ant 889t/697g). On air date: Sept 2, 1986. University Sq. (16541). (814) 871-7446. FAX: (814) 459-0996. Licensee: Gannon University Broadcasting Inc. Ownership: David A. Rubino (acq 6-3-93; 6-28-93). ■ Net: Fox. Rep: American Television Sls, Rgnl Reps, Commercial Media Sls. Wash atty: Haley, Bader & Potts. ■ Anthony J. Miceli, gen mgr; Art Arkelian, gen sls mgr; Judy Shannon, progmg dir; Doug Justham, chief engr. ■ On 7 CATVs—90,000 subs.

WICU-TV—ch 12, 316 kw vis, 31.6 kw aur, ant 1,000t/789g. TL: N42 03 52 W80 00 19. Stereo. On air date: March 15, 1949. 3514 State St. (16508). (814) 454-5201. FAX: (814) 455-0703; TWX: 510-696-6878. Licensee: Great Lakes Communications Inc. Ownership: Lamb Enterprises. ■ Net: NBC. Rep: Katz; Airtime TV Sls. Wash atty: Rosenman & Colin. News staff 18; news progmg 10 hrs wkly. ■ Priscilla Lamb Schwier, pres; Clarence Paolella, gen mgr, gen sls mgr & film buyer; Vince Ugoletti, stn mgr & chief engr; Betty McCleery, prom mgr; Bill Knupp, progmg dir. ■ On 59 CATVs—3,070,000 subs.

WJET-TV—ch 24, 1,100 kw vis, 110 kw aur, ant 960t/815g. TL: N42 02 24 W80 04 08. (CP: 1,120 kw vis, 112 kw aur, ant 955t). Hrs opn: 24. On air date: April 2, 1966. 8455 Peach St. (16509). (814) 864-2400. FAX: (814) 868-3041; TWX: 510-696-6877. Licensee: Jet Broadcasting Co. Group owner: The Jet Broadcasting Co. ■ Net: ABC. Rep: Blair. Wash atty: Reddy, Begley & Martin. News staff 18; news progmg 11 hrs wkly. ■ John Kanzius, pres & gen mgr; Mike George, gen sls mgr; Tom New, prom dir; Mary Scheuer, progmg dir; Chuck Jennings, engrg mgr. Co-owned radio: WJET-FM.

*WQLN—ch 54, 1,000 kw vis, 100 kw aur, ant 879t/679g. TL: N42 02 31 W80 03 57. On air date: Aug 13, 1967. 8425 Peach St. (16509). (814) 864-3001. FAX: (814) 864-4077. Licensee: Public Broadcasting of Northwest Pa. Inc. ■ Net: PBS, Pa. Pub Net. Wash atty: Dow, Lohnes & Albertson. ■ Paul Stankavich, pres & gen mgr; Ronald Daugherty, vp; Pat Combine, dev dir; Joe Mosier, prom mgr; Art Starkey, progmg dir & film buyer; Dennis Spagnolo, chief engr. ■ On 14 CATVs—105,800 subs. Co-owned radio: WQLN-FM.

WSEE-TV—ch 35, 1,170 kw vis, 117 kw aur, ant 941t/741g. TL: N42 02 20 W80 03 45. Hrs opn: 20. On air date: Apr 24, 1954. 1220 Peach St. (16501). (814) 455-7575. TWX: 510-696-6806. Licensee: NTG Inc. Group owner: Northstar Television Group Inc. (acq 9-11-89; grpsl; 9-25-89). ■ Net: CBS. Rep: Petry; Metrospot (Canada). News staff 28; news progmg 36 hrs wkly. ■ Robert Hoffman, vp & gen mgr; Jeff Gallop, gen sls mgr; Jim Larkin, prom mgr; Earl Kneissler, progmg dir; Pierre Bellieni, news dir; Dan Hungesser, chief engr. ■ On 18 CATVs—140,000 subs. ■ Rates: $400; 150; 35.

Greensburg

ADI No. 17; see Pittsburgh market

WPCB-TV—ch 40, 1,170 kw vis, 117 kw aur, ant 980t/839g. TL: N40 23 30 W79 46 51. Hrs opn: 24. On air date: Apr 15, 1979. Signal Hill Dr., Wall (15148-1499). (412) 824-3930. Licensee: Cornerstone Television Inc. (acq 7-78). Wash atty: Gammon & Grange. Sp, Greek, It one hr wkly. ■ R. Russell Bixler, pres; Oleen Eagle, exec vp & gen mgr; David Skeba, vp progmg & progmg dir; Blake Richert, vp engrg & engrg dir. ■ On 86 CATVs—750,000 subs. On one trans. ■ Rates: $60; 60; 60.

Harrisburg

ADI No. 44; see Harrisburg-York-Lancaster-Lebanon market

WHP-TV—ch 21, 1,200 kw vis, 245 kw aur, ant 1,220t/496g. TL: N40 20 44 W76 52 09. Stereo. Hrs opn: 20. On air date: Apr 15, 1953. Box 1507 (17105); 3300 N. Sixth St. (17110). (717) 238-2100. FAX: (717) 236-0198; TWX: 510-650-4925. Licensee: WHP Television L.P. Ownership: Ralph E. Becker. (Group owner: Farrow Communications. (acq 1993; $9.25 million; 9-6-93). ■ Net: CBS. Rep: Petry. Wash atty: Dow, Lohnes & Albertson. News staff 30; news progmg 14 hrs wkly. ■ Robert B. Farrow, pres & gen mgr; Matt Hope, opns mgr; Lee Smith, natl sls mgr; Jay Rabin, mktg dir; Katie Westerlund, prom mgr; Helen Young, progmg dir; Jon McCall, news dir; Rob Hershey, engrg dir. ■ On 62 CATVs—344,941 subs. ■ Rates: $1,500; 400; 45.

WHTM-TV—ch 27, 2,400 kw vis, 240 kw aur, ant 1,119t/608g. TL: N40 18 57 W76 57 02. Hrs opn: 21. On air date: June 19, 1953. Box 5860, 3235 Hoffman St. (17110-5860); NCNB National Bank Bldg., Suite 420, 3839 4th St. N., St. Petersburg, FL (33703). (717) 236-2727; (813) 821-7900. FAX: (717) 232-5272. Licensee: WHTM-TV Inc. Group owner: Smith Broadcasting Group Inc. (acq 4-17-86; $37 million; 12-16-85). ■ Net: ABC. Wash atty: Hogan & Hartson. News staff 30; news progmg 18 hrs wkly. ■ Robert N. Smith, pres; David Fitz, CFO; John Purcell, vp; Paul O'Dell, stn mgr, opns mgr & progmg mgr; Caroline Wilson, prom mgr; Holly Steuart, news dir; Donald Landis, chief engr. ■ On 96 CATVs—460,000 subs. On 3 trans. ■ Rates: $1,400; 350; 200.

***WITF-TV**—ch 33, 1,100 kw vis, 110 kw aur, ant 1,396t/724g. TL: N40 20 45 W76 52 06. On air date: Nov 22, 1964. Box 2954 (17105); 1982 Locust Ln. (17109). (717) 236-6000. FAX: (717) 236-4628. Licensee: WITF Inc. ■ Net: PBS; EEN. Wash atty: Dow, Lohnes & Albertson. ■ John Blair, vp opns; Michael Greenwald, vp dev; Constance Rannels, prom mgr; Thomas Keck, progmg dir; John A. Bosak, chief engr. ■ On 50 CATVs—170,000 subs. On 2 trans. Co-owned radio: *WITF-FM.

Hazleton

ADI No. 51; see Wilkes-Barre-Scranton market

WWLF-TV—ch 56, 1,000 kw vis, 100 kw aur, ant 1,079t/381g. TL: N41 02 13 W76 05 07. Stereo. Hrs opn: Sat-Thurs 6 AM-2 AM; Fri 24. On air date: June 3, 1985. 916 Oak St., Scranton (18508). (717) 347-9653. FAX: (717) 347-3141. Licensee: Pegasus Broadcast Television L.P. Group owner: Pegasus Broadcast Television. ■ Net: Fox. Rep: Seltel. Wash atty: Baraff, Koerner, Olender & Hochberg. ■ Peter Kilcullen, gen mgr & progmg dir; Jon Cadman, opns dir; Michael Yanuzzi, gen sls mgr; Raymond Gillette, rgnl sls mgr; Paul Silvestri, mktg dir & prom dir; Linda Greenwald, pub affrs dir; Rick Jordan, chief engr. ■ On 128 CATVS—150,000 subs. On 2 trans. Satellite of WOLF-TV Scranton. ■ Rates: $600; 135; 45.

Johnstown

ADI No. 89; see Johnstown-Altoona market

WJAC-TV—ch 6, 70.8 kw vis, 10.6 kw aur, ant 1,120t/175g. TL: N40 22 17 W78 58 58. Stereo. On air date: Sept 15, 1949. 1949 Hickory Ln. (15905). (814) 255-7600. TWX: 510-698-3274. Licensee: WJAC Inc. Ownership: Anderson H. Walters Estate, 61%. ■ Net: NBC. Rep: Harrington, Righter & Parsons. Wash atty: Wilkinson, Barker, Krauer & Quinn. ■ James M. Edwards Sr., pres & gen mgr; Richard D. Schrott, vp & gen sls mgr; Robert Maslak, opns mgr; Ken Degennaro, prom mgr; Jolene Courter, progmg dir & film buyer; Ronald Miller, news dir; Rob Abele, chief engr. ■ On 169 CATVs—700,905 subs.

WPTJ—ch 19, 1,660 kw vis, 166 kw aur, ant 1,191t/297g. TL: N40 10 53 W79 09 04. (CP: Ant 1,381t, TL: N40 17 29 W79 33 57). On air date: Oct 15, 1953. Box 985, Pittsburgh (15230); 2900 Gulf Tower, Pittsburgh (15219). (412) 471-5566. Licensee: WFAT Inc. Ownership: Leon A. Crosby, 100% (acq 2-1-83; $1.59 million). ■ Leon A. Crosby, pres; Silas Royster, gen mgr; Earl Garber, chief engr.

WWCP-TV—ch 8, 166 kw vis, 16.6 kw aur, ant 1,208t. TL: N40 10 53 W79 09 5. Hrs opn: 20. On air date: Oct 13, 1986. 1450 Scalp Ave. (15904). (814) 266-8088. FAX: (814) 266-7749. Licensee: Evergreen Broadcasting Corp. Group owner: Smith Broadcasting Group Inc. ■ Net: Fox. Rep: Katz. Wash atty: Hogan & Hartson. News staff 10; news progmg 5 hrs wkly. ■ Marty Ostrow, vp, gen mgr & gen sls mgr; Christopher J. Taylor, stn mgr; Ron Kabo, rgnl sls mgr; Jeff Alan, news dir; Jill Fondelier, pub affrs dir; Robert Andrade, chief engr. ■ On 114 CATVS—303,608 subs. On 4 trans.

Lancaster

ADI No. 44; see Harrisburg-York-Lancaster-Lebanon market

WGAL—ch 8, 112 kw vis, 21.4 kw aur, ant 1,361t/824g. TL: N40 02 04 W76 37 08. Stereo. On air date: Mar 18, 1949. Box 7127 (17604); 1300 Columbia Ave. (17603). (717) 393-5851. FAX: (717) 393-9484. Licensee: WGAL-TV Inc. Group owner: Pulitzer Broadcasting Co. ■ Net: NBC. Rep: Katz. Wash atty: Verner, Liipfert, Bernhard, McPherson & Hand. News staff 62; news progmg 16 hrs wkly. ■ Paul Quinn, vp & gen mgr; John Feeser, gen sls mgr; Tom VanBenschoten, rgnl sls mgr; Cil Frazier, mktg mgr & prom mgr; Nelson Sears, progmg dir; Ed Wickenheiser, news dir; Charlotte Asherman, pub affrs dir; Robert Good, chief engr. ■ On 121 CATVs—738,000 subs.

WLYH-TV—ch 15, 1,050 kw vis, 210 kw aur, ant 1,361t/1,059g. TL: N40 15 45 W76 27 53. Hrs opn: 6 AM-2 AM. On air date: Oct 15, 1953. Box 1283, Lebanon (17042). (717) 273-4551. FAX: (717) 270-0901. Licensee: Gateway Communications Inc. (group owner; acq 10-72; $14.4 million). ■ Net: CBS. Rep: Seltel. Wash atty: Wilner & Scheiner. News staff 5; news progmg 5 hrs wkly. ■ Lamont Pinker, pres; David F. Metz, vp, gen mgr & gen sls mgr; John McNally, natl sls mgr; Jan Hrabovsky, mktg mgr; Bob Patterson, progmg dir; Leilyn Perri, news dir; Tim Costley, chief engr. ■ On 90 CATVs—490,000 subs.

Lebanon

WGAL—See Lancaster.

WHTM-TV—See Harrisburg.

WLYH-TV—See Lancaster.

Satterfield & Perry, Inc.
Brokers • Consultants • Appraisers
Philadelphia • Kansas City • Denver
Jack Satterfield (215) 668-1168
John Weidman (215) 660-7760
Doug Stephens (913) 649-5103
Al Perry (303) 239-6670
Bob Austin (303) 740-8424

Philadelphia

ADI No. 4; see Philadelphia market

KYW-TV—ch 3, 100 kw vis, 10 kw aur, ant 1,000t/1,116g. TL: N40 02 39 W75 14 26. Stereo. On air date: Sept 3, 1941. Independence Mall E. (19106). (215) 238-4700. FAX: (215) 238-4907. Licensee: Westinghouse Broadcasting Inc. (group owner; acq 2-17-65; 3-1-65). ■ Net: NBC. Rep: Group W. Wash atty: Wilkes, Artis, Hedrick & Lane. ■ Jonathan Klein, pres; Anthony Vinciquerra, vp & gen mgr; Michael Colleran, gen sls mgr; Joanne Calabria, mktg dir; Steve Miller, prom mgr; Allen Murphy, progmg dir; Geaneen Rutledge, pub affrs dir; Bob Ross, engrg dir. Co-owned radio: KYW(AM).

WCAU-TV—ch 10, 191 kw vis, 19.1 kw aur, ant 1,160t/1,139g. TL: N40 02 36 W75 14 12. Stereo. On air date: Mar 15, 1948. City Ave. & Monument Rd. (19131). (215) 668-5510. FAX: (215) 668-5532. Licensee: CBS Inc. Group owner: CBS Broadcast Group (acq 7-3-58; grpsl; 8-4-58). ■ Net: CBS. ■ Eugene Lothery, vp & gen mgr; Jeffrey Cash, sls dir; Alex Dusek, prom dir; Dan Sitarski, progmg dir; Drew Berry, news dir; Joanne Wilder, pub affrs dir; Dave Harvey, engrg dir. Co-owned radio: WOGL-AM-FM.

WGBS-TV—ch 57, 5,000 kw vis, 500 kw aur, ant 1,160t/1,179g. TL: N40 02 21 W75 14 13. Stereo. On air date: June 15, 1981. 420 N. 20th St. (19130). (215) 563-5757. FAX: (215) 563-5786. Licensee: Combined Broadcasting Inc. (group owner). Rep: Katz. Wash atty: Fisher, Wayland, Cooper & Leader. ■ Robert E. O'Connor, gen mgr; Carol Healey, stn mgr & progmg dir; Edward Shaffer, gen sls mgr; Mark Cooper, prom mgr; Dick Quinto, chief engr.

***WHYY-TV**—See Wilmington, Del.

WPHL-TV—ch 17, 2,340 kw vis, 300 kw aur, ant 1,313t/1,092g. TL: N40 02 30 W75 14 24. On air date: Sept 17, 1965. 5001 Wynnefield Ave. (19131). (215) 878-1700. FAX: (215) 879-3665; TELEX: 497-6664. Licensee: Tribune Broadcasting Co. (group owner, see Cross-Ownership; acq 4-17-92; $19 million; FTR 5-18-92). Rep: TeleRep. Wash atty: Koteen & Naftalin. ■ Randall E. Smith, vp, gen mgr & stn mgr; Jan Dickler, gen sls mgr; Dan Reese, prom mgr; Trish Silvas, progmg dir; David Smith, chief engr. ■ On 1,540 CATVs—2,400,000 subs.

WPVI-TV—ch 6, 74.1 kw vis, 7.4 kw aur, ant 1,094t/1,111g. TL: N40 02 38 W75 14 25. Stereo. On air date: Sept 13, 1947. 4100 City Line Ave. (19131). (215) 878-9700. FAX: (215) 581-4515. Licensee: Capital Cities/ABC Inc. Group owner: Capital Cities/ABC Broadcast Group (acq 4-27-71; grpsl). ■ Net: ABC. Rep: CC/ABC Natl TV Sls. Wash atty: Wilmer, Cutler & Pickering. ■ Thomas Kane, pres & gen mgr; Charles R. Bradley, opns dir & progmg dir; Todd T. Wheeler, sls dir; Charles Dunn, natl sls mgr; Valari Dobson, mktg dir; William Burton, adv dir; Dave Davis, news dir; Irwin L. Ross, engrg dir.

WTXF—ch 29, 5,000 kw vis, 500 kw aur, ant 1,138t/1,188g. TL: N40 02 26 W75 14 20. Hrs opn: 24. On air date: May 18, 1965. 330 Market St. (19106). (215) 925-2929. FAX: (215) 925-2420. Licensee: Paramount Stations Group of Philadelphia Inc. Group owner: Paramount Stations Group. ■ Net: Fox. Rep: Seltel. Wash atty: Leventhal, Senter & Lerman. News progmg 7 hrs wkly. ■ Mike Conway, gen mgr; George Cummings, opns mgr; Bill Ballard, gen sls mgr; Scott Mayes, natl sls mgr; Bill Butler, mktg mgr & progmg mgr; Denise Rolfe, prom mgr; Roger C. LaMay, news dir; Diane E. Krach, chief engr.

***WYBE**—ch 35, 1,918 kw vis, ant 932t/920g. TL: N40 02 26 W75 14 20. Hrs opn: 8. On air date: June 10, 1990. Box 11896 (19128-1604). (215) 483-3900. FAX: (215) 483-6908. Licensee: Independence Public Media of Philadelphia Inc. ■ Net: PBS. Wash atty: Cohn & Marks. Sp 3 hrs wkly. ■ Daniel del Solar, gen mgr; Cicero Cadell, progmg dir.

Pittsburgh

ADI No. 17; see Pittsburgh market

KDKA-TV—ch 2, 100 kw vis, 10 kw aur, ant 995t/683g. TL: N40 29 38 W80 01 09. On air date: January 1949. One Gateway Ctr. (15222). (412) 575-2200. FAX: (412) 575-3207. Licensee: Group W Television Inc. Group owner: Westinghouse Broadcasting Inc. (acq 1-5-55; $9.75 million; 1-10-55). ■ Net: CBS. Wash atty: Wilkes, Artis, Hedrick & Lane. ■ Gary Cozen, vp & gen mgr; Jerry Kalke, opns dir; Bruce Kaplan, sls dir & mktg dir; Lorraine Snebold, prom dir; Jayne Adair, progmg dir; Sue McInerney, news dir; Dane Topich, pub affrs dir; Jack Cvetic, chief engr. ■ On 188 CATVs—527,840 subs. Co-owned radio: KDKA(AM).

WPCB-TV—See Greensburg.

WPGH-TV—ch 53, 2,340 kw vis, 117 kw aur, ant 1,010t/709g. TL: N40 29 43 W80 00 17. Hrs opn: 24. On air date: July 14, 1953. 750 Ivory Ave. (15214). (412) 931-5300. FAX: (412) 931-8029. Licensee: Sinclair Broadcast Group Inc. (group owner; acq 8-30-91; $55 million; 7-15-91). ■ Net: Fox. Rep: Petry. Wash atty: Fisher, Wayland, Cooper & Leader. ■ Alan Frank, gen mgr; Jim Lapiana, gen sls mgr; Kevin Moylan, natl sls mgr; Michael Wolff, mktg dir; Terry Caywood, prom mgr; Michael Karas, progmg dir; John Getz, chief engr. ■ On 129 CATVs—850,000 subs.

WPTT-TV—ch 22, 5,000 kw vis, 500 kw aur, ant 921t/829g. TL: N40 26 23 W79 43 11. Hrs opn: 24. On air date: Sept 26, 1978. Box 2809 (15230); 500 Seco Rd., Monroeville (15146). (412) 856-9010. TWX: 510-600-8950. Licensee: WPTT Inc. (acq 6-21-91; $7 million; 7-15-91). Rep: Seltel. Wash atty: Fisher, Wayland, Cooper & Leader. ■ Eddie Edwards, gen mgr; William Stanton, gen sls mgr; Michael Stephen, prom mgr; Kevin O'Leary, progmg dir & chief engr. ■ On 64 CATVs—680,000 subs. ■ Rates: $150; 100; 50.

Stations in the U.S.

WPXI—ch 11, 316 kw vis, 58.9 kw aur, ant 991t/849g. TL: N40 27 48 W80 00 18. Stereo. On air date: Sept 1, 1957. Box 1100, 11 Television Hill (15214). (412) 237-1100. FAX: (412) 323-8097; TWX: 710-664-4340. Licensee: WPXI Inc. Group owner: Cox Broadcasting (acq 1-1-65); $20.5 million; 11-30-64). ■ Net: NBC. Rep: TeleRep. Wash atty: Reed, Smith, Shaw & McClay. ■ John A. Howell III, vp & gen mgr; Howard Zeiden, sls dir; Steve Riley, prom dir; Mark W. Barash, progmg dir; Al Blinke, news dir; Glenn Romsos, engrg dir. ■ On 175 CATVs—515,442 subs.

*****WQED**—ch 13, 316 kw vis, 31.6 kw aur, ant 690t/600g. TL: N40 26 46 W79 57 51. On air date: Apr 1, 1954. 4802 Fifth Ave. (15213). (412) 622-1300. FAX: (412) 622-1488. Licensee: Metropolitan Pittsburgh Public Broadcasting Inc. ■ Net: PBS. Wash atty: Schwartz, Woods & Miller. ■ Margot Woodwell, gen mgr; Mark Muckler, gen sls mgr & progmg dir; Jack O'Donnell, chief engr. ■ On 185 CATVs.

*****WQEX**—ch 16, 667 kw vis, 66.1 kw aur, ant 705t/601g. TL: N40 26 46 W79 57 51. Hrs opn: 16. On air date: Sept 14, 1959. 4802 Fifth Ave. (15213). (412) 622-1550. FAX: (412) 622-1488. Licensee: QED Communications Inc. ■ Net: PBS. Wash atty: Schwartz, Woods & Miller. ■ Don Korb, pres; Michael Fields, gen mgr; Jim Wiener, opns mgr; Kweilin Nassar, mktg dir; Ida D'Errico, prom mgr & adv mgr; James Wiener, progmg dir & pub affrs dir; Myles Marks, chief engr. ■ On 55 CATVs.

WTAE-TV—ch 4, 100 kw vis, 20 kw aur, ant 960t/1,066g. TL: N40 16 49 W79 48 11. Stereo. Hrs opn: 24. On air date: Sept 14, 1958. 400 Ardmore Blvd. (15221). (412) 242-4300. FAX: (412) 244-4628. Licensee: Hearst Corp. Group owner: Hearst Broadcasting Group, see Cross-Ownership (acq 8-1-62); $10.6 million; 8-6-62). ■ Net: ABC. Rep: Katz. Wash atty: Harrington, Smith & Hargrove. ■ Jim Hefner, vp & gen mgr; Rick Henry, gen sls mgr; Dorothy Frank, natl sls mgr; Kirk Szesny, prom mgr; Viki Regan, progmg dir; Tom Petner, news dir; Martin Faubell, chief engr. ■ On 250 CATVs—1,137,143 subs. On one trans. Co-owned radio: WTAE(AM), WVTY(FM).

Reading

ADI No. 4; see Philadelphia market

WTVE—ch 51, 1,450 kw vis, 290 kw aur, ant 751t/125g. TL: N40 21 15 W75 53 56. (CP: 5,000 kw vis, 500 kw aur, 1,260t, TL: N40 20 47 W75 42 03). Hrs opn: 24. On air date: February 1980. 1729 N. 11th St. (19604). (215) 921-9181. FAX: (215) 921-9139. Licensee: Reading Broadcasting Inc. Ownership: Henry & Helen Aurandt, Robert Denby. Wash atty: Brown, Nietert & Kauffman. ■ Michael Parker, pres; George Mattmiller, stn mgr; Daniel Bendetti, opns mgr, sls dir & progmg mgr; Kimberley Bradley, pub affrs dir; Gibson White, chief engr. ■ On 5 CATVs—150,000 subs.

Red Lion

ADI No. 44; see Harrisburg-York-Lancaster-Lebanon market

WGCB-TV—ch 49, 617 kw vis, 114 kw aur, ant 581t/375g. TL: N39 54 18 W76 35 00. On air date: Apr 28, 1979. Box 88 (17356). (717) 246-1681. Licensee: Red Lion Broadcasting Co. Wash atty: Ben Cottone. ■ John H. Norris, CEO & gen mgr; John E. Stockstill, stn mgr & prom dir; Gordon Moul, natl sls mgr; Jerry Jacobs, mktg dir; Clyde Campbell, adv dir; John Banker, progmg dir; Fred Wise, chief engr.

Scranton

ADI No. 51; see Wilkes-Barre-Scranton market

WBRE-TV—(Wilkes-Barre). ch 28, 3,020 kw vis, 604 kw aur, ant 1,670t/870g. TL: N41 11 01 W75 52 02. On air date: Jan 1, 1953. 62 S. Franklin St., Wilkes-Barre (18773). (717) 823-2828. FAX: (717) 829-0440; TELEX: 62897160. Licensee: Northeastern TV Investors. Group owner: Pompadur-Becker Group (acq 8-22-84). ■ Net: NBC. Rep: Petry. Wash atty: Wiley, Rein & Fielding. ■ I. Martin Pompadur, pres; William W. Harper, vp & gen mgr; Kevin M. Mirek, gen sls mgr; Gregory Stetson, prom mgr & progmg dir; Larry Stirewalt, news dir; Barry Erick, chief engr. ■ On 120 CATVs—538,000 subs. On 4 trans. ■ Rates: $2,700; 550; 400.

WNEP-TV—ch 16, 1,268 kw vis, 127 kw aur, ant 1,666t/829g. TL: N41 01 58 W75 52 21. Stereo. On air date: Feb 9, 1954. 16 Montage Mountain Rd., Moosic (18507). (717) 346-7474. FAX: (717) 347-0359. Licensee: The New York Times Co. (group owner). (acq 12-30-85; $40 million; 9-23-85). ■ Net: ABC. Rep: Katz. Wash atty: Koteen & Naftalin. ■ Warren A. Reed, pres & gen mgr; Steve Gianacopoulos, prom mgr; Frank Andrews, news dir; Frank Chebalo, vp engrg & chief engr. ■ On 122 CATVs—695,000 subs. On 5 trans.

WOLF-TV—ch 38, 1,290 kw vis, 234 kw aur, ant 1,263t. TL: N41 26 09 W75 43 45. Hrs opn: Sat-Thurs 6 AM-2 AM; Fri 24. On air date: June 6, 1985. 916 Oak St. (18508). (717) 347-9653. FAX: (717) 347-3141. Licensee: Pegasus Broadcast Television L.P. (group owner). ■ Net: Fox. Rep: Scranton. Wash atty: Baraff, Koerner, Olender & Hochberg. ■ Peter Kilcullen, gen mgr & progmg dir; Jon Cadman, opns dir; Michael Yanuzzi, gen sls mgr & natl sls mgr; Raymond Gillette, rgnl sls mgr; Paul Silvestri, mktg dir & prom dir; Michael Tobias, film buyer; Linda Greenwald, pub affrs dir; Gary Blais, chief engr. ■ On 128 CATVs—450,000 subs. On 2 sat. ■ Rates: $600; 135; 45.

WSWB-TV—ch 64, 5,000 kw vis, 500 kw aur, ant 1,207t. TL: N41 26 09 W75 43 33. Not on air, target date unknown. Box 764, Clarks Summit (18411). Permittee: Ehrhardt Broadcasting. Wash atty: Schwartz, Woods & Miller. ■ Ted H. Ehrhardt, pres; Lynne Tatarowicz, gen mgr.

*****WVIA-TV**—ch 44, 1,000 kw vis, 100 kw aur, ant 1,670t/845g. TL: N41 10 55 W75 752 17. On air date: Sept 26, 1966. 70 Old Boston Rd., Pittston (18640). (717) 826-6144; (717) 344-1244. Licensee: Northeastern Pennsylvania Educational TV Assoc. ■ Net: PBS; EEN. Wash atty: Dow, Lohnes & Albertson. ■ A. William Kelly, CEO & pres; Thomas J. McHugh, vp; Raymond Boyle, dev dir; Judy Sedlak, dev mgr; Joy Evans, progmg dir; William L. Myers, engrg dir. ■ On 188 CATVs—813,244 subs. On 10 trans. Co-owned radio: *WVIA-FM.

WYOU—ch 22, 2,945 kw vis, 294 kw aur, ant 842g. TL: N41 10 58 W75 52 26. Stereo. Hrs opn: 24. On air date: June 7, 1953. 415 Lackawanna Ave. (18503). (717) 961-2222. FAX: (717) 342-1254. Licensee: Diversified Communications (group owner; acq 9-4-86); $22.8 million). ■ Net: CBS. Rep: Blair. News staff 38; news progmg 19 hrs wkly. ■ Bill Christian, vp & gen mgr; Harry McClintock, opns director, progmg dir & film buyer; Billy Huggins, gen sls mgr; Bob Fein, natl sls mgr; Timothy Mason, prom mgr; Mark Thomas, news dir; Linda Wallace, pub affrs dir; Joseph S. Balkan, chief engr. ■ On 114 CATVs—400,000 subs. On 5 trans.

Wilkes-Barre

WBRE-TV—Licensed to Wilkes-Barre. See Scranton.

Williamsport

ADI No. 51; see Wallkes-Barre-Scranton market

WILF—ch 53, 12.3 kw vis, 1.23 kw aur, ant 728t. TL: N41 11 57 W77 07 38. Not on air, target date unknown. 51 Academy Pl., Canandaigua, NY (14424). (716) 394-2795; (315) 536-0850. FAX: (315) 536-3299. Permittee: Pegasus Broadcast Associates L.P. Group owner: Pegasus Broadcast Television L.P. (acq 1993; $10,000; 2-15-93).

York

ADI No. 44; see Harrisburg-York-Lancaster-Lebanon market

WHTM-TV—See Harrisburg.

WPMT—ch 43, 2,140 kw vis, 214 kw aur, ant 1,361t/948g. TL: N40 01 38 W76 36 00. On air date: Dec 22, 1952. 2005 S. Queen St. (17403). (717) 843-0043. FAX: (717) 843-9741; TWX: 510-657-4217. Licensee: Channel 43 Licensee Inc. Group owner: Renaissance Communications (acq 3-30-90); $13,475,000). ■ Net: Fox. Rep: Petry. Wash atty: Nixon, Hargrave, Devans & Doyle. ■ Michael Filkenstein, pres; John A. Riggle, gen mgr; John Paiva, gen sls mgr; Dave Farish, prom mgr; John Sterling, chief engr. ■ On 68 CATVs—422,500 subs.

Rhode Island

Block Island

ADI No. 45; see Providence-New Bedford market

WOST-TV—ch 69, 17.8 kw vis, 1.8 kw aur, ant 125t. TL: N41 10 30 W71 34 10. On air date: April 2, 1992. 201 Power St., Providence (02906); Box 1239 (02807). (401) 455-0162; (401) 466-5222. Licensee: Offshore Broadcasting Corp. Ownership: Raymond Yorke, 100%. Wash atty: Cohn & Marks. ■ Ray Yorke, gen mgr.

Providence

ADI No. 45; see Providence-New Bedford market

WFDG—(New Bedford, MA). ch 28, 5,000 kw vis, 250 kw aur, ant 808t/833g. TL: N41 38 13 W70 55 41. Not on air, target date unknown. 39 Foster St. (02740). Permittee: Metrovision Inc. Wash atty: Keck, Mahin & Cate.

WJAR—ch 10, 316 kw vis, 50 kw aur, ant 1,000t/940g. TL: N41 51 54 W71 17 15. Stereo. On air date: July 10, 1949. 23 Kenney Dr., Cranston (02920). (401) 455-9100. TWX: 710-381-1765. Licensee: Outlet Communications Inc. (group owner; acq 7-30-86; grpsl). ■ Net: NBC. Rep: Katz. Spone hr monthly. ■ James G. Babb, CEO & chmn; Felix Oziemblewski, CFO; Linda Sullivan, gen mgr; Paul Pabis, opns mgr; Charles Compagnone, gen sls mgr; Paul Rossi, natl sls mgr; Ted Canova, news dir; Tim Chilinski, engrg dir. ■ On 79 CATVs.

WLNE—(New Bedford, MA). ch 6, 100 kw vis, 22.4 kw aur, ant 940t/996g. TL: N41 46 39 W70 55 41. On air date: Jan 1, 1963. 10 Orms St., Providence (02904). (401) 751-6666; (401) 453-8000. FAX: (401) 453-8088; TWX: 710-344-6898. Licensee: Freedom WLNE-TV Inc. Group owner: Freedom Newspapers Inc., Broadcast Division (acq 12-14-82; $15.5 million). ■ Net: CBS. Rep: Petry. ■ Paul B. Kilcullen, vp & gen mgr; Doreen Dawson-Wade, gen sls mgr; Truman Taylor, progmg dir; Scott James, news dir; Philip B. Taylor, chief engr.

WNAC-TV—ch 64, 3,720 kw vis, 372 kw aur, ant 1,033t/900g. TL: N41 52 14 W71 17 45. Stereo. On air date: December 1981. 33 Pine St., Rehoboth, MA (02769). (508) 252-9711. FAX: (508) 252-6210. Licensee: NTG Inc. Group owner: Northstar Television Group Inc. (acq 9-11-89; grpsl); 9-25-89). ■ Net: Fox. Rep: Seltel. Wash atty: Haley, Bader & Potts. ■ Richard F. Appleton, pres; John M. Fignar, vp & gen mgr; Keith Folz, opns mgr, progmg dir & film buyer; Craig Bachman, gen sls mgr; Jon Barcello, natl sls mgr; Deborah Koller, mktg dir; Charles Breeding, chief engr. ■ On 34 CATVs—638,000 subs.

WPRI-TV—ch 12, 316 kw vis, 31.6 kw aur, ant 910t/1,099g. TL: N41 52 37 W71 16 56. Stereo. On air date: March 27, 1955. 25 Catamore Blvd., East Providence (02914-1203). (401) 438-7200. FAX: (401) 434-3761. Licensee: Narragansett Television, L.P. Group owner: Narragansett Capital Inc. (acq 6-30-89). ■ Net: ABC. Wash atty: Reed, Smith, Shaw & McClay. News progmg 14 hrs wkly. ■ Robert F. Finke, vp, gen mgr, progmg dir & film buyer; Robert McCaughey, gen sls mgr; Michael Donahue, natl sls mgr; Margaret Hennessey-Nees, prom dir; Russell Kilgore, news dir; William Hague, chief engr. ■ On 48 CATVs—524,731 subs.

*****WSBE-TV**—ch 36, 1,230 kw vis, 123 kw aur, ant 597t/532g. TL: N41 48 18 W71 28 24. Stereo. Hrs opn: 7 AM-11 PM. On air date: June 5, 1967. 50 Park Ln. (02907). (401) 277-3636. FAX: (401) 277-3407. Licensee: Rhode Island Public Telecommunications Authority. ■ Net: PBS. Wash atty: Schwartz, Woods & Miller. ■ Susan L. Farmer, CEO & gen mgr; Edward P. Grace III, chmn; Albert Corrado, CFO; Dexter B. Merry, chief opns & engrg dir; Leila Mahoney, dev dir & mktg dir; Raymond Fass, progmg dir. ■ On 33 CATVs—230,000 subs. On one trans.

South Carolina

Allendale

ADI No. 110; see Augusta, GA market

*****WEBA-TV**—ch 14, 661 kw vis, 111 kw aur, ant 800t/809g. TL: N33 11 13 W81 23 54. On air date: Sept 5, 1967. Rt. 3, Box 380, Barnwell (29812). (803) 259-3245. Licensee: South Carolina ETV Commission. ■ Charles E. Cortez, stn mgr.

Anderson

ADI No. 35; see Greenville-Spartanburg-Asheville, NC-Anderson, SC market

WAXA—ch 40, 2,570 kw vis, 257 kw aur, ant 1,050t/1,020g. TL: N34 38 51 W82 16 13. Stereo. On air date: Dec 1, 1953. 520 U.S. Hwy. 29 Bypass N. (29621). (803) 226-9292. TWX: 810-283-2003. Licensee: WLOS TV Inc. Group owner: Continental Broadcasting Ltd. Rep: Adam Young. ■ Benjamin Diesback, pres; Pat Robinson, vp & gen mgr; Lou Anne Cox, gen sls mgr; Bob Mack, progmg dir; Jim Strigle, chief engr. ■ On 46 CATVs—140,000 subs.

Beaufort

ADI No. 101; see Savannah market

***WJWJ-TV**—ch 16, 851 kw vis, 169 kw aur, ant 1,279t/1,320g. TL: N32 42 44 W80 40 49. On air date: Sept 19, 1975. Box 1165 (29901). (803) 524-0808. FAX: (803) 524-1016. Licensee: South Carolina ETV Commission. ■ Net: PBS. ■ Ronald L. Schoenherr, gen mgr; Michael Brannen, stn mgr & progmg dir; Suzanne Sproatt, news dir; Harry Kramer, chief engr. Co-owned radio: WJWJ-FM.

Charleston

ADI No. 106; see Charleston, SC market

WCBD-TV—ch 2, 100 kw vis, 10 kw aur, ant 1,950t. TL: N32 56 24 W79 41 45. Stereo. Hrs opn: 24. On air date: Sept 25, 1954. Box 879 (29402); 210 W. Coleman Blvd., Mt. Pleasant (29464). (803) 884-2222. FAX: (803) 881-3410. Licensee: Charleston Television Inc. Group owner: Media General Broadcast Group (acq 3-1-83; $8 million; 1-24-83). ■ Net: ABC. Rep: MMT. Wash atty: Cohn & Marks. ■ J. William Evans III, pres & gen mgr; Richard Fordham, opns mgr; Douglas M. Pinkerton, gen sls mgr; Michael Cline, natl sls mgr; Stephen Gleason, prom mgr & progmg dir; Mac Thompson, news dir. ■ On 9 CATVs—83,724 subs.

WCIV—ch 4, 100 kw vis, 20 kw aur, ant 1,958t/1,958g. TL: N32 55 28 W79 41 58. Stereo. On air date: Oct 23, 1962. Box 22165 (29413); 888 Allbritton Blvd., Mt. Pleasant (29464). (803) 881-4444. FAX: (803) 849-2507. Licensee: First Charleston Corp. Group owner: Allbritton Communciations Co. (acq 1-26-76; grpsl). ■ Net: NBC. Rep: Katz Continental. Wash atty: Hogan & Hartson. ■ Stephen G. Brock, pres & gen mgr; Celia Shaw, stn mgr & progmg dir; Peter Carnes, gen sls mgr; Wendy Crandall, prom mgr; Deborah Tibbetts, news dir; Joe Papp, chief engr. ■ On 26 CATVs—15,000 subs. ■ Rates: $1,500; 350; 120.

WCSC-TV—ch 5, 100 kw vis, 20 kw aur, ant 1,958t. TL: N32 55 28 W79 41 58. Hrs opn: 24. On air date: June 19, 1953. 485 E. Bay St. (29402); Box 186 (29401). (803) 723-8371. FAX: (803) 723-0074; (803) 722-7537. Licensee: Jefferson-Pilot Communications Co. Ownership: William E. Blackwell (acq 9-3-93; $15.5 million; 9-27-93). ■ Net: CBS. Rep: Petry. Wash atty: Tierney & Swift. News staff 30; news progmg 17 hrs wkly. ■ James H. Smith, gen mgr; Charlie Thompson, opns mgr & progmg dir; Eddie Bolling, gen sls mgr; Andy Hunt, prom dir; Don Feldman, news dir; Beverly Pigg, pub affrs dir; Jack Becknell, engrg dir; Lowell Knouff, chief engr. ■ On 32 CATVs—124,498 subs.

WCTP—ch 36, 148 kw vis, 50 kw aur, ant 764t. TL: N32 47 15 W79 51 00. Not on air, target date unknown. 204 Grove St., (29403). Permittee: Caro Broadcasting Ltd. Ownership: Lee D. Andrews, 40%.; Elise Davis McFarland, 20%; David H. Wagner, 40%

***WITV**—ch 7, 310 kw vis, 31 kw aur, ant 1,850t. TL: N32 55 28 W79 41 58. On air date: Jan 19, 1964. Box 11000, Columbia (29211). (803) 737-3200; (803) 737-3500. Licensee: South Carolina ETV Commission. ■ Net: PBS. Wash atty: Dow, Lohnes & Albertson. ■ Henry J. Cauthen, gen mgr; Walter L. Morring, stn mgr.

WTAT-TV—ch 24, 5,000 kw vis, 497.5 kw aur, ant 1,800t/1,800g. TL: N32 56 24 W79 41 45. Stereo. On air date: Sept 7, 1985. 4301 Arco Ln. (29418). (803) 744-2424. FAX: (803) 554-9649; Licensee: Act III Broadcasting of Charleston Inc. Group owner: Act III Broadcasting Inc. (acq 9-14-89; $5 million; 10-2-89). ■ Net: Fox. Rep: Seltel. Wash atty: Minkin & Snyder. ■ P. J. Ryal, vp & gen mgr; William Littleton, opns mgr, progmg dir, news dir & pub affrs dir; Otis M. Pickett III, gen sls mgr; Jeff Tallman, mktg dir; Mark Bradley, prom dir; G. Clarke Holmes, chief engr. ■ On 15 CATVs—124,000 subs.

Columbia

ADI No. 86; see Columbia, SC market

WACH—ch 57, 5,000 kw vis, 500 kw aur, ant 633t/623g. TL: N34 02 39 W80 59 52. Stereo. On air date: Sept 1, 1981. 1221 Sunset Blvd., West Columbia (29169). (803) 791-5757. FAX: (803) 796-1120; TWX: 810-881-0003. Licensee: Elcom of South Carolina Inc. Group owner: Ellis Communications (acq 10-7-93; $15 million with WEVU(TV) Naples, FL; 10-25-93). ■ Net: Fox. Rep: Seltel. Wash atty: Cordon & Kelly. ■ Walter K. Flynn, pres; Murray Michaels, vp & progmg dir; C. Joseph Tonsing, gen mgr; Jack Colgrove, opns mgr; David Godbout, gen sls mgr; Lynn Rada, prom mgr; Lee Lathem, chief engr. ■ Rates: $400; 160; 75.

WIS—ch 10, 316 kw vis, 63.2 kw aur, ant 1,546t/1,526g. TL: N34 07 27 W80 45 25. Stereo. (CP: 316 kw vis, 63.1 kw aur) Hrs opn: 24. On air date: Nov 7, 1953. 1111 Bull St. (29201); Box 367 (29202). (803) 799-1010. FAX: (803) 758-1155. Licensee: Cosmos Broadcasting Corp. (group owner). ■ Net: NBC. Rep: Harrington, Righter & Parsons. Wash atty: Dow, Lohnes & Albertson. News staff 35; news progmg 15 hrs wkly. ■ Ron Loewen, vp & gen mgr; Coby Cooper, opns dir; David Harbert, gen sls mgr; Jenny Maxwell, prom mgr & adv dir; Diane K. Bagwell, progmg dir; Randy Covington, news dir; John Augustine, chief engr. ■ On 99 CATVs—351,000 subs.

WLTX—ch 19, 5,000 kw vis, 500 kw aur, ant 1,749t/1,706g. TL: N34 05 49 W80 45 51. On air date: Sept 1, 1953. Drawer M (29209). (803) 776-3600. FAX: (803) 783-2971; (803) 266-2629. Licensee: Lewis Broadcasting Corp. (group owner; acq 10-18-78; $3,987,500; 11-6-78). ■ Net: CBS. Rep: Petry. Wash atty: Pierson, Ball & Dowd. ■ J. Curtis Lewis Jr., pres; Richard Laughridge, gen mgr; Gene Upright, progmg dir & film buyer; Carolyn Powell, news dir; William F. Aull, chief engr. ■ On 20 CATVs—115,572 subs. On 5 trans.

WOLO-TV—ch 25, 3,550 kw vis, 355 kw aur, ant 830t. TL: N34 03 23 W80 58 49. On air date: Oct 1, 1961. Box 4217, 5807 Shakespeare Rd. (29240). (803) 754-7525. FAX: (803) 754-6147. Licensee: South Carolina Broadcasting Partners (acq 7-20-92). ■ Net: ABC. Rep: Katz. Wash atty: Jeff Malickson. ■ Cy N. Bahakel, pres; Carl V. Bruce, gen mgr; Dave Aiken, opns mgr & progmg mgr; Jerry Kelly, gen sls mgr; Steve Robertson, rgnl sls mgr; Pete Poore, news dir; Christy Mason, pub affrs dir; Scott Clarke, chief engr. ■ On 30 CATVs—140,000 subs. On one trans.

***WRLK-TV**—ch 35, 513 kw vis, 51 kw aur, ant 1,030t/999g. TL: N34 07 07 W80 56 12. Hrs opn: 18. On air date: Sept 5, 1966. Box 11000, (29201). (803) 737-3200; (803) 737-3500. Licensee: South Carolina ETV Commission. ■ Net: PBS. Wash atty: Dow, Lohnes & Albertson. ■ Henry J. Cauthen, pres; Ronald L. Schoenherr, sr vp; Thomas L. Clark, vp opns; Kathy Gardner-Jones, vp prom; Jesse Bowers, vp progmg; Tom Fowler, news dir; Charlton W. Bowers, vp engrg.

Conway

ADI No. 136; see Florence-Myrtle Beach market

***WHMC**—ch 23, 1,740 kw vis, 174 kw aur, ant 820t/839g. TL: N33 57 05 W79 06 31. On air date: Sept 2, 1980. Box 11000, Columbia (29211). (803) 737-3200; (803) 737-3500. Licensee: South Carolina Education TV Commission. ■ Net: PBS. ■ Henry J. Cauthen, gen mgr; Robert Cooper, stn mgr.

Florence

ADI No. 136; see Florence-Myrtle Beach market

WBTW—ch 13, 316 kw vis, 31.6 kw aur, ant 1,950t/2,000g. TL: N34 22 02 W79 19 22. On air date: Oct 18, 1954. 3430 TV Rd. (29501-0013). (803) 662-1565. TWX: 810-662-2212. Licensee: Spartan Radiocasting. Group owner: Spartan Radiocasting Co. Inc. ■ Net: CBS. Rep: Katz. Wash atty: Covington & Burling. ■ Jim Carthuers, gen mgr & film buyer; Luke Kirchen, gen sls mgr; Michelle Smith, prom mgr; Cecil Chandler, news dir; Doug Crall, chief engr. ■ On 22 CATVs. ■ Rates: $800; 500; 175.

WFIL—ch 21, 5,000 kw vis, 1,000 kw aur, ant 1,989t. TL: N33 55 14 W79 32 08. Not on air, target date unknown. Box 3806 (29502). (803) 669-2900. Permittee: Atlantic Media Group. Ownership: C. Lenoir Sturkie (acq 7-30-93; 8-23-93).

***WJPM-TV**—ch 33, 646 kw vis, 64.6 kw aur, ant 791t/798g. TL: N34 16 46 W79 44 37. On air date: Sept 3, 1967. Box 11000, Columbia (29211). (803) 737-3200; (803) 737-3500. Licensee: South Carolina ETV Commission. ■ Net: PBS. ■ Henry J. Cauthen, gen mgr; Ike Johnson, stn mgr.

WPDE-TV—ch 15, 1,290 kw vis, 129 kw aur, ant 1,948t/2,008g. TL: N34 21 53 W79 19 49. On air date: Nov 22, 1980. 3215 S. Cashua Dr. (29501). (803) 665-1515. TWX: 810-662-2205. Licensee: Diversified Communications (group owner; acq 8-13-85; $14.5 million; 6-3-85). ■ Net: ABC. Rep: Blair. Wash atty: Dow, Lohnes & Albertson. ■ Mike Reed, vp, gen mgr & gen sls mgr; Carl Jackson, opns mgr; Gary Nilsen, prom mgr; Linda McCaskill, progmg dir; Matt James, news dir; Bill Elks, chief engr. ■ On 33 CATVs—137,341 subs.

Greenville

ADI No. 35; see Greenville-Spartanburg-Asheville, NC-Anderson, SC market

WAXA—See Anderson.

WGGS-TV—ch 16, 1,120 kw vis, 112 kw aur, ant 1,151t/158g. TL: N34 56 26 W82 24 41. Hrs opn: 19. On air date: October 1972. Box 1616 (29602); 3409 Rutherford Rd., Taylors (29687). (803) 244-1616. FAX: (803) 292-8481. Licensee: Carolina Christian Broadcasting Inc. (group owner). Wash atty: Fisher, Wayland, Cooper & Leader. ■ James H. Thompson, pres & gen mgr; Joanne Thompson, vp; William A. Garthwaite, opns mgr; Bill Rainey, rgnl sls mgr; Greg West, prom dir; Hugh McLean, progmg dir; Gene Gibson, chief engr. ■ On 31 CATVs—181,000 subs.

WHNS—(Asheville, NC). ch 21, 3,390 kw vis, 398 kw aur, ant 2,509t/1,604g. TL: N35 10 56 W82 40 56. Hrs opn: 24. On air date: Apr 1, 1984. 21 Interstate Ct., Greenville, SC (29615); Central Office Park, Suite 105, 56 Central Ave., Asheville, NC (28801). (803) 288-2100; (704) 258-2100. FAX: (803) 297-0728; (704) 253-2570. Licensee: Cannell Communications L.P. (group owner; acq 10-10-90). ■ Net: Fox. Wash atty: Dow, Lohnes & Albertson. ■ William A. Schwartz, pres; R. Kent Replogle, vp & gen mgr; Joseph A. Shaffer, stn mgr & progmg dir; Rich Bunaro, gen sls mgr; Joe Chaplinski, natl sls mgr; Joe Heaton, prom mgr; Linda Nicodemus, pub affrs dir; Jerry Garvin, chief engr. ■ On 72 CATVs—381,747 subs.

WLOS—(Asheville, NC). ch 13, 170 kw vis, 19.6 kw aur, ant 2,804t/339g. TL: N35 25 32 W82 45 25. On air date: Sept 18, 1954. Box 1300, Asheville, NC (28802); 288 Macon Ave., Asheville, NC (28804). (704) 255-0013. FAX: (704) 255-4612. Licensee: WLOS Inc. Group owner: Continental Broadcasting Ltd. (acq 4-87; $50 million; 3-3-87). ■ Net: ABC. Rep: Harrington, Righter & Parsons. Wash atty: Hogan & Hartson. ■ Alan Henry, pres; James R. Conschafter, vp & gen mgr; J. David Bunnell, gen sls mgr; Bob Mackowiak, prom mgr; Clifford Pine, progmg dir; Alan Mason, news dir; James Carrier, chief engr. ■ On 65 CATVs—283,361 subs. On 19 trans.

***WNTV**—ch 29, 1,410 kw vis, 141 kw aur, ant 1,138t/149g. TL: N34 56 26 W82 24 38. (CP: 5,000 kw vis, 500 kw aur, ant 1,286t/297g). On air date: Sept 15, 1963. Box 11000, Columbia (29211). (803) 737-3200; (803) 737-5000. Licensee: South Carolina ETV Commission. ■ Net: PBS. ■ Henry J. Cauthen, gen mgr; David Harrell, stn mgr.

WSPA-TV—(Spartanburg). ch 7, 316 kw vis, 31.6 kw aur, ant 2,001t/258g. TL: N35 10 12 W82 17 27. On air date: Apr 29, 1956. Box 1717, 250 International Dr., Spartanburg (29304). (803) 576-7777. Licensee: Spartan Radiocasting Co. (group owner). ■ Net: CBS. Rep: Blair. Wash atty: Covington & Burling. ■ Nick Evans, pres; Jack West, gen mgr; Greg Rose, gen sls mgr; Bill Shatten, prom mgr; Jimmy Sanders, progmg dir; Ken Elmore, news dir; Bob Richardson, chief engr. ■ On 51 CATVs. On 18 trans. Co-owned radio: WSPA-AM-FM Spartanburg.

WYFF—ch 4, 100 kw vis, 20 kw aur, ant 2,000t/892g. TL: N35 06 40 W82 36 17. Stereo. Hrs opn: 24. On air date: Dec 31, 1953. 505 Rutherford St. (29602). (803) 242-4404. FAX: (803) 240-5329. Licensee: Pulitzer Broadcasting Co. (group owner; acq 2-17-83; grpsl; 3-14-83). ■ Net: NBC. Rep: Katz. Wash atty: Verner, Liipfert, Bernhard, McPherson & Hand. News staff 45; news progmg 15 hrs wkly. ■ David McAtee, vp & gen mgr; Ken Bauder, gen sls mgr; Katheryn Flanson, prom mgr; Kay Hall, progmg dir & film buyer; Jim Kollinger, chief engr. ■ On 62 CATVs—211,000 subs. On 14 trans.

Greenwood

ADI No. 35; see Greenville-Spartanburg-Asheville, NC-Anderson, SC market

***WNEH**—ch 38, 1,780 kw vis, 178 kw aur, ant 771t/691g. TL: N34 22 21 W82 10 03. On air date: Sept 10, 1984. Box 11000, Columbia (29211). (803) 737-3200; (803) 737-3500. Licensee: South Carolina Educational TV Commission. ■ Net: PBS. ■ Karl Leatherman, stn mgr.

Hardeeville

ADI No. 101; see Savannah market

WTGS—ch 28, 5,000 kw vis, 500 kw aur, ant 1,499t/1,527g. TL: N32 02 48 W81 20 27. Hrs opn: 24.

Stations in the U.S.   South Dakota

On air date: Nov 1, 1984. Box 718 (29927); 28 Broadcast Way, Ridgeland (29936). (803) 726-5244. FAX: (803) 726-5694. Licensee: Hilton Head Television Inc. Ownership: American Communications & Television Inc. ■ Net: Fox. Rep: Seltel. Wash atty: Bechtel, Borsari, Cole & Paxson. ■ Coy Eckland, chmn; C.O. Cliff Thompson, gen mgr; Sherrie Fowler, stn mgr; Menesa Pritchett, opns dir, prom mgr & progmg dir; Leon Spencer, rgnl sls mgr; Edward Youmans, chief engr. ■ On 33 CATVs—145,000 subs.

Myrtle Beach

ADI No. 136; see Florence-Myrtle Beach market

WBTW—See Florence.

WGSE—ch 43, 154 kw, ant 630t/600g. TL: N33 50 10 W78 51 08. On air date: July 5, 1984. Box 1243, 803-A Seaboard St. (29577). (803) 626-4300. Licensee: Carolina Christian Broadcasting Inc. (group owner). Wash atty: Fisher, Wayland, Cooper & Leader. ■ James Thompson, pres; Gene Gibson, gen mgr; Jim Simmons, gen sls mgr; Dana Anderson, prom mgr; Diane Barnhill, progmg mgr & pub affrs dir; Chris Hoopes, chief engr. ■ On 6 CATVs—1,350,000 subs. On one trans.

Rock Hill

ADI No. 30; see Charlotte market

WFVT—ch 55., Not on air, target date unknown. 201 S. College #1300, Charlotte, NC (28244). Permittee: Family Fifty-Five Inc. (acq 2-18-93; $314,000; 3-8-93).

*WNSC-TV—ch 30, 676 kw vis, 136 kw aur, ant 688t. TL: N34 50 24 W81 01 07. On air date: Jan 3, 1978. Box 11766 (29731). (803) 324-3184. Licensee: S.C. Educ TV Commission. ■ Net: PBS. ■ Henry J. Cauthen, pres; John Bullington, stn mgr; John Bambach, progmg dir; David Taylor, chief engr.

Spartanburg

ADI No. 35; see Greenville-Spartanburg-Asheville, NC-Anderson, SC market

WAXA—See Anderson.

*WNTV—See Greenville.

*WRET-TV—ch 49, 1,740 kw vis, 174 kw aur, ant 970t/859g. TL: N34 52 09 W81 49 15. On air date: Sept 4, 1980. Box 4069, Media Bldg., USCS (29305-4069). (803) 599-0201. FAX: (803) 578-6957. Licensee: South Carolina Educ TV Commission. ■ Net: PBS. Wash atty: Dow, Lohnes & Albertson. ■ Henry Cauthen, pres; William S. Hart, gen mgr; John Edwards, prom mgr & progmg dir; Don L. Fortner, chief engr.

WSPA-TV—Licensed to Spartanburg. See Greenville.

Sumter

ADI No. 86; see Columbia, SC market

*WRJA-TV—ch 27, 794 kw vis, 157 kw aur, ant 1,163t/1,200g. TL: N33 52 52 W80 16 14. On air date: Sept 7, 1975. Box 1836 (29151-1836). (803) 773-5546. Licensee: South Carolina ETV Commission. ■ Net: PBS. Progmg for the deaf 3 hrs wkly. ■ James L. Barnard, gen mgr & prom mgr; Ed Sexauer, progmg dir; Richard R. Seely, chief engr. ■ On 8 CATVs—47,000 subs. Co-owned radio: WRJA-FM.

South Dakota

Aberdeen

ADI No. 108; see Sioux Falls-Mitchell market

KABY-TV—ch 9, 316 kw vis, 31.6 kw aur, ant 1,401t. TL: N45 06 32 W97 53 30. On air date: Nov 28, 1958. Box 1520 (57401). (605) 225-9200. Licensee: New Vision Television I Inc. Group owner: New Vision Television Inc. (acq 9-7-93; $110 million as part of eight-stn sale; 9-27-93). ■ Net: ABC. ■ Denny Pitman, pres & gen mgr, stn mgr & gen sls mgr; Daryl Sundermeyer, chief engr. Satellite of KSFY-TV Sioux Falls.

*KDSD-TV—ch 16, 1,350 kw vis, 135 kw aur, ant 1,171t/1,062g. TL: N45 29 55 W97 40 35. On air date: Jan 1, 1972. Box 5000, Cherry & Dakota Sts., Vermillion (57069-5000). (605) 677-5861. Licensee: State Board of Directors for Educational TV. ■ Net: PBS. ■ Michelle Van Maanen, gen mgr. ■ On 22 CATVs—15,637 subs. Co-owned radio: KDSD-FM.

Brookings

ADI No. 108; see Sioux Falls-Mitchell market

*KESD-TV—ch 8, 245 kw vis, 51.3 kw aur, ant 751t/801g. TL: N44 20 10 W97 13 41. On air date: Feb 6, 1968. Box 5000, Cherry & Dakota Sts., Vermillion (57069-5000). (605) 677-5861. FAX: (605) 677-5010. Licensee: State Board of Directors for ETV. ■ Net: PBS; CEN. Wash atty: Cohn & Marks. ■ Michelle Van Maanen, gen mgr. ■ On 16 CATVs—26,000 subs. On one trans. Co-owned radio: *KESD-FM.

Deadwood

KIVV-TV—See Lead.

Eagle Butte

ADI No. 152; Minot-Bismarck-Dickinson, ND-Glendive, MT market

*KPSD-TV—ch 13, 316 kw vis, 31.6 kw aur, ant 1,700t/1,696g. TL: N45 03 20 W102 15 40. On air date: September 1973. Box 5000, Cherry & Dakota Sts., Vermillion (57069-5000). (605) 677-5861. Licensee: State Board of Directors for Educational TV. ■ Net: PBS. ■ Michelle Van Maanen, gen mgr. ■ On 9 CATVs—7,002 subs. On one trans. Co-owned radio: *KPSD-FM.

Florence

ADI No. 108; see Sioux Falls-Mitchell market

KDLO-TV—ch 3, 100 kw vis, 20 kw aur, ant 1,690t/1,710g. TL: N44 57 57 W97 35 22. On air date: September 1955. 501 S. Phillips, Sioux Falls (57102). (605) 336-1100. FAX: (605) 334-3447. Licensee: Midcontinent Television of South Dakota Inc. Group owner: Midcontinent Media Inc. ■ Net: CBS. Wash atty: Dow, Lohnes & Albertson. ■ Mike Braker, vp. Satellite of KELO-TV Sioux Falls. Co-owned radio: KDLO-FM.

Huron

ADI No. 108; see Sioux Falls-Mitchell market

KTTM—ch 12, 316 kw vis, 31.6 kw aur, ant 860t. TL: N44 11 39 W98 19 05. On air date: Sept 7, 1991. Suite M7, 375 Dakota S. (57350). (605) 338-0017. Licensee: Independent Communications Inc. Ownership: (group owner). ■ Net: Fox. ■ Charles Poppen, gen mgr; Ed Hoffman, prom dir.

Lead

ADI No. 168; see Rapid City market

KHSD-TV—ch 11, 316 kw vis, 31.6 kw aur, ant 1,890t/605g. TL: N44 19 36 W103 50 12. On air date: Nov 2, 1966. Box 1760, Rapid City (57709). (605) 342-2000. Licensee: Duhamel Broadcasting Enterprises (group owner). ■ Net: ABC. Rep: Katz. Wash atty: Fisher, Wayland, Cooper & Leader. ■ William F. Duhamel, pres & gen mgr; Wes Haugen, gen sls mgr; Monte Loos, progmg dir & film buyer; Helene Duhamel, news dir; Frank Etherington, chief engr. ■ On 12 CATVs—10,000 subs. On 10 trans. Satellite of KOTA-TV Rapid City.

KIVV-TV—ch 5, 100 kw vis, 10 kw aur, ant 1,851t/638g. TL: N44 19 30 W103 50 14. On air date: July 9, 1976. Box 677, Rapid City (57709). (605) 394-7777. FAX: (605) 348-9128. Licensee: KEVN Inc. Group owner: Heritage Media Corp. (acq 8-14-85; grpsl; 6-3-85). ■ Net: NBC. Rep: Petry. Wash atty: Sidley & Austin. ■ Gerry Fenske, pres & gen mgr; Don Nielsen, prom mgr; Bob Slocum, progmg dir; Mike Morgan, news dir; Harvey Sachau, chief engr. Satellite of KEVN-TV Rapid City.

Lowry

ADI No. 152; see Minot-Bismarck-Dickinson, ND-Glendive, MT market

*KQSD-TV—ch 11, 234 kw vis, 28 kw aur, ant 1,040t/826g. TL: N45 16 34 W99 59 03. On air date: Jan 1, 1976. Box 5000, Cherry & Dakota Sts., Vermillion (57069-5000). (605) 677-5861. Licensee: State Board of Directors for Educational TV. ■ Net: PBS. ■ Michelle Van Maanen, gen mgr. ■ On 11 CATVs—10,704 subs. Co-owned radio: *KQSD-FM.

Martin

ADI No. 168; see Rapid City market

*KZSD-TV—ch 8, 275 kw vis, 27.5 kw aur, ant 869t/571g. TL: N43 26 06 W101 33 14. On air date: Feb 8, 1978. Box 5000, Cherry & Dakota Sts., Vermillion (57069-5000). (605) 677-5861. Licensee: S.D. Board of Dir. for Ed. ■ Net: PBS. ■ Michelle Van Maanen, gen mgr. ■ On 10 CATVs—1,573 subs.

Mitchell

ADI No. 108; see Sioux Falls-Mitchell market

KDLT—ch 5, 100 kw vis, 10 kw aur, ant 1,510t/1,569g. TL: N43 37 56 W97 22 21. Stereo. Hrs opn: 19. On air date: June 12, 1960. 3600 S. Westport Ave. Sioux Falls (57116-0196). (605) 361-5555. FAX: (605) 361-3982. Licensee: Heritage Broadcasting Inc. Group owner: Heritage Media Corp. (acq 8-9-87; grpsl; 6-3-85). ■ Net: NBC. Rep: Petry. Wash atty: Akin, Gump, Strauss, Hauer & Feld. News staff 17; news progmg 7 hrs. wkly. ■ Steven M. Herman, pres & gen mgr; Wendy Miles, gen sls mgr; Candy Van Dam, prom mgr; Leslie Elliott, progmg dir; Terry Keegan, news dir; Don Sturzenbecher, chief engr. ■ On 176 CATVs—115,611 subs. On 8 trans. ■ Rates: $400; 50; 30.

Pierre

ADI No. 108; see Sioux Falls-Mitchell market

KPRY-TV—ch 4, 100 kw vis, 20 kw aur, ant 1,240t/1,089g. TL: N44 03 07 W100 05 03. On air date: February 1976. c/o SDTV Inc., Suite 100, 300 North Dakota Ave., Sioux Falls (57102). (605) 336-1300. Licensee: SDTV. Group owner: New Vision Television Inc. (acq 9-7-93; $110 million as part of eight-stn sale; 9-27-93). ■ Net: ABC. Wash atty: Arent, Fox, Kintner, Plotkin & Kahn. ■ Mike Smith, gen mgr.

*KTSD-TV—ch 10, 316 kw vis, 31.6 kw aur, ant 1,601t/1,327g. TL: N43 57 55 W99 35 56. On air date: Aug 1, 1970. Box 5000, Cherry & Dakota Sts., Vermillion (57069-5000). (605) 677-5861. Licensee: State Board of Directors for Educational TV. ■ Net: PBS. ■ Michelle Van Maanen, gen mgr. ■ On 19 CATVs—10,492 subs. On one trans. Co-owned radio: *KTSD-FM.

Rapid City

ADI No. 168; see Rapid City market

*KBHE-TV—ch 9, 39.8 kw vis, 7.2 kw aur, ant 649t/469g. TL: N44 03 09 W103 14 38. On air date: July 1967. Box 5000, Cherry & Dakota Sts., Vermillion (57069-5000). (605) 677-5861. FAX: (605) 677-5010. Licensee: State Board of Directors for Educational TV. ■ Net: PBS. ■ Craig Rasmussen, prom mgr; Michelle Van Maanen, progmg dir; Wayne Nelson, chief engr. ■ On 25 CATVs—23,177 subs. On 4 trans. Co-owned radio: *KBHE-FM.

KCLO-TV—ch 15, 690 kw vis, 69 kw aur, ant 520t/4,201g. TL: N44 04 14 W103 15 01. Stereo. On air date: November 1988. 2497 W. Chicago St. (57702). (605) 341-1500. FAX: (605) 348-5518. Licensee: Midcontinent Television of South Dakota Inc. Group owner: Midcontinent Media Inc. ■ Net: CBS. Rep: Blair. ■ Mike Braker, gen mgr; Pete Karn, opns mgr & chief engr; Perry Groten, news dir.

KEVN-TV—ch 7, 263 kw vis, 26.3 kw aur, ant 669t/623g. TL: N44 04 00 W103 15 01. On air date: July 11, 1976. Box 677 (57709). (605) 394-7777. FAX: (605) 348-9128. Licensee: KEVN Inc. Group owner: Heritage Media Corp. (acq 8-14-85; grpsl; 6-3-85). ■ Net: NBC. Rep: Petry Natl TV. Wash atty: Sidley & Austin. News staff 14; news progmg 6 hrs wkly. ■ Gerry Fenske, pres, gen mgr & gen sls mgr; Don Nielsen, prom mgr; Bob Slocum, progmg dir; Mike Morgan, news dir; Harvey Sachau, chief engr. ■ On 18 CATVs—22,000 subs. On 14 trans. ■ Rates: $425; 165; 65.

KOTA-TV—ch 3, 100 kw vis, 20 kw aur, ant 659t/606g. TL: N44 04 08 W103 15 03. On air date: July 1, 1955. Box 1760 (57709). (605) 342-2000. FAX: (605) 342-7305. Licensee: Duhamel Broadcasting Enterprises (group owner). ■ Net: ABC. Rep: Katz. Wash atty: Fisher, Wayland, Cooper, & Leader. ■ William F. Duhamel, pres & gen mgr; Wes Haugen, gen sls mgr; Monte Loos, progmg dir & film buyer; Helene Duhamel, news dir; Frank Etherington, chief engr. ■ On 9 CATVs—24,000 subs. On 40 trans. Co-owned radio: KOTA(AM).

Reliance

ADI No. 108; see Sioux Falls-Mitchell market

KPLO-TV—ch 6, 100 kw vis, 15 kw aur, ant 1,110t/711g. TL: N43 57 55 W99 36 11. On air date: July 1957. 501 S. Phillips, Sioux Falls (57102). (605) 336-1100. FAX: (605) 334-3447. Licensee: Midcontinent Broadcasting Co. Group owner: Midcontinent Media Inc. ■ Net: CBS. Wash atty: Dow, Lohnes & Albertson. ■ Mike Braker, vp & gen mgr. Satellite of KELO-TV Sioux Falls.

Sioux Falls

ADI No. 108; see Sioux Falls-Mitchell market

KDLT—See Mitchell.

KELO-TV—ch 11, 316 kw vis, 28.8 kw aur, ant 2,000t/1,985g. TL: N43 31 07 W96 32 05. Stereo. Hrs opn: 24. On air date: May 1953. 501 S. Phillips (57102). (605) 336-1100. FAX: (605) 334-3447. Licensee: Midcontinent Television of South Dakota. Group owner: Midcontinent Media Inc. ■ Net: CBS. Rep: Blair. Wash atty: Dow, Lohnes & Albertson. ■ Mike Braker, vp & film buyer; Jay Huizenga, gen sls mgr; Devin Duncan, prom mgr; Jennifer Townsend, progmg dir; Mark Millage, news dir; John Hertz, chief engr. ■ On 127 CATVs—50,000 subs. On 23 trans. Co-owned radio: KELO-AM-FM.

KSFY-TV—ch 13, 316 kw vis, 39.8 kw aur, ant 2,000t/1,985g. TL: N43 31 07 W96 32 05. On air date: July 31, 1960. Suite 100, 300 N. Dakota (57102). (605) 336-1300. FAX: (605) 336-1300. Licensee: New Vision Television I Inc. Group owner: New Vision Television Inc. (acq 9-7-93; $110 million as part of eight-stn sale; 9-27-93). ■ Net: ABC. Rep: Katz. Wash atty: Arent, Fox, Kintner, Plotkin & Kahn. ■ David Bradley Jr., pres; Mike Smith, gen mgr; Nick Kellen, gen sls mgr; Marge Hokenstad, progmg dir; Tom Claycomb, news dir; Gene Schultz, chief engr. ■ On 166 CATVs. On 7 trans.

KTTW—ch 17, 19.5 kw vis, 1.95 kw aur, ant 495t/499g. TL: N43 29 20 W96 45 40. Stereo. (CP: 196.7 kw vis). On air date: Nov 1, 1986. Box 5103 (57117-5103); Suite A, 2000 W. 42nd St. (57105). (605) 338-0017. Licensee: Independent Communications Inc. (acq 3-9-88). ■ Net: Fox. Wash atty: Reddy, Begley & Martin. ■ Charles Poppen, gen mgr; Ed Hoffman, prom dir. ■ On 9 CATVs.

Vermillion

ADI No. 140; see Sioux City, IA market

*KUSD-TV—ch 2, 100 kw vis, 20 kw aur, ant 760t/656g. TL: N43 03 00 W96 47 12. On air date: July 5, 1961. Box 5000, Cherry & Dakota Sts. (57069). (605) 677-5861. FAX: (605) 677-5010. Licensee: State Board of Directors for ETV. ■ Net: PBS, CEN. Wash atty: Cohn & Marks. ■ Craig Rasmussen, prom mgr; Michelle Van Maanen, progmg dir; Wayne Nelson, chief engr. ■ On 6 CATVs—24,233 subs. On 21 trans. Co-owned radio: KUSD-AM-FM.

Tennessee

Chattanooga

ADI No. 85; see Chattanooga market

WDEF-TV—ch 12, 316 kw vis, 37.1 kw aur, ant 1,260t/641g. TL: N35 08 06 W85 19 25. On air date: Apr 25, 1954. 3300 Broad St. (37408). (615) 267-3392. FAX: (615) 267-0009. Licensee: Roy H. Park Broadcasting of Tennessee Inc. Group owner: Park Communications Inc. (acq 2-12-64; grpsl; 2-24-64). ■ Net: CBS. Rep: Blair. Wash atty: Wiley, Rein & Fielding. ■ Mark Keown, vp & gen mgr; Chris Aldridge, gen sls mgr; Teresa Dinger, prom mgr; Doris Ellis, progmg dir & film buyer; Tony Windsor, news dir; William M. Christman, chief engr. ■ On 51 CATVs—200,104 subs. Co-owned radio: WDEF-AM-FM.

WDSI-TV—ch 61, 5,000 kw vis, 500 kw aur, ant 1,214t. TL: N35 12 34 W85 16 39. On air date: Jan 24, 1972. 2401 E. Main St. (37404). (615) 697-0661. FAX: (615) 697-0650. Licensee: Pegasus Broadcast Television L.P. (group owner; acq 2-18-93; $21 million with WDBD[TV] Jackson, MS; 3-8-93). ■ Net: Fox. Rep: Seltel. Wash atty: George Shapiro. ■ Bruce Lumpkin, gen mgr; Hoyt Andres, gen sls mgr; Jim Powell, prom dir; Cheryal Morgan, progmg dir; Glenn Coffey, chief engr. ■ On 15 CATVs—129,728 subs. ■ Rates: $150; 120; 50.

WRCB-TV—ch 3, 100 kw vis, 10 kw aur, ant 1,050t/281g. TL: N35 09 40 W85 18 52. Stereo. Hrs opn: 24. On air date: May 6, 1956. 900 Whitehall Rd. (37405-3247). (615) 267-5412. FAX: (615) 267-6840; (615) 756-3148 (NEWS). Licensee: Sarkes Tarzian Inc. (group owner; acq 10-82; $16 million; 10-18-82). ■ Net: NBC. Rep: Katz. Wash atty: Cohn & Marks. News progmg 20 hrs wkly. ■ Tom Tarzian, chmn; Tom Tolar, pres; Bob Davis, CFO; Vinnie Fusco, opns mgr; Doug Short, gen sls mgr; Cindy McCashin, prom mgr; Vinnie Fox, progmg dir; Bill Wallace, news dir; Judy Smith, pub affrs dir; Ed Aslinger, chief engr. ■ On 40 CATVs—200,000 subs.

*WTCI—ch 45, 1,480 kw vis, 148 kw aur, ant 1,200t. TL: N35 12 26 W85 16 52. Stereo. (CP: Ant 1,075t). Hrs opn: 18. On air date: Mar 8, 1970. 4411 Amnicola Hwy. (37406). (615) 629-0045. Licensee: The Greater Chattanooga PTV Corp. (acq 7-84). ■ Net: PBS. Wash atty: Dow, Lohnes & Albertson. ■ Victor A. Hogstrom, pres & gen mgr; Bob Williams, opns mgr; Yvonne Derrickson, vp dev; Brian Connell, mktg mgr; Marilyn Foresythe, prom mgr; Kelly Wilde, vp adv & vp progmg; J. Milton Greaves, pub affrs dir; Bryan Fuqua, vp engrg. ■ On 24 CATVs—250,090 subs.

WTVC—ch 9, 316 kw vis, 31.6 kw aur, ant 1,040t/278g. TL: N35 09 41 W85 19 03. Stereo. Hrs opn: 24. On air date: Feb 11, 1958. Box 1150 (37401); 410 W. Sixth St. (37402). (615) 756-5500. FAX: (615) 757-7400; (615) 757-7401. Licensee: Freedom TV-Sub Inc. Group owner: Freedom Newspapers Inc., Broadcast Division (acq 12-13-83; grpsl; 1-2-84). ■ Net: ABC. Rep: Petry. Wash atty: Latham & Watkins. News staff 50; news progmg 17 hrs wkly. ■ Jim Rosse, pres; Jerry Lingerfelt, gen mgr & gen sls mgr; Dennis W. Brown, opns mgr & chief engr; Ronnie Minton, prom mgr; Jim Church, news dir; Marcia Kling, pub affrs dir. ■ On 101 CATVs—137,838 subs.

Cleveland

ADI No. 85; see Chattanooga market

WFLI-TV—ch 53, 1,306 kw vis, 131 kw aur, ant 1,065t/1,016g. TL: N34 55 57 W84 58 32. Hrs opn: 24. On air date: May 25, 1987. Box 302, 4654 Cohutta-Varnell Rd., Cohutta, GA (30710). (706) 694-3337. FAX: (706) 694-4112. Licensee: WFLI Inc. Ownership: William E. Benns Jr., 24.4%; Ying Hua Benns, 70.7% Rep: Roslin. Wash atty: Mullin, Rhyne, Emmons & Topel. ■ Ying Hua Benns, pres & gen mgr; Dale Anthony, gen sls mgr & film buyer; Kim Duncan, prom mgr & progmg dir; Jeff Gregory, chief engr. ■ On 13 CATVs—150,000. Co-owned radio: WFLI(AM).

Cookeville

ADI No. 33; see Nashville market

*WCTE—ch 22, 1,320 kw vis, 77.6 kw aur, ant 1,394t/804g. TL: N36 10 26 W85 20 37. On air date: Aug 21, 1978. Box 2040 (38502). (615) 528-2222. Licensee: Upper Cumberland Broadcast Council (acq 12-20-85; 11-18-85). ■ Net: PBS. ■ Richard Castle, gen mgr & progmg dir; Donna Castle, prom mgr; Robert Huddleston, chief engr. ■ On 15 CATVs.

WKZX—ch 28, 229 kw vis, 22.9 kw aur, ant 869t/623g. TL: N36 07 33 W85 17 33. On air date: Sept 3, 1993. Television Station WKZX, 404 E. Broad (38501). (615) 520-0228. FAX: (615) 372-8917. Licensee: Inavision Broadcasting Inc. (acq 6-29-93; $100,000; 7-19-93). ■ Brian Welch, gen mgr.

Crossville

ADI No. 63; see Knoxville market

WINT-TV—ch 20, 14.8 kw vis, 1.4 kw aur, ant 157t. TL: N35 56 12 W85 00 46. Box 608 (38557). (615) 484-1220. Licensee: WINT-TV Inc. Ownership: Larry D. Hudson, 90%; John Cunningham, 10% (acq 6-3-83; 3-4-85). Wash atty: Dow, Lohnes & Albertson. ■ John A. Cunningham, gen mgr & chief engr; James Young, gen sls mgr; Rita L. Young, progmg dir; Robin Cunningham, film buyer; Wilda Gobb, news dir. ■ On 15 CATVs. On one trans.

Greeneville

ADI No. 91; see Bristol-Kingsport-Johnston City-Greenville market

WEMT—ch 39, 3,020 kw vis, 302 kw aur, ant 2,628t/141g. TL: N36 01 24 W82 42 56. Stereo. Hrs opn: 24. On air date: Nov 8, 1985. Box 3489 CRS, Johnson City (37601-3489); 3206 Hanover Rd., Johnson City (37602). (615) 283-3900. FAX: (615) 283-4938. Licensee: MaxEncore of Tri-Cities L.P. Ownership: John Trinder (acq 12-6-93; $3 million; 12-20-93). ■ Net: Fox. Rep: Katz. Wash atty: Larry Perry. ■ Ed Groves, vp & gen mgr; Paul Bantston, gen sls mgr; Gary Hlavacek, natl sls mgr; Matt Laws, prom dir; Julie Bestry, progmg dir; Jim Hartline, chief engr. ■ On 85 CATVs—200,000 subs. ■ Rates: $600; 150; 50.

Hendersonville

ADI No. 33; see Nashville market

WPGD—ch 50, 4,508 kw vis, 500 kw aur, ant 770t. TL: N36 28 02 W86 28 53. Hrs opn: 24. On air date: Sept 23, 1992. Not on air, target date unknown. Box 957, 221 Music Mountain Rd., Gallatin (37066-0957). (615) 230-9743. FAX: (615) 230-7372. Permittee: Sonlight Broadcasting System Inc. (acq 7-27-89; grpsl; 8-14-89). ■ Stuart J. Roth, CEO; Jay Sekulow, chmn; Stephen Box, CFO; J. Tom Park, stn mgr & chief engr. ■ On 24 CATVS—350,000 subs. On one trans.

Jackson

ADI No. 185; see Jackson, TN market

WBBJ-TV—ch 7, 316 kw vis, 31.6 kw aur, ant 1,060t/1,065g. TL: N35 38 15 W88 41 32. On air date: Mar 5, 1955. Box 2387 (38302); 346 Muse St. (38301). (901) 424-4515. FAX: (901) 424-9299. Licensee: Tennessee Broadcasting Partners (acq 7-20-92). ■ Net: ABC. Rep: Katz. Wash atty: Brown, Cahill, Kasswell, Bernstein & Effros. ■ Cy N. Bahakel, pres; Tommy Spain, gen mgr & film buyer; Pat McAlpin, prom mgr; Tom Britt, news dir; Rip Ward, chief engr. ■ On 35 CATVs—53,820 subs.

WMTU—ch 16, 589 kw vis, 58.9 kw aur, ant 1,932t. TL: N35 31 33 W88 47 10. (CP: 4,680 kw vis, 468 kw aur, ant 1,079t, TL: N35 47 22 W89 06 14). On air date: Apr 16, 1985. 2876 Directors Cove, Memphis (38131). (901) 664-1600. TWX: 810-591-0009. Licensee: Television Marketing Group of Jackson Inc. Group owner: Chesapeake Bay Holding Co. (acq 3-19-92; grpsl; 4-6-92). ■ Net: Fox. ■ Jack Peck, gen mgr; Joe Mazza, gen sls mgr. ■ On 14 CATVs—39,848 subs. ■ Rates: $70; 55; 25.

Jellico

ADI No. 63; see Knoxville market

WPMC—ch 54, 28.8 kw vis, 3.9 kw aur, ant 1,007t. TL: N36 30 26 W84 02 36. (CP: 20 kw vis, ant 1,296t, TL: N36 24 36 W84 10 38). Hrs opn: 24. On air date: Mar 12, 1991. Box 54, One Huddleston Cemetery Rd. (37762). Licensee: Pine Mountain Christian Broadcasting Inc. ■ Rev. Wayne Marler, CEO & pres; Joan Marler, vp; Wayne Marler, stn mgr & gen sls mgr. ■ On 4 CATVs—100,000 subs. ■ Rates: $50; 25; 10.

Johnson City

ADI No. 91; see Bristol-Kingsport-Johnson City-Greeneville market

WJHL-TV—ch 11, 245 kw vis, 30 kw aur, ant 2,320t/228g. TL: N36 25 55 W82 08 15. On air date: Oct 26, 1953. Box 1130 (37605). (615) 926-2151. TWX: 810-575-8551. Licensee: Roy H. Park Broadcasting of the Tri-Cities Inc. Group owner: Park Communications Inc. (acq 6-64; $2.5 million; 6-15-64). ■ Net: CBS. Rep: Blair. Wash atty: Wiley, Rein & Fielding. ■ Roy H. Park, pres; Jack Dempsey, gen mgr; Edward C. Herbert, gen sls mgr; Al Gregory, progmg dir & film buyer; Dennis Fisher, news dir; Carl Dickenson, chief engr. ■ On 73 CATVs—205,000 subs. On 3 trans. ■ Rates: $1,000; 400; 150.

WKPT-TV—See Kingsport, Tenn.

Kingsport

ADI No. 91; see Bristol-Kingsport-Johnson City-Greeneville market

WJHL-TV—See Johnson City, Tenn.

WKPT-TV—ch 19, 1,260 kw vis, 251 kw aur, ant 2,320t/225g. TL: N36 25 54 W82 08 15. Stereo. Hrs opn: 24. On air date: Aug 20, 1969. Box WKPT (37662); 222 Commerce St. (37660). (615) 246-9578. FAX: (615) 246-6261. Licensee: Holston Valley Broadcasting Corp. Group owner: The Home News Co. ■ Net: ABC. Rep: Seltel. Wash atty: Cordon & Kelly/Wiley, Rein & Fielding. News staff 15; news progmg 7 hrs wkly. ■ George E. DeVault Jr., pres & gen mgr; J. Raymond Walker, exec vp & stn mgr; Jack Jeter, rgnl sls mgr; Bob Lawrence, prom mgr; Fred Falin, progmg dir; Betty Payne, news dir

& pub affrs dir; Harold T. Dougherty, vp engrg. ■ On 100 CATVs—200,000 subs. On 10 trans. Co-owned radio: WKTP(AM)-WTFM(FM)-WKPT-AM. ■ Rates: $450; 250; 50.

Knoxville

ADI No. 63; see Knoxville market

WATE-TV—ch 6, 100 kw vis, 15 kw aur, ant 1,489t/1,152g. TL: N36 00 13 W83 56 35. Stereo. On air date: Oct 1, 1953. Box 2349 37901, 1306 N.E. Broadway (37917). (615) 637-6666. TWX: 810-583-0114. Licensee: Nationwide Communications Inc. Group owner: Nationwide Mutual Insurance Co. (acq 4-8-65; $6.8 million; 4-19-65). ■ Net: ABC. Rep: Blair. Wash atty: Fletcher, Heald & Hildreth. News staff 32; news progmg 15 hrs wkly. ■ Steve Berger, pres; Jim Mikels, gen mgr; John Mann, gen sls mgr; David Rosch, prom dir; Larry Cazavan, progmg dir; Bob Morford, news dir; Bob Williams, chief engr. ■ On 108 CATVs—389,608 subs. On 2 trans.

WBIR-TV—ch 10, 316 kw vis, 38 kw aur, ant 1,791t/1,505g. TL: N36 00 19 W83 56 23. On air date: Aug 13, 1956. 1513 Hutchison Ave. (37917). (615) 637-1010. FAX: (615) 637-6280. Licensee: Multimedia WBIR Inc. Group owner: Multimedia Broadcasting Co. (acq 11-16-60; grpsl; 11-21-60). ■ Net: NBC. Rep: Katz. Wash atty: Dow, Lohnes & Albertson. ■ James M. Hart, vp & gen mgr; Chris Gallu, gen sls mgr; Joe Cable, prom mgr; David Cowen, progmg dir; Jim Swinehart, news dir; Robert E. Horton, chief engr. ■ On 88 CATVs—208,162 subs. On 15 trans.

WKCH-TV—ch 43, 2,190 kw vis, 219 kw aur, ant 1,151t/1,080g. TL: N35 59 20 W83 57 45. Hrs opn: 20. On air date: Dec 31, 1983. Box 3809, 109 E. Churchwell St. (37917). (615) 971-4343. FAX: (615) 637-6957. Licensee: Ellis Communications. Group owner; (acq 10-7-93; $15 million; 10-25-93). ■ Net: Fox. Rep: Seltel. ■ Burt Ellis, pres; Ron Inman, vp & vp progmg; Dick Bradley, natl sls mgr; Brad Raney, rgnl sls mgr; Phil Rainey, progmg mgr, news dir & pub affrs dir; Jim Grimes, chief engr. ■ On 45 CATVs—254,600 subs.

***WKOP-TV**—ch 15, 2,240 kw vis, 224 kw aur, ant 1,683t/1,360g. TL: N36 00 19 W83 56 23. Stereo. Hrs opn: 15. On air date: Aug 15, 1990. 1611 E. Magnolia Ave. (37917). (615) 595-0220. FAX: (615) 595-0300. Licensee: East Tennessee Public Communications Corp. ■ Net: PBS, SECA. ■ E. Almer Curtis Jr., pres & gen mgr; Evelyn Clarke, prom mgr; Hop Edwards, progmg dir; Mike Knight, chief engr. ■ On 43 CATVs.

WKXT-TV—ch 8, 316 kw vis, 31.6 kw aur, ant 1,290t/1,073g. TL: N36 00 36 W83 55 57. Stereo. Hrs opn: 24. On air date: Dec 8, 1988. Box 59088 (37950); 6516 Papermill Rd. (37919). (615) 450-8888. FAX: (615) 450-8869. Licensee: Knoxville Channel 8 L.P. Ownership: Phipps Television of Tennessee Inc., 70%. ■ Net: CBS. Rep: Petry. News progmg 15 hrs wkly. ■ Lewis F. Cosby III, gen mgr; David Williams, opns mgr; Earl R. Taylor, gen sls mgr & progmg dir; Ranee Randby, prom mgr; Lewis Cosby, film buyer; Dick Hall, news dir; Robert Glenn, chief engr. ■ On 75 CATVs—275,000 subs.

Lebanon

ADI No. 33; see Nashville market

WJFB—ch 66, 251 kw vis, 528t. TL: N36 09 13 W86 22 46. (CP: 2,240 kw vis, 224 kw aur). On air date: 1989. 200 E. Spring St. (37087). (615) 244-5142. Licensee: Bryant Communications Inc. ■ Joe F. Bryant, gen mgr.

Lexington

ADI No. 185; see Jackson, TN market

***WLJT-TV**—ch 11, 316 kw vis, 63.1 kw aur, ant 640t/496g. TL: N35 45 12 W88 36 10. Stereo. Hrs opn: 17. On air date: Feb 1, 1968. Box 966, Clement Hall, Martin (38237-0966); U.T.-Martin, Martin (38238). (901) 587-7561. FAX: (901) 587-7566. Licensee: West Tennessee Public Television Council Inc. ■ Net: PBS. News staff one; news progmg one hr wkly. ■ Alice Houff, pres; Katrina Cobb, progmg dir; Wayne Gilmer, chief engr. ■ On 61 CATV's—67,000 subs.

Memphis

ADI No. 42; see Memphis market

WFBI—ch 50, 5,000 kw vis, 500 kw aur, ant 800t/768g. TL: N35 09 17 W89 49 20. Not on air, target date unknown. c/o Flinn Broadcasting Corp., 483 S. Highland (38111). (901) 458-8255. Permittee: Flinn Broadcasting Corp. (acq 8-27-90; $220,000; 11-19-90). ■ George S. Flinn, pres.

WHBQ-TV—ch 13, 316 kw vis, 63.2 kw aur, ant 1,000t/1,076g. TL: N35 10 28 W89 50 41. Hrs opn: 24. On air date: Sept 27, 1953. Box 11407, 485 S. Highland St. (38111). (901) 320-1313. FAX: (901) 323-0092; (901) 320-1366 (News). Licensee: Adams TV of Memphis Inc. Group owner: Adams Communications Corp. (acq 1-11-90; $39 million). ■ Net: ABC. Rep: Telerep. News staff 30; news progmg 19 hrs wkly. ■ Timothy M. Lynch, pres, gen mgr, progmg dir & film buyer; Susan Adams, gen sls mgr; John Koski, prom mgr; Dave Janecek, news dir; Larry Coughlan, chief engr. ■ On 110 CATVs—550,000 subs.

***WKNO-TV**—ch 10, 316 kw vis, 56.2 kw aur, ant 1,079t/1,113g. TL: N35 09 17 W89 49 20. Stereo. Hrs opn: 20. On air date: June 25, 1956. Box 241880 (38124-1880); 900 Getwell (38111). (901) 458-2521. FAX: (901) 458-2221. Licensee: Mid-South Public Communications Foundation. ■ Net: PBS. Wash atty: Schwartz, Woods & Miller. ■ Michael LaBonia, CEO & pres; Russ A. Abernathy, opns dir; Charles McLarty, dev dir; Debi Robertson, prom mgr & adv mgr; Rene Garza, progmg mgr; Arthur Smith, chief engr. ■ On 68 CATVs. Co-owned radio: *WKNO-FM, WKNA-FM, WKNP-FM, WKNQ-FM.

WLMT—ch 30, 5,000 kw vis, 500 kw aur, ant 1,000t/1,000g. TL: N35 09 17 W89 49 20. On air date: April 1983. Box 30030 (38130); 2876 Directors Cove (38131). (901) 346-3030. FAX: (901) 346-1451. Licensee: Television Marketing Group of Memphis Inc. Group owner: Chesapeake Bay Holding Co. (acq 3-19-92; debt grpsl; 4-6-92). Rep: Petry. Wash atty: McFadden, Evans & Sill. ■ Jack Peck, vp & gen mgr; Joe Mazza, gen sls mgr; Jim Wright, rgnl sls mgr; Greg Belz, prom mgr; Suzanne Pierce, progmg dir; Doug Henderson, chief engr. ■ On 35 CATVs—260,000 subs.

WMC-TV—ch 5, 100 kw vis, 20 kw aur, ant 1,010t/1,088g. TL: N35 10 09 W89 53 12. Stereo. On air date: Dec 11, 1948. 1960 Union Ave. (38104). (901) 726-0555. FAX: (901) 276-6851; TWX: 810-591-1710. Licensee: Elcom of Memphis Inc. Group owner: Ellis Communications (acq 10-7-93; $65 million with WMC-AM-FM Memphis; 10-25-93). ■ Net: NBC. Rep: Blair. Wash atty: Baker & Hostetler. ■ Richard J. Janssen, pres; Ronald G. Klayman, vp & gen mgr; Joe W. Cooper, gen sls mgr; Kathy Aicher, prom mgr; Bruce Whiteaker, news dir; Michael I. Schwartz, chief engr. ■ On 149 CATVs—383,493 subs. Co-owned radio: WMC-AM-FM.

WPTY-TV—ch 24, 3,020 kw vis, 600.6 kw aur, ant 1,011t/1,043g. TL: N35 12 11 W89 48 16. On air date: Sept 10, 1978. Box 42424, 2225 Union Ave. (38104). (901) 278-2424. TWX: 810-591-1201. Licensee: Clear Channel Television Licenses Inc. (group owner; acq 8-5-92). ■ Net: Fox. Rep: Seltel. Wash atty: Schnader, Harrison, Segal & Lewis. ■ Ed Karlik, pres; Jack Peck, gen mgr & gen sls mgr; Jon Keck, prom mgr; Marshall Hart, progmg dir & film buyer; Stephen W. Pickell, chief engr. ■ On 110 CATVs—372,115 subs. ■ Rates: $400; 200; 40.

WREG-TV—ch 3, 100 kw vis, 20 kw aur, ant 1,000t/1,077g. TL: N35 10 52 W89 49 56. On air date: Jan 1, 1956. 803 Channel 3 Dr. (38103). (901) 577-0100. FAX: (901) 577-0198. Licensee: The New York Times Co. (group owner; acq 8-8-71; $10,966,410). ■ Net: CBS. Rep: Katz. Wash atty: Koteen & Naftalin. ■ Olin F. Morris, pres & gen mgr; Peggy Vyncke, Ronald A. Walter, vps; Ronald A. Walter, stn mgr; Jim Anhalt, vp opns & vp engrg; Pat Schroeder, sls dir & mktg dir; Hugh Pulley, rgnl sls mgr; Stella Fields, progmg mgr; Tim Morrissey, news dir. ■ On 65 CATVs—155,000 subs.

Murfreesboro

ADI No. 33; see Nashville market

WHTN—ch 39, 5,000 kw vis, 500 kw aur, ant 820t/391g. TL: N36 04 54 W86 25 57. On air date: Dec 30, 1983. 14346 Lebanon Rd., Old Hickory (37138). (615) 754-0039. Licensee: Christian Television Network. Wash atty: Gammon & Grange. Sp progmg. News staff one; news progmg 2 hrs wkly. ■ Bob D'Andrea, gen mgr; Brian Glassford, stn mgr & progmg dir; Cardin Hesselton, natl sls mgr; Susan Meredith, pub affrs dir. ■ On 30 CATVs.

Nashville

ADI No. 33; see Nashville market

***WDCN**—ch 8, 295 kw vis, 29.5 kw aur, ant 1,280t/832.5g. TL: N36 02 49 W86 49 49. Stereo. On air date: Sept 10, 1962. Box 120609 (37212-0609). (615) 259-9325. FAX: (615) 248-6120. Licensee: Metropolitan Board of Public Education. ■ Net: PBS. Wash atty: Schwartz, Woods & Miller. ■ Robert L. Shepherd, vp & gen mgr; Diana C. Bayer, dev dir; Jean C. Reid, prom dir; Gaylord L. Ayers, progmg dir & film buyer; Ronald M. Sealy, chief engr. ■ On 60 CATVs—54,648 subs.

WHTN—See Murfreesboro.

WKRN-TV—ch 2, 100 kw vis, 10 kw aur, ant 1,350t/942g. TL: N36 02 49 W86 49 49. Hrs opn: 24. On air date: Nov 29, 1953. 441 Murfreesboro Rd. (37210); Box 2 (37202). (615) 259-2200; (615) 248-7222. FAX: (615) 248-7298; TWX: 810-371-1943. Licensee: Young Broadcasting of Nashville Inc. Group owner: Young Broadcasting Inc. (acq 4-17-89; $42 million; 5-8-89). ■ Net: ABC. Rep: Adam Young. Wash atty: Wiley, Rein & Fielding. News staff 45; news progmg 15 hrs wkly. ■ Vincent Young, chmn; Ronald J. Kwasnick, pres; Bob Cordell, sr vp; Deborah McDermott, vp & gen mgr; Dave Sankovich, gen sls mgr; Jan Wade, mktg dir & progmg dir; Perry Boxx, news dir; Evelyn Keller, pub affrs dir; Gene Parker, chief engr. ■ On 100 CATVs—376,600 subs.

WNAB—ch 58, 5,000 kw vis, 500 kw aur, ant 1,250t. TL: N35 49 03 W86 31 24. Not on air, target date unknown. Rt. 1, Box 63, Hartsville (37074). (615) 374-3170. Permittee: Ruth Payne Carman.

WSMV—ch 4, 100 kw vis, 10 kw aur, ant 1,424t/1,382g. TL: N36 08 27 W86 51 56. Stereo. On air date: Sept 30, 1950. Box 4 (37202); 5700 Knob Rd. (37209). (615) 353-4444. FAX: (615) 353-2343. Licensee: Cook Inlet Communications L.P. Ownership: CITP Holding Inc. (acq 6-17-92). ■ Net: NBC. Rep: TeleRep. Wash atty: Wilmer, Cutler & Pickering. ■ Mike Kettenring, pres & gen mgr; Larry Emsweller, opns mgr; Swan Burrus, gen sls mgr; Carolyn Lawrence, prom mgr; Brenda Jordan, progmg dir; Dan Akens, film buyer; Alan Griggs, news dir; Mike Nichols, chief engr. ■ On 41 CATVs—125,000 subs.

WTVF—ch 5, 100 kw vis, 10 kw aur, ant 1,390t/1,179g. TL: N36 16 05 W86 47 18. Stereo. On air date: Aug 6, 1954. 474 James Robertson Pkwy. (37219). (615) 244-5000. FAX: (615) 248-5207; TWX: 810-371-1168. Licensee: Landmark TV of Tennessee Inc. Group owner: Landmark Communications Inc. (acq 9-12-91; $46 million; 9-30-91). ■ Net: CBS. Rep: Petry. Wash atty: Hogan & Hartson. ■ Lem Lewis, pres & gen mgr; Charlie Orr, opns dir; Robert Clifft, gen sls mgr; Greg Hankins, mktg dir; Pam Case, prom mgr; Mark Binda, progmg dir; Robert Stoldal, news dir. ■ On 93 CATVs—311,928 subs.

WXMT—ch 30, 5,000 kw vis, 500 kw aur, ant 1,410t/1,244g. TL: N36 15 50 W86 47 38. Hrs opn: 24. On air date: Feb 18, 1984. 300 Peabody St. (37210). (615) 256-3030. Licensee: Central Tennessee Broadcasting Corp. Ownership: MT Communications (acq 12-22-88). Wash atty: Wiley, Rein & Fielding. ■ Michael Thompson, pres; Jerry Britton, gen mgr & gen sls mgr; Teresa Davidson, prom mgr; Tracy Stavros, progmg dir; Ray McInturff, chief engr. ■ On 57 CATVs—216,281 subs.

WZTV—ch 17, 3,266 kw vis, 326 kw aur, ant 1,161t/1,063g. TL: N36 08 27 W86 51 56. Stereo. (CP: 3,240 kw vis). On air date: March 1976. 631 Mainstream Dr. (37228); Box 1717 (37202). (615) 244-1717. FAX: (615) 259-3962. Licensee: Act III Broadcasting of Nashville. Group owner: Act III Broadcasting Inc. (acq 1988; $14 million). ■ Net: Fox. Rep: Seltel. Wash atty: Dow, Lohnes & Albertson. ■ Richard Ballinger, pres; Bob Jay, gen mgr & film buyer; Jim Bankston, natl sls mgr; Heidi Cooke, prom dir; Debbie Chadwell, progmg dir; Denise Ragland, pub affrs dir; Ed Murlatt, chief engr. ■ On 90 CATVs—225,000 subs.

Sneedville

ADI No. 63; see Knoxville market

***WSJK-TV**—ch 2, 100 kw vis, 20 kw aur, ant 1,760t/499g. TL: N36 22 52 W83 10 48. Hrs opn: 15. On air date: Mar 15, 1967. 1611 E. Magnolia Ave., Knoxville (37917). (615) 595-0220. FAX: (615) 595-0300. Licensee: East Tennessee Public Communications Corp. (acq 10-1-83). ■ Net: PBS; SECA. ■ E. A. Curtis, pres & gen mgr; Evelyn Clarke, prom mgr; Hop Edwards, progmg dir; Mike Knight, chief engr. ■ On 93 CATVs.

Texas

Abilene

ADI No. 157; see Abilene-Sweetwater market

KRBC-TV—ch 9, 316 kw vis, 31.6 kw aur, ant 851t/543g. TL: N32 17 13 W99 44 20. Stereo. On air date: Aug 31, 1953. Box 178 (79604). (915) 692-4242. FAX: (915) 692-8265. Licensee: Abilene Radio & TV Co. Group owner: Abilene Radio & TV Stns (acq 9-16-53; $500,000; 9-28-53). ■ Net: NBC. Rep: Blair. Wash atty: Kenkel, Barnard & Edmundson. ■ Ken Knox, gen mgr; Mary Cooksey, prom mgr; Jerry Shackleford, film buyer; Downing Bolls, news dir; James Tilley, chief engr. ■ On 40 CATVs. On 2 trans.

KTAB-TV—ch 32, 2,040 kw vis, 610.7 kw aur, ant 918t/757g. TL: N32 16 35 W99 35 39. On air date: Oct 6, 1979. Box 5309 (79608); 5401 S. 14th St. (79605). (915) 695-2777. TWX: 910-897-5439. Licensee: Big Country Television Co. of Abilene Inc. Group owner: Shamrock Broadcasting Inc. (acq 8-17-86; $15.75 million; 10-27-86). ■ Net: CBS. Rep: Katz. Wash atty: Fletcher, Heald & Hildreth. ■ Wayne Roy, gen mgr; Briana Brooks, prom mgr; Bryan Mundy, progmg dir & film buyer; Bob Bartlett, news dir; Leland Oldhausen, chief engr. ■ On 38 CATVs. ■ Rates: $350; 40; 35.

KTXS-TV—(Sweetwater). ch 12, 316 kw vis, 31.6 kw aur, ant 1,401t/1,070g. TL: N32 24 48 W100 06 25. On air date: Jan 30, 1956. Box 2997, Abilene (79604). (915) 677-2281. TWX: 910-897-5401. Licensee: Abilene-Sweetwater Broadcasting. Group owner: Lamco Communications Inc. ■ Net: ABC. Rep: Petry. Wash atty: Koteen & Naftalin. ■ Jackie Rutledge, gen mgr, gen sls mgr & film buyer; David Caldwell, prom mgr; Peggy Carpenter, news dir; Monte Williams, chief engr. ■ On 38 CATVs—83,502 subs. On 2 trans. ■ Rates: $500; 60; 30.

Alvin

ADI No. 10; see Houston market

KHSH-TV—ch 67, 5,000 kw vis, 500 kw aur, ant 1,781t/1,155g. TL: N29 34 06 W95 29 57. Stereo. On air date: Jan 27, 1986. 2522 Highland Sq. Mall (77511). (713) 331-8867. Licensee: Silver Broadcasting of Houston. Group owner: Silver King Communications Inc. (acq 11-13-86); $15 million; 9-29-86). ■ Jeff McGrath, pres; Debra Hunt, vp & gen mgr; Denise Dicks, progmg dir, film buyer & news dir; Glen Dingley, chief engr. ■ On 31 CATVs—243,644 subs.

Amarillo

ADI No. 129; see Amarillo market

*****KACV-TV**—ch 2, 100 kw vis, 10 kw aur, ant 1,499t/1,270g. Stereo. Hrs opn: 18. On air date: Aug 29, 1988. Box 447 (79178); 2408 S. Jackson (79109). (806) 371-5222; (806) 371-5230. FAX: (806) 371-5258. Licensee: Amarillo Junior College District. ■ Net: PBS. Wash atty: Roy Perkins. ■ Joyce Herring, gen mgr; Jeanette Moeller, opns dir; Hilda Patterson, dev dir; Linda Gutherie, dev mgr; Ellen Robertson-Neal, prom dir; Wendell Jones, progmg dir; Cathy Teague, pub affrs dir; Donald H. Ford, chief engr. ■ On 7 CATVs. On one trans. Co-owned radio: KACV-FM.

KAMR-TV—ch 4, 100 kw vis, 10 kw aur, ant 1,420t/1,440g. TL: N35 18 52 W101 50 47. Stereo. On air date: Mar 18, 1953. Box 751 (79189). (806) 383-3321. FAX: (806) 381-2943; TWX: 910-898-4146. Licensee: Cannan Communications Inc. Ownership: Darrold Cannan, 75.9%; Joe Sherrill, 5%; W.W Hamilton, 15%, Joe Protho, 5% (acq 9-1-74; $2.5 million; 8-12-74). ■ Net: NBC. Rep: Blair. Wash atty: Hogan & Hartson. ■ Darrold A. Cannan, pres; William M. Dunaway, vp, gen mgr & progmg dir; Michael DeLier, gen sls mgr; Cynthia Hunt, prom mgr; Lynn Walker, news dir; Ken High, chief engr. ■ On 58 CATVs—115,000 subs.

KCIT—ch 14, 1,280 kw vis, 128 kw aur, ant 1,521t/1,463g. TL: N35 20 33 W101 49 20. Hrs opn: 20. On air date: Oct. 1, 1982. Box 1414, 1015 S. Fillmore (79105). (806) 374-1414. FAX: (806) 371-0408; TWX: 910-898-4102. Licensee: KCIT Acquisition Co. Group owner: BSP Broadcasting Inc. (acq 3-11-91; $2.4 million; 3-25-91). ■ Net: Fox. Rep: Seltel. ■ Pete D'Acosta, pres & progmg dir; Joe Muller, gen mgr; Trent Poindexter, gen sls mgr; Mindy Carrier, prom mgr; Brian Weber, chief engr. ■ On 43 CATVs—95,000 subs. On 10 trans. ■ Rates: $200; 50; 25.

KFDA-TV—ch 10, 316 kw vis, 31.6 kw aur, ant 1,572t/1,493g. TL: N35 17 34 W101 50 42. Stereo. Hrs opn: 20. On air date: Apr 4, 1953. Box 10 (79105-0010); Cherry & Broadway (79108). (806) 383-1010; (806) 383-6397. Licensee: Panhandle Telecasting Co. Group owner: R.H. Drewry Group (acq 10-4-76; $3 million; 9-13-76). ■ Net: CBS. Rep: Petry. Wash atty: Arent, Fox, Kintner, Plotkin & Kahn. News staff 20; news progmg 13 hrs wkly. ■ R. H. Drewry, pres; Larry Patton, vp; Mike Lee, gen mgr, gen sls mgr & progmg dir; Lynne Groom, mktg dir, prom mgr & pub affrs dir; Walt Howard, news dir; Tim Winn, chief engr. ■ On 81 CATVs—146,000 subs. On 22 trans. ■ Rates: $400; 75; 70.

KVII-TV—ch 7, 316 kw vis, 31.6 kw aur, ant 1,703t/1,626g. TL: N35 22 29 W101 52 58. Stereo. On air date: Nov 1, 1957. One Broadcast Center (79101). (806) 373-1787. FAX: (806) 371-7329; TWX: 910-898-4136. Licensee: Marsh Media Inc. Group owner: Marsh Media (acq 3-1-68). ■ Net: ABC. Rep: Katz. Wash atty: Wiley, Rein & Fielding. Sp 2 hrs wkly. ■ James R. McCormick, pres, gen mgr, progmg dir & film buyer; Jackie Smith, opns mgr; John W. Patrick, gen sls mgr; John Morales, prom mgr; Steve Pritchett, news dir; Bill Canady, chief engr. ■ On 74 CATVs—138,372 subs.

Arlington

NEW TV—ch 68., Not on air, target date unknown. 1601 N. 29th, McAllen (78501). Permittee: Metroplex Communications Inc.

Austin

ADI No. 65; see Austin market

KBVO—ch 42, 2,510 kw vis, 251 kw aur, ant 1,290t/1,299g. TL: N30 19 10 W97 48 06. Hrs opn: 20. On air date: Dec 4, 1983. 10700 Metric Blvd. (78758); 10700 Metric Blvd. (78758). (512) 835-0042. FAX: (512) 837-6753. Licensee: Austin Television. ■ Net: Fox. Rep: Telerep. Wash atty: Hogan & Hartson. News staff one; news progmg one hr wkly. ■ Steve Beard, gen mgr, progmg dir & film buyer; Ray McEachern, stn mgr; Dusty Granberry, opns mgr; Joe Killebrew, gen sls mgr; Lori Leamons, prom mgr; Cindie Brooks, news dir; Jim Wynn, chief engr. ■ On 73 CATVs—314,955 subs.

KCFP—ch 54, 4,345 kw vis, ant 876t. TL: N30 19 20 W97 48 03. Not on air, target date unknown. 1702 Fawn Dr. (78741). Permittee: 54 Broadcasting Inc. (acq 3-26-92; 4-20-92).

*****KLRU-TV**—ch 18, 1,860 kw vis, 372.8 kw aur, ant 1,099t/1,183g. TL: N30 19 20 W97 48 10. Stereo. On air date: May 4, 1979. Box 7158 (78713). (512) 471-4811. FAX: (512) 322-3953. Licensee: Capital of Texas Public Broadcasting Council. ■ Net: PBS. Wash atty: Cohn & Marks. ■ Bill Arhos, pres & stn mgr; Judi Cantor, vp dev; Maria Rodriguez, vp progmg; Jack Wells, vp engrg. ■ On 52 CATVs—125,000 subs.

KTBC-TV—ch 7, 316 kw vis, 31.6 kw aur, ant 1,261t/1,114g. TL: N30 18 36 W97 47 33. On air date: Nov 27, 1952. 119 E. 10th St. (78701). (512) 476-7777. FAX: (512) 495-7001. Licensee: Argyle Television Inc. Group owner: Argyle Television Holding Inc. (acq 10-6-93; $335 million; as part of 4-stn sale; 10-25-93). ■ Net: CBS. Rep: Harrington, Righter & Parsons. Wash atty: Wilmer, Cutler & Pickering. Sp one hr wkly. News staff 40; news progmg 15 hrs wkly. ■ Jack Harrison, CEO, pres & gen mgr; Londa Trial, opns dir, progmg dir & film buyer; Steve McDonald, gen sls mgr; Stan Teater, prom mgr & adv dir; Deborah York, news dir; Victor Ovalle, pub affrs dir; Mario Lazzari, chief engr. ■ On 75 CATVs—236,801 subs. On 2 trans.

KVUE-TV—ch 24, 1,950 kw vis, 327 kw aur, ant 1,270t/1,184g. TL: N30 19 00 W97 48 10. Stereo. On air date: Sept 12, 1971. Box 9927 (78766); 3201 Steck Ave. (78758). (512) 459-6521. FAX: (512) 467-7503. Licensee: KVUE-TV Inc. Group owner: Gannett Broadcasting (division of Gannett Co. Inc.) (acq 2-18-86; grpsl; 1-13-86). ■ Net: ABC. Rep: Petry. Wash atty: Pierson, Ball & Dowd. ■ Ardyth R. Diercks, vp & gen mgr; Sam Rosenwasser, gen sls mgr; Debbie Brizendine, natl sls mgr; Dianne Downey, rgnl sls mgr; LisaBeth Schwenk, mktg mgr; Rick Muir, prom mgr; Craig Bean, progmg dir; Carole Kneeland, news dir; Pat Crovisier, pub affrs dir; Mike Wenglar, chief engr. ■ On 35 CATVs—170,000 subs. On one trans.

KXAN-TV—ch 36, 2,000 kw vis, 200 kw aur, ant 1,268t/1,168g. TL: N30 19 33 W97 47 58. Hrs opn: 24. On air date: Feb 12, 1965. Box 490 (78767); 908 W. Martin Luther King Blvd. (78701). (512) 476-3636. FAX: (512) 476-1520; (512) 469-0630. Licensee: Kingstip Communications Inc. Group owner: LIN Broadcasting Corp. (acq 1979; $4.5 million; 5-7-79). ■ Net: NBC. Rep: Blair. Wash atty: Covington & Burling. ■ Jane Wallace, pres, gen mgr & film buyer; Bob McAvoy, opns dir & engrg dir; Bob Stettner, gen sls mgr; Ross Newsome, natl sls mgr; Gwen Kinsey, mktg mgr; Margaret Mohr, prom mgr; Jeff Klotzman, news dir. ■ On 67 CATVs—262,440 subs.

Baytown

ADI No. 10; see Houston market

KRTW—ch 57, 5,000 kw vis, 500 kw aur, ant 1,919t. TL: N29 17 56 W95 14 11. On air date: 1987. 1050 Gemini St., Houston (77058). (713) 212-1077. FAX: (713) 212-1022. Licensee: Pray Inc. Ownership: Bess Harrison, 100% Wash atty: Ward & Mendelsohn. Sp 5 hrs wkly. ■ Eldred Thomas, pres & gen mgr; Leo Lesaca, gen sls mgr, prom mgr & progmg mgr; Linda Leon, pub affrs dir; Todd Loney, chief engr.

Beaumont

ADI No. 137; see Beaumont-Port Arthur market

KBMT—ch 12, 316 kw vis, 31 kw aur, ant 1,049t/1,022g. TL: N30 11 26 W93 53 08. On air date: June 18, 1961. Box 1550 (77704); 525 I-10 S. (77701). (409) 833-7512. FAX: (409) 833-4007. Licensee: Texas Telecasting. Group owner: McKinnon Broadcasting Co. (acq 11-1-76; $2.4 million; 11-15-77). ■ Net: ABC. Rep: Katz. Wash atty: Cohn & Marks. News staff 20; news progmg 7 hrs wkly. ■ Michael McKinnon, pres; Don Davis, opns mgr & prom mgr; Bob Wilson, gen sls mgr; Heather Russell, pub affrs dir; David Cunningham, engrg mgr. ■ On 35 CATVs—70,000 subs. On 5 trans. ■ Rates: $300; 90; 80.

KFDM-TV—ch 6, 100 kw vis, 20 kw aur, ant 960t/1,031g. TL: N30 08 24 W93 58 44. Hrs opn: 24. On air date: Apr 24, 1955. Box 7128, 2955 I-10 E. (77726-7128). (409) 892-6622. FAX: (409) 892-6665; (409) 892-7305 (News). Licensee: Freedom TV-Sub Inc. Group owner: Freedom Newspapers Inc., Broadcast Division (acq 1-4-84; grpsl; 1-2-84). ■ Net: CBS. Rep: Petry. Wash atty: Latham & Watkins. ■ Alan Bell, pres; Larry Beaulieu, gen mgr; Rix Garey, gen sls mgr; Suzanne Wolfrom, natl sls mgr; Gina Hinson, prom mgr; Karen Agnew, progmg dir & film buyer; David Lowell, news dir; Ed Smith, pub affrs dir; Richard Kihn, chief engr. ■ On 17 CATVs.

*****KITU**—ch 34, 1,170 kw vis, 117 kw aur, ant 1,023t/1,046g. TL: N30 10 41 W93 54 26. On air date: June 21, 1986. Box 158, Mauriceville (77626). (409) 745-3434. Licensee: Community Educational Television Inc. Wash atty: Colby May. ■ John DeCasoria, pres; Richard S. Tallent, gen mgr & chief engr; Martha Tallent, progmg dir.

KJAC-TV—(Port Arthur). ch 4, 100 kw vis, 20 kw aur, ant 1,184t/1,225g. TL: N30 09 31 W93 59 11. On air date: Oct 22, 1957. Box 3257, Port Arthur (77643); 2900 17th St., Port Arthur (77642). (409) 985-5557. Licensee: Southeast Texas Broadcasting Corp. Group owner: Price Communications Corp., debtor in possession (acq 7-16-87). ■ Net: NBC. Rep: Seltel. ■ Robert Price, pres; Robert Verde, vp, gen mgr & film buyer; Liz Stobart, rgnl sls mgr; Sarah Ivey, prom mgr & pub affrs dir; Bob Schnarr, progmg dir; Mark Clegg, news dir; Charles Ravell, chief engr. ■ On 38 CATVs—128,695 subs. ■ Rates: $550; 90; 60.

Belton

ADI No. 96; see Waco-Temple-Bryan market

*****KNCT**—ch 46, 479 kw vis, 67.6 kw aur, ant 1,261t/1,126g. TL: N30 59 12 W97 37 47. Hrs opn: 19. On air date: Nov 23, 1970. Box 1800, Telecommunications Bldg., U.S. Hwy. 190 W., Killeen (76540-9990); Hwy. 190 W., Killeen (76542). (817) 526-1176. FAX: (817) 526-4000. Licensee: Central Texas College. ■ Net: PBS. Wash atty: Arter & Hadden. News staff one; news progmg one hr wkly. ■ Max Rudolph, gen mgr; Bill Moss, stn mgr; Brent Moore, opns mgr; Dorothy Calhoon, gen sls mgr; Cliff McCartney, prom mgr; John Wheeler, progmg dir & film buyer; Jodi Ainsworth, pub affrs dir; Ed Loftis, engrg mgr. ■ On 19 CATVs. On one trans. Co-owned radio: *KNCT-FM.

Stations in the U.S.

Big Spring

ADI No. 149; see Odessa-Midland market

KWAB—ch 4, 12.9 kw vis, 1.5 kw aur, ant 380t/497g. TL: N32 15 14 W101 26 40. On air date: Jan 15, 1956. 2500 Kentucky Way (79720). (915) 263-4901. Licensee: MSP Television of Midland-Odessa Inc. Ownership: Midessa Television Co. (acq 9-9-91; $4.85 million with KTPX(TV) Odessa; 9-23-91). ■ Net: NBC. ■ John Foster, gen mgr. Satellite of KTPX(TV) Odessa.

Brownsville

ADI No. 113; see McAllen-Brownsville market

KGBT-TV—See Harlingen.

KRGV-TV—See Weslaco.

KVEO—ch 23, 2,570 kw vis, 1,000 kw aur, ant 1,460t/1,454g. TL: N26 05 59 W97 50 16. Hrs opn: 24. On air date: Dec 19, 1981. 394 N. Expressway (78521). (512) 544-2323. FAX: (512) 544-4636. Licensee: Associated Broadcasters Inc. Group owner: Tom Galloway (acq 10-31-90; grpsl; 11-19-90). ■ Net: NBC. Rep: Seltel. Wash atty: Fletcher, Heald & Hildreth. ■ Tom Galloway, pres; Wayne Elmore, CFO; Clark White, vp; Patti C. Smith, gen mgr, stn mgr & progmg dir; Zee Zepeda, gen sls mgr; Jeff DuBois, prom dir & progmg mgr; John Ross, chief engr. ■ On 5 CATVs—100,000 subs. ■ Rates: $275; 120; 35.

Bryan

ADI No. 96; see Waco-Temple-Bryan market

KBTX-TV—ch 3, 69.2 kw vis, 6.9 kw aur, ant 1,689t/1,544g. TL: N30 33 10 W96 01 50. On air date: May 22, 1957. Drawer 3730 (77805). (409) 846-7777. Licensee: Brazos Broadcasting Co. Ownership: KWTX Broadcasting Co. (KWTX-AM-TV Waco), 50%; Mrs. W.W. Callan, W.C. Mitchell, M.N. Bostick, and B. Varisco, estate, each 10%; John M. Lawrence III & Harry L. Eugene Estate, each 5%. ■ Net: CBS. Rep: Seltel. ■ Thomas Pears, pres; Jim Barroet, gen mgr; Bill Roberts, prom mgr; Lyn Wiland, progmg dir; Jeff Braun, news dir; John Bennett, chief engr. ■ On 22 CATVs—75,000 subs.

KYLE—ch 28, 3,000 kw vis, 500 kw aur, ant 777t. TL: N30 33 58 W95 59 24. Not on air, target date 1994. Box 3008, Suite 504, 1716 Briarcrest Dr. (77805). (409) 846-0165. FAX: (409) 846-0165; (409) 846-1933. Permittee: Silent Minority Group Inc. Wash atty: Gardner, Carton & Douglas. ■ Roger B. Watkins, pres.

College Station

ADI No. 96; see Waco-Temple-Bryan market

*KAMU-TV—ch 15, 22.9 kw vis, 2.29 kw aur, ant 390t/379g. TL: N30 37 48 W96 20 33. On air date: Feb 15, 1970. Texas A&M Univ. (77843). (409) 845-5611. TWX: 910-880-4425. Licensee: Texas A&M Univ. ■ Net: PBS. ■ Rodney L. Zent, gen mgr; Rodger Lewis, progmg dir; Wayne Pecena, chief engr. ■ On 6 CATVs—20,500 subs. Co-owned radio: KAMU-FM.

Conroe

ADI No. 10; see Houston market

NEW TV—ch 55, 5,000 kw vis, 500 kw aur, ant 1,132t. TL: N30 13 46 W95 54 33. Not on air, target date unknown. Apt 10 M, c/o 400 W. 43rd St., New York, NY (10036). Permittee: Carmen Matias.

KTFH—ch 49, 4,100 kw vis, 410 kw aur, ant 1,775t/1,200g. TL: N30 15 45 W95 14 50. Hrs opn: 18. On air date: June 16, 1989. Suite 49, 256 N. Belt, Houston (77060). (713) 820-4900. FAX: (713) 820-4048. Licensee: San Jacinto Television. Ownership: Arlens Insurance Co., 33.5%; Dupont Investment Group-'85, 30%; Timothy Lee Crosby, 24%; Max F. Vigil, 10.5%. Rep: Katz. Wash atty: Pepper & Corazzini. All Sp. ■ Max F. Vigil, pres; Timothy Lee Crosby, gen mgr; Dean Hava, gen sls mgr; Calvin Smith, chief engr. ■ On 43 CATVs—613,768 subs. On one trans.

Corpus Christi

ADI No. 123; see Corpus Christi market

*KEDT-TV—ch 16, 1,480 kw vis, 148 kw aur, ant 970t/996g. TL: N27 39 12 W97 33 15. On air date: Oct 15, 1972. Suite 38, 4455 S. Padre Island Dr. (78411). (512) 855-2213. FAX: (512) 855-3877. Licensee: South Texas Public Broadcasting System. ■ Net: PBS. Wash atty: Schwartz, Woods & Miller. ■ Robert Valerius, chmn; Peter A. Frid, pres & gen mgr; Don Dunlap, opns mgr; Myra Lombardo, dev dir; Anita Hebert, sls dir; Sylvia Coronado, progmg mgr; Jeff Felts, pub affrs dir; Mike Neibauer, chief engr. Co-owned radio: KEDT-FM.

KIII—ch 3, 100 kw vis, 10 kw aur, ant 860t/899g. TL: N27 39 29 W97 36 04. On air date: May 4, 1964. Box 6669 (78466). (512) 854-4733. TWX: 910-876-1470. Licensee: Channel 3 of Corpus Christi Inc. Group owner: McKinnon Broadcasting Co. (7-79; $171,720). ■ Net: ABC. Rep: Katz. Wash atty: Cohn & Marks. Sp 3 hrs wkly. ■ Michael D. McKinnon, pres; Bill Brotherton, vp, gen mgr & stn mgr; Kathryn Childers, prom mgr; Rob Dean, news dir; Fred Hoffman, chief engr. ■ On 12 CATVs. ■ Rates: $450; 275; 75.

KORO—ch 28, 1,450 kw vis, 146 kw aur, ant 762t/750g. TL: N27 45 11 W97 38 14. On air date: Apr 15, 1977. Box 2667 (78403); 102 N. Mesquite (78401). (512) 883-2823. Licensee: Telecorpus Inc. ■ Net: Univision. Rep: Univision. Wash atty: Mullin, Rhyne, Emmons and Topel. Sp 116 hrs wkly. News staff 5; news progmg 5 hrs wkly. ■ Jose R. De Leon, pres; Servando Caballero, gen mgr; Suzel Meadieta, stn mgr; Abel Pacheco, gen sls mgr; Lolly Vela, prom mgr; Javier Colmenero, news dir; Felipe Franco, chief engr. ■ On 10 CATVs.

KRIS-TV—ch 6, 100 kw vis, 10 kw aur, ant 987.5t/989.8g. TL: N27 44 28 W97 36 08. Stereo. On air date: May 22, 1956. Box 840 (78403); 409 S. Staples (78401). (512) 886-6100. TWX: 910-876-1442. Licensee: Gulf Coast Broadcasting Co. Ownership: T. Frank Smith Jr., 78%. ■ Net: NBC, Fox. Rep: Petry. Wash atty: Nixon, Hargrove, Devans & Doyle. News progmg 12 hrs wkly. ■ T. Frank Smith Jr., pres & gen mgr; Dorise Steele, vp & stn mgr; Charlie Brite, gen sls mgr; Manny Alvarez, prom mgr; Frank Smith, Jr., progmg dir; Fred Jordan, news dir; Steve West, chief engr. ■ On 5 CATVs. ■ Rates: $475; 160; 75.

KZTV—ch 10, 316 kw vis, 47.9 kw aur, ant 940t/984g. TL: N27 46 50 W97 38 03. On air date: Sept 30, 1956. Box TV-10, 301 Artesian (78403). (512) 883-7070. FAX: (512) 882-8553. Licensee: K-SIX Television Inc. Ownership: Corpus Christi Broadcasting Inc. (KSIX), 54.266%; Vann M. Kennedy, 29% & others. ■ Net: CBS. Rep: Seltel. Sp one hr wkly. News staff 18. ■ Vann M. Kennedy, pres & gen mgr; Jim Bixler, gen sls mgr; Mary L. Kennedy, prom mgr; Eugene M. Looper, progmg dir & film buyer; Walter Furley, news dir; Les Waters, chief engr. ■ On 10 CATVs. Co-owned radio: KSIX(AM).

Dallas

ADI No. 8; see Dallas-Ft. Worth market

KDAF—ch 33, 5,000 kw vis, 500 kw aur, ant 1,696t/1,529g. TL: N32 35 22 W96 58 10. On air date: July 29, 1984. 8001 Carpenter Freeway (75247). (214) 634-8833. FAX: (214) 905-3213. Licensee: Fox Television Stations Inc. (group owner; acq 3-17-86). ■ Net: Fox. Rep: Petry. Wash atty: Molly Pauker. ■ Kathy Saunders, vp & gen mgr; Carl Cramer, mktg dir; Chris Wolf, prom dir & progmg dir; Renee McmIllion, film buyer; Joe Maggio, chief engr.

KDFI-TV—ch 27, 5,000 kw vis, 500 kw aur, ant 1,690t/1,529g. TL: N32 35 22 W96 58 10. Stereo. On air date: Jan 26, 1981. Box 561427 (75356-1427). (214) 637-2727. FAX: (214) 637-2208 (Sales); (214) 905-1895 (Gen Mgr). Licensee: Dallas Media Investors Corp. (acq 6-27-84). Rep: Adam Young. Wash atty: Dow, Lohnes & Albertson. ■ John McKay, pres & stn mgr; Dan Corken, gen sls mgr; Joe Zambardino, natl sls dir; D. Boone Nerren, rgnl sls mgr; Kim Jenkins, prom mgr; Mark Lamberti, progmg dir; Lisa Attebery, pub affrs dir; Jim Kauffman, chief engr. ■ On 15 CATVs. ■ Rates: $500; 250; 75.

KDFW-TV—ch 4, 100 kw vis, 20 kw aur, ant 1,676t/1,517g. TL: N32 35 06 W96 58 41. Stereo. On air date: Dec 3, 1949. 400 N. Griffin (75202). (214) 720-4444. FAX: (214) 720-3207. Licensee: Argyle Television Inc. Group owner: Argyle Television Holding Inc. (acq 10-6-93; $335 million as part of 4-station sale; 10-25-93). ■ Net: CBS. Rep: Katz. Wash atty: Wilmer, Cutler & Pickering. ■ Jeff Rosser, CEO, pres & gen mgr; Howard Murphy, CFO; Jim Withers, opns dir & engrg dir; Frank Gregg, vp sls; Jim Monroe, mktg dir; Joe Bell, progmg dir; Mike Sechrist, news dir. ■ On 196 CATVs—724,713 subs.

*KDTX-TV—ch 58, 5,000 kw vis, 500 kw aur, ant 1,437t. TL: N32 35 22 W96 58 10. Hrs opn: 24. On air date: June 1986. 2823 W. Irving Blvd., Irving (75061-4236). (214) 313-1333. FAX: (214) 790-5853. Licensee: Trinity Broadcasting of Texas Inc. (group owner; acq 7-86; $1.6 million; 5-6-86). Wash atty: May & Dunne. ■ Paul F. Crouch, pres; Philip Crouch, gen mgr; Steve Fjordbak, progmg dir; Dana Hooper, pub affrs dir; Tee Thomas, chief engr. ■ On 4 CATVs—450,000 subs. ■ Rates: $95; 95.

*KERA-TV—ch 13, 316 kw vis, 31.6 kw aur, ant 1,540t/1,347g. TL: N32 34 43 W96 57 12. Stereo. On air date: Sept 14, 1960. 3000 Harry Hines Blvd. (75201). (214) 871-1390. FAX: (214) 754-0635. Licensee: North Texas Public Broadcasting Inc. ■ Net: PBS. Wash atty: Schwartz, Woods & Miller. ■ Richard J. Meyer, CEO; Michael M. Seymour, stn mgr; Patricia Callahan, vp dev; Don Boswell, vp sls; Roberta Wedlan, vp adv; Sylvia Komatsu, vp progmg; Bill Young, progmg dir; Yolette Garcia, news dir & pub affrs dir; Clyde Miller, vp engrg. ■ On 134 CATVs—63,634 subs. On one trans. Co-owned radio: *KERA-FM.

KHSX-TV—See Irving.

KTVT—See Fort Worth.

KXAS-TV—See Fort Worth.

KXTX-TV—ch 39, 4,470 kw vis, 447 kw aur, ant 1,679t/1,521g. TL: N32 35 07 W96 58 06. On air date: Feb 5, 1968. Box 190307, 3900 Harry Hines Blvd. (75219). (214) 521-3900. FAX: (214) 522-8311. Licensee: KXTX Inc. Ownership: U.S. Media Corp. (acq 1973). Rep: HRP Inc. Wash atty: Fisher, Wayland, Cooper & Leader. ■ Michael Carter, gen mgr; Deborah Murphy, natl sls mgr; Jeff Serio, rgnl sls mgr; Nelson Flanagan, prom mgr & progmg dir; Sarah Kirkham, pub affrs dir; Harold Nash, chief engr. ■ On 202 CATVs—904,000 subs.

WFAA-TV—ch 8, 316 kw vis, 31.6 kw aur, ant 1,680t/1,521g. TL: N32 35 06 W96 58 41. Stereo. Hrs opn: 24. On air date: Sept 17, 1949. Communications Ctr., 606 Young St. (75202-4810). (214) 748-9631; (214) 977-6491 (Traffic). FAX: (214) 977-6268; TWX: 910-861-4133. Licensee: WFAA-TV Inc. Group owner: A.H. Belo Corp., Broadcast Div. (acq 2-50). ■ Net: ABC. Rep: TeleRep. Wash atty: Dow, Lohnes & Albertson. News staff 87; news progmg 19 hrs wkly. ■ Cathy Creany, vp & gen mgr; Kathy Clements-Hill, gen sls mgr; Marc Montoya, natl sls mgr; Yvette Cook-Harris, rgnl sls mgr; Dave Muscari, prom mgr; David Walther, progmg dir; John Miller, news dir; Alva Goodall, pub affrs dir; Beaven Els, chief engr. ■ On 238 CATVs—1,100,000 subs.

Decatur

ADI No. 8; see Dallas-Ft. Worth market

KMPX—ch 29, 5,000 kw vis, 1,000 kw aur, ant 971t/788g. TL: N33 23 30 W97 33 49. On air date: Sept 15, 1993. Box 612066, Dallas (75261). 6221 N. O'Conner Blvd. #102, Irving (75039). (214) 432-0029. Licensee: Word of God Fellowship Inc. (acq 12-7-92). ■ Marcus D. Lamb, pres; John Murdock, progmg dir; David Thompson, chief engr.

Del Rio

ADI No. 36; see San Antonio-Victoria market

KTRG—ch 10, 316 kw vis, ant 1,155t. TL: N29 21 25 W100 22 16. Not on air, target date unknown. Box 246, Concan (78838). (210) 232-6700. FAX: (210) 232-6700. Permittee: Thomas Gilchrist (acq 9-24-93; $10; 10-18-93).

KXII—See Sherman.

Denton

ADI No. 8; see Dallas-Ft. Worth market

*KDTN—ch 2, 100 kw vis, 20 kw aur, ant 1,351t/1,204g. TL: N32 35 22 W96 58 10. On air date: Feb 2, 1988. 3000 Harry Hines Blvd., Dallas (75201). (214) 871-1390. FAX: (214) 754-0635. Licensee: North Texas Public Broadcasting. Ownership: Community Board of Directors, 100%. ■ Net: PBS. Wash atty: Wiley, Rein & Fielding. ■ Richard J. Meyer, CEO; Michael M. Seymour, stn mgr; Patricia Callahan, vp dev; Don Boswell, vp sls; Roberta Wedlan, vp prom & vp adv; Bill Young, progmg dir; Yolette Garcia, news dir & pub affrs dir; Clyde Miller, vp engrg. ■ On 230 CATVs. Co-owned radio: *KERA(FM).

Texas

Directory of Television

Eagle Pass

ADI No. 36; see San Antonio-Victoria market

KVAW—ch 16, 12.6 kw vis, 1.26 kw aur, ant 279t. TL: N28 43 32 W100 28 35. On air date: 1991. Box 788 (78852). (210) 757-0316. Licensee: Juan Wheeler Jr. ■ Juan Manuel Wheeler, gen mgr.

El Paso

ADI No. 100; see El Paso market

KCIK—ch 14, 398 kw vis, 39.8 kw aur, ant 1,981t/367g. TL: N31 48 55 W106 29 20. On air date: August 1979. 3100 N. Stanton St. (79902). (915) 533-1414. FAX: (915) 544-7463; TWX: 629-34797. Licensee: KCIK-TV Inc. (acq 9-25-88). ■ Net: Fox. Rep: ITS. Wash atty: Fisher, Wayland, Cooper & Leader. ■ Don Caparis, pres & gen mgr; Helen Barry, gen sls mgr & mktg mgr; Rebecca Benson, prom mgr; Larry Pepin, progmg dir; Ernie Hart, chief engr. ■ On 9 CATVs—97,000 subs. On one trans.

*__KCOS__—ch 13, 224 kw vis, 22.4 aur, ant 869t/342g. TL: N31 47 15 W106 28 47. On air date: Aug 18, 1978. Box 650, Education (79968); 206 Education Bldg., Univ. of Texas-El Paso (79902). (915) 747-6500. FAX: (915) 747-6605. Licensee: El Paso Public Television Foundation. ■ Net: PBS. Wash atty: Cohn & Marks. ■ Mike Bernstein, chmn; Robert Munoz, pres & gen mgr; Barbara Hakim, CFO; Jay Pilant, opns mgr; Harry Tyler, dev dir; John Schapiro, sls dir; Evelyn Aguilar Springer, mktg mgr; Wende Walker-Witus, progmg mgr; David Enchaniz, chief engr. ■ On 8 CATVs—102,000 subs.

KDBC-TV—ch 4, 100 kw vis, 10 kw aur, ant 1,563t/410g. TL: N31 47 46 W106 28 57. On air date: Dec 14, 1952. Box 1799 (79999); 2201 Wyoming (79903). (915) 532-6551. FAX: (915) 544-2591. Licensee: KDBC-TV L.P. Group owner: Imes Communications (acq 9-13-88). ■ Net: CBS. Rep: Seltel. Wash atty: Arent, Fox, Kintner, Plotkin & Kahn. News staff 25; news progmg 10 hrs wkly. ■ Stan Siegal, vp & gen mgr; Richard Pexton, opns mgr & chief engr; John M. Burton, gen sls mgr; Beverly Dudley, prom dir; Margaret Morgan, progmg dir; Bill Mitchell, news dir. ■ On 11 CATVs—180,000 subs. On 3 trans. ■ Rates: $550; 200; 60.

KINT-TV—ch 26, 2,240 kw vis, 224 kw aur, ant 1,499t/350g. TL: N31 47 46 W106 28 57. On air date: May 5, 1984. 5426 N. Mesa (79912). (915) 581-1126. FAX: (915) 581-1393. Licensee: Paso Del Norte Broadcasting Corp. Ownership: Jose A. Silva Jr., Richard Najera, Jose A. Silva Sr., Gus Rallis, Mary Ponce, Luz Candalaria, Angel Beltran, Jorge Salom, each 12.5%. ■ Net: Univision. Wash atty: Mullin, Rhyne, Emmons & Topel. Sp progmg. News staff 14; news progmg 10 hrs wkly. ■ Martino Silva, chmn; Gus Rallis, pres; Ron McDaniel, gen mgr; Rick Teplitz, rgnl sls mgr; Rene Canter, prom mgr; Sylvia Martinez, progmg dir; Roy Ortega, news dir; Alfredo Duran, chief engr. ■ On 4 CATVs—130,000 subs. Co-owned radio: KINT-FM, KSVE. ■ Rates: $200; 125; 55.

KJLF-TV—ch 65, 1,000 kw vis, 50 kw aur, ant 1,827t/199g. TL: N31 48 55 W106 29 17. On air date: 1991. 6529 Cromo Dr. (79912). (915) 833-0065. Licensee: UN2JC Communications Ltd. Ownership: Sara Diaz Warren, 46%; Jan A. Blomerth, 26%; Peggy A. Brown, 26%. Wash atty: Stuart B. Mitchell. ■ Sara Diaz Warren, pres; John Warren, gen mgr.

*__KSCE__—ch 38, 50.1 kw vis, 5 kw aur, ant 1,827t/172g. TL: N31 48 55 W106 29 17. Hrs opn: 18. On air date: April 15, 1989. 6400 Escondido Dr. (79912). (915) 585-8838. FAX: (915) 533-7403. Licensee: Channel 38 Christian Television. Sp 48 hrs wkly. News progmg 3 hrs wkly. ■ Andrew Paschall, chmn; Grace Rendall, gen mgr, adv dir & progmg dir; David Rendall, dev dir; Dorothy Begin, pub affrs dir; Ruben Madrid, chief engr. ■ Rates: $60; 30; 30.

KTSM-TV—ch 9, 316 kw vis, 42.7 kw aur, ant 1,910t/370g. TL: N31 48 18 W106 28 57. Stereo. Hrs opn: 20. On air date: Jan 4, 1953. 801 N. Oregon St. (79902). (915) 532-5421. FAX: (915) 532-6793. Licensee: Tri-State Broadcasting Co. Ownership: El Paso Community Foundation (acq 3-16-92; no financial consideration with KTSM-AM-FM; 4-6-92). ■ Net: NBC. Rep: Blair. Wash atty: Bryan, Cave, McPheeters & McReynolds. News staff 29; news progmg 7 hrs wkly. ■ Richard Pearson, CEO; Bonnie Barron, CFO; Dan Krieger, stn mgr; Larry Bracher, vp sls; Cathy Franco, prom dir; Udell Vigil, news dir; Cindy Collins, pub affrs dir; Oscar Medina, engrg dir. ■ On 9 CATVs. On 4 trans. Co-owned radio: KTSM-AM-FM. ■ Rates: $700; 225; 60.

KVIA-TV—ch 7, 316 kw vis, 31.6 kw aur, ant 820t/296g. TL: N31 47 15 W106 28 47. On air date: Sept 1, 1956. 4140 Rio Bravo (79902). (915) 532-7777. Licensee: Marsh Media of El Paso. Group owner: Marsh Media (acq 4-9-76; grpsl; 3-8-76). ■ Net: ABC. Rep: Katz Television. Wash atty: Wiley, Rein & Fielding. News staff 25; news progmg 10 hrs wkly. ■ Art Olivas, gen mgr; Dan Overstreet, gen sls mgr & mktg mgr; Jeanine French, prom dir; Jay Duncan, progmg dir; Gary Warner, news dir; Jack Wilkinson, chief engr. ■ On 8 CATVs—112,080 subs. On 5 trans.

XHIJ—(Ciudad Juarez, MX). ch 44, 240 kw vis, 60 kw aur, ant 1200t/150g. Stereo. Hrs opn: 20. On air date: Oct 16, 1980. Suite 200, 1790 Lee Trevino, El Paso, TX (79936). (915) 598-0440. FAX: (915) 598-1485. Licensee: Arnoldo Cabada De la O. Ownership: Arnoldo Cabada De la O, 52%; Luis Cabada Alvidrez, Sergio Cabada Alvidrez, & Jesus Cabada Alvidrez, each 16%. ■ Net: Telemundo. Sp 126 hrs wkly. News staff 20; news progmg 15 hrs wkly. ■ Sergio Cabada, pres; John Chapman, gen mgr; Abel Rodriguez, prom mgr; Armando Cabada, news dir; Gabriel Rios, chief engr. ■ On one CATV—89,707 subs. On one trans. ■ Rates: $250; 175; 125.

Farwell

ADI No. 129; see Amarillo market

KMZN—ch 18, 1,170 kw vis, 117 kw aur, ant 515t. TL: N34 26 18 W103 12 33. Not on air, target date unknown. Box 3757, Lubbock (79452). Permittee: Ramar Communications Inc. Ownership: Troy Ray Moran, 100%. ■ Troy Ray Moran, pres.

Fort Worth

ADI No. 8; see Dallas-Ft. Worth market

KDFW-TV—See Dallas.

*__KERA-TV__—See Dallas.

KFWD—ch 52, 5,000 kw vis, 500 kw aur, ant 1,076t. TL: N32 45 01 W97 16 07. On air date: Sept 1, 1988. 3000 W. Story Rd, Irving (75038). (214) 255-5200. Licensee: Interspan Communications, a California L.P. ■ Net: Telemundo. Sp progmg. ■ Arthur Gray, gen mgr; Marisa T. Martinez, opns mgr, progmg dir & news dir; Wayne Casa, gen sls mgr; Cerise Carter, natl sls mgr; Lori Prati, prom dir; Harley Engle, chief engr.

KHSX-TV—See Irving.

KTVT—ch 11, 316 kw vis, 31.6 kw aur, ant 1,670t/1,549g. TL: N32 34 43 W96 57 12. Stereo. On air date: Sept 11, 1955. Box 2495 (76113); 5233 Bridge St. (76103). (817) 451-1111; (817) 654-1100. FAX: (817) 457-1897. Licensee: Gaylord Broadcasting Co. (group owner; acq 8-1-62; $800,000; 8-6-62). Rep: MMT. Wash atty: Reed, Smith, Shaw & McClay. News staff 30; news progmg 7 hrs wkly. ■ Ed Trimble, vp & gen mgr; Brian Jones, stn mgr; Phil Crow, opns mgr; Kim Redmond, natl sls mgr; Stephanie Seywert, mktg mgr; Ken Foote, progmg mgr; Jim Holland, news dir; Clem Candelaria, pub affrs dir; Tom Daniels, chief engr.

KTXA—ch 21, 4,900 kw vis, 490 kw aur, ant 1,650t/1,489g. TL: N32 35 22 W96 58 10. On air date: Jan 4, 1981. 1712 E. Randol Mill Rd., Arlington (76011). (817) 265-2100. FAX: (817) 265-5949. Licensee: Paramount Stations Group of Fort Worth/Dallas Inc. Group owner: Paramount Communications Inc. (acq 2-28-91). Rep: Seltel. Wash atty: Leventhal, Senter & Lerman. ■ Walter DeHaven, vp & gen mgr; Rick Mills, gen sls mgr; Eric Lassberg, natl sls mgr; Sandy Cooke, Andre Woodson (loc), A. D. Huey (retail), rgnl sls mgrs; Rick Davey, prom mgr; Tammy Salinas, progmg dir; Beth Bowles, pub affrs dir; George DeLacerda, chief engr.

KXAS-TV—ch 5, 100 kw vis, 20 kw aur, ant 1,686t/1,527g. TL: N32 35 15 W96 57 59. Stereo. Hrs opn: 24. On air date: Sept 29, 1948. Box 1780 (76101); 3900 Barnett (76103). (817) 536-5555; (214) 745-5555. FAX: (817) 654-6362. Licensee: North Texas Broadcasting Corp. Group owner: LIN Broadcasting Corp. (acq 5-74; $35million; 5-27-74). ■ Net: NBC. Rep: Blair. Wash atty: Covington & Burling. ■ Doug Adams, pres & gen mgr; Patty Parker, gen sls mgr; Lee Spieckerman, mktg mgr; Brian Hocker, progmg dir; Dave Overton, news dir; Nada Ruddock, pub affrs dir; George C. Sahanin, engrg dir. ■ On 198 CATVs—690,866 subs.

KXTX-TV—See Dallas.

WFAA-TV—See Dallas.

Galveston

ADI No. 10; see Houston market

*__KLTJ__—ch 22, 5,000 kw vis, 500 kw aur, ant 1,873t/1,866g. TL: N29 17 16 W95 13 53. (CP: 1,857t, TL: N29 17 56 W95 14 11). Hrs opn: 24. On air date: July 22, 1989. 1050 Gemini, Houston (77058). (713) 212-1077. FAX: (713) 212-1022. Licensee: Galveston Educational TV Inc. Sp 10 hrs wkly. ■ Eldred Thomas, pres & gen mgr; Nathan Williams, opns dir; Leo S. Lesaca, sls dir & pub affrs dir; Linda Leon, progmg mgr & pub affrs dir; Ron Brown, chief engr. ■ On 13 CATVs—17,268 subs. ■ Rates: $50; 50; 50.

KTMD—ch 48, 5,000 kw vis, 500 kw aur, ant 1,199t/1,211g. TL: N29 27 57 W95 13 23. Hrs opn: 21. On air date: Dec 12, 1987. 3903 Stoney Brook, Houston (77063). (713) 974-4848. FAX: (713) 974-5875. Licensee: Telemundo of Galveston/Houston Inc. Group owner: Telemundo Group Inc. ■ Net: Telemundo. Wash atty: Hogan & Hartson. All Sp. News staff 14; news progmg 7 hrs wkly. ■ Enrique Perez, gen mgr; Blane Huhn, opns dir & engrg dir; Becky Diaz, gen sls mgr; Rebecca Diaz, mktg mgr; Nick Rivera, prom mgr; Marcello Marini, progmg dir & pub affrs dir; Cesar Rodriguez, news dir. ■ On 7 CATVs—450,000 subs.

Garland

ADI No. 8; see Dallas-Ft. Worth market

KUVN—ch 23, 5,000 kw vis, 1,000 kw aur, ant 1,142t. TL: N32 54 04 W96 41 14. On air date: Sept 25, 1986. 3720 Marquis Dr. (75042). (214) 494-0023. Licensee: Univision Station Group Inc. Group owner: Perenchio Television Inc. (acq 5-88; $5.2 million). ■ Net: Univision. Sp progmg. News progmg 10 hrs wkly. ■ Gayle Brammer, gen mgr & gen sls mgr; Roel Medina, stn mgr, prom mgr & news dir; Dan Kemper, natl sls mgr; Rosa Cuellar, rgnl sls mgr; Ken Savage, mktg dir; Arcilia Carrasco, pub affrs dir; Richard Craig, chief engr.

Greenville

ADI No. 8; see Dallas-Ft. Worth market

KTAQ—ch 47, 240 kw vis, 24 kw aur, ant 515t. TL: N33 09 32 W96 08 31. Not on air, target date unknown. Suite 101, 6801 Sanger, Waco (76710). (817) 751-7696. FAX: (817) 751-0322. Permittee: Mike Simons (acq 3-24-92; $50,000 for CP; 4-13-92).

Harlingen

ADI No. 113; see McAllen-Brownsville market

KGBT-TV—ch 4, 100 kw vis, 18.7 kw aur, ant 1,299t/1,293g. TL: N26 08 55 W97 49 17. Stereo. Hrs opn: 24. On air date: October 1953. 9201 W. Expressway 83 (78552). (210) 421-4444. FAX: (210) 421-2318. Licensee: Draper Communications Inc. (group owner; acq 4-13-86). ■ Net: CBS. Rep: Katz. Wash atty: Arent, Fox, Kintner, Plotkin & Kahn. Sp 2 hrs wkly. News staff 30; news progmg 15 hrs wkly. ■ Thomas H. Draper, pres; Vincent E. Donovan, gen mgr; Carrie Cox, opns mgr; James Lowder, gen sls mgr; Jim Chancey, prom mgr & progmg dir; Paul Shipley, news dir; Harry Thielemann, chief engr. ■ On 2 CATVs—110,000 subs.

*__KLUJ__—ch 44, 1,740 kw vis, 174 kw aur, ant 971t. TL: N26 13 00 W97 46 48. On air date: June 25, 1984. Box 1647, No. 117, 1920 Al Coneway Dr. (78550). (210) 425-4225. FAX: (210) 412-1740. Licensee: Community Educational TV Inc. (acq 4-84). Wash atty: May, Dunne & Gay. Sp 7 hrs wkly. ■ Dr. Reginald Cherry, pres; Maggie Combs, gen mgr; Mely DeLeon, pub affrs dir.

*__KMBH__—ch 60, 2,240 kw vis, 22.4 kw aur, ant 1,220t/1,169g. TL: N26 07 14 W97 49 18. On air date: Oct 8, 1985. Box 2147 (78551); 1701 Tennessee St. (78550). (210) 421-4111. FAX: (210) 421-4150. Licensee: RGV Educational Broadcasting Inc. ■ Net: PBS. Wash atty: Ross & Hardies. Sp 2 hrs wkly. ■ Darrell Rowlett, pres & gen mgr; John Harris III, vp; Thelma Comacho, mktg dir; Claudia Uresti, progmg mgr; Gilbert Resendez, chief engr. ■ On one CATV—69,780 subs. Co-owned radio: *KMBH-FM, KHID-FM.

KRGV-TV—See Weslaco.

Houston

ADI No. 10; see Houston market

*__KETH__—ch 14, 4,470 kw vis, 447 kw aur, ant 1,437t/1,470g. TL: N29 33 25 W95 30 04. On air date:

July 1987. 10902 S. Wilcrest Dr. (77099). (713) 561-5828. FAX: (713) 561-9793. Licensee: Community Educational Television of Houston Inc. Wash atty: May, Dunne & Gay. ■ Velma Marlin, stn mgr, progmg dir & pub affrs dir; Rod Hardy, chief engr.

KHOU-TV—ch 11, 316 kw vis, 47.9 kw aur, ant 1,870t/1,473g. TL: N29 33 40 W95 30 04. Stereo. On air date: Mar 22, 1953. Box 11 (77001-0011); 1945 Allen Pkwy. (77019). (713) 526-1111. FAX: (713) 521-4326. Licensee: KHOU-TV. Group owner: A.H. Belo Corp., Broadcast Division (acq 1984; grpsl; 11-17-83). ■ Net: CBS. Rep: TeleRep. Wash atty: Dow, Lohnes & Albertson. News progmg 19 hrs wkly. ■ Allan E. Howard, pres & gen mgr; Richard Keilty, sls dir & mktg dir; Garen VandeBeek, prom dir & adv dir; David Goldberg, news dir; Cris Perez, pub affrs dir; David Carr, chief engr. ■ On 91 CATVs.

KHSH-TV—See Alvin.

KHTV—ch 39, 5,000 kw vis, 500 kw aur, ant 1,950t/1,970g. TL: N29 34 06 W95 29 57. On air date: Jan 6, 1967. 7700 Westpark Dr. (77063). (713) 781-3939. FAX: (713) 781-3441. Licensee: Gaylord Broadcasting Co. (group owner; acq 10-13-65; $240,000). Rep: MMT. Wash atty: Reed, Smith, Shaw & McClay. ■ Paul Hastaba, vp & gen mgr; Lois Culpepper, gen sls mgr; Randy Wilkes, vp mktg; Sean Haley, prom mgr; Bob Clark, progmg dir; Jodie Sinclair, pub affrs dir; John R. Schilberg, chief engr. ■ On 48 CATVs—150,000 subs.

KPRC-TV—ch 2, 100 kw vis, 10 kw aur, ant 1,929t/1,969g. TL: N29 34 06 W95 29 57. Stereo. Hrs opn: 24. On air date: Jan 1, 1949. Box 2222 (77252). 8181 Southwest Frwy. (77074). (713) 771-4631. FAX: (713) 771-4653. Licensee: H & C Communications Inc. ■ Net: NBC. Rep: Petry. Wash atty: Dow, Lohnes & Albertson. News staff 80; news progmg 20 hrs wkly. ■ W. P. Hobby, chmn; Nolan Quam, pres & gen mgr; Dick Daggett, gen sls mgr; Pam Franco, mktg dir; Bruce Bryant, prom mgr; Lyle Schulze, progmg dir; Joe Nolan, news dir; Art Biggs, chief engr.

KRIV—ch 26, 5,000 kw vis, 500 kw aur, ant 1,948t/1,869g. TL: N29 34 28 W95 29 37. On air date: Aug 15, 1971. Box 22810 (77227); 3935 Westheimer Rd. (77027). (713) 626-2610. FAX: (713) 625-1809. Licensee: Fox Television Stations Inc. (group owner). ■ Net: Fox. Wash atty: Molly Paulker. ■ Jerry Marcus, vp & stn mgr; Debbie Benjamin, opns mgr; Craig Bland, gen sls mgr; Jose Oti, natl sls mgr; Nancy McNeil, rgnl sls mgr; Mary Delaney-Newton, prom mgr; Roz Brown, progmg dir; Margaret Garcia, pub affrs dir; Wendell Wybomy, chief engr.

KTRK-TV—ch 13, 316 kw vis, 39.8 kw aur, ant 1,929t. TL: N29 34 27 W95 29 37. On air date: Nov 20, 1954. 3310 Bissonnet (77005); Box 13 (77001). (713) 668-0024. Licensee: Capital Cities/ABC Inc. Group owner: Capital Cities/ABC Broadcast Group (acq 7-17-67). ■ Net: ABC. Rep: ABC Spot. News progmg 17 hrs wkly. ■ James Masucci, pres & gen mgr; Charles Wolf, opns mgr & film buyer; Jim Keeley, gen sls mgr; Margaret Shilstone, prom mgr; Kim Nordt Jackson, progmg dir; Richard Longorin, news dir; Cyndy Garza, pub affrs dir; J. L. Hamilton, chief engr. ■ On 40 CATVs-740,000 subs.

KTXH—ch 20, 5,000 kw vis, 500 kw aur, ant 1,811t/2,008g. TL: N29 34 34 W95 30 36. On air date: Nov 7, 1982. 8950 Kirby Dr. (77054). (713) 661-2020. FAX: (713) 665-3909. Licensee: Paramount Stations Group of Houston Inc. Group owner: Paramount Communications Inc. (acq 3-31-87; grpsl; 12-15-86). Rep: Seltel. Wash atty: Leventhal, Senter & Lerman. ■ Mike Dunlop, gen mgr; Linda Danna, gen sls mgr; Chris Wallace, prom mgr; Tom Zappala, progmg dir; Charles Hughes, chief engr.

***KUHT**—ch 8, 316 kw vis, 63.2 kw aur, ant 1,970t/2,049g. TL: N29 34 28 W95 29 37. Stereo. Hrs opn: 20. On air date: May 12, 1953. 4513 Cullen Blvd. (77004). (713) 748-8888; (800) 364-5848. FAX: (713) 749-8230. Licensee: Univ. of Houston System, Board of Regents. ■ Net: PBS. Sp, Fr, & Japanese 12 hrs wkly. ■ Jeff Clarke, gen mgr & stn mgr; Yvonne Menuet, dev dir & mktg dir; Jill Pickett, prom dir & adv dir; Ken Lawrence, progmg dir; Miriam Korshak, pub affrs dir; Andy Anderson, chief engr. ■ On 36 CATVs. Co-owned radio: *KUHF(FM).

KZJL—ch 61, 2,740 kw vis, 274 kw aur, ant 1,810t. TL: N29 33 40 W95 30 04. Not on air, target date unknown. No. 10J, 520 S. Burnside Ave., Los Angeles, CA (90036). Permittee: Urban Broadcasting Systems.

Irving

ADI No. 8; see Dallas-Ft. Worth market

KHSX-TV—ch 49, 5,000 kw vis, 500 kw aur, ant 1,200t/1,032g. TL: N32 35 24 W96 58 21. On air date: Apr 17, 1984. 1957 E. Irving Blvd. (75060). (214) 579-4900. FAX: (214) 579-1105. Licensee: Silver King Broadcasting of Dallas Inc. Group owner: Silver King Communications Inc. Wash atty: Dow, Lohnes & Albertson. ■ James J. Flynn, pres; Bradley Foltyn, vp & gen mgr; Tony Montes, progmg mgr; Art Runyon, chief engr. ■ On 39 CATVs.

Jacksonville

ADI No. 114; see Tyler-Longview-Jacksonville market

KETK-TV—ch 56, 5,000 kw vis, 500 kw aur, ant 1,583t/1,437g. TL: N32 03 40 W95 18 50. Stereo. Hrs opn: 24. On air date: March 1987. 4300 Richmond Rd., Tyler (75703). (903) 581-5656. FAX: (903) 561-1648. Licensee: Region 56 Network Inc. Group owner: Lone Star Broadcasting Inc. (acq 9-25-89; $7,452,323; 10-9-89). ■ Net: NBC, CBS. Rep: Blair. Wash atty: Winston & Strawn. News staff 24; news progmg 9 hrs wkly. ■ Philip H. Hurley, pres & gen mgr; Gary Swartz, opns dir; John Gaston, gen sls mgr; Tony Cruz, natl sls mgr; Jeff Miller, prom mgr; Carolyn Waters, progmg dir; Andy Shaw, news dir; Moe Strout, engrg dir; Steve Zanolini, chief engr. ■ On 114 CATVs—140,000 subs.

Katy

ADI No. 10; see Houston market

KNWS-TV—ch 51, 2,560 kw vis, 257 kw aur, ant 1,660t. TL: N29 33 40 W95 30 04. Stereo. Hrs opn: 20. On air date: Nov 3, 1993. 8440 Westpark, Houston (77063). (713) 974-5697. Licensee: Johnson Broadcasting Inc. Ownership: Douglas R. Johnson, 100%. Rep: TV Rep Inc. Wash atty: Arthur V. Belendiuk. ■ Douglas Johnson, pres & gen mgr.

Kerrville

ADI No. 36; see San Antonio-Victoria market

KRRT—ch 35, 5,000 kw vis, 500 kw aur, ant 1,758t. TL: N29 36 37 W98 53 35. Stereo. On air date: Nov 6, 1985. 6218 N.W. Loop 410, San Antonio (78238). (512) 684-0035. Licensee: Paramount Stations Group of Kerrville Inc. Group owner: Paramount Communications Inc. ■ Net: Fox. Rep: Seltel. Wash atty: Leventhal, Senter & Lerman. ■ David Boaz, gen mgr; Tom Hurley, gen sls mgr; Jennifer Allen, mktg dir; Vangie Mascorro, prom dir; Mel House, progmg dir; Patty Bissey, pub affrs dir; Kevin Busselman, chief engr. ■ On 26 CATVs—293,000 subs.

Lake Dallas

ADI No. 8; see Dallas-Ft. Worth market

KLDT—ch 55, 3,310 kw vis, 331 kw aur, ant 466t. TL: N33 00 19 W96 59 00. Not on air, target date unknown. Box 55, c/o Opal Thornton, Hurst (76053). (817) 267-9725. Permittee: Opal Thornton. ■ Opal Thornton, pres.

Laredo

ADI No. 198; see Laredo market

KGNS-TV—ch 8, 316 kw vis, 42.2 kw aur, ant 1,021t/1,049g. TL: N27 40 22 W99 39 23. Hrs opn: 20. On air date: Jan 6, 1956. Box 2829, 120 W. Del Mar Blvd. (78044). (210) 727-8888. FAX: (210) 727-5336; TWX: 910-870-1794. Licensee: Century Development Inc. (acq 12-86; $3.8 million). ■ Net: NBC, ABC. Rep: Katz. Wash atty: Dow, Lohn & Albertson. Sp 8 hrs wkly. ■ Malcom Glazer, pres; Jeff Pryor, gen mgr; Jeannette Puig, gen sls mgr & adv mgr; Leslie Brown, prom mgr; Velia Herrera, progmg dir; Richard Noriega, news dir; David York, chief engr. ■ On 5 CATVs—23,000 subs.

KLDO-TV—ch 27, 3,720 kw vis, 372 kw aur, ant 220t. TL: N27 30 03 W99 30 37. Hrs opn: 18. On air date: Dec 17, 1984. Riverdrive Mall, 1600 Water St. (78040). (210) 727-0027. FAX: (210) 727-2673. Licensee: Panorama Broadcasting Co. Ownership: Oscar M. Laurel, 18.3%; Hector H. Garcia, 18.3%; Eduardo Pena, 18.3%; Reynaldo Gonzalez 15.9%; Raymond Botello 15.9%; Oscar Larrel, Jr., 13%. ■ Net: Telemundo. Rep: Telemundo. Wash atty: Martin E. Firestone. Sp 126 hrs wkly. ■ Oscar M. Laurel, pres; Hector H. Garcia, vp; Elia Solis, gen mgr & film buyer; Elia Solis, Humberto Klee (loc), gen sls mgrs; Veronica Rabago, prom mgr & progmg dir; Merlin Miller, chief engr. ■ On 6 CATVs—29,102 subs. ■ Rates: $250; 75; 100.

KVTV—ch 13, 85.1 kw vis, 17.4 kw aur, ant 918t/1,033g. TL: N27 31 14 W99 31 19. On air date: Dec 29, 1973. Box 2039, 2600 Shea & Ana (78041). (210) 723-2923. FAX: (210) 723-0474. Licensee: K-SIX TV Inc. ■ Net: CBS. Rep: Seltel. ■ Vann M. Kennedy, pres & gen mgr; Debra S. Murphy, stn mgr; Joe Martinez, chief engr.

Llano

ADI No. 65; see Austin market

KXAM-TV—ch 14, 3,236 kw vis, 324 kw aur, ant 883t/459g. TL: N30 40 36 W98 33 59. Stereo. On air date: Sept 6, 1991. 908 W. Martin Luther King Jr. Blvd., Austin (78701); Box 490, Austin (78767). (512) 476-3636. FAX: (512) 476-1520. Licensee: KXAN Inc. ■ Net: NBC. ■ Jane Wallace, gen mgr.

Longview

ADI No. 114; see Tyler-Longview-Jacksonville market

KFXK-TV—ch 51, 4,680 kw vis, 36.70 kw aur, ant 1,249t/1,199g. TL: N32 15 35 W94 57 02. Hrs opn: 20. On air date: Sept 9, 1984. 701 N. Access Rd. (75602). (903) 236-0051. FAX: (903) 753-6637. Licensee: Warwick Communications Inc. (group owner; acq 5-13-92). ■ Net: Fox. Rep: Seltel. Wash atty: Fletcher, Heald & Hildreth. ■ Ed Stanton, pres; Mark McKay, gen mgr & progmg dir; Jim Prestwood, gen sls mgr; Brenda Mills, natl sls mgr; Richard Brooks, prom dir; Jan Maynard, pub affrs dir; Jay Rowe, chief engr. ■ On 41 CATVs—120,000 subs.

Lubbock

ADI No. 149; see Lubbock market

KAMC—ch 28, 2,000 kw vis, 374 kw aur, ant 840t/871g. TL: N33 30 57 W101 50 54. On air date: Nov 12, 1968. Box 3790 (79452-3790); 1201 84th St. (79423). (806) 745-2828. FAX: (806) 748-1080; (806) 745-2744. Licensee: McAlister TV Enterprises Inc. Ownership: Estate of B.B. McAlister, 75%; Majorie McAlister Thompson, 25%. ■ Net: ABC. Rep: Petry. Wash atty: Bryan, Cave, McPheeters & McRoberts. News staff 13; news progmg 8 hrs wkly. ■ Marjorie McAlister Thompson, chmn; Greg McAlister, pres & gen mgr; Gordon Thompson, vp; A.C. Wimberly, stn mgr & progmg dir; George Entz, opns dir; Chuck Spaugh, Sr., gen sls mgr; Bobbye Maxey, mktg dir; Bill Enloe, chief engr. ■ On 41 CATVs—65,000 subs. ■ Rates: $230; 120; 50.

KCBD-TV—ch 11, 316 kw vis, 60 kw aur, ant 804t/702g. TL: N33 32 32 W101 50 14. On air date: May 10, 1953. 5600 Avenue A (79404). (806) 744-1414. FAX: (806) 744-0449. Licensee: Holsum Inc. (acq 6-18-86). ■ Net: NBC. Rep: Katz. Wash atty: Dow, Lohnes & Albertson. ■ Bill deTournillon, vp & gen mgr; Craig Wells, stn mgr & gen sls mgr; Jeff Pitner, prom mgr; Diane Dotson, news dir; Sherrell Lambert, chief engr. ■ On 36 CATVs—80,000 subs. On 3 trans. ■ Rates: $700; 150; 100.

KJTV—ch 34, 3,720 kw vis, 372 kw aur, ant 840t/893g. TL: N33 30 08 W101 52 20. Stereo. Hrs opn: 24. On air date: Dec 10, 1981. Box 3757 (79452); 9800 Univ. Ave.(79423). (806) 745-3434. FAX: (806) 748-1949. Licensee: Ramar Communications Inc. Ownership: Ray Moran, 100% (acq 1-7-85; $1 million). ■ Net: Fox. Rep: Seltel. Wash atty: Fisher, Wayland, Cooper & Leader. ■ Ray Moran, pres; Brad Moran, gen mgr & progmg dir; Randy Roberts, gen sls mgr; Art Smith, chief engr. ■ On 58 CATVs—83,467 subs. On 9 trans.

KLBK-TV—ch 13, 316 kw vis, 25.1 kw aur, ant 880t/836g. TL: N33 31 33 W101 52 07. On air date: Nov 13, 1952. Box 1559, 7400 S. University Ave. (79408). (806) 745-2345. FAX: (806) 748-2250. Licensee: BA-NAM Broadcasting Inc. (group owner; acq 9-23-93; grpsl; 4-5-93). ■ Net: CBS. Rep: Blair. Wash atty: Kenkel & Assoc. News staff 20; news progmg 10 hrs wkly. ■ Paula Garrett, pres; Rick Lipps, vp, gen mgr & stn mgr; Philip Payne, gen sls mgr; Matt Hunter, prom mgr & pub affrs dir; Bill Blann, progmg mgr; Terry Graham, news dir; Don King, chief engr. ■ On 50 CATVs—114,000 subs. On 3 trans. ■ Rates: $300; 75; 75.

***KTXT-TV**—ch 5, 100 kw vis, 25 kw aur, ant 440t/817g. TL: N33 34 55 W101 53 25. On air date: Oct 16, 1962. Box 42161, Tech Station, 17th St. & Indiana Ave. (79409-2161). (806) 742-2209. FAX: (806) 742-1274. Licensee: Texas Tech U. ■ Net: PBS. ■ John Henson, gen mgr; Pat Cates, stn mgr; Helen Otken, dev dir & prom dir; James

Harris, progmg mgr; Robert Fusco, chief engr. ■ On 35 CATVs.

Lufkin

ADI No. 114; see Tyler-Longview-Jacksonville market

KTRE—ch 9, 158 kw vis, 31.7 kw aur, ant 670t. TL: N31 25 09 W94 48 02. Hrs opn: 24. On air date: Aug 31, 1955. Box 729 (75902). (409) 853-5873. FAX: (409) 853-3084. Licensee: TV-3 Inc. Group owner: Civic Communication Corp. (acq 5-16-89). ■ Net: ABC. Rep: Katz. Wash atty: Wiley, Rein & Fielding. Sp 1 hr wkly. News staff 15; news progmg 13 hrs wkly. ■ Frank Melton, CEO; J. Brad Streit, pres; Errol R. Kapellusch, sr vp, gen mgr & progmg dir; David Cantu, opns mgr; Gary Powers, gen sls mgr; Tina Alexander, news dir; Glenda Tharp, pub affrs dir; Dean Worley, chief engr. ■ On 50 CATVs—50,000 subs. ■

McAllen

ADI No. 113; see McAllen-Brownsville market

KNVO—ch 48, 3,162 kw vis, 316.2 kw aur, ant 524t/548g. TL: N26 05 20 W98 03 44. On air date: Oct 12, 1992. Suite 850, 1800 S. Main St. (78503). (210) 687-4848. FAX: (210) 687-7784. Licensee: Valley Channel 48 Inc. Ownership: Rosalie Goldberg (acq 3-24-92). ■ Net: Univision. Rep: Horizon Co-op Marketing. Wash atty: Barry Woods. Sp progmg. ■ Gloria Stromberg, pres; Larry Safir, gen mgr.

KVEO—See Brownsville.

Midland

ADI No. 149; see Odessa-Midland market

KMID—ch 2, 100 kw vis, 10 kw aur, ant 1,050t/1,147g. TL: N32 05 14 W102 17 12. Hrs opn: 24. On air date: Dec 18, 1953. Box 60230, 3200 Laforce Blvd. (79711). (915) 563-2222. FAX: (915) 563-5819; TWX: 910-897-5682. Licensee: KMID Licensee Co. Group owner: Davis-Goldfarb Co. (acq 1988). ■ Net: ABC. Rep: Katz. Wash atty: Leventhal, Senter & Lerman. News staff 19; news progmg 10 hrs wkly. ■ Stephen W. Dant, gen mgr; Al Nash, opns dir & news dir; Gisela Hughes, natl sls mgr; Amy Hancock, rgnl sls mgr; Marlo Alsup, progmg dir; Kyle Smith, chief engr. ■ On one trans. ■ Rates: $300; 30; 30.

KOSA-TV—See Odessa.

KWES-TV—See Odessa.

Monahans

KMID—See Midland.

KOSA-TV—See Odessa.

KWES-TV—See Odessa.

Nacogdoches

ADI No. 114; see Tyler-Longview-Jacksonville market

KLSB-TV—ch 19, 229 kw vis, ant 728t. TL: N31 24 28 W94 45 53. On air date: Sept 1, 1991. 204 W. Main St. (75961). (409) 564-1911. Licensee: Region 56 Television Network Inc. ■ Net: NBC. ■ Roby Somerford, gen mgr.

KTRE—See Lufkin.

Odessa

ADI No. 149; see Odessa-Midland market

KMID—See Midland.

KMLM—ch 42, 1,120 kw vis, 112 kw aur, ant 479t/473g. TL: N32 02 53 W102 17 44. On air date: Oct 18, 1988. Box 7708, Midland (79708); 10715 E. Browder, Gardendale (79758). (915) 563-4242; (915) 563-5656. FAX: (915) 561-8236. Licensee: Prime Time Christian Broadcasting Inc. ■ Paul Crouch, pres; Darlene Eve, gen mgr; Eddie Sills, chief engr.

*****KOCV-TV**—ch 36, 513 kw vis, 51.3 kw aur, ant 289t/306g. TL: N31 51 59 W102 22 50. On air date: Mar 24, 1986. 201 W. University (79764). (915) 335-6336; (915) 580-0036. FAX: (915) 337-0529. Licensee: Odessa Junior College District. ■ Net: PBS. Wash atty: Wayne Coy. ■ John McCarroll, gen mgr; Tom Hughes, stn mgr; Pam Six, dev mgr; Shorty Stokes, progmg dir; Al Harris, chief engr. ■ On 15 CATVs—60,000 subs. ■

KOSA-TV—ch 7, 316 kw vis, 39.8 kw aur, ant 741t/715g. TL: N31 51 50 W102 34 41. Hrs opn: 6 AM-1 AM. On air date: Jan 1, 1956. Box 4186.(79760); 1211 N. Whitaker (79763). (915) 337-8301. FAX: (915) 337-0536; TWX: 910-897-5504. Licensee: Brissette TV of Odessa Inc. Goup owner: Brissette Broadcasting Corp.; (acq 12-24-91; grpsl). ■ Net: CBS. Rep: Blair. Wash atty: Wiley, Rein & Fielding. Sp one hr wkly. News staff 18; news progmg 9 hrs wkly. ■ Paul Brissette, CEO & pres; Sheryl Jonsson, vp, gen mgr & progmg dir; Rick McGee, opns mgr; Tim Riggan, gen sls mgr; George Bugg, prom mgr; Kurt Kiser, news dir. ■ On 45 CATVs—109,690 subs. On one trans.

KPEJ—ch 24, 4,470 kw vis, 447 kw aur, ant 1,099t/1,196g. TL: N32 05 41 W102 17 21. Stereo. On air date: June 16, 1986. Box 11009 (79760); 1550 W. I-20 (79763). (915) 337-2424. FAX: (915) 337-3707. Licensee: Associated Broadcasters Inc. (group owner; acq 10-31-90; grpsl; 11-19-90). ■ Net: Fox. Rep: Seltel. Wash atty: Fletcher, Heald & Hildreth. ■ Joseph A. Sugg, gen mgr; James Beeghley, gen sls mgr; Rebecca Kelly-Norris, prom mgr; Ardelia Schmalz, progmg mgr & film buyer; Doug Faltus, chief engr. ■ On 42 CATVs—100,800 subs. ■ Rates: $350; 125; 40.

KWES-TV—ch 9, 316 kw vis, 45.7 kw aur, ant 1,269t/1,079g. TL: N31 59 17 W102 51 59. On air date: Dec 1, 1958. Box 60150, 11320 County Rd. 127 W. Midland (79711-0150). (915) 567-9999. FAX: (915) 561-5136; TWX: 910-895-5346. Licensee: MSP Television of Midland-Odessa. Ownership: Midessa Television Co. (acq 9-9-91; $4.85 million with KWAB(TV) Big Spring; 9-23-91). ■ Net: NBC. Rep: Seltel. ■ John L. Foster, gen mgr; Rick Wood, gen sls mgr; Kathy Williams, prom mgr; M. Gayle Hill, news dir; Chuck Cooper, chief engr. ■ On 35 CATVs—75,000 subs. On 3 trans.

Port Arthur

KJAC-TV—Licensed to Port Arthur. See Beaumont.

Rosenberg

ADI No. 10; see Houston market

KXLN-TV—ch 45, 2,100 kw vis, 210 kw aur, ant 1,450t/1,430g. TL: N29 33 25 W95 30 04. Hrs opn: 24. On air date: Sept 18, 1987. 9440 Kirby Dr., Houston (77054). (713) 662-4545. FAX: (713) 668-9054. Licensee: Pueblo Broadcasting Corp. Ownership: A.C. Pena, J.A. Trevino, V.M. Delgado, Mary Medina, C. Nava, G. Ponce, Mesbic Ventures Inc. ■ Net: Univision. Rep: Univision. Wash atty: Mullin, Rhyne, Emmons & Topel. Sp 165 hrs wkly. News staff 10; news progmg 4 hrs wkly. ■ Jose Adan Trevino, CEO & pres; Chris Brown, vp; Zanetta Kelley, gen sls mgr; Sandra Zavaleta, prom dir; Cindy Chisum, progmg dir; Beatriz de Alvarado, news dir; Stephen Looney, chief engr. ■ On 48 CATVs—500,000 subs. ■ Rates: $600; 500; 250.

San Angelo

ADI No. 190; see San Angelo market

KACB-TV—ch 3, 17.8 kw vis, 3.5 kw aur, ant 600t/469g. TL: N31 37 22 W100 26 14. On air date: Feb 8, 1962. 4510 S. 14th, Abilene (79605). (915) 692-4242. FAX: (915) 692-8265. Licensee: Abilene Radio & TV Co. (group owner). ■ Net: NBC. Wash atty: Kenkel & Barnard. ■ Ken Knox, gen mgr. ■ On 4 CATVs. Co-owned radio: Satellite of KRBC-TV Abilene.

KIDY—ch 6, 100 kw vis, 10 kw aur, ant 946t/1,000g. TL: N31 35 21 W100 31 00. Stereo. On air date: May 12, 1984. 406 S. Irving (76903); United Bank Centre, 1049 N. Third, Abilene (79604). (915) 658-2666; (915) 673-2345. FAX: (915) 655-8461; (915) 672-4816. Licensee: Sage Broadcasting Co. Ownership: Raymond Schindler. ■ Net: Fox. Wash atty: Rosenman & Colin. ■ Raymond Schindler, pres; Paris Schindler, exec vp; Bill Carter, vp & gen mgr; Lowell Wilks, stn mgr & gen sls mgr; Becky Sanchez, prom mgr; John Talley, progmg dir; Jodi Barton, pub affrs dir; Bill Brister, chief engr. ■ On 25 CATVs—68,329 subs. On 2 trans. ■ Rates: $425; 100; 65.

KLST—ch 8, 316 kw vis, 31.6 kw aur, ant 1,450t/1,500g. TL: N31 22 01 W100 02 48. Stereo. On air date: June 23, 1953. 2800 Armstrong (76903). (915) 949-8800. FAX: (915) 658-4006. Licensee: Jewell Television Corp. Ownership: Estate of T.B. Lanford (acq 2-1-71; $250,000). ■ Net: CBS. Rep: Katz. Wash atty: Wiley, Rein & Fielding. ■ Mary Jane Harper, pres; Tedford Kimbell, exec vp; Phil Brassie, vp; Glen Goode, stn mgr; Randy Aly, mktg dir; Kevin Settle, prom mgr; Gordon Hay, progmg dir; Lou Kordek, news dir; Bob Koob, pub affrs dir Larry White, chief engr. ■ On 17 CATVs—40,500 subs. ■ Rates: $435; 120; 115.

San Antonio

ADI No. 36; see San Antonio-Victoria market

KABB—ch 29, 5,000 kw vis, 500 kw aur, ant 1,503t/1,503g. TL: N29 17 27 W98 16 12. Stereo. On air date: Dec 17, 1987. 4335 N.W. Loop 410 (78229-5168). (210) 366-1129. FAX: (210) 377-4758. Licensee: Alamo Broadcasting Corp. Group owner: River City Broadcasting. Rep: Telerep. Wash atty: Schnader, Harrison, Segal & Lewis. ■ Paris R. Schindler, pres & film buyer; Mike Liff, stn mgr; Kevin Mirek, gen sls mgr; Scott Macaninch, prom mgr; Sam Bickel, progmg dir; David Osmo, chief engr. ■ On 26 CATVs—350,000 subs. ■ Rates: $400; 250; 100.

KENS-TV—ch 5, 100 kw vis, 10 kw aur, ant 1,390t/1,531g. TL: N29 16 10 W98 15 55. On air date: Feb 15, 1950. Box TV5 (78299); 5400 Fredericksburg Rd. (78229). (512) 366-5000. FAX: (512) 377-0740. Licensee: Harte-Hanks Television Inc. Ownership: Harte-Hanks Communications, see Cross-Ownership (acq 7-3-62; $6,256,000; 7-23-62). ■ Net: CBS. Rep: Blair. Wash atty: Arnold & Porter. ■ Michael J. Conly, pres & gen mgr; Jack W. Forehand, stn mgr & progmg dir; Michael Simpson, gen sls mgr; Marty Gamer, natl sls mgr; Bob Rogers, news dir; Henry Bonilla, pub affrs dir; Bob King, chief engr.

*****KHCE**—ch 23, 1,480 kw vis, 148 kw aur, ant 856t. TL: N29 31 25 W98 43 25. Hrs opn: 16. On air date: July 1989. 326 Sterling Browning Dr. (78232). (210) 496-2323. Licensee: Hispanic Community Educational Television Inc. ■ Delfino F. Sanchez, pres; Bruce Staffel, progmg dir; Gary Groth, chief engr.

*****KLRN**—ch 9, 302 kw vis, 30.2 kw aur, ant 960t/1,051g. TL: N29 19 33 W98 21 25. On air date: Sept 10, 1962. Box 9 (78291); 501 Broadway (78205). (210) 270-9000. FAX: (210) 270-9015; (210) 270-9077. Licensee: Alamo Public Telecommunications Council (acq 8-11-89). ■ Net: PBS. Wash atty: Cohn & Marks. ■ Victor Miramontes, chmn; Joanne Winik, pres & gen mgr; Bonnie Street, vp dev & mktg dir; Louisa Kerry-Rubenstein, natl sls mgr; Lewis Miller, vp engrg.

KMOL-TV—ch 4, 100 kw vis, 18 kw aur, ant 1,476t/1,531g. TL: N29 16 10 W98 15 55. Stereo. Hrs opn: 24. On air date: Dec 11, 1949. Box 2641 (78299); 1031 Navarro (78205). (210) 226-4444. FAX: (210) 223-5693. Licensee: United Television Inc. Group owner: Chris Craft Industries Inc. (acq 9-17-75; $9,300,000; 10-6-75). ■ Net: NBC. Rep: MMT. Wash atty: Wilmer, Cutler & Pickering. News staff 43; news progmg 11 hrs wkly. ■ Robert P. Donohue, vp, gen mgr & vp progmg; Kevin Donohue, gen sls mgr, adv mgr & progmg dir; Michael Stanford, prom dir; Tim Gardner, news dir; Harold Friesenhahn, chief engr. ■ On 86 CATVs—394,423 subs.

KSAT-TV—ch 12, 316 kw vis, 63.2 kw aur, ant 1,483t/1,505g. TL: N29 16 11 W98 15 31. Stereo. Hrs opn: 22. On air date: Jan 21, 1957. Box 2478 (78298); 1408 N. St. Mary's St. (78215). (512) 351-1200. FAX: (512) 351-1297. Licensee: H&C Communications Inc. (group owner; acq 4-29-86; $153 million; 3-24-86). ■ Net: ABC. Rep: Petry. Wash atty: Dow, Lohnes & Albertson. News progmg 21 hrs wkly. ■ James Joslyn, pres & gen mgr; Barbara Montemayor (loc sls mgr), rgnl sls mgr; Steve Wegner, prom mgr; Rick Andrycha, progmg dir & film buyer; Jim Boyle, news dir; Fred Lozano, chief engr.

KVDA—ch 60, 5,000 kw vis, 500 kw aur, ant 1,495t/1,025g. TL: N29 29 87 W98 29 53. Stereo. Hrs opn: Mon-Fri 5:30 AM-2:05 PM; Sat-Sun 5:30 AM-2 PM. On air date: Sept 10, 1989. 6234 San Pedro (78216). (210) 340-8860; (210) 340-8861. FAX: (210) 341-3962. Licensee: Telemundo of San Antonio. Group owner: Telemundo Group Inc. (acq 11-14-90; $1,275,000). ■ Net: Telemundo. Wash atty: Reddy, Begley & Martin. Sp 112 hrs wkly. News staff 7; news progmg 10 hrs wkly. ■ Arthur Emerson, pres; Armando M. Solis, opns dir & pub affrs dir; Nicole Smith, natl sls mgr; Luis F. Hernandez, rgnl sls mgr; Blanca Santos, prom mgr; Kathleen Sanchez, progmg mgr; Victor Landa, news dir; Roger Topping, chief engr. ■ On 20 CATVs—300,000 subs. ■ Rates: $600; 350; 200.

KWEX-TV—ch 41, 832 kw vis, 83.2 kw aur, ant 500t/604g. TL: N29 25 03 W98 29 26. Stereo. On air date: June 10, 1955. 411 E. Durango Blvd. (78204). (210) 227-4141. FAX: (210) 227-0469; TELEX: 76-7430. Licensee: KWEX L.P., G.P. Group owner: Perenchio Television Inc. (acq 7-86; grpsl). ■ Net: Univision. Wash atty: Wiley, Rein & Fielding. Sp progmg ■ Steve Giust, gen mgr; Scott Keeler, natl sls mgr; Irene Garza, mktg mgr; Martha

Stations in the U.S.

Solis, news dir; Amparo Ortiz, pub affrs dir; James Meek, chief engr. ■ Rates: $1,000; 500; 290.

San Benito

*KMBH—See Harlingen.

Sherman

ADI No. 156; see Sherman-Ada market

KXII—ch 12, 224 kw vis, 22.4 kw aur, ant 1,781t/1,698g. TL: N34 01 58 W96 48 00. Stereo. Hrs opn: 5:30 AM-1:30 AM. On air date: July 1956. Box 1175, 4201 Texoma Pkwy. (75090); Oklahoma Studios, 2624 S. Commerce, Ardmore, OK (73401). (903) 892-8123. FAX: (903) 893-7858; TWX: 910-860-5226. Licensee: KXII Broadcasters Inc. ■ Net: CBS, NBC. Rep: Seltel. Wash atty: Dow, Lohnes & Albertson. ■ M. N. Bostick, pres; Rich Adams, gen mgr & progmg dir; Lanny Pogue, gen sls mgr; Bruce Stidham, prom mgr; Loren Farr, news dir; Dennis Kite, chief engr. ■ On 47 CATVs—90,572 subs. On one trans.

Sweetwater

KTXS-TV—Licensed to Sweetwater. See Abilene.

Temple

ADI No. 96; see Waco-Temple-Bryan market

KCEN-TV—ch 6, 100 kw vis, 10 kw aur, ant 830t/833g. TL: N31 16 24 W97 13 14. Stereo. Hrs opn: 22. On air date: Nov 1, 1953. Box 6103 (76503); 17 S. 3rd Temple (76503-6103). (817) 773-6868; (817) 773-1633. FAX: (817) 773-1633. Licensee: Channel 6 Inc. Ownership: Anyse Sue Mayborn, 100%. ■ Net: NBC. Rep: Blair. Wash atty: Fisher, Wayland, Cooper & Leader. News staff 22; news progmg 12 hrs wkly. ■ Anyse Sue Maybom, pres; Daniel Lesmeister, vp & gen mgr; Raymond Britton, opns mgr & progmg dir; Larry Taylor, gen sls mgr; Cheryl Dorn, prom mgr; Catherine Peeples, news dir; Ken Smith, chief engr. ■ On 24 CATVs—72,500 subs. On one trans.

KWKT—See Waco.

Texarkana

KTAL-TV—Licensed to Texarkana. See Shreveport, La.

Tyler

ADI No. 114; see Tyler-Longview-Jacksonville market

KLTV—ch 7, 316 kw vis, 31.6 kw aur, ant 991t/1,079g. TL: N32 32 21 W95 13 16. On air date: Oct 15, 1954. Box 957 (75710); Loope 323 & Old Kilgore Hwy. (75701). (903) 597-5588. FAX: (903) 510-7847. Licensee: TV-3 Inc. Group owner: Civic Communication Corp. (acq 5-15-89). ■ Net: ABC. Rep: Katz. Wash atty: Wiley, Rein & Fielding. ■ Brad Streit, gen mgr; Shelley Martin, gen sls mgr; Charlie Lozano, prom mgr; Errol Kapellusch, progmg dir; Tom Moo, news dir; Butch Adair, chief engr. ■ On 15 CATVs. ■ Rates: $850; 225; 200.

Victoria

ADI No. 36; see San Antonio-Victoria market

KAVU-TV—ch 25, 2,140 kw vis, 2.14 kw aur, ant 1,020t/1,067g. TL: N28 48 06 W96 33 09. On air date: July 4, 1982. Box 4929 (77903); 3808 N. Navarro (77901). (512) 575-2500. FAX: (512) 575-2255. Licensee: Withers Broadcasting Co. of Texas Inc. Group owner: Withers Broadcasting Co. (acq 3-12-90; $1,076,241). ■ Net: ABC, NBC. Rep: Katz. Wash atty: Baraff, Koerner, Olender & Hochberg. News staff 13; news progmg 6 hrs wkly. ■ W. Russell Withers, Jr., CEO; Betty Grimsinger, stn mgr, gen sls mgr & film buyer; Heidi Garcia, progmg dir; Jerry Desmond, news dir; Gary Underwood, pub affrs dir; Ted Donnell, engrg dir. ■ On 14 CATVs—46,187 subs. ■ Rates: $150; 80; 50.

KVCT—ch 19, 155 kw vis, 15.5 kw aur, ant 489t/494g. TL: N28 46 41 W96 57 38. Hrs opn: 24. On air date: Nov 21, 1969. 980 FM 1746, Woodville (75979-9609). (512) 573-1900. FAX: (512) 575-1919. Licensee: KVCT(TV). Ownership: Jerianne Medley, 100% (acq 6-8-90). ■ On 15 CATVs—35,000 subs.

Waco

ADI No. 96; see Waco-Temple-Bryan market

KCEN-TV—See Temple.

*KCTF—ch 34, 79.4 kw vis, 7.9 kw aur, ant 508t/446g. TL: N31 30 31 W97 10 03. On air date: May 22, 1989. Box 304 (76703); 600 Austin Ave. (76701). (817) 757-3434. FAX: (817) 757-3437. Licensee: Brazos Valley Public Broadcasting Foundation (acq 12-6-93; $80,000; 12-20-93). ■ Net: PBS. Wash atty: Arter & Hadden. ■ Edward B. Jasuta Jr., gen mgr; Noel T. Smith, stn mgr; Don Julian, gen sls mgr; Recy Terry, prom mgr; Gordon Thornton, chief engr. ■ On one CATV. Co-owned radio: KNCT-FM, KNCT(TV).

KWKT—ch 44, 4,170 kw vis, 417 kw aur, ant 1,811t. TL: N31 18 52 W97 19 37. Hrs opn: 24. On air date: March 1988. Box 2544 (76702-2544); 8803 Woodway Dr. (76712). (817) 776-3844. FAX: (817) 776-8032. Licensee: Associated Broadcasters Inc. (group owner; acq 10-31-90; grpsl; 11-19-90). ■ Net: Fox. Wash atty: Fletcher, Heald & Hildreth. ■ Ron Crowder, gen mgr, progmg dir & film buyer; Charles K. Williams, opns dir; Jerry Clemmons, gen sls mgr; Duane Sartor, mktg mgr, prom dir & pub affrs dir; Charles Yoder, chief engr. ■ On 65 CATVs—168,471 subs.

KWTX-TV—ch 10, 209 kw vis, 21 kw aur, ant 1,820t/1,679g. TL: N31 19 19 W97 18 58. On air date: April 1955. Box 2636, 6700 American Plaza (76712). (817) 776-1330. FAX: (817) 751-1088. Licensee: KWTX Broadcasting Co. (group owner). ■ Net: CBS. Rep: Seltel. ■ Thomas G. Pears, pres; Ray Deaver, gen mgr; Pam Samford, gen sls mgr; Consuelo Amola, prom dir; Rick Bradfield, news dir; Kathryn Henson, pub affrs dir; Ken Musgrave, chief engr. ■ On 9 CATVs. Co-owned radio: KWTX-AM-FM.

KXXV—ch 25, 5,000 kw vis, 500 kw aur, ant 1,830t. TL: N31 20 15 W97 18 37. Stereo. On air date: Jan 1, 1985. Box 2522 (76702); 1909 S. New Rd. (76711). (817) 754-2525. Licensee: Shamrock Broadcasting Inc. (group owner; acq 10-87; $15,535,000). ■ Net: ABC. Rep: Katz. Wash atty: Steven A. Lerman. ■ Bob Good, gen mgr & stn mgr; Don Shores, gen sls mgr; Mark Puckett, prom mgr; Jinx Dennis, progmg dir; Don Marion, news dir; Lou Strowger, chief engr. ■ On 134 CATVs.

Weslaco

ADI No. 113; see McAllen-Brownsville market

KGBT-TV—See Harlingen.

KRGV-TV—ch 5, 100 kw vis, 19.1 kw aur, ant 950t/995g. TL: N26 09 54 W97 48 45. On air date: Apr 10, 1954. Box 5 (78596); 900 E. Expressway (78599). (210) 968-5555. FAX: (210) 968-5555, ext. 246; TWX: 910-870-1850. Licensee: Mobile Video Tapes Inc. Group owner: Manship Stns (acq 1-28-64); grpsl; 2-3-64). ■ Net: ABC. Rep: Blair. Wash atty: Cohn & Marks. Sp one hr wkly. News staff 28; news progmg 12 hrs wkly. ■ Douglas Manship, chmn; Richard Manship, pres; Ray Alexander, gen mgr; Julian Adame, opns mgr & progmg dir; Tom Hagner, gen sls mgr; John Kittleman, natl sls mgr; Mary Grace Landsberg, prom mgr; Rick Diaz, news dir; Bert Walling, chief engr. ■ On 20 CATVs.

Wichita Falls

ADI No. 141; see Wichita Falls-Lawton market

KAUZ-TV—ch 6, 100 kw vis, 20 kw aur, ant 1,021t/1,028g. TL: N33 54 04 W98 32 21. On air date: Mar 1, 1953. Box 2130 (76307). (817) 322-6957; (817) 322-1146. TWX: 910-890-5836. Licensee: Brissette TV of Wichita Falls Inc. Group owner: Brissette Broadcasting Corp. acq 12-24-91; grpsl). ■ Net: CBS. Rep: Blair. ■ Mark Cummings, pres, gen mgr & natl sls mgr; Gary Lucus, vp; Chuck Berthelot, opns mgr; Cindi Charlton, prom mgr; Darlene Collier, adv mgr; Linda Hilden, progmg dir; Ted Dyrda, news dir; Leon Hoeffner, chief engr. ■ On 24 CATVs—24,000 subs. On one trans. ■ Rates: $250; 45; 35.

KFDX-TV—ch 3, 100 kw vis, 20 kw aur, ant 1,000t/1,045g. TL: N33 53 23 W98 33 20. Stereo. Hrs opn: 19. On air date: Apr 12, 1953. 4500 Seymour Highway (76309); Box 4000 (76308). (817) 692-4530. Licensee: Texoma Broadcasting Corp. Group owner: Price Communications Corp., debtor in possession (acq 7-15-87). ■ Net: NBC. Rep: Katz. Wash atty: Roberts & Eckard. ■ Duane Lammers, vp & gen mgr; Dave Brott, opns mgr; Frank Forgey, gen sls mgr; Jeff Albert, prom mgr; Susana Schuler, news dir; Jim Smith, chief engr. ■ On 64 CATVs—114,500 subs. On one trans.

KJTL—ch 18, 2,820 kw vis, 282 kw aur, ant 1,079t/1,000g. TL: N34 12 06 W98 43 44. Stereo. Hrs opn: 20. On air date: May 18, 1985. Box 4865, 3800 Call Field Rd. (76308). (817) 691-1808. FAX: (817) 696-5766. Licensee: BSP Broadcasting Inc. (group owner; acq 8-16-89). ■ Net: Fox. Rep: Seltel. Wash atty: Spector & Goldberg. ■ Peter D'Acosta, pres & vp adv; Kyle Williams, gen mgr & gen sls mgr; Jeanette Hawkins, prom dir; Ken Bowman, progmg dir; Ken Thomason, chief engr. ■ On 80 CATVs—100,000 subs. On 5 trans. ■ Rates: $400; 150; 50.

KSWO-TV—See Lawton, Okla.

Utah

Cedar City

ADI No. 41; see Salt Lake City market

KSGI-TV—ch 4, 38 kw vis, 15.8 kw aur, ant 2,700t/360g. TL: N37 32 32 W113 04 05. Stereo. Hrs opn: 24. On air date: September 1985. Box 831, 1305 N. Airport Rd. (84721); Box 1450, 210 N. 1000 East St. George (84771). (801) 586-4900; (801) 628-1000. FAX: (801) 628-6636. Licensee: Liberty Broadcast Co. Ownership: Michael G. Golden, 55% and Vincent J. Carroll, 45% (acq 8-5-87). ■ E. Morgan Skinner, Jr., pres & gen mgr; Kyle Delange, opns dir; E. Morgan Skinner, gen sls mgr; Fred Kuenzi, mktg dir & prom mgr; Kent McGregor, news dir & pub affrs dir; Patrick O'Gara, engrg dir. ■ On 7 CATVs—39,000 subs. On 5 trans. Co-owned radio: KSGI-AM-FM. ■ Rates: $25; 18; 10.

Ogden

ADI No. 41; see Salt Lake City market

KOOG-TV—ch 30, 5,000 kw vis, 500 kw aur, ant 777t/347g. TL: N41 15 17 W112 14 13. (CP: 1,550 kw vis, 155 kw aur, ant 3,903t, TL: N40 39 25 W112 12 07). On air date: October 1985. 1309 16th St. (84404). (801) 621-3030. TELEX: 269213. Licensee: Miracle Rock Church (acq 7-14-93; $65,000; 8-2-93). ■ Vicky Bojanski, gen mgr; Curt Westphal, stn mgr, progmg dir & film buyer; Dale Bradshaw, prom mgr. ■ On 5 CATVs—100,000 subs. On one trans. ■ Rates: $130; 100; 45.

*KULC—ch 9, 166 kw vis, 16.6 kw aur, ant 2,882t/78g. TL: N40 36 30 W112 09 34. Hrs opn: 13. On air date: Dec 1, 1986. 101 Wasatch Dr., Salt Lake City (84112). (801) 581-4194. FAX: (801) 581-5620. Licensee: Utah State Board of Regents. ■ Net: PBS. Fr, Sp & Ger progmg. ■ Helen Lacy, gen mgr; Douglas E. Jones, prom mgr; Kathy M. Nelson, progmg dir & film buyer; Clark Rhoads, chief engr.

Provo

ADI No. 41; see Salt Lake City market

*KBYU-TV—ch 11, 162 kw vis, 35 kw aur, ant 2,941t/100g. TL: N40 36 28 W112 09 33. Stereo. Hrs opn: 18. On air date: Nov 15, 1965. C-302, HFAC, Brigham Young U. (84602). (801) 378-8450. FAX: (801) 378-8478. Licensee: Brigham Young U. ■ Net: PBS. Wash atty: Wilkinson, Barker, Knauer & Quinn. Ger 3 hrs, Fr 3 hrs, Sp 3 hrs wkly. News staff 3; news progmg 3 hrs wkly. ■ Mel Rogers, gen mgr; Norma Collett, stn mgr, dev dir & pub affrs dir; Larry Marsten, opns mgr; Derek Marquis, gen sls mgr; Sandra Ewing, prom mgr & adv mgr; Diena Simmons, progmg dir & film buyer; Lynn Edwards, engrg dir. ■ On 50 CATVs—500,000 subs. On 31 trans. Co-owned radio: *KBYU-FM.

St. George

ADI No. 41; see Salt Lake City market

KUSG—ch 12, 9.8 kw vis, ant 138t. TL: N37 03 49 W113 34 20. Not on air, target date unknown. c/o KUTV Inc., 2185 S. 3600 W., Salt Lake City (84119). (801) 973-3013. FAX: (801) 973-3387. Permittee: KUTV Inc. ■ William Bradford, chief engr.

Salt Lake City

ADI No. 41; see Salt Lake City market

*KBYU-TV—See Provo.

KJZZ-TV—ch 14, 1,637 kw vis, 163.7 kw aur, ant 3,847t/241g. TL: N40 39 12 W112 12 06. Stereo. On air date: Feb 10, 1989. 5181 Amelia Earhart Dr. (84116). (801) 537-1414. FAX: (801) 537-7084. Licensee: Larry H. Miller Communications Corp. (acq 2-12-93; $1.725 million; 3-15-93). Rep: Seltel. Wash atty: Kaye, Scholer, Fierman, Hays & Handler. ■ John C. Martin, vp & gen mgr; Christine Barnhurst, gen sls mgr, mktg mgr, prom mgr & adv mgr; Sheree Isom, natl sls mgr; Robert

Quigley, progmg dir. ■ On 14 CATVs—150,000 subs. On 2 trans.

KSL-TV—ch 5, 33.9 kw vis, 6.8 kw aur, ant 3,780t/219g. TL: N40 39 35 W112 12 05. Stereo. On air date: June 1, 1949. Box 1160, KSL-TV, Broadcast House (84110-1160). (801) 575-5500. FAX: (801) 575-5830. Licensee: Bonneville International Corp. (group owner). ■ Net: CBS. Rep: Petry. Wash atty: Wilkinson, Barker, Knauer & Quinn. Sp 5 hrs wkly. News staff 65; news progmg 21 hrs wkly. ■ Bruce Reece, exec vp; William Murdoch, gen mgr; Russ Wood, vp dev; Cliff Snyder, vp sls; Steve Lindsley, gen sls mgr; David R. Manookin, vp progmg; Greg James, news dir & engrg dir. ■ On 52 CATVs—125,000 subs. On 121 trans. Co-owned radio: KSL(AM).

KSTU—ch 13, 112 kw vis, 11.2 kw aur, ant 3,660t/144.3g. TL: N40 39 33 W112 12 08. Stereo. Hrs opn: 24. On air date: Oct 9, 1978. 5020 W. Amelia Earhart Dr. (84116). (801) 532-1300. FAX: (801) 537-5335. Licensee: Fox Television Stations Inc. (group owner; acq 2-26-90; $41 million). ■ Net: Fox. Rep: Telerep. ■ Steve Carlston, vp & gen mgr; Stanton Jones, gen sls mgr; Melanie Say, prom mgr; Christy Elswood, progmg dir; Al Schultz, chief engr. ■ On 70 CATVs—160,544 subs. On 53 trans. ■ Rates: $600; 400; 250.

KTVX—ch 4, 32.4 kw vis, 4.9 kw aur, ant 3,870t. TL: N40 36 50 W112 11 05. Stereo. On air date: Apr 15, 1948. 1760 Fremont Dr. (84104). (801) 975-4444. FAX: (801) 975-4442. Licensee: United Television Inc. Group owner: Chris Craft Industries Inc. (acq 10-75; $11 million; 9-1-75). ■ Net: ABC. Wash atty: Wilmer, Cutler & Pickering. News staff 50; news progmg 14 hrs wkly. ■ Evan C. Thompson, pres; Peter Mathes, vp & gen mgr; Dennis Shiner, opns mgr; Ron Fessenden, Tom Love (loc), gen sls mgrs; John Edwards, news dir; Jim McDermaid, chief engr. ■ On 42 CATVs—136,841 subs. On 115 trans.

***KUED**—ch 7, 155 kw vis, 15.5 kw aur, ant 3,030t/204g. TL: N40 36 29 W112 09 36. Stereo. On air date: Jan 20, 1958. 101 Wasatch Dr. (84112). (801) 581-7777. FAX: (801) 581-5620. Licensee: Univ. of Utah. ■ Net: PBS. Deaf progmg 7 hrs wkly. ■ Fred Esplin, gen mgr; Meg Wilson, dev dir & adv dir; Mary Dickson, prom dir; Scott Chaffin, progmg dir; Clark Rhoads, engrg dir. ■ On 53 CATVs—304,875 subs. On 56 trans. Co-owned radio: *KUER(FM).

KUTV—ch 2, 45.7 kw vis, 9.1 kw aur, ant 3,060t/233g. TL: N40 36 23 W112 09 47. Stereo. Hrs opn: 24. On air date: Sept 26, 1954. 2185 S. 3600 W. (84119). Box 30901 (84130). (801) 973-3000. FAX: (801) 973-3369. Licensee: KUTV L.P. (acq 3-7-56; $683,333; 3-12-56). ■ Net: NBC. Rep: Harrington, Righter & Parsons. Wash atty: Haley, Bader & Potts. News staff 56; news progmg 20 hrs wkly. ■ George C. Hatch, chmn; Jeffrey B. Hatch, pres & gen mgr; Wilda G. Hatch, vp; Tom Mitchell, opns dir; John Bailey, vp sls; Kent Crawford, gen sls mgr; John Greene, mktg dir; Betty Curtis, progmg mgr; Diane Orr, news dir; William Bradford, chief engr.

Vermont

Burlington

ADI No. 93; see Burlington-Plattsburgh market

WCAX-TV—ch 3, 38 kw vis, 7.25 kw aur, ant 2,739t. TL: N44 31 36 W72 48 57. On air date: Sept 26, 1954. Box 608 (05402). (802) 658-6300. TWX: 510-299-0026. Licensee: Mount Mansfield TV Inc. Ownership: S.T. Martin & family, 100%. ■ Net: CBS. Rep: Harrington, Righter & Parsons, Metrospot. Wash atty: Wilmer, Cutler & Pickering. News staff 27; news progmg 10 hrs wkly. ■ Stuart T. Martin, pres; Peter Martin, exec vp, gen mgr & progmg dir; Andrew Luchini, vp opns; Ken Jarvis, vp sls; Bruce Grindle, natl sls mgr; Marselis Parsons, news dir; Ken Greene, pub affrs dir; Ted Teffner, chief engr. ■ On 100 CATVs—130,000 subs. On 3 trans.

***WETK**—ch 33, 1,350 kw vis, 135 kw aur, ant 2,673t/87g. TL: N44 31 32 W72 48 54. Stereo. Hrs opn: 6:30 AM-2 AM Mon-Fri; Sat-Sun 7 AM-1 AM. On air date: Oct 16, 1967. 88 Ethan Allen Ave., Colchester (05446). (802) 655-4800. FAX: (802) 655-6593. Licensee: Vermont ETV Inc. (acq 11-6-89). ■ Net: PBS; EEN. Wash atty: Covington & Burling. ■ Hope S. Green, CEO & pres; Jack Candon, chmn; John E. King, CFO; Lee Ann Lee, vp dev; Ann Curran, mktg dir; Kenneth D. Schwab, progmg mgr & film buyer; Wayne Rosberg, vp engrg; Ronald Whitcomb, chief engr.

WVNY—ch 22, 1,000 kw vis, 100 kw aur, ant 2,739t/310g. TL: N44 31 40 W72 48 58. On air date: Aug 19, 1968. Box 22, 100 Market Sq. (05401). (802) 658-8022. FAX: (802) 865-9976. Licensee: Citadel Communications Ltd. Group owner: Citadel Communications Co. Inc., Coronet Communications Co. ■ Net: ABC. Rep: Katz, CC Communications (Toronto). Wash atty: Latham & Watkins. ■ Philip J. Lombardo, pres; William E. Bradley, gen mgr; Ken Kaszubowski, opns mgr & progmg dir; Charlie Cusimano, gen sls mgr; Jon Kontonleon, natl sls mgr; Linda Noyes, prom mgr; John Cavasos, news dir; Harold Sharland, chief engr. ■ On 49 CATVs—142,155 subs.

Hartford

ADI No. 93; see Burlington-Plattsburgh market

WNNE-TV—ch 31, 2,240 kw vis, 2.24 kw aur, ant 2,220t/149g. TL: N43 26 38 W72 17 17. On air date: Sept 27, 1978. Box 1310, White River Junction (05001). (802) 295-3100. Licensee: WNNE-TV. Group owner: Heritage Media Corp. (acq 12-15-91). ■ Net: NBC. ■ Robert Shields, gen mgr; Courtney Galluzzo, gen sls mgr; Bruce Lyndes, news dir; Stu Boughton, chief engr. ■ On 68 CATVs—88,000 subs. On one trans. ■ Rates: $130; 90; 20.

Rutland

ADI No. 93; see Burlington-Plattsburgh market

***WVER**—ch 28, 245 kw vis, 24.5 kw aur, ant 1,400t/297g. TL: N43 39 32 W73 06 25. Stereo. Hrs opn: 6 AM-2 AM Mon-Fri; 7 AM-1 AM Sat-Sun. On air date: Mar 18, 1968. 88 Ethan Allen Ave., Colchester (05446). Licensee: Vermont ETV Inc. (group owner; acq 11-6-89). ■ Hope S. Green, CEO & pres; Jack Candon, chmn; John E. King, CFO; Lee Ann Lee, vp dev; Ann Curran, mktg dir; Margery Hibberd Swim, vp progmg; Kenneth D. Schwab, film buyer; Joe Merone, pub affrs dir; Wayne Rosberg, vp engrg.

St. Johnsbury

ADI No. 93; see Burlington-Plattsburgh market

***WVTB**—ch 20, 589 kw vis, 58.9 kw aur, ant 1,940t/139g. TL: N44 34 15 W71 53 36. Stereo. Hrs opn: 6:30 AM-2 AM Mon-Fri; 7 AM-1 AM Sat-Sun. On air date: Feb 26, 1968. 88 Ethan Allen Ave., Colchester (05446). Licensee: Vermont ETV Inc. (group owner; acq 11-6-89). ■ Net: PBS. ■ Hope S. Green, CEO & pres; Jack Candon, chmn; John E. King, CFO; Lee Ann Lee, vp dev; Ann Curran, mktg dir; Margery Hibbard Swim, vp progmg; Kenneth D. Schwab, progmg mgr & film buyer; Wayne Rosberg, vp engrg.

Windsor

ADI No. 93; see Burlington-Plattsburgh market

***WVTA**—ch 41, 1,050 kw vis, 105 kw aur, ant 2,245t/414g. TL: N43 26 15 W72 27 09. Stereo. On air date: March 18, 1968. 88 Ethan Allen Ave., Colchester (05446). (802) 655-4800. Licensee: Vermont ETV Inc. (acq 11-27-89). ■ Hope S. Green, CEO; Margery Hibberd Swim, vp progmg; Ronald Whitcomb, chief engr. ■ On 2 trans. Satellite of *WETK Burlington.

Virginia

Arlington

ADI No. 7; see Washington, DC market

WTMW—ch 14, 129 kw vis, ant 718t. TL: N38 52 28 W77 13 24. Not on air, target date unknown. 3565 Lee Hwy. (22207). (703) 528-0051. Permittee: Urban Telecommunications Corp.

Ashland

ADI No. 61; see Richmond market

WZXK—ch 65, 1,581 kw vis, 158 kw aur, ant 892t/850g. TL: N37 44 32 W77 15 18. Stereo. (CP: Ant 859t). Hrs opn: 20. On air date: Mar 9, 1990. 4120 E. Parham Rd., Richmond (23228). (804) 672-6565. Licensee: Christel Broadcasting Inc. Wash atty: May & Dunne. News progmg 3 hrs wkly. ■ Jim Campana, pres & gen mgr; Bill Vansyock, chief engr. ■ On 16 CATVs—175,000 subs.

Bristol

ADI No. 91; see Bristol-Kingsport-Johnson City-Greeneville market

WCYB-TV—ch 5, 83.2 kw vis, 10.6 kw aur, ant 2,230t/90g. TL: N36 26 57 W82 06 31. Stereo. On air date: Aug 13, 1956. 101 Lee St. (24203). (703) 645-1555. FAX: (703) 645-1553; TWX: 510-580-2109. Licensee: Appalachian Broadcasting Corp. Group owner: Lamco Communications Inc. (acq 3-17-77; $8,618,636; 3-28-77). ■ Net: NBC. Rep: Petry. Wash atty: Koteen & Naftalin. ■ Joe Macione Jr., vp & gen mgr; Richard Torbett, gen sls mgr; Lisa Kelechava, prom mgr; Cheryl Stout, progmg dir; Steve Hawkins, news dir; Tom Cupp, chief engr. ■ On 118 CATVs—250,000 subs.

WJHL-TV—See Johnson City, Tenn.

WKPT-TV—See Kingsport, Tenn.

Charlottesville

ADI No. 197; see Charlottesville market

***WHTJ**—ch 41, 251 kw vis, 25.1 kw aur, ant 1,156t/237g. TL: N37 58 58 W78 29 00. (CP: TL: N37 59 00 W78 28 54). On air date: May 19, 1989. 23 Sesame St., Richmond (23235). (804) 320-1311. FAX: (804) 320-8729. Licensee: Central Virginia Educational Telecommunications Corp. ■ Net: PBS. Wash atty: Wiley, Rien & Fielding. ■ Dr. Charles W. Sydnor Jr., pres & gen mgr; Scott C. Arnold, CFO; Amy Chown, dev dir; Helene Funk, progmg dir; Judy Flanders, pub affrs dir; John Prather, vp engrg & chief engr. ■ On one CATV. Co-owned radio: WCVE-FM Richmond.

WVIR-TV—ch 29, 5,000 kw vis, 500 kw aur, ant 1,187t/289g. TL: N37 59 00 W78 28 54. Stereo. Hrs opn: 24. On air date: Mar 11, 1973. Box 769, 503 E. Market St. (22902). (804) 977-7082. FAX: (804) 977-2800. Licensee: Virginia Broadcasting Corp. Group owner: Waterman Broadcasting Corp. ■ Net: NBC. Rep: Katz. Wash atty: Cohn & Marks. ■ Harold B. Wright Jr., vp & gen mgr; Jim Fernald, gen sls mgr & adv mgr; Robert Van Winkle, mktg dir & prom dir; Bob Doyle, progmg dir; Sid Shumate, engrg dir; Dsave McGrady, chief engr. ■ On 12 CATVs—73,800 subs. On 5 trans. ■ Rates: $500; 250; 75.

Danville

ADI No. 66; see Roanoke-Lynchburg market

WDRG—ch 24, 5,000 kw vis, 1,000 kw aur, ant 522t. Not on air, target date unknown. 5902 Shakertown Drive, Canton, OH (44718). (703) 878-1228. Permittee: Danville Television Partnership (acq 6-12-92; $10,000; 6-29-92).

Fairfax

ADI No. 7; see Washington, DC market

***WNVC**—ch 56, 1,230 kw vis, 123 kw aur, ant 1,049t/689g. TL: N38 52 28 W77 13 24. (CP: 1,260 kw vis, 126 kw aur, ant 705t/345g). On air date: June 1, 1983. 8101A Lee Hwy., Falls Church (22042). (703) 698-9682. FAX: (703) 849-9796. Licensee: Central Virginia Educational Telecommunications Corp. Wash atty: Fisher, Wayland, Cooper & Leader. ■ B. W. Spiller, pres; Roger McIntosh, gen mgr; Joanne Meredith, prom mgr; Fred Thomas, progmg mgr; N. Bruce Miller, news dir; Garr Johnson, chief engr. ■ On 20 CATVs.

Goldvein

ADI No. 7; see Washington, DC market

***WNVT**—ch 53, 2,290 kw vis, 229 kw aur, ant 751t/651g. TL: N38 37 42 W77 26 20. On air date: Mar 1, 1972. 8101A Lee Hwy., Falls Church (22042). (703) 698-9682. FAX: (703) 849-9796. Licensee: Central Virginia Educational Telecommunications Corp. (acq 7-3-74; $550,000; 7-22-74). ■ Net: PBS. Wash atty: Wiley, Rein & Fielding. ■ Dr. Charles W. Sydnor Jr., pres; R. A. McIntosh, vp & gen mgr; Mike Baker, stn mgr; B.R. Hamlin, dev dir; Joanne Meredith, prom mgr; Beverly Himm, progmg dir; Dave Hurd, chief engr. ■ On one trans.

Grundy

ADI No. 91; see Bristol-Kingsport-Johnson City-Greeneville market

WLFG—ch 68, 1,150 kw vis, 115 kw aur, ant 2,503t. TL: N36 49 47 W82 04 45. Not on air, target date unknown.

c/o Rt. 460, Vansant (24656). (703) 935-7850. Permittee: Tookland Pentecostal Church. ■ Buford Smith, pres.

Hampton

WVEC-TV—Licensed to Hampton. See Norfolk.

Hampton-Norfolk

***WHRO-TV**—Licensed to Hampton-Norfolk. See Norfolk.

Harrisonburg

ADI No. 173; see Harrisonburg market

WHSV-TV—ch 3, 8.32 kw vis, 432 w aur, ant 2,130t/337g. TL: N38 36 05 W78 37 57. Hrs opn: 20. On air date: Oct 19, 1953. Box TV 3, Hwy. 33 W. (22801-0030). (703) 433-9191; (703) 433-2800. FAX: (703) 433-4028. Licensee: Benedek Broadcasting Corp. Group owner: Benedek Broadcasting Co. (acq 11-5-86; grpsl; 9-29-86). ■ Net: ABC. Rep: Katz. Wash atty: Covington & Burling. News staff 12; news progmg 7 hrs wkly. ■ Robert Ganzer, pres & gen mgr; Bob Bolyard, natl sls mgr; Dave Ford, rgnl sls mgr; Todd Jones, prom mgr; John Dodson, progmg dir; Steve Raml, news dir; Richard Hiett, chief engr. ■ On 40 CATVs—93,000 subs. ■ Rates: $750; 450; 190.

Lynchburg

ADI No. 66; see Roanoke-Lynchburg market

WJPR—ch 21, 4,170 kw vis, 417 kw aur, ant 1,640t/966g. TL: N37 19 14 W79 37 58. Stereo. (CP: 4,207 kw vis). Hrs opn: 20. On air date: February 1986. Box 2127, Roanoke (24009-2127); 2618 Colonial Ave. S.W., Roanoke (24015). (703) 344-2127. FAX: (703) 345-1912. Licensee: Grant Broadcasting System II Inc. (acq 5-21-93; $5.5 million with satellite station WFXR-TV Roanoke; 6-14-93). ■ Net: Fox. Rep: Seltel. Wash atty: Birch, Horton & Biitner. ■ Milt Grant, pres; Stan Marinoff, vp & gen mgr; Jim Prestwood, natl sls mgr; Tony Kahl, rgnl sls mgr; Kipp Preston, progmg mgr; Jill Thomas, pub affrs dir; Robert Jenkins, chief engr.

WSET-TV—ch 13, 302 kw vis, 50 kw aur, ant 2,050t/1,240g. TL: N37 18 52 W79 38 04. On air date: Feb 8, 1953. Box 11588 (24506-1588); 2320 Langhorne Rd. (24501). (804) 528-1313. FAX: (804) 847-0458. Licensee: WSET Inc. Group owner: Allbritton Communications Co. (acq 10-76; grpsl). ■ Net: ABC. Rep: Katz. Wash atty: Hogan & Hartson. News progmg 7 hrs wkly. ■ Jerry Heilman, pres & gen mgr; Mike Brunette, sls dir & mktg dir; John Crumpler, prom mgr; Roy Clem, news dir; Doug Daniel, chief engr.

Manassas

ADI No. 7; see Washington, DC market

WTKK—ch 66, 5,000 kw vis, 500 kw aur, ant 590t/409g. TL: N38 47 16 W77 19 49. On air date: Mar 26, 1978. 9008 Center St. (22110). (703) 631-2310. FAX: (703) 369-1910. Licensee: WTKK-TV Inc. Wash atty: John H. Midlen. Foreign lang progmg 125 hrs wkly. ■ Lester R. Raker, pres & gen mgr; Thomas L. Foltz, stn mgr; Bill Kilchenstein, gen sls mgr & mktg mgr; Kay Raker, vp progmg; Anthony Raker, news dir; Phil DeLorme, chief engr. ■ On 22 CATVs—50,000 subs. ■ Rates: $100; 60; 45.

Marion

ADI No. 91; see Bristol-Kingsport-Johnson City-Greeneville market

***WMSY-TV**—ch 52, 755 kw vis, 115 kw aur, ant 1,360t/247g. TL: N36 54 01 W81 32 35. Hrs opn: 18. On air date: Aug 1, 1981. Box 13246, 1215 McNeil Dr., Roanoke (24032). (703) 344-0991. FAX: (703) 344-2148. Licensee: Blue Ridge Public Television Inc. ■ Net: PBS. Wash atty: Cohn & Marks. ■ Donald Piedmont, chmn; Larry A. Dyer, pres & gen mgr; Randy Riggins, opns mgr; Barbara Landon, vp dev; Andre Burroughs, prom mgr; Jon Boettcher, vp progmg; Ronald B. Smith, vp engrg. ■ On 10 CATV—23,000 subs.

LAUREN A. COLBY
301-663-1086
COMMUNICATIONS ATTORNEY
Special Attention to Difficult Cases

Norfolk

ADI No. 40; see Norfolk-Portsmouth-Newport News-Hampton market

WAVY-TV—(Portsmouth). ch 10, 316 kw vis, 38.9 kw aur, ant 990t/1,026g. TL: N36 49 14 W76 30 41. Stereo. Hrs opn: 24. On air date: Sept 1, 1957. 300 Wavy St., Portsmouth (23704). (804) 393-1010. FAX: (804) 399-7628. Licensee: WAVY-TV Inc. Group owner: LIN Broadcasting Corp. (acq 3-27-68; $8 million; 4-11-68). ■ Net: NBC. Rep: Blair. Wash atty: Covington & Burling. News staff 45; news progmg 24 hrs wkly. ■ Lyle Banks, pres & gen mgr; Ed Munson, gen sls mgr; Mike A. Mastrullo, prom mgr; Jane Tucker, progmg dir; Bob Cashen, news dir; Les Garrenton, chief engr. ■ On 34 CATVs—40,000 subs. On 3 trans.

***WHRO-TV**—(Hampton-Norfolk). ch 15, 2,630 kw vis, 263 kw aur, ant 971t/949g. TL: N36 48 32 W76 30 13. Stereo. Hrs opn: 18. On air date: Oct 2, 1961. 5200 Hampton Blvd., Norfolk (23508). (804) 489-9476. FAX: (804) 489-0007. Licensee: Hampton Roads Educ. Telecommunications Assn Inc. ■ Net: PBS. Wash atty: Cohn & Marks. ■ John Morison, CEO & gen mgr; Kenneth B. Krall, exec vp; Lawrence E. Crum, srvp; Keith L. Massie, vp opns & vp engrg; Marguerite Vail, vp dev; Donna Hudgins, prom dir. ■ On 26 CATVs—387,600 subs. On 3 trans. Co-owned radio: WHRO(FM).

WJCB—ch 49, 501 kw vis, 50.1 kw aur, ant 508t. TL: N36 48 32 W76 30 13. On air date: unknown. Suite 600, 2501 Washington Ave., Newport News (23607). (804) 247-0049. Licensee: Tidewater Christian Communications (acq 3-22-85; $117,975; 4-8-85). ■ Bishop Samuel L. Green, chmn; Dwight L. Green, gen mgr; Andre Taylor, Terrell Melton, chiefs mgr.

WTKR-TV—ch 3, 100 kw vis, 20 kw aur, ant 980t/1,029g. TL: N36 48 56 W76 28 00. On air date: Apr 2, 1950. Box 2456 (23501); 720 Boush St. (23510). (804) 446-1000. FAX: (804) 622-1385. Licensee: Narragansett Television. Group owner: Narragansett Television L.P. ■ Net: CBS. Rep: Petry. Wash atty: Reed, Smith, Shaw & McClay; Pierson, Ball & Dowd. ■ Christopher W. Pike, vp & gen mgr; Dave Davis, gen sls mgr; Chris Dominici, prom mgr; Jack K. Welsby, progmg dir; Gene Gildow, chief engr. ■ On 11 CATVs.

WTVZ—ch 33, 5,000 kw vis, 500 kw aur, ant 909t/1,026g. TL: N36 48 32 W76 30 13. On air date: Sept 24, 1979. 900 Granby St. (23510). (804) 622-3333. FAX: (804) 623-1541. Licensee: WTVZ Inc. Ownership: Charles A. McFadden, 100% (acq 7-1-89; $10,750,000; 8-14-89). ■ Net: Fox, CBS. Rep: Seltel. Wash atty: Gardner, Carton & Douglas. ■ Charles A. McFadden, pres & gen mgr; Elise Kennett, gen sls mgr; Shelley Stiles, prom mgr; Mark Hudgins, progmg dir; Edward Cuthrell, chief engr. ■ On 28 CATVs—359,152 subs.

WVEC-TV—(Hampton). ch 13, 316 kw vis, 31.6 kw aur, ant 980t/1,028g. TL: N36 49 00 W76 28 05. (CP: Ant 987t). On air date: Sept 15, 1953. 613 Woodis Ave., Norfolk (23510). (804) 625-1313. FAX: (804) 628-6220. Licensee: WVEC Television Inc. Group owner: A.H. Belo Corp., Broadcast Division (acq 11-28-83; grpsl; 12-29-83). ■ Net: ABC. Rep: Telerep. Wash atty: Dow, Lohnes & Albertson. ■ Lee Salzberger, pres, gen mgr & progmg mgr; John Rizzuti, gen sls mgr; Chris Sniffen, natl sls mgr; Hal Brauer (local), rgnl sls mgr; Bud Brown, prom dir; Dave Cassidy, news dir; Sherri Brennen, pub affrs dir; Richard Cannon, chief engr. ■ On 62 CATVs—444,440 subs.

Norton

ADI No. 91; see Bristol-Kingsport-Johnson City-Greeneville market

***WSBN-TV**—ch 47, 690 kw vis, 61.7 kw aur, ant 1,940t/242g. TL: N36 53 52 W82 37 22. Hrs opn: 18. On air date: Mar 29, 1971. Box 13246, Roanoke (24032). (703) 344-0991. FAX: (703) 344-2148. Licensee: Blue Ridge Public Television Inc. ■ Net: PBS. Wash atty: Cohn & Marks. ■ Donald Piedmont, chmn; Larry A. Byer, pres; Larry A. Dyer, gen mgr; Randy Riggins, opns mgr; Barbara Landon, vp dev; Andre Burroughs, prom mgr; Jon Boettcher, progmg dir; Ronald Smith, chief engr. ■ On 17 CATVs—56,353 subs. On one trans.

Petersburg

WRIC-TV—Licensed to Petersburg. See Richmond.

Portsmouth

ADI No. 40; see Norfolk-Portsmouth-Newport News-Hampton market

WAVY-TV—Licensed to Portsmouth. See Norfolk.

WGNT—ch 27, 2,340 kw vis, 478 kw aur, ant 971t/1,026g. TL: N36 48 43 W76 27 49. On air date: Oct 1, 1961. 1318 Spratley St. (23704). (804) 393-2501. FAX: (804) 399-3303. Licensee: Centennial Communications Inc. Ownership: Raymond B. Bottom Jr., 63.6%; Robert L. Freeman Sr., 10.14% (acq 7-12-89); $10,690,000; 6-12-89). Rep: Katz. Wash atty: Cohen & Berfield. ■ Raymond Bottom, CEO; W. Howard Jernigan Jr., pres & gen mgr; Harry Doggette, opns dir; Ernest Harris, vp sls; Ruth Young, natl sls mgr; John Rezabeck, rgnl sls mgr; Jeanne Pennington, prom mgr; Scott Benton, Janell Alvarez, progmg mgrs; George Randell, chief engr. ■ On 37 CATVs.

WTVZ—See Norfolk.

Richmond

ADI No. 61; see Richmond market

***WCVE-TV**—ch 23, 2,290 kw vis, 351 kw aur, ant 1,079t/976g. TL: N37 30 46 W77 36 06. Stereo. On air date: Sept 14, 1964. 23 Sesame St. (23235). (804) 320-1301. FAX: (804) 320-8729. Licensee: Central Virginia Educational Telecommunications Corp. ■ Net: PBS. Wash atty: Wiley, Rien & Fielding. ■ Dr. Charles W. Sydnor Jr., pres & gen mgr; Scott Arnold, CFO; Amy Chown, dev dir; Helene Funk, progmg dir; Judy Flanders, pub affrs dir; John Prather, vp engrg & chief engr. ■ On 46 CATVs—193,730 subs. On 9 trans. Co-owned radio: WCVE-FM.

***WCVW**—ch 57, 1,000 kw vis, 100 kw aur, ant 961t/1,170g. TL: N37 30 46 W77 36 06. On air date: Dec 22, 1966. 23 Sesame St. (23235). (804) 320-1301. FAX: (804) 320-8729. Licensee: Central Virginia Educational Telecommunications Corp. ■ Net: PBS. Wash atty: Wiley, Rien & Fielding. Chinese 3 hrs wkly. ■ Dr. Charles W. Sydnor Jr., pres & gen mgr; Scott C. Arnold, CFO; Amy Chown, dev dir; Helene Funk, progmg dir; Judy Flanders, pub affrs dir; John Prather, vp engrg & chief engr. ■ On 9 CATVs—133,473 subs. On 4 trans.

WRIC-TV—(Petersburg). ch 8, 269 kw vis, 34.4 kw aur, ant 1,050t/999g. TL: N37 30 46 W77 36 06. Stereo. On air date: Aug 15, 1955. 301 Arboretum Pl., Richmond (23236-3464). (804) 330-8888. FAX: (804) 330-8882. Licensee: Nationwide Communications Inc. Group owner: Nationwide Mutual Insurance Co. (acq 11-3-67; $7,150,000; 11-13-67). ■ Net: ABC. Rep: Katz. Wash atty: Fletcher, Heald & Hildreth. ■ Benjamin McKeel, gen mgr; Sandhi Kozsuch, opns dir; Tim Frame, gen sls mgr; Lauren Bacigalupi, prom mgr; Joyce Reed, news dir; Tom Beauchamp, chief engr. ■ On 47 CATVs—282,745 subs.

WRLH-TV—ch 35, 2,588 kw vis, 259 kw aur, ant 1,259.2t. TL: N37 30 22 W77 42 30. Hrs opn: 24. On air date: Feb 20, 1982. 1925 Westmoreland St. (23230). (804) 358-3535; (804) 359-3510. FAX: (804) 358-1495. Licensee: WRLH Inc. Group Owner: Act III Broadcasting Inc. (acq 9-15-88). ■ Net: Fox. Rep: Seltel. Wash atty: Goldberg & Spector. ■ Don Richards, vp; Bill Finch, opns mgr & progmg dir; Brandt Minnick, gen sls mgr; Joe Bowman, natl sls mgr; Susan DeLong, rgnl sls mgr; Jeanine Joseph, prom mgr; Lori Antoniak, adv mgr; Marit Price, pub affrs dir; Eldon Brown, chief engr. ■ On 33 CATVs—230,000 subs. ■ Rates: $750; 200; 50.

WTVR-TV—ch 6, 100 kw vis, 15.1 kw aur, ant 1,049t/840g. TL: N37 34 00 W77 28 36. On air date: Apr 22, 1948. 3301 W. Broad St. (23230). (804) 254-3600. FAX: (804) 254-3699. Licensee: Roy H. Park Broadcasting of Va. Inc. Group owner: Park Communications Inc. (acq 11-65; $5,017,185; 10-25-65). ■ Net: CBS. Rep: Blair. Wash atty: Wiley, Rien & Fielding. ■ Richard Pegram, gen mgr; Tina Woody, opns mgr; Wanda Lewis, vp sls & vp adv; Armand Grez, natl sls mgr; Sandy Fowler-Jones, mktg dir; Matt Heffernan, progmg dir; Don LaCombe, film buyer; Elliott Wiser, news dir; Ken Miller, chief engr. ■ On 22 CATVs—100,120 subs. Co-owned radio: WTVR-AM-FM.

Washington

WWBT—ch 12, 316 kw vis, 63.1 kw aur, ant 790t/1,000g. TL: N37 30 23 W77 30 12. Stereo. On air date: Apr 29, 1956. Box 12 (23201); 5710 Midlothian Tpke. (23225). (804) 230-1212. FAX: (804) 230-2500. Licensee: Jefferson-Pilot Broadcasting Co. of Va. Group owner: Jefferson-Pilot Communications Co. (acq 1968; $5 million). ■ Net: NBC. Rep: Petry. Wash atty: Kirkland & Ellis. William E. Blackwell, pres; John Shreves, vp, gen mgr & progmg dir; Ellen Shuler, gen sls mgr; Mary MacMillan, mktg mgr; Harvey Powers, news dir; Dave Frasier, chief engr. ■ On 49 CATVs—218,853 subs.

Roanoke

ADI No. 66; Roanoke-Lynchburg market

*****WBRA-TV**—ch 15, 1,820 kw vis, 182 kw aur, ant 2,089t/265g. TL: N37 11 45 W80 09 18. Stereo. Hrs opn: 18. On air date: Aug 1, 1967. Box 13246 (24032); 1215 McNeil Dr. S.W. (24015). (703) 344-0991. FAX: (703) 344-2148. Licensee: Blue Ridge Public Television Inc. ■ Net: PBS. Wash atty: Cohn & Marks. ■ Donald Piedmont, chmn; Larry A. Dyer, pres & gen mgr; Randy Riggins, opns mgr; Barbara Landon, vp dev; Andre Burroughs, prom mgr; Jon Boettcher, vp progmg; Ronald Smith, vp engrg. ■ On 25 CATVs—137,009 subs. On 3 trans.

WDBJ—ch 7, 316 kw vis, 62.5 kw aur, ant 2,000t/78g. TL: N37 11 42 W80 09 22. Stereo. On air date: Oct 3, 1955. Box 7 (24022); 2001 Colonial Ave. (24015). (703) 344-7000. FAX: (703) 344-5097. Licensee: WDBJ Television Inc. Group owner: Schurz Communications Inc. (acq 11-1-69; $8.2 million; 11-10-69). ■ Net: CBS. Rep: Harrington, Righter & Parsons. Wash atty: Bryan, Cave, McPheeters & McRoberts. News staff 45; news progmg 18 hrs wkly. ■ Robert G. Lee, pres; Edward W. Allen, CFO; Carl W. Guffey, opns mgr; George V. Bassett, sls dir; Margie C. Burgess, prom mgr; Jim Shaver, vp progmg; Mike Bell, progmg mgr; Jim Kent, news dir; Kelly Zuber, pub affrs dir; Glenn Saunders, engrg mgr. ■ On 88 CATVs—346,743 subs. On one trans.

WEFC—ch 38, 1,350 kw vis, 135 kw aur, ant 2,021t. TL: N37 11 35 W80 09 29. Hrs opn: 24. On air date: Jan 3, 1986. 612 Bullitt Ave. S.E. (24013). (703) 982-3694. FAX: (703) 345-8568. Licensee: Vine & Branch Inc. ■ C. Kenneth Wright, pres; Andrew Wright, stn mgr & gen sls mgr; John Harqis, sls dir; Andy Wright, progmg dir; Scott Jordan, chief engr. ■ On 20 CATVs—150,000 subs.

WFXR-TV—ch 27, 1,230 kw vis, 123 kw aur, ant 2,001t/200g. TL: N37 11 46 W80 09 16. Stereo. Hrs opn: 20. On air date: March 1986. Box 2127 (24009-2127); 2618 Colonial Ave. S.W. (24015). (703) 344-2127. FAX: (703) 345-1912. Licensee: Grant Broadcasting System II Inc. (group owner; acq 9-93; $5.5 million with WJPR[TV] Lynchburg; 6-14-93). ■ Net: Fox. Rep: Seltel. Wash atty: Birch, Horton, Bittner & Cherot. ■ Milt Grant, pres; Stan Marinoff, vp & gen mgr; Tony Kahl, rgnl sls mgr; Kipp Preston, progmg dir; Jill Thomas, pub affrs dir; Robert Jenkins, chief engr. ■ On 32 CATVs—150,000 subs.

WSLS-TV—ch 10, 316 kw vis, 47 kw aur, ant 2,001t/242g. TL: N37 12 02 W80 08 55. On air date: Dec 11, 1952. Box 2161 (24009). (703) 981-9110. Licensee: Park Communications Inc. (group owner; acq 9-10-69; $7,050,000; 9-22-69). ■ Net: NBC. Rep: Blair. Wash atty: McKenna, Wilkinson & Kittner. News staff 33; news progmg 15 hrs wkly. ■ Mrs. Roy H. Park, CEO; Wright M. Thomas, pres; James L. DeSchepper, vp, gen mgr & film buyer; Pete Watkins, gen sls mgr; Mark Leslie, prom mgr; Kim Strickland, progmg dir; Bill Foy, news dir; Mike Berkey, chief engr. ■ On 66 CATVs—172,000 subs. On one trans.

Staunton

ADI No. 61; see Richmond market

*****WVPT**—ch 51, 525 kw vis, 67.6 kw aur, ant 2,230t/46g. TL: N38 09 54 W79 18 51. Stereo. On air date: Sept 9, 1968. 298 Port Republic Rd., Harrisonburg (22801). (703) 434-5391. Licensee: Shenandoah Valley ETV Corp. ■ Net: PBS. Wash atty: Covington & Burling. ■ Arthur E. Albrecht, pres; Amy Laser, dev dir; Wanda Swecker, progmg dir; Vincent O'Connell, engrg dir. ■ On 15 CATVs—94,000 subs. On 6 trans.

Washington

Bellevue

ADI No. 13; see Seattle-Tacoma market

KBEH—ch 51, 5,000 kw vis, 500 kw aur, ant 1,079t. TL: N47 36 17 W122 19 46. Not on air, target date unknown. c/o 980 W. Sunset Way, Isaquah (98027). Permittee: Bellevue Broadcasting Co. Ltd. Ownership: Darlene C. McHenry, gen ptnr, 20%; Marie G. O'Neill L.P., 30%; Jerry O'Neill L.P., 30%; Wayne D. Tanaka L.P., 10%; Dennis D. Sutter L.P., 10%.

Bellingham

ADI No. 13; see Seattle-Tacoma market

KBCB—ch 64, 42.7 kw vis, ant 2,217t. TL: N48 40 48 W122 50 23. Not on air, target date unknown. c/o Frank Washington Suite 237, 601 University Ave., Sacramento, CA (95825). (916) 921-2290. Permittee: Prism Broadcasting Corp.

KVOS-TV—ch 12, 234 kw vis, 45.7 kw aur, ant 2,368t/139g. TL: N48 40 40 W122 49 48. On air date: June 3, 1953. 1151 Ellis St. (98225). (206) 671-1212. FAX: (206) 647-0824; TELEX: 32-8812. Licensee: KVOS TV Inc. Group owner: Ackerley Communications Inc. (acq 6-5-85; $26 million). Rep: Seltel. Wash atty: Rubin, Winston & Dierks. News staff 10; news progmg 3 hrs wkly. ■ David Reid, vp, gen mgr & progmg dir; Margot Wilson, opns mgr & news dir; Chris Brown, vp sls; Duane Lee, natl sls mgr; T. S. Hunt, rgnl sls mgr; Berni Holsworth, mktg dir; Don Luchsinger, chief engr. ■ Rates: $500; 175; 75.

Centralia

ADI No. 13; see Seattle-Tacoma market

*****KCKA**—ch 15, 661 kw vis, 66.1 kw aur, ant 1,138t. TL: N46 33 16 W123 03 26. On air date: October 1982. 1101 S. Yakima, Tacoma (98405). (206) 596-1528. FAX: (206) 596-1623. Licensee: State Board for Community and Technical Colleges (acq 11-29-91; 12-16-91). ■ Net: PBS. Wash atty: McKenna, Wilkinson & Kittner. ■ Debbie Emond, gen mgr & stn mgr; Al Bednarczyk, chief engr. ■ On 10 CATVs—75,000 subs. On one trans.

Everett

ADI No. 13; see Seattle-Tacoma market

KONG-TV—ch 16, 5,000 kw vis, 500 kw aur, ant 1,079t/299g. TL: N47 32 34 W122 06 25. Not on air, target date unknown. Suite 521, 7700 Edgewater Dr., Oakland, CA (94621). (415) 632-3411. Permittee: Kong TV Inc. Ownership: C.D. Washington, 75%; Sam Schulman, 11%. Rep: ITS. Wash atty: Hunton & Williams. ■ Carl Washington, pres; Dan O'Brien, gen mgr; Bill Achatz, chief engr.

Kennewick

ADI No. 124; see Yakima-Pasco-Richland-Kennewick market

KVEW—ch 42, 501 kw vis, 39.8 kw aur, ant 1,280t/205g. TL: N46 06 11 W119 07 54. On air date: Oct 30, 1970. 601 N. Edison (99336). (509) 735-8369. Licensee: Apple Valley Broadcasting Inc. Group owner: Morgan Murphy Stns. ■ Net: ABC. ■ Darrell Blue, vp & gen mgr; Thom Spencer, news dir; Neil Bennett, chief engr. Satellite of KAPP Yakima.

Pasco

ADI No. 124; see Yakima-Pasco-Richland-Kennewick market

KEPR-TV—ch 19, 490 kw vis, 88.3 kw aur, ant 1,203t/354g. TL: N46 05 48 W119 11 36. On air date: Dec 28, 1954. Box 2648 (99302); 2807 W. Lewis (99301). (509) 547-0547. FAX: (509) 547-2845. Licensee: Retlaw Enterprises Inc. Group owner: Retlaw Broadcasting Co. (acq 12-28-86; grpsl; 10-27-86). ■ Net: CBS. Rep: Katz. Wash atty: Wiley, Rein, & Fielding. News staff 8; news progmg 8 hrs wkly. ■ Ben Tucker, pres; Ken Messer, vp & gen sls mgr; Steve Crow, stn mgr & adv mgr; Mary Beth Bradley, dev mgr; Dave Spraker, prom mgr; Stu Seibel, progmg dir; Jim Hall, news dir; Don Eckis, chief engr. ■ 85,000 subs. On 4 trans. ■ Rates: $120; 80; 30.

Pullman

ADI No. 78; see Spokane market

*****KWSU-TV**—ch 10, 117 kw vis, 11.7 kw aur, ant 1,350t/300g. TL: N46 51 43 W117 10 26. Hrs opn: 18. On air date: Sept 24, 1962. Murrow Communications Ctr., Washington State Univ. (99164-2530). (509) 335-6511. FAX: (509) 335-3772. Licensee: Washington State Univ. ■ Net: PBS. ■ Dennis Haarsager, gen mgr; Elizabeth Carroll, dev dir; Warren Wright, progmg dir; John Gray, engrg dir. ■ On 28 CATVs—116,000 subs. On one trans. Co-owned radio: *KWSU(AM).

Richland

ADI No. 124; see Yakima-Pasco-Richland-Kennewick market

KNDU—ch 25, 661 kw vis, 66.1 kw aur, ant 1,348t. TL: N46 06 11 W119 07 47. Hrs opn: 18. On air date: July 1, 1961. 3312 W. Kennewick Ave., Kennewick (99336). (509) 783-6151. FAX: (509) 783-3746; TWX: 510-777-5353. Licensee: Columbia Empire Broadcasting Corp., a Delaware Corp. Group owner: Farragut Communications (acq 3-24-88). ■ Net: NBC. Rep: Seltel; Art Moore. Wash atty: Wiley, Rein & Fielding. News staff 8; news progmg 7 hrs wkly. ■ Marvin L. Shapiro, pres; Elliot Kleeman, gen mgr; Dave Dalthrop, stn mgr; Dale Chaney, gen sls mgr; Robert Manderville, prom mgr; Rita Lockhart, progmg dir; Christine Brown, news dir; Dana Dwinell, pub affrs dir; Ed Lyon, chief engr. ■ On 27 CATVs—69,178 subs. On 2 trans.

*****KTNW**—ch 31, 53.5 kw vis, 5.35 kw aur, ant 1,198t/36g. TL: N46 06 23 W119 07 50. Hrs opn: 18. On air date: Oct 18, 1987. Murrow Communications Center, Washington State Univ., Pullman (99164-2530). (509) 335-6511. FAX: (509) 335-3772. Licensee: Washington State U. ■ Net: PBS. ■ Dennis L. Haarsager, gen mgr; Elizabeth Carroll, dev dir; Warren Wright, progmg dir; John Gray, engrg dir. Co-owned radio: KFAE-FM, KWSU (AM), KRFA-FM.

Seattle

ADI No. 13; see Seattle-Tacoma market

KCPQ—(Tacoma) ch 13, 316 kw vis, 31.6 kw aur, ant 2,000t/708g. TL: N47 32 53 W122 48 22. Stereo. (CP: Ant 1,191t; TL: N47 36 59 W122 18 23). Hrs opn: 24. On air date: 1954. Box 98828, 4400 Steilacoom Blvd. S.W., Tacoma (98499); Suite 405, 100 S. King St., Seattle (98104). (206) 582-8613. FAX: (206) 383-9551. Licensee: Kelly Television Co. Group owner: Kelly Broadcasting Co. (acq 1-21-81; $6.25 million). ■ Net: Fox, CBS, NBC. Rep: Telerep. Wash atty: Koteen & Naftalin. ■ Roger Ottenbach, gen mgr; Don Lacy, opns mgr; Greg Obata, gen sls mgr; Lloyd Low (west), Mike Seifert (east), natl sls mgrs; Dennis McCormick, rgnl sls mgr; Chris Kelly, mktg mgr; Robert Galvin, prom mgr; Robert E. Kelly, progmg dir; Keith Shipman, pub affrs dir; Larry Brandt, chief engr. ■ On 87 CATVs—868,135 subs. On 3 trans.

*****KCTS-TV**—ch 9, 316 kw vis, 50 kw aur, ant 830t/590g. TL: N47 36 58 W122 18 28. Stereo. Hrs opn: 24. On air date: Dec 7, 1954. 401 Mercer (98109). (206) 728-6463. FAX: (206) 443-6691. Licensee: KCTS Television (acq 7-15-87). ■ Net: PBS. Wash atty: Dow, Lohnes & Albertson. ■ Burnill Clark, CEO & pres; Walter Parsons, sr vp; Tom Howe, vp; Steve Welch, opns dir; Dorothy Paton, vp dev; Paula Nemzek, dev mgr; Michelle Barry, prom dir; Jane Sheridan, progmg mgr; Gary Gibson, pub affrs dir; Cliff Anderson, chief engr. ■ On 29 CATVs—1,070,393 subs. On 6 trans.

KHCV—ch 45, 5,000 kw vis, 500 kw aur, ant 1,289t. TL: N47 32 41 W122 06 28. Not on air, target date unknown. One W. Lone Cactus Dr., Phoenix, AZ (85027). Permittee: North Pacific International Television Inc. (acq 11-3-92; 11-23-92).

KING-TV—ch 5, 100 kw vis, 15.1 kw aur, ant 820t/570g. TL: N47 37 55 W122 20 59. Stereo. (CP: Ant 1,168t/918g). On air date: Nov 25, 1948. Box 24525 (98124); 333 Dexter Ave. N. (98109). (206) 448-5555. FAX: (206) 448-3936. Licensee: King Broadcasting Co. Group owner: Providence Journal Broadcasting Corp. (acq 8-27-91; $355 million; grpsl; 9-9-91). ■ Net: NBC. Rep: Blair, Paul Mulvihill (Canada). Wash atty: Fletcher, Heald & Hildreth. ■ Tony Twibell, pres & gen mgr; John Washington, gen sls mgr; D.J. Wilson, natl sls mgr; John Schuessler, rgnl sls mgr; Bob Casazza, mktg dir; Craig Smith, progmg dir; Andy Beers, news dir; Brian Lay, chief engr. ■ On 89 CATVs—954,264 subs. On 12 trans. ■ Rates: $4,000; 700; 200.

KIRO-TV—ch 7, 316 kw vis, 63.2 kw aur, ant 820t/599g. TL: N47 38 01 W122 21 20. Stereo. On air date: Feb 8, 1958. Box C 21326, 2807 3rd Ave. (98111-7000). (206) 728-7777. FAX: (206) 441-7905. Licensee: KIRO Inc. Group owner: Bonneville International Corp. (acq 12-17-83). ■ Net: CBS. Rep: Petry. Wash atty: Wilkinson, Barker, Knauer & Quinn. ■ Kenneth L. Hatch, pres; Glenn Wright, gen mgr; James "Sandy" Zogg, gen sls mgr; Dave Blakely, natl sls mgr; Gary Moore, mktg dir; Judy Law, prom mgr; John Reim, vp progmg; Bill Lord, news dir; Pamela Steele, pub affrs dir; Paul Polzin, chief engr. ■ On 83 CATVs—363,423 subs. On 8 trans. Co-owned radio: KIRO-AM-FM.

KOMO-TV—ch 4, 100 kw vis, 15 kw aur, ant 810t/550g. TL: N47 37 55 W122 21 09. Stereo. (CP: Ant 1,151t, TL: N47 37 56 W122 21 11). On air date: Dec 10, 1953. 100 4th Ave. N. (98109). (206) 443-4000. FAX: (206) 443-4014. Licensee: Fisher Broadcasting Inc. (group owner). ■ Net: ABC. Rep: Katz. Wash atty: Fisher, Wayland, Cooper & Leader. ■ Patrick Scott, CEO; John Behnke, chmn; Sherry Sharer, exec vp; Dick Warsinske, vp & gen mgr; Scott Hayner, vp sls; Phelps Fisher, vp mktg; Deborah Johnson, prom mgr; Jacques Natz, news dir; Don Wilkinson, vp engrg. ■ On 75 CATVs—416,651 subs. Co-owned radio: KOMO(AM). ■ Rates: $4,000; 1,200; 500.

KSTW—(Tacoma) ch 11, 316 kw vis, 47.8 kw aur, ant 891t/637g. TL: N47 36 56 W122 18 29. Stereo. Hrs opn: 24. On air date: Mar 1, 1953. Box 11411, Seattle (98122-0477); 2320 S. 19th St., Tacoma (98405). (206) 572-5789. FAX: (206) 272-7581. Licensee: Gaylord Broadcasting Co. (group owner; acq 3-1-74; $4.5 million). Rep: MMT. Wash atty: Reed, Smith, Shaw & McClay. News progmg 10 hrs wkly. ■ Gary Schneider, vp, gen mgr & progmg dir; Scott Bauer, gen sls mgr; Jim Cummings, Noreen King, natl sls mgrs; Steve Pickle, prom dir; Charles Johnson, news dir; Julie Furlong, pub affrs dir; Paul C. Crittenden, chief engr. ■ On 133 CATVs—1,868,592 subs. ■ Rates: $600; 1,000; 85.

KTZZ-TV—ch 22, 5,000 kw vis, 501 kw aur, ant 890t/639g. TL: N47 36 57 W122 18 26. Stereo. Hrs opn: 24. On air date: June 22, 1985. 945 Dexter Ave. N. (98109). (206) 282-2202. FAX: (206) 281-0207. Licensee: US TV of Washington State Inc. Group owner: Dudley Communications Corp. (acq 12-89). Rep: Seltel. Wash atty: Arter & Hadden. Japanese 5 hrs wkly. ■ Bob Dudley, chmn; John Dudley, pres; Wade Brewer, gen mgr & progmg dir; Greg Winston, gen sls mgr; John Schoonover, prom mgr; Bud Alger, pub affrs dir & chief engr. ■ On 57 CATVs—820,230 subs. On one trans. ■ Rates: $300; 200; 60.

Spokane

ADI No. 78; see Spokane market

KAYU-TV—ch 28, 1,200 kw vis, 240 kw aur, ant 2,001t/824g. TL: N47 34 44 W117 17 46. (CP: 2,400 kw vis, 120 kw aur, ant 1,998t/821g). On air date: Oct 31, 1982. Box 8115, S. 4600 Regal St. (99203). (509) 448-2828. FAX: (509) 448-3815. Licensee: KAYU-TV Partners Ltd. ■ Net: Fox. Rep: Petry; Tacher. Wash atty: Gardner, Carton & Douglas. News progmg 3 hrs wkly. ■ Robert J. Hamacher, pres, gen mgr & progmg dir; John R. Rowland, gen sls mgr; Val Putnam, prom mgr; Wanda Ferguson, pub affrs dir.

KHQ-TV—ch 6, 87.1 kw vis, 17.4 kw aur, ant 2,150t/904g. TL: N47 34 52 W117 17 47. Stereo. Hrs opn: 24. On air date: Dec 20, 1952. Box 8088 (99203-0088); 4202 S. Regal (99223-7738). (509) 448-6000. FAX: (509) 448-4694. Licensee: KHQ Inc. Ownership: James P. Cowles and William Stacey Cowles, co-trustees (acq 7-15-92; 8-3-92). ■ Net: NBC. Rep: Katz. Wash atty: Wiley, Rein & Fielding. News staff 35; news progmg 10 hrs wkly. ■ Lon C. Lee, pres; Scott Blair, opns mgr; Bill Storms, natl sls mgr; Larry McDaniels, prom mgr; Tom Cohrs, chief engr. ■ On 62 CATVs—183,750 subs. On 3 trans. ■ Rates: $450; 275; 70.

KREM-TV—ch 2, 84.7 kw vis, 15.5 kw aur, ant 2,200t/969g. TL: N47 35 42 W117 17 53. Stereo. Hrs opn: 24. On air date: Oct 31, 1954. Box 8037 (99203); 4103 S. Regal (99223). (509) 448-2000. FAX: (509) 448-2969 (NEWS). Licensee: King Broadcasting Co. Ownership: Providence Journal (acq 9-92; $355 million; grpsl; 9-16-91). ■ Net: CBS. Rep: Blair. Wash atty: Fletcher, Heald & Hildreth. News staff 36; news progmg 15 hrs wkly. ■ Jack Clifford, CEO; Paul McTear, pres; Barry Barth, gen mgr; Brooks Hoag, gen sls mgr; Meg Antonius, progmg dir & film buyer; Paul Brandt, news dir; Boyd Lundberg, chief engr. ■ On 110 CATVs—615,703 subs. On 92 trans.

KSKN—ch 22, 1,396 kw vis, 139.6 kw aur, ant 2,100t/900g. TL: N47 35 42 W117 17 53. (CP: 230 kw vis, ant 1,296t, TL: N47 36 04 W117 17 53). On air date: Oct 1, 1983. 408 Paseo Companeros, Chico, CA (95928). Licensee: KSKN Inc. (acq 2-15-91; 3-11-91).

***KSPS-TV**—ch 7, 316 kw vis, 31.6 kw aur, ant 1,830t/600g. TL: N47 34 34 W117 17 58. Stereo. Hrs opn: 18. On air date: April 24, 1967. S. 3911 Regal St. (99223). (509) 353-5777. TWX: 509-456-8785 Licensee: Spokane School District No. 81. ■ Net: PBS. Wash atty: Haley, Bader & Potts. News progmg 18 hrs wkly. ■ Claude Kistler, gen mgr; Bill Stanley, stn mgr & progmg dir; Patty Starkey, dev dir; Grant Smith, prom mgr; Sean Herrin, progmg mgr; Ron Valley, engrg dir. ■ On 40 CATV's—210,000 subs. On 20 trans.

KXLY-TV—ch 4, 47.9 kw vis, 9.55 kw aur, ant 3,060t/153g. TL: N47 55 18 W117 06 48. Stereo. Hrs opn: 24. On air date: Feb 22, 1953. 500 W. Boone Ave. (99201). (509) 324-4000. FAX: (509) 328-5274. Licensee: Spokane TV Inc. Group owner: Evening Telegram Company—Morgan Murphy Stns (acq 1-17-63; grpsl; 1-63). ■ Net: ABC. Rep: Harrington, Righter & Parsons. ■ Elizabeth M. Burns, pres; Steve Herling, vp & gen mgr; Brian Williams, opns mgr; Teddie Gibbon, gen sls mgr; Dawn Bayman, prom mgr; Eileen McKinnon, progmg dir; Robin Briley, news dir; Dean Moorehouse, pub affrs dir; Tim Anderson, chief engr. ■ On 150 CATVs—384,900 subs. Co-owned radio: KXLY-AM-FM.

Tacoma

ADI No. 13; see Seattle-Tacoma market

***KBTC-TV**—ch 28, 676 kw vis, 67.6 kw aur, ant 761t/326g. TL: N47 16 41 W122 30 42. On air date: Sept 25, 1961. 1101 S. Yakima Ave. (98405). (206) 596-1528. FAX: (206) 596-1623. Licensee: State Board for Community & Technical Colleges (acq 11-29-91; with KBTC-FM Tacoma; 12-16-91). ■ Net: PBS. Wash atty: McKenna, Wilkinson & Kittner. ■ Debbie Emond, gen mgr & stn mgr; Al Bednarczyk, chief engr. ■ On 27 CATVs—365,500 subs. On one trans. Co-owned radio: *KBTC-FM.

KCPQ—Licensed to Tacoma. See Seattle.

KSTW—Licensed to Tacoma. See Seattle.

KTBW-TV—ch 20, 3,550 kw max, 355 kw max aur, ant 1,670t/350g. TL: N47 32 50 W122 47 39. Hrs opn: 24. On air date: March 30, 1984. 1909 S. 341st Place, Federal Way (98003). (206) 927-7720; (206) 874-7420. Licensee: Trinity Broadcasting of Washington. Group owner: Trinity Broadcasting Network. Wash atty: Colby May. ■ Paul F. Crouch, pres; Mary Jane Allen, stn mgr; Kenny Witkoe, progmg mgr; Gene Glasunow, chief engr. ■ On 17 CATVs—500,000 subs.

***KWDK**—ch 56, 5,000 kw vis, 500 kw aur, ant 1,872t. TL: N47 32 53 W122 48 22. Not on air, target date unknown. c/o Suite 571, 2166 W. Broadway, Anaheim, CA (92804). Permittee: Korean-American Missions Inc.

Vancouver

ADI No. 27; see Portland, OR market

KPDX—ch 49, 2,612 kw vis, 216 kw aur, ant 1,785t/1,081g. TL: N45 31 22 W122 45 07. On air date: October 1983. 910 N.E. Martin Luther King Blvd., Portland, OR (97232); One Columbia River (98660). (503) 239-4949. (206) 254-4949. Licensee: Cannell Communications Ltd. (acq 11-6-92; $15 million; 11-23-92). ■ Net: Fox. Rep: Petry. Wash atty: Dow, Lohnes & Albertson. News progmg 3 hrs wkly. ■ William A. Schwartz, CEO; Cary D. Jones, vp; Cary D.D. Jones, gen mgr; Brian Benschoter, opns mgr & progmg dir; Anthony Thompson, gen sls mgr; Sunny Wetzel, natl sls mgr; Craig Miller, prom mgr; Bob Wyatt, chief engr. ■ On 81 CATVs—459,533 subs. On 12 trans.

Wenatchee

ADI No. 13; see Seattle-Tacoma market

KCWT—ch 27, 269 kw vis, 26.9 kw aur, ant 1,391t/190g. TL: N47 19 26 W120 13 55. On air date: Apr 9, 1984. Suite 707, 1200 Westlake Ave. N., Seattle (98109-3529). Licensee: Bingham Communications Group (acq 11-10-86; $2.3 million; 9-1-86). Wash atty: Fisher, Wayland, Cooper & Leader. ■ R. Craig Monson, pres.

Yakima

ADI No. 124; see Yakima-Pasco-Richland-Kennewick market

KAPP—ch 35, 646 kw vis, 64.6 kw aur, ant 961t. TL: N46 31 57 W120 30 33. On air date: Sept 21, 1970. 1610 S. 24th Ave. (98902). (509) 453-0351. FAX: (509) 453-3623. Licensee: Apple Valley Broadcasting Inc. ■ Net: ABC. Wash atty: Robert Rini. ■ Elizabeth M. Burns, pres; Darrell Blue, vp; Ron Simmons, stn mgr, progmg dir & film buyer; Judy Ernesti, gen sls mgr; Cassandra Soden, prom mgr & pub affrs dir; Dave Ettl, news dir; Bob Couchman, chief engr. ■ On 36 CATVs—112,163 subs. On 2 trans.

KIMA-TV—ch 29, 490 kw vis, 87.3 kw aur, ant 971t/67g. TL: N46 31 58 W120 30 26. Hrs opn: 19. On air date: July 19, 1953. Box 702 (98907); 2801 Terrace Heights Dr. (98901). (509) 575-0029. FAX: (509) 248-1218; TWX: 510-777-5356. Licensee: Retlaw Enterprises Inc. Group owner: Retlaw Broadcasting Co. (acq 12-28-86; grpsl; 10-27-86). ■ Net: CBS. Rep: Katz. Wash atty: Wiley, Rein & Fielding. News staff 10; news progmg 11 hrs wkly. ■ Ben Tucker, pres; Andy Mastauros, CFO; Ken Messer, vp, gen mgr & gen sls mgr; Karla Griffin, opns mgr; Steve Crow, mktg mgr; Stu Siebel, progmg dir; T. J. Close, news dir; Cliff Grady, chief engr. ■ On 11 CATVs—46,400 subs. On 8 trans. ■ Rates: $300; 200; 50.

KNDO—ch 23, 501 kw vis, 61 kw aur, ant 961/161g. TL: N46 31 59 W130 20 36. Hrs opn: 18. On air date: Oct 15, 1959. Box 10028 (98909); 1608 S. 24th Ave. (98902). (509) 248-2300. FAX: (509) 575-0266. Licensee: Columbia Empire Broadcasting Corp., a Delaware Corp. Group owner: Farragut Communications Inc. (acq 3-24-88; grpsl). ■ Net: NBC. Rep: Seltel; Art Moore. Wash atty: Wiley, Rein & Fielding. News staff 7; news progmg 5 hrs wkly. ■ Marvin L. Shapiro, pres; Elliot R. Kleeman, gen mgr; Dale Chaney, gen sls mgr; Robert Manderville, prom mgr; Rita Lockhart, progmg dir; Shelly Swanke, news dir; Dana Dwinell, pub affrs dir; Wayne Whitaker, engrg dir. ■ On 8 CATVs—40,885 subs. On one trans.

***KYVE**—ch 47, 640 kw vis, 64 kw aur, ant 918t/135g. TL: N46 31 58 W120 30 33. On air date: Nov 1, 1962. 1105 S. 15th Ave. (98902). (509) 452-4700. FAX: (509) 452-4704. Licensee: Central Washington Association for Public Telecommunications. ■ Net: PBS. Wash atty: Schwartz, Woods & Miller. Sp progmg. ■ Warren D. Starr, gen mgr; Barbara Greco, prom mgr; Diane Ulrich, progmg dir; Rod Venable, chief engr. ■ On 5 CATVs—9,000 subs. On 3 trans.

West Virginia

Beckley

WOAY-TV—See Oak Hill.

Bluefield

ADI No. 147; see Bluefield-Beckley-Oak Hill market

WLFB—ch 40, 1,000 kw vis, 200 w aur, ant 1,991t/544g. TL: N37 10 46 W81 22 41. Not on air, target date unknown. Box 151, Vansant, VA (24656). (703) 935-7850. Permittee: Living Faith Ministries Inc.

WVVA—ch 6, 50.1 kw vis, 6.03 kw aur, ant 1,220t/185g. TL: N37 15 21 W81 10 55. Stereo. On air date: July 31, 1955. Box 1930, Rt. 460 Bypass (24701). (304) 325-5487. FAX: (304) 327-5586; TWX: 710-938-8380. Licensee: WVVA TV Inc. Group owner: Quincy Newspapers Inc., see Cross-Ownership (acq 5-1-79; $8 million; 4-23-79). ■ Net: NBC. Rep: Petry. Wash atty: Wilkinson, Barker, Knauer & Quinn. News progmg 7 hrs wkly. ■ Thomas A. Oakley, pres; Charles E. Webb, vp & gen mgr; Larry Roe, opns mgr; Merry Ewing, gen sls mgr; James Riffe, prom mgr; Cheri Haag, news dir; Kenneth Dick, chief engr. ■ On 100 CATVs—130,000 subs.

Charleston

ADI No. 55; see Charleston-Huntington market

WCHS-TV—ch 8, 158 kw vis, 19.9 kw aur, ant 1,240t/999g. TL: N38 24 28 W81 54 13. On air date: Aug 15, 1954. 1301 Piedmont Rd. (25301). (304) 346-5358. FAX: (304) 346-4765; TWX: 710-930-8720. Licensee: WCHS Ltd. Ownership: Heritage Media Corp. (acq 6-26-87). ■ Net: ABC. Rep: Petry. Wash atty: Sidley & Austin. ■ Dennis Adkins, pres & gen mgr; Jo Corey, opns mgr & progmg dir; Bob Knowles, gen sls mgr; Michael Hooper, prom mgr; Tim Sharp, news dir; Robert Roush, chief engr. ■ On 53 CATVs—89,000 subs.

Wisconsin

WKRP-TV—ch 29, 5,000 kw vis, 500 kw aur, ant 1,491t. TL: N38 23 15W 81 25 24. Not on air, target date unknown. 10 Hail St. (25323). Permittee: P.S.A. Inc.

WVAH-TV—ch 11, 51 kw vis, 5.1 kw aur, ant 1,722t/1,552g. TL: N38 25 15 W81 55 27. Stereo. Hrs opn: 24. On air date: Sept 19, 1982. 11 Broadcast Plaza, Hurricane (25526). (304) 757-0011. FAX: (304) 757-7533. Licensee: ACT III Broadcasting of West Virginia Inc. Group owner: ACT III Broadcasting Inc. ■ Net: Fox. Rep: Seltel. Wash atty: Fisher, Wayland, Cooper & Leader. ■ Richard Ballinger, pres; Bill White, gen mgr; Steve Utt, opns mgr; Edwin Hill, gen sls mgr; Harold Cooper, natl sls mgr; Mindy Bradley, mktg mgr; John Fawcett, prom mgr; Rita Gazitano, progmg dir & pub affrs dir; George Parnicza, chief engr. ■ On 250 CATVs—465,000 subs. ■ Rates: $500; 175; 50.

Clarksburg

ADI No. 160; see Clarksburg-Weston market

WBOY-TV—ch 12, 263 kw vis; 42.5 kw aur, ant 860t/593g. TL: N39 17 06 W80 19 46. Stereo. On air date: Nov 17, 1957. Box 1590 (26302); 904 W. Pike St. (26301). (304) 623-3311. FAX: (304) 624-6152. Licensee: WBOY-TV Inc. Group owner: Imes Communications (acq 12-15-76; $750,000; 11-15-76). ■ Net: NBC. Rep: Seltel, Dome. Wash atty: Arent, Fox, Kintner, Plotkin & Kahn. ■ Birney Imes, pres; Gary R. Bowden, vp, gen mgr & gen sls mgr; Mike Simons, prom mgr; Frances Basile, progmg dir & film buyer; Jamie Logue, news dir & pub affrs dir; Ray Myers, chief engr. ■ On 75 CATVs—100,000 subs.

WLYJ—ch 46, 155 kw vis, 15.5 kw aur, ant 800t/632g. TL: N39 18 02 W80 20 37. On air date: Feb 8, 1981. Box 2544, 775 W. Pike St. (26302). (304) 623-5784. Licensee: Christian Communication Center Inc. Wash atty: Gammon & Grange. ■ Arthur Armstrong, pres; Jack L. Kincaid, gen mgr; Wayne Fast, chief engr. ■ Rates: $55; 40; 35.

Grandview

ADI No. 147; see Bluefield-Beckley-Oak Hill market

***WSWP-TV**—ch 9, 316 kw vis, 63.2 kw aur, ant 1,000t/488g. TL: N37 53 46 W80 59 21. On air date: Nov 1, 1970. Box A.H., Beckley (25802). (304) 255-1501. FAX: (304) 252-9797. Licensee: West Virginia Educational Broadcasting Authority. ■ Net: PBS. Wash atty: Blair, Joyce & Silva. ■ Rita Ray, gen mgr; Craig Lanham, progmg dir; Leon Drye, chief engr. ■ On 205 CATVs—140,000 subs. Co-owned radio: *WVPB(FM).

Huntington

ADI No. 55; see Charleston-Huntington market

WOWK-TV—ch 13, 141 kw vis, 26.3 kw aur, ant 1,269t/1,108g. TL: N38 30 21 W82 12 33. On air date: Oct 2, 1955. Box 13 (25706-0013); TV Center, 555 Fifth Ave. (25701). (304) 525-7661. FAX: (304) 529-4910. Licensee: Gateway Communications Inc. (group owner; acq 10-23-74; $7,424,000; 10-7-74). ■ Net: CBS. Rep: Blair. Wash atty: Wilner & Scheiner. ■ Lamont T. Pinker, pres; Gary H. Ritchie, gen mgr; Leo MacCourtney, vp opns; John Fusco, gen sls mgr; Cheryl Ayoub, mktg dir & prom dir; Leo MacCourtney, progmg dir; Ron Lease, chief engr. ■ On 242 CATVs—367,000 subs.

***WPBY-TV**—ch 33, 2,371 kw vis, 105 kw aur, ant 1,243t. TL: N38 29 41 W82 12 03. On air date: July 14, 1969. Box 7366, 1615 Third Ave. (25776-7366). (304) 696-6630. FAX: (304) 696-4343. Licensee: West Virginia Educational Broadcasting Authority. ■ Net: PBS; SECA. ■ Thomas K. Holleron, gen mgr; Jo Ellen Stephens, dev mgr; Sally Carico, prom mgr; William Russell, progmg dir. ■ On 118 CATVs—256,577 subs.

WSAZ-TV—ch 3, 42.7 kw vis, 7 kw aur, ant 1,273t/1,101g. TL: N38 30 34 W82 13 09. Stereo. On air date: Nov 15, 1949. Box 2115, 645 Fifth Ave. (25721). (304) 697-4780. FAX: (304) 697-4325. Licensee: Lee Enterprises Inc. (group owner; acq 4-28-71; $18 million; 3-1-71). ■ Net: NBC. Rep: Katz. Wash atty: Pierson, Ball & Dowd. ■ Richard D. Gottlieb, pres; Gary Schmedding, vp; Don Ray, gen mgr; Chris Leister, gen sls mgr; Bill Garten, natl sls mgr; Mickey Curry, prom mgr & progmg mgr; Ken Selvaggi, news dir; Bill Hayes, chief engr. ■ On 326 CATVs—422,500 subs.

WVAH-TV—See Charleston.

Lewisburg

ADI No. 147; see Bluefield-Beckley-Oak Hill market

WVGV-TV—ch 59, 70.9 kw vis, 7.9 aur, 1302t. TL: N37 57 13 W80 34 34. Not on air, target date Spring 1994. Box 371 (24901); Rt. 2, Box 365, Houfnagle Rd. (24901). Licensee: WVGV TV Corporation.

Martinsburg

ADI No. 7; see Washington, DC market

WYVN—ch 60, 3,890 kw vis, ant 1,717t/240g TL: N39 27 27 W78 03 53. Stereo. Hrs opn: 19. On air date: Oct 1, 1991. One Discovery Place (25401). (304) 267-6060. FAX: (304) 267-6180. Licensee: Green River Broadcasting of Martinsburg Inc. (acq 10-7-93). ■ Net: Fox. Wash atty: Cohn & Marks. News staff 9; news progmg 12 hrs wkly. ■ Ben Ewing, pres; Carol LaFever, stn mgr; Mary Huntsberry, gen sls mgr; Ralph Tobias, film buyer; Jeff Hertrick, news dir; Steve Salopek, chief engr. ■ On 13 CATVs—137,000 subs. ■ Rates: $65; 50; 35.

Morgantown

ADI No. 17; see Pittsburgh market

***WNPB-TV**—ch 24, 3,000 kw vis, 347 kw aur, ant 1,499t/515g. TL: N39 41 45 W79 45 45. On air date: Feb 23, 1969. Box TV-24 (26507); 191 Scott Ave. (26505). (304) 293-6511. FAX: (304) 293-2642. Licensee: West Virginia Educational Broadcasting Authority (acq 7-1-83). ■ Net: PBS; SECA. Wash atty: Cohn & Marks. ■ Carolyn Bailey Lewis, gen mgr; Charolette Bolyard, opns mgr; Albert H. Prichard, progmg dir; Mary Lucille DeBerry, pub affrs dir; Michael A. Galik, chief engr. ■ On 41 CATVs. On 7 trans.

Oak Hill

ADI No. 147; see Bluefield-Beckley-Oak Hill market

WOAY-TV—ch 4, 100 kw vis, 20 kw aur, ant 740t/688g. TL: N37 57 30 W81 09 03. On air date: Dec 14, 1954. Box 251 (25901). (304) 469-3361. FAX: (304) 465-1420. Licensee: Thomas Broadcasting Co. ■ Net: ABC. Rep: Katz. Wash atty: Fletcher, Heald & Hildreth. ■ Robert R. Thomas III, pres; Al Marra, vp, gen mgr & film buyer; John Price, news dir; James Martin, chief engr. ■ On 111 CATVs—157,000 subs.

Parkersburg

ADI No. 184; see Parkersburg market

WTAP-TV—ch 15, 234 kw vis, 41.1 kw aur, ant 620t/439g. TL: N39 20 59 W81 33 56. Hrs opn: 24. On air date: Oct 8, 1953. One Television Plaza (26101). (304) 485-4588. FAX: (304) 422-3920. Licensee: Benedek Broadcasting Co. (group owner; acq 10-3-79; $2.2 million). ■ Net: NBC. Rep: Katz. Wash atty: Covington & Burling. ■ Keith Bland, gen mgr & film buyer; Terry Cole, gen sls mgr; Joyce Ancrile, prom mgr & progmg dir; Roger Sheppard, news dir; Glenn Wilson, pub affrs dir; Gene Monday, chief engr. ■ On 37 CATVs—40,500 subs.

Weston

ADI No. 160; see Clarksburg-Weston market

WDTV—ch 5, 100 kw vis, 20 kw aur, ant 879t/503g. TL: N39 04 27 W80 25 28. On air date: June 1, 1960. Box 480, 5 Television Dr., Bridgeport (26330). (304) 623-5555. FAX: (304) 842-7501. Licensee: W. Russell Withers Jr. Group owner: Withers Broadcasting Co. (acq 5-8-73; $600,000; 4-16-73). ■ Net: CBS. Rep: Katz. Wash atty: Gardner, Carton & Douglas. ■ W. Russell Withers Jr., pres; Michael Smith, gen mgr & gen sls mgr; Deborah Gamblin, prom dir; Nick E. Pellegrin, progmg dir & film buyer; Mike Monseur, news dir; M. Gene Heskett, chief engr. ■ On 118 CATVs—172,892 subs. ■ Rates: $450; 125; 80.

Wheeling

ADI No. 144; see Wheeling-Steubenville market

WTOV-TV—See Steubenville, Ohio.

WTRF-TV—ch 7, 316 kw vis, 30.9 kw aur, ant 960t/740g. TL: N40 03 41 W80 45 08. Stereo. On air date: Oct 23, 1953. 96 16th St. (26003). (304) 232-7777. FAX: (304) 232-4975. Licensee: Brisstee TV of Wheeling Inc. Ownership: Paul A. Brissette (group owner; acq 12-24-91; grpsl). ■ Net: CBS, ABC. Rep: Blair. Wash atty: Wiley, Rein & Fielding. ■ Bill Rogala, gen mgr; Jim Roberts, gen sls mgr; Patrick Clutter, news dir; Joseph Dumas, chief engr. ■ On 160 CATVs—540,000 subs.

Wisconsin

Appleton

ADI No. 72; see Green Bay-Appleton market

WXGZ-TV—ch 32, 1,070 kw vis, 107 kw aur, ant 1,220t/1,026g. TL: N44 21 32 W87 58 58. Stereo. On air date: Mar 7, 1984. 170 Mitchell St. S.W., Atlanta, GA (30003-3424). (414) 864-8832. Licensee: Ace TV Inc. (acq 8-3-92); $505,000. Wash atty: Goldberg & Spector. ■ Carl J. Martin, pres; Bob Cox, gen mgr. ■ On 39 CATVs—116,800 subs. On one trans. ■ Rates: $160; 125; 40.

Chippewa Falls

ADI No. 128; see La Crosse-Eau Claire market

WEUX—ch 48, 60.3 kw vis, 6 kw aur, ant 321t. TL: N44 52 36 W91 18 22. Not on air, target date unknown. Box 19099, Green Bay (54307). Permittee: Aries Telecommunication Corp. (acq 4-9-91; grpsl; 4-22-91).

Eau Claire

ADI No. 72; see Green Bay-Appleton market

WEAU-TV—ch 13, 316 kw vis, 28.8 kw aur, ant 1,990t/2,000g. TL: N44 39 51 W90 57 41. Stereo. On air date: Dec 17, 1953. Box 47 (54702); 1907 S. Hastings Way (54701). (715) 835-1313. FAX: (715) 832-0246; TWX: 910-282-1633. Licensee: Busse Broadcasting Corp. (group owner; acq 8-28-87). ■ Net: NBC. Rep: Telerep. Wash atty: Pepper & Corazzini. News staff 22; news progmg 11 hrs wkly. ■ Cheri Weinke, gen mgr; Richard Dionne, opns mgr; Skip Dornseif, gen sls mgr; Joe Frank, natl sls mgr; Kris Lorentz, prom mgr & progmg dir; John Hoffland, news dir; Ron Weidemeier, chief engr. ■ On 109 CATVs—155,075 subs.

WQOW-TV—ch 18, 407 kw vis, 40.7 kw aur, ant 741t/507g. TL: N44 57 49 W91 40 05. Hrs opn: 19. On air date: Sept 20, 1980. 2881 S. Hastings Way (54701). (715) 835-1881. FAX: (715) 835-8009. Licensee: Tak Communications Inc. (group owner; acq 1-24-85; grpsl). ■ Net: ABC. Rep: Katz. Wash atty: Dow, Lohnes & Albertson. ■ Ron Montezon, gen mgr; Dave White, opns mgr & chief engr; Mark Golden, gen sls mgr; Ron Johnson, mktg mgr; Barb Bennett, progmg dir; Dave Marshall, film buyer; Sean Dwyer, news dir. ■ On 15 CATVs—35,000 subs.

Fond du Lac

ADI No. 72; see Green Bay-Appleton market

WMMF-TV—ch 68, 5,000 kw vis, 500 kw aur, ant 1,660t. TL: N43 21 44 W88 53 45. On air date: March 1994. Box 30, Skycom Inc., Lake Forest, IL (60045). (708) 234-4534. FAX: (708) 295-7780. Permittee: Skycom Inc.

Green Bay

ADI No. 72; see Green Bay-Appleton market

WBAY-TV—ch 2, 100 kw vis, 20 kw aur, ant 1,205t/1,149g. TL: N44 24 35 W88 00 05. Hrs opn: 24 Sun-Thurs, 19 Fri-Sat. On air date: Mar 17, 1953. 115 S. Jefferson (54301). (414) 432-3331; (800) 261-9229. FAX: (414) 432-7808. Licensee: Nationwide Communications. Group owner: Nationwide Mutual Insurance Co. (acq 12-27-74; $5,737,121; 1-13-75). ■ Net: ABC. Rep: Katz. Wash atty: Fletcher, Heald & Hildreth. ■ Don Carmichael, gen mgr; Robert Krieghoff, gen sls mgr; Jonie Paye, natl sls mgr; Richard Millhiser, progmg dir & pub affrs dir; Tom McCarey, news dir; Art Williams, chief engr. ■ On 73 CATVs—117,661 subs.

WFRV-TV—ch 5, 100 kw vis, 18.6 kw aur, ant 1,119t/998g. TL: N44 24 21 W88 00 19. On air date: May 21, 1955. Box 19055, 1181 E. Mason St. (54307-9055). (414) 437-5411. FAX: (414) 437-4576. Licensee: WFRV Television Inc. Group owner: CBS Inc. (acq 2-16-92; grpsl). ■ Net: CBS. Rep: McDermott (Canada). ■ R. Perry Kidder, vp & gen mgr; Alan Eaton, opns dir; Jackie Stewart, gen sls mgr; Gerald R. Jensen, news dir; Dan Ullmer, chief engr. ■ On 20 CATVs—58,000 subs. On 4 trans.

WGBA—ch 26, 2,510 kw vis, 251 kw aur, ant 1,181t/982g. TL: N44 21 30 W87 58 48. On air date: Dec 31, 1980. Box 19099, 1391 N. Rd. (54313). (414) 494-2626. FAX: (414) 494-7071; TWX: 510-600-6937. Licensee: Aries Telecommunication Corp. Ownership: Clark (acq 9-20-91; $7.6 million; grpsl; 10-14-91). Rep: Blair. ■ James L. Tomlin, gen mgr; Donna Kiley, progmg dir; Mark Cramer, chief engr. ■ On 45 CATVs—145,000 subs. On 4 trans.

WLUK-TV—ch 11, 316 kw vis, 47.4 kw aur, ant 1,260t/1,159g. TL: N44 24 31 W87 59 29. Stereo. On air date: Sept 11, 1954. Box 19011, 787 Lombardi Ave. (54307-9011). (414) 494-8711. FAX: (414) 494-8782. Licensee: WLUK-TV. Group owner: Burnham Broadcasting Co. (acq 8-2-84; $15,750,000). ■ Net: NBC. ■ William C. Fyffe, pres & gen mgr; Matthew Kreiner, vp sls & vp mktg; Steve Banka, natl sls mgr; Roxanne Bowers, rgnl sls mgr; Wendy Eisele, prom dir & pub affrs dir; Jan Wilson, progmg dir; Don Shafer, news dir; Jim Lueck, chief engr. ■ On 94 CATVs. On 3 trans.

***WPNE**—ch 38, 1,078 kw vis, 108 kw aur, ant 1,180t/1,149g. TL: N44 24 35 W88 00 05. 3319 W. Beltline Hwy., Madison (53713). (608) 264-9600. FAX: (608) 264-9622. Licensee: Educational Communications Board. ■ Net: PBS. Wash atty: Dow, Lohnes & Albertson. ■ Byron Knight, stn mgr; Michael Bridgeman, prom mgr; James Steinbach, progmg mgr; Don Moran, chief engr. Co-owned radio: *WPNE-FM.

Janesville

ADI No. 90; see Madison market

WJNW—ch 57, 646 kw vis, 64.6 kw aur, ant 403t. TL: N42 43 47 W89 10 10. Not on air, target date unknown. 26546 W. Ingleside Shore, Ingleside, IL (60041). (315) 525-6340. Permittee: Harish Puri (acq 6-14-93; $30,000; 7-12-93).

Kenosha

ADI No. 28; see Milwaukee market

WHKE—ch 55, 741 kw vis, 74.1 kw aur, ant 449t/349g. TL: N42 30 36 W87 53 11. Hrs opn: 24. On air date: June 1, 1988. 4300 43rd Ave. (53144). (414) 657-9453. FAX: (414) 656-7664. Licensee: LeSea Broadcasting Inc. Ownership: Dewayne Adamson (acq 7-29-92; $1.35 million; 8-24-92). Rep: Landin Media. Wash atty: Gardner, Carton & Douglas. ■ Lester Sumrall, pres; John R. Miller, gen mgr & film buyer; Dave Strash, gen sls mgr; Liz Provencher, progmg dir; Mijke Roggeveen, news dir; Doug Garlinger, chief engr.

La Crosse

ADI No. 128; see La Crosse-Eau Claire market

***WHLA-TV**—ch 31, 1,200 kw vis, 60 kw aur, ant 1,140t/831g. TL: N43 48 17 W91 22 06. On air date: Dec 3, 1973. 3319 W. Beltline Hwy., Madison (53713). (608) 264-9600. FAX: (608) 264-9622. Licensee: Educational Communications Board. ■ Net: PBS. Wash atty: Dow, Lohnes & Albertson. ■ Byron Knight, stn mgr; Michael Bridgeman, prom mgr; James Steinbach, progmg mgr; Don Moran, chief engr. ■ On 16 CATVs. Co-owned radio: *WHLA-FM.

WKBT—ch 8, 316 kw vis, 57.5 kw aur, ant 1,625t/1,540g. TL: N44 05 28 W91 20 15. Hrs opn: 20. On air date: Aug 8, 1954. 141 S. 6th St. (54601). (608) 782-4678. TWX: 910-28702572. Licensee: Young Broadcasting of La Crosse Inc. Group owner: Young Broadcasting Inc. (acq 9-15-86 grpsl; 4-14-86). ■ Net: CBS. Rep: Adam Young. ■ Ronald J. Kwasnick, pres; Bruce Pfeiffer, gen mgr & gen sls mgr; Dick Konrad, opns mgr; Larry Johnson, prom mgr; Maria Roswall, progmg dir. ■ On 144 CATVs—151,300 subs. On one trans. ■ Rates: $450; 100; 80.

WLAX—ch 25, 562 kw vis, 56.2 kw aur, ant 1,004t/674g. TL: N43 48 16 W91 22 18. On air date: Sept 28, 1986. 1305 Interchange Pl. (54603). (608) 781-0025. Licensee: Aries Telecommunications Corp. (acq 1-14-91; $7.6 million; grpsl 10-14-91). ■ Net: Fox. Rep: Seltel. ■ Nancy Martinsen, gen mgr; Kevin Gephart, gen sls mgr; Dave Shelly, prom mgr; Barbara Quillan, progmg dir; Mark Burg, chief engr. ■ On 75 CATVs.

WXOW-TV—ch 19, 631 vis, 63 aur, ant 1137t. TL: N43 48 23 W91 22 04. (CP: Ant 1,140t). On air date: March 7, 1970. Box C-4019 (54602-4019); 3705 County Hwy. 25, La Crescent, MN (55947). (507) 895-9969. FAX: (507) 895-8124. Licensee: Tak Communications Inc. (group owner; acq 3-4-85; grpsl). ■ Net: ABC. Rep: Katz. Wash atty: Dow, Lohnes & Albertson. ■ Chuck Roth, pres & gen mgr; Todd McWilliams, natl sls mgr; Dave Booth, rgnl sls mgr; David Marshall, prom mgr, progmg dir & film buyer; Sean Dwyer, news dir; Tom Sibenaller, chief engr. ■ On 120 CATVs—137,484 subs.

Madison

ADI No. 90; see Madison market

***WHA-TV**—ch 21, 759 kw vis, 75.9 kw aur, ant 1,250t/1,200g. TL: N43 03 18 W89 28 42. (CP: 1,020 kw vis, 102 kw aur, ant 1,529t, TL: N43 03 20 W89 32 07). On air date: May 3, 1954. 821 University Ave. (53706). (608) 263-2121. Licensee: Univ. of Wisconsin Board of Regents. ■ Net: PBS. Wash atty: Dow, Lohnes & Albertson. ■ Luke F. Lamb, gen mgr; Byron Knight, stn mgr; James Santulli, opns dir; Malcolm Brett, dev dir; Michael Bridgeman, prom dir; James Steinbach, progmg dir & film buyer; David Iverson, news dir & pub affrs dir; Ken Dixon, engrg dir. ■ On 141 CATVs—272,600 subs. On 2 trans. Co-owned radio: *WHA(AM).

WISC-TV—ch 3, 56.2 kw vis, 11 kw aur, ant 1,191t/1,108g. TL: N43 01 52 W89 30 18. Stereo. On air date: June 24, 1956. 7025 Raymond Rd. (53744); Box 44965 (53744-4965). (608) 271-4321. TWX: 910-286-2720. Licensee: TV Wisconsin Inc. Group owner: Morgan Murphy Stns. ■ Net: CBS. Rep: Harrington, Righter & Parsons. Wash atty: Rini & Coran. News staff 30; news progmg 30 hrs wkly. ■ Elizabeth Murphy Burns, pres; David Sanks, vp & gen mgr; Donna Kirner, gen sls mgr; Nan Roach, mktg dir & prom dir; Jill Koehn, progmg dir; Tom Bier, news dir; Chris Cain, chief engr. ■ On 15 CATVs—114,338 subs. ■ Rates: $1,200; 150; 150.

WKOW-TV—ch 27, 1,000 kw vis, 100 kw aur, ant 1,250t/1,182g. TL: N43 03 09 W89 28 42. Stereo. On air date: July 1953. Box 100, 5727 Tokay Blvd. (53701). (608) 274-1234. FAX: (608) 274-9514. Licensee: Tak Communications Inc. (group owner; acq 1-7-85; grpsl). ■ Net: ABC. Rep: Katz. Wash atty: Dow, Lohnes & Albertson. ■ Bob McCall, pres; Ken Simmons, gen sls mgr; Steve Olson, natl sls mgr; Jill Rabushka, prom mgr; Ellen Buss, progmg dir; Phil Hayes, news dir; Steve Biebel, pub affrs dir; Steve Zimmerman, chief engr. ■ On 24 CATVs—88,672 subs. On one trans.

WMSN-TV—ch 47, 1,000 kw vis, 100 kw aur, ant 1,006t. TL: N43 03 22 W89 32 07. Stereo. On air date: June 8, 1986. 7847 Big Sky Dr. (53719). (608) 833-0047. FAX: (608) 833-5055; (608) 833-0665 (Natl Sls). Licensee: Channel 47 L.P. Ownership: James L. Arnold, receiver (acq 6-17-92). ■ Net: Fox. Wash atty: Smithwick & Belendiuk. ■ Jim Arnold, gen mgr; Eric Jontra, gen sls mgr; Keith Triller, natl sls mgr; Mark Hodorowski, prom dir; Anita Meredith, prom mgr; John Noonan, progmg dir & film buyer; Julie Ganske, pub affrs dir; Jamie Nelson, engrg mgr; Kerry Maki, chief engr. ■ On 88 CATVs—166,365 subs.

WMTV—ch 15, 1,050 kw vis, 105 kw aur, ant 1,161t/1,101g. TL: N43 03 01 W89 29 15. Stereo. Hrs opn: 19. On air date: July 1953. 615 Forward Dr. (53711). (608) 274-1515; (608) 274-1500. FAX: (608) 271-5193. Licensee: Brissette TV of Madison Inc. Group owner: Brissette Broadcasting Corp. (acq 2-92; grpsl). ■ Net: NBC. Rep: Blair. Wash atty: Wiley, Rein & Fielding. ■ David Trabert, vp; Tom Weedon, opns mgr & chief engr; Sara McCormack, gen sls mgr; Perla Sarabia, prom mgr; Jim LeTourneau, news dir. ■ On 20 CATVs.

Mayville

ADI No. 28; see Milwaukee market

WWRS-TV—ch 52, 2,510 kw vis, 251 kw aur, ant 764t/530g. TL: N43 26 11 W88 31 33. Not on air, target date unknown. Box 1578, Fond Du Lac (53050). Permittee: TV-52 Inc. Ownership: Lyle R. Evans (acq 4-15-93; $850; 5-3-93). Wash atty: Mullin, Ryan, Emmons, Topel.

Menomonie

ADI No. 14; see Minneapolis-St. Paul market

***WHWC-TV**—ch 28, 1,100 kw vis, 54.5 kw aur, ant 1,151t/1197g. TL: N45 02 47 W91 51 42. On air date: Nov 18, 1973. 3319 W. Beltline Hwy., Madison (53713). (608) 264-9600. FAX: (608) 264-9622. Licensee: Educational Communications Board. ■ Net: PBS. Wash atty: Dow, Lohnes & Albertson. ■ Byron Knight, stn mgr & progmg dir; Michael Bridgeman, prom mgr; James Steinbach, progmg mgr; Don Moran, chief engr. ■ On 12 CATVs. Co-owned radio: *WHWC(FM).

Milwaukee

ADI No. 28; see Milwaukee market

WCGV-TV—ch 24, 3,000 kw vis, 300 kw aur, ant 1,030t/1,039g. TL: N43 05 15 W87 54 13. Stereo. On air date: Mar 17, 1980. 4041 N. 35th St. (53216). (414) 442-7050. FAX: (414) 874-1899. Licensee: BBM Partners. Group owner: ABRY Communications (acq 10-19-90; grpsl; 11-19-90). ■ Net: Fox. Rep: Katz. ■ Michael E. Schuch, stn mgr; Peter Stueck, opns mgr; Mitchell C. Nye, gen sls mgr; Nancy Stephens, natl sls mgr; Julie Stolper, mktg mgr; Lori Wucherer, prom mgr; Betty Hertz, progmg dir & film buyer; Walter White, chief engr. ■ On 37 CATVs—368,900 subs.

WDJT-TV—ch 58, 2,820 kw vis, 282 kw aur, ant 535t. TL: N43 02 20 W87 55 04. Stereo. On air date: November 1988. Suite 2500, 509 N. Wisconsin Ave. (53203). (414) 271-5800. FAX: (414) 272-1368. Licensee: Weigel Broadcasting. Rep: Roslin. Wash atty: Cohn & Marks. ■ Howard Shapiro, pres; Bill LeMonds, gen mgr; Karen Sheehan, opns mgr & progmg mgr; Jeff Raatz, dev dir; Sadie James, gen sls mgr; Gregg Schager, natl sls mgr; Kate Morgan, mktg mgr & prom dir; Eric Owens, chief engr. ■ On 8 CATVs. ■ Rates: $600; 300; 150.

WISN-TV—ch 12, 316 kw vis, 31.6 kw aur, ant 1,000t/1,105g. TL: N43 06 41 W87 55 38. Stereo. Hrs opn: 24. On air date: Oct 27, 1954. Box 402 (53201). (414) 342-8812. FAX: (414) 342-6490. Licensee: Hearst Corp. Group owner: Hearst Broadcasting Group, see Cross-Ownership (acq 3-2-55; $2 million; 3-14-55). ■ Net: ABC. Rep: Blair. Wash atty: Peper, Martin, Jensen, Maichel & Hetlage. ■ Howard Ritchie, vp & gen mgr; Peter Monfre, gen sls mgr; Pat Baldwin, prom mgr; Dean Maytag, progmg dir; Fred D'Ambrosi, news dir; Russ Elkin, chief engr. ■ On 48 CATVs—422,771 subs. On one trans. Co-owned radio: WISN(AM) and WLTQ(FM).

WITI-TV—ch 6, 100 kw vis, 10 kw aur, ant 1,000t/1,078g. TL: N43 05 24 W87 53 47. On air date: May 21, 1956. Box 17600, 9001 N. Green Bay Rd. (53217). (414) 355-6666. FAX: (414) 355-3263. Licensee: WITI License Inc. Group owner: SCI Television Inc. (acq 2-19-93; grpsl; 4-26-93). ■ Net: CBS. Rep: Telerep. Wash atty: Pepper & Corazzini. ■ Andrew P. Potos, pres & gen mgr; Maria Tully, sls dir; Jill Geisler, news dir; Donald Roering, chief engr. ■ On 19 CATVs—379,409 subs.

***WMVS**—ch 10, 309 kw vis, 30.9 kw aur, ant 1,010t/1,101g. TL: N43 05 48 W87 54 19. Stereo. On air date: Oct 28, 1957. 1036 N. 8th St., 4th Fl. (53233). (414) 271-1036. FAX: (414) 297-7536. Licensee: Milwaukee Area Dist Bd of Vocational, Technical & Adult Educ. ■ Net: PBS; CEN. Wash atty: Dow, Lohnes & Albertson. ■ William B. Combs, gen mgr; Tom Dvorak, prom mgr; John Pushkash, progmg dir; Luise Fuzy, news dir; David Felland, engrg dir. ■ On 25 CATVs—275,700 subs.

***WMVT**—ch 36, 2,340 kw vis, 234 kw aur, ant 928t/1,140g. TL: N43 05 48 W87 54 19. On air date: Jan 23, 1963. 4th Fl., 1036 N. 8th St. (53233). (414) 271-1036. FAX: (414) 297-7536. Licensee: Milwaukee Area Dist Bd of Vocational, Technical & Adult Educ. ■ Net: PBS. Wash atty: Dow, Lohnes & Albertson. Sp, Fr 4 hrs wkly. ■ William B. Combs, gen mgr; Lamont McLoughlin, dev dir; Tom Dvorak, prom dir; Kathleen Lenhardt, progmg dir; David Felland, engrg dir. ■ On 17 CATVs.

WTMJ-TV—ch 4, 100 kw vis, 20 kw aur, ant 1,000t/1,096g. TL: N43 05 29 W87 54 07. Stereo. On air date: December 1947. 720 E. Capitol Dr. (53212). (414) 332-9611. FAX: (414) 223-5255. Licensee: WTMJ Inc. (group owner). ■ Net: NBC. Rep: Petry. Wash atty: Hogan & Hartson. ■ Douglas G. Kiel, pres & gen mgr; Mark Strachota, gen sls mgr; Mike Stutz, progmg dir & film buyer; Jim Prather, news dir; Randy Price, chief engr. ■ On 12 CATVs. Co-owned radio: WTMJ(AM)-WKTI(FM).

WVCY-TV—ch 30, 1,070 kw vis, 55 kw aur, ant 961t. TL: N43 05 15 W87 54 19. Hrs opn: Mon-Fri Noon-11 PM; Sat-Sun 8 AM-11 PM. On air date: Jan 11, 1983. 3434 W. Kilborn Ave. (53208). (414) 935-3000. FAX: (414) 935-3015. Licensee: Wisconsin Voice of Christian Youth Inc. (group owner). Wash atty: Wiley, Rein & Fielding. ■ Randall Melchert, chmn; Vic Eliason, vp, gen mgr & stn mgr; Jim Cronin, opns mgr; Jim Schneider, progmg dir & pub affrs dir; Gordon Morris, news dir; Gary Piedot, chief engr. ■ On 23 CATVs. Co-owned radio: *WVCY(FM).

WVTV—ch 18, 5,000 kw vis, 500 kw aur, ant 1,008t/1,101g. TL: N43 05 48 W87 54 19. Stereo. Hrs opn: 24. On air date: July 1, 1959. 4041 N. 35th St. (53216). (414) 442-7050. FAX: (414) 874-1898; (414) 874-1999. Licensee: Gaylord Broadcasting Co. (group owner; acq 4-1-66; $500,000). Rep: Katz. Wash atty:

Reed, Smith, Shaw & McClay. News staff 18; news progmg 5 hrs wkly. ■ Michael E. Schuch, gen mgr; Sandra J. Graver, stn mgr; Mitch Nye, gen sls mgr; Lori Wucherer, prom mgr; Betty Hertz, progmg dir; Walter White, engrg dir. ■ On 56 CATVs—466,511 subs.

Park Falls

ADI No. 133; see Wausau-Rhinelander market

*WLEF-TV—ch 36, 741 kw vis, 74.2 kw aur, ant 1,468t/1,467g. TL: N45 56 43 W90 16 28. On air date: December 1977. 3319 W. Beltline Hwy., Madison (53713). (608) 264-9600. FAX: (608) 264-9622. Licensee: State of Wisconsin-Educational Communications Board. Wash atty: Dow, Lohnes & Albertson. ■ Byron Knight, stn mgr; Michael Bridgeman, prom mgr; James Steinbach, progmg mgr; Don Moran, chief engr.

Racine

ADI No. 28; see Milwaukee market

WJJA—ch 49, 2,690 kw vis, 260 kw aur, ant 435t/405g. TL: N42 51 18 W87 50 41. 24. On air date: Jan. 27, 1990. Box 92, 4311 E. Oakwood Rd., Oak Creek (53154). (414) 764-4953; (414) 632-4900. FAX: (414) 764-5190. Licensee: TV-49 Inc. Ownership: Joel Kinlow, 99%; Arvis Kinlow, 1%. ■ Joel J. Kinlow, pres; Willis Payne, prom mgr & film buyer. ■ On 2 CATVs. ■ Rates: $75; 40; 10.

Rhinelander

ADI No. 133; see Wausau-Rhinelander market

WJFW-TV—ch 12, 316 kw vis, 57.6 kw aur, ant 1,660t/1,677g. TL: N45 40 02 W89 12 27. On air date: Oct 20, 1966. Box 858, S. Oneida Ave. (54501). (715) 369-4700. FAX: (715) 369-1910. Licensee: Northland Television Inc. Group owner: Seaway Communications Inc. (acq 6-1-79; $912,588; 5-7-79). ■ Net: NBC. Rep: Seltel. Wash atty: Mullin, Rhyne, Emmons & Topel. ■ Marie Platteter, gen mgr & progmg dir; Susan Sharkey, prom mgr; Chris Oatman, news dir; Brian Henning, chief engr. ■ On 37 CATVs—48,727 subs. On one trans.

Superior

KBJR-TV—Licensed to Superior. See Duluth, Minn.

Suring

ADI No. 72; see Green Bay-Appleton market

WSCO—ch 14, 200 kw vis, 40 kw aur, ant 613t/544g. TL: N44 59 30 W88 23 55. On air date: Feb 22, 1984. c/o 3434 W. Kilbourn Ave., Milwaukee (53208). (414) 935-3000. FAX: (414) 935-3015. Licensee: Wisconsin Voice of Christian Youth Inc. (group owner). ■ Randall Melchert, pres; Vic Eliason, vp, gen mgr & stn mgr; Jim Schneider, progmg dir & pub affrs dir; Gary Piedot, chief engr.

Wausau

ADI No. 133; see Wausau-Rhinelander market

WAOW-TV—ch 9, 316 kw vis, 31.6 kw aur, ant 1,210t/647g. TL: N44 55 14 W89 41 31. On air date: May 7, 1965. 1908 Grand Ave. (54401). (715) 842-2251. FAX: (715) 848-0195. Licensee: Tak Communications Inc. (group owner; acq 3-5-85 grpsl). ■ Net: ABC. Rep: Katz. Wash atty: Dow, Lohnes & Albertson. ■ Laurin Jorstad, pres, gen mgr & film buyer; Marshall Porter, gen sls mgr; Suzanne Mueller, prom mgr; Sharon Reyer, progmg dir; Rick Moll, news dir; Russ Crass, chief engr. ■ On 29 CATVs. ■ Rates: $450; 135; 75.

*WHRM-TV—ch 20, 1,437 kw vis, 36.2 kw aur, ant 984t/977g. TL: N44 55 14 W59 41 31. On air date: 1975. 3319 W. Beltline Hwy., Madison (53713). (608) 264-9600. FAX: (608) 264-9622. Licensee: Educational Communications Board. ■ Net: PBS. Wash. atty: Dow, Lohnes & Albertson. ■ Byron Knight, stn mgr; Michael Bridgeman, prom mgr; James Steinbach, progmg dir; Don Moran, chief engr. Co-Owned radio: *WHRM (FM).

WSAW-TV—ch 7, 316 kw vis, 63.2 kw aur, ant 1,210t/647g. TL: N44 55 14 W89 41 31. On air date: Oct 23, 1954. 1114 Grand Ave. (54401). (715) 845-4211. FAX: (715) 845-2649. Licensee: Brissettte TV of Wausau Inc. Group Owner: Brissettte Broadcasting Corp. (acq 12-24-91; grpsl). ■ Net: CBS. Rep: Blair. ■ Scott Chorski, vp & gen mgr; Lee Klaus, opns mgr; Glen Moberg, news dir; Joe Kamenick, chief engr; ■ On 18 CATVs—58,559 subs. on one trans. ■ Rates: $590; 275; 50.

Wyoming

Casper

ADI No. 194; see Casper-Riverton market

KFNB-TV—ch 20, 1,550 kw vis, 155 kw aur, ant 1,748t. TL: N42 44 37 W106 18 26. Hrs opn: 20. On air date: Oct 31, 1984. Box 1, 7075 Salt Creek Hwy. (82601); 1865 Skyview Dr. (82601). (307) 577-5923; (307) 577-5924. FAX: (307) 577-5928; (307) 628-2238. Licensee: WyoMedia Corp. ■ Net: ABC. Rep: Savalli, Tacher, Art Moore. Wash atty: Dow, Lohnes & Albertson. ■ Mark Nalbone, gen mgr & gen sls mgr; Kelly Wright, prom mgr; Kim Ortega, progmg dir; Todd Martin, film buyer; Brian McCash, chief engr. ■ On 10 CATVs—37,500 subs. On one trans. ■ Rates: $150; 45; 35.

KGWC-TV—ch 14, 1,380 kw vis, 138 kw aur, ant 1,879t/242g. TL: N42 44 26 W106 21 34. On air date: Aug 12, 1981. Box 170 (82602); 304 N. Center (82601). (307) 234-1111. FAX: (307) 234-2835. Licensee: Stauffer Communications Inc. (group owner; acq 8-28-86; grpsl; 7-28-86). ■ Net: CBS, Fox. Rep: Katz. Wash atty: Dow, Lohnes & Albertson. ■ John H. Stauffer, pres; Tim Swanson, gen mgr & gen sls mgr; Jeremy Patey, opns mgr, progmg dir & film buyer; Bonnie Foster, natl sls mgr; Todd Senter, rgnl sls mgr; Ed Wiblemo, news dir; Tony Schafer, chief engr. ■ On 20 CATVs—38,800 subs.

KTWO-TV—ch 2, 100 kw vis, 10.2 kw aur, ant 2,001t/376g. TL: N42 44 03 W106 20 00. Hrs opn: 24. On air date: Mar 1, 1957. Box 2720 (82602); 4200 E. 2nd St. (82609). (307) 237-3711. FAX: (307) 234-9866. Licensee: KTWO Corp. Group owner: Dix Communications (acq 12-12-86; grpsl; 11-3-86). ■ Net: NBC. Rep: Seltel. Wash atty: Baker & Hostetler. News staff 13; news progmg 8 hrs wkly. ■ Stan Whitman, pres; Michelle Ferguson, gen mgr & stn mgr; Debbie McLemore, natl sls mgr; Tim Havasi, rgnl sls mgr; Roger Sewell, prom dir; Dave Borino, progmg dir & film buyer; Susan Anderson, news dir; Scott Barella, chief engr. ■ On 55 CATVs—85,000 subs. On 54 trans. ■ Rates: $400; 140; 110.

Cheyenne

ADI No. 196; see Cheyenne-Scotsbluff, NE market

KGWN-TV—ch 5, 100 kw vis, 10 kw aur, ant 620t/483g. TL: N41 06 01 W105 00 23. On air date: Mar 22, 1954. 2923 E. Lincolnway (82001). (307) 634-7755. FAX: (307) 637-8604; TWX: 910-949-4067. Licensee: Stauffer Communications Inc. (group owner; acq 7-22-86; grpsl). ■ Net: CBS, ABC. Rep: Katz. Wash atty: Dow, Lohnes & Albertson. News staff 11; news progmg 10 hrs wkly. ■ Frank Shepherd, CEO; John Stauffer, chmn; Gerald N. Holley, vp; Carl J. Occhipinti, gen mgr; Dusty Thein, gen sls mgr; Steve Van Court, opns mgr; Barbara Parenti, progmg dir; Brian Olson, news dir; Tim Akins, pub affrs dir; Tony Schaefer, chief engr. ■ On 20 CATVs—105,000 subs. on 2 trans. ■ Rates: $300; 150; 70.

KKTU—ch 33, 251 kw vis, 25.1 kw aur, ant 485t. TL: N41 08 55 W104 57 22. Stereo. Hrs opn: 20. On air date: Aug 28, 1987. Box 2720, Casper (82602); 4200 E. 2nd St. (82609). (307) 237-3711. FAX: (307) 234-9866. Licensee: KTWO Corp. Group owner: Dix Communications. ■ Net: NBC. Rep: Seltel. Wash atty: Baker & Hostetler. News staff 13; news progmg 8 hrs wkly. ■ Stan Whitman, pres; Michelle Ferguson, gen mgr & stn mgr; Tim Havasi, rgnl sls mgr; Roger Sewell, prom mgr; Dave Borino, progmg dir & film buyer; Susan Anderson, news dir; Scott Barella, chief engr. ■ On 4 CATVs—18,200 subs. On 2 trans.

KLWY—ch 27, 4,270 kw vis, 427 kw aur, ant 760t/635g. TL: N41 02 55 W104 53 28. Stereo. On air date: 1992. 7075 Salt Creek Hwy. #1, Casper (82601). (307) 577-5923. FAX: (307) 577-5928. Licensee: Wyomedia Corp. (acq 12-4-91; $100,000; 1-6-92). Rep: Adam Young, Bob Hix Co. Wash atty: Cordon & Kelly. ■ Mark Nalbone, gen mgr.

Jackson

ADI No. 158; see Idaho Falls-Pocatello

KJVI—ch 2, 178 w vis, 17.8 w aur, ant 997t. TL: N43 27 42 W110 45 10. Hrs opn: 5 AM-midnight. On air date: 1991. Box 7454 Powder Horn, 970 N. Broadway (83001). (307) 733-2066. FAX: (307) 733-4834. Licensee: Ambassador Media Corp. ■ Net: ABC. Rep: Seltel. News staff 3; news progmg 5 hrs wkly. ■ Bill Armstrong, CEO; Harry Neuhardt, exec vp; Kathy Brody, stn mgr, sls dir, adv dir & progmg dir; Roy Garton, prom dir & pub affrs dir; Bethany Nadel, news dir; Nick Davidson, engrg dir. ■ On one CATV. On one trans. ■ Rates: $125; 35; 30.

Lander

ADI No. 194; see Casper-Riverton market

*KCWC-TV—ch 4, 100 kw vis, 10 kw aur, ant 1,519t/199g. TL: N42 34 59 W108 42 36. On air date: January 1983. Central Wyoming College, 2660 Peck Ave., Riverton (82501). (307) 856-9291. FAX: (307) 856-3893. Licensee: Central Wyoming College. ■ Net: PBS. Wash atty: Fletcher, Heald & Hildreth. ■ Gregory T. Ray, gen mgr; Rubydee Calvert, progmg dir; Roger Hicks, chief engr.

KGWL-TV—ch 5, 100 kw vis, 10 kw aur, ant 269t/179g. TL: N42 53 43 W108 43 34. On air date: Sept 10, 1982. c/o 304 N. Center, Casper (82601). (307) 234-1111. FAX: (307) 234-2835. Licensee: Stauffer Communications Inc. (group owner; acq 8-28-86; grpsl; 7-28-86). ■ Net: CBS. Rep: Katz. Wash atty: Dow, Lohnes & Albertson. ■ John H. Stauffer, pres; Tim Swanson, gen mgr & gen sls mgr; Jeremy Patey, opns mgr, progmg dir & film buyer; Bonnie Foster, natl sls mgr & prom mgr; Todd Senter, rgnl sls mgr; Tony Schafer, chief engr. ■ On 7 CATVs—8,602 subs. On one trans. *KGWC

Rawlins

ADI No. 20; see Denver market

KFNR—ch 11, 1.66 kw vis, 166 w aur, ant 230t/449g. TL: N41 46 15 W107 14 25. On air date: Apr 16, 1986. Box 1, 7075 Salt Creek Rt., Casper (82601). (307) 577-5923; (307) 577-5924. FAX: (307) 577-5928. Licensee: Mark Nalbone, Receiver. ■ Net: ABC. Rep: Savalli, Tacher, Art Moore. Wash atty: Dow, Lohnes & Albertson. ■ Mark Nalbone, gen mgr & gen sls mgr; Kelly Wright, prom mgr; Kim Ortega, progmg dir; Todd Martin, film buyer; Brian McCash, chief engr. ■ On 3 CATVs—6,000 subs. ■ Rates: $110; 50; 35.

Riverton

ADI No. 194; see Casper-Riverton market

*KCWC-TV—See Lander.

KFNE—ch 10, 170 kw vis, 8.7 kw aur, ant 1,725t/174g. TL: N43 27 26 W108 12 02. On air date: Dec 22, 1957. Box 1, 7075 Salt Creek Rd., Casper (82601). (307) 577-5923; (307) 577-5924. FAX: (307) 577-5928. Licensee: Mark Nalbone, Receiver. ■ Net: ABC. ■ Mark Nalbone, gen mgr & gen sls mgr; Kelly Wright, prom mgr; Kim Ortega, progmg dir; Todd Martin, film buyer; Brian McCash, chief engr. ■ On 9 CATVs—20,000 subs. On 2 trans.

KGWL-TV—See Lander.

Rock Springs

ADI No. 41; see Salt Lake City market

KGWR-TV—ch 13, 209 kw vis, 10 kw aur, ant 1,624/1,669g. TL: N41 26 21 W109 06 42. (CP: Ant 1,709t, TL: N41 26 33 W109 06 28). On air date: Oct 21, 1977. Box 170, Casper (82602). (307) 234-1111. FAX: (307) 234-2835. Licensee: Stauffer Communications Inc. (group owner; acq 8-25-86; grpsl; 7-28-86). ■ Net: CBS. Rep: Katz. Wash atty: Dow, Lohnes & Albertson. News staff 7; news progmg 5 hrs wkly. ■ John H. Stauffer, pres; Tim Swanson, gen mgr & gen sls mgr; Jeremy Patey, opns mgr, progmg dir & film buyer; Bonnie Foster, natl sls mgr & prom mgr; Todd Senter, rgnl sls mgr; Tony Schafer, chief engr. ■ On 2 CATVs—13,000 subs. ■ Rates: $320; 100; 60.

Sheridan

ADI No. 168; see Rapid City market

KRBQ—ch 7, 316 kw vis, 31.6 kw aur, ant 955t. TL: N44 37 20 W107 06 55. Not on air, target date unknown. Box 80810, c/o KULR-TV, Billings, MT (59108-0810). (406) 656-8000. Permittee: KULR Corp. Group owner: Dix Communications (acq 1-12-93). ■ Stan Whitman, pres & gen mgr.

KSGW-TV—ch 12, 316 kw vis, 63.2 kw aur, ant 1,220t. TL: N44 37 20 W107 06 57. On air date: Oct 28, 1977. Box 1760, Rapid City, SD (57709). (605) 342-2000. FAX: (605) 342-7305. Licensee: Duhamel Broadcasting Enterprises (group owner). ■ Net: ABC. Rep: Katz, Soderlund. Wash atty: Fisher, Wayland, Cooper & Leader. ■ William Duhamel, pres & gen mgr; Wes Haugen, gen sls

American Samoa

Pago Pago

*KVZK-2—ch 2, 60 kw vis, 6.0 kw aur, ant 2,000t/400g. TL: W170 41 12 S14 16 14. KVZK-TV (96799). (684) 633-4191. FAX: (684) 633-1044. Licensee: The Government of American Samoa. ■ Net: PBS. Samoan 10 hrs, Chinese one hr, Korean one hr wkly. ■ Vaoita Savali, gen mgr; Nancy Satele, progmg dir; Tom Norman, chief engr. ■ On 3 trans.

*KVZK-4—ch 4, 72 kw vis, 7.2 kw aur. KVZK-TV (96799). (684) 633-4191. Licensee: The Government of American Samoa. ■ Net: ABC, CBS, NBC. ■ Vaoita Savali, gen mgr & news dir; Peni Failautusi, progmg dir; Tom Norman, chief engr.

*KVZK-5—ch 5, 72 kw vis, 7.2 kw aur, ant 2,000t/400g. On air date: Oct 5, 1964. KVZK-TV (96799). (684) 633-4191. FAX: (684) 633-1044; TELEX: 782-519. Licensee: The Government of American Samoa.■Net: ABC, CBS, NBC. Samoan 2 hrs wkly. ■ Vaoita Savali, gen mgr; Nancy Satele, progmg dir; Tom Norman, chief engr. ■ On 3 trans.

Guam

Agana

*KGTF—ch 12, 27.4 kw vis, 5.47 kw aur, ant 199t/187g. TL: N13 26 13 W144 48 17. Hrs opn: 18. On air date: Oct 30, 1970. Box 21449 (96921). (671) 734-2207. FAX: (671) 734-5483. Licensee: Guam Educational Telecommunications Corp. ■ Net: PBS. Wash atty: Cohn & Marks. ■ Joseph E. Tighe, gen mgr; H. Ed Davis, opns mgr; Doris T. Gallo, progmg dir; Mesengei Diaz, chief engr. ■ On one CATV—30,000 subs.

KUAM-TV—ch 8, 25.1 kw vis, 2.57 kw aur, ant 140t/320g. TL: N13 25 53 W144 42 36. On air date: Aug 5, 1956. Box 368 (96910). (671) 637-5826. FAX: (671) 637-9865. Licensee: Pacific Telestations Inc. Group owner: Micronesia Broadcasting Inc. (acq 1988).■Net: CBS, NBC. Rep: Intercontinental. Wash atty: Haley, Bader & Potts. Chamorro 10 hrs wkly. News staff 20; news progmg 14 hrs wkly. ■ Thomas J. Calvo, chmn; Jonathon M. Denight, pres; Jon Denight, gen mgr; Thomas Blaz, stn mgr; Michelle Benito, gen sls mgr; Annie San Nicholas, prom mgr; Ginger Cruz, progmg mgr; Nestor Licanto, news dir; Jim Bodein, chief engr. ■On 2 CATVs. On 2 trans. Co-owned radio: KUAM-AM-FM. ■ Rates: $75; 60; 50.

Tamuning

KTGM—ch 14, 12.8 kw vis, ant -52t/66g. TL: N13 30 09 W144 48 17. Stereo. On air date: Oct 19, 1988. Suite 308, 692 N. Marine Dr. (96911). (671) 646-4873. TELEX: 743-0830. Licensee: Island Broadcasting Inc. Ownership: David M. Larson, 66%; Edmund Y. Lee, 17%. ■Net: ABC, Fox. Wash atty: Mike Hirrel. ■ David M. Larson, pres & gen mgr; Marie L.G. Martin, opns dir; Ed Lee, chief engr. ■ On one CATV—35,500 subs.

Puerto Rico

Aguada

WQHA—ch 50, 2,000 kw vis, 200 kw aur, ant 1,122t. TL: N18 19 56 W67 11 16. Not on air, target date unknown. Box 846 (00602). Permittee: Aurio Matos dba Channel 50 TV.

Aguadilla

*WELU—ch 32, 9.33 kw vis, 933 kw aur, ant 971t/121g. TL: N18 18 46 W67 11 09. On air date: unknown. 1386 N. Reagan St. San Benito, TX (78586). (210) 412-5600. Licensee: Healthy Christian Family Media Inc. Ownership: Norman O. Gonzalez (acq 7-31-92; $500,000; 8-24-92). ■ Rene Hinojosa, pres.

WOLE-TV—ch 12, 316 kw vis, 31.6 kw aur, ant 1,250t/362g. TL: N18 18 51 W67 11 30. (CP: 275 kw vis, ant 2,181t., TL: N18 09 00 W66 59 00). On air date: May 13, 1960. Box 1200, Mayaguez (00709-1200). (809) 833-1200. FAX: (809) 831-6330. Licensee: Western Broadcasting Corp. of Puerto Rico. Ownership: Du Art Film Labs Inc., 61.2%; Jose Bechara, 30.6%; Alfonso Giminez-Aguayo, 8.2%. Wash atty: Dempsey & Koplovitz. Sp full time. ■ Irwin Young, pres; Luis A. Morales, gen mgr, gen sls mgr, prom mgr & film buyer; Lillian Gonzalez, progmg dir & news dir; Doel Oriol, chief engr. ■ On one translator.

WVEO—ch 44, 1,000 kw vis, 100 kw aur, ant 1,220t/235g. TL: N18 19 06 W67 10 42. On air date: October 1974. Box 1055 (00613). Licensee: Southwestern Broadcasting Corp. Sp full time. ■ Pablo Guardiola, pres; Hector Nicolau, chief engr.

Arecibo

WCCV-TV—ch 54, 11.7 kw vis, 2.34 kw aur, ant -220t. TL: N18 28 28 W66 43 36. (CP: 1,510 kw vis, 151 kw aur, ant 1,968t, TL: N18 14 06 W66 45 36). On air date: Nov 15, 1981. Box 949, Camuy (00627). (809) 898-5120. Licensee: Asociacion Evan. Cristo Viene Inc. Ownership: Francisco Valazquez, 88%; Wilfredo Almodovar, 6%; Juana Roman, 5%; Patricio R. Fermaintt, 2%. Rep: Schellenberg & Kirwan. Wash atty: A.L. Stein. ■ Francisco Valazquez, pres, gen mgr, gen sls mgr, progmg dir & film buyer; Juana Roman, prom mgr; Miguel Melendez, news dir; Hector Nicolau, chief engr. ■ Rates: $60; 40; 30.

WMEI—ch 60, 2,240 kw vis, 224 kw aur, ant 794t. TL: N18 27 21 W66 52 59. Not on air, target date unknown. GPO 7017, Caguas (00726). Permittee: Hector Negroni Cartagena.

Bayamon

WDWL—ch 36, 9.33 kw vis, 933 w aur, ant 1,079t/308g. TL: N18 16 40 W66 06 38. On air date: 1991. Box 50615, Levittown (00950). (809) 795-8181. Licensee: Bayamon Christian Network. Ownership: Felix Berrios, 20%; Simon Castillo, 20%; Wilfredo Diaz, 20%; David Perez, 20%; Luciano Rodriguez, 20%■Jesus Velez, pres; Jose Cortes, gen mgr.

Caguas

WLII—ch 11, 200 kw vis, 39.8 kw aur, ant 1,180t/240g. TL: N18 16 54 W66 06 46. Stereo. (CP: 316 kw vis, ant 1,135t). Hrs opn: 19. On air date: May 27, 1960. Box 10000, Santurce Stn., Ave. Condado No. 657, Santurce (00907). (809) 724-1111. FAX: (809) 385-9511. Licensee: Estrella Brilliante Ltd. Ownership: Malrite Communications Group Inc., 80%;TeleOnce Corp., 20% (acq 8-1-91; $3 million with WSUR-TV Ponce; 8-26-91). ■ Net: NBC. Rep: Katz. Wash atty: Kaye, Scholer, Fierman, Hays & Handler. Sp 140 hrs wkly. ■ David E. Murphy, vp & gen mgr; Santiago Rubin, sls dir; Hector Martinez, gen sls mgr; William Denizard, Manuel Santiago, prom dirs; Diana Hernandez (supv), progmg mgr; Linda Hernandez, news dir; Andres Diaz, chief engr. ■ Rates: $1,800; 750; 525.

*WUJA—ch 58, 55 kw vis, 5.5 kw aur, ant 1,078t/110g. TL: N18 16 40 W66 06 38. On air date: September 1985. Box 4039, Carolina (00985). (809) 750-4055. Licensee: Community TV of Caguas. ■ Lucy Villanueva, gen mgr.

Carolina

WDZE—ch 52, 663 kw vis, 66 kw aur, ant 1,919t/252g. TL: N18 16 44 W65 51 12. Not on air, target date unknown. Box 1833, Ceramica Annex (00984). (809) 762-5500. FAX: (809) 752-1825. Permittee: Enrique A. (Rickin) Sanchez and Blanche Vidal de Sanchez. Ownership: Enrique A. (Rickin) Sanchez, 50%; Blanche Vidal de Sanchez, 50%. Wash atty: John L. Tierney. Fr progmg. ■ Rickin Sanchez, pres & gen mgr; Blanche Sanchez, progmg dir; Jose Lara, chief engr.

Fajardo

*WMTJ—ch 40, 209 kw vis, 20.9 kw aur, ant 2,750t/259g. TL: N18 18 36 W65 47 41. On air date: January 1985. Box 21345, Rio Pedras (00928). (809) 766-2600. FAX: (809) 250-8546. Licensee: Fundacion Educativa Ana G. Mendez. Wash atty: Dow, Lohnes & Albertson. Sp 64 hrs wkly. ■ Jose F. Mendez, pres; Jose F. Mendez Jr., gen mgr; Emilio Sanchez, dev dir; Arnaldo Hernandez, prom mgr; Marilluz Gerena, progmg dir; Ariel Diaz, chief engr. ■ On 4 CATVs.

WPRV-TV—ch 13, 170 kw vis, 17 kw aur, ant 2,825t/210g. TL: N18 18 36 W65 47 41. (CP: 141 kw vis, 14.1 kw aur). On air date: 1991. Box 31313, Rio Pedras (00929). FAX: (809) 751-8154. Licensee: WPRV-TV Inc. Ownership: James C. Leake, 80%;Carmina M. Miller, 20%. Wash atty: Mullin, Rhyne, Emmons & Topel. ■ Evangelina Vives, pres; Nacha Rivera, gen mgr & gen sls mgr; Tony Puchola, progmg dir; Tony Lavey, news dir; Pedro Rivera, chief engr.

WRUA—ch 34, 50.1 kw vis, 5 kw aur, ant 2,877t. TL: N18 18 45 W65 47 32. Not on air, target date unknown. 101-1 107th St., Villa Carolina (00630). (809) 769-7783. Permittee: Damarys De Jesus, sole proprietor.

Guayama

WIDP—ch 46, 1,510 kw vis, 151 kw aur, ant 2,106t. TL: N18 16 48 W65 51 08. Not on air, target date unknown. Box 501, Cidra (00661). Permittee: Bocanegra/Girald Bcstg Group Corp.

Mayaguez

WIPM-TV—ch 3, 81.3 kw vis, 8.1 kw aur, ant 2,273t/382g. TL: N18 09 00 W66 59 00. (CP: 2,280t/389g). On air date: Apr 28, 1961. Box 449, Mayaguez (00681). (809) 834-0164. TELEX: 385-4401. Licensee: Puerto Rico Public Broadcasting Corp. ■ Net: PBS. Wash atty: Steptoe & Johnson. ■Alberto Acedevo, gen mgr.

WNJX-TV—ch 22, 200 kw vis, 20 kw aur, ant 1,137t/150g. TL: N18 19 06 W67 10 42. (CP: 1,550 kw vis, 155 kw aur, ant 2,033t, TL: N18 09 05 W66 59 20). On air date: Apr 27, 1986. Box 1030 (00681-1030). (809) 831-2222. FAX: (809) 834-2211. Licensee: WNJX-TV Inc. Ownership: Glenn A. Tryon & Ana J. Plaza, 33%;Michael Carter, 22.2%; T. Michael Whitney, 22.2%; David Peterson, 22.2%. Wash atty: Latham & Watkins. All Sp. ■ Ana J. Plaza, pres; Glenn A. Tryon, vp & gen mgr; Francis Irizarry, gen sls mgr; Ramon Rivera, chief engr. ■ On 4 CATVs—20,000 subs.

WOLE-TV—See Aguadilla.

WORA-TV—ch 5, 100 kw vis, 20 kw aur, ant 2,001t/241g. TL: N18 09 02 W66 59 20. On air date: Oct 1, 1955. Box 43 (00681). (809) 831-5555. FAX: (809) 833-0075. Licensee: Telecinco Inc. Ownership: Alfredo R. deArellano Jr. and family, 100%. Wash atty: Bryan, Cave, McPheeters & McRoberts. All Sp. ■ Alfredo R. deArellano, pres; Amado Martinez, CFO; Eduardo Bado, gen mgr & opns mgr; Benjamin Torres, opns dir; Ray Perez, progmg dir; Jesus Echavarria, chief engr. ■ On one trans. ■ Rates: $250; 150; 75.

WTRA—ch 16, 214 kw vis, 21.4 kw aur, ant 1,138t/148g. TL: N18 19 06 W67 10 42. Not on air, target date unknown. Calle Loiza 2432, Punta Maria (00917). Permittee: Bay Broadcasting Inc., Carlos J. Lastra, trustee.

Naranjito

WECN—ch 64, 1,000 kw vis, 100 kw aur, ant 466t/107g. TL: N18 17 34 W66 16 02. On air date: April 1986. Box 310, Bayamon (00960); Hwy. 167 (00957). (809) 799-6400. FAX: (809) 797-2450. Licensee: Encuentro Christian Net. Ownership: Rafael Torres Ortega, 11.11%;Iris Padilla, 11.11%;Ramon Luis Acevedo, 11.11%;Jofre Ayala, 11.11%;Daramid Ayala, 11.11% (acq 9-87; $175,000; 4-13-87). Wash atty: Mitchell, Fielstra & Assocs. Eng 5 hrs wkly. News progmg 6 hrs wkly. ■ Rafael Torres Ortega, pres; Iris Padilla, vp; Jofre Ayala, gen mgr; Rafael Torres Padilla, vp opns; Martin Scamaroni, natl sls mgr; Carmen Teresa Torres, mktg mgr; Mayra Marcial, vp adv; Yamil Ayala, progmg dir; Jose Antonio Ayala, news dir; Mickey Linares, chief engr. ■ On one CATV—100,000 subs. ■ Rates: $100; 75; 75.

Ponce

WKPV—ch 20, 100 kw vis, 10 kw aur, ant 850t/105g. TL: N18 04 50 W66 64 50. On air date: Aug 6, 1985. GPO Box 2556, San Juan (00936). Licensee: Multi Media Television Inc. (group owner). Wash atty: Dow, Lohnes & Albertson. ■ Franklin D. Lopez, pres; Tony Cardona, gen sls mgr; Magdalena Cuevas, prom mgr; Jorge Ariel Torres, news dir; Ricardo L. Alfaro, chief engr.

*WQTO—ch 26, 437 kw vis, 43.7 kw aur, ant 991t/246g. TL: N18 04 50 W66 44 54. On air date: November 1986. Box 21345, Rio Piedras (00928). (809) 766-2600. FAX: (809) 250-8546. Licensee: Fundacion Educativa Ana G. Mendez. Wash atty: Dow, Lohnes & Albertson. Sp 64 hrs wkly. ■ Jose F. Mendez, pres; Gloria Hernandez, gen mgr; Arnaldo Hernandez, prom mgr; Felix Vega, progmg dir; Ariel Diaz, chief engr.

WSTE—ch 7, 186 kw vis, 25.1 kw aur, ant 2,709t/439g. TL: N18 09 17 W66 33 16. On air date: Feb 2, 1958. Box A, Old San Juan Stn., San Juan (00902). (809) 724-7777. TWX: 325-2067. Licensee: Siete Grand Television Inc. Ownership: Jerry B.& Esther M. Hartman (acq 8-1-91; $6 million; 8-26-91). Sp full time.■Wanda Costanzo, gen mgr & film buyer; Margarita Silvestre, gen sls mgr;

Paul Moreno, prom mgr; Leandro Blanco, progmg dir; Doris Torres, news dir; Andres Diaz, chief engr.

WSUR-TV—ch 9, 58.9 kw vis, 5.89 kw aur, ant 2,270t/273g. TL: N18 10 10 W66 34 36. On air date: February 1958. Box 10000, Santurce Stn., Ave. Condado No. 657, Santurce (00907). (809) 724-1111. FAX: (809) 721-0777. Licensee: Estrella Brillante Ltd. Ownership: Malrite Communications Group Inc. (group owner; acq 8-1-91; $3 million with WLII(TV) Caguas; 8-26-91). Rep: Katz. Wash atty: Hamel & Park. Sp 140 hrs wkly. ■ Rafael Ruiz, vp; Eduardo Penedo, gen mgr; Hilary Hattler, gen sls mgr; Maggie Alonso, prom mgr; Guillermo Artau, progmg dir; Linda Hernandez, news dir; Jose A. Medina, chief engr. ■ Rates: $1,800; 750; 525.

WTIN—ch 14, 101.8 kw vis, 10 kw aur, ant 781t/53g. TL: N18 04 50 W66 44 50. On air date: unknown. c/o Hector Nicolau, AS-15 Rio Orocovis St., Bayamon (00619). Licensee: Hector Nicolau. Ownership: Hector Nicolau, 60%; P.R. Fermaintt, 40%. Wash atty: Baraff, Koerner & Oleander.

WVOZ-TV—ch 48, 61.7 kw vis, 6.2 kw aur, ant 810t/95g. TL: N18 04 50 W66 44 50. Not on air, target date unknown. 7425 S.W. 42nd St., Miami, FL (33155). Permittee: Canal 48 Inc. ■ Joseph F. Murphy, pres.

San Juan

WAPA-TV—ch 4, 53.7 kw vis, 8.13 kw aur, ant 2,865t/1,094g. TL: N18 06 42 W66 03 05. On air date: April 1954. GPO Box 362050 (00936-2050); State Rd. 19 (00657). (809) 792-4444. FAX: (809) 782-4420. TELEX: 345-0245. Licensee: Pegasus Broadcasting of San Juan Inc. Group owner: Pegasus Broadcasting Inc. (acq 9-11-90; grpsl; 10-1-90). Rep: Katz. Wash atty: Fletcher, Heald & Hildreth. Sp 133 hrs wkly. News staff 29; news progmg 8 hrs wkly. ■ John R. Bennett, pres & gen mgr; Enrique Cruz, exec vp & news dir; Cesar Maraver, prom dir & pub affrs dir; Giora Breil, progmg dir; Juan Abel Gonzalez, engrg dir. ■ Rates: $2,200; 700; 600.

*****WIPR-TV**—ch 6, 53.7 kw vis, 5.4 kw aur, ant 2,860t/1,094g. TL: N18 06 42 W66 03 05. (CP: 58.9 kw vis, 5.9 kw aur, ant 2,706t/940g). On air date: Jan 6, 1958. Box 909, Baldrich, Hato Rey (00919). (809) 766-0505. FAX: (809) 753-9846. Licensee: Puerto Rico Public Broadcasting Corp. ■ Net: PBS. Wash atty: Steven Huffines. Sp 40 hrs wkly. ■ Pedro Gonzalez Ramos, gen mgr; James Gillette, progmg dir. Co-owned radio: *WIPR-AM-FM.

WKAQ-TV—ch 2, 55 kw vis, 10.5 kw aur, ant 2,824t/1,099g. TL: N18 06 54 W66 03 10. On air date: Mar 28, 1954. Box 366222 (00936); 383 Roosevelt Ave., Hato Rey (00918). (809) 758-2222. FAX: (809) 759-9575. Licensee: TPR Television Inc. Group owner: Telemundo Group Inc. (acq 1-30-89; $160 million; 2-13-89). ■ Net: Telemundo. Wash atty: Hogan & Hartson. Sp 130 hrs wkly. News staff 40; news progmg 24 hrs wkly. ■ Joe Ramos, gen mgr; David Murphy, opns mgr; Gaspar Diaz, prom dir; Francisco Arrieta, vp progmg; Ileana Santiago, progmg dir & film buyer; Berta Castaner, news dir; Jose Medina, vp engrg. ■ On 5 trans. ■ Rates: $2,500; 1,000; 800.

WLII—See Caguas.

WRWR-TV—ch 30, 2,630 kw vis, 263 kw aur, ant 1,304t/196g. TL: N18 16 30 W66 05 36. Not on air, target date unknown. Calle No. One, No. 364 Hnas. Cavila, Bayamon (00629). Permittee: La Fe Del Progreso Bcstg Corp. Ownership: Ramon Rodriguez-Nieves. Wash atty: Gammon & Grange. ■ Ramon Rodriguez-Nieves, pres.

WSJN-TV—ch 24, 537 kw vis, 53.7 kw aur, ant 1,961t. TL: N18 16 47 W65 51 14. On air date: Feb 15, 1987. Box 2556 (00936). Licensee: Multi Media Television Inc. (group owner). Wash atty: Dow, Lohnes & Albertson. ■ Franklin D. Lopez, pres & gen mgr; Tony Cardona, gen sls mgr; Ricardo L. Alfaro, chief engr.

WSJU—ch 18, 759 kw vis, 75.9 kw aur, ant 2,778t/174g. TL: N18 18 36 W65 47 41. Stereo. On air date: Aug 19, 1984. Call Box 18, Carolina (00984). (809) 752-1800. Licensee: International Broadcasting Corp. ■ Net: NBC. Rep: Intercontinental Svcs Inc. Wash atty: Marmet & McComb. ■ Barakat Saleh, pres; Jerry Gervais, gen mgr. ■ Rates: $300; 125; 75.

San Sebastian

WJWN-TV—ch 38, 85.1 kw vis, 8.5 kw aur, ant 1,089t. TL: N18 19 06 W67 10 42. On air date: unknown. Box 4522, San Juan (00936). (809) 765-1810. Licensee: Tele 38 Inc.

Yauco

WIRS—ch 42, 1,510 kw vis, 151 kw aur, ant 1,961t. TL: N18 10 10 W66 34 36. On air date: Dec 1, 1991: Box 635, Bayamon (00960). (809) 799-6400. Licensee: Maranatha Christian Network. ■ Jofre Ayala, gen mgr.

Virgin Islands

Charlotte Amalie

WBNB-TV—ch 10, 2.51 kw vis, 251 w aur, ant 1,601t/298g. TL: N18 21 23 W64 56 42. On air date: July 22, 1961. Box 1947, St. Thomas (00801); 308 W. State St., Rockford, IL (61101). (212) 744-2333. TELEX: 347-0150. Licensee: Benedek Broadcasting of the Virgin Islands Inc. Group owner: Benadek Broadcasting Co. (acq 11-5-86; grpsl; 9-29-86). ■ Net: CBS. Rep: Katz. Wash atty: Wilner & Scheiner. ■ Richard Benedek, pres; Joseph Potter, vp; Page Stull, gen mgr; Lucette Mercer, gen sls mgr; Mari Morse, progmg dir; Yvonne Wright, news dir; Sam James, chief engr. ■ On 5 CATVs—150,000 subs.

*****WTJX-TV**—ch 12, 28.8 kw vis, 2.9 kw aur, ant 1,479t. TL: N18 21 26 W64 56 50. On air date: 1972. Box 7879 (00801). (809) 774-6255. Licensee: Virgin Islands Public Television System Board of Directors. ■ Net: PBS. Wash atty: Schwartz, Woods & Miller. ■ Patrick N. Williams, pres; Calvin F. Bastian, gen mgr; Leslie Hayes, opns mgr; Lori Elskoe, prom mgr & progmg mgr; Ron Traina, chief engr. ■ On 2 CATVs—15,000 subs. On 2 trans.

WVXF—ch 17, Not on air, target date unknown. Box 1605, c/o Atlantic Broadcasting Corp., Milwaukee WI (53201). Permittee: Atlantic Broadcasting Corp.

Christiansted

WSVI—ch 8, 200 kw vis, 20 kw aur, ant 1,144t/265g. TL: N17 45 20 W64 47 55. On air date: January 1966. Box 8ABC, Sunny Isle Shopping Ctr. (00823). (809) 778-5008. FAX: (809) 778-5011. Licensee: Antilles Broadcasting Corp. ■ Net: ABC. Rep: Roslin. Wash atty: Marmet & McCombs. Sp 5 hrs wkly. ■ Barakat Saleh, pres & gen mgr; Hilda Orengo, prom mgr; Barbara Shell, progmg dir; Eustace Browne, news dir; Chester Benjamin, chief engr. ■ On 6 CATVs—150,000 subs. On 2 trans. ■ Rates: $90; 70; 30.

Directory of Television Stations in Canada

Alberta

Ashmont

CFRN-TV-4—ch 12, 14.6 kw vis, 7.3 kw aur, ant 635t/590g. On air date: 1966. Box 5030, Station E, c/o CFRN-TV, Edmonton (T5S 1A8). Licensee: Sunwapta Broadcasting ■ Fred Filthaut, opns dir. Rebroadcasts CFRN-TV Edmonton.

Bonnyville

CBXFT-1—ch 6, 67 kw vis, 13.4 kw aur. Box 555, c/o CBXFT, Edmonton (T5J 2P4). (403) 468-7500. FAX: (403) 468-7792. Licensee: Canadian Broadcasting Corp. ■ Net: Radio Canada. ■ Denis Lord, opns dir. Rebroadcasts CBXFT Edmonton.

Calgary

CBRT—ch 9, 178 kw vis, 35.6 kw aur, ant 1,135t/845g. On air date: Sept 1, 1975. Box 2640, 1724 Westmount Blvd. N.W. (T2P 2M7). (403) 521-6000. TELEX: 038-21604. Licensee: CBC. ■ Net: CBC. ■ Ron Smith, gen mgr. ■ On 6 CATVs. On 16 trans.

CFCN-TV—ch 4, 100 kw vis, 27.5 kw aur, ant 623t/380g. TL: N52 03 37 W114 10 13. On air date: September 1960. Box 7060, Broadcast House, Postal Station E (T3C 3L9). (403) 240-5600. TELEX: 038-21637. Licensee: CFCN Communications Ltd. ■ Net: CTV. ■ Shawn Purdue, pres; Bruce Nelson, George Gonzo, exec vps; George Gonzo, vp sls; Don Thomas, prom mgr; Bruce Nelson, vp progmg; Pat McDougall, progmg mgr; Richard Coleman, chief engr. ■ On 9 CATVs—130,000 subs. On 16 trans.

CICT-TV—ch 2, 100 kw vis, 20 kw aur, ant 989t/633g. Stereo. Hrs opn: 24. On air date: October 1954. 222 23rd St. N.E. (T2E 7N2). (403) 235-7727. FAX: (403) 248-0252. Licensee: Calgary TV. Ownership: Westcom TV Group Ltd. Rep: Western. News staff 50; news progmg 13 hrs wkly. ■ J. Dagshaw, pres; N. Wagner, vp & stn mgr; D. Bates, vp sls; J. Eisler, mktg dir; B. Ash, progmg dir; W. Bill, news dir & pub affrs dir; W. McCambley, vp engrg.

Coronation

CKRD-TV-1—ch 10, 190 kw vis, 19 kw aur, ant 697t/240g. c/o RDTV, 2840 Bremner Ave., Red Deer (T4R 1M9). Licensee: Westcom TV Group Ltd. ■ Net: CBC. News staff 12; news progmg 5 hrs wkly. ■ Barry Duggan, gen mgr; Norman Michaelis, opns mgr; Larry Forster, rgnl sls mgr; Frank Thibault, progmg mgr; Neill Fitzpatrick, news dir; Gerald Cherepuschak, engrg mgr. Rebroadcasts CKRD-TV Red Deer.

Drumheller

CFCN-TV-1—ch 12, 14.1 kw vis, 7 kw aur. c/o CFCN-TV, Box 7060, Broadcast House, Postal Station E, Calgary (T3C 3L9). (403) 240-5600. FAX: (403) 240-5689. Licensee: CFCN TV Communications Ltd. ■ Net: CTV. ■ Shawn Purdue, pres; Bruce T. Nelson, exec vp. Rebroadcasts CFCN-TV Calgary.

Edmonton

CBXFT—ch 11, 90 kw vis, 18 kw aur. On air date: 1970. Box 555 (T5J 2P4); 8861 75th St. (T5C 4G8). (403) 468-7500. FAX: (403) 468-7792; TELEX: 037-2287. Licensee: Societe Radio-Canada/CBC. ■ Net: CBC. ■ Denis Lord, opns dir; Pierre Noel, prom mgr; Eric Batalla, news dir.

CBXT—ch 5, 318 kw vis, 34.3 kw aur. On air date: 1961. Box 555 (T5J 2P4). (403) 468-7500. FAX: (403) 468-7510. Licensee: CBC. ■ Net: CBC. ■ Ron Smith, gen mgr; Eric Upton, gen sls mgr; Glenn Luff, prom mgr; Bob McLaughlin, news dir; Mike Fallis, chief engr.

CFRN-TV—ch 3, 250 kw vis, 50 kw aur, ant 1,101t/260g. TL: N53 23 06 W113 12 48. Stereo. On air date: Oct 17, 1954. Box 5030, Station E, c/o CFRN-TV (T5P 4C2); 18520 Stony Plain Rd. (T5S 1A8). (403) 483-3311. FAX: (403) 484-8016. Licensee: Sunwapta Broadcasting Co. Ltd. ■ Net: CTV. Rep: Radio-TV Reps, Canada, Bolton Burchill, Harlan Oaks, U.S. News progmg 10 hrs wkly. ■ Fred Filthaut, vp & gen mgr; Jack Little, stn mgr; Brian Bolli, opns dir; Fred Vos, dev mgr; Alan Mabeee, gen sls mgr; Dennis Hendricks, rgnl sls mgr; Bob Gibson, progmg mgr; Steve Halinda, news dir; Stan Knaga, engrg dir. ■ On 13 trans.

CITV-TV—ch 13, 325 kw vis, 32.5 kw aur, ant 900t. TL: N53 23 06 W113 12 48. Stereo. On air date: 1974. 5325 Allard Way (T6H 5B8). (403) 436-1250. FAX: (403) 438-8448; (403) 434-4732. Licensee: Westcom TV Group Ltd. Ownership: WIC Western International Communications Ltd., 100% (acq 2-6-91). Rep: Western. Foreign lang progmg 137 hrs wkly. News staff 33; news progmg 11 hrs wkly. ■ Harold A. Roozen, pres; Wally Kirk, vp, gen mgr & vp progmg; Tom Climie, opns mgr; Art Eden, vp sls; Craig Roskin, rgnl sls mgr; Heather Grue, vp prom; Mark Jan Vrem, news dir; Mike Footz, engrg mgr. ■ On 4 CATVs. ■ Rates: C$4,000; 900; 800.

*****CJAL-TV**—ch 9, 8.2 kw vis. N53 24 19 W113 20 38. Hrs opn: 24. On air date: Apr 1, 1991. 3720 76th Ave. (T6B 2N9). (403) 440-7777. FAX: (403) 440-8899. Licensee: Alberta Educational Communications Corp. Ownership: Province of Alberta. ■ Don Thomas, pres; Malcolm Knox, gen mgr; Michael Schreiner, progmg dir; Neil Tegart, chief engr.

Fort McMurray

CBXFT-6—ch 12, 5.8 kw vis, 500 w aur, ant 200t/300g. On air date: Mar 1, 1970. Box 555, c/o CBXFT, Edmonton (T5J 2P4). (403) 468-7500. FAX: (403) 468-7792. Licensee: Canadian Broadcasting Corp. ■ Net: Radio Canada. ■ Denis Lord, opns dir. Rebroadcasts CBXFT Edmonton.

Grande Prairie

CBXAT—ch 10, 36 kw vis, 18 kw aur. Box 555, c/o CBXT, Edmonton (T5J 2P4); 8861 75th St. (T5C 4G8). (403) 468-7500. FAX: (403) 468-7893. Licensee: CBC. ■ Net: CBC. ■ Ron Smith, opns dir.

CBXFT-8—ch 19, 3.3 kw. Box 555, c/o CBXFT, Edmonton (T5J 2P4). (403) 468-7500. Licensee: CBC. ■ Net: Radio Canada. ■ Denis Lord, progmg dir. Rebroadcasts CBXFT Edmonton.

CFRN-TV-1—ch 13, 32 kw vis, 6.4 kw aur, ant 1,014t/641g. Box 5030, Station E, c/o CFRN-TV, Edmonton (T5P 4C2). Licensee: Sunwapta Broadcasting Ltd. ■ Net: CTV. ■ Fred Filthaut, opns dir. Rebroadcasts CFRN-TV Edmonton.

Grouard Mission-High Prairie

CFRN-TV-8—ch 18, 6 kw vis, 1 kw aur, ant 549t/369g. On air date: November 1981. Box 5030, Station E, c/o CFRN-TV, Edmonton (T5P 4C2). (403) 483-3311. Licensee: Sunwapta Broadcasting Ltd. ■ Net: CTV. ■ Fred Filthaut, opns dir. Rebroadcasts CFRN-TV Edmonton.

High Prairie

CBXAT-2—ch 2, 6.2 kw vis, 620 w aur. Box 555, c/o CBXT, Edmonton (T5J 2P4). (403) 468-7500. FAX: (403) 468-7893. ■ Net: CBC. ■ Ron Smith, opns dir. Rebroadcasts CBXAT Grand Prairie.

Lac La Biche

CFRN-TV-5—ch 2, 1,225 kw vis, 245 w aur, ant 126t/157g. Box 5030, Station E, c/o CFRN-TV, Edmonton (T5P 4C2). (403) 483-3311. Licensee: Sunwapta Broadcasting Ltd. ■ Net: CTV. ■ Fred Filthaut, opns dir. Rebroadcasts CFRN-TV Edmonton.

Lethbridge

CFCN-TV-5—ch 13, 47 kw vis, 7.34 kw aur. c/o CFCN-TV, Box 7060, Broadcast House, Postal Station E, Calgary (T3C 3L9). (403) 240-5600. Licensee: CFCN TV Communications Ltd. ■ Net: CTV. ■ Shawn Purdue, pres; Bruce T. Nelson, exec vp. Rebroadcasts CFCN-TV Calgary.

CISA-TV-7—ch 7, 167 kw vis, 33.4 kw aur, ant 662t/600g. TL: N49 47 01 W112 52 01. Stereo. On air date: 1955. Box 1120, 1401-28 Street N. (T1J 4A4). (403) 327-1521; (403) 320-2620; TELEX: 038-49130. Licensee: Lethbridge TV Ltd. Group owner: Westcom TV Group Ltd. Rep: Western. News staff 19; news progmg 12 hrs wkly. ■ R.C. Johnson, pres & gen mgr; Dennis Mathews, gen sls mgr; Terry Harrison, prom mgr; Kendall Gibson, progmg dir; Doug McArthur, news dir; Ron Joevenazzo, chief engr. ■ On 4 CATVs—24,500 subs. On 4 trans.

Lloydminster

CITL-TV—ch 4, 130 kw vis, 13 kw aur, ant 724t/708g. On air date: July 28, 1976. 5026 50 St. (T9V 1P3). (403) 875-3321. FAX: (403) 875-4704. Licensee: Midwest TV Ltd. ■ Net: CTV. ■ Mary L. Shortell, pres; Ken A. Ruptash, gen mgr; Graham Brown, gen sls mgr; Phil Manderson, prom mgr; Bob Cameron, progmg dir & film buyer; Michael Higgins, news dir; Raymond Green, chief engr.

CKSA-TV—ch 2, 116 kw vis, 23.2 kw aur. On air date: Sept 23, 1960. 5026 50th St. (T9V 1P3). (403) 875-3321. FAX: (403) 875-4704. Licensee: Midwest TV Ltd. ■ Net: CBC. ■ Mary L. Shortell, pres; Ken A. Ruptash, gen mgr; Graham Brown, gen sls mgr; Phil Manderson, prom mgr; Bob Cameron, progmg dir & film buyer; Michael Higgins, news dir; Raymond Green, chief engr.

Lougheed

CFRN-TV-7—ch 7, 5 kw vis, 500 w aur, ant 723t/517g. On air date: Sept 7, 1979. Box 5030, Station E, c/o CFRN-TV, Edmonton (T5P 4C2). (403) 483-3311. Licensee: Sunwapta Broadcasting Ltd. ■ Net: CTV. ■ Fred Filthaut, opns dir. Rebroadcasts CFRN-TV Edmonton.

Manning

CBXAT-3—ch 12, 1.77 kw vis, 177 w aur. Box 555, c/o CBXT, Edmonton (T5J 2P4). (403) 468-7500. FAX: (403) 468-7893. Licensee: CBC. ■ Net: CBC. ■ Ron Smith, opns dir; Bob McLaughlin, news dir; Mike Fallis, chief engr. Rebroadcasts CBXAT Grande Prairie.

Medicine Hat

CFCN-TV-8—ch 8, 6 kw vis, 600 w aur. c/o CFCN-TV, Box 7060, Broadcast House, Postal Station E, Calgary (T3C 3L9). (403) 240-5600. FAX: (403) 240-5689. Licensee: CFCN TV Ltd. ■ Net: CTV. ■ Shawn Purdue, pres; Bruce T. Nelson, exec vp.

CHAT-TV—ch 6, 58 kw vis, 5.8 kw aur, ant 700t/559g. On air date: 1956. Box 1270 (T1A 7H5). (403) 529-1270. FAX: (403) 529-1292. Licensee: Monarch Broadcasting Ltd. (group owner). ■ Net: CBC. Rep: Air Time. ■ W.H. Yuill, pres; Dwaine Dietrich, vp; Bryan Ellis, gen mgr; Ted Polish, gen sls mgr; Ken Poepping, prom mgr; Gary Rathwell, progmg dir; Brian Konrad, news dir; Bob Werre, chief engr. ■ On 6 CATVs—75,000 subs. Co-owned radio: CHAT(AM).

Peace River

CFRN-TV-2—ch 3, 2.4 kw vis, 240 w aur, ant 559t/351g. On air date: 1970. Box 5030, Station E, c/o CFRN-TV, Edmonton (T5P 4C2). (403) 483-3311. Licensee: Sunwapta Broadcasting Ltd. ■ Net: CTV. ■ Fred Filthaut, opns dir. Rebroadcasts CFRN-TV Edmonton.

Pivot

CHAT-TV-1—ch 4, 2.75 kw vis, 1.37 kw aur. Box 1270, c/o CHAT-TV, Medicine Hat (T1A 7H5). (403) 529-1270. FAX: (403) 529-1292. Licensee: Monarch Broadcasting Ltd. ■ Net: CBC. ■ Brian Ellis, gen mgr. Rebroadcasts CHAT-TV Medicine Hat.

Red Deer

CFRN-TV-6—ch 8, 24 kw vis, 4.8 kw aur, ant 882t/588g. Box 5030, Station E, c/o CFRN-TV, Edmonton (T5P 4C2). (403) 483-3311. Licensee: Sunwapta Broadcasting Ltd. ■ Net: CTV. ■ Fred Filthaut, opns dir. Rebroadcasts CFRN-TV Edmonton.

CKRD-TV—ch 6, 100 kw vis, 10 kw aur, ant 817t/570g. On air date: 1956. 2840 Bremner Ave. (T4R 1M9). (403) 346-2573. FAX: (403) 346-9980. Licensee: Westcom TV Group Ltd. Ownership: WIC Western International Communications Ltd. ■ Net: CBC. Rep: Alexander, Pearson & Dawson, WTR Media Sls. ■ Barry Duggan, gen mgr; Larry Foster, rgnl sls mgr; Frank Thibault, progmg mgr; Neill Fitzpatrick, news dir; Gerald Cherepuschak, chief engr. ■ On 7 CATVs—160,500 subs. On 2 trans.

Slave Lake

CFRN-TV-9—ch 4, 320 kw vis, 84 w aur, ant 1,101t/260g. On air date: November 1981. Box 5030, Station E, c/o CFRN-TV, Edmonton (T5P 4C2). (403) 483-3311. ■ Jack Little, gen mgr. Rebroadcasts CFRN-TV Edmonton.

British Columbia

Whitecourt

CFRN-TV-3—ch 12, 9.8 kw vis, ant 1,308t/160g. Box 5030, Station E, c/o CFRN-TV, Edmonton (T5P 4C2); 18520 Stony Plain Rd., Edmonton (T5S 1A8). (403) 483-3311. FAX: (403) 484-8016. Licensee: Sunwapta Ltd. ■ Net: CTV. ■ B.E. Cowie, pres; Jack Little, stn mgr; Fred Vos, opns mgr; Alan Mabee, gen sls mgr; Steve Lane, prom mgr & adv mgr; Bob Gibson, progmg mgr; Steve Halinda, news dir. Rebroadcasts CFRN-TV Edmonton.

British Columbia

Campbell River

CHEK-TV-5—ch 13, 3 kw vis, 300 w aur, ant 1493t/240g. c/o CHEK-TV, 780 King's Rd., Victoria (V8T 5A2). (604) 383-2435. FAX: (604) 384-7766. Licensee: CHEK-TV (div. of Westcom TV Group Ltd.) Group owner: BCTV, a division of Westcom TV Group Ltd. ■ Net: CTV. ■ Jim Nicholl, vp; Peter Gillespie, opns mgr; Neil Watson, gen sls mgr; Barry Dodd, prom mgr; Rick Wiertz, news dir; Dave Tidbury, chief engr.

Canal Flats

CBUBT-1—ch 12, 510 w vis, 51 w aur. Box 4600, c/o CBUT, Vancouver (V6B 4A2). (604) 662-6000. ■ Net: CBC. ■ John Kennedy, gen mgr. Rebroadcasts CBUBT-7 Cranbrook.

Courtenay

CHAN-TV-4—ch 11, 1.9 kw vis, 200 w aur, ant 1,321t/68g. Box 4700, c/o CHAN-TV, Vancouver (V6B 4A3). (604) 420-2288. FAX: (604) 421-9427. Licensee: British Columbia Television Broadcasting System Ltd. Group owner: BCTV, a division of Westcom TV Group Ltd. ■ Net: CTV. ■ T. Negoro, vp engrg.

Cranbrook

CBUBT-7—ch 10, 900 w vis, 90 w aur. On air date: 1962. c/o CBUT, Box 4600, Vancouver (V6B 4A2). Licensee: CBC. ■ Net: CBC. ■ John Kennedy, gen mgr. Rebroadcasts CBUT Vancouver.

Dawson Creek

CJDC-TV—ch 5, 10 kw vis, 5 kw aur, ant 1,500t/500g. On air date: 1958. 901-102nd Ave. (V1G 2B6). (604) 782-3341. FAX: (604) 782-1809; TELEX: 036-77127. Licensee: MEGA Communications Ltd. Ownership: J.L. Michaud, 40%; W.L. Michaud, 40%. ■ Net: CBC. ■ H.L. Michaud, pres & gen mgr; Alan Newby, opns dir; Peter Simons, gen sls mgr; Louise Perdue, vp prom; R.S. Hustak, progmg dir; E.R. Hall, film buyer; Dick Sequens, news dir; Morley Fountain, chief engr. ■ On 2 CATVs. On 8 trans. Co-owned radio: CJDC-AM-FM.

Kamloops

CBUFT-2—ch 50, 200 w. On air date: February 1979. 700 Hamilton St., Vancouver (V6B 2R5). (604) 662-6000. Licensee: Societe Radio Canada. ■ Net: CBC. ■ Pauline Sincennes, gen mgr. Rebroadcasts CBUFT Vancouver.

CFJC-TV—ch 4, 4.4 kw vis, 2.4 kw aur, ant 501t/114g. Stereo. On air date: 1957. 460 Pemberton Terr. (V2C 1T5). (604) 372-3322. FAX: (604) 374-0445. TELEX: 048-8148. Licensee: Jim Pattison Enterprises Ltd. Group owner: Jim Pattison Communications Group (acq 1987). ■ Net: CBC. Rep: Western. News staff 8; news progmg 14 hrs wkly. ■ Richard W. Arnish, vp & gen mgr; Dave Sommerton, opns mgr & progmg dir; Bryan White, gen sls mgr; Dave Somerton, program mgr; Dale Mortimer, adv mgr; Doug Collins, news dir; Kris Swamy, chief engr. ■ On 6 CATVs. Co-owned radio: CFJC(AM) & CIFM-FM.

CHKM-TV—ch 6, 4 kw vis, 400 w aur, ant 501t/114g. Box 4700, c/o CHAN-TV, Vancouver (V6B 4A3). (604) 420-2288. Licensee: British Columbia Television Broadcasting System Ltd. Group owner: BCTV, a division of Westcom TV Group Ltd. ■ Net: CTV. ■ T. Negoro, vp engrg. Rebroadcasts CHAN-TV Vancouver.

Kelowna

CHBC-TV—ch 2, 3.7 kw vis, 460 w aur, ant 2,704t/77g. TL: N49 58 00 W119 31 40. Hrs opn: 6 AM-2 AM. On air date: September 1957. 342 Leon Ave. (V1Y 6J2). (604) 762-4535. FAX: (604) 860-2422. TELEX: 048-5119. Licensee: Okanagan Valley Television Co. Ltd., a division of Westcom TV Group Ltd. ■ Net: CBC. Rep: Western. News staff 23; news progmg 12 hrs wkly. ■ R.K. Evans, pres & gen mgr; Terry Mahoney, vp opns, vp progmg & film buyer; Monty Cordingley, vp sls; Pat Vanderburg, prom mgr; Dennis Gabelhouse, adv mgr; Gordon Vizzutti, news dir; Larry Tisch, vp engrg. ■ On 16 CATVs—126,000 subs. On 22 trans. ■ Rates: $C200; 30; 60.

CHKL-TV—ch 5, 7 kw vis, 700 w aur, ant 1,672t/115g. Box 4700, c/o CHAN-TV, Vancouver (V6B 4A3). (604) 420-2288. Licensee: British Columbia Television Broadcasting System Ltd. Group owner: BCTV, a division of Westcom TV Group Ltd. ■ Net: CTV. ■ T. Negoro, vp engrg. Rebroadcasts CHAN-TV Vancouver.

Oliver-Osoyoos

CKKM-TV—ch 3, 1.0 kw vis, 100 w aur, ant 3,164t/110g. Box 4700, c/o CHAN-TV, Vancouver (V6B 4A3). (604) 420-2288. Licensee: British Columbia Television Broadcasting System Ltd. Group owner: BCTV, a division of Westcom TV Group Ltd. ■ Net: CTV. ■ T. Negoro, vp engrg.

100 Mile House

CITM-TV—ch 3, 1.3 kw vis, 130 w aur, ant 1,917t/134g. Box 4700, c/o CHAN-TV, Vancouver (V6B 4A3). (604) 420-2288. FAX: (604) 421-9427. Licensee: British Columbia Television Broadcasting System Ltd.(BCTV) (group owner). ■ Net: CTV. ■ T. Negoro, vp engrg. Rebroadcasts CHAN-TV Vancouver.

Penticton

CHKL-TV-1—ch 10, 1.0 kw vis, 100 w aur, ant 1,173t/67g. On air date: September 1970. Box 4700, c/o CHAN-TV, Vancouver (V6B 4A3). (604) 420-2288. Licensee: British Columbia Television Broadcasting System Ltd. Group owner: BCTV, a division of Westcom TV Group Ltd. ■ Net: CTV. Rep: Western Bcst Sls. ■ T. Negoro, vp engrg.

Prince George

CIFG-TV—ch 12, 4.7 kw vis, 500 w aur, ant 1,556t/91g. TL: N53 54 48 W122 27 10. Box 4700, c/o CHAN-TV, Vancouver (V6B 4A3). (604) 420-2288. Licensee: British Columbia Television Broadcasting System Ltd. Group owner: BCTV, a division of Westcom TV Group Ltd. ■ Net: CTV. Rep: Western Bcst Sls. ■ T. Negoro, vp engrg.

CKPG-TV—ch 2, 778 w vis, 389 w aur. On air date: 1961. 1220 6th Ave. (V2L 3M8). (604) 564-8861; (604) 562-8159. FAX: (604) 562-8768. Licensee: CKPG Television Ltd. Group owner: Monarch Broadcasting Ltd. (acq 1-74). ■ Net: CBC. Rep: Paul Mulvihill. ■ W. H. Yuill, pres; D. Dietrich, vp; G. M. Leighton, gen mgr & stn mgr; Thom Keene, opns mgr; B. Woodland, gen sls mgr; Brenda Levesque, progmg mgr; M. Woodworth, news dir; Ron Kellington, chief engr. Co-owned radio: CKPG(AM) and CIOI-FM.

Santa Rosa

CISR-TV—ch 68, 10 kw vis, 1 kw aur, ant 2,455t/30g. Box 4700, c/o CHAN-TV, Vancouver (V6B 4A3). (604) 420-2288. Licensee: British Columbia Television Broadcasting System Ltd. Group owner: BCTV, a division of Westcom TV Group Ltd. ■ Net: CTV. ■ T. Negoro, vp engrg. Rebroadcasting CHAN-TV Vancouver.

Terrace

CBUFT-3—ch 11, 500 w. On air date: Aug 27, 1979. 700 Hamilton, Vancouver (V6B 2R5). (604) 662-6000. Licensee: Societe Radio Canada. ■ Net: CBC. ■ Pauline Sincennes, gen mgr. Rebroadcasts CBUFT Vancouver.

CFTK-TV—ch 3, 13.8 kw vis, 1.38 kw aur, ant 1,488t/140g. On air date: 1962. 4625 Lazelle Ave. (V8G 1S4). (604) 635-6316. FAX: (604) 638-6320. Licensee: Skeena Broadcasters, a division of Okanagan Skeena Group Ltd. ■ Net: CBC. Rep: Mulvihill. ■ Bryan Edwards, pres; T. MacLean, gen mgr, gen sls mgr & film buyer; Chris Holtom, progmg dir & news dir; Harry Nutma, chief engr. ■ On 6 CATVs—12,088 subs. On 17 trans. Co-owned radio: CFTK(AM).

Trail

CKTN-TV—ch 8, 18 kw vis, 1.8 kw aur, ant 1,544t/60g. TL: N49 05 30 W117 49 10. Stereo. On air date: December 1976. Box 4700, Vancouver (V6B 4A3). (604) 420-2288. Licensee: BCTV, a division of Westcom TV Group Ltd. (group owner). ■ Net: CTV. Rep: Western. ■ Doug Holtby, chmn; Ron Bremner, pres; Bill Elliott, vp opns; Frank Babich, vp sls & vp mktg; Roy Gardner, vp progmg; T. Negoro, vp engrg. Rebroadcasts CHAN-TV Vancouver.

Vancouver

CBUFT—ch 26, 256 kw vis, ant 2,011t. TL: N49 21 12 W122 57 18. On air date: Sept 27, 1976. Box 4600 (V6B 4A2); 700 Hamilton St. (V6B 2R5). (604) 662-6170. Licensee: Societe Radio Canada. ■ Net: Radio Canada. ■ Pauline Sincennes, gen mgr.

CBUT—ch 2, 47.6 kw vis, 7.6 kw aur, ant 2,400t/190g. On air date: Dec 16, 1953. Box 4600 (V6B 4A2); 700 Hamilton St. (V6B 2R5). (604) 662-6000. TELEX: 04-51207. Licensee: CBC. ■ Net: CBC. ■ Doug Elthick, rgnl sls mgr; John H. Kennedy, progmg dir; Paul Patterson, news dir; Ian Munro, chief engr. ■ On 50 CATVs—750,000 subs. On 74 trans.

CHAN-TV—ch 8, 193.6 kw vis, 19.4 kw aur ant 2,315t/250g. Stereo. On air date: Oct 31, 1960. Box 4700 (V6B 4A3). (604) 420-2288. TELEX: 043-54784. Licensee: BCTV, a division of Westcom TV Group Ltd. (group owner). ■ Net: CTV. Rep: Western. ■ Doug Holtvy, CEO & chmn; R. Bremner, pres; F. Babich, vp sls & vp mktg; R. Gardner, vp progmg; T. Parsons, news dir; T. Negoro, vp engrg. ■ On 62 CATVs—985,300 subs. On 898 trans.

CKVU-TV—ch 10, 325 kw vis, 65 kw aur, ant 1,959t/159g. On air date: Sept 1, 1976. 180 W. Second Ave. (V5Y 3T9). (604) 876-1334. FAX: (604) 874-8225. Licensee: CanWest Pacific Television Inc. Rep: Can-Video TV Sls. ■ James W. Rusnak, pres & gen mgr; Haydn Kennard, chief opns & chief engr; Jack Tomik, gen sls mgr; Terry Leggett, rgnl sls mgr; Diane Johnson, prom mgr; Howard Slutsken, progmg dir & film buyer; Steve Wyatt, news dir.

Victoria

CHEK-TV—ch 6, 100 kw vis, 10 kw aur, ant 1,628t/380g. Stereo. Hrs opn: 24. On air date: 1956. 780 King's Rd. (V8T 5A2). (604) 383-2435. FAX: (604) 384-7766. Licensee: CHEK-TV. Group owner: BCTV, a division of Westcom TV Group Ltd. ■ Net: CTV. Rep: Western. ■ D.M. Smith, pres; Jim Nicholl, vp & gen mgr; Peter Gillespie, opns mgr; Neil Watson, gen sls mgr; Barry Dodd, prom mgr; Rick Wiertz, news dir; Dave Tiobury, chief engr.

Manitoba

Baldy Mountain

CBWST—ch 8, 120 kw vis, 12 kw aur. Box 160, c/o CBWT, Winnipeg (R3C 2H1). (204) 788-3222. ■ Net: CBC. ■ Marv Terhoch, opns dir. Rebroadcasts CBWT Winnipeg.

Brandon

CBWFT-10—ch 21, 9.4 kw, ant 340g. On air date: Feb 11, 1978. Box 160, c/o CBWFT, 541 Portage Ave., Winnipeg (R3C 2H1). (204) 788-3222. FAX: (204) 788-3639. Licensee: Societe Radio Canada. ■ Net: CBC. ■ Gilbert Teffaine, rgnl sls mgr. Rebroadcasts CBWFT Winnipeg.

CKX-TV—ch 5, 44 kw vis, 27 kw aur, ant 511t/525g. Hrs opn: 6 AM-2 AM. On air date: 1955. 2940 Victoria Ave. (R7B 0N2). (204) 728-1150; (204) 727-1150. FAX: (204) 727-2505. TELEX: 03-5016. Licensee: Craig Broadcast Systems Inc. Ownership: Craig Broadcast, 98%. ■ Net: CBC. Rep: Western. English progmg wkly. News staff 20; news progmg 15 hrs wkly. ■ A.S. Craig, pres; Boyd Craig, gen mgr & film buyer; Cam Cowies, vp sls; Mel Beatty, sls dir; Jacki Maginel, vp prom; Bob Bruce, news dir; Lawrence Dubois, chief engr. ■ On 15 CATVs—15,700 subs. Co-owned radio: CKX-AM-FM.

CKYB-TV—ch 4, 55 kw vis. c/o CKY-TV, Polo Park, Winnipeg (R3G 0L7). (204) 788-3300. FAX: (204) 783-4841. Licensee: Moffat Communications Ltd. ■ Net: CTV. ■ Vaughn Tozer, vp & gen mgr. Rebroadcasts CKY-TV Winnipeg.

Fisher Branch

CBWGT—ch 10, 27.4 kw vis, 5.48 kw aur, ant 559t/548g. Box 160, c/o CBWT, Winnipeg (R3C 2H1). (204) 788-3222. Licensee: CBC. ■ Net: CBC. ■ Marv Terhoch, rgnl sls mgr. Rebroadcasts CBWT Winnipeg.

Flin Flon

CBWBT—ch 10, 7.8 kw vis, 1.6 kw aur. Box 160, c/o CBWT, Winnipeg (R3C 2H1). (204) 788-3222. Licensee: CBC. ■ Net: CBC. ■ Marv Terhoch, rgnl sls mgr. Rebroadcasts CBWT Winnipeg.

Stations in Canada

Foxwarren

CKX-TV-1—ch 11, 46.8 kw vis, 3.48 kw aur. (CP: 56.8 kw vis). Box 1150, c/o CKX-TV, Brandon (R7A 6A5); c/o CKX-TV, 2940 Victoria Ave., Brandon (R7B 0N2). (204) 728-1150. Licensee: Western Manitoba Broadcasters Ltd. ■ Net: CBC. ■ Boyd Craig, gen mgr. Rebroadcasts CKX-TV Brandon.

Lac du Bonnet

CBWT-2—ch 4, 8.4 kw vis, 1.7 kw aur. Box 160, c/o CBWT, Winnipeg (R3C 2H1). (204) 788-3222. Licensee: CBC. ■ Net: CBC. ■ Marv Terhoch, rgnl sls mgr. Rebroadcasts CBWT Winnipeg.

Mafeking

CBWYT—ch 2, 4 kw vis, ant 370g. On air date: July 14, 1978. Box 160 c/o CBWT, Winnipeg (R3C 2H1). (204) 788-3222. Licensee: CBC. ■ Net: CBC. ■ Marv Terhoch, rgnl sls mgr. Rebroadcasts CBWT Winnipeg.

Minnedosa

CKND-TV-2—ch 2, 99 kw vis, 1,300t. On air date: Sept 1, 1982. c/o CKND-TV, 603 St. Mary's Rd., Winnipeg (R2M 3L8). (204) 233-3304. FAX: (204) 233-5615. TELEX: 07-55270. Licensee: CKND Television Inc. News progmg 12 hrs wkly. ■ Peter M. Liba, pres & gen mgr. Rebroadcasts CKND-TV Winnipeg.

Portage la Prairie

CHMI-TV—Licensed to Portage la Prairie. See Winnipeg.

Ste-Rose-du-Lac

CBWFT-4—ch 3, 1.2 kw, 120g. On air date: May 15, 1976. Box 160, c/o CBWFT, Winnipeg (R3C 2H1). (204) 788-3222. FAX: (204) 788-3639. Licensee: Societe Radio Canada. ■ Net: CBC. ■ Gilbert Teffaine, rgnl sls mgr. Rebroadcasts CBWFT Winnipeg.

Winnipeg

CBWFT—ch 3, 59 kw vis, 7.3 kw aur, ant 1,027t/1,020g. On air date: 1960. Box 160 (R3C 2H1). (204) 788-3222; (204) 788-3141. FAX: (204) 788-3639. Licensee: CBC. ■ Net: CBC. ■ Gilbert Teffaine, rgnl sls mgr.

CBWT—ch 6, 100 kw vis, 12 kw aur, ant 1,027t/1,020g. On air date: 1954. Box 160 (R3C 2H1). (204) 788-3222. TELEX: 07-57780. Licensee: CBC. ■ Net: CBC. ■ Anthony Manera, CEO; Pierre Juneau, pres; Kevin Comrie, gen sls mgr; Marv Terhoch, rgnl sls mgr; Martin Marcotte, chief engr. ■ On 4 CATVs—123,000 subs. On 54 Rebroadcasters.

CHMI-TV—(Portage la Prairie). ch 13, 325 kw vis, 32.5 kw aur, ant 1,029t/1,100g. Hrs opn: 24. On air date: Oct 17, 1986. Box 13000, 350 River Rd., Portage la Prairie (R1N 3V3). (204) 239-1113. FAX: (204) 239-5794. Licensee: Craig Broadcast Systems Inc. Rep: Western, Telerep. News staff 35; news progmg 34 hrs wkly. ■ A. Stuart Craig, pres; J. Drew Craig, gen mgr & vp progmg; Wayne Marks, opns mgr; Cam Cowie, gen sls mgr; Kevin Dunn, prom mgr; Pat Beswatknick, progmg mgr; Al Thorgerson, news dir; Vladimir Rybarczyk, chief engr.

CKND-TV—ch 9, 325 kw vis, 25 kw aur ant 500t/600g. Stereo. Hrs opn: 24. On air date: Sept 1, 1975. 603 St. Mary's Rd. (R2M 3L8). (204) 233-3304. FAX: (204) 233-5615; TELEX: 07-55270. Licensee: CKND Television Inc. Ownership: CanWest Communications Enterprises Inc. Rep: Canvideo, Metro Mktg West (Vancouver & West USA). News staff 19; news progmg 12 hrs wkly. ■ Peter M. Liba, pres & gen mgr; Stan Schmidt, gen sls mgr; Lloyd Lewis, prom mgr; Shelley Stuart, progmg dir & film buyer; Judy Waytiuk, news dir; Bob Hall, chief engr. ■ On 40 CATVs—220,000 subs. On one trans. ■ Rates: C$1,300; na; na.

CKY-TV—ch 7, 325 kw vis, 65 kw aur, ant 1,000g. On air date: 1960. Polo Park (R3G 0L7). (204) 788-3300. FAX: (204) 783-4841. TELEX: 07-57745. Licensee: Moffat Communications Ltd. (group owner). ■ Net: CTV. Rep: Alexander, Pearson & Dawson. ■ R.L. Moffat, pres; Vaughn Tozer, vp & gen mgr; J.S. Gibson, opns mgr; I.M. Lillie, gen sls mgr; B. Johnson, prom mgr; T.J. Smith, progmg dir; V.L. Merkeley, news dir; Michael Marshall, chief engr. ■ On 6 CATVs—190,000 subs. On 7 trans.

New Brunswick

Bon Accord

CHSJ-TV-1—ch 6, 54.7 kw vis, 27.3 kw aur. TL: N46 38 57 W67 35 35. c/o CHSJ-TV, Box 2000, Saint John (E2L 3T4); c/o CHSJ-TV, 335 Union St., Saint John (E2L 1B3). (506) 632-2222. FAX: (506) 632-3485. Licensee: New Brunswick Broadcasting Co. Ltd. ■ Net: CBC. Rep: Canvideo. ■ L.M. Nichols, pres & gen mgr. Rebroadcasts CHSJ-TV St. John.

Campbellton

CHCR-TV—ch 4, 25.12 kw vis, 3.71 kw aur, ant 1,354t/1,826g. TL: N48 08 07 W66 07 00. On air date: Nov 1, 1976. Box 2000, Saint John (E2L 3T4); 335 Union St., Saint John (E2L 1B3). (506) 632-2222. FAX: (506) 632-3485. Licensee: New Brunswick Broadcasting Co. Ltd. ■ Net: CBC. Rebroadcasts CHSJ-TV St. John.

CKCD-TV—ch 7, 920 w vis, 180 w aur, ant 75t. Box 5004, Moncton (E1C 8R6). (506) 857-2600. FAX: (506) 857-2618. Licensee: ATV New Brunswick (div. of CHUM Ltd.) Ownership: Atlantic TV System. ■ Net: CTV. Rep: Alexander, Pearson & Dawson. Rebroadcasts CKCW-TV Moncton.

Moncton

CBAFT—ch 11, 163 kw vis, 33 kw aur, ant 781t/394g. TL: N46 08 41 W64 54 14. On air date: 1959. Box 950, 250 Archibald St. (E1C 8N8). (506) 853-6725. FAX: (506) 853-6715. Licensee: Societe Radio-Canada. ■ Net: CBC. ■ Gerard Veillux, pres; Claude Bourque, gen mgr; Jacques Robichaud, opns mgr; Michel Bertin, gen sls mgr; Robert Nadeau, mktg dir; Louise Imbeault, progmg dir; Donald Langis, news dir; Michel LeBlanc, chief engr.

CHMT-TV—ch 7, 182 kw vis, 36.4 kw aur. TL: N45 48 32 W64 45 11. On air date: Sept 21, 1969. c/o CHSJ-TV, Box 2000, Saint John (E2L 3T4); c/o CHSJ-TV, 335 Union St., Saint John (E2L 1B3). (506) 632-2222. FAX: (506) 632-3485. Licensee: N.B. Broadcasting Co. Ltd. ■ Net: CBC. ■ L.M. Nichols, pres & gen mgr. Rebroadcasts CHSJ-TV St. John.

CKCW-TV—ch 2, 56 kw vis, 9.2 kw aur. On air date: 1954. Box 5004 (E1C 8R6). (506) 857-2600. FAX: (506) 857-2618. Licensee: ATV New Brunswick Ltd. Group owner: CHUM Ltd. ■ Net: CTV. Rep: Alexander, Pearson & Dawson. ■ F.G. Sherratt, pres; G. Mudry, vp & gen mgr; D. Eagles, stn mgr; J. Jay, opns mgr; N. Fuller, gen sls mgr; Anne-Marie Varner, prom mgr; R. Prat, progmg dir & film buyer; Bill Patrick, news dir; Larry Wartman, chief engr.

Saint John

CHSJ-TV—ch 4, 54.2 kw vis, 7.8 kw aur, ant 1,268t/1,631g. TL: N45 28 39 W66 14 03. On air date: 1954. Box 2000, 335 Union St. (E2L 3T4). (506) 632-2222. FAX: (506) 632-3485. TELEX: 014-47218. Licensee: New Brunswick Broadcasting Co. Ltd. ■ Net: CBC. Rep: Canvideo TV Sls, Brydson Spot Sls (East U.S.), Metro Mktg West (West U.S.). ■ L.M. Nichols, pres & gen mgr; Mel Johnston, opns mgr; Gary Murphy, gen sls mgr; Grace Craft, prom mgr; Dave Merzetti, progmg mgr & film buyer; David White, news dir; Ken Hauschildt, chief engr. Co-owned radio: CHSJ(AM).

CKLT-TV—ch 9, 162 kw vis, 32 kw aur, ant 1,361t/241g. Box 5004, Moncton (E1C 8R6). (506) 857-2600. FAX: (506) 857-2618. Licensee: ATV New Brunswick Ltd. Group owner: CHUM Ltd. ■ Net: CTV. ■ Fred Sherratt, pres; G. Mudry, vp & gen mgr; Colin Burns, gen sls mgr; Anne-Marie Varner, prom mgr; R. Prat, progmg dir & film buyer; W. Patrick, news dir; Larry Wartman, chief engr.

Upsalquitch Lake

CKAM-TV—ch 12, 280 kw vis, 141 kw aur. c/o CKCW-TV, Box 5004, Moncton (E1C 8R6). (506) 857-2600. FAX: (506) 857-2618. Licensee: ATV New Brunswick Ltd. Ownership: Atlantic TV Systems. ■ Net: CTV. Wash atty: Alexander, Pearson & Dawson. ■ D. Eagles, stn mgr; Larry Wartman, opns dir; David MacLeod, gen sls mgr; Claire Wright, prom dir. Rebroadcasts CKCW-TV Moncton.

Newfoundland

Argentia

CJAP-TV—ch 3, 6.7 kw vis, 3.4 kw aur, ant 275g. On air date: September 1957. Box 2020, c/o CJON-TV, St. John's (A1C 5S2). (709) 722-5015. FAX: (709) 726-5107. Licensee: Newfoundland Broadcasting Co. Ltd. (group owner; acq 9-1-77). ■ Net: CTV. ■ Brian Vallis, gen mgr. ■ On 5 trans. Rebroadcasts CJON-TV St. John's.

Baie Verte

CBNAT-1—ch 3, 3.4 kw vis. (CP: 8.8 kw vis). Box 12010, Stn A, c/o CBNT, St. John's (A1B 3T8). (709) 576-5000. Licensee: CBC. ■ Net: CBC. ■ Ron Croford, gen mgr. Rebroadcasts CBNT St. John's.

Bonavista

CJWB-TV—ch 10, 9.9 kw vis, 990 w aur, ant 539.55t/151.8g. TL: N48 37 30 W53 03 45. Stereo. Hrs opn: 1972. Box 2020, NTV Studios, 446 Logy Bay Rd., St. John's (A1C 5S2). (709) 722-5015. FAX: (709) 726-5107. Licensee: Newfoundland Broadcasting Co. Ltd. (group owner). ■ Net: CTV. ■ Brian Vallis, gen mgr. ■ On 7 CATVs. On 27 trans. Rebroadcasts CJON-TV St. John's.

Bonne Bay

CBYT-3—ch 2, 6.2 kw vis, 1.5 kw aur, ant 300t/300g. On air date: Aug 7, 1967. c/o CBNT, Box 12010, Station A, St. John's (A1B 3T8). (709) 576-5000. Licensee: CBC. ■ Net: CBC, CBC Northern Television Services. ■ Ron Croford, gen mgr. Rebroadcasts CBNT St. John's.

Corner Brook

CBYT—ch 5, 10.6 kw vis, 2.1 kw aur, ant 2,804t/300g. On air date: July 6, 1959. Box 610 (A2H 6G1). (709) 634-3141. FAX: (709) 634-8506. Licensee: CBC. ■ Net: CBC. ■ Walter Sheppard, stn mgr; Paula Giovanni, gen sls mgr; Bob Wakeham, news dir; Larry O'Brien, chief engr.

CJWN-TV—ch 10, 6.07 kw vis, 1 kw aur, ant 364t/300g. TL: N48 56 55 W57 58 23. Hrs opn: 24. On air date: December 1974. Box 2020, NTV Studios, 446 Logy Bay Rd., St. John's (A1C 5S2). (709) 722-5015. FAX: (709) 726-5107. Licensee: Newfoundland Broadcasting Co. Ltd. (group owner). ■ Net: CTV. ■ Brian Vallis, gen mgr. ■ On 7 CATVs. On 27 trans. Rebroadcasts CJON-TV St. John's.

Goose Bay-Labrador

CFLA-TV—ch 8, 1.9 kw vis, 536 w aur, ant 230t. On air date: October 1956. Box 1270, Station B, c/o CBNT, Happy Valley (A0P 1E0). (709) 737-4140. FAX: (709) 737-4212. Licensee: CBC (acq 7-1-73). ■ Net: CBC. ■ Jim Byrd, gen mgr. Rebroadcasts CBNT St. John's.

Grand Bank

CJOX-TV-1—ch 2, 4.67 kw vis, 470 w aur, ant 387t/287g. TL: N47 05 17 W55 46 23. Stereo. Hrs opn: 24. On air date: 1972. Box 2020, NTV Studio Bldg., 446 Logy Bay Rd., St. John's (A1C 5S2). (709) 722-5015. FAX: (709) 726-5107. Licensee: Newfoundland Broadcasting Co. Ltd. (group owner). ■ Net: CTV. ■ Brian Vallis, gen mgr. ■ On 7 CATVs. On 27 trans. Rebroadcasts CJON-TV St. John's.

Grand Falls

CBNAT—ch 11, 317 kw vis, 64 kw aur. Box 12010, Station A, c/o CBNT, St. John's (A1B 3T8). (709) 576-5000. Licensee: CBC. ■ Net: CBC. ■ Ron Croford, gen mgr. Rebroadcasts CBNT St. John's.

CJCN-TV—ch 4, 100 kw vis, 10 kw aur, ant 602.25t/376.2g. TL: N49 04 12 W55 16 54. Stereo. Hrs opn: 24. On air date: 1963. Box 2020, NTV Studio Bldg., 446 Logy Bay Rd., St. John's (A1C 5S2). (709) 722-5015. FAX: (709) 726-5107. Licensee: Newfoundland Broadcasting Co. (group owner). ■ Net: CTV. ■ Brian Vallis, gen mgr. ■ On 7 CATVs. On 27 trans. Rebroadcasts CJON-TV St. John.

Labrador City

*****CBNLT**—ch 13, 2 kw vis, 20 w aur, ant 100t. Box 12010, Station A, c/o CBNT, St. John's (A1B 3T8). (709) 576-5000. Licensee: CBC. ■ Net: CBC. ■ Ron Croford, gen mgr. Rebroadcasts CBNT St. John's.

Marystown

CBNT-3—ch 5, 2 kw vis, 200 w aur, ant 800t/372g. On air date: Oct 30, 1965. Box 12010, Station A, c/o CBNT, St. John's (A1B 3T8). (709) 576-5000. Licensee: Canadian Broadcasting Corp. ■ Net: CBC. ■ Ron Croford, gen mgr. Rebroadcasts CBNT St. John's.

Mount St. Margaret

CBNAT-9—ch 9, 29 kw vis. Box 12010, Station A, c/o CBNT, St. John's (A1B 3T8). (709) 576-5000. Licensee: CBC. ■ Net: CBC. ■ Ron Croford, gen mgr. Rebroadcasts CBNT St. John's.

Placentia

CBNT-2—ch 12, 150 w vis, 15 w aur. Box 12010, Station A, c/o CBNT, St. John's (A1B 3T8). Licensee: Canadian Broadcasting Corp. ■ Net: CBC. ■ Ron Croford, gen mgr. Rebroadcasts CBNT St. John's.

Port Rexton

CBNT-1—ch 8, 196 kw, 39.2 kw aur, ant 696t/636g. On air date: October 1964. Box 12010, Station A, c/o CBNT, St. John's (A1B 3T8). (709) 576-5000. Licensee: Canadian Broadcasting Corp. ■ Net: CBC. ■ Ron Croford, gen mgr; John Farrell, rgnl sls mgr; Bob Wagum, news dir. Rebroadcasts CBNT St. John's.

St. Anthony

CBNAT-4—ch 6, 6.54 kw vis, 650 w aur. Box 12010, Station A, c/o CBNT, St. John's (A1B 3T8). (709) 576-5000. Licensee: CBC. ■ Net: CBC. ■ Jim Byrd, gen mgr. Rebroadcasts CBNAT Grand Falls.

St. John's

CBNT—ch 8, 196 kw vis, 39 kw aur. On air date: 1964. Box 12010, Station A (A1B 3T8). (709) 576-5000. Licensee: CBC. ■ Net: CBC. ■ Ron Croford, gen mgr; John Farrell, rgnl sls mgr; John Ridge, progmg dir; Bob Wagum, news dir.

CJON-TV—ch 6, 80 kw vis, 8 kw aur, ant 825t/301.6g. TL: N47 31 36 W52 42 50. Stereo. Hrs opn: 24. On air date: September 1955. Box 2020, NTV Studios, 446 Logy Bay Rd. (A1C 5S2). (709) 722-5015. FAX: (709) 726-5107. Licensee: Newfoundland Broadcasting Co. Ltd. (group owner). ■ Net: CTV. Rep: Alexander, Pearson & Dawson. News staff 7; news progmg 7 hrs wkly. ■ Scott Stirling, CEO, pres & progmg dir; Geoffery Stirling, chmn; Frank Collins, CFO; Brian Vallis, gen mgr; Doug Neal, stn mgr & engrg dir; Ted Gardner, sls dir; Jim Furlong, news dir. ■ On 7 CATVs. On 27 trans. Co-owned radio: CHOZ-FM.

Stephenville

CBYT-1—ch 8, 11.6 kw vis, 2.32 kw aur, ant 200t/200g. On air date: Mar 11, 1967. c/o CBYT, Box 610, Corner Brook (A2H 6GI). (709) 634-3141. Licensee: CBC. ■ Net: CBC. ■ Walter Sheppard, stn mgr. Rebroadcasts CBYT Corner Brook.

CJSV-TV—ch 4, 5.56 kw vis, 560 w aur ant 439.7t/91g. TL: N48 31 09 W58 31 00. Hrs opn: 24. On air date: 1973. Box 2020, NTV Studio Bldg., 446 Logy Bay Rd., St. John's (A1C 5S2). (709) 722-5015. FAX: (709) 726-5107. Licensee: Newfoundland Broadcasting Co. Ltd. (group owner). ■ Net: CTV. ■ Brian Vallis, gen mgr. ■ On 7 CATVs. On 27 trans. Rebroadcasts CJON-TV St. John's.

Northwest Territories

Inuvik

***CHAK-TV**—ch 6, 3 kw vis, 300 w aur, ant 443t/360g. Bag Service No. 8 (X0E OTO). (403) 920-5400. FAX: (403) 979-4458. Licensee: CBC. ■ Net: CBC. News staff 2. ■ Gerard Veilleux, pres; Anne Crossman, gen mgr & progmg mgr; Lynn Nicol, news dir; Jack Delaney, chief engr.

Yellowknife

***CFYK-TV**—ch 8, 1 kw vis, 100w aur. On air date: 1968. Box 160 (X1A 2N2). (403) 920-5400. FAX: (403) 920-5489. TELEX: 034-44517. Licensee: CBC. ■ Net: CBC. ■ Craig Mackie, gen mgr & progmg mgr; Jim MacVicar, opns mgr; Marie Wilson, progmg dir; George Mount, chief engr. ■ On 1 CATV.

Nova Scotia

Antigonish

CJCB-TV-2—ch 9, 140 kw vis. c/o CJCB-TV, Box 469, Sydney (B1P 6H5). (902) 564-5596. ■ Net: CTV. ■ William Holmes, gen mgr. Rebroadcasts CJCB-TV Sydney.

Caledonia

CJCH-TV-6—ch 6, 100 kw vis, 20 kw aur, ant 630t/400g. Box 1653, 2885 Robie St., Halifax (B3J 2Z4). Rebroadcasts CJCH-TV Halifax.

Canning

CJCH-TV-1—ch 10, 18.1 kw vis, 3.62 kw aur, ant 886t/300g. Box 1653, 2885 Robie St., Halifax (B3J 2Z4). Rebroadcasts CJCH-TV Halifax.

Cheticamp

CBHFT-4—ch 10, 7.9 kw vis, 4 kw aur. c/o CBAFT, Box 950, Moncton, NB (E1C 8N8). (902) 420-4001. FAX: (902) 420-4278. Licensee: CBC. ■ Net: CBC. ■ Louise Imbeault, gen mgr. Rebroadcasts CBAFT Moncton, N.B.

CBIT-2—ch 2, 2.5 kw vis, 250 w aur, ant 150g. c/o CBIT 285 Alexandra St., Sydney (B1S 2E8). (902) 539-5050. FAX: (902) 562-7547. Licensee: CBC. ■ Net: CBC. ■ Craig Crinkley, gen mgr. Rebroadcasts CBIT Sydney.

Halifax

CBHFT—ch 13, 1.9 kw vis, 190 w aur. On air date: 1971. c/o CBAFT, Box 950, Moncton, NB (E1C 8N8). (902) 420-4001. FAX: (902) 420-4278. Licensee: CBC. ■ Net: CBC. ■ Louise Imbeault, gen mgr. Rebroadcasts CBAFT Moncton, N.B.

CBHT—ch 3, 56 kw vis, 11.2 kw aur, ant 866t/1,620g. On air date: 1954. Box 3000, 5600 Sackville St. (B3J 3E9). (902) 420-4001. FAX: (902) 420-4020. Licensee: CBC. ■ Net: CBC. ■ Bill Donovan, gen mgr.

CIHF-TV—ch 8, 8.2 kw vis, 1.6 aur, ant 691t/645g. TL: N44 39 03 W63 39 28. Stereo. On air date: Sept 5, 1988. 14 Akerley Blvd., Dartmouth (B3B 1J3). (902) 494-5200. FAX: (902) 468-2154. Licensee: New Brunswick Broadcasting Co. Ltd. News staff 28; news progmg 15 hrs wkly. ■ L. Nichols, pres; Ted Billo, vp; D. Verge, opns mgr; G. Murphy, gen mgr; B. Saunders, rgnl sls mgr; J. Morel, prom mgr; D. Merzetti, progmg dir & film buyer; John O'Brien, news dir; B. Graham, pub affrs dir; S. Wilson, chief engr.

CJCH-TV—ch 5, 100 kw vis, 10 kw aur, ant 822t/575g. On air date: Jan 1, 1961. Box 1653, 2885 Robie St. (B3J 2Z4). (902) 453-4000. FAX: (902) 454-3302; TELEX: 019-21826. Licensee: Atlantic Television System. Group owner: CHUM Ltd. ■ Net: CTV. Rep: Alexander, Pearson & Dawson (Canada); Hugh Wallace (Los Angeles). ■ Fred Sherratt, pres; G. Mudry, vp & gen mgr; Colin A. Burns, gen sls mgr; Anne-Marie Varner, prom mgr; Dick Prat, progmg dir; Bill Patrick, news dir; W.A. Robert, chief engr.

Inverness

CJCB-TV-1—ch 6, 9.4 kw vis, 4.7 kw aur. c/o CJCB-TV, Box 469, Sydney (B1P 6H5). (902) 562-5511. FAX: (902) 564-0495. Licensee: ATV Cape Breton. ■ Net: CTV. ■ William Holmes, gen mgr. Rebroadcasts CJCB-TV Sydney.

Mulgrave

CBHFT-2—ch 7, 106 kw vis. c/o CBAFT, Box 950, Moncton, NB (E1C 8N8). (902) 420-4001. FAX: (902) 420-4278. Licensee: CBC. ■ Net: CBC. ■ Louise Imbeault, gen mgr. Rebroadcasts CBAFT Moncton, N.B.

CBHT-11—ch 12, 129 kw vis, 12.9 kw aur. Box 3000, c/o CBHT, 5600 Sackville St., Halifax (B3J 3E9). (902) 420-4001. FAX: (902) 420-4278. Licensee: CBC. ■ Net: CBC. ■ Bill Donovan, gen mgr. Rebroadcasts CBHT Halifax.

Sheet Harbour

CBHT-4—ch 11, 9.07 kw vis, 1.814 kw aur. Box 3000, c/o CBHT, 5600 Sackville St., Halifax (B3J 3E9). (902) 420-4001. FAX: (902) 420-4278. Licensee: CBC. ■ Net: CBC. ■ Bill Donovan, gen mgr. Rebroadcasts CBHT Halifax.

Sydney

CBHFT-3—ch 13, 4.5 kw vis. c/o CBAFT, Box 950, Moncton, NB (E1C 8N8). (902) 420-4001. FAX: (902) 420-4278. Licensee: CBC. ■ Net: CBC. ■ Gerard Veilleux, chmn; Claude Bourque, opns mgr; Jacques Robichaud, opns mgr; Michel Berlin, natl sls mgr; Robert Nadeau, mktg mgr; Louise Imbeault, progmg mgr; Donald Langis, news dir; Michel LeBlanc, engrg mgr. Rebroadcasts CBAFT Moncton, N.B.

CBIT—ch 5, 54 kw vis, 5.4 kw aur. On air date: 1972. 285 Alexandra St. (B1S 2E8). (902) 539-5050. FAX: (902) 562-7547. Licensee: CBC. ■ Net: CBC. ■ Craig Crinkley, gen mgr; Brian Slemming, news dir; Sheldon McEwan, chief engr.

CJCB-TV—ch 4, 100 kw vis, 60 kw aur. On air date: 1954. Box 469 (B1P 6H5). (902) 562-5511. FAX: (902) 564-0495. Licensee: ATV Cape Breton. Group owner: CHUM Ltd. ■ Net: CTV. ■ F.G. Sherratt, pres; William Holmes, gen mgr; David Kerr, gen sls mgr; E.K. Williams, prom mgr; Bruce Hennessey, news dir; Edgar Bennett, chief engr.

Yarmouth

CBHFT-1—ch 3, 1.9 kw vis, 190 w aur. c/o CBAFT, Box 950, Moncton, NB (E1C 8N8). (902) 420-4001. FAX: (902) 420-4278. Licensee: CBC. ■ Net: CBC. ■ Louise Imbeault, gen mgr. Rebroadcasts CBAFT Moncton, N.B.

CBHT-3—ch 11, 15.7 kw vis, 3.3 kw aur. Box 3000, c/o CBHT, 5600 Sackville St., Halifax (B3J 3E9). (902) 420-4001. FAX: (902) 420-4278. Licensee: CBC. ■ Net: CBC. ■ Bill Donovan, gen mgr. Rebroadcasts CBHT Halifax.

Ontario

Bancroft

CIII-TV-2—ch 2, 100 kw vis, 15 kw aur, ant 1,279.2t/1,006.3g. Stereo. On air date: January 1974. c/o CIII-TV, 81 Barber Greene Rd., Don Mills (M3C 2A2). (416) 446-5311. FAX: (416) 446-5371. Licensee: Global Communications Ltd., div of CanWest Global Systems. Group owner: Global Television Network. ■ Net: Global. ■ Rodger Hone, sr vp; Doug Hoover, progmg dir. ■ On 201 CATVs—2,511,127 subs.

Barrie

CKVR-TV—ch 3, 100 kw vis, 12.5 kw aur, ant 820t/651g. On air date: Sept 28, 1955. Box 519, 33 Beacon Rd. (L4M 4T9). (705) 734-3300. FAX: (705) 733-0302; (705) 734-2061. Licensee: CKVR Ch 3 division of CHUM Ltd. Group owner: CHUM Ltd. ■ Net: CBC. Rep: Alexander, Pearson & Dawson. ■ Allan Waters, pres; Doug Garraway, gen mgr & stn mgr; Paul Miller, prom mgr; Peggy Hebden, progmg mgr & film buyer; Tony Panacci, news dir; Rod Reid, chief engr. ■ On 45 CATVs.

Chatham

***CICO-TV-59**—ch 59, 34.3 kw vis, 3.4 kw aur, ant 717t/718g. On air date: June 1976. Box 200, Stn Q, Toronto (M4T 2T1). (416) 484-2600. FAX: (416) 484-6285. Licensee: Ontario Educational Communications Authority. ■ Peter Hermdorf, CEO & pres; Don Duprey, Jacques Bensimon, progmg dirs; Bruce Read, engrg dir. Rebroadcasts *CICA-TV Toronto.

Cornwall

CJOH-TV-8—ch 8, 130 kw vis, 78 kw aur, ant 700t/681g. On air date: 1958. Box 5813, Station F, Merivale Depot, Ottawa (K2C 3G6). (613) 224-1313. FAX: (613) 224-7998; TELEX: 053-4294. Licensee: Nation's Capital Television Inc. Group owner: Baton Broadcasting Ltd. ■ Net: CTV. Rep: Alexander, Pearson, Dawson. ■ Bryn Matthews, gen mgr. ■ On 41 CATVs. Rebroadcasts CJOH-TV Ottawa.

Deseronto

CJOH-TV-6—ch 6, 55 kw vis, 5.5 kw aur, ant 671t/573g. On air date: September 1972. Box 5813, Station F, Merivale Depot, Ottawa (K2C 3G6). (613) 224-1313. FAX: (613) 224-7998; TELEX: 053-4294. Licensee: Nation's Capital Television Inc. Group owner: Baton Broadcasting Inc. ■ Net: CTV. Rep: Alexander, Pearson & Dawson. ■ Bryn Matthews, gen mgr. ■ On 41 CATVs.

Dryden

CBWDT—ch 9, 8.9 kw vis, 1.78 kw aur, ant 531.2t/531.2g. Box 936 (P8N 2Z5). (807) 938-6367. Licensee: CBC. ■ Net: CBC. ■ Marv Terhoch, gen mgr. ■ On one CATV. On 6 trans. Rebroadcasts CBWT Winnipeg, Man.

Stations in Canada — Ontario

Elliot Lake

CBLFT-6—ch 12, 18.6 kw vis, 3.72 kw aur. Box 3220, c/o CBOFT, Station C, Ottawa (K1Y 1E4). (613) 724-1200. FAX: (416) 975-5622. Licensee: Societe Radio-Canada. ■ Net: CBC French. ■ Pierre Fournier, progmg dir. Rebroadcasts CBLFT-1 Sturgeon Falls.

CICI-TV-1—ch 5, 19 kw vis, 1.9 kw aur, ant 576t/216g. On air date: 1958. c/o CICI-TV, 699 Frood Rd., Sudbury (P3C 5A3). (705) 674-8301. FAX: (705) 671-2444. Licensee: Mid Canada Communications Corp. Group owner: Baton Broadcasting Inc. ■ Net: CTV. Rep: Glen Warren. News staff 15; news progmg 10 hrs wkly. ■ George Lund, pres; Mike Fawcett, gen mgr & engrg dir; John Eddy, opns mgr; Pat Thompson, dev dir; Mary Lund, gen sls mgr; Scott Lund, rgnl sls mgr; Karen Thompson, mktg dir; Laird White, prom mgr & adv mgr; Bill Callendar, progmg dir; Marlene Moore, pub affrs dir. Rebroadcasts CICI-TV Sudbury.

CKNC-TV-1—ch 7, 12.5 kw vis, 1.3 kw aur. On air date: 1971. c/o CKNC-TV, 699 Frood Rd., Sudbury (P3C 5A3). (705) 674-8301. FAX: (705) 671-2444. Licensee: Mid Canada Communications Corp. Group owner: Baton Broadcasting Inc. ■ Net: CBC. Rep: Glen Warren Broadcast Sales. News staff 11; news progmg 6 hrs wkly. ■ Mike Fawcett, gen mgr. Rebroadcasts CKNC-TV Sudbury.

Fort Frances

CBWCT—ch 5, 20.2 kw vis, 4.04 kw aur, ant 660t. Box 500, Station A, Toronto (M5W 1E6). (416) 975-3311. Licensee: CBC. ■ Net: CBC. ■ Marv Terhoch, gen mgr.

Geraldton

CBLAT—ch 13, 22 kw vis, 4.4 aur, ant 598t/540g. Box 500, Station A, c/o CBLT, Toronto (M5W 1E6). (416) 205-5747. FAX: (416) 205-3311. Licensee: CBC. ■ Net: CBC. ■ Steve Sankar, stn mgr.

Hamilton

CHCH-TV—ch 11, 230 kw vis, 23 kw aur, ant 1,173t/1,054g. Stereo. Hrs opn: 24. On air date: June 4, 1954. 163 Jackson St. W. (L8N 3A6). (416) 522-1101. FAX: (416) 523-8011; TELEX: 061-8312. Licensee: Niagara Television Ltd. Ownership: Western International Communications Inc., 100% (acq 12-23-92). Rep: Western. ■ Steven M. Harris, pres; Reg McGuire, vp & gen mgr; Wilf Venne, opns mgr; Mike Sivems, vp sls; Ron Eberle, rgnl sls mgr; Ron Binns, prom mgr; Cheryle Heaney, progmg mgr; John Best, news dir; Jim Mercer, vp engrg. ■ On 78 CATVs—1,229,485 subs.

Hearst

CBLFT-5—ch 7, 8.4 kw vis, 1.68 kw aur. Box 3220, c/o CBOFT, Station C, Ottawa (K1Y 1E4). (613) 724-1200. FAX: (416) 975-5622. Licensee: Canadian Broadcasting Corp. ■ Net: Radio Canada. ■ Pierre Fournier, progmg dir. Rebroadcasts CBLFT-3 Timmins.

Kapuskasing

CBLFT-4—ch 12, 17.4 kw vis, 3.4 kw aur. Box 3220, c/o CBOFT, Station C, Ottawa (K1Y 1E4). (613) 724-1200. FAX: (416) 975-5622. Licensee: Canadian Broadcasting Corp. ■ Pierre Fournier, progmg dir. Rebroadcasts CBLFT-3 Timmins.

Kearns

CFCL-TV-2—ch 2, 38.5 kw vis, 3.85 aur, ant 736t/400g. c/o CFCL-TV, Box 620, Timmins (P4N 7G3). (705) 264-4211. Licensee: Mid-Canada Communications (Canada) Corp. Group owner: Baton Broadcasting Inc. ■ Net: CBC. ■ Scott Lund, gen mgr. Rebroadcasts CFCL-TV Timmins.

CITO-TV-2—ch 11, 325 kw vis, 32.5 kw aur, ant 734t/396g. Box 620, c/o CITO-TV, 681 Pine St. N., Timmins (P4N 7G3). (705) 264-4211. FAX: (705) 264-3266. Licensee: Mid-Canada Communications (Canada) Corp. Group owner: Baton Broadcasting Inc. ■ Net: CTV. ■ Scott Lund, gen mgr. Rebroadcasts CITO-TV Timmons.

Kenora

CBWAT—ch 8, 2 kw vis, 200 w aur, ant 433t/371g. Box 1890, c/o CBC, (P9N 3X8). (807) 468-6877. Licensee: CBC. ■ Net: CBC. ■ Marv Terhoch, gen mgr. Rebroadcasts CBWT Winnipeg, Man.

CJBN-TV—ch 13, 177 kw vis, 35 kw aur, ant 200g. On air date: April 1983. Box 1810 (P9N 3X8); 104 Tenth St., Keewatin (P0X 1C0). (807) 547-2852. FAX: (807) 547-2236. Licensee: Norcom Telecommunications Ltd. Ownership: Norcom Telecommunications Ltd. ■ Net: CTV. Rep: Metro Marketing West, Metro Spot, Brydson Media Sales. News staff 3; news progmg one hr wkly. ■ Warren Ritchie, gen mgr; Darryl Michaluk, natl sls mgr & progmg dir; Danielle McCulloch, rgnl sls mgr; Nick Chevrefils, mktg dir & news dir. ■ On 4 CATVs—4,500 subs. ■ Rates: C$175; 125; 95.

Kingston

CKWS-TV—ch 11, 325 kw vis, 32.5 kw aur, ant 830t/785g. TL: N44 10 02 W76 25 40. Stereo. Hrs opn: 24. On air date: 1954. 170 Queen St. (K7K 1B2). (613) 544-2340. FAX: (613) 544-5508. Licensee: Power Broadcasting Inc. Ownership: Power Corporation, 100%. ■ Net: CBC. Rep: Glen Warren Bcst Sls, CDN, Telerep, U.S. News progmg 12 hrs wkly. ■ John Tucker, pres & vp sls; Mike Tiernay, rgnl sls mgr; Warren Arsenault, vp progmg. ■ On 11 CATVs—200,000 subs. Co-owned radio: CFFX(AM), CFMK-FM

Kitchener

*****CICO-TV-28**—ch 28, 200 kw vis, 20 kw aur, ant 972t/904g. On air date: January 1976. Box 200 Stn. Q, Toronto (M4T 2T1). (416) 484-2600. FAX: (416) 484-6285. Licensee: Ontario Educational Communications Authority. ■ Peter Herrndorf, CEO & pres; Denis Hamel, adv dir; Don Duprey, Jacques Bensimon, progmg dirs; Christa Singer, pub affrs dir; Bruce Read, engrg dir. Rebroadcasts *CICA-TV Toronto.

CKCO-TV—ch 13, 325 kw vis, 32.5 kw aur, ant 954t/653g. TL: N43 24 15 W80 38 05. Stereo. Hrs opn: 24. On air date: Mar 1, 1954. 864 King St. W. (N2G 4E9). (416) 456-2930. FAX: (519) 743-0730. TELEX: 069-55432. Licensee: Electrohome Ltd. Ownership: Electrohome Ltd., 100%. ■ Net: CTV. ■ John Pollock, CEO & chmn; Bruce Cowie, pres; W.D. McGregor, sr vp; Don Willcox, vp & gen mgr; Peter Jackman, stn mgr & gen sls mgr; Ron Johnston, news dir; Joe Brenner, engrg mgr. ■ On 147 CATVs—1,963,858 subs. Co-owned radio: CKKW(AM), CFCA-FM.

London

CFPL-TV—ch 10, 325 kw vis, 43.2 kw aur, ant 1,000t/975g. On air date: Nov 28, 1953. Box 2880 (N6A 4H9). (519) 686-8810. TELEX: 064-5846. Licensee: South Western Ontario Broadcasting Inc. Group owner: Baton Broadcasting Inc. (acq 1-26-93). Rep: Glen-Warren. ■ E.W. "Ted" Eadinger, pres; Paul Harvey, opns mgr; Colleen Jones, gen sls mgr; Chris Cleaver, rgnl sls mgr; Don Mumford, prom dir; Lorne Freed, progmg dir; Derwyn Smith, news dir; George Clark, pub affrs dir; Don Wilson, engrg dir. ■ On 49 CATVs—545,000 subs.

*****CICO-TV-18**—ch 18, 34.9 kw vis, 3.5 kw aur, ant 1,029t/956.5g. On air date: April 1976. Box 200, Stn Q, Toronto (M4T 2T1). (416) 484-2600. FAX: (416) 484-6285. Licensee: Ontario Educational Communications Authority. ■ Peter Herrndorf, CEO & pres; Don Duprey, Jacques Bensimon, progmg dirs; Bruce Read, engrg dir. Rebroadcasts *CICA-TV Toronto.

Manitouwadge

CBLAT-1—ch 8, 22 kw vis, 4.4 kw aur. Box 500, Station A, c/o CBLT, Toronto (M5W 1E6). (416) 205-5747. FAX: (416) 205-3311. Licensee: Canadian Broadcasting Corp. ■ Net: CBC. ■ Steve Sankar, stn mgr. Rebroadcasts CBLT Toronto.

Marathon

CBLAT-4—ch 11, 7.5 kw vis, 1.532 kw aur, ant 599t. TL: N48 44 50 W86 34 00. Hrs opn: 17. On air date: May 16, 1968. Box 500, Station A, c/o CBLT, Geraldton (M5W 1E6). (416) 975-5747. FAX: (416) 975-3311. Licensee: Canadian Broadcasting Corp. ■ Net: CBC. ■ Steve Sankar, stn mgr. Rebroadcasts CBLT Toronto.

Midland

CIII-TV-7—ch 7, 325 kw vis, 48.8 kw aur, ant 1,132t/1,174g. Stereo. On air date: Nov 24, 1987. c/o CIII-TV, 81 Barber Greene Rd., Don Mills (M3C 2A2). (416) 446-5311. FAX: (416) 446-5371. Licensee: Global Communications Ltd., div of CanWest Global System. Group owner: Global Television Network Rep: Canvideo TV Sls. ■ Rodger Hone, sr vp; Doug Hoover, progmg dir. ■ On 201 CATVs—2,311,127 subs.

North Bay

CHNB-TV—ch 4, 60.9 kw vis, 6.1 kw aur, ant 730t/523g. Hrs opn: 6 AM-3 PM. On air date: 1955. Box 3220, 245 Oak St. E. (P1B 8P8). (705) 476-3111; (705) 476-3115. FAX: (705) 495-0922. Licensee: Mid Canada Communications Corp. Group owner: Baton Broadcasting Inc. ■ Net: CBC. Rep: Glen Warren. News progmg 8 hrs wkly. ■ George Lund, pres; Scott Lund, gen mgr; Jeff Turl, stn mgr & opns mgr; Brett Lund, gen sls mgr & adv mgr; Linda Holmes, prom mgr; Bill Callendar, progmg dir; Andy Bryce, news dir; Chuck Haskins, chief engr. ■ On 8 CATVs.

CKNY-TV—ch 10, 70.5 kw vis, 7.1 kw aur, ant 607t/1,165g. Hrs opn: 20. On air date: October 1981. 245 Oak St. E. (P1B 8P8). (705) 476-3111; (705) 476-3115. FAX: (705) 495-4474; (705) 495-0922. Licensee: Mid Canada Communications Corp. Group owner: Baton Broadcasting Inc. (acq 1991). ■ Net: CTV. Rep: Glen-Warren. News progmg 10 hrs wkly. ■ George Lund, pres; Scott Lund, gen mgr; Jeff Turl, stn mgr & opns mgr; Brett Lund, gen sls mgr & adv mgr; Dan Dolan, mktg mgr; Bill Callendar, progmg dir; Andrew Bryce, news dir; Chuck Haskins, chief engr. ■ On 9 CATVs.

Oil Springs

CIII-TV-29—ch 29, 370 kw vis, 55.5 kw aur, ant 685t/701g. Stereo. On air date: Jan 6, 1974. c/o CIII-TV, 81 Barber Greene Rd., Don Mills (M3C 2A2). (416) 446-5311. FAX: (416) 446-5371. Licensee: Global Communications, div of CanWest Global Systems. Group owner: Global Television Network. ■ Rodger Hone, sr vp; Doug Hoover, progmg dir. ■ On 201 CATVs—2,511,127 subs. Rebroadcasts CIII-TV Paris.

Ottawa

CBOFT—ch 9, 128 kw vis, 12.8 kw aur, ant 1,394t/702g. Box 3220, Station C, 250 Lanark (K1Y 1E4). (613) 724-1200. FAX: (613) 724-5074. Licensee: CBC. ■ Net: CBC. ■ Pierre Fournier, progmg dir.

CBOT—ch 4, 100 kw vis, 10 kw aur, ant 1,310t/618g. On air date: 1953. Box 3220, Station C, 250 Lanark Ave. (K1Y 1E4). (613) 724-5512. FAX: (613) 724-5023. TELEX: 013-4260. Licensee: CBC. ■ Net: CBC. ■ Carol Jones, prom dir; Marie Wilson, adv dir; Norm Bolen, progmg dir; Peter McNelly, news dir.

*****CICO-TV-24**—ch 24, 1,495 kw vis, 149.5 kw aur, ant 1,092t/400g. (CP: 855.1 kw vis). On air date: Oct 17, 1975. Box 200, Stn Q, c/o TV Ontario, Toronto (M4T 2T1). (416) 484-2600. FAX: (416) 484-6285. Licensee: Ontario Educational Communications Authority. ■ Peter Herrnsdorf, CEO & pres; Don Duprey, Jacques Bensimon, progmg dirs; Bruce Read, engrg dir. Rebroadcasts *CICA-TV Toronto.

CIII-TV-6—ch 6, 50 kw vis, 7.5 kw aur, ant 843t/750g. Stereo. On air date: Jan 6, 1974. c/o CIII-TV, 81 Barber Greene Rd., Don Mills (M3C 2A2). (416) 446-5311. FAX: (416) 446-5371. Licensee: Global Communications Ltd., div of CanWest Global System. Group owner: Global Television Network (acq 3-22-77). Rep: Canvideo TV Sls. ■ Rodger Hone, sr vp; Doug Hoover, progmg dir. ■ On 201 CATVs—2,511,127. Rebroadcasts CIII-TV Paris.

CJOH-TV—ch 13, 325 kw vis, 65 kw aur, ant 1,225t/533g. On air date: March 1961. Box 5813, Station F, Merivale Depot, Ottawa (K2C 3G6). (613) 224-1313. TELEX: (613) 224-7998. TELEX: 053-4294. Licensee: Baton Broadcasting Inc. (group owner). ■ Net: CTV. Rep: Canadian Standard Bcst Sls. ■ Bryn Matthews, gen mgr.

Owen Sound

CIII-TV-4—ch 4, 37 kw vis, 5.5 kw aur, ant 429t/477g. Stereo. On air date: June 27, 1988. c/o CIII-TV, 81 Barber Greene Rd., Don Mills (M3C 2A2). (416) 446-5311. FAX: (416) 446-5371. Licensee: Global Communications, div of CanWest Global System. Group owner: Global Television Network. ■ Rodger Hone, sr vp; Doug Hoover, progmg dir. ■ On 201 CATVs—2,311,127 subs. Rebroadcasts CIII-TV Paris.

Paris

CIII-TV—Licensed to Paris. See Toronto.

Pembroke

CHRO-TV—ch 5, 100 kw vis, 20 kw aur, ant 496t/520g. On air date: 1961. Box 1010, Forest Lea Rd. (K8A 7T3). (613) 735-1036. FAX: (613) 735-0022. TELEX: 013-34515. Licensee: Mid Canada Communications Ltd. Ownership: Baton Broadcasting Inc. ■ Net: CTV. Rep: Paul Mulvyhill. ■ Michael Keller, gen mgr.

Peterborough

CHEX-TV—ch 12, 325 kw vis, 32.5 kw aur, ant 772t/753g. TL: N44 19 45 W78 18 03. Stereo. On air date: 1955. Box 4150, 1925 Television Rd. (K9J 6Z9). (705) 742-0451. FAX: (705) 742-7274. Licensee: Power Broadcasting Inc. Ownership: Power Communications Corp. ■ Net: CBC. Rep: Glen-Warren Broadcast Sales, Telerep, U.S.A. East Indian, German, Greek progmg. News staff 27; news progmg 16 hrs wkly. ■ Peter Kruyt, CEO; Ted Eason, CFO; Dennis Watson, exec vp & gen mgr; Judy Carswell, prom dir; Wally Macht, news dir; Ben Wilke, vp engrg. ■ On 30 CATVs—1,084,774 subs. Co-owned radio: CKRU(AM), CKWF-FM. ■ Rates: C$850; 175; 65.

CIII-TV-27—ch 27, 2,535 kw vis, 380 aur, ant 913t/499g. Stereo. On air date: Oct 5, 1988. c/o CIII-TV, 81 Barber Greene Rd., Don Mills (M3C 2A2). (416) 446-5311. FAX: (416) 446-5371. Licensee: Global Communications, div of CanWest Global System. Group owner: Global Television Network. Rep: Canvideo TV Sls. ■ Rodger Hone, sr vp. Rebroadcasts CIII-TV Paris.

Sarnia

CKCO-TV-3—ch 42, 846 kw vis, 84.6 kw aur, ant 994t/985g. TL: N42 42 53 W82 08 12. Stereo. Hrs opn: 24. On air date: November 1975. c/o CKCO-TV, 864 King St. W., Kitchener (N2G 4E9). (416) 456-2930. FAX: (519) 743-0730. Licensee: Electrohome Ltd. ■ John Pollock, CEO & chmn; Bruce Cowie, pres; W.D. McGregor, sr vp; Don Willcox, vp & gen mgr; Peter Jackman, stn mgr & gen sls mgr; Alan Brooks, progmg mgr; Joe Brenner, engrg mgr. Rebroadcasts CKCO-TV Kitchener.

Sault Ste. Marie

CHBX-TV—ch 2, 100 kw vis, 10 kw aur, ant 600t/500g. On air date: September 1978. 119 East St. (P6A 3C7). (705) 759-8232. FAX: (705) 759-7783. Licensee: MCTV. Group owner: Baton Broadcasting Inc. ■ Net: CTV. Rep: All-Canada TV Sls. ■ W. A. Elgie, gen mgr.

***CICO-TV-20**—ch 20, 5.9 kw vis, 590 w aur, ant 650t/515g. On air date: October 1978. Box 200, Stn Q, c/o TVOntario, Toronto (M4T 2T1). (416) 484-2600. TELEX: 06-23547. Licensee: Ontario Educational Communications Authority. Group owner: Baton Broadcasting Inc. Rebroadcasts *CICA-TV Toronto.

CJIC-TV—ch 5, 38 kw vis, 8 kw aur, ant 600t/500g. On air date: 1954. 119 East St. (P6A 3C7). (705) 759-8232. FAX: (705) 759-7783. TELEX: 027-7716. Licensee: Mid-Canada Communications (Canada) Corp. Group owner: Baton Broadcasting Inc. ■ Net: CBC. Rep: All-Canada. ■ W. A. Elgie, gen mgr. ■ On 3 CATVs—26,500 subs.

Stevenson

CIII-TV-22—ch 22., Stereo. On air date: 1974. 81 Barber Greene Rd., Don Mills (M3C 2A2). (416) 446-5311. FAX: (416) 446-5371. Licensee: Global Communications Ltd. Group owner: Global Television Network.

Sturgeon Falls

CBLFT-1—ch 7, 9.75 kw vis, 1.95 kw aur. Box 3220, Station C, c/o CBOFT, Ottawa (K1Y 1E4). (613) 724-1200. FAX: (613) 724-5074. Licensee: Canadian Broadcasting Corp. ■ Net: Radio Canada. ■ Pierre Fournier, progmg dir.

Sudbury

CBLFT-2—ch 13, 271 kw vis, 27.1 kw aur. Box 3220, Station C, c/o CBOFT, Ottawa (K1Y 1E4). (613) 724-1200. FAX: (613) 724-5074. Licensee: Canadian Broadcasting Corp. ■ Net: Radio Canada. ■ Pierre Fournier, progmg dir. Rebroadcasts CBLFT-1 Sturgeon Falls.

CICI-TV—ch 5, 100 kw vis, 10 kw aur, ant 1,057t/975g. On air date: Oct 25, 1953. 699 Frood Rd. (P3C 5A3). (705) 674-8301. FAX: (705) 671-2444. Licensee: Mid Canada Communications Corp. Group owner: Baton Broadcasting Inc. (acq 4-1-80). ■ Net: CTV. Rep: Glen Warren. News staff 15; news progmg 10 hrs wkly. ■ George Lund, pres; Mike Fawcett, gen mgr & engrg dir; John Eddy, opns mgr; Pat Thomson, dev dir; Mary Lund, gen sls mgr; Scott Lund, rgnl sls mgr; Karen Thompson, mktg dir; Laird White, prom mgr & adv mgr; Bill Callendar, progmg dir; Mark Oldfield, news dir; Detlef Krumbacher, engrg mgr. ■ On 4 CATVs—88,000 subs.

***CICO-TV-19**—ch 19, 186.5 kw vis, 18.7 kw aur, ant 564t/497g. On air date: June 30, 1978. Box 200, Stn Q, Toronto (M4T 2T1). (416) 484-2600. FAX: (416) 484-6285. Licensee: Ontario Educational Communications Authority. ■ Peter Herrndorf, CEO & pres; Don Duprey, Jacques Bensimon, progmg dirs; Bruce Read, engrg dir. Rebroadcasts *CICA-TV Toronto.

CKNC-TV—ch 9, 115.5 kw vis, 29.3 kw aur, ant 627t/539g. On air date: Oct 4, 1971. 699 Frood Rd. (P3C 5A3). (705) 674-8301. FAX: (705) 671-2444. Licensee: MCTV Group owner: Baton Broadcasting Inc. ■ Net: CBC. Rep: Canvideo. News staff 15; news progmg 10 hrs wkly. ■ George Lund, CEO; Mike Fawcett, gen mgr & engrg dir; John Eddy, opns mgr; Pat Thomson, dev dir; Mary Lund, gen sls mgr; Karen Thomson, mktg dir; Laird White, prom mgr & adv dir; Bill Callendar, progmg dir; Mark Oldfield, news dir; Marlene Moore, pub affrs dir; Detlef Krumbacher, chief engr. ■ On 8 CATVs—88,000 subs.

The Muskokas

CKCO-TV-4—ch 11, 325 kw vis, 32.5 kw aur, ant 641t/599g. TL: N45 19 44 W78 57 56. Stereo. Hrs opn: 24. On air date: Feb 11, 1976. c/o CKCO-TV, 864 King St. W., Kitchener (N2G 4E9). (416) 456-2930. FAX: (519) 743-0730. Licensee: Electrohome Ltd. ■ John Pollock, CEO & chmn; Bruce Cowie, pres; W.D. McGregor, sr vp; Don Willcox, vp & gen mgr; Peter Jackman, stn mgr & gen sls mgr; Alan Brooks, progmg mgr; Joe Brenner, engrg mgr. Rebroadcasts CKCO-TV Kitchener.

Thunder Bay

CHFD-TV—ch 4, 56 kw vis, 10 kw aur, ant 1,202t/634g. TL: N48 31 30 W89 06 50. Hrs opn: 18. On air date: 1972. 87 N. Hill St. (P7A 5V6). (807) 344-9685. FAX: (807) 345-9923. Licensee: Thunder Bay Electronics Ltd. ■ Net: CTV. Rep: Mulvihill. ■ A. H. Seuret, vp & gen mgr. ■ On 9 CATVs—53,984. Co-owned radio: CKPR(AM), CJSD-FM. ■ Rates: C$600; 65; 155.

***CICO-TV-9**—ch 9, 32 kw vis, 3.2 kw aur, ant 780t/522g. On air date: June 1978. Box 200, Stn Q, c/o TVOntario, Toronto (M4T 2T1). (416) 484-2600. FAX: (416) 484-6285. Licensee: Ontario Educational Communications Authority. ■ Peter Herrndorf, CEO & pres; Don Duprey, Jacques Bensimon, progmg dirs; Bruce Read, engrg dir. Rebroadcasts *CICA-TV Toronto.

CKPR-TV—ch 2, 56 kw vis, 10 kw aur, ant 1,202t/643g. N48 31 30 W89 06 50. Hrs opn: 18. On air date: 1954. 87 N. Hill St. (P7A 5V6). (807) 344-9685. FAX: (807) 345-9923. Licensee: Thunder Bay Electronics Ltd. ■ Net: CBC. Rep: Mulvihill, Telerep. News staff 20; news progmg 11 hrs wkly. ■ H.F. Dougall, pres; A.H. Seuret, vp & gen mgr; W. Kallio, opns dir; S.E. Wiggins, mktg dir; M.E. LaBelle, prom mgr, progmg dir & film buyer; G. Rinne, news dir; M. Volbracht, engrg dir. ■ On 6 CATVs—50,150 subs. Co-owned radio: CKPR(AM)-CJSD-FM. ■ Rates: C$600; 65; 155.

Timmins

CBLFT-3—ch 9, 16 kw vis, 3.2 kw, ant 706t/525g. Box 3220, Station C, c/o CBOFT, Ottawa (K1Y 1E4). (613) 724-1200. FAX: (613) 724-5074. Licensee: CBC. ■ Pierre Fournier, progmg dir.

CFCL-TV—ch 6, 100 kw vis, 10 kw aur, ant 562t/508g. On air date: July 1, 1956. Box 620 (P4N 7G3). (705) 264-4211. FAX: (705) 264-3266. TELEX: 067-81539. Licensee: Mid-Canada Communications (Canada) Corp. Group owner: Baton Broadcasting Inc. ■ Net: CBC. Rep: Canvideo. ■ George Lund, CEO; Scott Lund, gen mgr; Ray Laneville, stn mgr; Pat Thomson, dev dir; Karen Thomson, mktg dir; Don Dewsbury, mktg mgr & pub affrs dir; Laird White, prom mgr; Bill Callendar, progmg dir; Greg Van Asperon, film buyer. Co-owned radio: CFCL(AM).

CITO-TV—ch 3, 100 kw vis, 10 kw aur, ant 544t/499g. Box 620, 681 Pine St. N. (P4N 7G3). (705) 264-4211. FAX: (705) 264-3266. Licensee: MCTV. Group owner: Baton Broadcasting Inc. ■ Net: CTV. Rep: Glenn Warren. ■ George Lund, pres; Scott Lund, gen mgr; Ray Laneville, stn mgr; Pat Thomson, dev dir; Ray Lanesville, sls dir; Karen Thomson, mktg dir; Michael Correlli, prom dir; Don Dewsbury, prom mgr; Bill Callendar, progmg dir; Marlene Moore, pub affrs dir; Mike Fawcett, engrg dir.

Toronto

CBLFT—ch 25, 1,760 kw vis, 182.7 kw aur, ant 1,602t/1,502g. On air date: Mar 23, 1973. Box 3220, Station C, c/o CBOFT, Ottawa (K1Y 1E4). (613) 724-1200. FAX: (613) 724-5074; TELEX: 06-23195. Licensee: CBC. ■ Net: CBC. ■ Pierre Fournier, progmg dir. Rebroadcasts CBOFT Ottawa.

CBLT—ch 5, 77 kw vis, 7 kw aur, ant 444t/541g. Box 500, Terminal A (M5W 1E6); 500 Church St. (M4Y 2C8). (416) 975-3311. TELEX: 06-23195. Licensee: CBC. ■ Net: CBC. ■ Steve Sankar, stn mgr.

CFMT-TV—ch 47, 807 kw vis, 80.7 kw aur, ant 1,600t/1,427g. Stereo. On air date: Sept 3, 1979. 545 Lakeshore Blvd. W. (M5V 1A3). (416) 260-0047. FAX: (416) 260-0509; TELEX: 06-23643. Licensee: Multilingual Television Ltd. Ownership: Rogers Communications Inc, 60%; Daisons Corp, 20% (acq 9-79). 18 ethnic languages 76 hrs wkly. ■ A.P. Viner, pres; Tom Ayley, CFO; Leslie Sole, exec vp & gen mgr; Kelly Colasanti, opns mgr; Farouk Muhammed, vp dev & vp progmg; James Macdonald, vp sls; Malcolm Dunlop, natl sls mgr; Farouk Muhammad, film buyer; Madelaine Ziniak, pub affrs dir; Steve Edwards, vp engrg. ■ On 56 CATVs—1,800,000 subs.

CFTO-TV—ch 9, 325 kw vis, 162 kw aur, ant 1815t/1614g. TL: N43 38 33 W79 23 15. Stereo. Hrs opn: 24. On air date: Jan 1, 1961. Box 9, Station O (M4A 2M9). (416) 299-2000. Licensee: CFTO-TV Ltd. Group owner: Baton Broadcasting Inc. ■ Net: CTV. Rep: Glen-Warren, Messner (Canada), Young Canadiens (U.S.). ■ Douglas G. Bassett, pres. ■ On 67 CATVs—2.2 million subs.

***CICA-TV**—ch 19, 1,080 kw vis, 108 kw aur, ant 1,605t/1,686g. (CP: 1,288.2 kw vis). On air date: Sept 27, 1970. Box 200, Station Q, c/o TVOntario (M4T 2T1). (416) 484-2600. FAX: (416) 484-6285. Licensee: Ontario Educational Communications Authority. ■ Peter Herrndorf, CEO & pres; Don Duprey, Jacques Bensimon, progmg dirs; Bruce Read, engrg dir.

CIII-TV—(Paris). ch 6, 100 kw vis, 15 kw aur, ant 1,037t/999g. Stereo. On air date: Jan 6, 1974. 81 Barber Greene Rd., Don Mills (M3C 2A2). (416) 446-5311. FAX: (416) 446-5371. Licensee: Global Communications Ltd., div of CanWest Global System. Group owner: Global Television Network (acq 3-22-77). ■ Net: Global. Rep: Canvideo Television Sls Ltd. ■ Dave Mintz, pres; Rodger Hone, sr vp; Doug Hoover, progmg dir; Doug Bonar, news dir. ■ On 201 CATVs—2,511,127 subs.

CIII-TV-41—ch 41, 732 kw vis, 221 kw aur, ant 1,644t/1,779g. TL: N43 38 33 W79 23 15. Stereo. On air date: Oct 22, 1987. c/o CIII-TV, 81 Barber Greene Rd., Don Mills (M3C 2A2). (416) 446-5311. FAX: (416) 446-5371. Licensee: Global Communications Ltd. Group owner: Global Television Network. ■ Rodger Hone, sr vp. Rebroadcasts CIII-TV Paris.

CITY-TV—ch 57, 280 kw vis, 28 kw aur, ant 1,690t/1,780g. Stereo. Hrs opn: 24. On air date: Sept 28, 1972. 299 Queen St. W. (M5V 2Z5). (416) 591-5757. Licensee: CITY-TV, div of Chum Ltd. Group owner: CHUM Ltd. (acq 1976). Rep: Alexander, Pearson & Dawson. News progmg 25 hrs wkly. ■ Moses Znaimer, pres; Ron Waters, gen mgr; Jay Switzer, stn mgr & vp progmg; Victor Rodriguez, gen sls mgr; Glenn Campbell, natl sls mgr; Mary Powers, prom dir; Ellen Baine, progmg mgr & film buyer; Stephen Hurlbut, news dir; Ron Reid, engrg dir. ■ On 200 CATVs—2,100,000 subs. On 1 trans. Co-owned radio: CHUM-AM-FM.

Wawa

CBLAT-3—ch 9, 16 kw vis, 3.2 kw aur, ant 581 ft. TL: N48 01 13 W84 45 00. Box 500, Station A, c/o CBLT, Geraldton (M5W 1E6). (416) 205-5747. FAX: (416) 205-3311. Licensee: Canadian Broadcasting Corp. ■ Net: CBC. ■ Steve Sankar, stn mgr. Rebroadcasts CBLAT Geraldton.

Wheatley

CHWI-TV—ch 16, 183 kw vis. On air date: Oct 18, 1993. 75 Riverside Dr. E., Windsor (N9A 7C4). (519) 977-7432. Licensee: South Western Ontario Broadcasting Inc. Group owner: Baton Broadcasting Inc. Rep: Glen-Warren. ■ Vivien Merkeley, gen mgr.

Wiarton

CKCO-TV-2—ch 2, 100 kw vis, 10 kw aur, ant 939t/789g. TL: N44 56 41 W81 07 55. Stereo. Hrs opn: 24. On air date: June 1, 1971. c/o CKCO-TV, 864 King St. W., Kitchener (N2G 4E9). (416) 456-2930. FAX: (519) 743-0730. Licensee: Electrohome Ltd. ■ John Pollock, CEO & chmn; Bruce Cowie, pres; W.D. McGregor, sr vp; Don Willcox, vp & gen mgr; Peter Jackman, stn mgr & gen sls mgr; Alan Brooks, progmg mgr; Joe Brenner, engrg mgr. Rebroadcasts CKCO-TV Kitchener.

Windsor

***CBEFT**—ch 54, 62.7 kw vis, 6.3 kw aur, ant 683g. On air date: July 17, 1976. 825 Riverside W. (N9A 5K9). (519) 255-3411. TELEX: 064-77-619. Licensee: Societe Radio Canada. ■ Net: Radio Canada. ■ Mina Grossman, stn mgr.

CBET—Licensed to Windsor. See Detroit, Mich.

Stations in Canada   **Quebec**

*CICO-TV-32—ch 32, 180 kw vis, 18 kw aur, ant 703t/703g. On air date: July 1976. Box 200, Station Q, Toronto (M4T 2T1). Licensee: Ontario Educational Communication Authority. Rebroadcasts *CICA-TV Toronto.

CIII-TV-1—ch 22, 218 kw vis, 33 kw aur, ant 367t/367g. Stereo. 81 Barber Greene Rd., Don Mills (M3C 2A2). (416) 446-5311. FAX: (416) 446-5371. Licensee: Global Communications, div of CanWest Global System. ■ Net: Global. Rep: Canvideo TV Sls. ■ David Mintz, pres; Rodger Hone, gen mgr; Doug Hoover, progmg dir; Doug Bonar, news dir. Rebroadcasts CIII-TV Paris.

Wingham

CKNX-TV—ch 8, 260 kw vis, 26 kw aur, ant 793t/623g. On air date: 1955. 215 Carling Terrace, Wingham (N0G 2W0). (519) 357-1310. FAX: (519)-357-1897. Licensee: South Western Ontario Broadcasting Inc. Group owner: Baton Broadcasting Inc. (acq 1-26-93). Rep: Western. ■ R.V. Elsden, pres; E.W. Eadinger, exec vp; Steve Young, gen mgr & news dir; Paul Mercey, gen sls mgr; Randy Jacobs, engrg dir. Co-owned radio: CKNX-AM-FM.

Prince Edward Island

Charlottetown

CBCT—ch 13, 320 kw vis, 30 kw aur, ant 918t/720g. On air date: 1968. Box 2230 (C1A 8B9). (902) 566-3591. TELEX: 014-44176. Licensee: CBC. Ownership: CBC (Crown Corp). ■ Net: CBC. ■ Barbara Trueman, stn mgr; John Stewart, opns mgr; Heather Boyce-MacLean, gen sls mgr; Jessie Clarey, prom mgr. ■ On 5 CATVs—45,000 subs. On 2 trans.

CKCW-TV-1—ch 8, 29 kw vis, 2.9 aur, ant 489t/250g. Box 5004, Moncton, NB (E1C 8R6). (506) 857-2600. FAX: (506) 857-2617. Licensee: ATV New Brunswick Ltd. (div. of CHUM). Group owner: CHUM Ltd. ■ Net: CTV. ■ Anne-Marie Nuyten, prom dir. Rebroadcasts CKCW-TV Moncton, N.B.

St. Edward

CKCW-TV-2—ch 5, 2.5 kw vis, 1.3 kw aur, ant 341t/356g. On air date: November 1982. Box 5004, Moncton, NB (E1C 8R6). (506) 857-2600. FAX: (506) 857-2617. Licensee: ATV New Brunswick (div. of CHUM). Group owner: CHUM Ltd. ■ Net: CTV. ■ Anne-Marie Nuyten, prom dir. Rebroadcasts CKCW-TV Moncton, N.B.

Quebec

Baie-Trinite

*CIVF-TV—ch 12, 62 kw vis, 2,001t. On air date: Nov 15, 1982. c/o Radio Quebec, 1000 rue Fullum, Montreal (H2K 3L7). (418) 364-7025. Licensee: Radio Quebec (group owner). ■ Francoise Bertrand, pres.

Bearn-Fabre

CKRN-TV-3—ch 3, 35 kw vis, 3.5 kw aur. c/o CKRN-TV, 380 Murdoch, Noranda (J9X 1G5). (819) 762-0741. Licensee: Radio-Nord, Inc. ■ Net: Radio Canada. ■ Bernard Gkuchier, gen mgr. Rebroadcasts CKRN-TV Rouyn.

Carleton

CHAU-TV—ch 5, 52.2 kw vis, 5.22 kw aur, ant 2,180t/475g. On air date: Oct 17, 1959. CP 100, 841 Route de LaMontagne (G0C 1G0). (418) 364-3344. FAX: (418) 364-7168; TELEX: 014-43126. Licensee: Television de la Baie des Chaleurs Inc. Group owner: Power Broadcasting Inc. ■ Net: TVA. Rep: Paul L'Anglais Inc. ■ Andre Desmarais, chmn; Pierre Harvey, pres & gen mgr; Yvon Chouinard, vp; Yvon Goulet, vp opns, progmg dir & film buyer; Jean Yves Ross, gen sls mgr; Normand LaFrance, vp mktg; Myriam Donaldson, news dir; Jean Fournier, chief engr. ■ On 11 CATVs—17,000 subs. On 12 trans.

Chapeau

*CIVP-TV—ch 23, 8.65 kw vis. c/o Radio Quebec, 800 rue Fullum, Montreal (H2K 3L7). (418) 364-7025. Licensee: Societe de radio-television du Quebec. Group owner: Radio Quebec. ■ Francoise Bertrand, pres. Rebroadcasts *CIVO-TV Hull.

Chicoutimi

CBJET—ch 58, 10 kw vis. c/o CBMT, 1400 boul. Rene Levesque E., Montreal (H2L 2M2). (514) 597-4450. ■ Net: CBC. ■ Tony Agostini, opns mgr. Rebroadcasts CBMT Montreal.

*CIVV-TV—ch 8, 278.1 kw vis, 27.8 kw aur, ant 1,948t/570g. On air date: November 1982. c/o Radio Quebec, 1000 rue Fullum, Montreal (H2K 3L7). (418) 364-7025. Licensee: Societe de radio-television du Quebec Group owner: Radio Quebec. ■ Francoise Bertrand, pres.

CJPM-TV—ch 6, 61 kw vis, 6.7 kw aur, ant 440t/190g. Stereo. On air date: Apr 14, 1963. Box 600 (G7H 5G3). (418) 549-2576. FAX: (418) 549-1130. Licensee: TM Multi-Regions Inc. Ownership: Tele Metropole, 100%. ■ Net: TVA. Rep: Paul L'Anglais (Canada), Metro Mktg West, Young Canadian Ltd. ■ Roger Jobyn, gen mgr. ■ On 6 CATVs. On 1 trans.

Gaspe-Nord

CFER-TV-2—ch 5, 100 kw vis, 10 kw aur, ant 706t/495g. On air date: Nov 13, 1981. c/o CFER-TV, 465 boul. Ste. Anne, Pointe-au-Pere (G5M 1G1). Licensee: TM Multi-Regions Inc. ■ Net: Reseau TVA. ■ Claude Auger, gen mgr & vp sls; Carol Bonin, sls dir; Christian LePage, news dir; Christian LaPage, pub affrs dir; Daniel LaVoie, engrg dir. Rebroadcasts CFER-TV Rimouski.

Hull

CFGS-TV—ch 49., On air date: Sept 7, 1986. 171 Jean Proulx (J8Z 1W5). (819) 776-4949. FAX: (819) 770-0272; (819) 770-1490 (News Room). Licensee: Radio Nord Inc. (group owner). ■ Net: Quatre Saisons. Rep: All-Canada. ■ Jean-Joffre Gourd, chmn; Gilles Poulin, pres & gen mgr; Robert H. Parent, stn opns dir & progmg mgr; Gaston Lavoie, sls dir & mktg dir; Robert Langdeau, news dir; Gerald Landry, engrg mgr.

CHOT-TV—ch 40, 1,022 kw vis, ant 1,184t. On air date: Oct 30, 1978. 171 Jean Proulx (J8Z 1W5). (819) 770-1040. FAX: (819) 770-0272; (819) 770-1490. Licensee: Radio Nord Inc. (group owner). ■ Net: TVA. Rep: Paul L'Anglais Inc. ■ Jean-Joffre Gourd, chmn; Gilles Poulin, pres & gen mgr; Robert H. Parent, stn opns dir & progmg mgr; Gaston Lavoie, sls dir & mktg dir; Robert Langdeau, news dir; Jean-Guy Langevin, vp engrg. ■ On 10 CATVs—791,000 subs.

*CIVO-TV—ch 30, 1,327.4 kw vis; 265.5 kw aur, ant 1,184t/465g. On air date: Aug 14, 1977. c/o CIVM-TV, 800 rue Fullum, Montreal (H2K 3L7). (418) 364-7025. Licensee: Societe de Radio-Television du Quebec. Group owner: Radio Quebec. ■ Francoise Bertrand, pres. Rebroadcasts *CIVM-TV Montreal.

Iles-de-la-Madeleine

CBIMT—ch 12, 2.8 kw vis, 280 kw aur, ant 750t/235g. On air date: Nov 9, 1964. Box 6000, c/o CBFT, Montreal (H3C 3A8); c/o CBFT, 1400 boul. Rene Levesque E., Montreal (H2L 2M2). (514) 597-4700. Licensee: Societe Radio Canada. ■ Net: Radio Canada. ■ Guy Gougeon, vp. Rebroadcasts CBFT Montreal.

Jonquiere

CFRS-TV—ch 4, 100 kw vis, 10 kw aur, ant 1,941t/460g. Stereo. On air date: Sept 7, 1986. 2303 rue Sir Wilfred Laurier (G7X 7X3). (418) 542-4551. FAX: (418) 542-7217. Licensee: Radio Saguenay Ltd. Ownership: Quatre Saisons. ■ Net: Quatre Saisons. Rep: Western, Publicite Select Inc. ■ Danille Samel, gen mgr. ■ On 12 CATVs—40,000 subs. On 4 trans. Co-owned radio: CKRS(AM).

La Tuque

CBVT-2—ch 3, 15.4 kw vis, 1.54 kw aur. c/o CBVT, Box 10400, Ste. Foy (G1V 2X2). ■ Net: Radio Canada. ■ Bertrand Emond, Andre Poirer, gen mgrs. Rebroadcasts CBVT Quebec City.

Malartic

CBVD-TV—ch 5, 9.35 kw vis, 4.675 kw aur. c/o CBMT, 1400 boul. Rene Levesque E., Montreal (H2L 2M2). (514) 597-4450. ■ Net: CBC. ■ Tony Agostini, opns mgr. Rebroadcasts CBMT Montreal.

Matane

CBGAT—ch 6, 1.3 kw vis, 130 w aur, ant 994t/228g. On air date: November 1978. 155 St. Sacrament St. (G4W 3P7). (418) 562-0290. Licensee: CBC. ■ Louis Pelletier, progmg dir.

Mont-Laurier

CBFT-2—ch 3, 28.2 kw vis, 2.8 kw aur, ant 509t/400g. On air date: Dec 3, 1962. c/o CBFT, 1400 Rene Levesque E., Montreal (H2L 2M2). (514) 597-4700. Licensee: Societe Radio Canada. ■ Net: Radio Canada. ■ Guy Gougeon, vp. Rebroadcasts CBFT-1 Mont Tremblant.

Montreal

CBFT—ch 2, 100 kw vis, 10 kw aur, ant 905t/252g. On air date: 1952. Box 6000 (H3C 3A8); 1400 boul. Rene Levesque E. (H2L 2M2). (514) 597-5970. TELEX: 052-67417. Licensee: CBC. Ownership: CBC. ■ Net: Radio Canada. ■ Guy Gougeon, vp.

CBMT—ch 6, 100 kw vis, 15 kw aur, ant 820t/167g. On air date: 1954. 1400 boul. Rene Levesque E. (H2L2M2). (514) 597-5970. TELEX: 052-67417. Licensee: CBC. ■ Net: CBC. ■ Tony Agostini, opns mgr.

CFCF-TV—ch 12, 325 kw vis, 33 kw aur, ant 1,032t/294g. Stereo. On air date: Jan 20, 1961. 405 Ogilvy Ave. (H3N 1M4). (514) 273-6311. TELEX: 05-826638. Licensee: CFCF Inc. (acq 7-6-79). ■ Net: CTV. Rep: Alexander, Pearson & Dawson (Canada), All-Canada (U.S.). ■ Chisto Georges, pres. ■ On 75 CATVs—900,000 subs.

CFJP-TV—ch 35, 697 kw vis, 70 kw aur, ant 900t/335g. TL: N45 35 20 W73 35 32. Stereo. On air date: Sept 7, 1986. 405 Ogilvy Ave. (H3N 2Y4). (514) 271-3535. FAX: (514) 271-6047 (SALES). TELEX: 05-825698. Licensee: Television Quatre Saisons Inc. Ownership: CFCF Inc., 100%. ■ Net: Quatre Saisons. News staff 51; news progmg 10 hrs wkly. ■ Charles Belanger, CEO & pres; Adrien D. Pouliot, chmn; Ghislain St. Pierre, vp opns & vp engrg; Francois Laganiere, vp sls; Carole Tessier, rgnl sls mgr; Josee Rochon, prom mgr; Luc Harvey, vp progmg. ■ On 140 CATVs—335,000 subs.

CFTM-TV—ch 10, 365 kw vis, 65 kw aur, ant 325t/1,068g. Box 170, Stn C (H2L4P6). (514) 526-9251. TELEX: 05-267329. Licensee: Tele-Metropole. ■ Net: TVA. Rep: Paul L'Anglais Inc. ■ Guy Cerevier, pres.

*CFTU-TV—ch 29, 10 kw vs, 1 kw aur, ant 604t/305g. Hrs opn: 24. On air date: Aug 20, 1986. CP 5250 Suc. C, Bureau 1840, 1001 Sherbrooke Est (H2X 3M4). (514) 527-3684; (514) 522-3540. FAX: (514) 525-7763. Licensee: Corp. pour l'Avancement de Nouvelles Aplication des Langages (acq 5-86). ■ On 11 CATVs—1,095,000 subs.

*CIVM-TV—ch 17, 1,212 kw vis, 242 kw aur. On air date: Jan 19, 1975. 800 rue Fullum (H2K 3L7). (514) 521-2424. TELEX: 05-25808. Licensee: Societe de radio-television du Quebec. Group owner: Radio Quebec. ■ Francoise Bertrand, pres. ■ On 50 CATVs—500,000 subs.

Noranda

CKRN-TV—See Rouyn.

Quebec City

CBVT—ch 11, 252 kw vis, 25.2 kw aur, ant 657t/541g. On air date: 1964. Box 10400, Ste-Foy (G1V 2X2). (418) 656-8500. FAX: (418) 656-8244. Licensee: CBC. ■ Net: CBC. ■ Bertrand Emond, Andre Poirer, gen mgrs.

CFAP-TV—ch 2, 70 kw vis, 7 kw aur, ant 551t/501g. TL: N46 48 27 W71 13 02. Stereo. Hrs opn: 11:30 AM-1:30 AM. On air date: Sept 7, 1986. Box 17500, 500 Bouvier St. (G2J 1E3). (418) 624-2222. FAX: (418) 624-3099; (418) 624-0162. Licensee: CFCF Inc. Ownership: CFCF Inc., 100%. Group owner: Reseau de Television Quatre Saisons Inc. ■ Net: Quatre Saisons. Rep: Premiere. Fr 105 hrs wkly. News staff 29; news progmg 9 hrs wkly. ■ Adrien D. Pouliot, chmn; Jean Fortier, pres; Gilles Gregoire, vp & gen mgr; Serge Matte, Richard Renaud, sls dirs; Renaud Francoeur, prom mgr & adv mgr; Jean-Pierre Pampalon, progmg dir; Jean-Pierre Pampalon, Pierre Taschereau (asst), news dirs; Jean-Pierre Pampalon, Pierre Taschereau (asst), pub affrs dirs; Jean Gagne, engrg dir. ■ On one CATV—220,000 subs. On 16 trans. ■ Rates: C$700; 400; 200.

CFCM-TV—ch 4, 100 kw vis, 15 kw aur, ant 460t/407g. On air date: July 17, 1954. 1000 Ave. Myrand, Sainte-Foy (G1V 2W3). (418) 688-9330. FAX: (418) 688-4239. Licensee: TM Multi-Regions Inc. (Group owner: Tele-Metropole Inc.). ■ Guy Crevier, pres; Agnes Jarnuszkiewicz, exec vp & progmg dir; Agnes Jarnuskiewicz, stn mgr; Raynald Savard, opns mgr; Jean-Claude Gendron, rgnl sls mgr; Claire Chasse, pub dir; Helene Pichette, news dir.

*CIVQ-TV—ch 15, 1,298 kw vis, 259 kw aur, ant 628t/576g. On air date: Jan 19, 1975. c/o CIVM-TV, 800

Saskatchewan

rue Fullum, Montreal (H2K 3L7). (514) 521-2424. Licensee: Societe de radio-television du Quebec. Group owner: Francoise Bertrand, pres. Rebroadcasts *CIVM-TV Montreal.

CKMI-TV—ch 5, 13.85 kw vis, 3.77 kw aur, ant 460t/407g. On air date: 1957. Box 2026, 1000 Myrand Ave. Ste.-Foy (G1V 2W3). (418) 688-9330. FAX: (418) 681-1252. Licensee: TM Multi-Regions Inc. (Group owner: Tele-Metropole; acq 1984). ■ Net: CBC. ■ Guy Crevier, pres; Agnes Jarnuszkiewicz, exec vp & stn mgr.

Rimouski

CFER-TV—ch 11, 325 kw vis, 32.5 kw aur, ant 1,420t/289g. On air date: June 4, 1978. 465 boul. Ste.-Anne, Poente-au-Pere (G5M 1G1). (418) 722-6011. FAX: (418) 724-7810. Licensee: TM Multi-Regions Inc. Group owner: Reseau TVA. ■ Net: TVA. ■ Claude Auger, gen mgr & prom dir; Guy Crevier, vp sls; Carol Dionne, sls dir; Christian LePage, news dir & pub affrs dir; Daniel Lavoea, engrg dir.

*CIVB-TV—ch 22, 55 kw vis, ant 300t. On air date: Oct 15, 1981. 79 Eveche E. (G5L 1X7). (514) 521-2424. Licensee: Societe de radio-television du Quebec. Group owner: Radio Quebec. ■ Francoise Bertrand, pres.

CJBRT—ch 2, 100 kw vis, 10 kw aur, ant 1,341t/204g. On air date: November 1954. c/o CBVT, Box 10400, Ste. Foy (G1V 2X2). (418) 654-1341. FAX: (418) 654-3207. Licensee: CBC. ■ Net: CBC. ■ Bertrand Emond, gen mgr. Rebroadcasts CBVT Quebec City.

Riviere-du-Loup

CIMT-TV—ch 9, 49 kw vis, 7.4 kw aur, ant 1,178t/200g. On air date: Sept 18, 1978. 15 Rue de la Chute (G5R 2V1). (418) 867-1341. FAX: (418) 867-4710. Licensee: Tele Inter-Rive Ltee. Group owner: Tele Metropole Inc. ■ Net: TVA. ■ Marc Simard, pres; Germain Gelinas, vp opns & engrg dir; Ginette Dumont, gen sls mgr; Nancy Fortin, mktg dir & prom dir; Linda Theriault, progmg dir & news dir.

CKRT-TV—ch 7, 49 kw vis, 24.5 kw aur, ant 1,156t/200g. On air date: 1961. 15 Rue de la Chute (G5R 2V1). (418) 867-1341. FAX: (418) 867-4710. Licensee: CKRT-TV Ltee. Ownership: Tele Inter-Rives Ltee, 100%. ■ Net: CBC. ■ Marc Simard, pres; Germain Gelinas, vp opns & engrg dir; Ginette Dumont, gen sls mgr; Nancy Fortin, mktg dir & prom dir; Linda Theriault, progmg dir.

Rouyn

CFVS-TV-1—ch 20., On air date: Jan 19, 1987. c/o CFVS-TV, 1729 3ieme Ave., Val d'Or (J9P 1W3). (819) 825-0010. Licensee: Radio Nord Inc. ■ Net: Quatre Saisons. Rep: All-Canada. ■ Bernard Gauchier, gen mgr.

*CIVA-TV—ch 8, 299.2 kw vis, 28.6 kw aur. On air date: Jan 18, 1980. 800 rue Fullum, Montreal (H2K 3L7). (514) 521-2424. Licensee: Quebec Broadcasting Bureau. Group owner: Radio Quebec. Radio Quebec. ■ Francoise Bertrand, pres. Rebroadcasts *CIVM-TV Montreal.

CKRN-TV—ch 4, 115 kw vis, 11.5 kw aur, ant 670g. On air date: 1957. 380 Murdoch, Noranda (J9X 1G5). (819) 762-0741. TELEX: 057-46526. Licensee: Groupe Radio Norde Inc. (group owner). ■ Net: Radio Canada. Rep: All-Canada. ■ Bernard Gauchier, gen mgr. ■ On 1 CATV.

Sept-Iles

CBST—ch 13, 3 kw vis, 300 w aur, ant 452g. On air date: Nov 1, 1982. c/o CBVT, Box 10400, Ste. Foy (G1V 2X2). (418) 654-1341. Licensee: Societe Radio Canada. Ownership: Societe Radio Canada. ■ Net: Radio Canada. ■ Bertrand Emond, gen mgr. Rebroadcasts CBVT Quebec City.

*CIVG-TV—ch 9, 246 kw vis, 49.2 kw aur, ant 943t/500g. On air date: Nov 5, 1982. 410 Evangeline (G4R 2N5). (418) 968-2240. FAX: (418) 968-2923. Licensee: Societe de radio-television du Quebec. Group owner: Radio Quebec. Fr 100 hrs wkly. ■ Francoise Bertrand, pres.

Sherbrooke

CFKS-TV—ch 30, 92.3 kw vis, ant 2,011t. TL: N45 18 43 W72 14 32. On air date: September 1986. 3720 Boul. Industriel (J1L 1Z9). (819) 565-9999. FAX: (819) 822-4205. TELEX: 05-836-133. Licensee: Cogeco Radio-Television Inc. Group owner: Cogeco Inc. ■ Net: Quatre Saisons. Rep: Paul Mulvihill. Fr. News progmg 3 hrs wkly. ■ Guy Godbout, gen mgr; Lucie Pelletier, opns mgr;

Marie Comtois, natl sls mgr; Alain Tetreault, rgnl sls mgr; Carole Beausejour, progmg dir; Marcel Courchesne, news dir. ■ Rates: C$400; 175; 175.

CHLT-TV—ch 7, 325 kw vis, 32.5 kw aur, ant 1,920t/106g. On air date: Aug 12, 1956. 3330 Ouest Rue King (J1L 1C9). (819) 565-7777. FAX: (819) 565-4650. Licensee: Pathonic Network Inc. (group owner; acq 1979). ■ Net: TVA. Rep: Paul L'Anglais Inc., Patcom. ■ Louise Coiscert, gen mgr.

*CIVS-TV—ch 24, 475 kw vis, 47.5 kw aur, ant 2,000t/90g. On air date: Feb 26, 1982. c/o Radio Quebec, 800 Rue Fullum, Montreal (H2K 3L7). (514) 521-2424. TELEX: 05-25808. Licensee: Societe de radio-television du Quebec. Group owner: Radio Quebec. ■ Net: Radio Canada. ■ Francoise Bertrand, pres. ■ On 15 CATVs—57,000 subs.

CKSH-TV—ch 9, 325 kw vis, 56 kw aur. On air date: Sept 1, 1974. 3720 boul. Industriel (J1L 1Z9). (819) 565-9999. FAX: (819) 822-4205. TELEX: 05-836133. Licensee: Cogeco Radio-Television Inc. Group owner: Cogeco Inc. ■ Net: CBC. Rep: Paul Mulvihill. ■ Danielle Chagnon, gen mgr. ■ On one CATV. On 13 trans.

Temiscaning

CBFST-2—ch 12, 6.9 kw vs, 1.416 kw aur. c/o CBOFT, Box 3220, Station C, 250 Lanark, Ottawa, ON (K1Y 1E4). (613) 724-1200. FAX: (613) 724-5074. ■ Net: Radio Canada. ■ Pierre Fournier, progmg dir. Rebroadcasts CBOFT Ottawa.

Trois-Rivieres

CFKM-TV—ch 16, 703.1 kw vis, 70.3 kw aur, ant 1,071g. Stereo. On air date: Sept 7, 1986. Box 277 (G9A 5G3). (819) 377-1441. FAX: (819) 377-1109. TELEX: 05-837-137. Licensee: Cogeco Radio-Television Inc. Group owner: Cogeco Inc. ■ Net: Quatre Saisons. Rep: Paul Mulvihill. ■ Michel Cloutier, gen mgr.

CHEM-TV—ch 8, 325 kw vis, 32.5 kw aur, ant 946t/698g. On air date: Aug 29, 1976. 3625 boul. Chanoine-Moreau (G8Y 5N6). (819) 376-8880. TELEX: 05-837212. Licensee: Pathonic Network Inc. (group owner; acq 1979). ■ Net: TVA. Rep: Paul L'Anglais, Patcom. ■ Lise Beaulieu, gen mgr.

*CIVC-TV—ch 45, 55 kw vis, 5 kw aur, ant 1,575t/1,000g. Hrs opn: Oct 7, 1981. c/o Radio Quebec, 800 rue Fullum, Montreal (H2K 3L7). (514) 521-2424. Licensee: Societe de radio-television du Quebec. Group owner: Radio Quebec. ■ Francoise Bertrand, pres.

CKTM-TV—ch 13, 325 kw vis, 65 kw aur, ant 1,660t/1,085g. Stereo. On air date: Apr 15, 1958. Box 277 (G9A 5G3). (819) 377-1441. TELEX: 05-837-137. Licensee: Cogeco Radio-Television Inc. Group owner: Cogeco Inc. ■ Net: CBC. Rep: Paul Mulvihill. ■ Michel Cloutier, gen mgr. ■ On 60 CATVs—561,000 subs.

Val d'Or

CFVS-TV—ch 25., On air date: Jan 19, 1987. 1729 troisieme Ave. (J9P 1W3). (819) 825-0010. Licensee: Radio Nord Inc. (group owner). ■ Net: Quatre Saisons. Rep: All-Canada. ■ Daniel Hamel, gen mgr.

Saskatchewan

Bellegarde

CBKFT-9—ch 26, 11.4 kw, ant 413t/416g. On air date: Mar 15, 1980. Box 540, 2440 Broad St., Regina (S4P 4A1). (306) 347-9540. FAX: (306) 347-9490. TELEX: 071-2289. Licensee: Societe Radio Canada. ■ Net: Radio Canada. ■ Gilbert Teffaine, gen mgr. Rebroadcasts CBWFT Winnipeg.

Colgate

CKCK-TV-1—ch 12, 84.8 kw vis, 8.5 kw aur, ant 532t/581g. TL: N49 26 16 W103 47 53. Hrs opn: 24. On air date: Dec 15, 1962. c/o CKCK-TV, Box 2000, Regina (S4P 3E5). ■ Leon Brin, gen mgr. Rebroadcasts CKCK-TV Regina.

Cypress Hills

CBCP-TV-2—ch 2, 2.4 kw, ant 395g. On air date: Oct 1, 1979. Box 540, 2440 Broad St., Regina (S4P 4A1). (306) 347-9540. FAX: (306) 347-9490. Licensee: CBC. ■ Net: CBC. ■ Brian Cousins, gen mgr. Rebroadcasts CJFB-TV Swift Current.

Debden

CBKFT-3—ch 22, 2.9 kw, ant 306t/310g. On air date: Dec 2, 1979. Box 540, 2440 Broad St., Regina (S4P 4A1). (306) 347-9540. FAX: (306) 347-9490. TELEX: 071-2289. Licensee: Societe Radio Canada. ■ Net: Radio Canada. ■ M. Raymond Marcotte, progmg dir. Rebroadcasts CBKFT-1 Saskatoon.

Golden Prairie

CKMC-TV-1—ch 10, 229 kw vis, 22.9 kw aur, ant 554t/600g. TL: N50 12 20 W109 35 43. Hrs opn: 24. On air date: Dec 15, 1988. c/o CKCK-TV, Box 2000, Regina (S4P 3E5). ■ Leon Brin, gen mgr. Rebroadcasts CKCK-TV Regina.

Gravelbourg

CBKFT-6—ch 39, 19 kw, ant 638t/615g. On air date: Mar 13, 1980. Box 540, 2440 Broad St., Regina (S4P 4A1). (306) 347-9540. FAX: (306) 347-9490. TELEX: 071-2289. Licensee: Societe Radio Canada. ■ Net: Radio Canada. ■ M. Raymond Marcotte, progmg dir. Rebroadcasts CBKFT Regina.

Greenwater Lake

CKBI-TV-3—ch 4, 6 kw vis, 600 w aur, ant 718t/514g. c/o CKBI-TV, 22 10th St. W., Prince Albert (S6V 3A5). (306) 922-6066. Licensee: STN Television Network, Inc. ■ Net: CBC. ■ Dennis Dunlop, gen mgr. Rebroadcasts CKBI-TV Prince Albert.

Marquis

CKMJ-TV—ch 7, 100 kw vis, 10 kw aur, ant 768t/810g. TL: N50 38 43 W105 46 06. Hrs opn: 24. On air date: Sept 18, 1964. c/o Box 2000, CKCK-TV, Regina (S4P 3E5). ■ Leon Brin, gen mgr. Rebroadcasts CKCK-TV Regina.

Melfort

CKBQ-TV—ch 2, 15.5 kw vis, 1.55 kw aur, ant 492t/490g. On air date: 1973. c/o CIPA-TV, 22 10th St. W., Prince Albert (S6V 3A5). (306) 922-6066. Licensee: STN Television Network Inc. (Group owner: Baton Broadcasting Inc.) ■ Net: CTV. ■ Dennis Dunlop, gen mgr. Rebroadcasts CIPA-TV Prince Albert.

Nipawin

CKBI-TV-4—ch 10, 8 kw vis, 800 w aur, ant 471t/405g. On air date: October 1978. c/o CKBI-TV, 22 10th St. W., Prince Albert (S6V 3A5). (306) 922-6066. Licensee: STN Television Network Inc. (Group owner: Baton Broadcasting Inc.) ■ Net: CBC. ■ Dennis Dunlop, gen mgr. Rebroadcasts CKBI-TV Prince Albert.

North Battleford

CFQC-TV-2—ch 6, 16.8 kw vis, 1.9 kw aur, ant 584t/350g. On air date: 1972. c/o CFQC-TV, 216 First Ave. N., Saskatoon (S7K 3W3). (306) 665-8600. Licensee: CFQC-TV Ltd. ■ Net: CTV. ■ Howard Cooper, pres & gen mgr. Rebroadcasts CFQC-TV Saskatoon.

Ponteix

CBCP-TV-3—ch 3, 10.5 kw, ant 650t/717g. On air date: November 1979. c/o CBVT, 2440 Broad St., Regina (S4P 4A1). (306) 347-9540. FAX: (306) 347-9490. Licensee: CBC. ■ Net: CBC. ■ Brian Cousins, gen mgr. Rebroadcasts CJFB-TV Swift Current.

Prince Albert

CIPA-TV—ch 9, 325 kw vis, 32.5 kw aur, ant 711t/460g. Stereo. Hrs opn: 24. On air date: Jan 12, 1987. 22 10th St. W. (S6V 3A5). (306) 922-6066. FAX: (306) 763-3041. Licensee: STN Television Network Inc. Group owner: Baton Broadcasting Inc. (acq 8-1-86). ■ Net: CTV. News staff 13. ■ Deryl Ring, pres; Dennis Dunlop, gen mgr; Brian Rock, opns mgr; Karen Newton, gen sls mgr; Rick Lewchuk, prom dir; Bill Stevenson, vp progmg; Dale Neufeld, news dir; Don Mitchell, pub affrs dir; Les Sampson, engrg dir. ■ On 15 CATVs—50,000 subs. On 7 trans.

CKBI-TV—ch 5, 61 kw vis, 12.2 kw aur, ant 1,300t/585g. Hrs opn: 20. On air date: 1958. 22 10th St. W. (S6V 3A5). (306) 922-6066. TELEX: 074-29130. Licensee: STN Television Network Inc. Group owner: Baton Broadcasting Inc. (acq 8-1-86). ■ Net: CBC. Rep: Glenn Warren. ■ Daryl Ring, pres; Dennis Dunlop, gen mgr & gen sls mgr; Brian Rock, opns mgr; Bill Stevenson, prom mgr, progmg dir & film buyer; Dale Neufeld, news dir; Les Samson, chief engr. ■ On 15 CATVs—50,000 subs. On 7 trans.

Regina

CBKFT—ch 13, 313 kw vis, 31.3 kw aur. On air date: Sept 27, 1976. Box 540, 2440 Broad St. (S4P 4A1). (306) 347-9540. FAX: (306) 347-9590. Licensee: Radio Canada. ■ Net: Radio Canada. ■ Raymond J. Marcotte, gen mgr; Brian Cousins, rgnl sls mgr.

CBKT—ch 9, 140 kw vis, 20 kw aur, ant 680t/698g. On air date: 1969. Box 540, 2440 Broad St. (S4P 4A1). (306) 347-9540. FAX: (306) 347-9490. Licensee: CBC. ■ Net: CBC. ■ Gerard Veilleux, pres; Brian Cousins, gen mgr; Bruce Rankin, opns mgr; Michael Landsberg, gen sls mgr; Mike Pietrus, news dir. ■ On 8 CATVs—67,000 subs. Co-owned radio: CBK(AM).

CFRE-TV—ch 11, 146 kw vis, ant 1,000g. Stereo. On air date: Sept 6, 1987. 370 Hoffer Dr. (S4N 7A4). (306) 721-2211. FAX: (306) 721-4817. Licensee: SaskWest Television Inc. Ownership: CanWest Broadcasting. Rep: CanVideo. ■ Jim Sward, pres; David Asper, gen mgr; Monte Graham, gen sls mgr; Stan Schmidt, mktg dir; Brent Toombs, prom mgr; Dean Parker, progmg dir; Stan Thomas, film buyer; Mark Evans, news dir; Brian Sather, chief engr. ■ On 2 CATVs.

CKCK-TV—ch 2, 100 kw vis, 10 kw aur, ant 588t/670g. TL: N50 26 52 W104 30 00. Stereo. Hrs opn: 24. On air date: July 28, 1954. Box 2000 (S4P 3E5). (306) 569-2000. FAX: (306) 569-2431. Licensee: STN Television Network Inc. Group owner: Baton Broadcasting Inc. ■ Net: CTV. ■ Leon Brin, gen mgr; Patricia Wourms, opns dir; Deryl Ring, vp sls; Glen Cave, rgnl sls mgr; Rick Lewchuck, prom mgr; Bill Stevenson, vp progmg & film buyer; Alex Docking, news dir & pub affrs dir; Richard Niebergall, chief engr.

St. Brieux

CBKFT-4—ch 7, 140 w, ant 200t/185g. On air date: Dec 17, 1979. Box 540, 2440 Broad St., Regina (S4P 4A1). (306) 347-9540. FAX: (306) 347-9490. TELEX: 071-2289. Licensee: Societe Radio Canada. ■ Net: Radio Canada. ■ M. Raymond Marcotte, gen mgr. Rebroadcasts CBKFT-1 Saskatoon.

Saskatoon

CBKST—ch 11, 325 kw vis, 32 kw aur, ant 559t/595g. Hrs opn: 20. On air date: Oct 17, 1971. 5th Fl., CN Tower (S7K 1J5). (306) 956-7400. FAX: (306) 956-7417 (NEWS); (306) 956-7476 (SALES). Licensee: CBC. ■ Net: CBC. ■ Gary Crippen, gen mgr, opns mgr, prom mgr & progmg dir; Don Burdego, gen sls mgr & adv mgr; Robert Osborne, news dir; Al Willems, chief engr. ■ On 3 CATVs—200,000 subs. On 14 trans.

CFQC-TV—ch 8, 325 kw vis, 180 kw aur, ant 891t/650g. On air date: 1954. 216 First Ave. N. (S7K 3W3). (306) 665-8600. TELEX: 074-2228. Licensee: CFQC Broadcasting Ltd. Group owner: Baton Broadcasting Inc. (acq 1972). ■ Net: CTV. Rep: Glen Warren. ■ Howard Cooper, pres & gen mgr; Jim Zaiachowski, gen sls mgr; Bruce Acton, prom mgr; Reed Brown, progmg dir; Jim Mattern, news dir; D. Polowick, chief engr.

CFSK-TV—ch 4, 54 kw vis, 5.4 kw aur, ant 455t/219g. Stereo. Hrs opn: 22. On air date: Sept 6, 1987. 218 Robin Cresc. (S7L 7C3). (306) 665-6969. FAX: (306) 665-6069; (306) 665-0058 (News). Licensee: SaskWest Television Inc. Ownership: CanWest Broadcasting Ltd., 100%. News staff 15; news progmg 10 hrs wkly. ■ Peter Liba, pres; Rick Friesen, gen mgr; Brian Taylor, opns mgr; Stan Schmidt, sls dir & mktg dir; Brent Toombs, prom mgr; Dean Parker, progmg mgr; Doug Hoover, film buyer; Lisa Ford, news dir; Len Virog, chief engr. ■ Rates: C$650; 175; 100.

Shaunavon

CBCP-TV-1—ch 7, 1,488 kw vis, 148.8 kw aur. Box 160, c/o CJFB-TV, Swift Current (S9H 3V7). (306) 773-7266. FAX: (306) 773-0123. Licensee: Swift Current Telecasting Co. Ltd. ■ Net: CBC. Rep: Airtime TV Sales. ■ William D. Forst, pres & gen mgr; Julie Forst, stn mgr. Rebroadcasts CJFB-TV Swift Current.

Stranraer

CBKST-1—ch 9, 323 kw vis, 32.3 kw aur. Hrs opn: 20. c/o CBKST, CN Tower, 5th Fl., Saskatoon (S7K 1J5). (306) 956-7400. FAX: (306) 956-7417. Licensee: CBC (group owner). ■ Gary Crippen, opns mgr; Don Burdego, gen sls mgr; Robert Osborne, news dir. Rebroadcasts CBKST Saskatoon.

CFQC-TV-1—ch 3, 10.3 kw vis, 1.8 kw aur. ant 930t/655g. On air date: 1961. c/o CFQC-TV, 216 First Ave. N., Saskatoon (S7K 3W3). (306) 665-8600. ■ Net: CTV. ■ Howard Cooper, pres & gen mgr. Rebroadcasts CFQC-TV Saskatoon.

Swift Current

CJFB-TV—ch 5, 13.3 kw vis, 2.5 kw aur, ant 511t/365g. On air date: Dec 23, 1957. Box 160 (S9H 3V7). (306) 773-7266. FAX: (306) 773-0123. Licensee: Swift Current Telecasting Co. Ltd. ■ Net: CBC. Rep: Airtime TV Sls. ■ William D. Forst, pres & gen mgr; Julie Forst, vp, stn mgr & progmg dir; Warren Carlson, gen sls mgr.

CKMC-TV—ch 12, 100 kw vis, 10 kw aur, ant 549t/390t. TL: N50 18 31 W107 52 35. Hrs opn: 24. On air date: Oct 20, 1976. c/o CKCK-TV, Box 2000, Regina (S4P 3E5). (306) 569-2000. Licensee: STN Television Network Inc. Group owner: Baton Broadcasting, Inc. ■ Leon Brin, gen mgr. Rebroadcasts CKCK-TV Regina.

Warmley

CIEW-TV—ch 7, 100 kw vis, 10 kw aur. c/o CICC-TV, 95 E. Broadway St., Yorkton (S3N 0L1). (306) 783-3685. Licensee: STN Television Network Inc. ■ Net: CTV. ■ Wilbur A. Westby, gen mgr. Rebroadcasts CICC-TV Yorkton.

Willow Bunch

CBKT-2—ch 10, 22.1 kw vis, 2.2 kw aur. Box 540, c/o CBKT, 2440 Broad St., Regina (S4P 4A1). (306) 947-9540. FAX: (306) 347-9490. ■ Net: CBC. ■ Brian Cousins, gen mgr. Rebroadcasts CBKT Regina.

CKCK-TV-2—ch 6, 17.5 kw vis, 8.75 kw aur, ant 864t/677g. (CP: 27.1 kw vis). On air date: May 29, 1963. c/o CKCK-TV, Box 2000, Regina (S4P 3E5). ■ Leon Brin, gen mgr. Rebroadcasts CKCK-TV Regina.

Wynyard

CHSS-TV—ch 6, 11 kw vis, 1.8 kw aur. c/o CKOS-TV, 95 E. Broadway, Yorkton (S3N 0L1). (306) 783-3685. Licensee: STN Television Network Inc. ■ Net: CBC. ■ Wilbur A. Westby, gen mgr. Rebroadcasts CKOS-TV Yorkton.

CICC-TV-1—ch 12, 140 kw vis, 27 kw aur. c/o CICC-TV, 95 E. Broadway, Yorkton (S3N 0L1). (306) 783-3685. FAX: (306) 782-3433; (306) 782-7212. Licensee: Shamrock Television Systems Inc. ■ Net: CTV. ■ Wilbur A. Westby, gen mgr. Rebroadcasts CICC-TV Yorkton.

Yorkton

CICC-TV—ch 10, 39.24 kw vis. On air date: 1974. 95 E. Broadway (S3N 0L1). (306) 783-3685. FAX: (306) 782-3433. Licensee: Shamrock Television Systems Inc. Group owner: Baton Broadcasting Inc. ■ Net: CTV. ■ R. L. Skinner, pres; Wilbur A. Westby, gen mgr; John Neufeld, gen sls mgr; Kim Balog, prom mgr; Elizabeth Popowich, news dir; Bob Maloney, pub affrs dir; Ken Golemba, engrg dir.

CKOS-TV—ch 5, 54.6 kw vis, 2.6 kw aur, ant 534t/525g. On air date: 1974. 95 E. Broadway (S3N 0L1). (306) 783-3685. FAX: (306) 782-3433; (306) 782-7212. Licensee: Shamrock Television Systems Inc. Group owner: Baton Broadcasting Inc. ■ Net: CBC. ■ Ronald L. Skinner, pres; Wilbur A. Westby, vp & gen mgr; John Neufeld, gen sls mgr.

Zenon Park

CBKFT-5—ch 21, 3 kw, ant 456t/310g. On air date: Feb 19, 1979. Box 540, c/o CBKFT, 2440 Broad St., Regina (S4P 4A1). (306) 347-9540. FAX: (306) 347-9490. Licensee: CBC. ■ Net: CBC. ■ Richard Marcotte, gen mgr. Rebroadcasts CBKFT-1 Saskatoon.

Yukon Territory

White Horse

CFWH-TV—ch 6, 441 w. vis, 30 w. aur, ant 1,248t/100g. 3103 Third Ave. (Y1A 1E5). (403) 668-8411. Licensee: CBC. ■ Net: CBC. ■ Don Irwin, gen mgr.

U.S. Television Stations by Call Letters

KAAL Austin MN
KAAS-TV Salina KS
KABB San Antonio TX
KABC-TV Los Angeles CA
KABY-TV Aberdeen SD
KACB-TV San Angelo TX
*KACV-TV Amarillo TX
KADE San Luis Obispo CA
KADN Lafayette LA
KADY-TV Oxnard CA
KAEF Arcata CA
*KAET Phoenix AZ
*KAFT Fayetteville AR
KAFU Enid OK
*KAID Boise ID
KAII-TV Wailuku HI
KAIL Fresno CA
KAIT-TV Jonesboro AR
*KAKM Anchorage AK
KALB-TV Alexandria LA
KAMC Lubbock TX
KAME-TV Reno NV
KAMR-TV Amarillo TX
*KAMU-TV College Station TX
KAPP Yakima WA
KARD-TV West Monroe LA
KARE Minneapolis MN
KARK-TV Little Rock AR
KASA-TV Santa Fe NM
KASN Pine Bluff AR
KATC Lafayette LA
KATN Fairbanks AK
KATU Portland OR
KATV Little Rock AR
KAUZ-TV Wichita Falls TX
KAVU-TV Victoria TX
KAWB Brainerd MN
KAWE Bemidji MN
KAYU-TV Spokane WA
*KAZQ Albuquerque NM
KBAK-TV Bakersfield CA
KBCB Bellingham WA
KBCI-TV Boise ID
*KBDI-TV Broomfield CO
KBEH Bellevue WA
KBFD Honolulu HI
*KBGH Filer ID
*KBHE-TV Rapid City SD
KBHK-TV San Francisco CA
KBIM-TV Roswell NM
*KBIN Council Bluffs IA
KBJR-TV Superior WI
KBLR Paradise NV
*KBME Bismarck ND
KBMT Beaumont TX
KBMY Bismarck ND
KBRR Thief River Falls MN
KBSD-TV Ensign KS
KBSH-TV Hays KS
KBSI Cape Girardeau MO
KBSL-TV Goodland KS
KBSP-TV Salem OR
*KBTC-TV Tacoma WA
KBTX-TV Bryan TX
KBVO Austin TX
KBVU Eureka CA
*KBYU-TV Provo UT
*KCAH Watsonville CA
KCAL Los Angeles CA
KCAN Albion NE
KCAU-TV Sioux City IA
KCBA Salinas CA
KCBD-TV Lubbock TX
KCBS-TV Los Angeles CA
KCBY-TV Coos Bay OR
KCCI-TV Des Moines IA
KCCN-TV Monterey CA
KCCO-TV Alexandria MN
KCCW-TV Walker MN
*KCDT Coeur d'Alene ID
KCEC Denver CO
KCEN-TV Temple TX
*KCET Los Angeles CA
KCFP Austin TX
KCFW-TV Kalispell MT
KCHF Santa Fe NM
*KCIK El Paso TX
KCIT Amarillo TX
*KCKA Centralia WA
KCLO-TV Rapid City SD
KCMY Sacramento CA
KCNC-TV Denver CO
KCNS San Francisco CA
KCOP Los Angeles CA
*KCOS El Paso TX
KCOY-TV Santa Maria CA
KCPM Chico CA
KCPQ Tacoma WA
KCPT Kansas City MO
KCRA-TV Sacramento CA
KCRG-TV Cedar Rapids IA
*KCSM-TV San Mateo CA
KCSO Modesto CA
*KCTF Waco TX
*KCTS-TV Seattle WA
KCTV Kansas City MO
KCTZ Bozeman MT
KCVU Paradise CA
*KCWC-TV Lander WY

KCWT Wenatchee WA
KDAF Dallas TX
KDBC-TV El Paso TX
KDEB-TV Springfield MO
KDFI-TV Dallas TX
KDFW-TV Dallas TX
*KDIN-TV Des Moines IA
KDKA-TV Pittsburgh PA
KDKF Klamath Falls OR
KDLH Duluth MN
KDLO-TV Florence SD
KDLT Mitchell SD
KDNL-TV St. Louis MO
KDOC-TV Anaheim CA
KDOR Bartlesville OK
KDRV Medford OR
*KDSD-TV Aberdeen SD
KDSE Dickinson ND
KDSM-TV Des Moines IA
*KDTN Denton TX
KDTV San Francisco CA
*KDTX-TV Dallas TX
KDUB-TV Dubuque IA
KDUH-TV Scottsbluff NE
KDVR Denver CO
KEBN Salem OR
KECI-TV Missoula MT
KECY-TV El Centro CA
*KEDT-TV Corpus Christi TX
*KEEF-TV Los Angeles CA
*KEET Eureka CA
KELO-TV Sioux Falls SD
*KEMV Mountain View AR
KENS-TV San Antonio TX
*KENW Portales NM
KEPB-TV Eugene OR
KEPR-TV Pasco WA
*KERA-TV Dallas TX
KERO-TV Bakersfield CA
*KESD-TV Brookings SD
KESQ-TV Palm Springs CA
*KETA Oklahoma City OK
*KETC St. Louis MO
*KETG Arkadelphia AR
*KETH Houston TX
KETK-TV Jacksonville TX
*KETS Little Rock AR
KETV Omaha NE
KEVN-TV Rapid City SD
KEVU Eugene OR
KEYC-TV Mankato MN
KEYT-TV Santa Barbara CA
KEZI Eugene OR
KFAA Rogers AR
KFBB-TV Great Falls MT
KFBT Las Vegas NV
KFCB Concord CA
KFCT Fort Collins CO
KFDA-TV Amarillo TX
KFDM-TV Beaumont TX
KFDX-TV Wichita Falls TX
KFMB-TV San Diego CA
*KFME Fargo ND
KFNB-TV Casper WY
KFNE Riverton WY
KFNR Rawlins WY
KFOR-TV Oklahoma City OK
KFSM-TV Fort Smith AR
KFSN-TV Fresno CA
KFTL Stockton CA
*KFTS Klamath Falls OR
KFTV Hanford CA
KFTY Santa Rosa CA
KFVE Honolulu HI
KFVS-TV Cape Girardeau MO
KFWD Fort Worth TX
KFWU Fort Bragg CA
KFXK-TV Longview TX
KFYR-TV Bismarck ND
KGAN Cedar Rapids IA
KGBT-TV Harlingen TX
KGET Bakersfield CA
*KGFE Grand Forks ND
KGIN Grand Island NE
KGLB-TV Okmulgee OK
KGMB Honolulu HI
KGMC Clovis CA
KGMD-TV Hilo HI
KGMV Wailuku HI
KGNS-TV Laredo TX
*KGTF Agana GU
KGTV San Diego CA
KGUN Tucson AZ
KGW-TV Portland OR
KGWC-TV Casper WY
KGWL-TV Lander WY
KGWN-TV Cheyenne WY
KGWR-TV Rock Springs WY
KHAS-TV Hastings NE
KHAW-TV Hilo HI
KHBB Helena MT
KHBC-TV Hilo HI
KHBS Fort Smith AR
*KHCE San Antonio TX
KHCV Seattle WA
KHDT-TV Caldwell ID
*KHET Honolulu HI
KHFT Hobbs NM

KHGI-TV Kearney NE
*KHIN Red Oak IA
KHIZ Barstow CA
*KHNE-TV Hastings NE
KHNL Honolulu HI
KHOG-TV Fayetteville AR
KHON-TV Honolulu HI
KHOU-TV Houston TX
KHQ-TV Spokane WA
KHQA-TV Hannibal MO
KHRR Tucson AZ
KHSC-TV Ontario CA
KHSD-TV Lead SD
KHSH-TV Alvin TX
KHSL-TV Chico CA
KHSX-TV Irving TX
KHTV Houston TX
KHVO Hilo HI
KICU-TV San Jose CA
KIDK Idaho Falls ID
KIDY San Angelo TX
KIEM-TV Eureka CA
KIFI-TV Idaho Falls ID
KIII Corpus Christi TX
*KIIN-TV Iowa City IA
KIKU Honolulu HI
KIMA-TV Yakima WA
KIMO Anchorage AK
KIMT Mason City IA
KING-TV Seattle WA
KINT-TV El Paso TX
KIPT Twin Falls ID
KIRO-TV Seattle WA
*KISU-TV Pocatello ID
KITN-TV Minneapolis MN
*KITU Beaumont TX
KITV Honolulu HI
KIVI Nampa ID
KIVV-TV Lead SD
*KIXE-TV Redding CA
KJAC-TV Port Arthur TX
KJCT Grand Junction CO
KJEO Fresno CA
KJLF-TV El Paso TX
KJMH Burlington IA
KJNP-TV North Pole AK
*KJRE Ellendale ND
KJRH Tulsa OK
KJRR Jamestown ND
KJTL Wichita Falls TX
KJTV Lubbock TX
KJUD Juneau AK
KJVI Jackson WY
KJWA Grand Junction CO
KJZZ-TV Salt Lake City UT
KKAK Porterville CA
KKFT Fort Scott KS
KKIK-TV Albuquerque NM
KKTM Flagstaff AZ
KKTU Cheyenne WY
KKTV Colorado Springs CO
KKVI Twin Falls ID
KLAS-TV Las Vegas NV
KLAX-TV Alexandria LA
KLBK-TV Lubbock TX
KLBY Colby KS
*KLCS Los Angeles CA
KLDO-TV Laredo TX
KLDT Lake Dallas TX
KLEI Kailua-Kona HI
*KLEP Newark AR
KLEW-TV Lewiston ID
KLFY-TV Lafayette LA
KLGT-TV Minneapolis MN
KLJB-TV Davenport IA
*KLNE-TV Lexington NE
KLPA-TV Alexandria LA
*KLPB-TV Lafayette LA
KLRN San Antonio TX
KLRT Little Rock AR
*KLRU-TV Austin TX
KLSB-TV Nacogdoches TX
KLSR-TV Roseburg OR
KLST San Angelo TX
*KLTJ Galveston TX
*KLTL-TV Lake Charles LA
*KLTM Monroe LA
*KLTS-TV Shreveport LA
KLTV Tyler TX
KLUJ Harlingen TX
KLUZ-TV Albuquerque NM
KLVX Las Vegas NV
KLWY Cheyenne WY
KLXO El Centro CA
KLXV-TV San Jose CA
KMAU Wailuku HI
KMBC-TV Kansas City MO
*KMBH Harlingen TX
KMCI Lawrence KS
KMCT-TV West Monroe LA
KMCY Minot ND
*KMEB Wailuku HI
KMEG Sioux City IA
KMEX-TV Los Angeles CA
KMGH-TV Denver CO
KMID Midland TX
KMIR-TV Palm Springs CA
KMIZ Columbia MO
KMLM Odessa TX
*KMNE-TV Bassett NE

KMNZ Oklahoma City OK
KMOH-TV Kingman AZ
KMOL-TV San Antonio TX
*KMOS-TV Sedalia MO
KMOT Minot ND
KMOV St. Louis MO
KMPH Visalia CA
KMPX Decatur TX
KMSB-TV Tucson AZ
KMSG-TV Sanger CA
KMSP-TV Minneapolis MN
KMSS-TV Shreveport LA
*KMTP-TV San Francisco CA
KMTR Eugene OR
KMTV Omaha NE
KMTX-TV Roseburg OR
KMTZ Coos Bay OR
KMVT Twin Falls ID
KMVU Medford OR
KMZN Farwell TX
KNAT Albuquerque NM
KNAZ-TV Flagstaff AZ
KNBC-TV Los Angeles CA
*KNCT Belton TX
KNDO Yakima WA
KNDU Richland WA
KNLC St. Louis MO
KNLJ Jefferson City MO
*KNME-TV Albuquerque NM
KNMT-TV Portland OR
KNOE-TV Monroe LA
KNOP-TV North Platte NE
*KNPB Reno NV
KNRR Pembina ND
KNSD San Diego CA
KNSO Merced CA
KNTV San Jose CA
KNVO McAllen TX
KNWS-TV Katy TX
*KNXT Visalia CA
KNXV-TV Phoenix AZ
KOAA-TV Pueblo CO
*KOAB-TV Bend OR
*KOAC-TV Corvallis OR
KOAM-TV Pittsburg KS
KOAT-TV Albuquerque NM
KOB-TV Albuquerque NM
KOBF Farmington NM
KOBI Medford OR
KOBN Honolulu HI
KOBR Roswell NM
KOCB Oklahoma City OK
*KOCE-TV Huntington Beach CA
KOCO-TV Oklahoma City OK
KOCR Cedar Rapids IA
*KOCT Carlsbad NM
*KOCV-TV Odessa TX
KODE-TV Joplin MO
*KOED-TV Tulsa OK
*KOET Eufaula OK
KOFT Gallup NM
KOFY-TV San Francisco CA
KOGG Wailuku HI
KOIN Portland OR
KOKH-TV Oklahoma City OK
KOKI-TV Tulsa OK
KOLD-TV Tucson AZ
KOLN Lincoln NE
KOLO-TV Reno NV
KOLR-TV Springfield MO
KOMO-TV Seattle WA
KOMU-TV Columbia MO
KONG-TV Everett WA
*KOOD Hays KS
KOOG-TV Ogden UT
*KOPB-TV Portland OR
KORO Corpus Christi TX
KOSA-TV Odessa TX
KOTA-TV Rapid City SD
KOTI Klamath Falls OR
KOTV Tulsa OK
*KOUS-TV Hardin MT
KOVR Stockton CA
KOVT Silver City NM
*KOZJ Joplin MO
*KOZK Springfield MO
KPAX-TV Missoula MT
*KPAZ-TV Phoenix AZ
*KPBS San Diego CA
KPDX Vancouver WA
KPEJ Odessa TX
KPHO-TV Phoenix AZ
KPIC Roseburg OR
KPIX San Francisco CA
KPLC-TV Lake Charles LA
KPLO-TV Reliance SD
KPLR-TV St. Louis MO
*KPNE-TV North Platte NE
KPNX Mesa AZ
KPOB-TV Poplar Bluff MO
KPOM-TV Fort Smith AR
KPRC-TV Houston TX
KPRY-TV Pierre SD
*KPSD-TV Eagle Butte SD
KPST-TV Vallejo CA
KPTM Omaha NE
*KPTS Hutchinson KS
KPTV Portland OR
KPVI Pocatello ID
KQCD-TV Dickinson ND

*KQCT Davenport IA
*KQED San Francisco CA
*KQSD-TV Lowry SD
KQTV St. Joseph MO
KRBC-TV Abilene TX
KRBK-TV Sacramento CA
KRBQ Sheridan WY
KRBR Duluth MN
KRCA Riverside CA
*KRCB-TV Cotati CA
KRCG Jefferson City MO
KRCR-TV Redding CA
KRDO-TV Colorado Springs CO
KREG-TV Glenwood Springs CO
KREM-TV Spokane WA
KREN-TV Reno NV
KREX-TV Grand Junction CO
KREY-TV Montrose CO
KREZ-TV Durango CO
KRGV-TV Weslaco TX
*KRIN Waterloo IA
KRIS-TV Corpus Christi TX
KRIV Houston TX
KRLR Las Vegas NV
*KRMA-TV Denver CO
*KRNE-TV Merriman NE
KRNV Reno NV
KRON-TV San Francisco CA
KRPA Rancho Palos Verdes CA
KRPV Roswell NM
KRQE Albuquerque NM
KRRT Kerrville TX
*KRSC-TV Claremore OK
KRTV Great Falls MT
KRTW Baytown TX
KRWF Redwood Falls MN
*KRWG-TV Las Cruces NM
KRXI Reno NV
KRZB-TV Hot Springs AR
KSAS-TV Wichita KS
KSAT-TV San Antonio TX
KSAX Alexandria MN
KSBI Oklahoma City OK
*KSBN-TV Springdale AR
*KSBS-TV Steamboat Springs CO
KSBW Salinas CA
*KSBY San Luis Obispo CA
KSCE El Paso TX
KSCH-TV Stockton CA
KSCI San Bernardino CA
KSDK St. Louis MO
KSEE Fresno CA
KSFY-TV Sioux Falls SD
KSGI-TV Cedar City UT
KSGW-TV Sheridan WY
KSHB-TV Kansas City MO
*KSIN Sioux City IA
KSKN Spokane WA
KSL-TV Salt Lake City UT
KSLA-TV Shreveport LA
KSMO-TV Kansas City MO
*KSMQ-TV Austin MN
KSMS-TV Monterey CA
KSNB-TV Superior NE
KSNC Great Bend KS
KSNF Joplin MO
KSNG Garden City KS
KSNK McCook NE
KSNT Topeka KS
KSNW Wichita KS
KSPR Springfield MO
*KSPS-TV Spokane WA
KSRE Minot ND
KSTF Scottsbluff NE
KSTP-TV St. Paul MN
KSTS San Jose CA
KSTU Salt Lake City UT
KSTV-TV Ventura CA
KSTW Tacoma WA
KSVI Billings MT
*KSWK Lakin KS
KSWO-TV Lawton OK
KSWT Yuma AZ
*KSYS Medford OR
KTAB-TV Abilene TX
KTAJ St. Joseph MO
KTAL-TV Texarkana TX
KTAQ Greenville TX
KTBC-TV Austin TX
KTBN-TV Santa Ana CA
*KTBO-TV Oklahoma City OK
KTBS-TV Shreveport LA
KTBW-TV Tacoma WA
KTBY Anchorage AK
*KTCA-TV St. Paul MN
*KTCI-TV St. Paul MN
*KTEH San Jose CA
*KTEJ Jonesboro AR
KTEN Ada OK
KTFH Conroe TX
KTFO Tulsa OK
KTGF Great Falls MT
KTGM Tamuning GU
*KTHI-TV Fargo ND
KTHV Little Rock AR
*KTIN Fort Dodge IA
KTIV Sioux City IA
KTKA-TV Topeka KS
KTLA Los Angeles CA
KTLC Oklahoma City OK

Broadcasting & Cable Yearbook 1994
C-90

U.S. Television Stations by Call Letters

KTMD Galveston TX
KTMF Missoula MT
*KTNE-TV Alliance NE
KTNL Sitka AK
KTNV Las Vegas NV
*KTNW Richland WA
*KTOO-TV Juneau AK
KTRE Lufkin TX
KTRG Del Rio TX
KTRK-TV Houston TX
KTRV Nampa ID
*KTSC Pueblo CO
*KTSD-TV Pierre SD
KTSF San Francisco CA
KTSM-TV El Paso TX
KTSP-TV Phoenix AZ
KTTC Rochester MN
KTTM Huron SD
KTTU-TV Tucson AZ
KTTV Los Angeles CA
KTTW Sioux Falls SD
KTTY San Diego CA
KTUL Tulsa OK
KTUU-TV Anchorage AK
KTVA Anchorage AK
KTVB Boise ID
KTVC Cedar Rapids IA
KTVD Denver CO
KTVE El Dorado AR
KTVF Fairbanks AK
KTVG Grand Island NE
KTVH Helena MT
KTVI St. Louis MO
KTVJ Boulder CO
KTVK Phoenix AZ
KTVL Medford OR
KTVM Butte MT
KTVN Reno NV
KTVO Kirksville MO
KTVQ Billings MT
*KTVR La Grande OR
KTVS Sterling CO
KTVT Fort Worth TX
KTVU Oakland CA
KTVW-TV Phoenix AZ
KTVX Salt Lake City UT
KTVZ Bend OR
KTWO-TV Casper WY
*KTWU Topeka KS
KTXA Fort Worth TX
KTXH Houston TX
KTXL Sacramento CA
KTXS-TV Sweetwater TX
*KTXT-TV Lubbock TX
KTZZ-TV Seattle WA
*KUAC-TV Fairbanks AK
KUAM-TV Agana GU
*KUAS-TV Tucson AZ
*KUAT-TV Tucson AZ
KUBD Denver CO
*KUED Salt Lake City UT
*KUFM-TV Missoula MT
*KUHT Houston TX
*KUID-TV Moscow ID
*KULC Ogden UT
KULR-TV Billings MT
KUMV-TV Williston ND
*KUON-TV Lincoln NE
KUPK-TV Garden City KS
KUSA-TV Denver CO
*KUSD-TV Vermillion SD
KUSG St. George UT
KUSI-TV San Diego CA
KUSK Prescott AZ
*KUSM Bozeman MT
KUTP Phoenix AZ
KUTV Salt Lake City UT
KUVN Garland TX
KUZZ-TV Bakersfield CA
KVAL-TV Eugene OR
KVAW Eagle Pass TX
KVBC Las Vegas NV
KVBM-TV Minneapolis MN
*KVCR-TV San Bernardino CA
KVCT Victoria TX
KVDA San Antonio TX
KVEA Corona CA
KVEO Brownsville TX
KVEW Kennewick WA
KVHP Lake Charles LA
KVIA-TV El Paso TX
*KVIE Sacramento CA
KVIH-TV Clovis NM
KVII-TV Amarillo TX
KVIQ Eureka CA
KVMD Twentynine Palms CA
KVOA-TV Tucson AZ
KVOS-TV Bellingham WA
*KVPT Fresno CA
KVRR Fargo ND
KVTN Pine Bluff AR
KVTV Laredo TX
KVUE-TV Austin TX
KVUT Little Rock AR
KVVU-TV Henderson NV
*KVZK-2 Pago Pago AS
*KVZK-4 Pago Pago AS
*KVZK-5 Pago Pago AS
KWAB Big Spring TX
*KWBI-TV Denver CO
*KWCH-TV Hutchinson KS
*KWCM-TV Appleton MN
KWCV Wichita KS
*KWDK Tacoma WA
KWES-TV Odessa TX

*KWET Cheyenne OK
KWEX-TV San Antonio TX
KWGN-TV Denver CO
KWHB Tulsa OK
KWHD Castle Rock CO
KWHE Honolulu HI
KWHH Hilo HI
KWHM Wailuku HI
KWHY-TV Los Angeles CA
KWKT Waco TX
KWLB Shreveport LA
KWMJ Tulsa OK
KWNB-TV Hayes Center NE
KWQC-TV Davenport IA
*KWSE Williston ND
*KWSU-TV Pullman WA
KWTV Oklahoma City OK
KWTX-TV Waco TX
KWWL Waterloo IA
KWYB Butte MT
KXAM-TV Llano TX
KXAN-TV Austin TX
KXAS-TV Fort Worth TX
KXGN-TV Glendive MT
KXGR Green Valley AZ
KXII Sherman TX
KXJB-TV Valley City ND
KXLF-TV Butte MT
KXLI St. Cloud MN
KXLN-TV Rosenberg TX
KXLT-TV Rochester MN
KXLY-TV Spokane WA
KXMA-TV Dickinson ND
KXMB-TV Bismarck ND
KXMC-TV Minot ND
KXMD-TV Williston ND
*KXNE-TV Norfolk NE
KXRM-TV Colorado Springs CO
KXTV Sacramento CA
KXTX-TV Dallas TX
KXXV Waco TX
KYES Anchorage AK
KYFC Kansas City MO
*KYIN Mason City IA
KYLE Bryan TX
KYMA Yuma AZ
*KYNE-TV Omaha NE
KYOU-TV Ottumwa IA
KYTV Springfield MO
*KYUK-TV Bethel AK
KYUS-TV Miles City MT
*KYVE Yakima WA
KYW-TV Philadelphia PA
KZIA Las Cruces NM
KZJC Flagstaff AZ
KZJG Longmont CO
KZJL Houston TX
KZKI San Bernardino CA
*KZSD-TV Martin SD
KZTV Corpus Christi TX
*KZXC Anchorage AK
NEW TV New Orleans LA
NEW TV Jonesboro AR
NEW TV Conroe TX
NEW TV Arlington TX
WAAP Burlington NC
WAAY-TV Huntsville AL
WABC-TV New York NY
WABG-TV Greenwood MS
WABI-TV Bangor ME
WABM Birmingham AL
WABU Boston MA
*WABW-TV Pelham GA
WACH Columbia SC
WACI Atlantic City NJ
WACN Raleigh NC
*WACS-TV Dawson GA
WACX Leesburg FL
WADL Mount Clemens MI
WAFB Baton Rouge LA
WAFF Huntsville AL
WAGA-TV Atlanta GA
WAGM-TV Presque Isle ME
WAGT Augusta GA
*WAIQ Montgomery AL
WAKA Selma AL
WAKC-TV Akron OH
WALA-TV Mobile AL
WALB-TV Albany GA
WAND Decatur IL
WANE-TV Fort Wayne IN
WAOM Morehead KY
WAOW-TV Wausau WI
WAPA-TV San Juan PR
WAPT Jackson MS
WAQP Saginaw MI
WASV-TV Asheville NC
*WATC Atlanta GA
WATE-TV Knoxville TN
WATL Atlanta GA
WATM-TV Altoona PA
WAVE Louisville KY
WAVY-TV Portsmouth VA
WAWD Fort Walton Beach FL
WAWS Jacksonville FL
WAXA Anderson SC
WAYQ Daytona Beach FL
WBAK-TV Terre Haute IN
WBAL-TV Baltimore MD
WBAY-TV Green Bay WI
WBBH-TV Fort Myers FL
WBBJ-TV Jackson TN
WBBM-TV Chicago IL
*WBCC Cocoa FL
WBFF Baltimore MD

WBFS-TV Miami FL
*WBGU-TV Bowling Green OH
WBHS-TV Tampa FL
*WBIQ Birmingham AL
WBIR-TV Knoxville TN
WBKB-TV Alpena MI
WBKO Bowling Green KY
WBMG Birmingham AL
WBNA Louisville KY
WBNB-TV Charlotte Amalie VI
WBNG-TV Binghamton NY
WBNS-TV Columbus OH
WBNX-TV Akron OH
WBOC-TV Salisbury MD
WBOY-TV Clarksburg WV
WBPH-TV Bethlehem PA
*WBRA-TV Roanoke VA
WBRC-TV Birmingham AL
WBRE-TV Wilkes-Barre PA
WBRZ Baton Rouge LA
WBSF Melbourne FL
WBSG-TV Brunswick GA
WBSV-TV Venice FL
WBSX Ann Arbor MI
WBTV Charlotte NC
WBTW Florence SC
WBUY Holly Springs MS
WBZ-TV Boston MA
WCAU-TV Philadelphia PA
WCAX-TV Burlington VT
*WCBB Augusta ME
WCBD-TV Charleston SC
WCBI-TV Columbus MS
WCBS-TV New York NY
WCCB Charlotte NC
WCCL New Orleans LA
WCCO-TV Minneapolis MN
WCCU Urbana IL
WCCV-TV Arecibo PR
WCDC Adams MA
WCEE Mount Vernon IL
*WCES-TV Wrens GA
*WCET Cincinnati OH
*WCEU New Smyrna Beach FL
WCFC-TV Chicago IL
WCFE-TV Plattsburgh NY
WCFN Springfield IL
WCFT-TV Tuscaloosa AL
WCGV-TV Milwaukee WI
WCHS-TV Charleston WV
WCIA Champaign IL
*WCIQ Mt Cheaha State Park AL
WCIU Chicago IL
WCIV Charleston SC
WCIX Miami FL
WCJB Gainesville FL
WCLF Clearwater FL
WCLJ Bloomington IN
*WCLP-TV Chatsworth GA
WCMH Columbus OH
*WCML-TV Alpena MI
*WCMU-TV Mount Pleasant MI
*WCMV Cadillac MI
*WCMW Manistee MI
WCNC-TV Charlotte NC
*WCNY-TV Syracuse NY
WCOV-TV Montgomery AL
*WCPB Salisbury MD
WCPO-TV Cincinnati OH
WCPX-TV Orlando FL
WCSC-TV Charleston SC
WCSH-TV Portland ME
WCTD Miami FL
*WCTE Cookeville TN
WCTI New Bern NC
WCTP Charleston SC
WCTV Thomasville GA
WCVB-TV Boston MA
WCVE-TV Richmond VA
*WCVN Covington KY
*WCVW Richmond VA
WCVX Vineyard Haven MA
WCYB-TV Bristol VA
WDAF-TV Kansas City MO
WDAM-TV Laurel MS
WDAU Ozark AL
WDAY-TV Fargo ND
WDAZ-TV Devils Lake ND
WDBB Tuscaloosa AL
WDBD Jackson MS
WDBJ Roanoke VA
WDCA Washington DC
*WDCN Nashville TN
*WDCO-TV Cochran GA
WDEF-TV Chattanooga TN
WDHN Dothan AL
WDHS Iron Mountain MI
WDIO-TV Duluth MN
*WDIQ Dozier AL
WDIV Detroit MI
WDJT-TV Milwaukee WI
WDKA Paducah KY
WDKY-TV Danville KY
WDLI Canton OH
*WDPB Seaford DE
WDRB-TV Louisville KY
WDRG Danville VA
*WDSE-TV Duluth MN
WDSI-TV Chattanooga TN
WDSU New Orleans LA
WDTN Dayton OH
WDTV Weston WV
WDWB Bayamon PR
WDZE Carolina PR
WDZL Miami FL

*WEAO Akron OH
WEAR-TV Pensacola FL
WEAU-TV Eau Claire WI
*WEBA-TV Allendale SC
WECN Naranjito PR
WECT Wilmington NC
*WEDH Hartford CT
*WEDN Norwich CT
*WEDU Tampa FL
*WEDW Bridgeport CT
*WEDY New Haven CT
WEEK-TV Peoria IL
WEFC Roanoke VA
WEHS-TV Aurora IL
WEHT Evansville IN
*WEIQ Mobile AL
*WEIU Charleston IL
WEJC Lexington NC
*WEKW-TV Keene NH
WELF Dalton GA
*WELU Aguadilla PR
WEMT Greeneville TN
*WENH-TV Durham NH
WENY-TV Elmira NY
WESH Daytona Beach FL
*WETA-TV Washington DC
WETG Erie PA
*WETK Burlington VT
WETM-TV Elmira NY
WEUX Chippewa Falls WI
WEVU Naples FL
WEVV Evansville IN
WEWS Cleveland OH
WEYI-TV Saginaw MI
WEYS Key West FL
WFAA-TV Dallas TX
WFAY Fayetteville NC
WFBI Memphis TN
WFDG New Bedford MA
WFFT-TV Fort Wayne IN
WFGC Palm Beach FL
WFGX Fort Walton Beach FL
WFHL Decatur IL
WFIE-TV Evansville IN
WFIL Florence SC
*WFIQ Florence AL
WFLA-TV Tampa FL
WFLD Chicago IL
WFLI-TV Cleveland TN
WFLX West Palm Beach FL
*WFME-TV West Milford NJ
WFMJ-TV Youngstown OH
WFMY-TV Greensboro NC
WFMZ-TV Allentown PA
*WFPT Frederick MD
WFRV-TV Green Bay WI
WFSB Hartford CT
*WFSG Panama City FL
*WFSU-TV Tallahassee FL
WFTE Salem IN
WFTS Tampa FL
WFTV Orlando FL
WFTX Cape Coral FL
WFTY Washington DC
*WFUM Flint MI
WFVT Rock Hill SC
*WFWA Fort Wayne IN
WFXG Augusta GA
WFXI Morehead City NC
WFXL Albany GA
WFXR-TV Roanoke VA
WFXT Boston MA
WFXU Live Oak FL
WFXV Utica NY
*WFYI Indianapolis IN
WGAL Lancaster PA
WGBA Green Bay WI
*WGBC Meridian MS
*WGBH-TV Boston MA
WGBO-TV Joliet IL
*WGBS-TV Philadelphia PA
*WGBX-TV Boston MA
*WGBY-TV Springfield MA
WGCB-TV Red Lion PA
WGEM-TV Quincy IL
WGFL High Springs FL
WGGB-TV Springfield MA
WGGN-TV Sandusky OH
WGGS-TV Greenville SC
WGGT Greensboro NC
WGHP-TV High Point NC
*WGIQ Louisville AL
WGKI Cadillac MI
*WGKU Vanderbilt MI
WGMB Baton Rouge LA
WGME-TV Portland ME
WGN-TV Chicago IL
WGNM Macon GA
WGNO New Orleans LA
WGNT Portsmouth VA
WGNX Atlanta GA
WGOT Merrimack NH
WGOX Inverness FL
WGPR-TV Detroit MI
*WGPT Oakland MD
WGRB Campbellsville KY
WGRZ-TV Buffalo NY
WGSE Myrtle Beach SC
*WGTE-TV Toledo OH
WGTJ Greenville NC
WGTQ Sault Ste. Marie MI
WGTU Traverse City MI
*WGTV Athens GA
WGTW Burlington NJ
*WGVK Kalamazoo MI

*WGVU-TV Grand Rapids MI
WGXA Macon GA
*WHA-TV Madison WI
WHAG-TV Hagerstown MD
*WHAI-TV Bridgeport CT
WHAS-TV Louisville KY
*WHBF-TV Rock Island IL
WHBI Lake Worth FL
WHBQ-TV Memphis TN
WHBR Pensacola FL
WHCT-TV Hartford CT
WHDH-TV Boston MA
WHEC-TV Rochester NY
WHFT Miami FL
WHIO-TV Dayton OH
*WHIQ Huntsville AL
WHIZ-TV Zanesville OH
WHKE Kenosha WI
WHKY-TV Hickory NC
*WHLA-TV La Crosse WI
WHLT Hattiesburg MS
WHMB-TV Indianapolis IN
*WHMC Conway SC
WHME-TV South Bend IN
*WHMM Washington DC
WHNS Asheville NC
WHNT-TV Huntsville AL
WHO-TV Des Moines IA
WHOA-TV Montgomery AL
WHOI Peoria IL
WHP-TV Harrisburg PA
WHRC Norwell MA
*WHRM-TV Wausau WI
*WHRO-TV Hampton-Norfolk VA
WHSE-TV Newark NJ
WHSG Monroe GA
WHSH-TV Marlborough MA
WHSI-TV Smithtown NY
WHSL East St. Louis IL
WHSP-TV Vineland NJ
WHSV-TV Harrisonburg VA
WHSW-TV Baltimore MD
*WHTJ Charlottesville VA
WHTM-TV Harrisburg PA
WHTN Murfreesboro TN
*WHWC-TV Menomonie WI
*WHYY-TV Wilmington DE
WIBW-TV Topeka KS
WICD Champaign IL
WICS Springfield IL
WICU-TV Erie PA
WICZ-TV Binghamton NY
WIDP Guayama PR
WIFR Freeport IL
WIIB Bloomington IN
*WIIQ Demopolis AL
WILF Williamsport PA
*WILL-TV Urbana IL
WILX-TV Onondaga MI
WINK-TV Fort Myers FL
WINM Angola IN
WINT-TV Crossville TN
*WIPB Muncie IN
WIPM-TV Mayaguez PR
*WIPR-TV San Juan PR
WIRB Melbourne FL
WIRS Yauco PR
WIRT Hibbing MN
WIS Columbia SC
WISC-TV Madison WI
WISH-TV Indianapolis IN
WISN-TV Milwaukee WI
*WITF-TV Harrisburg PA
WITI-TV Milwaukee WI
WITN-TV Washington NC
*WITV Charleston SC
WIVB-TV Buffalo NY
WIXT Syracuse NY
WJAC-TV Johnstown PA
WJAL Hagerstown MD
WJAR Providence RI
WJBF Augusta GA
*WJBK-TV Detroit MI
WJCB Norfolk VA
WJCL Savannah GA
*WJCT Jacksonville FL
*WJEB-TV Jacksonville FL
WJET-TV Erie PA
WJFB Lebanon TN
WJFW-TV Rhinelander WI
WJHG-TV Panama City FL
WJHL-TV Johnson City TN
WJJA Racine WI
WJKS Jacksonville FL
WJKA Wilmington NC
WJLA-TV Washington DC
WJMN-TV Escanaba MI
WJMY Marquette MI
WJNW Janesville WI
*WJPM-TV Florence SC
WJPR Lynchburg VA
WJRT-TV Flint MI
*WJSP-TV Columbus GA
WJSU-TV Anniston AL
WJTC Pensacola FL
WJTV Jackson MS
WJUE Battle Creek MI
WJW-TV Cleveland OH
WJWJ-TV Beaufort SC
WJWN-TV San Sebastian PR
WJXT Jacksonville FL
WJYS Hammond IN
WJZ-TV Baltimore MD
WJZY Belmont NC
WKAQ-TV San Juan PR

Broadcasting & Cable Yearbook 1994
C-91

U.S. Television Stations by Call Letters

*WKAR-TV East Lansing MI
*WKAS Ashland KY
WKAY Kannapolis NC
WKBD Detroit MI
WKBN-TV Youngstown OH
WKBS-TV Altoona PA
WKBT La Crosse WI
WKBW-TV Buffalo NY
WKCF Clermont FL
WKCH-TV Knoxville TN
WKEF Dayton OH
WKFT Fayetteville NC
*WKGB-TV Bowling Green KY
*WKHA Hazard KY
WKJG-TV Fort Wayne IN
*WKLE Lexington KY
WKMA Madisonville KY
WKMJ Louisville KY
WKMR Morehead KY
WKMU Murray KY
WKNO-TV Memphis TN
WKNT Bowling Green KY
WKOH Owensboro KY
WKOI Richmond IN
WKON Owenton KY
*WKOP-TV Knoxville TN
WKOW-TV Madison WI
*WKPC-TV Louisville KY
WKPD Paducah KY
WKPI Pikeville KY
WKPT-TV Kingsport TN
WKPV Ponce PR
WKRC-TV Cincinnati OH
WKRG-TV Mobile AL
WKRN-TV Nashville TN
WKRP-TV Charleston WV
WKSO-TV Somerset KY
WKTV Utica NY
WKXT-TV Knoxville TN
WKYC-TV Cleveland OH
WKYT-TV Lexington KY
*WKYU-TV Bowling Green KY
*WKZT-TV Elizabethtown KY
WKZX Cookeville TN
*WLAE-TV New Orleans LA
WLAJ Lansing MI
WLAX La Crosse WI
WLBT Jackson MS
*WLBZ-TV Bangor ME
WLCN Madisonville KY
*WLED-TV Littleton NH
*WLEF-TV Park Falls WI
WLEX-TV Lexington KY
WLFB Bluefield WV
WLFG Grundy VA
WLFI-TV Lafayette IN
WLFL Raleigh NC
WLIG Riverhead NY
WLII Caguas PR
WLIO Lima OH
*WLIW Garden City NY
WLJC-TV Beattyville KY
*WLJT-TV Lexington TN
WLKY-TV Louisville KY
WLLA Kalamazoo MI
WLMT Memphis TN
WLNE New Bedford MA
WLNS-TV Lansing MI
WLOS Asheville NC
WLOV-TV West Point MS
WLOX-TV Biloxi MS
*WLPB-TV Baton Rouge LA
*WLRN-TV Miami FL
WLS-TV Chicago IL
WLTV Miami FL
WLTX Columbia SC
WLTZ Columbus GA
WLUC-TV Marquette MI
WLUK-TV Green Bay WI
WLVI-TV Cambridge MA
*WLVT-TV Allentown PA
WLWT Cincinnati OH
WLXI-TV Greensboro NC
WLYH-TV Lancaster PA
WLYJ Clarksburg WV
*WMAB-TV Mississippi State MS
*WMAE-TV Booneville MS
*WMAH-TV Bude MS
*WMAO-TV Greenwood MS
WMAQ-TV Chicago IL
*WMAR-TV Baltimore MD
*WMAU-TV Bude MS
*WMAV-TV Oxford MS
*WMAW-TV Meridian MS
WMAZ-TV Macon GA
WMBB Panama City FL
WMBC-TV Newton NJ
WMBD-TV Peoria IL
WMC-TV Memphis TN
WMCC Marion IN
WMCF-TV Montgomery AL
WMDT Salisbury MD
*WMEA-TV Biddeford ME

*WMEB-TV Orono ME
*WMEC Macomb IL
*WMED-TV Calais ME
WMEI Arecibo PR
*WMEM-TV Presque Isle ME
WMFD-TV Mansfield OH
*WMFE-TV Orlando FL
WMFP Lawrence MA
WMGC-TV Binghamton NY
WMGM-TV Wildwood NJ
WMGT Macon GA
*WMHT Schenectady NY
WMMF-TV Fond du Lac WI
*WMPB Baltimore MD
*WMPN-TV Jackson MS
WMPT Annapolis MD
WMPV-TV Mobile AL
WMSN-TV Madison WI
*WMSY-TV Marion VA
*WMTJ-TV Fajardo PR
WMTU Jackson TN
WMTV Madison WI
*WMTW-TV Poland Spring ME
WMUR-TV Manchester NH
*WMVS Milwaukee WI
*WMVT Milwaukee WI
WNAB Nashville TN
WNAC-TV Providence RI
WNAL-TV Gadsden AL
WNBC New York NY
WNCT-TV Greenville NC
WNDS Derry NH
WNDU-TV South Bend IN
*WNED-TV Buffalo NY
*WNEG-TV Toccoa GA
*WNEH Greenwood SC
WNEM-TV Bay City MI
*WNEO Alliance OH
*WNEP-TV Scranton PA
*WNEQ-TV Buffalo NY
*WNET Newark NJ
WNFT Jacksonville FL
WNGM-TV Athens GA
WNGS Springfield NY
WNHT Concord NH
WNIN Evansville IN
*WNIT-TV South Bend IN
*WNJB New Brunswick NJ
*WNJM Montclair NJ
*WNJS Camden NJ
*WNJT Trenton NJ
WNJU Linden NJ
WNJX-TV Mayaguez PR
*WNMU-TV Marquette MI
WNNE-TV Hartford VT
*WNOL-TV New Orleans LA
*WNPB-TV Morgantown WV
*WNPE-TV Watertown NY
*WNPI-TV Norwood NY
WNPL-TV Naples FL
WNRW Winston-Salem NC
*WNSC-TV Rock Hill SC
*WNTV Greenville SC
WNTZ Natchez MS
WNUV-TV Baltimore MD
*WNVC Fairfax VA
*WNVT Goldvein VA
WNWO-TV Toledo OH
*WNYB-TV Buffalo NY
*WNYC-TV New York NY
*WNYE-TV New York NY
WNYT Albany NY
WNYW New York NY
WOAC Canton OH
WOAY-TV Oak Hill WV
WOCD Amsterdam NY
WOFL Orlando FL
WOGX Ocala FL
WOI-TV Ames IA
WOIO Shaker Heights OH
WOKR Rochester NY
WOLE-TV Aguadilla PR
WOLF-TV Scranton PA
WOLO-TV Columbia SC
WOOD-TV Grand Rapids MI
WORA-TV Mayaguez PR
WOST-TV Block Island RI
*WOSU-TV Columbus OH
WOTV Battle Creek MI
*WOUB-TV Athens OH
*WOUC-TV Cambridge OH
WOWK-TV Huntington WV
WOWL-TV Florence AL
WOWT Omaha NE
WPAN Fort Walton Beach FL
*WPBA Atlanta GA
WPBF Tequesta FL
WPBN-TV Traverse City MI
*WPBO-TV Portsmouth OH
*WPBT Miami FL
*WPBY-TV Huntington WV
WPCB-TV Greensburg PA
WPDE-TV Florence SC

WPEC West Palm Beach FL
*WPGA-TV Perry GA
WPGD Hendersonville TN
WPGH-TV Pittsburgh PA
WPGX Panama City FL
WPHL-TV Philadelphia PA
WPIX New York NY
WPLG Miami FL
WPMC Jellico TN
WPMI Mobile AL
WPMT York PA
*WPNE Green Bay WI
*WPPB-TV Boca Raton FL
WPRI-TV Providence RI
WPRV-TV Fajardo PR
WPSD-TV Paducah KY
*WPSX-TV Clearfield PA
WPTA Fort Wayne IN
*WPTD Dayton OH
WPTJ Johnstown PA
*WPTO Oxford OH
WPTT-TV Pittsburgh PA
WPTV West Palm Beach FL
WPTY-TV Memphis TN
WPTZ North Pole NY
WPVI-TV Philadelphia PA
WPWR-TV Gary IN
WPXI Pittsburgh PA
WPXT Portland ME
WQAD-TV Moline IL
*WQEC Quincy IL
*WQED Pittsburgh PA
*WQEX Pittsburgh PA
WQHA Aguada PR
*WQHS-TV Cleveland OH
*WQLN Erie PA
WQOW-TV Eau Claire WI
*WQPT-TV Moline IL
WQRF-TV Rockford IL
*WQTO Ponce PR
WRAL-TV Raleigh NC
WRBL Columbus GA
WRBW Orlando FL
WRC-TV Washington DC
WRCB-TV Chattanooga TN
WRDC Durham NC
WRDW-TV Augusta GA
WREG-TV Memphis TN
WRET-TV Spartanburg SC
WREX-TV Rockford IL
WRGB Schenectady NY
WRGT-TV Dayton OH
WRIC-TV Petersburg VA
*WRJA-TV Sumter SC
WRJM-TV Troy AL
WRKJ Dothan AL
WRLH-TV Richmond VA
WRLK-TV Columbia SC
WRMY Rocky Mount NC
WROC-TV Rochester NY
WRSP-TV Springfield IL
WRTV Indianapolis IN
WRUA Fajardo PR
WRWR-TV San Juan PR
WRXY-TV Tice FL
WSAV-TV Savannah GA
WSAW-TV Wausau WI
WSAZ-TV Huntington WV
WSB-TV Atlanta GA
*WSBE-TV Providence RI
WSBK-TV Boston MA
*WSBN-TV Norton VA
WSBT-TV South Bend IN
WSCO Suring WI
WSCV Fort Lauderdale FL
*WSEC Jacksonville IL
WSEE-TV Erie PA
WSET-TV Lynchburg VA
WSFA Montgomery AL
WSFJ Newark OH
*WSFP-TV Fort Myers FL
WSIL-TV Harrisburg IL
*WSIU-TV Carbondale IL
*WSJK-TV Sneedville TN
WSJN-TV San Juan PR
WSJU San Juan PR
WSJV Elkhart IN
*WSKG-TV Binghamton NY
WSLS-TV Roanoke VA
WSMH Flint MI
WSMV Nashville TN
WSNR-TV Syracuse NY
WSNS Chicago IL
WSOC-TV Charlotte NC
WSPA-TV Spartanburg SC
*WSRE Pensacola FL
WSST-TV Cordele GA
WSTE Ponce PR
WSTM-TV Syracuse NY
WSTR-TV Cincinnati OH
WSUR-TV Ponce PR
WSVI Christiansted VI
WSVN Miami FL

WSWB-TV Scranton PA
*WSWP-TV Grandview WV
WSWS-TV Opelika AL
WSYM-TV Lansing MI
WSYT Syracuse NY
WSYX Columbus OH
WTAE-TV Pittsburgh PA
*WTAJ-TV Altoona PA
WTAP-TV Parkersburg WV
WTAT-TV Charleston SC
WTBG-TV Bradenton FL
*WTBS Atlanta GA
*WTBU Indianapolis IN
WTBY Poughkeepsie NY
*WTCE Fort Pierce FL
*WTCI Chattanooga TN
WTCT Marion IL
WTEN Albany NY
WTGI-TV Wilmington DE
WTGL-TV Cocoa FL
WTGS Hardeeville SC
WTHI-TV Terre Haute IN
WTHR Indianapolis IN
WTIC-TV Hartford CT
WTIN Ponce PR
*WTIU Bloomington IN
WTJA Jamestown NY
WTJC Springfield IN
WTJP Gadsden AL
WTJR Quincy IL
*WTJX-TV Charlotte Amalie VI
WTKK Manassas VA
WTKR-TV Norfolk VA
WTLH Bainbridge GA
WTLJ Muskegon MI
WTLK-TV Marietta GA
WTLV Jacksonville FL
WTLW Lima OH
WTMJ-TV Milwaukee WI
WTMV Lakeland FL
WTMW Arlington VA
WTNH-TV New Haven CT
WTOC-TV Savannah GA
WTOG St. Petersburg FL
WTOK-TV Meridian MS
WTOL-TV Toledo OH
WTOM-TV Cheboygan MI
WTOV-TV Steubenville OH
WTRA Mayaguez PR
WTRF-TV Wheeling WV
WTSF Ashland KY
WTSP St. Petersburg FL
WTTA St. Petersburg FL
WTTE Columbus OH
WTTG Washington DC
WTTK Kokomo IN
WTTO Birmingham AL
WTTV Bloomington IN
*WTTW Chicago IL
WTVA Tupelo MS
WTVC Chattanooga TN
WTVD Durham NC
WTVE Reading PA
WTVF Nashville TN
WTVG Toledo OH
WTVH Syracuse NY
*WTVI Charlotte NC
WTVJ Miami FL
WTVM Columbus GA
WTVO Rockford IL
*WTVP Peoria IL
WTVQ-TV Lexington KY
WTVR-TV Richmond VA
*WTVS Detroit MI
WTVT Tampa FL
WTVU New Haven CT
WTVW Evansville IN
WTVX Fort Pierce FL
WTVY Dothan AL
WTVZ Norfolk VA
WTWC Tallahassee FL
WTWO Terre Haute IN
WTWS New London CT
WTXF Philadelphia PA
WTXL-TV Tallahassee FL
WTXX Waterbury CT
WTZA Kingston NY
WTZH Meridian MS
WUAB Lorain OH
WUBI Baxley GA
*WUCM-TV University Center MI
*WUCX-TV Bad Axe MI
*WUFT Gainesville FL
WUHF Rochester NY
*WUJA Caguas PR
*WUNC-TV Chapel Hill NC
*WUND-TV Columbia NC
*WUNE-TV Linville NC
*WUNF-TV Asheville NC
*WUNG-TV Concord NC
WUNI Needham MA
*WUNJ-TV Wilmington NC
*WUNK-TV Greenville NC

*WUNL-TV Winston-Salem NC
*WUNM-TV Jacksonville NC
*WUNP-TV Roanoke Rapids NC
WUPW Toledo OH
WUSA Washington DC
*WUSF-TV Tampa FL
*WUSI-TV Olney IL
WUTR Utica NY
WUTV Buffalo NY
WUXA Portsmouth OH
WVAH-TV Charleston WV
*WVAN-TV Savannah GA
WVCY-TV Milwaukee WI
WVEC-TV Hampton VA
WVEO Aguadilla PR
*WVER Rutland VT
WVEU Atlanta GA
WVGA Valdosta GA
WVGV-TV Lewisburg WV
*WVIA-TV Scranton PA
WVII-TV Bangor ME
WVIR-TV Charlottesville VA
WVIT New Britain CT
*WVIZ-TV Cleveland OH
WVLA Baton Rouge LA
WVNY Burlington VT
WVOZ-TV Ponce PR
*WVPT Staunton VA
*WVTA Windsor VT
*WVTB St. Johnsbury VT
WVTM-TV Birmingham AL
WVTV Milwaukee WI
WVUE New Orleans LA
WVUT Vincennes IN
WVVA Bluefield WV
WVXF Charlotte Amalie VI
WWAC-TV Atlantic City NJ
*WWAT Chillicothe OH
WWAY Wilmington NC
WWBT Richmond VA
WWCP-TV Johnstown PA
WWFD Key West FL
*WWL-TV New Orleans LA
WWLA Lewiston ME
WWLF-TV Hazleton PA
WWLP Springfield MA
WWMT Kalamazoo MI
*WWNY-TV Carthage NY
WWOR-TV Secaucus NJ
*WWPB Hagerstown MD
WWRS-TV Mayville WI
WWSB Sarasota FL
WWTI Watertown NY
WWTO-TV LaSalle IL
WWTV Cadillac MI
WWUP-TV Sault Ste. Marie MI
WXAE Toledo OH
*WXEL-TV West Palm Beach FL
*WXGA-TV Waycross GA
WXGZ-TV Appleton WI
WXIA-TV Atlanta GA
WXII Winston-Salem NC
WXIN Indianapolis IN
WXIX-TV Newport KY
WXMI Grand Rapids MI
WXMT Nashville TN
WXON Detroit MI
WXOW-TV La Crosse WI
WXTV Paterson NJ
WXTX Columbus GA
WXVT Greenville MS
WXXA-TV Albany NY
*WXXI-TV Rochester NY
WXXV-TV Gulfport MS
WXYZ-TV Detroit MI
*WYBE Philadelphia PA
*WYCC Chicago IL
WYDC Corning NY
*WYDN Worcester MA
WYDO Greenville NC
WYDP Orange Park FL
WYED Goldsboro NC
*WYES-TV New Orleans LA
WYFF Greenville SC
WYHS-TV Hollywood FL
*WYIN Gary IN
WYLE Florence AL
WYMT-TV Hazard KY
WYOU Scranton PA
WYTV Youngstown OH
WYVN Martinsburg WV
WYZZ-TV Bloomington IL
WZDX Huntsville AL
WZTV Nashville TN
WZWY Orlando FL
WZXK Ashland VA
WZZM-TV Grand Rapids MI

Canadian Television Stations by Call Letters

CBAFT Moncton NB
CBCP-TV-1 Shaunavon SK
CBCP-TV-2 Cypress Hills SK
CBCP-TV-3 Ponteix SK
CBCT Charlottetown PE
*CBEFT Windsor ON
CBET Windsor ON
CBFST-2 Temiscaning PQ
CBFT Montreal PQ
CBFT-2 Mont-Laurier PQ
CBGAT Matane PQ
CBHFT Halifax NS
CBHFT-1 Yarmouth NS
CBHFT-2 Mulgrave NS
CBHFT-3 Sydney NS
CBHFT-4 Cheticamp NS
CBHT Halifax NS
CBHT-3 Yarmouth NS
CBHT-4 Sheet Harbour NS
CBHT-11 Mulgrave NS
CBIMT Iles-de-la-Madeleine PQ
CBIT Sydney NS
CBIT-2 Cheticamp NS
CBJET Chicoutimi PQ
CBKFT Regina SK
CBKFT-3 Debden SK
CBKFT-4 St. Brieux SK
CBKFT-5 Zenon Park SK
CBKFT-6 Gravelbourg SK
CBKFT-9 Bellegarde SK
CBKST Saskatoon SK
CBKST-1 Stranraer SK
CBKT Regina SK
CBKT-2 Willow Bunch SK
CBLAT Geraldton ON
CBLAT-1 Manitouwadge ON
CBLAT-3 Wawa ON
CBLAT-4 Marathon ON
CBLFT Toronto ON
CBLFT-1 Sturgeon Falls ON
CBLFT-2 Sudbury ON
CBLFT-3 Timmins ON
CBLFT-4 Kapuskasing ON
CBLFT-5 Hearst ON
CBLFT-6 Elliot Lake ON
CBLT Toronto ON
CBMT Montreal PQ
CBNAT Grand Falls NF
CBNAT-1 Baie Verte NF
CBNAT-4 St. Anthony NF
CBNAT-9 Mount St. Margaret NF
*CBNLT Labrador City NF
CBNT St. John's NF
CBNT-1 Port Rexton NF
CBNT-2 Placentia NF
CBNT-3 Marystown NF
CBOFT Ottawa ON
CBOT Ottawa ON

CBRT Calgary AB
CBST Sept-Iles PQ
CBUBT-1 Canal Flats BC
CBUBT-7 Cranbrook BC
CBUFT Vancouver BC
CBUFT-2 Kamloops BC
CBUFT-3 Terrace BC
CBUT Vancouver BC
CBVD-TV Malartic PQ
CBVT Quebec City PQ
CBVT-2 La Tuque PQ
CBWAT Kenora ON
CBWBT Flin Flon MB
CBWCT Fort Frances ON
CBWDT Dryden ON
CBWFT Winnipeg MB
CBWFT-4 Ste-Rose-du-Lac MB
CBWFT-10 Brandon MB
CBWGT Fisher Branch MB
CBWST Baldy Mountain MB
CBWT Winnipeg MB
CBWT-2 Lac du Bonnet MB
CBWYT Mafeking MB
CBXAT Grande Prairie AB
CBXAT-2 High Prairie AB
CBXAT-3 Manning AB
CBXFT Edmonton AB
CBXFT-1 Bonnyville AB
CBXFT-6 Fort McMurray AB
CBXFT-8 Grande Prairie AB
CBXT Edmonton AB
CBYT Corner Brook NF
CBYT-1 Stephenville NF
CBYT-3 Bonne Bay NF
CFAP-TV Quebec City PQ
CFCF-TV Montreal PQ
CFCL-TV Timmins ON
CFCL-TV-2 Kearns ON
CFCM-TV Quebec City PQ
CFCN-TV Calgary AB
CFCN-TV-1 Drumheller AB
CFCN-TV-5 Lethbridge AB
CFCN-TV-8 Medicine Hat AB
CFER-TV Rimouski PQ
CFER-TV-2 Gaspe-Nord PQ
CFGS-TV Hull PQ
CFJC-TV Kamloops BC
CFJP-TV Montreal PQ
CFKM-TV Trois-Rivieres PQ
CFKS-TV Sherbrooke PQ
CFLA-TV Goose Bay-Labrador NF
CFMT-TV Toronto ON
CFPL-TV London ON
CFQC-TV Saskatoon SK
CFQC-TV-1 Stranraer SK
CFQC-TV-2 North Battleford SK
CFRE-TV Regina SK
CFRN-TV Edmonton AB

CFRN-TV-1 Grande Prairie AB
CFRN-TV-2 Peace River AB
CFRN-TV-3 Whitecourt AB
CFRN-TV-4 Ashmont AB
CFRN-TV-5 Lac La Biche AB
CFRN-TV-6 Red Deer AB
CFRN-TV-7 Lougheed AB
CFRN-TV-8 Grouard Mission-High Prairie AB
CFRN-TV-9 Slave Lake AB
CFRS-TV Jonquiere PQ
CFSK-TV Saskatoon SK
CFTK-TV Terrace BC
CFTM-TV Montreal PQ
CFTO-TV Toronto ON
*CFTU-TV Montreal PQ
CFVS-TV Val d'Or PQ
CFVS-TV-1 Rouyn PQ
CFWH-TV White Horse YT
*CFYK-TV Yellowknife NT
*CHAK-TV Inuvik NT
CHAN-TV Vancouver BC
CHAN-TV-4 Courtenay BC
CHAT-TV Medicine Hat AB
CHAT-TV-1 Pivot AB
CHAU-TV Carleton PQ
CHBC-TV Kelowna BC
CHBX-TV Sault Ste. Marie ON
CHCH-TV Hamilton ON
CHCR-TV Campbellton NB
CHEK-TV Victoria BC
CHEK-TV-5 Campbell River BC
CHEM-TV Trois-Rivieres PQ
CHEX-TV Peterborough ON
CHFD-TV Thunder Bay ON
CHKL-TV Kelowna BC
CHKL-TV-1 Penticton BC
CHKM-TV Kamloops BC
CHLT-TV Sherbrooke PQ
CHMI-TV Portage la Prairie MB
CHMT-TV Moncton NB
CHNB-TV North Bay ON
CHOT-TV Hull PQ
CHRO-TV Pembroke ON
CHSJ-TV Saint John NB
CHSJ-TV-1 Bon Accord NB
CHSS-TV Wynyard SK
CHWI-TV Wheatley ON
*CICA-TV Toronto ON
CICC-TV Yorkton SK
CICC-TV-1 Wynyard SK
CICI-TV Sudbury ON
CICI-TV-1 Elliot Lake ON
*CICO-TV-9 Thunder Bay ON
*CICO-TV-18 London ON
*CICO-TV-20 Sault Ste. Marie ON
*CICO-TV-24 Ottawa ON

*CICO-TV-28 Kitchener ON
*CICO-TV-32 Windsor ON
*CICO-TV-59 Chatham ON
CICT-TV Calgary AB
CIEW-TV Warmley SK
CIFG-TV Prince George BC
CIHF-TV Halifax NS
CIII-TV Paris ON
CIII-TV-1 Windsor ON
CIII-TV-2 Bancroft ON
CIII-TV-4 Owen Sound ON
CIII-TV-6 Ottawa ON
CIII-TV-7 Midland ON
CIII-TV-22 Stevenson ON
CIII-TV-27 Peterborough ON
CIII-TV-29 Oil Springs ON
CIII-TV-41 Toronto ON
CIMT-TV Riviere-du-Loup PQ
CIPA-TV Prince Albert SK
CISA-TV-7 Lethbridge AB
CISR-TV Santa Rosa BC
CITL-TV Lloydminster AB
CITM-TV 100 Mile House BC
CITO-TV Timmins ON
CITO-TV-2 Kearns ON
CITV-TV Edmonton AB
CITY-TV Toronto ON
*CIVA-TV Rouyn PQ
*CIVB-TV Rimouski PQ
*CIVC-TV Trois-Rivieres PQ
*CIVF-TV Baie-Trinite PQ
*CIVG-TV Sept-Iles PQ
*CIVM-TV Montreal PQ
*CIVO-TV Hull PQ
*CIVP-TV Chapeau PQ
*CIVQ-TV Quebec City PQ
*CIVS-TV Sherbrooke PQ
*CIVV-TV Chicoutimi PQ
*CJAL-TV Edmonton AB
CJAP-TV Argentia NF
CJBN-TV Kenora ON
CJBRT Rimouski PQ
CJCB-TV Sydney NS
CJCB-TV-1 Inverness NS
CJCB-TV-2 Antigonish NS
CJCH-TV Halifax NS
CJCH-TV-1 Canning NS
CJCH-TV-6 Caledonia NS
CJCN-TV Grand Falls NF
CJDC-TV Dawson Creek BC
CJFB-TV Swift Current SK
CJIC-TV Sault Ste. Marie ON
CJOH-TV Ottawa ON
CJOH-TV-6 Deseronto ON
CJOH-TV-8 Cornwall ON
CJON-TV St. John's NF
CJOX-TV-1 Grand Bank NF
CJPM-TV Chicoutimi PQ

CJSV-TV Stephenville NF
CJWB-TV Bonavista NF
CJWN-TV Corner Brook NF
CKAM-TV Upsalquitch Lake NB
CKBI-TV Prince Albert SK
CKBI-TV-3 Greenwater Lake SK
CKBI-TV-4 Nipawin SK
CKBQ-TV Melfort SK
CKCD-TV Campbellton NB
CKCK-TV Regina SK
CKCK-TV-1 Colgate SK
CKCK-TV-2 Willow Bunch SK
CKCO-TV Kitchener ON
CKCO-TV-2 Wiarton ON
CKCO-TV-3 Sarnia ON
CKCO-TV-4 The Muskokas ON
CKCW-TV Moncton NB
CKCW-TV-1 Charlottetown PE
CKCW-TV-2 St. Edward PE
CKKM-TV Oliver-Osoyoos BC
CKLT-TV Saint John NB
CKMC-TV Swift Current SK
CKMC-TV-1 Golden Prairie SK
CKMI-TV Quebec City PQ
CKMJ-TV Marquis SK
CKNC-TV Sudbury ON
CKNC-TV-1 Elliot Lake ON
CKND-TV Winnipeg MB
CKND-TV-2 Minnedosa MB
CKNX-TV Wingham ON
CKNY-TV North Bay ON
CKOS-TV Yorkton SK
CKPG-TV Prince George BC
CKPR-TV Thunder Bay ON
CKRD-TV Red Deer AB
CKRD-TV-1 Coronation AB
CKRN-TV Rouyn PQ
CKRN-TV-3 Bearn-Fabre PQ
CKRT-TV Riviere-du-Loup PQ
CKSA-TV Lloydminster AB
CKSH-TV Sherbrooke PQ
CKTM-TV Trois-Rivieres PQ
CKTN-TV Trail BC
CKVR-TV Barrie ON
CKVU-TV Vancouver BC
CKWS-TV Kingston ON
CKX-TV Brandon MB
CKX-TV-1 Foxwarren MB
CKY-TV Winnipeg MB
CKYB-TV Brandon MB

Low Power Television Stations

Alabama

BIRMINGHAM. W34BI, Whitehead Comm., Eddie L. Whitehead, pres, 12144 Classic Dr., Coral Springs, FL 33071.

BIRMINGHAM. W49AY, Glen Iris Baptist School, Jack Legrand, gen mgr, 1137 10th Pl. S., Birmingham, AL 35205.

FLORENCE. W03AW, Benny Carle Broadcasting Inc., Benny Carle, pres, Box 1316, Florence, AL 35631-1316.

FLORENCE. W05BB, Benny Carle Broadcasting Inc., Benny Carle, pres, Box 1316, Florence, AL 35631-1316.

GADSDEN. W15AP, Great American TV & Radio Co., 511 W. Adams St., Phoenix, AZ 85003.

GREENSBORO/MARION. W03BF, Dennis Adams, gen mgr, Box 154, Greensboro, AL 36744.

JASPER. W23AK, WMTY Inc., William Nichols, pres, Rt. 6 Box 156, Hamilton, AL 35570.

JASPER. W55BJ, Video Image Productions Inc., Lanny R. Capps, mgr, 1501 Gamble Ave., Jasper, AL 35501-4840.

MOBILE. W52BF, Penny C. Wilmoth, gen mgr, 1563 Laura St., Clearwater, FL 34615.

MOBILE. W69AU, John Franklin Ministries, John Franklin, pres, 3950 Hwy. 98 W., Navarre, FL 32569.

MONTGOMERY. W39AY, Sunbelt Media Group Inc., Bill Kitchen, pres, 3800 Arapahoe Ave., Boulder, CO 80303.

RUSSELLVILLE. W59CF, Unity Broadcasting Inc., Lealon Owens, pres, Box 111, Booneville, MS 38829.

SYLACAUGA. W04CB, Birmingham Television Corp.

Alaska

AKHIOK. K09UD, State of Alaska Div. of Telecommunications, John Morrone, deputy dir, 5900 E. Tudor Rd., Anchorage, AK 99507-1296.

AKIAK. K10MV, State of Alaska Div. of Telecommunications, John Morrone, deputy dir, 5900 E. Tudor Rd., Anchorage, AK 99507-1296.

AKUTAN. K09RH, State of Alaska Div. of Telecommunications, John Morrone, deputy dir, 5900 E. Tudor Rd., Anchorage, AK 99507-1296.

ALAKANUK. K08KD, State of Alaska Div. of Telecommunications, John Morrone, deputy dir, 5900 E. Tudor Rd., Anchorage, AK 99507-1296.

ALEKNAGIK. K13RP, State of Alaska Div. of Telecommunications, John Morrone, deputy dir, 5900 E. Tudor Rd., Anchorage, AK 99507-1296.

ALLAKAKET. K09QL, State of Alaska Div. of Telecommunications, John Morrone, deputy dir, 5900 E. Tudor Rd., Anchorage, AK 99507-1296.

AMBLER. K11QI, State of Alaska Div. of Telecommunications, John Morrone, deputy dir, 5900 E. Tudor Rd., Anchorage, AK 99507-1296.

ANAKTUVUK PASS. K09RS, State of Alaska Div. of Telecommunications, John Morrone, deputy dir, 5900 E. Tudor Rd., Anchorage, AK 99507-1296.

ANCHOR POINT. K51AF, State of Alaska Div. of Telecommunications, John Morrone, deputy dir, 5900 E. Tudor Rd., Anchorage, AK 99507-1296.

ANCHOR POINT/WRANGELL. K21AF, State of Alaska Div. of Telecommunications, John Morrone, deputy dir, 5900 E. Tudor Rd., Anchorage, AK 99507-1296.

ANCHORAGE. K14AP, N & K. L.P. of Alaska Inc., Ag Newmyer, pres, 12000 Biscayne Blvd., #600, Miami, FL 33181.

ANCHORAGE. K20AG, Alaska Broadcast Television Inc., Dr. Jeremy Prevo, pres, 6401 E. North Lights, Anchorage, AK 99504.

ANCHORAGE. K22AG, Green TV Corp., Box 255, Evergreen, CO 80439.

ANGOON. K09QF, State of Alaska Div. of Telecommunications, John Morrone, deputy dir, 5900 E. Tudor Rd., Anchorage, AK 99507-1296.

ANIAK. K02KY, State of Alaska Div. of Telecommunications, John Morrone, deputy dir, 5900 E. Tudor Rd., Anchorage, AK 99507-1296.

ANVIK. K07RE, State of Alaska Div. of Telecommunications, John Morrone, deputy dir, 5900 E. Tudor Rd., Anchorage, AK 99507-1296.

ARCTIC VILLAGE. K09RV, State of Alaska Div. of Telecommunications, John Morrone, deputy dir, 5900 E. Tudor Rd., Anchorage, AK 99507-1296.

ATKA. K09RX, State of Alaska Div. of Telecommunications, John Morrone, deputy dir, 5900 E. Tudor Rd., Anchorage, AK 99507-1296.

ATKASUK. K04NH, State of Alaska Div. of Telecommunications, John Morrone, deputy dir, 5900 E. Tudor Rd., Anchorage, AK 99507-1296.

ATMAUTLUAK. K12NP, State of Alaska Div. of Telecommunications, John Morrone, deputy dir, 5900 E. Tudor Rd., Anchorage, AK 99507-1296.

BARROW. K04KS, State of Alaska Div. of Telecommunications, John Morrone, deputy dir, 5900 E. Tudor Rd., Anchorage, AK 99507-1296.

BEAVER. K09QQ, State of Alaska Div. of Telecommunications, John Morrone, deputy dir, 5900 E. Tudor Rd., Anchorage, AK 99507-1296.

BETHEL. K21AO, State of Alaska Div. of Telecommunications, John Morrone, deputy dir, 5900 E. Tudor Rd., Anchorage, AK 99507-1296.

BETTLES. K09TE, State of Alaska Div. of Telecommunications, John Morrone, deputy dir, 5900 E. Tudor Rd., Anchorage, AK 99507-1296.

BUCKLAND. K09RI, State of Alaska Div. of Telecommunications, John Morrone, deputy dir, 5900 E. Tudor Rd., Anchorage, AK 99507-1296.

CANTWELL. K09SI, State of Alaska Div. of Telecommunications, John Morrone, deputy dir, 5900 E. Tudor Rd., Anchorage, AK 99507-1296.

CAPE POLE. K13SD, State of Alaska Div. of Telecommunications, John Morrone, deputy dir, 5900 E. Tudor Rd., Anchorage, AK 99507-1296.

CHALKYITSIK. K09QG, State of Alaska Div. of Telecommunications, John Morrone, deputy dir, 5900 E. Tudor Rd., Anchorage, AK 99507-1296.

CHAUTHBALUK. K06LG, State of Alaska Div. of Telecommunications, John Morrone, deputy dir, 5900 E. Tudor Rd., Anchorage, AK 99507-1296.

CHECKALOON. K10MT, State of Alaska Div. of Telecommunications, John Morrone, deputy dir, 5900 E. Tudor Rd., Anchorage, AK 99507-1296.

CHEFORNAK. K02LO, State of Alaska Div. of Telecommunications, John Morrone, deputy dir, 5900 E. Tudor Rd., Anchorage, AK 99507-1296.

CHENEGA. K13VV, State of Alaska Div. of Telecommunications, John Morrone, deputy dir, 5900 E. Tudor Rd., Anchorage, AK 99507-1296.

CHEVAK. K02KX, State of Alaska Div. of Telecommunications, John Morrone, deputy dir, 5900 E. Tudor Rd., Anchorage, AK 99507-1296.

CHIGNIK. K07RY, State of Alaska Div. of Telecommunications, John Morrone, deputy dir, 5900 E. Tudor Rd., Anchorage, AK 99507-1296.

CHIGNIK LAGOON. K09SO, State of Alaska Div. of Telecommunications, John Morrone, deputy dir, 5900 E. Tudor Rd., Anchorage, AK 99507-1296.

CHIGNIK LAKE. K02MR, State of Alaska Div. of Telecommunications, John Morrone, deputy dir, 5900 E. Tudor Rd., Anchorage, AK 99507-1296.

CHIGNIK LAKE. K13RQ, Chignik Lake Village Council, Lola A. Lind, sec, Box 24, Chignik Lake, AK 99502.

CHITINA. K13SB, State of Alaska Div. of Telecommunications, John Morrone, deputy dir, 5900 E. Tudor Rd., Anchorage, AK 99507-1296.

CIRCLE. K13SI, State of Alaska Div. of Telecommunications, John Morrone, deputy dir, 5900 E. Tudor Rd., Anchorage, AK 99507-1296.

CIRCLE HOT SPRINGS. K03GO, State of Alaska Div. of Telecommunications, John Morrone, deputy dir, 5900 E. Tudor Rd., Anchorage, AK 99507-1296.

CIRCLE HOT SPRINGS. K06LP, State of Alaska Div. of Telecommunications, John Morrone, deputy dir, 5900 E. Tudor Rd., Anchorage, AK 99507-1296.

CIRCLE HOT SPRINGS. K07SM, State of Alaska Div. of Telecommunications, John Morrone, deputy dir, 5900 E. Tudor Rd., Anchorage, AK 99507-1296.

CLARKS POINT. K12NL, State of Alaska Div. of Telecommunications, John Morrone, deputy dir, 5900 E. Tudor Rd., Anchorage, AK 99507-1296.

COFFMAN COVE. K09TV, State of Alaska Div. of Telecommunications, John Morrone, deputy dir, 5900 E. Tudor Rd., Anchorage, AK 99507-1296.

COLD BAY. K07TM, State of Alaska Div. of Telecommunications, John Morrone, deputy dir, 5900 E. Tudor Rd., Anchorage, AK 99507-1296.

COLD BAY. K13UO, State of Alaska Div. of Telecommunications, John Morrone, deputy dir, 5900 E. Tudor Rd., Anchorage, AK 99507-1296.

COOPER LANDING. K08KO, State of Alaska Div. of Telecommunications, John Morrone, deputy dir, 5900 E. Tudor Rd., Anchorage, AK 99507-1296.

COPPER CENTER. K12MO, State of Alaska Div. of Telecommunications, John Morrone, deputy dir, 5900 E. Tudor Rd., Anchorage, AK 99507-1296.

CORDOVA. K15AK, State of Alaska Div. of Telecommunications, John Morrone, deputy dir, 5900 E. Tudor Rd., Anchorage, AK 99507-1296.

COUNCIL. K09UK, State of Alaska Div. of Telecommunications, John Morrone, deputy dir, 5900 E. Tudor Rd., Anchorage, AK 99507-1296.

CRAIG. K61DE, State of Alaska Div. of Telecommunications, John Morrone, deputy dir, 5900 E. Tudor Rd., Anchorage, AK 99507-1296.

CROOKED CREEK. K07RZ, State of Alaska Div. of Telecommunications, John Morrone, deputy dir, 5900 E. Tudor Rd., Anchorage, AK 99507-1296.

CUBE COVE. K13TG, State of Alaska Div. of Telecommunications, John Morrone, deputy dir, 5900 E. Tudor Rd., Anchorage, AK 99507-1296.

DEERING. K09RN, State of Alaska Div. of Telecommunications, John Morrone, deputy dir, 5900 E. Tudor Rd., Anchorage, AK 99507-1296.

DELTA JUNCTION. K17AF, State of Alaska Div. of Telecommunications, John Morrone, deputy dir, 5900 E. Tudor Rd., Anchorage, AK 99507-1296.

DILLINGHAM. K02GU, State of Alaska Div. of Telecommunications, John Morrone, deputy dir, 5900 E. Tudor Rd., Anchorage, AK 99507-1296.

DILLINGHAM. K04KN, State of Alaska Div. of Telecommunications, John Morrone, deputy dir, 5900 E. Tudor Rd., Anchorage, AK 99507-1296.

DILLINGHAM. K10LD, State of Alaska Div. of Telecommunications, John Morrone, deputy dir, 5900 E. Tudor Rd., Anchorage, AK 99507-1296.

DIOMEDE. K13UX, State of Alaska Div. of Telecommunications, John Morrone, deputy dir, 5900 E. Tudor Rd., Anchorage, AK 99507-1296.

DOT LAKE. K13RM, State of Alaska Div. of Telecommunications, John Morrone, deputy dir, 5900 E. Tudor Rd., Anchorage, AK 99507-1296.

EAGLE VILLAGE. K09RF, State of Alaska Div. of Telecommunications, John Morrone, deputy dir, 5900 E. Tudor Rd., Anchorage, AK 99507-1296.

EEK. K09TN, State of Alaska Div. of Telecommunications, John Morrone, deputy dir, 5900 E. Tudor Rd., Anchorage, AK 99507-1296.

EEK. K11SD, State of Alaska Div. of Telecommunications, John Morrone, deputy dir, 5900 E. Tudor Rd., Anchorage, AK 99507-1296.

EGEGIK. K04KR, State of Alaska Div. of Telecommunications, John Morrone, deputy dir, 5900 E. Tudor Rd., Anchorage, AK 99507-1296.

EIGHT FATHOMS BIGHT. K09TA, State of Alaska Div. of Telecommunications, John Morrone, deputy dir, 5900 E. Tudor Rd., Anchorage, AK 99507-1296.

EKWOK. K11QW, State of Alaska Div. of Telecommunications, John Morrone, deputy dir, 5900 E. Tudor Rd., Anchorage, AK 99507-1296.

Low Power Television Stations

ELIM. K09QS, State of Alaska Div. of Telecommunications, John Morrone, deputy dir, 5900 E. Tudor Rd., Anchorage, AK 99507-1296.

EMMONAK. K05IH, State of Alaska Div. of Telecommunications, John Morrone, deputy dir, 5900 E. Tudor Rd., Anchorage, AK 99507-1296.

ENGLISH BAY. K31AG, State of Alaska Div. of Telecommunications, John Morrone, deputy dir, 5900 E. Tudor Rd., Anchorage, AK 99502-1296.

ERNESTINE. K11RI, State of Alaska Div. of Telecommunications, John Morrone, deputy dir, 5900 E. Tudor Rd., Anchorage, AK 99507-1296.

FAIRBANKS. K07UU, Tanana Valley TV Co., Box 84662, Fairbanks, AK 99708.

FALSE PASS. K09RP, State of Alaska Div. of Telecommunications, John Morrone, deputy dir, 5900 E. Tudor Rd., Anchorage, AK 99507-1296.

FORT YUKON. K07RC, State of Alaska Div. of Telecommunications, John Morrone, deputy dir, 5900 E. Tudor Rd., Anchorage, AK 99507-1296.

FRESHWATER BAY. K09TP, State of Alaska Div. of Telecommunications, John Morrone, deputy dir, 5900 E. Tudor Rd., Anchorage, AK 99507-1296.

GAKONA. K11RG, State of Alaska Div. of Telecommunications, John Morrone, deputy dir, 5900 E. Tudor Rd., Anchorage, AK 99507-1296.

GALENA. K04LZ, State of Alaska Div. of Telecommunications, John Morrone, deputy dir, 5900 E. Tudor Rd., Anchorage, AK 99507-1296.

GAMBELL. K09QR, State of Alaska Div. of Telecommunications, John Morrone, deputy dir, 5900 E. Tudor Rd., Anchorage, AK 99507-1296.

GIRDWOOD. K10MB, State of Alaska Div. of Telecommunications, John Morrone, deputy dir, 5900 E. Tudor Rd., Anchorage, AK 99507-1296.

GLENNALLEN/COPPER. K13UB, State of Alaska Div. of Telecommunications, John Morrone, deputy dir, 5900 E. Tudor Rd., Anchorage, AK 99507-1296.

GOLOVIN. K07QX, State of Alaska Div. of Telecommunications, John Morrone, deputy dir, 5900 E. Tudor Rd., Anchorage, AK 99507-1296.

GOODNEWS BAY. K04KT, State of Alaska Div. of Telecommunications, John Morrone, deputy dir, 5900 E. Tudor Rd., Anchorage, AK 99507-1296.

GRAVINA & PENNOCK ISLAND. K04NC, State of Alaska Div. of Telecommunications, John Morrone, deputy dir, 5900 E. Tudor Rd., Anchorage, AK 99507-1296.

GRAYLING. K11QH, State of Alaska Div. of Telecommunications, John Morrone, deputy dir, 5900 E. Tudor Rd., Anchorage, AK 99507-1296.

GUSTAVUS. K02LW, State of Alaska Div. of Telecommunications, John Morrone, deputy dir, 5900 E. Tudor Rd., Anchorage, AK 99507-1296.

HALIBUT COVE. K11QS, State of Alaska Div. of Telecommunications, John Morrone, deputy dir, 5900 E. Tudor Rd., Anchorage, AK 99507-1296.

HALIBUT COVE. K12NW, State of Alaska Div. of Telecommunications, John Morrone, deputy dir, 5900 E. Tudor Rd., Anchorage, AK 99507-1296.

HEALY. K58BI, State of Alaska Div. of Telecommunications, John Morrone, deputy dir, 5900 E. Tudor Rd., Anchorage, AK 99507-1296.

HOBART BAY. K09TB, State of Alaska Div. of Telecommunications, John Morrone, deputy dir, 5900 E. Tudor Rd., Anchorage, AK 99507-1296.

HOLLIA. K12NT, State of Alaska Div. of Telecommunications, John Morrone, deputy dir, 5900 E. Tudor Rd., Anchorage, AK 99507-1296.

HOLLIS. K08KP, State of Alaska Div. of Telecommunications, John Morrone, deputy dir, 5900 E. Tudor Rd., Anchorage, AK 99507-1296.

HOLLYCROSS. K07RJ, State of Alaska Div. of Telecommunications, John Morrone, deputy dir, 5900 E. Tudor Rd., Anchorage, AK 99507-1296.

HOMER/SELDOVIA. K11RK, State of Alaska Div. of Telecommunications, John Morrone, deputy dir, 5900 E. Tudor Rd., Anchorage, AK 99507-1296.

HOONAH. K07QV, State of Alaska Div. of Telecommunications, John Morrone, deputy dir, 5900 E. Tudor Rd., Anchorage, AK 99507-1296.

HOOPER BAY. K04MC, State of Alaska Div. of Telecommunications, John Morrone, deputy dir, 5900 E. Tudor Rd., Anchorage, AK 99507-1296.

HUALIA. K09QD, State of Alaska Div. of Telecommunications, John Morrone, deputy dir, 5900 E. Tudor Rd., Anchorage, AK 99507-1296.

HUGES. K09RY, State of Alaska Div. of Telecommunications, John Morrone, deputy dir, 5900 E. Tudor Rd., Anchorage, AK 99507-1296.

HYDABURG. K09QI, State of Alaska Div. of Telecommunications, John Morrone, deputy dir, 5900 E. Tudor Rd., Anchorage, AK 99507-1296.

HYDER. K02MJ, State of Alaska Div. of Telecommunications, John Morrone, deputy dir, 5900 E. Tudor Rd., Anchorage, AK 99507-1296.

IGUIGIG. K09SP, State of Alaska Div. of Telecommunications, John Morrone, deputy dir, 5900 E. Tudor Rd., Anchorage, AK 99507-1296.

ILIANMA. K04KO, State of Alaska Div. of Telecommunications, John Morrone, deputy dir, 5900 E. Tudor Rd., Anchorage, AK 99507-1296.

IVANOF BAY. K09SN, State of Alaska Div. of Telecommunications, John Morrone, deputy dir, 5900 E. Tudor Rd., Anchorage, AK 99507-1296.

KAKE. K09QP, State of Alaska Div. of Telecommunications, John Morrone, deputy dir, 5900 E. Tudor Rd., Anchorage, AK 99507-1296.

KAKHONAK. K09TM, State of Alaska Div. of Telecommunications, John Morrone, deputy dir, 5900 E. Tudor Rd., Anchorage, AK 99507-1296.

KAKTOVIK. K09QY, State of Alaska Div. of Telecommunications, John Morrone, deputy dir, 5900 E. Tudor Rd., Anchorage, AK 99507-1296.

KALSKAG. K09TR, State of Alaska Div. of Telecommunications, John Morrone, deputy dir, 5900 E. Tudor Rd., Anchorage, AK 99507-1296.

KALTAG. K09TX, State of Alaska Div. of Telecommunications, John Morrone, deputy dir, 5900 E. Tudor Rd., Anchorage, AK 99507-1296.

KARLUK. K09QK, State of Alaska Div. of Telecommunications, John Morrone, deputy dir, 5900 E. Tudor Rd., Anchorage, AK 99507-1296.

KARLUK. K09SM, State of Alaska Div. of Telecommunications, John Morrone, deputy dir, 5900 E. Tudor Rd., Anchorage, AK 99507-1296.

KASIGLUK. K09UE, State of Alaska Div. of Telecommunications, John Morrone, deputy dir, 5900 E. Tudor Rd., Anchorage, AK 99507-1296.

KENAI. K17AE, Tele-vu Partners, Denton Shelden, mgr, 500 Lake St., Kenai, AK 99611.

KENAI. K23AF, State of Alaska Div. of Telecommunications, John Morrone, deputy dir, 5900 E. Tudor Rd., Anchorage, AK 99507-1296.

KETCHIKAN. K21AH, State of Alaska Div. of Telecommunications, John Morrone, deputy dir, 5900 E. Tudor Rd., Anchorage, AK 99507-1296.

KIANA. K09RW, State of Alaska Div. of Telecommunications, John Morrone, deputy dir, 5900 E. Tudor Rd., Anchorage, AK 99507-1296.

KING COVE. K09QW, State of Alaska Div. of Telecommunications, John Morrone, deputy dir, 5900 E. Tudor Rd., Anchorage, AK 99507-1296.

KING SALMON. K04KM, State of Alaska Div. of Telecommunications, John Morrone, deputy dir, 5900 E. Tudor Rd., Anchorage, AK 99507-1296.

KING SALMON. K08KS, State of Alaska Div. of Telecommunications, John Morrone, deputy dir, 5900 E. Tudor Rd., Anchorage, AK 99507-1296.

KIPNUK. K04LM, State of Alaska Div. of Telecommunications, John Morrone, deputy dir, 5900 E. Tudor Rd., Anchorage, AK 99507-1296.

KIVALINA. K09QZ, State of Alaska Div. of Telecommunications, John Morrone, deputy dir, 5900 E. Tudor Rd., Anchorage, AK 99507-1296.

KLAWOCK. K07TI, State of Alaska Div. of Telecommunications, John Morrone, deputy dir, 5900 E. Tudor Rd., Anchorage, AK 99507-1296.

KLUKWAN. K04KQ, State of Alaska Div. of Telecommunications, John Morrone, deputy dir, 5900 E. Tudor Rd., Anchorage, AK 99507-1296.

KOBUK. K02KZ, State of Alaska Div. of Telecommunications, John Morrone, deputy dir, 5900 E. Tudor Rd., Anchorage, AK 99507-1296.

KODIAK. K09OS, Kodiak Public Broadcasting, Joe Stevens, eng, Box 484, Kodiak, AK 99507.

KODIAK. K13UY, State of Alaska Div. of Telecommunications, John Morrone, deputy dir, 5900 E. Tudor Rd., Anchorage, AK 99507-1296.

KOLIGANEK. K07QW, State of Alaska Div. of Telecommunications, John Morrone, deputy dir, 5900 E. Tudor Rd., Anchcrage, AK 99507-1296.

KONGIGANAK. K09RG, State of Alaska Div. of Telecommunications, John Morrone, deputy dir, 5900 E. Tudor Rd., Anchorage, AK 99507-1296.

KOTLIK. K09SL, State of Alaska Div. of Telecommunications, John Morrone, deputy dir, 5900 E. Tudor Rd., Anchorage, AK 99507-1296.

KOTZEBUE. K12UE, State of Alaska Div. of Telecommunications, John Morrone, deputy dir, 5900 E. Tudor Rd., Anchorage, AK 99507-1296.

KOTZEBUE. K13UE, State of Alaska Div. of Telecommunications, John Morrone, deputy dir, 5900 E. Tudor Rd., Anchorage, AK 99507-1296.

KOYUK. K02MB, State of Alaska Div. of Telecommunications, John Morrone, deputy dir, 5900 E. Tudor Rd., Anchorage, AK 99507-1296.

KOYUK. K09SA, Koyuk Village Council, Reginald M. Otitkon, city clerk, general Delivery, Koyuk, AK 99753.

KOYUKUK. K03FZ, State of Alaska Div. of Telecommunications, John Morrone, deputy dir, 5900 E. Tudor Rd., Anchorage, AK 99507-1296.

KWETHLUK. K09UJ, State of Alaska Div. of Telecommunications, John Morrone, deputy dir, 5900 E. Tudor Rd., Anchorage, AK 99507-1296.

KWIGILLINGOK. K11SC, State of Alaska Div. of Telecommunications, John Morrone, deputy dir, 5900 E. Tudor Rd., Anchorage, AK 99507-1296.

KWIGILLINGOK. K13UK, State of Alaska Div. of Telecommunications, John Morrone, deputy dir, 5900 E. Tudor Rd., Anchorage, AK 99507-1296.

LABOUCHERE BAY. K07SK, State of Alaska Div. of Telecommunications, John Morrone, deputy dir, 5900 E. Tudor Rd., Anchorage, AK 99507-1296.

LAKE LOUISE. K11RJ, State of Alaska Div. of Telecommunications, John Morrone, deputy dir, 5900 E. Tudor Rd., Anchorage, AK 99507-1296.

LARSEN BAY. K09QE, State of Alaska Div. of Telecommunications, John Morrone, deputy dir, 5900 E. Tudor Rd., Anchorage, AK 99507-1296.

LIME VILLAGE. K11RW, State of Alaska Div. of Telecommunications, John Morrone, deputy dir, 5900 E. Tudor Rd., Anchorage, AK 99507-1296.

LONG ISLAND. K05IR, State of Alaska Div. of Telecommunications, John Morrone, deputy dir, 5900 E. Tudor Rd., Anchorage, AK 99507-1296.

LONG ISLAND. K10MU, State of Alaska Div. of Telecommunications, John Morrone, deputy dir, 5900 E. Tudor Rd., Anchorage, AK 99507-1296.

LOVELOCK. K07TT, State of Alaska Div. of Telecommunications, John Morrone, deputy dir, 5900 E. Tudor Rd., Anchorage, AK 99507-1296.

MANLEY HOT SPRINGS. K07RX, State of Alaska Div. of Telecommunications, John Morrone, deputy dir, 5900 E. Tudor Rd., Anchorage, AK 99507-1296.

MANOKOTAK. K09TQ, State of Alaska Div. of Telecommunications, John Morrone, deputy dir, 5900 E. Tudor Rd., Anchorage, AK 99507-1296.

MARSHALL. K02KV, State of Alaska Div. of Telecommunications, John Morrone, deputy dir, 5900 E. Tudor Rd., Anchorage, AK 99507-1296.

MCGRATH. K09QC, State of Alaska Div. of Telecommunications, John Morrone, deputy dir, 5900 E. Tudor Rd., Anchorage, AK 99507-1296.

MCKINLEY PARK. K03GK, State of Alaska Div. of Telecommunications, John Morrone, deputy dir, 5900 E. Tudor Rd., Anchorage, AK 99507-1296.

MEKORYUK. K04MD, State of Alaska Div. of Telecommunications, John Morrone, deputy dir, 5900 E. Tudor Rd., Anchorage, AK 99507-1296.

Low Power Television Stations

MENTASTA LAKE. K09QJ, State of Alaska Div. of Telecommunications, John Morrone, deputy dir, 5900 E. Tudor Rd., Anchorage, AK 99507-1296.

METLAKATLA. K07SL, State of Alaska Div. of Telecommunications, John Morrone, deputy dir, 5900 E. Tudor Rd., Anchorage, AK 99507-1296.

MEYERS CHUCK. K09TI, State of Alaska Div. of Telecommunications, John Morrone, deputy dir, 5900 E. Tudor Rd., Anchorage, AK 99507-1296.

MINCHUMINA. K05IK, State of Alaska Div. of Telecommunications, John Morrone, deputy dir, 5900 E. Tudor Rd., Anchorage, AK 99507-1296.

MINCHUMINA. K09SZ, State of Alaska Div. of Telecommunications, John Morrone, deputy dir, 5900 E. Tudor Rd., Anchorage, AK 99507-1296.

MINTO. K13TK, State of Alaska Div. of Telecommunications, John Morrone, deputy dir, 5900 E. Tudor Rd., Anchorage, AK 99507-1296.

MOOSE PASS. K15AP, State of Alaska Div. of Telecommunications, John Morrone, deputy dir, 5900 E. Tudor Rd., Anchorage, AK 99507-1296.

MOSQUITO LAKE. K13UM, State of Alaska Div. of Telecommunications, John Morrone, deputy dir, 5900 E. Tudor Rd., Anchorage, AK 99507-1296.

MOUNTAIN VILLAGE. K13TJ, State of Alaska Div. of Telecommunications, John Morrone, deputy dir, 5900 E. Tudor Rd., Anchorage, AK 99507-1296.

N KENAI. K55BB, State of Alaska Div. of Telecommunications, John Morrone, deputy dir, 5900 E. Tudor Rd., Anchorage, AK 99507-1296.

NAKNEK. K13TZ, State of Alaska Div. of Telecommunications, John Morrone, deputy dir, 5900 E. Tudor Rd., Anchorage, AK 99507-1296.

NAPASKIAK. K02MZ, State of Alaska Div. of Telecommunications, John Morrone, deputy dir, 5900 E. Tudor Rd., Anchorage, AK 99507-1296.

NAPASKIAK. K07SJ, State of Alaska Div. of Telecommunications, John Morrone, deputy dir, 5900 E. Tudor Rd., Anchorage, AK 99507-1296.

NAPASKIAK. K10MR, State of Alaska Div. of Telecommunications, John Morrone, deputy dir, 5900 E. Tudor Rd., Anchorage, AK 99507-1296.

NAUKATI BAY. K09TJ, State of Alaska Div. of Telecommunications, John Morrone, deputy dir, 5900 E. Tudor Rd., Anchorage, AK 99507-1296.

NELSON LAGOON. K09QM, State of Alaska Div. of Telecommunications, John Morrone, deputy dir, 5900 E. Tudor Rd., Anchorage, AK 99507-1296.

NENANA. K55DE, State of Alaska Div. of Telecommunications, John Morrone, deputy dir, 5900 E. Tudor Rd., Anchorage, AK 99507-1296.

NEW STUYAHOK. K09QV, State of Alaska Div. of Telecommunications, John Morrone, deputy dir, 5900 E. Tudor Rd., Anchorage, AK 99507-1296.

NEWTOK. K02LN, State of Alaska Div. of Telecommunications, John Morrone, deputy dir, 5900 E. Tudor Rd., Anchorage, AK 99507-1296.

NIGHTMUTE. K10LU, State of Alaska Div. of Telecommunications, John Morrone, deputy dir, 5900 E. Tudor Rd., Anchorage, AK 99507-1296.

NIKOLAI. K04MB, State of Alaska Div. of Telecommunications, John Morrone, deputy dir, 5900 E. Tudor Rd., Anchorage, AK 99507-1296.

NIKOLSKI. K09RK, State of Alaska Div. of Telecommunications, John Morrone, deputy dir, 5900 E. Tudor Rd., Anchorage, AK 99507-1296.

NINILCHICK. K39AA, State of Alaska Div. of Telecommunications, John Morrone, deputy dir, 5900 E. Tudor Rd., Anchorage, AK 99507-1296.

NOATAK. K07RI, State of Alaska Div. of Telecommunications, John Morrone, deputy dir, 5900 E. Tudor Rd., Anchorage, AK 99507-1296.

NOME. K13UG, State of Alaska Div. of Telecommunications, John Morrone, deputy dir, 5900 E. Tudor Rd., Anchorage, AK 99507-1296.

NONDALTON. K09RQ, State of Alaska Div. of Telecommunications, John Morrone, deputy dir, 5900 E. Tudor Rd., Anchorage, AK 99507-1296.

NOORVIK. K09RU, State of Alaska Div. of Telecommunications, John Morrone, deputy dir, 5900 E. Tudor Rd., Anchorage, AK 99507-1296.

NORTHWAY. K02LB, Northway Village Council, Lorraine Felix, pres, Box 516, Northway, AK 99764.

NORTHWAY. K04KP, State of Alaska Div. of Telecommunications, John Morrone, deputy dir, 5900 E. Tudor Rd., Anchorage, AK 99507-1296.

NUIQSUT. K09RT, State of Alaska Div. of Telecommunications, John Morrone, deputy dir, 5900 E. Tudor Rd., Anchorage, AK 99507-1296.

NULATO. K02KW, State of Alaska Div. of Telecommunications, John Morrone, deputy dir, 5900 E. Tudor Rd., Anchorage, AK 99507-1296.

OLD HARBOR. K13RN, State of Alaska Div. of Telecommunications, John Morrone, deputy dir, 5900 E. Tudor Rd., Anchorage, AK 99507-1296.

OUZINKIE. K07QY, State of Alaska Div. of Telecommunications, John Morrone, deputy dir, 5900 E. Tudor Rd., Anchorage, AK 99507-1296.

PAXSON. K11QV, State of Alaska Div. of Telecommunications, John Morrone, deputy dir, 5900 E. Tudor Rd., Anchorage, AK 99507-1296.

PEDRO BAY. K13SV, State of Alaska Div. of Telecommunications, John Morrone, deputy dir, 5900 E. Tudor Rd., Anchorage, AK 99507-1296.

PELICAN. K09RM, State of Alaska Div. of Telecommunications, John Morrone, deputy dir, 5900 E. Tudor Rd., Anchorage, AK 99507-1296.

PERRYVILLE. K04MA, State of Alaska Div. of Telecommunications, John Morrone, deputy dir, 5900 E. Tudor Rd., Anchorage, AK 99507-1296.

PETERSBURG. K21CK, State of Alaska Div. of Telecommunications, John Morrone, deputy dir, 5900 E. Tudor Rd., Anchorage, AK 99507-1296.

PILOT POINT. K02LI, State of Alaska Div. of Telecommunications, John Morrone, deputy dir, 5900 E. Tudor Rd., Anchorage, AK 99507-1296.

PILOT STATION. K15AU, State of Alaska Div. of Telecommunications, John Morrone, deputy dir, 5900 E. Tudor Rd., Anchorage, AK 99507-1296.

PITKAS POINT. K02LV, State of Alaska Div. of Telecommunications, John Morrone, deputy dir, 5900 E. Tudor Rd., Anchorage, AK 99507-1296.

POINT BAKER. K09SY, State of Alaska Div. of Telecommunications, John Morrone, deputy dir, 5900 E. Tudor Rd., Anchorage, AK 99507-1296.

POINT HOPE. K09QN, State of Alaska Div. of Telecommunications, John Morrone, deputy dir, 5900 E. Tudor Rd., Anchorage, AK 99507-1296.

POINT LAY. K09UC, State of Alaska Div. of Telecommunications, John Morrone, deputy dir, 5900 E. Tudor Rd., Anchorage, AK 99507-1296.

PORT ALICE. K09TL, State of Alaska Div. of Telecommunications, John Morrone, deputy dir, 5900 E. Tudor Rd., Anchorage, AK 99507-1296.

PORT ALSWORTH. K07SH, State of Alaska Div. of Telecommunications, John Morrone, deputy dir, 5900 E. Tudor Rd., Anchorage, AK 99507-1296.

PORT GRAHAM. K09QB, State of Alaska Div. of Telecommunications, John Morrone, deputy dir, 5900 E. Tudor Rd., Anchorage, AK 99507-1296.

PORT GRAHAM. K13SC, State of Alaska Div. of Telecommunications, John Morrone, deputy dir, 5900 E. Tudor Rd., Anchorage, AK 99507-1296.

PORT HEIDEN. K13SA, State of Alaska Div. of Telecommunications, John Morrone, deputy dir, 5900 E. Tudor Rd., Anchorage, AK 99507-1296.

PORT LIONS. K07RG, State of Alaska Div. of Telecommunications, John Morrone, deputy dir, 5900 E. Tudor Rd., Anchorage, AK 99507-1296.

PORT MOLLER. K07SO, State of Alaska Div. of Telecommunications, John Morrone, deputy dir, 5900 E. Tudor Rd., Anchorage, AK 99507-1296.

PORT PROTECTION. K11QX, State of Alaska Div. of Telecommunications, John Morrone, deputy dir, 5900 E. Tudor Rd., Anchorage, AK 99507-1296.

QUINHAGAK. K09SX, State of Alaska Div. of Telecommunications, John Morrone, deputy dir, 5900 E. Tudor Rd., Anchorage, AK 99507-1296.

RAMPART. K09RD, State of Alaska Div. of Telecommunications, John Morrone, deputy dir, 5900 E. Tudor Rd., Anchorage, AK 99507-1296.

RED DEVIL. K02LA, State of Alaska Div. of Telecommunications, John Morrone, deputy dir, 5900 E. Tudor Rd., Anchorage, AK 99507-1296.

ROWAN BAY. K09TC, State of Alaska Div. of Telecommunications, John Morrone, deputy dir, 5900 E. Tudor Rd., Anchorage, AK 99507-1296.

RUBY. K04KU, State of Alaska Div. of Telecommunications, John Morrone, deputy dir, 5900 E. Tudor Rd., Anchorage, AK 99507-1296.

RUSSIAN MISSION. K09SH, State of Alaska Div. of Telecommunications, John Morrone, deputy dir, 5900 E. Tudor Rd., Anchorage, AK 99507-1296.

ST GEORGE. K09RE, State of Alaska Div. of Telecommunications, John Morrone, deputy dir, 5900 E. Tudor Rd., Anchorage, AK 99507-1296.

ST MARYS. K13SX, State of Alaska Div. of Telecommunications, John Morrone, deputy dir, 5900 E. Tudor Rd., Anchorage, AK 99507-1296.

ST MICHAEL. K09QX, State of Alaska Div. of Telecommunications, John Morrone, deputy dir, 5900 E. Tudor Rd., Anchorage, AK 99507-1296.

ST PAUL. K09RB, State of Alaska Div. of Telecommunications, John Morrone, deputy dir, 5900 E. Tudor Rd., Anchorage, AK 99507-1296.

SAND POINT. K09RA, State of Alaska Div. of Telecommunications, John Morrone, deputy dir, 5900 E. Tudor Rd., Anchorage, AK 99507-1296.

SAVOONGA. K07RD, State of Alaska Div. of Telecommunications, John Morrone, deputy dir, 5900 E. Tudor Rd., Anchorage, AK 99507-1296.

SCAMMON BAY. K02LS, State of Alaska Div. of Telecommunications, John Morrone, deputy dir, 5900 E. Tudor Rd., Anchorage, AK 99507-1296.

SELAWIK. K09RL, State of Alaska Div. of Telecommunications, John Morrone, deputy dir, 5900 E. Tudor Rd., Anchorage, AK 99507-1296.

SHAGELUK. K04KY, State of Alaska Div. of Telecommunications, John Morrone, deputy dir, 5900 E. Tudor Rd., Anchorage, AK 99507-1296.

SHAKTOOLIK. K07QU, State of Alaska Div. of Telecommunications, John Morrone, deputy dir, 5900 E. Tudor Rd., Anchorage, AK 99507-1296.

SHEEP MOUNTAIN. K12NO, State of Alaska Div. of Telecommunications, John Morrone, deputy dir, 5900 E. Tudor Rd., Anchorage, AK 99507-1296.

SHELDON POINT. K11QR, State of Alaska Div. of Telecommunications, John Morrone, deputy dir, 5900 E. Tudor Rd., Anchorage, AK 99507-1296.

SHISHMAREF. K09RZ, State of Alaska Div. of Telecommunications, John Morrone, deputy dir, 5900 E. Tudor Rd., Anchorage, AK 99507-1296.

SHUNGNAK. K07RA, State of Alaska Div. of Telecommunications, John Morrone, deputy dir, 5900 E. Tudor Rd., Anchorage, AK 99507-1296.

SITKA. K03GJ, State of Alaska Div. of Telecommunications, John Morrone, deputy dir, 5900 E. Tudor Rd., Abcgirage, AK 99507-1296.

SKAGWAY. K11QE, State of Alaska Div. of Telecommunications, John Morrone, deputy dir, 5900 E. Tudor Rd., Anchorage, AK 99507-1296.

SLANA. K04KX, State of Alaska Div. of Telecommunications, John Morrone, deputy dir, 5900 E. Tudor Rd., Anchorage, AK 99507-1296.

SLANA. K13SM, State of Alaska Div. of Telecommunications, John Morrone, deputy dir, 5900 E. Tudor Rd., Anchorage, AK 99507-1296.

SLEETMUTE. K07SX, State of Alaska Div. of Telecommunications, John Morrone, deputy dir, 5900 E. Tudor Rd., Anchorage, AK 99507-1296.

STEBBINS. K09RR, State of Alaska Div. of Telecommunications, John Morrone, deputy dir, 5900 E. Tudor Rd., Anchorage, AK 99507-1296.

STEVENS VILLAGE. K09SV, State of Alaska Div. of Telecommunications, John Morrone, deputy dir, 5900 E. Tudor Rd., Anchorage, AK 99507-1296.

STONY RIVER. K13SE, State of Alaska Div. of Telecommunications, John Morrone, deputy dir, 5900 E. Tudor Rd., Anchorage, AK 99507-1296.

TAKOTNA. K04LN, State of Alaska Div. of Telecommunications, John Morrone, deputy dir, 5900 E. Tudor Rd., Anchorage, AK 99507-1296.

Low Power Television Stations

TANANA. K07RB, State of Alaska Div. of Telecommunications, John Morrone, deputy dir, 5900 E. Tudor Rd., Anchorage, AK 99507-1296.

TANUNAK. K09SW, State of Alaska Div. of Telecommunications, John Morrone, deputy dir, 5900 E. Tudor Rd., Anchorage, AK 99507-1296.

TATITLEK. K13SJ, State of Alaska Div. of Telecommunications, John Morrone, deputy dir, 5900 E. Tudor Rd., Anchorage, AK 99507-1296.

TELIDA. K13RO, State of Alaska Div. of Telecommunications, John Morrone, deputy dir, 5900 E. Tudor Rd., Anchorage, AK 99507-1296.

TELLER. K09RO, State of Alaska Div. of Telecommunications, John Morrone, deputy dir, 5900 E. Tudor Rd., Anchorage, AK 99507-1296.

TENAKEE SPRINGS. K07RH, State of Alaska Div. of Telecommunications, John Morrone, deputy dir, 5900 E. Tudor Rd., Anchorage, AK 99507-1296.

TETLIN. K11QU, State of Alaska Div. of Telecommunications, John Morrone, deputy dir, 5900 E. Tudor Rd., Anchorage, AK 99507-1296.

THORNE BAY. K07SN, State of Alaska Div. of Telecommunications, John Morrone, deputy dir, 5900 E. Tudor Rd., Anchorage, AK 99507-1296.

TOGIAK. K09QU, State of Alaska Div. of Telecommunications, John Morrone, deputy dir, 5900 E. Tudor Rd., Anchorage, AK 99507-1296.

TOK. K13RR, State of Alaska Div. of Telecommunications, John Morrone, deputy dir, 5900 E. Tudor Rd., Anchorage, AK 99507-1296.

TOKSOOK BAY. K11QG, State of Alaska Div. of Telecommunications, John Morrone, deputy dir, 5900 E. Tudor Rd., Anchorage, AK 99507-1296.

TRAPPER CREEK. K24AG, State of Alaska Div. of Telecommunications, John Morrone, deputy dir, 5900 E. Tudor Rd., Anchorage, AK 99507-1296.

TULUKSAK. K08ID, State of Alaska Div. of Telecommunications, John Morrone, deputy dir, 5900 E. Tudor Rd., Anchorage, AK 99507-1296.

TUNTUTULIAK. K09TF, State of Alaska Div. of Telecommunications, John Morrone, deputy dir, 5900 E. Tudor Rd., Anchorage, AK 99507-1296.

TYONEK. K09QH, State of Alaska Div. of Telecommunications, John Morrone, deputy dir, 5900 E. Tudor Rd., Anchorage, AK 99507-1296.

UNALAKLEET. K09RC, State of Alaska Div. of Telecommunications, John Morrone, deputy dir, 5900 E. Tudor Rd., Anchorage, AK 99507-1296.

UNALASKA. K04KV, State of Alaska Div. of Telecommunications, John Morrone, deputy dir, 5900 E. Tudor Rd., Anchorage, AK 99507-1296.

UNALASKA. K08IW, Unalaska Community TV, Richard Hogarth, exec dir, Box 181, Unalaska, AK 99685.

VALDEZ. K15AI, State of Alaska Div. of Telecommunications, John Morrone, deputy dir, 5900 E. Tudor Rd., Anchorage, AK 99507-1296.

VENETIE. K09TW, State of Alaska Div. of Telecommunications, John Morrone, deputy dir, 5900 E. Tudor Rd., Anchorage, AK 99507-1296.

WAINWRIGHT. K09QO, State of Alaska Div. of Telecommunications, John Morrone, deputy dir, 5900 E. Tudor Rd., Anchorage, AK 99507-1296.

WALES. K02LT, State of Alaska Div. of Telecommunications, John Morrone, deputy dir, 5900 E. Tudor Rd., Anchorage, AK 99507-1296.

WHALES PASS. K07SI, State of Alaska Div. of Telecommunications, John Morrone, deputy dir, 5900 E. Tudor Rd., Anchorage, AK 99507-1296.

WHITE MOUNTAIN. K11QT, State of Alaska Div. of Telecommunications, John Morrone, deputy dir, 5900 E. Tudor Rd., Anchorage, AK 99507-1296.

WHITTIER. K09UB, State of Alaska Div. of Telecommunications, John Morrone, deputy dir, 5900 E. Tudor Rd., Anchorage, AK 99507-1296.

WOMENS BAY. K02ME, State of Alaska Div. of Telecommunications, John Morrone, deputy dir, 5900 E. Tudor Rd., Anchorage, AK 99507-1296.

YAKUTAT. K09UA, State of Alaska Div. of Telecommunications, John Morrone, deputy dir, 5900 E. Tudor Rd., Anchorage, AK 99507-1296.

Arizona

BULLHEAD CITY. K26AQ, Space Cable (Tri-State Broadcasting), Tom Titchen, pres, 1704 Arena Dr., Bullhead City, AZ 86442.

BULLHEAD CITY. K34DK, Patrick Salis, gen mgr, 2225 Avondale Dr., Alahambra, CA 91803.

CAMP VERDE. K18DD, Central States Comm., George Yount, owner, Box 461, Camp Verde, AZ 86322.

COTTONWOOD. K44CN, Scripps Howard Broadcasting Co., Jack R. Howard, pres, 1100 Central Trust Tower, Cincinati, OH 45201.

COTTONWOOD. K46CA, Yavapai College, 1100 E. Sheldon St., Prescott, AZ 56301.

DUNCAN. K17CM, Gospel Light Broadcasting, Box 520 Rt. 1, Stafford, AZ 85546.

DUNCAN. K33DA, Southern Greenlee City TV Inc., Milt Jensen, dir, 22 N. Hwy. 75, Duncan, AZ 85534.

DUNCAN. K35CP, Southern Greenlee City TV Inc., Milt Jensen, dir, 22 N. Hwy. 75, Duncan, AZ 85534.

DUNCAN. K39CM, Southern Greenlee City TV Inc., Milt Jensen, dir, 22 N. Hwy. 75, Duncan, AZ 85534.

DUNCAN. K41CV, Southern Greenlee City TV Inc., Milt Jensen, dir, 22 N. Hwy. 75, Duncan, AZ 85534.

DUNCAN. K43CN, Southern Greenlee City TV Inc., Milt Jensen, dir, 22 N. Hwy. 75, Duncan, AZ 85534.

DUNCAN. K47DA, Southern Greenlee City TV Inc., Milt Jensen, dir, 22 N. Hwy. 75, Duncan, AZ 85534.

DUNCAN. K49CH, Southern Greenlee City TV Inc., Milt Jensen, dir, 22 N. Hwy. 75, Duncan, AZ 85534.

DUNCAN. K53DL, Southern Greenlee City TV Inc., Milt Jensen, dir, 22 N. Hwy. 75, Duncan, AZ 85534.

DUNCAN. K55DM, Southern Greenlee City TV Inc., Milt Jensen, dir, 22 N. Hwy. 75, Duncan, AZ 85534.

DUNCAN. K57CU, Southern Greenlee City TV Inc., Milt Jensen, dir, 22 N. Hwy. 75, Duncan, AZ 85534.

DUNCAN. K67CP, Southern Greenlee City TV Inc., Milt Jensen, dir, 22 N. Hwy. 75, Duncan, AZ 85534.

DUNCAN/FRANKLIN. K65CM, Southern Greenlee City TV Inc., Milt Jensen, dir, 22 N. Hwy. 75, Duncan, AZ 85534.

DUNCAN/FRANKLIN. K69DG, Southern Greenlee City TV Inc., Milt Jensen, dir, 22 N. Hwy. 75, Duncan, AZ 85534.

FLAGSTAFF. K05HT, Russell Comm., James H. Russell Jr., pres, 407 E. Morningside Cir., Fullerton, CA 92635-3544.

GLOBE/MIAMI. K57BO, Community TV Project, Box 2750, Globe, AZ 85501.

HILLTOP. K36AX, Group Seven Comm. Inc., Maurice W. Coburn, pres, 1055 Empire Dr., #A, Lake Havasu City, AZ 86403-2400.

LAKE HAVASU. K23BJ, Group Seven Comm. Inc., Maurice W. Coburn, pres, 1055 Empire Dr., #A, Lake Havasu City, AZ 86403-2400.

LAKE HAVASU CITY. K25AL, Lake Havasu Christian TV, Richard Tatham, pastor, 510 North Acoma Blvd., Lake Havasu City, AZ 86403.

LAKE HAVASU CITY. K45AJ, Jeffrey W. Holmes, pres, Lake Havasu City, AZ 86403.

PARKER. K02MT, Hale Comm. Inc., Jerry Hale, pres, 912 Joshua St., Parker, AZ 85344.

PHOENIX. K25DM, Broadcasting Systems Inc., Kenneth Casey, pres, 21617 N. 9th Ave., #106, Phoenix, AZ 85027.

PHOENIX. K27AN, KUSK Inc., William H. Sauro, pres, 2809 Pine St., #A, San Francisco, CA 94115.

PHOENIX. K39BI, Arizona Christian TV System, Rick Hooton, gen mgr, Box 39, Phoenix, AZ 85001.

PHOENIX. K58DV, Atrium Broadcasting Co., Lawrence Rogow, pres, 23642 Calabasas Rd., Suite 104, Calabasas, CA 91302.

PHOENIX. K64DR, Hispanic Broadcasters of Tucson, William Arroyo, pres, 4228 First Ave., #15, Tucker, GA 30084.

PRESCOTT. K39CG, Yavapai College, 1100 E. Sheldon St., Prescott, AZ 56301.

QUARTZSITE. K39BV, American Television Network, Charles Cohen, pres, Box 832048, Delray Beach, FL 33483-0248.

QUARTZSITE. K41CE, American Television Network, Charles Cohen, pres, Box 832048, Delray Beach, FL 33483-0248.

QUARTZSITE. K43CA, Trinity Broadcasting Network, Jane Duff, vp, Box A, Santa Ana, CA 92711.

ROCK POINT. K56CC, Rock Point Community School, John Bieber, LPTV coord, Rock Point Community Schools, Rock Point, AZ 86545.

SHONTO. K40BZ, Gospel Overseas TV Net Inc., Martin Main, owner, Box 1606, Placerville, CA 95667.

SIERRA VISTA. K33CG, Richard Richards, owner.

SOUTH PHOENIX. K67FE, Polar Broadcasting of Arizona Inc., Warren Trumbly, pres, 1080 S. Los Molinos Way, Sacramento, CA 95864.

TUCSON. K14HR, Hispanic Broadcasters of Tucson, William Arroyo, pres, 4228 First Ave. #15, Tucker, GA 30084.

TUCSON. K21CX, West LPTV Inc., Jana Tucker, mgr, Box 36717, Tucson, AZ 85740.

TUCSON. K40AC, KTVW License Partnership, GP, 605 3rd Ave. 12th Fl., New York, NY 10158-0180.

TUCSON. K43CW, Polar Broadcasting of Arizona Inc., Warren Trumbly, pres, 1080 S. Los Molinos Way, Sacramento, CA 95864.

WINDOW ROCK. K44BB, The Navajo Nation, Box 2569, Window Rock, AZ 86515.

Arkansas

BATESVILLE. K12MY, Community Mgmt. Services Inc., Pat Lea, mgr, Box 2077 Channey Dr., Batesville, AR 72503.

BENTONVILLE. K67EO, The Times Southwest Broadcasting Inc., KFSM-TV, 318 N. 13th St., Fort Smith, AR 72902.

DEQUEEN. K08KF, Comm. Dynamics, Box 469, De Queen, AR 71832.

FAYETTEVILLE. K62DQ, The Times Southwest Broadcasting Inc., KFSM-TV 318 N. 13th St., Fort Smith, AR 72902.

FORT SMITH. K46BZ, Pharis Broadcasting Inc., Bill Pharis, pres, Box 573, Fort Smith, AR 72902-0573.

HARRISON. K23DU, Christians Inc. for Christ, Carlos Ortiz, pastor, 1108 S. Commerce St., Harlingen, TX 78550.

JONESBORO. K45AY, MG Productions, James McKee, pres, 207 E. Stroud, Jonesboro, AR 72401-5926.

LITTLE ROCK. K13UW, Jimmy C. Cowsert, owner, 121 Dexter Rd., North Little Rock, AR 72116.

LITTLE ROCK. K49CG, American Christian TV System, Michael Wright, mgr, Box 161098, Fort Worth, TX 76161.

LITTLE ROCK. K59DH, Talley Television Corp., 1740 Shadow Lawn St., Memphis, TN 38106.

PINE BLUFF. K65EK, Immanuel Broadcasting Corp., David Moore, gen mgr, 1801 W. 17th St., Pine Bluff, AR 71603.

SHERIDAN. K05IS, Glenda Ann Gray, owner,

SPRINGDALE. K15DR, Pharis Broadcasting Inc., Bill Pharis, pres, Box 573, Fort Smith, AR 72902-0573.

SPRINGDALE. K20CT, Christians Inc. for Christ, Carlos Ortiz, pastor, 1108 S. Commerce St., Harlingen, TX 78550.

TEXARKANA. K35CS, Beech Street Comm. Corp., Gary Underwood, vp, 516 Beech St., Texarkana, AR 75504.

California

ARROYO GRANDE. K66CY, Erwin Scala Broadcasting, Marty Scala, pres, 1263 Pomeroy Rd., Arroyo Grande, CA 93420.

BAKERSFIELD. K33BY, South West Broadcasting Co. Inc., Box 1723, Bellvue, WA 98004.

BAKERSFIELD. K39AB, KFTV License Partnership, GP, 605 3rd Ave. 12th Fl., New York, NY 10158-0180.

Low Power Television Stations

BAKERSFIELD. K58DJ, Park Place Broadcasting Co., Leo Kessleman, owner, 200 Glenridge Ave., Los Gatos, CA 95030.

BELRIDGE. K50CL, Belridge Elementary School Dist.

BLUE LAKE. K36BT, California Oregon Broadcasting Inc., Richard W. Green, vp, 755 Auditorium Dr., Redding, CA 96001.

CHICO. K15CX, California Oregon Broadcasting Inc., Richard W. Green, vp, 755 Auditorium Dr., Redding, CA 96001.

CHICO/PARADISE. K67DY, Butte Television, Carl Auel, partner, 4610 Briarwood Dr., Sacramento, CA 95821.

CHINA LAKE/SKY PLACE. K14AT, Indian Wells Valley TV Booster, Jan Thompson, gen mgr, Box 562, Ridgecrest, CA 93556-0562.

DAGGETT. K17CN, City of San Bernadino-area 40, Vern Knourek, off mgr, 157 W. 5th St., 2nd Fl., San Bernadino, CA 92415-0450.

DAGGETT. K67AZ, City of San Bernadino-area 40, Vern Knourek, off mgr, 157 W. 5th St., 2nd Fl., San Bernadino, CA 92415-0450.

DURHAM. K20CO, California Oregon Broadcasting Inc., Richard W. Green, vp, 755 Auditorium Dr., Redding, CA 96001.

EAGLEVILLE. K13IU, Surprise Valley Unif School Dist-Box 28 F, Cedarville, CA 96104.

EAST WEED. K33DI, California Oregon Broadcasting Inc., Richard W. Green, vp, 755 Auditorium Dr., Redding, CA 96001.

ESCONDIDO. K43DM, San Ysidro Broadcasting Corp., sec, 318 E. San Ysidro, San Ysidro, CA 92073.

FORT BRAGG. K48BQ, Family Television Inc., Joseph Perez, mgr, Box 272825, Concord, CA 94527-2825.

FORTUNA/RIO DELL. K20CN, California Oregon Broadcasting Inc., Richard W. Green, vp, 755 Auditorium Dr., Redding, CA 96001.

FRESNO. K04NJ, Gary Cocola, ceo, 706 W. Herndon Ave., Fresno, CA 93650.

FRESNO. K34AV, Gary Cocola, ceo, 706 W. Herndon Ave., Fresno, CA 93650.

FRESNO. K56DZ, National Minority TV Inc., Jane Duff, vp, Box A, Santa Ana, CA 92711.

GRASS VALLEY. K16CX, Sierra Joint Jr. College Dist., 5000 Rocklin Rd., Rocklin, CA 95677.

HEMET. K53DU, Buffalo Comm. Inc., Ray Wilson, sta mgr, 2336 San Jacinto St., San Jacinto, CA 92383.

INDIO. K04NT, Valley TV-4 KVER, Terry Ayers, gen mgr, 41701 Corporate Way #4, Palm Desert, CA 92253.

INDIO. K06MB, Park Place Broadcasting Co., Leo Kesselman, owner, 200 Glenridge Ave., Los Gatos, CA 95030.

INYOKERN. K19CL, William D. Britton, pres, 37428 3rd St. E., Palmdale, CA 93550.

INYOKERN/RIDGECREST. K43AG, Kitchen Productions Inc.

KLAMATH. K25CI, California Oregon Broadcasting Inc., William B. Smullin, sec, 125 S. Fir Box 5m, Medford, OR 97501.

LAKE SHASTINA. K27BH, California Oregon Broadcasting Inc., William B. Smullin, sec, 125 S. Fir Box 5m, Medford, OR 97501.

LAKEPORT. K33CH, The Lake County Television Club.

LAKEPORT. K52AJ, The Lake County Television Club.

LAKEPORT. K56AW, The Lake County Television Club.

LAKEPORT. K58AW, The Lake County Television Club.

LAKEPORT. K62AY, The Lake County Television Club.

LAKEPORT. K68AL, The Lake County Television Club

LAKEPORT/CLEARLAKE. K54CY, The Lake County Television Club.

LAYTONVILLE. K61CJ, Lester J. Dietz, pres, Box 637, Ukiah, CA 95482.

LITCHFIELD. K11RL, Honey Lake Community TV Corp., Box 963, Susanville, CA 96130.

LITCHFIELD. K13RZ, Honey Lake Community TV Corp., Box 963, Susanville, CA 96130.

LITCHFIELD. K48DI, Honey Lake Community TV Corp., Box 963, Susanville, CA 96130.

LITCHFIELD. K61EN, Honey Lake Community TV Corp., Box 963, Susanville, CA 96130.

LOS ANGELES. K38DL, Atrium Broadcasting Co., Lawrence Rogow, pres, 23642 Calabasas Rd. Suite 104, Calabasas, CA 91302.

MODESTO. K61FI, Telemundo of Northern California.

NEEDLES. K51AY, Garcia Broadcasting Assoc., Marta G. Garcia, owner, 44-551 Portola, Palm Desert, CA 92660.

NORTHRIDGE. K24CM, Northridge Community Broadcasting, 23642 Calabasas, Calabasas, CA 91302-1592.

OJAI. K33CC, Ojai Assembly of God, Rev. Frank Triggs, dir, 190 E. El Roblar Dr., Ojai, CA 93023-2398.

ONEALS. K66CQ, Gary Cocola, ceo, 706 W. Herndon Ave., Fresno, CA 93650.

OROVILLE. K18AO, Davis-Goldfarb Co., John A. Davis, pres, 2121 Ave. of the Stars #2800, Los Angeles, CA 90067.

PALM SPRINGS. K21DO, Ota Lee Babcock, owner, 34927 Merit, Cathedral City, CA 92234.

PALMDALE. K38CW, Four Pals Community Television.

PASO ROBLES. K36AL, Central Coast Good News Inc., Clyde F. Harmon, dir, 1027 N. Thornburg, Santa Maria, CA 93454.

PLACERVILLE. K62BT, Praise the Lord Chapel, John R. Hartman, pres, Box 1606, Placerville, CA 95667-1606.

REDDING. K34DF, Vibrant Living Broadcasting, Dick Seltzer, chairman, Box 493462, Redding, CA 96049-3462.

REDDING. K65DJ, Trinity Broadcasting Network, Jane Duff, vp, Box A, Santa Ana, CA 92711.

REDLANDS. K66ED, First Assembly of God, Claude E. Johnson, pastor, 1445 Ford St., Redlands, CA 92373.

RIVERSIDE/RAYMOND. K08IN, Riverside Television Assn..

SACREMENTO. K47DQ, Telemundo of N. CA, Paul Niedermeyer, vp, 2349 Bering Dr., San Jose, CA 95131.

SACREMENTO. K61DW, Dr. W.R. Portee, owner, 11243 S. Vermont Ave., Las Vegas, CA 90044.

SACREMENTO. K69FB, Trinity Broadcasting Network, Jane Duff, VP, Box A, Santa Ana, CA 92711.

SACREMENTO/STOCKTON. K08LC, Polar Broadcasting Inc., Warren Trumbly, pres, 1080 S. Los Molinas Way, Sacramento, CA 95864.

SACREMENTO/STOCKTON. K23DH, Polar Broadcasting Inc., Warren Trumbly, pres, 1080 S. Los Molinos Way, Sacramento, CA 95864.

SALINAS. K06LV, Lansman & Schatz Partners, Jeremy D. Lansman, owner, Box 240467, Anchorage, AK 99524.

SALINAS. K15CU, Telemundo of N. CA, Paul Niedermeyer, vp, 2349 Bering Dr., San Jose, CA 95131.

SAN DIEGO. K19BN, American Television Network, Philip Wilkinson, gen mgr, 720 Gateway Center Dr., San Diego, CA 92102.

SAN DIEGO. K57CD, Estrella License Corp. (Telemundo).

SAN DIEGO. K63EN, Civic Light Inc., John Wilkie, pres, Box 81146, San Diego, CA 92138.

SAN LUIS OBISPO. K15BD, Matrix Broadcasting, Hilding H. Larson, owner, 615 Tank Farm Rd., San Luis Obispo, CA 93401-7002.

SANTA BARBARA. K65BP, Harriscope of Los Angeles, Burt Harris, pres, 10920 Wilshire Blvd., Las Vegas, CA 90024.

SANTA CLARA/SAN JOSE. K22DD, Linda K. Trumbly, owner, 1080 S. Los Molinos Way, Sacramento, CA 96864.

SANTA MARIA. K25DX, Costa De Oro Television Inc., Walter F. Ulloa, pres, 6020 Nicolle St., Ventura, CA 93003.

SANTA MARIA. K27EI, Telemundo of N. CA, Nancy R. Alpert, vp, 1740 Broadway 18th Fl., New York, NY 10019.

SANTA MARIA/SAN LUIS OBISPO. K07TA, Ric Haley, gen mgr, 2325 Skyway Dr., #G, Santa Maria, CA 93455.

SANTA ROSA. K30DO, The Chronicle Publishing Co.

STOCKTON/LODI. K52CK, Telemundo of N. CA, Paul Niedermeyer, vp, 2349 Bering Dr., San Jose, CA 95131.

SUSANVILLE. K69FS, Honey Lake Community TV Corp., Box 963, Susanville, CA 96130.

SUSANVILLE/HERLONG. K65CC, Honey Lake Community TV Corp., Box 963, Susanville, CA 96130.

SUSANVILLE/HERLONG. K67BY, Honey Lake Commhnity TV Corp., Box 963, Susanville, CA 96130.

TWENTYNINE PALMS. K06KU, Moore Broadcasting Inc., Benjamin B. Moore, pres, Rt. 1 Box 1, Murfreesboro, TN 37130.

TWENTYNINE PALMS. K38AT, American Television Network, Charles Cohen, pres, Box 832048, Delray Beach, FL 33483-0248.

TWENTYNINE PALMS. K63CG, Morongo Basin TV Club Inc., E.W. Ball, pres, Box 864, Twentynine Palms, CA 92277-0864.

TYLER. K48DP, C-TEC Corporation, William S. Conley, Sr., ceo, 1037 N.N.E. Loop 323, Tyler, TX 75708.

UKIAH. K47AL, TV Improvement Assn., Harry Putnam, chairman, Box 342, Ukiah, CA 95482.

VENTURA. K47CL, Ojai Assembly of God, Rev. Frank Triggs, dir, 190 E. El Roblar Dr., Ojai, CA 93023-2398.

VICTORVILLE. K25AD, Victor Valley Public Translator.

VISTA/OCEANSIDE. K49BV, Lupian Warren Bernard Partners, c/o Richard Warren, pres, 8691 Echo Rd., La Mesda, CA 91941.

WILLOW CREEK. K34BW, California Oregon Broadcasting Inc., William B. Smullin, sec, 125 S. Fir Box 5m, Medford, OR 97501.

YUCCA VALLEY. K26BH, American Television Network, Charles Cohen, pres, Box 832048, Delray Beach, FL 33483-0248.

Colorado

AURORA. K36CP, Freeman Cosmo Harris,

AURORA. K38DF, Jean Bernard Van De Sande, pres, 2851 S. Parker Rd., #350, Aurora, CO 80014.

BOULDER. K54DK, 31 Licensee Inc.

CAHONE & DOVE CREEK. K02MF, Montezuma/Dolores City Metro, Box 158, Cortez, CO 81321.

COLORADO SPRINGS. K38CU, Beta Broadcasting Inc., Zenon Reynarowych.

COLORADO SPRINGS. K49CJ, Telemundo of Colorado Springs, c/o Telemundo Group-N Alpert, off mgr, 1740 Broadway 18th Fl., New York, NY 10019.

CORTEZ. K26CI, Montezuma/Dolores City Metro, Box 158, Cortez, CO 81321.

CORTEZ/MANCOS. K16CT, Southwest Colorado TV Translator, John Wayne, mgr, Box 158, Cortez, CO 81321.

CORTEZ/MANCOS. K41DE, Southwest Colorado TV Translator, John Wayne, mgr, Box 158, Cortez, CO 81321.

CRAIG. K55CI, Moffat County, 561 Russell St., Craig, CO 81011.

DENVER. K43DK, Golden Hills Broadcasting Corp.

DENVER. K47AQ, Trinity Broadcasting Network, Jane Duff, vp, Box A, Santa Ana, CA 92711.

DENVER. K57BT, Trinity Broadcasting Network, Jane Duff, vp, Box A, Santa Ana, CA 92711.

DOLORES. K02OG, Southwest Colorado TV Translator, John Wayne, mgr, Box 158, Cortez, CO 81321.

DURANGO. K39AH, KGSW-TV Inc., c/o Mountain States Broadcasting, gen mgr, Box 25200, Albuquerque, NM 87125.

FORT COLLINS. K54CQ, Echonet Corp., Charles Ergen, pres, 9805 E. Liff, Denver, CO 80231.

GLENWOOD SPRINGS. K25AH, Colorado West Broadcasting, Allen Bell, pres, 1322 1/2 Grand Ave., Glenwood Springs, CO 81601.

GLENWOOD SPRINGS. K65CK, Pikes Peak Broadcasting Co., Harry Hoth Jr., mgr, 399 S. 8th St., Colorado Springs, CO 80905.

GRAND VALLEY. K45AF, Pikes Peak Broadcasting Co., Harry Hoth Jr., mgr, 399 S. 8th St., Colorado Springs, CO 80905.

Low Power Television Stations

GUNNISON. K02LY, Gunnison City Metro Rec., Fred W. Henry, sec, Box 1382, Gunnison, CO 81230-1446.

MANCOS/CORTEZ. K24CH, Montezuma/Delores City Metro, Box 158, Cortez, CO 81321.

NEW CASTLE. K36AF, Pikes Peak Broadcasting Co., Harry Hoth Jr., mgr, 399 S. 8th St., Colorado Springs, CO 80905.

NUCLA. K49AX, Montrose County, Board of County Commisioners, Box 1289, Montrose, CO 81402.

PEETZ. K56EP, Board of Logan Co. Community, County Courthouse, Sterling, CO 80751.

PEETZ. K58DX, Board of Logan Co. Community, County Courthouse, Sterling, CO 80751.

RIFLE. K57CR, Pikes Peak Broadcasting Co., Harry Hoth Jr., mgr, 399 S. 8th St., Colorado Springs, CO 80905.

STERLING. K46CY, Board of Logan Co. Community, County Courthouse, Sterling, CO 80751.

Connecticut

GRANBY. W12CL, John Andrew Thompson, gen mgr, 28 Notch Rd., Grandby, CT 06035.

HARTFORD. W11BJ, Nat'l Black Media Coalition, David Honig, 38 New York Ave., N.E., Washington, DC 20002.

HARTFORD. W13BF, Channel 13 Television Inc., Paul D'Agostino, treas, 886 Maple Ave., Hartford, CT 06114.

HARTFORD. W47AD, WXTV License Partnership GP

NEW HAVEN. W06BP, Trident Broadcasting, Zenon Reynarowych, 8008 Margaret Pl., Glendale, NY 11385.

WEST HAVEN. W28AJ, Paging Assoc. Inc., Bob Knapp, sys eng, 24 Rockdale Rd., West Haven, CT 06516.

Delaware

DOVER. W27AJ, Delmarva Broadcast Service, 222 Pasadena Pl., Orlando, FL 32803.

NEWARK/BROOKSIDE. W14BG, Priority Commun. Ministries Inc., Francis J. Tareiski, owner, 1341 Lorewood Grove Rd., Middleton, DE 19709.

District of Columbia

WASHINGTON. W42AJ, Communicasting Corp., Christopher Sargent, pres, 150 S. Washington St. #401, Falls Church, VA 22046-2921.

WASHINGTON. W48AW, Los Cerezos Television Co., Antonio Guernica, gen mgr, 962 Wayne Ave. #900, Silver Spring, MD 20910-4433.

Florida

APALACHICOLA. W03AS, Richard L. Plessinger Sr., owner, 1591 Boyle Rd., Hamilton, OH 45013-1899.

COCOA/ROCKLEDGE. W04CN, Press Broadcasting Co., Perry Simon, pres, Box 1550, Neptune, NJ 07754-1550.

DAYTONA BEACH. W42AM, Channel America LPTV Licensed Subsidiary Inc., David Post, chairman, 19 W. 21st St., 2nd Fl., New York, NY 10019.

DE FUNIAK SPRINGS. W24AM, TV-24 Inc., Ashley N. Davis Jr., pres, Box 5180, Defuniak Springs, FL 32433.

DESTIN. W48BC, Beach TV Properties Inc., Jud Colley, pres, Box 9556, Panama City, FL 32407.

FORT LAUDERDALE. W27AQ, Skinner Broadcasting Inc., J. Rodger Skinner Jr., pres, 600 W. Hillsboro Blvd. #27, 3rd Fl., Deerfield Beach, FL 33441-1609.

FORT MYERS. W07BR, Tamiami Fort Myers Inc., Raymond A. Karpowicz, owner, One Outer Ladue, St. Louis, MO 63131.

FORT MYERS. W24AA, CFF Properties Inc., Nathan Price, pres, Box 5111, Lakeland, FL 33807-5111.

GAINESVILLE. W10BR, Board of Regents U. of Fla., John Morgese, stn mgr, 2000 Weimer Hall U. of Fla., Gainesville, FL 32611.

GAINESVILLE. W31AT, Video Jukebox Network Inc., LPTV coord, 12000 Biscayne Blvd., Miami, FL 33181-2742.

INGLIS/YANKEETOWN. W49AI, Citrus County Assn. for Retarded Children, Robert Thomas, pres, 1315 N. Van Nortwick Rd., Lecanto River, FL 32661-9710.

JACKSONVILLE. W36AJ, Trivest Financial Services, 2801 Fruitville Rd., #200, Sarasota, FL 34237.

JACKSONVILLE. W38AJ, M & M. Comm. Inc., J. Mccarthy Miller, pres, 606 Silvershore Dr., Pensacola, FL 32507.

JACKSONVILLE. W41BM, Jacksonville Translator Inc., Nathan Price, pres, Box 5111, Lakeland, FL 33807-5111.

JACKSONVILLE/BRENTWOOD/ARLINGTON W10AX, Video Jukebox Network Inc., LPTV coord, 12000 Biscayne Blvd., Miami, FL 33181-2742.

JUPITER. W09BU, Spirit Productions Inc., Pauline Therese Mantwill, gen mgr, Box 3161, Tequesta, FL 33469-0161.

KEY WEST. W34AD, Beach TV Properties Inc., Jud Colley, pres, Box 9556, Panama City, FL 32407.

KISSIMMEE. W19AX, Specialty Broadcasting Corp., Charles S. Namey, pres, 216 S. Center St., Winter Park, FL 32789-4374.

KISSIMMEE. W27BB, Specialty Broadcasting Corp., Charles S. Namey, pres, 216 S. Center St., Winter Park, FL 32789-4374.

LAKE CITY. W02BE, Woods Comm. Group, Charles Woods, pres, 3000 E. Cherry St., Springfield, MO 65802-2698.

LAKELAND. W14AC, Lakeland Translator Inc., Jim Mclennan, gen mgr, Box 314, Auburndale, FL 33823.

LIVE OAK. W02BH, Newsouth Broadcasting, Timothy S. Brumlik, mgr, Box 2271, Orlando, FL 32802.

LIVE OAK. W15AG, CFF Properties Inc., Nathan Price, pres, Box 5111, Lakeland, FL 33807-5111.

MADISON. W03AO, W03AO-TV, Billy G. Walker, owner, Drawer 772, Madison, FL 32340.

NAPLES. W09BS, Tamiami Naples Inc., Raymond A. Karpowicz, owner, One Outer Ladue, St. Louis, MO 63131.

NAPLES. W43AY, Russell R. Weddell, gen mgr, 87 Lake St., West Peabody, MA 01960.

OAKLAND PARK/CORAL SPRINGS. W55BO, CBS Inc., 51 West 52nd St., New York, NY 10019.

OCALA. W07BP, Marion County (FL) School Board.

ORLANDO. W04BN, Woods Comm. Group, Charles Woods, pres, 3000 E. Cherry St., Springfield, MO 65802-2698.

ORLANDO. W11BM, Video Jukebox Network Inc., LPTV coord, 12000 Biscayne Blvd., Miami, FL 33181-2742.

ORLANDO. W21AU, William K. Rowell, owner, 7575 Dr. Phillips Blvd., #300, Orlando, FL 32819.

ORLANDO. W31AU, CFF Properties Inc., Nathan Price, pres, Box 5111, Lakeland, FL 33807-5111.

ORLANDO. W63BH, Bahia Honda Inc., Enrique Perez, gen mgr, 2942 W. Columbus Dr., #204, Tampa, FL 33607.

PALATKA. W49AW, Pentecostal Revival Assn. Inc., James L. Harrell Jr., vp, Rt. 4, Box 1506, Palatka, FL 32177.

PALM BEACH. W19AQ, Main Street TV Inc., Raymond Horn, mgr, 1551 Forum Pl. #200e, West Palm Beach, FL 33401-2306.

PANAMA CITY BEACH. W46AN, Beach TV Properties Inc., Jud Colley, pres, Box 9556, Panama City, FL 32407.

PENSACOLA. W12CN, Vernon Watson, owner, 6582 Oakcliff Rd., Pensacola, FL 32526.

PENSACOLA. W31BB, John Walton, owner, 4434 4th Ave. South, St. Petersburg, FL 33711.

PENSACOLA. W63BK, Trinity Broadcasting Network, Jane Duff, vp, Box A, Santa Ana, CA 92711.

PERRY. W59BE, Perry Translators Inc., Nathan Price, pres, Box 5111, Lakeland, FL 33807-5111.

PERRY. W69AX, Perry Channel 69-TV Inc., Hudson Randall, gen mgr, Box 701, Perry, FL 32347.

PINEALLAS COUNTY. W14AW, Pinellas County Schools, 1960 E. Druid Rd., Clearwater, FL 33516.

ST AUGUSTINE. W22AN, Lumen Inc., Gino Andreani, gen mgr, 2507 U.S. 1 S. Suite 7712, St. Augustine, FL 32086.

ST PETERSBURG. W24BF, Southeast LPTV Inc., Michael Torici, asst sec, Box 9090, Clearwater, FL 34618.

ST PETERSBURG. W35AJ, Channel America Lic Subsid, David Post, chairman, 19 W. 21st St. 2nd Fl., New York, NY 10010.

ST PETERSBURG. W63BS, Henry Esteva, gen mgr, 201 2nd Ave. N., St. Petersburg, FL 33701.

SARASOTA. W24AT, TV-24 Sarasota Inc., Warren J. Cave, pres, Box 20596, Sarasota, FL 34238.

STUART. W16AR, Stuart Tower Corp., August F. Gabriel, pres, 126 Lucie Ln., Stuart, FL 34984.

TALLAHASSEE. W09BI, Assn. Christian TV, Clyde Bowers, gen mgr, 110 S. Monroe St., Tallahassee, FL 32301.

TALLAHASSEE. W17AB, Assn. Christian TV Systems Inc., Clyde Bowers, gen mgr, 110 S. Monroe St., Tallahassee, FL 32301.

TALLAHASSEE. W65BG, Temple Baptist Church, Jack Nichols, gen mgr, 3000 N. Meridian Rd., Tallahassee, FL 32312.

TAMPA. W06BE, WVJ-TV, Ronald D. Kniffen, pres, 449 Ave. A, Rochester, NY 14621.

TAMPA. W57BA, ZGS Television of Tampa Inc., Ronald J. Gordon, pres, 2300 Clarendon Blvd., #411, Arlington, VA 22201.

TAMPA. W61BL, Bahia Honda Inc., Enrique Perez, gen mgr, 2942 W. Columbus Dr., #204, Tampa, FL 33607.

TAMPA. W68CF, Trinity Broadcasting Network, Jane Duff, vp, Box A, Santa Ana, CA 92711.

VERO BEACH. W53AH, Maine Broadcasting Systems, Fredrick L. Thompson, pres, One Congress Sq., Portland, ME 04101.

VERO BEACH. W69BO, Vero Broadcasting Inc.

WEST PALM BEACH. W36AQ, Palm Beach Broadcasting Inc., Peter Clark, partner, 3180 Burgundy Dr. N., Palm Beach Gardens, FL 33410-1477.

Georgia

ALBANY. W12CH, Manuel A. Cantu, pres, Box 71162, Albany, GA 31707.

ALBANY. W35BD, Jesse Boone Productions, Jesse Boone Sr., owner, 313 Highland Ave., Albany, GA 31701.

ATHENS/WATKINSVILLE. W42AO, Georgia Regional Community TV, Stanley R. Pulliam, chairman, Box 454, Athens, GA 30603.

ATLANTA. W04BR, Woods Comm. Group, Charles Woods, pres, 3000 E. Cherry St., Springfield, MO 65802.

ATLANTA. W20AU, Valuevision International Inc., Robert Johander, pres, 5174 W. 76th St., Minneapolis, MN 55439-2300.

ATLANTA. W24AL, Southeast LPTV Inc., Michael Torici, asst sec, Box 9090, Clearwater, FL 34618.

ATLANTA. W42BQ, Frontier Broadcasting Inc., J. Mitchell Johnson, mng ptnr, Box 125, Fort Worth, TX 76101.

AUGUSTA. W67BE, Avn Inc., Jeremy Coghlan, gen mgr, 2827 Central Ave., Augusta, GA 30909.

CAMILLA. W02BS, McMinn Comm. Inc., Ed McMinn, pres, 692 Timothy Rd., Athens, GA 30606.

COLUMBUS. W07CP, Dr. Stephen Hollis, owner, Box 7008, Columbus, GA 31908.

COLUMBUS. W16AF, Dr. Stephen Hollis, owner, Box 7008, Columbus, GA 31908.

COLUMBUS. W22AH, Dr. Stephen Hollis, owner, Box 7008, Columbus, GA 31908.

DALTON. W43AT, Family Life TV 43, Doug Jensen, exec dir, 101 S. Spencer St., Dalton, GA 30721-3122.

DALTON. W66BA, Sudbrink Broadcasting of Ga, Hal Gore, pres, 200 N. Cobb Pky #114, Marietta, GA 30062-3538.

DUBLIN. W35BB, Gil Gillis, gen mgr, 211 South Monroe St., Dublin, GA 31021.

HAZLEHURST. W63AT, Jeff Davis Broadcasters Inc., John Hullett, pres, Box 757, Hazelhurst, GA 31539.

LA GRANGE. W33AT, Georgia-Alabama Broadcasting Inc., Sarah Beth Mallory, pres, Box 2830, La Grange, GA 30241.

MARIETTA. W55BM, Video Jukebox Network Inc., LPTV coord, 12000 Biscayne Blvd., Miami, FL 33181-2742.

Low Power Television Stations

ROME. W34AG, Prism Broadcasting Network Inc., Vince Castelli, pres,

ROME. W56CD, Prism Broadcasting Network Inc., Vince Castelli, pres,

ROSWELL. W67CI, Korean American TV Broadcasting, James Sim, pres, 250 Spring St. #6N302, Atlanta, GA 30303.

STATESBORO. W48BH, Carl L. Gillis Jr., owner, Box 2006, Dublin, GA 31021.

TIFTON. W05AZ, Moore Broadcasting Inc., Benjamin B. Moore, pres, Rt. 1 Box 1, Murfreesboro, TN 37130.

TIFTON. W51AR, Butterfly Broadcasting, 302 W. 20th St., Tifton, GA 31794.

VALDOSTA. W53HI, General Mgmt Consultants, Paul Lansat, pres, 5200 N. Ocean 318 B, Singer Island, FL 33404.

VIRGINIA CITY. W06BH, Greene Comm. Inc., 4207 W. Hartmant, Phoenix, AZ 85051.

Hawaii

HALEAKALA. K24CF, Oceania Broadcasting Network Inc., Christopher Racine, pres, 970 N. Kalaheo Ave. #c314, Kaliua, HI 96734.

HONOLULU. K50AP, Family Television Inc., Joseph Perez, mgr, Box 272825, Concord, CA 94527-2825.

MAUI. K61FE, ETV Hawaii/Elephant TV Inc., 147a-1 Kulalani Circle, Kula Isle of Maui, HI 96790.

WAILUKU. K21AG, King Broadcasting Co., Eric Bremner, vp, 333 Dexter Ave. N., Seattle, WA 98109.

WAILUKU. K59EI, Mauivision TV Broadcasting, Susan Durch, pres, 147a-1 Kulalani Circle, Kula Isle of Maui, HI 96790.

Idaho

ARCO. K13VK, Ambassador Media Corp., William L. Armstrong III, pres, 11 Carriage Ln., Littleton, CO 80121-2010.

ASHTON. K09VD, Ambassador Media Corp., William L. Armstrong III, pres, 11 Carriage Ln., Littleton, CO 80121-2010.

BLACKFOOT. K13VI, Ambassador Media Corp, William L. Armstrong III, pres, 11 Carriage Ln., Littleton, CO 80121-2010.

BOISE. K10MY, Women's LPTV Network, Janet L. Jacobsen, vp, 7860 N. Hayden Rd., #j101, Scottsdale, AZ 85258.

BOISE. K43BE, Kentel, Ken Jacobsen, mgr, 3242 Girard Ave. South #105, Minneapolis, MN 55408-3466.

BOISE. K47BE, Trinity Broadcasting Network, Jane Duff, vp, Box A, Santa Ana, CA 92711.

BURLEY. K07UL, Ambassador Media Corp., William L. Armstrong III, pres, 11 Carriage Ln., Littleton, CO 80121-2010.

BURLEY. K61AP, The Post Co., Box 2148, Idaho Falls, ID 83401.

CHALLIS. K08KU, Ambassador Media Corp., William L. Armstrong III, pres, 11 Carriage Ln., Littleton, CO 80121-2010.

COERR D'ALENE. K18DT, KHQ Inc., James P. Cowles, trustee, Box 8088, Spokane, WA 99203.

CROUCH. K13LB, Garden Valley Translator Dist., Roy Pleticha, chairman, Box 510, Garden Valley, ID 83662.

DRIGGS. K09UZ, Ambassador Media Corp., William L. Armstrong III, pres, 11 Carriage Ln., Littleton, CO 80121-2010.

FIRTH/BASALT. K12OE, Ambassador Media Corp., William L. Armstrong III, pres, 11 Carriage Ln., Littleton, CO 80121-2010.

GRIMES PASS. K08JA, Garden Valley Translator Dist., Roy Pleticha, chairman, Box 510, Garden Valley, ID 83662.

IDAHO FALLS. K12NZ, Ambassador Media Corp., William L. Armstrong III, pres, 11 Carriage Ln., Littleton, CO 80121-2010.

JEROME. K08KV, Ambassador Media Corp., William L. Armstrong III, pres, 11 Carriage Ln., Littleton, CO 80121-2010.

LEWISTON. K15CH, Orehards Community TV, Box 492, Lewiston, ID 83501.

LEWISTON. K21CC, Orehards Community TV, Box 492, Lewiston, ID 83501.

LEWISTON. K30BW, Spokane Television Inc.

LEWISTON. K35BW, Orehards Community TV, Box 492, Lewiston, ID 83501.

LEWISTON. K47BW, Inland Northwest TV Inc., Robert R. Bingham, pres, 1200 Westlake Ave. #707, Seattle, WA 98109.

LEWISTON. K66CE, Life of Victory TV Inc., David A. Tucker, owner, Box 421, Lewiston, ID 83501-0421.

LEWISTON. K68BC, Orehards Community TV, Box 492, Lewiston, ID 83501.

MONTPELIER. K31CI, Bear Lake County TV Dist., Williard G. Johnson, chairman, Box 184, Montpelier, ID 83254.

PAUL. K04ND, Ambassador Media Corp., William L. Armstrong III, pres, 11 Carriage Ln., Littleton, CO 80121-2010.

POCATELLO. K12OA, Ambassador Media Corp., William L. Armstrong III, pres, 11 Carriage Ln., Littleton, CO 80121-2010.

RUPERT. K02NO, Ambassador Media Corp., William L. Armstrong III, pres, 11 Carriage Ln., Littleton, CO 80121-2010.

ST ANTHONY. K12OB, Ambassador Media Corp., William L. Armstrong III, pres, 11 Carriage Ln., Littleton, CO 80121-2010.

SANDPOINT. K48DX, KHQ Inc., James P. Cowles, trustee, Box 8088, Spokane, WA 99203.

SHELLEY. K13VJ, Ambassador Media Corp., William L. Armstrong III, pres, 11 Carriage Ln., Littleton, CO 80121-2010.

TERRACE LAKES. K03ET, Garden Valley Translator Dist, Roy Pleticha, chairman, Box 510, Garden Valley, ID 83662.

TERRACE LAKES. K05EY, Garden Valley Translator Dist, Roy Pleticha, chairman, Box 510, Garden Valley, ID 83662.

TERRACE LAKES. K09LB, Garden Valley Translator Dist, Roy Pleticha, chairman, Box 510, Garden Valley, ID 83662.

TERRACE LAKES REC. RANCH. K11KS, Garden Valley Translator Dist, Roy Pleticha, chairman, Box 510, Garden Valley, ID 83662.

TWIN FALLS. K05IX, Ambassador Media Corp., William L. Armstrong III, pres, 11 Carriage Ln., Littleton, CO 80121-2010.

TWIN FALLS. K27AO, Linda D. Clevenger, pres, Box 44-A Rt. 2, Jefferson, TN 37760.

TWIN FALLS. K38AS, King Broadcasting Co., Eric Bremner, vp, 333 Dexter Ave. N., Seattle, WA 98109.

TWIN FALLS. K49AZ, American Comm. Broadcasting Co. Inc., 1317 F. St. N.W. #600, Washington, DC 20004.

TYGEE VALLEY. K10LO, Stump Tygee Trans. Station, Box 428, Auburn, WY 83111.

Illinois

BLUE ISLAND. W54AP, Catholic Views Broadcasts Inc., Rev Kenneth Baker, pres, 86 Riverside Dr., New York, NY 10024.

CHAMPAIGN. W39BH, Robert H. Shreffler, gen mgr, 1817 Northwood Dr., Clearwater, FL 34624-2461.

CHICAGO. W04CK, Silvia M. Landin, gen mgr, 8295 S.W. 48th St., Miami, FL 33155.

CHICAGO. W13BE, Woods Comm. Group, Charles Woods, pres, 3000 E. Cherry St., Springfield, MO 65802-2698.

CHICAGO. W23AT, Weigel Broadcasting Co., Ken Shapiro, pres, 141 W. Jackson Blvd., Chicago, IL 60604.

CHRISTIANSTED. W23AD, Blackhawk Broadcasting Corp., Joe Musser, pres, Box 4441, Rockford, IL 61110.

EFFINGHAM. W41BL, Lightning Broadcasting Co., 812 N. Olive St., St. Elmo, IL 62458.

FLORA. W24BP, H & R Comm., Box 368, Flora, IL 62839.

JOHNSTON CITY. W17AZ, Three Angels Broadcast Net Inc., Danny Shelton, pres, Box 220, West Frankfort, IL 62896.

MT CARMEL. W12CJ, Starlight Television Corp., John E. Rhine, pres, 230 E. 6th St., Mount Carmel, IL 62863.

PLANO. W30AL, WFXV-TV Inc., Larry Nelson, pres, One Broadcast Center, Plano, IL 60545.

ROBINSON. W57AO, Full Gospel Business Mens' Fellowship, Donald Badgley, gen mgr, Box 2357, Muncie, IN 47307.

ROCKFORD. W08CM, Blackhawk Broadcasting Corp., Joe Musser, pres, Box 4411, Rockford, IL 61110.

ROCKFORD. W45AJ, KATY Comm. Inc., John Shaller, gen mgr, 2200 E. Devon Ave. #220, Des Plaines, IL 60018-4501.

SALEM. W28AI, Three Angels Broadcast Network Inc., Danny Shelton, pres, Box 220, West Frankfort, IL 62896.

SPRINGFIELD. W28BE, The Marian Center, Mark Thomas, dir, 32 Birch Lake S., Sherman, IL 62684.

SPRINGFIELD. W33AY, North Central LPTV Inc., Michael Torici, asst sec, Box 9090, Clearwater, FL 34618.

SUGAR GROVE. W54BE, Waubonsee Community College, 6213 Middleton Springs Dr., Middleton, WI 53562.

Indiana

AUBURN. W07CL, CP Broadcasters Inc., Wayne H. Paradise, pres, 5446 County Rd., 29, Auburn, IN 46706.

CHESTERTON. W04CQ, TV-4 Indian Oak Corp., Winfield L. Chubb, pres, 348 Indian Boundary, Chesterton, IN 46304.

CHESTERTON. W54BK, Studio 5 Inc., Thomas W. Tittle, sec, 72 Hillcrest Rd., Portage, IN 46368.

EVANSVILLE. W04BV, South Central Comm. Corp., Robert O. Gathings, gen mgr, Box 3848, Evansville, IN 47736.

EVANSVILLE. W05BC, South Central Comm. Corp., Robert O. Gathings, gen mgr, Box 3848, Evansville, IN 47736.

EVANSVILLE. W52AZ, South Central Comm. Corp., John Reiplinger, gen mgr, Box 3848, Evansville, IN 47736.

FORT WAYNE. W45AG, Tran Star Inc., 716 N. Westwood Ave., Toledo, OH 43607.

FORT WAYNE. W68BN, Zonation Broadcasting, 350 Townsend St., San Francisco, CA 94107.

GARY. W18AT, Studio 5 Inc., Thomas W. Tittle, sec, 72 Hillcrest Rd., Portage, IN 46368.

INDIANAPOLIS. W11BV, Indiana Broadcasting Corp., Dave Smith, gen mgr, 7855 Teel Way, Indianapolis, IN 46256.

INDIANAPOLIS. W27AR, Videoindiana Inc., Michael Corken, gen mgr, 1000 N. Meridian St., Indianapolis, IN 46204.

INDIANAPOLIS. W47AZ, Video Jukebox Network Inc., LPTV coord, 12000 Biscayne Blvd., Miami, FL 33181-2742.

JASPER. W27BG, Paul E. Knies, owner, Jasper, IN 47546.

JEFFERSONVILLE/LOUISVILLE, KY. W05BE, Channel 5 Television, John W. Smith Jr., pres, Box 1226, Jeffersonville, IN 47131.

MARION. W25BN, Acts of Marion Inc., David Trimble, vp, 2172 Chapel Pike, Marion, IN 46952.

MARTINSVILLE. W15AY, Reporter Times Inc., 1420 S. Catherine St., Martinville, TN 46151.

MICHIGAN CITY. K24AI, Trinity Broadcasting Network, Jane Duff, vp, Box A, Santa Ana, CA 92711.

MUNCIE. W32AC, Full Gospel Business Mens' Fellowship, Donald Badgley, gen mgr, Box 2357, Muncie, IN 47307.

PORTAGE. W13BQ, Studio 5 Inc.

PRINCETON. W06BD, North Gibson School Corp., Bob Cloin, off mgr, Box 325, Princeton, IN 47670.

VALPARAISO. W24AW, Studio 5 Inc., Thomas W. Tittle, sec, 72 Hillcrest Rd., Portage, IN 46368.

Iowa

AMES. K52BH, TV-52 Inc., Box 203, Huxley, IA 50124-0203.

CEDAR RAPIDS. K61FF, Trinity Broadcasting Network, Jane Duff, vp, Box A, Santa Ana, CA 92711.

COUNCIL BLUFFS. K45CQ, R.B. Sheldahl, owner, 6825 N.W. 100th St., Johnston, IA 50131.

DAVENPORT. K58BX, Trinity Broadcasting Network, Jane Duff, vp, Box A, Santa Ana, CA 92711.

DES MOINES. K35CF, R.B. Sheldahl, owner, 6825 N.W. 100th St., Johnston, IA 50131.

DES MOINES. K41DD, Susan Webb, vp, 5301 Wisconsin Ave. #740, Washington, DC 20015.

IOWA CITY. K64DG, R.B. Sheldahl, owner, 6825 N.W. 100th St., Johnston, IA 50131.

KEOKUK. K60CL, Word Christ Vision, Rev. Harold Meyers, coord, Box 787, Keokuk, IA 52632-5603.

MARSHALLTOWN. K39AS, FM Iowa Inc., Mark Osmundson, gen mgr, Box 538, North Center, IA 50158.

OTTUMWA. K42AM, Trinity Broadcasting Network, Jane Duff, vp, Box A, Santa Ana, CA 92711.

SPENCER. K55FL, Maine Radio and TV Co., Fredrick L. Thompson, pres, Box 657, Sioux City, IA 51102.

STORM LAKE. K40CO, Maine Radio and TV Co., Fredrick L. Thompson, pres, Box 657, Sioux City, IA 51102.

WATERLOO. K65BY, Trinity Broadcasting Network, Jane Duff, vp, Box A, Santa Ana, CA 92711.

Kansas

JUNCTION CITY. K06KZ, Montgomery Publications Inc., Robert Raff, gen mgr, Box 129/222 W. 6th St., Junction City, KS 66441.

JUNCTION CITY. K26BZ, Trinity Broadcasting Network, Jane Duff, vp, Box A, Santa Ana, CA 92711.

JUNCTION CITY. K39BR, N.E. KS Broadcasting Services Inc., 222 Pasadena Pl., Orlando, FL 32853.

LAWRENCE. K58CX, N.E. KS Broadcasting Services Inc., 222 Pasadena Pl., Orlando, FL 32853.

MANHATTAN. K31BW, Trinity Broadcasting Network, Jane Duff, vp, Box A, Santa Ana, CA 92711.

OVERLAND PARK. K68DK, University of Kansas Medical Center, Breck Marion, media serv, Continuing Education Bldg., Lawrence, KS 66045.

SALINA. K15CN, Trinity Broadcasting Network, Jane Duff, vp, Box A, Santa Ana, CA 92711.

TOPEKA. K15BQ, Capitol City Broadcasting, Kelly Kraemer, dir, 601 S.W. Topeka Blvd., Topeka, KS 66603.

TOPEKA. K17CK, Generic Television, Eric Jacobsen, pres, 2818 E. Aster Dr., Phoenix, AZ 85032-6548.

WICHITA. K15DD, South Central LPTV Inc., Michael Torici, asst sec, Box 9090, Clearwater, FL 34618.

WICHITA. K51DN, River City Broadcasting, Larry Marcus, vp, 1215 Cole St., St. Louis, MO 63106.

WICHITA. K55FS, River City Broadcasting, Larry Marcus, vp, 1215 Cole St., St. Louis, MO 63106.

WICHITA. K59DA, Trinity Broadcasting Network, Jane Duff, vp, Box A, Santa Ana, CA 92711.

Kentucky

BOWLING GREEN/GLASGOW. W48BM, Jason Wilson, gen mgr, 9396 New Glasgow Rd., Scottsville, KY 42164.

CAMPBELLSVILLE. W04BP, Campbellsville College, Janet Graham, pgm dir, 200 W. College St., Campbellsville, KY 42718.

CORBIN. W20AS, Derek Ray Eubanks, owner, Drawer E., Corbin, KY 40702.

CORBIN. W48BD, Victory Training School, Charles E. Sivley, pres, R.R. 11 Box 381, Keavy, KY 40737.

HOPKINSVILLE. W43AG, TV-43, D.J. Everett, gen mgr, Box 4300, Hopkinsville, KY 42241.

LEBANON. K06AY, W & H. Broadcasting, J.T. Whitlock, ceo, Box 680, Lebanon, KY 40033.

LOUISVILLE. W13BZ, Video Jukebox Network Inc., LPTV coord, 12000 Biscayne Blvd., Miami, FL 33181-2742.

MOREHEAD. W10BM, Vearl Pennington, mgr, Box 968, Mount Sterling, KY 40353.

MOUNT STERLING. W02BP, McKinley Walker, gen mgr, Box 637, Mount Sterling, KY 40353.

MOUNT STERLING. W06BC, Vearl Pennington, mgr, Box 968, Mount Sterling, KY 40353.

MURRAY. W46BE, Keith Stubblefield, owner, 639 Rosemont Ave., Pasadena, CA 91103.

OWENSBORO. W12BJ, Commonwealth of KY/University of KY, Dr. John McGuire, pres, 4800 New Hartford Rd., Owensboro, KY 42301.

Louisiana

BATON ROUGE. K07UJ, Jeanne Conrad, owner, 2315 N. Granite Reef, Scottsdale, AZ 85257.

BATON ROUGE. K13VE, Classic Video Systems, Robert A. Hirschfeld, pres, 4723 N. 44th St., Phoenix, AZ 85018.

BATON ROUGE. K46CR, Patricia Screen, owner, 4693 N.W. 18th Ave., Miami, FL 33142.

BATON ROUGE. K52CQ, Capital Community Television, Samuel S. Di Maria, Box 45830, Baton Rouge, LA 70895.

BATON ROUGE. K65EF, Great Oaks Broadcasting Corp.

BATON ROUGE. W19AW, Great Oaks Broadcasting Corp., Louis Jenkins, pres, 914 N. Foster Dr., Baton Rouge, LA 70806.

BATON ROUGE. W39AT, American Television Network, Charles Cohen, pres, Box 832048, Delray Beach, FL 33483-0248.

CROWLEY. W65AS, TV-65 Inc. (full Gospel Int'l.), Lawrence M. Hollems, pres, Box 1304, Crowley, LA 70527.

JENNINGS. K13VG, Jennings Broadcasting Co. Inc., W. Bailey, pres, Drawer 1248, Jennings, LA 70546-1248.

LAFAYETTE. K21DM, Kare Network Management Inc., K Sandoval Burke, pres, Box 2295, Boulder, CO 80306.

LAFAYETTE. K62DW, Delta Management Corp., Eddie Blanchard, vp, 123 N. Easy St., Lafayette, LA 70506.

LAKE CHARLES. W63AQ, Full Gospel Business Mens' Fellowship, Richard Firmature, pres, Box 1014, Lake Charles, LA 70602.

MONROE. K22CQ, Telemedia Investors, 22 Hilltop Dr., Kimberling City, MO 65686.

MORGAN CITY. K39BJ, Ginger A. Price, gen mgr, Box 2642, Morgan City, LA 70381.

NEW ORLEANS. K14IE, South Central LPTV Inc., Michael Torici, asst sec, Box 9090, Clearwater, FL 34618.

NEW ORLEANS. K55EX, Sur Este Broadcasting Corp., Brian V. Wilder, pres, 16407 Ashwood Blvd., Tampa, FL 33624-1152.

NEW ORLEANS. W61AZ, Channel America LPTV Licensed Subsidiary Inc., David Post, chairman, 19 W. 21st St., 2nd Fl., New York, NY 10010.

SHREVEPORT. K67FD, Warren R. Wright, owner, 8714 Bay Crest Ln., Tampa, FL 33615.

SHREVEPORT. W61BC, Video Jukebox Network Inc., LPTV coord, 12000 Biscayne Blvd., Miami, FL 33181-2742.

Maine

BANGOR. W17BF, Craig Ministries Inc., Sherwood Craig, pres, 345 Main Rd., Orono, ME 04473.

CALAIS. W57AQ, Maine Broadcasting Co., Frederick L. Thompson, pres, One Congress Sq., Portland, ME 04101.

FALMOUTH. W57AP, Channel America LPTV Licensed Subsidiary Inc., David Post, chairman, 19 W. 21st St., 2nd Fl., New York, NY 10010.

PORTLAND. W45AL, Carter Broadcasting Corp., Ken Carter, pres, 20 Park Plaza #315, Boston, MA 02116.

WATERVILLE. W04AK, Maine Broadcasting Co., Frederick L. Thompson, pres, One Congress Sq., Portland, ME 04101.

WATERVILLE. W23AB, Russell Comm., James H. Russell Jr., pres, 407 E. Morningside Cir, Fullerton, CA 92635-3544.

WATERVILLE. W29AC, Russell Comm., James H. Russell Jr., pres, 407 E. Morningside Cir, Fullerton, CA 92635-3544.

Maryland

LEONARDTOWN. W52AX, Satellite Video Broadcasting, James Reichard, eng, 490 Jones Rd., Mechanicsville, MD 20659.

Massachusetts

BOSTON. W19AH, Channel 19 TV Corp., Peter N. Cuenca, pres, Box 850, Dorchester, MA 02125.

BOSTON. W33AV, Randolph M. Weigner, owner, 64 Douglas Dr., Meredith, NH 03253.

DENNIS. W58AO, Cape Television Inc., Fred Lungo, pres, 29 Bassett Ln., Hyannis, MA 02601.

DENNIS. W67BA, Cape Television Inc., Fred Lungo, pres, Box 1500, Valley Forge, PA 19842-1500.

FALL RIVER. W22AR, Freedom WLNE-TV Inc., D.R. Segal, pres, 430 County St., New Bedford, MA 02741.

HYANNIS. W08CH, WGBH Educational Foundation, John Lowell, chairman, 125 Western Ave., Boston, MA 02134.

NEW BEDFORD. W20AH, Freedom WLNE-TV Inc., D.R. Segal, pres, 430 County St., New Bedford, MA 02741.

SPRINGFIELD. W10BC, Harvard Broadcasting Inc., Louis Maisel, pres, Box 541, Harvard, MA 01451.

SPRINGFIELD. W65BX, Channel 13 Television Inc., Paul D. Agostino, treas, 886 Maple Ave., Hartford, CT 06114.

Michigan

BERRIEN SPRINGS. W25BM, Good News Television Inc., J.D. Wesley Hollingsworth, chairman, 9160 U.S. 31 Box 130, Berrien Springs, MI 49103-0130.

DETROIT. W05BN, Video Jukebox Network Inc.

DETROIT. W26AB, Channel America LPTV Licensed Subsidiary Inc., David Post, chairman, 19 W. 21st St., 2nd Fl., New York, NY 10010.

DETROIT. W36BD, Telethon TV Co. Inc., Robert Johander, pres, 8751 Red Oak Dr., Eden Prairie, MN 55347.

DETROIT. W44AR, Fairlane Assembly of God, Paul Bryant, pres, 22575 Ann Arbor Trail, Dearborne Hts., MI 48127.

DETROIT. W48AV, TV 48 Detroit Inc., Glenn R. Plummer, owner, Box 19700, Detroit, MI 48219.

GRAND RAPIDS. W59AZ, International Union UAW, Frank Joyce, mgr, 8000 E. Jefferson Ave., Detroit, MI 48214.

GRAND RAPIDS. W61BX, Good News Television Inc., J.D. Wesley Hollingsworth, chairman, 9150 U.S. 31 Box 130, Berrien Springs, MI 49103-0130.

IRON MOUNTAIN. K69BA, Bresnan Comm. Co. L.P., William J. Bresnan, pres, 709 Westchester Ave., White Plains, NY 10604.

IRON MOUNTAIN. W30AK, Bresnan Comm. Co. L.P., William J. Bresnan, pres, 709 Westchester Ave., White Plains, NY 10604.

IRON MOUNTAIN. W30AK, Bresnan Comm. Co. L.P., William J. Bresnan, pres, 709 Westchester Ave., White Plains, NY 10604.

IRON MOUNTAIN. W35AK, Bresnan Comm. Co. L.P., William J. Bresnan, pres, 709 Westchester Ave., White Plains, NY 10604.

IRON MOUNTAIN. W43AN, Bresnan Comm. Co. L.P., William J. Bresnan, pres, 709 Westchester Ave., White Plains, NY 10604.

IRON MOUNTAIN. W56BF, Bresnan Comm. Co. L.P., William J. Bresnan, pres, 709 Westchester Ave., White Plains, NY 10604.

IRON MOUNTAIN. W59AQ, Bresnan Comm. Co. L.P., William J. Bresnan, pres, 709 Westchester Ave., White Plains, NY 10604.

IRON MOUNTAIN. W63AW, Bresnan Comm. Co. L.P., William J. Bresnan, pres, 709 Westchester Ave., White Plains, NY 10604.

Low Power Television Stations

IRON MOUNTAIN. W65BN, Comm. Entertainment Inc. Co. Inc., Richard Abraham, owner, W. 8965 Frei Dr., Iron Mountain, MI 49801.

IRON MOUNTAIN. W67AO, Bresnan Comm. Co. L.P., William J. Bresnan, pres, 709 Westchester Ave., White Plains, NY 10604.

MUSKEGON. W40AK, Kelley Enterprises, Fenton Kelley, owner, 60 S. Milliron Rd., Muskegon, MI 49442.

REPUBLIC. W09AJ, Republic Township.

ST IGNACE. W13BH, Mighty Mac Broadcasting Co., Rod Kackley, mgr, 334 N. State, St. Ignace, MI 49781.

Minnesota

ALEXANDRIA. K16CO, Selective TV Inc., Barbara Beers, mgr, Box 665, Alexandria, MN 56308.

ALEXANDRIA. K18DG, Selective TV Inc., Barbara Beers, mgr, Box 665, Alexandria, MN 56308.

ALEXANDRIA. K24AE, Selective TV Inc., Charles G. Bundy, pres, Box 665, Alexandria, MN 56308.

ALEXANDRIA. K26CL, Selective TV Inc., Barbara Beers, mgr, Box 665, Alexandria, MN 56308.

ALEXANDRIA. K28BT, Selective TV Inc., Barbara Beers, mgr, Box 665, Alexandria, MN 56308.

ALEXANDRIA. K30AF, Hubbard Broadcasting Inc., 3415 University Ave., St. Paul, MN 55114.

ALEXANDRIA. K34AF, Selective TV Inc., Barbara Beers, mgr, Box 665, Alexandria, MN 56308.

ALEXANDRIA. K48DV, Selective TV Inc., Charles G. Bundy, pres, Box 665, Alexandria, MN 56038.

ALEXANDRIA. K50DB, Selective TV Inc., Charles G. Bundy, pres, Box 665, Alexandria, MN 56038.

ALEXANDRIA. K52DZ, Selective TV Inc., Charles G. Bundy, pres, Box 665, Alexandria, MN 56038.

ALEXANDRIA. K58DS, Selective TV Inc., Barbara Beers, mgr, Box 665, Alexandria, MN 56308.

APPLETON. K15DC, Prairieview TV Inc., Tamara K. Campbell, pres, 6545 Cecilia Circle, Minneaplois, MN 55439.

APPLETON. K17CS, Prairieview TV Inc., Tamara K. Campbell, pres, 6545 Cecilia Circle, Minneapolis, MN 55439.

APPLETON. K19CW, Prairieview TV Inc., Tamara K. Campbell, pres, 6545 Cecilia Circle, Minneapolis, MN 55439.

APPLETON. K23DF, Prairieview TV Inc., Tamara K. Campbell, pres, 6545 Cecilia Circle, Minneapolis, MN 55439.

APPLETON. K25EI, Prairieview TV Inc., Tamara K. Campbell, pres, 6545 Cecilia Circle, Minneapolis, MN 55439.

APPLETON. K29CC, Prairieview TV Inc., Tamara K. Campbell, pres, 6545 Cecilia Circle, Minneapolis, MN 55439.

APPLETON. K31BT, Prairieview TV Inc., Tamara K. Campbell, pres, 6545 Cecilia Circle, Minneapolis, MN 55439.

APPLETON. K33CR, Prairieview TV Inc., Tamara K. Campbell, pres, 6545 Cecilia Circle, Minneapolis, MN 55439.

AUSTIN. K43DH, Teleview Systems of MN, Dianne Noren, mgr, Box 112, Appleton, MN 56208.

AUSTIN. K45DF, Teleview Systems of MN, Dianne Noren, mgr, Box 112, Appleton, MN 56208.

AUSTIN. K49DB, Teleview Systems of MN, Dianne Noren, mgr, Box 112, Appleton, MN 56208.

AUSTIN. K51CY, Teleview Systems of MN, Dianne Noren, mgr, Box 112, Appleton, MN 56208.

AUSTIN. K53DI, Teleview Systems of MN, Dianne Noren, mgr, Box 112, Appleton, MN 56208.

AUSTIN. K55FJ, Teleview Systems of MN, Dianne Noren, mgr, Box 112, Appleton, MN 56208.

AUSTIN. K57EU, Teleview Systems of MN, Dianne Noren, mgr, Box 112, Appleton, MN 56208.

AUSTIN. K61EU, Teleview Systems of MN, Dianne Noren, mgr, Box 112, Appleton, MN 56208.

BEMIDJI. K26AC, Red River Broadcast Group, Ron Kunin, pres, 4015 9th Ave. S.W., Fargo, ND 58103.

BRAINERD. K54AT, Red River Broadcast Group, Ron Kunin, pres, 4015 9th Ave. S.W., Fargo, ND 58103.

DULUTH. K58CM, Trinity Broadcasting Network, Jane Duff, vp, Box A, Santa Ana, CA 92711.

EAGLE BEND. K45AR, Independent School Dist. 790, W. James, superinten, Box 299, Eagle Bend, MN 56446.

ELY. K30DX, Harry W. Reed II.

ELY. K32DH, Harry W. Reed II.

ELY. K34DS, Harry W. Reed II.

ELY. K36CY, Harry W. Reed II.

ERHARD. K31CH, Rural Services of Central MN Inc., Clarence Peterson, dir, Box 375, Pelican Rapids, MN 56572.

ERHARD. K39CJ, Rural Services of Central MN Inc., Clarence Peterson, dir, Box 375, Pelican Rapids, MN 56572.

ERHARD. K41CS, Rural Services of Central MN Inc., Clarence Peterson, dir, Box 375, Pelican Rapids, MN 56572.

ERHARD. K43CS, Rural Services of Central MN Inc., Clarence Peterson, dir, Box 375, Pelican Rapids, MN 56572.

ERHARD. K51DC, Rural Services of Central MN Inc., Clarence Peterson, dir, Box 375, Pelican Rapids, MN 56572.

FAIRMONT. K28AE, Ogden Broadcasting of MN Inc., David Ridgeway, mgr, Box 487, New Ulm, MN 56073.

GRAND RAPIDS. K18AI, Red River Broadcast Group, Ron Kunin, pres, 4015 9th Ave. S.W., Fargo, ND 58103.

GRANITE FALLS. K16CP, MN Valley TV Improvement, Daniel Richter, pres, Box A, Granite Falls, MN 56241.

GRANITE FALLS. K18DI, MN Valley TV Improvement, Daniel Richter, pres, Box A, Granite Falls, MN 56241.

GRANITE FALLS. K22DO, MN Valley TV Improvement, Daniel Richter, pres, Box A, Granite Falls, MN 56241.

GRANITE FALLS. K24CS, MN Valley TV Improvement, Daniel Richter, pres, Box A, Granite Falls, MN 56241.

GRANITE FALLS. K26DG, MN Valley TV Improvement, Daniel Richter, pres, Box A, Granite Falls, MN 56241.

GRANITE FALLS. K35DK, MN Valley TV Improvement, Daniel Richter, pres, Box A, Granite Falls, MN 56241.

GRANITE FALLS. K45DJ, MN Valley TV Improvement, Daniel Richter, pres, Box A, Granite Falls, MN 56241.

MINNEAPOLIS. K07UI, White Sage Broadcasting Co., Norman Houston, pres, 23642 Calabasas Rd., #104, Calabasas, CA 91302-1592.

MINNEAPOLIS. K13UT, Channel America LPTV Licensed Subsidiary Inc., David Post, chairman, 19 W. 21st St., 2nd Fl., New York, NY 10010.

MINNEAPOLIS. K35CY, North Central LPTV Inc., Michael Torici, asst sec, Box 9090, Clearwater, FL 34618.

MINNEAPOLIS. K62BD, Domsat of Minnesota Inc., Robert N. Johnson, pres, Box 7609, Naples, FL 33941.

MINNEAPOLIS. W62BD, Valuevision International Inc., Robert Johander, pres, 5174 W. 76th St., Minneapolis, MN 55439-2300.

MINNEAPOLIS/ST PAUL. K58BS, Trinity Broadcasting Network, Jane Duff, vp, Box A, Santa Ana, CA 92711.

NEW ULM. K22AE, Ogden Broadcasting of MN Inc., David Ridgeway, mgr, Box 487, New Ulm, MN 56073.

OLIVIA. K31CG, Renville County TV Corp., Box 378, Bird Island, MN 55310-0378.

OLIVIA. K33CT, Renville County TV Corp., Box 378, Bird Island, MN 55310-0378.

PARK RAPIDS. K05IV, Red River Broadcast Group, Ron Kunin, pres, 4015 9th Ave. S.W., Fargo, ND 58103.

REDWOOD FALLS. K15CE, Redwood TV Improvement Assn., Box 51, Redwood Falls, MN 56283.

REDWOOD FALLS. K17BV, Redwood TV Improvement Assn., Box 51, Redwood Falls, MN 56283.

REDWOOD FALLS. K19CV, Redwood TV Improvement Assn., Box 51, Redwood Falls, MN 56283.

REDWOOD FALLS. K21DJ, Redwood TV Improvement Assn., Box 51, Redwood Falls, MN 56283.

REDWOOD FALLS. K25DN, Redwood TV Improvement Assn., Box 51, Redwood Falls, MN 56283.

REDWOOD FALLS. K34DB, Redwood TV Improvement Assn., Box 51, Redwood Falls, MN 56283.

REDWOOD FALLS. K39CH, Redwood TV Improvement Assn., Box 51, Redwood Falls, MN 56283.

ROCHESTER. K60DS, Trinity Broadcasting Network, Jane Duff, vp, Box A, Santa Ana, CA 92711.

ST CLOUD. K19BG, Trinity Broadcasting Network, Jane Duff, vp, Box A, Santa Ana, CA 92711.

ST CLOUD/SARTELL. K13VS, Community Comm. Inc., Dennis Carpenter, pres, Box 699, St. Cloud, MN 56302.

ST JAMES. K16CG, Co-Op TV Assn. of S. Minnesota, Jeffrey Pelzel, mgr, Box 285, St. James, MN 56081.

ST JAMES. K19CA, United Comm., Box 128, Manakato, MN 56001.

ST JAMES. K21DG, Co-Op TV Assn. of S. Minnesota, Jeffrey Pelzel, mgr, Box 285, St. James, MN 56081.

ST JAMES. K24CP, Co-Op TV Assn. of S. Minnesota, Jeffrey Pelzel, mgr, Box 285, St. James, MN 56081.

ST JAMES. K26CS, Co-Op TV Assn. of S. Minnesota, Jeffrey Pelzel, mgr, Box 285, St. James, MN 56081.

ST JAMES. K35DC, Co-Op TV Assn. of S. Minnesota, Jeffery Pelzel, mgr, Box 285, St. James, MN 56081.

ST JAMES. K38CD, Co-Op TV Assn. of S. Minnesota, Jeffrey Pelzel, mgr, Box 285, St. James, MN 56081.

ST JAMES. K40BU, Co-Op TV Assn., of S. Minnesota, Jeffrey Pelzel, mgr, Box 285, St. James, MN 56081.

ST JAMES. K42AV, Co-Op TV Assn. of S. Minnesota, Jeffrey Pelzel, mgr, Box 285, St. James, MN 56081.

ST PAUL. K53CH, Catholic Views Broadcasts Inc., Rev. Kenneth Baker, pres, 86 Riverside Dr., New York, NY 10024.

WILLMAR. K27CK, West Central Christian Comm. Inc., Dale Lindquist, treas, Box 1739, Willmar, MN 56201.

WILLMAR. K34DG, UHF Television Inc., William C. Marcil, pres, Box 241, Willmar, MN 56201.

WILLMAR. K38CV, UHF Television Inc., William C. Marcil, pres, Box 241, Willmar, MN 56201.

WILLMAR. K66DN, UHF Television Inc., William C. Marcil, pres, Box 241, Wilmar, MN 56201.

Mississippi

BILOXI. W02BG, Trinity Broadcasting Network, Jane Duff, vp, Box A, Santa Ana, CA 92711.

BOONEVILLE. W53AF, Unity Broadcasting Inc., Lealon Owens, pres, Box 111, Booneville, MS 38829.

BRUCE. W07BN, Bruce Independent TV, William E. Morgan, mgr, Box 453, Bruce, MS 38915.

CLEVELAND. W08CQ, David Ellington, owner, Box 617, Webb, MS 38966.

JACKSON. K56BH, Sur Este Broadcasting Corp., Brian V. Wilder, pres, 16407 Ashwood Blvd., Tampa, FL 33624-1152.

JACKSON. W08CU, Video Jukebox Network Inc., LPTV coord, 12000 Biscayne Blvd., Miami, FL 33181-2742.

JACKSON. W10BD, Great Oaks Broadcasting Corp., Louis Jenkins, pres, 914 N. Foster Dr., Baton Rouge, LA 70806.

JACKSON. W64BB, Sur Este Broadcasting Corp., Brian V. Wilder, pres, 16407 Ashwood Blvd., Tampa, FL 33624-1152.

STARKVILLE. W05BV, First United Methodist Church, Marty Young, oper mgr, Drawer 728, Starkville, MS 39759.

WEBB. K11BU, David Ellington, owner, Box 617, Webb, MS 38966.

WEBB. W11BU, David Ellington, owner, Box 617, Webb, MS 38966.

Missouri

BRANSON. K05JQ, Lorianne Crook-Owens, owner, 1111 Wilson Pike, Brentwood, TN 37027.

BRANSON. K25BD, Christians Inc. for Christ, Carlos Ortiz, pastor, 1108 S. Commerce St., Harlingen, TX 78550.

CABOOL. K08AT, S. Central Missouri Broadcasting, Juanita Davis, mgr, Box 69, Houston, MO 65483.

Low Power Television Stations

CAMERON. K35CO, Eye 35-TV, Steve Hendrix, vp, Box 947, Cameron, MO 64429.

CAPE GIRARDEAU. K45CA, New Life World Outreach Ctr., Jack Cathcart, pastor, Box 182, Cape Girardeau, MO 63701-0182.

COLUMBIA. K02NQ, Karp-Comm Inc., Raymond A. Karpowicz, owner, One Outer Ladue, St. Louis, MO 63131.

COLUMBIA. K11SN, Koenig Broadcast Group, Richard E. Koenig, pres, Rt. 1 Box 123, Rocheport, MO 65279.

JOPLIN. K57DR, Board of Regents MO S. State College, Richard W. Massa, comm dept, Newman and Duquesne Rds., Joplin, MO 64801-1595.

JOPLIN/CARTHAGE. K09VM, Gary M. Kenny, owner, Box 817, Neosho, MO 64850.

KANSAS CITY. K26CR, North Central LPTV Inc.

KANSAS CITY. K29CF, Triangle TV Co. Inc., Gary O. Benson, owner, 2925 Dean Parkway, Minneapolis, MN 55416.

LEBANON. K24DF, New Life Evangelistic Center, Lawrence W. Rice Jr., pres, 1411 Locust, St. Louis, MO 63103.

MALDEN. K26DA, New York Times Broadcast Services Inc.

NEOSHO. K32CL, Gary M. Kenny, owner, Box 817, Neosho, MO 64850.

OSAGE BEACH. K44DO, New Life Evangelistic Center, Lawrence W. Rice Jr., pres, 1411 Locust, St. Louis, MO 63103.

ROLLA. K07SD, The Curators University of Mo., Carle Gustavison, off mgr, Video Comm. Ctr. G9, Rolla, MO 65401.

ROLLA. K19AN, Russell Comm., James H. Russell Jr., pres, 407 E. Morningside Cir., Fullerton, CA 92635-3544.

ST LOUIS. K07TV, Channel America LPTV Licensed Subsidiary Inc., David Post, chairman, 19 W. 21st St., 2nd Fl., New York, NY 10010.

ST LOUIS. K21OD, North Central LPTV Inc., Michael Torici, asst sec, Box 9090, Clearwater, FL 34618.

ST LOUIS. K52AY, Flor De Rio TV Co. Inc., Susan Catapano, pres, 300 E. 46th St., New York, NY 10017.

ST LOUIS. K56CA, Missouri Baptist College, Kent Kesterson, owner, 12542 Conway Rd., St. Louis, MO 63141.

ST LOUIS. K58DH, Kurt J. Petersen, owner, Box 1229, Eugene, OR 97440-1229.

ST LOUIS. K62EG, Catholic Views Broadcasts Inc., Rev. Kenneth Baker, pres, 86 Riverside Dr., New York, NY 10024.

ST LOUIS. K64DT, Valuevision International Inc., Robert Johander, pres, 5174 W. 76th St., Minneapolis, MN 55439-2300.

ST LOUIS/CLAYTON/JENNINGS. K13WA, KWA TV Inc., Jacquelyn Crallet, pres, Box 10434, Tampa, FL 33679.

SPRINGFIELD. K08LR, Pictures & Sound Inc., Paul G. Katona, pres, Rt. 1 Box 317, Fordland, MO 65652.

SPRINGFIELD. K15CZ, Nancy M. Kuni, owner, 5013 Meadowlark Ln., New Port Richey, FL 34653.

SPRINGFIELD. K39CI, TV-39 (Christian Life Comm), Robert Titus, gen mgr, 1601 Q. W. Sunshine, Springfield, MO 65807.

SPRINGFIELD. K49DG, Trinity Broadcasting Network.

SPRINGFIELD. K56FD, New Life Evangelistic Center, Lawrence W. Rice Jr., pres, 1411 Locust, St. Louis, MO 63103.

Montana

BELGRADE. K20DY, Big Horn Comm. Inc., Thomas Hendrickson, pres, Box 23309, Billings, MT 59102.

BILLINGS. K14AQ, Russell Comm., James H. Russell Jr., pres, 407 E. Morningside Cir., Fullerton, CA 92635-3544.

BILLINGS. K14IS, Yellowstone Valley Community TV, Samuel A. Benson, gen mgr, Box 21157, Billings, MT 59104.

BILLINGS. K25BP, Big Horn Comm. Inc., Thomas Hendrickson, pres, Box 23309, Billings, MT 59102.

BOULDER. K27CD, Boulder TV Translator Assn., Ralper R. Simons, pres, Box 146, Boulder, MT 59632.

BRIDGER. K63EA, Clarks Fork Valley TV Dist. #1, Box Q, Bridger, MT 53014.

BROWNING. K57FM, Browning Public School, 129 First Ave. S.E., Browning, MT 59417.

BUTTE. K43DU, Big Horn Comm. Inc., Thomas Hendrickson, pres, Box 23309, Billings, MT 59102.

CHINOOK. K59EM, Blaine County Public TV Inc., Richard C. King, chairman, Box 1343, Chinook, MT 59523.

CIRCLE. K14AG, Circle TV Booster Club Inc., Dale Bond, pres, Box 6, Brockway, MT 59214.

COLSTRIP. K28CB, Colstrip Public Schools, Judy Anderson, gen mgr, Box 159, Colstrip, MT 59323.

DARBY. K21AN, Bitteroot Valley Public TV, Box 588, Hamilton, MT 59840.

GLASGOW. K14AR, Valley County TV Dist. No. 1, Everett Breigenzer, chairman, Box 1129, Glasgow, MT 59230.

GLASGOW. K16AZ, Valley County TV Dist. No. 1, Everett Breigenzer, chariman, Box 1129, Glasgow, MT 59230.

GLASGOW. K18BN, Valley County TV Dist. No. 1, Everett Breigenzer, chairman, Box 1129, Glasgow, MT 59230.

GLASGOW. K19AC, Big Horn Comm. Inc., Thomas Hendrickson, pres, Box 23309, Billings, MT 59102.

HELENA. K41CX, Trinity Broadcasting Network, Jane Duff, vp, Box A, Santa Ana, CA 92711.

KALISPELL. K18AJ, KPAX Comm. Inc., William F. Sullivan, pres, 2204 Regent St., Missoula, MT 59801.

LAME DEER. K05BL, Dull Knife Memorial College, Ted Rowland, pres, Box 98, Lame Deer, MT 59043-0098.

LAME DEER. K13DF, Dull Knife Memorial College, Ted Rowland, pres, Box 98, Lame Deer, MT 59043-0098.

LEWISTOWN. K17AD, Big Horn Comm. Inc., Thomas Hendrickson, pres, Box 23309, Billings, MT 59102.

LIVINGSTON. K17BT, Shields Valley TV Tax Dist., Box 34, Clyde Park, MT 59018.

MALTA. K15AS, Phillips Co. TV Translator Dist., Ray Holzhey, chmn bd, Box 387, Malta, MT 59452.

MISSOULA/LOLO. K50CP, Life of Victory TV Inc., David A. Tucker, owner, Box 421, Lewiston, ID 83501-0421.

PABLO/RONAN. K25CL, Salish Kootenai College, Frank Tyro, TV dir, Box 117, Pablo, MT 59855.

PLAINS. K21CA, Plains/Paradise TV Dist., Richard Welty, gen mgr, Box 74, Paradise, CA 59586.

PLEVNA. K24DD, Plevna Public School Trustees Dist. #55 Box 158, Plevna, MT 59344.

ROUNDUP. K06KX, Roundup TV Tax Dist., Judge Nate Allen, chmn/trust, Box 448, Roundup, MT 59072.

ST. IGNATIUS. K28CF, Salish Kootenai College, Frank Tyro, TV dir, Box 117, Pablo, MT 59855.

THOMPSON FALLS. K36BW, Thompson Falls TV Dist., Box 515, Thompson Falls, MT 59873.

TOOLE. K40DG, East Butte TV Club Inc.

WHITE SULPHER. K57CX, Meagher County Public TV Inc., Robert Saunders, pres, Box 421, White Sulphur Springs, MT 59645.

WHITEHALL. K52CE, Whitehall Low Power TV Inc., Box 487, Whitehall, MT 59759.

Nebraska

LINCOLN. K61CU, Liberty Broadcasting of Nebraska, Steve Kafka, stn mgr, 941 O St. #902, Lincoln, NE 68508.

LINCOLN. K67CV, Channel America LPTV Licensed Subsidiary Inc., David Post, chairman, 19 W. 21st St., 2nd Fl., New York, NY 10010.

SCOTTSBLUFF. K42BG, Seven Star Television, Box 5527, Fullerton, CA 92635.

Nevada

BATTLE MOUNTAIN. K32CA, Lander County General Imp. Dist., Mark Lake, chairman, Box 565, Battle Mountain, NV 89820.

CARLIN. K30CD, Carlin Television Dist., Lois McKenzie, sec, Box 787, Carlin, NV 89822.

CARLIN. K35BR, Carlin Television Dist., Lois McKenzie, sec, Box 787, Carlin, NV 89822.

CARSON CITY. K15AN, Channel 5 Public Broadcasting Inc.

ELKO. K14AO, Elko Public Television, Eric Easterly, chairman, Box 2488, Elko, NV 89801.

ELY. K14AL, White Pine Television Dist. #1, R.E. Swain, chairman, Box 704, Ely, NV 89301.

EUREKA. K44CP, Eureka Television Dist., J.N. Rebaleatti, pres, Box 633, Eureka, NV 89316.

EUREKA. K47DG, Eureka Television Dist., J.N. Rebaleatti, pres, Box 633, Eureka, NV 89316.

FALLON. K25AK, Fallon Community TV Inc., Joe Ward, chairman, Box 2091, Fallon, NV 89406-0657.

HOT CREEK VALLEY. K09JC, Joe B. Fallini Jr.,

INCLINE VILLAGE. K14AJ, Lake Tahoe Public TV, John Campbell, gen mgr, Box 5570, Incline Village, NV 89450.

LAS VEGAS. K17CT, Tootlevision Broadcast Co., Charles K. Tootle, pres, 2606 S. Sheridan Rd., Tulsa, OK 74129.

LAS VEGAS. K19CS, Hey Buddy Broadcasting Co., Harry Tootle, vp, Box 33666, Las Vegas, NV 89133.

LAS VEGAS. K27AF, Las Tres Campanas TV, Walter F. Ulloa,

LAUGHLIN. K59EX, People's Comm., Richard W. Myers, gen mgr, 700 S. 3rd St., Las Vegas, NV 89102.

LOVELOCK. K18DP, Pershing County Public TV, Richard A. Wagner, dist atty, Courthouse Box 299, Lovelock, NV 89419.

MERCURY. K54BO, Comm. Engineering Inc., F.G. Fuson, pres, 3610 South Highland Dr., Las Vegas, NV 89103-5704.

MESQUITE. K45AI, MB Broadcasting, Wallace Brazzeal, pres, 95 E. Tabernacle Rd., #201, St. George, UT 84770.

PAHRUMP. K17CL, Town of Pahrump.

PAHRUMP. K19BU, Town of Pahrump.

PAHRUMP. K24BY, Town of Pahrump.

PAHRUMP. K28CS, Town of Pahrump.

PAHRUMP. K36BQ, Town of Pahrump.

PAHRUMP. K55EW, Comm. Engineering Inc., F.G. Fuson, pres, 3610 South Highland Dr., Las Vegas, NV 89103-5704.

RENO. K43CI, Kidd Comm., Chris Kidd, pres, 2470 Wrondel Way #202, Reno, NV 89502.

RENO. K43CT, HMC Comm. Inc.

RENO. K55DP, Galaxy Broadcasting Inc., 1600 S. Rock Blvd., #20, Reno, NV 89502.

RENO. K63DN, Generic Television, Eric Jacobsen, pres, 2818 E. Aster Dr., Phoenix, AZ 85032-6548.

RENO. K66CH, Women's LPTV Network, Janet L. Jacobsen, vp, 7860 N. Hayden Rd., #j101, Scottsdale, AZ 85258.

TONOPAH. K17AH, NYE County Public Television, c/o Robert B. Sorenson, chairman, Box 151, Tonopah, NV 89049.

WINNEMUCCA. K15AL, Northern Nevada Community College, Paul Burkholder, gen mgr, 25 W. 4th St., Winnemucca, NV 89445.

New Hampshire

CONCORD. W39AR, Center Broadcasting Corp. of NH, Gregory Uhrin, pres, 8 Commercial St., Concord, NH 03301.

NASHUA. W13BG, Center Broadcasting Corp. of NH, Gordon Jackson, mgr, 8 Commercial St., Concord, NH 03301.

NASHUA. W33AK, Center Broadcasting Corp. of NH, Gregory Uhrin, pres, 8 Commercial St., Concord, NH 03301.

New Jersey

CAPE MAY. W05AX, Beach TV Properties Inc., Jud Colley, pres, Box 9556, Panama City, FL 32407.

Low Power Television Stations

HAMMONTON/BERLIN/WILLIAMSTOWN. W08CC, Engle Broadcasting, Paul Engle, pres, Box 888, Hammonton, NJ 08037.

NEW BRUNSWICK. W36AS, Deepak Viswanth, pres, Box 286, East Elmhurst, NY 11369.

TRENTON. W25AW, Zantech Inc., Louis Zanoni, pres, 77 Shady Ln., Trenton, NJ 08619.

New Mexico

ALAMOGORDO. K53BM, Corinne Galt Acosta, owner, 6200 Valeria, El Paso, TX 79912.

ALAMOGORDO. K63CD, Vision Broadcasting Network Inc., Keith Gregory, gen mgr, 211 13th St., Alamogordo, NM 88310.

ALAMOGORDO/TULAROSA. K29BD, Prime Time Christian Broadcasting Inc., Albert O. Cooper, pres, Box 967, Roswell, NM 88202-0967.

ALBUQUERQUE. K59DB, Continental Broadcasting Corp., Jose Molina, pres, 6834 Hollywood Blvd., #300, Hollywood, CA 90028.

AMALIA. K08IM, Amalia TV Translator, Box 27, Costilla, NM 87524.

AMALIA. K10JL, Amalia TV Translator, Box 27, Costilla, NM 87524.

AMALIA. K12KB, Amalia TV Translator, Box 27, Costilla, NM 87524.

CARLSBAD. K63CK, Trinity Broadcasting Network, Jane Duff, vp, Box A, Santa Ana, CA 92711.

CLOVIS. K43BU, Marsh Media Inc., David Weir, gen mgr, 4140 Rio Bravo, El Paso, TX 79902.

FARMINGTON. K43AI, Regents of The University, Phillip Gonzales, gen mgr, 1130 University Blvd., N.E., Albuquerque, NM 87102.

FARMINGTON. K50BN, Channel 2 Assn. c/o KNMZ-TV, Edwin Bowen, gen mgr, 1311 Calle Anaya, Santa Fe, NM 87501.

HOBBS. K18DK, Prime Time Christian Broadcasting Inc., Albert O. Cooper, pres, Box 967, Roswell, NM 88202-0967.

LOVINGTON/HOBBS/CARLSBAD. K44DL, Prime Time Christian Broadcasting Inc., Albert O. Cooper, pres, Box 967, Roswell, NM 88202-0967.

NAVAJO. K13GX, The Navajo Nation, Box 2569, Window Rock, AZ 86515.

RODEO. K02IG, Rodeo TV Assn., Box 236, Rodeo, NM 88056.

RODEO. K07CW, Rodeo TV Assn., Box 236, Rodeo, NM 88056.

RODEO. K11FT, Rodeo TV Assn., Box 236, Rodeo, NM 88056.

ROSWELL. K15CV, Ramar Comm., Ray Moran, pres, Box 3757, Lubbock, TX 79452.

RUIDOSO. K35AN, Todd & Fugit, H. Leonard Todd, owner, 511 N. Lee, Odessa, TX 79761.

SANTA FE. K52BS, Continental Broadcasting Corp. of NM.

SHIPROCK. K48AW, The Navajo Nation, Box 2569, Window Rock, AZ 86515.

SOCORRO. K28CE, Son Broadcasting Inc., Benjamin B. Gonzales, pres, Box 4338, Albuquerque, NM 87106.

New York

AMITYVILLE/MINEOLA. W52BN, Amity Broadcasting Co., Michael Bogner, partner, Box 67, Valley Stream, NY 11582-0067.

ANDES. W83AL, WSKG Public T/C Council.

AUBURN. W48AO, Dr. Sonny Persad, gen mgr, Box 1100, Auburn, NY 13021-0016.

AUBURN. W54AK, Dr. Sonny Persad, gen mgr, Box 1100, Auburn, NY 13021-0016.

BELDEN. W62AX, WSKG Public T/C Council.

BINGHAMTON. W14AH, Trinity Broadcasting Network, Jane Duff, vp, Box A, Santa Ana, CA 92711.

BINGHAMTON. W57AF, A.

BLOOMVILLE ETC. W81AH, A.

BROWNSVILLE. W54AY, Island Broadcasting Co., Richard D. Bogner, partner, 25 Victoria Dr., Amityville, NY 11701.

BUFFALO. W58AV, Citizens TV Systems Inc. NY, Suzanne Chamberlain, gen mgr, 18 Agassiz Circle, Buffalo, NY 14214.

CAZENOVIA. W07CA, Metro TV Inc., Craig L. Fox, owner, 4853 Manor Hill Dr., Syracuse, NY 13215-1336.

CHERRY VALLEY. W83AT, WSKG Public T/C Council.

DEER PARK. W51BV, Zenia Renatta Izzo, owner, 409 W. 10th St., Long Beach, CA 90813.

DELHI. W67AD, WSKG Public T/C Council.

EAST BINGHAMTON. W63AG, WSKG Public T/C Council.

EDMESTON. W75AQ, WSKG Public T/C Council.

ENDICOTT. W67AM, WSKG Public T/C Council.

FABIUS. W60BC, Michael J. Devine.

FAYETTEVILLE. W54AL, AGK Comm., Craig L. Fox, owner, 4853 Manor Hill Dr., Syracuse, NY 13215-1336.

GLENS FALLS. W04BD, WMHT Educational T/C Inc.

GLENS FALLS. W08CJ, Grich Broadcasting Corp. D-I-P, James Edward Grich, pres, RR 1 Box 594, 28 Quaker Rd., Queensbury, NY 12804.

GLOVERSVILLE. W49BA, Michael A. Sleezer, gen mgr, 101 Park St., Gloversville, NY 12078.

HARPERSVILLE. W66AO, WSKG Public T/C Council.

HAWLEYTON. W66AE, A.

HOOSICK FALLS. W04AT, Brian A. Larson, owner.

HUNTER. W12AZ, WSKG Public T/C Council.

KATTLEVILLE. W65AK, WSKG Public T/C Council.

LAURENS/MOUNT VISION. W83AU, WSKG Public T/C Council.

LITTLE FALLS. W28AQ, Kevin O'Kane, gen mgr, 3353 Jenkins Rd., Vernon, NY 13476.

MAINE. W62AL, WSKG Public T/C Council.

MARGARETVILLE. W69AI, WSKG Public T/C Council.

MASSENA. W28BC, Watertown TV Corp. D-I-P, 1122 N. Calark #3903, Chicago, IL 60601.

MILFORD. W81AM, WSKG Public T/C Council.

MINEOLA. W57BC, Island Broadcasting Co., Richard D. Bogner, partner, 25 Victoria Dr., Amityville, NY 11701.

MORRIS. W04BG, WSKG Public T/C Council.

NEW YORK. W53AA, Panasian Comm. Inc., Charlotte Castillo, owner, 42-22 27th St., Long Island City, NY 11101.

NEW YORK. W60AI, Silver King Broadcasting of Nj Inc., Michael Torici, asst sec, Box 9090, Clearwater, FL 34618.

NEW YORK. W73AP, WPIX Inc.

NEWARK VALLEY. W65AN, WSKG Public T/C Council.

OLEAN. W20AB, Choice Olean TV Station Inc., Charles Bordonaro, pres, Box 606, Olean, NY 14760.

OLEAN. W51AN, Trinity Broadcasting Network, Jane Duff, vp, Box A, Santa Ana, CA 92711.

ONEIDA/WAMPSVILL. W13BR, Kevin O'Kane, gen mgr, 3353 Jenkins Rd., Vernon, NY 13476.

ONEONTA. W15AS, Rastus Broadcast, Walter Rasmussen, owner, Box 1115, Oneonta, NY 13820-5115.

OWEGO. W62AV, WSKG Public T/C Council.

PLAINVIEW. W44AI, Island Broadcasting Co., Richard D. Bogner, partner, 25 Victoria Dr., Amityville, NY 11701.

PLATTSBURGH. W27BI, Susan Clarke, partner, 225 N. Market St., Logan, OH 43138.

POUGHKEEPSIE. W42AE, Dutchess Comm. College-SUNY, Dr. Jerry Lee, chairman, 53 Pendell Rd., Poughkeepsie, NY 12601-1595.

PRATTSVILLE. W04AS, WSKG Public T/C Council.

ROCHESTER. W15AL, Metro TV Inc., Craig L. Fox, owner, 4853 Manor Hill Dr., Syracuse, NY 13215-1336.

ROCHESTER. W38AW, Hometown Vision Inc., Ronald D. Kniffen, pres, 449 Ave. A, Rochester, NY 14621.

ROCHESTER. W40AG, Channel America LPTV Licensed Subsidiary Inc., David Post, chairman, 19 W. 21st St., 2nd Fl., New York, NY 10010.

ROCHESTER. W63BM, George W. Kimble, pres, Box 1012, Canandaigua, NY 14424.

ROME. W12BZ, Kevin O'Kane, gen mgr, 3353 Jenkins Rd., Vernon, NY 13476.

SPRINGVILLE. W04BE, WSKG Public T/C Council.

SCHOHARIE. W04AJ, WMHT Educational T/C Inc.

SOUTH WORCESTER. W04AZ, WSKG Public T/C Council.

SOUTHAMPTON. W23AA, Channel America LPTV Licensed Subsidiary Inc., David Post, chairman, 19 W. 21st St., 2nd Fl., New York, NY 10010.

SPRINGFIELD CENTER. W67AA, WSKG Public T/C Council.

SPROUT BROOK. W07BF, WSKG Public T/C Council.

STAMFORD. W69BP, WSKG Public T/C Council.

SYRACUSE. W13BU, Metro TV Inc., Craig L. Fox, owner, 4853 Manor Hill Dr., Syracuse, NY 13215-1336.

SYRACUSE. W14AE, Channel America LPTV Licensed Subsidiary Inc., David Post, chairman, 19 W. 21st St., 2nd Fl., New York, NY 10010.

SYRACUSE. W18AL, Syracuse TV Corp., Craig L. Fox, pres, 4853 Manor Hill Dr., Syracuse, NY 13215-1336.

SYRACUSE. W35AQ, Craig L. Fox, owner, 4853 Manor Hill Dr., Syracuse, NY 13215-1336.

SYRACUSE. W49BF, Metro TV Inc., Craig L. Fox, owner, 4853 Manor Hill Dr., Syracuse, NY 13215-1336.

SYRACUSE/LIVERPOOL/MATTDALE. W11BP, Metro TV Inc., Craig L. Fox, owner, 4853 Manor Hill Dr., Syracuse, NY 13215-1336.

TIOGA CENTER. W64AP, WSKG Public T/C Council.

UTICA. K53AM, Kevin Okane, gen mgr, 3353 Jenkins Rd., Vernon, NY 13476.

UTICA/MARCY. W11BS, Kevin Okane, gen mgr, 3353 Jenkins Rd., Vernon, NY 13476.

WHITE LAKE. W51BN, Mesters TV, John Mester, pres, 971 Coney Island Ave., Brooklyn, NY 11218.

WHITNEY POINT. W66AG, A.

WORCESTER. W79AY, WSKG Public T/C Council.

North Carolina

DURHAM/CHAPEL HILL. W13BW, Video Jukebox Network Inc., LPTV coord, 12000 Biscayne Blvd., Miami, FL 33181-2742.

HENDERSON. W34AX, Taras Comm. Inc., Jim Terry, gen mgr, Box 1548, Henderson, NC 27536.

KINGSTON. W64AZ, Local TV Assoc. Inc., John W. Gainey III, pres, Box 2069, Morehead, NC 28557.

LENOIR. W53AO, AV Electronics, Ralph Gene Norman, owner, Rt. 10 Box 686-B, Lenoir, NC 28645.

LUMBERTON/PEMBROKE. W07CN, Billy Ray Locklear, owner, Box 2792, Pembroke, NC 28372.

RALEIGH. W13CI, Video Jukebox Network Inc., LPTV coord, 12000 Biscayne Blvd., Miami, FL 33181-2742.

RALEIGH. W58CD, Charles W. Williams, owner, 3728 Silina Dr., Virginia Beach, VA 23452.

RALEIGH. W68BK, Trustees St. Augustines College, Prezell R. Robinson, pres, 1315 Oakwood Ave., Raleigh, NC 27610-2298.

REIDSVILLE. W14AU, Community Broadcast Systems Inc., Robert Tudor, pres, 115 Gilmer St., Reidsville, NC 27320.

ROANOKE RAPIDS. W20AT, Moran Comm. Inc., Tim Moran, pres, Box 2017, Roanoke Rapids, NC 27870-2017.

ROCKY MOUNT. W47AG, Family Broadcasting Enterprises, Bob Pelletier, atty, Box 4750, Rocky Mount, NC 27803-0750.

SANFORD. W46BF, W46BF-TV, Burke Buchanan, owner, Box 1176, Sanford, NC 27331-1176.

SMITHFIELD/SELMA. W35AR, Waters & Brock Comm, Box 1, Selma, NC 25756.

WAYNESVILLE. W12AR, WLOS TV Inc.

Low Power Television Stations

WEAVERVILLE. W30AS, Rainbow Star Comm., Sidney Braverman, pres, 55 N. Main St. Box 947, Weaverville, NC 28787.

WILMINGTON. W10BZ, LP Comm. Inc., Phillip Bolton, pres, 5223 Market St., Wilmington, NC 28405.

North Dakota

BELCOURT. K53DH, Schindler Comm., Fred Schindler Sr., pres, Box 297, Belcourt, ND 58316-0297.

BELCOURT. K55FH, Schindler Comm., Fred Schindler Sr., pres, Box 297, Belcourt, ND 58316-0297.

BELCOURT. K57EV, Schindler Comm., Fred Schindler Sr., pres, Box 297, Belcourt, ND 58316-0297.

BELCOURT. K59DM, Schindler Comm., Fred Schindler Sr., pres, Box 297, Belcourt, ND 58316-0297.

BELCOURT. K61EF, Schindler Comm., Fred Schindler Sr., pres, Box 297, Belcourt, ND 58316-0297.

DEVILS LAKE. K23AJ, Red River Broadcast Group, Ron Kunin, pres, 4015 9th Ave. S.W., Fargo, ND 58103.

ROLETTE. K20AM, Full Gospel Business Mens' Fellowship, Raymond Quebedeaux, dir, 4710 Louisiana Ave., Lake Charles, LA 70605.

TURTLE MOUNT INDIAN RESERVATION. K65FE, Schindler Comm., Fred Schindler Sr., pres, Box 297, Belcourt, ND 58316-0297.

WILLISTON. K41BV, Trinity Broadcasting Network, Jane Duff, vp, Box A, Santa Ana, CA 92711.

WINDSOR/ELDRIDGE. K32AP, Cable Services Inc., Roy Sheppard, mgr, Box 608, 308 2nd St., Jamestown, ND 58402-0608.

Ohio

AKRON. W29AI, Media-Com Television Inc., Richard Klaus, pres, Box 2170, Akron, OH 44309.

ASHLAND. W59BP, North Central Ohio TV Corp., Walter Stampfli, pres, Box 311, Ashland, OH 44805.

BUCYRUS. W22AE, Allonas Comm. Inc., Bill Allonas, owner, 1820 E. Mansfield St., Bucyrus, OH 44820-0839.

BUCYRUS. W54AF, Allonas Comm. Inc., Bill Allonas, owner, 1820 E. Mansfield St., Bucyrus, OH 44820-0839.

CINCINNATI. W25AI, Block Video Productions, Elliott B. Block, pres, 2122 Losantiville Ave., Cincinnatti, OH 45237.

CLEVELAND. W53AX, Breckenridge Broadcasting Co. Inc., Mike Snow, gen mgr, 3300 Norwest Ctr., 90 S. 7th St., Minneapolis, MN 55402.

COLUMBUS. W08BV, CW Consultants Inc., Rev. Andy Lewter Jr., dir, 3556 Sullivant Ave. #205, Columbus, OH 43204-1153.

COLUMBUS. W13BN, North Central LPTV Inc., Michael Torici, asst sec, Box 9090, Clearwater, FL 34618.

COLUMBUS. W17AI, R B C Inc., Wendell A. Triplett, mgr, 1281 River Rd., Chillicothe, OH 45601-9027.

COLUMBUS. W62BE, Premier Broadcasting Co., James Pallone, ceo, 400 N. High St., Columbus, OH 43215.

COLUMBUS. W63BN, North Central LPTV Inc., Michael Torici, asst sec, Box 9090, Clearwater, FL 34618.

COLUMBUS. W64BG, James W. Feasel, owner, 13549 Morse Rd., Pataskale, OH 43062.

DEFIANCE. W19BN, Wolfe Comm. Inc., Robert R. Wolfe, pres, 118 Clinton St., Defiance, OH 43512.

DELAWARE. W56CA, Shaheen Broadcasters, James N. Shaheen, pres, Box 448, Delaware, OH 43015.

FINDLAY. W06BK, Findlay TV Corp., Mary F. Fleming, gen mgr, 418 S. Main St., 2nd Fl., Findlay, OH 45840.

FINDLAY. W47BD, Findlay TV Corp., Mary F. Fleming, gen mgr, 418 S. Main St., 2nd Fl., Findlay, OH 45840.

FREMONT. W02BY, Seeway Broadcasters, Bob Lee, pres, Box 543, Sandusky, OH 44870.

FREMONT. W21BF, Seway Broadcasters, Bob Lee, pres, Box 543, Sandusky, OH 44870.

MANSFIELD. W50BE, Mid-State Television Inc., Gunther Meisse, sta mgr, 2700 Bell Rd., Box 3030, Lexington, OH 44904.

MARIETTA. W26AL, The Christian Center Inc., Richard L. Jolliff,

MARION. W39AQ, Central OH Assn. of Christ, Rev. David R. Akin, sta mgr, 719 N. Main St., Marion, OH 43302.

PORTSMOUTH. W21AI, Trinity Broadcasting Network, Jane Duff, vp, Box A, Santa Ana, CA 92711.

SANDUSKY. W41AP, Register TV News, Robert Pifer, gen mgr, 314 West Market St., Sandusky, OH 44870.

SEAMAN. W17AY, Tranquility Community Church, Box 306, Seaman, OH 45679.

TOLEDO. W05BZ, Assal Broadcasting Co., Box 9225, Calabasas, CA 91372.

TOLEDO. W48AP, Ultravision, Bob Moore, pres, 716 N. Westwood Ave., Toledo, OH 43607.

TOLEDO. W60BJ, Tran Star Inc., 716 N. Westwood Ave., Toledo, OH 43607.

TOLEDO. W64BM, Lonnie James, owner, 700 Spottis Wood Ln., Clearwater, FL 34616.

Oklahoma

ARDMORE. K55DN, Moore Broadcasting Inc., Benjamin B. Moore, pres, Rt. 1 Box 1, Murfreesboro, TN 37130.

BROKEN BOW. K28DJ, Jewel B. Callahan, owner, 702 Circle Dr., Broken Bow, OK 74729.

ELK CITY. K02MU, Denero Dimensions Inc., Box 414, Elk City, OK 73648.

ELK CITY. K52AN, Northfolk TV Translator System, Arnold Cruze, pres, Box 397, Memphis, TX 79245.

ERICK. K58CS, Northfolk TV Translator System, Arnold Cruze, pres, Box 397, Memphis, TX 79245.

ERICK. K62BQ, Northfork TV Translator System, Arnold Cruze, pres, Box 397, Memphis, TX 79245.

GAGE. K20BR, Gage Translator System, Douglas Maupin, sta mgr, 618 9th St., Woodword, OK 73801.

LAWTON. K27AZ, Trinity Broadcasting Network, Jane Duff, vp, Box A, Santa Ana, CA 92711.

LAWTON. K53DS, BSP Broadcasting Inc., Pete D'Acosta, pres, 3800 Call Field Rd., Wichita Falls, TX 76308.

MAY. K22BR, Gage Translator System, Douglas Maupin, sta mgr, 618 9th St., Woodword, OK 73801.

MAY/FORT SUPPLY. K18BV, Gage Translator System, Douglas Maupin, sta mgr, 618 9th St., Woodword, OK 73801.

MUSKOGEE. K19CJ, American Indian TV & Radio, 2606 S. Sheridan Rd., Tulsa, OK 74129.

OKLAHOMA CITY. K07TX, Channel 7 Broadcasting, Jeffrey Bodley, gen mgr, 1425 Greenway Dr., #280, Irving, TX 75038.

OKLAHOMA CITY. K69EK, Le Sea Broadcasting Corp., Lester Sumrall, pres, Box 12, South Bend, IN 46624.

PONCA CITY. K12NE, Russell Comm., James H. Russell Jr., pres, 407 E. Morningside Cir., Fullerton, CA 92635-3544.

SEILING/TALOGA. K53CI, Shafer Translator Inc., Larry Miller, sec, 415 Barnes, Alva, OK 73717.

SEILING/VICI. K55EZ, Shafer Translator Inc., Larry Miller, sec, 415 Barnes, Alva, OK 73717.

SEILING/VICI. K57EA, Shafer Translator Inc., Larry Miller, sec, 415 Barnes, Alva, OK 73717.

STILLWATER. K07VB, Mike Veldman, owner, 1505 N. High Tower, Stillwater, OK 74075.

STILLWATER. K19DB, Heritage Media Corp., Ron Buck, 3600 S. West Port. Ave., Sioux Falls, SD 57116-0196.

STRONG CITY. K36AJ, Northfork TV Translator System, Arnold Cruze, pres, Box 397, Memphis, TX 79245.

SULPHUR. K20DQ, William Mayo, owner, 1010 W. 2nd St., Sulphur, OK 73086.

TAHLEQUAH. K21CS, Tahlequah TV-21, Dale Du Shane, mgr, 1511 Lawrence St., Tahlequah, OK 74454.

TULSA. K33DG, Toothlevision Broadcast Co., Charles K. Tootle, pres, 2606 S. Sheridan Rd., Tulsa, OK 74129.

TULSA. K39CW, South Central LPTV Inc., Michael Torici, asst sec, Box 9090, Clearwater, FL 34618.

TULSA/BROKEN ARROW/TURLEY. K04NZ, Gerald W. Brothers Jr., owner, 3512 E. 15th St., Tulsa, OK 74112.

WOODWARD. K23AD, Frontier Community Comm., Frank Rees Jr., pres, 511 Carpenter Freeway #222, Irving, TX 75062.

WOODWARD. K59EE, Shafer Translator Inc., Larry Miller, sec, 415 Barnes, Alva, OK 73717.

WOODWARD/MOORELAND. K69DH, OK-TV Translator System Inc., Douglas Maupin, pres, 618 9th St., Woodward, OK 73802-2612.

Oregon

ALTAMONT/KLAMATH FALLS. K52AS, Love Broadcasting Co., Aubrey L. Collum, partner, Box 728, Medford, OR 97501.

BAKER. K53EJ, Cannell Comm. L.P.

BEND. K11SE, Row River Comm TV Inc., Box 91, Dorena, OR 97434.

BEND. K33AG, Trinity Broadcasting Network, Jane Duff, vp, Box A, Santa Ana, CA 92711.

BROOKINGS. K49DH, Daniel C. Mcgrath, owner, Box 361, Brookings, OR 97415.

BROWNLEE/HALFWAY. K09OP, Idaho Power Co., Box 770, Boise, ID 83701.

CHILOQUIN. K59DW, Kurt J. Petersen, owner, Box 1229, Eugene, OR 97440-1229.

CHILOQUIN. K61FG, Three Rivers TV, Quentin L. Breen, pres, 36941 S. Chiloquin Rd., Chiloquin, OR 97624.

CHILOQUIN. K63EL, Three Rivers TV, Quentin L. Breen, pres, 36941 S. Chiloquin Rd., Chiloquin, OR 97624.

CHILOQUIN. K65EX, Three Rivers TV, Quentin L. Breen, pres, 36941 S. Chiloquin Rd., Chiloquin, OR 97624.

CHILOQUIN. K67FB, Three Rivers TV, Quentin L. Breen, pres, 36941 S. Chiloquin Rd., Chiloquin, OR 97624.

CHILOQUIN. K69GC, Three Rivers TV, Quentin L. Breen, pres, 36941 S. Chiloquin Rd., Chiloquin, OR 97624.

COOS BAY. K30BN, California Oregon Broadcasting Inc., Richard W. Green, vp, 755 Auditorium Dr., Redding, CA 96001.

COOS BAY. K33AO, Trinity Broadcasting Network, Jane Duff, vp, Box A, Santa Ana, CA 92711.

COOS BAY. K36BX, California Oregon Broadcasting Inc., William B. Smullin, sec, 125 S. Fir Box 5m, Medford, OR 97501.

COOS BAY. K46AS, KMTR Inc., Robert W. Davis, pres, Box 7308, Eugene, OR 97401-0208.

COOS BAY. K63DO, California/Oregon Broadcasting Inc., Patricia C. Smullin, 888 Goodpasture Island Rd., Eugene, OR 97401-1752.

DISSTON. K11KI, Row River Comm. TV Inc., Box 91, Dorena, OR 97434.

DORENA. K04GR, Row River Comm. TV Inc., Box 91, Dorena, OR 97434.

DORENA/CULP CREEK. K02GL, Row River Comm. TV Inc., Box 91, Dorena, OR 97434.

EUGENE. K25AS, California Oregon Broadcasting Inc., Patricia Smullin, 888 Goodpasture Island Rd., Eugene, OR 97401-1752.

EUGENE. K51DT, Gregory A. Petersen, sta mgr, Box 10674, Eugene, OR 97440.

EUGENE. K53EA, Gerald D. Kamp, owner, 1204 W. 4th Ave., Eugene, OR 97402.

EUGENE. K57EL, California/Oregon Broadcasting Inc., Richard W. Green, vp, 755 Auditorium Dr., Redding, CA 96001.

EUGENE/SPRINGFIELD. K59DJ, His Word Broadcasting Co., 875 Country Club Rd., Eugene, OK 97401.

EUGENE/SPRINGFIELD. K65ER, California/Oregon Broadcasting Inc., Patricia C. Smullin, 888 Goodpasture Island Rd., Eugene, OR 97401-1752.

GRANTS PASS. K38CP, California Oregon Broadcasting Inc., Richard W. Green, vp, 755 Auditorium Dr., Redding, CA 96001.

Low Power Television Stations

GRANTS PASS. K65EJ, Better Life Television, Robert L. Heisler, pres, 36505 Ditch Creek Rd., Rogue River, OR 97537.

KLAMATH FALLS. K56EW, Better Life Television, Robert L. Heisler, pres, 36505 Ditch Creek Rd., Rogue River, OR 97537.

LAGRANDE. K05HL, Big Horn Comm. Inc., Thomas Hendrickson, pres, Box 23309, Billings, MT 59102.

LAKEVIEW. K21BC, Trinity Broadcasting Network, Jane Duff, vp, Box A, Santa Ana, CA 92711.

LONG CREEK. K04AE, FLCR Community TV, Box 162, Long Creek, OR 97856.

LONG CREEK. K06AB, FLCR Community TV, Box 162, Long Creek, OR 97856.

LONG CREEK. K09AE, FLCR Community TV, Box 162, Long Creek, OR 97856.

LONG CREEK. K11AH, FLCR Community TV, Box 162, Long Creek, OR 97856.

MEDFORD. K26CH, California Oregon Broadcasting Inc., Richard W. Green, vp, 755 Auditorium Dr., Redding, CA 96001.

MEDFORD. K62DN, Better Life Television, Robert L. Heisler, pres, 36505 Ditch Creek Rd., Rogue River, OR 97537.

MILTON/FREEWATER. K63DA, Citizens TV Systems Inc. DC, Sam Simon, gen mgr, 901 15th St. N.W., Washington, DC 20036.

NEWBURG. K66EJ, Estate of A.B. Herman, Greg Herman, owner, 1628 N.W. Everett St., Portland, OR 97209.

NEWPORT. K29AZ, King Broadcasting Co., Eric Bremner, vp, 333 Dexter Ave. N., Seattle, WA 98109.

ONTARIO. K19AR, Tri County Comm., Box 234, Ontario, OR 97914.

PORTLAND. K16CB, KMST Television Inc., Kenneth J. Seymour, exec dir, Box 7205, Beaverton, OR 97007.

PORTLAND. K56EI, Greg Herman, owner, 1628 N.W. Everett St., Portland, OR 97209.

PORTLAND. K62DV, Greg Herman, owner, 1628 N.W. Everett St., Portland, OR 97209.

PRINEVILLE. K23CU, Christ Loves You Broadcasting, Box 7353, Bend, OR 97708.

ROGUE RIVER. K67EX, Better Life Television, Robert L. Heisler, pres, 36505 Ditch Creek Rd., Rogue River, OR 97537.

ROSEBURG. K14HA, Trinity Broadcasting Network, Jane Duff, vp, Box A, Santa Ana, CA 92711.

ROSEBURG. K62DR, California Oregon Broadcasting Inc., Richard W. Green, vp, 755 Auditorium Dr., Redding, CA 96001.

SALEM. K52DE, Cannell Comm. L.P.

SALEM. K61CC, Northwest Christian TV, Howard Nice, vp, 1310 Greenbriar Pl., McMinnville, OR 97128.

TERREBONNE/BEND. K42BR, Zentor Corp., Rodney Johnson, owner, Box 1, Powell Butte, OR 97753.

TERREBONNE/BEND. K48BL, Zentor Corp., Rodney Johnson, owner, Box 1, Powell Butte, OR 97753.

TILLAMOOK/LINCOLN CITY. K35CR, Cannell Comm. LP.

TRI-CITY. K19AD, KMTR Inc., Robert W. Davis, pres, Box 7308, Eugene, OR 97401-0208.

UMATILLA RIVER VALLEY. K03AX, Umatilla River TV Assn. Inc., Box 27, Cayuse, OR 97232.

YONCALLA. K39CL, California Oregon Broadcasting Inc., Richard W. Green, vp, 755 Auditorium Dr., Redding, CA 96001.

Pennsylvania

ALTOONA. W12BR, Silas F. Roystar, pres, 8650 Almendra Way, Tracy, CA 95376.

BERWICK. W41AQ, Diocese of Scranton, Maria Orzel, exec dir, 400 Wyoming Ave., Scranton, PA 18503-1272.

BERWICK. W47AO, Triple J Community Broadcasting Inc., Joseph S. Gans, pres, 217 E. 9th St., Hazelton, PA 18201.

BERWICK. W53AM, Joseph S. Gans, pres, 217 E. 9th St., Hazelton, PA 18201.

CLARK SUMMIT. W19AR, Diversified Comm..

DILLSBURG. W40AF, Raystay Co., George F. Gardner, pres, 1310 Holly Pike, Box 38, Carlisle, PA 17013-0038.

EAST STROUDSBURG. W24BB, Triple J Community Broadcasting Inc., Joseph S. Gans, pres, 217 E. 9th St., Hazelton, PA 18201.

HARRISBURG. W53HJ, Televisual Corp.

HARRISBURG. W65AV, Tele-Visual Corp., Jerry Gilbert, ceo, 50 Palmer Dr., Camp Hill, PA 17011.

HAZELTON. W35AT, Triple J Community Broadcasting Inc., Darlene Van Blargan, stn mgr, 217 E. 9th St., Hazelton, PA 18201.

HONESDALE. W08DF, Barbara J. Neuhaus, owner, 277 Garrison Ave., Staten Island, NY 10314.

KINGSTON. W54BO, Kathy Potera, owner, 157 Bunker Hill Rd., Wyoming, PA 15148.

MANSFIELD. W54AV, Diversified Comm..

MINERSVILLE. W66AI, Diversified Comm..

OIL CITY. W05AY, W05AY-TV, Jim Rodgers, gen mgr, rd 2 Box 43 A, Seneca, PA 16346.

PHILADELPHIA. W07CB, Morton Broadcasting Co., Ronald Joseph Caponigro, mgr, 44 Yale Ave., Morton, PA 19070.

PHILADELPHIA. W35AB, WXTV License Partnership GP, 605 3rd Ave. 12th Flr., New York, NY 10158-0180.

PITTSBURGH. W63AU, WNEU-TV, Nancy B. Hahn, pres, 1001 E. Entry Dr., Pittsburgh, PA 15216.

SHARON. W50BF, Cornerstone Television Inc., Russell Bixler, pres, Signal Hill Dr., Wall, PA 15148.

SHICKSHINNY. W68CE, Triple J Community Broadcasting Inc., Joseph S. Gans, pres, 217 E. 9th St., Hazelton, PA 18201.

STATE COLLEGE. W07CD, Moreland Broadcast Assoc., George W. Kimble, pres, Box 1012, Canandaigua, NY 14424.

STATE COLLEGE. W13BY, Moreland Broadcast Assoc., George W. Kimble, pres, Box 1012, Canandaigua, NY 14424.

STATE COLLEGE. W29AR, State College, Ann Elizabeth Plenderleith, owner, 390 McKinney Rd., Wexford, PA 15090.

STATE COLLEGE. W36BE, The New York Times Co., Frank Roberts, pres/broadcasting, 803 Channel Three Dr., Memphis, TN 38103.

STATE COLLEGE. W39BE, The New York Times Co., Frank Roberts, pres/broadcasting, 803 Channel Three Dr., Memphis, TN 38103.

STROUDSBURG. W60AH, Diversified Comm..

TOWANDA. W08CO, The New York Times Co.

WARMINSTER. W08CR, Charles W. Loughery, owner, 741 Cybus Way, South Hampton, PA 18996.

WILKESBARRE/PITTSTON. W07BV, Diocese of Scranton, Maria Orzel, exec dir, 400 Wyoming Ave., Scranton, PA 18503-1272.

WILLIAMSPORT. W05BG, Keystone Inspirational Network, John Stockstill, gen mgr, Windsor Rd., Red Lion, PA 17356.

WILLIAMSPORT. W09BL, Penn Central Broadcasting Inc., 15th & Hamilton Sts., Allenton, PA 18102.

WILLIAMSPORT. W13BJ, Mountain TV Network Inc., Dean Windsor, pres, 1140 N. Highley #109, Mesa, AZ 85202.

WILLIAMSPORT. W20AD, The New York Times Co., Frank Roberts, pres/broadcasting, c/o WREG-TV 803 Channel 3 Dr., Memphis, TN 38103.

WILLIAMSPORT. W26AT, Diversified Comm..

WILLIAMSPORT. W55AG, Diversified Comm..

YORK. W23AY, Grosat Broadcasting Inc., Dennis M. Grolman, gen mgr, 1902 Woodland Dr., York, PA 17403.

Rhode Island

PROVIDENCE. W23AS, Viking Comm. Inc., Philip R. Desano, pres, 10 Abbott Park, Providence, RI 02903.

PROVIDENCE. W48AE, Freedom WLNE-TV Inc.

South Carolina

FLORENCE. W56CC, Wely Inc., Frank Moore, mgr, 2361 Walker-Swinton Rd., Timmonsville, SC 29161.

GEORGETOWN. W51AT, Dove Broadcasting Inc., James H. Thompson, pres, Box 1616, Greenville, SC 29602.

HILTON HEAD ISLAND. W18BD, Timothy A. Pipher, owner, 1447 Dubonnet Ct, Fort Meyers, FL 33919.

HILTON HEAD ISLAND. W35AY, Myron K. Hines, owner, 8317 W. Alternate 98 #23, Panama, FL 32407.

MYRTLE BEACH. W08CV, Beach TV Properties Inc., Jud Colley, pres, Box 9556, Panama City, FL 32407.

MYRTLE BEACH. W11BR, Beach TV of South Carolina Inc., Jud Colley, pres, Box 9556, Panama City, FL 32407.

MYRTLE BEACH. W68BZ, Diversified Comm., Garry H. Ritchie, gen mgr, Box 7437, Portland, ME 04112.

South Dakota

ABERDEEN. K50AX, Classic Video Systems, Robert A. Hirschfeld, pres, 4723 N. 44th St., Phoenix, AZ 85018.

PIERRE. K18BC, Kay Cee Television, 1260 Lakeview Dr., La Mirada, CA 90638.

RAPID CITY. K24AM, Generic Television, Eric Jacobsen, pres, 2818 E. Aster Dr., Phoenix, AZ 85032-6548.

ROWENA. K52DI, Trinity Broadcasting Network, Jane Duff, vp, Box A, Santa Ana, CA 92711.

SIOUX FALLS. K07UP, Localvision, Harlan L. Jacobsen, pres, 318 South Main St., Sioux Falls, SD 57102.

SIOUX FALLS. K42CC, Localvision, Harlan L. Jacobsen, pres, 318 South Main St., Sioux Falls, SD 57102.

SIOUX FALLS. K44CW, Localvision, Harlan L. Jacobsen, pres, 318 South Main St., Sioux Falls, SD 57102.

SIOUX FALLS. K46CB, Heritage Broadcasting Group, James McCarter, owner, Box 627, Cadillac, MI 49601.

SIOUX FALLS. K48DK, Victory Television, Stuart E. Moen, mgr, 101 S. Main Avenue, Sioux Falls, SD 77090.

WATERTOWN. K32DK, Independent Comm. Inc., Thomas Whalen, sec, Box 5103, Sioux Falls, SD 57117-5103.

Tennessee

CHATTANOOGA. W06BG, Johnny Godgiben, mgr, 4707 12th Ave., Chatanooga, TN 37407.

CHATTANOOGA. W39AW, Ying Hua Benns, pres, Box 302, Cohutta, TN 30710.

COOKEVILLE. W07BM, Jason Wilson,

FARRAGUT/KNOXVILLE. W51BG, Dwight R. Magnuson, pres, Box 332, Seymour, TN 37865.

HARROGATE. W14AQ, Lincoln Memorial University, Harlod M. Finley, pres, Hwy. 25 East, Harrogate, TN 37752.

HARROGATE. W18AN, Lincoln Memorial University, Harold M. Finley, pres, Hwy. 25 East, Harrogate, TN 37752.

HEISKELL. W12BU, H. Earl Marlar, owner, Box 121, Heiskell, TN 37754.

HENDERSONVILLE. W11BZ, Hendersonville Div. of VTN, 3448 Columbus Rd., Wooster, OH 44691-9134.

JACKSON. W38AD, Blackhawk Broadcasting Corp., Joe Musser, pres, Box 4411, Rockford, IL 61110.

KINGSPORT. W30AP, Holston Valley Broadcasting Corp., Fred Falin, pgm dir, 222 Commerce St., Kingsport, TN 37662.

KNOXVILLE. W34BE, South Central Comm. Corp., Robert O. Gathings, gen mgr, Box 3848, Evansville, IN 47736.

KNOXVILLE. W50BK, Dwight R. Magnuson,

KNOXVILLE. W56CM, Southeast LPTV Inc., Michael Torici, asst sec, Box 9090, Clearwater, FL 34618.

KNOXVILLE. W60AX, Knoxville County Broadcasting Inc., Hugh T. Statum, pres, Box 740, Lenoir City, TN 37771.

LAWRENCEBURG. W10BV, Sarah Evetts, owner, 44 Marcella Rd., Ethridge, TN 38456.

LEBANON. W11BD, Bryant Comm., Dr. Joe F. Bryant, pres, 200 E. Spring St., Lebanon, TN 38087.

Low Power Television Stations

LENOIR CITY. W38AQ, Knox County Broadcasting, Mike Robinson, owner, Box 740 Martel Rd., Lenoir City, TN 37771.

MEMPHIS. W36AM, Video Jukebox Network Inc., LPTV coord, 12000 Biscayne Blvd., Miami, FL 33181-2742.

MEMPHIS. W61BP, Boyd Enterprises, Jimmy Boyd, pres, 4971 Vickie Dr., Memphis, TN 38109.

MURFREESBORO. W11BF, Channel 11 Inc., William O. Barry, pres, 1617 Lebanon Rd., Nashville, TN 37210.

MURFREESBORO. W27AN, WMTS-TV, John Thomas McCreery III, pres, box 860 1030 W. College, Murfreesboro, TN 37130-0860.

NASHVILLE. W10BI, TV-10 Inc., James W. Owens, owner, 1525 McGavock St., Nashville, TN 37203.

NASHVILLE. W12BV, South Central Comm Corp., Robert O. Gathings, gen mgr, Box 3848, Evansville, IN 47736.

NASHVILLE. W24AE, South Central Comm Corp., Robert O. Gathings, gen mgr, Box 3848, Evansville, IN 47736.

NASHVILLE. W52AY, Good News Television Inc., J.D. Wesley Hollingsworth, chmn, 9160 U. S.31 Box 130, Berrien Springs, MI 49103-0130.

NASHVILLE. W59AW, Microband Corp. of America, J. Patrick Dugan, pres, 286 Eldridge Rd., Fairfield, NJ 07006.

NASHVILLE. W61AR, TV-10 Inc., James W. Owens, owner, 1525 McGavock St., Nashville, TN 37203.

NASHVILLE. W68CG, South Central Comm. Corp., Tom Turpin, mgr, Box 3848, Evansville, IN 47736.

SELMER. W06AW, Wdtm Inc., David B. Jordan, pres, Box 629, Selmer, TN 38375.

SEVIERVILLE. W22AU, South Central Comm. Corp., Robert O. Gathings, gen mgr, Box 3848, Evansville, IN 47736.

SHARON/GREENFIELD. W02BT, Daystar Ministries, Pastor Ed Euband, pres, 102 N. Front St., Greenfield, TN 38230.

SOUTH PITTSBURGH. W36BG, M.D. Smith IV, owner.

UNION CITY. W09BM, Joseph H. Harpole Sr., owner, Box 709, Union City, TN 38261.

Texas

ABILENE. K07UF, Abilene Christian University, Dr. Larry Bradshaw, dir, Box 8051 ACU Station, Abilene, TX 79699-8051.

ABILENE. K51CK, Trinity Broadcasting Network, Jane Duff, vp, Box A, Santa Ana, CA 92711.

ABILENE. K56EJ, Sage Broadcasting Corp., Bill Carter, asst sec, 406 S. Irving, San Angelo, TX 76903.

AMARILLO. K56DF, Spectrum Media, Mary Helen Atkins, pres, 2921 Brown Trail #140, Bedford, TX 76021.

AUSTIN. K11SF, Telemundo of Austin Inc.

AUSTIN. K13VC, Global Information Tech Inc., Saleem Tawil, pres, 111 Congress Ave. #2530, Austin, TX 78701.

AUSTIN. K30CE, KWEX License Partnership, GP, 605 3rd Ave. 12th Fl., New York, NY 10158-0180.

AUSTIN. K49CY, WFIL Inc., 908 W. MLK Blvd., Austin, TX 78701.

AUSTIN. K63DR, Trinity Broadcasting Network, Jane Duff, vp, Box A, Santa Ana, CA 92711.

BEAUMONT. K09VO, WGS III Enterprises Inc.

BEAUMONT. K46CM, Faith Pleases God Church, Carlos Ortiz, pastor, 1108 S. Commerce St., Harlingen, TX 78550.

BEEVILLE. K14GX, Mountain TV Network Inc., Dean Windsor, pres, 1140 N. Highley #109, Mesa, AZ 85202.

BIG SPRINGS. K30DW, Prime Time Christian Broadcasting Inc., Albert O. Cooper, pres, Box 967, Roswell, NM 88202-0967.

BOOKER/DARROUZETT. K47BP, CL & O Translator System Inc., Robert R. Tripp, dir, Box 87, Lipscomb, TX 79056.

BROWNWOOD. K26AP, Trinity Broadcasting Network, Jane Duff, vp, Box A, Santa Ana, CA 92711.

BRYAN. K22DP, Faith Pleases God Church, Carlos Ortiz, pastor, 1108 S. Commerce St., Harlingen, TX 78550.

CANADIAN. K31CD, CL & O Translator System Inc., Robert R. Tripp, dir, Box 87, Lipscomb, TX 79056.

CLEAR LAKE. K05IL, Q Corp.

COLLEGE STATION. K28AK, Clear Channel Comm. Inc., J. Daniel Sullivan, pres, 7322 S.W. Fwy. #1100, Houston, TX 77074.

CORPUS CHRISTI. K07UD, TV-50 Inc., Christopher York, sta mgr, 5215 Embassy Dr., Corpus Christi, TX 78411.

CORPUS CHRISTI. K22BH, Nicolas Comm. Corp., Emilio R. Nicolas, pres, 111 Paseo Encinal, San Antonio, TX 78212.

CORPUS CHRISTI. K47DF, David Holley, pres, 2209 Padre Island Dr., #R, Corpus Christi, TX 78407.

CORPUS CHRISTI. K50AO, TV-50 Inc., Christopher York, sta mgr, 5215 Embassy Dr., Corpus Christi, TX 78411.

CORPUS CHRISTI. K55FX, Faith Pleases God Church, Carlos Ortiz, pastor, 1108 S. Commerce St., Harlingen, TX 78550.

CORPUS CHRISTI. K66EB, Hye Chin Lowery, owner, 5202 Gladehill Dr., Kingwood, TX 77345.

CORSICANA. K29AD, Navarro College, Jerry Zumwalt, pgm dir, W. Hwy. 31 Box 1170, Corsicana, TX 75110.

CROCKETT. K16BY, Jim Gibbs, owner, Box 1109, Crockett, TX 75835.

FAIRFIELD. K41AK, Navarro College, Jerry Zumwalt, pgm dir, W. Hwy. 31 Box 1170, Corsicana, TX 75110.

FALFURRIAS. K07TS, New Covenant Church, Box 566, Falfurrias, TX 78355.

GIDDINGS. K21DK, KXAN Inc. 908 W. Mlk Blvd., Austin, TX 78701.

GREENVILLE. K53ER, Bill R. Wright, owner, 3007 Maple, Greenville, TX 75401.

HOUSTON. K04NW, Gordon B. Madlock, owner, 1906 5th Ave. S.E., Cedar Rapids, IA 52403.

HOUSTON. K05HU, Wodlinger Broadcasting of Texas, Constance Wodlinger, pres, Box 572727, Houston, TX 77257-2727.

HOUSTON. K33DB, Dupont Investment GP 85, 2061 Business Center Dr., Irvine, CA 92715.

HOUSTON. K43DX, Third Coast Broadcasting Inc., Robert W. Fisher, mgr, 9315 Stockwell, Houston, TX 77083.

HOUSTON. K55FV, Breckenridge Broadcasting Co. Inc., Mike Snow, gen mgr, 3300 Norwest Ctr. 90 S. 7th St., Minneapolis, MN 55402.

HUNTSVILLE. K05IA, International Broadcasting Network, Dr. Paul Broyles, pres, Box 691111, Houston, TX 77269-1111.

HUNTSVILLE. K31AI, International Broadcasting Network, Dr. Paul Broyles, pres, Box 691111, Houston, TX 77269-1111.

KERRVILLE. K02MQ, International Broadcasting Network, Dr. Paul Broyles, pres, Box 691111, Houston, TX 77269-1111.

KILEEN. K31DG, Killeen Christian Broadcasting Corp., Catherine Mason, pres, 203 Evergreen, Harker Heights, TX 76543.

LA GRANGE. K32DA, KXAN Inc., 908 W. Mlk Blvd., Austin, TX 78701.

LIVINGSTON. K05HR, Polk County Broadcasting Co., Harold J. Haley, pres, Drawer 1236 Hwy. 35, Livingston, TX 77351.

LONGVIEW. K10NT, International Broadcasting Network, Dr. Paul Broyles, pres, Box 691111, Houston, TX 77269-1111.

LUBBOCK. K22BG, Ramar Comm. Inc., Ray Moran, pres, Box 3757, Lubbock, TX 79452-3757.

LUBBOCK. K40AN, Lubbock TV Co., Keith Sommer, gen mgr, 2124 15th St., Lubbock, TX 79401.

LUBBOCK. K46CS, Ramar Comm. Inc., Ray Moran, pres, Box 3757, Lubbock, TX 79452-3757.

LUBBOCK. K62DG, Ramar Comm. Inc., Ray Moran, pres, Box 3757, Lubbock, TX 79452-3757.

LUFKIN. K05HX, International Broadcasting Network, Dr. Paul Broyles, pres, Box 691111, Houston, TX 77269-1111.

LUFKIN. K11SI, International Broadcasting Network, Dr. Paul Broyles, pres, Box 691111, Houston, TX 77269-1111.

MEMPHIS/LAKEVIEW. K44AK, Cruze Electronics, Arnold Cruze, pres, Box 397, Memphis, TX 79245.

MOUNT PLEASANT. K54CB, F V. P Network Inc., Robert Palmer, pres, Box 390, Mount Pleasant, TX 75455.

MULLIN. K61CV, Pompey Mountain Broadcasting Co. Inc., Bruce Lethco, pres, Box 71, Mullin, TX 76864.

ODESSA. K49CD, Telemundo of Galveston-Houston, c/o Telemundo Group-N Alpert, off mgr, 1740 Broadway 18th Fl., New York, NY 10019.

ODESSA. K60EE, Telemundo of Galveston-Houston, c/o Telemundo Group-N Alpert, off mgr, 1740 Broadway 18th Fl., New York, NY 10019.

PARIS. K08KK, Eastern Oklahoma TV Co. Inc. D-I-P William E. Rutledge, trustee, Box 1450,

SAN ANTONIO. K02MX, San Antonio Channel 2 Inc., Bob Roth, pres, 121 Interpark #503, San Antonio, TX 78216.

SAN ANTONIO. K17BY, Nicolas Comm. Corp., Emilio R. Nicolas, pres, 111 Paseo Encinal, San Antonio, TX 78212.

SAN ANTONIO. K20BW, DCH Evangelism, Diana C. Hagee, pres, 600 N. Loop 1604 E., San Antonio, TX 78232.

SAN ANTONIO. K33CK, Dch Evangelism Television Inc., Diana C. Hagee, pres, 600 N. Loop 1604 E., San Antonio, TX 78232.

SAN ANTONIO. K52EA, Faith Pleases God Church, Carlos Ortiz, pastor, 1108 S. Commerce St., Harlingen, TX 78550.

SAN ANTONIO. K67DW, TVSA Inc., 407 6th St., San Antonio, TX 78215.

SAN MARCOS. K40CT, KXAN Inc., 908 W. Mlk Blvd., Austin, TX 78701.

SULPHUR SPRINGS. K18AL, H & B. Broadcasting, John Price, gen mgr, Box 4386, Tyler, TX 75702.

TURKEY. K60BW, Ramar Comm. Inc., Ray Moran, pres, Box 3757, Lubbock, TX 79452-3757.

TYLER. K45AN, Christian World Network, Box 8310, Jacksonville, TX 75766.

UVALDE. K15BV, Trinity Broadcasting Network, Jane Duff, vp, Box A, Santa Ana, CA 92711.

VICTORIA. K51BG, Community TV of Victoria, Dwight W. Strehon, pres, 1510 Coolidge, Deer Park, TX 77536.

VICTORIA. K53CZ, Community TV of Victoria, Dwight W. Strehon, pres, 1510 Coolidge, Deer Park, TX 77536.

VICTORIA. K55CP, Community TV of Victoria, Dwight W. Strehon, pres, 1510 Coolidge, Deer Park, TX 77536.

WELLINGTON/DODSON. K27BZ, Greenbelt TV Translator Systems, Marshall Peters, mgr, 1201 Floydada, Wellington, TX 79095.

WICHITA FALLS. K35BO, BSP Broadcasting Inc., Pete D. Acosta, pres, 3800 Call Field Rd., Wichita Falls, TX 76308.

WOODROW. K51BX, ZGS Broadcasting Inc., Ronald J. Gordon, pres, 2300 Clarendon Blvd., #411, Arlington, VA 22201.

Utah

APPLE VALLEY. K30DE, Washington County, Scott Hirschi, commiss, 197 E. Tabernacle, St. George, VT 84770.

APPLE VALLEY. K34CX, Washington County, Scott Hirschi, commiss, 197 E. Tabernacle, St. George, VT 84770.

AURORA. K53CF, KUTV, L.P. 2185 S. 3600 West, Salt Lake City, UT 84119.

BICKNEL/TEASDALE. K38CJ, University of Utah, Stephen H. Hess, dir, bldg. 002, Salt Lake City, UT 84112.

BONANZA. K39AK, Trinity Broadcasting Network, Jane Duff, vp, Box A, Santa Ana, CA 92711.

CEDAR CITY. K22AH, Russell Comm., James H. Russell Jr., pres, 407 E. Morningside Cir., Fullerton, CA 92635-3544.

Low Power Television Stations

DELTA. K64BO, KUTV, L.P., 2185 South 3600 West, Salt Lake City, UT 84119.

GARFIELD COUNTY. K27CE, Garfield County, Box 77 Courthouse Bldg., Panguitch, UT 84759.

GREEN RIVER. K30AG, Green River City TV, Blaine Silliman, mayor, Box 356, Green River, UT 84525.

KANAB. K12ND, Kanab Lions Club, Randy Cram, c/o NRC, 156 E. 100 S., Kanab, UT 84741.

MANTI/EPHRAIM. K28AG, Sanpete Television Corp., Steven K. Beazer, pres, 3882 S. 850 West, Bountiful, UT 84010.

MARYSVALE. K30CW, University of Utah, Stephen H. Hess, dir, Bldg. 2, Salt Lake City, UT 84112.

MARYSVALE. K32AL, University of Utah, Stephen H. Hess, dir, Bldg. 2, Salt Lake City, UT 84112.

MYTON. K43AE, KUTV, L.P., 2185 South 3600 West, Salt Lake City, UT 84119.

OGDEN. K64CJ, Trinity Broadcasting Network, Jane Duff, vp, Box A, Santa Ana, CA 92711.

PARK CITY. K45AX, Park City Television, Mike Philips, oper dir, Box 445 Luck John Dr., Park City, UT 84060.

RURAL GARFIELD. K25OC, University of Utah, Stephen H. Hess, dir, Bldg. 2, Salt Lake City, UT 84112.

ST GEORGE. K55DL, MB Broadcasting, Wallace Brazzeal, pres, 95 E. Tabernacle Rd., #201, St. George, UT 84770.

SALT LAKE CITY. K38CN, William Allen Marshall, gen mgr, Box 526175, Salt Lake City, UT 84152-6175.

SALT LAKE CITY. K46BJ, Scott Stuart, receiver, 1309 16th St., Ogden, UT 84404.

SPRING GLEN. K64AA, KUTV, L.P., 2185 South 3600 West, Salt Lake City, UT 84119.

TOOELE. K24CQ, University of Utah, Stephen H. Hess, dir, Bldg. 2, Salt Lake City, UT 84112.

Vermont

KILLINGTON. W18AE, Killington Ltd., Dave Hoot, gen mgr, Killington Rd., Killington, VT 05751.

MONKTON. W62BY, Vermont Wireless Cooperative, Box 221, East Corinth, VT 05040.

MONKTON. W64BP, Vermont Wireless Cooperative, Box 221, East Corinth, VT 05040.

MONKTON. W66BX, Vermont Wireless Cooperative, Box 221, East Corinth, VT 05040.

MONKTON. W68CK, Vermont Wireless Cooperative, Box 221, East Corinth, VT 05040.

Virginia

CHARLOTTESVILLE. W10CE, The Rector & Visitors of U. VA, Box 9011, Charlottesville, VA 22906.

CHESAPEAKE. W40AH, The Union Mission, Merton F. Basset, treas, 130 Brook Ave., Norfolk, VA 23510.

CONCORD. W33AD, Paul H. Passink, pres, Box 37, Concord, VA 24538.

DRIVER. W68BI, Cannel America LPTV Licensed Subsidiary Inc., David Post, chairman, 19 W. 21st St., 2nd Fl., New York, NY 10010.

FRONT ROYAL. W28AZ, Ruarch Assoc. Ltd., Dr. Arthur D. Stamler, partner, 123 E. Court. St., Woodstock, VA 22664-0010.

GLOUCESTER. W51BH, Lockwood Broadcasting Inc.

LYNCHBURG. W19BC, Liberty University Inc., Dr. A. Pierre Guillermin, dir, 3765 Candlers Mountain Rd., Lynchburg, VA 24506.

NORFOLK. W05BQ, The Union Mission, Merton F. Basset, treas, 130 Brook Ave., Norfolk, VA 23510.

PORTSMOUTH. W56CS, Whitehead Comm., Eddie L. Whitehead, pres, 12144 Classic Dr., Coral Springs, FL 33071.

ROANOKE. W56CP, Penny C. Wilmoth, gen mgr, 1563 Laura St., Clearwater, FL 34615.

WOODSTOCK/HARRISONBURG. W10AZ, Ruarch Assoc. Ltd., Dr. Arthur D. Stamler, partner, 123 E. Court. St., Woodstock, VA 22664-0010.

Washington

ABERDEEN. K23AS, Trinity Broadcasting Network, Jane Duff, vp, Box A, Santa Ana, CA 92711.

BELLINGHAM. K48DM, USTV of Washington State Inc., Robert L. Dudley, chairman, 500 3rd St. #208, Wausau, WI 54401.

CAMAS. K19CT, Estate of A.B. Herman, Greg Herman, owner, 1628 N.W. Everett St., Portland, OR 97209.

CHELAN. K44CK, KAYU-TV Partners Ltd., Robert J. Hamacher, pres, 4600 South Regal, Spokane, WA 99223.

COLVILLE. K09UP, KAYU-TV Partners Ltd., Robert J. Hamacher, pres, 4600 South Regal, Spokane, WA 99223.

CURLEW/MALO. K03EJ, Franson Peak TV Association, Box 55, Curlew, WA 99118.

CURLEW/MALO. K09MP, Franson Peak TV Association, Box 55, Curlew, WA 99118.

CURLEW/MALO. K11NB, Franson Peak TV Association, Box 55, Curlew, WA 99118.

CURLEW/MALO. K13NV, Franson Peak TV Association, Box 55, Curlew, WA 99118.

ELLENSBURG. K39DM, Christian Broadcasting of Yakima, David Eyles, mgr, 1700 South 24th Ave., Yakima, WA 98902.

ELLISFORD/OROVILLE. K35BJ, KAYU-TV Partners Ltd., Robert J. Hamacher, pres, 4600 South Regal, Spokane, WA 99223.

GRANT COUNTY AIRPORT. K11EY, Peoples TV Association Inc., Box AG, Moses Lake, WA 98837.

GRAYS RIVER/LEBAM. K63AW, Rural TV Cooperative, plan dir, 907 346th Pl., Ocean Park, WA 98460.

LARSON/MOSES LAKE. K13EP, Peoples TV Association Inc., Box AG, Moses Lake, WA 98837.

MOSES LAKE. K64AZ, Peoples TV Association Inc., Box AG, Moses Lake, WA 98837.

MOSES LAKE/EPHRATA. K08CN, Peoples TV Association Inc., Box AG, Moses Lake, WA 98837.

MOSES LAKE/WARDEN. K52AF, Peoples TV Association Inc., Box AG, Moses Lake, WA 98837.

MOSES LAKE/WARDEN. K55DJ, Peoples TV Association Inc., Box AG, Moses Lake, WA 98837.

MOSES LAKE/WARDEN. K58BL, Peoples TV Association Inc., Box AG, Moses Lake, WA 98837.

MOSES LAKE/WARDEN. K68BV, Peoples TV Association Inc., Box AG, Moses Lake, WA 98837.

OMAK/OKANOGAN. K31AH, KAYU-TV Partners Ltd., Robert J. Hamacher, pres, 4600 South Regal, Spokane, WA 99223.

OMAK/RIVERSIDE. K25CY, The Omak Chronicle, Box 273, Omak, WA 98841.

RICHLAND. K49CN, Radiant Light Broadcasting, Richard Tedeschi, mgr, 704 Symons St., Richland, WA 99352.

RICHLAND. K66BW, Triac Comm. Ltd., 4600 S. Regal St., Spokane, WA 99223.

SEATTLE. K68DL, Three Angels Broadcstg Network Inc.

SOAP LAKE/EPHRATA. K60AE, Peoples TV Association Inc., Box AG, Moses Lake, WA 98837.

SPOKANE. K14IF, Clarabelle F. Boone, gen mgr, 771 Preston Ave. S., St. Petersburg, FL 33701.

SPOKANE. K51CU, Edith C. Smith, gen mgr, 1524 Mill St., Belle Fourche, SD 57717-2302.

STEMILT/COLOCKUM. K63AO, KOIN-TV, Thomas W. Read, pres, 500 W. Boone Ave., Spokane, WA 99201.

SUNNYSIDE/GRANDVIEW. K08LU, Ronald Alan Bevins, owner, 713 W. Yakima Ave., Yakima, WA 98902-3046.

WALLA WALLA. K22BI, Blue Mountain Broadcasting Assn., Roger Johnson, pres, 12th St. & Larch Ave., College Place, WA 99324.

WALLA WALLA. K27DD, Blue Mountain Broadcasting Assn., Roger Johnson, pres, 12th St. & Larch Ave., College Place, WA 99324.

WENATCHEE. K14BF, Westcoast Broadcasting Co., J. Wallace, mgr, Box 159, Wenatchee, WA 98801.

WENATCHEE. K30AJ, Spokane Television Inc., Thomas W. Read, pres, 500 W. Boone Ave., Spokane, WA 99201.

YAKIMA. K53CY, KAYU-TV Partners Ltd., Robert J. Hamacher, pres, 4600 S. Regal, Spokane, WA 99223.

YAKIMA. K56EG, Ronald Alan Bevins, owner, 713 W. Yakima Ave., Yakima, WA 98902-3046.

YAKIMA. K64DH, Christian Broadcasting of Yakima, David Eyles, mgr, 1700 South 24th Ave., Yakima, WA 98902.

YAKIMA. K68EB, Triac Comm. Ltd., Robert J. Hamacher, gm, Yakima, WA 99223.

YAKIMA/TOPPENISH. K58DL, Three Angels Broadcast Net Inc., Danny Shelton, pres, Box 220, West Frankfort, IL 62896.

YAKIMA/WAPATO. K17CJ, Ronald Alan Bevins, owner, 713 W. Yakima Ave., Yakima, WA 98902-3046.

YAKIMA/WAPATO. K60EB, Ronald Alan Bevins, owner, 713 W. Yakima Ave., Yakima, WA 98902-3046.

West Virginia

HUNTINGTON. W14BI, Channel America LPTV Licensed Subsidiary Inc., David Post, chairman, 19 W. 21st St., 2nd Fl., New York, NY 10010.

HUNTINGTON. W17BH, Northeast LPTV Inc., Michael Torici, asst sec, Box 9090, Clearwater, FL 34618.

HUNTINGTON. W55AT, Channel America LPTV Holding Inc., David Post, chairman, 19 W. 21st St., 2nd Fl., New York, NY 10019.

Wisconsin

DARLINGTON. W56AB, City of Darlington.

DARLINGTON. W67AC, City of Darlington.

DARLINGTON. W69AB, City of Darlington.

GREEN BAY. W57BJ, Three Angels Broadcast Net Inc., Danny Shelton, pres, Box 220, West Frankfort, IL 62896.

LA CROSSE. W44BF, Douglas Sheldahl, owner, Box 201, Huxley, IA 50124-0201.

LAC DU FLAMBEAU. W23AH, Charles Francis Gauthier, gen mgr, Box 399 Hwy. 47, Lac du Flambeau, WI 54538.

LAC DU FLAMBEAU. W25AN, Charles Francis Gauthier, gen mgr, Box 399 Hwy. 47, Lac du Flambeau, WI 54538.

LAC DU FLAMBEAU. W27AP, Charles Francis Gauthier, gen mgr, Box 399 Hwy. 47, Lac du Flambeau, WI 54538.

LADYSMITH. W06AS, Bell Press Inc., Donald L. Bell, pres, 120 W. 3rd St. S., Ladysmith, WI 54848.

LAND O'LAKES. W16AC, Land O'Lakes Superstation, Violet Becker, pres, Box 115, Land O'Lakes, WI 54540.

MADISON. W05BD, Weather Central International, Daniel G. Dobrowolski, pres, Box 9089, Downers Grove, IL 60515-9089.

MADISON. W54BH, Three Angels Broadcast Net Inc., Danny Shelton, pres, Box 220, West Frankfort, IL 62896.

MADISON/MIDDLETON. W08CK, Healthys Inc., 2525 King St., Honolulu, HI 96826.

MILWAUKEE. W08BY, Woods Comm. Group, Charles Woods, pres, 3000 E. Cherry St., Springfield, MO 65802.

MILWAUKEE. W46AR, Weigel Broadcasting Co., Ken Shapiro, pres, 141 W. Jackson Blvd., Chicago, IL 60604.

MILWAUKEE. W65BT, TV-65 Inc., Ken Shapiro, pres, 509 W. Wisconsin Ave. #2500, Milwaukee, WI 53203.

MINOCQUA. W31BA, Ronald La Verne Myers, pres, 10196 Blue Lake Rd., Minocqua, WI 54548.

SHEBOYGAN. W08BW, Lakeshore Technical College, Charles Ma, media spec, 1290 North Ave., Cleveland, WI 53015.

WAUKESHA. W43AV, WCTV Inc., Lee Dolnick, gen mgr, Box 2232, Waukesha, WI 53187-2232.

Wyoming

BIG LARAMIE/BOSLER. K10FQ, Laramie Plains Antenna TV, Box 188, Laramie, WY 82070.

BIG LARAMIE/BOSLER. K12FY, Laramie Plains Antenna TV, Box 188, Laramie, WY 82070.

CASPER. K06KH, Casper Community College, 125 College Dr., Casper, WY 82601.

CASPER. K13UC, Manna Media Corp., John S. Runge, pres, Box 2595, Casper, WY 82602.

CHEYENNE. K11RP, Russell Comm., James H. Russell Jr., pres, 407 E. Morningside Cir., Fullerton, CA 92635-3544.

CHEYENNE. K49AY, Echonet Corp., Charles Ergen, pres, 9805 E. Liff, Denver, CO 80231.

CODY. K15AD, Rob-Art Inc., Robert K. Swanson, pres, Box 85, Cody, WY 82414.

DOUGLAS. K07RO, Sky-Window TV Inc., Lee Boyd Smathers, pres, Box 627, Douglas, WY 82633.

DUBOIS. K25AU, Central Wyoming College, Dr. Joanne McFarland, pres, 2660 Peck Ave., Riverton, WY 82501.

GILLETTE. K16AE, Big Horn Comm. Inc., Thomas Hendrickson, pres, Box 23309, Billings, MT 59102.

GILLETTE. K22AD, Summit Comm. Inc., James A. Hirshfield Jr., pres, 2814 Dogwood Ave., Gillette, WY 82716.

GILLETTE. K28CH, Central Wyoming College, Dr. Joanne McFarland, pres, 2660 Peck Ave., Riverton, WY 82501.

JACKSON. K48BM, Ambassador Media Corp., William L. Armstrong III, pres, 11 Carriage Ln., Littleton, CO 80121-2010.

LARAMIE. K57AF, Laramie Plains Antenna TV, Box 188, Laramie, WY 82070.

LARAMIE. K59AM, Laramie Plains Antenna TV, Box 188, Laramie, WY 82070.

RIVERTON/ARAPAHOE. K08GO, Riverton Fremont TV Club Inc., William Willman, pres, 113 S. 2nd E., Riverton, WY 82501.

ROCK SPRINGS. K22BK, Central Wyoming College, Dr. Joanne McFarland, pres, 2660 Peck Ave., Riverton, WY 82501.

RURAL WEST RIVERTON. K44AW, Riverton Fremont TV Club Inc., William Willman, pres, 113 S. 2nd E., Riverton, WY 82501.

SHERIDAN. K09UO, Russell Comm., James H. Russell Jr., pres, 407 E. Morningside Cir., Fullerton, CA 92635-3544.

SHERIDAN. K10KP, Sheridan TV Translator Inc., Box 150, Sheridan, WY 82801.

SHERIDAN. K26BE, Central Wyoming College, Dr. Joanne McFarland, pres, 2660 Peck Ave., Riverton, WY 82501.

SHOSHONI. K68DG, Riverton Fremont TV Club Inc., William Willman, pres, 113 S. 2nd E., Riverton, WY 82501.

Guam

TAMUNING. K14AM, Guahan Airwaves Corp., Edmund Y. Lee, pres, 692 N. Marine Dr., #305, Tamuning, GU 96911.

Puerto Rico

AGUADA. W63BF, Assn. Evangelistica Cristo Viene Evelyn Rivera, owner, Box 524 Carretera 411, Aguada, PR 00602.

ARECIBO. W28AH, Angel F. Ginorio, gen mgr, Antonio Lopez #117 Box 307, Humacao, PR 00661.

BAYAMON. W21AR, Three Angels Broadcasting Network.

ISABEL SEGUNDA. W28BA, Jose Julio Martinez Velilla, owner, 906 Quibrael, As, PR 00628.

MAYAGUEZ. W10BG, Telecinco Inc., Alfredo R. De Arellano, Box 43, Mayaguez, PR 00709.

MAYAGUEZ/ANASCO. W67CR, Assn. Evangelistica Cristo Viene Evelyn Rivera, owner, Bopiedrs. Blanco App. 846, Aguada, PR 00602.

QUEBRADILLAS. W66BM, Nelly Quiles, owner, Box 4173, Aquadilla, PR 00605.

YAUCO. W54AQ, Miguel Rodriguez Frias, owner, 17th St. V-20 Bay Gardens, Baymon, PR 00619.

Spanish-Language Television Stations

The following Spanish-language television stations operate within the United States or near the U.S. border.

For further information on individual stations, see *Directory of Television Stations in the U.S.* beginning on page C-3.

Arizona
Phoenix—KTVW-TV Phoenix (ch 33).
Tucson—KHRR(TV) Tucson (ch 40).

California
El Centro—KSWT(TV) Yuma, Ariz. (ch 13).
El Centro—XHBC-TV Mexicali, Mexico (ch 3).
Fresno—KFTV(TV) Hanford (ch 21).
Fresno—KMSG-TV Sanger (ch 59).
Los Angeles—KMEX-TV Los Angeles (ch 34).
Los Angeles—KSTV-TV Ventura (ch 57).
Los Angeles—KVEA(TV) Corona (ch 52).
Los Angeles—KWHY-TV Los Angelos (ch 22).
Sacramento—KCSO(TV) Modesto (ch 19).
Salinas-Monterey—KSMS-TV Monterey (ch 67).
San Diego—XEWT-TV Tijuana, Mexico (ch 12).
San Francisco—KDTV(TV) San Francisco (ch 14).
San Francisco—KSTS(TV) San Jose (ch 48).

Colorado
Denver—KCEC(TV) Denver (ch 50).
Denver—KUBD(TV) Denver (ch 59).

Florida
Fort Lauderdale—WSCV(TV) Fort Lauderdale (ch 51).
Miami—WLTV(TV) Miami (ch 23).

Illinois
Chicago—WCIU-TV Chicago (ch 26).
Chicago—WSNS(TV) Chicago (ch 44).

Massachusetts
Boston—WUNI(TV) Needham (ch 27).

Nevada
Reno—KREN-TV Reno (ch 27).

New Mexico
Albuquerque—KLUZ-TV Albuquerque (ch 41).

New York
New York—WNJU-TV Linden, N.J. (ch 47).
New York—WXTV(TV) Paterson, N.J. (ch 41).

Pennsylvania
Philadelphia—WTGI-TV Wilmington, Del. (ch 61).

Texas
Corpus Christi—KORO(TV) Corpus Christi (ch 28).
Dallas-Fort Worth—KFWD(TV) Fort Worth (ch 52).
Dallas-Fort Worth—KUVN(TV) Garland (ch 23).
El Paso—KINT-TV El Paso (ch 26).
El Paso—XEJ-TV Juarez, Mexico (ch 5).
El Paso—XEPM-TV Juarez, Mexico (ch 2).
El Paso—XHIJ-TV Juarez, Mexico (ch 44).
Houston—KTFH(TV) Conroe (ch 49).
Houston—KTMD(TV) Galveston (ch 48).
Houston—KXLN-TV Rosenberg (ch 45).
Laredo—KLDO-TV Laredo (ch 27).
Laredo—XEFE-TV Nuevo Laredo, Mexico (ch 2).
McAllen—KNVO McAllen (ch 48).
San Antonio—KVAW(TV) Eagle Pass (ch 16).
San Antonio—KVDA(TV) San Antonio (ch 60).
San Antonio—KWEX-TV San Antonio (ch 41).

Puerto Rico
Fajardo—*WMTJ(TV) Fajardo (ch 40).
Mayaguez—WNJX-TV Mayaguez (ch 22).
Mayaguez—WOLE-TV Aguadilla (ch 12).
Mayaguez—WORA-TV Mayaguez (ch 5).
Mayaguez—WVEO(TV) Aguadilla (ch 44).
Ponce—*WQTO(TV) Ponce (ch 26).
Ponce—WSTE(TV) Ponce (ch 7).
Ponce—WSUR-TV Ponce (ch 9).
San Juan—WAPA-TV San Juan (ch 4).
San Juan—*WIPR-TV San Juan (ch 6).
San Juan—WKAQ-TV San Juan (ch 2).
San Juan—WLII(TV) Caguas (ch 11).

Experimental Television Stations

The following is a list of the experimental television stations authorized by the FCC as of January 1994.

Advanced Television Test Center—Alexandria, Va. Private, nonprofit corporation that tests high definition (HDTV) transmission systems for new U.S. terrestrial TV standard. Provides testing & other support to FCC Advisory Committee on Advanced Television Service and to industry in evaluating advanced TV options. Members: Capital Cities/ABC, CBS, NBC, PBS, Electronic Industries Association, Association of Independent Television Stations, Association for Maximum Service Television, National Association of Broadcasters. Executives: Peter M. Fannon, exec dir; Charles W. Rhodes, chief scientist.

Blonder Broadcasting Corp.—WEXP-TV Hoboken, N.J., operates on UHF chs 27 & 28 with low power. Experimental testing of proposed HDTV systems, 3-D TV systems, terrestrial bcst reception, psychometric TV picture quality. Executive: Isaac S. Blonder, pres.

Channel 7 Inc.—WSTE(TV) Ponce, P.R., operates an experimental TV stn on ch 7 using 5.01 kw visual, 100 kw visual and 316 kw visual from three transmitter locations in Puerto Rico.

Dielectric Communications Antennas—KA2XZV Cherry Hill Twp., N.J. Chs 2 to 69, 54-88 mhz and 174-806 mhz, authorized to use up to 100 kw visual in the lower-VHF band, 316 kw visual in the upper-VHF band, and 5,000 kw on UHF chs up to ch 69.

King Broadcasting Co.—KHNL(TV) Honolulu (ch 13) operates a co-ch TV transmitter.

U.S. Independent Television Stations

KDMD Anchorage AK
KYES Anchorage AK
KJNP-TV North Pole AK
WABM Birmingham AL
WYLE Florence AL
WTJP Gadsden AL
WZDX Huntsville AL
WMPV-TV Mobile AL
WCOV-TV Montgomery AL
WMCF-TV Montgomery AL
*KLEP Newark AR
KASN Pine Bluff AR
KKTM Flagstaff AZ
KZJC Flagstaff AZ
KMOH-TV Kingman AZ
*KPAZ-TV Phoenix AZ
KPHO-TV Phoenix AZ
KUTP Phoenix AZ
KUSK Prescott AZ
KHRR Tucson AZ
KTTU-TV Tucson AZ
KDOC-TV Anaheim CA
KUZZ-TV Bakersfield CA
KHIZ Barstow CA
KGMC Clovis CA
KFCB Concord CA
KVEA Corona CA
KAIL Fresno CA
KCAL Los Angeles CA
KCOP Los Angeles CA
KTLA Los Angeles CA
KWHY-TV Los Angeles CA
KHSC-TV Ontario CA
KADY-TV Oxnard CA
KCVU Paradise CA
KKAK Porterville CA
KRPA Rancho Palos Verdes CA
KRCA Riverside CA
KCMY Sacramento CA
KRBK-TV Sacramento CA
KSCI San Bernardino CA
KTTY San Diego CA
KUSI-TV San Diego CA
KBHK-TV San Francisco CA
KCNS San Francisco CA
KOFY-TV San Francisco CA
KTSF San Francisco CA
KICU-TV San Jose CA
KTBN-TV Santa Ana CA
KFTY Santa Rosa CA
KFTL Stockton CA
KSCH Stockton CA
KPST-TV Vallejo CA
KSTV-TV Ventura CA
*KNXT Visalia CA
*KCAH Watsonville CA
KTVJ Boulder CO
KWHD Castle Rock CO
KTVD Denver CO
*KWBI-TV Denver CO
KWGN-TV Denver CO
KZJG Longmont CO
KSBS-TV Steamboat Springs CO
WHAI-TV Bridgeport CT
WHCT-TV Hartford CT
WTWS New London CT
WTXX Waterbury CT
WDCA Washington DC
WFTY Washington DC
WTGI-TV Wilmington DE

WTBG-TV Bradenton FL
WCLF Clearwater FL
WKCF Clermont FL
*WBCC Cocoa FL
WTGL-TV Cocoa FL
WAYQ Daytona Beach FL
WSCV Fort Lauderdale FL
WFGX Fort Walton Beach FL
WPAN Fort Walton Beach FL
WGFL High Springs FL
WYHS-TV Hollywood FL
WNFT Jacksonville FL
WEYS Key West FL
WWFD Key West FL
WHBI Lake Worth FL
WTMV Lakeland FL
WACX Leesburg FL
WBSF Melbourne FL
WIRB Melbourne FL
WBFS-TV Miami FL
WDZL Miami FL
WHFT Miami FL
WNPL-TV Naples FL
WYDP Orange Park FL
WHBR Pensacola FL
WTOG St. Petersburg FL
WTTA St. Petersburg FL
WBHS-TV Tampa FL
WBSV-TV Venice FL
WNGM-TV Athens GA
WGNX Atlanta GA
WTBS Atlanta GA
WVEU Atlanta GA
WUBI Baxley GA
WBSG-TV Brunswick GA
WSST-TV Cordele GA
WGNM Macon GA
WTLK-TV Marietta GA
WNEG-TV Toccoa GA
KHBC-TV Hilo HI
KWHH Hilo HI
KBFD Honolulu HI
KFVE Honolulu HI
KIKU Honolulu HI
KOBN Honolulu HI
KWHE Honolulu HI
KWHM Wailuku HI
WEHS-TV Aurora IL
WCFC-TV Chicago IL
WGN-TV Chicago IL
WFHL Decatur IL
WHSL East St. Louis IL
WGBO-TV Joliet IL
WWTO-TV LaSalle IL
WTCT Marion IL
WCEE Mount Vernon IL
WTJR Quincy IL
WCCU Urbana IL
WINM Angola IN
WCLJ Bloomington IN
WIIB Bloomington IN
WTTV Bloomington IN
WPWR-TV Gary IN
WJYS Hammond IN
WHMB-TV Indianapolis IN
*WTBU Indianapolis IN
WTTK Kokomo IN
WMCC Marion IN
WKOI Richmond IN
WFTE Salem IN

WHME-TV South Bend IN
KLBY Colby KS
*KSWK Lakin KS
KMCI Lawrence KS
KWCV Wichita KS
WTSF Ashland KY
WLJC-TV Beattyville KY
*WKGB-TV Bowling Green KY
*WCVN Covington KY
*WKZT-TV Elizabethtown KY
*WKHA Hazard KY
WBNA Louisville KY
WKMJ Louisville KY
*WKMA Madisonville KY
WLCN Madisonville KY
*WKMR Morehead KY
*WKMU Murray KY
*WKON Owenton KY
*WKPI Pikeville KY
*WKSO-TV Somerset KY
WCCL New Orleans LA
WGNO New Orleans LA
KMCT-TV West Monroe LA
WABU Boston MA
WSBK-TV Boston MA
WLVI-TV Cambridge MA
WMFP Lawrence MA
WHSH-TV Marlborough MA
WCVX Vineyard Haven MA
WHSW-TV Baltimore MD
WNUV-TV Baltimore MD
WJAL Hagerstown MD
WBSX Ann Arbor MI
WJUE Battle Creek MI
WGPR-TV Detroit MI
WXON Detroit MI
WDHS Iron Mountain MI
WLLA Kalamazoo MI
WJMY Marquette MI
WADL Mount Clemens MI
WTLJ Muskegon MI
WAQP Saginaw MI
KLGT-TV Minneapolis MN
KMSP-TV Minneapolis MN
KVBM-TV Minneapolis MN
KXLT-TV Rochester MN
KXLI St. Cloud MN
KNLJ Jefferson City MO
KSMO-TV Kansas City MO
KYFC Kansas City MO
KTAJ St. Joseph MO
KNLC St. Louis MO
KPLR-TV St. Louis MO
WNTZ Natchez MS
WASV-TV Asheville NC
WJZY Belmont NC
WAAP Burlington NC
WFAY Fayetteville NC
WKFT Fayetteville NC
WYED Goldsboro NC
WGGT Greensboro NC
WLXI-TV Greensboro NC
WYDO Greenville NC
WHKY-TV Hickory NC
WEJC Lexington NC
WNDS Derry NH
WGOT Merrimack NH
WWAC-TV Atlantic City NJ
WGTW Burlington NJ
WHSE-TV Newark NJ

WWOR-TV Secaucus NJ
WHSP-TV Vineland NJ
*KAZQ Albuquerque NM
KNAT Albuquerque NM
KOFT Gallup NM
KHFT Hobbs NM
KRPV Roswell NM
KASA-TV Santa Fe NM
KCHF Santa Fe NM
KRLR Las Vegas NV
KBLR Paradise NV
WOCD Amsterdam NY
*WNYB-TV Buffalo NY
*WLIW Garden City NY
WTZA Kingston NY
WPIX New York NY
WTBY Poughkeepsie NY
WLIG Riverhead NY
WHSI-TV Smithtown NY
WSNR-TV Syracuse NY
WBNX-TV Akron OH
WDLI Canton OH
WOAC Canton OH
WWAT Chillicothe OH
WSTR-TV Cincinnati OH
WQHS-TV Cleveland OH
WTLW Lima OH
WUAB Lorain OH
WSFJ Newark OH
WGGN-TV Sandusky OH
WTJC Springfield OH
KDOR Bartlesville OK
KOCB Oklahoma City OK
KOKH-TV Oklahoma City OK
KSBI Oklahoma City OK
KTFO Tulsa OK
KWHB Tulsa OK
KEVU Eugene OR
KNMT-TV Portland OR
KPTV Portland OR
KBSP-TV Salem OR
KEBN Salem OR
WFMZ-TV Allentown PA
WKBS-TV Altoona PA
WPCB-TV Greensburg PA
WPTJ Johnstown PA
WGBS-TV Philadelphia PA
WPHL-TV Philadelphia PA
WPTT-TV Pittsburgh PA
WTVE Reading PA
WGCB-TV Red Lion PA
*WELU Aguadilla PR
WOLE-TV Aguadilla PR
WVEO Aguadilla PR
WCCV-TV Arecibo PR
WDWL Bayamon PR
WDZE Carolina PR
WPRV-TV Fajardo PR
WRUA Fajardo PR
WNJX-TV Mayaguez PR
WORA-TV Mayaguez PR
WECN Naranjito PR
WKPV Ponce PR
*WQTO Ponce PR
WSTE Ponce PR
WSUR Ponce PR
WAPA-TV San Juan PR
WRWR-TV San Juan PR
WSJN-TV San Juan PR

WIRS Yauco PR
*WEBA-TV Allendale SC
WCTP Charleston SC
WGGS-TV Greenville SC
WGSE Myrtle Beach SC
WFLI-TV Cleveland TN
WPGD Hendersonville TN
WPMC Jellico TN
WFBI Memphis TN
WLMT Memphis TN
WHTN Murfreesboro TN
WXMT Nashville TN
KHSH-TV Alvin TX
KRTW Baytown TX
*KITU Beaumont TX
KYLE Bryan TX
KDFI-TV Dallas TX
*KDTX-TV Dallas TX
KXTX-TV Dallas TX
KVAW Eagle Pass TX
KTVT Fort Worth TX
KTXA Fort Worth TX
KTAQ Greenville TX
*KETH Houston TX
KHTV Houston TX
KTXH Houston TX
KHSX-TV Irving TX
KNWS-TV Katy TX
KLDT Lake Dallas TX
KLSB-TV Nacogdoches TX
KMLM Odessa TX
KABB San Antonio TX
KVCT Victoria TX
KSGI-TV Cedar City UT
KOOG-TV Ogden UT
WTMW Arlington VA
WZXK Ashland VA
*WNVC Fairfax VA
WLFG Grundy VA
WTKK Manassas VA
WJCB Norfolk VA
WGNT Portsmouth VA
WEFC Roanoke VA
*WVTA Windsor VT
KBCB Bellingham WA
KVOS-TV Bellingham WA
KONG-TV Everett WA
KTZZ-TV Seattle WA
KSKN Spokane WA
KSTW Tacoma WA
KTBW-TV Tacoma WA
KCWT Wenatchee WA
WMMF-TV Fond du Lac WI
WGBA Green Bay WI
WJNW Janesville WI
WDJT-TV Milwaukee WI
WVCY-TV Milwaukee WI
WVTV Milwaukee WI
*WLEF-TV Park Falls WI
WJJA Racine WI
WSCO Suring WI
WLYJ Clarksburg WV
KLWY Cheyenne WY

College, University and School-Owned Television Stations

*KZXC Anchorage AK
*KUAC-TV Fairbanks AK
*KLEP Newark AR
*KAET Phoenix AZ
*KUAS-TV Tucson AZ
*KUAT-TV Tucson AZ
*KOCE-TV Huntington Beach CA
*KLCS Los Angeles CA
*KVCR-TV San Bernardino CA
*KPBS San Diego CA
*KCSM-TV San Mateo CA
*KNXT Visalia CA
*KTSC Pueblo CO
*WHMM Washington DC
*WBCC Cocoa FL
*WUFT Gainesville FL
*WSRE Pensacola FL
*WFSU-TV Tallahassee FL
*WUSF-TV Tampa FL
*WPBA Atlanta GA
*KQCT Davenport IA

*KAID Boise ID
*KCDT Coeur d'Alene ID
*KBGH Filer ID
*KUID-TV Moscow ID
*KISU-TV Pocatello ID
*KIPT Twin Falls ID
*WSIU-TV Carbondale IL
*WEIU-TV Charleston IL
*WTTW Chicago IL
*WYCC Chicago IL
*WQPT-TV Moline IL
*WUSI-TV Olney IL
*WILL-TV Urbana IL
*WTIU Bloomington IN
*WTBU Indianapolis IN
*WIPB Muncie IN
WNDU-TV South Bend IN
*WVUT Vincennes IN
*KTWU Topeka KS
*WKYU-TV Bowling Green KY
WABU Boston MA

*WCML-TV Alpena MI
*WUCX-TV Bad Axe MI
*WCMV Cadillac MI
*WKAR-TV East Lansing MI
*WFUM Flint MI
*WGVU-TV Grand Rapids MI
*WGVK Kalamazoo MI
*WCMW Manistee MI
*WNMU-TV Marquette MI
*WCMU-TV Mount Pleasant MI
*WUCM-TV University Center MI
*KSMQ-TV Austin MN
*WDSE-TV Duluth MN
KOMU-TV Columbia MO
*KMOS-TV Sedalia MO
*KUSM Bozeman MT
*KUFM-TV Missoula MT
*WUNF-TV Asheville NC
*WUNC-TV Chapel Hill NC
*WUND-TV Columbia NC
*WUNG-TV Concord NC

*WUNK-TV Greenville NC
*WUNM-TV Jacksonville NC
*WUNE-TV Linville NC
*WUNP-TV Roanoke Rapids NC
*WUNJ-TV Wilmington NC
*WUNL-TV Winston-Salem NC
*KUON-TV Lincoln NE
*WENH-TV Durham NH
*WEKW-TV Keene NH
*WLED-TV Littleton NH
*KNME-TV Albuquerque NM
*KRWG-TV Las Cruces NM
*KENW Portales NM
*KLVX Las Vegas NV
*WNYE-TV New York NY
*WOUB-TV Athens OH
*WBGU-TV Bowling Green OH
*WOUC-TV Cambridge OH
*WOSU-TV Columbus OH
*WPBO-TV Portsmouth OH
*KRSC-TV Claremore OK

WETG Erie PA
*KACV-TV Amarillo TX
*KNCT Belton TX
*KAMU-TV College Station TX
*KUHT Houston TX
*KTXT-TV Lubbock TX
*KOCV-TV Odessa TX
*KBYU-TV Provo UT
*KUED Salt Lake City UT
*KCKA Centralia WA
*KWSU-TV Pullman WA
*KTNW Richland WA
*KSPS-TV Spokane WA
*KBTC-TV Tacoma WA
*WHA-TV Madison WI
*WMVS Milwaukee WI
*WMVT Milwaukee WI
*KCWC-TV Lander WY

U.S. Television Stations Broadcasting in Stereo

KTVA Anchorage AK
KYES Anchorage AK
WBMG Birmingham AL
WTTO Birmingham AL
WVTM-TV Birmingham AL
WTVY Dothan AL
WNAL-TV Gadsden AL
WAAY-TV Huntsville AL
WAFF Huntsville AL
WKRG-TV Mobile AL
WHOA-TV Montgomery AL
WDAU Ozark AL
WAKA Selma AL
WRJM-TV Troy AL
WDBB Tuscaloosa AL
KFSM-TV Fort Smith AR
KAIT-TV Jonesboro AR
KARK-TV Little Rock AR
*KETS Little Rock AR
KLRT Little Rock AR
KTHV Little Rock AR
KPNX Mesa AZ
*KAET Phoenix AZ
KPHO-TV Phoenix AZ
KUTP Phoenix AZ
KGUN Tucson AZ
KHRR Tucson AZ
KVOA-TV Tucson AZ
KSWT Yuma AZ
KDOC-TV Anaheim CA
KUZZ-TV Bakersfield CA
KCPM Chico CA
KFSN-TV Fresno CA
KSEE Fresno CA
*KVPT Fresno CA
KABC-TV Los Angeles CA
KCAL Los Angeles CA
KCBS-TV Los Angeles CA
KNBC-TV Los Angeles CA
KTLA Los Angeles CA
KTTV Los Angeles CA
KADY-TV Oxnard CA
KMIR-TV Palm Springs CA
KKAK Porterville CA
KCRA-TV Sacramento CA
KRBK-TV Sacramento CA
KXTV Sacramento CA
KCBA Salinas CA
KSBW Salinas CA
KFMB-TV San Diego CA
KGTV San Diego CA
KNSD San Diego CA
*KPBS San Diego CA
*KMTP-TV San Francisco CA
KOFY-TV San Francisco CA
KPIX San Francisco CA
*KQED San Francisco CA
KRON-TV San Francisco CA
KICU-TV San Jose CA
KSBY San Luis Obispo CA
KMSG-TV Sanger CA
KCOY-TV Santa Maria CA
KFTL Stockton CA
KOVR Stockton CA
KPST-TV Vallejo CA
KMPH Visalia CA
KCNC-TV Denver CO
KMGH-TV Denver CO
*KRMA-TV Denver CO
KTVD Denver CO
KUSA-TV Denver CO
KWGN-TV Denver CO
KJWA Grand Junction CO
KREX-TV Grand Junction CO
KOAA-TV Pueblo CO
*WEDH Hartford CT
WFSB Hartford CT
WHCT-TV Hartford CT
WTIC-TV Hartford CT
WVIT New Britain CT
WTXX Waterbury CT
WDCA Washington DC
*WETA-TV Washington DC
WJLA-TV Washington DC
WRC-TV Washington DC
*WHYY-TV Wilmington DE
WTGI-TV Wilmington DE
WESH Daytona Beach FL
WINK-TV Fort Myers FL
*WUFT Gainesville FL
WYHS-TV Hollywood FL
WAWS Jacksonville FL
WJKS Jacksonville FL
WTLV Jacksonville FL
WTMV Lakeland FL
WACX Leesburg FL
WCIX Miami FL
WCTD Miami FL
WLTV Miami FL
*WPBT Miami FL
WSVN Miami FL
WTVJ Miami FL
WFTV Orlando FL
*WFSG Panama City FL
*WSRE Pensacola FL
*WFSU-TV Tallahassee FL
*WEDU Tampa FL
WTVT Tampa FL

*WUSF-TV Tampa FL
WPBF Tequesta FL
WFLX West Palm Beach FL
WPEC West Palm Beach FL
WPTV West Palm Beach FL
*WXEL-TV West Palm Beach FL
*WGTV Athens GA
WATL Atlanta GA
WGNX Atlanta GA
*WPBA Atlanta GA
WSB-TV Atlanta GA
WVEU Atlanta GA
WXIA-TV Atlanta GA
WAGT Augusta GA
WFXG Augusta GA
WBSG-TV Brunswick GA
*WDCO-TV Cochran GA
*WJSP-TV Columbus GA
WLTZ Columbus GA
*WACS-TV Dawson GA
WMAZ-TV Macon GA
WMGT Macon GA
WTLK-TV Marietta GA
WJCL Savannah GA
*WCES-TV Wrens GA
KTGM Tamuning GU
KFVE Honolulu HI
KHON-TV Honolulu HI
WOI-TV Ames IA
KCRG-TV Cedar Rapids IA
KWQC-TV Davenport IA
KCCI-TV Des Moines IA
*KDIN-TV Des Moines IA
WHO-TV Des Moines IA
KTIV Sioux City IA
KWWL Waterloo IA
*KAID Boise ID
*KCDT Coeur d'Alene ID
KIFI-TV Idaho Falls ID
KIVI Nampa ID
KTRV Nampa ID
*KISU-TV Pocatello ID
WFLD Chicago IL
WGN-TV Chicago IL
WMAQ-TV Chicago IL
*WTTW Chicago IL
WAND Decatur IL
WSIL-TV Harrisburg IL
WMBD-TV Peoria IL
WICS Springfield IL
*WTIU Bloomington IN
WSJV Elkhart IN
WFIE-TV Evansville IN
*WNIN Evansville IN
WKJG-TV Fort Wayne IN
WPWR-TV Gary IN
*WFYI Indianapolis IN
WTHR Indianapolis IN
WXIN Indianapolis IN
WLFI-TV Lafayette IN
*WIPB Muncie IN
WNDU-TV South Bend IN
*WNIT-TV South Bend IN
WSBT-TV South Bend IN
KKFT Fort Scott KS
*KPTS Hutchinson KS
KWCH-TV Hutchinson KS
KMCI Lawrence KS
KOAM-TV Pittsburg KS
WIBW-TV Topeka KS
KAKE-TV Wichita KS
WDKY-TV Danville KY
WKYT-TV Lexington KY
WLEX-TV Lexington KY
WAVE Louisville KY
WDRB-TV Louisville KY
WHAS-TV Louisville KY
WXIX-TV Newport KY
WPSD-TV Paducah KY
KALB-TV Alexandria LA
*WLPB-TV Baton Rouge LA
WVLA Baton Rouge LA
KLFY-TV Lafayette LA
KPLC-TV Lake Charles LA
WCCL New Orleans LA
WDSU New Orleans LA
WNOL-TV New Orleans LA
WWL-TV New Orleans LA
*WYES-TV New Orleans LA
KMSS-TV Shreveport LA
KTBS-TV Shreveport LA
KARD-TV West Monroe LA
WBZ-TV Boston MA
WCVB-TV Boston MA
WFXT Boston MA
*WGBH-TV Boston MA
WHDH-TV Boston MA
WHSH-TV Marlborough MA
WGGB-TV Springfield MA
WWLP Springfield MA
WCVX Vineyard Haven MA
*WMPT Annapolis MD
WJZ-TV Baltimore MD
WMAR-TV Baltimore MD
*WMPB Baltimore MD
WNUV-TV Baltimore MD
*WFPT Frederick MD
WHAG-TV Hagerstown MD

*WWPB Hagerstown MD
*WGPT Oakland MD
*WCPB Salisbury MD
WMDT Salisbury MD
*WCBB Augusta ME
WCSH-TV Portland ME
WGME-TV Portland ME
WPXT Portland ME
*WUCX-TV Bad Axe MI
WGKI Cadillac MI
WTOM-TV Cheboygan MI
WDIV Detroit MI
WKBD Detroit MI
*WTVS Detroit MI
WXON Detroit MI
WXYZ-TV Detroit MI
*WFUM Flint MI
*WGVU-TV Grand Rapids MI
WOOD-TV Grand Rapids MI
*WGVK Kalamazoo MI
WLAJ Lansing MI
*WNMU-TV Marquette MI
WILX-TV Onondaga MI
*WUCM-TV University Center MI
WGKU Vanderbilt MI
*KAWE Bemidji MN
*WDSE-TV Duluth MN
KEYC-TV Mankato MN
KARE Minneapolis MN
KITN-TV Minneapolis MN
KLGT-TV Minneapolis MN
WCCO-TV Minneapolis MN
KTTC Rochester MN
KBRR Thief River Falls MN
KOMU-TV Columbia MO
KRCG Jefferson City MO
*KOZJ Joplin MO
*KCPT Kansas City MO
KCTV Kansas City MO
KSHB-TV Kansas City MO
*KMOS-TV Sedalia MO
KDEB-TV Springfield MO
KOLR-TV Springfield MO
*KOZK Springfield MO
KSPR Springfield MO
KDNL-TV St. Louis MO
*KETC St. Louis MO
KPLR-TV St. Louis MO
KSDK St. Louis MO
WLOX-TV Biloxi MS
WCBI-TV Columbus MS
WHLT Hattiesburg MS
WLBT Jackson MS
*WGBC Meridian MS
KTVQ Billings MT
KTVM Butte MT
KWYB Butte MT
KXLF-TV Butte MT
KFBB-TV Great Falls MT
KTGF Great Falls MT
KCFW-TV Kalispell MT
KECI-TV Missoula MT
KPAX-TV Missoula MT
KTMF Missoula MT
WJZY Belmont NC
*WUNC-TV Chapel Hill NC
WBTV Charlotte NC
WCNC-TV Charlotte NC
WSOC-TV Charlotte NC
*WTVI Charlotte NC
WRDC Durham NC
WKFT Fayetteville NC
WYED Goldsboro NC
WFMY-TV Greensboro NC
WFXI Morehead City NC
WLFL Raleigh NC
WRAL-TV Raleigh NC
WRMY Rocky Mount NC
WITN-TV Washington NC
WECT Wilmington NC
WXII Winston-Salem NC
KFYR-TV Bismarck ND
KQCD-TV Dickinson ND
*KFME Fargo ND
KTHI-TV Fargo ND
KVRR Fargo ND
KJRR Jamestown ND
KMOT Minot ND
KUMV-TV Williston ND
*KTNE-TV Alliance NE
*KMNE-TV Bassett NE
KHAS-TV Hastings NE
*KHNE-TV Hastings NE
*KLNE-TV Lexington NE
*KUON-TV Lincoln NE
*KRNE-TV Merriman NE
KNOP-TV North Platte NE
KETV Omaha NE
KMTV Omaha NE
KPTM Omaha NE
WOWT Omaha NE
*WENH-TV Durham NH
*WEKW-TV Keene NH
*WLED-TV Littleton NH
*WNJS Camden NJ
*WNJM Montclair NJ
WHSE-TV Newark NJ
*WNET Newark NJ

WWOR-TV Secaucus NJ
*WNJT Trenton NJ
WHSP-TV Vineland NJ
KOAT-TV Albuquerque NM
KOB-TV Albuquerque NM
KRQE Albuquerque NM
KVIH-TV Clovis NM
KOVT Silver City NM
KRLR Las Vegas NV
KTNV Las Vegas NV
KOLO-TV Reno NV
WBNG-TV Binghamton NY
WICZ-TV Binghamton NY
*WNED-TV Buffalo NY
*WNYB-TV Buffalo NY
WUTV Buffalo NY
WWNY-TV Carthage NY
WNBC New York NY
*WNYC-TV New York NY
WPIX New York NY
WPTZ North Pole NY
WROC-TV Rochester NY
WUHF Rochester NY
*WMHT Schenectady NY
WHSI-TV Smithtown NY
*WCNY-TV Syracuse NY
WSTM-TV Syracuse NY
WSYT Syracuse NY
WFXV Utica NY
WWTI Watertown NY
WAKC-TV Akron OH
*WEAO Akron OH
*WNEO Alliance OH
*WBGU-TV Bowling Green OH
*WCET Cincinnati OH
WCPO-TV Cincinnati OH
WKRC-TV Cincinnati OH
WSTR-TV Cincinnati OH
WKYC-TV Cleveland OH
WQHS-TV Cleveland OH
*WVIZ-TV Cleveland OH
WBNS-TV Columbus OH
WCMH Columbus OH
WHIO-TV Dayton OH
WKEF Dayton OH
*WPTD Dayton OH
WUAB Lorain OH
WOIO Shaker Heights OH
WTOV-TV Steubenville OH
*WGTE-TV Toledo OH
WNWO-TV Toledo OH
WTOL-TV Toledo OH
WTVG Toledo OH
WUPW Toledo OH
WFMJ-TV Youngstown OH
WHIZ-TV Zanesville OH
KSWO-TV Lawton OK
KFOR-TV Oklahoma City OK
KOCO-TV Oklahoma City OK
KWTV Oklahoma City OK
KJRH Tulsa OK
*KOAB-TV Bend OR
KTVZ Bend OR
KMTZ Coos Bay OR
KMTR Eugene OR
KOBI Medford OR
KATU Portland OR
KGW-TV Portland OR
KOIN Portland OR
KMTX-TV Roseburg OR
*WLVT-TV Allentown PA
WATM-TV Altoona PA
*WTAJ-TV Altoona PA
WICU-TV Erie PA
WHP-TV Harrisburg PA
WWLF-TV Hazleton PA
WJAC-TV Johnstown PA
WGAL Lancaster PA
KYW-TV Philadelphia PA
WCAU-TV Philadelphia PA
WGBS-TV Philadelphia PA
WPVI-TV Philadelphia PA
WPXI Pittsburgh PA
WTAE-TV Pittsburgh PA
WNEP-TV Scranton PA
WYOU Scranton PA
WLII Caguas PR
WSJU San Juan PR
WJAR Providence RI
WNAC-TV Providence RI
WPRI-TV Providence RI
*WSBE-TV Providence RI
WAXA Anderson SC
WCBD-TV Charleston SC
WCIV Charleston SC
WTAT-TV Charleston SC
WACH Columbia SC
WIS Columbia SC
WYFF Greenville SC
KDLT Mitchell SD
KCLO-TV Rapid City SD
KELO-TV Sioux Falls SD
KTTW Sioux Falls SD
WRCB-TV Chattanooga TN
*WTCI Chattanooga TN
WTVC Chattanooga TN
WEMT Greeneville TN
WKPT-TV Kingsport TN

WATE-TV Knoxville TN
*WKOP-TV Knoxville TN
WKXT-TV Knoxville TN
*WLJT-TV Lexington TN
*WKNO-TV Memphis TN
WMC-TV Memphis TN
*WDCN Nashville TN
WSMV Nashville TN
WTVF Nashville TN
WZTV Nashville TN
KRBC-TV Abilene TX
KHSH-TV Alvin TX
*KACV-TV Amarillo TX
KAMR-TV Amarillo TX
KFDA-TV Amarillo TX
KVII-TV Amarillo TX
*KLRU-TV Austin TX
KVUE-TV Austin TX
KRIS-TV Corpus Christi TX
KDFI-TV Dallas TX
KDFW-TV Dallas TX
*KERA-TV Dallas TX
WFAA-TV Dallas TX
KTSM-TV El Paso TX
KTVT Fort Worth TX
KXAS-TV Fort Worth TX
KGBT-TV Harlingen TX
KHOU-TV Houston TX
KPRC-TV Houston TX
*KUHT Houston TX
KETK-TV Jacksonville TX
KNWS-TV Katy TX
KRRT Kerrville TX
KXAM-TV Llano TX
KJTV Lubbock TX
KPEJ Odessa TX
KIDY San Angelo TX
KLST San Angelo TX
KABB San Antonio TX
KMOL-TV San Antonio TX
KSAT-TV San Antonio TX
KVDA San Antonio TX
KWEX-TV San Antonio TX
KXII Sherman TX
KCEN-TV Temple TX
KXXV Waco TX
KFDX-TV Wichita Falls TX
KJTL Wichita Falls TX
KSGI-TV Cedar City UT
*KBYU-TV Provo UT
KJZZ-TV Salt Lake City UT
KSL-TV Salt Lake City UT
KSTU Salt Lake City UT
KTVX Salt Lake City UT
*KUED Salt Lake City UT
KUTV Salt Lake City UT
WZXK Ashland VA
WCYB-TV Bristol VA
WVIR-TV Charlottesville VA
*WHRO-TV Hampton-Norfolk VA
WJPR Lynchburg VA
WRIC-TV Petersburg VA
WAVY-TV Portsmouth VA
*WCVE-TV Richmond VA
WWBT Richmond VA
*WBRA-TV Roanoke VA
WDBJ Roanoke VA
WFXR-TV Roanoke VA
*WVPT Staunton VA
*WETK Burlington VT
*WVER Rutland VT
*WVTB St. Johnsbury VT
*WVTA Windsor VT
*KCTS Seattle WA
KING-TV Seattle WA
KIRO-TV Seattle WA
KOMO-TV Seattle WA
KTZZ-TV Seattle WA
KHQ-TV Spokane WA
KREM-TV Spokane WA
*KSPS-TV Spokane WA
KXLY-TV Spokane WA
KCPQ Tacoma WA
KSTW Tacoma WA
WXGZ-TV Appleton WI
WEAU-TV Eau Claire WI
WLUK-TV Green Bay WI
WISC-TV Madison WI
WKOW-TV Madison WI
WMSN-TV Madison WI
WMTV Madison WI
WCGV-TV Milwaukee WI
WDJT-TV Milwaukee WI
WISN-TV Milwaukee WI
*WMVS Milwaukee WI
WTMJ-TV Milwaukee WI
WVTV Milwaukee WI
WVVA Bluefield WV
WVAH-TV Charleston WV
WBOY-TV Clarksburg WV
WSAZ-TV Huntington WV
WYVN Martinsburg WV
WTRF-TV Wheeling WV
KKTU Cheyenne WY
KLWY Cheyenne WY

U.S. Television Stations by Channel

Channel 2 (54-60 mhz)

KTUU-TV Anchorage AK
KATN Fairbanks AK
*WDIQ Dozier AL
*KETS Little Rock AR
*KVZK-2 Pago Pago AS
KNAZ-TV Flagstaff AZ
KCBS-TV Los Angeles CA
KTVU Oakland CA
KWGN-TV Denver CO
WESH Daytona Beach FL
*WPBT Miami FL
WSB-TV Atlanta GA
KHBC-TV Hilo HI
KHON-TV Honolulu HI
KGAN Cedar Rapids IA
KBCI-TV Boise ID
WBBM-TV Chicago IL
WTWO Terre Haute IN
KSNC Great Bend KS
WBRZ Baton Rouge LA
*WGBH-TV Boston MA
WMAR-TV Baltimore MD
WLBZ-TV Bangor ME
WJBK-TV Detroit MI
*KTCA-TV St. Paul MN
KQTV St. Joseph MO
KTVI St. Louis MO
*WMAB-TV Mississippi State MS
KTVQ Billings MT
*WUND-TV Columbia NC
WFMY-TV Greensboro NC
KXMA-TV Dickinson ND
*KGFE Grand Forks ND
KNOP-TV North Platte NE
KASA-TV Santa Fe NM
KTVN Reno NV
WGRZ-TV Buffalo NY
WCBS-TV New York NY
WKTV Utica NY
WDTN Dayton OH
KJRH Tulsa OK
KOTI Klamath Falls OR
KATU Portland OR
KDKA-TV Pittsburgh PA
WKAQ-TV San Juan PR
WCBD-TV Charleston SC
*KUSD-TV Vermillion SD
WKRN-TV Nashville TN
*WSJK-TV Sneedville TN
*KACV-TV Amarillo TX
*KDTN Denton TX
KPRC-TV Houston TX
KMID Midland TX
KUTV Salt Lake City UT
KREM-TV Spokane WA
WBAY-TV Green Bay WI
KTWO-TV Casper WY
KJVI Jackson WY

Channel 3 (60-66 mhz)

*KTOO-TV Juneau AK
KTVK Phoenix AZ
KIEM-TV Eureka CA
KCRA-TV Sacramento CA
KEYT-TV Santa Barbara CA
KREG-TV Glenwood Springs CO
KTVS Sterling CO
WFSB Hartford CT
WEAR-TV Pensacola FL
*WEDU Tampa FL
WRBL Columbus GA
WSAV-TV Savannah GA
KGMV Wailuku HI
KIMT Mason City IA
KIDK Idaho Falls ID
KLEW-TV Lewiston ID
WCIA Champaign IL
WSIL-TV Harrisburg IL
*KSWK Lakin KS
KSNW Wichita KS
WAVE Louisville KY
KATC Lafayette LA
KTBS-TV Shreveport LA
WJMN-TV Escanaba MI
WWMT Kalamazoo MI
KDLH Duluth MN
KTVO Kirksville MO
KYTV Springfield MO
WLBT Jackson MS
KRTV Great Falls MT
KYUS-TV Miles City MT
WBTV Charlotte NC
WWAY Wilmington NC
*KBME Bismarck ND
*KLNE-TV Lexington NE
KMTV Omaha NE
KOFT Gallup NM
*KENW Portales NM
KVBC Las Vegas NV
WSTM-TV Syracuse NY
WKYC-TV Cleveland OH
*KOET Eufaula OK
*KOAB-TV Bend OR
*WPSX-TV Clearfield PA
KYW-TV Philadelphia PA
WIPR-TV Mayaguez PR
KDLO-TV Florence SD

KOTA-TV Rapid City SD
WRCB-TV Chattanooga TN
WREG-TV Memphis TN
KBTX-TV Bryan TX
KIII Corpus Christi TX
KACB-TV San Angelo TX
KFDX-TV Wichita Falls TX
WHSV-TV Harrisonburg VA
WTKR-TV Norfolk VA
WCAX-TV Burlington VT
WISC-TV Madison WI
WSAZ-TV Huntington WV

Channel 4 (66-72 mhz)

KTBY Anchorage AK
*KYUK-TV Bethel AK
KJNP-TV North Pole AK
WTVY Dothan AL
KARK-TV Little Rock AR
*KVZK-4 Pago Pago AS
KZJC Flagstaff AZ
KVOA-TV Tucson AZ
KNBC-TV Los Angeles CA
KRON-TV San Francisco CA
KCNC-TV Denver CO
KJWA Grand Junction CO
WRC-TV Washington DC
WJXT Jacksonville FL
WTVJ Miami FL
KITV Honolulu HI
KTIV Sioux City IA
*KAID Boise ID
WHBF-TV Rock Island IL
WTTV Bloomington IN
KLBY Colby KS
WWL-TV New Orleans LA
WBZ-TV Boston MA
WTOM-TV Cheboygan MI
WDIV Detroit MI
WCCO-TV Minneapolis MN
WDAF-TV Kansas City MO
KMOV St. Louis MO
WCBI-TV Columbus MS
KXLF-TV Butte MT
KOUS-TV Hardin MT
*WUNC-TV Chapel Hill NC
KXJB-TV Valley City ND
*KWSE Williston ND
KDUH-TV Scottsbluff NE
KSNB-TV Superior NE
KOB-TV Albuquerque NM
KRNV Reno NV
WIVB-TV Buffalo NY
WNBC New York NY
WCMH Columbus OH
KFOR-TV Oklahoma City OK
KPIC Roseburg OR
WTAE-TV Pittsburgh PA
WAPA-TV San Juan PR
WCIV Charleston SC
WYFF Greenville SC
KPRY-TV Pierre SD
WSMV Nashville TN
KAMR-TV Amarillo TX
KWAB Big Spring TX
KDFW-TV Dallas TX
KDBC-TV El Paso TX
KGBT-TV Harlingen TX
KJAC-TV Port Arthur TX
KMOL-TV San Antonio TX
KSGI-TV Cedar City UT
KTVX Salt Lake City UT
KOMO-TV Seattle WA
KXLY-TV Spokane WA
WTMJ-TV Milwaukee WI
WOAY-TV Oak Hill WV
*KCWC-TV Lander WY

Channel 5 (76-82 mhz)

KYES Anchorage AK
WKRG-TV Mobile AL
KFSM-TV Fort Smith AR
*KVZK-5 Pago Pago AS
KPHO-TV Phoenix AZ
KTLA Los Angeles CA
KPIX San Francisco CA
KREX-TV Grand Junction CO
KOAA-TV Pueblo CO
WTTG Washington DC
*WUFT Gainesville FL
WPTV West Palm Beach FL
WAGA-TV Atlanta GA
KFVE Honolulu HI
WOI-TV Ames IA
WMAQ-TV Chicago IL
KALB-TV Alexandria LA
WCVB-TV Boston MA
WABI-TV Bangor ME
WNEM-TV Bay City MI
KSTP-TV St. Paul MN
KCTV Kansas City MO
KSDK St. Louis MO
KXGN-TV Glendive MT
KFBB-TV Great Falls MT
WRAL-TV Raleigh NC
KFYR-TV Bismarck ND
KHAS-TV Hastings NE
*KNME-TV Albuquerque NM
KVVU-TV Henderson NV

*KNPB Reno NV
WNYW New York NY
WPTZ North Pole NY
WTVH Syracuse NY
WLWT Cincinnati OH
WEWS Cleveland OH
KOCO-TV Oklahoma City OK
KOBI Medford OR
WORA-TV Mayaguez PR
WCSC-TV Charleston SC
KIVV-TV Lead SD
KDLT Mitchell SD
WMC-TV Memphis TN
WTVF Nashville TN
KXAS-TV Fort Worth TX
*KTXT-TV Lubbock TX
KENS-TV San Antonio TX
KRGV-TV Weslaco TX
KSL-TV Salt Lake City UT
WCYB-TV Bristol VA
KING-TV Seattle WA
WFRV-TV Green Bay WI
WDTV Weston WV
KGWN-TV Cheyenne WY
KGWL-TV Lander WY

Channel 6 (82-88 mhz)

WBRC-TV Birmingham AL
*KEMV Mountain View AR
KMOH-TV Kingman AZ
*KUAT-TV Tucson AZ
KVIQ Eureka CA
*KVIE Sacramento CA
KSBY San Luis Obispo CA
*KRMA-TV Denver CO
KREZ-TV Durango CO
WCIX Miami FL
WCPX-TV Orlando FL
WJBF Augusta GA
WCTV Thomasville GA
KLEI Kailua-Kona HI
KWQC-TV Davenport IA
KIVI Nampa ID
KPVI Pocatello ID
WRTV Indianapolis IN
KBSD-TV Ensign KS
WPSD-TV Paducah KY
WDSU New Orleans LA
WLNE New Bedford MA
WCSH-TV Portland ME
*WCML-TV Alpena MI
WLNS-TV Lansing MI
WLUC-TV Marquette MI
KAAL Austin MN
*KMOS-TV Sedalia MO
WABG-TV Greenwood MS
KSVI Billings MT
KTVM Butte MT
WECT Wilmington NC
WDAY-TV Fargo ND
*KSRE Minot ND
KWNB-TV Hayes Center NE
WOWT Omaha NE
KOCT Carlsbad NM
WRGB Schenectady NY
WSYX Columbus OH
KOTV Tulsa OK
KOIN Portland OR
WJAC-TV Johnstown PA
WPVI-TV Philadelphia PA
*WIPR-TV San Juan PR
KPLO-TV Reliance SD
WATE-TV Knoxville TN
KFDM-TV Beaumont TX
KRIS-TV Corpus Christi TX
KIDY San Angelo TX
KCEN-TV Temple TX
KTAL-TV Texarkana TX
KAUZ-TV Wichita Falls TX
WTVR-TV Richmond VA
KHQ-TV Spokane WA
WITI-TV Milwaukee WI
KBJR-TV Superior WI
WVVA Bluefield WV

Channel 7 (174-180 mhz)

*KAKM Anchorage AK
*WCIQ Mt Cheaha State Park AL
KATV Little Rock AR
KUSK Prescott AZ
KLXO El Centro CA
KABC-TV Los Angeles CA
KRCR-TV Redding CA
KGO-TV San Francisco CA
KMGH-TV Denver CO
WJLA-TV Washington DC
*WJCT Jacksonville FL
WSVN Miami FL
WJHG-TV Panama City FL
KAII-TV Wailuku HI
KWWL Waterloo IA
KTVB Boise ID
WLS-TV Chicago IL
WTVW Evansville IN
KBSH-TV Hays KS
KOAM-TV Pittsburg KS
*KIXE-TV Redding CA
KPLC-TV Lake Charles LA
WHDH-TV Boston MA
WVII-TV Bangor ME

WXYZ-TV Detroit MI
WPBN-TV Traverse City MI
KCCO-TV Alexandria MN
KHQA-TV Hannibal MO
WDAM-TV Laurel MS
KCTZ Bozeman MT
WITN-TV Washington NC
KQCD-TV Dickinson ND
KJRR Jamestown ND
*KMNE-TV Bassett NE
KETV Omaha NE
KOAT-TV Albuquerque NM
WKBW-TV Buffalo NY
WWNY-TV Carthage NY
WABC-TV New York NY
WHIO-TV Dayton OH
KSWO-TV Lawton OK
*KOAC-TV Corvallis OR
WSTE Ponce PR
*WITV Charleston SC
WSPA-TV Spartanburg SC
KEVN-TV Rapid City SD
WBBJ-TV Jackson TN
KVII-TV Amarillo TX
KTBC-TV Austin TX
KVIA-TV El Paso TX
KOSA-TV Odessa TX
KLTV Tyler TX
*KUED Salt Lake City UT
WDBJ Roanoke VA
KIRO-TV Seattle WA
*KSPS-TV Spokane WA
WSAW-TV Wausau WI
WTRF-TV Wheeling WV
KRBQ Sheridan WY

Channel 8 (180-186 mhz)

KJUD Juneau AK
WAKA Selma AL
KAIT-TV Jonesboro AR
*KAET Phoenix AZ
KFWU Fort Bragg CA
KSBW Salinas CA
KFMB-TV San Diego CA
KJCT Grand Junction CO
*KTSC Pueblo CO
WTNH-TV New Haven CT
WWFD Key West FL
WFLA-TV Tampa FL
*WGTV Athens GA
*WXGA-TV Waycross GA
KUAM-TV Agana GU
KCCI-TV Des Moines IA
KIFI-TV Idaho Falls ID
*WSIU-TV Carbondale IL
WQAD-TV Moline IL
WISH-TV Indianapolis IN
*KPTS Hutchinson KS
KNOE-TV Monroe LA
WVUE New Orleans LA
WMTW-TV Poland Spring ME
WAGM-TV Presque Isle ME
WOOD-TV Grand Rapids MI
*WDHS Iron Mountain MI
WGTQ Sault Ste. Marie MI
*WDSE-TV Duluth MN
KOMU-TV Columbia MO
KULR-TV Billings MT
KPAX-TV Missoula MT
WGHP-TV High Point NC
WFXI Morehead City NC
WDAZ-TV Devils Lake ND
KUMV-TV Williston ND
KCAN Albion NE
KSNK McCook NE
KOBR Roswell NM
KLAS-TV Las Vegas NV
KOLO-TV Reno NV
WROC-TV Rochester NY
WJW-TV Cleveland OH
KTUL Tulsa OK
*KSYS Medford OR
KGW-TV Portland OR
WWCP-TV Johnstown PA
WGAL Lancaster PA
*KESD-TV Brookings SD
*KZSD-TV Martin SD
WKXT-TV Knoxville TN
*WDCN Nashville TN
WFAA-TV Dallas TX
*KUHT Houston TX
KGNS-TV Laredo TX
KLST San Angelo TX
WRIC-TV Petersburg VA
WSVI Christiansted VI
WKBT La Crosse WI
WCHS-TV Charleston WV

Channel 9 (186-192 mhz)

*KZXC Anchorage AK
*KUAC-TV Fairbanks AK
*KETG Arkadelphia AR
KGUN Tucson AZ
KECY-TV El Centro CA
KCAL Los Angeles CA
*KIXE-TV Redding CA
*KQED San Francisco CA
KUSA-TV Denver CO
WUSA Washington DC

WFTV Orlando FL
WTVM Columbus GA
*WVAN-TV Savannah GA
KGMD-TV Hilo HI
KGMB Honolulu HI
KCRG-TV Cedar Rapids IA
KCAU-TV Sioux City IA
KHDT-TV Caldwell ID
WGN-TV Chicago IL
*WNIN Evansville IN
*KOOD Hays KS
WAFB Baton Rouge LA
WWTV Cadillac MI
*KAWE Bemidji MN
KMSP-TV Minneapolis MN
KMBC-TV Kansas City MO
*KETC St. Louis MO
WTVA Tupelo MS
*KUSM Bozeman MT
KCFW-TV Kalispell MT
WSOC-TV Charlotte NC
WNCT-TV Greenville NC
*KDSE Dickinson ND
*KPNE-TV North Platte NE
WMUR-TV Manchester NH
WWOR-TV Secaucus NJ
WIXT Syracuse NY
WCPO-TV Cincinnati OH
WTOV-TV Steubenville OH
KWTV Oklahoma City OK
KEZI Eugene OR
WSUR-TV Ponce PR
KABY-TV Aberdeen SD
*KBHE-TV Rapid City SD
WTVC Chattanooga TN
KRBC-TV Abilene TX
KTSM-TV El Paso TX
KTRE Lufkin TX
KWES-TV Odessa TX
*KLRN San Antonio TX
*KULC Ogden UT
*KCTS-TV Seattle WA
WAOW-TV Wausau WI
*WSWP-TV Grandview WV

Channel 10 (192-198 mhz)

*WBIQ Birmingham AL
WALA-TV Mobile AL
KTVE El Dorado AR
KTSP-TV Phoenix AZ
KXTV Sacramento CA
KGTV San Diego CA
KREY-TV Montrose CO
WPLG Miami FL
WTSP St. Petersburg FL
WALB-TV Albany GA
*KMEB Wailuku HI
*KISU-TV Pocatello ID
WGEM-TV Quincy IL
WTHI-TV Terre Haute IN
KBSL-TV Goodland KS
KAKE-TV Wichita KS
KLFY-TV Lafayette LA
*WCBB Augusta ME
*WMEM-TV Presque Isle ME
WILX-TV Onondaga MI
WWUP-TV Sault Ste. Marie MI
*KWCM-TV Appleton MN
WDIO-TV Duluth MN
KTTC Rochester MN
KBRR Thief River Falls MN
KOLR-TV Springfield MO
KHBB Helena MT
KMOT Minot ND
KOLN Lincoln NE
KSTF Scottsbluff NE
KBIM-TV Roswell NM
KOVT Silver City NM
KLVX Las Vegas NV
WTEN Albany NY
WHEC-TV Rochester NY
WBNS-TV Columbus OH
KTEN Ada OK
KTVL Medford OR
*KOPB-TV Portland OR
*WTAJ-TV Altoona PA
WCAU-TV Philadelphia PA
WJAR Providence RI
WIS Columbia SC
*KTSD-TV Pierre SD
WBIR-TV Knoxville TN
*WKNO-TV Memphis TN
KFDA-TV Amarillo TX
KZTV Corpus Christi TX
KTRG Del Rio TX
KWTX-TV Waco TX
WAVY-TV Portsmouth VA
WSLS-TV Roanoke VA
WBNB-TV Charlotte Amalie VI
*KWSU-TV Pullman WA
*WMVS Milwaukee WI
KFNE Riverton WY

Channel 11 (198-204 mhz)

KTVA Anchorage AK
KTVF Fairbanks AK
KTHV Little Rock AR
KMSB-TV Tucson AZ
KYMA Yuma AZ

U.S. Television Stations by Channel

KTTV Los Angeles CA
KNTV San Jose CA
KKTV Colorado Springs CO
WINK-TV Fort Myers FL
*WFSU-TV Tallahassee FL
WXIA-TV Atlanta GA
WTOC-TV Savannah GA
KHAW-TV Hilo HI
*KHET Honolulu HI
*KDIN-TV Des Moines IA
*WTTW Chicago IL
KSNG Garden City KS
*KTWU Topeka KS
WHAS-TV Louisville KY
WBAL-TV Baltimore MD
WBKB-TV Alpena MI
KARE Minneapolis MN
KPLR-TV St. Louis MO
WTOK-TV Meridian MS
*KUFM-TV Missoula MT
WTVD Durham NC
*KTHI-TV Fargo ND
KXMD-TV Williston ND
KGIN Grand Island NE
*WENH-TV Durham NH
*KCHF Santa Fe NM
KRXI Reno NV
WPIX New York NY
WTOL-TV Toledo OH
*KOED-TV Tulsa OK
KCBY-TV Coos Bay OR
WPXI Pittsburgh PA
WLII Caguas PR
KHSD-TV Lead SD
*KQSD-TV Lowry SD
KELO-TV Sioux Falls SD
WJHL-TV Johnson City TN
*WLJT-TV Lexington TN
KTVT Fort Worth TX
KHOU-TV Houston TX
KCBD-TV Lubbock TX
*KBYU-TV Provo UT
KSTW Tacoma WA
WLUK-TV Green Bay WI
WVAH-TV Charleston WV
KFNR Rawlins WY

Channel 12 (204-210 mhz)

WSFA Montgomery AL
KPNX Mesa AZ
KHSL-TV Chico CA
KCOY-TV Santa Maria CA
*KBDI-TV Broomfield CO
*WHYY-TV Wilmington DE
WTLV Jacksonville FL
WPEC West Palm Beach FL
WRDW-TV Augusta GA
*KGTF Agana GU
KMAU Wailuku HI
*KIIN-TV Iowa City IA
*KUID-TV Moscow ID
KTRV Nampa ID
*WILL-TV Urbana IL
KWCH-TV Hutchinson KS
*WYES-TV New Orleans LA
KSLA-TV Shreveport LA
*WMEB-TV Orono ME
WJRT-TV Flint MI
KEYC-TV Mankato MN
KCCW-TV Walker MN
KFVS-TV Cape Girardeau MO
KODE-TV Joplin MO
*WMAE-TV Booneville MS
WJTV Jackson MS
KTVH Helena MT
WCTI New Bern NC
WXII Winston-Salem NC
KXMB-TV Bismarck ND
KNRR Pembina ND
*KUON-TV Lincoln NE
*KRNE-TV Merriman NE
KVIH-TV Clovis NM
KOBF Farmington NM
WBNG-TV Binghamton NY
WKRC-TV Cincinnati OH
*KWET Cheyenne OK
KDRV Medford OR
KPTV Portland OR
WICU-TV Erie PA
WOLE-TV Aguadilla PR
WPRI-TV Providence RI
KTTM Huron SD
WDEF-TV Chattanooga TN
KBMT Beaumont TX
KSAT-TV San Antonio TX
KXII Sherman TX
KTXS-TV Sweetwater TX
KUSG St. George UT
WWBT Richmond VA
*WTJX-TV Charlotte Amalie VI
KVOS-TV Bellingham WA
WISN-TV Milwaukee WI
WJFW-TV Rhinelander WI
WBOY-TV Clarksburg WV
KSGW-TV Sheridan WY

Channel 13 (210-216 mhz)

KIMO Anchorage AK
KTNL Sitka AK
WVTM-TV Birmingham AL
*KAFT Fayetteville AR
KKTM Flagstaff AZ
KOLD-TV Tucson AZ

KSWT Yuma AZ
*KEET Eureka CA
KCOP Los Angeles CA
KOVR Stockton CA
KRDO-TV Colorado Springs CO
WMBB Panama City FL
WTVT Tampa FL
WMAZ-TV Macon GA
KHVO Hilo HI
KHNL Honolulu HI
WHO-TV Des Moines IA
*KIPT Twin Falls ID
WCEE Mount Vernon IL
WREX-TV Rockford IL
WTHR Indianapolis IN
KUPK-TV Garden City KS
WIBW-TV Topeka KS
WBKO Bowling Green KY
*KLTM-TV Monroe LA
WJZ-TV Baltimore MD
*WMED-TV Calais ME
WGME-TV Portland ME
WZZM-TV Grand Rapids MI
*WNMU-TV Marquette MI
WIRT Hibbing MN
KRCG Jefferson City MO
WLOX-TV Biloxi MS
KECI-TV Missoula MT
WLOS Asheville NC
*KFME Fargo ND
KXMC-TV Minot ND
*KTNE-TV Alliance NE
KHGI-TV Kearney NE
*WNET Newark NJ
KRQE Albuquerque NM
KTNV Las Vegas NV
WNYT Albany NY
WOKR Rochester NY
WTVG Toledo OH
*KETA Oklahoma City OK
KVAL-TV Eugene OR
*KTVR La Grande OR
*WQED Pittsburgh PA
WPRV-TV Fajardo PR
WBTW Florence SC
*KPSD-TV Eagle Butte SD
KSFY-TV Sioux Falls SD
WHBQ-TV Memphis TN
*KERA-TV Dallas TX
KTRK-TV Houston TX
KVTV Laredo TX
KLBK-TV Lubbock TX
KSTU Salt Lake City UT
WVEC-TV Hampton VA
WSET-TV Lynchburg VA
KCPQ Tacoma WA
WEAU-TV Eau Claire WI
WOWK-TV Huntington WV
KGWR-TV Rock Springs WY

Channel 14 (470-476 mhz)

KDTV San Francisco CA
KTVJ Boulder CO
WTLK-TV Marietta GA
*WABW-TV Pelham GA
KTGM Tamuning GU
KWHH Hilo HI
KWHE Honolulu HI
KMEG Sioux City IA
*WSEC Jacksonville IL
WFIE-TV Evansville IN
KARD-TV West Monroe LA
*WCMU-TV Mount Pleasant MI
*WMAW-TV Meridian MS
WYDO Greenville NC
WHKY-TV Hickory NC
KMCY Minot ND
*WPTO Oxford OH
KTBO-TV Oklahoma City OK
WTIN Ponce PR
*WEBA-TV Allendale SC
KCIT Amarillo TX
KCIK El Paso TX
*KETH Houston TX
KXAM-TV Llano TX
KJZZ-TV Salt Lake City UT
WTMW Arlington VA
WSCO Suring WI
KGWC-TV Casper WY

Channel 15 (476-482 mhz)

WOWL-TV Florence AL
WPMI Mobile AL
KNXV-TV Phoenix AZ
*KPBS San Diego CA
*WCEU New Smyrna Beach FL
KOGG Wailuku HI
KYOU-TV Ottumwa IA
WICD Champaign IL
WANE-TV Fort Wayne IN
*WKPC-TV Louisville KY
KADN Lafayette LA
*KSMQ-TV Austin MN
KPOB-TV Poplar Bluff MO
WXVT Greenville MS
KVRR Fargo ND
WLYH-TV Lancaster PA
WPDE-TV Florence SC
KCLO-TV Rapid City SD
*WKOP-TV Knoxville TN
*KAMU-TV College Station TX
*WHRO-TV Hampton-Norfolk VA
*WBRA-TV Roanoke VA

*KCKA Centralia WA
WMTV Madison WI
WTAP-TV Parkersburg WV

Channel 16 (482-488 mhz)

KLRT Little Rock AR
*WUSF-TV Tampa FL
*WUSI-TV Olney IL
WTJR Quincy IL
WNDU-TV South Bend IN
WBOC-TV Salisbury MD
KSNF Joplin MO
KTAJ St. Joseph MO
WAPT Jackson MS
KTGF Great Falls MT
WAAP Burlington NC
*WNPE-TV Watertown NY
*WPTD Dayton OH
KMTR Eugene OR
*WQEX Pittsburgh PA
WNEP-TV Scranton PA
WTRA Mayaguez PR
*WJWJ-TV Beaufort SC
*WGGS-TV Greenville SC
*KDSD-TV Aberdeen SD
WMTU Jackson TN
*KEDT-TV Corpus Christi TX
KVAW Eagle Pass TX
KONG-TV Everett WA

Channel 17 (488-494 mhz)

WDBB Tuscaloosa AL
*KLEP Newark AR
KGET Bakersfield CA
WJKS Jacksonville FL
*WLRN-TV Miami FL
WTBS Atlanta GA
KDSM-TV Des Moines IA
WAND Decatur IL
WTVO Rockford IL
WXMI Grand Rapids MI
*KTCI-TV St. Paul MN
KMIZ Columbia MO
*WMAU-TV Bude MS
WYED Goldsboro NC
*WUNE-TV Linville NC
KBMY Bismarck ND
KTVG Grand Island NE
*WNED-TV Buffalo NY
*WMHT Schenectady NY
WDLI Canton OH
KDOR Bartlesville OK
WPHL-TV Philadelphia PA
KTTW Sioux Falls SD
WZTV Nashville TN
WVXF Charlotte Amalie VI

Channel 18 (494-500 mhz)

WDHN Dothan AL
KTTU-TV Tucson AZ
*KVPT Fresno CA
KSCI San Bernardino CA
WHCT-TV Hartford CT
WKCF Clermont FL
*WCLP-TV Chatsworth GA
KLJB-TV Davenport IA
WLFI-TV Lafayette IN
KAAS-TV Salina KS
WLEX-TV Lexington KY
*KLTL-TV Lake Charles LA
*WMAV-TV Oxford MS
KWYB Butte MT
WCCB Charlotte NC
WETM-TV Elmira NY
*WNPI-TV Norwood NY
WHIZ-TV Zanesville OH
WSJU San Juan PR
*KLRU-TV Austin TX
KMZN Farwell TX
KJTL Wichita Falls TX
WQOW-TV Eau Claire WI
WVTV Milwaukee WI

Channel 19 (500-506 mhz)

WHNT-TV Huntsville AL
*KTEJ Jonesboro AR
KCSO Modesto CA
*KBGH Filer ID
WHOI Peoria IL
WLCN Madisonville KY
WXIX-TV Newport KY
WCDC Adams MA
WJMY Marquette MI
*WUCM-TV University Center MI
*KCPT Kansas City MO
*WMAH-TV Biloxi MS
*WUNM-TV Jacksonville NC
*KJRE Ellendale ND
*KXNE-TV Norfolk NE
WOIO Shaker Heights OH
WPTJ Johnstown PA
WLTX Columbia SC
WKPT-TV Kingsport TN
KLSB-TV Nacogdoches TX
KVCT Victoria TX
KEPR-TV Pasco WA
WXOW-TV La Crosse WI

Channel 20 (506-512 mhz)

WCOV-TV Montgomery AL
KOFY-TV San Francisco CA
KTVD Denver CO

WTXX Waterbury CT
WDCA Washington DC
WBBH-TV Fort Myers FL
WCJB Gainesville FL
*WCES-TV Wrens GA
KIKU Honolulu HI
*WYCC Chicago IL
WICS Springfield IL
*WFYI Indianapolis IN
KKFT Fort Scott KS
NEW TV New Orleans LA
WXON Detroit MI
WEJC Lexington NC
WUTR Utica NY
*WOUB-TV Athens OH
KAFU Enid OK
WKPV Ponce PR
WINT-TV Crossville TN
KTXH Houston TX
*WVTB St. Johnsbury VT
KBTW-TV Tacoma WA
*WHRM-TV Wausau WI
KFNB-TV Casper WY

Channel 21 (512-518 mhz)

WTTO Birmingham AL
WMPV-TV Mobile AL
*KPAZ-TV Phoenix AZ
KFTV Hanford CA
KXRM-TV Colorado Springs CO
WTCE Fort Pierce FL
WBSG-TV Brunswick GA
KWHM Wailuku HI
*KTIN Fort Dodge IA
WPTA Fort Wayne IN
WBNA Louisville KY
*WKMU Murray KY
*WCMW Manistee MI
KRBR Duluth MN
*KOZK Springfield MO
KRLR Las Vegas NV
KAME-TV Reno NV
*WLIW Garden City NY
*WXXI Rochester NY
WFMJ-TV Youngstown OH
KTVZ Bend OR
WHP-TV Harrisburg PA
WFIL Florence SC
KTXA Fort Worth TX
WJPR Lynchburg VA
*WHA-TV Madison WI

Channel 22 (518-524 mhz)

*KRCB-TV Cotati CA
KWHY-TV Los Angeles CA
KFCT Fort Collins CO
WCLF Clearwater FL
WEYS Key West FL
WJCL Savannah GA
*WMEC Macomb IL
WSBT-TV South Bend IN
*WVUT Vincennes IN
*WKPI Pikeville KY
WWLP Springfield MA
*WMPT Annapolis MD
*KAWB Brainerd MN
WHLT Hattiesburg MS
WLFL Raleigh NC
*KRWG-TV Las Cruces NM
WKEF Dayton OH
*KFTS Klamath Falls OR
KBSP-TV Salem OR
WPTT-TV Pittsburgh PA
WYOU Scranton PA
WNJX-TV Mayaguez PR
*WCTE Cookeville TN
KLTJ Galveston TX
WVNY Burlington VT
KTZZ-TV Seattle WA
KSKN Spokane WA

Channel 23 (524-530 mhz)

KAEF Arcata CA
KERO-TV Bakersfield CA
WLTV Miami FL
*WSRE Pensacola FL
WELF Dalton GA
WFHL Decatur IL
WIFR Freeport IL
WMCC Marion IL
*WKZT-TV Elizabethtown KY
*WKAR-TV East Lansing MI
KLGT-TV Minneapolis MN
KBSI Cape Girardeau MO
*WMAO-TV Greenwood MS
KTMF Missoula MT
*WNJS Camden NJ
KNAT Albuquerque NM
*WXXA-TV Albany NY
*WNEQ-TV Buffalo NY
WAKC-TV Akron OH
KOKI-TV Tulsa OK
KMTZ Coos Bay OR
WATM-TV Altoona PA
*WHMC Conway SC
KVEO Brownsville TX
KUVN Garland TX
*KHCE San Antonio TX
*WCVE-TV Richmond VA
KNDO Yakima WA

Channel 24 (530-536 mhz)

KPOM-TV Fort Smith AR
KCPM Chico CA
KSEE Fresno CA
*KVCR-TV San Bernardino CA
*KSBS-TV Steamboat Springs CO
*WEDH Hartford CT
*WMFE-TV Orlando FL
WGXA Macon GA
*KYIN Mason City IA
*WQPT-TV Moline IL
KSAS-TV Wichita KS
*WKYU-TV Bowling Green KY
*KLPB-TV Lafayette LA
*KLTS-TV Shreveport LA
WHSW-TV Baltimore MD
KNLC St. Louis MO
WTZH Meridian MS
*WCNY-TV Syracuse NY
WNWO-TV Toledo OH
KNMT-TV Portland OR
WJET-TV Erie PA
WSJN-TV San Juan PR
*WTAT-TV Charleston SC
WPTY-TV Memphis TN
KVUE-TV Austin TX
KPEJ Odessa TX
WDRG Danville VA
WCGV-TV Milwaukee WI
*WNPB-TV Morgantown WV

Channel 25 (536-542 mhz)

*WHIQ Huntsville AL
KVTN Pine Bluff AR
*KCAH Watsonville CA
KZJG Longmont CO
WYDP Orange Park FL
WPBF Tequesta FL
*WACS-TV Dawson GA
WEEK-TV Peoria IL
WEHT Evansville IN
*WKAS Ashland KY
*KLPA-TV Alexandria LA
WFXT Boston MA
WHAG-TV Hagerstown MD
*WEYI-TV Saginaw MI
KNLJ Jefferson City MO
WXXV-TV Gulfport MS
*WUNK-TV Greenville NC
*WNYE-TV New York NY
*WVIZ-TV Cleveland OH
KOKH-TV Oklahoma City OK
WOLO-TV Columbia SC
KAVU-TV Victoria TX
KXXV Waco TX
KNDU Richland WA
WLAX La Crosse WI

Channel 26 (542-548 mhz)

WYLE Florence AL
*WAIQ Montgomery AL
KRZB-TV Hot Springs AR
KTSF San Francisco CA
KMPH Visalia CA
WTWS New London CT
*WETA-TV Washington DC
WAYQ Daytona Beach FL
WEVU Naples FL
WAGT Augusta GA
KOBN Honolulu HI
KJMH Burlington IA
*KCDT Coeur d'Alene ID
WCIU-TV Chicago IL
WGNO New Orleans LA
*WMEA-TV Biddeford ME
*KOZJ Joplin MO
WJKA Wilmington NC
*WUNL-TV Winston-Salem NC
*KYNE-TV Omaha NE
WTJA Jamestown NY
WTJC Springfield OH
KMVU Medford OR
*WQTO Ponce PR
KINT-TV El Paso TX
KRIV Houston TX
WGBA Green Bay WI

Channel 27 (548-554 mhz)

*KUAS-TV Tucson AZ
WZWY Orlando FL
WTXL-TV Tallahassee FL
*KSIN Sioux City IA
WTCT Marion IL
*WQEC Quincy IL
WCCU Urbana IL
KSNT Topeka KS
WKYT-TV Lexington KY
*WLPB-TV Baton Rouge LA
WUNI Needham MA
*WCMV Cadillac MI
KDEB-TV Springfield MO
WLOV-TV West Point MS
KRPV Roswell NM
KREN-TV Reno NV
*WBGU-TV Bowling Green OH
WKBN-TV Youngstown OH
WHTM-TV Harrisburg PA
*WRJA-TV Sumter SC
KDFI-TV Dallas TX
KLDO-TV Laredo TX
WGNT Portsmouth VA
WFXR-TV Roanoke VA
KCWT Wenatchee WA

U.S. Television Stations by Channel

WKOW-TV Madison WI
KLWY Cheyenne WY

Channel 28 (554-560 mhz)

*KCET Los Angeles CA
WPGX Panama City FL
WFTS Tampa FL
*WJSP-TV Columbus GA
KOCR Cedar Rapids IA
WSJV Elkhart IN
WFDG New Bedford MA
*WCPB Salisbury MD
*WFUM Flint MI
WRDC Durham NC
WTTE Columbus OH
*KEPB-TV Eugene OR
WBRE-TV Wilkes-Barre PA
WTGS Hardeeville SC
WKZX Cookeville TN
KYLE Bryan TX
KORO Corpus Christi TX
KAMC Lubbock TX
*WVER Rutland VT
KAYU-TV Spokane WA
*KBTC-TV Tacoma WA
*WHWC-TV Menomonie WI

Channel 29 (560-566 mhz)

KHOG-TV Fayetteville AR
KBAK-TV Bakersfield CA
KBVU Eureka CA
KCMY Sacramento CA
WFLX West Palm Beach FL
*WDCO-TV Cochran GA
WTTK Kokomo IN
*WKPD Paducah KY
*WKSO-TV Somerset KY
KVHP Lake Charles LA
WGTU Traverse City MI
KITN-TV Minneapolis MN
*WMPN-TV Jackson MS
*KHNE-TV Hastings NE
KHFT Hobbs NM
WUTV Buffalo NY
WTXF Philadelphia PA
*WNTV Greenville SC
KMPX Decatur TX
KABB San Antonio TX
WVIR-TV Charlottesville VA
KIMA-TV Yakima WA
WKRP-TV Charleston WV

Channel 30 (566-572 mhz)

KFSN-TV Fresno CA
KCVU Paradise CA
KZKI San Bernardino CA
WVIT New Britain CT
*WSFP-TV Fort Myers FL
WAWS Jacksonville FL
*WPBA Atlanta GA
*WTIU Bloomington IN
KDNL-TV St. Louis MO
*WGBC Meridian MS
WUXA Portsmouth OH
*WGTE-TV Toledo OH
WRWR-TV San Juan PR
*WNSC-TV Rock Hill SC
WLMT Memphis TN
WXMT Nashville TN
KOOG-TV Ogden UT
WVCY-TV Milwaukee WI

Channel 31 (572-578 mhz)

WAAY-TV Huntsville AL
KRBK-TV Sacramento CA
KVMD Twentynine Palms CA
KDVR Denver CO
WFXL Albany GA
WMBD-TV Peoria IL
*WKOH Owensboro KY
KLAX-TV Alexandria LA
*WWPB Hagerstown MD
WBSX Ann Arbor MI
*WNYC-TV New York NY
WUHF Rochester NY
KDKF Klamath Falls OR
WNNE-TV Hartford VT
*KTNW Richland WA
*WHLA-TV La Crosse WI

Channel 32 (578-584 mhz)

WHOA-TV Montgomery AL
*KMTP-TV San Francisco CA
*WHMM Washington DC
WTMV Lakeland FL
WNEG-TV Toccoa GA
KBFD Honolulu HI
*KBIN Council Bluffs IA
*KRIN Waterloo IA
WFLD Chicago IL
WLKY-TV Louisville KY
*WLAE-TV New Orleans LA
*KAZQ Albuquerque NM
KEBN Salem OR
*WELU Aguadilla PR
KTAB-TV Abilene TX
WXGZ-TV Appleton WI

Channel 33 (584-590 mhz)

KDMD Anchorage AK
WCFT-TV Tuscaloosa AL
KTVW-TV Phoenix AZ
KADE San Luis Obispo CA
WBFS-TV Miami FL
WHBR Pensacola FL
WKJG-TV Fort Wayne IN
KWCV Wichita KS
WVLA Baton Rouge LA
KMSS-TV Shreveport LA
WGKI Cadillac MI
KSPR Springfield MO
*WUNF-TV Asheville NC
KFBT Las Vegas NV
WFXV Utica NY
WYTV Youngstown OH
*WITF-TV Harrisburg PA
*WJPM-TV Florence SC
KDAF Dallas TX
WTVZ Norfolk VA
*WETK Burlington VT
*WPBY-TV Huntington WV
KKTU Cheyenne WY

Channel 34 (590-596 mhz)

WDAU Ozark AL
KMEX-TV Los Angeles CA
WTVX Fort Pierce FL
WNGM-TV Athens GA
WUBI Baxley GA
*WNIT-TV South Bend IN
WGRB Campbellsville KY
WMGC-TV Binghamton NY
*WOSU-TV Columbus OH
KOCB Oklahoma City OK
KEVU Eugene OR
WRUA Fajardo PR
*KITU Beaumont TX
KJTV Lubbock TX
*KCTF Waco TX

Channel 35 (596-602 mhz)

KCBA Salinas CA
WFGX Fort Walton Beach FL
WCTD Miami FL
WOFL Orlando FL
KKVI Twin Falls ID
*WWTO-TV LaSalle IL
*WKHA Hazard KY
*WKMA Madisonville KY
WWLA Lewiston ME
*WUCX-TV Bad Axe MI
*WGVU-TV Grand Rapids MI
WLIO Lima OH
*KRSC-TV Claremore OK
WSEE-TV Erie PA
*WYBE Philadelphia PA
*WRLK-TV Columbia SC
KRRT Kerrville TX
WRLH-TV Richmond VA
KAPP Yakima WA

Channel 36 (602-608 mhz)

*WFIQ Florence AL
KMIR-TV Palm Springs CA
KICU-TV San Jose CA
WFTX Cape Coral FL
WATL Atlanta GA
*KQCT Davenport IA
*KHIN Red Oak IA
WTVQ-TV Lexington KY
*WGPT Oakland MD
WCNC-TV Charlotte NC
*WUNP-TV Roanoke Rapids NC
WENY-TV Elmira NY
WUPW Toledo OH
KLSR-TV Roseburg OR
WDWL Bayamon PR
*WSBE-TV Providence RI
WCTP Charleston SC
KXAN-TV Austin TX
*KOCV-TV Odessa TX
*WMVT Milwaukee WI
*WLEF-TV Park Falls WI

Channel 37 (608-614 mhz)

NOTE: Reserved for radio astronomy service.

Channel 38 (614-620 mhz)

KASN Pine Bluff AR
KCNS San Francisco CA
WTTA St. Petersburg FL
WLTZ Columbus GA
WCFC-TV Chicago IL
WBAK-TV Terre Haute IN
KMCI Lawrence KS
*WKMR Morehead KY
WNOL-TV New Orleans LA
WSBK-TV Boston MA
WADL Mount Clemens MI
WGTJ Greenville NC
WOLF-TV Scranton PA
WJWN-TV San Sebastian PR
*WNEH Greenwood SC
*KSCE El Paso TX
WEFC Roanoke VA
*WPNE Green Bay WI

Channel 39 (620-626 mhz)

KNSD San Diego CA
WDZL Miami FL
WQRF-TV Rockford IL
*WFWA Fort Wayne IN
*KMCT-TV West Monroe LA

*WUNJ-TV Wilmington NC
KBLR Paradise NV
*WLVT-TV Allentown PA
WEMT Greeneville TN
WHTN Murfreesboro TN
KXTX-TV Dallas TX
KHTV Houston TX

Channel 40 (626-632 mhz)

WJSU-TV Anniston AL
KHBS Fort Smith AR
KHRR Tucson AZ
KTXL Sacramento CA
KTBN-TV Santa Ana CA
WWSB Sarasota FL
WTWC Tallahassee FL
KDUB-TV Dubuque IA
WHMB-TV Indianapolis IN
WGGB-TV Springfield MA
WBUY Holly Springs MS
WDBD Jackson MS
WKFT Fayetteville NC
WMGM-TV Wildwood NJ
WICZ-TV Binghamton NY
WXAE Toledo OH
*WPCB-TV Greensburg PA
*WMTJ Fajardo PR
WAXA Anderson SC
WLFB Bluefield WV

Channel 41 (632-638 mhz)

*WIIQ Demopolis AL
*KWBI-TV Denver CO
WMGT Macon GA
WDRB-TV Louisville KY
WOTV Battle Creek MI
KXLI St. Cloud MN
KSHB-TV Kansas City MO
WXTV Paterson NJ
KLUZ-TV Albuquerque NM
KTFO Tulsa OK
KWEX-TV San Antonio TX
*WHTJ Charlottesville VA
*WVTA Windsor VT

Channel 42 (638-644 mhz)

WBMG Birmingham AL
*WEIQ Mobile AL
KVUT Little Rock AR
KFCB Concord CA
KESQ-TV Palm Springs CA
*WXEL-TV West Palm Beach FL
WCLJ Bloomington IN
KSAX Alexandria MN
*WTVI Charlotte NC
KPTM Omaha NE
*WPBO-TV Portsmouth OH
WIRS Yauco PR
KBVO Austin TX
KMLM Odessa TX
KVEW Kennewick WA

Channel 43 (644-650 mhz)

*WGIQ Louisville AL
KGMC Clovis CA
WHAI-TV Bridgeport CT
WBSF Melbourne FL
WYZZ-TV Bloomington IL
WKOI Richmond IN
WJUE Battle Creek MI
KRWF Redwood Falls MN
WSNR-TV Syracuse NY
WUAB Lorain OH
KTLC Oklahoma City OK
WPMT York PA
WGSE Myrtle Beach SC
WKCH-TV Knoxville TN

Channel 44 (650-656 mhz)

WNAL-TV Gadsden AL
KRPA Rancho Palos Verdes CA
KBHK-TV San Francisco CA
WJTC Pensacola FL
WTOG St. Petersburg FL
WVGA Valdosta GA
WSNS Chicago IL
WEVV Evansville IN
WGMB Baton Rouge LA
*WGBX-TV Boston MA
*WOUC-TV Cambridge OH
WTLW Lima OH
KGLB-TV Okmulgee OK
*WVIA-TV Scranton PA
WVEO Aguadilla PR
*KLUJ Harlingen TX
KWKT Waco TX

Channel 45 (656-662 mhz)

WMCF-TV Montgomery AL
KUTP Phoenix AZ
KUZZ-TV Bakersfield CA
WHFT Miami FL
KWLB Shreveport LA
WBFF Baltimore MD
WGKU Vanderbilt MI
KVBM-TV Minneapolis MN
WNRW Winston-Salem NC
WRGT-TV Dayton OH
*WTCI Chattanooga TN
KXLN-TV Rosenberg TX

KHCV Seattle WA

Channel 46 (662-668 mhz)

KXGR Green Valley AZ
KCCN-TV Monterey CA
KHSC-TV Ontario CA
WNPL-TV Naples FL
WGNX Atlanta GA
WHSL East St. Louis IL
WHME-TV South Bend IN
*WKLE Lexington KY
WHRC Norwell MA
WJZY Belmont NC
*WSKG-TV Binghamton NY
KMTX-TV Roseburg OR
WIDP Guayama PR
*KNCT Belton TX
WLYJ Clarksburg WV

Channel 47 (668-674 mhz)

KJEO Fresno CA
WNFT Jacksonville FL
*WTVP Peoria IL
WMDT Salisbury MD
WSYM-TV Lansing MI
KXLT-TV Rochester MN
WRMY Rocky Mount NC
WNJU Linden NJ
KWHB Tulsa OK
WKBS-TV Altoona PA
KTAQ Greenville TX
*WSBN-TV Norton VA
*KYVE Yakima WA
WMSN-TV Madison WI

Channel 48 (674-680 mhz)

WAFF Huntsville AL
NEW TV Jonesboro AR
KSTS San Jose CA
KTVC Cedar Rapids IA
*WYDN Worcester MA
WNTZ Natchez MS
WGGT Greensboro NC
WGTW Burlington NJ
KZIA Las Cruces NM
WYDC Corning NY
*WCET Cincinnati OH
WVOZ-TV Ponce PR
KTMD Galveston TX
KNVO McAllen TX
WEUX Chippewa Falls WI

Channel 49 (680-686 mhz)

*KNXT Visalia CA
*WEDW Bridgeport CT
WRXY-TV Tice FL
WTLH Bainbridge GA
WCFN Springfield IL
*WIPB Muncie IN
KTKA-TV Topeka KS
WDKA Paducah KY
WCCL New Orleans LA
WAQP Saginaw MI
*WLED-TV Littleton NH
*WNYB-TV Buffalo NY
WEAO Akron OH
WGCB-TV Red Lion PA
*WRET-TV Spartanburg SC
KTFH Conroe TX
KHSX-TV Irving TX
WJCB Norfolk VA
KPDX Vancouver WA
WJJA Racine WI

Channel 50 (686-692 mhz)

*KOCE-TV Huntington Beach CA
KFTY Santa Rosa CA
KCEC Denver CO
WFTY Washington DC
WBHS-TV Tampa FL
WPWR-TV Gary IN
WKBD Detroit MI
KYFC Kansas City MO
WACN Raleigh NC
WNDS Derry NH
*WNJM Montclair NJ
KKIK-TV Albuquerque NM
WWTI Watertown NY
WQHA Aguada PR
WPGD Hendersonville TN
WFBI Memphis TN

Channel 51 (692-698 mhz)

KFAA Rogers AR
KNSO Merced CA
KUSI-TV San Diego CA
WSCV Fort Lauderdale FL
WOGX Ocala FL
*WEIU-TV Charleston IL
WPXT Portland ME
WSFJ Newark OH
WTVE Reading PA
KNWS-TV Katy TX
KFXK-TV Longview TX
*WVPT Staunton VA
KBEH Bellevue WA

Channel 52 (698-704 mhz)

KVEA Corona CA
WTGL-TV Cocoa FL
*WKON Owenton KY

*WGVK Kalamazoo MI
*WEKW-TV Keene NH
*WNJT Trenton NJ
WGGN-TV Sandusky OH
KSBI Oklahoma City OK
WDZE Carolina PR
KFWD Fort Worth TX
*WMSY-TV Marion VA
WWRS-TV Mayville WI

Channel 53 (704-710 mhz)

KAIL Fresno CA
KWHD Castle Rock CO
*WEDN Norwich CT
WPAN Fort Walton Beach FL
WGFL High Springs FL
*WKGB-TV Bowling Green KY
WLAJ Lansing MI
WWAC-TV Atlantic City NJ
*WWAT Chillicothe OH
KWMJ Tulsa OK
WPGH-TV Pittsburgh PA
WILF Williamsport PA
*WFLI-TV Cleveland TN
WNVT Goldvein VA

Channel 54 (710-716 mhz)

WZDX Huntsville AL
*KTEH San Jose CA
WFXG Augusta GA
WXTX Columbus GA
*WCVN Covington KY
WNUV-TV Baltimore MD
WTLJ Muskegon MI
WTBY Poughkeepsie NY
*WQLN Erie PA
WCCV-TV Arecibo PR
WPMC Jellico TN
KCFP Austin TX

Channel 55 (716-722 mhz)

WACX Leesburg FL
WSST-TV Cordele GA
*WRSP-TV Springfield IL
WFFT-TV Fort Wayne IN
WOCD Amsterdam NY
WLIG Riverhead NY
WBNX-TV Akron OH
WFVT Rock Hill SC
NEW TV Conroe TX
KLDT Lake Dallas TX
WHKE Kenosha WI

Channel 56 (722-728 mhz)

KDOC-TV Anaheim CA
WIRB Melbourne FL
*WFSG Panama City FL
WYIN Gary IN
WDKY-TV Danville KY
WLVI-TV Cambridge MA
*WTVS Detroit MI
WWLF-TV Hazleton PA
KETK-TV Jacksonville TX
WNVC-TV Fairfax VA
*KWDK Tacoma WA

Channel 57 (728-734 mhz)

KSBN-TV Springdale AR
KSTV-TV Ventura CA
WFXU Live Oak FL
*WATC Atlanta GA
WYMT-TV Hazard KY
*WGBY-TV Springfield MA
*WCFE-TV Plattsburgh NY
WGBS-TV Philadelphia PA
WACH Columbia SC
KRTW Baytown TX
*WCVW Richmond VA
WJNW Janesville WI

Channel 58 (734-740 mhz)

*KLCS Los Angeles CA
KSCH-TV Stockton CA
WAWD Fort Walton Beach FL
WPGA-TV Perry GA
WFTE Salem IN
WCVX Vineyard Haven MA
*WUNG-TV Concord NC
*WNJB New Brunswick NJ
*WUJA Caguas PR
WNAB Nashville TN
*KDTX-TV Dallas TX
WDJT-TV Milwaukee WI

Channel 59 (740-746 mhz)

KMSG-TV Sanger CA
KUBD Denver CO
WTVU New Haven CT
*WJEB-TV Jacksonville FL
WXIN Indianapolis IN
WVGV-TV Lewisburg WV

Channel 60 (746-752 mhz)

WRKJ Dothan AL
WTJP Gadsden AL
*KCSM-TV San Mateo CA
WEHS-TV Aurora IL
WGOT Merrimack NH
WBPH-TV Bethlehem PA
WMEI Arecibo PR
*KMBH Harlingen TX

U.S. Television Stations by Channel

KVDA San Antonio TX
WYVN Martinsburg WV

Channel 61 (752-758 mhz)

KKAK Porterville CA
WTIC-TV Hartford CT
WTGI-TV Wilmington DE
WFGC Palm Beach FL
WTSF Ashland KY
WLXI-TV Greensboro NC
WQHS-TV Cleveland OH
WDSI-TV Chattanooga TN
KZJL Houston TX

Channel 62 (758-764 mhz)

KRCA Riverside CA
WBSV-TV Venice FL
WJYS Hammond IN
WMFP Lawrence MA
*WFPT Frederick MD

WGPR-TV Detroit MI
KSMO-TV Kansas City MO
WASV-TV Asheville NC
WFAY Fayetteville NC
WACI Atlantic City NJ
WTZA Kingston NY
KMNZ Oklahoma City OK

Channel 63 (764-770 mhz)

KADY-TV Oxnard CA
*WPPB-TV Boca Raton FL
WHSG Monroe GA
WINM Angola IN
WIIB Bloomington IN
WMBC-TV Newton NJ

Channel 64 (770-776 mhz)

KHIZ Barstow CA
KFTL Stockton CA
*WDPB Seaford DE
WGOX Inverness FL

WGNM Macon GA
WLLA Kalamazoo MI
WKAY Kannapolis NC
WSTR-TV Cincinnati OH
WSWB-TV Scranton PA
WECN Naranjito PR
WNAC-TV Providence RI
KBCB Bellingham WA

Channel 65 (776-782 mhz)

KLXV-TV San Jose CA
*WEDY New Haven CT
WRBW Orlando FL
WLJC-TV Beattyville KY
WHSP-TV Vineland NJ
KJLF-TV El Paso TX
WZXK Ashland VA

Channel 66 (782-788 mhz)

WSWS-TV Opelika AL
KPST-TV Vallejo CA

WTBG-TV Bradenton FL
WGBO-TV Joliet IL
WHSH-TV Marlborough MA
WSMH Flint MI
*WFME-TV West Milford NJ
WETG Erie PA
WJFB Lebanon TN
WTKK Manassas VA

Channel 67 (788-794 mhz)

WRJM-TV Troy AL
KSMS-TV Monterey CA
WHBI Lake Worth FL
WAOM Morehead KY
*WMPB Baltimore MD
WHSI-TV Smithtown NY
WNGS Springville NY
WOAC Canton OH
KHSH-TV Alvin TX

Channel 68 (794-800 mhz)

WABM Birmingham AL
*KEEF-TV Los Angeles CA
*WBCC Cocoa FL
WKMJ Louisville KY
WABU Boston MA
WJAL Hagerstown MD
WHSE-TV Newark NJ
WSYT Syracuse NY
WMFD-TV Mansfield OH
NEW TV Arlington TX
WLFG Grundy VA
WMMF-TV Fond du Lac WI

Channel 69 (800-806 mhz)

KTTY San Diego CA
WYHS-TV Hollywood FL
WVEU Atlanta GA
*WTBU Indianapolis IN
WFMZ-TV Allentown PA
WOST-TV Block Island RI

Canadian Television Stations by Channel

Channel 2
CICT-TV Calgary AB
CBXAT-2 High Prairie AB
CFRN-TV-5 Lac La Biche AB
CKSA-TV Lloydminster AB
CHBC-TV Kelowna BC
CKPG-TV Prince George BC
CBUT Vancouver BC
CBWYT Mafeking MB
CKND-TV-2 Minnedosa MB
CKCW-TV Moncton NB
CBYT-3 Bonne Bay NF
CJOX-TV-1 Grand Bank NF
CBIT-2 Cheticamp NS
CIII-TV-2 Bancroft ON
CFCL-TV-2 Kearns ON
CHBX-TV Sault Ste. Marie ON
CKPR-TV Thunder Bay ON
CKCO-TV-2 Wiarton ON
CBFT Montreal PQ
CFAP-TV Quebec City PQ
CJBRT Rimouski PQ
CBCP-TV-2 Cypress Hills SK
CKBQ-TV Melfort SK
CKCK-TV Regina SK

Channel 3
CFRN-TV Edmonton AB
CFRN-TV-2 Peace River AB
CITM-TV 100 Mile House BC
CKKM-TV Oliver-Osoyoos BC
CFTK-TV Terrace BC
CBWFT-4 Ste-Rose-du-Lac MB
CBWFT Winnipeg MB
CJAP-TV Argentia NF
CBNAT-1 Baie Verte NF
CBHT Halifax NS
CBHFT-1 Yarmouth NS
CKVR-TV Barrie ON
CITO-TV Timmins ON
CKRN-TV-3 Bearn-Fabre PQ
CBVT-2 La Tuque PQ
CBFT-2 Mont-Laurier PQ
CBCP-TV-3 Ponteix SK
CFQC-TV-1 Stranraer SK

Channel 4
CFCN-TV Calgary AB
CITL-TV Lloydminster AB
CHAT-TV-1 Pivot AB
CFRN-TV-9 Slave Lake AB
CFJC-TV Kamloops BC
CKYB-TV Brandon MB
CBWT-2 Lac du Bonnet MB
CHCR-TV Campbellton NB
CHSJ-TV Saint John NB
CJCN-TV Grand Falls NF
CJSV-TV Stephenville NF
CJCB-TV Sydney NS
CHNB-TV North Bay ON
CBOT Ottawa ON
CIII-TV-4 Owen Sound ON
CHFD-TV Thunder Bay ON
CFRS-TV Jonquiere PQ
CFCM-TV Quebec City PQ
CKRN-TV Rouyn PQ
CKBI-TV-3 Greenwater Lake SK
CFSK-TV Saskatoon SK

Channel 5
CBXT Edmonton AB
CJDC-TV Dawson Creek BC
CHKL-TV Kelowna BC
CKX-TV Brandon MB
CBYT Corner Brook NF
CBNT-3 Marystown NF
CJCH-TV Halifax NS
CBIT Sydney NS
CICI-TV-1 Elliot Lake ON
CBWCT Fort Frances ON
CHRO-TV Pembroke ON
CJIC-TV Sault Ste. Marie ON
CICI-TV Sudbury ON
CBLT Toronto ON
CKCW-TV-2 St. Edward PE
CHAU-TV Carleton PQ
CFER-TV-2 Gaspe-Nord PQ
CBVD-TV Malartic PQ
CKMI-TV Quebec City PQ
CKBI-TV Prince Albert SK
CJFB-TV Swift Current SK
CKOS-TV Yorkton SK

Channel 6
CBXFT-1 Bonnyville AB
CHAT-TV Medicine Hat AB
CKRD-TV Red Deer AB
CHKM-TV Kamloops BC
CHEK-TV Victoria BC
CBWT Winnipeg MB
CHSJ-TV-1 Bon Accord NB
CBNAT-4 St. Anthony NF
CJON-TV St. John's NF
CJCH-TV-6 Caledonia NS
CJCB-TV-1 Inverness NS
*CHAK-TV Inuvik NT
CJOH-TV-6 Deseronto ON
CIII-TV-6 Ottawa ON
CIII-TV Paris ON
CFCL-TV Timmins ON
CJPM-TV Chicoutimi PQ
CBGAT Matane PQ
CBMT Montreal PQ
CFQC-TV-2 North Battleford SK
CKCK-TV-2 Willow Bunch SK
CHSS-TV Wynyard SK
CFWH-TV White Horse YT

Channel 7
CISA-TV-7 Lethbridge AB
CFRN-TV-7 Lougheed AB
CKY-TV Winnipeg MB
CKCD-TV Campbellton NB
CHMT-TV Moncton NB
CBHFT-2 Mulgrave NS
CKNC-TV-1 Elliot Lake ON
CBLFT-5 Hearst ON
CIII-TV-7 Midland ON
CBLFT-1 Sturgeon Falls ON
CKRT-TV Riviere-du-Loup PQ
CHLT-TV Sherbrooke PQ
CKMJ-TV Marquis SK
CBCP-TV-1 Shaunavon SK
CBKFT-4 St. Brieux SK
CIEW-TV Warmley SK

Channel 8
CFCN-TV-8 Medicine Hat AB
CFRN-TV-6 Red Deer AB
CKTN-TV Trail BC
CHAN-TV Vancouver BC
CBWST Baldy Mountain MB
CFLA-TV Goose Bay-Labrador NF
CBNT-1 Port Rexton NF
CBNT St. John's NF
CBYT-1 Stephenville NF
CIHF-TV Halifax NS
*CFYK-TV Yellowknife NT
CJOH-TV-8 Cornwall ON
CBWAT Kenora ON
CBLAT-1 Manitouwadge ON
CKNX-TV Wingham ON
CKCW-TV-1 Charlottetown PE

*CIVV-TV Chicoutimi PQ
*CIVA-TV Rouyn PQ
CHEM-TV Trois-Rivieres PQ
CFQC-TV Saskatoon SK

Channel 9
CBRT Calgary AB
*CJAL-TV Edmonton AB
CKND-TV Winnipeg MB
CKLT-TV Saint John NB
CBNAT-9 Mount St. Margaret NF
CJCB-TV-2 Antigonish NS
CBWDT Dryden ON
CBOFT Ottawa ON
CKNC-TV Sudbury ON
*CICO-TV-9 Thunder Bay ON
CBLFT-3 Timmins ON
CFTO-TV Toronto ON
CBLAT-3 Wawa ON
CBET Windsor ON
CIMT-TV Riviere-du-Loup PQ
*CIVG-TV Sept-Iles PQ
CKSH-TV Sherbrooke PQ
CIPA-TV Prince Albert SK
CBKT Regina SK
CBKST-1 Stranraer SK

Channel 10
CKRD-TV-1 Coronation AB
CBXAT Grande Prairie AB
CBUBT-7 Cranbrook BC
CHKL-TV-1 Penticton BC
CKVU-TV Vancouver BC
CBWGT Fisher Branch MB
CBWBT Flin Flon MB
CJWB-TV Bonavista NF
CJWN-TV Corner Brook NF
CJCH-TV-1 Canning NS
CBHFT-4 Cheticamp NS
CFPL-TV London ON
CKNY-TV North Bay ON
CFTM-TV Montreal PQ
CKMC-TV-1 Golden Prairie SK
CKBI-TV-4 Nipawin SK
CBKT-2 Willow Bunch SK
CICC-TV Yorkton SK

Channel 11
CBXFT Edmonton AB
CHAN-TV-4 Courtenay BC
CBUFT-3 Terrace BC
CKX-TV-1 Foxwarren MB
CBAFT Moncton NB
CBNAT Grand Falls NF
CBHT-4 Sheet Harbour NS
CBHT-3 Yarmouth NS
CHCH-TV Hamilton ON
CITO-TV-2 Kearns ON
CKWS-TV Kingston ON
CBLAT-4 Marathon ON
CKCO-TV-4 The Muskokas ON
CBVT Quebec City PQ
CFER-TV Rimouski PQ
CFRE-TV Regina SK
CBKST Saskatoon SK

Channel 12
CFRN-TV-4 Ashmont AB
CFCN-TV-1 Drumheller AB
CBXFT-6 Fort McMurray AB
CBXAT-3 Manning AB
CFRN-TV-3 Whitecourt AB
CBUBT-1 Canal Flats BC
CIFG-TV Prince George BC
CKAM-TV Upsalquitch Lake NB
CBNT-2 Placentia NF
CBHT-11 Mulgrave NS

CBLFT-6 Elliot Lake ON
CBLFT-4 Kapuskasing ON
CHEX-TV Peterborough ON
*CIVF-TV Baie-Trinite PQ
CBIMT Iles-de-la-Madeleine PQ
CFCF-TV Montreal PQ
CBFST-2 Temiscaming PQ
CKCK-TV-1 Colgate SK
CKMC-TV Swift Current SK
CICC-TV-1 Wynyard SK

Channel 13
CITV-TV Edmonton AB
CFRN-TV-1 Grande Prairie AB
CFCN-TV-5 Lethbridge AB
CHEK-TV-5 Campbell River BC
CHMI-TV Portage la Prairie MB
*CBNLT Labrador City NF
CBHFT Halifax NS
CBHFT-3 Sydney NS
CBLAT Geraldton ON
CJBN-TV Kenora ON
CKCO-TV Kitchener ON
CJOH-TV Ottawa ON
CBLFT-2 Sudbury ON
CBCT Charlottetown PE
CBST Sept-Iles PQ
CKTM-TV Trois-Rivieres PQ
CBKFT Regina SK

Channel 15
*CIVQ-TV Quebec City PQ

Channel 16
CHWI-TV Wheatley ON
CFKM-TV Trois-Rivieres PQ

Channel 17
*CIVM-TV Montreal PQ

Channel 18
CFRN-TV-8 Grouard Mission-High Prairie AB
*CICO-TV-18 London ON

Channel 19
CBXFT-8 Grande Prairie AB
*CICO-TV-19 Sudbury ON
*CICA-TV Toronto ON

Channel 20
*CICO-TV-20 Sault Ste. Marie ON
CFVS-TV-1 Rouyn PQ

Channel 21
CBWFT-10 Brandon MB
CBKFT-5 Zenon Park SK

Channel 22
CIII-TV-22 Stevenson ON
CIII-TV-1 Windsor ON
*CIVB-TV Rimouski PQ
CBKFT-3 Debden SK

Channel 23
*CIVP-TV Chapeau PQ

Channel 24
*CICO-TV-24 Ottawa ON
*CIVS-TV Sherbrooke PQ

Channel 25
CBLFT Toronto ON
CFVS-TV Val d'Or PQ

Channel 26
CBUFT Vancouver BC
CBKFT-9 Bellegarde SK

Channel 27
CIII-TV-27 Peterborough ON

Channel 28
*CICO-TV-28 Kitchener ON

Channel 29
CIII-TV-29 Oil Springs ON
*CFTU-TV Montreal PQ

Channel 30
*CIVO-TV Hull PQ
CFKS-TV Sherbrooke PQ

Channel 32
*CICO-TV-32 Windsor ON

Channel 35
CFJP-TV Montreal PQ

Channel 39
CBKFT-6 Gravelbourg SK

Channel 40
CHOT-TV Hull PQ

Channel 41
CIII-TV-41 Toronto ON

Channel 42
CKCO-TV-3 Sarnia ON

Channel 45
*CIVC-TV Trois-Rivieres PQ

Channel 47
CFMT-TV Toronto ON

Channel 49
CFGS-TV Hull PQ

Channel 50
CBUFT-2 Kamloops BC

Channel 54
*CBEFT Windsor ON

Channel 57
CITY-TV Toronto ON

Channel 58
CBJET Chicoutimi PQ

Channel 59
*CICO-TV-59 Chatham ON

Channel 68
CISR-TV Santa Rosa BC

Television Assignments by State

The following table of assignments contains the channels designated for the listed communities in the United States, its territories, and possessions. Channels designated with an asterisk (*) are assigned for use by noncommercial educational broadcast stations only. A station on a channel identified by a plus (+) or minus (-) mark is required to operate with its carrier frequencies offset 10 khz above or below, respectively, the nominal carrier frequencies.

Footnotes: 1) Following the decision in Docket 18261 (amendment of rules regarding geographic reallocation of channels 1-20 to land mobile radio in the 25 largest urbanized areas of the U.S.) channels so indicated will not be available for use until further action by the FCC. 2) Operation on this channel is subject to the conditions, terms and requirements set out in the report and Order in Docket No. 19075, RM-1645, adopted Jan. 5, 1972, released Jan. 7, 1972, FCC 72-19 (Added 72-19, 1/7/72). 3) This channel is not available for Elgin, Ill., unless and until FCC determines it is not needed at Joliet, Ill. 4) Stations using these assignments shall limit radiation toward stations on the same channel in Puerto Rico to no more than the effective radiated power which would be radiated by an omnidirectional radio station using maximum permissible effective radiated power for antenna height above average terrain, at the minimum distances from such stations specified in §73.610(b). The FCC shall consider the status of the negotiations with the appropriate British authorities concerning these allotments when the applications for construction permits come before the FCC.

Alabama
Anniston: 40-
Arab: 56-
Birmingham: 6-, *10-, 13-, 42+, *62+, 68-
Demopolis: *41
Dothan: 4, 18, *39+, 60-
Dozier: *2-
Florence: 15, 26, *36-
Gadsden: 44+, 60
Gulf Shores: 55
Homewood: 21-
Huntsville: 19*, 25+, 31+, 48-
Huntsville/Decatur: 54
Louisville: *43+
Mobile: 5+, 10+, 15+, 21+, *31, *42, 61
Montgomery: 12, 20, *26+, 32, 45-, *63
Mt. Cheaha: *7-
Munford: *16-
Opelika: 50, 66
Ozark: 34
Selma: 8, 29-
Troy: 67
Tuscaloosa: 17, 33, *39-
Tuscumbia: 52+
Tuskegee: 22-

Alaska
Anchorage: 2-, 4-, 5, *7-, *9, 11, 13-,33
Bethel: *4
Dillingham: *2, 10
Fairbanks: 2+, 7+, *9+, 11+, 13+
Juneau: *3, 8, 10
Ketchikan: 2, 4, *9
North Pole: 4+
Seward: 3-
Sitka: 13

Arizona
Ajo: *23-
Coolidge: *43
Douglas: 3, *28
Flagstaff: 2, 4+, 9, 13, *16
Globe: *14+
Green Valley: 46
Holbrook: 11+, *18+
Kingman: 6-, *14-
Lake Havasu City: 34+
McNary: *22+
Mesa: 12-
Nogales: *16+
Page: *17
Parker: *17-
Phoenix: 3+, 5-, *8+, 10-, 15-, 21, 33, *39, 45, 61
Prescott: 7, *19
Safford: *23+
Sierra Vista: 58
Tolleson: 51
Tucson: 4-, *6+, 9-, 13-, 18-, *27-, 40
Tucson-Nogales: 11 (see note 2)
Yuma: 11-, 13+, *16-

Arkansas
Arkadelphia: *9+
El Dorado: 10-, *30+, 43-, 49-
Eureka Springs: 34+
Fayetteville: *13-, 36
Fort Smith: 5-, 24+, 40-
Gosnell: 46
Harrison: 31+
Hot Springs: *20, 26
Jonesboro: 8-, *19+, 48+
Little Rock: *2-, 4, 7-, 11, 16-, *36, 42
Mountain Home: 43+
Mountain View: *6-
Newark: *17
Pine Bluff: 25-, 38-
Rogers: 51-
Russellville: *28+
Springdale: 57

California
Alturas: 13+
Anaheim: 56-
Arcata: 23
Avalon: 54
Bakersfield: 17, 23-, 29, *39-, 45, 65+
Barstow: *35+, 64
Big Bear Lake: 59+
Bishop: *14-, 20+
Blythe: *22-
Brawley: *26
Calipatria: 54
Ceres: *23+
Chico: 12-, *18, 24+, *46
Clovis: 43
Coalinga: *27-
Concord: 42
Corona: 52
Cotati: *22-
El Centro: 7+, 9+
Eureka: 3-, 6-, *13-, 29
Fort Bragg: 8-
Fresno: *18+, 24, 30+, 47, 53
Hanford: 21
Huntington Beach: *50
Indio: *19+
Los Angeles: 2, 4, 5, 7, 9, 11, 13, 22, *28, 34, *58-, *68-
Merced: 51
Modesto: 19-
Norwalk:
Novato: 68
Oakland: 2+
Ontario: 46
Oroville: 28
Oxnard: 63+
Palm Springs: 36-, 42
Paradise: 30
Porterville: 61
Rancho Palos Verdes: 44+
Redding: 7, *9, 16
Ridgecrest: *25
Riverside: 62
Sacramento: 3, *6, 10, 29-, 31-, 40-, *52
Salinas-Monterey: 8+, 35-, 46-, *56, 67
San Bernardino: 18-, *24-, 30
San Diego: 8, 10, *15, 39, 51, 69
San Francisco: 4-, 5+, 7-, *9+, 14+, 20-, 26, *32+, 38, 44-
Sanger: 59
San Jose: 11+, 36, 48-, *54, 65
San Luis Obispo: 6+, *15+, 33
San Mateo: *60
Santa Ana: 40
Santa Barbara: 3-, 14, *20 (see note 1), 38, *55
Santa Cruz: *16-
Santa Maria: 12+, 42+
Santa Rosa: 50-, *62
Stockton: 13+, 58, 64
Susanville: *14
Twentynine Palms: 31
Vallejo-Fairfield: 66
Ventura: 57
Visalia: 26+, *49
Watsonville: *25+
Willits: 11-
Yosemite Valley: 41
Yreka City: *20+

Colorado
Alamosa: *16
Boulder: 14
Broomfield: *12
Castle Rock: 53
Colorado Springs: 11, 13, 21
Craig: *16-
Denver: 2, 4-, *6-, 7, 9-, 20, 31, *41, 50, 59
Durango: 6+, *20-, 33+
Fort Collins: 22-
Glenwood Springs: 3-, *19-
Grand Junction: *4, 5-, 8-, 11+, *18+
Gunnison: *17-
La Junta: *22+
Lamar: 12-, *14-
Leadville: *15-
Longmont: 25
Montrose: 10+, *22
Pueblo: 5, *8, 26+, 32-
Salida: *23+
Steamboat Springs: 24+
Sterling: 3, *18+
Trinidad: *24

Connecticut
Bridgeport: 43-, *49-
Hartford: 3+, 18-, *24, 61+
New Britain: 30+
New Haven: 8, 55, 59+
New London: 26+
Norwich: *53
Waterbury: 20

Delaware
Dover: *34
Seaford: 38, *64
Wilmington: *12, 61

District of Columbia
Washington: 4-, 5-, 7+, 9, 20+, *26-, *32+, 50

Florida
Boca Raton: *63
Bradenton: *19, 66
Bunnell: 58
Cape Coral: 36
Clearwater: 22
Clermont: 18-
Cocoa: 52, *68
Crystal River: 39-
Daytona Beach: 2-, 26
Destin: 64+
Fort Lauderdale: 51
Fort Myers: 11+, 20+, *30
Fort Pierce: *21-, 34
Fort Walton Beach: 35, 53, 58
Gainesville: *5-, 20, 61+
High Springs: 53+
Hollywood: 69
Inverness: 64
Islamorada: *9+
Jacksonville: 4+, *7, 12+, 17, 30+, 47-, *59
Kenansville: 31
Key West: 8, *13, 22+
Lake City: *41
Lake Worth: 67
Lakeland: 32
Leesburg: *45-, 55
Live Oak: 57-
Madison: *36-
Marathon: 16+
Marianna: *16+, 51
Melbourne: 43+, 56
Miami: *2, 4, 6, 7-, 10+, *17-, 23-, 33, 35, 39, 45+
Naples: 26-, 46
New Smyrna Beach: *15+
Ocala: *29, 51-
Orange Park: 25-
Orlando: 6-, 9, *24-, 27, 35+, 65
Palatka: *42, 65+
Palm Beach: 61
Panama City: 7+, 13, 28-, 46, *56
Panama City Beach: 46
Pensacola: 3-, *23, 33+, 44
St. Petersburg: 10-, 38, 44+
Sarasota: 40
Sebring: *48, 60
Stuart: 59
Tallahassee: *11-, 24, 27+, 40+
Tampa: *3, 8-, *13-, *16, 28, 50
Tequesta: 25
Tice: 49
Venice: 62
West Palm Beach: 5, 12, 29+, *42-

Georgia
Albany: 10, 19-, 31-, 52-
Ashburn: *23+
Athens: *8-, 34
Atlanta: 2, 5-, *11+, 17-, *30, 36, 46-, *57+, 69
Augusta: 6+, 12-, 26, 54-
Bainbridge: 49
Baxley: 34
Brunswick: 21+
Carnesville: *52
Carrollton: *49-
Cedartown: *65-
Chatsworth: *18-
Cochran: *29+
Columbus: 3, 9+, *28, 38+, *48, 54+
Cordele: 55+
Dalton: 23
Dawson: *25
Draketown: *27-
Elberton: *60+
Flintstone: 41-
Lafayette: *35
Macon: 13+, 24+, 41+, *47+, 64-
Monroe: 63
Pelham: *14-
Perry: 58+
Rome: 14+
Royston: *22+
Savannah: 3, *9-, 11, 22
Thomasville: 6
Toccoa: 32-, *68-
Valdosta: *33, 44-
Vidalia: *18+
Warner Robbins: 35-
Waycross: *8+
Wrens: *20-
Young Harris: *51-

Hawaii
Hilo (Hawaii): 2, *4, 9, 11, 13, 14, 20+, 26+, *32-, *38-
Honolulu (Oahu): 2+, 4-, 5, 9-, *11+, 13-, 14, 20, 26, 32, *38, *44
Kailua-Kona (Hawaii): 6
Lihue (Kauai): 3+, *8-, 10+, 12-, 15-, *21-, *27-, *67
Wailuku (Maui): 3, 7, *10, 12, 15, 21, *27, *33, 39

Idaho
Boise: 2, *4+, 7, 14
Burley: *17+
Caldwell: 9-
Coeur d'Alene: *26+
Filer: *19-
Grangeville: *15-
Idaho Falls: 3, 8+, 20, *33+
Lewiston: 3-
Moscow: *12-
Nampa: 6, 12+
Preston: *28
Pocatello: 6-, *10, 15, 25+, 31-
Sandpoint: *16+
Sun Valley: 5-
Twin Falls: 11, *13-, 35
Weiser: *17

Illinois
Aurora: 60
Bloomington: 43
Carbondale: *8
Champaign: 3+, 15-
Charleston: *51+
Chicago: 2-, 5, 7, 9+, *11, *20, 26, 32, 38-, 44
Danville: 68
Decatur: 17, 23-
DeKalb: *33, *48-
East St. Louis: 46
Edwardsville: *18-
Elgin: 66+ (see note 3)
Freeport: 23, *65-
Galesburg: 67
Harrisburg: 3
Jacksonville: *14
Joliet: 14- (see note 1), 66+
Kankakee: *54-
LaSalle: 35
Macomb: *22+
Marion: 27
Moline: 8, *24-
Mount Vernon: 13+
Olney: *16-
Paris: 46+
Peoria: 19, 25+, 31+, *47-, 59+
Pontiac: 53
Quincy: 10-, 16+, *27+
Rockford: 13, 17+, 39
Rock Island: 4+
Springfield: 20+, 49-, 55+, *65+
Streator: *63
Urbana: *12-, 27-
Vandalia: *21

Indiana
Anderson: 67+
Angola: 63
Bloomington: 4, *30-, 42+, 63+
Elkhart: 28+
Evansville: 7, *9+, 14-, 25-, 44
Fort Wayne: 15+, 21+, 33-, *39-, 55
Gary: 50, *56+
Hammond: 62+
Indianapolis: 6, 8-, 13-, *20-, 40, 59-, *69
Kokomo: 29-
Lafayette: 18, *24
Madison: *60+
Marion: 23
Muncie: 49, *61
Richmond: 43+
Salem: 58+
South Bend: 16, 22, *34-, 46
Terre Haute: 2+, 10, *26-, 38
Vincennes: *22+

Television Assignments by State

Iowa
Ames: 5, 23-, *34+
Burlington: 26-, *57-
Carroll: *18-, 30+, 52
Cedar Rapids: 2, 9-, 28+, 48-
Centerville: *31-
Council Bluffs: *32
Davenport: 6+, 18+, 30-, *36+
Decorah: *14+
Des Moines: 8-, *11+, 13-, 17+, *43-, 63-, 69
Dubuque: 16-, *29-, 40-
Estherville: *49+
Fort Dodge: *21
Fort Madison: *38+
Hampton: 50
High Point: *14-
Iowa City: *12+, 20-
Keokuk: *44+
Keosauqua: *54+
Lansing: *41+
Mason City: 3+, *24+
Mount Ayr: *25-
Newton: 39+
Ottumwa: 15-, *33-
Red Oak: *36
Rock Rapids: *25+
Sibley: *33
Sioux City: 4-, 9, 14, *27-
Spirit Lake: *38
Waterloo: 7+, 22-, *32-

Kansas
Chanute: *30+
Colby: 4
Columbus: *48-
Dodge City: *21-
Emporia: *25+
Ensign: 6+
Fort Scott: 20+
Garden City: 11+, 13-, *18
Goodland: 10
Great Bend: 2
Hays: 7-, *9
Hutchinson: *8, 12, 36+
Junction City: 31
Lakin: *3
Lawrence: 38
Liberal: 5+
Manhattan: *21
Oakley: *15-
Parsons: *39
Phillipsburg: *22-
Pittsburg: 7+, 14
Pratt: *32+
Salina: 18+, 34-, 44
Sedan: *28
Topeka: *11, 13+, 27, 43, 49
Wichita: 3-, 10-, *15+, 24-, 33, *42

Kentucky
Ashland: *25, 50-, 61+
Beattyville: 65
Blanco: 52+
Bowling Green: 13, *24-, 40+, *53-, 59+
Campbellsville: 34
Covington: *54+
Danville: 56
Elizabethtown: *23+
Harlan: 44
Hazard: *35-, 57-
Hopkinsville: 51
Lexington: 18+, 27-, 36, *46+, 62
Louisville: 3-, 11, *15, 21-, 32-, 41-, *68+
Madisonville: 19-, *35-, 57+
Morehead: *38+, 67-
Murray: *21-, 38
Newport: 19-
Owensboro: 31-, 48, 61+
Owenton: *52+
Paducah: 6+, 29, 49
Paintsville: 69+
Pikeville: *22-, 51+
Somerset: 16, *29-

Louisiana
Alexandria: 5, *25+, 31+, 41+
Baton Rouge: 2, 9-, *27-, 33-, 44+

Columbia: 11+
De Ridder: *23-
Hammond: 62+
Houma: 11
Lafayette: 3+, 10, 15, *24
Lake Charles: 7-, *18-, 29-
Minden: 21+
Monroe: 8+, *13
Morgan City: *14+
Natchitoches: *20+
New Iberia: 36-
New Orleans: 4+, 6, 8-, *12, 20-, 26, *32+, 38+, 49
Shreveport: 3-, 12, *24-, 33, 45+
Slidell: 54+
Tallulah: *19
West Monroe: 14-, 39+

Maine
Augusta: *10-
Bangor: 2-, 5+, 7-
Biddeford: *26-
Calais: *13-
Fort Kent: *46+
Fryeburg: *18+
Houlton: *25+
Kittery: *39
Lewiston: 35-
Millinocket: *44-
Orono: *12-
Poland Spring: 8-
Portland: 6-, 13+, 51
Presque Isle: 8, *10+, 62+
Rumford: *43+
Waterville: 23-

Maryland
Annapolis: *22+
Baltimore: 2+, 11-, 13+, 24+, 45, 54, *67-
Cumberland: 52+, 65
Frederick: *62
Hagerstown: 25-, *31, 68+
Oakland: *36+
Salisbury: 16+, *28-, 47-
Waldorf: *58+

Massachusetts
Adams: 19
Boston: *2+, 4+, 5-, 7+, 25+, 38, *44, 56, 68+
Cambridge: 56
Greenfield: 32+
Lawrence: 62
Marlborough: 66
New Bedford: 6+, 28-, *34
North Adams: *35
Norwell: 46+
Pittsfield: 51+
Springfield: 22, 40, *57+
Vineyard Haven: 58+
Worcester: 14, 27 (see note 1), *48+

Michigan
Alpena: *6, 11
Ann Arbor: 31+, *58+
Bad Axe: *15-, 41-
Battle Creek: 41+, 43-
Bay City: 5-, 61+
Cadillac: 9, *27, 33
Calumet: 5-, *22-
Cheboygan: 4+
Detroit: 2+, 4, 7-, 20+, 50-, *56, 62
East Lansing: *23-, *69-
Escanaba: 3+
Flint: 12-, *28-, 66-
Grand Rapids: 8+, 13+, 17-, *35+
Iron Mountain: 8-, *17+
Ironwood: *15-, 24+
Ishpeming: 10
Jackson: 18+
Kalamazoo: 3-, *52+, 64
Lansing: 6-, 47, 53-
Mainstee: 15+
Manistique: *15+
Marquette: 6-, *13, 19
Mount Clemens: 38+
Mount Pleasant: *14

Muskegon: 54+
Onondaga: 10-
Petoskey: *23+
Port Huron: 46+
Saginaw: 25-, 49-
Sault Ste. Marie: 8, 10+, *32-
Traverse City: 7+, 29-
University Center: *19-
West Branch: *24

Minnesota
Alexandria: 7, *24, 42
Appleton: *10-
Austin: 6-, *15-
Bemidji: *9, 26+
Brainerd: *22
Crookston: *33
Duluth: 3, *8, 10+, 21+, 27-
Ely: *17-
Fairmont: *16+
Hibbing: 13-, *18-
International Falls: 11, *35+
Mankato: 12, *26-
Marshall: *30-
Minneapolis-St. Paul: *2-, 4+, 5-, 9+, 11-, *17, 23+, 29+, 45
Redwood Falls: 43
Rochester: 10, 47-
St. Cloud: 19, *25-, 41
St. James: 32+
Thief River Falls: 10, *30
Vanderbilt: 45
Wadena: *20-
Walker: 12-, 38-
Willmar: *14-
Winona: *35+, 44-
Worthington: *20

Mississippi
Biloxi: 13+, *19-
Booneville: *12-
Bude: *17+
Clarksdale: *21
Cleveland: *31-
Columbia: *45
Columbus: 4-, *43
Greenville: 15-, 44
Greenwood: 6+, *23-
Grenada: 22+
Gulfport: 25-
Hattiesburg: 22, *47
Holly Springs: 40
Houston: 45+
Jackson: 3, 12+, 16, *29+, 40+, 51
Laurel: 7, 18+
Magee: 34+
Meridian: 11-, *14, 24-, 30-
Miss. State: *2+
Natchez: *42+, 48
Oxford: *18
Senatobia: *34-
Tupelo: 9-, 35+
Vicksburg: 35-
West Point: 27
Wiggins: 43-, 56+
Yazoo City: *32-

Missouri
Birchtree: *20-
Bowling Green: *35+
Cape Girardeau: 12, 23, *39
Carrollton: *18
Columbia: 8+, 17-, *23+
Flat River: *22
Hannibal: 7-
Jefferson City: 13, 25, *36-
Joplin: 12+, 16, *26-
Kansas City: 32-
King City: *28-
Kirksville: 3-
LaPlata: *21-
Lowry City: *15-
Poplar Bluff: 15+, *26+, 55
Rolla: *28
St. Joseph: 2-, 16-, 22
St. Louis: 2, 4-, 5-, *9, 11-, 24+, 30+, *40-, *46
Sedalia: 6

Sikeston: 45
Springfield: 3+, 10, *21-, 27-, 33-

Montana
Anaconda: 2+
Billings: 2-, 6, 8, *11, 14, 20+
Bozeman: 7-, *9
Butte: *2+, 4, 6+, 18, 24
Cut Bank: *14-
Dillon: *14+
Glendive: 5+, 13+, *16-
Great Falls: 3+, 5+, 16, 26, *32
Hardin: 4
Havre: 9+, 11-, *18-
Helena: 10+, 12, *15+
Joplin: 35-, 48, 54
Kalispell: 9-, *29-
Lewistown: 13
Miles City: 3-, *10
Missoula: 8-, *11+, 13-, 17-, 23-
Wolf Point: *17+

Nebraska
Albion: 18, *21+
Alliance: *13-
Bassett: *7-
Beatrice: 23+
Falls City: *24
Grand Island: 11-, 17
Hastings: 5-, *29+
Hayes Center: 6
Hay Springs-Scottsbluff: 4+
Kearney: 13
Lexington: *3+
Lincoln: 8+, 10+, *12-, 45, 51
McCook: 8-, 12, 16+
Merriman: *12
Norfolk: *19+
North Platte: 235, 246, 278
Omaha: 3, 6+, 7, 15, *26, 42+, *48-, 54
Orchard: 16
Pawnee City: 33+
Scottsbluff: 10-, 16
Superior: 4+

Nevada
Elko: 10-, *14+
Ely: 3-, 6+
Fallon: *25
Goldfield: 7-
Henderson: 5+
Las Vegas: 3, 8-, *10+, 13-, 15+, 21+, 33+
McGill: *13
Paradise: 39+
Pawnee City: *33+
Reno: 2, 4, *5, 8, 11, 21+, 27+
Tonopah: 9-, *17-
Winnemucca: 7+, *15-
Yerington: *16+

New Hampshire
Berlin: *40-
Concord: 21+
Derry: 50-
Durham: *11
Hanover: *15+
Keene: *52+
Littleton: 49+
Manchester: 9-
Merrimack: 60+
Portsmouth: 17- (see note 1)

New Jersey
Atlantic City: *36, 53+, 62-
Burlington: 48-
Camden: *23-
Linden-Newark: 47+
Montclair: *50+
Newark: 13-, 68
New Brunswick: *58
Newton: 63
Paterson: 41-
Secaucus: 9+
Trenton: *52-
Vineland: 59-, 65
West Milford: *66-
Wildwood: 40

New Mexico
Alamogordo: *18-
Albuquerque: 4+, *5+, 7+, 13+, 14-, 23-, *32+, 41, 50
Carlsbad: 6-, *15+, 25-
Clayton: *17
Clovis: 12-
Deming: *16
Farmington: 12+, *15+
Gallup: 3, *8-, 10
Hobbs: 29+
Las Cruces: *22-, 48+
Lovington: *19
Portales: *3+
Raton: *18-
Roswell: 8, 10-, 21-, 27-, *33-
Santa Fe: 2+, *9+, 11-, 19-
Silver City: 6, 10+, *12
Socorro: *15-
Tucumcari: *15

New York
Albany-Schenectady: 6, 10-, 13, *17+, 23-, *29+, 45
Amsterdam: *39+, 55
Arcade: 62-
Batavia: 51
Bath: 14-
Binghamton: 12+, 34, 40-, *46+
Buffalo: 2, 4, 7+, 17, *23, 29-, 49-
Carthage: 7-
Corning: *30, 48+
Elmira: 18+, 36-
Garden City: *21-
Glens Falls: *58-
Ilion: 67-
Ithaca: 52, *65+
Jamestown: *26+, *46
Kingston: 62+
Lake Placid: *34+
New York: 2, 4, 5+, 7, 11+, *25, 31-
North Pole: 5
Norwood: *18
Oneonta: 15 (see note 1), *42
Plattsburg: *57
Poughkeepsie: 54+
Riverhead: 55+
Rochester: 8, 10+, 13-, *21, 31+, *61+
Saranac Lake: 61-
Smithtown: 67
Springville: 67+
Syracuse: 3-, 5-, 9-, *24+, 43+, 56+, 62+
Utica: 2-, 4-, 20+, 33, *59
Watertown: *16, 50+

North Carolina
Andrews: *59
Asheville: 13-, 21+, *33, 62+
Belmont: 46+
Bryson City: *67
Burlington: 16
Canton: *27
Chapel Hill: *4+
Charlotte: 3, 9+, 18, 36, *42+
Columbia: *2
Concord: *58
Cullowhee: 50+
Durham: 11+, 28+
Fayetteville: 40+, 62
Forest City: *66
Franklin: *56+
Goldsboro: 17-
Greensboro: 2-, 48+, 61
Greenville: 9-, 14, *25, 38+
Hickory: 14-
High Point: 8-, *32+, 67+
Jacksonville: *19, 35
Kannapolis: 64-
Laurel Hill: 59+
Lexington: 20
Linville: *17
Lumberton: *31
Manteo: 4
Morehead City: 8+
Morgantown: 23-
New Bern: 12+
Raleigh: 5, 22, *34, 50+

Television Assignments by State

Roanoke Rapids: *36-
Rockingham: *53
Rocky Mount: 47+
Washington: 7
Waynesville: 59
Wilmington: 3-, 6, 26-, *39-
Wilson: 30-
Winston-Salem: 12, *26+, 45

North Dakota
Bismarck: *3, 5, 12-, 17-, 26+
Devils Lake: 8+, *22+
Dickinson: 2-, 7, *9-
Ellendale: *19-
Fargo: 6, 11+, *13, 15-
Grand Forks: *2, 14+, 27+
Jamestown: 7-, *23
Minot: *6+, 10-, 13-, 14-, 24
Pembina: 12
Valley City: 4-
Williston: *4, 8-, 11, *15-

Ohio
Akron: 23+, *49+, 55-
Alliance: *45+
Ashtabula: 15 (see note 1)
Athens: *20, 63-
Bowling Green: *27+
Cambridge: *44-
Canton: 17-, 67
Chillicothe: 53
Cincinnati: 5-, 9, 12, *48-, 64-
Cleveland: 3, 5+, 8, *25+, 61
Columbus: 4-, 6+, 10+, 28-, *34, *56-
Dayton: 2, 7+, *16+, 22+, 45
Defiance: 65+
Hillsboro: *24+, 55+
Lima: 17, 35-, 44+, *57+
Lorain: 43
Mansfield: *47+, 68
Newark: *31+, 51
Oxford: *14+
Portsmouth: 30, *42-
Sandusky: 52
Shaker Heights: 19
Springfield: 26+, *66
Steubenville: 9+, *62+
Toledo: 11-, 13, 24-, *30+, 36-, 40-
Xenia: 32
Youngstown: 21-, 27, 33, *58
Zanesville: 18-

Oklahoma
Ada: 10+, *22
Altus: *27
Ardmore: *17 (see note 1), *28-
Bartlesville: 17+
Cheyenne: 12+
Claremore: *35
Duncan: 40+
Elk City: *15-, 31
Enid: 20-, *26+
Eufaula: *3
Grove: 45+
Guymon: 9+, *16
Hugo: *15+ (see note 1), 42+, *48+
Lawton: 7+, 16-, *36-, 45
McAlester: *32-
Miami: *18-
Muskogee: 19
Norman: 46+
Oklahoma City: 4-, 5, 9-, *13, 14-, 25-, 34-, 43+, 52, 62+
Okmulgee: 44-
Sayre 8+
Shawnee: 30
Tulsa: 2+, 6+, 8-, *11-, 23, 41+, 47, 53, *63
Woodward: *17-

Oregon
Astoria: *21
Bend: *3+, *15, 21+
Brookings: *14-
Burns: *18
Coos Bay: 11, 23+, 41

Corvallis: *7-
Eugene: 9+, 13, 16+, *28-, 34
Grants Pass: *18+, 30+
Klamath Falls: 2-, *22+, 31
LaGrande: *13+, 16
Medford: 5, *8+, 10+, 12+, 26+
North Bend: *17+
Pendleton: 11-
Portland: 2, 6+, 8-, *10, 12, 24+, *30, 40-
Roseburg: 4+, 36, 46+
Salem: 22, 32
The Dalles: *17-

Pennsylvania
Allentown: *39, 69
Altoona: 10-, 23-, 47, *57+
Bethlehem: 60-
Clearfield: *3+
Erie: 12, 24, 35+, *54+, 66+
Greensburg: 40+
Harrisburg: 21+, 27-, *33+
Hazleton: 56
Johnstown: 6, 8-, 19+, *28+
Lancaster: 8+, 15+
Lebanon: 55-
Philadelphia: 3, 6-, 10, 17-, 29, *35-, 57
Pittsburgh: 2-, 4+, 11, *13-, *16, 22, 53+
Reading: 51
Red Lion: 49+
Scranton: 16-, 22-, 38+, *44-, 64
State College: 29+, *59+
Wilkes-Barre: 28
Williamsport: 20- (see note 1), 53-, *57
York: 43

Rhode Island
Block Island: 69-
Providence: 10+, 12+, 16 (see note 1), *36, 64+

South Carolina
Aiken: *44
Allendale: *14
Anderson: 40
Beaufort: *16-
Charleston: 2-, 4, 5+, *7-, 24, 36+
Columbia: 10-, 19+, 25-, *35+, 47, 57-
Conway: *23+
Florence: 13+, 15-, 21, *33+
Georgetown: *41-
Greenville: 4-, 16+, *29
Greenwood: *38, 48+
Hardeeville: 28-
Myrtle Beach: 32, 43+
Rock Hill: 30+, 55-
Spartanburg: 7+, 49
Sumter: *27-, 63-

South Dakota
Aberdeen: 9-, *16-
Allen: 22+
Brookings: *8
Eagle Butte: *13
Florence: 3-
Huron: 12+
Lead: 5-, 11+
Lowry: *11-, 56, 62+, 68
Martin: *8-
Mitchell: 5+
Pierre: 4, *10+
Rapid City: 3+, 7+, *9, 15-, 21-
Reliance: 6-
Seneca: *2-
Sioux Falls: 11, 13+, 17-, *23, 36+
Vermillion: *2+

Tennessee
Athens: *24
Chattanooga: 3+, 9, 12+, *45, 61-
Cleveland: 53
Cookeville: *22, 28+
Crossville: 20-, *55+
Fayetteville: *29-
Greeneville: 39-
Hendersonville: 50

Jackson: 7+, 16+, *32+
Jellico: 54-
Johnson City: 11-, *41
Kingsport: 19
Knoxville: 6, 8, 10+, *15-, 26-, 43+
Lebanon: 66
Lexington: *11+
Livingston: 60-
McMinnville: 33+
Memphis: 3-, 5+, *10+, 13+, *14+, 24, 30, 50+
Murfreesboro: 39+
Nashville: 2-, 4+, 5, *8+, 17+, 30+, *42, 58
Sneedville: *2+
Tullahoma: 64+
Union City: 41

Texas
Abilene: 9+, 15, *26+, 32+
Alpine: 12-
Alvin: 67
Amarillo: *2+, 4, 7, 10, 14+
Austin: 7+, *18+, 24, 36, 42-, 54
Bay City: *43+
Baytown: 57+
Beaumont: 6-, 12-, 21, *34-
Belton: 46-
Big Spring: 4-, *14
Blanco: 52+
Boquillas: 8-
Brady: 13
Brownsville: 23
Bryan: 3, 28
Childress: *21
College Station: *15, 50-
Conroe: 49+, 55+
Corpus Christi: 3-, 6, 10-, *16, 28-, 38+
Crockett: 40
Dallas: 4+, 8, *13+, 27-, 33+, 39, 58
Decatur: 29
Del Rio: 10, *24+
Denton: *2
Eagle Pass: 16+
El Paso: 4, 7, 9, *13, 14, 26+, *38-, 65
Farwell: 18+
Fort Stockton: 5+
Fort Worth: 5+, 11-, 21-, *31+, 52-
Fredricksburg: 2+
Galveston: *22, 48
Garland: 23
Greenville: 47+
Harlingen: 4+, *44, 60
Houston: 2-, *8, 11+, 13-, *14, 20, 26, 39-, 61
Irving: 49
Jacksonville: 56
Katy: 51+
Kennville: 35+
Killeen: 62
Lake Dallas: 55
Laredo: 8, 13, 27-, *39
Liano: 14-
Longview: 16+, 51-, 54+
Lubbock: *5, 11, 13-, 16+, 28, 34-
Lufkin: 9
McAllen: 48
Marfa: 3
Marshall: *22-, 35+
Midland: 2-, 18
Mineola: 64+
Monahans-Odessa: 9-
Nacogdoches: 19-, *32
Odessa: 7-, 24-, 30, *36+, 42
Palestine: 43
Paris: 36-, 42+
Port Arthur: -
Presidio: 7+
Rio Grande City: 40
Rosenberg: 45
San Angelo: 3-, 6, 8+, *21+
San Antonio: 4, 5, *9-, 12+, *23-, 29+, 41+, 60+
Sherman: 12-, 20-, *26-
Sonora: 11+

Sulphur Springs: 18
Sweetwater: 12
Temple: 6+
Texarkana: 6, 17-, *34
Tyler: 7, 14+, *38, 60
Uvalde: 26-
Victoria: 19+, 25, 31, *47
Waco: 10+, 25+, *34+, 44-
Weslaco: 5-
Wichita Falls: 3+, 6-, 18-, *24
Wolfforth: 22-

Utah
Cedar City: 4, *16+
Logan: 12-, *22
Moab: *14+
Monticello: *16-
Ogden: *9+, *18-, 24, 30
Price: 3+, *15
Provo: *11-, 16, 32
Richfield: 8+, *19
Salt Lake City: 2-, 4-, 5+, *7-, 13+, 14-, 20+, *26
St. George: 12, *18-
Vernal: 6, *17+

Vermont
Burlington: 3, 22+, *33-, 44+
Hartford: 31
Rutland: *28+
St. Johnsbury: *20-
Windsor: *41

Virginia
Arlington: 14-
Ashland: 65+
Blacksburg: *43, 65-
Bluefield: *63+
Bristol: 5+, *28-
Charlottesville: 29-, *41-, 64+
Courtland: *52
Danville: 24-, 44+, *56
Fairfax: *56-
Farmville: *31-
Fredericksburg: 69+
Front Royal: *42
Goldvein: *53
Grundy: 68
Harrisonburg: 3-
Lynchburg: 13, 21-, *54-
Manassas: 66+
Marion: *52-
Norfolk-Portsmouth-Newport News-Hampton: 3+, 10+, 13-, *15, 27, 33, 49-, *55+
Norton: *47-
Onancock: *25+
Petersburg: 8
Richmond: 6+, 12-, *23, 35+, *57-, 63
Roanoke: 7-, 10, *15+, 27+, 38-, 60
Staunton: *51-
Virginia Beach: 43+
West Point: *46

Washington
Anacortes: 64
Bellevue: 33+, 51+
Bellingham: 12+, 24, *34
Centralia: *15+
East Wenatchee: 249A
Everett: 16-
Kennewick: 42+
Morton: 39
Olympia: 67
Pasco: 19-
Pullman: *10-, 24+
Richland: 25, *31
Rochester: 26+
Seattle: 4, 5+, 7, *9, 22+, 45+, *62
Spokane: 2-, 4-, 6-, *7+, 22, 28-, 34-
Tacoma: 11+, 13-, 20, *28-, *56
Vancouver: *14, 49
Walla Walla: 14-
Wenatchee: *18+, 27
Yakima: 23+, 29+, 35, *47

West Virginia
Bluefield: 6-, 40-
Charleston: 8+, 11+, 23, 29, *49-
Clarksburg: 12+, 46-
Fairmont: 66

Grandview: *9-
Huntington: 3+, 13+, *33+
Keyser: *30+
Lewisburg: 59
Martinsburg: *44, 60+
Morgantown: *24-
Oak Hill: 4
Parkersburg: 15-, 39+, *57
Weirton: *50+
Weston: 5
Wheeling: 7, 14 (see note 1), *41
Williamson: *31+

Wisconsin
Appleton: 32+
Bloomington: *49
Chippewa Falls: 48
Crandon: 4
Eau Claire: 13+, 18
Fond du Lac: 68
Green Bay: 2+, 5+, 11+, 26+, *38, 44+
Highland: 31
Janesville: 57+
Kenosha: 55-
Kieler: *46+
LaCrosse: 8+, 19+, 25, *31
Madison: 3, 15, *21-, 27+, 47+
Manitowoc: 16+
Marshfield: 39-
Mayville: 52
Menomonie: *28-
Milwaukee: 4-, 6, *10+, 12, 18-, 24+, 30, *36, 58
Oshkosh: 22+, *50+
Park Falls: *36+
Racine: 49+
Rhinelander: 12+
Rice Lake: 16
Richland Center: 45+
Sheboygan: 28
Sturgeon Bay: 42
Superior: 6+, 40
Suring: 14-
Tomah: 43
Wausau: 7-, 9, *20+, 33-

Wyoming
Casper: 2+, *6+, 13+, 14-, 20-
Cheyenne: 5+, *17, 27-, 33-
Jackson: 2, 11+
Lander: *4, 5
Laramie: *8+
Rawlins: 11-
Riverton: 10+
Rock Springs: 13
Sheridan: 7, 9+, 12+

U.S. Territories and Possessions

Guam
Agana: *4, 8, 10, *12
Tamuning: 14, 20

Puerto Rico
Aguada: 50
Aguadilla: *32, 44
Arecibo-Aguadilla: 12+
Arecibo: 54, 60
Bayamon: 36
Caguas: 11-, *58
Carolina: 52
Fajardo: 13+, 34, *40
Guayama: 46
Humacoa: 68
Mayaguez: 3+, 5-, 16, 22
Naranjito: 64
Ponce: 7+, 9-, 14, 20, *26, 48
San Juan: 2+, 4-, *6+, 18, 24, 30, *62
San Sebastian: 38
Yauco: 42

Virgin Islands
Charlotte Amalie: 10-, 17, *23, 43
Charlotte Amalie-Christiansted: *3, *12 (see note 4)
Christiansted: 8+, 15, *21, 27

Arbitron ADI Market Atlas

The Area of Dominant Influence (ADI) is a geographic market design that defines each television market exclusive of others, based on measured viewing patterns. Each market's ADI consists of all the counties in which the home market stations receive a preponderance of viewing, and every county in the continental U.S. is allocated exclusively to one ADI—there is no overlap. The total of all ADIs represents the total television households in the U.S.

The ADI is a standard market definition. As a television buying tool it is a geographical and demographic means for maximum efficiency. As a station tool it is a geographic and demographic means for maximum efficiency. As a station tool it has applications for sales, programming and promotion planning.

Following, in alphabetical order, are Arbitron's 209 ADI markets for 1993–1994 with coverage maps for each, and county by county breakouts of TV households. Other data includes the markets' stations, their cities of license, channel numbers and network affiliations.

Coverage maps show total survey areas in light shading, the ADIs themselves outlined in black, and Arbitron Metro rating areas in white. The survey areas consist of all counties in which the home market stations are viewed to a significant extent, including via cable. The Metro Areas usually conform to U.S. Census Standard Metropolitan statistical areas.

Non-ADI markets do not meet Arbitron's criteria for having an ADI of their own. They are listed with the ADI of which they are a part.

A cross-reference list of cities in multi-city ADIs appears on C-201, and a listing of the non-ADI markets appears on C-202.

Abilene-Sweetwater, Tex. (157)

ADI TV Households: 108,200

KACB-TV San Angelo, Tex. ch. 3, satellite to KRBC-TV
KRBC-TV Abilene, Tex., ch. 9, NBC
KTXS-TV Sweetwater, Tex., ch. 12, ABC
KTAB-TV Abilene, Tex., ch. 32, CBS

ADI Counties	State	TV Households
Brown	TX	13,000
Callahan	TX	4,700
Coleman	TX	3,900
Eastland	TX	6,900
Fisher	TX	1,900
Haskell	TX	2,700
Jones	TX	5,800
Knox	TX	1,900
Mitchell	TX	2,900
Nolan	TX	5,900
Runnels	TX	4,200
Scurry	TX	6,000
Shackelford	TX	1,300
Stephens	TX	3,300
Stonewall	TX	800
Taylor	TX	43,000

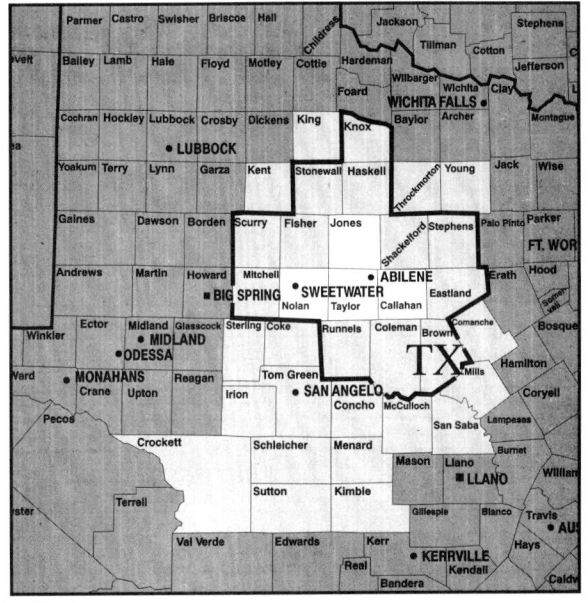

Albany (Cordele), Ga. (154)

ADI TV Households: 129,100

WALB-TV Albany, Ga., ch. 10, NBC
*WABW-TV Pelham, Ga., ch. 14, ETV
WFXL Albany, Ga., ch. 31, Fox
WVGA Valdosta, Ga., ch. 44, ABC
WSST-TV Cordele, Ga., ch. 55, IND

ADI Counties	State	TV Households
Atkinson	GA	2,100
Baker	GA	1,300
Ben Hill	GA	6,100
Berrien	GA	5,100
Calhoun	GA	1,700
Coffee	GA	10,800
Colquitt	GA	13,000
Cook	GA	4,700
Crisp	GA	7,400
Dougherty	GA	33,500
Irwin	GA	3,000
Lanier	GA	2,000
Lee	GA	5,500
Mitchell	GA	6,700
Terrell	GA	3,600
Tift	GA	12,500
Turner	GA	3,000
Worth	GA	7,100

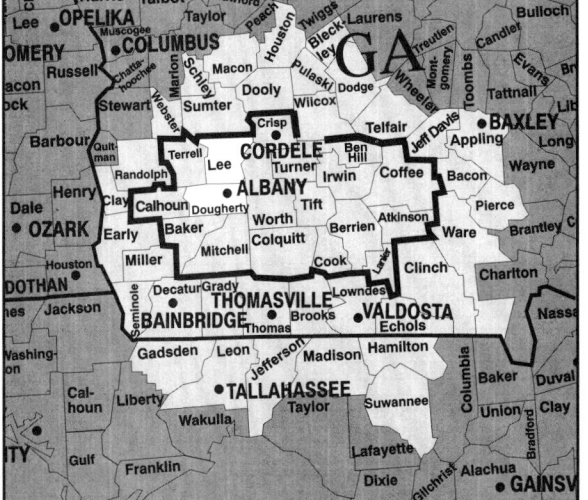

Arbitron ADI Market Atlas

Albany-Schenectady-Troy, N.Y. (53)

ADI TV Households: 507,300

WRGB Schenectady, N.Y., ch. 6, CBS
WTEN Albany, N.Y., ch. 10, ABC
WNYT Albany, N.Y., ch. 13, NBC
*WMHT Schenectady, N.Y., ch. 17, ETV
WCDC Adams, Mass., ch. 19, satellite to WTEN
WXXA-TV Albany, N.Y., ch. 23, Fox
*WMHX Schenectady, N.Y., ch. 45, ETV
WOCD Amsterdam, N.Y., ch. 55, IND

ADI Counties	State	TV Households
Berkshire	MA	52,500
Albany	NY	115,300
Columbia	NY	23,500
Fulton	NY	20,200
Greene	NY	16,600
Hamilton	NY	2,100
Montgomery	NY	19,800
Rensselaer	NY	57,700
Saratoga	NY	71,000
Schenectady	NY	59,600
Schoharie	NY	11,600
Warren	NY	23,000
Washington	NY	20,900
Bennington	VT	13,500

Albuquerque (Hobbs), N.M. (48)

ADI TV Households: 541,800

KKTO Santa Fe, N.M., ch. 2, IND
KOFT Gallup, N.M., ch. 3, IND
KOB-TV Albuquerque, N.M., ch. 4, NBC
*KNME-TV Albuquerque, N.M., ch. 5, ETV
KVIO-TV Carlsbad, N.M., ch. 6, ABC
New-TV Silver City, N.M., ch. 6, IND
KOAT-TV Albuquerque, N.M., ch. 7, ABC
KOBR Roswell, N.M., ch. 8, satellite to KCBD-TV
KBIM-TV Roswell, N.M., ch. 10, CBS
KOVT-TV Silver City, N.M., ch. 10, ABC
KCHF Santa Fe, N.M., ch. 11, IND
KOBF Farmington, N.M., ch. 12, NBC
KRQE-TV Albuquerque, N.M., ch. 13, CBS
KGSW-TV Albuquerque, N.M., ch. 14, Fox
KNAT Albuquerque, N.M., ch. 23, IND
KRPV Roswell, N.M., ch. 27, IND
KHFT Hobbs, N.M., ch. 29, IND
*KAZQ Albuquerque, N.M., ch. 32, ETV
KLUZ-TV Albuquerque, N.M., ch. 41, IND
KASC Albuquerque, N.M., ch. 50, IND

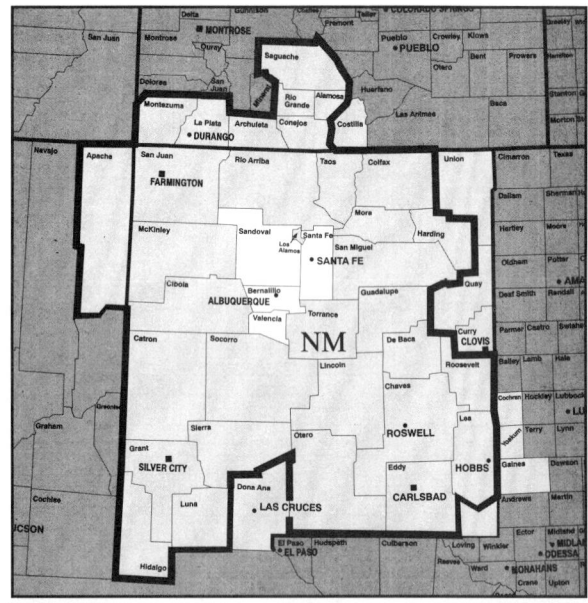

ADI Counties	State	TV Households
Apache North	AZ	12,700
Alamosa	CO	4,900
Archuleta	CO	2,200
Conejos	CO	2,500
La Plata	CO	12,700
Montezuma	CO	6,700
Rio Grande	CO	3,900
Saguache	CO	1,700
Bernalillo	NM	200,700
Catron	NM	900
Chaves	NM	21,000
Cibola	NM	7,000
Colfax	NM	4,700
De Baca	NM	900
Eddy	NM	17,800
Grant	NM	9,700
Guadalupe	NM	1,400
Harding	NM	400
Hidalgo	NM	1,900
Lea North	NM	15,800
Lincoln	NM	4,800
Los Alamos	NM	7,200
Luna	NM	7,300
McKinley	NM	16,700
Mora	NM	1,300
Otero	NM	18,800
Rio Arriba	NM	11,200
Roosevelt	NM	6,000
San Juan	NM	28,100
San Miguel	NM	8,400
Sandoval	NM	23,500
Santa Fe	NM	40,100
Sierra	NM	4,500
Socorro	NM	5,100
Taos	NM	8,600
Torrance	NM	4,000
Valencia	NM	16,700

Broadcasting & Cable Yearbook 1994

Alexandria, La. (Natchez, Miss.) (169)

ADI TV Households: 87,800

KALB-TV Alexandria, La., ch. 5, NBC
***KLPA-TV** Alexandria, La., ch. 25, ETV
KLAX-TV Alexandria, La., ch. 31, ABC

ADI Counties	State	TV Households
Avoyelles	LA	13,100
Grant	LA	6,500
Rapides	LA	46,400
Vernon	LA	21,800

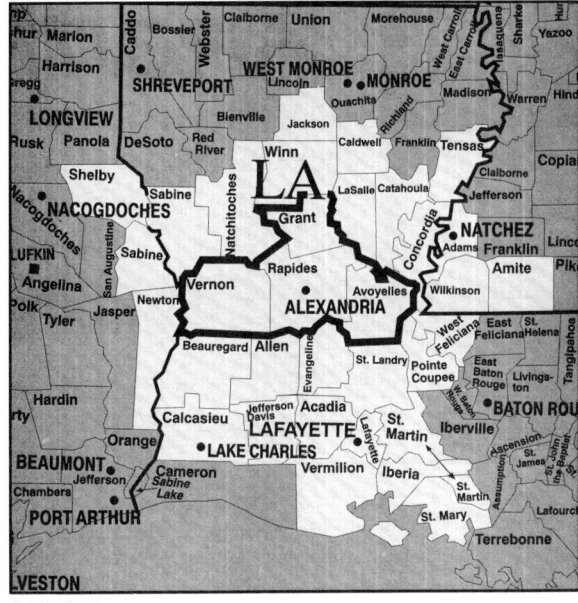

Alpena, Mich. (209)

ADI TV Households: 16,000

***WCML-TV** Alpena, Mich., ch. 6, ETV
WBKB-TV Alpena, Mich., ch. 11, CBS

ADI Counties	State	TV Households
Alcona	MI	4,400
Alpena	MI	11,600

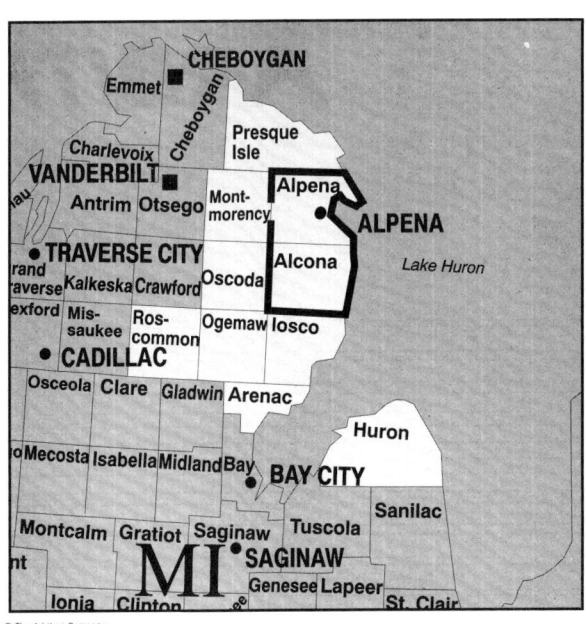

Arbitron ADI Market Atlas

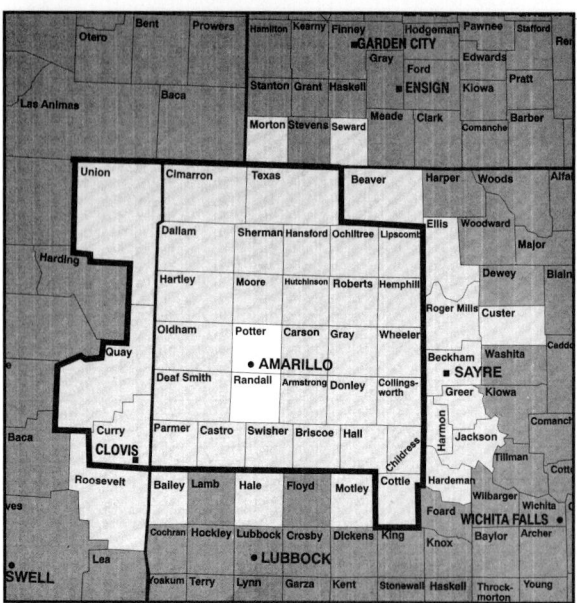

Amarillo, Tex. (129)

ADI TV Households: 168,900

*KACV-TV Amarillo, Tex., ch. 2, ETV
KAMR-TV Amarillo, Tex., ch. 4, NBC
KVII-TV Amarillo, Tex., ch. 7, ABC
KIVJ-TV Sayre, Okla., ch. 8, sat. to KVII-TV
KFDA-TV Amarillo, Tex., ch. 10, CBS
KCIT Amarillo, Tex., ch. 14, Fox
KMZN Farwell, Tex., ch 18, IND

ADI Counties	State	TV Households
Curry	NM	15,800
Quay	NM	3,900
Union	NM	1,500
Cimarron	OK	1,300
Texas	OK	5,900
Armstrong	TX	800
Briscoe	TX	800
Carson	TX	2,400
Castro	TX	2,900
Childress	TX	2,200
Collingsworth	TX	1,400
Cottle	TX	900
Dallam	TX	2,100
Deaf Smith	TX	5,900
Donley	TX	1,500
Gray	TX	8,900
Hall	TX	1,600
Hansford	TX	2,100
Hartley	TX	1,300
Hemphill	TX	1,300
Hutchinson	TX	9,300
Lipscomb	TX	1,200
Moore	TX	6,300
Ochiltree	TX	2,900
Oldham	TX	700
Parmer	TX	3,200
Potter	TX	37,400
Randall	TX	36,900
Roberts	TX	400
Sherman	TX	1,000
Swisher	TX	2,900
Wheeler	TX	2,200

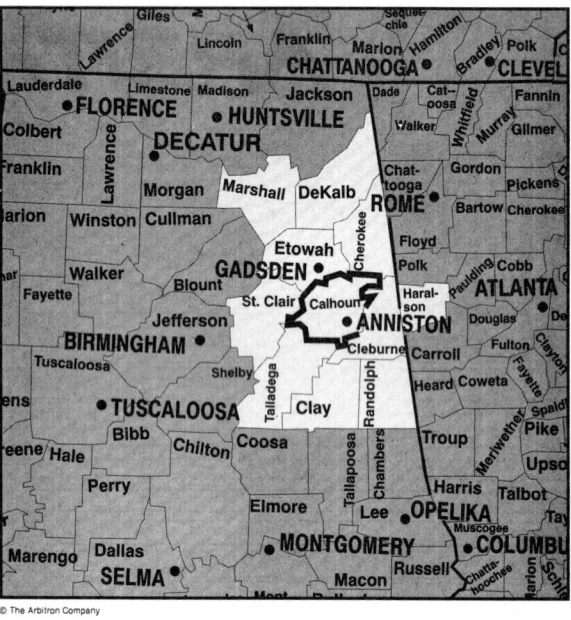

Anniston, Ala. (195)

ADI TV Households: 43,700

WJSU-TV Anniston, Ala., ch. 40, CBS

ADI Counties	State	TV Households
Calhoun	AL	43,700

Broadcasting & Cable Yearbook 1994
C-126

Arbitron ADI Market Atlas

Atlanta (Athens & Rome) (11)

ADI TV Households: 1,516,300

WSB-TV Atlanta, ch. 2, ABC
WAGA-TV Atlanta, ch. 5, CBS
***WGTV** Athens, Ga., ch. 8, ETV
WXIA-TV Atlanta, ch. 11, NBC
WTLK-TV Marietta, Ga., ch. 14, IND
WTBS Atlanta, ch. 17, IND
***WPBA** Atlanta, ch. 30, ETV
WNGM-TV Athens, Ga., ch. 34, IND
WATL Atlanta, ch. 36, Fox
WGNX Atlanta, ch. 46, IND
***WATC** Atlanta, ch. 57, ETV
WHSG Monroe, Ga., ch. 63, IND
WVEU Atlanta, ch. 69, IND

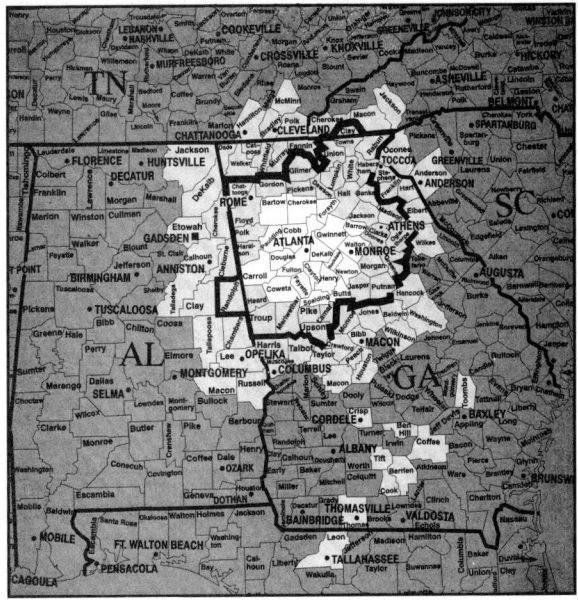

ADI Counties	State	TV Households
Randolph	AL	7,800
Banks	GA	3,800
Barrow	GA	11,700
Bartow	GA	22,200
Butts	GA	4,900
Carroll	GA	26,700
Chattooga	GA	8,600
Cherokee	GA	38,000
Clarke	GA	33,500
Clayton	GA	69,100
Cobb	GA	194,000
Coweta	GA	21,200
Dawson	GA	3,800
De Kalb	GA	221,600
Douglas	GA	26,600
Fayette	GA	25,000
Floyd	GA	30,500
Forsyth	GA	18,500
Fulton	GA	270,400
Gilmer	GA	5,500
Gordon	GA	13,100
Greene	GA	4,200
Gwinnett	GA	150,200
Habersham	GA	10,500
Hall	GA	37,300
Haralson	GA	8,300
Heard	GA	3,500
Henry	GA	23,600
Jackson	GA	11,400
Jasper	GA	3,100
Lamar	GA	4,900
Lumpkin	GA	5,300
Madison	GA	8,000
Meriwether	GA	7,600
Morgan	GA	4,300
Newton	GA	15,800
Oconee	GA	6,600
Oglethorpe	GA	3,600
Paulding	GA	16,800
Pickens	GA	5,700
Pike	GA	3,700
Polk	GA	12,800
Putnam	GA	5,700
Rabun	GA	4,800
Rockdale	GA	20,800
Spalding	GA	20,100
Towns	GA	2,900
Troup	GA	20,900
Union	GA	5,000
Upson	GA	9,800
Walton	GA	14,300
White	GA	5,200
Clay	NC	3,100

Augusta, Ga. (110)

ADI TV Households: 215,500

WJBF Augusta, Ga., ch 6, ABC
WRDW-TV Augusta, Ga., ch. 12, CBS
***WEBA-TV** Allendale, S.C., ch. 14, ETV
***WCES-TV** Wrens, Ga., ch. 20, ETV
WAGT Augusta, Ga., ch. 26, NBC
WFXG Augusta, Ga., ch. 54, Fox

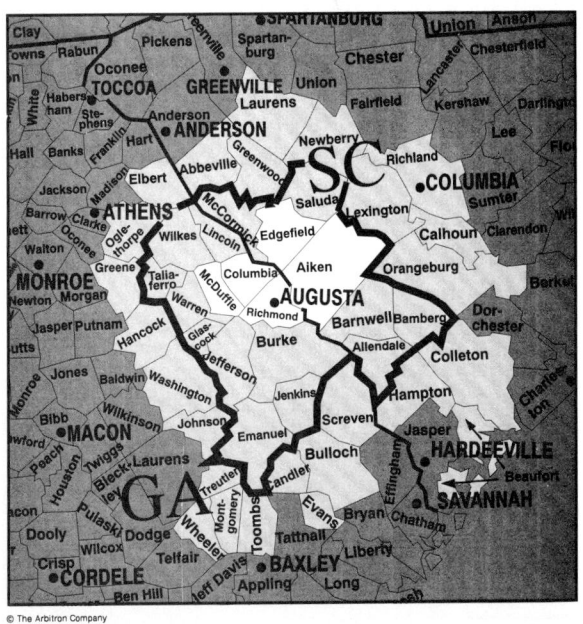

ADI Counties	State	TV Households
Burke	GA	6,800
Columbia	GA	25,100
Emanuel	GA	7,300
Glascock	GA	800
Jefferson	GA	6,100
Jenkins	GA	3,000
Lincoln	GA	2,800
McDuffie	GA	7,500
Richmond	GA	70,300
Taliaferro	GA	700
Warren	GA	2,100
Wilkes	GA	3,900
Aiken	SC	47,400
Allendale	SC	3,700
Bamberg	SC	5,700
Barnwell	SC	7,200
Edgefield	SC	6,700
McCormick	SC	2,700
Saluda	SC	5,700

Broadcasting & Cable Yearbook 1994

Arbitron ADI Market Atlas

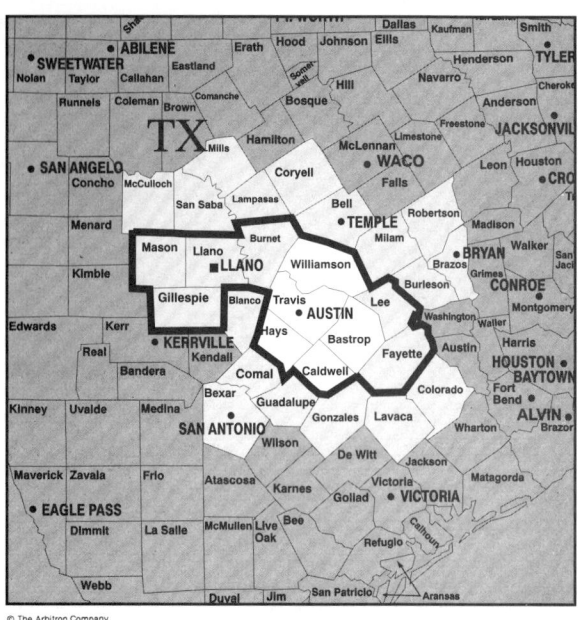

Austin, Tex. (65)

ADI TV Households: 392,400

KTBC-TV Austin, Tex., ch. 7, CBS
KXAM-TV Llano, Tex., ch. 14, satellite to KXAN-TV
*KLRU-TV Austin, Tex., ch. 18, ETV
KVUE-TV Austin, Tex., ch. 24, ABC
KXAN-TV Austin, Tex., ch. 36, NBC
KBVO Austin, Tex., ch. 42, Fox
KCFP Austin, Tex., ch. 54, IND

ADI Counties	State	TV Households
Bastrop	TX	14,000
Burnet	TX	9,400
Caldwell	TX	9,000
Fayette	TX	7,800
Gillespie	TX	6,900
Hays	TX	23,800
Lee	TX	4,600
Llano	TX	5,400
Mason	TX	1,400
Travis	TX	254,900
Williamson	TX	55,200

Bakersfield, Calif. (130)

ADI TV Households: 168,100

KGET Bakersfield, Calif., ch. 17, NBC
KERO-TV Bakersfield, Calif., ch. 23, CBS
KBAK-TV Bakersfield, Calif., ch. 29, ABC
KUZZ-TV Bakersfield, Calif., ch. 48, IND

ADI Counties	State	TV Households
Kern West	CA	168,100

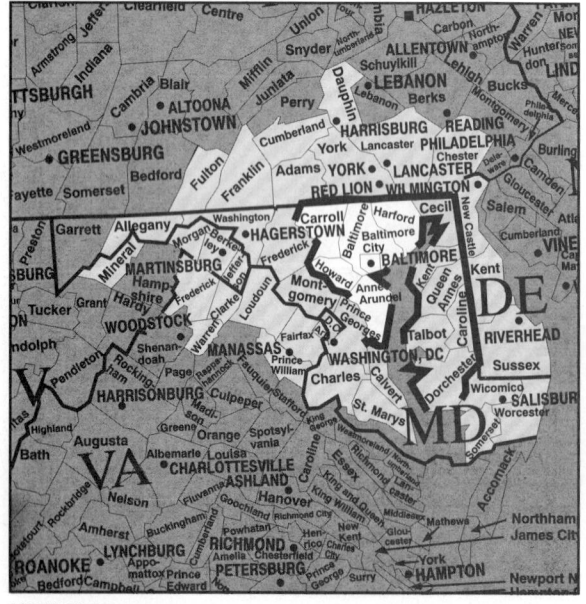

Baltimore (22)

ADI TV Households: 977,100

WMAR-TV Baltimore, ch. 2, NBC
WBAL-TV Baltimore, ch. 11, CBS
WJZ-TV Baltimore, ch. 13, ABC
*WMPT Annapolis, Md., ch. 22, ETV
WHSW Baltimore, ch. 24, IND
WBFF Baltimore, ch. 45, Fox
WNUV-TV Baltimore, ch. 54, IND
*WMPB Baltimore, ch. 67, ETV

ADI Counties	State	TV Households
Anne Arundel	MD	155,100
Baltimore	MD	278,200
Baltimore City	MD	270,500
Caroline	MD	10,100
Carroll	MD	46,000
Cecil	MD	26,400
Dorchester	MD	12,000
Harford	MD	69,500
Howard	MD	75,700
Kent	MD	6,900
Queen Annes	MD	13,500
Talbot	MD	13,200

Broadcasting & Cable Yearbook 1994
C-128

Arbitron ADI Market Atlas

Bangor, Me. (155)

ADI TV Households: 123,400

WLBZ-TV Bangor, Me., ch. 2, NBC
WABI-TV Bangor, Me., ch. 5, CBS
WVII-TV Bangor, Me., ch. 7, ABC
***WMEB-TV** Orono, Me., ch. 12, ETV
***WMED-TV** Calais, Me., ch. 13, ETV

ADI Counties	State	TV Households
Hancock	ME	18,400
Penobscot	ME	53,400
Piscataquis	ME	7,100
Somerset	ME	18,700
Waldo	ME	12,600
Washington	ME	13,200

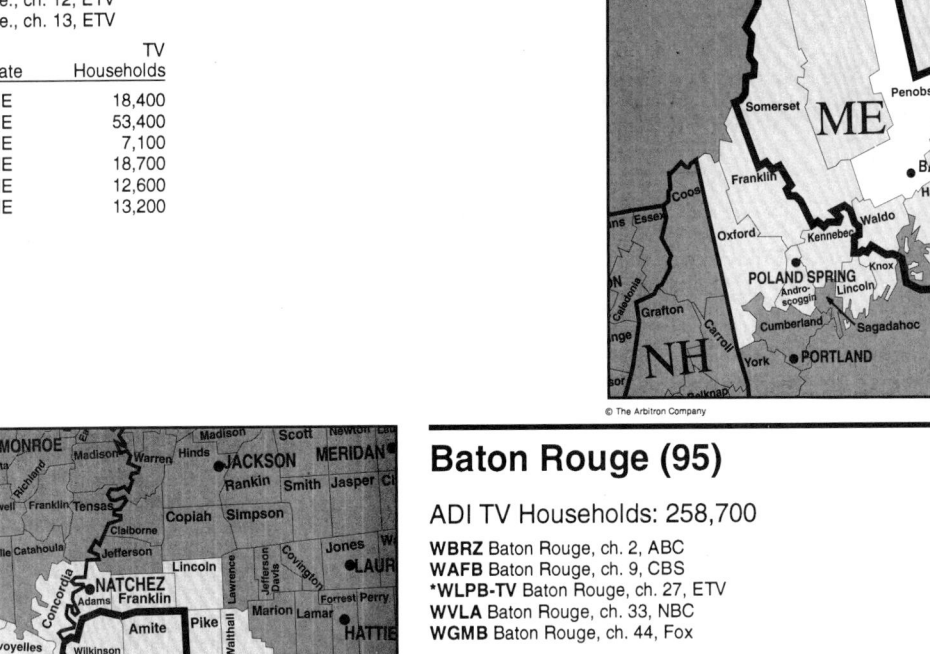

Baton Rouge (95)

ADI TV Households: 258,700

WBRZ Baton Rouge, ch. 2, ABC
WAFB Baton Rouge, ch. 9, CBS
***WLPB-TV** Baton Rouge, ch. 27, ETV
WVLA Baton Rouge, ch. 33, NBC
WGMB Baton Rouge, ch. 44, Fox

ADI Counties	State	TV Households
Ascension	LA	20,100
Assumption	LA	7,400
East Baton Rouge	LA	144,200
East Feliciana	LA	5,600
Iberville	LA	9,300
Livingston	LA	24,400
Pointe Coupee	LA	7,700
St. Helena	LA	3,200
St. Mary	LA	19,300
West Baton Rouge	LA	6,800
West Feliciana	LA	2,600
Amite	MS	4,900
Wilkinson	MS	3,200

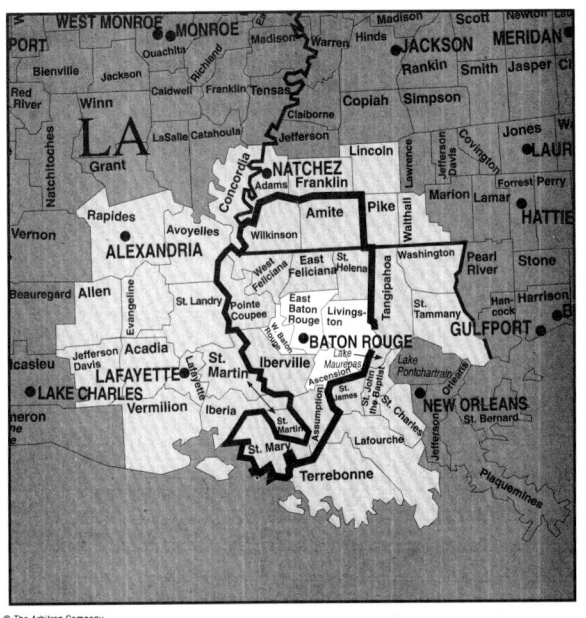

Beaumont-Port Arthur, Tex. (137)

ADI TV Households: 157,900

KJAC-TV Port Arthur, Tex., ch. 4, NBC
KFDM-TV Beaumont, Tex., ch. 6, CBS
KBMT Beaumont, Tex., ch. 12, ABC
***KITU** Beaumont, Tex., ch. 34, ETV

ADI Counties	State	TV Households
Hardin	TX	15,200
Jasper	TX	11,200
Jefferson	TX	91,400
Newton	TX	4,800
Orange	TX	29,500
Tyler	TX	5,800

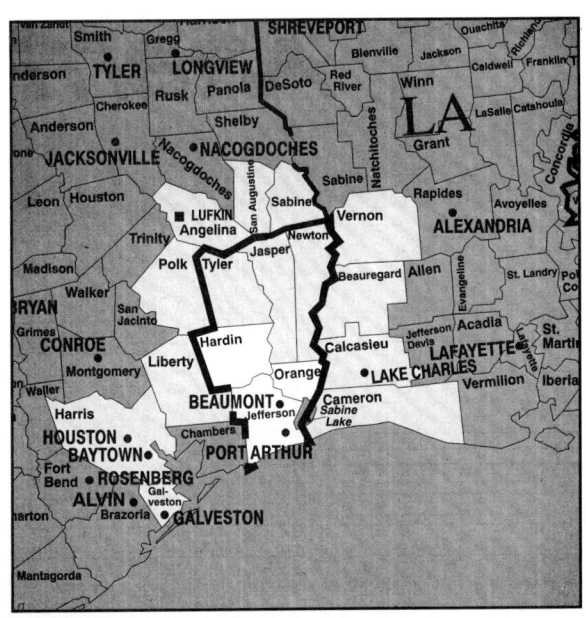

Broadcasting & Cable Yearbook 1994

Arbitron ADI Market Atlas

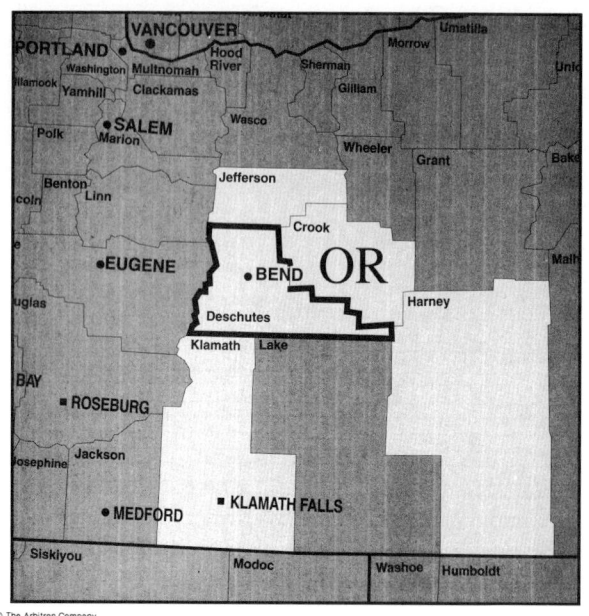

Bend, Ore. (202)

ADI TV Households: 31,900

*KOAB-TV Bend, Ore., ch. 3, ETV
KTVZ Bend, Ore., ch. 21, NBC

ADI Counties	State	TV Households
Deschutes	OR	31,900

Billings, Mont. (171)

ADI TV Households: 86,700

KTVQ Billings, Mont., ch. 2, CBS
KYUS-TV Miles City, Mont., ch. 3, NBC
KOUS-TV Hardin, Mont., ch. 4, ABC
KSVI-Billings, Mont., ch. 6, IND
KULR-TV Billings, Mont., ch. 8, NBC

ADI Counties	State	TV Households
Big Horn	MT	3,300
Carbon	MT	3,100
Custer	MT	4,400
Garfield	MT	500
Golden Valley	MT	300
Musselshell	MT	1,500
Park	MT	5,600
Petroleum	MT	200
Prairie	MT	500
Rosebud	MT	3,300
Stillwater	MT	2,700
Sweet Grass	MT	1,200
Treasure	MT	300
Wheatland	MT	900
Yellowstone	MT	46,000
Big Horn	WY	4,000
Park	WY	8,900

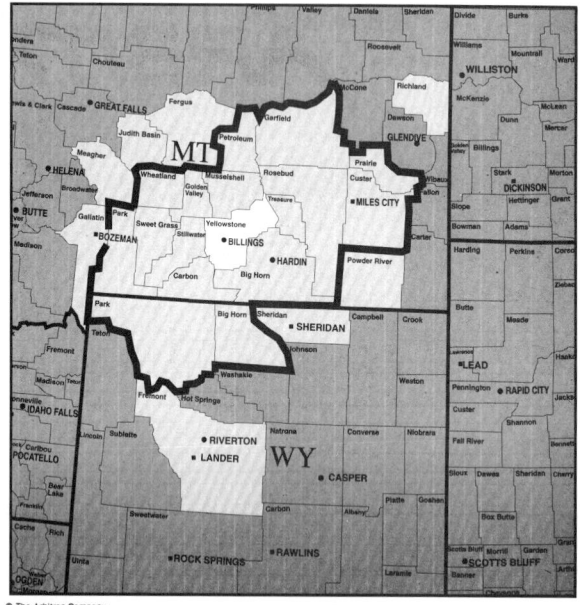

Biloxi-Gulfport-Pascagoula, Miss. (180)

ADI TV Households: 69,200

WLOX-TV Biloxi, Miss., ch. 13, ABC
*WMAH Biloxi, Miss., ch. 19, ETV
WXXV-TV Gulfport, Miss., ch. 25, IND

ADI Counties	State	TV Households
Greene	MS	3,300
Harrison	MS	62,000
Stone	MS	3,900

Broadcasting & Cable Yearbook 1994

Arbitron ADI Market Atlas

Binghamton, N.Y. (135)

ADI TV Households: 158,400

WBNG-TV Binghamton, N.Y., ch. 12, CBS
WMGC-TV Binghamton, N.Y., ch. 34, ABC
WICZ-TV Binghamton, N.Y., ch. 40, NBC
***WSKG** Binghamton, N.Y., ch. 46, ETV

ADI Counties	State	TV Households
Broome	NY	80,100
Chenango	NY	19,300
Delaware	NY	17,600
Tioga	NY	18,900
Bradford	PA	22,500

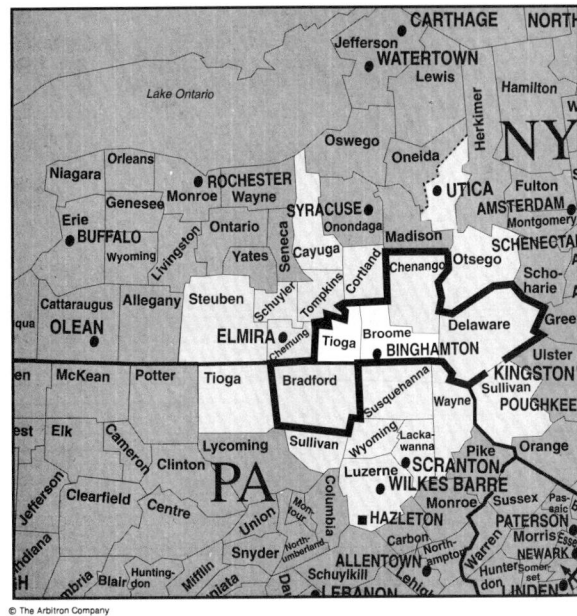

Birmingham (Gadsden), Ala. (50)

ADI TV Households: 531,400

WBRC-TV Birmingham, Ala., ch. 6, ABC
***WCIQ** Mt. Cheaha State Park, Ala., ch. 7, ETV
***WBIQ** Birmingham, Ala., ch. 10, ETV
WVTM-TV Birmingham, Ala., ch. 13, NBC
WTTO Birmingham, Ala., ch. 21, Fox
WBMG Birmingham, Ala., ch. 42, CBS
WNAL-TV Gadsden, Ala., ch. 44, Fox
WTJP Gadsden, Ala., ch. 60, IND
WABM Birmingham, Ala., ch. 68, IND

ADI Counties	State	TV Households			
Bibb	AL	6,000	Greene	AL	3,500
Blount	AL	15,100	Hale	AL	5,600
Cherokee	AL	7,600	Jefferson	AL	255,300
Chilton	AL	12,700	Marion	AL	11,200
Clay	AL	5,000	Pickens	AL	7,500
Cleburne	AL	4,800	St. Clair	AL	19,300
Coosa	AL	4,100	Shelby	AL	40,400
Cullman	AL	26,900	Talladega	AL	26,400
Etowah	AL	38,900	Walker	AL	25,800
Fayette	AL	6,900	Winston	AL	8,400

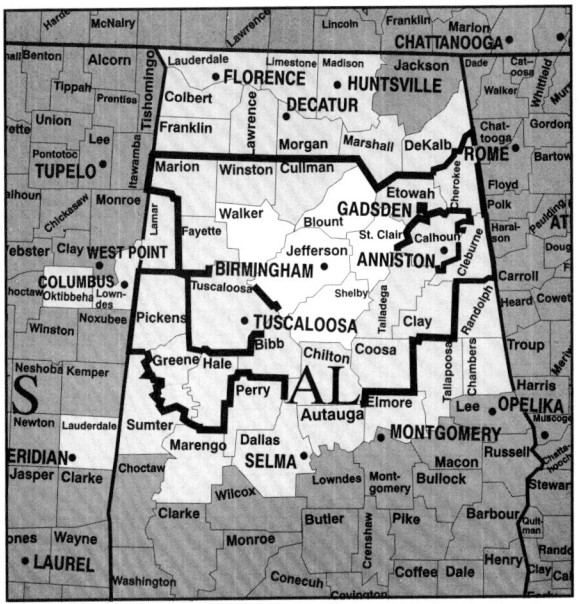

Bluefield-Beckley-Oak Hill, W. Va. (147)

ADI TV Households: 137,400

WOAY-TV Oak Hill, W. Va., ch. 4, ABC (CBS)
WVVA Bluefield, W. Va., ch. 6, NBC
***WSWP-TV** Grandview, W. Va., ch. 9, ETV
WLFB Bluefield, W.Va., ch. 40, IND
WVGV-TV Lewisburg, W.Va., ch. 59, IND

ADI Counties	State	TV Households
Bland	VA	2,100
Tazewell	VA	17,300
Fayette	WV	18,100
Greenbrier	WV	14,100
McDowell	WV	11,600
Mercer	WV	25,100
Monroe	WV	4,800
Raleigh	WV	29,000
Summers	WV	5,100
Wyoming	WV	10,200

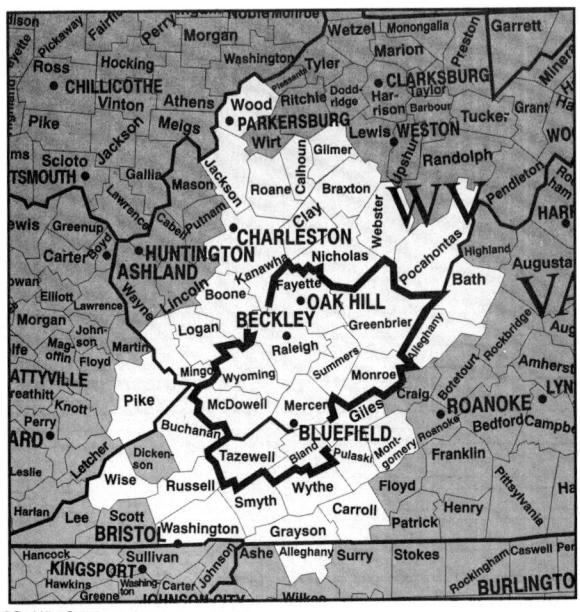

Broadcasting & Cable Yearbook 1994
C-131

Arbitron ADI Market Atlas

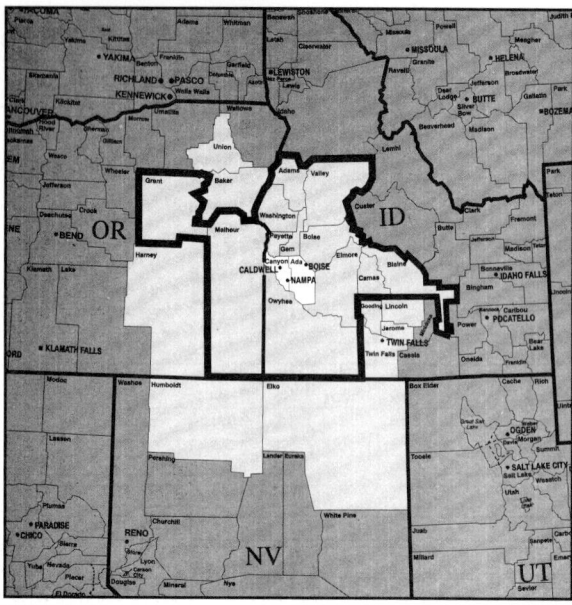

Boise, Idaho (132)

ADI TV Households: 167,700

KBCI-TV Boise, Idaho, ch. 2 CBS
***KAID** Boise, Idaho, ch. 4, ETV
KIVI Nampa, Idaho, ch. 6, ABC
KTVB Boise, Idaho, ch. 7, NBC
KHDT-TV Caldwell, Idaho, ch. 9, IND
KTRV Nampa, Idaho, ch. 12, Fox

ADI Counties	State	TV Households
Ada	ID	85,100
Adams	ID	1,200
Blaine	ID	6,400
Boise	ID	1,500
Camas	ID	300
Canyon	ID	33,700
Elmore	ID	7,000
Gem	ID	4,700
Owyhee	ID	2,800
Payette	ID	6,700
Valley	ID	2,700
Washington	ID	3,400
Grant	OR	3,000
Malheur	OR	9,200

Boston (Derry & Manchester, N.H., & Worcester, Mass.) (6)

ADI TV Households: 2,116,200

***WGBH-TV** Boston, ch. 2, ETV
WBZ-TV Boston, ch. 4, NBC
WCVB-TV Boston, ch. 5, ABC
WHDH-TV Boston, ch. 7, CBS
WMUR-TV Manchester, N.H., ch. 9, ABC
***WENH-TV** Durham, N.H., ch. 11, ETV
WNHT Concord, N.H., ch. 21, IND
WFXT Boston, ch. 25, Fox
WHLL Worcester, Mass., ch. 27, IND
WSBK-TV Boston, ch. 38, IND
***WGBX-TV** Boston, ch. 44, ETV
WHRC Norwell, Mass., ch. 46, IND
***WYDN** Worcester, Mass., ch. 48, ETV
WNDS Derry, N.H., ch. 50, IND
***WEKW-TV** Keene, N.H., ch. 52, ETV
WLVI-TV Cambridge, Mass., ch. 56, IND
WGOT Merrimack, N.H., ch. 60, IND
WMFP Lawrence, Mass., ch. 62, IND
WHSH Marlborough, Mass., ch. 66, IND
WQTV Boston, ch. 68, IND

ADI Counties	State	TV Households
Barnstable	MA	80,000
Essex	MA	249,100
Middlesex	MA	512,800
Nantucket	MA	2,500
Norfolk	MA	225,800
Plymouth	MA	149,400
Suffolk	MA	248,300
Worcester	MA	261,900
Belknap	NH	19,000
Cheshire	NH	26,900
Hillsborough	NH	132,500
Merrimack	NH	45,900
Rockingham	NH	92,300
Strafford	NH	39,200
Sullivan	NH	14,900
Windham	VT	15,700

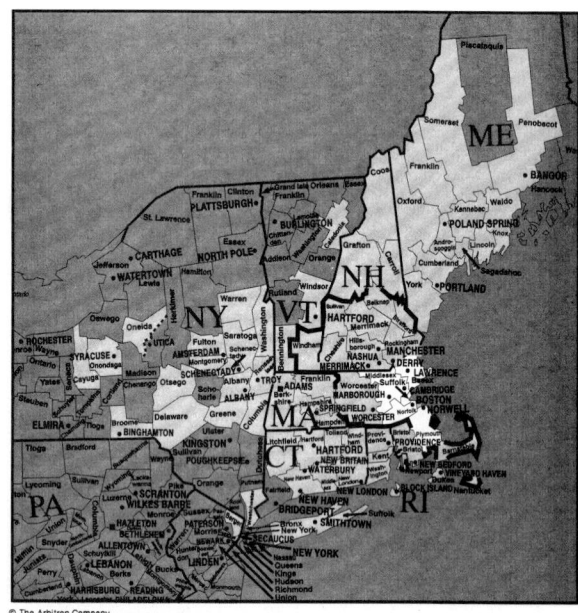

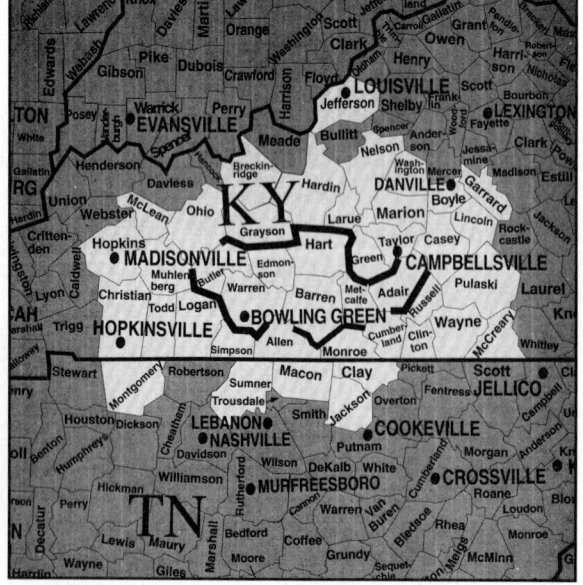

Bowling Green (Campbellsville), Ky. (181)

ADI TV Households: 66,300

WBKO Bowling Green, Ky., ch. 13, ABC
***WKYU-TV** Bowling Green, Ky., ch. 24, ETV
WGRB Campbellsville, Ky., ch. 34, sat. to WKNT
WKNT Bowling Green, Ky., ch. 40, FOX
***WKGB-TV** Bowling Green, Ky., ch. 53, ETV

ADI Counties	State	TV Households
Adair	KY	5,900
Barren	KY	13,300
Butler	KY	4,200
Edmonson	KY	3,700
Hart	KY	6,000
Metcalfe	KY	3,400
Warren	KY	29,800

Broadcasting & Cable Yearbook 1994
C-132

Arbitron ADI Market Atlas

Bristol, Va.-Kingsport, Johnson City & Greenville, Tenn.: Tri-Cities (91)

ADI TV Households: 278,600

WCYB-TV Bristol, Va., ch. 5, NBC
WJHL-TV Johnson City, Tenn., ch. 11, CBS
WLTK Somerset, Ky., ch. 16, IND
***WUNE-TV** Linville, N.C., ch. 17, ETV
WKPT-TV Kingsport, Tenn., ch. 19, ABC
WEMT Greeneville, Tenn., ch. 39, Fox
***WSBN-TV** Norton, Va., ch. 47, ETV
***WMSY-TV** Marion, Va., ch. 52, ETV
WLFG Grundy, Va., ch. 68, IND

ADI Counties	State	TV Households
Leslie	KY	4,600
Letcher	KY	9,500
Carter	TN	20,600
Greene	TN	21,800
Hawkins	TN	17,700
Johnson	TN	5,200
Sullivan	TN	58,300
Unicoi	TN	6,500
Washington	TN	37,200
Buchanan	VA	10,100
Dickenson	VA	6,400
Lee	VA	8,700
Russell	VA	10,300
Scott	VA	8,600
Smyth	VA	12,200
Washington	VA	24,900
Wise	VA	16,000

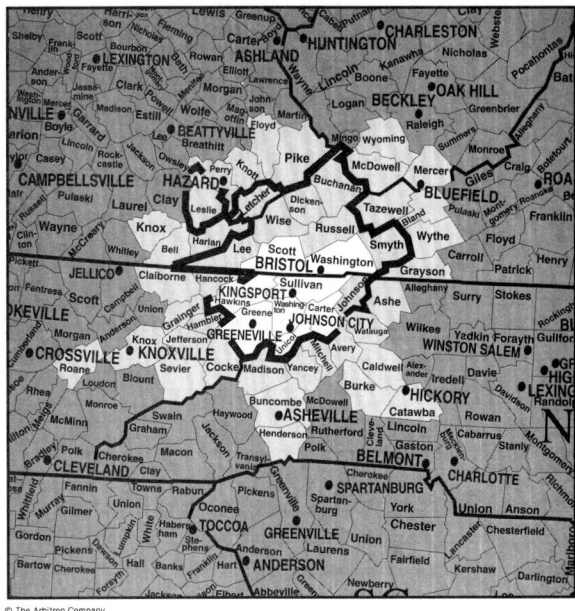

Buffalo (Jamestown), N.Y. (38)

ADI TV Households: 618,200

WGRZ-TV Buffalo, N.Y., ch. 2, NBC
WIVB-TV Buffalo, N.Y., ch. 4, CBS
WKBW-TV Buffalo, N.Y., ch. 7, ABC
***WNED-TV** Buffalo, N.Y., ch. 17, ETV
***WNEQ-TV** Buffalo, N.Y., ch. 23, ETV
WTJA Jamestown, N.Y., ch. 26, IND
WUTV Buffalo, N.Y., ch. 29, Fox
WNYB-TV Buffalo, N.Y., ch. 49, IND
WYDM Batavia, N.Y., ch. 51, IND

ADI Counties	State	TV Households
Allegany	NY	16,900
Cattaraugus	NY	30,300
Chautauqua	NY	52,700
Erie	NY	375,000
Genesee	NY	21,700
Niagara	NY	84,600
Wyoming	NY	13,900
McKean	PA	17,100
Potter	PA	6,000

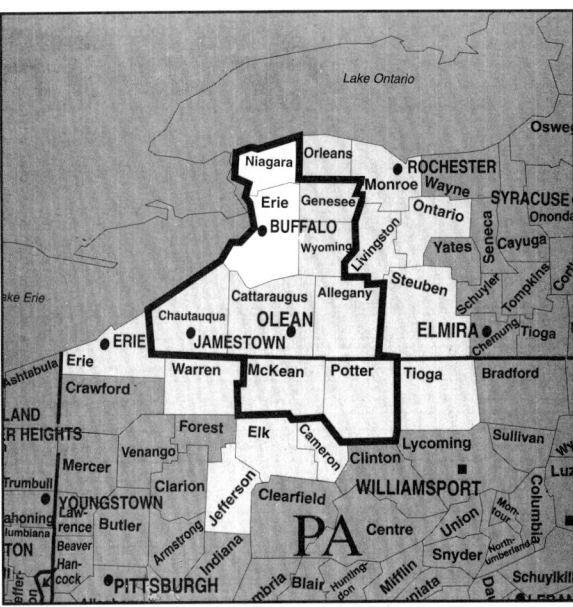

Burlington, Vt.-Plattsburgh, N.Y. (Hartford, Vt.) (93)

ADI TV Households: 271,300

WCAX-TV Burlington, Vt., ch. 3, CBS
WPTZ North Pole (Plattsburgh), N.Y., ch. 5, NBC
***WVTB** St. Johnsbury, Vt., ch. 20, ETV
WVNY Burlington, Vt., ch. 22, ABC
***WVER** Rutland, Vt., ch. 28, ETV
WNNE Hartford, Vt., ch. 31, NBC
***WETK** Burlington, Vt., ch. 33, ETV
***WVTA** Windsor, Vt., ch. 41, ETV
***WCFE-TV** Plattsburgh, N.Y., ch. 57, ETV

ADI Counties	State	TV Households
Grafton	NH	27,900
Clinton	NY	30,000
Essex	NY	13,400
Franklin	NY	15,700
Addison	VT	11,800
Caledonia	VT	10,600
Chittenden	VT	50,000
Essex	VT	2,500
Franklin	VT	14,800
Grand Isle	VT	2,100
Lamoille	VT	7,900
Orange	VT	9,500
Orleans	VT	8,900
Rutland	VT	23,700
Washington	VT	21,000
Windsor	VT	21,500

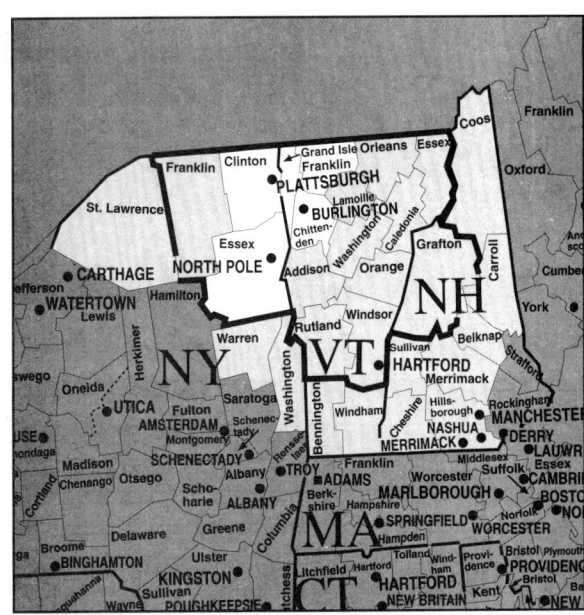

Broadcasting & Cable Yearbook 1994

Arbitron ADI Market Atlas

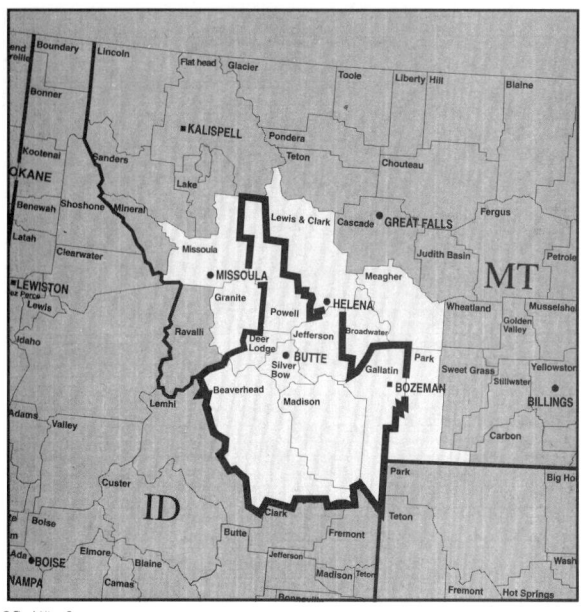

Butte, Mont. (189)

ADI TV Households: 49,300

KXLF-TV Butte, Mont., ch. 4, CBS
KTVM Butte, Mont., ch. 6, satellite to KECI-TV
KCTZ Bozeman, Mont., ch. 7, ABC
*****KUSM** Bozeman, Mont., ch. 9, ETV
KWYB Butte, Mont., ch. 18, IND

ADI Counties	State	TV Households
Beaverhead	MT	3,200
Deer Lodge	MT	4,000
Gallatin	MT	20,500
Jefferson	MT	3,100
Madison	MT	2,500
Powell	MT	2,100
Silver Bow	MT	13,900

Casper-Riverton, Wyo. (194)

ADI TV Households: 43,800

KTWO-TV Casper, Wyo., ch. 2, NBC
*****KCWC-TV** Lander, Wyo., ch. 4, ETV
KGWL-TV Lander, Wyo., ch. 5, CBS (ABC)
KFNE Riverton, Wyo., ch. 10, satellite to KFNB
KGWR-TV Rock Springs, Wyo., ch. 13, CBS
KGWC-TV Casper, Wyo., ch. 14, CBS
KFNB Casper, Wyo., ch. 20, ABC

ADI Counties	State	TV Households
Converse	WY	3,800
Fremont	WY	12,000
Hot Springs	WY	1,800
Natrona	WY	24,000

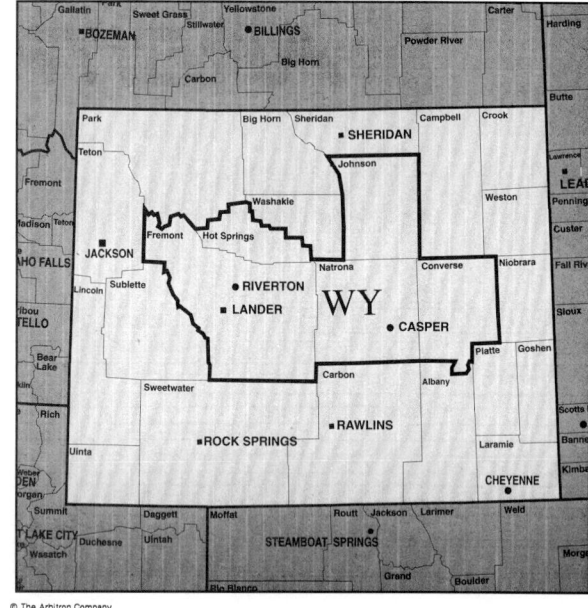

Cedar Rapids-Waterloo-Dubuque, Iowa (82)

ADI TV Households: 312,800

KGAN Cedar Rapids, Iowa, ch. 2, CBS
KWWL Waterloo, Iowa, ch. 7, NBC
KCRG-TV Cedar Rapids, Iowa, ch. 9, ABC
*****KIIN-TV** Iowa City, Iowa, ch. 12, ETV
KFSC Waterloo, Iowa, ch. 22, IND
KOCR Cedar Rapids, Iowa, ch. 28, IND
*****KRIN** Waterloo, Iowa, ch. 32, ETV
KDUB-TV Dubuque, Iowa, ch. 40, ABC
KTVC Cedar Rapids, Iowa, ch. 48, IND

ADI Counties	State	TV Households			
Allamakee	IA	5,200	Fayette	IA	8,300
Benton	IA	8,700	Grundy	IA	4,700
Black Hawk	IA	46,900	Iowa	IA	5,800
Bremer	IA	8,300	Johnson	IA	37,500
Buchanan	IA	7,500	Jones	IA	7,600
Butler	IA	6,000	Keokuk	IA	4,500
Cedar	IA	6,800	Linn	IA	67,300
Chickasaw	IA	4,900	Tama	IA	6,700
Clayton	IA	7,000	Washington	IA	7,600
Delaware	IA	6,600	Winneshiek	IA	7,000
Dubuque	IA	31,000	Grant	WI	16,900

Broadcasting & Cable Yearbook 1994

Arbitron ADI Market Atlas

Charleston, S.C. (106)

ADI TV Households: 230,100

WCBD-TV Charleston, S.C., ch. 2, ABC
WCIV Charleston, S.C., ch. 4, NBC
WCSC-TV Charleston, S.C., ch. 5, CBS
*****WITV** Charleston, S.C., ch. 7, ETV
WTAT-TV Charleston, S.C., ch. 24, Fox
WCTP Charleston, S.C., ch. 36, IND

ADI Counties	State	TV Households
Berkeley	SC	46,100
Charleston	SC	111,100
Colleton	SC	12,500
Dorchester	SC	31,000
Georgetown	SC	17,500
Williamsburg	SC	11,900

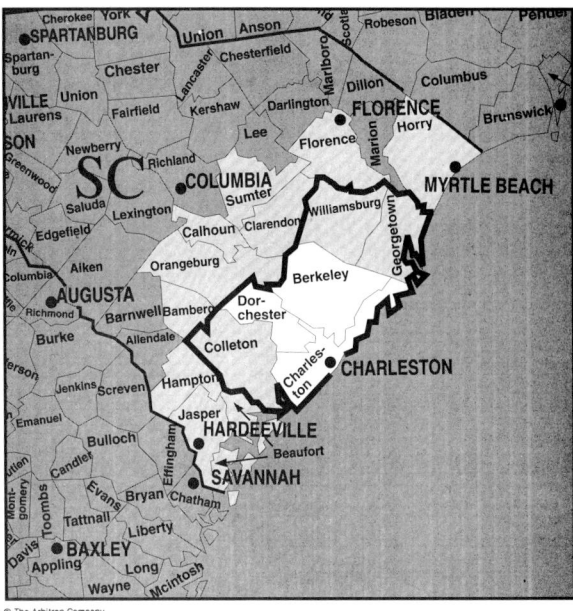

Charleston-Huntington, W. Va. (55)

ADI TV Households: 476,400

WSAZ-TV Huntington, W. Va., ch. 3, NBC
WCHS-TV Charleston, W. Va., ch. 8, ABC
WVAH-TV Charleston, W. Va., ch. 11, Fox
WOWK-TV Huntington, W. Va., ch. 13, CBS
*****WOUB-TV** Athens, Ohio, ch. 20, ETV
*****WKPI** Pikeville, Ky., ch. 22, ETV
*****WKAS** Ashland, Ky., ch. 25, ETV
WKRP-TV Charleston, W. Va., ch. 29, IND
WUXA Portsmouth, Ohio, ch. 30, IND
*****WPBY-TV** Huntington, W. Va., ch. 33, ETV
*****WPBO-TV** Portsmouth, Ohio, ch. 42, ETV
WTSF Ashland, Ky., ch. 61, IND

ADI Counties	State	TV Households
Boyd	KY	19,900
Carter	KY	8,900
Elliott	KY	2,300
Floyd	KY	15,700
Greenup	KY	13,400
Johnson	KY	8,400
Lawrence	KY	5,200
Lewis	KY	4,600
Magoffin	KY	4,300
Martin	KY	4,200
Morgan	KY	4,000
Pike	KY	26,000
Athens	OH	20,500
Gallia	OH	11,400
Jackson	OH	11,500
Lawrence	OH	23,100
Meigs	OH	8,600
Scioto	OH	29,900
Vinton	OH	4,200
Boone	WV	9,700
Braxton	WV	4,900
Cabell	WV	39,400
Calhoun	WV	2,900
Clay	WV	3,600
Jackson	WV	9,700
Kanawha	WV	85,100
Lincoln	WV	7,800
Logan	WV	15,200
Mason	WV	9,700
Mingo	WV	11,600
Nicholas	WV	10,000
Putnam	WV	17,000
Roane	WV	5,900
Wayne	WV	15,900

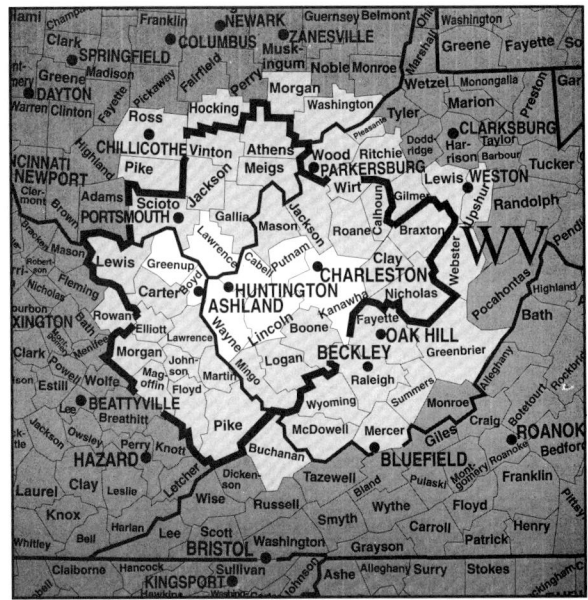

Charlotte (Hickory), N.C. (30)

ADI TV Households: 779,000

WBTV Charlotte, N.C., ch. 3, CBS
WSOC-TV Charlotte, N.C., ch. 9, ABC
WHKY-TV Hickory, N.C., ch. 14, IND
WCCB Charlotte, N.C., ch. 18, IND
*****WNSC-TV** Rock Hill, S.C., ch. 30, ETV
WCNC-TV Charlotte, N.C., ch. 36, NBC
*****WTVI** Charlotte, N.C., ch. 42, ETV
WJZY Belmont, N.C., ch. 46, IND
WFVT Rock Hill, S.C., ch. 55, IND
*****WUNG-TV** Concord, N.C., ch. 58, ETV
WKAY Kannapolis, N.C., ch. 64, IND

ADI Counties	State	TV Households
Alexander	NC	10,600
Anson	NC	8,400
Ashe	NC	9,000
Avery	NC	5,500
Burke	NC	29,600
Cabarrus	NC	39,600
Caldwell	NC	27,700
Catawba	NC	47,800
Cleveland	NC	32,700
Gaston	NC	67,000
Iredell	NC	37,400
Lincoln	NC	20,000
Mecklenburg	NC	219,700
Richmond	NC	17,000
Rowan	NC	44,300
Stanly	NC	20,300
Union	NC	31,700
Watauga	NC	13,900
Chester	SC	11,800
Chesterfield	SC	14,400
Lancaster	SC	20,300
York	SC	50,300

Broadcasting & Cable Yearbook 1994

Arbitron ADI Market Atlas

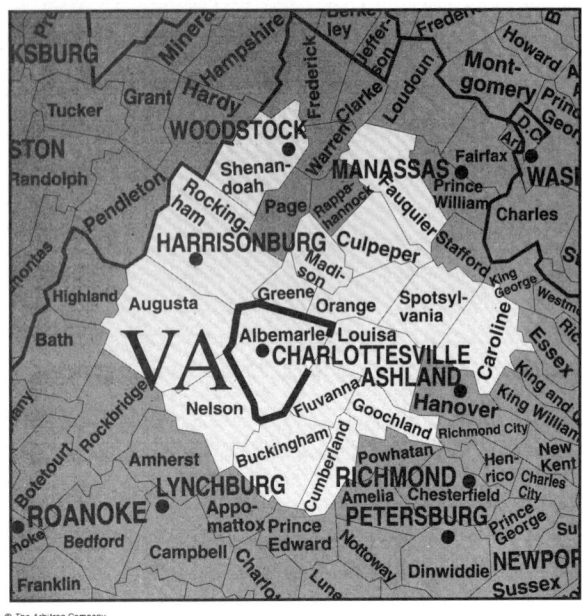

Charlottesville, Va. (197)

ADI TV Households: 41,700

WVIR-TV Charlottesville, Va., ch. 29, NBC
*WHTJ Charlottesville, Va., ch. 41, ETV

ADI Counties	State	TV Households
Albemarle	VA	41,700

Chattanooga (Cleveland), Tenn. (85)

ADI TV Households: 295,100

WRCB-TV Chattanooga, ch. 3, NBC
WTVC Chattanooga, ch. 9, ABC
WDEF-TV Chattanooga, ch. 12, CBS
*WCLP-TV Chatsworth, Ga., ch. 18, ETV
WELF Dalton, Ga., ch. 23, IND
*WTCI Chattanooga, ch. 45, ETV
WFLI-TV Cleveland, Tenn., ch. 53, IND
WDSI-TV Chattanooga, ch. 61, Fox

ADI Counties	State	TV Households
Catoosa	GA	16,400
Dade	GA	4,700
Fannin	GA	6,500
Murray	GA	10,400
Walker	GA	22,100
Whitfield	GA	27,500
Cherokee	NC	8,300
Bledsoe	TN	3,300
Bradley	TN	29,000
Grundy	TN	4,700
Hamilton	TN	114,700
Marion	TN	9,400
McMinn	TN	16,800
Meigs	TN	3,300
Polk	TN	5,100
Rhea	TN	9,600
Sequatchie	TN	3,300

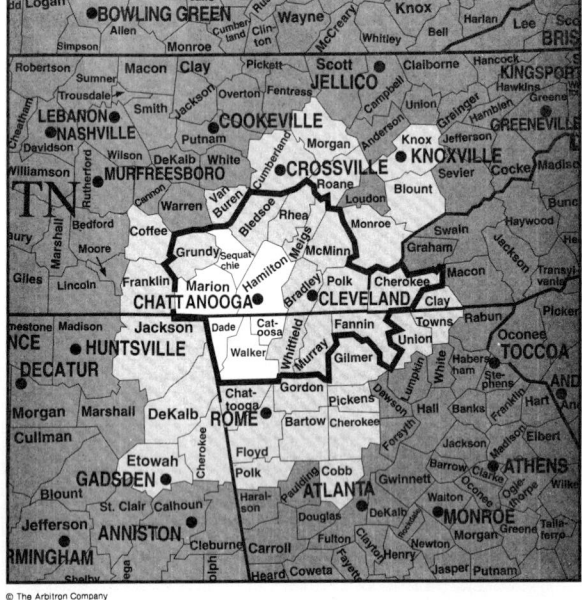

Cheyenne, Wyo.-Scottsbluff, Neb. (Sterling, Colo.) (196)

ADI TV Households: 43,400

KDUH-TV Scottsbluff, Neb., ch. 4, satellite to KOTA-TV
KGWN-TV Cheyenne, Wyo., ch. 5, CBS (ABC-NBC)
KTVS Sterling, Colo., ch. 3, satellite to KGWN-TV
KSTF Scottsbluff, Neb., ch. 10, satellite to KGWN-TV
KLWY Cheyenne, Wyo., ch. 27, IND
KKTU Cheyenne, Wyo., ch. 33, satellite to KTWO-TV

ADI Counties	State	TV Households
Scotts Bluff	NE	14,300
Laramie	WY	29,100

Broadcasting & Cable Yearbook 1994
C-136

Chicago (LaSalle) (3)

ADI TV Households: 3,076,500

WBBM-TV Chicago, ch. 2, CBS
WMAQ-TV Chicago, ch. 5, NBC
WLS-TV Chicago, ch. 7, ABC
WGN-TV Chicago, ch. 9, IND
*****WTTW** Chicago, ch. 11, ETV
*****WYCC** Chicago, ch. 20, ETV
WCIU-TV Chicago, ch. 26, IND
WFLD Chicago, ch. 32, Fox
WWTO-TV La Salle, Ill., ch. 35, IND
WCFC-TV Chicago, ch. 38, IND
WSNS Chicago, ch. 44, IND
WPWR-TV Gary, Ind., ch. 50, IND
WHKE Kenosha, Wis., ch. 55, IND
*****WYIN** Gary, Ind., ch. 56, ETV
WEHS Aurora, Ill., ch. 60, IND
WJYS Hammond, Ind., ch. 62, IND
WGBO-TV Joliet, Ill., ch. 66, IND

ADI Counties	State	TV Households			
Cook	IL	1,868,500	Lake	IL	188,000
Dekalb	IL	27,400	McHenry	IL	70,000
Dupage	IL	299,700	Will	IL	123,200
Grundy	IL	12,700	Jasper	IN	8,700
Iriquois	IL	11,600	La Porte	IN	38,800
Kane	IL	114,800	Lake	IN	170,500
Kankakee	IL	34,800	Newton	IN	4,900
Kendall	IL	14,000	Porter	IN	47,500
La Salle	IL	41,400			

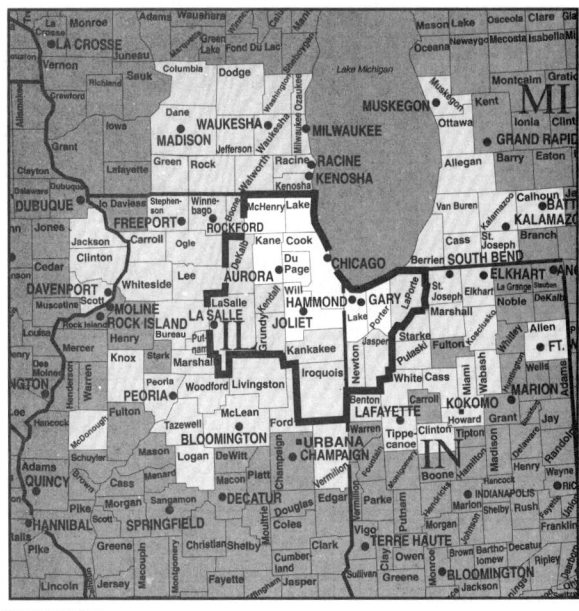

Chico-Redding, Calif. (125)

ADI TV Households: 171,000

KRCR-TV Redding, Calif., ch. 7, ABC
*****KIXE** Redding, Calif., ch. 9, ETV
KHSL-TV Chico, Calif., ch. 12, CBS
KCPM Chico, Calif., ch. 24, NBC
KCVU Paradise, Calif., ch. 30, IND

ADI Counties	State	TV Households
Butte	CA	75,000
Glenn	CA	9,100
Shasta	CA	61,900
Tehama	CA	20,100
Trinity	CA	4,900

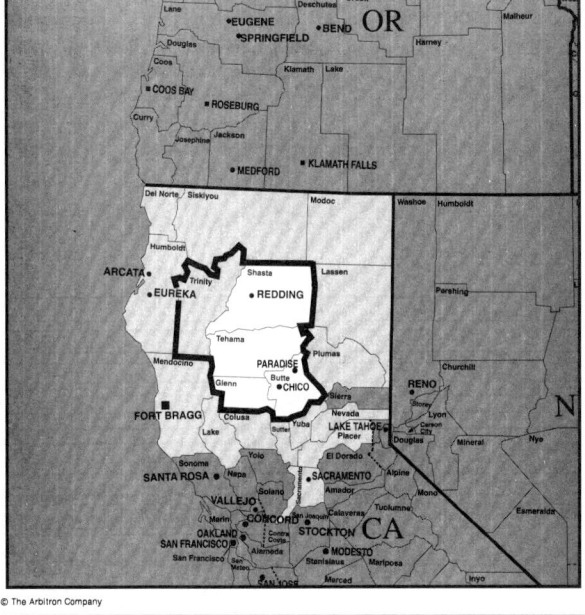

Cincinnati (31)

ADI TV Households: 771,000

WLWT Cincinnati, ch. 5, NBC
WCPO-TV Cincinnati, ch. 9, CBS
WKRC-TV Cincinnati, ch. 12, ABC
*****WPTO** Oxford, Ohio, ch. 14, ETV
WXIX-TV Newport, Ky., ch. 19, Fox
*****WCET** Cincinnati, ch. 48, ETV
*****WKON** Owenton, Ky., ch. 52, ETV
*****WCVN** Covington, Ky., ch. 54, ETV
WSTR-TV Cincinnati, ch. 64, IND

ADI Counties	State	TV Households			
Dearborn	IN	14,600	Mason	KY	6,600
Franklin	IN	6,900	Owen	KY	3,600
Ohio	IN	2,000	Pendleton	KY	4,700
Ripley	IN	9,000	Robertson	KY	800
Switzerland	IN	2,800	Adams	OH	9,500
Union	IN	2,500	Brown	OH	12,900
Boone	KY	22,800	Butler	OH	109,800
Bracken	KY	3,000	Clermont	OH	56,300
Campbell	KY	32,000	Clinton	OH	13,600
Gallatin	KY	2,000	Hamilton	OH	339,900
Grant	KY	6,000	Highland	OH	13,700
Kenton	KY	54,400	Warren	OH	41,600

Arbitron ADI Market Atlas

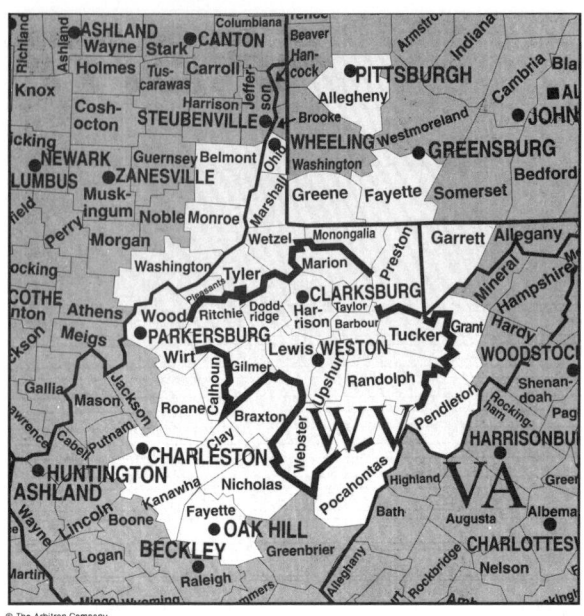

Clarksburg-Weston, W. Va. (160)

ADI TV Households: 102,600

WDTV Weston, W. Va., ch. 5, CBS (ABC)
WBOY-TV Clarksburg, W. Va., ch. 12, NBC (ABC)
WLYJ Clarksburg, W. Va., ch. 46, IND

ADI Counties	State	TV Households
Barbour	WV	5,700
Doddridge	WV	2,600
Gilmer	WV	2,700
Harrison	WV	27,500
Lewis	WV	6,400
Marion	WV	22,600
Randolph	WV	10,700
Ritchie	WV	3,800
Taylor	WV	5,600
Tucker	WV	3,100
Upshur	WV	8,100
Webster	WV	3,800

Cleveland (Akron, Canton, Mansfield & Sandusky, Ohio) (12)

ADI TV Households: 1,449,700

WKYC-TV Cleveland, ch. 3, NBC
WEWS Cleveland, ch. 5, ABC
WJW-TV Cleveland, ch. 8, CBS
WDLI Canton, Ohio, ch. 17, IND
WOIO Shaker Heights, Ohio, ch. 19, Fox
WAKC-TV Akron, Ohio, ch. 23, ABC
***WVIZ-TV** Cleveland, ch. 25, ETV
WUAB Lorain, Ohio, ch. 43, IND
***WEAO** Akron, Ohio, ch. 49, ETV
WGGN-TV Sandusky, Ohio, ch. 52, IND
WBNX-TV Akron, Ohio, ch. 55, IND
WQHS Cleveland, ch. 61, IND
WOAC Canton, Ohio, ch. 67, IND
WMFD-TV Mansfield, Ohio, ch. 68, IND

ADI Counties	State	TV Households
Ashland	OH	17,800
Ashtabula	OH	36,900
Carroll	OH	10,000
Cuyahoga	OH	560,500
Erie	OH	29,000
Geauga	OH	28,300
Holmes	OH	9,300
Huron	OH	20,900
Lake	OH	82,800
Lorain	OH	96,200
Medina	OH	44,200
Portage	OH	50,600
Richland	OH	48,500
Stark	OH	141,000
Summit	OH	204,700
Tuscarawas	OH	32,400
Wayne	OH	36,600

Colorado Springs-Pueblo, Colo. (97)

ADI TV Households: 252,000

KOAA-TV Pueblo, Colo., ch. 5, NBC
***KTSC** Pueblo, Colo., ch. 8, ETV
KKTV Colorado Springs, ch. 11, CBS
KRDO-TV Colorado Springs, ch. 13, ABC
KXRM-TV Colorado Springs, ch. 21, Fox

ADI Counties	State	TV Households
Baca	CO	1,600
Bent	CO	1,700
Cheyenne	CO	900
Costilla	CO	1,200
Crowley	CO	1,200
Custer	CO	800
El Paso	CO	164,600
Fremont	CO	11,700
Huerfano	CO	2,300
Kiowa	CO	700
Las Animas	CO	5,100
Otero	CO	7,400
Prowers	CO	4,800
Pueblo	CO	48,000

Broadcasting & Cable Yearbook 1994
C-138

Columbia, S.C. (86)

ADI TV Households: 290,600

WIS-TV Columbia, S.C., ch. 10, NBC
WLTX Columbia, S.C., ch. 19, CBS
WOLO-TV Columbia, S.C., ch. 25, ABC
*****WRJA-TV** Sumter, S.C., ch. 27, ETV
*****WRLK-TV** Columbia, S.C., ch. 35, ETV
WACH Columbia, S.C., ch. 57, IND
WQHB Sumter, S.C., ch. 63, IND

ADI Counties	State	TV Households
Calhoun	SC	4,400
Clarendon	SC	9,600
Fairfield	SC	7,700
Kershaw	SC	16,600
Lee	SC	6,000
Lexington	SC	65,000
Newberry	SC	12,800
Orangeburg	SC	29,900
Richland	SC	104,000
Sumter	SC	34,600

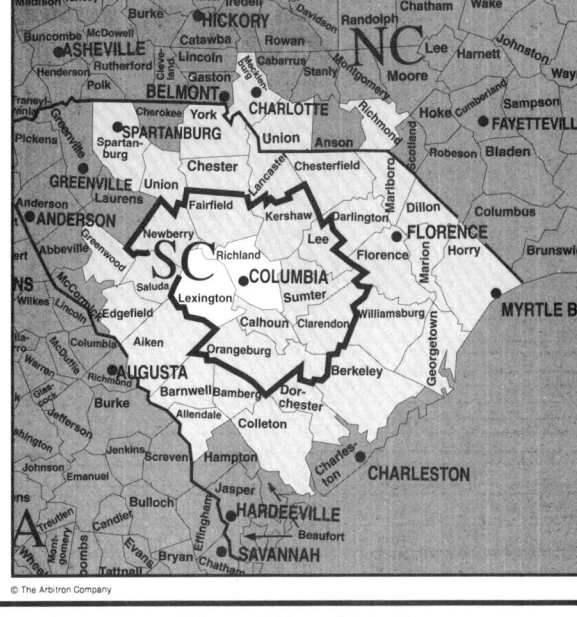

Columbia-Jefferson City, Mo. (151)

ADI TV Households: 135,300

KOMU-TV Columbia, Mo., ch. 8, NBC
KRCG Jefferson City, Mo., ch. 13, CBS
KMIZ Columbia, Mo., ch. 17, ABC
KNLJ Jefferson City, Mo., ch. 25, IND

ADI Counties	State	TV Households
Audrain	MO	8,900
Boone	MO	44,200
Callaway	MO	11,300
Chariton	MO	3,500
Cole	MO	24,000
Cooper	MO	5,100
Howard	MO	3,500
Maries	MO	3,000
Miller	MO	8,200
Moniteau	MO	4,500
Morgan	MO	6,300
Osage	MO	4,200
Randolph	MO	8,600

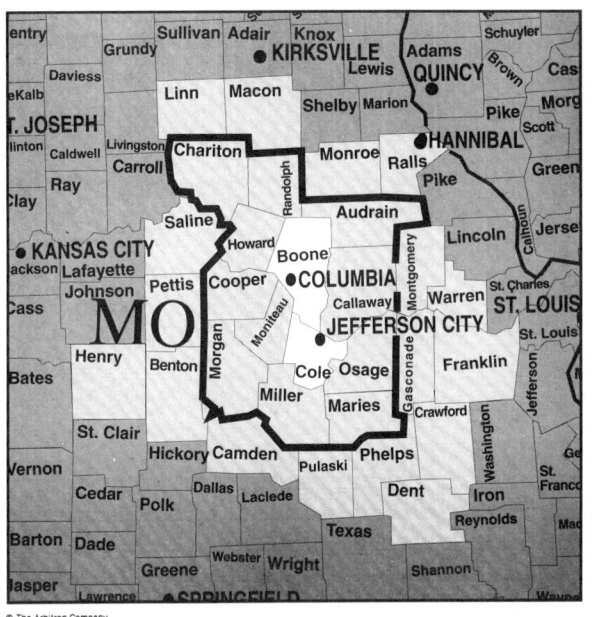

Columbus, Ga. (Opelika, Ala.) (122)

ADI TV Households: 180,700

WRBL Columbus, Ga., ch. 3, CBS
WTVM Columbus, Ga., ch. 9, ABC
*****WACS-TV** Dawson, Ga., ch. 25, ETV
*****WJSP-TV** Columbus, Ga., ch. 28, ETV
WLTZ Columbus, Ga., ch. 38, NBC
*****WGIQ** Louisville, Ala., ch. 43, ETV
WXTX Columbus, Ga., ch. 54, Fox
WSWS-TV Opelika, Ala., ch. 66, IND

ADI Counties	State	TV Households
Barbour	AL	8,900
Chambers	AL	13,900
Lee	AL	34,300
Russell	AL	18,500
Chattahoochee	GA	3,200
Clay	GA	1,200
Harris	GA	6,500
Macon	GA	4,300
Marion	GA	1,900
Muscogee	GA	67,600
Quitman	GA	900
Randolph	GA	2,800
Schley	GA	1,300
Stewart	GA	1,900
Sumter	GA	10,400
Talbot	GA	2,300
Webster	GA	800

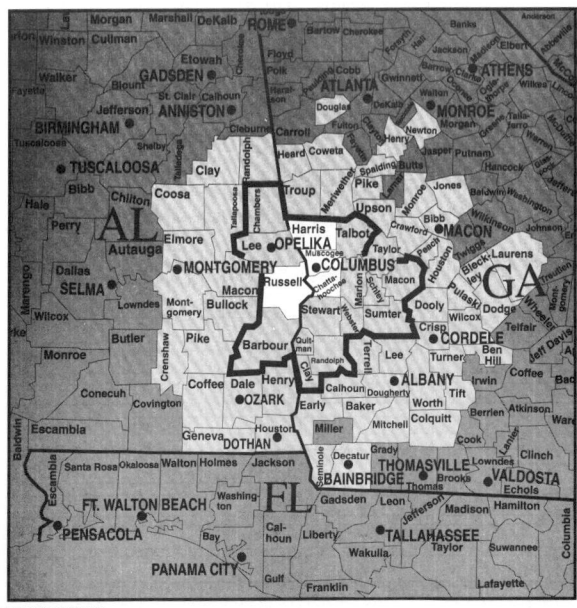

Arbitron ADI Market Atlas

Arbitron ADI Market Atlas

Columbus, Ohio (Chillicothe) (34)

ADI TV Households: 710,900

WCMH Columbus, Ohio, ch. 4, NBC
WSYX Columbus, Ohio, ch. 6, ABC
WBNS-TV Columbus, Ohio, ch. 10, CBS
WTTE Columbus, Ohio, ch. 28, Fox
*****WOSU-TV** Columbus, Ohio, ch. 34, ETV
WSFJ Newark, Ohio, ch. 52, IND
WWAT Chillicothe, Ohio, ch. 53, IND

ADI Counties	State	TV Households
Coshocton	OH	13,300
Crawford	OH	18,300
Delaware	OH	25,500
Fairfield	OH	37,900
Fayette	OH	10,300
Franklin	OH	395,500
Hardin	OH	11,200
Hocking	OH	9,500
Knox	OH	17,500
Licking	OH	49,100
Madison	OH	12,000
Marion	OH	23,500
Morgan	OH	5,100
Morrow	OH	10,000
Perry	OH	11,400
Pickaway	OH	15,500
Pike	OH	9,100
Ross	OH	24,500
Union	OH	11,700

Columbus-Tupelo (West Point), Miss. (127)

ADI TV Households: 170,300

*****WMAB-TV** Mississippi State, Miss., ch. 2, ETV
WCBI-TV Columbus, Miss., ch. 4, CBS
WTVA Tupelo, Miss., ch. 9, NBC
*****WMAE-TV** Booneville, Miss., ch. 12, ETV
WLOV-TV West Point, Miss., ch. 27, ABC

ADI Counties	State	TV Households
Lamar	AL	5,900
Calhoun	MS	5,700
Chickasaw	MS	6,500
Choctaw	MS	3,200
Clay	MS	7,300
Grenada	MS	7,700
Itawamba	MS	7,400
Lee	MS	26,200
Lowndes	MS	21,900
Monroe	MS	13,600
Montgomery	MS	4,400
Noxubee	MS	3,900
Oktibbeha	MS	13,000
Pontotoc	MS	8,600
Prentiss	MS	8,700
Tishomingo	MS	7,200
Union	MS	8,500
Webster	MS	3,700
Winston	MS	6,900

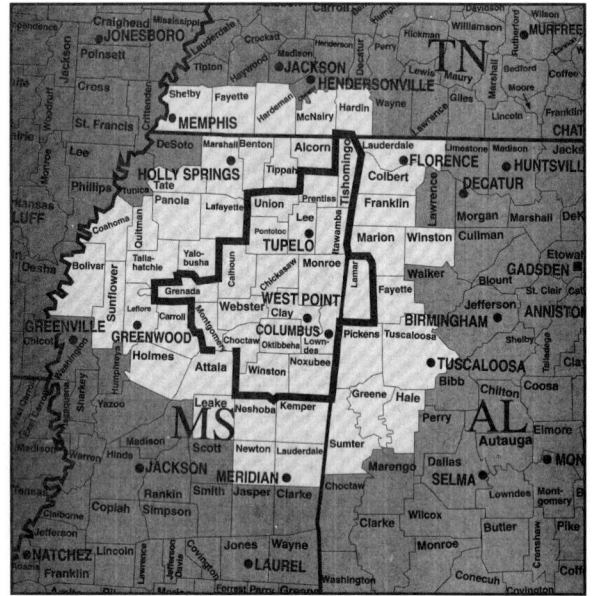

Corpus Christi, Tex. (123)

ADI TV Households: 173,800

KIII Corpus Christi, Tex., ch. 3, ABC
KRIS-TV Corpus Christi, Tex., ch. 6, NBC
KZTV Corpus Christi, Tex., ch. 10, CBS
*****KEDT-TV** Corpus Christi, Tex., ch. 16, ETV
KORO Corpus Christi, Tex., ch. 28, IND

ADI Counties	State	TV Households
Aransas	TX	7,400
Bee	TX	8,700
Brooks	TX	2,700
Duval	TX	4,000
Jim Hogg	TX	1,700
Jim Wells	TX	11,900
Kenedy	TX	100
Kleberg	TX	9,600
Live Oak	TX	3,200
Nueces	TX	102,900
Refugio	TX	2,900
San Patricio	TX	18,700

Broadcasting & Cable Yearbook 1994

Arbitron ADI Market Atlas

Dallas-Fort Worth (8)

ADI TV Households: 1,788,000

*KDTN Denton, Tex., ch. 2, ETV
KDFW-TV Dallas, ch. 4, CBS
KXAS-TV Fort Worth, ch. 5, NBC
WFAA-TV Dallas, ch. 8, ABC
KTVT Fort Worth, ch. 11, IND
*KERA-TV Dallas, ch. 13, ETV
KTXA Fort Worth, ch. 21, IND
KUVN Garland, Tex., ch. 23, IND
KDFI-TV Dallas, ch. 27, IND
KMPX Decatur, Tex., ch. 29, IND
KDAF Dallas, ch. 33, Fox
KXTX-TV Dallas, ch. 39, IND
KTAQ Greenville, Tex., ch. 47, IND
KHSX Irving, Tex., ch. 49, IND
KFWD Fort Worth, ch. 52, IND
KLDT Lake Dallas, Tex., ch. 55, IND
KDTX-TV Dallas, ch. 58, IND

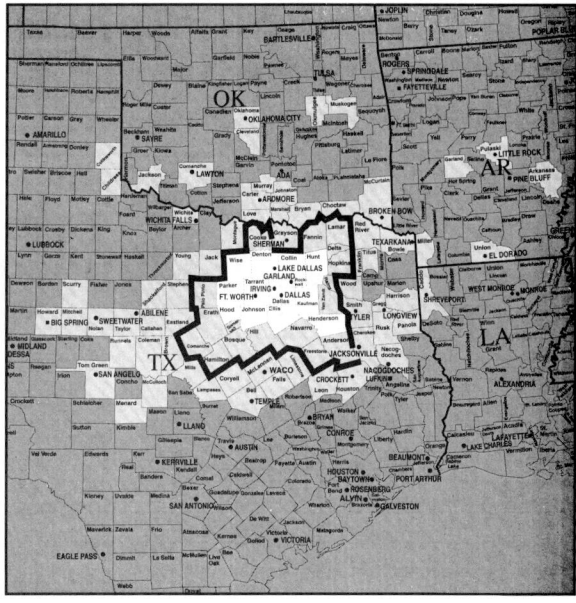

ADI Counties	State	TV Households
Anderson	TX	14,200
Bosque	TX	6,000
Collin	TX	110,700
Comanche	TX	5,200
Cooke	TX	11,600
Dallas	TX	737,100
Delta	TX	1,900
Denton	TX	116,200
Ellis	TX	31,100
Erath	TX	11,300
Fannin	TX	9,400
Freestone	TX	5,900
Hamilton	TX	3,100
Henderson	TX	23,800
Hill	TX	10,400
Hood	TX	13,200
Hopkins	TX	11,000
Hunt	TX	24,300
Johnson	TX	35,700
Kaufman	TX	19,500
Lamar	TX	16,600
Navarro	TX	14,600
Palo Pinto	TX	9,600
Parker	TX	25,300
Rains	TX	3,000
Rockwall	TX	10,400
Somervell	TX	2,100
Tarrant	TX	476,800
Van Zandt	TX	15,100
Wise	TX	12,900

Davenport, Iowa-Rock Island & Moline, Ill.: Quad City (Burlington, Iowa) (84)

ADI TV Households: 297,100

WHBF-TV Rock Island, Ill., ch. 4, CBS
KWQC-TV Davenport, Iowa, ch. 6, NBC
WQAD-TV Moline, Ill., ch. 8, ABC
KLJB-TV Davenport, Iowa, ch. 18, Fox
*WQPT-TV Moline, Ill., ch. 24, ETV
KJMH Burlington, Iowa, ch. 26, IND
*KQCT Davenport, Iowa, ch. 36, satellite to *WQPT-TV

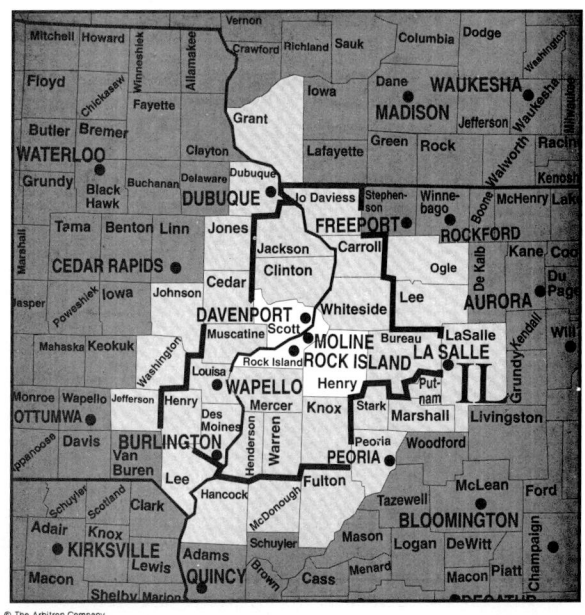

ADI Counties	State	TV Households
Clinton	IA	19,700
Des Moines	IA	17,000
Henry	IA	7,100
Jackson	IA	7,500
Louisa	IA	4,200
Muscatine	IA	15,400
Scott	IA	58,800
Bureau	IL	13,500
Carroll	IL	6,500
Henderson	IL	3,200
Henry	IL	18,100
Jo Daviess	IL	8,200
Knox	IL	21,600
Mercer	IL	6,500
Rock Island	IL	59,000
Warren	IL	7,200
Whiteside	IL	22,600

Broadcasting & Cable Yearbook 1994

Arbitron ADI Market Atlas

Dayton, Ohio (Richmond, Ind.) (52)

ADI TV Households: 509,500

WDTN Dayton, Ohio, ch. 2, ABC
WHIO-TV Dayton, Ohio, ch. 7, CBS
***WPTD** Kettering, Ohio, ch. 16, ETV
WKEF Dayton, Ohio, ch. 22, NBC
WTJC Springfield, Ohio, ch. 26, IND
WKOI Richmond, Ind., ch. 43, IND
WRGT-TV Dayton, Ohio, ch. 45, Fox

ADI Counties	State	TV Households
Wayne	IN	27,300
Auglaize	OH	16,600
Champaign	OH	13,700
Clark	OH	55,600
Darke	OH	19,600
Greene	OH	50,200
Logan	OH	16,600
Mercer	OH	13,700
Miami	OH	35,600
Montgomery	OH	229,700
Preble	OH	14,700
Shelby	OH	16,200

Denver (20)

ADI TV Households: 1,090,100

KWGN-TV Denver, ch. 2, IND
KREG-TV Glenwood Springs, Colo., ch. 3, CBS
KCNC-TV Denver, ch. 4, NBC
***KRMA-TV** Denver, ch. 6, ETV
KMGH-TV Denver, ch. 7, CBS
KUSA-TV Denver, ch. 9, ABC
KFNR Rawlins, Wyo., ch. 11, ABC
***KBDI-TV** Broomfield, Colo., ch. 12, ETV
***KTNE-TV** Alliance, Neb., ch. 13, ETV
KTVJ Boulder, Colo., ch. 14, IND
KTVD Denver, ch. 20, IND
KWXU Fort Collins, ch. 22, satellite to KDVR
KSBS-TV Steamboat Springs, Colo., ch. 24, IND
KZJG Longmont, Colo., ch. 25, IND
KDVR Denver, ch. 31, Fox
***KWBI-TV** Denver., ch. 41, ETV
KCEC Denver, ch. 50, IND
KWHD Castle Rock, Colo., ch. 53, IND
KUBD Denver, ch. 59, IND

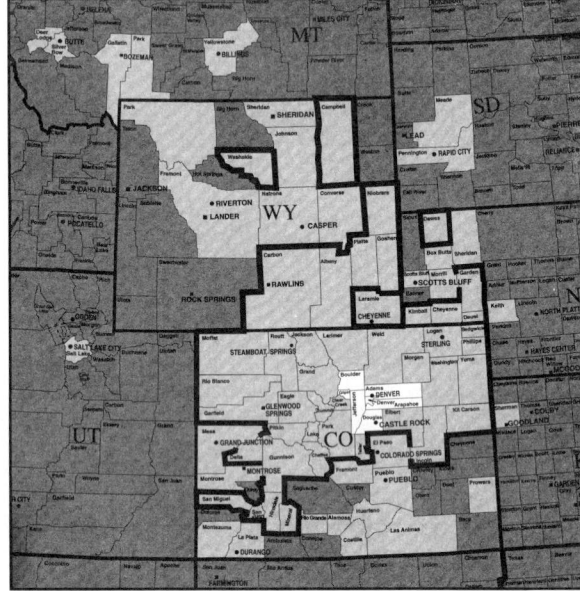

ADI Counties	State	TV Households
Adams	CO	103,000
Arapahoe	CO	172,400
Boulder	CO	95,500
Chaffee	CO	4,600
Clear Creek	CO	3,200
Delta	CO	8,400
Denver	CO	222,400
Douglas	CO	25,900
Eagle	CO	9,300
Elbert	CO	3,700
Garfield	CO	12,200
Gilpin	CO	1,400
Grand	CO	3,000
Gunnison	CO	3,700
Hinsdale	CO	200
Jackson	CO	600
Jefferson	CO	177,700
Kit Carson	CO	2,700
Lake	CO	2,400
Larimer	CO	78,600
Lincoln	CO	1,700
Logan	CO	6,700
Mineral	CO	200
Moffat	CO	3,900
Morgan	CO	8,700
Park	CO	3,100
Phillips	CO	1,700
Pitkin	CO	5,800
Rio Blanco	CO	2,200
Routt	CO	5,700
San Juan	CO	300
San Miguel	CO	1,800
Sedgwick	CO	1,100
Summit	CO	5,700
Teller	CO	5,300
Washington	CO	1,800
Weld	CO	49,300
Yuma	CO	3,400
Cheyenne	NE	3,900
Dawes	NE	3,000
Deuel	NE	900
Garden	NE	1,000
Kimball	NE	1,600
Albany	WY	12,600
Campbell	WY	9,900
Carbon	WY	5,700
Goshen	WY	4,900
Niobrara	WY	1,000
Platte	WY	3,200

Broadcasting & Cable Yearbook 1994

Des Moines, Iowa (68)

ADI TV Households: 380,800

WOI-TV Ames, Iowa, ch. 5, ABC
KCCI-TV Des Moines, Iowa, ch. 8, CBS
*****KDIN-TV** Des Moines, Iowa, ch. 11, ETV
WHO-TV Des Moines, Iowa, ch. 13, NBC
KDSM-TV Des Moines, Iowa, ch. 17, Fox
*****KTIN** Fort Dodge, Iowa, ch. 21, ETV

ADI Counties	State	TV Households
Adair	IA	3,400
Appanoose	IA	5,600
Audubon	IA	2,900
Boone	IA	9,800
Calhoun	IA	4,700
Carroll	IA	8,000
Clarke	IA	3,300
Dallas	IA	11,800
Decatur	IA	3,000
Franklin	IA	4,500
Greene	IA	4,100
Guthrie	IA	4,600
Hamilton	IA	6,300
Hardin	IA	7,400
Humboldt	IA	4,200
Jasper	IA	13,800
Lucas	IA	3,600
Madison	IA	4,900
Mahaska	IA	8,300
Marion	IA	11,400
Marshall	IA	14,800
Monroe	IA	3,200
Pocahontas	IA	3,800
Polk	IA	135,800
Poweshiek	IA	7,200
Ringgold	IA	2,200
Story	IA	26,900
Taylor	IA	2,700
Union	IA	5,100
Wapello	IA	14,300
Warren	IA	13,300
Wayne	IA	2,800
Webster	IA	15,800
Wright	IA	5,800
Mercer	MO	1,500

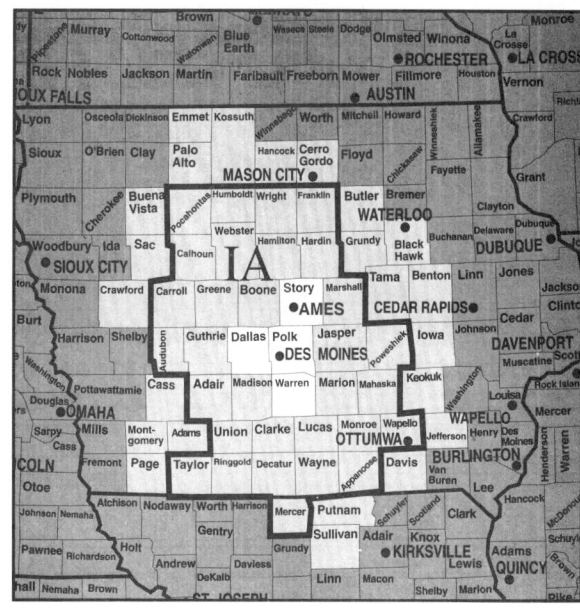

Detroit (9)

ADI TV Households: 1,739,100

WJBK-TV Detroit, ch. 2, CBS
WDIV Detroit, ch. 4, NBC
WXYZ-TV Detroit, ch. 7, ABC
CBET Windsor, Ont., ch. 9, CBC
WXON Detroit, ch. 20, IND
WADL Mount Clemens, Mich., ch. 38, IND
WKBD Detroit, ch. 50, IND, Fox
*****WTVS** Detroit, ch. 56, ETV
WGPR-TV Detroit, ch. 62, IND

ADI Counties	State	TV Households
Lapeer	MI	26,100
Livingston	MI	41,700
Macomb	MI	270,800
Monroe	MI	47,200
Oakland	MI	429,900
St. Clair	MI	54,900
Washtenaw	MI	107,600
Wayne	MI	760,900

Dothan, Ala. (165)

ADI TV Households: 94,700

WTVY Dothan, Ala., ch. 4, CBS
WDHN Dothan, Ala., ch. 18, ABC
WDAU Ozark, Ala., ch. 34, Fox
WRKJ Dothan, Ala., ch. 60, IND

ADI Counties	State	TV Households
Coffee	AL	15,800
Dale	AL	18,500
Geneva	AL	9,400
Henry	AL	5,900
Houston	AL	32,200
Holmes	FL	5,800
Early	GA	4,000
Seminole	GA	3,100

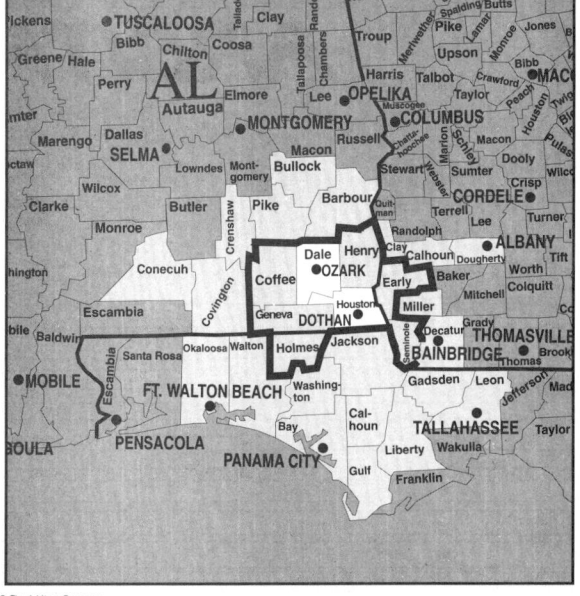

Broadcasting & Cable Yearbook 1994
C-143

Arbitron ADI Market Atlas

Duluth, Minn.-Superior, Wis. (126)

ADI TV Households: 170,900

KDLH Duluth, Minn., ch. 3, CBS
KBJR-TV Superior, Wis., ch. 6, NBC
*WDSE-TV Duluth, Minn., ch. 8, ETV
WDIO-TV Duluth, Minn., ch. 10, ABC
WIRT Hibbing, Minn., ch. 13, satellite to WDIO-TV
KRBR Duluth, Minn., ch. 21, IND

ADI Counties	State	TV Households
Gogebic	MI	7,300
Aitkin	MN	5,200
Carlton	MN	11,100
Cook	MN	1,800
Itasca	MN	15,300
Koochiching	MN	5,400
Lake	MN	4,100
St. Louis	MN	77,800
Ashland	WI	6,200
Bayfield	WI	5,800
Douglas	WI	16,900
Iron	WI	2,600
Sawyer	WI	5,700
Washburn	WI	5,700

El Centro, Calif.-Yuma, Ariz. (178)

ADI TV Households: 71,800

KLXO El Centro, Calif., ch. 7, IND
KECY-TV El Centro, Calif., ch. 9, CBS
KYMA Yuma, Ariz., ch. 11, NBC
KSWT Yuma, Ariz., ch. 13, ABC

ADI Counties	State	TV Households
Yuma	AZ	37,500
Imperial	CA	34,300

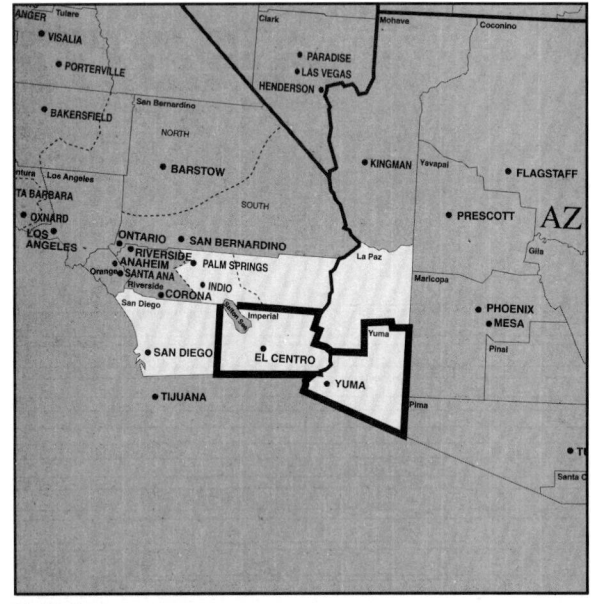

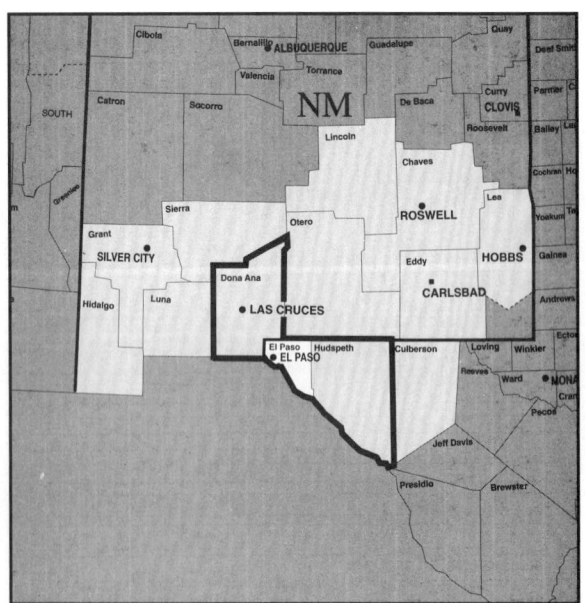

El Paso (Las Cruces, N.M.) (100)

ADI TV Households: 242,000

KDBC-TV El Paso, ch. 4, CBS
KVIA-TV El Paso, ch. 7, ABC
KTSM-TV El Paso, ch. 9, NBC
*KCOS El Paso, ch. 13, ETV
KCIK El Paso, ch. 14, Fox
*KRWG-TV Las Cruces, N.M., ch. 22, ETV
KINT-TV El Paso, ch. 26, IND
*KSCE El Paso., ch. 38, ETV
KASK-TV Las Cruces, N.M., ch. 48, IND
KJLF-TV El Paso, ch. 65, IND

ADI Counties	State	TV Households
Dona Ana	NM	48,700
El Paso	TX	192,400
Hudspeth	TX	900

Broadcasting & Cable Yearbook 1994
C-144

Arbitron ADI Market Atlas

Elmira, N.Y. (171)

ADI TV Households: 86,700

WETM-TV Elmira, N.Y., ch. 18, NBC
WENY-TV Elmira, N.Y., ch. 36, ABC
WYDC Corning, N.Y., ch. 48, IND

ADI Counties	State	TV Households
Chemung	NY	34,900
Steuben	NY	37,200
Tioga	PA	14,600

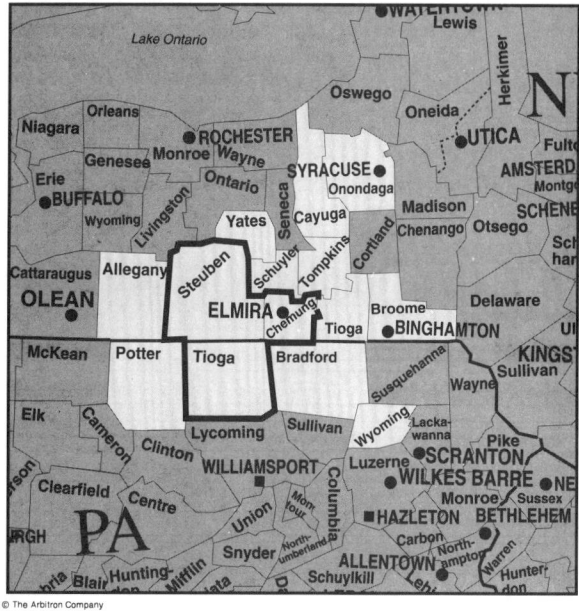

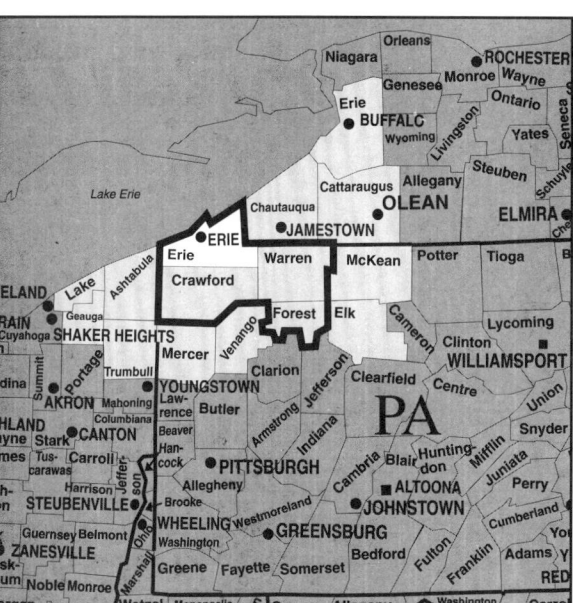

Erie, Pa. (142)

ADI TV Households: 152,600

WICU-TV Erie, Pa., ch. 12, NBC
WJET-TV Erie, Pa., ch. 24, ABC
WSEE-TV Erie, Pa., ch. 35, CBS
***WQLN** Erie, Pa., ch. 54, ETV
WETG Erie, Pa., ch. 66, Fox

ADI Counties	State	TV Households
Crawford	PA	31,700
Erie	PA	102,200
Forest	PA	1,900
Warren	PA	16,800

Eugene, Ore. (116)

ADI TV Households: 197,400

KEZI Eugene, Ore., ch. 9, ABC
KVAL-TV Eugene, Ore., ch. 13, CBS
KPIC Roseburg, Ore., ch. 4, satellite to KVAL-TV
KCBY-TV Coos Bay, Ore., ch. 11, satellite to KVAL-TV
KMTR Eugene, Ore., ch. 16, NBC
KMTZ Coos Bay, Ore., ch. 23, satellite to KMTR
***KEPB-TV** Eugene, Ore., ch. 28, ETV
KEVU Eugene, Ore., ch. 34, IND
KLSR-TV Roseburg, Ore., ch. 36, IND
KMTX-TV Roseburg, Ore., ch. 46, satellite to KMTR

ADI Counties	State	TV Households
Benton	OR	25,700
Coos	OR	23,500
Douglas	OR	35,700
Lane	OR	112,500

Broadcasting & Cable Yearbook 1994
C-145

Arbitron ADI Market Atlas

Eureka, Calif. (187)

ADI TV Households: 56,600

KIEM-TV Eureka, Calif., ch. 3, NBC
KVIQ Eureka, Calif., ch. 6, CBS
*KEET Eureka, Calif., ch. 13, ETV
KAEF Arcata, Calif., ch. 23, Fox
KBVU Eureka, Calif., ch. 29, IND

ADI Counties	State	TV Households
Del Norte	CA	8,500
Humboldt	CA	48,100

Evansville, Ind. (Madisonville, Ky.) (94)

ADI TV Households: 262,500

WTVW Evansville, Ind., ch. 7, ABC
*WNIN Evansville, Ind., ch. 9, ETV
WFIE-TV Evansville, Ind., ch. 14, NBC
WLCN Madisonville, Ky., ch. 19, IND
WEHT Evansville, Ind., ch. 25, CBS
*WKOH Owensboro, Ky., ch. 31, ETV
*WKMA Madisonville, Ky., ch. 35, ETV
WEVV Evansville, Ind., ch. 44, Fox

ADI Counties	State	TV Households
Edwards	IL	2,900
Wabash	IL	4,900
Wayne	IL	6,500
White	IL	6,400
Dubois	IN	13,500
Gibson	IN	12,300
Perry	IN	6,600
Pike	IN	4,800
Posey	IN	9,200
Spencer	IN	7,100
Vanderburgh	IN	66,800
Warrick	IN	16,400
Daviess	KY	33,800
Hancock	KY	2,800
Henderson	KY	16,700
Hopkins	KY	18,100
McLean	KY	3,700
Muhlenberg	KY	11,500
Ohio	KY	7,900
Union	KY	5,500
Webster	KY	5,100

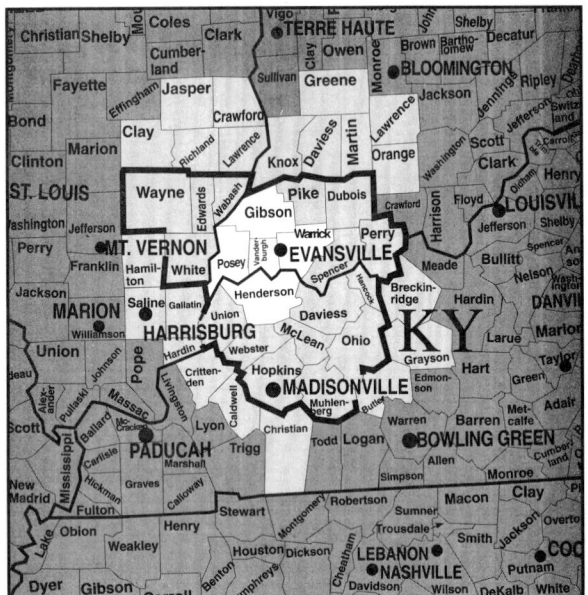

Fargo, N.D. (109)

ADI TV Households: 216,000

*KGFE Grand Forks, N.D., ch. 2, ETV
KXJB-TV Valley City, N.D., ch. 4, CBS
WDAY-TV Fargo, N.D., ch. 6, ABC
KJRR Jamestown, N.D., ch. 7, satellite to KVRR
WDAZ-TV Devils Lake, N.D., ch. 8, satellite to WDAY-TV
KBRR Thief River Falls, Minn., ch. 10, IND
KTHI-TV Fargo, N.D., ch. 11, NBC
KNRR Pembina, N.D., ch. 12, IND
*KFME Fargo, N.D., ch. 13, ETV
KVRR Fargo, N.D., ch. 15, Fox
*KJRE Ellendale, N.D., ch. 19, satellite to *KFME

ADI Counties	State	TV Households
Becker	MN	10,700
Clay	MN	17,700
Clearwater	MN	3,000
Kittson	MN	2,100
Lake of the Woods	MN	1,500
Mahnomen	MN	1,800
Marshall	MN	4,100
Norman	MN	2,900
Otter Tail	MN	19,700
Pennington	MN	5,000
Polk	MN	11,700
Red Lake	MN	1,700
Roseau	MN	5,600
Wilkin	MN	2,800
Barnes	ND	5,000
Benson	ND	2,300
Cass	ND	42,400
Cavalier	ND	2,000
Dickey	ND	2,300
Eddy	ND	1,200
Foster	ND	1,500
Grand Forks	ND	26,600
Griggs	ND	1,300
La Moure	ND	2,000
Nelson	ND	1,800
Pembina	ND	3,200
Ramsey	ND	4,800
Ransom	ND	2,300
Richland	ND	6,500
Sargent	ND	1,700
Steele	ND	1,000
Stutsman	ND	8,300
Towner	ND	1,400
Traill	ND	3,300
Walsh	ND	4,800

Flagstaff, Ariz. (204)

ADI TV Households: 30,600

KNAZ-TV Flagstaff, Ariz., ch. 2, NBC
KZJC Flagstaff, Ariz., ch. 4, IND
KVPY Flagstaff, Ariz., ch. 9, IND
KKTM Flagstaff, Ariz., ch. 13, IND

ADI Counties	State	TV Households
Coconino	AZ	30,600

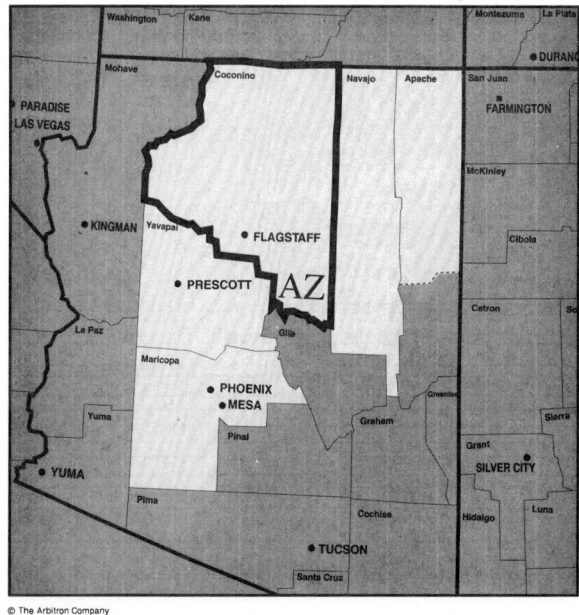

Arbitron ADI Market Atlas

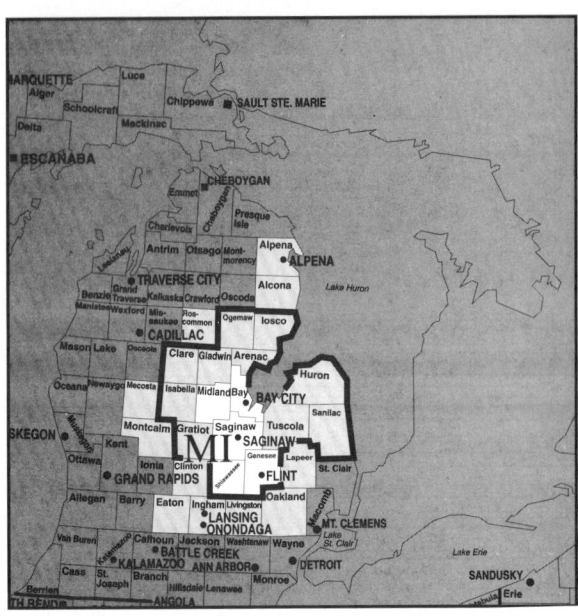

Flint-Saginaw-Bay City, Mich. (60)

ADI TV Households: 457,800

WNEM-TV Bay City, Mich., ch. 5, NBC
WJRT-TV Flint, Mich., ch. 12, ABC
*WCMU-TV Mt. Pleasant, Mich., ch. 14, ETV
*WUCM-TV University Center, Mich., ch. 19, ETV
WEYI-TV Saginaw, Mich., ch. 25, CBS
*WFUM Flint, Mich., ch. 28, ETV
*WUCX-TV Bad Axe, Mich., ch. 35, ETV
WAQP Saginaw, Mich., ch. 49, IND
WSMH Flint, Mich., ch. 66, Fox

ADI Counties	State	TV Households			
Arenac	MI	5,800	Isabella	MI	18,000
Bay	MI	41,800	Midland	MI	28,800
Clare	MI	10,400	Ogemaw	MI	7,600
Genesee	MI	160,700	Saginaw	MI	77,900
Gladwin	MI	8,600	Sanilac	MI	14,800
Gratiot	MI	13,600	Shiawassee	MI	25,200
Huron	MI	13,000	Tuscola	MI	19,600
Iosco	MI	12,000			

Florence-Myrtle Beach, S.C. (136)

ADI TV Households: 158,300

WBTW Florence, S.C., ch. 13, CBS
WPDE-TV Florence, S.C., ch. 15, ABC
WFIL Florence, S.C., ch. 21, IND
*WHMC Conway, S.C., ch. 23, ETV
*WJMP-TV Florence, S.C., ch. 33, ETV
WGSE Myrtle Beach, S.C., ch. 43, IND

ADI Counties	State	TV Households
Darlington	SC	22,600
Dillon	SC	10,000
Florence	SC	41,900
Horry	SC	62,000
Marion	SC	12,000
Marlboro	SC	9,800

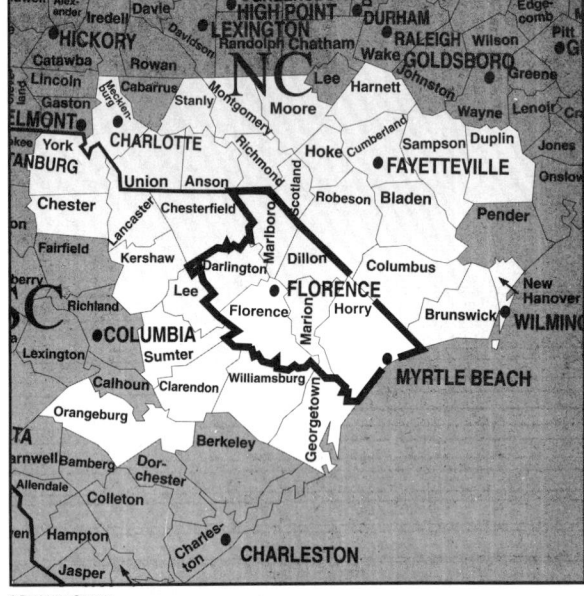

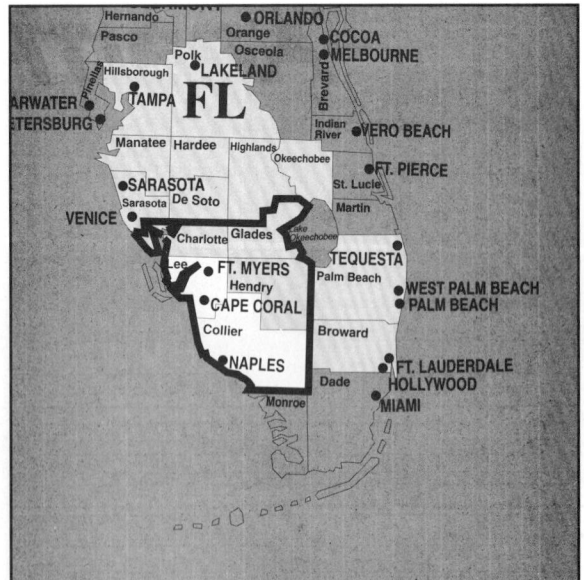

Ft. Myers-Naples, Fla. (87)

ADI TV Households: 290,500

WINK-TV Fort Myers, Fla., ch. 11, CBS
WBBH-TV Fort Myers, Fla., ch. 20, NBC
WEVU Naples, Fla., ch. 26, ABC
*WSFP-TV Fort Myers, Fla., ch. 30, ETV
WFTX Cape Coral, Fla., ch. 36, Fox
WNPL-TV Naples, Fla., ch. 46, IND
WRXY-TV Tice, Fla., ch. 49, IND

ADI Counties	State	TV Households
Charlotte	FL	55,100
Collier	FL	68,800
Glades	FL	2,700
Hendry	FL	9,200
Lee	FL	154,700

Arbitron ADI Market Atlas

Ft. Smith, Ark. (117)

ADI TV Households: 196,700

KFSM-TV Fort Smith, Ark., ch. 5, CBS
***KAFT** Fayetteville, Ark., ch. 13, ETV
KPOM-TV Fort Smith, Ark., ch. 24, NBC
KHBS Fort Smith, Ark., ch. 40, ABC
KHOG-TV Fayetteville, Ark., ch. 29, satellite to KHBS

ADI Counties	State	TV Households
Benton	AR	41,600
Crawford	AR	16,400
Franklin	AR	5,600
Logan	AR	7,500
Madison	AR	4,600
Scott	AR	4,000
Sebastian	AR	41,100
Washington	AR	46,600
LeFlore	OK	16,500
Sequoyah	OK	12,800

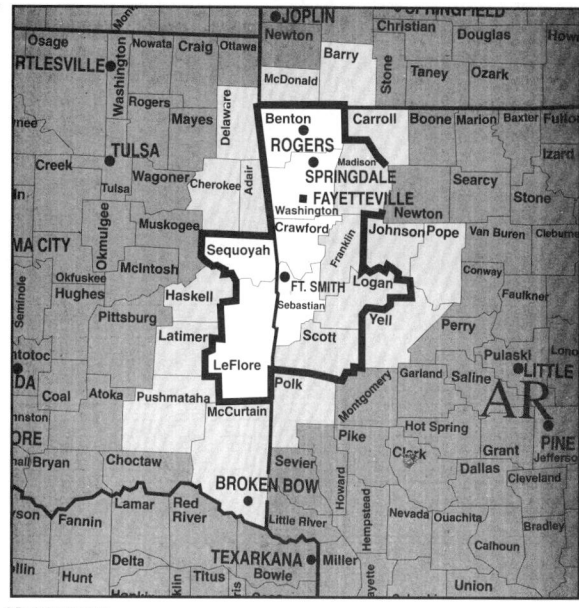

Ft. Wayne (Angola), Ind. (102)

ADI TV Households: 236,900

WANE-TV Fort Wayne, Ind., ch. 15, CBS
WPTA Fort Wayne, Ind., ch. 21, ABC
WKJG-TV Fort Wayne, Ind., ch. 33, NBC
***WFWA** Fort Wayne, Ind., ch. 39, ETV
WFFT-TV Fort Wayne, Ind., ch. 55, Fox
WINM Angola, Ind., ch. 63, IND

ADI Counties	State	TV Households
Adams	IN	10,800
Allen	IN	115,900
De Kalb	IN	13,300
Huntington	IN	13,300
Jay	IN	8,000
Noble	IN	13,700
Steuben	IN	11,000
Wabash	IN	12,300
Wells	IN	9,500
Whitley	IN	10,500
Paulding	OH	7,300
Van Wert	OH	11,300

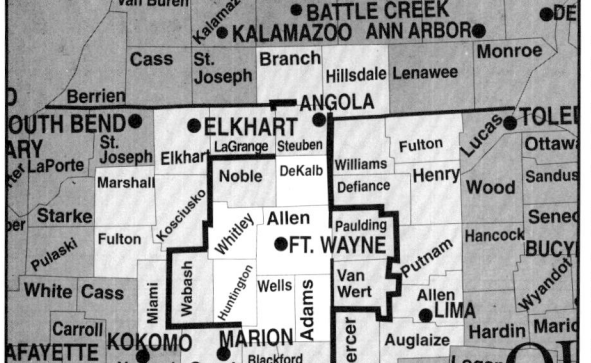

Fresno-Visalia (Hanford & Visalia-Porterville), Calif. (57)

ADI TV Households: 456,500

***KVPT** Fresno, Calif., ch. 18, ETV
KFTV Hanford, Calif., ch. 21, IND
KSEE Fresno, Calif., ch. 24, NBC
KMPH Visalia, Calif., ch. 26, IND
KFSN-TV Fresno, Calif., ch. 30, ABC
KSDI Clovis, Calif., ch. 43, IND
KJEO Fresno, Calif., ch. 47, CBS
***KNXT** Visalia, Calif., ch. 49, ETV
KNSO Merced, Calif., ch. 51, IND
KAIL Fresno, Calif., ch. 53, IND
KMSG-TV Sanger, Calif., ch. 59, IND
KKAK Porterville, Calif., ch. 61, IND

ADI Counties	State	TV Households
Fresno	CA	237,900
Kings	CA	29,700
Madera	CA	30,700
Mariposa	CA	6,000
Merced	CA	58,200
Tulare	CA	103,000

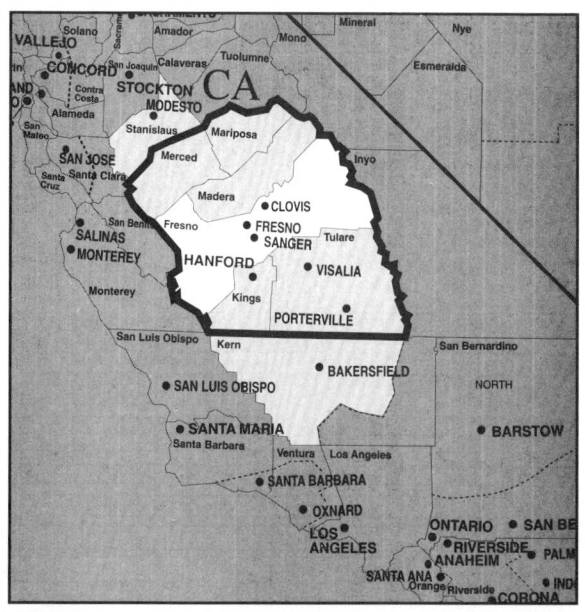

Broadcasting & Cable Yearbook 1994

Arbitron ADI Market Atlas

Gainesville (Ocala), Fla. (166)

ADI TV Households: 92,800

WUFT Gainesville, Fla., ch. 5, ETV
WCJB Gainesville, Fla., ch. 20, ABC
WOGX Ocala, Fla., ch. 51, IND
WGFL High Springs, Fla., ch. 53, IND

ADI Counties	State	TV Households
Alachua	FL	74,800
Dixie	FL	3,900
Gilchrist	FL	3,600
Levy	FL	10,500

Grand Junction-Durango, Colo. (188)

ADI TV Households: 49,700

KREX-TV Grand Junction, Colo., ch. 5, CBS (NBC)
KREZ-TV Durango, Colo., ch. 6, satellite to KREX-TV
KJCT Grand Junction, Colo., ch. 8, ABC
KREY-TV Montrose, Colo., ch. 10, satellite to KREX-TV

ADI Counties	State	TV Households
Mesa	CO	39,100
Montrose	CO	9,800
Ouray	CO	800

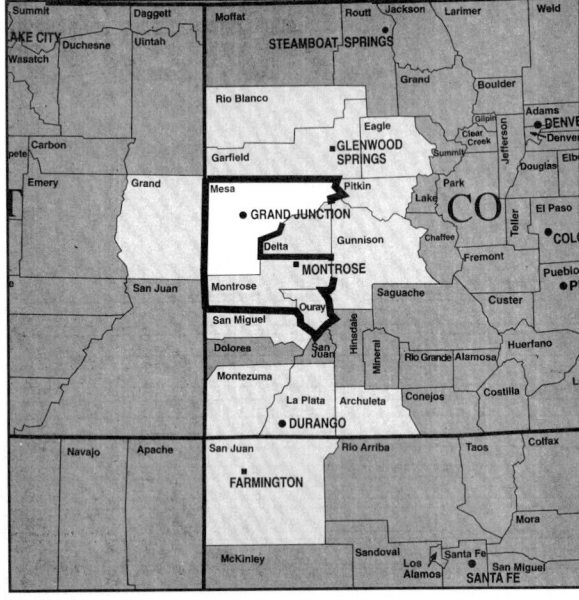

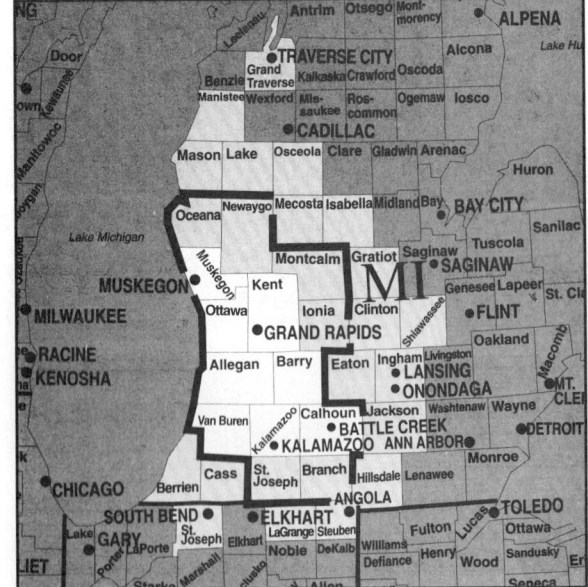

Grand Rapids-Kalamazoo-Battle Creek, Mich. (37)

ADI TV Households: 626,700

WWMT Kalamazoo, Mich., ch. 3, CBS
WOOD-TV Grand Rapids, Mich., ch. 8, NBC
WZZM-TV Grand Rapids, Mich., ch. 13, ABC
WXMI Grand Rapids, Mich., ch. 17, Fox
WGVU-TV Grand Rapids, Mich., ch. 35, ETV
WOTV Battle Creek, Mich., ch. 41, ABC
WJUE Battle Creek, Mich., ch. 43, IND
WGVK Kalamazoo, Mich., ch. 52, ETV

ADI Counties	State	TV Households			
Allegan	MI	33,300	Montcalm	MI	19,300
Barry	MI	18,200	Muskegon	MI	58,800
Branch	MI	14,500	Newaygo	MI	14,600
Calhoun	MI	52,900	Oceana	MI	8,200
Ionia	MI	18,600	Ottawa	MI	67,300
Kalamazoo	MI	84,400	St. Joseph	MI	22,000
Kent	MI	188,300	Van Buren	MI	26,300

Broadcasting & Cable Yearbook 1994
C-150

Great Falls, Mont. (182)

ADI TV Households: 65,800

KRTV Great Falls, Mont., ch. 3, CBS
KFBB-TV Great Falls, Mont., ch. 5, ABC
KTGF Great Falls, Mont., ch. 16, NBC

ADI Counties	State	TV Households
Blaine	MT	2,400
Cascade	MT	32,400
Chouteau	MT	2,000
Fergus	MT	4,700
Glacier	MT	3,700
Hill	MT	6,600
Judith Basin	MT	900
Liberty	MT	800
Meagher	MT	700
Phillips	MT	1,900
Pondera	MT	2,200
Teton	MT	2,300
Toole	MT	2,000
Valley	MT	3,200

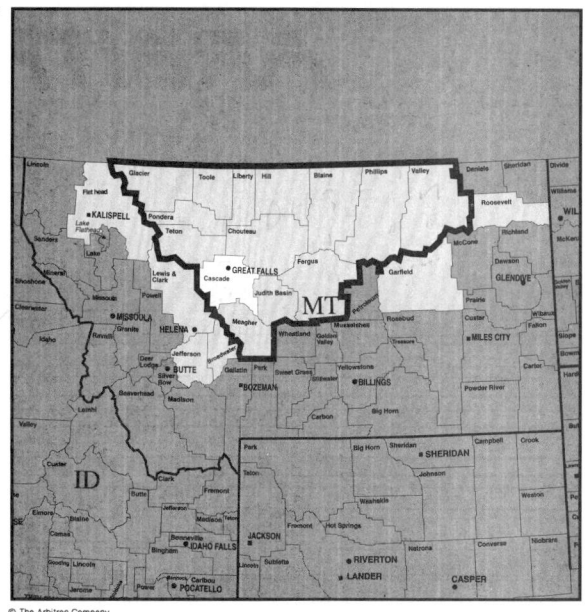

Green Bay-Appleton (Suring), Wis. (72)

ADI TV Households: 366,100

WBAY-TV Green Bay, Wis., ch. 2, CBS
WFRV-TV Green Bay, Wis., ch. 5, ABC
WJMN-TV Escanaba, Mich., ch. 3, satellite to WFRV-TV
WDHS Iron Mountain, Mich., ch. 8, IND
WLUK-TV Green Bay, Wis., ch. 11, NBC
WSCO Suring, Wis., ch. 14, IND
WGBA Green Bay, Wis., ch. 26, IND
WXGZ-TV Appleton, Wis., ch. 32, Fox
***WPNE** Green Bay, Wis.,, ch. 38, ETV
WMMF-TV Fond du Lac, Wis., ch. 68, IND

ADI Counties	State	TV Households			
Menominee	MI	9,700	Marinette	WI	16,000
Schoolcraft	MI	3,200	Menominee	WI	1,100
Brown	WI	75,900	Oconto	WI	11,400
Calumet	WI	12,200	Outagamie	WI	52,700
Door	WI	10,300	Shawano	WI	13,900
Fond du Lac	WI	33,400	Waupaca	WI	17,600
Green Lake	WI	7,400	Waushara	WI	7,900
Kewaunee	WI	6,900	Winnebago	WI	55,800
Manitowoc	WI	30,700			

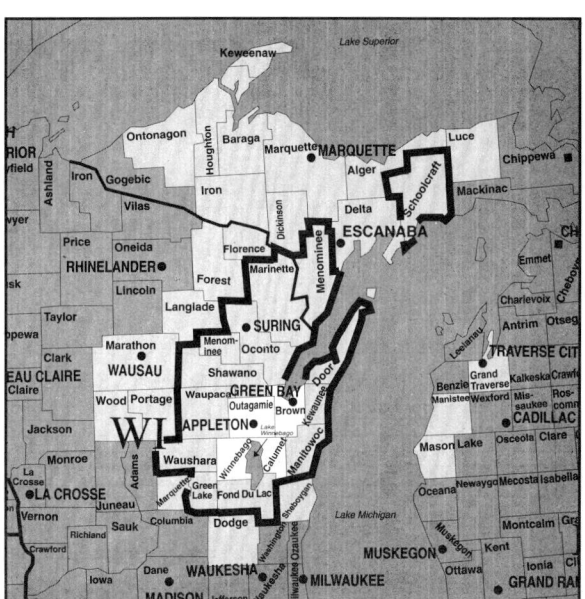

Greensboro-Winston Salem-High Point (Burlington), N.C. (49)

ADI TV Households: 540,900

WFMY-TV Greensboro, N.C., ch. 2, CBS
WGHP-TV High Point, N.C., ch. 8, ABC
WXII Winston-Salem, N.C., ch. 12, NBC
WAAP Burlington, N.C., ch. 16, IND
WEJC Lexington, N.C., ch. 20, IND
***WUNL-TV** Winston-Salem, N.C., ch. 26, ETV
WNRW Winston-Salem, N.C., ch. 45, Fox
WGGT Greensboro, N.C., ch. 48, Fox
WLXI-TV Greensboro, N.C., ch. 61, IND

ADI Counties	State	TV Households			
Alamance	NC	44,400	Randolph	NC	43,400
Alleghany	NC	4,000	Rockingham	NC	34,100
Caswell	NC	7,500	Stokes	NC	14,600
Davidson	NC	50,600	Surry	NC	24,800
Davie	NC	11,400	Wilkes	NC	23,100
Forsyth	NC	111,300	Yadkin	NC	12,700
Guilford	NC	144,100	Patrick	VA	6,800
Montgomery	NC	8,100			

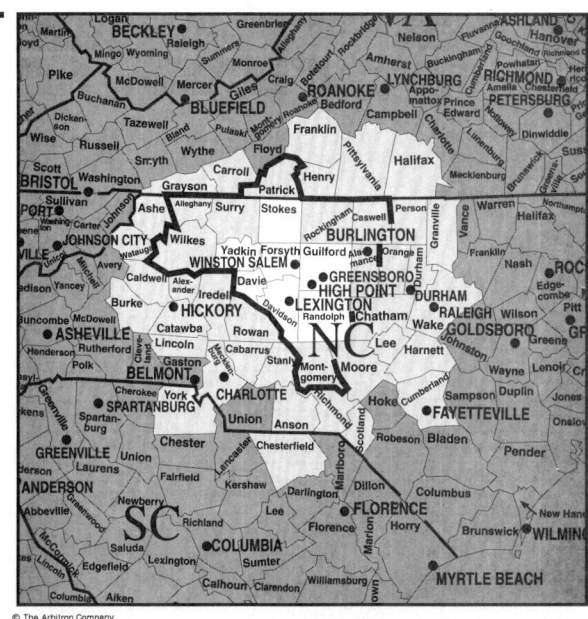

Broadcasting & Cable Yearbook 1994

Arbitron ADI Market Atlas

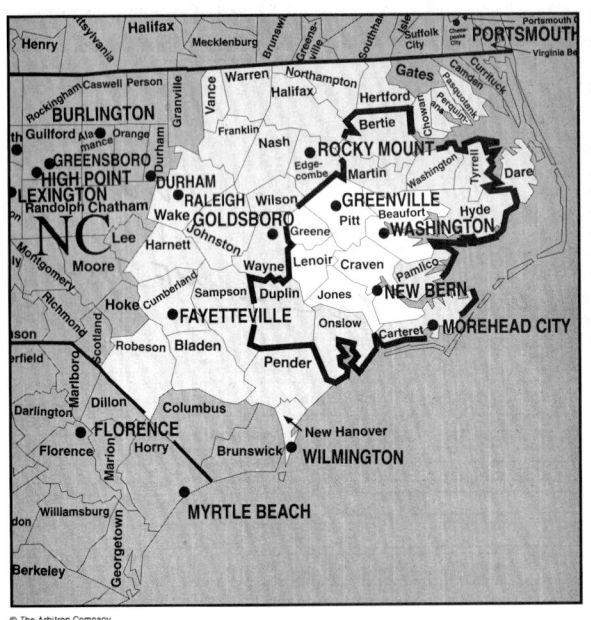

Greenville-New Bern-Washington (Morehead City), N.C. (104)

ADI TV Households: 230,300

*WUND-TV Columbia, N.C., ch. 2, ETV
WITN-TV Washington, N.C., ch. 7, NBC
WFXI Morehead City, N.C., ch. 8, IND
WNCT-TV Greenville, N.C., ch. 9, CBS
WCTI New Bern, N.C., ch. 12, ABC
WYDO Greenville, N.C., ch. 14, IND
*WUNM-TV Jacksonville, N.C., ch. 19, ETV
*WUNK-TV Greenville, N.C., ch. 25, ETV
WGTJ Greenville, N.C., ch. 38, IND

ADI Counties	State	TV Households
Beaufort	NC	16,600
Bertie	NC	7,300
Carteret	NC	22,700
Craven	NC	31,000
Duplin	NC	14,900
Greene	NC	5,500
Hyde	NC	2,000
Jones	NC	3,500
Lenoir	NC	22,100
Martin	NC	9,400
Onslow	NC	40,400
Pamlico	NC	4,700
Pitt	NC	43,500
Tyrrell	NC	1,500
Washington	NC	5,200

Greenville-Spartanburg-Anderson, S.C.-Asheville, N.C. (Toccoa, Ga.) (35)

ADI TV Households: 666,700

WYFF-TV Greenville, S.C., ch. 4, NBC
WSPA-TV Spartanburg, S.C., ch. 7, CBS
WLOS Asheville, N.C., ch. 13, ABC
WGGS-TV Greenville, S.C., ch. 16, IND
WHNS Asheville, N.C., ch. 21, Fox
*WNTV Greenville, S.C., ch. 29, ETV
WNEG-TV Toccoa, Ga., ch. 32, IND
*WUNF-TV Asheville, N.C., ch. 33, ETV
*WNEH Greenwood, S.C., ch. 38, ETV
WAXA Anderson, S.C., ch. 40, IND
*WRET-TV Spartanburg, S.C., ch. 49, ETV
WASV-TV Asheville, N.C., ch. 62, IND

ADI Counties	State	TV Households
Elbert	GA	7,000
Franklin	GA	6,500
Hart	GA	7,600
Stephens	GA	9,200
Buncombe	NC	73,800
Graham	NC	2,900
Haywood	NC	19,600
Henderson	NC	30,400
Jackson	NC	9,900
Macon	NC	10,200
Madison	NC	6,600
McDowell	NC	13,700
Mitchell	NC	5,800
Polk	NC	6,100
Rutherford	NC	22,700
Swain	NC	4,300
Transylvania	NC	10,400
Yancey	NC	6,400
Abbeville	SC	9,000
Anderson	SC	56,600
Cherokee	SC	17,100
Greenville	SC	127,400
Greenwood	SC	23,300
Laurens	SC	21,200
Oconee	SC	23,700
Pickens	SC	35,600
Spartanburg	SC	87,100
Union	SC	11,600

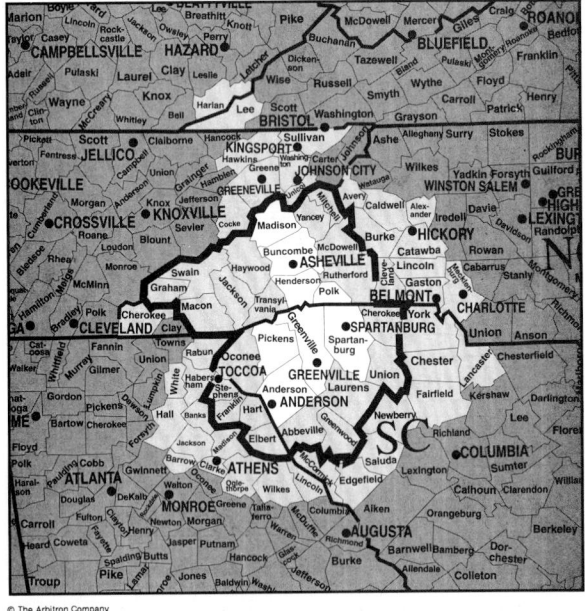

Greenwood-Greenville, Miss. (179)

ADI TV Households: 69,400

WABG-TV Greenwood, Miss., ch. 6, ABC
WXVT Greenville, Miss., ch. 15, CBS
*WMAO-TV Greenwood, Miss., ch. 23, ETV

ADI Counties	State	TV Households
Chicot	AR	5,200
Bolivar	MS	12,600
Carroll	MS	3,300
Leflore	MS	12,600
Sunflower	MS	8,700
Tallahatchie	MS	5,000
Washington	MS	22,000

Broadcasting & Cable Yearbook 1994
C-152

Hagerstown (Martinsburg), Md. (192)

ADI TV Households: 45,400

WHAG-TV Hagerstown, Md., ch. 25, NBC
***WWPB** Hagerstown, Md., ch. 31, ETV
WJAL Hagerstown, Md., ch. 68, IND

ADI Counties	State	TV Households
Washington	MD	45,400

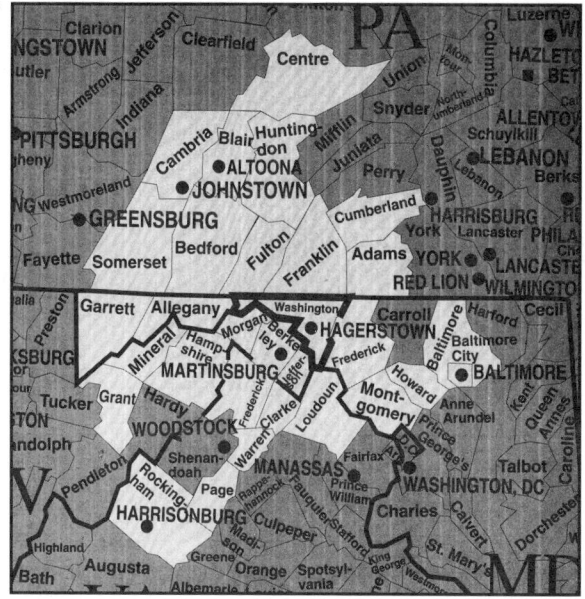

Harrisburg-York-Lancaster-Lebanon, Pa. (44)

ADI TV Households: 573,200

WGAL Lancaster, Pa., ch. 8, NBC
WLYH-TV Lancaster, Pa., ch. 15, CBS
WHP-TV Harrisburg, Pa., ch. 21, CBS
WHTM-TV Harrisburg, Pa., ch. 27, ABC
***WITF-TV** Harrisburg, Pa., ch. 33, ETV
WPMT York, Pa., ch. 43, Fox
WGCB-TV Red Lion, Pa., ch. 49, IND

ADI Counties	State	TV Households
Adams	PA	29,100
Cumberland	PA	75,700
Dauphin	PA	95,400
Juniata	PA	7,700
Lancaster	PA	156,100
Lebanon	PA	43,500
Mifflin	PA	17,500
Perry	PA	15,600
York	PA	132,600

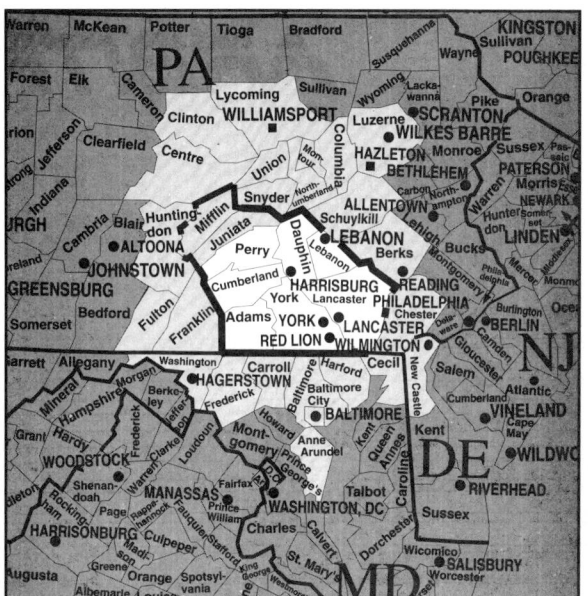

Harrisonburg, Va. (173)

ADI TV Households: 85,700

WHSV-TV Harrisonburg, Va., ch. 3, ABC

ADI Counties	State	TV Households
Augusta	VA	38,000
Page	VA	8,400
Rockingham	VA	32,200
Grant	WV	4,100
Pendleton	WV	3,000

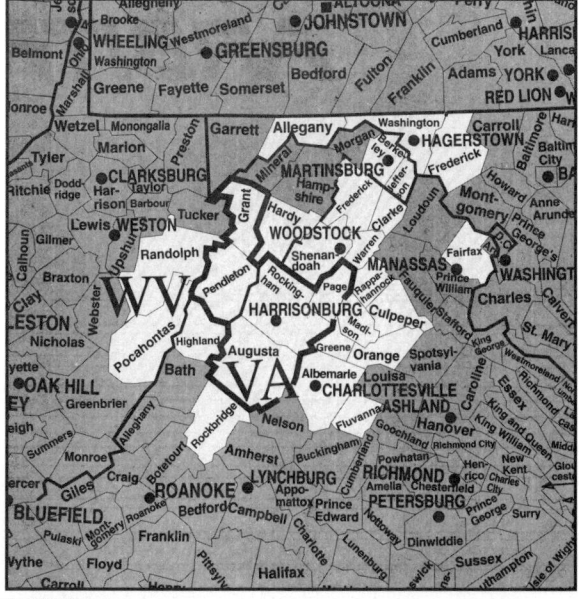

Arbitron ADI Market Atlas

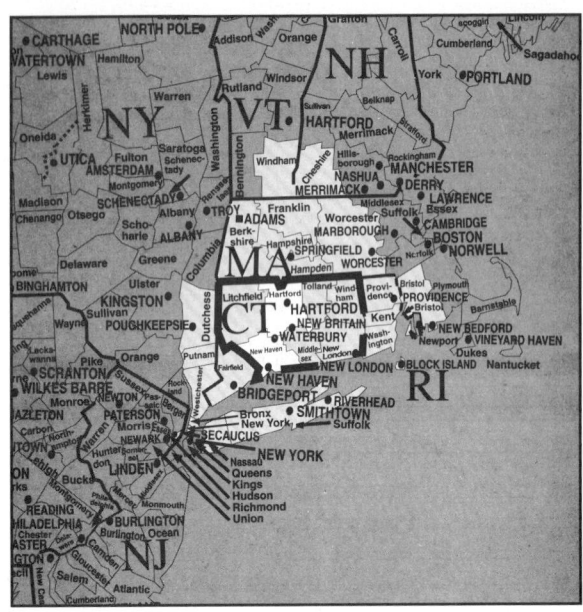

Hartford-New Haven (New London), Conn. (25)

ADI TV Households: 912,400

WFSB Hartford, Conn., ch. 3, CBS
WTNH-TV New Haven, Conn., ch. 8, ABC
WHCT-TV Hartford, Conn., ch. 18, IND
WTXX Waterbury, Conn., ch. 20, IND
***WEDH** Hartford, Conn., ch. 24, ETV
WTWS New London, Conn., ch. 26, IND
WVIT New Britain, Conn., ch. 30, NBC
***WEDN** Norwich, Conn., ch. 53, ETV
WTVU New Haven, Conn., ch. 59, IND
WTIC-TV Hartford, Conn., ch. 61, Fox
***WEDY** New Haven, Conn., ch. 65, ETV

ADI Counties	State	TV Households
Hartford	CT	318,100
Litchfield	CT	66,700
Middlesex	CT	54,800
New Haven	CT	300,000
New London	CT	91,400
Tolland	CT	44,100
Windham	CT	37,300

Helena, Mont. (207)

ADI TV Households: 20,700

KHBB Helena, Mont., ch. 10, IND
KTVH Helena, Mont., ch. 12, NBC

ADI Counties	State	TV Households
Broadwater	MT	1,200
Lewis and Clark	MT	19,500

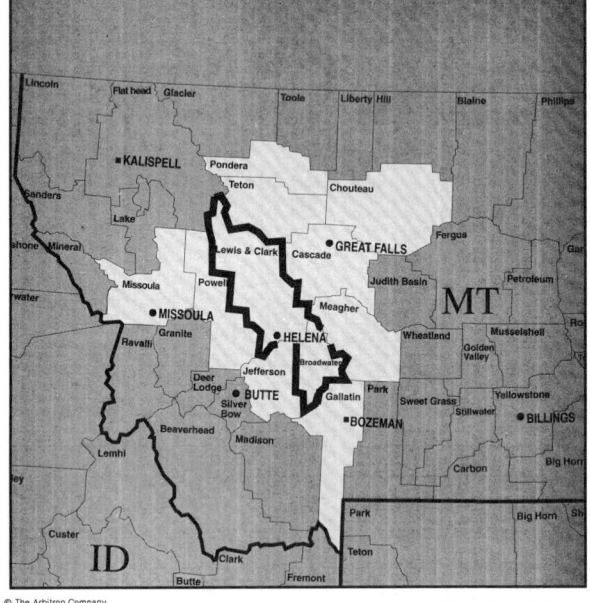

Houston (10)

ADI TV Households: 1,520,900

KPRC-TV Houston, ch. 2, NBC
***KUHT** Houston, ch. 8, ETV
KHOU-TV Houston, ch. 11, CBS
KTRK-TV Houston, ch. 13, ABC
***KETH** Houston, ch. 14, ETV
KTXH Houston, ch. 20, IND
***KLTJ** Galveston, Tex, ch. 22, ETV
KRIV-TV Houston, ch. 26, Fox

KHTV Houston, ch. 39, IND
KXLN-TV Rosenberg, Tex., ch. 45, IND
KTMD Galveston, Tex., ch. 48, IND
KTFH Conroe, Tex., ch. 49, IND
KNWS-TV Katy, Tex., ch. 51, IND
KRTW Baytown, Tex., ch. 57, IND
KZJL Houston, ch. 61, IND
KHSH Alvin, Tex., ch. 67, IND

ADI Counties	State	TV Households			
Austin	TX	7,400	Liberty	TX	18,400
Brazoria	TX	67,900	Matagorda	TX	13,100
Calhoun	TX	6,800	Montgomery	TX	71,000
Chambers	TX	6,800	Polk	TX	12,700
Colorado	TX	6,800	San Jacinto	TX	6,400
Fort Bend	TX	79,700	Walker	TX	15,600
Galveston	TX	85,100	Waller	TX	7,400
Grimes	TX	6,200	Washington	TX	9,500
Harris	TX	1,081,700	Wharton	TX	13,900
Jackson	TX	4,500			

Broadcasting & Cable Yearbook 1994

Huntsville-Decatur-Florence, Ala. (81)

ADI TV Households: 321,600

WOWL-TV Florence, Ala., ch. 15, NBC
WHNT-TV Huntsville, Ala., ch. 19, CBS
***WHIQ** Huntsville, Ala., ch. 25, ETV
WTRT Florence, Ala., ch. 26, IND
WAAY-TV Huntsville, Ala., ch. 31, ABC
***WFIQ** Florence, Ala., ch. 36, ETV
WAFF Huntsville, Ala., ch. 48, NBC
WZDX Huntsville, Ala., ch. 54, IND

ADI Counties	State	TV Households
Colbert	AL	20,300
De Kalb	AL	21,500
Franklin	AL	10,900
Jackson	AL	18,300
Lauderdale	AL	31,800
Lawrence	AL	11,700
Limestone	AL	21,300
Madison	AL	100,300
Marshall	AL	29,200
Morgan	AL	40,100
Lincoln	TN	11,100
Wayne	TN	5,100

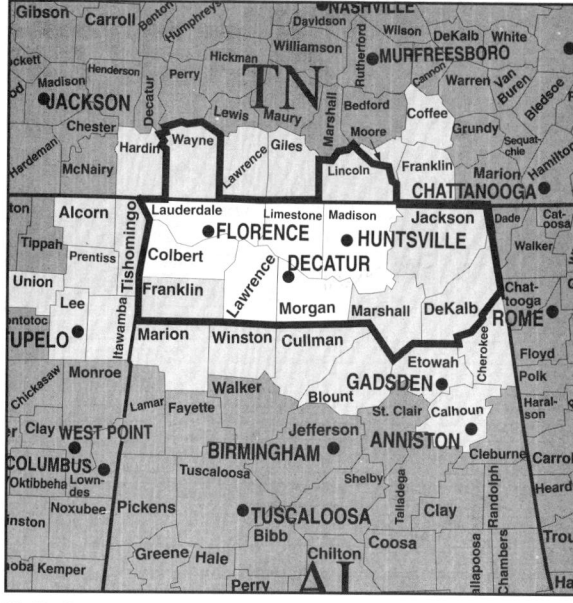

Idaho Falls-Pocatello, Idaho (158)

ADI TV Households: 108,000

KIDK Idaho Falls, Idaho, ch. 3, CBS
KPVI Pocatello, Idaho, ch. 6, ABC
KIFI-TV Idaho Falls, Idaho, ch. 8, NBC
***KISU-TV** Pocatello, Idaho, ch. 10, ETV

ADI Counties	State	TV Households
Bannock	ID	24,000
Bingham	ID	12,400
Bonneville	ID	26,800
Butte	ID	1,000
Caribou	ID	2,200
Cassia	ID	6,600
Clark	ID	300
Custer	ID	1,400
Fremont	ID	3,700
Jefferson	ID	5,300
Lemhi	ID	2,900
Madison	ID	5,900
Minidoka	ID	6,600
Power	ID	2,500
Teton	ID	1,200
Teton	WY	5,200

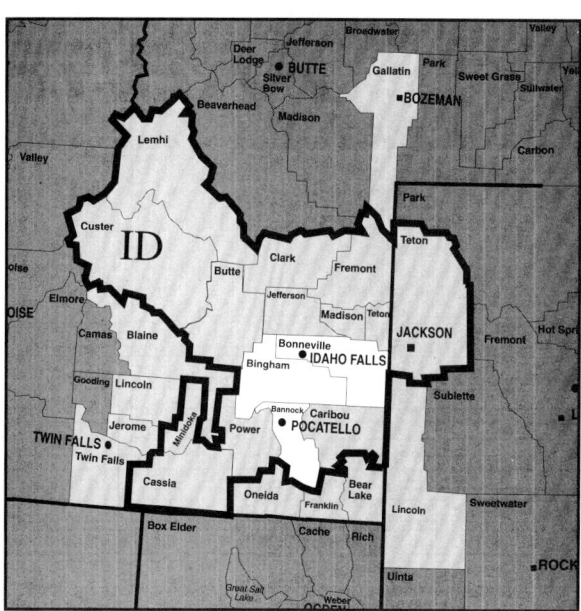

Arbitron ADI Market Atlas

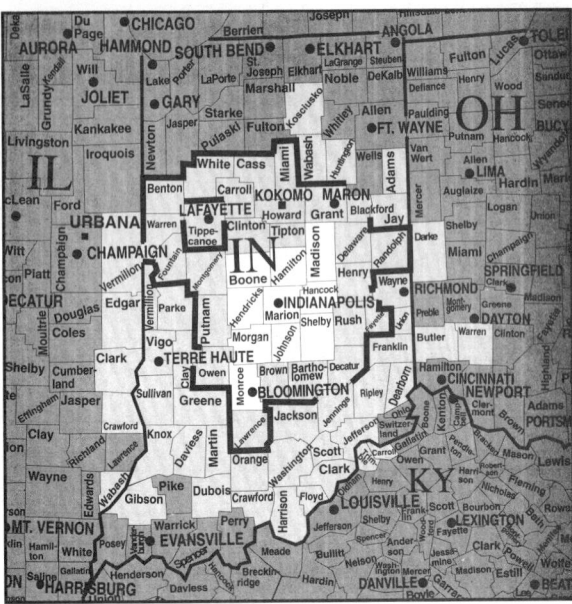

Indianapolis (Marion, Ind.) (26)

ADI TV Households: 905,000

WTTV Bloomington, Ind., ch. 4, IND
WRTV Indianapolis, ch. 6, ABC
WISH-TV Indianapolis, ch. 8, CBS
WTHR Indianapolis, ch. 13, NBC
*WFYI Indianapolis, ch. 20, ETV
WTTK Kokomo, Ind., ch. 29, satellite to WTTV
*WTIU Bloomington, Ind., ch. 30, ETV
WMCC Marion, Ind., ch. 23, IND
WHMB-TV Indianapolis, ch. 40, IND
WCLJ Bloomington, Ind., ch. 42, IND
*WIPB Muncie, Ind., ch. 49, ETV
WXIN Indianapolis, ch. 59, Fox
WIIB Bloomington, Ind., ch. 63, IND
*WTBU Indianapolis, ch. 69, ETV

ADI Counties	State	TV Households			
Bartholomew	IN	24,800	Howard	IN	31,700
Benton	IN	3,400	Johnson	IN	34,400
Blackford	IN	5,200	Lawrence	IN	16,300
Boone	IN	14,000	Madison	IN	49,600
Brown	IN	5,600	Marion	IN	327,800
Carroll	IN	7,300	Miami	IN	13,500
Cass	IN	14,600	Monroe	IN	40,300
Clinton	IN	11,900	Montgomery	IN	13,400
Decatur	IN	8,600	Morgan	IN	20,000
Delaware	IN	45,100	Owen	IN	6,800
Fayette	IN	9,900	Putnam	IN	10,400
Fountain	IN	6,700	Randolph	IN	10,300
Grant	IN	27,200	Rush	IN	6,400
Hamilton	IN	44,400	Shelby	IN	14,900
Hancock	IN	16,800	Tipton	IN	5,900
Hendricks	IN	27,500	Warren	IN	2,900
Henry	IN	18,400	White	IN	9,000

Jackson, Miss. (88)

ADI TV Households: 284,300

WLBT Jackson, Miss., ch. 3, NBC
WJTV Jackson, Miss., ch. 12, CBS
WAPT Jackson, Miss., ch. 16, ABC
*WMAU-TV Bude, Miss., ch. 17, ETV
WQHM McComb, Miss., ch. 28, IND
*WMPN-TV Jackson, Miss., ch. 29, ETV
WDBD Jackson, Miss., ch. 40, Fox
WNTZ Natchez, Miss., ch. 48, IND

ADI Counties	State	TV Households			
Adams	MS	13,000	Leake	MS	6,800
Attala	MS	7,000	Lincoln	MS	11,300
Claiborne	MS	3,100	Madison	MS	21,600
Copiah	MS	9,300	Pike	MS	13,100
Franklin	MS	3,100	Rankin	MS	32,000
Hinds	MS	90,900	Scott	MS	8,600
Holmes	MS	7,000	Sharkey	MS	2,100
Humphreys	MS	3,700	Simpson	MS	8,500
Issaquena	MS	600	Smith	MS	5,300
Jefferson	MS	2,600	Warren	MS	17,000
Jefferson Davis	MS	4,700	Yazoo	MS	8,600
Lawrence	MS	4,400			

Broadcasting & Cable Yearbook 1994
C-156

Arbitron ADI Market Atlas

Jackson, Tenn. (185)

ADI TV Households: 58,900

WBBJ-TV Jackson, Tenn., ch. 7, ABC
*WLJT-TV Lexington, Tenn., ch. 11, ETV
WMTU Jackson, Tenn., ch. 16, satellite to WLMT

ADI Counties	State	TV Households
Carroll	TN	10,900
Hardin	TN	9,100
Henderson	TN	8,500
Madison	TN	30,400

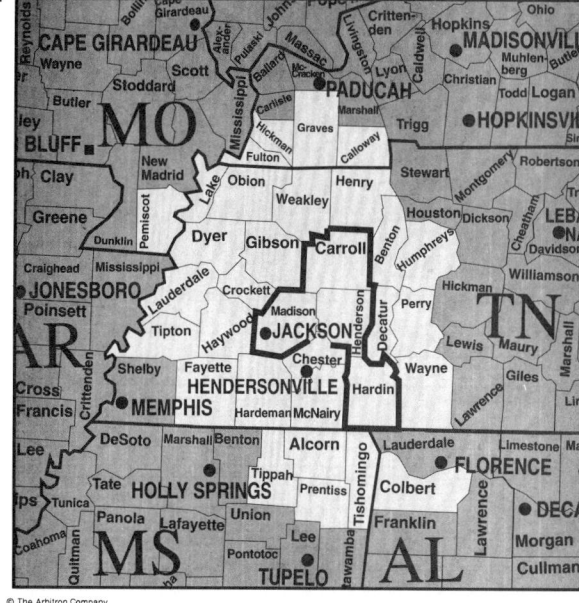

Jacksonville (Brunswick), Fla. (54)

ADI TV Households: 487,300

WJXT Jacksonville, Fla., ch. 4, CBS
*WJCT Jacksonville, Fla., ch. 7, ETV
*WXGA-TV Waycross, Ga., ch. 8, ETV
WTLV Jacksonville, Fla., ch. 12, NBC
WJKS Jacksonville, Fla., ch. 17, ABC
WBSG-TV Brunswick, Ga., ch. 21, IND
WYDP Orange Park, Fla., ch. 25, IND
WAWS Jacksonville, Fla., ch. 30, Fox
WNFT Jacksonville, Fla., ch. 47, IND
WDRU Bunnell, Fla., ch. 58, IND
*WJEB-TV Jacksonville, Fla., ch. 59, ETV
WAJM-TV Palatka, Fla., ch. 63, IND

ADI Counties	State	TV Households
Baker	FL	5,900
Bradford	FL	7,300
Clay	FL	40,300
Columbia	FL	16,500
Duval	FL	274,900
Nassau	FL	17,800
Putnam	FL	26,200
St. Johns	FL	37,300
Union	FL	2,700
Brantley	GA	3,900
Camden	GA	12,000
Charlton	GA	2,900
Clinch	GA	2,200
Glynn	GA	24,700
Ware	GA	12,700

Johnstown-Altoona, Pa. (89)

ADI TV Households: 283,400

*WPSX-TV Clearfield, Pa., ch. 3, ETV
WJAC-TV Johnstown, Pa., ch. 6, NBC
WWCP-TV Johnstown, Pa., ch. 8, Fox
WTAJ-TV Altoona, Pa., ch. 10, CBS
WPTJ Johnstown, Pa., ch. 19, IND
WATM-TV Altoona, Pa., ch. 23, ABC
WKBS-TV Altoona, Pa., ch. 47, IND

ADI Counties	State	TV Households
Bedford	PA	18,000
Blair	PA	50,100
Cambria	PA	60,600
Cameron	PA	2,400
Centre	PA	42,600
Clearfield	PA	29,200
Elk	PA	12,900
Fulton	PA	5,300
Huntingdon	PA	15,500
Jefferson	PA	17,500
Somerset	PA	29,300

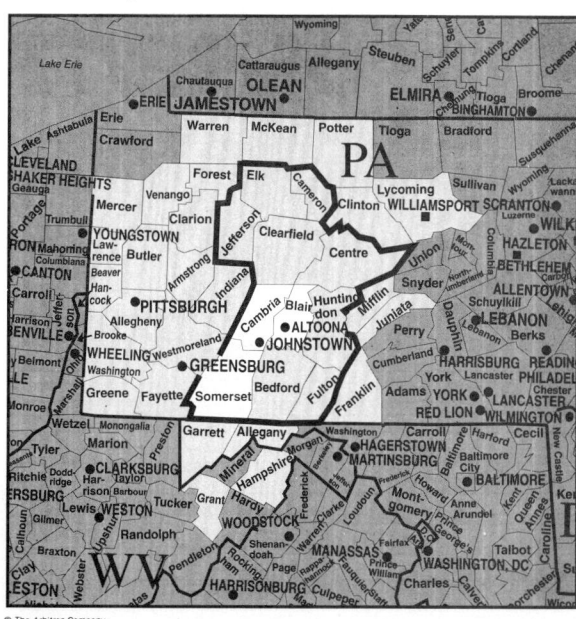

Broadcasting & Cable Yearbook 1994

Arbitron ADI Market Atlas

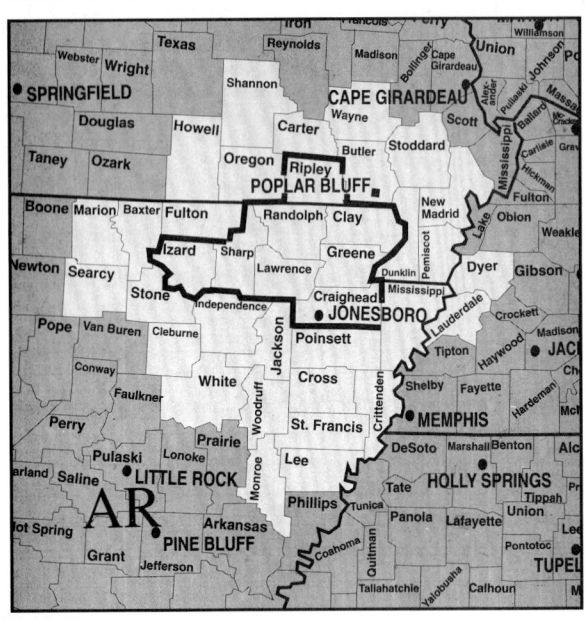

Jonesboro, Ark. (177)

ADI TV Households: 75,700

KAIT-TV Jonesboro, Ark., ch. 8, ABC
*KTEJ Jonesboro, Ark., ch. 19, ETV

ADI Counties	State	TV Households
Clay	AR	7,400
Craighead	AR	27,000
Greene	AR	12,500
Izard	AR	4,800
Lawrence	AR	6,700
Randolph	AR	6,400
Sharp	AR	6,000
Ripley	MO	4,900

Joplin, Mo.-Pittsburg, Kan. (146)

ADI TV Households: 139,100

KOAM-TV Pittsburg, Kan., ch. 7, CBS
KODE-TV Joplin, Mo., ch. 12, ABC
KSNF Joplin, Mo., ch. 16, NBC
KKFT Fort Scott, Kan., ch. 20, IND
*KOZJ Joplin, Mo., ch. 26, ETV
KFAA Rogers, Ark., ch. 51, IND

ADI Counties	State	TV Households
Allen	KS	5,400
Bourbon	KS	5,700
Cherokee	KS	8,300
Crawford	KS	14,500
Labette	KS	8,900
Neosho	KS	6,500
Wilson	KS	3,900
Woodson	KS	1,700
Barton	MO	4,700
Jasper	MO	36,400
McDonald	MO	6,400
Newton	MO	17,300
Vernon	MO	7,400
Ottawa	OK	12,000

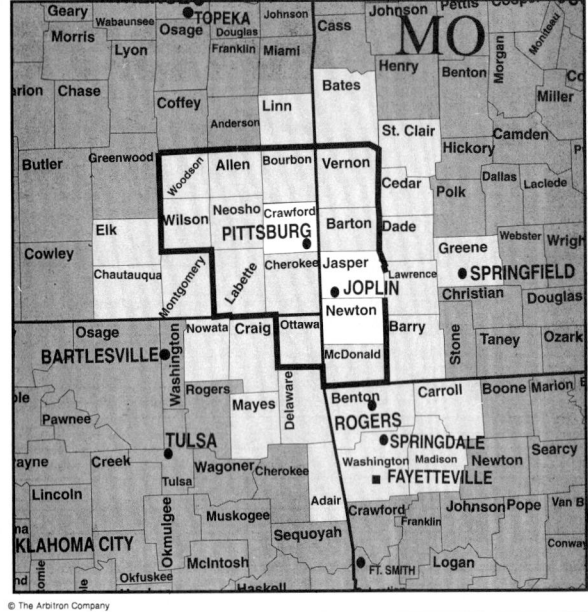

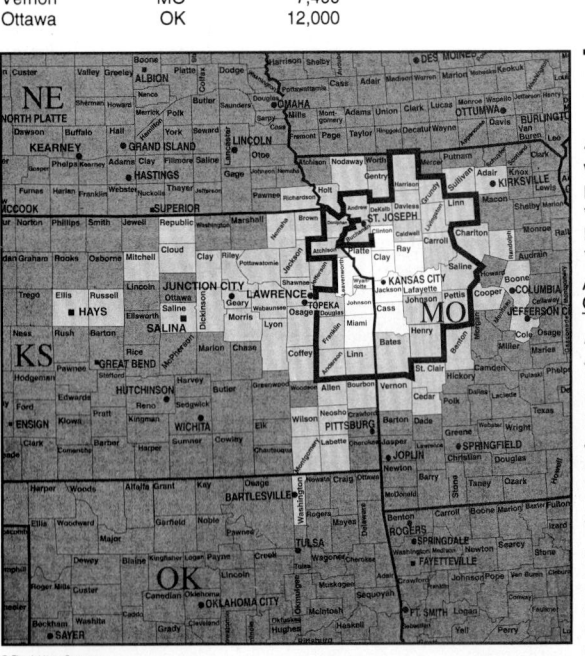

Kansas City, Mo. (Lawrence, Kan.) (29)

ADI TV Households: 780,700

WDAF-TV Kansas City, Mo., ch. 4, NBC
KCTV Kansas City, Mo., ch. 5, CBS
*KMOS-TV Sedalia, Mo., ch. 6, ETV
KMBC-TV Kansas City, Mo., ch. 9, ABC
*KCPT Kansas City, Mo., ch. 19, ETV
KMCI Lawrence, Kan., ch. 38, IND
KSHB-TV Kansas City, Mo., ch. 41, Fox
KYFC Kansas City, Mo., ch. 50, IND
KSMO-TV Kansas City, Mo., ch. 62, IND

ADI Counties	State	TV Households		ADI Counties	State	TV Households
Anderson	KS	3,000		Clinton	MO	6,400
Atchison	KS	6,100		Daviess	MO	3,000
Doniphan	KS	3,100		DeKalb	MO	3,000
Douglas	KS	32,400		Grundy	MO	4,200
Franklin	KS	8,200		Harrison	MO	3,400
Johnson	KS	153,400		Henry	MO	8,200
Leavenworth	KS	22,900		Jackson	MO	252,800
Linn	KS	3,200		Johnson	MO	15,100
Miami	KS	8,800		Lafayette	MO	11,800
Wyandotte	KS	59,900		Linn	MO	5,600
Andrew	MO	5,600		Livingston	MO	5,300
Bates	MO	5,900		Pettis	MO	14,100
Caldwell	MO	3,200		Platte	MO	24,200
Carroll	MO	4,200		Ray	MO	8,100
Cass	MO	24,900		Saline	MO	8,600
Clay	MO	62,100				

Broadcasting & Cable Yearbook 1994

Knoxville (Crossville & Jellico), Tenn. (63)

ADI TV Households: 423,400

*WSJK-TV Sneedville, Tenn., ch. 2, ETV
WATE-TV Knoxville, Tenn., ch. 6, ABC
WKXT-TV Knoxville, Tenn., ch. 8, CBS
WBIR-TV Knoxville, Tenn., ch. 10, NBC
*WKOP-TV Knoxville, Tenn., ch. 15, ETV
WINT-TV Crossville, Tenn., ch. 20, IND
WKCH-TV Knoxville, Tenn., ch. 43, IND
WPMC Jellico, Tenn., ch. 54, IND

ADI Counties	State	TV Households
Bell	KY	11,000
Harlan	KY	12,900
McCreary	KY	5,400
Whitley	KY	12,300
Anderson	TN	28,700
Blount	TN	35,300
Campbell	TN	13,100
Claiborne	TN	10,100
Cocke	TN	11,200
Cumberland	TN	14,600
Fentress	TN	5,700
Grainger	TN	6,600
Hamblen	TN	19,600
Hancock	TN	2,500
Jefferson	TN	13,200
Knox	TN	138,700
Loudon	TN	13,100
Monroe	TN	11,700
Morgan	TN	5,700
Roane	TN	18,900
Scott	TN	6,500
Sevier	TN	21,400
Union	TN	5,200

La Crosse-Eau Claire, Wis. (128)

ADI TV Households: 169,500

WKBT La Crosse, Wis., ch. 8, CBS
WEAU-TV Eau Claire, Wis., ch. 13, NBC
WQOW-TV Eau Claire, Wis., ch. 18, ABC
WXOW-TV La Crosse, Wis., ch. 19, ABC
WLAX La Crosse, Wis., ch. 25, Fox
*WHLA-TV La Crosse, Wis., ch. 31, ETV
WEUX Chippewa Falls, Wis., ch. 48, IND

ADI Counties	State	TV Households
Houston	MN	6,800
Winona	MN	16,800
Buffalo	WI	5,100
Chippewa	WI	19,600
Crawford	WI	6,100
Eau Claire	WI	32,200
Jackson	WI	6,200
La Crosse	WI	37,800
Monroe	WI	13,600
Rusk	WI	5,800
Trempealeau	WI	9,600
Vernon	WI	9,900

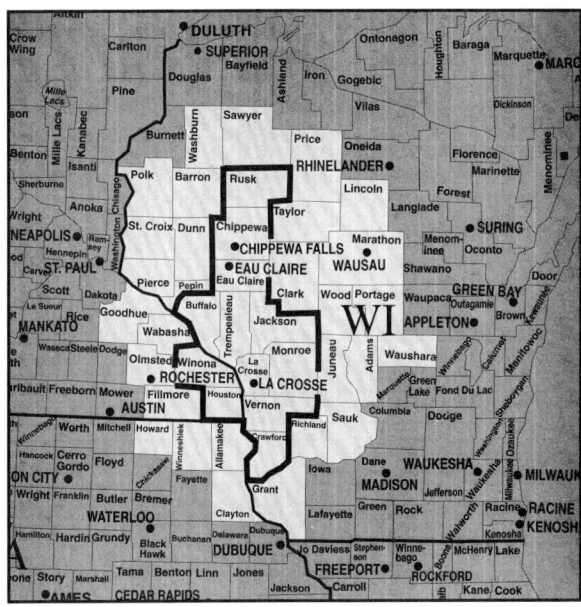

Lafayette, Ind. (191)

ADI TV Households: 46,900

WLFI-TV Lafayette, Ind., ch. 18, CBS

ADI Counties	State	TV Households
Tippecanoe	IN	46,900

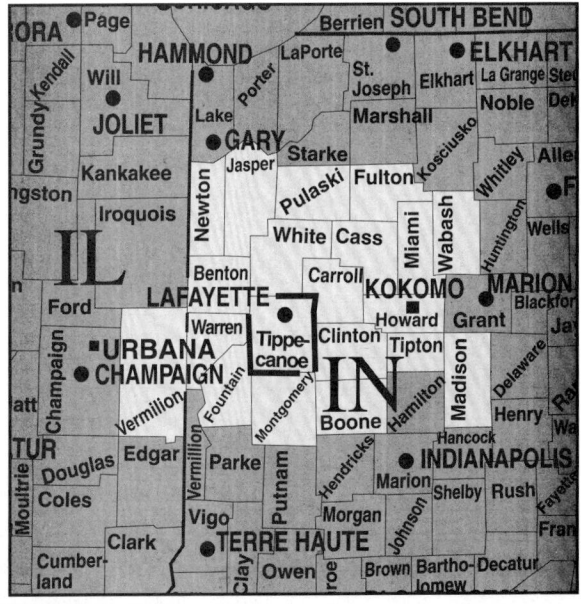

Arbitron ADI Market Atlas

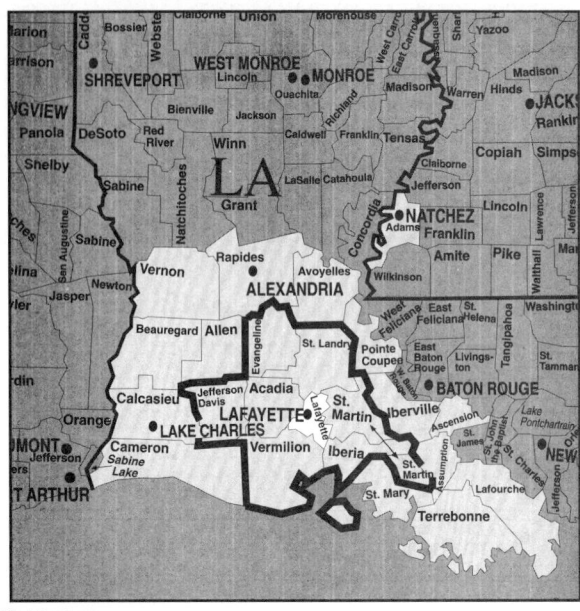

Lafayette, La. (120)

ADI TV Households: 188,400

KATC Lafayette, La., ch. 3, ABC
KLFY-TV Lafayette, La., ch. 10, CBS
KADN Lafayette, La., ch. 15, Fox
*KLPB-TV Lafayette, La., ch. 24, ETV

ADI Counties	State	TV Households
Acadia	LA	19,400
Evangeline	LA	11,500
Iberia	LA	23,200
Jefferson Davis	LA	10,800
Lafayette	LA	63,600
St. Landry	LA	27,400
St. Martin	LA	14,800
Vermilion	LA	17,700

Lake Charles, La. (174)

ADI TV Households: 82,200

KPLC-TV Lake Charles, La., ch. 7, NBC
*KLTL-TV Lake Charles, La., ch. 18, ETV
KVHP Lake Charles, La., ch. 29, IND

ADI Counties	State	TV Households
Allen	LA	6,700
Beauregard	LA	10,700
Calcasieu	LA	61,700
Cameron	LA	3,100

Lansing (Ann Arbor), Mich. (105)

ADI TV Households: 230,200

WLNS-TV Lansing, Mich., ch. 6, CBS
WILX-TV Onondaga, Mich., ch. 10, NBC
WHTV Jackson, Mich., ch. 18, IND
*WKAR-TV East Lansing, Mich., ch. 23, ETV
WBSX Ann Arbor, Mich., ch. 31, IND
WSYM-TV Lansing, Mich., ch. 47, Fox
WLAJ Lansing, Mich., ch. 53, ABC

ADI Counties	State	TV Households
Clinton	MI	21,100
Eaton	MI	35,400
Hillsdale	MI	16,000
Ingham	MI	103,100
Jackson	MI	54,600

Broadcasting & Cable Yearbook 1994
C-160

Arbitron ADI Market Atlas

Laredo, Tex. (198)

ADI TV Households: 40,300

KGNS-TV Laredo, Tex., ch. 8, NBC
KVTV Laredo, Tex., ch. 13, CBS
KLDO-TV Laredo, Tex., ch. 27, IND

ADI Counties	State	TV Households
Webb	TX	37,200
Zapata	TX	3,100

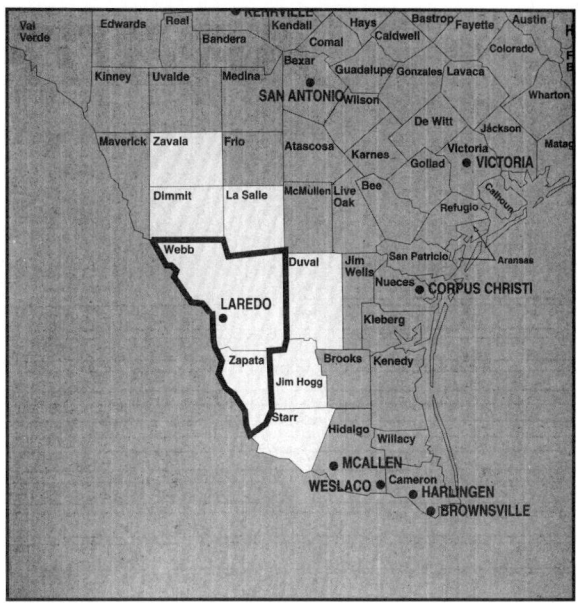

Las Vegas (74)

ADI TV Households: 343,600

KVBC Las Vegas, ch. 3, NBC
KVVU-TV Henderson, Nev., ch. 5, Fox
KLAS-TV Las Vegas, ch. 8, CBS
***KLVX** Las Vegas, ch. 10, ETV
KTNV Las Vegas, ch. 13, ABC
KRLR Las Vegas, ch. 21, IND
KFBT Las Vegas, ch. 33, IND
KBLR Paradise, Nev., ch. 39, IND

ADI Counties	State	TV Households
Clark	NV	337,600
Lincoln	NV	1,200
Nye South	NV	4,800

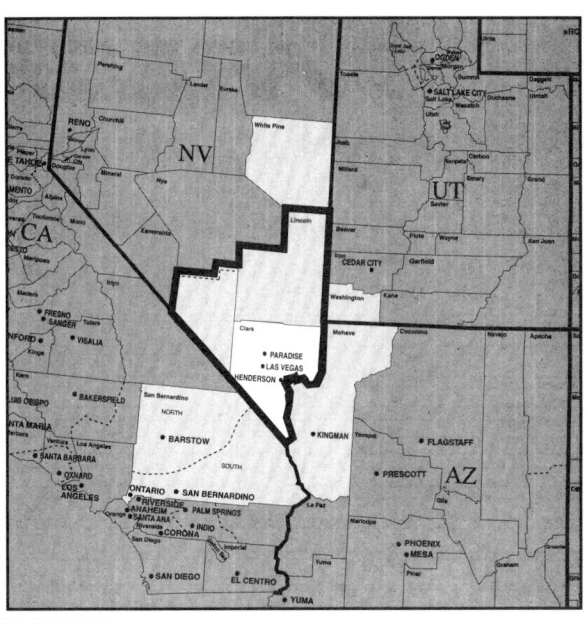

Laurel-Hattiesburg, Miss. (167)

ADI TV Households: 91,300

WDAM-TV Laurel, Miss., ch. 7, NBC
WHLT Hattiesburg, Miss., ch. 22, CBS

ADI Counties	State	TV Households
Covington	MS	5,800
Forrest	MS	25,700
Jasper	MS	5,900
Jones	MS	22,700
Lamar	MS	11,200
Marion	MS	9,000
Perry	MS	3,900
Wayne	MS	7,100

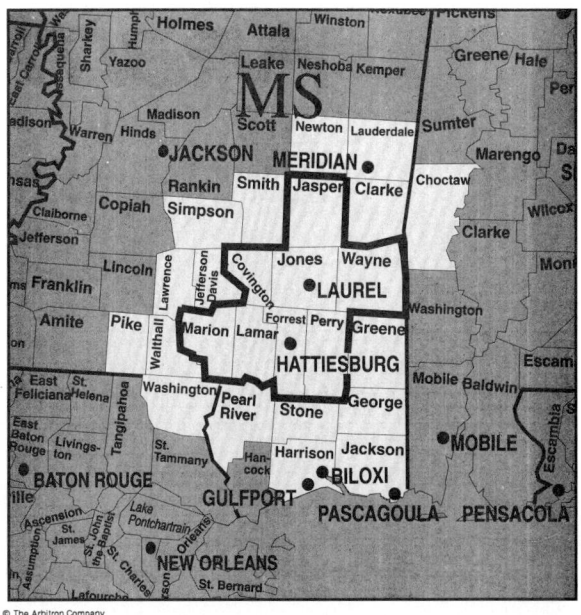

Broadcasting & Cable Yearbook 1994

Arbitron ADI Market Atlas

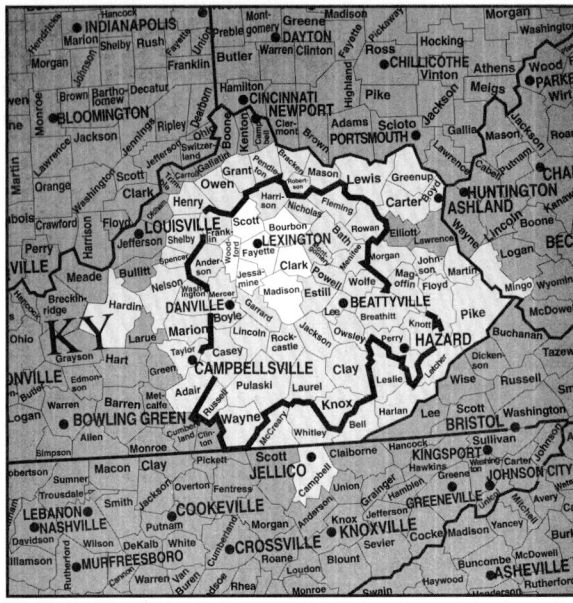

Lexington (Beattyville, Danville & Hazard), Ky. (70)

ADI TV Households: 371,300

WLEX-TV Lexington, Ky., ch. 18, NBC
WKYT-TV Lexington, Ky., ch. 27, CBS
*WKSO-TV Somerset, Ky., ch. 29, ETV
*WKHA Hazard, Ky., ch. 35, ETV
WTVQ-TV Lexington, Ky., ch. 36, ABC
*WKMR Morehead, Ky., ch. 38, ETV
*WKLE Lexington, Ky., ch. 46, ETV
WDKY-TV Danville, Ky., ch. 56, Fox
WYMT-TV Hazard, Ky., ch. 57, CBS
WLJC-TV Beattyville, Ky., ch. 65, IND
New TV Morehead, Ky., ch. 67, IND

ADI Counties	State	TV Households
Anderson	KY	6,000
Bath	KY	3,700
Bourbon	KY	7,300
Boyle	KY	9,400
Breathitt	KY	5,100
Casey	KY	5,400
Clark	KY	11,200
Clay	KY	7,400
Estill	KY	5,500
Fayette	KY	95,700
Fleming	KY	4,600
Franklin	KY	17,900
Garrard	KY	4,700
Harrison	KY	6,400
Jackson	KY	4,400
Jessamine	KY	11,500
Knott	KY	6,300
Knox	KY	10,800
Laurel	KY	16,500
Lee	KY	2,600
Lincoln	KY	7,700
Madison	KY	21,100
Menifee	KY	1,800
Mercer	KY	7,400
Montgomery	KY	7,200
Nicholas	KY	2,600
Owsley	KY	1,800
Perry	KY	10,600
Powell	KY	4,100
Pulaski	KY	19,700
Rockcastle	KY	5,700
Rowan	KY	7,000
Russell	KY	6,200
Scott	KY	9,100
Wayne	KY	6,700
Wolfe	KY	2,600
Woodford	KY	7,600

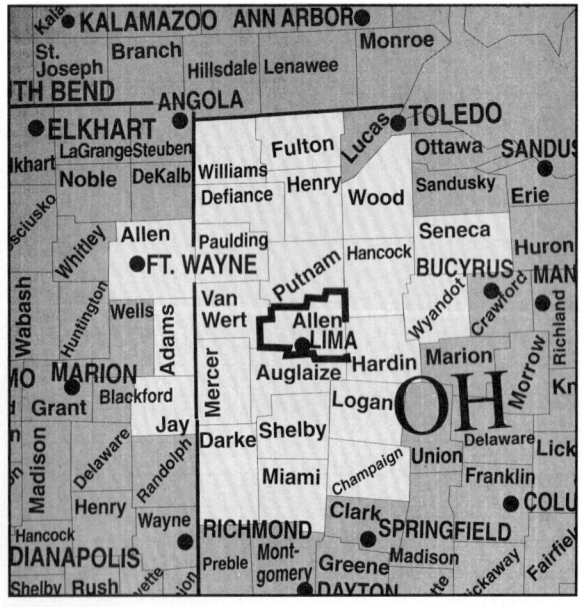

Lima, Ohio (199)

ADI TV Households: 38,800

WLIO Lima, Ohio, ch. 35, NBC (ABC)
WTLW Lima, Ohio, ch. 44, IND

ADI Counties	State	TV Households
Allen	OH	38,800

Broadcasting & Cable Yearbook 1994
C-162

Arbitron ADI Market Atlas

Lincoln-Hastings-Kearney, Neb. (99)

ADI TV Households: 245,400

*KLNE-TV Lexington, Neb., ch. 3, ETV
KHAS-TV Hastings, Neb., ch. 5, NBC
KSNB-TV Superior, Neb., ch. 4, satellite to KHGI-TV
KWNB-TV Hayes Center, Neb., ch. 6, satellite to KHGI-TV
*KMNE-TV Bassett, Neb., ch. 7, ETV
KCAN Albion, Neb., ch. 8, IND
KOLN Lincoln, Neb., ch. 10, CBS
KGIN Grand Island, Neb., ch. 11, satellite to KOLN
*KUON-TV Lincoln, Neb., ch. 12, ETV
KHGI-TV Kearney, Neb., ch. 13, ABC
KTVG Grand Island, Neb., ch. 17, Fox
*KHNE-TV Hastings, Neb., ch. 29, ETV
KGNQ Lincoln, Neb., ch. 51, IND

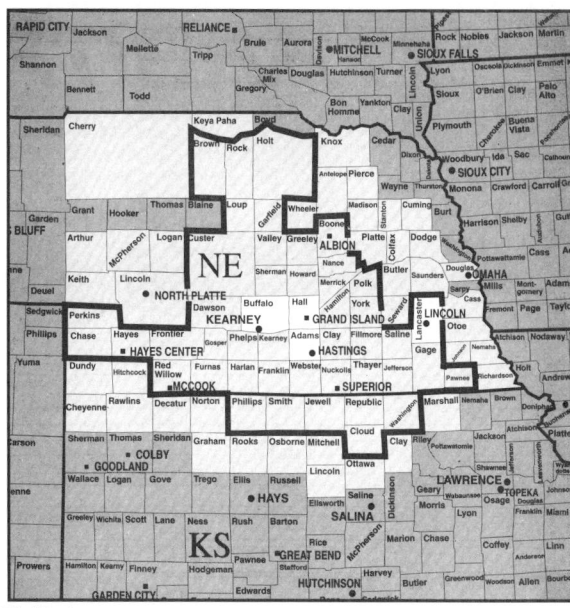

ADI Counties	State	TV Households
Cloud	KS	4,200
Jewell	KS	1,600
Phillips	KS	2,600
Republic	KS	2,600
Smith	KS	2,000
Washington	KS	2,700
Adams	NE	11,500
Boone	NE	2,500
Brown	NE	1,500
Buffalo	NE	14,400
Chase	NE	1,700
Clay	NE	2,700
Custer	NE	4,800
Dawson	NE	8,100
Fillmore	NE	2,800
Franklin	NE	1,600
Frontier	NE	1,200
Furnas	NE	2,500
Gage	NE	8,900
Garfield	NE	800
Gosper	NE	800
Greeley	NE	1,100
Hall	NE	19,000
Hamilton	NE	3,200
Harlan	NE	1,600
Hayes	NE	500
Holt	NE	4,600
Howard	NE	2,400
Jefferson	NE	3,600
Kearney	NE	2,500
Lancaster	NE	86,100
Loup	NE	300
Merrick	NE	3,000
Nance	NE	1,600
Nuckolls	NE	2,300
Pawnee	NE	1,400
Perkins	NE	1,300
Phelps	NE	3,800
Polk	NE	2,200
Red Willow	NE	4,600
Rock	NE	800
Saline	NE	4,600
Sherman	NE	1,400
Thayer	NE	2,700
Valley	NE	2,100
Webster	NE	1,700
York	NE	5,500

Little Rock, Ark. (56)

ADI TV Households: 466,000

*KETS Little Rock, Ark., ch. 2, ETV
KARK-TV Little Rock, Ark., ch. 4, NBC
*KEMV Mountain View, Ark., ch. 6, ETV
KATV Little Rock, Ark., ch. 7, ABC
*KETG Arkadelphia, Ark., ch. 9, ETV
KTHV Little Rock, Ark., ch. 11, CBS
KLRT Little Rock, Ark., ch. 16, Fox
*KLEP Newark, Ark., ch. 17, ETV
KVTN Pine Bluff, Ark., ch. 25, IND
KRZB-TV Hot Springs, Ark., ch. 26, IND
KASN Pine Bluff, Ark., ch. 38, IND
KVUT Little Rock, Ark., ch. 42, IND

ADI Counties	State	TV Households
Arkansas	AR	8,200
Bradley	AR	4,400
Calhoun	AR	2,200
Clark	AR	7,600
Cleburne	AR	8,400
Cleveland	AR	2,800
Conway	AR	7,300
Dallas	AR	3,500
Desha	AR	5,700
Drew	AR	6,200
Faulkner	AR	23,400
Garland	AR	31,900
Grant	AR	5,400
Hot Spring	AR	10,100
Independence	AR	11,900
Jackson	AR	7,300
Jefferson	AR	29,700
Johnson	AR	7,300
Lincoln	AR	3,700
Lonoke	AR	14,700
Monroe	AR	4,000
Montgomery	AR	3,000
Nevada	AR	3,700
Ouachita	AR	11,200
Perry	AR	3,100
Pike	AR	3,800
Polk	AR	6,900
Pope	AR	18,200
Prairie	AR	3,600
Pulaski	AR	140,600
Saline	AR	24,800
Stone	AR	4,100
Van Buren	AR	5,900
White	AR	20,800
Woodruff	AR	3,400
Yell	AR	7,200

Broadcasting & Cable Yearbook 1994

Arbitron ADI Market Atlas

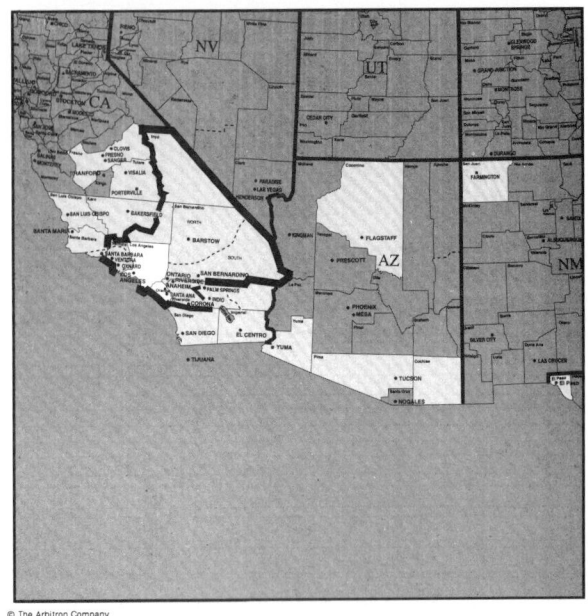

Los Angeles (Barstow, Corona & San Bernardino-Ontario), Calif. (2)

ADI TV Households: 4,978,800

KCBS-TV Los Angeles, ch. 2, CBS
KNBC-TV Los Angeles, ch. 4, NBC
KTLA Los Angeles, ch. 5, IND
KABC-TV Los Angeles, ch. 7, ABC
KCAL Norwalk, Calif., ch. 9, IND
KTTV Los Angeles, ch. 11, Fox
KCOP Los Angeles, ch. 13, IND
KSCI San Bernardino, Calif., ch. 18, IND
KWHY-TV Los Angeles, ch. 22, IND
***KVCR-TV** San Bernardino, Calif., ch. 24, ETV
***KCET** Los Angeles, ch. 28, ETV
KZKI San Bernardino, Calif., ch. 30, IND
KVMD Twentynine Palms, Calif., ch. 31, IND
KMEX-TV Los Angeles, ch. 34, IND
KTBN-TV Santa Ana, Calif., ch. 40, IND
KRPA Rancho Palos Verdes, Calif., ch. 44, IND
KHSC Ontario, Calif., ch. 46, IND
***KOCE-TV** Huntington Beach, Calif., ch. 50, ETV
KVEA Corona, Calif., ch. 52, IND
KDOC-TV Anaheim, Calif., ch. 56, IND
KSTV-TV Ventura, Calif., ch. 57, IND
***KLCS** Los Angeles, ch. 58, ETV
KBBL Big Bear Lake, Calif., ch. 59, IND
KRCA Riverside, Calif., ch. 62, IND
KHIZ Barstow, Calif., ch. 64, IND
***KEEF-TV** Los Angeles, ch. 68, ETV

ADI Counties	State	TV Households
Inyo	CA	7,200
Kern East	CA	30,000
Los Angeles	CA	3,003,400
Orange	CA	857,000
Riverside West	CA	347,200
San Bernardino N	CA	97,500
San Bernardino S	CA	416,800
Ventura East	CA	87,400
Ventura West	CA	132,300

Louisville, Ky. (47)

ADI TV Households: 545,200

WAVE Louisville, Ky., ch. 3, NBC
WHAS-TV Louisville, Ky., ch. 11, ABC
***WKPC-TV** Louisville, Ky., ch. 15, ETV
WBNA Louisville, Ky., ch. 21, IND
***WKZT-TV** Elizabethtown, Ky., ch. 23, ETV
WLKY-TV Louisville, Ky., ch. 32, CBS
WDRB-TV Louisville, Ky., ch. 41, Fox
WFTE Salem, Ind., ch. 58, IND
***WKMJ** Louisville, Ky., ch. 68, ETV

ADI Counties	State	TV Households
Clark	IN	33,500
Crawford	IN	3,600
Floyd	IN	25,400
Harrison	IN	11,000
Jackson	IN	14,400
Jefferson	IN	11,100
Jennings	IN	8,400
Orange	IN	6,800
Scott	IN	7,800
Washington	IN	8,800
Breckinridge	KY	6,400
Bullitt	KY	17,100
Carroll	KY	3,500
Grayson	KY	8,300
Green	KY	4,100
Hardin	KY	31,900
Henry	KY	5,100
Jefferson	KY	268,900
Larue	KY	4,800
Marion	KY	5,600
Meade	KY	9,000
Nelson	KY	11,300
Oldham	KY	11,900
Shelby	KY	9,500
Spencer	KY	2,500
Taylor	KY	8,500
Trimble	KY	2,300
Washington	KY	3,700

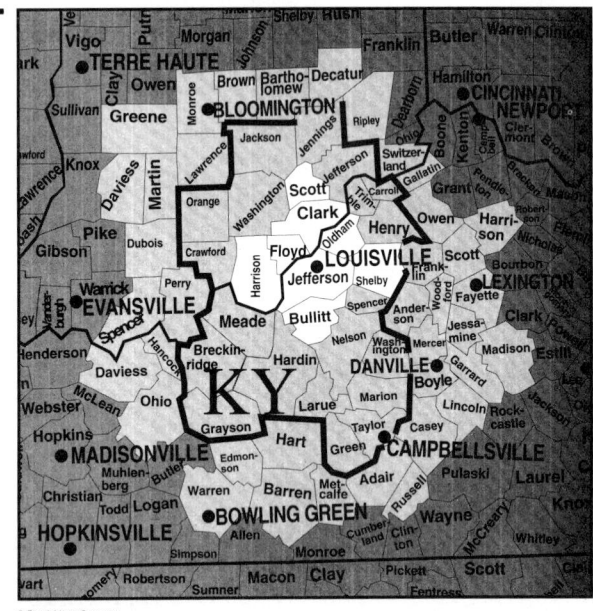

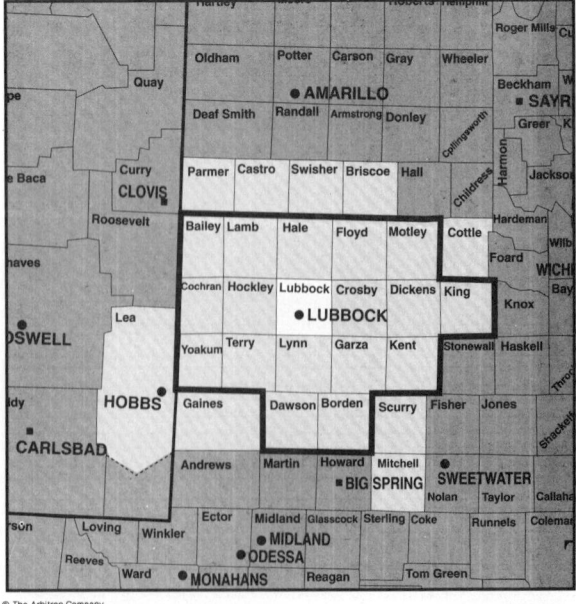

Lubbock, Tex. (149)

ADI TV Households: 136,100

***KENW** Portales, N.M., ch. 3, ETV
***KTXT-TV** Lubbock, Tex., ch. 5, ETV
KCBD-TV Lubbock, Tex., ch. 11, NBC
KVIH-TV Clovis, N.M., ch. 12, satellite to KVII-TV
KLBK-TV Lubbock, Tex., ch. 13, CBS
KAMC Lubbock, Tex., ch. 28, ABC
KJTV Lubbock, Tex., ch. 34, Fox

ADI Counties	State	TV Households
Bailey	TX	2,400
Borden	TX	300
Cochran	TX	1,300
Crosby	TX	2,500
Dawson	TX	4,700
Dickens	TX	1,000
Floyd	TX	2,900
Garza	TX	1,800
Hale	TX	11,900
Hockley	TX	7,900
Kent	TX	400
King	TX	100
Lamb	TX	5,300
Lubbock	TX	83,600
Lynn	TX	2,300
Motley	TX	600
Terry	TX	4,300
Yoakum	TX	2,800

Macon, Ga. (119)

ADI TV Households: 189,600

WMAZ-TV Macon, Ga., ch. 13, CBS
WGXA Macon, Ga., ch. 24, ABC
***WDCO-TV** Cochran, Ga., ch. 29, ETV
WMGT Macon, Ga., ch. 41, NBC
WPGA-TV Perry, Ga., ch. 58, IND
WGNM Macon, Ga., ch. 64, IND

ADI Counties	TV State	Households
Baldwin	GA	12,200
Bibb	GA	57,500
Bleckley	GA	3,700
Crawford	GA	3,200
Dodge	GA	6,500
Dooly	GA	3,300
Hancock	GA	2,900
Houston	GA	34,500
Johnson	GA	3,000
Jones	GA	7,500
Laurens	GA	14,700
Monroe	GA	6,100
Peach	GA	7,200
Pulaski	GA	3,000
Taylor	GA	2,800
Telfair	GA	3,900
Twiggs	GA	3,200
Washington	GA	6,600
Wheeler	GA	1,800
Wilcox	GA	2,500

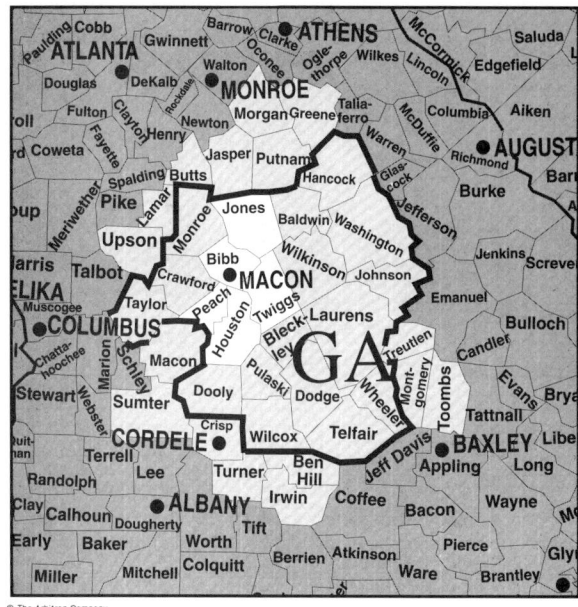

Madison, Wis. (90)

ADI TV Households: 281,300

WISC-TV Madison, Wis., ch. 3, CBS
WMTV Madison, Wis., ch. 15, NBC
***WHA-TV** Madison, Wis., ch. 21, ETV
WKOW-TV Madison, Wis., ch. 27, ABC
WMSN-TV Madison, Wis., ch. 47, Fox
WJNW Janesville, Wis., ch. 57, IND

ADI Counties	State	TV Households
Columbia	WI	17,700
Dane	WI	147,200
Green	WI	11,900
Iowa	WI	7,500
Juneau	WI	8,400
Lafayette	WI	5,700
Marquette	WI	5,100
Richland	WI	6,500
Rock	WI	53,200
Sauk	WI	18,100

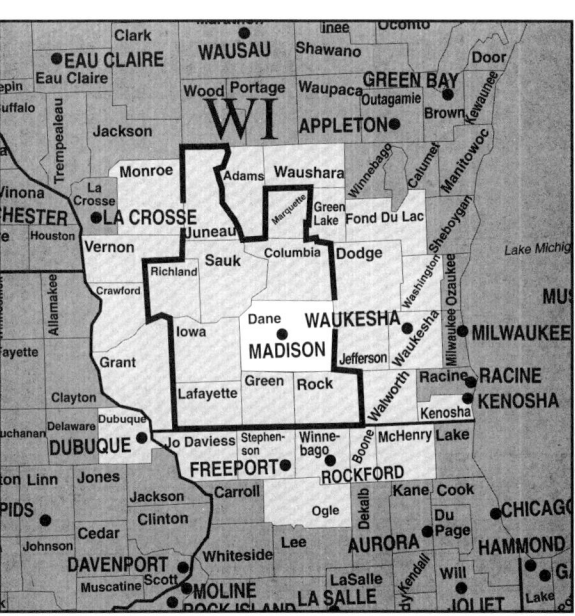

Mankato, Minn. (206)

ADI TV Households: 29,900

KEYC-TV Mankato, Minn., ch. 12, CBS

ADI Counties	State	TV Households
Emmet	IA	4,400
Blue Earth	MN	19,200
Faribault	MN	6,300

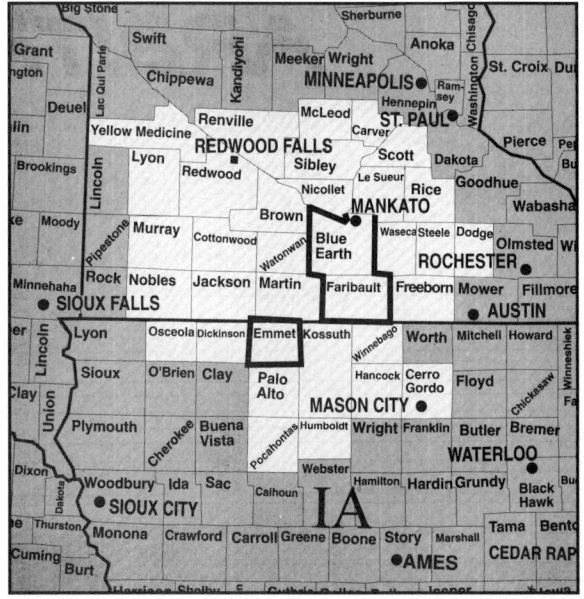

Broadcasting & Cable Yearbook 1994
C-165

Marquette (Escanaba), Mich. (175)

ADI TV Households: 82,100

WLUC-TV Marquette, Mich., ch. 6, CBS (NBC)
***WNMU-TV** Marquette, Mich., ch. 13, ETV
WJMY Marquette, Mich., ch. 19, IND

ADI Counties	State	TV Households
Alger	MI	3,300
Baraga	MI	3,200
Delta	MI	14,400
Dickinson	MI	10,700
Houghton	MI	13,100
Iron	MI	5,500
Keweenaw	MI	800
Marquette	MI	25,700
Ontonagon	MI	3,500
Florence	WI	1,900

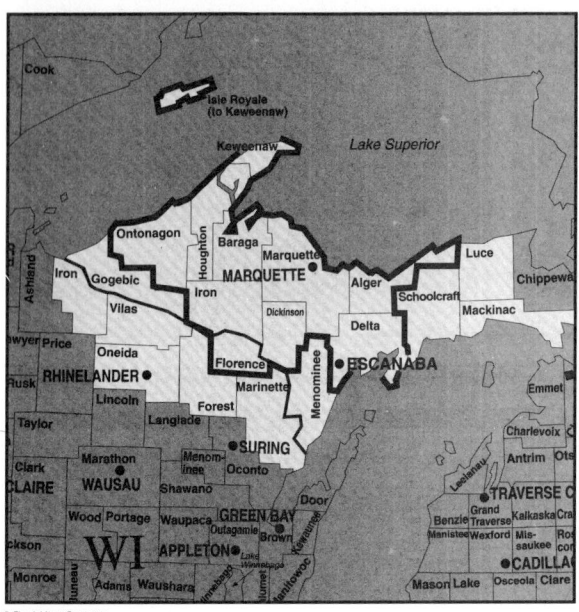

McAllen-Brownsville: Lower Rio Grande Valley, Tex. (113)

ADI TV Households: 205,800

KGBT-TV Harlingen, Tex., ch. 4, CBS
KRGV-TV Weslaco, Tex., ch. 5, ABC
KVEO Brownsville, Tex., ch. 23, NBC
***KLUJ** Harlingen, Tex., ch. 44, ETV
KNVO McAllen, Tex., ch. 48, IND
***KMBH** Harlingen, Tex., ch. 60, ETV

ADI Counties	State	TV Households
Cameron	TX	76,300
Hidalgo	TX	113,100
Starr	TX	11,400
Willacy	TX	5,000

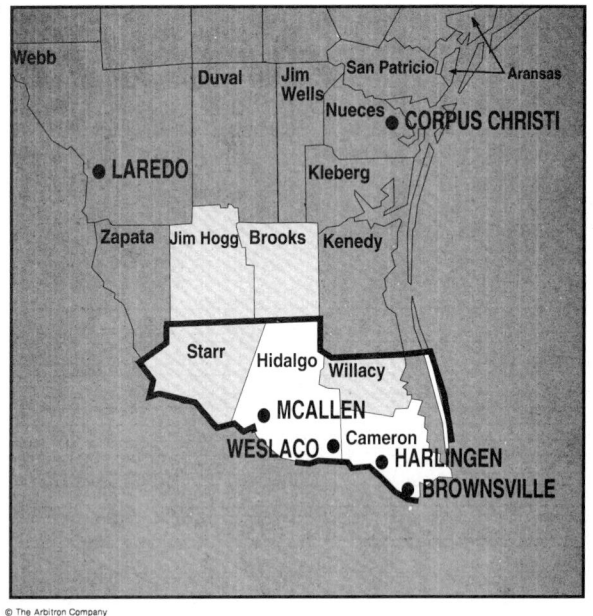

Medford, Ore. (145)

ADI TV Households: 140,000

KOBI Medford, Ore., ch. 5, NBC
KOTI Klamath Falls, Ore., ch. 2, satellite to KOBI
***KSYS** Medford, Ore., ch. 8, ETV
KTVL Medford, Ore., ch. 10, CBS
KDRV Medford, Ore., ch. 12, ABC
***KFTS** Klamath Falls, Ore., ch. 22, ETV
KMVU Medford, Ore., ch. 26, IND
KDKF Klamath Falls, Ore., ch. 31, ABC

ADI Counties	State	TV Households
Modoc	CA	3,600
Siskiyou	CA	17,200
Curry	OR	8,300
Jackson	OR	60,100
Josephine	OR	25,800
Klamath	OR	22,400
Lake	OR	2,600

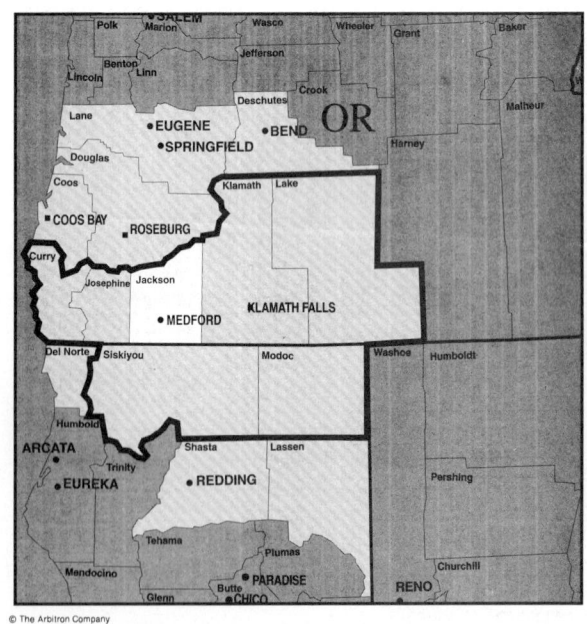

Memphis (Holly Springs, Miss.) (42)

ADI TV Households: 604,400

WREG-TV Memphis, ch. 3, CBS
WMC-TV Memphis, ch. 5, NBC
***WKNO-TV** Memphis, ch., 10, ETV
WHBQ-TV Memphis, ch. 13, ABC
***WMAV-TV** Oxford, Miss., ch. 18, ETV
WPTY-TV Memphis, ch. 24, IND
WLMT Memphis, ch. 30, IND
WBUY Holly Springs, Miss., ch. 40, IND
WFBI Memphis, ch. 50, IND

ADI Counties	State	TV Households
Crittenden	AR	16,900
Cross	AR	6,600
Lee	AR	4,400
Mississippi	AR	20,700
Phillips	AR	9,300
Poinsett	AR	9,000
St. Francis	AR	9,700
Pemiscot	MO	7,900
Alcorn	MS	12,600
Benton	MS	2,800
Coahoma	MS	9,900
De Soto	MS	27,100
Lafayette	MS	11,500
Marshall	MS	10,500
Panola	MS	10,700
Quitman	MS	3,300
Tate	MS	7,100
Tippah	MS	7,200
Tunica	MS	2,500
Yalobusha	MS	4,500
Chester	TN	4,600
Crockett	TN	5,300
Dyer	TN	13,800
Fayette	TN	8,700
Gibson	TN	18,400
Hardeman	TN	8,500
Haywood	TN	7,000
Lauderdale	TN	8,000
McNairy	TN	9,100
Shelby	TN	312,700
Tipton	TN	14,100

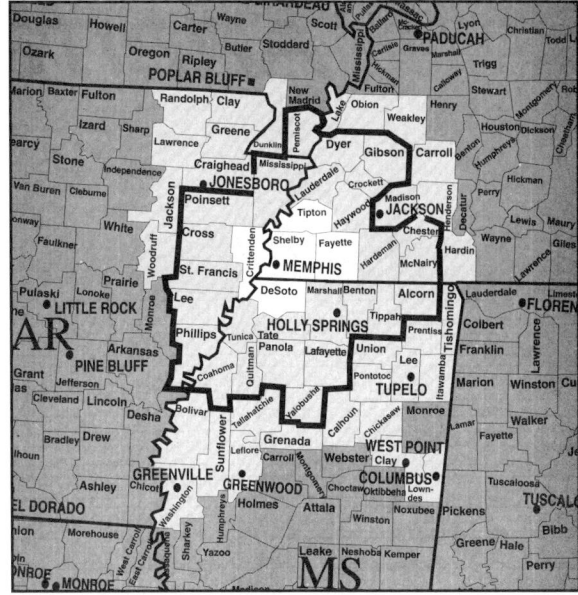

Meridian, Miss. (183)

ADI TV Households: 65,600

WTOK-TV Meridian, Miss., ch. 11, ABC
***WMAW-TV** Meridian, Miss., ch. 14, ETV
WTZH Meridian, Miss., ch. 24, CBS
WGBC Meridian, Miss., ch. 30, NBC
***WIIQ** Demopolis, Ala., ch. 41, ETV

ADI Counties	State	TV Households
Choctaw	AL	5,700
Sumter	AL	5,200
Clarke	MS	6,200
Kemper	MS	3,600
Lauderdale	MS	28,700
Neshoba	MS	8,800
Newton	MS	7,400

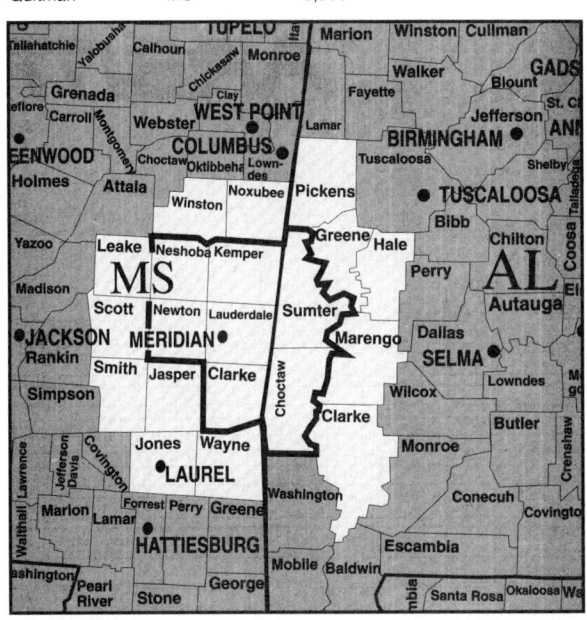

Miami-Ft. Lauderdale (Ft. Lauderdale-Hollywood), Fla. (15)

ADI TV Households: 1,308,200

***WPBT** Miami, ch. 2, ETV
WTVJ Miami, ch. 4, NBC
WCIX Miami, ch. 6, CBS
WSVN Miami, ch. 7, Fox
WWFD Key West, Fla., ch. 8, IND
WPLG Miami, ch. 10, ABC
WETV Key West, Fla., ch. 13, ETV
***WLRN-TV** Miami, ch. 17, ETV
***WKEB** Islamorada, Fla., ch. 18, ETV
WEYS Key West, Fla., ch. 22, IND
WLTV Miami, ch. 23, IND
WBFS-TV Miami, ch. 33, IND
WMLB-TV Miami, ch. 35, IND
WDZL Miami, ch. 39, IND
WHFT Miami, ch. 45, IND
WSCV Fort Lauderdale, Fla., ch. 51, IND

ADI Counties	State	TV Households
Broward	FL	565,900
Dade	FL	707,900
Monroe	FL	34,400

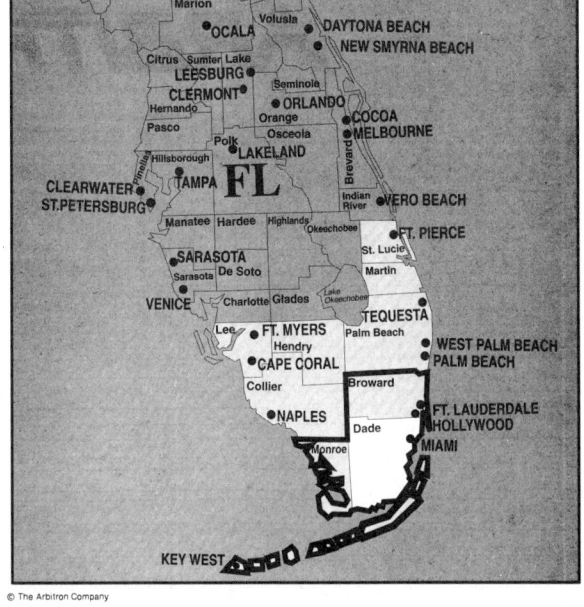

Arbitron ADI Market Atlas

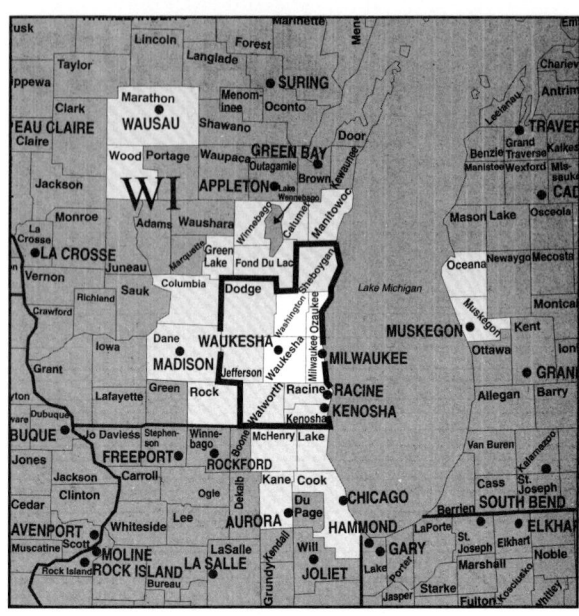

Milwaukee (Kenosha & Racine), Wis. (28)

ADI TV Households: 780,800

WTMJ-TV Milwaukee, ch. 4, NBC
WITI-TV Milwaukee, ch. 6, CBS
*WMVS Milwaukee, ch. 10, ETV
WISN-TV Milwaukee, ch. 12, ABC
WVTV Milwaukee, ch. 18, IND
WCGV-TV Milwaukee, ch. 24, Fox
WVCY-TV Milwaukee, ch. 30, IND
*WMVT Milwaukee, ch. 36, ETV
WJJA Racine, Wis., ch. 49, IND
WWRS-TV Mayville, Wis., ch. 52, IND
WDJT-TV Milwaukee, ch. 58, IND

ADI Counties	State	TV Households
Dodge	WI	27,400
Jefferson	WI	24,500
Kenosha	WI	48,900
Milwaukee	WI	373,300
Ozaukee	WI	27,200
Racine	WI	65,600
Sheboygan	WI	39,300
Walworth	WI	27,600
Washington	WI	35,400
Waukesha	WI	111,600

© The Arbitron Company

Minneapolis-St. Paul (St. Cloud), Minn. (14)

ADI TV Households: 1,418,100

*KTCA-TV St. Paul, ch. 2, ETV
WCCO-TV Minneapolis, ch. 4, CBS
KSTP-TV St. Paul, ch. 5, ABC
KCCO-TV Alexandria, Minn., ch. 7, CBS
*KAWE Bemidji, Minn., ch. 9, ETV
KMSP-TV Minneapolis, ch. 9, Fox
*KWCM-TV Appleton, Minn., ch. 10, ETV
KARE Minneapolis, ch. 11, NBC
KCCW-TV Walker, Minn., ch. 12, satellite to KCCO-TV
*KTCI-TV St. Paul, ch. 17, ETV
*KAWB Brainerd, Minn., ch. 22, ETV
KLGT-TV Minneapolis, ch. 23, IND
*WHWC-TV Menomonie, Wis., ch. 28, ETV
KITN-TV Minneapolis, ch. 29, IND
KXLI St. Cloud, Minn., ch. 41, IND
KSAX Alexandria, Minn., ch. 42, ABC
KRWF Redwood Falls, Minn., ch. 43, ABC
KVBM-TV Minneapolis, ch. 45, IND

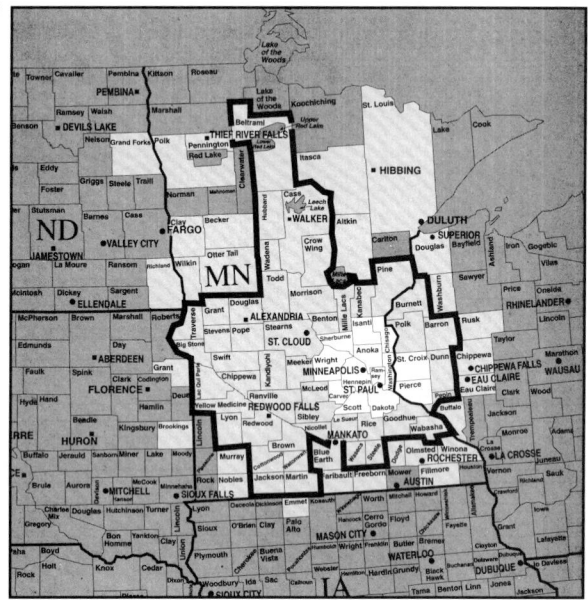

© The Arbitron Company

ADI Counties	State	TV Households
Anoka	MN	90,400
Beltrami	MN	12,200
Benton	MN	11,700
Big Stone	MN	2,400
Brown	MN	10,100
Carver	MN	18,800
Cass	MN	8,200
Chippewa	MN	5,000
Chisago	MN	11,400
Cottonwood	MN	4,500
Crow Wing	MN	18,000
Dakota	MN	112,900
Douglas	MN	11,200
Goodhue	MN	15,400
Grant	MN	2,400
Hennepin	MN	432,800
Hubbard	MN	5,900
Isanti	MN	9,400
Jackson	MN	4,300
Kanabec	MN	4,800
Kandiyohi	MN	14,700
Lac qui Parle	MN	3,300
Le Sueur	MN	8,600
Lyon	MN	8,900
Martin	MN	8,800
McLeod	MN	12,200
Meeker	MN	7,900
Mille Lacs	MN	7,100
Morrison	MN	10,300
Nicollet	MN	9,600
Pine	MN	7,800
Pope	MN	4,000
Ramsey	MN	193,100
Redwood	MN	6,200
Renville	MN	6,500
Rice	MN	17,000
Scott	MN	21,700
Sherburne	MN	15,000
Sibley	MN	5,200
Stearns	MN	41,100
Steele	MN	11,500
Stevens	MN	3,600
Swift	MN	4,000
Todd	MN	8,400
Traverse	MN	1,700
Wabasha	MN	7,400
Wadena	MN	4,800
Waseca	MN	6,800
Washington	MN	55,000
Watonwan	MN	4,400
Wright	MN	24,900
Yellow Medicine	MN	4,500
Barron	WI	15,800
Burnett	WI	5,400
Dunn	WI	12,600
Pepin	WI	2,500
Pierce	WI	11,400
Polk	WI	13,500
St. Croix	WI	19,100

Broadcasting & Cable Yearbook 1994

Arbitron ADI Market Atlas

Minot-Bismarck-Dickinson, N.D.-Glendive, Mont. (152)

ADI TV Households: 134,700

KXMA-TV Dickinson, N.D., ch. 2, satellite to KXMC-TV
***KBME** Bismarck, N.D., ch. 3, ETV
***KWSE** Williston, N.D., ch. 4, ETV
KXGN-TV Glendive, Mont., ch. 5, CBS (NBC)
KFYR-TV Bismarck, N.D., ch. 5, NBC
***KSRE** Minot, N.D., ch. 6, ETV
KQCD-TV Dickinson, N.D., ch. 7, NBC
KUMV-TV Williston, N.D., ch. 8, satellite to KFYR-TV
***KDSE** Dickinson, N.D., ch. 9, ETV
KMOT Minot, N.D., ch. 10, satellite to KFYR-TV
KXMD-TV Williston, N.D., ch. 11, satellite to KXMC-TV
***KQSD-TV** Lowry, S.D., ch. 11, ETV
KXMB-TV Bismarck, N.D., ch. 12, satellite to KXMC-TV
KXMC-TV Minot, N.D., ch. 13, CBS
KMCY Minot, N.D., ch. 14, ABC
KBMY Bismarck, N.D., ch. 17, ABC

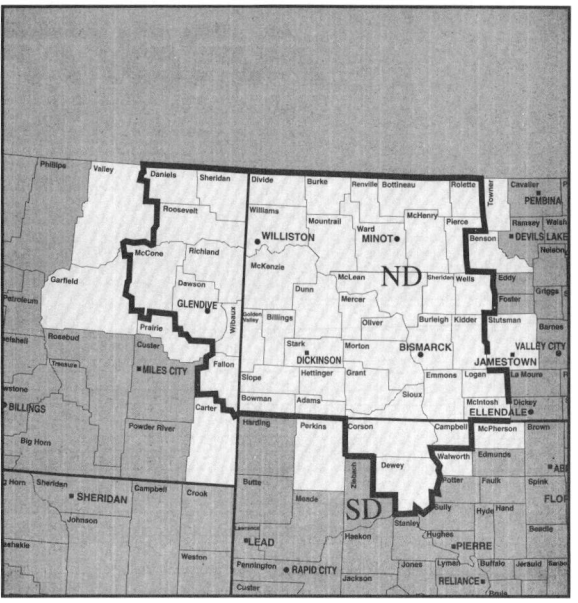

ADI Counties	State	TV Households
Daniels	MT	900
Dawson	MT	3,400
Fallon	MT	1,100
McCone	MT	800
Richland	MT	3,700
Roosevelt	MT	3,600
Sheridan	MT	1,900
Wibaux	MT	500
Adams	ND	1,200
Billings	ND	400
Bottineau	ND	3,100
Bowman	ND	1,400
Burke	ND	1,200
Burleigh	ND	23,500
Divide	ND	1,200
Dunn	ND	1,400
Emmons	ND	1,800
Golden Valley	ND	800
Grant	ND	1,400
Hettinger	ND	1,300
Kidder	ND	1,200
Logan	ND	1,100
McHenry	ND	2,500
McIntosh	ND	1,600
McKenzie	ND	2,200
McLean	ND	3,700
Mercer	ND	3,300
Morton	ND	8,200
Mountrail	ND	2,500
Oliver	ND	800
Pierce	ND	2,000
Renville	ND	1,200
Rolette	ND	4,200
Sheridan	ND	800
Sioux	ND	1,000
Slope	ND	300
Stark	ND	8,600
Ward	ND	21,800
Wells	ND	2,000
Williams	ND	7,500
Campbell	SD	800
Corson	SD	1,200
Dewey	SD	1,600

Missoula, Mont. (176)

ADI TV Households: 77,800

KPAX-TV Missoula, Mont., ch. 8, satellite to KXLF-TV
KCFW-TV Kalispell, Mont., ch. 9, satellite to KECI-TV
***KUFM-TV** Missoula, Mont., ch. 11, ETV
KECI-TV Missoula, Mont., ch. 13, NBC (ABC)
KTMF Missoula, Mont., ch. 23, IND

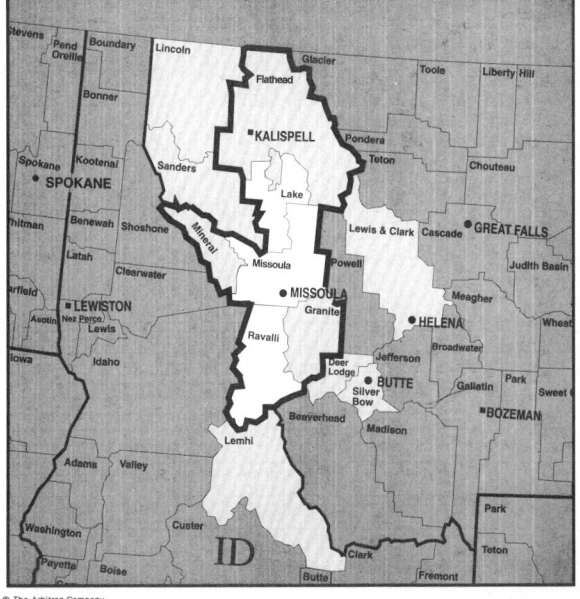

ADI Counties	State	TV Households
Flathead	MT	24,200
Granite	MT	1,000
Lake	MT	8,400
Mineral	MT	1,300
Missoula	MT	32,200
Ravalli	MT	10,700

Broadcasting & Cable Yearbook 1994

Arbitron ADI Market Atlas

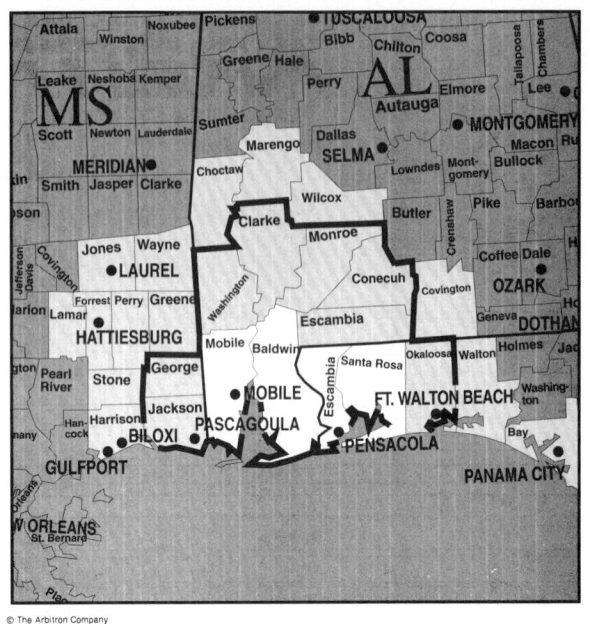

Mobile, Ala.-Pensacola, Fla. (Ft. Walton Beach, Fla.) (58)

ADI TV Households: 465,200

WEAR-TV Pensacola, Fla., ch. 3, ABC
WKRG-TV Mobile, Ala., ch. 5, CBS
WALA-TV Mobile, Ala., ch. 10, NBC
WPMI Mobile, Ala., ch. 15, Fox
WMPV-TV Mobile, Ala., ch. 21, IND
*****WSRE** Pensacola, Fla., ch. 23, ETV
WHBR Pensacola, Fla., ch. 33, IND
WFGX Fort Walton Beach, Fla., ch. 35, IND
*****WEIQ** Mobile, Ala., ch. 42, ETV
WJTC Pensacola, Fla., ch. 44, IND
WPAN Fort Walton Beach, Fla., ch. 53, IND
WAWD Fort Walton Beach, Fla., ch. 58, IND

ADI Counties	State	TV Households
Baldwin	AL	41,000
Clarke	AL	9,600
Conecuh	AL	5,200
Escambia	AL	12,500
Mobile	AL	141,600
Monroe	AL	8,400
Washington	AL	5,700
Escambia	FL	102,900
Okaloosa	FL	57,200
Santa Rosa	FL	33,200
George	MS	6,100
Jackson	MS	41,800

Monroe, La.-El Dorado, Ark. (131)

ADI TV Households: 167,800

KNOE-TV Monroe, La., ch. 8, CBS
KTVE El Dorado, Ark., ch. 10, NBC
*****KLTM-TV** Monroe, La., ch. 13, ETV
KARD West Monroe, La., ch. 14, ABC
KMCT-TV West Monroe, La., ch. 39, IND

ADI Counties	State	TV Households
Ashley	AR	8,700
Union	AR	17,600
Caldwell	LA	3,400
Catahoula	LA	3,800
Concordia	LA	7,000
East Carroll	LA	2,900
Franklin	LA	7,500
Jackson	LA	5,500
LaSalle	LA	5,100
Lincoln	LA	14,200
Madison	LA	4,100
Morehouse	LA	10,800
Ouachita	LA	50,700
Richland	LA	6,800
Tensas	LA	2,300
Union	LA	7,600
West Carroll	LA	4,300
Winn	LA	5,500

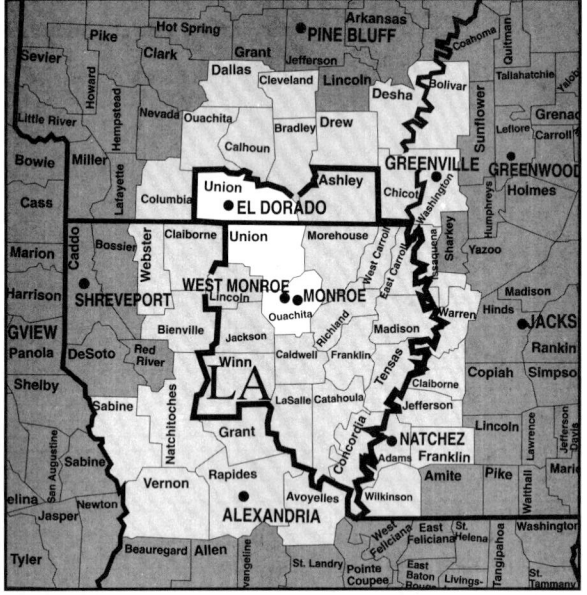

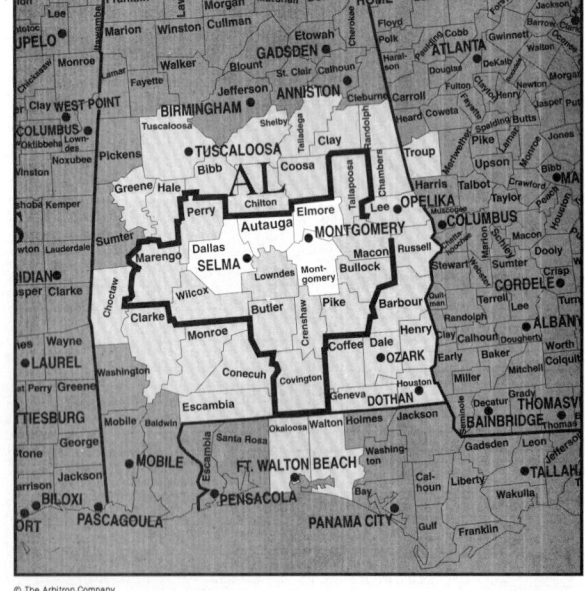

Montgomery-Selma, Ala. (111)

ADI TV Households: 212,500

*****WDIQ** Dozier, Ala., ch. 2, ETV
WAKA Selma, Ala., ch. 8, CBS
WSFA Montgomery, Ala., ch. 12, NBC
WCOV-TV Montgomery, Ala., ch. 20, Fox
*****WAIQ** Montgomery, Ala., ch. 26, ETV
WHOA-TV Montgomery, Ala., ch. 32, ABC
WMCF-TV Montgomery, Ala., ch. 45, IND
WRJM-TV Troy, Ala., ch. 67, IND

ADI Counties	State	TV Households
Autauga	AL	12,800
Bullock	AL	3,700
Butler	AL	7,800
Covington	AL	14,500
Crenshaw	AL	5,200
Dallas	AL	16,400
Elmore	AL	17,800
Lowndes	AL	3,900
Macon	AL	8,400
Marengo	AL	8,000
Montgomery	AL	79,900
Perry	AL	3,900
Pike	AL	10,800
Tallapoosa	AL	14,900
Wilcox	AL	4,500

Arbitron ADI Market Atlas

Nashville (33)

ADI TV Households: 731,400

WKRN-TV Nashville, ch. 2, ABC
WSMV Nashville, ch. 4, NBC
WTVF Nashville, ch. 5, CBS
*WDCN Nashville, ch. 8, ETV
WZTV Nashville, ch. 17, Fox
*WCTE Cookeville, Tenn., ch. 22, ETV
WMTT Cookeville, Tenn., ch. 28, IND
WXMT Nashville, ch. 30, IND
WHTN Murfreesboro, Tenn., ch. 39, IND
WPGD Hendersonville, Tenn., ch. 50, IND
WKKT-TV Hopkinsville, Ky., ch. 51, IND
WNAB Nashville, ch. 58, IND
WJFB Lebanon, Tenn., ch. 66, IND

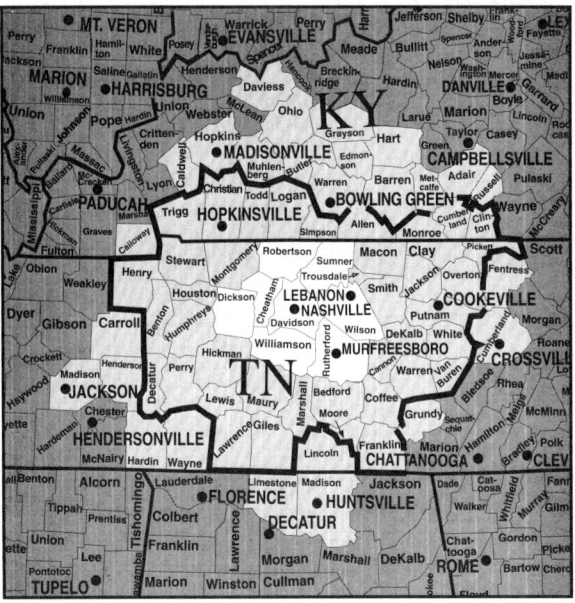

ADI Counties	State	TV Households
Allen	KY	5,700
Christian	KY	22,000
Clinton	KY	3,600
Cumberland	KY	2,700
Logan	KY	9,500
Monroe	KY	4,500
Simpson	KY	6,100
Todd	KY	4,100
Trigg	KY	4,300
Bedford	TN	12,300
Benton	TN	5,900
Cannon	TN	4,300
Cheatham	TN	10,300
Clay	TN	2,800
Coffee	TN	16,400
Davidson	TN	214,800
DeKalb	TN	5,900
Decatur	TN	4,200
Dickson	TN	14,100
Franklin	TN	13,200
Giles	TN	10,300
Henry	TN	11,500
Hickman	TN	6,500
Houston	TN	2,800
Humphreys	TN	6,200
Jackson	TN	3,500
Lawrence	TN	13,900
Lewis	TN	3,900
Macon	TN	6,400
Marshall	TN	8,900
Maury	TN	22,600
Montgomery	TN	37,700
Moore	TN	1,700
Overton	TN	7,000
Perry	TN	2,600
Pickett	TN	1,800
Putnam	TN	21,000
Robertson	TN	16,100
Rutherford	TN	47,800
Smith	TN	5,600
Stewart	TN	4,000
Sumner	TN	39,800
Trousdale	TN	2,300
Van Buren	TN	1,800
Warren	TN	13,000
White	TN	7,900
Williamson	TN	31,800
Wilson	TN	26,300

New Orleans (39)

ADI TV Households: 616,800

WWL-TV New Orleans, ch. 4, CBS
WDSU-TV New Orleans, ch. 6, NBC
WVUE New Orleans, ch. 8, ABC
*WYES-TV New Orleans, ch. 12, ETV
New TV New Orleans, ch. 20, IND
WGNO New Orleans, ch. 26, IND
*WLAE-TV New Orleans, ch. 32, ETV
WNOL-TV New Orleans, ch. 38, Fox
WCCL New Orleans, ch. 49, IND

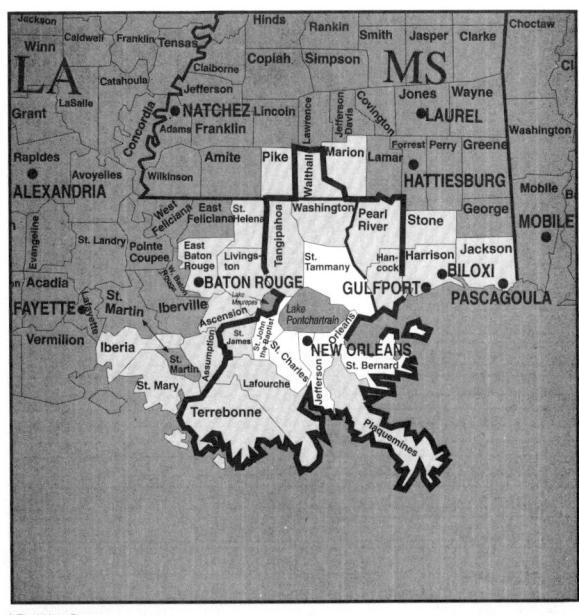

ADI Counties	State	TV Households
Jefferson	LA	172,000
Lafourche	LA	29,000
Orleans	LA	184,800
Plaquemines	LA	8,100
St. Bernard	LA	23,300
St. Charles	LA	15,200
St. James	LA	6,400
St. John the Baptist	LA	13,300
St. Tammany	LA	55,300
Tangipahoa	LA	30,000
Terrebonne	LA	32,200
Washington	LA	15,000
Hancock	MS	13,000
Pearl River	MS	14,400
Whithall	MS	4,800

Broadcasting & Cable Yearbook 1994

Arbitron ADI Market Atlas

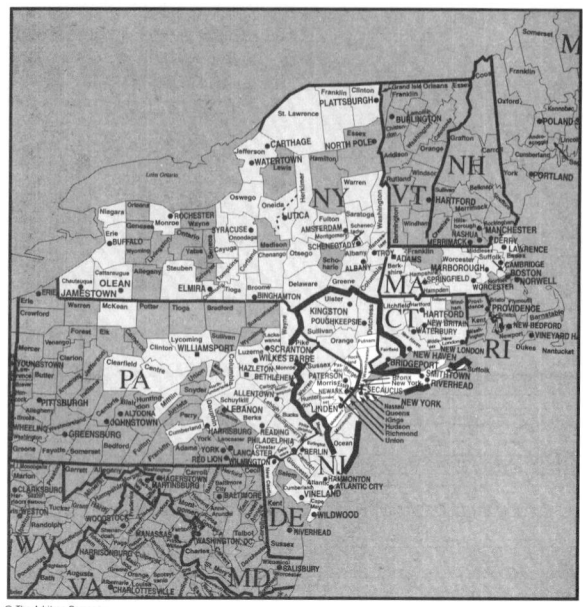

New York (Kingston, Newton & Poughkeepsie), N.Y. (1)

ADI TV Households: 6,723,700

WCBS-TV New York, ch. 2, CBS
WNBC-TV New York, ch. 4, NBC
WNYW New York, ch. 5, Fox
WABC-TV New York, ch. 7, ABC
WWOR-TV Secaucus, N.J., ch. 9, IND
WPIX New York, ch. 11, IND
*WNET Newark, N.J., ch. 13, ETV
*WLIW Garden City, N.Y., ch. 21, ETV
*WNYE-TV New York, ch. 25, ETV
*WNYC-TV New York, ch. 31, ETV
WXTV Paterson, N.J., ch. 41, IND

WHAI-TV Bridgeport, Conn., ch. 43, IND
WNJU Linden, N.J., ch. 47, IND
*WEDW Bridgeport, Conn., ch. 49, ETV
*WNJM Montclair, N.J., ch. 50, ETV
WTBY Poughkeepsie, N.Y., ch 54, IND
WLIG Riverhead, N.Y., ch. 55, IND
WMBC-TV Newton, N.J., ch. 63, IND
WTZA Kingston, N.Y., ch. 63, IND
*WFME-TV West Milford, N.J., ch. 66, ETV
WHSI Smithtown, N.Y., ch. 67, IND
WHSE Newark, N.J., ch. 68, IND

ADI Counties	State	TV Households
Fairfield	CT	295,100
Bergen	NJ	307,600
Essex	NJ	267,300
Hudson	NJ	202,600
Hunterdon	NJ	38,500
Middlesex	NJ	243,900
Monmouth	NJ	202,900
Morris	NJ	149,700
Ocean	NJ	175,200
Passaic	NJ	151,700
Somerset	NJ	94,300
Sussex	NJ	45,400
Union	NJ	176,800
Warren	NJ	34,500
Bronx	NY	412,200
Dutchess	NY	90,800
Kings	NY	802,200
Nassau	NY	428,800
New York	NY	693,500
Orange	NY	105,000
Putnam	NY	29,000
Queens	NY	708,700
Richmond	NY	134,000
Rockland	NY	84,400
Suffolk	NY	433,800
Sullivan	NY	24,700
Ulster	NY	60,300
Westchester	NY	318,500
Pike	PA	12,300

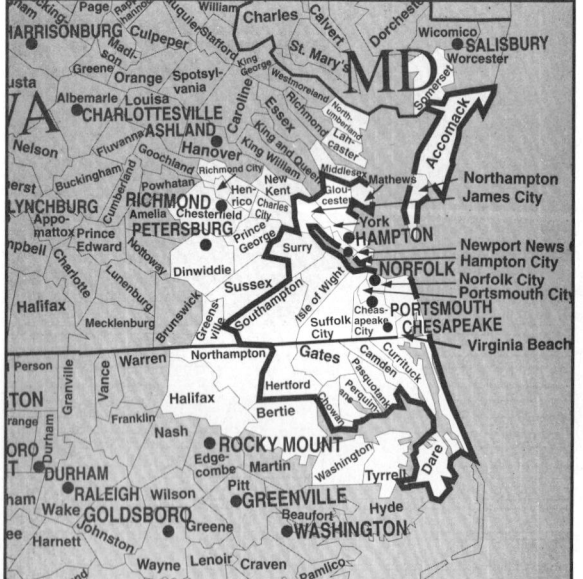

Norfolk-Portsmouth-Newport News-Hampton, Va. (40)

ADI TV Households: 616,400

WTKR-TV Norfolk, Va., ch. 3, CBS
WAVY-TV Portsmouth, Va., ch. 10, NBC
WVEC-TV Hampton, Va., ch. 13, ABC
*WHRO-TV Hampton-Norfolk, Va., ch. 15, ETV

WGNT Portsmouth, Va., ch. 27, IND
WTVZ Norfolk, Va., ch. 33, Fox
WJCB Norfolk, Va., ch. 49, IND

ADI Counties	State	TV Households
Camden	NC	2,200
Chowan	NC	5,300
Currituck	NC	5,400
Dare	NC	10,400
Gates	NC	3,300
Hertford	NC	8,300
Pasquotank	NC	11,900
Perquimans	NC	4,100
Accomack	VA	12,800
Chesapeake City	VA	58,900
Gloucester	VA	12,200
Hampton City	VA	51,900
Isle of Wight	VA	9,700
James City	VA	18,400
Mathews	VA	3,700
Newport News City	VA	67,600
Norfolk City	VA	87,400
Northampton	VA	5,000
Portsmouth City	VA	38,600
Southampton	VA	9,400
Suffolk City	VA	19,000
Surry	VA	2,300
Va Beach City	VA	148,300
York	VA	20,300

Broadcasting & Cable Yearbook 1994

Arbitron ADI Market Atlas

North Platte, Neb. (208)

ADI TV Households: 18,100

KNOP-TV North Platte, Neb., ch. 2, NBC
***KPNE-TV** North Platte, Neb., ch. 9, ETV

ADI Counties	State	TV Households
Arthur	NE	200
Blaine	NE	300
Hooker	NE	300
Keith	NE	3,400
Lincoln	NE	13,100
Logan	NE	300
McPherson	NE	200
Thomas	NE	300

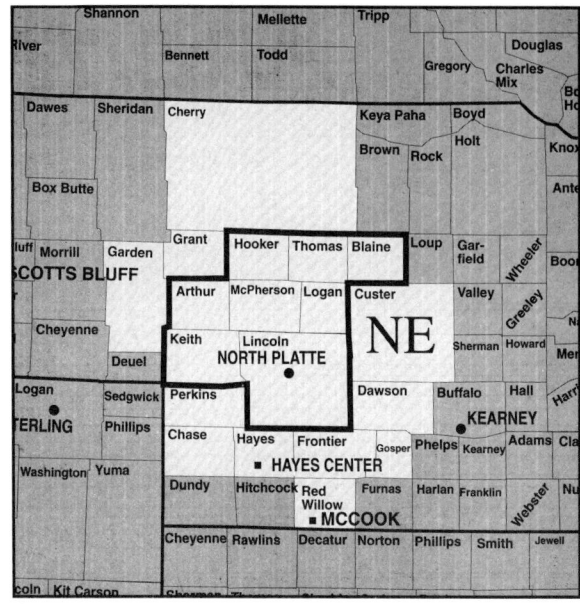

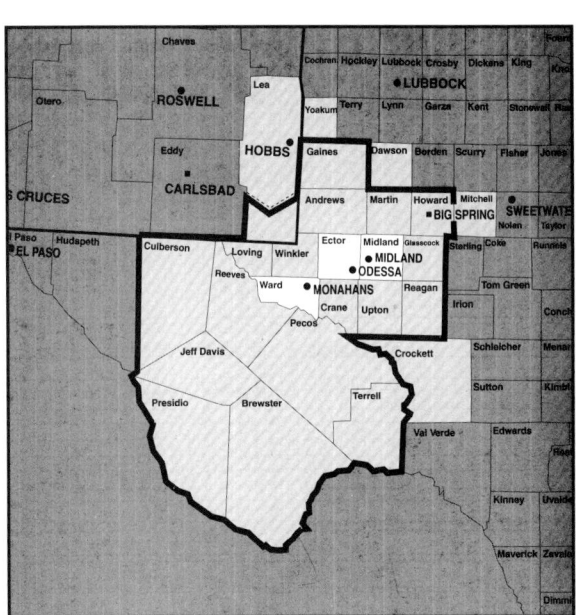

Odessa-Midland, Tex. (149)

ADI TV Households: 136,100

KMID-TV Midland, Tex., ch. 2, ABC
KOSA-TV Odessa, Tex., ch. 7, CBS
KTPX Odessa, Tex., ch. 9, NBC
KWAB Big Spring, Tex., ch. 4, satellite to KTPX
KPEJ Odessa, Tex., ch. 24, IND
*KOCV-TV Odessa, Tex., ch. 36, ETV
KMLM Odessa, Tex., ch. 42, IND

ADI Counties	State	TV Households			
Lea South	NM	2,500	Martin	TX	1,600
Andrews	TX	4,800	Midland	TX	40,800
Brewster	TX	3,400	Pecos	TX	4,300
Crane	TX	1,500	Presidio	TX	2,200
Culberson	TX	1,100	Reagan	TX	1,300
Ector	TX	42,500	Reeves	TX	4,600
Gaines	TX	4,500	Terrell	TX	500
Glasscock	TX	500	Upton	TX	1,500
Howard	TX	10,900	Ward	TX	4,000
Jeff Davis	TX	800	Winkler	TX	2,700
Loving	TX	100			

Oklahoma City (43)

ADI TV Households: 577,500

KFOR-TV Oklahoma City, ch. 4, NBC
KOCO-TV Oklahoma City, ch. 5, ABC
KWTV Oklahoma City, ch. 9, CBS
*KWET Cheyenne, Okla., ch. 12, ETV
*KETA Oklahoma City, ch. 13, ETV
KTBO-TV Oklahoma City, ch. 14, IND
KOKH-TV Oklahoma City, ch. 25, IND
KOCB Oklahoma City, ch. 34, IND
KAUT Oklahoma City, ch. 43, Fox
KSBI Oklahoma City, ch. 52, IND

ADI Counties	State	TV Households			
Alfalfa	OK	2,200	Kay	OK	18,900
Beckham	OK	6,800	Kingfisher	OK	4,800
Blaine	OK	4,400	Kiowa	OK	4,400
Caddo	OK	10,500	Lincoln	OK	11,100
Canadian	OK	26,900	Logan	OK	10,100
Cleveland	OK	69,000	Major	OK	3,000
Custer	OK	9,400	McClain	OK	8,500
Dewey	OK	2,200	Murray	OK	4,600
Ellis	OK	1,800	Noble	OK	4,300
Garfield	OK	21,500	Oklahoma	OK	243,200
Garvin	OK	10,100	Payne	OK	24,600
Grady	OK	15,400	Pottawatomie	OK	21,800
Grant	OK	2,300	Roger Mills	OK	1,500
Greer	OK	2,400	Seminole	OK	9,100
Harmon	OK	1,400	Washita	OK	4,300
Harper	OK	1,600	Woods	OK	3,700
Hughes	OK	5,200	Woodward	OK	6,500

Broadcasting & Cable Yearbook 1994

Arbitron ADI Market Atlas

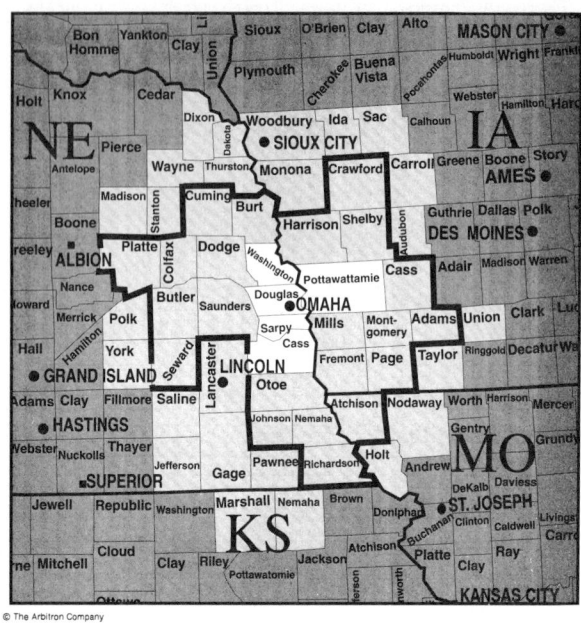

Omaha, Neb. (73)

ADI TV Households: 361,500

KMTV Omaha, ch. 3, CBS
WOWT Omaha, ch. 6, NBC
KETV Omaha, ch. 7, ABC
*****KYNE-TV** Omaha, ch. 26, ETV
*****KBIN** Council Bluffs, Iowa, ch. 32, ETV
*****KHIN** Red Oak, Iowa, ch. 36, ETV

ADI Counties	State	TV Households
Adams	IA	2,000
Cass	IA	6,100
Crawford	IA	6,400
Fremont	IA	3,200
Harrison	IA	5,500
Mills	IA	4,700
Montgomery	IA	4,800
Page	IA	6,500
Pottawattamie	IA	31,300
Shelby	IA	5,100
Atchison	MO	2,900
Burt	NE	3,100
Butler	NE	3,200
Cass	NE	8,100
Colfax	NE	3,500
Cuming	NE	3,800
Dodge	NE	13,400
Douglas	NE	165,900
Johnson	NE	1,900
Nemaha	NE	3,000
Otoe	NE	5,600
Platte	NE	11,300
Richardson	NE	4,000
Sarpy	NE	37,200
Saunders	NE	6,900
Seward	NE	5,700
Washington	NE	6,400

Orlando-Daytona Beach-Melbourne, Fla. (23)

ADI TV Households: 972,100

WESH Daytona Beach, Fla., ch. 2, NBC
WCPX-TV Orlando, Fla., ch. 6, CBS
WFTV Orlando, Fla., ch. 9, ABC
*****WCEU** New Smyrna Beach, Fla., ch. 15, ETV
*****WBCC** Cocoa, Fla., ch. 18, ETV
*****WMFE-TV** Orlando, Fla., ch. 24, ETV
WZWY Orlando, Fla., ch. 27, IND
WOFL Orlando, Fla., ch. 35, Fox
WBSF Melbourne, Fla., ch. 43, IND
WTGL-TV Cocoa, Fla., ch. 52, IND
WACX Leesburg, Fla., ch. 55, IND
WIRB Melbourne, Fla., ch. 56, IND
WKCF Clermont, Fla., ch. 68, IND

ADI Counties	State	TV Households
Brevard	FL	179,300
Flagler	FL	14,100
Lake	FL	70,000
Marion	FL	86,900
Orange	FL	277,500
Osceola	FL	45,100
Seminole	FL	120,200
Sumter	FL	12,700
Volusia	FL	166,300

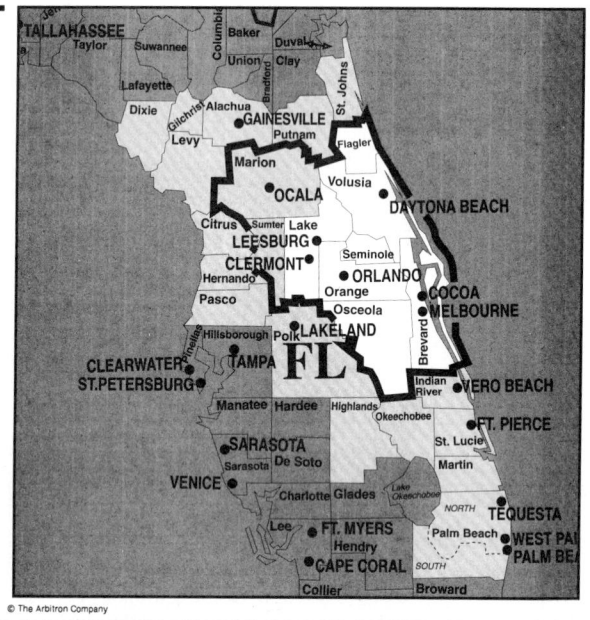

Ottumwa, Iowa-Kirksville, Mo. (Wapello, Iowa) (200)

ADI TV Households: 33,600

KTVO Kirksville, Mo., ch. 3, ABC
KYOU-TV Ottumwa, Iowa, ch. 15, IND

ADI Counties	State	TV Households
Davis	IA	3,100
Jefferson	IA	6,400
Van Buren	IA	3,000
Adair	MO	8,700
Macon	MO	6,000
Putnam	MO	2,100
Schuyler	MO	1,700
Sullivan	MO	2,600

Broadcasting & Cable Yearbook 1994

Paducah, Ky.-Cape Girardeau, Mo.-Harrisburg-Marion, Ill. (77)

ADI TV Households: 332,000

WSIL-TV Harrisburg, Ill., ch. 3, ABC
WPSD-TV Paducah, Ky., ch. 6, NBC
*WSIU-TV Carbondale, Ill., ch. 8, ETV
KFVS-TV Cape Girardeau, Mo., ch. 12, CBS
WCEE Mount Vernon, Ill., ch. 13, IND
KPOB-TV Poplar Bluff, Mo., ch. 15, satellite to WSIL-TV
*WKMU Murray, Ky., ch. 21, ETV
KBSI Cape Girardeau, Mo., ch. 23, Fox
WTCT Marion, Ill., ch. 27, IND
*WKPD Paducah, Ky., ch. 29, ETV
WDKA Paducah, Ky., ch. 49, IND

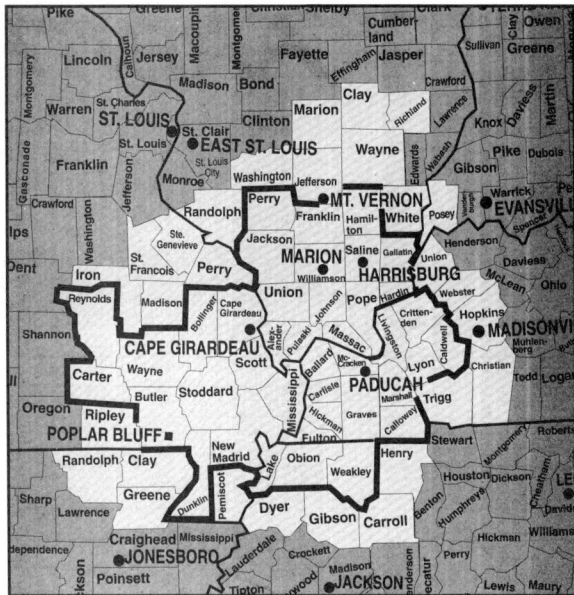

ADI Counties	State	TV Households
Alexander	IL	4,100
Franklin	IL	15,800
Gallatin	IL	2,600
Hamilton	IL	3,400
Hardin	IL	2,100
Jackson	IL	23,000
Johnson	IL	3,300
Massac	IL	5,800
Perry	IL	8,100
Pope	IL	1,500
Pulaski	IL	2,800
Saline	IL	10,600
Union	IL	7,000
Williamson	IL	23,000
Ballard	KY	3,100
Caldwell	KY	5,200
Calloway	KY	12,200
Carlisle	KY	2,100
Crittenden	KY	3,700
Fulton	KY	3,300
Graves	KY	13,700
Hickman	KY	2,200
Livingston	KY	3,600
Lyon	KY	2,300
Marshall	KY	11,200
McCracken	KY	26,200
Bollinger	MO	3,900
Butler	MO	15,200
Cape Girardeau	MO	24,200
Carter	MO	2,000
Dunklin	MO	12,400
Mississippi	MO	5,300
New Madrid	MO	7,300
Reynolds	MO	2,500
Scott	MO	14,600
Stoddard	MO	11,200
Wayne	MO	4,800
Lake	TN	2,400
Obion	TN	12,300
Weakley	TN	12,000

Palm Springs, Calif. (162)

ADI TV Households: 101,500

KMIR-TV Palm Springs, Calif., ch. 36, NBC
KESQ-TV Palm Springs, Calif., ch. 42, ABC

ADI Counties	State	TV Households
Riverside Central	CA	101,500

Arbitron ADI Market Atlas

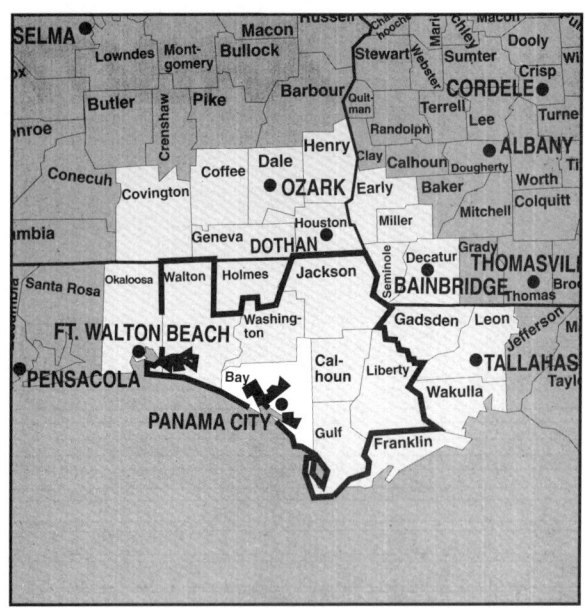

Panama City, Fla. (164)

ADI TV Households: 94,800

WJHG-TV Panama City, Fla., ch. 7, NBC
WMBB Panama City, Fla., ch. 13, ABC
WPGX Panama City, Fla., ch. 28, IND
*****WFSG** Panama City, Fla., ch. 56, ETV

ADI Counties	State	TV Households
Bay	FL	52,100
Calhoun	FL	4,000
Gulf	FL	4,100
Jackson	FL	14,500
Liberty	FL	1,700
Walton	FL	11,800
Washington	FL	6,600

Parkersburg, W. Va. (184)

ADI TV Households: 60,500

WTAP-TV Parkersburg, W. Va., ch. 15, NBC

ADI Counties	State	TV Households
Washington	OH	23,400
Pleasants	WV	2,800
Wood	WV	34,300

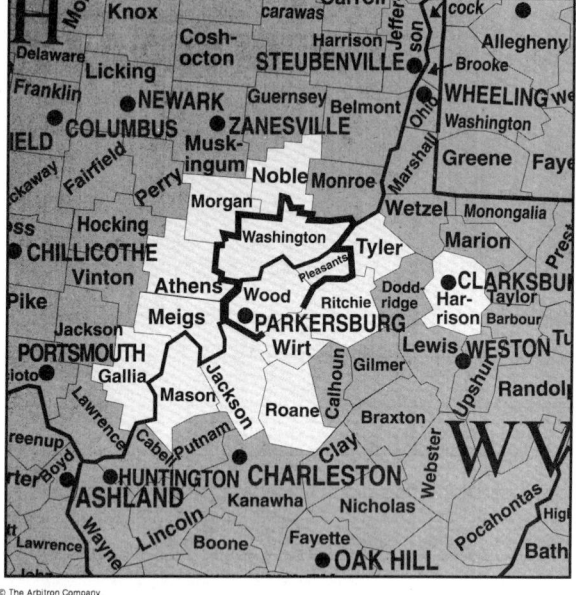

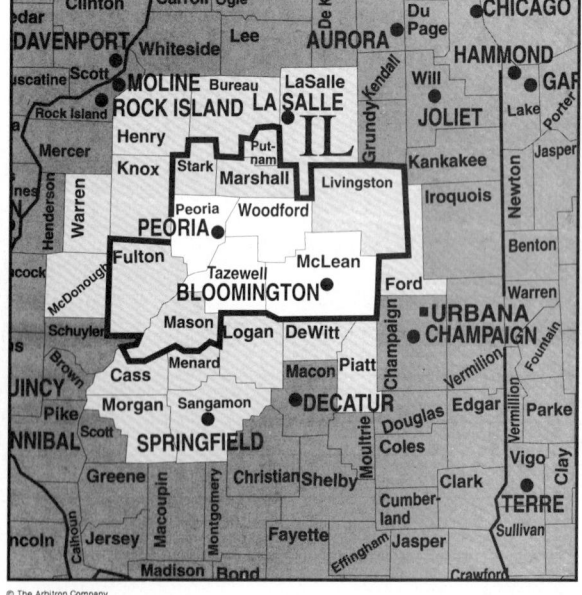

Peoria-Bloomington, Ill. (107)

ADI TV Households: 221,400

WHOI Peoria, Ill., ch. 19, ABC
WEEK-TV Peoria, Ill., ch. 25, NBC
WMBD-TV Peoria, Ill., ch. 31, CBS
WYZZ-TV Bloomington, Ill., ch. 43, Fox
*****WTVP** Peoria, Ill., ch. 47, ETV

ADI Counties	State	TV Households
Fulton	IL	14,300
Livingston	IL	13,400
Marshall	IL	4,800
Mason	IL	6,100
McLean	IL	48,500
Peoria	IL	70,500
Putnam	IL	2,100
Stark	IL	2,500
Tazewell	IL	47,600
Woodford	IL	11,600

Broadcasting & Cable Yearbook 1994
C-176

Arbitron ADI Market Atlas

Philadelphia (Allentown, Bethlehem & Reading, Pa.; Atlantic City, Vineland, Wildwood, N.J.; Wilmington, Del.) (4)

ADI TV Households: 2,661,800

KYW-TV Philadelphia, ch. 3, NBC
WPVI-TV Philadelphia, ch. 6, ABC
WCAU-TV Philadelphia, ch. 10, CBS
WHYY-TV Wilmington, Del., ch. 12, ETV
WPHL-TV Philadelphia, ch. 17, IND
*****WNJS** Camden, N.J., ch. 23, ETV
WTXF-TV Philadelphia, ch. 29, Fox
*****WYBE** Philadelphia, ch. 35, ETV
*****WLVT-TV** Allentown, Pa., ch. 39, ETV
WMGM-TV Wildwood, N.J, ch. 40, NBC
WGTW Burlington, N.J., ch. 48, IND
WTVE Reading, Pa., ch. 51, IND
*****WNJT** Trenton, N.J., ch. 52, ETV
WWAC-TV Atlantic City, N.J., ch. 53, IND
WGBS-TV Philadelphia, ch. 57, IND
*****WNJB** New Brunswick, N.J., ch. 58, ETV
WBPH-TV Bethlehem, Pa., ch. 60, IND
WTGI-TV Wilmington, Del., ch. 61, IND
WACI Atlantic City, N.J., ch. 62, IND
WHSP Vineland, N.J., ch. 65, IND
WFMZ-TV Allentown, Pa., ch. 69, IND

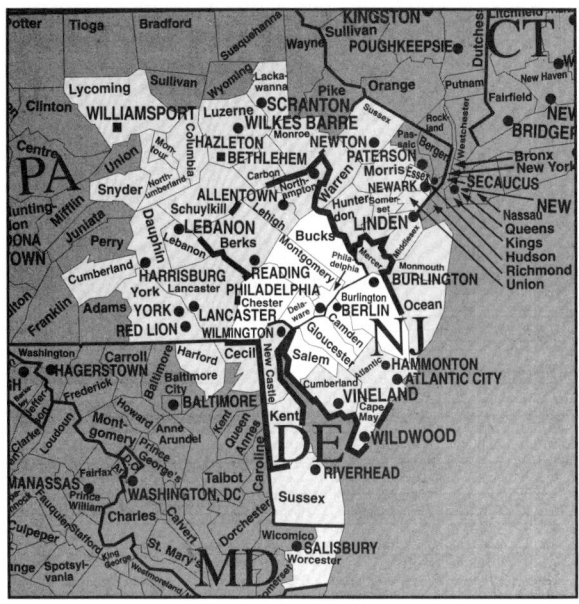

ADI Counties	State	TV Households
Kent	DE	40,900
New Castle	DE	172,000
Atlantic	NJ	86,700
Burlington	NJ	140,400
Camden	NJ	181,400
Cape May	NJ	38,400
Cumberland	NJ	46,300
Gloucester	NJ	81,800
Mercer	NJ	117,400
Salem	NJ	23,600
Berks	PA	130,700
Bucks	PA	199,400
Chester	PA	140,900
Delaware	PA	203,800
Lehigh	PA	116,000
Montgomery	PA	262,700
Northampton	PA	94,100
Philadelphia	PA	585,300

Phoenix (Kingman & Prescott), Ariz. (21)

ADI TV Households: 1,061,300

KTVK Phoenix, ch. 3, ABC
KPHO-TV Phoenix, ch. 5, IND
KMOH-TV Kingman, Ariz., ch. 6, IND
KUSK Prescott, Ariz., ch. 7, IND
*****KAET** Phoenix, ch. 8, ETV
KTSP-TV Phoenix, ch. 10, CBS
KPNX Mesa, Ariz., ch. 12, NBC
KNXV-TV Phoenix, ch. 15, Fox
KPAZ-TV Phoenix, ch. 21, IND
KTVW-TV Phoenix, ch. 33, IND
KUTP Phoenix, ch. 45, IND

ADI Counties	State	TV Households
Gila	AZ	15,900
Graham	AZ	8,100
Greenlee	AZ	2,700
La Paz	AZ	5,600
Maricopa	AZ	871,300
Mohave	AZ	41,100
Navajo	AZ	21,500
Pinal	AZ	40,800
Yavapai	AZ	48,200
Riverside East	CA	6,100

Arbitron ADI Market Atlas

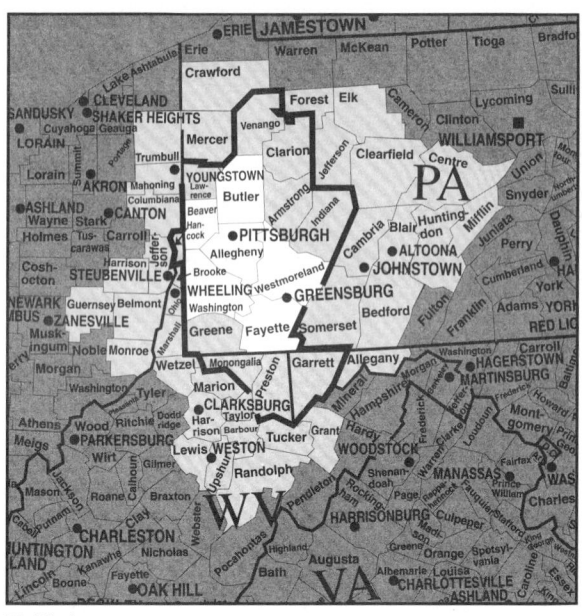

Pittsburgh (17)

ADI TV Households: 1,152,500

KDKA-TV Pittsburgh, ch. 2, CBS
WTAE-TV Pittsburgh, ch. 4, ABC
WPXI Pittsburgh, ch. 11, NBC
***WQED** Pittsburgh, ch. 13, ETV
***WQEX** Pittsburgh, ch. 16, ETV
WPTT-TV Pittsburgh, ch. 22, IND
***WNPB-TV** Morgantown, W. Va., ch. 24, ETV
***WGPT** Oakland, Md., ch. 36, ETV
WPCB-TV Greensburg, Pa., ch. 40, IND
WPGH-TV Pittsburgh, ch. 53, Fox

ADI Counties	State	TV Households			
Garrett	MD	10,300	Indiana	PA	31,400
Allegheny	PA	535,100	Lawrence	PA	35,800
Armstrong	PA	28,200	Venango	PA	21,600
Beaver	PA	71,800	Washington	PA	77,800
Butler	PA	57,200	Westmoreland	PA	143,900
Clarion	PA	14,800	Hancock	WV	13,800
Fayette	PA	55,400	Monongalia	WV	30,300
Greene	PA	14,200	Preston	WV	10,900

Portland, Ore. (27)

ADI TV Households: 886,600

KATU Portland, Ore., ch. 2, ABC
KOIN-TV Portland, Ore., ch. 6, CBS
***KOAC-TV** Corvallis, Ore., ch. 7, ETV
KGW-TV Portland, Ore., ch. 8, NBC
***KOPB-TV** Portland, Ore., ch. 10, ETV
KPTV Portland, Ore., ch. 12, IND
***KTVR** La Grande, Ore., ch. 13, ETV
KBSP-TV Salem, Ore., ch. 22, IND
KNMT Portland, Ore., ch. 24, IND
KEBN Salem, Ore., ch. 32, IND
KPDX Vancouver, Wash., ch. 49, Fox

ADI Counties	State	TV Households			
Baker	OR	5,900	Polk	OR	19,300
Clackamas	OR	109,100	Sherman	OR	800
Clatsop	OR	13,200	Tillamook	OR	8,700
Columbia	OR	14,500	Union	OR	8,800
Crook	OR	5,800	Wasco	OR	8,400
Gilliam	OR	700	Washington	OR	130,600
Harney	OR	2,700	Wheeler	OR	600
Hood River	OR	6,200	Yamhill	OR	23,300
Jefferson	OR	5,000	Clark	WA	96,500
Lincoln	OR	16,600	Cowlitz	WA	32,300
Linn	OR	35,100	Klickitat	WA	5,900
Marion	OR	86,000	Skamania	WA	3,100
Morrow	OR	2,800	Wahkiakum	WA	1,200
Multnomah	OR	243,500			

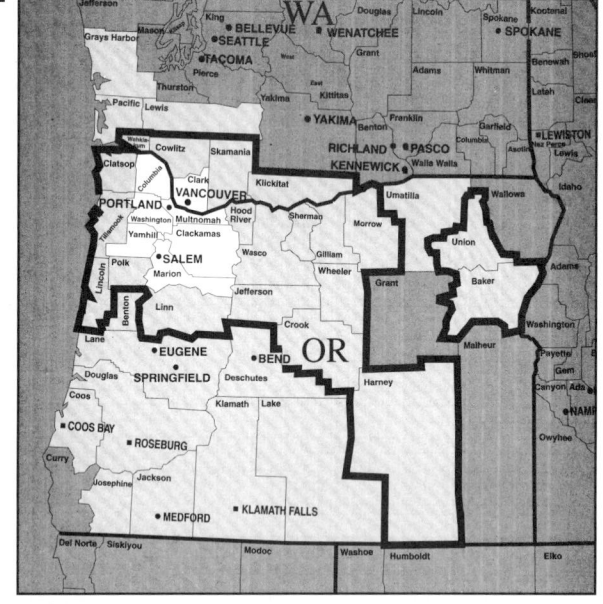

Portland-Poland Spring, Me. (76)

ADI TV Households: 338,200

WCSH-TV Portland, Me., ch. 6, NBC
WMTW-TV Poland Spring, Me., ch. 8, ABC
***WCBB** Augusta, Me., ch. 10, ETV
WGME-TV Portland, Me., ch. 13, CBS
***WMEA-TV** Biddeford, Me., ch. 26, ETV
WWLA Lewiston, Me., ch. 35, IND
***WLED-TV** Littleton, N.H., ch. 49, ETV
WPXT Portland, Me., ch. 51, Fox

ADI Counties	State	TV Households
Androscoggin	ME	39,400
Cumberland	ME	94,300
Franklin	ME	10,500
Kennebec	ME	44,000
Knox	ME	14,200
Lincoln	ME	11,900
Oxford	ME	19,900
Sagadahoc	ME	12,600
York	ME	62,500
Carroll	NH	15,100
Coos	NH	13,800

Broadcasting & Cable Yearbook 1994
C-178

Arbitron ADI Market Atlas

Presque Isle, Me. (205)

ADI TV Households: 30,100

WAGM-TV Presque Isle, Me., ch. 8, CBS (ABC, NBC)
***WMEM-TV** Presque Isle, Me., ch. 10, ETV

ADI Counties	State	TV Households
Aroostook	ME	30,100

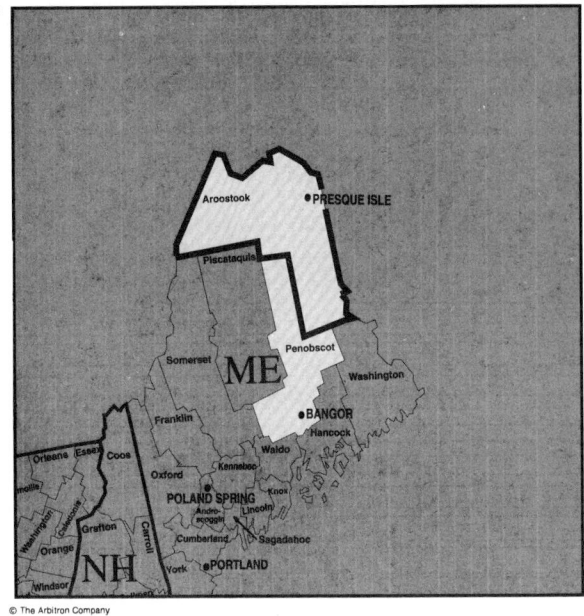

Providence, R.I.-New Bedford, Mass. (45)

ADI TV Households: 569,700

WLNE New Bedford, Mass., ch. 6, CBS
WJAR Providence, R.I., ch. 10, NBC
WPRI-TV Providence, R.I., ch. 12, ABC
WFDG New Bedford, Mass., ch. 28, IND
***WQEC** Quincy, Ill., ch. 27, ETV
WCVX Vineyard Haven, Mass., ch. 58, IND
WNAC-TV Providence, R.I., ch. 64, Fox
WOST-TV Block Island, R.I., ch. 69, IND

ADI Counties	State	TV Households
Bristol	MA	188,200
Dukes	MA	5,000
Bristol	RI	17,800
Kent	RI	62,800
Newport	RI	33,100
Providence	RI	222,400
Washington	RI	40,400

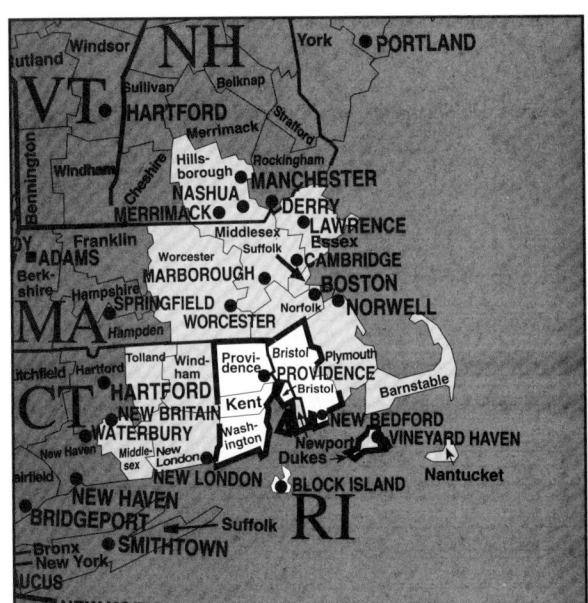

Quincy, Ill.-Hannibal, Mo. (159)

ADI TV Households: 104,400

KHQA-TV Hannibal, Mo., ch. 7, CBS
WGEM-TV Quincy, Ill., ch. 10, NBC
WTJR Quincy, Ill., ch. 16, IND
***WMEC** Macomb, Ill., ch. 22, ETV
***WQEC** Quincy, Ill., ch. 27, ETV

ADI Counties	State	TV Households			
Lee	IA	14,900	Clark	MO	2,800
Adams	IL	25,400	Knox	MO	1,800
Brown	IL	1,800	Lewis	MO	3,500
Hancock	IL	8,200	Marion	MO	10,500
McDonough	IL	12,000	Monroe	MO	3,500
Pike	IL	6,900	Ralls	MO	3,200
Schuyler	IL	3,000	Scotland	MO	1,900
Scott	IL	2,200	Shelby	MO	2,800

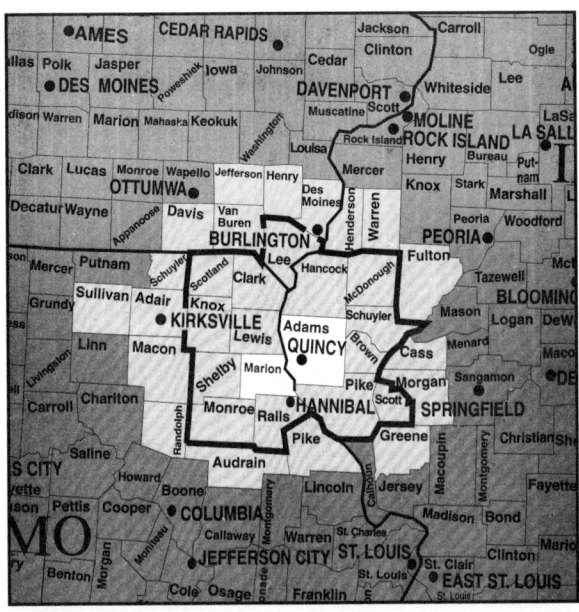

Arbitron ADI Market Atlas

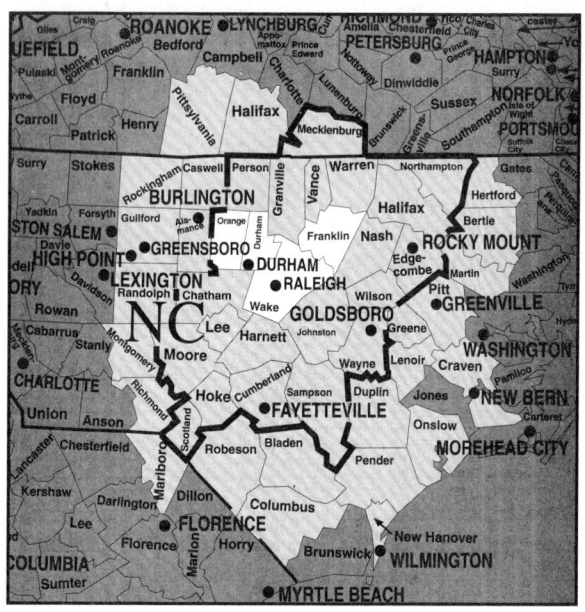

Raleigh-Durham (Fayetteville, Goldsboro & Rocky Mount), N.C. (32)

ADI TV Households: 769,300

*WUNC-TV Chapel Hill, N.C., ch. 4, ETV
WRAL-TV Raleigh, N.C., ch. 5, CBS
WTVD Durham, N.C., ch. 11, ABC
WYED Goldsboro, N.C., ch. 17, IND
WLFL-TV Raleigh, N.C., ch. 22, Fox
WRDC Durham, N.C., ch. 28, NBC
*WUNP-TV Roanoke Rapids, N.C., ch. 36, ETV
WKFT Fayetteville, N.C., ch. 40, IND
WRMY Rocky Mount, N.C., ch. 47, IND
WFCT Fayetteville, N.C., ch. 62, IND

ADI Counties	State	TV Households
Chatham	NC	15,900
Cumberland	NC	96,100
Durham	NC	77,300
Edgecombe	NC	20,200
Franklin	NC	14,300
Granville	NC	13,700
Halifax	NC	20,500
Harnett	NC	26,300
Hoke	NC	7,500
Johnston	NC	33,600
Lee	NC	16,400
Moore	NC	25,500
Nash	NC	30,400
Northampton	NC	7,400
Orange	NC	39,500
Person	NC	12,000
Sampson	NC	17,700
Scotland	NC	12,100
Vance	NC	14,400
Wake	NC	185,300
Warren	NC	6,300
Wayne	NC	40,100
Wilson	NC	25,600
Mecklenburg	VA	11,200

Rapid City, S.D. (168)

ADI TV Households: 91,100

KOTA-TV Rapid City, S.D., ch. 3, ABC
KIVV-TV Lead, S.D., ch. 5, satellite to KEVN-TV
KEVN-TV Rapid City, S.D., ch. 7, NBC
KRBQ Sheridan, Wyo., ch. 7, IND
*KZSD-TV Martin, S.D., ch. 8, ETV
*KBHE-TV Rapid City, S.D., ch. 9, ETV
KHSD-TV Lead, S.D., ch. 11, satellite to KOTA-TV
KSGW-TV Sheridan, Wyo., ch. 12, satellite to KOTA-TV
KCLO-TV Rapid City, S.D., ch. 15, IND

ADI Counties	State	TV Households
Carter	MT	600
Powder River	MT	700
Banner	NE	300
Box Butte	NE	4,800
Grant	NE	300
Morrill	NE	2,100
Sheridan	NE	2,600
Sioux	NE	600
Bennett	SD	1,000
Butte	SD	3,000
Custer	SD	2,300
Fall River	SD	2,700
Haakon	SD	900
Harding	SD	600
Jackson	SD	900
Lawrence	SD	8,200
Meade	SD	7,700
Pennington	SD	34,100
Perkins	SD	1,600
Shannon	SD	2,300
Ziebach	SD	600
Crook	WY	1,800
Sheridan	WY	9,100
Weston	WY	2,300

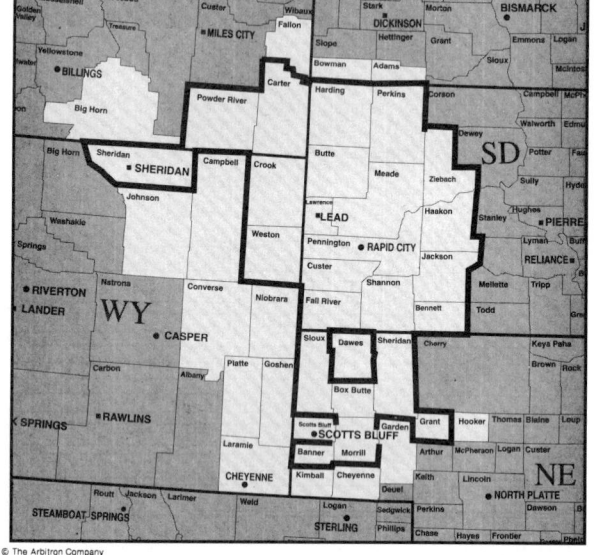

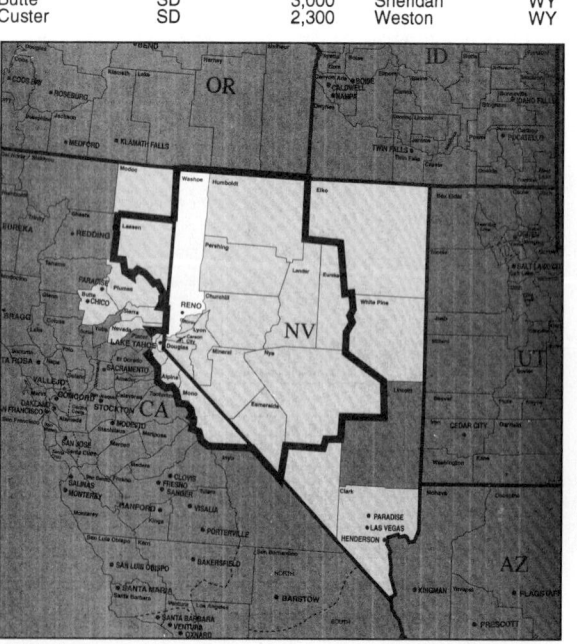

Reno, Nev. (118)

ADI TV Households: 195,100

KTVN Reno, ch. 2, CBS
KRNV Reno, ch. 4, NBC
*KNPB Reno, ch. 5, ETV
KOLO-TV Reno, ch. 8, ABC
KRXI Reno, ch. 11, IND
KAME-TV Reno, ch. 21, Fox
KREN-TV Reno, ch. 27, IND

ADI Counties	State	TV Households
Alpine	CA	400
El Dorado East	CA	13,200
Lassen	CA	8,600
Mono	CA	3,500
Placer East	CA	3,400
Carson City	NV	16,500
Churchill	NV	7,200
Douglas	NV	11,700
Esmeralda	NV	600
Eureka	NV	500
Humboldt	NV	5,000
Lander	NV	2,200
Lyon	NV	8,700
Mineral	NV	2,500
Nye North	NV	2,200
Pershing	NV	1,700
Storey	NV	1,000
Washoe	NV	106,200

Broadcasting & Cable Yearbook 1994
C-180

Richmond, Va. (61)

ADI TV Households: 448,900

WTVR-TV Richmond, Va., ch. 6, CBS
WRIC-TV Petersburg, Va., ch. 8, ABC
WWBT Richmond, Va., ch. 12, NBC
*WCVE-TV Richmond, Va., ch. 23, ETV
WRLH-TV Richmond, Va., ch. 35, Fox
*WVPT Staunton, Va., ch. 51, ETV
*WCVW Richmond, Va., ch. 57, ETV
WZXK Ashland, Va., ch. 65, IND

ADI Counties	State	TV Households			
Amelia	VA	3,000	King William	VA	4,200
Brunswick	VA	5,400	Lancaster	VA	4,600
Buckingham	VA	4,300	Louisa	VA	7,900
Caroline	VA	6,800	Lunenburg	VA	4,500
Charles City	VA	2,200	Middlesex	VA	3,600
Chesterfield	VA	88,200	Nelson	VA	4,900
Cumberland	VA	2,700	New Kent	VA	4,200
Dinwiddie	VA	22,000	Northumberland	VA	4,600
Essex	VA	3,200	Nottoway	VA	5,300
Fluvanna	VA	5,000	Orange	VA	8,600
Goochland	VA	5,200	Powhatan	VA	4,800
Greene	VA	3,900	Prince Edward	VA	5,300
Greensville	VA	4,600	Prince George	VA	17,300
Hanover	VA	25,100	Richmond	VA	2,700
Henrico	VA	93,800	Richmond City	VA	85,000
King and Queen	VA	2,300	Sussex	VA	3,700

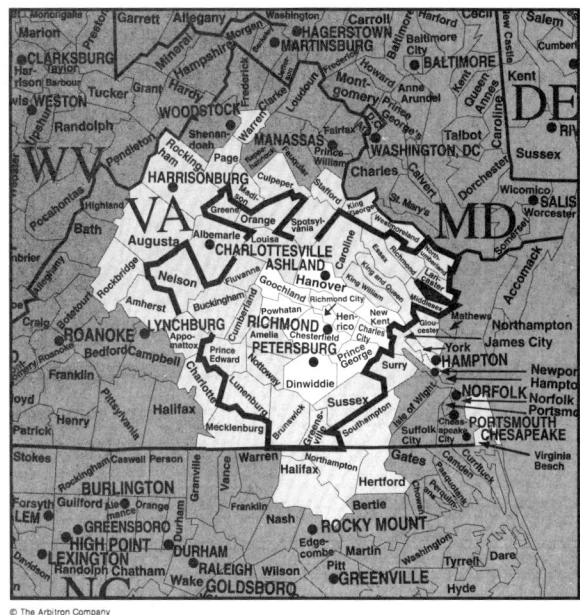

Roanoke-Lynchburg, Va. (66)

ADI TV Households: 387,200

WDBJ Roanoke, Va., ch. 7, CBS
WSLS-TV Roanoke, Va., ch. 10, NBC
WSET-TV Lynchburg, Va., ch. 13, ABC
*WBRA-TV Roanoke, Va., ch. 15, ETV
WJPR Lynchburg, Va., ch. 21, Fox
WPAJ Daneville, Va. ch. 24, IND
WVFT Roanoke, Va., ch. 27, satellite to WJPR
WEFC Roanoke, Va., ch. 38, IND
WPCT-TV Danville, Va., ch. 44, IND

ADI Counties	State	TV Households			
Alleghany	VA	9,600	Giles	VA	6,300
Amherst	VA	9,900	Grayson	VA	9,100
Appomattox	VA	4,600	Halifax	VA	13,400
Bath	VA	1,900	Henry	VA	28,500
Bedford	VA	21,200	Highland	VA	1,100
Botetourt	VA	9,400	Montgomery	VA	31,400
Campbell	VA	43,300	Pittsylvania	VA	41,900
Carroll	VA	10,100	Pulaski	VA	12,900
Charlotte	VA	4,200	Roanoke	VA	81,200
Craig	VA	1,700	Rockbridge	VA	11,600
Floyd	VA	5,000	Wythe	VA	10,000
Franklin	VA	15,400	Pocahontas	WV	3,500

Rochester, Minn.-Mason City, Iowa-Austin, Minn. (148)

ADI TV Households: 137,100

KIMT Mason City, Iowa, ch. 3, CBS
KAAL Austin, Minn., ch. 6, ABC
KTTC Rochester, Minn., ch. 10, NBC
*KSMQ-TV Austin, Minn., ch. 15, ETV
*KYIN Mason City, Iowa, ch. 24, ETV
KXLT-TV Rochester, Minn., ch. 47, IND

ADI Counties	State	TV Households			
Cerro Gordo	IA	19,500	Worth	IA	3,200
Floyd	IA	6,500	Dodge	MN	5,700
Hancock	IA	4,800	Fillmore	MN	7,700
Howard	IA	3,800	Freeborn	MN	12,900
Kossuth	IA	6,800	Mower	MN	14,800
Mitchell	IA	4,200	Olmsted	MN	42,500
Winnebago	IA	4,700			

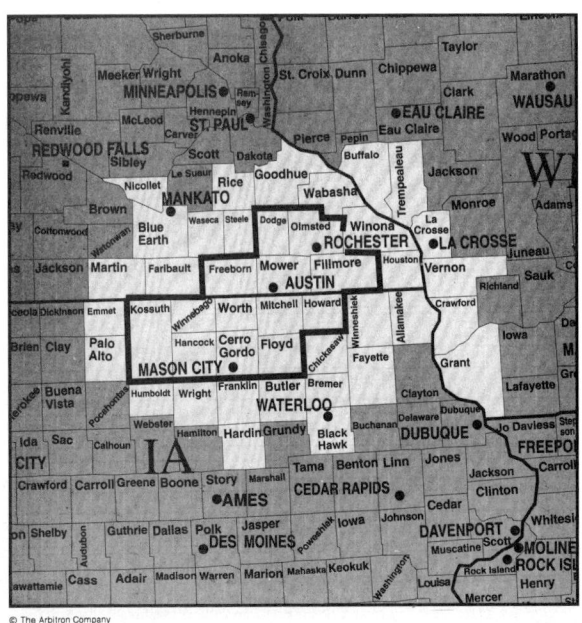

Arbitron ADI Market Atlas

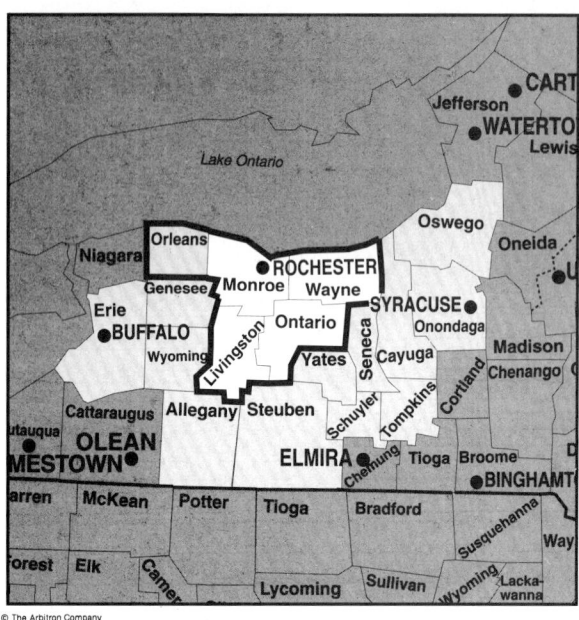

Rochester, N.Y. (69)

ADI TV Households: 377,300

WROC-TV Rochester, N.Y., ch. 8, CBS
WHEC-TV Rochester, N.Y., ch. 10, NBC
WOKR Rochester, N.Y., ch. 13, ABC
*WXXI-TV Rochester, N.Y., ch. 21, ETV
WUHF Rochester, N.Y., ch. 31, Fox

ADI Counties	State	TV Households
Livingston	NY	21,200
Monroe	NY	273,400
Ontario	NY	35,700
Orleans	NY	14,500
Wayne	NY	32,500

Rockford, Ill. (134)

ADI TV Households: 159,600

WREX-TV Rockford, Ill., ch. 13, ABC
WTVO Rockford, Ill., ch. 17, NBC
WIFR Rockford, Ill., ch 23, CBS
WQRF-TV Rockford, Ill., ch. 39, Fox

ADI Counties	State	TV Households
Boone	IL	11,500
Lee	IL	12,400
Ogle	IL	17,600
Stephenson	IL	18,900
Winnebago	IL	99,200

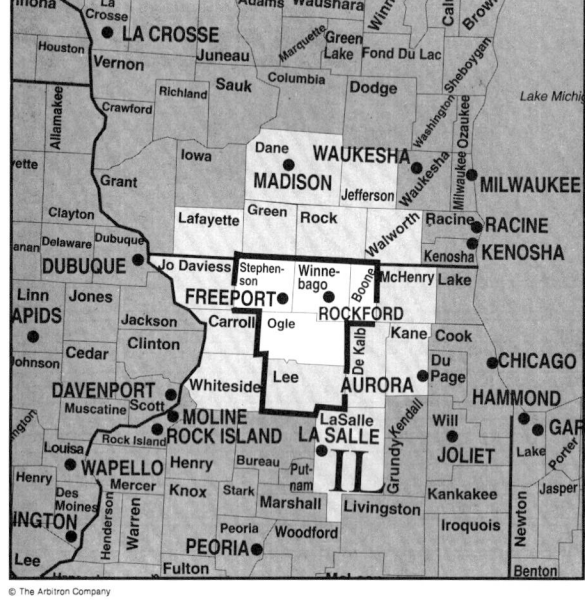

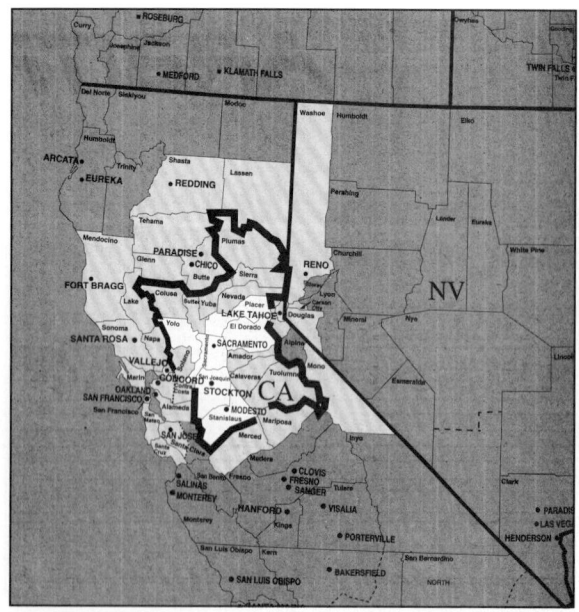

Sacramento-Stockton-Modesto, Calif. (19)

ADI TV Households: 1,093,000

KCRA-TV Sacramento, Calif., ch. 3, NBC
*KVIE Sacramento, Calif., ch. 6, ETV
KXTV Sacramento, Calif., ch. 10, CBS
KOVR Stockton, Calif., ch. 13, ABC
KCSO Modesto, Calif., ch. 19, IND
KCMY Sacramento, Calif., ch. 29, IND
KRBK-TV Sacramento, Calif., ch. 31, IND
KTXL Sacramento, Calif., ch. 40, Fox
KSCH-TV Stockton, Calif., ch. 58, IND
KFTL Stockton, Calif., ch. 64, IND

ADI Counties	State	TV Households			
Amador	CA	11,400	San Joaquin	CA	161,300
Calaveras	CA	14,400	Sierra	CA	1,200
Colusa	CA	5,700	Solano East	CA	73,500
El Dorado West	CA	39,400	Stanislaus	CA	134,000
Nevada	CA	32,800	Sutter	CA	25,400
Placer West	CA	67,800	Tuolumne	CA	18,900
Plumas	CA	8,400	Yolo	CA	53,100
Sacramento	CA	424,700	Yuba	CA	21,000

Broadcasting & Cable Yearbook 1994

Arbitron ADI Market Atlas

St. Joseph, Mo. (193)

ADI TV Households: 44,900

KQTV St. Joseph, Mo., ch. 2, ABC
KTAJ St. Joseph, Mo., ch. 16, IND

ADI Counties	State	TV Households
Buchanan	MO	31,800
Gentry	MO	2,600
Holt	MO	2,300
Nodaway	MO	7,200
Worth	MO	1,000

St. Louis (Mt. Vernon, Ill.) (18)

ADI TV Households: 1,114,200

KTVI St. Louis, ch. 2, ABC
KMOV St. Louis, ch. 4, CBS
KSDK St. Louis, ch. 5, NBC
*KETC St. Louis, ch. 9, ETV
KPLR-TV St. Louis, ch. 11, IND
KNLC St. Louis, ch. 24, IND
KDNL-TV St. Louis, ch. 30, Fox
WHSL East St. Louis, Ill., ch. 46, IND

ADI Counties	State	TV Households
Bond	IL	5,500
Calhoun	IL	2,000
Clinton	IL	11,400
Fayette	IL	7,500
Greene	IL	5,800
Jefferson	IL	14,200
Jersey	IL	7,600
Macoupin	IL	18,200
Madison	IL	96,200
Marion	IL	16,000
Monroe	IL	8,800
Randolph	IL	11,800
St. Clair	IL	94,100
Washington	IL	5,600
Crawford	MO	7,700
Franklin	MO	29,000
Gasconade	MO	5,800
Iron	MO	3,900
Jefferson	MO	62,700
Lincoln	MO	11,300
Madison	MO	4,400
Montgomery	MO	4,300
Perry	MO	6,100
Pike	MO	6,000
St. Charles	MO	84,500
St. Francois	MO	18,600
St. Louis	MO	387,400
St. Louis City	MO	157,100
Ste. Genevieve	MO	5,900
Warren	MO	7,700
Washington	MO	7,100

Salinas-Monterey, Calif. (103)

ADI TV Households: 233,100

KSBW Salinas, Calif., ch. 8, NBC
KNTV San Jose, Calif., ch. 11, ABC
*KCAH Watsonville, Calif., ch. 25, ETV
KCBA Salinas, Calif., ch. 35, Fox
KMST Monterey, Calif., ch. 46, CBS
KSMS-TV Monterey, Calif., ch. 67, IND

ADI Counties	State	TV Households
Monterey	CA	114,300
San Benito	CA	11,600
Santa Clara East	CA	26,400
Santa Cruz	CA	80,800

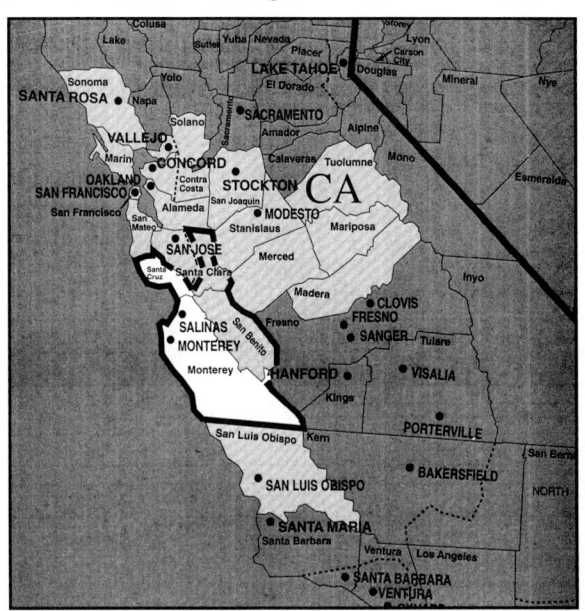

Broadcasting & Cable Yearbook 1994

Arbitron ADI Market Atlas

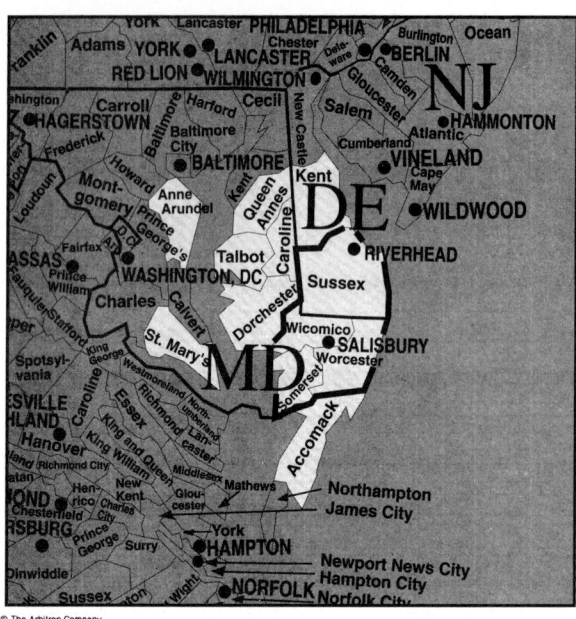

Salisbury, Md. (163)

ADI TV Households: 98,800

WBOC-TV Salisbury, Md., ch. 16, CBS (NBC)
*WCPB Salisbury, Md., ch. 28, ETV
WMDT Salisbury, Md., ch. 47, ABC (NBC)
*WDPB Seaford, Del., ch. 64, ETV

ADI Counties	State	TV Households
Sussex	DE	46,700
Somerset	MD	7,900
Wicomico	MD	29,100
Worcester	MD	15,100

Salt Lake City (Cedar City), Utah (41)

ADI TV Households: 614,700

KUTV Salt Lake City, ch. 2, NBC
KJVI Jackson, Wyo., ch. 2, ABC
KCCZ Cedar City, Utah, ch. 4, IND
KTVX Salt Lake City, ch. 4, ABC
KSL-TV Salt Lake City, ch. 5, CBS
*KUED Salt Lake City, ch. 7, ETV
*KULC Ogden, Utah, ch. 9, ETV
*KBYU-TV Provo, Utah, ch. 11, ETV
KUSG St. George, Utah, ch. 12, IND
KSTU Salt Lake City, ch. 13, Fox
KXIV Salt Lake City, ch. 14, IND
KOOG-TV Ogden, Utah, ch. 30, IND

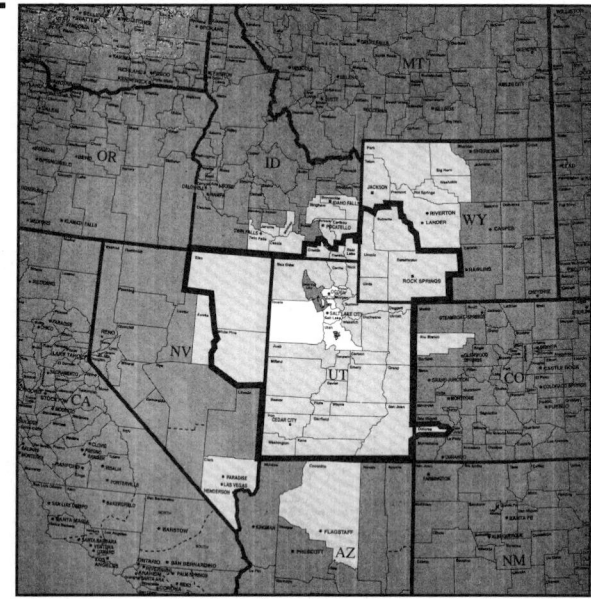

ADI Counties	State	TV Households
Dolores	CO	500
Bear Lake	ID	2,000
Franklin	ID	3,000
Oneida	ID	1,200
Elko	NV	12,600
White Pine	NV	3,100
Beaver	UT	1,600
Box Elder	UT	11,500
Cache	UT	21,200
Carbon	UT	6,700
Daggett	UT	300
Davis	UT	58,400
Duchesne	UT	3,600
Emery	UT	2,900
Garfield	UT	1,200
Grand	UT	2,300
Iron	UT	6,300
Juab	UT	1,800
Kane	UT	1,700
Millard	UT	3,200
Morgan	UT	1,600
Piute	UT	500
Rich	UT	500
Salt Lake	UT	255,000
San Juan	UT	2,900
Sanpete	UT	4,900
Sevier	UT	4,900
Summit	UT	6,000
Tooele	UT	9,100
Uintah	UT	6,900
Utah	UT	74,800
Wasatch	UT	3,300
Washington	UT	17,000
Wayne	UT	700
Weber	UT	56,100
Lincoln	WY	4,100
Sublette	WY	1,800
Sweetwater	WY	13,700
Uinta	WY	5,800

Arbitron ADI Market Atlas

San Angelo, Tex. (190)

ADI TV Households: 49,200

KIDY San Angelo, Tex., ch. 6, Fox
KLST San Angelo, Tex., ch. 8, CBS

ADI Counties	State	TV Households
Coke	TX	1,400
Concho	TX	1,000
Crockett	TX	1,400
Irion	TX	600
Kimble	TX	1,500
McCulloch	TX	3,100
Menard	TX	900
Schleicher	TX	1,000
Sterling	TX	500
Sutton	TX	1,500
Tom Green	TX	36,300

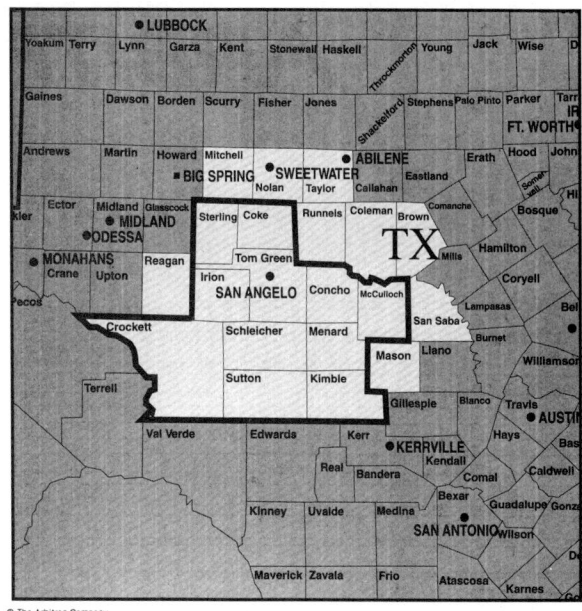

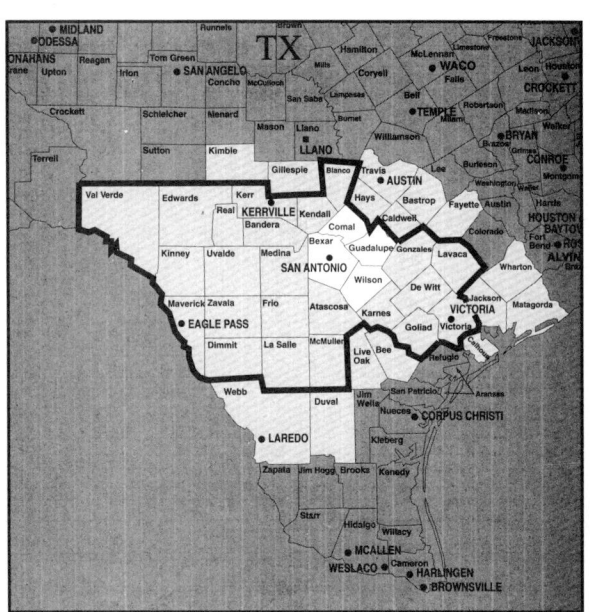

San Antonio-Victoria (Eagle Pass & Kerrville), Tex. (36)

ADI TV Households: 636,300

KMOL-TV San Antonio, Tex., ch. 4, NBC
KENS-TV San Antonio, Tex., ch. 5, CBS
*****KLRN** San Antonio, Tex., ch. 9, ETV
KTRG Del Rio, Tex., ch. 10, IND
KSAT-TV San Antonio, Tex., ch. 12, ABC
KVAW Eagle Pass, Tex., ch. 16, IND
*****KHCE** San Antonio, Tex., ch. 23, ETV
KABB San Antonio, Tex., ch. 29, IND
KRRT Kerrville, Tex., ch. 35, Fox
KWEX-TV San Antonio, Tex., ch. 41, IND
KVDA San Antonio, Tex., ch. 60, IND

ADI Counties	State	TV Households
Atascosa	TX	10,500
Bandera	TX	4,700
Bexar	TX	435,000
Blanco	TX	2,700
Comal	TX	21,300
DeWitt	TX	6,800
Dimmit	TX	3,100
Edwards	TX	800
Frio	TX	4,200
Goliad	TX	2,200
Gonzales	TX	6,200
Guadalupe	TX	24,100
Karnes	TX	4,200
Kendall	TX	6,200
Kerr	TX	15,200
Kinney	TX	1,200
LaSalle	TX	1,700
Lavaca	TX	7,100
Maverick	TX	10,300
McMullen	TX	300
Medina	TX	9,700
Real	TX	900
Uvalde	TX	7,700
Val Verde	TX	12,200
Victoria	TX	26,600
Wilson	TX	8,100
Zavala	TX	3,300

San Diego (24)

ADI TV Households: 919,900

XETV Tijuana, Mexico, ch. 6, Fox
KFMB-TV San Diego, ch. 8, CBS
KGTV San Diego, ch. 10, ABC
*****KPBS** San Diego, ch. 15, ETV
KNSD San Diego, ch. 39, NBC
KUSI-TV San Diego, ch. 51, IND
KTTY San Diego, ch. 69, IND

ADI Counties	State	TV Households
San Diego	CA	919,900

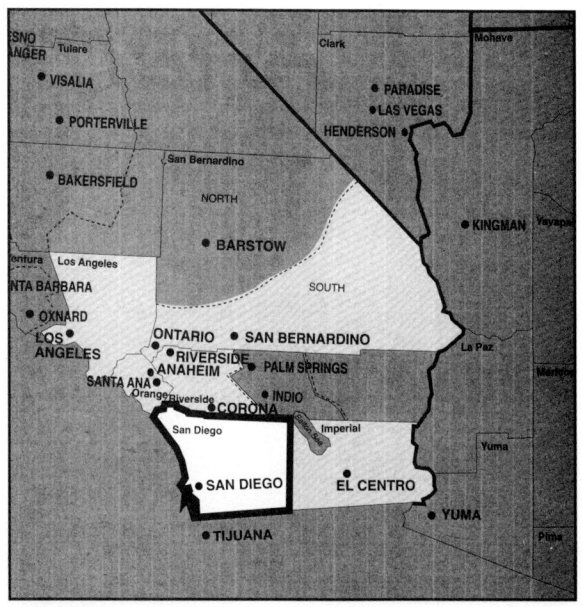

Arbitron ADI Market Atlas

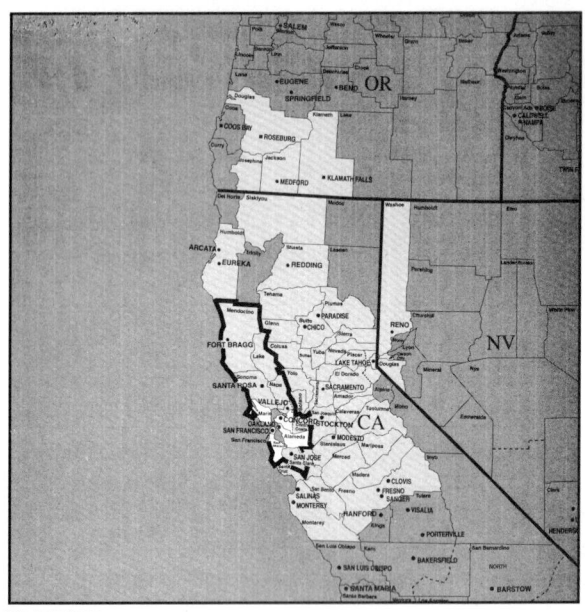

San Francisco-Oakland-San Jose (Santa Rosa & Vallejo), Calif. (5)

ADI TV Households: 2,225,500

KTVU Oakland, Calif., ch. 2, Fox
KRON-TV San Francisco, ch. 4, NBC
KPIX San Francisco, ch. 5, CBS
KGO-TV San Francisco, ch. 7, ABC
KFWU Fort Bragg, Calif., ch. 8, ABC
***KQED** San Francisco, ch. 9, ETV
KNTV San Jose, Calif., ch. 11, ABC
KDTV San Francisco, ch. 14, IND
KOFY-TV San Francisco, ch. 20, IND
***KRCB-TV** Cotati, Calif., ch. 22, ETV
KTSF San Francisco, ch. 26, IND
***KQEC** San Francisco, ch. 32, ETV
KICU-TV San Jose, Calif., ch. 36, IND
KCNS San Francisco, ch. 38, IND
KFCB Concord, Calif., ch. 42, IND
KBHK-TV San Francisco, ch. 44, IND
KSTS San Jose, Calif., ch. 48, IND
KFTY Santa Rosa, Calif., ch. 50, IND
***KTEH** San Jose, Calif., ch. 54, ETV
***KCSM-TV** San Mateo, Calif., ch. 60, ETV
KLXV-TV San Jose, Calif., ch. 65, IND
KPST-TV Vallejo, Calif., ch. 66, IND
KWOK Novato, Calif., ch. 68, IND

ADI Counties	State	TV Households
Alameda	CA	483,600
Contra Costa East	CA	47,900
Contra Costa West	CA	268,600
Lake	CA	22,100
Marin	CA	96,800
Mendocino	CA	30,300
Napa	CA	42,200
San Francisco	CA	292,900
San Mateo	CA	247,600
Santa Clara West	CA	487,500
Solano West	CA	50,800
Sonoma	CA	155,200

Santa Barbara-Santa Maria-San Luis Obispo (Oxnard), Calif. (112)

ADI TV Households: 210,700

KEYT-TV Santa Barbara, Calif., ch. 3, ABC
KSBY-TV San Luis Obispo, Calif., ch. 6, NBC
KCOY-TV Santa Maria, Calif., ch. 12, CBS
KADE San Luis Obispo, Calif., ch. 33, IND
KADY-TV Oxnard, Calif., ch. 63, IND

ADI Counties	State	TV Households
San Luis Obispo	CA	80,900
Santa Barbara N.	CA	60,600
Santa Barbara S.	CA	69,200

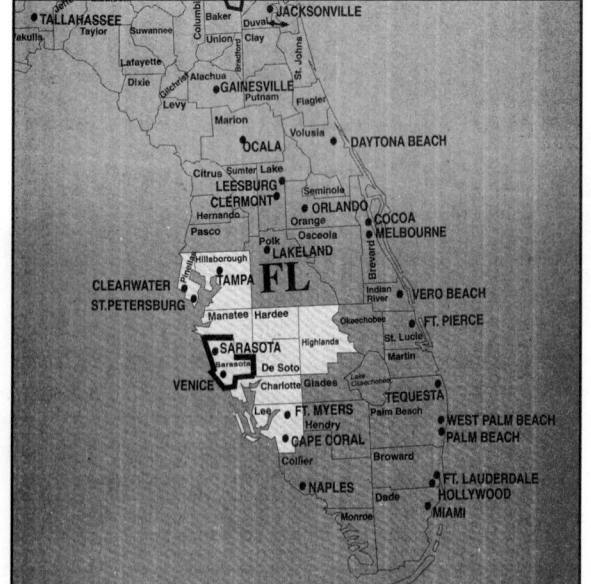

Sarasota, Fla. (153)

ADI TV Households: 133,500

WWSB Sarasota, Fla., ch. 40, ABC
WBSW-TV Venice, Fla., ch. 62, IND

ADI Counties	State	TV Households
Sarasota	FL	133,500

Broadcasting & Cable Yearbook 1994

Arbitron ADI Market Atlas

Savannah (Baxley), Ga. (101)

ADI TV Households: 238,200

WSAV-TV Savannah, Ga., ch. 3, ABC
***WVAN-TV** Savannah, Ga., ch. 9, ETV
WTOC-TV Savannah, Ga., ch. 11, CBS
***WJWJ-TV** Beaufort, S.C., ch. 16, ETV
WJCL Savannah, Ga., ch. 22, NBC
WTGS Hardeeville, S.C., ch. 28, Fox
WUBI Baxley, Ga., ch. 34, IND

ADI Counties	State	TV Households			
Appling	GA	6,100	McIntosh	GA	3,100
Bacon	GA	3,400	Montgomery	GA	2,400
Bryan	GA	6,000	Pierce	GA	4,800
Bulloch	GA	15,700	Screven	GA	4,900
Candler	GA	2,900	Tattnall	GA	5,600
Chatham	GA	83,200	Toombs	GA	8,900
Effingham	GA	9,600	Treutlen	GA	2,200
Evans	GA	3,300	Wayne	GA	8,200
Jeff Davis	GA	4,300	Beaufort	SC	33,400
Liberty	GA	16,200	Hampton	SC	6,300
Long	GA	2,200	Jasper	SC	5,500

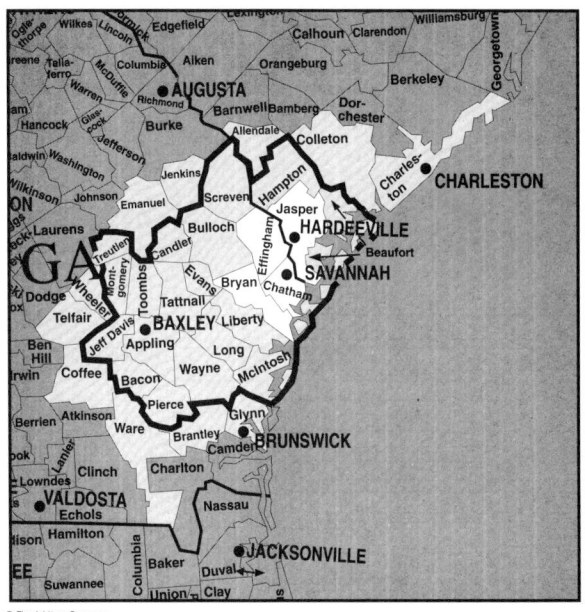

Seattle-Tacoma (Bellingham & Wenatchee), Wash. (13)

ADI TV Households: 1,438,600

KOMO-TV Seattle, ch. 4, ABC
KING-TV Seattle, ch. 5, NBC
KIRO-TV Seattle, ch. 7, CBS
***KCTS-TV** Seattle, ch. 9, ETV
KSTW Tacoma, Wash., ch. 11, IND
KVOS-TV Bellingham, Wash., ch. 12, CBS
KCPQ Tacoma, Wash., ch. 13, Fox
***KCKA** Centralia, Wash., ch. 15, ETV
KONG-TV Everett, Wash., ch. 16, IND

KTBW-TV Tacoma, Wash., ch. 20, IND
KTZZ-TV Seattle, ch. 22, IND
***KTBS** Tacoma, Wash., ch. 28, ETV
KBGE Bellevue, Wash., ch. 33, IND
KHCV Seattle, ch. 45, IND
KBEH Bellevue, Wash., ch. 51, IND
***KWDK** Tacoma, Wash., ch. 56 ETV
KBCB Bellingham, Wash., ch. 64, IND

ADI Counties	State	TV Households			
Chelan	WA	21,000	Lewis	WA	22,900
Clallam	WA	23,800	Mason	WA	15,800
Douglas	WA	10,700	Pacific	WA	7,600
Grays Harbor	WA	24,900	Pierce	WA	228,200
Island	WA	24,200	San Juan	WA	5,000
Jefferson	WA	9,500	Skagit	WA	33,100
King	WA	627,900	Snohomish	WA	185,200
Kitsap	WA	76,100	Thurston	WA	68,200
Kittitas West	WA	2,500	Whatcom	WA	52,000

Sherman-Ada, Okla. (156)

ADI TV Households: 108,600

KTEN Ada, Okla., ch. 10, ABC (NBC-CBS)
KXII Ardmore, Okla., ch. 12, CBS (NBC)

ADI Counties	State	TV Households
Atoka	OK	4,500
Bryan	OK	12,800
Carter	OK	16,300
Choctaw	OK	6,100
Coal	OK	2,300
Johnston	OK	3,700
Love	OK	3,000
Marshall	OK	4,600
Pontotoc	OK	13,600
Pushmataha	OK	4,300
Grayson	TX	37,400

Broadcasting & Cable Yearbook 1994
C-187

Arbitron ADI Market Atlas

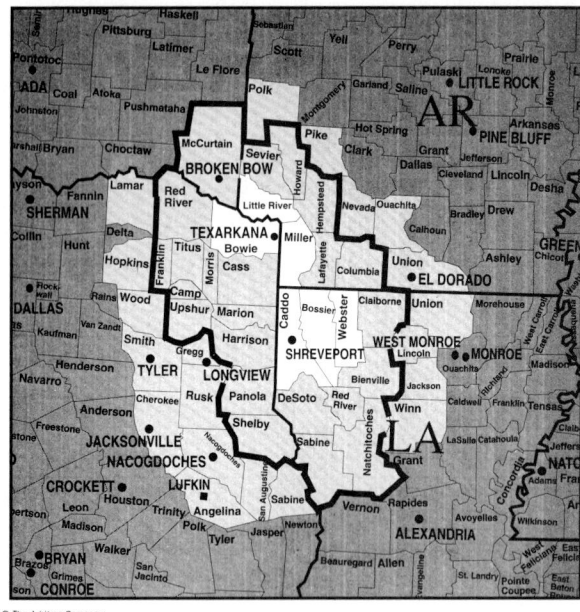

Shreveport, La.-Texarkana, Tex. (71)

ADI TV Households: 368,100

KTBS-TV Shreveport, La., ch. 3, ABC
KTAL-TV Texarkana, Tex., ch. 6, NBC
KSLA-TV Shreveport, La., ch. 12, CBS
***KLTS-TV** Shreveport, La., ch. 24, ETV
KMSS-TV Shreveport, La., ch. 33, Fox
KWLB Shreveport, La., ch. 45, IND

ADI Counties	State	TV Households
Columbia	AR	9,500
Hempstead	AR	8,300
Howard	AR	5,100
Lafayette	AR	3,500
Little River	AR	5,100
Miller	AR	14,400
Sevier	AR	5,200
Bienville	LA	5,900
Bossier	LA	31,200
Caddo	LA	92,900
Claiborne	LA	6,000
DeSoto	LA	8,800
Natchitoches	LA	12,500
Red River	LA	3,000
Sabine	LA	8,100
Webster	LA	15,800
McCurtain	OK	12,200
Bowie	TX	30,900
Camp	TX	3,800
Cass	TX	11,400
Franklin	TX	2,900
Harrison	TX	20,500
Marion	TX	3,900
Morris	TX	4,800
Panola	TX	8,400
Red River	TX	5,300
Shelby	TX	8,400
Titus	TX	8,400
Upshur	TX	11,900

Sioux City, Iowa (140)

ADI TV Households: 155,100

KTIV Sioux City, Iowa, ch. 4, NBC
KCAU-TV Sioux City, Iowa, ch. 9, ABC
KMEG Sioux City, Iowa, ch. 14, CBS
***KXNE-TV** Norfolk, Neb., ch. 19, ETV
***KSIN** Sioux City, Iowa, ch. 27, ETV

ADI Counties	State	TV Households
Buena Vista	IA	7,600
Cherokee	IA	5,300
Clay	IA	7,000
Dickinson	IA	6,500
Ida	IA	3,200
Monona	IA	4,000
O'Brien	IA	6,000
Palo Alto	IA	3,800
Plymouth	IA	8,400
Sac	IA	4,800
Sioux	IA	10,100
Woodbury	IA	37,900
Antelope	NE	2,900
Cedar	NE	3,600
Dakota	NE	6,100
Dixon	NE	2,300
Knox	NE	3,700
Madison	NE	12,400
Pierce	NE	2,900
Stanton	NE	2,200
Thurston	NE	2,300
Wayne	NE	3,200
Wheeler	NE	300
Clay	SD	4,500
Union	SD	4,100

Sioux Falls-Mitchell, S.D. (108)

ADI TV Households: 219,900

KUSD-TV Vermillion, S.D., ch. 2, ETV
KDLT Mitchell, S.D., ch. 5, NBC
*KESD-TV Brookings, S.D., ch. 8, ETV
*KTSD-TV Pierre, S.D., ch. 10, ETV
KELO-TV Sioux Falls, S.D., ch 11, CBS
KDLO-TV Florence, S.D., ch. 3, satellite to KELO-TV
KPLO-TV Reliance, S.D., ch. 6, satellite to KELO-TV
*KRNE-TV Merriman, Neb., ch. 12, ETV
KTTM Huron, S.D., ch. 12, Fox
*KPSD-TV Eagle Butte, S.D., ch. 13, ETV
KSFY-TV Sioux Falls, S.D., ch. 13, ABC
KPRY-TV Pierre, S.D., ch. 4, satellite to KSFY-TV
KABY-TV Aberdeen, S.D., ch. 9, satellite to KSFY-TV
*KDSD-TV Aberdeen, S.D., ch. 16, ETV
KTTW Sioux Falls, S.D., ch. 17, Fox

ADI Counties	State	TV Households
Lyon	IA	4,200
Osceola	IA	2,800
Lincoln	MN	2,700
Murray	MN	3,700
Nobles	MN	7,300
Pipestone	MN	4,000
Rock	MN	3,600
Boyd	NE	1,100
Cherry	NE	2,400
Keya Paha	NE	400
Aurora	SD	1,100
Beadle	SD	7,100
Bon Homme	SD	2,300
Brookings	SD	9,200
Brown	SD	14,100
Brule	SD	2,200
Buffalo	SD	500
Charles Mix	SD	3,100
Clark	SD	1,700
Codington	SD	9,000
Davison	SD	6,900
Day	SD	2,700
Deuel	SD	1,800
Douglas	SD	1,300
Edmunds	SD	1,600
Faulk	SD	1,000
Grant	SD	3,100
Gregory	SD	2,100
Hamlin	SD	1,900
Hand	SD	1,600
Hanson	SD	1,100
Hughes	SD	5,800
Hutchinson	SD	3,100
Hyde	SD	700
Jerauld	SD	1,000
Jones	SD	500
Kingsbury	SD	2,300
Lake	SD	4,000
Lincoln	SD	5,700
Lyman	SD	1,300
Marshall	SD	1,900
McCook	SD	2,100
McPherson	SD	1,300
Mellette	SD	700
Miner	SD	1,300
Minnehaha	SD	50,200
Moody	SD	2,400
Potter	SD	1,300
Roberts	SD	3,500
Sanborn	SD	1,000
Spink	SD	3,000
Stanley	SD	900
Sully	SD	600
Todd	SD	2,200
Tripp	SD	2,600
Turner	SD	3,300
Walworth	SD	2,300
Yankton	SD	7,300

South Bend-Elkhart, Ind. (83)

ADI TV Households: 299,600

WNDU-TV South Bend, Ind., ch. 16, NBC
WSBT-TV South Bend, Ind., ch. 22, CBS
WSJV Elkhart, Ind., ch. 28, ABC
*WNIT-TV South Bend, Ind., ch. 34, ETV
WHME-TV South Bend, Ind., ch. 46, IND

ADI Counties	State	TV Households
Elkhart	IN	57,800
Fulton	IN	7,300
Kosciusko	IN	23,600
Lagrange	IN	9,400
Marshall	IN	15,800
Pulaski	IN	4,600
St. Joseph	IN	94,300
Starke	IN	8,200
Berrien	MI	60,500
Cass	MI	18,100

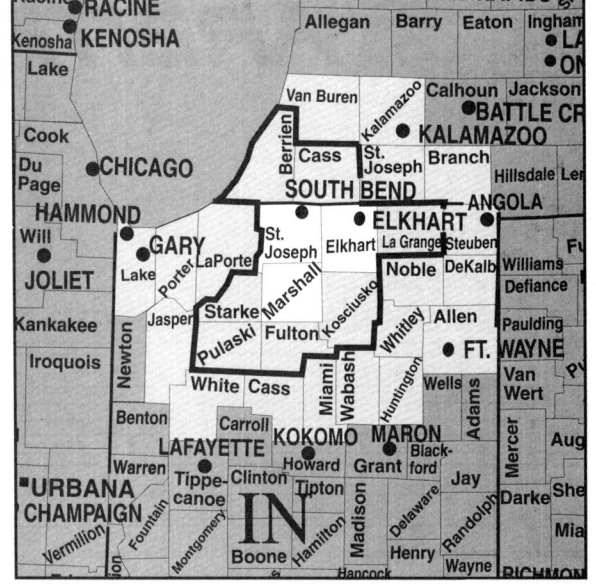

Arbitron ADI Market Atlas

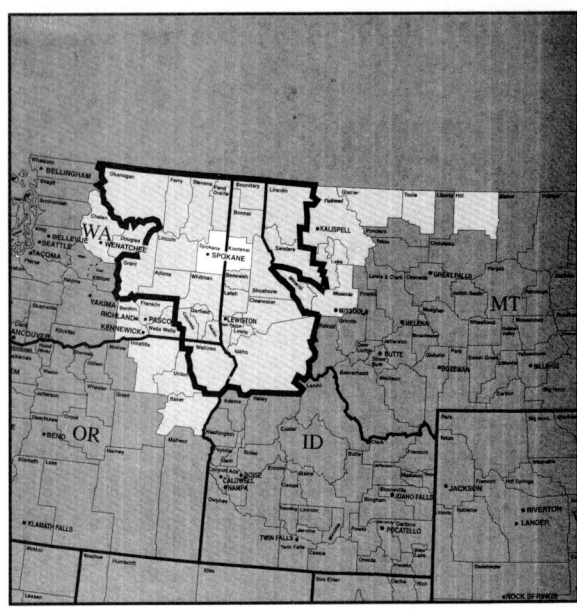

Spokane, Wash. (78)

ADI TV Households: 331,500

KREM-TV Spokane, Wash., ch. 2, CBS
KXLY-TV Spokane, Wash., ch 4, ABC
KHQ-TV Spokane, Wash., ch. 6, NBC
***KSPS-TV** Spokane, Wash., ch. 7, ETV
***KWSU-TV** Pullman, Wash., ch. 10, ETV
***KUID-TV** Moscow, Idaho, ch. 12, ETV
KSKN Spokane, Wash., ch. 22, IND
***KCDT** Coeur d'Alene, Idaho, ch. 26, ETV
KCWT Wenatchee, Wash., ch. 27, IND
KAYU-TV Spokane, Wash., ch. 28, Fox

ADI Counties	State	TV Households
Benewah	ID	3,200
Bonner	ID	11,300
Boundary	ID	3,100
Clearwater	ID	3,100
Idaho	ID	5,300
Kootenai	ID	29,900
Latah	ID	11,800
Lewis	ID	1,500
Nez Perce	ID	14,100
Shoshone	ID	5,500
Lincoln	MT	6,800
Sanders	MT	3,300
Wallowa	OR	2,700
Adams	WA	4,700
Asotin	WA	7,100
Columbia	WA	1,500
Ferry	WA	2,300
Garfield	WA	900
Grant	WA	20,700
Lincoln	WA	3,700
Okanogan	WA	12,400
Pend Oreille	WA	3,500
Spokane	WA	147,800
Stevens	WA	11,600
Whitman	WA	13,700

© The Arbitron Company

Springfield-Decatur-Champaign, Ill. (75)

ADI TV Households: 342,000

WCIA Champaign, Ill., ch. 3, CBS
***WILL-TV** Urbana, Ill., ch. 12, ETV
***WSEC** Jacksonville, Ill., ch. 14, ETV
WAND Decatur, Ill., ch. 17, ABC
WICS Springfield, Ill., ch. 20, NBC
WICD Champaign, Ill., ch. 15, satellite to WICS
WFHL Decatur, Ill., ch. 23, IND
WCCU Urbana, Ill., ch. 27, satellite to WRSP-TV
WCFN Springfield, Ill., ch. 49, IND
***WEIU-TV** Charleston, Ill., ch. 51, ETV
WRSP-TV Springfield, Ill., ch. 55, Fox

ADI Counties	State	TV Households			
Cass	IL	5,000	Macon	IL	45,400
Champaign	IL	64,500	Menard	IL	4,100
Christian	IL	13,200	Montgomery	IL	11,300
Coles	IL	19,000	Morgan	IL	13,300
DeWitt	IL	6,400	Moultrie	IL	5,000
Douglas	IL	7,100	Piatt	IL	5,800
Effingham	IL	11,500	Sangamon	IL	73,300
Ford	IL	5,400	Shelby	IL	8,400
Logan	IL	10,100	Vermilion	IL	33,200

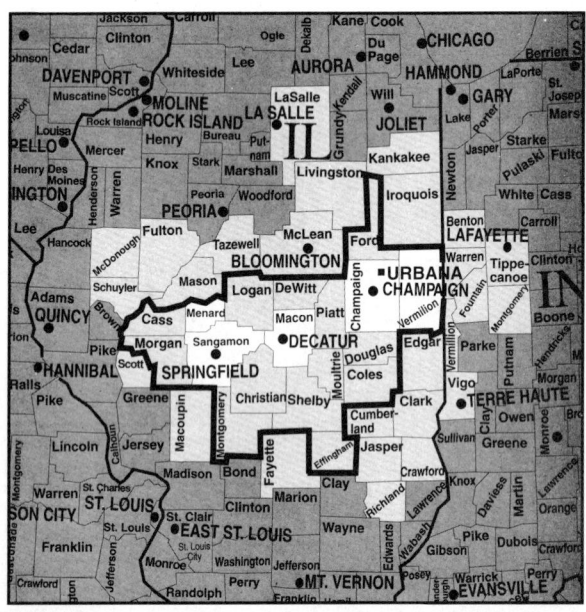

© The Arbitron Company

Broadcasting & Cable Yearbook 1994

Arbitron ADI Market Atlas

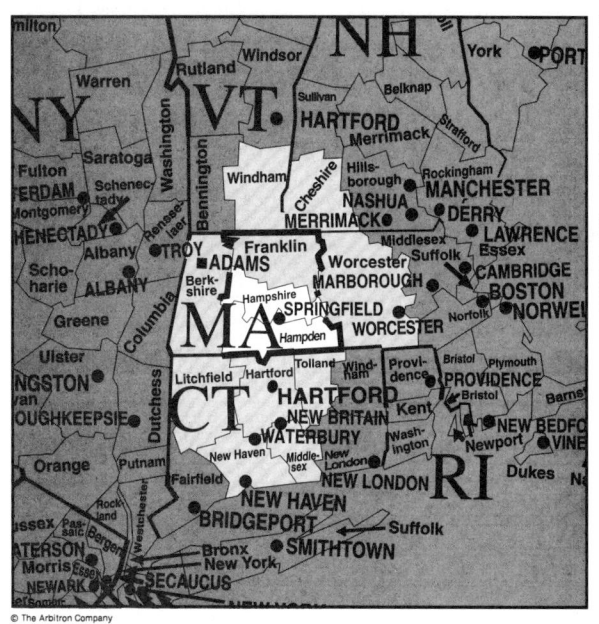

Springfield, Mass. (98)

ADI TV Households: 246,900

WWLP Springfield, Mass., ch. 22, NBC
WGGB-TV Springfield, Mass., ch. 40, ABC
***WGBY-TV** Springfield, Mass., ch. 57, ETV

ADI Counties	State	TV Households
Franklin	MA	27,700
Hampden	MA	168,700
Hampshire	MA	50,500

Springfield, Mo. (80)

ADI TV Households: 326,600

KYTV Springfield, Mo., ch. 3, NBC
KOLR Springfield, Mo., ch. 10, CBS
***KOZK** Springfield, Mo., ch. 21, ETV
KDEB-TV Springfield, Mo., ch. 27, Fox
KSPR Springfield, Mo., ch. 33, ABC

ADI Counties	State	TV Households
Baxter	AR	14,100
Boone	AR	11,400
Carroll	AR	7,900
Fulton	AR	4,000
Marion	AR	5,100
Newton	AR	2,700
Searcy	AR	2,900
Barry	MO	11,300
Benton	MO	5,900
Camden	MO	11,900
Cedar	MO	4,900
Christian	MO	13,500
Dade	MO	3,200
Dallas	MO	5,200
Dent	MO	5,100
Douglas	MO	4,600
Greene	MO	83,600
Hickory	MO	3,300
Howell	MO	12,400
Laclede	MO	10,500
Lawrence	MO	11,900
Oregon	MO	3,600
Ozark	MO	3,500
Phelps	MO	13,700
Polk	MO	8,300
Pulaski	MO	12,700
St. Clair	MO	3,400
Shannon	MO	2,800
Stone	MO	8,600
Taney	MO	11,100
Texas	MO	8,400
Webster	MO	8,700
Wright	MO	6,400

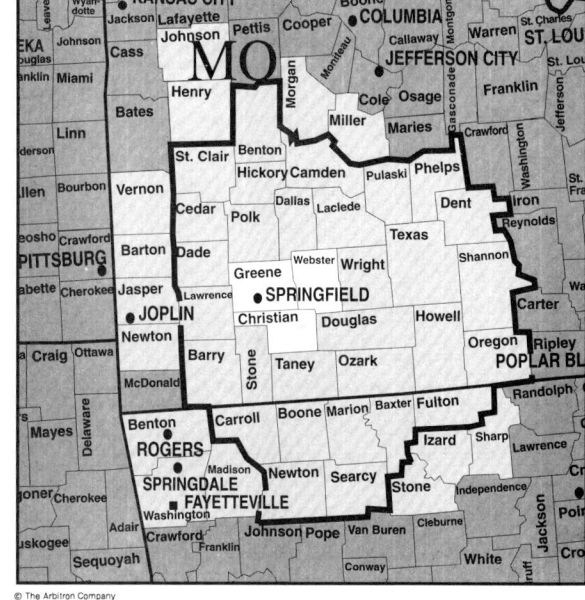

Syracuse, N.Y. (67)

ADI TV Households: 387,100

WSTM-TV Syracuse, N.Y., ch. 3, NBC
WTVH Syracuse, N.Y., ch. 5, CBS
WIXT Syracuse, N.Y., ch. 9, ABC
***WCNY-TV** Syracuse, N.Y., ch. 24, ETV
WSNR-TV Syracuse, N.Y., ch. 43, IND
WACA Ithaca, N.Y., ch. 52, IND
WSYT Syracuse, N.Y., ch. 68, Fox

ADI Counties	State	TV Households
Cayuga	NY	28,700
Cortland	NY	17,100
Madison	NY	23,800
Oneida West	NY	35,300
Onondaga	NY	178,500
Oswego	NY	43,500
Schuyler	NY	6,700
Seneca	NY	12,100
Tompkins	NY	32,800
Yates	NY	8,600

Broadcasting & Cable Yearbook 1994

Tallahassee, Fla.-Thomasville, Ga. (Bainbridge, Ga.) (115)

ADI TV Households: 201,100

WCTV Thomasville, Ga., ch. 6, CBS
*WFSU-TV Tallahassee, Fla., ch. 11, ETV
WTXL-TV Tallahassee, Fla., ch. 27, ABC
WTWC Tallahassee, Fla., ch. 40, NBC
WTLH Bainbridge, Ga., ch. 49, IND
WFXU Live Oak, Fla., ch. 57, IND

ADI Counties	State	TV Households
Franklin	FL	3,600
Gadsden	FL	13,700
Hamilton	FL	3,500
Jefferson	FL	3,900
Lafayette	FL	1,900
Leon	FL	80,000
Madison	FL	5,500
Suwannee	FL	10,700
Taylor	FL	6,500
Wakulla	FL	5,500
Brooks	GA	5,300
Decatur	GA	9,100
Echols	GA	800
Grady	GA	7,400
Lowndes	GA	26,900
Miller	GA	2,300
Thomas	GA	14,500

Tampa-St. Petersburg (Lakeland), Fla. (16)

ADI TV Households: 1,266,600

*WEDU Tampa, Fla., ch. 3, ETV
WFLA-TV Tampa, Fla., ch. 8, NBC
WTSP-TV St. Petersburg, Fla., ch. 10, ABC
WTVT Tampa, Fla., ch. 13, CBS
*WUSF-TV Tampa, Fla., ch. 16, ETV
WCLF Clearwater, Fla., ch. 22, IND
WFTS Tampa, Fla., ch. 28, Fox
WTMV Lakeland, Fla., ch. 32, IND
WTTA St. Petersburg, Fla., ch. 38, IND
WTOG St. Petersburg, Fla., ch. 44, IND
WBHS Tampa, Fla., ch. 50, IND
WGOX Inverness, Fla., ch. 64, IND
WTBG Bradenton, Fla., ch. 66, IND

ADI Counties	State	TV Households
Citrus	FL	45,500
De Soto	FL	8,600
Hardee	FL	6,500
Hernando	FL	48,400
Highlands	FL	31,800
Hillsborough	FL	341,500
Manatee	FL	97,100
Pasco	FL	129,200
Pinellas	FL	393,000
Polk	FL	165,000

Terre Haute, Ind. (138)

ADI TV Households: 156,100

WTWO Terre Haute, Ind., ch. 2, NBC
WTHI-TV Terre Haute, Ind., ch. 10, CBS
*WUSI-TV Olney, Ill., ch. 16, ETV
*WVUT Vincennes, Ind., ch. 22, ETV
WBAK-TV Terre Haute, Ind., ch. 38, ABC

ADI Counties	State	TV Households
Clark	IL	6,300
Clay	IL	5,500
Crawford	IL	7,400
Cumberland	IL	3,900
Edgar	IL	7,600
Jasper	IL	3,900
Lawrence	IL	6,000
Richland	IL	6,200
Clay	IN	9,400
Daviess	IN	9,900
Greene	IN	12,300
Knox	IN	15,000
Martin	IN	3,700
Parke	IN	5,700
Sullivan	IN	7,200
Vermillion	IN	6,500
Vigo	IN	39,600

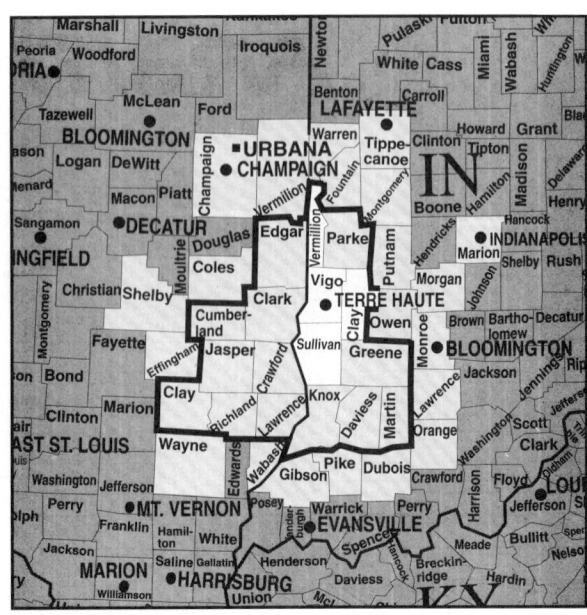

Arbitron ADI Market Atlas

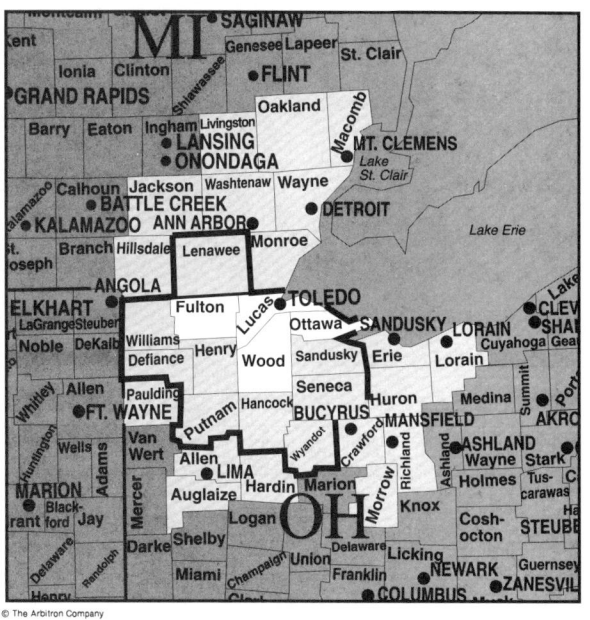

Toledo, Ohio (64)

ADI TV Households: 407,600

WTOL-TV Toledo, Ohio, ch. 11, CBS
WTVG Toledo, Ohio, ch. 13, NBC
WNWO-TV Toledo, Ohio, ch. 24, ABC
*WBGU-TV Bowling Green, Ohio, ch. 27, ETV
*WGTE-TV Toledo, Ohio, ch. 30, ETV
WUPW Toledo, Ohio, ch. 36, Fox
WXAE Toledo, Ohio, ch. 40, IND

ADI Counties	State	TV Households
Lenawee	MI	31,700
Defiance	OH	14,300
Fulton	OH	13,900
Hancock	OH	25,200
Henry	OH	10,500
Lucas	OH	178,400
Ottawa	OH	15,400
Putnam	OH	11,300
Sandusky	OH	22,900
Seneca	OH	21,300
Williams	OH	13,900
Wood	OH	40,700
Wyandot	OH	8,100

Topeka, Kan. (139)

ADI TV Households: 155,500

*KTWU Topeka, Kan., ch. 11, ETV
WIBW-TV Topeka, Kan., ch. 13, CBS
KSNT Topeka, Kan., ch. 27, NBC
KTKA-TV Topeka, Kan., ch. 49, ABC

ADI Counties	State	TV Households
Brown	KS	4,200
Clay	KS	3,500
Coffey	KS	3,200
Geary	KS	10,700
Jackson	KS	4,200
Jefferson	KS	6,000
Lyon	KS	12,800
Marshall	KS	4,300
Morris	KS	2,400
Nemaha	KS	3,900
Osage	KS	5,800
Pottawatomie	KS	6,100
Riley	KS	20,600
Shawnee	KS	65,400
Wabaunsee	KS	2,400

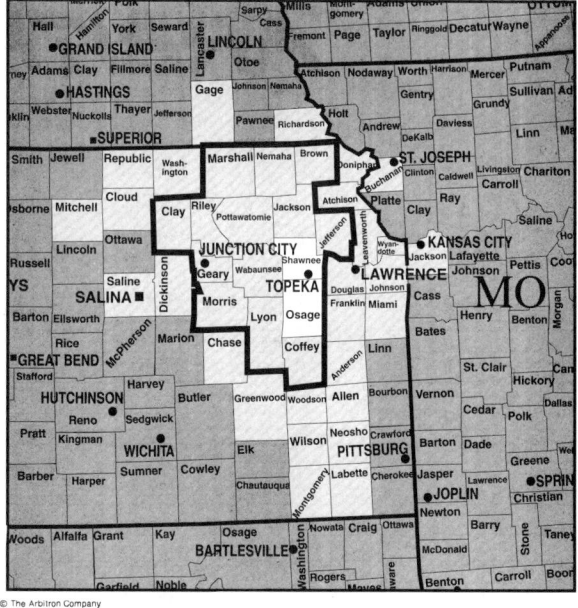

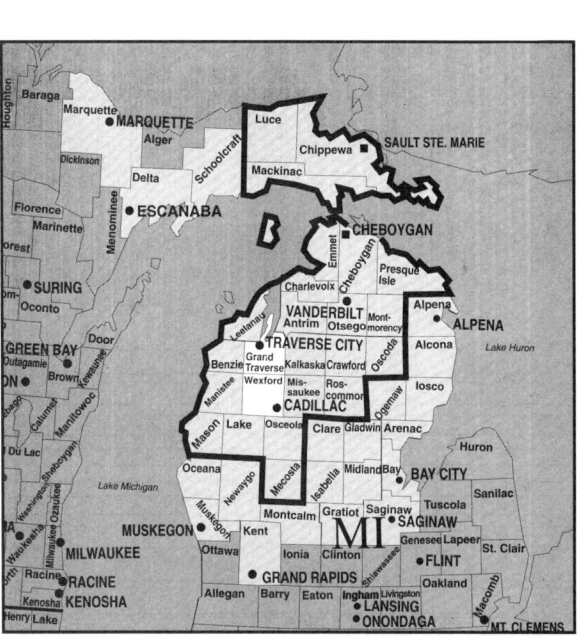

Traverse City-Cadillac, Mich. (121)

ADI TV Households: 185,200

WTOM-TV Cheboygan, Mich., ch. 4, satellite to WPBN-TV
WPBN-TV Traverse City, Mich., ch. 7, NBC
WGTQ Sault Ste. Marie, Mich., ch. 8, satellite to WGTU
WWTV Cadillac, Mich., ch. 9, CBS
WWUP-TV Sault Ste. Marie, Mich., ch. 10, satellite to WWTV
*WCMW Manistee, Mich., ch. 21, ETV
*WCMV Cadillac, Mich., ch. 27, ETV
WGTU Traverse City, Mich., ch. 29, ABC
WGKI Cadillac, Mich., ch. 33, Fox
WGKU Vanderbilt, Mich., ch. 45, IND

ADI Counties	State	TV Households			
Antrim	MI	7,300	Mackinac	MI	4,300
Benzie	MI	5,000	Manistee	MI	8,700
Charlevoix	MI	8,600	Mason	MI	10,000
Cheboygan	MI	8,100	Mecosta	MI	12,700
Chippewa	MI	11,800	Missaukee	MI	4,600
Crawford	MI	4,700	Montmorency	MI	3,500
Emmet	MI	10,000	Osceola	MI	7,600
Grand Traverse	MI	25,500	Oscoda	MI	3,400
Kalkaska	MI	5,200	Otsego	MI	7,100
Lake	MI	3,800	Presque Isle	MI	5,400
Leelanau	MI	6,500	Roscommon	MI	9,200
Luce	MI	2,000	Wexford	MI	10,200

Broadcasting & Cable Yearbook 1994

Arbitron ADI Market Atlas

Tucson, Ariz. (79)

ADI TV Households: 327,100

KVOA-TV Tucson, Ariz., ch. 4, NBC
*KUAT-TV Tucson, Ariz., ch. 6, ETV
KGUN Tucson, Ariz., ch. 9, ABC
KMSB-TV Tucson, Ariz., ch. 11, Fox
KOLD-TV Tucson, Ariz., ch. 13, CBS
KTTU-TV Tucson, Ariz., ch. 18, IND
*KUAS-TV Tucson, Ariz., ch. 27, ETV
KPOL Tucson, Ariz., ch. 40, IND
KXGR Green Valley, Ariz., ch. 46, IND

ADI Counties	State	TV Households
Apache South	AZ	2,600
Cochise	AZ	35,900
Pima	AZ	279,200
Santa Cruz	AZ	9,400

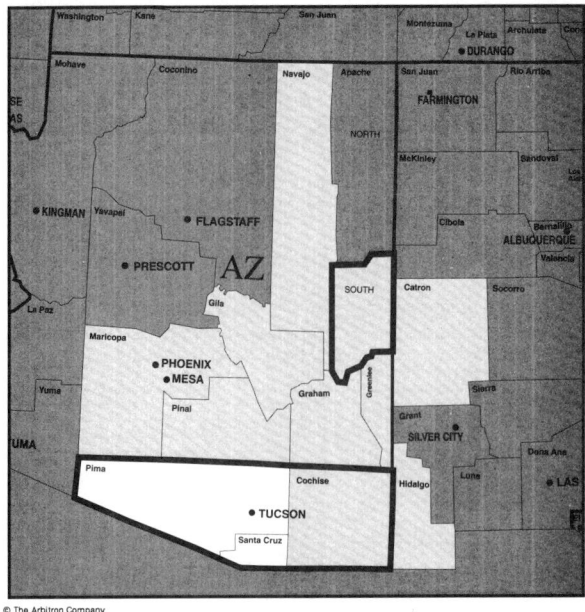

Tulsa (Bartlesville), Okla. (59)

ADI TV Households: 460,200

KJRH Tulsa, Okla., ch. 2, NBC
*KOET Eufaula, Okla., ch. 3, ETV
KOTV Tulsa, Okla., ch. 6, CBS
KTUL-TV Tulsa, Okla., ch. 8, ABC
*KOED-TV Tulsa, Okla., ch. 11, ETV
KDOR Bartlesville, Okla., ch. 17, IND

KOKI-TV Tulsa, Okla., ch. 23, Fox
*KRSC-TV Claremore, Okla., ch. 35, ETV
KTFO Tulsa, Okla, ch. 41, IND
KGLB-TV Okmulgee, Okla., ch. 44, IND
KWHB Tulsa, Okla., ch. 47, IND
New TV Tulsa, Okla., ch. 53, IND

ADI Counties	State	TV Households
Chautauqua	KS	1,800
Montgomery	KS	15,300
Adair	OK	6,500
Cherokee	OK	13,500
Craig	OK	5,200
Creek	OK	22,800
Delaware	OK	11,600
Haskell	OK	4,200
Latimer	OK	3,900
Mayes	OK	12,900
McIntosh	OK	7,100
Muskogee	OK	25,300
Nowata	OK	4,100
Okfuskee	OK	3,700
Okmulgee	OK	14,100
Osage	OK	15,000
Pawnee	OK	6,000
Pittsburg	OK	16,200
Rogers	OK	20,700
Tulsa	OK	212,900
Wagoner	OK	17,900
Washington	OK	19,500

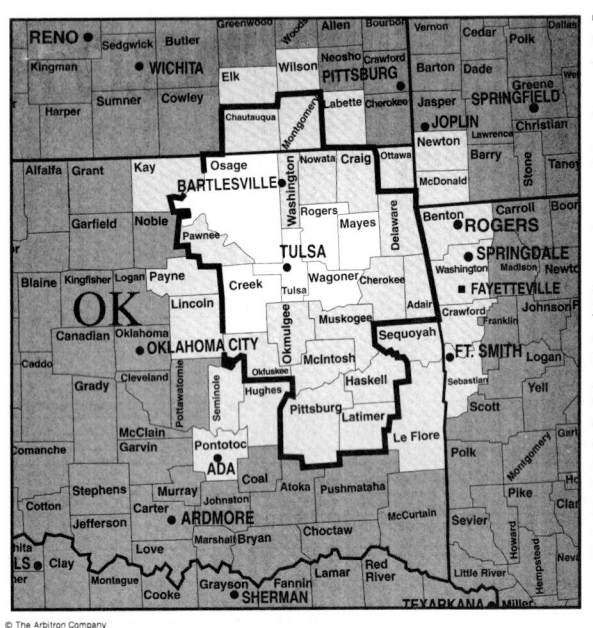

Tuscaloosa, Ala. (186)

ADI TV Households: 58,000

WDBB Tuscaloosa, Ala., ch. 17, Fox
WCFT-TV Tuscaloosa, Ala., ch. 33, CBS

ADI Counties	State	TV Households
Tuscaloosa	AL	58,800

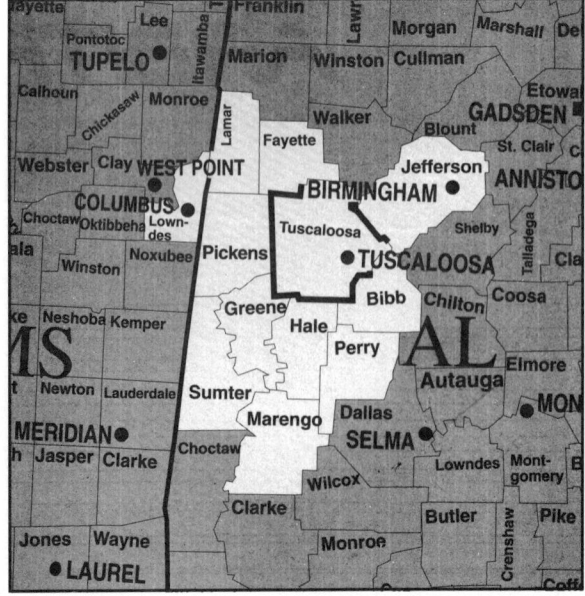

Broadcasting & Cable Yearbook 1994

Arbitron ADI Market Atlas

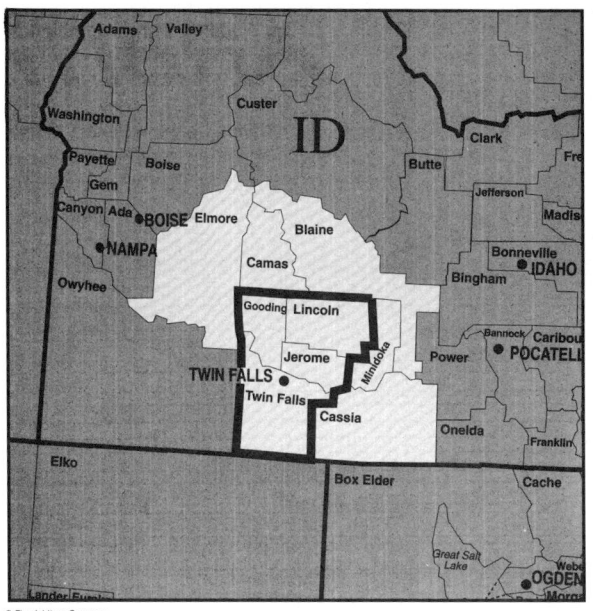

Twin Falls, Idaho (201)

ADI TV Households: 32,300

KMVT Twin Falls, Idaho, ch. 11, CBS
*KIPT Twin Falls, Idaho, ch. 13, satellite to *KAID
KKVI Twin Falls, Idaho, ch. 35, IND

ADI Counties	State	TV Households
Gooding	ID	4,700
Jerome	ID	5,600
Lincoln	ID	1,200
Twin Falls	ID	20,800

Tyler-Longview-Jacksonville, Tex. (114)

ADI TV Households: 204,000

KLTV Tyler, Tex., ch. 7, ABC
KTRE-TV Lufkin, Tex., ch. 9, satellite to KLTV
KLSB-TV Nacogdoches, Tex., ch. 19, NBC
KFXK Longview, Tex., ch. 51, Fox
KETK-TV Jacksonville, Tex., ch. 56, NBC

ADI Counties	State	TV Households
Angelina	TX	25,400
Cherokee	TX	14,800
Gregg	TX	41,500
Houston	TX	7,100
Nacogdoches	TX	20,400
Rusk	TX	16,500
Sabine	TX	4,200
San Augustine	TX	3,000
Smith	TX	59,100
Wood	TX	12,000

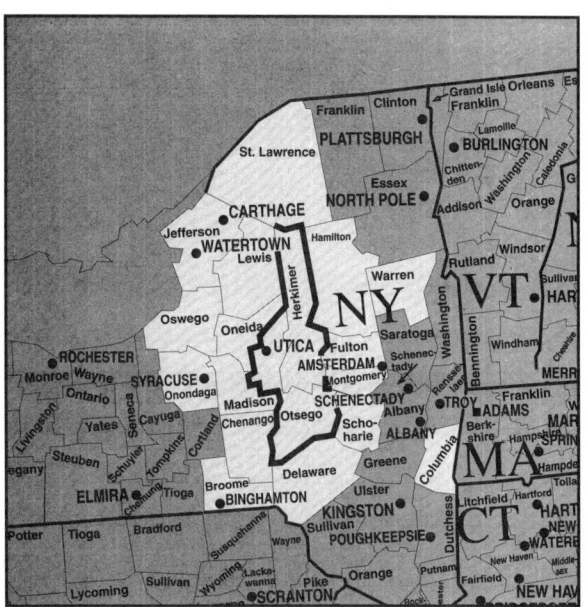

Utica, N.Y. (161)

ADI TV Households: 102,200

WKTV Utica, N.Y., ch. 2, NBC
WUTR Utica, N.Y., ch. 20, ABC
WFXV Utica, N.Y., ch. 33, Fox

ADI Counties	State	TV Households
Herkimer	NY	24,900
Oneida East	NY	55,400
Otsego	NY	21,900

Broadcasting & Cable Yearbook 1994
C-195

Arbitron ADI Market Atlas

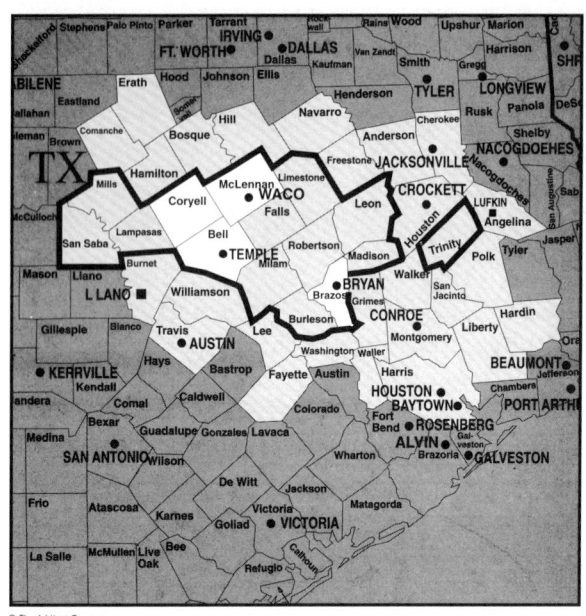

Waco-Temple-Bryan, Tex. (96)

ADI TV Households: 254,400

KCEN-TV Temple, Tex., ch. 6, ABC
KWTX-TV Waco, Tex., ch. 10, CBS
KBTX-TV Bryan, Tex., ch. 3, satellite to KWTX-TV
***KAMU-TV** College Station, Tex., ch. 15, ETV
KXXV Waco, Tex., ch. 25, NBC
KYLE Bryan, Tex., ch. 28, IND
***KCTF** Waco, Tex., ch. 34, ETV
KWKT Waco, Tex., ch. 44, IND
***KNCT** Belton, Tex., ch. 46, ETV

ADI Counties	State	TV Households
Bell	TX	65,800
Brazos	TX	45,000
Burleson	TX	5,300
Coryell	TX	17,100
Falls	TX	6,100
Lampasas	TX	5,100
Leon	TX	5,000
Limestone	TX	7,500
Madison	TX	3,000
McLennan	TX	71,900
Milam	TX	8,400
Mills	TX	1,800
Robertson	TX	5,500
San Saba	TX	2,100
Trinity	TX	4,800

Washington, D.C. (7)

ADI TV Households: 1,822,400

WRC-TV Washington, ch. 4, NBC
WTTG Washington, ch. 5, Fox
WJLA-TV Washington, ch. 7, ABC
WUSA Washington, ch. 9, CBS
WTMW Arlington, Va., ch. 14, IND
WDCA-TV Washington, ch. 20, IND
***WETA-TV** Washington, ch. 26, ETV
***WHMM** Washington, ch. 32, ETV
WFTY Washington, ch. 50, IND
***WNVT** Goldvein, Va., ch. 53, IND
***WNVC** Fairfax, Va., ch. 56, ETV
WYVN Martinsburg, W.Va., ch. 60, Fox
***WFPT** Frederick, Md., ch. 62, ETV
WTKK Manassas, Va., ch. 66, IND

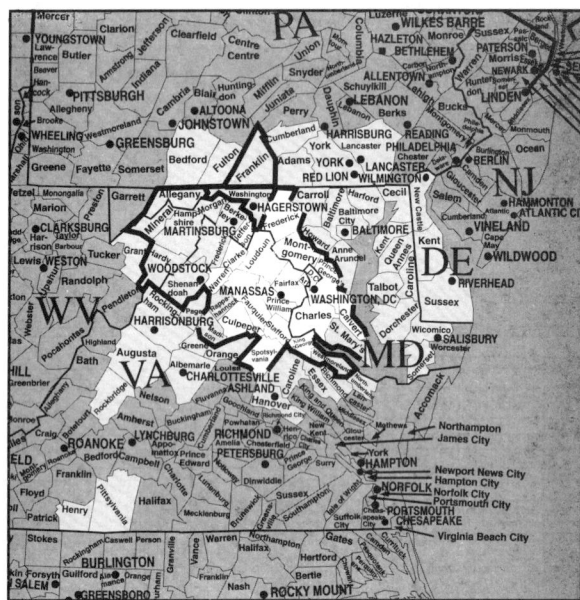

ADI Counties	State	TV Households
Dist of Columbia	DC	236,500
Allegany	MD	29,200
Calvert	MD	19,300
Charles	MD	35,800
Frederick	MD	57,000
Montgomery	MD	300,400
Prince Georges	MD	265,000
St. Marys	MD	27,500
Franklin	PA	46,500
Arlington	VA	134,800
Clarke	VA	4,200
Culpeper	VA	10,400
Fairfax	VA	328,600
Fauquier	VA	17,800
Frederick	VA	27,300
King George	VA	5,100
Loudoun	VA	34,100
Madison	VA	4,100
Prince William	VA	90,100
Rappahannock	VA	2,500
Shenandoah	VA	12,800
Spotsylvania	VA	29,300
Stafford	VA	22,100
Warren	VA	10,800
Westmoreland	VA	6,300
Berkeley	WV	24,300
Hampshire	WV	6,800
Hardy	WV	4,400
Jefferson	WV	13,800
Mineral	WV	10,400
Morgan	WV	5,200

Watertown-Carthage, N.Y. (170)

ADI TV Households: 87,200

WWNY-TV Carthage, N.Y., ch. 7, CBS (ABC, NBC)
***WNPE-TV** Watertown, N.Y., ch. 16, ETV
***WNPI-TV** Norwood, N.Y., ch. 18, ETV
WWTI Watertown, N.Y., ch. 50, IND

ADI Counties	State	TV Households
Jefferson	NY	39,600
Lewis	NY	9,600
St. Lawrence	NY	38,000

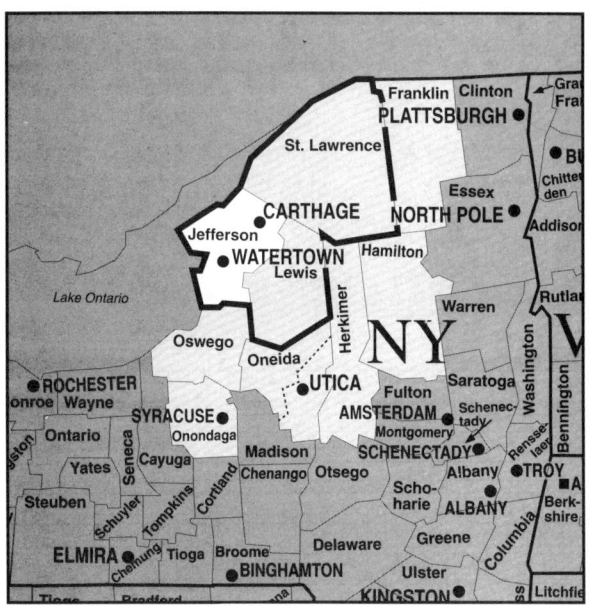

Wausau-Rhinelander, Wis. (133)

ADI TV Households: 165,900

WSAW-TV Wausau, Wis., ch. 7, CBS
WAOW-TV Wausau, Wis., ch. 9, ABC
WJFW-TV Rhinelander, Wis., ch. 12, NBC
***WHRM-TV** Wausau, Wis., ch. 20, ETV
***WLEF-TV** Park Falls, Wis., ch. 36, ETV

ADI Counties	State	TV Households
Adams	WI	6,100
Clark	WI	11,200
Forest	WI	3,400
Langlade	WI	7,800
Lincoln	WI	10,500
Marathon	WI	42,700
Oneida	WI	13,000
Portage	WI	22,500
Price	WI	6,100
Taylor	WI	6,900
Vilas	WI	7,500
Wood		28,200

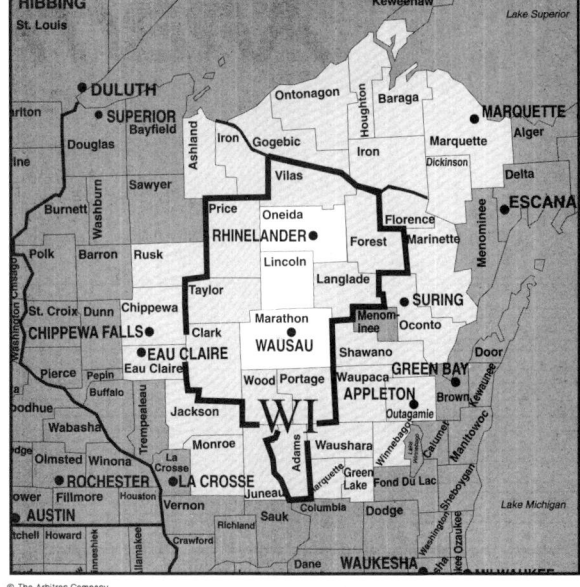

West Palm Beach-Ft. Pierce-Vero Beach, Fla. (46)

ADI TV Households: 569,100

WPTV West Palm Beach, Fla., ch. 5, NBC
WPEC West Palm Beach, Fla., ch. 12, CBS
***WTCE** Fort Pierce, Fla., ch. 21, ETV
WPBF Tequesta, Fla., ch. 25, ABC
WFLX West Palm Beach, Fla., ch. 29, Fox
WTVX Ft. Pierce, Fla., ch. 34, IND
***WXEL-TV** West Palm Beach, Fla., ch. 42, ETV
WFGC Palm Beach, Fla., ch. 61, IND
***WPPB-TV** Boca Raton, Fla., ch. 63, ETV
WHBI Lake Worth, Fla., ch. 67, IND
WCLU Clermont, Fla., ch. 68, IND

ADI Counties	State	TV Households
Indian River	FL	40,800
Martin	FL	46,600
Okeechobee	FL	10,800
Palm Beach North	FL	258,300
Palm Beach South	FL	147,800
St. Lucie	FL	64,800

Broadcasting & Cable Yearbook 1994

Arbitron ADI Market Atlas

Wheeling, W. Va.-Steubenville, Ohio (144)

ADI TV Households: 144,100

WTRF-TV Wheeling, W. Va., ch. 7, CBS (ABC)
WTOV-TV Steubenville, Ohio, ch. 9, NBC (ABC)
*WOUC-TV Cambridge, Ohio, ch. 44, ETV

ADI Counties	State	TV Households
Belmont	OH	27,400
Guernsey	OH	14,800
Harrison	OH	6,000
Jefferson	OH	30,800
Monroe	OH	5,600
Noble	OH	4,200
Brooke	WV	10,200
Marshall	WV	14,000
Ohio	WV	20,300
Tyler	WV	3,700
Wetzel	WV	7,100

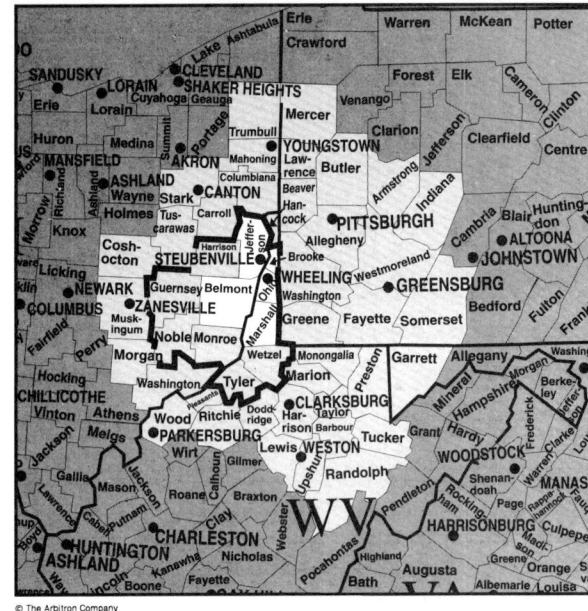

Wichita-Hutchinson, Kan. (62)

ADI TV Households: 430,200

KSNC Great Bend, Kan., ch. 2, satellite to KSNW
KSNW Wichita, Kan., ch. 3, NBC
*KSWK Lakin, Kan., ch. 3, ETV
KLBY Colby, Kan., ch. 4, ABC
KSWT Liberal, Kan., ch. 5, IND
KBSD-TV Ensign, Kan., ch. 6, satellite to KWCH-TV
KBSH-TV Hays, Kan., ch. 7, satellite to KWCH-TV
KSNK McCook, Neb., ch. 8, satellite to KSNW
*KOOD Hays, Kan., ch. 9, ETV
KAKE-TV Wichita, Kan., ch. 10, ABC
KBSL-TV Goodland, Kan., ch. 10, satellite to KBSH-TV
KSNG Garden City, Kan., ch. 11, satellite to KSNW
KWCH-TV Hutchinson, Kan., ch. 12, CBS
KUPK-TV Garden City, Kan., ch. 13, ABC
KAAS-TV Salina, Kan., ch. 18, IND
KSAS-TV Wichita, Kan., ch. 24, Fox
KWCV Wichita, Kan., ch. 33, IND

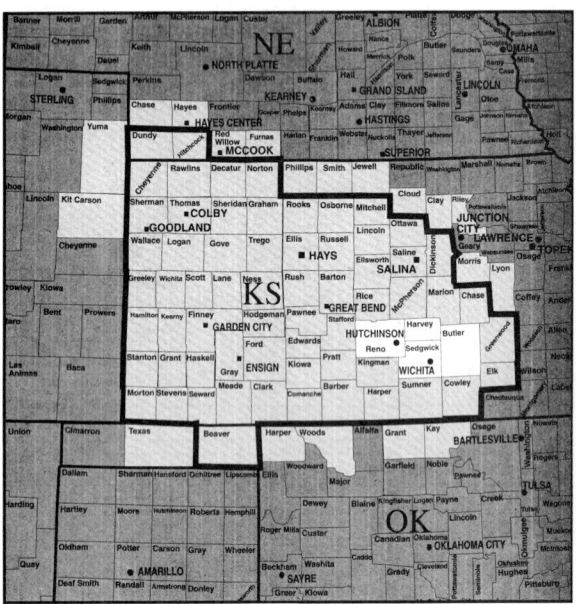

ADI Counties	State	TV Households
Barber	KS	2,200
Barton	KS	11,000
Butler	KS	19,400
Chase	KS	1,200
Cheyenne	KS	1,400
Clark	KS	1,000
Comanche	KS	900
Cowley	KS	13,500
Decatur	KS	1,600
Dickinson	KS	7,700
Edwards	KS	1,600
Elk	KS	1,400
Ellis	KS	9,900
Ellsworth	KS	2,500
Finney	KS	11,300
Ford	KS	10,200
Gove	KS	1,300
Graham	KS	1,400
Grant	KS	2,600
Gray	KS	1,900
Greeley	KS	700
Greenwood	KS	3,000
Hamilton	KS	900
Harper	KS	2,900
Harvey	KS	11,600
Haskell	KS	1,400
Hodgeman	KS	800
Kearny	KS	1,400
Kingman	KS	3,100
Kiowa	KS	1,400
Lane	KS	1,000
Lincoln	KS	1,500
Logan	KS	1,200
Marion	KS	4,800
McPherson	KS	10,000
Meade	KS	1,600
Mitchell	KS	2,700
Morton	KS	1,300
Ness	KS	1,700
Norton	KS	2,200
Osborne	KS	2,000
Ottawa	KS	2,200
Pawnee	KS	2,900
Pratt	KS	3,800
Rawlins	KS	1,400
Reno	KS	24,000
Rice	KS	4,000
Rooks	KS	2,300
Rush	KS	1,600
Russell	KS	3,100
Saline	KS	20,500
Scott	KS	2,000
Sedgwick	KS	164,900
Seward	KS	6,700
Sheridan	KS	1,200
Sherman	KS	2,700
Stafford	KS	2,200
Stanton	KS	800
Stevens	KS	1,900
Sumner	KS	9,800
Thomas	KS	3,000
Trego	KS	1,500
Wallace	KS	700
Wichita	KS	1,000
Dundy	NE	1,100
Hitchcock	NE	1,400
Beaver	OK	2,300

Arbitron ADI Market Atlas

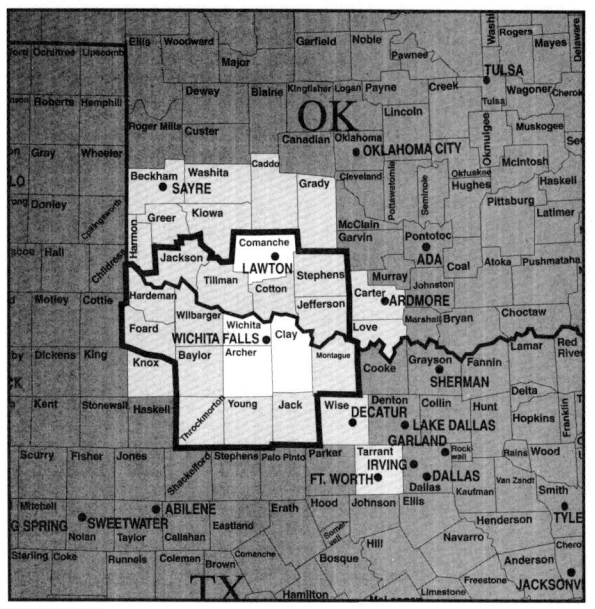

Wichita Falls, Tex.-Lawton, Okla. (141)

ADI TV Households: 154,300

KFDX-TV Wichita Falls, Tex., ch. 3, NBC
KAUZ-TV Wichita Falls, Tex., ch. 6, CBS
KSWO-TV Lawton, Okla., ch. 7, ABC
KJTL Wichita Falls, Tex., ch. 18, Fox
KTDA Lawton, Okla., ch. 45, IND

ADI Counties	State	TV Households
Comanche	OK	39,000
Cotton	OK	2,500
Jackson	OK	10,800
Jefferson	OK	2,800
Stephens	OK	17,100
Tillman	OK	3,900
Archer	TX	2,900
Baylor	TX	1,900
Clay	TX	3,700
Foard	TX	700
Hardeman	TX	2,000
Jack	TX	2,700
Montague	TX	6,700
Throckmorton	TX	800
Wichita	TX	44,800
Wilbarger	TX	5,400
Young	TX	6,600

Wilkes Barre-Scranton, Pa. (51)

ADI TV Households: 525,600

WNEP-TV Scranton, Pa., ch. 16, ABC
WYOU Scranton, Pa., ch. 22, CBS
WBRE-TV Wilkes-Barre, Pa., ch. 28, NBC
WOLF-TV Scranton, Pa., ch. 38, Fox
*WVIA-TV Scranton, Pa., ch. 44, ETV
WILF Williamsport, Pa., ch. 53, IND
WWLF-TV Hazleton, Pa., ch. 56, IND
WSWB-TV Scranton, Pa., ch. 64, IND

ADI Counties	State	TV Households
Carbon	PA	22,600
Clinton	PA	13,600
Columbia	PA	23,500
Lackawanna	PA	83,900
Luzerne	PA	128,200
Lycoming	PA	45,200
Monroe	PA	37,700
Montour	PA	6,400
Northumberland	PA	37,800
Schuylkill	PA	59,300
Snyder	PA	12,700
Sullivan	PA	2,200
Susquehanna	PA	15,300
Union	PA	11,500
Wayne	PA	15,400
Wyoming	PA	10,300

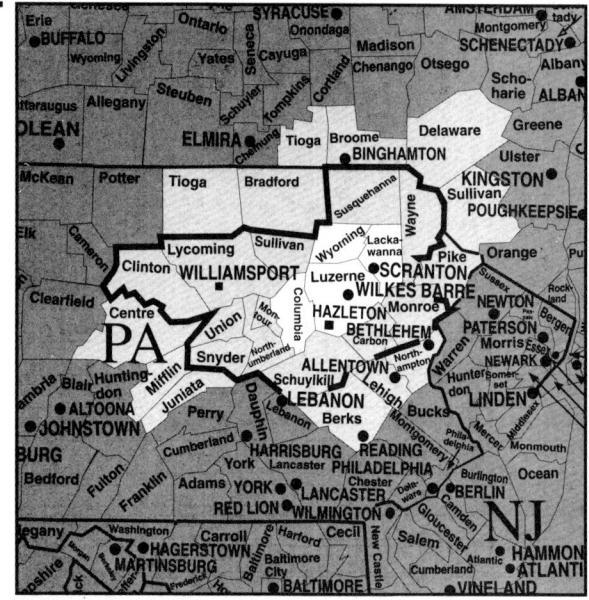

Wilmington, N.C. (142)

ADI TV Households: 152,600

WWAY Wilmington, N.C., ch. 3, ABC
WECT Wilmington, N.C., ch. 6, NBC
WJKA Wilmington, N.C., ch. 26, CBS
*WUNJ-TV Wilmington, N.C., ch. 39, ETV

ADI Counties	State	TV Households
Bladen	NC	10,800
Brunswick	NC	22,000
Columbus	NC	18,700
New Hanover	NC	52,000
Pender	NC	12,300
Robeson	NC	36,800

Broadcasting & Cable Yearbook 1994

Arbitron ADI Market Atlas

Yakima-Pasco-Richland-Kennewick, Wash. (124)

ADI TV Households: 171,400

KNDO Yakima, Wash., ch. 23, NBC
KNDU Richland, Wash., ch. 25, satellite to KNDO
KIMA-TV Yakima, Wash., ch. 29, CBS
KLEW-TV Lewiston, Idaho, ch. 3, satellite to KIMA-TV
KEPR-TV Pasco, Wash., ch. 19, satellite to KIMA-TV
*****KTNW** Richland, Wash., ch. 31, ETV
KAPP Yakima, Wash., ch. 35, ABC
KVEW Kennewick, Wash., ch. 42, satellite to KAPP
*****KYVE** Yakima, Wash., ch. 47, ETV

ADI Counties	State	TV Households
Umatilla	OR	21,300
Benton	WA	44,100
Franklin	WA	12,700
Kittitas East	WA	8,100
Walla Walla	WA	17,800
Yakima	WA	67,400

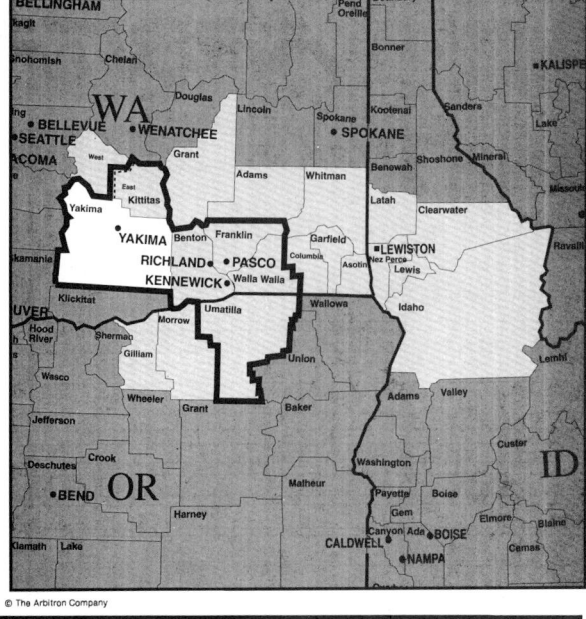

Youngstown, Ohio (92)

ADI TV Households: 274,500

WFMJ-TV Youngstown, Ohio, ch. 21, NBC
WKBN-TV Youngstown, Ohio, ch. 27, CBS
WYTV Youngstown, Ohio, ch. 33, ABC
*****WNEO** Alliance, Ohio, ch. 45, ETV

ADI Counties	State	TV Households
Columbiana	OH	41,500
Mahoning	OH	100,800
Trumbull	OH	86,800
Mercer	PA	45,400

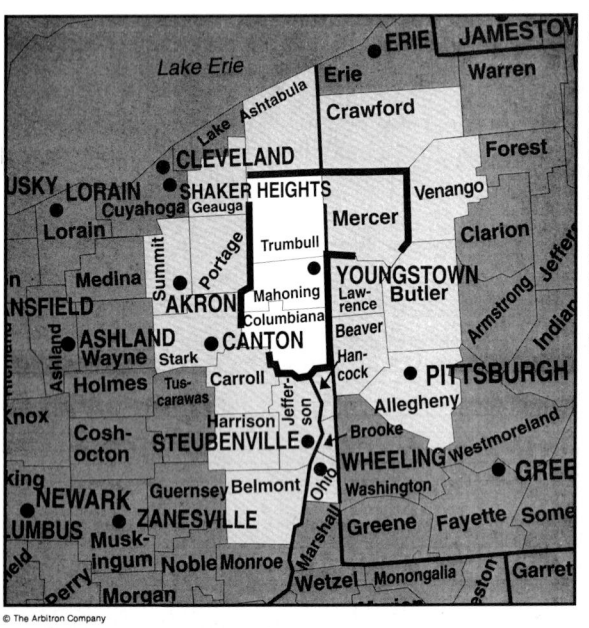

Zanesville, Ohio (203)

ADI TV Households: 30,900

WHIZ-TV Zanesville, Ohio, ch. 18, NBC

ADI Counties	State	TV Households
Muskingum	OH	30,900

Multi-City ADI Cross-Reference

The following cities are in hyphenated markets, but are not the first city given in such a market; i.e., Troy in Albany-Schenectady-Troy, N.Y. They are listed alphabetically.

Ada, OK	See Sherman-Ada
Altoona, PA	See Johnstown-Altoona
Anderson, SC	See Greenville-Spartanburg-Asheville-Anderson
Appleton, WI	See Green Bay-Appleton
Asheville, NC	See Greenville-Spartanburg-Asheville-Anderson
Austin, MN	See Rochester-Mason City-Austin
Battle Creek, MI	See Grand Rapids-Kalamazoo-Battle Creek
Bay City, MI	See Flint-Saginaw-Bay City
Beckley, WV	See Bluefield-Beckley-Oak Hill
Bismarck, ND	See Minot-Bismarck-Dickinson-Glendive
Bloomington, IL	See Peoria-Bloomington
Brownsville, TX	See McAllen-Brownsville
Bryan, TX	See Waco-Temple-Bryan
Cadillac, MI	See Traverse City-Cadillac
Cape Girardeau, MO	See Paducah-Cape Girardeau-Harrisburg-Marion
Carthage, NY	See Watertown-Carthage
Champaign, IL	See Springfield-Decatur-Champaign
Daytona Beach, FL	See Orlando-Daytona Beach-Melbourne
Decatur, AL	See Huntsville-Decatur-Florence
Decatur, IL	See Springfield-Decatur-Champaign
Dickinson, ND	See Minot-Bismarck-Dickinson-Glendive
Dubuque, IA	See Cedar Rapids-Waterloo-Dubuque
Durango, CO	See Grand Junction-Durango
Durham, NC	See Raleigh-Durham
Eau Claire, WI	See La Crosse-Eau Claire
El Dorado, AR	See Monroe-El Dorado
Elkhart, IN	See South Bend-Elkhart
Florence, AL	See Huntsville-Decatur-Florence
Ft. Lauderdale, FL	See Miami-Ft. Lauderdale
Ft. Pierce, FL	See West Palm Beach-Ft. Pierce-Vero Beach
Ft. Worth, TX	See Dallas-Ft. Worth
Glendive, ND	See Monot-Bismarck-Dickinson-Glendive
Greenville, MS	See Greenwood-Greenville
Greeneville, TN	See Bristol-Kingsport-Johnson City-Greeneville: Tri-Cities
Gulfport, MS	See Biloxi-Gulfport-Pascagoula
Hampton, VA	See Norfolk-Portsmouth-Newport News-Hampton
Hannibal, MO	See Quincy-Hannibal
Hardin, MT	See Billings-Hardin
Harrisburg, IL	See Paducah-Cape Girardeau-Harrisburg-Marion
Hastings, NE	See Lincoln-Hastings-Kearney
Hattiesburg, MS	See Laurel-Hattiesburg
High Point, NC	See Greensboro-Winston Salem-High Point
Huntington, WV	See Charleston-Huntington
Hutchinson, KS	See Wichita-Hutchinson
Jacksonville, TX	See Tyler-Longview-Jacksonville
Jefferson City, MO	See Columbia-Jefferson City
Johnson City, TN	See Bristol-Kingsport-Johnson City-Greeneville: Tri-Cities
Kalamazoo, MI	See Grand Rapids-Kalamazoo-Battle Creek
Kearney, NE	See Lincoln-Hastings-Kearney
Kennewick, WA	See Yakima-Pasco-Richland-Kennewick
Kingsport, TN	See Bristol-Kingsport-Johnson City-Greeneville: Tri-Cities
Kirksville, MO	See Ottumwa-Kirksville
Lancaster, PA	See Harrisburg-York-Lancaster-Lebanon
Lawton, OK	See Wichita Falls-Lawton
Lebanon, PA	See Harrisburg-York-Lancaster-Lebanon
Longview, TX	See Tyler-Longview-Jacksonville
Lynchburg, VA	See Roanoke-Lynchburg
Marion, IL	See Paducah-Cape Girardeau-Harrisburg-Marion
Mason City, IA	See Rochester-Mason City-Austin
Melbourne, FL	See Orlando-Daytona Beach-Melbourne
Midland, TX	See Odessa-Midland
Mitchell, SD	See Sioux Falls-Mitchell
Modesto, CA	See Sacramento-Stockton-Modesto
Moline, IL	See Davenport-Rock Island-Moline
Monterey, CA	See Salinas-Monterey
Myrtle Beach, SC	See Florence-Myrtle Beach
Naples, FL	See Ft. Myers-Naples
New Bedford, MA	See Providence-New Bedford
New Bern, NC	See Greenville-New Bern-Washington
New Haven, CT	See Hartford-New Haven
Newport News, VA	See Norfolk-Portsmouth-Newport News-Hampton
Oak Hill, WV	See Bluefield-Beckley-Oak Hill
Oakland, CA	See San Francisco-Oakland-San Jose
Pascagoula, MS	See Biloxi-Gulfport-Pascagoula
Pasco, WA	See Yakima-Pasco-Richland-Kennewick
Pensacola, FL	See Mobile-Pensacola
Pittsburg, KS	See Joplin-Pittsburg
Plattsburgh, NY	See Burlington-Plattsburgh
Pocatello, ID	See Idaho Falls-Pocatello
Poland Spring, ME	See Portland-Poland Spring
Port Arthur, TX	See Beaumont-Port Arthur
Portsmouth, VA	See Norfolk-Portsmouth-Newport News-Hampton
Pueblo, CO	See Colorado Springs-Pueblo
Redding, CA	See Chico-Redding
Rhinelander, WI	See Wausau-Rhinelander
Richland, WA	See Yakima-Pasco-Richland-Kennewick
Riverton, WY	See Casper-Riverton
Rock Island, IL	See Davenport-Rock Island-Moline
Saginaw, MI	See Flint-Saginaw-Bay City
St. Paul, MN	See Minneapolis-St. Paul
St. Petersburg, FL	See Tampa-St. Petersburg
San Jose, CA	See San Francisco-Oakland-San Jose
San Luis Obispo, CA	See Santa Barbara-Santa Maria-San Luis Obispo
Santa Maria, CA	See Santa Barbara-Santa Maria-San Luis Obispo
Schenectady, NY	See Albany-Schenectady-Troy
Scottsbluff, NE	See Cheyenne-Scottsbluff
Scranton, PA	See Wilkes Barre-Scranton
Selma, AL	See Montgomery-Selma
Spartanburg, SC	See Greenville-Spartanburg-Asheville-Anderson
Steubenville, OH	See Wheeling-Steubenville
Stockton, CA	See Sacramento-Stockton-Modesto
Superior, WI	See Duluth-Superior
Sweetwater, TX	See Abilene-Sweetwater
Tacoma, WA	See Seattle-Tacoma
Temple, TX	See Waco-Temple-Bryan
Texarkana, TX	See Shreveport-Texarkana
Thomasville, GA	See Tallahassee-Thomasville
Troy, NY	See Albany-Schenectady-Troy
Tupelo, MS	See Columbus-Tupelo
Vero Beach, FL	See West Palm Beach-Ft. Pierce-Vero Beach
Victoria, TX	See San Antonio-Victoria
Visalia, CA	See Fresno-Visalia
Washington, NC	See Greenville-New Bern-Washington
Waterloo, IA	See Cedar Rapids-Waterloo-Dubuque
Weston, WV	See Clarksburg-Weston
Winston Salem, NC	See Greensboro-Winston Salem-High Point
York, PA	See Harrisburg-York-Lancaster-Lebanon
Yuma, AZ	See El Centro-Yuma

Non-ADI Markets

The following single-county markets did not achieve ADI status because the preponderance of viewing is not to the home-market station. Neither did they meet the criteria of the 10% Rule to become an ADI. The home counties in Non-ADI markets are assigned to the ADIs that do receive the preponderance of viewing.

Non-ADI market	Home county	ADI where located
Akron, OH	Summit	Cleveland
Allentown, PA	Lehigh	Philadelphia
Angola, IN	Steuben	Ft. Wayne
Ann Arbor, MI	Washtenaw	Lansing
Athens, GA	Clarke	Atlanta
Atlantic City, NJ	Atlantic	Philadelphia
Bainbridge, GA	Decatur	Tallahassee-Thomasville
Barstow, CA	San Bernardino North	Los Angles
Bartlesville, OK	Washington	Tulsa
Baxley, GA	Appling	Savannah
Beattyville, KY	Lee	Lexington
Bellingham, WA	Whatcom	Seattle-Tacoma
Bethlehem, PA	Northampton	Philadelphia
Brunswick, GA	Glynn	Jacksonville
Burlington, IA	Des Moines	Davenport-Rock Island-Moline
Burlington, NC	Alamance	Greensboro-Winston Salem-High Point
Campbellsville, KY	Taylor	Bowling Green
Canton, OH	Stark	Cleveland
Cedar City, UT	Iron	Salt Lake City
Chillicothe, OH	Ross	Columbus, OH
Cleveland, TN	Bradley	Chattanooga
Cordele, GA	Crisp	Albany, GA
Corona, CA	Riverside West	Los Angeles
Crossville, TN	Cumberland	Knoxville
Danville, KY	Boyle	Lexington
Derry, NH	Rockingham	Boston
Eagle Pass, TX	Maverick	San Antonio-Victoria
Escanaba, MI	Delta	Marquette
Fayetteville, NC	Cumberland	Raleigh-Durham
Ft. Lauderdale-Hollywood, FL	Broward	Miami-Ft. Lauderdale
Ft. Walton Beach, FL	Okaloosa	Mobile-Pensacola
Gadsden, AL	Etowah	Birmingham
Glendive, MT	Dawson	Minot-Bismarck-Dickinson-Glendive
Goldsboro, NC	Wayne	Raleigh-Durham
Hanford, CA	Kings	Fresno-Visalia
Hartford, VT	Windsor	Burlington-Plattsburgh
*Hazard, KY	Perry	Lexington
Hickory, NC	Catawba	Charlotte
Hobbs, NM	Lea North	Albuquerque
Holly Springs, MS	Marshall	Memphis
Jamestown, NY	Chautauqua	Buffalo
Jellico, TN	Campbell	Knoxville
Kenosha, WI	Kenosha	Milwaukee
Kerrville, TX	Kerr	San Antonio-Victoria
Kingman, AZ	Mohave	Phoenix
Kingston, NY	Ulster	New York
La Salle, IL	La Salle	Chicago
Lakeland, FL	Polk	Tampa-St. Petersburg
Las Cruces, NM	Dona Ana	El Paso
Lawrence, KS	Douglas	Kansas City
Madisonville, KY	Hopkins	Evansville
Manchester, NH	Hillsborough	Boston
Mansfield, OH	Richland	Cleveland
Marion, IL	Williamson	Paducah-Cape Girardeau-Harrisburg-Marion
Marion, IN	Grant	Indianapolis
Martinsburg, WV	Berkeley	Hagerstown
Morehead City, NC	Carteret	Greenville-New Bern-Washington
Mt. Vernon, IL	Jefferson	St. Louis
Natchez, MS	Adams	Alexandria, LA
New London, CT	New London	Hartford-New Haven
Newton, NJ	Sussex	New York
Ocala, FL	Marion	Orlando (Ocala)
Opelika, AL	Lee	Columbus, GA
Oxnard, CA	Ventura West	Santa Barbara-Santa Maria-San Luis Obispo
Poughkeepsie, NY	Dutchess	New York
Prescott, AZ	Yavapai	Phoenix
Racine, WI	Racine	Milwaukee
Reading, PA	Berks	Philadelphia
Richmond, IN	Wayne	Dayton
Rocky Mount, NC	Edgecombe	Raleigh-Durham
Rome, GA	Floyd	Atlanta
St. Cloud, MN	Sterns	Minneapolis-St. Paul
San Bernardino-Ontario, CA	San Bernardino S.	Los Angeles
San Jose, CA	Santa Clara West	San Francisco-Oakland-San Jose
Sandusky, OH	Erie	Cleveland
Santa Rosa, CA	Sonoma	San Francisco-Oakland-San Jose
Sterling, CO	Logan	Cheyenne-Scottsbluff (Sterling)
Suring, WI	Oconto	Green Bay-Appleton
Toccoa, GA	Stephens	Greenville-Spartanburg-Asheville-Anderson
Vallejo, CA	Solano West	San Francisco-Oakland-San Jose
Victoria, TX	Victoria	San Antonio-Victoria
Vineland, NJ	Cumberland	Philadelphia
Visalia-Porterville, CA	Tulare	Fresno-Visalia
Wapello, IA	Wapello	Ottumwa-Kirksville
Wenatchee, WA	Chelan	Seattle-Tacoma
West Point, MS	Clay	Columbus-Tupelo
Wildwood, NJ	Cape May	Philadelphia
Wilmington, DE	New Castle	Philadelphia
Worcester, MA	Worcester	Boston

*Indicates ADI status achieved but elected to remain non-ADI.

Television Markets Ranked by Size

Listed here are the television markets of the United States ranked in descending order by the number of television homes they contain. Also shown are the numbers of women, men, teenagers and children in each market and the percentage of the total U.S. population each represents.

All data is from The Arbitron Company and represents the Arbitron television household and population estimates for the 1993-1994 season.

	ADI TV Households		ADI Women		ADI Men		ADI Teenagers		ADI Children	
1. New York	6,723,700	7.16	7,517,100	7.69	6,680,700	7.37	1,406,300	6.71	2,407,300	6.41
2. Los Angeles	4,978,800	5.30	5,500,400	5.62	5,428,600	5.99	1,225,500	5.85	2,318,100	6.18
3. Chicago	3,076,500	3.28	3,277,100	3.35	3,015,700	3.33	714,400	3.41	1,286,800	3.43
4. Philadelphia	2,661,800	2.83	2,875,500	2.94	2,575,600	2.84	551,100	2.63	1,007,000	2.68
5. San Francisco–Oakland–San Jose	2,225,500	2.37	2,327,700	2.38	2,272,300	2.51	418,600	2.00	799,300	2.13
6. Boston	2,116,200	2.25	2,287,700	2.34	2,079,100	2.29	401,300	1.92	744,400	1.98
7. Washington, D.C.	1,822,400	1.94	1,937,000	1.98	1,807,700	1.99	368,600	1.76	679,900	1.81
8. Dallas–Ft. Worth	1,788,000	1.90	1,782,200	1.82	1,704,800	1.88	396,900	1.90	763,500	2.03
9. Detroit	1,739,100	1.85	1,823,000	1.86	1,644,500	1.81	396,200	1.89	685,900	1.83
10. Houston	1,520,900	1.62	1,522,400	1.56	1,496,800	1.65	382,700	1.83	713,100	1.90
Markets 1–10	28,652,900	30.50	30,850,100	31.54	28,705,800	31.66	6,261,600	29.90	11,405,300	30.38
Cumulative Total	28,652,900	30.50	30,850,100	31.54	28,705,800	31.66	6,261,600	29.90	11,405,300	30.38
11. Atlanta	1,516,300	1.61	1,574,500	1.61	1,452,100	1.60	339,500	1.62	607,100	1.62
12. Cleveland	1,449,700	1.54	1,500,300	1.53	1,330,600	1.47	316,900	1.51	550,900	1.47
13. Seattle–Tacoma	1,438,600	1.53	1,396,600	1.43	1,358,900	1.50	280,300	1.34	550,800	1.47
14. Minneapolis–St. Paul	1,418,100	1.51	1,418,100	1.45	1,338,500	1.48	307,900	1.47	606,100	1.61
15. Miami–Ft. Lauderdale	1,308,200	1.39	1,388,100	1.42	1,243,400	1.37	244,000	1.16	442,100	1.18
16. Tampa–St. Petersburg	1,266,600	1.35	1,266,800	1.30	1,130,200	1.25	203,400	.97	362,900	.97
17. Pittsburgh	1,152,500	1.23	1,203,900	1.23	1,053,800	1.16	218,700	1.04	371,400	.99
18. St. Louis	1,114,200	1.19	1,141,400	1.17	1,018,900	1.12	247,700	1.18	451,400	1.20
19. Sacramento–Stockton–Modesto	1,093,000	1.16	1,121,200	1.15	1,089,700	1.20	251,100	1.20	502,700	1.34
20. Denver	1,090,100	1.16	1,033,700	1.06	997,600	1.10	218,100	1.04	421,300	1.12
Markets 11–20	12,847,300	13.67	13,044,600	13.35	12,013,700	13.25	2,627,600	12.53	4,866,700	12.97
Cumulative Total	41,500,200	44.17	43,894,700	44.89	40,719,500	44.91	8,889,200	42.43	16,272,000	43.35
21. Phoenix	1,061,300	1.13	1,044,800	1.07	1,002,900	1.11	227,400	1.09	433,900	1.16
22. Baltimore	977,100	1.04	1,040,100	1.06	949,800	1.05	193,400	.92	373,000	.99
23. Orlando–Daytona Beach–Melbourne	972,100	1.04	979,400	1.00	924,200	1.02	177,100	.85	323,200	.86
24. San Diego	919,900	.98	966,100	.99	1,001,700	1.10	190,300	.91	378,100	1.01
25. Hartford–New Haven	912,400	.97	966,200	.99	891,300	.98	172,700	.82	319,100	.85
26. Indianapolis	905,000	.96	927,600	.95	840,000	.93	203,100	.97	346,800	.92
27. Portland, Ore.	886,600	.94	873,100	.89	825,800	.91	190,600	.91	347,900	.93
28. Milwaukee	780,800	.83	803,500	.82	734,500	.81	174,800	.83	322,500	.86
29. Kansas City	780,700	.83	784,400	.80	716,300	.79	166,900	.80	310,800	.83
30. Charlotte	779,000	.83	808,100	.83	734,900	.81	170,100	.81	283,600	.76
Markets 21–30	8,974,900	9.55	9,913,300	9.40	8,621,400	9.51	1,866,400	8.91	3,438,900	9.17
Cumulative Total	50,475,100	53.72	53,088,000	54.29	49,340,900	54.42	10,755,600	51.34	19,710,900	52.52
31. Cincinnati	771,000	.82	793,100	.81	710,000	.78	176,100	.84	323,500	.86
32. Raleigh–Durham	769,300	.82	796,500	.81	734,100	.81	166,400	.79	289,300	.77
33. Nashville	731,400	.78	745,500	.76	690,700	.76	161,200	.77	275,000	.73
34. Columbus, OH	710,900	.76	726,100	.74	681,200	.75	155,700	.74	277,500	.74
35. Greenville–Spartanburg–Asheville–Anderson	665,700	.71	692,000	.71	621,300	.69	143,500	.69	228,200	.61
36. San Antonio–Victoria	636,300	.68	677,700	.69	620,400	.68	176,300	.84	313,900	.84
37. Grand Rapids–Kalamazoo–Battle Creek	626,700	.67	646,400	.66	605,500	.67	151,700	.72	284,700	.76
38. Buffalo	618,200	.66	641,100	.66	575,700	.63	127,000	.61	225,500	.60
39. New Orleans	616,800	.66	645,200	.66	570,600	.63	160,000	.76	282,700	.75
40. Norfolk–Portsmth–Newport News–Hamptn	616,400	.66	637,700	.65	626,300	.69	136,400	.65	267,100	.71
Markets 31–40	6,762,700	7.22	7,001,300	7.15	6,435,800	7.09	1,554,300	7.41	2,767,400	7.37
Cumulative Total	57,237,800	60.94	60,089,300	61.44	55,776,700	61.51	12,309,900	58.75	22,478,300	59.89

Television Markets Ranked by Size

	ADI TV Households		ADI Women		ADI Men		ADI Teenagers		ADI Children	
41. Salt Lake City	614,700	.65	631,300	.65	613,700	.68	229,600	1.10	417,300	1.11
42. Memphis	604,400	.64	637,100	.65	554,300	.61	155,800	.74	267,300	.71
43. Oklahoma City	577,500	.61	574,300	.59	528,200	.58	129,900	.62	231,300	.62
44. Harrisburg–York–Lancaster–Lebanon	573,200	.61	599,100	.61	550,300	.61	121,600	.58	215,700	.57
45. Providence–New Bedford	569,700	.61	614,700	.63	547,800	.60	113,600	.54	202,100	.54
46. West Palm Beach–Ft. Pierce–Vero Beach	569,100	.61	566,300	.58	518,500	.57	83,900	.40	159,900	.43
47. Louisville	545,200	.58	558,800	.57	507,700	.56	127,500	.61	212,400	.57
48. Albuquerque	541,800	.58	544,900	.56	514,300	.57	141,900	.68	263,100	.70
49. Greensboro–Winston Salem–High Point	540,900	.58	556,100	.57	496,000	.55	109,000	.52	175,000	.47
50. Birmingham	531,400	.57	554,800	.57	485,200	.54	123,700	.59	202,400	.54
Markets 41–50	**5,667,900**	**6.04**	**5,837,400**	**5.98**	**5,316,000**	**5.87**	**1,336,500**	**6.38**	**2,346,500**	**6.26**
Cumulative Total	**62,905,700**	**66.98**	**65,926,700**	**67.42**	**61,092,700**	**67.38**	**13,646,400**	**65.13**	**24,824,800**	**66.15**
51. Wilkes Barre–Scranton	525,600	.56	557,600	.57	498,200	.55	107,200	.51	179,000	.48
52. Dayton	509,500	.54	522,700	.53	472,700	.52	115,500	.55	201,700	.54
53. Albany–Schenectady–Troy	507,300	.54	526,500	.54	483,800	.53	104,100	.50	179,700	.48
54. Jacksonville	487,300	.52	491,100	.50	467,600	.52	107,900	.52	199,500	.53
55. Charleston–Huntington	476,400	.51	495,000	.51	446,900	.49	121,400	.58	179,600	.48
56. Little Rock	466,000	.50	478,700	.49	431,400	.48	110,400	.53	181,000	.48
57. Fresno–Visalia	465,500	.50	499,000	.51	492,500	.54	141,200	.67	278,600	.74
58. Mobile–Pensacola	465,200	.50	479,100	.49	439,200	.48	117,100	.56	196,400	.52
59. Tulsa	460,200	.49	455,500	.47	414,900	.46	103,300	.49	183,000	.49
60. Flint–Saginaw–Bay City	457,800	.49	469,700	.48	425,400	.47	115,100	.55	192,500	.51
Markets 51–60	**4,820,800**	**5.15**	**4,974,900**	**5.09**	**4,572,600**	**5.04**	**1,143,200**	**5.46**	**1,971,000**	**5.25**
Cumulative Total	**67,726,500**	**72.13**	**70,901,600**	**72.51**	**65,665,300**	**72.42**	**14,789,600**	**70.59**	**26,795,800**	**71.40**
61. Richmond	448,900	.48	472,300	.48	422,000	.47	92,600	.44	167,000	.44
62. Wichita–Hutchinson	430,200	.46	415,600	.42	389,300	.43	95,000	.45	181,200	.48
63. Knoxville	423,400	.45	436,600	.45	393,700	.43	93,900	.45	145,700	.39
64. Toledo	407,600	.43	422,200	.43	383,500	.42	98,900	.47	171,800	.46
65. Austin, TX	392,400	.42	377,500	.39	370,900	.41	78,700	.38	152,600	.41
66. Roanoke–Lynchburg	387,200	.41	410,200	.42	372,200	.41	78,700	.38	124,700	.33
67. Syracuse	387,100	.41	410,900	.42	379,600	.42	81,700	.39	153,000	.41
68. Des Moines	380,800	.41	383,100	.39	347,300	.38	78,900	.38	142,800	.38
69. Rochester, N.Y.	377,300	.40	394,500	.40	358,500	.40	76,600	.37	147,200	.39
70. Lexington	371,300	.40	390,500	.40	354,100	.39	88,500	.42	140,500	.37
Markets 61–70	**4,006,200**	**4.27**	**4,113,400**	**4.20**	**3,771,100**	**4.16**	**863,500**	**4.13**	**1,526,500**	**4.06**
Cumulative Total	**71,732,700**	**76.40**	**75,015,000**	**76.71**	**69,436,400**	**76.58**	**15,653,100**	**74.72**	**28,322,300**	**75.46**
71. Shreveport–Texarkana	368,100	.39	381,700	.39	335,100	.37	94,100	.45	161,300	.43
72. Green Bay–Appleton	366,100	.39	369,600	.38	348,700	.38	84,900	.41	155,100	.41
73. Omaha	361,500	.38	359,200	.37	329,600	.36	83,900	.40	153,300	.41
74. Las Vegas	343,600	.37	329,000	.34	339,700	.37	65,200	.31	128,600	.34
75. Springfield–Decatur–Champaign	342,000	.36	350,000	.36	321,900	.36	73,100	.35	127,500	.34
76. Portland–Poland Spring	338,200	.36	344,200	.35	315,100	.35	71,300	.34	128,000	.34
77. Paducah–Cp Girardeau–Harrsbrg–Marion	332,000	.35	339,600	.35	308,400	.34	72,700	.35	115,300	.31
78. Spokane	331,500	.35	321,700	.33	309,000	.34	76,600	.37	135,400	.36
79. Tucson	327,100	.35	321,800	.33	304,800	.34	69,500	.33	127,500	.34
80. Springfield, Mo.	326,600	.35	331,900	.34	308,700	.34	71,900	.34	118,600	.32
Markets 71–80	**3,436,700**	**3.65**	**3,448,700**	**3.54**	**3,221,000**	**3.55**	**763,200**	**3.65**	**1,350,600**	**3.60**
Cumulative Total	**75,169,400**	**80.05**	**78,463,700**	**80.250**	**72,657,400**	**80.13**	**16,416,300**	**78.37**	**29,672,900**	**79.06**
81. Huntsville–Decatur–Florence	321,600	.34	327,200	.33	301,700	.33	72,200	.34	118,000	.31
82. Cedar Rapids–Waterloo–Dubuque	312,800	.33	320,800	.33	298,600	.33	70,600	.34	123,200	.33
83. South Bend–Elkhart	299,600	.32	307,300	.31	281,500	.31	72,200	.34	127,600	.34
84. Davenprt–Rock Islnd–Moline: Quad City	297,100	.32	295,600	.30	271,200	.30	68,400	.33	116,300	.31
85. Chattanooga	295,100	.31	305,900	.31	274,600	.30	69,000	.33	107,000	.29
86. Columbia, SC	290.600	.31	315,600	.32	284,800	.31	74,000	.35	122,100	.33
87. Ft. Myers–Naples	290,500	.31	291,600	.30	272,600	.30	43,100	.21	79,600	.21
88. Jackson, Ms.	284,300	.30	307,100	.31	261,700	.29	81,000	.39	133,600	.36

Broadcasting & Cable Yearbook 1994

Television Markets Ranked by Size

	ADI TV Households		ADI Women		ADI Men		ADI Teenagers		ADI Children	
89. Johnstown–Altoona	283,400	.30	298,100	.30	280,500	.31	62,900	.30	99,800	.27
90. Madison	281,300	.30	282,500	.29	268,400	.30	57,100	.27	108,500	.29
Markets 81–90	**2,956,300**	**3.14**	**3,051,700**	**3.10**	**2,795,600**	**3.08**	**670,500**	**3.20**	**1,135,700**	**3.04**
Cumulative Total	**78,125,700**	**83.19**	**81,515,400**	**83.35**	**75,453,000**	**83.21**	**17,086,800**	**81.57**	**30,808,600**	**82.10**
91. Bristl–Kngspt–Jnsn Cty–Grnvl: Tri-City	278,600	.30	291,000	.30	264,100	.29	64,700	.31	93,100	.25
92. Youngstown	274,500	.29	284,900	.29	251,300	.28	62,500	.30	99,300	.26
93. Burlington–Plattsburgh	271,300	.29	281,300	.29	273,600	.30	59,100	.28	108,400	.29
94. Evansville	262,500	.28	267,000	.27	240,900	.27	61,300	.29	102,100	.27
95. Baton Rouge	258,700	.28	273,300	.28	253,400	.28	69,600	.33	127,000	.34
96. Waco–Temple–Bryan	254,400	.27	262,500	.27	266,200	.29	57,900	.28	110,800	.30
97. Colorado Springs–Pueblo	252,000	.27	246,600	.25	242,300	.27	57,600	.28	106,500	.28
98. Springfield, MA	246,900	.26	269,800	.28	236,600	.26	49,800	.24	92,300	.25
99. Lincoln–Hastings–Kearney	245,400	.26	242,200	.25	224,100	.25	51,900	.25	93,400	.25
100. El Paso	242,000	.26	277,200	.28	254,800	.28	87,100	.42	144,400	.38
Markets 91–100	**2,586,300**	**2.76**	**2,695,800**	**2.76**	**2,507,300**	**2.77**	**621,500**	**2.98**	**1,077,300**	**2.87**
Cumulative Total	**80,712,800**	**85.95**	**84,211,200**	**86.11**	**77,960,300**	**85.98**	**17,708,300**	**84.55**	**31,885,900**	**84.97**
101. Savannah	238,200	.25	249,300	.25	237,800	.26	59,000	.28	107,300	.29
102. Ft. Wayne	236,900	.25	240,900	.25	221,300	.24	59,700	.29	103,800	.28
103. Salinas–Monterey	233,100	.25	254,800	.26	265,000	.29	56,200	.27	110,000	.29
104. Greenville–New Bern–Washington	230,300	.25	240,000	.25	247,300	.27	53,500	.26	94,500	.25
105. Lansing	230,200	.25	241,200	.25	227,700	.25	53,200	.25	95,400	.25
106. Charleston, SC	230,100	.25	239,100	.24	230,400	.25	57,100	.27	108,900	.29
107. Peoria–Bloomington	221,400	.24	229,200	.23	208,300	.23	50,600	.24	84,900	.23
108. Sioux Falls–Mitchell	219,900	.23	216,100	.22	202,100	.22	51,700	.25	94,900	.25
109. Fargo	216,000	.23	212,100	.22	207,100	.23	48,600	.23	90,300	.24
110. Augusta	215,500	.23	226,400	.23	205,600	.23	57,000	.27	97,900	.26
Markets 101–110	**2,271,600**	**2.43**	**2,349,100**	**2.40**	**2,252,600**	**2.47**	**546,600**	**2.61**	**987,900**	**2.63**
Cumulative Total	**82,983,600**	**88.38**	**86,560,300**	**88.51**	**80,212,900**	**88.45**	**18,254,900**	**87.16**	**32,873,800**	**87.60**
111. Montgomery–Selma	212,500	.23	227,400	.23	195,400	.22	57,900	.28	91,700	.24
112. Snta Brbra–Snta Maria–Sn Luis Obispo	210,700	.22	224,700	.23	229,700	.25	40,700	.19	80,700	.21
113. McAllen–Brownsville: LRGV	205,800	.22	255,800	.26	224,800	.25	100,400	.48	153,100	.41
114. Tyler–Longview–Jacksonville	204,000	.22	209,800	.21	191,300	.21	48,300	.23	83,600	.22
115. Tallahassee–Thomasville	201,100	.21	212,700	.22	193,000	.21	48,600	.23	82,600	.22
116. Eugene	197,400	.21	194,900	.20	185,200	.20	41,100	.20	72,400	.19
117. Ft. Smith	196,700	.21	197,400	.20	183,600	.20	46,000	.22	76,900	.20
118. Reno	195,100	.21	185,700	.19	196,000	.22	37,400	.18	73,900	.20
119. Macon	189,600	.20	205,800	.21	182,200	.20	49,600	.24	82,200	.22
120. Lafayette, LA	188,400	.20	194,700	.20	173,600	.19	52,700	.25	97,600	.26
Markets 111–120	**2,001,300**	**2.13**	**2,108,900**	**2.15**	**1,954,800**	**2.15**	**522,700**	**2.50**	**894,700**	**2.37**
Cumulative Total	**84,984,900**	**90.51**	**88,669,200**	**90.66**	**82,167,700**	**90.60**	**18,777,600**	**89.66**	**33,768,500**	**89.97**
121. Traverse City–Cadillac	185,200	.20	186,400	.19	181,200	.20	42,100	.20	74,800	.20
122. Columbus, GA	180,700	.19	190,900	.20	179,400	.20	44,800	.21	75,800	.20
123. Corpus Christi	173,800	.19	183,500	.19	171,800	.19	52,100	.25	91,100	.24
124. Yakima–Pasco–Richland–Kennewick	171,400	.18	169,100	.17	166,800	.18	44,700	.21	81,600	.22
125. Chico–Redding	171,000	.18	169,000	.17	158,800	.18	35,900	.17	68,700	.18
126. Duluth–Superior	170,900	.18	165,500	.17	156,500	.17	37,500	.18	62,300	.17
127. Columbus–Tupelo	170,300	.18	179,800	.18	157,900	.17	45,100	.22	73,200	.20
128. La Crosse–Eau Claire	169,500	.18	174,500	.18	163,700	.18	38,500	.18	71,300	.19
129. Amarillo	168,900	.18	166,600	.17	153,200	.17	42,400	.20	77,000	.21
130. Bakersfield	168,100	.18	173,900	.18	177,700	.20	47,400	.23	99,100	.26
Markets 121–130	**1,729,800**	**1.84**	**1,759,200**	**1.80**	**1,667,000**	**1.84**	**430,500**	**2.05**	**774,900**	**2.07**
Cumulative Total	**86,714,700**	**92.35**	**90,428,400**	**92.46**	**83,834,700**	**92.44**	**19,208,100**	**91.71**	**34,543,400**	**92.04**
131. Monroe–El Dorado	167,800	.18	181,500	.19	157,000	.17	47,600	.23	78,500	.21
132. Boise	167,700	.18	164,100	.17	158,200	.17	42,900	.20	77,100	.21
133. Wausau–Rhinelander	165,900	.18	166,800	.17	161,300	.18	41,000	.20	70,300	.19
134. Rockford	159,600	.17	160,200	.16	149,100	.16	35,900	.17	64,100	.17

Television Markets Ranked by Size

		ADI TV Households		ADI Women		ADI Men		ADI Teenagers		ADI Children	
135.	Binghamton	158,400	.17	164,500	.17	150,900	.17	34,200	.16	61,100	.16
136.	Florence–Myrtle Beach	158,300	.17	167,400	.17	146,700	.16	42,400	.20	64,600	.17
137.	Beaumont–Port Arthur	157,900	.17	161,600	.17	145,300	.16	38,600	.18	68,500	.18
138.	Terre Haute	156,100	.17	162,000	.17	147,200	.16	34,900	.17	58,600	.16
139.	Topeka	155,500	.17	156,300	.16	153,300	.17	33,400	.16	64,700	.17
140.	Sioux City	155,100	.17	156,300	.16	142,800	.16	37,600	.18	67,500	.18
	Markets 131–140	**1,602,300**	**1.73**	**1,640,700**	**1.69**	**1,511,800**	**1.66**	**388,500**	**1.85**	**675,000**	**1.80**
	Cumulative Total	**88,317,000**	**94.08**	**92,069,100**	**94.15**	**85,346,500**	**94.10**	**19,596,600**	**93.56**	**35,218,400**	**93.84**
141.	Wichita Falls–Lawton	154,300	.16	155,400	.16	149,500	.16	36,300	.17	65,800	.18
142.	Erie	152,600	.16	158,200	.16	143,300	.16	35,200	.17	60,000	.16
143.	Wilmington	152,600	.16	157,900	.16	138,600	.15	37,700	.18	57,300	.15
144.	Wheeling–Steubenville	144,100	.15	150,100	.15	131,500	.15	32,600	.16	50,100	.13
145.	Medford	140,000	.15	135,500	.14	128,600	.14	29,900	.14	51,200	.14
146.	Joplin–Pittsburg	139,100	.15	139,700	.14	123,800	.14	30,500	.15	52,200	.14
147.	Bluefield–Beckley–Oak Hill	137,400	.15	143,500	.15	125,100	.14	36,900	.18	48,200	.13
148.	Rochester–Mason City–Austin	137,100	.15	134,900	.14	122,600	.14	29,400	.14	55,900	.15
149.	Lubbock	136,100	.14	138,900	.14	130,700	.14	34,300	.16	64,100	.17
150.	Odessa–Midland	136,100	.14	135,600	.14	128,300	.14	38,300	.18	73,300	.20
	Markets 141–150	**1,429,400**	**1.51**	**1,449,700**	**1.48**	**1,322,000**	**1.46**	**341,100**	**1.63**	**578,100**	**1.55**
	Cumulative Total	**89,746,400**	**95.59**	**93,518,800**	**95.63**	**86,668,500**	**95.56**	**19,937,700**	**95.19**	**35,796,500**	**95.39**
151.	Columbia–Jefferson City	135,300	.14	140,700	.14	135,200	.15	29,000	.14	52,700	.14
152.	Minot–Bismarck–Dickinson–Glendive	134,700	.14	128,800	.13	123,600	.14	34,900	.17	62,000	.17
153.	Sarasota	133,500	.14	133,100	.14	114,400	.13	15,400	.07	26,400	.07
154.	Albany, GA	129,100	.14	138,100	.14	119,600	.13	37,500	.18	61,700	.16
155.	Bangor	123,400	.13	126,400	.13	119,000	.13	28,300	.14	47,600	.13
156.	Sherman–Ada	108,600	.12	110,500	.11	98,600	.11	25,200	.12	40,900	.11
157.	Abliene–Sweetwater	108,200	.12	110,100	.11	100,500	.11	25,400	.12	45,700	.12
158.	Idaho Falls–Pocatello	108,000	.12	108,300	.11	106,300	.12	38,100	.18	66,000	.18
159.	Quincy–Hannibal	104,400	.11	107,500	.11	98,500	.11	23,000	.11	39,100	.10
160.	Clarksburg–Weston	102,600	.11	107,600	.11	95,600	.11	23,900	.11	35,800	.10
	Markets 151–160	**1,187,800**	**1.27**	**1,211,100**	**1.23**	**1,111,300**	**1.24**	**280,700**	**1.34**	**477,900**	**1.28**
	Cumulative Total	**90,934,200**	**96.86**	**94,729,900**	**96.86**	**87,779,800**	**96.80**	**20,218,400**	**96.53**	**36,274,400**	**96.67**
161.	Utica	102,200	.11	108,300	.11	101,200	.11	22,000	.11	39,100	.10
162.	Palm Springs	101,500	.11	108,800	.11	108,800	.12	26,600	.13	55,800	.15
163.	Salisbury	98,800	.11	103,500	.11	95,700	.11	19,500	.09	35,600	.09
164.	Panama City	94,800	.10	96,300	.10	94,200	.10	22,000	.11	35,900	.10
165.	Dothan	94,700	.10	97,000	.10	88,500	.10	24,200	.12	38,700	.10
166.	Gainesville	92,800	.10	93,600	.10	90,700	.10	16,700	.08	31,600	.08
167.	Laurel–Hattiesburg	91,300	.10	96,700	.10	83,700	.09	25,100	.12	41,000	.11
168.	Rapid City	91,100	.10	87,800	.09	86,700	.10	23,400	.11	44,400	.12
169.	Alexandria, LA	87,800	.09	92,200	.09	89,200	.10	24,000	.11	44,300	.12
170.	Watertown–Carthage	87,200	.09	91,800	.09	95,100	.10	22,300	.11	39,300	.10
	Markets 161–170	**942,200**	**1.01**	**976,000**	**1.00**	**933,800**	**1.03**	**225,800**	**1.09**	**405,700**	**1.07**
	Cumulative Total	**91,876,400**	**97.87**	**95,705,900**	**97.86**	**88,713,600**	**97.83**	**20,444,200**	**97.62**	**36,680,100**	**97.74**
171.	Billings–Hardin	86,700	.09	84,800	.09	79,300	.09	21,500	.10	37,200	.10
172.	Elmira	86,700	.09	88,600	.09	82,100	.09	20,300	.10	34,700	.09
173.	Harrisonburg	85,700	.09	92,800	.09	86,300	.10	17,700	.08	30,200	.08
174.	Lake Charles	82,200	.09	85,200	.09	81,000	.09	22,400	.11	39,400	.10
175.	Marquette	82,100	.09	80,800	.08	81,400	.09	18,600	.09	31,600	.08
176.	Missoula	77,800	.08	74,100	.08	70,900	.08	18,300	.09	32,000	.09
177.	Jonesboro	75,700	.08	77,400	.08	69,400	.08	17,000	.08	26,400	.07
178.	El Centro–Yuma	71,800	.08	77,900	.08	78,000	.09	24,300	.12	41,500	.11
179.	Greenwood–Greenville	69,400	.07	77,900	.08	67,800	.07	24,100	.12	39,900	.11
180.	Biloxi–Gulfport–Pascagoula	69,200	.07	70,100	.07	69,100	.08	17,300	.08	31,100	.08
	Markets 171–180	**787,300**	**.83**	**809,600**	**.83**	**765,300**	**.86**	**201,500**	**.97**	**344,000**	**.91**
	Cumulative Total	**92,663,700**	**98.70**	**96,515,500**	**98.69**	**89,478,900**	**98.69**	**20,645,700**	**98.59**	**37,024,100**	**98.65**

Television Markets Ranked by Size

	ADI TV Households		ADI Women		ADI Men		ADI Teenagers		ADI Children	
181. Bowling Green	66,300	.07	70,000	.07	62,600	.07	15,700	.07	24,300	.06
182. Great Falls	65,800	.07	63,300	.06	60,700	.07	16,000	.08	30,200	.08
183. Meridan	65,600	.07	69,400	.07	59,700	.07	18,400	.09	29,000	.08
184. Parkersburg	60,500	.06	61,900	.06	54,800	.06	14,100	.07	21,700	.06
185. Jackson, TN	58,900	.06	61,100	.06	53,200	.06	13,400	.06	21,800	.06
186. Tuscaloosa	58,000	.06	62,600	.06	56,800	.06	13,100	.06	21,100	.06
187. Eureka	56,600	.06	54,300	.06	56,000	.06	11,500	.05	23,100	.06
188. Grand Junction–Durango	49,700	.05	48,100	.05	44,600	.05	11,200	.05	20,300	.05
189. Butte	49,300	.05	47,300	.05	49,000	.05	10,600	.05	18,500	.05
190. San Angelo	49,200	.05	51,600	.05	47,500	.05	11,500	.05	22,000	.06
Markets 181–190	**579,900**	**.60**	**589,600**	**.59**	**544,900**	**.60**	**135,500**	**.63**	**232,000**	**.62**
Cumulative Total	**93,243,600**	**99.30**	**97,105,100**	**99.28**	**90,023,800**	**99.29**	**20,781,200**	**99.22**	**37,256,100**	**99.27**
191. Lafayette, IN	46,900	.05	51,800	.05	52,700	.06	8,900	.04	16,400	.04
192. Hagerstown	45,400	.05	47,200	.05	48,300	.05	8,900	.04	16,300	.04
193. St. Joseph	44,900	.05	46,800	.05	40,800	.04	9,800	.05	16,900	.05
194. Casper–Riverton	43,800	.05	41,800	.04	39,500	.04	11,300	.05	20,300	.05
195. Anniston	43,700	.05	46,400	.05	42,100	.05	10,600	.05	16,400	.04
196. Cheyenne–Scottsbluff (Sterling)	43,400	.05	41,300	.04	39,300	.04	10,400	.05	18,000	.05
197. Charlottesville	41,700	.04	46,200	.05	42,100	.05	6,900	.03	13,900	.04
198. Laredo	40,300	.04	52,400	.05	45,500	.05	19,500	.09	32,200	.09
199. Lima	38,800	.04	40,000	.04	38,400	.04	10,000	.05	16,800	.04
200. Ottumwa–Kirksville	33,600	.04	34,700	.04	31,100	.03	7,000	.03	11,200	.03
Markets 191–200	**422,500**	**.46**	**448,600**	**.46**	**419,800**	**.45**	**103,300**	**.48**	**178,400**	**.47**
Cumulative Total	**93,666,100**	**99.76**	**97,553,700**	**99.74**	**90,443,600**	**99.74**	**20,884,500**	**99.70**	**37,434,500**	**99.74**
201. Twin Falls	32,300	.03	31,300	.03	30,000	.03	9,200	.04	15,400	.04
202. Bend	31,900	.03	30,400	.03	29,600	.03	6,700	.03	12,200	.03
203. Zanesville	30,900	.03	32,500	.03	28,300	.03	7,500	.04	12,600	.03
204. Flagstaff	30,600	.03	34,000	.03	33,200	.04	9,700	.05	17,900	.05
205. Presque Isle	30,100	.03	30,200	.03	29,600	.03	7,600	.04	11,800	.03
206. Mankato	29,900	.03	31,900	.03	30,000	.03	6,600	.03	11,700	.03
207. Helena	20,700	.02	19,400	.02	18,200	.02	4,800	.02	8,500	.02
208. North Platte	18,100	.02	16,900	.02	15,400	.02	4,300	.02	7,700	.02
209. Alpena	16,000	.02	15,900	.02	14,700	.02	3,600	.02	5,800	.02
Markets 201–209	**240,500**	**.24**	**242,500**	**.24**	**229,000**	**.25**	**60,000**	**.29**	**103,600**	**.27**
Cumulative Total	**93,906,600**	**100.00**	**97,796,200**	**99.98**	**90,672,600**	**99.99**	**20,944,500**	**99.99**	**37,538,100**	**100.01**

Broadcasting & Cable Yearbook 1994

TV Markets by Nielsen Marketing Research Territory

Nielsen Marketing Research territory groups are another standard way of reporting sales data. The following table ranks TV markets, known as Designated Market Areas (DMAs), within each Nielsen territory. This provides a yardstick for determining the number of spot markets needed to achieve a given coverage of territory. For example, if the national media are not delivering sufficient advertising weight in New England, the planner will find that three TV markets, (Boston, Hartford and Providence) contain over 75% of New England territory households. The planner can also use the table to get a better idea of what TV markets are needed to cover all of New England. Data is from the Nielsen Station Index with tabulations based on a January 1994 estimate.

DMA	TV Households	Territory %	Total U.S.%	Rank
New England				
Boston	2,104,900	45.6	2.247	6
Hartford & New Haven	915,110	19.8	.977	25
Providence–New Bedford	565,460	12.3	.604	46
Portland–Auburn	341,080	7.4	.364	79
Burlington–Plattsburgh	282,740	6.1	.302	92
Springfield–Holyoke	247,300	5.4	.264	99
Bangor	123,820	2.7	.132	155
Presque Isle	30,300	.7	.033	206
Total	**4,610,710**	**100.0**	**4.923**	
Metropolitan New York				
New York	6,692,370	100.0	7.146	1
Total	**6,692,370**	**100.0**	**7.146**	
Middle Atlantic				
Philadelphia	2,661,360	28.6	2.842	4
Washington, D.C.	1,855,440	19.9	1.981	7
Baltimore	970,030	10.5	1.036	22
Buffalo	633,560	6.8	.676	37
Harrisburg–Lancaster–Lebanon–York	569,920	6.1	.609	44
Wilkes Barre–Scranton	549,770	5.9	.587	47
Albany–Schenectady–Troy	508,820	5.5	.543	52
Syracuse	384,800	4.2	.411	67
Rochester, N.Y.	363,620	3.9	.388	71
Johnstown–Altoona	283,950	3.0	.303	91
Binghamton	136,120	1.5	.146	148
Salisbury	98,310	1.0	.105	163
Utica	97,900	1.1	.104	164
Elmira	93,850	1.0	.100	166
Watertown	87,430	1.0	.094	170
Total	**9,294,880**	**100.0**	**9.925**	
East Central				
Detroit	1,735,340	13.7	1.853	9
Cleveland	1,446,970	11.5	1.545	12
Pittsburgh	1,141,830	9.1	1.219	17
Indianapolis	912,190	7.2	.974	26
Cincinnati	770,400	6.1	.823	30
Columbus, Ohio	710,910	5.7	.759	34
Grand Rapids–Kalamazoo–Battle Creek	638,940	5.1	.682	36
Louisville	533,170	4.2	.569	49
Dayton	508,500	4.0	.543	53
Charleston–Huntington	473,200	3.8	.506	56
Flint–Saginaw–Bay City	447,670	3.5	.478	60
Toledo	407,850	3.3	.435	63
Lexington	378,720	3.0	.404	69
South Bend–Elkhart	299,050	2.4	.320	84
Youngstown	274,570	2.1	.293	94
Evansville	268,930	2.2	.287	95
Ft. Wayne	237,090	1.9	.253	103
Lansing	229,780	1.8	.246	104
Traverse City–Cadillac	183,800	1.4	.196	121
Wheeling–Steubenville	157,600	1.3	.168	138
Erie	151,100	1.2	.162	141
Terre Haute	150,560	1.2	.160	143
Bluefield–Beckley–Oak Hill	134,620	1.0	.144	150
Clarksburg–Weston	101,580	.9	.109	161
Marquette	60,360	.4	.064	183
Parkersburg	56,390	.5	.060	187
Bowling Green	52,260	.4	.056	190
Lafayette, Ind.	46,670	.4	.050	194
Lima	38,750	.3	.041	200
Zanesville	30,990	.2	.033	204
Alpena	16,240	.2	.018	209
Total	**12,596,030**	**100.0**	**13.450**	
Metropolitan Chicago				
Chicago	3,070,830	100.0	3.279	3
Total	**3,070,830**	**100.0**	**3.279**	
West Central				
Minneapolis–St. Paul	1,389,420	11.5	1.483	14
St. Louis	1,109,090	9.2	1.184	18
Denver	1,090,970	9.0	1.165	21
Milwaukee	780,350	6.5	.834	28
Kansas City	767,930	6.4	.820	31
Wichita–Hutchinson Plus	423,920	3.5	.452	61
Green Bay–Appleton	391,650	3.3	.419	65
Des Moines–Ames	362,520	3.0	.387	72
Omaha	359,610	2.9	.384	73
Paducah–Cape Girardeau–Harrisburg	345,970	2.9	.369	76
Champaign & Springfield–Decatur	343,300	2.9	.367	77
Springfield, Mo.	325,260	2.7	.347	80
Cedar Rapids–Waterloo & Dubuque	300,880	2.5	.321	83
Madison	297,970	2.4	.318	86
Davenport–Rock Island–Moline	296,850	2.5	.317	88
Lincoln & Hastings–Kearney Plus	250,580	2.1	.268	97
Colorado Springs–Pueblo	245,350	2.0	.262	100
Sioux Falls (Mitchell)	219,700	1.8	.234	107
Fargo–Valley City	215,660	1.8	.231	108
Peoria–Bloomington	207,930	1.8	.222	113
Duluth–Superior	169,860	1.4	.181	128
Wausau–Rhinelander	166,590	1.3	.178	133
La Crosse–Eau Claire	163,540	1.4	.175	135
Rockford	159,750	1.3	.170	137
Topeka	150,970	1.3	.161	142
Sioux City	150,550	1.2	.161	144
Rochester–Mason City–Austin	141,240	1.2	.151	146
Joplin–Pittsburg	138,670	1.2	.148	147
Columbia–Jefferson City	134,340	1.1	.144	151
Minot–Bismarck–Dickinson	131,040	1.1	.139	153
Quincy–Hannibal–Keokuk	109,950	.9	.118	157
Billings	86,790	.7	.093	172
Rapid City	84,520	.7	.090	173
Missoula	77,310	.6	.082	174
Great Falls	65,550	.6	.070	180
Grand Junction–Montrose	58,110	.5	.062	184
St. Joseph	57,660	.4	.062	185

TV Markets by Nielsen Marketing Territory

DMA	TV Households	Territory %	Total U.S.%	Rank
Mankato	53,990	.5	.058	189
Butte	50,350	.4	.053	191
Cheyenne–Scotsbluf–Strlng	48,370	.4	.052	192
Casper–Riverton	47,010	.4	.050	193
Ottumwa–Kirksville	41,360	.3	.044	198
Helena	19,620	.2	.021	208
North Platte	14,550	.1	.016	210
Glendive	3,920	.1	.004	211
Total	**12,050,520**	**100.0**	**12.867**	

Southeast

DMA	TV Households	Territory %	Total U.S.%	Rank
Atlanta	1,510,340	8.3	1.613	11
Tampa–St. Petersburg, Sarasota	1,384,150	7.7	1.478	15
Miami–Ft. Lauderdale	1,296,800	7.2	1.384	16
Orlando–Daytona Beach–Melbourne	967,360	5.4	1.033	23
Charlotte	774,760	4.3	.828	29
Raleigh–Durham	753,570	4.1	.804	32
Nashville	737,810	4.1	.788	33
Greenville–Spartanburg–Asheville	669,090	3.7	.715	35
Norfolk–Portsmouth–Newport News	612,880	3.4	.654	39
Memphis	595,380	3.3	.636	42
West Palm Beach–Ft. Pierce	566,140	3.2	.604	45
Greensboro–High Point–Winston Salem	538,090	3.0	.575	48
Birmingham	522,420	2.9	.558	51
Jacksonville–Brunswick	484,220	2.6	.517	54
Richmond–Petersburg	484,030	2.7	.517	55
Mobile–Pensacola	422,340	2.4	.450	62
Knoxville	404,020	2.2	.432	64
Roanoke–Lynchburg	386,300	2.2	.412	66
Chattanooga	310,680	1.7	.332	82
Fort Myers–Naples	298,920	1.6	.319	85
Huntsville–Decatur, Florence	296,930	1.7	.317	87
Columbia, S.C.	295,640	1.6	.316	89
Jackson, Miss.	286,200	1.6	.306	90
Tri-Cities, Tenn.-Va.	278,870	1.6	.297	93
Savannah	238,210	1.3	.255	102
Charleston, S.C.	229,740	1.2	.245	105
Greenville–New Bern–Washington	228,530	1.3	.244	106
Montgomery	210,590	1.2	.225	111
Augusta	208,320	1.1	.222	112
Tallahassee–Thomasville	198,760	1.1	.213	116
Columbus, Ga.	181,950	1.1	.194	122
Macon	178,610	.9	.191	124
Florence–Myrtle Beach	169,960	1.0	.181	127
Columbus–Tupelo–West Point	165,550	.9	.177	134
Wilmington	151,790	.8	.162	140
Albany, Ga.	128,790	.8	.138	154
Biloxi–Gulfport	106,450	.5	.113	159
Dothan	99,710	.6	.107	162
Gainesville	91,610	.5	.097	167
Hattiesburg–Laurel	90,150	.5	.097	168
Panama City	89,340	.5	.095	169
Greenwood–Greenville	76,340	.4	.082	175
Meridian	64,870	.4	.069	181
Jackson, Tenn.	62,180	.3	.066	182
Tuscaloosa	57,370	.4	.062	186
Charlottesville	44,320	.2	.047	196
Anniston	43,440	.2	.046	197
Harrisonburg	38,090	.3	.041	201
Total	**18,031,610**	**100.0**	**19.254**	

Southwest

DMA	TV Households	Territory %	Total U.S.%	Rank
Dallas–Ft. Worth	1,816,700	17.3	1.940	8
Houston	1,510,580	14.4	1.613	10
San Antonio	610,660	5.9	.652	40
New Orleans	609,000	5.8	.650	41
Oklahoma City	572,300	5.4	.611	43
Albuquerque–Santa Fe	530,040	5.1	.566	50
Little Rock–Pine Bluff	463,630	4.4	.495	58
Tulsa	456,430	4.4	.488	59
Austin	383,230	3.7	.409	68
Shreveport	351,650	3.3	.375	74
Baton Rouge	258,180	2.5	.276	96
Waco–Temple	247,620	2.3	.264	98
El Paso	241,980	2.4	.259	101
Tyler–Longview	213,520	2.0	.228	109
Harlingen–Weslaco–Brnsvlle	202,940	1.9	.216	115
Ft. Smith	195,490	1.9	.209	118
Lafayette, La.	194,500	1.9	.208	120
Corpus Christi	169,180	1.6	.181	129
Amarillo	168,690	1.6	.180	130
Monroe–El Dorado	167,060	1.6	.178	132
Beaumont–Port Arthur	160,480	1.5	.171	136
Wichita Falls & Lawton	152,200	1.5	.163	139
Lubbock	134,730	1.3	.144	149
Odessa–Midland	132,800	1.2	.142	152
Abilene–Sweetwater	106,680	1.0	.113	158
Alexandria, La.	87,040	.9	.093	171
Jonesboro	75,370	.7	.081	176
Lake Charles	74,890	.7	.080	177
Ada–Ardmore	70,480	.7	.075	179
San Angelo	45,730	.4	.049	195
Laredo	39,980	.4	.043	199
Victoria	26,400	.3	.028	207
Total	**10,470,160**	**100.0**	**11.180**	

Greater Los Angeles

DMA	TV Households	Territory %	Total U.S.%	Rank
Los Angeles	5,006,380	98.1	5.346	2
Palm Springs	93,990	1.9	.100	165
Total	**5,100,370**	**100.0**	**5.446**	

Remaining Pacific

DMA	TV Households	Territory %	Total U.S.%	Rank
San Francisco–Oak–San Jose	2,253,220	19.2	2.406	5
Seattle–Tacoma	1,427,750	12.1	1.524	13
Sacramento–Stockton–Modesto	1,099,950	9.4	1.175	19
Phoenix	1,097,480	9.3	1.172	20
San Diego	920,570	7.9	.983	24
Portland, Ore.	890,120	7.6	.950	27
Salt Lake City	616,720	5.2	.659	38
Fresno–Visalia	473,020	4.1	.505	57
Las Vegas	346,710	2.9	.370	75
Spokane	341,630	2.9	.365	78
Tucson (Nogales)	322,750	2.8	.345	81
Santa Barbara–Sanmar–Sanluob	211,640	1.8	.225	110
Monterey–Salinas	206,960	1.7	.221	114
Eugene	198,710	1.7	.213	117
Reno	194,600	1.7	.207	119
Yakima–Pasco–Rchlnd–Knnwck	179,630	1.5	.192	123
Chico–Redding	172,560	1.5	.185	125
Bakersfield	172,550	1.5	.184	126
Boise	167,660	1.4	.179	131
Medford–Klamath Falls	141,870	1.2	.151	145
Idaho Falls–Pocatello	104,050	.9	.111	160
Yuma–El Centro	73,490	.6	.079	178
Eureka	55,740	.5	.059	188
Twin Falls	32,600	.3	.035	202
Bend, Ore.	32,140	.3	.035	203
Total	**11,734,120**	**100.0**	**12.530**	

Continental U.S. Total 93,651,600   100.0

The Top 100 Companies

The following charts list the top 100 companies publicly reporting electronic communications-related operations for 1992. The companies are separated into specific categories including Broadcasting, Programming, Technology, Cable, and Agencies and Services. ECI revenue comprises a company's business interest in radio, TV, cable, satellite, allied services and manufacturing. Items not included in ECI revenue for programmers include revenue from theatrical releases and the home video market. For manufacturers, it includes revenue from sales of television sets or products for the general public not built specifically or primarily for Fifth Estate commercial use. All data was obtained from *Broadcasting Magazine's* "Top 100 Companies in Electronic Communications". ECI estimates were provided by the companies, securities analysts and industry associations. NM=not meaningful.

Broadcasting

ECI Rank	'92 ECI Revenue (in millions)	% Chg. in ECI Rev. from '91	ECI as % of total Revenue	'92 ECI Income (in millions)	'92 total Net Earnings (in millions)	% Chg. in Net from '91
1. Capital Cities/ABC	$4,265.6	–1%	80%	$619.3	$246.1	–28%
2. CBS	$3,503.0	15%	100%	$180.1	$81.0	NM
3. General Electric	$3,363.0	8%	6%	$204.0	$4,725.0	80%
4. News Corp.	$1,480.0	3%	19%	$291.0	$457.0	NM
5. Westinghouse	$725.0	2%	9%	$157.0	($1,291.0)	NM
6. Tribune	$684.1	11%	32%	$121.3	$119.8	–16%
7. Multimedia	$444.3	12%	77%	$146.5	$60.5	25%
8. Scripps-Howard	$389.8	12%	100%	$90.2	$36.8	127%
9. Gannett Co.	$370.6	4%	11%	$66.2	$199.7	–34%
10. BHC Communications	$307.9	17%	100%	$22.4	$109.3	1%
11. SCI Television	$221.2	6%	100%	$38.4	($47.0)	NM
12. Great American Communications	$210.8	5%	100%	$25.6	($560.0)	NM
13. A.H. Belo	$201.1	11%	39%	$56.5	$37.2	200%
14. Univision	$190.3	6%	95%	$15.0	($28.2)	NM
15. Infinity Broadcasting	$171.8	27%	100%	$35.4	($9.4)	NM
16. Telemundo Group	$153.6	14%	100%	$10.8	($26.7)	NM
17. LIN Broadcasting Corp.	$142.9	10%	25%	$53.0	($90.1)	NM
18. Jefferson-Pilot	$129.7	4%	11%	$24.3	$203.2	16
19. Pulitzer	$113.4	4%	28%	$23.3	($1.2)	NM
20. Meredith Corp.	$106.0	–3%	15%	$17.3	($6.3)	NM
21. McGraw-Hill	$103.7	6%	5%	$29.2	$28.6	–81%
22. Clear Channel	$94.5	27%	100%	$13.5	$4.3	281%
23. Allbritton Communications	$84.8	1%	100%	$24.7	$3.1	NM
24. Lee Enterprises	$79.1	14%	22%	$14.5	$38.5	22%
25. Park Communications	$77.3	15%	48%	$22.6	$17.2	45%
26. Liberty Corp.	$74.9	5%	22%	$14.7	$40.5	35%
27. Burnham Broadcasting	$72.8	8%	100%	$3.4	($18.2)	NM
28. Jacor Communications	$70.5	9%	100%	($3.2)	($23.7)	NM
29. Ackerley Communications	$67.9	2%	41%	$21.0	($14.5)	NM
30. AFLAC Broadcast	$66.3	3%	2%	$18.3	$183.4	23%
31. Heritage Media	$64.4	26%	27%	$14.6	($18.6)	NM
32. The New York Times Co.	$62.0	9%	3%	$8.1	($44.7)	NM
33. Silver King Communications	$46.8	76%	100%	$4.3	($15.2)	NM

The Top 100 Companies

Programming

ECI Rank	'92 ECI Revenue (In millions)	% Chg. in ECI Rev. from '91	ECI as % of Total Revenue	'92 Total Net Earnings (In millions)	% Chg. in Net from '91
1. Viacom	$1,864.7	9%	100%	$49.0	NM
2. Turner Broadcasting	$1,641.4	18%	93%	$77.6	−10%
3. Paramount	$1,216.4	50%	28%	$261.4	113%
4. QVC Networks	$1,070.6	16%	100%	$55.1	81%
5. Home Shopping Network	$1,053.9	2%	96%	$37.3	NM
6. Walt Disney Co.	$761.0	1%	10%	$816.7	28%
7. King World Productions	$503.1	6%	100%	$94.9	5%
8. Gaylord Entertainment	$392.2	9%	61%	$29.4	1,533%
9. Spelling Entertainment	$258.5	111%	100%	$10.0	−23%
10. Liberty Media	$156.5	47%	100%	$13.9	−68%
11. Westwood Inc.	$137.7	−5%	100%	($24.1)	−174%
12. International Family Entertainment	$131.7	16%	100%	$29.6	49%
13. BET Holdings	$61.7	21%	99%	$11.7	26%
14. RHI Entertainment	$56.5	70%	100%	$5.6	133%
15. All American Communications	$45.3	80%	78%	$0.9	NM
16. dick clark productions	$34.8	−17%	95%	$3.1	7%
17. Playboy Enterprises	$32.5	30%	17%	$3.7	−18%
18. Republic Pictures	$25.3	−47%	36%	($3.5)	NM

Technology

ECI Rank	'92 ECI Revenue (In millions)	% Chg. in ECI Rev. from '91	ECI as % of Total Revenue	'92 Total Net Earnings (In millions)	% Chg. in Net from '91
1. Sony	$3,098.0	21.5%	9%	$312.6	−65.4%
2. Matsushita	$2,443.0	15.9%	4%	$331.0	−66.9%
3. GI	$849.0	14.0%	79%	$109.7	NM
4. Harris	$450.6	−14.3%	15%	$75.2	55.7%
5. Scientific-Atlanta	$406.6	14.3%	70%	$16.3	1,381.8%*
6. Ampex	$404.1	18.1%	94%	($71.5)	NM
7. Tektronix	$285.4	−2.8%	22%	$19.8	−59.0%
8. 3M	$277.7	4.1%	2%	$1,233.0	6.8%
9. Kodak	$201.8	42.6%	1%	$1,146.0	**
10. Varian	$90.2	−10.4%	7%	$38.6	−32.9%
11. Zenith	$74.6	−6.8%	6%	($109.0)	NM
12. Chyron Pesa Group	$43.3	−72.0%	100%	($172.2)	NM†
13. C-COR	$41.7	59.2%	80%	$2.3	NM
14. Motorola	$39.8	17.0%	1%	$453.0	−0.2%

**Kodak went from a net of only $17 million last year to $1.1 billion this year, an apparent jump of almost 7,000%. The numbers make more sense, however, when one accounts for a $1.032 billion write-off from 1991. Without the '91 write-off, Kodak's performace improved about 11% in 1992.
†Negative earnings reflect interest payments to Spanish parent company Pesa, not actual losses, according to the company.

Broadcasting & Cable Yearbook 1994

The Top 100 Companies

Cable

ECI Rank	'92 ECI Revenue (in millions)	% Chg. in ECI Rev. from '91	ECI as % of Total Revenue	'92 ECI Income (in millions)	'92 Total Net Earnings (in millions)	% Chg. in Net from '91
1. Time Warner	$5,590.0	18%	43%	$767.0	$86.0	NM
2. TCI	$3574.0	11%	100%	$956.0	($49.0)	NM
3. Continental	$1,113.5	7%	100%	$488.3	($103.0)	NM
4. Comcast	$728.2	13%	81%	$203.4	($270.2)	NM
5. Cablevision Systems	$572.5	–5%	100%	$79.1	($250.5)	NM
6. Times Mirror	$546.5	10%	15%	$112.9	($66.1)	NM
7. Cablevision Industries	$441.9	9%	100%	$37.2	($86.7)	NM
8. Washington Post	$336.2	4%	23%	$93.5	$128.8	80%
9. Century	$281.2	9%	93%	$68.0	($66.0)	NM
10. Adelphia	$276.7	10%	100%	$72.7	($121.6)	NM
11. Media General	$169.9	6%	24%	$25.9	19.0	NM
12. TCA Cable	$138.8	9%	100%	$37.6	$15.0	4%
13. Jones Intercable	$131.0	32%	100%	$35.6	$19.6	NM
14. ML Media	$100.6	1%	100%	$3.1	($9.3)	NM
15. C-TEC	$85.3	12%	33%	$30.1	($2.0)	NM
16. ML Opportunity	$53.6	27%	100%	($6.4)	($38.4)	NM
17. Falcon	$50.6	10%	100%	$7.7	($9.0)	NM

Agencies & Services

ECI Rank	'92 ECI Revenue (in millions)	% Chg. in ECI Rev. from '91	ECI as % of Total Revenue	'92 Total Net Earnings (in millions)	% Chg. in Net from '91
1. Interpublic	$1,020.0	10%	55%	$111.9	18%
2. Saatchi & Saatchi	$1,003.0	1%	76%	($1,259.9)	NM
3. WPP*	$674.8	–9%	35%	($180)†	NM
4. Omnicom	$567.9	23%	41%	$69.2	21%
5. Grey	$378.2	9.5%	73%	$16.5	283%
6. GM Hughes	$245.9	6.5%	2%	($921.6)	NM
7. Dun & Bradstreet	$188.0	8%	4%	$4,750.7	.1%
8. Ceridian	$178.3	–9%	21%	($392.5)	NM
9. FCB	$125.1	–	35%	$21.7	213.2%
10. Comsat	$120.0	55%	27%	$42.9	NM
11. Reuters*	$88.2	–2%	4%	$2,367.1†	13.6%
12. IDB	$75.0	9%	49%	$8.5	449%
13. Associated Press	$63.5	–	17%	$5.3	NM
14. Unitel Video	$63.0	37%	100%	$1.73	66%

*ECI revenue numbers reflect U.S. operations only. U.S. dollar has been converted at a rate of $1.51 to £1.
†Profit attributable to ordinary shareholders.

How Network Delivery Varies by Market

National advertisers use spot television to increase network advertising weight in specific markets to achieve a predetermined level. These market goals are derived from the advertising budget and the market's share of the brand's projected sales. Thus, a spot schedule is usually indicated where a market has an unusually high brand-sales potential, or where the network weight delivered for the brand is below the national average used in planning, or both.

The first factor, market brand potential, varies by product and is difficult to generalize. The second factor, local market network audiences, must be generalized because planning is based upon next season's *anticipated* network performance. The prevalence of network package buys, which tends to deliver average audience levels, supports the use of average data.

The following tabulation, chosen especially for *Broadcasting & Cable Yearbook* shows Arbitron Television's Areas of Dominant Influence (ADI) in total number of U.S. TV households. Also listed, in percentage, are the network audiences in each ADI market during prime-time hours. It is this market audience figure, when compared to the market's share of the population, that indicates whether the network commitment will perform above or below the national plan average in that market.

		ADI TV Hseholds	ADI% of U.S. TV Hseholds	—ABC— % of U.S.	Index	—CBS— % of U.S.	Index	—FOX— % of U.S.	Index	—NBC— % of U.S.	Index
1.	New York	6,760,400	7.29	7.69	105	6.39	88	9.47	130	7.34	101
2.	Los Angeles	4,962,300	5.35	5.05	94	4.12	77	7.10	133	4.90	92
3.	Chicago	3,023,600	3.26	3.53	109	2.78	85	3.21	99	3.72	114
4.	Philadelphia	2,659,700	2.87	3.54	124	2.93	102	3.63	127	2.89	101
5.	San Francisco–Oakland–San Jose	2,236,700	2.41	2.42	100	2.01	83	3.09	128	1.90	79
6.	Boston	2,121,400	2.29	2.36	103	2.29	100	2.26	99	2.43	106
7.	Washington, DC	1,812,500	1.95	1.80	92	1.84	94	2.79	143	1.77	90
8.	Dallas–Ft. Worth	1,803,200	1.94	2.39	123	2.18	112	1.96	101	2.16	111
9.	Detroit	1,728,100	1.86	2.33	125	2.13	114	2.14	115	2.17	117
10.	Atlanta	1,483,400	1.60	1.68	105	1.71	107	2.17	136	1.56	98
	Markets 1–10	28,591,300	30.82	32.79	106	28.38	92	37.82	123	30.84	100
	Cumulative Total	28,591,300	30.82	32.79	106	28.38	92	37.82	123	30.84	100
11.	Houston	1,465,000	1.58	1.82	116	1.70	107	2.08	131	1.56	99
12.	Cleveland	1,418,100	1.53	2.01	131	1.66	109	1.76	115	1.82	119
13.	Minneapolis–St. Paul	1,400,500	1.51	1.22	81	1.50	99	.88	58	1.24	82
14.	Seattle–Tacoma	1,399,100	1.51	1.30	86	1.03	69	1.41	93	1.35	90
15.	Miami–Ft. Lauderdale	1,301,900	1.40	1.27	91	.94	67	2.12	151	1.21	86
16.	Tampa–St. Petersburg (Sarasota)	1,258,500	1.36	1.40	103	1.44	106	1.17	86	1.56	115
17.	Pittsburgh	1,137,900	1.23	1.42	115	1.17	95	1.46	119	1.29	105
18.	St. Louis	1,108,300	1.19	1.10	92	1.33	111	1.41	118	1.59	133
19.	Sacramento–Stockton	1,073,700	1.16	.98	84	1.03	89	1.40	121	.92	79
20.	Phoenix	1,040,300	1.12	1.07	95	1.18	105	1.35	121	1.26	112
	Markets 11–20	12,604,000	13.59	13.59	100	12.98	96	15.04	111	13.80	102
	Cumulative Total	41,195,300	44.41	46.38	104	41.36	93	52.86	119	44.64	101
21.	Denver	1,031,700	1.11	1.04	94	.97	87	.81	73	1.13	102
22.	Baltimore	973,000	1.05	1.32	126	1.25	120	1.62	155	1.02	97
23.	Orlando–Daytona Beach–Melbourne	952,100	1.03	1.01	98	.88	86	1.08	106	1.08	105
24.	Hartford–New Haven	928,000	1.00	.93	93	.98	98	.93	93	.91	91
25.	San Diego	909,500	.98	.72	73	.82	84	1.07	109	.73	74
26.	Portland, OR	887,900	.96	.86	90	.80	84	.65	68	.82	85
27.	Indianapolis	881,200	.95	.84	88	.97	102	.91	96	.87	91
28.	Kansas City	772,900	.83	1.06	128	1.04	125	1.00	120	.89	107
29.	Milwaukee	772,200	.83	.87	105	.89	106	.77	92	.99	119
30.	Charlotte	756,700	.82	.75	92	.90	111	.79	97	.56	69
	Markets 21–30	8,865,000	9.56	9.40	98	9.50	99	9.63	101	9.00	94
	Cumulative Total	50,060,300	53.97	55.78	103	50.86	94	62.49	116	53.64	99
31.	Cincinnati	756,400	.82	.83	102	.94	116	.78	95	.75	93
32.	Raleigh–Durham	751,100	.81	.88	108	.85	106	.80	99	.61	75
33.	Nashville	731,000	.79	.77	98	.92	116	.67	85	.88	111
34.	Columbus, OH	696,800	.75	.76	101	.85	113	.61	82	.86	114
35.	Greenville–Spartanburg–Asheville	666,400	.72	.59	82	.78	109	.59	82	.70	98
36.	San Antonio	626,700	.68	.58	86	.69	103	.59	88	.71	105
37.	Grand Rapids–Kalamazoo–Battle Creek	623,000	.67	.68	101	.66	99	.66	98	.69	103
38.	Buffalo	613,900	.66	.74	111	.64	97	.50	76	.70	106
39.	Norfolk–Portsmth–Newport News–Hamptn	611,200	.66	.64	97	.66	100	.76	116	.68	104
40.	New Orleans	603,900	.65	.59	91	.85	131	.66	101	.69	107
	Markets 31–40	6,680,400	7.21	7.06	98	7.84	109	6.62	92	7.27	101
	Cumulative Total	56,740,700	61.18	62.84	103	58.70	96	69.11	113	60.91	100
41.	Salt Lake City	597,600	.64	.56	88	.51	79	.62	96	.55	85
42.	Memphis	595,200	.64	.60	94	.74	116	.65	101	.72	111
43.	Providence–New Bedford	571,500	.62	.62	101	.48	78	.61	100	.74	120
44.	Harrisburg–York–Lancaster–Lebanon	567,700	.61	.57	94	.52	86	.59	96	.61	99
45.	Oklahoma City	563,000	.61	.53	88	.68	113	.51	84	.65	107
46.	W. Palm Beach–Ft. Pierce–Vero Beach	563,000	.61	.43	70	.57	94	.66	108	.58	96
47.	Louisville	545,400	.59	.63	107	.69	117	.63	108	.57	96
48.	Greensboro–Winston Salem–High Point	533,300	.57	.58	101	.63	109	.53	92	.52	90
49.	Birmingham	523,700	.56	.59	104	.45	81	.64	113	.60	107
50.	Wilkes Barre–Scranton	521,600	.56	.68	122	.61	109	.43	77	.62	110
	Markets 41–50	5,582,000	6.01	5.79	96	5.88	98	5.87	98	6.16	102
	Cumulative Total	62,322,700	67.19	68.63	102	64.58	96	74.98	112	67.07	100

How Network Delivery Varies by Market

		ADI TV Hseholds	ADI% of U.S. TV Hseholds	ABC % of U.S.	ABC Index	CBS % of U.S.	CBS Index	FOX % of U.S.	FOX Index	NBC % of U.S.	NBC Index
51.	Albuquerque	519,000	.56	.56	100	.48	85	.46	82	.50	90
52.	Albany–Schenectady–Troy	506,400	.55	.52	96	.61	112	.39	71	.55	100
53.	Dayton	504,400	.54	.56	102	.62	113	.55	102	.49	90
54.	Jacksonville	475,700	.51	.40	78	.60	116	.67	130	.48	93
55.	Charleston–Huntington	471,200	.51	.47	92	.47	92	.53	105	.64	126
56.	Fresno–Visalia	456,900	.49	.48	97	.43	87	.68	138	.45	92
57.	Flint–Saginaw–Bay City	453,900	.49	.56	115	.48	98	.49	100	.62	127
58.	Little Rock	450,800	.49	.56	116	.55	114	.41	85	.52	107
59.	Tulsa	448,700	.48	.53	110	.57	118	.52	106	.48	99
60.	Richmond	441,800	.48	.50	105	.47	99	.41	85	.47	98
	Markets 51–60	4,728,400	5.10	5.14	101	5.28	104	5.11	100	5.20	102
	Cumulative Total	67,051,100	72.29	73.77	102	69.86	97	80.09	111	72.27	100
61.	Wichita–Hutchinson	422,500	.46	.40	87	.50	110	.31	67	.45	99
62.	Knoxville	415,700	.45	.40	90	.41	92	.38	85	.41	92
63.	Mobile–Pensacola	414,100	.45	.41	93	.54	120	.40	90	.48	107
64.	Toledo	405,900	.44	.39	89	.54	124	.39	88	.50	114
65.	Green Bay–Appleton	385,400	.42	.47	113	.46	110	.34	81	.50	122
66.	Austin, TX	385,300	.42	.35	85	.44	106	.44	106	.37	89
67.	Roanoke–Lynchburg	383,700	.41	.33	79	.50	122	.22	52	.40	96
68.	Syracuse	382,000	.41	.44	108	.42	101	.36	88	.43	106
69.	Rochester, NY	373,400	.40	.41	102	.39	96	.38	95	.39	97
70.	Des Moines	372,700	.40	.38	96	.48	119	.26	64	.44	109
	Markets 61–70	3,940,900	4.26	3.98	93	4.68	110	3.48	82	4.37	103
	Cumulative Total	70,992,000	76.55	77.75	102	74.54	97	83.57	109	76.64	100
71.	Shreveport–Texarkana	368,300	.40	.46	115	.44	112	.32	80	.40	100
72.	Lexington	363,700	.39	.37	94	.43	109	.38	96	.36	92
73.	Omaha	358,000	.39	.47	122	.41	105	.34	89	.38	98
74.	Springfield–Decatur–Champaign	350,700	.38	.32	85	.40	105	.25	67	.40	107
75.	Portland–Poland Spring	343,300	.37	.30	82	.34	93	.25	68	.32	85
76.	Paducah–Cape Girardeau–Harrisburg–Marion	329,900	.36	.26	73	.45	126	.25	71	.35	97
77.	Las Vegas	328,900	.35	.28	78	.39	110	.57	161	.37	105
78.	Springfield, MO	321,700	.35	.29	83	.49	142	.30	85	.43	125
79.	Tucson	320,400	.35	.30	87	.30	87	.32	93	.34	97
80.	Spokane	315,600	.34	.33	97	.37	109	.22	64	.30	88
	Markets 71–80	3,400,500	3.68	3.38	92	4.02	109	3.20	87	3.65	99
	Cumulative Total	74,392,500	80.23	81.13	101	78.56	98	86.77	108	80.29	100
81.	Huntsville–Decatur–Florence	308,600	.33	.27	82	.33	100	.31	92	.29	87
82.	Cedar Rapids–Waterloo–Dubuque	300,800	.32	.33	102	.31	97	.08	25	.39	120
83.	South Bend–Elkhart	298,500	.32	.35	109	.38	119	.13	40	.38	119
84.	Davenport–Rock Islnd–Moline: Quad-Cty	298,300	.32	.33	102	.32	101	.32	101	.35	110
85.	Chattanooga	292,000	.31	.35	113	.29	92	.25	81	.31	97
86.	Columbia, SC	291,300	.31	.25	80	.31	98	.33	106	.38	120
87.	Jackson, MS	287,600	.31	.25	81	.34	110	.26	83	.38	124
88.	Ft Myers–Naples	284,700	.31	.27	88	.37	119	.28	90	.35	114
89.	Johnstown–Altoona	281,100	.30	.22	74	.34	113	.18	60	.34	113
90.	Bristol–Kingsport–Johnson City:Tri-Cty	280,700	.30	.21	71	.35	116	.15	49	.36	119
	Markets 81–90	2,923,600	3.13	2.83	90	3.34	107	2.29	73	3.53	113
	Cumulative Total	77,316,100	83.36	83.96	101	81.90	98	89.06	107	83.82	101
91.	Madison	276,300	.30	.29	97	.33	112	.27	90	.25	84
92.	Youngstown	270,000	.29	.33	113	.35	120	.17	60	.34	116
93.	Burlington–Plattsburgh	268,500	.29	.22	78	.32	110	.01	4	.27	92
94.	Evansville	260,000	.28	.31	112	.29	104	.29	103	.28	100
95.	Baton Rouge	253,300	.27	.33	121	.31	115	.21	76	.24	87
96.	Waco–Temple–Bryan	253,200	.27	.24	86	.34	125	.27	98	.24	89
97.	Springfield, MA	247,400	.27	.24	91	.22	84	.24	91	.25	94
98.	Colorado Springs–Pueblo	243,600	.26	.32	123	.27	104	.24	91	.25	94
99.	Lincoln–Hastings–Kearney	241,900	.26	.24	94	.30	115	.13	48	.19	72
100.	El-Paso	236,500	.25	.17	68	.21	84	.27	104	.24	95
	Markets 91–100	2,550,700	2.74	2.69	98	2.94	107	2.10	77	2.55	93
	Cumulative Total	79,866,800	86.10	86.65	101	84.84	99	91.16	106	86.37	100
101.	Ft. Wayne	235,900	.25	.30	120	.27	104	.16	61	.24	96
102.	Savannah	234,400	.25	.19	75	.27	108	.35	137	.20	81
103.	Greenville–New Bern–Washington	228,900	.25	.24	98	.30	122	.19	79	.25	103
104.	Lansing	228,700	.25	.23	93	.28	112	.27	109	.27	111
105.	Charleston, SC	225,700	.24	.25	104	.27	111	.27	110	.23	196
106.	Peoria–Bloomington	218,100	.24	.23	96	.24	100	.22	95	.24	101
107.	Sioux Falls–Mitchell	218,000	.23	.26	109	.29	123	.09	39	.17	73
108.	Fargo	214,100	.23	.22	94	.22	96	.15	64	.18	78
109.	Santa Brbra–Santa Maria–San Luis Obispo	210,000	.23	.18	81	.19	82	.17	74	.21	93
110.	Montgomery–Selma	209,100	.23	.15	68	.25	110	.24	107	.27	120
	Markets 101–110	2,222,900	2.40	2.25	94	2.58	108	2.11	88	2.26	94
	Cumulative Total	82,089,700	88.50	88.90	100	87.42	99	93.27	105	88.63	100

Broadcasting & Cable Yearbook 1994

How Network Delivery Varies by Market

		ADI TV Hseholds	ADI% of U.S. TV Hseholds	ABC % of U.S.	ABC Index	CBS % of U.S.	CBS Index	FOX % of U.S.	FOX Index	NBC % of U.S.	NBC Index
111.	Augusta	207,200	.22	.24	107	.24	107	.32	144	.16	71
112.	Tyler–Longview–Jacksonville	206,400	.22	.31	141	.16	74	.15	69	.21	94
113.	Salinas–Monterey	206,300	.22	.18	81	.14	61	.24	110	.18	81
114.	McAllen–Brownsville (LRGV)	201,500	.22	.20	92	.21	96	xx	xx	.17	77
115.	Tallahassee–Thomasville	196,600	.21	.13	63	.26	125	.20	93	.15	71
116.	Reno	195,400	.21	.23	111	.18	86	.22	104	.19	91
117.	Ft. Smith	191,800	.21	.23	109	.27	131	.09	45	.18	87
118.	Lafayette, LA	184,300	.20	.23	115	.31	154	.29	147	.15	77
119.	Traverse City–Cadillac	182,200	.20	.18	90	.24	122	.09	47	.19	98
120.	Macon	181,700	.20	.18	94	.25	127	.07	37	.14	71
	Markets 111–120	1,953,400	2.11	2.11	100	2.26	107	1.67	79	1.72	82
	Cumulative Total	84,043,100	90.61	91.01	100	89.68	99	94.94	105	90.35	100
121.	Columbus, Ga	181,400	.20	.21	109	.19	99	.21	108	.15	75
122.	Columbus–Tupelo	172,200	.19	.10	52	.23	124	.04	19	.24	131
123.	Corpus Christi	170,400	.18	.22	122	.21	112	.08	43	.22	121
124.	Eugene	168,700	.18	.17	91	.20	109	.13	71	.15	84
125.	Duluth–Superior	168,100	.18	.23	128	.22	122	.02	13	.22	123
126.	La Crosse–Eau Claire	167,900	.18	.15	81	.20	111	.10	55	.20	111
127.	Yakima-Pasco-Richland-Kennewick	167,500	.18	.16	87	.19	104	.13	72	.18	98
128.	Amarillo	167,400	.18	.20	113	.19	107	.15	86	.17	95
129.	Monroe–El Dorado	167,300	.18	.14	77	.27	152	.01	8	.20	110
130.	Chico–Redding	166,900	.18	.21	116	.16	87	.11	59	.14	78
	Markets 121–130	1,697,800	1.83	1.79	98	2.06	113	.98	54	1.87	102
	Cumulative Total	85,740,900	92.44	92.80	100	91.74	99	95.92	104	92.22	100
131.	Bakersfield	164,000	.18	.15	85	.16	92	.16	89	.17	95
132.	Wausau–Rhinelander	162,500	.18	.24	135	.26	146	.04	23	.18	100
133.	Boise	158,400	.17	.15	90	.14	80	.17	97	.18	106
134.	Binghamton	158,300	.17	.15	90	.19	113	.08	48	.16	95
135.	Wichita Falls–Lawton	156,500	.17	.15	87	.19	111	.18	106	.18	108
136.	Rockford	156,300	.17	.15	90	.16	97	.20	116	.18	107
137.	Topeka	154,700	.17	.13	79	.21	125	.09	53	.15	88
138.	Terre Haute	154,100	.17	.14	82	.24	144	.04	26	.19	115
139.	Florence–Myrtle Beach	154,000	.17	.16	97	.25	149	.06	37	.13	80
140.	Beaumont–Port Arthur	153,900	.17	.17	104	.24	144	.12	71	.18	110
	Markets 131–140	1,572,700	1.72	1.59	92	2.04	119	1.14	66	1.70	99
	Cumulative Total	87,313,600	94.16	94.39	100	93.78	100	97.06	103	93.92	100
141.	Sioux City	153,400	.17	.19	116	.17	103	.01	7	.19	118
142.	Wheeling–Steubenville	152,800	.16	.12	71	.26	155	.11	69	.19	116
143.	Erie	150,500	.16	.18	114	.18	108	.09	58	.19	119
144.	Wilmington	148,700	.16	.19	119	.16	98	.06	39	.18	110
145.	Medford	137,900	.15	.14	92	.15	104	.04	30	.15	98
146.	Joplin–Pittsburg	137,500	.15	.18	124	.18	123	.04	25	.17	113
147.	Rochester–Mason City–Austin	135,500	.15	.15	104	.17	114	.03	20	.15	100
148.	Bluefield–Beckley–Oak Hill	135,000	.15	.14	95	.12	85	.06	41	.18	123
149.	Lubbock	135,000	.15	.13	87	.16	113	.16	111	.17	114
150.	Minot–Bismarck–Dickinson–Glendive	134,900	.15	.08	52	.14	97	xx	xx	.17	116
	Markets 141–150	1,421,200	1.55	1.50	97	1.69	109	.60	39	1.74	112
	Cumulative Total	88,734,800	95.71	95.89	100	95.47	100	97.66	102	95.66	100
151.	Columbia–Jefferson City	133,200	.14	.14	95	.16	113	.03	19	.15	103
152.	Odessa–Midland	133,000	.14	.13	92	.13	92	.12	87	.12	85
153.	Sarasota	131,600	.14	.15	109	.16	112	.07	52	.14	102
154.	Albany, GA	127,800	.14	.06	42	.10	74	.16	113	.19	141
155.	Bangor	124,400	.13	.13	95	.15	113	.03	19	.12	90
156.	Abilene–Sweetwater	107,900	.12	.11	99	.15	129	.04	32	.12	102
157.	Idaho Falls–Pocatello	107,800	.12	.11	92	.13	111	xx	xx	.13	112
158.	Biloxi–Gulfport–Pascagoula	107,000	.12	.15	133	.10	88	.15	130	.09	77
159.	Quincy–Hannibal	103,900	.11	.06	52	.15	135	.03	29	.14	128
160.	Utica	102,500	.11	.10	86	.10	90	.09	78	.14	127
	Markets 151–160	1,179,100	1.27	1.14	90	1.33	105	.72	57	1.34	106
	Cumulative Total	89,913,900	96.98	97.03	100	96.80	100	98.38	101	97.00	100
161.	Clarksburg–Weston	101,300	.11	.06	58	.16	143	.07	60	.11	105
162.	Salisbury	97,000	.10	.11	101	.16	157	.06	58	.06	56
163.	Panama City	96,900	.10	.09	89	.10	100	.09	83	.12	115
164.	Gainesville	91,000	.10	.12	122	.06	61	.12	125	.05	56
165.	Laurel–Hattiesburg	90,400	.10	.07	71	.09	93	.07	74	.15	156
166.	Palm Springs	90,400	.10	.09	89	.08	85	.07	72	.09	94
167.	Dothan	89,400	.10	.07	70	.13	137	.07	77	.08	85
168.	Watertown–Carthage	87,400	.09	.06	60	.12	123	.04	44	.04	44
169.	Rapid City	87,000	.09	.13	141	.06	61	xx	xx	.10	107
170.	Elmira	86,500	.09	.11	115	.09	98	.06	63	.10	107
	Markets 161–170	917,300	.98	.91	93	1.05	107	.65	66	.90	92
	Cumulative Total	90,831,200	97.96	97.94	100	97.85	100	99.03	101	97.90	100

Broadcasting & Cable Yearbook 1994

How Network Delivery Varies by Market

		ADI TV Hseholds	ADI% of U.S. TV Hseholds	ABC % of U.S.	ABC Index	CBS % of U.S.	CBS Index	FOX % of U.S.	FOX Index	NBC % of U.S.	NBC Index
171.	Alexandria, LA	85,200	.09	.08	87	.08	83	.06	61	.15	161
172.	Harrisonburg	84,500	.09	.12	131	.07	80	.05	60	.07	77
173.	Billings–Hardin	83,800	.09	.07	72	.11	125	xx	xx	.10	114
174.	Jonesboro	81,800	.09	.16	180	.06	74	.04	40	.06	70
175.	Lake Charles	81,300	.09	.07	85	.08	97	.11	120	.13	149
176.	Missoula	73,800	.08	.05	58	.09	116	xx	xx	.09	112
177.	Ardmore–Ada	70,800	.08	.03	42	.13	173	.02	20	.10	132
178.	Greenwood–Greenville	69,900	.08	.08	113	.07	97	.01	11	.05	71
179.	El Centro–Yuma	68,600	.07	.05	72	.04	59	.07	92	.06	82
180.	Meridian	64,700	.07	.11	158	.05	74	.02	33	.06	88
	Markets 171–180	**764,400**	**.83**	**.82**	**99**	**.78**	**94**	**.38**	**46**	**.87**	**105**
	Cumulative Total	**91,595,600**	**98.79**	**98.76**	**100**	**98.63**	**100**	**99.41**	**101**	**98.77**	**100**
181.	Jackson, TN	62,300	.07	.11	165	.04	66	.02	26	.05	77
182.	Great Falls	62,200	.07	.07	108	.08	119	xx	xx	.07	99
183.	Grand Junction–Durango	60,900	.07	.08	116	.07	103	xx	5	.05	73
184.	Parkersburg	57,100	.06	.06	92	.05	86	.07	106	.08	127
185.	Tuscaloosa	56,600	.06	.04	67	.07	115	.05	86	.05	76
186.	Eureka	56,000	.06	.04	65	.06	106	.04	65	.06	106
187.	Marquette	56,000	.06	.08	134	.05	85	.03	52	.05	79
188.	San Angelo	49,400	.05	.03	53	.08	141	.04	83	.03	61
189.	Butte	48,400	.05	.03	62	.07	134	xx	xx	.05	103
190.	Lafayette, IN	45,900	.05	.03	71	.05	104	.05	99	.04	80
	Markets 181–190	**554,800**	**.60**	**.57**	**95**	**.62**	**103**	**.30**	**50**	**.53**	**88**
	Cumulative Total	**92,150,400**	**99.39**	**99.33**	**100**	**99.25**	**100**	**99.71**	**100**	**99.30**	**100**
191.	Bowling Green	45,800	.05	.09	186	.04	83	.03	63	.03	60
192.	Hagerstown	45,000	.05	.05	93	.05	101	.04	91	.05	108
193.	St. Joseph	44,800	.05	.07	147	.05	97	.03	70	.04	82
194.	Anniston	43,000	.05	.05	101	.04	97	.03	75	.04	83
195.	Cheyenne–Scottsbluff (Sterling)	42,400	.05	.05	99	.06	130	xx	xx	.04	96
196.	Charlottesville	41,200	.04	.03	71	.03	71	.03	70	.05	110
197.	Casper–Riverton	40,200	.04	.04	84	.04	93	.01	18	.05	117
198.	Laredo	39,100	.04	.01	35	.03	68	xx	xx	.04	88
199.	Lima	39,100	.04	.03	66	.04	93	.02	55	.06	144
200.	Ottumwa–Kirksville	33,600	.04	.05	145	.03	74	.02	42	.03	77
	Markets 191–200	**414,200**	**.45**	**.47**	**104**	**.41**	**91**	**.21**	**47**	**.43**	**96**
	Cumulative Total	**92,564,600**	**99.84**	**99.80**	**100**	**99.66**	**100**	**99.92**	**100**	**99.73**	**100**
200.	Twin Falls	30,800	.03	.02	73	.05	155	.01	44	.03	94
203.	Zanesville	30,700	.03	.02	71	.03	96	.02	68	.05	152
202.	Presque Isle	30,400	.03	.02	57	.06	173	xx	xx	.03	81
206.	Bend	29,900	.03	.03	78	.03	80	.02	54	.04	120
204.	Mankato	29,800	.03	.03	104	.04	123	.02	59	.02	66
205.	Flagstaff	29,700	.03	.02	67	.03	81	.02	61	.03	102
208.	Helena	18,700	.02	.01	58	.01	74	xx	xx	.03	135
209.	North Platte	17,700	.02	.02	81	.01	65	xx	xx	.03	147
210.	Alpena	15,600	.02	.01	76	.03	178	.01	38	.01	84
	Markets 201–210	**233,300**	**.24**	**.18**	**75**	**.29**	**121**	**.10**	**42**	**.27**	**113**
	Cumulative Total	**92,797,900**	**100.08**	**99.98**	**100**	**99.95**	**100**	**100.02**	**100**	**100.00**	**100**

U.S. Sales of Television Receivers 1983–1992

Data compiled by Electronic Industries Association.

Year	Portable & Table Color TV Units	Dollars	Console Color TV Units	Dollars	Stereo Color TV Units	Dollars	Monochrome TV Units	Dollars
1983	11,179	3,443	2,807	1,443	n/a	n/a	5,697	465
1984	13,092	3,875	2,991	1,484	n/a	n/a	4,909	419
1985	13,993	4,114	3,002	1,408	n/a	n/a	3,754	308
1986	15,399	4,481	2,805	1,355	n/a	n/a	3,959	333
1987	16,805	4,890	2,525	1,257	4,349	n/a	3,570	328
1988	17,768	4,691	2,448	1,217	5,090	2,428	2,580	196
1989	19,557	5,359	2,149	1,062	6,043	2,737	1,656	116
1990	18,453	5,148	1,931	950	6,655	2,928	1,411	99
1991	17,951	5,134	1,523	818	7,377	3,209	784	61
1992	19,717	5,757	1,339	754	8,534	3,729	633	47

Dollar figures are in millions and represent factory sales price multiplied by unit sales to dealers.

Unit figures include distributor sales and factory direct sales to dealers.

n/a=not available

Record of Television Station Growth Since Television Began

	TV Authorized	On Air
Jan. 1, 1946*	9	6
June 30, 1946*		
Jan. 1, 1947*	52	
June 30, 1947		
Jan. 1 1948*	73	17
Jan. 1, 1949	124	50
Jan. 1, 1950	111	97
Jan. 1, 1951	109	107
Jan. 1, 1952	108	108
Jan. 1, 1953*	273	129
June 30, 1953*		
Jan. 1, 1954	567	356
Jan. 1, 1955	576	439[1]
Jan. 1, 1956	590	482[2]
Jan. 1, 1957	631	511
Jan. 1, 1958	657	544[3]
Jan. 1, 1959	666	562[4]
Jan. 1, 1960	673	573[5]
Jan. 1, 1961	634	583
Jan. 1, 1962	654	563
Jan. 1, 1963	662	579
Jan. 1, 1964	661	582
Jan. 1, 1965	676	586
Jan. 1, 1966	702	596
Jan. 1, 1967	769	623
Jan. 1, 1968	818	644
Jan. 1, 1969	834	672
Jan. 1, 1970	1,038	872
Jan. 1, 1971	1,025	892
Jan. 1, 1972	1,004	905
Jan. 1, 1973	1,001	922
Jan. 1, 1974	1,002	938
Jan. 1, 1975	1,010	952
Jan. 1, 1976	1,030	962
Jan. 1, 1977	1,029	984
Jan. 1, 1978	1,045	986
Jan. 1, 1979	1,059	992
Jan. 1, 1980	1,094	1,013
Jan. 1, 1981	1,143	1,019
Jan. 1, 1982	1,168	1,020
Jan. 1, 1983	1,276	1,090
Jan. 1, 1984	1,318	1,149
Jan. 1, 1985	1,505	1,194
Oct. 30, 1986	1,493	1,220
Oct. 31, 1986	1,558	1,285
Jan. 1, 1988	1,615	1,342
Jan. 1, 1989	1,683	1,395
Jan. 1, 1990	1,684	1,436
Jan. 1, 1991	1,690	1,469
Jan. 1, 1992	1,688	1,488
Jan. 1, 1993	1,688	1,505
Jan. 1, 1994		**1,518**

*Comparable figures for all services not available at this date.
[1] Includes stations with Special Temporary Authorizations, which either had not started operations as of this date, had started but had gone dark, or had received authorizations but turned them back with or without operating.
[2] Includes 2 licensees that had suspended operation and 37 stations with STAs in same category as footnote 1.
[3] Includes 7 licensees that had suspended operation and 40 stations with STAs in same category as footnote 1.
[4] Includes 6 licensees that had suspended operation and 38 stations with STAs in same category as footnote 1.
[5] Includes 10 licensees that had suspended operation and 38 stations with STAs in same category as footnote 1.

U.S. Television Audiences

According to Nielsen Media Research, 98.3% of all U.S. homes (including Alaska and Hawaii) were television equipped as of October 1993. Homes equipped with color television sets totaled 91.5 million or 98% of all television homes. The extent to which television sets were used is indicated in the following tables.

Television Usage per Home per Week (hours and minutes)

	7 am-1 pm	1 pm-4:30 pm	4:30 pm-7:30 pm	7:30 pm-8 pm	8 pm-11 pm	11 pm-1 am	1 am-7 am
Monday-Friday	6:41	4:54	6:25	1:23	9:10	3:27	3:24
Saturday	1:26	1:07	1:12	0:15	1:39	0:46	:42
Sunday	1:26	1:21	1:26	0:18	1:56	0:41	:34
All Days	9:34	7:22	9:03	1:56	12:45	4:54	4:40

Television Audience Composition

	Homes Using TV	Viewers Per 1,000 Viewing Homes	Men	Women	Teens	Children
Monday-Friday 10 am-1 pm	22.8	1,249	30%	54%	3%	12%
Monday-Friday 1-4:30 pm	28.0	1,267	29%	56%	5%	10%
All Nights 8-11 pm	60.6	1,634	39%	46%	6%	9%

(% of Audience per Average Minute for Men, Women, Teens, Children)

Types of Regular Network TV Shows and Their Audiences (7-11 pm)

	Number of Programs	% of Average Audience	% Share of Programming
Suspense and Mystery	11	10.7	13%
General Drama	13	10.7	14%
Situation Comedy	41	12.0	30%
Adventure	2	—	3%
Feature Films	7	11.2	18%
Variety	4	8.2	3%
All Programs	92	11.3	—

Source: Nielsen Media Research National Audience
Demographics Report—October 1993
COPYRIGHT 1993—NIELSEN MEDIA RESEARCH

Section D

Cable

Table of Contents

Table of Contents.	D-1
Key to Listings.	D-2
Directory of Multiple Systems Operators (MSOs), Independent Owners & Cable Systems in the U.S. and Canada.	D-3
Geographical Index to Large Cable Systems & MSOs in the U.S. and Canada.	D-55
Broadcasters in Cable Television.	D-66
Cable Market Statistics	
Cable Penetration by Market.	D-68
Top 50 DMA Ranked by Percentage of Cable Penetration.	D-72
Top 50 DMA Ranked by Cable Television Households.	D-73
Top 50 DMA Ranked by Television Households.	D-74
Bottom 50 DMA Ranked by Percentage of Cable Penetration.	D-75
Top 50 MSOs.	D-76

Key to Cable Listings

Multicable Inc.

(1) R.R. 1, 15 Maple St., Edgemont, CT 02244. (232) 555-6262; FAX: (232) 555-0111. **(2)** James Armstrong, pres/CEO; Robert Sawyer, vp opns; Anita Morris, vp mktg. **(3)** Owned by Johnson Communications Corp. **(4)** Total Basic Subscribers: 2,200,000; Pay Cable Subscribers: 1,250,000; **(5)** Number of Cable Systems: 62.

(6) REGIONS

Northeast: 65 Main St., Rolling Hills, NY 12166; (212) 625-0000; Margaret Avery, gen mgr. *West:* 144 Hwy. 56, Glendale, CA 14628; (415) 689-0000; Peter Steeves, gen mgr.

SYSTEMS WITH OVER 20,000 SUBSCRIBERS

(7) Multicable Associates (35,000 subscribers). **(8)** 2708 Grand Ave., Des Moines, IA 50312. (414) 234-0000; FAX: (414) 234-1000. **(9)** Dan Smith, gen mgr; Jean Jones, mktg dir. **(10)** *Area(s) Served:* IA. County: Dubuque. Serving Center Grove, Dubuque, E. Dubuque. Pop: 63,000. **(11)** Miles of Plant: 150. **(12)** Homes Passed: 90,000. **(13)** Homes Served: 35,000. **(14)** *Channel Capacity:* 22. In Use: 18. **(15)** *Basic Service:* Subscribers: 35,000; 03/10/93. Programming (via satellite): 8 chs. **(16)** *Pay Services:* Total Pay Subscribers: 13,000; 03/10/93. *(1)* Pay Units: 2,000; 3/10/93. Programming (via satellite): Disney. *(2)* Pay Units: 6,000; 3/10/93. Programming (via satellite): Showtime. *(3)* Pay Units: 5,000; 3/10/93. Programming (via satellite): SportsChannel. **(17)** Pay Per View Subscribers: 12,500; 6/15/93. **(18)** *Local Advertising Accepted.* **(19)** *Equipment:* Catel & Scientific-Atlanta headend; Times Cable; Scientific-Atlanta set top converters.

(20) SMALLER SYSTEMS

Connecticut - Multicable Inc., 65 Essex Ave., Canterbury, CT 02241; (424) 885-1000; 2,900 subs. **Ohio** - Multicable of Ohio, 404 Grove Blvd., Milltown, OH 66002; (929) 333-1000; 1,000 subs.

---

(1) Address, telephone and fax information for the Multiple Systems Operator (MSO).

(2) Names and titles of key personnel.

(3) Ownership information. Percentage of ownership may also be included.

(4) Total multiple systems operator subscribers and number of pay subscribers.

(5) The number of cable systems belonging to the multiple systems operator.

(6) Address, telephone and contact information for the multiple systems operator's regional offices.

(7) Name of large cable system (20,000 subscribers or more) and number of subscribers.

(8) Large cable system address, telephone and fax information.

(9) Names and titles of key large cable system personnel.

(10) States, counties, cities and towns of area served and service area population.

(11) Miles of cable installed.

(12) The number of homes the large cable system passes by.

(13) The number of homes receiving the large cable system's service.

(14) The maximum number of channels the large cable system can simultaneously carry and the number of channels currently in use.

(15) The number of subscribers receiving basic cable service. The number of channels or actual stations and how they are transmitted, i.e. via satellite, may also be listed. Effective dates are also included.

(16) The number of subscribers receiving premium channels for an additional charge over the basic service fee. The number of pay units, effective dates and types of programming may also be listed.

(17) The number of pay per view subscribers and effective date.

(18) The large cable system offers local advertising opportunities on its channels.

(19) The type of equipment used to operate the large cable system.

(20) Smaller cable systems with less than 20,000 subscribers. State, name of cable system, address, telephone and number of subscribers are listed when available.

Multiple Systems Operators, Independent Owners & Cable Systems in the U.S. and Canada

A.D. Management Inc.

Box 932, Fayette, AL 35555. (205) 932-7264; FAX: (205) 932-7280. Joe D. Acker, CEO & vp; Bob Dailey, pres. Total Basic Subscribers: 5,032; Number of Cable Systems: 1.

Adams CATV Inc.

9 N. Main St., Carbondale, PA 18407-2395. (717) 282-6121; FAX: (717) 282-3787. David Adams, CEO & pres; Doug Adams, vp opns & vp mktg. Owned by Adams CATV Inc. Total Basic Subscribers: 16,000; Number of Cable Systems: 1.

Adams Telcom Inc.

Box 248, Golden, IL 62339. (217) 696-2701; FAX: (217) 696-4811. Walter Rowland, vp opns. Owned by Adams Telephone Cooperative. Total Basic Subscribers: 1,200; Number of Cable Systems: 1.

Adelphia Communications

Box 472, 5 W. 3rd St., Coudersport, PA 16915. (814) 274-9830; FAX: (814) 274-8631. John Rigas, CEO, chmn & pres; Timothy J. Rigas, CFO; James Boso, vp opns; John Adduci, vp mktg; Jack Olson, vp adv; John Abplananlp, vp progmg; Dave Scott, vp; Daniel Milliard, vp; Daniel Liberatore, vp. Owned by Adelphia Communications Corporation. Total Basic Subscribers: 1,238,022; Pay Cable Subscribers: 608,038; Number of Cable Systems: 50.

SYSTEMS WITH OVER 20,000 SUBSCRIBERS

Adelphia Cable (51,619 subscribers). 7378 Lake Worth Rd., Lake Worth, FL 33467. (407) 439-5970; FAX: (407) 845-7709. Cathy Wolosin, mktg dir.
Area(s) Served: FL. Serving Atlantis, Boca Raton, Boyton, Delray Beach, Green Acres, Lake Worth, Las Verdes, Palm Springs, St. Andrews in Edgewater, Woodfield. Homes Served: 51,619. *Basic Service:* Subscribers: 51,619; 08/31/93.

Adelphia Cable (38,846 subscribers). 91 Industrial Park Rd., Plymouth, MA 02360. (508) 747-3300; FAX: (508) 747-0731. Jim Sweeney, gen mgr; Trisha Hastings, mktg dir; Jim Sullivan, loc adv dir; Michael McNamara, chief tech; Trudy Bennett, cust svc dir.
Area(s) Served: MA. Counties: Barnstable, Plymouth. Serving Carver, Duxbury, Falmouth, Kingston, Marshfield, Plymouth. Miles of Plant: 1,250. Homes Passed: 45,000. Homes Served: 38,846. *Channel Capacity:* 61. In use: 61. *Basic Service:* Subscribers: 38,846; 11/15/92. *Local Advertising Accepted.*

Adelphia Cable (67,000 subscribers). Box 198, One Apollo Rd., Plymouth Meeting, PA 19462. (215) 828-3932; FAX: (215) 941-9943. Rick Conrad, gen mgr; Charles Balestri, mktg dir; Joe Ruff, chief tech; Grace Herman, cust svc dir.
Area(s) Served: PA. Counties: Delaware, Montgomery. Serving Ambler Borough, Broomall, Hatboro, Haverford, Horsham Twp., Lansdale, Lower Gwynedd Twp., Marple Twp., Montgomery Twp., North Wales, Plymouth Twp., Radnor, Springfield Twp., Towamencin, Upper Dublin Twp., Upper Gwynedd Twp., Whitemarsh Twp., Whitpain Twp. Miles of Plant: 1,300. Homes Passed: 106,000. Homes Served: 67,000. *Channel Capacity:* 36. In use: 36. *Basic Service:* Subscribers: 67,000; 10/15/93. *Pay Services:* Total Pay Subscribers: 36,593; 10/15/93. *Local Advertising Accepted.*

Adelphia Cable (27,033 subscribers). 324 W. Main St., Charlottesville, VA 22901. (804) 977-7845; FAX: (804) 293-9263. Dell Hanley, gen mgr; Patrick Hogan, mktg dir; Gary Bennett, chief tech; M. Suzanne Henning, cust svc dir.
Area(s) Served: VA. Counties: Albemarle, Fluvonna. Serving Lake Monticello. Homes Passed: 32,200. Homes Served: 27,033. *Channel Capacity:* 36. In use: 36. *Basic Service:* Subscribers: 27,033; 10/15/93. *Pay Services:* Total Pay Subscribers: 12,075; 08/15/91. Pay Per View Subscribers: 15,100; 08/15/91. *Local Advertising Accepted.*

Adelphia Cable (26,000 subscribers). 18 Ave. B, Williston, VT 05495. (802) 658-1249; FAX: (802) 658-5488.
Philip Hughes, gen mgr; Scott Bill, mktg dir; John Rivolta, chief tech; Joe Davison, cust svc dir.
Area(s) Served: VT. Counties: Addison, Chittenden. Serving Burlington. Pop: 65,000. Miles of Plant: 425. Homes Passed: 36,000. Homes Served: 26,000. *Channel Capacity:* 52. In use: 50. *Basic Service:* Subscribers: 26,000; 10/15/93. *Pay Services:* Total Pay Subscribers: 14,000; 09/30/92. Pay Per View Subscribers: 14,000; 09/30/92. *Local Advertising Accepted.*

Adelphia Cable Communications (150,000 subscribers). 789 Indian Church Rd., West Seneca, NY 14224. (716) 827-9444; FAX: (716) 827-3890. Thomas Haywood, gen mgr; Steve Pawlik, chief tech; Tracy Gilano, cust svc dir.
Area(s) Served: NY. Counties: Erie, Niagara. Serving Amherst, Blasdell, Boston, Cheektowaga, Depew, Eden, Hamburg, Kenmore, Lackawanna, North Tonawanda, Pendleton, Sloan, West Seneca, Wheatfield, Williamsville. Miles of Plant: 1,790. Homes Served: 150,000. *Channel Capacity:* 36. In use: 36. *Basic Service:* Subscribers: 150,000; 10/15/93. *Pay Services:* Total Pay Subscribers: 80,000; 10/15/93. *Local Advertising Accepted.*

Adelphia Cable Communications (30,000 subscribers). 1575 Lexington Ave., Mansfield, OH 44907. (419) 756-3333; FAX: (419) 756-5319. Erv Davis, gen mgr; Sebio DeLuciano, mktg dir; Charles W. Jones, loc adv dir; Larry Nelson, chief tech.
Area(s) Served: OH. County: Richland. Serving Lexington, Lucas, Madison, Mansfield, Mifflin, Ontario, Springfield, Troy, Washington, Weller. Pop: 75,000. Miles of Plant: 480. Homes Passed: 33,000. Homes Served: 30,000. *Channel Capacity:* 38. In use: 38. *Basic Service:* Subscribers: 30,000; 10/5/93. *Pay Services:* Total Pay Subscribers: 10,530; 11/09/91. *Local Advertising Accepted.*

Adelphia Cable Communications of Syracuse (40,000 subscribers). 500 S. Salina St., Syracuse, NY 13202. (315) 471-1911; FAX: (315) 471-1502. Tim Henderson, gen mgr; Kathleen Kires, mktg dir; Mary Francis Sabins, loc adv dir; William Taddeo, chief tech; Gail Cawley, cust svc dir.
Area(s) Served: NY. County: Onondaga. Serving Syracuse. Pop: 200,000. Miles of Plant: 314. Homes Passed: 66,670. Homes Served: 40,000. *Channel Capacity:* 39. In use: 39. *Basic Service:* Subscribers: 40,000; 10/15/93. Programming (via satellite): 32 chs. Programming (via microwave): 32 chs. Programming (off air): 5 chs. *Pay Services:* Total Pay Subscribers: 34,987; 10/30/92. (1) Pay Units: 16,096; 10/30/92. Programming (via satellite): HBO. (2) Pay Units: 4,333; 10/30/92. Programming (via satellite): Cinemax. (3) Pay Units: 2,320; 10/30/92. Programming (via satellite): Showtime. (4) Pay Units: 1,810; 10/30/92. Programming (via satellite): The Movie Channel. Pay Per View Subscribers: 13,640; 10/30/92. *Local Advertising Accepted. Equipment:* Jerrold converters; Jerrold trunk amps; DBC line extenders; Scientific-Atlanta headend; Comm/Scope cable.

Adelphia Cable, South East Florida (165,000 subscribers). 2129 Congress Ave., Riviera Beach, FL 33404. (407) 863-5701; FAX: (407) 845-7709. Mark Galloway, gen mgr; Cathy Wolosin, mktg dir; Barry Rhodes, chief tech.
Area(s) Served: FL. Counties: Martin, Palm Beach, St. Lucie. Homes Passed: 214,632. Homes Served: 165,000. *Basic Service:* Subscribers: 165,000; 10/15/93. *Local Advertising Accepted.*

Adelphia Cable-Northeast (34,000 subscribers). 1100 Clay Ave., Dunmore, PA 18510. (717) 342-2270; FAX: (717) 344-4573. Robert G. Wahl, gen mgr; Richard Hoteck, mktg dir; Frank Hanczyk, chief tech; Marianne Presken, cust svc dir.
Area(s) Served: PA. Counties: Lackawana, Luzerne, Wyoming. Miles of Plant: 729. Homes Passed: 43,474. Homes Served: 34,000. *Channel Capacity:* 37. In use: 37. *Basic Service:* Subscribers: 34,000; 09/01/93. Pay Per View Subscribers: 3,000; 11/15/92. *Local Advertising Accepted. Equipment:* Scientific-Atlanta addressable converters; Hamlin converters.

Adelphia Cable-Niagara (30,000 subscribers). 2604 Seneca Ave., Niagara Falls, NY 14305. (716) 297-6900; FAX: (716) 297-0616. Vincent Laurendi Jr., gen mgr &
mktg dir; Sam Granieri, loc adv dir; Ray Szyjka, chief tech.
Area(s) Served: NY. County: Niagara. Serving Lewiston, Niagara Falls, Niagara, Porter, Sanborn, Wilson, Youngstown. Miles of Plant: 438. Homes Served: 30,000. *Channel Capacity:* 62. In use: 56. *Basic Service:* Subscribers: 30,000; 10/1/93. *Local Advertising Accepted.*

Adelphia Cable-South Dade (58,000 subscribers). 20800 Southwest 167 Ave., Miami, FL 33187. (305) 255-3770; FAX: (305) 238-3770. Lynn Whisenhunt, gen mgr & chief tech; John Wattick, mktg dir; Jorge Fittere, loc adv dir; Douglas Vaughn, cust svc dir.
Area(s) Served: FL. County: Dade. Pop: 350,000. Miles of Plant: 1,400. Homes Passed: 140,000. Homes Served: 58,000. *Channel Capacity:* 62. In use: 58. *Basic Service:* Subscribers: 58,000; 10/3/93. *Local Advertising Accepted.*

Adelphia Communications-Clear (90,000 subscribers). Box 847, 830 Hwy. 37 W., Toms River, NJ 08755. (908) 286-2971; FAX: (908) 286-2914. William B. Scott, gen mgr; Rick Hoteck, mktg dir; Henry DeBianchi, loc adv dir; Ray Manuwald, chief tech; Diane Kelly, cust svc dir.
Area(s) Served: NJ. County: Ocean. Serving Barnegat Twp., Beachwood, Eagleswood Twp., Island Heights, Lace Twp., Lakehurst, Little Egg Harbor Twp., Manahawkin, Manchester, Ocean Gate, Ocean Twp., Pine Beach, Stafford Twp., Toms River, Tuckerton, Waretown. Miles of Plant: 1,500. Homes Passed: 106,000. Homes Served: 90,000. *Channel Capacity:* 80. In use: 50. *Basic Service:* Subscribers: 90,000; 10/15/93. *Pay Services:* Total Pay Subscribers: 50,000; 10/30/91. Pay Per View Subscribers: 22,000; 10/30/91. *Local Advertising Accepted.*

SMALLER SYSTEMS

Massachusetts - Adelphia Cable, Highfield Deport Ave., Falmouth, MA 02541; (508) 548-7784. Adelphia Cable-Berkshire, 225 N. Hodges Crossroad, North Adams, MA 01247; (413) 664-4011. **Michigan -** Adelphia Cable-Kalamazoo, 11921 M-89, Richland, MI 49083; (616) 731-2121. **New York -** Adelphia Cable-Harbor Vue, 23 Wright St., Dunkirk, NY 14048; (716) 366-8484. Adelphia Cable-Resort, Lake Colby Dr., Saranac Lake, NY 12983; (518) 891-2810. **North Carolina -** Adelphia Cable, 1537-A North Rd., St. Elizabeth City, NC 27909; (919) 338-1091. Adelphia Cable-Ahoskie/Murfreesboro, 118 N. Mitchell St., Ahoskie, SC 27910; (919) 332-4746. **Ohio -** Adelphia Cable, Box 300, 5335 Enterprise Blvd., Bethel Park, PA 15102; (412) 831-1337. Adelphia Cable, 114 W. Warren St., Bucyrus, OH 44820; (419) 562-8068. Adelphia Cable, 82, N. Main St., Fredericktown, OH 43019; (614) 684-0091. Adelphia Cable, 1801 Elyria Ave., Lorain, OH 44052; (216) 245-3535. Adelphia Cable, 59 E. Main St., Shelby, OH 44875; (419) 342-3286. Adelphia Cable-Western Reserve, 885 E. Highland Rd., Macedonia, OH 44056; (216) 467-1804. **Pennsylvania -** Adelphia Cable, 5 W. Third St., Coudersport, PA 16915; (814) 274-9830. Adelphia Cable, 215 E. North St., New Castle, PA 16101; (412) 658-2501. Adelphia Cable, Box 198, Plymouth Meeting, PA 19462; (215) 828-3932. Adelphia Cable, 234 N. Findley St., Punxsutawney, PA 15767; (814) 938-6139. Adelphia Cable, 367 Cleveland St., Rochester, PA 15074; (412) 775-2814. Adelphia Cable-William Penn, One Adelphia Dr., Blairsville, PA 15717; (412) 459-5400. **South Carolina -** Adelphia Cable, Box 6652, Hilton Head, SC 29936; (803) 785-5175. **Vermont -** Adelphia Cable, Granger Rd., Montpelier, VT 05601; (802) 223-2852. Adelphia Cable, 299 N. Main St., Rutland, VT 05702; (802) 773-2755. Adelphia Cable-Bennington/Hosick Falls, 107 McKinley St., Bennington, VT 05201; (802) 442-9395. **Virginia -** Adelphia Cable, 2154 Sycamore Ave., Buena Vista, VA 24416; (703) 261-3626. Adelphia Cable, 15 N. Royal Ave., Front Royal, VA 22630; (703) 635-1568. Adelphia Cable, 112 Washington St., Galax, VA 24333; (703) 236-7171. Adelphia Cable, 5 W. Nelson St., Lexington, VA 24450; (703) 464-5893. Adelphia Cable, 125 E. Main St., Marion, VA 24354; (703) 783-6182. Adelphia Cable, 390 Commonwealth Blvd., Martinsville, VA 24112; (703) 638-6422. Adelphia Cable, 25225 Harwell Dr., Petersburg, VA 23803; (804) 733-7031; 2,200 subs. Adelphia Cable, 641 E. Main St., Pulaski, VA 24301; (703) 980-2206. Adelphia Cable, 306 Suffolk Ave., Richlands, VA 24641; (703) 963-

Multiple Systems Operators, Independent Owners & Cable Systems

0148. Adelphia Cable, 1711 Seymour Dr., South Boston, VA 24592; (804) 575-7368. Adelphia Cable, 308 N. Central Ave., Staunton, VA 24401; (703) 886-4520. Adelphia Cable, 417 N. Delphine Ave., Waynesboro, VA 22980; (703) 943-9218. Adelphia Cable, 971 N. Frederick Pike, Winchester, VA 22601; (703) 667-6055.

Alabama TV Cable Co.

Box 369, 213-B Broad St., Aliceville, AL 35442. (205) 373-8701; FAX: (205) 373-8894. Theresa Dunlap, pres; J.R. Ball, vp opns. Owned by R.E. Hook, 90%; C.S. Sterling 10%. Total Basic Subscribers: 6,800; Number of Cable Systems: 1.

Alaskan Cable Network

21221 Oxnard St., Woodland Hills, CA 91367. (818) 713-3800; FAX: (818) 713-0057. Jack K. Cooke, pres; Brad Ogden, CFO; James Lacher, vp. Owned by Jack K. Cooke. Total Basic Subscribers: 24,500; Number of Cable Systems: 4.

SMALLER SYSTEMS

Alaska - Alaska Cable Network Inc., Fairbanks, AK. Alaska Cable Network Inc., Juneau, AK. Alaska Cable Network Inc., Ketchikan, AK. Alaska Cable Network Inc., Sitka, AK.

ALEXCOM Inc.

Suite 1701, 745 Fifth Ave., New York, NY 10151. (212) 421-9870; FAX: (212) 688-3043. Richard Treibick, CEO & chmn; Rust Muirhead, pres; Rory Phillips, CFO; Wendell Dean, vp opns. Owned by Richard Treibick. Total Basic Subscribers: 45,000; Number of Cable Systems: 2.

SYSTEMS WITH OVER 20,000 SUBSCRIBERS

Smyrna Cable TV (23,000 subscribers). Box 1587, 3773 S. Cobbs Dr., Smyrna, GA 30081-1587. (404) 433-2338; FAX: (404) 433-3430. Wendell Dean, gen mgr; Rhonda Mcglamry, mktg dir & cust svc dir. *Area(s) Served:* GA. County: Cobb. Homes Served: 23,000. *Basic Service:* Subscribers: 23,000; 10/31/93.

SMALLER SYSTEMS

Tennessee - Tennessee Cablevision Inc., 120 Randolph Rd., Oak Ridge, TN 37830; 17,500 subs.

Allen's TV Cable Service Inc.

Box 2643, 611 Everett St., Morgan City, LA 70381. (504) 384-8335; FAX: (504) 384-5243. Greg Price, pres; Chris Price, vp opns & vp mktg. Number of Cable Systems: 1.

ALLTEL

218 E. Broadway, Bolivar, MO 65613. (417) 326-5214. Kenneth Deane, pres. Owned by AllTel, Little Rock, AK. Total Basic Subscribers: 3,002; Pay Cable Subscribers: 819; Number of Cable Systems: 2.

SMALLER SYSTEMS

Missouri - AllTel, Bolivar, MO 65613. Missouri Telephone Co., Stockton, MO.

ALLTEL - Western Division

Suite 400, 2121 N. California Blvd., Walnut Creek, CA 94596-8192. (510) 295-9500; FAX: (510) 945-4996. David L. Thomas, pres; Larry Schafer, vp mktg; Francis Mike, vp; Robert Cori, vp. Owned by AllTel, Little Rock, AK. Total Basic Subscribers: 9,059; Pay Cable Subscribers: 5,438; Number of Cable Systems: 2.

SMALLER SYSTEMS

Arizona - NCC Systems Inc., Drawer CC, Window Rock, AZ 86512. **California** - Cablevision of Needles, 911 Broadway, Needles, CA 92363.

AMC Cablevision

Box 7, Redwood, VA 24146. (703) 489-1300; FAX: (703) 489-6250. Eddy Martinez, CEO & vp opns; Kelvin Bowles, pres; Jim Lusk, vp mktg. Owned by Atlantic Metrovision Corp. Total Basic Subscribers: 5,455; Pay Cable Subscribers: 4,911; Number of Cable Systems: 1.

Americable International

Suite A104, 10711 Southwest 216th St., Miami, FL 33170. (305) 232-9208; FAX: (305) 252-9097. Charles Hermanowski, pres; Rick Hensley, vp opns; Joe Riccuia, vp mktg. Total Basic Subscribers: 55,000; Number of Cable Systems: 34.

American Cable Communications

Suite 14A, 95 Morgan St., Stamford, CT 06905. (203) 323-7800; FAX: (203) 323-3972. Rick Perone, vp opns; Ken Makowski, vp mktg. Owned by American Cable Communications L.P. Total Basic Subscribers: 3,000; Number of Cable Systems: 4.

SMALLER SYSTEMS

Connecticut - American Cable Communications, 95 Morgan St., Suite 14A, Stamford, CT. **Maine** - American Cable Communications, Sheepscot Rd., Newcastle, ME 04553. **Maryland** - American Cable Communications, 10800 Hanna St., Suite U, Beltsville, MD 20705. American Cable Communications, Bolin Airforce Base, MD.

Amery Telephone Co.

116 N. Harriman Ave., Amery, WI 54001. (715) 268-7101; FAX: (715) 268-9194. Michael Jensen, pres; Michael Griffin, vp opns. Total Basic Subscribers: 1,500; Number of Cable Systems: 4.

SMALLER SYSTEMS

Wisconsin - Northwest Community Communications, 116 N. Harriman Ave., Avery, WI 54001.

Amrac Cable Television

470 Totten Pond Rd., Waltham, MA 02154. (617) 890-9191. David Sifka, vp opns. Owned by Sidney Whiting, gen ptnr. Total Basic Subscribers: 4,000; Number of Cable Systems: 1.

Wilbur L. Anderson

Box 2040, San Angelo, TX 76902. (915) 658-6539; FAX: (915) 655-8511. Wilbur L. Anderson, pres; Daniel Anderson, vp opns & vp mktg. Total Basic Subscribers: 1,070; Number of Cable Systems: 2.

SMALLER SYSTEMS

Texas - Western Community TV Service, Box 2040, San Angelo, TX 76902.

Annox Inc.

Box 230, 6509 Hwy. 41A, Pleasant View, TN 37146. (615) 746-8927; FAX: (615) 746-3409. Tom Lender, CEO & pres; Lisa Rhoads, vp mktg. Total Basic Subscribers: 4,667; Number of Cable Systems: 1.

Apollo CableVision Inc.

13100 Alondra Blvd., Cerritos, CA 90703-3307. (310) 802-2253; FAX: (310) 926-8017. Thomas Roback, CEO & pres; Charlotte Roback, chmn, vp sls, vp mktg & vp prom; Lisa Dumas, CFO & vp progmg; Gil Lucero, vp adv; Michael Garcia, vp; Denise Retmier, vp. Owned by T.L. Roback, Inc. Total Basic Subscribers: 7,300; Pay Cable Subscribers: 4,100; Number of Cable Systems: 1.

Armstrong Communications Inc.

One Armstrong Pl., Butler, PA 16001. (412) 283-0925. Jay Sedwick, CEO; Jud Sedwick, chmn; Kirby Campbell, vp opns; Jud D. Stewart, vp mktg. Owned by Yolando G. Barco, Jud L. Sedwick. Total Basic Subscribers: 39,046; Pay Cable Subscribers: 17,580; Number of Cable Systems: 4.

SYSTEMS WITH OVER 20,000 SUBSCRIBERS

Armstrong Communications Inc. (26,000 subscribers). 259 E. Crawford Ave., Connellsville, PA 15425. (412) 628-5462; FAX: (412) 628-4963. William Corbett, gen mgr. *Basic Service:* Subscribers: 26,000; 10/31/93.

SMALLER SYSTEMS

Pennsylvania - Armstrong Communications Inc., Bear Rocks, PA. Armstrong Communications Inc., California, PA. Armstrong Communications Inc., Weadville, PA.

Armstrong Utilities Inc.

One Armstrong Pl., Butler, PA 16001. (412) 283-0925; FAX: (412) 283-2602. Jay Sedwick, CEO & pres; Jud L. Sedwick, chmn; Kirby Campbell, CFO; A. Dean Busatto, vp opns; Jud Stewart, vp mktg; William Stewart, vp. Total Basic Subscribers: 180,000; Pay Cable Subscribers: 97,000; Number of Cable Systems: 14.

SYSTEMS WITH OVER 20,000 SUBSCRIBERS

Armstrong Cable Services (38,500 subscribers). 9328 Woodworth Rd., North Lima, OH 44452. (216) 758-6411; FAX: (216) 726-0117. Paul Wachtel, gen mgr; Joe Battista, chief tech; Sharon Turney, cust svc dir. *Area(s) Served:* OH. Counties: Mahoning, Trumbull. Serving Austintown, Beaver, Boardman, Campbell, Canfield, McDonald, Poland, Weathersfield. Miles of Plant: 690. Homes Passed: 47,982. Homes Served: 38,500. *Channel Capacity:* 35. In use: 35. *Basic Service:* Subscribers: 38,500. Programming (via satellite): 27 chs. Programming (via microwave): 1 ch. Programming (off air): 7 chs. *Pay Services:* Total Pay Subscribers: 26,095; 11/20/92. (1) Pay Units: 13,989; 11/20/92. Programming (via satellite): HBO. (2) Pay Units: 7,900; 11/20/92. Programming (via satellite): Cinemax. *Local Advertising Accepted.*

Armstrong Utilities Inc. (22,000 subscribers). 390 Beubrook Rd., Butler, PA 16001. (412) 283-4480; FAX: (412) 482-4884. Richard L. Ross, gen mgr; Jud D. Stewart, mktg dir; Pat Mills, chief tech. *Basic Service:* Subscribers: 22,000; 10/15/93.

Arvig Telephone Co.

101 Main St., Pequot Lakes, MN 56472. (218) 568-4115; FAX: (218) 568-2125. Bruce Brunes, pres; Mike Arvig, vp opns. Total Basic Subscribers: 3,500; Number of Cable Systems: 1.

SMALLER SYSTEMS

Minnesota - Inter Lake CableVision, Box 27, Pequot Lakes, MN 56472.

Atlantic Telephone Membership Corporation

Box 3198, 620 Whiteville Rd. N.W., Shallotte, NC 28459. (919) 754-4311. Carol Danford, pres; Percy Woodard, vp mktg. Total Basic Subscribers: 10,814; Number of Cable Systems: 1.

Attleboro Radio Association Inc.

8 N. Main St., Attleboro, MA 02703. (508) 222-1320; FAX: (508) 761-9239. Peter H. Ottmar, CEO & pres; Jerome Ottmar, chmn; Richard Behlman, CFO; Stephen Cronin, vp opns; Donald Charlebois, vp mktg. Total Basic Subscribers: 12,500; Pay Cable Subscribers: 12,253; Number of Cable Systems: 1.

SMALLER SYSTEMS

Massachusetts - Inland Cable Communication, 8 N. Main St., Attleboro, MA 02703. (508) 222-1320; 12,500 subs.

Avatar Properties Inc.

255 Alhambra Cir., Coral Gables, FL 33134. (407) 933-5308; FAX: (407) 870-5006. Larry Wilkov, pres; Jeff Pashley, vp opns; Jeanette Coughenour, vp mktg. Total Basic Subscribers: 2,700; Number of Cable Systems: 1.

SMALLER SYSTEMS

Florida - American Cable Vision, 24 Doverplum Ctr., Kissimee, FL 34759.

Avenue TV Cable Service Inc.

Box 1458, 1954 E. Main St., Ventura, CA 93002-2324. (805) 643-9971; FAX: (805) 643-1284. Johnny George, pres; Steve George, vp opns. Total Basic Subscribers: 10,500; Pay Cable Subscribers: 3,000; Number of Cable Systems: 2.

B & L Communications

Box 970, Andalusia, AL 36420. (205) 222-6110; FAX: (205) 222-2159. Chris Alexander, pres; Maurice Rabren, vp opns; Allen Sharp, vp mktg. Total Basic Subscribers: 4,400; Number of Cable Systems: 2.

Multiple Systems Operators, Independent Owners & Cable Systems

SMALLER SYSTEMS

Utah - B & L Communications - Cleveland, Box 580, Orangeville, UT 84537.

Bachow Communications Inc.

Suite 502, 3 Bala Plaza E., Bala Cynwyd, PA 19004. (215) 660-4900; FAX: (215) 660-4930. Owned by Bachow & Associates. Total Basic Subscribers: 4,700; Number of Cable Systems: 1.

SMALLER SYSTEMS

Mississippi - Cable Cast Advertising, 16 1st St., Grenada, MS 38906; (601) 226-1120.

Bainbridge Cable Co.

28 Juliand St., Bainbridge, NY 13733. (607) 967-2012. Frank Boyle, pres; David Coe, vp opns & vp mktg. Owned by Frank Boyle. Total Basic Subscribers: 1,750; Number of Cable Systems: 1.

Baldwin Telecom Inc.

930 Maple St., Baldwin, WI 54002. (715) 684-3346; FAX: (715) 684-4747. William C. Hawley, pres; Larry Konigendorf, vp opns. Total Basic Subscribers: 1,250; Number of Cable Systems: 1.

Barden Communications Inc.

243 W. Congress, Detroit, MI 48226. (313) 963-5010; FAX: (313) 963-5274. Don H. Barden, CEO & pres; Yvonne Penn, vp opns; John Barden, vp mktg. Owned by Don H. Barden. Total Basic Subscribers: 4,500; Number of Cable Systems: 1.

SMALLER SYSTEMS

Michigan - Barden Cable Vision of Inkster, 2680 Michigan Ave., Inkster, MI 48141; (313) 561-5252.

City of Bardstown

Box 368, 220 N. 5th St., Bardstown, KY 40004. (502) 348-9711; FAX: (502) 348-2433. Larry Hamilton, vp opns; Bobbie Blincow, vp mktg. Total Basic Subscribers: 5,000; Number of Cable Systems: 1.

SMALLER SYSTEMS

Kentucky - Bardstown Cable TV, 220 N. 5th St., Bardstown, KY 40004.

Barry Electronics Inc.

Box 144, Commodore, PA 15729. (412) 254-9626. Carl Barry, pres; Dan Barry, vp mktg. Total Basic Subscribers: 1,571; Pay Cable Subscribers: 559; Number of Cable Systems: 1.

Bath TV Service Corporation

45 Liberty St., Bath, NY 14810. (607) 776-4861; FAX: (607) 776-1152. William G. Conelley, pres; Harold L. Brown, vp mktg. Total Basic Subscribers: 3,875; Number of Cable Systems: 1.

Bay Cable Inc.

Suite 202, 2444 Solomons Island Rd., Annapolis, MD 21401. (410) 266-9393; FAX: (410) 266-9054. Roye Hayes Jr., pres; Charles Hookey, vp opns. Total Basic Subscribers: 9,000; Number of Cable Systems: 35.

Bayside Cable TV

Box 2330, Gulf Shores, AL 36547. (205) 968-5414; FAX: (205) 968-5415. Greg Armstrong, pres. Owned by Cable Management Group. Total Basic Subscribers: 3,300; Number of Cable Systems: 2.

SMALLER SYSTEMS

Alabama - Bayside Cable TV, Baldwin County, AL. **Oklahoma** - Buntz Vision, Tulsa, OK.

Bee Line Inc.

Box 859, 22 N. St., Houlton, ME 04730. (207) 532-7060; FAX: (207) 532-7062. Paul Hannigan, pres; George Allen, vp opns & vp mktg. Total Basic Subscribers: 9,984; Number of Cable Systems: 2.

SMALLER SYSTEMS

Maine - Bee Line Inc., 232 Penobscot, Millinocket, ME 04462. Bee Line Inc., Lake Wood Ave., Skowhegan, ME 04976.

Belhaven Cable TV Inc.

Box 8, 3 Foodlion Plaza, Belhaven, NC 27810. (919) 943-3736; FAX: (919) 943-3738. Guinn Leveritt, pres; Corky Leveritt, vp mktg. Total Basic Subscribers: 1,100; Number of Cable Systems: 1.

Belisle Communications Inc.

Box 1203, Coraopolis, PA 15108. (412) 262-5517; FAX: (412) 262-5518. Helen P. Belisle, CEO & pres; B.R. Belisle, vp opns & vp mktg. Total Basic Subscribers: 7,200; Number of Cable Systems: 15.

SMALLER SYSTEMS

Indiana - Concept Cable Vision of Indiana, 106 Main St., Sheridan, IN 46069. **South Carolina** - Concept Cable Vision-South Carolina, 1068 State St., Holly Hill, SC 29059.

Benchmark Communications

21545 Ridgetop Cir., Sterling, VA 20166. (703) 444-1800; FAX: (703) 444-9797. Max Kipher, CEO & vp opns; Michael Santille, CFO; Tania R. Mennes, vp mktg. Total Basic Subscribers: 58,325; Pay Cable Subscribers: 45,905; Number of Cable Systems: 5.

SMALLER SYSTEMS

California - Benchmark Cablevision, 543 Inyokern Rd., Ridgecrest, CA 93555; (619) 446-5500; 11,948 subs. **Florida** - Palm Cablevision, 211 Joe Plaza Dr., Palm Coast, FL 32137; (904) 445-5464; 7,502 subs. **Virginia** - Cablevision of Loudoun, 207 E. Holly Ave., Suite 206, Stirling, VA 22170; (703) 438-3501; 12,629 subs. Cablevision of Manassas, 9540 Center St., Manassas, VA 22110; (703) 368-4227; 19,399 subs. Cablevision of Manassas Park, 9102 Manassas Dr., Manassas Park, VA 22111; (703) 368-4227; 4,167 subs.

Bend Cable Communications Inc.

Box 5067, 63090 Sherman Rd., Bend, OR 97708. (503) 382-5551; FAX: (503) 385-3271. Don Tykeson, pres; Mike Puckett, vp mktg. Owned by Tykeson Communications. Total Basic Subscribers: 17,500; Number of Cable Systems: 1.

Berkeley Cable TV Co. Inc.

Box 1257, Moncks Corner, SC 29461. (803) 761-8188; FAX: (803) 761-9120. Robert L. Helmley Sr., CEO & pres; Robert Helmley Jr., vp opns; Claude Sykes, vp mktg. Total Basic Subscribers: 4,736; Number of Cable Systems: 1.

Biltmore-Holiday Corporation

300 E. 3rd St., Lordsburg, NM 88045. (505) 542-3584; FAX: (505) 542-3535. Soila DePaoli, pres; Francis Rosales, vp opns. Total Basic Subscribers: 1,030; Number of Cable Systems: 1.

SMALLER SYSTEMS

New Mexico - City TV & Cable Services, 300 E. Third St., Lordsburg, NM 88045.

Joseph R. Biondo

605 Pennsylvania Ave., Matamoras, PA 18336. (717) 491-4837; FAX: (717) 491-2742. Joseph R. Biondo, CEO & pres. Total Basic Subscribers: 2,800; Number of Cable Systems: 1.

SMALLER SYSTEMS

Pennsylvania - Matamoras Video Cable, 605 Pennsylvania Ave., Matamoras, PA 18336.

Blade Communications Inc.

541 Superior St., Toledo, OH 43660. (419) 245-6000; FAX: (419) 245-6167. William Block, chmn; William Block Jr., pres; Gary J. Blair, CFO; John R. Block, vp; Allan Block, vp. Total Basic Subscribers: 148,000; Pay Cable Subscribers: 69,000; Number of Cable Systems: 3.

SYSTEMS WITH OVER 20,000 SUBSCRIBERS

Buckeye Cablevision Inc. (120,000 subscribers). 5566 Southwyck Blvd., Toledo, OH 43614. (419) 866-5802; FAX: (419) 866-7074. David G. Huey, gen mgr; Ellen Jackson, mktg dir; Steve Piller, loc adv dir; James Dryden, chief tech; Linda Mayberry, cust svc dir. *Area(s) Served:* OH. Counties: Lucas, Wood. Pop: 450,000. Miles of Plant: 1,800. Homes Passed: 185,000. Homes Served: 120,000. Channel Capacity: 54. In use: 50. *Basic Service:* Subscribers: 120,000; 09/30/93. Programming (via satellite): 43 chs. Programming (off air): 7 chs. *Pay Services:* Total Pay Subscribers: 56,000; 09/30/93. Pay Per View Subscribers: 86,000; 09/30/93. Local Advertising Accepted. *Equipment:* Tocom converter.

Blakely Cable Television Inc.

41 Court Sq., Blakely, GA 31723. (912) 723-3555; FAX: (912) 723-3800. W.C. Deloach Jr., pres; Wayne R. Foster, vp opns. Owned by Blakely Cable Television Inc. Total Basic Subscribers: 2,600; Pay Cable Subscribers: 850; Number of Cable Systems: 6.

SMALLER SYSTEMS

Alabama - Blakely Cable, Columbia, AL; 329 subs. **Georgia** - Blakely Cable, Baconton, GA; 142 subs. Blakely Cable, Blakely, GA; 1,713 subs. Blakely Cable, Leary, GA; 129 subs. Blakely Cable, Morgan, GA; 57 subs. Blakely Cable, Newton, GA; 136 subs.

Bledsoe Telephone Cooperative

Box 609, 203 Cumberland Ave., Pikeville, TN 37367. (615) 447-2121; FAX: (615) 447-2498. John L. Downey, pres; Robert Clemons, vp opns. Total Basic Subscribers: 3,709; Pay Cable Subscribers: 567; Number of Cable Systems: 1.

Bley Family

121 W. Main St., Beardstown, IL 62618. (217) 323-3400; FAX: (217) 323-2252. Mary A. Bley, pres; Nancy Bley, vp progmg. Total Basic Subscribers: 2,400; Number of Cable Systems: 1.

SMALLER SYSTEMS

Illinois - Bley Cable Inc., 121 W. Main St., Beardstown, IL 62618.

Blue Mountain TV Cable Co.

Box 267, Mount Vernon, OR 97865. (503) 932-4613. Owned by Jack McKenna. Total Basic Subscribers: 1,800; Number of Cable Systems: 4.

Blytheville TV Cable Co.

Box 127, 121 S. Second St., Blytheville, AR 72315. (501) 763-6688; FAX: (501) 763-8459. Harold L. Sudburg Jr., pres; Carl Bishop, vp opns. Owned by Harold L. Sundburg Jr. Total Basic Subscribers: 7,000; Number of Cable Systems: 1.

Booth American Co.

333 W. Fort St., Detroit, MI 48226. (313) 965-3360; FAX: (313) 965-1160. John L. Booth Sr., chmn; John L. Booth II, pres; Ralph H. Booth, CFO; Richard Lesky, vp opns; James H. Milford Jr., vp mktg; Chris Ciak, vp. Owned by John L. Booth Sr., John L. Booth II, Ralph H. Booth. Total Basic Subscribers: 139,935; Pay Cable Subscribers: 72,000; Number of Cable Systems: 9.

SYSTEMS WITH OVER 20,000 SUBSCRIBERS

Booth Communications of Birmingham (24,589 subscribers). 645 S. Eton, Birmingham, MI 48009. (313) 540-6110; FAX: (313) 540-6739. Hugh Jencks, gen mgr; Suzanne Harwood, mktg dir; Tim Funk, chief tech. *Basic Service:* Subscribers: 24,589; 10/15/93.

Hi-Desert Cablevision (32,514 subscribers). 12490 Business Center Dr., Victorville, CA 92392. (619) 241-7848; FAX: (619) 241-7659. Tom Burka, gen mgr; Dave Elliott, loc adv dir; Don Williams, chief tech; Monica Velarde, cust svc dir. *Area(s) Served:* CA. County: San Bernardino. Serving Apple Valley, Hesperia, Spring Valley Lake, Victorville. Pop: 200,000. Miles of Plant: 830. Homes Passed: 41,000. Homes Served: 32,514. Channel Capacity: 43. In use: 43. *Basic Service:* Subscribers: 32,514; 10/13/93. Programming (via satellite): 37 chs. Program-

Multiple Systems Operators, Independent Owners & Cable Systems

ming (via microwave): 8 chs. Programming (off air): 1 ch. *Local Advertising Accepted.*

High Country Cable TV (22,000 subscribers). Box 1219, 220 Postal St., Boone, NC 28607. (704) 264-9411; FAX: (704) 262-5705. Len Hagaman, gen mgr; Dawn Marie Gaid, mktg dir; Kenny Arnold, vp opns; Steve Foote, chief tech; Deborah Bruce, cust svc dir. *Area(s) Served:* NC, TN. Counties: Avery, Carter, Watauga. Serving Ashe, Caldwell. Pop: 50,000. Miles of Plant: 850. Homes Passed: 22,000. Homes Served: 22,000. *Channel Capacity:* 42. In use: 42. *Basic Service:* Subscribers: 22,000; 09/01/93. *Local Advertising Accepted.*

Boulder Ridge Cable TV dba Starstream Communications

Box 3129, 590 Kelly Ave., Half Moon Bay, CA 94019. (415) 726-1305; FAX: (415) 726-9571. Dean Hazen, pres; Jack Stock, CFO; Dean Henderson, vp opns; Zoe Hazen, vp. Total Basic Subscribers: 16,000; Pay Cable Subscribers: 9,400; Number of Cable Systems: 3.

SMALLER SYSTEMS

California - Boulder Ridge Cable TV/Starstream Communications, Box 767, Redway, CA 95560. Boulder Ridge Cable TV/Starstream Communications, Box 637, 4120 Citrus Ave., Rocklin, CA 95677. **Hawaii** - Cable TV Services, Box 618 C, Honolulu, HI 96818.

Branch Cable Inc.

Suite 1306, 125 S. Congress, Jackson, MS 39201. (601) 355-1522; FAX: (601) 355-0950. James H. Creekmore, pres; Brooks Derryberry, vp adv. Owned by The Potosi Company. Total Basic Subscribers: 2,800; Number of Cable Systems: 1.

Bresnan Communications Co.

709 Westchester Ave., White Plains, NY 10604. (914) 997-5656; FAX: (914) 997-6871. William J. Bresnan, pres; Jeffrey S. Demond, CFO; Michael Bresnan, vp opns; Patrick J. Bresnan, vp mktg. Owned by William J. Bresnan, 51%; Tele-Communications Inc., 49%. Total Basic Subscribers: 160,000; Pay Cable Subscribers: 62,000; Number of Cable Systems: 11.

SYSTEMS WITH OVER 20,000 SUBSCRIBERS

Bresnan Communications Co. (21,518 subscribers). Box 0190, Marquette, MI 49855. (906) 228-2900. Rex Buettgenbach, gen mgr. *Basic Service:* Subscribers: 21,518; 10/15/93.

Bresnan Communications Co. (44,000 subscribers). Box 445, Essexville, MI 48732. (517) 893-6355; FAX: (517) 893-1122. William Black, gen mgr; Jody Valerio, mktg dir; Ray Snyder, chief tech. *Basic Service:* Subscribers: 44,000; 10/15/93. *Local Advertising Accepted.*

Bresnan Communications Co. (25,000 subscribers). 300 E. Superior St., Duluth, MN 55802. (218) 722-2815. Michael J. McPhee, gen mgr; Steve Netzel, mktg dir; James Matuszewski, chief tech. *Area(s) Served:* WI. Serving Superior. Homes Served: 25,000. *Channel Capacity:* 60. In use: 55. *Basic Service:* Subscribers: 25,000; 12/01/92. *Local Advertising Accepted.*

Brockway TV Inc.

501 Main St., Brockway, PA 15824. (814) 268-6565. L.F. Robertson, pres; Christine Judice, vp. Owned by Borough of Brockway. Total Basic Subscribers: 1,452; Pay Cable Subscribers: 426; Number of Cable Systems: 1.

Brownwood TV Cable Service Inc.

Box 1149, 310 Carnegie, Brownwood, TX 76804. (915) 646-3576. Johnny Andrew, pres. Total Basic Subscribers: 12,000; Number of Cable Systems: 8.

Buena Vision Telecommunications Corporation

912 N. Eastern Ave., Los Angeles, CA 90063. (213) 269-0391; FAX: (213) 269-8257. Montezuma Esparza, pres; Ben O. Choa, vp opns; Hector Gonzalez, vp mktg. Total Basic Subscribers: 7,025; Pay Cable Subscribers: 5,397; Number of Cable Systems: 1.

Buford Television Inc.

Box 9090, Tyler, TX 75711. (903) 561-4411. Robert Buford, CEO; June Predue, vp mktg; Sandy Douglas, vp progmg. Total Basic Subscribers: 85,000; Pay Cable Subscribers: 54,000; Number of Cable Systems: 165.

REGIONS

Arkansas: Friendship Cable, Box 730, Danville, AR 72833. *South Carolina:* Friendship Cable, Box 4620, Columbia, SC 29240. *Texas:* Friendship Cable, Box 7389, Beaumont, TX 77726. Friendship Cable, Box 800609, Balch Spring, TX 75180-0609.

Gary Burtoft

211 E. Flaget, Bardstown, KY 40004. (502) 348-4074; FAX: (502) 348-4074. Gary Burtoft, CEO. Owned by Gary Burtoft. Total Basic Subscribers: 1,280; Number of Cable Systems: 2.

SMALLER SYSTEMS

Kentucky - B & G Cable TV Inc., Apt. C2E, 205 W. Broadway, Bardstown, KY 40004; (502) 348-4074; 300 subs. Clear Cable TV Inc., Apt. C2E, 205 W. Broadway, Bardstown, KY 40004; (502) 348-4074; 980 subs.

Paul Butcher

Box 956, Paintsville, KY 41240. (606) 789-3455; FAX: (606) 789-5352. Paul Butcher, chmn & pres; David Butcher, vp opns. Owned by Paul Butcher. Total Basic Subscribers: 2,600; Number of Cable Systems: 1.

SMALLER SYSTEMS

Kentucky - Big Sandy TV Cable, Box 956, Paintsville, KY 41240.

Arthur M. Bye

30 W. Main, Crosby, MN 56441. (218) 546-6225. Arthur M. Bye, pres & vp opns. Total Basic Subscribers: 1,250; Number of Cable Systems: 1.

SMALLER SYSTEMS

Minnesota - Bye Cable Inc., 30 W. Main, Crosby, MN 56441.

C & W Cable Inc.

7920 Hwy. 30 W., Annville, KY 40402-9748. (606) 364-5357. Don Williams, pres; Judy C. Williams, vp opns & vp mktg. Total Basic Subscribers: 1,621; Number of Cable Systems: 1.

C-TEC Cable Systems Inc.

120 Lake St., Dallas, PA 18612. (717) 675-5822; FAX: (717) 675-1853. Michael J. Mahoney, pres; Loraine Reddington, CFO; John J. Gdovin, vp opns; Mark Haverkate, vp; Robin R. Troop, vp. Owned by C-TEC Corporation. Total Basic Subscribers: 263,076; Pay Cable Subscribers: 135,698; Number of Cable Systems: 68.

REGIONS

Michigan: 814 S. Main St., Lapeer, MI 48446; John Kopacka. 315 Davis St., Grand Haven, MI 49417; Robert Ritzel. 701 S. Airport Rd. W., Traverse City, MI 49684; Dave McManus. 1145 S. Telegraph Rd., Monroe, MI 48161; Cliff Cleland. *New Jersey:* 279 Amwell Rd., Somerville, NJ 08876; Mark Haverkate. *New York:* 21 Old Rt. 6, Carmel, NY 10512; Glenn Bisogno.

SYSTEMS WITH OVER 20,000 SUBSCRIBERS

C-TEC Cable Systems (62,500 subscribers). 279 Amwell Rd., Somerville, NJ 08876. (908) 281-3200; FAX: (908) 359-0142. Mark Haverkate, gen mgr; Marie DeWees, mktg dir & loc adv dir; Jim Witterschein, chief tech. *Basic Service:* Subscribers: 62,500; 10/13/93.

C-TEC Cable Systems of New York Inc. (26,000 subscribers). 21 Old Rt. 6, Carmel, NY 10512. (914) 225-2343; FAX: (914) 225-1802. Glenn Bisogno, gen mgr & mktg dir; Kevin Bailey, loc adv dir; Michael Massimo, chief tech; Denise Moccio, cust svc dir. *Area(s) Served:* NY. Counties: Dutchess, Putnam, Westchester. Serving Beekman, Brewster, Carmel, Kent, Patterson, Pawling, Putnam Valley, Somers, Southeast. Pop: 120,000. Miles of Plant: 1,100. Homes Passed: 29,600. Homes Served: 26,000. *Channel Capacity:* 52. In use: 52. *Basic Service:* Subscribers: 26,000; 10/15/93. *Pay Services:* Total Pay Subscribers: 17,800; 12/01/92. Pay Per View Subscribers: 17,800; 12/01/92. *Local Advertising Accepted.*

SMALLER SYSTEMS

Florida - St. Lucie Cablevision, 590 N.W. Peacock Loop, Suite 3, Port St. Lucie, FL 34986; 667 subs. **Michigan** - C-TEC Cable Systems, 1039 N. Mitchell, Box 578, Cadillac, MI 49601; (616) 755-9745; 4505 subs. C-TEC Cable Systems, 1202 W. Benton, Box 187, Greenville, MI 48838; (616) 754-3651; 5,472 subs. C-TEC Cable Systems, 247 James St., Holland, MI 49424; (616) 399-0220; 10,886 subs. C-TEC Cable Systems, 1213 Manistee Hwy., Manistee, MI 49660; (616) 723-2549; 3,930 subs. C-TEC Cable Systems, 700 Columbus Dr., West Branch, MI 48661; (517) 345-1704; 8,895 subs. **New Jersey** - C-TEC Cable Systems, 601 Ewing St., Princeton, NJ 08540; 5,187 subs. **Pennsylvania** - C-TEC Cable Systems, 521 Maple St., Forest City, PA 18421; (717) 785-9200; 1,287 subs.

C.P.S. Cable Vision Inc.

Box 336, Maine & Filbert Sts., Coalport, PA 16627. (814) 672-5393. Richard L. Ginter, CEO & pres. Total Basic Subscribers: 2,001; Number of Cable Systems: 1.

Cable America Corporation

Suite 160 K, 4250 E. Camelback Rd., Phoenix, AZ 85018-8394. (602) 952-0471; FAX: (602) 952-0458. William G. Jackson, CEO & pres; Christopher Dyrek, CFO; Richard Houghton, vp opns; William H. Lewis, vp. Total Basic Subscribers: 54,000; Pay Cable Subscribers: 37,000; Number of Cable Systems: 6.

SYSTEMS WITH OVER 20,000 SUBSCRIBERS

Cable Alabama (25,316 subscribers). Suite F, 1035 Putnam Dr., Huntsville, AL 35816. (205) 895-9966. William Lewis, gen mgr. *Basic Service:* Subscribers: 25,316; 10/31/93.

SMALLER SYSTEMS

Arizona - Cable America, 350 E. 10th Dr., Mesa, AZ 85210; (602) 461-0715; 15,000 subs. **California** - Cable America, 10398 Rockingham Dr., Suite 6, Sacramento, CA 95827. **Michigan** - Cable America, Box 268M, Eagle Harbor, MI 49950; 100 subs. **Missouri** - Cable America, 229 Millwell Dr., Maryland Heights, MO 63043; 16,000 subs. **New Mexico** - Cable New Mexico, 8 Cable Dr., Placitas, NM 87043; (505) 867-3500; 600 subs.

Cable Communications Cooperative of Palo Alto Inc.

3200 Park Blvd., Palo Alto, CA 94306. (415) 856-8181; FAX: (415) 856-8244. John Kelly, chmn & pres; Steve Opson, vp opns; Carolyn Hillman, vp mktg; Pat Odenthal, vp. Total Basic Subscribers: 21,500; Pay Cable Subscribers: 13,000; Number of Cable Systems: 1.

Cable Cooperative Inc.

23 E. College St., Oberlin, OH 44074. (216) 775-4001; FAX: (216) 775-1635. Carlton Schumate, pres. Total Basic Subscribers: 1,479; Number of Cable Systems: 1.

Cable Management

Box 802068, Noel Rd., Dallas, TX 75380. (214) 233-9616; FAX: (214) 701-8332. Nathan A. Levine, chmn; Charles Friel, pres. Owned by Nathan A. Levine. Total Basic Subscribers: 37,000; Number of Cable Systems: 20.

Cable Services Inc.

Box 608, 308 Second St. N.W., Jamestown, ND 58401. (701) 252-5281; FAX: (701) 252-1105. Roy Sheppard, pres; Barbara Lang, vp mktg. Total Basic Subscribers: 5,200; Number of Cable Systems: 1.

Cable Synergy L.P.

Box 876, Ridgefield, CT 06877. (203) 438-6051; FAX: (203) 438-6599. Mike Hilton, chmn; John McNitt, pres. Owned by Brookridge Inc. Total Basic Subscribers: 3,450; Number of Cable Systems: 1.

Cable Systems Inc.

Box 206, Huxley, IA 50124. (515) 597-3385. Doug Sheldahl, pres; Ken Thompson, vp opns. Owned by

Multiple Systems Operators, Independent Owners & Cable Systems

Doug Sheldahl. Total Basic Subscribers: 917; Number of Cable Systems: 8.

Cable Systems Management of Iowa Inc.

Box 163, 1805 Okoboji Ave., Milford, IA 51351. (712) 338-4967; FAX: (712) 338-4719. Robert Smith, pres; Cliff Plagman, vp opns. Total Basic Subscribers: 1,800; Number of Cable Systems: 7.

Cable TV del Noroeste

Box 5229, Aguadilla, PR 00605. (809) 882-1625; FAX: (809) 882-3404. Janice Fuellhart, CEO & chmn; Ricardo Ruiz, pres; Vivian Smith, vp mktg. Owned by Cable Systems USA, Partners. Total Basic Subscribers: 22,500; Pay Cable Subscribers: 8,800; Number of Cable Systems: 1.

Cable TV of East Providence Inc.

One Office Pkwy., East Providence, RI 02914. (401) 438-7953; FAX: (401) 438-8905. Peter Brubaker, pres; James Munchel, vp opns. Owned by Susquehanna Pfaltzgraff Co. Total Basic Subscribers: 15,053; Number of Cable Systems: 1.

Cable TV of Georgia & Assoc.

Box 99, Dahlonega, GA 30533. (706) 864-7474; FAX: (706) 864-4605. Jim Whicht, pres; Virginia Beard, vp sls. Total Basic Subscribers: 4,800; Number of Cable Systems: 1.

Cable TV of the Kennebunks

35 Beach St., Kennebunk, ME 04043. (207) 967-5212; FAX: (207) 967-0591. Ken Thompson, pres; Claudia Richards, vp opns & vp mktg. Owned by Ken Thompson. Total Basic Subscribers: 6,600; Number of Cable Systems: 1.

Cable TV Services

Box 420, 399 W. Jasper Hwy. 24 W., Goodland, IN 47958. (219) 297-3400; FAX: (219) 474-6332. Richard Mailloux, pres & vp opns. Total Basic Subscribers: 1,650; Pay Cable Subscribers: 250; Number of Cable Systems: 1.

Cable Video Enterprises Inc.

Suite 550, 7007 College Blvd., Overland Park, KS 66211. (913) 469-1700; FAX: (913) 469-1888. Rodney Weary, CEO & pres; Rick McGee, vp mktg. Owned by Rodney Weary. Total Basic Subscribers: 11,000; Pay Cable Subscribers: 4,188; Number of Cable Systems: 5.

SMALLER SYSTEMS

Missouri - Cable Video Enterprises, 130 E. Davis St., Fayette, MO 65248. Cable Video Enterprises, 536 S. Hwy. 13, Lexington, MO 64067. **Oklahoma -** Cable Vision Enterprises, 729 Petree Plaza, Anadarko, OK 73005; (405) 247-7477. **Texas -** Cable Video Enterprises, Box 668, 103 E. Buck St., Caldwell, TX 77836. Cable Video Enterprises, 129 W. Cameron St., Rockdale, TX 76567.

Cable-Vision Ltd.

Box 757, Gatesville, TX 76528. (817) 865-6542. Phil Bone, pres; Chris Bone, vp; Jan Bone, vp; Martha Bone, vp. Total Basic Subscribers: 3,000; Number of Cable Systems: 1.

Cablesouth Inc.

Suite 405, 600 Luckie Dr., Birmingham, AL 35223. (205) 879-8884; FAX: (205) 879-5613. Paul Mass, CEO; Michael Dailey, pres; Tony Farwell, vp opns & vp mktg; Judy Cannon, vp. Total Basic Subscribers: 27,000; Number of Cable Systems: 9.

SMALLER SYSTEMS

Alabama - Albertville System, Conway Rd., Albertville, AL; (205) 878-3802; 9,807 subs. Arab System, Tower St., Arab, AL; (205) 878-3802; 3,433 subs. Heflin System, Evans Bridge Rd., Heflin, AL; (205) 837-3802; 1,033 subs. Henagar System, Lovin Brothers Park, Henagar, AL; (205) 878-3802; 2,135 subs. Hokes Bluff System, 278 Main St., Hokes Bluff, AL; (205) 878-3802. Northport System, County Rd. 22, Northport, AL; (205) 339-7972; 3,292 subs. Southside System, Guyn Dr., Southside, AL; (205) 878-3802; 1,675 subs. Taylorville System, Bear Mount Rd., Taylorville, AL; (205) 339-7972; 2,481 subs. West End System, Unity Rd, Tuscaloosa, AL; (205) 339-7972; 320 subs.

Cablevision Industries Inc.

Box 311, One Cablevision Ctr., Liberty, NY 12754. (914) 292-7550; FAX: (914) 295-2761. Alan Gerry, CEO & chmn; Rocco B. Commisso, CFO; Fred H. Schulte, vp opns; Bill Doten, vp mktg; Michael Egan, vp progmg; Philip I. Dropkin, vp; David L. Testa, vp; Mark Halpin, vp. Total Basic Subscribers: 1,307,760; Pay Cable Subscribers: 422,356; Number of Cable Systems: 81.

REGIONS

Northeast: One Cablevision Ctr., Liberty, NY 12754; (914) 292-7550; Donald L. Rafferty. *Mid-Atlantic/Midwest:* 1700 N. 49th St., Philadelphia, PA 19131; Stephen Joyce. *Louisiana:* 1304 Ridgefield Rd., Thibodaux, LA 70301; Andrew Angelette. *California:* 9260 Topanga Canyon Rd., Chatsworth, CA 91311; (818) 700-0551; Tom Belcher.

SYSTEMS WITH OVER 20,000 SUBSCRIBERS

Cablevision Industries (28,500 subscribers). 844 McGuire, Ocoee, FL 34761. (407) 656-3327; FAX: (407) 656-1162. J.W. Taylor, gen mgr; Carl Newberry, chief tech; Judi Everson, cust svc dir.
Area(s) Served: FL. County: Orange. Serving Clermont, Ocoee, St. Cloud, Winter Garden. Pop: 95,000. Miles of Plant: 625. Homes Passed: 38,000. Homes Served: 28,500. *Channel Capacity:* 60. In use: 53. *Basic Service:* Subscribers: 28,500; 10/31/93. *Pay Services:* Total Pay Subscribers: 7,500; 12/01/92. (1) Pay Units: 5,200; 10/01/91. Programming (via satellite): HBO. (2) Pay Units: 2,200; 10/01/91. Programming (via satellite): Cinemax. (3) Pay Units: 2,000; 10/01/91. Programming (via satellite): Showtime. *Local Advertising Accepted. Equipment:* Jerrold; Scientific-Atlanta; Magnavox.

Cablevision Industries (56,000 subscribers). 85 E. Belcher Rd., Foxboro, MA 02035. (508) 543-8650; FAX: (508) 698-0601. Steve Grossman, gen mgr; Mary Anderson, mktg dir; Brian Joyce, chief tech; Erin Bedard, cust svc dir.
Area(s) Served: MA. Counties: Bristol, Middlesex, Norfolk, Plymouth. Serving Ashland, Bellingham, Bridgewater, Canton, Dover, Foxboro, Holliston, Hopedale, Mansfield, Medfield, Medway, Mendon, Norfolk, Seekonk, Sharon, Walpole, Wrentham. Pop: 233,222. Miles of Plant: 1,500. Homes Passed: 76,436. Homes Served: 56,000. *Channel Capacity:* 66. In use: 59. *Basic Service:* Subscribers: 56,000; 10/31/93. *Pay Services:* Total Pay Subscribers: 37,500; 12/01/92. (1) Pay Units: 17,328. Programming (via satellite): HBO. (2) Pay Units: 4,651. Programming (via satellite): Showtime. (3) Pay Units: 4,963. Programming (via satellite): Cinemax. (4) Pay Units: 2,566. Programming (via satellite): The Movie Channel. (5) Pay Units: 6,789. Programming (via satellite): SportsChannel. (6) Pay Units: 10,348. Programming (via satellite): NESN. *Local Advertising Accepted. Equipment:* Impulse ANI 071.

Cablevision Industries (25,172 subscribers). 1006 S.W. Maynard Rd., Cary, NC 27511. (919) 467-2800; FAX: (919) 467-3586. Hugh MacEachren, gen mgr; Paul Stephens, chief tech.
Area(s) Served: NC. County: Wake. Serving Apex, Cary, Fuquay-Varina, Holly Springs, Morrisville. Pop: 56,300. Miles of Plant: 738. Homes Passed: 33,109. Homes Served: 25,172. *Channel Capacity:* 36. In use: 36. *Basic Service:* Subscribers: 25,172; 10/31/93. *Pay Services:* Total Pay Subscribers: 6,800; 12/01/92. (1) Pay Units: 4,089; 10/09/91. Programming (via microwave): HBO. (2) Pay Units: 930; 10/09/91. Programming (via microwave): Cinemax. (3) Pay Units: 1,396; 10/09/91. Programming (via microwave): Showtime. (4) Pay Units: 1,278; 10/09/91. Programming (via microwave): Disney. *Local Advertising Accepted.*

Cablevision Industries - DeLand (48,000 subscribers). Box 6001, 1655 State Rd. 472, DeLand, FL 32723-6001. (904) 775-4444; FAX: (904) 775-9303. Robert A. Bevis, gen mgr; Marcia Mayls, mktg dir; Karen D'Agostino, loc adv dir; Joe Cordaro, chief tech; Val Gabaree, cust svc dir.
Area(s) Served: FL. County: Volusia. Serving DeLand, Edgewater, Holly Hill, Lake Helen, New Smyrna Beach, Oak Hill, Orange City. Miles of Plant: 1,410. Homes Passed: 89,000. Homes Served: 48,000. *Channel Capacity:* 54. In use: 52. *Basic Service:* Subscribers: 48,000; 11/01/92. Pay Per View Subscribers: 13,000; 11/01/92. *Local Advertising Accepted.*

Cablevision Industries - Finger Lakes (46,000 subscribers). 3518 Sutton Rd., Geneva, NY 14456. (315) 781-1551; FAX: (315) 781-0231. Louis A. McGuigan, gen mgr; Sue Maha, mktg dir; Bill Kimble, loc adv dir; Tom Allen, chief tech; Shelia Clingerman, cust svc dir.
Area(s) Served: NY. Counties: Cayuga, Ontario, Schuyler, Seneca, Wayne. Serving Auburn, Aurora, Canandaigua, Cayuga, Clifton Springs, Clyde, Dix, East Bloomfield, Farmington, Fayette, Geneva, Gibson, Holcomb, Interlaken, Lodi, Lyons, Manchester, Marion, Montour Falls, Newark, N. Rose, Odessa, Ontario, Ovid, Palmyra, Phelps, Port Macedon, Red Creek, Romulus, Rose, Savannah, Seneca Castle, Seneca Falls, Shortsville, Sodus, Sodus Point, Stanley, Union Springs, Varick, Victor, Walworth, Waterloo, Watkins Glen, Willard, Williamson, Wolcott. Miles of Plant: 1,040. Homes Passed: 60,843. Homes Served: 46,000. *Channel Capacity:* 38. In use: 38. *Basic Service:* Subscribers: 46,000; 10/31/93. Programming (via satellite): 19 chs. Programming (off air): 10 chs. *Pay Services:* Total Pay Subscribers: 26,914; 10/01/92. (1) Pay Units: 4,411. Programming (via satellite): Showtime. (2) Pay Units: 3,280. Programming (via satellite): Disney. (3) Pay Units: 7,294. Programming (via satellite): Madison Square Garden. (4) Pay Units: 3,581. Programming (via satellite): Cinemax. (5) Pay Units: 1,006. Programming (via satellite): Playboy. *Local Advertising Accepted. Equipment:* Hughes; Scientific-Atlanta; DX; Jerrold; ISS.

Cablevision Industries - Oneida/Seneca Division (20,100 subscribers). Box 510, 426 Fairview Ave., Oneida, NY 13421. (315) 363-4832; FAX: (315) 363-4618. Henry Pearl, gen mgr; Sue Maha, mktg dir; Cathleen Dolan, loc adv dir; Mike Fuller, chief tech; Nancy Verkler, cust svc dir.
Area(s) Served: NY. Counties: Madison, Oneida, Onondaga, Oswego. Serving Canastota, Constantia, Lenox, Lincoln, Lysander, Munnsville, Oneida, Sherrill, Stockbridge, Van Buren, Vernon, Verona, Wampsville, West Monroe. Miles of Plant: 521. Homes Passed: 26,468. Homes Served: 20,100. *Channel Capacity:* In use: 29. *Basic Service:* Subscribers: 20,100; 10/31/93. Programming (via satellite): 27 chs. Programming (via microwave): 2 chs. Programming (off air): 8 chs. *Pay Services:* Total Pay Subscribers: 17,900; 11/01/92. (1) Pay Units: 7,276; 10/18/91. Programming (via satellite): HBO. (2) Pay Units: 2,701; 10/18/91. Programming (via satellite): Cinemax. (3) Pay Units: 1,573; 10/18/91. Programming (via satellite): Showtime. (4) Pay Units: 1,868; 10/18/91. Programming (via satellite): Disney. Pay Per View Subscribers: 6,000; 12/01/92. *Local Advertising Accepted. Equipment:* Scientific-Atlanta converters & software.

Cablevision Industries - Orange County Division (52,000 subscribers). Box 887, Industrial Dr., Middletown, NY 10940. (914) 692-5339; FAX: (914) 692-0778. William V. Jensen, gen mgr; Michael Maguire, mktg dir & loc adv dir; Al Vance, chief tech; Sharlene Helfgott, cust svc dir.
Area(s) Served: NY. Counties: Orange, Sullivan, Ulster. Serving Bloomingburg, Blooming Grove, Crawford, Deer Park, Gardiner, Goshen, Goshen Village, Hamptonburgh, Highlands, Highland Falls, Lloyd, Mamakating, Maybrook, Middletown, Montgomery, Montgomery Village, Mount Hope, Newburgh, New Paltz, Otisville, Plattekill, Port Jervis, Shawangunk, Walden, Wallkill, Washingtonville, Wawayanda, Wurtsboro. Pop: 162,600. Miles of Plant: 1,015. Homes Passed: 56,000. Homes Served: 52,000. *Channel Capacity:* 39. In use: 39. *Basic Service:* Subscribers: 52,000; 10/31/93. Programming (via satellite): 32 chs. Programming (off air): 10 chs. Pay Per View Subscribers: 20,000; 10/01/92. *Local Advertising Accepted. Equipment:* Jerrold addressable converters; Cable Service Group billing system.

Cablevision Industries - West Columbia (93,705 subscribers). Box 2989, West Columbia, SC 29171. (803) 791-4670; FAX: (803) 794-4399. Rick Keyser, gen mgr; Hal Schlenger, mktg dir; Venus Baughman, cust svc dir.
Area(s) Served: SC. Counties: Lexington, Richland. Serving Arcadia Lakes, Eastover, Forest Acres, Fort Jackson. Pop: 196,000. Miles of Plant: 1,737. Homes Passed: 90,674. Homes Served: 93,705. *Channel Capacity:* 36. In use: 36. *Basic Service:* Subscribers: 93,705; 10/31/93. Programming (via satellite): 31 chs. Programming (off air): 5 chs. *Local Advertising Accepted. Equipment:* Jerrold Satcom 6 converters; Jerrold A-H 4 controller.

Cablevision Industries - West Valley (94,000 subscribers). 9260 Topanga Canyon Blvd., Chatsworth, CA 91311. (818) 700-6500; FAX: (818) 998-2310. Tom Belcher, gen mgr; Bob Helmuth, mktg dir; Gary Miller, loc adv dir; Mike Rush, chief tech; Fran Smith, cust svc dir.

Multiple Systems Operators, Independent Owners & Cable Systems

Area(s) Served: CA. County: Los Angeles. Serving Western San Fernando Valley. Miles of Plant: 1,260. Homes Passed: 186,328. Homes Served: 94,000. *Channel Capacity:* 60. In use: 60. *Basic Service:* Subscribers: 94,000; 10/31/93. Programming (via satellite): 40 chs. Programming (off air): 13 chs. *Pay Services:* Total Pay Subscribers: 65,800; 12/01/92. (1) Pay Units: 30,922; 09/30/91. Programming (via satellite): HBO. (2) Pay Units: 12,746; 09/30/91. Programming (via satellite): Cinemax. (3) Pay Units: 9,795; 09/30/91. Programming (via satellite): Showtime. (4) Pay Units: 9,250; 09/30/91. Programming (via satellite): Disney. (5) Pay Units: 2,085; 09/30/91. Programming (via satellite): Playboy. (6) Pay Units: 5,475; 09/30/91. Programming (via satellite): Sports Channel. (7) Pay Units: 2,359; 09/30/91. Programming (via satellite): Bravo. *Local Advertising Accepted. Equipment:* Jerrold Starphone 7000 series; DP5 sidecar.

Cablevision Industries Ltd. (25,290 subscribers). 560 Patton St., Danville, VA 24541. (804) 797-4135; FAX: (804) 793-6920. Mark Mayhook, gen mgr; Jerry Lesser, mktg dir; Jim Linley, chief tech; Kathy S. Thomas, cust svc dir.
Area(s) Served: VA, NC. Counties: Cambell, Caswell, Pittsylvania. Serving Altavista, Chatham, Danville, Gretna. Pop: 45,000. Miles of Plant: 625. Homes Passed: 35,874. Homes Served: 25,290. *Channel Capacity:* 60. In use: 42. *Basic Service:* Subscribers: 25,290; 10/31/93. Programming (via satellite): 28 chs. Programming (via microwave): 1 ch. Programming (off air): 12 chs. *Pay Services:* Total Pay Subscribers: 10,300; 12/01/92. (1) Pay Units: 9,657; 10/05/91. Programming (via satellite): HBO. (2) Pay Units: 2,834; 10/05/91. Programming (via satellite): Cinemax. (3) Pay Units: 1,544; 10/05/91. Programming (via satellite): Showtime. *Local Advertising Accepted.*

Cablevision Industries of Cape Coral (30,000 subscribers). 1418 S.E. 10th St., Cape Coral, FL 33990. (813) 574-2020; FAX: (813) 574-2813. Sandy Vale, gen mgr; Marcia Mayls, mktg dir; Carl Spradlin, chief tech; Debbie White, cust svc dir.
Area(s) Served: FL. Counties: Charlotte, Lee. Serving Cape Coral, Fort Myers, Punta Gorda. Pop: 105,000. Miles of Plant: 609. Homes Passed: 34,000. Homes Served: 30,000. *Channel Capacity:* 60. In use: 60. *Basic Service:* Subscribers: 30,000; 10/31/93. Programming (via satellite): 48 chs. Programming (off air): 7 chs. *Pay Services:* Total Pay Subscribers: 11,917; 10/01/92. (1) Pay Units: 6,158; 10/24/91. Programming (via satellite): HBO. (2) Pay Units: 3,054; 10/24/91. Programming (via satellite): Showtime. (3) Pay Units: 2,593; 10/24/91. Programming (via satellite): Cinemax. (4) Pay Units: 1,204; 10/24/91. Programming (via satellite): The Movie Channel. *Local Advertising Accepted. Equipment:* Jerrold/OEC A114C converter control system; Jerrold DPV7 addressable impulse converters with built-in telephone modems for purchase reporting.

Cablevision Industries of Dearborn/Wayne (28,000 subscribers). 15200 Mercantile Dr., Dearborn, MI 48120. (313) 336-4300; FAX: (313) 271-2600. Rick Clark, gen mgr; Francis Tuck, cust svc dir.
Area(s) Served: MI. County: Wayne. Serving Dearborn, Wayne. Pop: 125,000. Miles of Plant: 478. Homes Passed: 43,100. Homes Served: 28,000. *Channel Capacity:* 54. In use: 53. *Basic Service:* Subscribers: 28,000; 10/31/93. Programming (via satellite): 33 chs. Programming (off air): 10 chs. *Local Advertising Accepted. Equipment:* Jerrold AH4E; MVP encoder; TelVue ANI ordering system.

Cablevision Industries of Saratoga Associates (26,900 subscribers). 174 West Ave., Saratoga Springs, NY 12866. (518) 587-7993; FAX: (518) 587-0223. Mark Loreno, gen mgr; George Shin, mktg dir; Molly Brindele, loc adv dir; Phil Piscitelli, chief tech; Barbara Munch, cust svc dir.
Area(s) Served: NY. Counties: Saratoga, Schenectady. Serving Ballston, Ballston Spa, Charlton, Glenville, Greenfield, Malta, Milton, Round Lake, Saratoga Springs, Wilton. Miles of Plant: 567. Homes Passed: 36,168. Homes Served: 26,900. *Channel Capacity:* 37. In use: 37. *Basic Service:* Subscribers: 26,900; 10/31/93. Programming (via microwave): 3 chs. Programming (off air): 5 chs. *Local Advertising Accepted. Equipment:* Jerrold converters and controller; Scientific-Atlanta headend; Magnavox line equipment.

Cablevision Industries of St. Tammany Division (30,000 subscribers). Box 890, Slidell, LA 70458. (504) 641-9251; FAX: (504) 649-3250. Kelly A. LeBouef, gen mgr; George Yelder, mktg dir & loc adv dir; Charles Thibodaux, chief tech; Diane Uli, cust svc dir.
Area(s) Served: LA. County: St. Tammany Parish. Serving Abita Springs, Covington, Lacombe, Madisonville, Mandeville, Pearl River, Slidell. Pop: 144,000. Miles of Plant: 1,034. Homes Passed: 34,766. Homes Served: 30,000. *Channel Capacity:* 35. In use: 35. *Basic Service:* Subscribers: 30,000; 10/31/93. *Pay Services:* Total Pay Subscribers: 20,542; 10/01/92. (1) Pay Units: 10,156; 10/01/91. Programming (via satellite): HBO. (2) Pay Units: 4,350; 10/01/91. Programming (via satellite): Showtime. (3) Pay Units: 3,865; 10/01/91. Programming (via satellite): Disney. *Local Advertising Accepted. Equipment:* Jerrold addressable converters.

Cablevision Industries of Tennessee (31,753 subscribers). 2177 Christmasville Rd., Jackson, TN 38305. (901) 424-3213; FAX: (901) 424-4257. Kim Kersey, gen mgr; Ron Crowder, chief tech.
Area(s) Served: TN. Counties: Benton, Crockett, Madison, McNairy, Obion, Pryor. Serving Adamsville, Alamo Bells, Bethel Springs, Camden, Jackson, Maury City, Newbern, Obion, Selmer, Trimble, Troy. Pop: 119,000. Miles of Plant: 750. Homes Passed: 34,000. Homes Served: 31,753. *Channel Capacity:* 60. In use: 48. *Basic Service:* Subscribers: 31,753; 10/31/93. Programming (via satellite): 4 chs. Programming (via microwave): 2 chs. Programming (off air): 6 chs. *Pay Services:* Total Pay Subscribers: 14,023; 10/01/92. (1) Pay Units: 7,051; 09/24/91. Programming (via satellite): HBO. (2) Pay Units: 3,488; 09/24/91. Programming (via satellite): Cinemax. (3) Pay Units: 2,380; 09/24/91. Programming (via satellite): Showtime. (4) Pay Units: 726; 09/24/91. Programming (via satellite): The Movie Channel. *Local Advertising Accepted.*

CVI (26,427 subscribers). 5615 Sapp Rd., Greensboro, NC 27409. (919) 854-3035; FAX: (919) 294-7957. Wayne Wright, gen mgr; John Smith, mktg dir; Randy Mims, chief tech; Zelda Lewis, cust svc dir.
Area(s) Served: NC. Counties: Guilford, Rockingham. Serving Greensboro, High Point. Miles of Plant: 1,300. Homes Passed: 41,580. Homes Served: 26,427. *Channel Capacity:* 52. *Basic Service:* Subscribers: 26,427; 09/07/93. Programming (via satellite): 37 chs. Programming (off air): 7 chs. *Pay Services:* Total Pay Subscribers: 13,450; 12/02/92. (1) Pay Units: 8,005; 10/04/91. Programming (via satellite): HBO. (2) Pay Units: 1,484; 10/04/91. Programming (via satellite): Disney. (3) Pay Units: 1,457; 10/04/91. Programming (via satellite): Showtime. (4) Pay Units: 1,219; 10/04/91. Programming (via satellite): Cinemax. (5) Pay Units: 809; 10/04/91. Programming (via satellite): The Movie Channel. *Local Advertising Accepted. Equipment:* Jerrold time equipment; Scientific-Atlanta headend.

CVI - Evans Division (30,689 subscribers). 10376 E. Colonial Dr., Orlando, FL 32817. (407) 277-4782; FAX: (407) 380-3174. Linda Shaffer, gen mgr; Lennie Baer, chief tech; Wanda Brownson, cust svc dir.
Area(s) Served: FL. Counties: Orange, Seminole. Serving Oviedo. Pop: 80,000. Miles of Plant: 668. Homes Passed: 45,628. Homes Served: 30,689. *Channel Capacity:* 52. In use: 50. *Basic Service:* Subscribers: 30,689; 10/31/93. Programming (via satellite): 35 chs. Programming (off air): 10 chs. *Pay Services:* Total Pay Subscribers: 14,299; 10/01/92. (1) Pay Units: 6,627; 10/01/91. Programming (via satellite): HBO. (2) Pay Units: 2,407; 10/01/91. Programming (via satellite): Showtime. (3) Pay Units: 1,271; 10/01/91. Programming (via satellite): The Movie Channel. (4) Pay Units: 2,655; 10/01/91. Programming (via satellite): Cinemax. *Local Advertising Accepted. Equipment:* CAK programmable converters; Jerrold addressable converters; Scientific-Atlanta tuners.

CVI of Long Beach (66,400 subscribers). 2931 Redondo Ave., Long Beach, CA 90806. (310) 424-4657; FAX: (310) 490-9981. Frank McNellis, gen mgr; Wm. Steve Rohan, mktg dir; David Kydd, loc adv dir; Jeremy Hooper, chief tech; Linda Edwards, cust svc dir.
Area(s) Served: CA. Serving Long Beach, Signal Hill. Pop: 360,000. Miles of Plant: 751. Homes Passed: 185,800. Homes Served: 66,400. *Channel Capacity:* 61. In use: 61. *Basic Service:* Subscribers: 66,400; 08/31/93. Programming (via satellite): 37 chs. Programming (off air): 17 chs. *Pay Services:* Total Pay Subscribers: 49,300; 08/31/93. (1) Pay Units: 8,500; 08/31/93. Programming (via satellite): The Movie Channel. (2) Pay Units: 7,600; 08/31/93. Programming (via satellite): Showtime. (3) Pay Units: 6,200; 08/31/93. Programming (via satellite): Disney. (4) Pay Units: 18,300; 08/31/93. Programming (via satellite): HBO. *Local Advertising Accepted. Equipment:* Provided by Scientific-Atlanta, Jerrold, Lemming & Catel.

CVI-LaFourche Division (20,000 subscribers). 1306 Ridgefield Rd., Thibodaux, LA 70301. (504) 446-8444; FAX: (504) 446-9849. Andrew Angelette, gen mgr; George Yelder, mktg dir. *Basic Service:* Subscribers: 20,000.

Genesee/Tri-County Cablevision (37,885 subscribers). 29 Cedar St., Batavia, NY 14020. (716) 344-2186; FAX: (716) 344-0913. Kathy Conley, gen mgr; Sue Maha, mktg dir; Mark Napoleone, loc adv dir; Dale Tompkins, chief tech; Fran Sprague, cust svc dir.
Area(s) Served: NY. Counties: Erie, Genesee, Livingston, Monroe, Niagara, Ontario, Orleans, Wyoming. Serving Albion, Alden, Alexander, Akron, Attica, Avon, Batavia, Bergen, Bloomfield, Caledonia, Carlton, Castile, Churchville, Conesus, Corfu, Elba, Gaines, Gainesville, Genesee, Genesee Falls, Groveland, Hartland, Honeoye Falls, Kendall, Leicester, Leroy, Lima, Livonia, Lyndonville, Marilla, Medina, Mendon, Middleport, Mount Morris, Mumford, Newstead, Nunda, Oakfield, Pavilion, Pembroke, Perry, Portage, Ridgeway, Royalton, Rush, Scottsville, Shelby, Silver Springs, Stafford, York, West Pavilion. Miles of Plant: 900. Homes Passed: 43,152. Homes Served: 37,885. *Channel Capacity:* 60. In use: 44. *Basic Service:* Subscribers: 37,885; 10/31/93. Programming (via satellite): 33 chs. Programming (off air): 13 chs. *Local Advertising Accepted. Equipment:* Eastern Microwave.

Wade Cablevision (56,000 subscribers). 1700 N. 49th St., Philadelphia, PA 19131. (215) 871-7870; FAX: (215) 581-6909. Joseph Candile, gen mgr; Victoria Milner, mktg dir; Irene Foster-James, cust svc dir.
Area(s) Served: PA. County: Philadelphia. Serving Philadelphia. Pop: 573,500. Miles of Plant: 597. Homes Passed: 155,000. Homes Served: 56,000. *Channel Capacity:* 78. In use: 77. *Basic Service:* Subscribers: 56,000; 10/31/93. Programming (via satellite): 48 chs. Programming (via microwave): 1 ch. Programming (off air): 10 ch. *Local Advertising Accepted. Equipment:* Tocom converters with VHPIII; Telvue ANI ordering system.

SMALLER SYSTEMS

Alabama - CVI-Daleville Division, Box 698, Daleville, AL 36322; (205) 598-6333. CVI-Dothan Division, Box 8247, Dothan, AL 36304; (205) 793-3383. **Florida** - CVI-Apollo Division, Box 68, Wimauma, FL 33598; (813) 633-1455. CVI-Belle Glade/Pahokee Division, 417 N.W. 16th St., Belle Glade, FL 33430; (407) 996-3086. CVI-Clewiston Division, 306 Bond St., Clewiston, FL 33440; (813) 983-9131. CVI-Golden Gate Division, 1610 40th Terr. S.W., Golden Gate, FL 33999; (813) 455-4114. CVI-LaBelle Division, 459 Devil's Garden Rd., LaBelle, FL 33935; (813) 675-4241. CVI-Live Oak Division, Box 419, Live Oak, FL 32068; (904) 362-3535. CVI-Lynn-Marion County Division, R.D. 2, Box 504 HA, E. State Rd. 40, Silver Springs, FL 32688; (904) 625-1640. CVI-Moore Haven Division, Box 159, Moore Haven, FL 33471; (813) 946-0580. CVI-Okeechobee Division, 107 N.W. Seventh Ave., Okeechobee, FL 33935; (813) 763-5566. CVI-Palatka Division, 507 St. John's Ave., Palatka, FL 32077; (904) 328-1567. CVI-Palmetto Division, Box 68, Wimauma, FL 33598; (800) 255-7856. CVI-St. Augustine Division, Box 1269, 801 S. Ponce DeLeon Blvd., St. Augustine, FL 32084; (904) 824-2813. **Georgia** - CVI-Fort Benning Division, Box 2008, Fort Benning, GA 31995; (404) 687-6324. Kansas - CVI-Colby Division, Box 587, Colby, KS 67701; (913) 462-7523. **Louisana** - CVI-Church Point Division, Box 297, Church Point, LA 70525; (318) 684-6301. CVI-Eunice Division, Box 1047, LA 70535; (318) 457-3058. CVI-Jennings Division, Box 100, Jennings, LA 70456; (318) 824-2981. CVI-LaFourche Division, Box 5178, Thibodaux, LA 70302; (504) 446-8444. CVI-Mandeville Division, Box 610, Mandeville, LA 70448; (504) 893-0212. CVI-Opelousas Division, Box 7187, Opelousas, LA 70571; (318) 948-3653. CVI-Pointe Coupee Division, Drawer 410, New Roads, LA 70760; (504) 638-9049. CVI-St. Tammany Division, Box 2470, Covington, LA 70434; (504) 892-6886. **Massachusetts** - CVI-Bridgewater Division, 86 Spring St., Bridgewater, MA 02324; (508) 697-6200. CVI-Fairhaven/Acushnet Division, Box D-10, Fairhaven, MA 02719; (508) 997-9407. **Mississippi** - CVI-Picayune Division, Box 667, Picayune, MS 39466; (601) 798-8080. New York - CVI-Oneida Seneca Division, Box 257, Baldwinsville, NY 13027; (315) 635-5514. CVI-Saugerties Division, 124 Partition St., Saugerties, NY 12477; (914) 246-2700. **North Carolina** - CVI-Carrboro Division, Box 309, Carrboro, NC 27510; (919) 967-7068. CVI-Elizabethtown Division, Box 2128, Elizabethtown, NC 28337; (919) 862-2006. CVI-Farmville Division, Box 52, Farmville, NC 27828; (919) 753-5522. CVI-Garner Division, Box 364, Garner, NC 27529; (919) 772-2553. CVI-Goldsboro Division, Box 2103, Goldsboro, NC 27530; (919) 735-2221. CVI-Red Springs Division, Box 751, Red Springs, NC 28377; (919) 843-3452. CVI-Reidsville Division, Box 4, Reidsville, NC 28377; (919) 843-3452. CVI-Selma Division, Box 99, Selma, NC 27576; (919) 965-6651. CVI-Wake Forest Division, NC

27587; (919) 556-6011. CVI-Wendell Division, Box 745, Wendell, NC 27591; (919) 365-9010. CVI-Wilson Division, Box 427, Wilson, NC 27893; (919) 291-0069. **Oklahoma** - CVI-Pryor Division, Box 279, Pryor, OK 74362; (918) 825-5975. **Pennsylvania** - CVI-Corry Division, 122 N. Center St., Corry, PA 16407; (814) 664-2411. CVI-Greenville Division, Box 264, Greenville, PA 16125; (412) 588-8000. CVI-Sayre Division, 142 W. Lockhart St., Sayre, PA 18840; (717) 888-9331. **South Carolina** - CVI-Batesburg/Twin Cities Division, Box 631, Batesburg, SC 29006; (803) 532-3814. CVI-Georgetown Division, Box 695, Georgetown, SC 29440; (803) 546-2475. CVI-Kingstree Division, Box 128, Kingstree, SC 29556; (803) 354-6842. CVI-Lake City Division, Box 1043, Lake City, SC 29560; (803) 394-8231. CVI-Manning Division, SC 29102; (803) 435-8051. CVI-St. Matthews Division, 125 E. Bridge St., St. Matthews, SC 29135; (803) 655-5703. CVI-Summerville Division, Box 2080, Summerville, SC 29484; (803) 871-7000. West Virginia - CVI-Clarksburg Division, Box 2508, Clarksburg, WV 26301; (304) 623-6792. CVI-Fairmont Division, Box 907, Fairmont, WV 26554; (304) 366-2881.

Cablevision Systems Corporation

One Media Crossways, Woodbury, NY 11797. (516) 364-8450; FAX: (516) 496-1780. Charles F. Dolan, CEO & chmn; James A. Kofalt, pres; William J. Bell, CFO; William J. Quinn, vp opns; Tim Williams, vp adv; Peter Low, vp progmg. Total Basic Subscribers: 1,979,209; Pay Cable Subscribers: 3,570,452; Number of Cable Systems: 25.

SYSTEMS WITH OVER 20,000 SUBSCRIBERS

A-R Cable Services Inc. (22,500 subscribers). 121 Mill St., Auburn, ME 04210. (207) 783-2023; FAX: (207) 786-2563. Rita Rossignol, gen mgr; Dan McManus, mktg dir; Jeff Grabarz, loc adv dir.
Area(s) Served: ME. Counties: Androscoggin, Oxford. Serving Auburn, Lewiston, Lisbon, Lisbon Falls, Mechanic Falls, Oxford, Sabattus. Pop: 84,000. Miles of Plant: 365. Homes Passed: 35,000. Homes Served: 22,500. *Channel Capacity:* 33. In use: 33. *Basic Service:* Subscribers: 22,500; 10/15/93. *Pay Services:* Total Pay Subscribers: 2,000; 10/15/93. Pay Per View Subscribers: 2,000; 10/15/93. *Local Advertising Accepted.*

A-R Cable Services-Maine Inc. (26,000 subscribers). Box 1405, 149 Target Industrial Cir., Bangor, ME 04401. (207) 942-4661; FAX: (207) 942-5426. William Fay, gen mgr; Deborah Chapman, mktg dir; Jeff Gabarz, loc adv dir; Robert Jones, chief tech; Patricia Rollins, cust svc dir.
Area(s) Served: ME. Counties: Hancock, Penobscot, Piscataquis, Somerset, Waldo. Serving Bangor, Bar Harbor, Belfast, Bradley, Brewer, Bucksport, Corrina, Dexter, Dover, Eddington, Ellsworth, Foxcroft, Hampton, Indian Island, Lincoln, Milford, Newport, Old Town, Orono, Orrington, Seasport, Southwest Harbor, Tremont, Winterport, Veazie, Verona Island, Winterport. Miles of Plant: 615. Homes Passed: 47,918. Homes Served: 26,000. *Channel Capacity:* 41. In use: 41. *Basic Service:* Subscribers: 26,000; 09/28/93. Programming (via satellite): 31 chs. Programming (via microwave): 6 chs. Programming (off air): 4 chs. *Local Advertising Accepted. Equipment:* Scientific-Atlanta 8536 converters; Scientific-Atlanta 6350 modulators; Scientific-Atlanta 6680 satellite receivers; Jerrold scramblers; Zenith PM1 converters.

Cablevision (180,000 subscribers). 7 Severance Cir., Cleveland Heights, OH 44118. (216) 291-4006; FAX: (216) 291-1631. Richard A. Coplan Jr., gen mgr; Barbara Brewer, mktg dir; Jeff Smith, loc adv dir; Sam Morabith, chief tech.
Area(s) Served: OH. Counties: Cuyahoga, Geauga, Lorain, Medina, Summit. Serving Gibsonburg. Pop: 724,500. Miles of Plant: 4,169. Homes Passed: 303,350. Homes Served: 180,000. *Channel Capacity:* 52. In use: 52. *Basic Service:* Subscribers: 180,000; 10/15/93. *Local Advertising Accepted. Equipment:* Jerrold & Scientific-Atlanta headend; Zenith, Jerrold & Scientific-Atlanta converters.

Cablevision of Boston (125,000 subscribers). 28 Travis St., Allston, MA 02134. (617) 787-6600; FAX: (617) 787-6606. Henry J. Ferris, gen mgr; John Hauenstein, mktg dir; Frank Vogelle, chief tech.
Area(s) Served: MA. County: Suffolk. Serving Allston, Back Bay, Beacon Hill, Brighton, Charleston, Chinatown, Dorchester, East Boston, Hyde Park, Jamaica Plain, Mattapan, North End, Penway, Roslindale, Roxbury, South Boston, South End, West Roxbury. Pop: 580,000. Homes Passed: 248,000. Homes Served: 125,000. *Channel Capacity:* 104. In use: 100. *Basic Service:* Subscribers: 125,000; 10/15/93. Pay Per View Subscribers: 100,266; 10/15/93. *Local Advertising Accepted.*

Cablevision of Chicago (77,000 subscribers). 820 Madison St., Oak Park, IL 60302. (708) 383-5850; FAX: (708) 383-9625. William P. Morton, gen mgr; Bob Lindenfelzer, mktg dir; Kenn Geer, loc adv dir; Don Ashton, chief tech; James Saunders, cust svc dir.
Area(s) Served: IL. Counties: DuPage, Cook. Serving Bedford Park, Bridgeview, Broadview, Burbank, Burnham, Cicero, Country Club Hills, Darien, Dixmoor, Downers Grove, East Hazel Crest, Evanston, Forest View, Hodgkins, Homewood, Justice, Lincolnwood, Lyons, McCook, Merrionette Park, Niles, North Riverside, Oak Park, Palos Heights, River Forest, Sauk Village, Stone Park, Summit, Willow Springs, Woodridge. Miles of Plant: 13,008. Homes Passed: 193,043. Homes Served: 77,000. *Channel Capacity:* 55. In use: 51. *Basic Service:* Subscribers: 77,000; 10/15/93. Programming (via satellite): 8 chs. Programming (off air): 8 chs. *Local Advertising Accepted. Equipment:* Pink Label; White Label; B-Max; Chro-Maxz; ciphers; scramblers.

Cablevision of Conneticut (100,000 subscribers). 28 Cross St., Norwalk, CT 06851. (203) 846-4700; FAX: (203) 846-9412. Irene McPhail Tripodi, gen mgr; Dom Garaffa, mktg dir; John Oleynick, loc adv dir; Tim Nagel, chief tech; Scott Allison, cust svc dir.
Area(s) Served: CT. County: Fairfield. Serving Darien, Easton, Greenwich, New Canaan, Norwalk, Redding, Stamford, Weston, Westport, Wilton. Homes Served: 100,000. *Basic Service:* Subscribers: 100,000; 10/15/93. *Local Advertising Accepted.*

Cablevision of Long Island (392,300 subscribers). One Media Crossways, Woodbury, NY 11797. (516) 364-8450; FAX: (516) 364-8026. Joe Azznara, gen mgr; Stephanie Reina, mktg dir; Shirley Stiles, cust svc dir.
Area(s) Served: NY. Counties: Nassau, Suffolk. Serving Babylon, Huntington, Islip. Homes Served: 392,300. *Channel Capacity:* 56. In use: 55. *Basic Service:* Subscribers: 392,300; 10/15/93. *Local Advertising Accepted.*

Cablevision of Long Island/Hauppauge (151,000 subscribers). 1600 Motor Pkwy., Hauppauge, NY 11788. (516) 348-6800; FAX: (516) 348-6872. Kate Adams, gen mgr; Thomas DeMarinis, mktg dir; Andrew Heeren, chief tech; Janet Andreassi, cust svc dir.
Area(s) Served: NY. County: Suffolk. Homes Served: 151,000. *Basic Service:* Subscribers: 151,000; 10/15/93.

Cablevision of Massachusetts (32,500 subscribers). 762 N. Main St., Leominster, MA 01453. (508) 537-4186; (508) 562-1675; FAX: (508) 537-4821; (508) 562-7591. Penny Contos, gen mgr; Dan Predegast, mktg dir; Thomas Garcia, chief tech; Rosemary Centola, cust svc dir.
Area(s) Served: MA. County: Worcester. Serving Fitchburg, Gardner, Leominster, Lunenburg, Templeton, Westminster. Miles of Plant: 480. Homes Passed: 44,743. Homes Served: 32,500. *Channel Capacity:* 62. In use: 62. *Basic Service:* Subscribers: 32,500; 10/15/93. Programming (via satellite): 39 chs. Programming (via microwave): 2 chs. Programming (off air): 12 chs. *Local Advertising Accepted. Equipment:* Scientific-Atlanta 6350 modulator, 9040 satellite receiver, encoder.

Cablevision of Michigan (46,000 subscribers). 4176 Commerical Ave., Kalamazoo, MI 49001. (616) 323-2236; FAX: (616) 323-0580. Tony Ruopoli, gen mgr; Jud Henrie, loc adv dir; Gary Wightman, chief tech; Denise Webber, cust svc dir.
Area(s) Served: MI. County: Kalamazoo. Serving Comstock, Cooper, Kalamazoo, Ohstemo, Parchment, Portage. Miles of Plant: 740. Homes Served: 46,000. *Channel Capacity:* 44. In use: 44. *Basic Service:* Subscribers: 46,000; 10/15/93. *Local Advertising Accepted.*

Cablevision of New Jersey Inc. (49,000 subscribers). 5 Legion Dr., Cresskill, NJ 07626. (201) 569-3720; FAX: (201) 569-3082. Richard N. Rasmus, gen mgr; Mark Quirk, chief tech.
Area(s) Served: NJ. Serving Bergenfield, Closter, Cresskill, Demarest, Dumont, Emerson, Fair Lawn, Harrington Park, Haworth, Hillsdale, New Milford, Northvale, Norwood, Old Tappan, Oradell, Paramus, River Vale, Rockleigh, Saddle River, Tenafly, Woodcliff Lake. Homes Served: 49,000. *Basic Service:* Subscribers: 49,000; 10/15/93.

Cablevision of Newark (43,776 subscribers). 360 Central Ave., Newark, NJ 07103. (201) 622-1727; FAX: (201) 642-2221. George Booth, gen mgr; Michael Casillo, mktg dir. *Basic Service:* Subscribers: 43,776; 10/15/93.

Cablevision of Rockford/Park (59,500 subscribers). 227 N. Wyman St., Rockford, IL 61109. (815) 962-4400; FAX: (815) 962-4400. Wiley Jones, gen mgr; K.C. McWilliams, mktg dir; Ellen Puckett, loc adv dir; Chuck Gelazus, chief tech; Nancy Berg, cust svc dir.
Area(s) Served: IL. County: Winnebago. Serving Loves Park, Machesney Park, New Milford, Rockford. Pop: 250,000. Miles of Plant: 989. Homes Passed: 91,000. Homes Served: 59,500. *Channel Capacity:* 35. In use: 35. *Basic Service:* Subscribers: 59,500; 12/31/92. Programming (via satellite): 22 chs. Programming (off air): 7 chs. *Pay Services:* Total Pay Subscribers: 18,000; 12/31/92. Pay Per View Subscribers: 17,500; 12/31/92. *Local Advertising Accepted.*

Cablevision of Southern Connecticut (84,000 subscribers). 122 River St., Bridgeport, CT 06604. (203) 333-5883. Irene McPhail Tripodi, gen mgr; Dom Garaffa, mktg dir; John Oleynick, loc adv dir; Scott Allison, cust svc dir.
Area(s) Served: CT. Counties: Fairfield, New Haven. Serving Fairfield, Milford, Orange, Stratford, Woodbridge. Homes Served: 84,000. *Basic Service:* Subscribers: 84,000; 9/30/93. *Local Advertising Accepted.*

Cablevision Systems of Westchester (40,500 subscribers). 6 Executive Plaza, Yonkers, NY 10701. (914) 378-8960; FAX: (914) 378-8974. Robert L. Brewer, gen mgr; Pete Frasca, mktg dir; Jeff Cardoso, chief tech; Bill Shelley, cust svc dir.
Area(s) Served: NY. County: Westchester. Serving Yonkers. Pop: 72,000. Miles of Plant: 412. Homes Passed: 72,000. Homes Served: 40,500. *Channel Capacity:* 39. In use: 39. *Basic Service:* Subscribers: 40,500; 10/15/93. *No Local Advertising Accepted.*

Cablevision's East End System (58,059 subscribers). 254 Old Country Rd. (Rt. 58), Riverhead, NY 11901. (516) 727-6300; FAX: (516) 727-3186. Thomas Dolan, gen mgr; Jerry Corsaletti, mktg dir; Kevin Lanzer, chief tech; Allen Earle, cust svc dir.
Area(s) Served: NY. County: Suffolk. Serving East Hampton, Riverhead. Miles of Plant: 1,400. Homes Passed: 73,923. Homes Served: 58,059. *Channel Capacity:* 60. In use: 60. *Basic Service:* Subscribers: 58,059; 10/15/93. *Local Advertising Accepted.*

U.S. Cable (Gulf Coast) (75,998 subscribers). 4435 Gulf Breeze Pkwy., Gulf Breeze, FL 32561. (904) 932-5208; FAX: (904) 932-9237. David Fyffe, gen mgr. *Basic Service:* Subscribers: 75,998; 10/15/93.

U.S. Cable of North Carolina (44,100 subscribers). 512B N. Main St., Hendersonville, NC 28792. (704) 693-1959; FAX: (704) 692-2253. Craig Simon, gen mgr; Bill Barbour, mktg dir. *Basic Service:* Subscribers: 44,100; 10/15/93.

SMALLER SYSTEMS

Arkansas - Paragould Cablevision Inc., Box 1365, Valley S. Shopping Ctr., Paragould, AR 72451; (501) 239-2185. **Kentucky** - US Cable, 76 North Main, Benton, KY 42025; (800) 999-8028. **Missouri** - Bootheel Video, Inc., 501 Ward Ave., Caruthersville, MO 63830; (314) 333-1148. US Cable, 218 South St., 2nd Fl., Excelsior Springs, MO 64024; (816) 637-4500. **New York** - Cablevision, R.D. #2, 3 Agway Dr., Rensselaer, NY 12144; (518) 283-3653. Cablevision, 3458 Riverside Dr., Wellsville, NY 14895; (716) 593-1310. **Ohio** - Cablevision, 300 W. Cedar St., Gibsonburg, OH 43431; (419) 637-2189. Nath Coast Cable, 3300 Lakeside Ave., Cleveland, OH 44114; (216) 575-8016.

Calavision

Suite 104, 23642 Calabasas Rd., Calabasas Park, CA 91302-1592. (818) 222-5366; FAX: (818) 222-5377. Ira Weschlei, pres; Gary Spire, vp opns; Barry Spero, vp mktg. Owned by Ira Weschlei. Total Basic Subscribers: 2,698; Pay Cable Subscribers: 1,756; Number of Cable Systems: 2.

Calco Cable Co. Inc.

Box 988, 202 S. Ann St., Port Lavaca, TX 77979. (512) 552-6342. George F. Rhodes, pres; Marion A. Rhodes, vp. Total Basic Subscribers: 1,276; Number of Cable Systems: 2.

SMALLER SYSTEMS

Texas - Bloomington Cable Co., Box 988, Port Lavaca, TX 77979. Kennedy Cable Co., Box 988, Port Lavaca, TX 77979.

Multiple Systems Operators, Independent Owners & Cable Systems

California-Oregon Broadcasting Inc.

Box 5M, 125 S. Fir St., Medford, OR 97501. (503) 779-5555; FAX: (503) 779-5564. Patsy Smullin, pres; Roger Harris, vp. Total Basic Subscribers: 9,300; Number of Cable Systems: 3.

SMALLER SYSTEMS

Oregon - Crestview Cable TV, 103 Hwy. 82, Suite 1-A, Enterprise, OR 97828. Crestview Cable TV, 35 S.E. C St., Suite E, Madras, OR 97741. Crestview Cable TV, 190 W. 4th, Prineville, OR 97754.

Jewel B. Callaham

Box 817, 108 N. Park Dr., Broken Bow, OK 74728. (405) 584-3340. Jewel B. Callaham, pres; Angela Whisenhunt, vp opns & vp mktg. Total Basic Subscribers: 1,840; Number of Cable Systems: 1.

SMALLER SYSTEMS

Oklahoma - Broken Bow TV, 108 N. Park Dr., Broken Bow, OK 74728.

Callais Cablevision Inc.

Drawer 788, Golden Meadow, LA 70357. FAX: (504) 475-7111. Harold Callais, pres; Corey Callais, vp opns & vp mktg. Total Basic Subscribers: 10,500; Number of Cable Systems: 1.

Cambridge Communications

Suite 204, 7031 Orchard Lake Rd., West Bloomfield, MI 48322. (313) 855-9448; FAX: (313) 855-0835. Glenn Healey, vp; Don Arndt, vp; Tom Gelardi, vp. Total Basic Subscribers: 16,000; Number of Cable Systems: 3.

SMALLER SYSTEMS

New Mexico - Valencia County Cable TV, 106 N. Sixth St., Belen, NM 87002; (505) 864-2226. **Oregon** - Columbia Basin Cable TV, 611 Sixth St., Vmitilla, OR 97882; (503) 922-5759. **Texas** - Willow Park Cable TV, 100D El Chico Trail, Willow Park, TX 76087; (817) 441-8073.

Caribbean Communications Corporation

One Beltjen Pl., St. Thomas, VI 00802. (809) 776-2150; FAX: (809) 776-5029. Norman Knight, chmn; Randolph H. Knight, pres; Andrea L. Martin, vp opns; Jacob S. Kohn, vp. Total Basic Subscribers: 16,098; Pay Cable Subscribers: 13,843; Number of Cable Systems: 1.

SMALLER SYSTEMS

Virgin Islands - St. Thomas-St. John Cable TV, One Beltjen Pl., St. Thomas, VI 00802; (809) 776-2150; 16,098 subs.

Carlys Cable Vision

Box 222, Sulphur, LA 70664. (318) 583-4973; FAX: (318) 583-2089. John Henning, pres; Raymond Hennigan, vp mktg. Total Basic Subscribers: 1,479; Pay Cable Subscribers: 1,289; Number of Cable Systems: 1.

Cass Cable TV Inc.

Box 200, Virginia, IL 62691. (217) 452-7725. Gerald Gill, pres; Russell Decker, vp opns; Donna Troutman, vp mktg. Total Basic Subscribers: 13,000; Pay Cable Subscribers: 12,666; Number of Cable Systems: 4.

Catalina Cable TV Co.

222 Metropole Ave., Avalon, CA 90704. (310) 510-0255; FAX: (310) 510-2565. Ralph J. Morrow Jr., CEO & vp opns; Sandra Enos, vp mktg. Total Basic Subscribers: 1,118; Number of Cable Systems: 1.

Catawba Services Inc.

203 Saluda St., Rock Hill, SC 29731; (803) 329-9000; FAX: (803) 329-2600. William Baty, pres; Bill Baty Jr., vp opns; John M. Barnes Jr., vp mktg. Total Basic Subscribers: 19,075; Pay Cable Subscribers: 10,109; Number of Cable Systems: 4.

SMALLER SYSTEMS

South Carolina - Lancaster Cable, 209 Wylie St., Lancaster, SC 29270; (803) 283-1000. Rock Hill Cable, 203 Saluda St., Rock Hill, SC 29731; (803) 329-9000. Winnsboro Cablevision Inc., Box 3-F, Rt. 3, Winnsboro, SC 29180; (803) 635-6459. York Cable TV, Box 98, 730 Hwy., 321 Bypass, York, SC 29745; (803) 684-1012.

CATV Service Inc.

115 Mill St., Danville, PA 17821. (717) 275-8410; FAX: (717) 275-3888. Margaret Walsonavich, pres; Ron Podlesny, vp opns. Total Basic Subscribers: 16,500; Pay Cable Subscribers: 3,800; Number of Cable Systems: 1.

Center Broadcasting Co.

307 San Augustine St., Center, TX 75935. (409) 598-2333; FAX: (409) 598-9537. Dan Dillinger, vp opns & vp mktg. Total Basic Subscribers: 2,690; Number of Cable Systems: 2.

SMALLER SYSTEMS

Texas - Center Cable TV, 307 San Augustine St., Center, TX 75935. San Augustine Cable TV, San Augustine, TX.

Century Communications Corporation

50 Locust Ave., New Canaan, CT 06840. (203) 972-2000; FAX: (203) 966-9228. Leonard Tow, CEO & chmn; Bernard P. Gallagher, pres; Walter A. Kinash, vp opns; Robert E. Morrison, vp; Claire L. Tow, vp; Andrew Tow, vp. Total Basic Subscribers: 907,000; Pay Cable Subscribers: 453,000; Number of Cable Systems: 55.

REGIONS

National: Century Cable Television Division, 111 Presidential Blvd., Bala Cynwyd, PA 19004; Daniel E. Gold. *Southeast:* Century Cable Television Division, 1967 Glenn Ave., Brunswick, GA 31520; Kenneth P. Rhoades. *Southwest:* Century Cable Television Division, 2939 Nebraska Ave., Santa Monica, CA 90404; William J. Rosendahl.

SYSTEMS WITH OVER 20,000 SUBSCRIBERS

Cable TV of Greater San Juan (102,000 subscribers). One Manuel Camanas St., Tres Monjitas Industrial Park, San Juan, PR 00918. (809) 766-0909; FAX: (809) 250-6532. Francisco Toste, gen mgr; Juliet Giamartino, mktg dir; Francisco Framic, loc adv dir; Guillermo Schwartz, chief tech; Rita Roman, cust svc dir.
Area(s) Served: PR. Serving Bayamon, Carolina, Guaynabo, San Juan, Trujillo Alto. Pop: 1,500,000. Miles of Plant: 1,300. Homes Passed: 230,000. Homes Served: 102,000. *Channel Capacity:* 56. In use: 52. *Basic Service:* Subscribers: 102,000; 08/30/93. Programming (via satellite): 44 chs. Programming (off air): 11 chs. *Pay Services:* Total Pay Subscribers: 71,000; 08/30/93. Pay Per View Subscribers: 45,000; 08/30/93. *Local Advertising Accepted. Equipment:* Scientific-Atlanta headend; Magnavox & Texscan amplifiers.

Century Cable (20,000 subscribers). Box 1945, 313 N. Eighth St., El Centro, CA 92244. (619) 352-8663; FAX: (619) 353-8800. Tom Mixon, gen mgr; Shirley Elmore, mktg dir; Lulu Montes, cust svc dir.
Area(s) Served: CA. County: Imperial. Serving Brawley, Calexico, El Centro, Heber, Holtville, Imperial, Seeley, Westmorland. Pop: 100,000. Miles of Plant: 280. Homes Passed: 30,000. Homes Served: 20,000. *Channel Capacity:* 40. In use: 40. *Basic Service:* Subscribers: 20,000; 11/15/93. Programming (via satellite): 16 chs. Programming (via microwave): 6 chs. Programming (off air): 3 chs. *No Local Advertising Accepted. Equipment:* Magnavox line equipment; Jerrold headend.

Century Cable (23,000 subscribers). Box 1798, 100 Industrial Dr., Owensboro, KY 42301. (502) 685-2991; FAX: (502) 685-0854. Scott Douglas, gen mgr; Barbara Taylor, mktg dir.
Area(s) Served: KY. Counties: Daviess, Henderson, Webster. Serving Clay, Corydon, Dixon, Henderson, Maceo, Masonville, Newman, Owensboro, Philpot, Poole, Reed, Smithmills, Sorgho, Stanley, Thruston, Utica, Wheatcroft. Miles of Plant: 635. Homes Passed: 32,000. Homes Served: 23,000. *Channel Capacity:* 46. In use: 45. *Basic Service:* Subscribers: 23,000; 11/30/92. *Pay Services:* Total Pay Subscribers: 6,000; 09/15/91. *Local Advertising Accepted.*

Century Cable Television (42,000 subscribers). 2767 N. Mayfair Rd., Wauwatosa, WI 53222. (414) 259-1233. James T. Hough, gen mgr; Sandy Fast, mktg dir; Jeff Miskie, chief tech; Sharon Steinhart, cust svc dir.
Area(s) Served: WI. Counties: Milwaukee, Ozaukee, Washington, Waukesha. Serving Brookfield, Butler, Delafield, Elm Grove, Germantown, Hartland, Merton, Mukwonago, Pewaukee, Port Washington, St. Francis, Saulkville, Theinsville, Waukesha, Wauwatosa, West Milwaukee. Pop: 200,000. Miles of Plant: 1,000. Homes Passed: 80,000. Homes Served: 42,000. *Channel Capacity:* 45. In use: 45. *Basic Service:* Subscribers: 42,000; 11/15/93. Pay Per View Subscribers: 8,000; 11/15/91. *Local Advertising Accepted.*

Century Cable TV - Van Nuys, CA (36,649 subscribers). 14165 Bessemer St., Van Nuys, CA 91401. (818) 374-1200; FAX: (818) 988-8038. Rick Mathis, gen mgr; Lynn Balsamo, mktg dir; Mary Foster, cust svc dir.
Area(s) Served: CA. Counties: Los Angeles, Ventura. Serving Bel Air, Bell Canyon, Encino, Los Angeles, North Hollywood, Sherman Oaks, Studio City, Tarzana, Woodland Hills. Homes Served: 36,649. *Channel Capacity:* 41. In use: 41. *Basic Service:* Subscribers: 36,649; 11/30/92. *Pay Services:* Total Pay Subscribers: 30,182; 11/30/92. *Local Advertising Accepted.*

Century Cable TV - West Hollywood, CA (20,458 subscribers). 14165 Bessemer St., Van Nuys, CA 91401. (818) 374-1200; FAX: (818) 988-8038. Rick Mathis, gen mgr; Lynn Balsamo, mktg dir; Mary Foster, cust svc dir.
Area(s) Served: CA. County: Los Angeles. Serving Beverly Hills, West Hollywood. Homes Served: 20,458. *Basic Service:* Subscribers: 20,548; 11/30/92. *Pay Services:* Total Pay Subscribers: 10,893; 11/30/92.

Century Cable TV of Huntington (21,500 subscribers). 51 W. Sixth Ave., Huntington, WV 25701. (304) 522-8226; FAX: (304) 523-5493. Stephen Frantela, gen mgr; Stacey Grounds, mktg dir & loc adv dir; Joe Jarrell, chief tech.
Area(s) Served: WV. County: Cabell. Serving Barbourville, East Pea Ridge, Guyan Estates, Lesage, West Pea Ridge. Miles of Plant: 370. Homes Passed: 41,000. Homes Served: 21,500. *Channel Capacity:* 36. In use: 36. *Basic Service:* Subscribers: 21,500; 11/15/93. *Pay Services:* Total Pay Subscribers: 4,400; 11/01/92. *Local Advertising Accepted. Equipment:* Scientific-Atlanta headend.

Century Cable TV of Longview (22,000 subscribers). 750 11th Ave., Longview, WA 98632. (206) 577-2599. Jim Elliot, gen mgr; Crystal Meade, mktg dir; Dave Andrew, loc adv dir.
Area(s) Served: WA. County: Cowlitz. Serving Castle Rock, Kalama, Kelso, Rose Valley, Silver Lake, Toutle, Woodland. Pop: 45,000. Miles of Plant: 300. Homes Passed: 25,500. Homes Served: 22,000. *Channel Capacity:* 38. In use: 38. *Basic Service:* Subscribers: 22,000; 11/01/92. *Local Advertising Accepted.*

Century Cable TV of Morgantown (31,000 subscribers). Box 599, Dellslow, WV 26531. (304) 292-6561; FAX: (304) 296-6518. Mark Lustfield, gen mgr & loc adv dir; Tammy Straface, mktg dir; Doug Lanham, chief tech; Linda Simon, cust svc dir.
Area(s) Served: WV. Counties: Harrison, Marion, Moongalia, Preston, Taylor. Serving Carolina, Fairmont, Grafton, Grenville, Monongah, Morgantown, Osage, Rivesville, Rowlesburg, Star City, Worthington. Miles of Plant: 901. Homes Passed: 40,150. Homes Served: 31,000. *Channel Capacity:* 36. In use: 36. *Basic Service:* Subscribers: 31,000; 11/15/93. *Pay Services:* Total Pay Subscribers: 6,300; 11/01/92. *Local Advertising Accepted.*

Century Cable TV of Muncie (28,875 subscribers). 3601 W. Eighth St., Muncie, IN 47307. (317) 284-3357; FAX: (317) 284-9536. Phil Hopkins, gen mgr; Jennifer Marcum, mktg dir; Bill Derringer, chief tech.
Area(s) Served: IN. Counties: Delaware, Randolph. Serving Cowan, Daleville, Desoto, Farmland, Muncie, Oakville, Parker City, Selma, Yorktown. Homes Served: 28,875. *Channel Capacity:* 38. In use: 38. *Basic Service:* Subscribers: 28,875; 11/15/93. *Local Advertising Accepted.*

Century Cable TV of Yuma (24,000 subscribers). 1289 Second Ave., Yuma, AZ 85364. (602) 782-9853; FAX: (602) 783-0329. Karen Fleetwood, gen mgr; Melanie Richardson, mktg dir; Glenn Montgomery, chief tech.
Area(s) Served: AZ, CA. Counties: Imperial, Yuma. Serving Marine Corps Air Station, San Luis, Somerton, Winterhaven, Yuma, Yuma Proving Ground. Pop: 58,000. Homes Served: 24,000. *Channel Capacity:* 36. In use: 35. *Basic Service:* Subscribers: 24,000; 11/15/93. *Local Advertising Accepted. Equipment:* RCA & Scientific-Atlanta headends; Magnavox amplifiers; Comm/Scope cable.

Century S.W. Cable TV Inc. (57,476 subscribers). 2939 Nebraska Ave., Santa Monica, CA 90404. (310) 829-7079; FAX: (310) 315-0405. Greg Boucher, mktg dir; Helen Shepard, cust svc dir.

Multiple Systems Operators, Independent Owners & Cable Systems

Area(s) Served: CA. County: Los Angeles. Serving Brentwood, Marina Del Rey, Pacific Palisades, Santa Monica, West Los Angeles, Westwood. Homes Served: 57,476. *Channel Capacity:* 50. In use: 50. *Basic Service:* Subscribers: 57,476; 11/30/92. *Pay Services:* Total Pay Subscribers: 32,103; 11/30/92. Pay Per View Subscribers: 1,200; 09/07/93. *Local Advertising Accepted.*

Century S.W. Cable TV Inc. - Eagle Rock, CA (38,361 subscribers). 4344 Eagle Rock Blvd., Los Angeles, CA 90041. (213) 258-3252; FAX: (213) 255-1901. Manuel Martinez, gen mgr; Vicki Call, mktg dir; Steve Silveira, chief tech; Delia Sanchez, cust svc dir.
Area(s) Served: CA. County: Los Angeles. Serving Atwater, China Town, Eagle Rock, Echo Park, El Sereno, Glassel Park, Highland Park, Hollywood, Las Feliz, Lincoln Heights, Montecito, Monterey Hills, Mount Silver Lake, Washington. Homes Served: 38,361. *Channel Capacity:* 40. In use: 40. *Basic Service:* Subscribers: 38,361; 11/15/93. *Pay Services:* Total Pay Subscribers: 16,870; 11/30/92. *Local Advertising Accepted.*

Colorado Cablevision Inc. (90,000 subscribers). 213 N. Union Blvd., Colorado Springs, CO 80909. (719) 633-6616; FAX: (719) 633-0085. Kevin Hyman, gen mgr; Becky Hurley, mktg dir; Dave Brickhaus, loc adv dir; Al Fulk, chief tech; Sally Candelario, cust svc dir.
Area(s) Served: CO. County: El Paso. Serving Colorado Springs, Fountain, Green Mountain Falls, Manitou Springs, U.S. Air Force Academy. Homes Served: 90,000. *Channel Capacity:* 60. In use: 60. *Basic Service:* Subscribers: 90,000; 11/15/93.

SMALLER SYSTEMS

Alabama - Century Alabama Corp., Box 889, 613 Gault Ave. N., Fort Payne, AL 35967. Century Cullman Corp., 1854 Hwy. 69 N.E., Cullman, AL 36331. Century Enterprise Cable, Box 870, 205 Ouida St., Enterprise, AL 36331. **California -** Century Cable of Northern California, Box 807, 175 East N. St., Benicia, CA 94510. Century Cable Of Northern California, Box 758, 5327 Jacuzzi St., Richmond, CA 94804. Century Cable of Northern Califomia, 6650 Crescent, #11, Ventura, CA 93003. Century Cable of Southern California, Box 547, 185 E. Alder St., Brea, CA 92621. Century Cable of Southern California, 2923/25 W. 182nd St., Redondo Beach, CA 90278. Century Mendocino Cable TV Inc., Box 178, 1060 N. State St., Ukiah, CA 95482. Hi-Desert Cable, 7500 Kickapoo Trail, Yucca Valley, CA 92286-0280. **Connecticut -** Century Cable Management Corp., One Hill Top Rd., Norwich, CT 08360. Century Norwich Corp., One Hill Top Rd., Norwich, CT 08360. **Florida -** Century Cable, 218 W. Pennsylvania, Dunnelon, FL 32630. Century Cable, Box 1377, Nassau Plaza-Suite & Hwy. A1A, Yulee, FL 32097. **Georgia -** Rentavision of Brunswick, Box 1319, 1967 Glenn Ave., Brunswick, GA 31521. **Idaho -** Century Cable, Box 668, 345 E. Second N., Mountain Home, ID 83647. **Indiana -** Huntington CATV Inc., Box 761, 812 W. Tipton, Huntington, IN 46750. Warrick Cablevision, Box 305, 5088 S. Plaza Dr., Newburgh, IN 47380. **Kansas -** Century Kansas Cable Corp., 110 W. Second St., Liberal, KS 67901-0069. **Massachusetts -** Century Berkshire Cable, Box 667, Silver St. & Rt. 20, Lee, MA 01238. **Mississippi -** Century Greenwood Corp., Box 1119, 622 Hwy. 82 W., Greenwood, MS 38930. **New Mexico -** Century New Mexico Cable, Box 941, 622 W. Ave. D, Lovington, NM 88260. Century New Mexico Cable, Box 885, 708 E. Second St., Portales, NM 88130. Century New Mexico Cable, Box 1320, 1014 Pope St., Silver City, NM 88062. Century New Mexico Cable, Box 1428, 1808 S. First St., Tucumcari, NM 88401. Clear Site Cable Inc., 2530 Hot Springs Blvd., Las Vegas, NM 88701. Los Alamos Cable TV, Box 1250, 1225 Diamond Dr., Los Alamos, NM 87544. Sun Cable TV, 109 N. Silver, Deming, NM 88030. Taos Cable TV, Box 1854, S. Santa Fe Rd., Taos, NM 87571. **New York -** Valley Video Inc., Box 551, R.D. #1, River Rd., Norwich, NY 13815. **North Carolina -** Century Cable, Box 109, 222 Wilkinson Dr. N., Laurinburg, NC 28353-1109. **Ohio -** Century Ohio Cable TV Corp., Box 1508, 807 Washington St., Portsmouth, OH 45662. Century Ohio Cable TV Corp., Box 149, 289 Elm St., Struthers, OH 44471. **Pennsylvania -** Century Lykens Cable Corp., 690 N. Second St., Lykens, PA 17048. Century Shenango Cable TV Inc., Box 1008, 155 Snyder Rd., Hermitage, PA 18148. **Virginia -** Century Virginia Corp., Box 1300, 838 Park Ave. N.E., Norton, VA 24273. **West Virginia -** Wilderness Cable Co., Box 100, Rt. 34 N., Red House, WV 25168. **Wyoming -** Century Wyoming Cable Corp., 1020 Main St., Evanston, WY 82930.

Chambers Communications Corp.

Box 7009, 2225 Coburg Rd., Eugene, OR 97401. (503) 485-5611; FAX: (503) 342-2695. Carolyn S. Chambers, pres; Jim Plummer, CFO; Robert D. Towe, vp opns; Sylvia Sycamore, vp; Scott D. Chambers, vp. Owned by Carolyn S. Chambers. Total Basic Subscribers: 90,000; Pay Cable Subscribers: 32,000; Number of Cable Systems: 9.

SYSTEMS WITH OVER 20,000 SUBSCRIBERS

Chambers Cable (30,000 subscribers). Box 1559, Chico, CA 95927. (916) 342-4242; FAX: (916) 343-3818. Cort C. Schreiber, gen mgr; Sue Linders, mktg dir; Gary Harmon, chief tech; Paula Murphy, cust svc dir.
Area(s) Served: CA. Counties: Butte, Glenn, Tehema. Serving Chico, Corning, Durham, Hamilton City, Willows. Pop: 74,000. Miles of Plant: 427. Homes Passed: 47,000. Homes Served: 30,000. *Channel Capacity:* 31. In use: 31. *Basic Service:* Subscribers: 30,000; 10/15/93. Programming (via satellite): 23 chs. Programming (via microwave): 3 chs. Programming (off air): 7 chs. *Local Advertising Accepted.*

Channelvision Cable TV Inc.

No. 7, 2525 East St., Texarkana, AR 75502. (501) 772-8028; FAX: (501) 773-2105. Sharon Hamilton, vp opns. Total Basic Subscribers: 4,198; Number of Cable Systems: 1.

Charter Cable Inc.

300 Main St., Cincinnati, OH 45202. (513) 421-7373; FAX: (513) 421-0718. J. Grant Troja, pres; Ken Jaskot, vp opns; Tom Fischer, vp mktg. Total Basic Subscribers: 7,000; Pay Cable Subscribers: 1,400; Number of Cable Systems: 4.

Cherokee Cablevision Inc.

Box 487, Cherokee, NC 28719. (704) 497-4861; FAX: (704) 497-4983. Ken Blankenship, pres; Delores Murphy, vp opns. Total Basic Subscribers: 2,500; Number of Cable Systems: 1.

Chibardun Cable TV Cooperative

Box 164, 110 N. Second Ave., Dallas, WI 54733. (715) 837-1011; FAX: (715) 837-1196. Merlin Haugestuin, CEO; Rick Vergin, vp opns. Owned by Chibardun Telephone Cooperative. Total Basic Subscribers: 1,850; Pay Cable Subscribers: 1,027; Number of Cable Systems: 1.

Cim Tel Cable Inc.

Box 266, Manford, OK 74044. (918) 865-3314. H.Z. Gotcher, pres; Robert Berryman, vp opns & vp mktg. Total Basic Subscribers: 4,123; Pay Cable Subscribers: 1,800; Number of Cable Systems: 1.

Citizens Telephone Co.

Box 1177, Brevard, NC 28712. (704) 884-9011; FAX: (704) 885-2300. C.W. Pickelseimer Jr., pres. Total Basic Subscribers: 7,900; Number of Cable Systems: 1.

SMALLER SYSTEMS

North Carolina - Sylvan Valley CATV, Box 1177, Brevard, NC 28712.

City of Baxter Springs CATV

Box 577, Baxter Springs, KS 66713. (316) 856-2114; FAX: (316) 856-5483. Jim Thiele, vp opns; Beth Johnson, vp mktg; Darla Snook, vp. Owned by City of Baxter Springs. Total Basic Subscribers: 1,473; Pay Cable Subscribers: 447; Number of Cable Systems: 1.

Clearview Cable TV Inc.

Box 247 AA, Rt. 4, Lewisburg, WV 24901. (304) 645-1397. Van James II, pres & vp opns. Total Basic Subscribers: 1,200; Number of Cable Systems: 1.

Clearview CATV Inc.

394 Highland Dr., Mountville, PA 17554. (717) 285-3746. Owned by William Domurad, Alvin Miller, Brandt Warner. Total Basic Subscribers: 4,674; Number of Cable Systems: 1.

SMALLER SYSTEMS

Maryland - Clearview CATV, 2242 Conowingo Rd., Bel Air, MD 21015.

Clearwater Cablevision

Box 484, 112 S. Lee St., Clearwater, KS 67026. (316) 584-2077. Gordon Mikesell, pres; Maxine Mikesell, vp mktg; Kendall Mikesell, vp. Total Basic Subscribers: 1,529; Number of Cable Systems: 1.

Clinton Cable TV Co. Inc.

355 S. Main, Clinton, IN 47842. (317) 832-3586. George Nicholls, pres. Total Basic Subscribers: 4,400; Number of Cable Systems: 1.

Coaxial Cable TV Corporation

Suite 130, 220 W. Plum St., Edinboro, PA 16412. (814) 734-1424; FAX: (814) 734-8898. Michael Meade, pres. Owned by Times Publishing Co. Total Basic Subscribers: 4,000; Pay Cable Subscribers: 950; Number of Cable Systems: 1.

Coaxial Communications

3770 E. Livingston Ave., Columbus, OH 43227. (614) 236-1292; FAX: (614) 236-1737. Joel S. Rudich, CEO & pres; Nick Nicholls, vp mktg & vp progmg; Daniel McKay, vp; Tom Wilson, vp; Don Lewis, vp. Owned by Barry Silverstein, Dennis McGillicuddy, Steve McVoy. Total Basic Subscribers: 107,000; Pay Cable Subscribers: 83,000; Number of Cable Systems: 8.

SYSTEMS WITH OVER 20,000 SUBSCRIBERS

Coaxial Communications of Central Ohio Inc. (79,000 subscribers). 3770 E. Livingston Ave., Columbus, OH 43227. (614) 236-1292; FAX: (614) 236-1737. Joel S. Rudich, gen mgr; Harry "Nick" E. Nicholls, mktg dir; William Gilbert, loc adv dir; Daniel McKay, chief tech; Steve Crane, cust svc dir.
Area(s) Served: OH. Counties: Delaware, Fairfield, Franklin, Licking, Pickaway. Serving Amanda, Berlin, Blendon, Bloom, Brice, Brown, Canal Winchester, Columbus, Delaware Twp., Enta, Gahanna, Genoa, Greenfield, Hamilton, Harlem, Harrison, Jefferson, Jersey, Liberty, Lima, Lithopolis, Madison, Monroe, New Albany, Orange, Pikerington, Plain, Whitehall, Reynoldsburg, Saint Albans, Violet, Walnut, Westerville, Whitehall. Miles of Plant: 2,129. Homes Passed: 143,830. Homes Served: 79,000. *Channel Capacity:* 54. In use: 54. *Basic Service:* Subscribers: 79,000; 10/15/93. Programming (via satellite): 42 chs. Programming (via microwave): 42 chs. Programming (off air): 11 chs. *Pay Services:* Total Pay Subscribers: 65,826; 10/01/92. Pay Per View Subscribers: 61,245; 10/01/92. *Local Advertising Accepted.*

Coaxial Communications of Southern Ohio (28,000 subscribers). 3416 State Rt.132, Amelia, OH 45102. (513) 797-4400; FAX: (513) 797-8625. Art Loescher, gen mgr.
Area(s) Served: OH. Serving Amelia, Coveland, Lebanon. Homes Served: 28,000. *Basic Service:* Subscribers: 28,000; 10/15/93.

Colony Communications Inc.

20 Washington Pl., Providence, RI 02903. (401) 277-7400; FAX: (401) 277-7694. Jack C. Clifford, CEO & chmn; Bruce A. Clark, pres; John Van Luling, CFO; Paul A. Silva, vp opns; Jeffrey C. Wayne, vp mktg & vp adv; Daniel V. Donohue, vp; Michael J. Angi, vp. Owned by Providence Journal Co. Total Basic Subscribers: 761,802; Pay Cable Subscribers: 444,032; Number of Cable Systems: 27.

REGIONS

West: 575 Anton Blvd., Suite 1000, Costa Mesa, CA 92626; (714) 434-3232; Jim Petro, mgr. *Southeast:* 2151 W. 62nd St., Hialeah, FL 33016; (305) 828-4220; Glenn Schein, mgr. *Northeast:* 421 Founch Corner Rd., North Dartmouth, MA 02747; (508) 997-5572; Richard Wadman, mgr.

SYSTEMS WITH OVER 20,000 SUBSCRIBERS

Colony Cablevision Inc. (76,000 subscribers). Box 368, 41-725 Cook St., Palm Desert, CA 92261. (619) 340-2225; FAX: (619) 340-2384. Stephen B. Merritt, gen mgr; Virginia Blake, mktg dir; Mark Merritt, chief tech.
Area(s) Served: CA. County: Riverside. Serving Banning, Beaumont, Cathedral City, Coachella, Indian

Multiple Systems Operators, Independent Owners & Cable Systems

Wells, Indio, La Quinta, Palm Desert, Palm Springs, Rancho Mirage, Thermal, Thousand Palms. Miles of Plant: 1,160. Homes Passed: 104,458. Homes Served: 76,000. *Channel Capacity:* 55. *Basic Service:* Subscribers: 76,000; 10/31/93. *Pay Services:* Total Pay Subscribers: 31,415; 12/09/92. Pay Per View Subscribers: 9,000; 10/30/91. *Local Advertising Accepted.*

Colony Cablevision Inc. (120,000 subscribers). Box 413018, Naples, FL 33941. (813) 793-9600; FAX: (813) 793-1317. Ken Fuchs, gen mgr; Fritz Hoehne, mktg dir; John Garbo, loc adv dir; Duke McNaughton, chief tech; Michelle Oswalt, cust svc dir.
Area(s) Served: FL. Counties: Collier, Lee. Serving Bonita Springs, Captiva Island, Estero, Everglades City, Fort Myers, Fort Myers Beach, Marco Island, Naples, Pine Island, San Carlos Park, Sanibel Island. Miles of Plant: 1,863. Homes Passed: 162,440. Homes Served: 120,000. *Channel Capacity:* 62. In use: 56. *Basic Service:* Subscribers: 120,000; 10/31/93. Programming (via satellite): 46 chs. Programming (via microwave): 1 ch. Programming (off air): 6 chs. *Pay Services:* Total Pay Subscribers: 42,707; 12/03/92. (1) Pay Units: 16,739; 10/31/92. Programming (via satellite): HBO. (2) Pay Units: 9,277; 10/31/92. Programming (via satellite): Showtime. (3) Pay Units: 6,213; 10/31/92. Programming (via satellite): Cinemax. (4) Pay Units: 5,300; 10/31/92. Programming (via satellite): Disney. Pay Per View Subscribers: 21,000; 10/31/92. *Local Advertising Accepted.*

Copley/Colony Cablevision of Costa Mesa, Inc. (22,600 subscribers). 200 Paularino Ave., Costa Mesa, CA 92626. (714) 549-4242; FAX: (714) 549-4805. George Noel, gen mgr; Bill Erickson, mktg dir; Sean Flynn, chief tech.
Area(s) Served: CA. County: Orange. Serving Cypress, Irving, Lakewood, Newport Beach, Wilmington. Miles of Plant: 332. Homes Passed: 39,629. Homes Served: 22,600. *Channel Capacity:* 62. In use: 62. *Basic Service:* Subscribers: 22,600; 10/31/93. *Pay Services:* Total Pay Subscribers: 16,900; 12/09/92.

Copley/Colony Harbor Cablevision Inc. (21,223 subscribers). 605 E. G St., Wilmington, CA 90744. (310) 513-0600; FAX: (310) 549-5102. Tim Kelly, gen mgr; Randall Hicks, mktg dir; Rich Miller, chief tech; Michelle Lindsey, cust svc dir.
Area(s) Served: CA. County: Los Angeles. Serving Harbor City, Lomita, San Pedro. Miles of Plant: 323. Homes Passed: 53,285. Homes Served: 21,223. *Channel Capacity:* 60. In use: 60. *Basic Service:* Subscribers: 21,223; 10/31/93. *Pay Services:* Total Pay Subscribers: 24,676; 12/03/92. *Local Advertising Accepted. Equipment:* Magnavox amplifiers; Sony VTRs; Compuvid character generator; Scientific-Atlanta set top converters, addressable set top converters, headend; Simulsat satellite antenna; ChannelMatic commercial insert.

Dynamic Cablevision of Florida Ltd. (72,600 subscribers). 2151 W. 62nd St., Hialeah, FL 33016. (305) 558-2112; FAX: (305) 828-4418. Henry Martinez, gen mgr; Al Perez de la Mesa, mktg dir; Ellen Wedner, loc adv dir; Hector Hernandez, chief tech; Thomas Free, cust svc dir.
Area(s) Served: FL. County: Dade. Serving Coral Gables, Hialeah, Hialeah Gardens, Medley, Miami Springs, Sweetwater, Virginia Gardens, West Miami. Miles of Plant: 991. Homes Passed: 136,995. Homes Served: 72,600. *Channel Capacity:* 54. In use: 54. *Basic Service:* Subscribers: 72,600; 09/01/93. Programming (via satellite): 42 chs. Programming (off air): 12 chs. *Pay Services:* Total Pay Subscribers: 59,100; 09/01/93. Pay Per View Subscribers: 63,100; 09/01/93. *Local Advertising Accepted. Equipment:* Provided by Scientific-Atlanta.

Greater Fall River Cable TV (26,906 subscribers). Box 671, 800 Warren St., Fall River, MA 02722. (508) 675-1171; FAX: (508) 679-5662. Janice Rogers, gen mgr.
Area(s) Served: MA. County: Bristol. Serving Fall River. Homes Passed: 42,683. Homes Served: 26,906. *Basic Service:* Subscribers: 26,906; 10/31/93. *Pay Services:* Total Pay Subscribers: 17,231; 12/09/92.

King Videocable (24,000 subscribers). 556 Birch St., Lake Elsinore, CA 92530. (909) 674-7741; FAX: (909) 674-0895. Tom Thomas, gen mgr; Jennifer McElmeel, mktg dir; Chuck Barthauer, chief tech.
Area(s) Served: CA. County: Riverside. Serving Lake Elsinore. Pop: 34,000. Homes Passed: 32,245. Homes Served: 24,000. *Channel Capacity:* 42. In use: 42. *Basic Service:* Subscribers: 24,000; 10/31/93. *Pay Services:* Total Pay Subscribers: 13,734; 12/09/92. *Local Advertising Accepted.*

King Videocable (27,241 subscribers). 22620 Market St., Newhall, CA 91321. (805) 259-6909; FAX: (805) 259-0199. Shirley Aronson, gen mgr; Virginia Blake, mktg dir; Tom Holcomb, loc adv dir; Randy Harris, chief tech; Evelyn Arnold, cust svc dir.
Area(s) Served: CA. County: Los Angeles. Serving Castaic, Newhall, Saugus, Stevenson Ranch, Valencia. Pop: 130,000. Miles of Plant: 318. Homes Passed: 31,799. Homes Served: 27,241. *Channel Capacity:* 78. In use: 49. *Basic Service:* Subscribers: 27,241; 08/31/93. Programming (via satellite): C-Span, TV Food Net, TBN, HSN, The Weather Channel, USA, ESPN, Nickelodeon, CNN, Prime Ticket, A&E, Lifetime, MTV, CNN Headline News, Nashville, The Discovery Channel, TBS, TNT, Family Channel, Sci-Fi Channel, CNBC, VH-1, Encore, Court TV. Programming (off air): 2, 4, 5, 7, 9, 11, 13, 10-KEET, 8-KLCS, 12-KMEX, KWHY, HSC. *Pay Services:* Total Pay Subscribers: 13,734; 12/09/92. (1) Pay Units: 1,774; 08/31/93. Programming (via satellite): Cinemax. (2) Pay Units: 2,995; 08/31/93. Programming (via satellite): Disney. (3) Pay Units: 4,960; 08/31/93. Programming (via satellite): HBO. (4) Pay Units: 1,051; 08/31/93. Programming (via satellite): The Movie Channel. (5) Pay Units: 3,841; 08/31/93. Programming (via satellite): Showtime. Pay Per View Subscribers: 1,855; 08/31/93. *Local Advertising Accepted. Equipment:* Jerrold addressable; Hamlin decoders, remotes & standard converters; Pioneer & Regal remotes.

King Videocable (25,094 subscribers). 7584 80th St. S., Cottage Grove, MN 55016. (612) 458-3411; FAX: (612) 458-4016. Charlie Foukes, gen mgr.
Area(s) Served: MN, WI. Counties: Dakota, Washington, Pierce, St. Croix. Serving Afton, Bayport, Cottage Grove, Denmark, Grey Cloud, Hastings, Hudson, Lakeland, Lakeland Shore, Lake St. Croix Beach, Marshan, Newport, North Hudson, Oak Park Heights, Prescott, River Falls, St. Mary's Point, St. Paul Park, Stillwater, Woodbury. Miles of Plant: 750. Homes Passed: 47,119. Homes Served: 25,094. *Channel Capacity:* 64. *Basic Service:* Subscribers: 25,094; 10/31/93. *Pay Services:* Total Pay Subscribers: 15,198; 12/09/92. *No Local Advertising Accepted. Equipment:* Scientific-Atlanta headend, amplifiers, set top converters; Comm/Scope cable; MSI & Compuvid character generator; Simulsat satellite antenna; Avantik satellite receivers.

King Videocable Co. (30,280 subscribers). 10000 Commerce Ave., Tujunga, CA 91042. (818) 352-8621; FAX: (818) 352-7745. Robert Brown, gen mgr; Conrad Villegas, chief tech; Elizabeth Braga, cust svc dir.
Area(s) Served: CA. County: Los Angeles. Serving Kagel Canyon, Lakeview Terrace, Los Angeles, Pacoima, Sun Valley, Sunland, Sylmar, Tujunga. Miles of Plant: 330. Homes Passed: 43,628. Homes Served: 30,280. *Channel Capacity:* 62. In use: 48. *Basic Service:* Subscribers: 30,280; 12/03/92. Programming (via satellite): 26 chs. Programming (off air): 13 chs. *Pay Services:* Total Pay Subscribers: 13,910; 12/03/92. (1) Pay Units: 1,874; 10/31/92. Programming (via satellite): Disney. (2) Pay Units: 2,887; 10/31/92. Programming (via satellite): Showtime. (3) Pay Units: 2,274; 10/31/92. Programming (via satellite): Cinemax. (4) Pay Units: 1,721; 10/31/92. Programming (via satellite): The Movie Channel. (5) Pay Units: 617; 10/31/92. Programming (via satellite): SportsChannel. *Local Advertising Accepted.*

King Videocable Co. (50,104 subscribers). 6901 Winnetka Ave. N., Brooklyn Park, MN 55428. (612) 533-8020; FAX: (612) 531-4445. James Commers, gen mgr; Gary Houston, mktg dir; Alan Featherstone, chief tech.
Area(s) Served: MN. County: Hennepin. Serving Brooklyn Center, Corcoran, Crystal, Golden Valley, Maple Grove, Medicine Lake, New Hope, Osseu, Plymouth, Robbinsdale, Rogers. Homes Passed: 103,368. Homes Served: 50,104. *Basic Service:* Subscribers: 50,104; 10/31/93. *Pay Services:* Total Pay Subscribers: 28,469; 12/09/92.

Lowell Cable Televison Inc. (42,284 subscribers). Box 1121, 12 Washer St., Lowell, MA 01853. (508) 459-3313; FAX: (508) 454-6910. Donald R. Ratte, gen mgr; Peggy Nickerson, mktg dir; Mike O'Brien, loc adv dir; Kevin Siebert, chief tech; Michele Spinney, cust svc dir.
Area(s) Served: MA. County: Middlesex. Serving Chelmsford, Lowell, Tewksbury. Pop: 150,000. Miles of Plant: 520. Homes Passed: 65,041. Homes Served: 42,284. *Channel Capacity:* 52. In use: 52. *Basic Service:* Subscribers: 42,284; 09/09/93. *Pay Services:* Total Pay Subscribers: 33,113; 09/09/93. (1) Pay Units: 8,542; 09/09/93. Programming (via satellite): HBO. (2) Pay Units: 2,597; 09/09/93. Programming (via satellite): Cinemax. (3) Pay Units: 5,023; 09/09/93. Programming (via satellite): Showtime. (4) Pay Units: 3,949; 09/09/93. Programming (via satellite): Disney. (5) Pay Units: 2,675; 09/09/93. Programming (via satellite): SportsChannel. (6) Pay Units: 4,564; 09/09/93. Programming (via satellite): The Movie Channel. *Local Advertising Accepted. Equipment:* Scientific-Atlanta headend; GTE Sylvania & Scientific-Atlanta amplifiers; Times cable; Hitachi, Ikegami & Sony cameras; JVC & Sony VTRs; Chyron data systems; 3M character generator; Scientific-Atlanta addressable set top converters; Scientific-Atlanta satellite antenna & receivers; Pico traps; M/A-Com satellite receivers; Adams-Russell commercial insert.

U.S. Cablevision Corp. (60,562 subscribers). Box 889, 38 Old Rt. 9, Wappingers Falls, NY 12590. (914) 297-3333; FAX: (914) 297-9364. Mari Sevey, gen mgr; Elizabeth Gloede, mktg dir; Bud Brehenney, loc adv dir; Albert Perotti, chief tech; Marie Milligan, cust svc dir.
Area(s) Served: NY. Counties: Duchess, Orange, Putnam, Ulster. Serving Beacon, Blooming Grove, Clintondale, Cold Spring, East Fishkill, Fishkill, Gardner, Harriman, Highland Mills, Hyde Park, Lagrange, Lagrangeville, Lloyd, Marlboro, Modena, Monroe, Nelsonville, Philipstown, Plattekill, Poughkeepsie, Staatsburg, Storriville, Walkill, Wappingers Falls. Miles of Plant: 1,192. Homes Passed: 65,721. Homes Served: 60,562. *Channel Capacity:* 39. In use: 39. *Basic Service:* Subscribers: 60,562; 10/31/93. *Pay Services:* Total Pay Subscribers: 40,334; 10/31/92. *Local Advertising Accepted.*

Whaling City Cable TV Inc. (37,362 subscribers). 700 Kempton St., New Bedford, MA 02740. (508) 999-1390; FAX: (508) 992-7365. Janice Rogers, gen mgr; Arthur Tower, mktg dir; Adam Hamblett, loc adv dir; Thomas Kennedy, chief tech.
Area(s) Served: MA. County: Bristol. Serving New Bedford, North Dartmouth, South Dartmouth. Pop: 135,000. Miles of Plant: 417. Homes Passed: 54,459. Homes Served: 37,362. *Channel Capacity:* 41. In use: 41. *Basic Service:* Subscribers: 37,362; 10/31/93. *Pay Services:* Total Pay Subscribers: 21,071; 12/03/92. *Local Advertising Accepted.*

SMALLER SYSTEMS

California - Colony Cablevision of Lakewood, 5595 Corporate Dr., Cypress, CA 90630; 13,793 subs. Copley/Colony Cablevision of Cypress Inc., 5595 Corporate Dr., Cypress, CA 90630; 10,899 subs. King Videocable Company, 1521 S. Stockton St., Lodi, CA 95240 (209) 369-2426; 14,284 subs. King Videocable Company, Lake Mary Rd., Mammoth Lakes, CA 93546; (619) 934-8553; 6,980 subs. King Videocable Company, 219 E. Alma St., Mt. Shasta, CA 96067; (916) 926-6120; 5,506 subs. King Videocable Company, 21 N. Main St., San Andreas, CA 95249; (209) 754-4266; 11,039 subs. King Videocable Company-Placerville, 6517 Commerce Way, Diamond Springs, CA 95619; (916) 622-7503; 17,358 subs. **Idaho** - King Videocable Company, 261 Eastland Dr., Twin Falls, ID 83303; (208) 733-6230; 14,308 subs. King Videocable Company-American Falls, 261 Eastland Dr., Twin Falls, ID 83303; (208) 733-6230; 1,107 subs. **Rhode Island** - Vision Cable TV of RI Inc., 670 Narragansett Park Dr., Pawtucket, RI 02861; (401) 728-7904; 17,994 subs. Westerly Cable TV Inc., 415 Canal St. Westerly, RI 02891; (401) 596-1779; 15,225 subs. **Washington** - King Videocable Company, 1105 E. Tenth, Ellensburg, WA 98926; (509) 925-6565; 6,615 subs.

Colorado Springs Cablevision

213 N. Union Blvd., Colorado Springs, CO 80909. (719) 633-6616; FAX: (719) 633-0085. Ken Lore, CFO; Kevin Hyman, vp opns; Becky Hurley, vp mktg; Jeffrey B. Tarbert, vp. Owned by Time Warner Cable, 50%; Century Communications Corp., 50%. Total Basic Subscribers: 90,000; Number of Cable Systems: 1.

Columbia International Inc.

Box 4624, 9 Greenwich Office Park, Greenwich, CT 06830. (203) 661-1509; FAX: (205) 661-7651. Robert M. Rosencrans, CEO & pres; Scott N. Ledbetter, CFO; Kenneth S. Gunter, vp; Calvin D. Brousard, vp; Homer E. Harmon, vp. Total Basic Subscribers: 250,000; Pay Cable Subscribers: 190,000; Number of Cable Systems: 9.

SYSTEMS WITH OVER 20,000 SUBSCRIBERS

Columbia Cable of Michigan (65,000 subscribers). Box 998, 2505 S. Industrial Hwy., Ann Arbor, MI 48106. (313) 973-2266; FAX: (313) 973-0078. Ron Harmon, gen mgr; Richard Allen, mktg dir; Jim Bowen, chief tech. *Basic Service:* Subscribers: 65,000; 12/01/92.

Multiple Systems Operators, Independent Owners & Cable Systems

Columbia Cable of Oregon (67,034 subscribers). 14200 S.W. Brigadoon Ct., Beaverton, OR 97005. (503) 644-3188; FAX: (503) 646-8004. Frank Settle, gen mgr; Bryon Allen, mktg dir. *Basic Service:* Subscribers: 67,034; 10/01/93.

Columbia Cable of Virginia (45,500 subscribers). 4391 Dale Blvd., Woodbridge, VA 22193. (703) 670-0189; FAX: (703) 670-5479. Troy Fitzhugh, gen mgr; Mike Draughon, mktg dir; Scott Weber, chief tech.
Area(s) Served: VA. County: Price William. Serving Dumfries, Lake Ridge, Woodbridge. Miles of Plant: 835. Homes Passed: 61,000. Homes Served: 45,500. *Channel Capacity:* 64. In use: 64. *Basic Service:* Subscribers: 45,500; 09/01/93. Programming (off air): 12 chs. *Pay Services:* Total Pay Subscribers: 45,600; 09/01/93. Pay Per View Subscribers: 31,000; 09/01/93. *Local Advertising Accepted. Equipment:* Provided by Scientific-Atlanta.

Columbia Cable of Washington (53,000 subscribers). 6916 N.E. 40th St., Vancouver, WA 98661. (206) 254-0771; FAX: (206) 892-8744. Calvin D. Broussard, gen mgr; Michael L. Williams, mktg dir & cust svc dir; Norrie R. Bush, chief tech.
Area(s) Served: WA, OR. Counties: Clark, Multnomah. Serving Battle Ground, Camas, Hayden Island, Lacenter, Ridgefield, Vancouver, Washougal. Pop: 257,500. Miles of Plant: 1,290. Homes Passed: 88,000. Homes Served: 53,000. *Channel Capacity:* 56. In use: 56. *Basic Service:* Subscribers: 53,000; 10/01/93. Programming (via microwave): KCTS-9, Seattle; KING-5, Seattle; KSTW-11, Seattle; KIRO-7, Seattle. Programming (off air): KATU-2, Portland; KOIN-6, Portland; KGW-8, Portland; KOPB-10, Portland; KPTV-12, Portland; KNMT-24, Portland; KPDX-49, Vancouver. *Pay Services:* Total Pay Subscribers: 35,213; 10/31/92. (1) Pay Units: 12,854; 10/31/92. Programming (via satellite): HBO. (2) Pay Units: 11,022; 10/31/92. Programming (via satellite): Showtime. (3) Pay Units: 2,817; 10/31/92. Programming (via satellite): The Movie Channel. (4) Pay Units: 3,396; 10/31/92. Programming (via satellite): Cinemax. (5) Pay Units: 4,959; 10/31/92. Programming (via satellite): Disney. *Local Advertising Accepted. Equipment:* Scientific-Atlanta, General Instruments & Pioneer headends; Texscan & Scientific-Atlanta plants; Pioneer & General Instrument converters.

Columbus TV Cable Corporation

Box 1468, 319 College Ave., Columbus, MS 39701. (601) 328-1786; FAX: (601) 329-8481. Janice Matthews, vp mktg. Total Basic Subscribers: 15,000.

Comcast Cable Communications

16th Fl., 1234 Market St., Philadelphia, PA 19107-3723. (215) 665-1700; FAX: (215) 981-7790. Thomas G. Baxter, pres; Richard S. Sperry, vp sls; Steven M. Brookstein, vp mktg; Michael H. Young, vp progmg; Michael S. Tallent, vp. Owned by Comcast Corporation. Total Basic Subscribers: 2,764,500; Pay Cable Subscribers: 1,800,000; Number of Cable Systems: 63.

REGIONS

South Central: 1312 22nd Ave., Meridian, MS 39301; Glenn A. Colvin. *Midwest:* 20000 Pleasant Ave., St. Clair Shores, MI 48080-0207; Gary L. Mizga. *Northeast:* 1234 Market St., Philadelphia 19107. *Atlantic/Western Area:* 1234 Market St., Philadelphia 19107; Michael A. Dayle. *Southeast:* 1401 Northpoint Pkwy., 2nd Fl., W. Palm Beach, FL 33407; William R. Goetz Jr.

SYSTEMS WITH OVER 20,000 SUBSCRIBERS

Chesterfield Cablevision Inc. (56,000 subscribers). 6510 Ironbridge Rd., Richmond, VA 23234. (804) 743-1171; FAX: (804) 743-1613. Buck Dopp, gen mgr; Erin Ratliff, mktg dir; Barry Coffman, loc adv dir.
Area(s) Served: VA. County: Chesterfield. Miles of Plant: 1,500. Homes Passed: 84,000. Homes Served: 56,000. *Channel Capacity:* 41. In use: 41. *Basic Service:* Subscribers: 56,000; 11/15/93. *Local Advertising Accepted.*

Comcast Cablevision of Howard County (46,000 subscribers). 3417 Plumtree Dr., Ellicott City, MD 21042. (410) 461-1156; FAX: (410) 461-4731. Tom Beach, gen mgr; Jim Homer, mktg dir; Mike Manz, chief tech; Rose Westfall, cust svc dir.
Area(s) Served: MD. County: Howard. Serving Columbia, Ellicott City. Pop: 63,553. Miles of Plant: 832. Homes Passed: 61,394. Homes Served: 46,000. *Channel Capacity:* 46. In use: 46. *Basic Service:* Subscribers: 46,000; 11/15/93. *Pay Services:* Total Pay Subscribers: 36,500; 11/15/93. *Local Advertising Accepted.*

Comcast Cablevision of Baltimore County (170,000 subscribers). 8031 Corporate Dr., Baltimore, MD 21236. (410) 931-4600; FAX: (410) 931-6345. Curt Pendleton, gen mgr; Paul Chiamulera, mktg dir; Mike Vince, loc adv dir; Julie Cox, cust svc dir.
Area(s) Served: MD. County: Baltimore. Homes Served: 170,000. *Channel Capacity:* 45. In use: 45. *Basic Service:* Subscribers: 170,000; 11/15/93. *Local Advertising Accepted.*

Comcast Cablevision of Danbury (33,000 subscribers). 5 Shelter Rock Rd., Danbury, CT 06810. (203) 792-0900; FAX: (203) 792-9396. Jim Francisco, gen mgr; Debbie Joyce, mktg dir; Dawn Trohalis, loc adv dir; Robert Gabriele, chief tech.
Area(s) Served: CT. County: Fairfield. *Channel Capacity:* 39. In use: 39. *Basic Service:* Subscribers: 33,000; 11/15/93. *Local Advertising Accepted.*

Comcast Cablevision of Flint (82,272 subscribers). 3008 Airpark Dr., Flint, MI 48507. (313) 235-6112; FAX: (313) 235-9205. Les Jakobsen, gen mgr; John Reinhart, mktg dir; Bob Jenkins, loc adv dir; Janice Zaiglin, cust svc dir.
Area(s) Served: MI. County: Genesee. Serving Burton, Clio, Flint, Flint Twp., Flushing, Flushing Twp., Genesee, Grand Blanc, Grand Blanc Twp., Holly, Holly Twp., Mt. Morris, Mt. Morris Twp., Mundy, Rose, Swartz Creek, Vienna. Homes Served: 82,272. *Channel Capacity:* 55. In use: 44. *Basic Service:* Subscribers: 82,272; 11/15/93. *Local Advertising Accepted.*

Comcast Cablevision of Florence (29,000 subscribers). 116 S. Pine St., Florence, AL 35630. (205) 767-3200; FAX: (205) 767-3326. Jim Pickens, gen mgr; Derrick Robinson, loc adv dir.
Area(s) Served: AL. Counties: Colbert, Lauderdale. Serving Colbert Heights, Florence, Muscle Sheffield, St. Florian, Shoals, Tuscumbia, Wilson Lake Shores. Homes Served: 29,000. *Channel Capacity:* 37. In use: 37. *Basic Service:* Subscribers: 29,000; 11/15/93. *Local Advertising Accepted.*

Comcast Cablevision of Fort Wayne (64,000 subscribers). 720 Taylor St., Fort Wayne, IN 46802. (219) 456-9474; FAX: (219) 458-5138. Linda Hossinger, gen mgr; Gary Harrington, mktg dir; Craig Ruble, loc adv dir; Lillie Cantrell, cust svc dir.
Area(s) Served: IN, OH. Counties: Allen, Huntington, Noble, Wells, Whitley. Serving Avilla, Convoy, Ft. Wayne, Huntertown, Monroeville, New Haven, Ossian, Payne, Roanoke, Woodburn. Homes Served: 64,000. *Channel Capacity:* 37. In use: 37. *Basic Service:* Subscribers: 64,000; 11/15/93. *Local Advertising Accepted.*

Comcast Cablevision of Gadsden (20,000 subscribers). 241 S. Third St., Gadsden, AL 35999. (205) 547-6821; FAX: (205) 547-4062. Ellen Coffey, gen mgr; Susan Morris, loc adv dir.
Area(s) Served: AL. County: Etowah. Serving Gadsden, Glencoe, Rainbow. Homes Served: 20,000. *Channel Capacity:* 54. In use: 54. *Basic Service:* Subscribers: 20,000; 11/15/93. *Local Advertising Accepted.*

Comcast Cablevision of Harford County (42,000 subscribers). 30 N. Park St., Aberdeen, MD 21001. (410) 272-7500; FAX: (410) 272-6203. Brian A. Lynch, gen mgr; Mark Watts, mktg dir; Rick Otenasek, loc adv dir; Karen LaCoste, cust svc dir.
Area(s) Served: MD. County: Harford. Serving Aberdeen, Bel Air, Havre de Grace. Homes Served: 42,000. *Channel Capacity:* 60. In use: 50. *Basic Service:* Subscribers: 42,000; 11/15/93. *Local Advertising Accepted.*

Comcast Cablevision of Huntsville (45,553 subscribers). 2047 Max Luther Dr., Huntsville, AL 35810. (205) 859-7828; FAX: (205) 852-5599. C. Thomas Hill, gen mgr; Mary Dean, mktg dir; Linda Persall, loc adv dir; Patricia Clark, cust svc dir.
Area(s) Served: AL. Serving Huntsville. Homes Served: 45,553. *Channel Capacity:* 42. In use: 42. *Basic Service:* Subscribers: 45,553; 11/15/93. *Local Advertising Accepted.*

Comcast Cablevision of Indianapolis (127,000 subscribers). 5330 E. 65th St., Indianapolis, IN 46220-0911. (317) 353-2225; FAX: (317) 842-5143. Jerry Murray, gen mgr; Rise Helgemo, loc adv dir; Randy Sheets, chief tech; Nancy Long, cust svc dir.
Area(s) Served: IN. Counties: Hamilton, Hancock, Hendricks, Merion, Morgan, Shelby. Serving Beech Grove, Brownsburg, Clermont, Crows Nest, Cumberland, Danville, Homecroft, Indianapolis, Lawrence, Meridian Hills, Mooresville, North Crows Nest, Plainfield, Ravenswood, Southport, Speedway, Warren Park, Williams Creek, Wynnedale. Homes Served: 127,000. *Channel Capacity:* 37. In use: 37. *Basic Service:* Subscribers: 127,000; 11/15/93. *Local Advertising Accepted.*

Comcast Cablevision of Meadowlands (28,000 subscribers). 171 River Rd., North Arlington, NJ 07031. (201) 997-7522; FAX: (201) 997-5257. Don Daniels, gen mgr; Linda Avlon, mktg dir; Barry Martin, loc adv dir.
Area(s) Served: NJ. Counties: Bergen, Hudson. Serving Carlstadt, East Newark, East Rutherford, Kearny, Lyndhurst, North Arlington, Rutherford, Wallington. Homes Served: 28,000. *Channel Capacity:* 43. In use: 43. *Basic Service:* Subscribers: 28,000; 11/15/93. *Local Advertising Accepted.*

Comcast Cablevision of Middletown (22,700 subscribers). 19 Tuttle Pl., Middletown, CT 06457. (203) 632-0517; FAX: (203) 632-2871. Tom Coughlin, gen mgr; Debbie Joyce, mktg dir; Rebecca Usenia, loc adv dir; Peter Sarkisian, chief tech; Joann King, cust svc dir.
Area(s) Served: CT. Serving Cromwell, East Hampton, Middlefield, Middletown, Portland. Miles of Plant: 495. Homes Passed: 28,800. *Channel Capacity:* 41. In use: 41. *Basic Service:* Subscribers: 22,700. *Local Advertising Accepted.*

Comcast Cablevision of Mobile (57,000 subscribers). 3257 Moffette Rd., Mobile, AL 36607. (205) 476-2190; FAX: (205) 478-7809. Richard H. Almand III, gen mgr; Elaine Tilley, mktg dir; Lionel Robitaille, loc adv dir.
Area(s) Served: AL. County: Mobile. Serving Chickasaw, Dauphin Island, Mobile, Prichard, Saraland. Homes Served: 57,000. *Channel Capacity:* 38. In use: 36. *Basic Service:* Subscribers: 57,000; 11/15/93. *Local Advertising Accepted.*

Comcast Cablevision of Orange County (88,393 subscribers). Suite 220, 1000 E. Santa Ana Blvd., Santa Ana, CA 92701. (714) 285-2000; FAX: (714) 285-2014. Jeff Carlson, gen mgr; David Barford, mktg dir; Mike Szczechura, loc adv dir; Frank Maldonado, chief tech; Kathy Teff, cust svc dir.
Area(s) Served: CA. County: Orange. Serving Buena Park, Fullerton, Newport Beach, Placentia, Santa Ana, Seal Beach. Homes Served: 88,393. *Basic Service:* Subscribers: 88,393; 11/15/93. *Local Advertising Accepted.*

Comcast Cablevision of Paducah (24,000 subscribers). 800 Broadway, Paducah, KY 42001. (502) 442-8144; FAX: (502) 442-4071. Ed Mount, gen mgr; Dan Daniels, loc adv dir.
Area(s) Served: KY, IN. Counties: Livingston, Massac, McCraken. Serving Brookport, Metropolis, Paducah. Homes Served: 24,000. *Channel Capacity:* 41. In use: 37. *Basic Service:* Subscribers: 24,000; 11/15/93. *Local Advertising Accepted.*

Comcast Cablevision of Panama City (26,000 subscribers). 1316 Harrison Ave., Panama City, FL 32401. (904) 769-2929; FAX: (904) 769-8074. Russell Byrd, gen mgr; Cil Schnitker, mktg dir.
Area(s) Served: FL. County: Bay. Serving Callaway, Cedar Grove, Lynn Haven, Panama City, Parker, Springfield. Homes Served: 26,000. *Channel Capacity:* 62. In use: 46. *Basic Service:* Subscribers: 26,000; 11/15/93. *Local Advertising Accepted.*

Comcast Cablevision of Philadelphia (157,000 subscribers). 11400 Northeast Ave., Philadelphia, PA 19116. (215) 673-6600; FAX: (215) 961-3875. Jim Riesenbach, mktg dir; Nancy Fallis, cust svc dir.
Area(s) Served: PA. County: Philadelphia. Serving Philadelphia. Homes Served: 157,000. *Channel Capacity:* 82. In use: 82. *Basic Service:* Subscribers: 157,000; 11/15/93. *Local Advertising Accepted.*

Comcast Cablevision of Pontiac (29,200 subscribers). 1300 Crescent Lake Rd., Waterford, MI 48327. (313) 674-0500; FAX: (313) 673-7572. Donald Ivey, gen mgr; Dave Ugorowski, chief tech; Marsha Burtch, cust svc dir.
Area(s) Served: MI. County: Oakland. Serving Lake Angelus, Pontiac, Waterford. Homes Served: 29,200. *Channel Capacity:* 54. In use: 52. *Basic Service:* Subscribers: 29,200; 11/15/93. *Local Advertising Accepted.*

Comcast Cablevision of Santa Maria (25,000 subscribers). 309 W. Main St., Santa Maria, CA 93454. (805) 925-9504; FAX: (805) 922-6794. Richard Korwes, gen mgr; Pat Bierend, mktg dir; Bob Sorrells, chief tech; Minnie Peinado, cust svc dir.
Area(s) Served: CA. County: Santa Barbara. Serving Santa Maria. *Channel Capacity:* 40. In use: 38. *Basic Service:* Subscribers: 25,000; 11/30/92. *Local Advertising Accepted.*

Comcast Cablevision of Simi Valley (27,000 subscribers). 485 Easy St., Simi Valley, CA 93065. (805) 526-5721; FAX: (805) 526-0832. Greg Mackney, gen mgr; Doris Engelman-Sale, mktg dir; Ron Ambroff, loc adv dir; Maryanne Castilo, cust svc dir.

Area(s) Served: CA. County: Ventura. Serving Simi Valley. Pop: 100,000. Miles of Plant: 370. Homes Passed: 26,000. Homes Served: 27,000. *Channel Capacity:* 40. In use: 40. *Basic Service:* Subscribers: 27,000; 11/15/93. Programming (via satellite): 28 chs. Programming (via microwave): 1 ch. Programming (off air): 11 chs. *Local Advertising Accepted.*

Comcast Cablevision of Southeast Michigan (120,000 subscribers). 6095 Wall St., Sterling Heights, MI 48312. (313) 978-0467; FAX: (313) 978-1511. Dave Wells, gen mgr; David Bologna, mktg dir; Christine Dick, cust svc dir.
Area(s) Served: MI. County: Macomb. Serving Clinton, Fraser, Grosse Pointe Shores, Macomb, Mt. Clemens, St. Clair Shores, Shelby, Sterling Heights, Utica, Warren. *Channel Capacity:* 60. In use: 52. *Basic Service:* Subscribers: 120,000; 11/30/92. *Local Advertising Accepted.*

Comcast Cablevision of Tallahassee (56,000 subscribers). 3760 Hartsfield Rd., Tallahassee, FL 32303. (904) 574-4016; FAX: (904) 574-4030. Patrick Keating, gen mgr; Kevin Gardner, mktg dir; Bill Lickson, loc adv dir.
Area(s) Served: FL. County: Leon. Serving Tallahassee. Homes Served: 56,000. *Channel Capacity:* 37. In use: 37. *Basic Service:* Subscribers: 56,000; 11/15/93. *Local Advertising Accepted.*

Comcast Cablevision of the Inland Empire (46,600 subscribers). 1205 DuPont St., Ontario, CA 91761. (909) 988-8322; FAX: (909) 988-8432. Michael Schenker, gen mgr; David Rosenbloom, mktg dir; K.C. Muller, cust svc dir.
Area(s) Served: CA. County: San Bernardino. Serving Fontana, Grand Terrace, Highland, Loma Linda, Montclair, Ontario, Rancho Cucamonga, San Bernardino, Upland. Homes Served: 46,600. *Channel Capacity:* 49. In use: 45. *Basic Service:* Subscribers: 46,600; 11/15/93. *Local Advertising Accepted.*

Comcast Cablevision of Trenton (38,000 subscribers). 940 Prospect St., Trenton, NJ 08628. (609) 394-8635; FAX: (609) 392-2325. Michael J. Simmons, gen mgr; Juanita Johnson, mktg dir; Anne Sherwood, loc adv dir; Doug Cooper, chief tech; Mary Ann La Sardo, cust svc dir.
Area(s) Served: NJ. County: Mercer. Serving Ewing, Hopewell, Lawrence, Pennington, Trenton. *Channel Capacity:* 54. In use: 54. *Basic Service:* Subscribers: 38,000; 11/30/92. *Local Advertising Accepted.*

Comcast Cablevision of Tuscaloosa (33,000 subscribers). 700 Parkview Ctr., Tuscaloosa, AL 35401. (205) 345-0424; FAX: (205) 345-8223. Scott Randall, gen mgr; Susan Richards, loc adv dir; Sue Elmore, cust svc dir.
Area(s) Served: AL. County: Tuscaloosa. Serving Northport, Tuscaloosa. *Channel Capacity:* 42. In use: 39. *Basic Service:* Subscribers: 33,000; 09/15/92. *Local Advertising Accepted.*

Comcast Cablevision of West Palm Beach (95,000 subscribers). First Fl., 1401 Northpoint Pkwy., West Palm Beach, FL 33407. (407) 478-8399; FAX: (407) 686-9499. Len Rozek, gen mgr; Gene Shatlock, mktg dir; Rosie Wills, loc adv dir; Carroll Esco, cust svc dir.
Area(s) Served: FL. County: Palm Beach. Serving Boynton Beach, Cloud Lake, Glen Ridge, Gulfview, Haverhill, Hypoluxo, Jupiter, Lake Clark Shores, Lake Worth, Lantana, Manalapan, Mangonia Park, Palm Beach, Palm Springs, Riviera Beach, South Palm Beach, West Palm Beach. *Channel Capacity:* 48. In use: 47. *Basic Service:* Subscribers: 95,000; 11/15/92. *Local Advertising Accepted.*

Comcast Cablevision of Westmoreland (40,000 subscribers). 890 Constitution Blvd., New Kensington, PA 15068. (412) 335-9188; FAX: (412) 335-6648. Rick Ricchuito, gen mgr; Al Malmaux, mktg dir; Wesley Sapp, loc adv dir; Jim Moore, chief tech; Betty Jenkins, cust svc dir.
Area(s) Served: PA. County: Allegheny. Serving Arnold, Blawnox, Brackenridge, Buffalo, Cheswick, East Deer, Fawn, Frazer, Hampton, Harmar, Harrison, Indiana, Lower Burrell, New Kensington, O'Hara, Oakmont, Richland, Springdale, Springdale Twp., Tarentum, Verona, West Deer. Homes Served: 40,000. *Channel Capacity:* 54. In use: 46. *Basic Service:* Subscribers: 40,000; 11/15/93. *Local Advertising Accepted.*

Comcast Cablevision of Willow Grove (35,000 subscribers). 29 York Rd., Willow Grove, PA 19090. (215) 657-6970; FAX: (215) 657-7096. Randall Johnson, gen mgr; Donna McCarthy, mktg dir; Denise Koller, cust svc dir.
Area(s) Served: PA. County: Montgomery. Serving Abington, Bryn Athyn, Cheltenham, Jenkintown, Lower Moreland, Rockledge, Upper Moreland. Homes Served: 35,000. *Channel Capacity:* 44. In use: 42. *Basic Service:* Subscribers: 35,000; 11/15/93. *Local Advertising Accepted.*

Storer Cable (27,892 subscribers). 4609 Camp Robinson Rd., North Little Rock, AR 72118. (501) 758-3490; FAX: (501) 375-1042. Mike Wilson, gen mgr; Dottie Lane, mktg dir; Mary Thompson, loc adv dir; Lonnie Elswick, chief tech.
Area(s) Served: AR. County: Pulaski. Miles of Plant: 557. Homes Passed: 50,563. Homes Served: 27,892. *Channel Capacity:* 37. In use: 36. *Basic Service:* Subscribers: 27,892; 09/30/91. *Pay Services:* Total Pay Subscribers: 16,588; 09/30/91. *Local Advertising Accepted. Equipment:* Jerrold & Scientific-Atlanta headends; C-COR & Magnavox amplifiers; Comm/Scope cable; Andrew satellite antenna.

Storer Cable (48,960 subscribers). 801 Scott St., Little Rock, AR 72201. (501) 375-5755; FAX: (501) 375-1042. Mike Wilson, gen mgr; Dottie Lane, mktg dir; Mary Thompson, loc adv dir; Lonnie Elswick, chief tech.
Area(s) Served: AR. Counties: Pulaski, Saline. Serving Bryant, Commack Village. Miles of Plant: 1,068. Homes Passed: 86,684. Homes Served: 48,960. *Channel Capacity:* 41. In use: 41. *Basic Service:* Subscribers: 48,960; 09/30/91. *Pay Services:* Total Pay Subscribers: 27,515; 09/30/91. *Local Advertising Accepted.*

Storer Cable (50,500 subscribers). Box 790, 90 Lake Dr., East Windsor, NJ 08520. (609) 443-1970; FAX: (609) 443-0611. Michael Simmons, gen mgr; Alvin Albert, mktg dir; Raphael Arocho, chief tech.
Area(s) Served: NJ. Counties: Mercer, Middlesex, Monmouth. Serving Cranbury, Dayton, East Brunswick, East Windsor, Helmetta, Hightstown, Jamesburg, Kendall Park, Kingston, Monmouth Junction, Monroe, Plainsboro, Princeton Junction, Roosevelt, South Brunswick, Spotswood, West Windsor. Miles of Plant: 977. Homes Passed: 68,032. Homes Served: 50,500. *Channel Capacity:* 50. In use: 50. *Basic Service:* Subscribers: 50,000; 11/15/93. *Pay Services:* Total Pay Subscribers: 22,768; 11/15/93. Pay Per View Subscribers: 36,400; 11/15/93. *Local Advertising Accepted. Equipment:* Jerrold headend; Jerrold amplifiers; Jerrold set top converters; Times cable; Video Data Systems character generator; Scientific-Atlanta satellite antenna.

Storer Cable Communications (27,599 subscribers). 22266 Edgewater Dr., Port Charlotte, FL 33980. (813) 625-6000; FAX: (813) 624-5862. Maureen Cestari, gen mgr; Jay Crawford, chief tech.
Area(s) Served: FL. County: Charlotte. Serving Punta Gorda, Windmill Village. Miles of Plant: 871. Homes Passed: 39,905. Homes Served: 27,599. *Channel Capacity:* 31. In use: 31. *Basic Service:* Subscribers: 27,599; 09/30/92. *Pay Services:* Total Pay Subscribers: 10,919; 09/30/91.

Storer Cable Communications of Burlington County (35,000 subscribers). 21 Beverley-Rancocas Rd., Willingboro, NJ 08046. (609) 871-6900; FAX: (609) 871-1147. Edward Pardini, gen mgr; Kathy Banco, mktg dir; Theresa Simons, chief tech.
Area(s) Served: NJ. County: Burlington. Serving Beverly, Bordentown, Bordentown Twp., Burlington, Burlington Twp., Cinnaminson, Delanco, Delran, Edgewater Park, Palmyra, Riverside, Riverton, Westampton, Willingboro. Miles of Plant: 549. Homes Passed: 49,000. Homes Served: 35,000. *Channel Capacity:* 36. In use: 36. *Basic Service:* Subscribers: 35,000; 11/15/93. *Pay Services:* Total Pay Subscribers: 27,000; 11/15/93. Pay Per View Subscribers: 8,300; 11/15/93. *Local Advertising Accepted. Equipment:* Times Fiber cable; Video Data Systems character generator; Jerrold set top converters, addressable converters; DX antenna; Scientific-Atlanta satellite receivers; Texscan commercial insert.

Storer Cable Communications of Gloucester County Inc. (33,000 subscribers). 304 S. Broad St., Woodbury, NJ 08096. (609) 853-9217; FAX: (609) 853-7206; (609) 853-7200. Kevin R. Smith, gen mgr; Harry Griffith, chief tech.
Area(s) Served: NJ. County: Gloucester. Serving Clayton, Deptford, East Greenwich, Glassboro, Greenwich, Mantua, National Park, Paulsboro, Wenonah, West Deptford, Westville, Woodbury, Woodbury Heights. Miles of Plant: 610. Homes Passed: 39,300. Homes Served: 33,000. *Channel Capacity:* 38. In use: 38. *Basic Service:* Subscribers: 33,000; 11/15/93. *Pay Services:* Total Pay Subscribers: 23,477; 10/26/91. Pay Per View Subscribers: 4,000; 10/26/91. *Local Advertising Accepted. Equipment:* Jerrold headend; Jerrold amplifiers; Jerrold set top converters; Comm/Scope cable; Hitachi & Skegami cameras; Sony VTRs; Video Data Systems character generator; Buehl film chain; Andrew & Microdyne satellite antenna.

Storer Cable of Carolina Inc. (75,000 subscribers). Box 63407, North Charleston, SC 29419. (803) 747-1403; FAX: (803) 747-0546. Roddy Edge, gen mgr; Jim Richardson, loc adv dir; Marc Billingsley, chief tech.
Area(s) Served: SC. Counties: Berkeley, Charleston, Dorcester. Serving Goose Creek, Hanahan, Hunley Park, Isle of Palms, Mt. Pleasant, North Charleston, Sullivan's Island, Summerville. Miles of Plant: 1,617. Homes Passed: 133,450. Homes Served: 75,000. *Channel Capacity:* 36. In use: 36. *Basic Service:* Subscribers: 75,000; 11/15/93. *Pay Services:* Total Pay Subscribers: 56,493; 11/15/93. *Local Advertising Accepted.*

Storer Cable of Houston (54,412 subscribers). 2505 Bisbee, Houston, TX 77017. (713) 645-3738; FAX: (713) 645-3821. Gary Pomonis, gen mgr; Mark Peebles, mktg dir; Dan Schmitz, chief tech.
Area(s) Served: TX. County: Harris. Serving Clear Lake City, Sage Glen, Sage Meadow, Scarsdale. Miles of Plant: 2,004. Homes Passed: 195,970. Homes Served: 54,412. *Channel Capacity:* 41. In use: 41. *Basic Service:* Subscribers: 54,412; 11/30/92. *Pay Services:* Total Pay Subscribers: 52,866; 09/30/91. *Local Advertising Accepted.*

Storer Cable of Monmouth County (63,000 subscribers). 403 South St., Eatontown, NJ 07724. (908) 542-8107; FAX: (908) 389-0289. Steve Randell, gen mgr; Maureen Dalton, mktg dir; Pete Frascella, chief tech.
Area(s) Served: County: Monmouth. Serving Allenhurst, Atlantic Highlands, Belford, Deal, East Keansburg, Eatontown, Fair Haven, Ft. Monouth, Freehold, Hazlet, Highlands, Holmdel, Leonardo, Lincroft, Little Silver, Loch Arbour, Locust, Long Branch, Middletown, Monmouth Beach, Navesink, New Monmouth, Oceanport, Port Monmouth, Red Bank, Rumson, Sea Bright, Shrewsbury Borough, Shrewsbury Twp., Tinton Falls. Homes Passed: 90,000. Homes Served: 63,000. *Channel Capacity:* 40. In use: 40. *Basic Service:* Subscribers: 63,000; 11/15/93. *Local Advertising Accepted.*

Storer Cable of Ocean County (35,000 subscribers). 751 Brick Blvd., Brick, NJ 08723. (908) 920-6010; FAX: (908) 920-6017. Steven Randell, gen mgr; Lynn Fliedner, mktg dir; Randy Adams, chief tech.
Area(s) Served: NJ. County: Ocean. Serving Brick, Lakewood. Miles of Plant: 447. Homes Passed: 44,258. Homes Served: 35,000. *Channel Capacity:* 45. In use: 45. *Basic Service:* Subscribers: 35,000; 11/15/93. *Local Advertising Accepted. Equipment:* Jerrold headend; Jerrold & Kaiser amplifiers; Comm/Scope cable; Panasonic cameras; JVC VTRs; Scientific-Atlanta satellite antenna.

Storer Cable TV of Connecticut Inc. (67,400 subscribers). 190 Whalley Ave., New Haven, CT 06511. (203) 865-0429; FAX: (203) 865-3170. Rick Germano, gen mgr; Charles Goodman, mktg dir; John Bean, chief tech.
Area(s) Served: CT. County: New Haven. Serving Hamden, New Haven, West Haven. Miles of Plant: 730. Homes Passed: 105,000. Homes Served: 67,400. *Channel Capacity:* 40. In use: 40. *Basic Service:* Subscribers: 67,400; 11/15/93. *Pay Services:* Total Pay Subscribers: 18,500; 10/25/91. *Local Advertising Accepted.*

Storer Cable TV of Florida Inc. (76,000 subscribers). Box 1178, 5205 Fruitville Rd., Sarasota, FL 34232. (813) 371-4444; FAX: (813) 371-5097. Rod Dagenais, gen mgr; Jerry Norris, mktg dir; Andrew Behn, chief tech.
Area(s) Served: FL. Counties: Manatee, Sarasota. Serving Longboat Key. Miles of Plant: 1,274. Homes Passed: 107,400. Homes Served: 76,000. *Channel Capacity:* 38. In use: 38. *Basic Service:* Subscribers: 76,000; 11/15/93. *Pay Services:* Total Pay Subscribers: 30,294; 09/30/91. *Local Advertising Accepted.*

Storer Cable TV of Florida Inc. (34,257 subscribers). 214 W. Miami Ave., Venice, FL 34285. (813) 484-0602; FAX: (813) 485-9165. Gary Waterfield, gen mgr; Jerry Norris, mktg dir; Dave Wood, chief tech.
Area(s) Served: FL. Counties: Charlotte, Sarasota. Serving Boca Grande, Casey Key, Englewood, Laurel, Nokomis, North Port, Rotonda, Venice. Miles of Plant: 870. Homes Passed: 57,874. Homes Served: 34,257. *Channel Capacity:* 36. In use: 36. *Basic Service:* Subscribers: 34,257; 09/30/91. *Pay Services:* Total Pay Subscribers: 12,361; 09/30/91. *Local Advertising Accepted.*

Storer Communications of Groton Inc. (28,500 subscribers). 401 Gold Star Hwy., Groton, CT 06340. (203) 445-7727; FAX: (203) 445-4800. Rae Abate, gen mgr; Michael Ligouri, mktg dir & loc adv dir; Bill Golden, chief tech.
Area(s) Served: CT. County: New London. Serving Groton, Ledyard, Mystic, North Stonington, Stonington, Voluntown. Pop: 93,600. Miles of Plant: 650. Homes Passed: 28,500. Homes Served: 28,500. *Channel Capacity:* 80. In use: 54. *Basic Service:* Subscribers: 28,500; 11/15/93. *Local Advertising Accepted. Equipment:* Scientific-Atlanta headend; Jerrold amplifiers; Times cable; Chyron character generator; Oak, Jerrold & Pioneer set top converters; Andrew satellite antenna; Hughes satellite receivers; Texscan commerical insert.

SMALLER SYSTEMS

Alabama - Comcast Cablevision of Dothan/Marianna, 509 S. Oates St., Dothan, AL 36301; (205) 754-3171. **California -** Comcast Cablevision of Lompoc, 626 N. H St., Lompoc, CA 93436; (805) 736-8836. **Florida -** Comcast Cablevision of Boca Raton, 1830 N.W. Second Ave., Boca Raton, FL 33432; (407) 391-7556. Comcast Cablevision of Perry, 107 N. Jefferson St., Perry, FL 32347; (904) 584-4249. **Michigan -** Comcast Cablevision of Grosse Pointe, 15001 Charlevoix Ave., Grosse Pointe Park, MI 48230; (313) 822-9200. Comcast Cablevision of Hillsdale, 63 N. Howell St., Hillsdale, MI 49242; (517) 437-3288. **Mississippi -** Comcast Cablevision of Laurel, 1225 W. Fifth St., Laurel, MS 39440; (601) 649-7234. Comcast Cablevision of Meridian, 909 24th Ave., Meridian, MS 39301; (601) 693-2366. Comcast Cablevision of Tupelo, 357 N. Gloster St., Tupelo, MS 38801; (601) 844-8760. **Pennsylvania -** Comcast Cablevision of Lower Merion, 205 E. Levering Mill Rd., Bala Cynwyd, PA 19004; (215) 667-8917.

Command Cable Corporation

Suite B, 10 W. Railroad Ave., Jamesburg, NJ 08831. (908) 656-0006; FAX: (908) 6566-0257. Robert Sentora, pres; David Mandell, vp opns. Total Basic Subscribers: 11,000.

Communication Systems Inc.

Suite 211, 2712 Middleburg Dr., Columbia, SC 29204. (803) 799-6460. Tom Mauldin, pres; Michael Fowler, vp opns; Martha Myers, vp mktg. Total Basic Subscribers: 2,700; Number of Cable Systems: 1.

Community Antenna System Inc.

655 Hill Ave., Hillsboro, WI 54634. (608) 489-2321. Eugene J. Kubarski, chmn; Bernice E. Kubarski, pres; Randall Kubarski, vp; Gregory Kubarski, vp. Owned by Community Antenna System Inc. Total Basic Subscribers: 1,508; Number of Cable Systems: 4.

SMALLER SYSTEMS

Wisconsin - Community Antenna System Inc., Cazenovia, WI; 104 subs. Community Antenna System Inc., Elroy, WI; 591 subs. Community Antenna System Inc., Hillsboro, WI; 627 subs. Community Antenna System Inc., Kendall, WI; 196 subs.

Community Cable Service Division

315 W. 2nd St., Frankfort, KY 40601. (502) 223-3401; FAX: (502) 223-3887. Bruce Dungan, chmn. Owned by Frankfort Electric & Water Plant Board. Total Basic Subscribers: 16,158; Number of Cable Systems: 1.

Community Cablevision Co.

Box 307, 1550 W. Rogers Blvd., Skiatook, OK 74070. (918) 396-3019. George E. Hamilton, chmn; Mrs. George E. Hamilton, pres; Ray Soule, vp opns. Total Basic Subscribers: 4,650; Number of Cable Systems: 1.

Community Communications Co.

Box 558, Hwy. 425 N., Monticello, AR 71655. (501) 367-7300; FAX: (501) 367-9770. Paul Gardner, CEO; Bill Copeland, pres. Total Basic Subscribers: 11,732; Pay Cable Subscribers: 1,072; Number of Cable Systems: 1.

Community TV Co.

5 College St., Ellijay, GA 30540. (706) 276-2288; FAX: (706) 276-2298. Doug Harrison, pres. Total Basic Subscribers: 1,750.

Community TV Corporation

408 Union Ave., Laconia, NH 03246. (603) 524-4425. Harmon White, pres; William Schmalberger, vp opns; Lawrence A. Patten, vp mktg. Total Basic Subscribers: 39,000; Number of Cable Systems: 4.

Comserv Ltd.

Box 310, 111 W. 2nd St., Schaller, IA 51053. (712) 275-4215; FAX: (712) 275-4121. Glen Rymers, pres. Total Basic Subscribers: 1,841; Pay Cable Subscribers: 630; Number of Cable Systems: 6.

SMALLER SYSTEMS

Iowa - Comserv, Cushing, IA; 78 subs. Comserv, Ida Grove, IA; 735 subs. Comserv, Kiron, IA; 76 subs. Comserv, Lake View, IA; 420 subs. Comserv, Odebolt, IA; 277 subs. Comserv, Schaller, IA; 246 subs.

Consolidated Cable Partners

206 W. Main St., Benton Harbor, MI 49022. (616) 926-1197; FAX: (616) 926-2582. Bill James, pres; Greg Smith, vp opns; Dorothy DeYoung, vp mktg. Total Basic Subscribers: 8,510; Pay Cable Subscribers: 4,950; Number of Cable Systems: 1.

Continental Cablevision Inc.

The Pilot House, Lewis Wharf, Boston, MA 02110. (617) 742-9500; FAX: (617) 742-0530. Amos B. Hostetter Jr., CEO & chmn; Michael J. Ritter, pres; Nancy Hawthorne, CFO; Frederick C. Livingston, vp mktg; Robert A. Stengel, vp progmg; Robert J. Sachs, vp; Richard A. Hoffstein, vp. Total Basic Subscribers: 2,900,000; Pay Cable Subscribers: 2,600,000; Number of Cable Systems: 152.

REGIONS

Chicago/St. Paul: 688 Industrial Dr., Elmhurst, IL 60126; Emmett White, Sr VP. *Florida:* Box 17613F, 5934 Richard Rd., Jacksonville, FL 32245; Jeff DeLorme, Sr VP. *Illinois/Iowa/Missouri:* 1000 Des Peres Rd., Suite 300, St. Louis, MO 63131; James Wand, Sr VP. *Michigan:* 1111 Michigan Ave., Suite 200, E. Lansing, MI 48823; Richard Weigand, Sr VP. *New England:* 180 Greenleaf Ave., Portsmouth, NH 03801; William Schleyer, Exec VP. *Ohio:* Box CS-2015, 211 W. Main Cross St., Finlay, OH 45839; Charles Younger, Exec VP. *Sierra Valleys/California:* 445 W. Weber, Suite 226, Stockton, CA 95203; Steve Martin, Sr VP. *Southern California:* 6133 Bristol Pkwy., Suite 100, Culver City, CA 90230; Ron Cooper, Sr VP. *Virginia:* 1520 W. Main St., Suite 201, Richmond, VA 23220-4697; H.W. Goodall, Sr VP. *Western New England/New York:* 17 Connecticut S. Dr., E. Granby, CT 06026; Russel Stephens, Sr VP.

SYSTEMS WITH OVER 20,000 SUBSCRIBERS

Continental Cablevision (25,000 subscribers). 111 N. Mooney Blvd., Tulare, CA 93274. (209) 688-7593; FAX: (209) 688-0867. Len Falter, gen mgr; Scott Barbee, mktg dir; Bob Guzman, chief tech; Lynn Roberts, cust svc dir.
Area(s) Served: CA. Counties: Kings, Tulare. Serving Tulare, Visalia. Miles of Plant: 430. Homes Passed: 44,123. Homes Served: 25,000. *Channel Capacity:* 41. In use: 41. *Basic Service:* Subscribers: 25,000; 11/15/93. Programming (via satellite): 25 chs. Programming (off air): 11 chs. Pay Per View Subscribers: 13,781; 09/30/91. *Local Advertising Accepted.*

Continental Cablevision (66,580 subscribers). 6505 Tam O'Shanter Dr., Stockton, CA 95210. (209) 473-4955; FAX: (209) 473-8177. John Pezzini, gen mgr; Brian Caldwell, mktg dir; Ballard Warkentin, chief tech; Bill Haeffner, cust svc dir.
Area(s) Served: CA. County: San Joaquin. Serving French Camp, Lathrop, Lincoln Village West, Linden, Manteca, Stockton. Pop: 259,896. Miles of Plant: 800. Homes Passed: 118,221. Homes Served: 66,580. *Channel Capacity:* 66. In use: 60. *Basic Service:* Subscribers: 66,580; 11/15/93. Programming (via satellite): 41 chs. Programming (via microwave): 7 chs. Programming (off air): 9 chs. *Pay Services:* Total Pay Subscribers: 55,389; 10/31/92. Pay Per View Subscribers: 43,117; 10/31/92. *Local Advertising Accepted.*

Continental Cablevision (102,000 subscribers). 1945 N. Helm Ave., Fresno, CA 93727. (209) 252-8210; FAX: (209) 456-1544. Jamie Howard, gen mgr; Scott Barbee, mktg dir; Ann Vaia, loc adv dir; Horacio Guzman, chief tech.
Area(s) Served: CA. Counties: Fresno, Madera. Serving Clovis, Fresno, Madera. Miles of Plant: 1,516. Homes Passed: 176,584. Homes Served: 102,000. *Channel Capacity:* 48. In use: 48. *Basic Service:* Subscribers: 102,000; 11/15/93. Programming (via satellite): 22 chs. Programming (via microwave): 22 chs. Programming (off air): 9 chs. *Pay Services:* Total Pay Subscribers: 95,264; 09/30/91. (1) Pay Units: 38,603; 09/30/91. Programming (via satellite): HBO. (2) Pay Units: 21,206; 09/30/91. Programming (via satellite): Cinemax. (3) Pay Units: 25,892; 09/30/91. Programming (via satellite): Showtime. *Local Advertising Accepted.*

Continental Cablevision (71,000 subscribers). 6314 Arizona Pl., Westchester, CA 90045. (310) 216-3500. Matt McGinnity, gen mgr; Dan Boyle, mktg dir.
Area(s) Served: CA. County: Los Angeles. Serving Mar Vista, Marina Del Rey, Playa Del Rey, Venice, Westchester. Miles of Plant: 463. Homes Passed: 206,000. Homes Served: 71,000. *Channel Capacity:* 54. In use: 54. *Basic Service:* Subscribers: 71,000; 11/15/93. *Local Advertising Accepted. Equipment:* Zenith set top converters.

Continental Cablevision (44,400 subscribers). 10839 LaReina Ave., Downey, CA 90241. (310) 869-5301; FAX: (310) 861-4522. Vic Pascarelli, gen mgr; Mark Billnitzer, mktg dir; Mary Thompson, loc adv dir; Chuck Harper, chief tech; Ron Morin, cust svc dir.
Area(s) Served: CA. County: Los Angeles. Serving Bell Gardens, Bellflower, Downey, La Mirada, Lynwood, Maywood, Paramount, Santa Fe Springs, South El Monte. Pop: 396,405. Miles of Plant: 730. Homes Passed: 117,590. Homes Served: 44,400. *Channel Capacity:* 53. In use: 52. *Basic Service:* Subscribers: 44,400; 11/15/93. Programming (via satellite): 26 chs. Programming (off air): 16 chs. Pay Per View Subscribers: 40,665. *Local Advertising Accepted. Equipment:* Zenith PM system with PCII remote controls & Universal remote; TOCOM converters.

Continental Cablevision (66,500 subscribers). 900 N. Cahuenga Blvd., Los Angeles, CA 90048. (213) 993-8000; FAX: (213) 993-8197. Deborah Picciolo, gen mgr; Scott Gretencord, mktg dir; Mary Thompson, loc adv dir; Joe Casasanta, chief tech.
Area(s) Served: CA. County: Los Angeles. Serving Hollywood, Los Angeles, Wilshire. Miles of Plant: 454. Homes Passed: 201,009. Homes Served: 66,500. *Channel Capacity:* 56. In use: 56. *Basic Service:* Subscribers: 66,500; 11/15/93. *Pay Services:* Total Pay Subscribers: 39,190; 10/31/91. Pay Per View Subscribers: 64,450; 10/31/91. *No Local Advertising Accepted. Equipment:* Tocom converters; Scientific-Atlanta headend; Scientific-Atlanta earth stations; Comm/Scope cable; Jerrold amplifiers, Sony VTRs.

Continental Cablevision (21,605 subscribers). 2204 N. Long Beach Blvd., Compton, CA 90221. (310) 537-7212; FAX: (310) 604-4083. Joseph Lawson, gen mgr; Carra Wallace, chief tech.
Area(s) Served: CA. County: Los Angeles. Miles of Plant: 386. Homes Passed: 67,522. Homes Served: 21,605. *Channel Capacity:* 53. In use: 53. *Basic Service:* Subscribers: 21,605; 11/15/93. *Local Advertising Accepted.*

Continental Cablevision (32,000 subscribers). 311 B St., Yuba City, CA 95991. (916) 674-9173; FAX: (916) 671-3822. DeeDee Brady, gen mgr; Judy Dayton, mktg dir; Debbie Watkins, loc adv dir; Rick Adams, chief tech; Sally Green, cust svc dir.
Area(s) Served: CA. Counties: Sutter, Yuba. Serving Beale Air Force Base, Linda Olivehurst, Live Oak, Marysville, Sutter City, Wheatland, Yuba City. Pop: 138,963. Miles of Plant: 411. Homes Passed: 40,628. Homes Served: 32,000. *Channel Capacity:* 54. *Basic Service:* Subscribers: 32,000; 11/15/93. Programming (via satellite): 28 chs. Programming (via microwave): 4 chs. Programming (off air): 11 chs. Pay Per View Subscribers: 1,124; 09/30/91. *Local Advertising Accepted. Equipment:* A/B switches; Scientific-Atlanta converters.

Continental Cablevision (62,000 subscribers). 2900 Crenshaw Blvd., Los Angeles, CA 90016. (213) 730-9500. Pamela Smith, gen mgr; Bob Nelson, mktg dir; Steve Repech, chief tech.
Area(s) Served: CA. County: Los Angeles. Serving Englewood, Los Angeles. Miles of Plant: 836. Homes Passed: 209,555. Homes Served: 62,000. *Channel Capacity:* 60. In use: 53. *Basic Service:* Subscribers: 62,000; 11/15/93. Pay Per View Subscribers: 58,109; 10/31/91. *No Local Advertising Accepted.*

Continental Cablevision (207,941 subscribers). 5934 Richard St., Jacksonville, FL 32216. (904) 731-7700; FAX: (904) 448-3758. Scott Westerman, gen mgr; George Thorry, mktg dir; Bud Campbell, chief tech.

Area(s) Served: FL, GA. Counties: Camden, Duval. Serving Baldwin, Cecil Field Naval Air Station, Crescent City, Folkston, Jacksonville Beach, Jacksonville Naval Air Station, Kings Bay, Lake Butter, Mayport Naval Air Station, McClenny, Nahunta, Waldo, Welaka. Miles of Plant: 4,700. Homes Passed: 335,000. Homes Served: 207,941. *Channel Capacity:* 52. In use: 52. *Basic Service:* Subscribers: 207,941; 11/15/93. *Pay Services:* Total Pay Subscribers: 180,000; 11/11/91. Pay Per View Subscribers: 72,000; 11/11/91. *Local Advertising Accepted.*

Continental Cablevision (74,386 subscribers). 688 Industrial Dr., Elmhurst, IL 60126. (708) 530-4477; FAX: (708) 530-8654. Bill Connors, gen mgr; Terry Dowling, mktg dir; Tom Broadwater, loc adv dir.
Area(s) Served: IL. Counties: Cook, DuPage. Serving Bensenville, Berkeley, Burr Ridge, Clarendon Hills, Countryside, Elmwood Park, Lemont, Leyden, Lyons, Forest Park, Franklin Park, Hillside, Hinsdale, Lombard, Oak Brook, Oak Brook Terrace, River Grove, Rosemont, Schiller Park, Westchester, Westmont, Willowbrook. *Basic Service:* Subscribers: 74,386; 11/13/92. *Local Advertising Accepted.*

Continental Cablevision (50,000 subscribers). 1575 Rohlwing Rd., Rolling Meadows, IL 60008. (708) 577-1818; FAX: (708) 577-1187. Rhonda Christenson, gen mgr; Melony Griffin, mktg dir.
Area(s) Served: IL. Counties: Cook, DuPage, Lake. Serving Buffalo Grove, Elk Grove, Hoffman Estates, Palantine. Homes Passed: 78,877. Homes Served: 50,000. *Channel Capacity:* 52. In use: 52. *Basic Service:* Subscribers: 50,000; 11/15/93. *Pay Services:* Total Pay Subscribers: 31,992; 10/31/91. Pay Per View Subscribers: 34,304; 10/31/91. *Local Advertising Accepted. Equipment:* Zenith set top converters.

Continental Cablevision (21,000 subscribers). 201 Boston Post Rd. W., Marlborough, MA 01752. (508) 481-2503; FAX: (508) 481-0205. Paul Cronin, gen mgr; Susan Tabb, mktg dir; Charles Crook, loc adv dir; Brian Bane, chief tech.
Area(s) Served: MA. Counties: Middlesex, Worcester. Serving Bolton, Clinton, Lancaster, Marlborough, Phillipston, Sterling, Winchendon. Miles of Plant: 516. Homes Passed: 26,600. Homes Served: 21,000. *Channel Capacity:* 54. In use: 54. *Basic Service:* Subscribers: 21,000; 11/15/93. Pay Per View Subscribers: 3,700; 10/31/91. *Local Advertising Accepted. Equipment:* Scientific-Atlanta headend, amplifiers, satellite antenna & satellite receivers; Comm/Scope cable; Video Data Systems character generator; Jerrold set top converters; General Instrument addressable set top converters; Gamco & Alcon traps; Sony commercial insert.

Continental Cablevision (42,696 subscribers). 81 School St., Quincy, MA 02169. (617) 471-3200; FAX: (617) 472-7350. Stephen J. Farquhar, gen mgr; Kathleen Taraschi, mktg dir; William Snowling, chief tech; Allyn McManmon, cust svc dir.
Area(s) Served: MA. County: Norfolk. Serving Milton, Quincy, Randolph. Pop: 131,000. Miles of Plant: 386. Homes Passed: 55,000. Homes Served: 42,696. *Channel Capacity:* 54. In use: 54. *Basic Service:* Subscribers: 42,696; 11/15/93. Programming (via satellite): 35 chs. Programming (via microwave): 1 ch. Programming (off air): 14 chs. *Local Advertising Accepted.*

Continental Cablevision (33,000 subscribers). 88 Sherman St., Cambridge, MA 02140. (617) 876-5005; FAX: (617) 876-8613. Joyce Conroy-Hillcoat, gen mgr; Anthony Price, mktg dir; Scott Nickerson, chief tech.
Area(s) Served: MA. County: Middlesex. Serving Arlington, Cambridge. Homes Served: 33,000. *Channel Capacity:* 67. In use: 67. *Basic Service:* Subscribers: 33,000; 11/15/93. Pay Per View Subscribers: 5,000; 11/14/91. *Local Advertising Accepted.*

Continental Cablevision (22,000 subscribers). 15 Farrar Farm Rd., Norwell, MA 02061. (617) 659-0502; FAX: (617) 659-2448. Joseph Hayes, gen mgr; Gail Pearson, mktg dir; Peter LePage, chief tech; Mary Connolly, cust svc dir.
Area(s) Served: MA. Serving Cohasset, Hanover, Hingham, Hull, Norwell, Scituate. Miles of Plant: 640. Homes Passed: 31,000. Homes Served: 22,000. *Channel Capacity:* 66. In use: 63. *Basic Service:* Subscribers: 22,000; 11/04/93. *Local Advertising Accepted. Equipment:* Jerrold 2-way addressable converters; Impulse PPV.

Continental Cablevision (46,500 subscribers). 12 Tozer Rd., Beverly, MA 01915. (508) 927-5700; FAX: (508) 927-6074. David A. Dane, gen mgr; Tami Benedick, mktg dir; Mike Allen, chief tech; Deborah Capobianco, cust svc dir.
Area(s) Served: MA. Counties: Essex, Suffolk. Serving Beverly, Hamilton, Marblehead, Nahant, Revere, Rexford, Saugus, Topsfield, Wenham. Miles of Plant: 720. Homes Passed: 63,120. Homes Served: 46,500. *Channel Capacity:* 60. In use: 54. *Basic Service:* Subscribers: 46,500; 11/15/93. Pay Per View Subscribers: 28,000. *Local Advertising Accepted. Equipment:* Jerrold headend & converters - DRV, DPV; Magnavox 450 MHZ amplifier; Scientific-Atlanta 550 amplifiers.

Continental Cablevision (127,567 subscribers). 1110 E. Mountain Rd., Westfield, MA 01085. (413) 562-9923; FAX: (413) 568-6625. Greg A. Wells, mktg dir; Cecelia Lang, loc adv dir; David J. Miller, chief tech; Jean Rines, cust svc dir.
Area(s) Served: MA. Counties: Hampden, Hampshire. Serving Agawam, Granby, Granville, Holyoke, South Haldey, Southwick, West Springfield, Westfield. Miles of Plant: 850. Homes Passed: 71,700. Homes Served: 127,567. *Channel Capacity:* 60. In use: 56. *Basic Service:* Subscribers: 127,567; 11/15/93. Programming (via satellite): 43 chs. Programming (off air): 9 chs. *Pay Services:* Total Pay Subscribers: 20,771; 11/21/92. (1) Pay Units: 13,374; 09/30/91. Programming (via satellite): HBO. (2) Pay Units: 5,245; 09/30/91. Programming (via satellite): Showtime. (3) Pay Units: 4,499; 09/30/91. Programming (via satellite): Cinemax. (4) Pay Units: 3,144; 09/30/91. Programming (via satellite): The Movie Channel. (5) Pay Units: 5,417; 09/30/91. Programming (via satellite): Disney. (6) Pay Units: 4,615; 09/30/91. Programming (via satellite): NESN. Pay Per View Subscribers: 21,614; 11/21/92. *Local Advertising Accepted. Equipment:* Magnavox distribution plant; Scientific-Atlanta addressable converters; Jerrold converters; Catel, Standard & Scientific-Atlanta headends.

Continental Cablevision (18,000 subscribers). 27432 Grossbeck Hwy., Roseville, MI 48066. (313) 779-3421; FAX: (313) 779-0635. Joe Geroux, gen mgr; Ray Segler, mktg dir; John Rill, chief tech; Jean Klwalczwyk, cust svc dir.
Area(s) Served: MI. County: Macomb. Serving Hazelpack, Madison Heights, Roseville. Miles of Plant: 300. Homes Passed: 40,000. Homes Served: 18,000. *Channel Capacity:* 54. In use: 50. *Basic Service:* Subscribers: 18,000; 11/15/93. *Local Advertising Accepted.*

Continental Cablevision (49,645 subscribers). 27800 Franklin Rd., Southfield, MI 48034. (313) 353-3905; FAX: (313) 353-0141. Walter Maude, gen mgr; Beth Segler, mktg dir; Wayne Hindmarsh, loc adv dir; Richard Smith, chief tech.
Area(s) Served: MI. County: Oakland. Serving Keego Harbor, Lathrup Village, Lake, Oak Park, Orchard Lake, Royal Oak Twp., Southfield, Sylvan, West Bloomfield. Miles of Plant: 887. Homes Passed: 72,900. Homes Served: 49,645. *Channel Capacity:* 49. In use: 49. *Basic Service:* Subscribers: 49,645; 11/15/93. Pay Per View Subscribers: 22,800; 11/12/91. *Local Advertising Accepted. Equipment:* Scientific-Atlanta headend; Magnavox amplifiers; Comm/Scope cable; Sony cameras; Sony VTRs; Video Data Systems & Quanta character generators; Jerrold & Scientific-Atlanta set top converters; Scientific-Atlanta addressable set-top converters; Eagle traps; Ziemak film chain; Scientific- Atlanta satellite antenna; Scientific-Atlanta satellite receivers.

Continental Cablevision (61,000 subscribers). Union Depot Place, 214 E. Fourth St., St. Paul, MN 55101. (612) 224-2697; FAX: (612) 298-9520. Randall Coleman, gen mgr; Fran Zeuli, mktg dir; Mike Solac, loc adv dir; Dick Behr, chief tech.
Area(s) Served: MN. Counties: Dakota, Ramsey. Serving Inver Grove Heights, Lilydale, Mendota, Mendota Heights, South St. Paul, Sunfish Lake, West St. Paul. Miles of Plant: 850. Homes Passed: 144,000. Homes Served: 61,000. *Channel Capacity:* 62. In use: 62. *Basic Service:* Subscribers: 61,000; 11/15/93. *Pay Services:* Total Pay Subscribers: 53,000. Pay Per View Subscribers: 58,000. *Local Advertising Accepted.*

Continental Cablevision (22,000 subscribers). 1315 Granville Pike, Lancaster, OH 43130. (614) 653-6899; FAX: (614) 653-0019. Dave Johnston, gen mgr; Mike Bash, chief tech.
Area(s) Served: OH. Counties: Fairfield, Licking, Pickaway. Serving Ashville, Baltimore, Berne, Bloom, Bremen, Carrcll, Circleville, Creek, Grenfield, Harrison, Hocking, Liberty, Lima, Millersport, Pataskala, Pickaway, Pleasant, Rush, South Bloomfield, Stoutsville, Sugar Grove, Thurston, Walnut, Washington. Miles of Plant: 505. Homes Passed: 33,685. Homes Served: 22,000. *Channel Capacity:* 30. In use: 29. *Basic Service:* Subscribers: 22,000; 11/15/93. *Pay Services:* Total Pay Subscribers: 11,212; 10/31/91. *Local Advertising Accepted. Equipment:* Scientific-Atlanta headend; Scientific-Atlanta amplifiers; Comm/Scope cable; Panasonic set top converters.

Continental Cablevision (79,486 subscribers). 3914 Wistar Rd., Richmond, VA 23228. (804) 262-4004; FAX: (804) 264-8435. David Lee, gen mgr; Kenneth Dye, mktg dir; Matthew Zoller, loc adv dir; Bill Watson, chief tech; Barbara Parker, cust svc dir.
Area(s) Served: VA. Counties: Goochland, Hanover, Henrico. Serving Ashland. Homes Passed: 107,000. Homes Served: 79,486. *Channel Capacity:* 38. In use: 38. *Basic Service:* Subscribers: 79,486; 11/15/93. *Pay Services:* Total Pay Subscribers: 54,500; 10/31/91. *Local Advertising Accepted.*

Continental Cablevision Inc. (83,485 subscribers). 760 Main St., Wilmington, MA 01887. (508) 658-0400; FAX: (508) 657-3885. Greg Brenner, gen mgr; Tom Cagney, mktg dir; George Picariello, chief tech.
Area(s) Served: MA. County: Middlesex. Serving Billerica, Burlington, Reading, Stoneheart, Wilmington, Winchester, Woburn. Miles of Plant: 754. Homes Passed: 64,652. Homes Served: 83,485. *Channel Capacity:* 54. In use: 54. *Basic Service:* Subscribers: 83,485; 11/15/93. *Pay Services:* Total Pay Subscribers: 44,756; 10/22/91. Pay Per View Subscribers: 42,333; 10/22/91. *Local Advertising Accepted.*

Continental Cablevision Inc. of Springfield (44,911 subscribers). 3303 Main St., Springfield, MA 01107. (413) 733-5121; FAX: (413) 734-9243. Richard F. Orr, gen mgr; Mark Smith, mktg dir.
Area(s) Served: MA. County: Hampden. Serving Long Meadow, Springfield. Miles of Plant: 620. Homes Passed: 69,561. Homes Served: 44,911. *Channel Capacity:* 80. In use: 60. *Basic Service:* Subscribers: 44,911; 11/15/93. *No Local Advertising Accepted. Equipment:* Jerrold headend; Magnavox amplifiers; Times cable; Hitachi & Sony cameras; Sony VTRs; Compuvid character generator; Regency, Oak, Hamlin & Scientific-Atlanta set top converters; Regency & Jerrold addressable set top converters; Eagle traps; Ziemark film chain; Microdyne satellite antenna & satellite receivers.

Continental Cablevision of Brockton (51,000 subscribers). 4 Main St., Brockton, MA 02401. (508) 588-9290; FAX: (508) 588-5168. Richard Donahue, gen mgr; T.J. Lacey, mktg dir; Jack Orpen, chief tech; Renea Jeffers, cust svc dir.
Area(s) Served: MA. Counties: Norfolk, Plymouth. Serving Avon, Brockton, East Bridgewater, Easton, Hanson, Holbrook, Raimen, Stoten, West Bridgewater, Whitman. Miles of Plant: 938. Homes Passed: 55,666. Homes Served: 51,000. *Channel Capacity:* 70. In use: 59. *Basic Service:* Subscribers: 51,000; 11/15/93. Programming (via satellite): 25 chs. Programming (via microwave): 1 ch. Programming (off air): 16 chs. Pay Per View Subscribers: 29,382; 09/30/91. *Local Advertising Accepted.*

Continental Cablevision of Broward County (155,140 subscribers). 141 N.W. 16th St., Pompano Beach, FL 33060. (305) 946-7011; FAX: (305) 782-5781. Ellen Filipiak, gen mgr; Larry Hoepfner, mktg dir; Michael Anapolsky, loc adv dir; Andy McCarthy, chief tech; Bill Shaw, cust svc dir.
Area(s) Served: FL. County: Broward. Serving Deerfield Beach, Hillsboro Beach, Lauderhill, Lazy Lake, Lighthouse Point, Oakland Park, Plantation, Pompano Beach, Sunrise, Tamarac, Wilton Manors. Miles of Plant: 1,507. Homes Passed: 227,021. Homes Served: 155,140. *Channel Capacity:* 54. In use: 52. *Basic Service:* Subscribers: 155,140; 11/15/93. *Local Advertising Accepted.*

Continental Cablevision of Connecticut (33,266 subscribers). 5 Niblick Rd., Enfield, CT 06082. (203) 741-3531; FAX: (203) 741-6249. Mark Smith, mktg dir; Mark Clark, chief tech.
Area(s) Served: CT, MA. Counties: Hartford, Hampden, Toland. Serving East Granby, East Windsor, Enfield, Granby, Hartland, Holland, Somers, Stafford, Suffield, Union, Windsor Locks. Miles of Plant: 899. Homes Passed: 45,327. Homes Served: 33,266. *Channel Capacity:* 54. In use: 54. *Basic Service:* Subscribers: 33,266; 9/30/93. *Pay Services:* Total Pay Subscribers: 29,092. Pay Per View Subscribers: 19,000. *Local Advertising Accepted.*

Continental Cablevision of Lake County Inc. (38,374 subscribers). 7820 Division Dr., Mentor, OH 44060. (216) 974-7000; FAX: (216) 974-3201. Michael F. Battel, gen mgr; Joyce Rinear, mktg dir; David Sanders, chief tech; Bonnie Gross, cust svc dir.
Area(s) Served: OH. County: Lake. Serving Eastlake, Fairport Harbor, Grand River, Lakeline, Mentor, Paines-

Multiple Systems Operators, Independent Owners & Cable Systems

ville, Timberlake, Wickliffe, Willoughby, Willoughby Hills. Miles of Plant: 681. Homes Passed: 52,427. Homes Served: 38,374. *Channel Capacity:* 43. In use: 43. *Basic Service:* Subscribers: 38,374; 09/30/93. *Local Advertising Accepted.*

Continental Cablevision of Lansing Inc. (59,285 subscribers). 1401 E. Miller, Lansing, MI 48909. (517) 394-0001. Patricia Wilson, gen mgr; Dave Childs, mktg dir; Joe Boullion, chief tech.
Area(s) Served: MI. Counties: Clinton, Eaton, Ingham. Serving Alaiedon, Delhi, Delta, DeWitt, Eaton Rapids, Grand Ledge, Hamlin, Lansing, Lansing Twp., Oneida, Watertown, Windsor. Miles of Plant: 880. Homes Passed: 87,500. Homes Served: 59,285. *Channel Capacity:* 41. In use: 41. *Basic Service:* Subscribers: 59,285; 11/15/93. *Local Advertising Accepted.*

Continental Cablevision of Massachusetts Inc. (56,515 subscribers). 95 Wexford St., Needham, MA 02194. (617) 449-7080; FAX: (617) 455-8693. Anthony D. Doar, gen mgr; Karen Sennott, mktg dir; Joe Guariglia, chief tech.
Area(s) Served: MA. Counties: Middlesex, Norfolk. Serving Natick, Needham, Newton, Sherbon, Watertown, Wayland, Wellesley, Weston. Miles of Plant: 306. Homes Served: 56,515. *Channel Capacity:* 61. In use: 61. *Basic Service:* Subscribers: 56,515; 11/15/93.

Continental Cablevision of Massachusetts Inc. (85,000 subscribers). 92 Glenn St., Lawrence, MA 01843. (508) 687-2288; FAX: (508) 687-7932. Greg Brenner, gen mgr; Barbara Moschetto, cust svc dir.
Area(s) Served: MA. County: Essex. Serving Lawrence, Methuen, North Andover. Miles of Plant: 1,144. Homes Passed: 95,687. Homes Served: 85,000. *Channel Capacity:* 77. In use: 36. *Basic Service:* Subscribers: 85,000; 11/15/93. *Pay Services:* Total Pay Subscribers: 31,433; 11/13/91. Pay Per View Subscribers: 11,000; 11/13/91. *Local Advertising Accepted. Equipment:* Jerrold headend; Magnavox amplifiers; Times cable; Ikegami, Shibadin & Hitachi cameras; Sony VTRs; Texscan character generator; Jerrold set top converters; Vitek & Pico traps; Microdyne satellite antenna; Scientific-Atlanta satellite receivers; Catel commercial insert.

Continental Cablevision of Michigan Inc. (40,700 subscribers). 2800 S. Gulley Rd., Dearborn Heights, MI 48125. (313) 277-1050; FAX: (313) 277-1796. Kay'elen Perry, gen mgr; Sue Ruwe, mktg dir; Nancy Meledosian, loc adv dir; Robert M. Anderson, chief tech; Carrell Bouchard, cust svc dir.
Area(s) Served: MI. County: Wayne. Serving Dearborn Heights, Westland. Pop: 149,771. Miles of Plant: 500. Homes Passed: 57,859. Homes Served: 40,700. *Channel Capacity:* 62. In use: 58. *Basic Service:* Subscribers: 40,700; 11/15/93. Programming (via satellite): 40 chs. Programming (off air): 10 chs. *Pay Services:* Total Pay Subscribers: 48,067; 10/23/92. (1) Pay Units: 8,415; 09/30/91. Programming (via satellite): HBO. (2) Pay Units: 5,371; 09/30/91. Programming (via satellite): Cinemax. (3) Pay Units: 5,564; 09/30/91. Programming (via satellite): Showtime. (4) Pay Units: 3,229; 09/30/91. Programming (via satellite): The Movie Channel. (5) Pay Units: 3,374; 09/30/91. Programming (via satellite): Disney. Pay Per View Subscribers: 38,764; 10/23/92. *Local Advertising Accepted. Equipment:* Scientific-Atlanta 8500, 8580, 8590 converters.

Continental Cablevision of New England (26,751 subscribers). 8 Commercial St., Concord, NH 03301. (603) 224-1984; FAX: (603) 226-0764. Mary J. Colletti, gen mgr; Jeff Vandeberghe, mktg dir; Dan Cannon, chief tech; Debra Repoza, cust svc dir.
Area(s) Served: NH. Counties: Belknap, Grafton, Hillsborough, Merrimack. Serving Alexandria, Allenstown, Antrim, Boscawen, Bow, Bridgewater, Bristol, Canterbury, Chichester, Concord, Deering, Hebron, Henniker, Hillsboro, Hopkinton, Loudon, New Hampton, Pembroke, Weare. Miles of Plant: 801. Homes Passed: 38,469. Homes Served: 26,751. *Basic Service:* Subscribers: 26,751; 08/21/93. *Pay Services:* Total Pay Subscribers: 13,239; 08/21/93. Pay Per View Subscribers: 9,459; 08/21/93. *Local Advertising Accepted. Equipment:* Jerrold headend; Jerrold & Century III amplifiers; Times cable; Sony VTRs; Scientific-Atlanta addressable set top converters; Microdyne & Scientific-Atlanta satellite antenna; Microdyne satellite receivers.

Continental Cablevision of New England Inc. (22,576 subscribers). Bldg. E, 8 Industrial Way, Salem, NH 03079. (603) 893-1648; FAX: (603) 894-4889. Greg Sanders, gen mgr; Heather King, mktg dir; Al Grabowski, chief tech.
Area(s) Served: NH. County: Rockingham. Serving Derry, Hampstead, Plaistow, Salem, Sandown. Miles of Plant: 484. Homes Passed: 28,691. Homes Served: 22,576. *Channel Capacity:* 52. In use: 46. *Basic Service:* Subscribers: 22,576; 11/15/93. *Pay Services:* Total Pay Subscribers: 15,000; 10/21/91. Pay Per View Subscribers: 12,000; 10/21/91. *Local Advertising Accepted. Equipment:* Catel headend; Magnavox amplifiers; Times cable; Sony VTRs; Compuvid character generator; Jerrold set top converters; Scientific-Atlanta addressable set top converters; Eagle traps.

Continental Cablevision of New Hampshire Inc. (43,000 subscribers). 155 Commerce Way, Portsmouth, NH 03801. (603) 436-6050; FAX: (603) 431-0083. Glenn Tamaro, gen mgr; Lisa Clark, mktg dir; John Dowd, chief tech; Eileen Blanchard, cust svc dir.
Area(s) Served: NH, ME. Counties: Rockingham, York. Serving Eliot, Exeter, Greenland, Hampton, Kittery, New Castle, Newington, Portsmouth, Rye, Stratham. Miles of Plant: 425. Homes Passed: 31,000. Homes Served: 43,000. *Channel Capacity:* 59. In use: 56. *Basic Service:* Subscribers: 43,000; 11/15/93. Pay Per View Subscribers: 7,500; 11/14/91. *Local Advertising Accepted.*

Continental Cablevision of New York (57,000 subscribers). One Van Cortlandt Ave., Ossining, NY 10562. (914) 762-8684; FAX: (914) 762-0799. Douglas R. Guthrie, gen mgr; D.J. Shugars, mktg dir; Diane Rainey, loc adv dir; Elmo Ortiz, chief tech; Tara Cohen, cust svc dir.
Area(s) Served: NY. County: Westchester. Serving Bedford, Briarcliff Manor, Buchanan, Cortlandt, Croton, Mt. Pleasant, New Castle, North Tarrytown, Ossining, Peekskill, Philipstown, Pleasantville. Pop: 150,000. Miles of Plant: 730. Homes Passed: 58,255. Homes Served: 57,000. *Channel Capacity:* 41. In use: 41. *Basic Service:* Subscribers: 57,000; 11/15/93. Programming (via satellite): 15 chs. Programming (off air): 11 chs. Pay Per View Subscribers: 24,500; 10/15/91. *Local Advertising Accepted. Equipment:* Magnavox & Sylvania line equipment; Jerrold headend; Jerrold converters; Panasonic non-addressable converters; Cabledata billing; Telecorp ARU; TelVue ANI.

Continental Cablevision of Ohio (66,000 subscribers). 4333 Display Ln., Kettering, OH 45429. (513) 294-6800; FAX: (513) 294-3994. Cathy Schelb, mktg dir; Debbie Bowser, cust svc dir.
Area(s) Served: OH. Counties: Greene, Montgomery, Warren. Serving Beavercreek, Bellbrook, Centerville, Clear Creek, Corwin, Franklin, Kettering, Miami, Miamisburg, Moraine, Oakwood, Spring Valley, Springboro, Sugar Creek, Wayne, Waynesville, West Carrollton. Homes Served: 66,000. *Channel Capacity:* 37. In use: 37. *Basic Service:* Subscribers: 66,000; 11/30/92.

Continental Cablevision of Ohio Inc. (23,700 subscribers). 576 Ternes Ave., Elyria, OH 44035. (216) 365-1861. Larry Williamson, gen mgr; Susan St. Clair, mktg dir; Bill Keslar, chief tech.
Area(s) Served: OH. County: Lorain. Serving Amherst, Amherst Twp., Carlisle Twp., Elyria, Elyria Twp., North Ridgeville, South Amherst. Miles of Plant: 520. Homes Passed: 40,800. Homes Served: 23,700. *Channel Capacity:* 61. In use: 42. *Basic Service:* Subscribers: 23,700; 10/31/92. Programming (via satellite): 31 chs. Programming (off air): 11 chs. *Pay Services:* Total Pay Subscribers: 19,800; 10/31/92. *Local Advertising Accepted. Equipment:* Scientific-Atlanta headend; Magnavox amplifiers; Comm/Scope cable; Panasonic cameras; Sony VTRs; Video Data Systems character generator; Jerrold set top converters; Eagle traps; Scientific-Atlanta & Fort Worth Tower satellite antennas; Microdyne satellite receivers.

Continental Cablevision of Ohio Inc. (38,221 subscribers). 4166 Little York Rd., Dayton, OH 45424. (513) 294-6400; FAX: (513) 890-4951. Robert E. Pugh, gen mgr; Darrell Pugh, chief tech.
Area(s) Served: OH. Counties: Greene, Montgomery. Serving Bath, Butler, Clay, Clayton, Dayton, Englewood, Harrison, Huber Heights, Madison, Randolph, Trotwood, Union, Vandalia. Miles of Plant: 670. Homes Served: 38,221. *Channel Capacity:* 37. In use: 37. *Basic Service:* Subscribers: 38,221; 11/30/92. *Pay Services:* Total Pay Subscribers: 30,163; 11/18/91. *Local Advertising Accepted. Equipment:* RCA headend; Sylvania amplifiers; General, Comm/Scope & Theta-Com cables; Video Data Systems, 3M character generator; Jerrold & Panasonic set top converters; Eagle traps; Microdyne, Scientific-Atlanta & RCA satellite antennas; Microdyne, Sony & Scientific-Atlanta satellite receivers.

Continental Cablevision of Ohio Inc. (26,057 subscribers). 75 W. Main St., Springfield, OH 45502. (513) 325-7001; FAX: (513) 325-9844. Bob Pugh, gen mgr; Timothy J. Kuss, chief tech.
Area(s) Served: OH. Counties: Clark, Madison. Serving Catawba, Clifton, Green, Harmony, Moorefield, Pleasant, South Charleston Village, South Solon, South Vienna, Springfield, Springfield Twp. Homes Served: 26,057. *Channel Capacity:* 45. In use: 45. *Basic Service:* Subscribers: 26,057; 11/30/92. *Local Advertising Accepted.*

Continental Cablevision of Richmond (41,000 subscribers). 918 North Blvd., Richmond, VA 23230. (804) 355-2124; FAX: (804) 353-0285. Leonardo A. Chappelle, gen mgr; Kenneth Dye, mktg dir; Matthew Zoller, loc adv dir; James Wilson, chief tech; Nancy Hamner, cust svc dir.
Area(s) Served: VA. Serving Richmond. Pop: 205,000. Miles of Plant: 724. Homes Passed: 90,752. Homes Served: 41,000. *Channel Capacity:* 38. In use: 38. *Basic Service:* Subscribers: 41,000; 11/15/93. Programming (via satellite): 25 chs. Programming (off air): 7 chs. *Local Advertising Accepted. Equipment:* Magnavox line equipment; Scientific-Atlanta & Pioneer converters.

Continental Cablevision of St. Louis County (28,665 subscribers). 317 W. Main St., Belleville, IL 62220. (618) 277-7820; FAX: (618) 277-6751. Mary Harp, gen mgr; Bob Krahman, mktg dir; Ivan Parrish, chief tech; Glenda Riley, cust svc dir.
Area(s) Served: IL. County: St. Clair. Serving Belleville, Fairview Heights, O'Fallon, St. Claire, Swanesa. Miles of Plant: 590. Homes Passed: 47,410. Homes Served: 28,665. *Channel Capacity:* 40. In use: 40. *Basic Service:* Subscribers: 28,665; 11/15/93. Programming (via satellite): 22 chs. Programming (via microwave): 1 ch. Programming (off air): 8 chs. *Local Advertising Accepted.*

Continental Cablevision of St. Louis County Inc. (41,452 subscribers). 2411 Verona Ave., St. Louis, MO 63114. (314) 428-0915; FAX: (314) 428-4235. Thomas Hopfinger, gen mgr; Pat Koch, mktg dir; Richard Bizan, loc adv dir; Chuck Prossez, chief tech; Cathy Statler, cust svc dir.
Area(s) Served: MO. County: St. Louis. Serving Breckenridge Hills, Chesterfield, Clayton, Edmundson, Maplewood, Overland, Stann, University City. Pop: 200,000. Miles of Plant: 826. Homes Passed: 78,000. Homes Served: 41,452. *Channel Capacity:* 39. In use: 39. *Basic Service:* Subscribers: 41,452; 09/30/93. Programming (via satellite): 28 chs. Programming (off air): 7 chs. *Local Advertising Accepted. Equipment:* Magnavox & Scientific-Atlanta line equipment; Panasonic, Jerrold & Scientific-Atlanta remote boxes.

Continental Cablevision of Will County (66,580 subscribers). 1304 Marquette Dr., Romeoville, IL 60441. (708) 759-4600; FAX: (708) 759-2611. William J. Shreffler, gen mgr; Chuck Bernard, mktg dir; Tom Broadwater, loc adv dir; Jim Bragg, chief tech; Adriana Johnson, cust svc dir.
Area(s) Served: IL. County: Will. Serving Beecher, Bolingbrook, Crest Hill, Fairmont, Frankfort, Frankfort Twp., Homer Twp., Joliet, Joliet Twp., Lockport, Lockport Twp., Manteno, Mokena, Monee, Monee Twp., New Lenox, New Lenox Twp., Peotone, Plainfield, Plainfield Twp., Rockdale, Romeoville, Shorewood, Troy Twp., Wheatland Twp. Pop: 310,000. Miles of Plant: 1,394. Homes Passed: 104,934. Homes Served: 66,580. *Channel Capacity:* 56. In use: 56. *Basic Service:* Subscribers: 66,580; 07/31/93. *Pay Services:* Total Pay Subscribers: 54,157; 07/31/93. Pay Per View Subscribers: 63,398; 07/31/93. *Local Advertising Accepted. Equipment:* Provided by Tocom.

SMALLER SYSTEMS

California - Continental Cablevision of California, 20930 Bonita Ave., Suite Z, Carson, CA 90746; (213) 515-1303. Continental Cablevision of California, 189 Business Ctr. Dr., Corona, CA 91720; (714) 735-6767. Continental Cablevision of California, 302 E. Rowland St., Covina, CA 90723; (818) 915-6031. Continental Cablevision of California, 129 E Ctr., Suite 4, Manteca, CA 95336; (209) 239-4959. Continental Cablevision of California, 2808 Metropolitan Pl., Pomona, CA 91767; (714) 596-3859. Continental Cablevision of California, 13816 Red Hill Ave., Tustin, CA 92680; (714) 731-6793. **Illinois -** Continental Cablevision of Cook County, 14150 Chicago Rd., Dolton, IL 60419; (708) 841-9606. Continental Cablevision of Illinois, Box 629, 109 W. Main St., Freeport, IL 60132; (815) 235-7183. Continental Cablevision of Illinois, Box 629, 213 W. Second St., Kewanee, IL 61443; (309) 852-3316. Continental Cablevision of Illinois, Box 570, 125 N. Kickapoo, Lincoln, IL 62656; (217) 735-3448. Continental Cablevision of Illinois, 300 S. Main St., Morton, IL 61550; (309) 263-2721. Continen-

Multiple Systems Operators, Independent Owners & Cable Systems

tal Cablevision of Illinois, Box 309, 1617 Valle Vista Blvd., Pekin, IL 61554; (309) 347-7071. Continental Cablevision of Illinois, 115 N. Fifth St., Quincy, IL 62301; (217) 222-5388. Continental Cablevision of Morton Grove, 8101 N. Austin Ave., Morton Grove, IL 60053; (708) 470-0803. Continental Cablevision of St. Louis County, 4336 E. Hwy. 161, Belleville, IL 62221; (618) 566-2218. **Iowa** - Continental Cablevision of Illinois, Box 407, 411 Main St., Keokuk, IA 52632; (319) 524-8544. **Maine** - Continental Cablevision of New England, 42 Industrial Park Rd., Saco, ME 04072; (207) 282-5916. **Massachusetts** - Cable Advertising, 110 Antwerp St., Milton, MA 02186; (617) 698-0814. Continental Cablevision, 27 Hale St., Newburyport, MA 01950; (508) 465-2230. Continental Cablevision of Massachusetts, 149 Wareham Rd., Marion, MA 02738; (508) 748-2400. Continental Cablevision of Massachusetts, Box 643, 172 Central St., Milford, MA 01757; (508) 478-0087. Continental Cablevision of Massachusetts, 249 W. Chestnut St., Natick, MA 01760; (617) 651-0022. Continental Cablevision of Massachusetts, Box 1678, 15 Locust Rd., Orleans, MA 02653; (508) 255-7300. Continental Cablevision of Massachusetts, 89 N. Main St., Randolph, MA 02368; (617) 986-7505. Continental Cablevision of Massachusetts, 41 Marble St., Revere, MA 02151; (617) 289-4103. Continental Cablevision of Needham, 95 Wexford St., Needham, MA 02194; (617) 449-7080. Continental Cablevision of Southern Massachusetts, 169 N. Franklin St., Holbrook, MA 02343; (617) 767-1405. Continental Cablevision of Southern Massachusetts, 159 E. Grove St., Drawer B, Middleboro, MA 02346; (508) 824-1457. Continental Cablevision of Western New England, 71 Bradford St., Northampton, MA 01060; (413) 584-8661. **Michigan** - Continental Cablevision of Michigan, 162 E. 19th St., Holland, MI 48423; (616) 392-7071. Continental Cablevision of Michigan, 2000 Cooper St., Jackson, MI 49202; (517) 787-2000. Continental Cablevision of Michigan, 333 Washington Sq. N., Lansing, MI 48933; (517) 485-5940. Continental Cablevision of Michigan, 32090 John R. Rd., Madison Heights, MI 48071; (313) 583-1354. **Missouri** - Continental Cablevision of St. Louis County, 7053 Emma Ave., Jennings, MO 63136; (314) 389-0914. Continental Cablevision of St. Louis County, 1194 Lake St. Louis Blvd., Lake St. Louis, MO 63367; (314) 625-1611. Continental Cablevision of St. Louis County, 11838 Borman Dr., St. Louis, MO 63146 (314) 569-2111. **Nevada** - Continental Cablevision of Nevada, Box 18198, 7111 A 15 S. Virginia St., Reno, NV 89511; (702) 851-3110. **New Hampshire** - Continental Cablevision of New England, 79 Main St., Dover, NH 03820; (603) 742-2234. Continental Cablevision of New England, Box 1010, 115 Epping Rd., Exeter, NH 03833; (603) 772-4732. **Ohio** - Continental Cablevision of Ohio, One Mound St., Athens, OH 45701; (614) 592-4435. Continental Cablevision of Ohio, 209 W. Main St., Finley, OH 45840; (419) 423-8515. Continental Cablevision of Ohio, 21 Public Sq., Galion, OH 44833; (419) 468-2000. Continental Cablevision of Ohio, 29 E. Main St., Norwalk, OH 44857; (419) 668-8111. Continental Cablevision of Ohio, 90 S. Washington St., Tiffin, OH 44883; (419) 447-7328. **Virginia** - Continental Cablevision of Virginia, Box 1926, 417 Old York Hampton Rd., Grafton, VA 23692; (804) 898-4626. Continental Cablevision of Virginia, 112 Newquarter Rd., Drawer G, Williamsburg, VA 23185; (804) 229-7622.

Conway Corporation

Box 99, 1319 Prairie St., Conway, AR 72032. (501) 450-6000. W.M. Hegeman, pres, vp opns & vp mktg. Total Basic Subscribers: 9,896; Pay Cable Subscribers: 2,800; Number of Cable Systems: 1.

Cooney Cable Associates Inc.

228 Park Ave., Worcester, MA 01609. (508) 754-5865; FAX: (508) 752-7342. John Cooney, pres. Total Basic Subscribers: 2,650; Pay Cable Subscribers: 950; Number of Cable Systems: 4.

SMALLER SYSTEMS

West Virginia - Cooney Cable Associates of West Virginia, Delbarton, WV; (304) 475-2081.

Coosa Cable Co.

1701 Cogswell Ave., Pell City, AL 35125. (205) 884-4545. Art Smith, pres; Wanda McGowen, vp mktg; Jeffrey Smith, vp. Owned by Art Smith. Total Basic Subscribers: 5,900; Number of Cable Systems: 1.

Phyllis Cordova

Box 1007, Clove Rd., Montague, NJ 07827. (201) 293-7474. Teresa Gurdineer, vp. Owned by Joseph Biondo & Phyllis Cordova. Total Basic Subscribers: 1,282; Number of Cable Systems: 1.

SMALLER SYSTEMS

New Jersey - Montague Cable Company, Box 1007, Clove Rd., Montague, NJ 07827.

Country Cable Inc.

6839 Convoy Ct., San Diego, CA 92111. (619) 789-2663; FAX: (619) 292-1116. Bruce Witte, pres; C.G. Pappas, vp opns. Total Basic Subscribers: 2,400; Pay Cable Subscribers: 1,400; Number of Cable Systems: 1.

Covington Cable TV

1167 Pace St., Covington, GA 30209. (404) 787-4444. Gary Curtiss, vp opns; Barbara Cruse, vp. Owned by City of Covington. Total Basic Subscribers: 6,800; Number of Cable Systems: 1.

Cox Cable Communications

1400 Lake Hearn Dr., Atlanta, GA 30319. (404) 843-5000; FAX: (404) 843-5777. James O. Robbins, pres; Jimmy Hayes, CFO; Barry R. Elson, vp opns; Ajit M. Dalvi, vp mktg & vp progmg; Patrick J. Esser, vp adv; Robert O'Leary, vp; David Woodrow, vp; Alex Best, vp. Owned by Cox Enterprises Inc. Total Basic Subscribers: 1,764,562; Pay Cable Subscribers: 1,243,957; Number of Cable Systems: 24.

SYSTEMS WITH OVER 20,000 SUBSCRIBERS

Cox Cable Bakersfield (21,972 subscribers). 820 22nd St., Bakersfield, CA 93301. (805) 327-0821. Jill Campbell, gen mgr; Debbie Hernstedt, mktg dir.
Area(s) Served: CA. County: Kern. Serving Bakersfield. Homes Served: 21,972. *Channel Capacity:* 54. In use: 50. *Basic Service:* Subscribers: 21,972; 10/31/93. *Pay Services:* Total Pay Subscribers: 7,900. Pay Per View Subscribers: 8,300. *No Local Advertising Accepted.*

Cox Cable Cedar Rapids Inc. (43,118 subscribers). 6300 Council St. N.E., Cedar Rapids, IA 52402. (319) 395-9699; FAX: (319) 393-7017. Mike Horan, gen mgr; Arlene Heck, mktg dir; Bob Hanson, loc adv dir; Connie Fulton, cust svc dir.
Area(s) Served: IA. County: Linn. Serving Cedar Rapids, Hiawath, Marion, Toddville. Homes Passed: 60,135. Homes Served: 43,118. *Channel Capacity:* 35. In use: 35. *Basic Service:* Subscribers: 43,118; 10/31/93. *Pay Services:* Total Pay Subscribers: 24,709. (1) Pay Units: 16,394. Programming (via satellite): HBO. (2) Pay Units: 3,123. Programming (via satellite): Cinemax. (3) Pay Units: 2,655. Programming (via satellite): Showtime. Pay Per View Subscribers: 2,000. *Local Advertising Accepted.*

Cox Cable Cleveland Area Inc. (64,000 subscribers). 12221 Plaza Dr., Parma, OH 44130. (216) 676-8300; FAX: (216) 676-8689. Ron Hammaker, gen mgr; Kevin Killen, mktg dir; Kevin Haynes, cust svc dir.
Area(s) Served: OH. County: Cuyahoga. Serving Broadview Heights, Brooklyn Heights, Fairview Park, Lakewood, Olmsted Falls, Olmsted, Parma, Parma Heights, Rocky River, Seven Hills. Miles of Plant: 750. Homes Passed: 98,000. Homes Served: 64,000. *Channel Capacity:* 39. In use: 39. *Basic Service:* Subscribers: 64,000; 10/31/93. *Pay Services:* Total Pay Subscribers: 39,000. Pay Per View Subscribers: 11,000; 12/01/92. *Local Advertising Accepted.*

Cox Cable Greater Hartford (57,695 subscribers). 801 Parker St., Manchester, CT 06045-0310. (203) 646-6289; FAX: (203) 643-4041. Jayson Juraska, gen mgr; Frank Naples, mktg dir; Bill Farina, loc adv dir; John Roberts, chief tech; Robyn King, cust svc dir.
Area(s) Served: CT. Serving Glastonburg, Manchester, Newington, Rocky Hill, South Windsor, Wethersfield. Miles of Plant: 900. Homes Served: 57,695. *Basic Service:* Subscribers: 57,695; 10/31/93. Pay Per View Subscribers: 18,000; 10/15/91. *Local Advertising Accepted.*

Cox Cable Greater Ocala Inc. (28,000 subscribers). Box 2318, 2410 S.W. 27th Ave., Ocala, FL 34478-2318. (904) 237-1111; FAX: (904) 237-6706. Gary Cassard, gen mgr; Doris Young, loc adv dir; Kenneth Parnell, chief tech; Jamie Cherlin, cust svc dir.
Area(s) Served: FL. County: Marion. Serving Ocala. Homes Served: 28,000. *Channel Capacity:* 35. In use: 35. *Basic Service:* Subscribers: 28,000; 10/31/93. *Local Advertising Accepted.*

Cox Cable Hampton Roads Inc. (190,000 subscribers). 225 Clearfield Ave., Virginia Beach, VA 23462. (804) 497-1071; FAX: (804) 671-1501. Franklin Bowers, gen mgr; Larry Michel, mktg dir; Eric Zitron, loc adv dir; Dana Coltrin, chief tech; Bruce Williams, cust svc dir.
Area(s) Served: VA, NC. County: Currituck. Serving Norfolk, Portsmouth, Virginia Beach. Pop: 315,000. Homes Served: 190,000. *Channel Capacity:* 54. In use: 52. *Basic Service:* Subscribers: 190,000; 11/31/92. *Local Advertising Accepted.*

Cox Cable Humboldt Inc. (30,500 subscribers). 911 W. Wabash, Eureka, CA 95501. (707) 443-3128; FAX: (707) 444-9017. Dorothy Lovfald, gen mgr; Wendy Purnell, mktg dir; Dwayne Darnell, chief tech; Sharon Knife, cust svc dir.
Area(s) Served: CA. County: Humboldt. Serving Arcata, Bayside, Big Lagoon, Blue Lake, Carlotta, Eureka, Ferndale, Fields Landing, Fortuna, Hydesville, King Salmon, Lolita, Rio Dell, Scotia, Trinidad. Homes Served: 30,500. *Channel Capacity:* 42. In use: 37. *Basic Service:* Subscribers: 30,500; 10/31/93. Pay Per View Subscribers: 2,500. *Local Advertising Accepted.*

Cox Cable Jefferson Parish (225,000 subscribers). 338 Edwards Ave., Harahan, LA 70123. (504) 733-5680; FAX: (504) 734-0869. Ray K. Nagin, gen mgr; Fred Bristol, mktg dir; Michael Salgado, loc adv dir; Warren Herkes, chief tech.
Area(s) Served: LA. County: Jefferson Parish. Homes Served: 225,000. *Channel Capacity:* 47. In use: 47. *Basic Service:* Subscribers: 225,000; 10/31/93. *Local Advertising Accepted.*

Cox Cable Lubbock (41,574 subscribers). 6710 Hartford Ave., Lubbock, TX 79413. (806) 793-2222; (806) 793-7381; FAX: (806) 793-7818. Randy Wink, gen mgr; Phil Maddern, loc adv dir; Dave Mothershed, chief tech; Christy Meriwether, cust svc dir.
Area(s) Served: TX. County: Lubbock. Serving Lubbock. Pop: 185,000. Miles of Plant: 640. Homes Passed: 78,000. Homes Served: 41,574. *Channel Capacity:* 52. In use: 46. *Basic Service:* Subscribers: 41,574; 09/07/93. Programming (via satellite): Prevue, CSPAN I, CSPAN II, TBN, WOR, WGN, WTBS, ESPN, USA, Discovery, Nickelodeon, CNN, A&E, TNN, MTV, Family Channel, HNN, TNT, QVC, CNBC, E!, Comedy Central, HSE, Cinemax, HBO, Disney, Showtime, TMC, Viewer's Choice. Programming (off air): CBS, ABC, NBC, Fox, K40AN, Telemundo, Univision. *Pay Services:* Total Pay Subscribers: 35,827; 04/01/92. (1) Pay Units: 14,023; 04/01/92. Programming (via satellite): HBO. (2) Pay Units: 8,495; 04/01/92. Programming (via satellite): Showtime. (3) Pay Units: 5,763; 04/01/92. Programming (via satellite): Cinemax. (4) Pay Units: 3,492; 04/01/92. Programming (via satellite): The Movie Channel. Pay Per View Subscribers: 37,498; 04/01/92. *Local Advertising Accepted.*

Cox Cable Middle Georgia Inc. (68,699 subscribers). Box 10278, 6601 Hawkinsville Rd., Macon, GA 31206. (912) 784-8010; FAX: (912) 784-5100. Claus Kroeger, gen mgr; Charles Moore, mktg dir & cust svc dir; Tim Morgan, loc adv dir; Mark Williams, chief tech.
Area(s) Served: GA. Counties: Bibb, Houston, Jones, Peach. Serving Byron, Centerville, Macon, Warner-Robins. Homes Served: 68,699. *Channel Capacity:* 54. In use: 53. *Basic Service:* Subscribers: 68,699; 09/03/93. *Pay Services:* Total Pay Subscribers: 42,137; 11/12/92. Pay Per View Subscribers: 41,172; 09/03/93. *Local Advertising Accepted.*

Cox Cable New Orleans Inc. (90,000 subscribers). 2120 Canal St., New Orleans, LA 70112. (504) 522-3838; FAX: (504) 529-2394. C. Ray Nagin, gen mgr; Fred Bristol, mktg dir; Margaret King, cust svc dir.
Area(s) Served: LA. County: Orleans Parish. Serving Algiers, Gretna. Homes Served: 90,000. *Channel Capacity:* 54. In use: 54. *Basic Service:* Subscribers: 90,000; 10/31/93. *Local Advertising Accepted.*

Cox Cable Oklahoma City Inc. (98,000 subscribers). 2312 N.W. 10th St., Oklahoma City, OK 73107. (405) 525-2771; FAX: (405) 525-8030. David Bialis, gen mgr; Jim Lisko, mktg dir; Mark Kanter, loc adv dir; Kent Morris, cust svc dir.
Area(s) Served: OK. Counties: Canadian, Cleveland, Oklahoma. Serving Oklahoma City. Homes Served: 98,000. *Channel Capacity:* 38. In use: 38. *Basic Service:* Subscribers: 98,000; 10/31/93. *Pay Services:* Total Pay Subscribers: 82,800; 10/31/92. Pay Per View Subscribers: 11,700; 10/31/92. *Local Advertising Accepted.*

Multiple Systems Operators, Independent Owners & Cable Systems

Cox Cable Omaha (88,046 subscribers). 11505 W. Dodge Rd., Omaha, NE 68154. (402) 330-6770; FAX: (402) 330-6528. Richard Hook, gen mgr; Mark Caniglia, mktg dir; Bob Sebby, cust svc dir.
Area(s) Served: NE, IA. Counties: Douglas; Pottowatamie. Serving Carter Lake, Millard, Omaha. Homes Served: 88,046. *Channel Capacity:* 55. In use: 55. *Basic Service:* Subscribers: 88,046; 10/31/93. *Pay Services:* Total Pay Subscribers: 65,079; 10/24/91. (1) Pay Units: 29,460; 10/15/91. Programming (via satellite): HBO. (2) Pay Units: 4,850; 10/15/91. Programming (via satellite): The Movie Channel. (3) Pay Units: 6,660; 10/15/91. Programming (via satellite): Showtime. (4) Pay Units: 1,005; 10/15/91. Programming (via satellite): Playboy. (5) Pay Units: 17,470; 10/15/91. Programming (via satellite): Cinemax. (6) Pay Units: 275; 10/15/91. Programming (via satellite): Bravo. Pay Per View Subscribers: 26,000; 11/20/92. *Local Advertising Accepted.*

Cox Cable Quad Cities (58,500 subscribers). 3900 26th Ave., Moline, IL 61265. (309) 797-2580; FAX: (309) 797-2414. Kay Galligan, gen mgr; Doug Pauley, mktg dir; Mike Miller, loc adv dir; Mitch Carlson, chief tech; Dan Mills, cust svc dir.
Area(s) Served: IL, IA. Counties: Rock Island, Scott. Serving Bettendorf, Davenport, East Moline, Eldridge, Hampton, Long Grove, Moline, Pleasant Valley, Panorama Park, Parkview, Riverdale, Rock Island Arsenal, Silvis. Homes Passed: 91,214. *Channel Capacity:* 44. In use: 44. *Basic Service:* Subscribers: 58,500; 12/15/92. Pay Per View Subscribers: 16,432. *Local Advertising Accepted.*

Cox Cable Rhode Island Inc. (38,870 subscribers). 111 Comstock Pkwy., Cranston, RI 02921. (401) 943-6993; FAX: (401) 946-3830. Gary Perrelli, gen mgr; Genny Plas, mktg dir & cust svc dir; James Kelly, chief tech.
Area(s) Served: RI. County: Providence. Serving Burrillville, Cranston, Glocester, Johnston, Scituate. Homes Served: 38,870. *Channel Capacity:* 56. In use: 56. *Basic Service:* Subscribers: 38,870; 10/31/93. *Pay Services:* Total Pay Subscribers: 37,774; 10/31/92. Pay Per View Subscribers: 32,321; 10/15/91. *Local Advertising Accepted.*

Cox Cable Roanoke Inc. (53,000 subscribers). Box 13726, 1909 Salem Ave., Roanoke, VA 24036. (703) 982-1110; FAX: (703) 342-9172. Gretchen Shine, gen mgr; Bill Sledd, mktg dir; Fred Mareia, loc adv dir; Johnny Benson, chief tech; Barbara Robertson, cust svc dir.
Area(s) Served: VA. County: Roanoke. Serving Roanoke, Vinton. Homes Served: 53,000. *Channel Capacity:* 35. In use: 35. *Basic Service:* Subscribers: 53,000; 10/31/93. *Pay Services:* Total Pay Subscribers: 41,000. Pay Per View Subscribers: 16,000. *Local Advertising Accepted.*

Cox Cable Saginaw Inc. (32,032 subscribers). 720 N. Bates St., Saginaw, MI 48602. (517) 799-8030; FAX: (517) 799-7829. Phil Ahlschlager, gen mgr; Keir Daviol, chief tech.
Area(s) Served: MI. County: Saginaw. Serving Bridgeport, Buena Vista, Carrollton, Kochville, Saginaw, Spaulding, Zilwaukee. Homes Served: 32,032. *Channel Capacity:* 54. In use: 51. *Basic Service:* Subscribers: 32,032; 12/15/92. *Pay Services:* Total Pay Subscribers: 19,000; 11/15/91. Pay Per View Subscribers: 9,500; 11/15/91. *Local Advertising Accepted.*

Cox Cable San Diego (325,000 subscribers). 5159 Federal Blvd., San Diego, CA 92105. (619) 263-9251; FAX: (619) 266-5540. Robert McRann, gen mgr; Art Reynolds, mktg dir; Moya Gollaher, loc adv dir; Steve Gautereaux, chief tech; Ron Hummel, cust svc dir.
Area(s) Served: CA. County: San Diego. Serving Alpine, Bonita, Chula Vista, El Cajun, Imperial Beach, La Mesa, Lemon Grove, National City, Pine Valley, San Diego, San Ysidro, Santee. Pop: 1,861,846. Miles of Plant: 2,784. Homes Passed: 480,606. Homes Served: 325,000. *Channel Capacity:* 62. In use: 60. *Basic Service:* Subscribers: 325,000; 10/31/93. *Pay Services:* Total Pay Subscribers: 211,363; 10/31/92. Pay Per View Subscribers: 110,815; 10/31/92. *Local Advertising Accepted.*

Cox Cable Santa Barbara Inc. (62,600 subscribers). 22 S. Fairview Ave., Goleta, CA 93117. (805) 683-7751; FAX: (805) 964-6069. Duffy Leone, gen mgr; Bill Monser, mktg dir; Ray Briare, loc adv dir.
Area(s) Served: CA. County: Santa Barbara. Serving Carpinteria, Goleta, Isla Vista, Montecito, Santa Barbara, Summerland. Pop: 200,000. Miles of Plant: 700. Homes Passed: 80,000. Homes Served: 62,600. *Channel Capacity:* 46. In use: 46. *Basic Service:* Subscribers: 62,600; 10/31/93. *Local Advertising Accepted.*

Cox Cable South Carolina Inc. (23,400 subscribers). 1901 Oak St., Myrtle Beach, SC 29577. (803) 448-7196; FAX: (803) 626-2922. Darrell Wells, gen mgr; Carol Harvill-Vaughn, mktg dir; Linda Kohlhagen, loc adv dir; Mike Hagg, chief tech.
Area(s) Served: SC. County: Horry. Serving Conway, Myrtle Beach. Homes Passed: 28,700. Homes Served: 23,400. *Channel Capacity:* 54. *Basic Service:* Subscribers: 23,400; 10/31/93. *Pay Services:* Total Pay Subscribers: 12,300; 11/20/92. Pay Per View Subscribers: 3,500; 11/20/92. *Local Advertising Accepted.*

Cox Cable Spokane (82,463 subscribers). Box HAYC-1, E. 1717 Buckeye Ave., Spokane, WA 99207. (509) 484-4900; FAX: (509) 483-7502. Alan D. Collins, gen mgr; Dale Tapley, mktg dir; Jeff T. Johnson, loc adv dir; Chuck McDowell, chief tech.
Area(s) Served: WA. County: Spokane. Serving Spokane. Homes Served: 82,463. *Channel Capacity:* 38. In use: 38. *Basic Service:* Subscribers: 82,463; 10/31/93. *Pay Services:* Total Pay Subscribers: 46,500. *Local Advertising Accepted.*

Cox Cable TV of Pensacola (72,187 subscribers). 2205 La Vista Ave., Pensacola, FL 32504. (904) 477-2695; FAX: (904) 479-3912. Larry F. Lewis, gen mgr; John Bowen, mktg dir.
Area(s) Served: FL. County: Escambia. Homes Served: 72,187. *Channel Capacity:* 35. In use: 35. *Basic Service:* Subscribers: 72,187; 9/30/93. *Pay Services:* Total Pay Subscribers: 47,500. Pay Per View Subscribers: 10,500. *Local Advertising Accepted.*

Cox Cable University City Inc. (46,000 subscribers). Box 147012, 6020 N.W. 43rd St., Gainesville, FL 32614-7012. (904) 377-1741. Gary Cassard, gen mgr; Dana Nemenyi, mktg dir; Kenneth Williams, chief tech; Ruby Sullivan, cust svc dir.
Area(s) Served: FL. County: Alachua. Serving Gainesville. Homes Served: 46,000. *Channel Capacity:* 35. In use: 35. *Basic Service:* Subscribers: 46,000; 10/31/93. *Pay Services:* Total Pay Subscribers: 33,000; 12/15/92. *Local Advertising Accepted.*

Emerald Coast Cable Television (61,745 subscribers). Box 2827, 784 N. Beal Pkwy., Fort Walton Beach, FL 32549. (904) 862-4142. Mike Holmes, gen mgr; John Bowen, mktg dir; Richard See, chief tech; Jackie Wortham, cust svc dir.
Area(s) Served: FL. Counties: Okaloosa, Walton. Serving Choctaw Beach, Cinco Bayou, Destin, Hurlburt Field, Mary Esther, Okaloosa Island, Shalimar, Villa Tasso. Miles of Plant: 951. Homes Passed: 77,000. Homes Served: 61,745. *Basic Service:* Subscribers: 61,745; 10/31/93. *Pay Services:* Total Pay Subscribers: 16,000; 10/31/92. (1) Pay Units: 4,300; 10/31/92. Programming (via satellite): The Movie Channel. (2) Pay Units: 12,800; 10/31/92. Programming (via satellite): HBO. (3) Pay Units: 7,200; 10/31/92. Programming (via satellite): Showtime. (4) Pay Units: 4,300; 10/31/92. Programming (via satellite): Disney. (5) Pay Units: 5,000; 10/31/92. Programming (via satellite): Cinemax. Pay Per View Subscribers: 19,600; 10/31/92. *Local Advertising Accepted.*

Crosslake Telephone & Cablevision Co.

Box 70, Crosslake, MN 56442. (218) 692-2777; FAX: (218) 692-2410. Marty Heino, pres. Owned by Town of Crosslake. Total Basic Subscribers: 1,700; Number of Cable Systems: 1.

Crown Media Inc.

Suite 1650, 13355 Noel Rd., Dallas, TX 75240. (214) 702-7380; 702-7308; FAX: (214) 960-4800. James M. Hoak, CEO & chmn; Robert J. Druten, CFO; Rod G. Thole, vp opns; John D. Clark, vp mktg & vp progmg; Wayne L. Kern, vp; Steve Brockett, vp. Total Basic Subscribers: 835,399; Pay Cable Subscribers: 446,000; Number of Cable Systems: 85.

REGIONS

Wisconsin: 314 Main St., Box 279, Onalaska, WI 54650; Dale Clements. 1138 S. 108th St., Box 14129, West Allis, WI 53214; Joe Zuravle. 400 Scott St., Box 1818, Wausau, WI 54402; Jim Blakey. *California:* Cencom Cable Television, 6680 View Park Ct., Riverside, CA 92503; James Bray. Cencom Cable Television, Box 1451, Alhambra, CA 91802; Craig Watson. *South Carolina:* 1115 N.E. Main, Box 850, Simpsonville, SC 29681; David McCall. *Alabama:* Crown Cable, 3524 DeCatur Hwy., Suite 302, Fultondale, AL 35068; Dave Troxel.

SYSTEMS WITH OVER 20,000 SUBSCRIBERS

Crown Cable (71,507 subscribers). Suite 302, 3524 Decatur Hwy., Fulton Dale, AL 35068. (205) 631-9681; FAX: (205) 631-6609. David Troxel, gen mgr; Bruce Williams, mktg dir; Rick Barnett, chief tech.
Area(s) Served: AL. Counties: Jeffeson, Shelby, Talladega, Tuscaloosa, Walker. Serving Alabaster, Blockton, Columbiana, Gardendale, Helena, Hoover, Jasper, Leeds, Pelham, Talladega, Trussville. Pop: 375,000. Miles of Plant: 2,630. Homes Passed: 120,000. Homes Served: 71,507. *Channel Capacity:* 36. In use: 35. *Basic Service:* Subscribers: 71,507; 10/31/93. Programming (via satellite): 27 chs. Programming (off air): 7 chs. *Pay Services:* Total Pay Subscribers: 31,900; 12/01/92. (1) Pay Units: 11,098; 12/01/92. Programming (via satellite): HBO. (2) Pay Units: 11,955; 12/01/92. Programming (via satellite): Showtime. (3) Pay Units: 908; 12/01/92. Programming (via satellite): The Movie Channel. (4) Pay Units: 3,275; 12/01/92. Programming (via satellite): Cinemax. Pay Per View Subscribers: 12,000; 12/01/92. *Local Advertising Accepted. Equipment:* Scientific-Atlanta headend; Scientific-Atlanta converters; Jerrold, Magnavox, Scientific-Atlanta & Texscan line equipment.

Crown Cable (106,000 subscribers). 2215 W. Mission Rd., Alhambra, CA 91802. (818) 300-6100; FAX: (818) 300-6112. Craig L. Watson, gen mgr; Kevin Maguire, mktg dir; Joe Slavin, loc adv dir; Lennie Smith, chief tech; C.C. Holmberg, cust svc dir.
Area(s) Served: CA. Counties: Los Angeles. Serving Alhambra, Altadena, Azusa, Chapman Woods, Commerce, Huntington Park, La Canada Flintridge, Montebello, Monterey Park, Norwalk, Pasadena, Rosemead, San Gabriel, Temple City, Walnut, West Covina. Miles of Plant: 1,879. Homes Passed: 290,000. Homes Served: 106,000. *Channel Capacity:* 63. In use: 63. *Basic Service:* Subscribers: 106,000; 10/31/93. Programming (via satellite): 45 chs. Programming (via microwave): 18 chs. *Pay Services:* Total Pay Subscribers: 90,000; 09/01/93. (1) Pay Units: 38,000; 09/01/93. Programming: HBO. (2) Pay Units: 23,000; 09/01/93. Programming: Showtime. (3) Pay Units: 11,000; 09/01/93. Programming: Cinemax. (4) Pay Units: 5,000; 09/01/93. Programming: The Movie Channel. *Local Advertising Accepted. Equipment:* Scientific-Atlanta headend & amplifiers.

Crown Cable (44,000 subscribers). 6680 View Park Ct., Riverside, CA 92503. (909) 687-2721; FAX: (909) 353-1228. Doug Montandon, gen mgr & mktg dir.
Area(s) Served: CA. County: Riverside. Serving Mira Loma, Norco, Riverside. Homes Passed: 106,000. Homes Served: 44,000. *Channel Capacity:* 54. In use: 54. *Basic Service:* Subscribers: 44,000; 10/31/93. Programming (via satellite): 35 chs. Programming (via microwave): 5 chs. Programming (off air): 13 chs. *Local Advertising Accepted. Equipment:* Jerrold & Scientific-Atlanta converter boxes.

Crown Cable (46,000 subscribers). 11 Commerce Rd., Newtown, CT 06470-1655. (203) 270-8665; FAX: (203) 350-8828. Steve Reifschneider, gen mgr; Dave Elmore, mktg dir; Jess Ballew, loc adv dir; Robert Sereday, chief tech; Sharon Roehm, cust svc dir.
Area(s) Served: CT. Counties: Fairfield, Litchfield, New Haven. Serving Bridgewater, Brookfield, Kent, Monroe, Newtown, New Fairfield, New Milford, Roxbury, Sherman, Southbury, Trumbull, Washington. Miles of Plant: 1,688. Homes Passed: 58,138. Homes Served: 46,000. *Basic Service:* Subscribers: 46,000; 08/01/93. *Pay Services:* Total Pay Subscribers: 44,000; 08/01/93. *Local Advertising Accepted.*

Crown Cable (29,317 subscribers). Box 280, 90 S. Park St., Willimantic, CT 06226. (203) 456-4191; FAX: (203) 456-4130. Steve Reifschneider, gen mgr; Dick Elwell, mktg dir & loc adv dir; Laurel Haas, chief tech.
Area(s) Served: CT. County: Windham. Serving Brooklyn, Canterbury, Chaplin, Columbia, Coventry, Eastford, Hampton, Lebanon, Mansfield, Pomfret, Scotland, Thompson, Willimantic, Willington, Windham, Woodstock. Miles of Plant: 1,000. Homes Passed: 62,000. Homes Served: 29,317. *Channel Capacity:* 53. In use: 53. *Basic Service:* Subscribers: 29,317; 9/30/93. *Pay Services:* Total Pay Subscribers: 8,319; 11/30/92. *Local Advertising Accepted. Equipment:* Scientific-Atlanta headend; C-COR amplifiers; Comm/Scope & Times Fiber cable.

Crown Cable (37,800 subscribers). Box 540, 210 W. Division St., Maryville, IL 62062. (618) 345-8121; FAX: (618) 345-6234. Dave Miller, gen mgr.
Area(s) Served: IL. Counties: Bonn, Madison, St. Clair. Serving Alhanibra, Caseyville, Collinsville, Columbia, Edwardsville, Glenn Carbon, Granite City Depot,

Multiple Systems Operators, Independent Owners & Cable Systems

Hamel, Highland, Hollywood Heights, Madison, Marine, Millstadt, New Douglas, Pontoon Beach, St. Jacobs, Sorento, Troy, Venice, Warden, Waterloo Depot. Homes Passed: 67,000. *Channel Capacity:* 37. *Basic Service:* Subscribers: 37,800; 10/31/93. *Pay Services:* Total Pay Subscribers: 21,000; 10/31/93.

Crown Cable (157,300 subscribers). 9358 Dielman Industrial Dr., St. Louis, MO 63132. (314) 997-7570. David Niswonger, gen mgr; E.J. Glaser, mktg dir.
Area(s) Served: MO. County: St. Louis. Serving Badwin, Bella Villa, Black Jack, Brentwood Village, Charluck, Country Life Estates, Crestwood, Crieve Couer, Crystal Lake, Des Peres, Eureka, Fenton, Frontenac, Huntlugh, Kirkwood, Ladue, Lakeshire, Mackenzie, Marlborough, Oakland, Redmond Heights, Rock Hill, St. George, Sunset Hills, Sycamore Hills, Times Beach, Twin Oaks, Valley Park, Venita Park, Westwood, Winchester, Webster Groves, Woodson Terrace. Homes Served: 157,300. *Basic Service:* Subscribers: 157,300; 9/30/93. *Pay Services:* Total Pay Subscribers: 86,000; 11/30/91.

Crown Cable (25,700 subscribers). Suite 101, 1850 Business Park Dr., Clarksville, TN 37040. (615) 552-2288; FAX: (615) 648-9255. Chris Ginn, gen mgr; Christy Poole, mktg dir; Bob Beldins, loc adv dir.
Area(s) Served: TN. Counties: Chatham, Montgomery. Serving Ashland City, Clarksville. Miles of Plant: 700. Homes Passed: 30,000. Homes Served: 25,700. *Channel Capacity:* 35. In use: 35. *Basic Service:* Subscribers: 25,700; 10/31/93. *Pay Services:* Total Pay Subscribers: 12,000; 10/30/91. *Local Advertising Accepted.*

Crown Cable (26,371 subscribers). 320 N. Wisconsin Ave., DePere, WI 54115. (414) 337-2300; FAX: (414) 337-9251. Jim Blakey, gen mgr; Julie Stadtmueller, mktg dir. *Basic Service:* Subscribers: 26,371; 9/30/93.

Crown Cable (20,000 subscribers). Box 1818, 400 Scott St., Wausau, WI 54402-1818. (715) 845-4222; FAX: (715) 848-0081. Jim Blakey, gen mgr; Susan Jirgl, mktg dir; Brian Bertrand, loc adv dir; Bruce Waslesye, chief tech; Connie Van Zummeren, cust svc dir.
Area(s) Served: WI. County: Marathon. Serving Mosinee, Rothschild, Schofield, Wausau. Pop: 36,000. Homes Passed: 29,700. Homes Served: 20,000. *Channel Capacity:* 36. In use: 36. *Basic Service:* Subscribers: 20,000; 08/31/93. Programming (via satellite): 26 chs. Programming (via microwave): 2 chs. Programming (off air): 5 chs. *Pay Services:* Total Pay Subscribers: 4,656; 08/31/93. (1) Pay Units: 3,991; 08/31/93. Programming (via satellite): HBO. (2) Pay Units: 2,917; 08/31/93. Programming (via satellite): Cinemax. *Local Advertising Accepted. Equipment:* Provided by Magnavox.

Crown Cable (32,077 subscribers). 1348 Plainfield Ave., Janesville, WI 53545. (608) 754-3644; FAX: (608) 754-8107. Joe Zuravle, gen mgr. *Basic Service:* Subscribers: 32,077.

Crown Cable (52,178 subscribers). Box 14129, 1138 S. 108th St., West Allis, WI 53214. (414) 771-2954; FAX: (414) 453-5405. Joe Zuravle, gen mgr. *Basic Service:* Subscribers: 52,178.

SMALLER SYSTEMS

Colorado - Crown Cable, 1441 Specker Ave., Fort Carson, CO 80913; (719) 579-8227; 1,655 subs. **Georgia -** Crown Cable, Box 329, Grovetown, GA 30813-0329; (706) 860-1580. **Kentucky -** Crown Cable, Box 569, 614 N. Main St., Hopkinsville, KY 42240; (502) 886-3932; 9,758 subs. **Missouri -** Crown Cable, 3300 Sunswept Park Dr., Florissant, MO 63033. Crown Cable, 143 W. Clinton Pl., Kirkwood, MO 63122. **North Carolina -** Crown Cable, Box 6445, Asheville, NC 28816; (704) 252-8522. Crown Cable, Box 2128, 697 Pennton Ave., Lenoir, NC 28645; (704) 754-2191. Crown Cable, 1804 J. Colonial Village, Lincolnton, NC 28092; (704) 735-8784. Crown Cable, 2516 Sayetteville St., Sanford, NC 27330; (919) 774-3700; 10,981 subs. Crown Cable, Box 214, Bldg. TT44, Tarawa Terrace, NC 28543; (314) 476-4446; 5,300 subs. **South Carolina -** Crown Cable, Box 396, Pelzer, SC 29669; (803) 947-9084. Crown Cable, Box 367, Simpsonville, SC 29681; (803) 963-3676. **Texas -** Crown Cable, 139 E. Myrtle, Angleton, TX 77515; (409) 849-5728. Crown Cable, 18 N. Holland, Box 639, Bellville, TX 77418; (409) 826-3502; 1,850 subs. Crown Cable, 1010 W. Jasper, Suite 9, Killeen, TX 76541; (817) 554-6404. Crown Cable, 516 E. Kleberg, Kingsville, TX 78363; (512) 595-0100; 5,202 subs. Crown Cable, 114 W. Main, Box 282, Madisonville, TX 77864; (409) 348-3173; 1,300 subs. Crown Cable, 247 Live Oak, Marlin, TX 76661; (817) 883-2597; 1,600 subs.

Bill Daniels

Box 344, 5720 El Camino Real, Carlsbad, CA 92008-3845. (619) 438-7741; FAX: (619) 438-8461. Tony Acone, pres; Joni Odum, vp opns. Owned by Bill Daniels. Total Basic Subscribers: 60,000; Number of Cable Systems: 2.

Davis Communications Inc.

Box 117, 1630 1st St., Cheney, WA 99004. (509) 235-5144; FAX: (509) 235-5158. Thomas Davis, pres. Total Basic Subscribers: 2,700; Pay Cable Subscribers: 1580; Number of Cable Systems: 1.

SMALLER SYSTEMS

Washington - Cheney Cable TV Co., 1630 1st St., Cheney, WA 99004; (509) 235-5144.

DCA Cablevision

1836 Union St., San Francisco, CA 94123. (415) 563-2288; FAX: (415) 563-2351. William J. Marks, pres; R. Thomas Goodrich, vp; Albert Bracht, vp; William D. Marks, vp. Owned by West Coast Cable Partners, Dickinson California Arizona Assoc. Ltd. Total Basic Subscribers: 11,401; Pay Cable Subscribers: 6,390; Number of Cable Systems: 8.

De-Cal Cable Company Inc.

Box 988, 202 S. Ann St., Port Lavaca, TX 77979. (512) 552-6342. George F. Rhodes, pres; Marion Rhodes, CFO; George F. Rhodes Jr., vp. Total Basic Subscribers: 2,215; Pay Cable Subscribers: 490; Number of Cable Systems: 4.

SMALLER SYSTEMS

Texas - Hudson Cable TV, Hudson, TX. Runge Cable, 309 S. Third St., Kennedy, TX 78119; (210) 583-9466. Karne City Cable TV, 309 S. Third St., Kennedy, TX 78119; (210) 583-9466. Yorktown Cable Co., 131 E. Main St., Yorktown, TX 78164; (512) 564-3241.

Delta County Tele-Comm Inc.

132 Grand Ave., Paonia, CO 81428. (303) 527-4801; FAX: (303) 527-3313. Don Reynolds, vp opns. Owned by TDS Tele-Data Systems Inc. Total Basic Subscribers: 2,400; Pay Cable Subscribers: 1,500; Number of Cable Systems: 3.

SMALLER SYSTEMS

Colorado - Delta County Tele-Comm, Cedaridge, CO. Delta Tele-Comm, Crawford, CO. Delta Tele-Comm, Hotch Kiss, CO.

Dixie Cable TV Inc.

Box 97, Alma, GA 31510. (912) 632-4241; FAX: (912) 632-8855. Jack Bennett, pres; Kevin Brooks, vp opns & vp mktg. Total Basic Subscribers: 1,600; Number of Cable Systems: 1.

John Donofrio Jr. dba Full Channel TV Inc.

57 Everett St., Warren, RI 02885. (401) 247-2250; FAX: (401) 247-0191. John Donofrio Jr., pres; Michael Davis, vp. Owned by John Donofrio Jr. Total Basic Subscribers: 11,047; Pay Cable Subscribers: 7,407; Number of Cable Systems: 1.

SMALLER SYSTEMS

Rhode Island - Full Channel, 57 Everett St., Warren, RI 02885.

Donrey Cablevision

Box 410, Las Vegas, NV 89125. (702) 452-2060; FAX: (702) 452-7569. Fred W. Smith, CEO & pres; E.H. Patterson, CFO; Don R. Burris Sr., vp. Owned by Donrey Media Group. Total Basic Subscribers: 55,009; Pay Cable Subscribers: 24,801; Number of Cable Systems: 5.

SYSTEMS WITH OVER 20,000 SUBSCRIBERS

Donrey Cablevision (25,872 subscribers). 460 Curtola Pkwy., Vallejo, CA 94591. (707) 553-9562; FAX: (707) 552-4156. W.R. Kostrzewski, gen mgr; Karen West, mktg dir & loc adv dir; Stas Mills, chief tech; Mike Urick, cust svc dir.

Area(s) Served: CA. County: Solano. Serving Vallejo. Pop: 110,000. Miles of Plant: 294. Homes Passed: 45,000. Homes Served: 25,872. *Channel Capacity:* 104. In use: 67. *Basic Service:* Subscribers: 25,872; 10/31/93. Programming (via satellite): 42 chs. Programming (off air): 22 chs. *Pay Services:* Total Pay Subscribers: 7,378; 10/15/92. Pay Per View Subscribers: 7,378; 10/15/92. *Local Advertising Accepted. Equipment:* Scientific-Atlanta addressable converters.

SMALLER SYSTEMS

Arkansas - Donrey Cablevision, 1401 S. 8th, Rogers, AR 72756. **Oklahoma -** Donrey Cablevision, 4127 Nowata Rd., Bartlesville, OK 76006. Donrey Cablevision, 1105 W. 9th, Blackwell, OK 74631. Donrey Cablevision, 215 W. 5th, Guymon, OK 73962.

Boyce Dooley dba Clear-Vu

Box 368, 101 N. Commerce St., Summerville, GA 30747. (706) 857-2551; FAX: (706) 857-2194. Boyce Dooley, pres. Owned by Boyce Dooley. Total Basic Subscribers: 5,600; Number of Cable Systems: 5.

SMALLER SYSTEMS

Georgia - Clear-Vu-Cable, 101 N. Commerce St., Summerville, GA 30747.

Douglas Communication V L.P.

600 S. Catury, Rantoul, IL 61866. (217) 892-9333; FAX: (217) 893-1036. Douglas H. Dittrick, CEO & pres; Jay E. Ricks, chmn; Calvin G. Craib, CFO; Robert E. Probert, vp opns. Owned by Douglas Communications Corp. II. Total Basic Subscribers: 9,050; Pay Cable Subscribers: 3,950; Number of Cable Systems: 50.

SMALLER SYSTEMS

Illinois - Douglas Communications V, Bismark, IL; 364 subs. Douglas Communications V, Braceville, IL; 171 subs. Douglas Communications V, Brocton, IL; 83 subs. Douglas Communications V, Buckley, IL; 205 subs. Douglas Communications V, Carlock, IL; 100 subs. Douglas Communications V, Cissna Park, IL; 21 subs. Douglas Communications V, East Brooklyn, IL; 18 subs. Douglas Communications V, Essex, IL; 78 subs. Douglas Communications V, Gifford, IL; 277 subs. Douglas Communications V, Godley, IL; 86 subs. Douglas Communications V, Gulfport, IL; 114 subs. Douglas Communications V, Highland Heights, IL; 129 subs. Douglas Communications V, Hume, IL; 118 subs. Douglas Communications V, Joy, IL; 93 subs. Douglas Communications V, Keithsburg, IL; 140 subs. Douglas Communications V, Kirkwood, IL; 180 subs. Douglas Communications V, Lake Camelot, IL; 282 subs. Douglas Communications V, Ludlow, IL; 159 subs. Douglas Communications V, Mazon, IL; 233 subs. Douglas Communications V, Metcalf, IL; 54 subs. Douglas Communications V, New Boston, IL; 194 subs. Douglas Communications V, Oakrun, IL; 126 subs. Douglas Communications V, Pinewood Park, IL; 130 subs. Douglas Communications V, Potomac, IL; 239 subs. Douglas Communications V, Rankin, IL; 63 subs. Douglas Communications V, Rantoul, IL; 2,184 subs. Douglas Communications V, South Wilmington, IL; 203 subs. **Indiana -** Douglas Communications V, Dana, IN; 179 subs. Douglas Communications V, Newport, IN; 197 subs. Douglas Communications V, West Lebanon, IN; 223 subs. **Iowa -** Douglas Communications V, Batavia, IA; 135 subs. Douglas Communications V, Biggsville, IA; 104 subs. Douglas Communications V, Birmingham, IA; 107 subs. Douglas Communications V, Cantril, IA; 52 subs. Douglas Communications V, Crawfordsville, IA; 71 subs. Douglas Communications V, Denmark, IA; 98 subs. Douglas Communications V, Donnellson, IA; 254 subs. Douglas Communications V, Franklin, IA; 43 subs. Douglas Communications V, Grandview, IA; 130 subs. Douglas Communications V, Hillsboro, IA; 60 subs. Douglas Communications V, Letts, IA; 93 subs. Douglas Communications V, M&W Trailer Park, IA; 42 subs. Douglas Communications V, Milton, IA; 107 subs. Douglas Communications V, Muscatine County, IA; 183 subs. Douglas Communications V, Oakville, IA; 123 subs. Douglas Communications V, Ripley's, IA; 198 subs. Douglas Communications V, Salem, IA; 138 subs. Douglas Communications V, Sidell, IA; 178 subs. Douglas Communications V, Stockport, IA; 89 subs. Douglas Communications V, Winfield, IA; 257 subs.

Multiple Systems Operators, Independent Owners & Cable Systems

Douglas Communications Corporation II

East Wing, Suite 3D, 1200 E. Ridgewood Ave., Ridgewood, NJ 07450. (201) 444-1700; FAX: (201) 444-5092. Douglas H. Dittrick, CEO & pres; Michael J. Pohl, vp mktg. Total Basic Subscribers: 106,000; Pay Cable Subscribers: 35,000; Number of Cable Systems: 350.

Dowden Communications Investors

Suite 1735, 1100 Abernathy Rd., Atlanta, GA 30328. (404) 396-1088. Thomas C. Dowden, CEO & pres; Nancy Wood, vp opns. Owned by Stewart Corbett, Lloyd Counter, Thomas C. Dowder, Stuart V. Gibson, Peter Knowles, M. Kent Sharp, Raymond C. Smucker, Nancy Wood, Centennial Fund. Total Basic Subscribers: 1,067; Pay Cable Subscribers: 902; Number of Cable Systems: 6.

Durand Cable Co. Inc.

320 Third Ave. W., Durand, WI 54736. (715) 672-5966; FAX: (715) 672-4344. Henry W. Niehoff, pres; Gerald Hanson, vp. Owned by Henry W. Niehoff, Gerald Hanson. Total Basic Subscribers: 2,000; Pay Cable Subscribers: 500; Number of Cable Systems: 1.

Eagle Communications Inc.

Box 817, 2300 Hall, Hays, KS 67601. (913) 625-4000; FAX: (913) 625-8030. Robert E. Schmidt, pres; Kenneth R. Braun, CFO. Total Basic Subscribers: 12,642; Pay Cable Subscribers: 4,791; Number of Cable Systems: 7.

SMALLER SYSTEMS

Kansas - Brewster Cable TV Co., Brewster, KS; (913) 694-2838; 103 subs. Eagle Communications Inc., Box 817, 2703 Hall St., Hays, KS; (913) 625-4000; 103 subs. Ellis Cable TV Co., Ellis, KS; (913) 726-3291; 673 subs. Goodland Cable TV Co., Goodland, KS; (913) 899-3371; 1,886 subs. Hays Cable TV Co., Hays, KS; (913) 625-5910; 6,834 subs. Hoxie Cable TV Co., Hoxie, KS; (913) 675-2310; 539 subs. Russell Cable TV Co., Russell, KS; (913) 483-3244; 1,739 subs. Wakeeney Cable TV Co., Wakeeney, KS; (913) 743-5616; 868 subs.

Eastern Connecticut Cable TV Inc.

61 Myrock Ave., Waterford, CT 06385. (203) 442-8525; FAX: (203) 443-6031. Edmund W. O'Brien, CEO; Ralph A. Mariani, pres; Glen Lyon, vp opns; Katherine Occhionero, vp mktg; Janet B. Pawlikowski, vp; Michael J. Byrne, vp. Total Basic Subscribers: 42,835; Pay Cable Subscribers: 17,451; Number of Cable Systems: 2.

SYSTEMS WITH OVER 20,000 SUBSCRIBERS

Eastern Connecticut Cable TV Inc. (42,741 subscribers). Box 6001, Waterford, CT 06385. (203) 442-8525; FAX: (203) 443-6031. Linda Misiaszek, gen mgr; Kathy Occhionero, mktg dir; Glen Lyon, chief tech. *Area(s) Served:* CT. Counties: New London, Windham. Serving East Lyme, Griswold, Killingly, Montville, New London, Plainfield, Putnam, Sterling, Waterford. Miles of Plant: 1,003. Homes Passed: 52,265. Homes Served: 42,741. *Channel Capacity:* 44. In use: 44. *Basic Service:* Subscribers: 42,741; 08/31/93. Programming (via satellite): 28 chs. Programming (off air): 13 chs. *Pay Services:* Total Pay Subscribers: 11,961; 08/31/93. Pay Per View Subscribers: 29,739; 08/31/93. *Local Advertising Accepted.*

Eastern Telecom Corporation

453 Davidson Rd., Pittsburgh, PA 15239. (412) 795-3930; FAX: (412) 795-5798. Mary Chiodo-Finchman, CEO; Mary Chiodo-Fincham, pres; Henry M. Yocco, vp. Total Basic Subscribers: 19,000; Pay Cable Subscribers: 7,200; Number of Cable Systems: 6.

REGIONS

Pennsylvania: Nanty Glo Cable TV, 891 Chestnut St., Nanty Glo, PA; (814) 749-8619.

Easton Utilities Commission

Box 1189, 142 N. Harrison St., Easton, MD 21601. (410) 822-6110; FAX: (410) 822-0743. Roger Judd, CEO; Bill Russell, vp opns; Nancy Brinson, vp mktg; Mark Heckler, vp; Scott Pallman, vp. Owned by Town of Easton. Total Basic Subscribers: 4,100; Pay Cable Subscribers: 2,410; Number of Cable Systems: 1.

L.E Elliot dba Firestone Cable

Box 368, 115 N. Main St., Ripley, MS 38663. (601) 837-4881. L.E. Elliott, pres; Leon Bailey, vp opns. Owned by L.E. Elliott. Total Basic Subscribers: 2,000; Pay Cable Subscribers: 550; Number of Cable Systems: 1.

SMALLER SYSTEMS

Mississippi - Ripley Video Cable Co., Inc., Box 368, Ripley, MS 38663.

Entertainment Express Ltd.

11404 Broadview Dr., Moorpark, CA 93021. (805) 529-0218; FAX: (805) 529-4584. Marc Sklar, pres; Laura Iannetta, vp opns. Total Basic Subscribers: 1,560; Number of Cable Systems: 1.

Ervin Cable

212 E. Lincoln Blvd., Shawneetown, IL 62984. (618) 269-3119. Gary Ervin, pres; Glinda Baker, vp mktg. Owned by Gary Ervin, Tim Ervin, Robert Ervin. Total Basic Subscribers: 1,119; Pay Cable Subscribers: 850; Number of Cable Systems: 5.

SMALLER SYSTEMS

Illinois - Ervin Cable, Equality, IL. Ervin Cable, Ridgway, IL. Ervin Cable, Shawneetown, IL. **Kentucky** - Ervin Cable, Henderson, KY.

Dallas R. Eubanks dba Eastern Cable

Box 126, 701 South Ln., Corbin, KY 40701. (606) 528-6400; FAX: (606) 523-0427. Dallas R. Eubanks, pres. Owned by Dallas R. Eubanks. Total Basic Subscribers: 2,500; Pay Cable Subscribers: 450; Number of Cable Systems: 1.

Eyecom

2121 Abbott Rd., Anchorage, AK 99507. (907) 349-2400; FAX: (907) 349-1858. Jack Ryner, pres & vp opns; Michael Burke, CFO; Penny LaChapelle, vp mktg. Owned by Telalaska. Total Basic Subscribers: 1,544; Pay Cable Subscribers: 2,053; Number of Cable Systems: 4.

SMALLER SYSTEMS

Alaska - Eyecom, Galena, AK. Alyeska Cable, Girdwood, AK. Eyecom, Port Lions, AK. Eyecom, Un-Alaska, AK.

Fairbanks Communications Inc.

Suite 202 E, 1601 Belvedere Rd., West Palm Beach, FL 33406. (407) 838-4370; FAX: (407) 689-9957. Richard M. Fairbanks, pres; Roger S. Snowdon, CFO; James C. Hilliard, vp opns; Richard Smart, vp; Richard Hindes, vp. Total Basic Subscribers: 47,738; Pay Cable Subscribers: 19,050; Number of Cable Systems: 2.

REGIONS

Indiana: 50 Randall Ave., Aurora, IN 47001; Warren Evans. *Florida:* 1595 S.W. 4th Ave., Delray, FL 33444; Gene Strickland.

SYSTEMS WITH OVER 20,000 SUBSCRIBERS

Leadership Cablevision (39,500 subscribers). Box 250, 1595 S.W. Fourth Ave., Delray Beach, FL 33444. (407) 272-2521; FAX: (407) 272-8776. Gene Strickland, gen mgr; Patricia O'Brien, mktg dir. *Basic Service:* Subscribers: 39,500; 09/01/93. *Pay Services:* Total Pay Subscribers: 8,300; 12/01/92. *Local Advertising Accepted.*

Falcon Cable TV

15th Fl., 10900 Wilshire Blvd., Los Angeles, CA 90024. (310) 824-9990; FAX: (310) 208-3655. Mark Nathanson, CEO & pres; Joe Johnson, vp opns; Skip Harris, vp mktg; Tom Hatchell, vp. Owned by Falcon Holding Group Inc. Total Basic Subscribers: 794,000; Number of Cable Systems: 350.

SYSTEMS WITH OVER 20,000 SUBSCRIBERS

Falcon Cable Systems (31,000 subscribers). 7640 Eigleberry St., Gilroy, CA 95020. (408) 842-5653; FAX: (408) 848-2391. Bruce Williams, gen mgr; Filomena Fagundes, mktg dir; Eric Hart, chief tech. *Area(s) Served:* CA. Counties: Monterey, San Benito, Santa Clara. Serving Aromas, Castroville, Gilroy, Gonzalez, Greenfield, Holister, King City, Los Lomas, Morgan Hill, Moss Landing, Oakhills, Prunedale, Ridgemark, Salinas, San Benito, San Juan Bautista, San Martin, Soledad. Miles of Plant: 672. Homes Passed: 50,200. Homes Served: 31,000. *Channel Capacity:* 35. In use: 35. *Basic Service:* Subscribers: 31,000; 11/15/93. *Pay Services:* Total Pay Subscribers: 15,500; 10/31/91. *Local Advertising Accepted. Equipment:* Scientific-Atlanta & Jerrold amplifiers; Times cable; Scientific-Atlanta set top converters; Scientific-Atlanta satellite antenna.

Falcon/Capital Cable Partners L.P. (34,655 subscribers). 150 N. Meramec, St. Louis, MO 63105. (314) 726-0099; FAX: (314) 726-4880. Scott R. Widham, gen mgr; Mary Meier, mktg dir; Edward Trower, chief tech. *Area(s) Served:* IL, IA, KY, MO, KS, IN. Homes Served: 34,655. *Basic Service:* Subscribers: 34,665; 07/31/93. *Pay Services:* Total Pay Subscribers: 16,159; 07/31/93.

SMALLER SYSTEMS

California - Falcon Cablevision, Box 1771, 41490 Big Bear Blvd., Big Bear Lake, CA 92315; (909) 866-3416; 12,600 subs. **Kentucky** - Falcon Cable, 4815 S. Hwy. 27, Somerset, KY 42501; (606) 679-8308. **North Carolina** - Falcon Cable, 1000 Main St. W., Valdese, NC 28690; (704) 874-4146. **Oregon** - Falcon Cable, 601 Railroad St., Brookings, OR 97415; (503) 469-4911; 4,000 subs. **Virginia** - Falcon Cable, 216 Moore Ave., Suffolk, VA 23434; (804) 539-8307; 8,300 subs.

Fanch Communications Inc.

Suite 1550, 1873 S. Bellaire St., Denver, CO 80222. (303) 756-5600; FAX: (303) 756-5774. Robert C. Fanch, CEO & chmn; Thomas W. Binning, pres; Dean Wandry, vp opns; Suzanne Cyman, vp mktg. Owned by Robert C. Fanch. Total Basic Subscribers: 200,000; Pay Cable Subscribers: 105,000; Number of Cable Systems: 300.

SYSTEMS WITH OVER 20,000 SUBSCRIBERS

Davison/Fenton (20,000 subscribers). 14300 Fenton Rd., Fenton, MI 48430. (313) 750-9965. Harold McNeill, gen mgr. *Basic Service:* Subscribers: 20,000; 11/15/93.

SMALLER SYSTEMS

Ohio - Wood Cable TV Inc, 118 Main St., Bowling Green, OH 43402; (419) 352-8424; 9,900 subs.

Fannon Cable TV Systems Inc.

Box 526, 120 Main St., New Tazewell, TN 37825. (615) 626-9107; FAX: (615) 626-6304. Ray Fannon, CEO & pres; Alice Breeding, vp. Owned by Ray Fannon, Bill Fannon, Bob Fannon, Hollis Bush, Letton Bush, Charles Chadwell. Total Basic Subscribers: 5,544; Pay Cable Subscribers: 1,200; Number of Cable Systems: 2.

First Cable of Missouri Inc.

Box 1010, 605 Concannon, Moberly, MO 65270. (816) 263-6300; FAX: (816) 263-3238. Alan D. Steinbach, pres; Jesse W. Wamsley, vp; Craig H. Plaster, vp. Owned by Alan D. Steinbach, Jesse W. Wamsley, Craig H. Plaster. Total Basic Subscribers: 1,009; Pay Cable Subscribers: 490; Number of Cable Systems: 15.

First Carolina Communications Inc.

Suite 310, 108 S. Frontage Rd., Vail, CO 81657. (303) 476-2002; FAX: (303) 476-0200. E.B. Chester, CEO & chmn; C. David Smith, pres; Pat Warren, vp opns. Owned by E.B. Chester, C. David Smith. Total Basic Subscribers: 29,865; Pay Cable Subscribers: 14,000; Number of Cable Systems: 2.

SMALLER SYSTEMS

New Hampshire - First Carolina Cable, Box 222, Campton, NH 03223; (603) 726-3611. 1,750 subs. First Carolina New England L.P., Peterboro, NH. **Vermont** - First Carolina Cable TV, 539 Charleston Rd., Box 520, Springfield, VT 05150; (802) 885-4529; (800) 356-2966.

First Commonwealth Communications Inc.

Box 857, Summerville Plantation, Gloucester, VA 23061. (804) 693-3535; FAX: (804) 693-2885. Donald A. Perry, CEO & chmn; Brinton Belyea, vp; Patricia Gibbs, vp. Owned by First Commonwealth Communications Inc. Total Basic Subscribers: 12,935; Pay Cable Subscribers: 7,014; Number of Cable Systems: 5.

Multiple Systems Operators, Independent Owners & Cable Systems

SMALLER SYSTEMS

Virginia - Gloucester Cablevision, Box 857, Gloucester, VA; 6,681 subs. Middlesex Cablevision, Box 857, Gloucester, VA; 1,629 subs. New Kent Cablevision, Box 857, Gloucester, VA; 1,549 subs. Northern Neck Cablevision, Box 857, Gloucester, VA; 1,879 subs. West Point Cablevision, Box 857, Gloucester, VA; 1,063 subs.

Kevin Flannigan dba Grafton Cable

Box 67, 419 N. Main St., Grafton, OH 44044. (216) 926-3230; FAX: (216) 926-3305. Kevin Flannigan, CEO. Owned by Kevin Flannigan. Total Basic Subscribers: 3,500; Pay Cable Subscribers: 2,500; Number of Cable Systems: 2.

SMALLER SYSTEMS

Ohio - South Shore Cable T.V. Services, Box 67, 419 N. Main Graston, OH 44044. Wellington Cable Communications, 100 S. Main, Wellington, OH 44090; (216) 647-6445.

Frankfort Cable Communication

Box 9, 251 E. Clinton St., Frankfort, IN 46041. (317) 659-4678; FAX: (317) 654-7031. Ken Bronson, CEO & pres; Ron Emrick, vp opns & vp progmg; Terri Bowles, vp sls & vp mktg. Owned by Nixon Newspapers Inc. Total Basic Subscribers: 5,100; Pay Cable Subscribers: 2,000; Number of Cable Systems: 1.

Harold Freeman dba Troy Cable

Box 1228, 1006 S. Brundige St., Troy, AL 36081. (205) 566-3310; FAX: (205) 566-3304. Harold Freeman, pres. Owned by Harold Freeman. Total Basic Subscribers: 2,705; Pay Cable Subscribers: 1,411; Number of Cable Systems: 1.

Futurevision

Box 2058, 1308 1/2 W. Pine St., Hattiesburg, MS 39403. (601) 545-3800; FAX: (601) 584-8320. B.L. Chain, CEO & pres. Owned by Chain Electric. Total Basic Subscribers: 2,957; Pay Cable Subscribers: 1,194; Number of Cable Systems: 3.

SMALLER SYSTEMS

Mississippi - Futurevision of Brookhaven, 116 E. Cherokee St., Brookhaven, MS 39601; (601) 833-4089. Futurevision of Bruce, Hwy. 32 E., Bruce, MS 38915; (601) 983-4883.

G H Cable Arizona L.P.

Box 38, Carlisle, PA 17013-0038. (717) 245-0040; FAX: (717) 245-9277. George F. Gardner, pres; David Gardner, vp. Owned by George F. Gardner. Total Basic Subscribers: 52,311; Pay Cable Subscribers: 8,000; Number of Cable Systems: 7.

Galaxy Cablevision

1220 N. Main, Sikeston, MO 63801. (314) 471-3080; FAX: (314) 471-0119. Tommy L. Gleason Jr., CEO & pres; J. Keith Davidson, CFO; Larry Eby, vp mktg. Owned by Galaxy Cablevision Management Inc., Tommy L. Gleason. Total Basic Subscribers: 56,500; Number of Cable Systems: 91.

Garden State Cable TV

1250 Haddonfield-Berlin Rd., Cherry Hill, NJ 08034. (609) 354-1880; FAX: (609) 354-1459. John Barrett, CFO; Patrick McCall, vp opns; Barry Bella, vp mktg. Owned by Comcast Corp., Lenfest Communications Inc. & Llewellyn. Total Basic Subscribers: 189,346; Pay Cable Subscribers: 147,331; Number of Cable Systems: 1.

Garden Valley Telephone Co.

201 Ross Ave., Erskine, MN 56535. (218) 687-5251; FAX: (218) 687-9980. Edgar Olson, chmn & pres; Joe Sandberg, vp; Raymond J. Voxland, vp. Total Basic Subscribers: 1,830; Pay Cable Subscribers: 460; Number of Cable Systems: 6.

SMALLER SYSTEMS

Minnesota - Garden Valley Telephone Co., Clearbrook, MN. Garden Valley Telephone Co., Erskine, MN. Garden Valley Telephone Co., Grygla, MN. Garden Valley Telephone Co., Oklee, MN. Garden Valley Telephone Co., Shevlin, MN. Garden Valley Telephone Co., St. Hilaire, MN.

Gateway Cablevision Corporation

6 Genessee Ln., Amsterdam, NY 12010. (518) 842-6803; FAX: (518) 842-0737. Joseph M. Isabel, pres; Jeffrey T. Kozlowski, vp; Ernest W. Scialabba, vp. Owned by Joseph M. Isabel. Total Basic Subscribers: 4,714; Number of Cable Systems: 4.

REGIONS

Gateway Chesterfield Cablevision: 132-2 Monadnock Hwy., East Swanzey, NH 03446; (603) 357-9962. *Gateway Area Telecable:* Box 271, Rt. 100 N. Commercial Plaza, West Dover, VT 05356; (802) 464-5200.

GCTV (Georgia Cable TV & Communications)

1018 W. Peachtree St., Atlanta, GA 30309. (404) 874-8000; FAX: (404) 873-5216. William R. Proud, vp opns; Pat Koutrag, vp. Owned by Georgia Cable Partners, Atlanta Cable Partners L.P. & Bass Group (RMB Inc.), 80%; Prime Cable, 20%. Total Basic Subscribers: 219,526; Number of Cable Systems: 3.

Genesis Cable Corporation

Suite C, One Boar's Head Pl., Charlottesville, VA 22903-4612. (804) 977-7404; FAX: (804) 977-7904. Smedley D. Butler, pres; George L. Jones, vp opns. Owned by Smedley D. Butler, George L. Jones. Total Basic Subscribers: 13,500; Pay Cable Subscribers: 6,200; Number of Cable Systems: 7.

Nadine Colem Gill dba Mobridge Cable

Box 205, 118 Third St. E., Mobridge, SD 57601. (605) 845-3227; FAX: (605) 845-3656. Nadine C. Gill, pres; William F. Duhamel, vp opns. Owned by Nadine Colem Gill, William F. Duhamel. Total Basic Subscribers: 1,400; Pay Cable Subscribers: 400; Number of Cable Systems: 1.

SMALLER SYSTEMS

South Dakota - Mobridge Cable TV, 118 Third St. E., Mobridge, SD 57601; (605) 845-3227.

Glasgow Electric Plant Board - CATV Division

Box 1809, 100 Mallory Dr., Glasgow, KY 42141. (502) 651-8341; FAX: (502) 651-1638. William J. Ray, CEO; Jim Searcy, CFO; Charles Rice, vp opns. Owned by Community of Glasgow. Total Basic Subscribers: 2,000; Pay Cable Subscribers: 1,200; Number of Cable Systems: 1.

Golden West Telecommunications Cooperative Inc.

Box 411, Wall, SD 57790-0411. (605) 279-2161; FAX: (605) 279-2727. Dwight Flatt, vp opns; Gwen Davis, vp mktg. Owned by Golden Telecommunications Co-Operative. Total Basic Subscribers: 2,500; Pay Cable Subscribers: 1,800; Number of Cable Systems: 13.

Grassroots Cable Systems

Box 280, Exeter, NH 03833. (603) 772-4600; FAX: (603) 772-4650. W. Robert Felder, pres; Marsha B. Felder, vp opns. Owned by W. Robert Felder, Marsha B. Felder. Total Basic Subscribers: 6,399; Pay Cable Subscribers: 4,753; Number of Cable Systems: 21.

SMALLER SYSTEMS

Maine - Grassroots Cable Systems, Franklin, ME; 200 subs. Grassroots Cable Systems, Friendship, ME; 284 subs. Grassroots Cable Systems, Greenbrush, ME; 212 subs. Grassroots Cable Systems, Lovell, ME; 213 subs. Grassroots Cable Systems, New Sharon, ME; 286 subs. Grassroots Cable Systems, Northport, ME. Grassroots Cable Systems, Rangeley, ME; 267 subs. Grassroots Cable Systems, Searsmont, ME; 57 subs. Grassroots Cable Systems, Sorrento, ME; 61 subs. Grassroots Cable Systems, Temple, ME; 111 subs. Grassroots Cable Systems, Union, ME; 343 subs. Grassroots Cable Systems, Weld, ME; 79 subs. **New Hampshire** - Grassroots Cable Systems, Bath, NH; 79 subs. Grassroots Cable Systems, Carroll, NH; 258 subs. Grassroots Cable Systems, Hill, ME; 121 subs. Grassroots Cable Systems, Madison, NH; 693 subs. Grassroots Cable Systems, Monroe, NH; 178 subs. Grassroots Cable Systems, Plainfield, NH; 503 subs. Grassroots Cable Systems, Stratford, NH; 265 subs. Grassroots Cable Systems, Sugar Hill, NH; 83 subs. Grassroots Cable Systems, Wakefield, NH; 1,332 subs. Grassroots Cable Systems, Wentworth, NH; 772 subs.

Great Plains Cable TV

Box 600, 1635 Front St., Blair, NE 68008. (402) 426-9511; FAX: (402) 426-6475. Timothy J. Garrigan, vp. Owned by Great Plains Communications Inc. Total Basic Subscribers: 1,800; Pay Cable Subscribers: 162; Number of Cable Systems: 5.

SMALLER SYSTEMS

Nebraska - Great Plains Cable TV, 1122 W. 2nd St., Box 170, Crofton, NE 68730; (402) 388-4312. Great Plains Cable TV, 338 Washington Ave., Box 127, Grant, NE 69140; (308) 352-2400. Great Plains Cable TV, 817 Broadway, Box 610, Imperial, NE 69033; (308) 882-5221.

Great Southern Printing & Manufacturing Co.

438 W. Patrick St., Frederick, MD 21701. (301) 662-6822; FAX: (301) 662-1307. George B. Delaplaine Jr., pres; Robert Cole, vp opns; Robert Krebs, vp mktg. Total Basic Subscribers: 61,464; Pay Cable Subscribers: 36,199; Number of Cable Systems: 3.

SYSTEMS WITH OVER 20,000 SUBSCRIBERS

Frederick Cablevision Inc. (41,288 subscribers). Box 398, 442 W. Patrick St., Frederick, MD 21705. (301) 662-6822; FAX: (301) 662-1307. Robert W. Cole, gen mgr; Robert G. Krebs, mktg dir & loc adv dir; James Delaplaine, chief tech; Thom Roach, cust svc dir.
Area(s) Served: MD. County: Frederick. Serving Brunswick, Burkittsville, Emmitsburg, Frederick, Middletown, Mount Airy, Myersville, New Market, Thurmont, Walkersville, Woodsboro. Miles of Plant: 1,050. Homes Passed: 48,400. Homes Served: 41,288. *Channel Capacity:* 60. In use: 56. *Basic Service:* Subscribers: 41,288; 8/30/93. Programming (via satellite): 34 chs. Programming (off air): 16 chs. *Pay Services:* Total Pay Subscribers: 26,781; 10/31/92. (1) Pay Units: 12,067; 10/31/92. Programming (via satellite): HBO. (2) Pay Units: 9,511; 10/31/92. Programming (via satellite): Cinemax. (3) Pay Units: 4,500; 10/31/92. Programming (via satellite): Disney. Pay Per View Subscribers: 1,800; 10/31/92. Local Advertising Accepted.

SMALLER SYSTEMS

Pennsylvania - G.S. Communications, Box 98, Glen Rock, PA 17327; 11,572 subs. **West Virginia** - C/R TV Cable, 302 N. Mildred St., Ranson, WV 25438; 6,569 subs.

Greater Media Inc.

Box 1059, 2 Kennedy Blvd., East Brunswick, NJ 08816. (908) 247-6161; FAX: (908) 247-0215. Peter Bordes, chmn; Frank Kabela, pres; Jim Higgins, vp mktg; Walter Veth, vp; Ronald Eckhart, vp. Total Basic Subscribers: 224,000; Pay Cable Subscribers: 193,700; Number of Cable Systems: 3.

SYSTEMS WITH OVER 20,000 SUBSCRIBERS

Greater Philadelphia Cablevision Inc. (77,400 subscribers). 1351 S. Delaware Ave., Philadelphia, PA 19147. (215) 463-1100; FAX: (215) 463-2330. Stanley Greene, gen mgr; Bobbie Herbs, mktg dir; John Pitts, loc adv dir. *Basic Service:* Subscribers: 77,400; 10/1/93. *Pay Services:* Total Pay Subscribers: 85,605; 12/04/92.

Greater Worcester Cablevision Inc. (110,000 subscribers). 95 Higgins St., Worcester, MA 01606. (508) 853-1515; FAX: (508) 854-5042. Richard Tuthill, gen mgr; Arthur F. Goody, mktg dir; Allan Eisenberg, loc adv dir; Brian Bedard, chief tech.
Area(s) Served: MA. County: Worcester. Homes Served: 110,000. *Channel Capacity:* 58. In use: 58. *Basic Service:* Subscribers: 110,000; 11/30/92. Local Advertising Accepted.

Green River Cable TV Inc.

40 Hwy. 910, Russell Springs, KY 42642. (502) 866-2655; FAX: (502) 866-2655. Gary Yocom, pres; Clarence

Multiple Systems Operators, Independent Owners & Cable Systems

Reid Jr., vp opns. Total Basic Subscribers: 1,450; Pay Cable Subscribers: 290; Number of Cable Systems: 3.

Greene Inc.

Box 337, Maringouin, LA 70757. (504) 625-2311; FAX: (504) 625-2311. Craig Greene, pres; Mark Greene, vp. Owned by Craig Greene, Mark Greene. Total Basic Subscribers: 1,500; Pay Cable Subscribers: 700; Number of Cable Systems: 1.

SMALLER SYSTEMS

Louisiana - Stillway Cablevision, Box 337, Maringouin, LA 70757; (504) 625-2311.

Roy M. Greene

Box 130, 2400 Sportsman Dr., Phenix City, AL 36867. (205) 298-7000; FAX: (205) 298-0833. Roy M. Greene, CEO; Lynne Heard, vp mktg. Total Basic Subscribers: 14,000; Pay Cable Subscribers: 3,300; Number of Cable Systems: 1.

SMALLER SYSTEMS

Alabama - Phenix Cable, 2400 Sportsman Dr., Phenix City, AL; (404) 298-7000; 13,600 subs.

Guadalupe Valley Telephone Cooperative Inc.

100 FM 3159, New Braunfels, TX 78130. (210) 885-4411; FAX: (210) 885-2100. Ken D. Brannies, CEO & pres; C.W. Bremer, chmn; Malford Jost, vp opns. Owned by Community of New Braunfels. Total Basic Subscribers: 5,000; Pay Cable Subscribers: 2,700; Number of Cable Systems: 2.

SMALLER SYSTEMS

Texas - Guadalupe Valley Communications Systems Inc., 211 N. Main St., Boerne, TX 78006; (210) 249-8181. Guadalupe Valley Communications Systems Inc., Canyon Lake, TX.

Gulf American Cable Group

9111 Interline Ave., Baton Rouge, LA 70809. (504) 928-4137; FAX: (504) 925-5271. Andrew E. Ezell, pres; Larry Massey, vp opns. Total Basic Subscribers: 12,000; Pay Cable Subscribers: 5,000; Number of Cable Systems: 1.

GWC Communications Co. L.P.

Box 166, 201 Church St., Lake Waccamaw, NC 28450. (919) 646-3041. Charles Gree, pres; Warren Love, CFO. Owned by Amcom Inc., gnl ptnr; Guinn O. Leverett Jr., Warren Love, Walter R. Muluis, ltd. ptnrs. Total Basic Subscribers: 2,500; Number of Cable Systems: 4.

SMALLER SYSTEMS

North Carolina - Lake Waccamaw Cable TV, Lake Waccamaw, NC. Roland Cable TV, Raland, NC. Rural Cable TV, Rural, NC. Taber City Cable TV, Taber City, NC.

H.L.M. Cable Co.

Suite A, 2305 Parview Rd., Middleton, WI 53562. (608) 831-7044. David Walsh, CEO; Robert E. Ryan, CFO & vp opns. Owned by D.G. Walsh, Olena Miller. Total Basic Subscribers: 1,617; Pay Cable Subscribers: 901; Number of Cable Systems: 8.

SMALLER SYSTEMS

Illinois - Walworth County Cablevision, Gem Suburban Mobile Home Park, Rockford, IL 61102. **Wisconsin** - Blufview Acres Cable, Faulk County, WI 53951. Dodge County Cablevision, Dodge County, WI. H.L.M. Cable, Arpin, WI 54410. H.L.M. Cable, Auburndale, WI 54412. H.L.M. Cable, Hewitt, WI 54441. H.L.M. Cable, Junction City, WI 54443. H.L.M. Cable, Marshfield Twp., WI 54449. H.L.M. Cable, Rudolph, WI 54475. H.L.M. Cable, Vesper, WI 54489. Pittsville Cable, Pittsville, WI 54466. Walworth County Cablevision, Darien, WI.

Haefele TV Inc.

Box 368, 24 E. Tioga St., Spencer, NY 14883. (607) 589-6235; FAX: (607) 587-7211. Lee Haefele, CEO & pres. Owned by Lee Haefele. Total Basic Subscribers: 4,600; Pay Cable Subscribers: 4,801; Number of Cable Systems: 9.

Halcyon Communication Partners

Suite 312, 4823 S. Sheridan, Tulsa, OK 74145. (918) 627-9406; FAX: (918) 627-9407. Robert E. Price, pres. Total Basic Subscribers: 6,100; Number of Cable Systems: 1.

SMALLER SYSTEMS

Arkansas - WestArk Cablesystems, 731 Fayetteville St., Alma, AR 72921; (501) 632-5197. **Nevada** - Nevada Cable, Box 450, Ely, NV 89301; (702) 289-8374; 2,400 subs.

Hamilton County Cable TV Inc. dba Gore Mountain Cable TV

1430 Balltown Rd., Schenectady, NY 12309. (518) 381-4833; FAX: (518) 381-4855. Paul F. Schonewolf, pres; George Williams, CFO. Total Basic Subscribers: 1,400; Pay Cable Subscribers: 850; Number of Cable Systems: 2.

SMALLER SYSTEMS

New York - Hamilton County Cable TV, Box 275, Wells, NY 12190; (516) 924-2013; 1,400 subs.

Hanover Cable TV Inc.

Box 717, 505 Baltimore St., Hanover, PA 17331. (717) 637-2268; FAX: (717) 637-6950. Joan McAnall, chmn; William H. Hafer, vp; Edgar E. Howe, vp. Owned by Joan McAnall, Barbara McLaughlin. Total Basic Subscribers: 13,457; Pay Cable Subscribers: 4,308; Number of Cable Systems: 1.

Harlan Community TV Inc.

Box 592, First & Eversole Sts., Harlan, KY 40831. (606) 573-2945; FAX: (606) 573-6959. Raymond Cole, pres; James Morgan, vp. Total Basic Subscribers: 3,300; Pay Cable Subscribers: 600; Number of Cable Systems: 1.

Harmon Cable Communications

Suite 6900, 8480 E. Orchard Rd., Englewood, CO 80111. (303) 773-3821; FAX: (303) 773-0839. Alan R. Harmon, chmn & pres; Robert M. Fukumoto, CFO; James R. Jackman, vp opns; Laura Olson, vp mktg. Owned by Alan R. Harmon. Total Basic Subscribers: 33,000; Pay Cable Subscribers: 17,000; Number of Cable Systems: 23.

SMALLER SYSTEMS

Minnesota - Harmon Cable Communications, Tracy, MN. **Nebraska** - Harmon Cable Communications, Ashland, NE. Harmon Cable Communications, Elkhorn, NE. Harmon Cable Communications, Greenwood, NE. Harmon Cable Communications, Gretna, NE. Harmon Cable Communications, Lake Ventura, NE. Harmon Cable Communications, Plattsmouth, NE. Harmon Cable Communications, Wahoo, NE. Harmon Cable Communications, Waverly, NE. **North Dakota** - Harmon Cable Communications, West Fargo, ND. **Oklahoma** - Harmon Cable Communications, Elmore City, OK. Harmon Cable Communications, Roff, OK. Harmon Cable Communications, Sulphur, OK. **Texas** - Harmon Cable Communications, Haskell, TX. Harmon Cable Communications, Munday, TX. Harmon Cable Communications, Stanford, TX. **West Virginia** - Harmon Cable Communications, Nitro, WV.

Harold's TV

Box 190, Grantsville, MD 21536. (301) 895-5830. Owned by Garnett Lipscomb, Harold Lipscomb. Total Basic Subscribers: 1,500; Pay Cable Subscribers: 300; Number of Cable Systems: 1.

Harron Communications Corp.

70 E. Lancaster Ave., Frazer, PA 19355. (215) 644-7500; FAX: (215) 644-2790. Paul F. Harron, CEO; Joel C. Cohen, pres & CFO; Gregory J. Raymond, vp opns; Linda C. Stuchell, vp mktg & vp progmg; Alan H. Eisenstein, vp; Wayne Hall, vp; John F. Quigley, vp. Total Basic Subscribers: 224,322; Pay Cable Subscribers: 152,498; Number of Cable Systems: 12.

REGIONS

Delaware Valley: 111 Ruthland Ave., Malvern, PA 19355; Andrew J. Walton. *Michigan:* 55800 New Haven Rd., Box 368, Chesterfield, MI 48051; John Ogren. *New England:* 333 Weymouth St., Rockland, MA 02370; Terry Hicks.

New York: 1000 Firehouse Rd., Utica, NY 13502; Gerald T. Kelley. *Texas:* F.M. 813 at Lakeshore Dr., Box 2628, Waxahachie, TX 75165; Kevin Lyngaas.

SYSTEMS WITH OVER 20,000 SUBSCRIBERS

Harron Cable of New York (45,467 subscribers). Box 105, Utica, NY 13503. (315) 797-8111; FAX: (315) 797-9722. Gerald T. Kelley, gen mgr; Bruce Davis, mktg dir; Terry Murphy, chief tech. *Basic Service:* Subscribers: 45,467; 10/31/93. *Pay Services:* Total Pay Subscribers: 22,688; 10/15/92.

Harron Cable TV (21,897 subscribers). Box 611008, 2780 Beach Rd., Port Huron, MI 48060. (313) 987-7880. John Ogren, gen mgr; Bernard Ravine, mktg dir; Russ Mitchell, chief tech. *Basic Service:* Subscribers: 21,897; 10/31/93.

Harron Cable TV Co. Inc. (25,000 subscribers). 111 Ruthland Ave., Malvern, PA 19355. (215) 296-5100; FAX: (215) 296-7060. Andrew Walton, gen mgr; Patricia Sincavage, mktg dir; James Mellon, chief tech; Hugh Scott, cust svc dir. *Channel Capacity:* 56. In use: 56. *Basic Service:* Subscribers: 25,000; 10/31/93. Programming (via satellite): 41 chs. Programming (via microwave): 1 ch. Programming (off air): 12 chs. *Pay Services:* Total Pay Subscribers: 19,268; 07/01/93. Pay Per View Subscribers: 11,500; 07/01/93. *Local Advertising Accepted.*

Harron Cable TV-Chesterfield (31,079 subscribers). 55800 New Haven Rd., Chesterfield, MI 48051. (313) 749-9561; FAX: (313) 749-9140. John Ogren, gen mgr; Bernard Ravine, mktg dir; Bill Stahlman, chief tech. *Basic Service:* Subscribers: 31,079; 10/31/93.

SMALLER SYSTEMS

Massachusetts - Harron Cable-Bourne, 49 Herring Pond Rd., Bourne, MA 02532; (508) 888-9255; 10,633 subs. Harron Cable-Rockland, 333 Weymouth St., Rockland, MA 02370; (617) 871-6097; 14,356 subs. **Michigan** - Harron Cable-Caseville, 6912 Main St., Caseville, MI 48725; (517) 856-2231; 48725 subs. Harron Cable-New Haven, 55800 New Haven Rd., Box 368, Chesterfield, MI 48051; (313) 749-9561. Harron Cable-Port Huron, 2780 Beach Rd., Box 61008, Port Huron, MI 48060; (313) 987-7844. **New Hampshire** - Harron Cable-Londonderry, 184A Rockingham Rd., Londonderry, NH 03053; (603) 432-0382; 15,052 subs. **New Jersey** - Harron Cable TV-New Jersey, 415 N. High St., Box 843, Millville, NJ 08332; (609) 825-5399; 7,348 subs. **New York** - Harron Cable-Adirondack Region, 227 Dix Ave., Glens Falls, NY 12801; (518) 793-0192. Harron Cable-Utica, 1000 Firehouse Rd., Utica, NY 13502; (315) 797-7111. **Pennsylvania** - Harron Cable-Kennett Square, 116 S. Broad St., Kennett Square, PA 19348; (215) 444-1225; 8,124 subs. Harron Cable-Malvern, 111 Ruthland Ave., Malvern, PA 19355; (215) 296-5111. **Texas** - Harron Cablevision of Texas Inc., F.M. 813 at Lakeshore Dr., Box 2628, Waxahachie, TX 75165; (214) 938-9288; 13,733 subs.

Hauser Communications Inc.

712 5th Ave., New York, NY 10019-4102. (212) 956-5665; FAX: (212) 956-1413. Gustave M. Hauser, CEO & chmn; John D. Evans, pres; Shu Y. Wong, CFO; John R. Eddy, vp; Robert J. Gordon, vp. Total Basic Subscribers: 231,000; Pay Cable Subscribers: 226,000; Number of Cable Systems: 2.

SYSTEMS WITH OVER 20,000 SUBSCRIBERS

Arlington Cable Partners (51,037 subscribers). 2707 Wilson Blvd., Arlington, VA 22201. (703) 841-7700. Robert J. Gordon, gen mgr; Amy Belson, mktg dir; Scott Shelley, chief tech. *Basic Service:* Subscribers: 51,037; 10/15/93. *Pay Services:* Total Pay Subscribers: 30,000; 12/15/92.

Montgomery Cablevision Company (174,141 subscribers). 20 W. Gude Dr., Rockville, MD 20850. (301) 294-7600. John R. Eddy, gen mgr; Phil Roter, mktg dir; Bruce Weintraub, chief tech. *Basic Service:* Subscribers: 174,141; 10/15/93. *Pay Services:* Total Pay Subscribers: 79,000; 12/15/92.

Jim Hays

Box 186, 232 Broadway, Irvine, KY 40336. (606) 723-4240. Total Basic Subscribers: 1,200; Pay Cable Subscribers: 1,200; Number of Cable Systems: 1.

Multiple Systems Operators, Independent Owners & Cable Systems

SMALLER SYSTEMS

Kentucky - McKee Television Enterprises, Box 186, 232 Broadway, Irvine, KY 40336.

Helicon Corporation

630 Palisades Ave., Englewood Cliffs, NJ 07632. (201) 568-7720; FAX: (201) 568-6228. Theodore B. Baum, CEO & chmn; Herbert J. Roberts, CFO; Gregory A. Kriser, vp opns; David M. Baum, vp mktg & vp progmg; Thomas L. Gimbel, vp. Total Basic Subscribers: 82,831; Pay Cable Subscribers: 18,716; Number of Cable Systems: 5.

REGIONS

Pennsylvania: 66 N. Gallatin Ave., Uniontown, PA 15401; Craig Tomchik. *West Virginia:* 150 N. Pinch Rd., Pinch, WV 25156; Jack Wade. *North Carolina:* 1144 N. Main St., Roxboro, NC 27573; Tom Kalisz. *Louisana:* 4549 Hwy. 24, Bourg, LA 70343; Laban Bergeron. *Vermont:* 20 Maple St., St. Johnsbury, VT 05819; Mark Ellingwood.

SYSTEMS WITH OVER 20,000 SUBSCRIBERS

Helicon Cablevision (37,614 subscribers). 320 Bailey Ave., Uniontown, PA 15401. (412) 437-9875; FAX: (412) 437-6910. Craig S. Tomchik, gen mgr; Fred Davies, chief tech. *Basic Service:* Subscribers: 37,614; 10/31/93. *Pay Services:* Total Pay Subscribers: 8,000; 12/01/92.

SMALLER SYSTEMS

Louisana - Terrebonne Cablevision, 4549 Hwy. 24, Bourg, LA 70343; (504) 594-4910; 10,241 subs. **North Carolina -** Roxboro Cablevision, 1144 N. Main St., Roxboro, NC 27573; (919) 599-1128; 6,172 subs. **Vermont -** Helicon Cablevision, 20 Maple St., St. Johnsbury, VT 05819; (802) 748-8917; 12,552 subs. **West Virginia -** Helicon Cablevision, 150 N. Pinch St., Pinch, WV 25156; (304) 965-6104; 13,715 subs.

Hereford Cable Vision

Box 1656, 119 E. Fourth, Hereford, TX 79045. (806) 364-3912; FAX: (806) 364-7147. Clint Formby, CEO & chmn. Owned by Hereford Clearvideo, Inc., James Witherspoon. Total Basic Subscribers: 3,950; Pay Cable Subscribers: 1,350; Number of Cable Systems: 1.

Herr Cable Co.

Box 717, R.R. 4, Montoursville, PA 17754. (717) 435-2780. Owned by Alden Herr, Rita Herr. Total Basic Subscribers: 1,500; Pay Cable Subscribers: 300; Number of Cable Systems: 3.

Edward Hewson

Box 1569, Ocean Shores, WA 98569. (206) 289-2252; FAX: (206) 289-2750. Edward Hewson, pres; Ron Thomason, vp opns. Total Basic Subscribers: 3,000; Pay Cable Subscribers: 900; Number of Cable Systems: 1.

SMALLER SYSTEMS

Washington - Coast Communications Co. Inc., Pacific Beach, WA.

Higgins Lake Cable TV Inc.

Box 338, 5939 W. Higgins Lake Dr., Higgins Lake, MI 48627. (517) 821-5567. Jim Brandt, pres; Steve Collin, vp opns. Total Basic Subscribers: 2,835; Pay Cable Subscribers: 835; Number of Cable Systems: 1.

Russell G. Hilliard dba Cable USA, Inc.

Box 2299, 1722 First Ave., Scottsbluff, NE 69361. (308) 635-2363; FAX: (308) 635-2721. Russ Hilliard, pres; Craig Auer, CFO. Owned by Russell G. Hillard. Total Basic Subscribers: 24,403; Number of Cable Systems: 47.

Honeoye Cable TV Inc.

Box 706, 31 E. Main St., Honeoye, NY 14471. (716) 229-2650. Paul Cipro, pres. Total Basic Subscribers: 1,400; Pay Cable Subscribers: 507; Number of Cable Systems: 1.

Honesdale TV Service

Box 1085, 1040 Main St., Honesdale, PA 18431. (717) 253-3451. Patricia McGinnis, CEO & chmn. Owned by Patricia McGinnis. Total Basic Subscribers: 3,116; Pay Cable Subscribers: 388; Number of Cable Systems: 1.

Horizon Cable TV Inc.

Box 937, Fairfax, CA 94978. (415) 456-1280; FAX: (415) 382-0814. Kevin Daniel, pres; Susan Daniel, CFO. Owned by Kevin Daniel. Total Basic Subscribers: 2,300; Number of Cable Systems: 3.

Horizon Cablevision Inc.

2598 Lansing Rd., Charlotte, MI 48813. (517) 543-1245; FAX: (517) 543-8057. Glenn Friedly, chmn & CFO; Alan Baird, vp. Pay Cable Subscribers: 25,000; Number of Cable Systems: 16.

Hornell TV Service Inc.

166 Main St., Hornell, NY 14843. (607) 324-4611. John A. Pryor, pres; Susan P. Lynch, vp; Linda L. Berlin, vp. Owned by John A. Pryor, Susan P. Lynch. Total Basic Subscribers: 6,197; Pay Cable Subscribers: 1,486; Number of Cable Systems: 1.

Horry Telephone Cooperative Inc.

Drawer 1820, Conway, SC 29526. (803) 365-2151; FAX: (803) 365-1111. Curley Huggins, CEO; H.G. McNeill, chmn & pres; O'Neal Miller, CFO. Total Basic Subscribers: 14,300; Pay Cable Subscribers: 14,300; Number of Cable Systems: 1.

Martin Howser

729 S. Bernard St., Spokane, WA 99204. (509) 624-4140; FAX: (509) 624-7372. Martin Howser, CEO & pres. Total Basic Subscribers: 3,950; Pay Cable Subscribers: 2,525; Number of Cable Systems: 11.

SMALLER SYSTEMS

Washington - Community Antenna Systems, Connell, WA. Community Antenna Systems, Ione, WA. Community Antenna Systems, Kahlotus, WA. Community Antenna Systems, Liberty Lake, WA. Community Antenna Systems, Lind, WA. Community Antenna Systems, Metaline, WA. Community Antenna Systems, Metaline Falls, WA. Community Antenna Systems, Odessa, WA. Community Antenna Systems, Ritzville, WA. Community Antenna Systems, Tekoa, WA. Community Antenna Systems, Warden, WA.

Huntingdon TV Cable Co. Inc.

170 Penn St., Huntington, PA 16652. (814) 643-3498; FAX: (814) 643-2830. J. Melvin Isett, pres; Beulah Isett, vp; Chester Isett, vp. Total Basic Subscribers: 7,000; Number of Cable Systems: 2.

Illini Cablevision

595 San Antonio Ave., Many, LA 71449. (318) 256-2097. Edwin T. Baldrige, pres; Tedd W. Dumas, vp. Owned by Edwin T. Baldrige, Tedd W. Dumas. Total Basic Subscribers: 3,800; Pay Cable Subscribers: 1,250; Number of Cable Systems: 5.

Ind. Co. Cable TV Inc.

Box 3799, 2700 N. St. Louis St., Batesville, AR 72501. (501) 793-4174; FAX: (501) 793-7439. J.D. Pierce, pres; Boyce E. Barnett, vp. Owned by J.D. Pierce, Boyce E. Barnett. Total Basic Subscribers: 7,600; Pay Cable Subscribers: 2,300; Number of Cable Systems: 24.

Insight Communications Co.

126 E. 56th St., New York, NY 10022. (212) 371-2266. Sidney R. Knafel, chmn; Michael S. Willner, pres; Kim D. Kelly, CFO; Roger Worboys, vp opns; Pamela N. Euler, vp mktg; James Steward, vp. Total Basic Subscribers: 140,000; Pay Cable Subscribers: 90,000; Number of Cable Systems: 9.

SYSTEMS WITH OVER 20,000 SUBSCRIBERS

Insight Cablevision (22,852 subscribers). 21200 N. Black Canyon Hwy., Phoenix, AZ 85027. (602) 780-2222. Pam MacKenzie, gen mgr; Mark St. Cyr, mktg dir. *Basic Service:* Subscribers: 22,852; 10/15/93.

Insight Cablevision (22,000 subscribers). 15229 Stoney Creek Way, Noblesville, IN 46060. (317) 776-0660. Doug Smith, gen mgr; Dave Beasley, mktg dir & loc adv dir. *Basic Service:* Subscribers: 22,000; 10/15/93.

Insight Cablevision (24,369 subscribers). 3408 Industrial Pkwy., Jeffersonville, IN 47130. (812) 288-6471. Sandra Edgmon, gen mgr; Chuck Moss, mktg dir; David Brown, chief tech; Edie Smith, cust svc dir.
Area(s) Served: IN, KY. Counties: Clark; Henry, Oldham, Tremble. Serving Borden, Charlestown, Clarksville, Hamburg, Jeffersonville, Marysville, Memphis, Nabb, New Washington, Otisco, Sellersburg, Utica; Bedford, Campbellsburg, Crestwood, Goshen, Lagrange, Peewee Valley, Pendleton, Prospect, Smithfield, Westport. *Basic Service:* Subscribers: 24,369; 09/21/93.

Insight Cablevision (26,000 subscribers). 9075 South 700 West, Sandy, UT 84070. (801) 561-9275; FAX: (801) 255-2711. Marg Rhodes, gen mgr; Chris Jeffers, mktg dir; Roger Scheaer, loc adv dir; Richard LaJeunesse, chief tech; Ann Izzo, cust svc dir.
Area(s) Served: UT. Counties: Salt Lake, Utah. Serving Alpine, American Fork, Copperton, Highland, Lehi, Linden, Mapleton, Midvale, Orem, Pleasant Grove, Sandy, Springville, West Jordan. Miles of Plant: 870. Homes Passed: 66,250. Homes Served: 26,000. *Channel Capacity:* 45. In use: 42. *Basic Service:* Subscribers: 26,000; 09/01/93. Programming (via satellite): 34 chs. Programming (off air): 7 chs. *Pay Services:* Total Pay Subscribers: 19,000; 09/01/93. (1) Pay Units: 4,609; 09/01/93. Programming (via satellite): HBO. (2) Pay Units: 1,900; 09/01/93. Programming (via satellite): Cinemax. (3) Pay Units: 3,240; 09/01/93. Programming (via satellite): Showtime. (4) Pay Units: 3,500; 09/01/93. Programming (via satellite): Disney. (5) Pay Units: 60; 09/01/93. Programming (via satellite): The Movie Channel. Pay Per View Subscribers: 10,500; 09/01/93. *Local Advertising Accepted. Equipment:* Provided by Jerrold.

SMALLER SYSTEMS

California - Insight Cable, 212 S. Indian Hill Rd., Claremont, CA 91711; (714) 624-5566; 8,500 subs. **Georgia -** Insight Cable, 1150 Everee Inn Rd., Griffin, GA 30223; (404) 228-3333; 10,500 subs. **Utah -** Insight Cable, 45 East 200 South, Brigham City, UT 84302; (801) 723-8548; 9,700 subs. Insight Cable, 9075 S. 700 West, Sandy, UT 84070; (801) 561-9275. Insight Cable, 35 N. 100 West, Vernal, UT 84078; 6,500 subs. **Virginia -** Insight Cable, 408 Franklin St., Franklin, VA 23851; (804) 569-9122; 7,200 subs.

InterMedia Partners

235 Montgomery St., San Francisco, CA 94104. (415) 616-4600; FAX: (415) 397-3406. Leo J. Hindery Jr., CEO; David G. Rozzelle, pres; Edward G. Liebst Jr., CFO; Terry C. Cotten, vp opns; Richard J. Maul, vp mktg; David J. Large, vp. Total Basic Subscribers: 542,052; Pay Cable Subscribers: 190,746; Number of Cable Systems: 18.

REGIONS

Southeast: 482 Hwy. 74 N., Box 2670, Peachtree City, GA 30269; John Southard. *West:* 235 Mongomery St., San Francisco, CA 94104; Alan Mutter. *Tennessee:* 1722 Gen. George Patton Dr., Brentwood, TN 37027; Dave Maney.

SYSTEMS WITH OVER 20,000 SUBSCRIBERS

Desert Cablevision (20,000 subscribers). 150 E. Wilcox Dr., Sierra Vista, AZ 85635. (602) 458-4705; FAX: (602) 452-4423. Marshall Greyson, gen mgr; Chip Spann, mktg dir; Mike Gargiulo, cust svc dir. *Basic Service:* Subscribers: 20,000; 10/31/93.

East Tennessee Cablevision (51,342 subscribers). Box 600, Alcoa, TN 37701. (615) 983-8200; FAX: (615) 982-4974. Dennis Marmon, gen mgr. *Basic Service:* Subscribers: 51,342; 10/31/93.

Gainesville Cablevision (20,960 subscribers). Box 2535, Gainesville, GA 30503. (404) 532-9961; FAX: (404) 532-0455. Sonny Seneker, gen mgr; Elizabeth Dycus, chief tech. *Basic Service:* Subscribers: 20,960; 10/31/93.

Midwest Cablevision (118,000 subscribers). 4062 W. County Rd. 42, Savage, MN 55037. (612) 895-1530; FAX: (612) 895-1812. John Brinker, gen mgr. *Basic Service:* Subscribers: 118,000; 10/31/93.

Multiple Systems Operators, Independent Owners & Cable Systems

North Arundel Cable Television (44,100 subscribers). Suite 201, 406 Headquarters Rd., Millersville, MD 21108. (410) 987-8400; FAX: (410) 987-4890. Rick Oldenburg, gen mgr; Paul Janson, mktg dir; Craig Malang, chief tech; Trish Archibald, cust svc dir.
Area(s) Served: MD. County: Anne Arundel. Serving Arnold, Brooklyn Park, Glen Burnie, Linthium, Millersville, Pasadena, Severn, Sevena Park. Miles of Plant: 950. Homes Passed: 70,700. Homes Served: 44,100. Channel Capacity: 54. In use: 51. *Basic Service:* Subscribers: 44,100; 09/01/93. Programming (via satellite): 37 chs. Programming (off air): 14 chs. *Local Advertising Accepted.*

Palmetto Cablevision (23,300 subscribers). Box 151, 3060 Cablevision Rd., Aiken, SC 29802. (803) 648-8361; FAX: (803) 649-1002. Larry Greenberg, gen mgr; Richelle Eckles, mktg dir; Gordy McMillan, chief tech. *Basic Service:* Subscribers: 23,300; 10/31/92. *Pay Services:* Total Pay Subscribers: 12,408; 11/15/92.

Sonic Cable Television (35,000 subscribers). 1031 Triangle Ct., West Sacramento, CA 95605. (916) 372-2221; FAX: (916) 372-3865. John Adams, gen mgr; Heinz Ludke, mktg dir; Eric Brownell, chief tech. *Basic Service:* Subscribers: 35,000; 10/31/93.

Sonic Cable Television of San Luis Obispo (46,000 subscribers). Box 1205, San Luis Obispo, CA 93406. (805) 544-1962; FAX: (805) 541-6042. Steve Burrell, gen mgr; Jeff Fox, mktg dir; Stephen P. Gorden, chief tech. *Basic Service:* Subscribers: 46,000; 12/01/92.

South Bay Cablevision (65,000 subscribers). 2700 Scott Blvd., Santa Clara, CA 95050. (408) 727-5295; FAX: (408) 988-3723. William Haggerty, gen mgr; Cindy Weintraub, mktg dir. *Basic Service:* Subscribers: 65,000; 10/31/93.

Tennessee Valley Cablevision and InterMedia Co. (30,000 subscribers). 1722 General George Patton Dr., Brentwood, TN 37027. (615) 377-3680; FAX: (615) 377-3683. Dave Maney, gen mgr; Sandra K. Staggs, mktg dir; Dan Winkler, chief tech. *Basic Service:* Subscribers: 30,000; 10/31/93.

Tucson Cablevision (76,200 subscribers). 1440 E. 15th St., Tucson, AZ 85719. (602) 629-8410; FAX: (602) 624-5918. Wendell Owen, gen mgr. *Basic Service:* Subscribers: 76,200; 10/31/93. Programming (via satellite): 37 chs. Programming (off air): KTTU, KVOA, KUAT, KGUN, KHR, KMSB, KOLD, KTVW, Galavision. *Pay Services:* Total Pay Subscribers: 69,719; 10/15/92. (1) Pay Units: 22,852; 10/15/92. Programming (via satellite): HBO. (2) Pay Units: 3,748; 10/15/92. Programming (via satellite): Cinemax. (3) Pay Units: 7,057; 10/15/92. Programming (via satellite): The Movie Channel. (4) Pay Units: 5,247; 10/15/92. Programming (via satellite): Disney. (5) Pay Units: 1,058; 10/15/92. Programming (via satellite): Playboy. (6) Pay Units: 17,575; 10/15/92. Programming (via satellite): Encore. *Local Advertising Accepted.*

Volunteer Cable (43,000 subscribers). 307 Circle Dr., McKenzie, TN 38201. (901) 352-3304; FAX: (901) 352-3164. Billy Barksdale, gen mgr; Craig Forstrom, mktg dir. *Basic Service:* Subscribers: 43,000; 10/31/93.

SMALLER SYSTEMS

California - Sonic Communications Santa Cruz, 475 Airport Blvd., Watsonville, CA; 14,260 subs. **Georgia** - Peachstate Cablevision, 482 Hwy. 74 N., Peachtree City, GA; (404) 487-5011; 18,000 subs. **Hawaii** - Kanai Cable TV, 3-1866 Kaumualii, Lihue, HI 96766; (808) 245-7720; 8,000 subs. **North Carolina** - McDowell County Cablevision, 12 S. Garden, Marrion, NC; (704) 652-3818; 4,800 subs. Tri-County Cablevision, 153 N. Main, Mt. Arry, NC; (917) 789-5000; 6,200 subs. **South Carolina** - Greenwood Cablevision, 235 N. Creek Blvd., Greenwood, SC 229-5421; 13,800 subs. **Utah** - Sonic Communications, 1350 N. 200 W., Box 488, Logan, UT 84321; 13,245 subs.

InterMedia Partners II L.P.

235 Montgomery St., San Francisco, CA 94104. (415) 616-4600; FAX: (415) 397-3406. David G. Rozzelle, CEO; Terry C. Cotten, vp opns; Richard J. Maul, vp mktg; David J. Large, vp. Owned by InterMedia Partners. Total Basic Subscribers: 119,893; Pay Cable Subscribers: 48,067; Number of Cable Systems: 4.

REGIONS

Midwest: 4062 W. Country Rd. 42, Savage, MN 55378; John Brinker.

InterMedia Partners V L.P.

235 Montgomery St., San Francisco, CA 94104. (415) 616-4600; FAX: (415) 397-3406. Leo J. Hindery Jr., CEO; David G. Rozzelle, pres; Karen J. Linder, CFO; Terry C. Cotten, vp opns; Richard J. Maul, vp mktg; David J. Large, vp. Owned by InterMedia Partners. Total Basic Subscribers: 160,810; Pay Cable Subscribers: 99,591; Number of Cable Systems: 7.

REGIONS

Southeast: 482 Hwy. 74 N., Box 2670, Peachtree City, GA 30269; John Southard. *Tennessee:* 1722 General George Patton Dr., Brentwood, TN 37027; Dave Maney.

SMALLER SYSTEMS

Georgia - Royston Cablevision, 737 Cook St., Box 115, Royston, GA 30662; (706) 245-9336; 1,449 subs. Toccoa Cablevision, 303 N. Broad St., Suite 3, Toccoa, GA 30577-2303; (706) 245-9336; 4,832 subs. **Tennessee** - Central Cablevision, 4056 N. Mount Juliet Rd., Mount Juliet, TN 37122; (615) 754-2338; 15,889 subs.

Iron River Cooperative TV Antenna Corp.

Box 132, 420 W. Genesee St., Iron River, MI 49935. (906) 265-3810. Bernard Johnson, pres. Total Basic Subscribers: 1,478; Pay Cable Subscribers: 750; Number of Cable Systems: 1.

Jackson Cable TV Inc.

Box 8196, Clinton, LA 70722. (504) 683-9297; FAX: (504) 683-9297. V.F. Jackson Jr., CEO; James G. Jackson, chmn; V.F. Jackson Sr., pres. Total Basic Subscribers: 1,585; Pay Cable Subscribers: 586; Number of Cable Systems: 1.

Jackson Municipal TV System

80 W. Ashley St., Jackson, MN 56143. (507) 847-3225. Curt Egeland, vp. Total Basic Subscribers: 1,580; Number of Cable Systems: 1.

Lynda & Robert Jacobson

Box 759, Ranchester, WY 82839. (307) 655-9011. Robert Jacobson, CEO. Total Basic Subscribers: 1,300; Number of Cable Systems: 4.

SMALLER SYSTEMS

Wyoming - Sundance Cable Vision Inc., Sundance, WY. Tongue River Cable TV Inc., Ranchester, WY. Tongue River Cable TV Inc., Story, WY. Tongue River Cable TV Inc., Hulett, WY.

James Cable Partners L.P.

Suite 180, 710 N. Woodward, Bloomfield Hills, MI 48304. (313) 647-1080; FAX: (313) 647-1321. William R. James, CEO & pres; Daniel K. Shoemaker, chmn & CFO. Total Basic Subscribers: 79,427; Pay Cable Subscribers: 29,850; Number of Cable Systems: 9.

SMALLER SYSTEMS

Alabama - Better Vision Cable, 707 N. Main St., Roanoke, AL 36274; (205) 863-8112; 5,120 subs. Tri County Cable, 12th Ave. West, Guin, AL 35563; (205) 468-3601; 3,390 subs. **Colorado** - Platte River Cablevision, 113 S. College, Suite A, Fort Collins, CO 80524; (303) 224-3325; 10,300 subs. **Florida** - Cable Florida, 2025 N.E. Santa Fe Blvd., High Springs, FL 32643; (904) 454-2299; 6,600 subs. **Georgia** - Midstate Cable TV, Eatonton, GA 31024; (706) 485-2288; 13,700 subs. **Louisiana** - Video Design, 2504 Westwood Rd., Westlake LA 70669; (318) 433-0892; 12,200 subs. **Tennessee** - Big South Fork Cablevision, 1106 Hwy. 62, Box 465, Wartburg, TN 37887; (615) 346-6674; 9,800 subs. **Texas** - Southwest Cablevision, 28048 FM51 I, Box 869, Decatur, TX 76234; (817) 627-3099; 17,700 subs.

Jefferson County Cable Inc.

116 S. Fourth St., Toronto, OH 43964. (614) 537-2214; FAX: (614) 537-2802. Marvin Bates, CEO & pres. Owned by Marvin Bates. Total Basic Subscribers: 4,000; Pay Cable Subscribers: 1,513; Number of Cable Systems: 1.

Johnsonburg Community TV Co. Inc.

424 Center St, Johnsonburg, PA 15845. (814) 965-4888; FAX: (814) 965-4040. Roy Nelson, pres; Harry Horne, vp opns, vp sls & vp progmg. Total Basic Subscribers: 1,641; Pay Cable Subscribers: 1,315; Number of Cable Systems: 1.

Jones Intercable Inc.

9697 E. Mineral Ave., Englewood, CO 80112. (303) 792-3111; FAX: (303) 790-0533. Glenn R. Jones, CEO & chmn; James O'Brien, pres; Kevin Coyle, CFO; Ruth Warren, vp opns; Jerry Czuchna, vp adv. Total Basic Subscribers: 1,300,000; Number of Cable Systems: 59.

SYSTEMS WITH OVER 20,000 SUBSCRIBERS

Jones Intercable (51,000 subscribers). 8251 N. Cortaro Rd., Tucson, AZ 85743. (602) 744-2657; FAX: (602) 744-4737. Kenna Smith, gen mgr & mktg dir; Allen Showalter, chief tech.
Area(s) Served: AZ. County: Pima. Serving Catalina, Marana, Oro Valley. Miles of Plant: 930. Homes Passed: 73,400. Homes Served: 51,000. Channel Capacity: 54. In use: 53. *Basic Service:* Subscribers: 51,000; 11/15/93. *Pay Services:* Total Pay Subscribers: 15,230; 11/15/93. Pay Per View Subscribers: 31,071; 12/01/92. *Local Advertising Accepted.*

Jones Intercable (55,700 subscribers). 41551 10th St. W., Palmdale, CA 93551. (805) 273-1890; FAX: (805) 273-6439. John Woody Hutton, gen mgr; Dennis Beaulieu, mktg dir; Craig Chase, chief tech.
Area(s) Served: CA. Counties: Kern East, Los Angeles. Serving California City, Edwards, Elizabeth Lake, Green Valley, Lancaster, Leona Valley, Palmdale, Quartz Hill. Homes Passed: 81,272. Homes Served: 55,700. Channel Capacity: 60. In use: 46. *Basic Service:* Subscribers: 55,700; 11/15/93. *Pay Services:* Total Pay Subscribers: 22,500; 11/30/92. *Local Advertising Accepted.*

Jones Intercable (35,256 subscribers). 2212 McGregor Blvd., Fort Myers, FL 33901. (813) 334-8055; FAX: (813) 334-7023. Andy Anderson, gen mgr; Steve Bumm, mktg dir; Scott Nordstrom, loc adv dir; Will Truckenmiller, chief tech.
Area(s) Served: FL. County: Lee. Serving Ft. Myers. Pop: 138,000. Miles of Plant: 682. Homes Passed: 63,493. Homes Served: 35,256. Channel Capacity: 60. In use: 57. *Basic Service:* Subscribers: 35,256; 10/15/92. Programming (via satellite): 46 chs. Programming (off air): 7 chs. Pay Per View Subscribers: 10,942; 08/31/93. *Local Advertising Accepted. Equipment:* Provided by Scientific-Atlanta, Jerrold, Magnavox & Texscan.

Jones Intercable (60,000 subscribers). 4400 W. Dr. Martin Luther King Jr. Blvd., Tampa, FL 33614. (813) 877-6805; FAX: (813) 875-2507. Gail Hisle, mktg dir; Ken Hisle, chief tech.
Area(s) Served: FL. County: Hillsborough. Serving Tampa. Miles of Plant: 1,100. Homes Served: 60,000. Channel Capacity: 60. In use: 60. *Basic Service:* Subscribers: 60,000; 11/15/93. *Local Advertising Accepted. Equipment:* Scientific-Atlanta headend; Texscan amplifiers; Trilogy cable; MSI character generator; Jerrold set top and addressable set top converters; Arcom traps; DX Engineering satellite receivers; ChannelMatic commercial insert.

Jones Intercable (64,000 subscribers). Box 3576, 1424 Monte Sano Ave., Augusta, GA 30904. (706) 733-7712; FAX: (706) 736-7287. George Paschall, gen mgr; Kathy Carr Hammon, mktg dir; Mike Scott, chief tech.
Area(s) Served: GA. Counties: Burke, Columbia, Richmond. Serving Hephzibah. Homes Passed: 94,754. Homes Served: 64,000. Channel Capacity: 78. In use: 54. *Basic Service:* Subscribers: 64,000; 11/15/93. *Pay Services:* Total Pay Subscribers: 51,701; 09/15/92. *Local Advertising Accepted. Equipment:* Scientific-Atlanta, Catel & Hughes headend; Scientific-Atlanta amplifiers; Times cable; JVC cameras; Sony VTRs; Texscan & MSI character generators; Zenith, Panasonic & Scientific-Atlanta set top converters; Eagle & Arcom traps; Scientific-Atlanta satellite antenna and receivers; ChannelMatic commercial insert.

Jones Intercable (45,000 subscribers). 1101 E. Roosevelt Rd., Wheaton, IL 60187. (708) 690-3500; FAX: (708) 690-8648. Wayne Vestal, gen mgr; Joanie Brooke, mktg dir.
Area(s) Served: IL. Counties: Du Page, Kane. Serving Addison, Chicago, Geneva, Glen Ellyn, St. Charles, Warrenville, West Chicago, Wheaton, Winfield. Miles of Plant: 1,195. Homes Passed: 78,300. Homes Served:

45,000. *Channel Capacity:* 56. In use: 56. *Basic Service:* Subscribers: 45,000; 09/01/93. *Pay Services:* Total Pay Subscribers: 34,800; 12/01/92. Pay Per View Subscribers: 20,200; 09/01/93. *Local Advertising Accepted.*

Jones Intercable (74,000 subscribers). Box 2000, 4700 Selsa Rd., Independence, MO 64055. (816) 795-8377; FAX: (816) 795-0946. Douglas Johnson, gen mgr; Dwayne Lewis, mktg dir; Ken Covey, chief tech; Denise Stout, cust svc dir.
Area(s) Served: KS, MO. Counties: Cass, Clay, Jackson, Johnson. Serving Baldwin Park, Blue Springs, Blue Summit, Grain Valley, Greenwood, Lake Lotawana, Lake Tapawingo, Lake Winnebago, Lee's Summit, Oak Grove, Odessa, Olathe, Peculiar, Pleasant Hill, Raytown, Sugar Creek. Miles of Plant: 1,500. Homes Passed: 126,000. Homes Served: 74,000. *Channel Capacity:* 35. In use: 35. *Basic Service:* Subscribers: 74,000; 10/01/93. *Pay Services:* Total Pay Subscribers: 54,919; 10/01/93. *Local Advertising Accepted.*

Jones Intercable (107,000 subscribers). 4611 Montbel Pl. N.E., Albuquerque, NM 87107. (505) 761-6200; FAX: (505) 761-6273. Kevin Bethke, gen mgr; Linda Rosenberg, loc adv dir; Brian Throp, chief tech; Lynne Lofton, cust svc dir.
Area(s) Served: NM. Counties: Bernalillo, Sandoval, Valencia. Serving Bernalillo, Bosque Farms, Corrales, Los Ranchos, North Valley, Paradise Hills, Peralta, South Valley, Taylors Ranch. Pop: 420,000. Homes Passed: 200,000. Homes Served: 107,000. *Channel Capacity:* 43. In use: 43. *Basic Service:* Subscribers: 107,000; 11/15/93. *Pay Services:* Total Pay Subscribers: 62,000; 11/30/92. Pay Per View Subscribers: 5,500; 11/30/92. *Local Advertising Accepted.*

Jones Intercable (35,200 subscribers). 617A S. Pickett St., Alexandria, VA 22304. (703) 751-7710; FAX: (703) 823-3061. Jeff Spiegleman, gen mgr; Steven Apodaca, mktg dir; Carl Elieff, chief tech.
Area(s) Served: VA. Serving Alexandria. Homes Served: 35,200. *Channel Capacity:* 51. *Basic Service:* Subscribers: 35,200; 11/15/93. *Pay Services:* Total Pay Subscribers: 35,127; 11/15/93. *Local Advertising Accepted. Equipment:* Scientific-Atlanta headend; Jerrold amplifiers; Comm/Scope cable; Hitachi cameras; Sony VTRs; Video Data Systems character generator; Scientific-Atlanta set top and addressable set top converters; Scientific-Atlanta satellite antenna and satellite receivers; ChannelMatic commercial insert.

Jones Intercable Inc. (50,500 subscribers). 6565 Nova Dr., Davie, FL 33317. (305) 731-7100; FAX: (305) 452-4411. Tom Horne, gen mgr; Brad Goar, mktg dir; Lorett Breznikar, loc adv dir; George Stickler, chief tech; Tom Autry, cust svc dir.
Area(s) Served: FL. County: Broward. Serving Cooper City, Dania, Davie, Lauderdale Lakes. Miles of Plant: 900. Homes Passed: 87,000. Homes Served: 50,500. *Channel Capacity:* 55. In use: 55. *Basic Service:* Subscribers: 50,500; 08/31/93. Pay Per View Subscribers: 5,900; 08/31/93. *Local Advertising Accepted.*

Jones Intercable Inc. (34,000 subscribers). 8 E. Galena, Aurora, IL 60506. (708) 897-2288; FAX: (708) 897-8521. Paul Vasek, gen mgr; Ed Zamirippa, mktg dir; John Green, chief tech.
Area(s) Served: IL. Counties: Du Page, Kane, Kendall. Serving Boulder Hill, Montgomery, North Aurora, Oswego. Homes Served: 34,000. *Channel Capacity:* 54. In use: 54. *Basic Service:* Subscribers: 34,000; 11/15/93. *Local Advertising Accepted.*

Jones Intercable Inc. (42,500 subscribers). Box 267, 815 Rt. 3, Gambrills, MD 21054. (410) 987-3900; FAX: (410) 923-3568. Gary Massaglia, gen mgr; Ben Painter, mktg dir; Nancy Valle, loc adv dir; Tom Gorman, chief tech; Lea Rigby, cust svc dir.
Area(s) Served: MD. County: Anne Arundel. Serving Annapolis, Arnold, Cape St. Claire, Crofton, Crownsville, Glen Burnie, Jessup, Laurel, Maryland City, Millersville, Pasadena, Severna Park. Miles of Plant: 1,170. Homes Passed: 86,600. Homes Served: 42,500. *Channel Capacity:* 60. In use: 53. *Basic Service:* Subscribers: 42,500; 11/15/92. Pay Per View Subscribers: 37,800; 11/15/92. *Local Advertising Accepted. Equipment:* Scientific-Atlanta headend; Texscan & Magnavox amplifiers; Times Fiber cable; Sony VTRs; Hamlin & Scientific-Atlanta set top converters; Scientific-Atlanta addressable set top converters; Eagle traps; Scientific-Atlanta satellite antenna; Scientific-Atlanta satellite receivers; ChannelMatic commercial insert.

Jones Intercable Inc. (31,945 subscribers). Box 775, Black Horse Pike & Cable TV Ln., Turnersville, NJ 08012. (609) 728-8251; FAX: (609) 875-1390. Irene C. Picard, gen mgr; Maureen Cooper, mktg dir; James Cushman, loc adv dir; Dave Lisco, chief tech; Lisa Bryden, cust svc dir.
Area(s) Served: NJ. Counties: Atlantic, Camden, Gloucester. Serving Buena Vista, Chesilhurst, Folsom, Monroe Twp., Washington Twp., Waterford, Winslow. Miles of Plant: 721. Homes Passed: 43,331. Homes Served: 31,945. *Channel Capacity:* 60. In use: 60. *Basic Service:* Subscribers: 31,945; 09/03/93. Programming (via satellite): 43 chs. Programming (via microwave): 4 chs. Programming (off air): 11 chs. *Pay Services:* Total Pay Subscribers: 16,352; 09/03/93. (1) Pay Units: 9,139; 09/03/93. Programming (via satellite): HBO. (2) Pay Units: 7,349; 09/03/93. Programming (via satellite): Showtime. (3) Pay Units: 8,053; 09/03/93. Programming (via satellite): The Movie Channel. (4) Pay Units: 7,078; 09/03/93. Programming (via microwave): Prism. Pay Per View Subscribers: 31,945; 09/03/93. *Local Advertising Accepted. Equipment:* Scientific-Atlanta headend; Magnavox amplifiers; Comm/Scope cable; Sony & JVC cameras; Sony VTRs; Laird character generator; Scientific-Atlanta addressable set top converters; AFC, M/A-Com & Scientific-Atlanta satellite antenna; DX satellite receivers; ChannelMatic commercial insert.

Jones Intercable of Oxnard (35,650 subscribers). 721 Mulhardt Ave., Oxnard, CA 93030. (805) 485-3888; FAX: (805) 485-6710. Jeff Jones, gen mgr; Dede Tanner, mktg dir; Dan Wong, loc adv dir; Paul Olivares, chief tech; Steve Naber, cust svc dir.
Area(s) Served: CA. Counties: Ventura, West. Serving El Rio, Oxnard, Port Hueneme. Miles of Plant: 366. Homes Passed: 52,000. Homes Served: 35,650. *Channel Capacity:* 55. In use: 55. *Basic Service:* Subscribers: 35,650; 12/01/92. *Pay Services:* Total Pay Subscribers: 14,000; 12/01/92. Pay Per View Subscribers: 25,500; 12/01/92. *Local Advertising Accepted. Equipment:* Scientific-Atlanta headend; Century III & C-COR amplifiers; Times, M/A-Com & Comm/Scope cable; Sony cameras; Sony VTRs; Chyron character generator; Zenith set top and addressable set top converters; Scientific-Atlanta satellite antenna; Prodelin and Scientific-Atlanta satellite receivers; ChannelMatic commercial insert.

Billy R. Jones

Box 1470, 10 Wilson Rd., Stockbridge, GA 30281. (404) 389-9999; FAX: (404) 389-0166. Billy R. Jones, pres; Carl Krutchfeld, vp opns. Total Basic Subscribers: 1,700; Number of Cable Systems: 1.

SMALLER SYSTEMS

Georgia - Bijo Cablevision, 10 Wilson Rd., Stockbridge, GA 30281. **Virginia -** King George Cablevision, Box 558, King George, VA 22485; (703) 775-5313.

Kan-D Land Inc.

605 W. Seventh Ave., Corsicana, TX 75110. (903) 872-3131; FAX: (903) 872-6623. Richard Parker, pres; Bob Belcher, vp opns; Greg Mitchell, vp mktg. Total Basic Subscribers: 5,000; Pay Cable Subscribers: 3,500; Number of Cable Systems: 1.

SMALLER SYSTEMS

Texas - Corsicana Cable TV, 605 W. Seventh Ave., Corsicana, TX 75110; (903) 872-3131.

KBLCOM

Suite 1800, 1200 Smith St., Houston, TX 77002. (713) 659-5411; FAX: (713) 651-2700. Don D. Jordan, CEO & chmn; Gary G. Weik, pres; Jim Bryan, CFO; John R. Bickham, vp opns; Frank Hosea, vp sls; Dean Gilbert, vp. Owned by Houston Industries. Total Basic Subscribers: 571,000; Pay Cable Subscribers: 424,954; Number of Cable Systems: 6.

SYSTEMS WITH OVER 20,000 SUBSCRIBERS

Paragon Cable (103,000 subscribers). 801 Plymouth Ave., Minneapolis, MN 55411. (612) 522-2000; FAX: (612) 521-7626. Wayne Nighton, gen mgr; Bruce Baumhardt, loc adv dir; Matt Haviland, chief tech; Rick Braemer, cust svc dir.
Area(s) Served: MN. County: Hennepin. Serving Eden Prairie, Edina, Hopkins, Minnetonka, Richfield, Minneapolis. Homes Passed: 254,026. Homes Served: 103,000. *Basic Service:* Subscribers: 103,000; 10/01/93. *Pay Services:* Total Pay Subscribers: 57,869; 10/24/91. (1) Pay Units: 23,411; 10/24/91. Programming (via satellite): HBO. (2) Pay Units: 12,616; 10/24/91. Programming (via satellite): Showtime. (3) Pay Units: 13,110; 10/24/91. Programming (via satellite): The Movie Channel. (4) Pay Units: 7,928; 10/24/91. Programming (via satellite): Cinemax. *Local Advertising Accepted.*

Paragon Cable (110,000 subscribers). 3075 N.E. Sandy Blvd., Portland, OR 97232. (503) 230-2099; FAX: (503) 230-2218. Kevin Kidd, gen mgr; Jeff Henry, mktg dir; Lois Petrik, loc adv dir; Ken Gores, chief tech; Sandy Moran, cust svc dir.
Area(s) Served: OR. Counties: Clackamas, Multnomah. Serving Boring, Corbett, Damascus, Fairview, Gresham, Happy Valley, Linnton, Orient, Portland, Springdale, Troutdale, Woodvillage. Miles of Plant: 1,800. Homes Passed: 220,000. Homes Served: 110,000. *Channel Capacity:* 59. In use: 59. *Basic Service:* Subscribers: 110,000; 09/01/93. Programming (via satellite): 29 chs. Programming (off air): 17 chs. *Pay Services:* Total Pay Subscribers: 79,316; 09/01/93. (1) Pay Units: 4,614; 09/01/93. Programming (via satellite): Cinemax. (2) Pay Units: 10,980; 09/01/93. Programming (via satellite): Disney. (3) Pay Units: 26,137; 09/01/93. Programming (via satellite): HBO. (4) Pay Units: 19,274; 09/01/93. Programming (via satellite): The Movie Channel. Pay Per View Subscribers: 75,000; 09/01/93. *Local Advertising Accepted.*

Paragon Cable (25,500 subscribers). 1313 W. Calton Rd., Laredo, TX 78041. (210) 721-0600; FAX: (210) 721-0612. Carlos Del Castillo, gen mgr; Lisa Rogerio, mktg dir; John Speer, loc adv dir; Olga Guerra, cust svc dir.
Area(s) Served: TX. County: Webb. Serving Laredo, Rio Bravo. Pop: 110,000. Miles of Plant: 400. Homes Passed: 39,600. Homes Served: 25,500. *Channel Capacity:* 38. In use: 38. *Basic Service:* Subscribers: 25,500; 10/01/93. Programming (via satellite): 34 chs. Programming (via microwave): 4 chs. Programming (off air): 2 chs. *Pay Services:* Total Pay Subscribers: 23,932; 10/24/91. (1) Pay Units: 10,869; 10/24/91. Programming (via satellite): HBO. (2) Pay Units: 3,562; 10/24/91. Programming (via satellite): Showtime. (3) Pay Units: 3,555; 10/24/91. Programming (via satellite): The Movie Channel. (4) Pay Units: 1,824; 10/24/91. Programming (via satellite): Cinemax. Pay Per View Subscribers: 10,465; 10/24/91. *Local Advertising Accepted. Equipment:* Provided by Jerrold & Hamlin.

Paragon Cable T.V. (93,000 subscribers). 7441 Chapman Ave., Garden Grove, CA 92641. (714) 895-6886; FAX: (714) 898-1524. Mark Mangolia, gen mgr; Mariann Belmonte, mktg dir; Camille Whelen, loc adv dir; Mike McDonald, chief tech; Kathy Carr, cust svc dir.
Area(s) Served: CA. County: Orange. Serving Cypress, Fountain Valley, Garden Grove, Huntington Beach, Los Alamitos, Midway City, Rossmoor, Stanton, Westminster. Homes Served: 93,000. *Channel Capacity:* 45. In use: 45. *Basic Service:* Subscribers: 93,000; 09/14/93. *Local Advertising Accepted.*

Paragon Cable-San Antonio (240,000 subscribers). Box 761, 415 N. Main St., San Antonio, TX 78205. (210) 222-9912; FAX: (210) 222-2402. Navarra Williams, gen mgr; Tom Owen, mktg dir; Bill Brestridge, chief tech.
Area(s) Served: TX. Counties: Bexar, Comal, Guadalupe. Serving Alamo Heights, Balcones Heights, Brooks Air Force Base, Castle Hills, Cibolo, Converse, Fort Sam Houston, Grey Forest, Guadalupe, Helotes, Hill Country Village, Hollywood Park, Kelly Air Force Base, Kirby, Lackland Air Force Base, Leon Valley, Live Oak, Olmos Park, Randolph Air Force Base, Schertz, Selma, Shavano Park, Terrell Hills, Timberwood Park, Universal City, Windcrest. Miles of Plant: 4,300. Homes Passed: 471,000. Homes Served: 240,000. *Channel Capacity:* 43. In use: 43. *Basic Service:* Subscribers: 240,000; 10/01/93. *Pay Services:* Total Pay Subscribers: 111,390; 11/30/91. Pay Per View Subscribers: 78,000; 11/30/91. *Local Advertising Accepted.*

J. Roger Kennedy Jr.

Box 2069, Hwy. 280 W., Reidsville, GA 30453. (912) 557-6133; FAX: (912) 557-4039. J. Roger Kennedy, pres; Paul Font, vp. Owned by J. Roger Kennedy. Total Basic Subscribers: 2,259; Pay Cable Subscribers: 2,000; Number of Cable Systems: 2.

SMALLER SYSTEMS

Georgia - Cablevision of Pembroke, Box 2069, Reidsville, GA 30453. Kennedy Cablevision Inc., Box 2069, Reidsville, GA 30453.

William L. Kepper

Box 636, McHenry, IL 60051-0636. (815) 344-0242. William L. Kepper, CEO; Robert Van Der Heyden, vp. Total Basic Subscribers: 2,300; Number of Cable Systems: 1.

Multiple Systems Operators, Independent Owners & Cable Systems

SMALLER SYSTEMS

Illinois - Full Circle Communications, Inc., McHenry, IL.

Keystone Cable TV Inc.

222 Kohler Rd., Kutztown, PA 19530. (215) 683-6055; FAX: (215) 683-7715. William D. George, pres. Owned by William D. George, Allen George. Total Basic Subscribers: 6,050; Pay Cable Subscribers: 2,080; Number of Cable Systems: 1.

REGIONS

Pennsylvania: Box 263, Kutztown, PA 19530-0263; Michael G. Starner.

King Cable

2931 Paces Ferry Rd., Atlanta, GA 30339. (404) 432-3405; FAX: (404) 432-3419. Kim King, pres; Guy Lee, vp opns; Edward Saffell, vp. Total Basic Subscribers: 10,450; Pay Cable Subscribers: 2,500; Number of Cable Systems: 2.

REGIONS

Georgia: 327 E. 1st Ave., Rome, GA 30161; (404) 234-9546. *South Carolina:* Wild Dunes, Isle of Palms, SC 29451; (803) 886-2400.

King Communications Inc.

2800 Big Oaks Dr., King, NC 27021. (919) 983-2121; FAX: (919) 983-0980. Ruth Thompson, pres. Owned by Ruth Thompson. Total Basic Subscribers: 5,000; Number of Cable Systems: 1.

J.R. King Enterprises Inc.

919 Ranch Rd. 620 S., Austin, TX 78734. (512) 263-9194; FAX: (512) 263-3445. Jess King, pres; Suzanne King, vp. Owned by Jess & Suzanne King. Total Basic Subscribers: 3,500; Number of Cable Systems: 1.

SMALLER SYSTEMS

Texas - Cable Vision of White Travis, 919 Ranch Rd. 620 S., Austin, TX.

Ron Klingenstein

Box 148, 204 E. Main St., Dayton, WA 99328. (509) 382-2132. Ron Klingenstein, CEO & pres. Total Basic Subscribers: 1,100; Number of Cable Systems: 1.

SMALLER SYSTEMS

Washington - Touchet Valley Earth Station, 802 N. 1st St., Dayton, WA 99328.

Arthur J. Krause

Box 11, 305 State St., Manhattan, IL 60442. (815) 357-6678. Arthur J. Krause, pres. Owned by Arthur J. Krause. Total Basic Subscribers: 1,300; Number of Cable Systems: 1.

SMALLER SYSTEMS

Illinois - Krause Cable TV, 305 State St., Manhattan, IL 60442.

KRM Cablevision

Box 648, Mellen, WI 54546. (715) 274-7631. Stan Rheinholtz, pres. Owned by Stan Rheinholtz. Total Basic Subscribers: 1,900; Pay Cable Subscribers: 600; Number of Cable Systems: 10.

KTS Corporation

2267 E. Washington Blvd., Pasadena, CA 91104. (818) 798-6298; FAX: (818) 798-2832. Melvin L. Matthews, CEO & pres. Owned by Melvin L. Matthews. Total Basic Subscribers: 4,000; Number of Cable Systems: 2.

SMALLER SYSTEMS

Connecticut - Duarte Cable Communication, 1628 3rd St., Duarte, CT 91010.

Kuhn Communications

Box 277, 301 W. Main St., Walnut Bottom, PA 17266. (717) 532-8857; FAX: (717) 532-5563. Earl Kuhn, CEO & pres. Owned by Earl Kuhn. Total Basic Subscribers: 1,100; Number of Cable Systems: 3.

SMALLER SYSTEMS

Pennsylvania - Kuhn Communications, Newburg, PA. Kuhn Communications, Orrstown, PA. Kuhn Communications, Walnut Bottom, PA.

Lake Champlain Cable TV Corp.

Box 808, 72 W. Milton Rd., Milton, VT 05468. (802) 893-1551; FAX: (802) 893-7310. Raymond Pecor Jr., pres. Total Basic Subscribers: 7,363; Number of Cable Systems: 2.

SMALLER SYSTEMS

Vermont - Lake Champlain Cable TV, 72 W. Milton Rd., Milton, VT 05468. Richmond Cable TV, Richmond, VT.

Laurel Highland Television Co.

Box 168, Stahlstown, PA 15687. (412) 593-2411. J. Paul Kalp, pres; M. Graham Hunter, vp. Owned by J. Paul Kalp, Graham Hunter, Mary Lou Baruhart, Morgan F. Whithrow, William I. Piper. Total Basic Subscribers: 3,300; Number of Cable Systems: 3.

SMALLER SYSTEMS

Pennsylvania - Laurel Highland Television, Indian Creek, PA. Laurel Highland Television, Mill Run, PA. Laurel Highland Television, Stahlstown, PA.

Lenfest Group

202 Shoemaker Rd., Pottstown, PA 19464. (215) 327-0965; FAX: (215) 327-6340. H.F. Lenfest, CEO, chmn & pres; Harry Brooks, CFO; JoAnne Carter, vp mktg; Debra Krzywicki, vp progmg. Owned by Lenfest Communications. Total Basic Subscribers: 482,262; Pay Cable Subscribers: 398,114; Number of Cable Systems: 13.

SYSTEMS WITH OVER 20,000 SUBSCRIBERS

Bay Cablevision (47,500 subscribers). 2900 Technology Ct., Richmond, CA 94806. (510) 262-1825. Dahlia Moodie, gen mgr; Robin Jones, mktg dir; Dennis Jones, chief tech; Bridgett Cook, cust svc dir.
Area(s) Served: CA. Counties: Alomeda, Contra Costa. Serving Berkeley, El Cerrito, Hercules, Richmond. Miles of Plant: 360. Homes Passed: 74,000. Homes Served: 47,500. *Channel Capacity:* 60. *Basic Service:* Subscribers: 47,500; 10/01/93. *Pay Services:* Total Pay Subscribers: 37,000; 11/15/91. Pay Per View Subscribers: 37,000; 11/15/91. *Local Advertising Accepted.*

Cable Oakland (72,400 subscribers). 4215 Foothill Blvd., Oakland, CA 94601. (510) 534-3364; FAX: (510) 436-7531. Clay Owens, gen mgr; Maxine Ashcraft, mktg dir; John Newby, loc adv dir; James Thomas, chief tech.
Area(s) Served: CA. Counties: Alameda, San Francisco. Serving Oakland, Emeryville, Piedmont, Treasure Island. Miles of Plant: 715. Homes Passed: 145,000. Homes Served: 72,400. *Channel Capacity:* 53. In use: 53. *Basic Service:* Subscribers: 72,400; 11/30/92. *Local Advertising Accepted.*

Suburban Cable - Lancaster (74,296 subscribers). Box 120, 1131 S. Duke St., Lancaster, PA 17608. (717) 291-3000; FAX: (717) 299-4511. Phillip Ressler, gen mgr; Joe Parkyn, chief tech.
Area(s) Served: PA. County: Lancaster. Serving Columbia, Conestoga, Drumore, East Hempfield, East Lampeter, East Petersburg, Eden, Fulton, Lancaster, Leacock, Manheim, Manor, Martic, Millersville, Mountville, Pequea, Providence, Strasburg, Strasburg Twp., West Hempfield, West Lampeter. Miles of Plant: 1,077. Homes Served: 74,296. *Channel Capacity:* 43. In use: 43. *Basic Service:* Subscribers: 74,296; 10/01/93. *Pay Services:* Total Pay Subscribers: 25,040; 11/01/92. (1) Pay Units: 9,901; 11/01/92. Programming (via satellite): HBO. (2) Pay Units: 3,739; 11/01/92. Programming (via microwave): Prism. (3) Pay Units: 2,961; 11/01/92. Programming (via satellite): Disney. (4) Pay Units: 3,077; 11/01/92. Programming (via satellite): Showtime. Pay Per View Subscribers: 15,540; 11/01/92. *Local Advertising Accepted. Equipment:* Jerrold & C-Cor amplifiers; Scientific-Atlanta labels; Tocom addressable.

Suburban Cable TV (25,200 subscribers). 237 W. Germantown Pike, Norristown, PA 19401. (215) 279-7200; FAX: (215) 279-7969. Tom Stowell, gen mgr. *Basic Service:* Subscribers: 25,200; 11/15/93.

Suburban Cable TV - Pottstown (40,190 subscribers). 202 Shoemaker Rd., Pottstown, PA 19464. (215) 323-6400; FAX: (215) 327-6395. David Heffline, gen mgr; JoAnne Carter, mktg dir; Henry Petri, chief tech.
Area(s) Served: PA. Counties: Berks, Chester, Montgomery. Serving Bally, Bechtelsville, Boyertown, Charleston, Colebrookdale, Douglass, Earl, East Coventry, East Greenville, East Pikeland, East Vincent, Hereford, Limerick, Limerick Twp., Lower Pottsgrove, New Hanover, North Coventry, Oley, Pennsburg, Phoenixville, Red Hill, Royersford, Schuylkill, Spring City, Upper Hanover, Upper Pottsgrove, Upper Providence, Washington, West Pottsgrove. Miles of Plant: 785. Homes Served: 40,190. *Channel Capacity:* 38. In use: 38. *Basic Service:* Subscribers: 40,190; 10/01/93. Pay Per View Subscribers: 6,500; 10/31/91. *No Local Advertising Accepted.*

Suburban Cable TV - Sellersville (31,537 subscribers). Box 620, 114 Ridge Rd., Sellersville, PA 18960. (215) 257-8046; FAX: (215) 257-1867. Marc Lockard, gen mgr; JoAnne Carter, mktg dir; Greg Siewert, chief tech; Lori Davidson, cust svc dir.
Area(s) Served: PA. Counties: Bucks, Montgomery. Serving Bedminster, Dublin, East Rockhill, Franconia, Green Lake, Hatfield, Hatfield Twp., Hilltown, Lower Frederick, Lower Salford, Marlborough, Milford, Perkasie, Quakertown, Richland, Richlandtown, Salford, Silverdale, Soudertown, Telford, Trumbauersville, Upper Frederick, Upper Salford, West Rockhill. Miles of Plant: 897. Homes Passed: 46,300. Homes Served: 31,537. *Channel Capacity:* 40. In use: 40. *Basic Service:* Subscribers: 31,537; 10/01/93. *Pay Services:* Total Pay Subscribers: 22,100; 09/30/91. (1) Pay Units: 10,300; 09/30/91. Programming (via satellite): HBO. (2) Pay Units: 7,400; 09/30/91. Programming (via satellite): Prism. (3) Pay Units: 1,400; 09/30/91. Programming (via satellite): Disney. (4) Pay Units: 1,100; 09/30/91. Programming (via satellite): Showtime. (5) Pay Units: 1,200; 09/30/91. Programming (via satellite): Cinemax. Pay Per View Subscribers: 5,300; 09/30/91. *Local Advertising Accepted.*

Suburban Cable TV Co. Inc. (112,000 subscribers). 3 Moore Rd., Wallingford, PA 19086. (215) 876-5000; FAX: (215) 876-8755. Joseph DiJulio, gen mgr; John Murawski, mktg dir; Louis Perrotta, loc adv dir; Christopher Patterson, chief tech; Diane Harlow, cust svc dir.
Area(s) Served: PA. County: Delaware. Serving Aldan, Aston, Bethel, Brookhaven, Chester, Chester Heights, Chester Twp., Clifton Heights, Collingdale, Colwyn, Concord, Darby, Darby Twp., East Lansdowne, Eddystone, Folcroft, Glenolden, Lansdowne, Lower Chichester, Marcus Hook, Media, Middletown, Millbourne, Morton, Nether Norwood, Parkside, Prospect Park, Providence, Ridley Park, Ridley Twp., Rose Valley, Sharon Hill, Swarthmore, Tinicum Twp., Trainer, Upland, Upper Chichester, Upper Darby, Upper Providence, Yeadon. Pop: 454,999. Homes Passed: 179,563. Homes Served: 112,000. *Channel Capacity:* 47. In use: 47. *Basic Service:* Subscribers: 112,000; 10/01/93. Programming (via satellite): 27 chs. Programming (off air): 9 chs. *Pay Services:* Total Pay Subscribers: 67,644; 11/30/92. Pay Per View Subscribers: 15,700; 11/30/92. *Local Advertising Accepted.*

Suburban Cable TV Co. Inc. (27,150 subscribers). The Warwick Bldg., 2319 York Rd., Jamison, PA 18929. (215) 343-5425; FAX: (215) 343-2766. John D. Mohn, gen mgr; Julie D. Eble, mktg dir; Deborah Stevens, loc adv dir; John Wolf, chief tech; Margie Stevenson, cust svc dir.
Area(s) Served: PA. County: Bucks. Serving Buckingham, Chalfont, Doylestown, Ivyland, New Britain, Newtown, Northampton Twp., Plumstead, Solebury, Tinicum, Warrington, Warwick. Pop: 110,544. Miles of Plant: 856. Homes Passed: 36,848. Homes Served: 27,150. *Channel Capacity:* 54. In use: 48. *Basic Service:* Subscribers: 27,150; 10/07/93. Programming (via satellite): 42 chs. Programming (via microwave): 1 ch. Programming (off air): 10 chs. *Pay Services:* Total Pay Subscribers: 23,445; 09/30/91. (1) Pay Units: 7,541; 09/30/91. Programming (via satellite): HBO. (2) Pay Units: 6,687; 09/30/91. Programming (via microwave): Prism. (3) Pay Units: 2,565; 09/30/91. Programming (via satellite): Disney. (4) Pay Units: 2,810; 09/30/91. Programming (via satellite): Showtime. (5) Pay Units: 2,454; 09/30/91. Programming (via satellite): Cinemax. Pay Per View Subscribers: 6,000; 09/30/91. *Local Advertising Accepted. Equipment:* Jerrold DPV 7000 addressable converters.

Suburban Cable TV of Chester County (46,157 subscribers). Box 351, Rt. 82 at Monacy Rd., Coatesville, PA 19320. (215) 383-4383; FAX: (215) 384-3804. David Heffline, gen mgr; JoAnne Carter, mktg dir; Ron Correll, chief tech; Lee Javens, cust svc dir.

Broadcasting & Cable Yearbook 1994
D-27

Multiple Systems Operators, Independent Owners & Cable Systems

Area(s) Served: PA. Counties: Chester, Delaware. Serving Atglen, Birmingham, Cain, Coatesville, Downingtown, East Bradford, East Brandywine, East Cain, East Fallowfield, East Goshen, Modena, Parkesburg, Sadsbury, South Coatesville, Thornbury, Upper Uwchlan, Uwchlan Twp., Valley, Wallace, West Bradford, West Brandywine, West Cain, West Chester, West Goshen, West Nantmeal, West Pikeland, West Sadsbury, West Whitehead, Westtown. Pop: 250,000. Miles of Plant: 900. Homes Passed: 65,000. Homes Served: 46,157. *Channel Capacity:* 42. In use: 38. *Basic Service:* Subscribers: 46,157; 10/07/93. *Local Advertising Accepted.*

SMALLER SYSTEMS

New Jersey - Bridge Cable TV, 30-1/2 Coryell St., Lambertville, NJ 08530; 6,860 subs. **Pennsylvania -** Suburban Cable TV Co. Inc., 441 W. Chocolate Ave., Box 438, Hershey, PA 17033; 17,721 subs. Suburban Cable TV Co. Inc., 251 W. DeKalb Pike, Suite EG 2, King of Prussia, PA 19406; 13,205 subs.

Leonard Communications Inc.

13780 E. Rice Pl., Aurora, CO 80015. (303) 693-0900; FAX: (303) 690-4192. Roger Leonard, chmn; Jane Meuret, CFO; Peter Locke, vp mktg. Owned by Roger Leonard. Total Basic Subscribers: 66,000; Number of Cable Systems: 124.

Longfellow Cable Co. Inc.

Box 949, Farmington, ME 04938. (207) 778-4200; FAX: (207) 778-3639. Frederick Leighton, CEO & pres; James Lingley, vp opns. Owned by Frederick Leighton, George Carneal, Larry Warren. Total Basic Subscribers: 5,200; Number of Cable Systems: 5.

SMALLER SYSTEMS

Maine - Longfellow Cable Co. Inc., Belgrade, ME. Longfellow Cable Co. Inc., Carrabassett Valley, ME. Longfellow Cable Co. Inc., Norridgewock, ME. Longfellow Cable Co. Inc., Phillips, ME.

Lovelock Cable

Box 1077, Lovelock, NV 89419. (702) 273-2020. Tom Mitchell, CEO & pres; John Hamilton, vp opns. Owned by Tom Mitchell, Unev Communications. Total Basic Subscribers: 850; Number of Cable Systems: 1.

Lowell Light & Power Co.

127 N. Broadway, Lowell, MI 49331. (616) 897-8402. Paul Christman, vp. Owned by City of Lowell. Pay Cable Subscribers: 1,900; Number of Cable Systems: 1.

SMALLER SYSTEMS

Michigan - Lowell Cable TV, 121 Lafayette St., Lowell, MI; (616) 897-8405; 1,960 subs.

M-Tek Systems

Box 129, 200 Lake Dr., Redwood Falls, MN 56283. (507) 637-8351; FAX: (507) 637-8351. LuVerne Maserek, chmn; Magdalen Maserek, CFO; Laura Maserek, vp mktg. Owned by LuVerne Maserek, Magdalen Maserek. Total Basic Subscribers: 870; Pay Cable Subscribers: 145; Number of Cable Systems: 7.

SMALLER SYSTEMS

Minnesota - M-Tek Systems, Belview, MN; 58 subs. M-Tek Systems, Comfrey, MN; 86 subs. M-Tek Systems, Courtland, MN; 105 subs. M-Tek Systems, Echo, MN; 97 subs. M-Tek Systems, Hanska, MN; 125 subs. M-Tek Systems, Nicollet, MN; 245 subs. M-Tek Systems, Wood Lake, MN; 145 subs.

M.C.T. Cablevision L.P.

Vista Verde Shopping Ctr., Rte. 2, Mayaguez, PR 00680. (809) 834-8550. Howard Verlin, pres; Roger Skidmore, vp opns & vp mktg. Owned by Pegasus Capital Management. Total Basic Subscribers: 11,300; Number of Cable Systems: 1.

Maclean Hunter Cable TV

80 Worcester Rd., Etobicoke, ON M9W 1K7. (416) 675-5930; FAX: (416) 675-2436. J. Barry Gage, CEO & pres; John Haughey, CFO; Donald H. Hinds, vp opns; Gord Corlett, vp mktg; R. Merle Zoerb, vp progmg; R. Scott Colbran, vp; Philip R. Patterson, vp; Ralph Von Eppinghoven, vp. Owned by Maclean Hunter Ltd. Total Basic Subscribers: 1,234,261; Pay Cable Subscribers: 699,926; Number of Cable Systems: 44.

SYSTEMS WITH OVER 20,000 SUBSCRIBERS

Barden Cablevision (114,538 subscribers). 12775 Lyndon Ave., Detroit, MI 48227. (313) 934-2600; FAX: (313) 934-9490. John Rawcliffe, gen mgr; Gary Dusa, mktg dir; Charles Welch, loc adv dir; Mark Francisco, chief tech; Evylon Hubbard, cust svc dir.
Area(s) Served: MI. County: Wayne. Serving Detroit. Pop: 1,027,974. Miles of Plant: 2,050. Homes Passed: 410,027. Homes Served: 114,538. *Channel Capacity:* 78. In use: 66. *Basic Service:* Subscribers: 114,538; 08/25/93. Programming (via satellite): 45 chs. Programming (via microwave): 2 chs. Programming (off air): 11 chs. *Pay Services:* Total Pay Subscribers: 236,753; 08/25/93. (1) Pay Units: 78,257; 08/25/93. Programming (via satellite): HBO. (2) Pay Units: 54,770; 08/25/93. Programming (via satellite): Showtime. (3) Pay Units: 41,195; 08/25/93. Programming (via satellite): Cinemax. (4) Pay Units: 27,955; 08/25/93. Programming (via satellite): The Movie Channel. (5) Pay Units: 11,444; 08/25/93. Programming (via satellite): Disney. (6) Pay Units: 3,370; 08/25/93. Programming (via satellite): Playboy. Pay Per View Subscribers: 105,000; 08/25/93. *Local Advertising Accepted.*

Cable TV of Jersey City (31,043 subscribers). 2121 Kennedy Blvd., Jersey City, NJ 07305. (201) 915-0508; FAX: (201) 434-5870. William Lester, gen mgr; Arnold McKinnon, mktg dir; Steven Bis, loc adv dir; James Guarino, chief tech; Michael DeRose, cust svc dir.
Area(s) Served: NJ. County: Hudson. Serving Jersey City. Pop: 228,156. Miles of Plant: 167. Homes Passed: 90,600. Homes Served: 31,043. *Channel Capacity:* 78. In use: 73. *Basic Service:* Subscribers: 31,043; 09/01/93. Pay Per View Subscribers: 26,579; 09/01/93. *Local Advertising Accepted.*

Maclean Hunter Cable TV (123,966 subscribers). 475 Richmond Rd., Ottawa, ON K24 3Y8. (613) 722-1111; FAX: (613) 725-2223. Barry Chapman, gen mgr; Bill Kincaid, mktg dir; Dave Nash, chief tech; Pat Madge, cust svc dir.
Area(s) Served: ON. Serving Arnprior, Carp, Ottawa, Pembroke, Renfren. Pop: 350,000. Miles of Plant: 1,491. Homes Passed: 160,829. Homes Served: 123,966. *Channel Capacity:* 46. In use: 46. *Basic Service:* Subscribers: 123,966; 10/01/93. *Pay Services:* Total Pay Subscribers: 17,487; 10/31/92. (1) Pay Units: 15,903; 10/18/91. Programming (via satellite): First Choice. (2) Pay Units: 615; 10/18/91. Programming (via satellite): Super Ecran. Pay Per View Subscribers: 4,300; 10/18/91. *No Local Advertising Accepted.*

Maclean Hunter Cable TV (178,086 subscribers). 80 Worcester Rd., Etobicoke, ON M9W 1K7. (416) 675-5930; FAX: (416) 675-4254. Charles Elliott, gen mgr; Sue Prigge, mktg dir; Wally Hartwick, chief tech.
Area(s) Served: ON. Serving Etobicoke, Mississauga, Parkdale, Toronto. Homes Passed: 230,696. Homes Served: 178,086. *Channel Capacity:* 60. In use: 53. *Basic Service:* Subscribers: 178,086; 08/31/93. *Pay Services:* Total Pay Subscribers: 19,979; 08/31/93. *No Local Advertising Accepted.*

Maclean Hunter Cable TV Inc. (69,015 subscribers). 24744 Eureka Rd., Taylor, MI 48180. (313) 946-6010; FAX: (313) 946-4421. Kathleen Ebli, gen mgr; Kathy Harrison, mktg dir; Rob Summers, chief tech; Joe Poletti, cust svc dir.
Area(s) Served: MI. Serving Allen Park, Berlin Twp., Brownstown Twp., Centerline, Eastpointe, Ecorse, Flat Rock, Garden City, Grosse Ile, Melvindale, River Rouge, Rockwood, South Rockwood, Southgate, Taylor. Miles of Plant: 1,097. Homes Passed: 108,241. Homes Served: 69,015. *Channel Capacity:* 56. In use: 56. *Basic Service:* Subscribers: 69,015; 08/17/93. Programming (via satellite): 50 chs. Programming (via microwave): 10 chs. Programming (off air): 11 chs. *Pay Services:* Total Pay Subscribers: 54,600; 08/17/93. (1) Pay Units: 22,729; 08/17/93. Programming (via satellite): HBO. (2) Pay Units: 9,666; 08/17/93. Programming (via satellite): Showtime. (3) Pay Units: 5,283; 08/17/93. Programming (via satellite): Cinemax. (4) Pay Units: 3,115; 08/17/93. Programming (via satellite): The Movie Channel. (5) Pay Units: 4,795; 08/17/93. Programming (via satellite): Disney. (6) Pay Units: 672; 08/17/93. Programming (via satellite): Playboy. Pay Per View Subscribers: 28,463; 08/17/93. *Local Advertising Accepted. Equipment:* Scientific-Atlanta satellite video recievers model 9640; Video Cypher II descrambler; Oak stereo sigma encoder; Scientific-Atlanta modules 6350.

Selkirk Communications (83,000 subscribers). 644 S. Andrews Ave., Fort Lauderdale, FL 33301. (305) 527-6620; FAX: (305) 527-4039. Richard Kreeger, gen mgr; David Lucoff, mktg dir & loc adv dir; Marc Ayo, chief tech; Jane Hepp, cust svc dir.
Area(s) Served: FL. County: Broward. Serving Hallendale, Lauderdale-by-the-Sea, Oakland Park, Sea Ranch Lakes. Pop: 250,000. Miles of Plant: 630. Homes Passed: 150,000. Homes Served: 83,000. *Channel Capacity:* 88. In use: 63. *Basic Service:* Subscribers: 83,000; 08/30/93. Programming (off air): 16 chs. *Pay Services:* Total Pay Subscribers: 48,530; 10/31/92. Pay Per View Subscribers: 32,500; 11/30/92. *Local Advertising Accepted.*

Suburban Cablevision (235,650 subscribers). 800 Rahway Ave., Union, NJ 07083. (908) 602-7444; FAX: (908) 851-8888. Frank DeJoy, gen mgr; Jane A. Bulman, mktg dir; Laura Johnson, loc adv dir; Larry Beauchamp, chief tech; Allison Lamers, cust svc dir.
Area(s) Served: NJ. Counties: Essex, Hudson, Middlesex, Union. Serving Belleville, Berkeley Heights, Bloomfield, Caldwell, Carteret, Clark, Cranford, Essex Falls, Fairfield, Fanwood, Garwood, Glen Ridge, Harrison, Hillside, Irvington, Kenilworth, Linden, Livingston, Maplewood, Millburn, Montclair, Mountainside, New Providence, Orange, Perth Amboy, Rahway, Roseland, Roselle, Roselle Park, Scotch Plains, Secaucus, South River, Springfield, Summit, Union, Verona, West Caldwell, West Orange, Westfield, Winfield, Woodbridge. Pop: 986,277. Miles of Plant: 2,500. Homes Passed: 403,563. Homes Served: 235,650. *Channel Capacity:* 56. In use: 56. *Basic Service:* Subscribers: 235,650; 10/01/93. *Pay Services:* Total Pay Subscribers: 233,334; 10/31/92. Pay Per View Subscribers: 99,276; 10/14/91. *Local Advertising Accepted.*

SMALLER SYSTEMS

U.S.: Florida - Selkirk Communications Inc., 900 S. Dixie Hwy., Hallandale, FL 33301; (305) 454-0990; 13,222 subs. **Michigan -** Maclean Hunter Cable TV Inc., 20936 Kelly Rd., Eastpointe, MI 48021; (313) 772-1023; 10,229 subs. Maclean Hunter Cable TV Inc., 29141 Pardo Rd., Garden City, MI 48135; (313) 427-4940; 7,936 subs. **CANADA: Ontario -** Maclean Hunter Cable TV, 700 Finley Ave., Unit No. 5, Ajax, ON L1S 3Z2; (416) 683-1751; 17,271 subs. Maclean Hunter Cable TV, 4 Sandford Fleming Dr., Collingwood, ON L9Y 4V9; (705) 445-3400; 13,375 subs. Maclean Hunter Cable TV, 135 James St. S., Suite 105, Hamilton, ON L8P 4V7; (415) 522-0123; 10,675 subs. Maclean Hunter Cable TV, 1444 Aberdeen St., Hawkesbury, ON K6A 1K7; (613) 632-8531; 8,997 subs. Maclean Hunter Cable TV, 20 West St. S., Box 370, Huntsville, ON P0A 1K0; (705) 789-2731; 3,146 subs. Maclean Hunter Cable TV, Box 489, Balm Beach Rd., Midland, ON L4R 4L3; (705) 526-5031; 10,187 subs. Maclean Hunter Cable TV, 240 Fee St., Box 370, North Bay, ON P1B 8S4; (705) 472-6580; 18,119 subs. Maclean Hunter Cable TV, 1040 20th St. E., Box 440, Owen Sound, ON N4K 5P7; (519) 376-5195; 11,273 subs. Maclean Hunter Cable TV, 185 Lake St., Pembroke, ON K8A 5M1; (613) 735-6819; 14,314 subs. Maclean Hunter Cable TV, Wallacburg, ON; 2,350 subs.

Marcus Cable Partners L.P.

Suite 1300, 2911 Turtle Creek Blvd., Dallas, TX 75219. (214) 521-7898; FAX: (214) 526-2154. Jeffrey A. Marcus, CEO & pres; Mark A. Biersmith, CFO; Louis A. Borrelli Jr., vp opns; John Pietri, vp; Cynthia J. Mannes, vp. Total Basic Subscribers: 140,000; Pay Cable Subscribers: 80,510; Number of Cable Systems: 3.

REGIONS

Wisconsin: 3300 Birch St., Eau Claire, WI 54703; Dave Hanson, VP optns. *Texas:* 28 W. Concho, San Angelo, TX 76903; Mark Poche, gen mgr. *Delaware/Maryland:* R.D. 4, Box 255, Harrington, DE 19952; Chris Fenger, gen mgr.

SYSTEMS WITH OVER 20,000 SUBSCRIBERS

Marcus Cable of Delaware & Maryland L.P. (18,470 subscribers). R.D. 4, Box 255, Harrington, DE 19952. (302) 398-4714; FAX: (302) 398-4762. Chris Fenger, gen mgr; Paul Joiner, mktg dir; Scott LaShier, chief tech; Elizabeth Butler, cust svc dir.
Area(s) Served: DE, MD. Counties: Kent, Sussex; Caroline, Dorchester, Wiscomico. Serving Bowers Beach, Bridgeville, Ellendale, Farmington, Felton, Frederica, Greenwood, Harrington, Hartly, Houson, Kenton, Magnolia, Milton, Slaughter Beach, Viola; Brookview, Cambridge, Church Creek, Denton, Eldorado, Federalsburg, Galestown, Goldsboro, Henderson, Hillsboro, Hurlock, Mardela Springs, Marydel,

Multiple Systems Operators, Independent Owners & Cable Systems

Preston, Queen Anne, Ridgely, Secretary, Sharptown. Miles of Plant: 1,116. Homes Passed: 30,891. Homes Served: 18,470. *Channel Capacity:* 42. In use: 38. *Basic Service:* Subscribers: 18,470; 10/31/93. Programming (via satellite): 38 chs. Programming (off air): 34 chs. *Pay Services:* Total Pay Subscribers: 22,924; 12/31/92. (1) Pay Units: 3,328; 12/31/92. Programming (via satellite): HBO. (2) Pay Units: 3,383; 12/31/92. Programming (via satellite): Showtime. (3) Pay Units: 2,137; 12/31/92. Programming (via satellite): Cinemax. *Local Advertising Accepted.*

Marcus Cable of San Angelo L.P. (30,357 subscribers). 28 W. Concho, San Angelo, TX 76903. (915) 655-8911; FAX: (915) 655-4848. Mark Poche, gen mgr; Rachel Rybarczyk, mktg dir & cust svc dir; Susan Winn, loc adv dir; Bob Arno, chief tech.
Area(s) Served: TX. Counties: Andrews, Runnels, Tom Green. Serving Andrews, Ballinger, Miles, San Angelo, Winters. Miles of Plant: 575. Homes Passed: 47,009. Homes Served: 30,357. *Channel Capacity:* 38. In use: 38. *Basic Service:* Subscribers: 30,357; 10/31/93. Programming (via satellite): Prevue Guide, CNN, ESPN, Disney, TMC, Showtime, USA, MTV, TNN, VISN/ACTS, TNT, VH-1, Family, CNN HL, A&E, QVC, TDC, HSE, TBN, Galavision, Univision, BET, HBO. Programming (via microwave): WFAA, KERA, Satellite-C-Span, TWC, Nickelodeon, Request I, Cinemax. Programming (off air): KLST, KACB, KIDY, KTXS. *Pay Services:* Total Pay Subscribers: 13,506; 10/31/92. (1) Pay Units: 7,540; 10/24/92. Programming (via satellite): HBO. (2) Pay Units: 895; 10/24/92. Programming (via satellite): Cinemax. (3) Pay Units: 1,151; 10/24/92. Programming (via satellite): The Movie Channel. (4) Pay Units: 837; 10/24/92. Programming (via satellite): Digital Music Express. (5) Pay Units: 1,552; 10/24/92. Programming (via satellite): Disney. Pay Per View Subscribers: 5,382; 10/24/92. *Local Advertising Accepted.* Equipment: Jerrold DP-7; Scientific-Atlanta 8511; Jerrold DRX, PRZ.

SMALLER SYSTEMS

Wisconsin - Marcus Cable, 2230 Neva Rd., Antigo, WI 54409; (715) 627-4817; 8,003 subs. Marcus Cable, 516 W. Main St., Ashland, WI 54806; (715) 682-2166; 7,859 subs. Marcus Cable, 364 S. Pine St., Burlington, WI 53105; (414) 763-8158; 13,225 subs. Marcus Cable, 219 W. Miner, Ladysmith, WI 54848; (715) 532-6796; 6,393 subs. Marcus Cable, 394 Red Cedar St., Menomonie, WI 54751; (715) 235-6837; 4,883 subs. Marcus Cable, 530 N. Main, Rice Lake, WI 54868; (715) 234-3821; 7,502 subs. Marcus Cable, 208 E. Jackson, Tomah, WI 54660; (608) 372-2999; 6,318 subs. Marcus Cable, 3315 Lincoln Ave., Tow Rivers, WI 54241; (414) 793-2213; 8,170 subs. Marcus Cable, 612 E. Main, Waunakee, WI 53597; (608) 849-8033; 12,000 subs. Marcus Cable, Hwy. 21 & 73 E., Wautoma, WI 54982; (414) 787-4608; 9,026 subs.

Marks Cablevision

Suite H, 9155 Archibald Ave., Rancho Cucamonga, CA 91730. (909) 794-4427; FAX: (909) 980-8678. Sam Johnston, vp opns. Owned by Marks Group. Total Basic Subscribers: 744; Number of Cable Systems: 2.

Marshall C. Martin

106 E. 6th St., Luverne, AL 36049. (205) 335-5059. Marshall C. Martin, CEO & pres. Owned by Marshall C. Martin, Marsha Baines, William Baines, Wendy Baines. Total Basic Subscribers: 1,300; Number of Cable Systems: 2.

SMALLER SYSTEMS

Alabama - Brantley TV Cable, Brantley, AL; 3,000 subs. Luverne TV Cable Service, Luverne, AL; (205) 335-5059; 1,000 subs.

Masada Corporation

Suite 301, 3900 Montclair Rd., Birmingham, AL 35213. (205) 871-3470; FAX: (205) 871-3574. Terry W. Johnson, CEO & pres; Joseph E. Gibbs, CFO; Doug Barlow, vp opns; Kemp Delo, vp mktg. Owned by Joseph E. Gibbs, Daryl E. Harms, Terry W. Johnson. Total Basic Subscribers: 68,034; Pay Cable Subscribers: 30,000; Number of Cable Systems: 42.

SMALLER SYSTEMS

Alabama - Premiere Cable of Hartselle, 134 W. Main St., Hartselle, AL 35640; (205) 773-6537. **Georgia** - Barnesville System, 342 College St., Barnesville, GA 30204; (404)358-3719. Premiere Cable Communications, 31 Griffin St., McDonough, GA 30253; (404) 954-4589.

Montana - Premiere Communications, 7905 Zaugg Dr., Missoula, MT 59802; (406) 258-6701. Ronan Pablo Cable, 210 Main St. S.W., Ronan, MT 59864; (406) 676-2445. **Missouri** - Premiere Cable of St. Louis, 6981 Hwy. 21, Barnhart, MO 63012; (314) 942-3901. **South Carolina** - Premiere Cable, 202 Campbell St., Belton, SC 29627; (803) 338-9975. Premiere Cable, 101 Cestrian Sq., Chester, SC 29706; (803) 377-1181. Premiere Cable, 124 Willis St., Gaffney, SC 29340; (803) 489-3186.

Massillon Cable TV Inc.

814 Cable Ct. N.W., Massillon, OH 44647. (216) 833-4134; FAX: (216) 833-7522. Richard W. Gessner, pres & CFO; Robert B. Gessner, vp mktg; Richard Reichel, vp. Owned by Richard W. Gessner, Susan R. Gessner, principals. Total Basic Subscribers: 38,500; Pay Cable Subscribers: 17,000; Number of Cable Systems: 2.

SYSTEMS WITH OVER 20,000 SUBSCRIBERS

Massillon Cable TV Inc. (26,000 subscribers). Box 814, 814 Cable Ct., Massillon, OH 44648. (216) 833-4134; FAX: (216) 833-7522. Robert Gessner, gen mgr & mktg dir; Tom Mogus, chief tech. *Basic Service:* Subscribers: 26,000; 08/31/93. *Local Advertising Accepted.*

Matrix Cablevision Inc.

12333 S. Saratoga-Sunnyvale Rd., Saratoga, CA 95070. (408) 253-6590; FAX: (408) 253-6591. Brad Daniel, CEO; Carol Ortiz, vp mktg & vp adv. Owned by Video Engineering Inc, Matrix Inc. Total Basic Subscribers: 1,000; Pay Cable Subscribers: 210; Number of Cable Systems: 2.

SMALLER SYSTEMS

California - Aldercroft Heights Cable, Parorama Dr., Los Gatos, CA. Menlo Park Cable, 1670 El Camino Real, Menlo Park, CA.

M.K. McDaniel

Box 839, Georgetown, TX 78627. (512) 869-1505; FAX: (512) 869-2962. M.K. McDaniel, pres; Dale Hoffman, vp opns. Total Basic Subscribers: 10,500; Pay Cable Subscribers: 6,900; Number of Cable Systems: 3.

SMALLER SYSTEMS

Texas - Williamson County Cablevision, Georgetown, TX. Williamson County Cablevision, Leander, TX. Williamson County Cablevision, Pflugerville, TX.

McDonald Investment Co.

Suite 300, One Office Park Cir., Birmingham, AL 35223. (205) 879-0456. William W. McDonald, pres. Owned by William W. McDonald. Total Basic Subscribers: 74,327; Number of Cable Systems: 6.

MCT Communications Inc.

11 Kearsarge Ave., Contoocook, NH 03229. (603) 456-2211; FAX: (604) 746-3567. Paul Violette, pres. Total Basic Subscribers: 2,072; Pay Cable Subscribers: 917; Number of Cable Systems: 1.

McVay Communications Inc.

100 First St., Coalinga, CA 93210. (209) 935-1674; FAX: (209) 935-9040. Joan B. McVay, pres; Judy Price, vp opns. Owned by Joan B. McVay. Total Basic Subscribers: 2,700; Number of Cable Systems: 2.

SMALLER SYSTEMS

California - McVay Communications, Coalinga, CA. McVay Communications, Huron, CA.

Media General Inc.

Box 85333, Richmond, VA 23293-0001. (804) 649-6000; FAX: (804) 649-6898. J. Stewart Bryan III, CEO & pres; M.N. Morton, CFO; Robert W. Pendergast, vp. Total Basic Subscribers: 215,000; Pay Cable Subscribers: 189,200; Number of Cable Systems: 2.

SYSTEMS WITH OVER 20,000 SUBSCRIBERS

Media General Cable of Fairfax Inc. (203,000 subscribers). 14650 Old Lee Rd., Chantilly, VA 22021-1799. (703) 378-8400; FAX: (703) 378-3840. Thomas E. Waldrop, gen mgr; Don Mathison, mktg dir; Mike Nelson, chief tech.

Area(s) Served: VA. County: Fairfax. Serving Clifton, Fairfax, Falls Church, Herndon, Vienna. Miles of Plant: 3,900. Homes Passed: 303,000. Homes Served: 203,000. *Channel Capacity:* 120. In use: 100. *Basic Service:* Subscribers: 203,000; 09/30/93. *Pay Services:* Total Pay Subscribers: 188,000; 09/30/93. (1) Pay Units: 68,866; 08/31/93. Programming (via satellite): HBO. (2) Pay Units: 28,875; 08/31/93. Programming (via satellite): Showtime. (3) Pay Units: 33,167; 08/31/93. Programming (via satellite): Cinemax. (4) Pay Units: 10,227; 08/31/93. Programming (via satellite): The Movie Channel. Pay Per View Subscribers: 190,000; 09/30/93. *Local Advertising Accepted.*

SMALLER SYSTEMS

Virginia - Media General of Fredericksburg, 1310 Belman Rd., Fredericksburg, VA 22401; (703) 373-6343.

MetroVision Inc.

Suite 550, 115 Perimeter Center Pl., Atlanta, GA 30346. (404) 394-8837; FAX: (404) 698-0228. Henry Harris, pres; Donald A. Smith, vp opns. Owned by Newhouse Broadcasting. Total Basic Subscribers: 480,930; Pay Cable Subscribers: 442,972; Number of Cable Systems: 20.

SYSTEMS WITH OVER 20,000 SUBSCRIBERS

KBC Cablevision (35,000 subscribers). Box 579, 309 N. College St., Killeen, TX 76540. (817) 634-3145. Chuck Davis, gen mgr; David Cochran, mktg dir; J.D. Lartcher, chief tech. *Basic Service:* Subscribers: 35,000; 10/15/93. *Pay Services:* Total Pay Subscribers: 10,000; 12/15/92.

Lincoln Cablevision (70,500 subscribers). 5400 S. 16th St., Lincoln, NE 68512. (402) 421-0330; FAX: (402) 421-0305. Richard Bates, gen mgr; Jeff Varecke, mktg dir; Jim Bothe, loc adv dir; Tom Coleman, chief tech; Scott Anderson, cust svc dir.
Area(s) Served: NE. County: Lancaster. Serving Lincoln. Pop: 180,000. Miles of Plant: 786. Homes Passed: 94,000. Homes Served: 70,500. *Channel Capacity:* 78. In use: 65. *Basic Service:* Subscribers: 70,500; 09/01/93. *Pay Services:* Total Pay Subscribers: 32,000; 12/31/92. *Local Advertising Accepted.* Equipment: Scientific-Atlanta 8600 converter.

MetroVision of DuPage County (24,242 subscribers). Box 29, Bloomingdale, IL 60108. (708) 894-4949; FAX: (708) 894-5598. Rich Lyons, gen mgr; Rob Hill, chief tech.
Area(s) Served: IL. Serving Glendale Heights. Homes Served: 24,242. *Basic Service:* Subscribers: 24,242; 10/15/93. *Local Advertising Accepted.*

MetroVision of Livonia Inc. (25,000 subscribers). Box CN3305, 14525 Farmington Rd., Livonia, MI 48151. (313) 422-2810; FAX: (313) 422-2239. Carol Gibson, gen mgr; Dan Dinsmore, mktg dir; Gary Nauman, chief tech. *Basic Service:* Subscribers: 25,000; 10/15/93.

MetroVision of Oakland County (33,192 subscribers). 37635 Enterprise Ct., Farmington Hills, MI 48331. (313) 553-7300; FAX: (313) 553-4829. Bob McKeon, gen mgr; Dan Dinsmore, mktg dir; Clay Collins, chief tech. *Basic Service:* Subscribers: 33,192; 10/15/93.

MetroVision of Prince Georges County (66,318 subscribers). 9315 Largo Dr. W., Landover, MD 20785. (301) 499-2930; FAX: (301) 336-7490. Roger Wells, gen mgr; Chuck Mann, mktg dir; Doug Worley, chief tech. *Basic Service:* Subscribers: 66,318; 10/15/93. *Pay Services:* Total Pay Subscribers: 54,000; 11/30/92.

MetroVision Southwest Cook County (58,124 subscribers). 7720 W. 98th St., Hickory Hills, IL 60457. (708) 430-4840; FAX: (708) 430-1870. Ron Murray, gen mgr; Mary Battaglia, mktg dir. *Basic Service:* Subscribers: 58,124; 10/15/93.

Waco Cablevision (42,436 subscribers). Box 7852, Waco, TX 76714. (817) 776-1141; FAX: (817) 776-8651. John Mankin, gen mgr; Bill Hughes, mktg dir; Ron Brush, loc adv dir; James Jones, chief tech; Debbie Hughes, cust svc dir.
Area(s) Served: TX. County: McLonnan. Serving Behrmead, Beverly Hills, Hewitt, Lacy Lakeview, McGregor, North Crest, Robinson, Waco, Woodway. Pop: 150,000. Miles of Plant: 830. Homes Passed: 67,099. *Channel Capacity:* 36. In use: 36. *Basic Service:* Subscribers: 42,436; 11/01/92. Programming (via satellite): 27 chs. Programming (via microwave): 4 chs. Programming (off air): 5 chs. *Pay Services:* Total Pay Subscribers: 24,000; 12/15/92. *Local Advertising Accepted.*

Multiple Systems Operators, Independent Owners & Cable Systems

SMALLER SYSTEMS

Indiana - MetroVision of Indiana, Box 6000, 2225 Locust Ct., Portage, IN 46368; (219) 762-9511; 8,641 subs.
Texas - Cablevision, Box 1195, 4520 Stonewall, Greenville, TX 75401; (903) 455-0012; 7,472 subs.

Mid-Atlantic Cable

Suite 750, 5335 Wisconsin Ave. N.W., Washington, DC 20015. (202) 364-3511; FAX: (202) 364-3520. John C. Norcutt, CEO & pres; Joan H. Miller, vp opns; Jim Chadwick, vp mktg; David C. Knolls, vp; Nancy Moyer, vp; John Lubitkin, vp. Total Basic Subscribers: 23,000; Pay Cable Subscribers: 12,000; Number of Cable Systems: 29.

Mid Coast Cable TV Inc.

Box 1269, 1905 W. Loop, El Campo, TX 77437. (409) 543-6858. Clive Runnels, chmn; J.H. Landrum, vp opns. Owned by Clive Runnels. Total Basic Subscribers: 3,800; Pay Cable Subscribers: 1,375; Number of Cable Systems: 2.

SMALLER SYSTEMS

Texas - Mid Coast Cable TV Inc., El Campo, TX. Mid Coast Cable TV Inc., Louise, TX.

Mid-Hudson Cablevision Inc.

Box 399, 200 Jefferson Heights, Catskill, NY 12414. (518) 943-6600; FAX: (518) 943-6603. James M. Reynolds, CEO; Stuart W. Smith, vp opns. Owned by James M. Reynolds. Total Basic Subscribers: 17,146; Number of Cable Systems: 1.

Mid South Cable TV Inc.

Box 910, McKenzie, TN 38201. (901) 352-2980; FAX: (901) 352-3533. Gary Blount, pres. Owned by Gary Blount, Paul Field, Dave Pardouner, John Flanagan Jr., Joseph Arms. Total Basic Subscribers: 7,659; Pay Cable Subscribers: 2,250; Number of Cable Systems: 6.

SMALLER SYSTEMS

New York - Mid-Hudson Cablevision Inc., Catskill, NY 12414.

Mid-State Community TV Inc.

1001 12th St., Aurora, NE 68818. (402) 694-5101; FAX: (402) 694-2848. Phillip C. Nelson, pres. Owned by Phillip Nelson. Total Basic Subscribers: 2,013; Pay Cable Subscribers: 799; Number of Cable Systems: 6.

SMALLER SYSTEMS

Nebraska - Mid-State Community TV Inc., Aurora, NE. Mid-State Community TV Inc., Domphan, NE. Mid-State Community TV Inc., Giltner, NE. Mid-State Community TV Inc., Hordville, NE. Mid-State Community TV Inc., Marquette, NE. Mid-State Community TV Inc., Trumbull, NE.

Midcontinent Cable Co.

Box 910, 24 First Ave. N.E., Aberdeen, SD 57402. (605) 229-1775; FAX: (605) 229-0478. Joe H. Floyd, CEO; N.L. Bentson, pres; Rick Reed, vp opns; Colleen Goodman, vp mktg; Lloyd D. Wetenkamp, vp. Owned by Midcontinent Media Inc. Total Basic Subscribers: 73,000; Pay Cable Subscribers: 22,000; Number of Cable Systems: 175.

SYSTEMS WITH OVER 20,000 SUBSCRIBERS

Sioux Falls Cable TV (28,662 subscribers). 3507 S. Duluth Ave., Sioux Falls, SD 57105. (605) 339-3339; FAX: (605) 335-1987. Rod Carlson, gen mgr; Lee Johnson, mktg dir; Tim Evans, loc adv dir; Ken Dickinson, chief tech.
Area(s) Served: SD. County: Minnehaha. Serving Sioux Falls. Pop: 105,000. Miles of Plant: 407. Homes Passed: 42,508. Homes Served: 28,662. *Channel Capacity:* 38. In use: 37. *Basic Service:* Subscribers: 28,662; 08/31/93. Programming (via microwave): KUSD. Programming (off air): CBS, NBC, ABC, Fox. *Pay Services:* Total Pay Subscribers: 13,669; 08/31/93. (1) Pay Units: 7,368; 08/31/93. Programming (via satellite): HBO. (2) Pay Units: 2,721; 08/31/93. Programming (via satellite): Showtime. (3) Pay Units: 1,900; 08/31/93. Programming (via satellite): Disney. Pay Per View Subscribers: 773; 08/31/93. *Local Advertising* Accepted.

Midwest Cable Communications Inc.

Box 337, 314 Third St., Bemidji, MN 56601. (218) 751-5507. Jon P. Langhout Sr., pres; Ada Langhout, vp opns; Jon P. Langhout Jr., vp. Owned by Jon P. Langhout Sr. Total Basic Subscribers: 5,500; Number of Cable Systems: 2.

Midwest I Cablesystems Inc.

35 Industrial Dr., Martinsville, IN 46151. (317) 342-1370; FAX: (317) 342-4919. Mark J. Rekers, pres; Richard Chandler, vp mktg & vp adv; Bob Cagle, vp; John Hagstrom, vp; Paul Scott, vp. Total Basic Subscribers: 38,000; Number of Cable Systems: 440.

Midwest Video Electronics Inc.

Box 6478, Rochester, MN 55903-6478. (507) 287-0880. Patricia P. Likos, pres. Owned by Irene & John Dohrmann, Plunkett Children's Trust. Total Basic Subscribers: 6,000; Number of Cable Systems: 4.

SMALLER SYSTEMS

Wisconsin - Midwest Video Electronics Inc., Crandon, WI. Midwest Video Electronics Inc., Rhinelander, WI. Midwest Video Electronics Inc., Tomahawk, WI. Midwest Video Electronics Inc., Wabeus, WI.

Millersburg TV Co.

Box 66, 804 Plum St., Millersburg, PA 17061. (717) 692-4772. William B. Helwig, CEO & pres; Donald B. Herrold, vp. Owned by David Hawley, Leah R. Long, Robert E. Woodside, George Helwig, Donald Miller. Total Basic Subscribers: 4,303; Pay Cable Subscribers: 409; Number of Cable Systems: 1.

SMALLER SYSTEMS

Pennsylvania - Millersburg TV Co., 804 Plum St., Millersburg, PA 17061; (717) 692-4772; 4,303 subs.

Millington CATV Inc.

Box 399, 5115 Easley Rd., Millington, TN 38053. (901) 872-3600. Holly Starnes, pres. Owned by Holly Starnes. Total Basic Subscribers: 6,544; Number of Cable Systems: 1.

Mission Cable

Suite 1550, 1873 S. Bellaire St., Denver, CO 80222. (303) 756-5600. Tom Benning, pres; Suzanne Cyman, vp mktg. Owned by Managed by Fanch Communications Inc. Total Basic Subscribers: 76,000; Number of Cable Systems: 1.

Mobile Park Properties Inc.

950 Ridgewood Ave., Venice, FL 34292-1799. (813) 485-5441. William Dorsey, pres. Owned by English S. Deschaups, James M. Doss, Fred H. Lendstrom, John M. Miller, Wesley L. Peterson, Colleen Wilson, Stuart W. Gregory. Total Basic Subscribers: 1,309; Pay Cable Subscribers: 731; Number of Cable Systems: 1.

Moffat Communications Ltd.

Box 220, Station L, Winnipeg, MB R3H 0Z5. (204) 788-3440; FAX: (204) 956-2710. Randall L. Moffat, CEO & pres; William A. Davis, vp. Total Basic Subscribers: 37,986; Pay Cable Subscribers: 18,463; Number of Cable Systems: 4.

SMALLER SYSTEMS

Florida - Florida Satellite Network, 8949 Gall Blvd., Zephyr Hills, FL 34248; (813) 788-7634. **Texas** - Kingwood Cablevision, 4103 W. Lake Houston Pkwy., Kingwood, TX 77339; (713) 360-7500. Lakewood Cablevision, 1895 Yaupon Core, Box 1689, Onalaska, TX 77360; (409) 646-5227. Lakewood Cablevision - Walden Office, 12-504 Walden Rd., Montgomery, TX 77356; (409) 582-4855.

Monmouth Cablevision Associates

Box 58, Belmar, NJ 07719. (908) 681-3400; FAX: (908) 681-5458. Joe Fischer, pres; Mary Tassini, vp mktg; Dave S. Kaykendall, vp. Total Basic Subscribers: 110,000.

Monroe Cable Vision

9795 E. Caron, Scottsdale, AZ 85258-5602. (602) 391-1904. La Junta Monroe, CEO & pres; James Monroe, vp. Owned by James Monroe, La Junta Monroe. Total Basic Subscribers: 1,727; Pay Cable Subscribers: 1,092; Number of Cable Systems: 4.

SMALLER SYSTEMS

Arizona - Apache Cable Vision, San Carlos, AZ.
California - Julian Cable Vision, Julian, CA.

Montgomery Cablevision & Entertainment Inc.

1450 Ann St., Montgomery, AL 36107. (205) 262-4004; FAX: (205) 262-3726. William B. Blunt, pres; Alice Jackson, vp. Owned by William B. Blunt. Total Basic Subscribers: 5,600; Pay Cable Subscribers: 4,200; Number of Cable Systems: 1.

Moosehead Enterprises Inc.

Box 526, Lakeview St., Greenville, ME 04441. (207) 695-3337. Scott Richardson, CEO; Earl Richardson Jr., pres & CFO; Earl Richardson, vp opns. Owned by Earl Richardson. Total Basic Subscribers: 2,500; Pay Cable Subscribers: 800; Number of Cable Systems: 6.

Mount Vernon Cablevision

Box 191, 111 S. Mulberry, Mount Vernon, OH 43050. (614) 397-2288; FAX: (614) 397-3730. Jonathan Zelkowitz, CEO. Owned by Jonathan Zelkowitz. Total Basic Subscribers: 6,500; Number of Cable Systems: 1.

Mountain Zone TV Systems

307 East Ave. E., Alpine, TX 79830. (915) 837-5423. Janet Neu, pres; Steve Neu, vp opns & vp. Owned by Neu Family. Total Basic Subscribers: 1,400; Number of Cable Systems: 7.

SMALLER SYSTEMS

Texas - Mountain Zone TV Systems, Balmorhea, TX. Mountain Zone TV Systems, Chisos Basin, TX. Mountain Zone TV Systems, Fort Davis, TX. Mountain Zone TV Systems, Marathon, TX. Mountain Zone TV Systems, Panther Junction, TX. Mountain Zone TV Systems, Presidio, TX. Mountain Zone TV Systems, Valentine, TX. Mountain Zone TV Systems, West Alpine, TX.

Multi-Cablevision Co. of Livingston/Washtenaw

8505 E. M36, Whitmore Lake, MI 48189. (313) 231-1872; FAX: (313) 231-9760. Gilbert R. Clark, pres; William Batey, vp. Owned by Gilbert R. Clark Jr. Total Basic Subscribers: 11,500; Pay Cable Subscribers: 9,000; Number of Cable Systems: 1.

SMALLER SYSTEMS

Michigan - Multi-Cablevision Co. of Livingston/Washtenaw, Green Oak Township, MI 48189.

Multimedia Cablevision Inc.

Box 3027, 701 E. Douglas, Wichita, KS 67201. (316) 262-4270. Don Sbarra, CEO; Mike Burrus, pres; Tom Smith, vp mktg. Total Basic Subscribers: 401,370; Pay Cable Subscribers: 310,036; Number of Cable Systems: 4.

SYSTEMS WITH OVER 20,000 SUBSCRIBERS

Multimedia Cablevision of Greenville (20,000 subscribers). 517 Arlington Blvd., Greenville, NC 27834. (919) 756-3559; FAX: (919) 756-4954. Bill Paramore, gen mgr; Scott Joseph, mktg dir. *Basic Service:* Subscribers: 20,000; 10/31/93.

Multimedia Cablevision of Oak Lawn (27,003 subscribers). 10545 S. Cicero Ave., Oak Lawn, IL 60453. (708) 636-9573. Cliff Waggoner, gen mgr; Karen Krivsky, mktg dir; David Reyment, loc adv dir. *Basic Service:* Subscribers: 27,003; 10/31/93. *Pay Services:* Total Pay Subscribers: 27,842; 12/01/92.

Multimedia Cablevision of Rocky Mount (24,500 subscribers). 1509 Westmount Dr., Rocky Mount, NC 27801. (919) 443-4019; FAX: (919) 443-5932. Tom Edwards, gen mgr; Scott Joseph, mktg dir. *Basic Service:* Subscribers: 24,500; 10/31/93.

Multiple Systems Operators, Independent Owners & Cable Systems

Multimedia Cablevision of Wichita (96,943 subscribers). Box 3027, 701 E. Douglas, Wichita, KS 67201. (316) 262-4270; FAX: (316) 262-0676. Ronald R. Marnell, gen mgr; Ben Sciortino, mktg dir; Dick Abraham, chief tech; Linda Jurgensen, cust svc dir. *Channel Capacity:* 36. In use: 36. *Basic Service:* Subscribers: 96,943; 07/31/93. *Pay Services:* Total Pay Subscribers: 65,229; 07/31/93. *Local Advertising Accepted.*

SMALLER SYSTEMS

Illinois - Multimedia Cablevision of Villa Park, 44 S. Villa, Villa Park, IL 60181; (708) 941-7925; 4,700 subs.

MultiVision

321 Railroad Ave., Greenwich, CT 06830. (203) 622-4860; FAX: (203) 622-4876. I. Martin Pompadur, CEO & chmn; David R. Van Valkenburg, pres; Ewan A. Mirylees, vp sls & vp mktg; Richard Hainbach, vp; Rick Sander, vp. Owned by MultiVision Cable TV. Total Basic Subscribers: 211,800; Pay Cable Subscribers: 156,273; Number of Cable Systems: 6.

REGIONS

Capitol: 9609 Annapolis Rd., Lanham, MD 20706; David A. Wilson, VP & rgnl gen mgr. *Northern California:* 2250 Boynton Ave., Fairfield, CA 94533; Frances Parkey, VP & rgnl gen mgr. *Southern California:* 3041 Miraloma Ave., Anaheim, CA 92806; Donald Granger, VP & rgnl gen mgr.

SYSTEMS WITH OVER 20,000 SUBSCRIBERS

MultiVision Cable TV (52,000 subscribers). 595 Martin Ave., Rohnert Park, CA 94928. (707) 584-4617; FAX: (707) 585-7547. Frances A. Parkey, gen mgr; Dennis F. Davis, mktg dir; Thomas A. Ansel, loc adv dir; Dale Ulrich, chief tech; Nadine E. Martindale, cust svc dir.
Area(s) Served: CA. Counties: Napa, Sonoma. Serving Calistoga, Cotati, Rohnert Park, St. Helena, Santa Rosa, Sebastopol, Sonoma, Yountville. Miles of Plant: 900. Homes Passed: 63,000. Homes Served: 52,000. *Channel Capacity:* 41. In use: 41. *Basic Service:* Subscribers: 52,000; 10/07/93. Programming (via satellite): 27 chs. Programming (via microwave): 27 chs. Programming (off air): 13 chs. *Pay Services:* Total Pay Subscribers: 23,000; 12/01/92. (1) Pay Units: 7,900; 09/30/91. Programming (via satellite): HBO. (2) Pay Units: 3,400; 09/30/91. Programming (via satellite): Cinemax. (3) Pay Units: 4,300; 09/30/91. Programming (via satellite): Showtime. (4) Pay Units: 2,600; 09/30/91. Programming (via satellite): The Movie Channel. *Local Advertising Accepted.*

MultiVision Cable TV (42,100 subscribers). 3041 Miraloma Ave., Anaheim, CA 92806. (714) 632-9222; FAX: (714) 630-4353. Donald R. Granger, gen mgr; Rick Cable, mktg dir & loc adv dir; William P. Snyder, chief tech; Chris Miller, cust svc dir.
Area(s) Served: CA. County: Orange. Serving Anaheim, Villa Park. Miles of Plant: 780. Homes Passed: 87,800. Homes Served: 42,100. *Channel Capacity:* 60. In use: 60. *Basic Service:* Subscribers: 42,100; 09/01/93. Programming (via satellite): 28 chs. Programming (via microwave): 28 chs. Programming (off air): 15 chs. *Local Advertising Accepted.*

MultiVision Cable TV (27,000 subscribers). 2250 Boynton Ave., Fairfield, CA 94533. (707) 422-1183; FAX: (707) 422-2070. Frances A. Parkey, gen mgr; Dennis F. Davis, mktg dir; Thomas A. Ansel, loc adv dir; William A. Christensen, chief tech; George Serio, cust svc dir.
Area(s) Served: CA. County: Solano. Serving Cordellia, Fairfield, Solano, Suisin City. Miles of Plant: 303. Homes Passed: 32,420. Homes Served: 27,000. *Channel Capacity:* 41. In use: 41. *Basic Service:* Subscribers: 27,000; 10/01/93. Programming (via satellite): 22 chs. Programming (via microwave): 1 ch. Programming (off air): 16 chs. *Local Advertising Accepted.*

MultiVision Cable TV (75,000 subscribers). 9609 Annapolis Rd., Lanham, MD 20706. (301) 731-5560; FAX: (301) 731-7822. David A. Wilson, gen mgr; Elizabeth Wilson, mktg dir; Lucinda Peters, loc adv dir; Keith Hennek, chief tech; Lisa Allen, cust svc dir.
Area(s) Served: MD. County: Prince George. Serving Berwyn Heights, Bladensburg, Bowie, Brentwood, Cheverly, College Park, Colmar Manor, Cottage City, Edmonston, Glenarden, Greenbelt, Hyattsville, Landover Hills, Laurel, Mount Rainier, New Carollton, North Brentwood, Riverdale, University Park. Miles of Plant: 1,154. Homes Passed: 140,000. Homes Served: 75,000. *Channel Capacity:* 78. In use: 75. *Basic Service:* Subscribers: 75,000; 09/03/93. Programming (via satellite): 36 chs. Programming (off air): 18 chs. *Pay Services:* Total Pay Subscribers: 76,000; 09/03/93. (1) Pay Units: 33,350; 09/30/91. Programming (via satellite): HBO. (2) Pay Units: 14,775; 09/30/91. Programming (via satellite): Cinemax. (3) Pay Units: 17,450; 09/30/91. Programming (via satellite): Showtime. (4) Pay Units: 8,850; 09/30/91. Programming (via satellite): The Movie Channel. (5) Pay Units: 7,900; 09/30/91. Programming (via satellite): Disney. *Local Advertising Accepted.*

SMALLER SYSTEMS

California - Multivision Cable TV, 1529 Valley Dr., Hermosa Beach, CA 90254; (310) 318-3423; 18,896 subs.
Virginia - Multivision Cable TV, 310 Parker Ct., Leesburg, VA 22075; (703) 478-1106; 5,122 subs.

N-Com

11401 Joseph Campau, Hamtramck, MI 48212. (313) 365-0760; FAX: (313) 365-2170. Harry Surri, pres; Cathy Hughes, vp mktg. Total Basic Subscribers: 47,803; Pay Cable Subscribers: 19,000; Number of Cable Systems: 4.

SYSTEMS WITH OVER 20,000 SUBSCRIBERS

Omnicom Cablevision (38,695 subscribers). 8465 Ronda Dr., Canton, MI 48187. (313) 459-7300. Lisa Boland, gen mgr; Cathy Hughes, mktg dir; Warren Jones, chief tech. *Basic Service:* Subscribers: 38,695; 10/15/93. *Pay Services:* Total Pay Subscribers: 16,000; 11/01/92.

SMALLER SYSTEMS

Michigan - Clear Cablevision, Box 248, 813 W. Michigan Ave., Saline, MI 48176; (313) 429-4923. Omnicom CATV, 12750 Huron River Dr., Romulus, MI 48174.

Nashoba Cable Services

4 Lyberty Way, Westford, MA 01886. (508) 692-1906; FAX: (508) 692-9491. Alan S. Davis, CEO; William A. Schuler, chmn; Sharon M. Levesque, CFO; Lisa Keegan, vp mktg. Owned by Alan S. Davis, William A. Schuler, gen ptnrs. Total Basic Subscribers: 32,000; Pay Cable Subscribers: 18,000; Number of Cable Systems: 2.

SMALLER SYSTEMS

Massachusetts - Nashoba Cable Services, Danvers, MA; 7,000 subs. Nashoba Cable Services, Westford, MA; 25,000 subs.

City of Negaunee Cable TV

Box 70, City Hall, Silver St., Negaunee, MI 49866. (906) 475-7700; FAX: (906) 475-4880. Kenneth Huber, vp. Owned by City of Negaunee. Total Basic Subscribers: 1,417; Pay Cable Subscribers: 447; Number of Cable Systems: 1.

Nelsonville TV Cable Inc.

One W. Columbus St., Nelsonville, OH 45764. (614) 753-2686. Eugene R. Edwards, pres; Betty Edwards, vp. Owned by Eugene R. Edwards, Betty Edwards. Total Basic Subscribers: 6,000; Number of Cable Systems: 1.

SMALLER SYSTEMS

Ohio - Nelsonville TV Cable Inc., Nelsonville, OH 45764.

NEPSK Inc.

Box 610, 6 Water St., Houlton, ME 04730. (207) 532-2579; FAX: (207) 532-4025. Pete Kozloski, pres. Total Basic Subscribers: 2,950; Pay Cable Subscribers: 758; Number of Cable Systems: 3.

Netarts Cable TV Inc.

4970 Crab Ave., Netarts, OR 97143. (503) 842-4943. Ronald Groshong, pres; Donald Groshong, vp opns. Owned by Harold L. Groshong, Donald Groshong, Ronald Groshong. Total Basic Subscribers: 1,131; Number of Cable Systems: 1.

New England Cablevision Massachusetts

38 Blackburn Ctr., Gloucester, MA 01930. (508) 281-0811; FAX: (508) 281-8679. Lee K. Stanley, CEO & pres; Donna Washburn, vp mktg. Owned by Diversified Communications. Total Basic Subscribers: 44,713; Number of Cable Systems: 4.

SMALLER SYSTEMS

Maine - New England Cablevision, 72 Pleasant St., Springvale, ME 04083; (207) 324-3700.
Massachusetts - New England Cablevision, 194A Main St., Amesbury, MA 01913; (508) 388-3335. New England Cablevision, 38 Blackburn Ctr., Gloucester, MA 01930; (508) 281-0811. **New Hampshire** - 22 Farmington Rd., Rochester, NH 03867; (603) 332-5466.

New Heritage Associates

Suite 301, 2600 Grand Ave., Des Moines, IA 50312. (515) 246-1750. James Cownie, chmn; Nile McDonald, vp opns; Dale Parker, vp mktg; David Lundguist, vp; Kim McAdams, vp. Owned by Meredith/New Heritage Strategic Partnership. Total Basic Subscribers: 123,573; Number of Cable Systems: 2.

SYSTEMS WITH OVER 20,000 SUBSCRIBERS

Meredith Cable (103,714 subscribers). 934 Woodhill Dr., Roseville, MN 55113. (612) 483-3233. Kevin Griffin, gen mgr; Scott Melter, chief tech. *Basic Service:* Subscribers: 103,714; 10/31/93. *Pay Services:* Total Pay Subscribers: 31,155; 12/11/92.

Meredith Cable (22,579 subscribers). 318 E. Broadway, Bismarck, ND 58501. (701) 223-4000; FAX: (701) 258-8751. Jot Turner, gen mgr; Marcia Huey, mktg dir; Paul Frank, loc adv dir; Dennis Hilfer, chief tech; Kathy Nagel, cust svc dir.
Area(s) Served: ND. Counties: Burleigh, Morton. Serving Bismarck, Mandon. Pop: 65,000. Miles of Plant: 477. Homes Passed: 32,000. Homes Served: 22,579. *Channel Capacity:* In use: 40. *Basic Service:* Subscribers: 22,579; 10/31/93. Programming (via satellite): 29 chs. Programming (off air): 4 chs. *Pay Services:* Total Pay Subscribers: 7,716; 12/21/92. (1) Pay Units: 5,293; 12/21/92. Programming (via satellite). (2) Pay Units: 2,163; 12/21/92. Programming (via satellite): Disney. (3) Pay Units: 2,692; 12/21/92. Programming (via satellite): Showtime. (4) Pay Units: 769; 12/21/92. Programming (via satellite): The Movie Channel. (5) Pay Units: 1,365; 12/21/92. Programming (via satellite): Cinemax. Pay Per View Subscribers: 14,219; 12/21/92. *No Local Advertising Accepted.*

New Hope Telephone Cooperative

Box 452, New Hope, AL 35760. (205) 723-4211. Larry Martin, pres; Loyd Athley, vp opns. Owned by New Hope Telephone Co. Total Basic Subscribers: 2,900; Pay Cable Subscribers: 875; Number of Cable Systems: 1.

SMALLER SYSTEMS

Alabama - New Hope Telephone Cooperative, Grant, AL. New Hope Telephone Cooperative, New Hope, AL. New Hope Telephone Cooperative, Owens Cross Roads, AL.

New Richmond Cable Co.

Box 318, 154 E. Second St., New Richmond, WI 54017. (715) 246-2145; FAX: (715) 246-7111. Michael Walsh, vp. Owned by Rochester Telephone. Total Basic Subscribers: 1,850; Pay Cable Subscribers: 620; Number of Cable Systems: 1.

NewChannels Corporation

Box 4872, 5015 Campuswood Dr., Syracuse, NY 13221. (315) 463-2288; FAX: (315) 463-6584. Leo Calistri, pres; Thomas Kirkwood, vp mktg; Daniel Cavallo, vp progmg; Mary Cotter, vp; William Doolittle, vp; William Futera, vp. Owned by Newhouse Broadcasting Corp. Total Basic Subscribers: 391,000; Pay Cable Subscribers: 255,000; Number of Cable Systems: 19.

SYSTEMS WITH OVER 20,000 SUBSCRIBERS

Anniston NewChannels Corporation (32,554 subscribers). 620 Noble St., Anniston, AL 36201. (205) 238-1144; FAX: (205) 236-4475. Don Richey, gen mgr; Tim Roden, mktg dir; Mike Parris, loc adv dir; Bill Reynolds, chief tech; Gayla Craig, cust svc dir.
Area(s) Served: AL. Counties: Calhoun, Talladega. Serving Annistown, Bynum, Choccolocco, DeArmanville, Eastaboga, Ft. McClellan, Jacksonville, Munford, Ohatchee, Oxford, Saks, Weaver. Pop: 120,000. Miles of Plant: 705. Homes Passed: 35,156. Homes Served: 32,554. *Channel Capacity:* In use: 41. *Basic Service:* Subscribers: 32,554; 11/15/93. Programming (via satellite): 30 chs. Programming (via microwave): 10 chs. Pay Per View Subscribers: 11,334; 10/25/91. *Local Advertising Accepted. Equipment:* Scientific-Atlanta re-

Multiple Systems Operators, Independent Owners & Cable Systems

ceivers, processors, modulators, satellite receiver antennas & converters.

Binghamton NewChannels (61,485 subscribers). Box 2208, Binghamton, NY 13902. (607) 798-0422; FAX: (607) 770-8639. James A. Streevy, gen mgr; Joyce Price, mktg dir; David J. Whalen, loc adv dir; Al Collingwood, chief tech; Dave Levenson, cust svc dir.
Area(s) Served: NY. County: Broome. Serving Binghamton, Binghamton Twp., Chenango, Conklin, Dickinson, Endicott, Fenton, Johnson City, Kirkwood, Maine, Nanticoke, Owego, Port Dickinson, Union, Vestal. Miles of Plant: 890. Homes Passed: 80,161. Homes Served: 61,485. *Channel Capacity:* 45. In use: 42. *Basic Service:* Subscribers: 61,485; 10/24/91. Programming (via satellite): 2 chs. Programming (via microwave): 3 chs. Programming (off air): 4 chs. *Local Advertising Accepted. Equipment:* Scientific-Atlanta 6600 video receiver; Scientific-Atlanta 6350 modulator; VideoCipher II general instrument; Jerrold DSE encoder.

NewChannels (53,000 subscribers). 59 Leversee Rd., Troy, NY 12182. (518) 237-3740; FAX: (518) 237-1217. William Mitch, gen mgr; Mike Smith, mktg dir; Charles O'Brien, chief tech; Carole Vozzy, cust svc dir.
Area(s) Served: NY. Counties: Albany, Rensselaer, Saratoga, Washington. Serving Brunswick, Cambridge, Clifton Park, Cohoes, East Greenbush, Easton, Greenwich, Halfmoon, Jackson, Mechanicville, Northumberland, Pittstown, Salem, Saratoga, Schagticoke, Stillwater, Troy, Valley Falls, Victory Mills, Waterford. Pop: 161,162. Miles of Plant: 957. Homes Passed: 67,151. Homes Served: 53,000. *Channel Capacity:* 42. In use: 42. *Basic Service:* Subscribers: 53,000; 11/15/93. Programming (via satellite): 30 chs. Programming (via microwave): 4 chs. Programming (off air): 5 chs. Pay Per View Subscribers: 26,128; 09/01/91. *Local Advertising Accepted. Equipment:* Scientific-Atlanta converters.

Syracuse NewChannels (82,000 subscribers). Box 4791, 6154 Thompson Rd., Syracuse, NY 13221. (315) 437-1401; FAX: (315) 463-8020. Mark H. Ganley, gen mgr; Terry Brennan, mktg dir; Robyn Bombard, loc adv dir; Michael J. Kennedy, chief tech; Karen Caporizzo, cust svc dir.
Area(s) Served: NY. Counties: Brutus, Madison, Onondaga. Serving Brutus, Camillus, Cato, Cicero, Clay, Dewitt, East Syracuse, Elbridge, Fayetteville, Field, Geddes, Hancock Field, Ira, Jordan, Lafayette, Liverpool, Lysander, Madison, Manlius, Marcellus, Meridian, Minoa, North Syracuse, Onondaga, Otisco, Phoenix, Pompey, Port Byron, Salina, Skaneateles, Solvay, Tully, Van Buren, Weedsport. Pop: 400,000. Miles of Plant: 1,640. Homes Passed: 114,110. Homes Served: 82,000. *Channel Capacity:* 41. In use: 41. *Basic Service:* Subscribers: 82,000; 11/15/93. Programming (via satellite): 32 chs. Programming (via microwave): 4 chs. Programming (off air): 5 chs. Pay Per View Subscribers: 43,877; 10/24/91. *Local Advertising Accepted. Equipment:* Jerrold & Regency addressable converters; Jerrold & Regency non-addressable converters.

SMALLER SYSTEMS

Alabama - Alabama NewChannels, Box 290, Rt. 2 & Hwy. 431 N., Eufaula, AL 36027; (205) 687-5555. Alabama NewChannels, 3996 US Hwy. 231, Wetumpka, AL 36092; (205) 567-4344. **New York** - Battenkill NewChannels, 75 Main St., Greenwich, NY 12834; (518) 692-9691. Carthage NewChannels, Box 470, 10 N. Broad St., Carthage, NY 13619; (315) 493-3520. Champlain NewChannels, Box 757, 42 Champlain St., Rouses Pt., NY 12979; (518) 297-6688. Corning NewChannels, 50 Ferris St., Corning, NY 14830; (607) 936-3722. Fulton NewChannels, 417 S. Second St., Fulton, NY; (315) 593-7918. Malone NewChannels, Box 7, E. Main St., Malone, NY 12953; (518) 483-1010. Massena NewChannels, Box 180, 277 Andrews St. Rd., Massena, NY 13662; (315) 764-0244. Ogdensburg NewChannels, Box 979, One Fine St., Ogdensburg, NY 13669; (315) 393-3090. Oneonta New Channels, 21 Elm St., Oneonta, NY 13820; (607) 432-0500. Potsdam New Channels, 1 Corporate Dr., R.D. #4, Potsdam, NY 13676; (315) 265-8300. Rome NewChannels, Box 711, Rome, NY 13440; (315) 337-1120. **Pennsylvania** - NewChannels, Box 360, Canonsburg, PA 15317; (412) 745-4734. NewChannels, 644 Stoops Ferry Rd., Coraopolis, PA 15108; (412) 264-6600.

Newport Cablevision Inc.

90 Main St., Newport, VT 05855. (802) 334-2614. Sam Scherrer, CEO; Phil Hughes, pres. Owned by Phil Hughes, Sam Scherrer. Total Basic Subscribers: 3,387; Number of Cable Systems: 1.

North Coast Cable

3300 Lakeside Ave., Cleveland, OH 44114. (216) 575-8016; FAX: (216) 575-0212. Lee Howley, pres; James K. Anderson, vp opns; Vicky Green, vp mktg. Total Basic Subscribers: 75,082; Pay Cable Subscribers: 120,000; Number of Cable Systems: 1.

SYSTEMS WITH OVER 20,000 SUBSCRIBERS

North Coast Cable Ltd. (82,000 subscribers). 3300 Lakeside Ave., Cleveland, OH 44114. (216) 575-8016; FAX: (216) 575-0212. James K. Anderson, gen mgr; Vicky Green, mktg dir. *Channel Capacity:* 79. In use: 60. *Basic Service:* Subscribers: 82,000. *Pay Services:* Total Pay Subscribers: 115,000. *Local Advertising Accepted.*

Northland Communications Corp.

Suite 3600, 1201 Third Ave., Seattle, WA 98101. (206) 621-1351; FAX: (206) 623-9015. John S. Whetzell, CEO, chmn & pres; Gary S. Jones, CFO; Richard J. Dyste, vp; James E. Hanlon, vp. Total Basic Subscribers: 151,000; Pay Cable Subscribers: 45,281; Number of Cable Systems: 77.

Northwest Cable L.P.

E. 4013 Mission Ave., Spokane, WA 99202. (509) 534-3766. Bill Yusko, pres. Owned by Bill Yusko, gen. ptnr. Total Basic Subscribers: 1,425; Pay Cable Subscribers: 545; Number of Cable Systems: 10.

SMALLER SYSTEMS

Idaho - Northwest Cable L.P., Worley, ID. **Washington** - Northwestern Cable L.P., Fairfield, WA. Northwestern Cable L.P., Garfield, WA. Northwestern Cable L.P., Harrington, WA. Northwestern Cable L.P., Oakesdale, WA. Northwestern Cable L.P., Reardan, WA. Northwestern Cable L.P., Rosalia, WA. Northwestern Cable L.P., Spangle, WA. Northwestern Cable L.P., Sprague, WA. Northwestern Cable L.P., Springdale, WA.

Northwest Communications Inc.

Box 186, Havelock, IA 50546. (712) 776-2222; FAX: (712) 776-4444. Don Miller, vp opns. Owned by Northwest Telephone Co-op. Total Basic Subscribers: 1,000; Number of Cable Systems: 4.

SMALLER SYSTEMS

Iowa - Northwest Communications, Inc., Havelock, IA. Northwest Communications Inc., Mallard, IA. Northwest Communications Inc., Rolfe, IA. Northwest Communications Inc., West Bank, IA.

City of Norway CATV

Box 99, Norway, MI 49870. (906) 563-9641; FAX: (906) 563-7502. Mark Bretchi, vp opns; Tom Pearman, vp. Owned by City of Norway. Total Basic Subscribers: 1,460; Pay Cable Subscribers: 400; Number of Cable Systems: 1.

Nova Cable Management Inc.

Box 793, 228-1/2 Washington Ave., Grand Haven, MI 49417. (616) 847-0072; FAX: (616) 847-9409. Gary Van Volkenburg, pres; Christine Munn, vp mktg; Edward Francke, vp. Owned by Gary Van Volkenburg. Total Basic Subscribers: 5,655; Pay Cable Subscribers: 2,769; Number of Cable Systems: 19.

SMALLER SYSTEMS

Michigan - Nova Cable Management Inc., Ashley, MI. Nova Cable Management Inc., Barry County, MI. Nova Cable Management Inc., Barryton, MI. Nova Cable Management Inc., Big Prairie Twp., MI. Nova Cable Management Inc., Billings, MI. Nova Management Inc., Bingham Township, MI. Nova Cable Management Inc., Broomfield Valley Trailpark, MI. Nova Cable Management Inc., Chester Township, MI. Nova Cable Management Inc., Garfield Twp., MI. Nova Cable Management Inc., Johnstown Twp., MI. Nova Cable Management Inc., Lake George, MI. Nova Cable Management Inc., Maple Rapids, MI. Nova Cable Management Inc., Marxing Twp., MI. Nova Cable Management Inc., Perinton, MI. Nova Cable Management Inc., Remus, MI. Nova Cable Management Inc., Surrey Twp., MI. Nova Cable Management Inc., Weidman, MI. Nova Cable Management Inc., Woodland (Village), MI. Nova Cable Management Inc., Gilmore Twp., MI.

Oak Cable Systems Inc.

Box 206, 700 North Hwy. 69, Huxley, IA 50124. (515) 597-3385; FAX: (515) 597-2437. Douglas Shedahl, pres; Ken Thompson, vp opns. Owned by Douglas Shedahl. Total Basic Subscribers: 1,000; Number of Cable Systems: 8.

OCB Cablevision Inc.

Suite 2, 3706 Atlanta Hwy., Athens, GA 30606. (706) 353-2972. Lawrence R. Waltz, pres; Charles K. Lindsey, vp. Owned by Lawrence R. Waltz. Total Basic Subscribers: 4,997; Pay Cable Subscribers: 1,970; Number of Cable Systems: 1.

Omega Communications Inc.

Box 1766, 29 E. Maryland St., Indianapolis, IN 46206. (317) 264-4000. Robert E. Schloss, CEO & pres; James Jones, CFO; Merle Frey, vp. Owned by Schloss Family. Total Basic Subscribers: 50,000; Number of Cable Systems: 14.

SMALLER SYSTEMS

California - Schloss Bros. Family Investment Management, 655 Deep Valley Dr., Suite 220, Rolling Hills Estates, CA 90274; (303) 377-0405 **Illinois** - Cardinal Telecable Corp., 1010 Alexander, Box 187, Paris, IL 61944; (217) 465-4121. Hoopeston Cable TV Co., 326 W. Main, Box 325, Hoopestown, IL 64952; (217) 283-9181. See-More TV Corp., 1209 N. State, Box 129, Westville, IL 61883; (217) 276-3195. **Indiana** - Cable Brazil Inc., 604 E. National Ave., Box 485, Brazil, IN 47834; (812) 448-8308. Moosier Mills Cable Co., 1201 W. Main St., Mitchell, IN 47446; (812) 849-2200. Omega of Brown County, Old State Rd. 46 E., Box 685, Nashville, IN 47448; (812) 988-6696. **Michigan** - Cable Vision Inc., 1250 E. Superior, Box 168, Alma, MI 48801; (517) 463-4988. Cable Vision Inc., 93 N. Division B, Box 356, Hesperia, MI 49421; (616) 854-1515. Cable Vision Inc., 590 S. Pere Marquette HW, Ludington, MI 49431; (616) 843-3461. Cable Vision Inc., 915 Broomfield, Mt. Pleasant, MI 48858; (517) 772-0956. Cable Vision Inc., 218 N. Clinton Ave., Suite 3, Box 8, St. Johns, MI 48879; (517) 224-8914. **Missouri** - Mineral Area Cablevision, 106 W. Main, Flat River, MO 63601; (314) 431-5902. **Pennsylvania** - Clear Channels Cable Co., 154-56 S. Jefferson St., Rittanning, PA 16201; (412) 548-1536.

Oneonta Telephone Co. Inc.

Box 550, 505 Third Ave. E., Oneonta, AL 35121. (205) 625-3591. R.C. Corr, CEO; Bryan Corr, vp opns. Owned by R.C. Corr. Total Basic Subscribers: 2,072; Number of Cable Systems: 1.

OPP Cablevision

Box 311, 108 N. Main St., Opp, AL 36467. (205) 493-4571; FAX: (205) 493-6666. Mike Russell, vp opns; Mildred Rogers, vp mktg. Owned by Utilities of Opp. Total Basic Subscribers: 3,420; Pay Cable Subscribers: 1,500; Number of Cable Systems: 1.

Orwell Telephone Co.

70 S. Maple St., Orwell, OH 44076-0337. (216) 437-6111. Donald Pokorny, pres. Total Basic Subscribers: 2,200; Pay Cable Subscribers: 1,345; Number of Cable Systems: 2.

SMALLER SYSTEMS

Ohio - Orwell Cable Television Co., Leipsie, OH. Orwell Cable Television Co., Orwell, OH.

Frederick Osborne dba Auburn Cablevision Inc.

32 Owasco St., Auburn, NY 13021. (315) 252-7563; FAX: (315) 252-9514. Frederick Osborne, pres; Rita M. Valentino, vp. Owned by Frederick Osborne, principal. Total Basic Subscribers: 14,000; Pay Cable Subscribers: 5,000; Number of Cable Systems: 1.

Dominic Padilla dba Dom's Cable TV

Box 360, San German, PR 00683. (809) 892-5606; FAX: (809) 892-4263. Jorge Rivera, vp opns; Maria Frontera, vp mktg; Greg Hernandez, vp. Owned by Dominic Padilla, Three Sixty Corp. Total Basic Subscribers: 15,600; Number of Cable Systems: 1.

Multiple Systems Operators, Independent Owners & Cable Systems

SMALLER SYSTEMS

Puerto Rico - Dom's Cable TV, Box 360, San German, PR 00753; (809) 892-5606.

Pagosa Vision Inc.

1500 E. Conecuh, Union Springs, AL 36089. (205) 738-2204; FAX: (205) 738-5555. Mrs. Billy Pimie, pres; Andy Williams, vp. Owned by Ropir Industries, R.M. Pimie. Total Basic Subscribers: 3,000; Number of Cable Systems: 8.

Palmetto Cable TV Inc.

101 Allison St., Fort Mill, SC 29715. (803) 548-6000. W.C. Baty Jr., pres; John M. Barnes Jr., vp mktg. Owned by Robert Helmly, 50%; Springs Co., 50%. Total Basic Subscribers: 5,472; Pay Cable Subscribers: 2,311; Number of Cable Systems: 1.

SMALLER SYSTEMS

South Carolina - Fort Hill Cable TV, 101 Allison St., Fort Hill, SC 29715.

Panther Valley Services Inc.

10 Corporate Pl. S., Piscataway, NJ 08854. (800) 553-7899. Dennis Shea, vp. Total Basic Subscribers: 3,200; Pay Cable Subscribers: 1,600; Number of Cable Systems: 4.

Par Cable Inc.

Box 260, Jackson, MS 39205-0260. (601) 354-5300; FAX: (601) 354-4609. Rea Hederman, pres; Glen Dowe, vp opns; Robert Hederman, vp. Owned by Hederman Family. Total Basic Subscribers: 35,000; Pay Cable Subscribers: 17,000; Number of Cable Systems: 4.

Paradigm Communications Inc.

124 W. Putnam Ave., Greenwich, CT 06830-5436. (203) 622-1888; FAX: (203) 622-1887. James Kingsdale, pres. Owned by James Kingsdale, 50%; Memorial Drive Trust & Schooner Capital Corp., 50%. Total Basic Subscribers: 7,000; Pay Cable Subscribers: 3,000; Number of Cable Systems: 3.

Paxton Cable Television Inc.

Box 621, Hilliard, OH 43026. (614) 876-7190. Susan McVoy, pres & CFO; Steve McVoy, vp opns. Owned by Steve McVoy, Susan McVoy. Total Basic Subscribers: 2,000; Pay Cable Subscribers: 1,200; Number of Cable Systems: 1.

Peach State Cable Co.

Box 1198, 910 Carrol St., Perry, GA 31069. (912) 987-3444. Bill Mitchell, pres; Sandy Head, vp. Owned by Mansfield Jennings. Total Basic Subscribers: 5,060; Pay Cable Subscribers: 1,455; Number of Cable Systems: 1.

Peachtree Cable TV Inc.

Box 340, 212 S. Jefferson St., Dublin, GA 31021. (912) 453-9448. D.F. Bryan, CEO & pres; Richard Cofer, vp. Total Basic Subscribers: 14,000; Number of Cable Systems: 2.

Pecoco Inc. dba TV Horizons

121 Williams St., Randolph, WI 53956. (414) 326-5808; FAX: (414) 326-4125. Thomas S. Sanderson, CEO & chmn; Elizabeth J. Burke, pres; Bryan Woltman, CFO; Gary Perleberg, vp opns; Jeffrey E. Beck, vp sls, vp prom & vp progmg; Mike Petrouske, vp. Total Basic Subscribers: 2,948; Pay Cable Subscribers: 1,150; Number of Cable Systems: 2.

SMALLER SYSTEMS

Wisconsin - People's Broadband Communications, 121 Williams St., Randolph, WI 53956; 2,882 subs. People's Broadband Communications-Fairwater, 121 Williams St., Randolph, WI 53956; 66 subs.

Pencor Services Inc.

Box 215, 471 Delaware Ave., Palmerton, PA 18071. (215) 826-2551; FAX: (215) 826-7626. Donald G. Reinhard, pres; Jeff Gehman, vp opns. Total Basic Subscribers: 139,669; Pay Cable Subscribers: 60,400; Number of Cable Systems: 20.

SYSTEMS WITH OVER 20,000 SUBSCRIBERS

Blue Ridge Cable TV Inc. (39,306 subscribers). 920 Ehler St., Stroudsburg, PA 18360. (717) 421-0780. John Kintner, gen mgr; Dave Transu, chief tech. *Basic Service:* Subscribers: 39,306; 10/15/93.

Blue Ridge Cable TV Inc. (27,430 subscribers). Box 215, 471 Delaware Ave., Palmerton, PA 18071. (215) 826-2551. Richard Semmel, gen mgr; Jeff Reinhard, mktg dir. *Basic Service:* Subscribers: 27,430; 10/15/93.

Blue Ridge CATV Inc. (27,617 subscribers). Box 150, 804 Academy Heights Ave., Ephrata, PA 17522. (717) 733-4111; FAX: (717) 733-3245. Robert Miller, gen mgr; Lisa Maragioglio, mktg dir; Terry Connelly, loc adv dir; Jeff Oberholtzer, chief tech; Sharon Blechschmidt, cust svc dir.
Area(s) Served: PA. County: Lancaster. Homes Served: 27,617. *Basic Service:* Subscribers: 27,617; 10/15/93. *Local Advertising Accepted.*

Pennsylvania Classic Cable

209 Locust St., East Berlin, PA 17316. (215) 667-9600; FAX: (215) 667-9603. John Bamback Jr., CEO & chmn; Frank Vitale, CFO. Total Basic Subscribers: 13,000; Pay Cable Subscribers: 6,500; Number of Cable Systems: 2.

SMALLER SYSTEMS

Florida - Jackson County Classic Cable, Jackson County, FL; 1,100 subs. **Pennsylvania** - Pennsylvania Classic Cable, East Berlin, PA; 11,300 subs.

Peoples Telephone Co. Inc.

Box 310, Main St., Erin, TN 37061. (615) 289-4221; FAX: (615) 289-4220. Joseph D. Fail, chmn & pres; Harvey Poole, CFO. Owned by Telephone Electronics Inc. Total Basic Subscribers: 1,500; Pay Cable Subscribers: 580; Number of Cable Systems: 2.

Philippi Communications System

Box 460, 108 N. Main St., Philippi, WV 26416. (304) 457-3700; FAX: (304) 457-2703. Carl Radcliff, vp opns. Owned by City of Philippi. Total Basic Subscribers: 1,472; Number of Cable Systems: 1.

Phoenix Cable Inc.

10 S. Franklin Tpk., Ramsey, NJ 07446. (201) 825-9090; FAX: (201) 825-8794. Charles Himelrick Jr., vp opns; John E. Finley, vp mktg; James S. Fenney, vp. Owned by Phoenix Leasing Inc. Total Basic Subscribers: 29,306; Pay Cable Subscribers: 15,500; Number of Cable Systems: 43.

Pine State Management

Suite 233, 724 W. Lancaster Ave., Wayne, PA 19087. (215) 688-6051; FAX: (215) 975-0123. Walter Kemerer, CEO; Britton Smith, vp opns; James Lingley, vp. Owned by Walter Kemerer L.P. Total Basic Subscribers: 5,400; Number of Cable Systems: 1.

SMALLER SYSTEMS

Maine - Pine Tree Cablevision, Box 68, Rt. 1 & Rt. 214, Penbrook, ME.

Pioneer Cable Inc.

Box 39, 183 Washington, Monument, CO 80132. (719) 481-2451; FAX: (719) 481-2211. Stan Searle, pres; Rebecca Hendricks, vp. Owned by Stan Searle. Total Basic Subscribers: 3,000; Pay Cable Subscribers: 1,920; Number of Cable Systems: 3.

SMALLER SYSTEMS

Colorado - Tri-Lakes Cable, Cuchara Valley, CO. Tri-Lakes Cable, Gleneagle, CO. Tri-Lakes Cable, Monument, CO.

Pioneer Communications Co.

Suite 200, 1907 N. Lamar, Austin, TX 78705. (512) 477-6866; FAX: (512) 476-1879. Wendell Mayes Jr., pres; Cathey Mayes, vp. Owned by Mayes Family, 100%. Total Basic Subscribers: 8,250; Pay Cable Subscribers: 5,000; Number of Cable Systems: 2.

Plains Cable Systems

Box 267, Spirit Lake, IA 51360. (712) 336-5151; FAX: (712) 336-5687. E.M. Parsens, CEO & pres; Jerry Kittelson, vp. Owned by E.M. Parsens, 90%; Jerry Kittelson, 10%. Total Basic Subscribers: 800; Pay Cable Subscribers: 750; Number of Cable Systems: 1.

SMALLER SYSTEMS

South Dakota - Plains Cable Systems, Oacoma, SD.

Platteville Cable TV Corp.

135 N. Bonson St., Platteville, WI 53818. (608) 348-3048; FAX: (608) 348-2679. Gary McFall, vp. Owned by PTI Communications. Total Basic Subscribers: 3,200; Pay Cable Subscribers: 1,500; Number of Cable Systems: 1.

Post Communications Inc.

Suite 11-B, 14828 W. 6th Ave., Golden, CO 80401. (303) 278-9660; FAX: (303) 278-9685. John Post, pres. Owned by John Post, 100%. Total Basic Subscribers: 2,000; Pay Cable Subscribers: 1,000; Number of Cable Systems: 9.

Post-Newsweek Cable Inc.

Suite 270, 4742 N. 24th St., Phoenix, AZ 85016. (602) 468-1177; FAX: (602) 468-9216. Howard E. Wall, CEO & chmn; Thomas O. Might, pres; Ronald Pancratz, vp adv; Peter Newell, vp; Thomas Basinger, vp; Harvey Boyd, vp. Owned by The Washington Post Co. Total Basic Subscribers: 479,000; Pay Cable Subscribers: 301,000; Number of Cable Systems: 52.

SYSTEMS WITH OVER 20,000 SUBSCRIBERS

Post-Newsweek Cable (45,450 subscribers). 3242 Airway Dr., Santa Rosa, CA 95403. (707) 544-7337; FAX: (707) 544-3703. John Gosch, gen mgr; Lisa Alexander, mktg dir; George Moody, loc adv dir; Charlie Fleshman, chief tech.
Area(s) Served: CA. County: Sonoma. Serving Fulton, Kenwood, Oakmont, Santa Rosa. Pop: 135,500. Miles of Plant: 630. Homes Passed: 56,800. Homes Served: 45,450. *Channel Capacity:* 53. In use: 53. *Basic Service:* Subscribers: 45,450; 10/01/93. Pay Per View Subscribers: 46,200; 12/01/92. *Local Advertising Accepted.*

Post-Newsweek Cable (52,134 subscribers). 1639 Princeton Ave., Modesto, CA 95350. (209) 577-3456; FAX: (209) 529-6636. Ken Berns, gen mgr; Rick Lang, mktg dir; Barbara Etrick, loc adv dir; Jim Blackwell, chief tech; Jack McHugh, cust svc dir.
Area(s) Served: CA. County: Stanislaus. Serving Modesto, Oakdale. Pop: 200,000. Miles of Plant: 714. Homes Passed: 79,000. Homes Served: 52,134. *Channel Capacity:* 78. In use: 72. *Basic Service:* Subscribers: 52,134; 10/01/93. Programming (via satellite): 42 chs. Programming (off air): 12 chs. *Pay Services:* Total Pay Subscribers: 21,000; 12/15/92. (1) Pay Units: 11,698; 12/15/92. Programming (via satellite): HBO. (2) Pay Units: 9,230; 12/15/92. Programming (via satellite): Disney. (3) Pay Units: 8,093; 12/15/93. Programming (via satellite): Showtime. (4) Pay Units: 4,105; 12/15/93. Programming (via satellite): Cinemax. (5) Pay Units: 2,845; 12/15/93. Programming (via satellite): SportsChannel. Pay Per View Subscribers: 24,000; 12/15/92. *Local Advertising Accepted. Equipment:* Scientific-Atlanta headend & amplifiers; Zenith converters.

Post-Newsweek Cable (21,314 subscribers). 3415 Hewes Ave., Gulfport, MS 39507. (601) 864-1506; FAX: (601) 865-9476. Ray Clemons, gen mgr; Michael Woods, mktg dir; Louis Jones, chief tech; Retha Karnes, cust svc dir.
Area(s) Served: MS. County: Harrison. Serving Gulfport. Pop: 102,000. Miles of Plant: 420. Homes Passed: 26,000. Homes Served: 21,314. *Channel Capacity:* 39. In use: 39. *Basic Service:* Subscribers: 21,314; 12/01/92. *Pay Services:* Total Pay Subscribers: 8,674; 12/01/92. Pay Per View Subscribers: 4,561; 11/15/91. *Local Advertising Accepted. Equipment:* Scientific-Atlanta headend.

Post-Newsweek Cable (20,000 subscribers). 3720 Texoma Pkwy., Sherman, TX 75090. (903) 893-6548; FAX: (903) 868-2754. Claude H. Edwards, gen mgr; Charlie Downs, mktg dir; Cecil Miller, chief tech.
Area(s) Served: TX. County: Grayson. Serving Denison, Sherman. Pop: 62,000. Miles of Plant: 400. Homes Passed: 27,000. Homes Served: 20,000. *Channel Capacity:* 78. In use: 70. *Basic Service:* Subscribers: 20,000; 11/01/92. Pay Per View Subscribers: 11,400;

Multiple Systems Operators, Independent Owners & Cable Systems

11/01/92. *Local Advertising Accepted. Equipment:* Scientific-Atlanta headend; Scientific-Atlanta amplifiers; Comm/Scope & Scientific-Atlanta cable.

Post-Newsweek Cable (24,500 subscribers). 315 W. Eighth St., Odessa, TX 79761. (915) 334-7200; FAX: (915) 334-7216. Bruce Tipi, gen mgr; June Baumann, mktg dir; Nathan Hankins, chief tech.
Area(s) Served: TX. County: Ector. Pop: 132,000. Miles of Plant: 444. Homes Passed: 44,000. Homes Served: 24,500. *Channel Capacity:* 52. In use: 51. *Basic Service:* Subscribers: 24,500; 08/26/93. *Pay Services:* Total Pay Subscribers: 8,900; 08/26/93. Pay Per View Subscribers: 6,547; 08/26/93. *Local Advertising Accepted. Equipment:* Scientific-Atlanta headend; Jerrold addressable boxes.

Sooland Cablecom (22,000 subscribers). 900 Steuben St., Sioux City, IA 51101. (712) 233-2000; FAX: (712) 233-2235. Joel H. Durham, gen mgr; Kevin Lloyd, mktg dir; Claudia Killinger, loc adv dir; Bud Kumpf, chief tech; Paula Todd, cust svc dir.
Area(s) Served: IA, SD, NE. Counties: Woodbury, Union, Dakota. Serving Sergeant Bluff, Sioux City, Dakotabones, McCouk Lake, North Sioux City, Dakota City, South Sioux City. Pop: 110,000. Miles of Plant: 400. Homes Passed: 32,000. Homes Served: 22,000. *Channel Capacity:* 42. In use: 42. *Basic Service:* Subscribers: 22,000; 11/01/92. Programming (via satellite): 35 chs. Programming (off air): 4 chs. *Pay Services:* Total Pay Subscribers: 7,135; 10/31/92. (1) Pay Units: 2,500; 12/15/91. Programming (via satellite): Cinemax. (2) Pay Units: 4,200; 12/15/91. Programming (via satellite): HBO. (3) Pay Units: 1,300; 12/15/91. Programming (via satellite): Disney. (4) Pay Units: 1,200; 12/15/91. Programming (via satellite): The Movie Channel. Pay Per View Subscribers: 5,600; 10/31/92. *Local Advertising Accepted. Equipment:* Scientific-Atlanta & GTE line amps; RCA & Scientific-Atlanta headend; Magnovox line extenders; Jerrold boxes.

SMALLER SYSTEMS

Mississippi - Coast TV, 19201 Pineville Rd., Long Beach, MS 39560; (601) 864-4380; 10,000 subs.

Premiere Cable I Ltd.

212 S. 11th St., Coeur'd Alene, ID 83814. (208) 664-3370; FAX: (208) 664-5888. Sharon Shull, CFO; Ted W. Hughett, vp opns; Kevin Sharrai, vp mktg. Owned by Stratlyn Inc., gen. ptnr. Total Basic Subscribers: 14,400; Number of Cable Systems: 59.

REGIONS

Idaho: 61 W. Center St., Box 655, Soda Springs, ID 83276; (208) 547-4341. *California:* 415 N. Mt. Shasta Blvd., Suite 2, Mt. Shasta, CA 96067; (916) 926-6593.

Prestige Cable TV Inc.

Box 785, 156 Morningside Dr., Cartersville, GA 30120. (404) 382-0531. Jon Oscher, CEO & chmn; Rob Buckfelder, CFO; Lorri Oscher, vp opns. Owned by Prestige Cable TV. Total Basic Subscribers: 103,974; Pay Cable Subscribers: 41,783; Number of Cable Systems: 10.

REGIONS

Virginia: Fredericksburg, VA; Bill Smith. *Maryland:* Westminster, MD; Bill Bethune. *North Carolina:* Mooresville, NC; Danny Heath. *Georgia:* Cartersville, GA; Joe Keenan.

Prime Cable

One American Ctr., Suite 3000, 600 Congress Ave., Austin, TX 78701. (512) 476-7888; FAX: (512) 476-4869. Robert W. Hughes, CEO & chmn; Gregory Marchbanks, pres; Jerry Lindauer, vp; Allan Barnes, vp; William Glasgow, vp. Owned by Robert W. Hughes. Total Basic Subscribers: 526,552; Pay Cable Subscribers: 490,000; Number of Cable Systems: 7.

SYSTEMS WITH OVER 20,000 SUBSCRIBERS

Catawba Valley Cable TV (33,000 subscribers). Box 2989, Hickory, NC 28602. (704) 322-3875; FAX: (704) 322-5492. Bill Hysell, gen mgr; Tom Tierney, chief tech.
Area(s) Served: NC. Counties: Burke, Caldwell, Catawba. Serving Brookford, Claremont, Conover, Granite Falls, Hickory, Hildebran, Longview, Maiden, Newton, Rhodhiss. Miles of Plant: 950. Homes Passed: 49,000. Homes Served: 33,000. *Channel Capacity:* 36. In use: 36. *Basic Service:* Subscribers: 33,000. *Local Advertising Accepted. Equipment:* Jerrold headend; Magnovox amplifiers; Comm/Scope cable; Chyron character generator; Jerrold set top converters; Scientific-Atlanta satellite antenna; Scientific-Atlanta receivers; Texscan commercial insert.

Prime Cable (Eastern & Western Suburbs) (115,000 subscribers). 13700 Veterans Memorial Blvd., Houston, TX 77014. (713) 537-2900; FAX: (713) 586-5338. Robert M. Burns, gen mgr; Karen Alexander, mktg dir; Ray Searcy, chief tech; Brenna Clendaniel, cust svc dir.
Area(s) Served: TX. Counties: Fort Bend, Harris. Serving Barrett Station, Channelview, Crosby, Deer Park, Ft. Bend, Highlands, Humble, Katy, La Porte, Morgans Point, Needville, Pasadena, Richmond, Shore Acres, S. Houston, Sugar Land. Homes Passed: 220,000. Homes Served: 115,000. *Channel Capacity:* 44. In use: 44. *Basic Service:* Subscribers: 115,000; 09/01/93. *Local Advertising Accepted.*

Prime Cable of Alaska Inc. (54,911 subscribers). 5151 Fairbanks St., Anchorage, AK 99503. (907) 562-2400; FAX: (907) 561-4396. Marty Robinson, gen mgr; Dave Paeth, mktg dir.
Area(s) Served: AK. Counties: Anchorage, Bethel, Kenai Peninsula. Serving Chugiak, Eagle River, Elmendorf Air Force Base, Fort Richardson, Kenai, Kenai Peninsula, Ridgeway, Soldotna. Miles of Plant: 944. Homes Passed: 103,709. Homes Served: 54,911. *Channel Capacity:* 53. In use: 53. *Basic Service:* Subscribers: 54,911; 10/31/93. *Pay Services:* Total Pay Subscribers: 56,918; 12/04/92. *Local Advertising Accepted. Equipment:* Scientific-Atlanta & Zenith headend; Scientific-Atlanta & RCA amplifiers; Cerro & Comm/Scope cable; Sony cameras VTRs; Video Data Systems character generator; Zenith addressable set top converters; AFC & Microdyne satellite antenna; Microdyne satellite receivers; ChannelMatic commercial insert.

Prime Cable of Chicago Inc. (118,000 subscribers). 3970 N. Milwaukee Ave., Chicago, IL 60641. (312) 202-3000; FAX: (312) 794-2291. W.A. Chain, gen mgr; Dana Dejanovich-Maragos, mktg dir; Don Murphy, loc adv dir; Steve Price, chief tech; Carolyn Mitchell, cust svc dir.
Area(s) Served: IL. County: Cook. Serving Chicago. Miles of Plant: 1,000. Homes Passed: 410,000. Homes Served: 118,000. *Channel Capacity:* 61. In use: 61. *Basic Service:* Subscribers: 118,000; 09/01/92. *Pay Services:* Total Pay Subscribers: 154,000; 11/01/91. *Local Advertising Accepted. Equipment:* Scientific-Atlanta & K-Tel headend; Texscan amplifiers; Times & Comm/Scope cable; JVC & Sony cameras; Sony VTRs; MSI character generator; Pioneer & Jerrold set top converters; Pioneer & Jerrold addressable set top converters; Scientific-Atlanta satellite receivers; Adams-Russell commercial insert.

Prime Cable of Las Vegas (211,819 subscribers). 121 S. Martin Luther King, Las Vegas, NV 89106. (702) 383-4000; FAX: (702) 383-6014. Harris H. Bass, gen mgr; Mary Alice Bauchman, mktg dir.
Area(s) Served: NV. Serving Boulder City, Clark City, Henderson, Las Vegas, North Las Vegas. Homes Served: 211,819. *Channel Capacity:* 52. In use: 52. *Basic Service:* Subscribers: 211,819; 10/31/93.

Public Service TV Co.

Box 669, Reynolds, GA 31076. (912) 847-3101; FAX: (912) 847-4106. Donald Bond, pres. Total Basic Subscribers: 1,493; Number of Cable Systems: 4.

SMALLER SYSTEMS

Georgia - Flint Cable TV, Box 669, Reynolds, GA; 31076.

Quincy Community TV Association Inc.

Box 834, 81 Bradley St., Quincy, CA 95971. (916) 283-2330; FAX: (916) 283-2330. Max Frantz, pres; Terry Kidd, CFO; Art Griffin, vp. Owned by Community of Quincy. Total Basic Subscribers: 2,039; Pay Cable Subscribers: 694; Number of Cable Systems: 1.

Range TV Cable Co. Inc.

Box 189, 1818 3rd Ave. E., Hibbing, MN 55746. (218) 262-1071; FAX: (218) 263-8340. Frank Befera, pres; Linda Ritz, vp mktg; Robert S. Nickoloff, vp. Owned by F. Befera, 54%; R.S. Nickoloff, 26.8%; B.P. Owens, 10%; J. Parise, 5%; C. Henry, 2.1%; J. Klungness, 2.1%. Total Basic Subscribers: 5,600; Pay Cable Subscribers: 1,200; Number of Cable Systems: 1.

Raystay Co.

Box 38, Carlisle, PA 17013. (717) 243-4918. George F. Gardner, pres; David A. Gardner, vp; Lee Sandifer, vp. Total Basic Subscribers: 40,000; Pay Cable Subscribers: 17,000; Number of Cable Systems: 5.

Leon Reed

15 Crofton St., Wellsboro, PA 16901. (717) 724-4516; FAX: (717) 724-2562. Leon Reed, pres. Total Basic Subscribers: 3,500; Number of Cable Systems: 2.

SMALLER SYSTEMS

Pennsylvania - Reed Cable TV, Arnot, PA. Reed Cable TV, Wellsboro, PA.

Retel TV Cable Co. Inc.

1836 Hayes Ave., Williamsport, PA 17701. (717) 494-1809. George L. Hughes, pres; Vera P. Hughes, vp. Owned by Hughes Family, 100%. Total Basic Subscribers: 2,454; Number of Cable Systems: 4.

Rifkin & Associates

Suite 600, 360 S. Monroe St., Denver, CO 80209. (303) 333-1215; FAX: (303) 322-3553. Monroe M. Rifkin, CEO & chmn; June E. Travis, pres; Dale P. Wagner, CFO; Paul S. Bambei, vp; Steve Hattrup, vp; Jack T. Pottle, vp. Owned by Rifkin & Assoc. L.P. Total Basic Subscribers: 360,000; Pay Cable Subscribers: 183,000; Number of Cable Systems: 45.

SYSTEMS WITH OVER 20,000 SUBSCRIBERS

Clay Cablevision (23,500 subscribers). Box 1451, 357 College, Orange Park, FL 32067-1451. (904) 272-5711; FAX: (904) 272-3945. Paul Hoffman, gen mgr; Bob Riegal, mktg dir; Larry May, chief tech. *Basic Service:* Subscribers: 23,500; 10/31/93.

Gold Coast Cablevision (50,000 subscribers). Suite 201, 1440 79th St. Causeway, North Bay Village, FL 33141. (305) 864-7824; (305) 861-8069; FAX: (305) 861-9047. Kevin Grossman, gen mgr; Terese Delgado, mktg dir; Marty Mohr, chief tech. *Basic Service:* Subscribers: 50,000; 10/31/93.

NE Roswell Cablevision (38,000 subscribers). Suite 450, 3075 Breckinridge Blvd., Duluth, GA 30136. (404) 806-7060; FAX: (404) 806-7099. Mike Champagne, gen mgr; Robin Crick, mktg dir; Chris White, chief tech. *Basic Service:* Subscribers: 38,000; 10/31/93.

West Boca Cablevision (33,000 subscribers). 23123 State Rd. 7, Boca Raton, FL 33428. (407) 487-2200; FAX: (407) 479-2446. John W. Gash, gen mgr; Lisa Treloar, mktg dir; Jim McClellan, chief tech. *Basic Service:* Subscribers: 33,000; 10/31/93.

Riviera Utilities Cable TV

Box 550, 413 E. Laurel Ave., Foley, AL 36536. (205) 943-5001; FAX: (943) 943-5275. Charles J. Ebert Jr., chmn; H. Sewell St. John Jr., pres; Cecil M. Hinote, CFO; Trond Manskow, vp opns. Owned by Community of Foley. Total Basic Subscribers: 4,066; Pay Cable Subscribers: 1,819; Number of Cable Systems: 1.

Rock Assoc.

Suite 400, 5808 Lake Washington Blvd., Kirkland, WA 98033. (206) 822-0254; FAX: (206) 828-0226. Gordon Rock, chmn; Dean Barney, CFO; Jim Uebelner, vp opns. Owned by Gordon Rock, Bob Allison, Sam Evans, Bob Nagel. Total Basic Subscribers: 60,000; Pay Cable Subscribers: 35,000; Number of Cable Systems: 20.

Rogers Cablesystems Limited

One Valleybrook Dr., 5th Fl., Toronto, ON M3B 2S7. (416) 447-5500; FAX: (416) 391-7261. Colin D. Watson, CEO & pres; Mark C. Steinman, CFO; Peter J. Irwin, vp mktg; Nicholas F. Hamilton-Piercy, vp; Paul J. Temple, vp; Donald W. Smith, vp. Owned by Rogers Communications Inc. Total Basic Subscribers: 1,843,892; Pay Cable Subscribers: 227,840; Number of Cable Systems: 14.

REGIONS

Eastern: 855 York Mills Rd., Toronto, ON M3B 1Z1; Rudolph Engel, exec VP & COO. *Western:* Rogers Cantel Twr., 1600-4710 Kingsway, Burnaby, BC V5H 4M5; (604) 436-1111; Frank Eberdt, exec VP & COO.

Multiple Systems Operators, Independent Owners & Cable Systems

SYSTEMS WITH OVER 20,000 SUBSCRIBERS

Rogers Cable TV - Abbotsford (27,506 subscribers). Box 2125, 31450 Marshall Rd., Abbotsford, BC V2T 3X8. (604) 856-0776; FAX: (604) 850-2517. Scott Atkinson, gen mgr; Susanna Reardon, chief tech.
Area(s) Served: BC. Serving Abbotsford, Matsqui, Sumas. Homes Served: 27,506. *Channel Capacity:* 38. In use: 38. *Basic Service:* Subscribers: 27,506; 09/10/93. *Pay Services:* Total Pay Subscribers: 1,911; 11/27/92. *Local Advertising Accepted.*

Rogers Cable TV - Calgary (107,548 subscribers). 3003 MacLeod Trail S.W., Calgary, AB T2G 2P8. (403) 261-4200; FAX: (403) 263-6076. Donald E. Taylor, gen mgr; John Harrison, chief tech.
Area(s) Served: AB. Serving Crossfield, South Calgary. Homes Served: 107,548. *Channel Capacity:* 44. In use: 42. *Basic Service:* Subscribers: 107,548; 10/15/93. *Pay Services:* Total Pay Subscribers: 14,039; 11/27/92. *Local Advertising Accepted.*

Rogers Cable TV - Cornwall (22,089 subscribers). 517 Pitt St., Cornwall, ON K6J 3R4. (613) 932-5966; FAX: (613) 932-3176. Carol Ring, gen mgr; Andre Cayer, chief tech.
Area(s) Served: ON. Serving Cornwall, Ingleside, Long Sault, St. Andrews. Pop: 50,000. Homes Passed: 26,003. Homes Served: 22,089. *Channel Capacity:* 49. In use: 47. *Basic Service:* Subscribers: 22,089; 10/15/93. *Pay Services:* Total Pay Subscribers: 3,360; 11/27/92. *Local Advertising Accepted.*

Rogers Cable TV - Fraser (78,000 subscribers). 1820 Kingsway Ave., Port Coquitlam, BC V3C 1S5. (604) 941-0461; FAX: (604) 941-2477. R.C. "Bob" Leslie, gen mgr, mktg dir & cust svc dir; Robert Johnston, loc adv dir.
Area(s) Served: BC. Serving Anmore, Belcarra, Coquitlam, Hatzlic Lake, Ioco, Maple Ridge, Mission, Pitt Meadows, Port Coquitlam, Port Moody. Miles of Plant: 1,200. Homes Passed: 80,000. Homes Served: 78,000. *Channel Capacity:* 46. In use: 44. *Basic Service:* Subscribers: 78,000; 10/15/93. Programming (via microwave): 50 chs. *Pay Services:* Total Pay Subscribers: 7,792; 11/27/92. *Local Advertising Accepted.*

Rogers Cable TV - Grand River (173,000 subscribers). P.O. Box 488, 85 Grand Crest Pl., Kitchener, ON N2G 4A8. (519) 893-2101; FAX: (519) 893-5861. Robert Shaw, gen mgr; Maurice Lovelock, chief tech.
Area(s) Served: ON. Serving Brantford, Cambridge, Kitchener, St. Mary's, Stratford, Waterloo. Homes Served: 173,000. *Channel Capacity:* 54. In use: 54. *Basic Service:* Subscribers: 173,000; 10/15/93. *Pay Services:* Total Pay Subscribers: 25,693; 11/27/93. Pay Per View Subscribers: 27,467; 11/27/93. *Local Advertising Accepted.*

Rogers Cable TV - Hamilton/Niagara (59,332 subscribers). 695 Lawrence Rd., Hamilton, ON L8K 6P1. (416) 547-7836; FAX: (416) 547-5237. Vinnie Welsh, gen mgr.
Area(s) Served: ON. Serving Hamilton, Niagara, Stoney Creek. Homes Served: 59,332. *Channel Capacity:* 55. In use: 55. *Basic Service:* Subscribers: 59,332; 10/15/93. *Pay Services:* Total Pay Subscribers: 10,252; 11/27/92. Pay Per View Subscribers: 10,715; 11/27/92. *Local Advertising Accepted.*

Rogers Cable TV - London (74,985 subscribers). P.O. Box 5800, 800 York St., London, ON N6A 5B1. (519) 672-0030; FAX: (519) 672-0199. Richard Harding, gen mgr; Harry Davis, chief tech.
Area(s) Served: ON. Serving Arva, Dorchester, Hyde Park, Kilworth, Komoka, London, Thamesford. Homes Passed: 91,574. Homes Served: 74,985. *Channel Capacity:* 53. In use: 52. *Basic Service:* Subscribers: 74,985. *Pay Services:* Total Pay Subscribers: 10,778. Pay Per View Subscribers: 11,897. *Local Advertising Accepted.*

Rogers Cable TV - Newmarket (23,337 subscribers). 20 Gladman Ave., Newmarket, ON L3Y 2N2. (416) 895-1604; FAX: (416) 898-7577. Dennis Rosenberg, gen mgr.
Area(s) Served: ON. Serving Ansnorveldt, Bradford, East Gwillimbury, Holland Landing, Mount Albert, Newmarket, River Drive Park, Queensville, Sharon, West Gwillimbury. Homes Served: 23,337. *Channel Capacity:* 51. In use: 51. *Basic Service:* Subscribers: 23,337; 11/27/92. *Pay Services:* Total Pay Subscribers: 4,206; 11/27/92. Pay Per View Subscribers: 4,575; 11/27/92. *Local Advertising Accepted.*

Rogers Cable TV - Ottawa (127,752 subscribers). 1810 St. Laurent Blvd., Ottawa, ON K1G 0N2. (613) 739-5000; FAX: (613) 731-4369. Carol Ring, gen mgr; Wayne Cramp, chief tech.
Area(s) Served: ON. Serving Carleton, Cumberland, Gloucester, Nepean, Osgoode, Ottawa, Rideau, Rockliffe Park, Russell, Vanier. Homes Served: 127,752. *Channel Capacity:* 58. In use: 57. *Basic Service:* Subscribers: 127,752; 10/15/93. *Pay Services:* Total Pay Subscribers: 13,727; 11/27/92. Pay Per View Subscribers: 14,455; 11/27/92. *Local Advertising Accepted.*

Rogers Cable TV - Peel (170,274 subscribers). 3573 Wolfedale Rd., Mississauga, ON L5C 3T6. (416) 273-8000; FAX: (416) 273-9661. George Vehi, gen mgr; Dave Tavenor, chief tech.
Area(s) Served: ON. Serving Brampton, Caledon, Milton, Mississauga. Pop: 300,000. Homes Passed: 188,633. Homes Served: 170,274. *Channel Capacity:* 60. In use: 58. *Basic Service:* Subscribers: 170,274; 08/27/93. *Pay Services:* Total Pay Subscribers: 27,354; 08/27/93. Pay Per View Subscribers: 14,183; 10/31/92. *Local Advertising Accepted.*

Rogers Cable TV - Pine Ridge (72,600 subscribers). 301 Marwood Dr., Oshawa, ON L1H 1J4. (905) 579-1601; FAX: (905) 579-5559. Paul Coleman, gen mgr; Jim Scott, chief tech.
Area(s) Served: ON. Serving Bowmanville, Hampton, Newcastle, Orono, Oshawa, Whitby. Homes Served: 72,600. *Channel Capacity:* 53. In use: 53. *Basic Service:* Subscribers: 72,600; 10/15/93. *Pay Services:* Total Pay Subscribers: 12,240; 08/31/93. Pay Per View Subscribers: 13,280; 11/27/92. *Local Advertising Accepted.*

Rogers Cable TV - Surrey (115,042 subscribers). 10445 - 138th St., Surrey, BC V3T 4X3. (604) 588-1229; FAX: (604) 588-6448. Peter Davison, gen mgr; Susanna Reardon, chief tech.
Area(s) Served: BC. Serving Aldergrove, Langley, New Minster, Surrey. Homes Served: 115,042. *Channel Capacity:* 42. In use: 42. *Basic Service:* Subscribers: 115,042; 10/15/93. *Pay Services:* Total Pay Subscribers: 10,968; 11/27/92. *Local Advertising Accepted.*

Rogers Cable TV - Toronto (409,134 subscribers). 855 York Mills Rd., Don Mills, ON M3B 1Z1. (416) 446-6500; FAX: (416) 446-6003. Dennis Rosenberg, gen mgr; Peter O'Brien, loc adv dir; John Heslip, chief tech.
Area(s) Served: ON. Serving Downsview, East York, North York. Homes Served: 409,134. *Channel Capacity:* 57. In use: 57. *Basic Service:* Subscribers: 409,134; 10/15/93. *Pay Services:* Total Pay Subscribers: 68,983; 11/27/92. Pay Per View Subscribers: 75,200; 11/27/92. *Local Advertising Accepted.*

Rogers Cable TV - Vancouver (291,602 subscribers). Eaton Centre Metrotown, 1600-4710 Kingsway, Burnaby, BC V5H 4M5. (604) 436-1111; FAX: (604) 436-1000. Michael Black, gen mgr; Dennis Davies, chief tech.
Area(s) Served: BC. Serving Burnaby, Kitsilano, Richmond, Vancouver. Homes Served: 291,602. *Channel Capacity:* 46. In use: 44. *Basic Service:* Subscribers: 291,602; 10/15/93. *Pay Services:* Total Pay Subscribers: 34,522; 11/27/92. *Local Advertising Accepted.*

Rogers Cable TV - Victoria (89,252 subscribers). 861 Cloverdale Ave., Victoria, BC V8X 4S7. (604) 381-5050; FAX: (604) 381-4190. Glen Terrell, gen mgr; John Foss, chief tech.
Area(s) Served: BC. Serving Esquimalt, Oak Bay, Saanich, Victoria, View Royal. Homes Served: 89,252. *Channel Capacity:* 50. In use: 48. *Basic Service:* Subscribers: 89,252; 11/27/92. *Pay Services:* Total Pay Subscribers: 6,500; 11/27/92. *Local Advertising Accepted.*

David E. Rolan

Box 56339, Phoenix, AZ 85079. (602) 248-8333; FAX: (602) 248-0690. David E. Rolan, pres. Total Basic Subscribers: 3,000; Pay Cable Subscribers: 900; Number of Cable Systems: 7.

John M. Roskowski

2113 Marydale Ave., Williamsport, PA 17701. (717) 323-8518; FAX: (717) 322-5373. John M. Roskowski, pres. Total Basic Subscribers: 8,900; Pay Cable Subscribers: 3,500; Number of Cable Systems: 2.

SMALLER SYSTEMS

Pennsylvania - Cable Services Co., Inc., 2113 Marydale Ave., Williamsport, PA 17701. River Valley Cable Co., 11 Main St., Millhall, PA 17751; (717) 726-4700.

Rural Missouri Cable TV Inc.

310 Walnut Extension, Branson, MO 65616. (417) 334-7897; FAX: (417) 334-7899. Larry Frazier, CEO & pres; Kay Russell, vp. Total Basic Subscribers: 5,003; Pay Cable Subscribers: 1,391; Number of Cable Systems: 1.

Saguaro Cable Investors L.P.

Suite 230, 513 Wilcox St., Castle Rock, CO 80104. (303) 688-4462; FAX: (303) 688-5001. Owned by Western Cable Inc. Total Basic Subscribers: 7,400; Pay Cable Subscribers: 3,300; Number of Cable Systems: 4.

St. Joseph Cablevision

Box 8069, 102 N. Woodbine, St. Joseph, MO 64506. (816) 279-1234; FAX: (816) 279-8773. Henry H. Bradley, CEO; Douglas Fuller, pres; Elaine Miller, vp opns. Owned by News Press & Gazette Co. Total Basic Subscribers: 26,347; Pay Cable Subscribers: 7,852; Number of Cable Systems: 5.

SYSTEMS WITH OVER 20,000 SUBSCRIBERS

St. Joseph Cablevision (33,000 subscribers). 102 N. Woodbine, St. Joseph, MO 64506. (816) 279-1234; FAX: (816) 279-8773. Douglas Fuller, gen mgr; Dave Wattenbarger, mktg dir; Nancy Black, loc adv dir; Larry Douglas, chief tech; Elaine Miller, cust svc dir.
Area(s) Served: MO. Counties: Andrew, Buchanan, DeKalb. Serving Agency, Country Club Village, Savannah, Union Star. Miles of Plant: 400. Homes Passed: 33,000. Homes Served: 33,000. *Channel Capacity:* 36. In use: 36. *Basic Service:* Subscribers: 26,700; 09/01/93. Programming (via satellite): 28 chs. Programming (off air): 8 chs. *Pay Services:* Total Pay Subscribers: 11,270; 09/01/93. (1) Pay Units: 3,600; 09/01/93. Programming (via satellite): HBO. (2) Pay Units: 2,530; 09/01/93. Programming (via satellite): Showtime. (3) Pay Units: 1,730; 09/01/93. Programming (via satellite): Disney. (4) Pay Units: 1,450; 09/01/93. Programming (via satellite): The Movie Channel. *Local Advertising Accepted. Equipment:* Provided by Jerrold & Zenith.

Sammons Communications Inc.

Suite 800, 3010 LBJ Fwy., Dallas, TX 75234. (214) 484-8888; FAX: (214) 919-5799. Mark S. Weber, pres; Don Amick, vp opns; Sherry Wilson, vp mktg; Geary Stills, vp; Ed Comstock, vp; Sandra Turley, vp. Owned by Sammons Enterprises Inc. Total Basic Subscribers: 1,025,000; Number of Cable Systems: 55.

SYSTEMS WITH OVER 20,000 SUBSCRIBERS

Oxford Valley Cablevision Inc. (42,135 subscribers). Box 445, 1750 Byberry Rd., Bensalem, PA 19020. (215) 638-7770. Alane Sica, gen mgr; Lil Ouslager, mktg dir; Michael Sinback, chief tech.
Area(s) Served: PA. County: Lower Bucks. Serving Bensalem, Falls, Lower Southampton, Morrisville, Tullytown, Upper Southampton, Warminster. Homes Passed: 58,000. Homes Served: 42,135. *Channel Capacity:* 36. In use: 36. *Basic Service:* Subscribers: 42,135; 10/15/93. *Local Advertising Accepted.*

Sammons Cable (21,000 subscribers). 5100 MacPelah Rd., Pascagoula, MS 39567. (601) 769-1121; FAX: (601) 769-6216. Cindy Scearce, gen mgr; Tammy Moore, mktg dir & loc adv dir.
Area(s) Served: MS. County: Jackson. Serving Escatawapa, Gautier, Hurley, Moss Point, Pascagaoula, Wade. Homes Served: 21,000. *Channel Capacity:* 33. *Basic Service:* Subscribers: 21,000; 10/15/93. *Local Advertising Accepted. Equipment:* Provided by Scientific-Atlanta & Maganavox.

Sammons Cable Services (107,000 subscribers). 4528 W. Vickery St., Fort Worth, TX 76107. (817) 737-4731; FAX: (817) 738-7472. Tom Soulsby, gen mgr; Kristie Empey, mktg dir; Doug Wiggins, loc adv dir; John Fram, chief tech.
Area(s) Served: TX. Counties: Johnson, Tarrant. Serving Banbrook, Blue Mound, Burleson, Crowley, Edgecliff, Everman, Forest Hill, Haltom City, Hurst, Keller, Kennedale, Lake Worth, Mansfield, North Richland Hills, Richland Hills, Saginaw, Tarrant, Watauga, Westover Hills, White Settlement. Homes Served: 107,000. *Channel Capacity:* 55. In use: 55. *Basic Service:* Subscribers: 107,000; 10/15/93. *Local Advertising Accepted.*

Sammons Communications (33,903 subscribers). 1846 N. West Blvd., Vineland, NJ 08360. (609) 692-2100; FAX: (609) 692-3971. Michael Taylor, gen mgr; Kelly Tistan, mktg dir; Alex Swider, chief tech.
Area(s) Served: NJ. Counties: Atlantic, Cumberland, Gloucester. Serving Bridgeton, Buena, Hammontown, Hopewell, Millville, Newfield, Shiloh, Upper Deerfield. Miles of Plant: 647. Homes Passed: 49,000. Homes

Multiple Systems Operators, Independent Owners & Cable Systems

Served: 33,903. *Channel Capacity:* 52. In use: 43. *Basic Service:* Subscribers: 33,903; 10/15/93. *Pay Services:* Total Pay Subscribers: 15,000; 12/01/92. *Local Advertising Accepted. Equipment:* Jerrold & Scientific-Atlanta headend; Jerrold, Scientific-Atlanta & Texscan amplifiers; Times & Comm/Scope cable; Sony cameras; Sony VTRs; Atari character generator; Scientific-Atlanta set top converters; Jerrold addressable set top converters; Vitek traps; Andrew, M/A-Com & Microdyne satellite antenna; Andrew, Scientific-Atlanta & Microdyne satellite receivers.

Sammons Communications (24,000 subscribers). Box 1620, Morristown, TN 37816. (615) 586-8700; FAX: (615) 586-9065. Mike Hill, gen mgr; Janie Beck, mktg dir.
Area(s) Served: TN. Counties: Cacke, Grainger, Hamblen, Hancock, Jefferson. Serving Hawkins. Homes Served: 24,000. *Basic Service:* Subscribers: 24,000; 10/15/93. *Local Advertising Accepted.*

Sammons Communications Inc. (73,691 subscribers). Box 5104, 6246 San Fernando Rd., Glendale, CA 91201. (818) 246-1091; FAX: (818) 242-9553. Shirley Orr, gen mgr; Maria Palma, mktg dir; Irv Hammock, chief tech.
Area(s) Served: CA. County: Los Angeles. Serving Burbank, Glendale, La Canada, La Crescenta. Miles of Plant: 603. Homes Passed: 120,900. Homes Served: 73,691. *Channel Capacity:* 40. In use: 40. *Basic Service:* Subscribers: 73,691; 10/15/93. *Local Advertising Accepted.*

Sammons Communications Inc. (24,530 subscribers). 918 Rander Ave., Turlock, CA 95380. (209) 667-5003; FAX: (209) 667-0520. Peggy Thurner, gen mgr; Edward McLean, mktg dir; George Vandell, chief tech.
Area(s) Served: CA. Counties: Merced, Stanislau. Serving Ceres, Delhi, Denair, Nilmar, Stanislau, Turlock. Homes Served: 24,530. *Channel Capacity:* 54. In use: 40. *Basic Service:* Subscribers: 24,530; 10/15/93.

Sammons Communications Inc. (21,366 subscribers). 2302 S. Roan St., Johnson City, TN 37601. (615) 929-2101; FAX: (615) 929-7230. Steve Pollock, gen mgr; George Page, mktg dir; Larry Sparks, chief tech.
Area(s) Served: TN. Counties: Carter, Elizabethton, Johnson City, Washington. Homes Served: 21,366. *Channel Capacity:* 61. In use: 44. *Basic Service:* Subscribers: 21,366; 10/15/93. *Local Advertising Accepted.*

Sammons Communications of Connecticut Inc. (44,214 subscribers). 695 Huntingdon Ave., Waterbury, CT 06708. (203) 755-1178; FAX: (203) 756-1321. Ernest Magaro, gen mgr; Mary Beall, mktg dir; Tom Wolff, chief tech.
Area(s) Served: CT. Counties: Litchfield, New Haven. Serving Middlebury, Platts Mills, Plymouth, Prospect, Terryville, Waterbury, Wolcott. Miles of Plant: 631. Homes Passed: 63,121. Homes Served: 44,214. *Channel Capacity:* 35. In use: 35. *Basic Service:* Subscribers: 44,214; 10/15/93. *Pay Services:* Total Pay Subscribers: 15,260; 11/30/92. Pay Per View Subscribers: 200; 11/30/92. *Local Advertising Accepted. Equipment:* Scientific-Atlanta headend; Magnavox amplifiers; Comm/Scope cable; JVC & Sony cameras; JVC & Sony VTRs; Quanta character generator; Hamlin, Jerrold & Oak set top converters; Simulsat satellite antenna; Scientific-Atlanta satellite receivers; Adams-Russel & Arris commercial insert.

Sammons Communications of Illinois Inc. (24,000 subscribers). Box 218, 401 W. Washington St., Ottawa, IL 61350. (815) 433-1163; FAX: (815) 433-1288. Charlotte Bragg, gen mgr; Debbie Draper, mktg dir; Arnie Brown, chief tech.
Area(s) Served: IL. Serving Dayton, Maneilles, Naplate, Ottawa. Homes Served: 24,000. *Channel Capacity:* 35. In use: 33. *Basic Service:* Subscribers: 24,000; 10/15/93. *Local Advertising Accepted.*

Sammons Communications of New Jersey Inc. (96,151 subscribers). 901 W. Leeds Ave., Absecon, NJ 08201. (609) 641-6700; FAX: (609) 272-0452. Pamela Winand, gen mgr; Michele Miklovich, mktg dir; Thomas Young, chief tech.
Area(s) Served: NJ. Counties: Atlantic, Cape May. Serving Absecon, Atlantic City, Brigantine, Corbin City, Dennis, Egg Harbor, Galloway, Linwood, Longport, Margate City, Northfield, Ocean City, Pinehurst, Port Republic, Somers Point, Upper Twp., Ventnor City, Woodbine. Miles of Plant: 1,075. Homes Served: 96,151. *Channel Capacity:* 47. In use: 47. *Basic Service:* Subscribers: 96,151; 10/15/93. *Local Advertising Accepted. Equipment:* Jerrold & Scientific-Atlanta headend; Magnavox & Scientific-Atlanta amplifiers; Comm/Scope cable; JVC cameras; JVC & Sony VTRs; Texscan & Jerrold addressable set top converters; Hughes, Scientific-Atlanta & Simulsat satellite antenna; Microdyne, Scientific-Atlanta & Standard Communications satellite receivers.

Sammons Communications of New Jersey Inc. (98,000 subscribers). 160 E. Blackwell St., Dover, NJ 07801. (201) 361-6955; FAX: (201) 361-4879. Alan Goldenberg, gen mgr; Diane Kohn, mktg dir; Donald Palmer, chief tech.
Area(s) Served: NJ. Counties: Morris, Sussex. Serving Boonton, Chatham, Denville, East Hanover, Florham Park, Hanover, Hopatcong, Jefferson, Madison, Mine Hill, Montville, Morris Plains, Morristown, Morris, Mount Arlington, Mount Olive, Mountain Lakes, Netcong, Parsippany, Picatinny Arsenal, Randolph, Rockaway, Roxbury, Stanhope, Victory Gardens, Wharton. Miles of Plant: 1,578. Homes Passed: 122,837. Homes Served: 98,000. *Channel Capacity:* 37. In use: 37. *Basic Service:* Subscribers: 98,000; 10/15/93. Pay Per View Subscribers: 33,000; 11/01/91. *Local Advertising Accepted.*

Sammons Communications of Pennsylvania (93,107 subscribers). 4601 Smith St., Harrisburg, PA 17109-1597. (717) 540-8900; FAX: (717) 657-3926. H.E. Lockard, gen mgr; Lynn Wadley, mktg dir; Hank Hall, chief tech.
Area(s) Served: PA. Counties: Adams, Cumberland, Dauphin, Gettysberg, Perry, York. Serving Camp Hill, Carroll, Dauphin, East Pennsboro, Fairview, Hampden, Highspire, Lemoyne, Lower Allen, Lower Paxton, Lower Swatara, Marysville, Mechanicsburg, Middle Paxton, Middletown, Monroe, New Cumberland, New Cumberland Army Depot, Paxtang, Penbrook, Royalton, Shiremanstown, Silver Spring, Steelton, Susquehanna, Swatara, Upper Allen, West Fairview, West Hanover, Wormleysburg. Homes Passed: 120,000. Homes Served: 93,107. *Channel Capacity:* 42. In use: 42. *Basic Service:* Subscribers: 93,107; 10/15/93. *Pay Services:* Total Pay Subscribers: 35,000; 10/31/92. Pay Per View Subscribers: 1,200; 10/31/92. *Local Advertising Accepted.*

Sammons Communications of Pennsylvania, Inc. (26,199 subscribers). Box 639, 1604 Sullivan Trail, Easton, PA 18042. (215) 253-6174; FAX: (215) 253-4301. Mary Vongas, gen mgr; Kim Vitelli, mktg dir; John Turner, chief tech.
Area(s) Served: PA, NJ. Counties: Northampton, Warren. Serving Alpha, Bethlehem, Bloomsbury, Forks, Greenwich, Harmony, Lopatcong, Palmer, Phillipsburg, Plainfield, Pohatcong, Stewartsville, Stockertown, West Easton, Williams, Wilson. Miles of Plant: 459. Homes Passed: 35,000. Homes Served: 26,199. *Channel Capacity:* 54. In use: 46. *Basic Service:* Subscribers: 26,199; 10/15/93. *Pay Services:* Total Pay Subscribers: 10,000; 10/30/92. Pay Per View Subscribers: 1,400; 10/30/92. *Local Advertising Accepted.*

City of San Bruno Municipal Cable TV

567 El Camino Real, San Bruno, CA 94066. (415) 877-8889; FAX: (415) 871-5526. David Thomas, vp opns. Owned by City of San Bruno. Total Basic Subscribers: 11,400; Number of Cable Systems: 1.

Satcom Inc.

Box 427, 220 W. First St., Laurel, MT 59044. (406) 628-2100; FAX: (406) 628-8181. L.P. Hilliard, pres; Ken Young, vp opns; Margaret Hilliard, vp. Owned by L.P. Hilliard, Margaret Hilliard. Total Basic Subscribers: 7,500; Pay Cable Subscribers: 2,250; Number of Cable Systems: 9.

Satellite Cable Services Inc.

Drawer U, De Smet, SD 57231. (605) 854-9133. Richard Cutler, pres & vp opns; Doug Bierschbach, vp. Owned by Richard Cutler, Robert Hayes, David Knutson, Demming Smith. Total Basic Subscribers: 9,200; Pay Cable Subscribers: 2,500; Number of Cable Systems: 57.

Savage Communications Inc.

Suite 216, 4756 Banning Ave., White Bear Lake, MN 55110. (612) 426-9323; FAX: (612) 426-9328. Ron Savage, pres. Owned by Ron Savage, Principal; Mike Danielson, Pat McCabe, Jerry Meier, ltd. ptnrs. Total Basic Subscribers: 6,022; Pay Cable Subscribers: 2,900; Number of Cable Systems: 33.

Schurz Communications Inc.

225 W. Colfax Ave., South Bend, IN 46626. (219) 287-1001. Franklin D. Schurz Jr., pres; James C. Young Jr., CFO. Owned by Franklin D. Schurz, 25%; James M. Schurz, 25%; Mary Schurz, 25%; Scott C. Schurz, 25%. Total Basic Subscribers: 55,000; Number of Cable Systems: 2.

SYSTEMS WITH OVER 20,000 SUBSCRIBERS

Antietam Cable TV (30,000 subscribers). 1000 Willow Cir., Hagerstown, MD 21740. (301) 733-3635; FAX: (301) 797-4829. Gene Hager, gen mgr; Greg Davis, mktg dir & chief tech. *Basic Service:* Subscribers: 30,000; 10/15/93.

Cable TV of Coral Springs Inc. (26,432 subscribers). 12409 N.W. 35th St., Coral Springs, FL 33065. (305) 753-0100; FAX: (305) 345-8164. Wally Snedeker, gen mgr; Michele Fitzpatrick, mktg dir; Rick Scheller, chief tech.
Area(s) Served: FL. County: Broward. Serving Coral Springs. Pop: 88,000. Homes Passed: 35,000. Homes Served: 26,432. *Channel Capacity:* 63. In use: 63. *Basic Service:* Subscribers: 26,432; 09/01/93. *Pay Services:* Total Pay Subscribers: 23,004; 09/01/93. Pay Per View Subscribers: 13,000; 09/01/93. *Local Advertising Accepted.*

Schuylkill Valley Trans Video Corp.

Box 233, Brockton, PA 17925. (717) 668-4460. Dominic A. Vitelli, pres. Total Basic Subscribers: 1,570; Number of Cable Systems: 1.

SCI Investments Inc.

4359 Shire Cove Rd., Hilliard, OH 43026. (614) 771-0504. Michael D. Mahaffey, pres; Dan Borders, vp. Total Basic Subscribers: 1,700; Number of Cable Systems: 7.

Scope Cable TV of Nebraska

Box 600, 1635 Front St., Blair, NE 68008. (402) 426-6434; FAX: (402) 426-6475. Lea Ann Quist, vp. Owned by P.J. Garrigan, S.M. Jensen. Total Basic Subscribers: 6,000; Pay Cable Subscribers: 2,000; Number of Cable Systems: 16.

Scott Telecom Electronics Inc.

Box 489, 125 Woodland St., Gate City, VA 24251. (703) 452-9119; FAX: (703) 452-2447. Lloyd Porter, pres; Ron Schlegel, vp mktg. Owned by Scott Telephone Cooperative. Total Basic Subscribers: 3,000; Pay Cable Subscribers: 750; Number of Cable Systems: 1.

Scripps Howard Cable Co.

Box 5380, Cincinnati, OH 45201. (513) 977-3000; FAX: (513) 977-3768. Larry Leser, pres; Wayne Vowell, vp mktg; F. Steven Crawford, vp. Owned by The E.W. Scripps Company. Total Basic Subscribers: 677,000; Pay Cable Subscribers: 517,100.

SYSTEMS WITH OVER 20,000 SUBSCRIBERS

Atlanta Cluster (66,255 subscribers). 3425 Malone Dr., Atlanta, GA 30341. (404) 451-4788; FAX: (404) 455-0235. Martin O'Keefe, gen mgr; Sandy Eide, mktg dir; Jim Sherman, chief tech; Gale Hovey, cust svc dir.
Area(s) Served: GA, SC, FL. Serving Elberton, Homerville, Louisville, Mount Vernon, North DeKalb, Quitman, Waynesboro; Newberry; Jasper, Madison. Homes Served: 66,255. *Channel Capacity:* 54. In use: 54. *Basic Service:* Subscribers: 66,255; 10/01/93. *Pay Services:* Total Pay Subscribers: 17,000; 11/15/91. *Local Advertising Accepted. Equipment:* Scientific-Atlanta headend & amplifiers.

Chattanooga Cable TV Co. (78,578 subscribers). Box 182249, 2030 E. Polymer Dr., Chattanooga, TN 37422. (615) 855-3900; FAX: (615) 892-5893. James H. Crowdis, gen mgr; Paul A. Maynard, mktg dir; Diana Ward, loc adv dir; Hal Dickey, chief tech; Anita Martin, cust svc dir.
Area(s) Served: TN, GA. Counties: Dade, Hamilton. Serving Chattanooga; Battlefield, Blue Ridge, LaFayette. Pop: 284,000. Miles of Plant: 2,694. Homes Passed: 141,850. Homes Served: 78,578. *Channel Capacity:* 80. In use: 57. *Basic Service:* Subscribers: 78,578; 08/31/93. Programming (via satellite): 49 chs. Programming (via microwave): 1 ch. Programming (off air): 7 chs. *Pay Services:* Total Pay Subscribers: 63,560; 08/31/91. (1) Pay Units: 22,811; 07/24/93. Programming (via satellite): HBO. (2) Pay Units: 17,277; 07/24/93. Programming (via satellite): Showtime. (3) Pay Units: 6,831; 07/24/93. Programming (via satellite): The Movie Channel. (4) Pay Units: 6,279; 07/24/93. Programming (via satellite): Cinemax. Pay Per View

Multiple Systems Operators, Independent Owners & Cable Systems

Subscribers: 26,935; 09/30/93. *Local Advertising Accepted.*

Florida Cluster (45,000 subscribers). Box 490919, Leesburg, FL 34749. (904) 787-7875; FAX: (904) 365-6279. Philip R. Yapkowitz, gen mgr; Randy Ittner, mktg dir; Craig Baggs, loc adv dir; John Wilde, chief tech. *Area(s) Served:* FL. Counties: DeBary, Lake. Serving DeBary, Eustis, Fruitland, Howey-in-the-Hills, Lady Lake, Leesburg, Monteverde, Mount Dora, Mount Plymouth, Sorrento, Tavares, Umatilla. Pop: 200,000. Miles of Plant: 1,235. Homes Passed: 63,000. Homes Served: 45,000. *Channel Capacity:* 36. In use: 36. *Basic Service:* Subscribers: 45,000; 10/01/93. *Pay Services:* Total Pay Subscribers: 15,000; 11/15/91. *Local Advertising Accepted. Equipment:* Scientific-Atlanta headend & amplifiers.

Sacramento Cable (210,570 subscribers). 4350 Pell Dr., Sacramento, CA 95838. (916) 927-2225; FAX: (916) 923-1706. R. Kim Rueckert, gen mgr; Ruth Blank, mktg dir & loc adv dir; Cindy Simonsen, cust svc dir. *Area(s) Served:* CA. County: Sacramento. Serving Citrus Heights, Galt, North Highlands, Orangevale, Sacramento. Miles of Plant: 3,730. Homes Passed: 417,000. Homes Served: 210,570. *Channel Capacity:* 68. In use: 66. *Basic Service:* Subscribers: 210,570; 10/01/93. Programming (via satellite): 41 chs. Programming (off air): 12 chs. *Local Advertising Accepted.*

Scripps Howard Cable Co. of Colorado (31,000 subscribers). 434 Kimbark St., Longmont, CO 80501. (303) 776-6600; FAX: (303) 678-5302. Gregory E. Griffin, gen mgr; Tim Burke, mktg dir; Stan Reifschneider, loc adv dir; Ian Thomas, chief tech. *Area(s) Served:* CO. Counties: Boulder, Garfield, Larimer, Weld. Serving Battlement Mesa, Berthoud, Erie, Fort Lupton, Lafayette, Longmont, Louisville, Loveland, Parachute, Superior. Miles of Plant: 900. Homes Passed: 50,000. *Basic Service:* Subscribers: 31,000; 10/1/93. *Local Advertising Accepted.*

Scripps Howard Cable of Northwest Georgia (42,684 subscribers). 707 E. 1st St., Rome, GA 30161. (706) 291-7288; FAX: (706) 291-3830. Neal Fondren, gen mgr; Greg Hartel, mktg dir; Jackie Moreland, loc adv dir; Billy Gadd, chief tech; Wanda Smith, cust svc dir. *Area(s) Served:* GA. Serving Calhoun, Dallas, Rome, Tallapoosa. Miles of Plant: 1,381. Homes Passed: 52,187. Homes Served: 42,684. *Basic Service:* Subscribers: 42,684; 10/01/93. *Pay Services:* Total Pay Subscribers: 10,630; 09/15/91. *Local Advertising Accepted.*

Scripps Howard Cable TV Co. of Knoxville (95,832 subscribers). 614 N. Central Ave., Knoxville, TN 37917. (615) 637-5411; FAX: (615) 637-8805. Barbara Lewis, gen mgr; Angela Bush, mktg dir; Tim Kiser, loc adv dir; Willy Porter, chief tech; Patsy Harris, cust svc dir. *Area(s) Served:* TN, KY. Serving Knoxville, LaFollette; Barbourville. Miles of Plant: 2,400. Homes Passed: 144,742. Homes Served: 95,832. *Channel Capacity:* 36. In use: 36. *Basic Service:* Subscribers: 95,832; 08/31/93. *Pay Services:* Total Pay Subscribers: 40,520; 11/11/91. *Local Advertising Accepted.*

TeleScripps Cable (50,336 subscribers). 1901 Leatherwood Ln., Bluefield, WV 24701. (304) 325-6206; FAX: (304) 325-7376. Don Kersey, gen mgr. *Area(s) Served:* WV, TN. Serving Bluefield; Glade Spring, Gray, Greenville. Homes Served: 50,336. *Basic Service:* Subscribers: 50,336; 10/01/93.

TeleScripps Cable of Western Kentucky (39,676 subscribers). 2919 Ring Rd., Elizabethtown, KY 42701. (502) 765-2731; FAX: (502) 737-3379. Doug McMillan, gen mgr. *Area(s) Served:* KY, IN, TN. Serving Campbellsville, Elizabethtown, Glasgow, Greenville-Central City; Tell City; Livingston. Homes Served: 39,676. *Basic Service:* Subscribers: 39,676; 10/01/93.

Semo Communications Inc.

Box C, Sikeston, MO 63801. (314) 471-6594; FAX: (314) 471-6878. Travis E. Garrett, pres. Owned by Travis E. Garrett. Total Basic Subscribers: 1,470; Pay Cable Subscribers: 400; Number of Cable Systems: 7.

Service Electric Cablevision Inc.

Suite 255, 1259 S. Cedar Crest Blvd., Allentown, PA 18103. (215) 432-2210; FAX: (215) 438-8262. Hoyt D. Walter, pres. Owned by Service Electric Cable T.V. Inc. Total Basic Subscribers: 205,300; Pay Cable Subscribers: 21,000; Number of Cable Systems: 7.

SYSTEMS WITH OVER 20,000 SUBSCRIBERS

Service Electric Cable TV Inc. (82,000 subscribers). 2260 Ave. A, Bethlehem, PA 18017. (215) 865-9100; FAX: (215) 865-5031. Jack Capparell, gen mgr. *Basic Service:* Subscribers: 82,000; 11/30/93.

Service Electric Cable TV of NJ Inc. (34,801 subscribers). Suite 303, 270 Sparta Ave., Sparta, NJ 07871. (201) 729-7653. Ron Debelko, gen mgr. *Basic Service:* Subscribers: 34,801; 11/30/93.

Service Electric Cablevision, Inc. (22,000 subscribers). Box R, Hazleton, PA 18201-0076. (717) 454-3841; FAX: (717) 454-3652. Robert Trently, gen mgr. *Basic Service:* Subscribers: 22,000; 11/30/93.

Service Electric Co. (28,292 subscribers). 15 J Campbell Collins Dr., Wilkes-Barre, PA 18702. (717) 825-8508. Ed Ganc, gen mgr. *Basic Service:* Subscribers: 28,292; 11/30/93.

SMALLER SYSTEMS

Pennsylvania - Service Electric Cablevision, Box 8, Birdsboro, PA 19508; (215) 582-5317; 14,000 subs. Service Electric Cablevision, Box 587, Bloomsburg, PA 17815; (717) 784-5979; 7,000 subs. Service Electric Co., 201 W. Centre St., Mahanoy City, PA 17948. (717) 773-2585; 17,282 subs.

Shen-Heights TV Associates Inc.

38 N. Main St., Shenandoah, PA 17976. (717) 462-1911; FAX: (717) 462-1948. Martin Brophy, pres. Owned by Martin Brophy. Total Basic Subscribers: 4,000; Pay Cable Subscribers: 500; Number of Cable Systems: 1.

Shenandoah Telecommunications Inc.

Box 459, Edinburg, VA 22824. (703) 984-4140. Christopher French, pres; Dave Fergerson, vp prom; Gail Payne, vp. Total Basic Subscribers: 2,500; Pay Cable Subscribers: 519; Number of Cable Systems: 1.

John P. Shoemaker Jr. dba Chatmoss Cablevision

Box 5064, Martinsville, VA 24115. (804) 685-1521. John P. Shoemaker Jr., pres; Charles Lewis, vp opns. Owned by John P. Shoemaker Jr. Total Basic Subscribers: 1,215; Pay Cable Subscribers: 627; Number of Cable Systems: 1.

Showcase Communications II Inc.

37 N. Fullerton Ave., Montclair, NJ 07042. (201) 744-5540; FAX: (201) 744-5563. Richard Levinson, pres. Owned by Richard Levinson. Total Basic Subscribers: 5,800; Number of Cable Systems: 17.

Shrewsbury's Community Cablevision

100 Maple Ave., Shrewsbury, MA 01545. (508) 845-4881; FAX: (508) 842-9419. Wayne Collen, vp opns; Suzanne Foley, vp mktg; Thomas Josie, vp. Owned by Municipality of Shrewsbury. Total Basic Subscribers: 8,700; Pay Cable Subscribers: 4,043; Number of Cable Systems: 1.

Simmons Communications Inc.

Suite 400, One Landmark Sq., Stamford, CT 06901. (203) 359-0455; FAX: (203) 325-3110. Steve Simmons, CEO & chmn; Bruce Armstrong, pres & vp mktg; John Flanagan, CFO; Day Patterson, vp; Jerry Earl, vp; Steve Fox, vp. Owned by Steve Simmons. Total Basic Subscribers: 178,133; Number of Cable Systems: 26.

John Sinclair dba AAA Cable TV Inc.

Box 604, Brownsburg, IN 46112. (317) 745-7368; FAX: (317) 745-2189. John Sinclair, pres; David Sinclair, vp opns. Owned by John Sinclair. Total Basic Subscribers: 3,000; Pay Cable Subscribers: 500; Number of Cable Systems: 1.

Sjoberg's Cable TV Inc.

315 N. Main St., Thief River Falls, MN 56701. (218) 681-3044; FAX: (218) 681-6801. Richard Sjoberg, pres; Stan Sjoberg, vp. Owned by Richard Sjoberg, 50%; Stan Sjoberg, 50%. Total Basic Subscribers: 8,000; Pay Cable Subscribers: 2,000; Number of Cable Systems: 11.

SLT Cable TV

Box 432, Mexia, TX 76667. (817) 562-5359; FAX: (817) 562-9254. R.C. Brown III, CEO & pres; Charles Schuchard, CFO; Terry Beeler, vp opns. Owned by SLT Communications Inc. Total Basic Subscribers: 6,600; Number of Cable Systems: 12.

Small Cities Cable TV Ltd.

Box 190, 2050 Shelburne Rd., Shelburne, VT 05482. (802) 985-3308; FAX: (802) 985-2872. Paul J. Growald, chmn; Sharon Arnell, vp opns; Steve Schouten, vp mktg; Steve Schuyler, vp. Total Basic Subscribers: 4,000; Pay Cable Subscribers: 1,700; Number of Cable Systems: 1.

Souris River Tele-Communications Cooperative

Box 2027, Minot, ND 58702-2027. (701) 852-1151; FAX: (701) 722-2290. Clayton Fegley, pres; Donovan Arnold, vp. Total Basic Subscribers: 1,500; Pay Cable Subscribers: 400; Number of Cable Systems: 14.

South Dakota Cable Inc.

Box 309, R.R. 8C55 Box 400, Sturgis, SD 57785. (800) 658-3456; FAX: (605) 347-3499. William Duhamel Jr., pres; Steve Duffy, vp opns. Owned by Helen & William Duhamel. Total Basic Subscribers: 14,000; Pay Cable Subscribers: 5,000; Number of Cable Systems: 8.

SMALLER SYSTEMS

South Dakota - South Dakota Cable, Belle Fourche, SD. South Dakota Cable, Blackhawk, SD. South Dakota Cable, Custer, SD. South Dakota Cable, Deadwood, SD. South Dakota Cable, Hot Springs, SD. South Dakota Cable, Piedmont, SD. South Dakota Cable, Spearfish, SD. South Dakota Cable, Sturgis, SD.

Southeast Cable TV Inc.

Box 584, 107 S. Main St., Boston, GA 31626. (912) 498-4191; FAX: (912) 498-1026. James F. Cavanaugh, pres; Bob Heide, vp opns. Owned by James F. Cavanaugh, 50%; Bob Heide, 50%. Total Basic Subscribers: 1,500; Pay Cable Subscribers: 500; Number of Cable Systems: 7.

SMALLER SYSTEMS

Florida - Southeast Cable, Hosford, FL. Southeast Cable, Keaton Beach, FL. Southeast Cable, White Springs, FL. **Georgia** - Southeast Cable, Boston, GA. Southeast Cable, Coolidge, GA. Southeast Cable, Ochlocknee, GA. Southeast Cable, Pavo, Ga.

Southern Cable Communications

Box 1998, Georgetown, SC 29442. (803) 546-2200; FAX: (803) 527-2314. Ronald J. Charlton, CEO & pres; Ronand J. Charlton, chmn; Keith Harper, CFO; Rita Wilson, vp opns; Bonnie Charlton, vp mktg; Robert Adkison, vp. Total Basic Subscribers: 3,000; Pay Cable Subscribers: 900; Number of Cable Systems: 6.

SMALLER SYSTEMS

North Carolina - Bald Head Island-Southern Cable Communications, Georgetown, SC; 400 subs. **South Carolina** - Clarendon County-Southern Cable Communications, Georgetown, SC; 800 subs. Dunes West-Southern Cable Communications, Georgetown, SC; 150 subs. Lakeview/Nicoles-Southern Cable Communications, Georgetown, SC; 800 subs. Little River-Southern Cable Communications, Georgetown, SC; 250 subs. Marion County-Southern Cable Communications, Georgetown, SC; 600 subs.

Southland Cablevision Inc.

Box 1348, 127 Jackson St., Vidalia, GA 30474. (912) 537-3996; FAX: (912) 537-7233. Wade O'Neal, pres; Charles P. Gillis, vp opns. Owned by Wade O'Neal, 100%. Total Basic Subscribers: 2,500; Pay Cable Subscribers: 3,000; Number of Cable Systems: 1.

Southwest Missouri Cable TV Inc.

Box 696, Carthage, MO 64836. (417) 358-3002; FAX: (417) 358-1845. Ruth I. Kolpin, CEO & vp progmg; Dean Petersen, pres & vp opns; John Burken, CFO; Ralph Latimer, vp mktg; Craig Burford, vp adv. Owned by Ruth I. Kolpin, Dean Petersen. Total Basic Subscribers:

Multiple Systems Operators, Independent Owners & Cable Systems

10,000; Pay Cable Subscribers: 3,900; Number of Cable Systems: 1.

Southwestern Cable Investments Corporation

Box 1656, 119 E. Fourth, Hereford, TX 79045. (806) 364-3912; FAX: (806) 364-7147. Wendell Mayes Jr., CEO; Lloyd Ames, vp opns. Total Basic Subscribers: 3,950; Pay Cable Subscribers: 1,350; Number of Cable Systems: 1.

Southwestern CATV Inc.

Box 171, No. 1 Big Rock Blvd., Medicine Park, OK 73557. (405) 529-2288; FAX: (405) 529-5225. Steven Hillary, pres. Owned by Edward & Steven Hillary. Total Basic Subscribers: 1,500; Number of Cable Systems: 5.

Splitrock Telecom Cooperative Inc.

Box 349, 612 3rd St., Garretson, SD 57030. (605) 594-3411; FAX: (605) 594-6776. Don Snyders, vp opns. Total Basic Subscribers: 1,725; Pay Cable Subscribers: 1,725; Number of Cable Systems: 1.

SRW Inc.

71 Cedar Ave., Hershey, PA 17033. (717) 533-3322; FAX: (717) 533-3344. Richard Snyder, pres; Paul Whipple, CFO; John Weidman, vp; Fred G. Vogelsong, vp. Owned by Richard Snyder, Paul Whipple, John Weidman. Total Basic Subscribers: 11,905; Pay Cable Subscribers: 3,252; Number of Cable Systems: 17.

SMALLER SYSTEMS

Maryland - SRW Cablevision, Deep Creek Lake, MD; 1,408 subs. **North Carolina** - SRW Cablevision, Creston, NC; 332 subs. SRW Cablevision, Meat Camp, NC; 229 subs. SRW Cablevision, Roan Fork, NC; 43 subs. SRW Cablevision, Zionville, NC; 1,209 subs. **Ohio** - SRW Cablevision, Albany, OH; 1,600 subs. **Pennsylvania** - Broad Top Cable TV, Broad Top City, PA; 656 subs. Broad Top Cable TV, Defiance, PA; 725 subs. Broad Top Cable TV, SWR Mill Creek, PA; 380 subs. Broad Top Cable TV, Williamsburg, PA; 887 subs. SRW Cable TV, Messiah Village, PA; 401 subs. SRW Cablevision, Meyersdale, PA; 1,488 subs. **Tennessee** - SRW Cablevision, Butler/Stoney Creek, TN; 1,256 subs. SRW Cablevision, Crackers Neck, TN; 326 subs. SRW Cablevision, Erwin, TN; 179 subs. SRW Cablevision, Laurel Bloomery, TN; 337 subs. SRW Cablevision, Simerly Creek, TN; 449 subs.

St. Croix Cable TV

Box 5968, Heron Commercial Park, St. Croix, VI 00823. (809) 778-6701; FAX: (809) 778-5230. John Klindworth, pres; Keith A. Kirkman, vp opns. Number of Cable Systems: 1.

St. Marys TV

314 S. Michael St., St. Marys, PA 15857. (814) 781-1466; FAX: (814) 834-1706. Frank Vitarelli, pres. Owned by Vitarelli Family, Cletas Heller. Total Basic Subscribers: 6,700; Number of Cable Systems: 1.

Standard Tobacco Co. Inc.

Box 100, 626 Forest Ave., Maysville, KY 41056. (606) 564-5678; FAX: (606) 564-4291. James A. Finch Jr., CEO & pres; Ronald Buerkley, vp opns; Ivan Cracraft, vp; Pauline H. Bierlin, vp. Owned by James A. Finch Jr., 90%; Barbara Tucker, 10%. Total Basic Subscribers: 5,500; Number of Cable Systems: 2.

Star Cable Associates

Suite 100, 381 Mansfield Ave., Pittsburgh, PA 15220. (412) 937-0099; FAX: (412) 937-0145. James C. Roddey, pres; Richard W. Talarico, CFO; Michael R. Haislip, vp opns; Matthew M. Polka, vp. Owned by Star Cable Associates. Total Basic Subscribers: 61,568; Pay Cable Subscribers: 34,398; Number of Cable Systems: 6.

SMALLER SYSTEMS

Louisiana - Star Cable Associates, 1000 W. Lasalle, Ville Platte, LA 70586; 7,823 subs. **North Carolina** - Star Cable Associates, 651 S. Main, Box 950, Dobson, NC 27017; 15,782 subs. **Ohio** - Star Cable Associates, 5537 Mahoning Ave., Box 4458, Youngstown, OH 44515; 8,780 subs. **South Carolina** - 101 W. Park Blvd., Columbia, SC 29210; 8,091 subs. **Texas** - Star Cable Associates, 800 Hwy. 36 N., Bldg. 3, Suite 132, Drawer 1570, Brazoria, TX 77422; 15,018 subs. Star Cable Associates, 200 Scurry St., Box 626, Daingerfield, TX 75638; 4,040 subs.

Starwest Inc.

Box 177, Atkins, IA 52206. (319) 446-7858; FAX: (319) 446-7858. John Stookesberry, pres. Owned by John Stookesberry. Total Basic Subscribers: 1,250; Pay Cable Subscribers: 936; Number of Cable Systems: 8.

SMALLER SYSTEMS

Iowa - Starwest Inc., Atkins, IA. Starwest Inc., Brighton, IA. Starwest Inc., Fairfax, IA. Starwest Inc., Farmington, IA. Starwest Inc., Fremont, IA. Starwest Inc., Hedrick, IA. Starwest Inc., Keosauqua, IA. Starwest Inc., Richland, IA.

State Cable TV Corporation

261 State St., Augusta, ME 04330. (207) 623-5145; FAX: (207) 623-3407. Michael Angelakis, CEO & pres; Edward Barlow, chmn; Kenneth E. Danielson, CFO; Perian Phillips, vp mktg. Owned by Whitney Communication Corporation. Total Basic Subscribers: 62,800; Pay Cable Subscribers: 25,500; Number of Cable Systems: 11.

SMALLER SYSTEMS

Maine - State Cable TV Corp., Augusta, ME. State Cable TV Corp., Jay, ME. State Cable TV Corp., Norway, ME. State Cable TV Corp., Pittsfield, ME. State Cable TV Corp., Rumford, ME. State Cable TV Corp., Waterville, ME. **New Hampshire** - State Cable TV Corp., Conway, NH. State Cable TV Corp., Freedom, NH. State Cable TV Corp., Lincoln, NH. State Cable TV Corp., Littleton, NH. State Cable TV Corp., Plymouth, NH.

Staten Island Cable

100 Cable Way, Staten Island, NY 10303. (718) 447-7000; FAX: (718) 816-8433. Stephen Pagano, pres; Chris Van Name, vp mktg. Owned by 50% owned by Cox Cable Communications; 50% owned by Time Warner Cable. Total Basic Subscribers: 80,000; Number of Cable Systems: 1.

Stephen Cable TV Inc.

Box 9, Stephen, MN 56757. (218) 478-3074; FAX: (218) 478-3074. David Sunsdahl, pres. Owned by David Sunsdahl. Total Basic Subscribers: 1,000; Pay Cable Subscribers: 320; Number of Cable Systems: 6.

SMALLER SYSTEMS

Minnesota - Stephen Cable TV, Alvarado, MN; 125 subs. Stephen Cable TV, Argyle, MN; 217 subs. Stephen Cable TV, Kennedy, MN; 115 subs. Stephen Cable TV, Lake Bronson, MN; 115 subs. Stephen Cable TV, Lancaster, MN; 136 subs. Stephen Cable TV, Stephen, MN; 290 subs.

Stuck Electric Inc.

147 W. Main, Sheridan, OR 97378. (503) 843-2322. Donald Stuck, pres; Velna Stuck, vp. Owned by Donald & Velna Stuck. Total Basic Subscribers: 1,750; Number of Cable Systems: 1.

Sully Buttes Telephone Cooperative Inc.

218 Commercial S.E., Highmore, SD 57345. (605) 852-2224; FAX: (605) 852-2404. Total Basic Subscribers: 1,211; Pay Cable Subscribers: 303; Number of Cable Systems: 12.

SMALLER SYSTEMS

South Dakota - Sully Buttes Telephone Cooperative, Blunt, SD; 130 subs. Sully Buttes Telephone Cooperative, Harrold, SD; 62 subs. Sully Buttes Telephone Cooperative, Highmore, SD; 334 subs. Sully Buttes Telephone Cooperative, Hitchcock, SD; 54 subs. Sully Buttes Telephone Cooperative, Hoven, SD; 199 subs. Sully Buttes Telephone Cooperative, Langford, SD; 124 subs. Sully Buttes Telephone Cooperative, Onaka, SD; 21 subs. Sully Buttes Telephone Cooperative, Ree Heights, SD; 27 subs. Sully Buttes Telephone Cooperative, Seneca, SD; 27 subs. Sully Buttes Telephone Cooperative, Tolstoy, SD; 27 subs. Sully Buttes Telephone Cooperative, Tulare, SD; 98 subs. Sully Buttes Telephone Cooperative, Wessington, SD; 108 subs.

Summit Communications Group Inc. (Atlanta, GA)

115 Perimeter Ctr. Pl., Atlanta, GA 30346. (404) 394-0707; FAX: (404) 394-9778. James Wesly Jr., CEO, chmn & pres; Adrian Cox, vp. Owned by Gordon Gray Family. Total Basic Subscribers: 151,727; Pay Cable Subscribers: 92,391; Number of Cable Systems: 3.

SYSTEMS WITH OVER 20,000 SUBSCRIBERS

Summit Cable Services of Forsyth County Inc. (78,682 subscribers). Box 2954, Winston-Salem, NC 27102. (919) 785-3390; FAX: (919) 785-9899. Adrian E. Cox, gen mgr; Jackie Johnson, mktg dir; David B. Schien, chief tech; Vicky Thaxton, cust svc dir.
Area(s) Served: NC. County: Forsyth. Serving Bermuda Run, Clemmons, Kernersville, Lewisville, Rural Hall, Winston-Salem. Pop: 218,713. Miles of Plant: 1,909. Homes Passed: 121,740. Homes Served: 78,682. *Channel Capacity:* 54. In use: 46. *Basic Service:* Subscribers: 78,682; 08/31/93. *Pay Services:* Total Pay Subscribers: 50,564; 08/31/93. (1) Pay Units: 22,777; 08/31/93. Programming (via satellite): HBO. (2) Pay Units: 15,441; 08/31/93. Programming (via satellite): Showtime. (3) Pay Units: 5,537; 08/31/93. Programming (via satellite): Cinemax. Pay Per View Subscribers: 616; 08/31/93. *Local Advertising Accepted.*

Summit Cable Services of Georgia Inc. (56,500 subscribers). Box 220, Woodstock, GA 30188. (404) 926-0334; FAX: (404) 924-0429. John C. Howell, gen mgr; Eleanor McClintock, mktg dir; Glyndell Moore, chief tech.
Area(s) Served: GA. Counties: Cobb, Cherokee, Fulton. Serving Roswell, Woodstock. *Basic Service:* Subscribers: 56,500; 12/31/93.

SMALLER SYSTEMS

North Carolina - Summit Cable Services of Thom-A-Lex Inc., Box 667, Lexington, NC 27293; (704) 249-7444.

Summit Communications Inc. (Bellevue, WA)

Suite 107, 3633 136th Pl. S.E., Bellevue, WA 98006. (206) 747-4600; FAX: (206) 644-4621. James A. Hirschfield, pres; Robert J. Erickson, CFO; Wilmot Lilly, vp opns. Owned by James A. Hirshfield, 92%. Total Basic Subscribers: 30,865; Pay Cable Subscribers: 12,000; Number of Cable Systems: 30.

Sumner Cable TV Co.

117 W. Harvey, Wellington, KS 67152. (316) 326-8989; FAX: (316) 326-3290. Philip Brown, vp opns. Total Basic Subscribers: 3,100; Number of Cable Systems: 1.

Susquehanna Cable Co.

140 E. Market St., York, PA 17401. (717) 848-5500; FAX: (717) 771-1439. Louis J. Appell Jr., chmn; Peter B. Brubaker, pres. Owned by Susquehanna Pfaltzgraff. Total Basic Subscribers: 111,000; Number of Cable Systems: 7.

SYSTEMS WITH OVER 20,000 SUBSCRIBERS

Cable TV of York (50,000 subscribers). 1050 E. King St., York, PA 17403. (717) 854-1912; FAX: (717) 843-5400. James D. Munchel, gen mgr; Brad Schofield, mktg dir; Wayne Stambaugh, chief tech; Brenda Winter, cust svc dir.
Area(s) Served: PA. County: York. Serving Dallastown, Dover, Hellam, Manchester, Spring Garden, Spring-Ettsbury, West York, York, York Twp. Miles of Plant: 900. Homes Passed: 68,000. Homes Served: 50,000. *Channel Capacity:* 41. In use: 41. *Basic Service:* Subscribers: 50,000; 10/31/93. Programming (via satellite): 30 chs. Programming (via microwave): 1 ch. Programming (off air): 10 chs. *Pay Services:* Total Pay Subscribers: 17,000; 10/24/92. Pay Per View Subscribers: 28,500; 10/24/92. *Local Advertising Accepted.*

SMALLER SYSTEMS

Maine - Casco Cable, 192 Front St., Bath, ME 04530; (207) 443-2231; 14,000 subs.

Multiple Systems Operators, Independent Owners & Cable Systems

Sutton Capital Group

231 E. 35th St., New York, NY 10016. (212) 686-8022; FAX: (212) 686-8083. William H. Ingram, pres; Cathy M. Brienza, vp. Owned by William H. Ingram & Cathy M. Brienza. Total Basic Subscribers: 175,000; Pay Cable Subscribers: 168,500; Number of Cable Systems: 3.

SYSTEMS WITH OVER 20,000 SUBSCRIBERS

Riverview Cablevision Associates L.P. (44,700 subscribers). 360 1st St., Hoboken, NJ 07030. (201) 798-1614; FAX: (201) 798-4163. Gregory Arnold, gen mgr; Tina Segali, mktg dir; Gregory Maugeri, loc adv dir; Michael Lotempio, chief tech.
Area(s) Served: NJ. County: Hudson. Serving Hoboken, North Bergen, Union City, Weehawken, West New York. Pop: 150,000. Miles of Plant: 127. Homes Passed: 85,000. Homes Served: 44,700. *Channel Capacity:* 41. In use: 41. *Basic Service:* Subscribers: 44,700; 11/20/92. Programming (via satellite): NICK, CNBC, AMC, ESPN, TNT, MSG, VH-1, QVC, Headline News, CNN, WTBS, MTV, Galavision, Lifetime, Weather, USA, Learning, Discovery, A&E, Travel Channel, Valuevision, Sci-Fi Channel, E!-TV, Video Juke-Box. Programming (off air): WCBS, WNBC, WNYW, WABC, WXTV, NPIX, WNET, WNTV, WNJM, WNYC, WWOR, WPIX, WNJV, WHSE. *Pay Services:* Total Pay Subscribers: 38,000; 11/20/92. (1) Pay Units: 21,000; 11/20/92. Programming (via satellite): HBO. (2) Pay Units: 7,000; 11/20/92. Programming (via satellite): Cinemax. (3) Pay Units: 6,000; 11/20/92. Programming (via satellite): Disney. (4) Pay Units: 2,000; 11/20/92. Programming (via satellite): SportsChannel. (5) Pay Units: 1,000; 11/20/92. Programming (via satellite): Playboy. Pay Per View Subscribers: 42,800; 11/20/92. *Local Advertising Accepted. Equipment:* Provided by Jerrold.

Sweetwater Cable TV Co. Inc.

Box 8, 602 Broadway, Rock Springs, WY 82901. (307) 362-3773; FAX: (307) 382-2781. Albert M. Carollo Sr., chmn; Albert M. Carollo Jr., pres; James R. Carollo, vp; John B. Carollo, vp; Leona Carollo, vp. Owned by Albert M. Carollo Jr., 25%; James R. Carollo, 25%; John B. Carollo, 25%; Albert M. Carollo Sr., 17%; Leona Carollo, 8%. Total Basic Subscribers: 12,923; Pay Cable Subscribers: 9,325; Number of Cable Systems: 3.

SMALLER SYSTEMS

Wyoming - Sweetwater Cable TV, Green River, WY. Sweetwater Cable TV, Rock Springs, WY. Sweetwater Cable TV, Wamsutter, WY.

Taconic Technology Corporation

Taconic Pl., Chatham, NY 12037. (518) 392-3500; FAX: (518) 392-3699. Lorinda Ackley, pres; Dan Yamin, vp opns. Owned by Taconic Telephone Co. Total Basic Subscribers: 4,234; Pay Cable Subscribers: 1,100; Number of Cable Systems: 1.

TBA Inc.

1975 Taylor Rd., East Cleveland, OH 44112. (216) 851-9423; FAX: (216) 851-1445. Alfred H. Quarles, pres; Louis Rivituso, vp mktg. Owned by Alfred H. Quarles. Total Basic Subscribers: 5,500; Number of Cable Systems: 3.

TCA Cable TV Inc.

Box 130489, 3015 ESE Loop 323, Tyler, TX 75713-0489. (903) 595-3701; FAX: (903) 595-1929. Robert M. Rogers, CEO; Fred Nichols, pres; Jimmy Taylor, CFO; Sue Saxenmeyer, vp mktg; Martha S. Hensley, vp. Total Basic Subscribers: 420,000; Number of Cable Systems: 54.

SYSTEMS WITH OVER 20,000 SUBSCRIBERS

Lafayette Cable TV (48,000 subscribers). 714 Eraste Landry Rd., Lafayette, LA 70506. (318) 232-6323; FAX: (318) 234-8376. Steve Creeden, gen mgr; Nicole Blair, mktg dir; Shanna Higgin Botham, loc adv dir; Harvard Bryan, chief tech; Greg Uselton, cust svc dir.
Area(s) Served: LA. Counties: Lafayette, St. Martin, Vermilion. Serving Broussard, Carencro, Duson, Maurice, Milton, Scott. Miles of Plant: 1,200. Homes Passed: 72,000. Homes Served: 48,000. *Channel Capacity:* 45. In use: 45. *Basic Service:* Subscribers: 48,000; 10/15/93. Pay Per View Subscribers: 38,000; 11/15/92. *Local Advertising Accepted. Equipment:* Scientific-Atlanta headend; C-COR amplifiers; Tocom set top converters; Scientific-Atlanta satellite antenna; Scientific-Atlanta satellite receivers.

TCA Cable of Amarillo (44,000 subscribers). 5880 W. 45th St., Amarillo, TX 79109. (806) 358-4801; FAX: (806) 354-7419. Brady DeBord, gen mgr; Vel Allen, mktg dir; Troy Grider, chief tech; Dan Spoelman, cust svc dir.
Area(s) Served: TX. Counties: Potter, Randall. Serving Amarillo, Canyon. Pop: 170,000. Miles of Plant: 900. Homes Passed: 77,000. Homes Served: 44,000. *Channel Capacity:* 40. In use: 36. *Basic Service:* Subscribers: 44,000; 09/01/93. Programming (via satellite): 31 chs. Programming (off air): 5 chs. *Pay Services:* Total Pay Subscribers: 27,000; 11/25/92. (1) Pay Units: 7,576; 11/25/92. Programming (via satellite): HBO. (2) Pay Units: 6,323; 11/25/92. Programming (via satellite): Showtime. (3) Pay Units: 4,067; 11/25/92. Programming (via satellite): The Movie Channel. (4) Pay Units: 4,483; 11/25/92. Programming (via satellite): Cinemax. *Local Advertising Accepted. Equipment:* Jerrold converters; C-COR line equipment; Scientific-Atlanta headend.

TCA Cable TV - Bryan (33,000 subscribers). 4114 E. 29th St., Bryan, TX 77802. (409) 846-2229; FAX: (409) 268-0139. Randy Rogers, gen mgr; Jeanne Kipp, mktg dir; Pat Clark, chief tech; Sharon Streger, cust svc dir.
Area(s) Served: TX. County: Brazos. Serving Bryan, College Station. Homes Passed: 45,000. Homes Served: 33,000. *Channel Capacity:* 39. In use: 39. *Basic Service:* Subscribers: 33,000; 10/15/93. *Pay Services:* Total Pay Subscribers: 13,000; 12/15/92. Pay Per View Subscribers: 10,000; 09/30/91. *Local Advertising Accepted.*

SMALLER SYSTEMS

Texas - TCA Cable, 209 W. 4th St., Hearne, TX 77859-2507; (409) 279-5201; 1,500 subs.

Tekstar Cablevision Inc.

150 2nd Ave. S.W., Perham, MN 56573. (218) 346-2288; FAX: (218) 346-5510. Eleanor Arvig, chmn; Allen Arvig, pres. Owned by Arvig Enterprises Inc. Total Basic Subscribers: 13,842; Pay Cable Subscribers: 3,800; Number of Cable Systems: 6.

SMALLER SYSTEMS

Minnesota - Tekstar Cablevision, Tower Rd., Detroit Lakes, MN 56501. Tekstar Cablevision, New York Mills, MN 56567. Tekstar Cablevision, Perham, MN 56573. Tekstar Cablevision, Twin Valley, MN 56584. Tekstar Cablevision, Walker, MN 56484. Tekstar Cablevision, Wall Lake, MN 56515.

Tel-Com Inc.

Box 159, Harold, KY 41635. (606) 478-9406; FAX: (606) 478-3650. Paul Gerhart, pres; James Cambell, vp opns. Total Basic Subscribers: 23,000; Number of Cable Systems: 1.

Tele-Cable Service Corporation

2455 Stirrup Rd., Borrego Springs, CA 92004. (619) 767-5607; FAX: (619) 767-3609. A.A. Burnand III, pres; Dorothy J. Barnett, CFO; Arthur C. Barnett, vp. Owned by A.A. Burnand III. Total Basic Subscribers: 1,400; Number of Cable Systems: 1.

Tele-Communications Inc.

Box 5630, Denver, CO 80217. (303) 721-5500; FAX: (303) 488-3209. John C. Malone, CEO & pres; Bob Magness, chmn; Stephen Brett, vp; Larry Romrell, vp; Robert Lewis, vp. Total Basic Subscribers: 10,200,000; Pay Cable Subscribers: 7,668,215; Number of Cable Systems: 692.

SYSTEMS WITH OVER 20,000 SUBSCRIBERS

American Cable L.P. Five (25,000 subscribers). 113 Country Village Rd., Dagsboro, DE 19939. (302) 732-6600. Dave Kane, gen mgr. *Basic Service:* Subscribers: 25,000; 11/30/93.

Billings Tele-Communications Inc. (24,000 subscribers). Suite 6, 1124 16th St. W., Billings, MT 59102. (406) 245-3051. Kenneth Watts, gen mgr; Vicky Wynne, mktg dir; Randi Frieze, cust svc dir.
Area(s) Served: MT. County: Yellowstone. Miles of Plant: 450. Homes Passed: 42,000. Homes Served: 24,000. *Pay Services:* Total Pay Subscribers: 11,000; 11/15/91. *Local Advertising Accepted. Equipment:* Jerrold headend.

Cablevision of Baton Rouge Ltd. (97,700 subscribers). 5428 Florida Blvd., Baton Rouge, LA 70806. (504) 923-0256; FAX: (504) 925-1668. Mike Ross, gen mgr; Gary Galle, mktg dir; Randy Harman, loc adv dir; Dave Matthews, chief tech.
Area(s) Served: LA. County: Baton Rouge Parish. Serving Baton Rouge. Pop: 380,000. Miles of Plant: 1,600. Homes Passed: 154,500. Homes Served: 97,700. *Channel Capacity:* 39. In use: 39. *Basic Service:* Subscribers: 97,700; 10/31/91. *Local Advertising Accepted. Equipment:* Scientific-Atlanta, RCA & Tocom headend; C-COR & Century III amplifiers; Comm/Scope cable.

Chicago Cable TV (200,000 subscribers). 5711 South-western Ave., Chicago, IL 60636. (312) 434-6976. Morgan McChesney, gen mgr; Sandra Jostes, mktg dir; Tom Scanlin, chief tech.
Area(s) Served: IL. Serving Chicago (zones 1,4,5). Homes Passed: 540,000. Homes Served: 200,000. *Channel Capacity:* 60. *Basic Service:* Subscribers: 200,000; 11/30/93.

Daniels Cablevision Inc. (50,000 subscribers). 5720 El Camino Real, Carlsbad, CA 92008. (619) 438-7741; FAX: (619) 438-8461. Joni Odum, gen mgr; Susan Otto, mktg dir; Mike Canizaro, loc adv dir; Don Williams, chief tech; Jeff Nyberg, cust svc dir.
Area(s) Served: CA. County: San Diego. Serving Carlsbad, Del Mar, Encinitas, Fallbrook, Lake San Marcos. Pop: 150,000. Miles of Plant: 675. Homes Passed: 65,000. Homes Served: 50,000. *Channel Capacity:* 62. In use: 56. *Basic Service:* Subscribers: 50,000. Programming (via satellite): 43 chs. Programming (via microwave): 1 ch. Programming (off air): 12 chs. Pay Per View Subscribers: 20,000. *Local Advertising Accepted. Equipment:* Scientific-Atlanta headend & converters; Texscan inserters; C-COR amplifiers; Sony decks.

District Cablevision (259,000 subscribers). 900 Michigan Ave., Washington, DC 20017. (202) 332-7000; FAX: (202) 462-4064. Mike Mason, gen mgr; Don Fitzgerald, chief tech.
Area(s) Served: DC. Pop: 660,000. Miles of Plant: 901. Homes Passed: 259,000. Homes Served: 259,000. *Channel Capacity:* 60. In use: 57. *Basic Service:* Subscribers: 79,547; 10/20/91. *Local Advertising Accepted.*

Foothills Cablevision Ltd. (50,500 subscribers). 1041 E. Alosta Ave., Glendora, CA 91740. (818) 914-4382; FAX: (818) 335-9581. Thomas A. Prevette, gen mgr; Jessica Barcena, mktg dir; Jose Leon, chief tech.
Area(s) Served: CA. Counties: Los Angeles, San Bernardino. Serving Arcadia, Bradburg, Glendora, La Verne, Monrovia, Rialto, San Bernardino, San Dimas, Sierra Madre. Pop: 400,000. Miles of Plant: 1,100. Homes Passed: 112,000. *Channel Capacity:* 60. In use: 54. *Basic Service:* Subscribers: 50,500; 10/31/91. Pay Per View Subscribers: 36,000. *Local Advertising Accepted. Equipment:* Jerrold addressable converters; Scientific-Atlanta, RCA & Texscan amplifiers.

Miami Tele-Communications Inc. (39,000 subscribers). 1306 N.W. 7th Ave., Miami, FL 33106. (305) 326-1574; FAX: (305) 325-8741. Don Foster, gen mgr; Sonny Malone, chief tech; Gladys Espinoza, cust svc dir.
Area(s) Served: FL. Serving Miami, Opalocka. Homes Passed: 166,000. *Channel Capacity:* 52. In use: 52. *Basic Service:* Subscribers: 39,000; 10/15/91. *Pay Services:* Total Pay Subscribers: 27,000; 10/15/91.

Mile Hi Cablevision (91,556 subscribers). 1617 S. Acoma St., Denver, CO 80223. (303) 744-9696; FAX: (303) 778-2912. Stephen Santambria, gen mgr; Rhonda Dorchester, mktg dir; Deborah Friday, loc adv dir.
Area(s) Served: CO. Counties: Arapahoe, Denver. Serving Denver, Glendale, Lowry Air Force Base. Pop: 600,000. Miles of Plant: 1,200. Homes Passed: 240,000. Homes Served: 91,556. *Channel Capacity:* 62. In use: 62. *Basic Service:* Subscribers: 91,565; 10/15/91. *Pay Services:* Total Pay Subscribers: 70,788; 10/15/91. (1) Pay Units: 5,582; 10/15/91. Programming (via satellite): Disney. (2) Pay Units: 33,921; 10/15/91. Programming (via satellite): HBO. (3) Pay Units: 18,878; 10/15/91. Programming (via satellite): Cinemax. (4) Pay Units: 3,577; 10/15/91. Programming (via satellite): The Movie Channel. (5) Pay Units: 6,882; 10/15/91. Programming (via satellite): Showtime. *Local Advertising Accepted.*

Newport News Cablevision (47,000 subscribers). 179 Louise Dr., Newport News, VA 23601. (804) 595-6969; FAX: (804) 595-2396. Bill Moore, gen mgr; Beth Matthews, mktg dir; Brian Saunders, loc adv dir; Brian Schade, chief tech; Catherine Gunderson, cust svc dir.
Area(s) Served: VA. Serving Newport News. Pop: 355,000. Miles of Plant: 752. Homes Passed: 74,000. Homes Served: 47,000. *Channel Capacity:* 55. In use:

Multiple Systems Operators, Independent Owners & Cable Systems

55. *Basic Service:* Subscribers: 47,000. Programming (off air): 9 chs. *Pay Services:* Total Pay Subscribers: 45,500; 11/15/91. *Local Advertising Accepted. Equipment:* Scientific-Atlanta & Jerrold headend; GTE & Jerrold amplifiers; Comm/Scope & Times Fiber cable.

Southland Cablevision (44,000 subscribers). 1722 Orange Tree Ln., Redlands, CA 92373. (909) 798-3588; FAX: (909) 793-8941. Kathy Ouillette, gen mgr; Bob Stice, mktg dir; Robert Haithcook, chief tech; Laurie Maynard, cust svc dir.
Area(s) Served: CA. Counties: Riverside, San Bernardino. Serving Beaumont, Calimesa, Colton, East Highland, Loma Linda, March Air Force Base, Mentone, Moreno Valley, Perris, Redlands, Yucaipa. Pop: 220,000. Miles of Plant: 760. Homes Passed: 84,000. Homes Served: 44,000. *Channel Capacity:* 36. In use: 36. *Basic Service:* Subscribers: 44,000; 10/15/91. *Local Advertising Accepted. Equipment:* Jerrold & Scientific-Atlanta headend; C-COR & Scientific-Atlanta amplifiers; Comm/Scope cable.

St. Louis Tele-Communications Inc. (55,000 subscribers). 4940 Delmar Blvd., St. Louis, MO 63108. (314) 361-7300. Greg Schacher, gen mgr; Debra Sanders, loc adv dir.
Area(s) Served: MO. Serving St. Louis. Homes Served: 55,000. *Channel Capacity:* 52. *Basic Service:* Subscribers: 55,000; 11/30/93. *Local Advertising Accepted.*

Storer Cable (46,000 subscribers). 9825 S.W. 72nd St., Miami, FL 33173. (305) 595-0924; FAX: (305) 598-3944. Maureen O'Neill, gen mgr; Leslie Brown, chief tech.
Area(s) Served: FL. County: Dade. Miles of Plant: 886. Homes Passed: 82,376. Homes Served: 46,000. *Channel Capacity:* 51. In use: 51. *Basic Service:* Subscribers: 46,000; 09/30/92. *Pay Services:* Total Pay Subscribers: 23,351; 09/30/91. *Local Advertising Accepted. Equipment:* Microdyne & Phasecom headend; RCA amplifiers; Comm/Scope cable; Sony VTRs; Compuvid character generator; Jerrold & Scientific-Atlanta set top converters.

Storer Cable Communications Inc. (50,000 subscribers). 5990 S. Monticello Dr., Montogomery, AL 36117. (205) 277-4455; FAX: (205) 260-8333. Jack Gilbert, gen mgr; Cass Chandler, mktg dir; Jack Clarke, loc adv dir; Gerald Williams, chief tech.
Area(s) Served: AL. County: Montgomery. Pop: 275,000. Miles of Plant: 1,000. Homes Passed: 70,000. Homes Served: 50,000. *Channel Capacity:* 61. In use: 61. *Basic Service:* Subscribers: 50,000; 11/30/93. *Local Advertising Accepted.*

TCI Cable (33,511 subscribers). 1275 N. Water St., Decatur, IL 62521. (217) 424-8450; FAX: (217) 429-0170. Fred Furnish, gen mgr; Al Waterman, mktg dir; Ralph Duff, chief tech; Sharon Froan, cust svc dir.
Area(s) Served: IL. County: Macon. Serving Decatur, Elwin, Forsyth, Mount Zion. Pop: 100,000. Miles of Plant: 503. Homes Passed: 43,000. Homes Served: 33,511. *Channel Capacity:* 31. In use: 31. *Basic Service:* Subscribers: 33,511. Programming (via satellite): 25 chs. Programming (off air): 6 chs. *Local Advertising Accepted.*

TCI Cable (43,000 subscribers). 1900 N. Fares Ave., Evansville, IN 47711. (812) 422-1167; FAX: (812) 428-2427. Delores Gatlin, gen mgr; Brett A. Pfender, mktg dir; Doris Dausman, cust svc dir.
Area(s) Served: IN. County: Vanderburgh. Serving Darmstadt, Vanderburgh. Pop: 169,000. Miles of Plant: 702. Homes Passed: 70,000. Homes Served: 43,000. *Channel Capacity:* 54. In use: 46. *Basic Service:* Subscribers: 43,000; 11/15/91. *Local Advertising Accepted. Equipment:* Scientific-Atlanta headend; C-COR amplifiers; Times cable.

TCI Cable (25,000 subscribers). Box 23, St. Joseph, MI 49085. (616) 429-3265; FAX: (616) 429-3749. Ronald Linn, gen mgr; Wendy Henry, mktg dir; Ron Sevison, chief tech.
Area(s) Served: MI. Counties: Berrien, Van Buren. Serving Bainbridge, Berrien Springs, Berrien Twp., Lincoln, Oronoko, Royalton, St. Joseph, Shoreham, Sodus, Stevensville. Miles of Plant: 863. Homes Passed: 43,475. Homes Served: 25,000. *Channel Capacity:* 35. In use: 35. *Basic Service:* Subscribers: 25,000; 11/30/93. *Pay Services:* Total Pay Subscribers: 13,398; 11/30/93. *Local Advertising Accepted.*

TCI Cable (30,000 subscribers). 1441 Woodward St., Abilene, TX 79605. (915) 698-3585; FAX: (915) 698-0319. Don Thornton, gen mgr.
Area(s) Served: TX. Counties: Taylor, Tye. *Basic Service:* Subscribers: 30,000.

TCI Cable of Brookhaven (65,000 subscribers). Industrial Rd., Port Jefferson Station, NY 11776. (516) 928-4900; FAX: (516) 928-5712. Scott D. Neesley, gen mgr; Edward O'Hare, mktg dir; Christopher Raskopf, loc adv dir; Leonard T. Muscato, chief tech; Nancy Duran, cust svc dir.
Area(s) Served: NY. County: Suffolk. Serving Bellport, Lake Grove, Patchogue, Poquott. Pop: 420,000. Miles of Plant: 1,000. Homes Passed: 82,600. Homes Served: 65,000. *Channel Capacity:* 60. In use: 54. *Basic Service:* Subscribers: 65,000; 11/30/93. Pay Per View Subscribers: 17,500; 12/11/91. *Local Advertising Accepted. Equipment:* Scientific-Atlanta headend; Scientific-Atlanta amplifiers; Comm/Scope & Times Fiber cable.

TCI Cable of Central Indiana (26,755 subscribers). 633 Jackson St., Anderson, IN 46016. (317) 649-0407; FAX: (317) 649-1532. Craig McCrystal, gen mgr; Rich DeMarco, loc adv dir; Mike Etherington, chief tech; Kathy Norton, cust svc dir.
Area(s) Served: IN. County: Madison. Serving Anderson, Chesterfield, Edgewood, Pendleton. Pop: 85,000. Miles of Plant: 545. Homes Served: 26,755. *Channel Capacity:* 47. In use: 47. *Basic Service:* Subscribers: 26,755; 11/15/91. *Local Advertising Accepted. Equipment:* Scientific-Atlanta headend; C-COR amplifiers; Times Fiber cable.

TCI Cable of Colorado (37,000 subscribers). 2190 E. 104th Ave., Thornton, CO 80233. (303) 450-2200; FAX: (303) 790-0550. Art Lee, gen mgr; Rhonda Dorchester, mktg dir; Debbie Friday, loc adv dir.
Area(s) Served: CO. Counties: Adams, Arapahoe, Douglas, Jefferson. Serving Northglenn, Highlands Ranch, Littleton, Thornton, Wheat Ridge. Homes Passed: 66,000. Homes Served: 37,000. *Channel Capacity:* 52. In use: 52. *Basic Service:* Subscribers: 37,000; 12/01/92. *Pay Services:* Total Pay Subscribers: 30,000; 09/15/91. *Local Advertising Accepted.*

TCI Cable of Georgia (28,550 subscribers). Box 1707, 509 Flint Ave., Albany, GA 31703. (912) 883-4414; FAX: (912) 883-2086. James M. Walker, gen mgr; Jeff Cochran, mktg dir; Ron Hoover, chief tech.
Area(s) Served: GA. Counties: Dougherty, Lee. Serving Albany, Leesburg, Pine Glen, Putney. Miles of Plant: 839. Homes Passed: 43,891. Homes Served: 28,550. *Channel Capacity:* 64. In use: 60. *Basic Service:* Subscribers: 28,550; 11/30/93. *Pay Services:* Total Pay Subscribers: 16,000; 10/15/91. *Local Advertising Accepted. Equipment:* Jerrold headend; AEL & GTE Sylvania amplifiers; Times cable; Sony VTRs; MSI character generator; Comtech satellite antenna.

TCI Cable of Louisiana (20,000 subscribers). 725 Benton Rd., Bossier City, LA 71111. (318) 747-1666; FAX: (318) 746-2186. Jim Niswender, gen mgr; Lee Anderson, chief tech; Joe Tabuchi, cust svc dir.
Area(s) Served: LA. County: Bossier Parish. Serving Barksdale Air Force Base, Fillmore, Haughton, Princeton. Miles of Plant: 500. Homes Passed: 31,000. Homes Served: 20,000. *Channel Capacity:* 33. In use: 32. *Basic Service:* Subscribers: 20,000; 11/15/91. *Pay Services:* Total Pay Subscribers: 17,000; 11/15/91. Pay Per View Subscribers: 17,000; 11/15/91. *Local Advertising Accepted.*

TCI Cable of Oklahoma (160,000 subscribers). 6650 E. 44th St., Tulsa, OK 74145. (918) 665-1990; FAX: (918) 665-0590. Rick Comfort, gen mgr; Kelly Schneider, mktg dir; Vic Bailey, loc adv dir; Ernest Staten, chief tech; Pat Ross, cust svc dir.
Area(s) Served: OK. Counties: Creek, Rogers, Tulsa, Wagner. Serving Bristow, Broken Arrow, Claremore, Drumright, Jenks, Owasso, Sapulpa, Tulsa. Pop: 500,000. Miles of Plant: 2,900. Homes Passed: 260,000. Homes Served: 160,000. *Channel Capacity:* 40. In use: 40. *Local Advertising Accepted.*

TCI Cable of Scottsdale (40,800 subscribers). 7661 E. Gray Rd., Scottsdale, AZ 85260. (602) 948-8355; FAX: (602) 483-1359. Nancy Schamadan, gen mgr; Dan Hayes, mktg dir; Dan Myers, chief tech; Dan Corbelli, cust svc dir.
Area(s) Served: AZ. County: Maricopa. Serving Carefree, Scottsdale. Pop: 133,000. Miles of Plant: 852. Homes Passed: 73,200. Homes Served: 40,800. *Channel Capacity:* 60. In use: 60. *Basic Service:* Subscribers: 40,800. Programming (via satellite): 50 chs. Programming (via microwave): 1 ch. Programming (off air): 8 chs. *Local Advertising Accepted.*

TCI Cable of the Midlands (32,000 subscribers). 1500 Wall St., Bellevue, NE 068005. (402) 292-4044; FAX: (402) 292-9366. Julie Breeling, mktg dir; J. Liebenguth, loc adv dir; Randy Parker, chief tech; Kit Timmons, cust svc dir.
Area(s) Served: NE. Counties: Douglas, Sarpy. Serving Bellevue, La Vista, Omaha, Papillion, Ralston. Pop: 150,000. Miles of Plant: 500. Homes Passed: 45,000. Homes Served: 32,000. *Channel Capacity:* 36. *Basic Service:* Subscribers: 32,000; 11/15/91. Pay Per View Subscribers: 28,000; 11/15/91. *Local Advertising Accepted. Equipment:* Scientific-Atlanta & Jerrold headend; Scientific-Atlanta & Jerrold amplifiers; Comm/Scope & Times Fiber cable.

TCI Cable of Westchester (80,000 subscribers). 609 Center Ave., Mamaroneck, NY 10543. (914) 899-9020; FAX: (914) 381-5650. Scott Brown, gen mgr; Sam Pizzano, mktg dir; Marguerite Tolliver, loc adv dir; Cameron Gough, chief tech; Kevin Liga, cust svc dir.
Area(s) Served: NY. County: Westchester. Serving Ardsley, Bronxville, Dobbs Ferry, East Chester, Elmsford, Greenburg, Hastings-on-Hudson, Irvington, Larchmont, Mamaroneck, New Rochelle, New Castle, Pelham, Pelham Manor, Rye, Rye Brook, Scarsdale, Tuckahoe, White Plains. Miles of Plant: 1,000. Homes Passed: 120,000. Homes Served: 80,000. *Channel Capacity:* 78. In use: 41. *Local Advertising Accepted.*

TCI Cablevision (82,388 subscribers). Suite E, 2840 Howe Rd., Martinez, CA 94553. (510) 372-0290. Joe Haber, gen mgr; Terry Hamlin, mktg dir; John Goucher, chief tech.
Area(s) Served: CA. Serving Alamo, Blackhawk, Clyde, Concord Naval Weatpon Station, Contra Costa, Danville, Diablo, Lafayette, Martinez, Marago, Orinda, Pleasant Hill, San Roman, Walnut Creek Station. Homes Passed: 96,437. *Channel Capacity:* 43. *Basic Service:* Subscribers: 82,388. *Local Advertising Accepted.*

TCI Cablevision (59,033 subscribers). Box 667, Branford, CT 06405. (203) 481-3434. Blaine Randles, gen mgr; Kelly Hulin, mktg dir; Frank Yaskin, chief tech.
Area(s) Served: CT. County: New Haven. Serving Branford, East Haven, Guilford, Madison, North Branford, North Haven, Wallingford. Homes Passed: 71,262. Homes Served: 59,033. *Channel Capacity:* 64. *Basic Service:* Subscribers: 59,033; 11/30/93. *Pay Services:* Total Pay Subscribers: 27,724; 11/30/93. *Local Advertising Accepted.*

TCI Cablevision (28,525 subscribers). 940 12th St., Vero Beach, FL 32960. (407) 567-3444; FAX: (407) 778-9635. James Foody, gen mgr; David Davis, mktg dir; Jim Goins, chief tech; Akemi Walker, cust svc dir.
Area(s) Served: FL. Counties: Indian River, St. Lucie. Miles of Plant: 500. Homes Passed: 35,000. Homes Served: 28,525. *Channel Capacity:* 52. In use: 48. *Basic Service:* Subscribers: 28,525; 11/30/93. *Local Advertising Accepted. Equipment:* Scientific-Atlanta headend; Jerrold amplifiers; Comm/Scope & Times Fiber cable.

TCI Cablevision (41,627 subscribers). 300 Carpenter Blvd., Carpentersville, IL 60110. (708) 428-6171; FAX: (708) 428-8560. Darrell Schmitz, gen mgr; Ben McConnell, loc adv dir; Les Wood, chief tech; Jill Bures, cust svc dir.
Area(s) Served: IL. Counties: Kane, McHenry. Serving Algonquin, Cady, Carpentersville, Crystal Lake, Dundee, Fox River Grove, Huntley. Pop: 100,000. Miles of Plant: 569. Homes Passed: 41,627. Homes Served: 41,627. *Channel Capacity:* 53. In use: 53. *Basic Service:* Subscribers: 31,965; 11/30/93. Programming (via satellite): 39 chs. Programming (off air): 14 chs. *Pay Services:* Total Pay Subscribers: 20,969; 10/26/91. (1) Pay Units: 11,668; 10/26/91. Programming (via satellite): HBO. (2) Pay Units: 2,332; 10/26/91. Programming (via satellite): Cinemax. (3) Pay Units: 2,067; 10/26/91. Programming (via satellite): Showtime. (4) Pay Units: 982; 10/26/91. Programming (via satellite): The Movie Channel. (5) Pay Units: 3,704; 10/26/91. Programming (via satellite): Disney. Pay Per View Subscribers: 15,796; 10/26/91. *Local Advertising Accepted. Equipment:* Jerrold Starcom VII.

TCI Cablevision (39,000 subscribers). Box 978, Muskegon, MI 49443. (616) 733-0818; FAX: (616) 733-0426. Jim Flood, gen mgr.
Area(s) Served: MI. Counties: Muskegon, Newaygo, Ottawa. Serving Brooks, Cedar Creek, Dalton, Dayton, Egelston, Everett, Fremont, Ferrysburg, Fruitland, Fruitport, Garfield, Holton, Laketon, Muskegon, Muskegon Heights, Muskegon Twp., North Muskegon, Norton Shores, Roosevelt Park, Sheridan, Sherman, Spring Lake, Spring Lake Twp., Sullivan. Homes Served: 39,000. *Channel Capacity:* 35. In use: 35. *Basic Service:* Subscribers: 39,000; 11/30/93. *Local Advertising Accepted. Equipment:* Scientific-Atlanta headend; Theta-Com amplifiers; Belden & CCS Hatfield cable;

Multiple Systems Operators, Independent Owners & Cable Systems

Sony VTRs; Jerrold & Standard Components set top converters; Andrew & Scientific-Atlanta satellite antenna; Andrew, Scientific-Atlanta satellite receivers.

TCI Cablevision (26,000 subscribers). 820 N.W. Cornell, Corvallis, OR 97330. (503) 758-8808. Gary Hofstettler, gen mgr; Anita Jackson, mktg dir.
Area(s) Served: OR. Serving Adair Village, Corvallis, Millersburg, Philomath. *Channel Capacity:* 34. *Basic Service:* Subscribers: 26,000; 11/15/91.

TCI Cablevision (100,000 subscribers). 934 E. Centerville Rd., Garland, TX 75041. (214) 840-2388; FAX: (214) 271-4535. Theresa Kirk-Fowler, gen mgr; Wanda Dorchester, mktg dir; Paul Arvin, chief tech.
Area(s) Served: TX. Counties: Dallas, Rockwell. Serving Rowlett, Sunnyvale. Miles of Plant: 2,388. Homes Passed: 205,985. Homes Served: 100,000. *Channel Capacity:* 46. In use: 46. *Basic Service:* Subscribers: 100,000; 11/30/93. *Pay Services:* Total Pay Subscribers: 88,544; 09/30/91. *Local Advertising Accepted.*

TCI Cablevision (20,000 subscribers). 451 S. Durbin, Casper, WY 82601. (307) 265-3130; FAX: (307) 266-6821. Jeff Frankenberger, gen mgr; Debbie Ridgely, mktg dir; Dick Monahan, loc adv dir; John Miller, chief tech.
Area(s) Served: WY. County: Natrona. Serving Bar Nunn, Casper, Evansville, Mills, Paradise Valley. Pop: 50,000. Miles of Plant: 300. Homes Passed: 30,000. Homes Served: 20,000. *Channel Capacity:* 40. In use: 40. *Basic Service:* Subscribers: 20,000; 09/15/93. *Pay Services:* Total Pay Subscribers: 10,500; 09/15/93. Pay Per View Subscribers: 5,800; 09/15/93. *Local Advertising Accepted. Equipment:* Jerrold headend; Magnavox amplifiers; Comm/Scope & Times cable.

TCI Cablevision of Alabama Inc. (20,000 subscribers). Box 360268, Hoover, AL 35236. (205) 822-8731; FAX: (205) 823-0353. Barry Kerr, gen mgr; Sherry Brewer, mktg dir.
Area(s) Served: AL. Counties: Calhoun, Cherokee, Jefferson, Shelby. Serving Bluff Park, Center Point, Centre, Fairfield, Hoover, Hueytown, Midfield, Piedmont, Pleasant Grove, Riverchase, Rocky Ridge, Shades Mountain, Tarrant, Vestavia Hills. *Channel Capacity:* 60. *Local Advertising Accepted.*

TCI Cablevision of Alameda (20,000 subscribers). 2061 Challenger Dr., Alameda, CA 94501. (510) 865-2917; FAX: (510) 522-2481. Elaine Barden, gen mgr; Jack Morton, chief tech; Elaine Tirsell, cust svc dir.
Area(s) Served: CA. County: Alameda. Serving Alameda. Pop: 77,500. Miles of Plant: 148. Homes Passed: 31,781. Homes Served: 20,000. *Channel Capacity:* 78. In use: 65. *Basic Service:* Subscribers: 20,000; 10/25/91. *Pay Services:* Total Pay Subscribers: 7,742; 10/25/91. (1) Pay Units: 5,957; 10/25/91. Programming (via satellite): HBO. (2) Pay Units: 3,097; 10/25/91. Programming (via satellite): Showtime. (3) Pay Units: 2,547; 10/25/91. Programming (via satellite): Disney. (4) Pay Units: 2,203; 10/25/91. Programming (via satellite): Cinemax. (5) Pay Units: 2,105; 10/25/91. Programming (via satellite): Encore. (6) Pay Units: 816; 10/25/91. Programming (via satellite): SportsChannel. Pay Per View Subscribers: 14,798; 10/25/91. *Local Advertising Accepted. Equipment:* Jerrold Starcom VI, VI+, VII.

TCI Cablevision of Annapolis (21,435 subscribers). 914 Bay Ridge Rd., Annapolis, MD 21403. (410) 268-7551; FAX: (410) 268-1758. William Forest, gen mgr; Sharon DeArmond, mktg dir; Jim Scott, chief tech; Toni Scarborough, cust svc dir.
Area(s) Served: MD. County: Anne Arundel. Serving Annapolis. Miles of Plant: 485. Homes Passed: 35,605. Homes Served: 21,435. *Channel Capacity:* 54. In use: 54. *Basic Service:* Subscribers: 21,435. Programming (via satellite): 25 chs. Programming (off air): 14 chs. *Local Advertising Accepted. Equipment:* Jerrold addressable converters.

TCI Cablevision of Asheville (27,000 subscribers). 172 Charlotte St., Asheville, NC 28801. (704) 255-0000; FAX: (704) 253-4236. Dan Martin, gen mgr; Sabrina Williams, mktg dir; Steve Curtis, loc adv dir; Dean McCracken, chief tech.
Area(s) Served: NC. County: Buncombe. Serving Arden, Ashville, Biltmore Forest, Fairview, Skyland. Pop: 80,000. Miles of Plant: 550. Homes Passed: 39,000. Homes Served: 27,000. *Channel Capacity:* 38. In use: 38. *Basic Service:* Subscribers: 27,000; 11/15/91. *Pay Services:* Total Pay Subscribers: 18,500; 11/15/91. Pay Per View Subscribers: 16,000; 11/15/91. *Local Advertising Accepted. Equipment:* Jerrold & Scientific-Atlanta headend; Jerrold & Scientific-Atlanta amplifiers; Comm/Scope & Times Fiber cable.

TCI Cablevision of California (48,445 subscribers). 106 Whispering Pines Dr., Scotts Valley, CA 95066. (408) 439-5000; FAX: (408) 439-5065. Stewart Butler, gen mgr; Mary C. Schlotterer, mktg dir; Jack Yearwood, loc adv dir; Lori Eddlemon, cust svc dir.
Area(s) Served: CA. County: Santa Cruz. Serving Aptos, Ben Lomand, Scotts Valley. Miles of Plant: 789. Homes Passed: 67,360. Homes Served: 48,445. *Channel Capacity:* 78. In use: 64. *Basic Service:* Subscribers: 48,445; 11/15/91. Pay Per View Subscribers: 33,000; 11/15/91. *Local Advertising Accepted. Equipment:* Jerrold headend.

TCI Cablevision of California Inc. (36,700 subscribers). 47770 Westinghouse Dr., Fremont, CA 94539. (510) 490-8445; FAX: (510) 490-1627. Lee Perron, gen mgr; Rebecca Haugh, mktg dir; Rick Schick, chief tech.
Area(s) Served: CA. County: Alameda. Serving Fremont. Homes Passed: 64,000. Homes Served: 36,700. *Channel Capacity:* 32. In use: 32. *Basic Service:* Subscribers: 36,700; 11/15/92. *Pay Services:* Total Pay Subscribers: 33,000.

TCI Cablevision of Cape Cod (48,000 subscribers). 10 Old Townhouse Rd. E., South Yarmouth, MA 02664. (508) 771-3700; (508) 432-6900; FAX: (508) 394-1015. Joseph Pietrowski, chief tech.
Area(s) Served: MA. County: Barnstable. Serving Barnstable, Chatham, Dennis, Harwich, Yarmouth. Miles of Plant: 1,100. Homes Served: 48,000. *Channel Capacity:* 50. In use: 50. *Basic Service:* Subscribers: 48,000; 11/30/93. *Pay Services:* Total Pay Subscribers: 17,000; 11/19/91. *Local Advertising Accepted. Equipment:* Jerrold & Scientific-Atlanta headend; Jerrold & Scientific-Atlanta amplifiers; Comm/Scope & Times cable; Ikegami cameras; JVC VTRs; Texscan character generator; Jerrold & Pioneer set top converters; Anixter, Harris & Scientific-Atlanta satellite antennas; Texscan commercial insert.

TCI Cablevision of Central Connecticut (167,914 subscribers). 91 Shield St., West Hartford, CT 06110. (203) 677-9599; FAX: (203) 548-2052. Ron Roe, gen mgr; Peter Cirelli, mktg dir; Ray Kowalinski, chief tech; Dianne Deutchman, cust svc dir.
Area(s) Served: CT. Counties: Hartford, Tolland. Serving Andover, Avon, Berlin, Bloomfield, Bolton, Bristol, Burlington, Canton, East Hartford, Ellington, Farmington, Hebron, Marlborough, New Britian, Plainville, Simsbury, Tolland, Vernon, West Hartford, Windsor. Miles of Plant: 2,753. Homes Passed: 263,099. Homes Served: 167,914. *Channel Capacity:* 46. In use: 46. *Basic Service:* Subscribers: 167,914; 10/15/91. *Local Advertising Accepted. Equipment:* Scientific-Atlanta headend; Magnavox & Jerrold amplifiers; Times Fiber & Belden Wire cable.

TCI Cablevision of Central Illinois (56,589 subscribers). 3517 N. Dries Ln., Peoria, IL 61604. (309) 686-2600; FAX: (309) 688-9828. Jeanne Coleman, gen mgr; Michelle Heap, mktg dir; Kent Furnish, chief tech; Mary Jo Roberts, cust svc dir.
Area(s) Served: IL. Counties: Peoria, Tazewell, Woodford. Serving Bartonville, Bellevue, Creve Coeur, East Peoria, Hollis, Kickapoo, Limestone, Medina, Norwood, Peoria Heights, Richwoods, Sunnyland, Tazewell, Washington, West Peoria. Pop: 386,000. Miles of Plant: 920. Homes Passed: 83,000. Homes Served: 56,589. *Channel Capacity:* 27. *Basic Service:* Subscribers: 56,589; 11/15/91. Programming (via satellite): 29 chs. Programming (via microwave): 5 chs. Programming (off air): 5 chs. *Pay Services:* Total Pay Subscribers: 41,000; 11/15/91. *Local Advertising Accepted. Equipment:* Scientific-Atlanta headend; Jerrold, Scientific-Atlanta & C-COR amplifiers; Times cable; ANI pay per view; ARU digital phone switch; Zeinth scrambling PM-Z system.

TCI Cablevision of Colorado Inc. (25,000 subscribers). Box 576, 620 W. Ninth St., Pueblo, CO 81003. (719) 546-1090; FAX: (719) 546-1597. Joseph Stackhouse, gen mgr; Jim Bell, loc adv dir; Sid Maddux, chief tech.
Area(s) Served: CO. County: Pueblo. Miles of Plant: 617. Homes Passed: 46,500. Homes Served: 25,000. *Channel Capacity:* 40. In use: 40. *Basic Service:* Subscribers: 25,000; 10/24/91. Pay Per View Subscribers: 3,500; 10/24/91. *Local Advertising Accepted. Equipment:* Jerrold headend; Jerrold amplifiers, Times cable.

TCI Cablevision of Dallas (105,000 subscribers). 1565 Chenault St., Dallas, TX 75228. (214) 328-2882; FAX: (214) 320-7336. Steve Crawford, gen mgr; Bennie Wilcox, chief tech.
Area(s) Served: TX. County: Dallas. Serving Dallas, Farmers Branch, Mesquite. Miles of Plant: 4,386. Homes Passed: 438,079. *Channel Capacity:* 100. In use: 100. *Basic Service:* Subscribers: 105,000; 10/31/91. *Pay Services:* Total Pay Subscribers: 90,000; 11/15/91. *Local Advertising Accepted.*

TCI Cablevision of Dubuque Inc. 3033 Asbury Rd., Dubuque, IA 52001. (319) 557-8020. Pat Dunn, chief tech.
Area(s) Served: IA.

TCI Cablevision of East Texas (34,000 subscribers). 322 N. Glenwood Blvd., Tyler, TX 75702. (903) 595-4321; FAX: (903) 593-6189. Vince Thomas, gen mgr; Kathy Lasater, mktg dir; Mogan Porter, loc adv dir; Dennis Watts, chief tech; Polly Beckley, cust svc dir.
Area(s) Served: TX. Counties: Cuerokee, Smith. Serving Jacksonville, Tyler, Whitehouse. Pop: 85,000. Miles of Plant: 745. Homes Passed: 49,000. Homes Served: 34,000. *Channel Capacity:* 60. In use: 52. Programming (off air): 10 chs. *Local Advertising Accepted. Equipment:* Jerrold & Scientific-Atlanta headend; Magnavox amplifiers; Times Fiber cable; Anixter-Andrews satellite antenna; Standard satellite receivers.

TCI Cablevision of Eastern Shore (31,633 subscribers). 8301 Coastal Hwy., Ocean City, MD 21842. (410) 524-3401; FAX: (410) 524-2335. David Kane, gen mgr; Karen Clayland, mktg dir; Bob Hammond, loc adv dir; Jack Evans, chief tech.
Area(s) Served: MD, DE. Counties: Sussex, Worcester. Serving Berlin, Fenwick Island, Ocean City, Selbyville, West Ocean City. Miles of Plant: 280. Homes Passed: 35,018. Homes Served: 31,633. *Channel Capacity:* 60. In use: 56. *Basic Service:* Subscribers: 31,633; 10/30/93. Programming (via satellite): 36 chs. Programming (via microwave): 5 chs. Programming (off air): 3 chs. *Pay Services:* Total Pay Subscribers: 16,393; 09/15/91. (1) Pay Units: 8,622; 09/15/91. Programming (via satellite): HBO. (2) Pay Units: 1,463; 09/15/91. Programming (via satellite): Cinemax. (3) Pay Units: 2,511; 09/15/91. Programming (via satellite): Disney. (4) Pay Units: 347; 09/15/91. Programming (via satellite): Playboy. (5) Pay Units: 1,217; 09/15/91. Programming (via satellite): Showtime. (6) Pay Units: 1,006; 09/15/91. Programming (via satellite): The Movie Channel. Pay Per View Subscribers: 4,255; 09/15/91. *Local Advertising Accepted. Equipment:* Jerrold addressable converters; Jerrold remotes.

TCI Cablevision of Florida (38,500 subscribers). Box 290098, 209 Dunlawton, Port Orange, FL 32127. (904) 760-9950. Jackson Hatton, gen mgr; Karl Memig, chief tech.
Area(s) Served: FL. Serving Daytona Beach, Ponce, Port Orange, South Daytona, Volusia. Homes Passed: 67,396. *Channel Capacity:* 36. *Basic Service:* Subscribers: 38,500; 10/15/91. *Pay Services:* Total Pay Subscribers: 18,637; 10/15/91.

TCI Cablevision of Georgia (25,500 subscribers). Suite 102, 495 Hawthorne Ave., Athens, GA 30606. (706) 543-6585. Woody Wood, gen mgr; Merry Beth Edwards, mktg dir; Michelle Minchew, loc adv dir; Tony Houser, chief tech.
Area(s) Served: GA. Counties: Clarke, Madison, Oconee. Homes Passed: 39,286. Homes Served: 25,500. *Channel Capacity:* 39. *Basic Service:* Subscribers: 25,500; 11/30/93. *Pay Services:* Total Pay Subscribers: 16,966; 10/15/91. *Local Advertising Accepted.*

TCI Cablevision of Greater Michigan Inc. (24,000 subscribers). 350 N. 22nd St., Battle Creek, MI 49015. (616) 962-6216; FAX: (616) 962-5934. Catalina Salley, gen mgr; Tina Lewis, mktg dir & cust svc dir; Greg Culver, chief tech.
Area(s) Served: MI. County: Calhoun. Serving Battle Creek, Bedford, Ceresco, East LeRoy, Emmett, LeRoy, Marshall, Newton, Pennfield, Springfield. Miles of Plant: 592. Homes Passed: 32,826. Homes Served: 24,000. *Channel Capacity:* 37. In use: 37. *Basic Service:* Subscribers: 24,000; 10/20/91. *Pay Services:* Total Pay Subscribers: 22,493; 10/20/91. Pay Per View Subscribers: 1,200. *Local Advertising Accepted.*

TCI Cablevision of Hayward (69,680 subscribers). 23525 Clawiter Rd., Hayward, CA 94545. (510) 785-6077; FAX: (510) 732-1045. Lee Perron, gen mgr; Jackie Lopey, mktg dir; Kathy Wilson, loc adv dir; Jeff Coffman, chief tech; Michelle Pestana, cust svc dir.
Area(s) Served: CA. Counties: Alameda, San Mateo. Serving Foster City, Hayward, Hillsborough, San Leandro, San Lorenzo. Pop: 272,177. Miles of Plant: 732. Homes Passed: 114,472. Homes Served: 69,680. *Channel Capacity:* 78. In use: 61. *Basic Service:* Subscribers: 69,680; 10/10/91. *Pay Services:* Total Pay Subscribers: 34,460; 10/10/91. (1) Pay Units: 29,539; 10/10/91. Programming (via satellite): HBO. (2) Pay Units: 15,566; 10/10/91. Programming (via satellite): Showtime. (3) Pay Units: 11,178; 10/10/91. Program-

Multiple Systems Operators, Independent Owners & Cable Systems

ming (via satellite): Disney. (4) Pay Units: 7,929; 10/10/91. Programming (via satellite): Cinemax. (5) Pay Units: 13,431; 10/10/91. Programming (via satellite): Encore. Pay Per View Subscribers: 59,509; 10/10/91. *Local Advertising Accepted. Equipment:* Jerrold Starcom VI, VI+, VII.

TCI Cablevision of Houston (46,370 subscribers). 7033 Airport Blvd., Houston, TX 77565. (713) 326-1343; FAX: (713) 644-5109. Gary Pomonis, gen mgr; Mark Peebles, mktg dir; Dan Schmitz, chief tech.
Area(s) Served: TX. Counties: Brazoria, Galveston, Harris, Montogomery. Serving Albin, Clear Lake, Dickinson, Friendswood, Hitchcock, Houston, LaMarque, League City, Nassau Bay, Pearland, Santa Fe, Seabrook, Texas City, Tomball, Webster. Miles of Plant: 1,205. Homes Passed: 96,374. Homes Served: 46,370. *Channel Capacity:* 38. In use: 38. *Basic Service:* Subscribers: 46,370; 11/15/93. *Pay Services:* Total Pay Subscribers: 40,682; 09/30/91. *Local Advertising Accepted.*

TCI Cablevision of Idaho Inc. (22,000 subscribers). 1480 Lincoln Rd., Idaho Falls, ID 83401. (208) 523-4567. Dean Jones, gen mgr; Linda Patrick, loc adv dir. *Basic Service:* Subscribers: 22,000; 12/15/92.

TCI Cablevision of Los Angeles County (33,800 subscribers). 15255 Salt Lake Ave., City of Industry, CA 91745. (818) 961-3622; FAX: (818) 961-3389. Kurt Taylor, gen mgr; Alan Krazlow, mktg dir; Patrice Painter, loc adv dir; Richard Olson, chief tech; Danielle Guzman, cust svc dir.
Area(s) Served: CA. County: Los Angeles. Serving Baldwin Park, Bassett, La Puenta, Pico Rivera, South Whittier, West Whittier. Pop: 310,000. Miles of Plant: 850. Homes Passed: 101,000. Homes Served: 33,800. *Channel Capacity:* 60. In use: 60. *Basic Service:* Subscribers: 33,800; 12/01/92. *Local Advertising Accepted.*

TCI Cablevision of Maryland Inc. (24,174 subscribers). 201 S. Mechanic St., Cumberland, MD 21502. (301) 722-6540; FAX: (301) 722-0158. Richard Angarman, gen mgr; Bob Hidey, loc adv dir.
Area(s) Served: MD, PA, WV. Counties: Allegany, Bedford, Mineral. Serving Bowling Green, Centerville, Corriganville, Cresaptown, Cumberland Valley Twp., Eckhart, Ellerslie, Fort Ashby, LaVale, Londonderry Twp., Mount Savage, Potomac Park, Rawlings, Ridgeley, Southampton, Southampton Twp., Wiley Ford. Miles of Plant: 176. Homes Passed: 29,582. Homes Served: 24,174. *Channel Capacity:* 36. In use: 36. *Basic Service:* Subscribers: 24,174; 10/15/91. *Pay Services:* Total Pay Subscribers: 9,701; 10/15/91. *No Local Advertising Accepted. Equipment:* RCA headend; Magnavox & SKL amplifiers; Times cable; Hitachi & Sony cameras; Sony VTRs; RMS satellite antenna; Microdyne satellite receivers.

TCI Cablevision of Medford Inc. (31,178 subscribers). Box 399, 926 S. Grape St., Medford, OR 97501. (503) 779-1851; FAX: (503) 776-2278. Glenn Rierson, gen mgr; Vince Zauskey, mktg dir; Mike Dadaos, loc adv dir; Bob Thomas, chief tech.
Area(s) Served: OR. County: Jackson. Serving Ashland, Central Point, Eagle Point, Gold Hill, Jacksonville, Medford, Phoenix, Talent, White City. Miles of Plant: 624. Homes Passed: 49,500. Homes Served: 31,178. *Channel Capacity:* 26. In use: 26. *Basic Service:* Subscribers: 31,178; 11/30/93. *No Local Advertising Accepted. Equipment:* Scientific-Atlanta headend; Century III & Texscan amplifiers; Comm/Scope cable; Sony VTRs; Multi-Image photo advertising; Jerrold & Texscan set top converters; Jerrold addressable set top converters; Microwave Assoc. & Prodelin satellite antenna; Scientific-Atlanta set top receivers.

TCI Cablevision of Merced County (27,000 subscribers). Box 680, 1343 W. Main St., Merced, CA 95340. (209) 384-1881; FAX: (209) 383-0497. Dean Dealin, gen mgr; Warren Mitchell, mktg dir; Toni Ekas, loc adv dir; Dick Jackson, chief tech; Suzi Balestra, cust svc dir.
Area(s) Served: CA. County: Merced. Serving Atwater, Castle Air Force Base, Le Grand, Winton. Pop: 50,000. Homes Passed: 38,000. Homes Served: 27,000. *Channel Capacity:* 35. In use: 35. *Basic Service:* Subscribers: 27,000; 10/15/91. *Local Advertising Accepted.*

TCI Cablevision of Michigan (26,200 subscribers). 21170 Allen Rd., Woodhaven, MI 48183. (313) 675-8304; FAX: (313) 692-1987. Deborah Mesnick, gen mgr; Mark Hughes, chief tech.
Area(s) Served: MI. County: Wayne. Serving Gibraltar, Lincoln Park, Riverview, Trenton, Woodhaven. Pop: 100,000. Miles of Plant: 334. Homes Served: 26,200. *Channel Capacity:* 57. In use: 57. *Local Advertising Accepted. Equipment:* Scientific-Atlanta headend; Jerrold amplifiers; Comm/Scope cable.

TCI Cablevision of Mid-Michigan (20,000 subscribers). 1070 Trowbridge, East Lansing, MI 48823. (517) 351-8080; FAX: (517) 351-5126. John R. Liskey, gen mgr; Linda Janesky, mktg dir; Keith Jones, chief tech; Sandra Weicher, cust svc dir.
Area(s) Served: MI. County: Ingham. Serving Haslett, Okmes. Pop: 72,000. Miles of Plant: 321. Homes Passed: 30,600. Homes Served: 20,000. *Channel Capacity:* 37. In use: 37. *Basic Service:* Subscribers: 20,000; 09/15/91. *Pay Services:* Total Pay Subscribers: 11,000; 09/15/91. (1) Pay Units: 5,584; 09/15/91. Programming (via satellite): HBO. (2) Pay Units: 1,632; 09/15/91. Programming (via satellite): Cinemax. (3) Pay Units: 940; 09/15/91. Programming (via satellite): Showtime. (4) Pay Units: 1,390; 09/15/91. Programming (via satellite): Disney. *Local Advertising Accepted. Equipment:* Jerrold Starcom V, VI.

TCI Cablevision of Missouri Inc. (37,000 subscribers). 4160 Old Mill Pkwy., St. Peters, MO 63376. (314) 441-7737; FAX: (314) 939-0148. Tim Chaffin, gen mgr; Mike Hoffey, mktg dir; Debra Sanders, loc adv dir; Russ Pritchett, chief tech; Bonnie Blevins, cust svc dir.
Area(s) Served: MO. Counties: St. Charles, St. Peters. Serving Cottleville, Dardenne Praire, O'Fallon, St. Charles, St. Peters. Miles of Plant: 875. Homes Passed: 68,000. *Channel Capacity:* 39. In use: 39. *Basic Service:* Subscribers: 37,000; 08/20/93. Programming (via satellite): 29 chs. Programming (off air): 8 chs. *Pay Services:* Total Pay Subscribers: 45,000; 08/20/93. (1) Pay Units: 13,600; 08/20/93. Programming (via satellite): HBO. (2) Pay Units: 5,050; 08/20/93. Programming (via satellite): Showtime. (3) Pay Units: 2,200; 08/20/93. Programming (via satellite): The Movie Channel. (4) Pay Units: 3,130; 08/20/93. Programming (via satellite): Disney. Pay Per View Subscribers: 1,000; 08/20/93. *Local Advertising Accepted. Equipment:* Provided by Jerrold, Scientific-Atlanta, Regal, C-Cor & Standard Communications.

TCI Cablevision of New Castle County (127,197 subscribers). 4008 N. Dupont Hwy., New Castle, DE 19720. (302) 652-1454; FAX: (302) 652-0774. Jon Danielson, gen mgr; A. Miles McNamee, mktg dir; Bruce Meisterman, loc adv dir; Don Pittman, chief tech; Denise Troise, cust svc dir.
Area(s) Served: DE. County: New Castle. Serving Arden, Ardencroft, Ardentown, Bellefonte, Elsmere, Newark, New Castle, Newport, Wilmington. Pop: 444,996. Miles of Plant: 2,144. Homes Passed: 183,052. Homes Served: 127,197. *Channel Capacity:* 52. In use: 52. *Basic Service:* Subscribers: 127,197; 11/30/92. Programming (via satellite): 38 chs. Programming (via microwave): 1 ch. Programming (off air): 9 chs. *Pay Services:* Total Pay Subscribers: 133,069; 11/30/92. Pay Per View Subscribers: 61,326; 11/30/92. *Local Advertising Accepted.*

TCI Cablevision of New England (93,378 subscribers). Box 518, Rt. 146 Eddy Dowling Hwy., Lincoln, RI 02865. (401) 765-3802; FAX: (401) 766-9043. Andy Jennison, gen mgr; Jim Robinson, mktg dir; William Everett, loc adv dir; Russell Stephens, chief tech; Liz Carnevale, cust svc dir.
Area(s) Served: RI, MA. County: Newport. Serving Blackstone, Central Falls, Cumberland, Exeter, Franklin, Jamestown, Lincoln, Little Compton, Middletown, Millis, Narragansett, Newport, North Kingston, North Smithfield, Norton, Plainville, Portsmouth, Smithfield, Somerset, South Kingston, Swansea, Tiverton, West Greenwich, Woonsocket. Homes Passed: 160,320. *Basic Service:* Subscribers: 93,378; 08/23/93. *Pay Services:* Total Pay Subscribers: 92,887; 08/23/93. *Local Advertising Accepted.*

TCI Cablevision of North Seattle (63,000 subscribers). 1140 N. 94th St., Seattle, WA 98102. (206) 525-0332; FAX: (206) 526-1618. William Bennett, gen mgr; Lori Shelden, mktg dir; Anne McMullen, cust svc dir.
Area(s) Served: WA. County: King. Serving Seattle. Homes Passed: 120,000. Homes Served: 63,000. *Channel Capacity:* 37. In use: 37. *Basic Service:* Subscribers: 63,000; 12/15/93. *Local Advertising Accepted.*

TCI Cablevision of Oakland County (78,300 subscribers). 4500 Delemere Blvd., Royal Oak, MI 48073. (313) 549-8288; FAX: (313) 549-6289. Mike Cleland, gen mgr; Karen Coranado, mktg dir; Elaine Goode, loc adv dir; Dan Leith, chief tech; Deborah Messerknect, cust svc dir.
Area(s) Served: MI. County: Oakland. Serving Auburn Heights, Berkley, Clarkston, Clawson, Ferndale, Huntington Woods, Independence, Oakland, Orion, Orion Twp., Pleasant Ridge, Rochester, Rochester Hills, Troy. Pop: 135,000. Miles of Plant: 1,700. Homes Passed: 132,000. Homes Served: 78,300. *Channel Capacity:* 120. In use: 93. *Basic Service:* Subscribers: 78,300; 11/15/91. *Pay Services:* Total Pay Subscribers: 47,000; 11/15/91. *Local Advertising Accepted. Equipment:* RCA headend; Jerrold amplifiers; Comm/Scope & Times cable.

TCI Cablevision of Ohio Inc. (42,000 subscribers). 2650 Weir Rd. N.E., Warren, OH 44483. (216) 372-1112; FAX: (216) 372-9520. Marion Schultz, gen mgr.
Area(s) Served: OH. County: Trumbull.

TCI Cablevision of Ohio, Inc. (66,634 subscribers). Box 710, 341 City Centre Mall, Middletown, OH 45044. (513) 424-2408; FAX: (513) 424-6555. Jeff Heinrich, gen mgr.
Area(s) Served: OH. Counties: Butler, Montgomery, Warren. Miles of Plant: 600. Homes Passed: 85,000. Homes Served: 66,634. *Channel Capacity:* 60. In use: 56. *Basic Service:* Subscribers: 66,634; 11/30/93. *Pay Services:* Total Pay Subscribers: 37,116; 11/30/93. (1) Pay Units: 4,204; 09/15/91. Programming (via satellite): Cinemax. (2) Pay Units: 8,566; 09/15/91. Programming (via satellite): HBO. (3) Pay Units: 1,750; 09/15/91. Programming (via satellite): Disney. (4) Pay Units: 2,631; 09/15/91. Programming (via satellite): Showtime. *Local Advertising Accepted. Equipment:* Jerrold & Scientific-Atlanta headend.

TCI Cablevision of Oregon (72,000 subscribers). 3500 S.W. Bond Ave., Portland, OR 97201. (503) 243-7426; FAX: (503) 243-7413. William J. Tierney, gen mgr; Brad Nosler, mktg dir; Jim Warhurst, chief tech; Steve Peterson, cust svc dir.
Area(s) Served: OR. Miles of Plant: 1,200. Homes Passed: 130,000. Homes Served: 72,000. *Channel Capacity:* 62. In use: 58. *Basic Service:* Subscribers: 72,000; 11/30/93. Programming (via satellite): 35 chs. Programming (off air): 6 chs. *Pay Services:* Total Pay Subscribers: 48,000; 11/30/93. *Local Advertising Accepted.*

TCI Cablevision of Oregon Inc. (53,000 subscribers). 990 Garfield St., Eugene, OR 97402. (503) 484-3000. Mike White, gen mgr; Jacqueline Johnson, mktg dir; Todd Wylie, loc adv dir; Mike Vaughn, chief tech; Loretta Moorhead, cust svc dir.
Area(s) Served: OR. Counties: Lane, Linn. Serving Eugene, Harrisburg, Junction City, Springfield. Miles of Plant: 826. Homes Passed: 86,000. Homes Served: 53,000. *Channel Capacity:* 36. In use: 36. *Basic Service:* Subscribers: 53,000; 09/1/93. Programming (via satellite): 22 chs. Programming (via microwave): 2 chs. Programming (off air): 6 chs. *Pay Services:* Total Pay Subscribers: 21,000; 09/01/93. *Local Advertising Accepted. Equipment:* Scientific-Atlanta headend; Jerrold amplifiers; Times Fiber & Comm/Scope cable.

TCI Cablevision of Pasco County (50,000 subscribers). 10555 Moon Lake Rd., New Port Richey, FL 34654. (813) 856-3278. Vickie D. Chansler, gen mgr; Jerry Pesce, chief tech.
Area(s) Served: FL. County: Pasco. Serving Bayonet Point, Elfers, Holiday, Hudson, New Port Richey. Homes Passed: 100,000. *Local Advertising Accepted.*

TCI Cablevision of San Jose (280,000 subscribers). Box 114, San Jose, CA 95103-0114. (408) 452-9100; FAX: (408) 452-5720. Tom Lacey, gen mgr; Ernie Villicana, mktg dir; Dave Carlsen, chief tech.
Area(s) Served: CA. Serving Cupertino, Pacifica, San Jose, San Mateo, Sunnyvale. Homes Passed: 500,000. Homes Served: 280,000. *Channel Capacity:* 64. *Basic Service:* Subscribers: 280,000; 11/30/93. *Pay Services:* Total Pay Subscribers: 188,000; 11/30/93.

TCI Cablevision of Santa Fe (20,000 subscribers). 1414 Luisa St., Santa Fe, NM 87501. (505) 982-1968; FAX: (505) 983-4088. Joe Wilcox, gen mgr; Doug Brown, chief tech; Eric Erb, cust svc dir.
Area(s) Served: NM. County: Santa Fe. Serving Santa Fe. Pop: 80,000. Miles of Plant: 357. Homes Passed: 30,200. Homes Served: 20,000. *Channel Capacity:* 43. In use: 43. *Basic Service:* Subscribers: 20,000; 11/15/91. *Pay Services:* Total Pay Subscribers: 10,282; 11/15/91. (1) Pay Units: 1,098; 11/15/91. Programming (via satellite): Cinemax. (2) Pay Units: 1,228; 11/15/91. Programming (via satellite): Encore. (3) Pay Units: 4,358; 11/15/91. Programming (via satellite): HBO. (4) Pay Units: 2,052; 11/15/91. Programming (via satellite): Showtime. *Local Advertising Accepted. Equipment:* Jerrold & Scientific-Atlanta headend; Magnavox amplifiers; Times cable.

TCI Cablevision of Southeast Washington (34,500 subscribers). 639 N. Kellogg St., Kennewick, WA 99336. (509) 783-0123; FAX: (509) 735-3795. Ronald A.

Multiple Systems Operators, Independent Owners & Cable Systems

Asplund, gen mgr; Pat Young, mktg dir; Lynn Bousquet, loc adv dir; John Jagelski, cust svc dir.
Area(s) Served: WA. Serving Kennewick, Pasco, Richland. Pop: 120,000. Miles of Plant: 672. Homes Passed: 53,000. Homes Served: 34,500. *Channel Capacity:* 53. In use: 51. *Basic Service:* Subscribers: 34,500; 11/30/93. *Pay Services:* Total Pay Subscribers: 17,000; 11/15/91. Pay Per View Subscribers: 9,000; 11/15/91. *Local Advertising Accepted. Equipment:* RCA & Scientific-Atlanta headends; Century III amplifiers; Comm/Scope cable.

TCI Cablevision of Tacoma Inc. (45,000 subscribers). Box 11209, Tacoma, WA 98411. (206) 383-4311; FAX: (206) 627-0433. Barbara Wyatt, gen mgr; Bart Christensen, mktg dir; Ted Axtell, chief tech; Kathy Parhomsky, cust svc dir.
Area(s) Served: WA. County: Pierce. Miles of Plant: 618. Homes Passed: 78,000. Homes Served: 45,000. *Channel Capacity:* 38. In use: 38. *Basic Service:* Subscribers: 45,000. *Pay Services:* Total Pay Subscribers: 23,000; 11/15/92. Pay Per View Subscribers: 900; 11/15/92. *Local Advertising Accepted.*

TCI Cablevision of Texas (79,000 subscribers). 2921 S. Expressway 83, Harlingen, TX 78550. (210) 425-7880; FAX: (210) 425-5756. Neil Haman, gen mgr; Robert Villarreal, mktg dir.
Area(s) Served: TX, CA. Serving Alamo, Alice, Alton, Brownsville, Combes, Donna, Edouch, Edinburg, Elsa, Falfurrias, Harlingen, Hildalgo, Indian Lakes, La Feria, Laguna Heights, Laguna Vista, La Joya, La Villa, Las Milpas, Lopezville, Los Fresnos, Lyford, McAllen, Mercedes, Mission, Olmito, Palm Valley, Palm View, Penitas, Pharr, Port Isabel, Premont, Primera, Rancho Viejo, Raymondville, Rio Del Sol, Rio Grande City, Rio Hondo, San Benito, San Diego, San Juan, Santa Rosa, South Padre Island, Sullivan City, Weslaco. Pop: 408,000. Homes Passed: 168,000. *Channel Capacity:* 35. In use: 27. *Basic Service:* Subscribers: 79,000.

TCI Cablevision of Texas (28,607 subscribers). 5330 Twin City Hwy., Port Arthur, TX 77642. (409) 962-0234; FAX: (409) 962-3424. Mike McKee, gen mgr; Joe Walker, loc adv dir; Bob Hollis, chief tech.
Area(s) Served: TX. County: Jefferson. Serving Groves, Nederland, Port Arthur, Port Neches. Miles of Plant: 500. Homes Passed: 49,547. Homes Served: 28,607. *Channel Capacity:* 35. In use: 35. *Basic Service:* Subscribers: 28,607; 11/15/91. *Local Advertising Accepted. Equipment:* Scientific-Atlanta headend; Jerrold & Scientific-Atlanta amplifiers; Comm/Scope cable; Scientific-Atlanta satellite antenna; Scientific-Atlanta satellite receivers.

TCI Cablevision of Texas Inc. (48,600 subscribers). Box 6607, Corpus Christi, TX 74811. (512) 857-5000; FAX: (512) 857-5868. Dennis Moore, gen mgr; Jerri Coppedge, mktg dir; John Bolles, loc adv dir; Rich Rowe, chief tech; Jesse Barrios, cust svc dir.
Area(s) Served: TX. Counties: Nueces, San Patricio. Serving Corpus Christi, Robstown. Miles of Plant: 1,114. Homes Passed: 87,100. *Channel Capacity:* 53. In use: 39. *Basic Service:* Subscribers: 48,600; 11/30/92. Programming (via satellite): 35 chs. Programming (off air): 6 chs. *Pay Services:* Total Pay Subscribers: 66,000; 11/30/92. Pay Per View Subscribers: 2,000; 11/30/92. *Local Advertising Accepted. Equipment:* Jerrold headend; Anaconda amplifiers; Anaconda cable; Comtech & Scientific-Atlanta satellite antenna; Microdyne satellite receivers.

TCI Cablevision of Texas Inc. (28,000 subscribers). 1460 Calder Ave., Beaumont, TX 77701. (409) 839-4601; FAX: (409) 839-4215. Pat Morrow, gen mgr; Danny Green, chief tech.
Area(s) Served: TX. Serving Beaumont. Miles of Plant: 800. Homes Passed: 46,000. Homes Served: 28,000. *Channel Capacity:* 35. In use: 35. *Pay Services:* Total Pay Subscribers: 17,000; 11/15/91. *Local Advertising Accepted. Equipment:* Scientific-Atlanta headend.

TCI Cablevision of Treasure Valley (55,000 subscribers). 8400 Westpark St., Boise, ID 83704. (208) 377-2491; FAX: (208) 375-7500. Wayne H. Watson, gen mgr; Steve Hawley, mktg dir & cust svc dir; Bruce Whitten, loc adv dir; Dave Rehder, chief tech.
Area(s) Served: ID. Counties: Ada, Canyon. Serving Caldwell, Eagle, Garden City, Kuna, Meridian, Nampa. Pop: 250,000. Miles of Plant: 1,500. Homes Passed: 115,000. Homes Served: 55,000. *Channel Capacity:* 37. In use: 37. *Basic Service:* Subscribers: 55,000; 09/30/93. Pay Per View Subscribers: 12,000; 09/30/93. *Local Advertising Accepted. Equipment:* Jerrold headend; Jerrold amplifiers; Comm/Scope & Times Fiber cable.

TCI Cablevision of Utah Inc. (25,000 subscribers). 1649 W. 4200 South, Salt Lake City, UT 84123. (801) 261-2662; FAX: (801) 261-8862. Richard Friedman, gen mgr; Jeff Raddatz, mktg dir.
Area(s) Served: UT. Serving West Valley.

TCI Cablevision of Utah Inc. (50,000 subscribers). 1350 E. Miller Ave., Salt Lake City, UT 84106. (801) 485-0500; FAX: (801) 487-1887. Dan Sutton, gen mgr; Leslie White, mktg dir; Everett Preece, chief tech; Becky Ruley, cust svc dir.
Area(s) Served: UT. County: Salt Lake. Serving Midvale City, Murray City, Salt Lake City, Sandy City, South Salt Lake. Pop: 315,000. Miles of Plant: 1,208. Homes Passed: 148,000. Homes Served: 50,000. *Channel Capacity:* 36. In use: 36. *Basic Service:* Subscribers: 50,000; 11/15/91. Programming (via satellite): 27 chs. Programming (off air): 9 chs. *Pay Services:* Total Pay Subscribers: 36,500; 11/15/91. *Local Advertising Accepted. Equipment:* Jerrold headend.

TCI Cablevision of Utah Inc. (25,549 subscribers). Suite 100, 3585 Harrison Blvd., Ogden, UT 84403-2048. (801) 621-8844; FAX: (801) 621-0601. Cory Mauchley, gen mgr; Lisa Robinson, mktg dir & loc adv dir; Jeff Rosenquist, chief tech; Paulette Vigoreu, cust svc dir.
Area(s) Served: UT. Counties: Davis, Morgan, Weber. Serving Harrisville, Mountain Green, North Ogden, Ogden Canyon, Riverdale, Roy, South Ogden, South Weber, Vintah City, Washington Terrace. Homes Passed: 52,000. Homes Served: 25,549. *Channel Capacity:* 32. In use: 32. *Basic Service:* Subscribers: 25,549; 11/30/93. *Pay Services:* Total Pay Subscribers: 15,500; 11/15/91. *Local Advertising Accepted.*

TCI Cablevision of Walnut Creek (21,300 subscribers). Box 4308, 1267 Arroyo Way, Walnut Creek, CA 94596. (510) 933-1212; FAX: (510) 933-0324. Gene Cook, gen mgr; Florence Raleigh, mktg dir; Jeff Sellstrom, chief tech.
Area(s) Served: CA. County: Contra Costa. Serving Walnut Creek. Pop: 55,000. Miles of Plant: 223. Homes Passed: 24,300. Homes Served: 21,300. *Channel Capacity:* 62. In use: 59. *Basic Service:* Subscribers: 21,300; 11/30/93. *Local Advertising Accepted. Equipment:* Scientific-Atlanta headend & amplifiers; Scientific-Atlanta, Times Fiber & Comm/Scope cable; Tocom converters.

TCI Cablevision of Washington (34,483 subscribers). 777 W. Horton Rd., Bellingham, WA 98226. (206) 734-5522; FAX: (206) 647-8967. Dan Crocker, gen mgr; Ms. Jay Burse, mktg dir.
Area(s) Served: WA. County: Whatcom. Miles of Plant: 400. Homes Passed: 28,500. Homes Served: 34,483. *Channel Capacity:* 35. In use: 35. *Basic Service:* Subscribers: 34,483; 11/30/93. *Pay Services:* Total Pay Subscribers: 9,000; 11/15/91. *Local Advertising Accepted. Equipment:* Jerrold headend.

TCI Cablevision of Washington (41,000 subscribers). Box 129, Olympia, WA 98507. (206) 357-3364; FAX: (206) 754-5811. Bill Lawson, gen mgr; Linda Gowdy, mktg dir; Kevin Ware, chief tech; Lynn Peets, cust svc dir.
Area(s) Served: WA. Counties: Mason, Pierce, Thurston. Serving Lacey, Scott Lake, Steamboat Island, Summit Lake, Turnwater. Miles of Plant: 908. Homes Passed: 42,000. Homes Served: 41,000. *Basic Service:* Subscribers: 41,000.

TCI Cablevision of West Michigan (122,000 subscribers). 955 Century Ave. S.W., Grand Rapids, MI 49503. (616) 247-0575; FAX: (616) 247-0932. Donald N. Stephan, gen mgr; Cindy Rosloniec, mktg dir; Ruth Anne Karnes, loc adv dir; George J. Michas, chief tech; Carol Perkins, cust svc dir.
Area(s) Served: MI. Counties: Alegan, Kent, Ottawa. Serving Ada, Alpine, Byron, Cannon, Cascade, Dorr, East Grand Rapids, Jenison, Gaines, Georgetown, Grand Rapids, Grandville, Grattan, Kentwood, Jamestown, Lowell, Oakfield, Plainfield, Sparta, Tallmadge, Vergennes, Walker, Wright, Wyoming. Miles of Plant: 2,223. Homes Passed: 185,764. Homes Served: 122,000. *Channel Capacity:* 47. In use: 47. *Basic Service:* Subscribers: 122,000; 10/15/91. Programming (via satellite): 46 chs. Programming (via microwave): 1 ch. *Local Advertising Accepted. Equipment:* Scientific-Atlanta headend; C-COR amplifiers; Comm/Scope & Times Fiber Cable; Simulsat satellite dish; Catel FM gear; Scientific-Atlanta satellite antenna; Scientific-Atlanta satellite receivers.

TCI Cablevision of Western Colorado Inc. (25,000 subscribers). 2502 Foresight Cir., Grand Junction, CO 81505. (303) 245-8750; FAX: (303) 245-6803. Tom Worster, gen mgr; Jerry Morgan, loc adv dir; Darrel Phelps, chief tech.
Area(s) Served: CO. County: Mesa. Serving Fruita, Grand Junction, Orchard Mesa, Palisade. Homes Passed: 39,500. Homes Served: 25,000. *Channel Capacity:* 35. In use: 35. *Basic Service:* Subscribers: 25,000; 11/30/93. *Local Advertising Accepted. Equipment:* RCA & Scientific-Atlanta headend; Jerrold & Magnavox amplifiers; Times & Comm/Scope cable; addressable pay per view.

TCI Cablevision of Wisconsin (70,000 subscribers). 5723 Tokay Blvd., Madison, WI 53719. (608) 274-3822; FAX: (608) 274-1436. Maury Lee, gen mgr; Linda Lawson, mktg dir; Kent Schneider, chief tech.
Area(s) Served: WI. County: Madison.

TCI Cablevision of Wyoming (23,000 subscribers). 1415 E. 13th St., Cheyenne, WY 82001. (307) 632-8114; FAX: (307) 637-5973. Randy Robinson, gen mgr; J.J. Johnson, chief tech.
Area(s) Served: WY. Homes Served: 23,000. *Basic Service:* Subscribers: 23,000; 11/30/93. *Pay Services:* Total Pay Subscribers: 14,000; 11/15/91. *No Local Advertising Accepted. Equipment:* Jerrold & Scientific-Atlanta headend.

TCI Cablevision of Yakima (32,000 subscribers). 1005 N. 16th Ave., Yakima, WA 98902. (509) 575-1697; FAX: (509) 575-1749. Gary Bailey, gen mgr; Shelly Bjornson, mktg dir.
Area(s) Served: WA. County: Yakima. Serving Prosser. Miles of Plant: 600. Homes Passed: 56,000. Homes Served: 32,000. *Channel Capacity:* 35. In use: 35. *Basic Service:* Subscribers: 32,000; 11/30/93. *Pay Services:* Total Pay Subscribers: 12,000; 11/15/91. *Local Advertising Accepted.*

TCI of Arkansas (28,700 subscribers). 1520 S. Caraway Rd., Jonesboro, AR 72401. (501) 935-3615; FAX: (501) 972-8141. Garry Bowman, gen mgr; Bill Little, loc adv dir; Thersa Woodruff, cust svc dir.
Area(s) Served: AR. Counties: Craighead, Crittenden, Cross, Mississippi, Poinsett. Serving Bay, Cherry Valley, Dell, Earle, Harrisburg, Hoxie, Inboden, Jonesboro, Keiser, Lake City, Leachville, Luxora, Manila, Marked Tree, Osceola, Parken, Revenden, Walnut Ridge, Weiner. Pop: 46,000. Miles of Plant: 750. Homes Passed: 32,000. Homes Served: 28,700. *Channel Capacity:* 62. In use: 54. *Basic Service:* Subscribers: 28,700; 11/30/93. *Local Advertising Accepted. Equipment:* Scientific-Atlanta, Jerrold & RCA headend; Jerrold amplifiers; Comm/Scope & Times Fiber cable.

TCI of Arkansas Inc. (28,346 subscribers). Box 3408, Fort Smith, AR 72913. (501) 782-8941; FAX: (501) 783-7892. Craig Stensaas, gen mgr; John Mosher, mktg dir; Saundra Julian, loc adv dir; Paul Lander, chief tech.
Area(s) Served: AR, OK. Serving Bonanza, Greenwood, Hackett, Jenny Lind, Le Flore, Muldrow, Old Jenny Lind, Poland, Sebastian, Sequoyah. Homes Passed: 35,954. *Channel Capacity:* 40. *Basic Service:* Subscribers: 28,346; 10/15/91. *Pay Services:* Total Pay Subscribers: 13,052; 10/15/91.

TCI of Central Iowa (80,000 subscribers). 2205 Ingersoll, Des Moines, IA 50312. (515) 246-1890; FAX: (515) 246-2211. Llyod S. Riddle, gen mgr; Leann Treloar, mktg dir; Rich Gilman, loc adv dir; Mike Brose, chief tech; Shirley Galvin, cust svc dir.
Area(s) Served: IA. Counties: Polk, Warren. Serving Altoona, Ankeny, Bondurant, Carlisle, Clive, Des Moines, Grimes, Johnston, Lakewood, Norwalk, Pleasant Hill, Urbandale, West Des Moines, Windsor Heights. *Channel Capacity:* 37. In use: 37. *Local Advertising Accepted.*

TCI of Colorado (240,000 subscribers). 6850 S. Tuscon Way, Englewood, CO 80112. (303) 930-2000; FAX: (303) 790-0550. Dan Hebert, gen mgr; Ronda Dorchester, mktg dir; Ken Hilliard, chief tech; Paula Trustdorf, cust svc dir.
Area(s) Served: CO. Counties: Adams, Arapahoe, Boulder, Denver, Douglas, Jefferson. Serving Acres Green, Applewood, Arvada, Aurora, Bennett, Boulder, Byers, Castle Pines, Castle Rock, Cherry Hills Village, Commerce City, Cottonwood, Englewood, Federal Heights, Foxridge Farm, Franktown, Golden, Greenwood Village, Highlands Ranch, Lakewood, Littleton, Northglenn, Parker, Perry Park, Roxborough Park, Sedalia, Sheridan, Strasburg, Surrey Ridge, The Pinery, Thornton, Westminster, Wheat Ridge. Pop: 1,000,000. Homes Passed: 460,000. Homes Served: 240,000. *Channel Capacity:* 49. In use: 49. *Basic Service:* Subscribers: 240,000; 11/30/93. *Pay Services:* Total Pay Subscribers: 250,000; 11/30/93. *Local Advertising Accepted. Equipment:* Scientific-Atlanta headend; Jerrold,

Multiple Systems Operators, Independent Owners & Cable Systems

Scientific-Atlanta & Magnavox amplifiers; Trilogy, Comm/Scope & Times Fiber cable.

TCI of Greensburg (47,000 subscribers). Box 1167, Greensburg, PA 15601. (412) 834-6990; FAX: (412) 834-8983. Jeff Harshman, gen mgr; Rich McCready, mktg dir; Russ Duecot, chief tech; Brigid Steffey, cust svc dir.
Area(s) Served: PA. County: Westmoreland. Serving Adamsburg, Arona, East Huntingdon, Hempfield, Hunter, Irwin, Jeannette, Madison, Manor, Mount Pleasant, New Alexandria, New Stanton, North Huntingdon, North Irwin, Penn, Salem, Sewickley, South Greensburg, South Huntingdon, South Versailles, Southwest Greensburg, Unity, Youngwood. Miles of Plant: 760. Homes Passed: 57,500. Homes Served: 47,000. *Channel Capacity:* 36. In use: 36. *Basic Service:* Subscribers: 47,000; 11/15/91. *Pay Services:* Total Pay Subscribers: 4,500; 11/15/91. *Local Advertising Accepted.*

TCI of Illinois Inc. (91,300 subscribers). 1201 Feehanville Dr., Mount Prospect, IL 60056. (708) 299-9220; FAX: (708) 299-4086. Kelvin Fee, gen mgr; Diane Siles, mktg dir; David Starr, chief tech; Kristine Grill, cust svc dir.
Area(s) Served: IL. Counties: Cook, DuPage, Lake. Serving Arlington Heights, Bartlett, Des Plaines, Glenview, Golf, Hanover Park, Maywood, Mount Prospect, Northbrook, Park Ridge, Prospect Heights, Streamwood Schaumbury, Wheeling. Miles of Plant: 2,200. Homes Passed: 191,00. Homes Served: 91,300. *Channel Capacity:* 60. In use: 60. *Basic Service:* Subscribers: 91,300; 11/15/92. *Local Advertising Accepted.*

TCI of Illinois Inc. (23,000 subscribers). 6 Dearborn Sq., Kankakee, IL 60901. (815) 937-2700; FAX: (815) 937-2714. John Niebur, gen mgr; Laura Fransen, loc adv dir; Jim Brandt, chief tech.
Area(s) Served: IL. Counties: Iroquois, Kankakee. Serving Aroma Park, Aroma Twp., Ashkum, Bourbonnais, Bourbanais Twp., Bradley, Chebanse, Clifton, Danforth, Gilman, Herscher, Kankakee, Kankakee Twp., Limestone Twp., Onarga, Piper City, St. Anne, Sun River Terrace. Pop: 65,000. Miles of Plant: 370. Homes Passed: 27,000. Homes Served: 23,000. *Channel Capacity:* 35. In use: 35. *Basic Service:* Subscribers: 23,000; 11/01/92. *Local Advertising Accepted.*

TCI of Kansas Inc. (40,00 subscribers). 1615 Washburn Ave., Topeka, KS 66604. (913) 233-5018. Todd Kruthird, gen mgr; John Hicks, chief tech; Becky Sullivan, cust svc dir.
Area(s) Served: KS. Counties: Shawnee, Wabaunsee. Serving Maplehill.

TCI of Louisiana (33,000 subscribers). Box 5365, 413 E. Prien Lake Rd., Lake Charles, LA 70601. (318) 477-9674; FAX: (318) 474-3436. Glenn Williams, gen mgr; Darren Ryder, loc adv dir; Keith Vidrine, chief tech.
Area(s) Served: LA. County: Calcasieu Parish. Serving Lake Charles, Sulphur. Pop: 66,000. Miles of Plant: 233. Homes Passed: 45,000. Homes Served: 33,000. *Channel Capacity:* 37. In use: 37. *Basic Service:* Subscribers: 33,000; 10/01/93. Programming (via satellite): 30 chs. Programming (off air): 8 chs. *Pay Services:* Total Pay Subscribers: 15,000; 10/01/93. *Local Advertising Accepted.*

TCI of Michiana (79,000 subscribers). 815 W. Edison Rd., Mishawaka, IN 46545. (219) 258-5858; FAX: (219) 255-2423. Rick Tuttle, gen mgr; Leslie White, mktg dir; Tom White, chief tech.
Area(s) Served: IN. Counties: Elkhart, Marshall, St. Joseph. Serving Goshen, Mishawaka, Osceola, Plymouth, Roseland, South Bend. Homes Passed: 135,000. *Channel Capacity:* 36. In use: 36. *Basic Service:* Subscribers: 79,000; 10/15/91. *Pay Services:* Total Pay Subscribers: 40,000; 10/15/91. Pay Per View Subscribers: 25,000; 09/08/93. *Local Advertising Accepted.*

TCI of New York Inc. (85,000 subscribers). 2585 Main St., Buffalo, NY 14214. (716) 862-4600; FAX: (716) 835-8035. Paul J. Meegan, gen mgr; Dennis M. Sprole, mktg dir; Dan Ziolkowski, chief tech; Loretta Brehm, cust svc dir.
Area(s) Served: NY. County: Buffalo. Homes Served: 85,000. *Channel Capacity:* 61. In use: 56. *Basic Service:* Subscribers: 85,000; 11/30/93. *Local Advertising Accepted.*

TCI of New York Inc. (30,000 subscribers). 100 Bigelow Ave., Schenectady, NY 12304. (518) 370-2525; FAX: (518) 370-4808. Allan Sagendorf, gen mgr; Armand Mastroianni, chief tech; Marilyn Howland, cust svc dir.
Area(s) Served: NY. County: Schenectady. Miles of Plant: 500. Homes Passed: 48,000. Homes Served: 30,000. *Channel Capacity:* 35. In use: 35. *Basic Service:* Subscribers: 30,000; 11/15/91. *Local Advertising Accepted.*

TCI of Northern Colorado (20,000 subscribers). 3737 W. 10th St., Greeley, CO 80634. (303) 351-0669; FAX: (303) 353-4363. Kathy Stewart, gen mgr; Karen Height, loc adv dir; John Harris, chief tech.
Area(s) Served: CO. County: Weld. Pop: 58,000. Miles of Plant: 300. Homes Passed: 33,000. Homes Served: 20,000. *Channel Capacity:* 36. In use: 36. *Basic Service:* Subscribers: 20,000; 11/15/91. *Local Advertising Accepted. Equipment:* Scientific-Atlanta headend; Scientific-Atlanta amplifiers; Comm/Scope cable.

TCI of Northern Indiana (23,200 subscribers). 844 169th St., Hammond, IN 46324. (219) 932-4111; FAX: (219) 931-4827. Manuel Longoria, gen mgr; Sheila McMillior, mktg dir; Mike Wilczynski, loc adv dir; Chris Foor, chief tech; John Reyes, cust svc dir.
Area(s) Served: IN. County: Lake. Serving East Chicago, Hammond. Pop: 140,000. Miles of Plant: 267. Homes Passed: 44,331. Homes Served: 23,200. *Channel Capacity:* 54. In use: 52. *Basic Service:* Subscribers: 23,230; 10/31/91. Programming (via satellite): 37 chs. Programming (off air): 12 chs. *Pay Services:* Total Pay Subscribers: 20,371; 10/31/91. Pay Per View Subscribers: 18,522; 10/31/91. *Local Advertising Accepted. Equipment:* Jerrold Starcom VI, VI+, VII.

TCI of Northern Iowa (32,591 subscribers). Box 2457, Waterloo, IA 50704. (319) 232-8800; FAX: (319) 232-7841. Darrel Wenzel, gen mgr; Chris Vokaty, mktg dir; Mike Goar, loc adv dir; Kevin Elston, chief tech.
Area(s) Served: IA. Counties: Benton, Blackhawk, Buchannon, Fayette, Floyd, Grundy, Hardin. Serving Cedar Falls, Charles City, Elk Run Heights, Evansdale, Floyd, Gilbertville, Hazelton, Independence, Iowa Falls, Oelwein, Raymond, Reinbeck, Washburn, Waterloo, Vinton. Miles of Plant: 797. Homes Passed: 55,467. Homes Served: 32,591. *Channel Capacity:* 35. In use: 35. *Basic Service:* Subscribers: 32,591; 10/24/91. *Pay Services:* Total Pay Subscribers: 14,521; 10/24/91. *Local Advertising Accepted.*

TCI of Northern New Jersey (196,643 subscribers). 40 Potash Rd., Oakland, NJ 07436. (201) 337-1550; FAX: (201) 405-0490. Henry Magers, gen mgr; Jay Kirschner, mktg dir; Lenny Melamedas, loc adv dir; Peter Psirogianes, chief tech; Dan Perillo, cust svc dir.
Area(s) Served: NJ. Counties: Bergen, Essex, Morris, Passaic. Serving Allandale, Alpine, Bloomingdale, Bogota, Butler, Cedar Grove, Clifton, Elmwood Park, Franklin Lakes, Garfield, Glen Rock, Hackensack, Haledon, Hasbrouck Heights, Hawthorne, Hillsdale, Hohokus, Kinnelon, Lincoln Park, Little Falls Twp., Lodi, Maywood, Midland Park, Montville Twp., North Caldwell, North Haledon, Nutley, Paramus, Park Ridge, Passaic, Pequannock, Pompton Lakes, Prospect Park, Ramsey, Ridgewood, Ringwood, Riverdale, River Edge, Rochelle Park, Saddle Brook, South Hackensack Twp., Teaneck, Totowa, Upper Saddle River, Waldwick, Wanaque, Washington Twp., Wayne, West Paterson, Westwood, Woodridge, Wyckoff. Miles of Plant: 2,700. Homes Passed: 323,610. Homes Served: 196,643. *Channel Capacity:* 60. In use: 60. *Basic Service:* Subscribers: 196,643; 09/22/93. Programming (via satellite): 27 chs. Programming (via microwave): Cable Television Network of New Jersey. Programming (off air): WCBS, WNBC, WNYW, WABC, WWOR, WPIX, WNJM, WNET, WNYC, WLIW, WNJV. *Pay Services:* Total Pay Subscribers: 285,984; 11/18/92. (1) Pay Units: 113,945; 11/18/92. Programming (via satellite): HBO. (2) Pay Units: 114,862; 11/18/92. Programming (via satellite): Encore. (3) Pay Units: 13,733; 11/18/92. Programming (via satellite): Cinemax. (4) Pay Units: 16,089; 11/18/92. Programming (via satellite): Showtime. (5) Pay Units: 10,204; 11/18/92. Programming (via satellite): Disney. (6) Pay Units: 4,009; 11/18/92. Programming (via satellite): The Movie Channel. Pay Per View Subscribers: 53,124; 11/18/92. *Local Advertising Accepted. Equipment:* Catel, RCA & Scientific-Atlanta headend; Jerrold, Magnavox & RCA amplifiers; Belden, Comm/Scope & Times Fiber cable.

TCI of Pennsylvania (32,000 subscribers). Box 7129, 5651 Jordan Rd., Erie, PA 16510. (814) 899-0625; FAX: (814) 898-1540. Tom Carey, gen mgr; Bob Westland, chief tech.
Area(s) Served: PA. Counties: Crawford, Erie. Serving Albion, Cranesville, Conneautville, Fairview, Girard, Greene Twp., Lake City, Lawrence Park, McKeon, Mill Creek, Northeast, Platea, Springboro, Summit, Waterford. Miles of Plant: 660. Homes Passed: 40,344. *Channel Capacity:* 35. In use: 35. *Local Advertising Accepted.*

TCI of Pennsylvania (385,000 subscribers). 300 Corliss St., Pittsburgh, PA 15283. (412) 771-8700; FAX: (412) 331-7452. James Mazur, gen mgr; Andrew Field, mktg dir; John Olander, chief tech; David Wittman, cust svc dir.
Area(s) Served: PA. Serving Pittsburgh. Homes Passed: 520,000. Homes Served: 385,000. *Channel Capacity:* 80. In use: 65. *Basic Service:* Subscribers: 385,000; 11/30/93. *Pay Services:* Total Pay Subscribers: 220,000; 11/30/93. *Local Advertising Accepted.*

TCI of Pennsylvania Inc. (25,000 subscribers). 1155 Benner Pike, State College, PA 16801. (814) 238-3096. Jeffrey B. Fisher, gen mgr; Neil Jones, mktg dir.
Area(s) Served: PA. County: Centre.

TCI of Reno (53,000 subscribers). Box 11860, 1250 Terminal Way, Reno, NV 89502. (702) 329-9695; FAX: (702) 788-5021. LaFawn VanNest, gen mgr; Paul Stager, chief tech.
Area(s) Served: NV, CA. Counties: Lyon, Sierra, Washoe. Serving Cold Springs Valley, Mogul, Peavine, Reno, Reno Cascade, Sierra Royal, Spanish Springs Valley, Sparks, Sparks City, Verdi, Wadsworth. Homes Served: 53,000. *Channel Capacity:* 60. In use: 60. *Basic Service:* Subscribers: 53,000; 10/31/91. *Local Advertising Accepted.*

TCI of South Florida (29,000 subscribers). 18601 N.W. 2nd Ave., Miami, FL 33169. (305) 921-1770; FAX: (305) 925-8178. Don Foster, gen mgr; Jim Simpson, chief tech.
Area(s) Served: FL. County: Broward. Serving Hollywood. Pop: 128,000. Miles of Plant: 368. Homes Passed: 58,000. Homes Served: 29,000. *Channel Capacity:* 57. In use: 57. *Basic Service:* Subscribers: 29,000; 11/30/92. *Pay Services:* Total Pay Subscribers: 9,800; 10/15/91. *Local Advertising Accepted.*

TCI of South Florida Inc. (88,612 subscribers). 18601 N.W. Second Ave., Miami, FL 33169. (305) 653-5541; FAX: (305) 654-6718. Steve Friedman, gen mgr; David Bromberg, loc adv dir; Paula Davidson, cust svc dir.
Area(s) Served: FL. Counties: Broward, Dade. Serving Biscayne Park, El Portal, Miami Shores, Miramar, North Miami Beach, Pembroke Park, Pembroke Pines. Miles of Plant: 1,480. Homes Passed: 164,791. Homes Served: 88,612. *Channel Capacity:* In use: 39. *Basic Service:* Subscribers: 88,612; 09/30/91. *Pay Services:* Total Pay Subscribers: 60,295; 09/30/91. *Local Advertising Accepted.*

TCI of South Mississippi (30,000 subscribers). 786 Washington Loop, Biloxi, MS 39530. (601) 374-5900; FAX: (601) 435-3939. John F. Humphries, gen mgr; Georgia Storey, mktg dir; August Taconi, loc adv dir; Mellonee Kingsley, cust svc dir.
Area(s) Served: MS. Counties: Harrison, Jackson. Serving Biloxi, D'Iberville, Keesler Air Force Base, Ocean Springs. Miles of Plant: 600. Homes Passed: 34,500. Homes Served: 30,000. *Channel Capacity:* 39. In use: 39. *Basic Service:* Subscribers: 30,000; 11/15/93. *Local Advertising Accepted. Equipment:* Scientific-Atlanta headend; C-COR amplifiers; Times & Comm/Scope cable; Oak addressable set top converters; Scientific-Atlanta satellite antenna; Simulsat satellite dish; Alpha power supply (battery-backed power supply).

TCI of South Seattle (89,000 subscribers). 15241 Pacific Hwy. S., Seattle, WA 98188. (206) 433-3401; (206) 433-3434; FAX: (206) 433-5103. Gary Hokenson, gen mgr; Joe Webster, mktg dir; Bruce Boutilier, cust svc dir.
Area(s) Served: WA. Homes Passed: 141,000. Homes Served: 89,000. *Channel Capacity:* 38. In use: 38. *Basic Service:* Subscribers: 89,000; 11/15/93. *Pay Services:* Total Pay Subscribers: 21,000; 11/15/93. *Local Advertising Accepted.*

TCI of Southern Minnesota (32,500 subscribers). Box 69, 117 E. Center St., Rochester, MN 55904. (507) 289-1611; FAX: (507) 289-1958. Robert Loos, gen mgr; Sherry Dostal, mktg dir; Daryl Glassmaker, chief tech.
Area(s) Served: MN. Counties: Dodge, Goodhue, Olmstead. Serving Byron, Cascade, Eyota, Haverhill, Kasson, Marion, Oronoco, Rochester, Rochester Twp., Stewartville, Zumbrota. Miles of Plant: 450. Homes Passed: 39,500. Homes Served: 32,500. *Channel Capacity:* 60. In use: 49. *Basic Service:* Subscribers: 32,500; 10/31/91. *Pay Services:* Total Pay Subscribers: 12,500; 10/31/91. Pay Per View Subscribers: 6,300; 10/31/91. *Local Advertising Accepted. Equipment:* Scientific-Atlanta headend; C-COR amplifiers; Times cable; Hitachi cameras; Sony VTRs; Texscan character generator; Jerrold set top converters; Jerrold addressable set top converters; Scientific-Atlanta satellite an-

tennas; Hughes & Scientific-Atlanta satellite receivers; Falcone International commercial insert.

TCI of Virginia Inc. (33,600 subscribers). 1828 S. Military Hwy., Chesapeake, VA 23320. (804) 424-6660; FAX: (804) 420-8648. Donald Deal, gen mgr; Larry Cox, chief tech.
Area(s) Served: VA. Serving Chesapeake City. Homes Served: 33,600. *Channel Capacity:* 52. *Basic Service:* Subscribers: 33,600; 10/15/91. *Local Advertising Accepted. Equipment:* Jerrold headend; Jerrold amplifiers; Comm/Scope cable; Hitachi cameras; Sony VTRs; Video Data Systems character generator; Jerrold set top converters; Scientific-Atlanta satellite antenna; Scientific-Atlanta satellite receivers.

TCI of West Virginia Inc. (25,000 subscribers). 1737 E. Seventh St., Parkersburg, WV 26101. (304) 485-7433; FAX: (304) 428-8579. Terry White, gen mgr; Donna Maston, mktg dir; Jerry Buskirk, chief tech.
Area(s) Served: WV, OH.

United Artists Cable (20,000 subscribers). 340 New Salem Hwy., Murfreesboro, TN 37129. (615) 896-2981; FAX: (615) 896-6112.
Area(s) Served: TN. County: Rutherford. Serving Christiana, Murfreesboro, Rockvale. Pop: 100,000. Miles of Plant: 500. Homes Passed: 26,000. Homes Served: 20,000. *Channel Capacity:* 35. In use: 35. *Basic Service:* Subscribers: 20,000; 11/15/93. *Pay Services:* Total Pay Subscribers: 12,500; 11/15/91. *Local Advertising Accepted. Equipment:* Scientific-Atlanta headend; Scientific-Atlanta amplifiers; Comm/Scope cable; Texscan 8 ch. commercial inserter.

United Artists Cable of Baltimore (101,209 subscribers). 2525 Kirk Ave., Baltimore, MD 21218. (410) 338-2777; FAX: (410) 366-7469. Euan Fannell, gen mgr; Gary MacGregor, mktg dir; Jay Cleaver, loc adv dir.
Area(s) Served: MD. County: Baltimore. Serving Baltimore. Pop: 750,000. Miles of Plant: 1,100. Homes Passed: 300,000. Homes Served: 101,209. *Channel Capacity:* 78. In use: 66. *Basic Service:* Subscribers: 101,209; 11/15/91. *Local Advertising Accepted. Equipment:* Jerrold headend; Jerrold amplifiers; Standard receivers; M/A-Com video cipher 2; Starcom VI & VII; Harris & Scientific-Atlanta satellite antenna; synchronous fiber optic equipment.

United Artists Cable/TCI (86,000 subscribers). 15055 Oxnard St., Van Nuys, CA 91411. (818) 778-5000; FAX: (818) 376-0555. Rhonda Cohn, gen mgr.
Area(s) Served: CA. County: Los Angeles. Serving Arleta, Mission Hills, North Hollywood, Pacioma, Panorama City, San Fernando, Sepulveda, Sherman Oaks, Studio City, Sun Valley, Sylmar, Toluca Lake, Van Nuys. Homes Passed: 195,000. Homes Served: 86,000. *Channel Capacity:* 78. In use: 77. *Basic Service:* Subscribers: 86,000; 11/15/93. *Local Advertising Accepted.*

SMALLER SYSTEMS

California - TCI Cablevision of Alameda, 2061 Challenger Dr., Alameda, CA 94501; (501) 865-2917; 15,316 subs. **Colorado -** Sterling Cable Fund Inc., Suite 320, 9137 E. Mineral Circle, Englewood, CO 80112; (303) 799-6833; Joseph R. Bruning; 4,000 subs. TCI of Northern Colorado, 3737 W. 10th St., Greeley, CO 80634; (303) 351-0669; 17,100 subs. **Hawaii -** Hawaiian Cablevision Company, Suite 6, 910 Honoapiilani Hwy., Lahaina, Maui, HI 96761; (808) 661-4607; 16,259 subs. **Kentucky -** R.V. Cable-Vision Inc., Box 218, 108 N. Greenville St., Harrodsburg, KY 40330. **Louisiana -** TCI Cable of Louisiana, 725 Benton Rd., Bossier City, LA 71111; (318) 747-1666; 19,500 subs. TCI of Louisiana, 7509 East St., Bernard Hwy., Violet, LA 70092; (504) 682-4684; 15480 subs. **Massachusetts -** TCI Cablevision of Waltham, Box 9000, Waltham, MA 02254-9000; (617) 893-6447; David Sartori. **Michigan -** TCI Cablevision of Mid-Michigan, 1070 Trowbridge, East Lansing, MI 48823; (517) 351-8080; 19,300 subs. **New Mexico -** TCI Cablevision of Santa Fe, 1414 Luisa St., Santa Fe, NM 87501; (505) 982-1968; 15,967 subs. **Puerto Rico -** TCI Cablevision de PR Inc., 2nd St. Ctr. Comm. Bresas del Mar, Luquillo, PR 00773; (809) 889-5804; Paco Gonzalez; 16,839 subs. **Tennessee -** TCI of Tennessee, 340 New Salem Hwy., Murfreesboro, TN 37129; (615) 896-2981; 16,800 subs. **Texas -** TCI Cablevision of South Texas, Box 928, 703 Grant, Roma, TX 78584; (512) 849-1523; 4,900 subs. TCI Cable, Box 1764, San Marcos, TX 78667-1764; (512) 353-3456; 13,000 subs. **Utah -** American Televenture Corporation, Box 69 A, Rt. 1, Fairview, UT 84629. **Wyoming -** TCI Cablevision, 451 S. Durbin, Casper, WY 82601; (307) 265-3130; 16,000 subs.

Tele-Media Corporation of Delaware

2151 E. College Ave., State College, PA 16801. (814) 238-8314; FAX: (814) 231-6742. Robert E. Tudek, CEO & chmn; Everett I. Mundy, pres; Thomas F. Kenly, vp opns; Robert R. Shepherd, vp mktg; Robert H. Stewart, vp progmg; Jon A. Allegretti, vp; Robert D. Stemler, vp; Richard W. Shore, vp. Owned by Robert E. Tudek, 50%; Everett I. Mundy, 50%. Total Basic Subscribers: 443,688; Pay Cable Subscribers: 139,749; Number of Cable Systems: 157.

REGIONS

Ohio: 1156-B Alum Creek Dr., Columbus, OH 43209; Gerald P. Corman. *Pennsylvania:* 320 W. College Ave., Pleasant Gap, PA 16823; Charles J. Hilderbrand. *Florida:* 6833 Vista Pkwy. N., West Palm Beach, FL 33411; Tony S. Swain. *Massachusetts:* Merchant's Mart State Rd., Vineyard Haven, MA 02568; Douglas F. Best. *Virginia:* 3971 Deep Rock Rd., Richmond, VA 23233; Frank R. Vicente. *Texas:* 605 Lake Bardwell Dr., Suite C, Ennis, TX 75119; Robert R. Shock.

SYSTEMS WITH OVER 20,000 SUBSCRIBERS

Tele-Media Co. of Southern Florida (43,000 subscribers). 19146 Lyons Rd., Boca Raton, FL 33434. (407) 482-2500. Nancy Yamotsky, gen mgr. *Basic Service:* Subscribers: 43,000; 12/15/92.

Tele-Media Company of Western Connecticut (42,000 subscribers). 80 Great Hill Rd., Seymour, CT 06483. (203) 736-2691; FAX: (203) 734-3425. Harold Kramer, gen mgr; Denise Hudson, mktg dir; Miriam Cantor, loc adv dir; Joseph Goertz, chief tech; Richard Brinker, cust svc dir.
Area(s) Served: CT. Counties: New Haven, Fairfield. Serving Ansonia, Beacon Falls, Bethany, Derby, Naugatuck, Oxford, Seymour, Shelton. Miles of Plant: 667. Homes Passed: 51,343. Homes Served: 42,000. *Channel Capacity:* 66. In use: 66. *Basic Service:* Subscribers: 42,000; 06/30/93. Programming (via satellite): 19 chs. Programming (via microwave): 1 ch. Programming (off air): 13 chs. *Pay Services:* Total Pay Subscribers: 31,828; 07/31/93. (1) Pay Units: 9,954; 07/31/93. Programming (via satellite): HBO. (2) Pay Units: 2,765; 07/31/93. Programming (via satellite): Cinemax. (3) Pay Units: 4,631; 07/31/93. Programming (via satellite): Showtime. (4) Pay Units: 4,068; 07/31/93. Programming (via satellite): The Movie Channel. (5) Pay Units: 5,127; 07/31/93. Programming (via satellite): Encore. Pay Per View Subscribers: 27,836; 08/31/93. *Local Advertising Accepted. Equipment:* Scientific-Atlanta headend; Texscan amplifiers; Comm/Scope cable.

TeleCable Corporation

Suite 900, 999 Waterside Dr., Norfolk, VA 23510-3306. (804) 624-5000; FAX: (804) 624-5079. Richard D. Roberts, CEO & pres; Frank Batten, chmn; Alfred Ritter, CFO; Dan Basnight, vp mktg. Owned by Frank Batten, majority stockholder. Total Basic Subscribers: 663,974; Number of Cable Systems: 21.

SYSTEMS WITH OVER 20,000 SUBSCRIBERS

Arlington TeleCable Inc. (58,500 subscribers). 2421 Matlock Rd., Arlington, TX 76015. (817) 265-7766; FAX: (817) 548-7420. Tony Carolla, gen mgr; Lydia Hall, mktg dir; Gary Hill, loc adv dir; Larry Dehmel, chief tech.
Area(s) Served: TX. County: Tarrant. Serving Arlington, Dalworthington Gardens, Pantego. Miles of Plant: 1,111. Homes Passed: 113,856. Homes Served: 58,500. *Channel Capacity:* 63. In use: 63. *Basic Service:* Subscribers: 58,500; 10/15/93. Pay Per View Subscribers: 53,750; 10/15/93. *Local Advertising Accepted.*

Racine TeleCable (38,000 subscribers). 5812 21st St., Racine, WI 53406. (414) 637-9637; FAX: (414) 637-7375. Kevin Anthony, gen mgr; Davis Driver, mktg dir; Lynn Zook, loc adv dir; Kelly Klenzer, cust svc dir.
Area(s) Served: WI. County: Racine. Serving Caledonia, Elmwood Park, Mt. Pleapant, North Bay, Racine, Sturtevant, Wind Point. Pop: 132,000. Miles of Plant: 500. Homes Passed: 49,000. Homes Served: 38,000. *Channel Capacity:* 55. In use: 55. *Basic Service:* Subscribers: 38,000; 11/15/93. *Local Advertising Accepted. Equipment:* Zenith & Scientific-Atlanta headend; Jerrold & Scientific- Atlanta amplifiers; Comm/Scope cable.

TeleCable of Beckley Inc. (22,250 subscribers). 113 First Ave., Beckley, WV 25802. (304) 252-6358; FAX: (304) 253-6843. Brenda McNutt, gen mgr; Dan Basnight, mktg dir.
Area(s) Served: WV. Homes Served: 22,250. *Basic Service:* Subscribers: 22,250; 11/15/93. *Pay Services:* Total Pay Subscribers: 15,252; 11/15/93.

TeleCable of Bloomington-Normal Inc. (30,619 subscribers). Box 1386, 1202 W. Division St., Bloomington, IL 61702. (309) 454-3350; FAX: (309) 452-6271. Tom Piazza, gen mgr.
Area(s) Served: IL. *Basic Service:* Subscribers: 30,619. *Pay Services:* Total Pay Subscribers: 23,625.

TeleCable of Broward County (32,000 subscribers). 950 N.W. 66th Ave., Margate, FL 33063. (305) 972-7500; FAX: (305) 977-9174. Anthony Genova, gen mgr; Karen Bartel, mktg dir; Joseph Genova, chief tech.
Area(s) Served: FL. County: Broward. Serving Coconut Creek, Margate, North Lauderdale, Parkland. Miles of Plant: 350. Homes Passed: 45,000. Homes Served: 32,000. *Channel Capacity:* 51. In use: 51. *Basic Service:* Subscribers: 32,000; 11/15/92. *Pay Services:* Total Pay Subscribers: 5,000; 11/15/91. *Local Advertising Accepted.*

TeleCable of Columbus Inc. (30,000 subscribers). 6700 Macon Rd., Columbus, GA 31907. (706) 569-5900; FAX: (706) 568-8270. Tom Tidd, gen mgr; John Anglin, mktg dir.
Area(s) Served: GA. Homes Served: 30,000. *Basic Service:* Subscribers: 30,000; 11/15/93.

TeleCable of Greenville Inc. (64,500 subscribers). 17 Lindsay Ave., Greenville, SC 29607. (803) 271-8526; FAX: (803) 242-4029. Vic Nicholls, gen mgr; Garnette H. Bane, mktg dir.
Area(s) Served: SC. Counties: Greenville, Pickens, Spartanburg. Serving City View, Easley, Greer. Pop: 250,000. Homes Passed: 91,840. Homes Served: 64,500. *Channel Capacity:* 40. In use: 40. *Basic Service:* Subscribers: 64,500; 11/15/93. Pay Per View Subscribers: 53,700; 11/15/93. *Local Advertising Accepted.*

TeleCable of Kokomo Inc. (26,500 subscribers). Box 2246, Kokomo, IN 46904. (317) 453-9075; FAX: (317) 455-4340. Rick Hamilton, gen mgr; Jeff Stamm, chief tech.
Area(s) Served: IN. Counties: Cass, Howard, Miami, Tipton. Serving Galveston, Greentown, Kokomo, Russianville, Sharpsville, Windfall. Miles of Plant: 432. Homes Passed: 30,194. Homes Served: 26,500. *Channel Capacity:* 46. In use: 46. *Basic Service:* Subscribers: 26,500; 11/15/93. Programming (via satellite): 36 chs. Programming (off air): 10 chs. *Local Advertising Accepted.*

TeleCable of Lexington Inc. (75,500 subscribers). 2544 Palumbo Dr., Lexington, KY 40509. (606) 268-1123. Max Hertweck, gen mgr; Brooke McDaniel, mktg dir; Bas Mattingly, loc adv dir; Billy Grubbs, chief tech.
Area(s) Served: KY. Counties: Fayette, Jessamine. Pop: 270,000. Miles of Plant: 970. Homes Passed: 100,700. Homes Served: 75,500. *Channel Capacity:* 45. In use: 45. *Basic Service:* Subscribers: 75,500; 10/15/93. *Local Advertising Accepted. Equipment:* Scientific-Atlanta headend; Jerrold amplifiers; Times fiber cable.

TeleCable of Overland Park Inc. (82,500 subscribers). Box 25567, Overland Park, KS 66225. (913) 451-5858. James Pimer, gen mgr.
Area(s) Served: KS. County: Johnson. Homes Served: 82,500. *Basic Service:* Subscribers: 82,500; 10/15/93. *Pay Services:* Total Pay Subscribers: 56,000; 10/15/93.

TeleCable of Richardson-Plano Inc. (53,400 subscribers). 1414 Summit Ave., Plano, TX 75074. (214) 578-7573; FAX: (214) 423-2248. J.T. Hendricks, gen mgr.
Area(s) Served: TX. Homes Served: 53,400. *Basic Service:* Subscribers: 53,400; 09/01/93.

TeleCable of Spartanburg (39,500 subscribers). 725 Union St., Spartanburg, SC 29304. (803) 585-0354; FAX: (803) 585-7701. Kirby Brooks, gen mgr.
Area(s) Served: SC. Homes Served: 39,500. *Channel Capacity:* 37. *Basic Service:* Subscribers: 39,500; 11/15/93. *Pay Services:* Total Pay Subscribers: 29,998.

TeleCable of Springfield (47,846 subscribers). 1533 S. Enterprise, Springfield, MO 65804. (417) 883-7557; FAX: (417) 883-0265. Jerry Rutherford, gen mgr; Stan Melton, mktg dir; Gary Banner, loc adv dir; Rick Pool, chief tech; Judy Dean, cust svc dir.
Area(s) Served: MO. County: Greene. Serving Battlefield, Springfield. Pop: 200,000. Miles of Plant: 964. Homes Passed: 69,334. Homes Served: 47,846. *Channel Capacity:* 61. In use: 61. *Basic Service:* Subscribers: 47,846; 09/11/93. Pay Per View Subscribers: 35,976; 09/11/93. *Local Advertising Accepted. Equipment:* Sci-

Multiple Systems Operators, Independent Owners & Cable Systems

entific-Atlanta headend; Jerrold amplifiers; Comm/Scope cable.

Telephone & Data Systems Inc.

301 S. Westfield Rd., Madison, WI 53717-1707. (608) 845-4500; FAX: (608) 845-4809. Leroy Carlson Jr., CEO; Vince Reed, vp opns; Jerry Masters, vp mktg. Total Basic Subscribers: 2,700; Pay Cable Subscribers: 1,000; Number of Cable Systems: 5.

Teleponce Cable TV Inc.

Box 204, Mercedita, PR 00715-0204. (809) 848-7745; FAX: (809) 848-7757. Hector R. Gonzalez, CEO & chmn; Albert N. Ferraro, CFO; Jose Mendez, vp opns; Jacqueline Ramos, vp sls; Lourdes Estrada, vp mktg; Bob Ritchie, vp adv; Enid Anglero, vp progmg; Ivo Graciani, vp. Owned by TPC Communications PR Inc. Total Basic Subscribers: 25,000; Pay Cable Subscribers: 18,000; Number of Cable Systems: 1.

REGIONS

Ponce: Plaza Nuevo Mundo Shopping Ctr., Ponce, PR 00715; (809) 844-7700; Arlene Trizarry. *Yauco:* Yauco Plaza Shopping Ctr., Yauco, PR 00698; (809) 856-6024; Cindy Correa.

Telepro Communications

Suite 310, 4122 128th Ave. S.E., Bellevue, WA 98006. (206) 957-4730; FAX: (206) 957-0119. John F. Craig, pres. Owned by John F. Craig. Total Basic Subscribers: 3,500; Pay Cable Subscribers: 1,700; Number of Cable Systems: 11.

Telesat Cablevision Inc.

Suite 600 A, 2101 NW 33rd St., Pompano Beach, FL 33069. (305) 978-1218; FAX: (305) 971-8019. Harry F. Cushing, pres; Richard M. Schorr, CFO. Owned by FPL Group Capital Inc. Total Basic Subscribers: 41,000; Pay Cable Subscribers: 36,000.

Teleview Systems Corporation

Box 35, 207 W. Pearl St., Decorah, IA 52101. (319) 382-3560. Robert E., Houlihan, pres; John E. Anundsen, vp. Owned by Robert E. Houlihan, John E. Anundsen. Total Basic Subscribers: 3,160; Pay Cable Subscribers: 1,000; Number of Cable Systems: 1.

Televista Communications Inc.

Box 604, 37269 Huron River Dr., New Boston, MI 48164. (313) 753-3450; FAX: (313) 753-9891. Michael E. Turner, CEO & pres. Total Basic Subscribers: 6,500; Pay Cable Subscribers: 3,500; Number of Cable Systems: 2.

SMALLER SYSTEMS

Michigan - North Oakland Cable, New Boston, MI; 3,500 subs. Televista Cable TV, New Boston, MI: 3,000 subs.

Terril Telephone Co.

Box 100, 107 S. State St., Terril, IA 51364. (712) 853-6121; FAX: (712) 853-6185. Douglas R. Nelson, CEO; Douglas Nelson, vp opns; Dana Loring, vp mktg; Geraldine Zelinsky, vp progmg; Steve Oleson, vp. Owned by Ter Tel Enterprises Inc. Total Basic Subscribers: 1,310; Pay Cable Subscribers: 550; Number of Cable Systems: 5.

SMALLER SYSTEMS

Iowa - Terril Cable Systems, Terril, IA. Terril Cable Systems, Ruthven, IA. **Minnesota** - Terril Cable Systems, Trimont, MN. Terril Cable Systems, Truman, MN. Terril Cable Systems, Welcome, MN.

Ben Terry

Box 1436, Henderson, NC 27536. (919) 492-0427; FAX: (919) 492-9013. Ben Terry, CEO; John Terry, vp. Total Basic Subscribers: 14,000; Number of Cable Systems: 4.

SMALLER SYSTEMS

North Carolina - Franklin Cablevision, Franklin, NC. Henderson Cable TV, Henderson, NC. Oxford Cable TV, Oxford, NC. Warren Cable TV, Warren, NC.

Terry Thomas

Box 8, 124 E. 7th Ave., Redfield, SD 57469. (605) 472-3415. Total Basic Subscribers: 1,800; Pay Cable Subscribers: 1,400; Number of Cable Systems: 1.

SMALLER SYSTEMS

South Dakota - Village Cable, 124 E. 7th Ave., Redfield, SD 57469.

Thompson Cablevision Co. Inc.

Box 13309, Sissonville, WV 25360. (304) 984-0025; FAX: (304) 984-0002. Allen D. Thompson, pres; Anthony Cochran, vp. Owned by Allen D. Thompson. Total Basic Subscribers: 15,238; Pay Cable Subscribers: 3,692; Number of Cable Systems: 10.

Time Warner Cable

300 First Stamford Pl., Stamford, CT 06902. (203) 328-0600; FAX: (203) 328-4887. Joseph J. Collins, CEO & chmn; James H. Doolittle, pres; Tom Harris, CFO; Kevin Leddy, vp mktg; Fred Dressler, vp progmg; John F. Gault, vp; Kevin H. Rorke, vp; James P. Cottingham, vp. Total Basic Subscribers: 7,100,000.

SYSTEMS WITH OVER 20,000 SUBSCRIBERS

American Cablevision (28,000 subscribers). 1605 Wabash Ave., Terre Haute, IN 47807. (812) 232-5013; FAX: (812) 232-7453. Rick Orr, gen mgr; Phaedra Hyche, mktg dir; Al Winn, chief tech.
Area(s) Served: IN. County: Vigo. Serving Riley, West Terre Haute. Homes Served: 28,000. *Channel Capacity:* 42. In use: 42. *Basic Service:* Subscribers: 28,000; 11/15/93. *Local Advertising Accepted.*

American Cablevision (174,000 subscribers). 6550 Winchester, Kansas City, MO 64133. (816) 358-5360; FAX: (816) 358-5815. Robert B. Niles, gen mgr; Jeff Johnston, mktg dir; Alan T. Schimer, chief tech.
Area(s) Served: KS, MO. Homes Passed: 330,000. Homes Served: 174,000. *Channel Capacity:* 35. *Basic Service:* Subscribers: 174,000; 11/15/93.

American Cablevision of Indianapolis (81,000 subscribers). 3030 Roosevelt Ave., Indianapolis, IN 46218. (317) 632-2288; FAX: (317) 632-5311. Jay Satterfield, gen mgr; Bob Roelfs, mktg dir; Nick Arnold, loc adv dir; Bob Jones, chief tech; Sue Cloyed, cust svc dir.
Area(s) Served: IN. Counties: Hendricks, Marion. Serving Browsburg, Danville. Miles of Plant: 1,140. Homes Passed: 165,500. Homes Served: 81,000. *Channel Capacity:* 42. In use: 41. *Basic Service:* Subscribers: 81,000; 11/15/93. *Pay Services:* Total Pay Subscribers: 77,000; 09/15/91. *Local Advertising Accepted.*

American Cablevision of Monroeville (32,000 subscribers). 200 James Pl., Monroeville, PA 15146. (412) 856-7140; FAX: (412) 856-7650. Barbara Lukens, gen mgr; Mary Millar, mktg dir; Jason Martin, loc adv dir; Mike Matthyse, chief tech; Russ Williams, cust svc dir.
Area(s) Served: PA. County: Allegheny. Serving Braddock, Churchill, East McKeesport, East Pittsburgh, Monroeville, North Braddock, North Huntingdon, North Versailles, Ronkin, Swissvale, Trafford, Turtlecreek, Wilkins. Miles of Plant: 315. Homes Passed: 41,800. Homes Served: 32,000. *Channel Capacity:* 38. In use: 38. *Basic Service:* Subscribers: 32,000; 11/15/93. *Pay Services:* Total Pay Subscribers: 21,600; 10/15/91. Pay Per View Subscribers: 6,000; 10/15/91. *Local Advertising Accepted.*

American Community Cablevision (26,000 subscribers). 519 W. State St., Ithaca, NY 14850. (607) 272-3456; FAX: (607) 277-5404. Raymond McCabe, gen mgr; Tom Downey, mktg dir; Paula Tarallo, loc adv dir; David Huff, chief tech; Doc McQuade, cust svc dir.
Area(s) Served: NY. Counties: Tioga, Tompkins. Serving Candor, Caroline, Cayuga Hgts., Danby, Dryden, Freeville, Groton, Ithaca, Lansing, Newark Valley, Newfield, Trumansburg, Ulysses. Miles of Plant: 500. Homes Passed: 30,000. Homes Served: 26,000. *Channel Capacity:* 60. In use: 51. *Basic Service:* Subscribers: 26,000; 11/15/93. Pay Per View Subscribers: 18,000; 11/15/91. *Local Advertising Accepted.*

ATC - Cablevision (21,200 subscribers). 18356 Soledad Canyon Rd., Canyon Country, CA 91351. (805) 252-2318; FAX: (805) 251-6181. Scott Binder, gen mgr; Debbie Worden, mktg dir; Craig Ziofanni, chief tech.
Area(s) Served: CA. County: Los Angeles. Serving Newhall, Santa Clarita, Saugus. Homes Served: 21,200. *Basic Service:* Subscribers: 21,200; 11/15/93.

Austin Cablevision (190,000 subscribers). 2191 Woodward Ave., Austin, TX 78744. (512) 448-8100; FAX: (512) 448-8191. Tom Rutledge, gen mgr; Judy Walsh, mktg dir; Jim Norton, loc adv dir; Reggie Workman, chief tech; Cheryl Rummel, cust svc dir.
Area(s) Served: TX. Counties: Bastrop, Caldwell, Fayette, Gonzales, Travis, Williamson. Serving Austin, Bastrop, Cedar Park, Davenport Ranch, Elgin, Flatonia, Hudson Bend, Lost Creek, Lulins, Nixon, Rollingwood, Round Rock, San Leonna, Sunset Valley, Taylor, Wells Branch, West Lake Hills. Pop: 800,000. Miles of Plant: 2,500. Homes Passed: 264,000. Homes Served: 190,000. *Channel Capacity:* 57. In use: 57. *Basic Service:* Subscribers: 190,000; 08/31/93. Programming (via satellite): 44 chs. Programming (off air): 6 chs. *Pay Services:* Total Pay Subscribers: 88,700; 08/31/93. (1) Pay Units: 44,600; 08/31/93. Programming (via satellite): HBO. (2) Pay Units: 28,500; 08/31/93. Programming (via satellite): Cinemax. (3) Pay Units: 8,300; 08/31/93. Programming (via satellite): Showtime. (4) Pay Units: 5,200; 08/31/93. Programming (via satellite): Disney. (5) Pay Units: 1,700; 08/31/93. Programming (via satellite): Playboy. Pay Per View Subscribers: 43,000; 08/31/93. *Local Advertising Accepted.*

Berks Cable (63,000 subscribers). 400 Riverfront Dr., Reading, PA 19602. (215) 378-4600; FAX: (215) 378-4668. Jon Scott, gen mgr; Marilyn Garcia, mktg dir; Don Wynen, chief tech; Tony Castner, cust svc dir.
Area(s) Served: PA. Counties: Berks, Lebanon. Miles of Plant: 729. Homes Passed: 82,000. Homes Served: 63,000. *Channel Capacity:* 42. In use: 41. *Basic Service:* Subscribers: 63,000; 11/15/93. *Pay Services:* Total Pay Subscribers: 45,997; 07/15/91. Pay Per View Subscribers: 7,157; 07/15/91. *Local Advertising Accepted.*

Birmingham Cable Communications (72,000 subscribers). 6429 First Ave. S., Birmingham, AL 35212. (205) 591-6880; FAX: (205) 599-5641. Michael D'Ambra, gen mgr; Julia Muscari, mktg dir; Rod Clark, loc adv dir; Brian Merrill, cust svc dir.
Area(s) Served: AL. County: Jefferson. Serving Brighton, Brownville, Irondale, Lipscomb, Roosevelt City. Miles of Plant: 1,100. Homes Passed: 146,000. Homes Served: 72,000. *Channel Capacity:* 42. In use: 42. *Basic Service:* Subscribers: 72,000; 11/15/93. Pay Per View Subscribers: 11,000; 09/15/91. *Local Advertising Accepted.*

C.V. - Cablevision of Central Florida (66,000 subscribers). 2850 S. Leconto Hwy., Leconto, FL 32661. (904) 746-7664; FAX: (904) 746-7353. John Doctor, gen mgr; Lisa Daniel, mktg dir; Don Koehler, loc adv dir; Scott Twyman, chief tech; Karen Sheppard, cust svc dir.
Area(s) Served: FL. County: Citrus. Serving Beverly Hill, Citrus Springs, Crystal River, Hernando, Homosassa, Homosassa Springs, Iverness. Homes Served: 66,000. *Basic Service:* Subscribers: 66,000; 11/15/93.

C.V. - Cablevision of Central Florida (140,400 subscribers). 720 Magnolia Ave., Melbourne, FL 32935. (407) 254-3300. Troy Harville, gen mgr; Elaine Kowalski, mktg dir; Robert Sell, chief tech; Debbie Kelly, cust svc dir.
Area(s) Served: FL. County: Brevard. Serving Cocoa, Indiatlantic, Indian Harbor Beach, Kochledge, Mulayar, Melbourne Beach, Melbourne Village, Merritt Island, Palm Bay, Palm Shores, Satellite Beach, West Melbourne. Homes Served: 140,400. *Basic Service:* Subscribers: 140,400; 11/15/93.

Cablevision of Alamance County (22,000 subscribers). 316 Huffman Mill Rd., Burlington, NC 27215. (919) 584-1383; FAX: (919) 584-3262. Diane Blackwood, gen mgr.
Area(s) Served: NC. Counties: Alamance, Guilford. Serving Alamance, Burlington, Elon College, Gibsonville, Graham, Haw River. Miles of Plant: 582. Homes Passed: 33,000. Homes Served: 22,000. *Channel Capacity:* 42. In use: 42. *Basic Service:* Subscribers: 22,000; 09/01/93. *Pay Services:* Total Pay Subscribers: 15,800; 11/15/91. Pay Per View Subscribers: 14,000; 09/01/93. *Local Advertising Accepted.*

Cablevision of Appleton (34,000 subscribers). 1001 Kennedy Ave., Kimberly, WI 54136. (414) 738-3160; FAX: (414) 749-0618. Kathy Keatina, gen mgr; Jim Reinl, mktg dir; Ann Whisler, loc adv dir.
Area(s) Served: WI. Counties: Calumet, Outagamie, Winnebago. Serving Greater Appleton. Miles of Plant: 700. Homes Served: 34,000. *Channel Capacity:* 40. In use: 40. *Basic Service:* Subscribers: 34,000; 11/15/93. *Pay Services:* Total Pay Subscribers: 11,700; 11/15/91. *Local Advertising Accepted.*

Multiple Systems Operators, Independent Owners & Cable Systems

Cablevision of Central Florida (190,000 subscribers). 3767 All American Blvd., Orlando, FL 32810. (407) 295-9119; FAX: (407) 298-5904. David Spencer, gen mgr; Heather Grasso, mktg dir; John Walsh, chief tech; Allan Herring, cust svc dir.
Area(s) Served: FL. Counties: Orange, Osceola, Seminole. Serving Apopka, Belle Isle, Casselberry, Eatonville, Edgewood, Kissimmee, Longwood, Maitland, Sanford, Windermere, Winter Park, Winter Springs. *Basic Service:* Subscribers: 190,000; 11/15/93.

CableVision of Central Florida (53,000 subscribers). 2806 Recker Hwy., Winter Haven, FL 33880. (813) 293-4319; FAX: (813) 294-2318. Jack Jessen, gen mgr; Gaynelle Henderson, mktg dir; Don Koehler, loc adv dir; Scott Henry, chief tech; Robin Pinks, cust svc dir.
Area(s) Served: FL. Counties: Hardee, Pinellas. Serving Auburndale, Bowling Green, Eagle Lake, Lake Alfred, Lakeland, Mulberry, Winter Haven. Homes Served: 53,000. *Channel Capacity:* 53. In use: 53. *Basic Service:* Subscribers: 53,000; 11/15/93. *Local Advertising Accepted.*

Cablevision of Champaign-Urbana (37,500 subscribers). 303 Fairlawn Dr., Urbana, IL 61801. (217) 384-2530; FAX: (217) 384-2021. Stan Cochran, gen mgr; William W. Rouggly, mktg dir; Lynn Wombacher, loc adv dir; Tom Loveay, chief tech; Leslie Grayson, cust svc dir.
Area(s) Served: IL. County: Champaign. Serving Bondville, Champaign, Savoy, Urbana. Miles of Plant: 425. Homes Passed: 50,600. Homes Served: 37,500. *Channel Capacity:* 36. In use: 36. *Basic Service:* Subscribers: 37,500; 11/15/93. *Pay Services:* Total Pay Subscribers: 17,600; 12/15/91. Pay Per View Subscribers: 7,000; 12/15/91. *Local Advertising Accepted.*

Cablevision of Charlotte (103,000 subscribers). 316 E. Morehead, Charlotte, NC 28202. (704) 377-2228; FAX: (704) 332-4550. Jeff King, gen mgr; Peter Gulla, mktg dir; Walt Colquilt, chief tech.
Area(s) Served: NC. County: Mecklenburg. Serving Matthews. Homes Passed: 155,000. Homes Served: 103,000. *Channel Capacity:* 38. In use: 38. *Basic Service:* Subscribers: 103,000; 11/15/93. Pay Per View Subscribers: 35,000; 11/15/91. *Local Advertising Accepted.*

Cablevision of Eau Claire (26,000 subscribers). Box 125, 2207 Heimstead Rd., Eau Claire, WI 54703. (715) 836-8580; FAX: (715) 836-8591. Leslie Grayson, gen mgr; Brad Elbers, mktg dir; Tim Normand, chief tech; Marge Vlasak, cust svc dir.
Area(s) Served: WI. Counties: Chippewa, Dunn, Eau Claire. Serving Altoona, Chippewa Falls, Eagle Point, Elk Mound, Hallie, Pleasant Valley, Seymour, Tilden, Union, Washington, Wheaton. Miles of Plant: 490. Homes Passed: 35,750. Homes Served: 26,000. *Channel Capacity:* 36. In use: 36. *Basic Service:* Subscribers: 26,000; 11/15/93. *Pay Services:* Total Pay Subscribers: 9,000; 11/15/91. *Local Advertising Accepted.*

Cablevision of Fayetteville (76,800 subscribers). Box 40508, Fayetteville, NC 28309. (919) 864-2004; FAX: (919) 864-8878. Bill Carey, gen mgr; Vic Scarborough, mktg dir; John Nicholas, chief tech; Trish Harleston, cust svc dir.
Area(s) Served: NC. Counties: Cumberland, Harnett, Robeson, Sampson. Serving Autryville, Dunn, Erwin, Falcon, Fort Bragg, Godwin, Hope Mills, Parkton, Spring Lake, Stedmare, Wade. Homes Served: 76,800. *Channel Capacity:* In use: 38. *Basic Service:* Subscribers: 76,800; 11/15/93. *Pay Services:* Total Pay Subscribers: 52,000; 10/15/91. Pay Per View Subscribers: 40,000; 10/15/91. *Local Advertising Accepted.*

Cablevision of Green Bay (28,300 subscribers). 2580 W. Mason, Green Bay, WI 54303. (414) 496-2040; FAX: (414) 496-0814. Patrick Hourigan, gen mgr; Nancy Crabbs, mktg dir; Ann Whisler, loc adv dir.
Area(s) Served: WI. Counties: Brown, Outagamie. Serving Green Bay. Homes Served: 28,300. *Channel Capacity:* 36. In use: 36. *Basic Service:* Subscribers: 28,300; 11/15/93. *Pay Services:* Total Pay Subscribers: 14,000; 11/15/91. *Local Advertising Accepted.*

Cablevision of Greensboro (50,000 subscribers). Box 5487, 1813 Spring Garden St., Greensboro, NC 27103. (919) 379-0220; FAX: (919) 274-9609. D.K. McLaughlin, gen mgr; Linda White, mktg dir; Ray Standridge, chief tech; Karen Kearney, cust svc dir.
Area(s) Served: NC. County: Guilford. Serving Greensboro. *Channel Capacity:* 38. In use: 38. *Basic Service:* Subscribers: 50,000; 11/30/92. *Local Advertising Accepted.*

Cablevision of Orange (25,600 subscribers). 154 N. Glassell St., Orange, CA 92666. (714) 771-4910; FAX: (714) 771-3369. Steve Everett, gen mgr; Shelly Trainor, mktg dir; Ken Eldridge, chief tech.
Area(s) Served: CA. County: Orange. Homes Passed: 40,000. Homes Served: 25,600. *Channel Capacity:* 46. In use: 46. *Basic Service:* Subscribers: 25,600; 11/15/93. *Pay Services:* Total Pay Subscribers: 22,000; 09/15/91. Pay Per View Subscribers: 11,000; 09/15/91. *Local Advertising Accepted.*

Cablevision of Savannah (59,300 subscribers). Box 22879, 5515 Abercorn St., Savannah, GA 31405. (912) 354-7531; FAX: (912) 353-6045. Beth Scarborough, gen mgr; Larry Peterson, mktg dir; Tommy Murphy, chief tech; Carolyn Laws, cust svc dir.
Area(s) Served: GA, SC. Counties: Bryan, Chatham, Effingham, Hampton, Liberty. Serving Bloomingdale, Brunson, Garden City, Hampton, Midway, Pooler, Port Wentworth, Rincon, Springfield, Thunderbolt, Varnville, Vernonbury. Miles of Plant: 1,147. Homes Passed: 94,702. Homes Served: 59,300. *Channel Capacity:* 30. In use: 30. *Basic Service:* Subscribers: 59,300; 11/15/93. *Pay Services:* Total Pay Subscribers: 38,972; 11/15/91. Pay Per View Subscribers: 10,250; 11/15/91. *Local Advertising Accepted.*

Cablevision of Shreveport (60,000 subscribers). 6529 Quilen Rd., Shreveport, LA 71108. (318) 631-3060; FAX: (318) 631-1027. Mike Hugunin, gen mgr; Caroline Flaton, mktg dir; Darrell Eichelberger, chief tech; Ruby Hawkins, cust svc dir.
Area(s) Served: LA, TX. Counties: Caddo, DeSoto, Harrison. Serving Bethany, Greenwood, Waskom. Miles of Plant: 1,300. Homes Passed: 103,000. Homes Served: 60,000. *Channel Capacity:* 37. In use: 37. *Basic Service:* Subscribers: 60,000; 11/15/93. *Pay Services:* Total Pay Subscribers: 30,000; 10/15/91. Pay Per View Subscribers: 14,000; 10/15/91. *Local Advertising Accepted.*

Capitol Cablevision (74,000 subscribers). Box 9426, 5375 Executive Pl., Jackson, MS 39206. (601) 982-1187; FAX: (601) 982-9532. Steve McMahon, gen mgr; Paul Hardin, mktg dir; Glenn Whitfield, chief tech; Ernestine Jackson, cust svc dir.
Area(s) Served: MS. Counties: Hinds, Madison, Rankin. Serving Bolton, Cleary Heights, Clinton, Edwards, Florence, Jackson, Lake Ridgelea, Madison, Pearl River Valley Water Supply District, Richland, Ridgeland. Miles of Plant: 1,411. Homes Passed: 109,685. Homes Served: 74,000. *Channel Capacity:* 41. In use: 40. *Basic Service:* Subscribers: 74,000; 11/15/93. Programming (off air): 5 chs. *Pay Services:* Total Pay Subscribers: 46,467; 10/31/92. Pay Per View Subscribers: 20,000; 10/31/92. *Local Advertising Accepted.*

Capitol Cablevision (33,500 subscribers). Box 2673, 209 Broad St., Charleston, WV 25330. (304) 345-8483; FAX: (304) 357-6707. Thomas L. Kinney, gen mgr; Michael Kelemen, mktg dir; Ron Batson, chief tech.
Area(s) Served: WV. County: Kanawha. Serving Dunbar, Institute, Ruthdale, South Charleston. Miles of Plant: 450. Homes Passed: 43,000. Homes Served: 33,500. *Channel Capacity:* 60. In use: 55. *Basic Service:* Subscribers: 33,500; 11/15/93. *Pay Services:* Total Pay Subscribers: 13,000; 10/15/91. Pay Per View Subscribers: 3,000; 10/15/91. *Local Advertising Accepted.*

Capitol Cablevision Systems Inc. (65,000 subscribers). 130 Washington Ave. Ext., Albany, NY 12203. (518) 869-5500. Tony Esposito, gen mgr; Stuart Gorenstein, mktg dir; Charmene Ushkow, loc adv dir; Mark S. Miller, chief tech; Victor Mahoney, cust svc dir.
Area(s) Served: NY. County: Albany. Serving Altamont, Colonie, Green Island, Guilderland, Menands. Miles of Plant: 789. Homes Passed: 88,700. Homes Served: 65,000. *Channel Capacity:* 37. In use: 37. *Basic Service:* Subscribers: 65,000; 11/15/93. *Pay Services:* Total Pay Subscribers: 45,000; 10/15/91. Pay Per View Subscribers: 26,000; 10/15/91. *Local Advertising Accepted.*

Durham Cablevision (52,800 subscribers). 708 E. Club Blvd., Durham, NC 27704. (919) 220-4145; FAX: (919) 220-3822. Willis G. Smith, gen mgr; Terrell Mayton, mktg dir; Bob Hermann, chief tech.
Area(s) Served: NC. Counties: Durham, Granville. Miles of Plant: 1,200. Homes Passed: 77,000. Homes Served: 52,800. *Basic Service:* Subscribers: 52,800; 11/15/93. *Pay Services:* Total Pay Subscribers: 33,000; 11/15/91. *No Local Advertising Accepted.*

Erie Cablevision (30,000 subscribers). 823 Peach St., Erie, PA 16501. (814) 453-4553; FAX: (814) 456-5162. Kevin Nolan, gen mgr; Peggy Bach, mktg dir; Keith Krueger, chief tech.
Area(s) Served: PA. County: Erie. Miles of Plant: 267. Homes Passed: 45,850. Homes Served: 30,000. *Channel Capacity:* 84. In use: 84. *Basic Service:* Subscribers: 30,000; 11/15/93. *Pay Services:* Total Pay Subscribers: 17,000; 11/15/91. Pay Per View Subscribers: 6,000; 11/15/91. *Local Advertising Accepted.*

Greater Rochester Cablevision (192,000 subscribers). 71 Mount Hope Ave., Rochester, NY 14620. (716) 325-1111; FAX: (716) 454-3321. Frank Chiaino, gen mgr; Tony Marino, mktg dir; Deborah Cuffaro, loc adv dir; Paul Gemme, chief tech; Greg Hunt, cust svc dir.
Area(s) Served: NY. Counties: Genesee, Monroe, Orleans. Serving Brighton, Brockport, Byron, Chili, Churchville, Clarendon, Clarkson, East Rochester, Fairport, Gates, Greece, Hamlin, Henrietta, Hilton, Holley, Irondequoit, Murray, Ogden, Parma, Penfield, Perinton, Pittsford, Riga, Scottsville, Spencerport, Sweden, Webster. Homes Served: 192,000. *Basic Service:* Subscribers: 192,000; 11/15/93.

Laurel Cablevision (25,300 subscribers). 622 Torrington Rd., Litchfield, CT 06759. (203) 567-3103; FAX: (203) 567-8531. Joshua L. Jamison, gen mgr; Pamela Little, mktg dir; Robert W. Bailey, chief tech.
Area(s) Served: CT. County: Litchfield. Serving Burrville, Litchfield, Morris, Northfield, Oakville, Thomaston, Warren, Waterton. Miles of Plant: 604. Homes Passed: 32,000. Homes Served: 25,300. *Channel Capacity:* 37. In use: 37. *Basic Service:* Subscribers: 25,300; 11/15/93. *Pay Services:* Total Pay Subscribers: 11,316; 09/15/91. *Local Advertising Accepted.*

Lebanon Valley Cable (31,500 subscribers). 1220 Mifflin St., Lebanon, PA 17042. (717) 273-8511; FAX: (717) 273-0702. Lee Glowacki, gen mgr; Kim Dehart, mktg dir; Barry Stephenson, chief tech.
Area(s) Served: PA. Counties: Berks, Lebanon, Schuylkill. Serving Annville, Bethel, Cornwall, East Hanover, Heidelbergs, Jackson, Jonestown, Lebanon City, Millcreek, Mount Gretna, Myerstown, North Annville, North Cornwall, North Lebanon, Pine Grove, Richland Cleona, South Annville, South Heidelberg, South Lebanon, South Londonderry, Strausstown, Swatara, Tremont, Tulpehocken, Union, Upper Tulpehocken, Washington, West Lebanon, West Cornwall, Womelsdorf Robesonia. Miles of Plant: 733. Homes Passed: 42,456. Homes Served: 31,500. *Channel Capacity:* 35. In use: 34. *Basic Service:* Subscribers: 31,500; 11/15/93. Programming (via satellite): CNN, HSN, Headline News, A&E, C-SPAN, Lifetime, Weather Channel, ESPN, TNT, USA, Family Channel, Nickelodeon, Discovery Channel, MTV, AMC, CNBC, TBS. Programming (via microwave): WVIA. Programming (off air): WLYH, KYW, WHP, WPVI, WPHL, WGAL, WGCB, WGBS, WHTM, WITF, WLVT, WCAU. *Pay Services:* Total Pay Subscribers: 13,500; 11/30/92. (1) Pay Units: 5,508; 10/30/92. Programming (via satellite): HBO. (2) Pay Units: 2,646; 10/30/92. Programming (via satellite): Cinemax. (3) Pay Units: 2,199; 10/30/92. Programming (via satellite): Disney. *Local Advertising Accepted.*

Lower Bucks Cablevision Inc. (38,000 subscribers). 2320 Trenton Rd., Levittown, PA 19056. (215) 547-3819; FAX: (215) 943-2528. Frank J. Moore, gen mgr; Linda Shibanak, mktg dir; Thomas Kolenda, chief tech.
Area(s) Served: PA. County: Bucks. Serving Bristol, Bristol Twp., Hulmeville, Langhorne, Langhorne Manor, Lower Makefield, Middletown, Penndel, Yardley. Miles of Plant: 600. Homes Passed: 51,720. Homes Served: 38,000. *Channel Capacity:* 35. In use: 35. *Basic Service:* Subscribers: 38,000; 11/15/93. *Pay Services:* Total Pay Subscribers: 23,855; 11/15/91. Pay Per View Subscribers: 5,200; 11/15/91. *Local Advertising Accepted.*

Lynchburg Cablevision (21,000 subscribers). 2820 Linkhorne Dr., Lynchburg, VA 24503. (804) 384-1000; FAX: (804) 384-1199. Regina Martin, gen mgr; Mike Tilley, mktg dir; Dale Pollard, chief tech; Pamela Shackleford, cust svc dir.
Area(s) Served: VA. Counties: Bedford, Campbell. Homes Served: 21,000. *Basic Service:* Subscribers: 21,000; 11/15/93.

Memphis Cablevision (200,000 subscribers). Suite 400, 6555 Quince Rd., Memphis, TN 38119. (901) 365-1770; FAX: (901) 369-4515. Dean Deyo, gen mgr; Steven Stiger, mktg dir; Greg Hamilton, loc adv dir; Don Shackelford, chief tech; Jo Cossart, cust svc dir.
Area(s) Served: TN, AK, MS. Counties: Alcorn, Crittedon, DeSoto, Fayette, Hardeman, Haywood, Marshall, Shelby, Tate, Tippah. Serving Renove, Southaven. Miles of Plant: 3,000. Homes Passed: 350,000. Homes Served: 200,000. *Channel Capacity:* 37. In use: 37. *Basic Service:* Subscribers: 200,000; 11/15/93. *Pay Services:* Total Pay Subscribers: 140,000; 11/15/91.

Broadcasting & Cable Yearbook 1994
D-47

Multiple Systems Operators, Independent Owners & Cable Systems

Pay Per View Subscribers: 25,000; 11/15/91. *Local Advertising Accepted.*

Oceanic Cablevision Inc. (231,438 subscribers). 200 Akamainui St., Mililani, HI 96789. (808) 625-2100; FAX: (808) 625-5888. Don E. Carroll, gen mgr; Bill Butts, mktg dir; Nitzi Lehano, loc adv dir; Mike Goodish, chief tech; Sandy Davis, cust svc dir.
Area(s) Served: HI. County: Honolulu. Serving Ahuimanu, Aiea, Aliamunu Government Reserve, Diamond Head/Wilhelmina, Enchanted Hills, Ewa, Ewa Beach, Foster Village, Halawa Heights, Haleiwa, Hauula, Kaaawa, Kahaluu, Kahuku, Kaimuki, Kapahulu, Kapalama, Kapiolani, Kuliouou Valley, Laie, Maili, Makaha, Makakilo City, Makiki, Manoa, Maunawili, McCully, Mililani, Moanalua, Moiliili, Mokuleia, Nanakuli, North Shore, Nuuanu, Pacific Heights, Pauoa, Pearl City, Pearl Harbor Government Reserve, Punchbowl, Pupukea, St. Louis Heights, Sunset Beach, Wahiawa, Waialua, Waipahu, Waipio. Pop: 900,000. Miles of Plant: 1,710. Homes Passed: 301,913. Homes Served: 231,438. *Channel Capacity:* 36. In use: 34. *Basic Service:* Subscribers: 231,438; 11/15/93. *Pay Services:* Total Pay Subscribers: 194,723; 11/15/91. Pay Per View Subscribers: 147,695; 11/15/91. *Local Advertising Accepted.*

Paragon Cable (119,000 subscribers). 11500 Ninth St. N., St. Petersburg, FL 33716. (813) 579-8600; FAX: (813) 579-4981. Robert J. Barlow, gen mgr; John Nix, mktg dir; Jack Taylor, loc adv dir; Steve Eichler, chief tech; Wanda Hayes, cust svc dir.
Area(s) Served: FL. County: Pinellas. Serving Belleair Beach, Belleair Bluffs, Belleair Shores, Gulfport, Indian Rocks Beach, Indian Shores, Largo, St. Petersburg, St. Petersburg Beach, Seminole, South Pasedena, Treasure Island. Miles of Plant: 1,460. Homes Passed: 195,000. *Channel Capacity:* 78. In use: 62. *Basic Service:* Subscribers: 119,000. *Local Advertising Accepted.*

Paragon Cable (122,000 subscribers). 520 Grand Regency Blvd., Brandon, FL 33510. (813) 684-6100; FAX: (813) 651-1597. Harry F. Sheraw, gen mgr; Dan Wright, mktg dir; Nick Smith, loc adv dir; Mike Vanderkodde, chief tech; Sue Thrower, cust svc dir.
Area(s) Served: FL. Counties: Hillsborough, Pasco. Serving Plant City, Temple Terrace. Miles of Plant: 3,000. Homes Passed: 215,000. Homes Served: 122,000. *Channel Capacity:* 54. In use: 54. *Basic Service:* Subscribers: 122,000; 11/15/93. *Pay Services:* Total Pay Subscribers: 72,000; 12/01/92. Pay Per View Subscribers: 23,000; 12/01/92. *Local Advertising Accepted.*

Paragon Cable (60,900 subscribers). Suite A, 3526 9th St. W., Bradenton, FL 34205. (813) 748-3816; FAX: (813) 747-0005. Rosemary Carlson, gen mgr; Colleen Tomisiea, mktg dir; Dane Hall, loc adv dir; Rick Hoffmeister, chief tech; Jane Waldo, cust svc dir.
Area(s) Served: FL. County: Manatee. Serving Anna Maria, Bradenton Beach, Holmes Beach. Homes Served: 60,900. *Basic Service:* Subscribers: 60,900; 11/15/93.

Paragon Cable (25,000 subscribers). Box 3800, Lakeland, FL 33802-9966. (813) 683-6451; FAX: (813) 687-6998. Ray Graber, gen mgr; Roy Russell, mktg dir.
Area(s) Served: FL. County: Polk. Homes Served: 25,000. *Basic Service:* Subscribers: 25,000; 11/15/93.

Paragon Cable (22,900 subscribers). 610 W. Third St., Jamestown, NY 14701. (716) 664-7310; FAX: (716) 664-3123. Allan Hall, gen mgr; Dan Swakhemmer, mktg dir; Rich Flanders, chief tech; Joan Barton, cust svc dir.
Area(s) Served: NY. County: Chautauqua. Serving Bemus Point, Busti, Carroll, Celoron, Ellery, Ellicott, Falconer, Gerry, Kiantone, Lakewood, Maple Springs, North Harmony, Poland, Sinclair. Miles of Plant: 300. Homes Passed: 26,000. Homes Served: 22,900. *Channel Capacity:* 60. In use: 42. *Basic Service:* Subscribers: 22,900; 11/15/93. *Pay Services:* Total Pay Subscribers: 6,000; 11/15/91. Pay Per View Subscribers: 6,000; 11/15/91. *Local Advertising Accepted.*

Paragon Cable (95,700 subscribers). 7010 Airport Rd., El Paso, TX 79906-4943. (915) 772-1123; FAX: (915) 772-4605. John Neal, gen mgr; Norm Knoeble, mktg dir; Susie Shumaker, loc adv dir; Ramon Diaz, chief tech; Pat Mareno, cust svc dir.
Area(s) Served: TX, NM. Counties: Dona Ana, El Paso. Serving Canutillo, Fabens, Socorro. Miles of Plant: 1,677. Homes Passed: 165,000. Homes Served: 95,700. *Channel Capacity:* 42. In use: 42. *Basic Service:* Subscribers: 96,000; 11/15/93. *Pay Services:* Total Pay Subscribers: 39,250; 05/15/91. Pay Per View Subscribers: 18,000; 05/15/91. *Local Advertising Accepted.*

Paragon Cable Los Angeles (62,000 subscribers). 1511 Cravens Ave., Torrance, CA 90501. (310) 618-9496; FAX: (310) 328-7628. Paul Fisher, gen mgr; Bob Green, mktg dir; Steve Miller, loc adv dir; Louis Di Giandeomenico, cust svc dir.
Area(s) Served: CA. County: Los Angeles. Serving El Segundo, Gardena, Hawthorne, Lawndale, North Torrance, Redondo Beach, Torrance. Homes Passed: 123,934. Homes Served: 62,000. *Channel Capacity:* 60. In use: 60. *Basic Service:* Subscribers: 62,000; 11/15/93. *Pay Services:* Total Pay Subscribers: 53,480; 10/15/91. Pay Per View Subscribers: 44,000; 10/15/91. *Local Advertising Accepted.*

Paragon Cable Manhattan (190,313 subscribers). 5120 Broadway, New York, NY 10034. (212) 304-3000; FAX: (212) 304-3111. John Rigsby, gen mgr; Peter Rubin, mktg dir; Larry Pestana, chief tech; Susan Curtis-Miller, cust svc dir.
Area(s) Served: NY. Serving New York City. Miles of Plant: 1,492. Homes Passed: 345,379. *Channel Capacity:* 77. In use: 77. *Basic Service:* Subscribers: 190,313; 09/09/93. Programming (via satellite): 41 chs. Programming (off air): 13 chs. *Pay Services:* Total Pay Subscribers: 187,076; 08/31/93. (1) Pay Units: 68,851; 09/09/93. Programming (via satellite): HBO. (2) Pay Units: 40,152; 09/09/93. Programming (via satellite): Showtime. (3) Pay Units: 25,102; 09/09/93. Programming (via satellite): Cinemax. (4) Pay Units: 17,019; 09/09/93. Programming (via satellite): SportsChannel. (5) Pay Units: 6,376; 09/09/93. Programming (via satellite): Bravo. (6) Pay Units: 14,497; 09/09/93. Programming (via satellite): Disney. (7) Pay Units: 12,906; 09/09/93. Programming (via satellite): The Movie Channel. Pay Per View Subscribers: 185,083; 08/31/93. *No Local Advertising Accepted.*

Paragon Communications (25,500 subscribers). Box 188, Waldbaum's Plaza, Rt. 94 & Temple Hill Rd., Vails Gate, NY 12584. (914) 565-6882; FAX: (914) 565-6818. Henry Zemsky, gen mgr; Melinda Vickerman, mktg dir; Jane Sehr, loc adv dir; Kevin Trohalis, chief tech; Kathy Fabrizo, cust svc dir.
Area(s) Served: NY. Counties: Orange, Ulster. Serving Cornwall, Marlboro, Newburgh, New Windsor. Miles of Plant: 490. Homes Passed: 32,500. Homes Served: 25,500. *Channel Capacity:* 60. In use: 53. *Basic Service:* Subscribers: 25,500; 10/15/92. *Pay Services:* Total Pay Subscribers: 19,275; 10/15/92. Pay Per View Subscribers: 10,250; 10/15/92. *Local Advertising Accepted.*

Paragon Communications (60,000 subscribers). 209 S. Rogers Rd., Irving, TX 75060. (214) 221-6531; FAX: (214) 221-1525. Walter Nesbit, gen mgr; Steve Hellebush, mktg dir; Philip Haley, loc adv dir; Mildred Sutton, cust svc dir.
Area(s) Served: TX. Counties: Dallas, Denton, Tarrant. Serving Coppell, Grapevine, Irving, Lewisville. Miles of Plant: 1,100. Homes Passed: 110,000. Homes Served: 60,000. *Channel Capacity:* 60. In use: 57. *Basic Service:* Subscribers: 60,000. *Pay Services:* Total Pay Subscribers: 46,000; 11/15/91. *Local Advertising Accepted.*

Public Cable Co. (58,000 subscribers). 118 Johnson Rd., Portland, ME 04102. (207) 775-3431; FAX: (207) 775-6422. Jerome Ramsey, gen mgr; Lee Fischer, mktg dir; Bill McEnaney, loc adv dir; Jim Kersnowski, chief tech; Kristy Tibbetts, cust svc dir.
Area(s) Served: ME. County: Cumberland. Serving Cape Elizabeth, Casco, Cumberland, Falmouth, Gorham, Gray, New Gloucester, North Yarmouth, Portland, Pownal, Raymond, Scarborough, South Portland, Westbrook, West Pownal, Windham, Yarmouth. Homes Passed: 70,000. Homes Served: 58,000. *Channel Capacity:* 42. In use: 42. *Basic Service:* Subscribers: 58,000; 11/15/93. Pay Per View Subscribers: 11,500; 11/15/92. *Local Advertising Accepted.*

Southwestern Cable TV (156,854 subscribers). 8949 Ware Ct., San Diego, CA 92121. (619) 695-3110; FAX: (619) 536-8203. Ann Burr, gen mgr; Jim Fellhauer, mktg dir; Rick Winet, loc adv dir; Roger Kramer, chief tech; Lisa Stewart, cust svc dir.
Area(s) Served: CA. County: San Diego. Serving Carriage Hills, Clairemont, Delmar Heights, La Jolla, Linda Vista, Mira Mesa, Mission Beach, North City West, North Poway, Pacific Beach, Poway, Rancho Bernardo, Rancho Penas Quitos, Scripps Ranch, Tierra Santa, University City. Miles of Plant: 14,000. Homes Passed: 208,911. Homes Served: 156,854. *Channel Capacity:* 45. In use: 42. *Basic Service:* Subscribers: 160,000; 11/15/93. *Pay Services:* Total Pay Subscribers: 96,121; 11/15/91. Pay Per View Subscribers: 62,000; 11/15/91. *Local Advertising Accepted.*

Time Warner Cable (20,700 subscribers). 163 Fourth St., Pittsfield, MA 01201. (413) 443-4755; FAX: (413) 499-2774. Sal Grenillo, gen mgr; Fran Markham, chief tech.
Area(s) Served: MA. County: Berkshire. Serving Dalton, Pittsfield, Richmond. Miles of Plant: 278. Homes Passed: 24,939. Homes Served: 20,700. *Channel Capacity:* 60. In use: 51. *Basic Service:* Subscribers: 20,700; 11/15/93. Pay Per View Subscribers: 7,229; 11/15/91. *Local Advertising Accepted.*

Time Warner Cable (81,600 subscribers). 2505 Atlantic Ave., Raleigh, NC 27604. (919) 821-7925; FAX: (919) 829-2670. Jimmy White, gen mgr; Terrell Mayton, mktg dir & cust svc dir; Chris Barker, chief tech.
Area(s) Served: NC. County: Wake. Miles of Plant: 1,331. Homes Passed: 107,672. Homes Served: 81,600. *Basic Service:* Subscribers: 81,600; 11/15/93. *Pay Services:* Total Pay Subscribers: 54,574; 11/01/91. Pay Per View Subscribers: 56,801; 11/01/91. *Local Advertising Accepted.*

Time Warner Cable (39,300 subscribers). Box 2330, 2200 Beale Ave., Altoona, PA 16601. (814) 946-5491; FAX: (814) 943-1721. Craig Thompson, gen mgr; John Cappi, mktg dir; George Kimberly, chief tech.
Area(s) Served: PA. County: Blair. Serving Allegheny, Antis, Bellwood, Blair, Claysburg, Ducansville, East Freedom, Frankstown, Hollidaysburg, Juniata, Logan, Martinsburg, Roaring Spring, Tyrone. Miles of Plant: 650. Homes Passed: 43,500. Homes Served: 39,300. *Channel Capacity:* 60. In use: 56. *Basic Service:* Subscribers: 39,300; 11/15/93. Programming (via satellite): 47 chs. Programming (off air): 9 chs. *Pay Services:* Total Pay Subscribers: 7,058; 11/01/92. (1) Pay Units: 4,582; 11/01/92. Programming (via satellite): HBO. (2) Pay Units: 3,095; 11/01/92. Programming (via satellite): Showtime. (3) Pay Units: 1,536; 11/01/92. Programming (via satellite): The Movie Channel. (4) Pay Units: 2,419; 11/01/92. Programming (via satellite): Cinemax. Pay Per View Subscribers: 9,569; 11/01/92. *Local Advertising Accepted. Equipment:* Pioneer standard & owa converters.

Time Warner Cable (Greater Boston Division) (119,353 subscribers). Suite 12, 300 Commercial St., Malden, MA 02148. (617) 397-2600; FAX: (617) 397-0416. Terry O'Connell, gen mgr; Frank Lagona, loc adv dir; Carol Rice, chief tech; Beth Romanelli, cust svc dir.
Area(s) Served: MA. Counties: Essex, Middlesex, Suffolk. Serving Chelsea, Everett, Lynn, Malden, Medford, Melrose, Salem, Somerville, Swampscott, Winthrop. Miles of Plant: 839. Homes Passed: 226,939. Homes Served: 119,353. *Channel Capacity:* 54. In use: 54. *Basic Service:* Subscribers: 119,353; 11/15/93. *Local Advertising Accepted.*

Time Warner Cable of Bakersfield (70,372 subscribers). 3600 N. Sillect Ave., Bakersfield, CA 93308. (805) 327-9935; FAX: (805) 327-4074. Bill Grinstead, gen mgr; Rich Cozzi, mktg dir; Don Stone, loc adv dir; Kevin O'Connor, chief tech; Becky Mitchell, cust svc dir.
Area(s) Served: CA. Counties: Kern, Kings. Serving Arvin, Avenal, Bakersfield, Delano, Lamont, McFarland, Shafter, Taft, Tehachani, Wasco. Pop: 500,000. Miles of Plant: 1,041. Homes Passed: 113,853. Homes Served: 70,372. *Channel Capacity:* 61. In use: 56. *Basic Service:* Subscribers: 70,372; 11/15/93. Programming (via satellite): 35 chs. Programming (via microwave): 5 chs. Programming (off air): 8 chs. *Pay Services:* Total Pay Subscribers: 22,800; 11/23/92. (1) Pay Units: 15,654; 08/31/93. Programming (via satellite): HBO. (2) Pay Units: 6,672; 08/31/93. Programming (via satellite): The Movie Channel. (3) Pay Units: 7,944; 08/31/93. Programming (via satellite): Showtime. (4) Pay Units: 9,442; 08/31/93. Programming (via satellite): Disney. (5) Pay Units: 911; 08/31/93. Programming (via satellite): Playboy. Pay Per View Subscribers: 24,015; 08/31/93. *Local Advertising Accepted. Equipment:* Scientific-Atlanta & Jerrold headends; Scientific-Atlanta & Pioneer converters; Scientific-Atlanta distribution; Hughes microwave.

Time Warner Cable of Greater Johnstown (33,000 subscribers). 120 Southmont Blvd., Johnstown, PA 15905. (814) 535-3506; FAX: (814) 535-7749. Karen Broach, gen mgr; Natalie Johns, mktg dir; James Reesman, loc adv dir; Charles Sorchilla, chief tech; Gloria Robine, cust svc dir.
Area(s) Served: PA. Counties: Cambria, Somerset. Serving Benson, Brownstown, Conemaugh Twp., Daisytown, Dale, East Taylor, Ferndale, Franklin, Geistown, Jackson, Jenner, Lorain, Lower Yoder, Middle Taylor, Paint, Quemahoning, Quemahoneny, Richland, Southmont, Stoneycreek, Upper Yoder, Westmont, West Taylor. Miles of Plant: 494. Homes Passed: 39,472. Homes Served: 33,000. *Channel Capacity:* 44. In use: 44. *Basic Service:* Subscribers: 33,000; 11/15/93. *Pay Services:* Total Pay Subscribers: 5,000;

Multiple Systems Operators, Independent Owners & Cable Systems

11/15/91. Pay Per View Subscribers: 8,500; 11/15/91. *Local Advertising Accepted.*

Time Warner Cable of New York City (945,000 subscribers). 120 E. 23rd St., New York, NY 10010. (212) 598-7200; FAX: (212) 420-4809. Barry Rosenblum, gen mgr; Hugh Panero, mktg dir; Roosevelt Mikhale, chief tech; Barbara Kelly, cust svc dir.
Area(s) Served: NY. Serving Brooklyn, Manhattan, Queens. Miles of Plant: 2,333. Homes Passed: 1,444,093. Homes Served: 945,000. *Channel Capacity:* 76. In use: 76. *Basic Service:* Subscribers: 945,000; 11/15/93. *Pay Services:* Total Pay Subscribers: 382,079; 12/15/92. *Local Advertising Accepted.*

Vista Cablevision Inc. (25,000 subscribers). 3225 Maurine St., Wichita Falls, TX 76305. (817) 855-5700; FAX: (817) 855-0465. Bert Bucher, gen mgr; Natalie Dorlan, mktg dir; Milt Slavin, chief tech.
Area(s) Served: TX. Counties: Archer, Wichita. Serving Holiday, Lakeside City, Sheppard Air Force Base. Homes Served: 25,000. *Basic Service:* Subscribers: 25,000; 11/15/93.

Warner Cable (27,031 subscribers). Box 1177, 3100 Elida Rd., Lima, OH 45802. (419) 331-3333; FAX: (419) 331-1573. Jeff Parker, gen mgr; Sandy Bayliff, mktg dir; John Quatman, loc adv dir; Larry D. Bryan, chief tech; Margory Thompson, cust svc dir.
Area(s) Served: OH. County: Allen. Serving Amanda, American, Auglaize, Bath, Beaverdam, Cairo, Elida, Gomer, Harrod, Jackson, Lafayette, Marion, Monroe, Perry, Richland, Shawnee, Spencer, Spencerville, Sugar Creek, Westminster. Miles of Plant: 504. Homes Passed: 36,932. Homes Served: 27,031. *Channel Capacity:* 41. In use: 41. *Basic Service:* Subscribers: 27,031; 11/15/93. *Pay Services:* Total Pay Subscribers: 15,000; 11/15/91.

Warner Cable Communications (102,000 subscribers). 1655 Brittain Rd., Akron, OH 44310. (216) 633-9203; FAX: (216) 633-7970. Steven Fry, gen mgr; Robert P. Nyitray, chief tech; Bob Walcot, cust svc dir.
Area(s) Served: OH. Counties: Medina, Portage, Summit, Wayne. Serving Barberton, Cuyahoga Falls, Doylestown, Fairlawn, Lakemore, Mogadore, Muroe Falls, Norton, Silver Lake, Springfield, Stow, Tallmadge, Wadsworth. Miles of Plant: 1,500. Homes Passed: 175,000. Homes Served: 102,000. *Channel Capacity:* 39. In use: 39. *Basic Service:* Subscribers: 102,000; 11/15/93. *Pay Services:* Total Pay Subscribers: 30,000; 10/31/91. Pay Per View Subscribers: 40,000; 10/31/91. *Local Advertising Accepted.*

Warner Cable Communications - Kingsport (29,000 subscribers). Box 3608, 105 Jack White Dr., Kingsport, TN 37664. (615) 247-2183; FAX: (615) 247-1807. Craig Perica, gen mgr; Tim Miller, mktg dir; Grant Evans, chief tech; Mark Taillard, cust svc dir.
Area(s) Served: TN. Counties: Hawkins, Sullivan. Serving Church Hill, Mount Carmel, Sullivan Gardens. Miles of Plant: 664. Homes Passed: 100,000. Homes Served: 29,000. *Channel Capacity:* 51. In use: 46. *Basic Service:* Subscribers: 29,000; 11/15/93. *Pay Services:* Total Pay Subscribers: 7,778; 09/15/91. Pay Per View Subscribers: 12,400; 09/15/91. *Local Advertising Accepted.*

Warner Cable Communications Inc. (30,452 subscribers). 1050 N. Palm Canyon Rd., Palm Springs, CA 92262. (619) 320-8810; FAX: (619) 323-7589. Michael Bawerfeind, gen mgr; Dave Grace, chief tech; Joy Alvarez, cust svc dir.
Area(s) Served: CA. County: Riverside. Serving Cathedral City, Palm Springs. Miles of Plant: 439. Homes Passed: 37,045. Homes Served: 30,452. *Channel Capacity:* 61. In use: 55. *Basic Service:* Subscribers: 30,452; 11/15/93. *Pay Services:* Total Pay Subscribers: 7,875; 11/15/91. Pay Per View Subscribers: 10,000; 11/15/91. *Local Advertising Accepted.*

Warner Cable Communications Inc. (185,000 subscribers). 11252 Cornell Park Dr., Cincinnati, OH 45242. (513) 489-5000; FAX: (513) 489-5065. Virgil M. Reed, gen mgr; Dennis Holzmeier, mktg dir; Dan O'Brien, chief tech.
Area(s) Served: OH. Counties: Butler, Clermont, Hamilton, Warren. Homes Passed: 366,000. Homes Served: 185,000. *Channel Capacity:* 60. In use: 60. *Basic Service:* Subscribers: 185,000; 11/15/93. *Pay Services:* Total Pay Subscribers: 80,000; 11/15/91. Pay Per View Subscribers: 145,000; 11/15/91. *Local Advertising Accepted.*

Warner Cable Communications Inc. (240,000 subscribers). 8400 W. Tidwell, Houston, TX 77040. (713) 462-1900; FAX: (713) 895-2612. Ron McMillan, gen mgr; Marc Hertz, mktg dir; Joan Bean, loc adv dir; Bill Arnold, chief tech; Bob Bates, cust svc dir.
Area(s) Served: TX. Counties: Ft. Blend, Harris. Serving Bellaire, Jersey Village, Meadows, Memorial Village, Missouri City, West University Place. Miles of Plant: 4,700. Homes Passed: 580,000. Homes Served: 240,000. *Channel Capacity:* 43. In use: 43. *Basic Service:* Subscribers: 240,000; 11/15/93. *Pay Services:* Total Pay Subscribers: 185,600; 11/15/91. Pay Per View Subscribers: 185,600; 11/15/91. *Local Advertising Accepted.*

Warner Cable Communications Inc.- Youngstown (22,000 subscribers). 755 Wick Ave., Youngstown, OH 44501. (216) 747-2550; FAX: (216) 747-5003. Daryl Morrison, gen mgr; Dan Bates, mktg dir; Russell Hickenbottom, chief tech; Mike McNair, cust svc dir.
Area(s) Served: OH. County: Mahoning. Miles of Plant: 348. Homes Passed: 36,000. Homes Served: 22,000. *Channel Capacity:* 36. In use: 36. *Basic Service:* Subscribers: 22,000; 11/15/93. *Pay Services:* Total Pay Subscribers: 8,950; 11/15/91. Pay Per View Subscribers: 11,000; 11/15/91. *Local Advertising Accepted.*

Warner Cable Communications of Milwaukee (185,800 subscribers). 1610 N. Second St., Milwaukee, WI 53212. (414) 277-4000; FAX: (414) 224-6155. Thomas E. Sharrard, gen mgr; Alan Hall, mktg dir; Dick Olmstead, loc adv dir; Joe Huzecker, chief tech; Bob Bates, cust svc dir.
Area(s) Served: WI. Counties: Milwaukee, Ozaki, Waukesha, Washington. Serving Milwaukee. Homes Served: 185,800. *Channel Capacity:* 55. In use: 55. *Basic Service:* Subscribers: 185,800; 11/15/93. *Local Advertising Accepted.*

Warner Cable of Canton (73,000 subscribers). Box 9902, Canton, OH 44711-0902. (216) 494-0095; FAX: (216) 497-6397. Bill Farmer, gen mgr; Jim Nicholas, mktg dir; Barbara Steill, loc adv dir; Tod Dean, chief tech; Cindy McAfee, cust svc dir.
Area(s) Served: OH. Counties: Carroll, Stark, Tuscarawas. Miles of Plant: 1,359. Homes Passed: 109,000. Homes Served: 73,000. *Channel Capacity:* 38. In use: 38. *Basic Service:* Subscribers: 73,000; 11/15/93. *Pay Services:* Total Pay Subscribers: 17,000; 11/15/91. Pay Per View Subscribers: 24,000; 11/01/91. *Local Advertising Accepted.*

Warner Cable of Columbus (166,874 subscribers). 1266 Dublin Rd., Columbus, OH 43215. (614) 481-5000; FAX: (614) 481-5044. John Porter, gen mgr; Mark Psigoda, mktg dir; Joe Salerno, loc adv dir; Randy Hall, chief tech; Ronda Milby, cust svc dir.
Area(s) Served: OH. Counties: Delaware, Franklin. Serving Beechwold, Bexley, Briggsdale, Canal Winchester, Columbus, Concord Twp., Delaware Twp., Dublin Twp., Eastland, Gahanna, Galloway, Grandview Heights, Grove City, Groveport, Hilliard Twp., Jackson Twp., Lincoln Village, Marble Cliff, Minerva Park, Mount Vernon, Norwich Twp., Obetz, Ostrander, Perry Twp., Plain City, Pleasant Twp., Powell, Radnor, Riverside, Upper Arlington, Valleyview, Westerville, West Worthington, Worthington. Miles of Plant: 2,988. Homes Passed: 314,931. Homes Served: 166,874. *Channel Capacity:* 77. In use: 65. *Basic Service:* Subscribers: 166,874; 08/31/93. *Pay Services:* Total Pay Subscribers: 140,155; 08/31/93. Pay Per View Subscribers: 110,152; 08/31/93. *Local Advertising Accepted.*

Warner Cable of Hampton (41,900 subscribers). 1323 W. Pembroke Ave., Hampton, VA 23661. (804) 722-2851; FAX: (804) 728-0515. William T. Day, gen mgr; Greg DiPaolo, mktg dir; Ron Horchler, chief tech; Glen Chalmers, cust svc dir.
Area(s) Served: VA. Counties: Poquoson, Williamsburg. Serving Fort Monroe, Hampton, Langley Air Force Base, Poquoson. Miles of Plant: 674. Homes Passed: 62,207. Homes Served: 41,900. *Channel Capacity:* 35. In use: 32. *Basic Service:* Subscribers: 41,900; 11/15/93. *Pay Services:* Total Pay Subscribers: 17,912; 10/15/92. Pay Per View Subscribers: 13,642; 10/15/92. *Local Advertising Accepted.*

Warner Cable of Nashua (23,702 subscribers). 460 Amherst St., Nashua, NH 03063. (603) 889-6694; FAX: (603) 882-4415. Doug Whiting, gen mgr; David Gray, mktg dir; David Hevey, chief tech; Victoria Jepson, cust svc dir.
Area(s) Served: NH. County: Hillsborough. Miles of Plant: 285. Homes Passed: 33,801. Homes Served: 23,702. *Channel Capacity:* 60. In use: 54. *Basic Service:* Subscribers: 23,702; 11/15/93. *Pay Services:* Total Pay Subscribers: 9,500; 11/15/91. Pay Per View Subscribers: 11,000; 11/15/91. *Local Advertising Accepted.*

SMALLER SYSTEMS

Mississippi - Cable of Olive Brunch, Box 9, Olive Branch, MS 38654; (601) 895-7979; 6,000 subs.

Times Mirror Cable Television

2381-2391 Morse Ave., Irvine, CA 92714-6233. (714) 660-0500; FAX: (714) 660-0501. Larry W. Wangberg, CEO & pres; James H. Smith III, vp opns; Christopher B. Forgy, vp sls & vp mktg; Kent D. Franke, vp progmg. Owned by The Times Mirror Co. Total Basic Subscribers: 1,183,587; Number of Cable Systems: 61.

REGIONS

Northeast: 1484 Highland Ave., Cheshire, CT 06410.
Central: 105 N. 11th St., Newark, OH 43055.

SYSTEMS WITH OVER 20,000 SUBSCRIBERS

Dimension Cable Services (375,000 subscribers). 17602 N. Black Canyon Hwy., Phoenix, AZ 85023. (602) 866-0072; FAX: (602) 863-3532. Gregg Holmes, gen mgr; Paul Gregg, mktg dir; Steve Rizley, loc adv dir; Alan Sparks, chief tech; Sylvia Coccagna, cust svc dir.
Area(s) Served: AZ. County: Maricopa. Serving Buckeye, Casa Grande, Chandler, Fountain Hills, Glendale, Goodyear, Guadalupe, Litchfield Park, Mesa, Paradise Valley, Peoria, Phoenix, Sun City, Sun City West, Sun Lakes, Surprise, Tempe, Youngtown. Pop: 2,000,000. Miles of Plant: 6,900. Homes Passed: 772,042. Homes Served: 375,000. *Channel Capacity:* 52. In use: 45. *Basic Service:* Subscribers: 375,000; 11/30/92. Programming (via satellite): WTBS, WGN, Prevue Guide, QVC, VH-1, MTV, Family Channel, Lifetime, USA, ESPN, CNBC, CSPAN, CNN, Nickelodeon, Telemundo, A & E, Weather Channel, Pay Per View Guide. Programming (via microwave): Arizona Sports Programming Network. Programming (off air): KTVK, KPHO, KTSP, KPNX, KNXV, KUTP, KPAZ, KTVW. *Pay Services:* Total Pay Subscribers: 148,000; 09/13/93. (1) Pay Units: 83,937; 09/13/93. Programming (via satellite): HBO. (2) Pay Units: 61,814; 09/13/93. Programming (via satellite): Showtime. (3) Pay Units: 23,045; 09/13/93. Programming (via satellite): The Movie Channel. (4) Pay Units: 17,037; 09/13/93. Programming (via satellite): Cinemax. Pay Per View Subscribers: 134,000; 09/13/93. *Local Advertising Accepted.*

Dimension Cable Services (140,000 subscribers). 26181 Avenida Aeropuerto, San Juan Capistrano, CA 92675. (714) 240-1212; (714) 240-8828; FAX: (714) 661-7297. Leo Brennan, gen mgr; David Limebrook, mktg dir; Mitch Seigal, loc adv dir; Len White, chief tech; Karen Kranick, cust svc dir.
Area(s) Served: CA. Counties: Orange, San Diego. Serving Capistrano Beach, Coto de Caza, Dana Point, El Toro, Laguna Beach, Laguna Hills, Laguna Niguel, Mission Viejo, Modjeska Canyon, Rancho Santa Margarita, San Clemente, San Juan Capistrano, San Onofre, Silverado Canyon, South Laguna, Trabuco Canyon, Tustin. Pop: 450,000. Miles of Plant: 1,600. Homes Passed: 180,000. Homes Served: 140,000. Channel Capacity: 54. In use: 54. Basic Service: Subscribers: 140,000; 08/31/93. Programming (via satellite): 36 chs. Programming (via microwave): 1 ch. Programming (off air): 17 chs. Pay Services: Total Pay Subscribers: 90,200; 08/31/93. Pay Per View Subscribers: 80,000; 08/31/93.No Local Advertising Accepted. Equipment: Pioneer BA5000 & BA6000 series converters.

Dimension Cable Services (28,000 subscribers). 43 Peninsula Ctr., Rolling Hills Estates, CA 90274. (310) 377-1800; FAX: (310) 544-2546. Steve G. Fowler, gen mgr; Robert J. Bloom, mktg dir; Mary J. Schoenheider, loc adv dir; Larry Shaw, chief tech; Karen Zweep, cust svc dir.
Area(s) Served: CA. County: Los Angeles. Serving Palos Verdes Estates, Rancho Palos Verdes, Rolling Hills, Rolling Hills Estates, San Pedro. Pop: 270,000. Homes Passed: 45,000. Homes Served: 28,000. *Channel Capacity:* 50. In use: 50. *Basic Service:* Subscribers: 28,000; 10/31/93. *Pay Services:* Total Pay Subscribers: 14,000. Pay Per View Subscribers: 17,400. *Local Advertising Accepted.*

Dimension Cable Services (130,000 subscribers). 2790 Business Park Dr., Vista, CA 92083-7860. (619) 599-6060; FAX: (619) 598-0132. Thomas R. Tomkins, gen mgr; James E. Crawford, mktg dir; Jan Cherry, loc adv dir; Russell Bottjer, chief tech; Bob Rubery, cust svc dir.
Area(s) Served: CA. County: San Diego. Serving Camp Pendleton, Encinitas, Escondio, Oceanside, Ramona, San Marcos, Solana Beach, Vista. Miles of Plant: 1,800. Homes Passed: 178,000. Homes Served: 130,000. *Channel Capacity:* 54. In use: 48. *Basic Service:* Subscribers: 130,000; 10/31/93. *Pay Services:* Total Pay Subscribers: 72,742; 11/30/92. Pay Per View Subscribers: 60,600; 11/30/92. *No Local Advertising Accepted.*

Dimension Cable Services (38,500 subscribers). 683 E. Main St., Meriden, CT 06450. (203) 634-4435; FAX: (203) 238-4686. Vincent Caramenello, gen mgr; Kelly Margaro, mktg dir & cust svc dir; Fred Bucchieri, chief tech.
Area(s) Served: CT. Counties: Hartford, New Haven. Serving Cheshire, Meriden, Southington. Homes Passed: 49,800. Homes Served: 38,500. *Channel Capacity:* 36. In use: 36. *Basic Service:* Subscribers: 38,500; 10/31/93. *Pay Services:* Total Pay Subscribers: 17,621. Pay Per View Subscribers: 8,500. *Local Advertising Accepted.*

Dimension Cable Services (50,740 subscribers). Box 3066, 711 S. Dirksen Pkwy., Springfield, IL 62703. (217) 788-5656; FAX: (217) 788-8093. Greg Capranica, gen mgr; David Smith, mktg dir; Cal Coleman, loc adv dir; John Linton, chief tech; Libbie Stehn, cust svc dir.
Area(s) Served: IL. County: Sangamon. Serving Grandview, Jerome, Leland Grove, Rochester, Springfield, Southern View, Woodside Twp. Pop: 120,000. Miles of Plant: 635. Homes Passed: 70,518. Homes Served: 50,740. *Channel Capacity:* 60. In use: 42. *Basic Service:* Subscribers: 50,740; 10/31/93. Programming (via satellite): 34 chs. Programming (off air): 8 chs. *Pay Services:* Total Pay Subscribers: 17,328; 11/01/91. (1) Pay Units: 1,804; 11/01/91. Programming (via satellite): The Movie Channel. (2) Pay Units: 7,864; 11/01/91. Programming (via satellite): Showtime. (3) Pay Units: 6,309; 11/01/91. Programming (via satellite): HBO. (4) Pay Units: 5,157; 11/01/91. Programming (via satellite): Cinemax. Pay Per View Subscribers: 20,179; 11/01/91. *Local Advertising Accepted. Equipment:* Scientific-Atlanta, Jerrold & Leaming headend; Jerrold converters.

Dimension Cable Services (39,000 subscribers). Box 4609, 325 S. Creasy Ln., Lafayette, IN 47903. (317) 447-6886; FAX: (317) 447-7622. Brett McKee, gen mgr; Don Deiley, mktg dir; Kathy Roudebush, loc adv dir; Chet Day, chief tech; Velicia Glass, cust svc dir.
Area(s) Served: IN. Counties: Clinton, Tippecanoe. Serving Battle Ground, Dayton, Lafayette, Mulberry, West Lafayette. Pop: 120,000. Miles of Plant: 500. Homes Passed: 49,435. Homes Served: 39,000. *Channel Capacity:* 52. In use: 46. *Basic Service:* Subscribers: 39,000; 10/31/93. Programming (via satellite): 32 chs. Programming (via microwave): 1 ch. Programming (off air): 7 chs. *Pay Services:* Total Pay Subscribers: 11,434; 11/01/91. (1) Pay Units: 1,623; 11/01/91. Programming (via satellite): The Movie Channel. (2) Pay Units: 5,642; 11/01/91. Programming (via satellite): Showtime. (3) Pay Units: 6,873; 11/01/91. Programming (via satellite): HBO. (4) Pay Units: 3,072; 11/01/91. Programming (via satellite): Cinemax. Pay Per View Subscribers: 13,432; 11/01/91. *Local Advertising Accepted.*

Dimension Cable Services (27,000 subscribers). 111 N. 11th St., Newark, OH 43055. (614) 345-4000; FAX: (614) 345-7670. Judy Pierce, gen mgr; Roy Lucas, mktg dir.
Area(s) Served: OH. County: Licking. Serving Buckeye Lake, Franklin, Granville, Hanover, Heath, Hebron, Licking, Madison, Newark, St. Louisville, Union. Homes Served: 27,000. *Channel Capacity:* 35. In use: 35. *Basic Service:* Subscribers: 27,000; 10/31/93.

Dimension Cable Services (21,000 subscribers). 617 Tuscarawas Ave., New Philadelphia, OH 44663. (216) 364-6634. Bruno Masdea, gen mgr; Rich Lutze, mktg dir; Carey Gardner, loc adv dir.
Area(s) Served: OH. County: Tuscarawas. Serving Barnhill, Columbia, Dennison, Dover, Gradenhutton, Midvale, New Philadelphia, Parral, Roswell, Strasburg, Sugarcreek, Uhricsville, Wainwright. Homes Served: 21,000. *Channel Capacity:* 60. In use: 35. *Basic Service:* Subscribers: 21,000; 10/31/93. *Pay Services:* Total Pay Subscribers: 7,385; 09/30/91. *Local Advertising Accepted.*

Dimension Cable Services (25,200 subscribers). 330 Basin St., Williamsport, PA 17701. (717) 326-3384; FAX: (717) 326-7833. Carol Rosebrough, gen mgr; Mike Lee, mktg dir; Seth Burch, loc adv dir; Tom Girton, chief tech; Laurie Howe, cust svc dir.
Area(s) Served: PA. County: Lycoming. Serving Armstrong, Dubolstown, Fairfield, Hepburn, Loyalsock, Lycoming, Montoursville, Old Lycoming, South Williamsport, Susquehanna, Williamsport, Woodward. Homes Served: 25,200. *Channel Capacity:* 36. In use: 36. *Basic Service:* Subscribers: 25,200; 10/31/93. *Pay Services:* Total Pay Subscribers: 9,300. *Local Advertising Accepted.*

Dimension Cable Services (86,500 subscribers). 9 J.P. Murphy Hwy., West Warwick, RI 02893-2381. (401) 828-2288; FAX: (401) 828-3835. Don Layher, mktg dir; Don Civalier, chief tech; Jean Fournier, cust svc dir.
Area(s) Served: RI. Counties: Kent, Providence. Serving Coventry, East Greenwich, Warwick, West Warwich. Homes Served: 86,500. *Channel Capacity:* 52. In use: 52. *Basic Service:* Subscribers: 86,500; 10/31/93. *Pay Services:* Total Pay Subscribers: 69,000. Pay Per View Subscribers: 32,000. *Local Advertising Accepted.*

Dimension Cable Services (25,106 subscribers). 221 Texas Blvd., Texarkana, TX 75501. (903) 794-3426. Jay Butler, gen mgr; Kevin Canal, mktg dir; Mark Glorioso, loc adv dir; John Lanier, chief tech; Lillian Martin, cust svc dir.
Area(s) Served: TX, AR. Counties: Bowie; Miller. Serving Nash, Texarkana, Wake Village. Pop: 55,000. Miles of Plant: 430. Homes Passed: 35,354. Homes Served: 25,106. *Channel Capacity:* 54. In use: 34. *Basic Service:* Subscribers: 25,106; 10/31/93. Programming (via satellite): 27 chs. Programming (via microwave): 5 chs. Programming (off air): 2 chs. *Pay Services:* Total Pay Subscribers: 7,026; 11/01/91. (1) Pay Units: 1,479; 11/01/91. Programming (via satellite): The Movie Channel. (2) Pay Units: 1,682; 11/01/91. Programming (via satellite): Showtime. (3) Pay Units: 3,057; 11/01/91. Programming (via satellite): HBO. (4) Pay Units: 2,020; 11/01/91. Programming (via satellite): Cinemax. *Local Advertising Accepted. Equipment:* Scientific-Atlanta headend; Scientific-Atlanta converters.

Dimension Cable Services (30,000 subscribers). 2530 S. Midkiff, Midland, TX 79701. (915) 694-7721; FAX: (915) 694-3267. Missy Orr-Ryan, gen mgr; Terry Harris, mktg dir; Mike Simons, chief tech.
Area(s) Served: TX. Serving Midland. Homes Served: 30,000. *Channel Capacity:* 54. In use: 42. *Basic Service:* Subscribers: 30,000; 10/31/93. *Local Advertising Accepted.*

TKR Cable Co.

678 Mountain Blvd., Warren, NJ 07060. (908) 356-1010; FAX: (908) 356-9087. Paul Freas, pres; William Mitchell, CFO; Judi Heady, vp sls & vp adv; Brian Hickey, vp mktg; Peter Luscombe, vp. Owned by Tele-Communications Inc., Knight-Ridder Newspapers Inc. Total Basic Subscribers: 600,000; Number of Cable Systems: 11.

SYSTEMS WITH OVER 20,000 SUBSCRIBERS

TKR Cable Company (30,000 subscribers). 2137 Hamilton Ave., Hamilton Township, NJ 08619. (609) 586-2288; FAX: (609) 586-2478. Dwayne Patterson, gen mgr; Karen Horvath, mktg dir; Dave Farrow, chief tech.
Area(s) Served: NJ. Counties: Mercer, Monmouth. Homes Served: 30,000. *Channel Capacity:* 54. *Basic Service:* Subscribers: 30,000; 10/31/93. *Local Advertising Accepted.*

TKR Cable Company of Rockland (58,000 subscribers). 25 Smith St., Nanuet, NY 10954. (914) 624-8200; FAX: (914) 623-5619. Jim Helfgott, gen mgr; Laura Bachert, mktg dir; Kevin Hewett, chief tech.
Area(s) Served: NJ, NY. Counties: Bergen; Orange, Rockland. Miles of Plant: 1,200. Homes Passed: 90,000. *Channel Capacity:* 62. In use: 58. *Basic Service:* Subscribers: 58,000; 11/30/92. *Local Advertising Accepted.*

TKR Cable Company Tri-System (146,000 subscribers). CN 6805, 275 Centennial Ave., Piscataway, NJ 08855. (908) 457-0131; FAX: (908) 885-3889. Charles Barlotta, gen mgr; Donna Alda, mktg dir; Larry Rutter, chief tech.
Area(s) Served: NJ. Counties: Middlesex, Monmouth, Somerset. Homes Served: 146,000. *Channel Capacity:* 41. In use: 41. *Basic Service:* Subscribers: 146,000; 10/31/93. *Local Advertising Accepted.*

TKR Cable of Greater Louisville (183,000 subscribers). 1536 Story Ave., Louisville, KY 40206. (502) 448-7336; FAX: (502) 447-2477. Charlie King, gen mgr; Daniel Coe, mktg dir; Chris Bowling, chief tech.
Area(s) Served: KY. County: Jefferson. Serving Louisville. Homes Passed: 300,000. Homes Served: 183,000. *Channel Capacity:* 43. In use: 42. *Basic Service:* Subscribers: 183,000; 10/31/93. *Pay Services:* Total Pay Subscribers: 80,000; 10/30/91. *Local Advertising Accepted.*

TKR Cable of Northern Kentucky (56,000 subscribers). 717 Madison Ave., Covington, KY 41011. (606) 431-0300; FAX: (606) 431-3464. Debbie Cummings, mktg dir; Tom Diamante, chief tech.
Area(s) Served: KY. Counties: Boone, Campbell, Kenton. Serving Bromley, Burlington, Crescent Park, Crescent Springs, Crestview Hills, Edgewood, Elsemere, Erlanger, Fairview, Florence, Fort Mitchell, Fort Wright, Independence, Kenton Vale, Lakeside Park, Latonia Lakes, Ludlow, Park Hills, Ridgeview Heights, Ryland Heights, Taylor Mill, Union, Villa Hills, Visalia, Walton, Winston Park. Homes Passed: 101,000. Homes Served: 56,000. *Channel Capacity:* 82. In use: 64. *Basic Service:* Subscribers: 56,000; 10/31/93. *Pay Services:* Total Pay Subscribers: 22,000; 11/08/91. Pay Per View Subscribers: 4,900; 11/08/91. *Local Advertising Accepted.*

TKR Cable of Wildwood (33,900 subscribers). 4315 New Jersey Ave., Wildwood, NJ 08260. (609) 522-0103; FAX: (609) 522-0707. Peter Berkowitz, gen mgr; Victoria Hendley, mktg dir; John Faley, chief tech.
Area(s) Served: NJ. County: Cape May. Homes Served: 33,900. *Channel Capacity:* 44. In use: 44. *Basic Service:* Subscribers: 33,900; 10/31/93. *Local Advertising Accepted.*

SMALLER SYSTEMS

Kentucky - TKR Cable Co., Bowling Green, KY. **New Jersey** - TKR Cable Co., Elizabeth, NJ. TKR Cable Co., Gloucester City/Maple Shade Township, NJ. TKR Cable Co., Long Beach Township, NJ. **New York** - TKR Cable Co., Warwick, NY.

Tomoka Cable TV

1951 State Road 40, Ormond Beach, FL 32174. (904) 672-7573; FAX: (904) 677-5707. Owned by J. Stanley Shirah, Steve P. Shirah. Total Basic Subscribers: 2,100; Pay Cable Subscribers: 900; Number of Cable Systems: 2.

SMALLER SYSTEMS

Florida - Tomoka Cable T.V., Port Orange, FL.

Total TV of California Inc.

27-700 Avenida Belleza, Cathedral City, CA 92234. (619) 325-5125; FAX: (619) 325-4012. James F. Fitzgerald Sr., chmn; James F. Fitzgerald Jr., pres; Pete Bongard, vp mktg. Owned by James F. Fitzgerald Sr., James F. Fitzgerald Jr., Brian Fitzgerald. Total Basic Subscribers: 4,000; Pay Cable Subscribers: 500; Number of Cable Systems: 2.

SMALLER SYSTEMS

California - Total TV of California, Inc., 27-700 Avenida Belleza, Cathedral City, CA 92234. Total TV of Fort Irwin, N.W. Corner Inner Loop and Barstow, Fort Irwin, CA 92310; (619) 386-2392.

Trans-Video Inc.

37 Depot Sq., Northfield, VT 05663. (802) 485-3811. George Goodrich, pres; Robert Goodrich, vp opns. Owned by George Goodrich, Robert Goodrich. Total Basic Subscribers: 1,600; Pay Cable Subscribers: 600; Number of Cable Systems: 1.

Transwestern Video Inc.

Suite 139, 4405 N.W. 4th St., Oklahoma City, OK 73107. (405) 948-8947. Joe D. Davis, pres; Joe D. Davis Jr., vp. Owned by William H. Davis, Susan Lee C. Coffee, Joe D. Davis Jr. Total Basic Subscribers: 13,500; Pay Cable Subscribers: 5,000; Number of Cable Systems: 20.

Trenton TV Cable

Box 345, Hwy. 45, Trenton, TN 38382. (901) 855-2808. Harold Norvell, pres; Stephen Norvell, vp. Owned by Harold Norvell, Stephen Norvell, ptnrs. Total Basic Subscribers: 2,060; Number of Cable Systems: 1.

Triax Communications Corporation

Suite 600, 100 Fillmore St., Denver, CO 80206. (303) 333-2424; FAX: (303) 333-1110. James De Sorrento, CEO & chmn; Jay Busch, pres; Jim Vaughn, vp opns; Dave Downey, vp mktg & vp progmg; Christopher O'Toole, vp. Owned by James De Sorrento. Total Basic Subscribers: 339,000; Pay Cable Subscribers: 153,000; Number of Cable Systems: 459.

Tri-County Communications Corporation

Box 186, New Richmond, IN 47967. (317) 339-4651; FAX: (317) 339-7999. Ben Miller, pres; Helen Widmer, vp mktg. Owned by Tri-County Telephone Co. Inc. Total

Multiple Systems Operators, Independent Owners & Cable Systems

Basic Subscribers: 1,356; Pay Cable Subscribers: 584; Number of Cable Systems: 1.

The Tulalip Tribes Cablevision Company

6326 33rd Ave. N.E., Marysville, WA 98271. (206) 653-0235; FAX: (206) 653-5397. Richard Brown, vp opns. Owned by Tulalip Reservation. Total Basic Subscribers: 1,200; Pay Cable Subscribers: 600; Number of Cable Systems: 1.

TV Cable Co. of Andalusia Inc.

Box 34, Andalusia, AL 36420. (205) 222-6464; FAX: (205) 222-7226. J. Dige Bishop, pres; Ivan H. Bishop, vp. Owned by J. Dige Bishop. Total Basic Subscribers: 4,100; Pay Cable Subscribers: 750; Number of Cable Systems: 1.

TV Cable of Rensselaer

Suite 19, 215 W. Kellner St., Rensselaer, IN 47978. (219) 866-7101. Charlotte Filson, CEO; Steven T. Filson, pres & vp opns. Owned by Theodore W. Filson. Total Basic Subscribers: 3,983; Pay Cable Subscribers: 666; Number of Cable Systems: 2.

SMALLER SYSTEMS

Indiana - TV Cable of Rensselaer, 215 W. Kellner St., Rensselaer, IN 47978; (219) 866-7101; 1,364 subs. TV Cable of Winamac, 110 E. Adams, Winamac, IN 46996; (219) 946-3813; 1,346 subs.

TV Service Inc.

Box 698, Hindman, KY 41822. (606) 785-3450; FAX: (606) 785-3110. Robert C. Thacker, pres; Eddie Tiller, vp mktg; Archie W. Everage, vp adv. Owned by Robert C. Thacker. Total Basic Subscribers: 6,000; Pay Cable Subscribers: 550; Number of Cable Systems: 3.

Twin County Trans Video Inc.

5508 Nor-Bath Blvd., Northampton, PA 18067. (215) 262-6100; FAX: (215) 261-5099. Bark L. Yee, CEO & pres; Stella C. Yee, CFO; Tina M. Fritzinger, vp mktg; Susan C. Yee, vp; Kenneth C. Yee, vp; Raymond C. Yee, vp. Owned by Bark L. Yee, Kenneth Yee, Raymond Yee, Stella C. Yee, Susan Yee. Total Basic Subscribers: 56,000; Number of Cable Systems: 1.

SYSTEMS WITH OVER 20,000 SUBSCRIBERS

Twin County Cable TV (56,000 subscribers). 5508 Nor-bath Blvd., Northampton, PA 18067. (215) 264-5141; FAX: (215) 261-5099. Bark L. Yee, gen mgr. *Area(s) Served:* PA. Counties: Lehigh, Northampton. Homes Served: 56,000. *Basic Service:* Subscribers: 56,000; 10/31/93.

Union CATV Inc.

Box 2C, 531 U.S. Hwy. 60 E., Morganfield, KY 42437-1275. (502) 389-1818; FAX: (502) 389-2459. Alan E. Reed, CEO, pres & vp opns; Millie M. Reed, vp. Owned by Alan E. Reed, Millie M. Reed. Total Basic Subscribers: 2,700; Pay Cable Subscribers: 1,200; Number of Cable Systems: 2.

United Artists Cable

2407-A Timberloch Pl., The Woodlands, TX 77380. (713) 363-0975; FAX: (713) 292-1088. Bill Helmbold, vp opns. Owned by The Woodlands Communications Network, TCI Inc., ptnrs. Total Basic Subscribers: 10,800; Number of Cable Systems: 1.

United Broadcasting Co.

Suite 808, 4733 Bethesda Ave., Bethesda, MD 20814. (301) 652-7707; FAX: (301) 652-4614. Gerald Hroblak, pres; Arthur Rawson, CFO. Owned by Nations Bank, Richard Eaton Estate, Daniel Eaton, Pierre Eaton, Gerald Hroblak, William Paris, Samuel Phillips, Joseph Schweighart. Total Basic Subscribers: 42,934; Number of Cable Systems: 2.

SYSTEMS WITH OVER 20,000 SUBSCRIBERS

United Cable Company of New Hampshire Inc. (41,869 subscribers). Box 658, 751 E. Industrial Park Dr., Manchester, NH 03109. (603) 669-2115; FAX: (603) 641-2996. Samuel E. Phillips, gen mgr. *Area(s) Served:* NH. Counties: Hillsborough, Merrimack, Rockingham. Homes Served: 41,869. *Channel Capacity:* 35. In use: 35. *Basic Service:* Subscribers: 41,869; 10/31/93. *Local Advertising Accepted.*

SMALLER SYSTEMS

Vermont - G.O. Enterprises Inc., R.D. 1, Graniteville, VT 05654.

United Cable Management

Box 487, Grand Forks, ND 58201. (701) 772-7191. David A. Ramage, pres. Owned by David A. Ramage. Total Basic Subscribers: 2,300; Pay Cable Subscribers: 600; Number of Cable Systems: 5.

United Cable Systems Inc.

Box 698, Hwy. 550, Hindman, KY 41822. (606) 785-3450; FAX: (606) 785-3110. Eddie Tiller, vp mktg; Roger Fannin, vp adv; Archie W. Everage, vp progmg. Total Basic Subscribers: 4,200; Pay Cable Subscribers: 390; Number of Cable Systems: 1.

United Communications Association Inc.

Box 117, 1107 McArtor Rd., Dodge City, KS 67801. (316) 227-8645; FAX: (316) 227-7032. Laurence Vierthaler, pres; Don Howell, vp; Emma Jo Smith, vp. Total Basic Subscribers: 1,400; Pay Cable Subscribers: 650; Number of Cable Systems: 8.

United Video Cablevision Inc.

Box 420, 100 1st Stamford Pl., Stamford, CT 06904-0420. (203) 363-0200; FAX: (203) 363-0349. Lawrence Flinn Jr., pres; Robert Sullivan, CFO. Owned by Lawrence Flinn Jr. Total Basic Subscribers: 150,000; Pay Cable Subscribers: 77,200; Number of Cable Systems: 79.

US Cable Corporation

28 W. Grand Ave., Montvale, NJ 07645. (201) 930-9000; FAX: (201) 930-9232. Stephen E. Myers, chmn; James D. Pearson, pres; John C. Fletcher, vp opns; Michael C. Anderson, vp. Total Basic Subscribers: 197,316; Pay Cable Subscribers: 124,852; Number of Cable Systems: 49.

SYSTEMS WITH OVER 20,000 SUBSCRIBERS

US Cable of Lake County (55,000 subscribers). 3233 W. Grand Ave., Waukegan, IL 60085. (708) 336-7200; FAX: (708) 336-6233. Paul Ashley, gen mgr; Steve Tracy, mktg dir; Diane Schepis, loc adv dir; Jim Emrick, chief tech; Lynn Farias, cust svc dir. *Area(s) Served:* IL. County: Lake. Serving Antioch, Fox Lake, Gurnee, Lake Bluff, Lake Forest, Lindenhurst, North Chicago, Park City, Wadsworth, Waukegan, Winthrop Harbor, Zion. Miles of Plant: 1,300. Homes Passed: 95,000. Homes Served: 55,000. *Channel Capacity:* 52. In use: 52. *Basic Service:* Subscribers: 55,000; 09/01/93. Programming (via satellite): 28 chs. Programming (via microwave): 1 ch. Programming (off air): 11 chs. *Pay Services:* Total Pay Subscribers: 35,000; 12/01/92. Pay Per View Subscribers: 44,000; 12/01/92. *Local Advertising Accepted.*

US Cable of Northern Indiana (75,000 subscribers). 6161 Cleveland St., Merrillville, IN 46410. (219) 887-2011; FAX: (219) 887-3070. Michael Zimmer, gen mgr; John Gauder III, mktg dir & loc adv dir; Jeff Spence, chief tech; Janet Frageman, cust svc dir. *Area(s) Served:* IN, IL, MI. Counties: Jasper, Lake, Laporte, Porter, Cook, WI; Berrien. Serving Cedar Lake, Crown Point, Demotte, Duneland Beach, Dyer, Griffith, Hebron, Highland, Hobart, Keener Twp., Lake of Four Seasons, Lake Station, Long Beach, Lowell, Michiana Shores, Michigan City, Munster, New Chicago, North Chicago, Pine Twp., Pottawatomi Park, Schererville, Shorewood Estates, St. John, Trail Creek, Uninc, Whiting; Bloom Twp., Crete Twp., Ford Heights, Glenwood, Lynwood; Grand Beach, New Buffalo Twp., Michiana. Miles of Plant: 1,829. Homes Passed: 128,562. Homes Served: 75,000. *Channel Capacity:* 53. In use: 52. *Basic Service:* Subscribers: 75,000; 10/31/93. Programming (via satellite): 41 chs. Programming (off air): 11 chs. *Pay Services:* Total Pay Subscribers: 25,043; 10/31/92. (1) Pay Units: 18,645; 10/31/92. Programming (via satellite): HBO. (2) Pay Units: 7,811; 10/31/92. Programming (via satellite): Showtime. (3) Pay Units: 7,249; 10/31/92. Programming (via satellite): Cinemax. (4) Pay Units: 3,040; 10/31/92. Programming (via satellite): The Movie Channel. (5) Pay Units: 5,712; 10/31/92. Programming (via satellite): Disney. Pay Per View Subscribers: 45,720; 10/31/92. *Local Advertising Accepted. Equipment:* Scientific-Atlanta receivers; Jerrold modulators; Jerrold processors.

US Cable of Paterson (22,200 subscribers). 137-141 Ellison St., Paterson, NJ 07505. (201) 279-6600; FAX: (201) 279-3071. Thomas Meli, gen mgr; Earnest Roy, mktg dir; Fred Stillman, chief tech. *Area(s) Served:* NJ. County: Passaic. Homes Served: 22,200. *Channel Capacity:* 77. In use: 77. *Basic Service:* Subscribers: 22,200; 12/15/92. *Local Advertising Accepted.*

Valley Cable Systems

Box 78, Doylesburg, PA 17219. (717) 349-7717. Barry L. Kepner, chmn. Owned by Barry L. Kepner. Total Basic Subscribers: 1,370; Pay Cable Subscribers: 250; Number of Cable Systems: 8.

Valley Cable TV Inc.

602 College St., Fort Valley, GA 31030. (912) 825-3626. Fletcher Barnes, pres. Owned by Fletcher Barnes. Total Basic Subscribers: 1,900; Number of Cable Systems: 1.

Valparaiso Communication Systems

Box 296, 465 Hwy. 190, Valparaiso, FL 32580. (904) 729-5404; FAX: (904) 678-4553. Faye B. Floyd, CFO; Burt Bennett, vp opns. Owned by City of Valparaiso. Total Basic Subscribers: 1,575; Pay Cable Subscribers: 1,070; Number of Cable Systems: 1.

Vantage Cable Associates L.P.

Suite 200, 1025 Ashworth Rd., West Des Moines, IA 50265-3542. (515) 224-7220; FAX: (515) 224-9656. Douglas Hradek, pres; Marlyn Shaffer, vp; John Kilian, vp. Total Basic Subscribers: 31,000; Pay Cable Subscribers: 16,000; Number of Cable Systems: 126.

Norman S. Vaughan

Box 1459, 101 E. Wiygul, Fulton, MS 38843. (601) 862-5333; FAX: (601) 862-5388. Marty McDowell, pres; Steve Vaughan, vp. Owned by Norman Vaughan, H.D. McGee, Steve Vaughan, ptnrs. Total Basic Subscribers: 3,120; Pay Cable Subscribers: 550; Number of Cable Systems: 1.

Stephen W. Vaughan

Box 660, Fayette, AL 35555. (205) 932-4700. Steve Vaughan, pres. Total Basic Subscribers: 6,500; Pay Cable Subscribers: 1,800; Number of Cable Systems: 3.

SMALLER SYSTEMS

Alabama - West Alabama TV Cable Company, Fayette, AL. West Alabama TV Cable Company, Hamilton, AL. West Alabama TV Cable Company, Winfield, AL. **Michigan** - West Alabama TV Cable Company, Detroit, MI.

Vento Cable Management Inc.

Suite 1207, 5610 Wisconsin Ave., Chevy Chase, MD 20815. (301) 951-6222; FAX: (301) 656-0398. Gerald T. Vento, pres; John Vento, vp opns. Total Basic Subscribers: 25,000; Number of Cable Systems: 2.

SMALLER SYSTEMS

New Jersey - Atlantic Cable Television, Box 699, Mullica Hill, NJ 08062; (800) 228-5318; 5,000 subs. South Jersey Cablevision, Box 85, Swedesboro, NJ 08085; (609) 467-0275.

Verto Cable TV Corp.

140 N. Washington Ave., Scranton, PA 18503. (717) 342-0285; FAX: (717) 342-6517. James J. Tedesco Sr., chmn; Joseph Pagnotti, pres; James Peters, vp. Owned by Pagnotti Enterprises. Total Basic Subscribers: 54,000; Pay Cable Subscribers: 20,000; Number of Cable Systems: 1.

SYSTEMS WITH OVER 20,000 SUBSCRIBERS

Verto Cable TV (53,946 subscribers). Box 918, Scranton, PA 18503. (717) 342-0285. Marlene T. Miller, gen mgr.

Multiple Systems Operators, Independent Owners & Cable Systems

Area(s) Served: PA. Counties: Lackawanna, Luzerne. Homes Served: 53,946. *Channel Capacity:* 35. In use: 35. *Basic Service:* Subscribers: 53,946; 11/15/92. *Pay Services:* Total Pay Subscribers: 20,000; 11/15/92. *Local Advertising Accepted.*

Viacom Cable Inc.

Box 13, 5924 Stoneridge Dr., Pleasanton, CA 94566. (510) 463-0870; FAX: (510) 463-3241. John W. Goddard, CEO & pres; John Kopchik, CFO; Garrett J. Girovan, vp opns; Diane Schneiderjohn, vp mktg; Stephanie Storms, vp; Susan Dolce, vp. Owned by Viacom International Inc. Total Basic Subscribers: 1,081,700; Pay Cable Subscribers: 737,900; Number of Cable Systems: 14.

REGIONS

Bay Region: 2333 Nissen Dr., Livermore, CA; Kurt Jorgensen, mgr. *One-Cal Region:* 5797 Eastside Rd., Redding, CA; Kent Rasmussen, mgr. *Pacific Northwest:* 900 132nd St. N.W., Everett, WA; Eric Knudnen, mgr. *Midwest:* 660 Mainstream Dr., Nashville, TN; Stan Smith, mgr.

SYSTEMS WITH OVER 20,000 SUBSCRIBERS

Viacom Cable (24,800 subscribers). 1289 N. McDowell Blvd., Petaluma, CA 94594. (707) 763-9626; FAX: (707) 763-2074. Tim Rae, gen mgr.
Area(s) Served: CA. County: Sonoma. Serving Cloverdale, Forestville, Guerneville, Healdsburg, Petaluma, Windsor. Homes Served: 24,800. *Channel Capacity:* 36. In use: 36. *Basic Service:* Subscribers: 24,800; 11/15/93. *Pay Services:* Total Pay Subscribers: 10,237; 12/15/92. *No Local Advertising Accepted.*

Viacom Cable (39,700 subscribers). 550 Garcia Ave., Pittsburg, CA 94565. (510) 432-0500. Dee Trotta, gen mgr; Ken Gurgone, mktg dir; Marv Hansen, chief tech.
Area(s) Served: CA. County: Contra Costa. Serving Antioch, West Pittsburg. Miles of Plant: 400. Homes Passed: 52,600. Homes Served: 39,700. *Channel Capacity:* 40. In use: 40. *Basic Service:* Subscribers: 39,700; 11/15/93. Pay Per View Subscribers: 26,000; 11/15/91.

Viacom Cable (42,200 subscribers). 1710 Salem Industrial Dr. N.E., Salem, OR 97303. (503) 370-2770; FAX: (503) 370-2751. Terry Dillon, gen mgr; Dave Ramsey, mktg dir; Paul Kalkman, loc adv dir; Randy Love, chief tech; Diane Reeves, cust svc dir.
Area(s) Served: OR. Counties: Marion, Polk, Yamhill. Serving Amity, Keizer, Salem. Pop: 150,000. Miles of Plant: 550. Homes Passed: 72,000. Homes Served: 42,200. *Channel Capacity:* 37. In use: 37. *Basic Service:* Subscribers: 42,200; 11/15/93. Programming (via microwave): KTVU. *Pay Services:* Total Pay Subscribers: 12,000; 12/01/92. Pay Per View Subscribers: 7,500; 12/01/92. *Local Advertising Accepted. Equipment:* Scientific-Atlanta headend; GTE amplifiers; Cerro & Comm/Scope cables; Texscan character generator; Hamlin & Jerrold set top converters; Scientific-Atlanta satellite antenna; Hughes & Scientific-Atlanta satellite receivers; ChannelMatic commercial insert.

Viacom Cable (266,300 subscribers). 900 132nd St. S.W., Everett, WA 98204. (206) 745-8400; FAX: (206) 745-8360. Eric Kronen, gen mgr; Colette Jelineo, mktg dir; Art Hedstrom, chief tech.
Area(s) Served: WA. Counties: Island, King, Snohomish. Serving Beaux Arts Village, Bellevue, Bothell, Brier, Everett, Gold Bar, Granite Falls, Kirkland, Lake Forest Park, Lake Stevens, Lynwood, Mercer Island, Mill Creek, Monroe, Mountlake Terrace, Mukilteo, Oak Harbor, Redmond, Seattle, Snohomish, Startup, Sultan, Whidbey Island Naval Air Station. Homes Served: 266,300. *Channel Capacity:* 35. In use: 35. *Basic Service:* Subscribers: 266,300; 11/15/93. *Local Advertising Accepted.*

Viacom Cable Inc. (25,000 subscribers). 2128 Myers St., Oroville, CA 95966. (916) 533-3017. Jim Ragland, gen mgr; Bret Rios, mktg dir; Nick Clark, loc adv dir; Bob Forde, chief tech; Linda Kelly, cust svc dir.
Area(s) Served: CA. Counties: Butte, Colusa. Serving Biggs, Colusa, Gridley, Oroville, Paradise. Pop: 175,000. Miles of Plant: 500. Homes Passed: 38,000. *Channel Capacity:* 36. In use: 36. *Basic Service:* Subscribers: 25,000; 09/01/93. Programming (via satellite): 26 chs. Programming (via microwave): 2 chs. Programming (off air): 9 chs. *Local Advertising Accepted. Equipment:* Hughes, Jerrold & Scientific-Atlanta headend; Jerrold amplifiers; Cerro, Comm/Scope & Times cable; Hamlin & Jerrold set top converters; Harris & Scientific-Atlanta satellite antenna; Scientific-Atlanta satellite receivers.

Viacom Cable-San Francisco (160,000 subscribers). 2055 Folson St., San Francisco, CA 94110. (415) 863-8500; FAX: (415) 863-1659. Jon Marx, gen mgr; Patrick O'Hare, chief tech.
Area(s) Served: CA. County: San Francisco. Serving San Francisco. Homes Served: 160,000. *Channel Capacity:* 52. In use: 49. *Basic Service:* Subscribers: 160,000; 11/15/93. *No Local Advertising Accepted.*

Viacom Cablevision (57,000 subscribers). 6640 Sierra Ln., Dublin, CA 94568. (510) 828-8520; FAX: (510) 828-6112. Jon Marx, gen mgr; Ken Gurgone, mktg dir; Bob Brightenstine, chief tech.
Area(s) Served: CA. Counties: Alameda, Contra Costa. Serving Castro Valley, Dublin, Livermore, Pleasanton, San Leandro, San Ramon, Sunol. Miles of Plant: 567. Homes Passed: 80,000. Homes Served: 57,000. *Channel Capacity:* 36. In use: 36. *Basic Service:* Subscribers: 57,000; 11/15/93. *Pay Services:* Total Pay Subscribers: 53,000; 12/15/92. Pay Per View Subscribers: 28,000; 10/30/91. *Local Advertising Accepted. Equipment:* Hughes & Scientific-Atlanta headends; Jerrold, GTE & Theta-Com amplifiers; Comm/Scope cable; Sony VTRs; Panasonic character generator; Hamlin set top converters; Zenith addressable set top converters; Scientific-Atlanta satellite receivers.

Viacom Cablevision (126,000 subscribers). 660 Mainstream Dr., Nashville, TN 37208-0570. (615) 244-7462; FAX: (615) 255-6528. Stan Smith, gen mgr; Debbye Bettis, mktg dir; Fritz Baker, chief tech.
Area(s) Served: TN. County: Davidson. Homes Passed: 212,000. Homes Served: 126,000. *Channel Capacity:* 36. In use: 36. *Basic Service:* Subscribers: 126,000; 11/15/93. *Pay Services:* Total Pay Subscribers: 82,000; 11/15/92. Pay Per View Subscribers: 86,000; 11/12/91. *Local Advertising Accepted.*

Viacom Cablevision (139,000 subscribers). 2316 S. State St., Tacoma, WA 98405. (206) 597-7800; FAX: (206) 272-4062. Julie McGovern, gen mgr; Colette Jelineo, mktg dir; Greg Nissen, chief tech.
Area(s) Served: WA. Counties: King, Pierce, Thurston. Serving Bonny Lake, Federal Way, Fife, Fircrest, Fort Lewis, Fox Island, Gig Harbor, Gig Harbor Peninsula, Graham, Lakebay, Lake Holliday, Lake Minterwood, Lakewood Center, Lake of the Woods, McKenna, Milton, Peninsula, Puyallup, Rainier, Roy, South Prairie, Spanaway, Steilacoom, Summit, Sumner, Tacoma, Vashon, Yelm. Homes Served: 139,000. *Channel Capacity:* 35. In use: 35. *Basic Service:* Subscribers: 139,000; 11/15/93. *Local Advertising Accepted.*

Viacom Cablevision Inc. (35,400 subscribers). 5797 Eastside Rd., Redding, CA 96001. (916) 241-7300; FAX: (916) 241-0278. Kent Rasmussen, gen mgr; Bret Rios, mktg dir; Walt Mortimer, chief tech.
Area(s) Served: CA. Counties: Shasta, Tehama. Serving Anderson, Cottonwood, Red Bluff, Redding. Homes Passed: 56,000. Homes Served: 35,400. *Channel Capacity:* 36. In use: 36. *Basic Service:* Subscribers: 35,400; 11/15/93. *Pay Services:* Total Pay Subscribers: 10,300; 11/11/91. *Local Advertising Accepted.*

Viacom Cablevision of Dayton Inc. (52,000 subscribers). 275 Leo St., Dayton, OH 45404. (513) 223-4077; FAX: (513) 461-1838. John Wise, gen mgr; Beverly Wall, mktg dir; Greg Coherd, chief tech.
Area(s) Served: OH. County: Montgomery. Serving Butler Twp., Dayton, Mad River, Riverside. Miles of Plant: 621. Homes Passed: 93,900. Homes Served: 52,000. *Channel Capacity:* 35. In use: 35. *Basic Service:* Subscribers: 52,000; 11/15/93. *Local Advertising Accepted.*

Viacom Cablevision of Marin County (61,600 subscribers). 1111 Anderson Dr., San Rafael, CA 94901. (415) 457-9100; FAX: (415) 258-0136. Tim Rae, gen mgr; Greg Johnson, chief tech.
Area(s) Served: CA. County: Marin. Serving Belvedere, Corte Madera, Fairfax, Forest Knolls, Green Brae, Kentfield, Lagunitas, Larkspur, Marin City, Mill Valley, Ross, San Anselmo, San Geronimo, San Quentin, San Rafael, Sausalito, Tiburon, Woodacre. Homes Served: 61,600. *Channel Capacity:* 37. In use: 37. *Basic Service:* Subscribers: 61,600; 11/15/93. *Pay Services:* Total Pay Subscribers: 32,511; 12/15/92.

Viacom Cablevision of Napa (22,900 subscribers). 2260 Brown St., Napa, CA 94558. (707) 255-8543; FAX: (707) 255-0812. Shirley Gulbransen, gen mgr; David Fox, mktg dir; Tom Toutriella, chief tech.
Area(s) Served: CA. County: Napa. Miles of Plant: 250. Homes Passed: 27,500. Homes Served: 22,900. *Channel Capacity:* 60. In use: 40. *Basic Service:* Subscribers: 22,900; 11/15/93. *Pay Services:* Total Pay Subscribers: 13,341; 12/15/92. *Local Advertising Accepted. Equipment:* Hughes & Jerrold headends; Hughes & Jerrold amplifiers; JVC & Telemation VTRs; Shibaden character generator; Starcom & Jerrold remote; Oak, Sigma & Texscan set top converters; Andrew & Scientific-Atlanta satellite antennas; Scientific-Atlanta satellite receivers.

SMALLER SYSTEMS

California - Viacom Cable, 498D Moone Ln., Healdsburg, CA 95448; 16,400 subs. Viacom Cable, 1289 N. McDowell Blvd., Petaluma, CA 94594; (707) 763-9626; 17,900 subs. Viacom Cable, 751 Belmont Way, Pinole, CA 94564; 14,500 subs. Viacom Cable, 2166 Rheem Dr., Pleasanton, CA 94588; 12,700 subs.

Vidacable CATV Systems

6 Fairview Ave., High Falls, NY 12440. (914) 687-9695. Sue Ellen Sheeley, pres. Owned by Ellen Sheeley. Total Basic Subscribers: 3,300; Number of Cable Systems: 1.

Video Inc.

Box 708, Bay Springs, MS 39422. (601) 764-2121; FAX: (601) 764-4900. Joseph D. Fail, CEO; R.A. McFarland, vp opns; Betty Hinton, vp mktg. Owned by Telephone Electronics Corp. Total Basic Subscribers: 1,742; Number of Cable Systems: 2.

Viking Electronic Inc.

Box 35, 818 4th St., Park River, ND 58270. (701) 284-7111. Lawrence F. Deutz, vp opns. Owned by Polar Communications Mutual Aid Corp. Total Basic Subscribers: 3,000; Pay Cable Subscribers: 1,000; Number of Cable Systems: 12.

Vision Cable Communications Inc.

One Coliseum Centre, 2300 Yorkmont Rd., Charlotte, NC 28217. (704) 357-6900; FAX: (704) 329-7580. Mitchell Roberts, pres; Charles Dietz, vp; Ron Summow, vp. Owned by Newhouse Broadcasting Co. Total Basic Subscribers: 506,000; Number of Cable Systems: 15.

SYSTEMS WITH OVER 20,000 SUBSCRIBERS

Vision Cable (49,280 subscribers). 200 Roosevelt Pl., Palisades Park, NJ 07650. (201) 592-7600; FAX: (201) 592-7736. Ed Rose, gen mgr; Phil Giordano, mktg dir; Dane Terry, loc adv dir; Bob Higgins, chief tech; Joann Schriever, cust svc dir.
Area(s) Served: NJ. Counties: Bergen, Hudson. Serving Cliffside Park, Edgewater, Englewood, Englewood Cliffs, Fairfiew, Fort Lee, Guttenberg, Leonia, Little Ferry, Moonachie, Palisades Park, Ridgefield, Ridgefield Park, Teterboro. Miles of Plant: 362. Homes Served: 49,280. *Channel Capacity:* 46. In use: 46. *Basic Service:* Subscribers: 49,280; 11/21/92. Programming (via satellite): 35 chs. Programming (via microwave): 1 ch. Programming (off air): 13 chs. *Pay Services:* Total Pay Subscribers: 50,450; 11/21/92. (1) Pay Units: 28,200; 11/21/92. Programming: HBO. (2) Pay Units: 6,550; 11/21/92. Programming: Cinemax. (3) Pay Units: 5,850; 11/21/92. Programming: Showtime. (4) Pay Units: 3,000; 11/21/92. Programming: Disney. Pay Per View Subscribers: 31,330; 11/21/92. *Local Advertising Accepted.*

Vision Cable of Alpine Inc. (27,300 subscribers). 3250 Donahue Ferry Rd., Pineville, LA 71360. (318) 640-2892; FAX: (318) 640-6951. Mike Burns, gen mgr; Diana Rogers-Deville, mktg dir & cust svc dir. *Basic Service:* Subscribers: 27,300; 9/30/93.

Vision Cable of Metrolina (32,000 subscribers). 909 Kansas St., Kannapolis, NC 28083. (704) 938-5156; FAX: (704) 938-6916. Robert Melton, gen mgr; Shirley Hurlocker, mktg dir; Dennis Butta, loc adv dir; Joe Dickens, chief tech; Priscilla Williams, cust svc dir.
Area(s) Served: NC. Counties: Cabarrus, Rowan. Serving China Grove, Concord, Harrisburg, Kannapolis, Landis, Mount Pleasant. Pop: 100,000. Miles of Plant: 1,010. Homes Passed: 46,250. Homes Served: 32,000. *Channel Capacity:* 46. In use: 44. *Basic Service:* Subscribers: 32,000; 10/15/93. *Local Advertising Accepted.*

Vision Cable of Newport Inc. (28,000 subscribers). 500 Vision Cable Dr., Newport, NC 28570. (919) 223-5011; FAX: (919) 223-3208. Mike Williams, gen mgr. *Basic Service:* Subscribers: 28,000; 10/31/93.

Multiple Systems Operators, Independent Owners & Cable Systems

Vision Cable of North Carolina (45,000 subscribers). 4606 Margaret Wallace Rd., Matthews, NC 28105. (704) 545-0136; FAX: (704) 545-1460. James Molt, gen mgr; Sherry Kronjaeger, mktg dir; Roger Martin, chief tech. *Area(s) Served:* NC, SC. Counties: Mecklenburg, Union; Lancaster. Homes Passed: 57,000. Homes Served: 45,000. *Basic Service:* Subscribers: 45,000; 10/31/93.

Vision Cable of Pinellas Inc. (133,500 subscribers). 2530 Drew St., Clearwater, FL 34625. (813) 797-1818; FAX: (813) 797-9629. James Waldo, gen mgr; Dennis Kapp, mktg dir; Matt Pautin, chief tech. *Area(s) Served:* FL. County: Pinellas. Serving Belleair, Clearwater, East Lake Woodlands, Kenneth City, Largo, Pinellas Park, Seminole. Homes Served: 133,500. *Channel Capacity:* 63. In use: 63. *Basic Service:* Subscribers: 133,500; 10/14/93. *Local Advertising Accepted.*

Vision Cable of South Carolina Inc. (26,527 subscribers). Box 3948, 3232 Bryson Dr., Florence, SC 29501. (803) 662-8191; FAX: (803) 665-5483. Kurt Newber, gen mgr; Joe Pariano, mktg dir; Tommy Martin, chief tech; Robin Weaver, cust svc dir. *Area(s) Served:* SC. Counties: Darlington, Florence. Serving Darlington, Florence, Pamplico, Quinby, Timmonsville. Pop: 90,000. Miles of Plant: 812. Homes Passed: 35,500. Homes Served: 26,527. *Channel Capacity:* 42. In use: 41. *Basic Service:* Subscribers: 26,527; 09/01/93. Programming (via satellite): 34 chs. Programming (off air): 7 chs. *Pay Services:* Total Pay Subscribers: 17,126; 09/01/93. (1) Pay Units: 9,439; 09/01/93. Programming (via satellite): HBO. (2) Pay Units: 3,424; 09/01/93. Programming (via satellite): Cinemax. (3) Pay Units: 2,297; 09/01/93. Programming (via satellite): Showtime. Pay Per View Subscribers: 12,704; 09/01/93. *Local Advertising Accepted. Equipment:* Jerrold convertor & line equipment.

Vision Cable of Wilmington (50,000 subscribers). 1949 Dawson St., Wilmington, NC 28403. (919) 763-4638; FAX: (919) 762-3641. William Greene, gen mgr; Rob Flinchum, mktg dir; Dennis Flowers, chief tech. *Area(s) Served:* NC. Counties: Brunswick, New Hanover, Peuder. Homes Served: 50,000. *Channel Capacity:* 45. In use: 45. *Basic Service:* Subscribers: 50,000; 10/15/93. *Local Advertising Accepted.*

Vision Electronics

14707 N. 72nd St., Omaha, NE 68122. (402) 571-7590; FAX: (402) 571-2801. John W. Smith, pres; Trace Smith, vp opns. Owned by John W. Smith. Total Basic Subscribers: 3,844; Pay Cable Subscribers: 1,000; Number of Cable Systems: 30.

Vista Communications

33 Nagog Park, Acton, MA 01720. (508) 263-0467; FAX: (508) 635-9488. Neil McHugh, pres; Richard Singer, CFO; Charles Davis, vp. Owned by Charles Davis, Neil McHugh, Richard Singer. Total Basic Subscribers: 18,959; Pay Cable Subscribers: 8,206; Number of Cable Systems: 35.

Volcano Communications Inc.

Box 890, Pine Grove, CA 95665. (209) 296-2288; FAX: (209) 296-1471. James Welch Jr., & chmn; Sharon Lundgren, CFO; James C. Graves, vp opns; Jay Lucke, vp; Ray Crabtree, vp. Total Basic Subscribers: 3,400; Number of Cable Systems: 1.

SMALLER SYSTEMS

California - Volcano Vision, Box 890, Pine Grove, CA 95665.

W.K. Communications Inc.

Box 309, 922 Rich Ave., Iron Mountain, MI 49801. (906) 774-1120; FAX: (906) 774-8233. Robert K. Weary Jr., chmn; Robert Knoke, pres. Owned by Robert Knoke, Robert K. Weary Jr. Total Basic Subscribers: 20,700; Number of Cable Systems: 12.

Waitsfield-Fayston Telephone Co.

Box 9, Waitsfield, VT 05673. (802) 496-5800; FAX: (802) 496-5811. Dana Haskin, pres; John Simms, vp opns. Owned by Dana Haskin. Total Basic Subscribers: 3,000; Number of Cable Systems: 1.

SMALLER SYSTEMS

Vermont - Waitsfield Cable, Box 9, Waitsfield, VT 05673.

Wander Telecommunications

Box 368, Gualala, CA 95445. (707) 884-4111; FAX: (707) 884-4116. Dr. Gerhard J. Hanneman, pres; Poppy Faldutos, vp opns; Russ Jarvis, vp. Total Basic Subscribers: 2,300; Pay Cable Subscribers: 500; Number of Cable Systems: 1.

SMALLER SYSTEMS

California- Wander Cable Television, Gualala, CA.

Warmath Communications Inc.

Box 760, Humboldt, TN 38343. (901) 784-5000; FAX: (901) 784-2533. John F. Warmath, pres; Frank Warmath, vp opns. Owned by J. Frank Warmath Estate, John F. Warmath, James C. Warmath. Total Basic Subscribers: 3,600; Pay Cable Subscribers: 1,000; Number of Cable Systems: 2.

SMALLER SYSTEMS

Tennessee - Warmath Communications Inc., Box 760, Humboldt, TN 38343. Warmath Communications Inc., Medina, TN.

Brandt R. & Madeline C. Warner

901 Delta Rd., Red Lion, PA 17356. (717) 246-0456. Brandt R. Warner, pres; Madeline C. Warner, vp. Total Basic Subscribers: 3,200; Pay Cable Subscribers: 1,650; Number of Cable Systems: 2.

SMALLER SYSTEMS

Maryland - Cecilton CATV Inc., Cecilton, MD.
Pennsylvania - Airview CATV Inc., 901 Delta Rd., Red Lion, PA 17356.

Warsaw TV Cable Corp.

Box 225, 10 W. Buffalo St., Warsaw, NY 14569. (716) 786-5638. Irving J. Toner, pres; Iris C. Toner, vp. Owned by Irving J. Toner, Iris C. Toner. Total Basic Subscribers: 1,600; Number of Cable Systems: 1.

Water, Light & Gas Commission - City of Monroe

Box 725, 215 N. Broad St., Monroe, GA 30655. (404) 267-3429; FAX: (404) 267-3698. James Salter, vp opns. Owned by City of Monroe. Total Basic Subscribers: 4,427; Pay Cable Subscribers: 2,404; Number of Cable Systems: 1.

SMALLER SYSTEMS

Georgia - Water, Light & Gas Commission, Box 725, Monroe, GA.

Waycross Cable Co. Inc.

Box 37, 126 Havanna Ave., Waycross, GA 31501. (912) 283-2332; FAX: (912) 285-9836. John Stembler, pres; John Harrison, vp opns. Total Basic Subscribers: 10,977; Pay Cable Subscribers: 2,500; Number of Cable Systems: 1.

Robert K. Weary Jr. dba Belleville Community Antenna Systems, Inc.

1809 N St., Belleville, KS 66935. (913) 527-2226. Robert K. Weary Jr., pres; Judy Bizner, vp. Owned by Robert K. Weary Jr. Total Basic Subscribers: 3,084; Pay Cable Subscribers: 1,122; Number of Cable Systems: 2.

SMALLER SYSTEMS

Kansas - Belleville Community Antenna Systems Inc., 1809 N St., Belleville, KS 66935; (913) 527-2226. Wamego Community Antenna Systems, Box 187, Junction City, KS 66441.

WEHCO Video Inc.

Box 2221, Little Rock, AR 72203. (501) 378-3529; FAX: (501) 376-8594. Walter E. Hussman Jr., CEO; Jim Wilbanks, vp opns & vp mktg. Owned by KCMC Inc. Total Basic Subscribers: 106,829; Number of Cable Systems: 14.

SYSTEMS WITH OVER 20,000 SUBSCRIBERS

Longview Cable TV Co. Inc. (22,300 subscribers). Box 4399, Longview, TX 75606. (903) 758-9991; FAX: (903) 758-3083. Robert Durham, gen mgr; Gail Bennett Tedder, mktg dir; Robert Young, chief tech. *Area(s) Served:* TX. County: Gregg. Serving Longview. Homes Served: 22,300. *Channel Capacity:* 54. In use: 46. *Basic Service:* Subscribers: 22,300; 10/31/93. *Pay Services:* Total Pay Subscribers: 10,700; 10/31/93. *Local Advertising Accepted.*

Robert Weisberg dba Mountain Cable

Suite PHA, 145 E. 92nd St., New York, NY 10128. (212) 722-2990. Robert Weisberg, CEO. Owned by Robert Weisberg. Total Basic Subscribers: 885; Pay Cable Subscribers: 325; Number of Cable Systems: 2.

SMALLER SYSTEMS

New York - Mountain Cablevision, Inc., New York, NY.

Western Cabled Systems

818 Douglas Ave., Redwood City, CA 94063. (415) 366-8294; FAX: (415) 366-0678. Jeff Stevens, pres; Larry D. Whitney, vp opns. Owned by Balkar Cable Holdings Inc. Total Basic Subscribers: 11,000; Pay Cable Subscribers: 6,403; Number of Cable Systems: 9.

SMALLER SYSTEMS

California - Western Cabled Systems, Belmont, CA; (415) 366-8294; 400 subs. Western Cabled Systems, Esparto, Yolo County, CA; (916) 787-4553; 500 subs. Western Cabled Systems, Mariwa Bay, Richmond, CA; (800) 698-8830; 900 subs. Western Cabled Systems, Portola Valley, CA; (415) 851-3945; 750 subs. Western Cabled Systems, San Mateo, CA; (415) 366-8294; 6,700 subs. Western Cabled Systems, San Mateo County, CA; (415) 851-3945; 350 subs. Western Cabled Systems, Santa Cruz County, CA; (408) 734-1868; 250 subs. Western Cabled Systems, Westlake, Daily City, CA; (415) 755-2958; 4,000 subs. Western Cabled Systems, Woodside, CA; (415) 851-3945; 700 subs.

Western Cablesystems Inc.

Suite 230, 513 Wilcox, Castle Rock, CO 80104. (303) 688-4462. Michael Kruger, CEO & pres; Denise Rucker, vp. Owned by Michael Kruger. Total Basic Subscribers: 10,000; Number of Cable Systems: 3.

Western Cablevision Inc.

5773 W. Lazy Heart, Tucson, AZ 85713. (602) 578-0382; FAX: (602) 578-0758. Joe Gans III, pres & vp opns; Dennis E. Snow, vp mktg. Owned by Joseph S. Gans. Total Basic Subscribers: 1,700; Pay Cable Subscribers: 600; Number of Cable Systems: 3.

Western Communications

2 Rincon Center, Suite 203, 121 Spear St., San Francisco, CA 94105. (415) 896-5000; FAX: (415) 896-0236. John Sias, CEO; Christopher J. Lammers, pres; Robert M. Stoops, vp mktg. Owned by Chronicle Publishing Co. Total Basic Subscribers: 320,855; Number of Cable Systems: 7.

SYSTEMS WITH OVER 20,000 SUBSCRIBERS

Chronicle Cablevision (26,804 subscribers). 350 Hoohana St., Kahului, HI 96732. (808) 877-4425; FAX: (808) 877-3534. Ross Waggoner, gen mgr; Wendy Wells, mktg dir; Gerrianne Sakamoto, loc adv dir; Howard Feig, chief tech. *Area(s) Served:* HI. County: Hawaii. Homes Served: 26,804. *Channel Capacity:* 24. In use: 24. *Basic Service:* Subscribers: 26,804; 10/31/93.

Concord TV Cable (41,460 subscribers). 2450 Whitman Rd., Concord, CA 94518. (510) 685-2330; FAX: (510) 686-1257. Alexander Zwissler, gen mgr; Leslie Blankenstip, mktg dir; Mark Spencer, chief tech; Cindy Graffort, cust svc dir. *Area(s) Served:* CA. County: Contra Costa. Serving Clayton, Concord. Homes Served: 41,460. *Channel Capacity:* 54. In use: 52. *Basic Service:* Subscribers: 41,460; 10/31/93. *Pay Services:* Total Pay Subscribers: 16,561; 10/31/93. *Local Advertising Accepted.*

Inland Valley Cablevision (48,000 subscribers). 4077 W. Stetson Ave., Hemet, CA 92545. (909) 766-4270; FAX: (909) 766-4289. Thomas R. Unglaub, gen mgr; Cindy Harrington, mktg dir; Terry Cordell, chief tech; Nancy Null, cust svc dir. *Area(s) Served:* CA. County: Riverside. Serving Hemet, Idyllwild, Murrata, San Jacinto, Temecula, Winchester. Homes Served: 48,000. *Channel Capacity:* 62. In use:

Multiple Systems Operators, Independent Owners & Cable Systems

54. *Basic Service:* Subscribers: 48,000; 09/30/93. *Local Advertising Accepted.*

Las Cruces TV Cable (23,300 subscribers). Box J, 110 E. Idaho, Las Cruces, NM 88004. (505) 523-2531; FAX: (505) 523-7208. John Christopher, gen mgr; Paula Anzell, mktg dir; Drew Flynt, loc adv dir; Bud Tleimat, chief tech; Ruth Clark, cust svc dir.
Area(s) Served: NM. County: Dona Ana. Serving Las Cruces, Mesilla. Pop: 62,000. Miles of Plant: 566. Homes Passed: 35,500. Homes Served: 23,300. *Channel Capacity:* 43. In use: 43. *Basic Service:* Subscribers: 23,300; 09/07/93. Programming (via satellite): Prevue, ESPN, USA, TNT, CNN, Lifetime, QVC, KTLA, WTBS, WGN, WOR, C-SPAN, TNN, Discovery, A&E, CNBC, Weather Channel, Nickelodeon. Programming (via microwave): KOAT. Programming (off air): KRWG, KDBC, KCOS, KVIA, KCIK, KTSM, KINT, KZIA, KERM, KJLF. *Pay Services:* Total Pay Subscribers: 12,055; 09/07/93. (1) Pay Units: 4,416; 09/07/93. Programming (via satellite): HBO. (2) Pay Units: 1,557; 09/07/93. Programming (via satellite): Disney. (3) Pay Units: 915; 09/07/93. Programming (via satellite): The Movie Channel. (4) Pay Units: 2,751; 09/07/93. Programming (via satellite): Showtime. Pay Per View Subscribers: 3,000; 09/07/93. *Local Advertising Accepted. Equipment:* Zenith addressable converters & remotes.

Monterey Peninsula TV Cable (75,200 subscribers). Box 1711, 2455 Henderson Way, Monterey, CA 93940. (408) 649-9105; FAX: (408) 649-8680. Minni Marshall, mktg dir; Dave Walton, chief tech.
Area(s) Served: CA. County: Monterey. Homes Served: 75,200. *Channel Capacity:* 40. In use: 38. *Basic Service:* Subscribers: 75,200; 10/31/93. *Local Advertising Accepted.*

Ventura County Cablevision (107,000 subscribers). Suite 200, 2645 Townsgate Rd., Westlake Village, CA 91361. (805) 379-5300; FAX: (805) 379-5321. Dave La Rue, gen mgr; Richard Yelen, mktg dir; Jerry Sanders, chief tech.
Area(s) Served: CA. Counties: Los Angeles, Ventura. Homes Served: 107,000. *Channel Capacity:* 55. In use: 50. *Basic Service:* Subscribers: 90,000; 10/31/93. *Local Advertising Accepted.*

Western Wisconsin Communications Cooperative

Box 846, 202 Whitehall Rd., Independence, WI 54747. (715) 985-3004; FAX: (715) 985-3261. Mark Schroeder, vp opns. Total Basic Subscribers: 6,100; Pay Cable Subscribers: 2,200; Number of Cable Systems: 4.

Westfield Community Antenna Association Inc.

121 Strang St., Westfield, PA 16950. (814) 367-5190. Total Basic Subscribers: 1,060.

Weststar Communications Inc.

2nd Fl., Suite 250, 2200 Sunrise Blvd., Rancho Cordova, CA 95670. (916) 631-9100; FAX: (916) 631-8160. Eugene A. Iacopi, pres; Barry K. Hyne, CFO. Total Basic Subscribers: 42,766; Pay Cable Subscribers: 22,914; Number of Cable Systems: 9.

SMALLER SYSTEMS

California - WestStar Lake of the Pines, 10062 Streeter Rd., Suite 2, Auburn, CA 95603. Westar Cable TV, 10062 Streeter Rd., Suite 2, Suburn, CA 95603. WestStar Communications III, 201 E. Line St., Bishop CA 93514. WestStar Shaver Lake Inc., 201 E. Line St., Bishop, CA 93514. Coastside Cable TV Inc., 525 Obispo Rd., El Granada, CA 94018. Coastside Cable TV Inc., 1-A 142 Fourth Ave., Fort Ord, CA 93941. Tahoeview Cablevision Inc., 2200 Sunrise Blvd., Suite 250, Rancho Cordova, CA 95670. WestStar Communications I, 10418 Donner Pass Rd., Truckee, CA 96161. **Idaho -** WestStar Communications I, 816 E. Mullan St., Osburn, ID 83849. **Montana -** WestStar Group North Inc., 816 E. Mullan St., Osburn, ID 83849.

White Mountain Cablevision

Box 66, N. Main St., Colebrook, NH 03576. (603) 237-5573; FAX: (603) 237-8256. William Hinton, vp opns. Owned by William Hinton, Dennis Nolin, David Pouliotte. Total Basic Subscribers: 1,569; Number of Cable Systems: 1.

Windom Cable Communications

Box 38, 444 9th St., Windom, MN 56101. (507) 831-2363; FAX: (507) 831-3340. Dennis Purrington, vp opns; Gene Sunstrom, vp progmg; Dennis Nelson, vp. Owned by Community of Windom. Total Basic Subscribers: 1,500; Pay Cable Subscribers: 400; Number of Cable Systems: 1.

Wire Tele-View Corporation

603 E. Market St., Pottsville, PA 17901. (717) 622-4501. Deborah A. Stabinsky, pres; Mary L. Schoffstall, vp. Owned by Deborah A. Stabinsky, J. Richard Kim, Mary Louise Schoffstall. Total Basic Subscribers: 2,600; Pay Cable Subscribers: 450; Number of Cable Systems: 2.

Wolfe Broadcasting Corporation

905 W. State St., Fremont, OH 43420. (419) 332-6972; FAX: (419) 332-9341. Margaret Wolfe, CEO; Tim Wolfe, pres. Owned by Margarat Wolfe. Total Basic Subscribers: 6,500; Pay Cable Subscribers: 2,300; Number of Cable Systems: 1.

SMALLER SYSTEMS

Ohio - Fremont Cablevision, 905 W. State St., Fremont, OH 43420; (419) 332-6972; Tim Wolfe.

Wometco Cable Corporation

Box 562205, Suite 800, 9500 S. Dadeland Blvd., Miami, FL 33156. (305) 670-1105. John M. Lewis, CEO & pres; Gerald V. Cheney, vp opns; James F. Brown, vp mktg. Total Basic Subscribers: 215,580; Number of Cable Systems: 8.

SYSTEMS WITH OVER 20,000 SUBSCRIBERS

Wometco Cable (67,655 subscribers). Box 1049, Suite 440, 1780 Corporate Dr., Millcross, GA 30093. (404) 921-0010; FAX: (404) 279-9423. Floye Hewatt, gen mgr; JoAnn Robertson, mktg dir; Mitch Jones, chief tech.
Area(s) Served: GA. County: Gwinett. Serving Berkeley Lake, Grayson, Lidburn, Norcross, Snellville. Homes Served: 67,655. *Channel Capacity:* 61. In use: 43. *Basic Service:* Subscribers: 67,655; 10/31/93. *Local Advertising Accepted.*

Wometco Cable TV of Clayton County Inc. (39,107 subscribers). Suite 22, 6435 Tara Blvd., Jonesboro, GA 30236. (404) 478-0010; FAX: (404) 471-6639. Chris W. Cofty, gen mgr; Nancy Palmatter, mktg dir & loc adv dir; J.C. Kirkland, chief tech; Susan Crutchfield, cust svc dir.
Area(s) Served: GA. Counties: Clayton, Fulton, Henry. Serving Conley, Ellenwood, Forest Park, Hapeville, Jonesboro, Lovejoy, Morrow, Rex, Riverdale, Stockbridge. Homes Served: 39,107. *Channel Capacity:* 60. In use: 53. *Basic Service:* Subscribers: 39,107; 10/31/93. *Pay Services:* Total Pay Subscribers: 24,788; 11/20/92. Pay Per View Subscribers: 11,062; 10/24/92. *Local Advertising Accepted.*

Wometco Cable TV of Cobb (70,000 subscribers). 1145 Powder Springs Rd., Marietta, GA 30064. (404) 427-0010; FAX: (404) 425-7524. Greg Ownby, gen mgr; Peter W. Tinkham, mktg dir & loc adv dir; Joe Zeller, chief tech; Joslyn Ward, cust svc dir.
Area(s) Served: GA. County: Cobb. Serving Kennesaw, Marbleton, Marietta. Miles of Plant: 2,000. Homes Passed: 109,664. Homes Served: 70,000. *Channel Capacity:* 63. In use: 59. *Basic Service:* Subscribers: 70,000; 10/31/93. Programming (via satellite): 28 chs. Programming (off air): 9 chs. *Pay Services:* Total Pay Subscribers: 30,900; 10/24/92. (1) Pay Units: 13,520; 10/24/92. Programming (via satellite): HBO. (2) Pay Units: 9,110; 10/24/92. Programming (via satellite): Showtime. (3) Pay Units: 5,550; 10/24/92. Programming (via satellite): Disney. (4) Pay Units: 1,400; 10/24/92. Programming (via satellite): Cinemax. (5) Pay Units: 1,000; 10/24/92. Programming (via satellite): The Movie Channel. Pay Per View Subscribers: 13,000; 10/24/92. *Local Advertising Accepted. Equipment:* Scientific-Atlanta & Jerrold headend; Scientific-Atlanta addressable converters; Scientific-Atlanta system controllers.

World Co.

Box 888, 609 New Hampshire St., Lawrence, KS 66044. (913) 843-2100; FAX: (913) 843-4512. Dolph C. Simons Jr., pres; Ralph Gage, vp opns. Total Basic Subscribers: 56,000; Pay Cable Subscribers: 20,000; Number of Cable Systems: 2.

SYSTEMS WITH OVER 20,000 SUBSCRIBERS

Columbine Cablevision (30,500 subscribers). 1201 University Ave., Fort Collins, CO 80521. (303) 493-7400; FAX: (303) 493-4958. Bob Carnahan, gen mgr; Phil Johnson, mktg dir; Dan Kuntz, loc adv dir; Rick Montoya, chief tech.
Area(s) Served: CO. County: Larimer. Serving Fort Collins. Pop: 90,000. Miles of Plant: 650. Homes Passed: 35,000. Homes Served: 30,500. *Channel Capacity:* 52. In use: 46. *Basic Service:* Subscribers: 30,500; 10/31/93. Programming (via satellite): 25 chs. Programming (off air): 9 chs. *Pay Services:* Total Pay Subscribers: 8,000; 07/01/92. Pay Per View Subscribers: 8,000; 07/01/92. *Local Advertising Accepted.*

Wyandotte Municipal Services, CATV Dept.

3005 Biddle Ave., Wyandotte, MI 48192. (313) 282-7100; FAX: (313) 282-7100. Thomas Daily, vp opns; Bill Booker, vp mktg. Owned by Community of Wyandotte. Total Basic Subscribers: 9,800; Pay Cable Subscribers: 11,300; Number of Cable Systems: 1.

Y Co. Inc.

Box 6478, 215 Rochester Bank & Trust, 331 16th Ave. N.W., Rochester, MN 55903-6478. (507) 287-0880; FAX: (507) 288-9207. Rick Plunkett, CEO. Owned by Rick Plunkett. Total Basic Subscribers: 3,950; Pay Cable Subscribers: 950; Number of Cable Systems: 1.

SMALLER SYSTEMS

Minnesota - Fairmont Cable TV, Rochester, MN.

Youngsville TV Corporation

140 Davis St., Youngsville, PA 16371. (814) 563-3336. Felix Matthews, pres; Raymond Walter, vp opns. Total Basic Subscribers: 1,187; Pay Cable Subscribers: 653; Number of Cable Systems: 1.

Roger E. Zylstra Trust

Box 178, Eighth & Douglas, Yankton, SD 57078. (605) 665-8030; FAX: (605) 665-0683. J.W. Abbott, pres; Brian Steward, CFO & vp opns. Owned by J.W. Abbott. Total Basic Subscribers: 13,000; Pay Cable Subscribers: 4,900; Number of Cable Systems: 6.

SMALLER SYSTEMS

Iowa - Orange City-Alton Cable TV, Orange City-Alton, IA. **Minnesota -** Luverne Cable TV, Luverne, MN. Worthington Cable TV, Worthington, MN. **South Dakota -** Canton Cable TV, Canton, SD. Vermillion Cable TV, Vermillion, SD. Yankton Cable TV, Yankton, SD.

Geographical Index to Large Cable Systems & MSOs in the U.S. & Canada

ALABAMA

Anniston
Anniston NewChannels Corporation
 (NewChannels Corporation)

Birmingham
Birmingham Cable Communications
 (Time Warner Cable)

Florence
Comcast Cablevision of Florence
 (Comcast Cable Communications)

Fulton Dale
Crown Cable
 (Crown Media Inc.)

Gadsden
Comcast Cablevision of Gadsden
 (Comcast Cable Communications)

Hoover
TCI Cablevision of Alabama Inc.
 (Tele-Communications Inc.)

Huntsville
Cable Alabama
 (Cable America Corporation)
Comcast Cablevision of Huntsville
 (Comcast Cable Communications)

Mobile
Comcast Cablevision of Mobile
 (Comcast Cable Communications)

Montgomery
Storer Cable Communications Inc.
 (Tele-Communications Inc.)

Tuscaloosa
Comcast Cablevision of Tuscaloosa
 (Comcast Cable Communications)

ALASKA

Anchorage
Prime Cable of Alaska Inc.
 (Prime Cable)

ARIZONA

Phoenix
Dimension Cable Services
 (Times Mirror Cable Television)
Insight Cablevision
 (Insight Communications Co.)

Scottsdale
TCI Cable of Scottsdale
 (Tele-Communications Inc.)

Sierra Vista
Desert Cablevision
 (InterMedia Partners)

Tucson
Jones Intercable
 (Jones Intercable Inc.)
Tucson Cablevision
 (InterMedia Partners)

Yuma
Century Cable TV of Yuma
 (Century Communications Corporation)

ARKANSAS

Fort Smith
TCI of Arkansas Inc.
 (Tele-Communications Inc.)

Jonesboro
TCI of Arkansas
 (Tele-Communications Inc.)

Little Rock
Storer Cable
 (Comcast Cable Communications)

North Little Rock
Storer Cable
 (Comcast Cable Communications)

CALIFORNIA

Alameda
TCI Cablevision of Alameda
 (Tele-Communications Inc.)

Alhambra
Crown Cable
 (Crown Media Inc.)

Anaheim
MultiVision Cable TV
 (MultiVision)

Bakersfield
Cox Cable Bakersfield
 (Cox Cable Communications)
Time Warner Cable of Bakersfield
 (Time Warner Cable)

Canyon Country
ATC - Cablevision
 (Time Warner Cable)

Carlsbad
Daniels Cablevision Inc.
 (Tele-Communications Inc.)

Chatsworth
Cablevision Industries - West Valley
 (Cablevision Industries Inc.)

Chico
Chambers Cable
 (Chambers Communications Corp.)

City of Industry
TCI Cablevision of Los Angeles County
 (Tele-Communications Inc.)

Compton
Continental Cablevision
 (Continental Cablevision Inc.)

Concord
Concord TV Cable
 (Western Communications)

Costa Mesa
Copley/Colony Cablevision of Costa Mesa Inc.
 (Colony Communications Inc.)

Downey
Continental Cablevision
 (Continental Cablevision Inc.)

Dublin
Viacom Cablevision
 (Viacom Cable Inc.)

El Centro
Century Cable
 (Century Communications Corporation)

Eureka
Cox Cable Humboldt Inc.
 (Cox Cable Communications)

Fairfield
MultiVision Cable TV
 (MultiVision)

Fremont
TCI Cablevision of California Inc.
 (Tele-Communications Inc.)

Fresno
Continental Cablevision
 (Continental Cablevision Inc.)

Garden Grove
Paragon Cable TV
 (KBLCOM)

Gilroy
Falcon Cable Systems
 (Falcon Cable TV)

Glendale
Sammons Communications Inc.
 (Sammons Communications Inc.)

Glendora
Foothills Cablevision Ltd.
 (Tele-Communications Inc.)

Goleta
Cox Cable Santa Barbara Inc.
 (Cox Cable Communications)

Hayward
TCI Cablevision of Hayward
 (Tele-Communications Inc.)

Hemet
Inland Valley Cablevision
 (Western Communications)

Lake Elsinore
King Videocable
 (Colony Communications Inc.)

Long Beach
CVI of Long Beach
 (Cablevision Industries Inc.)

Los Angeles
Century S.W. Cable TV Inc. - Eagle Rock, CA
 (Century Communications Corporation)
Continental Cablevision
 (Continental Cablevision Inc.)
Continental Cablevision
 (Continental Cablevision Inc.)

Martinez
TCI Cablevision
 (Tele-Communications Inc.)

Merced
TCI Cablevision of Merced County
 (Tele-Communications Inc.)

Modesto
Post-Newsweek Cable
 (Post-Newsweek Cable Inc.)

Monterey
Monterey Peninsula TV Cable
 (Western Communications)

Napa
Viacom Cablevision of Napa
 (Viacom Cable Inc.)

Newhall
King Videocable
 (Colony Communications Inc.)

Oakland
Cable Oakland
 (Lenfest Group)

Ontario
Comcast Cablevision of the Inland Empire
 (Comcast Cable Communications)

Orange
Cablevision of Orange
 (Time Warner Cable)

Broadcasting & Cable Yearbook 1994
D-55

Geographical Index to Large Cable Systems & MSOs

Oroville
Viacom Cable Inc.
(Viacom Cable Inc.)

Oxnard
Jones Intercable of Oxnard
(Jones Intercable Inc.)

Palm Desert
Colony Cablevision Inc.
(Colony Communications Inc.)

Palm Springs
Warner Cable Communications Inc.
(Time Warner Cable)

Palmdale
Jones Intercable
(Jones Intercable Inc.)

Petaluma
Viacom Cable
(Viacom Cable Inc.)

Pittsburg
Viacom Cable
(Viacom Cable Inc.)

Redding
Viacom Cablevision Inc.
(Viacom Cable Inc.)

Redlands
Southland Cablevision
(Tele-Communications Inc.)

Richmond
Bay Cablevision
(Lenfest Group)

Riverside
Crown Cable
(Crown Media Inc.)

Rohnert Park
MultiVision Cable TV
(MultiVision)

Rolling Hills Estates
Dimension Cable Services
(Times Mirror Cable Television)

Sacramento
Sacramento Cable
(Scripps Howard Cable Company)

San Diego
Cox Cable San Diego
(Cox Cable Communications)
Southwestern Cable TV
(Time Warner Cable)

San Francisco
Viacom Cable-San Francisco
(Viacom Cable Inc.)

San Jose
TCI Cablevision of San Jose
(Tele-Communications Inc.)

San Juan Capistrano
Dimension Cable Services
(Times Mirror Cable Television)

San Luis Obispo
Sonic Cable Television of San Luis Obispo
(InterMedia Partners)

San Rafael
Viacom Cablevision of Marin County
(Viacom Cable Inc.)

Santa Ana
Comcast Cablevision of Orange County
(Comcast Cable Communications)

Santa Clara
South Bay Cablevision
(InterMedia Partners)

Santa Maria
Comcast Cablevision of Santa Maria
(Comcast Cable Communications)

Santa Monica
Century S.W. Cable TV Inc.
(Century Communications Corporation)

Santa Rosa
Post-Newsweek Cable
(Post-Newsweek Cable Inc.)

Scotts Valley
TCI Cablevision of California
(Tele-Communications Inc.)

Simi Valley
Comcast Cablevision of Simi Valley
(Comcast Cable Communications)

Stockton
Continental Cablevision
(Continental Cablevision Inc.)

Torrance
Paragon Cable Los Angeles
(Time Warner Cable)

Tujunga
King Videocable Co.
(Colony Communications Inc.)

Tulare
Continental Cablevision
(Continental Cablevision Inc.)

Turlock
Sammons Communications Inc.
(Sammons Communications Inc.)

Vallejo
Donrey Cablevision
(Donrey Cablevision)

Van Nuys
Century Cable TV - Van Nuys, CA
(Century Communications Corporation)
Century Cable TV - West Hollywood, CA
(Century Communications Corporation)
United Artists Cable/TCI
(Tele-Communications Inc.)

Victorville
Hi-Desert Cablevision
(Booth American Co.)

Vista
Dimension Cable Services
(Times Mirror Cable Television)

Walnut Creek
TCI Cablevision of Walnut Creek
(Tele-Communications Inc.)

West Sacramento
Sonic Cable Television
(InterMedia Partners)

Westchester
Continental Cablevision
(Continental Cablevision Inc.)

Westlake Village
Ventura County Cablevision
(Western Communications)

Wilmington
Copley/Colony Harbor Cablevision Inc.
(Colony Communications Inc.)

Yuba City
Continental Cablevision
(Continental Cablevision Inc.)

COLORADO

Colorado Springs
Colorado Cablevision Inc.
(Century Communications Corporation)

Denver
Mile Hi Cablevision
(Tele-Communications Inc.)

Englewood
TCI of Colorado
(Tele-Communications Inc.)

Fort Collins
Columbine Cablevision
(World Co.)

Grand Junction
TCI Cablevision of Western Colorado Inc.
(Tele-Communications Inc.)

Greeley
TCI of Northern Colorado
(Tele-Communications Inc.)

Longmont
Scripps Howard Cable Co. of Colorado
(Scripps Howard Cable Company)

Pueblo
TCI Cablevision of Colorado Inc.
(Tele-Communications Inc.)

Thornton
TCI Cable of Colorado
(Tele-Communications Inc.)

CONNECTICUT

Branford
TCI Cablevision
(Tele-Communications Inc.)

Bridgeport
Cablevision of Southern Connecticut
(Cablevision Systems Corporation)

Danbury
Comcast Cablevision of Danbury
(Comcast Cable Communications)

Enfield
Continental Cablevision of Connecticut
(Continental Cablevision Inc.)

Groton
Storer Communications of Groton Inc.
(Comcast Cable Communications)

Litchfield
Laurel Cablevision
(Time Warner Cable)

Manchester
Cox Cable Greater Hartford
(Cox Cable Communications)

Meriden
Dimension Cable Services
(Times Mirror Cable Television)

Middletown
Comcast Cablevision of Middletown
(Comcast Cable Communications)

New Haven
Storer Cable TV of Connecticut Inc.
(Comcast Cable Communications)

Newtown
Crown Cable
(Crown Media Inc.)

Norwalk
Cablevision of Conneticut
(Cablevision Systems Corporation)

Seymour
Tele-Media Company of Western Connecticut
(Tele-Media Corporation of Delaware)

Waterbury
Sammons Communications of Connecticut Inc.
(Sammons Communications Inc.)

Waterford
Eastern Connecticut Cable TV Inc.
(Eastern Connecticut Cable TV Inc.)

West Hartford
TCI Cablevision of Central Connecticut
(Tele-Communications Inc.)

Willimantic
Crown Cable
(Crown Media Inc.)

DELAWARE

Dagsboro
American Cable L.P. Five
(Tele-Communications Inc.)

Harrington
Marcus Cable of Delaware & Maryland L.P.
(Marcus Cable Partners L.P.)

New Castle
TCI Cablevision of New Castle County
(Tele-Communications Inc.)

DISTRICT OF COLUMBIA

Washington
District Cablevision
(Tele-Communications Inc.)

FLORIDA

Boca Raton
Tele-Media Co. of Southern Florida
(Tele-Media Corporation of Delaware)
West Boca Cablevision
(Rifkin & Associates)

Bradenton
Paragon Cable
(Time Warner Cable)

Brandon
Paragon Cable
(Time Warner Cable)

Cape Coral
Cablevision Industries of Cape Coral
(Cablevision Industries Inc.)

Clearwater
Vision Cable of Pinellas Inc.
(Vision Cable Communications Inc.)

Coral Springs
Cable TV of Coral Springs Inc.
(Schurz Communications Inc.)

Davie
Jones Intercable Inc.
(Jones Intercable Inc.)

DeLand
Cablevision Industries - DeLand
(Cablevision Industries Inc.)

Delray Beach
Leadership Cablevision
(Fairbanks Communications Inc.)

Fort Lauderdale
Selkirk Communications
(Maclean Hunter Cable TV)

Fort Myers
Jones Intercable
(Jones Intercable Inc.)

Fort Walton Beach
Emerald Coast Cable Television
(Cox Cable Communications)

Gainesville
Cox Cable University City Inc.
(Cox Cable Communications)

Gulf Breeze
U.S. Cable (Gulf Coast)
(Cablevision Systems Corporation)

Hialeah
Dynamic Cablevision of Florida Ltd.
(Colony Communications Inc.)

Jacksonville
Continental Cablevision
(Continental Cablevision Inc.)

Lake Worth
Adelphia Cable
(Adelphia Communications)

Lakeland
Paragon Cable
(Time Warner Cable)

Leconto
C.V. - Cablevision of Central Florida
(Time Warner Cable)

Leesburg
Florida Cluster
(Scripps Howard Cable Company)

Margate
TeleCable of Broward County
(TeleCable Corporation)

Melbourne
C.V.- Cablevision of Central Florida
(Time Warner Cable)

Miami
Adelphia Cable-South Dade
(Adelphia Communications)
Miami Tele-Communications Inc.
(Tele-Communications Inc.)
Storer Cable
(Tele-Communications Inc.)
TCI of South Florida
(Tele-Communications Inc.)
TCI of South Florida Inc.
(Tele-Communications Inc.)

Naples
Colony Cablevision Inc.
(Colony Communications Inc.)

New Port Richey
TCI Cablevision of Pasco County GP
(Tele-Communications Inc.)

North Bay Village
Gold Coast Cablevision
(Rifkin & Associates)

Ocala
Cox Cable Greater Ocala Inc.
(Cox Cable Communications)

Ocoee
Cablevision Industries
(Cablevision Industries Inc.)

Orange Park
Clay Cablevision
(Rifkin & Associates)

Orlando
Cablevision of Central Florida
(Time Warner Cable)
CVI - Evans Division
(Cablevision Industries Inc.)

Panama City
Comcast Cablevision of Panama City
(Comcast Cable Communications)

Pensacola
Cox Cable TV of Pensacola
(Cox Cable Communications)

Pompano Beach
Continental Cablevision of Broward County
(Continental Cablevision Inc.)

Port Charlotte
Storer Cable Communications
(Comcast Cable Communications)

Port Orange
TCI Cablevision of Florida
(Tele-Communications Inc.)

Riviera Beach
Adelphia Cable, South East Florida
(Adelphia Communications)

St. Petersburg
Paragon Cable
(Time Warner Cable)

Sarasota
Storer Cable TV of Florida Inc.
(Comcast Cable Communications)

Tallahassee
Comcast Cablevision of Tallahassee
(Comcast Cable Communications)

Tampa
Jones Intercable
(Jones Intercable Inc.)

Venice
Storer Cable TV of Florida Inc.
(Comcast Cable Communications)

Vero Beach
TCI Cablevision
(Tele-Communications Inc.)

West Palm Beach
Comcast Cablevision of West Palm Beach
(Comcast Cable Communications)

Winter Haven
CableVision of Central Florida
(Time Warner Cable)

GEORGIA

Albany
TCI Cable of Georgia
(Tele-Communications Inc.)

Athens
TCI Cablevision of Georgia
(Tele-Communications Inc.)

Atlanta
Atlanta Cluster
(Scripps Howard Cable Company)

Augusta
Jones Intercable
(Jones Intercable Inc.)

Columbus
TeleCable of Columbus Inc.
(TeleCable Corporation)

Duluth
NE Roswell Cablevision
(Rifkin & Associates)

Gainesville
Gainesville Cablevision
(InterMedia Partners)

Jonesboro
Wometco Cable TV of Clayton County Inc.
(Wometco Cable Corporation)

Macon
Cox Cable Middle Georgia Inc.
(Cox Cable Communications)

Marietta
Wometco Cable TV of Cobb
(Wometco Cable Corporation)

Millcross
Wometco Cable
(Wometco Cable Corporation)

Rome
Scripps Howard Cable of Northwest Georgia
(Scripps Howard Cable Company)

Savannah
Cablevision of Savannah
(Time Warner Cable)

Smyrna
Smyrna Cable TV
(ALEXCOM Inc.)

Geographical Index to Large Cable Systems & MSOs

Woodstock
Summit Cable Services of Georgia Inc.
 (Summit Communications Group Inc. (Atlanta, GA))

HAWAII

Kahului
Chronicle Cablevision
 (Western Communications)

Mililani
Oceanic Cablevision Inc.
 (Time Warner Cable)

IDAHO

Boise
TCI Cablevision of Treasure Valley
 (Tele-Communications Inc.)

Idaho Falls
TCI Cablevision of Idaho Inc.
 (Tele-Communications Inc.)

ILLINOIS

Aurora
Jones Intercable Inc.
 (Jones Intercable Inc.)

Belleville
Continental Cablevision of St. Louis County
 (Continental Cablevision Inc.)

Bloomingdale
MetroVision of DuPage County
 (MetroVision Inc.)

Bloomington
TeleCable of Bloomington-Normal Inc.
 (TeleCable Corporation)

Carpentersville
TCI Cablevision
 (Tele-Communications Inc.)

Chicago
Chicago Cable TV
 (Tele-Communications Inc.)
Prime Cable of Chicago Inc.
 (Prime Cable)

Decatur
TCI Cable
 (Tele-Communications Inc.)

Elmhurst
Continental Cablevision
 (Continental Cablevision Inc.)

Hickory Hills
MetroVision Southwest Cook County
 (MetroVision Inc.)

Kankakee
TCI of Illinois Inc.
 (Tele-Communications Inc.)

Maryville
Crown Cable
 (Crown Media Inc.)

Moline
Cox Cable Quad Cities
 (Cox Cable Communications)

Mount Prospect
TCI of Illinois Inc.
 (Tele-Communications Inc.)

Oak Lawn
Multimedia Cablevision of Oak Lawn
 (Multimedia Cablevision Inc.)

Oak Park
Cablevision of Chicago
 (Cablevision Systems Corporation)

Ottawa
Sammons Communications of Illinois Inc.
 (Sammons Communications Inc.)

Peoria
TCI Cablevision of Central Illinois
 (Tele-Communications Inc.)

Rockford
Cablevision of Rockford/Park
 (Cablevision Systems Corporation)

Rolling Meadows
Continental Cablevision
 (Continental Cablevision Inc.)

Romeoville
Continental Cablevision of Will County
 (Continental Cablevision Inc.)

Springfield
Dimension Cable Services
 (Times Mirror Cable Television)

Urbana
Cablevision of Champaign-Urbana
 (Time Warner Cable)

Waukegan
US Cable of Lake County
 (US Cable Corporation)

Wheaton
Jones Intercable
 (Jones Intercable Inc.)

INDIANA

Anderson
TCI Cable of Central Indiana
 (Tele-Communications Inc.)

Evansville
TCI Cable
 (Tele-Communications Inc.)

Fort Wayne
Comcast Cablevision of Fort Wayne
 (Comcast Cable Communications)

Hammond
TCI of Northern Indiana
 (Tele-Communications Inc.)

Indianapolis
American Cablevision of Indianapolis
 (Time Warner Cable)
Comcast Cablevision of Indianapolis
 (Comcast Cable Communications)

Jeffersonville
Insight Cablevision
 (Insight Communications Co.)

Kokomo
TeleCable of Kokomo Inc.
 (TeleCable Corporation)

Lafayette
Dimension Cable Services
 (Times Mirror Cable Television)

Merrillville
US Cable of Northern Indiana
 (US Cable Corporation)

Mishawaka
TCI of Michiana
 (Tele-Communications Inc.)

Muncie
Century Cable TV of Muncie
 (Century Communications Corporation)

Noblesville
Insight Cablevision
 (Insight Communications Co.)

Terre Haute
American Cablevision
 (Time Warner Cable)

IOWA

Cedar Rapids
Cox Cable Cedar Rapids Inc.
 (Cox Cable Communications)

Des Moines
TCI of Central Iowa
 (Tele-Communications Inc.)

Dubuque
TCI Cablevision of Dubuque Inc.
 (Tele-Communications Inc.)

Sioux City
Sooland Cablecom
 (Post-Newsweek Cable Inc.)

Waterloo
TCI of Northern Iowa
 (Tele-Communications Inc.)

KANSAS

Overland Park
TeleCable of Overland Park Inc.
 (TeleCable Corporation)

Topeka
TCI of Kansas Inc.
 (Tele-Communications Inc.)

Wichita
Multimedia Cablevision of Wichita
 (Multimedia Cablevision Inc.)

KENTUCKY

Covington
TKR Cable of Northern Kentucky
 (TKR Cable Co.)

Elizabethtown
TeleScripps Cable of Western Kentucky
 (Scripps Howard Cable Company)

Lexington
TeleCable of Lexington Inc.
 (TeleCable Corporation)

Louisville
TKR Cable of Greater Louisville
 (TKR Cable Co.)

Owensboro
Century Cable
 (Century Communications Corporation)

Paducah
Comcast Cablevision of Paducah
 (Comcast Cable Communications)

LOUISIANA

Baton Rouge
Cablevision of Baton Rouge Ltd.
 (Tele-Communications Inc.)

Bossier City
TCI Cable of Louisiana
 (Tele-Communications Inc.)

Harahan
Cox Cable Jefferson Parish
 (Cox Cable Communications)

Lafayette
Lafayette Cable TV
 (TCA Cable TV Inc.)

Lake Charles
TCI of Louisiana
 (Tele-Communications Inc.)

New Orleans
Cox Cable New Orleans Inc.
 (Cox Cable Communications)

Pineville
Vision Cable of Alpine Inc.
 (Vision Cable Communications Inc.)

Shreveport
Cablevision of Shreveport
(Time Warner Cable)

Slidell
Cablevision Industries of St. Tammany Division
(Cablevision Industries Inc.)

Thibodaux
CVI-LaFourche Division
(Cablevision Industries Inc.)

MAINE

Auburn
A-R Cable Services Inc.
(Cablevision Systems Corporation)

Bangor
A-R Cable Services-Maine Inc.
(Cablevision Systems Corporation)

Portland
Public Cable Co.
(Time Warner Cable)

MARYLAND

Aberdeen
Comcast Cablevision of Harford County
(Comcast Cable Communications)

Annapolis
TCI Cablevision of Annapolis
(Tele-Communications Inc.)

Baltimore
Comcast Cablevision of Baltimore County
(Comcast Cable Communications)
United Artists Cable of Baltimore
(Tele-Communications Inc.)

Cumberland
TCI Cablevision of Maryland Inc.
(Tele-Communications Inc.)

Ellicott City
Comcast Cablevision of Howard County
(Comcast Cable Communications)

Frederick
Frederick Cablevision Inc.
(Great Southern Printing & Manufacturing Co.)

Gambrills
Jones Intercable Inc.
(Jones Intercable Inc.)

Hagerstown
Antietam Cable TV
(Schurz Communications Inc.)

Landover
MetroVision of Prince Georges County
(MetroVision Inc.)

Lanham
MultiVision Cable TV
(MultiVision)

Millersville
North Arundel Cable Television
(InterMedia Partners)

Ocean City
TCI Cablevision of Eastern Shore
(Tele-Communications Inc.)

Rockville
Montgomery Cablevision Company
(Hauser Communications Inc.)

MASSACHUSETTS

Allston
Cablevision of Boston
(Cablevision Systems Corporation)

Beverly
Continental Cablevision
(Continental Cablevision Inc.)

Brockton
Continental Cablevision of Brockton
(Continental Cablevision Inc.)

Cambridge
Continental Cablevision
(Continental Cablevision Inc.)

Fall River
Greater Fall River Cable TV
(Colony Communications Inc.)

Foxboro
Cablevision Industries
(Cablevision Industries Inc.)

Lawrence
Continental Cablevision of Massachusetts Inc.
(Continental Cablevision Inc.)

Leominster
Cablevision of Massachusetts
(Cablevision Systems Corporation)

Lowell
Lowell Cable Televison Inc.
(Colony Communications Inc.)

Malden
Time Warner Cable (Greater Boston Division)
(Time Warner Cable)

Marlborough
Continental Cablevision
(Continental Cablevision Inc.)

Needham
Continental Cablevision of Massachusetts Inc.
(Continental Cablevision Inc.)

New Bedford
Whaling City Cable TV Inc.
(Colony Communications Inc.)

Norwell
Continental Cablevision
(Continental Cablevision Inc.)

Pittsfield
Time Warner Cable
(Time Warner Cable)

Plymouth
Adelphia Cable
(Adelphia Communications)

Quincy
Continental Cablevision
(Continental Cablevision Inc.)

South Yarmouth
TCI Cablevision of Cape Cod
(Tele-Communications Inc.)

Springfield
Continental Cablevision Inc. of Springfield
(Continental Cablevision Inc.)

Westfield
Continental Cablevision
(Continental Cablevision Inc.)

Wilmington
Continental Cablevision Inc.
(Continental Cablevision Inc.)

Worcester
Greater Worcester Cablevision Inc.
(Greater Media Inc.)

MICHIGAN

Ann Arbor
Columbia Cable of Michigan
(Columbia International Inc.)

Battle Creek
TCI Cablevision of Greater Michigan Inc.
(Tele-Communications Inc.)

Birmingham
Booth Communications of Birmingham
(Booth American Co.)

Canton
Omnicom Cablevision
(N-Com)

Chesterfield
Harron Cable TV-Chesterfield
(Harron Communications Corp.)

Dearborn
Cablevision Industries of Dearborn/Wayne
(Cablevision Industries Inc.)

Dearborn Heights
Continental Cablevision of Michigan Inc.
(Continental Cablevision Inc.)

Detroit
Barden Cablevision
(Maclean Hunter Cable TV)

East Lansing
TCI Cablevision of Mid-Michigan
(Tele-Communications Inc.)

Essexville
Bresnan Communications Co.
(Bresnan Communications Co.)

Farmington Hills
MetroVision of Oakland County
(MetroVision Inc.)

Fenton
Davison/Fenton
(Fanch Communications Inc.)

Flint
Comcast Cablevision of Flint
(Comcast Cable Communications)

Grand Rapids
TCI Cablevision of West Michigan
(Tele-Communications Inc.)

Kalamazoo
Cablevision of Michigan
(Cablevision Systems Corporation)

Lansing
Continental Cablevision of Lansing Inc.
(Continental Cablevision Inc.)

Livonia
MetroVision of Livonia Inc.
(MetroVision Inc.)

Marquette
Bresnan Communications Co.
(Bresnan Communications Co.)

Muskegon
TCI Cablevision
(Tele-Communications Inc.)

Port Huron
Harron Cable TV
(Harron Communications Corp.)

Roseville
Continental Cablevision
(Continental Cablevision Inc.)

Royal Oak
TCI Cablevision of Oakland County
(Tele-Communications Inc.)

Saginaw
Cox Cable Saginaw Inc.
(Cox Cable Communications)

St. Joseph
TCI Cable
(Tele-Communications Inc.)

Southfield
Continental Cablevision
(Continental Cablevision Inc.)

Geographical Index to Large Cable Systems & MSOs

Sterling Heights
Comcast Cablevision of Southeast Michigan
 (Comcast Cable Communications)

Taylor
Maclean Hunter Cable TV Inc.
 (Maclean Hunter Cable TV)

Waterford
Comcast Cablevision of Pontiac
 (Comcast Cable Communications)

Woodhaven
TCI Cablevision of Michigan
 (Tele-Communications Inc.)

MINNESOTA

Brooklyn Park
King Videocable Co.
 (Colony Communications Inc.)

Cottage Grove
King Videocable
 (Colony Communications Inc.)

Duluth
Bresnan Communications Co.
 (Bresnan Communications Co.)

Minneapolis
Paragon Cable
 (KBLCOM)

Rochester
TCI of Southern Minnesota
 (Tele-Communications Inc.)

Roseville
Meredith Cable
 (New Heritage Associates)

St. Paul
Continental Cablevision
 (Continental Cablevision Inc.)

Savage
Midwest Cablevision
 (InterMedia Partners)

MISSISSIPPI

Biloxi
TCI of South Mississippi
 (Tele-Communications Inc.)

Gulfport
Post-Newsweek Cable
 (Post-Newsweek Cable Inc.)

Jackson
Capitol Cablevision
 (Time Warner Cable)

Pascagoula
Sammons Cable
 (Sammons Communications Inc.)

MISSOURI

Independence
Jones Intercable
 (Jones Intercable Inc.)

Kansas City
American Cablevision
 (Time Warner Cable)

St. Joseph
St. Joseph Cablevision
 (St. Joseph Cablevision)

St. Louis
Continental Cablevision of St. Louis County Inc.
 (Continental Cablevision Inc.)
Crown Cable
 (Crown Media Inc.)
Falcon/Capital Cable Partners L.P.
 (Falcon Cable TV)
St. Louis Tele-Communications Inc.
 (Tele-Communications Inc.)

St. Peters
TCI Cablevision of Missouri Inc.
 (Tele-Communications Inc.)

Springfield
TeleCable of Springfield
 (TeleCable Corporation)

MONTANA

Billings
Billings Tele-Communications Inc.
 (Tele-Communications Inc.)

NEBRASKA

Bellevue
TCI Cable of the Midlands
 (Tele-Communications Inc.)

Lincoln
Lincoln Cablevision
 (MetroVision Inc.)

Omaha
Cox Cable Omaha
 (Cox Cable Communications)

NEVADA

Las Vegas
Prime Cable of Las Vegas
 (Prime Cable)

Reno
TCI of Reno
 (Tele-Communications Inc.)

NEW HAMPSHIRE

Concord
Continental Cablevision of New England
 (Continental Cablevision Inc.)

Manchester
United Cable Company of New Hampshire Inc.
 (United Broadcasting Co.)

Nashua
Warner Cable of Nashua
 (Time Warner Cable)

Portsmouth
Continental Cablevision of New Hampshire Inc.
 (Continental Cablevision Inc.)

Salem
Continental Cablevision of New England Inc.
 (Continental Cablevision Inc.)

NEW JERSEY

Absecon
Sammons Communications of New Jersey Inc.
 (Sammons Communications Inc.)

Brick
Storer Cable of Ocean County
 (Comcast Cable Communications)

Cresskill
Cablevision of New Jersey Inc.
 (Cablevision Systems Corporation)

Dover
Sammons Communications of New Jersey Inc.
 (Sammons Communications Inc.)

East Windsor
Storer Cable
 (Comcast Cable Communications)

Eatontown
Storer Cable of Monmouth County
 (Comcast Cable Communications)

Hamilton Township
TKR Cable Co.
 (TKR Cable Co.)

Hoboken
Riverview Cablevision Associates L.P.
 (Sutton Capital Group)

Jersey City
Cable TV of Jersey City
 (Maclean Hunter Cable TV)

Newark
Cablevision of Newark
 (Cablevision Systems Corporation)

North Arlington
Comcast Cablevision of Meadowlands
 (Comcast Cable Communications)

Oakland
TCI of Northern New Jersey
 (Tele-Communications Inc.)

Palisades Park
Vision Cable
 (Vision Cable Communications Inc.)

Paterson
US Cable of Paterson
 (US Cable Corporation)

Piscataway
TKR Cable Company Tri-System
 (TKR Cable Co.)

Somerville
C-TEC Cable Systems
 (C-TEC Cable Systems Inc.)

Sparta
Service Electric Cable TV of NJ Inc.
 (Service Electric Cablevision Inc.)

Toms River
Adelphia Communications-Clear
 (Adelphia Communications)

Trenton
Comcast Cablevision of Trenton
 (Comcast Cable Communications)

Turnersville
Jones Intercable Inc.
 (Jones Intercable Inc.)

Union
Suburban Cablevision
 (Maclean Hunter Cable TV)

Vineland
Sammons Communications
 (Sammons Communications Inc.)

Wildwood
TKR Cable of Wildwood
 (TKR Cable Co.)

Willingboro
Storer Cable Communications of Burlington County
 (Comcast Cable Communications)

Woodbury
Storer Cable Communications of Gloucester County Inc.
 (Comcast Cable Communications)

NEW MEXICO

Albuquerque
Jones Intercable
 (Jones Intercable Inc.)

Las Cruces
Las Cruces TV Cable
 (Western Communications)

Santa Fe
TCI Cablevision of Santa Fe
 (Tele-Communications Inc.)

Geographical Index to Large Cable Systems & MSOs

NEW YORK

Albany
Capitol Cablevision Systems Inc.
(Time Warner Cable)

Batavia
Genesee/Tri-County Cablevision
(Cablevision Industries Inc.)

Binghamton
Binghamton NewChannels
(NewChannels Corporation)

Buffalo
TCI of New York Inc.
(Tele-Communications Inc.)

Carmel
C-TEC Cable Systems of New York Inc.
(C-TEC Cable Systems Inc.)

Geneva
Cablevision Industries - Finger Lakes
(Cablevision Industries Inc.)

Hauppauge
Cablevision of Long Island/Hauppauge
(Cablevision Systems Corporation)

Ithaca
American Community Cablevision
(Time Warner Cable)

Jamestown
Paragon Cable
(Time Warner Cable)

Mamaroneck
TCI Cable of Westchester
(Tele-Communications Inc.)

Middletown
Cablevision Industries - Orange County Division
(Cablevision Industries Inc.)

Nanuet
TKR Cable Company of Rockland
(TKR Cable Co.)

New York
Paragon Cable Manhattan
(Time Warner Cable)
Time Warner Cable of New York City
(Time Warner Cable)

Niagara Falls
Adelphia Cable - Niagara
(Adelphia Communications)

Oneida
Cablevision Industries - Oneida/Seneca Division
(Cablevision Industries Inc.)

Ossining
Continental Cablevision of New York
(Continental Cablevision Inc.)

Port Jefferson Station
TCI Cable of Brookhaven
(Tele-Communications Inc.)

Riverhead
Cablevision's East End System
(Cablevision Systems Corporation)

Rochester
Greater Rochester Cablevision
(Time Warner Cable)

Saratoga Springs
Cablevision Industries of Saratoga Associates
(Cablevision Industries Inc.)

Schenectady
TCI of New York Inc.
(Tele-Communications Inc.)

Syracuse
Adelphia Cable Communications of Syracuse
(Adelphia Communications)
Syracuse NewChannels
(NewChannels Corporation)

Troy
NewChannels
(NewChannels Corporation)

Utica
Harron Cable of New York
(Harron Communications Corporation)

Vails Gate
Paragon Communications
(Time Warner Cable)

Wappingers Falls
U.S. Cablevision Corporation
(Colony Communications Inc.)

West Seneca
Adelphia Cable Communications
(Adelphia Communications)

Woodbury
Cablevision of Long Island
(Cablevision Systems Corporation)

Yonkers
Cablevision Systems of Westchester
(Cablevision Systems Corporation)

NORTH CAROLINA

Asheville
TCI Cablevision of Asheville
(Tele-Communications Inc.)

Boone
High Country Cable TV
(Booth American Co.)

Burlington
Cablevision of Alamance County
(Time Warner Cable)

Cary
Cablevision Industries
(Cablevision Industries Inc.)

Charlotte
Cablevision of Charlotte
(Time Warner Cable)

Durham
Durham Cablevision
(Time Warner Cable)

Fayetteville
Cablevision of Fayetteville
(Time Warner Cable)

Greensboro
Cablevision of Greensboro
(Time Warner Cable)
CVI
(Cablevision Industries Inc.)

Greenville
Multimedia Cablevision of Greenville
(Multimedia Cablevision Inc.)

Hendersonville
U.S. Cable of North Carolina
(Cablevision Systems Corporation)

Hickory
Catawba Valley Cable TV
(Prime Cable)

Kannapolis
Vision Cable of Metrolina
(Vision Cable Communications Inc.)

Matthews
Vision Cable of North Carolina
(Vision Cable Communications Inc.)

Newport
Vision Cable of Newport Inc.
(Vision Cable Communications Inc.)

Raleigh
Time Warner Cable
(Time Warner Cable)

Rocky Mount
Multimedia Cablevision of Rocky Mount
(Multimedia Cablevision Inc.)

Wilmington
Vision Cable of Wilmington
(Vision Cable Communications Inc.)

Winston-Salem
Summit Cable Services of Forsyth County Inc.
(Summit Communications Group Inc. (Atlanta, GA))

NORTH DAKOTA

Bismarck
Meredith Cable
(New Heritage Associates)

OHIO

Akron
Warner Cable Communications
(Time Warner Cable)

Amelia
Coaxial Communications of Southern Ohio
(Coaxial Communications)

Canton
Warner Cable of Canton
(Time Warner Cable)

Cincinnati
Warner Cable Communications Inc.
(Time Warner Cable)

Cleveland
North Coast Cable Ltd.
(North Coast Cable)

Cleveland Heights
Cablevision
(Cablevision Systems Corporation)

Columbus
Coaxial Communications of Central Ohio Inc.
(Coaxial Communications)
Warner Cable of Columbus
(Time Warner Cable)

Dayton
Continental Cablevision of Ohio Inc.
(Continental Cablevision Inc.)
Viacom Cablevision of Dayton Inc.
(Viacom Cable Inc.)

Elyria
Continental Cablevision of Ohio Inc.
(Continental Cablevision Inc.)

Kettering
Continental Cablevision of Ohio
(Continental Cablevision Inc.)

Lancaster
Continental Cablevision
(Continental Cablevision Inc.)

Lima
Warner Cable
(Time Warner Cable)

Mansfield
Adelphia Cable Communications
(Adelphia Communications)

Massillon
Massillon Cable TV Inc.
(Massillon Cable TV Inc.)

Mentor
Continental Cablevision of Lake County Inc.
(Continental Cablevision Inc.)

Middletown
TCI Cablevision of Ohio Inc.
(Tele-Communications Inc.)

New Philadelphia
Dimension Cable Services
(Times Mirror Cable Television)

Geographical Index to Large Cable Systems & MSOs

Newark
Dimension Cable Services
　(Times Mirror Cable Television)

North Lima
Armstrong Cable Services
　(Armstrong Utilities Inc.)

Parma
Cox Cable Cleveland Area Inc.
　(Cox Cable Communications)

Springfield
Continental Cablevision of Ohio Inc.
　(Continental Cablevision Inc.)

Toledo
Buckeye Cablevision Inc.
　(Blade Communications Inc.)

Warren
TCI Cablevision of Ohio Inc.
　(Tele-Communications Inc.)

Youngstown
Warner Cable Communications Inc.- Youngstown
　(Time Warner Cable)

OKLAHOMA

Oklahoma City
Cox Cable Oklahoma City Inc.
　(Cox Cable Communications)

Tulsa
TCI Cable of Oklahoma
　(Tele-Communications Inc.)

OREGON

Beaverton
Columbia Cable of Oregon
　(Columbia International Inc.)

Corvallis
TCI Cablevision
　(Tele-Communications Inc.)

Eugene
TCI Cablevision of Oregon Inc.
　(Tele-Communications Inc.)

Medford
TCI Cablevision of Medford Inc.
　(Tele-Communications Inc.)

Portland
Paragon Cable
　(KBLCOM)
TCI Cablevision of Oregon
　(Tele-Communications Inc.)

Salem
Viacom Cable
　(Viacom Cable Inc.)

PENNSYLVANIA

Altoona
Time Warner Cable
　(Time Warner Cable)

Bensalem
Oxford Valley Cablevision Inc.
　(Sammons Communications Inc.)

Bethlehem
Service Electric Cable TV Inc.
　(Service Electric Cablevision Inc.)

Butler
Armstrong Utilities Inc.
　(Armstrong Utilities Inc.)

Coatesville
Suburban Cable TV of Chester County
　(Lenfest Group)

Connellsville
Armstrong Communications Inc.
　(Armstrong Communications Inc.)

Dunmore
Adelphia Cable - Northeast
　(Adelphia Communications)

Easton
Sammons Communications of Pennsylvania Inc.
　(Sammons Communications Inc.)

Ephrata
Blue Ridge CATV Inc.
　(Pencor Services Inc.)

Erie
Erie Cablevision
　(Time Warner Cable)
TCI of Pennsylvania
　(Tele-Communications Inc.)

Greensburg
TCI of Greensburg
　(Tele-Communications Inc.)

Harrisburg
Sammons Communications of Pennsylvania
　(Sammons Communications Inc.)

Hazleton
Service Electric Cablevision Inc.
　(Service Electric Cablevision Inc.)

Jamison
Suburban Cable TV Co. Inc.
　(Lenfest Group)

Johnstown
Time Warner Cable of Greater Johnstown
　(Time Warner Cable)

Lancaster
Suburban Cable - Lancaster
　(Lenfest Group)

Lebanon
Lebanon Valley Cable
　(Time Warner Cable)

Levittown
Lower Bucks Cablevision Inc.
　(Time Warner Cable)

Malvern
Harron Cable TV Co. Inc.
　(Harron Communications Corporation)

Monroeville
American Cablevision of Monroeville
　(Time Warner Cable)

New Kensington
Comcast Cablevision of Westmoreland
　(Comcast Cable Communications)

Norristown
Suburban Cable TV
　(Lenfest Group)

Northampton
Twin County Cable TV
　(Twin County Trans Video Inc.)

Palmerton
Blue Ridge Cable TV Inc.
　(Pencor Services Inc.)

Philadelphia
Comcast Cablevision of Philadelphia
　(Comcast Cable Communications)
Greater Philadelphia Cablevision Inc.
　(Greater Media Inc.)
Wade Cablevision
　(Cablevision Industries Inc.)

Pittsburgh
TCI of Pennsylvania
　(Tele-Communications Inc.)

Plymouth Meeting
Adelphia Cable
　(Adelphia Communications)

Pottstown
Suburban Cable TV - Pottstown
　(Lenfest Group)

Reading
Berks Cable
　(Time Warner Cable)

Scranton
Verto Cable TV
　(Verto Cable TV Corporation)

Sellersville
Suburban Cable TV - Sellersville
　(Lenfest Group)

State College
TCI of Pennsylvania Inc.
　(Tele-Communications Inc.)

Stroudsburg
Blue Ridge Cable TV Inc.
　(Pencor Services Inc.)

Uniontown
Helicon Cablevision
　(Helicon Corporation)

Wallingford
Suburban Cable TV Co. Inc.
　(Lenfest Group)

Wilkes-Barre
Service Electric Co.
　(Service Electric Cablevision Inc.)

Williamsport
Dimension Cable Services
　(Times Mirror Cable Television)

Willow Grove
Comcast Cablevision of Willow Grove
　(Comcast Cable Communications)

York
Cable TV of York
　(Susquehanna Cable Co.)

RHODE ISLAND

Cranston
Cox Cable Rhode Island Inc.
　(Cox Cable Communications)

Lincoln
TCI Cablevision of New England
　(Tele-Communications Inc.)

West Warwick
Dimension Cable Services
　(Times Mirror Cable Television)

SOUTH CAROLINA

Aiken
Palmetto Cablevision
　(InterMedia Partners)

Florence
Vision Cable of South Carolina Inc.
　(Vision Cable Communications Inc.)

Greenville
TeleCable of Greenville Inc.
　(TeleCable Corporation)

Myrtle Beach
Cox Cable South Carolina Inc.
　(Cox Cable Communications)

North Charleston
Storer Cable of Carolina Inc.
　(Comcast Cable Communications)

Spartanburg
TeleCable of Spartanburg
　(TeleCable Corporation)

West Columbia
Cablevision Industries - West Columbia
　(Cablevision Industries Inc.)

SOUTH DAKOTA

Sioux Falls
Sioux Falls Cable TV
(Midcontinent Cable Co.)

TENNESSEE

Alcoa
East Tennessee Cablevision
(InterMedia Partners)

Brentwood
Tennessee Valley Cablevision and InterMedia Co.
(InterMedia Partners)

Chattanooga
Chattanooga Cable TV Co.
(Scripps Howard Cable Company)

Clarksville
Crown Cable
(Crown Media Inc.)

Jackson
Cablevision Industries of Tennessee
(Cablevision Industries Inc.)

Johnson City
Sammons Communications Inc.
(Sammons Communications Inc.)

Kingsport
Warner Cable Communications - Kingsport
(Time Warner Cable)

Knoxville
Scripps Howard Cable TV Co. of Knoxville
(Scripps Howard Cable Company)

McKenzie
Volunteer Cable
(InterMedia Partners)

Memphis
Memphis Cablevision
(Time Warner Cable)

Morristown
Sammons Communications
(Sammons Communications Inc.)

Murfreesboro
United Artists Cable
(Tele-Communications Inc.)

Nashville
Viacom Cablevision
(Viacom Cable Inc.)

Oak Ridge
Tennessee Cablevision Inc.
(ALEXCOM Inc.)

TEXAS

Abilene
TCI Cable
(Tele-Communications Inc.)

Amarillo
TCA Cable of Amarillo
(TCA Cable TV Inc.)

Arlington
Arlington TeleCable Inc.
(TeleCable Corporation)

Austin
Austin Cablevision
(Time Warner Cable)

Beaumont
TCI Cablevision of Texas Inc.
(Tele-Communications Inc.)

Bryan
TCA Cable TV - Bryan
(TCA Cable TV Inc.)

Corpus Christi
TCI Cablevision of Texas Inc.
(Tele-Communications Inc.)

Dallas
TCI Cablevision of Dallas
(Tele-Communications Inc.)

El Paso
Paragon Cable
(Time Warner Cable)

Fort Worth
Sammons Cable Services
(Sammons Communications Inc.)

Garland
TCI Cablevision
(Tele-Communications Inc.)

Harlingen
TCI Cablevision of Texas
(Tele-Communications Inc.)

Houston
Prime Cable (Eastern & Western Suburbs)
(Prime Cable)
Storer Cable of Houston
(Comcast Cable Communications)
TCI Cablevision of Houston
(Tele-Communications Inc.)
Warner Cable Communications Inc.
(Time Warner Cable)

Irving
Paragon Communications
(Time Warner Cable)

Killeen
KBC Cablevision
(MetroVision Inc.)

Laredo
Paragon Cable
(KBLCOM)

Longview
Longview Cable TV Co. Inc.
(WEHCO Video Inc.)

Lubbock
Cox Cable Lubbock
(Cox Cable Communications)

Midland
Dimension Cable Services
(Times Mirror Cable Television)

Odessa
Post-Newsweek Cable
(Post-Newsweek Cable Inc.)

Plano
TeleCable of Richardson-Plano Inc.
(TeleCable Corporation)

Port Arthur
TCI Cablevision of Texas
(Tele-Communications Inc.)

San Angelo
Marcus Cable of San Angelo L.P.
(Marcus Cable Partners L.P.)

San Antonio
Paragon Cable-San Antonio
(KBLCOM)

Sherman
Post-Newsweek Cable
(Post-Newsweek Cable Inc.)

Texarkana
Dimension Cable Services
(Times Mirror Cable Television)

Tyler
TCI Cablevision of East Texas
(Tele-Communications Inc.)

Waco
Waco Cablevision
(MetroVision Inc.)

Wichita Falls
Vista Cablevision Inc.
(Time Warner Cable)

UTAH

Ogden
TCI Cablevision of Utah Inc.
(Tele-Communications Inc.)

Salt Lake City
TCI Cablevision of Utah Inc.
(Tele-Communications Inc.)
TCI Cablevision of Utah Inc.
(Tele-Communications Inc.)

Sandy
Insight Cablevision
(Insight Communications Co.)

VERMONT

Williston
Adelphia Cable
(Adelphia Communications)

VIRGINIA

Alexandria
Jones Intercable
(Jones Intercable Inc.)

Arlington
Arlington Cable Partners
(Hauser Communications Inc.)

Chantilly
Media General Cable of Fairfax Inc.
(Media General Inc.)

Charlottesville
Adelphia Cable
(Adelphia Communications)

Chesapeake
TCI of Virginia Inc.
(Tele-Communications Inc.)

Danville
Cablevision Industries Ltd.
(Cablevision Industries Inc.)

Hampton
Warner Cable of Hampton
(Time Warner Cable)

Lynchburg
Lynchburg Cablevision
(Time Warner Cable)

Newport News
Newport News Cablevision
(Tele-Communications Inc.)

Richmond
Chesterfield Cablevision Inc.
(Comcast Cable Communications)
Continental Cablevision
(Continental Cablevision Inc.)
Continental Cablevision of Richmond
(Continental Cablevision Inc.)

Roanoke
Cox Cable Roanoke Inc.
(Cox Cable Communications)

Virginia Beach
Cox Cable Hampton Roads Inc.
(Cox Cable Communications)

Woodbridge
Columbia Cable of Virginia
(Columbia International Inc.)

Geographical Index to Large Cable Systems & MSOs

WASHINGTON

Bellingham
TCI Cablevision of Washington
(Tele-Communications Inc.)

Everett
Viacom Cable
(Viacom Cable Inc.)

Kennewick
TCI Cablevision of Southeast Washington
(Tele-Communications Inc.)

Longview
Century Cable TV of Longview
(Century Communications Corporation)

Olympia
TCI Cablevision of Washington
(Tele-Communications Inc.)

Seattle
TCI Cablevision of North Seattle
(Tele-Communications Inc.)
TCI of South Seattle
(Tele-Communications Inc.)

Spokane
Cox Cable Spokane
(Cox Cable Communications)

Tacoma
TCI Cablevision of Tacoma Inc.
(Tele-Communications Inc.)
Viacom Cablevision
(Viacom Cable Inc.)

Vancouver
Columbia Cable of Washington
(Columbia International Inc.)

Yakima
TCI Cablevision of Yakima
(Tele-Communications Inc.)

WEST VIRGINIA

Beckley
TeleCable of Beckley Inc.
(TeleCable Corporation)

Bluefield
TeleScripps Cable
(Scripps Howard Cable Co.)

Charleston
Capitol Cablevision
(Time Warner Cable)

Dellslow
Century Cable TV of Morgantown
(Century Communications Corporation)

Huntington
Century Cable TV of Huntington
(Century Communications Corporation)

Parkersburg
TCI of West Virginia Inc.
(Tele-Communications Inc.)

WISCONSIN

DePere
Crown Cable
(Crown Media Inc.)

Eau Claire
Cablevision of Eau Claire
(Time Warner Cable)

Green Bay
Cablevision of Green Bay
(Time Warner Cable)

Janesville
Crown Cable
(Crown Media Inc.)

Kimberly
Cablevision of Appleton
(Time Warner Cable)

Madison
TCI Cablevision of Wisconsin
(Tele-Communications Inc.)

Milwaukee
Warner Cable Communications of Milwaukee
(Time Warner Cable)

Racine
Racine TeleCable
(TeleCable Corporation)

Wausau
Crown Cable
(Crown Media Inc.)

Wauwatosa
Century Cable Television
(Century Communications Corporation)

West Allis
Crown Cable
(Crown Media Inc.)

WYOMING

Casper
TCI Cablevision
(Tele-Communications Inc.)

Cheyenne
TCI Cablevision of Wyoming
(Tele-Communications Inc.)

PUERTO RICO

Tres Monjitas Industrial Park, San Juan
Cable TV of Greater San Juan
(Century Communications Corporation)

Canada

ALBERTA

Calgary
Rogers Cable TV - Calgary
(Rogers Cablesystems Limited)

BRITISH COLUMBIA

Abbotsford
Rogers Cable TV - Abbotsford
(Rogers Cablesystems Limited)

Burnaby
Rogers Cable TV - Vancouver
(Rogers Cablesystems Limited)

Port Coquitlam
Rogers Cable TV - Fraser
(Rogers Cablesystems Limited)

Surrey
Rogers Cable TV - Surrey
(Rogers Cablesystems Limited)

Victoria
Rogers Cable TV - Victoria
(Rogers Cablesystems Limited)

ONTARIO

Cornwall
Rogers Cable TV - Cornwall
(Rogers Cablesystems Limited)

Don Mills
Rogers Cable TV - Toronto
(Rogers Cablesystems Limited)

Etobicoke
Maclean Hunter Cable TV
(Maclean Hunter Cable TV)

Hamilton
Rogers Cable TV - Hamilton/Niagara
(Rogers Cablesystems Limited)

Kitchener
Rogers Cable TV - Grand River
(Rogers Cablesystems Limited)

London
Rogers Cable TV - London
(Rogers Cablesystems Limited)

Mississauga
Rogers Cable TV - Peel
(Rogers Cablesystems Limited)

Newmarket
Rogers Cable TV - Newmarket
(Rogers Cablesystems Limited)

Oshawa
Rogers Cable TV - Pine Ridge
(Rogers Cablesystems Limited)

Ottawa
Maclean Hunter Cable TV
(Maclean Hunter Cable TV)
Rogers Cable TV - Ottawa
(Rogers Cablesystems Limited)

It's all the business of show business.

Showbiz news reaches far beyond the borders of Hollywood. And so does the need for up-to-the minute show business information.

Daily Variety has been breaking showbiz news since 1933. And for people in the film, television, video and cable industries, knowing what's happening quickly is *essential* to getting ahead *and* staying ahead.

It's all in Daily Variety: the most complete listing of films and television currently in production (both cable and network) and weekly film box office reports. You'll also find reviews of current films, network and cable programs, a detailed listing of showbiz stock transactions and even international showbiz news.

Get your showbiz news when it breaks, instead of when it's recent history.

Call **1-800-552-3632**
to order your subscription *today!*

GB99

Broadcasters in Cable Television

Note: The MSO (Multiple System Operator) directory lists in detail all cable holdings.

Bahakel Communications Ltd. WAKA(TV) Selma, Ala.; KILO(FM) Colorado Springs; WRSP-TV Springfield & WCCU(TV) Urbana, both Ill.; WBAK-TV Terre Haute, Ind.; KXEL(AM) & KOKZ(FM) Waterloo, Iowa; WLBJ(AM) Bowling Green, Ky.; WABG-AM-TV Greenwood, Miss.; WCCB(TV) Charlotte & WPET(AM)-WKSI(FM) Greensboro, both N.C.; WOLO-TV Columbia, S.C.; WDOD-AM-FM Chattanooga & WBBJ-TV Jackson, both Tenn.; & WWOD(AM) Lynchburg, Va. (All 100% owned.) Owns cable systems in Appomattox, Bedford County, Blackstone-Crewe, Burkeville & Campbell County, all Va.; Bailysville, Brenton, Cub Creek, Fanrock, Glover, Meeting House Branch, Oceana, Pineville, Ramey, Sun Hill & Toney Fork Junction, all W.V. (All 100% owned.) Hqtrs: Box 32488, Charlotte, N.C. 28232. (704) 372-4434. FAX: (704) 335-9904. Beverly Poston, VP.

Baum Broadcast Group Inc. WLMX-AM-FM Rossville, Ga.; WOMP-AM-FM Bellaire, Ohio; & WMFX(FM) St. Andrews, S.C. Baum Broadcast Group Inc., an operating entity of limited partnerships, is affiliated with Helicon Corp. Hqtrs: 630 Palisade Ave., Englewood Cliffs, N.J. 07632. (201) 568-7720. FAX: (201) 568-6228. David Baum, VP progmg.

A.H. Belo Corp. WFAA-TV Dallas; KHOU-TV Houston; KXTV(TV) Sacramento, Calif.; WVEC-TV Norfolk, Va.; KOTV(TV) Tulsa, Okla. (All 100% owned.) Hqtrs: 400 S. Record St., Dallas 75202. (214) 977-8730. FAX: (214) 977-8209.

Blade Communications Inc. KTRV(TV) Nampa, Idaho; WLFI-TV Lafayette, Ind.; WDRB-TV Louisville, Ky.; & WLIO(TV) Lima, Ohio. (All 100% owned.) Owns Buckeye Cablevision Inc., Toledo, Ohio; Erie County Cablevision Inc., Sandusky, Ohio; & Monroe Cablevision Inc., Monroe, Mich. (All 100% owned.) Hqtrs: 541 Superior St., Toledo, Ohio 43660. (419) 245-6000. FAX:(419) 245-6167. Gary Blair, treas.

Booth American Co. WZPL(FM) Greenfield & WRBR(FM) South Bend, both Ind.; WIOG(FM) Bay City, WJLB(FM) Detroit & WSGW(AM) Saginaw, all Mich.; WSAI(AM)-WWNK-FM Cincinnati, WWWE(AM)-WLTF(FM) Cleveland & WTOD(AM)-WKKO(FM) Toledo, all Ohio. Booth American Co. also owns Genesis Broadcasting (see listing). Booth American Co. owns cable systems in California, Florida, Michigan, North Carolina, South Carolina, South Dakota & Virginia. Hqtrs: 333 W. Fort St., Suite 1230, Detroit 48226. (313) 965-3360. FAX: (313) 965-1160. Mr. Shefferly, asst.

CJBN Broadcasting Ltd. CJBN-TV Kenora, Ont. Owned by Norcom Telecommunications Ltd., which owns systems in Ontario. Hqtrs: Box 1810, Kenora, Ont., Canada P9N 3X1.

CableSouth Inc. KSJX(AM) & KSJO(FM) San Jose, Calif. (pending FCC approval). Owns cable systems in Alabama serving 46,226 subs & 21,184 pay-cable subs. Hqtrs: 600 Luckie Dr., Suite 405, Birmingham, Ala. 35223. (205) 879-8884. FAX: (205) 879-5613. Jack Landham, dir mktg.

Center Broadcasting Co. Inc. KDET(AM) & KLCR(FM) Center, Tex. (100%). Owns cable systems in Center & San Augustine, both Tex. (Both 100% owned.) Hqtrs: 307 San Augustine St., Center, Tex. 75935. (409) 598-3304. FAX: (409) 598-9537. Dan Dillinger, stn mgr.

Chambers Communications Corp. KEZI(TV) Eugene, KDRV (TV) Medford, KDKF (TV) Klamath Falls, all Ore., (100%). Chambers Communications Corp. owns systems serving communities by cable in California, Idaho, Oregon & Washington. Hqtrs: Box 7009, Eugene, Ore. 97401. (503) 485-5611. FAX: (503) 342-2695. Bruce Liljegren, stn mgr.

The Chronicle Publishing Co. KRON-TV San Francisco; KLBY(TV) Colby, KUPK-TV Garden City & KAKE-TV Wichita, all Kan. & WOWT(TV) Omaha, Neb. (All 100% owned.) The Chronicle Publishing Co., also owns 100% of Western Communications. Western Communications, owns cable systems in California, Hawaii & New Mexico. Hqtrs: 901 Mission St., San Francisco 94103. (415) 777-1111. FAX: (415) 512-8196.

Cogeco Inc. CHLC(AM) Baie-Comeau, CFRP(AM) Forestville, CFGL-FM Laval (Montreal), CJMF-FM Quebec, CFEI-FM St. Hyacinthe, CFKS-TV & CKSH-TV Sherbrooke, & CFKM-TV & CKTM-TV Trois-Rivieres, all Quebec. (All 100% owned.) Cogeco Telecom Inc., 100% owned by Cogeco Inc., owns 100% of Beauce Video Inc., Cablestrie Inc., Cablovision Alma Inc., Compagnie de Television de Sept-Iles Ltee., La Belle Vision Inc. & Thetford Video Inc. Cogeco Inc. also owns Cablenet Ltd. & 01 Cablesystems Inc. Hqtrs: One Place Ville-Marie, Bureau 3636, Montreal, Que. Canada H3B 3P2. (514) 874-2600. FAX: (514) 874-2625.

Cox Enterprises Inc. WSB-AM-FM-TV Atlanta; WSOC-TV Charlotte, N.C.; WHQT(FM) Coral Gables, Fla.; KLRX(FM) Dallas; WHIO-AM-TV & WHKO(FM) Dayton, Ohio; WCKG(FM) Elmwood Park, Ill. (Chicago); KFI(AM) & KOST(FM) Los Angeles; KTVU(TV) Oakland, Calif.; WIOD(AM) & WFLC(FM) Miami, Fla.; WFTV(TV) Orlando, Fla.; WSUN(AM) & WCOF(FM) St. Petersburg, Fla.; & WPXI(TV) Pittsburgh. Note: Group has bought WYAI(FM) La Grange, Ga.; WYSY-FM Aurora, Ill.; & KTXQ(FM) Fort Worth & sold WSUN(AM) & WCOF(FM) St. Petersburg, Fla., subject to FCC approval. Cox Enterprises Inc. owns 100% of Cox Cable Communications Inc. (see MSO listing). Hqtrs: Box 105357, Atlanta 30348. (404) 843-5000. FAX: (404) 843-5777. Ajit Dalvi, opns mgr.

Diversified Communications. WCJB(TV) Gainesville, Fla.; WABI-AM-TV & WYOU-FM Bangor, Me.; WYOU(TV) Scranton, Pa.; & WPDE-TV Florence, S.C. Owns New England Cablevision Inc., operator of 23 cable systems in Maine, Massachusetts & New Hampshire. Hqtrs: Box 7437, Portland, Me. 04112. (207) 774-5981. FAX: (207) 761-7915. Paul Clancy, pres.

Donrey Media Group. KOLO-TV Reno (100%). Owns cable systems in Rogers, Ark. (100%); Vallejo, Calif. (100%); Bartlesville, Blackwell & Guymon, all Oklahoma (all 100%); & Kilgore, Tex. (34%). Administrative center: Box 17017, Fort Smith, Ark. 72917-7017. (501) 785-7810. FAX: (501) 785-9467.

R.H. Drewry Group. KRHD-AM-FM Duncan & KSWO-AM-TV Lawton, both Okla.; KFDA-TV Amarillo, KWAB(TV) Big Spring & KWES-TV Odessa, all Tex. R. H. Drewry owns a cable system in Lawton, Okla. (100%). Hqtrs: Box 708 A, Lawton, Okla. 73502. (405) 353-0820. FAX: (405) 355-7531. R.H. Drewry, pres.

William F. Duhamel. Owns 63% of KDUH-TV Scottsbluff, Neb.; KHSD-TV Lead & KOTA-AM-TV Rapid City, both S.D.; & KSGW-TV Sheridan, Wyo. Group has purchased KEZV(FM) Spearfish, S.D. Owns 4.8% of cable systems in Belle Fourche, Central City, Custer, Deadwood, Hot Springs, Lead, Spearfish, Piedmont & Sturgis, all S.D. owns 3% of Telecab in Mexico City, Mexico. Hqtrs: c/o Duhamel Broadcasting Enterprises, Box 1760, Rapid City, S.D. 57709.

Fairbanks Communications Inc. WJNX(AM) Fort Pierce, WRMF(FM) Palm Beach & WJNO(AM) West Palm Beach, all Fla.; WKOX(AM) & WCLB-FM Framingham, Mass. (Boston). (All 100% owned.) Owns cable systems in Delray Beach, Fla., & Lawrenceburg, Ind. Hqtrs: 1601 Belvedere Rd., No. 202E, West Palm Beach, Fla. 33406. (407) 838-4370. FAX: (407) 689-9957.

James A. Finch. WFTM-AM-FM Maysville, Ky. (90%). Mr. Finch owns 90% of Standard Tobacco Inc., which operates cable systems in Kentucky serving Augusta, Bracken County, Brooksville, Germantown, Mason County & Maysville. Hqtrs: c/o Standard Tobacco Inc., 626 Forest Ave., Maysville, Ky. 41056. (606) 564-5678. FAX: (606) 564-4291.

Fundy Cable Ltd. (Broadcasting Division). CFBC(AM) & CJYC-FM Saint John, N.B.; CJCB(AM) & CKPE-FM Sydney, N.S. (All 100% owned.) Affiliated with Fundy Cable Ltd., operator of 19 cable systems in New Brunswick. Hqtrs: Box 930, Saint John, N.B., Canada E2L 4E2. (506) 658-2330. FAX: (506) 658-2320.

Gateway Broadcasting Corp. WCSS(AM) & WKOL-FM Amsterdam, N.Y. Gateway Broadcasting Corp. owns 100% of WKOL-FM & 96.4% of Community Service Broadcasting Corp., licensee of WCSS(AM). Joseph M. Isabel, owner of Gateway Broadcasting Corp., also owns 70% of Gateway Cablevision Corp., operator of cable systems in Amsterdam & Northville, both New York. Hqtrs: 6 Genesee Ln., Amsterdam, N.Y. 12010-1892. (518) 842-5942. FAX: (518) 842-0737.

Genesis Broadcasting. KSMJ(AM) Sacramento & KSFM(FM) Woodland, both Calif.; KMJI(FM) Denver & KRZN(AM) Thornton, both Colo. Booth American Co., principal owner of Genesis Broadcasting, owns cable systems in California, Florida, Michigan, North Carolina, South Carolina, South Dakota & Virginia. Hqtrs: 5949 Sherry Ln., Suite 935, Dallas 75225. (214) 361-2932. FAX: (214) 987-2524.

Greater Media Inc. KLSX(FM) Los Angeles & KRLA(AM) Pasadena, both Calif.; WWRC(AM) & WGAY(FM) Washington, D.C.; WBCS(FM) & WMEX(AM)-WMJX(FM) Boston; WCSX(FM) Birmingham & WHND(AM) Monroe, both Mich.; WCTC(AM) & WMGQ(FM) New Brunswick, N.J.; WGSM(AM) Huntington & WMJC(FM) Smithtown, both New York; WPEN(AM) & WMGK(FM) Philadelphia. (All 100% owned.) Greater Media Inc. owns cable systems in Massachusetts & Pennsylvania. Hqtrs: Box 1059, 2 Kennedy Blvd., East Brunswick, N.J. 08816. (908) 247-6161. FAX: (908) 247-0215.

Harron Communications Corp. WMTW-TV Poland Spring, Me.(100%), WKTV-TV Utica (40%), & WETM (TV) Elmira (40%), both N.Y.; KCCN-TV Monterey, Calif. (90%). Owns cable systems in Abington, Bourne, Pembroke, Plymouth, Sandwich & Rockland, all Mass.; Caseville, Chesterfield Twp., Port Huron & St. Clair Twp., all Mich.; Londonderry, N.H.; Carrollton, Waxahachie/Midlothian, Crandall, Godley, Hubbard/Dawson, Rockett, Alverado, Whitney, Frost/Blooming Grove, all headends of the Texas Region (100% owned); Canajoharie, Granville, Queensbury & Utica, all N.Y.; Kennett Square & Malvern, both Pa.; & Wells, Vt. (All 100% owned.) Hqtrs: 70 E. Lancaster Ave., P.O. Box 3022, Frazer, Pa. 19355. (215) 644-7500. FAX: (215) 644-2790. Greg Raymonds, VP opns.

High Communications Partnership. WCKU(FM) Nicholasville, Ky., & WCYK-AM-FM Crozet, Va. High Communications is a division of High Industries, which operates High Media Group (with cable systems in Ky.). Hqtrs: 1853 William Penn Way, Lancaster, Pa. 17605-0008. (717) 293-4410. FAX: (717) 293-4444.

Roth E. Hook. WQST-AM-FM Forest, Miss. (80%). Mr. Hook owns 80% of Alabama TV Cable Co. Hqtrs: Box 309, Aliceville, Ala. 35442. (205) 373-2390.

Landmark Communications Inc. KLAS-TV Las Vegas; WTVF(TV) Nashville; WTAR (AM) & WLTY(FM) Norfolk, Va. (All 100% owned.) Owns 100% of The Weather Channel & The Travel Channel (Atlanta). Hqtrs: 150 W. Brambleton Ave., Norfolk, Va. 23510. (804) 446-2000. FAX: (804) 446-2489. John Wynne, pres/CEO.

Le Groupe Videotron Ltee. CFTM-TV Montreal (40.8%). Le Groupe Videotron Ltee. owns Videotron Inc., operator of cable systems in Alberta & Quebec serving 1,056,372 subs & 259,327 pay-cable subs. Hqtrs: 2000 Berri St., Montreal, Que. Canada H2L 4V7. (514) 281-1232. FAX: (514) 985-8794.

H.F. (Gerry) Lenfest. WCOJ(AM) Coatesville, Pa. H.F. (Gerry) Lenfest & family own 50% of Lenfest Communications Inc., operator of cable systems in California, New Jersey & Pennsylvania. Hqtrs: 202 Shoemaker Road, Pottstown, Pa. 19464. (215) 327-0965. FAX: (215) 327-6340. H.F. (Gerry) Lenfest, pres.

ML Media Partners L.P. KORG(AM) & KEZY(FM) Anaheim, Calif.; WICC(AM) Bridgeport & WEBE(FM) Westport, both Conn.; WREX-TV Rockford, Ill.; WCKN(AM) & WRZX (FM) Indianapolis; (100%) KATC(TV) Lafayette, La.; WQAL(FM) Cleveland; WFID(FM) Rio Piedras & WUNO(AM) San Juan, both P.R. (All 50% owned.) Owns systems managed by MultiVision Cable TV Corp. (see MSO). See also RP Companies Inc. Hqtrs: 321 Railroad Ave., Greenwich, Conn. 06830. (203) 622-4860. FAX: (203) 622-4876.

Maclean Hunter Limited. CFCN-AM-TV/CJAY-FM Calgary & CHED(AM)-CKNG-FM Edmonton (30%), both Alta; CKNB(AM) Campbellton, CKCW(AM)-CFQM-FM Moncton, CFAN(AM) Newcastle, CIOK-FM Saint John & CJCW(AM) Sussex, all N.B.; CKDH(AM) Amherst & CHNS(AM)-CHFX-FM Halifax, both N.S.; CFNY-FM Brampton (Toronto), CFCO(AM) Chatham, CHYM(AM)-CKGL-FM Kitchener, CHYR(AM) Leamington, CIWW(AM)-CKBY-FM Ottawa, CKTY(AM)-CFGX-FM Sarnia & CKYC(AM) Toronto, all Ont.; CFCY(AM) & CHLQ-FM Charlottetown, P.E.I. Note: CFCO(AM) Chatham, Ont., has been sold, subject to CRTC approval. Owns 100% of Maclean Hunter Cable TV (see MSO). Hqtrs: 777 Bay St., Toronto, Ont., Canada M5W 1A7. (416) 596-5103. FAX: (416) 593-3175. Ronald W. Osborne, pres.

Wendell Mayes Stations. KCRS-AM-FM Midland (85%), KSNY-AM-FM Snyder (32.5%), KAMG(AM) & KVIC(FM) Victoria (90.9%), all Tex. Owns interests in cable systems in Corsicana (25%) & Hereford (minority interest), both Tex. Hqtrs: Box 50030, 1907 N. Lamar, Austin, Tex. 78705. (512) 477-6866. FAX: (512) 476-1879.

Media General Inc. WJKS(TV) Jacksonville & WFLA-TV Tampa, both Fla; & WCBD-TV Charleston, S.C. (All 100% owned.) Owns cable systems in Fairfax County and Fredericksburg (including Spotsylvania & Stafford counties), both Va. (Both 100% owned.) Hqtrs: Box 85333, 333 E. Grace St. Richmond, Va. 23293. (804) 649-6000. FAX: (804) 775-8059. J. Stewart Bryan, pres.

Meyer Broadcasting Co. KFYR-AM-TV & KYYY(FM) Bismarck, KQCD-TV Dickinson, KMOT(TV) Minot, & KUMV-TV Williston, all N.D. (100%). Hqtrs: Box 1738, Bismarck, N.D. 58502. (701) 255-5757. FAX: (701) 255-4921. Judy E. Johnson, pres/CEO.

Mid Canada Television. CHBX-TV Sault Ste. Marie & CJIC-TV Sault Ste. Marie, both Ont. (Both 100% owned.) Owns 100% of a cable system in Sault Ste. Marie, Ont. Hqtrs: Box 370, 119 E. St., Sault Ste. Marie, Ont. Canada P6A 5M2. (705) 759-8232. FAX: (705) 759-7783. Michael Elgie, gen mgr.

Midcontinent Media Inc. KXLK(FM) Haysville & KFH(AM) Wichita, both Kan.; WDGY-AM Minneapolis & KDWB-FM Richfield, both Minn.; KDLO-TV Florence, KCLO-TV Rapid City, KELO-AM-FM-TV Sioux Falls & KDLO-FM Watertown, all S.D.; WTSO(AM) & WZEE(FM) Madison, Wis. Midcontinent Cable Co. operates cable systems in Minnesota, Montana, Nebraska, North Dakota & South Dakota. Hqtrs: 7900 Xerxes Ave., S. Suite 1100, Minneapolis 55431-11108. (612) 844-2600. FAX: (612) 844-2660. Cable Hqtrs: Box 910, Aberdeen, S.D. 57401. Joe H. Floyd, exec VP.

Midwest Communications Inc. WJMN-TV Escanaba, Mich.; KCCO-TV Alexandria, WCCO-AM-TV & WLTE(FM) Minneapolis, & KCCW-TV Walker, all Minn.; & WFRV-TV Green Bay, Wis. Midwest Communications Inc. also owns 100% of Midwest Cable & Satellite Inc., which operates a teleport at Lino Lakes, Minn., & which provides complete turnkey services, fixed local loop services, microwave interconnect to 16 cable TV companies in the Twin City area, common carrier services. Midwest Communications Inc. also owns Midwest Sports Channel, a 24-hour cable regional sports network serving Iowa, Minnesota, North Dakota, South Dakota & Wisconsin. Midwest Communications Inc. is an affiliate of CBS Hqtrs: 90 S. 11th St., Minneapolis 55403. (612) 330-2400. FAX: (612) 330-2603. John Culliton, gen mgr.

Moffat Communications Ltd. CKY (TV) Winnipeg, Man. Owns cable systems in Pinawa & Winnipeg, both Man.; Pasco county (90%) & Zephyrhills (100%), both Fla.; Kingwood, Tex. (100%); & Lakewood Cablevision (100%) in Tex. Hqtrs: CKY Building, Polo Park, Winnipeg, Man., Canada R3G 0L7. (204) 788-3440. FAX: (204) 956-2710. Bill Davis vp/U.S. Cable.

Monarch Communications Inc. CJXX(AM) Grande Prairie, CKRZ(AM) Lethbridge, CHAT-AM-TV Medicine Hat, CKRD(AM) Red Deer & CKTA(AM) Taber, all Alta.; CKMK(AM) Mackenzie, CKPG-AM-TV-CIOI-FM Prince George, all B.C. (All 100% owned.) Owns Monarch Cable TV Ltd., which operates 22 cable systems in Alberta. Hqtrs: 361 First St. S.E., Medicine Hat, Alta., Canada T1A 0A5. (403) 526-4529. FAX: (403) 526-4000.

Multimedia Broadcasting Co. WMAZ-AM-TV & WAYS(FM) Macon, Ga.; KEEL(AM) & KITT(FM) Shreveport, La.; KSDK(TV) St. Louis; WLWT(TV) Cincinnati & WKYC-TV Cleveland; WFBC-AM-FM Greenville & WORD(AM) Spartanburg, both S.C.; WBIR-TV Knoxville, Tenn.; & WEZW(FM) Wauwatosa, Wis. (Milwaukee). Multimedia Broadcasting Co. is a division of Multimedia Inc., which owns 100% of Multimedia Cablevision Inc. (see MSO). Broadcasting hqtrs: 140 W. 9th St., Cincinnati 45202. (513) 352-5070. FAX: (513) 352-5969.

Nationwide Communications Inc. KVRY(FM) Mesa (Phoenix), Ariz.; KNCI(FM) Sacramento, Calif. (100%); WOMX-AM-FM Orlando, Fla.; WPOC(FM) Baltimore; KITN-TV Minneapolis; KLUC-FM/KXNO-AM Las Vegas (100%); WGAR-FM Cleveland, WCOL-AM-FM Columbus & WNCI(FM) Columbus, all Ohio; WATE-TV Knoxville, Tenn.; KDMX(FM) Dallas & KHMX(FM) Houston; WRIC-TV Petersburg (Richmond), Va.; KISW(FM) Seattle; & WBAY-TV Green Bay, Wis. (All 100% owned.) Note: KITN-TV Minneapolis has been sold, subject to FCC approval. Nationwide Communications Inc. dba EagleVision owns private cable systems in Texas. Hqtrs: One Nationwide Plaza, 27th Fl., Columbus, Ohio 43216. (614) 249-7676. FAX: (614) 249-6995. Steve Berger, pres.

Nelsonville TV Cable Inc. WAIS(AM) Buchtel & WSEO(FM) Nelsonville, both Ohio. Owns a cable system in Nelsonville, Ohio. Hqtrs: One W. Columbus St., Nelsonville, Ohio 45764. (614) 753-2686. FAX: (614) 753-4963. Eugene R. Edwards, pres.

Palmer Communications Inc. WCVU(FM) & WNOG-AM-FM Naples, Fla. (100%); WHO-AM-TV & KLYF(FM) Des Moines, Iowa; & KFOR-TV Oklahoma City. (All 100% owned.) Palmer Communications Inc. owns cable systems in California. Hqtrs: 12800 University Dr., Suite 500, Fort Myers, Fla. 33907-5333. (813) 433-4350. FAX: (813) 433-8213.

James D. Popwell. WCEH-AM-FM Hawkinsville, Ga. (100%). Owns a cable systems in Perry (including Marshallville), Ga. (50%). Hqtrs: c/o WCEH-AM-FM, Box 489, Hawkinsville, Ga. 31036. (912) 892-9061. FAX: (912) 892-9063. Jay Braswell, gen mgr.

Post-Newsweek Stations Inc. WFSB(TV) Hartford, Conn.; WJXT(TV) Jacksonville & WPLG(TV) Miami, both Fla; & WDIV(TV) Detroit. Owned by the Washington Post Co., which also owns Post-Newsweek Cable Inc. (see MSO). Note: Post-Newsweek Stations also owns 100% of PASS, Inc., a regional sports cable channel. Hqtrs: 1150 15th St. N.W., Washington 20071. (202) 334-4600. FAX: (202) 334-4605. G. William Ryan, pres/CEO; Catherine Nierle, VP business affrs.

Providence Journal Co. KMSB-TV Tucson, Ariz.; WHAS-TV Louisville, Ky.; KASA-TV Santa Fe/Albuquerque, N.M.; & WCNC-TV Charlotte, N.C. (All 100% owned.) Owns 100% of Colony Communications Inc. (see MSO). Note: Providence Journal Co. and Kelso & Co., New York, have purchased the following stns: KHBC-TV Hilo, KHNL(TV) Honolulu & KOGG(TV) Wailuku, all Hawaii; KTVB(TV) Boise, Idaho; KGW-TV Portland, Ore.; KING-TV Seattle & KREM-TV Spokane, both Wash. Providence Journal Co. and Kelso & Co., New York, also have purchased King Videocable, consisting of 12 systems (232,000 subs) in five states. Hqtrs: 75 Fountain St., Providence, R.I. 02902. (401) 277-7000. FAX: (401) 274-2076.

RP Companies Inc. KORG(AM) & KEZY(FM) Anaheim, Calif.; WICC(AM) Bridgeport & WEBE(FM) Westport, both Conn.; WREX-TV Rockford, Ill.; WFXF-AM-FM Indianapolis; KATC(TV) Lafayette, La.; WQAL(FM) Cleveland; WFID(FM) Rio Piedras & WUNO(AM) San Juan, both Puerto Rico. Owns cable systems managed by MultiVision Cable TV Corp. (see MSO). Hqtrs: 350 Park Ave., 16th Fl., New York 10022. (212) 980-7110. FAX: (212) 980-8374. Martin Pompadur, CEO.

David A. Ramage. KDMA(AM) & KMGM(FM) Montevideo, Minn. (66 2/3%). David A. Ramage owns cable systems in North Dakota. Hqtrs: Box 487, Grand Forks, N.D. 58201. (701) 772-4305. Mrs. Ramage, owner.

Rogers Broadcasting Ltd. CFTR(AM), CHFI-FM & CFMT-TV (80%) Toronto, both Ont. Owned by Rogers Communications Inc., which operates 15 cable systems (1,772,538 subs) in Alberta, British Columbia & Ontario. Hqtrs: 25 Adelaide St. E., Toronto, Canada M5C 1H3. (416) 864-2000. FAX: (416) 363-2387. Andy Sanderson, gen mgr.

Robert E. Schmidt. KLOE(AM)-KKCI(FM) Goodland, KAYS(AM)-KHAZ(FM) Hays, KHOK(FM) Hoisington & KWBW(AM)-KHUT(FM) Hutchinson, all Kan.; KFEQ(AM) St. Joseph & KSJQ(FM) Savannah, both Mo.; KCOW(AM)-KAAQ(FM) Alliance, KQSK(FM) Chadron & KOOQ(AM)-KELN(FM) North Platte, all Neb. (All 100% owned.) Owns cable systems in Brewster, Ellis, Goodland, Hays, Hoxie, Russell & Wakeeney, all Kan. Hqtrs: c/o KAYS Inc., Box 817, Hays, Kan. 67601. (913) 625-2578. FAX: (913) 625-3632.

Schurz Communications Inc. WAGT(TV) Augusta, Ga.; WASK-AM-FM Lafayette & WSBT-AM-TV & WNSN(FM) South Bend, all Ind.; KYTV(TV) Springfield, Mo.; & WDBJ(TV) Roanoke, Va. (All 100% owned.) Owns cable systems in Coral Springs, Fla., & Hagerstown, Md. (Both 100% owned.) Hqtrs: 225 W. Colfax Ave., South Bend, Ind. 46626. (219) 287-1001. Franklin D. Schurz Jr., pres.

Scripps Howard Broadcasting Co. KNXV-TV Phoenix; WFTS(TV) Tampa & WPTV(TV) West Palm Beach, both Fla.; WMAR-TV Baltimore; WXYZ-TV Detroit; KSHB-TV Kansas City, Mo.; WCPO-TV Cincinnati & WEWS(TV) Cleveland; KJRH(TV) Tulsa, Okla.; & KUPL-AM-FM Portland, Ore. Owns 100% of Scripps Howard Cable Co. (see MSO). Hqtrs: Box 5380, Cincinnati 45201. (513) 977-3000. FAX: (513) 977-3728. Barbara Elslager.

Skeena Broadcasters, a division of Okanagan Skeena Group Ltd. CKTK(AM) Kitimat, CFTK-AM-TV & CJFW-FM Terrace, CHTK(AM) & CFTK-TV-1 Prince Rupert, all B.C. Okanagan Skeena Group Ltd. also owns Okanagan Radio Ltd., which operates CJOR(AM) Osoyoos, CKOR(AM)-CJMG-FM Penticton, CIOR(AM) Princeton & CHOR(AM) Summerland, all B.C.; & owns 49% of CJCD(AM) Yellowknife, N.W.T. Skeena Broadcasters, a division of Okanagan Skeena Group Ltd., owns cable systems in British Columbia. Hqtrs: 4625 Lazelle Ave., Terrace, B.C., Canada V8G 1S4. (604) 635-6316. FAX: (604) 638-6320.

Standard Tobacco Co. WFTM-AM-FM Maysville, Ky. (100%). Standard Tobacco Co. owns cable systems in Augusta, Bracken County, Brooksville, Germantown, Mason County & Maysville, all Ky. Hqtrs: Box 100, 626 Forest Ave., Maysville, Ky. 41056. (606) 564-5678; (800) 264-3572. FAX: (606) 564-4291. James A. Finch, own.

Summit Communications Group Inc. WAOK(AM) & WVEE(FM) Atlanta (100%); WCAO(AM) & WXYV(FM) Baltimore (100%); KJMZ(FM) & KHVN(AM) Dallas (100%); WONE(AM) & WTUE(FM) Dayton, Ohio; & WRKS-FM New York. Summit Communications Group Inc. owns cable systems in Georgia & North Carolina. Hqtrs: 115 Perimeter Ctr. Pl., Suite 1150, Atlanta 30346. (404) 394-0707. FAX: (404) 394-9778.

Susquehanna Radio Corp. KNBR(AM) & KFOG(FM) San Francisco; WNNX(FM) Atlanta; WFMS(FM) Indianapolis; WRRM(FM) Cincinnati; WARM(AM) Scranton, WMGS(FM) Wilkes-Barre & WSBA(AM)-WARM-FM York, all Pennsylvania; KLIF(AM) Dallas, KPLX(FM) Fort Worth & KRBE-AM-FM Houston; & WGH-AM-FM Newport News, Va. Note: Group has purchased WAJC(FM) Indianapolis, subject to FCC approval. Owned by Susquehanna Pfaltzgraff Co., which also owns Susquehanna Cable Co. (see MSO listing). Group also operates WBHT(FM) Mountaintop, Pa., & WGRL(FM), Indianapolis, under a local marketing agreement. Hqtrs: 140 E. Market St., York, Pa. 17401. (717) 848-5500. M. Sue Krom.

TMZ Broadcasting Co. WTAD(AM) & WQCY(FM) Quincy, Ill.; WEST(AM)-WLEV(FM) Easton, WQKK(FM) Ebensburg & WRKZ(FM) Hershey, all Pa.; WLKW(AM)-WWLI(FM) & WPRO-AM-FM Providence, R.I. TMZ Broadcasting Co. is owned 33 1/3% by Robert E. Tudek & 33 1/3% by Everett I. Mundy, who each own 50% of Tele-Media Corp. (see MSO listing). Box 39, Bellefonte, Pa. 16823. (814) 353-2081. FAX: (814) 353-2072.

Times Mirror Broadcasting. KTBC-TV Austin & KDFW-TV Dallas, both Tex. (both 100% owned.) The Times Mirror Co. also owns Times Mirror Cable Television Inc. (see MSO). Hqtrs: 780 3rd Ave., New York 10017. (212) 418-9600. FAX: (212) 319-6294.

United Broadcasting Co. Owns 100% of KALI(AM) San Gabriel, Calif. & WKDM(AM) New York; & WJMO-AM-FM Cleveland Heights, Ohio. Owns cable systems in Auburn, Bedford, Candia, Goffstown, Hooksett, Manchester & Piermont, all N.H.; Bradford, Chelsea & South Royalton, all Vt. (All 100% owned.) Hqtrs: 4733 Bethesda Ave., Suite 808, Bethesda, Md. 20814. (301) 652-7707. FAX: (301) 652-4614. Gerald Hroblak, pres.

Venture Technologies Group. WHTV(TV) Jackson, Mich. (95%); KBCB(TV) Bellingham, Wash. (44%); plus low power TV stns: K25DJ Tucson, Ariz. (100%); W29AY East Lansing, Mich. (95%); K07UI Minneapolis (100%); & W29AH Pittsburgh. Venture Technologies Group owns 66.67% of CalaVision Inc., which operates cable systems in Calabasas & Thousand Palms, both Calif. Hqtrs: 23642 Calabasas Rd., Suite 104, Calabasas, Calif. 91302-1592. (818) 222-5390. FAX: (818) 222-5377. Gary Spire, mgr.

Viacom International Inc. KXEZ(FM) & KYSR(FM) Los Angeles, KSRY(FM) San Francisco, KOFY(AM) San Mateo & KSRI(FM) Santa Cruz, all Calif.; WVIT(TV) New Britain (Hartford-New Haven), Conn.; WMZQ-FM Washington, D.C.; WLIT-FM Chicago; KSLA-TV Shreveport, La.; WLTI(FM) Detroit; KMOV(TV) St. Louis; WNYT(TV) Albany, WLTW(FM) New York & WHEC-TV Rochester, all N.Y.; KIKK(AM) Pasadena & KIKK-FM Houston, both Tex.; WMZQ(AM) Arlington, Va. (Washington); KBSG(AM) Auburn, KNDD(FM) Seattle & KBSG-FM Tacoma, all Wash. Note: Group has bought WCPT(AM) Alexandria & WCXR-FM Woodbridge, both Va., & sold KIKK(AM) Pasadena & KIKK-FM Houston, both Tex., subject to FCC approval. Viacom International operates cable systems through a division, Viacom Cable (see MSO). Hqtrs: 1515 Broadway, New York 10036. (212) 258-6000. FAX: (212) 258-6244.

WKEY Inc. WKEY(AM) & WIQO-FM Covington, Va. (100%). Owns a cable system in Bath County, Va. (100%). Hqtrs: Box 710, Covington, Va. 24426. (703) 962-1133.

Wolfe Broadcasting Corp. WFRO-AM-FM Fremont, Ohio (100%). Owns a cable system in Fremont, Ohio (100%). Hqtrs: 905 W. State St., Fremont, Ohio 43420. (419) 332-7381. FAX: (419) 332-9341.

Cable Penetration by Market

Listed below are the A.C. Nielsen Company's Designated Market Areas (DMAs) with the number of cable homes and the percentage of penetration. The estimates are from November 1993. (Copyright 1993 Nielsen Media Research.)

Designated Market Area	Cable Households	Cable Penetration (%)
Abilene-Sweetwater	72.160	67.6
Ada-Ardmore	37,700	53.5
Albany, Ga.	76,220	59.2
Albany-Schenectady-Troy	347,730	68.3
Albuquerque-Santa Fe	288,530	54.4
Alexandria, La.	59,140	67.9
Alpena	10,110	62.3
Amarillo	113,340	67.2
Anchorage	60,760	50.8
Anniston	34,080	78.5
Atlanta	916,500	60.7
Augusta	126,310	60.6
Austin	243,450	63.5
Bakersfield	118,890	68.9
Baltimore	567,630	58.5
Bangor	58,580	47.3
Baton Rouge	184,220	71.4
Beaumont-Port Arthur	102,550	63.9
Bend, Ore.	22,970	70.5
Billings	48,990	56.4
Biloxi-Gulfport	81,710	76.8
Binghamton	98,790	72.6
Birmingham	325,360	62.3
Bluefield-Beckley-Oak Hill	100,010	74.3
Boise	83,040	49.5
Boston	1,537,060	73.0
Bowling Green	26,580	50.9
Buffalo	449,560	71.0
Burlington-Plattsburgh	168,500	59.6
Butte	27,650	54.9
Casper-Riverton	31,490	67.0
Cedar Rapids-Waterloo & Dubuque	179,110	59.5
Champaign & Springfield-Decatur	244,840	71.3
Charleston, S.C.	135,500	59.0
Charleston-Huntington	340,110	71.9
Charlotte	491,950	63.5
Charlottesville	27,820	62.8
Chattanooga	197,690	63.6
Cheyenne-Scottbluff-Sterling	33,080	68.4
Chicago	1,688,040	55.0
Chico-Redding	103,900	60.2
Cincinnati	448,980	58.3
Clarksburg-Weston	70,170	69.1
Cleveland	933,040	64.5
Colorado Springs-Pueblo	155,140	61.9
Columbia, S.C.	163,350	55.3
Columbia-Jefferson City	74,700	55.6
Columbus, Ga.	118,400	65.1
Columbus, Ohio	421,490	59.3
Columbus-Tupelo-West Point	87,680	53.0

Cable Penetration by Market

Designated Market Area	Cable Households	Cable Penetration (%)
Corpus Christi	106,650	63.0
Dallas-Fort Worth	891,470	49.1
Davenport-Rock Island-Moline	183,070	61.7
Dayton	339,340	66.7
Denver	632,910	58.0
Des Moines-Ames	202,860	56.0
Detroit	1,091,640	62.9
Dothan	59,970	60.1
Duluth-Superior	83,380	49.1
El Paso	135,720	56.1
Elmira	68,350	72.8
Erie	97,240	64.4
Eugene	126,760	63.8
Eureka	41,430	74.3
Evansville	154,140	57.3
Fairbanks	10,370	33.6
Fargo-Valley City	120,750	56.0
Flint-Saginaw-Bay City	259,450	58.0
Florence-Myrtle Beach	115,480	67.9
Fresno-Visalia	238,800	50.5
Fort Myers-Naples	216,660	72.5
Fort Smith	119,900	61.3
Fort Wayne	122,040	51.5
Gainesville	56,760	62.0
Glendive	2,700	68.9
Grand Junction-Montrose	35,000	60.2
Grand Rapids-Kalamazoo-Battle Creek	377,880	59.1
Great Falls	35,560	54.2
Green Bay-Appleton	205,620	52.5
Greensboro-High Point-Winston Salem	311,690	57.9
Greenville-New Bern-Washington	137,180	60.0
Greenville-Spartanburg-Asheville-Anderson	358,990	53.7
Greenwood-Greenville	52,550	68.8
Harlingen-Weslaco-Brownsville-McAllen	93,030	45.8
Harrisburg-Lancaster-Lebanon-York	399,330	70.1
Harrisonburg	24,460	64.2
Hartford & New Haven	763,390	83.4
Hattiesburg-Laurel	45,380	50.3
Helena	12,490	63.7
Honolulu	309,930	82.8
Houston	771,010	51.0
Huntsville-Decatur, Florence, Ala.	199,300	67.1
Idaho Falls-Pocatello	53,200	51.1
Indianapolis	559,940	61.4
Jackson, Miss.	156,360	54.6
Jackson, Tenn.	35,940	57.8
Jacksonville, Brunswick	348,120	71.9
Johnstown-Altoona	225,270	79.3
Jonesboro	49,760	66.0
Joplin-Pittsburg	75,730	54.6
Kansas City	462,910	60.3
Knoxville	252,630	62.5
La Crosse-Eau Claire	94,860	58.0
Lafayette, Ind.	37,260	79.8
Lafayette, La.	127,100	65.3

Cable Penetration by Market

Designated Market Area	Cable Households	Cable Penetration (%)
Lake Charles	52,080	69.5
Lansing	141,550	61.6
Laredo	30,550	76.4
Las Vegas	201,840	58.2
Lexington	255,100	67.4
Lima	29,260	75.5
Lincoln & Hastings-Kearney Plus	163,600	66.7
Little Rock-Pine Bluff	272,490	58.8
Los Angeles	2,949,710	58.9
Louisville	313,740	58.8
Lubbock	78,680	58.4
Macon	120,540	67.5
Madison	174,840	58.7
Mankato	36,630	67.8
Marquette	44,460	78.8
Medford-Klamath Falls	83,830	59.1
Memphis	343,420	57.7
Meridian	32,220	49.7
Miami-Fort Lauderdale	853,740	65.8
Milwaukee	411,040	52.7
Minneapolis-St. Paul	658,780	47.4
Minot-Bismarck-Dickinson	78,020	59.5
Missoula	41,120	53.2
Mobile-Pensacola	276,050	65.4
Monroe-El Dorado	100,510	60.2
Monterey-Salinas	168,710	81.5
Montgomery	128,030	60.8
Nashville	418,990	56.8
New Orleans	412,780	67.8
New York	4,293,190	64.2
Norfolk-Portsmouth-Newport News	427,060	69.7
North Platte	9,080	62.4
Odessa-Midland	95,790	72.1
Oklahoma City	338,490	59.1
Omaha	223,590	62.2
Orlando-Daytona Beach-Melbourne	705,720	73.0
Ottumwa-Kirksville	24,480	59.2
Paducah-Cape Girardeau-Harrisburg-Mt. Vernon	188,200	54.4
Palm Springs	83,980	89.3
Panama City	58,280	65.2
Parkersburg	43,470	72.0
Peoria-Bloomington	135,360	65.1
Philadelphia	1,891,030	71.1
Phoenix	586,710	53.5
Pittsburgh	856,390	75.0
Portland, Ore.	510,040	57.3
Portland-Auburn	239,120	70.1
Presque Isle	20,290	67.0
Providence-New Bedford	405,920	71.8
Quincy-Hannibal-Keokuk	61,320	55.8
Raleigh-Durham	438,350	58.2
Rapid City	46,820	55.4
Reno	134,260	69.0
Richmond-Petersburg	270,290	55.8
Roanoke-Lynchburg	232,520	60.2

Cable Penetration by Market

Designated Market Area	Cable Households	Cable Penetration (%)
Rochester, N.Y.	249,150	68.5
Rochester-Mason City-Austin	84,460	59.8
Rockford	99,360	62.2
Sacramento-Stockton-Modesto	665,390	60.5
Salisbury	70,630	71.8
Salt Lake City	312,230	50.6
San Angelo	37,040	81.0
San Antonio	385,810	63.2
San Diego	729,090	79.2
San Francisco-Oakland-San Jose	1,510,060	67.0
Santa Barbara-Santa Maria-San Luis Obispo	176,800	83.5
Savannah	151,850	63.7
Seattle-Tacoma	966,560	67.7
Shreveport	204,210	58.1
Sioux City	89,100	59.2
Sioux Falls (Mitchell)	126,860	57.7
South Bend-Elkhart	167,330	56.0
Spokane	197,870	57.9
Springfield, Mo.	150,860	46.4
Springfield-Holyoke	194,720	78.7
St. Joseph	38,950	67.6
St. Louis	541,080	48.8
Syracuse	263,510	68.5
Tallahassee-Thomasville	118,200	59.5
Tampa-St. Petersburg, Sarasota	929,070	67.1
Terre Haute	89,710	59.6
Toledo	265,200	65.0
Topeka	108,960	72.2
Traverse City-Cadillac	98,820	53.8
Tri-Cities, Tenn.-Va.	193,640	69.4
Tucson (Nogales)	190,390	59.0
Tulsa	276,450	60.6
Tuscaloosa	44,690	77.9
Twin Falls	16,080	50.0
Tyler-Longview (Lufkin & Nacogdoches)	128,550	60.2
Utica	72,830	74.4
Victoria	20,590	78.0
Waco-Temple-Bryan	163,320	66.0
Washington, D.C.	1,148,900	61.9
Watertown	61,890	70.8
Wausau-Rhinelander	76,940	46.2
West Palm Beach-Fort Pierce	434,670	76.8
Wheeling-Steubenville	114,030	72.4
Wichita Falls & Lawton	103,450	68.0
Wichita-Hutchinson Plus	278,250	65.6
Wilkes Barre-Scranton	417,130	75.9
Wilmington	89,490	59.0
Yakima-Pasco-Richland-Kennewick	107,640	59.9
Youngstown	181,870	66.2
Yuma-El Centro	52,900	72.0
Zanesville	21,490	69.3

Top 50 DMA Ranked by Percentage of Cable Penetration

Listed below are the A.C. Nielsen Company's Designated Market Areas (DMAs) ranked by percentage of cable penetration. The estimates are from November 1993. (Copyright 1993 Nielsen Media Research.)

Rank	Designated Market Area	Cable Penetration (%)
1	Palm Springs	89.3
2	Santa Barbara-Santa Maria-San Luis Obispo	83.5
3	Hartford & New Haven	83.4
4	Honolulu	82.8
5	Monterey-Salinas	81.5
6	San Angelo	81.0
7	Lafayette, Ind.	79.8
8	Johnstown-Altoona	79.3
9	San Diego	79.2
10	Marquette	78.8
11	Springfield-Holyoke	78.7
12	Anniston	78.5
13	Victoria	78.0
14	Tuscaloosa	77.9
15	Biloxi-Gulfport	76.8
15	West Palm Beach-Fort Pierce	76.8
17	Laredo	76.4
18	Wilkes Barre-Scranton	75.9
19	Lima	75.5
20	Pittsburgh	75.0
21	Utica	74.4
22	Bluefield-Beckley-Oak Hill	74.3
22	Eureka	74.3
24	Boston	73.0
24	Orlando-Daytona Beach-Melbourne	73.0
26	Elmira	72.8
27	Binghamton	72.6
28	Fort Myers-Naples	72.5
29	Wheeling-Steubenville	72.4
30	Topeka	72.2
31	Odessa-Midland	72.1
32	Parkersburg	72.0
32	Yuma-El Centro	72.0
34	Charleston-Huntington	71.9
34	Jacksonville, Brunswick	71.9
36	Providence-New Bedford	71.8
36	Salisbury	71.8
38	Baton Rouge	71.4
39	Champaign & Springfield-Decatur	71.3
40	Philadelphia	71.1
41	Buffalo	71.0
42	Watertown	70.8
43	Bend, Ore.	70.5
44	Harrisburg-Lancaster-Lebanon-York	70.1
44	Portland-Auburn	70.1
46	Norfolk-Portsmouth-Newport News	69.7
47	Lake Charles	69.5
48	Tri-Cities, Tenn.-Va.	69.4
49	Zanesville	69.3
50	Clarksburg-Weston	69.1

Top 50 DMA Ranked by Cable Television Households

Listed below are the A.C. Nielsen Company's Designated Market Areas (DMAs) ranked by number of cable television households. The estimates are from November 1993. (Copyright 1993 Nielsen Media Research.)

Rank	Designated Market Area	Cable Television Households
1	New York	4,293,190
2	Los Angeles	2,949,710
3	Philadelphia	1,891,030
4	Chicago	1,688,040
5	Boston	1,537,060
6	San Francisco-Oakland-San Jose	1,510,060
7	Washington, D.C.	1,148,900
8	Detroit	1,091,640
9	Seattle-Tacoma	966,560
10	Cleveland	933,040
11	Tampa-St. Petersburg-Sarasota	929,070
12	Atlanta	916,500
13	Dallas-Fort Worth	891,470
14	Pittsburgh	856,390
15	Miami-Fort Lauderdale	853,740
16	Houston	771,010
17	Hartford & New Haven	763,390
18	San Diego	729,090
19	Orlando-Daytona Beach-Melbourne	705,720
20	Sacramento-Stockton-Modesto	665,390
21	Minneapolis-St. Paul	658,780
22	Denver	632,910
23	Phoenix	586,710
24	Baltimore	567,630
25	Indianapolis	559,940
26	St. Louis	541,080
27	Portland, Ore.	510,040
28	Charlotte	491,950
29	Kansas City	462,910
30	Buffalo	449,560
31	Cincinnati	448,980
32	Raleigh-Durham	438,350
33	West Palm Beach-Fort Pierce	434,670
34	Norfolk-Portsmouth-Newport News	427,060
35	Columbus, Ohio	421,490
36	Nashville	418,990
37	Wilkes Barre-Scranton	417,130
38	New Orleans	412,780
39	Milwaukee	411,040
40	Providence-New Bedford	405,920
41	Harrisburg-Lancaster-Lebanon-York	399,330
42	San Antonio	385,810
43	Grand Rapids-Kalamazoo-Battle Creek	377,880
44	Greenville-Spartanburg-Asheville-Anderson	358,990
45	Jacksonville-Brunswick	348,120
46	Albany-Schenectady-Troy	347,730
47	Memphis	343,420
48	Charleston-Huntington	340,110
49	Dayton	339,340
50	Oklahoma City	338,490

Top 50 DMA Ranked by Television Households

Listed below are the A.C. Nielsen Company's Designated Market Areas (DMAs) ranked by television households. The estimates are from September 1993. (Copyright 1993 Nielsen Media Research.)

Rank	Designated Market Area	Television Households	Cable Penetration	Cable TV Households
1	New York	6,692,370	64.2	4,293,190
2	Los Angeles	5,006,380	58.9	2,949,710
3	Chicago	3,070,830	55.0	1,688,040
4	Philadelphia	2,661,360	71.1	1,891,030
5	San Francisco-Oakland-San Jose	2,253,220	67.0	1,510,060
6	Boston	2,104,900	73.0	1,537,060
7	Washington, D.C.	1,855,440	61.9	1,148,900
8	Dallas-Fort Worth	1,816,700	49.1	891,470
9	Detroit	1,735,340	62.9	1,091,640
10	Houston	1,510,580	51.0	771,010
11	Atlanta	1,510,340	60.7	916,500
12	Cleveland	1,446,970	64.5	933,040
13	Seattle-Tacoma	1,427,750	67.7	966,560
14	Minneapolis-St. Paul	1,389,420	47.4	658,780
15	Tampa-St. Petersburg, Sarasota	1,384,150	67.1	929,070
16	Miami-Fort Lauderdale	1,296,800	65.8	853,740
17	Pittsburgh	1,141,830	75.0	856,390
18	St. Louis	1,109,090	48.8	541,080
19	Sacramento-Stockton-Modesto	1,099,950	60.5	665,390
20	Phoenix	1,097,480	53.5	586,710
21	Denver	1,090,970	58.0	632,910
22	Baltimore	970,030	58.5	567,630
23	Orlando-Daytona Beach-Melbourne	967,360	73.0	705,720
24	San Diego	920,570	79.2	729,090
25	Hartford & New Haven	915,110	83.4	763,390
26	Indianapolis	912,190	61.4	559,940
27	Portland, Ore.	890,120	57.3	510,040
28	Milwaukee	780,350	52.7	411,040
29	Charlotte	774,760	63.5	491,950
30	Cincinnati	770,400	58.3	448,980
31	Kansas City	767,930	60.3	462,910
32	Raleigh-Durham	753,570	58.2	438,350
33	Nashville	737,810	56.8	418,990
34	Columbus, Ohio	710,910	59.3	421,490
35	Greenville-Spartanburg-Asheville-Anderson	669,090	53.7	358,990
36	Grand Rapids-Kalamazoo-Battle Creek	638,940	59.1	377,880
37	Buffalo	633,560	71.0	449,560
38	Salt Lake City	616,720	50.6	312,230
39	Norfolk-Portsmouth-Newport News	612,880	69.7	427,060
40	San Antonio	610,660	63.2	385,810
41	New Orleans	609,000	67.8	412,780
42	Memphis	595,380	57.7	343,420
43	Oklahoma City	572,300	59.1	338,490
44	Harrisburg-Lancaster-Lebanon-York	569,920	70.1	399,330
45	West Palm Beach-Ft. Pierce	566,140	76.8	434,670
46	Providence-New Bedford	565,460	71.8	405,920
47	Wilkes Barre-Scranton	549,770	75.9	417,130
48	Greensboro-High Point-Winston Salem	538,090	57.9	311,690
49	Louisville	533,170	58.8	313,740
50	Albuquerque-Santa Fe	530,040	54.4	288,530

Bottom 50 DMA Ranked by Percentage of Cable Penetration

Listed below are A.C. Nielsen Company's Designated Market Areas (DMAs) ranked by percentage of cable penetration. Fairbanks has the lowest percentage. The estimates are from November 1993. (Copyright 1993 Nielsen Media Research.)

Rank	Designated Market Area	Cable Penetration (%)
1	Fairbanks	33.6
2	Harlingen-Weslaco-Brownsville-McAllen	45.8
3	Wausau-Rhinelander	46.2
4	Springfield, Mo.	46.4
5	Bangor	47.3
6	Minneapolis-St. Paul	47.4
7	St. Louis	48.8
8	Duluth-Superior	49.1
8	Dallas-Fort Worth	49.1
10	Boise	49.5
11	Meridian	49.7
12	Twin Falls	50.0
13	Hattiesburg-Laurel	50.3
14	Fresno-Visalia	50.5
15	Salt Lake City	50.6
16	Anchorage	50.8
17	Bowling Green	50.9
18	Houston	51.0
19	Idaho Falls-Pocatello	51.1
20	Fort Wayne	51.5
21	Green Bay-Appleton	52.5
22	Milwaukee	52.7
23	Columbus-Tupelo-West Point	53.0
24	Missoula	53.2
25	Phoenix	53.5
25	Ada-Ardmore	53.5
27	Greenville-Spartanburg-Asheville-Anderson	53.7
28	Traverse City-Cadillac	53.8
29	Great Falls	54.2
30	Paducah-Cape Girardeau-Harrisburg-Mt. Vernon	54.4
30	Albuquerque-Santa Fe	54.4
32	Joplin-Pittsburg	54.6
32	Jackson, Miss.	54.6
34	Butte	54.9
35	Chicago	55.0
36	Columbia, S.C.	55.3
37	Rapid City	55.4
38	Columbia-Jefferson City	55.6
39	Richmond-Petersburg	55.8
39	Quincy-Hannibal-Keokuk	55.8
41	South Bend-Elkhart	56.0
41	Fargo-Valley City	56.0
41	Des Moines-Ames	56.0
44	El Paso	56.1
45	Billings	56.4
46	Nashville	56.8
47	Portland, Ore.	57.3
47	Evansville	57.3
49	Sioux Falls (Mitchell)	57.7
49	Memphis	57.7

Top 50 MSOs

The following list ranks MSOs by number of basic subscribers as reported by the MSOs themselves. For more information on these and other MSOs, see *Multiple Systems Operators, Independent Owners & Cable Systems in the U.S. & Canada*, this section.

Rank	MSO	Total Basic Subscribers
1	Tele-Communications Inc.	10,200,000
2	Time Warner Cable	7,100,000
3	Continental Cablevision Inc.	2,900,000
4	Comcast Cable Communications	2,764,500
5	Cablevision Systems Corporation	1,979,209
6	Rogers Cablesystems Limited	1,843,892
7	Cox Cable Communications	1,764,562
8	Cablevision Industries Inc.	1,307,760
9	Jones Intercable Inc.	1,300,000
10	Adelphia Communications	1,238,022
11	Maclean Hunter Cable TV	1,234,261
12	Times Mirror Cable Television	1,183,587
13	Viacom Cable Inc.	1,081,700
14	Sammons Communications Inc.	1,025,000
15	Century Communications Corporation	907,000
16	Crown Media Inc.	835,399
17	Falcon Cable TV	794,000
18	Colony Communications Inc.	761,802
19	Scripps Howard Cable Co.	677,000
20	TeleCable Corporation	663,974
21	TKR Cable Co.	600,000
22	KBLCOM	571,000
23	InterMedia Partners	542,052
24	Prime Cable	526,552
25	Vision Cable Communications Inc.	506,000
26	Lenfest Group	482,262
27	MetroVision Inc.	480,930
28	Post-Newsweek Cable Inc.	479,000
29	Tele-Media Corporation of Delaware	443,688
30	TCA Cable TV Inc.	420,000
31	Multimedia Cablevision Inc.	401,370
32	NewChannels Corporation	391,000
33	Rifkin & Associates	360,000
34	Triax Communications Corporation	339,000
35	Western Communications	320,855
36	C-TEC Cable Systems Inc.	263,076
37	Columbia International Inc.	250,000
38	Hauser Communications Inc.	231,000
39	Harron Communications Corporation	224,322
40	Greater Media Inc.	224,000
41	GCTV (Georgia Cable TV & Communications)	219,526
42	Wometco Cable Corporation	215,580
43	Media General Inc.	215,000
44	MultiVision	211,800
45	Fanch Communications Inc.	200,000
46	US Cable Corporation	197,316
47	Garden State Cable TV	189,346
48	Armstrong Utilities Inc.	180,000
49	Simmons Communications Inc.	178,133
50	Sutton Capital Group	175,000

Section E
Satellites and Other Carriers

Table of Contents

Table of Contents	E-1
Satellite Owners and Operators	E-2
Satellite Guide to the Sky	E-3
Satellite Resale and Common Carriers	E-4
Direct Broadcast Satellites	E-9
Teleports	E-10
Microwave	E-12
Wireless Cable Operators	E-13
Multipoint Distribution Services	E-14
Multichannel Multipoint Distribution Services	E-17

Satellite Owners and Operators

AT&T. Box 752, 900 Rt. 202-206 N., Bedminster, N.J. 07921-0752. (908) 234-4000. FAX: (908) 234-7940. Ernie G. DeNigris, gen mgr, SKYNET Satellite Services & Telestar 4 Program, Rm. 4C114, (908) 234-8667; Paul F. Coffey, district mgr, SKYNET Transponder Services Product Management, Rm. 2A108, (908) 234-6265; Joan M. Byrnes, prod mgr, SKYNET Transponder Services, Ancillary Services, Rm. 2A112, (908) 234-7843.

New York 10007: 195 Broadway, 14th Fl., John J. Cappadona, natl acct mgr, (212) 335-8255; Jim Pantazis, branch sys mgr, (212) 387-5100.

Svcs provided on three AT&T-owned Telstar satellites & on Satcom K-2 satellite. AT&T's SKYNET C-band & Ku-band satellite svcs complement AT&T's terrestrial net svcs. SKYNET Digital Service offers C-band voice, data, image & video transmission. SKYNET Star Network Service offers Ku-band bcst or interactive data as well as video capabilities. SKYNET Transponder Service offers space segment capability on either a part-time or full-time basis. SKYNET Television Service links with SKYNET Transponder Service for end-to-end bcst, cable or closed-circuit TV transmission. SKYNET Video Conferencing Service packages any special video event in the U.S. or internationally.

COMSAT Corp. 6560 Rock Spring Rd., Bethesda, Md. 20817. (301) 214-3000. FAX: (301) 214-7100. Bruce L. Crockett, pres/CEO.

COMSAT Technology Services. 22300 Comsat Dr., Clarksburg, Md. 20871-9475. (301) 428-4704. FAX: (301) 540-6271. John Morris, actg pres/VP business planning & dev.

CSD specializes in the engrg & integration of systems & nets for the movement & mgmt of info. Telecommunications & info systems tech & svcs, to govt, coml & international customers.

COMSAT Video Enterprises Inc. 6560 Rock Spring Dr., Bethesda, Md. 20817. (301) 214-3000. FAX: (301) 214-7100. Charlie Lyons, pres/CEO; Robert Myer, VP opns.

Hotel entertainment svcs, videoconferencing, special events & satellite bcst distribution svcs.

COMSAT World Systems. 6560 Rock Spring Dr., Bethesda, Md. 20817. (301) 214-3000. FAX: (301) 214-7100. Betty C. Alewine, pres; Patricia Benton, VP/gen mgr; Joanne Tanner, dir bcst svc.

Through 19 INTELSAT satellites, COMSAT World Systems offers news, sports & entertainment customers analog & digital TV, newsgathering, business TV & digital audio distribution svcs that interconnect the U.S. with over 185 countries.

ENSR Corp. 3000 Richmond Ave., Houston 77098. (713) 520-9900. FAX: (713) 520-6802. Robert Zoch, pres; Dick Brown, exec VP.

GE American Communications Inc. 4 Research Way, Princeton, N.J. 08540. (609) 987-4000. FAX: (609) 987-4440. John F. Connelly, chmn/CEO; Walter Braun, sr VP govt/tech opns; John C. DiMarco, VP financial opns.

Owns & operates the SATCOM domestic satellite system which offers video, audio, voice & data transmission svcs to business, govt & electronic media. Seven SATCOM satellites serve cable TV programmers, radio nets, TV bcstrs, wire svcs, syndicated bcstrs & international/occasional video/audio users.

Satcom C-5 carries the company's Digital Audio Transmission Service (DATS) for radio net prog distribution & transmission svcs for occasional TV. Satcom C-5 also carries long distance telephone traf for Alascom Inc. & provides data & video distribution for the govt. Satcom IIR is used for govt video data & occasional TV svcs. Satcom C-1, C-3 & C-4 carry cable TV progmg. Two 45-watt Ku-band satellites, designated Satcom K-1 & K-2, were launched in 1986. K-2 is the bcst satellite with NBC & syndicated TV svc downlinking to more than 700 antennas. K-1 is used for video, VSAT/business svc. GE Americom will launch a new hybrid satellite, GE-1, early in 1996. GE-1 will serve bcst, cable, educ, govt & private business.

GTE Spacenet Corp. (A wholly-owned subsidiary of GTE Corp.) 1700 Old Meadow Rd., McLean, Va. 22102. (703) 848-1000. FAX: (703) 848-0004; (703) 848-0005. Howard Svigals, pres.

Supplies telecommunications svcs & systems to business, news organizations & govt agencies across the U.S. & around the globe. GTE Spacenet operates a multisatellite system offering both C- & Ku-band transmission svcs. These include analog & digital video, audio, voice & data to a var of customers such as specialized common carriers & resellers, cable & TV bcstrs, govt agencies, educ institutions, business users, corporations & international entities. Affiliated satellite company was founded in 1972, with GTE Spacenet incorporated in 1983. Special GTE Spacenet svcs include News Express℠, for satellite news gathering, & Skystar Network Services, for interactive & bcst point-to-point or point-to-multipoint data communications applications, & Skystar® Television. Full-time transponders are dedicated seven days a week, 24 hours a day. Partial or fractional transponder svcs provide bandwidth & power options for customers with lesser volume requirements. Occasional use allows the scheduling of time increments as brief as five minutes for news event coverage, news exchange, pay-per-view progmg, videoconferencing & other regular distribution.

Global Access Telecommunications Services. 101 Federal St., Suite 1900, Boston 02110. (617) 423-3274. Jack Morse, pres.

Hughes Communications Inc. Box 92424, El Segundo, Calif. 90245. (310) 607-4000. FAX: (310) 607-4065. Stephen J. Petrucci, pres/CEO; Fred L. Judge, sr VP/COO; Eddy W. Hartenstein, sr VP; Jerald F. Farrell, sr VP; Floyd Stewart, VP opns.

Provides satellites for cable, TV & radio distribution; video time-sharing, videoconferencing, satellite news gathering, business TV & very small aperture terminal business nets. Medium-power direct-to-home TV systems.

International Telecommunications Satellite Organization (INTELSAT). 3400 International Dr. N.W., Washington 20008-3098. (202) 944-6800. FAX: (202) 944-7890. TELEX: (WUI) 64290; (WUT) 89-2707. Irving Goldstein, dir gen/CEO; John Hampton, exec VP/COO; David T. Tudge, VP/CFO; Edith W. Martin, VP/chief info off; Pierre Madon, VP engrg/rsch; Francis Latapie, dir international rel; Tony A. Trujillo Jr., mgr public/external rel; Arnie Meyers, mgr bcst svcs.

INTELSAT is an international coml, not-for-profit cooperative of 126 member nations that owns & operates the global communications satellite system used worldwide by countries for their international & domestic communications.

The INTELSTAT system is a major provider of transoceanic, rgnl & domestic telephone & TV svcs. It also offers, via its 19 satellite global system, business svcs such as international video, teleconferencing, facsimile, data & telex.

Mobile Communications. (A subsidiary of Bell South.) 25 Rockwood Pl., Englewood, N.J. 07631. (201) 894-8000. FAX: (201) 871-3469. Steve Pazian, pres; Tom Eberle, gen mgr.

Holds construction permit for DBS satellite; has radio paging business, two cellular telephone partnerships and serves the corporate syndicate communications needs of the country's investment banking community.

PanAmSat. One Pickwick Plaza, Suite 270, Greenwich, Conn. 06830. (203) 622-6664. FAX: (203) 622-9163. Rene Anselmo, chmn/CEO; Fred Landman, pres/COO; Mike Antonovich, VP bcst svcs; Guy Lanni, VP digital net svcs.

Owns transoceanic international satellite which provides bcstg, business communications & telephony into or within Europe, North America, South America & the Caribbean.

Telesat Canada. 1601 Telesat Ct., Gloucester, Ont., Canada K1B 5P4. (613) 748-0123. Laurier J. Boisvert, pres/COO; F. Bartlett, VP finance/administration & treas; G. Fraser, VP net svcs; J. Perkins, sec/gen counsel; L. Stass, VP space systems; S.B. Turner, VP sls/mktg; D. Weese, VP engrg.

Communications via satellite, consulting, satellite earth stn nets.

Satellite Guide to the Sky

Carrier Satellite	[1]C-band	Ku-band	Approximate end-of-life	Orbital slot[2]
AT&T				
Telestar 301	24	–	Nov. 1993	96
Telestar 302	24	–	Sept. 1994	85
Telestar 303	24	–	April 1995	123*
GE Americom				
Satcom C-1	24	–	Nov. 2000	137
Satcom II-R	24	–	Jan. 1995	72
Satcom C-3	24	–	Sept. 2004	131
Satcom C-4	24	–	Aug. 2004	135
Satcom C-5	24	–	Jan. 2001	139
Satcom K-1	–	16	Dec. 1996	85
Satcom K-2	–	16	April 1997	81
GTE Spacenet[3]				
Spacenet II	18	6	Nov. 1994	69
Spacenet III	18	6	March 1998	87
Spacenet IV	18	6	April 2001	101
GStar I	–	16	May 1995	103
GStar II	–	16	March 1996	125
GStar III	–	16	Sept. 1994	93
GStar IV	–	16	Nov. 2002	105
ASC I	18	6	Aug. 1995	128
Hughes Communications				
Galaxy I	24	–	June 1993	133
Galaxy II	24	–	Sept. 1993	74
Galaxy III	24	–	Sept. 1994	93.5
Galaxy IV	24	24	Scheduled for June '93 launch	93
Galaxy V	24	–	March 2002	125
Galaxy VI	24	–	Nov. 2000	99
Galaxy VII	24	24	2005	91
SBS 5	–	14	Sept. 1998	123
SBS 6	–	19	Nov. 2000	99

[1] C-band and Ku-band columns indicate numbers of transponders on each satellite. End-of-life estimates are based on launch date plus average 10 years, although several of the newer satellites are built to last 12 years.

[2] Orbital slots are in degrees west longitude.

[3] GTE and Contel merged in March 1991. Contel ASC's second satellite, ASC II, was renamed Spacenet IV.

* 125 prior to June 1992.

Satellite Resale and Common Carriers

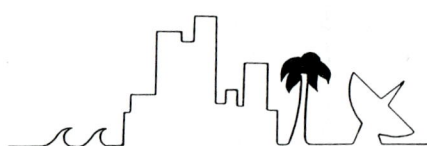

VISION ACCOMPLISHED INC.

AT&T. Rts. 202 & 206, Room 2A115M, Bedminster, N.J. 07921. (908) 234-7546. T. Corus, prod mgr.
Full- & part-time inter-exchange common carrier terrestrial facilities used in the transmission of coml, educ & CATV bcsts.

Alascom Inc. (A wholly-owned subsidiary of Pacific Telecom Inc.) Box 196607, Anchorage 99519-6607. (907) 264-7000. FAX: (907) 274-5029. C.E. Robinson, pres/CEO; John Ayers, exec VP/gen mgr; C.L. Wareham, VP opns; R.R. Ownbey, VP sls & mktg; J. Gore, VP admin.
Telecommunications, long-distance telephone carrier for the state of Alaska offering bcst, voice, data, WATS, Alaskanet & dedicated private line long-distance svcs.

Alpha Lyracom Space Communications Inc. One Pickwick Plaza, Suite 270, Greenwich, Conn. 06830. (203) 622-6664. FAX: (203) 622-9163.

BAF Communications Corp. 316 Northstar Ct., Sanford, Fla. 32771. (407) 324-8250; (800) 633-8223. Charles G. Angelakis, pres/CEO; Bob King, VP sls & mktg; James Vautrot, gen mgr satellite svcs.
Manufactures mobile Ku- & C-band satellite uplinks. Broker of satellite transponder time for Ku- & C-band users, including bcst news organizations & private nets.

British Aerospace Communications Defense Ltd.—BAe COM. (Dynamics Division). Box 19, Six Hills Way, Stevenage, Hertford, England SG1 2DA. 0438 312422. David Layboum, mgng dir.
Satellite svcs company providing data bcst, business TV, international VSAT nets & unlink facilities.

Channel America Television Networks. 19 W. 21st St., New York, 10010. (212) 366-9880. FAX: (212) 366-9890. David A. Post, CEO/vice chmn.
24-hour-a-day bcst TV net; provides classic movies, sports, syndicated comedy & drama, & first-run progs.

Communications III. 1201 Olentangy River Rd., Columbus, Ohio 43212. (614) 294-4445. FAX: (614) 297-1616. Scott Halliday, pres.
Common carrier/C-band uplink svcs. Video conferencing, business communicative, coml & prog prod facilities. Full soundstages, three on-line & off-line edit suites.

Continental Satellite Corp. 402 Nevada Hwy., Boulder City, Nev. 89005. (805) 822-6971. FAX: (805) 822-4981. James H. Schollard, CEO; William P. Welty, pres.
Info intermediators offering 130+ w DBS transponders in half-CONUS svc starting second quarter 1996 (anticipated). Ground system anticipated in central Utah.

Conus Communications Inc. 3415 University Ave., Minneapolis 55414. (612) 642-4645. FAX: (612) 642-4680. Charles H. Dutcher III, VP/gen mgr; Tim Rudell, VP/bureau chief Conus Washington; Ray Conover, VP/dir engrg.
Satellite News Gathering (SNG), news feeds, complete satellite svcs & transponder booking.

Crawford Satellite Services. 535 Plasamour Dr., Atlanta 30324. (404) 876-7149. FAX: (404) 876-8956. Jesse Crawford, own/pres; Candy Alger, VP.
Teleport C- & Ku-band, satellite networking, spec event bcstg, ad-hoc teleconferencing, news feeds, private networking, satellite time, prog distribution, transportable uplink & postprod svcs.

Cycle Sat Inc. 119 John K. Hanson Dr., Forest City, Iowa 50436. (800) 622-1865. FAX: (515) 582-6998. Loren A. Swenson, pres; Joycelyn Steil, exec VP; Tom O. Mikkelsen, dir opns; Mark Cooper, mgr prod svcs.
F/T K2 lease, time available. Two SNV units. C- & Ku-band earth stns, turnaround. Complete prod facility; multi-format duplication.

The Family Channel. (A subsidiary of International Family Entertainment Inc. "NYSE FAM".) 1000 Centerville Tpke., Virginia Beach, Va. 23463. (804) 523-7301. FAX: (804) 532-7880. Tim Robertson, pres; Rick Busciglio, VP mktg; Paul Krimsier, VP progmg; Steve Lentz, VP natl sls; Larry Dantzler, CFO; Craig Sherwood, VP affil rel.
Produces original comedies, adventures, dramatic series & movies. 56 million subs.

GE American Communications Inc. 4 Research Way, Princeton, N.J. 08540. (609) 987-4000. FAX: (609) 987-4517. John F. Connelly, chmn/CEO; Walter H. Braun, sr VP/gen mgr govt & tech opns; John C. DiMarco, VP financial opns.
Provides svc to both coml & govt customers through its fleet of Satcom satellites.

GTE Spacenet Corp. 1700 Old Meadow Rd., McLean, Va. 22102. (703) 848-1000. FAX: (703) 848-0004; (703) 848-0005. Harry Mahon, dir bcst svcs.
Comprehensive range of satellite-based communication svcs. Satellite news gathering svcs & complete satellite bcst svcs.

Global Access Telecommunications Services. 205 Portland St., Boston 01224. (617) 367-0500. FAX: (617) 720-0803. Jack Morse, VP/gen mgr; Dick King, natl sls mgr; Scott Lenahan, mgr opns; Fred Healy, Karla Silas, Tim Smith, Kathy Sohar, opns coords; Carol McGrath, mgr syndication svcs; Jessica Lynn, syndication coord; Mary Beth Karr, business mgr.
Washington: Susan Cecala, rgnl mgr.
Kansas City, Mo.: Bud Turner, rgnl mgr.
Los Angeles: Carol Tucker, rgnl mgr.
Transmission svcs provider—fiber optics & satellite. All fiber carriers (all transmission rates) & all domestic satellites, both C-Band & Ku band. Prog syndication distribution svcs, news & sports distribution & full video conference coordination. Teleports available in Kansas City & Birmingham.

Group W Satellite Communications. 250 Harbor Dr., Stamford, Conn. 06904. (203) 965-6388. FAX: (203) 965-6320. Don Mitzner, pres; Altan C. Stalker, VP/gen mgr; James Crowe, exec dir opns; Peter A. Concelmo, dir sls & mktg; Cheryl Daly, VP pub rels.
C- & Ku-band domestic & international transmission svc; connectivity to metro New York via microwave/fiber cable origination, bcst, business TV, transponder availability, studios & postprod.

COMMITMENT TO QUALITY AND SERVICE
30 years of experience
Satellite/Videotape Distribution
Standards Conversion
Video Duplication
Film to Tape Transfers

GROUP W VIDEOSERVICES

Ted Barajas, (800) 245-4463
310 Parkway View Dr., Pittsburgh, PA 15205
Lee Salas, (213) 850-3851
3801 Barham Blvd., Suite 200, Los Angeles, CA 90068

Group W Video Services. 310 Parkway Dr., Pittsburgh, Pa. 15205. (412) 747-4726. FAX: (412) 747-4726. Ted Barajas, VP/gen mgr; Lee R. Salas, natl sls mgr (213) 850-3851.
Satellite & syndication servicing; international standards conversion.

Home Shopping Network. Box 9090, Clearwater, Fla. 34618-9090. (813) 572-8585. FAX: (813) 572-8585, ext. 4103. Robert Bennett, chmn of bd; Gerry Hogan, pres/CEO; Todd Cralley, VP bcst affil; Scott Cooper, sr VP tech svcs.
Svcs include C- & Ku-band transmissions from Tampa, C-band transmissions from New York and Los Angeles, & postprod.

Hughes Communications Inc. (HCI). Box 92424, Los Angeles 90009. (310) 607-4511. FAX: (310) 607-4065. Stephen J. Petrucci, pres/CEO; Eddy W. Hartenstein, pres DirecTv Inc.; Fred L. Judge, sr VP/COO; Jerald F. Farrell, sr VP Galaxy Satellite Svcs; Kevin N. McGrath, sr VP/CFO.
Satellite nets providing video, voice & data communications svcs, domestic & international.

IDB Communications Group Inc. 10525 W. Washington Blvd., Culver City, Calif. 90232. (213) 870-9000. FAX: (213) 240-3901. Jeffrey P. Sudikoff, chmn/CEO; Edward R. Cheramy, pres; Peter F. Hartz, sr VP sls & mktg; Dave Anderson, VP opns.
Transmission & distribution svcs for domestic & international radio, TV & data/voice communications. IDB's svcs include Hughes Television Network's TV sports transmissions & digital compression svcs. IDB is the largest U.S. reseller of satellite time. Facilities include IDB's teleports in Los Angeles, New York & Houston, The Sports Satellite Interconnect uplink net, transcontinental & oceanic fiber, "flyway" earth stns in the U.S. & extensive international links. Svcs include those for net, news, syndicated & spec event progmg, plus teleconferencing, phone & fax support svcs.

INET Communications Corp. 950 Office Park Rd., Suite 308, W. Des Moines, Iowa 50265-2548. (515) 222-0725. Art Hutzler, pres.
Long-distance telephone.

Integrity Communications. 6360-1 E. Thomas Rd., Suite 318, Scottsdale, Ariz. 85251. (602) 955-5700. FAX: (602) 955-1454. Doug Meece, pres/CEO; Peggy Rowe, VP media; Eugene A. Sauder, VP finance.
Full-svc agency including media scheduling & buying, stn coordination, videotape duplication & shipping, satellite transmission & transponder time, & full prod svcs.

KEYSTONE COMMUNICATIONS
C- and Ku-Band Space Segment
C- and Ku-Band Uplink
Studios in L.A. and D.C.
1-800-752-8469

Keystone Communications. 303 E. South Temple St., Salt Lake City 84111-1226. (801) 322-4400. FAX: (801) 531-7375. TELEX: 910-925-4069. David E. Simmons, chmn/CEO; Peter Marshall, pres; Barry McCann, VP natl division; Bret Leifson, CFO; Gary Horrocks, VP engrg; Blaine Colton, sr VP Network Services Group; Douglas Jessop, dir mktg.
Keystone Communications provides end-to-end video bcst & transmission svcs through its own net of origination facilities, fiber-optic & microwave sys-

INTERNATIONAL SATELLITE DIRECTORY

THE COMPLETE GUIDE TO THE SATELLITE COMMUNICATIONS INDUSTRY

Over 1,200 page Directory covering 380 satellites, 5,000 companies, their products and services - In fact over 25,000 entries. The 1994 all new 9th edition is organized so that you can reference any subject, company, name, address, product or service in Satellite Communications in seconds!

Inside the Directory you'll find -

INTERNATIONAL ORGANIZATIONS. Government Regulators and Administrators worldwide; all the PTT's - every contact you'd need to set up satellite communications with details on video standards, electrical systems used etc.

SATELLITE OPERATORS. Intelsat, Inmarsat, Intersputnik, Arabsat, Aussat, Eutelsat etc. Extensive information on Regional, Domestic and Planned satellite systems. Every Satellite Operator worldwide is covered in detail.

SPACECRAFT. Manufacturers and a detailed description of rockets & launch vehicles, launch schedules 1994-1997.

MANUFACTURERS . Manufacturers of satellites & satellite components. Ground transmit & receive equipment; Consumer systems; DBS and Commercial systems; VSAT's etc. - in fact complete coverage of all manufacturers worldwide.

GPS & MOBILE SYSTEMS. Satellite Positioning & Tracking systems, Mobile telephones, Data and voice systems, Transportable Uplinks and other mobile equipment.

UPLINK EARTH STATIONS. Details on most International and most US domestic earth stations including capabilities, interconnectivity, which satellites they access and contact information.

NETWORK SYSTEMS. Integrated satellite systems, System Integrators, Corporate networks & VSAT users, VSAT System Managers & Operators, Videoconferencing & Teleconferencing networks.

USERS OF SATELLITE SERVICES. Satellite Programmers; Broadcasters (Radio & TV); Educational & Religious Programmers, Complete world transponder listings of TV & Radio programs; Videotex; Major Cable Companies.

PROVIDERS OF SATELLITE SERVICES. Distributors, Common Carriers; Transponder Brokers; Transmission and Downlink Services & Teleports.

GENERAL SERVICES. Technical and Consulting Services; Installation and Maintenance Services; Associations; Legal, Licensing and Insurance Services; Research, Educational and Technical Centers; Publishers and Publications; Financial Institutions.

GEOSYNCHRONOUS SATELLITES. Information such as Location, Prime Contractors, Owner/Operator, Operating Frequencies, Number & Type of Transponders, Polarization, TWTA/SSPA Power etc. is included in this exceedingly informative chapter. There are over 350 pages of information with maps showing the EIRP, G/T & SFD of satellites worldwide.

INDEX, BUYERS GUIDE & GENERAL INFORMATION. - A very comprehensive glossary of satellite terms, statistics and an extensive index cross referenced by all the thousands of companies that are detailed in the Directory & a helpful and exhaustive product cross reference guide.

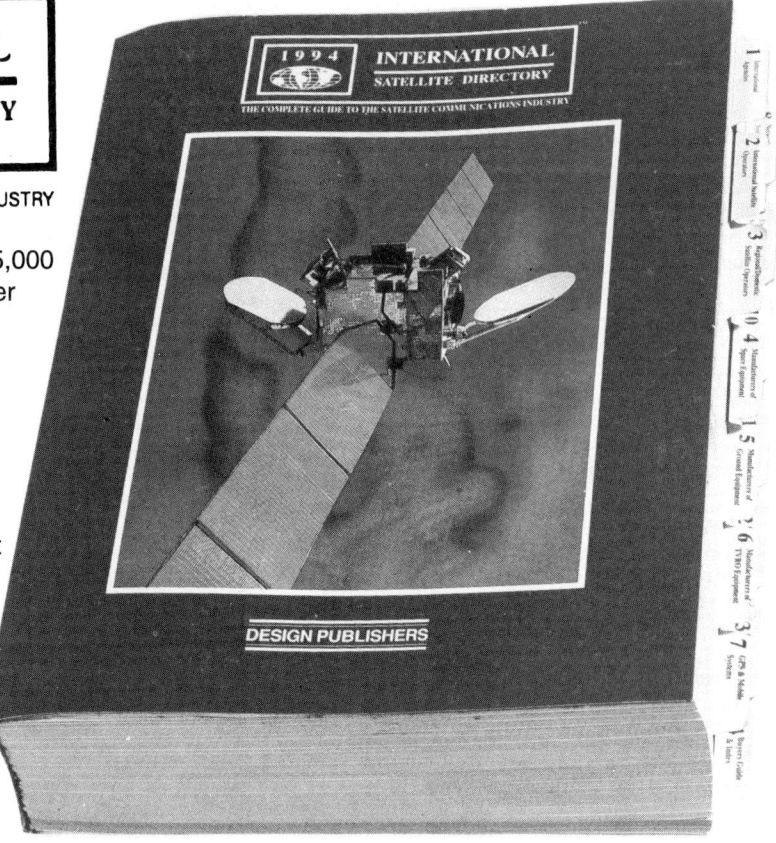

YES! Please send me more details:

Name:_____
Company:_____
Address:_____
_____
_____

DESIGN PUBLISHERS
800 Siesta Way • Sonoma
CA 95476 • USA
Tel: (707) 939-9306
Fax: (707) 939-9235

Satellite Resale and Common Carriers

tems, switching centers, teleports & satellite transponders. Keystone Communications owns & operates C- & Ku-band facilities in New York; Los Angeles; Washington, D.C.; San Diego; and Salt Lake City. Keystone's Washington, D.C., facility, complete with studio, is just blocks from Capitol Hill. Keystone's Los Angeles facility offers studio, editing & tape playback svcs. Keystone also publishes a bimonthly reference guide, *The Keystone Communications North American Satellite Guide©*, an up-to-date, easy to understand guide to video traffic on North American satellites.

Keystone Communications. 6430 Sunset Blvd., Suite 1400, Los Angeles 90028. (213) 467-8900. FAX: (213) 465-8750. Charles A. Fedorko Jr., VP/gen mgr western rgn; Keith Buckley, dir sls, western rgn; Gene Deck; chief engr; Craig Rees, studio mgr; Matthew Hutchings, dir international business dev; Teresa Botello, mgr administration.

The Los Angeles office is home to Keystone's unique 24-hour Network Control Center where both domestic & international satellite transmissions are coordinated & monitored. In addition to both C- & Ku-band uplink & downlink svcs, Keystone's Los Angeles facility also offers studio, editing & tape playback svcs. Los Angeles is home to Keystone's Standard "A" Intelsat earth stn for optimum coverage of the Pacific Rim. Keystone's Los Angeles facility also serves as the main gateway for K2 Skylink, the first full-time circuit for occasional video between Asia & North America.

Keystone Communications provides end-to-end video bcst & transmission svcs through its own net of origination facilities, fiber-optic & microwave systems, switching centers, teleports & satellite transponders. Keystone Communications owns & operates facilities in New York; Los Angeles; Washington, D.C.; San Diego; & Salt Lake City.

Keystone Communications. 400 North Capitol N.W., Suite 177, Washington 20001. (202) 737-4440. FAX: (202) 783-5166. Peter Marshall, pres; Harley Shuler, VP/gen mgr eastern rgn; John Turell, dir sls D.C.

Just one block from the U.S. Capitol Building, Keystone's Washington, D.C., facility offers "one stop" satellite svcs. A three-camera studio is directly tied to uplinking & space segment for media tours & newscasts. Keystone also offers a rooftop shot with the Capitol Building in the background. Full-time transmit boxes also operate on the Senate & House sites.

Keystone Communications provides end-to-end video bcst & transmission svcs through its own net of origination facilities, fiber-optic & microwave systems, switching centers, teleports & satellite transponders. Keystone Communications owns & operates C- & Ku-band facilities in New York; Los Angeles; Washington, D.C.; San Diego; & Salt Lake City.

Keystone Communications. 45 W. 45th St., Suite 905, New York, 10036. (212) 869-4575. FAX: (212) 921-0301. Russell Bittner, sls dir N.Y.; Steve Ludwig, opns mgr N.Y.

Keystone's New York Technical Operating Center, on the 82nd floor of the Empire State Building, offers connectivity to all major venues in the tri-state area. Access to INTELSAT K & PanAmSat for feeds to Europe & South America. C- to Ku-band & Ku- to C-band turnarounds are available through Keystone's New York facility.

Keystone Communications provides end-to-end video bcst & transmission svcs through its own net of origination facilities, fiber-optic & microwave systems, switching centers, teleports, & satellite transponders. Keystone Communications owns & operates C- & Ku-band facilities in New York; Los Angeles; Washington, D.C.; San Diego; & Salt Lake City.

Keystone Communications. 9670 Aero Dr., San Diego 92123. (619) 569-8451. FAX: (619) 569-9248.

Keystone's San Diego facility is the only "one call" uplink & space segment provider in the San Diego area. With connectivity to major sports venues & mobile microwave, Keystone effectively blankets the five-county southern California area. San Diego is home to Keystone's "Mobile Link" Ku-band uplink/production truck.

Keystone Communications provides end-to-end video bcst & transmission svcs through its own net of origination facilities, fiber-optic & microwave systems, switching centers, teleports, & satellite transponders. Keystone Communications owns & operates C- & Ku-band facilities in New York; Los Angeles; Washington, D.C.; San Diego; and Salt Lake City.

Massachusetts Corp. for Educational Telecommunications (MCET). 38 Sidney St., Cambridge, Mass. 02139-4135. (617) 621-0290. FAX: (617) 621-0291. Dr. Inabeth Miller, exec dir; Linda DiRocco, dir educ progmg & net opns; Joseph Schabhetl, dir of engrg.

Operates the Mass LearnPike satellite bcst net providing 1,000 hours of live interactive progmg for K-12 & the Mass LearnNet computer net.

Michigan Information Technology Network (MITN). 4660 S. Hagadorn Rd., Suite 230, East Lansing, Mich. 48823. (517) 351-1100. FAX: (517) 336-1006. Brian Raymond, pres; Dave Fleig, dir telecommunications.

Five redundant Ku-band steerable uplinks (Detroit, Ann Arbor, East Lansing, Kalamazoo & Hougton) & one redundant Ku-band uplink/prod truck.

The Microband Companies Inc. 286 Eldridge Rd., Fairfield, N.J. 07004. (201) 808-3700. FAX: (201) 227-2612. J. Patrick Dugan, pres/CEO.

SNI is an ind common carrier providing satellite earth stn facilities & interconnection & loc distribution svcs for video & audio point-to-point or multi-point nets. SNI is a joint venture of Microband National System Inc., Satellite Network Services Inc., & Oak Industries.

Modern Telecommunications Inc. (MTI). 885 2nd Ave., Level C, New York 10017. (212) 355-0510. FAX: (212) 722-6505. William A. Dalessandro, pres.

New York 10029: 1443 Park Ave. (212) 722-1818. MTI TV City.

Prod & postprod svcs, including remotes, computer animation, scenic svcs, satellite transmissions & networking.

National Gateway Video. Box 420, 27 Randolph St., Carteret, N.J. 07008. (908) 969-3700. FAX: (908) 969-3983. Bill Kopacka, VP video/audio svcs.

Operates teleport facilities serving New York City. Videotape svcs; satellite transmission for the bcst, CATV & videoconferencing industries. International wideband voice, data & videoconferencing svcs overseas.

National Public Radio Satellite Services. 635 Massachusetts Ave. N.W., Washington 20001. (202) 414-2000. DeLano Lewis, pres; John Dingess, dir news & info; Peter J. Lowenstein, VP distribution.

Full-time wideband chs for stereo audio transmission & narrow-band chs for voice nets. Audio distribution via analog or digital transponders, ad-hoc nets including domestic & international back hauling, 20 uplinks & 30 downlinks, transportable uplinking facilities, troubleshooting & maintenance, engrg consulting & tech support, equipment leasing. Svcs provided to public radio & other noncoml & coml users.

Novanet Communications Ltd. 1340 Phillip Murray Ave., Oshawa, Ont., Canada L1J 6Z9. (905) 686-6666. FAX: (905) 723-0662. Randolph A. Zedic, pres; Michael S. Taylor, sr VP; Donald G. Witzel, natl sls mgr.

Provides info distribution svcs; audio svcs from 3.5 khz to 20 khz in analog or digital formats, also a line of data bcst offerings ranging in speed from 75 baud to T-1; & "Satpac," a packet-switched data net using receiver technology.

PanAmSat. One Pickwick Plaza, Suite 270, Greenwich, Ct. 06830. (203) 622-6664. FAX: (203) 622-9163. Rene Anselmo, chmn/CEO; Fred Landman, pres/COO; Mike Antonovich, VP bcstg svcs; Guy Lanni, VP digital net svcs.

Owners of transoceanic international satellite providing bcstg, business communications & telephony into or within Europe, North America, South America & the Carribean.

PROSTAR. 12831 Royal Dr., Stafford, Tex. 77477. (713) 240-2800. FAX: (713) 240-1447. John C. Parks, pres; D. Scott Hofmann, dir engrg; Brent Shannon, dir opns.

Provides satellite encryption systems for bus, entertainment & sports use.

PVS (Professional Video Services). 2030 M St. N.W., Washington 20036. (202) 775-0894. FAX: (202) 775-1288. Robert Grevemberg, pres; Steve Tello, VP/gen mgr.

TV & prod studios, multi-format edit suites, computer animation, graphics, Ku-band truck, Ku-band redundant flyaway. Capitol Hill studios, ImMIX non-linear editing.

Pacific Satellite Connection Inc. (PASCAT). 1121 L St., Suite 109, Sacramento, Calif. 95814. (916) 446-7890. FAX: (916) 446-7893. Steve Mallory, pres; Keith Feldkamp, opns mgr.

Provides transportable Ku-band uplinks & video prod for sports, news & corporate clients from opns in Los Angeles, Phoenix, Seattle & Sacramento.

Production & Satellite Services Inc. (PSSI). 11860 Mississippi Ave., Los Angeles, 90025. (310) 575-4400. FAX: (310) 575-4451. Robert C. Lamb, VP prod/opns; Charles P. Storlie, VP sls/engrg; Nancy M. Lurie, dir opns.

Ku-band transportable uplinks, domestic & international satellite transmission svcs, private net instal & maintenance, teleconferencing, video projection & prod svcs.

Pyramid Video Inc. 480 National Press Bldg., Washington 20045. (202) 783-5030. FAX: (202) 628-7228. Christopher Cates, pres; Nicola Frost, dir transmission svcs.

TV prod facilities include studios, editing & transmission facilities to Ku-band & C-band satellites. Interconnect to major news-gathering points in Washington at the National Press Bldg.

Ray Communications Inc. 179 Lovers Ln., Suite B, Elizabeth City, N.C. 27909. (919) 335-7294. FAX: (919) 335-2496. William S. Ray, pres; Gregory Gingery, VP; Scott Fortenberry, chief engr; Lisa Ray, sls.

24-hour turnkey C-band satellite transmission svc for radio news, sports, syndicated prog distribution, audio conferencing; transportable bcst studio/uplinks for remote bcsts & domestic back hauling; net coord svcs & space segment bookings available.

Satellite Resale and Common Carriers

Reuters Television/BrightStar. 1333 H St. N.W., Washington 20005. (202) 842-8410. FAX: (202) 898-1241. William J. Page, VP mktg/sls.
Operates international bcst center; 24-hour satellite, prod, engrg & news facilities; five edit suites, two studios & rooftop teleport.

Reuters Television International. International Ctr., Rockefeller Ctr., 630 5th Ave., Suite 700, New York 10111. (212) 698-4500. FAX: (212) 698-2367. Chris Travers, exec VP; Richard Frisch, corporate TV svcs.
Satellite svcs for news departments; satellite prod & communication departments handle satellite feed requirements from anywhere in the world. Satellite coords, video crews & major studios on six continents. Standards conversion.

Rose Telecom. 15 East Ave., Mount Carmel, Pa. 17851. (717) 339-0210. FAX: (215) 639-0211. Carmine D. Scicchitano III, pres; Paul "ACE" McCabe, dir engrg.
Offers international video & fdm links between the U.S., Europe & Mexico. Two 4.5-meter C-band transportable earth stns. Contract svc only. Parent company of Fire Fighter Productions, Ltd., specializing in live concerts for TV. Owner: Philadelphia Teleport Inc.

Satellite Network Systems Inc. 2375 University Ave. W., St. Paul, Minn. 55114. (612) 644-2200. FAX: (612) 644-8025. Paul R. Heinerscheid, pres/CEO; Edwin S. Van Hamm, exec VP; Susan S. Broadribb, mgr net svcs; Fred Hamilton, dir sls; Matt Barrett, engr.
Provides occasional & recurring time on a wide range of satellites. Provides prod & transmission svcs to international bcstrs. Installs & manages private TV nets for businesses & assns.

Southeast Agrinet/Sunstar Satellite. 3621 N.W. 10th St., Ocala, Fla. 34475. (904) 629-7400. Gary Cooper, pres.
Farm radio net; satellite audio uplinking svcs (Galaxy 2).

Southern Satellite Systems Inc. (A subsidiary of Liberty Media Corp.) 2232 Dell Range Blvd., Suite 209, Cheyenne, Wyo. 82009. (307) 771-3800. FAX: (307) 771-3819. Peter Barton, pres; Jody Kaveney, dir opns.
Satellite transmission.

SpaceCom Systems Inc. 3801 S. Sheridan Rd., Tulsa, Okla. 74145. (800) 950-6690; (918) 488-4800. FAX: (918) 488-4848. Al Stem, VP/gen mgr.
Provides high-quality satellite transmission svcs & space segment on C- & Ku-Band for point-to-multipoint applications including paging nets, bcst radio, audio tests, real estate, finance & many other info distribution markets.

Telemundo Network. 2470 W. 8th Ave., Hialeah, Fla. 33010. (305) 884-8200. FAX: (305) 884-4722. Joaquim Blaya, pres; Al Lewerenz, chief engr.
Prod capabilities & svcs. Uplink & video transmission. C- & Ku-band uplink & downlink. Ku-band transportable, mobile prod vehicles, studio facilities & editing. Fiber & microwave also available.

Teleport Chicago. (A service of MRC Telecommunications.) 275 N. Corporate Dr., Brookfield, Wis. 53045. (414) 792-9700. FAX: (414) 792-7717. Nancy Carey, pres; Michael J. Turnbull, gen sls mgr; Robert E. Rogers, VP opns & engrg; Jim Doherty, video traf mgr.
A full-svc teleport serving the upper Midwest via the MRC Telecommunications microwave & fiber-optic transmission system.

Tempo Satellite Inc. 5619 DTC Pkwy., Englewood, Colo. 80111-3000. (303) 267-5600. FAX: (303) 779-1228. John Malone, pres.
Satellite progmg.

Ti-In Network Inc. 1303 Marsh Ln., Carrollton, Tex. 75006. (800) 999-8446. FAX: (214) 716-5427. Roger J. Benavides, gen mgr; Robert Nelson, prog dir; John Erickson, natl sls mgr.
Ku-band distance learning, Ku transponder time, prog/prod svcs.

United Video Inc. 3801 S. Sheridan Rd., Tulsa, Okla. 74145. (918) 665-6690; (800) 331-4806. FAX: (918) 663-6228. Roy L. Bliss, pres; Jeff Treeman, COO; Dave Wheaton, CFO; Jerry Henshaw, VP science & technology; Mike Peyton, sr VP transmission svcs.
Ind satellite carrier serving CATV, SMATV, TVRO, & business-to-business audio & data. Distributes WGN, WPIX, KTVT, KTLA, & Prevue Network, the Electronic Program Guide & Cable SportsTracker.

VTC Satellite Network. (VTC Division of Starcom Television Services Inc.) 10523 Burbank Blvd., North Hollywood, Calif. 91601. (818) 753-3000. FAX: (818) 985-0614. Gary Worth, CEO; David Lister, VP/gen mgr; Jon Schwenzer, VP; Dolly Kerkes, satellite svcs mgr.

Satellite Resale and Common Carriers

New York 10017: One Dag Hammarskjold Plaza. (212) 207-9872. FAX: (212) 702-4810.

Satellite & videotape transfer/duplication svcs for syndicators, coml advertisers & producers of industrial progmg.

Vision Accomplished Inc. 550 Maulhardt Ave., Oxnard, Calif. 93030. (805) 981-8740. FAX: (805) 981-8738. Kimithy Vaughan, mgng dir.

12 transportable & satellite transmission facilities (video, audio, voice, data). Flypack prod & SNG svcs.

Vision Communications Inc. (A subsidiary of WTVS/Detroit Public Television.) 7441 2nd Blvd., Detroit 48202. (313) 873-7200. FAX: (313) 876-8118. Robert Larson, pres/gen mgr.

Provides uplinks & downlinks. Complete prod, videoconferencing & postprod facilities.

Vyvx Inc. 111 E. 1st St., Tulsa, Okla. 74103-2808. (800) 324-8686. FAX: (918) 588-5761. Del Bothof, pres; Jim Trecek, VP sls; Howard Meiseles, VP engrg; Indra Paul, VP opns.

Full-motion, bcst-quality, switched DS-3 TV & video net. One-way & two-way occasional & dedicated transmission for all types of TV progmg & business TV/video conferencing.

WHYY Inc. Independence Mall W., 150 N. 6th St., Philadelphia 19106. (215) 351-1200. FAX: (215) 351-0398. Rick Breitenfield, pres; David Othmer, VP/stn mgr; William Weber, VP tech/engrg administration; Nessa Forman, VP communications.

Occasional video, encryption svcs, & transponder time available. Interconnect with Telco, & on-site prod facilities & teleconferencing. Ku-band transportable earth stn available. C- or Ku-band uplinking.

WRS Channel One Ltd. 1000 Napor Blvd., Pittsburgh, 15205. (412) 937-7700. FAX: (412) 922-1020. F. Jack Napor, pres; Edward Janow, VP/gen mgr; Greg Thomas, VP admin svcs.

Videotape & satellite distribution svc; satellite transponder time, uplinking & downlinking. Tape duplication in all formats.

WTVS(TV). 7441 2nd Blvd., Detroit 48202. (313) 876-8104; (313) 876-8110. FAX: (313) 876-8118. Dr. Robert F. Larson, pres/gen mgr; Daniel Alpert, sr VP/asst gen mgr; Ron Herman, dir enterprises.

Offers C- & Ku-band uplinking to any satellite; uplink, downlink, prod, postprod & teleconference svcs available.

Wold International Inc. 3440 Motor Ave., Suite 200, Los Angeles 90034. (310) 842-6900. FAX: (310) 842-6903. TELEX: 49609810. Robert E. Wold, pres/CEO; Richard H. Caldwell, exec VP; Irene M. Escardo, Latin American affrs; Julian Chan, Chinese affrs; Edilberto G. Sarango, controller; Mayumi Austin, Kathleen Laundy, Carol Granlund, Christopher Maes, Jessica Payne, Sean Sullivan, William Wilson, Peter Wold, opns mgmt team.

Worldwide prog transmission, booking & monitoring for international bcstrs, utilizing international video carriers. Provides 24-hour PBC & Net Control Center.

World Satellite Network. 821 Marquette Ave., Suite 700, Minneapolis 55402. (612) 339-9018; (800) 367-3193. FAX: (612) 371-8218. Jeffrey Maxwell, pres; Steve Porter, VP mktg.

Full-svc provider (progmg, brokerage, seminars, publishing, consulting, tradeshows) to private cable/wireless cable industry.

Direct Broadcast Satellites

Access America D.B.N. 3200 Chartres St., New Orleans 70117. (504) 942-9200. FAX: (504) 942-9204. Barbara Lamont, pres; Herb Devlin, dir mktg; Shaun Scott, account exec.

A direct-to-home medium power DBS svc. Unscrambled, free svc for advertisers, corporate & personal video messages, & prog distribution. Business-to-business progs, long-distance learning, mini-nets, classic movies, bilingual spots & other progs. Reaches all of North & Central America & the Caribbean.

Advance Inc. (Computer System Immigration.) 2200 Wilson Blvd., Suite 700, Arlington, Va. 22201. (703) 358-9100. FAX: (703) 358-9199 Dennis J. Brownlee, pres.

Satellite net designs & implementation; ADP engrg.

Canadian Satellite Communications Inc. (CANCOM). 50 Burnhamthorpe Rd. W., 10th Fl., Mississauga, Ont., Canada L5B 3C2. (416) 272-4960. FAX: (416) 272-3399. Sheelagh Whittaker, pres/CEO; Claude Lewis, exec VP.

Full-time user of satellite capacity for the extension of TV & radio bcst svcs to individual homes & cable users.

Child of God Broadcasting Network. (A division of Holy Bible Gospel Ministry.) 429 Cliffside, Houston 77076. Lawrence Herbst, pres.

Continental Satellite Corp. 402 Nevada Hwy., Boulder City, Nev. 89005. (805) 822-6971. FAX: (805) 822-4981. James H. Schollard, CEO; William P. Welty, pres. FCC counsel: Brinig & Bernstein, (202) 331-7050.

DBS licensee for svc on 11 transponders. Anticipates second-quarter 1996 launch of constellation of four DBS spacecraft to operate 130+ w transponders in the Ku-band. Vendor: INTRASPACE Corp. of North Salt Lake City, Utah.

Direct Broadcasting Satellite Corp. 4401-A Connecticut Ave. N.W., Suite 400, Washington 20008. Harley W. Radin, chmn/CEO; Charles A. Kase, corporate sec.

DBS system providing leased transponders for use with small home receiving antennas (15 to 24 inches diameter). Satellites planned for launch in 1994. System ideal for HDTV & incorporates capability for rgnl progmg.

DirecTv Inc. (A subsidiary of Hughes Communications Inc., a unit of GM Hughes Electronics.) Box 92424, Los Angeles 90245. (310) 535-5000. Eddy Hartenstein, pres; Bill Butterworth, Jim Ramo, sr VPs; Steve Ste. Marie, VP sls /mktg; Thomas Bracken, mgr communications.

DirecTv™ is a high-power DBS progmg distribution svc that delivers approximately 150 chs of digital entertainment & informational progmg to 18-inch satellite dishes.

Dominion Video Satellite Inc. 5551 Ridgewood Dr., Suite 505, Naples, Fla. 33963. (813) 597-3320. FAX: (813) 597-6478. Robert W. Johnson, chmn/CEO; Allen Rundle, pres/COO; Pelle Karlsson, VP; Charles Duke, dir; Clinton Schultz, VP; Randall Swanson, gen counsel.

High-power DBS permittee. Provides educ, family, childrens, religious progmg to 18-inch antennas.

GBI/Gear Broadcasting International Inc. Box 23172, Weybosset St., Providence, R.I. 02903. (401) 331-6072; (401) 274-5121. News office: 94 Calverly St., Providence, R.I. 02908. Edward R. Robalisky, chmn/pres; Jack G. Thayer, exec VP; G.A. Rainone, VP finance; Noel Howard, VP engrg.

Gear Syndicated Program Services: *Classic Rock Revue, News This Week, News Pondering* commentaries, *Magazine Reports on Radio, Sports Broadcast Capsule, Government Information Update,* holiday mus progs, *GBI on Entertainment, Gear Science & Technology.*

The SuperNetwork GBI provides news, talk, sports & entertainment progmg to wireless cable operators (MMDS), TVRO operators & radio stns in a delivered simulcasted format. Satellite: GTE Spacenet II.

Primestar Partners. 100 N. Presidential Blvd., 4th Fl., Bala Cynwyd, Pa. 19004. (215) 660-6100. FAX: (215) 660-6112. John Cusick, pres/CEO; David Beddow, exec VP/COO.

Ten-ch mid-power Ku-band.

United States Satellite Broadcasting Co. Inc. 3415 University Ave., St. Paul, Minn. 55114. (612) 645-4500. FAX: (612) 642-4578. Stanley S. Hubbard, pres/CEO; Stanley E. Hubbard, pres/COO; Rob Hubbard, exec VP; Jim Blake, Ralph Dolan, VPs.

DBS svcs: direct-to-home delivery of video (primary svc), audio & data (secondary svc).

WorldSpace Inc. 1730 Rhode Island Ave. N.W., Washington 20036. (202) 408-8071. FAX: (202) 408-5292. Noah A. Samara, pres; Wilbur Pritchard, chief tech off; Eyob Samara, CFO.

Satellite sound radio bcstg.

Teleports

C- and Ku-Band Space Segment
C- and Ku-Band Uplink
Studios in L.A. and D.C.
1-800-752-8469

Los Angeles—Keystone Communications. 6430 Sunset Blvd., Suite 1400, Los Angeles 90028. (213) 467-8900. FAX: (213) 465-8750. Charles Fedorko, VP/gen mgr western rgn; Keith Buckley, dir sls western rgn; Gene Deck, chief engr; Craig Rees, studio mgr.

The Los Angeles office is home to Keystone's unique 24-hour Network Control Center where both domestic & international satellite transmissions are coordinated & monitored. In addition to both C-band & Ku-band uplink & downlink svcs, Keystone's Los Angeles facility also offers studio, editing & tape playback svcs. Los Angeles is home to Keystone's Standard "A" Intelsat earth stn for optimum coverage of the Pacific Rim. Keystone's Los Angeles facility also serves as the main gateway for K2 Skylink, the first full-time circuit for occasional video between Asia & North America.

Keystone Communications provides end-to-end video bcst & transmission svcs through its own network of origination facilities, fiber-optic & microwave systems, switching centers, teleports & satellite transponders. Keystone Communications owns & operates facilities in New York; Los Angeles; Washington, D.C.; San Diego; and Salt Lake City.

Los Angeles—IDB Communications Group Inc. 10525 W. Washington Blvd., Culver City, Calif. 90232. (213) 870-9000. FAX: Sales (213) 240-3901. Jeffrey Sudikoff, chmn/CEO; John Tagliaferro, pres IDB Broadcast; Howard Miller, VP/gen mgr IDB Broadcast; Phil McInnes, exec VP IDB Broadcast-International Sls.

IDB's Los Angeles International Teleport offers on-line, Ku- & C-band satellite transmission svcs for audio, video & data/voice. Domestically & internationally; uplink & downlink capabilities, microwave & fiber-optic connectivity; full fleet of "fly-away" earth stations.

San Diego—Keystone Communications. 9670 Aero Dr., San Diego 92123. (619) 569-8451. FAX: (619) 569-9248. David Simmons, pres.

Uplink & space segment provider. Connectivity to major sports venues & mobile microwave. San Diego is home to Keystone's "Mobile Link" Ku-band uplink/production truck.

San Francisco—Bay Area Teleport. 1141 Harbor Bay Pkwy., Suite 260, Alameda, Calif. 94501. (800) 621-5003; (415) 769-5300. FAX: (510) 769-5737. Michael Bacich, exec pres/gen mgr; Steve Bowen, gen counsel.

Alternative Access Carrier. Bay Area Teleport provides communications svcs at DS0, T1 or T3 levels for primary or alternative access applications. Bay Area Teleport's system connects 12 counties in northern California. The system includes a fiber-optic net in San Francisco & across to Oakland as well as access to satellite svcs through its earth stn complex in Niles Canyon.

San Francisco—San Francisco Satellite Center Inc. 101 California St., Suite 2025, San Francisco 94111. (415) 616-9680. FAX: (415) 616-9676. Jay S. Watson, pres; Jim Von Striver, VP; Cindy Okazaki, dir mktg & sls.

C- & Ku-band uplinks from teleports located at San Bruno Mountain, seven miles from San Francisco's financial district, & Sky Valley. Total capacity of 22 satellite slips, two zoned for Intelsat, & innerconnect to Pac Bell, AT&T & 40 terrestrial microwave sites.

Englewood—Teleport Denver Inc. 9174 S. Jamica St., Englewood, Colo. 80112. (303) 397-4100. FAX: (303) 799-8325. William Becker, CEO.

Fiber-optic & satellite svcs.

Stamford, Conn.—Group W Satellite Communications. 250 Harbor Dr., Stamford, Conn. 06904. (203) 965-6388. FAX: (203) 965-6320. Don Mitzner, pres; Altan C. Stalker, VP/gen mgr; James Crowe, exec dir opns; Peter Concelmo, dir sls/mktg; Cheryl Daly, VP PR.

C- & Ku-band domestic & international transmission svc; connectivity to metro New York via microwave/fiber cable origination, bcst, bus TV, transponder availability; studio & postprod.

Washington—Keystone Communications. 400 N. Capitol N.W., Suite 177, Washington 20001. (202) 737-4440. FAX: (202) 783-5166. Peter Marshall, pres; Harley Shuler, VP/gen mgr eastern rgn; John Turell, dir sls D.C.

Just one block from the U.S. Capitol Building. A three-camera studio is directly tied to uplinking & space segment for media tours & newscasts. Also offers a rooftop shot with the Capitol Building in the background. Full-time transmit boxes also operate on the Senate & House sites.

Washington—Washington International Teleport. 5600 General Washington Dr., Suite B210, Alexandria, Va. 22312. (703) 914-0014; (800) 243-1995; (24-hour opns ctr). (703) 750-0010; FAX: (703) 658-4919. Steven G. Tom, CEO. Ownership: Midcontinent Media.

On-line. Multiple C- & Ku-band uplinks; full domestic arc access; direct international AOR coverage; full net mgmt; 24-hour opns & traf; tape playback; standards conversion; transportables.

North Miami, Fla.—TLC Productions Inc. North Miami International Teleport, 14833 N.E. 20th Ave., North Miami, Fla. 33181-1150. (305) 944-9424. FAX: (305) 944-1906. Vernon Oliver, pres; Terry Kirk, pres; Irene Pace, sec/dir.

Mobile/fixed uplinks & downlinks, connectivity via fiber & microwave, turnaround, full prod.

Orlando, Fla.—The Florida Teleport/Sky^Sat. Box 1311, Orlando, Fla. 32801-1311. (407) 422-7518. John Whathaway, VP.

Prod facilities & tape playback, C- & Ku-band uplinking & downlinking, turnaround svcs, direct PanAmSat access via Ku-band, mobile Ku trucks, telephone interconnects, transponder coord, net consultation.

Atlanta—Crawford Satellite Services. 535 Plasamour Dr., Atlanta 30324. (404) 876-7149; (800) 831-8027. FAX: (404) 876-8956. Jesse Crawford, own/pres; Candy Alger, VP. Ownership: Crawford Satellite Services.

On-line.

Atlanta—Megastar Inc. 701 Desert Ln., #4, Las Vegas 89106. (702) 386-2844. Nigel Macrae, pres.

International teleport, both domestic & international svcs, offering Ku- & C-band.

Atlanta—Turner Teleport Inc. One CNN Ctr., Atlanta 30348. (404) 827-1500. Terry McGuirk, pres Turner Teleport; Gene Wright, VP engrg. Ownership: Turner Broadcasting System Inc.

On-line.

Atlanta—UpSouth Corp. Box 15498, 1802 Briarcliff Rd., Atlanta 30333. (404) 325-0818. FAX: (404) 325-3949. Robert J. Doty Sr., VP/gen mgr; Robert J. Doty Jr., dir opns; Cary M. McDaniel, dir engrg. Ownership: Pacific Telecom Inc.

Full-svc teleport with C- & Ku-band uplinks & downlinks; tape playback; metro Atlanta microwave systems; fiber & telco full-time connections; common carrier.

Douglasville, Ga.—Southern Satellite Systems Inc. 3530 Bomar Rd., Douglasville, Ga. 30135. (404) 949-6600. FAX: (404) 942-6653. Adam Grow III, gen mgr/dir engrg; Owned by Tele-Communications Inc.

Videocipher II & encryption/satellite time purchasing; video/audio/data C-band uplinking/downlinking; Teletext origination. WTBS uplink site; custom videocipher II interfacing svcs. Ku to C-band turnaround.

Chicago—Chicago International Teleport. (A United Video company.) 6723 W. Steger Rd., Monee, Ill. 60449. (708) 534-2400. FAX: (708) 534-0060. Bill Hartanovich, gen mgr; Michael T. Peyton, VP telecommunication svcs. Ownership: United Video Inc.

C- & Ku-band satellite transmission svcs. Audio-video-data uplink/downlink communication.

Chicago—Teleport Chicago. 3717 Oakton St., Milwaukee 60076. (414) 792-7723. Robert E. Roger, VP; Nancy Carey.

Digital message svc, satellite uplink, downlink, turnaround, encryption, tape playback, rgn access on Midwestern Relay Company Interstate Net. VSAT svc available.

Lagrange, Ill.—Centel Videopath Inc. 8935 55th St., McCook, Ill. 60525. (708) 387-0127. FAX: (708) 485-9449. John C. Tammen, gen mgr; Ed Kane, mgr sls mktg; Jon C. Tammen, dir engrg. Ownership: Centel Communications Co.

Uplink/downlink svcs, videoconferencing, hard cable interconnect, loc progmg distribution, data transmissions.

Monee, Ill.—Chicago International Teleport. 6723 W. Steger Rd., Monee, Ill. 60449. (708) 534-2400. FAX: (708) 534-0060. Lawrence Flynn Jr., own; Michael Peyton, VP telecommunications svcs; Bill Hartanovich, teleport gen mgr.

On-line. Common carrier of audio-video data. VA, telco, microwave or satellite. C- & Ku-band satellite transmission svcs.

New Orleans—Network Teleports Inc. 3200 Chartres St., New Orleans 70117. (504) 942-9200. FAX: (504) 942-9204. Barbara Lamont, pres; Ludwig Gelobter, VP; C.E. Feltner, chmn of bd; Noily Paul, VP satellite svcs; Kirk Savoy, dir maintenance. Ownership: Gibraltar Holdings Ltd., Network Teleport.

C-band voice/video, Ku-band data/voice, B-MAC encryption, newsfeeds, prod, fiber-optic links, DBS net, audio-subcarrier & shore-to-ship Inmarsat svc.

Boston—Videocom Satellite Associates Inc. 502 Sprague St., Dedham, Mass. 02026. (617) 329-4080. FAX: (617) 329-8534. Bob Hanson, opns mgr; Frank Cavallo, gen mgr.

Videocom Teleport Boston. Steerable C- & Ku-band antennas interconnected via private microwave & telco loops co-located with single- & multiple-camera prod facility. Receives & transmits all formats of videotape; transportable uplinks; bcst news distribution; link with Canadian satellites.

Jackson, Miss.—Jackson Teleport Inc. 916 Foley St., Jackson, Miss. 39202. (601) 352-6673. FAX: (601) 948-6052. Edward St. Pé, pres; Dave Barber, opns; Deborah St. Pé, administration. Ownership: Edward St. Pé (100%).

On-line Ku-band uplinking. Video satellite transmission & reception. Videoconferencing, business TV, news-sports, weathercast feed, origination, prog distribution & syndication svcs.

Kansas City, Mo.—Kansas City Teleport. (A satellite division of Global Access Telecom in Boston.) 3030 Summit, Kansas City, Mo. 64108. (816) 753-0020. Bud Turner, mgr. Ownership: Great American TV & Radio Co.

On-line; uplinks, downlinks, prog distribution, sports events, news feeds, teleconferences.

Carteret, N.J.—Satellite City. National Gateway Video. Box 420, 27 Randolph St., Carteret, N.J. 07008. (908) 969-3191; (908) 969-3700. FAX: (908) 969-3983. W. Kopacka, VP video/audio svcs. Owned by Pacific Telecom Inc.

TV uplink & downlink svcs, C- & Ku-band, videotape playback svcs, fiber & microwave interconnect with major New York City studios & TV stns.

New York—IDB Communications Group Inc. New York Teleport, 5 Teleport Dr., Staten Island, N.Y. 10311. (718) 983-0800. FAX: (718) 983-2403. Jeffrey Sudikoff, chmn/CEO; Gabrielle Snyder, gen mgr.

IDB's New York Teleport offers on-line Ku- & C-band satellite transmission svcs for audio, video & data/voice domestically & internationally; uplink & downlink capabilities, fiber-optic connectivity.

New York—The Teleport. Teleport Communications, One Teleport Dr., Staten Island, N.Y. 10311. (718) 983-2180. FAX: (718) 983-2147. John Reiser, VP corporate quality & real estate; Howard W. Bruhnke, VP engrg. Ownership: Joint venture of Port Authority of New York & New Jersey, Merrill Lynch & Co. Inc., & City of New York.

On-line.

New York—Rainbow Network Communications. 35 N. Tyson Ave., Floral Park, N.Y. 11001. (516) 328-6710. FAX: (516) 328-6760. Thomas Greco, dir sls & mktg; Steven Pontillo, dir engrg; Doug Keck, VP/gen mgr.

Multiple 11 meter & 9 meter uplinking antennas, multiple downlinking antennas, both servicing the entire satellite arc. Connectivity in & out of New York & metropolitan area, Ku transportable, origination/editing svcs, full & occasional transponders available in C- & Ku-band.

New York—Keystone Communications. 45 W. 45th St., Suite 905, New York 10036. (212) 869-4575. (212) 921-0301. Russell Bittner, dir sls; Steve Ludwig, opns mgr.

Keystone's New York Technical Operating Center on the 82nd floor of the Empire State Building offers connectivity to all major venues in the tri-state area. Access to INTELSAT K & PanAmSat for feeds to Europe & South America. C- to Ku-band & Ku- to C-band turnarounds are available through Keystone's New York facility.

Provides end-to-end video bcst & transmission svcs through its own network of orgination facilities, fiber-optic & microwave systems, switching centers, teleports & satellite transponders.

Raleigh, N.C.—Capitol Satellite and Communications Systems. 3100 Highwoods Blvd., Suite 110, Raleigh, N.C. 27604. (919) 834-3265. FAX: (919) 850-4554. Paul Pope, gen mgr; Bonnie Sullivan, sls/mktg; Irene Joiner, opns mgr; George T. Spence, engrg mgr. Ownership: Capitol Broadcasting Co. Inc.

Fixed & transportable video satellite transmission & reception, C- & Ku-band, domestic/international, videoconferencing business TV, news/sports feed origination, prog distribution, fiber & microwave nets.

Cincinnati—WLWT-TV. 140 W. 9th St., Cincinnati 45202. (513) 352-5000. FAX: (513) 352-5028. Owned by Multimedia Inc.

On-line. Provides occasional C-band uplinking svcs.

Oklahoma City—UPLINK 43. Box 14190, Oklahoma City 73113. (405) 858-8501. FAX: (405) 821-9282. Robert L. Allen, exec dir; Mike Palmer, opns mgr. Ownership: Oklahoma Educational Television Authority.

Ku-band uplink, C- & Ku-band downlinking on-site & remote prod facilities available.

Catawissa, Pa.—Roaring Creek International Teleport/AT&T. Rd. 3, Box 49, Catawissa, Pa. 17820. (717) 799-1000; (717) 799-1025; (717) 799-1020. FAX: (717) 799-1042. TWX: 5106652400. Ray Odonnell, opns mgr. Ownership: AT&T.

Antennas 1, 2, 3, 4, 5. G/T 40.91 international voice, data, video to primary path, major path 1 & 2, 307 degree, international satellites, Mexico & all U.S. domestic satellites. D5-3 fiber to both New York & D.C. Facilities are available for transportable interconnect or permanent transmission space/facilities to be constructed. All C-band antennas are Intelesat standard A-30 meters & all Ku-band antennas are standard C-30 meters. Intelsat master TDMA & FDMA earth stn.

Philadelphia—Philadelphia Teleport Inc. 15 East Ave., Mount Carmel, Pa. 17851. (717) 339-0210. FAX: (215) 639-0211. Carmine Scicchitano, pres; Paul "Ace" McCabe, dir engrg. Ownership: Rose Telecom Ltd.

Offers international video links between the U.S., Europe & Mexico. Two 4.5-meter C-band transportable earth stns along with lietch, Mac-B, OakOrion encryption systems. Live off-track wagering nets, Philadelphia park live. Contract svc only. Live entertainment provided by Fire Fighter Productions Ltd.

Pittsburgh—Group W Videoservices. 310 Parkway View Dr., Pittsburgh 15205. (412) 747-4700; (800) 245-4463. FAX: (412) 747-4726. Ted Barajas, VP/gen mgr; Lee Salas, West Coast sls mgr.

On-line. Distribution of syndicated progmg, coml spots, videotape, subcarrier, satellite svcs, mus svcs, standards conversion, film transfer.

Pittsburgh—Pittsburgh International Teleport. Box 14070, Pittsburgh 15239. (800) 634-6530. George Sperry, gen mgr.

Fixed & remote uplinking & downlinking, turnarounds, space segment, microwave & fiber interconnects, point-to-point & VSAT svcs.

Powell, Tenn.—Tennessee Teleport Inc./Video Catalog Channel Inc. 7613 Blueberry Road, Powell, Tenn. 37849. (615) 938-5101. FAX: (615) 938-1210. John W. Pirkle, pres; W. Kent Blackwelder, gen mgr; C.W. Wells, VP. Ownership: John W. Pirkle, Dr. Charles Wells, Emil Cerney.

Home shopping, data delivery, audio subcarrier svcs, full-svc C-band uplink, satellite time available.

Dallas—Dallas-Fort Worth Teleport Ltd. 3838 Leone Dr., Irving, Tex. 75039. (214) 869-1800. FAX: (214) 869-2302. Dean G. Popps, pres; John Hatem, VP/gen mgr. Ownership: Crow Communications Co., Trammell S. Crow, chmn.

On-line. C- & Ku-band transmission for business TV, cable TV sports, news, entertainment. Also transponder sls, prod, turnarounds, local transmission, occasional events.

Dallas—Megastar Inc. 701 Desert Ln., #4, Las Vegas 89106. (702) 386-2844. Nigel Macrae, pres.

International teleport, both domestic & international svcs, offering Ku- & C-band.

Houston—Megastar Inc. 701 Desert Ln., #4, Las Vegas 89106. (702) 386-2844. Nigel Macrae, pres.

International teleport, both domestic & international svcs, offering Ku- & C-band.

Houston—IDB Communications Group Inc. Houston Teleport, 3003 Moffet Ln., Missouri City, Tex. 77489. (713) 438-3600. FAX: (713) 438-9407. Jeffrey Sudikoff, chmn/CEO; John Overstreet, gen mgr; Jim Weitzel, project mgmt.

CAPITOL SATELLITE

- C and Ku band Fixed and Transportable Uplinking
- Videoconferencing • Business Television
- Program Distribution • Encryption
- Domestic and International Service
- Coast to Coast Fiber Interconnect

SATELLITE SERVICES YOU CAN COUNT ON!

3100 Highwoods Blvd., Raleigh, NC 27604

919-834-3265

IDB's Houston Teleport svcs include all Intelsat offerings, access to Morelos, VSAT shared hub, uplink/downlink tape duplications editing, playback & distribution.

Salt Lake City—Keystone Communications. 303 E. South Temple St., Salt Lake City 84111-1226. (801) 322-4400. FAX: (801) 531-7375. TELEX: 910-925-4069. David E. Simmons, chmn/CEO; Peter Marshall, pres; Brett Leifson, CFO; Barry McCann, VP natl div; Gary Horrocks, VP engrg; Baline Colton, sr VP net svcs group; Douglas Jessop, dir mktg.

Provides end-to-end video bcst & transmission svcs through its own net of origination facilities, fiber-optic & microwave systems, switching centers, teleports & satellite transponders. Keystone publishes a bimonthly reference guide, The Keystone Communications North American Satellite Guide©, a guide to video traffic on North American satellites.

Richmond, Va.—Ray Communications Inc. 1850 Centennial Park Dr., Suite 650, Ruston, Va. 22091. (703) 242-0850. William S. Ray, pres.

C-band stationary & transportable uplinks; 24-hour opns; full prod & syndication svcs available.

Calgary, Alta.—Calgary Teleport. Telesat Canada. 1601 Telesat Ct., Gloucester, Ont. Canada K1B 5P4. (613) 748-0123. FAX: (613) 748-8712. Larry Boisvere, pres; Barry Tumer, VP business dev.

Access to all Telesat Anik satellites & most U.S. domestic satellites.

Edmonton, Alta.—Edmonton Teleport. Telesat Canada. 5311 Allaro Way, Edmonton, Alta., Canada T6H 5B8. (403) 437-6167. FAX: (403) 436-5667. L.J. Boisvert, pres/COO; B. Turner, VP domestic bus; G. Fraser, VP net svcs.

Major bcst teleport offering full North American arc at C-band, & Anik E1 & E2 at Ku-band for occasional use needs.

Vancouver, B.C.—Vancouver Teleport. Telesat Canada. 1601 Telesat Ct., Gloucester, Ont. Canada K1B 5P4. (613) 748-0123. FAX: (613) 748-8712. Larry Boisvert, pres; Barry Turner, VP bus dev.

Teleport under dev. Receive svcs & some transmit svcs available to Telesat's Anik satellites.

Toronto, Ont.—Toronto Teleport. Telesat Canada. 1601 Telesat Ct., Gloucester, Ont. Canada K1B 5P4. (613) 748-0123. FAX: (613) 748-8712. Larry Boisvert, pres; Barry Turner, VP business dev; Jane R. Logan, VP teleport dev, Telesat Enterprises Inc.

Access to all Telesat Anik satellites & most U.S. domestic satellites.

Montreal, Que.—Montreal Teleport. Telesat Canada. 1601 Telesat Ct., Gloucester, Ont. Canada K1B 5P4. (613) 748-0123. FAX: (613) 748-8712. Larry Boisvert, pres; Barry Turner, VP business dev; Jane R. Logan, VP teleport dev, Telesat Enterprises Inc.

Access to all Telesat Anik satellites & most U.S. domestic satellites. Bcst studios available.

Microwave

American Microwave & Communications Inc. (A division of TCI.) 2510 W. Main St., Lansing, Mich. 48917. (517) 485-3000. FAX: (517) 485-6010. Terry Trentman, gen mgr.

Microwave delivery of distant signals to CATV systems; net TV & radio svc to bcst stns.

California Microwave Inc. 985 Almanor Ave., Sunnyvale, Calif. 94086. (408) 732-4000. Phil Otto, pres.

DCT Communications Inc. 229 Quaker Rd., Chappequa, N.Y. 10514. (914) 238-4375. FAX: (914) 238-1213. Jim Wiesenberg Sr., VP.

Omni-directional microwave provider for metro wide analog, digital audio, data or video delivery to end users or as interconnect.

EMI Communications Corp. Box 4872, 5015 Campuswood Dr., East Syracuse, N.Y. 13057. (315) 433-0022. FAX: (315) 433-9137. Dennis Dundon, pres/CEO.

Serves Pennsylvania Public Television Network, Pennsylvania, Ohio, New Jersey, Vermont, New Hampshire, New York & Massachusetts. CATV systems with a variety of svcs.

East Texas Transmission Co. 1351 S. Hwy. 19, Canton, Tex. 75103. (903) 595-1207. Jim Roby, pres/gen mgr.

Video relay svc.

Hi-Desert Microwave Inc. Box 1031, 92 W. Adams St., Burns, Ore. 97720. (503) 573-2936. A.L. Runnels, pres; F.V. Des Ilets, sec/treas.

Point-to-point video svc.

Keystone Communications. 303 E. South Temple St., Salt Lake City 84111-1226. (801) 322-4400. FAX: (801) 531-7375. TELEX: 910-925-4069. David E. Simmons, chmn/CEO; Peter Marshall, pres; Barry McCann, VP natl div; Bret Leifson, CFO; Gary Horrocks, VP engrg; Blaine Colton, sr VP net svcs group; Douglas Jessop, dir mktg.

Los Angeles 90028: 6430 Sunset Blvd., Suite 1400. (213) 467-8900. FAX: (213) 465-8750. Charles Fedorko, VP/gen mgr western rgn; Keith Buckley, dir sls western rgn; Gene Deck, chief engr; Craig Rees, studio mgr.

Washington 20001: 400 N. Capitol N.W., Suite 177. (202) 737-4440. FAX: (202) 783-5166. Peter Marshall, pres; Harley Shuler, VP/gen mgr eastern rgn; John Turrell, dir sls D.C.

New York 10036: 45 W. 45th St., Suite 905. (212) 869-4575. FAX: (212) 921-0301. Russell Bittner, sls dir N.Y.; Steve Ludwig, opns mgr N.Y.

San Diego 92123: 9670 Aero Dr. (619) 569-8451. FAX: (619) 569-9248.

Provides end-to-end video bcst & transmission svcs through its own net or origination facilities, fiber-optic & microwave systems, switching centers, teleports & satellite transponders. Owns & operates C- & Ku-band facilities in New York; Los Angeles; Washington, D.C.; San Diego; & Salt Lake City. Keystone's Washington, D.C. facility, complete with studio, is just blocks from Capitol Hill. Los Angeles facility also offers studio, editing & tape playback svcs. Keystone also publishes a bimonthly reference guide, the *Keystone Communications North American Satellite Guide* ©, a guide to video traffic on North American satellites.

MCI Telecommunications Corp. (A subsidiary of MCI Communications Corp.) 1801 Pennsylvania Ave. N.W., Washington 20006. (202) 872-1600. Bert C. Roberts, chmn of bd/CEO.

Intercity long-distance govt, business & residential telecommunications svcs throughout the U.S.

MRC Telecommunications. 275 N. Corprit Dr., Brookfield, Wis. 53045-5818. (414) 792-9700. FAX: (414) 792-7733. Nancy B. Carey, pres; Michael J. Turnbull, gen sls mgr; Robert E. Rogers, VP opns & engrg.

Specialized common carrier providing transmission & tech svcs to natl telecommunications community. Svcs include digital transmission capacity; video, audio & data svcs & tech engrg; installation & maintenance svcs.

Megastar Inc. 701 Desert Ln., #4, Las Vegas 89106. (702) 386-2844. FAX: (702) 388-1250. Nigel Macrae, pres.

Microwave system serving all major cities in Texas & Oklahoma. Teleports located in Dallas; Houston; Austin & Georgia.

MicroNet Inc. 2370 York Rd., Bldg. B, Jamison, Pa. 18929. (215) 491-7400. FAX: (215) 491-0260. Carl Cangelosi, pres; James Innes, mktg mgr; Wayne Johnson, dir sls; Linda Watts, Bob Thiebaut, account execs; Dan Adickes, gen mgr, Southwest MicroNet.

Provides switched video transmission in New York; Philadelphia; Baltimore; Washington, D.C.; Dallas; Houston; San Antonio. Uplink/downlink Los Angeles, Dallas, New York. Local loop access available all locations. International & domestic video transmission available New York & Dallas.

Microwave Networks Inc. 10795 Rockley Rd., Houston Tex. 77099. (713) 495-7123. FAX: (713) 879-4728. Arthur Epley, pres; Allen Lamberti, VP sls & mktg; Charles Bentley, VP mfg; James R. Gordon, VP bus dev; Brian Belcher, dir sls US/Canada; Bill Torbert, dir Latin America/Caribbean.

Microwave Service Co. Box 163, Tupelo, Miss. 38802. (601) 842-7620, ext. 30. FAX: (601) 844-7061. Frank K. Spain, pres; James D. Green, VP/chief engr.

Point-to-point transmission of video by microwave.

Multicomm Sciences International Inc. (MSI). 266 W. Main St., Denville, N.J. 07834. (201) 627-7400. FAX: (201) 625-1002. Victor J. Nexon Sr., pres; Victor Nexon Jr., VP.

Satellite, microwave, lightwave, radio, cable. Market info, field surveys, system design, feasibility studies, frequency coordination, project mgmt.

Pacific Microwave Joint Venture 940 S. Grape St., Medford, Ore. 97501. (503) 773-4171. Cecil Emory, tech mgr.

Penn Service Microwave Co. Inc. 115 Mill St., Danville, Pa. 17821. (717) 275-1431. FAX: (717) 275-3888. Margaret Walsonavich, pres; Ron Podlesny, gen mgr.

Video distribution of TV signals to various CATV companies in Pennsylvania.

Time Warner Cable. 160 Inverness Dr. W., Englewood, Colo. 80112. (303) 799-1200. FAX: (303) 799-0202.

Common carrier & other loc area net svcs in California; Washington; Minnesota; Virginia; & North & South Carolina.

Western Tele-Communications Inc. Terrace Tower II, 5619 DTC Pkwy., Englewood, Colo. 80111-3000. (303) 267-5500. FAX: (303) 488-3225. Larry Romrell, pres; Bob Lemming, exec VP; Ben Summers, VP engrg.

Microwave for net TV; radio carrier-MCI; SPCC; govt svcs; satellite svcs; special projects; consulting; remote site voice & data svcs; fixed & transportable uplink svcs & transponder brokerage.

Wireless Cable Operators

ACS Enterprises Inc. 2510 Metropolitan Dr., Trevose, Pa. 19053. (215) 396-9400. FAX: (215) 396-9550. Alan Sonnenberg, CEO; Walt Mecleary, exec VP; Charles Mallon, CFO; Mike Lovella, VP engrg; Tom Bird, VP field svcs.

Philadelphia chs: 3,6,10,12,17,29,35,48 & 57; BET, USA Network, ESPN, The Family Channel, WTBS, WWOR, CNN, CNBC, LIFETIME Television, The Discovery Channel, HBO, PRISM, Cinemax, SportsChannel, Philadelphia Park Racing, Arts & Entertainment Network, Nostalgia Television, MTV, TNN (The Nashville Network), Showtime, Nickelodeon, The Disney Channel, C-SPAN, QVC, & The International Channel.

American Telecasting Inc. 4065 N. Sinton Rd., Suite 201, Colorado Springs 80907. (719) 632-5544. FAX: (719) 632-5549. Brian Gast, pres/CEO; John Hager, controller; Chris Clark, dir mktg; Jon Schumacher, dir engrg.

Operates microwave bcst systems.

American Wireless Systems Inc. 11811 N. Tatum Blvd., Suite 1060, Phoenix 85028. (602) 494-7003; (800) 886-7003. FAX: (602) 494-7377. William R. Jenkins, CEO.

Wireless cable opns in Dallas-Fort Worth, Memphis, Minneapolis-St. Paul & Pittsburg (some operated in conjunction with certain joint ventures).

Cross Country Wireless Cable 67-A Mountain Blvd., Warren, N.J. 07059. (908) 271-4880. FAX: (908) 271-8778. George M. Ring, chmn/CEO.

Offering state-of-the-art info & entertainment.

Fort Wayne Telsat Inc. (dba Choice TV.) 1909 Production Rd., Fort Wayne, Ind. 46808. (219) 482-2020. FAX: (219) 484-4547. David Bradford, gen mgr; Sally Kang, opns mgr.

Wireless cable TV svc, 14 basic chs & three premium svcs.

Gear Wireless Cable. Box 28404, Providence, R.I. 02908. (401) 331-6072. Jack G. Thayer, pres/CEO.

TV progmg; 15,000 subs; news, mus, movies, pay-per-view, sports, etc.

Liberty Cable Television. 575 Madison Ave., New York 10022. (212) 891-7771. FAX: (212) 891-7790. P. Price, pres.

Cable TV svcs.

The Microband Companies Inc. 286 Eldridge Rd., Fairfield, N.J. 07004. (201) 227-8700. FAX: (201) 227-2612. J. Patrick Dugan, pres/CEO; William K. Hoffman, sr VP/gen counsel; Mary Ellen Bauman, VP/CFO; Alfred Dalimonte, sr VP/chief scientist.

Transmits cable TV progmg to subs in New York City & owns common carrier stns throughout the country.

TV Communications Network Inc. (TVCN). 10020 E. Girard Ave., Denver 80231. (303) 751-2900. FAX: (303) 751-1081. Omar A. Duwaik, chmn of bd/pres/CEO; Kenneth D. Roznoy, VP/sec; Jacob A. Duwaik, VP/treas.

Wireless cable TV svc in the following locations: Denver; Detroit; Washington, D.C.; San Luis Obispo, Calif.; Salina & Hays, Kan.; Mobile, Ala.; state of Quatar (Arabian Gulf).

Valley Wireless TV. 5610 District Blvd., Suite 101, Bakersfield, Calif. 93313-2178. (805) 397-2222. FAX: (805) 397-2223. Dan Crisp, VP/CEO.

Wireless cable TV svc.

Wireless Cable of Florida Inc. 1950 Landings Blvd., Suite 110, Sarasota, Fla. 34231-3310. (813) 924-2400. FAX: (813) 924-1650. Jim Hall, chmn; Rod Warner, pres; Paul Manning, sec/treas.

Operation & mgmt of wireless cable systems. Consulting or by mgmt contract. Dev of new mkts.

Multipoint Distribution Services

Alabama

Huntsville. WDU266; Channel 1. MDS Service Co. c/o Microband Corp. of America. 655 3rd Ave., New York, N.Y. 10017.

Alaska

Anchorage. KFC63; Channel 1. MDS Systems c/o James R. Hendershot. Box 190929, Anchorage, Alaska. 99519.

Fairbanks. WPY44; Channel 1. Tundra Microwave Inc. 2841 Debarr Rd., Suite 22, Anchorage, Alaska. 99508.

Arizona

Phoenix. WHB522; Channel 2. Phoenix MDS Co. c/o Howard S. Klotz. 145 Huguenot St., New Rochelle, N.Y. 10801.

Phoenix. WPF47; Channel 1. Microband Corp. of America. 286 Eldridge Rd., Fairfield, N.J. 07004.

Tucson. WMH229; Channel 1. People's Choice TV Partnership. 201 S. Wilmot Rd., Tucson, Ariz. 85711-4002.

Tucson. WMI956; Channel 2A. People's Choice TV Partnership. 201 S. Wilmot Rd., Tucson, Ariz. 85711-4002.

California

Anaheim. KFI79; Channel 1. Microband Corp. of America. 286 Eldridge Rd., Fairfield, N.J. 07004.

Anaheim. WGX394; Channel 2. Anaheim MDS Co. c/o Broadcast Data Corp. 25 Rockwood Pl., Englewood, N.J. 07631.

Bakersfield. WMH877; Channel 1. Valley Wireless Cable Inc. 5610 District Blvd., Suite 101, Bakersfield, Calif. 93313-2178.

Bakersfield. WMI942; Channel 2A. Tharrell D. Ming. 5610 District Blvd., Suite 101, Bakersfield, Calif. 93313-2178.

Contra Costa. KFF68; Channel 1. Hydra Communications Inc. 26573 Basswood Ave., Rancho Palos Verdes, Calif. 90274.

El Centro. WGW408; Channel 1. Hydra Communications Inc. 26573 Basswood Ave., Rancho Palos Verdes, Calif. 90274.

Fresno. KNJ21; Channel 1. Fresno MDS Co. c/o Microband Corp. of America. 655 3rd Ave., New York, N.Y. 10017.

Lancaster. WGW239; Channel 1. Hydra Communications Inc. 26573 Basswood Ave., Rancho Palos Verdes, Calif. 90274.

Los Angeles. KFF79; Channel 1. Earl S. Kim. 10837 Farralone Ave., Chatsworth, Calif. 91311.

Los Angeles. WHD479; Channel 2. Los Angeles MDS Co. Inc. 26573 Basswood Ave., Rancho Palos Verdes, Calif. 90274.

Monterey. WPX66; Channel 1. Broadcast Data Corp. 189 Berdan Ave., Suite 247, Wayne, N.J. 07470.

Oro Grande. WDU486; Channel 1. Warren Electronics. 421 Via La Selva, Redondo Beach, Calif. 90277.

Palm Springs. WSL86; Channel 1. Desert MDS Co. Box 163, Tupelo, Miss. 38801.

Palo Alto. WJL36; Channel 1. Microband Corp. of America. 286 Eldridge Rd., Fairfield, N.J. 07004.

Riverside. WPW94; Channel 1. Riverside MDS Co. 189 Berdan Ave., Suite 242, Wayne, N.J. 07470.

Sacramento. WGW352; Channel 2. Broadcast Data Corp. 189 Berdan Ave., Suite 247, Wayne, N.J. 07470.

Sacramento. WSL88; Channel 1. Sacramento Microband Inc. c/o Microband Corp. of America. 655 3rd Ave., New York, N.Y. 10017.

San Bernadino. WHT573; Channel 2. Microband Corp. of America. 286 Eldridge Rd., Fairfield, N.J. 07004.

San Diego. WFY435; Channel 1. Tekkom Inc. 2550 5th Ave., Suite 5, San Diego, Calif. 92103.

San Diego. WHT559; Channel 2. San Diego MDS Co. 3660 Maguire Blvd., #200, Orlando, Fla. 32803.

San Francisco. KFF81; Channel 1. Microband Pacific Corp. 286 Eldridge Rd., Fairfield, N.J. 07004.

San Francisco. WGW270; Channel 1. Microband Pacific Corp. 286 Eldridge Rd., Fairfield, N.J. 07004.

San Francisco. WLK228; Channel 2. San Francisco MDS Co. Box 19768, Orlando, Fla. 32814.

San Marcos. WPX85; Channel 1. Hydra Communications Inc. 26573 Basswood Ave., Rancho Palos Verdes, Calif. 90274.

San Pedro. WPY40; Channel 1. Microband Corp. of America. 286 Eldridge Rd., Fairfield, N.J. 07004.

Wishon. WGW311; Channel 1. Mountain Broadcasters. 32169 Marantha Dr., Box 618, North Fork, Calif. 93643.

Colorado

Colorado Springs. WPG39; Channel 2A. American Telecasting of Colorado Springs Inc. 1800 Diagonal Rd., Suite 230, Alexandria, Va. 22314.

Colorado Springs. WPW97; Channel 1. American Telecasting of Colorado Springs Inc. 1800 Diagonal Rd., Suite 230, Alexandria, Va. 22314.

Denver. WPY32; Channel 1. Microvision. 836 E. Washington St., San Diego, Calif. 92103.

District of Columbia

Washington. WHT747; Channel 2. Washington MDS Co. c/o Boyd King. Box 206, Prince Fredrick, Md. 20678.

Washington. WOI93; Channel 1. Washington Microband Inc. 655 3rd Ave., New York, N.Y. 10017.

Florida

Bonito Springs. WQQ76; Channel 1. Palmer Communications Inc. 1801 Grand Ave., Des Moines, Iowa 50308.

Marco Island. WFY577; Channel 1. Marco Island MDS Co. 4426 Cleveland Ave., Fort Myers, Fla. 33901.

Miami. WLJ79; Channel 1. Microband Corp. of America. 286 Eldridge Rd., Fairfield, N.J. 07004.

Orlando. WFY742; Channel 1. Contemporary Communications Corp. c/o Howard S. Klotz. 145 Huguenot St., New Rochelle, N.Y. 10801.

Orlando. WGW518; Channel 2A. Contemporary Communications Corp. c/o Howard S. Klotz. 145 Huguenot St., New Rochelle, N.Y. 10801.

Pensacola. WDU502; Channel 1. Contemporary Communications Corp. c/o Howard S. Klotz. 145 Huguenot St., New Rochelle, N.Y. 10801.

Pompano Beach. KFJ28; Channel 1. Contemporary Communications Corp. c/o Howard S. Klotz. 145 Huguenot St., New Rochelle, N.Y. 10801.

Stuart. WFY650; Channel 1. MDS Services of Stuart Inc. 4363 10th Ave. N., Box 5568, Lake Worth, Fla. 33461.

Tampa. WOF43; Channel 1. Contemporary Communications Corp. c/o Howard S. Klotz. 145 Huguenot St., New Rochelle, N.Y. 10801.

West Palm Beach. WGW504; Channel 2A. Contemporary Communications Corp. c/o Howard S. Klotz. 145 Huguenot St., New Rochelle, N.Y. 10801.

West Palm Beach. WPY38; Channel 1. Communication Innovations Corp. 145 Huguenot St., Suite 401, New Rochelle, N.Y. 10801.

Georgia

Atlanta. WGW309; Channel 2. Atlanta MDS Co. Inc. c/o M.C.C.A. Service Corp. 1500 Capital Towers, Jackson, Miss. 39201.

Atlanta. WQR43; Channel 1. Microband United Corp. 286 Eldridge Rd., Fairfield, N.J. 07004.

Valdosta. WLW877; Channel 1. Russel Acree. Box 656, Office #901, Adel, Ga. 31620.

Idaho

Twin Falls. WKR64; Channel 1. Channel View Inc. Box 2787, El Cajon, Calif. 92021.

Illinois

Casey. WLW800; Channel 1. Bolin Enterprises Inc. Box 133, Casey, Ill. 62420.

Casey. WLW804; Channel 2A. Bolin Enterprises Inc. Box 133, Casey, Ill. 62420.

Champaign. WLW763; Channel 1. Specchio Developers Ltd. 233 N. Garrard, Rantoul, Ill. 61866.

Chicago. WHT562; Channel 2. Chicago MDS Co. Box 19768, Orlando, Fla. 32814.

Chicago. WOF49; Channel 1. Microband Corp. of America. 286 Eldridge Rd., Fairfield, N.J. 07004.

Creve Coeur. WPX72; Channel 1. Evans Microwave Inc. Box 181, Savoy, Ill. 61874.

Salem. WMH485; Channel 1. Southern Illinois Wireless Cable Co. Inc. Box 429, Salem, Ill. 62881-0429.

Urbana. KEW94; Channel 2A. Board of Trustees of the University of Illinois, a Public Corp. 506 Wright St., Urbana, Ill. 61801.

Waukegan. WGW344; Channel 1. Microband Corp. of America. 286 Eldridge Rd., Fairfield, N.J. 07004.

Indiana

Fort Wayne. WGW300; Channel 1. James A. Simon. 3526 Stellhorn Rd., Fort Wayne, Ind. 46815.

Fort Wayne. WHD358; Channel 2A. James A. Simon. 3526 Stellhorn Rd., Fort Wayne, Ind. 46815.

Indianapolis. WLK246; Channel 2. Indianapolis MDS Co. c/o Private Networks Inc. 57 E. 11th St., 6th Fl., New York, N.Y. 10003.

Indianapolis. WPX33; Channel 1. Microband Corp. of America. 286 Eldridge Rd., Fairfield, N.J. 07004.

Iowa

Davenport. WFY595; Channel 1. Contemporary Communications Corp. c/o Howard S. Klotz. 145 Huguenot St., New Rochelle, N.Y. 10801.

Des Moines. WMH232; Channel 2A. Distinctive Sound. 1205 31st, W. Des Moines, Iowa 50265.

Kansas

Erie. NEW; Channel 1. Larry D. Hudson. R.R. #4, Chanute, Kan. 66720.

Manhattan. WMH881; Channel 2A. Grand Alliance Manhattan (F) Partnership. 1920 N St. N.W., Suite 660, Washington, D.C. 20036.

Kentucky

Louisville. KOA86; Channel 1. Microband Corp. of America. 286 Eldridge Rd., Fairfield, N.J. 07004.

Louisiana

Alexandria. WFY645; Channel 1. Satellite Vision Broadcasting Co. 801 3rd St., Bentley Hotel, Alexandria, La. 71301.

Baton Rouge. WPW96; Channel 1. K-Towers Partnership. 123 N. Easy St., Lafayette, La. 70506.

New Orleans. WKR26; Channel 1. Microband Corp. of America. 286 Eldridge Rd., Fairfield, NJ 07004.

New Orleans. WLK290; Channel 2. Radiofone Inc. c/o James D. and Lawrence D. Garvey. 3131 N. I-10 Service Rd., Metairie, La. 70815.

Rayville. WFY896; Channel 1. Communications Towers Inc. of Texas. 7855 Airline Hwy., Baton Rouge, La. 70815.

Maryland

Baltimore. WHT571; Channel 2. Microband Corp. of America. 286 Eldridge Rd., Fairfield, N.J. 07004.

Multipoint Distribution Services

Massachusetts

Boston. WGW339; Channel 2. Boston MDS Co. Rockwood IV Corporate Ctr., 25 Rockwood Pl., Englewood, N.J. 07631.

Boston. WSL33; Channel 1. Microwave Distribution Services Inc. c/o Microband Corp. of America. 655 3rd Ave., New York, N.Y. 10017.

Hyannis. WFY616; Channel 1. Dynamic Sound c/o Donald E. & L. Bernadine Hartley. 4910 Aircenter Cir., #108, Reno, Nev. 89502.

Michigan

Detroit. WJM22; Channel 1. Motor City MDS Inc. 286 Eldridge Rd., Fairfield, N.J. 07004.

Saginaw. WMI947; Channel 2A. Microcom Inc. 3735 Bern St., Bay City, Mich. 48706.

Minnesota

Minneapolis. WCU552; Channel 2. Minneapolis MDS Co. 189 Berdan Ave., Suite 247, Wayne, N.J. 07470.

Minneapolis. WPE99; Channel 1. Microband Corp. of America. 286 Eldrige Rd., Fairfield, N.J. 07004.

Mississippi

Tupelo. WGW671; Channel 1. Microwave Service Co. c/o Frank K. Spain. Box 163, Tupelo, Miss. 38801.

Missouri

Carthage. WDU466; Channel 1. Southwest Missouri Cable TV Inc. Box 696, Carthage, Mo. 64836.

Kansas City. KOB43; Channel 1. Microband Corp. of America. 286 Eldridge Rd., Fairfield, N.J. 07004.

Lake of Ozarks. WOG68; Channel 1. Richard W. Rohde. 3489 Delmar Dr., Rocky River, OH 44116.

St. Louis. WHT702; Channel 2. St. Louis MDS Co. c/o Private Networks Inc. 157 W. 57th St., #109, New York, N.Y. 10019.

St. Louis. WQQ64; Channel 1. Microband Corp. of America. 286 Eldridge Rd., Fairfield, N.J. 07004.

Montana

Billings. WFY748; Channel 1. Phoebe Virginia Stiles. 3441 Poly Dr., Suite 10, Billings, Mont. 59102.

Nebraska

Kearney. WFY431; Channel 1. Mid-Nebraska Telecommunications Inc. Box 1159, 1100 E. 25th, Kearney, Neb. 68847.

Nevada

Carson City. WJL89; Channel 1. Jonsson Communications Corp. 233 Wilshire Blvd., Suite 900, Santa Maria, Calif. 90401.

Las Vegas. WKR65; Channel 2A. Carl B. Hilliard Jr. 2550 5th Ave., Suite 5, San Diego, Calif. 92103.

Las Vegas. WWZ51; Channel 1. Tekkom Inc. 2550 5th Ave., Suite 5, San Diego, Calif. 92103.

Reno. WFY434; Channel 1. Jonsson Communications Corp. 233 Wilshire Blvd., Suite 900, Santa Maria, Calif. 90401.

Reno. WFY553; Channel 2A. Dynamic Sound. c/o Donald E. & L. Bernadine Hartley, 4910 Aircenter Cir., #108, Reno, Nev. 89502

New Jersey

New Brunswick. WCU573; Channel 1. Microband Corp. of America. 286 Eldridge Rd., Fairfield, N.J. 07004.

New Mexico

Albuquerque. KFK32; Channel 1. Contemporary Communications Corp. c/o Howard S. Klotz, 145 Huguenot St., New Rochelle, N.Y. 10801.

Albuquerque. WLW898; Channel 2A. Cox Music and Sound. 8024 Chico Rd. N.E., Albuquerque, N.M. 87108.

Las Cruces. WJM88; Channel 1. Las Cruces MDS Co. Box 2787, El Cajon, Calif. 92021.

Santa Fe. WGW413; Channel 1. Santa Fe MDS Co. c/o Richard E. Vail, Box 2787, El Cajon, Calif. 92021.

New York

Albany. WHI966; Channel 2. George W. Bott. Box 186, Rexford, N.Y. 12148.

Elmira. WMH869; Channel 1. KA3B2 Television Partnership. 2219 Thousand Oaks Blvd., #238, Thousand Oaks, Calif. 91362.

Long Island. WJM64; Channel 1. Lipper Communications Inc. 74 Trinity Pl., New York, N.Y. 10006.

New York. WLK227; Channel 2. New York MDS Inc. Box 19768, Orlando, Fla. 32814.

New York. WQQ79; Channel 1. Microband Corp. of America. 286 Eldridge Rd., Fairfield, N.J. 07004.

Syracuse. WHC998; Channel 1. Contemporary Communications Corp. c/o Howard S. Klotz, 145 Huguenot St., New Rochelle, N.Y. 10801.

North Carolina

Charlotte. WGW715; Channel 1. T.V. Signal Co. c/o Allen Guin, 3301 Woodwardia Dr., Charlotte, N.C. 28210.

Greensboro. WFY738; Channel 1. Contemporary Communications Corp. c/o Howard S. Klotz, 145 Huguenot St., New Rochelle, N.Y. 10801.

Ohio

Cincinnati. WOG60; Channel 1. Microband Corp. of America. 286 Eldridge Rd., Fairfield, N.J. 07004.

Cleveland. WQQ66; Channel 1. Cleveland Microband Teleservices Inc. 286 Eldridge Rd., Fairfield, N.J. 07004.

Columbus. WDU606; Channel 2. Broadcast Data Corp. 189 Berdan Ave., Suite 247, Wayne, N.J. 07470.

Lima. WMI386; Channel 1. W.A.T.C.H. TV Co. 2323 Allentown Rd., Lima, Ohio 45805.

Lima. WMI390; Channel 2A. W.A.T.C.H. TV Co. 2323 Allentown Rd., Lima, Ohio 45805.

Toledo. KFK31; Channel 1. Media Broadcasting Inc. 2049 Robinwood Ave., Toledo, Ohio 43620.

Youngstown. WDU693; Channel 1. WKBN Broadcasting Corp. 3930 Sunset Blvd., Youngstown, Ohio 44501

Oklahoma

Ada. WMI932; Channel 1. Barry James. 202 N. 3rd St., Durant, Okla. 74701.

Enid. WLW787; Channel 1. James Douglas King. 707 N.W. 64th St., Oklahoma City, Okla. 73116.

Oklahoma City. WFY642; Channel 2. Broadcast Data Corp. 189 Berdan Ave., Suite 247, Wayne, N.J. 07470.

Oklahoma City. WJL99; Channel 1. Contemporary Communications Corp. c/o Howard S. Klotz. 145 Huguenot St., New Rochelle, N.Y. 10801.

Tulsa. WPG45; Channel 2A. Contemporary Communications Corp. c/o Howard S. Klotz, 145 Huguenot St., New Rochelle, N.Y. 10801.

Oregon

Bend. WHA674; Channel 1. West Indian Group Inc. Box 939, Portland, Ore. 97207.

Portland. WPY39; Channel 1. Microband Corp. of America. 286 Eldridge Rd., Fairfield, N.J. 07004.

Pennsylvania

Philadelphia. WPE97; Channel 1. Micro TV Inc. 3600 Conshohocken Ave., Philadelphia, Pa. 19131.

Pittsburgh. WPF48; Channel 1. Microband Corp. of America. 286 Eldridge Rd., Fairfield, N.J. 07004.

Rhode Island

Providence. KNV65; Channel 1. Colony Microband of Rhode Island Inc. 286 Eldridge Rd., Fairfield, N.J. 07004.

Tennessee

Chattanooga. WPE83; Channel 1. Contemporary Communications Corp. c/o Howard S. Klotz, 145 Huguenot St., New Rochelle, N.Y. 10801.

Memphis. WJM63; Channel 1. Microband Corp. of America. 286 Eldridge Rd., Fairfield, N.J. 07004.

Union City. WGW505; Channel 1. Union City Microvision. Box 709, Union City, Tenn. 38261.

Texas

Amarillo. WCZ53; Channel 1. Supreme Cable Co. Inc. 100 Congress Ave., Suite 1910, Austin, Tex. 78701.

Austin. WJM66; Channel 1. Texas Wired Music Inc. Box 8278, San Antonio, Tex. 78208.

Austin. WLW975; Channel 2A. Cable Maxx Inc. 5910 Courtyard Dr., Suite 100, Austin, Tex. 78731.

Bay City. WHT625; Channel 1. Communication Security Enterprises. Box 2193, 2525 Ave. D, Bay City, Tex. 77414.

Beaumont. WJL88; Channel 1. Beaumont MDS Co. c/o Microband Corp. of America, 655 3rd Ave., New York, N.Y. 10017.

Brady. WMI987; Channel 1. Central Texas Telephone Cooperative Inc. Box 627, Goldthwaite, Tex. 76844.

Corpus Christi. WDU282; Channel 1. Texas Wired Music Inc. Box 8278, San Antonio, Tex. 78208.

Dallas. WHT564; Channel 2. Texas MDS Co. 286 Eldridge Rd., Fairfield, N.J. 07004.

Dallas. WQQ65; Channel 1. Taft Broadcasting Co. 4808 San Felipe Rd., Houston, Tex. 77056.

El Paso. WSL59; Channel 1. Texas Wired Music Inc. Box 8278, San Antonio, Tex. 78208.

Fort Worth. WFY900; Channel 2. Texas MDS Co. 286 Eldridge Rd., Fairfield, N.J. 07004.

Fort Worth. WJM75; Channel 1. Taft Broadcasting Co. 4808 San Felipe Rd., Houston, Tex. 77056.

Galveston. WDU206; Channel 1. Taft Broadcasting Co. 4808 San Felipe Rd., Houston, Tex. 77056.

Goldthwaite. WMI991; Channel 2A. Central Texas Telephone Cooperative Inc. Box 627, Goldthwaite, Tex. 76844.

Goldthwaite. WMI995; Channel 1. Central Texas Telephone Cooperative Inc. Box 627, Goldthwaite, Tex. 76844.

Houston. WHT570; Channel 2. Private Networks Inc. 57 E. 11th St., 6th Fl., New York, N.Y. 10003.

Houston. WOF76; Channel 1. Taft Broadcasting Co. 4808 San Felipe Rd., Houston, Tex. 77056.

Killeen. WDU302; Channel 1. Texas Wired Music Inc. Box 8278, San Antonio, Tex. 78208.

Lubbock. WDU247; Channel 1. Lubbock MDS Co. 655 3rd Ave., New York, N.Y. 10017.

McAllen. WDU443; Channel 1. Specialty Broadcasting Corp. c/o Henry Colgate, 4068 Dietz Farm Cir. N.W., Albuquerque, N.M. 87107.

Pampa. WLW861; Channel 1. Alton Dale Greenhouse. 1701 Evergreen, Pampa, Tex. 79065.

San Angelo. WML478; Channel 1. Charles R. Jones. Box 609, Lindsay, Okla. 73052.

San Antonio. WFY852; Channel 2. Supreme Cable Texas Inc. 5910 Courtyard Dr., Suite 100, Austin, Tex. 78731.

San Antonio. WJM80; Channel 1. Texas Wired Music Inc. Box 8278, San Antonio, Tex. 78208.

San Saba. WMI944; Channel 1. Central Texas Telephone Cooperative Inc. Box 627, Goldthwaite, Tex. 76844.

Victoria. WGW374; Channel 1. Texas Wired Music Inc. Box 8278, San Antonio, Tex. 78208.

Utah

Ogden. WFY786; Channel 1. Ogden MDS Co. c/o Telecommunicatons Systems Inc., Fischer Medical Publications Inc. 280 Madison Ave., New York, N.Y. 10016.

Park City. WGW291; Channel 1. Channel View Inc. Box 2787, El Cajon, Calif. 92021.

Provo. WFY865; Channel 1. Channel View Inc. Box 2787, El Cajon, Calif. 92021.

Multipoint Distribution Services

St. George. WMI946; Channel 1. American Wireless Inc. Box 1207, St. George, Utah 84770-7101.

Salt Lake City. KEW74; Channel 1. Channel View Inc. Box 2787, El Cajon, Calif. 92021.

Vermont

Rutland. WMH868; Channel 1. Sanguinetti Investment Corp. 168 N. Main St., Rutland, Vt. 05701.

Rutland. WMI343; Channel 2A. Sanguinetti Investment Corp. 168 N. Main St., Rutland, Vt. 05701.

Virginia

Charlottesville. WPX69; Channel 1. Microband of Virginia Inc. 286 Eldridge Rd., Fairfield, N.J. 07004.

Washington

Bellingham. WDU571; Channel 1. Telecommunications Systems Inc. Box 7222, Menlo Park, Calif. 94026.

Yakima. WKR57; Channel 1. Summit Communications Inc. 3633 136th Pl. S.E., Suite 107, Bellevue, Wash. 98006.

West Virginia

Shannondale. WHT629; Channel 1. Shannondale Wireless. 3623 Park Ln., Fairfax, Va. 22030.

Shannondale. WLK242; Channel 2A. Shannondale Wireless. 3623 Park Ln., Fairfax, Va. 22030.

Wisconsin

Green Bay. WQQ77; Channel 1. Gallery Productions c/o Joseph L. Roffer. Box 443, Depere, Wis. 54155.

Madison. WPY30; Channel 1. Madison MDS Co. c/o Tel-Radio Communications Properties Inc. 517 N. Segoe Rd., Madison, Wis. 53705.

Milwaukee. WHT566; Channel 2. Milwaukee MDS Co. c/o Broadcast Data Corp., 25 Rockwood Pl., Englewood, N.J. 07631.

Milwaukee. WKR27; Channel 1. Microband Corp. of America. 286 Eldridge Rd., Fairfield, N.J. 07004.

Wyoming

Evanston. WMI408; Channel 1. G/S Evanston F Settlement Group. c/o Step 9 MMDS Partners, MGP, 11600 Pine Haven Ave., Bakersfield, Calif. 93312.

Riverton. WMI404; Channel 1. G/S Evanston F Settlement Group. c/o C.M.G. Enterprises, MGP, 2120 E. Prien Lake Rd., Lake Charles, La. 70601.

Multichannel Multipoint Distribution Services

Alabama

Huntsville. WLR564; Channel E. Theodore D. Little. 5310 Waupaca Rd., Rancho Palos Verdes, Calif. 90274.

Huntsville. WLW773; Channel F. Private Networks Inc. 57 E. 11th St., 6th Fl., New York, N.Y. 10003.

Mobile. WHT773; Channel E. Multichannel Distribution of America (MDA). 10020 E. Girard, #300, Denver, Colo. 80231.

Arizona

Casa Grande. WMI344; Channel F. MWTV Inc. 3401 E. Cholla St., Phoenix, Ariz. 85028.

Casa Grande. WMI839; Channel E. Virginia Communications Inc. 6330 E. Mockingbird Ln., Scottsdale, Ariz. 85253.

Flagstaff. WLW970; Channel F. Multi-Micro Inc. 1223 W. 10th St., Tempe, Ariz. 85281-5318.

Flagstaff. WMI320; Channel E. Kannew Broadcast Technologies. c/o Terry Newmyer, 1220 L St. N.W., #425, Washington, D.C. 20005.

Tucson. WHK994; Channel F. Omega Radiotelephone. c/o David Hernandez, 1601 Neptune Dr., San Leandro, Calif. 94577.

Verde Valley. WMI827; Channel E. Virginia Communications Inc. 6330 E. Mockingbird Ln., Scottsdale, Ariz. 85253.

Verde Valley. WMI864; Channel F. Mettler Communications Inc. c/o Lyle W. Mettler, Pres., 1453 E. Ivyglen, Mesa, Ariz. 85203.

Yuma. WLW826; Channel F. B.F. Investments Inc. 7521 E. Edgemont, Scottsdale, Ariz. 85257.

Yuma. WLW829; Channel E. Microwave Video Services Inc. c/o Philip C. Merrill, 331 Sea Ridge Dr., La Jolla, Calif. 92037.

Arkansas

Decatur/Jay, Okla. WLW846; Channel E. Grand Telephone Company Inc. Box 308, Jay, Okla. 74346.

Fayetteville. WMI881; Channel F. Krisar Inc. Box 186, Rexford, N.Y. 12148.

Fort Smith. WLK312; Channel E. Virginia Communications Inc. 6330 E. Mockingbird Ln., Scottsdale, Ariz. 85253.

Fort Smith. WLK316; Channel F. MWTV Inc. 3401 E. Cholla St., Phoenix, Ariz. 85028.

California

Bakersfield. WHT584; Channel E. Haddonfield Wireless Co. 400 Merion Ave., Haddonfield, N.J. 08033.

Bakersfield. WHT585; Channel F. Multi-Micro Inc. 1223 W. 10th St., Tempe, Ariz. 85281-5318.

Fresno. WHT715; Channel E. VIA/NET Companies. 836 E. Washington St., San Diego, Calif. 92103.

Fresno. WLW816; Channel F. Video/Multipoint Inc. 2809 Pine St., Suite A, San Francisco, Calif. 94115.

Los Angeles. WHT637; Channel F. Metrocall of Nevada Partnership II. 6677 Richmond Hwy., Alexandria, Va. 22306.

Mammoth Lake. WMI385; Channel F. Government Enterprise Inc. 279 S. Beverly Hills, Suite 1035, Beverly Hills, Calif. 90212.

Mammoth Lake. WMI389; Channel E. Government Enterprise Inc. 279 S. Beverly Hills, Suite 1035, Beverly Hills, Calif. 90212.

Sacramento. WHT689; Channel E. Steven C. Bailey. 7120 Calcite St., Diamond Springs, Calif. 95619.

Sacramento. WHT690; Channel F. Multi-Micro Inc. 1223 W. 10th St., Tempe, Ariz. 85281-5318.

San Francisco. WHT701; Channel F. East-West Communications Inc. 1682 E. Guide Dr., Suite 102D, Rockville, Md. 20850.

San Luis Obispo. WGW606; Channel E. Multichannel Distribution of America (MDA). 10020 E. Girard, #300, Denver, Colo. 80231.

Visalia. WGW280; Channel E. Walter Communications Inc. 1223 W. 10th St., Tempe, Ariz. 85281-5318.

Yuba City. WMH381; Channel F. Sutter-Buttes Cablevision. 1513 Sports Dr., Suite 9, Sacramento, Calif. 95834.

Colorado

Colorado Springs. WHT756; Channel E. Thomas Glab. 2129 San Marcos Pl., Claremont, Calif. 91711.

Colorado Springs. WHT758; Channel F. American Telecasting of Colorado Springs Inc. 1800 Diagonal Rd., Suite 230, Alexandria, Va. 22314.

Denver. WHK938; Channel F. Heritage Broadcasting Group Inc. 2509 Commercial Dr., Auburn Hills, Mich. 48057.

Denver. WLK321; Channel E. Midwest Cable & Satellite Inc. c/o CBS Inc., 51 W. 52 St., 36th Fl., New York, N.Y. 10019.

Greeley. WMH425; Channel F. Debra Chavez. Box 2268, Denver, Colo. 80201.

Wray. WHK934; Channel E. Southwest Telecommunications Cooperative Association Inc. Box N, Palisade, Neb. 69040.

Wray. WHK935; Channel F. Nebraska Telecommunications Inc. 616 Chestnut Dr., Loveland, Colo. 80538.

Connecticut

Hartford. WHT672; Channel F. Lawrence N. Brandt. 3201 New Mexico Ave. N.W., Suite 220, Washington, D.C. 20016.

District of Columbia

Washington. WHT659; Channel F. F Corp. c/o The Capitol Connection, Kelley Dr., George Mason University, Fairfax, Va. 22030.

Florida

Bradenton. WLW830. Channel F. MWTV Inc. 3401 E. Cholla St., Phoenix, Ariz. 85028.

Bradenton. WMH513. Channel E. Fortuna Systems Corp. c/o Philip C. Merrill, 3312 Garrison St., San Diego, Calif. 92106.

Daytona Beach. WHT761; Channel E. Line of Site Inc. 6048 E. Kathleen Rd., Scottsdale, Ariz. 85254.

Daytona Beach. WHT762; Channel F. Multi-Micro Inc. 1223 W. 10th St., Tempe, Ariz. 85281-5318

Fort Myers. WHK973; Channel F. Columbia Wireless Corp. 1629 K. St. N.W., Suite 600, Washington, D.C. 20006

Fort Myers. WHK974; Channel F. MDS Signal Group/ McFadden, Evans & Sill. 1627 Eye St. N.W., Suite 810, Washington, D.C. 20006.

Fort Pierce. WLK308; Channel F. MMDS Fort Pierce Inc. 1220 19th St. N.W., Suite 501, Washington, D.C. 20036.

Fort Pierce. WLW758; Channel E. Multi-Point Television Distributors Inc./ Philip C. Merrill. 2000 L St. N.W., Suite 200, Washington, D.C. 20036.

Jacksonville. WHT675; Channel E. WJCT Inc. 100 Festival Park Ave., Jacksonville, Fla. 32202.

Jacksonville. WHT676; Channel F. Sunbelt Entertainment Corp. Oakland-Alameda Coliseum, Oakland, Calif. 94621.

Lakeland. WHK925; Channel E. Lakeland BDC-MMDS Co. c/o Broadcast Data Corp., 25 Rockwood Pl., Englewood, N.J. 07631.

Lakeland. WHK958; Channel F. Delta Band Services, Ltd. Suess Path, Box 1241, Quogue, N.Y. 11909.

Orlando. WHT731; Channel E. Line of Site Inc. 6048 E. Kathleen Rd., Scottsdale, Ariz. 85254.

Orlando. WHT732; Channel F. Orlando BDC-MMDS Co./William Walker. 57 E. 11th St., New York, N.Y. 10003.

Tampa. WHT699; Channel F. Mars Communications. 101 E. Kennedy Blvd., Suite 3300, Tampa, Fla. 33603.

Tampa. WHT700; Channel E. Paul Communications Inc. 1223 W. 10th St., Tempe, Ariz. 85281-5318.

Georgia

Athens. WMI284; Channel E. Kannew Broadcast Technologies. c/o Terry Newmyer, 1220 L St. N.W., #425, Washington, D.C. 20005.

Athens. WMI824; Channel F. Multichannel Media Inc. 2219 California St. N.W., Washington, D.C. 20008.

Atlanta. WHT663; Channel E. Stephen Communications Inc. c/o Phil Merrill, 2135 S. 2200 E., Salt Lake City, Utah 84109.

Atlanta. WHT664; Channel F. National Television Co. Meeting House Farm, Lincoln, Va. 22078.

Macon. WMH545; Channel E. Paul Communications Inc. 1223 W. 10th St., Tempe, Ariz. 85281-5318.

Macon. WMI857; Channel F. Krisar Inc. Box 186, Rexford, N.Y. 12148.

Valdosta. WLW848; Channel F. James Jackson Eldridge. Rte. 2, Box 2273, Ocilla, Ga. 31774.

Valdosta. WLW881; Channel E. Russel Acree. Box 656, Office #901, Adel, Ga. 31620.

Hawaii

Honolulu. WHT718; Channel F. Red Honolulu F Partnership. 2219 California St. N.W., Washington, D.C. 20008.

Idaho

Twin Falls. WLW965; Channel E. Charles William Mogensen Jr. c/o Idaho Home Theatre, Box 1508, Twin Falls, Idaho 83301.

Illinois

Bloomington. WHI964; Channel F. Krisar Inc. Box 186, Rexford, N.Y. 12148.

Bloomington. WHI968; Channel E. Prairieland Cable Partnership #1. 215 E. Douglas, Bloomington, Ill. 61701.

Casey. WLW821; Channel E. Ray Finney. Box 150, Casey, Ill. 62420.

Casey. WMI896; Channel F. Bolin Enterprises Inc. Box 133, Casey, Ill. 62420.

Champaign. WLK292; Channel F. Presco Corp. c/o Lowell H. Press, 4547 4th Ave. N.E., Seattle, Wash. 98105.

Champaign. WLW779; Channel E. Line of Site Inc. 6048 E. Kathleen Rd., Scottsdale, Ariz. 85254.

Chicago. WHK999; Channel F. Arnold Malkan. 304 Crestwood Dr., Fort Worth, Tex. 76107.

Peoria. WMH200; Channel F. Stephanie Engstrom. 111 Arlington Blvd., West Bldg. #732, Arlington, Va. 22209.

Peoria. WMH380; Channel E. Jack G. Hubbard. 8793 Ranch Dr., Chesterland, Ohio 44026.

Rockford. WMH333; Channel E. Walter Communications Inc. 1223 W. 10th St., Tempe, Ariz. 85281-5318.

Indiana

Anderson. WMH569; Channel E. Walter Communications Inc. 1223 W. 10th St., Tempe, Ariz. 85281-5318.

Elkhart. WMH360; Channel E. Paul Communications Inc. 1223 W. 10th St., Tempe, Ariz. 85281-5318.

Evansville. WLW799; Channel F. Multi-Micro Inc. 1223 W. 10th St., Tempe, Ariz. 85281-5318.

Fort Wayne. WHT767; Channel E. Figgie Communications Inc. c/o Alfred E. Ventola, 1063 Technology Park Dr., Glen Allen, Va. 23060.

Fort Wayne. WHT768; Channel F. T/V Communications Associates. 2550 5th Ave., Suite 124, San Diego, Calif. 92103.

Indianapolis. WHT674; Channel F. Red Indianapolis F Partnersip. 2219 California St. N.W., Washington, D.C. 20008.

Multichannel Multipoint Distribution Services

Kokomo. WMI877; Channel F. Krisar Inc. Box 186, Rexford, N.Y. 12148.

Lafayette. WLW814; Channel F. MWTV Inc. 3401 E. Cholla St., Phoenix, Ariz. 85028.

Muncie. WMH689; Channel E. Century Microwave Corp. 51 Locust Ave., New Canaan, Conn. 06840.

South Bend. WMI853; Channel F. Krisar Inc. Box 186, Rexford, N.Y. 12148.

Terre Haute. WMI833; Channel E. People's Choice TV Inc. Box 846, 233 N. Garrard, Rantoul, Ill. 61866.

Iowa

Palmer. WLK383; Channel E. Todd Communications Inc. 6545 Cecilia Cir., Minneapolis, Minn. 55435-2722.

Palmer. WLK386; Channel F. Evertek Inc. 216 N. Main St., Everly, Iowa 51338

Sioux City. WLW956; Channel F. Pro-Communications Inc. 233 N. Garrard, Rantoul, Ill. 61866.

Sioux City. WMH468; Channel E. Grand Alliance Sioux City (E) Partnership. c/o Rhonda L. Neil, Esq., 1920 N St. N.W., Suite 660, Washington, D.C. 20036

Spencer. WLK267; Channel F. Evertek Inc. 216 N. Main St., Everly, Iowa 51338.

Spencer. WLK403; Channel E. Todd Communications Inc. 6545 Cecilia Cir., Minneapolis, Minn. 55435-2722

Waterloo. WHK956; Channel E. Group Communications Inc. 1463 Oak Crest St., Waterloo, Iowa 50701.

Kansas

Erie. NEW; Channel F. John C. Rubow. R.R. 4, Chanute, Kan. 66720.

Hays. WHT621; Channel E. Multichannel Distribution of America (MDA). 10020 E. Girard, #300, Denver, Colo. 80231.

Salina. WHT623; Multichannel Distribution of America (MDA). 10020 E. Girard, #300, Denver, Colo. 80231.

Wichita. WHT743; Channel E. Paging Systems Inc. Box 4249, Burlingame, Calif. 94010.

Wichita. WHT744; Channel F. Omega Radiotelephone. c/o David Hernandez, 1601 Neptune Dr., San Leandro, Calif. 94577.

Kentucky

Louisville. WHT725; Channel E. VIA/NET Companies. 836 E. Washington St., San Diego, Calif. 92103.

Paducah. WLW755. Channel F. Baypoint TV Inc./McFadden, Evans & Sill. 1627 Eye St. N.W., Suite 810, Washington, D.C. 20006.

Paducah. WLW995. Channel E. Kannew Broadcast Technologies. c/o Terry Newmyer, 1220 L St. N.W., #425, Washington, D.C. 20005.

Louisiana

Baton Rouge. WHT707; Channel E. William Erdman & Max Hugel. 261 Dolfin Cove Quay, Stamford, Conn. 06902.

Houma. WMI831; Channel E. Virginia Communications Inc. 6330 E. Mockingbird Ln., Scottsdale, Ariz. 85253.

Lafayette. WMH361; Channel F. MWTV Inc., 3401 E. Cholla St., Phoenix, Ariz. 85028.

Lake Charles. WMH708; Channel E. Edna Comaggia. 4095 Fruit St., Space 345, La Verne, Calif. 91750.

Monroe. WMH357; Channel E. National Wireless Video Inc. c/o Walter Daniels, 24 Oak Dr., Durham, N.C. 27707.

New Orleans. WHT681; Channel E. Gold Star Communications. 1465 Greenbriar Dr., Green Oak, Ill. 60048.

New Orleans. WLW963; Channel F. WGNO Inc. 2 Canal St., Suite 2800 WTC, New Orleans, La. 70130.

Rayville. WMH413; Channel F. MDS of Louisiana. Box 454, Rayville, La. 71269.

Shreveport. WLK223; Channel E. Line of Site Inc. 6048 E. Kathleen Rd., Scottsdale, Ariz. 85254.

Maryland

Baltimore. WHT630; Channel E. Gay & Destefano Feasel. 156 Lazelle Rd., Worthington, Ohio 43085.

Baltimore. WHT631; Channel F. Multi-Micro Inc. 1223 W. 10th St., Tempe, Ariz. 85281-5318.

Massachusetts

Boston. WMI863; Channel E. Virginia Communications Inc. 6330 E. Mockingbird Ln., Scottsdale, Ariz. 85253.

Pittsfield. WMI289; Channel E. Belwen Inc. 7 Boyle Rd., Scotia, N.Y. 12302.

Springfield. WLK226; Channel F. Connecticut Home Theater. 1024 Coney Island Ave., Brooklyn, N.Y. 11230.

Worcester. WMH752; Channel E. DKB-GP Holding Corp., General Partner. 1800 Diagonal Rd., Suite 230, Alexandria, Va. 22314.

Worcester. WMI893; Channel E. Multi-Micro Inc. 1223 W. 10th St., Tempe, Ariz. 85281-5318.

Michigan

Detroit. WLK238; Channel F. Microband Wireless Cable of Detroit Inc. 286 Eldridge Rd., Fairfield, N.J. 07004.

Detroit. WLK367; Channel E. Daniels Entertainment Group Inc. 1880 Veteran Ave., #311, Los Angeles, Calif. 90025.

Flynt. WLK200; Channel F. B.F. Investments Inc. 7521 E. Edgemont, Scottsdale, Ariz. 85257.

Jackson. WMH517; Channel F. Mettler Communications Inc. c/o Lyle W. Mettler, Pres., 1453 E. Ivyglen, Mesa, Ariz. 85203.

Minnesota

Austin. WMH316; Channel E. Todd Communications Inc. 6545 Cecilia Cir., Minneapolis, Minn. 55435-2722.

Austin. WMH332; Channel F. Walter L. Bush Jr. 5704 Camelback Dr., Minneapolis, Minn. 55436.

Fairmont. WLW834; Channel E. Todd Communications Inc. 6545 Cecilia Cir., Minneapolis, Minn. 55435-2722.

Fairmont. WMH424; Channel F. Walter L. Bush Jr. 5704 Camelback Dr., Minneapolis, Minn. 55436.

Garfield. WLW783; Channel E. CMS Ltd. c/o Viking Vision, Box 963, 213 Lincoln Ave., Alexandria, Va. 56308.

Garfield. WLW784; Channel F. Marilyn Rouse. 807 S. Blackford, Algona, Iowa 50511.

Mankato. WLW853; Channel F. MDS Signal Group/McFadden, Evans & Sill. 1627 Eye St. N.W., Suite 810, Washington, D.C. 20006.

Minneapolis. WHT677; Channel E. Theodore D. Little. 5310 Waupaca Rd., Rancho Palos Verdes, Calif. 90274.

Minneapolis. WHT678; Channel F(1). Scollard Communications Inc. 3049 Las Vegas Blvd. S., Suite 432, Las Vegas, Nev. 89109.

St. Cloud. WMI286; Channel F. MWTV Inc. 3401 E. Cholla St., Phoenix, Ariz. 85028.

Windom. WLW989; Channel F. Wireless Cable Network. Box 337, Mitchell, S.D. 57301.

Windom. WLW990; Channel E. Georgia Livesay. Box 783, Mitchell, S.D. 57301.

Mississippi

Jackson. WLK203; Channel E. Virginia Communications Inc. 6330 E. Mockingbird Ln., Scottsdale, Ariz. 85253.

Missouri

Kansas City. WHT790; Channel E. Evans Microwave Inc. Box 181, Savoy, Ill. 61874.

Kansas City. WLK282; Channel F. BA-United Services Corp. Inc. 4363 10th Ave. N., Box 6486, Lake Worth, Fla. 33461.

Sikeston. WMH440; Channel E. Jerry Albert Payne. 1640 Barron Rd., Poplar Bluff, Mo. 63907.

St. Louis. WHT651; Channel E. Louis R. Dutreil/Dutreil, Lunding & Rackly Inc. 240 N. Washington Blvd., Suite 700, Sarasota, Fla. 34236.

St. Louis. WLK422; Channel F. Baypoint TV Inc./McFadden, Evans & Sill. 1627 Eye St. N.W., Suite 810, Washington, D.C. 20006.

Montana

Billings. WFY603; Channel E. Phoebe Virginia Stiles. 3441 Poly Dr., Suite 10, Billings, Mont. 59102.

Billings. WLW837; Channel F. Allaire Capital Corp. 1325 Warren Ave., Spring Lake, N.J. 07762.

Nebraska

Bartley. WHK929; Channel F. Southwest Telecommunications Cooperative Association Inc. Box N, Palisade, Neb. 69040.

Bartley. WLW999; Channel E. Nebraska Telecommunications Inc. 616 Chestnut Dr., Loveland, Colo. 80538.

Grand Island. WLW922; Channel F. Broadcast Data Corp. 189 Berdan Ave., Suite 247, Wayne, N.J. 07470.

Grand Island. WLW974; Channel E. Kannew Broadcast Technologies. c/o Terry Newmyer, 1220 L St. N.W., #425, Washington, D.C. 20005.

North Platte. WHK923; Channel F. Southwest Telecommunications Cooperative Association Inc. Box N, Palisade, Neb. 69040.

North Platte. WHK928; Channel E. Nebraska Telecommunications Inc. 616 Chestnut Dr., Loveland, Colo. 80538.

Omaha. WHT777; Channel E. Line of Site Inc. 6048 E. Kathleen Rd., Scottsdale, Ariz. 85254.

Omaha. WLW992; Channel F. Ron Abboud. 3208 S. 121st St., Omaha, Neb. 68137.

Oshkosh. WLW964; Channel F. Southwest Telecommunications Cooperative Association Inc. Box N, Palisade, Neb. 69040.

Oshkosh. WLW997; Channel E. Nebraska Telecommunications Inc. 616 Chestnut Dr., Loveland, Colo. 80538.

Wauneta. WHK926; Channel F. Southwest Telecommunications Cooperative Association Inc. Box N, Palisade, Neb. 69040.

Wauneta. WLW998; Channel E. Nebraska Telecommunications Inc. 616 Chestnut Dr., Loveland, Colo. 80538.

Nevada

Carson City. WMH705; Channel E. Lawrence N. Brandt. 3201 New Mexico Ave. N.W., Suite 220, Washington, D.C. 20016.

Carson City. WMH709; Channel F. Broadcast Data Corp. 189 Berdan Ave., Suite 247, Wayne, N.J. 07470.

Las Vegas. WHT722; Channel F. MMDS-Las Vegas Inc./McFadden, Evans & Sill. 1220 19th St. N.W., Suite 501, Washington, D.C. 20036.

Reno. WHT781; Channel E. Jonsson Communications Corp. 233 Wilshire Blvd., Suite 900, Santa Maria, Calif. 90401.

Reno. WHT782; Channel F. Michael O'Brien. 230 Sandburg Dr., Sacramento, Calif. 95819.

New Jersey

Atlantic City. WHT752; Channel E. Walter Communications Inc. 1223 W. 10th St., Tempe, Ariz. 85281-5318.

Atlantic City. WHT753; Channel F. Lehigh Valley Mobile Telephone Co. E. Rock Rd., Allentown, Pa. 18103.

Atlantic City. WMI280; Channel F. Orion Broadcasting Systems Inc. 2700 E. Sunset Blvd., Suite B-14, Las Vegas, Nev. 89120.

New Mexico

Albuquerque. WHT661; Channel E. Multichannel MDS Inc. R.D. 2, Elverson, Pa. 19520.

Albuquerque. WHT662; Channel F. Paul M. Kimball. Box 54526, Oklahoma City, Okla. 73154.

Las Cruces. WHK961; Channel F. Hazel & Walter Mickelson. 1709 Moon N.E., Albuquerque, N.M. 87112.

Las Cruces. WHK962; Channel E. National Wireless Video Inc. c/o Walter Daniels, 24 Oak Dr., Durham, N.C. 27707.

Santa Fe. WLW782; Channel E. Ted & Nancy Phillips Co. Box 431, Seminole, Okla. 74868.

Santa Fe. WMI325; Channel F. New Mexico Media Ltd. c/o Lee Brown, Gen. Ptnr., Box 4816, Santa Fe, N.M. 87502.

Multichannel Multipoint Distribution Services

Socorro. WMI416; Channel E. Socorro Satellite Systems Inc. 215 E. Manzanares Ave., Socorro, N.M. 87801.

Socorro. WMI417; Channel F. Socorro Satellite Systems Inc. 215 E. Manzanares Ave., Socorro, N.M. 87801.

New York

Albany. WHT750; Channel E. Affiliated MDS Corp./Brown, Rudnick, Freed & Gesmer. One Financial Center, 18th Fl., Boston, Mass. 02110.

Albany. WHT751; Channel F. John Hobart Wilson. Box 2978, Florence, Ore. 97439.

Binghamton. WLK276; Channel F. Krisar Inc. Box 186, Rexford, N.Y. 12148.

Buffalo. WHT665; Channel E. Lawrence N. Brandt. 3201 New Mexico Ave. N.W., Suite 220, Washington, D.C. 20016.

Glens Falls. WMI301; Channel F. Glens Falls BDC-MMDS Co. c/o Richard L. Vega & Associates, Box 19769, Orlando, Fla. 32814.

Syracuse. WHT739; Channel E. Line of Site Inc. 6048 E. Kathleen Rd., Scottsdale, Ariz. 85254.

Utica. WMI820; Channel F. Multi-Micro Inc. 1223 W. 10th St., Tempe, Ariz. 85281-5318.

North Carolina

Wilmington. WMI295; Channel F. Broadcast Data Corp. 189 Berdan Ave., Suite 247, Wayne, N.J. 07470.

North Dakota

Bowbells. WLW987; Channel E. Burke-Divide Electric Cooperative Inc. Box 6, Columbus, N.D. 58727.

Bowbells. WLW988; Channel F. Northwest Communications Cooperative. Box 38, Ray, N.D. 58849.

Cando. WLW982; Channel F. Cavalier Rural Electric Cooperative Inc. Box 749, Langdon, N.D. 58249.

Cando. WLW986; Channel E. United Telephone Mutual Aid Corp. Box 729, 411 7th Ave., Langdon, N.D. 58249.

Carrington. WLW751; Channel E. Tri-County Electric Cooperative Inc. Box 180, Carrington, N.D. 58421.

Carrington. WLW752; Channel F. Dakota Central Rural Telephone Cooperative Association Inc. Box 299, Carrington, N.D. 58421.

Fargo. WLK300; Channel F. Joseph W. Hubbard. 26573 Basswood Ave., Rancho Palo Verdes, Calif. 90274.

Fargo. WLW839; Channel E. Broad Inc. 11601 Wilshire Blvd., Los Angeles, Calif. 90025.

Fort Ransom. WMI875; Channel E. Cass County Electric Cooperative Inc. Box 676, Kindred, N.D. 58051-0008.

Fort Ransom. WMI879; Channel F. Cass County Electric Cooperative Inc. Box 676, Kindred, N.D. 58051-0008.

Killdeer. WLW765; Channel F. West Plains Electric Cooperative Inc. Box 1038, Dickinson, N.D. 58602.

Killdeer. WLW766; Channel E. Consolidated Telephone Cooperative Inc. Box 1077, Dickinson, N.D. 58602.

Langdon. WLW984; Channel E. United Telephone Mutual Aid Corp. Box 729, 411 7th Ave., Langdon, N.D. 58249.

Langdon. WLW984; Channel F. Cavalier Rural Electric Cooperative Inc. Box 749, Langdon, N.D. 58249.

Lefor. WLW764; Channel F. West Plains Electric Cooperative Inc. Box 1038, Dickinson, N.D. 58602.

Lefor. WLW771; Channel E. Consolidated Telephone Cooperative Inc. Box 1077, Dickinson, N.D. 58601.

Minot. WLC269; Channel F. Broadcast Data Corp. 189 Berdan Ave., Suite 247, Wayne, N.J. 07470.

Minot. WMI313; Channel E. Lawrence N. Brandt. 3201 New Mexico Ave. N.W., Suite 220, Washington, D.C. 20016.

Scranton. WLW769; Channel F. Slope Electric Cooperative Inc., Box 338, New England, N.D. 58647.

Scranton. WLW770; Channel E. Consolidated Telephone Cooperative Inc. Box 1077, Dickinson, N.D. 58601.

Williston. WLW748; Channel E. Williams Electric Cooperative Inc. Box 1346, Williston, N.D. 58647.

Williston. WLW968; Channel F. Northwest Communications Cooperative. Box 38, Ray, N.D. 58849.

Ohio

Cincinnati. WHT632; Channel E. Charter Cable Inc. 300 Main St., 2nd Fl., Cincinnati, Ohio 45202.

Cincinnati. WHT633; Channel F. Superior Broadcasting Corp. 27181 Euclid Ave., Euclid, Ohio 44132

Cleveland. WLK306; Channel F. Krisar Inc. Box 186, Rexford, N.Y. 12148.

Cleveland. WLK310; Channel E. Lawrence N. Brandt. 3201 New Mexico Ave. N.W., Suite 220, Washington, D.C. 20016.

Columbus. WHT669; Channel E. Columbus Wireless Cable TV Inc. 156 Lazelle Rd., Worthington, Ohio 43085.

Columbus. WHT670; Channel F. Champion Industries Inc. 300 W. Mission Dr., Chandler, Ariz. 85225.

Dayton. WHT713; Channel E. Stephen Communications Inc. c/o Phil Merrill, 2135 South 2200 East, Salt Lake City, Utah 84109.

Dayton. WHT714; Channel F. Progressive MDS & Associates. 1920 N Street N.W., Suite 620, Washington, D.C. 20036.

Lima. WMH228; Channel E. Line of Site Inc. 6048 E. Kathleen Rd., Scottsdale, Ariz. 85254.

Lima. WMH528; Channel F. Hisol Limited Partnership. 7521 E. Edgemont, Scottsdale, Ariz. 85257.

Toledo. WHT741; Channel E. Jody Barnes. 690 Sycamore, Claremont, Calif. 91711.

Toledo. WHT742; Channel F. B.F. Investments Inc. 7521 E. Edgemont, Scottsdale, Ariz. 85257.

Oklahoma

Ada. WMH336; Channel F. Frankie Cornelison. 1948 W. Live Oak, Durant, Okla. 74701.

Ada. WMH337; Channel E. Barry James. 202 N. 3rd St., Durant, Okla. 74701.

Broken Bow/Idab. WHM376; Channel E. Jewel B. Callaham. Box 548, Broken Bow, Okla. 74728.

Clayton. WLK328; Channel E. Oklahoma Western Telephone. Box 399, Clayton, Okla. 74536.

Colony. WMI311; Channel F. Hinton Telephone Co. of Hinton Oklahoma Inc. 120 W. Main, Hinton, Okla. 73047.

Enid. WMH701; Channel F. Baypoint TV Inc./McFadden, Evans & Sill. 1627 Eye St. N.W., Suite 810, Washington, D.C. 20006.

Lindsay. WLW828; Channel E. Charles R. Jones. Box 609, Lindsay, Okla. 73052.

Lindsay. WLW983; Channel F. Rural Electric Cooperative Inc. Box 609, Lindsay, Okla. 73052.

Oklahoma City. WHT683; Channel E. John J. O'Loughlin. 15 Wheeler Ct., Deer Park, N.Y. 11729.

Oklahoma City. WHT684; Channel F. Starchannels Associates L.P. One Huntington Quadrangle, Suite 2, South 9, Melville, N.Y. 11747.

Oregon

Medford. WLK249; Channel E. Fortuna Systems Corp. c/o Philip C. Merrill, 3312 Garrison St., San Diego, Calif. 92106.

Medford. WLK253; Channel F. Mettler Communications Inc. c/o Lyle W. Mettler, Pres., 1453 E. Ivyglen, Mesa, Ariz. 85203.

Portland. WHT647; Channel E. Red Portland E Partnership. 2219 California St. N.W., Washington, D.C. 20008.

Portland. WHT648; Channel F. Champion Industries Inc. 300 W. Mission Dr., Chandler, Ariz. 85225.

Prineville. WHK953; Channel E. West Indian Group Inc. Box 939, Portland, Ore. 97207.

Prineville. WLW954; Channel F. Terracomm Partnership. c/o Robert T. Stenson, 700 Larkspur Landing Cir., Suite 175, Larkspur, Calif. 94939.

Pennsylvania

Altoona. WLK302; Channel E. Virginia Communications Inc. 6330 E. Mockingbird Ln., Scottsdale, Ariz. 85253.

Philadelphia. WHT643; Channel E. ACS Enterprises Inc. 2064 State Rd., Bensalem, Pa. 19020.

Philadelphia. WHT644; Channel F. Northwest Communications Inc. 7900 Germantown Ave., Philadelphia, Pa. 19118.

Pittsburgh. WHT645; Channel E. Pro-Communications Inc. 233 N. Garrard, Rantoul, Ill. 61866.

Pittsburgh. WHT646; Channel F. Champion Industries Inc. 300 W. Mission Dr., Chandler, Ariz. 85225.

Reading. WMI314; Channel E. Paul Communications Inc. 1223 W. 10th St., Tempe, Ariz. 85281-5318.

State College. WMI366; Channel F. Krisar Inc. Box 186, Rexford, N.Y. 12148.

South Dakota

Aberdeen. WLK408; Channel E. Northern Rural Cable TV Cooperative Inc. Box 488, Bath, S.D. 57427.

Aberdeen. WLK409; Channel F. FEM Electric Association Inc. Box 468, Ipswich, S.D. 57451.

Colman. WHI959; Channel F. Sioux Valley Rural Television Inc. Colman, S.D. 57017.

Mitchell. WGW419; Channel E. Charles Mauszycki. 210 N. Main, Mitchell, S.D. 57301.

Mitchell. WHD364; Channel F. Kevin Johnson. Box 126, Mitchell, S.D. 57301.

Rapid City. WMI825; Channel E. People's Choice TV Inc. Box 846, 233 N. Garrard, Rantoul, Ill. 61866.

Sioux Falls. WLK285; Channel F. Warren F. Ache. 3206 Rustic Villa Dr., Kingwood, TX 77345.

Sisselton. WLK365; Channel E. Coteau Multipoint Corp. Box 880, Watertown, S.D. 57201.

Sisselton. WLK366; Channel F. Prairie Multipoint Corp. Box 850, Watertown, S.D. 57201.

Watertown. WLK327; Channel F. Prairie Multipoint Corp. Box 850, Watertown, S.D. 57201.

Watertown. WLK330; Channel E. Coteau Multipoint Corp. Box 880, Watertown, S.D. 57201.

Willow Lake. WLK319; Channel F. Prairie Multipoint Corp. Box 850, Watertown, S.D. 57201.

Willow Lake. WLK323; Channel E. Codington-Clark Electric Cooperative Inc. Box 880, Watertown, S.D. 57201.

Yankton. WLK328; Channel F. Kevin Johnson. Box 126, Mitchell, S.D. 57301.

Yankton. WLK384; Channel F. E.M. Parsens. Box 1043, Pierre, S.D. 57501.

Tennessee

Clarksville. WLW966; Channel E. Virginia Communications Inc. 6330 E. Mockingbird Ln., Scottsdale, Ariz. 85253.

Clarksville. WLW969; Channel F. Multi-Micro Inc. 1223 W. 10th St., Tempe, Ariz. 85281-5318.

Knoxville. WHT720; Channel F. Captial Cities Entertainment Systems Inc. Capital Cities/ABC Inc. 77 W. 66th St., 16th Fl., New York, N.Y. 10023.

Knoxville. WLW953; Channel E. Belwen Inc. 7 Boyle Rd., Scotia, N.Y. 12302.

Nashville. WHT679; Channel F. Presco Corp. c/o Lowell H. Press, 4547 4th Ave. N.E., Seattle, Wash. 98105.

Nashville. WHT680; Channel E. Jack G. Hubbard. 8793 Ranch Dr., Chesterland, Ohio 44026.

Union City. WGW628; Channel E. Union City Microvision. Box 709, Union City, Tenn. 38261.

Union City. WMI844; Channel F. Steven J. Harpole. Box 709, Union City, Tenn. 38261.

Texas

Amarillo. WHT794; Channel E. Microwave Video Services Inc. c/o Philip C. Merrill, 331 Sea Ridge Dr., La Jolla, Calif. 92037.

Austin. WHT705; Channel E. Grand MMDS Alliance Austin E/P Partnership. 1920 N St. N.W., Suite 660, Washington, D.C. 20036.

Austin. WHT706; Channel F. Columbia Wireless Corp. 1629 K St. N.W., Suite 600, Washington, D.C. 20006.

Broadcasting & Cable Yearbook 1994

Multichannel Multipoint Distribution Services

Bryan. WLW978; Channel F. Becker Broadcasting. Box 12641, 106 Castellano, El Paso, Tex. 79912.

Bryan. WLW979; Channel E. Teltran Communications Inc. 8850 Kenton Dr., Dallas, Tex. 75213.

Corpus Christi. WHT711; Channel E. Fortuna Systems Corp. c/o Philip C. Merrill, 3312 Garrison St., San Diego, Calif. 92106.

Corpus Christi. WHT712; Channel F. Starchannels Associates L.P. One Huntington Quadrangle, Suite 2, South 9, Melville, N.Y. 11747.

Dallas. WHT789; Channel F. BA United Service Corp. Inc. 233 N. Garrard, Rantoul, Ill. 61866.

El Paso. WHK950; Channel E. T/V Communications Associates. 2550 5th Ave., Suite 124, San Diego, Calif. 92103.

El Paso. WHT766; Channel F. Red El Paso F Partnership. 1220 19th St. N.W., Washington, D.C. 20036.

Falfurrias. WLW892; Channel E. Ultra Vision of Texas Inc. 602 Barracuda, Corpus Christie, Tex. 78411.

Falfurrias. WLW896; Channel F. Ultra Vision of Texas Inc. 602 Barracuda, Corpus Christie, Tex. 78411.

George West. WLW900; Channel E. Ultra Vision of Texas Inc. 602 Barracuda, Corpus Christie, Tex. 78411.

George West. WLW904; Channel F. Ultra Vision of Texas Inc. 602 Barracuda, Corpus Christie, Tex. 78411.

Houston. WLK305; Channel E. Block & Associates. 3777 Boise Ave., Los Angeles, Calif. 90066.

Killeen. WMI835; Channel E. Visionaire Inc. R.R. 4, Box 206, Pound Ridge, N.Y. 10576.

Killeen. WMI869; Channel F. Krisar Inc. Box 186, Rexford, N.Y. 12148.

Longview. WMH477; Channel E. Fortuna Systems Corp. c/o Philip C. Merrill, 3312 Garrison St., San Diego, Calif. 92106.

Roma. WLW940; Channel E. Tele-View Inc. Box 186, Roma, Tex. 78584.

Roma. WLW941; Channel F. Valley Wireless Cable Inc. 5610 District Blvd., Suite 101, Bakersfield, Calif 93313-2178.

San Angelo. WLW827; Channel F. Joseph Louis Calibani. 5222 N. Bentwood Dr., San Angelo, Tex. 76904.

San Antonio. WHT693; Channel E. Ralph Larsen & Son Inc. 1849 Old Bayshore Hwy., Suite 321, Burlingame, Calif. 94010.

San Antonio. WHT694; Channel F. Omega Radiotelephone. c/o David Hernandez, 1601 Neptune Dr., San Leandro, Calif. 94577.

San Saba. WMH724; Channel F. Central Texas Telephone Cooperative Inc. Box 627, Goldthwaite, Tex. 76844.

San Saba. WMH728; Channel E. Central Texas Telephone Cooperative Inc. Box 627, Goldthwaite, Tex. 76844.

Sherman. WLW760; Channel F. Broadcast Data Corp. 189 Berdan Ave., Suite 247, Wayne, N.J. 07470.

Waco. WHI625; Channel E. People's Choice TV Inc. Box 846, 233 N. Garrard, Rantoul, Ill. 61866.

Waco. WMI865; Channel F. Mettler Communications Inc. c/o Lyle Mettler, Pres., 1453 E. Ivyglen, Mesa, Ariz. 85203.

Utah

St. George. WMI363; Channel F. American Wireless Inc. Box 1207, St. George, Utah 84770-7101.

St. George. WMI367; Channel E. American Wireless Inc. Box 1207, St. George, Utah 84770-7101.

Salt Lake City. WLW775; Channel E. Affiliated Communications Corp. 333 Jericho Tpke., Jericho, N.Y. 11753.

Vermont

Cornwall. WMH308; Channel E. Satellite Signals of New England Inc. Box 608, Barre, Vt. 05641.

Rutland. WLK341; Channel E. Satellite Signals of New England Inc. Box 608, Barre, Vt. 05641.

Virginia

Charlottesville. WLW840; Channel F. Desert Communications Inc. 1414 Valley Bank Plaza, 300 S. 4th St., Las Vegas, Nev. 89101.

Charlottesville. WMH388; Channel E. Charlottesville Quality Cable Corp. 1147 River Rd., Suite 7, Charlottesville, Va. 22901.

Lynchburg. WMI288; Channel F. G/S Lynchburg F Settlement Group. c/o Paul L. Yoquelet, Mgng. Ptnr., 3423 Rolston St., Fort Wayne, Ind. 46805.

Roanoke. WGW371; Channel F. Microwave Television Inc. Medical Arts Bldg., 3708 S. Main St., Suite F, Blacksburg, Va. 24060.

Washington

Seattle. WHT656; Channel E. Jack G. Hubbard. 8793 Ranch Dr., Chesterland, Ohio 44026.

Spokane. WHT783; Channel F. Haddonfield Wireless Co. 400 Merion Ave., Haddonfield, N.J. 08033.

Spokane. WHT784; Channel F. Stephanie Engstrom. 1111 Arlington Blvd., West Bldg. #732, Arlington, Va. 22209.

Yakima. WLK396; Channel E. Microwave Video Services Inc. c/o Philip C. Merrill, 331 Sea Ridge Dr., La Jolla, Calif. 92037.

Yakima. WLW944; Channel F. Presco Corp. c/o Lowell H. Press, 4547 4th Ave. N.E., Seattle, Wash. 98105.

West Virginia

Parkersburg. WMI413; Channel F. Multi-Micro Inc. 1223 W. 10th St., Tempe, Ariz. 85281-5318.

Wheeling. WLK289; Channel E. Paul Communications Inc. 1223 W. 10th St., Tempe, Ariz. 85281-5318.

Wheeling. WLK293; Channel F. Mettler Communications Inc. c/o Lyle Mettler, Pres., 1453 E. Ivyglen, Mesa, Ariz. 85203.

Wisconsin

Green Bay. WLW980; Channel F. MWTV Inc. 3401 E. Cholla St., Phoenix, Ariz. 85028.

Green Bay. WLW981; Channel E. Fortuna Systems Corp. c/o Philip C. Merrill, 3312 Garrison St., San Diego, Calif. 92106.

Janesville. WMI326; Channel F. Multi-Micro Inc. 1223 W. 10th St., Tempe, Ariz. 85281-5318.

La Crosse. WMH472; Channel F. Grand Alliance La Crosse (F) Partnership. 1920 N St. N.W., Suite 660, Washington, D.C. 20036.

Madison. WDU380; Channel E. Edna Comaggia. 4095 Fruit St., Space 345, La Verne, Calif. 91750.

Madison. WHT772; Channel F. Skyview Inc. 171 Industrial Ave., Belleville, Wis. 53508.

Milwaukee. WHT641; Channel F. John Hobart Wilson. Box 2978, Florence, Ore. 97439.

Sheboygan. WMH688; Channel F. Broadcast Data Corp. 189 Berdan Ave., Suite 247, Wayne, N.J. 07970.

Wyoming

Sheridan. WLW820; Channel F. Dana Kathleen Wyatt. 844 Greystone, Sheridan, Wyo. 82801.

Sheridan. WLW824; Channel E. Elaine Vestesen Abdallah. 3404 Sharp Rd. Glenwood, Md. 21738.

Puerto Rico

San Juan. WHT654; Channel F. Victor Ginorio Gomez. Epedregel #7, Box 307, Humacao, P.R. 00661.

San Juan. WHT655; Channel F. Sala Foundation Inc. 43 Concordia, Suite 105, Ponce, P.R. 00731.

Section F

Advertising and Marketing Services

Table of Contents

Table of Contents	F-1
Advertising Agencies Handling Major Radio and Television Accounts	F-2
Independent Media Buying/Planning Services	F-8
Barter Service Companies	F-9
Radio, Television and Cable Representatives	
United States	F-10
Canada	F-20
Public Relations, Publicity and Promotion Services	F-21

Advertising Agencies Handling Major Radio and Television Accounts

AC & R Advertising Inc. 16 E. 32nd St., New York 10016. (212) 685-2500. FAX: (212) 689-2258. Alvin Chereskin, chmn; Steve Bennett, pres/CEO.
Radio-TV media dept: Randy Novick, VP/media dir; Linda Melman, assoc media dir.

Abramson, Ehrlich-Manes, Co. 1275 K St., Washington 20005. (202) 289-6900. David Abramson, pres/CEO.

Ally & Gargano Inc. 805 3rd Ave., New York 10022. (212) 688-5300. FAX: (212) 418-6875. Mal Macdougall, chmn; William Luceno, CEO; Warren Dechter, pres/COO.
Radio-TV media dept: Dawn Sibley, exec VP/dir media & communications svcs.

Ammirati & Puris Inc. 100 5th Ave., New York 10011. (212) 206-0500. FAX: (212) 337-9481. Ralph Ammirati, chmn/creative dir; Martin Ford Puris, pres/CEO.
Radio-TV media dept: Michael Lotito, sr VP/media dir.

Athletes in Advertising. 18 Tomney Rd., Greenwich, Conn. 06830. (203) 629-9098. FAX: (203) 869-0416. Albert S. Kestnbaum, pres.

N.W. Ayer Inc. 825 8th Ave., New York 10019-7498. (212) 474-5000. FAX: (212) 474-5400. Jerry J. Siano, chmn/pres/CEO; Dominick Rossi, pres Ayer New York.
Radio-TV media dept: Beth Gordon, sr VP/N.Y. media dir; Aaron Cohen, sr VP dir bcstg progmg.
Chicago 60610: 515 State St. (312) 644-2937. Frank Maher, gen mgr. Zwiren & Ayer.
Los Angeles 90036: 5900 Wilshire Blvd. (213) 931-6301. Dick Fried, pres. Ayer Tuttle.
Detroit 48202: 2000 Fisher Bldg. (313) 874-8500. Danielle Colliver, pres/mngng dir; Robert Reuschle, media dir. Ayer Detroit.

BBDO Chicago Inc. 410 N. Michigan Ave., Chicago 60611. (312) 337-7860. FAX: (312) 337-6871. Eric Harkna, pres/CEO; Mike Hedge, sr VP/dir media svcs; Bob Bailey, Ernie Stern, Phil Gant, exec VPs; David Quinnert, sr VP/CFO.
Radio-TV media dept: Maureen Gorman, Nancy Swiet, Deb Nevin, VPs.

BBDO South. 1600 Monarch Plaza, 3414 Peachtree Rd. N.E., Atlanta 30326. (404) 231-1700. FAX: (404) 841-1788. Donald C. Mitchum, pres/CEO; Jack V. Walz, exec VP/dir account mgmt; Virgil Shutze, chmn/chief creative off.
Radio-TV media dept: Allen Ginsberg, sr VP media dir; Sara Walker, VP/dir bcst buying; Nik Mainthia, VP/assoc media dir.

BBDO Worldwide. 1285 Ave. of the Americas, New York 10019. (212) 459-5000. Allen G. Rosenshine, chmn/CEO; Bruce Crawford, pres; E.E. Norris, exec VP/chmn adv strategy review bd; Richard B. White, exec VP; Robert H. Ellis, exec VP/mgmt supvr; Larry Light, exec VP/dir mktg, media svcs & bus dev; J. Thomas Clark, exec VP; Arnold Semsky, sr VP/dir media & net progmg; Philip Dusenberry, sr VP/creative off; Karl Fischer, sr VP/dir radio-TV prod & art svcs.
Minneapolis 55415: Lutheran Brotherhood Bldg., 625 4th Ave. S., Suite 900. (612) 338-8401. John Firestone, sr VP/gen mgr.

Backer Spielvogel Bates Worldwide Inc. Crysler Bldg. 405 Lexington Ave., New York 10174. (212) 297-7000. FAX: (212) 297-8637. Carl Spielvogel, chmn/CEO; William Backer, vice-chmn/exec creative dir; John Citron, exec VP finance & admin; Anne Melanson, sr VP/dir human resources. Backer Spielvogel Bates Inc. (U.S.): Stephen M. Leff, vice-chmn/dir media & admin svcs; Jay Schoenfeld, exec VP/media dir; Gerald Bonsaing, sr VP/dir local bcst & field opns; Leslie Wood, VP media rsch.
Dublin, Ohio 43017: 94 N. High St. (614) 792-0555.

Bailey, Klepinger & Medrich. 130 S. 1st St., Ann Arbor, Mich. 48104. (313) 769-6771. FAX: (313) 769-3713. Melvin L. Medrich, chmn; Robert L. Klepinger, pres.
Radio-TV media dept: Karen M. Tucker, media dir.

Walter Bennett Communications. 13355 Noel Rd., Suite 1815, Dallas 75240. (214) 661-1122. FAX: (214) 980-0640. Ted Dienert, pres; Larry Ross, mgr PR; Vin Bell, exec VP/financial VP.
Chicago 60606: 20 N. Wacker, Suite 2245. (312) 372-1131. Jan Kluts, TV media dir; Marie Molsen, asst media dir.
Fort Washington, Pa. 19034: 7111 Valley Green Rd., Suite 220. (215) 836-2727. Fred Dienert, chmn of bd; Bob Straton, sr VP/mktg dir radio bcst svc.

Biederman, Kelly & Shaffer Inc. 475 Park Ave. S., New York 10016. (212) 213-5500. Barry Biederman, chmn; John F. Kelly, pres; Joanne Veloudos, sr VP/media dir.
Radio-TV media dept: Lisa Bifulco, dir bcst prod; Kelly DesRoches, bcst traf coord.

Bigelow & Eigel Inc. 2 Executive Pk. W., Atlanta 30329. (404) 320-7260. FAX: (404) 320-7381. Thomas G. Bigelow, pres/exec creative dir; Stephen C. Eigel, chmn.
Radio-TV media dept: Michael Green, gen mgr/exec VP.

Ralph Bing Advertising Co. 16109 Selva Dr., San Diego 92128. Ralph S. Bing, pres.
Radio-TV media dept: Ralph S. Bing.

Bozell Inc. 40 W. 23rd St., New York 10010. (212) 727-5000. FAX: (212) 645-9262. Charles D. Peebler Jr., CEO; David Bell, pres; Ron Anderson, exec VP/chief creative off; Leo Arthur Kelmenson, chmn exec committee; Ron DeLuca, vice-chmn; Sid Marshall, exec VP; Murray L. Smith, pres international; Lawrence Dobrow, exec VP/dir corporate communications media dept.
Radio-TV media dept: Michael Drexler, exec VP/natl media dir.
Atlanta 30305: One Securities Ctr., 3490 Piedmont Rd. (404) 226-2221. David Strauss, gen mgr; Bob Scott, media dir.
Chicago 60611: 625 N. Michigan Ave. (312) 988-2000. Ric Cooper, pres Midwest; Diane Niederman, media dir.
Irving, Tex. 75062: 201 E. Carpenter Fwy. (214) 556-1100. Leiner Temerlin, chmn of bd; Dennis McClain, pres Southwest. Dallas office.
Birmingham, Mich. 48010: 30600 Telegraph Rd. (313) 645-6170. George Beech, exec VP; Phil Matz, media dir. Detroit office.
Los Angeles 90025: 2121 Wilshire Blvd. (310) 442-2400. Renee Fraser, gen mgr; Ben Benya, media dir.
Minneapolis 55403: 100 N. 6th St. (612) 371-7500. Ron Benza, gen mgr; Jeanette Gordon, media dir.
Omaha, Neb. 68131-2453: 800 Blackstone Centre, 302 S. 36th St. (402) 345-3400. Tim Stickinger, gen mgr; Lynda Alvarez, media dir.
Tampa 33607: 3030 N. Rocky Point Dr. W. (813) 281-0477. William Diaz, gen mgr; Rue Ann Porter, media dir.
Alexandria, Va. 22314: 99 Canal Ctr. Plaza. (703) 549-0600. Bill Burling, gen mgr. Washington office.

Brugnatelli & Partners Inc. 555 W. 57th St., New York 10019. (212) 586-1020. FAX: (212) 586-1362. Bruno E. Brugnatelli, pres; F. Malcolm Minor, exec VP; Gerald Weinman, sr VP; Mitchell Siegel, sr VP.
Radio-TV media dept: Debra Dubin, media dir.
Rome, Italy: Via Aquilania, 27-100177. 06-290325. Giuseppe Lucci, pres.
Madrid, Spain 28033: Garcia Plata S.A. Calle Marquez De Urquijo 10.

Howard Burkat Communications. 11 Rectory Ln., Scarsdale, N.Y. 10583. (914) 723-2657. FAX: (914) 472-6225. Howard Burkat, owner.
Consulting, mktg, promoting & adv—international & domestic—for cable, TV, satellite, video. Plans, analyses, campaigns, ads, brochures, recruiting.

Leo Burnett Co. Inc. 35 W. Wacker Dr., Chicago 60601. (312) 220-5959. FAX: (312) 220-6566. Hall Adams, CEO; Rick Fizdale, pres/chief creative off; Bill Lynch, pres USA.
Radio-TV media dept: Willard Hadlocks, exec VP media svcs; Jayne Zenatry, VP/dir media research; Marla Johnson, VP bcst bus.
New York 10022: 767 5th Ave. (212) 759-5959. Eugene Accas, Gary Press, VPs net rel.
Los Angeles 90068: 3801 Barham Blvd. (213) 876-5959. Wil Fieldhouse, VP/mgr TV svcs.
Toronto, Ont., Canada M5H 3C1: 165 University Ave. (416) 366-5801. Tony Houghton, mngng dir. Leo Burnett Co. Ltd.

Burson - Marsteller. 230 Park Ave. S., New York 10013. (212) 614-4000. Harold Burson, chmn; Larry Snodden, pres.
Chicago 60601: One E. Wacker Dr. (312) 329-1100. R. Milton Lynnes, VP/gen mgr.
Pittsburgh 15219: 600 Grant St. (412) 456-2500. Richard Farrell, VP/gen mgr.
Los Angeles 90010: 3600 Wilshire Blvd. (213) 386-8600. Donald Brashears, VP/mgr client svcs.

Lawrence Butner Advertising Inc. 228 E. 45th St., New York 10017. (212) 682-3200. Lawrence Butner, pres; Eleanor Butner, exec VP; Nevil Cross, sr VP; Robin Butner, sr VP/gen mgr.
Radio-TV media dept: Henry Bartolf, VP/media dir; Felicia Harris & Michelle Branciforte, media svcs reps.

CME-KHBB. 222 S. 9th St., Minneapolis 55402. (612) 347-1000. FAX: (612) 347-1515. Bill Dunlap, CEO.
Radio/TV media dept: Earl Herzog, media dir.
Chicago 60611: 737 N. Michigan Ave. (312) 266-5100. Tess Zych, media dir.
Southfield, Mich. 48034: 27777 Franklin Blvd., Suite 1000. (313) 354-5400. Randy Schroeder, media dir.
New York 10174: Chrysler Bldg., 405 Lexington Ave. (212) 856-4500.

Cable Networks Inc. 260 Madison Ave., 12th Fl., New York 10016. (212) 889-4670. FAX: (212) 689-0952. Peter J. Moran, sr VP; Stacie M. Colbeth, dir sls eastern rgn.
Atlanta 30305: 7 Piedmont Ctr., Suite 420. (404) 266-3885. Jenny Hazelry, sls mgr.
Boston 02116: 855 Boylston St., 3rd Fl. (617) 266-7711. Bill Wayland, sls mgr.
Dallas 75247: 8150 Brook River Dr., Suite 202. (214) 905-9966. Ray Gaskin, sls mgr.
Santa Monica, Calif. 90404: Colorado Pl., 2450 Broadway Ave., Suite 500. (310) 828-1142. Ilise Welter, sls mgr.
Cleveland 44114: 3400 Lakeside Ave. (216) 621-2221. Mark Dolan, sls mgr. N.O.I./CNI.

Calet, Hirsch & Ferrell. 250 Park Ave. S., New York 10003. (212) 777-0666. FAX: (212) 529-3496. Ricardo C. Calvillo, chmn; Peter Hirsch, vice chmn/exec creative dir; John Ferrell, pres/chief creative off; Donald S. Wergeles, pres.
Radio-TV media dept: Lori O' Rourke, VP assoc media dir; Gloria Peterkin, media dir.

Carden & Cherry Advertising Agency. 1220 McGavock St., Nashville 37203. (615) 255-6694. FAX: (615) 255-9302. Jerry Carden, pres; Tom Sparks, sr VP.

Chestnut Communications Inc. 18 Tomney Rd., Greenwich, Conn. 06830. (203) 629-9098. FAX: (203) 869-0416. Albert S. Kestnbaum, pres.

Chiat/Day/Mojo Inc. 340 Main St., Venice, Calif. 90291. (310) 314-5000. FAX: (310) 314-6166. Jay Chiat, CEO/chmn of bd (worldwide); Lee Clow, exec VP/chief creative dir.
New York 10003: 79 5th Ave., 15th Fl. (212) 807-4000. Jay Chiat, chmn.

Cole & Weber. 308 Occidental Ave. S., Seattle 98104. (206) 447-9595. FAX: (206) 447-1944. Austin McGhie, chmn/pres/CEO; Jim Christensen, VP/CFO.
Radio-TV media dept: Sam Walsh, sr prod; Shirley Radebaugh, prod; Ron Jaco, sr VP/mgnng dir (media); Mary Jane Keehn, VP/dir media planning.
Portland, Ore. 97204: 55 S.W. Yamhill St. (503) 226-2821. Debby Kennedy, mngng dir.

Colle & McVoy Advertising Agency Inc. 7900 International Dr., Suite 700, Minneapolis 55425. (612) 851-2500. Clarence M. Thompson Jr., chmn of bd; Al Hietala, CEO; Jim Bergeson, pres.
Radio-TV media dept: Merry Johnson, media dir; Rose Chick, bcst prod mgr; Mona Morgan, bcst traf mgr.

Cove, Cooper, Lewis Inc. 135 E. 55th St., New York 10022. (212) 371-9583. FAX: (212) 371-9583. Bernard Cooper, pres.
Radio-TV media dept: Francesca Lupo, media dir.

The Cramer-Krasselt Co. 733 N. Van Buren St., Milwaukee 53202. (414) 227-3500. FAX: (414) 276-8710. Paul Consell, CEO.
Radio-TV media dept: Donald E. Pom, VP TV/radio.
Chicago 60601: 225 N. Michigan Ave. (312) 977-9600. P.G. Krivkovich, pres.
Radio-TV media dept: Bill Blaha, VP/media dir.
Phoenix 85014: 1420 E. Missouri Ave. (602) 277-0600. R.G. Normann, exec VP/gen mgr.
Radio-TV media dept: Ginny Michaelson, media dir.
Orlando, Fla. 32802: 225 E. Robinson. (407) 236-8300. Fran Mathews, VP/gen mgr.
Radio-TV media dept: Pam Taylor, media dir.

Advertising Agencies

Creative Media Associates Inc. 1219 Florida Ave., Palm Harbor, Fla. 34683. (813) 785-3888. FAX: (813) 785-6757. James Doulgeris, pres; William Clark, exec VP.

Creswell, Munsell, Fultz & Zirbel Inc. (CMF&Z). (A Young & Rubicam Co.) Box 2879, 4211 Signal Ridge Rd. N.E., Cedar Rapids, Iowa 52406. (319) 395-6500. FAX: (319) 395-6575. Frank C. Baker, pres/CEO; William Fritz, sr VP/exec creative dir.
 Radio-TV media dept: Diane E. Stadlen, sr VP/dir media svcs.
 Des Moines 50306: Box 4807, 600 E. Court Ave., Suite E. (515) 246-3500. William Fultz, chmn.
 Washington 20006: 1667 K St. N.W., Suite 430. (202) 862-4990. Susan Neely, sr VP/gen mgr.
 Raleigh, N.C. 27604: 3100 Smoketree Ct., Suite 803. (919) 872-1477. Al Schoneman, gen mgr.

Cuneo Sullivan Dolabany. 745 Boylston St., Suite 201, Boston 02116. (617) 262-1616. FAX: (617) 262-5850. John R. Cuneo, pres/CEO; Paul J. Sullivan, Dana J. Dolabany, exec VPs.
 Radio-TV media dept: Michael Jarmolowsky, media dir; Rhonda Curtis, Michelle Carideo, media buyers.

DDB Needham Worldwide Inc. 437 Madison Ave., New York 10022. (212) 415-2000. (212) 415-2715. FAX: (212) 415-3591. Keith Reinhard, chmn & CEO, John Bernbach, pres; Page Thompson, exec VP media progmg.
 Radio-TV media dept: Daniel F. Rank, sr VP/dir. (212-415-2756. FAX: 212-415-3443).
 Dallas 75201: 200 Crescent Ct. (214) 885-2300. FAX: (214) 885-2394. Greg Taucher, sr VP/gen mgr. DDB Needham Worldwide Inc.
 Dallas 75201: 200 Crescent Ct., Suite 900. (214) 969-9000. Mike Rawlings, pres/CEO. Tracy Locke Inc.
 Los Angeles 90025: 11601 Wilshire Blvd. (310) 996-5700. FAX: (310) 996-5890. Ken Kaess, pres; Gary Fountain, sr VP mgmt/supvr entertainment division; Sandi Coryell, VP media dir. DDB Needham Worldwide Inc.
 Seattle 98104: 1008 Western Ave., Suite 601. (206) 442-9900. FAX: (206) 223-6309. Ron Elgin, pres. Elgin Syferd DDB Needham.
 Chicago 60601: 303 E. Wacker Dr., (312) 552-1504. FAX: (312) 552-2370. Susan Gillette, pres; Michael S. White, exec VP/dir media dept. DDB Needham Worldwide Inc.
 Troy, Mich. 48084: 755 W. Big Beaver Rd., Suite 900. (313) 362-2339. FAX: (313) 362-4012. Detroit—DDB Needham Worldwide Inc.
 Honolulu 96813: 700 Bishop St., 12th Fl. (808) 536-0881. Nick Ng Pack, pres. Millci Valenti Gabriel/DDB Needham Inc.

DMB&B (D'Arcy, Masius, Benton & Bowles Inc.) 1675 Broadway, New York 10019. (212) 468-3622. FAX: (212) 468-4385. Roy J. Bostock, CEO; Clayton Wilhite, pres.

Wesley Day Advertising. 1441 29th St., Suite 111, West Des Moines, Iowa 50266. (515) 224-9330. (515) 224-6737. David A. Sanderson, pres; Wil Steinhart, exec VP.

Del Rey Communications. Box 5274, Oakbrook, Ill. 60522. (708) 655-0020. John R. Hamilton, pres.

Dentsu Inc. 1-11, Tsukiji, Chuo-ku, Tokyo, 104, Japan. 3-3544-5599. FAX: 3-3546-2967. Gohei Kogure, chmn; Yutaka Nanta, pres; Minoru Kamata, Akitoshi Ishihara, Toshiro Toyota, Shunya Hashiguchi, exec VPs.
 Radio-TV media dept: Tsuyashi Takeuchi, dir TV division; Nariyuki Nabeshima, dir radio division; Kotaro Wakui, dir new electronics division.
 New York 10036: Grace Bldg., 1114 Ave. of Americas, 30th Fl. (212) 869-8318. Koicli Arai, pres.
 Los Angeles 90010: 4751 Wilshire Blvd., Suite 203. (213) 939-3857. Hideo Hosiba, pres.

Doe-Anderson Advertising Agency Inc. 620 W. Main St., Louisville, Ky. 40202. (502) 589-1700. FAX: (502) 587-8349. David G. Wilkins, chmn/CEO; James S. Lindsey, Philip D. Payne, exec VPs; Marty Jewett, exec art dir; Thomas A. Mudd, sec/treas; Gary Sloboda, VP/creative dir.
 Radio-TV media dept: Julia Hopper, Glenn Culver, media planners; Debbie Wilson, assistant media planner; Tom Walthall, Tina Goldberg, media buyers.

Domain Audio Services. Box 337, Wheaton, Ill. 60187. (708) 668-5300. FAX: (708) 668-0158. Edward A. Elliott, pres; R. David Morris, COO; Jim Draper, VP sls.

The Domain Group. 720 Olive Way, Suite 1700, Seattle 98101. (206) 682-3035. FAX: (206) 612-0139. Edward Elliott, pres/ptnr; Richard Perry, VP/mgng ptnr; Timothy Burgess, ptnr.

Strategic Marketing Maneuvers

For years, marketers dreamed of having America on one, tremendous database, with each individual listed with real psychographic, demographic and geographic details! Today, **RadioBase** is the best answer to this desire to have America at your fingertips. **RadioBase** makes possible instantaneous market research on any specific group or area.

- 95 Million Households
- 295 Million Viewers/Listeners/Consumers
- 36 Million Cable Subscribers

RADIOBASE

Put an end to the old methods of market research! Call today to find out how RadioBase can revolutionize your next marketing campaign!

167 Crary-On-The-Park • Mount Vernon, NY 10550
Phone: (914) 668-3563 • Fax: (914) 668-4247

RAD MARKETING AND RADIOBASE

 Radio-TV media dept: Daniel Balow, account exec; Julie Volchko, media dir.
 London, England.

W.B. Doner & Co. 25900 Northwestern Hwy., Southfield, Mich. 48075. (313) 354-9700. FAX: (313) 827-8448. Alan Kalter, pres/COO; John Decerchio, vice chmn/exec creative dir; H. Barry Levine, exec VP/CFO; John Considine, exec VP/dir strategic dev.
 Baltimore 21218: 2305 N. Charles St. (301) 338-1600. Herbert D. Fried, chmn exec committee; Jim Dale, chmn of bd/CEO.
 Arlington, Tex. 76011: 600 Six Flags Dr. (817) 695-1705. Clair Kelling, VP/mgmt supvr.
 St. Petersburg, Fla. 33716: 100 Carillon Pkwy. (813) 573-4333. Virginia Vonckx, sr VP/mgmt supvr.
 Boston 02166: One Exeter Plaza, 699 Boylston St. (617) 267-8989. Tim Blett, VP/mgmt supvr.
 London U.K. W1: Oriel Bldg., 10-11 Margaret St. (011) 4471-436-7195. Don Riesett, pres Donner International; David Foxon, sr VP/gen mgr.
 Cleveland 44114-2301: 200 Public Sq. (216) 771-5700. Jerry Preyss, exec VP/gen mgr.
 Montreal, Que., Canada H3A 2A5: 2020 University, Suite 2320. (514) 842-3757. Marie Gordon, VP/exec media dir.
 Toronto, Ont., Canada M4R 2E7: 90 Eglinton Ave. W. (416) 485-9901. Dan Peppler, chmn/natl creative dir.

Doremus & Co. 200 Varick St., 11th & 12th Fls., New York 10014. (212) 366-3000. FAX: (212) 366-3632. Carl Anderson, pres; Parry Merkley, exec VP/creative dir.
 Radio-TV media dept: David Brown, media dir.
 Chicago 60606: 10 S. Riverside Plaza. (312) 321-1377. FAX: (312) 993-7851. James Kross, VP finance & adv.
 Boston 02116: 855 Boylston St. (617) 859-3500. FAX: (617) 859-3535. Robert Jaczko, gen mgr.
 Los Angeles 90025: Doremus/Pondel & Parsons. 12100 Wilshire Blvd. (310) 207-3210. FAX: (310) 447-8195. Roger Pondel, gen mgr.
 London U.K. W1P 4FL: 14-17 Wells Mews. (011-4471)-436-3421. FAX: (011-4471)-436-3170. Michael Callahan, sr VP/mgng dir.
 San Francisco 94108: 530 Busch, 5th Fl. (415) 398-5699. Steve Rosenblum, mgr.

Draper Daniels Media Services Inc. 2525 Armitage Ave., Melrose Park, Ill. 60160. (708) 450-3390. Bill Behrmann, VP.
 Radio-TV media dept: Rita Hart, assoc media dir.

Duboy Automotive Advertising. 9211 Arboretum Pkwy., Suite 300, Richmond, Va. 23236. (804) 320-2277. FAX: (804) 320-0052. Jess Duboy, pres; William M. Allen, exec VP; David M. Barnett, sr VP; Charles P. Bowles, sec/treas.
 Radio-TV media dept: Donna D. Spurrier, media dir.

Earl, Palmer & Brown. 1710 E. Franklin St., Richmond, Va. 23223. (804) 775-0700. Bill Bergman, chmn.

A. Elcoff & Co. 401 N. Michigan Ave., Chicago 60611. (312) 527-7100. FAX: (312) 527-7192. Ron Bliwas, pres.
 TV media dept: Francie Barson, sr VP/media dir; Linda Aitken, Ken Houdek, VPs/assoc media dirs.

Eisaman, Johns & Laws Inc. 5700 Wilshire Blvd., 6th Fl., Los Angeles 90036. (213) 932-1234. Dennis Coe, Dean Laws, corporate presidents.
 Radio-TV media dept: Rod Damrow, sr VP.
 Chicago 60611: 401 N. Michigan Ave. (312) 263-3474. Mike deMaio, pres.
 Houston 77056: 2121 Sage Rd. (713) 961-4355. Richard Westman, pres Southwest division.

Elkman Advertising & Public Relations. 150 Monument Rd., Bala Cynwyd, Pa. 19004. (215) 668-1100. FAX: (215) 668-2586. Stanley Elkman, chmn; Donald M. Tuckerman, pres/CEO; Donald Rosenblit, sr exec VP.
 Radio-TV media dept: Marc Goldstein, VP/media dir.

Evans Group. 110 Social Hall Ave., Salt Lake City 84111. (801) 364-7452. FAX: (801) 364-7484. Glenn Snarr, chmn of bd/CEO; Chuck Bartholomew, pres; Dennis Newbold, VP/media dir.
 Seattle 98119: 190 Queen Anne. (206) 284-8383. Richard Jennings, chmn of bd; Frank Horsley, pres/gen mgr. Evans/Pacific.
 Portland, Ore. 97205: 308 S.W. 1st Ave. (503) 227-3921. Everett Mitchell, chmn of bd; Delivan Nelson, pres.
 Los Angeles 90036: 5757 Wilshire Blvd. (213) 954-3000. Bernard Weinberg, chmn; Gordon Hearne, pres (Evans/Weinberg).
 San Francisco 94107: 690 5th St. (415) 957-0300. James Elder, pres.
 Denver 80202: 1050 17th St., Suite 700. (303) 534-2343. Charles Bartholomew, pres (Evans & Bartholomew).
 Dallas 75204: 4131 N. Central Expwy., Suite 510. (214) 521-9460. Phil Motta, CEO; George Arnold, COO; Andrea Winans, media supvr.

FCB/LGK. (A Foote, Cone & Belding Communications Co.) 200 S. Broad St., Philadelphia 19102. (215) 790-4100. FAX: (215) 790-4373. Brian Gail, pres/CEO; Michael J. Daly, sr VP/media dir.

F/S Reilly Media. 3717 Buchanan, San Francisco 94123. (415) 346-1956. FAX: (415) 346-0250. Frank E. Reilly, pres; Sharon S. Reilly, exec VP.

Fahlgren Martin. 120 E. 4th St., Cincinnati 45202-4070. (513) 241-9200. FAX: (513) 241-5982. Martin Schwalhe, sr VP; Mary Ann Terlinden, dir radio/TV.
 Atlanta 30339: 2727 Paces Ferry Rd., Suite 1800. (404) 434-2424. Ralph Thompson, pres.
 Dublin, Ohio 43017-7159: 655 Metro Pl. S., Suite 700. (614) 766-3500. Lisa Hamilton, exec partner.
 Parkersburg, W.V. 26101: Rosemar Rd. & Seminary Dr. (304) 423-4591. John Ferry, pres.
 Toledo 43604: One SeaGate, Suite 901. (419) 247-5200. Jim Miller, pres.

Broadcasting & Cable Yearbook 1994

Advertising Agencies

Ft. Lauderdale, Fla. 33309: 899 W. Cypress Creek Rd., Suite 800. (303) 776-6886. Joe Talcott, sr. VP.

Tampa 33609: 600 N. Westshore. (813) 287-8200. Bob Doyle, gen mgr.

Feitz Advertising. 2470 Cheremoya Ave., Los Angeles 90068. (213) 957-9229. FAX: (213) 463-7725. Bill Feitz.

Full-svc advertising agency specializing in bcst-related products.

Film House Inc. 230 Cumberland Bend, Nashville 37228. (615) 255-4000. FAX: (615) 256-3380. Curt Hahn, pres; Wayne Campbell, VP mktg.

Fitzgerald Advertising Inc. 1055 Saint Charles Ave., Suite 615, New Orleans 70130. (504) 529-3161. Donald C. Smith, chmn of bd; Ronald J. Thompson, pres.

Foltz-Wessinger Inc. Box 1297, 800 New Holland Ave., Lancaster, Pa. 17608. (717) 392-2105. Thomas R. Farrow, pres.

Radio/TV media dept: Deb Parrish, media dir.

Foote, Cone & Belding Communications Inc. 101 E. Erie St., Chicago 60611-2897. (312) 751-7000. Mitchell Engel, exec VP/mng dir.

Chicago 60611-2897: FCB Direct. 101 E. Erie St. (312) 751-7000. Jim Tennant, pres.

Chicago 60611-2897: IMPACT. 101 E. Erie St. (312) 751-7000. Joseph Flanagan, pres/CEO.

Chicago 60611-2897: Wahlstrom Chicago. 101 E. Erie St. (312) 751-7000. Roy Beatty, VP/mng dir.

Chicago 60611-2897: FCB Communications Inc. 101 E. Erie St. (312) 751-7000. Bruce Mason, chmn/CEO.

New York 10153: FCB Database Marketing Group. 767 5th Ave. (212) 705-1000. Gary Beck, sr VP/gen mgr.

New York 10153: FCB Direct. 767 5th Ave. (212) 705-1000. Jonathon Adams, pres.

New York 10153: FCB/LKP. 767 5th Ave. (212) 705-1000. Charles Taney, pres/COO; J. Brendan Ryan, pres/CEO.

New York 10022: Krupp/Taylor USA. 505 Park Ave., 17th Fl. (212) 980-9800. Jim Schwantner, mng dir.

New York 10017: VICOM/FCB Consumer. 304 E. 45th St., 15th Fl. (212) 983-1560. Douglas Bruce, sr VP/mgng dir.

New York 10178-0065: FCB NBU. 101 Park Ave. (212) 907-7000. Fred Wray, sr VP/media dir North America; Alison Danzberger.

New York 10178: FCB SBU. 101 Park Ave. (212) 907-7000. Fred Wray, sr VP/media dir North America; Howard Nass.

New York 10019: Publicis Inc. 1675 Broadway, 30th Fl. (212) 956-8550. Frederick Rhines, pres/CEO.

New York 10016: Siboney Advertising. 2 Park Ave., Suite 1420. (212) 213-6640. Gustavo Foldvari, gen mgr.

New York 10178-0065: FCB Corporate Media. 101 Park Ave. (212) 907-7000. Joseph Ostrow, exec VP/corp dir media; Joanne Burke, sr VP/corp dir media research; Tim Zagin, VP/mgr international media.

New York 10153: FCB International. 767 5th Ave., 16th Fl. (212) 705-1000. Craig Wiggins, chmn.

Philadelphia 19102: Foote, Cone & Belding. 200 S. Broad St. (215) 790-4100. Brian Gail, pres/CEO.

Philadelphia 19106: Wahlstrom Philadelphia. The Bourse Building. (215) 351-0470. Donald Racer, mng dir.

Stamford, Ct. 06902: Wahlstrom & Co. 1290 E. Main St. (203) 348-7347. Frank Barton, pres.

Atlanta 30328: FCB Atlanta - TBSO. 5 Concourse Pkwy., Suite 320. (404) 395-3990. George Antonini, VP/dir field opns.

Dallas 75204: FCB Dallas - TBSO. 3232 McKinney Ave., Suite 1110. (214) 871-7707. Barbara Schwartzman, VP/mgmt supvr.

Dallas 75219: Siboney USA. 3500 Maple Ave., 1070. (214) 521-6060. Tory Syvrud, pres.

Denver 80222: FCB Denver - TBSO. 600 S. Cherry St., Suite 510. (303) 321-7949. Gretchen Miller, account supvr.

Los Angeles 90025-1772: FCB Direct West. 11601 Wilshire Blvd. (310) 312-7000. Chirstopher LaBonge, exec VP/mktg dir.

Los Angeles 90025-1772: Foote, Cone & Belding. 11601 Wilshire Blvd. (310) 312-7000. Richard Edler, exec VP/mgng dir.

Los Angeles 90025: Krupp/Taylor USA. 11601 Wilshire Blvd. (310) 312-7000. Patrick Coll, pres.

Burbank, Calif. 91505: FCB Entertainment. 3601 W. Olive Ave., Suite 480. (818) 848-3330. Jack McQueen, pres.

Dominguez Hills, Calif. 90220: Wahlstrom West. 2200 W. Artesia Blvd., Suite 106. (310) 635-8030. Sandra Hall, VP/mgng dir.

Santa Ana, Calif. 92707-0505: Foote, Cone & Belding. 4 Hutton Centre Dr., Suite 900. (714) 662-6500. William Hagelstein, exec VP/gen mgr.

San Francisco 94111-1176: FCB Direct West. 1160 Battery St. (415) 398-5200. Michael Feld, gen mgr.

San Francisco 94111: FCB Pacific Group - TBSO. 1255 Battery St. (415) 398-5200. Dan Odishoo, sr VP/gen mgr.

San Francisco 94111-1176: FCB Technology. 1160 Battery St. (415) 398-5200. David Clauson, sr VP/gen mgr.

San Francisco 94111: Foote, Cone & Belding. 1255 Battery St. (415) 398-5200. Richard Ward, exec VP/gen mgr; Jack Balousek, pres.

San Francisco 94111-1176: IMPACT West. 1160 Battery St. (415) 398-5200. Lori Rathje, sr VP/gen mgr.

San Francisco 94111: Pro/Health. 15 Lombard. (415) 788-1775. David Rossini, sr VP/mgng dir.

San Francisco 94111: VICOM/FCB. One Lombard, 3rd Fl. (415) 391-8700. Lester Barnett, exec VP; John Loden, pres/CEO.

Miami, Fla. 33131: FCB Latin America. 1401 Brickell Ave., Suite 1100. (305) 372-8855. Jose Cubas, pres/CEO.

Miami, Fla. 33131: Siboney. 1401 Brickell Ave., Suite 1100. (305) 372-8855. Oscar Corea, gen mgr.

Toronto, Ont., Canada M4P 3C2: FCB Canada Ltd. 245 Eglinton Ave. E., Suite 300. (416) 438-3600. David Haan, pres/CEO.

Toronto, Ont., Canada M4P 3C2: FCB Direct. 245 Eglinton Ave. E., Suite 300. (416) 483-3600. Paul Nelson, sr VP/mgng dir.

Toronto, Ont., Canada M4P 3C2: Optimedia. 245 Eglinton Ave. E., Suite 200. (416) 483-3600. Sunni Boot, sr VP/mgng dir.

Montreal, Que., Canada H2W 1M5: Auger Babeux/FCB. 225 rue Roy E., Bureau 100. (514) 499-1964. Paul Auger, pres/co-creative dir.

Montreal, Que., Canada H3A 2N4: FCB Direct. 1801 McGill College Ave., Suite 1335. (514) 849-7055. FAX: (514) 849-7142. Mark Goodman, sr VP/mgng dir.

Vancouver, B.C., Canada V6G 2Z6: FCB Canada Ltd. 1500 W. Georgia St., Suite 450. (604) 684-8311. Donald Panton, sr VP/gen mgr.

Paris, France 75380 Cedex 08: Publicis - FCB Communications. 133 Champs-Elysees. (33-1) 47 20 78 00. Maurice Levy, chmn/CEO.

FCB/European Offices: Amsterdam, Ancona, Athens, Bologna, Brussels, Budapest, Casablanca, Copenhagen, Dublin, Dusseldorf, Frankfurt, Hague, Hamburg, Helsinki, Istanbul, Lausanne, Lisbon, London, Madrid, Milan, Munich, Oslo, Paris, Prague, Rome, Rotterdam, Stockholm, Tel Aviv, Vienna, Warsaw, Zagreb and Zurich.

FCB/Latin American Offices: Bogata, Buenos Aires, Caracas, Guatemala City, Guayaquil, Kingston, Medellin, Mexico City, Port of Spain, Quito, Rio de Janeiro, Sao Paulo, San Jose, San Juan, San Pedro, San Salvador, Santo Domingo, Tegucigalpa.

FCB/International Offices: Auckland, Bangkok, Brisbane, Christchurch, Dunedin, Hong Kong, Jakarta, Johannesburg, Kuala Lumpur, Manila, Melbourne, Sydney, Taipei, Tokyo, Wellington, West Perth.

Albert Frank-Guenther Law Inc. (A Foote, Cone and Belding Communications Co.) 71 Broadway, New York 10006. (212) 248-5200. Paul Lucy, chmn; Walt Guarino, pres.

San Francisco 94111: 244 California St., Suite 310. Vicky Quattro, sr VP/mgr. Albert Frank Guenther Law Inc.

Erwin Frankel Productions. 127 W. 72nd St., New York 10023. (212) 873-1222. FAX: (212) 873-1245. Erwin Frankel, Ellen Rafel, David Crommett, exec prods.

Sheldon Fredericks Adv. Inc. 655 Washington Blvd., Stamford, Conn. 06901. (203) 324-0051. FAX: (203) 324-0520. Frederick A. Schwartz, pres; Charles Ryan, VP.

Radio-TV media dept: Dean Adams, VP.

Freed & Associates Inc. 3600 Clipper Mill Rd., Suite 220, Baltimore 21211. (410) 243-1421. FAX: (410) 235-2108. Gloria Freed, pres; Cindy Butta, media dir; Jane Morrison, media buyer.

GGH&M Advertising Co. 11500 Olive Blvd., Suite 136, St. Louis 63141. (314) 991-5311. Irven Hammerman, pres; Louis Myers, VP/creative dir.

Radio-TV media dept: Carla Cox.

G.M. Communications Ltd. 304 E. 55th St., New York 10022. (212) 593-3088. FAX: (212) 751-2087. Jack Bratman, pres; Carolyn Lizzo, VP sls; Honey Franklin, prod dir; Robin Zucker, sr account exec; Nina Kennedy, creative dir; Al Saura, VP exec; Mike Jimenez, sr art dir.

Radio-TV media dept: Gail Juris, media dir.

Garrett Media Services Inc. 1119 San Antonio, El Paso, Tex. 79901. (915) 533-4700. FAX: (915) 533-3640. Garrett W. Haston, pres.

Gerber Advertising Agency. 209 S.W. Oak St., Portland, Ore. 97204. (503) 221-0100. FAX: (503) 228-7471. Phil Stevens, pres/CEO.

Radio-TV media dept: Betty Chimenti, VP/media dir.

Gober Advance Inc. 2620 San Mateo Blvd. N.E., Suite F&G, Albuquerque 87110. (505) 881-5107. FAX: (505) 881-4252. Angie McKinstry, media buyer.

Golin/Harris Communications. (A Shandwick Co.) 500 N. Michigan Ave., Chicago 60611. (312) 836-7100. FAX: (312) 836-7170. Alvin Golin, chmn; Rich Jernstedt, pres/CEO; Richard S. Kline, COO; Dave Gilbert, gen mgr Chicago.

New York 10017: 666 3rd Ave. (212) 697-9191. Golin/Harris Communications.

Philadelphia 19102: 200 S. Broad St. (215) 790-7800. Kate Allison, gen mgr.

Los Angeles 90071: One Bunker Hill, 601 W. 5th St. (213) 623-4200. Fred Cooke, exec VP/co-gen mgr; Maureen B. Crow, exec VP/ co-gen mgr.

Toronto Ont., Canada M5B 2E7: 415 Yonge St. (416) 598-8988. Christopher Bunting, chmn/CEO. Continental PIR Communications.

London U.K. WC2E 8RJ: 43 King St., Covent Garden. (011) 4471-836-6677. John Martin, CEO. Welbeck Golin/Harris.

Bellevue, Wash. 98004: 800 Bellevue Way, Suite 400. (206) 462-4220. Don Yaryu, VP.

Washington, 20007: 1025 Thomas Jefferson St. N.W., Suite 301 W. (202) 625-7100. Kathy Foster, VP.

Gray Kirk/VanSant Advertising Inc. World Trade Ctr., Baltimore 21202. (410) 539-5400. FAX: (410) 234-2441. Roger L. Gray, pres/CEO; Graham V. Kirk, sr exec VP/COO; John McLaughlin, exec VP/dir client svcs.

Radio-TV media dept: Sheldon T. Taule, sr VP/dir media svcs.

Grey Advertising Inc. 777 3rd Ave., New York 10017. (212) 546-2000. Edward H. Meyer, chmn of bd; Robert L. Berenson, exec VP admin; Richard Karp, Stephan Novick, exec VPs creative svcs.

Radio-TV media dept: Alec Gerster, exec VP/dir media & progmg svcs.

San Francisco 94111: 2 Embarcardero Ctr., Suite 200. (415) 421-1000. Warren Peterson, exec VP/mgng dir.

Los Angeles 90048: 6100 Wilshire Blvd., Suite 900. (213) 936-6060. Miles Turpin, chmn/CEO (western division).

Griswold Inc. 101 Prospect Ave. W., Cleveland 44115. (216) 696-3400. FAX: (216) 696-3405. Patrick J. Morin, chmn/CEO; Neal B. Davis, exec VP/dir client svcs; Robert J. Clancy, exec VP/ creative dir.

Radio-TV media dept: Norman Olson, exec VP/media dir.

Hall, Haerr, Peterson & Harney Inc. 6907 N. Knoxville Ave., Suite 200, Peoria, Ill. 61614. (309) 692-7011. FAX: (309) 692-0934. J. Philip Harney, chmn of bd; Richard A. Hall, pres.

Radio-TV media dept: Kathy Baker, media dir.

Jefferson City, Mo. 65102: Box 207, 415 E. McCarty St. (314) 636-3107.

Margret Haney of Graham-Haney. 2995 Woodside Rd., Woodside, Calif. 94062. (415) 325-5552. FAX: (415) 325-5556. Margret Haney, pres; Sondra Carver, J.D. law & taxes.

Media brokerage/consulting, advertising, media buyers.

C.J. Herrick Associates Inc. 2 W. 45th St., New York 10036. (212) 840-6090. Clarence Herrick, pres.

Radio-TV media dept: David Crowell.

Bernard Hodes Advertising Inc. 555 Madison Ave., New York 10022. (212) 935-4000. FAX: (212) 755-7324. Bernard S. Hodes, pres/CEO; Alan V. Schwartz, exec VP/CFO/COO; Jo Bredwell, sr VP/natl dir client svc.

Atlanta 30342: Bldg. C, Suite 175, 5775 Peachtree Dunwoody Rd. (404) 250-8400. FAX: (404) 250-8411; (404) 250-8412. Carol Barber, VP/district mgr; Kevin Hensley, branch mgr.

Cambridge, Mass. 02142: 215 1st St. (617) 576-2131. FAX: (617) 576-2361; (617) 576-6981. David A. Dwyer, sr VP/branch mgr. Boston office.

Chicago 60606: 10 S. Riverside Plaza. (312) 258-9000. FAX: (312) 258-8510. Kristin Swanson, VP/branch mgr.

Dallas 75231: 7424 Greenville Ave., Suite 203. (214) 361-9986. FAX: (214) 369-5124; (214) 361-5241. Wanda Bravata, branch mgr.

Englewood, Colo. 80111: 5655 S. Yosemite. (303) 773-0111. FAX: (303) 773-0236. Robert Feese, VP/branch mgr. Denver office.

Advertising Agencies

Houston 77040: 7676 Hillmont, Suite 290. (713) 690-0272. FAX: (713) 690-5272; (713) 690-5278. Barry Siegel, exec VP southern rgn.
Los Angeles 90025: 11755 Wilshire Blvd. (310) 575-4000. FAX: (310) 312-6028. Steven Petersen, sr VP/rgnl mgr.
Irvine, Calif. 92715: 19700 Fairchild, Suite 180. (714) 955-2324. FAX: (714) 955-2366. Suzi Lathrop, account supvr.
Fort Lauderdale, Fla. 33312: 2901 Stirling Rd., Suite 210. (305) 966-3500. FAX: (305) 966-1462; (305) 966-4155. Carol Barber, VP/district mgr. Miami office.
New York 10022: 555 Madison Ave. (212) 758-2600. FAX: (212) 486-4049; (212) 832-9516. Marion Starr, exec VP.
Orlando, Fla. 32809: 280 W. Canton Ave., Suite 420. (407) 740-5002. FAX: (407) 740-8725.
Palo Alto, Calif. 94303: 1101 Embarcadero Rd. (415) 856-1000. FAX: (415) 856-1181; (415) 856-1182. Bruce Skillings, exec VP western rgn.
Philadelphia 19017: 834 Chestnut St. (215) 351-0041. FAX: (215) 351-0087; (215) 351-0266. Tom DeSimone, Maryalice Doria, VPs/branch managers.
Phoenix 85016: 2111 E. Highland Ave., Suite 280B. (602) 956-8989. FAX: (602) 956-9142. Vicki Cichocki, VP/branch mgr.
San Francisco 94108: 530 Bush St. (415) 394-0770. FAX: (415) 394-0780; (415) 394-0781. Linda Such, mgmt supvr.
Arlington, Va. 22209: 1600 Wilson Blvd. (703) 528-6253. FAX: (703) 528-6308; (703) 528-6311. John Swirchak, Rosemary Peluso, VPs/branch managers. Washington office.
Sacramento, Calif. 95827: 3909 Fite Cir., Suite 104. (916) 362-1993. FAX: (916) 362-2075. Laura Duffin, branch mgr.
Tucson 85715: 1161 N. El Dorado Pl. (602) 721-1844. FAX: (602) 721-1834. Vicki Cichocki, VP/branch mgr; Margie Kasse, account exec.
Tampa 33618: 14502 N. Dale Mabry. (813) 961-9255. FAX: (813) 963-3664. Carol Barber, district mgr; Tracy Mounsour, dir accounting & dev.
Toronto Ont., Canada M5C 1M1: 2 Lombard St. (416) 362-7999. FAX: (416) 367-9895. Steven Wills, pres.
London U.K. W6 8BS: Griffin House, 161 Hammersmith Rd. (081) 846-9666. FAX: (081) 748-0311. John Stainer, chief exec; Kevin Turner, mgng dir.
Birmingham, U.K. 5B 7AS: Monaco House, Bristol St. (021) 666-6700. FAX: (021) 622-6971. David Morris.
Bristol, U.K. BS1 4XG: 2 St. Augustine's Parade. (027) 227-2983. FAX: (027) 229-0932. Chris Samuel, rgnl dir.
Manchester, U.K. M2 5WS: Television House, Mount St. (061) 833-0042. FAX: (061) 832-9972. Maureen O'Connor.
Cardiff, Wales, U.K. CF1 3DN: Royal Chambers, 2nd Fl., Park Pl. (022) 222-9469. FAX: (022) 222-9598. Chris Samuel, rgnl dir; Michelle Lewis, rgnl mgr.
Seattle 98104: 1008 Western Ave. (206) 621-6480. FAX: (206) 583-0308. Dennis Graham, branch mgr.
Raleigh, N.C. 27612: 3717 National Dr. (919) 571-0180. FAX: (919) 571-2986. Laura Lewis, branch mgr.
Vancouver, B.C., Canada V6E 3X3: 1066 W. Hastings St. (604) 682-0313. FAX: (604) 687-2766. Robin Wyss, gen mgr.

Hoffman, York & Compton Inc. Plaza East, 330 E. Kilbourn Ave., Milwaukee 53202. (414) 289-9700. FAX: (414) 289-0417. Eugene Gilmartin, pres/CEO.
Radio-TV media dept: Frank Label, VP/dir media; Phil Backe, sr media planner

Hutchins/Young & Rubicam Inc. 400 Midtown Tower, Rochester, N.Y. 14604. (716) 546-6480. James Morey, chmn; M.A. Sapos, pres/CEO; Charles Reller, sr VP/treas/gen mgr.
Radio-TV media dept: Tracy Till, media dir.

IMPACT. (A Foote, Cone and Belding Communications Co.) 101 E. Erie St., Chicago 60611-2897. (312) 751-3500. Joseph Flanagan, pres.

The Ideasmiths Co. 133 John St., Oakville, Ont., Canada L6K 1H3. (905) 844-7604. FAX: (905) 844-7650. P.M. Festing-Smith, pres; P.C. Festing-Smith, VP.
Radio-TV media dept: P.M. Festing-Smith, media dir.

Innerwest. 550 California Ave., Reno, Nev. 89509. (702) 323-4500. FAX: (702) 323-5572. Cindi Murin, sec/treas/media dir.

The Interpublic Group of Companies Inc. 1271 Ave. of the Americas, New York 10020. (212) 399-8000. FAX: (212) 399-8130. Philip Geier Jr., chmn of bd/CEO.
Parent company of McCann-Erickson Worldwide; Lintas: Worldwide; Dailey & Associates; & The Lowe Group.

Jacobs & Gerber Inc. 731 N. Fairfax Ave., Los Angeles 90046-7293. (213) 655-4082. FAX: (213) 655-0195. Albert B. Litewka, pres/CEO; Stefan Gerber, sr VP/exec creative dir.
Radio-TV media dept: Reggie Lundin, media coord.

Bob Jones Associates. 102 Woodmont Blvd., Suite 100, Nashville 37205. (615) 298-5448. FAX: (615) 298-5621. Bob Jones, pres; Doti Jones, pres.
Radio-TV media dept: Bob Jones.

Jordan Advertising Inc. 1100 Wheaton Oaks Ct., Wheaton, Ill. 60187. (708) 665-4965. FAX: (708) 665-4966. Grace R. Jordan, pres.
Radio-TV media dept: Grace Jordan, media dir.

Henry J. Kaufman & Assocs Inc. 2233 Wisconsin Ave. N.W., Washington 20007. (202) 333-0700. Michael G. Carberry, chmn.
Radio-TV media dept: Maria Ivancin, media planner; Amy Carden, sr media buyer.

Ketchum Advertising. 220 E. 42nd St., New York 10017. (212) 907-9388. Steve Penchina, chmn exec.

Ketchum Communications Inc. 6 PPG Pl., Pittsburgh 15222. (412) 456-3500. (412) 456-3588. Paul Alvarez, chmn/CEO/pres; Mike Walsh, media dir.
Chicago 60606-7272: 111 N. Canal St., Suite 1150. (312) 715-9200. Lee Lippman, pres; Bob Johnson, media dir.
Los Angeles 90025: 11755 Wilshire Blvd. (310) 444-5000. Craig Mathieson, pres; Cherie Crane, media dir.
New York 10017: 220 E. 42nd St. (212) 907-9300. William Perkins, pres; Jim McHugh, media dir.
Philadelphia 19103: Bell Atlantic Tower, 1717 Arch St., 33rd Fl. (215) 656-8000. Sam Rand, pres; Bill Melnick, media dir.
San Francisco 94111: 55 Union St. (415) 984-6100. Dianne Snedaker, pres; Mary Murphy, media dir.
New York 10017: 220 E. 42nd St. (212) 907-9300. John Curran, sr VP/dir net progmg.

Ketchum/Mandabach & Simms. 111 N. Canal St., Chicago 60606. (312) 902-1300. Tim Dorgan, Corey Phillips, exec VPs; Kevin Beauseigneur, sr VP creative.
Radio-TV media dept: Robert Johnson, media dir.

Klemtner Advertising Inc. 375 Hudson St., New York 10014. (212) 463-3400. FAX: (212) 463-3541.

Krupp/Taylor USA. (A Foote, Cone and Belding Communications Co.) 5405 Jandy Pl., Los Angeles 90066. (310) 306-3646.

Landin Media Sales Inc. 3033 N. 44th St., Suite 375, Phoenix 85018-7229. (602) 553-4080. FAX: (602) 553-4090. Larry L. Cummings, pres/CEO; Dennis Hart, VP.

Larson-Marvine Inc. 4031 Sunset Ln., Northbrook, Ill. 60062. (708) 498-2080. FAX: (708) 498-2000. Kim Larson, pres; Paul Marvine, VP/chief creative off.

Lavidge & Associates Inc. 409 Bearden Park Cir., Knoxville, Tenn. 37919. (615) 584-6121. FAX: (615) 584-6756. Arthur W. Lavidge, pres; Hal Ernest, exec VP; Pat Dawson, sr VP.
Radio-TV media dept: Pat Dawson, sr VP.

J. Richard Lee Inc. 700 1st St., Oceanside, Calif. 92054. (619) 722-8232. J. Richard Lee, pres.
Radio-TV media dept: Dorothy Lee, media dir.

Al Paul Lefton Co. Inc. Rohm and Hass Bldg., Independence Mall W., Philadelphia 19106. (215) 923-9600. FAX: (215) 351-4298. Al Paul Lefton Jr., pres/CEO; John M. Evans, sr VP pub rels; Steven E. Yarrow, VP.
Radio-TV media dept: Steve Zartarian, VP/media dir.

Liggett-Stashower Inc. 1228 Euclid Ave., Cleveland 44115. (216) 348-5800. FAX: (216) 861-1284. David L. Stashower, chmn/CEO; C. Henry Foltz, pres/COO.
Radio-TV media dept: Charles D. Knepper, sr VP/media dir.

Lintas: USA. One Dag Hammarskjold Plaza, New York 10017-2203. (212) 605-8000. FAX: (212) 935-2164. Spencer Plavoukos, chmn/CEO; Cathy A. St. Jean, sr VP/mgr; Marc Goldstein, exec VP/dir natl bcst; Gary Carr, sr VP/mgr; Anthony DeGregorio, exec VP/chief creative off.
Atlanta 30339: 2727 Paces Ferry Rd., Suite 1800. (404) 434-2424. FAX: (404) 438-8508.
Los Angeles 90025: 11100 Santa Monica Blvd., Suite 600. (213) 914-2200.
Warren, Mich. 48093: 30400 VanDyke Ave. (313) 558-6302. Detroit office.

Lois USA. 40 W. 57th St., 6th Fl., New York 10019. (212) 373-4700. FAX: (212) 757-6707. Ted Veru, pres/media dir; Jon Tracosas, exec VP account svcs.
Radio-TV media dept: Chris Tinkham, media planning supvr.

Manheim Advertising Inc. Tower East, Suite 901, 20600 Chagrin Blvd., Cleveland 44122-5334. (216) 991-1184. FAX: (216) 991-9633. Kenneth Manheim, pres; John Slosar, exec VP; Robert Volek, sr VP/creative dir.
Radio-TV media dept: Debbie Bozich, Patty Jones, Patricia Hylkema, Bee Burgess, Susan Olevitch.

Marcus Advertising Inc. Landmark Ctr., 25700 Science Park Dr., Cleveland 44122. (216) 292-4700. FAX: (216) 292-7219. Donald H. Marcus, chmn; Harvey Scholnick, pres; William Greenwald, Donald Campbell, exec VPs; Harlan Miller, sr VP; James Reed, VP; Mark Davis, VP/creative dir; King Hill, VP/pub rels dir.
Radio-TV media dept: Charles Ford, VP.

McCaffrey and McCall Inc. 575 Lexington Ave., New York 10022. (212) 350-1000. FAX: (212) 355-0224. Robert Henry, CFO; Mike Robertson, chmn; Dany Khosrovani, planning dir.
Radio-TV media dept: Tom Wilson, exec VP media dir.

McCann Direct. 750 3rd Ave., New York 10017. (212) 286-0460. FAX: 212-867-5177. William Morrissey, exec VP.
Radio-TV media dept: Donna Maynes, media dir.

McCann-Erickson Worldwide. 750 Third Ave., New York 10017. (212) 984-3004. FAX: (212) 984-2858. Robert L. James, chmn/CEO; John J. Dooner Jr., pres/COO; Ira Carlin, exec VP dir Worldwide Media.
Affiliated companies in 64 countries including Switzerland, Belgium, France, Germany, Great Britain, Italy, Netherlands, Spain, Costa Rica, El Salvador, Guatemala, Mexico, Panama, Puerto Rico, Argentina, Brazil, Colombia, Ecuador, Peru, Uruguay, Venezuela, Australia, Hong Kong, Japan and Philippines.

McConnaughy Stein, Schmidt & Brown. North Pier, 401 E. Illinois St., Suite 500, Chicago 60611. (312) 321-8000. FAX: (312) 321-8008. Thomas McConnaughy, chmn/CEO; Bill Stein, pres/CEO.

McKinney Advertising & Public Relations. 1904 Terminal Tower, 50 Public Sq., Cleveland 44113. (216) 621-5133. FAX: (216) 621-1181. Judy Cerne, exec VP/gen mgr.
Philadelphia 19106: Independence Mall W. (215) 922-2635. David Hammer, exec VP/gen mgr.
Chicago 60610: 430 W. Erie, #310. (312) 944-6784. Frank Callahan, pres.

Meldrum & Fewsmith Communications Inc./Meldrum & Fewsmith Advertising Inc. 1350 Euclid Ave., Cleveland 44115. (216) 241-2141. FAX: (216) 479-2437. M & F Communications: Chris N. Perry, chmn/CEO; Robert P. Huddilston, exec VP/CFO. M & F Advertising: William C. Waldman, pres.
Radio-TV media dept: Virginia E. Carmichael, VP dir bcst svcs/creative svcs.

Message on Hold. Box 1001, Hendersonville, N.C. 28793. (800) 223-1930. Ellis Molton, own.

Messner, Vetere, Berger, McNamee, Schmetterer. 350 Hudson St., New York 10014. (212) 886-4100. FAX: (212) 886-4415. Louise McNamee, pres.
Radio-TV media dept: Jack Curtis, COO.
Los Angeles 90036: 5900 Wilshire Blvd. (213) 937-8540. Alan Pando, pres.

Milici Valenti Gabriel DDB Needham Inc. 700 Bishop St., 12th Fl., Honolulu 96813. (808) 536-0881. FAX: (808) 529-6208. Nick Ng Pack, pres.
Radio-TV media dept: Joan Gregory, VP/media dir.

Miller Advertising Agency Inc. 71 5th Ave., New York 10003. (212) 929-2200. FAX: (212) 727-4734. Leonard J. Miller, chmn of bd; Robert Miller, pres.

Mincom. 30 E. 60th St., New York 10022. (212) 355-3289. FAX: (212) 758-9659. Stuart Minton Jr., pres; Hillary Jaffe, account supvr; John DiQuarto, dir commercial prod.

Moret Advertising Inc. 940 N. Finance Center Dr., Suite 240, Tuscon, Ariz. 85710. (602) 721-8811. FAX: (602) 296-7506. Rich Moret, pres/chmn of bd; Mike Mundy, VP/CFO.
Adv, mktg, pub rels. Full-svc agency emphasizing results.

Advertising Agencies

Moroch & Associates Inc. 3625 N. Hall St., Suite 1200, Dallas 75219. (214) 520-9700. FAX: (214) 520-6464. Tom Moroch, chmn; Pat Kemps, pres.
Radio-TV media dept: Gayle Smiley, media dir.
Tulsa, Okla. 64135: 5800 E. Skelly Dr. (918) 663-1050. Doris Coon, admin asst.
Oklahoma City, Okla. 73116: 6801 N. Broadway, Suite 200. (405) 848-6800. Rob Bossell, VP/gen mgr.

Moss and Co. Inc. 49 W. 38th St., New York 10018. (212) 575-0808. FAX: (212) 730-6020. Murray Brauman, chmn; Steven Hunter, sr VP/creative dir; Tony Micale, exec VP/art dir.
Radio-TV media dept: Peter Beiro.

Mouncey Ferguson & Associates. One W. Market St., Suite 200, Leesburg, Va. 22075. (703) 777-6795. FAX: (703) 771-8709. Mouncey Ferguson, pres; Judith Ross Ferguson, Bill Replogle, VPs.
Full-svc agency, offering adv, pub rels, mktg & event mgmt.

John F. Murray Advertising Agency Inc. 685 3rd Ave., New York 10017. (212) 878-5000. FAX: (212) 878-5062. Richard Feldheim, pres; Ingrid Loeuis, VP/treas.
Radio-TV media dept: Marianne McArdle, sr VP/dir natl TV; Kathleen Margaritov, Patricia Stern, Kenneth Lagana, VPs natl TV; Matthew Feinberg, dir spec projects; Emma Salgado, VP traf.

Myers Advertising Inc. 1440 Kapiolani Blvd., Suite 920, Honolulu 96814. (808) 949-3531. FAX: (808) 946-5034. Jean K. Myers, pres; James Effler, media dir.

Myers Reports. 322 Rt. 46 W., Parsippany, N.J. 07054. (201) 808-7333. FAX: (201) 882-3651. Jack Meyers, pres.

Newmark, Posner & Mitchell Inc. 300 E. 42nd St., New York 10017. (212) 867-3900. FAX: (212) 818-0083. Peter S. Posner, pres; Robert S. Posner, Charles Barber, VPs.
Radio-TV media dept: Pearl Grossberg.

New York Communications Inc. 207 S. State Rd., Upper Darby, Pa. 19082. (215) 352-5505. FAX: (215) 352-6225. Michael Davis, pres.
Philadelphia office.

Northlich Stolley LaWarre. 200 W. 4th St., Cincinnati 45202. (513) 421-8840. FAX: (513) 287-1855. William M. LaWarre, pres/CEO; Mark A. Serrianne, exec VP; Cynthia Hardie, VP/gen mgr.
Radio-TV media dept: Carole Walters, VP/media dir.

Ogilvy & Mather Inc. 309 W. 49th St., New York 10019. (212) 237-4000. FAX: (212) 237-5123. Charlotte Beers, chmn.
Radio-TV media dept: Lawrence Cole, sr VP/dir media svcs.
Los Angeles 90025: 11766 Wilshire Blvd. (310) 996-0400.
Atlanta 30308: 401 W. Peachtree. (404) 262-3764. Neill Cameron, VP/gen mgr.
Houston 77002: 1415 Louisiana, St., Suite 2700. (713) 659-6688. Ralph Lefevre, sr VP/gen mgr.
Toronto, Ont., Canada M5E 1X6: 33 Younge St. (416) 367-3573. Andy Watson, CEO.
Montreal, Que., Canada H3A 2P6: Place du Canada. (514) 849-3601.

Old City Group Inc. 7755 Belle Point Dr., Greenbelt, Md. 20770. (301) 220-2100. FAX: (301) 220-3044. Therese M. Seidel, pres/CEO; Bill Santry, creative dir.
Radio-TV media dept: Diane Levant, radio/TV buyer; Pamela Peseux, sr media planner.

Paragon Advertising Inc. 580 Centre View Blvd., Crestview Hills, Ky. 41017. (606) 344-1617. FAX: (606) 344-8562. John L. Pierce, pres/CEO; Dan Hubbard, exec VP; Joanne E. Page, VP client svcs.

The Patten Corp. (Retail Automotive Advertising Agency.) Box 2150, 27255 Lahser Rd., Southfield, Mich. 48037. (313) 353-4520. FAX: (313) 358-5514. Thomas Beauvais, pres.

Phillips-Ramsey. 6863 Friars Rd., San Diego 92108. (619) 574-0808. FAX: (619) 291-4132. Jim King, media.

Quartet International Inc. 20 Butternut Dr., Pearl River, N.Y. 10965. (914) 735-8700. FAX: (914) 735-8999. Harvey Chertok, pres; Barbara Ann Chertok, exec VP.

Quinlan Advertising. 11555 N. Meridian, Carmel, Ind. 46032. (317) 573-5080. Telex: 317-573-5088. John McCaig, pres.
Radio-TV media dept: Karen Wehman.

RAD

MARKETING AND RADIOBASE

RAD Marketing & Radiobase. 167 Crary-on-the-Park, Mount Vernon, N.Y. 10550. (212) 274-0640. FAX: (212) 274-0646. Bob Dadarria, pres; Marc Dadarria, VP; Kathy Kruver, Hank Tooley, account execs.

RAD Marketing began with the unique idea of being able to provide marketers of any size with the largest, most ideal audience available. Through a variety of strategic mktg svcs, RAD Marketing can help companies identify & reach a mkt for their product—which can range from soup to soap, radio stns to cable nets, & more. If you're looking for a unique & guaranteed method of locating your mkt, RAD Marketing can offer strategic solutions to your mktg needs. Other svcs include: Age Segmentation, Audio Duping/Voice Overs, Brand Name Modeling, Billing Insert Programs, Cable TV Direct, Computer Enhancement of Mailing Lists, Computerization, Custom Database Design, Data Entry, Direct Mail, Radio, TV, Fulfillment and Reporting, Fundraising, Laser Printing, List Management, List Order Fulfillment, Local Area Markets, Mapping, Merge Purge, Product Models—Regional/National, Product & Promotional Sweepstakes, Radio-Base, Sweepstakes Mail Pick-Up Control, & TV Commercial Duping.

RadioMail/TV Mail. 11300 Sorrento Valley Rd., Suite 255, San Diego 92121. (619) 597-0263. FAX: (619) 597-0992 Peter D. Hobbs, pres.

Rainbow Advertising Sales Co. 260 Madison Ave., New York 10016. (212) 889-3380. FAX: (212) 725-6949. Robert T. Fennimore, pres/COO; Phil DeCabia, VP/sls dir; Peter J. Moran, sr VP Cable Netwks Inc. (CNI).

L.W. Ramsey Advertising Agency. 111 E. 3rd St., Davenport, Iowa 52801. (319) 326-0157. David A. Pautsch, pres; Gordon S. Fowler, chmn of bd.
Radio-TV media dept: Brenda Spencer, admin media; Joseph Elceser, mktg dir.

Rapp, Collins & Marcoa. 488 Madison Ave., New York 10022. (212) 725-8100. FAX: (212) 371-9270. David Scholes, pres.

Russ Reid Co. 2 N. Lake Ave., Suite 600, Pasadena, Calif. 91101. (818) 449-6100. FAX: (818) 577-5048. Russ Reid, chmn/CEO; Keith Jespersen, pres; Jerry B. McClun, sr VP media; Stan Bruckheim, media dir; Cynthia Liebling, bcst mgr.

Rives Carlberg. 5599 San Felipe, Houston 77056-2721. (713) 965-0764. FAX: (713) 965-0135. Chuck Carlberg, pres/CEO; Alice Michalec, exec VP/gen mgr; Carl Whitmire, VP/group mgmt supv; Judi Maddrey, VP/group mgmt supv; Cynthia Koplos, VP/dir account planning; Tom Adkins, VP/dir strategic planning; Sherri Oldman, VP/creative dir; Mark Rice, VP finance & admin.
Radio-TV media dept: Sandy Pardo, VP/media dir; Maria Hale, assoc media dir.

Robetta Corp. 1817 S. Neil St., Champaign, Ill. 61820. (217) 359-0641. Robert F. Grubb, pres; John A. Grubb, sr consultant.
Mktg & adv consultants, trade show displays, creative & graphic svcs.

Rosenfeld, Sirowitz, Humphrey & Strauss Advertising Inc. 111 5th Ave., New York 10003. (212) 505-0200. FAX: (212) 505-7309. Leonard Sirowitz, co-chmn/chief creative off; Harold L. Strauss, co-chmn/CFO.
Radio-TV media dept: Leslie Jacobus, exec VP/media dir.
Phoenix, 85012: 3200 N. Central Ave. (602) 274-7707. Fred Brownfeld, pres. Rosenfeld, Sirowitz, Humphrey & Strauss Inc. (Patchen Brownfeld Division).

The Alan Rothman Co. Inc. 18 Corporate Hill Dr., Suite 101, Little Rock, Ark. 72205. (501) 224-4808. FAX: (501) 224-7418. Alan Rothman, pres; Scotty Scholl, sr VP.
Radio-TV media dept: Debbie Dollar, VP/media dir.

Morgan Rothschild & Co. Inc. 220 W. 93rd St., New York 10025. (212) 595-5292. FAX: (212) 595-5343. Daniel Flamberg, mng dir; Jane Shahmanesh, dir.

Ross Roy Inc. 100 Bloomfield Hills Pkwy., Bloomfield Hills, Mich. 48304. (313) 433-6000. FAX: (313) 433-6669. TELEX: 023-5521. Peter Mills, pres/CEO.
Radio-TV media dept: Patricia Cuda, group media dir.

Rubin Reid Noto & Ehrenthal Inc. 100 6th Ave., New York 10013. (212) 966-5550. FAX: (212) 966-5546. Mel Rubin, pres; Herb Ehrenthal, exec VP/COO.
Radio-TV media dept: David Michaelson, dir media svcs.

S S D & W. 350 Main Rd., Montville, N.J. 07045. (201) 299-8000. FAX: (201) 299-7937. Andrew F. Scelba, chmn of bd/pres/account exec.
Radio-TV media dept: David F. Scelba, VP/account exec.

Saatchi & Saatchi Advertising. (A Division of Saatchi and Saatchi Advertising Inc. North America.) 375 Hudson St., New York 10014-3620. (212) 463-2000. FAX: (212) 463-9855. Joseph P. Mack, chmn/CEO; Michael Keeshan, pres/COO; Stuart Upson, chmn Saatchi & Saatchi Advertising Inc.; Edward L. Wax, pres/CEO Saatchi & Saatchi Advertising Inc.

Scali, McCabe, Sloves Inc. 800 3rd Ave., New York 10022. (212) 735-8000. FAX: (212) 735-8418. Marvin Sloves, chmn of bd; Sam Scali, pres.
Radio-TV media dept: Alan Jumaim, exec VP/dir media & prog.
Toronto Ont., Canada M4T 2T5: 2 St. Claire Ave. E. (416) 961-3817. Richard Kelly.
Melbourne, Australia 3004: 390 St. Kilda Road. 267-1344. William Shannon, mgng dir.
London, U.K. W1M J13: 32 Ayerbrook St. 839-6361. Peter Mead, mgng dir.
Lafayette 88 Colonia Anzures, Mexico 5 D.F. David Hart, pres.

Sherwood & Partners. 411 Lafayette St., 3rd Fl., New York 10003. (212) 254-7800. FAX: (212) 254-8893. Lew Sherwood, pres.
Radio-TV media dept: Bob McDonald, art dir.

Simons Michelson Zieve Inc. 900 Wilshire Dr., Suite 102, Troy, Mich. 48084. (313) 362-4242. Morton Zieve, chmn of bd; James A. Michelson, pres; Helen Charewych, VP finance.
Radio-TV media dept: Kyra Kinney, media dir.

Smith/Greenland Advertising Inc. 555 W. 57th St., 11th Fl., New York 10019. (212) 757-3200. FAX: (212) 757-7217. Leo Greenland, CEO; Drew Greenland, Bert Rosenberg, exec VPs.
Radio-TV media dept: Glen Ascher, prod; Marcia Birnbaum, prod; Beryl Seidenberg, sr VP/media dir.

The Softness Group Inc. 381 Park Ave. S., New York 10016. (212) 696-2444. Carol Blades, pres.

Steen Advertising Corp. 1975 Linden Blvd., Elmont, N.Y. 11003. (516) 285-3900. FAX: (516) 285-3904. Norman Steen, pres.

Steppin' Out & See America. 3655A Old Court Rd., Suites 1 & 2, Pikesville, Md. 21208. (410) 653-2616. FAX: (410) 653-2687. Bob Colton, CEO; Eli Colton, pres; Ray Grauer, dir mktg & prom.

Sudler & Hennessey Inc. 1633 Broadway, New York 10019. (212) 969-5800. FAX: (212) 969-5991. William B. Gibson, chmn/pres/CEO.
Radio-TV media dept: Kenneth Kopas Sr., VP/media dir.
New York 10036: 1180 Ave. of the Americas. (212) 827-6500. Arthur M. Rosen, exec VP/dir.

Sunbow Productions International. 130 5th Ave., New York 10011. (212) 337-6100. FAX: (212) 366-4242. C.J. Kettler, exec VP/mgng dir; David Wollos, VP sls & opns; Ellen Postman, mgr international sls.

Talkline Communications Advertising Agency. Box 20108, Parkwest Station, New York 10025-1510. (212)

Advertising Agencies

769-1925; (800) 628-TALK. FAX: (212) 799-4195. Zev J. Brenner, pres.

Target & Response Inc. 620 N. Michigan Ave., Suite 500, Chicago 60611. (312) 573-0500. FAX: (312) 573-0516. Laurence Levis, pres/gen mgr; Gary Kretchmer, VP/account mgr.

Radio-TV media dept: Susanne Jonson, media svcs mgr; Geri Marmo Lawrin, sr media svcs rep; Karen Johnson-Jickling, off mgr.

Tatham Euro RSCG. 980 N. Michigan Ave., Chicago 60611. (312) 337-4400. FAX: (312) 337-5930. Ralph Rydholm, CEO/chmn.

Radio-TV media dept: Phillip Gerber, sr ptnr/media opns dir; Eileen McKnight, group media dir.

J. Walter Thompson Co. 466 Lexington Ave., New York 10017. (212) 210-7000. FAX: (212) 210-6889. Burton J. Manning, chmn/CEO.

Radio-TV media dept: Jean Pool, sr VP US bcst; Marion Preston, sr VP/ dir bus affrs & US media; Robert Warrens, sr VP US media rsch.

Atlanta 30326: One Atlanta Plaza, 950 E. Paces Ferry Rd. (404) 365-7300. Jeff White, exec VP/gen mgr.

Chicago 60611: 900 N. Michigan Ave., Fls. 22-27. (312) 951-4000. J. Steve Davis, gen mgr.

Detroit 48226-3428: One Detroit Ctr., 500 Woodward Ave. (313) 964-3800. Peter Schweitzer, vice chmn agency opns.

Los Angeles 90025: 6500 Wilshire Blvd. (213) 951-1500.

San Francisco 94111: 4 Embarcadero Ctr., Suite 900. (415) 955-2000. Stephen Darland, gen mgr.

New York 10017: 466 Lexington Ave. (212) 210-7000. Jim Heekin, gen mgr.

Washington 20005: 1156 15th St. N.W. (202) 331-1990. Rich O'Leary, mgr.

Charlotte, N.C. 28212: 4801 E. Independence Blvd., Suite 708. (704) 536-9091. Scott Adkins, rep.

Dallas 75251: 12700 Park Central Dr. (214) 386-7202. Pam Kitkoski, supvr.

Denver 80202: 1401 17th St., Suite 1500. (303) 296-7668. Steve Blasing, sr VP/off mgr.

Houston 77042: 10777 Westheimer, Suite 718. (713) 995-9595. Ted Thompson, rep.

Indianapolis 46260: 9292 N. Meridian, Suite 111. (317) 844-5181. Rob Hopman, rep.

Memphis 38157: 5050 Poplar St., Suite 1000. (901) 682-9656. Paul Jackson, rep.

New Orleans 70001: One Galleria Blvd., Suite 1701. (504) 836-5136. Pat Gebhardt, rep.

Overland Park, Kan. 66211: 6900 College Blvd., Suite 550. (913) 339-6300. Sam Chiodo, rep.

Salt Lake City 84116: Lakeside Plaza, Building #1, 5215 W. Wiley Post Way, Suite 100. (801) 363-0310. Jeff Creer, rep.

Scottsdale, Ariz. 85253: 7373 N. Scottsdale Rd., Suite C-136. (602) 443-0702. Trey Curtola, rep. Phoenix office.

Glenn Allen, Va. 23060: The Colonnade Bldg., 4050 Innslake Dr., Suite 262. (804) 527-0075. Mark Tinsey, rep. Richmond office.

St. Ann, Mo. 63074: 500 Northwest Plaza, Suite 809. (314) 291-4540. George Willing, rep.

Cincinnati 45255: Waycross North, 431 Ohio Pike, Suite 110. (513) 528-4555. Frank Bodewell, VP/rep.

Columbus, Ohio 43229: 1601 Schrock Rd., Suite B2. (614) 523-3016. Patrick Doran II, rep.

Miami, Fla. 33131: One Brickell Sq., 801 Brickell Ave., Suite 15. (305) 789-6630. Carlos Thompson, regional account dir.

Minneapolis 55437: Southgate Office Plaza, 5001 W. 80th St., Suite 835. (612) 835-7991. Brian Dressel, rep.

East Brunswick, N.J. 08816: 3A Aver Ct. (908) 390-9322. Newark office.

Philadelphia 19087: 2 Radnor Corporate Ctr., 100 Matsonford Rd., Suite 835. (215) 995-0616. Anthony Accurso, rep.

Fairport, N.Y. 14450: 890 Cross Keys Office Park. (716) 223-0875. Cary S. Chaitoff, account mgr. Rochester office.

Tulsa, Okla. 74133: 7666 E. 61st St., Suite 130. (918) 250-1884. Kyle McQuaid, account mgr.

Tracy-Locke. Box 50129, 200 Crescent Ct., Dallas 75250. (214) 969-9000. FAX: (214) 855-2137. Howard Davis, chmn/pres/CEO; David Hudnall, CFO; Robert Largen, exec VP/dir mktg, planning & rsch; Ron Askew, exec VP/mgmt supvr.

Radio-TV media dept: Mike Rawlings; pres/chmn/CEO; Judy Miller, sr VP; Lora Funderburk, VP/assoc media dir; Carol Castellano, VP/spot buying dir.

Denver 80265: Prudential Plaza Bldg., 1050 17th St., Suite 700. (303) 892-4500.

Los Angeles 90025: 12100 Wilshire Blvd., Suite 1800. (310) 207-1002.

Atlanta 30305: One Buckhead Plaza, 3060 Peachtree Rd. N.E. (404) 396-9007.

Tucker Wayne/Luckie & Co. 1100 Peachtree St. N.E., Suite 1800, Atlanta 30309. (404) 347-8700. FAX: (404) 347-8800. Knox Massey Jr., CFO; Sidney L. Smith, pres. Atlanta office.

Radio-TV media dept: Richard O'Gorman, sr VP/media dir; Bill Zuspan Sr., media info & research; Jill Ditton, VP/assoc media dir; Linda Rountree, media dir Birmingham office.

Birmingham, Ala. 35223: 600 Luckie Dr. (205) 879-2121. Robert Luckie Jr., chmn of bd; Frank M. Lee, pres.

U.S./Mexico Travel Exchange. 1119 San Antonio, El Paso, Tex. 77901. (915) 533-4700. FAX: (915) 533-3640. Garrett W. Haston, pres; Jeffrey Peters, exec VP.

Vicom/FCB. (A Foote, Cone and Belding Communications Co.) One Lombard St., San Francisco 94111. (415) 391-8700. FAX: (415) 391-1042. John Loden, chmn.

Wahlstrom and Co. Inc. (A Foote, Cone and Belding Communications Co.) Box 1211, 1290 E. Main St., Stamford, Conn. 06904. (203) 348-7347. FAX: (203) 348-7350. Frank Barton, pres.

Waring & LaRosa Inc. 909 3rd Ave., New York 10022. (212) 755-0700. FAX: (212) 644-6980. Joseph LaRosa, chmn/co-CEO/pres; Saul Waring, vice-chmn/co-CEO; Morton Grossman, treas; James Caporimo, creative dir.

Radio-TV media dept: Caroline Coleman, sr prod radio & TV; Joe LaRosa Jr., sr prod radio & TV; Robert Steinhilber, assoc media dir.

Warwick Baker & Fiore Inc. 100 Ave. of the Americas, New York 10013. (212) 941-4200. FAX: (212) 941-4277; (212) 941-4342. Wilder D. Baker, chmn of bd/CEO; Rogert J. Fiore, pres/COO; John P. Warwick, honorary chmn of bd; Ronald S. Fierman, exec VP/gen mgr; Susan Small-Weil, exec VP/chief planning off; Andrew Mendolsohn, exec VP/creative dir; Jerry Prestomburgo, exec VP/creative dir; Alden Ludlow III, exec VP/mgr creative svcs; Michael A. Haggerty, group sr VP/media dir.

San Diego 92103: 2900 4th Ave. (619) 293-7720. Sheila Fox, pres. Chapman/Warwick Advertising.

The Weightman Group. 1818 Market St., Philadelphia 19103. (215) 561-6100. FAX: (215) 496-9195. Charles Coffey, chmn; John Goodchild, pres; Mark Plamondon, exec VP.

Radio-TV media dept: Neil Harrison, exec media dir; Edward O'Keefe, VP strategic planning.

Wells, Rich, Greene B.D.D.P. 9 W. 57th St., New York 10019. (212) 303-5000. FAX: (212) 758-4381. Ken Olsham, CEO; Mark Buttitta, media dir.

Los Angeles 90067: 1900 Ave. of the Stars. (310) 277-3200. Ray Townsend, chmn.

Larry John Wright Advertising. 1045 E. University Dr., Mesa, Ariz. 85203. (602) 833-8111. FAX: (602) 969-2895. Larry F. John, CEO; John N. Wright, pres.

Full-svc advertising agency specializing in film & video commercials, radio commercials, jingles & TV shows.

Wunderman, Ricotta & Kline Inc. 675 6th Ave., New York 10010. (212) 941-3000. FAX: (212) 627-8379. Lester Wunderman, chmn/CEO; Mitch Kurz, CEO.

Radio-TV media dept: Hal Zwick, media dir.

Wyse Advertising Inc. 24 Public Sq., Cleveland 44113. (216) 696-2424. FAX: (216) 621-2950. Marc A. Wyse, chmn; Lois Wyse, corporate pres; Carl E. Camden, Michael C. Marino, pres Cleveland.

Radio-TV media dept: Jim Pockmire, exec VP media. New York 10003: 79 5th Ave., 11th Fl. John Lippman, exec VP account svcs; Nat Gayster, sr VP media.

Cleveland 44141: 24 Public Sq. (212) 689-3939. Errol W. Dengler, pres. Pinnacle Media.

Young & Rubicam Inc. 285 Madison Ave., New York 10017-6486. (212) 210-3000. FAX: (212) 490-9073. Alexander Kroll, chmn/CEO; Peter A. Georgescu, pres.

Radio-TV media dept: Joe Philport, sr VP/dir loc bcst & net radio; Paul Isacsson, exec VP/dir bcst progmg & purchasing.

Chicago 60606: One S. Wacker Dr. (312) 845-4000. Pat Casserata, pres.

Detroit 48243-1283: 200 Renaissance Ctr., Suite 1000. (313) 446-8600. Mike Howue, pres/CEO.

San Francisco 94105: 100 1st St., 18 Fl. (415) 882-0600. Craig Branigan, sr VP/gen mgr.

Zeitgeist Inc. 9903 Santa Monica Blvd., Suite 431, Beverly Hills, Calif. 90212. (310) 553-7788. FAX: (310) 553-7799. Sam Lee, pres; Susan Lee, John Joseph Lee, VPs.

Century City, Calif. 90067: Century City Park E., Suite 1810. (310) 553-7781. Joe Walters, VP.

Holbrook, N.Y. 11741: Box 600.

The Zimmerman Group. 701 4th Ave. S., Suite 1330 Minneapolis 55415. (612) 341-1100. FAX: (612) 341-0323. Jim Zimmerman, pres.

Independent Media Buying/Planning Services

Advanswers Media/Programming. 10 Broadway, St. Louis 63102. (314) 444-2100. FAX: (314) 444-2199. Donald Stork, pres; John Marlow, sr exec off; Joe Rousseau, sr VP/exec group dir; Fred Webber, sr VP/exec group dir; Charles Haines, sr VP/corporate rsch & dev; Gordon Hendry, sr VP/dir spec projects; Kathy Lawson, sr VP/exec dir bcst; Ray Ruzicka, sr VP/project group dir; Carol Raack Watkins, VP/assoc group dir; Dave Hatt, VP/dir bcst proms; John Lenzini, VP/assoc group dir.
New York 10019: 1740 Broadway. (212) 581-4087.
Net subsidiary: Paul Schulman Co., New York; Paul Schulman, pres.
Complete start-to-finish media svc, including media planning, technology, cable, syndication & net bcst negotiation; also bcst prom unit.

American Telecast Corp. 16 Industrial Blvd., Paoli Corporate Ctr., Suite 200, Paoli, Pa. 19301. (215) 251-9933. FAX: (215) 251-9256. John Marsh, pres.

Atwood Richards Inc. 99 Park Ave., New York 10016. (212) 490-9200.

Clifford A. Botway Inc. 747 3rd Ave., New York 10017. (212) 421-4200. FAX: (212) 421-8258. Clifford A. Botway, chmn of bd; Arthur N. Schreibman, pres.
Comprehensive natl net TV, radio, cable & syndication svcs specialists.

CPM Inc. 515 N. State St., Chicago 60610. (312) 527-2100. FAX: (312) 527-1506; (312) 527-1507. Norman M. Goldring, pres; Michael Willner, exec VP/COO; Roger Casty, exec VP.
Planning & buying of media; spot bcst, print, net, out-of-home, direct response.

CSI International Corp. 800 2nd Ave., New York 10017. (212) 687-5600. FAX: (212) 983-1186. Steven Geller, chmn; June Brody, vice chmn; Bill Schachter, pres; David Rapaport, VP natl bcstg; Sue Harris, VP spot bcstg; Fran Feinstein, VP print svcs.
Media buying specializing in reciprocal trade.

Gaynor Media Corp. 488 Madison Ave., New York 10022. (212) 755-9494. Lee Gaynor, pres; Joy Uniss, media dir.
Planning & buying all media, primarily bcst.

Greenstripe Media Inc. 1300 Quail St., Suite 209, Newport Beach, Calif. 92660. (714) 752-9277. Joe Winkelmann, pres/time buyer; Tony DeDios, gen mgr; George Benedict, bcst coord; Julie Bohne, syndication & cable mgr.
Planning, placement & syndication.

Margret Haney of Graham-Haney. 2995 Woodside Rd., Woodside, Calif. 94062. (415) 325-5552. FAX: (415) 325-5556. Margret Haney, pres; Sondra Carver, J.D. law & taxes.
Media adv, buying, brokerage & consulting.

Independent Media Services Inc. 770 Lexington Ave., New York 10021. (212) 836-8900. FAX: (212) 593-3687. Neil L. Aronstam, pres; Robert L. Petizon, exec VP; Leslie Holasek, sr VP; Frank Reynolds, controller.
All media buying & planning with experience in package goods, retail, co-op, circ bldg & direct response.

Kelly, Scott & Madison Inc. 35 E. Wacker Dr., Suite 1150, Chicago 60601. (312) 977-0772. FAX: (312) 977-0874. Leonard Cohen, pres; Herb Isaacs, exec VP; Leonard Kay, sr VP.

Landin Media Sales. 3033 N. 44th St., Suite 375, Phoenix 85018. (602) 553-4080. FAX: (602) 553-4090. Larry Cummings, pres; Dennis Hart, VP.
TV stn rep & discounted barter time.

MJP Carat International. Broadway House, 2-6 Fulham Broadway, London, U.K. SW6 1AA. 071-381-8010. FAX: 071-385-3233; TELEX: 298775.

Media Corporate Inventory. 114 E. 32nd St., New York 10016. (212) 832-6500. FAX: (212) 447-5973. Michael Nichter, pres; Helene Cella, VP/mgng dir.
Media buying & mktg.

Perry Enterprises. 827 ½ N. Judge Ely Blvd., Abilene, Tex. 79601. (915) 676-7330. David R. Perry, own.
Loc direct-mail lists. Mktg includes convenience stores, & water & air filtration systems for hospitals, hotels.

Rapp Collins Worldwide. 488 Madison Ave., 4th Fl., New York 10012. (212) 725-8100. G. Steven Dapper, corp CEO; Emily Soell, corp CCO; David Scholes, pres/CEO; Ed McNally, corp CFO.
Full-svc direct response agency.

SFM Media Corp. 1180 Ave. of the Americas, New York 10036. (212) 790-4800. Walter Staab, chmn/pres; Robert A. Frank, Stanley H. Moger, exec VPs; Jordan Ringel, David Tabin, Bob Perlstein, sr VPs; Joe Gerard, sr VP/treas.

SMY Inc. 333 N. Michigan Ave., Chicago 60601. (312) 621-9600. A.E. Staley III, chmn/pres; Virginia L. Shirley, exec VP; Peg Bartelson, sr VP/dir media svcs; Steven Schroeppel, sr VP.
Planning, analysis of markets & media, media rsch, trafficking, billing, evaluation. Emphasis on negotiation & generated time.

Time Buying Services Inc. 10 Columbus Cir., New York 10019. (212) 765-7710. FAX: (212) 245-6591. Frank Muratore, CEO; Stanley Leipzig, pres; Robert Kresch, treas; Nicholas Gerrasi, comptroller.
Rsch, planning, buying & post-analysis for all media. Merchandise & media barter svcs.

Vitt Media International Inc. 1114 Ave. of the Americas, New York 10036. (212) 921-0500. FAX: (212) 575-4700. Sam B. Vitt, chmn emeritus; Roy A. Muro, chmn; Robert Calandruccio, pres; Leonard Lieboff, Sheldon Kawer, Steve Berger, exec VPs.
Specialists in media planning, buying, rsch, traf, merchandise for all media for advertisers & adv agencies, plus bcst syndicating.

Barter Service Companies

Action Media Group. 5855 Topanga Canyon Blvd., Suite 210, Woodland Hills, Calif. 91367. (818) 592-2900. FAX: (818) 592-2913. Rick Pack, pres/CEO; Len Materna, VP Midwest sls; Robert Chenoff, VP eastern sls.
 Natl barter time sls company for syndicated TV.

Andrews Entertainment & Club Golf. 6311 N. O'Connor, #214 LB-93, Irving, Tex. 75039. (214) 869-4653. FAX: (214) 869-1818. Max Andrews, pres.
 TV syndication & prod, & foreign distribution.

Buena Vista Television Advertising Sales. 500 Park Ave., New York 10022. (212) 735-7400. FAX: (212) 735-7402. Michael Shaw, sr VP; Howard Levy, VP sls; Jim Engleman, VP Midwest sls; Norman Lesser, VP eastern sls.
 Natl adv sls for all Buena Vista TV properties & selected acquired progmg.

Camelot Entertainment Sales Inc. 1700 Broadway, 35th Fl., New York 10019. (212) 315-4747. FAX: (212) 247-7674. Steve Hirsch, pres; Michael Auerbach, sr VP.
 A barter subsidiary of Kingworld selling natl adv time in Kingworld & other TV progmg.

Group W Productions Media Sales. 888 7th Ave., New York 10106. (212) 307-3264. FAX: (212) 307-3930. Dan Cosgrove, pres; Glen Burnside, VP eastern mgr; Patricia Brown, VP Midwest mgr.

International Family Entertainment Advertiser Sales. 1140 Ave. of the Americas, 11th Fl., New York 10036. (212) 997-1842. FAX: (212) 997-1843. Robert C. Dahill, VP sls; Steven Lenta, sr VP sls; James Harder, dir Midwest sls; Chris Monteferrante, account exec.
 Chicago 60611: 444 N. Michigan, Suite 1000. (312) 222-0043. Bob Dahill, VP advertiser sls; Chris Monteferrante, account exec; James Harder, Midwest account exec; Chris Bolte, sls planner; Amy Shigo, sr sls asst.
 Fully integrated barter sls & mktg company with the resources to develop, distribute & market progs from many sources.

Kassel Marketing. 150 E. 52nd St., 7th Fl., New York 10022. (212) 980-1555. FAX: (212) 758-1982. Terry Kassel, pres; George Giatzis, eastern sls mgr; Ken Ripley, account exec.
 Full svc TV ad sls agency specializing in sports, entertainment & news.

Landin Media Sales Inc. 3033 N. 44th St., Suite 375, Phoenix 85018-7229. (602) 553-4080. FAX: (602) 553-4090. Larry Cummings, pres; Dennis Hart, VP.
 TV stn rep & discounted barter time.

One World Entertainment. (A division of MTV Networks.) 1515 Broadway, New York 10036. (212) 258-8142. FAX: (212) 258-8103. Rick Levy, sr VP; Michael Spalding, VP; Tom Burke, dir mktg & rsch; Christopher Pearse, dir Midwest sls; Chip Meehan, dir western sls.
 Sls & mktg of original, first-run & represented bartered syndication inventory with franchises among kids, young adult & female demographics.

Select Media Communications Inc. 152 W. 57th St., New York 10019. (212) 765-1020. FAX: (212) 765-2943. Mitch Gutkowski, pres; Claire Scully, exec VP; Marc Juris, VP creative svcs; Carol Blank, dir adv & sls; Linda Yaccarino, dir stn sls/adv sls exec.
 TV prog distribution & prod.

Twentieth Television. 1211 Ave. of the Americas, 3rd Fl. New York 10036. (212) 556-2520. FAX: (212) 869-7840. Bob Cesa, sr VP adv sls; Jon Barovick, VP adv sls.
 Creator, prod & distributor of net, first-run & off-net progmg & feature TV films.

Worldvision Enterprises Advertising Sales. 1700 Broadway, New York 10019-5992. (212) 261-2700. FAX: (212) 261-2724. Gary G. Montanus, sr VP mktg; Doreen Muldoon, dir sls administration; Mirka Cigan, sls coord; Tim Davis, account exec; Pam Eaton, dir sls planning.
 Represents natl availabilities in Worldvision's domestic & international progmg, as well as availabilities in outside distributors progmg.

U.S. Radio, Television and Cable Representatives

ABN Radio & TV. 1515 W. Lane Ave., Columbus, Ohio 43221. (614) 486-9577. FAX: (614) 487-8205. Ed Johnson, pres/farm dir; Grant Neilley, opns dir; Dale Minyo, assoc farm dir; Doug Tanner, studio pro.

A/D Media Sales. 2755 Franklin St., San Francisco 94123. (415) 441-3955. Al Dougherty, mgr.

Advertising Sales West. 2755 Franklin St., San Francisco 94123. (415) 441-3955. Al Dougherty, mgr.

Agri Broadcasting Network Representatives. 1515 W. Lane Ave., Columbus, Ohio 43221. (614) 486-9577.

BRI Inc. Box 100, Little Rock, Ark. 72203. (501) 372-7780. FAX: (501) 372-7787. Wally Tucker, pres; Peg Tucker, VP.

Banner Radio. 125 W. 55th St., 4th Fl., New York 10019. (212) 424-6160. FAX: (212) 424-6180. Mike L. Chires, pres; Robert F. Ferraro, exec VP; Rosemary Zimmerman, VP; Mike Moran VP/rgnl mgr NY; Chuck Fleming, VP/mgr; Til Levesque VP/mgr spec sls.
  Atlanta 30305: 6 Piedmont Ctr., Suite 712. (404) 365-3060. FAX: (404) 816-5708. Glen R. Woosley, VP/mgr.
  Boston 02116: Statler Office Bldg., Suite 216. (617) 357-1670. FAX: (617) 357-1658. Jane Doherty Rodophele, VP/mgr.
  Chicago 60611: 455 N. Cityfront Plaza Dr., Suite 1700. (312) 755-3960. FAX: (312) 755-0876. Greg Jankowski, VP/mgr; Bob McArthur, VP stns.
  Dallas 75201: 300 Crescent Ct., Suite 420. (214) 999-2148. FAX: (214) 855-5204. Martin J. Toole, VP/mgr.
  Troy, Mich. 48084: 3310 W. Big Beaver Rd., Suite 513. (313) 643-4061. FAX: (313) 643-9486. Ann Pantalone, mgr; Mitch Kline, VP/gen sls mgr. Detroit office.
  Houston 77027: 2900 Weslayan, Suite 625. (713) 961-2974. FAX: (713) 629-0303. Gregory Stroud, mgr.
  Los Angeles 90048: 6500 Wilshire Blvd., Suite 320. (213) 966-5000. FAX: (213) 852-0956. Ira Wechsler, VP; Bill Freund, sls mgr.
  Minneapolis 55402: Piper Jaffray Tower, Suite 2990. (612) 339-9904. FAX: (612) 339-2005. Dennis Sternitzky, mgr.
  Portland, Ore. 97201: Crown Plaza, 1500 S.W. 1st Ave., Suite 320. (503) 222-2122. FAX: (503) 222-1474. David Lichtman, mgr. Portland & Seattle offices.
  Philadelphia 19103: 8 Penn Ctr., Suite 1350. (215) 564-2533. FAX: (215) 567-5850. Vince Gambino, VP/mgr.
  St. Louis 63102: 10 S. Broadway, Equitable Bldg., Suite 560. (314) 421-0888. FAX: (314) 621-8357. Stanley B. Greenberg, VP/mgr.
  San Francisco 94105: 100 Spear St., Suite 1900. (415) 281-2477. FAX: (415) 974-1871. Nancy Meyer, mgr.

John Blair Communications Inc. 1290 Ave. of the Americas, New York 10104. (212) 603-5000. FAX: (212) 603-5453/5423/5003/5501. Tim McAuliff, chmn/CEO; Ronald J. Brooks, gen counsel; Sanford S. Ackerman, sr VP finance & admin/CFO; Kenneth P. Donnellon, VP adv & communication.

Blair Television. (A subsidiary of John Blair Communications Inc.) 1290 Ave. of the Americas, New York 10104. (212) 603-5000. FAX: (212) 603-5453. TWX: 710-581-4351. Timothy M. McAuliff, chmn/CEO; James R. Kelly, sr VP/dir client svcs; Sanford S. Ackerman, sr VP finance & admin/CFO; George G. Dallas, VP/dir info systems; Kenneth P. Donnellon, VP adv & communication; Robert R. Saracen, VP sls admin; Steven A. Murphy, VP/dir sls analysis & planning; James P. Murtagh, VP corporate dev. Blair USA: Leo M. MacCourtney Jr., pres; David R. Bisceglia, VP (Red Division); Ronald Cochran, mgr (Red Division/Knicks); Al J. Ferrara, mgr (Red Division/Nets); Charles W. Holmes, VP (White Division); William J. Acker, mgr (White Division/Islanders); David C. Crawford, VP/mgr (White Division/Mets); Thomas F. McGarrity, sr VP (Blue Division); Paul Wilson, mgr (Blue Division/Rangers); Peter H. Senseney, VP/mgr (Blue Division/Yankees); Donald K. Williams, VP/dir mktg (Blue Division). Blair America: Floyd J. Gelini, pres; David J. Herman, sr VP/dir sls; Richard M. Morris, VP (Red Division); James V. Catalano, mgr (Red Division/Bills); Linda A. Scutari, VP (White Division); Don H. Levinson, mgr (White Division/Giants); Philip B. Kirk, VP (Blue Division); Jeffrey A. Lingg, mgr (Blue Division/Jets). Sales Support Division: John B. Poor Jr., sr VP/dir support svcs; John A. Rohr, VP/dir progmg; Alan B. Picozzi, VP/dir sls rsch; Eugene M. Cunningham, VP/rsch dir; Cora N. Enriquez, VP/rsch.
  Atlanta 30305: 7 Piedmont Ctr., Suite 610. (404) 231-0232. FAX: (404) 231-0797. Denny Godwin, VP/mgr; Cynthia Morris, sls mgr.
  Boston 02116: Heritage-on-the-Garden, 75 Park Plaza. (617) 695-2180. FAX: (617) 695-2190. Carole J. Aaron, VP/mgr.
  Charlotte, N.C. 28211: 2101 Rexford Rd., Suite 119E. (704) 365-4747. FAX: (704) 365-8460. Gayle Rabon, VP/mgr.
  Chicago 60611: 455 N. Cityfront Plaza Dr., Suite 800. (312) 321-6600. FAX: (312) 321-6797. Sidney "Sid" C. Brown, sr VP/reg sls; Mike Mougey, sls mgr (Bulls); D. William Ross, sls mgr (Bears); Jan Barkell, sls mgr (Cubs); James E. Jump, VP/sls mgr (Power); Robert T. Jacobs, VP/sls mgr (Blackhawks); Tara Kovach, sls mgr (White Sox); Steve Dillworth, rgnl sls mgr.
  Dallas 75240: One Lincoln Centre, 5400 LBJ Fwy., Suite 975/LB #7. (214) 239-9600. FAX: (214) 770-2420. Michael C. Howe, VP/mgr; James McGuire, VP/sls mgr.
  Aurora, Colo. 80014: 2851 S. Parker Rd., Suite 800. (303) 337-1308. FAX: (303) 337-0089. Scott Blackett, VP/mgr. Denver office.
  Detroit 48202: 225 Fisher Bldg. (313) 871-3060. FAX: (313) 871-5803. Kathy Zimmerman, VP/mgr.
  Houston 77027: 5 Post Oak Park, Suite 1740. (713) 552-0600. FAX: (713) 552-1712. Barry Maxwell, mgr.
  Jacksonville, Fla. 32207: Gulf Life Tower, Suite 1626. (904) 399-1900. FAX: (904) 398-6598. Glenna S. Pluchak, VP/mgr.
  Los Angeles 90025: Westwood Gateway Bldg., 11111 Santa Monica Blvd., Suite 1900. (310) 444-3500. FAX: (310) 575-9140. Allan E. Keir, VP/mgr; Mike Dempsey, rgnl sls mgr; Aleyne Larner, sls mgr (Lakers); Janet Cutler, sls mgr (Kings); Al DeFlorio, sls mgr (Raiders); Nancy Dodson, sls mgr (Dodgers).
  Miami, Fla. 33131: One Bayfront Plaza, 100 S. Biscayne Blvd., Suite 1103. (305) 358-9911. FAX: (305) 374-6426. Alan Brittain, mgr.
  Minneapolis 55402: 60 S. 6th St., Suite 2450. (612) 376-7969. FAX: (612) 376-7970. Bradd Lasch, VP/mgr.
  Philadelphia 19103: 1800 Kennedy Blvd., 4th Fl. (215) 568-6540. FAX: (215) 568-1845. Mike Murphy, VP/mgr; Kevin Branigan, VP/sls mgr.
  Portland, Ore. 97201: 1501 S.W. Jefferson St. (503) 226-5090. FAX: (503) 220-1806. JoAnne James, mgr.
  St. Louis 63102: The Equitable Bldg., 10 Broadway, Suite 1620. (314) 421-5262. FAX: (314) 421-6529.
  San Francisco 94111: 505 Sansome St. (415) 434-2393. FAX: (415) 392-1943.
  Seattle 98109: 333 Dexter Ave. N. (206) 448-3620. FAX: (206) 441-5620. Pam Guinn, sls mgr.
  Tampa 33607: 5005 W. Laurel St., Suite 205. (813) 289-3979. FAX: (813) 286-2412. Sarah Tyrrell, VP/mgr.

Broadcast Representatives Radio & TV. 1705 S. 116th St., Omaha, Neb. 68144. (402) 333-2636. FAX: (402) 333-2638. Howard Anderson, pres.

Brydson Media Sales International Inc. 330 W. 56th St., Suite 7E, New York 10019. (212) 586-7773. FAX (212) 582-6353. David G. Brydson, pres; Tom McCoughlin, Maddy Boos, Marie Boroes.

CBS Radio Representatives. 51 W. 52nd St., New York 10019. (212) 975-1877; (212) 975-5354. FAX: (212) 975-2003. Raif S. D'Amico, VP/gen mgr; Marc Gross, sls mgr/eastern rgnl mgr.
  Atlanta 30305: 11 Piedmont Ctr., Suite 608. (404) 233-8281. Chad Brown, sls mgr.
  Boston 02108: 30 Winter St., 12th Fl. (617) 728-1916. Amy Caplan, sls mgr.
  Chicago 60611: 630 N. McClurg Ct. (312) 951-3286. Rocky Cosgrove, sls mgr/central rgnl mgr.
  Dallas 75204: 4131 N. Central Expwy., Suite 820. (214) 526-0557. Linda Weaver, sls mgr.
  Detroit 48034: 26877 Northwestern Hwy., Suite 421. (313) 351-2161. David Rice, sls mgr.
  Los Angeles 90028: 6121 Sunset Blvd. (213) 460-3705; (213) 460-3703. Rich Allen, western rgnl mgr; Scott Sringer, sls mgr.
  Minneapolis 55402: 625 2nd Ave. S., Suite 417. (612) 371-9051. Karen Miller, sls mgr.
  Philadelphia 19131: City Ave. & Monument Rd. (215) 688-5990. Michael Garrity, sls mgr.
  St. Louis 63102: One Memorial Dr. (314) 444-3221. David Brennan, sls mgr.
  San Francisco 94111: One Embarcadero Ctr. (415) 765-4006. Marco Camacho, sls mgr.
  Seattle 98101: 1191 2nd Ave., Suite 1960. (206) 654-4104. Larry Adams, sls mgr.
  St. Louis 63102: One Memorial Dr. (314) 444-3221. David Brennan, sls mgr.

U.S. Radio, Television and Cable Representatives

CBS Television Stations National Sales. 51 W. 52nd St., New York 10019. (212) 975-4321. FAX: (212) 975-4005. Philip Press, VP/gen mgr sls & mktg; Melinda Duchak, dir rsch.

Atlanta 30305: 11 Piedmont Ctr. (404) 261-2227. Gene McHugh, office mgr.

Chicago 60611: 630 N. McClurg Ct. (312) 944-6000. Terry Dunning, mgr Midwest sls.

Boston 02116: 218 Newbury St., 3rd Fl. (617) 262-7337. Diane Cipriani, office mgr.

Dallas 75062: 545 E. John Carpenter Fwy., Suite 1540. (214) 556-1245. Sandy Delaunay, office mgr.

Detroit 48034: 26877 Northwest Hwy. Elaine Carpenter, office mgr.

Los Angeles 90028: 6121 Sunset Blvd. (313) 352-2800. Julie Ballard, office mgr.

San Francisco 94111: One Embarcadero Ctr., Suite 3237. (415) 433-0500. Frank Wheeler, office mgr.

Washington 20036: 1800 M St. N.W., Suite 300N. (202) 457-4509. Sonja Milliner, office mgr.

CC/ABC National Television Sales. 77 W. 66th St., New York 10023. (212) 456-7777. FAX: (212) 456-7607. John B. Watkins, pres; Philip J. Sweenie, VP; Ed Pearson, gen sls mgr.

Atlanta 30305: 3060 Peachtree Rd. N.W., Suite 1470. (404) 266-1750. Debbie Shay, sls mgr.

Boston 02116: One Exeter Plaza. (617) 262-8989.

Charlotte, S.C. 28211: 6525 Morrison Blvd., Suite 201. (704) 364-6767. Scott Dempsey, sls mgr.

Chicago 60601: 190 N. State St. (312) 899-4200. Scott Thomas, sls mgr.

Dallas 75251: 12222 Merit Dr., Suite 1760. (214) 960-7981. Mike Irvine, sls mgr.

Detroit 48075: 3000 Town Ctr., Suite 2001. (313) 355-4490. Hyla Kelly, sls mgr.

Los Angeles 90067: 2020 Ave. of the Stars. (310) 557-6241. Michael Jack, sls mgr.

Philadelphia 19131: 4100 City Line Ave. (215) 879-3100. Bernie Prazencia, sls mgr.

St. Louis 63102: One Metropolitan Sq., Suite 1630. (314) 231-6050.

San Francisco 94111-1450: 900 Front St. (415) 954-7810. Donna Assumma, sls mgr.

CTV Media Inc. 5900 Roche Dr., Suite 600, Columbus, Ohio 43229. (614) 848-5800. FAX: (614) 848-4099. Kathryn C. Dixon, pres/CEO; Kim Miller, VP opns; Liz Holbert, VP financial.

Cincinnati 45210: 1110 Pendleton St., #22. (513) 241-5144. Pat Preziosi, Midwest division sls mgr.

Amherst, N.Y. 14226: 4476 Main St., Suite 207. (716) 839-3464. Barbi Johnson, eastern division sls mgr.

Caballero Spanish Media. 261 Madison Ave., 18th Fl., New York 10016. (212) 697-4120. FAX: (212) 697-9151. Eduardo Caballero, CEO; Joe Antelo, pres; Manny Ballestero, sr VP natl sls; David Haymore, VP N.Y. rgnl sls; Lionel Benn, account exec; Oscar Ramos, sls asst; Francisco Martinez, controller/CFO; Jose LaCosta, accounting department; Elaine Cruz, traf; Maria Turchiano, asst Caballero/Antelo; Lilyvette Serrano, receptionist; Glenda Villanueva, dir sls; Eric Bench, account exec.

Los Angeles 90024: 10880 Wilshire Blvd., Suite 1215. (310) 475-0033. FAX: (310) 474-3454. Mike Nelson, dir sls; Andi Kushner, sls asst.

Charlotte, N.C. 28212: 6407 Idlewild Rd., Suite 112. (704) 568-8111. FAX: (704) 568-0043. Jim Peacock, dir sls; Karen (Ragan) Wood, sls asst.

Chicago 60601: 205 N. Michigan Ave, Suite 2015. (312) 861-9385. FAX: (312) 938-0152. Beth Vander Bergh, account exec; Margi McGuire, sls asst.

Larkspur, Colo. 80118: 14693 Spring Valley Rd. (303) 688-4370. FAX: (303) 688-3085. Debbie Lang, dir sls. Denver office.

San Francisco 94111: 750 Battery St., Suite 340. (415) 772-2740. FAX: (415) 772-2758. John Hurlburt, dir sls.

Marietta, Ga. 30067: 1640 Powers Ferry Rd., Bldg. 5, Suite 300. (404) 953-1111. FAX: (404) 953-0417. Charles Maisano, dir sls; Pat Morino, sls asst. Atlanta office.

Southfield, Mich. 48075: 4000 Town Center, Suite 290. (313) 357-7711. FAX: (313) 357-2610. Jennifer Van Vallis, dir sls; Judy Hitt, sls asst. Detroit office.

Houston 77057: MCO Plaza, 5718 Westheimer, Suite 1705. (713) 266-7667. FAX: (713) 266-6925. Jill Garlarneau, dir sls; Marlea Zwiebel, sls asst.

Boston 02116: 31 St. James Ave., Suite 809. (617) 426-3374. FAX: (617) 451-0067. Greg Martin, dir sls; Karen "Ragan" Wood, sls asst.

Minneapolis 55404: 1111 3rd Ave. S., Suite 450. (612) 333-8717. FAX: (612) 341-9832. Kate Hesslan-Miller, dir sls; Tracey Eden, sls asst.

Philadelphia 19102: The Bellevue, Broad & Walnut St., 9th Fl. (215) 732-3380. FAX: (215) 732-1329. Charles Reilly, dir sls; Kathleen O'Connor, sls asst.

Portland, Ore. 97201: 4700 S.W. Macadam Ave., Suite 303. (503) 223-1700. FAX: (503) 223-4580. Georgia Hess, dir sls; Sandy Stein, sls asst.

Richmond, Va. 23255-0608: Box 70608. (804) 360-0433. FAX: (804) 360-1251. Tena Lustig, dir sls.

Seattle 98121: 2505 2nd Ave., Suite 515. (206) 441-3401. FAX: (206) 443-1872. Jenny Hill, account exec.

St. Louis 63102: 10 S. Broadway, Suite 500. (314) 231-0000. FAX: (314) 241-0049. Mark Riordan, account exec; Stephanie Kunz, sls asst.

Cable AdNet. 1332 Enterprise Dr., Suite 300, West Chester, Pa. 19380: (215) 344-9000. FAX: (215) 429-5181. David P. McGlade, pres.

Billings, Mont. 59102: 1925 Grand Ave., Suite 123. (406) 252-6911. FAX: (406) 252-6763.

Reno, Nev. 89502: 3100 Mill St., Suite 104. (702) 348-2772. FAX: (702) 348-7294.

Carnegie, Pa. 15106: 700 N. Bell Ave., Bldg. 4, Suite 280. (412) 276-7200. FAX: (412) 276-7915. Pittsburgh office.

Charlotte, N.C. 28212: 6407 Idlewild Rd., Suite 431. (704) 537-8000. FAX: (704) 537-0497.

Dallas 75247: 8150 Brookriver Dr., Suite S-700. (214) 637-7744. FAX: (214) 638-8402.

Hurst, Tex. 76054: 1865 Norwood Plaza. (817) 282-8113. FAX: (817) 282-8119.

Williston, Vt. 05495: 18 Blair Park Rd., Suite 200. (802) 879-5377. FAX: (802) 878-5398. Vermont/New Hampshire office.

Cable Advantage. (A division of Holson Valley Broadcasting Corp.) Box WKPT, Kingsport, Tenn. 37662. (615) 246-9578. FAX: (615) 246-1863. George E. DeVault Jr., pres/gen mgr; J. Raymond Walker, exec VP.

Cable Media. 789 Indian Church Rd., West Seneca, N.Y. 14224. (716) 827-1113. FAX: (716) 827-1333. Richard Lewis, opns mgr; Ron Gotti, gen sls mgr.

Cable Networks Inc. 260 Madison Ave., New York 10016. (212) 889-4670. FAX: (212) 689-0952. Robert Fennimore, pres/COO; Peter J. Moran, sr VP; Stacie M. Colbeth, VP eastern sls; Eglon Simons, gen mgr New York Interconnect; Bill Fagan, dir sls WNYI; Ed Renicker, sls mgr New York Interconnect; Jim McDaniels, natl sls mgr.

Atlanta 30305: 7 Piedmont Ctr., Suite 420. (404) 266-3885. FAX: (404) 266-3938. Jenny Hazelrig, sls dir southern rgn.

Boston 02116: 855 Boylston St., 3rd Fl. (617) 266-7711. FAX: (617) 266-7853. William Wayland, natl sls mgr.

Chicago 60611: 625 N. Michigan Ave., Suite 1701. (312) 335-0870. FAX: (312) 335-5456. Dan McTigue.

Cleveland 44114: 3400 Lakeside Ave. (216) 621-2221. FAX: (216) 621-4982. Mark Dolan, natl sls mgr.

Dallas 75247: 8150 Brookriver Dr., Suite 202. (214) 905-9966. FAX: (214) 688-7472. Ray Gaskin, natl sls mgr.

San Francisco 94111: 901 Battery Pl., Suite 204. (415) 392-0222. FAX: (415) 392-4921. Frank Angelo.

Santa Monica, Calif. 90404: 2425 W. Olympic Blvd., Suite 5050. (310) 828-1142. FAX: (310) 828-1232. Wylie Drummond, VP western division; Illise Welter, dir sls western rgn. Los Angeles office.

Southfield, Mich. 48075: 2000 Town Center, Suite 1900. (313) 351-8728. FAX: (313) 351-8729. Laura Blake, natl sls mgr. Detroit office.

CableOne. 322 Rt. 46 W., Parsippany, N.J. 07054. (201) 808-7333. Jack Meyers, pres.

CableTime of San Francisco. 350 Sansome St., Suite 200, San Francisco 94104. (415) 392-0222. FAX: (415) 392-4921. Frank D. Angelo, pres.

Sacramento, Calif. 95821: CableTime of Sacramento. 3323 Watt Ave., Suite 102. (916) 887-1212. Dede Nieto, sls mgr.

Carey, Bladon, McDonald & McKernan Inc. 10 Piedmont Ctr., Suite 406, 3495 Piedmont Rd., Atlanta 30305. (404) 237-5141. FAX: (404) 237-5592. Joseph H. Carey, pres; Ron Bladon, VP.

Dallas 75240: One Galleria Tower, Suite 1865, 13355 Noel Rd. (214) 701-8585. Steve McDonald, mgr.

Carolina Spot Sales. Box 75, Powder Horn Mountain, Deep Gap, N.C. 28618. (919) 467-8645. Barry A. Noll, pres.

Don Cavitt. 6404 Washburn Ave. S., Minneapolis 55423. (612) 866-7660. Don Cavitt.

CharterDirect. 4400 Coldwater Canyon, Suite 127, Studio City, Calif. 91604. (818) 505-9222. FAX: (818) 505-0909. Terence J. Kollman, pres; Stephen Reiss, CFO; Mark Alyn, assoc creative dir bcst; Jim Graca, assoc creative dir print; Angelo Grillo, sr copywriter; Barbara Denzer, dir mktg & business dev; Robert Houghland, dir mktg & rsch.

Christal Radio. 125 W. 55th St., 6th Fl., New York 10019. (212) 424-6500. FAX: (212) 424-6507. Bill Fortenbaugh, pres; Ken Davidman, VP stns; Stephen Shaw, VP/gen sls mgr; Jennifer Haynes, Thomas Flood, sls mgrs.

Atlanta 30305: 6 Piedmont Ctr., Suite 722. (404) 365-3040. FAX: (404) 816-5543. Hunter Meadows, VP stns; Daren Leoci, sls mgr.

Boston 02116: Statler Office Bldg., 20 Park Plaza, Suite 227. (617) 357-1660. FAX: (617) 357-1667. Richard Higgins, mgr.

Chicago 60611: 455 N. Cityfront Plaza Dr., Suite 1700. (312) 755-3920. FAX: (312) 755-0877. David K. Winston, VP stns; Kathy Houlihan, mgr.

Dallas 75201: 300 Crescent Ct., Suite 430. (214) 999-2166. FAX: (214) 855-5227. Bill Tichenor, mgr.

Troy, Mich. 48084: 3310 W. Big Beaver Rd., Suite 110. (313) 649-3230. FAX: (313) 649-2870. John M. Fouts, VP stn dev; Christy Torgler, VP/mgr. Detroit office.

Los Angeles 90048: 6500 Wilshire Blvd, Suite 200. (213) 966-5180. FAX: (213) 658-6804. Robert Gad, VP stns west division; William Denton, VP/mgr.

Minneapolis 55402: Piper Jaffray Tower, Suite 2855. (612) 333-8833. FAX: (612) 339-3053. Steve Plotkin, VP/mgr.

Philadelphia 19103: 8 Penn Ctr., Suite 1330. (215) 564-4561. FAX: (215) 567-3167. Rotha Maddox, VP/mgr.

Portland, Ore. 97201: 1500 S.W. 1st Ave., Suite 320. (503) 222-2122. FAX: (503) 222-1474. David Lichtman, mgr.

St. Louis 63102: Equitable Bldg., 10 S. Broadway, Suite 575. (314) 421-4946. FAX: (314) 421-0392. Sherri Sadon, mgr.

U.S. Radio, Television and Cable Representatives

San Francisco 94105: 100 Spear St., Suite 1980. (415) 957-9960. FAX: (415) 974-1744. Ellen Sutherland, mgr.

Seattle 98121: 3131 Elliot Ave., Suite 620. (206) 284-5088. FAX: (206) 284-4770. Kim Jack, VP/mgr.

Toronto, Ont., Canada M4W 3C7: 920 Yonge St., Suite 512. (416) 923-1239. Richard A. Sienko, mgr.

Clayton-Davis & Associates Inc. 8229 Maryland, St. Louis 63105. (314) 862-7800.

Clem & Lowrance Inc. 75 Forrest Lake Dr. N.W., Atlanta 30327. (404) 255-6416. Clyde L. Clem Jr., pres; Joe H. Carey, VP.

Commercial Media Sales Inc. 1439 Denniston Ave., Pittsburgh 15217. (412) 421-2600. FAX: (412) 421-6001. Roger Rafson, pres.

Dallas 75244: 14330 Midway Rd., Suite 207. (214) 788-1630. Jack Riley.

Communications Fund Inc. Stations. 8081 Manchester Rd., St. Louis 63144. (314) 781-9600. FAX: (314) 781-0422. Richard J. Miller, pres; Gary Lewis, gen sls mgr.

Concert Music Broadcast Sales Inc. 271 Madison Ave., New York 10016. (212) 532-1900. FAX: (212) 532-1647. Peter J. Cleary, pres; Roy Lindau, exec VP.

Chicago 60611: 500 N. Michigan Ave., Suite 507. (312) 744-1144. Chuck Duncan, mgr.

Santa Monica, Calif. 90401: 528 Arizona Ave., Suite 316. (310) 260-3232. Mark E. Benenson, account exec.

Atlanta 30305: 110 E. Andreaus Dr., Suite 309. (404) 237-9791. Terry Scalcucci, account exec.

Dallas 75226: c/o WRR, Fair Park Station. (214) 421-9848. Gordon McCaw, account exec.

Southfield, Mich. 48034: c/o WQRS, 28588 N. Western Hwy., Suite 200. (313) 352-1390. Kay Sullivan, Rita Starr, account execs.

San Francisco 94109: 2822 Van Ness Ave. (415) 474-0254. Catherine Berryessa, account exec.

Continental Cablevision Advertising-Jacksonville. 1902 2nd Ave. N., Jacksonville Beach, Fla. 32250. (904) 730-7020. FAX: (904) 249-6100. Michael A. Anapolsky, rgnl dir adv sls; Theresa H. Fletcher, gen mgr adv sls.

Creative Communicators. 4125 Victoria Dr., Fort Wayne, Ind. 46815. (219) 483-3882. FAX: (219) 484-2316. Gene Pyle, pres/gen mgr.

Cyr Associates Inc. 20 Westland St., Bangor, Me. 04401. (207) 947-8849. FAX: (207) 947-8862. Barbara Cyr, pres.

D&R Radio. 205 N. Michigan, #2015, Chicago 60601. (212) 309-9000. Anthony Durpetti, chmn of bd/CEO; Kirk Combs (Atlanta), exec VP/client svc.

New York 10017: 100 Park Ave., 5th Fl. (212) 309-9000. FAX: (212) 309-9055; (212) 309-9030. Jacqui Rossinsky, pres/COO; John Fabian, exec VP/client dev; Marcia Herman, sr VP/rgnl mgr; Andy Lipset, Peggy Kafka, co-dirs sls; JoAnn Goldberg, Ron Potts, VPs sls; Robert Fabian, Joe Leake, Sue McNamara, Carol Rosenberg, Jessica Silver, Leon Van Gelder, John Viola, account execs.

Marietta, Ga. 30067: 1640 Powers Ferry Rd., Bldg. 5, Suite 380. (404) 859-0026. FAX: (404) 953-0417. Kirk Combs, exec VP/client svc; Chris Tsltouris, VP/dir sls; Sheila Oliver, VP sls; Tammie Gleti, Jeanne Jones, account execs. Atlanta office.

Boston 02116: 31 St. James Ave., Suite 809. (617) 426-8487. FAX: (617) 451-2343. Kathy Crowley, dir sls.

Chicago 60601: 205 N. Michigan Ave., Suite 2015. (312) 819-0100. FAX: (312) 819-1970. Anthony Durpetti, bd chmn/CEO; Robert Neville, dir sls; Zina Meggas, Deborah McGowan, account execs.

Las Colinas, Tex. 75038: 1350 Walnut Hill Ln., Suite 100. (214) 518-9620. FAX: (214) 518-8094. Kevin Cassidy, sr VP/rgnl mgr; Susan Bessire, Lee Ann Longinotti, Lulie Lane, account execs. Dallas office.

Southfield, Mich. 48075: 4000 Town Ctr., Suite 290. (313) 357-0900. FAX: (313) 358-2468. Jay Kirchmaier, VP/rgnl exec; Jim Watts, VP/dir sls; Tom Howe, Richelle Zonca, account execs.

Los Angeles 90024: 10880 Wilshire Blvd., Suite 1215. (310) 470-7178. FAX: (310) 475-2721. Sharon Wiensveg, sr VP/rgnl mgr; Dan Chambers, Eric Ronning, co-dirs sls; Darren McMillan, Jolie deSedas, Cindy Cohen, account execs.

Minneapolis 55404: 1111 3rd Ave. S., Suite 450. (612) 339-2626. FAX: (612) 341-9832. Tracy Eiden, dir sls.

Philadelphia 19102: The Bellevue, Broad & Walnut Sts., 9th Fl. (215) 985-1494. FAX: (215) 985-0282. Eric Perry, VP/rgnl exec; Tom Byrne, dir sls; Adele Eglin, account exec.

St. Louis 63102: 10 S. Broadway, Suite 500. (314) 241-7799. FAX: (314) 241-0049. Linda Thompson, dir sls; Robin Vorel, account exec.

San Francisco 94111: 750 Battery St., Suite 340. (415) 772-2735. FAX: (415) 772-2758. Victoria Yereance, dir sls; Andy Salvas, account exec.

Sherman Oaks, Calif. 91403: 1409 Ventura Blvd., Suite 210. FAX: (818) 501-8654. Debbie Goodman, rsch dir (818-501-6016); Craig Sasaki, rsch analyst (818-501-6042).

Dome & Associates Inc. 8450 Ardleigh St., Philadelphia 19118. (215) 242-3660. FAX: (215) 242-4028. Robert S. Dome, pres.

Allison Park, Pa. 15101: 4018 Mt. Royal Blvd. (412) 486-8166. FAX: (412) 486-1143. Steve Rooney, pres. Pittsburgh office.

Doorley & Associates. 183 N. Mansfield Ave., Los Angeles 90036. (213) 936-8009. Marilyn Doorley, pres.

Dora-Clayton Agency Inc. Box 33100, Decatur, Ga. 30033. (404) 373-2662. FAX: (404) 373-4658. Danial A. Haight Sr., pres.

Eastman Radio. 125 W. 55th St., 5th Fl., New York 10019. (212) 424-6410. FAX: (212) 424-6415 (corp); (212) 424-6407 (sls). Carl Butrum, pres; Steve Moskowitz, VP/gen sls mgr; Lindsay Berry, VP/mgr; Charlie Sislen, VP rsch & mktg.

Atlanta 30305: 6 Piedmont Ctr., Suite 720. (404) 365-3090. FAX: (404) 816-5703. Marlene Kunis-Poehler, VP; Rich Farquhar, VP/mgr.

Boston 02116-4396: Statler Office Bldg., Suite 225. (617) 357-1666. FAX: (617) 357-1665. S. Peter Kadetsky, VP/mgr.

Chicago 60611: 455 N. Cityfront Plaza Dr., Suite 1700. (312) 755-3940. FAX: (312) 755-0875. Diane Nader, VP/mgr.

Dallas 75201: 300 Crescent Ct., Suite 410. (214) 999-2127. FAX: (214) 855-1473. Mark Hawkins, VP/mgr.

Troy, Mich. 48084: 3310 W. Big Beaver Rd., Suite 545. (313) 643-7555. FAX: (313) 643-6339. Tom O'Brien, VP/mgr. Detroit office.

Los Angeles 90048: 6500 Wilshire Blvd., Suite 330. (213) 966-5108. FAX: (213) 852-0961. Andy Rosen, mgr.

Philadelphia 19103: 8 Penn Ctr., Suite 1320. (215) 557-6610. FAX: (215) 557-7313. Karen Crane, VP/mgr.

St. Louis 63102: 10 S. Broadway, Equitable Bldg., Suite 570. (314) 241-7040. FAX: (314) 241-9031. Brett Cervantes, mgr.

Seattle 98121: 2200 6th Ave., Suite 707. (206) 441-6773. FAX: (206) 441-6819. Sandy Runnion, mgr.

San Francisco 94104: 100 Spear St., Suite 1950. (415) 512-9320. FAX: (415) 512-9013. Brian Robinson, VP/mgr.

Toronto, Ont., Canada M4W 3C7: 920 Yonge St., Suite 512. (416) 923-1239. Richard A. Sienko, mgr.

Portland, Ore. 97201: 1500 S.W. 1st St., Suite 320. (503) 222-2122. FAX: (503) 222-1474. Dave Lichtman, mgr.

Minneapolis 55402: Piper Jaffray Tower, Suite 2860. (612) 339-8941. FAX: (612) 339-3053. Carl Riis, mgr.

Family Enterprises Inc. Box 5700, Huntington Beach, Calif. 92615. (714) 963-7763. FAX: (714) 963-7171. Tom Benvenuti, pres; Tom Benvenuti Jr., VP.

J.L. Farmakis Inc. Box 1004, New Canaan, Conn. 06840. (203) 966-1746. FAX: (203) 966-0473. Jack Farmakis, pres; Jan Anderson, VP/gen mgr.

Mt. Vernon, Iowa 52314: Box 100. (319) 895-6723. Russ Parker, VP.

J.C. Gates & Co. c/o The Jockey Club, Suite J, 3700 Las Vegas Blvd. S., Las Vegas 89109. (702) 795-7600. FAX: (702) 795-7132. James C. Gates, own; Juanita Haddy Landon, natl sls mgr.

Gentile, Larry Associates. 288 Fisher Rd., Grosse Point Farms, Mich. 48230. (313) 885-0252. Larry Gentile, pres.

Gillis Broadcasting Representatives. 10153 ½ Riverside Dr., Suite 181, Toluca Lake, Calif. 91602. (818) 505-1097. FAX: (818) 505-1099. Jim Gillis, pres.

Eugene F. Gray Co. 1156 W. 103rd St., Suite 215, Kansas City, Mo. 64114. (816) 471-5502. Gene Gray, pres; N.K. Gray.

Greater Dayton Cable. 4162 Little York Rd., Dayton, Ohio 45414. (513) 890-0965. FAX: (513) 890-4286. Clete Buddelmeyer, sls mgr.

Herbert E. Groskin & Co. Inc. 280 Madison Ave., Suite 1011, New York 10016. (212) 689-5850. FAX: (212) 689-5885. H. Groskin, pres; D. Groskin, VP; Vicki Paige, sls mgr.

Group W Radio Sales. 100 Park Ave., New York 10017. (212) 818-8990. FAX: (212) 818-8989. Tony Miraglia, pres.

Group W Television Sales. 90 Park Ave., New York 10016. (212) 883-6100. FAX: (212) 856-8144. Joseph Berwanger, pres; Joel Segall, sr VP/gen sls mgr; Greg Schaefer, N.Y. sls mgr; Bob Kaplan, N.Y. group sls mgr; Joseph Piccirillo, dir rsch; Joseph Piccirillo, VP/dir.

Boston 02134: 1170 Soldiers Field Rd. (617) 787-7000. Scott Brady, sls mgr.

Chicago 60611: NBC Tower, 455 Cityfront Plaza. (312) 245-4830. Diane Weeks.

Los Angeles 90048: 6500 Wilshire Blvd., Suite 1850. (213) 655-3556. David Morris, mgr.

Baltimore 21211: Television Hill. (410) 466-0013. Steve Smith, sls mgr.

Birmingham, Mich. 48010: 31000 Telegraph Rd., Suite 200. (313) 647-8960. Robert Newsham, office mgr.

Philadelphia 19106: Independence Mall E. (215) 238-4700. Gary Herman, sls mgr.

Harrington, Righter & Parsons Inc. 805 3rd Ave., New York 10022. (212) 756-3600. FAX: (212) 756-3668/3669/3670/3671. John J. Walters Jr., chmn; Peter F. Ryan, pres.

Atlanta 30326: 3340 Peachtree Rd. N.E., Suite 1910. (404) 237-7768. FAX: (404) 365-8139. John Radovich, VP/Atlanta sls mgr.

Boston 02116: One Exeter Plaza. (617) 247-4004. FAX: (617) 421-0933. Catherine Shaffer, VP/New England sls mgr.

Charlotte, N.C. 28210: 6100 Fairview Rd., Suite 1460. (704) 553-7799. FAX: (704) 553-2824. Mark Chapman, VP/Charlotte sls mgr.

Chicago 60611: 444 N. Michigan Ave., Suite 3500. (312) 222-5500. FAX: (312) 222-4103. Steve Shadid, sr VP/Chicago sls mgr.

Cleveland 44114: 815 Superior Ave. N.E., Suite 1725. (216) 861-2265. FAX: (216) 861-5946. Gerry Pas, VP/Cleveland sls mgr.

Dallas 75206: 8350 N. Central Expwy., Suite 420. (214) 369-3925. FAX: (214) 373-3101. Larry Ramsey, VP/Dallas sls mgr.

Southfield, Mich 48075: 4000 Town Ctr., Suite 202. (313) 353-3370. FAX: (313) 353-9237. Douglas Christie, VP/Detroit sls mgr. Detroit office.

Los Angeles 90211: 8484 Wilshire Blvd., Suite 630. (213) 653-5900. FAX: (213) 653-5995. Jan Eggers, sr VP/Los Angeles sls mgr.

Minneapolis 55402: 105 S. 5th St., Suite 730. (612) 332-2446. FAX: (612) 332-6741. James Jowett, VP/Minneapolis sls mgr.

Philadelphia 19103: One Penn Ctr., 1617 JFK Blvd., Suite 1640. (215) 665-1170. FAX: (215) 665-1301. Michael D. Miglino, VP/Philadelphia sls mgr.

St. Louis 63101: 720 Olive St., Suite 2206. (314) 231-9797. FAX: (314) 231-5414. Bruce Butler, VP/St. Louis sls mgr.

San Francisco 94104: 235 Montgomery St., Suite 925. (415) 781-4125. FAX: (415) 781-1908. William Wexelblatt, VP/San Francisco sls mgr.

Seattle 98101: Plaza 600, 6th & Stewart Sts., Suite 1307. (206) 443-1700. FAX: (206) 443-8859. Cara O'Donnell, VP/Seattle sls mgr.

Tampa 33609: 4830 W. Kennedy Blvd., Suite 400. (813) 287-0204 FAX: (813) 286-1465. Ron Schrutt, VP/Tampa sls mgr.

U.S. Radio, Television and Cable Representatives

Hyett/Ramsland Inc. 630 Baker Bldg., Minneapolis 55402. (612) 339-7179. FAX: (612) 339-7182. James O. Ramsland, pres.

The Integrity Communications. 6360-1 E. Thomas Rd., Suite 318, Scottsdale, Ariz. 85251. (602) 955-5700. FAX: (602) 955-1454. Douglas Neece, pres.

New York 10168: 122 E. 42nd St. (212) 949-3400. FAX: (212) 949-7534. Jerry Wolff.

Highland Park, Ill. 60035: 344 Oakland Dr. (708) 926-9100. FAX: (708) 926-9101. Barry Lunenfeld.

Intercontinental Services Ltd. 347 5th Ave., Suite 1007, New York 10016. (212) 679-3910. FAX: (212) 679-3912. Elaine Herzstein, pres.

Santurce, P.R.: Box 8961. (809) 722-5665. Alicia Irizarry. Schellenberg & Kirwan.

San Francisco 94133: 559 Pacific Ave. (415) 391-1984. Sam Posner, pres. Radio Time Sales International.

Katz Communications

Precision media for reaching today's consumer.

The Interep Radio Store. 100 Park Ave., 5th Fl., New York 10017. (212) 916-0700. FAX: (212) 916-0772.

Marietta, Ga. 30067: 1640 Powers Ferry Rd. (404) 933-4248. FAX: (404) 953-0417. Tony Maisano. Atlanta office.

Boston 02116: 31 St. James Ave. (617) 451-1395. FAX: (617) 542-5270. Tom Poulos.

Charlotte, N.C. 28212: 6407 Idelwild. (704) 568-0202. FAX: (704) 568-0043. Rosalyn Morton.

Chicago 60601: 205 N. Michigan Ave. (312) 819-0702. FAX: (312) 819-1970. Michael Weiss.

Milford, Conn. 06460: 10 Weeping Willow Ln. (203) 877-3978. FAX: (203) 877-4092. Sharon Siegal.

Irving, Tex. 75038: 1350 Walnut Hill Ln. (214) 518-9625. FAX: (214) 518-1729. Don Hall. Dallas office.

Larkspur, Colo. 80118: 14693 Spring Valley Rd. (303) 688-4370. FAX: (303) 688-3085. Debby Lang. Denver office.

Southfield, Mich. 48075: 4000 Town Center. (313) 358-2081. FAX: (313) 358-2468. Jay Kirchmaier. Detroit office.

Los Angeles 90024: 10880 Wilshire Blvd. (310) 474-6356. FAX: (310) 474-3454. Jeff Dashev.

Lubbock, Tex. 79493-6060: Box 6060. (806) 792-2000. FAX: (806) 792-9200. Lloyd Senn.

Minneapolis 55404: 1111 3rd Ave. S. (612) 333-8033. FAX: (612) 341-9832. Kate Hesslau-Miller.

Philadelphia 19102: The Bellevue, Broad & Walnut Sts. (215) 545-5380. FAX: (215) 985-0282. Eric Perry.

Portland, Ore. 97201: 4700 S.W. Macadam Ave. (503) 223-1707. FAX: (503) 223-4580. Georgia Hess.

Richmond, Va. 23255-0608: Box 70608. (804) 360-0433. FAX: (804) 360-1251. Tena Lustig.

San Francisco 94111: 750 Battery St. (415) 772-2717. FAX: (415) 772-2758. Austin Walsh.

Seattle 98121: 2505 2nd Ave. (206) 443-1774. FAX: (206) 443-1872. Michelle Robinson.

St. Louis 63102: 10 S. Broadway. (314) 231-0114. FAX: (314) 241-0049.

The Interep Radio Store is a full-service sls & mktg company for radio adv with offices in 19 cities. It is the parent company that owns & operates five natl representation firms: D&R Radio, Group W Radio Sales, Major Market Radio Sales, McGavren Guild Radio, The Torbet Radio Group as well as the Interep Radio Store Networks, Caballero/MG Spanish Media (a joint venture with Caballero Spanish Media), Interep Sports & support svcs including Research, Promotion Marketing & our new business development team, The Radio Marketing Specialists.

Intermoutain Network. 575 East 4500 South, Suite B-200, Salt Lake City 84107. (801) 266-1480. FAX: (801) 266-2365. Kathy Bingham, pres.

Hooper Jones Assoc. Inc. 1920 Waukegan Rd., Suite 211, Glenview, Ill. 60025. (708) 486-1021. FAX: (708) 486-1025. Hooper R. Jones, pres.

Katz American Television. 125 W. 55th St., New York 10019-5366. (212) 424-6331. FAX: (212) 424-6389. Michael F. Hugger, pres; Jay Friesel, VP/gen sls mgr; Bruce Kallner, VP/natl sls mgr (White Team); Sharon Korn, mgr (White Team); Kenneth Perren, VP/natl sls mgr (Blue Team); Jay Zeitchik, VP/mgr (Blue Team); Swain Weiner, VP/natl sls mgr (Eagles Team); Bill Carroll, VP/dir progmg; Len Graziano, VP/natl sls mgr (Stars Team); Bob Scutari, VP/mgr (Eagles Team); Keith Green, VP/mgr (Stars Team); Chickie Bucco, VP/dir direct-response sls; Lisa Schoenback, VP/dir rsch.

Atlanta 30305-1579: 6 Piedmont Ctr., Suite 710. (404) 365-3100. FAX: (404) 816-5548. Michael Panethere, mgr.

Boston 02116-4396: Statler Office Bldg., Suite 220. (617) 542-5466. FAX: (617) 357-1677. TWX: 710-321-0516. Ruth Robertson, VP/mgr.

Charlotte, N.C. 28209-3514: 5821 Fairview Rd., Suite 407. (704) 553-0220. FAX: (704) 553-1547. TWX: 810-621-0427. Mark Turner, VP/mgr.

Chicago 60611: 455 N. Cityfront Plaza Dr., Suite 1700. (312) 755-3800. FAX: (312) 755-0872. TWX: 910-221-4425. Tom Morrisey, VP/mgr (Red Team); John Crenna, VP/mgr (White Team); Bob Johnston, VP/mgr (Eagles Team).

Cleveland 44115-2107: Keith Bldg., 1621 Euclid Ave., Suite 1718. (216) 621-7924. FAX: (216) 623-8363. TWX: 810-421-8238. Stephen Thompson, VP/mgr.

Dallas 75201-1817. 300 Crescent Ct., Suite 400. (214) 999-2014. FAX: (214) 855-7801. TWX: 910-861-4173. Don Adams, mgr.

Englewood, Colo. 80111-2702: One DTC, 5251 DTC Pkwy., PH5. (303) 740-8765. FAX: (303) 796-2930. TWX: 910-935-0880. Scott Gudzak, VP/mgr. Denver office.

Troy, Mich. 48084-2870: 3310 W. Big Beaver Rd., Suite 501. (313) 649-6390. FAX: (313) 649-2086. Karen Nielsen, VP/mgr. Detroit office.

Houston 77027-5150: 2900 Weslayan, Suite 625. (713) 961-5195. FAX: (713) 961-5814. Ron Speck, mgr.

Jacksonville, Fla. 32202-5015: 2201 Independent Sq., Suite 2201. (904) 358-2914. FAX: (904) 632-2347. Greg MacGregor, mgr.

Kansas City, Mo. 64105-2112: 1100 Main St., Suite 1890. (816) 842-2606. FAX: (816) 221-7731. TWX: 910-771-0556. Peter A. Logli, VP/mgr.

Los Angeles 90048-4922: 6500 Wilshire Blvd., Suite 200. (213) 966-5000. FAX: (213) 658-6901. TWX: 910-321-3734. Shelly Adrian, mgr (Red Team); Linda Delaurentis, mgr (White Team), Ed Robertson, mgr prog time sls.

Hollywood, Fla. 33021-6927: 3440 Hollywood Blvd., Suite 480. (305) 961-3881. FAX: (305) 964-4518. Benjamin Wolf, VP/mgr. Miami office.

Minneapolis 55402-3385: Piper Jaffray Tower, Suite 2885. (612) 339-4405. FAX: (612) 339-1335. TWX: 910-576-2852. Debra Ryan, mgr.

Philadelphia 19103-2113: 8 Penn Ctr., Suite 1050. (215) 567-7590. FAX: (215) 567-6338. Joe Eisberg, mgr.

Portland, Ore. 97201: 1500 S.W. 1st Ave., Suite 320. (503) 226-3973. FAX: (503) 228-4967. Jodi Rogaway, VP/mgr.

St. Louis 63102-1795: 10 S. Broadway, Suite 550. (314) 231-1868. FAX: (314) 231-3620. Gina Richardson, mgr.

San Francisco 94105-1575: 100 Spear St., Suite 1900. (415) 777-3377. FAX: (415) 978-9657. Karen Baner-Orofino, VP/mgr.

Seattle 98121: 3131 Elliot Ave., Suite 620. (206) 284-3088. FAX: (206) 284-5733. Kevin Cahill, VP/mgr.

Tampa 33607-1462: 7650 W. Courtney Campbell Causeway, Suite 450. (813) 287-8686. FAX: (813) 287-0953. Tom Barrett, VP/mgr.

Washington 20036-2304: 1233 20th St. N.W., Suite 203. (202) 872-5880. FAX: (202) 872-0263. Cliff McKinney, mgr.

Toronto, Ont., Canada M4P IE4: Box 2384, 2300 Yonge St., Suite 807. (416) 488-6835. FAX: (416) 488-

U.S. Radio, Television and Cable Representatives

8283. Fraser Gordon, pres/gen mgr. Canadian Communications Co.

Katz Communications Inc. 125 W. 55th St., New York 10019. (212) 424-6000. FAX: (212) 424-6489. James Greenwald, chmn; Peter Goulazian, pres/CEO; Arnold Sheiffer, exec VP/COO; Harvey Fenster, sr VP/CFO; Maria Busi, VP/controller; Paul Belitz, pres media data; Lucille Luongo, sr VP corporate communications; Paul Arnzen, sr VP bcst opns; Jim Belitz, VP/gen mgr media data; Joe Wisn, VP corporate administration & facilities planning; Richard Weinstein, VP planning & dev; Susan Wagner, VP corporate mktg; Nancy Williams, VP per.

Katz Continental Television. 125 W. 55th St., New York 10019. (212) 424-6061. FAX: (212) 424-6030. Jack Higgins, pres; Chris Jordan, VP/natl sls mgr east; Michael Spiesman, VP/natl sls mgr southeast; Bob Swan, VP/natl sls mgr east central; Brad Siegel, VP/mgr east central; Meg Courtney, VP/mgr east; Gerry Spinoso, VP/mgr south central; Ardie Bialek, VP/natl sls mgr west central; Mark Ryan, VP/mgr west & west central; Paul Bolwin, VP/mgr southeast; Chickie Bucco, VP/dir direct-response sls; Ruth Lee, VP/dir prog; Jon Johannan, VP/dir mktg svcs; Michael Steinberg, VP/dir rsch.

Atlanta 30305-1579: 6 Piedmont Ctr., Suite 710. (404) 233-0203. FAX: (404) 261-2258. Don Kirk, VP/mgr.

Boston 02116-4396: Statler Office Bldg., Suite 220. (617) 542-5458. FAX: (617) 357-1677. David Henderson, VP/mgr.

Charlotte, N.C. 28209-3649: 5821 Fairview Rd., Suite 407. (704) 553-0220. FAX: (704) 553-1547. Mark Turner, VP/mgr.

Chicago 60611-3964: 455 N. Cityfront Plaza Dr., Suite 1700. (312) 755-3800. FAX: (312) 755-0870. TWX: 910-221-4425. Beth Wagner, VP/mgr (Silver Team); John Wall, VP/mgr (Gold Team); Judson Beck, mgr (Olympic Team).

Cleveland 44115-2107: Keith Bldg., 1621 Euclid Ave., Suite 1718. (216) 621-7924. FAX: (216) 623-8363. Steve Thompson, VP/mgr.

Dallas 75201-1817: 300 Crescent Ct., Suite 400. (214) 978-4900. FAX: (214) 978-4992. Candy Orem, mgr.

Englewood, Colo. 80111-2702: One DTC, 5251 DTC Pkwy., PH5. (303) 740-8765. FAX: (303) 796-2930. TWX: 910-935-0880. Scott Gudzak, VP/mgr.

Troy, Mich. 48084-2870: 3310 W. Big Beaver Rd., Suite 501. (313) 649-6381. FAX: (313) 649-2086. John Hoffman, VP/mgr. Detroit office.

Houston 77027-5150: 2900 Weslayan, Suite 625. (713) 961-5195. FAX: (713) 961-5814. Ron Speck, mgr.

Jacksonville, Fla. 32202-5015: 2201 Independent Sq. (904) 358-2914. FAX: (904) 632-2347. Greg MacGregor, mgr.

Kansas City, Mo. 64105-2112: 1100 Main St., Suite 1890. (816) 842-2606. FAX: (816) 221-7731. Peter Logli, VP/mgr.

Los Angeles 90048-4922: 6500 Wilshire Blvd., Suite 200. (213) 966-5000. FAX: (213) 658-6443. Rick Schwartz, natl sls mgr (West Station Group); Terry Dreher, VP/mgr (Silver Team); Jeff Maloney, mgr (Gold Team); Ed Robertson, mgr prog time sls.

Hollywood, Fla. 33021-6927: 3440 Hollywood Blvd., Suite 480. (305) 961-3881. FAX: (305) 964-4518. Benjamin Wolf, VP/mgr. Miami office.

Minneapolis 55402-3385: Piper Jaffray Tower, Suite 2885. (612) 339-7711. FAX: (612) 339-1335. John C. Aronson, VP/mgr.

Philadelphia 19103-2113: 8 Penn Ctr., Suite 1350. (215) 567-7950. FAX: (215) 567-6338. Joe Eisberg, mgr.

Portland, Ore. 97204-1461: 111 S.W. 5th Ave., Suite 1440. (503) 226-3973. FAX: (503) 228-4967. Jodi Rogaway, VP/mgr.

St. Louis 63102-1795: Equitable Bldg., Suite 550, 10 S. Broadway. (314) 231-1868. FAX: (314) 231-3620. Ed Adams, VP/mgr.

San Francisco 94105-1575: 100 Spear St., Suite 1900. (415) 777-3377. FAX: (415) 978-9657; Karen Baner-Orofino, VP/mgr.

Seattle 98121-1438: 4th & Battery Bldg., Suite 950. (206) 441-6400. FAX: (206) 728-2536. Kevin Cahill, VP/mgr.

Tampa 33607-1462: 7650 W. Courtney Campbell Causeway, Suite 450. (813) 287-8686. FAX: (813) 287-0953. Tom Barrett, VP.

Washington 20036-2304: 1233 20th St. N.W., Suite 203. (202) 872-5880. FAX: (202) 872-0263. Cliff McKinney, mgr.

Toronto, Ont., Canada M4P IE4: Box 2384, 2300 Yonge St., Suite 807. (416) 488-6835. FAX: (416) 488-8283. Fraser Gordon, pres/gen mgr.

Katz Hispanic Radio Sales. 125 W. 55th St., 7th Fl., New York 10019. (212) 424-6250; (212) 424-6200. Eugene Bryan, VP/gen sls mgr.

Atlanta 30305-1579: 6 Piedmont Ctr., Suite 722. (404) 365-3060. FAX: (404) 876-5708. Glen Woosley, sls mgr.

Boston 02116-4396: Statler Office Bldg., 20 Park Plaza, Suite 227. (617) 357-1670. FAX: (617) 357-1658. Jane Rodophele, sls mgr.

Chicago 60611: 455 N. Cityfront Plaza Dr., Suite 1700. (312) 755-3800. FAX: (312) 755-0877. Jodi Desser.

Dallas 75201: 300 Crescent Ct., Suite 430. (214) 999-2091. FAX: (214) 855-7854. Leslie Falmar, account exec.

Troy, Mich. 48084: 3310 W. Big Beaver Rd., Suite 545. (313) 643-7555. FAX: (313) 643-6339. Tom O'Brien, sls mgr.

Houston 77027-5150: 2900 Weslayan, Suite 625. (713) 960-1252. FAX: (713) 960-8861. Steve Johnson.

Los Angeles 90048: 6500 Wilshire Blvd. (213) 966-5000. FAX: (213) 658-6701. Ed D'Abate, VP/western division mgr; Gaby Donitz, Kim Lipitz, Rebecca Viramontes, account execs.

Minneapolis 55402-3385: Piper Jaffray Tower, Suite 2990. (612) 339-9904. FAX: (612) 339-2005. Dennis Sternitzky, sls mgr.

New York 10019-5366: 125 W. 55th St. (212) 424-6500. FAX: (212) 424-6507/6508. Michelle Snyder, sr account exec; Dominic Amarito, Roberto Rafalowsky, Mitch Korn, Louis Romero, Lisa Montemarano, account execs.

Philadelphia 19103: 8 Penn Ctr., Suite 1330. (215) 564-2533. FAX: (215) 567-5850. Vince Gambino, sls mgr.

Portland, Ore. 97201-5829: 1500 S.W. First Ave., Suite 320. (503) 222-2122. FAX: (503) 222-1474. Dave Lichtman, sls mgr.

St. Louis 63102-1795: Equitable Bldg., 10 S. Broadway, Suite 570. (314) 421-7040. FAX: (314) 241-9031. Brett Cervantes, sls mgr.

San Francisco 94105: 100 Spear St., Suite 1980. (415) 777-3327. FAX: (415) 974-1744. Doreen Cappelli, sls mgr.

Seattle 98121-1438: 3131 Elliot Ave., Suite 620. (206) 284-5088. FAX: (206) 284-4770. Larry Lustig, VP/mgr.

Katz Hispanic Media. 125 W. 55th St., New York 10019. (212) 424-6497. FAX: (212) 424-6264. Elena Soto, pres; Michelle Snyder, sr account exec; Julisa Diaz, sls coord.

Atlanta 30305-1579: 6 Piedmont Ctr., Suite 710. (404) 233-0203. FAX: (404) 261-2258. Sant Perez.

Boston 02116-4396: Statler Office Bldg., Suite 220. (617) 542-5458. FAX: (617) 357-1677. David Henderson, VP/mgr.

Charlotte, N.C. 28209-3649: 5821 Fairview Rd., Suite 407. (704) 553-0220. FAX: (704) 553-1547. Bob Schellenberg.

Chicago 60611-3964: 444 N. Michigan Ave., Suite 3200. (312) 836-0500. FAX: (312) 836-5489. Doug Cook.

Cleveland 44115-2107: Keith Bldg., 1621 Euclid Ave., Suite 1718. (216) 621-7924. FAX: (216) 623-8363. Ray Mendelsohn.

Dallas 75201-1817: 300 Crescent Ct., Suite 400. (214) 978-2090. FAX: (214) 978-4992. Leslie Falmar, account exec.

Englewood, Colo. 80111-2702: One DTC, 5251 DTC Pkwy., PH5. (303) 740-8765. FAX: (303) 796-2930. Scott Gudzak, VP/mgr. Denver office.

Troy, Mich. 48084-2870: 3310 W. Big Beaver Rd., Suite 501. (313) 649-6381. FAX: (313) 649-2086. David Blaszkowski. Detroit office.

Houston 77027-5150: 2900 Weslayan, Suite 625. (713) 961-5195. FAX: (713) 961-5814. Ron Speck, mgr.

Jacksonville, Fla. 32202-5015: 2201 Independent Sq. (904) 358-2914. FAX: (904) 632-2347. Greg MacGregor, mgr.

Kansas City, Mo. 64105-2112: 1100 Main St., Suite 1890. (816) 842-2606. FAX: (816) 221-7731. Pete Logli, mgr.

Los Angeles 90048-4922: 6500 Wilshire Blvd., Suite 200. (213) 966-5000. FAX: (213) 658-6443. Kim Lipit, account exec (213-966-5095).

Hollywood, Fla. 33021-6927: 3440 Hollywood Blvd., Suite 480. (305) 961-3881. FAX: (305) 964-4518. Jay Doro.

Minneapolis 55402-3385: Piper Jaffray Tower, Suite 2885. (612) 339-7711. FAX: (612) 339-1335. Anne Malvaney.

Philadelphia 19103-2113: 8 Penn Ctr., Suite 1350. (215) 567-7590. FAX: (215) 567-6338. David Handler.

Portland, Ore. 97204-1461: 111 S.W. 5th Ave., Suite 1440. (503) 226-3973. FAX: (503) 228-4967. Jodi Rogaway, VP/mgr.

St. Louis 63102-1795: Equitable Bldg., Suite 550, 10 S. Broadway. (314) 231-1868. FAX: (314) 231-3620. Ed Adams, VP/mgr.

San Francisco 94105-1575: 100 Spear St., Suite 1900. (415) 777-3388. FAX: (415) 974-1744. Doreen Capelli, mgr.

Seattle 98121-1438: 4th & Battery Bldg., Suite 950. (206) 441-6400. FAX: (206) 728-2536. Kevin Cahill, mgr (206-284-3088; FAX 206-284-5733).

Tampa 33607-1462: 7650 W. Courtney Campbell Causeway, Suite 450. (813) 287-8686. FAX: (813) 287-0953. Tom Barrett, VP.

Washington 20036-2304: 1233 20th St. N.W., Suite 203. (202) 872-5880. FAX: (202) 872-0263. Cliff McKinney, mgr.

Katz National Television. 125 W. 55th St., New York 10019. (212) 424-6611. FAX: (212) 424-6685. Marty Ozer, pres; Craig Broitman, natl sls mgr (Lancers Team); Kaye Fox, team mgr (Lancers Team); Michael Raounas, VP/natl sls mgr (Sabers Team); Paul Wilson, VP/team mgr (Sabers Team); Stuart Zuckerman, VP/natl sls mgr (Swords Team); Larry Maloney, VP/natl sls mgr (Swords Team); Donna McCarty, VP/dir mktg; John von Soosten, VP/dir progmg; Chickie Bucco, VP/dir direct-response sls; Bob Einhorn, VP/dir rsch.

Atlanta 30305-1579: 6 Piedmont Ctr., Suite 710. (404) 233-0203. FAX: (404) 261-2258. Sant Perez, mgr.

Boston 02116-4396: Statler Office Bldg., Suite 220. (617) 542-0955. FAX: (617) 357-1677. Alan Friedman, mgr.

Charlotte, N.C. 28209-3649: 5821 Fairview Rd., Suite 407. (704) 553-0220. FAX: (704) 553-1547. Mark Turner, VP/mgr.

Chicago 60611: 455 N. Cityfront Plaza Dr., Suite 1700. (312) 755-3800. FAX: (312) 755-0871. Denise Roggensack, mgr (Swords Team); Stephen King, mgr (Lancers/Sabres Teams).

Cleveland 44115-2107: Keith Bldg., 1621 Euclid Ave., Suite 1718. (216) 621-7755. FAX: (216) 623-8363. Dennis Taylor, mgr.

Dallas 75201-1817: 300 Crescent Ct., Suite 400. (214) 978-4900. FAX: (214) 978-4992. Melba Meade, VP/mgr.

Englewood, Colo. 80111-2702: One DTC, 5251 DTC Pkwy., PH5. (303) 740-8765. FAX: (303) 796-2930. Scott Gudzak, VP/mgr. Denver office.

Troy, Mich. 48084-2870: 3310 W. Big Beaver Rd., Suite 501. (313) 649-5472. FAX: (313) 649-2086. Kristi Heft, mgr. Detroit office.

Jacksonville, Fla. 32202-5015: 2201 Independent Sq. (904) 358-2914. FAX: (904) 632-2347. Greg MacGregor, mgr.

Los Angeles 90048-4922: 6500 Wilshire Blvd., Suite 200. (213) 966-5000. FAX: (213) 658-6901. Mickey Colen, VP/rgnl sls mgr; Izzy Rostovsky, VP/mgr (Swords); Tom Maney, mgr sports sls; Ed Robertson, mgr prog time sls.

Hollywood, Fla. 33021-6927: 3440 Hollywood Blvd., Suite 480. (305) 961-3881. FAX: (305) 964-4518. Benjamin Wolf, VP/mgr. Miami office.

Minneapolis 55402-3385: Piper Jaffray Tower, Suite 2885. (612) 339-8734. FAX: (612) 339-1335. Peg Schabes, VP/mgr.

Philadelphia 19103-2113: 8 Penn Ctr., Suite 1350. (215) 567-7590. FAX: (215) 567-6338. David Handler, mgr.

St. Louis 63102-1795: 10 S. Broadway, Suite 550. (314) 241-3282. FAX: (314) 231-3620. Steve Shenkan, mgr.

San Francisco 94105-1575: 100 Spear St., Suite 1900. (415) 777-3377. FAX: (415) 978-9657. Tony Santino, VP/mgr.

U.S. Radio, Television and Cable Representatives

Seattle 98121-1438: 4th & Battery Bldg., Suite 950. (206) 441-6400. FAX: (206) 728-2536. Kevin Cahill, VP/mgr.

Tampa 33607-1462: 7650 W. Courtney Campbell Causeway, Suite 450. (813) 287-8686. FAX: (813) 287-0953. Tom Barrett, VP.

Washington 20036-2304: 1233 20th St. N.W., Suite 203. (202) 872-5880. FAX: (202) 872-0263. Karen Meister, mgr.

Houston 77027-5150: 2900 Weslayan, Suite 625. (713) 961-5195. FAX: (713) 961-5814. Ron Speck, mgr.

Toronto, Ont., Canada M4P IE4: Box 2384, 2300 Yonge St., Suite 807. (416) 488-6835. FAX: (416) 488-8283. Fraser Gordon, pres/gen mgr. Canadian Communications Company.

Katz Radio. 125 W. 55th St., 7th Fl., New York 10019-5366. (212) 424-6212. FAX: (212) 424-6230. Bob McCurdy, pres; Mike Agovino, VP/gen sls mgr; Glenn Corneliess, Mark Gray, Dominick Milano, mgrs; Elizabeth Haban, rsch mgr.

Atlanta 30305-1579: 6 Piedmont Ctr., Suite 722. (404) 365-3060. FAX: (404) 876-5708. Glen Woosley, sls mgr.

Boston 02116-4396: Statler Office Bldg., 20 Park Plaza, Suite 227. (617) 357-1670. FAX: (617) 357-1658. Jane Rodophele, sls mgr.

Chicago 60611: 455 N. Cityfront Plaza Dr., Suite 1700. (312) 755-3800. FAX: (312) 755-0877. Jodi Desser.

Dallas 75201: 300 Crescent Ct., Suite 430. (214) 999-2091. FAX: (214) 855-7854. Leslie Falmar, account exec.

Troy, Mich. 48084: 3310 W. Big Beaver Rd., Suite 545. (313) 643-7555. FAX: (313) 643-6339. Tom O'Brien, sls mgr.

Houston 77027-5150: 2900 Weslayan, Suite 625. (713) 960-1252. FAX: (713) 960-8861. Steve Johnson.

Los Angeles 90048: 6500 Wilshire Blvd. (213) 966-5000. FAX: (213) 658-6102. Ed D'Abate, VP/western division mgr; Gaby Donitz, Kim Lipitz, Rebecca Viramontes, account execs.

Minneapolis 55402-3385: Piper Jaffray Tower, Suite 2990. (612) 339-9904. FAX: (612) 339-2005. Dennis Stemitzky, sls mgr.

New York 10019-5366: 125 W. 55th St. (212) 424-6500. FAX: (212) 424-6507/6508. Michelle Snyder, sr account exec; Dominic Amarito, Roberto Rafalowsky, Mitch Korn, Louis Romero, Lisa Montemarano, account execs.

Philadelphia 19103: 8 Penn Ctr., Suite 1330. (215) 564-2533. FAX: (215) 567-5850. Vince Gambino, sls mgr.

Portland, Ore. 97201-5829: 1500 S.W. First Ave., Suite 320. (503) 222-2122. FAX: (503) 222-1474. Dave Lichtman, sls mgr.

St. Louis 63102-1795: Equitable Bldg., 10 S. Broadway, Suite 570. (314) 421-7040. FAX: (314) 241-9031. Brett Cervantes, sls mgr.

San Francisco 94105: 100 Spear St., Suite 1980. (415) 777-3327. FAX: (415) 974-1744. Doreen Cappelli, sls mgr.

Seattle 98121-1438: 3131 Elliot Ave., Suite 620. (206) 284-5088. FAX: (206) 284-4770. Larry Lustig, VP/mgr.

Katz Radio Group. 125 W. 55th St., New York 10019. (212) 424-6212. Gordon Hastings, pres; Stu Olds, exec VP/gen mgr; Bonnie Press, sr VP/gen mgr Katz Radio Group sls; Gerry Boehme, sr VP/dir rsch.

Katz Television Group. 125 W. 55th St., New York 10019. (212) 424-6212. FAX: (212) 424-6489. Tom Olson, pres; Jim Beloyianis, sr VP; Mark Shottland, VP mktg & net sls; Dick Goldstein, VP; John von Soosten, VP/dir progmg.

Katz & Powell. 470 Park Ave. S., Suite 1400, New York 10016. (212) 545-0600. FAX: (212) 889-6370. Shelly Katz, pres.

Chicago 60611: 435 N. Michigan Ave. (312) 467-0200. Doug Levy, Midwest mgr.

Los Angeles 90069: 200 N. Roberton Blvd. (310) 274-8885. Susan Laronge, western mgr.

Dallas 75234: 3001 LBJ Fwy., Suite 127. (214) 243-8770. Tissie Hauan, Southwest mgr.

Kettell-Carter Inc. 31 St. James Ave., Boston 02116. (617) 423-3535. FAX: (617) 423-4604. John D. Kettell, pres; Beth M. Kettell, VP opns.

Knight Radio Sales. 63 Bay State Rd., Boston 02215. (617) 262-1950. FAX: (617) 267-5160. N. Scott Knight, pres; Paul Haley, gen sls mgr.

The L.A. East Group. Box 1189, Ozark, Ala. 36361-1189. (205) 774-7212. FAX: (205) 774-5623. Julian H. Brown, pres.

Landin Media Sales. 3033 N. 44th St., Suite 375, Phoenix 85018-7229. (602) 553-4080. FAX: (602) 553-4090. Larry Cummings, pres/CEO; Dennis Hart, VP.

New York 10168: 122 E. 42nd St. (212) 682-1515. FAX: (212) 949-7534. Jerry Wolff.

Chicago 60611: 625 N. Michigan Ave. (312) 751-5410. FAX: (312) 482-9695. Barry Lunenfeld.

Lenawee Broadcasting Co. Box 687, Adrian, Mich. 49221. (517) 263-1039. FAX: (517) 265-5362. Julie M. Koehn, pres/gen mgr.

Lotus Hispanic Reps. 50 E. 42nd St., Suite 2301, New York 10017. (212) 697-7601. FAX: (212) 697-8215; (212) 467-8256. Richard B. Kraushaar, pres; Yvonne Luna, account exec; Robert Albright, exec VP; Brad Snyder, Beth Sanchez, sls assts.

Hollywood, Calif. 90028: 6777 Hollywood Blvd., Suite 400. (213) 464-1311. Lucy Martinez, bus mgr; Veronica Rodriguez, accounts receivable supvr. Accounting office.

Chicago 60601: 203 N. Wabash Ave. (312) 346-8442. FAX: (312) 346-6580. Julie Sayre, account exec.

Dallas 75251: 7616 LBJ Frwy., Suite 702. (214) 960-1707. FAX: (214) 960-1721. Mark Munoz, mgr; Kimberly Coleman, sls asst.

San Francisco 94111: 447 Battery St. (415) 773-8244. FAX: (415) 788-8812. David A. Specland, mgr.

Los Angeles 90028: 6777 Hollywood Blvd., Suite 400. (213) 464-1311. FAX: (213) 464-0549. Peggy Martin, VP western mgr; Vicki Kramer, Mary Hawley, account execs; Felipa Barriga, sls asst.

St. Claire Shore, Mich. 48080: 22971 Nine Mile Rd. (313) 773-7700. FAX: (313) 774-4489. Ken Patt, mgr; Mike Martin, account exec. Detroit office.

MMT Sales Inc. 150 E. 52nd St., New York 10022. (212) 319-8008. FAX: (212) 838-1315. Jack Oken, pres; Charles Lizzo, exec VP; Don Gorman, sr VP/dir sls; Ted Van Erk, sr VP/dir sls; Murray Berkowitz, sr VP/dir sls; Al Cannarella, corporate VP rsch; Bruce Mitchel, VP/CFO; Dolores White, corporate VP bus opns; Maureen Boylan, corporate VP computer opns; Carmen King, dir computer opns; Joan Dowd, mgr computer opns; Ken Better, VP mktg & bus dev; Lou Dennig, assoc prog dir; Matt Shapiro, corporate VP/dir progmg; Jean McCrann-Benesch, dir rsch; Michael Markowitz, mgr (Team A); Brian Monihan, mgr (Team B); Ken Gelb, mgr (Team C); Julie Holmberg, mgr (Team D).

Atlanta 30326: 950 E. Paces Ferry Rd., Suite 2145. (404) 365-2088. FAX: (404) 365-2089. Kris Karavitis-Goff, branch mgr.

Boston 02116: 38 Newberry St., Suite 502. (617) 267-7707. FAX: (617) 267-4714. Mo Peck, branch mgr.

Charlotte, N.C. 28211: 2101 Rexford Rd., Suite 320. (704) 365-4700. Robbie Horn, branch mgr.

Chicago 60611: 444 N. Michigan Ave., Suite 100. (312) 467-9810. FAX: (312) 467-9808. Michael Held, VP/rgnl group mgr; Dianne Downey, sls mgr (Team A); Sharon Weiler, sls mgr (Team B); Ward Lewis, sls mgr (Team C).

Cleveland 44114: Ohio Bldg., 1717 E. 9th St., Suite 907. (216) 621-1933. FAX: (216) 621-8145. Georgiann Pace, branch mgr.

Dallas 75251: 12790 Merit Dr. (214) 980-9855. FAX: (214) 991-8479. Peter Uzelac, VP/branch mgr.

Troy, Mich. 48084: 50 W. Big Beaver Rd. (313) 680-1300. FAX: (313) 680-1867. Steve Ryckman, branch mgr. Detroit branch.

Houston 77057: 5847 San Felipe Rd., Suite 4242, (713) 266-9705. FAX: (713) 266-3039. Doug Sallows, branch mgr.

Los Angeles 90036: 5900 Wilshire Blvd., Suite 2130. (213) 937-5434. FAX: (213) 935-8591. Karen Schmidtke, VP/rgnl group mgr; Kyle Sherman, sls mgr (Team A); Joan Eckersley, sls mgr (Team B); Jason Kleinhein, sls mgr (Team C).

Edina, Minn. 55436: 5100 Eden Ave. S. (612) 929-8571. DuAnn Junis, branch mgr. (Minneapolis office).

St. Louis 63101: One Boatmen's Plaza. (314) 421-5360. FAX: (314) 421-1733. Nick Alvernia, branch mgr.

Tampa 33618: 10008 N. Dale Mabry, Suite 112. (813) 264-1706. FAX: (813) 960-3459. Kitty Hutchens, branch mgr.

San Francisco 94111: 353 Sacramento St. (415) 434-9023. FAX: (415) 434-1358. Ron Garfield, branch mgr.

Philadelphia 19102: 2 Penn Ctr., Suite 1004. (215) 568-6570. FAX: (215) 568-2523. Jim Ross, branch mgr.

Major Market Radio Inc. 100 Park Ave., 5th Fl., New York 10017. (212) 818-8900. FAX: (212) 818-8910. Warner Rush, chmn/CEO; Dave Kaufman, pres; Brian Knox, VP/rgnl mgr/DOS; John Feyer, Rosemary Anselmo, Diane Finch, Andrea Barone, Rhona Waxenberg, Nancy Kahn, account execs; Barbara Hogan, exec dir; Marie Austin, corp opns; Debbie Lidsky, office mgr.

Marietta, Ga. 30067: 1640 Powers Ferry Rd., Bldg. 5, Suite 360. (404) 859-0075. FAX: (404) 953-0417. Bonnie Chapman, rgnl mgr; Judy Maloney, account exec. Atlanta office.

Boston 02116: 31 St. James Ave., Suite 809. (617) 426-6796. FAX: (617) 426-4599. Donald St. Sauveur, rgnl mgr/DOS.

Chicago 60601: 205 N. Michigan Ave., Suite 2015. (312) 938-0999. FAX: (312) 938-0152. Steve Jonsen, rgnl mgr/DOS; Tim Weil, Susie Stewart, account execs; Laura Treacy, office mgr.

Las Colinas, Tex. 75038: 1350 Walnut Hill Ln., Suite 100. (214) 518-9635. FAX: (214) 518-8090. Karin Haubner, rgnl mgr/DOS; Lance Aldridge, Shauri Wood, Kay Bordelon, account execs. Dallas office.

Southfield, Mich. 48075: 4000 Town Ctr., Suite 290. (313) 358-2060. FAX: (313) 358-2468. Tom Perry, rgnl mgr/DOS; Beth Chaklos, account exec; Jan Young, office mgr. Detroit office.

Larkspur, Colo. 80118: 14549 S. Perry Park Rd. (303) 688-4370. FAX: (303) 688-3085. Debbie Lang, Interep DOS. Denver office.

Los Angeles 90024: 10880 Wilshire Blvd., Suite 1212. (310) 474-5311. FAX: (310) 474-7620. Larry Muller, rgnl mgr/DOS; Jill Albert, sr account exec; Kim Hallisay, Jana Cosgrove, account execs.

Philadelphia 19102: The Bellevue, Broad & Walnut Sts., 9th Fl. (215) 985-1330. FAX: (215) 735-5478. Marianne Zaren, rgnl mgr/DOS; Jeanne Scheier, sls assoc.

Portland, Ore. 97201: 4700 S.W. Macadam Ave., #303. (503) 222-4892. FAX: (503) 223-4580. Debbie Wood, rgnl mgr/DOS.

San Francisco 94111: 750 Battery St. (415) 772-2710. FAX: (415) 772-2758. Austin Walsh, exec VP western division mgr; Kevin Dakis, DOS/account exec; Elizabeth Dasher, account exec; Jan Thomas, office mgr; Kate Butler, sls assoc.

St. Louis 63102: 10 S. Broadway, Suite 500. (314) 231-9005. FAX: (314) 241-0049. Leona Dunsmoor, rgnl mgr/DOS; Kelly Phillips, office mgr.

Seattle 98121: 2505 2nd Ave., Suite 515. (206) 728-8016. FAX: (206) 728-1680. Doug Frame, rgnl mgr/DOS; Cindy Bowers, account exec; Vickie Eksevics, office mgr.

Marsh Radio Marketing. 1030 E. Alosta Ave., #F, Glendora, Calif. 91740-6330. (818) 914-7717. FAX: (818) 963-7086. Dick Marsh, pres.

Bill Masi Network. 788 Hwy. 434, Suite 102-A, Altamonte Springs, Fla. 32714. (800) 275-6274; (407) 788-0777. FAX: (407) 869-9019. Bill Masi, CEO; John Ondo, pres.

Metrobase Cable Advertising. 70 E. Lancaster Ave., Frazer, Pa. 19355. (215) 640-1340. FAX: (215) 644-5407. Alan Eisenstein, VP/gen mgr; Lee Stein, natl sls mgr; Philip W. Salas, gen sls mgr.

Indianola, Pa. 15051: 207 Rt. G10. (412) 727-3500. Terry Myers, rgnl gen mgr.

Utica, N.Y. 13501: 1415 Genesee St. (315) 797-0037. Todd Kuhn, rgnl gen mgr.

McGavren Guild Radio. 100 Park Ave., 5th Fl., New York 10017. (212) 916-0500. FAX: (212) 916-0759/0772/0790. Peter Doyle, pres.

U.S. Radio, Television and Cable Representatives

Marietta, Ga. 30067: Bldg. 5, Suite 300, 1640 Powers Ferry Rd. (404) 953-1111. Anthony Maisano, pres.
Boston 02116: 31 St. James Ave., Suite 809. (617) 423-0606. Tom Poulos, VP/rgnl mgr.
Charlotte, N.C. 28210: 6135 Park Rd., Suite 103. (704) 552-7761. Jim Peacock, sls mgr.
Chicago 60601: 205 N. Michigan Ave., Suite 2015. (312) 565-4888. Gene Noack, exec VP central div.
Irving, Tex. 75038: 1350 Walnut Hill Ln., Suite 100. (214) 580-8336. Tom Dolliff, rgnl mgr.
Southfield, Mich. 48075: 4000 Town Ctr., Suite 290. (313) 358-8500.
Houston 77057: MCO Plaza, 5718 Westheimer, Suite 1705. (713) 266-7667. Jill Galarneau, sls mgr.
Los Angeles 90024: 10880 Wilshire Blvd., Suite 1215. (310) 470-3383. Jeff Dashev, exec VP western division.
Minneapolis 55404: 1111 3rd Ave., Suite 450. (612) 333-8717. Kate Hesslau-Miller, sls mgr.
Philadelphia 19102: The Bellevue, Broad & Walnut Sts., 9th Fl. (215) 732-3380. Charles Reilly, mgr.
Portland, Ore. 97201: 4700 S.W. Macadam Ave., Suite 303. (503) 223-1700. Georgia Hess, sls mgr.
St. Louis 63102: 10 S. Broadway, Suite 500. (314) 231-0000. Gary Ahrens, VP/rgnl mgr.
San Francisco 94111: 750 Battery St., Suite 340. Michael Nelson, sls mgr.
Seattle 98121: 2505 2nd Ave., Suite 515. (415) 772-2700. Michelle Robinson, sls mgr.
Denver 80231: Suite 247, Bldg. C, 10200 E. Girard Ave. (303) 368-0334. Jeff Edley, sls mgr.

Michigan Spot Sales. 44958 Ford Rd., Canton Township, Mich. 48187. (313) 454-4100. Mike Toth, pres.

Mid American Media Services Inc. 7324 Valleyview Dr., Independence, Ohio 44131. (216) 524-2088. N.J. Kocab, pres.

Midsouth Spot Sales Inc. 5050 Poplar, Suite 521, Memphis 38157. (901) 685-6962. FAX: (901) 685-6965. Carol Chisholm, pres.

Milwaukee Cable Advertising 1610 N. 2nd St., Milwaukee 53212-3980. (414) 277-4200. FAX: (414) 277-9420. Richard N. Olmsted, gen mgr/sls mgr; David J. De Grace, rgnl sls mgr.

Art Moore, Inc.

Art Moore Inc. 2200 6th Ave., Suite 707, Seattle 98121-1823. (206) 443-9991. FAX: (206) 443-9998. Greg Smith, CEO/pres; Ruth Hallett, COO/sr VP; Sandra Runnion, mgr.
Portland, Ore. 97201: 4800 S.W. Macadam Blvd., Suite 200. (503) 228-0016. FAX: (503) 228-0556. Teddi Jones, mgr.
Denver 80206: 222 Milwaukee St., Suite 209. (303) 321-2354. FAX: (303) 321-1087. Gerriann Sullivan-Ward, VP/mgr.
Salt Lake City 84107-2972: 575 East, 4500 South, Suite B200. (801) 266-3576. FAX: (801) 266-2365. Kathy Bingham, mgr.

Tracy Moore & Associates. 535 Alta Vista Ave., South Pasadena, Calif. 91030. (213) 257-4627. Tracy Moore, Jerome A. Moore, ptnrs.

Mountain Media Inc. 2878 W. Long Cr., Unit B, Littleton, Colo. 80120. (303) 797-8594. Gordon Myers, pres.

Myers Marketing & Research. 322 Rt. 46 W., Parsippany, N.J. 07054. (201) 808-7333. FAX: (201) 882-3651. Jack Myers, pres; Leah Leznick, account svcs.

NBC Spot Television Sales. GE Bldg., 30 Rockefeller Plaza, 51st Fl., New York 10112. (212) 664-4444. Monte Newman, exec VP sls & mktg (212-664-3688); Andrew Capone, dir sls & mktg (212-664-7066); Marc Wollis, dir sls planning & mkt analysis (212-664-3417); Kathy Lenard, VP rsch (212-664-3445).
Represented nationally by:
New York 10022: 805 3rd Ave. (212) 756-3600. Representing WMAQ Chicago, WNBC New York, KNBC Los Angeles. HRP.
New York 10022: 3 E. 54th St. (212) 688-0200. Representing WRC Washington, D.C., KCNC Denver, WTVJ Miami, Fla. Petry.

National Cable Advertising. 137 Newbury St., Boston 02116. (617) 267-8582. FAX: (617) 247-2069. Robert Williams, pres; Linda Williams, VP; Robin Rosen, sls mgr.
Atlanta 30305: 10 Piedmont Ctr., Suite 518. (404) 231-3652. FAX: (404) 231-5072. Al Strada, sls mgr.
Chicago 60611: 444 N. Michigan Ave., Suite 950. (312) 527-5755. FAX: (312) 527-4794. Jim Mittal, sls mgr.
Irving, Tex. 75062: 511 E. John Carpenter Frwy., Suite 200. (214) 869-9811. FAX: (214) 869-9039. Lou Conover, sls mgr. Dallas office.
Southfield, Mich. 48075: 4000 Town Ctr., Suite 670. (313) 357-2200. FAX: (313) 357-2206. Kim Sharp, sls mgr. Detroit office.
Los Angeles 90025: 11150 Santa Monica Blvd., Suite 900. (310) 996-1025. FAX: (310) 996-1034. Doug Fleming, sls mgr.
New York 10036: 114 W. 47th St., 17th Fl. (212) 840-1710. FAX: (212) 840-1492. Gig Barton, Tracey Tynan, Dan Thomas, Sue Schmatzback, sls mgrs.
Philadelphia 19103: 1515 Market St., Suite 822. (215) 977-7766. FAX: (215) 977-8898. Victor Branch, sls mgr.
San Francisco 94133: 50 Francisco St., Suite 267. (415) 399-0400. FAX: (415) 399-9560. David Klein, sls mgr.
McLean, Va. 22102: 1650 Tysons Blvd., Suite 600. (703) 506-0660. FAX: (703) 506-9292. Matt Stanton, sls mgr. Washington office.

Jim Neidigh Co. 10037 N.E. 13th St., Bellevue, Wash. 98004. (206) 451-2921. Jim Neidigh, pres.

New England Spot Sales Inc. 100 Boylston St., Boston 02116. (617) 482-4370. FAX: (617) 482-4369. George C. Bingham, pres; Carolyn S. Bingham, admin asst; Gretchen L. Soter, office mgr.

Northwest Cable Advertising. 18 W. Mercer, Seattle 98119. (206) 286-1818. FAX: (206) 286-9010. Penny Taylor, mktg mgr.

NuAd Inc. Box 710, 348 Washington St., Leonardtown, Md. 20650. (301) 475-7900. FAX: (301) 475-7902. Al Dailey, VP mktg.

O'Malley Communications. 332 Minnesota St., Suite E-1318, St. Paul, Minn. 55101. (612) 292-9412; (612) 292-9321. Scot O'Malley, pres.

PTS Advertising. 590 G St., Suite 8, Chula Vista, Calif. 91910. (619) 691-5378. FAX: (619) 691-5967.

Pan American Broadcasting. 10201 Torre Ave., Suite 320, Cupertino, Calif. 95014-2132. (408) 996-2033. FAX: (408) 252-6855. G. Bernald, J. Manero, C. Jung, M. Sanchez.

Patt Media Sales. Box 691, 22971 Nine Mile Rd., St. Clair Shores, Mich. 48080. (313) 773-7700. FAX: (313) 774-4889. Kenneth D. Patt, pres; Michael A. Martin, VP.

Pembrook Pines Mass Media. 94 Cedar St., Corning, N.Y. 14830. (607) 733-5627; (607) 962-1400. Robert Pfuntner, pres.

Perry Enterprises. 827 ½ N. Judge Ely Blvd., Abilene, Tex. 79601. (915) 676-7330. FAX: (915) 676-7332. David R. Perry, own.

PETRY
first in spot television.

Petry Inc. 3 E. 54th St., New York 10022. (212) 688-0200. FAX: (212) 230-5876. TWX: 710-581-2135. PETRY CORPORATE: David S. Allen, chmn; Thomas F. Burchill, pres/CEO; James R. Ganley, exec VP/CFO; John I. Heise, exec VP/pres Petry Television; William P. Shaw, exec VP/pres Petry National Television; Harry R. Stecker, exec VP/pres Petry Communications. PETRY COMMUNICATIONS: Harry Stecker, pres Petry Communications; Jack Fentress, VP/progmg dir Petry National; Richard Kurlander, VP/progmg dir Petry Television; Ronald Martzolf, progmg dir Petry National; Rob Hebenstreit, VP/rsch dir Petry Television; Jeff Rosenberg, VP/rsch dir Petry National; Gail Healy, progmg dir Petry National; Jim Joyella, sr VP mktg. PETRY TELEVISION: John Heise, pres Petry Television; Jerry Linehan, sr VP/gen sls mgr; Donald O'Toole, VP/sls dir; Richard Larcade, VP/sls dir; Kevin Nugent, VP/sls dir; Tom Belviso, VP/sls dir; Steve Eisenberg, VP/sls dir; Tom Fleming, group mgr (Thunderbirds); Craig Riedell, group mgr (Ravens); John Shannon, group mgr (Eagles); Susan Perelson, VP/group mgr (Falcons); Fran Gennarelli, VP/group mgr (Hawks); Don Brownstein, VP/rgnl area mgr; Val Napolitano, VP/rgnl area mgr; Laverne Cole, VP/rgnl area mgr; Patrick McNew, VP/rgnl area mgr. PETRY NATIONAL: William P. Shaw, pres Petry National; William Hahn, sr VP/gen sls mgr; Paul Morrissey, sr VP/sls dir; Joseph Lyons, VP/dir sls; Dede Lyons, VP/group mgr (Green); Elizabeth Apelles, VP/group mgr (White); T.J. Connolly, group mgr (Red); Barry Offitzer, VP/group mgr (Blue); Don Brownstein, VP/rgnl area mgr; Val Napolitano, VP/rgnl area mgr; Laverne Cole, VP/rgnl area mgr; Patrick McNew, VP/rgnl area mgr.

Chicago 60611-4243: 410 N. Michigan Ave., Suite 1180. (312) 644-9660. FAX: (312) 644-9774. TWX: 624-429-10. Bill

U.S. Radio, Television and Cable Representatives

Carney, VP/gen mgr/group mgr Petry Television; Lynn Evans, Stu Lutz, group mgrs Petry Television; James Ottolin, Stewart R. Strizak, group mgrs Petry National.

Beverly Hills, Calif. 90211-2405: 8383 Wilshire Blvd., Suite 626. (213) 655-3353. FAX: (213) 655-2862. TWX: 910-321-4180. Don Brownstein, VP/rgnl area mgr; John Callari, Jim Baral, group mgrs Petry Television; James Valice, Monika Alexenko, group mgrs Petry National. Los Angeles office.

Atlanta 30326-1115: 950 E. Paces Ferry Rd., Suite 2940. (404) 237-5727. FAX: (404) 261-0586. TWX: 810-751-8523. Val Napolitano, VP/rgnl area mgr/group mgr Petry Television; Chris Teter, Scott Jolles, group mgrs Petry National.

Boston 02116-3305: 419 Boylston St. (617) 353-1100. FAX: (617) 353-0280. TWX: 710-321-6708. M.P. Kelleher, VP/sls mgr.

Charlotte, N.C. 28210-3102: 2 Fairview Plaza, 5950 Fairview Rd., Suite 804. (704) 554-8134. FAX: (704) 553-0529. TWX: 810-621-0390. Stockton Holt, VP/sls mgr.

Cleveland 44114-2507: 1111 Superior Ave., Suite 970. (216) 861-2252. FAX: (216) 861-0914. TWX: 810-421-8275. Roger Stepic, sls mgr.

Dallas 75204-2915: 2711 N. Haskell Ave., Suite 2000, LB #23. (214) 821-8200. FAX: (214) 821-4120. TWX: 910-860-9308. Laverne Cole, VP/rgnl area mgr; Cynthia White, group mgr Petry Television; John White, group mgr Petry National.

Denver 80209-3817: 3773 Cherry Creek N. Dr., Suite 750. (303) 399-3030. FAX: (303) 399-9316. TWX: 910-931-2299. Brook A. Willardsen, sls mgr.

Troy, Mich. 48084-2859: 3221 W. Big Beaver Rd., Suite 102. (313) 649-0100. FAX: (313) 649-0866. TWX: 810-232-4802. Patrick L. McNew, VP/rgnl area mgr; J. Patrick O'Donnell, group mgr Petry Television; Carol Charron, group mgr Petry National. Detroit office.

Houston 77056-6501: 3000 Post Oak Blvd., Suite 1590. (713) 850-0194. FAX: (713) 850-8609. TWX: 910-881-4372. Chuck Sitta, VP/sls mgr.

Minneapolis 55402-3092: 706 2nd Ave. S., Suite 1138. (612) 339-6606. FAX: (612) 339-9330. TWX: 910-576-3177. Dan Mayasich, VP/sls mgr.

Philadelphia 19103: 7 Penn Ctr., Suite 420, 1635 Market St. (215) 567-6005. FAX: (215) 567-5938. TWX: 710-670-1437. Dave Bell, VP/sls mgr.

Portland, Ore. 97258-2005: One S.W. Columbia, Suite 437. (503) 228-0200. FAX: (503) 228-1060. TWX: 910-997-5132. Nancy Deitz, sls mgr.

St. Louis 63102-1732: 10 S. Broadway, Suite 525. (314) 241-2445. FAX: (314) 241-9215. TWX: 910-761-0447. Bruce Farber, VP/sls mgr.

San Francisco 94133-4693: 909 Montgomery St., Suite 402. (415) 781-3363. FAX: (415) 781-2419. TWX: 910-372-7712. Lori Gravino, VP/sls mgr.

Seattle 98121-3958: 1600 Westin Bldg., 2001 6th Ave. (206) 728-1747. FAX: (206) 728-4479. TWX: 901-444-4188. Carol Smith, sls mgr.

St. Petersburg, Fla. 33702-2457: 9800 4th St. N., Suite 108. (813) 576-1780. FAX: (813) 577-3911. TWX: 810-863-0416. Mary Louise Word, sls mgr. Tampa/St. Petersburg office.

Promotores Asociados Inc. Box 5738, San Jaun, P.R. 00906. (809) 723-9791. FAX: (809) 726-0640. Charles Slavin, pres; Abilio Felipe, VP.

Radio Time Sales/International. 559 Pacific Ave., San Francisco 94133. (415) 391-1984. Sam Posner, own/pres; Audrey Posner, VP.
  Decatur, Ga. 30033: Drawer 33100. (404) 633-9080. Dan Haight. Atlanta office.
  Chicago 60601: 333 N. Michigan, Suite 2032. (312) 346-3334. John F. Murphy, mgr.
  Dallas 75236: 3008 LBJ Fwy. (214) 243-8764. Tamela Benbenek, mgr.
  Detroit 48226: 1553 Woodward Ave., Suite 925. (313) 961-3353. Eleanor Krupp, Mary George, mgrs.
  Glendale, Calif. 91208: 1383 Opechee Way. (818) 500-7201. Jack Kabateck, mgr.
  New York 10016: 347 5th Ave., Suite 1007. (212) 679-3910. Elaine Herzstein, mgr.
  Portland, Ore. 97201: 1512 S.W. 18th. (503) 226-2911. Sanna Hern, mgr.
  St. Louis 63105: Box 50269. (314) 991-4261. Bruce Schneider.
  Seattle 98109: 701 Dexter N., Suite 216. (206) 285-1913. Kelly Chandler, mgr.

Read & Read. Box 31000, Spokane, Wash. 99223-3016. (509) 448-7400. FAX: (509) 448-3811. Thomas W. Read, pres.
  Sun Valley, Idaho 83353: Box 1572. (509) 448-7400. Thomas W. Read, pres.

Regional Reps Corp. 1100 Chester Ave., #100, Cleveland 44115-1404. (216) 781-0030. Stuart J. Sharpe, pres; Rebecca L. Sharpe, sec/treas.
  Cincinnati 45203: Holiday Park Tower, 644 Linn St. (513) 651-1511. Joseph C. Hearn, VP.
  Cleveland 44115-1404: 1100 Chester Ave., #100. (216) 781-0035. Robert A. Stern, rgnl mgr.
  Atlanta 30338: 4480 N. Shallowford Rd. (404) 394-7377. Michael E. Povlo, rgnl mgr; Jack DeHaven, sls mgr.

The Resort Representatives Inc. 425 Club Ln., Louisville, Ky. 40207-1801. (502) 895-5661. William J. Conway, pres.
  New York. (212) 772-8356.

Riley Representatives. 14330 Midway Rd., Suite 207, Dallas 75244. (214) 788-1630. Jack Riley, own.
  Decatur, Ga. 30033: Drawer 33100. (404) 633-9080. Dan Haight. Atlanta office.
  Chicago 60606: 20 N. Wacker Dr., Suite 540. (312) 263-3340. Howard Weiss.
  St. Clair Shores, Mich. 48080: 22971 Nine Mile Rd. (313) 773-7700. Ken Patt, Mike Martin. Detroit office.
  Toluca Lake, Calif. 91602: 10153 ½ Riverside Dr., Suite 181. (818) 505-1097. Jim Gillis. Los Angeles office.
  Pittsburgh 15217: 6326 Forward Ave. (412) 421-2600. Roger Rafson.
  San Francisco 94133: 559 Pacific Ave. (415) 391-1984. Sam Posner.
  New York 10001: ll Penn Plaza. (212) 239-3288. Joe Hoffman.

Roslin Radio Sales Inc. 515 Madison Ave., Suite 1104, New York 10022. (212) 486-0720. FAX: (212) 486-1958. Marvin Roslin, pres; Allan S. Korowitz, VP/gen sls mgr; Frank Truglio, N.Y. sls mgr; George Pafitis, Richard Filapelli, account execs.
  Atlanta 30326: 3355 Lenox Rd. N.E., Suite 750. (404) 266-0614. FAX: (404) 266-9169. Lisa Hanrahan, sls mgr.
  Boston 02116: 229 Berkeley St., #31. (617) 262-3400. FAX: (617) 262-5066. Jeff Finkel, sls mgr. Office serves Boston, Philadelphia, Baltimore, Washington & Toronto.
  Chicago 60610: 54 W. Hubbard St., Suite 100. (312) 644-0267. FAX: (312) 644-9249. Chris Brandli, sls mgr. Office serves Chicago, Detroit, Minneapolis & St. Louis.
  Dallas 75204: 4144 N. Central Expwy., Suite 660. (214) 823-7092. FAX: (214) 823-7094. Shanon Clark, sls mgr. Dallas/Houston office.
  Beverly Hills, Calif. 90211: 200 N. Robertson. (310) 278-8098. FAX: (310) 278-8153. Barry Poles, sls mgr. Los Angeles/San Francisco office.
  Phoenix 85018: (Paid religous prog rep.) 3326 E. Orange Dr. (602) 956-5837. FAX: (602) 956-3514. Eldon Wyant, sls mgr. Phoenix office.
  Chicago 60614: ("SHOWPLACE.") 1962 N. Bissel. (312) 472-8828. FAX: (312) 929-1108. Hal Pontious, pres Television Programming Dept.

SBS Network. 26 W. 56th St., New York 10019. (212) 541-6700. FAX: (212) 541-8535. Carroll Larkin, VP/gen sls mgr; Frank Soricelli, comptroller.
  Los Angeles 90028: 5700 Sunset Blvd. (213) 466-3001. Peter Pilcher, Peter Bellas.
  Miami, Fla. 33145: 1411 Coral Way. (305) 854-1830. Alina de Varona, Claudia Puig.

SJL Broadcast Management Corp. Box 2557, Billings, Mont. 59103. (406) 256-0705. FAX: (406) 252-9144. George D. Lilly, pres; Dave McCurdy, VP/controller.
  Montecito, Calif. 93108: 633 Picacho Ln. (805) 969-9278. FAX: (805) 969-2399. George D. Lilly.

The Sandeberg-Glenn Co. 666 Wall Rd., Napa, Calif. 94558. (707) 944-9115. Ward Glenn.

Savalli Broadcast Sales. 11 Penn Plaza, Suite 962, New York 10001. (212) 239-3288. FAX: (212) 563-1301. Howard Weiss, own; Joseph Savalli, Tom Pazler, Joseph Hoffman, gen mgrs.
  Decatur, Ga. 30033: Box 33100. (404) 373-2662. Dan Haight. Atlanta office.
  Chicago 60606: 20 N. Wacker Dr. (312) 263-3340. FAX: (312) 263-8494. Howard Weiss.
  Dallas 75244: 14330 Midway Rd. (214) 788-1630. FAX: (214) 490-6438. Jack Riley.
  Grosse Point Park, Mich. 48230: 874 Westchester. (313) 821-4604. Bud Pearse. Detroit office.
  Toluca Lake, Calif. 91602: 10153 ½ Riverside Dr. (818) 505-1097. Jim Gillis. Los Angeles office.
  Napa, Calif. 94558: 666 Wall Rd. (707) 944-9115. Ward Glenn. San Francisco office.
  Detroit 48080: 22971 Nine Mile Shore. (313) 773-7700. FAX: (313) 774-4889. Ken Patt, Mike Martin.
  Los Angeles 91208: 1383 Opechee Way. (818) 500-7201. FAX: (818) 244-9483. Jack Kabatech.

Bruce Schneider & Co. Inc. Box 411186, St. Louis 63141. (314) 991-4261; (314) 991-5249. Bruce Schneider, pres; Donna L. Schneider, sls asst/sec.

Schubert Radio Sales. 100 Park Ave., New York 10017. (212) 916-0780. FAX: (212) 916-0790. Jerry Schubert, pres; Erica Farber, exec VP mktg.
  Southfield, Mich. 48075: 4000 Town Ctr., Suite 290. (313) 357-0903. FAX: (313) 358-2468. Cynthia McGuineas. Detroit office.
  Chicago 60601: 205 N. Michigan Ave., Suite 2015. (312) 819-0485. FAX: (312) 819-1970. Lynn Kite.
  Los Angeles 90024: 10880 Wilshire Blvd., Suite 1215. (310) 470-3383. FAX: (310) 474-3454. Leslie Scheinman.
  Irving, Tex. 75038: 1350 Walnut Hill Ln., Suite 100. (214) 518-9628. FAX: (214) 518-1729. Julie Lane. Dallas office.
  Atlanta: TBA.

Seltel Inc. 575 5th Ave., New York 10017. (212) 476-9400. FAX: (212) 476-9630; (212) 476-9625; (212) 687-4234. TWX: 710-581-6768. L. Donald Robinson, pres/CEO; Raymond J. Johns, exec VP/COO; Maria-

U.S. Radio, Television and Cable Representatives

Luise Busi, VP/treas; David F. Schwartz, sr VP domestic sls; Michael Rix, dir manpower dev; Dan Parisi, VP/natl sls mgr (Indy-Rockets & Renegades Teams); Bob Webb, VP/natl sls mgr (Indy-Raiders & Renegades Teams); Carl Mathis, VP/natl sls mgr (Indy-Rangers Team); Mark Goldstein, natl sls mgr (Indy-Rebels & Racers Teams); Judy Kleinberger, natl sls mgr affil (White Team); Michael Rix, VP/natl sls mgr affil (Red Team); Janeen Bjork, VP/dir progmg; Lois Friedman, dir rsch.

Atlanta 30309: 3490 Piedmont Rd. N.E., Suite 1206. (404) 233-3906. FAX: (404) 233-5440. Dan Griffin, gen mgr.

Boston 02116: 38 Newbury St., Suite 603. (617) 236-8666. FAX: (617) 236-4927. Rosemarie Ferrara, gen mgr.

Charlotte, N.C. 28209: 5821 Fairview Rd., Suite 308. (704) 554-7124. (704) 553-7320. FAX: (704) 553-7320. TWX: 810-621-7832. Suzy Plettner, gen mgr.

Chicago 60611: 211 E. Ontario, Suite 700. (312) 642-2450. FAX: (312) 642-1631. Michael Custardo, gen mgr; Michael Terenzio, sls mgr (Indy-Raiders Team); Barbara Bruns, sls mgr (Indy-Rangers Team); Dan Trapani, sls mgr (Indy-Rockets Team); Randy Brown, sls mgr affil (Red & White Teams).

Dallas 75204: 3131 McKinney Ave., Suite 240. (214) 720-0070. FAX: (214) 720-0111. Michael Girocco, gen mgr.

Denver 80206: 222 Milwaukee St., Suite 210. (303) 333-4845. FAX: (303) 321-1087. Gerriann Sullivan-Ward, gen mgr.

Southfield, Mich. 48076: 26211 Central Park Blvd., Suite 202. (313) 354-3611. (313) 354-2405. FAX: (313) 354-2405. TWX: 810-224-4502. David Brangan, gen mgr. Detroit office.

Houston 77081: 4848 Loop Central Dr., Suite 710. (713) 660-8881. FAX: (713) 666-9586. Michael Thomas, gen mgr.

Los Angeles 90036: 5757 Wilshire Blvd., Suite One. (213) 930-2450. FAX: (213) 931-0567; (213) 931-2561. TWX: 910-321-4124. David Ware, gen mgr; Lee Winikoff, sls mgr (Indy-Raiders Team); Maria Giovenco, sls mgr (Indy-Rangers); Bill Dietz, sls mgr (Indy-Rockets Team); John Wahlert, sls mgr affil (Red & White Teams).

Miami 33126: 6100 Blue Lagoon Dr., Suite 340. (305) 266-4066. FAX: (305) 266-7713. Enid Bluestone, gen mgr.

Minneapolis 55402: 120 S. 6th St., Suite 2005. (612) 338-7017. FAX: (612) 349-6261. Essie Dalton, gen mgr.

Philadelphia 19103: 1760 Market St., 7th Fl. (215) 563-5400. FAX: (215) 563-2974. Rickie Ellis, gen mgr.

Portland, Ore. 97201: 1512 S.W. 18th Ave. (503) 226-2911. FAX: (503) 226-6596. Richard Gohlman, gen mgr.

St. Louis 63102: St. Louis Pl., 200 N. Broadway, Suite 1620. (314) 241-4193. FAX: (314) 241-9849. Richard J. Quigley III, gen mgr.

San Francisco 94111: 444 Market St., Suite 1520. (415) 391-8890. FAX: (415) 391-4252. Steve Jones, gen mgr.

Seattle 98109: 211 6th Ave. N., Suite 200. (206) 727-2222. FAX: (206) 441-2738. Bob Tacher, gen mgr.

Cleveland 44114: East Ohio Bldg., Suite 1625, 171 E. 9th St. (216) 696-0500. FAX: (216) 696-0505; John F. Ahlin, gen mgr.

Detroit 48084: 2075 W. Beaver, Suite 310. (313) 649-5222. FAX: (313) 649-5877. David Brangan, gen mgr.

Tampa 33607: 3507 Frontage Rd., Suite 130. (813) 286-9689. FAX: (813) 282-3045. Steve Henderson, gen mgr.

Frederick W. Smith Station Representative. Box 459, Bellport, N.Y. 11713. (212) 840-0614.

Soderlund Co. 5901 Garfield St., Lincoln, Neb. 68506-1448. Harold A. Soderlund.

Southern Television System. Box 2220, Florence, Ala. 35630. (205) 764-7711; (205) 764-1122. FAX: (205) 764-7750. Richard B. Biddle, pres/CEO/VP opns.

Bruce C. Staffel Co. 326 Sterling Browning, San Antonio 78232. (210) 490-4000. FAX: (210) 496-5661. Bruce C. Staffel, own.

State Nets (National Association of State Radio Networks). 18216 Harwood Ave., Homewood, Ill. 60430. (708) 799-6676. FAX: (708) 799-6698. Thomas F. Dobrez, pres.

Atlanta 30329: 4 Executive Park Dr., Suite 1217. (404) 636-8676. FAX: (404) 636-9033. Ann Defforge, account exec.

TBG Communications Inc. 161 S. Lincolnway, Suite 211, North Aurora, Ill. 60542. (708) 844-3313. FAX: (708) 844-9291. Jim Burkhardt, CEO.

TCI. 1801 E. 4th Ave., Olympia, Wash. 98506. (206) 754-7081. FAX: (206) 943-5911. Matt Bien, VP; Kathryn Nevin, gen sls mgr.

Seattle 98102: 2359 Yale Ave. E. (206) 323-4716. Tinsley Palmer, rgnl/natl sls mgr.

Bellingham, Wash. 98225: 119 N. Commercial, #660. (206) 734-2150. Bill Gorman, loc sls mgr.

Bremerton, Wash. 98312: 5610 Kitsap Way, #320. (206) 479-8486. Linda Boysen, loc sls mgr.

Port Angeles, Wash. 98362: 725 E. First St. (206) 452-8466.

Mount Vernon, Wash. 98273: 1107 W. Division. (206) 424-6446. Chuck Payne, loc sls mgr.

T N Spot Sales - Agricultural and Retail. Box 12800, 711 Hillsborough St., Raleigh, N.C. 27605. (919) 890-6046 (agriculture division); (919) 890-6076 (retail division). FAX: (919) 890-6024. Agriculture division: Ray Wilkinson, VP/gen mgr; Andy Roat, natl sls mgr; Susan Hill, opns mgr; Lesa Hudson, account exec.

TV Rep Inc. Box 708, Bloomfield Hills, Mich. 48303-0708. (313) 355-2020. FAX: (313) 355-0368. Douglas Johnson, pres.

New York 10017: 212 E. 47th St. (212) 888-7377; (800) 752-8320. Howard Levinson, natl sls mgr.

Chicago 60611: 440 N. Wabash, Suite 3006. (312) 923-0101; (800) 752-8321. Joseph Antelo, rgnl sls mgr.

Beverly Hills, Calif. 90210: 316 N. Oakhurst, Suite 301. (310) 859-8880; (800) 752-8323. John Hughes, rgnl sls mgr.

Tacher Co. Inc. 211 6th Ave. N., Suite 200, Seattle 98109-5005. (206) 727-2222. FAX: (206) 441-2738. Mick Tacher, pres/CEO; Bob Tacher, VP; Greg Tacher, Denise Norman, account execs.

Portland, Ore. 97201: 1512 S.W. 18th Ave. (503) 226-2911. FAX: (503) 226-6596. Richard Gohlman, VP; Karen Le Gore, Laurie Ware, account execs.

Tampa Bay Interconnect. 5201 W. Kennedy Blvd., Suite 930, Tampa 33609. (813) 281-2662. FAX: (813) 281-2663. Paul "Siracuse" Siragusa, gen mgr.

Target Radio. 2200 6th Ave., Suite 707, Seattle 98121. (206) 443-9925. FAX: (206) 443-9998. Greg Smith, pres; Ruth Hallett, mgr.

Portland, Ore. 97201: 4800 S.W. Macadam Blvd., Suite 200, (503) 228-0016. FAX: (503) 228-0556. Barbara Barry, account exec.

Denver 80206: 222 Milwaukee St., Suite 209. (303) 368-0334. FAX: (303) 321-1087. Adriana Vernon, account exec.

Salt Lake City 84107: 575 East, 4500 South, Suite B-200. (801) 266-1986. FAX: (801) 266-2365. Kathy Bingham, account exec.

Telemundo Group Inc. 1740 Broadway, New York 10019. (212) 492-5500. FAX: (212) 265-4092; (212) 459-9498. Saul P. Steinberg, chmn of bd; Joaquin F. Blaya, pres/CEO; Peter J. Housman, pres bus & corporate affrs/CFO; Jose C. Cancela, pres stn group; Marisa Chaves, sr VP sls; Saul Rosenthal, VP natl spot sls; Maureen Allegro, VP net sls; Emily Phillips, natl spot sls mgr.

Chicago 60611: 435 N. Michigan Ave., Suite 1310. (312) 321-1911. FAX: (312) 321-1916. Michael O'Shea, sls mgr.

Los Angeles 90048: 6500 Wilshire Blvd., Suite 1220. (213) 658-6868. FAX: (213) 653-2367. Hilary Dubin, West Coast rgnl mgr.

Hialeah, Fla. 33010: 2300 W. 8th Ave. (305) 889-7586. FAX: (305) 888-0236. Julyanne Trullunque, sls mgr. Miami office.

Dallas 75240: 1860 Two Lincoln Center, 5420 LBJ Fwy. (214) 661-2560. FAX: (214) 661-2605. Jose Chapa, sls mgr.

Irvine, Calif. 92715: 18101 Von Karman, Suite 660. (714) 252-0552. FAX: (714) 440-2814. Karl Meyer, sls mgr.

San Francisco 94104: 250 Montgomery St., Suite 510. (415) 421-6071. FAX: (415) 421-6602. Joe Corderi, sls mgr.

TeleRep

THE LEADER FOR OVER 25 YEARS

DEDICATED TO EXCELLENCE
COMMITTED TO RESULTS

TeleRep Inc. One Dag Hammarskjold Plaza, 25th Fl., New York 10017. (212) 759-8787. Steven Herson, pres/gen mgr; Thomas Tilson, VP/dir sls; Larry Goldberg, VP/gen sls mgr (Cougar & Wildcat stns); Lisa Brown, VP/gen sls mgr (Tiger stns); Amy Carney, VP/gen sls mgr (Jaguar stns); Andy Feinstein, VP/gen sls mgr (Lion stns); Murray Berkowitz, VP/gen sls mgr (Leopard stns); Patricia Prie, VP/CFO; Jay Isabella, VP/dir progmg; Jim Monahan, VP/dir spec projects & audience dev; Dan Kelly, VP/dir prom & PR; Dave Hills, VP sls dev.

Atlanta 30309: 1605 W. Peachtree St. N.E. (404) 881-1948. Bill Hoffman, sls mgr.

Chicago 60611: 401 N. Michigan Ave., Suite 3300. (312) 329-1515. Jim Jordan, VP/Midwest mgr.

Detroit 48202: 1400 Fisher Bldg. (313) 873-6664. Ed Kroninger, VP/Midwest mgr.

Los Angeles 90036: 5900 Wilshire Blvd., Suite 800. (213) 937-4644. Bob Miggins, VP/West Coast mgr.

Minneapolis 59415: 701 4th Ave. S. (612) 332-7333. Cathy Faulkner, sls mgr.

St. Louis 63101: Equitable Bldgs., Suite 920, 10 S. Broadway. (314) 241-7979. Dennis Leonard, sls mgr.

U.S. Radio, Television and Cable Representatives

San Francisco 94111: One California St., Suite 2250. (415) 433-1966. Steve Lane, sls mgr.

Philadelphia 19103: 1601 Market St., Suite 1090. (215) 564-1206. Joe Hockenjos, sls mgr.

Boston 02116: 399 Boylston St. (617) 247-2555. MaryJane Kelley, VP/East Coast mgr.

Dallas 75206: 6500 Greenville Ave., Suite 770. (214) 987-0991. Alan Sawyer, sls mgr.

Cleveland 44114: One Cleveland Ctr., 1375 E. 9th St., Suite 1970. (216) 566-8282. Bill Young, sls mgr.

Houston 77046: 11 Greenway Plaza, Suite 2116. (713) 627-7791. Charlene Salvato, sls mgr.

Miami, Fla. 33126: 6303 Blue Lagoon Dr., Suite 460. (305) 262-3133. Steve Bluestone, sls mgr.

Charlotte, N.C. 29210: 2 Fairview Plaza, 5950 Fairview Rd., Suite 705. (704) 552-8862. Patti Markham, sls mgr.

Seattle 98121: 2025 1st Ave. (206) 443-3939. Jeanine Newhall, sls mgr.

Torbet Radio Group. 100 Park Ave., 5th Fl., New York 10017. (212) 916-0700. FAX: (212) 309-9079. Jerry Schubert, chmn; Anthony Fasolino, pres/CEO; Michael Bellantoni, exec VP; Sally Alzapiedi, exec asst. Sls/Rsch: Mariann Deluca, sr VP/dir sls; Ernie Metcalf, VP/account exec; Caryn Jacoby, sr account exec; Amy FitzGerald, Adam Millinger, Valerie Gerena, Pam Burkle, sls assts; Stefanie Schwartz, Tony Battiato, Tracy Marraccini, Linda Madonna, Louise Kalechstein Zagnit, account execs; Katrina Liendecker, rsch dir; Stephanie Nussbaum, rsch/sls asst. The Interep Radio Store: Bob Lion, VP/rgnl exec; Amy Greenstein, account mgr; Debbie Lombardo, sls assoc. The Interep Radio Information Services: Jane Greenfield, mgr info svcs. Accounting: Joe Kruszewski, accounting; Louise Gongora, Interep Radio nets accounting SVSR; Theresa Williams-Cruz, AR analyst. Support Services: Joyce Jimenez, receptionist; John Lynch, mail room supvr; Freddie Arocho, computer operator.

Marietta, Ga. 30067: Bldg. 5, 1640 Powers Ferry Rd. (404) 951-8114. FAX: (404) 953-0417. Jim Peacock, rgnl mgr/DOS; Sharon Sigler, account exec; Tara Blahnik, sls asst. Atlanta office.

Los Angeles 90024: 10880 Wilshire Blvd., Suite 1215. (310) 475-0033. FAX: (310) 474-3454. Leslie Scheinman, VP/rgnl mgr/DOS; Michael Nelson, Lori Perman, Jeanne Lindholm, account execs; Lisa Smith, Andi Kushner, sls assts. Los Angeles office.

Boston 02116: 31 St. James Ave., Suite 809. (617) 426-3374. FAX: (617) 451-0067. Greg Martin, rgnl mgr/DOS; Carol Firicano, office mgr/sls asst.

Chicago 60601: 205 N. Michigan Ave., Suite 2015. (312) 819-0088. FAX: (312) 819-1970. Bob Lurito, sr VP/MW division mgr/DOS; Mary Lou Hamburger, Karla Sanders, account execs; Nada Kreger, Lucia Bertrand, sls assts.

Las Colinas, Tex. 75038: 1350 Walnut Hill Ln., Suite 100. (214) 518-9630. FAX: (214) 518-8091. Barbara Longoria, rgnl mgr/DOS; Susan Hegmann, account exec; Fernando Laclette, sls asst. Dallas office.

Southfield, Mich. 48075: 4000 Town Ctr., Suite 290. (313) 353-0400. FAX: (313) 358-2468. Eve Haley, rgnl mgr/DOS; Michael Maiorano, account exec; Valerie Wilson, sls assoc. Detroit office.

San Francisco 94111: 750 Battery St., Suite 340. (415) 772-2707. FAX: (415) 362-3903. Joni Fausone, rgnl mgr/DOS; Kris Lee, sls asst. San Francisco/Seattle office.

Lubbock, Tex. 79424: Box 6060, 4418 74th St., Suite 54. (806) 792-2000. FAX: (806) 792-9200. Loyd Senn, dir agri-mktg; Julia Childs, asst.

Philadelphia 19102: The Bellevue, Broad & Walnut, 9th Fl. (215) 732-9532. FAX: (215) 546-8313. Jerry Gubin, VP/rgnl mgr/DOS; Michelle Quinn, sls asst.

Larkspur, Colo. 80118: Interep/The Torbet Radio Group. 14693 Spring Valley Rd. (303) 688-4370. FAX: (303) 688-3085. Debby Lang, rgnl mgr/DOS. Denver office.

United Television Broadcasting Systems Inc. 1670 W. Beverly Blvd., Los Angeles 90026-5733. (213) 483-2929. FAX: (213) 483-3438. John Y. Haneda, pres.

Tokyo 107, Japan: United Television International Inc. 401, 8-5-9, Akasaka, Minato-Ku. 03-3403-6495. Rumiko Naito, exec VP.

Univision Network. 605 3rd Ave., 12th Fl., New York 10158-0180. (212) 455-5200. FAX: (212) 867-6710. Jaime Davila, chmn/CEO; Ray Rodriquez, pres/COO; Raul Torano, pres sls; Peter von Gal, VP/dir sls; Carlos Deschapelles, mgr natl spot sls; Guillermo Martinez, sr VP news & sports; Andrew Hobson, exec VP; Stephen Hammond, corporate communications.

Bingham Farms, Mich. 48025: 30700 Telegraph Rd., Suite 3640. (313) 540-5705. FAX: (313) 540-2419. Mark Brown, sls mgr.

Chicago 60611-4305: 401 E. Illinois St., Suite 325. (312) 321-8200. FAX: (312) 321-8223. Brian Pussilano, sls mgr.

Irvine, Calif. 92714: 2030 Main St., Suite 235. (714) 474-8585. FAX: (714) 474-8385. Steve Mandala, sls mgr.

Irving, Tex. 75039: 600 E. Las Colinas Blvd., Suite 566. (214) 869-0202. FAX: (214) 869-2635. Jack Hobbs, sls mgr.

Los Angeles 90045: 6701 Center Dr. W., 15th Fl. (310) 338-0700. FAX: (310) 348-3619. Patricia Testa, sls mgr.

Miami, Fla. 33178: 9405 N.W. 41st St. (305) 471-3900. FAX: (305) 471-4027. Evelyn Castillo, sls mgr.

San Francisco 94124: 2200 Palou Ave. (415) 824-4384. FAX: (415) 824-1906. Rodolfo Balderrama, sls mgr.

Hugh Wallace Inc. 11332 Camarillo St., North Hollywood, Calif. 91602. (818) 980-3212. FAX: (818) 980-8464. Hugh Wallace, sls mgr; Bill Mendell, Bruce Gold, Mary Williams.

Chicago 60606: 20 N. Wacker Dr., Suite 562. (312) 263-3340. Howard Weiss, Jeff Brunstein.

Western Regional Broadcast Sales. 1383 Opechee Way, Glendale, Calif. 91208. (818) 500-7201. FAX: (818) 244-9483. Jack J. Kabateck, principal own.

San Francisco 94133: 559 Pacific Ave. (415) 391-1984. Sam Posner, rgn mgr.

New York 10001: 11 Penn Plaza, Suite 2219. (212) 239-3288. Joe Hoffman, rgn mgr.

Atlanta 30033: Drawer 33100. (404) 373-2662. Dan Haight, Arletta Haight.

Detroit 48081: 21714 Lakeland. (313) 445-0491. Ken Patt, rgn mgr.

Dallas 75244: 14330 Midway Rd., Suite 207. (214) 788-1630. Jack Riley, rgn mgr.

Williams Radio Sales Inc. 157 W. 57th St., Suite 604, New York 10019-2210. (212) 757-6868. FAX: (212) 956-0235. Melvin Williams Jr., pres/CEO; Rosanna Lau, Joel Lass, mktg consultants.

Chicago office: (312) 641-2412. FAX: (312) 641-2413.

Adam Young Inc. (Television). 599 Lexington Ave., 47th Fl., New York 10022. (212) 688-5100. Adam Young; Vincent J. Young, chmn; Arthur W. Scott, pres.

Atlanta 30305: 4 Piedmont Ctr., Suite 711. (404) 261-8800. Tom Durr, mgr.

Boston 02116: 31 St. James Ave., 9th Fl. (617) 423-4987. John D. Kettell, mgr.

Chicago 60611: 444 N. Michigan Ave., Suite 3470. (312) 744-1313. Lois Hamelin, mgr.

Dallas 75204-2423: 3232 McKinney Ave., Suite 670. (214) 871-2988. Lynda Shotwell, mgr.

Troy, Mich. 48084: 2855 Coolidge, Suite 222. (313) 649-3999. Allan Baur, mgr.

Los Angeles 90048: 6100 Wilshire Blvd., Suite 320. (213) 938-2081. Thomas Camarda, West Coast mgr.

Minneapolis 55402: 630 Baker Bldg. (612) 339-3397. James O. Ramsland, mgr.

New York 10022: 599 Lexington Ave. (212) 688-5100. Steven Mullen, account exec. Philadelphia/Pittsburgh territory.

St. Louis 63141: Box 411186. (314) 991-5249. Bruce W. Schneider, mgr.

San Francisco 94104: 155 Montgomery St., Suite 406. (415) 986-5366. Andrew Rosenfeld, mgr.

Canadian Radio, Television and Cable Representatives

Airtime Broadcast Sales Ltd. 1037 W. Broadway, #104, Vancouver, B.C. V6H 1E3. (604) 736-6634. FAX: (604) 736-8059. Frank Jobes, pres.

AirTime Television Sales. 6 Crescent Rd., 2nd, Toronto, Ont. M4W 1T1. (416) 923-7177. FAX: (416) 923-7620. Bernie Ziegler, pres; John Aonso, Mark Burko, VPs.
   Vancouver, B.C.: (604) 736-6634.
   Montreal, Que.: (514) 282-1510. FAX: (514) 849-8366.

Alexander, Pearson & Dawson Inc. 2 Bloor St. E., 31st Fl., Toronto, Ont. M4W 1A8. (416) 928-0044. R.G. Alexander, pres; J. Hurley, VP/group mgr; Ken Lydford, group mgr; J. Lynn, VP.
   Montreal, Que. H3A 1Y9: 2050 Mansfield St., Suite 1400. (514) 842-1945. M. Mezzaluna, Montreal mgr.
   Vancouver, B.C. V7Y 1A1: 701 W. Georgia St., Suite 510. (604) 689-0027.

All-Canada Radio & Television. 1000 Yonge St., Toronto, Ont. M4W 2K2. (416) 963-7800. FAX: (416) 963-4367. John F. Gorman, pres; Victor Dann, VP natl sls; Terri Fedoruk, office/traf supvr; Wendy Maude, Word Pro coord; Jane Martindale, mktg mgr; Jim Whelan, sls supvr (metro); Hedy Bouthillier, sls supvr (non-metro); Dennis Horlick, satellite radio sls mgr.
   Dartmouth, N.S. B2Y 2N6: 615-45 Aldemay Dr. (902) 465-6881. FAX: (902) 465-9796. Greg Asling, mgr Atlantic rgn; Krita Reynolds-Lingley, sls rep. Halifax office.
   Montreal, Que. H3A 2N3: 1155 rue Sherbrooke Ouest., Bureau 1605. (514) 284-1344. FAX: (514) 284-3057. Mike Laframboise, sls supvr; Brigitte Henri, Gianna Ciancio, sls reps; Jacques Goulet, consultant (non-metro).
   Calgary, Alta. T3E 6X6: 3320 17th Ave. S.W. (403) 686-1000. FAX: (403) 686-1003. J. Dunlop, mgr Prairie rgn; Krista Fordham, sls rep.
   Vancouver, B.C. V5Z 4J6: 2440 Ash St. (604) 876-3990. FAX: (604) 876-8035. Gary Milne, mgr Pacific rgn; Tony Prinzen, Stephen Thomas, sls reps.
   Winnipeg, Man. R3G 0L7: 1440 Rapelje Ave. (204) 788-3411. FAX: (201) 788-0284. Jim Dunlop, mgr Prairie rgn; John Brown, dir sls.

Broadcast Representatives, Canada Ltd. 159 Scotia St., Winnepeg, Man. R2W 3X2. (204) 586-7755. Helen Kolomaya, pres.

Brydson Media Sales International Inc. 330 W. 56th St., Suite 7E, New York 10019. (212) 586-7773. FAX: 212-582-6353. David Brydson, pres; Rebecca LaBrecque, Maddy Boos, acct execs.
   Montreal, Ont. H3A 1S5: 1411 Peel St. (514) 987-1220. FAX: (514) 987-1188.

Canvideo Television Sales. 2200 Yonge St., Suite 1300, Toronto, Ont. M4S 2C6. (416) 482-6200. David Mintz, chmn; Rodger Hone, pres/CEO; Edward Wood, sr VP/gen mgr.
   Montreal, Que. H3A 1S5: 1411 Peel St., Suite 600. (514) 787-1515. Henry Mauer, gen mgr.

Glen-Warren Broadcast Sales. (A division of Baton Broadcasting Inc.) 2 Bloor St. W., Suite 300, Toronto, Ont. M4W 3L2. (416) 963-9898. William H. Cox, pres; Steve Hand, VP/gen sls mgr.
   Montreal, Que. H3A 2R7: 1010 Sherbrooke St. (514) 282-1845.
   Vancouver, B.C. V7Y 1C6: Box 10149, Pacific Ctr. (604) 682-8404.

Golden West Media. 305-326 Broadway, Winnipeg, Man. R3C 0S5. (204) 943-9574. FAX: (204) 943-6016. Elmer Hildebrand, pres; Henry Boschman, account exec.

Paul L'Anglais Inc. 1600 De Maisonneuve Blvd. Est, 6th Fl., Montreal, Que. H2L 4P2. (514) 526-9201. FAX: (514) 526-6133. Jean Vurecher, pres/gen mgr.
   Toronto, Ont. M4S 1V6: 30 Soudan Ave., 4th Fl. (416) 487-1551. Vic Menage, VP.

Metro Marketing West Inc. 680C Leg-in-Boot Sq., False Creek, Vancouver, B.C. V5Z 4B5. (604) 874-8463. FAX: (604) 874-9300. James D. McLennan, CEO; Tracy L. Fraser, natl accounts supvr.

Metrospot Television. Box 2003, 20 Eglinton Ave. W., Suite 1902, Toronto, Ont. M4R 1K8. (416) 322-9404. FAX: (416) 322-9405. Norman Bain, pres; Les Salnick, VP.
   Lachine, Que. H8T 3H5: 3160 Rue Joseph Debreuil. (514) 697-4850. FAX: (514) 426-5608. Tom Flaherty.
   West Vancouver, B.C. V7T 1A7: Stuart Bldg., 935 Marine Dr., #403. (604) 926-9493. Doug Davis.

Paul Mulvihill Ltd. 45 St. Claire Ave. W., 3rd Fl., Toronto, Ont. M4V 1K9. (416) 962-0080. FAX: (416) 962-6883. Norman Bonnell, pres; Ed Volton, TV mgr; Joe Mulvihill, VP/radio mgr.
   Montreal, Que. H3B 2L3: 1155 René-Lévesque Blvd. W., Suite 2920. (514) 393-4101. Luc Leduc, mgr.
   Vancouver, B.C. V6E 1M7: 1033 Davie St., Suite 518. (604) 684-6277. John Grant, mgr.
   Dartmouth, N.S. B3B 1T5: 202 Brownlow Ave., Tower D, Suite 205. (902) 468-8928. Stephen Feswick, mgr.

Myers Marketing. (A division of Jack Myers Marketing Communications.) 322 Rt. 46 W., Parsippany, N.J. 07054. (201) 882-6602. Jack Myers, pres; Leah Reznick, VP.

National Cable Network. One Valleybrook Dr., Toronto, Ont. M3B 2S7. (416) 391-7238. FAX (416) 441-9963. Jean Thomas, gen mgr; Bob Tadman, account mgr.

Opex Communications/Telemedia Division. 1411 rue Peel, Suite 300, Montreal, Que. H3A 3L5. (514) 845-8191. FAX: (514) 845-0122. Marc Paris, VP/gen mgr.
   Toronto, Ont. M4S 3C3: 40 Holly St., 9th Fl. (416) 482-9383. Marc Paris, VP/gen mgr.

Starcom Broadcast Sales. 2722 Allwood St., Abbotsford, B.C. V2T 3R8. (604) 859-5277. FAX: (604) 859-9907. Bill Coombes, pres/CEO; Peter Alpen, VP mktg; Bob Singleton, VP admin.

Target Broadcast Sales. 1867 Yonge St., Suite 905, Toronto, Ont. M4S 1Y5. (416) 932-2202. FAX: (416) 932-2336. Richard Sienko, pres.
   Montreal, Que. H3C 1L9: 640 St. Paul St. W., #204. (514) 397-8615. FAX: (514) 397-8617. Richard LeBrun, mgr.
   Winnipeg, Man. R3C 0S5: 326 Broadway, #305. (204) 943-9574. FAX: (204) 943-6016. Henry Boschman, mgr.

Telemedia Radio Sales. 40 Holly St., Toronto, Ont. M4S 3C3. (416) 482-9383. FAX: (416) 482-9469. Marc Paris, VP/gen mgr; Warren Locke, sls mgr.
   Vancouver, B.C. V6E 4A4: Mediagroup West. 1130 W. Pender St., Suite 301. (604) 685-5747. David St. Laurent, sls mgr.
   Montreal, Que. H3A 1S5: 1411 Peel St., Suite 300. (514) 845-8191. Lucie Veillet, sls mgr.

Western Broadcast Sales Ltd. 55 Bloor St. W., Suite 1600, Toronto, Ont. M4W 1A5. (416) 960-9205. FAX: (416) 960-0257. Keith Morrison, pres/CEO.
   Vancouver, B.C. V7X 1M6: 505 Burrard St., Suite 1960. (604) 687-2844. Joe Balango, sls mgr western Canada.
   Montreal, Que. H3A 1G8: 1250 René-Lévesque Blvd. W., Suite 4035. (514) 937-8376. Paul LaBarbera, sls mgr Quebec.

Public Relations, Publicity and Promotion Services

A&R Partners. 509 Seaport Ct., Port of Redwood City, Calif. 94063. (415) 363-0982.

Adams Sandler Inc. 1901 Research Blvd., Rockville, Md. 20850. (301) 279-5555. FAX: (301) 424-6722. Kevin O'Keefe, pres.
Pub rels, adv & mktg firm.

Advocate Associates Inc. 180 Mohegan Tr., South Windsor, Conn. 06074. (203) 644-2100. Sherman Tarr, pres.
Pub rels counseling, speeches, mailings, polls.

American Radio Brokers Inc/SFO. 1255 Post St., San Francisco 94109. (415) 441-3377. Chester P. Coleman, pres; Kathleen O'Donnell, office mgr; Richard "Julio" Haskey, tech consultant; Warren Earl, consultant; Marlo Holmes, dir opns Alaska.

Artisans Public Relations. 1800 S. Robertson Blvd., #932, Los Angeles 90034. (310) 837-6008. FAX: (310) 837-2286. Linda A. Rosner, pres; Keith Gayhart, creative dir.
Pub rels & adv.

Associated Essentials. Box 8135, Chicago 60680. (312) 224-5612. Frank Howard Jr., chmn; R.C. Hillsman, co-chmn.
Pub rels to the cable, TV, radio, video, film & entertainment industries.

Banner & Greif Ltd. 370 Lexington Ave., New York 10017-6589. (212) 687-7730. FAX: (212) 949-9806. Ed Greif, chmn; Jim Greif, pres.
Pub rels consulting & publ svcs on annual retainer or project basis.

The Barash Group. Box 77, State College, Pa. 16804. (814) 238-5051. FAX: (814) 237-4327. Mimi U. Coppersmith Fredman, pres; Dick Hall, sr VP; Ronald Shroyer, VP/creative dir; Nan R. Barash, VP.
Full agency svcs & spec promotions, billboards & specialties.

Baron Video Productions. 301 E. 47th St., Suite 10M, New York 10017. (212) 223-1826. FAX: (212) 223-3737. Jed Canaan, pres/exec prod.
Video news releases, satellite media tours, mktg videos, TV news monitoring.

Aleon Bennett Promotions/Public Relations. 13455 Ventura Blvd., Suite 212, Sherman Oaks, Calif. 91423. (818) 990-8070. Aleon Bennett, pres; Vonne Godfrey, VP; Kenneth Cullen, assoc.

Edward L. Bernays. 7 Lowell St., Cambridge, Mass. 02138. (617) 547-6258. Edward L. Bernays.
Counsel in pub rels.

Robert W. Bloch Public Relations. 30 E. 60th St., New York 10022. (212) 755-8047. FAX (212) 758-1558. Robert W. Bloch, own/mgr.
International pub rels, communications & mktg consultant svcs.

Braun Ketchum Public Relations. 11755 Wilshire Blvd., Suite 2300, Los Angeles 90025. (310) 444-5000. FAX: (310) 312-8943. Larry Fisher, pres; Doug Jeffe, exec VP; Christine Lewis, Billie C. Greer, sr VPs; Keven Bellows, Evon Gotlieb, Sydney Dailey, VPs/group mgrs; Jennifer Floto-Katz, VP.
Full range of natl & international pub rels, publ, govt rel, corporate & financial rel svcs.

Bridal Fair Inc. 11248 John Galt Blvd., Omaha, Neb. 68137. (402) 592-8200. FAX: (402) 592-2991. Bruce E. Thiebauth, pres; Sherry Edwards, VP admin; Cary Kruger, sr rgnl mgr; Les Steffen, sec/treas; E. Donald Donaldson, rgnl sls rep.
Self-liquidating syndications to radio & TV stns providing substantial first-quarter revenues from loc retail sources.

Broadcast Interview Source. 2233 Wisconsin Ave. N.W., Suite 540, Washington 20007. (202) 333-4904. FAX: (202) 342-5411. Mitchell P. Davis, publisher; Loretta Rogers, mgng edit.
Publishers of the *Yearbook of Experts, Authorities, and Spokespersons* ®, an encyclopedia of sources available for interviews with the media.
Also publishers of *Talk Show Selects*, a directory of more than 700 radio & TV talk shows (local & natl), & *Power Media Selects*, a directory of media outlets in the U.S. Both directories are available as mailing labels & computer disks.

George Burns International. 6965 El Camino Real, Suite 105-229, Rancho La Costa, Calif. 92009. (619) 746-7993. FAX: (619) 739-8303. George Burns, gen ptnr; Larry Lakoduk, mgng editing ptnr; Todd Stewart, VP progmg.
Radio management & consulting.

Burson-Marsteller. 230 Park Ave. S., New York 10003-1566. (212) 614-4444. FAX: (212) 614-4263. James H. Dowling, chmn; Harold Burson, founder chmn; Larry Snodden, pres/CEO; Thomas Mosser, pres North America; Trudi Schutz, mgng dir media svcs.
International pub rels, pub affrs, mkt support.

Carl Byoir & Associates Inc. 420 Lexington Ave., New York 10017. (212) 210-6000. Chamelle Hardy, pres.
Radio features, series; TV news; video/film/slide industrials; sls/mktg presentations; videoconferencing; guest for radio & TV talk/news/magazine progs; electronic press kits.

CMI (Celestial Mechanix Inc.). 612 Hampton Dr., Venice, Calif. 90291. (310) 392-8771. FAX: (310) 392-9179. Robert Benderson, pres.
Creates, develops & markets TV prom campaigns.

COMAC Corp. 565 Sinclair Rd., Milpitas, Calif. 95035-5470. (408) 945-1600. FAX: (408) 945-1135.
Literature distribution.

Camelot Entertainment Sales. 1700 Broadway, 35th Fl., New York 10019. (212) 315-4747. FAX: (212) 247-7674. Steven R. Hirsch, pres; Michael Auerbach Sr., VP eastern sls.
Full-svc sls & mktg rep.

Canaan Public Relations. 301 E. 47th St., New York 10017. (212) 223-0100; FAX: (212) 223-3737. Lee Canaan, pres.; Jed Canaan, VP.
Pub rels for diverse clientele: TV, hotels, spas, authors & performing artists.

Catspaw Productions Inc. 560 Dutch Valley Rd., Atlanta 30324. (404) 876-CATS. FAX: (404) 881-8409. G. Douglas Paul, pres; Sharon V. Paul, sec/treas/gen mgr; Ralph J. Destito, VP sls & mktg; Larry Melnick, VP bcst sls.

Celebrity Service International Inc. 1780 Broadway, Suite 300, New York 10019. (212) 245-1460. Vicki Bagley, pres.
Clearinghouse of info & rsch. Contact & access to celebrities & famous persons through a number of svcs & publications. Publ; can get celebrities for spec events.

The Cellular Group Inc./Wireless Cable Division. 205 N. Orange Ave., Sarasota, Fla. 34236. (813) 957-0065. FAX: (813) 955-6586. David Bednarsh, pres; Henry Kavett, VP mktg; Joanne Bednarsh, VP finance & admin.
Wireless communications operators; cellular telephone systems; wireless cable systems; wireless communications mktg svcs.

Communication Bridges. 180 Harbor Dr., #204A, Sausalito, Calif. 94965. (415) 331-3133. FAX: (415) 331-3141. Jon Leland, pres/creative dir.
Video communication design, full creative svcs, animation design & prod including Mac II FX, scripts, concepts, live action.

Communication Planners Inc. Three Wedgewood Ct., Great Neck, N.Y. 11023. (212) 724-1204; (516) 487-1221. Martin G. Waldman, pres; Sandra Nemser Waldman, VP.
Pub rels, adv & communications counseling for corporations & organizations; pub affrs & campaign planning.

CommunicationMasters. Corporate Communications Ctr., 2900 Cole Ct., Norcross, Ga. 30071. (404) 263-6464. FAX: (404) 263-6624. Gerald A. Decker, pres.
Pub rels & mktg representation for companies involved in bcst, cable & other tech fields.

Community Club Awards Inc. Box 151, Corporate Communication Ctr., Westport, Conn. 06881. (203) 226-3377. FAX: (203) 222-0779. John C. Gilmore, pres; Bess Gilmore, exec VP; William Romot, comptroller; Tom Boone, VP sls.
Radio, TV, cable & nwspr sls prom campaigns.

The Hal Copeland Co. Inc. 314 Meadows Bldg., 5646 Milton St., Dallas 75206. (214) 361-8788. FAX: (214) 691-1573. Hal E. Copeland, pres; Ann Bryan Copeland, exec VP.
"Crisis Communications," "Motivational Station Breaks," & other svcs for prom & sponsorships. Rsch, writing & pub rels projects.

Creamer, Dickson, Basford Inc. 1000 Turks Head Bldg., Providence, R.I. 02903. (401) 456-1555. FAX: (401) 456-1538. Donald J. Goncolves, VP bus mgmt & client svcs; Ellen Miller, John Nero, VPs.
Natl firm specializing in business-to-business mktg, pub rels & communications.

DWJ Television. 16 E. 65th St., New York 10021. (212) 772-6600. FAX: (212) 772-6715. Daniel G. Johnson, pres; Michael L. Friedman, exec VP.
Specializing in TV pub rels; video news release prod & placement.

Steve Davis Public Relations. 320 E. 42nd St., New York 10017. (212) 697-3521. FAX: (212) 697-3522. Steve Davis, pres.
General pub rels agency with spec emphasis on sports, travel, fashion, bcstg & business svcs; spec events.

Direct Marketing Results (DMR). 1463 E. Galbraith Rd., Cincinnati 45215-5607. (513) 761-1463. FAX: (513) 761-0596. Jay Williams Jr., CEO; Michael Eisele, pres; Catherine Jung, VP radio; Lou Josephs, rsch dir; Brad Butler, mgr new technologies; Judy Baldwin, Perry Frey, mktg consultants.
Wayland, Mass. 01778: 35 Main St. (508) 653-7200. FAX: (508) 653-4088.
Full-svc mktg, consulting & prod firm offering custom direct mail, telemktg & database mgmt svcs to bcstrs exclusively.

Ditingo Media Enterprises. 100 Park Ave., New York 10017. (212) 308-8810; Vincent M. Ditingo, pres.
Media & mktg consulting, corporate writing, books, profiles, articles, speeches, brochures, video scripts, newsletters & periodicals for bcstg & cable.

Explosive Promotions Inc. 4801 S. University Dr., West Tower, Davie, Fla. 33328. (305) 680-8485. FAX: (305) 434-7594. Roy Rose, pres; Karen Demuth, account exec.
Value-added mktg by use of incentive/prom travel to top sport & mus events.

Faraone Communications Inc. 162 W. 56th St., Suite 1203, New York 10019. (212) 489-1313. FAX: on request. Jennie Faraone, chmn; Ted Faraone, pres.
Media rel & publ svcs for bcst industry clients on consulting or full-svc basis.

Milton Fenster Associates Inc. 540 Madison Ave., New York 10022. (212) 759-3540. Milton Fenster, pres.
Pub rels consultants.

First Marketing Co. 3300 Gateway Dr., Pompano Beach, Fla. 33069. (305) 979-0700. FAX: (303) 971-4707. Robert Legler, pres; W. Dale Martin, exec VP/dir sls & mktg; Thomas P. Johnson, VP/natl sls mgr; Neil L. Rosenblum, dir cable publications.
Publisher of customized newsletters (research, writing, design & printing).

Daniel Fox & Associates. 4121 W. Magonila Blvd., Burbank, Calif. 91505. (818) 841-3221. FAX: (818) 841-2166. Daniel Fox, pres.
Promotional announcements for game, talk, var, sports, etc., progs.

Freed & Associates Inc. 3600 Clipper Mill Rd., Suite 220, Baltimore 21211. (410) 243-1421. FAX: (410) 235-2108. Gloria Freed, pres; William Costello, exec VP; Steven Cline, VP account svcs; Robert Canale, VP/creative dir.

Fun Industries. 627 15th Ave., East Moline, Iowa 61244. (800) 747-1144. Melvin W. LaForce, co-own.
Cash cube "Money Machine" available for spec promotions. (Participants try to catch swirling money inside Plexiglass booth.)

GPR International Co. Three W. 51st St., Suite 605, New York 10019. (813) 923-0009. FAX: (212) 247-8759. John P. Grimaldi, pres/CEO.

Frank Gari Productions Inc. 10999 Riverside Dr., Suite 300, North Hollywood, Calif. 91602. (818) 509-0007. FAX: (818) 980-7888. Frank Gari, pres; Dick Glasser,

Public Relations, Publicity and Promotion Services

exec dir opns; Chris Gari, exec prod; Kimberly Gari, accounts exec; Lisa Baker, sls rep; Gordon Smith, dir creative svcs; Gary Young, southeastern sls dir.
Full-svc mus prod company.

Garrett Media Services Inc. 1119 San Antonio, El Paso, Tex. 79901. (915) 533-4700. Garrett W. Haston, pres.
Specializing in bcstg & entertainment fields.

Gold Nugget. Box 13 EE, San Antonio 78201. (512) 336-2739. Bobby L. Watson, pres; Martina Watson, VP.
Manufacturer & wholesaler of 14- & 18-carat gold jewelry, custom manufacturer of company logos & trademarks for use as sls incentives & awards.

S.J. Golden Associates. 300 E. 34th St., New York 10016. (212) 683-9672. Sherri Golden, pres.
Pub rels & mktg consultants specializing in the video & film industries.

William Hatfield. 212 Whitestone Rd., Silver Spring, Md. 20901. (301) 593-0184. William Hatfield, pres.

Hazel's Fantasy Factory. 1515 N. Portland, Oklahoma City, Okla. 73107. (405) 942-9960. FAX: (405) 943-9643. Claudia Lancaster, Diane Beleele, sls & mktg.
Specializes in custom walking character costumes, used for promotions & adv.

Hedicke & Associates Public Relations. 2277 Fair Oaks Blvd., Suite 330, Sacramento, Calif. 95825. (916) 641-6115. FAX: (916) 641-6277. Kathy Hedicke, pres.

Hill and Knowlton Public Affairs Worldwide. 901 31st St. N.W., Washington 20007. (202) 333-7400. FAX: (202) 333-1638. Tom Hoog, chmn/gen mgr; James C. Jennings, exec VP; Frank Mankiewicz, vice-chmn pub affrs; Gary Hymel, vice-chmn govt affrs.
International pub rels & pub affrs; planning & counseling for TV, radio & cable industries; creative svcs for prom & radio/TV prod.

Holman Communications. 1667 K St. N.W., Suite 390, Washington 20006. (202) 822-6804. FAX: (202) 822-0667. Diana Holman, pres.
A communications consulting firm emphasizing TV & CATV with capacity for video & film prod.

Horizon Media. 630 3rd Ave., New York 10017. (212) 916-8600. FAX: (212) 916-8669. Bill Koenigsberg, pres.
Media placement.

IGC/The Independent Group of Companies Inc. 971 Stuyvesant Ave., Union, N.J. 07083-6909. (908) 964-7111. FAX: (908) 964-5046. Henry C. Kavett, pres.
Wireless communications svcs; bcst & cable prom svcs.

Jacobs & Gerber Inc. 731 N. Fairfax Ave., Los Angeles 90046. (213) 655-4082. FAX: (213) 655-0195. Albert B. Litewka, pres/CEO; Stefan Gerber, sr VP/exec creative dir; Barbara Breest, VP finance & admin; Reggie Lundin, media dir.
Net, stn & entertainment company adv & prom; on-air; radio; nwspr & trade consumer magazines; collateral materials & outdoor adv/creative prod; animation; mus & lyrics.

Jennifer Jones Booking Agency. 523 Dumaine, Suite 6, New Orleans 70116. (504) 529-2543. FAX: (818) 899-4457. Jennifer Jones, pres.
Pub rels for diverse clientele—authors & performing artists, restaurants, hotels & spas.

Joe Jones & Marion Jones' Service. 10556 Arnwood Rd., Lake View Terrace, Calif. 91342. (818) 890-0730. FAX: (818) 899-4457. Marion Jones, pres; Joe Jones, dir mktg & promotions.
Clearance house of info to recording artists & celebrities.

The Kalmus Corp. 425 Madison Ave., 4th Fl., New York 10021. (212) 421-1122. Allan H. Kalmus, pres.
Pub rels & sports mktg firm.

M.A. Kempner Inc. 11820 Fountainside Cir., Boynton Beach, Fla. 33437. (407) 732-8895. FAX: (305) 360-7534. Marvin A. Kempner, pres/CEO.
Bcst syndication & specialty electronic equipment for media.

Klein. 1111 S. Robertson Blvd., Los Angeles 90035. (310) 278-5600. FAX: (310) 278-1454. Bob Klein, pres.
Bcst prom consultants.

The Philip Lesly Company. 155 N. Harbor Dr., Suite 5311, Chicago 60601. (312) 819-3590. FAX (312) 819-3592. Philip Lesly, pres.
Counsel & key creative svcs in pub rels, pub affrs & mass communications.

The Lippin Group. 6100 Wilshire Blvd., 4th Fl., Los Angeles 90048. (213) 965-1990. FAX: (213) 965-1993.
New York 10169: 230 Park Ave., 5th Fl. (212) 986-7080. FAX: (212) 986-2354.

Nancy Low & Associates Inc. 5454 Wisconsin Ave., Suite 1300, Chevy Chase, Md. 20815. (301) 951-9200. FAX: (301) 986-1641. Nancy O. Low, pres/creative dir; J. Michael Cosgrove, COO.
Pub rels, issues & svcs, mktg, communications counsel.

MJM Research & Programming. 11539 W. 83rd Terr., Lenexa, Kan. 66214. (800) 945-4MJM; (913) 888-3366. FAX: (913) 888-4423. C.C. McCartney, pres; Clark Roberts, VP.
Provides hook-tape prod, listener screening, fielding, & tabulation for all music testing, perceptual studies, focus groups, & promotional telemarketing.

Manning, Selvage & Lee. 79 Madison Ave., New York 10016. (212) 213-0909. Jim Grag, pres-USA; Kirk Stewart, chmn/CEO.
Pub rels svcs for all media.

Marcus Public Relations. 25700 Science Park Dr., Landmark Ctr., Cleveland 44122. (216) 292-4700. FAX: (216) 292-7219. King J. Hill, VP/dir.
An independent unit of Marcus Advertising Inc. handling media rel, publ & mktg communications.

May Co. 920 W. 7th St., Los Angeles 90017. (213) 627-8043.

Kenneth R. Meades. Box 1469, Los Angeles 90053. (213) 669-9670. Kenneth R. Meades, own.

Media Travel Services. 1119 E. San Antonio, El Paso 79901. (915) 533-4700. Michelle A. Haston, pres.
Provide promotional & travel incentives for bcstrs.

Howard Mendelsohn & Co. Inc. 500 N. Michigan Ave., Suite 1400, Chicago 60611. (312) 329-1815. Howard Mendelsohn, pres.
Pub rels & adv counsel.

Jay Mitchell Associates. Box 1285, Fairfield, Iowa 52556. (515) 472-4087. Jay Mitchell, pres; Lori Morgan, opns mgr; Dawn Bergendahl, speech & language therapist; Jeffrey Hedquest, sweeper & IDs.

Model/Auerbach & Co. 37 Riverside Dr., New York 10023. (212) 362-5141. FAX (212) 362-8373. F.P. Model, ptnr.
Sherman Oaks, Calif. 91423: 3887 Dixie Canyon Ave. (818) 501-4221. FAX: (818) 501-4211. Alexander Auerbach, ptnr.
Corporate & institutional pub rels, edit svcs, film/video scripts for bus, industry & nonprofit sectors.

Florence Morrison - Richard Roffman. *Cover The News,* 170 Westend Ave., New York 10023. (212) 724-9365. Florence Morrison, host/co-producer; Richard H. Roffman, co-producer.
Pub rels, publ, prom, personal representation, press releases, spec events, radio & TV prods, editorial svcs. *Florence Morrison/Richard Roffman Cover The News* WNWK/FM radio (Paragon & Manhattan cable) ch 16.

Network Ink Public Relations. 1101 18th Ave. S., Nashville 37212. (615) 320-5727. FAX: (615) 321-4569. Elizabeth Thiels, pres; Bunny Snow office mgr; Ellen Jones Pryor, account exec; Kevin Lane, Ray Crabtree, Calvin Gilbert, publicists.
Full-svc pub rel and entertainment mktg firm.

New York Communications Inc. 207 S. State Rd., Upper Darby, Pa. 19082. (215) 352-5505. FAX: (215) 352-6225. Michael Davis, pres.
Mktg, adv & prom consulting svcs to TV stns nationwide in all size markets. Philadelphia office.

North America Network. 7910 Woodmont Ave., Suite 1400, Bethsesda, Md. 20814. (301) 654-9810. FAX: (301) 654-9828. Tom Sweeney, pres; Julie Brown, VP opns; Steve Murphy, dir sls & stn svcs; Lisa Brusio Coster, stn svcs mgr.
Radio communications company providing media rel support to corporations, govt agencies & assns. Also audio news releases, talk show interviews, PSAs & syndicated progs.

Northern Lights Communications Inc. 10925 Valley View Rd., Suite 204, Eden Prairie, Minn. 55344. (612) 941-1254. FAX: (612) 941-1931. Jason Gould, CEO/dir media svcs; Dixon Gould, CFO/dir prog svcs; Jan Baaden Gee, account exec bcst progmg group.
Northern Lights Communications, a mktg communications company, works with bcstrs to generate new revenue sources through a var of media options.

Page Communications Inc. 111 Cloister Ct., Suite 120, Chapel Hill, N.C. 27514. (919) 967-1134. Robert C. Page III, pres/accounts mgr.

Partnership of Packer, Oesterling & Smith Inc. 124 State St., Harrisburg, Pa. 17101. (717) 232-1898. FAX: (717) 236-6793. Donald O. Oesterling, chmn; Carolyne L. Smith, pres; Virginia A. Roth, ptnr.
Adv, pub affrs, pub rels svcs, specializing in the cable TV industry.

Pittelli & Partners Inc. 414 Main St., Laurel, Md. 20707. (301) 206-5393. FAX: (301) 206-9112. Mary Pittelli, pres; Judith Williams, VP; Paul Jay Rodriguez, dir edit svcs; Lisa Sloan, dir media rel.

Porter/Novelli, Omnicom PR Network. 1633 Broadway, New York 10019. (212) 315-8000. FAX: (212) 315-8107. Bob Druckenmiller, pres.
Pub rels svcs for all media; contests & promotions for stns & sponsors.

Precious Products Corp. 366 5th Ave., New York 10001. (212) 947-4930. Edward K. Stupell, pres; Ruth Weinflash, dir sls.
Microphone I.D. flags, newscaster I.D. pins.

Pro-Media Network. Box 1122, Carlsbad, Calif. 92018. (619) 434-1308. FAX: (619) 434-1905.
Develops complete imprinted stickers, pens, key chains, mugs, etc. Adv, sls, promotional campaigns specializing in remotes, sports, concerts & safety progs.

Promotional Consideration Inc. 4121 W. Magnolia Blvd., Burbank, Calif. 91505. (818) 841-9053. FAX: (818) 841-2166. Arthur A. Alisi, pres; Daniel Fox, VP.

Publishers Support Services, a Division of Five Star Publications. 4696 W. Tyson St., Chandler, Ariz. 85226-2903. (602) 940-8182. FAX: (602) 940-8787. Linda F. Radke, publishing consultant.
Assists publishers with natl book publ, prom, mktg, & fulfillment. Also provides dev of promotional materials.

RPS Communications. 3 Bittersweet Ct., Centerport, N.Y. 11721. (516) 754-3300. FAX: (516) 754-8168. Randolph P. Savicky, pres; Dr. Barbara Panos-Savicky, VP; Stan Zlotnick, art dir.
Pub rels, mktg, adv & support svcs for the bcst, film, video & professional audio marketplaces, including prog prom.

RRN Inc. 111 5th Ave., Suite 1300, New York 10003. (212) 995-9800; (800) 451-3622. FAX: (212) 995-9848. Anthony S. Niskanen, pres; Patricia M. Barnes, opns mgr.
Sls promotions for radio & TV.

Radio Etcetera. 1000 Business Center Cir., Suite 213, Newbury Park, Calif. 91320. (800) 767-1267; (805) 499-8848. FAX: (805) 499-9971. Rick Lemmo, pres.
Produces direct mail & P.O.S. sls & progmg concepts to build revenue & ratings. Products include "Letter Perfect the Radio Game," "Radio Census," "Music Trivia Scratch & Win" in addition to customized concepts.

The Radioguide People Inc. 24725 W. 12 Mile Rd., Suite 316, Southfield, Mich. 48034. (810) 355-0022. FAX: (810) 353-0660. Arthur R. Vuolo Jr., pres; Barry M. Grant C.P.A., sr VP.
Publishes travel radio guides in assn with AM/FM stns.

Ridini & Associates. 335 N. Maple Dr., Suite 350, Beverly Hills, Calif. 90210. (310) 285-6306. FAX: (310) 285-6190. TELEX: (213) 493-8846. Maryann Ridini.

Martin Roberts & Associates Inc. 270 N. Canon Dr., Suite 103, Beverly Hills, Calif. 90210. (310) 273-0381. FAX: (818) 990-6802. Martin Roberts, pres; Robert Loper, VP.
Adv, pub rels, & rsch in motion picture, TV & home video.

George Rodman Associates. 3785 Via Nona Marie, Suite 310, Carmel, Calif. 93923. (408) 626-1630. FAX: (408) 625-1250. George T. Rodman, pres; Sally M. Rodman, VP/client svcs mgr.
Provides complete mktg counseling, materials, adv campaigns, logos, video design, image campaigns, animation, & spots to stns, nets, groups & prog suppliers.

Rogers & Cowan Inc. 10000 Santa Monica Blvd., Los Angeles 90067. (310) 201-8800. FAX: (310) 552-0412. Thomas A. Tardio, pres/CEO; Paul Bloch, vice-chmn.

Daniel S. Roher Inc. Public Relations. 228 E. 45th St., New York 10017. (212) 986-6668. Daniel S. Roher, pres; Richard S. Roher, COO.
Mktg, corporate communications & market rsch in business to busines & consumer industries. Partner: PR Organization International.

Public Relations, Publicity and Promotion Services

Rosen & Associates Ltd.(Marketing/Public Relations). 200 Park Ave., New York 10025-6658. (212) 751-2970. Fred Rosen.
Pub rels (professional & association) for non-profit organizations, & healthcare mktg for pharmaceutical companies, hospitals, & physicians.

William Russell & Associates Inc. 5340 Holmes Pkwy., Suite 712, Alexandria, Va. 22304. (703) 751-8610. FAX: (703) 751-8611. William A. Russell Jr., pres; Garrett N. Scalera, Asia rep.
Govt rel & mktg consultants specializing in telecommunications & international trade.

Ryder Communications Inc. 3111 University Dr., Suite 406, Coral Springs, Fla. 33065. (305) 753-6666. FAX: (305) 753-9505. David Ryder, pres.
Value-added viewer/advertiser telephone info systems on 800 or 900. Turnkey for contesting, info, rsch & polling.

SCA Promotions Inc. 8300 Douglas Ave., Suite 625, Dallas 75225. (800) 527-5409. FAX: (214) 691-3071. Robert D. Hamman, pres; Doug McCrum, exec VP.

Arnold Singer Co. 733 3rd Ave., 9th Fl., New York 10017. (212) 297-0133. FAX: (212) 297-0139.
Pub rels & mktg communications.

The Wayne Smith Co. Inc. 1300 L St. N.W., Suite 1050, Washington 20005-4107. (202) 484-5620. FAX: (202) 898-0484. Wayne J. Smith, pres; Leslie Milsten, account exec.
Adv, pub rels, & publ.

The Solomen Agency Inc. 25454 Hardy Pl., Stevenson Ranch, Calif. 91381-1504. (805) 255-9956. FAX: (805) 255-9957. Jack Solomen, pres.
Complete mktg & pub rels svcs.

Stone/Hallinan Public Relations Associates Inc. 1350 Ave. of the Americas, Suite 1800, New York 10019. (212) 489-5590. FAX: (212) 582-4802.
Los Angeles 90046: 7449 Melrose Ave. (213) 655-8970.

TV Cableguide. 2069 Zumbehl Rd., Suite 81, St. Charles, Mo. 63303. (314) 949-8000. Annette Brooks, VP/mktg dir; Franklin Brooks, pres.
Customized or generic magazines tailored to individual CATV systems.

TV Data Technologies. Northway Plaza, Queensbury, N.Y. 12804. (800) 833-9581. FAX: (518) 793-2852. Kathleen Wern, sls mgr; Lawrence Shulman, dir new bus dev; Richard Guay, market dev specialist.
Svcs include custom-formatted TV listings delivered via overnight courier (camera-ready), electronic modem (MacIntosh computer) or dedicated phone lines.

Talkline Communications Advertising Agency. Box 20108, Parkwest Station, New York 10025-1510. (212) 769-1925; (800) 628-TALK. FAX: (212) 799-4195. Zev J. Brenner, pres.
Specializes in radio promotion & advertising geared to the Jewish & ethnic markets.

TeleWords Corporate Communications. 1011 4th St., Santa Monica, Calif. 90403. (310) 451-9851. FAX: (310) 394-0454. Ruth Macy, pres.
Press releases, corporate communications, mktg communications & editorial svcs for companies in the bcstg, CATV & satellite communications industries.

Tracy-Locke Inc. Box 50129, 200 Crescent Ct., Dallas 75250. (214) 969-9000. FAX: (214) 855-2479. Mike Rawlings, pres/CEO; David Fowler, chmn/chief creative off.
Full-svc community rels company with specialty svcs in sls prom, pub rels, direct mktg, business-to-business communications & Hispanic mktg.

Trylon Communications Inc. 231 W. 29th St., Suite 205, New York 10001. (212) 268-3888. FAX: (212) 643-0688. Lloyd Trufelman, pres.
Arranges media tours, produces video news releases, spec event planning, specialty publishing, direct mail, & communications rsch & audits. Areas of expertise include cable nets & MSOs, TV prods, radio programmers, equipment manufacturers, media brokerage, & financial & legal firms.

21st Century Robotics. 3042 Adriatic Ct., Norcross, Ga. 30071. (404) 448-6348. FAX: (404) 446-6295. Thomas P. Zaken, pres.
Robots for promotional use, sale or rent.

2B System Corp. 6575 Arrow Dr., Sterling Heights, Mich. 48078. (313) 254-6900. FAX: (313) 254-1765. Scott Smith, chmn; Matthew Mrowczynski, dir bcst prom.
Manufacturer of plastic card promotions for radio & TV stns.

Vibration Promotions Inc. 500 5th Ave., Suite 1021, New York 10110. (212) 764-2555. FAX: (212) 764-2558. Ronald M. Cohen, pres.
T-shirts, jackets, buttons, & other promotional merchandise. Barter svcs.

A.G. Visk. 2973 Evans Oaks Ct., Atlanta 30340. (404) 939-5657. Tony Visk, pres/own.
Promotional concepts, scripts & publications for the bcstg & entertainment industries.

Visual Resources Inc. 1556 N. Fairfax Ave., Los Angeles 90046. (213) 851-6688. FAX: (213) 876-5396.
Specializes in mktg, adv & sls prom.

Vonco Products. 201 Park Ave., Lake Villa, Ill. 60046. (708) 356-2323. L.L. Laske, pres.
Manufacturers of premium items, puppets, kites.

Morton Dennis Wax & Associates Inc. 1560 Broadway, New York 10036. (212) 302-5360. FAX: (212) 302-5364. Morton Dennis Wax, pres; Sandra Wax, treas.
Consumer & financial pub rels, including sponsorship & tie-ins.

Wishner Communications Ltd. 440 Park Ave. S., New York 10016. (212) 725-0006. FAX: (212) 545-0446. Howard E. Wishner, pres.
Corporate communications, pub rels & mktg.

Section G
Programming Services

Table of Contents

Table of Contents G-1
Producers, Distributors, Production and Other Services
   Subject Index G-2
   Alphabetical Index G-9
Radio Programming Services
   Major National Radio Networks G-36
   Public Broadcasting - Radio G-48
   Radio Program Networks G-49
   Regional Radio Networks G-51
   Unwired Radio Networks G-54
   Canadian Radio Networks G-55
   Radio News Services G-56
   Radio Format Providers G-59
Television Programming Services
   Major National Television Networks G-62
   Public Broadcasting - Television G-68
   Television Program Networks G-69
   Regional Television Networks G-70
   Unwired Television Networks G-71
   Canadian Television Networks G-72
   Television News Services G-74
   Closed Circuit Television G-77
Cable Programming Services
   Pay Cable Services G-78
   Basic Cable Services G-79
   Automated Cable Channel Programmers G-83
   Audio Cable Programming Services G-84
   Regional Cable Television News Services G-85
   Cable Sports Services G-86
   Canadian Cable Programming Services G-88
Other Programming Services
   Music Licensing Groups G-89
   Videotext Operations G-90
   Teletext Operations G-91
   Subcarrier/VBI Services G-92

Broadcasting & Cable Yearbook 1994

Producers, Distributors, Production and Other Services Subject Index

Companies are generally classified under their primary services and may be listed under one or more subject areas. Refer to the *Alphabetical Index* for complete company information.

3-D FILMS
3-D Video Corp.
Jack Lieb Productions
Spatial Technologies Inc.

3-D TV SYSTEMS
3-D Video Corp.
Spatial Technologies Inc.

AGRICULTURAL PROGRAMMING, RADIO
Hometown Illinois Radio Network
Israel Broadcasting Service
Radio Sound Network
Ray Communications Inc.
Tribune Radio Networks

ANIMATION
Buzzco Associates Inc.
Calico Entertainment
Caridi Entertainment
Cascom International Inc.
Chicago Symphony Orchestra/Amoco Radio Network
Cinema Concepts Communications Inc.
Digital Animation Corp.
Devlin Design Group
Electric Paint and Design
Northwest Imaging & F.X.
Pantomime Pictures
Paragon International Inc.
Pike Productions Inc.

AUDIO PRODUCTION
All Productions
Armedia Communications
Audio Creations
The Audio Department Inc.
Century III at Universal Studios
Clausen Communications Inc.
Command Productions
Continental Recordings Inc.
Cornell University Media Services
Creative Media Associates Inc.
D-V-X International
Ecumenical Communications
Editel-Chicago
Four Star Media
Horizon Audio Creations
Irving Productions Inc.
Larsong Productions
MPL Film & Video
Ben Manilla Productions
William Mauldin Productions Inc.
MediaTracks Inc.
Ellis Molton Advertising
MotorNet
MotorPro
New Dimensions Radio
PAMS Productions/PAMS Jingles
Perceptions
Players Music Inc.
Protestant Radio and Television Center Inc.
Radio Spirits Inc.
Radio Today Entertainment
Reizner & Reizner Film & Video
Strand Broadcast Services
SyberVision Systems Inc.
TeleScene
Toes Productions Inc.
Morrie Trumble & Associates
U.S. Air Force Recruiting Service
United Sound Systems Inc.
WFMT Fine Arts Network
WNGN-FM Hoosick Falls, N.Y.
ZBS Foundation

AUDIO PRODUCTION LIBRARY
Center City Film & Video
FirstCom Broadcast Services
Happi Associates
Man From Mars Productions
Ray Norman Productions Inc.
Omnimusic
SyberVision Systems Inc.
United Sound Systems Inc.

AUDIO RECORDING SERVICES
The Audio Department Inc.
Command Productions
D-V-X International
Horizon Audio Creations
House of Music
Irving Productions Inc.
Lion & Fox Recording Inc.
R & M Productions
Radio Production Services Inc.
Ross-Gaffney Inc.
Shield Productions Inc.
Toes Productions Inc.
United Sound Systems Inc.

AUDIO/VISUAL SERVICES
Academy Film Productions Inc.
Thomas Craven Film Corp.
Encore Teleproductions Corp.
Image Devices International Inc.
Irving Productions Inc.
Protestant Radio and Television Center Inc.
SWTV Production Services Inc.

BACKGROUND MUSIC
Airforce Broadcast Services Inc.
Combs Music
Horizon Audio Creations
Eddy Manson Productions/Margery Music Co.
Ray Norman Productions Inc.
TRF Production Music Libraries

CD PRODUCTION LIBRARY
Airforce Broadcast Services Inc.
FirstCom Broadcast Services
Manhattan Production Music
Ray Norman Productions Inc.
Omnimusic

CAMERA OPERATORS
African Family Films
Bell Foto Art Productions
FTC/New York
FTC/Orlando
Image Devices International Inc.
Larsong Productions
Limelight Communication Inc.
Lindberg Productions Inc.
Nemo News
Reizner & Reizner Film & Video
The Seattle Bureau
Sullivan Video Services Inc.
Worldwide Television News
Sandy Zimmerman Productions

CASSETTE DUPLICATING
Command Productions
Cornell University Media Services
DeLuxe Laboratories Inc.
HAVE Inc.
Tom Jones Recording Studios
Lion & Fox Recording Inc.
MPL Film & Video
Protestant Radio and Television Center Inc.
R & M Productions
Teleworld Inc.
United Sound Systems Inc.
Video West
WRS/Channel One-Division of WRS

CHILDREN'S PROGRAMMING, RADIO
American International Productions
We Like Kids!

CHILDREN'S PROGRAMMING, RADIO & TV
KIDSNET
Story Time Stories That Rhyme

CHILDREN'S PROGRAMMING, TV
BBC Lionheart Television
S. Banks (In Television) Ltd.
Buzzco Associates Inc.
Calico Entertainment
Caridi Entertainment
Children's Media Productions
Films for Educators Inc./Films for Television
Glenray Productions Inc.
Hearst Entertainment
Janson Associates
MTM Enterprises Inc.
Maryland Public Television
Muller Media Inc.
Pantomime Pictures
Redwood Entertainment Inc.
Vide-U Productions
World Wide Syndications Corp.

COMMERCIAL DISTRIBUTION, RADIO
Al Ham Productions dba Music of Your Life
KJD Teleproductions
Larsong Productions
Dick Orkin's Amazing Radio
Radio America
Strand Broadcast Services
Teleworld Inc.

COMMERCIAL DISTRIBUTION, RADIO & TV
All Productions
Vitt Media International Inc.

COMMERCIAL DISTRIBUTION, TV
Classic Films International Inc.
Fishing the West
Thomas Horton Associates Inc.
KJD Teleproductions
National Film Board of Canada
Northwest Imaging & F.X.
Video-Cinema Films Inc.

COMMERCIAL PRODUCTION, RADIO
Audio Creations
The Audio Department Inc.
Continental Recordings Inc.
Creative Media Associates Inc.
Globe Productions
KJD Teleproductions
William Mauldin Productions Inc.
MotorNet
MotorPro
Dick Orkin's Amazing Radio
Perceptions
Protestant Radio and Television Center Inc.
Radio America
Radio Today Entertainment
Strand Broadcast Services
Time Capsule Inc.
WNGN-FM Hoosick Falls, N.Y.

COMMERCIAL PRODUCTION, RADIO & TV
Academy Film Productions Inc.
Airwaves Audio Inc.
The Church of Jesus Christ of Latter-Day Saints
Goodman Productions
Irving Productions Inc.
Eddy Manson Productions/Margery Music Co.
Maysles Films Inc.
Metro Studios & Post Production Inc.
New York Communications Inc.
Perceptions
Prime Productions

Producers, Distributors, Production and Other Services Subject Index

R & M Productions
TeleScene

COMMERCIAL PRODUCTION, TV
9KUSA Productions
ADCO Productions
Bell Foto Art Productions
Buzzco Associates Inc.
Calico Entertainment
Circle Video Productions
Consumer Savings Network
Creative Media Associates Inc.
Encore Teleproductions Corp.
Fishing the West
Thomas Horton Associates Inc.
Independent Artists
KJD Teleproductions
Longworth Communications Inc.
MRG Production Associates Inc.
Maysles Films Inc.
Miller & Luria
Warren Miller Entertainment
Montgomery Community Television Inc.
Nemo News
New York Communications Inc.
Pantomime Pictures
Pegasus Broadcasting of San Juan Inc.
ProVideo
Quality Film and Video
Carl Ragsdale Associates Inc.
Sullivan Video Services Inc.
Video West
WO4AT - Hoosick Falls, N.Y.
Welwood International Film Production/Syndication
Worldwide Television News

COMPUTER GRAPHICS
Atlantic Video Inc.
Calico Entertainment
Century III at Universal Studios
Cinema Concepts Communications Inc.
Editel-Chicago
Electric Paint and Design
MPL Film & Video
Pike Productions Inc.
RW VIDEO Inc.
Rampion Visual Productions
Yada/Levine Productions

CREATIVE SERVICES
American Video Productions
Gene Bayliss
Bonneville Communications
Calico Entertainment
Cinema Concepts Communications Inc.
Consumer Savings Network
Creative Media Associates Inc.
Devlin Design Group
Focal Point Film Productions
Globe Net Productions
Happi Associates
Imero Fiorentino Associates Inc.
Independent Artists
KIDSNET
Klein &
Lindberg Productions Inc.
Eddy Manson Productions/Margery Music Co.
Ellis Molton Advertising
New York Communications Inc.
Dick Orkin's Amazing Radio
Pantomime Pictures
Peters Productions Inc.
Pike Productions Inc.
Prime Productions
ProCom Associates Inc.
ProVideo
Russ Reid Company
Sound of Birmingham Productions
Talco Productions
Toes Productions Inc.
Ventures in Media
Welwood International Film Production/Syndication
World Wide Syndications Corp.
Sandy Zimmerman Productions

DEVELOPMENT, FILMS
Caridi Entertainment
Ebbets Field Productions Ltd.
Focal Point Film Productions
Fries Entertainment Inc.
Hargrove Entertainment Inc.
Lighthorse Productions
ProVideo

DEVELOPMENT, FILMS, TV SERIES & VIDEO
9KUSA Productions
ADCO Productions
Academy Film Productions Inc.
All Media Productions Inc.
Anderson Productions Ltd.
BBC Lionheart Television
Dave Bell Associates Inc.
Circle Video Productions
Fries Entertainment Inc.
Glenray Productions Inc.
Independent Artists
International Program Consultants Inc.
Jack Lieb Productions
Lighthorse Productions
Marquee Entertainment Inc.
Maysles Films Inc.
New York Communications Inc.
Pantomime Pictures
Redwood Entertainment Inc.
Turner Entertainment Co.
V.I.E.W. Video Inc.
Ventures in Media
Video/Films International Inc. (VFI)
Vitt Media International Inc.

DEVELOPMENT, TV FILMS, SERIES
ADCO Productions
S. Banks (In Television) Ltd.
Dave Bell Associates Inc.
CanLib
Capital Cities/ABC Video Enterprises
Ebbets Field Productions Ltd.
Sandy Frank Entertainment Inc.
Hargrove Entertainment Inc.
Independent Artists
Janson Associates
MAN QC Creations Inc.
MRG Production Associates Inc.
MTM Enterprises Inc.
Paramount Television Group
Rysher TPE
VPI - Videfilm Producers International, Ltd.
Ventures in Media
Vide-U Productions

DEVELOPMENT, VIDEO
Agency for Instructional Technology (AIT)
Anderson Productions Ltd.
Beach Associates
Hargrove Entertainment Inc.
Lindberg Productions Inc.
MAN QC Creations Inc.
Montgomery Community Television Inc.
Reiss Media Enterprises Inc.
SyberVision Systems Inc.

DISTRIBUTION, AUDIO
Radio Sound Network
Ray Communications Inc.
ZBS Foundation

DISTRIBUTION, CABLE
Anderson Productions Ltd.
Broadcast Programming
Bruder Releasing Inc. (BRI)
Cable Films
Capital Cities/ABC Video Enterprises
Favorite TV
Hargrove Entertainment Inc.
Hearst Entertainment
Marquee Entertainment Inc.
National Film Board of Canada
Pro Am Sports System/Pass Sports
Reel Movies International Inc.
SFM Entertainment
Video-Cinema Films Inc.
Virginia Tech, CNS (Communications Network Services)

DISTRIBUTION, CARTOONS
Classic Films International Inc.
Favorite TV
Hearst Entertainment
Paragon International Inc.
Reel Movies International Inc.
Turner Program Services

DISTRIBUTION, FILM AND VIDEO
African Family Films
All Media Productions Inc.
Asia Pacific Productions
Bruder Releasing Inc. (BRI)
Cable Films
Children's Media Productions
The Cinema Guild Inc.
Classic Films International Inc.
Favorite TV
Films for Educators Inc./Films for Television
Films for the Humanities Inc./FFH Video
Fries Entertainment Inc.
Group W Video Services
Handel Film Corporation
Hargrove Entertainment Inc.
Hearst Entertainment
Raymond Horn Syndication Inc.
INTERAMA Inc.
Janson Associates
Walter J. Klein Co. Ltd.
Marquee Entertainment Inc.
National Film Board of Canada
New Century Telecommunications
New City Releasing Inc.
New Visions Entertainment
Pike Productions Inc.
Reel Movies International Inc.
SyberVision Systems Inc.
Teleworld Inc.
Turner Entertainment Co.
V.I.E.W. Video Inc.
VPI - Videfilm Producers International, Ltd.
Video-Cinema Films Inc.
WRS/Channel One Division of WRS

DISTRIBUTION, MUSIC
Reel Movies International Inc.

DISTRIBUTION, RADIO & TV PROGRAMMING
All Productions
Bonneville Communications
The Church of Jesus Christ of Latter-Day Saints
Goodman Productions
Lutheran Hour Ministries
Russ Reid Company
Tutman Productions
World Wrestling Federation

DISTRIBUTION, RADIO PROGRAMMING
Daynet Radio
Fred Hall Productions
Happi Associates
Heil Enterprises
Host Communications Inc.
J&H Music Programming Inc.
Ben Manilla Productions
MotorNet
MotorPro
Music Director Programming Service
New Dimensions Radio
Dick Orkin's Amazing Radio
PAMS Productions/PAMS Jingles
Premiere Radio Networks Inc.
RPM-Radio Programming & Management Inc.
Radio America
Radio Production Services Inc.
Radio Spirits Inc.
Ray Communications Inc.
Sound Source
Sports Entertainment Network
Tribune Radio Networks
Tutman Productions
WFMT Fine Arts Network

DISTRIBUTION, TV PROGRAMMING
BBC Lionheart Television
Bruder Releasing Inc. (BRI)
Bill Burrud Productions Inc.
CS Associates
Cable Films
CanLib
Capital Cities/ABC Video Enterprises International
Children's Media Productions
Classic Films International Inc.
Ellis Enterprises Ltd.
Favorite TV
Films for Educators Inc./Films for Television
Sandy Frank Entertainment Inc.

Producers, Distributors, Production and Other Services Subject Index

Freedom Sports Network
Fries Entertainment Inc.
GalaVision Inc.
Genesis Entertainment
Gray-Schwartz Enterprises Inc.
Group W Video Services
Hargrove Entertainment Inc.
Hearst Entertainment
Raymond Horn Syndication Inc.
Host Communications Inc.
INTERAMA Inc.
ITC Television/Cinema Distribution Inc.
International Program Consultants Inc.
Longworth Communications Inc.
MGM/Television Canada
MTM Enterprises Inc.
Marquee Entertainment Inc.
Maryland Public Television
Muller Media Inc.
National Film Board of Canada
New Century Telecommunications
New Visions Entertainment
Paragon International Inc.
Paramount Television Group
Prime Cut Productions Inc.
Pro Am Sports System/Pass Sports
Promark
Reel Movies International Inc.
Reiss Media Enterprises Inc.
Reuters Television
Rhodes Productions
Richter Productions Inc.
Roberts Television International Inc.
Rysher TPE
SFM Entertainment
Turner Program Services
VPI - Videfilm Producers International, Ltd.
Video-Cinema Films Inc.
Wold Productions Co.
World Wide Syndications Corp.
Worldview Entertainment Inc.
Worldvision Enterprises Inc.
Worldwide Television News

DUBBING SERVICES

Audio Creations
Glenray Productions Inc.
Group W Video Services
House of Music
Irving Productions Inc.
Quality Film and Video
Video/Films International Inc. (VFI)

DUPLICATION SERVICES

American International Productions
Audio Creations
The Audio Department Inc.
Daley Tele-Video Productions
Film/Audio Services Inc.
HAVE Inc.
Highland Laboratories
Tom Jones Recording Studios
MPL Film & Video
Metro Studios & Post Production Inc.
Northwest Imaging & F.X.
Pro Video
Quark Video
Sifford Video Services Inc.
Teleworld Inc.
Video West
Sandy Zimmerman Productions

EDITING SERVICES

American Video Productions
Center City Film & Video
Century III at Universal Studios
Circle Video Productions
Crystal Productions
Editel-Chicago
Electric Paint and Design
Globe Net Productions
HAVE Inc.
Image Devices International Inc.
Walter J. Klein Co. Ltd.
MRG Production Associates Inc.
Montgomery Community Television Inc.
Pro Video
ProCom Associates Inc.
Riviera Productions
Ross-Gaffney Inc.
Sullivan Video Services Inc.
Teleworld Inc.

Trick Bag
Video I-D Inc.
Yada/Levine Productions

EDUCATIONAL PROGRAMMING, RADIO

Endless Mountains Radio Productions Inc.
KCSN 88.5 FM
Little Chicago
National Federation of Community Broadcasters
New Dimensions Radio
Sound Source
Souvenirs of the 60's
Strand Broadcast Services

EDUCATIONAL PROGRAMMING, RADIO & TV

All Productions
Army Reserve Pentagon, Office of the Chief
BBC Lionheart Television
The Church of Jesus Christ of Latter-Day Saints
Faith for Today
KIDSNET
Story Time Stories That Rhyme
University of Detroit Mercy

EDUCATIONAL PROGRAMMING, TV

9KUSA Productions
Agency for Instructional Technology (AIT)
All Media Productions Inc.
Bill Burrud Productions Inc.
Buzzco Associates Inc.
Capital Cities/ABC Video Enterprises
ETN - Educational Telecommunications Network
Films for Educators Inc./Films for Television
Globe Net Productions
Hamilton Productions Inc.
Ivanhoe Broadcast News Corporation
Janson Associates
Longworth Communications Inc.
MRG Production Associates Inc.
Maryland Public Television
Maysles Films Inc.
Modern Sound Pictures Inc.
Burt Munk & Co.
National Film Board of Canada
Scola
WO4AT - Hoosick Falls, N.Y.
WTOB Channel 2 - Public/Government Access T.V.

ENTERTAINMENT PROGRAMMING, RADIO

American International Productions
Broadcast Programming
Fred Hall Productions
Happi Associates
KCSN 88.5 FM
Little Chicago
Ben Manilla Productions
MediaTracks Inc.
Premiere Radio Networks Inc.
Radio Production Services Inc.
Sam Shad Productions
Sound Source
Souvenirs of the 60's
Time Capsule Inc.
Trick Bag
Morrie Trumble & Associates
U.S. Air Force Recruiting Service
WFMT Fine Arts Network

ENTERTAINMENT PROGRAMMING, RADIO & TV

Bailey Broadcasting Services
Barnes Communications Inc.
Faith for Today
Arthur Henley Productions
Pantomime Pictures
Redwood Entertainment Inc.
Sam Shad Productions
Story Time Stories That Rhyme
World Wide Syndications Corp.
World Wrestling Federation

ENTERTAINMENT PROGRAMMING, TV

9KUSA Productions
Anderson Productions Ltd.
BBC Lionheart Television
Bill Burrud Productions Inc.
Cable Films
Calico Entertainment
Channel America Television Network

Circle Video Productions
Consumer Savings Network
Daynet Radio
Favorite TV
Sandy Frank Entertainment Inc.
GEMS Television
Glenray Productions Inc.
Gray-Schwartz Enterprises Inc.
Reg Grundy Productions Inc.
International Program Consultants Inc.
Janson Associates
Lighthorse Productions
MAN QC Creations Inc.
MTM Enterprises Inc.
Modern Sound Pictures Inc.
Muller Media Inc.
National Film Board of Canada
New City Releasing Inc.
New York Communications Inc.
Prime Cut Productions Inc.
Reel Movies International Inc.
Reid/Land Productions Inc.
Reiss Media Enterprises Inc.
Rhodes Productions
The Seattle Bureau
Telepros
V.I.E.W. Video Inc.
Ventures in Media
WO4AT - Hoosick Falls, N.Y.
WTOB Channel 2 - Public/Government Access T.V.
Wold Productions Co.

FILM LABORATORIES

DeLuxe Laboratories Inc.
MPL Film & Video
Quality Film and Video
WRS/Channel One-Division of WRS

FILM PRESERVATION/RESTORATION

Turner Entertainment Co.

FILM AND TAPE TRANSFERS (FILM-TO-TAPE)

Atlantic Video Inc.
Center City Film & Video
Century III at Universal Studios
DWJ Television
DeLuxe Laboratories Inc.
Editel-Chicago
Film/Audio Services Inc.
HAVE Inc.
TeleScene

GRAPHIC EFFECTS LIBRARY

Cascom International Inc.

GRAPHICS

Atlantic Video Inc.
Center City Film & Video
Devlin Design Group
Editel-Chicago
Electric Paint and Design
The Image Group
Ellis Molton Advertising
Peters Productions Inc.
Videosmith Inc.

INDUSTRIAL FILMS

Academy Film Productions Inc.
D-V-X International
Encore Teleproductions Corp.
Imero Fiorentino Associates Inc.
Independent Artists
Jack Lieb Productions
Limelight Communication Inc.
Lindberg Productions Inc.
Mason Video
Burt Monk & Co.
Nemo News
Prime Productions
Quality Film and Video
Talco Productions

INFLIGHT AUDIO PROGAMMING

All Productions
Combs Music
Endless Mountains Radio Productions Inc.
Horizon Audio Creations
House of Music
MSE

Producers, Distributors, Production and Other Services Subject Index

Sound Source
Time Capsule Inc.

INTERACTIVE TELEVISION

Interactive Network Inc.

INTERACTIVE TELEVISION PROGRAMMING

ACTV Inc.

JINGLES

Audio Creations
Tim Cissell Music
Command Productions
Continental Recordings Inc.
Goodman Productions
Happi Associates
PAMS Productions/PAMS Jingles
Peters Productions Inc.
Premiere Radio Networks Inc.
R & M Productions
Shield Productions Inc.
Sound of Birmingham Productions
Station Break Music Productions

LIBRARIES, FILM

Caridi Entertainment
Classic Films International Inc.
Walter J. Klein Co. Ltd.
Warren Miller Entertainment
New Century Telecommunications
New Visions Entertainment
Turner Entertainment Co.
Worldwide Television News

LIBRARIES, TV

BBC Lionheart Television
Thomas Horton Associates Inc.
New Century Telecommunications
New Visions Entertainment
Reuters Television
Turner Entertainment Co.
Worldvision Enterprises Inc.
Worldwide Television News

LIBRARIES, VIDEO

Cascom International Inc.
Handel Film Corporation
Story Time Stories That Rhyme

LICENSING SERVICES

Barnes Communications Inc.
Manhattan Production Music
Turner Entertainment Co.

LOCATION SERVICES

MRG Production Associates Inc.

MEDICAL PROGRAMMING, RADIO

MediaTracks Inc.

MEDICAL PROGRAMMING, RADIO & TV

Faith for Today
MSE
Tutman Productions

MEDICAL PROGRAMMING, TV

Bell Foto Art Productions
Hamilton Productions Inc.
Ivanhoe Broadcast News Corporation
Mason Video
Maysles Films Inc.
Metro Studios & Post Production Inc.
Nemo News

MOBILE PRODUCTION UNITS

American Video Productions
Nemo News
The Seattle Bureau
Teletainment Inc.

MUSIC COMPOSITION

Tim Cissell Music
Combs Music
Eddy Manson Productions/Margery Music Co.
Players Music Inc.
R & M Productions
Station Break Music Productions
Sutcliffe Music Inc.

MUSIC LIBRARIES

Airforce Broadcast Services Inc.
Associated Production Music
FirstCom Broadcast Services
Fred Hall Productions
Manhattan Production Music
Music Director Programming Service
Omnimusic
Promusic Inc.
SoperSound Music Library
Sound Ideas
Station Break Music Productions
TRF Production Music Libraries

MUSIC LYRICS

Audible Advertising Productions Inc.
Cummings Productions
Lone Star Humor Consulting & Creative Services
Wawatay Native Communication Society

MUSIC PRODUCTION

Airforce Broadcast Services Inc.
Armedia Communications
Chicago Symphony Orchestra/Amoco Radio Network
Combs Music
Eddy Manson Productions/Margery Music Co.
Music Director Programming Service
PAMS Productions/PAMS Jingles
Protestant Radio and Television Center Inc.
SoperSound Music Library
Sound of Birmingham Productions
Station Break Music Productions
United Sound Systems Inc.

MUSIC PRODUCTION, FILM AND VIDEO

Tim Cissell Music
Players Music Inc.

MUSIC PRODUCTION, RADIO

Cadena Radio Centro (CRC Radio Network)
Continental Recordings Inc.
Globe Productions
J&H Music Programming Inc.
Music Director Programming Service
Ray Norman Productions Inc.
Premiere Radio Networks Inc.
Radio Today Entertainment
SoperSound Music Library
Morrie Trumble & Associates

MUSIC PRODUCTION, RADIO & TV

Tim Cissell Music
Al Ham Productions dba Music of Your Life
Peters Productions Inc.
Players Music Inc.
Shield Productions Inc.
Sutcliffe Music Inc.

MUSIC PRODUCTION, TV

Caridi Entertainment
Continental Recordings Inc.

MUSIC PROGRAMMING, RADIO

Broadcast Programming
Globe Productions
Horizon Audio Creations
House of Music
J&H Music Programming Inc.
Little Chicago
Ben Manilla Productions
Music Director Programming Service
Radio Today Entertainment
Sing for Joy
Souvenirs of the 60's
Trick Bag
WFMT Fine Arts Network
WNGN-FM Hoosick Falls, N.Y.

MUSIC SCORING

Associated Production Music
Cinema Concepts Communications Inc.
Lion & Fox Recording Inc.
R & M Productions
Station Break Music Productions
Sutcliffe Music Inc.
TRF Production Music Libraries

MUSIC SERVICES

House of Music
Manhattan Production Music
Music Director Programming Service
PAMS Productions/PAMS Jingles
Promusic Inc.

RPM-Radio Programming & Management Inc.
SoperSound Music Library

MUSIC AND SOUND EFFECTS

Associated Production Music
Films for the Humanities Inc./FFH Video
FirstCom Broadcast Services
Lion & Fox Recording Inc.
Ray Norman Productions Inc.
Omnimusic
PAMS Productions/PAMS Jingles
Promusic Inc.
Ross-Gaffney Inc.
SoperSound Music Library
Sound Ideas
Sutcliffe Music Inc.
TRF Production Music Libraries

MUSIC VIDEO PRODUCTION

African Family Films
Circle Video Productions
Redwood Entertainment Inc.
Vide-U Productions

NATURE PROGRAMMING, TV

Bill Burrud Productions Inc.
Films for Educators Inc./Films for Television
Thomas Horton Associates Inc.

NEWS PROGRAMMING, RADIO

American Stock Exchange - Radio AMEX
Bailey Broadcasting Services
Broadcast News Service
Cadena Radio Centro (CRC Radio Network)
Daynet Radio
Ecumedia News Service
KCSN 88.5 FM
Ben Manilla Productions
Metro Networks
Radio America
Ray Communications Inc.
Sound Source
Sports Entertainment Network
Morrie Trumble & Associates

NEWS PROGRAMMING, RADIO & TV

American Stock Exchange - Radio AMEX
Army Reserve Pentagon, Office of the Chief
Goodman Productions
Israel Broadcasting Service
MSE
News/Broadcast Network
Sam Shad Productions
Talco Productions
Tutman Productions

NEWS PROGRAMMING, TV

American Stock Exchange - Radio AMEX
Anderson Productions Ltd.
Bell Foto Art Productions
DWJ Television
Globe Net Productions
Hamilton Productions Inc.
Limelight Communication Inc.
Mason Video
Northern California News Satellite Inc.
Paramount Television Group
The Seattle Bureau
WO4AT - Hoosick Falls, N.Y.
Worldwide Television News

ORIGINAL MUSIC SCORING

Airforce Broadcast Services Inc.
Tim Cissell Music
Continental Recordings Inc.
Al Ham Productions dba Music of Your Life
Eddy Manson Productions/Margery Music Co.
Players Music Inc.
Sutcliffe Music Inc.
TRF Production Music Libraries

PERFORMING ARTS PROGRAMMING, RADIO

Chicago Symphony Orchestra/Amoco Radio Network
KCSN 88.5 FM
WFMT Fine Arts Network

PERFORMING ARTS PROGRAMMING, TV

Bell Foto Art Productions
Reiss Media Enterprises Inc.
V.I.E.W. Video Inc.
VPI - Videfilm Producers International, Ltd.

Producers, Distributors, Production and Other Services Subject Index

WTOB Channel 2 - Public/Government Access T.V.
Wold Productions Co.

PHOTOGRAPHIC SERVICES

3-D Video Corp.
Spatial Technologies Inc.
Virginia Tech, CNS (Communications Network Services)
Sandy Zimmerman Productions

POSTPRODUCTION FACILITIES

9KUSA Productions
American Video Productions
Associated Production Music
Century III at Universal Studios
Cornell University Media Services
D-V-X International
Daley Tele-Video Productions
ESPI Video
Encore Teleproductions Corp.
HAVE Inc.
Thomas Horton Associates Inc.
Image Devices International Inc.
Northwest Imaging & F.X.
Quark Video
RW VIDEO Inc.
Rampion Visual Productions
Ross-Gaffney Inc.
TeleScene
Teletainment Inc.
Video I-D Inc.
Video West
Videosmith Inc.
Yada/Levine Productions

POSTPRODUCTION SERVICES

3-D Video Corp.
Associated Production Music
Atlantic Video Inc.
D-V-X International
Daley Tele-Video Productions
Hal Dennis Post Production Rentals
Editel-Chicago
Electric Paint and Design
HAVE Inc.
Montgomery Community Television Inc.
ProCom Associates Inc.
Quark Video
RW VIDEO Inc.
Ross-Gaffney Inc.
Spatial Technologies Inc.
TeleScene
VTC a Division of Starcom Televison Services
Video I-D Inc.
Videosmith Inc.
Virginia Tech, CNS (Communications Network Services)
Yada/Levine Productions

PROCESSING LABS

DeLuxe Laboratories Inc.

PRODUCERS, DOCUMENTARIES

African Family Films
Asia Pacific Productions
Dave Bell Associates Inc.
Brillig Productions Inc.
Ellis Enterprises Ltd.
FTC/New York
FTC/Orlando
Globe Net Productions
Walter J. Klein Co. Ltd.
Jack Lieb Productions
Lindberg Productions Inc.
Longworth Communications Inc.
MAN QC Creations Inc.
Maryland Public Television
Burt Monk & Co.
Carl Ragsdale Associates Inc.
Restivo Communications Group
Richter Productions Inc.
Spencer Productions Inc.
Talco Productions
VPI - Videfilm Producers International, Ltd.

PRODUCERS, FILM

ADCO Productions
Academy Film Productions Inc.
African Family Films
Dave Bell Associates Inc.
Brillig Productions Inc.
Thomas Craven Film Corp.
Custom Films/Video Inc.
Ebbets Field Productions Ltd.
FTC/New York
FTC/Orlando
Fries Entertainment Inc.
Handel Film Corporation
Walter J. Klein Co. Ltd.
The Landsburg Company
Jack Lieb Productions
Burt Monk & Co.
New City Releasing Inc.
Pike Productions Inc.
Prime Productions
ProVideo
Carl Ragsdale Associates Inc.
Rampion Visual Productions
Restivo Communications Group
Richter Productions Inc.
Riviera Productions
Spencer Productions Inc.
Warren Miller Entertainment
Worldview Entertainment Inc.

PRODUCERS, MULTIMEDIA

Jack Lieb Productions
Burt Monk & Co.
Rampion Visual Productions
Restivo Communications Group
V.I.E.W. Video Inc.

PRODUCERS, RADIO PROGRAMMING

Armedia Communications
Barnes Communications Inc.
Call for Action Inc.
Creative Media Associates Inc.
Daynet Radio
ESPN Radio Network
Earthwatch Radio
Ecumedia News Service
Ecumenical Communications
Endless Mountains Radio Productions Inc.
Faith for Today
Four Star Media
Globe Productions
Good News Broadcasting Association Inc.
Fred Hall Productions
Al Ham Productions dba Music of Your Life
Heil Enterprises
Arthur Henley Productions
Israel Broadcasting Service
J&H Music Programming Inc.
KJD Teleproductions
Lutheran Hour Ministries
Ben Manilla Productions
William Mauldin Productions Inc.
MediaTracks Inc.
MotorNet
MotorPro
New Dimensions Radio
Premiere Radio Networks Inc.
Radio America
Radio Production Services Inc.
Radio Sound Network
Radio Spirits Inc.
Radio Today Entertainment
Ray Communications Inc.
Russ Reid Company
Restivo Communications Group
Sam Shad Productions
Spencer Productions Inc.
Sports Entertainment Network
Strand Broadcast Services
Talco Productions
Time Capsule Inc.
Ukrainian Melody Hour
WFMT Fine Arts Network
World Wrestling Federation
ZBS Foundation

PRODUCERS, TV PROGRAMMING

9KUSA Productions
ADCO Productions
Agency for Instructional Technology (AIT)
Barnes Communications Inc.
Beach Associates
Dave Bell Associates Inc.
Brillig Productions Inc.
Broadcast News Service
Capital Cities/ABC Video Enterprises International
Children's Media Productions
Consumer Savings Network
Creative Media Associates Inc.
Ebbets Field Productions Ltd.
Ellis Enterprises Ltd.
FTC/New York
FTC/Orlando
Faith for Today
Fishing the West
Sandy Frank Entertainment Inc.
Fries Entertainment Inc.
Genesis Entertainment
Glenray Productions Inc.
Hamilton Productions Inc.
Hearst Entertainment
Arthur Henley Productions
Israel Broadcasting Service
KJD Teleproductions
The Landsburg Company
Limelight Communication Inc.
Longworth Communications Inc.
Lutheran Hour Ministries
MAN QC Creations Inc.
MTM Enterprises Inc.
Warren Miller Entertainment
Montgomery Community Television Inc.
Muller Media Inc.
Paramount Television Group
Perceptions
Prime Cut Productions Inc.
ProVideo
Reid/Land Productions Inc.
Russ Reid Company
Restivo Communications Group
Rhodes Productions
Roberts Television International Inc.
Rysher TPE
SFM Entertainment
SWTV Production Services Inc.
Sam Shad Productions
Spencer Productions Inc.
Talco Productions
Telepros
Teletainment Inc.
Turner Program Services
Ukrainian Melody Hour
VPI - Videfilm Producers International, Ltd.
Ventures in Media
Video/Films International Inc. (VFI)
Wold Productions Co.
World Wrestling Federation

PRODUCERS, VIDEO

ADCO Productions
Academy Film Productions Inc.
All Media Productions Inc.
Anderson Productions Ltd.
Asia Pacific Productions
Gene Bayliss
Beach Associates
Bell Foto Art Productions
Capital Cities/ABC Video Enterprises
Center City Film & Video
Children's Media Productions
Thomas Craven Film Corp.
Creative Sports
Custom Films/Video Inc.
D-V-X International
DWJ Television
Daley Tele-Video Productions
Ebbets Field Productions Ltd.
Encore Teleproductions Corp.
FTC/New York
FTC/Orlando
Imero Fiorentino Associates Inc.
Glenray Productions Inc.
Good News Broadcasting Association Inc.
Great Plains National (GPN)
Al Ham Productions dba Music of Your Life
Hamilton Productions Inc.
Handel Film Corporation
Limelight Communication Inc.
Lindberg Productions Inc.
MSE
MAN QC Creations Inc.
Mason Video
Nemo News
Prime Cut Productions Inc.
Prime Productions
Quality Film and Video
RW VIDEO Inc.
Rampion Visual Productions
Redwood Entertainment Inc.
Restivo Communications Group
Richter Productions Inc.

Producers, Distributors, Production and Other Services Subject Index

Riviera Productions
The Seattle Bureau
Spencer Productions Inc.
Story Time Stories That Rhyme
SyberVision Systems Inc.
Telepros
Teletainment Inc.
Tutman Productions
Vide-U Productions
Video/Films International Inc. (VFI)
Video I-D Inc.
Yada/Levine Productions

PRODUCTION MUSIC LIBRARIES

Airforce Broadcast Services Inc.
Associated Production Music
Globe Productions
Fred Hall Productions
Manhattan Production Music
Omnimusic
RPM-Radio Programming & Management Inc.
Riviera Productions
Virginia Tech, CNS (Communications Network Services)

PRODUCTION SERVICES

3-D Video Corp.
American Video Productions
Asia Pacific Productions
Barnes Communications Inc.
Cornell University Media Services
Thomas Craven Film Corp.
Creative Sports
Crystal Productions
Custom Films/Video Inc.
ESPI Video
FTC/Orlando
Film House Inc.
Imero Fiorentino Associates Inc.
Fishing the West
Freedom Sports Network
Larsong Productions
Maysles Films Inc.
Kenneth R. Meades
Dick Orkin's Amazing Radio
ProCom Associates Inc.
RW VIDEO Inc.
Reizner & Reizner Film & Video
The Seattle Bureau
Spatial Technologies Inc.
Teletainment Inc.
Video I-D Inc.
Videosmith Inc.

PROMOTION DESIGN

Film House Inc.
KIDSNET
Ellis Molton Advertising
Peters Productions Inc.

PROMOTION FILM DISTRIBUTION/PRODUCTION

Asia Pacific Productions
Pike Productions Inc.

PROMOTION PRODUCTION, RADIO

Command Productions
Custom Films/Video Inc.
Film House Inc.
Good News Broadcasting Association Inc.
Radio Production Services Inc.
Tribune Radio Networks

PROMOTION PRODUCTION, RADIO & TV

CanLib
Clausen Communications Inc.
Custom Films/Video Inc.
Endless Mountains Radio Productions Inc.
Film House Inc.
Metro Studios & Post Production Inc.
New York Communications Inc.
Peters Productions Inc.
Prime Productions
Toes Productions Inc.

PROMOTION PRODUCTION, TV

Bell Foto Art Productions
Caridi Entertainment
Consumer Savings Network
Creative Sports
SWTV Production Services Inc.

PUBLIC SERVICE ANNOUNCEMENTS

Army Reserve Pentagon, Office of the Chief
Bonneville Communications
The Church of Jesus Christ of Latter-Day Saints
Thomas Craven Film Corp.
Four Star Media
KIDSNET
William Mauldin Productions Inc.
MediaTracks Inc.
News/Broadcast Network
Tutman Productions
U.S. Air Force Recruiting Service
WTOB Channel 2 - Public/Government Access T.V.

PUBLISHING, VIDEO AND PRINT

Agency for Instructional Technology (AIT)
Blues City Journal
Children's Media Productions
DWJ Television
Dhanus Music Publishing
ETN - Educational Telecommunications Network
Faraone Communications Inc.
Good News Broadcasting Association Inc.
Host Communications Inc.
Lord Hume Music
Story Time Stories That Rhyme
SunGuard Mailing Service
V.I.E.W. Video Inc.
Video/Films International Inc. (VFI)
What's Happening

RECORDING STUDIOS

Airwaves Audio Inc.
The Audio Departmen Inc.
Horizon Audio Creations
Tom Jones Recording Studios
Lion & Fox Recording Inc.
William Mauldin Productions Inc.
Message on Hold Inc.
New Dimensions Radio
Sound of Birmingham Productions
Time Capsule Inc.
ZBS Foundation

RELIGIOUS PROGRAMMING, RADIO

Broadcast News Service
Child of God Broadcasting Network
Christian TV Services of Ellicottville Inc.
Ecumedia News Service
Heil Enterprises
International Broadcasting Network
Sing For Joy
WNGN-FM Hoosick Falls, N.Y.

RELIGIOUS PROGRAMMING, RADIO & TV

Bonneville Communications
Evangelical Lutheran Church in America
Faith for Today
Larsong Productions
Protestant Radio and Television Center Inc.

RELIGIOUS PROGRAMMING, TV

Child of God Broadcasting Network
Christian TV Services of Ellicottville Inc.
Modern Sound Pictures Inc.
Virginia Tech, CNS (Communications Network Services)
WO4AT - Hoosick Falls, N.Y.

REMOTE FACILITIES

Black Audio Devices
The Image Group
Tom Jones Recording Studios
Pro Am Sports System/Pass Sports
Reizner & Reizner Film & Video
SWTV Production Services Inc.
Sullivan Video Services Inc.

SATELLITE UPLINK SERVICES

Century III at Universal Studios
Chicago Symphony Orchestra/Amoco Radio Network
Communications III Inc.
Cornell University Media Services
DWJ Television
Daley Tele-Video Productions
Globe Net Productions
Group W Video Services
Hughes Television Network
The Image Group
International Broadcasting Network
Pro Am Sports System/Pass Sports

Radio Sound Network
Reuters Television
Roberts Television International Inc.
SWTV Production Services Inc.
Sullivan Video Services Inc.
WRS/Channel One Division of WRS

SCRIPTWRITERS

All Media Productions Inc.
Beach Associates
Ebbets Field Productions Ltd.
Arthur Henley Productions
Lighthorse Productions
Limelight Communication Inc.
MSE
Paramount Television Group
ProVideo
Redwood Entertainment Inc.
Vide-U Productions
World Wide Syndications Corp.

SET DESIGN

Devlin Design Group

SOUND DESIGN

Tim Cissell Music
The Image Group
Players Music Inc.
Station Break Music Productions
Sutcliffe Music Inc.
Videosmith Inc.

SOUND EFFECTS/SOUND EFFECT LIBRARIES

The Audio Department Inc.
Films for the Humanities Inc./FFH Video
FirstCom Broadcast Services
Manhattan Production Music
Ray Norman Productions Inc.
Omnimusic
Promusic Inc.
Ross-Gaffney Inc.
Shield Productions Inc.
SoperSound Music Library
Sound Ideas
TRF Production Music Libraries

SOUND RECORDING

Tom Jones Recording Studios
Lion & Fox Recording Inc.
New Dimensions Radio
Shield Productions Inc.
Toes Productions Inc.
United Sound Systems Inc.
ZBS Foundation

SOUND STAGES

Atlantic Video Inc.
Center City Film & Video

SPECIAL EFFECT LIBRARIES

Cascom International Inc.
FirstCom Broadcast Services

SPECIAL EFFECTS

3-D Video Corp.
Spatial Technologies Inc.
Videosmith Inc.
Sandy Zimmerman Productions

SPORTS PROGRAMMING, RADIO

Cadena Radio Centro (CRC Radio Network)
ESPN Radio Network
Host Communications Inc.
Metro Networks
MotorNet
MotorPro
Radio Sound Network
Sports Entertainment Network
Tribune Radio Networks

SPORTS PROGRAMMING, RADIO & TV

Jerry M. Gross Productions Inc.
NCAA Productions
Phoenix Communications Group
World Wrestling Federation

SPORTS PROGRAMMING, TV

Creative Sports
Freedom Sports Network
Thomas Horton Associates Inc.

Producers, Distributors, Production and Other Services Subject Index

Mason Video
Warren Miller Entertainment
Pro Am Sports System/Pass Sports
Reid/Land Productions Inc.
Roberts Television International Inc.
Telepros
WO4AT - Hoosick Falls, N.Y.
Wold Productions Co.

STAGE AND STUDIO RENTAL
Devlin Design Group
Rampion Visual Productions
Sak Entertainment

STANDARDS CONVERSION
Group W Video Services
Prime Cut Productions Inc.
Quark Video
Sifford Video Services Inc.

STOCK FOOTAGE/TAPE
African Family Films
Archive Films Inc.
Bill Burrud Productions Inc.
Film/Audio Services Inc.
Host Communications Inc.
Image Devices International Inc.
Worldview Entertainment Inc.

STUDIO FACILITIES
Circle Video Productions
Encore Teleproductions Corp.
Metro Studios & Post Production Inc.
Quark Video
Video West

SYNDICATION, CABLE
Cable Films
Creative Sports
Sandy Frank Entertainment Inc.
Gaylord Syndicom
The Image Group
Muller Media Inc.
New Century Telecommunications
New Visions Entertainment
Pro Am Sports System/Pass Sports
SFM Entertainment
Video-Cinema Films Inc.
Vitt Media International Inc.

SYNDICATION, RADIO
Armedia Communications
Audio Creations
Bailey Broadcasting Services
Barnes Communications Inc.
Broadcast Programming
Cadena Radio Centro (CRC Radio Network)
Daynet Radio
Four Star Media
Happi Associates
International Broadcasting Network
Jameson Broadcast Inc.
Little Chicago
MediaTracks Inc.
Ellis Molton Advertising
Orange Productions Inc.
Dick Orkin's Amazing Radio
Premiere Radio Networks Inc.
Radio America
Radio Production Services Inc.
Radio Spirits Inc.
Radio Today Entertainment
Ray Communications Inc.
Russ Reid Company
Sam Shad Productions
Sound Source

Souvenirs of the 60's
Sports Entertainment Network
Sports Final Radio Network Inc.
Strand Broadcast Services
Time Capsule Inc.
Tribune Radio Networks
Trick Bag
Morrie Trumble & Associates
University of Detroit Mercy
Vitt Media International Inc.

SYNDICATION, TV
Cable Films
CanLib
Classic Films International Inc.
Creative Sports
Endless Mountains Radio Productions Inc.
Sandy Frank Entertainment Inc.
Freedom Sports Network
Gray-Schwartz Enterprises Inc.
Hughes Television Network
International Program Consultants Inc.
Ivanhoe Broadcast News Corporation
King World Productions Inc.
Lutheran Hour Ministries
MTM Enterprises Inc.
Muller Media Inc.
New Century Telecommunications
New Visions Entertainment
Paramount Television Group
Russ Reid Company
Rhodes Productions
Rysher TPE
SFM Entertainment
Turner Program Services
Video-Cinema Films Inc.
Vitt Media International Inc.
WRS/Channel One Division of WRS
Warner Bros. Domestic Pay-TV, Cable & Network Features Distribution
Wold Productions Co.
World Wide Syndications Corp.
World Wrestling Federation
Worldvision Enterprises Inc.

TELECONFERENCES
Atlantic Video Inc.
Communications III Inc.
Imero Fiorentino Associates Inc.
Hamilton Productions Inc.
Hughes Television Network
KIDSNET
MRG Production Associates Inc.
Maryland Public Television
Northwest Imaging & F.X.
Teletainment Inc.
Virginia Tech, CNS (Communications Network Services)

TRAINING FILM PRODUCTIONS
All Media Productions Inc.
Bell Foto Art Productions
Thomas Craven Film Corp.
MSE
Burt Monk & Co.
ProCom Associates Inc.
Video/Films International Inc. (VFI)

TRAINING FILMS
Films for the Humanities Inc./FFH Video
Walter J. Klein Co. Ltd.
Riviera Productions
SyberVision Systems Inc.

TRAVEL PROGRAMMING, TV
All Productions

Bill Burrud Productions Inc.
Consumer Savings Network
Warren Miller Entertainment
Prime Cut Productions Inc.
Reizner & Reizner Film & Video
Sandy Zimmerman Productions

TRAVELOGUES
Modern Sound Pictures Inc.
Riviera Productions

VIDEO CONFERENCES
Gene Bayliss
Communications III Inc.
Cornell University Media Services
Imero Fiorentino Associates Inc.
Hughes Television Network
Reizner & Reizner Film & Video
SWTV Production Services Inc.
Scola
Telepros

VIDEOTAPE EDITING
Asia Pacific Productions
Custom Films/Video Inc.
DWJ Television
Daley Tele-Video Productions
Image Devices International Inc.
The Image Group
Longworth Communications Inc.
MPL Film & Video
Metro Studios & Post Production Inc.
Montgomery Community Television Inc.
Northwest Imaging & F.X.
ProCom Associates Inc.
Quality Film and Video
Quark Video
RW VIDEO Inc.
Sullivan Video Services Inc.
TeleScene
Telepros
Teleworld Inc.
Vide-U Productions
Video I-D Inc.
Video West
Yada/Levine Productions

VOICE-OVERS
Airwaves Audio Inc.
American International Productions
American Video Productions
Clausen Communications Inc.
Command Productions
Globe Productions
Goodman Productions
Irving Productions Inc.
Larsong Productions
William Mauldin Productions Inc.
MotorPro
Perceptions
Shield Productions Inc.
Sound of Birmingham Productions
Toes Productions Inc.

WEATHER PROGRAMMING
Skywatch Weather Center
Morrie Trumble & Associates

WEATHER PROGRAMMING, RADIO
Metro Networks
Metro Weather Service Inc.
Skywatch Weather Center
WRS/Channel One-Division of WRS

Producers, Distributors, Production and Other Services
Alphabetical Index

A

ABC Distribution Co. 825 7th Ave., New York 10019. (212) 456-1725. FAX: (212) 456-1708. Archie C. Purvis Jr., pres; Joseph Y. Abrams, sr VP; Paul D. Coss, VP prog acquisitions & dev; Michael J. Dragotto, VP worldwide cable/home video mktg; Maria D. Komodikis, VP international TV sls; Sharon R. Rehme, VP sls admin & opns; June Shelley, dir theatrical sls & adv promotion; Melanie Topp, dir prog acquisition & dev; Patricia E. Vance, VP ancillary mkt sls; Mara Stemthal, mgr international TV sls; Dan Willis, dir international TV sls; Celeste Papepinto, dir international news mktg.
TV-CATV only.
Licenses all rights worldwide to all media: prod, co-prod, acquisition, dev & distribution of progmg. TV-CATV only.

ABC Watermark. 3575 W. Cahuenga Blvd., Suite 555, Los Angeles 90068. (213) 882-8330. FAX: (213) 850-5832. Corinne Baldassano, VP progmg.
Radio prod & distribution.

ABN Radio & TV. 1515 W. Lane Ave., Columbus, Ohio 43221. (614) 486-9577. FAX: (614) 487-8205. Ed Johnson, pres; Grant Neilley, opns dir; Randall Helt, gen sls mgr.
Agricultural radio net serving Ohio farmers & consumers via satellite.

ACTV Inc. 1270 Ave. of the Americas, Suite 2401, New York 10020. (212) 262-2570. FAX: (212) 459-9548. Dr. Michael J. Freeman, chmn of bd; William C. Samuels, pres/CEO; David Reese, CFO.
TV-CATV only.
Interactive TV progmg for educ & entertainment.

ADCO Productions. 7101 Biscayne Blvd., Miami, Fla. 33138. (305) 751-3118; (800) 777-FILM. FAX: (305) 751-6080. Earl Wainwright, pres; Barbara Hillman, prod mgr.
TV/film prod, remote facilities, ENG/EFP crews, film/tape editing. Florida, Caribbean & South America location svcs.

AEI Music Network Inc. 3716 National Dr., Suite 210, Raleigh, N.C. 27612-4863. (919) 571-1590. FAX: (919) 781-5056. Michael Malone, own/pres.
Programmer & supplier of satellite delivered mus svcs for business & cable TV. Available satellite direct or through FM subcarrier.

AKO Video Productions Inc. 43 Colborne St., 2nd Fl., Toronto, Ont., Canada M5E 1E3. (416) 862-7100. FAX: (416) 862-5578. Stan Czudek, mgr.
TV-CATV only.
Interformat video postprod facilities, duplication in all formats for TV-CATV only. Studio also available.

ALIN TV. 149 Madison Ave., Suite 804, New York 10016. (212) 889-1327. FAX: (212) 213-6968. Alan Steinberg, chmn; John Giebel, pres; Alan Cohen, exec VP.
TV-CATV only.
Unwired TV natl net.

ALL POST Inc. 1133 N. Hollywood Way, Burbank, Calif. 91505. (818) 841-7440. FAX: (818) 842-8409. Larry Kingen, pres/CEO; Gary Costanzo, exec VP/COO; Jim Bullard, sr VP/CFO; John Knowles, VP sls.
TV-CATV only.
Burbank, Calif. 91505: 2660 W. Olive. (818) 840-8060. FAX: (818) 840-8594. Dennis Imbler, gen mgr; Bob Franchini, VP sls & prod; Jim Livolsi, creative dir/postprod.
Videotape postprod facility. Film to tape mastering, on-line editing, videotape duplication in all formats, standards conversion & audio svcs for TV-CATV only.

AMA Radio News. 515 N. State St., 17th Fl., Chicago 60610. (312) 464-4449. FAX: (312) 464-5839. Bruce K. Dixon, prod.
One-minute medical news reports in wrap form free to radio stns via 800 number & wkly satellite feed.

AMI News. 50 Vashell Way, Suite 300, Orinda, Calif. 94563-3020. (510) 254-4456. FAX: (510) 254-6135. John Hamilton, pres; Rob Brown, VP.
Eastern Bureau. (800) 736-0370. Claire Diepenbrock.
Produce & package outdoor recreation reports of 30-, 60-, 90-seconds in length. Also deliver ski reports via phone, computer & facsimilie.

APA International Film Distributors Inc. 7400 SW 50th Terrace, Suite 202, Miami, Fla. 33155. (305) 663-3204. FAX: (305) 663-2618. Rafael Fusaro, pres.
TV prog prod & distribution.

ARP Films Inc./Centaur Distribution Corp. 18 E. 41st St., Suite 1605, New York 10017. (212) 685-7100. FAX: (212) 685-7106. Claude S. Hill, pres; Anne B. Cody, opns mgr.
TV-CATV only.
TV prog distribution company.

Academy Film Productions Inc. 3918 W. Estes Ave., Lincolnwood, Ill. 60645. (708) 674-2122. Bernard Howard, pres/exec prod.
Offers clients & agencies creative svcs in all aspects of radio, TV, video & audio-visual prod.

Academy of Religious Broadcasting. 500 Wall St., Suite 415, Seattle 98121. (206) 441-6110. J. Graley Taylor, exec dir.
TV prog, promotion film prod & distribution; prod svcs; rgnl award prog, ARBY Awards.

Accuracy in Media Inc. 4455 Connecticut Ave. N.W., #330, Washington 20008. (202) 364-4401. FAX: (202) 364-4098. Reed Irvine, chmn; Joseph C. Goulden, dir media analysis; Deborah Lambert, pub affrs dir; Bernard Yoh, communications dir; Don Irvine, exec sec.
Nationwide media monitoring organization. Produces documentary TV films counteracting biased reporting. Produces five days per week, a three minute radio commentary, *Media Monitor* as a pub svc.

Ad Vantage Audio. Box 8057, Pensacola, Fla. 32505. (904) 438-8054. Frederic T.C. Brewer, pres.
Radio prog, coml prod & distribution.

Adler Video Marketing Ltd./Adler Enterprises Ltd. 6849 Old Dominion Dr., Suite 360, McLean, Va. 22101. (703) 556-8880. FAX: 703-556-9288. Larry Adler, pres; Michael du Monceau, sr VP/Adler Enterprises; LaLee Downey Du Moneau, dir international sls.
TV-CATV only.
Prog distributors to TV, cable & home video mkts worldwide. Handles series, documentaries, mus & children's features completed or in dev.

Advertisers Broadcasting Co. Box 191, Ghent, N.Y. 12075. (518) 392-2193. FAX: (518) 392-2193. Sholom Rubinstein, exec prod.
Offers TV & radio prog, coml prod.

African Family Films. Box 630, Santa Cruz, Calif. 95061-0630. (408) 426-3133. Taale Laafi Rosellini, founder/dir.
TV-CATV only.
Prod & distribution of films & videotapes promoting African family life & culture.

Agency for Instructional Technology (AIT). Box A, Bloomington, Ind. 47402-0120. (812) 339-2203; (800) 457-4509. FAX: (812) 333-4218. Michael F. Sullivan, exec dir.
TV-CATV only.
Produces, acquires & distributes technology-based learning resources—including video, videodisc, software & print—for all K-12 curricular areas, voc ed/tech prep, early childhood & professional dev.

Agrinet Farm Radio Network. 179 Lovers Ln., Suite A, Elizabeth City, N.C. 27909. (919) 335-7294. FAX: (919) 335-2496. Bill Ray, farm dir; Harvey Jernigan, chief engr.
State, rgnl & natl agricultural news, mkts & weather.

Ailes Communications Inc. 440 Park Ave. S., New York 10016. (212) 685-8400. FAX: (212) 689-3701. Roger E. Ailes, chmn & CEO; Kathy Ardleigh, VP creative dir.
TV prog, coml, promotional film prod; prod svcs.

Airforce Broadcast Services Inc. 216 Carlton St., Main Fl., Toronto, Ont., Canada M5A 2L1. (416) 961-2541. FAX: (416) 961-7754. Mort Ross, pres; Jennifer Ward, sls opns mgr.
Prod of mus for radio/TV. The NEW Production Library & POWERPLAY Library on CD. Also NEW Christmas library.

Airwaves Audio Inc. 15 Toronto St. (lower level), Toronto, Ont., Canada. (416) 863-6881. FAX: (416) 867-9107. Al Staruch, pres; Cathy Onyskiw, office mgr.
Audiovisual & industrial postprod. Audio recording & mixing for radio & TV.

The Album Network Inc. 120 N. Victory Blvd., 3rd Fl., Burbank, Calif. 91502. (818) 955-4000. FAX: (818) 955-8048. Elias N. Bird, CEO; Stephen R. Smith, pres; Tommy Nast, VP radio.
Radio prod & distribution, rsch svcs.

Alden Electronics Inc. 40 Washington St., Westboro, Mass. 01581. (508) 898-3511. FAX: (508) 836-3711. Kevin A. Porreco, division mgr; Cindy D. Leader, account mgr.
Distributors of natl weather svc facsimile & text svcs; color weather satellite imagery, graphics & other specialized weather products.

Alden Films. Box 449, Clarksburg, N.J. 08510. (908) 462-3522. FAX: (908) 294-0330. Paul Weinberg, pres; Maureen Mitnick, admin asst.
TV-CATV only.
Distributes nearly 600 films & videos on Israel & Judaica. Official distributor for State of Israel.

All American Television Inc. 875 3rd Ave., 9th Fl., New York 10022. (212) 418-3000. FAX: (212) 418-3010. Henry Siegel, pres; George Back, chmn AATV distribution; Joseph E. Kovacs, pres AATV distribution; Paul Siegel, pres international ancilliary enterprises; Mike Weiden, pres adv sls.
TV prog distribution & co-prod, natl advertisers, sls domestically & worldwide.
Los Angeles 90066: 5301 Beethoven St., Suite 224. (310) 301-1721.

All Media Productions Inc. 1708 Baldwin St., Jenison, Mich. 49428. (616) 457-7030. FAX: (616) 457-7033. Linda Langs, pres.
TV-CATV only.
Prod svcs, instructional design for training, interactive laser disc, video, film & educ progmg for TV/CATV.

All My Features Inc. 6001 Lake Side Ave., Suite 20, Richmond, Va. 23228. (804) 264-7406. FAX: (804) 264-0536. Marc C. Guncheon, pres.
Provides daily entertainment news & entertainment-related features via audio & computer feeds.

All Post. 2660 W. Olive St., Burbank, Calif. 91505. (818) 840-8060. FAX: (818) 840-8594. Dennis Imbler, gen mgr; Bob Franchini, VP sls/producer; Jim Livolsi, creative dir/postprod.
TV stage prod, postprod & duplication.

All Productions. 7025 Regner Rd., San Diego 92119-1941. Box 19153, San Diego CA 92159-0153. (619) 460-4837. FAX: (619) 460-6160. Stephen A. All, CEO; Jean M. All, pres; George Kirazian, prod/dir.
TV & radio prog prod & distribution; cable-ready TV progmg; promotional film prod, prod svcs; TV & radio spots; coml announcers.

Allegro Productions Inc. 1000 Clint Moore Rd., Suite 211, Boca Raton, Fla. 33487. (407) 994-9111. FAX: (407) 241-0707. Jerome G. Forman, pres.
TV-CATV only.
Provides TV coml prod & distribution; promotional film prod; prod svcs including on-line editing & duplication.

Allied Film & Video. 7375 Woodward Ave., Detroit 48202. (313) 871-2222. FAX: (313) 871-4120. James Merkle, sr VP & gen mgr; Jack Spring, dir sls & mktg.
TV-CATV only.
Film processing, film to tape transfers, video editing, videocassette duplication, packaging & fulfillment.

Producers, Distributors, Production and Other Services

Allied Production and Distribution Services. 135 W. Hancock St., Decatur, Ga. 30030. (404) 373-1227. FAX: (404) 373-1227. Edwin Clark, pres.
TV-CATV only.
TV prog prod & distribution.

Altman Productions. 3401 Macomb St. N.W., Washington 20016. (202) 362-0234. Sophie B. Altman, exec prod; Susan Altman, prod.
TV & radio prog prod.

Altschul Group Corp. 1560 Sherman Ave., Suite 100, Evanston, Ill. 60201. (708) 328-6700. FAX: (708) 328-6706. Joel Altschul, chmn; Joe Farragher, pres.
TV-CATV only.
Educ prog, series & documentaries.

Ambea International Ltd. 233 E. Erie, Suite 300, Chicago 60611-2906. (312) 664-8944. FAX: (312) 664-6361. Bill Archer & Angelo Bosco, business & sls admin.

America On The Road-Mutual Broadcasting System. 1020 Riverside Dr., Suite 45, Burbank, Calif. 91506. (818) 843-5951. FAX: (818) 558-3993. Ed Yelin, prod; Steven Parker & Mike Anson, co-hosts.
One hour wkly, 2.5 minute daily automotive consumer show.

American Chiropractic Association Inc. 1701 Clarendon Blvd., Arlington, Va. 22209. (703) 276-8800. FAX: (703) 243-2593. J. Ray Morgan, exec VP; David Shingler, dir communications.
TV & radio prog distribution; professional membership organization.

American Farm Bureau Federation. 225 Touhy Ave., Park Ridge, Ill. 60068. (312) 399-5700. FAX: (312) 399-5896. Stewart Truelsen, dir bcst svcs.
Food & agriculture newsline, daily feed & insight commentary for radio, Ku-band uplink, video news releases, documentaries & stock tape for TV.

American Foundation for the Blind. 15 W. 16th St., New York 10011. (212) 620-2000. FAX: (212) 727-7418. Carl Augusto, pres/exec dir; Susan J. Spungin, assoc exec dir of prog svcs; Liz Grecco, pub rels mgr.
Provides consultation & referrals, social rsch, technological rsch & dev, publications, info svcs, pub educ, govt rels, consumer products, talking books.

American Heart Association. 7272 Greenville Ave., Dallas 75231-4596. (214) 706-1340. FAX: (214) 706-1551. Carol Floyd, bcst news prod; Howard L. Lewis, dir health & science news div.
TV prog prod, animated video news releases & stock footage related to heart & diet.

American International Productions. Box 31000, Spokane, Wash. 99223. (509) 534-6000. FAX: (509) 448-3811. Thomas Wilmot Read, pres.
Nostalgic radio prod & distribution; children's radio progmg; duplication svcs; entertainment radio progmg; voice overs.

American Medical Television. 515 N. State St., Chicago 60610. (312) 464-5395. FAX: (312) 464-4190. Dan Hoort, CEO; Wendy Borow, pres; Leona Doyle, VP/opns mgr.
TV-CATV only.
Ten hours of medical & health info for physicians & consumers every weekend (10am - 3pm ET) on CNBC.

The American Network Group Inc. 621 Mainstream Dr., Suite 230, Nashville 37228. (615) 742-6105. FAX: (615) 742-6124. John Casey, chmn; Robert J. Williamson, pres; C. Donald Williams, VP sports opns; Dan Gordon, VP net opns.
State radio networking, collegiate radio & TV networking.

American Program Service. 120 Boylston St., Boston 02116. (617) 338-4455. FAX: (617) 338-5369. John S. Porter, pres.
Serves all public TV stns.

American Stock Exchange - Radio AMEX. 86 Trinity Pl., New York 10006. (212) 306-1637. Tom Mariam, dir.
Provides wkly talk show & daily stock market reports tailored for ind stns & nets for TV/CATV & radio.

American Stock Exchange - Video AMEX. 86 Trinity Place, New York 10006. (212) 306-1637. Tom Mariam, mgr.
Provides live daily video feeds from the American Stock Exchange trading floor to TV nets & stns.

American Video Productions. 123 E. Dania Beach Blvd., Dania, Fla. 33004. (305) 921-1111. FAX: (305) 922-4222. Michael Mancusi, pres; Sherie Lynn Kelley, creative dir.
TV-CATV only.
World wide on-location prod; complete Beta SP prod & post-prod svcs; studio facility; TV progmg, corporate & industrial.

America's Most Wanted. 5151 Wisconsin Ave. N.W., Washington 20016. (202) 895-3103. FAX: (202) 895-3096. Lance Heflin, exec prod; John Walsh, host; Joe Russin, supervising prod; Paul Sparrow, prod; Nan Allendorfer, coord/prod; Phil Lerman, mgng edit.
Wkly reality-based program for Fox TV.

Ken Anderson Films. Box 618, Winona Lake, Ind. 46590. (219) 267-5774. FAX: (219) 267-5876. Ken Anderson, pres/prod supvr; Lane Anderson, VP.
TV prog prod & distribution.

Anderson Productions Ltd. 51 W. 81st St., Suite 1B, New York 10024. (212) 769-2501. FAX: (212) 769-2993. Steven C. F. Anderson, pres/exec prod.
TV-CATV only.
TV prog prod & consulting firm specializing in info progmg for cable TV.

Robert Anderson Associates Ltd. 500 Kenwood Ave., Ottawa, Ont., Canada K2A 0L3. (613) 722-1962. Robert Anderson, pres.
Film & TV prog prod.

Antenne 2 - French TV 2. 1290 Ave. of the Americas, Suite 2720, New York 10104. (212) 581-1771. FAX: (212) 541-4309. Nicole Devilaine, dir.
TV prog prod.

Archive Films Inc. 530 W. 25th St., New York 10001. (212) 620-3955. FAX: (212) 645-2137. Patrick Montgomery, pres.
TV-CATV only.
Stock footage library providing all types of historical footage for use in prods for TV/CATV.

Armedia Communications. Box 257, Postal Stn. C, Toronto, Ont., Canada M6J 3P4. (905) 507-2973. FAX: (905) 507-4329. David Mazmanian, own.
Audio, video, mus prod & bcst svcs.

Army Reserve Pentagon, Office of the Chief. 1815 N. Fort Myer Dr., Arlington, Va. 22209-1805. (703) 696-3963. FAX: (703) 696-3745. Al Schilf, actg dir pub affrs; Mark Zimmer, mktg dir.
Audio & TV progmg, VNRs, RNRs, PSAs.

The Kay Arnold Group. 34 Kramer Dr., Paramus, N.J. 07652. (201) 652-6037. FAX: (201) 612-8578. Kay Arnold, pres.
TV-CATV-Radio.
Prod & distribution of film & tape progs for TV, satellite, cable, home video & non-theatrical.

J. Arnold Productions. 440 Totten Pond Rd., Waltham, Mass. 02154. (617) 890-0129. FAX: (617) 890-2991. James Arnold, pres; Stephanie Berger, prod mgr.
TV-CATV only.
Full-svc video prod & postprod facility.

Toby Arnold and Associates Inc. 3234 Commander Dr., Carrollton, Tex. 75006. (800) 527-5335. FAX: (214) 250-6014. Toby Arnold, pres; Dolly Arnold, VP/COO; Larry Mangiameli, VP/creative dir.
Audio prod libraries for TV & radio. Custom & syndicated mus for TV, radio & local advertisers. Programs include *The Ultimate, Attitude* & *Visions*.

Asia Pacific Productions. 3-17 Higashimaruyama Cho, Nagata-ku, Kobe, Japan 653. (78) 691-2450. FAX: (78) 641-3394. Thomas F. Hopkins, pres; Miyuki Shigeji, VP/comptroller.
TV-CATV only.
Provides news, documentary & prog prod, distribution; coml prod; business/prom film & video prod & distribution; prod svcs for TV/CATV.

Associated Production Music. 6255 Sunset Blvd., Suite 820, Hollywood, Calif. 90028. (213) 461-3211; (800) 543-4276. FAX: (213) 461-9102. Cassie Lord, natl sls dir; Connie Red, bcst sls dir.
Supplies *Broadcast One, Two & Three* prod music libraries, as well as sound effects, to radio & TV for use in promotions, progs, news & comls.

Atlantic Video Inc. 650 Massachusetts Ave. N.W., Washington 20091-0904. (202) 408-0900. FAX: (202) 408-8496. Dong Moon Joo, pres; Christopher Cates, VP/gen mgr; Craig George, dir mktg.

Washington 20001: 650 Massachusetts Ave. N.W. (202) 408-0900. FAX: (202) 408-8496.
Alexandria Va. 22304: 150 S. Gordon St. (703) 823-2800. Lee Lindbloom, asst gen mgr.
Postprod, graphics, duplication, remote, satellite uplink, videoconferencing & sound stages.

Atlantis Audio and Video. 2602 San Joaquin Hills Rd., Corona del Mar, Calif. 92625-1127. Art Kemp, own.
Editing 3/4" - 1", soundstage, ENG, duplication, audio recording, mixing, 19 mus libraries (compact discs).

Atwood-Richards Inc. 99 Park Ave., 15th Fl., New York 10016. (212) 490-1414. FAX: (212) 867-8450. Moreton Binn, chmn & pres.
Irvine, Calif. 92715: 2600 Mitchellson Dr. (714) 251-8555.
TV prog distribution.

Auburn Television. (A division of Telecommunications.) Auburn University, Corner of Samford & Donahue, Auburn, Ala. 36849-5423. (205) 844-4110. FAX: (205) 844-9360. James H. Stone, exec dir; Terry Harper, chief engr.
TV/studio/remote prod, promotional film prod, satellite uplink/downlink, photographic svcs.

Audible Advertising Productions Inc. Desota Bldg., 215 W. 91st St., Suite 25, New York 10024. (212) 873-1238. Mary Hurt, exec prod.
Musical comls for radio; syndicated orchestrations with original lyrics for each client.

Audio Action. 4444 Lakeside Dr., Suite 340, Burbank, Calif. 91505. (800) 533-1293. FAX: (818) 845-8039. Rhona Nici Parry, CEO.
Provides prod mus library & sound effects.

Audio Control Techniques. 1124 Princeton Dr., Glendale, Calif. 91205. (818) 246-0366. Robert Doherty, own.
Radio prog distributors including *Day in Court* & *Doctor's House Call*.

Audio Creations. 801 Starmount Ave. N.W., Roanoke, Va. 24019. (703) 343-7109. FAX: (703) 343-2306 Ben Peyton, pres.
TV & radio coml prog prod, distribution & jingles. Religious prog & distribution.

The Audio Department Inc. 119 W. 57th St., New York 10019. (212) 582-1303. FAX: (212) 245-1675. Joe Danis, pres.
Audio & audio for video, for adv & media promotion.

Audio Production Services, University of Colorado. Campus Box 379, 313 Stadium Bldg., Boulder, Colo. 80309. (303) 492-2675. FAX: (303) 492-7071. Richard Borkowski, studio mgr.
Radio prog prod.

Australian Tourist Commission. 489 5th Ave., 31st Fl., New York 10017. (212) 687-6300. FAX: (212) 661-3340. Lindel Gray, mgr eastern rgn.
Los Angeles 90010: (213) 380-6060. Steve Bowman, mgr western rgn.
Chicago 60601: (312) 329-0314. Steve Bowman, mgr central rgn.
TV prog distribution.

Avid Technology Inc. One Metropolitan Park W., Tewksbury, Mass. 01876. (800) 949-AVID; (508) 851-0418. FAX: (508) 851-0418. Anthony J. Mark, VP/gen mgr bcst prods; Mark P. Overington, dir worldwide svcs bcst prods.
Avid's networked bcst news prods are designed to facilitate the process of digital news gathering (DNG).

Axcess Broadcast Services Inc. 4801 Spring Valley, Suite 105-B, Dallas 75244. (214) 386-6847. FAX: (214) 386-5207. Otis Conner, pres.
Exclusive sls consulting for new businesses in the top 100 markets. CD production library, radio & TV promotions & IDs.

B

BBC Enterprises Ltd. Woodlands, 80 Wood Ln., London W12 0TT. 081-576-2000. FAX: 081-749-0538. John Thomas, mgng dir; Jackie Alexander, dir resources; Graham Massey, dir international; Keith Owen, dir cable & satellite TV; Ken Wright, dir finance; Nick Chapman, dir consumer products.
TV prog distribution & co-prod; sale & licensing of sports, news, current affrs & excerpts; video, print & magazine publishing.

Producers, Distributors, Production and Other Services

BBC Lionheart Television. 630 5th Ave., Suite 2220, New York 10111. (212) 373-4100. FAX: (212) 956-2399. Sarah Frank, pres/CEO; Eileen Opatut, exec VP, co-prod/sls.
TV-CATV only.
TV prog prod & distribution.

BC Television Productions/International Television Film & Video Production Associates. 4550 Via Marina, Suite 105, Marina del Rey, Calif. 90292. (310) 578-1480. FAX: (310) 578-5114. Bud Connell, exec prod.
Film & video prod & duplication for corporate, industrial & entertainment clients.

BES Teleproductions. 6829 E. Atmore Rd., Richmond, Va. 23225. (804) 276-5110. FAX: (804) 276-1982. Guy Spiller, pres; Derrell Harman, vp opns; Karen Abse, business mgr.
Film & video prod; creative svcs; film transfer; post prod; animation; audio prod; mus composition; duplication. All formats including 2-inch.

BGM International. Box 8057, Pensacola, Fla. 32505. (904) 434-1953. FAX: (904) 433-7932. Frederic T.C. Brewer, own.
Computer-based system for mus & coml auto playback control of CD, DAT & digital voice for bcst & satellite interface.

BNA Communications Inc. 9439 Key West Ave., Rockville, Md. 20850. (301) 948-0540; (800) 233-6067. FAX: (301) 948-2085. Robert L. Velte, pres; George Stillman, VP.
Video-based training progs in Equal Employment Opportunity, mgmt dev, labor rels & safety.

Backer, Spielvogel & Bates. 405 Lexington, New York 10174. (212) 297-7000. FAX: (212) 986-0270. Carl Spielvogel, chmn & CEO; Michael Bundy, pres/COO; Richard Wysocki, sr VP/dir bcst prod & mgr creative svcs.
TV & radio coml prod & distribution.

Bailey Broadcasting Services 3151 Cattuenga Blvd., W. #200, Los Angeles 90068-1768. (213) 969-0011. FAX: (213) 969-8474. Lee Bailey, pres/exec prod; Diane Blackmon-Bailey, exec VP; Greg Johnson, dir sls & mktg.
Prod of ongoing short & long form progs & seasonal specials for domestic & international urban/CHR radio markets.

Balanced Living Communications. 5430 Fredericksburg Rd., Suite 510, San Antonio, 78229. (210) 349-6551. FAX: (210) 349-0713. Harry A. Croft M.D., pres; Myong H. Covert, mgr.
Offering full length & drop-in medical features; prod & syndicates The Mind is Powerful Medicine psychiatric series. Available in Sp.

S. Banks (In Television) Ltd. 20 Holly St., Suite 300, Toronto, Ont., Canada M4W 3M5. (416) 484-8000. FAX: (416) 484-8001. Sydney Banks, pres.
TV-CATV only.
TV prog prod.

Barnes Communications Inc. 19 W. 44th St., Suite 705, New York 10036. (212) 302-3399. FAX: (212) 302-3402. Gene Barnes, pres; Wade Barnes, chmn.
Prods, writers, personal reps, pub rels-publicity-mktg, special events & new product introduction for corps & personalities for TV/CATV & radio.

Robert Baron & Associates. 63-33 98th Pl., Forest Hills, N.Y. 11374. (718) 275-4349. Robert Baron, exec prod; Robert Braverman, dir; Hanh Nadler, edit; Jack Godler, writer.
Film & video prod.

Baruch Entertainment. 1331 F St. N.W., Suite 800, Washington 20004. (202) 833-1777. FAX: (202) 737-0725. Ed Baruch, pres; Mark Dorf, VP; Steve Smallwood, mktg dir.
Mktg, syndication & prod/distribution of progmg to net syndication, cable, home video & international.

Baton Broadcasting Inc. Box 9, Station O, Toronto, Ont., Canada M4A 2M9. (416) 299-2000. FAX: (416) 299-2220. Douglas G. Bassett, pres/CEO; Joseph J. Garwood, exec VP/COO.
TV-CATV only.
TV bcstng, prog prod & distribution.

Gene Bayliss. 16 Burritts Landing, Westport, Conn. 06880. (203) 227-7521. FAX (203) 454-1032. Gene Bayliss, prod/consultant.
Produces & directs video conferences & video tapes for corporations & industries.

Beach Associates. 370 S. Washington St., Suite 400, Falls Church, Va. 22046. (703) 536-0444. Frank Beach, pres/sr prod & dir; Kay Leonard, exec VP/gen mgr; Jane Bergamin, dir mktg.
A full-svc vis communications firm. Staff prods, writers & dirs provide full creative direction & project mgmt from concept dev, treatment, scripting & graphics design to prod & delivery. Offers videotape, live event prod, consulting svcs for organizational communications. Provides comprehensive prod svcs for videotape, special event & live business TV-video conference progmg. Also offers media training, video news release prod, video press tours & consulting for private nets.

Beethoven Satellite Network (Classical Music Format Service). c/o WFMT Fine Arts Radio, 303 E. Wacker Dr., Chicago 60601. (312) 565-5000; (800) USA-WFMT. FAX: (312) 565-5169. David Levin, dir; Scott Kuiper, prog dir; Carol Martinez, opns mgr.
Prog prod & distribution; 83 hours per week classical mus format with prog hosts in one-hour modules, loc sound included.

Dave Bell Associates Inc. 3211 Cahuenga Blvd. W., Hollywood, Calif. 90068. (213) 851-7801. FAX: (213) 851-9349. David L. Bell, pres; Cynthia B. Shapiro, VP; Dennis Bogorad, VP dev; Judith Auberjonois, dev; Lesley Jacobs, dev assoc; Shari Cookson, prod/dir documentaries.
TV-CATV only.
Dev & prod of TV movies, series, feature films, documentaries & game shows.

Bell Foto Art Productions. 5 S. Cherry St., Denver 80222-1028. (303) 377-4606. FAX: (303) 322-2443. Chris Bell, own/chief cameraman; Katie Bell, prod/sound recordist.
TV-CATV only.
News video prod with overseas specialty; corporate, medical & legal video prod; underwater video & still photography.

Bellon Enterprises Ltd. 137 5th Ave., 8th Fl., New York 10010. (212) 477-2850. FAX: (212) 477-3203. Joseph P. Bellon, pres; Gregory P. Bellon, VP.
TV-CATV only.
Develop TV & home video series for worldwide distribution.

William Benton Broadcast Project of the University of Chicago. 5737 S. University Ave., Chicago 60637. (312) 702-9024. FAX: (312) 702-4517. John Callaway, dir; Frederick Schneider, project mgr.
TV & radio prod.

Best Film & Video Corp. 108 New South Rd., Hichsville, N.Y. 11801. (516) 931-6969. FAX: (516) 931-5959. Roy B. Winnick, pres; Arlene S. Winnick, VP.
TV prog prod & distribution.

Bevtel Programs Inc. 285 Forest Hill Rd., Toronto, Ont., Canada M5P 2N3. (416) 484-8000. FAX: (416) 484-8001. Beverly Fein, pres.
TV-CATV only.
TV prog distribution.

Bird Nest Inc. 1995 N.E. 150th St., North Miami, Fla. 33181. (305) 944-1006. FAX: (305) 949-7014. Randy Bird, pres.
Coml prod & original mus tracks for TV/CATV & Radio.

Black Audio Devices. Box 106, Ventura, Calif. 93002-0106. (805) 653-5557. FAX: (805) 653-5557. Bruce Black, pres.

The Blackwell Corp. USA Today Bldg, 1000 Wilson Blvd., Arlington, Va. 22209. (703) 524-2300. FAX: (703) 841-4340. Neal B. Freeman, chmn.
TV prod & distribution.

Blanc Communications Corp. 8306 Wilshire Blvd., Suite 8075, Beverly Hills, Calif. 90211. (310) 278-2600. FAX: (310) 271-5308. Noel Blanc, pres; Patrick Bailey, exec VP.
TV prog prod; TV & radio coml prod & distribution.

Chuck Blore & Bill McDonald Inc. 1606 N. Argyle, Hollywood, Calif. 90028. (213) 462-0944. FAX: (213) 462-3822. Chuck Blore, CEO; William McDonald, pres.
TV progs & commercial prod svcs. Radio coml prod svcs.

Blue Canyon Productions. Box 6622, Santa Fe, N.M. 87502. (505) 989-9298. Jim Terr, pres.
Award-winning, nationally-bcst jingle, PSA & radio spot prod, as well as music prod & scoring, scripting, voice-overs & video prod.

Blue Sky Productions Inc. 100 Executive Blvd., Ossing, N.Y. 10562. (914) 941-5260. FAX: (914) 923-9058. David B. Brown, pres; Alison Brown, exec prod; Chris Wedge, creative dir; Michael Ferraro, Carl Ludwig & Eugene Troubetzkoy, VPs.
Design & prod of high-end computer-generated animation, created on proprietary software.

Blues City Journal. Box 2147, Sioux City, Iowa 51104-0147. (712) 276-2295. "Morrie" Miller, mus edit.
Offers advance print reviews to radio prods, distributors & syndicators of new prods.

Robert L. Bocchino. Box 99, Haverford, Pa. 19041-0099. (610) 649-0993; FAX: (610) 649-0895. Robert L. Bocchino, principal.
TV & radio coml prod svcs for cultural organizations & corporate communications.

Bonneville Broadcasting System. 4080 Commercial Ave., Northbrook, Ill. 60062-1829. (800) 631-1600; (708) 291-0110. FAX: (708) 291-0841. John Patton, pres/CEO; Bud Stiker, exec VP; Walter Powers, VP opns; Ford Colley, VP consulting; Michael Krafcisin, VP opns & mktg svcs; Dave Verdery, prog dir easy listening; Jon Radford, Joe Cassady, progmg consultants; Jeff Dear, prod mgr; Mindy Herman, office mgr.
Radio progmg, opns, mgmt, finance, duopoly & LMA consultants. Progmg prod & distribution. Signature Series includes a variety of formats. Adult Contemporary CD music libraries. Auditorium music testing. Talent resources & creative spot copywriting/prod svcs. Digital audio playback systems. Custom strategic mapping market analysis.

Bonneville Communications. 179 Social Hall Ave., Salt Lake City 84111. (801) 237-2600. FAX: (801) 237-2696. Richard D. Alsop, pres; Walter H. Canals, VP media svcs; Gary J. Dixon, VP creative svcs; Gregg D. Garber, dir account svcs; Casey C. Jones, VP account dev; Delon W. Williams, VP/controller.
A values-driven adv agency engaged in communications for quality life.

Boston Symphony Orchestra. Boston Symphony Hall, 301 Massachusetts Ave., Boston 02115. (617) 266-1492. FAX: (617) 638-9223. Ken Haas, gen mgr; Michael McDonough, dir business affrs; Caroline Smedvig, dir pub rels/mktg.
Evening at Pops TV series & other special TV prods. Originates regular radio bcst of BSO concerts.

Robert Braverman Productions. 366 N. Broadway, Jericho, N.Y. 11753. (516) 939-2990. Robert Braverman, exec prod; Paul Fritz-Nemeth, special projects; John Ruvolo, rep.
TV-CATV only.
TV prog prod; prod svcs; dubbing into English & other languages.

Bray Studios Inc. 19 Ketchum, Westport, Conn. 06880. (203) 226-3777. FAX: (203) 226-6368. Paul Bray Jr., pres.
TV coml prod & distribution; promotional film prod; prod svcs, all specializing in aviation.

Breath of Life. 1100 Rancho Conejo Blvd., Newbury Park, Calif. 91320. (805) 373-7600. FAX: (805) 373-7701. Charles D. Brooks, speaker; Walter E. Arties, prod & ministry coord.
TV prog prod & distribution.

Dick Brescia Associates. 164 Garfield St. Haworth, N.J. 07641. (201) 385-6566. Dick Brescia, pres; David West, exec VP.
Radio shows: When Radio Was, Stan Freberg Here & Walter Cronkite's Twentieth Century.

Brillig Productions Inc. 770 Amalfi Dr., Pacific Palisades, Calif. 90272. (310) 459-4450. FAX: (310) 459-4456. Barry Brown, pres.
Feature films, TV features, TV commercials & documentaries.

British Broadcasting Corp. (Fine Arts Programs.) c/o WFMT Fine Arts Network, 303 E. Wacker Dr., Chicago 60601. (312) 565-5000. FAX: (312) 565-5169. David Levin, dir; Carol Martinez, opns mgr; Barry Hochman, prod mgr.
Produce wkly series including My Music, & My Word for coml & pub stns, distributed in U.S. by WFMT Fine Arts Network.

Producers, Distributors, Production and Other Services

From The Producers Of Radio's Best Features

Leonard Maltin On Video
THE DAILY :60 RADIO FEATURE ABOUT HOME VIDEO

And

FACE OFF
With Senators
Ted Kennedy and Alan Simpson

America's Most Entertaining Computer Talk Show!

OnLine
TONIGHT
LIVE Coast-To-Coast Sunday Nights Via Satellite

The Broadcast Group

Call Now For Demo Tapes and Complete Information

The Broadcast Group. 3333 K St. N.W., Suite 77, Washington 20007. (202) 337-3111. FAX: (202) 337-2567. Pegge Goertzen, pres; Chris Lauterbach, prod; Matthew H. Coates, dir special projects, prod.
 Prod & distribution of radio features including *Face Off* & *Leonard Maltin On Video.*

Broadcast News Service. Box 1008, Boston 02103. P.J. Romano, dir.
 Radio & TV features & prods.

Broadcast Productions & Services Inc. 2230 Gallows Rd., Suite 310, Dunn Loring, Va. 22027. (703) 204-4462. FAX: (703) 207-9503. Robert Johnson, pres.
 Film & video prog prod, radio prog prod & distribution.

Broadcast Programming. 2211 5th Ave., Seattle 98121. (206) 728-2741; (800) 426-9082. FAX: (206) 441-6582. Edith N. Hilliard, pres; John Carlile, mgr; Becky Brenner, progmg mgr; Jim LaMarca, sls mgr; Keith Chambers, mktg mgr.
 Radio mus formats on CD & reel-to-reel. Offering 35 different radio formats. Automation equipment & consulting.

Brockway Broadcasting Corp. 755 New York Ave., Huntington, N.Y. 11743. (516) 673-4400. FAX: (516) 673-4468. Richard S. Brockway, chmn; William J. Maier, exec VP mktg; Andrew Mancini, VP postprod.
 TV prog, coml, promotional film prod & distribution.

Brown Berry Productions. 1300 Mercantile Ln., Suite 126, Landover, Md. 20785. (301) 925-4513. FAX: (301) 925-2040. Carol Gordon-Berry, pres/CEO.
 Develops & mkts consumer & public interest progmg to Hispanic & African-American audiences for radio, TV & video distribution.

Himan Brown. 285 Central Park W., New York 10024. (212) 724-4333. Himan Brown, own.
 Radio prog prod; TV & film prog prod.

Bruder Releasing Inc. (BRI). 2020 Broadway, Santa Monica, Calif. 90404. (310) 829-2222. FAX: (310) 829-0202. Marc Bruder, pres; Kimberly Rowe, VP.
 TV-CATV only.
 Supplies ind films to pay-per-view, cable, bcst & video markets.

Buena Vista Television. 500 S. Buena Vista St., Burbank, Calif. 91521. (818) 560-1000. FAX: (818) 563-2601. Robert Jacquemin, pres
 The Walt Disney Co. subsidiary; develops & syndicates first-run adult & children's progmg, off-network progmg & feature film packages.

Bill Burrud Productions Inc. 16902 Bolsa Chica St., Huntington Beach, Calif. 92649. (714) 846-7174. FAX: (714) 846-4814. John Burrud, pres; Linda Hecomovich, VP prod; Bill MacDonald, prod; Karl Deeds, assoc prod.
 TV-CATV only.
 Feature film & TV prod of animal, wildlife, human adventure, documentaries & world exploration.

Business Education Films. Box 449, Clarksburg, N.J. 08510. (908) 462-3522. FAX: (908) 294-0330. Paul Weinberg, pres.
 TV-CATV only.
 Films & videos of Scandinavia & other specialized titles.

Buzzco Associates Inc. 33 Bleecker St., Suite 5A, New York 10012. (212) 473-8800. FAX: (212) 473-8891. Vincent Cafarelli, Candy Kugel, dirs/prods.
 TV-CATV only.
 A full range of animation from traditional cell through sophisticated design, MTV & beyond.

C

C.B. Distribution Co. 5750 Wilshire Blvd., Suite 590, Los Angeles 90036. (213) 937-1552. FAX: (213) 937-6532. Deidre Baxter.
 TV-CATV only.
 TV syndication.

CBS Entertainment Productions. CBS Television City, 7800 Beverly Blvd., Los Angeles 90036. (213) 852-4251. FAX: (213) 460-3733. Jeff Sagansky, pres; Peter Tortorici, VP.

C.D. Media Inc. 380 Madison Ave., 7th Fl., New York 10017. (212) 856-4435. FAX: (212) 697-5490. Rick Dees, chmn; Tom Shovan, VP/gen mgr.
 Offers *Rick Dees Weekly Top 40*, a four-hour CHR countdown wkly; *Satellite Comedy Network*, daily comedy vignettes & parody songs via satellite.

CDR Communications Inc. 9310-B Old Keene Mill Rd., Burke, Va. 22015. (703) 569-3400. FAX: (703) 569-3448. Christopher D. Rogers, pres; Nancy B. Rogers, VP.
 TV & video prod: documentaries, ad campaigns, PSAs; promotion & training; news progmg; mktg.

CEL Communications Inc. 477 Madison Ave., New York 10022. (212) 557-3400. FAX: (212) 752-2756. Martin L. Waldman, chmn/CEO.
 Provides original progmg for coml, pub & cable TV; also for home & educ mkts.

CKW & Associates. 4769 Elmer Ave., North Hollywood, Calif. 91602. (818) 985-4743. FAX: (818) 985-3779. Charles K. Whaley, pres.
 Radio prog supplier/barter syndication of dramatic radio series. Prog titles: *Louis L'Amour Theater*, *Milford Haven*.

COMPRO Productions Inc. 2080 Peachtree Industrial Ct., Suite 114, Atlanta 30341. (404) 455-1943. FAX: (404) 455-3356. Nels Anderson, pres; Steve Brinson, VP; Kim Anderson, VP; Kerrie Lupica, prod.
 TV-CATV only.
 Full-svc specializing in film & video prod for corporate & bcst communications. Features a fully component Betacam SP on-line editing system, 16mm film editing, studio facilities, 3/4-inch off-line editing, video duplication & distribution, & location vehicles.

CRM Films. 2215 Faraday Ave., Carlsbad, Calif. 92008-7295. (800) 421-0833. FAX: (619) 931-5792. Peter J. Jordan, CEO/pres; Stephanie R. Glidden, founding principal.
 TV-CATV only.
 Prod & distributor of business training films.

CRN International. One Circular Ave., Hamden, Conn. 06514. (203) 288-2002. FAX: (203) 281-3291. Barry Berman, pres; S. Richard Kalt, sr VP.
 Short-form customized radio progs & productions; Wimbledon radio net; UCONN football & basketball, Skiwatch, Beachwatch & On the Go.

C.R.N. Media Inc. 124 W. 60th St., Suite 33F, New York 10023. (212) 765-2587. FAX: (212) 586-8797. Tom Shovan, pres.
 Produces, distributes & consults loc & syndicated progmg, consults for progmg suppliers for radio only.

CS Associates. 102 E. Blithedale, Mill Valley, Calif. 94941. (415) 383-6060. FAX: (415) 383-2520. Charles Schuerhoff, pres.
 TV-CATV only.
 Prog distribution, specializing in documentaries, foreign & domestic TV & cable; broker co-prods.

Cable Advertising. (A division of Continental Cablevision.) One Gateway Ctr., Newton, Mass. 02158. (617) 244-4880. FAX: (617) 964-4406. Steve Feingold, gen mgr.

Cable Alternatives Inc. Box 1141, Toms River, N.J. 08753. (908) 929-0110. Greg Koziar, chmn of bd.
 Offers mus progmg & coml prod for radio & cable TV alphanumeric chs.

Cable Films. Box 7171, Country Club Station, Kansas City, Mo. 64113. (913) 362-2804. FAX: (913) 341-7365. Herbert Miller, VP mktg; Todd Randall, gen mgr; Marc Stevens, mktg mgr.
 TV-CATV only.
 Feature film distributor for TV & cable; available on 16mm, 3/4" U-Matic (NTSC & PAL) & one-inch tape.

CTN
Proudly Serves New Jersey
124 West State Street
Trenton, NJ 08608
1-800-421-0443   (fax) 609-392-8682

Cable Television Network of New Jersey Inc. 124 W. State St., Trenton, N.J. 08608. (609) 392-4360; (800) 421-0443. FAX: (609) 392-8682. James A. DeBold, exec dir.
 TV-CATV only.
 A 24-hour statewide net providing community svc & coml progmg.

Cadena Radio Centro (CRC Radio Network). 1645 N. Vine St., Suite 220, Hollywood, Calif. 90028. (213) 463-3800. FAX: (213) 463-5724. Carlos Aguirre, vice chmn; Barrett L. Alley, pres; Tony Hernandez, VP/gen sls mgr; Ilia Leon, affil rels dir; Richard Santiago, news dir.
 A 24-hour Spanish radio net featuring news, mus, talk, sports. Hispanic coverage 87%.

Calico Entertainment. 8843 Shirley Ave., Northridge, Calif. 91324. (818) 701-5862. FAX: (818) 772-1484. Tom Burton, pres/CEO.
 Total prod source in animation, special effects, computer graphics & live-action for TV/CATV & radio.

Call for Action Inc. 3400 Idaho Ave. N.W., Suite 101, Washington 20016. (202) 537-0585. TDD: (202) 537-1551. FAX: (202) 244-4881. Shirley L. Rooker, pres.
 Provides nationwide info & assistance to individuals & small businesses unable to solve their consumer problems.

Camelot Entertainment Sales. 1700 Broadway, 35th Fl., New York 10019. (212) 315-4747. FAX: (212) 247-7674. Steven R. Hirsch, pres; Michael Auerbach, sr VP east coast sls; Robin King, dir midwest sls; Jay Leon, VP rsch.
 TV-CATV only.
 Barter syndication sls for King World Productions, Claster Television, MGM-Pathe, Western International & others.

Candid Productions Inc. 250 W. 57th St., Suite 1818, New York 10107. (212) 581-9450. FAX: (212) 581-9373. Richard T. Button, pres; Michael J. Mathis, VP prod & mktg; Miriam Chaban, controller.
 Produces TV prog & promotional films.

CanLib Inc. 19324 Santa Rita St., Tarzana, Calif. 91356. (818) 705-7843. FAX: (818) 881-1013. Gene Accas, pres; Carol Stevens, exec VP; Stephanie Finamore, sec/treas.
 TV-CATV only.
 Bcstg & media consulting: rsch, sls dev, sls promotion & tailor-made creative material for prods, distributors, advertisers & agencies.

Cannell Distribution Co. 7083 Hollywood Blvd., Hollywood, Calif. 90028. (213) 465-5800. FAX: (213) 856-7987. Pat Kenney, pres.
 TV-CATV only.
 Syndicated TV distribution.

Cannell Studios. 7083 Hollywood Blvd., Hollywood, Calif. 90028. (213) 465-5800. FAX: (213) 856-7454. Stephen J. Cannell, chmn/CEO; Michael J. Dubelko, pres; Howard D. Kurtzman, sr VP business & legal affrs; Joseph C. Kaczorowski, sr VP/CFO.
 TV-CATV only Stephen J. Cannell Productions (a subsidiary company). Kim LeMasters, pres.

Capital Cities/ABC Video Enterprises. 77 W. 66th St., New York 10023. (212) 456-7777. FAX: (212) 456-7635. Herbert A. Granath, pres; Bruce Maggin, exec VP; Jack Healy, pres Capital Cities/ABC Video Enterprises International; Archie Purvis, pres ABC Distribution Company.
 Prog supplier for cable, home video, educ & theatrical mkts. Involved in developing communication technologies.

Producers, Distributors, Production and Other Services

Capital Cities/ABC Video Enterprises International. 825 7th Ave., 5th Fl., New York 10019. (212) 456-1725. FAX: (212) 456-1708. John T. Healy, pres Video Enterprises International; Joseph Y. Abrams, pres ABC Distribution Co.

Capital Communications. Box 70188, Nashville 37207. (615) 868-2040. FAX (615) 868-5239. James Springer, pres/COO; Robert Springer, CEO.
TV-CATV only.
International distributor of pre-packaged TV prog.

Capitol Production Music. 6922 Hollywood Blvd., Suite 718, Hollywood, Calif. 90028. (213) 461-2701; (800) 421-4163. Fax: (213) 461-1543. Ole Georg, pres/sls mgr.
Produces mus for bcstg, film & video; CDs & LPs; longer versions & edited sound beds. Custom scoring is available.

The Caption Center. 125 Western Ave., Boston 02134. (617) 492-9225. FAX: (617) 562-0590. Trisha O'Connell, dir.
Offices in New York & Los Angeles.
Provides captioning, subtitling & consulting.

Carden & Cherry Inc. 1220 McGavock St., Nashville 37203. (615) 255-6694. FAX: (615) 255-9302. Jerry Carden, pres; Tom Sparks, sr VP; John R. Cherry III, exec VP.
TV & radio coml prod & distribution; prod svcs.

Caridi Entertainment. 250 W. 57th St., Suite 1416, New York 10107. (212) 581-2277. FAX: (212) 581-2278. Carmella Caridi, pres/CEO; Peter M. Hargrove, VP sls & acquisitions.
Full-svc international distributor & prod company.

Carleton Productions Inc. 1500 Merivale Rd., Nepean, Ont., Canada K2E 6Z5. (613) 224-1313. FAX: (613) 224-9074. Wayne Hicks, VP/gen mgr; Dianne van Velthoven, Bill Graham, Randi Hansen, Mark Ross, prod & account execs.
TV & radio prog & coml prod & distribution; prod svcs.

George Carlson & Associates. 2512 2nd Ave., #306, Seattle 98121. (206) 441-1466. George Carlson, prod.
TV-CATV only.
Prods & distributes 1/2 hour color, true life, travel adventure series to all parts of the world called *The Traveler & Northwest Traveler.*

Carolco Television Inc. 8800 Sunset Blvd., Los Angeles 90069. (310) 859-8800. FAX: (310) 657-1629. Jeffrey Kazmar, VP TV; Paula Ely, sls support.
TV-CATV only.
Pay-per-view prods & distributors for cable TV.

Carpel Video Inc. 429 E. Patrick St., Frederick, Md. 21701. (800) 238-4300. FAX: (301) 694-9510. Andy Carpel, pres.
Videotape recyclers; prod svcs.

Carriage House Studios. 119 W. Hill Rd., Stamford, Conn. 06902. (203) 358-0065. FAX: (203) 964-4988. John Montagnese, pres; Patricia Spicer, studio mgr.
TV & radio prog, coml prod; promotional film prod; prod svcs.

Casablanca Productions. 8544 Sunset Blvd., Los Angeles 90069. (310) 659-2067. FAX: (310) 285-0965. David Nelson, pres/dir; Lisa Shanks, exec prod; Penny Johnson, postprod supvr; Stu Berg, dir.
TV coml prod & postprod.

Cascom International Inc. 806 4th Ave. S., Nashville 37210. (615) 242-8900. FAX: (615) 256-7890. Victor Rumore, pres.
Graphic effects library, animated film elements, custom prod, stock comls, newsreel & archival footage, mus & sound effects libraries for TV, radio & corporate prods.

Cass Broadcasting Inc. Murray Hill Station 367, New York 10156. (212) 982-7699. Gregory H. Castello, pres/CEO.
Radio prog prod, distribution & syndication svcs.

Castle Hill Productions Inc. 1414 Ave. of the Americas, New York 10019. (212) 888-0080. FAX: (212) 644-0956. Julian Schlossberg, pres; Mel Maron, mktg & distribution; Barbara Karmel, sr acct exec; Milly Sherman, dir sls svcs.
TV prog prod & distribution.

Catholic Communication Campaign. 3211 4th St. N.E., Washington 20017. (202) 541-3355. FAX: (202) 541-3129. Ramon Rodriguez, dir.
TV & radio prod & distribution.

Catholic Communications Office. 65 Elliot St., Springfield, Mass. 01101. (413) 732-4546. FAX: (413) 747-0273. Michael A. Graziano, coord communications.
TV & radio prod svcs.

Celebrities Productions. 8229 Maryland Ave., St. Louis 63105. (314) 721-1247. I.J. Davis, pres; David Dovich & Walt Williams, VPs.
Creation & prod of radio & TV spots, progs & audio visuals; arrangement for celebrity talent, mus, syndication & video conference prod.

Celtic Eye Television. 300 E. 42nd St., New York, 10017. (212) 818-0700. FAX: (212) 370-3859. Patrick Murphy, pres.

Center City Film & Video. 1503-05 Walnut St., Philadelphia 19102. (215) 568-4134. FAX: (215) 568-6011. Jordan M. Schwartz, chmn; Frank C. Beazley Jr., pres.
TV-CATV only.
Video, film prod & postprod, bcst, corporate, studio, remote, film-to-tape, motion control, AVID.

Century Features Inc. Box 597, Pittsburgh 15230. (412) 471-6533. FAX: (412) 281-7227. Charles Reichblum, pres.
Syndicates radio/TV progs *Teasers & Nuggets of Knowledge.*

Century III at Universal Studios. 2000 Universal Studios Plaza, Orlando, Fla. 32819-7606. (407) 354-1000. FAX: (407) 352-8662. Ross M. Cibella, pres; Winston Shepherd, dir postprod opns; Pamela Warren, VP sls & mktg.
Full-svc postprod facility, audio dept, custom high-end graphics, digital recording capabilities, mobile facilities & satellite uplink for TV/CATV & radio.

Channel America Television Network. 19 W. 21st St., New York 10010. (212) 366-9880. FAX: (212) 366-9890. Ted Kavanau, pres; David A. Post, vice chmn; Veronica Albrecht, VP.
TV-CATV only.
Family oriented progmg via satellite; movies, sports, drama, animation, talk shows.

Channel One Inc. 1727 Clifton Rd. N.E., Atlanta 30329-4099. (404) 634-3324. FAX: (404) 634-3326. William W. Horlock, pres.
TV & radio prog & coml, promotional film prod & distribution; audio prod svcs.

Sam Chase Associates Inc. 118 W. 79th St., New York 10024. (212) 799-4455. Sam Chase, pres.
TV prog prod; radio prog prod & distribution.

Ramon Cheber Enterprises. 1600 Broadway, Office 1006, New York 10019. (212) 581-2252. FAX: (212) 765-5430. Ramon Cheber, pres.
Film, video & TV prog distribution.

Chicago Radio Syndicate Inc. 1140 N. La Brea, Los Angeles 90038. (800) 621-6949. FAX: (213) 460-4280. Sandy Orkin, pres.
Syndication of Dick Orkin comedy features—Chickenman, Tooth Fairy & Mini-People.

Chicago Symphony Orchestra/Amoco Radio Network. c/o WFMT Fine Arts Network. 303 E. Wacker Dr., Chicago 60601. (312) 565-5000. FAX: (312) 565-5169. Daniel J. Schmidt, sr VP; David Levin, dir; Carol Martinez, opns mgr; Jim Barker, gen sls mgr; Norman Pellegrini, prod/host.
Wkly series of concerts from Chicago's Orchestra Hall & Ravinia Festival.

Child of God Broadcasting Network. (A division of Holy Bible Gospel Ministry). 429 Cliffside, Houston 77076. Dr. Lawrence Herbst, pres/chmn of bd; Ruth Gray, VP.
Gospel radio & TV DBS stn, recording studio, satellite dish manufacturer/inventor.

Children's Media Productions. Box 40400, Pasadena, Calif. 91114. (818) 797-5462. FAX: (818) 797-7524. C. Ray Carlson, pres; Joy Carlson, pub rels.
Prod & distributor of children's progs, videos & feature films.

Children's Television Workshop. One Lincoln Plaza, New York 10023. (212) 595-3456. FAX: (212) 875-6110. David Britt, pres.
TV prog prod.

Christian Children's Associates. Box 446, Toms River, N.J. 08754. (908) 240-3003. Jean Donaldson, exec dir; Frank Troilo, VP; Gertrude McCandless, treas; Richard Trotter, prod.
Prod & distribution of radio & TV progmg for children; new prog for grandparents.

The Christian Science Publishing Society. One Norway St., C-20, Boston 02115-3122. (617) 450-2000. FAX: (617) 450-2905. David Cook, editor radio bcstg; David Creigh, exec prod radio bcstg.
Radio programs.

Christian TV Services of Ellicottville Inc. Box 209, 12 Elizabeth St., Ellicottville, N.Y. 14731-0209. (716) 699-2549. Rev. George A. Thayer, pres/CEO; Roger A. Thayer, VP; Joyce Thayer, sec/treas; Randy Thayer & Robert A. Thayer, exec offs.
Religious radio & TV prod; satellite consultants.

The Christophers Inc. 12 E. 48th St., New York 10017. (212) 759-4050. FAX: (212) 838-5073. Rev. John T. Catoir, dir; Cecilia Harriendorf, exec prod radio & TV.
TV & radio prod & distribution.

The Church of Jesus Christ of Latter-day Saints. 15 East South Temple St., Salt Lake City 84150. (801) 240-4612; (801) 240-4397. FAX: (801) 240-1167. Don Russell, mgr electronic media mktg.
Offers free pub affrs, news & feature progmg, & guests for talk shows. Pub affrs progmg is not "church-oriented."

Maria Chychula Ukrainian Radio. 2224 W. Chicago Ave., Chicago 60622. (312) 276-3747. Maria Chychula, prog dir.
Radio prog, coml prod & distribution.

Cimarron/Bacon/O'Brien. 758 N. Highland Ave., Hollywood, Calif. 90038. (213) 461-5850. FAX: (213) 461-1025. Linda Brady, mktg dir; Jeffrey Bacon, Chris Arnold, Bob Farina, John O'Brien, ptnrs.
TV promotions, special shoots, graphics, sls presentations, trade & consumer print design, title treatment & image campaigns.

Cinecraft Productions Inc. 2515 Franklin Blvd., Cleveland 44113. (216) 781-2300. FAX: (216) 781-1067. Neil G. McCormick, chmn; Maria E. Keckan, pres.
TV-CATV only.
Betacam SP field prod, 60'x 80' studio with hard cyc. Betacam SP, 3/4 SP & 1" to 1" edit suites.

CineFilm Laboratory Inc. 2156 Faulkner Rd. N.E., Atlanta 30324. (404) 633-1448. FAX: (404) 633-3867. William G. Thornton, pres.
TV-CATV only.
16-35mm negative processing, 16-35mm liquid gate printing, internegatives, dup negatives, feature dailies & screening.

Cinema Circle Productions Ltd. 162 W. 56th St., Suite 707, New York 10019. (212) 757-7662. Anthony P. LaMarca, pres.
TV progs, comls, promotional films, home video prod & gen prod svcs.

Cinema Concepts Animation Studio. 2030 Powers Ferry Rd., #214, Atlanta 30339. (404) 956-7460. FAX: (404) 956-8358. Stuart D. Harnell, CEO; Sharron A. Harnell, VP/gen mgr; Richard Neville, studio dir; Chris Glass, art dir.
Animated corporate IDs, presentation/policy trailers for TV, cable & motion picture theaters.

Cinema Consulting Group. Box 93, 8033 Sunset Blvd., Los Angeles 90046. (213) 650-5646. FAX: (213) 650-2006. Michael F. Goldman, pres.
TV-CATV only.
Consultant, theatrical features; mktg, distribution, all media-international.

Cinema Great Inc. 118 E. 65th St., New York 10021. (212) 628-8600. Bernard L. Schubert, pres.
TV-CATV only.
TV prog distribution.

The Cinema Guild Inc. 1697 Broadway, Suite 506, New York 10019. (212) 246-5522. FAX: (212) 246-5525. Gary Crowdus, pres; Philip Hobel, chmn; Mary Ann Hobel, co-chmn.
TV-CATV only.
Film & video distribution to theatrical, non-theatrical, TV & home video mkts.

Cinema Sound Ltd. 311 W. 75th St., New York 10023. (212) 799-4800. FAX (212) 799-2057. Joan S. Franklin, pres; John S. Rockwell, prod dir.
Radio prog prod & distribution; gen prod svcs.

Cine-Tele Productions. Box 270693, San Diego 92128-0987. (619) 673-5151. Harry J. Lehman, own/mgr.
Business & training films.

Circle Oak Productions Inc. 33 N. Birch Hill Rd., Patterson, N.Y. 12563. (914) 878-9017. Peter J. Lodge, pres.
Educ & industrial film prod; TV & radio adv prod.

Producers, Distributors, Production and Other Services

Circle Video Productions. 631 Mainstream Dr., Nashville 37228. (615) 244-1717. FAX: (615) 259-3962. Rich Sublett, prod svc mgr.
TV-CATV only.
Full range video & film prod facility; 25 x 40 studio & 60 x 60 studio soundstage; betacams & a var of tape formats for TV/CATV.

Tim Cissell Music. 604 Newberry Dr., Richardson, Tex. 75080-5621. (214) 680-0817. Tim Cissell, own.
Offers mus composition & prod for media (TV/CATV & radio): jingles, IDs, film & video.

City Film Center. (A division of City Film Productions.) 64-12 65th Pl., Middle Village, N.Y. 11379-1624. (718) 456-5050. John R. Gregory, exec prod; Herbert Avvenire, prod.
TV prog, coml, promotional film prod; prod svcs.

The Dick Clark Productions. 3003 W. Olive Ave., Burbank, Calif. 91505. (818) 841-3003. FAX: (818) 954-8609. Dick Clark, chmn/CEO; Francis C. Lamaina, pres/COO; Kenneth Ferguson, CFO.
TV prod for nets, cable & syndication. Produces series, specials & movies for TV.
TV-CATV only.

Wally Clark Productions. 380 Madison Ave., 7th Fl. New York 10017. (212) 856-4428. FAX: (212) 697-5490. Wally Clark, pres.
Provides daily satellite comedy svcs, radio stn liner & "attitude" voices & syndicated radio progmg.

Classic Films International Inc. Box 446, Lovingston, Va. 22949-0446. (804) 263-5000. FAX: (804) 456-2199. Joseph Clement, CEO/pres.
TV-CATV only.
TV & film library; archival footage available.

Claster Television Inc. 9630 Deereco Rd., Timonium, Md. 21093. (410) 561-5500. FAX: (410) 561-5509. John Claster, pres; Sally C. Bell, exec VP; Janice Carter, sr VP sls; Terri Akman, prog dir; Peggy Powell, acct exec/dir creative svcs; Dana Feldman, distribution; Ann Vickers, acct exec.
TV prog distribution.

Clausen Communications Inc. 23 Phillips Rd., Nahant, Mass. 01908-1123. (617) 593-2437. FAX: (617) 592-1150. Henry Barentz, CEO; C. Clausen, pres; Chris Clausen, VP.
Net quality voice-overs for TV & radio stns. Digital or analog delivery.

Clayton-Davis & Associates Inc. 8229 Maryland Ave., St. Louis 63105. (314) 862-7800. FAX: (314) 721-5171. Irvin Davis, pres; Steve Pezold, VP.
Prog prod, syndication & barter.

Club Theatre Network Inc. 2095 N. Andrews Ave. Extension, Pampano Beach, Fla. 33069. (305) 946-2341. FAX: (305) 979-6372. Larry Glauber, gen mgr.
Prod & postprod for video & film. HDTV film to tape transfers. Symbolics computer graphics.

Coe Film Associates Inc. 65 E. 96th St., New York 10128. (212) 831-5355. FAX: (212) 996-6728. Bernice Coe, pres; Mignon Levey, dir sls.
TV-CATV only.
TV prog distribution.

Joel Cohen Productions & Distribution Inc. 11500 Olympic Blvd., Suite 418, Los Angeles 90064. (310) 473-7444. FAX: (310) 473-7091. Joel Cohen, pres; Michael Cohen, VP sls worldwide; Larry Cohen, VP production/co-production.
TV-CATV only.
Prods & distributors for TV, syndication, cable & home video; domestically & internationally.

Colbert Television Sales. 1835 Centinela Ave. Santa Monica, Calif. 90404. (310) 998-5828. FAX: (310) 998-9194. Richard H. Colbert, own; Meri Hillier, pres.
TV-CATV only.
Syndication: *Rifleman*.

Collector Watch TV Show. Box 2777, Alexandria, Va. 22301. (703) 548-8007. Clayton Willis, pres/exec prod/critic/White House correspondent.
TV prod company produces documentaries on collectors, collections & art. Library of historical footage; camera; prod facilities.

Columbia Pictures Television. Sony Pictures Plaza, 10202 W. Washington Blvd., Culver City Calif. 90232. (310) 280-8000. Gary Lieberthal, chmn; Mel Harris, pres; Robert Cook, sr VP rsch; David Mumford, sr VP rsch; Ed Wilson, sr VP syndication; Francine Beougher, VP syndication opns; Alan Daniels, VP creative svcs; Lon Feldman, VP motion picture syndication prod; Elise Keen, VP syndication contracts; Terry Mackin, VP eastern rgn; Leslie Tobin, VP motion picture & TV sls.

New York 10022: 711 5th Ave. (212) 702-2920. FAX: (212) 702-6239. Terry Mackin, VP syndication eastern rgn; David Ozer, div mgr; Gerry Stynes, div mgr.
Chicago 60611: 455 N. Cityfront Plaza Dr., Suite 3120. (312) 644-0770. FAX: (312) 644-0781. Stuart Walker, div mgr midwestern rgn; Tom Cauldo, acct exec.
Atlanta 30309: 1201 W. Peachtree St., No. 4820. (404) 892-2725. Susan Grant, VP southeastern rgn; Steve Maddox, account exec southeastern rgn.
Dallas 75225: 8117 Preston Rd., Suite 510. (214) 987-3671. Joe Kissack, mgr syndication southwestern rgn.

Combs Music. 313 Beechcliff Ct., Winston-Salem, N.C. 27104. (919) 760-3855. FAX: (919) 760-3855. David M. Combs, own.
Composes, produces, publishes & distributes easy lstng instrumental mus, e.g. "Rachel's Song."

Command Productions. Box 2824, San Francisco 94126. (415) 332-3161. FAX: (415) 332-1901. Warren Weagant, pres; Kitt Weagant, VP.
Radio prog, coml prod & distribution; distribution svcs.

Communication Bridges. 180 Harbor Dr., Suite 204A, Sausalito, Calif. 94965. (415) 331-3133. FAX: (415) 331-3141. Jon Leland, pres/creative dir; Lisa Reutter, prod mgr.
TV-CATV only.
Educ video progs, including *The Desktop Video-Video*, a 20-minute overview of the advantages of the latest low cost prod tools.

Communications Associates. Broadcasting House, Monte Rio, Calif. 95462-0250. (707) 865-2623. Lt. Col. Clifford Anchor, Robert J. Booth.
Radio only.
Provides radio prog prod & distribution. Offers antenna site use for western Sonoma county, Santa Rosa & the northern San Francisco rgn.

Communications III Inc. 1201 Olentangy River Rd., Columbus, Ohio 43212. (614) 294-4445. FAX: (614) 297-1616. Scott Halliday, pres; Elizabeth Seacrist, office mgr; Mark Alphin, chief engr.
TV-CATV only.
C-Band satellite uplink svcs for TV/CATV. Central Ohio PictureTel videoconferencing dealers.

Communi-Creations Inc. 2130 S. Bellaire St., Denver 80222. (303) 759-1155. FAX: (303) 757-1832. Don Spencer, pres.
TV & radio coml, promotional film prod & distribution; prod svcs.

Compact Video Services Inc. 2813 W. Alameda Ave., Burbank, Calif. 91505. (818) 840-7000; (800) 423-2277. FAX: (818) 846-5197. Robert K. Glassenberg, VP sls & mktg.

Compu-Weather Inc. Box 1122, 29-50 Union St., Flushing, N.Y. 11354. (718) 961-4242. FAX: (718) 353-1294. Jeff Wimmer, pres; Todd Gross, VP; Peter Muldavin, sls mgr.
Weather & environmental features, actualities, forecasts & info.

Com/Tech Communication Technologies Inc. 770 Lexington Ave., New York 10021. (212) 826-2935. FAX: (212) 688-4264. Gregory W. Harer, pres; Ellen Rae Zalk, VP.
TV-CATV only.
Full-svc prod company providing both prod & postprod facilities & svcs for TV/CATV. Wall Street & Midtown studio facilities with two-way fiber optic & microwave linkage to Waterfront Communications.

Concept Productions. 120 Main St., Roseville, Calif. 95678. (916) 782-7754; (800) 783-3454. FAX: (916) 786-8304. Dick Wagner, pres; Mary Wagner, VP.
Produces five mus formats: AC, Country, Gold, CHR, MOR on reels or DAT; plus voice-tracks by major market announcers.

Consolidated Film Industries (CFI). 959 N. Seward St., Hollywood, Calif. 90038. (213) 960-7444. FAX: (213) 460-4885. Jerry Virnig, pres; George Hutchison, exec VP; Michel Papadaki, VP sls & mktg.
TV-CATV only.
Film processing; titles & opticals; videotape transfers; stage & office rentals.

Consumer Information Center. GSA Bldg., 18th & F Sts. N.W., Washington 20405. FAX: (202) 501-4281. Teresa Nasif, dir.

Consumer Savings Network. 40 Sheppard Ave. W., 8th Fl., Toronto, Ont., Canada M2N 6K9. (416) 730-8414. FAX: (416) 730-8591. Dennis Kwasnicki, pres; Janice Lee, dir sls.
TV-CATV only.
New Canadian TV net with scheduled 15 & 30 minute infomercial progs for TV/CATV. Digital signal. In-house creative & prod.

Continental Recordings Inc. 230 Adams St., Newton, Mass. 02158. (617) 630-0007. FAX: (617) 630-0019. L. Daniel Flynn, pres.
TV-CATV-Radio
Coml jingles, stn IDs, original mus creation & prod, cassette duplication.

William F. Cooke Television Programs. 890 Yonge St., Suite 800, Toronto, Ont., Canada M4W 3P4. (416) 967-6141. FAX: (416) 967-5133. William F. Cooke, pres; Clifford H. Wilson, VP sls.
TV-CATV only.
TV prog prod & distribution.

Coote Communications. 9 Trailsmoke Cres., Etobicoke-Toronto, Ont., Canada M9C 1L9. (416) 621-2565. Morgan Coote, pres; Donald Coote, VP.
TV-CATV only.
Complete film & videotape prod from script to screen.

Coral Pictures Corp. 6101 Blue Lagoon Dr, Miami, Fla. 33126. (305) 261-9660. FAX: (305) 261-9490. Marcel Granier, pres/CEO; German Perez, exec VP/gen mgr; Gustavo Basalo, exec VP mktg & sls; T. Sheila Hall, dir mktg communications; Marco Lovera, atty/sec.
TV-CATV only.
TV prog prod & distribution.

Cori Films International. 2049 Century Park E., Suite 1100, Los Angeles 90067. (310) 557-0173. FAX: (310) 785-0016. Marie Hoy, pres; Graham King, servicing.
TV & film distribution.

Cornell University Media Services. NB 13 MVR Hall, Ithaca, N.Y. 14853-4401. (607) 255-5431. FAX: (607) 255-1533. David O. Watkins Jr., dir media svcs; Glen Palmer, mgr business & prod svcs.
Satellite uplinks, Betacam video prod & postprod, audio prod.

Corporate Communications Inc. (A division of the Rockey Co.) 2121 5th Ave., Seattle 98121. (206) 728-1778. FAX: (206) 728-2464. Robley W. Sundmacher, pres; Susan A. McAllister, VP.
Corporate & financial film prod.

The Cramer Co. 4605 Lankershim Blvd., Suite 617, North Hollywood, Calif. 91602. (213) 877-7027. FAX: (213) 877-0159. Douglas S. Cramer, pres; Dennis L. Hammer, supvr prod.
TV prog prod.

Thomas Craven Film Corp. 5 W. 19th St., New York 10011-4016. (212) 463-7190. FAX: (212) 627-4761. Michael Craven, pres; Ernest Barbieri, VP.
Complete film & video prod svcs from scripting through shooting, editing & distribution.

Crawford Communications. 535 Plasamour Dr., Atlanta 30324. (404) 876-7149. FAX: (404) 876-8956. Jesse C. Crawford, pres; Steve Carlisle, exec VP; Susan Shipsky, mgr bcst sls; Randy Bishop, mktg dir.
Computer graphics, animation, prod & postprod svcs, satellite teleport addressing the entire domestic arc.

Creative International Activities Ltd. 372 Central Park W., New York 10025. (212) 663-8944. FAX: (212) 724-1436. TWX: 423 409 ITTUI. Klaus J. Lehmann, pres.
International TV prog distribution.

Creative Marketing & Communications Corp. 3914 Miami Rd., Cincinnati 45227. (513) 271-6632; (800) 845-8477. FAX: (513) 271-6651. Terry Dean, pres; Joyce Koop, Kevin Foss, account executives.
Syndicated 30- to 60-second features & 30-second coml wrap-arounds™.

Creative Media Associates Inc. 1219 Florida Ave., Palm Harbor, Fla. 34683. (813) 785-3888. FAX: (813) 785-6757. James Doulgeris, pres; William Clark, exec VP.
Conception, creation, dev, prod & placement of transactional & entertainment progmg.

Producers, Distributors, Production and Other Services

Creative Production Services Inc. Halle Bldg., 1228 Euclid Ave., Suite 820, Cleveland 44115. (216) 771-7711. FAX: (216) 566-8901. Mike H. Shields, pres.
Meeting mgmt; audio & visual svcs; radio & TV prod; special events mgmt.

Creative Productions Inc. 200 Main St., Orange, N.J. 07050. (201) 676-4422. FAX: (201) 676-0868. Gus J. Nichols, pres; Marcia Nichols, VP.
Video prod & postprod, computer generated speaker support slides, script writing, sound recording, photography, photo lab, modem slide imaging.

Creative Radio Network. Box 7749, Thousand Oaks, Calif. 91359. (805) 379-4012. FAX: (805) 379-1741. Darwin Lamm, pres.
Radio prog prod & syndication - all formats; holiday & artist specials.

Creative Sports. 7621 Little Ave., Suite 516, Charlotte, N.C. 28226. (704) 541-6600. FAX: (704) 541-6666. Bray Cary, pres/CEO; Mike Wells, exec VP prod; Robert Barnwell, comptroller; Greg Walter, affil rels; Tony Renaud, dir sls; Armando Fitz, VP racing.
TV-CATV-Radio
Prod & distributor of TV sports events including college & professional basketball, boxing & auto racing for over the air & cable.

Crest National Videotape & Film Laboratories. 1000 N. Highland Ave., Hollywood, Calif. 90038. (213) 466-0624. FAX: (213) 461-8901. Ron Stein, VP/gen mgr.
TV-CATV only.
Full videotape postprod including film transfer, processing, sweetening & duplication.

The Crime Channel. 13601 Ventura Blvd., Suite 103, Sherman Oaks, Calif. 91423. (818) 907-5769. FAX: (818) 907-5997. Amie Frank, pres; Sheldon Altfeld, VP net opns; Joan Frank, dir mktg.
TV-CATV only.
TV prog distribution.

Criterion Productions Inc. 331 Melrose Dr., Suite 100, Richardson, Tex. 75080. (214) 907-2525. FAX: (214) 669-0677. Robert B. May Jr., pres/CEO.
TV-CATV only.
Ind video prod company offering video editing & duping svcs. Prods of natl cable TV progmg.

Ben Cromer Productions. 1802 Key Blvd., No. 481, Arlington, Va. 22201. (703) 528-8670. Ben Cromer, prod/writer/editor.
Feature writing & script preparation for print & bcst media; specializing in the mus & entertainment industry.

Cross Country Entertainment. 609 Shendoah Dr., Brentwood, Tenn. 37027. (615) 373-4600. (615) 370-5656. Robert Porter, chmn; Steve Saslow, pres; June Brody, VP.
Prod of radio progs specializing in the country radio format.

Crown International Pictures Inc. 8701 Wilshire Blvd., Beverly Hills, Calif. 90211. (310) 657-6700. FAX: (310) 657-4489. Scott Schwimer, VP business affrs & TV syndication; Mark Tenser, pres/CEO.
Promotional film prod & distribution.

Crown International Television. (A division of Crown International Pictures Inc.) 8701 Wilshire Blvd., Beverly Hills, Calif. 90211. (310) 657-6700. FAX: (310) 657-4489. Sy Shapiro, gen sls mgr.
TV prog prod & distribution.

Crystal Pictures Inc. 1560 Broadway, Suite 503, New York 10036. (212) 840-6181. FAX: (212) 840-6182. Joshua Tager, pres; Sidney Tager, gen sls mgr.
TV-CATV only.
Charlotte, N.C. 28207: 725 Providence Rd. (704) 335-0671. FAX: (704) 333-0672.
Distribution of feature film & svcs to all TV outlets in U.S. & abroad.

Crystal Productions. 1024 Blouin Dr., Dolton, Ill. 60419. (708) 841-2622. FAX: (708) 841-2721. Tim Dwyer, opns mgr.
Full prod & editing; mobile prod for TV/CATV.

Cummings Media Inc. (A division of Integrity Communications.) 2929 E. Camelback Rd., Suite 220, Phoenix 85016. (602) 955-5700. FAX: (602) 955-1454. Douglas Neece, pres; Peggy Kinner, VP media; Eugene Sauder, VP finance.
TV & radio prog distribution.

Cummings Productions. Box 313, Arlington, Vt. 05250. (802) 375-6367. Ralph Waldo Cummings, own.
Mus, lyrics, plus copy for radio & TV comls with prod assistance.

Dan Curtis Distribution Corp. 10000 W. Washington Blvd., Suite 3014, Culver City, Calif. 90232. (310) 280-6567. FAX: (310) 558-5946. Dan Curtis, pres.
TV-CATV only.
Film distribution for TV & home video markets.

Custom Films/Video Inc. 11 Cob Dr., Westport, Conn. 06880. (203) 226-0300. FAX: (203) 227-9435. Lester S. Becker, pres.
TV-CATV only.
TV prog, promotional film prod & distribution; prod svcs.

Custom Productions Inc. 1776 Massachusetts Ave. Cambridge, Mass. 02140. (617) 354-5556. FAX: (617) 354-9776. Steve Stockman, pres.
Creation & prod of custom TV campaigns for radio stns in the top 50 mkts.

Cycle Sat Inc. 119 John K. Hanson Dr., Forest City, Iowa 50436. (800) 622-1865. FAX: (515) 582-6998. Loren A. Swenson, pres; Joycelyn Steil, exec VP; Tom O. Mikkelsen, dir opns; Peter Kenne, mgr tech opns & prod svcs; Mark Cooper, mgr SNV opns.
Distributor of TV comls/traffic via satellite by remote VTR control to 500 stns; radio coml distribution; prod, postprod. Multi-format duplication.

D

DC Audio (Dryden Clarke Audio). 1137 5th St. N.E. Washington 20002. (202) 544-2533. FAX: (202) 544-3048. John Dryden, pres.
Produces *The Daily Feed*, a 90-second political, social radio satire commentary, bcst prod, comedy soundtrack, consultation.

DESIGNefx. (A division of Crawford Communications Inc.) 535 Plasamoore Dr., Atlanta 30324. (404) 876-7149. FAX: (404) 876-8956. Jesse C. Crawford, pres; Steve Carlisle, VP; Susan Shipsky & Bill Sobel, bcst sls.
Design & animation for bcst TV stns & cable nets; svcs include design, 2D & 3D cel animation & motion control cinematography.

DIC Enterprises Inc. 3601 W. Olive Ave., Burbank, Calif. 91505. (818) 955-5400. FAX: (818) 955-5696. Andy Heyward, pres.
TV prog prod.

DLT Entertainment Ltd. 31 W. 56th St., New York 10019. (212) 245-4680. FAX: (212) 315-1132. Donald L. Taffner; John Fitzgerald, CEO; Bob Peyton, exec VP/mgng dir domestic syndication; David Dreilinger, VP business & legal affrs.
TV-CATV only.
TV prog prod & distribution.

DRDP. 3700 Durham Rd., Guilford, Conn. 06437. (203) 457-1032 FAX: (203) 457-1855. Bob Nary, own/pres.
Audio duplication svs. Premium quality cassette, CD-R, DAT & reel to reel. Mastering, printing, packaging, fulfillment, blank tapes & supplies. TV/CATV & radio.

D-V-X International. (A division of Demo-Vox Sound Studio Inc.) 1038 Bay Ridge Ave., Brooklyn, N.Y. 11219. (718) 680-7234. FAX: (718) 680-7234. Frank J. Grassi, pres/dir; Laura B. Grassi, sec-treas/prod coord.
Sound & video recording, creative prod & postprod svcs.

DWJ Television. 16 E. 65th St., New York 10021. (212) 772-6600. FAX: (212) 772-6715. Daniel G. Johnson, pres; Michael L. Friedman, exec VP.
TV & radio progmg & prod; promotional video prod & prod svcs.

Daley Tele-Video Productions. Box 830, Concord, Calif. 94522. (510) 676-7260. FAX: (510) 798-0660. Greg A. Daley, own.
TV-CATV only.
D2, Betacam SP, 1", & 3/4" postprod; TV prod; satellite uplinking; stages & set design.

Darino Films/Library of Special Effects. 222 Park Ave. S., New York 10003. (212) 228-4024. FAX: (212) 473-7448. Ed Darino, CEO.
Special visual effects, stock background footage, ID logos, business courses, English educ tapes, cartoons, children's films & cartoons anthology.

Allan Davidson Associates. 1425 Hopkins St. N.W., Suite 401, Washington 20036. (202) 296-2022. FAX: (202) 775-0580. Allan Davidson, own/pres.
Computer radio show prog prod & syndication.

Daynet Radio. 125 W. End Ave., 6th Fl., New York 10023. (212) 456-5595. Michael A. Castello, pres; Miguel LaBoy, chief engr.
Personality driven, caller intensive, satellite delivered, barter based, talk-radio progmg.

De Wolfe Music Library Inc. 25 W. 45th St., New York 10036. (212) 382-0220. FAX: (212) 382-0278. Andrew M. Jacobs, pres; Mitchel J. Greenspan, VP.
Prod svcs.

DeLuxe Laboratories Inc. 1377 N. Serrano Ave., Hollywood, Calif. 90027. (213) 462-2671; (213) 462-6171. FAX: (213) 461-0608. Burton Stone, pres; Jim Hannafin, exec VP mktg.
Motion picture processing lab with video facility.

Hal Dennis Post Production Rentals. 6314 La Mirada Ave., Hollywood, Calif. 90038. (213) 467-7146. FAX: (213) 467-7235. Harold J. Dennis, pres; D.M. Hill, sec/treas.
TV-CATV only.
Rentals, sls, svc for post prod i.e. Moviolas, flatbeds, splicers, synchronizers & editing tables. TV/CATV only.

Devillier-Donegan Enterprises. 4401 Connecticut Ave. N.W., Suite 601, Washington 20009. (202) 686-3980. FAX: (202) 686-3999. Ronald J. Devillier, pres; Brian Donegan, exec VP; Joane Lanigan, VP business legal affrs; Linda Ekizian, VP international sls.
TV-CATV only.
Worldwide distribution of quality progmg: international & ind documentaries, Hollywood profiles, science series, animation, drama & performing arts.

Devlin Design Group. 12526 High Bluff Dr., 3rd Fl., San Diego Calif. 92130. (619) 792-3676. FAX: (619) 942-2664. Dan Devlin, pres; Carol Vandervelden, VP design svcs; David Smaw, lighting direction; Jerry Chauvin, project mgmt.
TV-CATV only.
Designs, builds & installs news sets & newsrooms. Facility planning, bcst consulting, tech & lighting direction. TV/CATV only.

Dhanus Music Publishing (BMI). Box 2147, Sioux City, Iowa 51104-0147. (712) 276-2295. "Morrie" Miller, professional creative mgr.
Music Publishing.

Dialing for Dollars. (A division of Newhoff Blumberg Inc.) 8203 Arodene Rd., Pikesville, Md. 21208. (410) 486-5718. Frank L. Blumberg, chmn.
TV prog prod & distribution.

Diamond P Sports Inc. 9675 4th Station, St. Petersburg, Fla. 33702. (813) 570-2200. (813) 570-2233. George Orgera, pres; George Elliott, VP/gen mgr.
TV prog prod & distribution.

Digital Animation Corp. 24445 Northwestern Hwy., Suite 105, Southfield, Mich. 48075. (800) 572-0098; (313) 354-0890. FAX: (313) 354-0796. Tom Hamill, pres.
Packaged animations include backgrounds, holidays, adv, corporate, adv & globes, maps & flags.

Disc-Location. Box 155, Whitehall, Mich. 49461. (616) 894-9092. Jim Schlichting, pres; Linda Schlichting, VP.
Radio prog prod & distribution.

The Disney Channel. 3800 W. Alameda Ave., Burbank, Calif. 91505. (818) 569-7500. FAX: (818) 566-1518. John F. Cooke, pres.
Original TV prog prod & distribution.

Walt Disney Co. 500 S. Buena Vista St., Burbank, Calif. 91521. (818) 560-1000. Michael Eisner, chmn/CEO; Jeffrey Katzenberg, chmn/CEO Walt Disney Studios; Richard H. Frank, pres Walt Disney Studios; John Cooke, pres The Disney Channel.

William Ditzel Productions. 933 Shroyer Rd., Dayton, Ohio 45419. (513) 298-5381. FAX: (513) 298-6672. William G. Ditzel, own.
TV prog, coml, promotional film prod; prod svcs.

The Dolmatch Group Ltd. Box 12077, Marina del Rey, Calif. 90295-3077. (310) 306-7566. FAX: (310) 306-3284. Murray Dolmatch, pres; Sandra Dolmatch, VP.
TV-CATV only.
Represents German, French & Italian prods for non-English TV progs in U.S.

The Domain Group. 289 Main Pl., Carol Stream, Ill. 60188. (708) 668-5300. FAX: (708) 668-0158. Edward Elliott, mgng ptnr; Tim Burgess, ptnr; Richard Perry, ptnr.
Recording studios, media agency, high-speed cassette duplicating & fund-raising.

W.P. Donnelly & Associates. 7507 Sunset Blvd., Suite 202, Los Angeles 90046. (213) 850-5861. FAX: (213) 850-5866. W.P. Donnelly, pres.
TV-CATV only.
Mktg & licensing films to pay-TV; net & syndication packages.

Producers, Distributors, Production and Other Services

Doorbell Productions Inc. 370 Windsor Rd., Englewood, N.J. 07631. (201) 569-2562. Bill Britten, pres.
Prod & creation of TV progs & comls.

Drake-Chenault/Jones Satellite Services. Box 9101, Albuquerque 87119-9101. (505) 247-3303. FAX: (505) 247-9964. J. Chris Aschenbeck, group VP/COO; T.J. Lambert, sr VP sls & mktg; Phil Barry, VP progmg & opns; Marlene Maywood, media rels.
Live 24-hour progmg; rsched mus library; matchup playlist. Computer generated song by song list for every hour of the wk. Prog consulting available.

Mark Druck Productions Inc. 300 E. 40th St., New York 10016. (212) 682-5980. Mark Druck, pres; Lisa Dodenhoff, prod.
TV & radio progmg, promotional film prod & distribution.

E

E.F.M. Media Management. 342 Madison Ave., Suite 920, New York 10173. (212) 661-7500. FAX: (212) 661-7945. Edward F. McLaughlin, CEO; John Axten, pres; Stewart Krane, VP/ptnr.
Radio prog prod & distribution.

ESPI Video. 3500 Maple Ave., #400, Dallas Tex. 75219. (214) 522-6699. FAX: (214) 522-7699. Gary Sleeper, pres; Kimball Anderson, sr VP; Mike Pirrello, sr prod.
TV-CATV only.
Full-svc prod company specializing in corporate video prod. Postprod facilities & on-location svcs also available. TV/CATV only.

ESPN Radio Network. ESPN Plaza, Bristol, Conn. 06010. (203) 585-2000. FAX: (203) 589-5523. John A. Walsh, exec edit; Mark W. Mason, gen mgr; Shelby Whitfield, exec prod/dir ABC radio sports.
Sportsbeat with Brent Musburger; sportsbreak covering all major sporting events. Radio only.

ETN - Educational Telecommunications Network. (An ETV svc of the Los Angeles County Office of Education.) The Los Angeles County Office of Education, 9300 Imperial Hwy., Downey, Calif. 90242-2890. (310) 922-6668. FAX: (310) 803-1885. Patricia H. Cabrera, Ph.D., exec dir.
ETN develops & transmits educ progs in the major K-12 curriculum areas as well as adult educ & parent educ progs (via satellite over Ku-Band) to schools, homes & offices nationwide.

EUE Screen Gems/Video Services. 222 E. 44th St., New York 10017. (212) 867-4030. George Cooney, CEO; Jay Kenny, exec VP/gen mgr; Nicholas Bavaro, VP/opns dir; John Clarke, VP finance; Lee Davis, exec prod; Tim Merjos, sls rep; David Elliot, Mike Elliot, Ashley Lazarus, Howard Blume, Mickey Trenner, dirs.
TV prog, coml prod & distribution.

Eagle Media Productions Ltd. Rt. 121, Box 430, Grant Rd., North Salem, N.Y. 10560. (914) 669-5277. Louis C. Adler, pres; Thalia Adler, VP.
Radio prog syndication, prog & news consultant. Prods of *Medical Journal*, *A Matter of Law* & other short form info features offered on barter.

Earthwatch Radio. 10 Science Hall, 550 N. Park St., Madison, Wis. 53706. (608) 263-3063. FAX: (608) 262-2273. Steve Pomplun & Richard Hoops, co-prods.
Daily two-minute radio features on environment & science. Ten progs distributed on cassette bi-weekly.

Ebbets Field Productions Ltd. Box 42, Wykagyl Station, New Rochelle, N.Y. 10804. (914) 636-1281. David Saperstein, pres.
Writers, directors & prods of film (features, TV, cable) & video.

Ecumedia News Service. 475 Riverside Dr., Rm. 856, New York 10115. (212) 870-2312; (212) 870-2227. FAX: (212) 870-2030. Roy T. Lloyd, dir.
News stories, features & actualities about ethics & relg produced for radio.

Ecumenical Communications. Box 270999, West Hartford, Conn. 06127-0999. (203) 521-3573. Robert J. Geckler, own.
Radio prog prod & distribution; prod svcs.

Edit Masters. 324 cooper Rd., Berlin, N.J. 08009. (609) 784-1177. FAX: (609) 346-2697. Michelle Pruyn, pres.
TV-CATV only.
TV prog, coml prod & distribution; prod svcs. Prog dubbing & stn distribution.

Editel-Chicago. 301 E. Erie St., Chicago 60611. (312) 440-2360. FAX: (312) 440-1573. Richard Mandeberg, pres; D.L. Bean, gen mgr.
TV-CATV only.
Postprod: FTT/Renaissance Color Correction, editorial, animation, special audio effects, design prod, EADG at Editel.

Educational Media Australia Pty Ltd. 7 Martin St., South Melbourne, Victoria, Australia 3205. (61) (3) 699-7144. FAX: (61) (3) 699-4947. Ken Widdowson, pres/dir.
TV & hard copy distribution of educ & training progs in Australia, New Zealand & internationally.
TV-CATV only.

Ed-Venture Films. Box 23214, 1122 Calada St., Los Angeles 90023. (213) 261-1885. William E. Hines, pres; Robert E. Hines, VP.
TV prog, coml, promotional film prod; prod svcs & consultation.

Electric Paint & Design. (Lake Tahoe.) Box 8822, Incline Village, Nev. 89452-8822. (702) 323-6868. Jon Paul Davidson, dir/designer; Beth Davidson, writer/prod.
TV-CATV only.
Animation, computer graphics & non-linear editing. TV & CATV.

Ellis Enterprises Ltd. 1231 Yonge St., Suite 201, Toronto, Ont., Canada M4T 2T8. (416) 924-2186. FAX: 416-924-6115. Ralph C. Ellis, chmn; R. Stephen Ellis, pres; M. Kelly Warner, sr sls exec.
TV-CATV only.
Full-svc TV & CATV domestic & foreign prog distribution house, featuring a specialized on-line computer system.

Encore Video Productions Inc. 811 Main St., Myrtle Beach, S.C. 29577. (803) 448-9900. FAX: (803) 448-9235. Rik Dickinson, pres; Frank Payne, VP; Tim Hellaby, prod mgr.
TV-CATV only.
Location & studio prod, specializing in EFP/ENG 1-Camera prods, full script to screen svc, VNR, satellite media tours, teleconferences & magazine TV prod. Betagami SP, 3/4" prod & postprod.

Endless Mountains Radio Prod Inc. R.D. 2, Box 157K, New Milford, Pa. 18834. (717) 465-7712. FAX: (717) 465-7712. Kim Ezra Shienbaum, Ph.D., pres/CEO.
Co-prod/syndication Endless Mountains success stories, radio & inflight audio business info progmg.

Entertainment Programming Services Ltd. (EPS). Box 787 BCE Pl., Suite 100, Toronto, Ont., Canada M5J 2T3. (416) 956-2000. FAX: (416) 956-2020. David W. Jackson, pres; Nat Abraham, VP sls; Jean Bureau, VP sls; Vanda Macura, dir mktg; Donna Schweitzer, mktg coord.
TV-CATV only.
TV prog distribution.

Episcopal Church Center. 815 2nd Ave., New York 10017. (212) 867-8400. FAX: (212) 949-8059. Clement W.K. Lee, electronic media dir; Gary F. Filsinger, media resources mgr.
Spokespersons for church & society issues.

Essence Television Productions Inc. 1500 Broadway, New York 10036. (212) 642-0600. FAX: (212) 921-5173. Clarence O. Smith, pres.
TV prog prod.

European Television Inc. R.D. 1, Westfield, Vt. 05874. (802) 744-6100. Timothy D. McInerny, chmn/CEO; Robert G. Sholty, VP mktg; Jochen G. Balan, VP/European dir.
TV prog prod & distribution.

Evangelical Lutheran Church in America. 8765 W. Higgins Rd., Chicago 60631. (312) 380-2952. FAX: (312) 380-2406. John L. Peterson, dir pub media.
TV & radio progmg, promotional film prod & distribution; prod svcs.

Evening News Broadcasting Co. Box 2777, Alexandria, Va. 22301. (703) 548-8007. Clayton Willis, pres/White House correspondent.
TV prog company & ind Washington news bureau; historical tape library for dubbing; camera crew & prod facilities available.

Excel Telemedia International Corp. 900 Park Ave., Suite 5D, New York 10021. (212) 288-6980. Ken Israel, pres.
TV-CATV only.
TV prog prod & distribution worldwide.

The Exxel Co. 102 N. Ditmar St., Oceanside, Calif. 92054. (619) 722-8284. FAX: (619) 722-8234. J.Richard Lee, pres; William Kottcamp, mgr.
Radio prog, coml prod & distribution.

F

FTC/New York. 155 W. 18th St., New York 10011. (800) 683-1156. FAX: (212) 633-2301. A. J. Foresta, K. Armstrong.
Full-svc film & TV prod company. Specializing in feature & coml prod. Area of specialty: steadicam.

FTC/Orlando. 503 W.Robinson St., Orlando, Fla. 32801. (407) 422-8246. FAX: (407) 843-0738. A.J. Foresta, pres; K. Armstrong, corp sec; K. Fisher, prod mgr.
Full-svc film & TV prod company specializing in coml & feature prod. Area specialty: steadicam.

Faith for Today. 1100 Rancho Conejo Blvd., Newbury Park, Calif. 91320. (805) 373-7686. (805) 373-7701. Daniel Matthews, exec prod.
TV-CATV only.
Prod & distributer of *Lifestyle Magazine* TV.

The Family Channel. 1000 Centerville Tpke., Virginia Beach, Va. 23463. (804) 523-7300. FAX: (804) 523-7880. Timothy B. Robertson, pres; Ron Harris, VP mktg & corporate communictions; Paul Krimsier, VP progmg; Steve Lentz, VP sls; Craig Sherwood, VP affils.
TV-CATV only.
Family entertainment with original series, movies, comedies, dramas, westerns & children's shows.

Family Stations Inc. 290 Hegenberger Rd., Oakland, Calif. 94621. (510) 568-6200. FAX: (510) 633-7983. Harold E. Camping, pres/gen mgr; Scott Smith, VP; Rick Brine, tech dir; W. Craig Hulsebos, prog mgr.
Radio prog prod & distribution.

Faraone Communications Inc. 162 W. 56th St., Suite 1203, New York 10019. (212) 489-1313. Jennie Faraone, chmn; Ted Faraone, pres.
Media rels svcs to prods & distributors of radio & TV progs.

Favorite TV. (A division of ATA Trading Corp.) 50 W. 34th St., Suite 5C6, New York 10001. (212) 594-6460. FAX: (212) 594-6461. Harold G. Lewis, pres; Susan Lewis, VP.
Worldwide distributors for ind prods in all areas of feature films, made for TV prods, series, documentaries & children's prog.

Features International Ltd. Box 3140, Chesapeake, Va. 23320. (804) 523-0523. FAX: (804) 523-5500. Lynn Hodge, pres; Steve Newton, VP media; Rick Milam, VP prod; Rick Seeberger, VP mktg.
Prod, post prod, media placement, printing & consulting. TV/CATV/Radio

Don Fedderson Productions Inc. 16255 Ventura Blvd., Suite 205, Encino, Calif. 91436. (818) 986-3118. FAX: (818) 986-5328. Don Fedderson, chmn of bd.
TV prog prod.

Toni Ficalora Productions. 10 Castle Rd., Irvington, N.Y. 10533. (914) 591-7344. FAX: (914) 591-8055. Toni Ficalora, pres; Michael A. Ficalora, exec prod.
TV coml prod.

Film House Inc. 230 Cumberland Bend, Nashville 37228. (615) 255-4000. FAX: (615) 256-3380. Curt Hahn, pres; Ron Routson, sr VP; Wayne Campbell, VP mktg; Eric Stein, VP creative dir; Andy Cohen, VP finance; Philip Cheney, VP prod.
Specializing in creating & producing TV mktg campaigns for radio & TV stns worldwide.

Film Service Lab Inc. 95 Harvey St., Cambridge, Mass. 02140. (617) 876-5876. FAX: (617) 497-0151. Lisa Mattei, lab mgr.
Super 8 motion picture lab.

Film/Audio Services Inc. 430 W. 14th St., Suite 311, New York 10014. (212) 645-2112. (212) 255-4220. Bob Summers, pres.
TV-CATV only.
Stock footage library & rsch svcs specializing in historical footage & rsch. Representation of materials on behalf of prods & camera people. TV & CATV.

Films Five Inc. 42 Overlook Rd., Great Neck, N.Y. 11020. (516) 487-5865. Walter Bergman, pres.
TV-CATV only.
Pre- & postprod: film & video comls, documentaries, sls films.

Producers, Distributors, Production and Other Services

Films for Educators Inc./Films for Television. 420 E. 55th St., Suite 6U, New York 10022. (212) 486-6577. FAX: (212) 980-9826. Rochelle Bebell, pres.
Worldwide distribution of documentary, educ & features. Large environmental video series.

Films for the Humanities Inc./FFH Video. Box 2053, Princeton, N.J. 08543. (609) 275-1400. FAX: (609) 275-3767. Harold Mantell, pres; Lisa Schmucki, dir mktg; Marianne Mantell, exec VP.
Distributes progs for bcst & cable industries to nontheatrical, institutional, home video & business mkts.

Films of India. Box 48303, Los Angeles 90048. (213) 383-9217. R.M. Bagai, pres.
Distributes 35mm & 16mm theatrical, educ & documentary films from India for theatres & TV stns in the US & Canada.

Films of the Nations. Box 449, Clarksburg, N.J. 08510. (908) 462-3522. FAX: (908) 294-0330. Paul Weinberg, pres.
TV-CATV only.
TV prog, promotional & educ film distribution.

Financial Media Services Inc. 70 Fairlie St., Suite 350, Atlanta 30303. (404) 524-3830. FAX: (404) 524-3851. Charles Ross, pres/CEO; Larry Culhoun, VP pub rels & promotion; Richard Jordan, VP sls & mktg.
Produces & syndicates nationally syndicated radio show *Your Personal Finance*.

Finger Lakes Productions. Box I, Ithaca, N.Y. 14851. (607) 273-0317. FAX: (607) 277-0961. Paul Bartishevich, pres; Bob Kantor, VP; James Wolff, affil rels dir.
Full-svc radio mktg, prod & syndication.

Fiore & Lane Films. 118 Mallory Ave., Jersey City, N.J. 07304. (201) 432-4474. Albert A. Fiore, pres.
TV coml & promotional film prod & distribution.

Imero Fiorentino Associates Inc. 33 W. 60th St., New York 10023. (212) 246-0600. FAX: (212) 246-6408. Imero Fiorentino, pres; James Hartzer, exec VP/COO; Anthony Salerno Jr., sr VP prod.
TV-CATV only.
TV prod, creative svcs, lighting design, tech supervision svcs & video conferencing.

Firestone Communications Inc. One Maxwell St., East Rockaway, N.Y. 11518. (516) 887-5100. FAX: (516) 887-5157. Jack Firestone, Brian Firestone, ptnrs.
TV-CATV only.
TV prog distribution.

First Marketing Co. 3300 Gateway Dr., Pompano Beach, Fla. 33069. (305) 979-0700. FAX (305) 971-4707. Robert Legler, pres; W. Dale Martin, exec VP/dir sls & mktg; Thomas P. Johnson, VP/national sls mgr; Neil L. Rosenblum, VP cable publications.
Publishes customized newsletters (rsch, write, design & print).

FirstCom Broadcast Services. (A division of Jim Long Companies Inc., a Zomba Co.) 13747 Montfort, Suite 220, Dallas 75240. (214) 934-2222; (800) 858-8880. FAX: (214) 404-9656. Jim Long, chmn; Cecelia Garr, pres/CEO.
Prod & SFX libraries; advertiser creative sls consulting prog; stn IDs; promotions. TV/CATV/Radio.

Fishing the West. Box 46, Oregon City, Ore. 97045. (503) 654-0092. FAX: (503) 654-1690. Larry Schoenborn, exec prod & host; Jeff Boyer, co-host, Lana LaVoie, dir syndication.
TV-CATV only.
TV prog, coml prod & distribution; prod svcs.

Flagg Films Inc. Box 1107, Studio City, Calif. 91614. (818) 985-5050. Don Flagg, pres; Helen Mazeika Flagg, VP.
TV prog, coml, promotional film prod & distribution.

Focal Point Film Productions. 35 Sutton Place, New York 10022. (212) 759-6222. John P. Strang, pres.
TV-CATV only.
Dev of film & TV properties.

Forde Motion Picture Labs. 306 Fairview Ave. N., Seattle 98109. (206) 682-2510; (800) 682-2510. FAX: (206) 682-2560. Richard E. Vedvick, pres.
TV-CATV only.
Overnight processing of 35mm/16mm Eastman color negative dailies; release printing; film to tape transfers.

Four Star International Inc. 1440 S. Sepulveda Blvd., Los Angeles 90025. (310) 444-8400. FAX (310) 444-8696. Alfred Markim, chmn/CEO; Lance Thompson, sr VP; Robert Neece, VP domestic sls; Kristie Smith, VP international sls.
TV-CATV only.
Prods & distributors of TV progs including over 30 classic series & 200 feature films.

Four Star Media. 373 Park Ave. S., 8th Fl., New York 10016. (212) 889-9863. FAX: (212) 685-2714. Ellen M. Silver, own.
Radio progmg prod, distribution & mktg.

Fox Lorber Associates Inc. 419 Park Ave. S., New York 10016. (212) 686-6777. FAX: (212) 685-2625. Richard Lorber, pres/CEO; Kiyoshi Watanabe, COO; Michael Oliveri, exec VP domestic HV; Sheri Levine, sr VP international distribution; Nancy Silverside, dir international sls; Mickie Steinmann, dir international sls; Krysanne Katsoolis, dir acquisitions; Cynthia Barach, dir opns.
Worldwide distributors of film & video properties for home video, standard & non-standard TV.

FoxTape. Fox Television Center, 5746 Sunset Blvd., Los Angeles 90028. (213) 856-1420. FAX: (213) 463-6239. Monte Kuklenski, dir opns.
Videotape prod facilities, stages, equipment, per, rehearsal halls.

Fox 29 WUTV. (Act III Broadcasting). Grand Island, N.Y. 14072. (716) 773-7531. FAX: (716) 773-5753. Willard Stone, VP & gen mgr; Don Moran, gen sls mgr; Dennis Cruz, natl sls mgr; Lois Ringle, prog & mktg dir; Mike Anger, chief engr; Lee Mc Enery, mktg mgr; Robert Bart, controller; Deborah Cardarella, creative svcs dir.
TV-CATV only.
TV coml prod; US rep, SELTEL; Canadian rep, Airtime.

Franciscan Communications. 1229 S. Santee St., Los Angeles 90015. (213) 746-2916. FAX: (213) 747-9126. Cullen Schippe, pres/CEO; Karl Holtsnider, VP product dev; William A. Sheck, VP opns.
TV & radio coml, promotional film prod & distribution; prod svcs.

Sandy Frank Entertainment Inc. 750 Lexington Ave., Suite 1402, New York 10022. (212) 759-9199. FAX: (212) 308-5034. Sandy Frank, chmn/CEO; Maury Shields, VP admin; Joe Fisher, dir mktg; Sandra Spidell, VP opns; Barbara Kal, Eastern European sls rep.
TV-CATV only.
TV prog prod & distribution. *You Asked For It, Name That Tune, Face The Music, & International Psychic Mysteries*.

Erwin Frankel Productions. 127 W. 72nd St., Rm. 2R, New York 10023. (212) 873-1222. FAX: (212) 873-1245. Erwin Frankel, pres; Ellen Rafel, VP.
TV & radio coml, radio prog prod & distribution.

Freedom Sports Network. 30 E. Kiowa, Suite 101, Colorado Springs 80903. (719) 635-8447. FAX: (719) 635-8202. Ron DeLorenzo, pres.
TV prog syndication, prod mgmt svcs, sports & events mktg.

Fremantle International Inc./Talbot Television Ltd. 70 E. 55 St., 18th Fl., New York 10022. (212) 421-4530. FAX: (212) 207-8357. Paul Talbot, pres.
TV prog distribution.

Fries Entertainment Inc. 6922 Hollywood Blvd., 12th Fl., Hollywood, Calif. 90028. (213) 466-2266. FAX: (213) 462-0881. Charles W. Fries, chmn/CEO; Chris Fries, VP dev; Neal Smaler, CFO; Mike Murashko, VP domestic sls; Tony Ginnane, international sls agent.
Domestic & international TV, home video, & feature film prod & distribution.

G

GBI/Gear Broadcasting International Inc. Box 23172, Weybosset St., Providence, R.I. 02902. (401) 274-5121. FAX: (401) 231-0255. Edward R. Robalisky, chmn/pres; Jack G. Thayer, exec VP; G.A. Rainone, VP finance; Noel Howard, VP engrg.
Syndicated prog svcs; SuperNetwork GBI provides news, talk, sports & entertainment progmg to MMDS, TVRO operators & radio stns in a delivered simulcasted format. Provides Gear Super TV to wireless cable operators. Satellite: GTE Spacenet II.

GGP/GGP Sports. 400 Tamal Plaza, Corte Madera, Calif. 94925. (415) 924-7500. FAX: (415) 924-0264. Robert C. Horowitz, pres; Franklin Lowe, VP/gen sls mgr; Jay Elliot, VP prod svc; Ted D. Griggs, VP/sr prod; Hillary Mandel, VP/gen mgr/dir acquisitions & distribution; John Dick, events mgr.
TV-CATV only.
Sports & non-sports TV progmg, distribution & sls; sports mktg & event staging; full-svc prod facilities.

GLL TV Enterprises Inc. 8009 Via Fiore, Sarasota, Fla. 34238. (813) 925-4339. FAX: (813) 925-3976. Gunther L. Less, pres; Ellen G. Less, sec treas; Sharyn Fitter, assoc prod & dir syndication.
TV-CATV only.
TV prog, coml, promotional film prod & distribution.

GMI Media Group. 2012 S. 314th, Suite 121, Federal Way, Wash. 98003. (206) 839-9414. FAX: (206) 839-5112. Ron Erak, pres.
Custom ID jingle packages for AC, country & soft AC. CD prod libraries & voice talent bank. Complete digital liner & ID prod svcs.

GTG Entertainment. Culver Studios. 9336 W. Washington Blvd., Culver City, Calif. 90232. (310) 202-3300. FAX: (310) 202-3559. Grant Tinker, pres; Robert Kaplan, VP.
TV-CATV only.

GWSC Post. 250 Harbor Dr., Stamford, Conn. 06904. (203) 965-6388. FAX: (203) 965-6320. Altan C. Stalker, VP & gen mgr; James Crowe, exec dir opns; Peter Concelmo, dir sls & mktg.
Postprod editing, graphics creation, studio prod, teleconference svcs, duplication & transfer, satellite distribution.

Galavision. 605 3rd Ave., 12th Fl., New York 10158-0180. (212) 455-5200. FAX: (212) 867-6710. Stuart Livingston, VP affil opns; Javier Saralegui, gen mgr adv sls; Luly Estevez, affil sls & mktg; Elena Niell, affil sls & mktg; Olivia Lanza, affil rels coord.
Los Angeles 90045: 6701 Center Dr. W., 15th Fl. (310) 338-0700. FAX: (310) 348-3643. Daniel Huertas, affil sls & mktg; Vera Gonzalez, affil sls & mktg.
Spanish TV prog distribution.

Gannet Productions Inc. 535 Madison Ave., New York 10022. (212) 715-5300. FAX: (212) 715-5358. John Curly, pres.
TV prog, coml & promotional film prod; general prod svcs.

Garrett Entertainment Corp. 1119 E. San Antonio, El Paso, Tex. 79901. (915) 533-4700. FAX: (915) 533-3640. Garrett W. Haston, pres.
TV & radio prog & coml prod; general prod svcs.

Gaylord Syndicom. 65 Music Square W., Nashville 37203. (615) 327-0110. FAX: (615) 320-7473. Jane D. Grams, VP/gen mgr.
TV-CATV only.
TV prog distribution.

Gems Television. 4380 N.W. 128 St., Opa Locka, Fla. 33054. (305) 769-4555. FAX (305) 681-0412. W. Gary McBride, pres; M. Alexander Berger, COO; Mari Carmen Villanveva, dir prog & promotion; Grace Santana, dir mktg svcs; Eduardo Ruiz, dir affil sls international; Thomas Morrison, dir affil sls U.S.
TV-CATV only.
International Sp language multichannel cable prog svc targeted specifically at women. Featuring novellas, mini-series, films, musicals & informational vignettes.

General Broadcasting Co. Inc. 1000 Brown St., Suite 106, Wauconda, Ill. 60084. (708) 526-6655. FAX: (708) 526-9367. Robert E. Potter, pres; Charles E. Maples, VP.
Radio prog prod & distribution; background mus, sound system instal.

General Conference of Seventh-day Adventists. 12501 Old Columbia Pike, Silver Spring, Md. 20904-6600. (301) 680-6300. FAX: (301) 680-6312. Shirley Burton, dir communication; Walter R.L. Scragg, dir Adventist World Radio; David Brillhart, dir media svcs.
Radio & TV prog prod & distribution.

General Media Corp. Inc. 1065 Park Ave., New York 10128. (212) 534-0855. Richard Hall, pres/exec prod; Thomas A. Kennedy, VP/prom mgr.
TV prog, coml, promotional film prod; prod svcs.

Broadcasting & Cable Yearbook 1994

Producers, Distributors, Production and Other Services

General Television Network (GTN). 13320 Northend Ave., Oak Park, Mich. 48237. (313) 548-2500. FAX: (313) 548-8614. Doug Cheek, pres.
Studios, remote equipment, multi-format editing, film transfer, audio & duplication svcs; on site satellite svcs & graphics.

Genesis Entertainment. 30501 Agoura Rd., Suite 200, Agoura Hills, Calif. 91301. (818) 706-6341. FAX: (818) 707-0785. Wayne Lepoff, pres/COO; Gary Gannaway, chmn/CEO.
TV prog prod & distribution.

Girard Video Inc. 1331 F St. N. W., Suite 250, Washington 20004. (202) 393-6666. FAX: (202) 393-1247. Jacques Girard, pres; Andy Hemmendinger, VP.
Video field prod & postprod; computer graphics; random access editing; duplication; satellite transmission.

Gladney Communications Ltd. 85 Old Shore Rd., Port Washington, N.Y. 11050. (516) 767-1955. FAX: (516) 767-1957. Norman Gladney, pres; Marion Gladney, exec VP.
TV & radio prod & distribution.

Glenray Productions Inc. Box 40400, Pasadena, Calif. 91114. (818) 797-5462. FAX: (818) 797-7524. C. Ray Carlson, pres.
TV-CATV only.
Films, TV series & video distribution.

Glen-Warren Productions Ltd. 9 Channel Nine Ct., Scarborough, Ont., Canada M1S 4B5. (416) 291-7571. FAX: (416) 299-2067. Allan P. Chapman, pres.
Co-prod; distributor.

Global Satellite Network. 14958 Ventura Blvd., Sherman Oaks, Calif. 91403. (818) 906-1888. FAX: (818) 906-9736. Howard Gillman, pres.; George Taylor Morris, VP progmg; Nan Kingsley, VP sls.
Radio prog syndicator, young adult mus specialist providing long form & special event progs both live & pre-recorded. Country format progmg & news/talk prog *Food For Thought*.

Globe Net Productions. NTV - Yonbancho-Bekkan, 5-6 Yonbancho, Chiyoda-ku, Tokyo, Japan 102. (813) 3221-1551. FAX: (813) 3221-6143. Bruce MacDonell, exec prod.
Full svcs: prod, writing, shooting, VTR editing, rsch, satellite feeds, fixing. Covers all Asia.

Globe Productions. Box 20465, Roanoke, Va. 24018. (703) 344-3283. J.W. Shepherd, own.
Full-svc automated/live assist mus; full wk, covering 51 yrs of mus, without repeats for radio.

Jeff Gold Productions Inc. 13900 Panay Way, M-319, Marina del Rey, Calif. 90292. (310) 827-9165. Jeff Gold, dir.
TV prog, coml, promotional film prod; prod svcs.

The Samuel Goldwyn Co. 10203 Santa Monica Blvd., Los Angeles 90067. (310) 552-2255. FAX: (310) 284-8493. Samuel Goldwyn Jr., chmn/CEO; Meyer Gottlieb, pres/COO; Jeri Sacks, VP cable & ancillary sls; Dan Gelfand, VP adv; Ron Wanless, sr VP worldwide mktg; Mike Byrd, sr VP international TV sls; Richard H. Askin Jr., pres TV distribution; Leonie de Picciotto, VP publ.
TV prog distribution.

Good Life Associates. Box 81803, Lincoln, Neb. 68501. (402) 474-6440. FAX: (402) 474-4519. Thomas C. Schindler, pres; Martin Jones, mgr.
Radio prog, coml prod & distribution; distribution svcs.

Good News Broadcasting Association Inc. Box 82808, Lincoln, Neb. 68501. (402) 474-4567. FAX: (402) 474-4519. Dr. Woodrow Kroll, gen dir; Brian Erickson, exec dir.
Radio prog prod & distribution.

Good News Video Network. 785 Crossover Ln., Suite 257, Memphis, Tenn. 38117. (901) 685-5884. FAX: (901) 762-8038. Basil Hero, pres; Norfleet Turner, chmn.
TV-CATV only.
Prod & distribution of mthy video magazine licensed to TV stn in each market & distributed through Blockbuster video chain.

Goodman Productions Nashville. Box 23652, Nashville 37202. (615) 746-4789. FAX: (615) 259-4462. Tony Goodman, Rene Goodman, co-exec prods.
Produces TV & radio progs for net, cable, syndication, plus news breaks *Inside Country Music with Rene Goodman* & specs.

Mark Goodson Productions. 375 Park Ave., New York 10152. (212) 751-0600. FAX: (212) 319-0013. Jonathan Goodson, pres; Giraud Chester, exec VP; Alan Sandler, VP finance.
Los Angeles 90036: 5750 Wilshire Blvd. (213) 965-6500. Jonathan Goodson, VP; Michael Brockman, VP.
TV prog prod.

Call Now for Latest Demo at 1-800-814-5588

gordon communications

ERIC GORDON
Television Promotion Announcer

Available for Your Station on a Market Exclusive Basis

Affordable Monthly Retainer

FREE DEMO SESSIONS

Gordon Communications. 1182 Brookhaven Woods Ct., Atlanta 30319. (404) 261-0581. FAX: (404) 816-0449. Eric Gordon.
TV promotion announcements.

Gordon Productions. Box 640549, San Francisco 94164; 1557 Pine St., San Francisco 94109. (415) 776-7484. John Gordon, pres; Jerry Gordon, CEO; Les Lieurance, VP.
Prod & distribution of video news releases, TV pub svc announcements, radio news actualities. Distribution via satellite & cassette.

Gould Entertainment Corp. 101 W. 57th St., New York 10019. (212) 586-5760. Michael J. Gould, pres.
TV-CATV only.
Consultants, packages, distributors of progmg; specialists in mktg foreign progs; non-theatrical distribution.

Gray-Schwartz Enterprises Inc. 4507 Park Allegra, Calabasas, Calif. 91302. (818) 222-6500. Marv Gray, pres.
TV-CATV only.
TV prog syndication rep.

Great Plains National (GPN). Box 80669, Lincoln, Neb. 68501. (800) 228-4630. FAX: (402) 472-1785. Lee Rockwell, dir; Stephen C. Lenzen, assoc dir; Larry Aemi, mktg coord.
TV-CATV only.
Acquires, produces, promotes & distributes videotaped instructional videos for bcst, cablecast & audiovisual use.

Merv Griffin Enterprises. 9860 Wilshire Blvd., Beverly Hills, Calif. 90210. (310) 859-0188. FAX: (310) 859-4998. Robert J. Murphy, pres; Peter Barsocchini, VP dev MP & Primetime.
Full-svc prod company; slate includes *Wheel of Fortune, Jeopardy!* & other series, specials & films.

Sherman Grinberg Film Libraries Inc. 1040 N. McCadden Pl., Hollywood, Calif. 90038. 630 9th Ave., New York NY 10036. (213) 464-7491. (212) 765-5170. FAX: (213) 462-5352; (212) 262-1532. Bernard Chertok, pres (N.Y.); Linda Grinberg, chmn/CEO (Hollywood).
TV-CATV only.
Stock footage & news library.

Jerry M. Gross Productions Inc. Box 2925, La Jolla, Calif. 92038. (619) 459-4448. Jerry Gross, pres/CEO/prod/sportscaster.
TV & radio prog prod & distribution. Sports; play-by-play, anchor, sports talk show host.

Group W Productions Inc. One Lakeside Plaza, 3801 Barham Blvd., Suite 200, Los Angeles 90068. (213) 850-3800. (213) 850-3889. Derk Zimmerman, pres/CEO; Lynn Alford, VP/controller; Stephanie Drachkovitch, VP progmg; Esther Grief, VP prod; Owen S. Simon, VP creative svcs; Barry Stoddard, VP mktg & prog rsch; Brock Kruzic, western rgnl mgr; Karyn Bolger, client rels & promotion mgr; Dana Moorehead, mgr mktg & prog rsch.
New York 10106: 888 7th Ave. (212) 307-3000. FAX: (212) 307-3930. Richard Sheingold, exec VP; Peter Gimber, VP/natl sls mgr syndication sls; Jim Blueweiss, eastern rgnl mgr; Robert Liuag, account exec eastern rgnl syndication sls; Maryann Martin, mktg mgr; Dan Cosgrove, pres media sls; Glen Burnside, VP media sls; Steve Parker, sr account exec media sls; Liz Koman, sr account exec media sls; Scott Collins, jr account exec media sls.
Chicago 60611: 455 Cityfront Plaza Dr. (312) 245-4820. FAX: (312) 245-4826. Patricia Brown, VP midwest media sls; Sean A. O'Boyle, midwest rgnl mgr syndication sls; Brian R. Fleming, midwest div mgr syndication sls.
Atlanta 30328: Concourse Bldg, # 185, 2 Concourse Pkwy. (404) 392-9044. FAX: (404) 671-1607. Jeff Hoops, southern rgnl mgr syndication sls; Tim Lavender, southern div mgr syndication sls.
Pittsburgh 15205: Group W Videoservices. 310 Parkway View Dr. (412) 850-3800. FAX: (412) 747-4726.
Los Angeles 90068: Group W Videoservices & Westinghouse Broadcasting International. 3801 Barham Blvd. (213) 850-3800. FAX: (213) 850-3889. Group W Videoservices: Lee Salas, mgr West Coast sls. Westinghouse Broadcasting International: Catherine Malatesta, VP international; Joseph G. Matesevac, mgr international admin; Sanja Broda, distribution coord international; Barbara Bocek, contract administration international; Ling Chan, international sls asst.
TV prog prod & distribution.

Group W Satellite Communications. 250 Harbor Dr., Stamford, Conn. 06904. (203) 965-6388. FAX: (203) 965-6320. Don Mitzner, pres; Altan C. Stalker, VP/gen mgr; James Crowe, exec dir opns; Peter Concelmo, dir sls & mktg; Cheryl Daly, VP pub rels.
Postprod editing, graphics creation, studio prod, teleconference svcs, duplication & transfer, satellite distribution.

Group W Videoservices. 310 Parkway View Dr., Pittsburgh 15205. (412) 747-4700. FAX: (412) 747-4726. Lee R. Salas, West Coast client svcs, (213) 850-3851; April Hodgson, East Coast client svcs.
TV-CATV only.
Satellite & syndication servicing; international standards conversion; industrial duplication.

Growise Radio Network. 179 Lovers Ln., Elizabeth City, N.C. 27909. (919) 335-7294. FAX (919) 335-2496. Dr. Marc Cathy, Bill Ray, co-hosts.
Growise Garden show, Saturday a.m.; *The Growise Minute*, Monday through Saturday radio only. Popular daily tips by Dr. Cathy, pres of the American Horticultural Society & former dir of the National Arboretom.

Gruen Communications. 136 W. 75th St., New York 10023. (212) 580-0271. David Gruen, own.
TV-CATV only.
TV prod for bcst cable/satellite & distribution.

Reg Grundy Productions Inc. 9911 W. Pico Blvd., Suite 1200, Los Angeles 90035. (310) 557-3555. FAX: (310) 277-1687. Reg Grundy, pres/chmn; Richard Barovick, CEO; Robert Crystal, sr VP admin.
TV-CATV only.
Produce both light entertainment shows & serialized drama for TV & cable bcst.

H

HEA Productions Inc. 1616 Butler Ave., West Los Angeles, Calif. 90025. (310) 478-8769. FAX: (310) 478-2414. Susan Hamilton, pres.
Radio & TV coml prod & distribution.

Alfred Haber Inc. 321 Commercial Ave., Palisades Park, N.J. 07650. (201) 224-8000. FAX: (201) 947-4500. Alfred Haber, pres.
TV prog distribution.

Fred Hall Productions. Box 612478, South Lake Tahoe, Calif. 96152. (916) 573-0709. FAX: (916) 573-0712. Fred M. Hall, pres; Clyde Hendricks, sls mgr.
Prog: *Fred Hall's Swing Thing*, barter/cash. Format: Great times. 3,600 basic selections, big band nostalgia. Radio only.

Halland Broadcast Services Inc. 1289 E. Alosta Ave., Glendora, Calif. 91740. (818) 963-6300; (800) HALLAND. FAX: (818) 963-2070. Hank Landsberg, pres; Steve Steinberg, VP/gen mgr.
Rock 'n' Roll Graffiti, oldies library on compact disc; *The Eighties Plus* AC/CHR library on compact disc & *The Seventies* AC/CHR gold library on compact disc.

Al Ham Productions. (The Music of Your Life.) 90 Soundview Ave., Huntington, Conn. 06484. (203) 929-6395. FAX: (203) 929-6023. Al Ham, pres; Joe Restifo, exec VP.
Radio prog prod & distribution.

Producers, Distributors, Production and Other Services

Hamilton Productions Inc. 6848 Elm St., McLean, Va. 22102. (703) 734-5444. FAX: (703) 734-5449. John Hamilton, pres; Nancy Bradsher, sr VP; Jay Hamilton & Anne Hamilton, VPs.
TV-CATV only.
Independent TV prod firm.

Handel Film Corp. 8730 Sunset Blvd., West Hollywood, Calif. 90069. (310) 657-8990. FAX: (310) 657-2746. Leo A. Handel, pres; Peter Mertens, VP.
TV-CATV only.
TV prog prod/distribution.

Hanna-Barbera Productions Inc. 3400 Cahuenga Blvd., Hollywood, Calif. 90068. (213) 851-5000. FAX: (213) 882-1606. William Hanna, Joseph Barbera, cochmns; David Kirschner, CEO; Fred Seibert, pres; Joy Every, sr VP TV; Buzz Potamkin, sr VP prod; Paul Gertz, sr VP business & legal affrs; Jack Morrow Jr., sr VP/gen mgr licensing; Laura Moskowitz, sr VP motion pictures; Bruce Johnson, sr VP syndication & CATV; Jayne Barbera, sr VP animation prod; Iwao Takamoto, VP creative design; Ray Paterson, VP animation dir; Terry Moore, VP postprod; Jill Jones; VP creative svcs; Stephen Muirhead, sr VP international; Mark Young, sr VP animation dev; Julie Steward, VP retail; Gary Berberet, VP mktg; Tom Brocato, VP publ & pub rels.
TV prog prod.

Happi Associates. Box 110892, Nashville 37222. (615) 331-8570; (800) 624-0018. FAX: (615) 331-8571. Skeeter Dodd, gen mgr.
Radio prog & mgmt; country formats; motivational speaking, jingles ID & coml, prod mus, features, customized prods.

Hargrove Entertainment Inc. Box 338, Forest Hills, N.Y. 11375-9998. (718) 657-0542. FAX (718) 657-0543. Peter M. Hargrove, pres.
TV-CATV only.
International distributor of films & TV progmg.

Larry Harmon Pictures Corp. 7080 Hollywood Blvd., Suite 202, Hollywood, Calif. 90028. (213) 463-2331. FAX: (213) 463-7219. Larry Harmon, pres; Susan Harmon, exec VP; Jerry Digney, VP mktg.
TV-CATV only.
Own & distributor of *Bozo* cartoons & live show franchise, *Laurel & Hardy* cartoons.

Harmony Gold Pictures Inc. 7655 Sunset Blvd., Los Angeles 90046. (213) 851-4900. FAX: (213) 851-5599. Frank Agrama, CEO.
TV-CATV only.
TV prod.

Harpo Productions. 110 N. Carpenter, Chicago 60607. (312) 633-1000.

Harris Communications. 1907 Darby Rd., Havertown, Pa. 19083. (215) 789-0100. FAX: (215) 789-2184. George Harris, pres; Tom Evans, VP progmg; Rob Lipshutz, progmg assoc.
Natl radio programmers. AOR progmg consultants.

Con Hartsock & Co. Inc. 10564 Linbrook Dr., Los Angeles 90024. (310) 208-6091. FAX: (310) 208-1247. Con Hartsock, pres; Joyce Killingsworth, opns mgr; Merry Hartsock, treas.
TV-CATV only.
Worldwide exclusive ind TV distribution & prod.

Have Inc. 309 Power Ave., Hudson, N.Y. 12534. (518) 828-2000. FAX: (518) 828-2008. Nancy Gordon, pres; Paul Swedenburg, VP.
TV-CATV only.
Nashville 37214: 606 Lincoya Bay Dr. Dr. Agatha Brown, southern rgnl sls mgr.
Distribution of audio & videotape, equipment, accessories & supplies, featuring CANARE cable. Duplication, postprod svcs & international standards conversion svcs.

Hayes Productions. 21384 Milsa, San Antonio 78249. (512) 698-3627. Jerry M. Hayes, pres.
TV-CATV only.
TV & CATV crews plus stock footage.

Hearst Entertainment. 235 E. 45th St., New York 10017. (212) 455-4000; (800) 526-5464. FAX: (212) 983-6379. Bruce L. Paisner, chmn/CEO; Gerald Isenberg, pres/COO; William E. Miller, co-chmn/Hearst Entertainment Distribution & chmn/Hearst Animation Productions; Terry Botwick, pres HED & natl progmg.
TV-CATV only.
Prod & distributor of feature-length films, series, documentaries & animated series.

Hearts of Space. Box 31321, San Francisco 94131. (415) 759-1130. FAX: (415) 759-1166. Stephen M. Hill, pres/prod; Leyla Rael Hill, VP/gen mgr.
Syndicted one hour prog of new age/space mus via NPR satellite transmission.

Heil Enterprises. Box 1372, Lancaster, Pa. 17608-1372. (717) 898-9100. FAX: (717) 898-6600. Paul Heil, own/exec prod; Shelia Heil, admin mgr.
Radio prog prod & distribution.

Arthur Henley Productions. 175 5th Ave., Suite 2462, New York 10010. (718) 263-0136. Arthur Henley, pres.
TV & radio prog prod; radio prog distribution.

Herald Broadcasting Syndicate. 1660 Soldiers Field Rd., Boston 02135. (617) 562-4210. FAX: (617) 562-4280. Al Carnesciali, pres; Kathryn Dearborn, VP finance.
International sw bcstng; radio & TV progmg & distribution to MONITORadio, WQTV & THE MONITOR CHANNEL (a natl cable ch).

Hi Ho Teleproductions. (Formerly Soundmasters.) Box 8135, Chicago 60680. (312) 224 5612. Frank Howard Jr, pres; R.C. Hillsman, VP.
Stage & studio rental.

Highland Laboratories. 840 Battery St., San Francisco 94111. (415) 981-5010. B.J. Brose, pres.
Video, audio, film duplication, film transfers: D-2, Betacam, 2", 1", 3/4", 1/2".

Hilton/Sucherman Productions. 230 Park Ave., Suite 805, New York 10169. (212) 687-2002. (212) 697-9008. Jack Hilton, chmn; Stuart Sucherman, pres; Marc Morgenstern, exec VP.
TV & video prods.

Hit Video USA. 510 Bering, Suite 300, Houston 77057. (713) 785-9100. Constance J. Wodlinger, own/CEO; Scott Assyia, CFO; Laura Dodge, VP affl rels & opns; Lou Robinson, prog dir.
Provides 24-hour Top 40 contemp hit mus video progmg with live 800 call-in number; five special feature shows.
Satellite: Satcom F1R, transponder 10.

Hollywood Video Library. 1831 Hyperion Ave., Hollywood, Calif. 90027. (213) 664-7234. FAX: (310) 559-5957. Chaba Mehes, pres.
TV-CATV only.
Motion picture distribution.

Hometown Illinois Radio Network. Box 169, 111 W. Main Cross, Taylorville, Ill. 62568-0169 (217) 824-3395. FAX: (217) 824-3301. Randal J. Miller, pres/gen mgr.
Wired net providing live coverage of Ill. high school basketball via satellite; loc reports from State Fair & Ill. Farm Bureau Convention.

Horizon Audio Creations. Box 486, 74 Chemin De Lanse, Hudson Heights-Rigaud, Que., Canada J0P 1J0. (514) 451-4549. FAX: (514) 451-4549. Craig W. Cutler, pres; Victoria Dodd, prod; Greg Stewart, mgr rsch; Marguerite Blais, mgr international progs; Mary-Lou Dodd, opns mgr.
Radio prog, coml prod; prod svcs; inflight audio progmg & adv.

Horizons Television Inc. 9305 Monalaine Ct., Great Falls, Va. 22066. (703) 759-7500. FAX: (703) 759-1620. Timothy E. Donner, exec dir; Leesa Kelly, creative dir.
TV-CATV only.
Creative dev & fullsvc prod of reality based TV progs & commissioned videos for non-profit organizations & assns.

Raymond Horn Syndication Inc. 841 W. Palmdale Blvd., Palmdale, Calif. 93551. (805) 272-5882. FAX: (805) 266-3800. Raymond Horn, pres; Gloria Horn, VP.
TV-CATV only.
Syndicator of TV & CATV progs.

Thomas Horton Associates Inc. 222 Sierra Rd., Ojai, Calif. 93023. (805) 646-7866. FAX: (805) 646-3600. Thomas F. Horton, prod; Jean Horton Garner, VP mktg; Thomas F. Horton Jr., VP opns.
Video & TV prog prod & distribution, postprod svcs.

Host Communications Inc. 546 E. Main St., Lexington, Ky. 40507. (606) 253-3230. FAX: (606) 254-7419. W. James Host, CEO; Charles L Jarvie, COO.
TV & radio prod & syndication. Handle college sports including NCAA Radio Network.

House of Music. 92 Corporate Pk., Suite C300, Irvine, Calif. 92714. (714) 641-8000; (800) 641-8000. FAX: (714) 552-8000. Douglas J. Peck, pres.
Radio progmg.

Howard Radio-TV Productions. 3918 W. Estes Ave., Lincolnwood, Ill. 60645. (708) 674-2122. Bernard Howard, own.
TV & radio prog; coml & promotional film prod; prod svcs.

Hughes Communications Inc. Box 92426, Los Angeles 90009. (310) 607-4000. FAX: (310) 364-4758. Stephen J. Petrucci, pres/CEO; Fred L. Judge, sr VP/COO; Jerald F. Farrell, sr VP; Eddy Hartenstein, sr VP.
Domestic satellite communications svcs; cable & bcst TV distribution, radio distribution & international TV svcs; video time sharing svcs; high-power direct to home TV svcs; satellite newsgathering & business TV.

Hughes Television Network. (A division of IDB Communications Group Inc.) 380 Madison Ave., New York 10017. (212) 478-6100. FAX: (212) 478-6101. John Tagliaferro, pres; J. Gordon Bridge, VP communication svcs; William Hyland, VP business affrs.
TV-CATV only.
Supplier of communication svcs including satellite time, uplinking, downlinking & encryption. TV & CATV only.

Lord Hume Music (ASCAP). Box 2147, Sioux City, Iowa 51104-0147. (712) 276-2295. T.H. Eglin, pres; "Morrie" Miller, professional creative mgr.
Mus publishing.

Huntridge Video Productions Inc. Box 3813, Greenville, S.C. 29608-3813. (803) 271-3348. FAX: (803) 232-4462. Mat Hunt, pres.
TV-CATV only.
TV prod & postprod.

I

IBS/Trimark. (A division of Trimark Holdings.) 2644 30th St., Santa Monica, Calif. 90405. (310) 314-3053. FAX: 310-452-8909. Marc Amin, chmn/CEO; Jim Keegan, sr VP/CFO; Kenneth Lameiras, VP sls; Ronald E. Alexander, sls mgr; Jorge Serrano, mgng dir South America; Cristian Vergara, sls mgr South America; Christine Cosse, sls mgr French speaking countries; Alison Lightbourn, prog acquisitions mgr; Isis Moussa, adv & promotion mgr; Stephen Williams, prod mgr.
TV-CATV only.
International TV, film & video distribution & adv sls firm. Builds, manages & invests in domestic & foreign bcst networks.

IFEX International Inc. 159 W. 53rd St., Suite 19 B, New York 10019-6050. (212) 582-4318. FAX: (212) 956-2257. Gerald J. Rappoport, pres; Beulah Rappoport, VP business affrs; Suzanne Fedak, VP mktg.
TV-CATV only.
Distributor of quality foreign-language feature films, animated & live-action short films & documentaries; extensive library of Soviet films.

I.N.I. Entertainment Group Inc. 11150 Olympic Blvd., Suite 700, Los Angeles 90064. (310) 479-6755. FAX: (310) 479-3475. Irv Holender, chmn/CEO; Michael R. Ricci, pres; Stephanie Zill, VP accounting & admin; Sy Samuels, exec VP sls & distribution.
We have a complete library available for your progmg needs.
An international producer, synidcator & distributor of quality features, animated features & other taped shows for TV & video.
Shows currently in our line up & available:
Animation—*Sparky's Magic Piano, Alice Through the Looking Glass, The Return to Treasure Island, The New Adventures of Oliver Twist*, THE INTER-

Producers, Distributors, Production and Other Services

NATIONAL FAMILY CLASSICS I (14x1 hour), *THE INTERNATIONAL FAMILY CLASSICS II* (13x1 hour), *ENVIRO MEN* (26x1 hour).

Features—*Any Man's Death, The Return of Superfly, THE JOHN WAYNE FAMILY THEATRE* (13x1 hour - colorized), *The Most Dangerous Woman Alive, Bullet Down Under.*

Sports—*G.L.O.W. (Gorgeous Ladies of Wresting)* (104-1 hour), *Slam Dunk* (26x½ hour).

INTERAMA Inc. 301 W. 53rd St., Suite 19-E, New York 10019. (212) 977-4830. FAX: (212) 581-6582. Nicole Jouve, pres.
TV-CATV only.
Distribution of films (theatrical, non-theatrical, TV & video); prod of TV progs.

ITC Entertainment Group (ITC Distribution). 12711 Ventura Blvd., Studio City, Calif. 91604. (818) 760-2110. FAX: (818) 506-8189. Mike Russo, sr exec VP domestic; Lori Shakel, VP mktg domestic TV; Matt Hornstein, VP domestic TV Eastern sls; James P. Marrinan, sr exec VP international; Armando Nunez, exec VP foreign sls; Doralea Rosenberg, gen mgr foreign sls; Edward Gilbert, VP legal & business affrs; Lori Bardwil, mgr worldwide adv/prom/publicity.
TV-CATV only.
TV prog prod & distribution.

ITC Television/Cinema Distribution Inc. 55 Bloor St. W., Suite 1203, Toronto, Ont., Canada M4W 1A5. (416) 964-7795. FAX: (416) 964-0981. Doralea Rosenberg, gen mgr.
TV-CATV only.
TV prog distribution.

ITP-Paulist Communications. 818 Roeder Rd., Suite 600, Silver Spring, Md. 20910-4423. (301) 588-0505. FAX: (301) 565-2015. John Geaney C.S.P., dir; Larry Rice C.S.P., assoc dir.
Prod & distribution of relg radio progs; video prod for TV & teleconferencing.

Icarus Films International. 153 Waverly Pl., 6th Fl., New York 10014. (212) 645-8653. FAX: (212) 989-7649. James Lee, pres/prod.
TV-CATV only.
International TV prog distribution: documentaries, current affrs, mus, arts, cultural progs.

Image Devices International Inc. 1825 N.E. 149th St., Miami, Fla. 33181. (305) 945-1111. FAX: (305) 945-1117. David Haylock, pres.
Atlanta 30337: 1941 Providence Ct. (404) 977-1111. FAX: (404) 977-1114.
Rental, sls, svc & maintenance of prog motion picture, TV & video prod equipment.

The Image Generators. Box 742, Olney, Md. 20830. (301) 924-5700. FAX: (301) 570-8916. Michael J. Weiner, pres/CEO.
Natl voice overs & radio spot prod; image & promotional voicers; digital editing; concept to completion.

The Image Group. 305 E. 46th St., New York 10017. (212) 752-3010. FAX: (212) 752-3745. Kassie Caffiero, gen mgr; Chuck Hoyer, dir engrg.
Complete postprod svcs; film to tape, editing & graphics.

Images Communication Arts Corp. 366 N. Broadway, Suite 310, Jericho, N.Y. 11753. (516) 939-2990. Robert Braverman, pres; Joseph Bellucci, special projects.
Syndication & co-prod of TV & radio prog series & specials. Syndication of "old-time-radio" dramas.

Imperial Entertainment Corp. 4640 N. Lankershim Blvd., 4th Fl., North Hollywood, Calif. 91602. (818) 762-0005. FAX: (818) 762-0006. Sunil R. Shah, pres; Sundip R. Shah, exec VP; Ash R. Shah, exec VP prod; James G. Slater, VP TV sls.
TV-CATV only.
Syndication sls feature film packages: Action Pak I & II & the Imperial Ninja Theatre.

Independent Artists. (A division of Screen Gems Pictures Inc.) 16 W. 56th St., New York 10019. (212) 765-4640. FAX: (212) 765-4686. Herb Sidel, gen mgr/exec prod.
TV coml prod.

Info World. 7210 Jordan Ave., Canoga Park, Calif. 91303. (213) 990-4595; (818) 704-7051. Lee Hansen, pres/CEO.
Dev & prod svcs for radio & TV comls, features & documentaries.

IntelliPrompt. 1555 Cassil Pl., Hollywood, 90028. (213) 461-3113. FAX: (213) 461-1264. Jeff Accardi, gen mgr.
Tele-promoting svcs.

Interactive Network Inc. 1991 Landings Dr., Mountain View, Calif. 94043. (415) 960-1000. FAX (415) 960-3331. David B. Lockton, pres/CEO; Bow Rodgers, VP sls & mktg; Jerry Frazee, VP opns & admin; Bob Brown, VP engrg & admin; Robert Mahoney, VP finance; Terry Donaher, VP bcst net.
TV-CATV only.
Chicago Ill. 60601.
Digital bcst net supplying interactive progmg to all TV homes. Currently in Nothern Calif. & Chicago.

International Broadcasting Network. Box 36096, Denver 80236. (303) 980-1211. Bob Larson, pres; Pam Koczman, VP.
175 U.S. affils: one in Ala., eight in Alaska., seven in Ariz., two in Ark., eight in Calif., two in Colo., one in Conn., eight in Fla., three in Ga., one in Idaho, one in Ill., two in Ind., three in Iowa, two in Kan., four in Ky., four in La., two in Me., three in Md., three in Mass., six in Mich., two in Minn., four in Mo. three in Mont., two in Neb., three in Nev., one in N.H., one in N.J., two in N.M., three in N.Y., four in N.C., two in N.D., ten in Ohio, two in Okla., 24 in Ore., five in Pa., one in R.I., three in S.C., five in Tenn., nine in Tex., three in Utah, four in Va., four in Wash., five in W. Va., one in Wis. & one in Wyo.
Seven Canadian affils: one in B.C., two in Man., one in Ont., one in Que., two in Sask.
One short wave international affil bcstg to Western Europe, Mediterranian, North Africa & South America.

International Media Associates Inc. 101 W. 57th St., New York 10019. (212) 247-3760. FAX: (212) 247-3778. David T. Menair, mgng dir; Nina C. Berry, VP.
TV-CATV only.
TV prog distribution, TV & home video prod.

International Program Consultants Inc. 52 E. End Ave., New York 10028. (212) 734-9096. FAX: (212) 734-6495. Russell J. Kagan, mgng dir.
TV-CATV only.
International TV distribution, TV progmg & home video aquisition consultation, co-prod consultation.

International Tele-Film Enterprises Ltd. 5090 Explorer Dr., Toronto Ont., Canada L4W 4T9. (905) 629-3313. FAX: (905) 629-3453. Stuart Grant, pres; Steve Sweigman, VP; Randi Perry, VP mktg.
TV-CATV only.
Distributor for documentaries, features, series & specials in Canada & worldwide.

Ion Weather Network. Morristown Municipal Airport, Morristown, N.J. 07960. (201) 267-6800. FAX: (201) 267-0428. Stephen Pellettiere, pres/certified consulting meteorologist; Madeline Petho, VP/media rels dir.
Gen weather forecasts, science info.

Irving Productions Inc. 3202 E. 21st, Tulsa, Okla. 74114. (918) 744-1221. FAX: (918) 744-1223. Dick Schmitz, pres/owner. Barry Evans, chief engr.
Audio recording & prod svcs for all media.

Israel Broadcasting Service. 800 2nd Ave., New York 10017. (212) 867-7584. Myra Cohen, dir.
TV & radio progmg from & about Israel.

The It Is Written Telecast. 1100 Rancho Conejo Blvd., Newbury Park, Calif. 91320. (805) 373-7733. FAX: (805) 373-7702. Mark Finley, speaker; George Vandeman, speaker emeritus; Glenn Aufderhar, exec prod; David L. Jones, prod/dir; Sheridan Adams, assoc prod/dir; Randy Stout assoc prod; David Smith, dir pub rels; Royce Williams, mgr.
TV & radio prog prod & distribution.

Italian Radio TV System. See RAI Corp.

Italtoons Corp. 32 W. 40th St., New York 10018. (212) 730-0280. FAX: (212) 730-0313. Giuliana Nicodemi, pres; Luisa Rivosecchi, international sls exec; Ken Priester, gen mgr.
TV-CATV only.
TV prog prod & distribution.

Ivanhoe Broadcast News Corp. 401 S. Rosalind Ave., Orlando, Fla. 32801. (407) 423-8045. FAX: (407) 425-2413. Marjorie BeKaert Thomas, CEO; Bette Bon Fleur, pres; John Cherry, VP syndication sls.
Prod & distributors of medical & educ news series, half-hour documentaries & vignettes. TV & CATV only.

J

JAM Creative Productions Inc. 5454 Parkdale Dr., Dallas 75227. (214) 388-5454. FAX: (214) 381-4647. Jonathan M. Wolfert, pres; Mary Lyn Wolfert, sr VP; Fred Hardy, VP sls; Randy Bell, VP sls; Chris Kershaw, VP/creative dir; Tom Parma, sls rep.
ID jingle & coml prod for radio & TV, prod mus libraries, custom mus & prod svcs.

JC Productions Inc. Box 1902, New York 10156. (212) 532-2820. FAX: (212) 532-3301. Joe Conforti, dir.
TV-CATV only.

J.E.D. Productions Corp. 140 E. 56th St., Suite 11-E, New York 10022. (212) 826-1221. FAX: (212) 826-3129. Jackson E. Dube, pres.
TV-CATV only.
TV prog prod & distribution.

J&H Music Programming Inc. Box 1697, Marco Island, Fla. 33969. (813) 642-6899. Joseph V. Gelo, pres; Helen J. Gelo, VP.
Radio prog distribution.

Riley Jackson Productions. 6353 Homewood Ave., Hollywood, Calif. 90028. (213) 464-4708. Riley Jackson, own.
TV prog prod; prod svcs.

James & Aster Music Inc. 115 E. 23rd St., New York 10010. (212) 982-0300. FAX: (212) 505-0959. Robert Aster, pres; Thomas James, VP; Michael C. Lau, mus mktg dir.
The Music Source for all bcst media; svcs include mus libraries in CD format, original scores, postprod & clearances.

Jameson Broadcast Inc. 1700 Connecticut Ave. N.W., Washington 20009. (202) 328-3283. FAX: (202) 332-6810. Jamie G. Jameson, pres; Trulee C. Burns, VP.
Radio prog prod, syndication & special projects.

Janson Associates Inc. Plaza W., 88 Semmens Rd., Harrington Park, N.J. 07640. (201) 784-8488. FAX: (201) 784-3993. Stephen Janson, pres; Zara Janson, VP; Cathy L. Nesi, sls assoc; Jessica Spillane, opns mgr; Kathleen Janson, editorial dir.
TV-CATV only.
International TV & video prog distribution & prod; video publishing.

Japan Network Group Inc. 1325 Ave. of the Americas, 8th Fl., New York 10019. (212) 262-3377. FAX: (212) 262-5577. Masakazu Ohtsu, CEO; Takao Yoneyama, COO/pres; Toru Okabe, exec VP.
Distributes progmg, such as *TV-Japan* & *Japan Cable Radio*, directly from Japan via satellite.

Jefferson-Pilot Sports. One Julian Price Pl., Charlotte, N.C. 28208. (704) 374-3664. FAX: (704) 374-3859. Edward M. Hull, pres/gen mgr; Grady Pridgen Jr., VP/gen sls mgr; Powell Kidd, asst VP/tech opns mgr; Charlie Pittman, mktg dir.
TV-CATV only.
TV & CATV sports prod & syndication.

Jerusalem Radio Productions. 545 W. 111th St., Suite 8-I, New York 10025. (212) 666-2144. Jon Schachter, pres.
Radio prog prod & distribution; prod svcs.

Joe Jones Productions. 10556 Arnwood Rd., Lake View Terrace, Calif. 91342. (818) 890-0730. FAX: (818) 899-4457. Joe Jones, exec prod; Marion Jones, VP opns.
TV & radio coml & prog prod; jingle prod & prod svcs.

Jones Satellite Networks. 9697 E. Mineral Ave., Englewood, Colo. 80112. (800) 876-3303. FAX: (303) 784-8786. Roy Simpson, exec VP/gen mgr; Phil Barry, VP progmg & opns.
Live 24-hour progmg; rsched mus library; matchup playlist; computer-generated song by song list for every hour of the week; prog consulting available.

Tom Jones Recording Studios. 1620 Greenview Dr. S.W., Rochester, Minn. 55902. (507) 288-7711. FAX: (507) 288-4531. Thomas H. Jones, pres; Aaron Manthei, mgr.
Recording studio, cassette duplication, CD recording svcs. Radio prog & coml prod.

Producers, Distributors, Production and Other Services

K

KCRA-TV. (Kelly Broadcasting Co.) 3 Television Cir., Sacramento, Calif. 95814-0794. (916) 446-3333. Jon S. Kelly & Robert E. Kelly, ptnrs; John A. Serrao, gen mgr.
TV- CATV only.
TV prog & coml prod; prod svcs.

KCSN 88.5 FM California State University, Northridge, 18111 Nordhoff St., Northridge, Calif. 91330. (818) 885-3090. FAX: (818) 885-3069. Teresa Rogers, gen mgr; Jared Charles, prog dir; Tessa Marshal, dir dev & pub rels; Michael Worrall, chief engr; Fred Fichman, business mgr.
Public radio serving most of L.A.: classical weekdays & eclectic weekends. Distributes wkly *Classical Countdown*. NPR affil.

KEG Productions Ltd. 1231 Yonge St., Suite 201, Toronto, Ont., Canada M4T 2T8. (416) 924-2186. FAX: 416-924-6115. Ralph C. Ellis, chmn; R. Stephen Ellis, pres.
TV-CATV only.
Prods of nature oriented TV progs.

KIDSNET. 6856 Eastern Ave. N.W., Suite 208, Washington, 20012. (202) 291-1400. FAX: (202) 882-7315. Karen Jaffe, exec dir; Liz Kline, project mgr; Beth Steingard, rsch mgr; E.J. Hovey, office administrator.
Information clearing house of TV, radio, audio & video for children; prog-related study guides; moly print & electronic publications.

KJD Teleproductions. 30 Whyte Dr., Voorhees, N.J. 08043. (609) 751-3500. FAX: (609) 751-7729. Larry Scott, pres/CEO.
TV & radio prog & coml, promotional film prod & distribution; prod svcs; TV processing lab.

M.A. Kempner Inc. 11820 Fountain Side Cir., Boynton Beach, Fla. 33437. (407) 736-3463. FAX: (407) 732-8895. Marvin A. Kempner, pres; Glenn A. Seger, VP.
TV-CATV only.
Syndicated progs; game shows; electronic automated polling equipment.

The Kenwood Group. 139 Townsend St., Suite 505, San Francisco 94107-1922. (415) 957-5333. FAX: (415) 777-0428. Christina Crowley, pres; Larry Behrs, VP.
Creative svcs & prod of comls & corporate communications, film, video, multimedia, meetings & events.

Keystone Communications. 303 E. South Temple, Salt Lake City 84111. (801) 322-4400. FAX: (801) 531-7375. David E. Simmons, chmn; Barry McCann, VP sls & mktg; Blaine D. Colton, VP business TV/sr VP net svc group; Douglas Jessop, dir mktg.
TV-CATV only.
Domestic & international telecommunication svcs; uplink, downlink, space segment, microwave, fiber; studios: LA & DC; prog distribution, news, sports, BTV.

Killer Music. 6532 Sunset Blvd., Hollywood, Calif. 90028. (213) 464-6333. FAX: (213) 464-5931. Ron Hickin, pres.
Original, custom & syndicated radio jingle packages; news, weather & sports mus packages for TV; pre- & post-scoring mus prod library.

Killer Tracks. 6534 Sunset Blvd., Hollywood, Calif. 90028. (800) 877-0078. FAX: (213) 957-4470. Sam Trust, pres.
CD mus prod library; multi-year licenses available; over 10 updates per year; 50 CDs in initial package.

King World Productions Inc. 12400 Wilshire Blvd., #1200, West Los Angeles, Calif. 90025-1006. (310) 826-1108. FAX: (310) 447-8057. Roger King, chmn of bd; Michael King, pres/CEO; Stephen W. Palley, COO/exec VP; Scott Towle, pres domestic TV sls; Jonathan Birkhahn, gen counsel; Steven A. LoCascio, VP/controller; Diana King, VP/sec; E.V. DiMassa Jr., sr VP progmg & dev; Moira Farrell, sr VP corporate rsch & sls mktg; Steven Hirsch, pres Camelot Entertainment Sales Inc.; Jeffrey E. Epstein, CFO; Fred Cohen, pres international division; Allyson Kossow Felix, VP pub rels; Donald Prijatel, VP creative svcs.
TV-CATV only.
New York 10019: 1700 Broadway, 35th Fl. (212) 315-4000.
TV prog prod & distribution.

Kingsbury Broadcast Consultants. 933 E. Kingsbury St., Springfield, Mo. 65807. (417) 881-1955. Bert Buhrman, pres; Gary G. Reynolds, VP/prod mgr; Denise Gorringe, treas.

Create Killer spots and promos with

Killer Tracks

Production Music Library
Call 1-800-877-0078
Not the same tired sound.
Surprisingly affordable.

Radio prog prod, distribution & syndication, holiday specials, coml background mus.

The Klages Group Inc. 1438 N. Gower St., Hollywood, Calif. 90028. (213) 856-9191. FAX: (213) 856-9258. Bill Klages, chmn of bd; S.L."Penney" Dodson, pres.
TV-CATV only.
TV lighting design, industrial prod, TV prod & tech supervision svcs.

Klein &. 1111 S. Robertson, Los Angeles 90035. (310) 278-5600. FAX: (310) 278-1454. Bob Klein, creative dir.
TV-CATV only.
Creative svcs agency & cross-ch tune in consultant.

Jordan Klein Productions. (Jordan Klein Film & Video.) 10197 S.E. 144th Pl., Summerfield, Fla. 34491. (904) 288-6060. FAX: (904) 288-5673. Jordan Klein, pres; Gloria Holloway, sec.
Underwater & on the water prod; rental film & video housing & crews; Bahamas specialist.

Walter J. Klein Co. Ltd. Box 472087, 6311 Carmel Rd., Charlotte, N.C. 28247-2087. (704) 542-1403. FAX: (704) 542-0735. Walter J. Klein, chmn; Richard A. Klein, pres; Terry Losardo, VP prod; Elizabeth Klein, VP.
TV-CATV only.
Prod & free distribution of TV specials & sponsored motion pictures for industry, organizations & govt.

Krypton International Corp. 3681 Prospect Dr., Riviera Beach, Fla. 33404. (407) 842-1558. FAX: (407) 842-1558. C.E. Feltner Jr., chmn/pres; Robert Marcella, exec VP sls.
TV-CATV only.
TV prog prod & distribution.

Kultur International Films Ltd. 121 Hwy. 36, West Long Branch, N.J. 07764. (908) 229-2343; (800) 458-5887. FAX: (908) 229-0066. Dennis Hedlund, pres; Pearl Lee, VP; Johanna Kelly, sls mgr; Ronald Davis, mgng dir; Lynne Zecca, business affrs mgr.
Suppliers of performing arts progs on home video cassette in North America; selection includes opera, ballets, class mus performances, documentaries & profiles.

L

Lakeside Television Co. Inc. 18 Crescent Ln., Dobbs Ferry, N.Y. 10522. (914) 693-4643. Bernard Schulman, pres.
TV prog distribution.

The Landsburg Co. 11811 W. Olympic Blvd., Los Angeles 90064. (310) 478-7878. FAX: (310) 477-7166. Alan Landsburg, chmn/CEO; Howard Lipstone, pres/COO; Kay Hoffman, exec VP prod; Sandra Gong, VP finance; Victor Paddock, VP business affrs; Laurie Goldstein, VP creative affrs.
TV prog prod; prod svcs.

Larsong Productions. RD 1, Box 152, Valley Falls, N.Y. 12185. (518) 753-6310; (518) 753-4117. Brian A. Larson, pres.
Audio prod & audio for video; creative writing, campaign mgmt & design. Studio layout & bcst consulting.

Learn Incorporated. 113 Gaither Dr., Mt. Laurel, N.J. 08054. (609) 234-6100. FAX: (609) 273-7766. Bruce E. Corley, pres; William Kelley, VP sls.
Publisher & distributor of audio-print exec training self-study progs. TV INFOmercial on Speed Learning available.

Legacy Audio/Video Specialists Inc. 7666-H Fullerton Rd., Suite 101, Springfield, Va. 22153. (703) 536-9000. FAX: (703) 569-3262. Blake B. Stamler, pres; Bert B. Stamler, exec prod.
Specialists in creation, prod, mfg & distribution of PSAs to radio & TV stns.

John Lemmon Films. 1216 Pinecrest Ave., Charlotte, N.C. 28205. (704) 532-1944. John Lemmon, pres; Mike Rosinski, head animator.
TV-CATV only.
Clay animation for TV specials, comls, prog openings & on-air IDs.

Les Productions SDA Ltee. 1425 Rene-Levesque Blvd. W., 10th Fl., Montreal, Que., Canada H3G 1T7. (514) 866-1761. FAX: (514) 866-0331. Francois Champagne, pres; Daniel Proulx; admin dir.
TV prog & coml, promotional film prod & distribution; prod svcs; TV processing lab.

Gene Lester Productions. 4918 Alcove Ave., Sherman Village, Calif. 91607. (818) 769-6160. Gene Lester, prod/dir; Dan Bresler, asst.
TV-CATV only.
TV prog prod: short subjects & documentaries.

Leukemia Society of America. 600 3rd Ave., New York 10016. (212) 573-8484. FAX: (212) 972-5776; (212) 856-9686. Timothy Powers, VP & dir communications.
Produces & distributes TV progs to inform & educate viewers about leukemia & related diseases & available treatment.

Lexicon Music Inc./Light Records. 2001 Butterfield Rd., #1400, Downers Grove, Ill. 60515. (708) 769-0033. FAX: (708) 769-0049.
Manufactures, distributes & promotes recording artists & their products.

Liberty Hill Broadcasting. 31800 Northwestern Hwy., Suite 100, Farmington Hills, Mich. 48018. (313) 737-3000. Ronald Zate, sr VP project dev; Leonard Jacobson, sr VP sports; Phillis Shapiro, stn svcs; Barry Zate, sr VP progmg; Carol Cunningham, natl sls dir; Gina Ratliffe, affil rels.
Prod/syndicator of radio featues: news, sports, entertainment & information. Short & long form progmg. Prog distribution svcs.

Producers, Distributors, Production and Other Services

Liberty Studios Inc. 238 E. 26th St., New York 10010. (212) 532-1865. FAX: (212) 779-2207. Anthony Lover, exec prod.
TV prog, coml prod.

Jack Lieb Productions. 216 N. May St., Chicago 60607. (312) 226-7660. FAX: (312) 226-7740. Warren H. Lieb, pres; Charles R. Kite, chief edit.
TV coml prod & distribution; promotional film prod; prod svcs.

Lifestyle Magazine. Box 320, Newbury Park, Calif. 91320. (805) 373-7686. FAX: (805) 373-7701. Daniel G. Matthews, exec prod; Jerry Chudleigh, mgr.
TV prog prod & distribution.

Lifetime Television Network. 34-12 36th St., Astoria, N.Y. 11106. (718) 706-3513. FAX: (718) 706-3589. Stuart M. Lefkowitz, sr VP net opns & engrg; Lew Herman, dir studio opns.
TV-CATV only.
Two TV studios (8,000 & 4,000 sq. ft.) & support facilities for makeup room, green room, dressing rooms & prod offices.

Lighthorse Productions. Box 203, Rocky Point, N.Y. 11778. (516) 744-1188. FAX: (516) 744-1131. L. Harry Lee, pres/exec prod; James G. Kingston, Ken Copel, dirs; Patti Roenbeck, prod; Katie Polk, Frank Klotz, assoc prods; Cami Callirgos, Ed Van Bomel, mktg dirs.
TV-CATV only.
Produces feature motion pictures, news, TV comls, TV pilot demo tapes, sit coms, industrials, educ, corporate videos. Modelling & casting.

LightYear Entertainment L.P. Empire State Bldg., 350 5th Ave., Suite 5101, New York 10118. (212) 563-4610. (212) 563-1932. Arne Holland, pres.
TV prog prod & distribution.

Limelight Communication Inc. 2532 W. Meredith Dr., Vienna, Va. 22181. (703) 242-4596. FAX: (703) 242-0324. Kenneth Reff, pres.
Writing, producing & editing svcs for bcst & industrial clients. Available as sub-contractors for specific svcs, or to fully produce complete shows. TV-CATV & radio.

Lindberg Productions Inc. 49 W. 46th St., New York 10036. (212) 719-2060. FAX: (212) 719-2061. Larry Lindberg, pres; Erika Lindberg, prod.
TV-CATV only.
Video prod for business & industry.

Lintas Campbell-Ewald. 30400 Van Dyke, Warren, Mich. 48093. (313) 574-3400. FAX: (313) 575-9925. R.D. O'Connor, chmn/CEO; P.A. Dow, vice-chmn/COO; A.J. Hopp, pres; S.H. Gilbert, exec VP/CFO; J.T.L. Homan, D.A. Karnowsky, W.J. Ludwig, I. McGregor, L.M. Schultz, J.T. Seregny, exec VPs.
New York 10017: One Dag Hammarskjold Plaza. (212) 605-8000.
Los Angeles 90025: 11100 Santa Monica Blvd., 6th Fl. (213) 914-2200.
Chicago 60611: One Magnificent Mile, 930 N. Michigan Ave., Suite 1060. (312) 587-2650.
TV prog, TV & radio coml, promotional film prod.

Lion & Fox Recording Inc. 1905 Fairview Ave. N.E., Washington 20002. (202) 832-7883. Harold Lion, chmn; James Fox, pres; Sally Lion, VP.
Audio prod & post prod for TV & radio; Music & EFX libraries; reel & cassette duplication; location audio.

Little Chicago. Box 2147, Sioux City, Iowa 51104-0147. "Daddy Blues", prod & co-host; "L.C.", co-host.
Contemporary & traditional American Blues radio prog available to public, college & coml radio stns for syndication.

Lobo Productions. 2304 Gardner, Glendale, Calif. 91206. (818) 549-0568. Pepe Lobo, pres.
TV progs, corporate video, consumer audio prod.

London Weekend Television International. South Bank Television Ctr., Upperground, London SE19LT 011-44-71-6201620. Greg Dyke, mgr dir.
TV-CATV only.
New York 10110: 500 5th Ave., Suite 1710. (212) 682-3055. FAX: (212) 869-3693. Ellis Bell, CPA.
TV prog prod & distribution.

Lone Star Humor Consulting & Creative Services. Box 29000, #103, San Antonio 78229. Lauren Barnett, head creative svcs.
Prod svcs for TV-CATV & Radio.

Longhorn Radio Network. (University of Texas at Austin.) Communication Bldg. B, University of Texas, Austin, Tex. 78712-1090. (512) 471-8704. FAX: (512) 471-3700. John L. Hanson Jr., exec prod; William F. Grimes, distribution mgr.
Radio series for a var of formats: current affrs, drama, science, music (blues to new age).

Longworth Communications Inc. 230 S. Crater Rd., Petersburg, Va. 23803. (804) 748-2512; (804) 862-9967. FAX: (804) 733-0355. James L. Longworth Jr., pres; Joanne H. Williimas, VP.
Dev & prod of TV progmg; educ, health, economic, develop industrial videos; corporate video news releases; bcst comls & PSAs. 74x48 foot studio.

Louisville Productions. 940 Starks Bldg., Louisville, Ky. 40202. (502) 581-1900. FAX: (502) 581-0408. Edward W. Tonini, pres; Denise Mitchell, VP creative.
TV-CATV only.
TV & cable progmg, ind films, film/tape prods, prod svcs, TV coml prod.

Lutheran Hour Ministries. 2185 Hampton Ave., St. Louis 63139. (314) 647-4900; (800) 944-3450. FAX: (314) 647-6923. Ken Peterson, dir; Allan Admire, mgr; Violet Knickrehm, acct exec radio sls; Sandi Clement, acct exec TV sls.
TV & radio prod & distribution (English & Spanish).

Lyric Opera of Chicago/Nuveen Radio Network. c/o WFMT Fine Arts Radio, 303 E. Wacker Dr., Chicago 60601. (312) 565-5000. FAX: (312) 565-5169. David Levin, dir; Daniel J. Schmiat, sr VP; Carol Martinez, opns mgr; Jim Barker, sls mgr.
Prod of eight grand operas each spring. Radio prog prod & distribution.

M

MAKEWIDE Productions. 10556 Amwood Rd., Lake View Terrace, Calif. 91342. (818) 890-0730. FAX: (818) 899-4457. Marion Jones, pres; Dwayne Jones, dir sls & mktg; Keith Jones, CEO; Detra Jones, opns mgr; Joe Jones, international.
TV coml prod, radio prog, coml & jingle prod.

MAN QC Creations Inc. 123 E. Dania Beach Blvd., Dania, Fla. 33004. (305) 921-1111. FAX: (305) 922-4222. Joseph Mancusi, pres; Michael Mancusi, sr prod; Sherie Lynn Kelley, creative dir.
TV-CATV only.
Prods of TV progmg, documentaries, series, travelogues; dev, prod, postprod & promotion.

MCA Inc. 100 Universal City Plaza, Universal City, Calif. 91608. (818) 777-1000. Lew R. Wasserman, chmn & CEO; Sidney J. Scheinberg, pres & COO; Al Rush, chmn MCA TV Group; Robert Harris, pres MCA TV Group.

MCA TV. 1755 Broadway, 6th Fl., New York 10019. (212) 841-8000. FAX: (212) 841-8687. Shelly Schwab, pres MCA TV.
TV prog prod & distribution.

MCEG Sterling. 188 Century Park E., Suite 1777, Los Angeles 90067. (310) 282-0871. FAX: (310) 282-8303. John W. Hyde, CEO; Kathryn Cass, COO.
Film, video & TV prod & distribution worldwide.

MCP DaviSound. Box 521, 1504 Sunset, Newberry, S.C. 29108. (803) 276-0639. Hayne Davis, prod/dir; Annette Davis, opns mgr.
Coml & promotional writing & prod for radio, jingles & prog prod & distribution.

MGM Inc. 2500 Broadway, Santa Monica, Calif. 90404. (310) 449-3000. FAX: (310) 836-1680. Sidney Cohen, pres domestic TV distribution.
TV prog distribution.

MGM TV Canada. 720 King St. W., Suite 611. Toronto, Ont., Canada M5V 2T3. (416) 865-9579. FAX: (416) 361-3216. William F. Wineberg, VP sls; Mira Quinn, admin mgr/sls asst.
TV-CATV only.
Film distribution for all MGM, Pathe & UA features & series; representing Turner Entertainment Co. for Canada only (Hanna Barbera Product - Canada).

MG/Perin Inc. 104 E. 40th St., New York 10016. (212) 697-8687. FAX: (212) 949-8140. Marvin Grieve, pres; Richard Perin, exec VP; Stephanie Beatty, VP western rgn; Charlotte Sweet, VP southeastern rgn; Steven Blechman, dir sls eastern rgn.
TV-CATV only.
TV prog prod & distribution.

MGS Services. 619 W. 54th St., New York 10019. (212) 765-4500. FAX: (212) 586-3771. R.A. Russell, pres.
Offices in Chicago & Los Angeles. Duplication, distribution & storage—all formats videotape, cassettes, film & radio tapes.

MHL Productions Inc. 609 Brickville Rd., Sycamore, Ill. 60178. (815) 895-3561. Michael Lazar, pres.
Radio coml prod & distribution; prod svcs.

MJM Research & Programming. 11539 W. 83rd Terr., Lenexa, Kan. 66214. C.C. McCartney, pres; Clark Roberts, VP.
Provides hook-tape prod, listener screening, fielding & tabulation for all music testing, perceptual studies, focus groups & promotional telemarketing.

MPL Film & Video. 781 S. Main St., Memphis 38106. (901) 774-4944. FAX: (901) 774-4526. Blaine Baker, pres; Steve LeSage, gen mgr; Larry Jackson, CFO.
16/35 color negative processing, rank cintel transfer, video edit, graphics, VHS duplication.

MRC Films. 21 W. 46th St., New York 10036. (212) 730-7705. Larry Mollot, exec prod.
Prods of original progmg for bcst, cablecast, TV comls & PSAs.

MRG Production Associates Inc. 95 Colony Dr., Holbrook, N.Y. 11741. (516) 447-1041. FAX: (516) 447-1042. Michael R. Glaser, pres/exec prod/dir Media Enterprises; Barbara Centrella, VP prog dev.
Complete prod svcs from dev to syndication in natl & international markets.

MRN Radio. 1801 International Speedway Blvd., Daytona Beach, Fla. 32114. (904) 254-6760. FAX: (904) 254-6716. John McMullin, pres/gen mgr; Allen Bestwick, asst gen mgr; David Hyatt, dir affils.
Live coverage of NASCAR stock car racing plus NASCAR Live wkly telephone talk, NASCAR Today daily news prog via satellite.

MSE. 41 RiverColony, Guilford, Conn. 06437. (203) 453-8538. FAX: (203) 458-8538. Marcia Simon, pres.
Health & medical progs for radio & TV, lifestyle, health, sports medicine, corporate video prod & writing.

MTI Television City. 1443 Park Ave., New York 10011. (212) 722-1818. FAX: (212) 722-6505. William Dalessandro, pres; Charles Pontillo, exec VP & COO.
TV prog prod; prod svcs.

MTI/The Image Group. 885 2nd Ave., New York 10017. (212) 355-0510. FAX: (212) 759-7465. William Dalessandro, pres; Charles Pontillo, exec VP & COO.
Twelve online suites, six Avid/EMC2, 2D/3D graphics, two SSL Scenarias, three film transfer, four stages, one remote unit, duplication.

MTM Enterprises Inc. 4024 Radford Ave., Studio City, Calif. 91604. (818) 760-5942. FAX: (818) 760-5250. William C. Allen, pres MTM TV; Greg Phillips, pres MTM Internatl.
TV-CATV only.
TV prog prod & distribution.

MVI Post. 2701-C Wilson Blvd., Arlington, Va. 22201. (703) 525-6476. FAX: (703) 525-0949. Frank Maniglia Jr., pres; Craig Maniglia, VP.
Full-svc video, audio & graphics postprod; features screensound digital audio system & velocity animation system.

MacNeil/Lehrer Productions. 1775 Broadway, Suite 608, New York 10019. (212) 560-3131. FAX: (212) 560-3102. Al Vecchione, pres; Bill Lynch, VP; Harold Crawford, controller; Chris Ramsey, dir communications & mktg; Diedra Cox, admin mgr.
Produces news & info progs for public TV & other coml & cable nets. Prod of MacNeil/Lehrer NewsHour.

Madison Square Garden Event Productions. 5750 Wilshire Blvd., Suite 225, Los Angeles 90036. (213) 965-0800. FAX: (213) 965-0926. Michael Walker, pres; Gail Rosenblum, dir legal & business affrs; Martin Kip, VP prod.
TV-CATV only.
TV prog prod.

Madison Square Garden Network. 2 Penn Plaza, New York 10121. (212) 465-6000. FAX: (212) 465-6021. Doug Moss, pres; Martin Brooks, sr VP progmg & prod; Peter Silverman, VP TV opns; Andi Poch, VP adv sls; Paul Schneider, VP pub rels; Mike McCarthy, Joe Townley, exec prods.
NY Knicks, NY Rangers & NY Yankee games; boxing, college football & basketball; exclusive Garden events; original series.

Producers, Distributors, Production and Other Services

Magic Lantern Productions. 9 E. 19th St., New York 10007. (212) 254-5035; (212) 677-3500. Ben Oliver, exec prod.
 TV-CATV only.
 Audio & vis svcs; promotional & video training films.

Magno Sound & Video. 729 7th Ave., New York 10019. (212) 302-2505. FAX: (212) 819-1282. Robert Friedman, pres; David Friedman, VP.
 Complete film, TV & radio prod & postprod svcs. Agencies, features, net, corporate, industrial.

Man From Mars Productions. 159 Orange St., Manchester, N.H. 03104. (603) 668-0652. FAX: (603) 666-4878. Ed Brouder, own.
 Aircheck sls for radio collectors; coml prod.

Manhattan Production Music. 311 W. 43rd St., Suite 702, New York 10036. (212) 333-5766; (800) 227-1954. FAX:(212) 262-0814; Ron Goldberg, natl sls mgr; Mark Zguro, account exec.
 50 CD mus library, five CD sound effects library, 50 CD classical mus library.

Ben Manilla Productions. 111 Sutter St., Suite 2130, San Francisco 94104. (415) 421-1220. FAX: (415) 421-4749. J. Ben Manilla, pres.
 Audio prod & progmg for a var of formats.

Eddy Manson Productions/Margery Music Co. 7245 Hillside Ave., Suite 216, Los Angeles 90046-2329. (213) 874-9318. Eddy Lawrence Manson, pres/creative dir; Paula Dorne, VP/treas.
 Mus composition, prod & publishing for all media.

Marquee Entertainment Inc. (formerly Lway Entertainment.) 9044 Melrose Ave., 3rd Fl., Los Angeles 90069. (310) 859-6050. FAX: (310) 274-6731. Hal Brown, chmn of bd; Ralph Smith, pres.
 International film distribution.

Maryknoll World Productions. Box 308, Media Relations Dept., Maryknoll, N.Y. 10545-0308. (914) 941-7590. FAX: (914) 945-0670. William J. Grimm, M.M.; dir; Ronald Hines, promotion coord.
 Offers a library of video & film prods featuring Third World countries; radio & TV progs also available.

Maryland Public Television. 11767 Owings Mills Blvd., Owings Mills, Md. 21117. (410) 356-5600. FAX: (410) 581-4338. Raymond K.K. Ho, pres/CEO; Leo Eaton, sr VP natl/international prods; Norm Silverstein, sr VP admin support svcs; Dr. Archie Buffkins, sr VP bcstg; Bruce Herget, VP engrg; Tom Bohn, VP opns; Joan Frangos, VP dev.
 TV prog prod & distribution.

Masai Films Inc. 6922 Hollywood Blvd., Suite 401, Hollywood, Calif. 90028. (213) 466-5451. FAX: (213) 466-2440. Fritz Goode, prod, dir & writer; Denise Nicholas, actress, writer & prod; Joseph Wilcots, dir photography & prod.
 TV & radio prog & coml prod; prod svcs.

Mason Video. 9632 N. 34th St., Omaha, Neb. 68112. (402) 455-9422. Pager: (402) 221-9860. Mele Mason, principal own.
 TV-CATV only.
 Offers complete Betacam SP prod. Equipment includes SONY 400 Betacam.

Matchframe Video. 610 N. Hollywood Way, Suite 101, Burbank, Calif. 91505. (818) 840-6800. FAX: (818) 840-2726. Howard Brock, mng ptnr; Brian Roberts, ptnr; Pam Hollander, gen mgr.
 TV-CATV only.
 In-house editing suites; audio sweetening; portable on-line/off-line editing systems.

William Mauldin Productions Inc. 1010 Canonero Dr., Greensboro, N.C. 27410-4611. Box 49944, Guilford Finance Station, Greensboro, N.C. NC 27419. (910) 632-9801. FAX: (910) 632-9801. William D. Mauldin, pres & CEO.
 Specialty voice tracks, narrations, audio tracks for comls, info radio, training & convention presentations, stn ID voice tracks.

Maximum Marketing Services Inc. 430 W. Erie, Suite 400, Chicago 60610. (312) 587-1200. FAX: (312) 587-2180. John McGowan, pres.
 TV & Radio prog, prod & distribution.

Maysles Films Inc. 250 W. 54th St., New York 10019. (212) 582-6050. FAX: (212) 586-2057. Albert Maysles, pres/dir/cinematographer; Henry Corra, dir; Susan Froemke, exec prod/dir; Sam Telerico, dir sls.
 Full prod svcs for theatrical & TV non-fiction films; adv comls; industrial films, including pre- & postprod.

McClain Enterprises. Box 23344, Nashville 37202. 10 Music Circle E., Nashville 37203. (615) 254-2060. FAX: (615) 254-0642. Carolyn McClain, pres.
 Custom & syndicated TV mktg for radio; sls consulting, sls & promotional projects for radio & TV stns.

Kenneth R. Meades. Box 1469, Los Angeles 90053. (213) 669-9670. Kenneth R. Meades, own.
 Consulting & prod svc for small mkt radio stns.

Medallion TV Enterprises Inc. 8831 Sunset Blvd., No. 100, West Hollywood, Calif. 90069. (310) 652-8100. FAX: (310) 659-8512. Shanna O'Brien, pres.
 Distribution of movies & specs throughout the world. Home video & bcst.

Media Action Research Center Inc. 475 Riverside Dr., #1901, New York 10115. (212) 865-6690. FAX: (212) 663-2746. Wilford Bane, pres.
 TV coml prod.

Media Associates Inc. Box 5747, 7400 Fullerton Rd., Suite 105, Springfield, Va. 22153-5747. (703) 866-6100; (800) 628-3556. FAX: (703) 866-6109. Debbie Wiater, pres.
 Provides full-svc video duplication, packaging, warehousing & complete order fulfilment.

The Media Group Inc. 70 Birch Hill Rd., Weston, Conn. 06883. (203) 227-7555. FAX: (203) 221-7299. Harvey F. Bellin, Tom Kieffer, ptnrs/exec prods.
 TV-CATV only.
 TV, video, film prod, writing, directing & editing; oxberry cinematography; TV, corporate & govt svcs offered.

Media Production. 197 W. 12th Ave., Eugene, Ore. 97401. (503) 687-2068. FAX: (503) 686-0248. Stan Garrett, pres; Jeff Powell, VP syndication.
 Producing syndicator/advertiser-based target markets; loc co-op coordination svcs.

Medialink. 708 3rd Ave., 21st Fl., New York 10017. (212) 682-8300. FAX: (212) 682-2370. Laurence Moskowitz, pres; Nick Peters, VP opns; Mark Manoff, VP sls.
 Chicago 60601: The Time & Life Bldg., 541 N. Fairbanks Ct. (312) 222-9850. FAX: (312) 222-9810.
 Washington 20005: 1401 New York Ave. N.W., Suite 520. (202) 628-3800. FAX: (202) 628-2377.
 Los Angeles 90028: 6430 Sunset Blvd. (213) 465-0111. FAX: (213) 465-9230.
 London WC2 7LJ: 38 Maiden Ln. (011-44-71) 240-3923. FAX: (011-44-71) 240-3921.
 Video news release distributor with dedicated newswire in TV stns throughout the U.S. & Europe.

Mediatech Inc. 110 W. Hubbard St., Chicago 60610. (312) 828-1146. FAX: (312) 828-9874. Thomas H. Baur, pres; Bob Semmer, exec VP sls; Shirley Danko, VP mktg. Mediatech East: (212) 463-8300. Mediatech West: (213) 466-6442.
 Duplication & distribution of corporate training & educ TV & radio progs. Distribution of syndicated TV progs via satellite & videotape.

MediaTracks Inc. 1235 Wood Ave., Deerfield, Ill. 60015. (708) 317-1515. FAX: (708) 317-1570. Shel Lustig, pres; Reed Pence, VP; Susan Glick, VP.
 Produce, syndicate & distribute radio progmg, comls & PSAs. Specialists in health & medicine, news & public affrs.

Medstar Communications Inc. 5920 Hamilton Blvd., Allentown, Pa. 18106. (215) 395-1300. FAX: (215) 391-1556. William P. Ferretti, CEO; Paul Dowling, pres; Julio Bermudez, dir sls; Bill Lynch, chief mktg off; Tom Hauff, medical news consultant; Peter Pellegrino, medical news dir.
 TV-CATV only.
 Health & medical news progmg includes one-hour specs, *Health Matters* TV series, *Med*Source* & *Advances Plus* news svcs.

Melcor Broadcasting Co. 245 E. 63rd St., New York 10021. (212) 759-1030. FAX: (212) 759-0446. George S. Kalman, pres.
 Syndicate radio progs: *Perry Como Specials* & *Moment of Musical History*.

Bill Melendez Productions Inc. 439 N. Larchmont Blvd., Los Angeles 90004. (213) 463-4101. FAX: (213) 469-0195. Bill Melendez, pres.
 TV prog, coml animation prod.

Message on Hold Inc. Box 1001, Hendersonville, N.C. 28793-1001. (704) 692-7200; (800) 223-1930. FAX: (704) 693-1662. J. Ellis Molton, pres; Randy Molton, opns mgr.

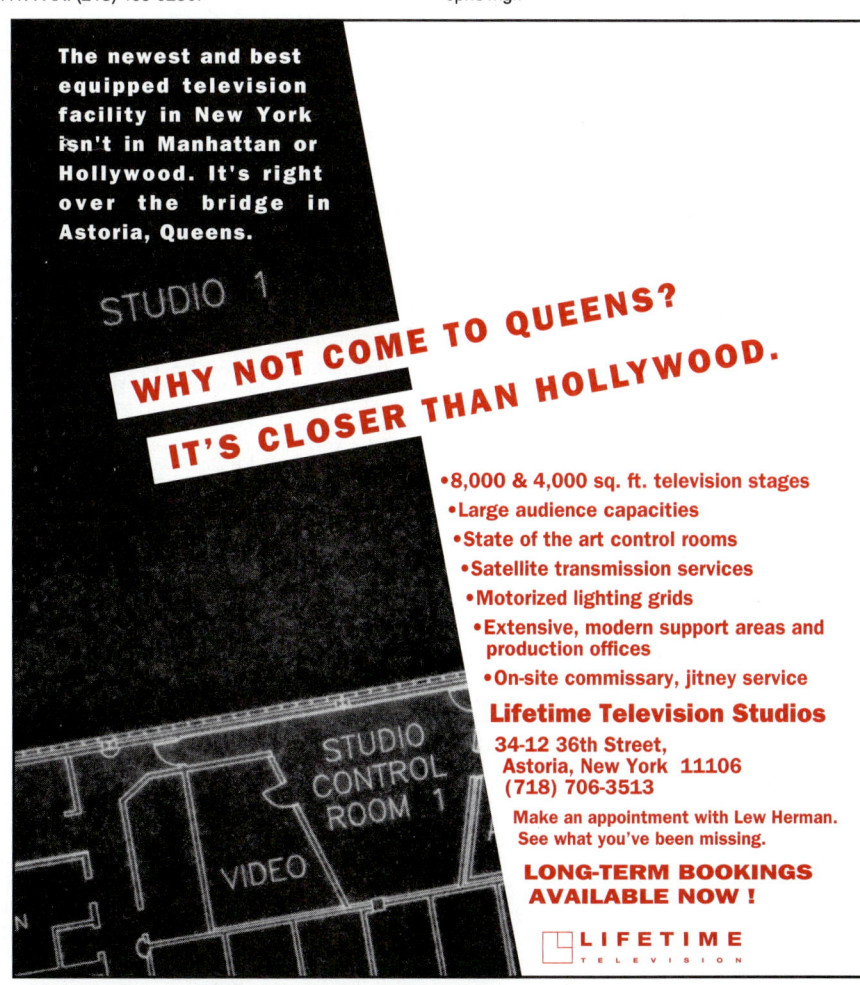

The newest and best equipped television facility in New York isn't in Manhattan or Hollywood. It's right over the bridge in Astoria, Queens.

**WHY NOT COME TO QUEENS?
IT'S CLOSER THAN HOLLYWOOD.**

- 8,000 & 4,000 sq. ft. television stages
- Large audience capacities
- State of the art control rooms
- Satellite transmission services
- Motorized lighting grids
- Extensive, modern support areas and production offices
- On-site commissary, jitney service

Lifetime Television Studios
34-12 36th Street,
Astoria, New York 11106
(718) 706-3513

Make an appointment with Lew Herman.
See what you've been missing.

**LONG-TERM BOOKINGS
AVAILABLE NOW !**

LIFETIME TELEVISION

Producers, Distributors, Production and Other Services

Prod of high quality comls for telephone "hold" lines. Specializing in automotive, financial, morticians & pharmacies.

Metro Networks. 2700 Post Oak Blvd., Suite 1400, Houston 77056. (800) 800-NEWS. FAX: (215) 668-9868. David Vanderslice, dir opns; Bill Yeager, VP of news, sports & weather.

Customized progmg of news, sports, weather & traffic for stns in 50 cities in the US & three foreign countries.

Metro Studios & Post Production Inc. 240 E. 45th St., New York 10017. (212) 986-8270. FAX: (212) 986-8279. Gene Tulchin, pres; Peter Valasiadas, opns.

Total prod & postprod facilities including fully equipped stage, on- & off-line & interformat computerized editing AVID, location capabilities.

Metro Weather Service Inc. 507-535 Rockaway Ave., Suite 3, Valley Stream, N.Y. 11581. (800) 488-SUNNY. FAX: (516) 568-8853. Pat Pagano, pres.

Provides accurate understandable weather forecasts; radio personalities. Serves any part of the nation.

Charles Michelson Inc. 9350 Wilshire Blvd., Beverly Hills, Calif. 90212. (310) 278-4546. FAX: (310) 278-7932. Charles Michelson, pres.

Prog buyers for overseas TV stns. Distributors of half-hour radio progs. Cash not barter.

Robert Michelson Inc. 127 W. 26th St., New York 10001. (212) 243-2702. FAX: (212) 691-5531. Robert Michelson, pres; Susan Scharf, VP.

TV coml prod; radio prog prod & distribution.

Midwest Video Communications Inc. Box 11627, Omaha 68111. (402) 453-2450. FAX: (402) 451-2876. John S. Turner, pres; Gay H. Turner, VP; John Lott, prod/dir.

TV-CATV only.

TV prog & distribution; coml prod, satellite teleconference prods; business & promotional film prods; prod svcs.

Mighty Minute Programs. 840 Battery St., San Francisco 94111. (415) 788-1211. FAX: (415) 788-1139. Andrew Meblin, pres; David Meblin, sr VP; Bob Kizer, VP/sls mgr; Elaine Smith, Vivian Batty, Al Larson, sls reps.

Distributors of newsfeature series: *Produce Man, You Be the Doctor, Planetary Pets, Earth Beat, Consumer Pharmacist, Travel Takes,* & *TatleTale Tillie.*

Miller Broadcast Management Inc. 708 N. Dearborn, Chicago 60610. (312) 266-6665. FAX: (312) 266-6632. Lisa Miller, pres.

Produces & syndicates progs nationally including *Kidsradio, Danny Bonaduce, Ramsey Lewis* & *Walton & Johnson.*

Miller & Luria. 100 N. Hope Ave., Suite 14, Santa Barbara, Calif., 93110. (805) 898-2660. FAX: (805) 569-3935. James Miller, gen ptnr; Cynthia Luria, gen ptnr.

TV-CATV only.

Consulting svcs on effective use of prog length comls; media negotiation for natl placement of these comls.

Robin Miller, Filmaker Inc. 606 W. Broad St., Bethlehem, Pa. 18018. (215) 691-0900. FAX: (215) 865-3732. Robin Miller, pres.

TV prog, promotional film prod; prod svcs.

Warren Miller Entertainment. 505 Pier Ave., Hermosa Beach, Calif. 90254. (310) 379-2494. FAX: (310) 374-4042. Peter Speck & Kurt Miller, co-owns; Don Brolin, VP prod; Brian Sisselman, dir/cameraman.

TV-CATV only.

Second unit feature, coml, TV prog, promotion; film prod & distribution specializing in snow & outdoor adventure sports.

Mission City Television Inc. Box 701028, San Antonio 78270-1028. 326 Sterling Browning Dr. San Antonio 78232 (512) 490-4000. FAX: (512) 496-5661. Bruce C. Staffel, pres.

TV-CATV-only.

Studio prod, postprod & TV prog distribution.

Mobile Video Services Ltd. 1620 Eye St. N.W., Washington 20006. (202) 331-8882. FAX: (202) 331-9064. Lawrence J. VanderVeen, pres; Stephen W. Meeks, sls & mktg.

TV-CATV only.

Bcst prod svcs, project design & prod svcs of all types; live, taped & postprod svcs.

Modern Sound Pictures Inc. 1402 Howard St., Omaha, Neb. 68102. (402) 341-8476. FAX: (402) 341-8487. Keith T. Smith, pres; Sandra L. Smith, VP.

TV-CATV only.

TV prog distribution.

Modern Talking Picture Service. 5000 Park St. N., St. Petersburg, Fla. 33709. (813) 541-7571. FAX: (813) 545-2380. Nina Thorbecke, division mgr.

Distribution & monitoring of pub rels TV progmg, video news releases, PSAs.

Modern TV. 5000 Park St. N., St. Petersburg, Fla. 33709. (813) 541-7571. FAX: (813) 545-2380. Eugene A. Cafiero, pres; Nina Thorbecke, mgr TV opns.

Distribution & monitoring pub rels, TV, VNR, PSAs & series.

Ellis Molton Advertising. Box 1001, Hendersonville, N.C. 28793-1001. (704) 692-7200; (800) 223-1930. FAX: (704) 693-1662. Ellis Molton, own.

Syndicated radio & nwspr series for loc use.

Montgomery Community Television Inc. 7548 Standish Pl., Rockville, Md. 20855. (301) 424-1730. FAX: (301) 294-7476. Ralph N. Malvik, exec dir; Don Katzen, mktg dir; Todd Van Gelder, prod dir.

TV-CATV only.

Full-svc video prod & postprod 2,400 sq ft. studio including complete control room, GVG200 switcher, DVE, on & off line editing.

Moody Broadcasting Network. 820 N. LaSalle Blvd., Chicago 60610-3284. (312) 329-4433. FAX: (312) 329-4339. Robert Neff, VP bcstg; Robert West, dir net dev; David Woodworth, administrator affil dev.

Radio prog prod, full-svc religious stereo audio progmg via satellite & syndicated tape distribution.

Charles Morrow Associates Inc. 611 Broadway, Suite 817, New York 10012. (212) 529-4550. FAX: (212) 529-9885. Charlie Morrow, pres; Jeff Christianson, sls rep.

Cultural bcst for radio & TV; soundtracks, comls & worldwide distribution.

Motivision Ltd. 2 Beechwood Rd., Hartsdale, N.Y. 10530. (914) 684-0110. FAX: (914) 684-0431. Richard S. Milbauer, pres.

TV & radio prog, & promotional film prod; gen prod svcs.

MotorNet. Box 69, Farmingdale, N.J. 07727-0069. (908) 938-2662. FAX: (908) 294-0398. Charlie Roberts, pres/exec prod.

Radio prog prod & distribution.

MotorPro. Box 69, Farmingdale, N.J. 07727-0069. (908) 938-2662. FAX: (908) 294-0398. Charlie Roberts, pres/exec prod.

Radio coml prod & distribution; prod svcs.

Muller Media Inc. 23 E. 39th St., New York 10016. (212) 683-8220. FAX: (212) 661-0572. Robert B. Muller, pres; Daniel E. Mulholland, exec VP.

TV-CATV only.

TV distribution/prod to bcst syndication, cable & home video.

Multi Market Media. 14677 Midway Rd., Suite 200, Dallas 75244. (214) 392-7571. FAX: (214) 392-7316. Terry Doane, mgr.

Mktg svcs firm providing adv, promotions, sports & event mktg, media buying & consulting svcs.

Multimedia Entertainment Inc. 45 Rockefeller Plaza, 35th Fl., New York 10011. (212) 332-2000. FAX: (212) 332-2010. Robert L. Turner, pres; Richard C. Thrall, sr VP opns & admin; Richard Coveny, exec VP; Thomas Shannon, sr VP stn sls; Norman Hayes, VP stn sls Southeast; Gerry Philpott, VP stn sls West; Fred Patrosino, VP/natl sls mgr; Elizabeth Allen, VP business affrs/gen counsel; Ethan Podell, VP internatl dev.

TV & cable prog prod, sls & distribution.

Multimedia Television Productions. (A division of Multimedia Entertainment.) 8439 Sunset Blvd., Suite 200, Los Angeles 90069. (213) 848-3100. Neil Russell, pres; Adina Savin, sr VP business & legal affrs; Brenda Miao, VP creative affrs.

TV prog prod, sls & distribution.

Burt Munk & Co. 666 Dundee Rd., Suite 501, Northbrook, Ill. 60062. (708) 564-0855. Burton M. Munk, pres; Mary C. Abraham, sec/treas.

Promotional film prod & distribution; gen prod svcs.

Music Director Programming Service. Box 51978, Indian Orchard, Mass. 01151. (413) 783-4626. FAX: (413) 783-3168. Budd Clain, gen mgr; Bill Schoenborn, prod mgr; Richard Bosse, chief engr; Carl Drake, country consultant; Brenda Clain, office mgr.

Mus libraries on CD, DAT or analog reels for A/C, CHR & Country formats. Mus rsch books & currents available for A/C.

Music Springs Corp. Box 128, Matawan, N.J. 07747. (908) 566-9600. FAX: (908) 566-0451. Gloria Bolendz, pres; John H. Bolendz, VP.

Leased tape libraries of programmed mus for transmission via SCA, cable or on-site systems to subscribing coml locations.

Musical Starstreams. Box 1989, Sedona, Ariz. 86339. (602) 204-1989. FAX: (602) 204-1990. F. Forest, prod/host.

Two-hour wkly syndicated instrumental-based progsv mus progmg also available as a full-time format; radio adv prod.

Musivision. 185 E. 85th St., New York 10028. (212) 860-4420. Fred Kessler, pres.

TV-CATV-Radio

Design & prod of computer graphics & animation for stn IDs, promotions, show openings & coml applications.

N

NASA Broadcast & Imaging Branch. NASA Headquarters (PMD), 300 E. St. S.W., Room 8G82, Washington 20546. (202) 358-1733. FAX: (202) 358-4333. J.L. Headlee, chief bcst & imaging branch.

Aeronautics & Space Report, a ¼-hour magazine quarterly (Betacam SP) to media & prods only.

NCAA Productions. 6201 College Blvd., Overland Park, Kan. 66211-2422. (913) 339-1906, ext. 7611. FAX: (913) 339-0027. James Marchiony, dir communications.

TV prog prod & distribution.

NCAA TV News. 119 W. 57th St., New York 10019. (212) 541-8840. Ron Schwartz, dir.

TV-CATV-Radio only.

TV prog prod & distribution. News clips.

NFL Films Video. 330 Fellowship Rd., Mt. Laurel, N.J. 08054. (609) 778-1600. Steve Sabol, pres; Harlan Sugerman, VP sls; Jay Gerber, VP prod; Hal Lipman, VP facilities; Jim Obrien, VP finance; Phil Tuckett, VP entertainment videos; Jeff Howard, VP video opns.

Teleprod facility: interformat edit suites, 16mm & 35mm film processing, film-to-tape transfer, studio & remote prod, sound studios, animation & paintbox.

NGBA. 111 S. George Mason Dr., Arlingotn, Va. 22204.

NHK Japan Broadcasting Corp. 2030 M St. N.W., Suite 706, Washington 20036. (202) 828-5180. FAX: (202) 828-4571. Hidetoshi Fujisawa, bureau chief.

TV & radio prog distribution.

9Kusa Productions. 500 Speer Blvd., Denver 80203. (303) 871-1899. FAX: (303) 871-1801. Jim Berger, mgr prod & prog dev.

TV-CATV only.

Prod of TV comls, progmg, corporate videos & satellite tele-conferences. Facilities include prod & postprod svcs & prod studios.

NTV International Corp. 50 Rockefeller Plaza, Suite 845, New York 10020. (212) 489-8390. FAX: (212) 489-8395. Takao Sumii, pres; Yasuo Ema, sr VP; Nobuo Katsura, VP/chief engr.

TV-CATV only.

Complete video prod & postprod facility; satellite transmission capabilities worldwide; ENG packages, TV prod, internatl TV coord.

NUS Training Corp. Box 6032, 910 Clopper Rd., Gaithersburg, Md. 20878-1399. (800) 848-1717. FAX: (301) 258-1205. Ronald E. Burdge, pres; John R. Polli, VP sls & mktg; Diane E. Langeloh, VP product prod.

Video-based training progs for industry, utilities & govt relating to maintenance, opns & safety.

NVC Arts. The Forum, 74-80 Camden St., 4th Fl., London NW1 OJL. (071) 388-3833. FAX: (071) 383-5332. John Kelleher, mgng dir; Robin Scott, head prod.

TV-CATV only.

Prod & distributors of opera, ballet & performing arts progs for world TV.

Narwood Productions Inc. 211 E. 43rd, Rm. 603, New York 10017. (212) 983-3320. FAX: (212) 983-3325. David LeVan, pres.

Radio prog, coml prod & distribution.

National Association of Home Builders. 1201 15th St. N.W., Washington 20005. (202) 822-0200. FAX: (202) 861-2131. Tommy Thompson, pres; Kent W. Colton, exec VP/CEO; Spencer Levine, exec prod *Right at Home.*

Free daily consumer-oriented radio prog on home care, repair, maintenance, improvements & issues important to owns, renters, buyers & sellers.

National Collegiate Athletic Association. 6201 College Blvd., Overland Park, Kan. 66211. (913) 339-1906. FAX: (913) 339-0027. Joseph N. Crowley, pres; Cedric W. Dempsey, sec/treas; Richard D. Schultz, exec dir.

Prod of selected NCAA championships.

Producers, Distributors, Production and Other Services

National Council of Churches Communications Unit. 475 Riverside Dr., Rm. 850, New York 10115. (212) 870-2227. FAX: (212) 870-2030. J. Martin Bailey, assoc gen sec communication; David W. Pomeroy, dir media resources; Roy T. Lloyd, dir bcst news svcs; Carol J. Fouke, dir news svcs.
Bcst prod, distribution & assistance to reporters, nets, stns; prepared radio reports & actualities without chg from bcst news professionals.

National Federation of Community Broadcasters (NFCB). 666 11th St. N.W., Suite 805, Washington 20001. (202) 393-2355. FAX: (202) 393-2357. Lynn Chadwick, pres/CEO; David LePage, VP member svcs.
Natl representation, policy dev, publications, individual consulting & training for community-oriented radio stns.

National Film Board of Canada. 1251 Ave. of the Americas, 16th Fl., New York 10020-1173. (212) 596-1770. FAX: (212) 596-1779. Mary Jane Terrell, U.S. mktg mgr TV.
TV-CATV only.
TV prog distribution.

National Public Radio. 635 Massachusetts Ave. N.W., Washington 20001. (202) 414-2000. Douglas J. Bennet, pres; William E. Buzenberg, VP news & info; Peter J. Loewenstein, VP distribution; Barbara Hall, VP dev; Sidney Brown, VP finance & admin; Peter Pennekamp, VP culture progs & prog svcs; Midge Ramsey, VP representation.
Radio prog prod & distribution.

N W N - T V
TV Weathercast Via Satellite
On/Air Weather Talent!
Localized, customized, TV weathercast for your market. Limited clients, now being accepted. Reserve your market for AM, PM, weekend, or drop-in weathercast.
Call National Weather Network: 601/352-6673
Edward St. Pe'

National Weather Network. Box 786, Jackson, Miss. 39205. (601) 352-6673. FAX: (601) 948-6052. Edward St. Pé, pres.
TV weathercasts with on-camera meteorologist fed to affil via satellite daily.

Nationality Broadcasting Network-NBN Radio/TV. 11906 Madison Ave., Lakewood, Ohio 44107. (216) 221-0330. FAX: (216) 221-3638. Miklos Kossanyi, pres; Maria Kossanyi, gen mgr; Sheila Calanni, stn mgr; Attila Kossanyi, VP.
TV & radio prog & coml; promotional film prod & distribution; prod & adv svcs.

Naval Reserve Recruiting. 4400 Dauphine St., Code 41, New Orleans 70145-5001. (504) 948-5839. FAX: (504) 948-1013.

Nemo News. 7179 Via Maria, San Jose, Calif. 95139. (408) 226-6339. FAX: (408) 226-6403. Dick Reizner, news edit/own.
ENG unit (all formats) covering assignments worldwide.

Network Music Inc. 15150 Ave. of Science, San Diego 92128. (619) 451-6400. FAX: (619) 451-6409. Robert M. Skomer, pres; Ken Berkowitz, VP sls.
Prod mus, sound effects & prod elements libraries.

Network Video Services. 1600 Broadway, Suite 307, New York 10019. (212) 581-7108. FAX: (212) 582-7940. Francisco Ramirez, pres; Joseph Jackson, VP sls & mktg.
TV-CATV only.
ENG/EPP remote crews & equipment supplies, film, documentaries, trainings, educ, coml PSAs, VNRs, mus videos.

New Century Telecommunications. 9911 W. Pico Blvd., Suite 980, Los Angeles 90035. (310) 552-8460. FAX: (310) 552-0031. Samuel Schulman, chmn of bd; Bernard Tabakin, vice chmn.
Motion picture prod & distribution.

New City Releasing Inc. 15445 Ventura Blvd., Sherman Oaks, Calif. 91403. (818) 508-5353. FAX: (818) 508-0190. Alan B. Bursteen, pres.
TV-CATV only.
Film prod as well as distribution of films, videos & TV entertainment progmg.

New Dimension Media Inc. 85803 Lorane Hwy., Eugene, Ore. 97405. (503) 484-7125. FAX: (503) 484-5267. Steve Raymen, pres; Janet Brock, gen mgr.
Educ TV & cable distribution. Svcs libraries, health & social svc mkts.

New Dimensions Radio. Box 410510, San Francisco 94141. (415) 563-8899. Michael A. Toms, pres; Justine Toms, exec dir; Jane Heaven, dir bcstg.
Radio prog prod & distribution.

New Visions Entertainment. 9911 W. Pico Blvd., Suite 980, Los Angeles 90035. (310) 552-8460. FAX: (310) 552-0031. Samuel Schulman, chmn of bd; Bernard Tobakin, vice chmn.
Distribution of motion pictres to TV & video.

New World Television. 625 Madison Ave., 11th Fl., New York 10022. (212) 527-4800. FAX: (212) 527-4801. James M. McNamara, pres/CEO.
TV-CATV only.
TV prog prod & distribution.

New York Communications Inc. 207 S. State Rd., Upper Darby, Pa. 19082. (215) 352-5505. FAX: (215) 352-6225. Michael Davis, pres; Don Creamer, prod mgr. Philadelphia office.
Creates, produces & distributes TV & cable progmg, value-added TV progmg, TV & radio promotional campaigns.

New Zoo Revue. 9301 Wilshire Blvd., Suite 509, Beverly Hills, Calif. 90210. (310) 247-8167. FAX: (310) 247-0309. Barbara Atlas, pres.
TV-CATV only.
TV prog prod & distribution.

News Travel Network. 747 Front St., San Francisco 94111. (415) 397-2876. FAX: (415) 421-4982. Jim Hornthal, chmn; Roy Walkenhorst, pres.
TV-CATV only.
Daily 90-second consumer travel reports; wkly day & date 30-minute travel news magazine; custom travel promotions; daily 90-second environmental reports; daily 90-second Dr. Dean Edell medical reports.

News/Broadcast Network. 149 Madison Ave., New York 10016. (212) 889-0888. FAX: (212) 696-4611. Mike Hill, pres; Jim Hill, sr chmn; Robert L. Kimmel, sr VP; Robert Hill, sr VP; Tom Hill, VP; James Hill Jr., VP.
Produce & distribute news & feature material to TV & radio stns.

Nightingale-Conant Corp. 7300 N. Lehigh Ave., Niles, Ill. 60714. (708) 647-0300. FAX: (708) 647-7145. Vic Conant, pres.
Radio prog prod & distribution.

Nine Network Australia. 6255 Sunset Blvd., Suite 1500, Los Angeles 90028. (213) 461-3853. FAX: (213) 462-4849. Mark Burrows, bureau chief; Noel Masson, opns mgr; Phil Storey, chief engr.
Studio prod facility, standard conversion & all format tape facilities.

No Soap Productions. 1600 Broadway, New York 10019. (212) 581-5572. FAX: (212) 586-0045. Dan Aron, pres/creative dir; Ann Aron, VP/gen mgr; Syd Weiss, VP/sls dir; Dawn Mjoen, asst prod.
Radio comls, sound design for radio & TV, voicecasting.

Ray Norman Productions Inc. 11 Glenwood Rd., Toms River, N.J. 08753. (908) 349-8569. Ray Norman, pres.
Nostalgia mus prods, LP & CD masters made.

North American Network Inc. 7910 Woodmont Ave., Suite 1400, Bethesda, Md. 20814. (301) 654-9810. FAX: (301) 654-9828. Thomas P. Sweeney, pres; Stephen F. Murphy, VP mktg; Lisa Brusio Coster, dir stn svcs.
Full-svc radio net providing progmg, news, promotional campaigns & sls opportunities to stns nationwide.

North Star Records Inc. 95 Hathaway St., Providence, R.I. 02907. (401) 785-8400. FAX: (401) 785-8404. Richard R. Waterman, VP; Virginia E. Shea, dir publ & promotion VP.
Prod, distribution, mktg & promotion of recorded mus.

Northern California News Satellite Inc. 1121 L St., Suite 109, Sacramento, Calif. 95814. (916) 446-7890. FAX: (916) 446-7893. Steve Mallory, pres; Bill Branch, bureau chief.
TV-CATV only.
Video wire svc providing daily news coverage, via satellite of California's capitol for TV stns statewide.

Northwest Imaging & F.X. 2339 Columbia St., Suite 100, Vancouver, B.C. V5Y 3Y3. (604) 873-9330. FAX: (604) 873-9339. Alex Tkach, gen mgr.
Shooting, special effects, animation, digital editing suites, audio sweetening, Betacam Sp & 1", five camera jet pack plus crews.

Northwest Mobile Television. 379 W. 60th St., Minneapolis 55419. (612) 869-1119. FAX: (612) 869-5105. Mike Koenig, gen mgr.
Mobile TV facilities for remote prod of multi-camera events.

Northwestern Inc. 15938 S.W. 72nd Ave., Portland, Ore. 97224. (503) 624-7800; (800) 547-2252. FAX: (503) 624-2185. Jeanne Alldredge, pres; Ken Thompson & Kathleen Lawrence, sls.
Audio/videotape & supplies; custom load audio/videocassettes & audio duplication; audio bk & ITC carts.

O

Olympia Networks. 7745 Carondelet Ave., St. Louis 63105-3315. (314) 727-8900. FAX: (314) 727-4115. Stephen Bunyard, pres; Bill Latz, John McElfresh, VPs.
Sports progmg syndication.

OMNIMUSIC
The fine art of library music
1-800-828-6664
6255 Sunset Blvd   Suite 803   Hollywood   California   90028

Omnimusic. 6255 Sunset Blvd., Suite 803, Hollywood, Calif. 90028. (213) 962-6494. FAX: (213) 962-4556. Jerry Burnham, dir natl sls & customer svc.
Digitally-produced mus & sound effect libraries for TV, radio & cable featuring real instruments in various styles & orchestrations.

Oppix & Hider Inc. 1501 Lee Hwy., Arlington, Va. 22139. (703) 524-3000. Bob Hider & James Oppenheimer, principals.
TV-CATV only.
Full-svc creative video & film prod firm serving corps, assns, nonprofit organizations & govt.

Optimedia Systems Inc. 373 Rt. 46 W., Fairfield, N.J. 07004. (201) 227-8822. FAX: (201) 227-0586. George Hoffman, pres; Steven Hoffman, gen mgr.
TV prod & postprod; 1" Betacam interformat for bcst & cable.

Orange Productions Inc. 105 Forrest Ave., Narberth, Pa. 19072. (215) 667-8620. FAX: (215) 667-8939. Sid Mark, pres; Jon Harmelin, VP/gen mgr; Brian Mark, opns mgr.
Prod & distribution of a wkly two-hour prog *Sounds of Sinatra*.

Orion Pictures Corp. 1888 Century Park E., Suite 600, 7th Fl., Los Angeles 90067. (310) 282-0550. FAX: (310) 201-0798. Debra Stasson, VP business affrs & legal; Joseph D. Indelli, exec VP domestic TV distribution; Kimberle Lynch, sr VP business affrs Home Video; Rochel Blachman, sr VP business affrs Orion Pictures.
TV & theatrical distribution.

Dick Orkin's Amazing Radio. 1140 N. Labrea, Los Angeles 90038. (213) 462-4966. FAX: (213) 460-4280. John N. Tierney, pres; Sanford Orkin, dir sls.
Syndicated packages of Dick Orkin comls customized for loc advertisers. Available in six categories.

Our Daily Bread. Box 2222, Grand Rapids, Mich. 49555. (616) 942-6770. FAX: (616) 957-5741. Martin De Haan, pres; Richard W. Mason, exec VP.
Radio prod & distribution.

Jim Owens & Associates Inc. 1525 McGavock St., Nashville 37203. (615) 256-7700. FAX: (615) 256-7779. Jim Owens, pres; Jerry W. Fox, VP/gen mgr.
TV & radio prog prod company for syndication & net cable outlets.

Broadcasting & Cable Yearbook 1994
G-25

Producers, Distributors, Production and Other Services

P

PAMS Productions/PAMS Jingles (A division of CPMG Inc.) 4631 Insurance Ln., Dallas 75205. (800) 522-PAMS. FAX: (214) 521-8578. Benjamin R. Freedman, pres; Richard Kaufman, VP.
 Provides hundreds of famous radio ID jingles, being used by more than 200 oldies stns.

PBS Video. 1320 Braddock Pl., Alexandria, Va. 22314. (703) 739-5000. FAX: (703) 739-0775. Dan Hamby, dir acquisitions; Eric Sass, VP/pres video/mktg & per.
 Handles videocassette sls, rental & licensing of selected PBS progs to schools, colleges, libraries, hospitals & other institutions.

Palace Production Center. 29 N. Main St., South Norwalk, Conn. 06854. (203) 853-1740. FAX: (203) 855-9608. George Battocchio, COO; Wendy Lambert, VP mktg.
 TV-CATV only.
 On-air promotional design & animation; prog opns; identity packages; special effects; postprod; motion control animation; Quantel HAL digital compositing.

Pandora International. 10 Rockefeller Plaza, Suite 609, New York 10020. (212) 373-1900. FAX: (212) 373-1910. Howard J. France, VP opns & dev; Kenneth DuBow, head of sls; Jesse Weatherby, western sls.
 TV-CATV only.
 TV prog distribution.

Pandora S.A. 23 Ave. de Neuilly, Paris 75116. (1) 40-67-77-77. FAX: (1) 40-67-74-10. Christian Bourguignon, pres; Edwin Joory, dir finance; Peter Tomlinson, dir sls.
 TV-CATV only.
 International TV & video distributor.

Pantomime Pictures Inc. 12144 Riverside Dr., North Hollywood, Calif. 91607. (818) 980-5555. FAX: (818) 984-3470 Fred Crippen, creative dir; Jack Hadley, exec prod; Matt Crippen, prod.
 TV-CATV only.
 Animation prod & design for TV comls, educ & industrial use. Animation camera for 35 mm & 16 mm.

Paragon International Inc. 119 Spadina Ave., Suite 900, Toronto, Ont., Canada M5V 2L1. (416) 595-6300. FAX: (416) 977-0489. Isme Bennie, pres; Kirstine Layfield, dir international sls.
 TV-CATV only.
 TV prog distribution.

Paramount Domestic Television. 5555 Melrose Ave., Los Angeles 90038. (213) 956-5000. FAX: (213) 956-2007. Dick Montgomery, sr VP/western rgnl mgr.
 New York 10023: 15 Columbus Cir. (212) 373-7000. Joel Berman, sr VP/natl sls mgr; John Nogawski, VP/eastern rgnl mgr.
 Chicago 60611: 737 N. Michigan Ave. (312) 951-0100. Gerald Noonan, sr VP/central rgnl mgr.
 Fort Lauderdale, Fla. 33301: One E. Broward Blvd. (305) 463-8388. Albert Rothstein, sr VP/southern rgnl mgr.
 Dallas 75225: 5949 Sherry La. (214) 696-6823. Mark Dvornik, southwestern div mgr.
 Sydney, Australia N.S.W. 2000: Suite 3209, Australia Sq. (011) 61-2-2479367. George Mooratoff, VP Far East sls.
 Hamilton, Bermuda HM CX: One Parliament St. (809) 29-28255. Bruce Gordon, pres international TV.
 Toronto, Ont., Canada M5S 1M4: 146 Bloor St. W. (416) 922-3600. Malcolme Orme, VP TV sls.
 London W1X 8J8: 23 Berkeley House, Hay Hill. (011) 44-71-629-1150. Peter Cary, VP international.
 Domestic Ops: Steven Goldman, pres; Howard Green, VP administration; Meryl Cohen, sr VP adv & promotion; Robert Sheehan, exec VP business affrs & finance; Vance Van Petten, sr VP business affrs legal; Emeline Davis, VP finance; Tom Fortuin, VP legal affrs; Phil Murphy, VP opns; Frank Kelly, exec VP progmg; Jim Martz, VP rsch & sls dev; Greg Meidel, exec VP/gen mgr sls.
 Network TV: John Pike, pres; John Wentworth, VP adv, publ & promotion; Cecelia Andrews, exec VP business affrs; John Symes, exec VP creative affrs; Gerald Goldman, VP finance; Howard Barton, sr VP legal affrs; Timothy Iacofano, VP progs; Helen Mossler, VP talent & casting.
 Video: Robert Klingensmith, pres; Timothy Clott, exec VP; Hollace Brown, VP adv & sls promotion home video; Eric Doctorow, sr VP/gen mgr home video; Steven Madoff, VP legal affrs; Alan Perper, sr VP mktg home video; Harold Fraser, VP opns; Jack Kanne, sr VP sls home video.

Paramount Television Group. 5555 Melrose Ave., Los Angeles 90038. (213) 956-5000. FAX: (213) 956-5555. Kerry McCluggage, chmn.
 TV prog prod.

Parkway/Muse Inc. Box 5123, Springfield, Va. 22150. (301) 460-7626; (703) 569-2469. FAX: (301) 460-0043. Uldis Adamsons, chmn; Roger E. Elm Jr., VP.
 Fifty-six hours classical, two-hours folk & one-hour Big Band nostalgia wkly.

Parrot Communications International Inc. 2917 N. Ontario St., Burbank, Calif. 91504. (818) 567-4700. FAX: (818) 567-4600. Robert W. Mertz, pres/CEO; Rae Ann Mertz, exec VP; Greg Julian, sr VP corporate dev.
 Data base mgmt, direct-mail svcs, promotional fulfillment, warehousing, contest fulfillment & bcst faxing.

Patrick Productions. 8302 Professional Hill Dr., Fairfax, Va. 22031. (703) 938-4477. FAX: (703) 641-9853. Mike Patrick, chmn; Janet Bishop Patrick, pres; Cathrine Clark, mgr.
 Prod & distribution of TV & radio spots; PSAs & assn; corporate presentations.

Paulist Productions. Box 1057, Pacific Palisades, Calif. 90272. (310) 454-0688. FAX: (310) 459-6549. Ellwood E. Kieser, pres; John J. Furia Jr., VP; Paul A. Weber, sec/treas.
 TV prog prod.

Peckham Productions. 65 S. Broadway, Tarrytown, N.Y. 10591. (914) 631-5050. Peter H. Peckham, pres.
 TV-CATV only.
 Full-svc film & video prod facility.

Pegasus Broadcasting of San Juan Inc. Box 2050, San Juan, Puerto Rico 00936-2050. (809) 792-4444. FAX: (809) 782-4420. John Bennett, pres/gen mgr; Enrique Cruz, VP news; Jonathan Garcia, VP sls mgr; Gloria Breil, prog dir.
 TV-CATV only.
 Coml TV bcstg.

Penta Corp. 2505 S. Neil St., Champaign, Ill. 61820. (217) 351-4940. FAX: (217) 351-7783. Bala RamaKrishnan, pres; Russ Proch, VP.

People's Network Inc. 3 River St., White Springs, Fla. 32096. (904) 397-4145. FAX: (904) 397-4149. Charles Harder, pres.
 Radio prog: *For the People*.

Perceptions. 200 Grand Ave., Suite 110, Grand Junction, Colo. 81501. (303) 242-0405. FAX: (303) 241-9774. Rand Taylor, pres; Kim Martens, prod; Terry Tormey, prod; Butch Terrill, photographer; Kim Martens, prod.
 Net quality Betacam SP video prod, digital audio coml prod.

Peters Productions Inc. 9655 Granite Ridge Dr., San Diego 92123. (619) 565-8511. FAX: (619) 565-7218. Edward J. Peters, pres.
 Media mktg consultants providing rsch, concept, mktg plan, mus, graphics & animation.

Philadelphia Flyers Hockey Club. The Spectrum, Pattison Pl., Philadelphia 19148. (215) 465-4500. FAX: (215) 389-9403. Edward M. Sinder, chmn; Jay Snider, pres; Keith Allen, exec VP; Ron Ryan, COO; Mark Piazza, VP pub rels; Dick Deleguadia, VP sls & mktg; Dan Clemmens, VP finance; Rich Oriolo, VP mktg.
 TV & radio prog prod.

PHoenix Communications Group. 3 Empire Blvd., South Hackensack, N.J. 07606. (201) 807-0888. FAX: (201) 807-0272. Joe Podesta, chmn; Jim Holland, pres; Peggy White, VP sls; Geoff Belinfante, sr VP & exec prod.
 Major League Baseball Prods, Sports Newsatellite, NHL Prods; TV & video prod & distribution; stock footage licensing.

Pied Piper Films. Shelburne, Ont., Canada L0N 1S6. (519) 925-6558. FAX: (519) 925-6558. Allan Wargon, exec prod; Esther Israelski, prod.
 TV-CATV only.
 Motion picture prod.

Pike Productions Inc. Box 300, 11 Clark St., Newport, R.I. 02840. (401) 846-8890. FAX: (401) 847-0070. James A. Pike, pres; Cornelia M. Pike, sls mgr; Gregory M. Pike, tech dir.
 Custom ads & special announcement trailers produced & distributed in all formats—35mm, 185x1, Scope, mono or stereo, 70MM stereo.

Platinum Radio Partners, II. 3135 Industrial Rd., Suite 218, Las Vegas 89109. (702) 369-0096. FAX: (702) 791-5828. Andrew Fonfa, CEO; Bill Lastra, pres/sls mgr; Cheryl E. Cohen, exec prod; David Host, host.
 Produces, markets & distributes *Sports Overnight*, a full-svc sports-talk prod.

Playboy Entertainment Group. 9242 Beverly Blvd., Beverly Hills, Calif. 90210. (310) 246-4000. FAX: (310) 246-4050. Tony Lynn, pres; Dick Sowa, pres distribution/COO; Michael Fleming, sr VP/gen mgr pay TV; Richard Rosetti, pres prod.
 TV prog prod & distribution.

Players Music Inc. 216 Carlton St., Toronto, Ont., Canada M5A 2L1. (416) 961-5290. FAX: (416) 961-7754. Mort Ross, pres; Brian Gagnon, mus dir; Jennifer Ward, prod mgr.
 Provides original mus for comls, TV; radio & TV v/0 prod; sound design; stock mus; customization of stock.

Playhouse Pictures. 1401 N. La Brea Ave., Hollywood, Calif. 90028. (213) 851-2112. FAX: (213) 851-2117. Ted Woolery, prod; Gerry Woolery, dir.
 Animated TV coml prod.

Potomac TV/Communications. 500 N. Capitol St. N.W., Suite 800, Washington 20001. (202) 783-8000. FAX: (202) 783-1861. Bruce Finland, pres; Michelle LeCompte, dir sls & mktg.
 Full-svc TV prod facility. C- & Ku-band satellite transmit/receive svcs.

Power Play Music Video Television. 223-225 Washington St., Newark, N.J. 07102. (201) 642-5132. FAX: (201) 623-8458. Greg F. Ferguson, pres; Michelle Miller, mktg dir.
 TV & radio prog; coml prod & distribution; prod svcs.

Praxis Media Inc. 18 Marshall St., South Norwalk, Conn. 06854. (203) 866-6666. FAX: (203) 853-8299. Christopher Campbell, pres/creative dir; Deborah Weingrad, VP/edit dir; Dorria DiManno, VP opns.
 TV-CATV only.
 TV prog, coml & promotional film prod; gen prod svcs.

Premier Film Video & Recording Corp. 3033 Locust St., St. Louis 63103. (314) 531-3555. FAX: (314) 531-9588. Robert Heuermann, pres/gen mgr; Grace Dalzell, sec/treas.
 TV & radio prog & spots; video, film, scripting, graphics, editing, screening room, shipping.

Premiere Home Video Inc. 755 N. Highland, Hollywood, Calif. 90038. (213) 934-8903. FAX: (213) 934-8910. Cynthia Gaske, mktg dir.
 TV-CATV only.
 Prod & distribution of home video products.

Premiere Radio Networks Inc. 15260 Ventura Blvd., 5th Fl., Sherman Oaks, Calif. 91403-5339. (818) 377-5300. FAX: (818) 377-5333. Steve Lehman, pres/CEO; Tim Kelly, exec VP; Kraig T. Kitchin, sr VP sls.
 Supplier of 14 wkly progs, in short & long form, from Comedy Networks & Plain-Wrap Countdowns to short-form features that include News from the Boonies, The Cla'ence Update of the Young & the Restless & On the Phone with Ti-Rone. Syndicates Morning Show: Gerry House & The House Foundation, distributes Mediabase rsch & produces Anti-Jingles & Pure Impact I & II Jingles. All features & svcs offered on a barter basis.

Presbyterian Church (U.S.A.). 100 Witherspoon St., Louisville, Ky. 40202-1396. (502) 569-5211. FAX: (502) 569-5018. Ann Gillies, coord media svcs.
 Radio & TV prod, video prod, distribution, mktg.

Presentation Services Inc. 22 7th St. N.E., Atlanta 30308. (404) 873-5353. Thomas S. Lines, own.
 TV coml prod & distribution; promotional film prod; prod svcs.

Richard Price Television Associates. 444 Madison Ave., 24th Fl., New York 10022. (212) 980-6960. FAX: (212) 832-7397. Christina Thomas, U.S. opns.
 TV-CATV only.
 TV prog distribution.

Prime Cut Productions Inc. 1550 Bayside Dr., Corona del Mar, Calif. 92625. (714) 760-6059. FAX: (714) 760-6053. Edward Flaherty, pres; Jan Kaplan, VP.
 TV-CATV only.
 Paris, France 75004: 4 Quai des Celestins. 42-78-70-00.
 NTSC Betacam European prod for American TV; bilingual location professionals; distribution, co-prod, stock footage.

Prime Productions. 207 S. State Rd., Upper Darby, Pa. 19082. (215) 352-8288. FAX: (215) 352-6225. Michael Davis, pres; Don Creamer, gen mgr; Bill Groce, dir sls. Philadelphia office.
 Prod of net-quality TV & cable progmg, comls, corporate films & videos.

Prime Ticket Network. 10000 Santa Monica Blvd., Suite 200, Los Angeles 90067. (310) 286-3800. FAX: (310) 286-3703. Roger Werner, pres.
 TV prog prod & distribution.

Broadcasting & Cable Yearbook 1994
G-26

Producers, Distributors, Production and Other Services

Primedia Inc. Cinevillage 65 Heward Ave., Ste. A-109, Toronto, Ont., Canada M4M 2T5. (416) 466-1600. FAX: (416) 466-1333. W. Paterson Ferns, pres; Doug Dales, chmn; Jacqueline Kelly, finance; Pam Devenport, business affrs.
TV-CATV only.
TV prog prod & distribution.

Primetime Entertainment Inc. 444 Madison Ave., New York 10022. (212) 980-6960. FAX: (212) 832-7397. Christina Thomas, dir U.S. opns.
International TV co-prod & packaging.

Pro Am Sports System/Pass Sports. Box 3040 550 W. Lafayette Blvd., Detroit 48231-3040. (313) 222-7277. FAX: (313) 223-2299. William J. Wischman Jr., gen mgr; Kathleen Hunt, CFO; Annette Mansfield, dir mktg; Denise McGee, net mgr; William P. Glenn, prod mgr.
TV-CATV only.
Cable net covering rgnl sports (Mich., Ohio & Ind.) Professional, collegiate & amateur sports.

Pro Video. 801 N. La Brea Ave., Hollywood, Calif. 90038. (213) 934-8840. FAX: (213) 934-8837. Joel Webb, chmn.
TV-CATV only.
Custom duplication & post-prod: comls, mus videos & trailers.

ProCom Associates Inc. 1300-G First State Blvd. Wilmington, Del. 19804-3538. (800) PROCOM-4. (302) 633-0300; FAX: (302) 633-0336. Thomas J. Mitten, pres.
TV-CATV
Creative svcs for bcst & business communications; Abekas effects, interformat Betacam SP/S-VHS, prod & postprod; Maxell tape products distributor.

Producer Service Group Inc. 1284 Beacon St., Suite 110, Brookline, Mass. 02146. (617) 730-8430. FAX: (617) 730-8131. Louise Rosen, pres.
TV-CATV only.
London NW5 3BT: 35 Inkerman Rd., (71) 916-1090. FAX: (71) 916-4695.
Worldwide TV distributor for cable, pay TV, satellite, home video: theatrical documentaries, children's, arts, mus, drama.

Producers Group Ltd. 7440 N. Figueroa St., Suite 102, Los Angeles 90041 FAX: (213) 550-1251. Lee W. Gluckman Jr., pres/exec prod.
Dev & prod of theatrical TV films & series.

Production Garden Music Libraries. Box 781388, San Antonio 78278. (800) 247-5317. FAX: (512) 599-1254. Mel Taylor, pres; Carmen Andrade, account exec.
Production Garden mus libraries include the *Broadcast 100 Series* featuring more than 2,000 cuts on 22 CDs & the *AV/Video 200 Series* featuring more than 330 themes on 21 CDs. Also, a library from Europe featuring 20 CDs & eight sep sound-effect libraries.

The Production Group. Box 20004, Alexandria, Va. 22320-1004. (703) 660-9522. James Morris, pres; Jim Simpson, VP.
TV & radio prog & coml, promotional film prod.

Production & Satellite Services Inc. (PSSI). 1860 Mississippi Ave., Los Angeles 90025. (310) 575-4400. FAX: (310) 575-4451. Robert C. Lamb, VP prod & opns; Charles P. Storlie, VP sls & engrg.
TV-CATV only.
Prod & satellite transmission svcs including Ku-band transportable uplink/prod trucks with Skywitch in Los Angeles, San Francisco & San Diego.

Productions SDA Ltee. 1425 René-Lévesque Blvd. O., 10e Etage, Montreal, Que., Canada H3G 1T7. (514) 866-1761. FAX: (514) 866-0331. Francois Champagne, pres; Daniel Proulx, VP.
TV prod co offering a full range of svcs, from producing to postprod facilities.

Professional Video Services Corp. 2030 M St. N.W., Washington 20036. (202) 775-0894; (800) 232-0894. FAX: (202) 775-1288. Robert L. Grevemberg, pres; Larry Tyler & Larry D'Anna, VPs.
Full-svc prod/postprod facility, camera crews, equipment rental, TV studios & satellite facilities.

The Program Entertainment Group Inc. 16255 Ventura Blvd., Suite 710, Encino, Calif. 91436. (818) 981-4344. FAX: (818) 981-2890. William D. Morrison & James A. Sowards, co-chairs.
TV-CATV only.
TV prog prod & distributor. Movie Greats Network.

The Program Exchange. 375 Hudson St., New York 10014. (212) 463-3500. FAX: (212) 463-2662. Chris Hallowell, sr VP/mgng dir; Susan Radden, VP stn rels & client rels.
TV prog distribution.

Program Syndication Services Inc. 375 Hudson St., New York 10014-3620. (212) 463-3900. FAX: (212) 463-3170. Peggy Green, pres; Suzanne Crowe, sr VP/dir sls.
TV prog distribution.

ProgramLink. (A division of Video Broadcasting Corp.) 708 3rd Ave., 21st Fl., New York 10017. (212) 682-8300; (800) 843-0677. FAX: (212) 682-2370. Larry Moskowitz, pres; Nick Peters, VP.
TV-CATV only.
A natl syndicators' newswire; high-speed printer net for delivery of progmg data directly to TV stns nationwide.

Promark. 777 N. Palm Canyon Dr., Suite 101, Palm Springs, Calif. 92262-5534. (619) 322-7776. FAX: (619) 322-6440. David Levine, pres.
TV prog prod & distribution.

ProMedia. 170 Ludlow Ave., Northvale, N.J. 07647. (201) 768-7900. FAX: (201) 768-7908. June Brody, pres; Beverly Padratzck, VP affil rels; Frank Guida, VP prod.
Comedy svcs for radio.

Promusic Inc. 941 A Clint Moore Rd., Boca Raton, Fla. 33487. (407) 995-0331. FAX: (407) 995-8434; (800) 322-7879. Alain Leroux, pres; Cheryl Mathauer, mgr; David Walters, account exec.
Prod mus library; licensing per needle drop, prod blanket or annual license.

ProServ Television. 10935 Estate Ln., Suite 100, Dallas 75238. (214) 343-1400. FAX: (214) 343-2068. Donald L. Dell, chmn; Robert A. Briner, pres; Dennis N. Spencer, sr VP; Herbert K. Swan, sr VP international; John Humphrey, assoc VP.
TV prog prod & distribution.

Protestant Radio and Television Center Inc. 1727 Clifton Rd. N.E., Atlanta 30329. (404) 634-3324. FAX: (404) 634-3326. William W. Horlock, pres.
Radio prog prod & distribution; prod svcs.

ProVideo. 2242 E. 4500 S., #12, Salt Lake City 84117. (801) 277-9368. John Rasmussen, prod dir.
TV-CATV only.
Develops, produces & distributes films & other progmg for theatrical & TV release.

Public Interest Affiliates Inc. 680 N. Lake Shore Dr., Suite 1230, Chicago 60611. (312) 943-8888. FAX: (312) 943-5464. Bradley Saul, pres; Sandra Kramer, VP/exec prod.
Radio prog, coml prod & distribution, inflight audio & video.

Public Media Incorporated Television. 5547 N. Ravenswood Ave., Chicago 60640. (312) 878-7300. Charles Benton, chmn; Betty McLean, dir TV.

Purcell Productions Inc. 484 W. 43rd St., Suite 23-M, New York 10036. (212) 279-0795. FAX: (212) 594-7224. Don Purcell, pres; Lou Carter, VP.
Prod of radio jingles, comedy spots & PSAs. Publisher of *Not for Me!* drug & alcohol educ curriculum for grades 3-6.

Q

QED Communications Inc. (WQED), 4802 5th Ave., Pittsburgh 15213. (412) 622-1300. FAX: (412) 622-1488. Lloyd Kaiser, pres; Thomas Skinner, exec VP; Jay Rayvid, sr VP.
TV & radio prog, promotional film prod & distribution; prod svcs.

QED Enterprises. 4802 5th Ave., Pittsburgh 15213. (412) 622-1500. FAX: (412) 622-6413. James C. Rogal, VP.
Full-svc operation providing svc from conception to completion, film or video.

Quality Film and Video. 232 Cockeysville Rd., Hunt Valley, Md. 21030. (410) 785-1920. Peter A. Garey, pres; Guy G. Garey, VP.
Offers 16mm Ektachrome film processing, 16mm B&W reversal film processing, video prod & postprod svcs & video tape duplication.

Quark Video. 109 W. 27th St., New York 10001. (212) 807-7711. Michael Levin, pres.
TV-CATV only.
On-line & off-line postprod, videotape duplication, stage with hard cyc.

Quartet Films Inc. 12417 Ventura Blvd., Studio City, Calif. 91604. (818) 509-0100. FAX: (818) 509-0103. Michael R. Lah, pres.
TV-CATV only.
Prod of animation & live-action comls.

R

R & M Productions. 569 Warren Ave., East Providence, R.I. 02914. (401) 434-1549. Myron Arnold, dir/prod/mgr/treas.
Audio recording svcs, cassette duplicating, coml prod: radio & TV, jingles, mus composition & mus scoring.

RAD MARKETING AND RADIOBASE

RAD Marketing & Radiobase. 167 Crary-on-the-Park, Mount Vernon, N.Y. 10550. (212) 274-0640. FAX: (212) 274-0646. Bob Dadarria, pres; Marc Dadarria, VP; Kathy Kruver, Hank Tooley, account execs.

RAD Marketing began with the unique idea of being able to provide marketers of any size with the largest, most ideal audience available. Through a variety of strategic mktg svcs, RAD Marketing can help companies identify & reach a market for their product—which can range from soup to soap, radio stns to cable nets & more. If you're looking for a unique & guaranteed method of locating your market, RAD Marketing can offer strategic solutions to your mktg needs. Other svcs include: Age Segmentation, Audio Duping/Voice Overs, Brand Name Modeling, Billing Insert Programs, Cable TV Direct, Computer Enhancement of Mailing Lists, Computerization, Custom Database Design, Data Entry, Direct Mail, Radio, TV, Fulfillment & Reporting, Fundraising, Laser Printing, List Management, List Order Fulfillment, Local Area Markets, Mapping, Merge Purge, Product Models—Regional/Natl, Product & Promotional Sweepstakes, Radio-Base, Sweepstakes Mail Pick-Up Control & TV Commercial Duping.

RAI Corp. (Italian Radio TV System). 1350 Ave. of the Americas, 21st Fl., New York 10019. (212) 468-2500. FAX: (212) 247-5450. Umberto Bonetti, pres; Antonio Devita, exec VP; Gul Wines, VP progmg.
Italian natl radio & TV.

RMD & Associates Inc. 214 State Rd., Media, Pa. 19063. (215) 566-3799. FAX: (215) 891-0348. Dick D'Anjolell, exec prod; Hank Shaw, tech support svcs; Celeste Walsh, prod coord.
Prog creative svcs, prod & distribution, specializing in promotion & business info.

RPM-Radio Programming & Management Inc. 4198 Orchard Lake Rd., Orchard Lake, Mich. 48323. (313) 681-2660; (800) 521-2537. FAX: (313) 681-3936. Thomas M. Krikorian, pres.
Chicago 60461: 3521 Ithaca Rd., Olympia Fields. (800) 621-5699; (708) 748-9444. FAX: (708) 503-0001. Ray Lowy.
Wkly CD svc top hits U.S.A. & CD mus libraries.

RW Video Communications. 4902 Hammersley Rd., Madison, Wis. 53711. (608) 274-4000. Robert C. Wickhem, pres; Andrew Garcia, gen mgr.
Video/film prod, video postprod, duplication, staging, computer graphics, in-house audio prod & sweetening svcs.

The Radio Almanac. 107 Jensen Cir, West Springfield, Mass. 01089-4451. (413) 737-7600. Charles G. Spencer, editor/publisher.
Lifestyle info; special rsch; writing, voice & prod projects. Monthly filler material publication featuring events, sports, bio sketches & other info.

Producers, Distributors, Production and Other Services

Radio America. 1030 15th St., N.W., Suite 700, Washington 20005. (202) 408-0944. FAX: (202) 408-1087. James C. Roberts, pres; Marc A. Lipsitz, VP; Brett Moss, prod.
News & feature svc providing daily, wkly & special progs (90 seconds to one hour) & multi-part documentaries.

Radio Bible Class Inc. Box 22, Grand Rapids, Mich. 49555. (616) 942-6770. FAX: (616) 957-5741. Martin DeHaan II, pres; Richard W. Mason, exec VP.
TV & radio prod & distribution.

Radio Canada International/Canadian Broadcasting Corp. Box 6000, Montreal, Que., Canada H3C 3A8. (514) 597-7555. FAX: (514) 284-2052. Allan Familiant, prog dir; Terry Hargreaves, exec dir; Jacques Bouliane, dir engrg.
Daily sw radio bcsts around the world in 7 languages; recorded material distributed to foreign AM & FM stns.

Radio City Music Hall Productions. 1260 Ave. of the Americas, Rockefeller Plaza, New York 10020. (212) 632-4000. FAX: (212) 956-2544. Jay Winuk, dir publ; Annie Fort, Stephen Henderson, publicists.
Los Angeles 90067: 2049 Century Park E., Suite 1200. (310) 551-2721.
TV prog prod; prod svcs.

Radio Express Inc. 3575 Cahuenga Blvd. W., Suite 390, Los Angeles 90068. (213) 850-1003. FAX: (213) 874-7753. Tom Rounds, pres; John Fodor, VP/gen mgr.
International representation & distribution of radio progmg, mus & prod libraries, jingles & software.

Radio Production Services Inc. Box 3887, Park Place Station, Greenville, S.C. 29608. (803) 859-7930. (803) 859-7930 ext. 21. R. Kenneth Rogers, pres; G. Leighton Grantham III, VP/CFO; Glen R. Rice Jr., business & legal VP; Clemson H. Key, dir engrg; Lisa N. Cooley, mgr communications; Dennis DeMichele, stn sls.
Radio Prog prod specializing in early R&B & Oldies formats. Radio & TV coml prod & distribution. Stn ID packages, jingles, consultation svcs in sls & progmg.

Radio Sound Network. 1515 W. Lane Ave., Columbus, Ohio 43221. (614) 481-6003. FAX: (614) 487-8205. Ed Johnson, pres; Steve Clawson, dir engrg; Joe Karoscik, studio prod.
Satellite distribution & prod, svc to radio; audio news release-press conferences.

Radio Spirits Inc. 3150 River Rd., Suite 11, Des Plaines, Ill. 60018. (708) 635-8978. FAX: (708) 635-8943. Carl Amari, pres; Roy P. Millonzi, VP.
Syndicated radio prod. Specializing in *Golden Age of Radio*. Prod of *When Radio Was* with Art Fleming, bartered to 100 affls.

Radio Sweden. c/o Swedish Broadcasting Co. 12 W. 37th St., New York 10018-7404. (212) 643-8855. FAX: (212) 594-6413. Elisabeth Johansson, exec dir/NY office.
Prod & distributor.

Radio & TV Roundup Productions. 426 Sunset Blvd., Cape May, N.J. 08204. (609) 884-0620; (212) 749-3647. Bill Bertenshaw, exec prod; Bobbi Cherrelle, CEO; Fred Long, TV dir; Dan Frercks, radio dir; B.C. Slachofsky, business mgr; Dick Roffman, cable prod.
Prod & placement of TV & radio progmg including comls & PSAs.

Radio Today Entertainment. 1776 Broadway, 4th Fl., New York 10019. (212) 581-3962. FAX: (212) 459-9343. Geoff Rich, pres; Tom Powell, VP prod; Ramona Rideout, VP affil rels.
Prod of award-winning natl & international radio features, such as Flashback, Flashback Pop Quiz & Rock Slides.

Radioguide People Inc. 24725 W. 12 Mile Rd., Suite 316, Southfield, Mich. 48034. (313) 355-0022. FAX: (313) 353-0660. Arthur R. Vuolo Jr., pres; Barry M. Grant, sr VP.
Publishers of radio stn guides for the gen public; co-sponsored by loc stns & natl advertisers.

Radio-TV Commission of the Southern Baptist Convention. 6350 W. Freeway, Fort Worth, Tex. 76150. (817) 737-4011; (800) 292-2287 for progs. FAX: (817) 737-8209. Jack Johnson, pres; Richard T. McCartney, exec VP; Debrah Key, VP net opns; Robert Thornton, VP TV svcs; Glenn McEowen, VP engrg; Ed Malone, VP radio svcs; Doug Dillard, VP external rels; Jerry Stamps, VP business svcs.
TV & radio prod & distribution.

Carl Ragsdale Associates Inc. 4725 Stillbrooke, Houston 77035-4911. (713) 729-6530. Diane Ragsdale, chmn of bd; Carl V. Ragsdale, pres.
Promotional film prod.

Rampion Visual Productions. 316 Stuart St. in Park Square, Boston 02116. (617) 574-9601. FAX: (617) 574-9604. Randel F. Cole, dir/writer; Steven Tringali, camera; Joe Benson, VP dev.
TV-CATV only.
ENG, EFP, Beta SP to D2 editing, 2D & 3D computer graphics, 20' by 28' studio.

Ray Communications Inc. 179 Lovers Ln., Suite B, Elizabeth City, N.C. 27909. (919) 335-7294. Bill Ray, pres; Harvey Jernegan, chief engr.
Radio prog syndication & distribution. Moble satellite uplink svcs.

Ray Sports Network. 179 Lovers Ln., Suite C, Elizabeth City, N.C. 27909. (919) 335-7294. FAX: (919) 335-2496. Bill Ray, pres; Bob DeBlois, sports dir; Harvey Jernegan, chief engr.
TV prog & coml prod, distribution. Radio prog & coml prod, distribution. Prod svcs.

Raycom Inc. Box 33367, 412 East Blvd., Charlotte, N.C. 28203-5136. (704) 378-4400. FAX: (704) 378-4461. Rick Ray, CEO; Dee Ray, pres; Ken Haines, exec VP; Pat LaPlatney, VP stn sls & mktg; Jim Duncan, dir net opns; Ray Warren, exec VP sls & mktg.
Prod, market & distribute sports & entertainment progmg nationally & internationally.

Real Deal Productions. Box 2147, Sioux City, Iowa 51104-0147. (712) 276-2295. "Morrie" Miller, dir.
Produces & distributes radio progs: *Little Chicago* (contempory & traditional American Blues), *Souvenirs of the 60's* (60's rock), *Trick Bag* (60's soul).

Redwood Entertainment Inc. 71 Ayers Ct., Suite 3A, Teaneck, N.J. 07666. (201) 833-4368. FAX: (201) 833-4072. Janet E. Castiel, pres.
TV prog, film prod, mus videos.

Reel Movies International Inc. 8235 Douglas Ave., Suite 770, Dallas 75225. (214) 363-4400. FAX: (214) 739-3456. Tom T. Moore, pres; Dena Moore, contract servicing.
TV-CATV only.
Worldwide distributor of motion pictures & TV series. Servicing all rights.

Reeves Entertainment. 10877 Wilshire Blvd., 9th Fl. Westwood, Calif. 90024. (310) 209-2200. FAX: (818) 953-7684. Merrill Grant, chmn of bd; Richard S. Reisberg, pres/COO.
TV prog prod.

Regal Studios. 1349 Regal Row, Dallas 75247. (214) 634-8511. FAX: (214) 638-5724. Pat Hogan, pres.
TV/radio comls; various bcst & prod svcs film score.

Reid/Land Productions Inc. 70-25 Yellowstone Blvd., No. 15C, Forest Hills, N.Y. 11375. (718) 793-3880. Allen Reid, pres; Mady Land, exec VP.
TV-CATV only.
Nashville 37214: 2806 Opryland Dr. (615) 885-1545. FAX: (615) 391-4380.
Packaging, creation & prod of TV progs: var, entertainment, mus, games, sports & cooking.

Russ Reid Co. 2 N. Lake Ave., Suite 600, Pasadena, Calif. 91101. (818) 449-6100. FAX: (818) 449-5773. Russ Reid, chmn/CEO; Keith Jespersen, pres; Jerry McClun, sr VP media; Terry Cavin, sr VP/COO; Tom Harrison, sr VP pub rels; Gary Evans, sr VP/chief creative off.
Specializes in fund-raising, direct-response adv, direct mail, TV & radio prog prod & placement, & pub rels for non-profit organizations.

Reiss Media Enterprises Inc. 5619 DTC Pkwy., Denver 80111. (303) 267-6101. FAX: (303) 267-6199. Jeffrey C. Reiss, chmn/CEO; Bruce T. Karpas, pres/COO & pres/CEO Reiss Media International & Reiss Media Entertainment Corp; Hugh Panero, pres/CEO Request TV.
TV-CATV only.
Distributes special events, licenses ind films for pay-per-view exhibition & licenses pay-per-view rights of films internationally.

Reizner & Reizner Film & Video. 7179 Via Maria, San Jose, Calif. 95139. (408) 226-6339. FAX: (408) 226-6403. Dick Reizner, own.
Bcst & industrial prod in all formats. Certified Legal Video Specialist. Gyrozoom rental.

Reliance Audio Visual Corp. 1600 Broadway, New York 10019. (212) 586-5000. FAX: (212) 586-5002. Gil M. Meyer, pres; Norma E. Matthews, exec VP.
Audio & video permanent instals & design, consultation, rentals, staging multimedia & video projection, dealerships, leasing, display design.

Religious Television Associates. 315 Queen St. E., Toronto, Ont., Canada M5A 1S7. (416) 366-9221. FAX: (416) 368-9774. Rodney M. Booth, exec dir.
TV-CATV only.
TV prog prod & distribution.

Republic Pictures Corp. 12636 Beatrice St., Los Angeles 90066. (310) 306-4040. FAX: (310) 306-2203. Russell Goldsmith, CEO.
TV-CATV only.
TV prog, prod & distribution.

Restivo Communications Group. 107 S. West St., Suite 199, Alexandria, Va. 22314. (703) 461-0767. Peter J. Restivo, pres.
TV prod & concept. News & info progmg.

Reuters Satellite Services. 1333 H St. N.W., Washington 20005. (202) 898-0058. William J. Page, VP/North America; Jay Lebowitz, opns mgr/North America.
International satellite carrier of news, sports, entertainment & business TV progmg with domestic & international satellite & TV opn centers.

Reuters Television. International Bldg., Rockefeller Ctr., 630 5th Ave., Suite 700, New York 10111. (212) 698-4500. FAX: (212) 698-2367. Chris Travers, sr VP; Laura Brandt IR mgr N. America; Richard Frisch, VP corporate TV.
TV-CATV only.
International news svc. Provides location crews & engr facilities worldwide. World's largest TV news archive. Services 650 bcstrs in over 80 countries.

Rhodes Productions. 124 11th St., Manhattan Beach, Calif. 90266. (310) 379-3686. FAX: (310) 376-2625. Jack E. Rhodes, pres; Ralph V. Cunningham, exec VP; Willis R. Tomlinson, sr VP; Jack E. Rhodes Jr., pres syndicated svcs division; Rhian R. Rhodes, VP special projects.
TV-CATV only.
TV prog prod & distribution.

Richardy Productions. 3239 S. 90th E. Ave., Tulsa, Okla. 74145. (918) 627-4607. FAX: (918) 627-4607. Richard G. Hardy, pres.
TV & radio prod & distribution.

Richter Productions Inc. 330 W. 42nd St., New York 10036. (212) 947-1395. FAX: (212) 643-1208. Robert Richter, pres; Madeleine Solano, dir mktg.
TV-CATV only.
TV prog & promotional film prod & distribution, film & video.

Riden International Inc. 6024 Paseo Palmilla, Goleta, Calif. 93117. (805) 964-1338. Richard Dennison, pres.
TV prog prod & distribution.

The Riviera Library. 31628 Saddletree Dr., Westlake Village, Calif. 91361. (818) 889-5778. F.W. Zens, pres.
Prod svcs.

Riviera Productions. 31628 Saddletree Dr., Westlake Village, Calif. 91361. (818) 889-5778. Wil Zens, prod/dir.
TV-CATV only.
Motion picture prod.

Roberts Television International Inc. 4170 S. Decatur Blvd., Suite C-7, Las Vegas 89103. (702) 365-1875. FAX: (702) 365-6815. Tommy Roberts, pres; Todd Roberts, exec VP.
Prog prod & distribution. Satellite transmission, encoding & decoding svcs. Exclusive rights ownship of various prog & sporting events worldwide.

Richard H. Roffman Associates Inc. 697 W. End Ave., Suite 6A, New York 10025. (212) 749-3647; (212) 749-3648. Richard H. Roffman, pres/co-prod; Florence Morrison, host/co-prod; Evelyn Neinken, VP.
AM & FM radio, cable & TV prods; pub rels & publ legal svcs, talent representation, editorial svcs for publishers, books, magazines & nwsprs.

Romano & Associates Inc. 10630 Little Patuxent Pkwy., Suite 313, Columbia, Md. 21044. (410) 730-4133. FAX: (301) 621-4622. Neil Romano, prod/dir; John Saint-John, asst prod; Jim Carroll, account exec/writer; Tina Guisto, writer.
Full-svc prod company specializing in issue-oriented short-feature films & documentaries, as well as PSAs; prod of children's educ videos & comls.

Rosler Creative. 4624 Cherokee Trail, Dallas 75209. (214) 357-2005. FAX: (214) 357-1255. Peter Rosler, own.
TV comls, creative dev & prod.

Producers, Distributors, Production and Other Services

Ross-Gaffney Inc. 21 W. 46th St., New York 10036. (212) 719-2744. FAX: (212) 944-8539. James Gaffney, pres; Tony Cacioppo, opns mgr; Kathryn Grassi, sec/treas.
Motion picture postprod svcs. Film editing & cutting room svcs. Sound mixing & sound recording; mus & FX library.

Jack Rourke Productions. Box 1705, Burbank, Calif. 91507. (818) 843-4839. Jack Rourke, pres; Henry Edwards, VP adv & promotion.
TV & radio prog prod.

Rowe International Inc. 75 Troy Hills Rd., Whippany, N.J. 07981. (201) 887-0400. FAX: (201) 887-2399. Dave Markowitz, sls mgr mus division.
Suppliers of various types of mus to coml enterprises.

Ruby-Spears Productions Inc. 3575 Cahuenga Blvd., Hollywood, Calif. 90068. (213) 874-5100. Joe Ruby, pres/exec prod; Ken Spears, VP/exec prod.
TV-CATV only.
Animation & live action prod studio; Saturday morning & prime-time syndication.

Russian-American Broadcasting Co. One Bridge Plaza, Suite 145, Fort Lee, N.J. 07024. (201) 461-6667. FAX: (201) 461-6227. David A. Moro, CEO; James W. Barry Grau, VP/gen mgr.
Provides Russian language radio & TV prog via DBS & through cable systems thoughout North America.

Rysher TPE. One Dag Hammarskjold Plaza, New York 10017. (212) 750-9190. FAX: (212) 752-2759. Keith Samples, pres; Tim Helfet, COO; Ira Bernstein, exec VP; Harvey Garmm, sr VP/gen sls mgr; Marc Solomon, sr VP ad sls; Jim Burke, sr VP sls; Henry Urick, sr VP worldwide mktg.
TV-CATV only.
Burbank, Calif. 91505: 3400 Riverside Dr., (818) 846-0030. FAX: (818) 846-1163.
Prod & distributor of first-run progs.

S

SATVIEW PLUS. 723 Port Richmond Ave., Staten Island, N.Y. 10302. (212) 978-3375. FAX: (718) 876-7928. Charles J. Hargrove, pres/CEO.
TV-CATV only.
Satellite delivered video distribution svcs for both corporations & non-profit institutions.

SBS Network. 26 W. 56th St., New York 10019. (212) 541-6700. FAX: (212) 541-8535; (212) 541-9236. Mickie Reyes, mgng dir; Carroll Larkin, gen sls mgr.
Spanish progmg syndication.

SESAC Inc. 421 W. 54th St., New York 10019. (212) 586-3450. FAX: (212) 489-5699. Freddie Gershon, Ira Smith, co-chmn; Vincent Candilora, pres/CEO.
Nashville 30723: 55 Music Sq. E. (375) 320-0055. FAX: (375) 329-9627. Natl office.
Mus rights organization representing the performance, mechanical & synchronization rights of affil composers, authors & publishers.

1776 Productions. 5 Sparrow Dr., Livingston, N.J. 07039. (212) 736-1776. Ralph Weisinger, pres.
Promotional film prod.

SFM Entertainment. (A division of SFM Media Corp.). 1180 Ave. of the Americas, New York 10036. (212) 790-4800. FAX: (212) 790-4897. Stanley H. Moger, pres; Jordan Ringel, exec VP; Cyndy Wynne, VP/syndication; Frank Campisi, sr dir rsch.
TV-CATV-Radio.
Producer & distributor of TV prog package & videocassettes.

SJS Radio Networks Ltd. 800 2nd Ave., New York 10017. (212) 370-9460. FAX: (888) 883-1186. Steve Saslow, chmn; June Brody, pres; Beverly Padratzek, VP prog dev.
Prod, affil rels and/or sls representation.

S.L.P. Production. 19 W. 36th St., 11th Fl., New York 10018. (212) 714-1710. FAX: (212) 714-0132. Shelton Leigh Palmer, pres; Liz Harwell, creative dir; Jason Baker, chief recording engr.
Mus prod & promotional svcs; campaigns, themes, jingles, sound effects, prod mus, frame accurate on-line video editing; natl & loc coml prod.

S/M Communications. 780 E. 700 N., Logan, Utah 84321. USU Box 1920, Logan, Utah 84322-0199. (801) 752-7000. FAX: (801) 753-8211. Stephen W. Skinner, pres; Marlene McCausland, bcst coord; Keith Christensen, engr; Bob Appuhn, Voice of the Aggies.
Produces & distributes football & basketball play-by-play via satellite; wkly radio & TV coach's show & select games via satellite for cable systems.

STARNET. Box 7341, 10523 Burbank Blvd., N. Hollywood, Calif. 91603. (818) 753-3042. FAX: (818) 508-4541. Gary J. Worth, pres/CEO; Alan Maretsky, VP opns.
New York 10017: One Dag Hammarkjold Plaza, 7th Fl., (212) 207-9872. FAX: (212) 702-4810.
Daily motion picture & shopping svc. Satellite: Telstar 302, transponder 8H.

SWTV Production Services Inc. Box 62013, Phoenix 85082-2013. (602) 244-1982. FAX: (602) 244-1813. L.E. Meyers, pres.
TV-CATV only.
Mobile TV prod.

Saban Entertainment. 4000 W. Alameda Ave., Burbank, Calif. 91505. (818) 972-4800. FAX: (818) 972-4895. Haim Saban, chmn/CEO; Mel Woods, pres/COO; Stan Golden, pres international; Lance Robbins, sr VP prod.
TV-CATV only.
Entertainment company specializing in the creation, prod, acquisition & distrubution of all forms of TV progmg & mus for the worldwide market.

Sacred Heart Program Inc. 3900 Westminster Pl., St. Louis 63108. (800) 747-7692. FAX: (314) 533-0335. Rev. Michael V. Tueth, S.J., exec dir; Donald L. Merl, dir radio & mktg/distribution.
Produces inspirational radio & TV progs using a documentary prod style & offering them to stns free of chg.

Sak Entertainment. 45 E. Church St., Orlando, Fla. 32801. (407) 648-0001. FAX: (407) 648-1333. R. Will Sera, pres; Terry Olson, mgng dir.
Professional comedy actors, dirs, prods & writers. Entertainment consultants for WDW, Universal Studio, Harrahs Corp & Busch Gardens.

Alan Sands Productions. 6 E. 45th St., New York 10017. (212) 286-8805. Alan Sands, pres; C. Diamond, VP sls; L. Stix, VP progmg.
Syndication of radio & TV progs.

Satellite Music Network Inc. 12655 N. Central Expwy., Suite 600, Dallas 75243. (800) 527-4892; (214) 991-9200. FAX: (214) 991-1071. David Cantor, chmn; David Hubschman, exec VP; Frank Woodbeck, VP assoc sls.
Live 24 hours a day premium progmg available featuring 10 radio formats. Also includes SMN PRIZM rsch clustering.

The Saturday Evening Post Television Division. (Benjamin Franklin Literary & Medical Society.) 1100 Waterway Blvd., Indianapolis 46202. (317) 636-8881. Rick Maultra, dir communications.
Produces & distributes health shows for radio & TV.

Scola. Box 619, McClelland, Iowa 51548-0619. (712) 566-2202. FAX: (712) 566-2502. Lee Lubbers, S.J., pres; Francis Lajba, exec dir.
Satellite retransmission of TV news from 40 countries in original languages for schools & cables.

The Seattle Bureau. 2700 4th Ave., Suite 607, Seattle 98121. (206) 448-2500. FAX: (206) 728-0878. David Oglevie, pres; Kevin Ely, VP.
TV-CATV only.
Location video prod for bcst news, corporate & industrial mktg & medical news. BETACAM SP or 3/4" SP formats.

Hal Seeger Studios Inc. 45 W. 45th St., New York 10036. (212) 391-1020. FAX: (212) 768-1302. Hal Seeger, pres.
Prod svcs.

Select Media Communications Inc. 152 W. 57th St., New York 10019. (212) 765-1020. FAX: (212) 765-2943. Mitch Gutkowski, pres; Claire Scully, exec VP; Marc Juris, VP creative svcs; Carol Blank, dir adv sls; Linda Yaccarino, dir stn & adv sls.
TV-CATV only.
TV prog, prod & distribution.

Semiaphore Entertainment Group. 32 E. 57th St., New York 10022. (212) 371-6850. FAX: (212) 888-8650. Robert B. Meyrowitz, pres; Michael Abramson, exec VP mktg & distribution; Michael Pillot, VP prod.
TV prog prod, radio prog prod & distribution.

Seraphim Communications Inc. 1568 Eustis St., St. Paul, Minn. 55108. (612) 645-9173. FAX: (612) 645-3515. Hal Dragseth, own/pres; Don Oberdorfer, own/sec/treas.
Full-svc audio, video & AV capabilities. Emphasis on video prod from concept through final product.

Seven Network Australia Inc. 10100 Santa Monica Blvd., Suite 2060, Los Angeles 90067. (310)-553-3445. FAX: (310) 553-4812. Zane Bair, U.S. rep/mgr; Paul Marshall, bureau chief.
TV-CATV only.
US office & news bureau of Channel 7, Australia (a major coml TV net of Australia).

Seven Oaks Productions. 9145 Sligo Creek Pkwy., Silver Spring, Md. 20901. (301) 587-0030. FAX: (301) 587-8649. M.A. Marlow, CEO; Gene Starbecker, pres.
Manitou Springs, Colo. 80829: 1154 Manitou Ave. (719) 685-5549. Gene Starbecker, pres.
TV & radio prog, comls, & promotional films produced & distributed; gen prod svcs.

Seventh Day Adventists. Box 10853 Reno, Nev. 89510. (702) 857-2244. FAX: (702) 857-2272. Sam Shad, pres; Bonnie McCorkle, prog dev.
Radio progmg & coml prod, TV progmg & coml prod, TV & radio progmg concepts dev from start to finish.

Shadow Broadcast Services/Shadow Traffic Network. 5700 Florida Blvd., Suite 210, Baton Rouge 70806. (504) 926-7152. FAX: (504) 923-0704. Carole Marshall, pres/gen mgr; Jay Trotsky, dir opns.
Traffic reports & news info to radio & news stns.

Sheridan-Elson Communications Inc. 20 W. 37th St., New York 10018. (212) 239-2000. FAX: (212) 629-4417. Robert E. Elson, pres.
TV & radio progs, comls, & promotional film prod & distribution; gen prod svcs.

Shield Productions Inc. 161 E. Grand Ave., Chicago 60611. (312) 644-1666. James C. Dolan Sr, pres.
Creation & prod of radio & TV comls.

Shop Television Network. 1845 Empire, Burbank, Calif. 91504. (818) 840-1400.
TV-CATV only.

Showcase Productions International. Tribeca Film Center, 6 E. 39th St., New York 10006. (212) 679-8230. FAX: (212) 686-0801. Sandra J. Birnhak, chmn/CEO; David R. Ames, pres; Marcy Stuzin, VP dev.
Prod of theatrical feature films & TV movies, TV series. Distributes TV product worldwide. Also does co-prod ventures in U.S. & abroad.

Sidewater Enterprises Inc. 2647 Laurel Pass, Los Angeles 90046. (213) 650-1902. FAX: (213) 656-7853. Frederic M. Sidewater, pres; Rosalyn G. Sidewater, exec VP.
TV-CATV only.
Consulting regarding financing & distribution for ind prods.

Sierra Equipment Inc. 2401 N.W. 42nd Ave., Miami 33142. (305) 871-5523. FAX: (305) 871-5437. Santiago Sierra, pres; Juan Sierra, sec.
TV prog prod & distribution; prod svcs.

Sifford Video Services Inc. 121 Lyle Ln., Nashville. 37210. (800) 251-1009. FAX: (615) 244-5712. Gary Cornstubble, pres; Lawson Turk, VP.
Videotape duplication, standard conversions.

The Silverbach-Lazarus Group. 9911 W. Pico Blvd. Penthouse M, Los Angeles 90035. (310) 552-2660. FAX: (310) 552-9039. Alan Silverbach, chmn; Herb Lazarus, pres.
TV prog distribution (U.S. & international).

The Fred Silverman Co. 12400 Wilshire Blvd, Suite 920, Los Angeles 90025. (310) 826-6050. FAX: (310) 207-5357. Fred Silverman, pres; Michael Frankel, dir finance & business affrs.
TV-CATV only.
TV prog prod.

Silverman Productions Inc. 106 E. Cary St., Richmond, Va. 23219. (804) 343-1934. Donald Silverman, pres.
TV & radio coml prods & sponsored videos for corporations & assns.

Sing For Joy. Saint Olaf College, Northfield, Minn. 55057. (507) 646-3071. Alvin Rueter, host/prod.
Vocal church mus with comments relating the mus to ecumenical scriptures; 29 minutes wkly.

Skywatch Weather Center. 347 Prestley Rd., Bridgeville, Penn. 15017. (412) 221-6000; 1-800-SKY-WATCH. FAX: (412) 221-3160. Dick Mancini, pres.
Specially formatted weathercasts produced in the Skywatch Weather Center.

Producers, Distributors, Production and Other Services

Smith/Lee Productions. 7420 Manchester Rd., St. Louis 63143. (314) 647-3900. FAX: (314) 647-3959. David Smith, pres; Barry Lee, VP.
TV & radio coml promotional film prod; prod svcs.

Smithsonian Institution, Office of TeleCommunications. National Museum of American History Bldg., Rm. BB40, Washington 20560. (202) 357-2985. FAX: (202) 357-1565. Paul Johnson, dir.
Provides TV documentaries, radio progmg, home video & educ media products.

Soldiers Radio & Television, U.S. Army Command Information Unit. 2320 Mill Rd., Alexandria, Va. 22314. (703) 325-5535. FAX: (703) 325-5834. Clark Taylor, dir; MSG Dave Foster, opns mgr; Ralph R. Fick, chief engr; SFC Elba Kunsman, dir radio & TV news.
Radio & TV news bureau, soldiers radio satellite net.

Solid Color Productions. Box 1100, Fremont, Calif. 94538. (510) 656-8660. FAX: (510) 505-0666. Andrew J. deBruyn, own/videographer/edit; Carolyn Harvey, edit.
TV-CATV only.
Engrg, EFP & edit svcs.

SONY Trans Com Entertainment Programming. 1833 Alton Ave., Irvine, Calif. 92714. (714) 252-6565. FAX: (714) 252-0721. Ron Romano, prod; Liliane Aouizerat, progmg mgr.
Inflight audio progmg & prod for airlines.

SoperSound Music Library. Box 498, Palo Alto, Calif. 94301. (415) 321-4022; (800) 227-9980. FAX: (415) 321-9261. Dennis Reed, pres.
Contemp prod mus library for all prod needs. Available on CDs & tapes.

Sound Idea Productions. 405 14th St., Suite 612, Oakland, Calif. 94612. (510) 832-5178. FAX: (510) 832-5178. Glenn Davidson, pres.
Telephone-hold tapes for cable operators. Radio prod & syndication.

Sound Ideas. 105 W. Beaver Creek Rd., Suite 4, Richmond Hill, Ont., Canada L4B 1C6. (416) 886-5000. FAX: (416) 886-6800. Brian Nimens, pres; Mike Bell, gen mgr.
Sound effects & prod mus libraries designed for bcst prod needs.

Sound of Birmingham Productions. 3625 5th Ave. S., Birmingham, Ala. 35222. (205) 595-8497. Don Mosley, pres; Betty Mosley, VP/office mgr; Noah White, chief engr.
Radio & TV voice-overs, jingles, video sweetening, custom mus, recording studios.

Sound Source. 2 St. Clair Ave. W., Toronto, Ont., Canada M4V 1L6. (416) 922-1290. FAX: (416) 323-6834. J.M. Heimrath, VP/gen mgr; L. Soldat, VP affil rels.
Produces, markets & distributes radio progs nationally.

Sound*Bytes. 1425 Hopkins St. N.W., Suite 401, Washington 20036. (202) 296-2022. FAX: (202) 775-0580. Jan Ziff, pres.
Computer audio show prod & syndication.

Soundmasters. See Hi Ho Teleproductions.

Sounds of the Times (Radio Bible Class). Box 2222, Grand Rapids, Mich. 49555. (616) 942-6770. FAX: (616) 957-5741. Martin Dehaan, pres.
TV prog prod; TV & radio coml prod & distribution.

The Soundshop Inc. 1307 Division St., Nashville 37203. (615) 244-4149. FAX: (615) 242-8759. Buddy Killen, pres; Mike Bradley, mgr.
TV & radio prod & distribution.

Southcott Productions. Box 33185, Granada Hills, Calif. 91344; 131 S. Abbot Kinney Blvd., Venice, Calif. 90291. (818) 368-4938; (800) 356-9107. FAX: (818) 368-4938. Chuck Southcott, own.
Radio prog, coml prod & distribution.

Southern Trax Productions. Box 3511, Muscle Shoals, Ala. 35662. (800) 462-4420; FAX also. Clete Quick, sls & mktg.
Muscle Shoals Magic CD prod library, stn IDs, coml jingles produced professionally.

Souveniors of the 60's. Box 2147, Sioux City, Iowa 51104-0147. (712) 276-2295. "Sky King", prod/host.

Spatial Technologies Inc. 801 N. La Brea Ave., Suite 104, Hollywood, Calif. 90038. (818) 772-8425. FAX: (818) 592-0987. Daniel L. Symmes, pres.
TV-CATV only.
3D (stereoscopic) TV & film systems.

Spectrum Associates Inc. 536 W. 29th St., New York 10001. (212) 563-1680. FAX: (212) 563-1683. George Pitt, pres; Rudy Tomasselli, VP.
TV coml, promotional film prod & distribution.

Spelling Television Inc. 5700 Wilshire Blvd., Suite 575, Los Angeles 90036. (213) 965-5888. Aaron Spelling, chmn of bd; E. Duke Vincent, vice chmn; Gail Paterson, VP prod.
TV prog prod.

Charlie Spencer Productions. 107 Jensen Cir., West Springfield, Mass. 01089-4451. (413) 737-7600. Charlie Spencer, prod/dir.
Specializes in nature & environmental progmg, outdoor recreation & nature travel. Svcs include: producing, directing, rsch/writing & narration. Award-winning progs include *The Urban Canoeist* & *American Waste*.

Spencer Productions Inc. 234 5th Ave., Suite 301, New York 10001. (212) 677-2200; (212) 865-8829. FAX: (212) 779-3443. Bruce Spencer, exec prod; Alan Abel, creative dir.
Comedy prog created for TV, cable & radio by Alan Abel.

Spiritual World Network. 1088 Bishop St., Suite 204, Honolulu 96813. (808) 522-5100. Triaka Don Smith, pres; Steve Tedrahn, mgng dir; Karen Schipani, VP TV progmg.
Produces TV & radio progs & develops ind net that impartially reflects spiritual activity.

Sportlite Films/Video. 641 N. Ave., Glendale Heights, Ill. 60139. (708) 790-3300. FAX: (708) 790-3325. Alfred D. LeVine, gen mgr/prod; Robert Erinberg, comptroller; Jack Paige; sls mgr.
TV prog, promotional film prod & distribution, prod svcs & sports pro-action videos.

Sports Byline U.S.A. 300 Broadway, Suite 8, San Francisco 94133. (415) 434-8300. FAX: (415) 391-2569. Ron Barr, chmn; Kevin Mulligan, CEO; Charlie Coane, pres; Steve Block, sls mgr.
Satellite-delivered nationwide radio sports talk show, listener 800 number, Mon.-Fri., 7-10 PM (West Coast), barter.

Sports Entertainment Network. 3333 Cambridge St., Las Vegas 89109. (702) 731-5200. FAX: (702) 731-4200. Jerry Kutner, pres; Bill Wright, opns dir; Rodd Stowell, prog dir.
America's only 24-hour sports talk radio net with an interactive 800 phone number & top interviews.

Sports Final Radio Network. (Talk America Radio Network.) Box 697, 48 Fitchburg St., Marlboro, Mass. 01752. (508) 460-0588. FAX: (508) 624-6496. John Crohen, pres; Tom Star, VP; Bob Long, stn rels.
Bcstg 24 hours a day, 7 days a week on stn C-5 & Galaxy 2.

Spotmaker Studio. Box 1065, Del Mar, Calif. 92014. (619) 296-0181. Gary Seger, proprietor.
Radio prog & coml prod.

Al Stahl Animated. 1600 Broadway, New York 10019. (212) 265-2942. FAX: (212) 265-2944. Al Stahl, pres; J. Stahl, VP.
TV prog, coml, & promotional film prod & distribution; gen prod svcs.

Star Date. The University of Texas at Austin, RLM 15.308, Austin, Texas 78712. (512) 471-5285. FAX: (512) 471-5060. Sandra Barnes, exec prod; Damond Benningfield, prod.
365 syndicated two-minute radio progs on stars & planets visible in the night sky. Each prog is date specific.

Starborne Productions Corp. Box 155, Whitehall, Mich. 49461. (616) 894-9092. James P. Schlichting, pres; Linda Schlichting, VP.
Radio prog prod & distribution.

Starcom Entertainment. Box 7341, 10523 Burbank Blvd., North Hollywood, Calif. 91603. (818) 753-3042. FAX: (818) 508-4541. Gary J. Worth, pres/CEO; Alan Maretsky, VP opns.
TV-CATV only.
New York 10017: One Dag Hammarskjold Plaza, 7th Fl. (212) 207-9872. FAX: (212) 702-4810.
TV prog distribution via TV, cable & satellite.

Station Break Music Productions. 103 Southwood Cir., Syosset, N.Y. 11791. (516) 496-1012; (212) 444-5239. FAX: (516) 496-8426. Steve Meyers, pres.
Original mus composition, prod & design, radio & TV spots, stn IDs, openers, themes, stingers, customized stock mus.

Charles H. Stern Agency Inc. 11755 Wilshire Blvd., Suite 2320, Los Angeles 90025. (310) 479-1788. Charles H. Stern, pres.
Radio coml prod & distribution.

Steven B. Stevens Production. 2077 Edinburg Ln., Fairfield, Ohio 45014. (513) 829-1211. (513) 829-5002. Steven B. Stevens, pres.
Provides documentary prod, award-winning travelogues, fund raisers, infomercials & direct response comls.

Stewart Digital Video. 525 Mildred Ave., Primos, Pa. 19018. (215) 626-6500. FAX: (215) 626-2638. David Bowers, gen mgr; Mark Von Zech, sls mgr; Stan Leshner, sls mgr.
TV-CATV only.
Coml & industrial video & audio prod, multi-camera remote & studio prod, mobile unit, on-line editing & animation.

Story Time Stories That Rhyme. Box 416, Denver 80201-0416. (303) 575-5676. Alfreda C. Doyle, own.
Prod & supplier of children's TV progs for cable TV starting in Denver. Progs are entitled *Stories That Rhyme* & *Story Time Stories That Rhyme*. They are 10-30 minutes in length & are educ, entertaining & inspirational.

Marty Stouffer Productions Inc. 300 S. Spring St., Aspen, Colo. 81611. (303) 925-5536. FAX: (303) 920-3820. Marty Stouffer, pres/treas.
TV prog prod.

Strand Broadcast Services. 1461 9th St., Manhattan Beach, Calif. 90266. (310) 318-1666. FAX: (310) 372-6282. Mike Carruthers, pres.
Radio prog, coml prod & distribution; media training.

Studio Center Corp. 200 W. 22nd St., Norfolk, Va. 23517. (804) 622-2111. FAX: (804) 623-5512. Bob Jump, pres/exec prod.
Radio & TV comls, stn promotions, TV voice-over svcs.

Studio 5 Productions. 5 TV Pl., Needham, Mass. 02192. (617) 433-4139. FAX: (617) 433-4198. William Lowell, exec dir.
Full-svc prod company. Prog dev for corporate communications. Home video & bcst prod facilities. Multi format post, studio & location packages. Satellite uplinking.

Studio M Productions Unlimited. 8715 Waikiki St., Honolulu 96830-0715. (808) 734-3345; (800) 443-3345. FAX: (808) 734-3299. Mike Michaels, own/sr engr/prod; Hugo Buehring, prod mgr.
Hollywood, Calif. 90038: 1041 N. Orange Dr. (213) 462-7372; (800) 762-7372. FAX: (213) 462-8556.
TV & radio prog prod, tape, film & live; prod svcs. Live remotes for TV & radio, news & sports.

Studio 6 Productions. 4466 John Young Pkwy., Orlando, Fla. 32804. (407) 291-6000. FAX: (407) 578-1321. Len DePanicis, prod; Mike Schweitzer, gen mgr.
TV prog, coml, promotional film prod; prod svcs.

Subito Studios. 367 N. Hwy. 101, Solana Beach, Calif. 92075. (619) 259-9339. FAX: (619) 755-6562. Cam MacMillan, own/exec prod.
TV-CATV only.
Design & prod bcst 3-D computer graphics. Logo animation, stn packages. All tape formats supported. Prod Subito Studio Video Graphics Volumes.

Sullivan Productions Inc. 340 W. Main, Missoula, Mont. 59806 (406) 721-2063. Robert H. Precht, pres; Marcy Levine, VP.
TV prog prod.

Sullivan Video Services Inc. 111 S. Bedford St., Suite 205, Burlington, Mass. 01803. (617) 229-7799. FAX: (617) 229-1533. John M. Sullivan, pres; Thomas F. Clark, rental opns mgr.
TV-CATV only.
Full-svc video prod & equipment rental house. Provides ENG/EFP news crews & Ku satellite svcs.

Sundial Productions. 24 Commerce St., Suite 1426, Newark, N.J. 07102. (201) 624-1085. FAX: (201) 624-1281. Jack Kreismer, principal; David Lapidus, principal.
TV & radio prog, telephone feature prod.

SunGard Mailing Service. 210 Automation Way, Birmingham, Ala. 35210. (205) 956-7803. FAX: (205) 956-7834. Michael L. Dikeman, pres; Johnny R. Harbison.
Laser statement printing & mailing svcs, including zip plus six delivery point barcoding & carrier route postal optimization. Custom statements, formats, conversions & data transmissions.

Producers, Distributors, Production and Other Services

Sunny Day Productions. 1931 S.E. Morrison, Portland, Ore. 97214. (503) 238-4525. FAX: (503) 236-8347. Russell E. Gorsline, pres; Greg Branson, VP/studio mgr.
TV & radio prod; audio recording.

Suntree Corp. Box 1335, Hampton Bays, N.Y. 11946. (516) 283-7089. FAX: (516) 287-3348. David Funt, pres; Roslyn Baws, exec VP.
TV-CATV only.
Infomercial specialists; design, prod & consulting.

Superior Promotions Inc. Box 249, 687 Bent Ridge Ln., Barrington, Ill. 60010. (708) 381-0909. FAX: (708) 381-1178. Thomas Edinger, pres; Ralph Polan, sls mgr; Pat Kelly, gen mgr.
Direct response TV/radio mktg & coml prod. Special interest video distribution, syndication, international distribution & video duplication sourcing.

Sutcliffe Music Inc. 8 W. 19th St., 2nd Fl., New York 10011. (212) 989-9292. FAX: (212) 989-5195. Gary S. Sutcliffe, pres/exec prod; Jennifer Countryman, business mgr; Annlee Diamant, April Jaffee, Jerry Winkowski reps; Angella Dryden, chief engr; Ned Davis, sound designer composer; Jon Cobert, David Immer, composer/arrangers.
Chicago: (312) 902-3456. Valerie Gobos Stewart, rep.
Los Angeles: (619) 770-7700. Layne Allyson, rep.
Original mus, sound design & scoring for TV & radio comls & films. State of the art 24 track & digital recording facility.

Swell Pictures Inc. 233 E. Wacker Dr., Chicago 60601. (312) 649-9000. FAX: (312) 649-0096. Michael Topel, pres; Sid Kavenow, sr VP/business mgr; Joe Flores, sr VP/chief engr; Brian Clark, exec VP; Dave Mueller, VP client svcs; Radi Akel, opns mgr.
TV-CATV only.
Film-to-tape transfer, videotape editing, digital sound editing & original mus. Avid, 3D graphics & compositing.

The Sweney Group Inc. Box 5608, Santa Barbara, Calif. 93150. (805) 565-3445. FAX: (805) 565-1036. William Sweney, pres; Kimberly May, VP.
Radio & TV prog prod, mus videos, documentaries, comls.

The Sweney Group Inc. Box 80177, South Dartmouth, Mass. 02748. (508) 992-0533. FAX: (508) 992-6886. W.H. Sweney, CEO.
Net progs, documentaries, mus, childrens, wildlife, sports.

SyberVision Systems Inc. One Sansome St., Suite 1610, San Francisco 94104. (415) 677-8616. FAX: (415) 433-3047. Paul Eisele, pres; David Bannon, VP product dev.
TV-CATV-Radio.
Publisher of self-improvement video & audio progs on health & fitness, sports, business, personal dev, family & language.

Syndicom. Box 12837, San Luis Obispo, Calif. 93406. (805) 543-9214. FAX: (805) 543-9243. Mike Hesser, pres; Sharon Miller, exec asst.
Produces *Red Neckerson*, one-minute comedy editorial; *Kaleidophonic Jazz*, three hours wkly; *Countryphonics, Sound Bite Trivia-Original*, authentic voices & themes.

T

30 Minutes TV Show. Box 2777, Alexandria, Va. 22301. (703) 548-8007. FAX: (703) 548-8007. Clayton Willis, pres/White House correspondent.
TV prod company which does documentaries on a wide range of topics. Extensive tape & film library, camera & prod facilities.

3D Video Corp. 801 N. La Brea Ave., Suite 104, Hollywood, Calif. 90038. (818) 772-8425. FAX: (818) 592-0987. Daniel L. Summes, pres.
TV-CATV only.
3D (stereoscopic) TV & film systems.

TM Century Inc. 2002 Academy, Dallas 75234. (214) 934-2121; (800) 937-2100. FAX: (800) 749-2121. P. Craig Turner, pres/CEO; Stuart McRae, VP sls.
Radio mus & prod libraries on CDs, TV prod & media placement.

TNN - The Nashville Network. 2806 Opryland Dr., Nashville 37214. (615) 889-6840. FAX: (615) 871-6698. Tom Griscom, VP/Gaylord Entertainment Co.; Kevin Hale, VP/gen mgr; C. Paul Corbin, dir progmg.
TV-CATV only.
Offers original concert specs, exclusive sports coverage, entertainment news & interview, info, live var & class western movies.

TR Productions. 1031 Commonwealth Ave., Boston 02215. (617) 783-0200. FAX: (617) 783-4844. Ross P. Benjamin, exec VP.
Prod svcs.

TRF Production Music Libraries. 747 Chestnut Ridge Rd., Chestnut Ridge, N.Y. 10977. (800) 899-MUSIC. (914) 356-0895. Michael Nurko, pres/CEO; Kenneth Gilman, VP.
Over 50,000 selections (4,000 discs) of both contemp & traditional mus. Includes BMG/RCA, Bosworth, Image, MP 2000, Music Scene, Prime time, TRF Alpha, Tele Music & the new Pyramid mus libraries. Also includes complete classical series & sound effects library, international ethnic series.

TRI-COMM Productions Inc. Box 21120, 11 Palmetto Pkwy., Hilton Head, S.C. 29925. (803) 681-5000. FAX: (803) 681-2945. William J. Robinson, pres; Stuart R. Silver, VP.
TV-CATV only.
Full-svc video & film prods, bcst & non-bcst.

Tri Video Teleproduction. (Lake Tahoe). Box 8822, Incline Village, Nev. 89452-8822. (702) 323-6868. Jon Paul Davidson, dir/designer; Beth Davidson, writer/prod.
TV-CATV only.
Animation, computer graphics & non-linear editing.

TTS Inc. 1790 Platte St., Denver 80202. (303) 480-0800. FAX: (303) 480-1733. F.R. Wurpel, pres/prod/consultant; Peter England, VP prod.
Worldwide TV full-svc event consulting, developing, designing, budgeting, accounting, scripting, sponsorship, talent procurement, live TV events, mgmt & prod.

T.V. Productions Inc. 1015 N. Cahuenga Blvd., Hollywood, Calif. 90038. (213) 461-3288. FAX: (213) 461-3280. TWX: 650-3162325. Charlene Eber, pres; Kenneth S. Eber, VP.
Betacam 3/4 inch.

Talco Productions. 279 E. 44th St., New York 10017. (212) 697-4015. Alan Lawrence, pres; Marty Holberton, VP.
TV & radio prog & film prod (concept through post-prod). Documentaries, ind, educ prod, pub rels consultation & gen prod svcs.

Talkline Communications Radio Network. Box 20108, Parkwest Stn., New York 10025-1510. (212) 769-1925; (800) 628-8255. FAX: (212) 799-4195. Zev J. Brenner, pres/exec prod.
Natl Jewish radio net. Contemp Jewish progmg; newsmaker guests; call-in format. Live segments from Israel. Available on barter. Satellite delivered.

Talkline Communications Television Network. Box 20108, Parkwest Stn., New York 10025-1510. (212) 769-1925; (800) 628-8255. Zev J. Brenner, pres/exec prod.
TV & CATV only.
Natl Jewish TV net. Carried in over 2500 markets. Interview format with newsmaker guests from politics, entertainment & Israel. Available on barter.

Tamouz Media. 123 W. 93rd St., Suite 5B, New York 10025. (212) 864-7603. FAX: (212) 666-2686. Ilan Ziv, prod.
TV prog prod.

The Tape House Editorial Co. 216 E. 45th St., New York 10017. (212) 557-4949. FAX: (212) 983-4083. Mark Polyocan, principal; John Dowdell III, VP; Michelle Brunwasser, VP; Tase O'Connor, VP.
Video postprod. Film to tape, film & video editing. Paintbox/Harry. Progmg & comls.

Tape Networks Inc. 1305 Glenwood, Delano, Calif. 93215-2040. (805) 725-2599. FAX: (805) 725-2609. Richard Palmquist, pres.
Consulting, equipment package (audio only) & mus for 24-hour daily sacred mus progmg.

Target Sports Video. 400 E. Lancaster Ave., Wayne, Pa. 19087. (215) 688-9233. FAX: (215) 688-2879. W.W. Orr, pres; Don Kimberling, creative dir; Marie Teeters, prod coord.
TV & radio coml promotional film & video prod; prod svcs.

Taurus Communications Inc. Taurus Teleport, 15 Forest Ave., Ashland, Mass. 01721. (508) 877-2210. FAX: (508) 877-1760. Dudley C. Freeman, pres; Al Potter, exec prod; Mark Lewis, dir engr.
TV-CATV only.
Transportable uplink svc Ku- & C-band, transponder brokerage, portable prod enquipment; full-svc satellite & prod svcs.

Technisonic Studios. 500 S. Ewing Ave., Suite G, St. Louis 63103. (314) 533-1777. FAX: (314) 533-6527. Michael Rosenthal, own/operator; Roel Van de Wijngaard, dir photography.
16 & 35 mm film prod; full sound studios; video prod; film & video editing.

Teeman Sleppin Enterprises Inc. 147 W. 26th St., New York 10001. (212) 243-7836. FAX: (212) 206-7457. Bob Teeman, prod/writer; Stu Sleppin, dir/writer.
Create, produce & distribute TV shows, features, shorts & corporate-sponsored prods.

Teen Talk Communications. 451 Buckminster Dr., T6, Norwood, Mass. 02062. (617) 255-0123. FAX: (617) 255-0822. Jason R. Rich, exec prod.
Radio Arcade, syndicated one-minute radio spots about the latest home video games, including news & game reviews combined with playing tips.

Tel-Air Interests Inc. 1755 N.E. 149th St., Miami, Fla. 33181. (305) 944-3268. FAX: (305) 944-1143. Grant H. Gravitt, pres; Grant H. Gravitt Jr, VP; M.L. Gravitt, sec/treas.
TV-CATV only.
Syndicated TV specs (sports & mus), contract prod, theatrical short subjects & documentary TV & films.

TeleCom Productions Inc. 2300 Peachford Rd., Suite 3000, Atlanta 30338. (404) 455-4666. FAX: (404) 455-3938. Budd O. Libby, pres; Roger B. Clark, chmn, Derek P. Borg, VP.
Prod & syndicator of *Let's Go to the Races* & *Post Time* retail prize promotions.

Telegenic Programs Inc. 20 Holly St., Suite 300, Toronto Ont., Canada M4S 3B1. (416) 484-8000. FAX: (416) 484-8001. H. Lawrence Fein, pres; Michael J. Taylor, VP; L. LePage-Chown, prog coord; R. Fein, booking/prom; A. Smit, treas.
TV-CATV only.

TelePost Inc. 24479 W. 10 Mile Rd., Southfield, Mich. 48034. (313) 355-3090. FAX: (313) 355-3493. Larry M. Phipps, pres/own; Janet S. Buchanan, VP mktg & pub rels.
TV-CATV only.
Abekas A-82/D-2 editing suite for no generation loss, 1-inch suite, DFX paintbox/compositing suite, IMC motion stand/slides, art, product ultimate, stage, 3/4 inch & SP, Betacam & SP, announce booth.

Teleprograms Marketing Inc. 8500 Melrose Ave., Suite 213, Los Angeles 90069. (310) 854-4475. FAX: (310) 854-5979. Jim Hampton, CEO; Robert Nieto, pres; Karen Draper, VP business dev.
Radio mktg firm specializing in orchestrated pros which include direct mail, custom radio shows, radio/TV spots, sweepstakes & contests in an integrated format.

Telepros. Box 1116, Belmont, Calif. 94002. (415) 345-0505. Niels Melo, pres.
TV-CATV only.
Prods of entertainment & sports TV progs, video conferences & industrial videos.

TeleScene. 3487 W. 2100 S., Salt Lake City 84119. (800) 562-9884. FAX: (801) 973-3297. Rick Larsen, gen mgr; Bill Lines, dir sls & mktg.
Complete digital editing. Audio, D-1, D-2I multiple postprod digital audio suites; digital film transfer; 2-D/3-D animated graphics.

Teletainment Inc. (Crystal Productions Division.) 1024 Blouin Dr., Dolton, Ill. 60419. (708) 841-2622. FAX: (708) 841-2721. Timothy Dwyer, pres/opns mgr; Jeffrey J. Babick, exec prod/sr dir; Robert J. Liptack, chief engr.
TV-CATV only.
Full-svc TV prod including scriptwriters, ENG & EFP crews, multi-camera remote prods.

Televents Ltd. 2450 Virginia Ave. N.W., Washington 20037. (202) 296-0541. James Avis, mgr.
TV prog prod & distribution.

TeleVideo Productions. 611 S. Farwell St., Eau Claire, Wis. 54701. (715) 833-9269. FAX: (715) 833-9273. Mark Atkinson, gen mgr; Jim Paulson, prod coord; Don Byrne, prod mgr.
TV coml & corp video prod.

Television & Radio Features Inc. 1910 1st St., Suite 300, Highland Park, Ill. 60035. (708) 432-6565. (708) 432-1223. FAX: (708) 432-1223. Morton A. Small, pres.
Promotions, prize svcs.

Producers, Distributors, Production and Other Services

Teleworld Inc. 245 W. 55th St., New York 10019. (212) 489-9310. FAX: (212) 262-9395. Robert Seidelman, pres.
TV prog distribution.

Telfax Inc. 3305 Pleasant Valley Ln., Arlington, Tex. 76015. (817) 468-0070. FAX: (817) 468-0111. Tony Symanovich, pres.
Remote TV prod svcs.

Telstar Inc. Box 388, Westport, Conn. 06881. (203) 226-3379. FAX: (203) 222-0779. Bess Gilmore, pres; John C. Gilmore, exec VP; Douglas Gilmore, VP/exec prod; Keith Gilmore, VP/chief engr; Tom Boone, sr exec VP sls.
TV prod, sls & distribution.

Thames Television PLC. Broom Rd., Teddington Lock, Teddington, Middlesex, U.K. TW11 9N10. 01-387-9494. R.J. Dunn, mgng dir; Mike Phillips, dir overseas sls.
British coml TV company. Overseas sls through Thames Television International.

Danny Thomas Productions. 1888 Century Park E., Suite 400, Los Angeles 90067. (310) 277-4866. FAX: (310) 286-1963.
TV progs, features, coml prod.

Thompson Creative. 4631 Insurance Ln., Dallas Tex. 75205. (800) 723-4643. FAX: (214) 521-8578. Larry Thompson, CEO; Ben Freeman, VP/gen sls mgr.
Contemp radio ID jingles for all formats.

Time Capsule Inc. 124 Cottonwood Ln., Centerville, Mass. 02632. (508) 775-5100-demo; (800) 822-7785-sales; (508) 775-5100-country demo. FAX: (508) 778-5590. Richard T. Teimer, pres/dir sls; Nancy Q. Proctor, VP affil rels; Bill Stephens, VP special project.
Guess the month & year quizzes for contemp, oldies & country formats (90-seconds daily).

Time Rite Inc. 2500 Ridgmar Plaza, Fort Worth, Tex. 76116. (817) 377-8463. FAX: (817) 737-7853. Jack B. Johnson, pres; Steve J. Roberson, exec VP; Susan Venturini, natl sls rep.
TV prog prod & distribution.

Times Square Studios Inc. 1481 Broadway, New York 10036. (212) 704-9700. FAX: (212) 704-9812. Marcelino Miyares, pres; Richard Neuman, dir mktg & sls.
Midtown Manhattan TV prod, postprod, graphic arts & bcst facility. Teleport & ATT Loops. ENG & full remote prods.

Titansports Inc. Titan Tower, 1241 E. Main St., Stamford, Conn. 06902. (203) 352-8600. FAX: (203) 359-5111. Vincent K. McMahon, pres/CEO; Linda E. McMahon, exec VP; Basil Devito, sr VP mktg & promotion.
World Wrestling Federation progs: WWF Super Stars, Wrestling Challenge & Wrestling Spotlight - all 60 minute progs. Straight barter, 7/5 split.

Toes Productions Inc. 1701 N. Pelham Rd. N.W., Atlanta 30324. (404) 875-1563. FAX: (404) 875-9984. Brad Abelle, pres; Joe Camoosa, dir opns.
Offers voice-overs for net, cable net, syndication, trailers, comls. Represnted by Don Buchwald, N.Y.C., (212) 867-1070.

Tomwil Inc. 4621 Cahuenga Blvd., Toluca Lake, Calif. 91602. (818) 760-4523. FAX: (818) 769-0887. James R. Rokos, pres; Wilda A. Rokos, VP.
Distributors of features, light entertainment, sports, series & documentaries to all media in the world mkt.

Toucan Productions. 315 W. End Ave., Suite 2C, New York 10023. (212) 580-4882. FAX: (212) 580-8434. Fred Margulies, exec prod.
Corporate video prods from conception to completion.

Traffax Traffic Network. 300 Bridge St., New Cumberland, Pa. 17070-2144. (717) 774-8150. FAX: (717) 774-8160. Brian William Freeman, CEO (founder); Jeffrey G. Schatzer, pres/dir opns.
TV & radio net; radio prod & distribution.

The Transfer Zone. 13251 Northend, Oak Park, Mich. 48237-3212. (313) 548-7580. FAX: (313) 548-0924. Roxane B.Nusholtz, dir mktg; Robert Nusholtz, dir tech.
TV-CATV only.
Intercontinental video standard conversions, duplication, film/slide transfers: 1/2 & 3/4, A-B roll editing, video slide/film.

TransStar Television Sales. 1119 San Antonio, El Paso, Tex. 79901. (915) 533-4700. Garrett W. Haston, pres.
TV & radio prog & coml prod & distribution.

Tri Video Teleproduction. Box 8822, Incline Village, Nev. 89452-8822. (702) 323-6868. Jon Paul Davidson, dir/designer; Beth Davidson, writer/prod. Lake Tahoe office.
TV-CATV only.
Animation, computer graphics & non-linear editing.

Tribune Entertainment Co. 435 N. Michigan Ave., Suite 1800, Chicago 60611. (312) 222-4441. FAX: (312) 222-9065. Donald Hacker, pres; David Sifford, exec VP mktg & sls; Marcy Abelow, VP adv sls; Carol Forace, VP rsch & sls dev; James Lutton, VP progmg; George Paris, VP progmg; Greg Miller, VP prog dev; Allan Grafman, VP project dir; Bill Lyall, VP finance & admin; Jim Corboy, VP creative svcs; Mary Beth Hughes, dir creative svcs; Maryann Schulze, dir stn rels; Michael Adinamis, VP bcst opns; Megan Bueschel dir pub rels; Rick North, supvr adv sls.
New York 10019: 712 5th Ave., 14th Fl. (212) 554-1650.
Chicago 60611: 435 N. Michigan Ave. (312) 222-4441.
Nashville 37210: 117 Lyle Ln. (615) 242-7017.
Acquires, develops, produces & distrbutes progmg for TV. Produces more than 20 shows including *Geraldo*, *The Joan Rivers Show* & *Tribune Premiere Network*.

Tribune Radio Networks. 435 N. Michigan Ave., Chicago 60611. (312) 222-3342. FAX: (312) 222-4876. Kenton Morris, gen mgr; Jack Rosenberg, mgr sports; Barb Atsaves, admin mgr.
Tape & satellite-delivered farm, sports & specialty progs including: Chicago Cubs Network, Chicago Bears Network, The Dave Wannstedt Show, Pro Football Weekly, Agri-Voice, National Farm Report, Farming America, John Block Reports & The Thoroughbred Connection.

Trick Bag. Box 2147, Sioux City, Iowa 51104-0147. (712) 276-2295.

Troika Productions Inc. 355 W. 52nd St., New York 10019. (212) 974-0606. FAX: (212) 974-0976. Charles N. Gelber, pres; Alan J. Weiss, exec VP.
TV prog, coml prod & distribution; prod svcs.

Morrie Trumble & Associates. 139 Fulton St., Suite 917, New York 10038. (212) 233-1736. FAX: (212) 571-1422. Morrie Trumble, pres; Danny Toy, prod.
News, lifestyle & localized leisure events progmg for radio & TV. Mus specials & syndicated progs for radio.

Turner Entertainment Co. 1888 Century Park E., 12th Fl., Los Angeles 90006. (310) 788-6800. Roger L. Mayer, pres & COO; James Gentilcone, VP film & tape svcs.
TV prog prod & distribution.

Turner International Sales Ltd. 19-22 Rathbone Pl., London, U.K. W1P 1DF1. 4471-637-6700. FAX: 4471-637-6768; 4471-637-6713. Howard Karshan, pres.
TV prog distribution.

Turner Program Services. One CNN Center, Atlanta 30348; 1875 Century Park E., Suite 320, Los Angeles CA 90067. (404) 827-2085; (310) 551-6300. FAX: (404) 827-2373; (310) 551-6315. Bill Grumbles, chmn of bd; W. Russell Barry, pres; John Walden, sr VP mktg & sls; Tony Bauer, VP/gen sls mgr eastern rgn; Lynn Lazaroff, VP adv & promotion.
TV-CATV only.
TV prog prod & distribution.

Tutman Productions. 551 Commerce Dr., Suite B, Upper Marlboro, Md. 20772. (301) 249-8200. FAX: (301) 249-3613. Fred Tutman, pres; Mary Levock, business mgr.
TV-CATV only.
Video & film prod svcs operating in the Washington & Baltimore area. Industrial, corporate, bcst.

Twentieth Television. 10201 W. Pico Blvd., Los Angeles 90035. (310) 203-2211. FAX: (310) 203-2141. Lucy Salhany, chmn; Edward Nassour, VP postprod; Gary Newman, sr VP business affrs; Walter Swanson, VP legal affrs; Michael Lambert, pres domestic syndication; Leonard Grossi, exec VP admin & opns; Fred Bierman, sr VP mktg; William Saunders, pres international TV; James Griffiths, sr VP pay TV & home video.
Produces & distributes progmg for net TV & domestic & international TV markets.

U

U Network. 71 George St., Providence, R.I. 02912-1824. (401) 863-1834. FAX: (401) 863-2221. Glenn Gutmacher, pres.
Syndicates student-produced & selected independently-produced radio & TV progs oriented to a natl college-age audience through college & coml stn affils.

Progs include comedy, drama, mus/interview, environmental, pub affs, documentary, etc. Satellite: Galaxy VI.

UPA Productions of America. 14101 Valley Heart Dr., Suite 200, Sherman Oaks, Calif. 91423. (818) 990-3800. FAX: (818) 990-4854. Henry G. Saperstein, pres; Dorothy Schechter, VP financial; Patricia Saperstein, mktg dir; S. Richard Krown, VP prod.
TV-CATV only.
TV prog & coml, promotional film prod & distribution.

U.S. Air Force Recruiting Service. Randolph AFB, Tex. 78150-5421. (210) 652-3937. FAX: (210) 652-3935. TSgt. Clayton Edens (RSAACB), NCOIC bcdst opns; SrA Lori Singer, staff announcer.
Prod radio PSA's for Air Force Recruiting. Prod *Country Music Time* prog for country radio.

U.S. Army Reserve. Army Reserve Support Center, Public Affairs Office, 1815 N. Fort Myer Dr., Rm. 203, Arlington, Va. 22209. (703) 696-3963. FAX: (703) 696-5300. Mark Zimmer, info off.
PSAs, UNRs, short subjects & radio progmg.

Ukrainian Melody Hour. Box 2257, Washington 20013. (202) 529-7606. Roman V. Marynowych, prod/dir; Odile E. Marynowych, exec sec.
Ukrainian radio, TV & cable prog prods.

Ukrainian Variety Hour. 2224 W. Chicago Ave., Chicago 60622. (312) 276-3747. Maria Chychula, prog dir.
Radio & TV prog, coml prod & distribution.

Unheard Of, The Radio Broadcasts. 12007 Red Oak Court N., Burnsville, Minn. 55337. (612) 894-8792. Leo Clark, mktg dir.
Provides wkly syndicated mus prog spotlighting unheard of artists; all songs tested for adult contemp compatibility.

Unistar Radio Network. 1675 Broadway, 17th Fl., New York 10019. (212) 247-1600. FAX: (212) 247-0393. Bill Hogan, pres.
Net radio news; 24-hour satellite radio formats; radio progmg prod & distribution.

United Church Television. 315 Queen St. E., Toronto Ont., Canada M5A 1S7. (416) 366-9221. FAX: (416) 368-9774. Rodney M. Booth, exec prod.
TV prog prod & distribution; prod svcs.

United Film Enterprises Inc. 120 W. Park Ave., Suite 3F, Long Beach, N.Y. 11561. (516) 431-2687. FAX: (516) 431-2805. Munio Podhorzer, pres; Nathan Podhorzer, VP.
TV-CATV only.
Representing motion picture prods & distributors throughout the world in the sale & purchase of feature films, home video & TV progs.

United Methodist Communications. 475 Riverside Dr., Suite 1901, New York 10115. (212) 663-8900. Wil Bane, exec prod.
TV & radio prod & distribution.

United Sound Systems Inc. 5840 2nd. Blvd., Detroit 48202. (313) 832-3313. FAX: (313) 832-5666. Donald Davis, pres; Willie Davis, VP; Mattie Winters, studio mgr.
Audio & duplicating recording; postprod audio facilties & svcs; mus prod.

University of Colorado Television. Campus Box 379, Boulder, Colo. 80309. (303) 492-1857. FAX: (303) 492-7017. Bud Leonard, sr prod/dir.
TV & radio prog prod & distribution; prod svcs.

University of Detroit Mercy. Box 19900, Communication Studies Dept., 4001 W. McNichols, Detroit 48219-0900. (313) 993-1173. FAX: (313) 993-1120. Jerry Curtsinger, audio technician.
Radio prog syndication.

University of Kentucky Public Relations & Radio-TV News Bureau. Mathews Bldg., Rm. 4, Lexington, Ky. 40506. (606) 257-1754. FAX: (606) 257-4017. Bernie Vonderheide, dir; Carl Nathe, dir radio & TV news bureau.
TV & radio prog & coml, promotional film prod & distribution.

Univision. 605 3rd Ave., New York 10158. (212) 455-5200. FAX: (212) 867-6710. Jaime Davila, pres/CEO; Ray Rodriguez, pres/COO; Hector Beltran, sr VP/ dir creative svcs; Raul Torano, pres net sls; Mario Rodgriguez, VP progmg.
TV-CATV only.
TV prog prod & distribution.

Producers, Distributors, Production and Other Services

V

VA-Tech University Television. (CNS-Communications Network Services.) 1700 Pratt Dr., Blacksburg, Va. 24061-0506. (703) 231-6460. FAX: (703) 231-3928. Judy Lilly, dir.
TV & radio prod & distribution.

V.I.E.W. Video Inc. 34 E. 23rd St., New York 10010. (212) 674-5550. FAX: (212) 979-0266; Telex: 291354 IVE UR. Bob Karcy, pres; Jack Arel, VP European opns; Stephen R. Kates, dir mktg; Karen Rabinowicz, VP sls & mktg; Christopher Johns, dir opns; James Reilly, sls mgr; Dorian Karchman, new project dev.
TV-CATV only.
International home video prod & distribution of special interest progs in the areas of art, jazz, pop mus, opera, dance, children's interactive sports & modern lifestyle progs.

VPI-Videfilm Producers International Ltd. 250 W. 57th St., Suite 1701, New York 10107. (212) 581-0400. FAX: (212) 581-2752. Kirk D'Amico, pres; Adam Rogers, dir distribution; Marc J. Zand, VP legal & business affrs, Ingrid Enzelsberger, mgr acquisitions.
TV-CATV only.
An ind TV co-prod & distribution company specializing in mus series, features, documentaries & drama for the international market.

VTC. (A Division of STARCOM TV Services.) 10523-45 Burbank Blvd., North Hollywood, Calif. 91601. (818) 753-3000. FAX: (818) 985-0614. Gary J. Worth, pres/CEO; David Lister, VP/gen mgr; Jon Schwenzer, VP.
TV-CATV only.
New York 10017: One Dag Hammarskjold Plaza, 7th Fl. (212) 207-9872. FAX: (212) 702-4810.
Satellite & videotape TV prog delivery, standards conversion, videocassette duplication & film-to-tape transfer.

Valentino Music and Sound Effect Libraries. 500 Executive Blvd., Elmsford, N.Y. 10523. (914) 347-7878; (800) 223-6278. FAX: (914) 347-4764. Thomas J. Valentino, pres; Francis T. Valentino, VP.
Compact disc mus & sound effects libraries.

Vanguard Audio Features Inc. 4348 Cliff Rd., Birmingham, Ala. 35222. (205) 592-3000. FAX: (205) 592-6300. Greg Wonble, pres; Aaron Beam Jr., VP.
Produces & syndicates progmg for radio, audio cable & cassette distribution.

Steve Vaus Productions. Box 288017, San Diego 92128. (619) 674-4444. FAX: (619) 674-1114. Steve Vaus, own.
Stn ID packages, coml jingles, promotional theme songs; custom cassettes & CDs.

Ventures in Media Inc. 32107 W. Lindero Cayon Rd., Suite 133, Westlake Village, Calif. 91361. (818) 991-1648. FAX: (818) 991-1649. Morrie Gelman, pres; Adam Gelman, VP/sec; Robert A. Finlayson, VP/CFO & pub rels.
TV & cable prog dev, mkt rsch info packaging & consulting.

David Verner Inc. Six Lake View St., Lake Placid, N.Y. 12946. (518) 523-1431. FAX: (518) 523-9431. David Verner, pres.
TV-CATV only.
Complete prod & postprod svcs & support. Mobile & in-house prod facilities. TV sports progmg & show packaging & multimedia svcs.

Viacom International Inc. 1515 Broadway, New York 10036. (212) 258-6000. FAX: (212) 258-6100. Sumner M. Redstone, chmn; Frank J. Biondi, pres/CEO; Raymond A. Boyce, sr VP corporate rels; Neil S. Braun, chmn/CEO Viacom Entertainment; Winston H. (Tony) Cox, chmn/CEO Showtime & The Movie Channel Inc.; Mark W. Weinstein, VP/gen counsel; George S. Smith Jr., VP/CFO; Thomas E. Dooley, VP finances/treas. Viacom Enterprises: Joseph Zaleski, pres domestic syndication; Dennis Gillespie, sr VP mktg; John D. Kelly, VP/gen sls mgr; Raul Levkovich, VP internatl; Michael Gerber, sr VP; Toby Martin, VP prog dev & prod; Lisa Merians, dir creative svcs; Paul Kalvin, sr VP sls; Eric Veale, VP opns; Joseph DiSalvo, sls mgr northeast; Sean Denny, sls mgr mid-atlantic div; William Theis, dir tech & international svcs; Howard Berk, dir mdse & licensing; Beth McTigue, assoc dir international sls admin; Andrew Spitzer, VP first-run sls; Gerald Pinks, dir domestic sls svc; Elissa Lebeck, VP rsch & mktg svcs. Viacom Productions: Thomas D. Tannenbaum, pres; Roger P. Kirman, VP business affrs; George Faber, dir communications.
Universal City, Calif. 91608-1097: 10 Universal City Plaza. (818) 505-7500. Brooks Carroll, VP western div; Al Miller, sls exec western div.
Atlanta 30346: 400 Perimeter Center Terr. (404) 395-7795. Frank Flanagan, VP southern div.
Irving, Tex. 75039: 433 E. Las Colinas Blvd. (214) 556-2255. Dave Campbell, VP southwest div.
Chicago 60606: 10 South Riverside Plaza. (312) 648-5858. Dennis Emerson, VP central div.
London W1R 9FB: Viacom International Ltd., 40 Conduit St. (011-411) 434-4483. Peter Press, VP/mgng dir.
North Sydney NSW 2000, Australia: Viacom International, Martin's Tower, 31 Market St. (612) 261-5391. Tony Manton VP/mgng dir.
Sao Paolo, 01420 Brazil: Viacom Video-Audio C Communicacoes Ltda., Alameda Jau 1742-11 Andar, Caixa Postal 51521. (55-11) 853-4633. Ivan Aragon, mgng dir.
Tokyo 104: Viacom Japan Inc. 4F, Mitsuwa Bldg., 7-2 Ginza 6-Chome, Chuo-Ku. (813) 3573-0551. Hiro Kuno, VP/mgng dir.
Toronto, Ont., Canada M4Y 1S2: Viacom Enterprises Canada Ltd., 45 Charles St. E. (416) 925-3161. Alistair Banks, VP/gen mgr.
TV prog prod & distribution.

Victory Television. 1001 Franklin Ave., Garden City, N.Y. 11031. (516) 739-0770. James T. Victory, pres.
TV-CATV only.
TV prog distribution.

Video Dub Inc. 423 W. 55th St., New York 10019. (212) 757-3300. FAX: (212) 489-6186. Leonard Schwartz, VP/gen mgr; Steven A. Gabrielli, dir opns.
TV-CATV only.
Duplication in all formats, film to tape transfers, syndication/satellite distribution & editing.

Video 8 Productions/KPTS-TV. Box 288, Wichita, Kan. 67201. (316) 838-3090. FAX: (316) 838-8586. Carl E. Chance, VP/dir contract svcs.
TV-CATV only.
Industrial video prod for corporate training & mktg communications.

Video Enterprises Inc. 11340 Olympic Blvd., Suite 365, Los Angeles 90064. (301) 312-1500. FAX: (301) 312-1568. Heidi Lane-Ambrose, pres; Carol Munson, office mgr.
Placement of natl ten second promotional spots on game shows, talk, variety & sports prog.

Video I-D Inc. 105 Muller Rd., Washington, Ill. 61571. (309) 444-4323. Sam B. Wagner, pres; Gwen Wagner, mktg mgr; Rick Holman, chief edit, Bob Pyle, sls dir.
TV-CATV only.
Full teleprod svcs, location prod, computer editing, remote truck, live multi-camera sports bcst & teleconferencing, training, sls promotion.

Video Program Network. 3075 Cohasset Rd., Chico, Calif. 95926. (916) 894-1000. FAX: (916) 894-8888. Rolfe Auerbach, pres; Roy Dankman, gen mgr; Laura Schwartz, sls mgr; Bob Sands, prog dir.
TV-CATV only.
TV net comprised of 28 ind TV stns located throughout U.S. major markets.

Video Techniques Inc. Box 9649, Bradenton, Fla. 34206. (813) 746-4949. FAX: (813) 746-1937. Bob Lorentzen, pres/exec prod.
TV-CATV only.
Beta SP & MII field & postprod facilities.

Video West. Broadcast House, 5 Triad Ctr., Salt Lake City 84110-1160. (801) 575-7400. FAX: (801) 575-7449. Al Henderson, VP/gen mgr; Jim Yorgason, VP/mgr opns.
Film & video prod & postprod, video duplication, TV progmg.

Video-Cinema Films Inc. 510 E. 86th St., New York 10028. (212) 734-1632. Larry Stern, pres/sls mgr.
TV-CATV only.
Distributor of motion pictures to all forms of TV.

Video/Films International Inc. (VFI). Box 40400, Pasadena, Calif. 91114. (818) 797-5462. FAX: (818) 797-7524. C. Ray Carlson, pres.
TV-CATV only.
Prod, distributor, ADR language dubbing.

Videographics Corp. 441 E. Erie St., Suite 1804, Chicago 60611. (312) 642-6652. FAX: (312) 642-6608. Brian Shaw, pres.
TV-CATV only.
Sells PC- & Mactinosh-based graphics systems for video systems for video prod.

Video-It Post. 5000 Overland Ave., Suite 6, Culver City, Calif. 90230. (301) 280-0505. FAX: (301) 280-0193. John Kohan-Matlick, pres; Felisa Kohan-Matlick, VP; Keith Manasco, gen mgr.
TV-CATV only.
On-line interformat editing specializing in D-2 digital mastering with the Ampex 100 ADO. Bulk duplication available from D-2. Digital Paint, non-linear off-line.

Videomasters. See Hi Ho Teleproductions.

Videosmith Inc. 520 N. Delaware Ave., Philadelphia 19123. (215) 238-5050. FAX: (215) 238-5055. Steven T. Smith, pres.
TV progmg, comls, 35mm film prod; video prod & post-prod, 3 animation, equipment rental.

Vide-U Productions. 612 N. Sepuleuida Blvd., Los Angeles 90035. (310) 657-4385. FAX: (310) 657-4385. Bradley Friedman, pres; Sabel Tyree, COO, David Temianka, dir.
Feature film & TV prod, mus videos, children's progmg, comls, robotics, scipting, fairlight CUI.

Vidistrib Inc. 4209 Troost Ave., Studio City, Calif. 91604. (818) 762-2559. John P. Ballinger, pres; Rita M. Ballinger, VP/treas; Rita Cross, VP/ traf mgr.
TV-CATV only.
TV show sls, syndication, barter sls, consultation svcs & distribution.

Norm Virag Productions. 3415 N. East St., Lansing, Mich. 48906. (517) 374-8193. FAX: (517) 374-9073. Norm Virag, own; Cheryl Virag, treas.
TV & radio progs & comls, promotional film prod & distribution; prod svcs.

Virginia Tech, CNS (Communications Network Services). 1700 Pratt Dr., Blacksburg, Va. 24061-0506. (703) 231-6460. FAX: (703) 231-3928. Judy L. Lilly, dir communications net svcs; Thomas Head, dir media svcs.
TV-CATV-Radio.
Provides TV & radio prod & distribution.

Vision Broadcasting Network. Box 478, Grand Central Station, New York 10163. (212) 765-3827. Floyd E. Vasquez, pres; Roy Hendrickson, dir audio prod.
Prod & distributor of radio-based progmg. Products include UBN Presents™ series of radio progs, & Breakthrough Tour™.

Visual Projects Ltd. 67 Yale St., Roslyn Heights, N.Y. 11577. (516) 621-5285. FAX: (516) 484-1249. Newton E. Meltzer, exec prod; Barbara L. Brilliant, creative dir.
TV prog & documentary promotional film prod.

Vitt Media International Inc. 1114 Ave. of the Americas, New York 10036. (212) 921-0500. FAX: (212) 575-4709. Roy Muro, chmn/CEO; Robert Calandruccio, pres/CEO; Leonard Lieboff, sr exec VP; Sheldon Kawer, William Morton, Steve Berger, exec VPs; Arnold Chase, Group VP.
TV & radio prog distribution.

Vuolo Video Air-Chex. Box 219, Ypsilanti, Mich. 48197. (313) 434-2712; (313) 355-0022. Arthur R. Vuolo, prod/dir.
Video air checks of American radio stns; an *Inside Look*.

W

WFMT Fine Arts Network. 303 E. Wacker Dr., Chicago 60601. (312) 565-5000. Daniel J. Schmidt, sr VP.
Produces wkly series including Chicago Symphony Orchestra & lyric opera for coml & pub stns.

WGN Television. 2501 W. Bradley Pl., Chicago 60618. (312) 528-2311. FAX: (312) 528-6857. Peter Walker, VP/gen mgr; James Zerwekh, progmg dir; Pam Pearson, creative svcs dir; John Vitanoveo, stn mgr; Merri Dee, community rels dir; John Poelking, controller; Jennifer Schulze, news dir; David Tynan, sls dir.
TV-CATV only.
TV progs & comls; promotional film prod & distribution; prod svcs.

WMAQ-TV. NBC Tower 454 N. Columbus Dr., Chicago 60611-5555. (312) 836-5555. Patrick T. Wallace, pres/gen mgr; Lisa Churchville, dir sls; Rich Brase, dir bcdst & promotion; Diana Borri, dir regulatory affrs; Tom Powers, dir bcdst opns & engrg.
TV-CATV only.
TV prog prod; prod svcs.

WNGN-FM Hoosick Falls N.Y. Box 36, Kings Rd., Bushkirk, 12028. (518) 686-0975. FAX: (518) 686-0975. Brian A. Larson, pres/gen mgr; Peter Morton, chief engr.
A 24-hour Christian radio stn.

WNN Winners News Network. 6699 N. Federal Hwy., Boca Raton, Fla. 33487. (407) 997-0074. FAX: (407) 997-0476. Howard Goldsmith, pres.
Worldwide 24-hour format of motivational speakers & self help info.

Producers, Distributors, Production and Other Services

W04AT-Hoosick Falls N.Y.(VHF-TV-4). Box 36, Kings Rd., Buskirk, N.Y. 12028. (518) 686-0975. FAX: (518) 686-0975. Brian A. Larson, pres/gen mgr; Peter Morton, chief engr.
24-hour community TV on VHF-TV-4 serving Hoosick Falls, Cambridge, Eagle Ridge & Buskirk, N.Y. & Bennington, Vt.

The WPA Film Library. 5525 W. 159th. St., Oak Forest, Ill. 60658. (708) 535-1540. FAX: (708) 535-1541. Matthew White, pres; Lou Zucaro, dir opns; Michael F. Mertz, archivist; Jeff Martin, rsch coord.
TV-CATV-Radio
From 1895-1992, WPA has a stock & archival footage with thousands of hours of 35mm originals remastered onto D2.

WQED Communication Inc. (The Metropolitan Pittsburgh Public Broadcasting Station.) 4802 5th Ave., Pittsburgh 15213. (412) 622-1300. FAX: (412) 622-1488. Don Korp, CEO; Jay Rayvid, sr VP; Dan Fales, VP.
TV & radio prog prod & distribution; prod svcs.

WQXR Syndication. 122 5th Ave., 3rd Fl., New York 10011. (212) 633-7600. FAX: (212) 633-7666. Warren G. Bodow, pres; Larry Krents, VP.
Radio prog prod.

WRS/Channel One. (A division of WRS Inc.) 1000 Napor Blvd., Pittsburgh 15205. (412) 937-7700. FAX: (412) 922-1020. F. Jack Napor, pres; Ed Janow, VP/gen mgr; Monica Cecchini, syndication sls mgr; Nick Farrell, syndication distribution mgr.
TV-CATV only.
Complete syndication & distribution svcs via satellite & tape. Integration, AMOL encoding, duplication, uplink/downlink fulfillment, audio, film to tape transfer.

WTOB Channel 2 - Public/Government Access TV. Box 90003, Blacksburg, Va. 24062-9003. (703) 961-1199. FAX: (703) 951-2180. Susan W. Huff, stn mgr.
TV-CATV only.
Locally originated progmg, live town meetings, equipment training & loan svcs in 3/4", S-VHS & VHS formats.

WYHC. 6707-C Fairview Rd., Charlotte, N.C. 28210. (704) 362-0400. FAX: (704) 362-2279. Marc H. Silverman, pres.
Travel radio. Tourist & traf info with emphasis on traf conditions, transmitted through cells along the interstate highway.

Wade Productions Inc. 15 W. 44th St., New York 10036. (212) 575-9111. FAX: (212) 764-4178. Carolyn J. Wade, pres; Ronni Goldfarb, account mgr; Patricia Monahan, account mgr.
TV-CATV only.
Meetings, video, slide prods; staging & teleconferencing for corporations & assns.

Warner Bros. Bldg. 10, 300 Television Plaza, Burbank, Calif. 91505. (818) 954-7500. Leslie Moonves, pres.
TV-CATV only.
TV prog prod & distribution.

Warner Bros. Animation. 15303 Ventura Blvd., Suite 1200, Sherman Oakes, Calif. 91403. (818) 379-9401. FAX: (818) 905-1692. Jean MacCurdy, pres; Kathleen Helpie, VP prod & admin.
TV prog prod & distribution.

Warner Bros. Distributing (Canada) Ltd. 4576 Yonge St., 2nd Fl., North York, Ont., Canada M2N 6P1. (416) 250-8384. FAX: (416) 250-8598. Michael J. Solomon, pres worldwide TV distribution; Jeff Schlesinger, sr VP (Burbank); Kevin M. Byles, gen mgr Canadian opns (Toronto); Sally Thoun, promotions; Don Dennis, booking.
TV prog distribution & promotion.

Warner Bros. Domestic Pay TV, Cable & Network Features. 75 Rockefeller Plaza, New York 10019. (212) 484-8000. FAX: (212) 397-0728. Edward Bleier, pres; Eric Frankel, sr VP mktg; Jeffrey Calman, VP sls planning & business affrs; J.T. Shadoan, VP finance affrs; Tony Cochi, dir finance affrs; Gary Hahn, dir adv publ & promotion; Timothy Ramirez, mgr pay-per-view; Stacey Nagel Galper, mgr progmg & inventory; Charlotte Mulford Marlis, mgr net & admin.
TV-CATV only.

Warner Bros. Domestic Television Distribution. 4000 Warner Blvd., Burbank, Calif. 91522. (818) 954-6000. FAX: (818) 954-5820 Dick Robertson, pres; Scott Carlin, sr VP sls; Mark Robbins, VP/gen sls mgr; Mary Voll, Damian Riordan, Andrew Weir, Eric Strong, Chris Smith, Bill Hague, Jacqueline Hartley, Jeff Hufford, Mark O'Brien, VPs; Vince Messina, VP western sls & feature fillm mktg; Dave Hedrick, acct exec.
Print Department - Burbank: Bud Rowe, foreign TV print administrator. (818) 954-3731.
TV prog syndication.

Warner Bros. International Television. 4000 Warner Blvd., Burbank, Calif. 91522. (818) 954-6000. FAX: (818) 954-6539. Michael Jay Solomon, pres; Jeffrey Schlesinger, sr VP; Michael Lecourt, VP France; Wayne Broun, VP Australia & Far East; Jorge Sanchez, VP Latin America; Rosario Ponzio, mng dir Italy; Greg Robertson, sls exec Australia & Far East; Mauro Sardi, VP special projects & pay TV; David Peebler, sls dir Scandanavia, Benelux, Israel; Donna Brett, sls dir Eastern Europe, Africa, Greece, Middle East; Richard Milnes, mng dir U.K.; Lisa Gregonan, dir international rsch & mktg prog distributor.

Warner Bros. Television Production. 4000 Warner Blvd., Burbank, Calif. 91522. (818) 954-6000. FAX: (818) 954-4539. Leslie Moonves, pres; Tony Jonas, exec VP creative affrs; Art Stoinitz, exec VP business & financial affrs; Billy Campbell, sr VP drama dev; David Janollari, sr VP comedy dev; Gregg Maday, sr VP movies & miniseries; Barbara Miller, sr VP talent & casting; Steve Pearlman, sr VP current progs; Robert Rosenbaum, sr VP net prod; David Sacks, sr VP current progmg; Paul Stager, sr VP studio gen counsel; Julie Waxman, sr VP business affrs.
TV-CATV only.
TV prog prod.

Washington International Teleport Inc. (WIT). 5600 General Washington Dr., Suite B-210, Alexandria, Va. 22312. (703) 914-0014. FAX: (703) 658-4919. Stephen Tom, pres/CEO; Henry Clark, VP sls & mktg; Peter Brown, VP opns & engineering; Andrew Cassells, traffic mgr.
Full domestic arc, satellite uplinking/downlinking & turnaround, fiber & microwave interconnects; direct international satellite access on Intelsat 332.5, 335.5, K & PAS-1.

Wawatay Native Communication Society. Box 1180, 165th Ave., Sioux Lookout, Ont., Canada P8T 1B7. (807) 737-2951. FAX: (807) 737-3224. Lawrence Martin, exec dir; Arthur Beardy, pres.
Radio & TV (Cree, Djibway & English) net, portable Ku-band uplink, bi-lingual nwspr, aboriginal language translations, multi-track audio recording.

M.D. Wax Courier Films. 1560 Broadway, New York 10036. (212) 302-5360. FAX: (212) 302-5364. Mort Wax, pres.
Supplier of high-quality foreign films & progmg to ethnic markets.

Wax Works Radio Network Inc. 11130 Holmes Rd., Kansas City, Kan. 64131. (800) 279-2702. FAX: (816) 942-1288. Bill Miller, VP/gen mgr.
Offers the Wax Works Radio Show; big band & var wkly series with host, Bill Miller Barter.

We Like Kids! 224 4th St., Juneau, Alaska 99801. (907) 586-1670. FAX: (907) 586-3612. Jeff Brown, prod.
A natl radio prog highlighting contemp mus & stories for children.

Weiss Global Enterprises. Box 20360, Oxnard, Calif. 93034-0360. (805) 486-4495. FAX: (805) 487-3330. Adrian Weiss, pres; Ethel L. Weiss, sec; Alex Gordon, info svcs.
TV-CATV only.
Distributor of syndicated TV series, features, documentaries, cartoons & westerns.

Welwood International Film Production/Syndication. 160 Washington S.E., Suite 138, Albuquerque 87108. (505) 242-5644. FAX: (505) 242-5661. Bill Swortwood, pres; Barbara Ferrel, VP.
TV coml prod for radio stns; custom & syndicated spots from concept to completion.

West Hills Centre. 1020 Beers School Rd., Coraopolis, Pa. 15108-2502. (412) 264-4800. FAX: (412) 264-2436. John H. Swartz Jr., exec admin.
Nashville 37207: 827 Meridian St. (615) 226-1122. Aubrey Mayhew, sr prod.
Produces & syndicates a var of quality, low-cost radio shows for all formats.

Westwood One Co. 9540 Washington Blvd., Culver City, Calif. 90232. (310) 840-4000. FAX: (310) 840-4052. Norman J. Pattiz, chmn/CEO; Gregory P. Batusic, pres/Net Radio Division.
Radio progmg, prod & distribution on NBC Radio Networks, Talknet, Source, Mutual Broadcasting System & Westwood One Radio Networks.

What's Happening. Box 2147, Sioux City, Iowa 51104-0147. (712) 276-2295. Morrie Miller, mus editor.
Entertainment publication, reviews of mus related news, recordings & events.

Daniel Wilson Productions Inc. 300 W. 55th St., New York 10019. (212) 765-7148. FAX: (212) 765-7916. Daniel Wilson, pres.
TV & theatrical film prod & distribution.

Wilson & Peck Inc. 2425 Maryland Ave., Baltimore 21218. (410) 889-9300. FAX: (410) 889-9396. William A. Peck, pres; William J. Wilson Jr., VP.
Radio coml prod & distribution.

Windstar Studios Inc. 525 Communications Cir., Colorado Springs 80905. (719) 635-0422. FAX: (719) 635-7119. Dale Mitchell, pres; Dane Scott, VP.
Film & video prod with postprod facilities, animation & sound stage.

Witt/Thomas/Harris Productions. 846 N. Cahuenga, Bldg. D, Los Angeles 90038. (213) 464-1333. FAX: (213) 960-1855. Paul Junger Witt, Tony Thomas, Susan Harris, ptnrs.
TV-CATV only.
TV prod company.

Wold Productions Co. 814 Amherst Ave., Los Angeles 90049-5292. (310) 826-0487. FAX: (310) 447-5954. Robert N. Wold, pres.
TV-CATV only.
Special-interest & entertainment progmg for bcst & cable TV.

Fred Wolf Films. 4222 W. Burbank Blvd., Burbank, Calif. 91505. (818) 846-0611. FAX: (818) 846-0979. Fred Wolf, pres.
TV prog prod & distribution.

World Events Productions Ltd. 4935 Lindell Blvd., St. Louis 63108. (314) 454-6475. FAX: (314) 454-6428. Edward J. (Ted) Koplar, pres; Edward R. Ascheman, VP/COO; Kevin Harlan, mgr dir.
TV-CATV only.
TV prog prod & distribution.

World Wide Syndications Corp. 781 58th Ave. S., St. Petersburg, Fla. 33705. (813) 867-5845. FAX: (813) 866-2743. Arthur N. Millman, pres.
TV & radio prog syndication. TV series, feature films, radio vignetts.

World Wrestling Federation. 1241 E. Main St., Stamford, Conn. 06902. (203) 352-8600. Vincent K McMahon, CEO; Linda McMahon, pres; Basil V. DeVito Jr, exec VP sls & mktg; Michael Ortman, VP affil rels; Ann Bojack, VP international opns; John Howard, gen sls mgr; Skip Desjardin, PPV.
Exclusive prods & distributors of WWF live events, TV & radio progmg.

Worldview Entertainment Inc. 6 E. 39th St., Suite 502, New York 10016. (212) 679-8230. FAX: (212) 686-0801. Sandra J. Birnhak, CEO; Marcy Stuzin, VP.
Stock footage library; distribution to international bcstrs.

Worldvision Enterprises Inc. 1700 Broadway, New York 10019. (212) 261-2700. FAX: (212) 261-2788. TWX: 52491 WOR UW. John D. Ryan, pres/CEO; Bert Cohen, exec VP/COO; Lawrence Gottlieb, exec VP finance & admin; Tony Colabaro, sr VP finance & admin; Philip Marella, sr VP legal & business affrs; Karen Miller, sr VP prog; Gary G. Montanus, sr VP mktg; Charles Quinones, sr VP opns; Robert E. Raleigh, sr VP domestic sls; Bill Baffi, VP Cable/New Technologies; Mitch Black, VP opns; Brian O'Sullivan, VP eastern div; Rita Scarfone, VP adv & promotion; Alan Winnikoff, VP/dir communications; Frank L. Browne, David McNaney, account exec eastern div; Jacqueline Comeau, account exec adv sls; Doreen Muldoon, dir adv sls mgmt; Andy Samet, dir promotion; Marybeth Strambi, dir rsch; Linda Tobin, dir international sls admin WV Home Video: Robert W. Sigman, exec VP/gen mgr; Gary Delfiner, dir mktg; Michael Thornton, dir international sls.
TV-CATV only.
Atlanta 30346: 400 Perimeter Center Terr., Suite 150. (404) 394-3967 (Latin American business). FAX: (404) 394-9002. Mary Ann Pasante, Leticia Estrada.
Chicago 60610: 515 N. State St., Suite 2305. (312) 527-0461. FAX: (312) 527-0688. Gary Butterfield, VP central division mgr.
Beverly Hills, Calif. 90036: 5700 Wilshire Blvd., 5th Fl. (213) 965-5910. FAX: (213) 965-5915. Paul Danylik, VP western division mgr; Ed O'Brien, acct exec western division.
London, England SW1X OAE: Worldvision Enterprises U.K. Ltd. 54 Pond St. 011-44-71-584-5357. FAX: 011-44-71-581-3483. TWX: (815) 8812754 (WORVIS G); CABLE: WORLVIFILM, LONDON via ITT. Bill Peck; Janice Wilson; Evelyn Leonard.
Sydney, Milsons Point, Australia 2061: Worldvision Enterprises of Australia PTY Ltd., 5-13 Northcliff St. 011-61-2-922-4722. FAX: 011-61-2-955-8207. TWX:

Producers, Distributors, Production and Other Services

(790) 70474; CABLE: WORLDVISION, SYDNEY, AUSTRALIA. Brian Rhys-Jones; Charmaine Williamson; Karen Zylstra.
Paris, France 75008: Worldvision Enterprises S.A.R.L. 28, Rue Bayard. 011-33-1-4723-3995. FAX: 011-33-1-4070-9269. TWX: (842) 648218 WOLFRA. Mary Jane Fourniel; Catherine Molinier; John Hernan.
Rio de Janeiro, Brazil CEP 22271: Rua Macedo Sobrinho 50., Botafogo. 011-55-21-286-8992. FAX: 011-55-21-266-4737. TWX: (391) 2123321 WFBR BR; WORFILMES, RIO DE JANEIRO. Raymondo Rodriguez; Maria Alice Freire.
Rome, Italy 00186: Adalia Anstalt, Via del Corso, 22/Int 10. 011-39-6-67-87-056. FAX: 011-39-6-322-6450. CABLE: Lt: Kiwe: Via del Corso 22 Rome, Italy. Michael Kiwe; Andrea Migliori; Dorothy Shaw; Adalia Anstalt.
Tokyo, Japan 104: Tsukiji Hamarikyu Bldg., 7th Fl., 5-3-3 Tsukiji, Chou-ku. 011-81-3-3545-3978. FAX: 011-81-3-3545-3964. TWX: (781) 2525077 (Amcast J); CABLE: AMOCAST, Tokyo, Japan. Ms. Mie Horasawa; Ms. Asae Iijima.
Toronto, Ont., Canada M5R 2A5: Worldvision Enterprises of Canada. 1200 Bay St., Suite 203. (416) 967-1200. FAX: (416) 967-0521. TWX: (369) 6524659. Bruce Swanson; Suzanne Lisi.
TV prog distribution for ind prods.

Worldwide Television News. 1705 DeSales St. N.W., Suite 300, Washington 20036. (202) 835-0750. FAX: (202) 887-7891. Paul C. Sisco, Washington bureau mgr.
TV-CATV only.
TV news prod, news library, video editing, ENG prod.

The Worship Network. 14444 66th St. N., Clearwater, Fla. 34624. (813) 536-0036. FAX: (813) 530-0671. James West, pres; Lowell W. Paxson, chmn of bd stewards; Larry Sims, VP opns; Lee Nagelhout, VP progmg; Bob Shreffler, VP finance & MIS; Gil McDowell, VP ministry.
TV-CATV only.
Live, interactive worship & praise svc 24 hours a day.

Carter Wright Enterprises. 6533 Hollywood Blvd., Suite 201, Hollywood, Calif. 90028. (213) 469-0944. FAX: (213) 464-3781. Carter Wright, pres.
Agency franchising with SAG, AFTRA, Musician's Local 47, Writer's Guild, Equity; vocal prod coaching.

Larry John Wright Film, Video & Entertainment. 1045 E. University Dr., Suite 4, Mesa, Ariz. 85203. (602) 833-8111. FAX: (602) 969-2895. Larry F. John, CEO; John N. Wright, pres.
Owns & operates prod studios; produces film & video comls, radio comls, jingles & TV shows.

Doug Wyles Productions Inc. 2109 Broadway, Suite 202A, New York 10023. (212) 877-4800. FAX: (212) 877-2157. John Zaff.

Y

Yada/Levine Productions. 346 N. Larchmont Blvd., Los Angeles 90004. (213) 461-1616. FAX: (213) 461-2288. Wayne M. Levine, exec creative dir; Dana Ware, exec prod.
TV-CATV only.

Betacam SP prod, camera crews with equipment packages, location travel. Full prod staff, non-linear off-line bays.

Yale Video Inc. 1360 N. Hancock St., Anaheim, Calif. 92807. (714) 693-5300. FAX: (714) 693-5395. Burton A. Yale, pres; Chris Wagner, gen mgr/VP finance.
Offers the latest in editing technology; from D-2 to Hi8.

Z

ZBS Foundation. R.R. One, Box 1201, Fort Edward, N.Y. 12828. (518) 695-6406. FAX: (518) 695-4041. Thomas Lopez, pres.
Prod of audio drama.

Zachry Associates. 709 N. 2nd St., Abilene, Tex. 79601. (915) 677-1342. FAX: (915) 672-2001. H.C. Zachry, pres; Paul Fulham, VP.
TV & radio progs, comls, & promotional film prod & distribution; gen prod svcs.

Sandy Zimmerman Productions. 3535 Cambridge, Suite 206, Las Vegas 89109. (702) 731-6491. Sandy Zimmerman, prod/own; Robert Gonzales, prod mgr; Rita Sparling, prog coord.
Prod from script to finished product. Syndication of one-, two- & five-minute prog fillers as well as ½-hour progs: TV progs, documentaries, informercials, travel specials, industrial & corporate videos, & TV comls.

Major National Radio Networks

ABC

Capital Cities/ABC Inc.

Headquarters: 77 W. 66th St., New York 10023-6298. (212) 456-7777. West Coast: 2040 Ave. of the Stars, Century City, Calif. 90067. (213) 557-7777.

Board of Directors: Thomas S. Murphy, Robert P. Bauman, Nicholas F. Brady, Warren E. Buffett, Frank T. Cary, John B. Fairchild, Leonard H. Goldenson, Frank S. Jones, Ann Dibble Jordan, John H. Muller Jr., Wyndham Robertson, M. Cabell Woodward Jr.

Officers: Thomas S. Murphy, chmn of the bd/CEO; John B. Fairchild, exec VP; Robert A. Iger, exec VP/pres ABC Television Network Group; Ronald J. Doerfler, sr VP/CFO; Herbert A. Granath, sr VP/pres ABC Cable & International Broadcast Group; Michael P. Mallardi, VP/pres Broadcast Group; Phillip J. Meek, sr VP/pres Publishing Group; Stephen A. Weiswasser, sr VP/pres Multimedia Group; David Westin, VP/gen counsel; Allan J. Edelson, VP/controller/asst sec; Joseph M. Fitzgerald, VP investor rels; James M. Goldberg, VP taxes; Robert T. Goldman, VP; and Andrew E. Jackson, VP; Patricia J. Matson, VP corporate communications; Jeffrey Ruthizer, VP labor rels; David J. Vondrak, VP/treas; William J. Wilkinson, VP human resources; Philip R. Farnsworth, sec; Allen S. Bomes, asst treas.

Capital Cities/ABC Radio Division: James P. Arcara, pres; Alfred E. Resnick, VP/dir engrg.

Eastern Region Headquarters: 125 West End Ave., New York 10023. (212) 456-5200.

West Region Headquarters: 12655 N. Central Expwy., Suite 600, Dallas 75243. (800) 527-4892; (214) 991-9200.

ABC Radio Networks: Robert F. Callahan Jr., pres; Bart W. Catalane, exec VP; Robert Connelly, sr VP engrg; Richard Martinez, VP engrg; William T. McClenaghan, sr VP rsch; Ralph Modugno, VP finance; John McConnell, VP radio news; David Kantor, exec VP; Frank Raphael, VP line net progmg; Corinne L. Baldassano, VP syndicated & long form progmg; Robert Hall, VP progmg 24-hour formats; Darryl E. Brown, sr VP affil mktg; Lyn Andrews, sr VP adv sls & mktg; Frank Woodbeck, VP affil mktg western rgn; Karen Freeman, VP affil mktg eastern rgn; Martin Raab, VP mktg; Bob Donnelly, VP engrg; Derek Berghuis, sr VP new bus dev; Susan Love, VP eastern sls; Dennis Glynn, VP Midwest sls; Dick Grunow, VP Detroit sls; Dan Perry, VP western sls; Rhonda Munk, VP southwestern sls.

ABC Radio Networks serves over 3,400 radio stations and is the largest radio network in the U.S. reaching an estimated 97.5 million listeners per week. ABC Radio broadcasts six full-service line networks, the ESPN Radio Network, long-form progmg (American Top 40, Paul Harvey News & Commentary, and American Country Countdown), ABC/SMN 24-hour formats, news, sports and daily & weekly features.

Capital Cities/ABC-Owned Radio Stations: Don P. Bouloukos, pres Group I; Norman S. Schrutt, pres Group II.

Group I:

WABC New York: Don P. Bouloukos, pres/gen mgr.

WPLJ New York: Mitch Dolan, pres/gen mgr.

WJR Detroit: James E. Long, pres/gen mgr.

WHYT-FM Detroit: John E. Cravens, pres/gen mgr.

KABC-AM Los Angeles: George Green, pres/gen mgr.

KLOS-FM Los Angeles: Bill Sommers, pres/gen mgr.

KGO-AM San Francisco: Michael Luckoff, pres/gen mgr.

Group II:

WYAY-AM-FM Atlanta.

WKHX-AM-FM Atlanta: Norman S. Schrutt, pres/gen mgr.

WBAP-AM Fort Worth-Dallas: William S. Hare, pres/gen mgr.

KSCS(FM) Fort Worth-Dallas: Victor Sansone, pres/gen mgr.

KQRS-AM-FM Minneapolis: Mark S. Steinmetz, pres/gen mgr.

WLS Chicago: Thomas R. Tradup, pres/gen mgr.

WYTZ-FM Chicago: Thomas R. Tradup, pres/gen mgr.

WRQX(FM) Washington: Jim Robinson, pres/gen mgr.

WMAL(AM) Washington: Thomas J. Bresnahan, pres/gen mgr.

Capital Cities/ABC Broadcast Group: Michael P. Mallardi, pres Broadcast Group; James P. Arcara, pres radio div; Norman S. Schruth, pres Capital Cities/ABC-Owned Radio Stations-Group II; Robert F. Callahan Jr., pres ABC Radio Networks Inc.

Capital Cities/ABC Publishing Group: Ann Maynard Gray, VP/pres Diversified Publishing Group; David S. Loewith, VP.

Corporate Divisions:

Legal: Stephen A. Weiswasser, sr VP/pres Capital Cities/ABC Multimedia Group; Griffith Foxley, VP corporate legal affrs; Andrew J. Jackson, VP corp affrs; Jeffrey S. Rosen, VP litigation; Mark MacCarthy, VP Washington, D.C.; Larry M. Loeb, VP legal affrs, video enterprises & publishing; Samuel Antar, VP law & regulation; Charles L. Stanford, VP legal & bus affrs bcstg; Jeffrey Ruthizer, VP labor rels.

Broadcast Standards & Practices: Christine Hikawa, VP; Harvey Cary Dzodin, VP coml standards; Brett White, VP prog standards.

Financial: Ronald J. Doerfler, sr VP/CFO; Allan J. Edelson, VP/controller; David J. Vondrak, VP/treas; Joseph M. Fitzgerald, VP investor rels; Mark Hasson, VP/asst controller; Kerry A. Carr, VP internal audit; James M. Goldberg, VP taxes; Andrew G. Governali, VP tax planning & admin; Alan S. Bomes, asst treas.

Administration: Robert T. Goldman, VP admin; Richard E. Hockman, VP real estate & construction; Roger Lund, VP admin West Coast; Bruce Phillips, design & dev, & real estate & construction; Andrew Pucher, VP facilities & security East Coast; Marion Roder Capriglione, VP travel & conference admin.

Corporate Communications: Patricia J. Matson, VP corporate communications ABC Inc.; Julie Tarachow Hoover, VP corporate projects; Veronica Pollard, dir corporate communications.

Office of Corporate Initiatives: Charles Keller, VP corporate initiatives; Dr. John E. Harr, VP office of communications.

Human Resources: William J. Wilkinson, VP human resources; Anita Hecht, VP employee rels; Anthony D. Sproule, VP per West Coast; Warren Salerno, VP employee benefits.

Affiliate Relations: George H. Newi, exec VP affil rels; Buzz Mathesius, VP/dir affil opns; Bryce Rathbone, VP/dir stn rels; Mike Nissenblatt, VP affil mktg & rsch svcs.

Public Relations & Affiliate Marketing Services: Pete Barrett, sr VP; Jerry Hellard, VP pub rels West Coast; Janice Gretemeyer, VP/dir pub rels East Coast; Alan R. Morris, VP/dir affil mktg svcs; Sherrie Berger, VP/dir prog publ & photography.

Business Affairs: Ronald V. Sunderland, exec VP bus affrs & contracts; Mark Pedowitz, sr VP bus affrs; Barry Gordon, VP bus affrs West Coast; Ronald Pratz, VP bus affrs admin West Coast; Anthony Farinacci, VP bus affrs East Coast; David Sherman, music & bus affrs.

ABC News: Roone Arledge, pres; Paul Friedman, exec VP; Richard C. Wald, sr VP editorial quality; William N. Temple, sr VP finance; Alan Wurtzel, VP magazines & long-form progmg; Michael Duffy, VP opns; William Moore, VP news opns Washington, D.C.; Steven Sadicario, VP bus affrs; Mimi Gurbst, VP news coverage; Don Dunphy Jr., VP affil news svcs; Joanna Bistany, VP/asst to the pres; Amy Entelis, VP talent recruitment & dev;

William Nagy, VP prod control; Robin Sproul, VP news coverage Washington, D.C.

Radio: John McConnell, VP ABC News; Richard Rosenbaum, gen mgr radio news & progmg; John Lyons, gen mgr radio news opns.

ABC Sports: Dennis Swanson, pres; Dennis Lewin, sr VP prod; Bob Apter, sr VP financial & admin; David Downs, VP progmg; Jack O'Hara, exec prod; Keith Ritter, VP mktg; Jonathan Leess, VP prod planning; Tom Remiszewski, VP adv & prom; Lydia Stephans, VP progmg.

Production: David Westin, pres Ambroco Media Group Inc.; Archie C. Purvis, pres; Paul D. Coss, VP prog acquisitions & dev; Dennis B. Kane, pres ABC/Kane Productions International.

ABC Productions: Brandon Stoddard, pres; Michael Ross, sr VP bus affrs; Ada Goldberg, VP bus & legal affrs; Jeffrey Offsay, exec VP; Amy Adelson, sr VP creative affrs; John Schwartz, VP finance; Thomas H Brokek, sr VP prod; Jim Painten, VP prod.

Broadcast Operations and Engineering: Preston A. Davis, pres; Michael Lang, VP bus affrs; Neil MacLeod, VP admin, finance & planning; David Elliott, VP engrg svcs East Coast; Mary Frost Distler, VP/gen mgr net opns East Coast; Jim Truelove, VP bcst opns & engrg opns Washington, D.C.; Robert A. Young, VP bcst opns & engrg West Coast.

Capital Cities/ABC Broadcasting Group: Michael P. Mallardi, pres.

Capital Cities/ABC Publishing Group: 77 W. 66th St., New York 10023. Phillip J. Meek, pres.

Specialized Publications:

Fairchild Publications (New York): John B. Fairchild, chmn/editorial dir; Michael F. Coady, pres.

Diversified Publishing Group: Ann Maynard Gray, pres.

Financial Services and Medical Group: Peter Derow, pres.

Daily Newspapers:

The Kansas City Star (Kansas City, Mo.): James H. Hale, chmn of bd/publisher.

Fort Worth Star-Telegram (Fort Worth, Tex.): Richard L. Connor, pres/publisher.

The Oakland Press (Pontiac, Mich.): Bruce H. McIntyre, pres/publisher.

Belleville News-Democrat (Belleville, Ill.): Gary L. Berkley, pres/publisher.

The Times Leader (Wilkes-Barre, Pa.). Dale A. Duncan, pres/publisher.

Albany Democrat-Herald (Albany, Ore.): John Buchner, publisher.

The Daily Tidings (Ashland, Ore.): Michael O'Brien, publisher.

Milford Citizen (Milford, Ct.): Richard Backer, publisher.

St. Louis Daily Record (St. Louis, Mo.): Sue Tedesco, publisher.

St. Louis Countian (St. Louis, Mo.): Sue Tedesco, publisher.

St. Peters Courier Post (St. Peters, Mo.): Sue Tedesco, publisher.

Weekly Newspapers and Shopping Guides: in eight states.

ABC Cable and International Broadcast Group: Herbert A. Granath, pres; John T. Healy, pres CC/ABC Video Enterprises International; Richard F. Spinner, mgng dir/CEO European opns; Jeremiah G. Sullivan, sr VP finance & admin.

ABC Distribution Co.: Joseph Y. Abrams, pres; Carol Brokaw, VP sls opns & admin.

American Urban Radio Networks

Headquarters: 463 7th Ave., New York 10018. (212) 714-1000.

Officers: Ronald Davenport, co-chmn; Sydney Small, co-chmn; Jack Bryant, pres.

Satellite: Spacenet 3R, Transponder 5H, Channel 6.30 Left and 6.48 Right.

American Urban Radio Networks

The following stations, according to American Urban Radio Networks, were affiliates as of November 1993.

New York
WLIB New York
WMCA New York
WWRL New York

Chicago
WGCI-AM-FM Chicago
WIMG-AM Chicago
WWCA Gary, Ind.

Los Angeles
KGFJ Los Angeles

Philadelphia
WDAS-AM-FM Philadelphia
WUSS Atlantic City, N.J.
WNAP Norristown, Pa.
WIMG Trenton, N.J.

Washington D.C.
WOL Washington, D.C.
WUST Washington, D.C.
WYCB Washington, D.C.

Detroit
WGPR-FM Detroit
WCHB Inkster, Mich.
WMKM Inkster, Mich.

Atlanta
WIGO Atlanta
WXAG Athens, Ga.
WXLL Decatur, Ga.
WTJH East Point, Ga.
WMXY Hogansville, Ga.

Houston
KCOH Houston
KWWJ Baytown, Tex.
KANI Wharton, Tex.

Baltimore
WBGR Baltimore
WEBB Baltimore

Dallas-Ft. Worth
KGGR Dallas

Memphis
WLOK Memphis
WXSS Memphis
WBOL Bolivar, Tenn.
WWUN-FM Clarksdale, Miss.
WURC-FM Holly Springs, Miss.
KFTH-FM Marion, Ark.
KCLT-FM West Helena, Ark.

Raleigh-Durham
WCLY Raleigh, N.C.
WLLE Raleigh, N.C.
WDUR Durham, N.C.
WFXC-FM Durham, N.C.
WSRC Durham, N.C.
WIDU Fayetteville, N.C.
WAUG New Hope, N.C.
WRSV-FM Rocky Mount, N.C.
WGTM Wilson, N.C.

San Francisco
KDIA Oakland, Calif.

Miami
WMBM Miami Beach
WYFX Boynton Beach, Fla.
WRBD Pompano Beach, Fla.

New Orleans
WBOK New Orleans

Norfolk-Portsmouth
WZAM Norfolk, Va.
WPCE Portsmouth, Va.
WBXB-FM Edenton, N.C.
WTJZ Newport News, Va.

Cleveland
WABQ Cleveland

St. Louis
KATZ St. Louis
KATZ-FM Alton, Ill.
WESL East St. Louis, Mo.

Charlotte, N.C.
WGSP Charlotte, N.C.

Richmond, Va.
WANT Richmond, Va.
WFTH Richmond, Va.
WPAK Farmville, Va.
WCLM Highland Springs, Va.

Jackson, Miss.
WKXI Jackson, Miss.
WJMG-FM Hattiesburg, Miss.
WONG Canton, Miss.
WLTD-FM Lexington, Miss.
WMJW-FM Magee, Miss.
WMIS Natchez, Miss.
WTYJ-FM Natchez, Miss.

Birmingham
WAGG Birmingham, Ala.
WATV Birmingham, Ala.
WAYE Birmingham, Ala.
WENN-FM Birmingham, Ala.
WJLD Fairfield, Ala.
WMGJ Gadsen, Ala.
WAJO Marion, Ala.

Tampa-St. Petersburg
WRXB St. Petersburg, Fla.
WTMP Tampa, Fla.
WWAB Lakeland, Fla.

Columbia, S.C.
WKWQ-FM Batesburg, S.C.
WTGH Cayce, S.C.
WSSB-FM Orangeburg, S.C.
WQIZ St. George, S.C.
WQKI St. Matthews, S.C.

Shreveport-Texarkana
KOKA Shreveport, La.
KXAR-FM Hope, Ark.
KBWC-FM Marshall, Tex.

Jacksonville, Fla.
WCGL Jacksonville
WSVE Jacksonville

Orlando
WWKO Cocoa, Fla.
WPUL South Daytona, Fla.

Greenville-Spartanburg
WHYZ Greenville, S.C.
WASC Spartanburg, S.C.
WABV Spartanburg, S.C.
WLWZ-FM Easley, S.C.
WFGN Gaffney, S.C.
WGSW Greenwood, S.C.

Greensboro-High Point-Winston-Salem
WNAA-FM Greensboro, N.C.
WQMG Greensboro, N.C.
WAAA Winston-Salem, N.C.
WSMX Winston-Salem, N.C.
WSNC-FM Winston-Salem, N.C.
WVST Petersburg, Va.
WTNC Thomasville, N.C.

Mobile
WGOK Mobile, Ala.

Montgomery, Ala.
WENN-FM Birmingham, Ala.
WCOX Camden, Ala.
WTQX Selma, Ala.
WBIL-AM-FM Tuskegee, Ala.
WSFU-FM Union Springs, Ala.
WAPZ Wetumpka, Ala.

Nashville
WNAH Nashville
WQKS Hopkinsville, Tenn.

Baton Rouge
WXOK Baton Rouge, La.
KQXL-FM New Roads, La.

Greenville-New Bern-Washington, N.C.
WOOW Greenville, N.C.
WRSV-FM Rocky Mount
WGTM Wilson

Charleston, S.C.
WPAL Charleston, S.C.
WVBX Georgetown, S.C.
WTUA-FM St. Stephens, S.C.
WWWZ-FM Summerville, S.C.

Little Rock
KMZX-FM Lonoke, Ark.
KCAT Pine Bluff, Ark.

Savannah
WSOK Savannah, Ga.
WVGB Beaufort, S.C.

Boston
WILD Boston

Indianapolis
WPZZ-FM Franklin, Ind.

Augusta
WKZK North Augusta, S.C.
WBRO Waynesboro, Ga.

Kansas City
KPRS-FM Kansas City
KPRT Kansas City

Cincinnati
WCIN Cincinnati

Pittsburgh
WAMO-FM Pittsburgh
WYJZ Pittsburgh
WCXJ Braddock, Pa.

Columbus, Ga.
WFXE-FM Columbus, Ga.
WOKS Columbus, Ga.

Macon, Ga.
WDDO Macon, Ga.
WIBB Macon, Ga.
WFXM-FM Forsyth, Ga.
WXKO Fort Valley, Ga.

Hartford-New Haven, Conn.
WKND Windsor, Conn.

Tallahassee
WFHT-FM Quincy, Fla.
WWSD Quincy, Fla.
WHGH Thomasville, Ga.
WJEM Valdosta, Ga.

Roanoke-Lynchburg
WJJS Lynchburg, Va.
WKBY Chatham, Va.
WILA Danville, Va.
WTOY Salem, Va.

West Palm Beach
WYFX Boynton Beach, Fla.
WMBM Miami Beach, Fla.
WRBD Pompano Beach, Fla.
WPOM Riviera Beach, Fla.

Milwaukee
WNOV Milwaukee
WGLB-FM Port Washington, Wisc.

Columbus, Ohio
WCKX-FM London, Ohio

Monroe-El Dorad, La.
KTRY-AM-FM Bastrop, La.
KXLA Rayville, La.
KYEA-FM West Monroe, La.

Major National Radio Networks

Florence, S.C.
WYNN-AM-FM Florence, S.C.

Louisville
WLLV Louisville, Ky.
WLOU Louisville, Ky.

Greenwood-Greenville, Miss.
WKXG Greenwood, Miss.
WDTL-AM-FM Cleveland, Miss.
WBAD-FM Leland, Miss.
WESY Leland, Miss.

Lafayette, La.
KFXZ-FM Maurice, La.
KQXL-FM New Roads, La.

Dayton
WDAO Dayton

Columbus-Tupelo, Miss.
WACR-AM-FM Columbus, Miss.

Buffalo
WUFO Amherst, N.Y.

Flint-Saginaw
WTLZ-FM Saginaw, Mich.

Seattle-Tacoma
KNHC-FM Seattle
KRIZ Renton, Wash.

Huntsville-Decatur, Ala.
WENN-FM Birmingham, Ala.
WEUP Huntsville, Ala.
WZZA Tuscumbia, Ala.

Wilmington, N.C.
WBMS Wilmington, N.C.
WVOE Chadbourn, N.C.

Grand Rapids-Kalamazoo
WKWM Kentwood, Mich.
WMHG-FM Muskegon, Mich.

Las Vegas
KCEP-FM Las Vegas

Tulsa
KXOJ Sand Springs, Okla.

Chattanooga
WNOO Chattanooga

Toledo
WVOI Toledo

Laurel-Hattiesburg, Miss.
WJMG-FM Hattiesburg
WORV Hattiesburg

Alexandria, La.
KBCE-FM Boyce, La.

Salisbury, Md.
WJDY Salisbury, Md.
WESM-FM Princess Anne, Md.

Biloxi-Gulfport, Miss.
WQFX-FM Gulfport, Miss.

Harrisburg-York
WWEC-FM Elizabeth City, Pa.

Springfield-Decatur, Ill.
WBCP Urbana, Ill.

Tuscaloosa, Ala.
WENN-FM Birmingham, Ala.
WTSK Tuscaloosa, Ala
WIDO-FM Eutaw, Ala.

Lake Charles, La.
KXZZ Lake Charles, La.
KALO Port Arthur, Tex.

Wichita-Hutchinson
KBUZ-FM El Dorado, Kan.

Syracuse
WOLF Syracuse

Portland, Ore.
KBGR Battle Ground, Wash.
KBMS Vancouver, Wash.

Fort Wayne
WJFX-FM New Haven, Ind.

Topeka
KPRS-FM Kansas City, Mo.

Albuquerque
KANW-FM Albuquerque, N.M.

Des Moines
KUCB-FM Des Moines, Iowa

Cedar Rapids-Waterloo, Iowa
KBBG-FM Waterloo, Iowa

Utica, N.Y.
WPNR-FM Utica, N.Y.

Wheeling, W.V.-Steubenville, Ohio
WAMO-FM Pittsburgh, Pa.

Rockford, Ill.
WGCI-FM Chicago

Associated Press Network News

Associated Press Broadcast Division

Broadcast News Center: 1825 K St. N.W., Washington, D.C. 20006-1253. (800) 821-4747; (202) 736-1100. Fax: (202) 736-1199, news; (202) 736-1124, administration; (202) 736-1107, VP's office.

Officers: Louis D. Boccardi, pres/CEO; Jim Williams, VP/dir, (202) 736-1108.

News & Programming

Deputy Director & Managing Editor: Brad Kalbfeld (202) 736-1170.

Assistant Managing Editors: Ed Tobias, news (202) 736-1172; Wally Hindes, prog, (202) 736-1171; Barbara Worth, bcst wires (202) 736-1173.

Chief Supervisor: Steve Katz (202) 736-9505.

Assignment Editors: Kate McKenna, Lauri Schwartz (202) 736-9520.

Business: Paul Courson, edit (202) 736-9548.

Sports: Dave Lubeski, dir (202) 736-9540.

Entertainment: Michael Weinfeld, edit (202) 736-9515.

National Correspondents: Bob Moon, Los Angeles (213) 346-0223; Mark Smith, Washington, D.C. (202) 736-9522.

Regional Correspondents: Warren Levinson, New York (212) 621-1524; Ted Hampson, Chicago (312) 781-0909; Amanda Barnett, Dallas (214) 991-2020; Brian Bland, Los Angeles (213) 748-3590; Tony Winton, Miami, Fla. (305) 591-1488.

European Coordinator: Karen Sloan, London (44-71) 353-3692.

Engineering: George Mayo, chief engr (202) 736-1161; Greg Crowley, asst chief engr (202) 736-1162.

Sales & Marketing

Director of Sales & Marketing: Daryl Staehle (202) 736-1145.

Radio Sales Manager, Eastern Division: Matt Hoff (202) 736-1147.

Regional Radio Executives, Eastern Division: Jerry Jackson (Alabama, Kentucky & Tennessee), 1100 Broadway, Nashville, Tenn. 37203, (615) 244-2205; John Willis (Florida & southern Georgia), 47 E. Robinson St., Orlando, Fla. 32801, (407) 425-3169; John Harris (North Carolina, South Carolina & northern Georgia), 4020 W. Chase Blvd., Raleigh, N.C. 27607-3922, (919) 833-8687; Carol Robinson (District of Columbia, Maryland, Virginia & West Virginia), 1825 K St. N.W., Washington 20006-1253, (202) 736-1154; Joyce Belmonte (Delaware, New Jersey & Pennsylvania), One Franklin Plaza, Suite 250, Philadelphia 19102, (215) 567-2727; Richard Shafer (Connecticut & New York), Box 11010, Albany, N.Y. 12211-0010, (518) 458-7821; Maine, Massachusetts, New Hampshire, Rhode Island & Vermont, 184 High St., Boston 02110, (617) 357-8524; Arkansas, Louisiana & Mississippi, Capital Towers, 125 S. Congress, Suite L-170, Jackson, Miss. 39201, (601) 948-2034.

Radio Sales Manager, Western Division: Steve Crowley, 215 W. Pershing Rd., Kansas City, Mo. 64108-1850, (816) 421-4792.

Regional Radio Executives, Western Division: Sherry Duncan (Alaska, Idaho, Montana, Oregon, Washington), Box 2144, Seattle 98111-2144, (206) 623-1754; John Folger (northern California, northern Nevada, Utah), Box 7247, San Francisco 94120-7247, (415) 621-7432; Dave Tyler (Arizona, southern California, Hawaii, southern Nevada), 1111 S. Hill St., Room 263, Los Angeles 90015-2296, (213) 626-1200; Colorado, Nebraska, New Mexico, Wyoming, 1444 Wazee St., Suite 130, Denver 80202-1395, (303) 825-0123; John Schweitzer (Iowa, Minnesota, North Dakota, South Dakota), 511 11th Ave. S., Suite 404, Minneapolis 55415, (612) 332-2727; Dave Rizzo(Kansas, Missouri, Oklahoma), 215 W. Pershing Rd., Kansas City, Mo. 64108-1850, (816) 421-6725; Doug Kienitz (Texas), 4851 LBJ Freeway, Suite 300, Dallas 75244-6002, (214) 991-7766; Susan Spaulding (Illinois, Indiana, Wisconsin), 230 N. Michigan Ave., Chicago 60601-5960, (312) 781-0500; Ken Charbat (Michigan & Ohio), 300 River Pl., Suite 2400, Detroit 48207, (313) 259-0650.

Networks: Dave Polyard, dir (202) 736-1150.

Technology Services: Bob Feldman, mktg mgr (202) 736-1151.

Technology: Lee Perryman, deputy dir (202) 736-1135; Sue Mosher, asst dir technology dev (202) 736-1136; John Morrissey, info systems mgr (202) 736-1137; Lori McCafferty, prod mgr (202) 736-1140.

Station Services: Evelyn Cassidy, dir (202) 736-1152; Kelly Malone, mktg coord (202) 736-1153.

Administration: Greg Groce, dir (202) 736-1110; Wayne Chin, asst dir (202) 736-1111.

Bureau Chiefs: Alabama/Georgia: Gary Clark, Atlanta (404) 522-8971; **Alaska:** Dean Fosdick, Anchorage (907) 272-7549; **Arizona:** Charlotte Porter, Phoenix (602) 258-8934; **Arkansas:** Bill Simmons, Little Rock (501) 374-5536; **Southern California/Southern Nevada:** Andrew Lippman, Los Angeles (213) 626-1200; **Northern California/Northern Nevada:** Dan Day, San Francisco (415) 621-7432; **Colorado/Wyoming:** Joseph McGowan Jr., Denver (303) 825-0123; **Connecticut:** Mary Ann Rhyne, Hartford (203) 246-6876; **Delaware/Maryland:** Linda Stowell, Baltimore (301) 539-3524; **District of Columbia:** Jon Wolman, Washington (202) 828-6400; **Florida:** James Reindl, Miami (305) 594-5825; **Hawaii:** Howard Graves, Honolulu (808) 536-5510; **Idaho/Utah:** William R. Beecham, Salt Lake City (801) 322-3405; **Illinois:** Jim Wilson, Chicago (312) 781-0500; **Indiana:** Robert Shaw, Indianapolis (317) 639-5501; **Iowa:** Kristi Umbreit, Des Moines (515) 243-3281; **Kansas/Missouri:** Paul Stevens, Kansas City (816) 421-4844; **Kentucky:** Ed Staats, Louisville (502) 583-7718; **Louisiana/Mississippi:** Patrick Arnold, New Orleans (504) 523-3931; **Maine/New Hampshire/Vermont:** Larry Laughlin, Concord, N.H. (603) 224-3327; **Massachusetts/Rhode Island:** Michael Short, Boston (617) 357-8100; **Michigan:** Charles Hill, Detroit (313) 259-0650; **Minnesota:** Dave Pyle, Minneapolis (612) 332-2727; **Montana:** John Kuglin, Helena (406) 442-7440; **Nebraska:** Paul Simon, Omaha (402) 341-4963; **New Jersey:** Mark Mittelstadt, Trenton (609) 392-3622; **New Mexico:** David Sedeno, Albuquerque (505) 822-9022; **New York City:** Sam Boyle (212) 621-1670; **New York State:** Lew Wheaton, Albany (518) 458-7821; **North Carolina:** Ambrose Dudley, Raleigh (919) 833-8687; **North Dakota/South Dakota:** Tena Haraldson, Sioux Falls, S.D. (605) 322-2111; **Ohio:** Jake Booher, Columbus (614) 855-2727; **Oklahoma:** Lindel Hutson, Oklahoma City (405) 525-2121; **Oregon:** Eva Parziale, Portland (503) 228-2169; **Pennsylvania:** George Zucker, Philadelphia (215) 561-1133; **South

Carolina: John Shurr, Columbia (803) 799-6418; **Tennessee:** Kent Flanagan, Nashville (615) 224-2205; **Texas:** John Lumpkin, Dallas (214) 991-2100; **Virginia:** Dorothy Abernathy, Richmond (804) 643-6646; **Washington:** Dale Leach, Seattle (206) 682-1812; **West Virginia:** Pete Mattiace, Charleston (304) 346-0897; **Wisconsin:** T. Lee Hughes, Milwaukee (414) 225-3580.

Board of Directors

Chairman: Frank A. Daniels Jr., pres/publisher News & Observer, Raleigh, N.C.

Vice Chairman: James K. Batten, chmn/CEO Knight-Ridder Inc., Miami, Fla.

Directors: David R. Bradley Jr., pres/editor News-Press & Gazette Co., St. Joseph, Mo.; J. Stewart Bryan III, chmn/publisher Richmond Times-Dispatch, Richmond, Va.; William R. Burleigh, exec VP Scripps Howard Inc., Cincinnati; David E. Easterly, pres Cox Newspapers, Atlanta; Stephen Hamblett, chmn/CEO/publisher Providence Journal Co., Providence, R.I.; Robert H. Hartmann, chmn/publisher Evansville Press, Evansville, Ind.; Edwin L. Heminger, chmn The Findlay Publishing Co., Findlay, Ohio; Ruth S. Holmberg, publisher The Chattanooga Times, Chattanooga, Tenn.; Gregg K. Jones, co-publisher The Greeneville Sun, Greeneville, Tenn.; Harold R. Lifvendahl, pres/publisher The Orlando Sentinel, Orlando, Fla.; Kenneth H. Maness, pres Tri-Cities Radio Corp., Gray, Tenn.; Francis A. Martin III, pres/CEO Chronicle Broadcasting Co., San Francisco; John G. Montgomery, pres/publisher Montgomery Publications Inc., Junction City, Kan.; Donald E. Newhouse, pres The Star-Ledger, Newark, N.J.; Eric Ober, pres CBS News, New York; Roger L. Ogden, pres/gen mgr KCNC-TV Denver; Mary Schurz, editor/publisher The Advocate-Messenger, Danville, Ky.; Joe D. Smith Jr., chmn Alexandria Daily Town Talk, Alexandria, La.; David J. Whichard II, chmn The Daily Reflector, Greenville, N.C.; George W. Wilson, pres Concord Monitor, Concord, N.H.

AP Broadcasters Inc.

President: Roger Ogden, pres/gen mgr KCNC-TV Denver.

President-Elect: Kenneth Maness, pres WJCW-AM/WQUT-FM Gray, Tenn.

Vice President for Television: John Corporon, sr VP news WPIX-TV New York.

Vice President for Radio: Treeda Smith, news dir WRVQ-FM & WRXL-FM Richmond, Va.

Secretary: Scott Herman, news dir KYW-AM & KYW-TV Philadelphia.

Directors: Allan Buch, VP/gen mgr KSNW-TV Wichita, Kan.; Terry Duffie, exec VP WKMX-FM Enterprise, Ala.; Dan Halyburton, VP/gen mgr KLIF-AM/KPLX-FM Dallas; Kenneth L. Hatch, pres/CEO KIRO-AM/KSEA-FM/KIRO-TV Seattle; Mike Kettenring, pres/gen mgr WSMV-TV Nashville; Robert Krueger, VP/gen mgr KTVB-TV Boise, Idaho; Fred Lark, pres/gen mgr KXLO-AM/KLCM-FM Lewistown, Mont.; Adrienne Laurent, asst news dir KMST-TV Monterey, Calif.; Dave Maurer, news dir WSGW-AM & WIOG-FM Saginaw, Mich.; Richard Moore, news dir WSB-TV Atlanta; Robert M. Rogers, VP news dir KENS-TV San Antonio; Carol Rueppel, news dir WDIV-TV Detroit; William R. Sanders, pres/own/gen mgr KICD-AM/FM Spencer, Iowa; Eric Seidel, stn mgr WGST-AM Atlanta.

State APB Presidents: Alabama: Henry Roddam, WBRC-TV Birmingham; **Arizona:** Tim Walters, KATO-AM; **Arkansas:** Kein Inman, KAAB-AM Batesville; **California/Nevada:** John Paminteri, KEYT-TV Santa Barbara, Calif.; **Colorado:** Paul MacGregor, KOA-AM Denver; **Connecticut:** James Sweeney, Cablevision News 12 Norwalk; **Delaware/D.C./Maryland:** Bill Grant, WDEL-AM/WSTW-FM Wilmington, Del.; **Florida:** Peter Neumann, WEAR-TV Pensacola, Fla.; **Georgia:** Peter Michenfelder, WJBF-TV Augusta; **Idaho:** Mark Maier, KBAR-AM Burley; **Illinois:** Jennifer McCarthy, WGIL-AM Galesburg; **Indiana:** Lloyd Winnecke, WEHT-TV Evansville; **Iowa:** J.K. Martin, KBUR-AM Burlington, Iowa; **Kansas:** Richard Baker, KKSU-AM Manhattan; **Kentucky:** Beth Merrell, WHAS-AM Louisville; **Louisiana:** Sam Moore, WBRZ-TV Baton Rouge; **Massachusetts:** Brian Whitimore, WBZ-AM Boston; **Michigan:** Jeff Gilbert, WWJ-AM Southfield; **Minnesota:** John Schadl, KDAL-AM Duluth; **Mississippi:** Joe Norwood, WTOK-TV Meridian; **Missouri:** Becky Hostetter, KTVO-TV Kirksville; **Montana:** Mark Daniels, KSEN-AM/KZIN-FM Shelby; **Nebraska:** Kevin Mooney, KNEB-AM/FM Scottsbluff; **New Hampshire:** Carl Cameron, WMUR-TV Manchester; **New Jersey:** Drew Jacobs, WPSC-FM Wayne; **New Mexico:** Scott Michlin, KOBF-TV Farmington; **New York:** John Butler, WSYR-AM Syracuse; **North Carolina:** Michael Kronley, WSOC-TV Charlotte; **North Dakota:** Mark Narum, KXMC-TV Minot; **Ohio:** Ron Robertson, WONE-AM/WTUE-FM Dayton; **Oklahoma:** Brian Gann, KVOO-AM/FM Tulsa; **Oregon:** Gayle Mitchell, KTVL-TV Medford; **Pennsylvania:** Pierre Bellicini, SEE-TV Erie; **South Carolina:** Deborah Tibbetts, WCIB-TV Charleston; **South Dakota:** Tom Sorenson, KUSD-AM/FM Vermillion; **Tennessee:** Jim Ellis, WLAC-AM/FM Nashville; **Texas:** Dan Potter, WBAP-AM Fort Worth; **Vermont:** Bruce Lyndes, WNNE-TV Hartford; **Virginia:** Steve Hawkins, WCYB-TV Bristol; **West Virginia:** Jim Reader, WSAZ-TV Charleston; **Wisconsin:** Rick Cohler, WDUZ-AM/WQLH-FM Green Bay; **Wyoming:** Dave Lerner, KGWN-TV Cheyenne.

CBS Inc.

Headquarters: 51 W. 52nd St., New York 10019 (212) 975-4321. 7800 Beverly Blvd., Los Angeles 90036. (213) 852-2345.

Officers: Laurence A. Tisch, chmn/pres/CEO; Jay L. Kriegel, sr VP; Martin D. Franks, VP Washington, D.C.; Mark B. Pearlman, VP planning & bus dev; Edward Grebow, sr VP opns & admin; Peter W. Keegan, sr VP finance; Louis J. Rauchenberger Jr., VP/treas; Keith Fawcett, asst treas; Dennis D'Oca, VP risk mgmt; Alvan L. Bobrow, VP/dir taxes; Anton W. Guitano, VP/gen auditor; James B. Sirmons, sr VP industrial rels; Leon Schulzinger, VP industrial rels East Coast; John M. McLean, VP industrial rels West Coast; Ellen O. Kaden, VP/gen counsel/sec.

CBS Operations & Administration

Edward Grebow, sr VP opns & admin; Joan Showalter, sr VP human resources; Karen Beldegreen, VP compensation & policy, & per; Thomas F. McVeigh, VP per benefits; James Halsey, VP mgmt info systems CBS Inc.; John Lalli, VP opns; Thomas C. Maile, VP telecommunications; Robert Monaghan, VP admin svcs CBS Inc.; Joseph A. Flaherty, sr VP tech; Dave White, VP special projects; Jay Fine, VP bcst opns East Coast; Brent Stranathan, VP bcst distribution; Robert Mauro, VP prod mgmt; Charles Dages, VP engrg; Richard Streeter, VP sys engrg; Robert P. Seidel, VP bcst svcs engrg; Darcy Antonellis, VP, tech opns; Charles Cappleman, VP bcst opns West Coast; Ken Cooper, VP facilities opns New York.

CBS/Broadcast Group

Howard Stringer, pres; Beth Waxman Bressan, VP/asst to the pres; Matthew Margo, VP prog practices New York; Carol A. Altieri, VP prog practices Hollywood, Calif.; Peter A. Lund, exec VP CBS Broadcast Group/pres CBS mktg div; George F. Schweitzer, sr VP mktg & communications; Ann Morfogen, VP media rels; Susan Tick, VP publ West Coast; Tom Goodman, VP communications CBS News & CBS TV stns; Michael Mischler, VP adv & promotion Los Angeles; Kathie Culleton, VP media & planning, & adv & promotion; John Bradford Crum, VP affil adv & prom; John Luma, VP on-air prom; Jerold Goldberg, VP creative svcs; David F. Poltrack, sr VP planning & rsch; Jay D. Gold, VP finance; Bruce C. Taub, VP financial planning; Gary McCarthy, VP finance Hollywood, Calif.

CBS Enterprises Division

James A. Warner, pres; Rainer Siek, sr VP sls & mktg CBS Broadcast International; David P. Berman, VP prod & admin CBS Broadcast International; Kenneth Ross, VP/gen mgr CBS Video, CBS Enterprises; Tom Newell, VP bus affrs & opns.

CBS Affiliate Relations Division

Anthony C. Malara, pres; Scott T. Michels, VP/dir.

CBS Entertainment Division

Jeff Sagansky, pres; Peter F. Tortorici, exec VP; Steve Warner, VP prog planning; Madalene Horne, VP current progs; Madeline Peerce, VP creative svcs/artist rels; Suzan Mischer, VP entertainment & info specials; Andy Hill, exec VP CBS Entertainment Productions; Robert Gros Sr., sr VP CBS Entertainment Productions; Timothy Flack, VP comedy prog dev; Jonathan Levin, VP dramatic prog dev; Lisa Freiberger, VP talent & casting; William B. Klein, sr VP bus affrs; Leola Gorius, VP bus affrs; Layne Britton, VP bus affrs West Coast; Sidney Lyons, VP bus affrs, long form contracts & acquisitions; James F. McGowan, VP bus affrs admin.

CBS Marketing Division

Peter A. Lund, exec VP CBS Broadcast Group/pres CBS Marketing Div; Mary Lou Jennerjahn, VP admin; Daniel J. Koby, VP/group head/natl sls mgr; W. Scott McGraw, VP/dir sls & mktg; Duncan E. Ryder, VP/dir sls & mktg; John R. Kelly, VP/dir sls & mktg; John P. O'Sullivan, VP/dir sls & mktg; Martin B. Daly, VP/dir sls & mktg; Dorothy S. Schwartz, VP/group head planning, admin & mkt resources; Richard J. Blangiardi, VP new bus dev; Ann E. Harkins, VP sls svcs; Kenneth J. Wachtel, VP/dir sls planning & proposals; Bonnie Hiramoto, VP mkt resources; William G. Cecil, VP prog sls; John Gray, VP West Coast sls; John Ginway, VP central sls; Richard Masilotti, VP Detroit sls; JoAnn C. Ross, VP Olympic sls; Michael A. Guariglia, VP sports sls; Jane P. Davey, VP news sls; John K. Brooks, VP/dir sports sls.

CBS News Division

Eric Ober, pres; Joseph Peyronin, VP CBS News Prime Time/asst to pres; Donald E. DeCesare, VP opns; Lane Venardos, VP hard news & special events; John Frazee, VP news svcs; Linda Mason, VP pub affrs; James M. McKenna, VP finance & admin; Robert E. McCarthy, VP bus affrs; Barbara Cochran, VP/bureau mgr CBS News Washington, D.C.; Al Ortiz, VP/bureau chief London & Europe; Larry D. Cooper, VP CBS News Radio.

CBS Sports Division

Neal H. Pilson, pres; Jay B. Rosenstein, VP progmg; Len DeLuca, VP prog planning; Jeremy Handelman, VP prog planning; Rick Gentile, sr VP prod; Mark H. Harrington III, VP Olympics; James F. Harrington, VP prog admin & opns; Raymond Harmon, VP bus planning; Noel B. Berman, VP sports bus affrs & compliance.

CBS Radio Division

Nancy C. Widmann, pres; Anna Mae Sokusky, VP CBS-owned AM stns; Dan Griffin, VP/gen mgr WCBS; Frank Oxarart, VP/gen mgr KCBS; Steve Carver, VP/gen mgr WBBM; George Nicholaw, VP/gen mgr KNX; Rod Zimmerman, VP/gen mgr KMOX; Roger Nadel, VP/gen mgr WWJ/WJOI-FM; Rand Gottlieb, VP/gen mgr WCCO; Rod Calarco, VP CBS-owned FM stns; Maire Mason, VP/gen mgr WCBS-FM; Tom Matheson, VP/gen mgr WBBM-FM; Dennis Begley, VP/gen mgr WOGL-AM-FM; Rod Zimmerman, VP/gen mgr KLOU-FM; Clinton Culp, VP/gen mgr KTXQ-FM; Donald Marion, VP/gen mgr KRQR-FM; Dave Van Dyke, VP/gen mgr KCBS-FM; Sarah Taylor, VP/gen mgr WLTT-FM; Shawn Portmann,

Major National Radio Networks

VP/gen mgr WYNF-FM; Bob Pates, VP/gen mgr WODS-FM; John D. Hiatt, VP/gen mgr KLTR-FM; Rolf Pepple, VP/gen mgr WLTE-FM; Robert P. Kippermann, VP/gen mgr CBS Radio Networks; Frank D. Murphy, VP progs CBS Radio Networks; Nicholas Kieman, VP affil sls CBS Radio Networks; Larry Cooper, VP CBS News Radio; Richard Silipigni, VP sls CBS Radio Networks; Paul Bronstein, VP rsch CBS Radio Networks; Raif D'Amico, VP/gen mgr CBS Radio reps; Elizabeth Hayter, VP media practices; Michael H. O'Neal, VP/controller; Anthony Masiello, VP tech opns.

CBS-Owned AM-FM Stations:

WCBS(AM): 51 W. 52nd St., New York 10019. (212) 975-4321. Dan Griffin, VP/gen mgr.

WCBS(FM): 51 W. 52nd St., New York 10019. (212) 975-4321. Maire Mason, VP/gen mgr.

WBBM(AM): 630 N. McClurg Ct., Chicago 60011. (312) 944-6000. Steve Carver, VP/gen mgr.

WBBM(FM): 630 N. McClurg Ct., Chicago 60011. (312) 944-6000. Thomas A. Matheson, VP/gen mgr.

KNX(AM): 6121 Sunset Blvd., Los Angeles 90028. (213) 460-3000. George Nicholaw, VP/gen mgr.

KCBS(FM): 6121 Sunset Blvd., Los Angeles 90028. (213) 460-3000. Dave Van Dyke, VP/gen mgr.

WOGL(AM): City & Monument Aves., Philadelphia 19131. (215) 668-5800. Dennis Begley, VP/gen mgr.

WOGL(FM): City & Monument Aves., Philadelphia 19131. (215) 668-5800. Dennis Begley, VP/gen mgr.

WODS(FM): 30 Winter St., Boston 02108. (617) 426-2200. Bob Pates, VP/gen mgr.

KMOX(AM): 1 Memorial Dr., St. Louis 63102. (314) 621-2345. Rod Zimmerman, VP/gen mgr.

KLOU(FM): 1 Memorial Dr., St. Louis 63102. (314) 621-2345. Rod Zimmerman, VP/gen mgr.

KCBS(AM): 1 Embarcadero Ctr., San Francisco 94111. (415) 765-4000. Frank J. Oxarart Jr., VP/gen mgr.

KRQR(FM): 1 Embarcadero Ctr., San Francisco 94111. (415) 765-4000. Don Marion, VP/gen mgr.

WLTT(FM): 5912 Hubbard Dr., Rockville, Md. 20852. (301) 984-6000. Sarah Taylor, VP/gen mgr.

WYNF(FM): 9720 Executive Center Dr. N., St. Petersburg 33702. (813) 576-6090. Shawn V. Portmann, VP/gen mgr.

KTXQ(FM): 4131 N. Central Expy., Suite 1200, Dallas 75204. (214) 528-5500. Clinton Culp, VP/gen mgr.

KLTR(FM): 10333 Richmond Ave., Suite 693, Houston 77042. (713) 780-0937. John Hiatt, VP/gen mgr.

WWJ/WJOI(FM): 16550 W. Nine Mile Rd., Southfield, Mich. 48086. (313) 423-3300. Roger Nadel, VP/gen mgr.

WCCO(AM): 625 2nd Ave. S., Minneapolis 55402. (612) 370-0611. Rand Gottlieb, VP/gen mgr.

WLTE(FM): 1111 3rd Ave. S., Suite 470, Minneapolis 55404. (612) 339-1029. Rolf Pepple, VP/gen mgr.

CBS Radio Network

The following stations, according to CBS, were affiliates as of September 1993.

Alabama
WDNG Anniston
WYDE Birmingham
WWNT Dothan
WZOB Fort Payne
WRSA-FM Huntsville
WKRG Mobile
WACV Montgomery
WJDB-AM-FM Thomasville

Alaska
KBYR Anchorage
KCBF Fairbanks
KJNO Juneau

Arizona
KJAA Globe
KTAR Phoenix
KYCA Prescott
KTUC Tucson
KINO Winslow

Arkansas
KURM Fayetteville
KWXI Glenwood
KWXE-FM Glenwood
KARN Little Rock
KARV Russellville
KFCM-FM Salem

California
KNZR Bakersfield
KHSL Chico
KXO El Centro
KINS Eureka
KMPH Fresno
KRKC Kings City
KNX Los Angeles
KNRY Monterey
KEDY-FM Mount Shasta
KTOX Needles
KCMJ Palm Springs
KPRL Paso Robles
KPCO Quincy
KSHA-FM Redding
KLOA Ridgecrest
KRAK-AM-FM Sacramento
KFMB San Diego
KCBS San Francisco
KSMA Santa Maria
KTHO S. Lake Tahoe
KKBN-FM Twain Harte
KUKI-AM-FM Ukiah

Colorado
KRLN Canon City
KVOR Colorado Springs
KYBG Denver
KIUP Durango
KBRU-FM Fort Morgan
KFTM Fort Morgan
KNZZ Grand Junction
KVLE-FM Gunnison
KSEC-FM Lamar
KCSJ Pueblo

Connecticut
WTIC Hartford
WZBG-FM Litchfield
WNLC New London
WATR Waterbury

Delaware
WYUS Milford
WILM Wilmington

District of Columbia
WTOP Washington

Florida
WAAZ-FM Crestview
WJSB Crestview
WNDB Daytona Beach
WDBF Delray Beach
WINK Fort Myers
WJNX Fort Pierce
WRUF Gainesville
WZNZ Jacksonville
WKIZ Key West
WLBE Leesburg
WTAI Melbourne
WINZ Miami
WNOG Naples
WWNZ-AM-FM Orlando
WCCF Punta Gorda
WFOY St. Augustine
WTAL Tallahassee
WFNS Tampa
WHNZ Tampa
WTTB Vero Beach
WJNO West Palm Beach

Georgia
WGPC-AM-FM Albany
WGAU Athens
WGUN Atlanta
WGAC Augusta
WGIG Brunswick
WYXC Cartersville
WRCG Columbus
WGFS Covington
WLSQ Dalton
WXLI Dublin
WGGA Gainesville
WWIQ-FM Macon
WWYQ-FM Macon
WMGA Moultrie
WLAQ Rome
WBMQ Savannah
WWNS Statesboro
WPAX Thomasville
WTIF Tifton
WVLD Valdosta
WCJM-FM West Point
WPLV West Point

Guam
KGUM Agana

Hawaii
KPUA Hilo
KGU Honolulu
KMVI Wailuku

Idaho
KID Idaho Falls
KATW-FM Lewiston
KART Twin Falls

Illinois
WQRL-FM Benton
WDWS Champaign
WBBM Chicago
WDAN Danville
WSOY Decatur
WFRL Freeport
WLDS Jacksonville
WMBD Peoria
WPOK Pontiac
WTAD Quincy
WTAX Springfield
WSDR Sterling

Indiana
WHBU Anderson
WYNG-FM Evansville
WOWO Fort Wayne
WTLC Indianapolis
WBAT Marion
WLBC Muncie
WSBT South Bend
WAOV Vincennes

Iowa
KCPS Burlington
KCIM Carroll
WMT-AM-FM Cedar Rapids
KJOC Davenport
KRNT Des Moines
KDTH Dubuque
KVFD Fort Dodge
KGLO Mason City
KBIZ Ottumwa
KOAK-AM-FM Red Oak
KICD-AM-FM Spencer
KNEI-AM-FM Waukon

Kansas
KABI Abilene
KNCK Concordia
KIUL Garden City
KLOE Goodland
KKOW Pittsburg
WIBW Topeka
KFH Wichita

Kentucky
WKCT Bowling Green
WCCK-FM Calvert City
WCKQ-FM Campbellsville
WTCO-AM-FM Campbellsville
WFKY Frankfort
WCLU Glasgow
WGOH Grayson
WUGO-FM Grayson
WHOP Hopkinsville
WAVG Louisville
WFTM-FM Maysville
WMOK Paducah
WTKY-AM-FM Tompkinsville
WTCW Whitesburg
WEKC Williamsburg

Major National Radio Networks

Louisiana
WJBO Baton Route
KWJM-FM Farmerville
KPEL-AM-FM Lafayette
WWL New Orleans
KVLA Vidalia

Maine
WFAU Augusta
WKCG-FM Augusta
WZON Bangor
WDEA Ellsworth
WSYY-AM-FM Millinocket
WGAN Portland
WOZI Presque Isle

Maryland
WBAL Baltimore
WFMD Frederick
WJEJ Hagerstown
WMSG Oakland
WSBY-FM Salisbury

Massachusetts
WHDH Boston
WHAI-AM-FM Greenfield
WBRK Pittsfield
WNNZ Springfield
WTAG Worcester

Michigan
WWJ Detroit
WDBC Escanaba
WFDF Flint
WGHN-AM-FM Grand Haven
WHTC Grand Rapids
WJMS Ironwood
WJCO Jackson
WKZO Kalamazoo
WAIR-FM Petoskey
WJML Petoskey
WSGW Saginaw
WDBI-FM Tawas

Minnesota
WJJY Brainerd
KDLM Detroit Lakes
KDAL Duluth
WCCO Minneapolis
KTRF Thief River Falls

Mississippi
WHSY Hattiesburg
WJNT Jackson
WHNY McComb

Missouri
KOMC Branson
KBFL-FM Buffalo
KZIM Cape Girardeau
KWOS Jefferson City
KCMO Kansas City
KMMO-AM-FM Marshall
KWIX Moberly
KFEQ St. Joseph
KMOX St. Louis
KDRO Sedalia

Montana
KBOZ Bozeman
KBOW Butte
KRYK-FM Chinook
KCAP Helena
KGEZ Kalispell
KMTA Miles City
KGVO Missoula

Nebraska
KHAS Hastings
KGFW Kearney
KLIN Lincoln
KKAR Omaha

Nevada
KNUU Las Vegas
KOH Reno

New Hampshire
WKXL Concord
WTSL Hanover
WKNE Keene
WEMJ Laconia
WFEA Manchester

New Jersey
WFPG Atlantic City

New Mexico
KKOB Albuquerque
KGAK Gallup
KOBE Las Cruces
KRSN Los Alamos

New York
WGY Albany
WAUB Auburn
WABH Bath
WVIN-FM Bath
WINR Binghampton
WBEN Buffalo
WVNC-FM Canton
WELM Elmira
WHCU Ithaca
WKSN Jamestown
WKNY Kingston
WIRD Lake Placid
WLPW-FM Lake Placid
WCBS New York
WMNS Olean
WGFB Plattsburgh
WHAM Rochester
WHEN Syracuse
WIBX Utica
WTNY Watertown

North Carolina
WZKY Albemarle
WSKY Asheville
WBT Charlotte
WFNC Fayetteville
WGLD Greensboro
WNCT Greenville
WLAS Jacksonville
WVOD-FM Manteo
WMNC Morganton
WPTF Raleigh-Durham
WMPM Smithfield
WTOE Spruce Pine
WAME Statesville
WMFD Wilmington

North Dakota
KDIX Dickinson
KFGO Fargo
KCNN Grand Forks
KQDJ Jamestown
KNDK-AM-FM Langdon
KCJB Minot
KTGO Tioga

Ohio
WNIR-FM Akron
WATH Athens
WQEL Bucyrus
WBEX Chillicothe
WCKY Cincinnati
WKNR Cleveland
WBNS Columbus
WING Dayton
WDOH-FM Delphos
WFOB Fostoria
WCIT Lima
WNDH-FM Napoleon
WLEC Sandusky
WBTC Urichsville
WKOV-FM Wellston
WKBN Youngstown

Oklahoma
KICM-FM Ardmore
KWON Bartlesville
KGWA Enid
KOMA-AM-FM Oklahoma City
KWOX-FM Oklahoma City
WWLS Oklahoma City
KQLL Tulsa
KTFX Tulsa

Oregon
KVAS Astoria
KBND Bend
KFAT-FM Corvallis
KLOO Corvallis
KUGN Eugene
KOHU Hermiston
KQFM-FM Hermiston
KAGO Klamath Falls
KMED Medford
KZUS-AM-FM Newport
KZUS-FM Newport
KBBR North Bend
KXL Portland
KRNR Roseburg
KMCQ-FM The Dalles

Pennsylvania
WAEB Allentown
WFBG Altoona
WPSE Erie
WCMB Harrisburg
WDAD Indiana
WOGL Philadelphia
KQV Pittsburgh
WPPA Pottsville
WGBI Scranton
WMAJ State College
WKOK Sunbury
WMBS Uniontown
WWPA Williamsport

Puerto Rico
WOSO San Juan

Rhode Island
WOON Woonsocket

South Carolina
WSCQ Columbia
WLMA Greenwood
WRNN-FM Myrtle Beach
WBFM-FM Seneca
WSNW Seneca
WSPA Spartanburg

South Dakota
KKAA Aberdeen
KCCR Pierre
KOTA Rapid City
KQKD Redfield
KWSN Sioux Falls
KWAT Watertown
WNAX Yankton

Tennessee
WDEF-AM-FM Chattanooga
WKRM Columbia
WHUB Cookeville
WIRJ Humboldt
WJCW Johnson City
WKIN Johnson City
WUTK Knoxville
WZLT-FM Lexington
WREC Memphis
WLAC Nashville
WDLY-FM Sevierville
WSEV Sevierville

Texas
KGNC Amarillo
KLBJ Austin
WTAW Bryan
KSIX Corpus Christi
KRLD Dallas
KTSM El Paso
KTRH Houston
KLAR Laredo
KFRO Longview
KFYO Lubbock
KURV McAllen-Brownsville
KYCX-FM Mexia
KRIL Odessa-Midland
WOAI San Antonio
KTEM Temple
KCMC Texarkana
KWFT Wichita Falls

Utah
KUTA Blanding
KSUB Cedar City
KSL Salt Lake City
KSGI St. George

Broadcasting & Cable Yearbook 1994

Major National Radio Networks

Vermont
WSNO Barre
WKVT Brattleboro
WFAD Middlebury

Virginia
WAXM-FM Big Stone Gap
WLSD Big Stone Gap
WFNR Blacksburg
WXLZ Castlewood
WINA Charlottesville
WDVA Danville
WEVA Emporia
WFLO-FM Farmville
WHAP Hopewell
WKWI-FM Kilmarnock
WLCC-FM Luray
WRAA Luray
WHEE Martinsville
WNIS Norfolk
WRVA Richmond
WFIR Roanoke
WTON-AM-FM Staunton
WQRA-FM Warrenton
WYVE Wytheville

Virgin Islands
WVWI St. Thomas

Washington
KBAM Longview
KSWW-FM Raymond
KIRO-AM-FM Seattle
KXLY Spokane
KREW Sunnyside
KIT Yakima

West Virginia
WCHS Charleston
WTBZ-FM Grafton
WMTD-FM Hinton
WEPM Martinsburg
WADC Parkersburg-Marietta
WYKM Rupert
WCWV-FM Summersville

Wisconsin
WHBY Appleton
WGEZ Beloit
WWIS-AM-FM Black River Falls
WNFL Green Bay
WIBA Madison
WOMT Manitowoc
WEMP Milwaukee
WTMJ Milwaukee
WRCO-AM-FM Richland Center
WCWC Ripon
WTCH Shawano
WJJQ-AM-FM Tomahawk
WXCO Wausau
WFHR Wisconsin Rapids

Wyoming
KTWO Casper
KRAE Cheyenne
KDLY-FM Lander
KOVE Lander
KROE Sheridan

Unistar Radio Networks

Headquarters: 1675 Broadway, 17th Fl., New York 10019. (212) 247-1600. FAX: (212) 247-0393.

Formats Division: 25060 West Ave. Stanford, Valencia, Calif. 91355. (805) 294-9000. FAX: (805) 294-9380.

News Bureau: 2000 N. 15th St., Suite 200, Arlington, Va. 22201. (703) 276-2900. FAX: (703) 276-2947.

Executives: Mel Karmazin, CEO; William Hogan, pres/gen mgr; Ed Salamon, pres progmg; Jim Higgins, sr VP sls; Kirk Stirland, sr VP affil rels; Rich Rieman, VP news & sports; Denise Oliver, VP progmg.

Legal Counsel: Martin Weisberg Esq., Snea & Gould, 1251 Ave. of the Americas, New York 10020-1193.

Sales Offices:

New York 10019: 1675 Broadway, 17th Fl. (212) 247-1600. Dick Kelley, exec VP.

Chicago 60611: 401 N. Michigan Ave., Suite 3100. (312) 836-8300. Ted S. Jakubiak, VP midwest sls.

Roanoke, Tex. 76262 (Dallas): 562 Timber Ridge Dr. (817) 430-8111. Cris Crisafulli.

Troy, Mich. 48084 (Detroit): 3221 W. Big Beaver, Suite 200A. (313) 649-0960. Dave A. Gneiser, VP Detroit sls.

Valencia, Calif. 91355: West Ave., Stanford. (805) 294-9000. Kevin J. Paradis, mgr western sls.

90's Country: Wkly one-hour series profiling contemporary country stars through interviews & music.

Academy of Country Music Awards Nominations Special: Annual special preceding the televised awards featuring interviews with top country stars hosted by Gene Wood.

The Beach Boys: Three-hour prod reuniting Beach Boys Brian Wilson, Mike Love, Carl Wilson, Bruce Johnston and Al Jardine.

Classic Artist Specials: Monthly three-hour restrospective featuring important artists & themes in rock history.

Countdown America: Three-hour prog hosted by Dick Clark showcasing the top 20 AC hits and the artists who created them.

Country Gold Saturday Night: Five-hour nationwide country oldies request prog with host Mike Fitzgerald.

Country Six Pack: Annual holiday weekend country series featuring six three-hour theme specials beginning on Memorial Day.

Dick Clark's Rock, Roll And Remember: Four hours of oldies hits and artists hosted by Dick Clark.

Last Night on Tonight: Weekday morning presentation of the best minute of Jay Leno's Tonight Show monologue from the previous night.

Memories of Elvis: Unistar's annual three-hour tribute reuniting Elvis' friends & collaborators.

Rock Quotes: The stars "drop by" Unistar affiliates each day with comments on rock classics in this svc designed for local customization.

Rockin' in the '70s: A look back at rock's classic decade one year at a time in a wkly 10-part summertime series of one-hour specials.

Solid Gold Saturday Night: America's original live Saturday night call-in request show featuring five hours of oldies music with a contemporary approach from host Bob Worthington.

Super Gold: Five-hour live weekend broadcast from Disney World hosted by Mike Harvey with a blend of oldies, requests and dedications.

Super Gold New Year's Eve: Miek Harvey hosts a special edition of his live oldies request show from Disney World from 7 pm to Midnight EST.

The Weekly Country Music Countdown: Host Chris Charles counts down the week's top 30 country hits and gets the behind-the-hits story from today's country artists in this three-hour special.

Unistar Radio Programming Division offers the following personality & talk shows:

Don & Mike: Each show features stunts, listener games and on-air antics.

The G. Gordon Liddy Show: An intelligent alternative to traditional talk radio, G. Gordon Liddy maneuvers on-air guests and listener phone calls into an entertaining midday show.

Imus in the Morning: Don Imus attracts the 25-54 demographics with popular guests, controversial topics & satire.

Unistar Radio Programming Division offers the following sports:

Inside the NFL: Based on the HBO series, hosts Len Dawson, Nick Buoniconti and Cris Collinsworth offer 30 minutes of gridiron action and analysis, with interviews, commentary and predictions, every weekend beginning mid-September.

This Is The NFL: Daily one-minute vignettes featuring the greatest moments from NFL games, hosted by Steve Sabol. Available mid-August through the Pro-Bowl.

Unistar Radio Programming Division offers the following news programs:

CNBC Business Radio: Business news reports twice an hour, 24-hours-a-day during the business week, plus weekend reports, an annual Tax tips series and rgnl Marketscan reports. Daily news insert material.

CNN Headline News: 24-hour audio from the CNN TV news channel, now available for an Adult 25-54 radio news format.

CNN Radio News: Top- and bottom-of-the-hour newscasts 24-hours-a-day, plus business, sports and lifestyle updates that blend smoothly with Unistar formats.

Unistar News: Top-and-bottom-of-the-hour newscasts 24 hours a day presented by anchors targeted to contemporary demographics. 18 newscall and 2 sportscall feeds each weekday, and 12 on the weekends, with sound from our own correspondents based in Washington as well as CNN's worldwide bureaus. Live special event coverage on a separate channel, plus daily health and business reports and an entertainment news feed.

United Press International

Headquarters: 1400 Eye St. N.W., Washington 20005. (202) 898-8000; (800) 777-5532.

Executives: L. Brewster Jackson, CEO; Steve Geimann, exec edit; I.J. Vidacovich, dir client rels; Mike Aulabaugh, mgr bcst svcs; Gene Puschel, natl sls mgr corporate & pub sector; L. Thomas Adams, VP sls (202) 898-8221; Peter T. Leach, VP mktg (202) 898-8200.

Editorial Executives: Vince Mannino, gen mgr news pictures (202) 898-8071; Jerry Kronenberg, bus news mgr (202) 898-8021; Ian Love, natl sports mgr (202) 898-8150; Andrea Varin, natl news mgr (202) 898-8015; Robert A. Martin, international editor; Tobin C. Beck, deputy editorial mgr (202) 898-8015.

UPI Radio Network

Headquarters: 1400 Eye St. N.W., Washington 20005. (202) 898-8111. FAX: (202) 898-8124.

Executive: Howard Dicus, gen mgr.

UPI Radio Noticias (Spanish Language Service): Armando Trull, news dir (202) 898-8148.

UPI Radio (English): Ron Colbert, news dir (202) 898-8111.

Northeastern Division: 2 Penn Plaza, (212) 560-1190.

Central Division: 203 N. Wabash, Suite 600, Chicago 60601. (312) 781-1617. Jay Sapir, bureau mgr.

Western Division: 361 W. 2nd St., 6th Fl., Los Angeles 90012. (213) 620-0977. Pat Nason, bureau mgr.

USA Radio Networks

Headquarters: 2290 Springlake Rd., Dallas 75234. (214) 484-3900; (800) 829-8111. FAX: (214) 243-3489.

Executives: Marlin Maddoux, pres; J.W. Brinkley, VP dev; John Clemens, news dir USA News; Grant Boone, sports dir USA Sports; Al Ross, natl dir USA affil rels; Mike Sala, dir USA natl sls; Chuck Roberts, dir opns; Tim Maddoux, dir USA engrg.

USA News: five minutes of news at the top of the hour, 24 hours a day.

USA Updates: two-minute news reports on the half hour, 24 hours a day.

USA Sports: 17 weekday & nine weekend three-minute sports reports on the 45-minute mark.

Point-of-View Talk Show: weekday natl telephone talk show. Ken Dowe Daily Magazine: weekday natl personality-driven talk show. Golden Age of Radio Theatre: old time radio at its best.

Svc available via SpaceNet 3R and through other nets via Satcom 1R, Galaxy 2, Galaxy 3, and Aurora 2 (Satcom C-5).

The USA Radio Network includes 1100 affiliated radio stations.

Westwood One Inc.

Headquarters: 9540 Washington Blvd., Culver City, Calif. 90232. (310) 204-5000. FAX: (310) 840-4052.

Offices:
New York 10019: 1700 Broadway. (212) 237-2500. FAX: (212) 581-4699.
Arlington, Va. 22202 (Washington): 1755 S. Jefferson Davis Hwy. (703) 413-8300. FAX: (703) 413-8445.
Chicago 60601: 111 E. Wacker Dr., Suite 1321. (312) 938-0222.
Dallas 75231: 10000 N. Central Expy., Suite 1438. (214) 373-0022.
Troy, Mich. 48084 (Detroit): 3250 W. Big Beaver, Suite 125. (810) 649-6300.
Toronto M5V 1W5: 260 Richmond St. W., Suite 400. (416) 597-8529.

Executives: Norman J. Pattiz, chmn/CEO; Bruce Kanter, exec VP/CFO; Gregory P. Batusic, pres radio net div; Jack B. Clements, VP net opns; Thomas C.N. Evans, VP rsch; Eric R. Weiss, VP bus & legal affrs; Gary J. Yusko, VP finance; Laurie Peters, pub rels dir.

Advertiser Sales Divisions: William M. Rosalie, exec VP/dir natl sls; Frank Leoce, VP/dir sls eastern rgn; Blaise Leonardi, VP/dir sls eastern rgn; Jack Patterson, VP/dir sls Detroit rgn; Richard Ziltz, VP/dir sls Midwest rgn; Trish Healy, dir sls, planning & admin; Ira Berger, VP/dir sls western & southwestern.

Westwood One Radio Network: Thomas A. Ferro, exec VP/gen mgr; Craig Whetstine, VP/dir affil rels; Andrew Denemark, dir progmg; Bill Stolier, dir international affil rels; Rob Tonkin, dir artist rels, mktg & prom; Dwight Kuhlman, dir talent & music mktg.

NBC Radio Network: Jack B. Clements, VP net opns; George Barber, VP stn rels; Margaret M. Solomon, VP opns; Barton J. Tessler, VP news; Larry Michael, dir sports.

NBC's The Source: George Barber, VP affil rels; Andrew J. Denemark, prog dir; Dia Stein, mgr progmg.

NBC's Talknet: Margaret M. Solomon, VP opns; George Barber, VP stn rels.

Mutual Broadcasting System Inc.

Headquarters: 1755 S. Jefferson Davis Hwy., Arlington, Va. 22202. (703) 685-2000. FAX: (703) 685-2145.

Executives: Jack B. Clements, pres; George Barber, VP stn rels; Margaret M. Solomon, VP opns; Barton J. Tessler, VP news; Larry Michael, sports dir.

Mutual Advisory Board: Russ Withers (chmn), WMIX Mt. Vernon, Ill.; Bob Pricer (vice chmn), WCLT Newark, Ohio; Phil Nolan (treas), KAUS Austin, Minn.; Rod Burnham, WGET Gettysburg, Pa.; C.J. Jones, Jones Eastern Radio, Wilmington, N.C.; Tom Kennedy, WNOE New Orleans; Dennis Rumsey, WLKM-AM-FM Three Rivers, Mich.; Charles Wilson, KBOI Boise, Idaho; Catherine Meloy, WGMS Rockville, Md.

NBC Radio Network

Headquarters: 1755 S. Jefferson Davis Hwy., Arlington, Va. 22202. (703) 685-2000. FAX: (703) 685-2145.

Executives: Jack B. Clements, VP net opns; George Barber, VP stn rels; Barton J. Tessler, VP news; Margaret M. Solomon, VP opns; Larry Michael, dir sports.

NBC Affiliate Executive Committee: Paul Hedberg (chmn), Hedberg Broadcasting Group; Allan Land (vice chmn), WHIZ Zanesville, Ohio; Dennis Curley (sec/treas), WCXU Caribou, Me.; Roy Shapiro, KYW Philadelphia; Ray Saadi, KHOM Houma, La.; Barbara Beddor, KJRB Spokane, Wash.; Michael Shott, Adventure Communications, Bluefield, W.V.; John Wilks, KNWZ Palm Desert, Calif.; Dick Rakovan, WGAY/WRC Silver Spring, Md.

NBC's The Source: Thomas Ferro, VP/gen mgr; Andrew J. Denemark, prog dir; Dia Stein, mgr progmg.

NBC's Talknet: Margaret M. Solomon, VP opns.

Mutual Broadcasting System

Alabama
WATV Birmingham
WJOX Birmingham
WCKO-FM Carrolton
WXAL Demopolis
WZNJ-FM Demopolis
WOOF-FM Dothan
WTVY-FM Dothan
WJLD Fairfield
WABF Fairhope
WHEP Foley
WJBB Haleyville
WTKI Huntsville
WAVH-FM Mobile
WKRG Mobile
WLWI-FM Montgomery
WLAY-AM-FM Muscle Shoals
WJHO Opelika
WGSY-FM Phenix City
WPID Piedmont
WWIC Scottsboro
WMRK Selma
WFEB Sylacauga
WTBF Troy
WTSK Tuscaloosa

Alaska
KYAK Anchorage
KIAK Fairbanks

Arizona
KCUZ Clifton
KCKY Coolidge
KNNS Glendale
KDJI Holbrook
KTAR Phoenix
KONC-FM Sun City
KFMM-FM Thatcher
KNST Tucson
KRQQ-Fm Tucscon

Arkansas
KAMD Camden
KWEH-FM Camden
KFCA Conway
KTOD-FM Conway
KFFA Helena
KFTH-FM Marion

California
KJAZ-FM Alameda
KPAY Chico
KRGO Fowler
KHSJ Hemet
KVLI Lake Isabella
KNTI-FM Lakeport
KGFJ Los Angeles
KMMT-FM Mammoth Lakes
KATM-FM Modesto
KOCN-FM Pacific Grove
KNWZ Palm Desert
KPRL Paso Robles
KRDX Rancho Cordova
KQMS Redding
KSHA-FM Redding
KPRO Riverside
KGIL San Fernando
KFRC San Francisco
KZOZ-FM San Luis Obispo
KJAX Stockton
KSUE-AM-FM Susanville
KFIY Tulare
KMIX-AM-FM Turlock

Canada
CKLW Windsor

Colorado
KHOW-AM-FM Denver
KIUP Durango
KLMR Lamar
KLOV Loveland
KJCO-FM Yuma

Connecticut
WBIS Bristol
WLAD Danbury
WSNG Torrington

Delaware
WNRK Newark
WILM Wilmington

District of Columbia
WGMS-FM Washington
WYCB Washngton

Florida
WWBF Bartow
WDUV-FM Bradenton
WOLZ-FM Fort Myers
WJAX Jacksonville
WOKV Jacksonville
WSVE Jacksonville
WKWF Key West
WGGD Melbourne
WIOD Miami
WXBM-FM Milton

Major National Radio Networks

WGUL-FM New Port Richey
WSBB New Smyrna Beach
WWNZ Orlando
WPBR Palm Beach
WTKN Pinellas Park
WKXY Sarasota
WSUN St. Petersburg

Georgia
WJIZ-FM Albany
WJYZ Albany
WAOK Atlanta
WGST Atlanta
WJYA Buford
WLKQ-FM Buford
WPBE Conyers
WBLJ Dalton
WBKZ Jefferson
WPEH-AM-FM Louisville
WAYS-FM Macon
WDDO Macon
WMLS Monroe
WMTM-FM Moultrie
WCOH Newnan
WPGA-AM-FM Perry
WSGC-FM Ringold
WKCX-FM Rome
WEAS-FM Savannah
WJAT-FM Swainsboro
WTWA Thomson
WAYX-FM Waycross
WLET Toccoa
WZLI-FM Toccoa

Hawaii
KUAI Eleele
KHVH Honolulu
KMVI Wailuku Maui
KDEO-FM Waipahu

Idaho
KBOI Boise
KQFC-FM Boise
KSEI-AM-FM Pocatello
KBBK Rupert
KNAQ-FM Rupert

Illinois
WIBV Belleville
WJJD Chicago
WJMK-FM Chicago
WPNT-FM Chicago
WVON Chicago
WESL East St. Louis
WRMN Elgin
WAAG-FM Galesburg
WGIL Galesburg
WJPF Herrin
WAKO-AM-FM Lawrenceville
WSMI Litchfield
WCFL-FM Morris
WCSJ Morris
WTAZ-FM Morton
WMIX-AM-FM Mount Vernon
WIKK-FM Newton
WIRL Peoria
WZOE-FM Princeton
WTAX Springfield
WKMQ-FM Winnebago

Indiana
WRBI-FM Batesville
WHON Centerville
WCSI Columbus
WKKG-FM Columbus
WWJY-FM Crown Point
WNJY-FM Delphi
WCMR Elkhart
WFRN-FM Elkhart
WBDC-FM Huntingburg
WNDE Indianapolis
WBTU-FM Kendallville
WBTO Linton
WQTY-FM Linton
WMDH-FM New Castle
WPGW-AM-FM Portland
WAMJ South Bend
WTHI-AM-FM Terre Haute
WAYT Wabash

Iowa
WMT-AM-FM Cedar Rapids
KROS Clinton
KOKX-AM-FM Keokuk
KDLS-AM-FM Perry
KMNS Sioux City
KUOO-FM Spirit Lake
KWLO Waterloo

Kansas
KLLS-FM Augusta
KQLS-FM Colby
KXXX Colby
KEGS-FM Emporia
KIND-AM-FM Independence
KNHN Kansas City
KSLS-FM Liberal
KYUU Liberal
KMAN Manhattan
KQNK Norton
KFNF-FM Oberlin
KGLS-FM Pratt
KWLS Pratt
KYEZ-FM Salina
KTOP Topeka
KQAM Wichita

Kentucky
WLBN Lebanon
WLSK-FM Lebanon
WLSY Louisville
WFTM Maysville
WDDJ-FM Paducah
WPAD Paducah
WLSI Pikeville
WSEK-FM Somerset
WLKS West Liberty

Louisiana
WKJN-FM Hammond
KVOL-FM Lafayette
KVVP-FM Leesville
KASO-AM-FM Minden
WBOK New Orleans
WNOE-AM-FM New Orleans
KVOL Opelousas
KQLD-FM Pt. Sulphur
KWKH-AM-FM Shreveport
WSLA Slidell
KLAA-FM Tioga

Maryland
WBAL Baltimore
WITH Baltimore
WLIF-FM Baltimore
WWIN Baltimore
WCTR Chestertown
WARX-FM Hagerstown
WETT Ocean City

Massachusetts
WHDH Boston
WRKO Boston
WGAW Gardner
WBRK Pittsfield
WMAS Springfield

Mexico
XTRA Tijuana

Michigan
WLEN-FM Adrian
WBCM-FM Boyne City
WMTG Dearborn
WGPR-FM Detroit
WJZZ-FM Detroit
WQBH Detroit
WGRY Grayling
WCXT-FM Hart
WHTC Holland
WKEZ-FM Holland
WIMI-FM Ironwood
WSMA Marine City
WFXD-FM Marquette
WCEN Mount Pleasant
WAOR-FM Niles
WNIL Niles
WGER-FM Saginaw
WSDS Salem
WKNW Sault Ste. Marie
WSTD Standish
WLKM-AM-FM Three Rivers
WTCM-AM-FM Traverse City
WEFG-AM-FM Whitehall

Minnesota
KAUS-FM Austin
KBHP-FM Bemidji
WJJY-FM Brainerd
KRWC Buffalo
KROX Crookston
WELY Ely
KBRF Fergus Falls
KGHS International Falls
KSDM-FM International Falls
KEYL Long Prairie
KEEZ-FM Mankato

KBBJ-FM Marshall
KFAN Minneapolis
KOLV-FM Olivia
KDIO Ortonville
KFIL-AM-FM Preston
KOLM Rochester
KWWK-FM Rochester
KMSR-FM Sauk Center
KXAX-FM St. James
WCDK-FM Virginia
WHLB Virginia
KOWO-AM-FM Waseca

Mississippi
WFFF-AM-FM Columbia
WKCU Corinth
WXRZ-FM Corinth
WZMP-FM Marion

Missouri
KRZK-FM Branson
KGMO-FM Cape Girardeau
KCRV Caruthersville
KLOW-FM Caruthersville
KCHR Charleston
KFMO Flat River
KMBZ Kansas City
KIRX Kirksville
KLWT-AM-FM Lebanon
KWWR-FM Mexico
KXEO Mexico
KZNN-FM Rolla
KUSA St. Louis
KWTO Springfield
KOKO Warrensburg

Montana
KGHL Billings
KMMS Bozeman
KXTL Butte
KAAK-FM Great Falls
KOFI Kalispell
KMSO-FM Missoula
KGCH-FM Sidney
KGCX Sidney

Nebraska
KKAR Bellevue
KSDZ-FM Gordon
KMMJ Grand Island
KLIN Lincoln
KNCY-AM-FM Nebraska City
KEXL-FM Norfolk
WJAG Norfolk
KODY North Platte
KNEB Scottsbluff
KRFS-AM-FM Superior

Nevada
KNUU Las Vegas
KOH Reno
KROW Reno

New Hampshire
WNTK-FM Lebanon
WSMN Nashua
WNTK Newport

New Jersey
WSNJ-AM-FM Bridgeton
WSUS-FM Franklin

New Mexico
KPSA Almogordo
KCCC Carlsbad
KLMX Clayton
KWKA Clovis
KGAK Gallup
KKEL Hobbs
KASK-FM Las Cruces
KNYN-FM Santa Fe

New York
WHRL-FM Albany
WPTR Albany
WBEN Buffalo
WSCM Cobleskill
WCLI Corning
WZKZ-FM Corning
WDNY Dansville
WFLR-AM-FM Dundee
WBZA Glens Falls
WHUC Hudson
WRVW-FM Hudson
WHVW Hyde Park
WXRL Lancaster
WYNY-FM Lake Success
WEVD New York
WNEW New York

Major National Radio Networks

WOR New York
WWRL New York
WEBO Oswego
WGES-FM Oswego
WSGO Oswego
WIRY Plattsburgh
WADR Remsen
WRNY Rome
WTRY-FM Rotterdam
WLNG-AM-FM Sag Harbor
WCDO-AM-FM Sidney
WSYR Syracuse
WTRY Troy
WIBX Utica
WTNY Watertown
WJQZ-FM Wellsville

North Carolina
WKJV Asheville
WWNC Asheville
WBBB Burlington
WPCM-FM Burlington
WCHL Chapel Hill
WCSL Cherryville
WRSF-FM Columbia
WTIK Durham
WGNC Gastonia
WKTC-FM Goldsboro
WKOO-FM Jacksonville
WNNC Newton
WKIX Raleigh
WSTP Salisbury
WOHS Shelby
WIOZ-FM Southern Pines
WTLK Taylorsville
WTHP-FM Thomasville
WVOT Wilson
WSJS Winston-Salem
WMQX-AM-FM Winston-Salem
WTQR-FM Winston-Salem

North Dakota
KDLR Devils Lake

Ohio
WAKR Akron
WNCO-AM-FM Ashland
WXTQ-FM Athens
WWKC-FM Caldwell
WILE Cambridge
WKKJ-FM Chillicothe
WSAI Cincinnati
WERE Cleveland
WNCX-FM Cleveland
WMNI Columbus
WONW Defiance
WMQH Hamilton
WMRN-AM Marion
WCLT-AM-FM Newark
WLEC Sandusky
WMVR-AM-FM Sidney
WBLY Springfield
WSTV Steubenville
WKBN Youngstown

Oklahoma
KEYB-FM Altus
KXLS-FM Alva
KFXI-FM Marlow
KMCO-FM McAlester
KQLL-FM Owasso
WBBZ Ponca City
KSPI Stillwater

Oregon
KUGN-AM-FM Eugene
KUIK Hillsboro
KIHR Hood River
KSXM-FM Pendleton
KEX Portland
KKEY Portland
KIJK-FM Prineville
KRCO Prineville
KWBY Woodburn

Pennsylvania
WAEB Allentown
WRAX-FM Bedford
WBUT Butler
WLER-FM Butler
WFRA Franklin
WGET Gettysburg
WGTY-FM Gettysburg
WHJB Greensburg
WADV Lebanon
WMLP Milton
WIP Philadelphia
WTAE Pittsburgh

WKXU-FM Portage
WZGO Portage
WPAM Pottsville
WDSN-FM Reynoldsville
WTIV Titusville
WJPA Washington
WAYZ-FM Waynesboro
WCHE West Chester
WILK Wilkes-Barre

Rhode Island
WICE Pawtucket

South Carolina
WKXC-FM Aiken
WAIM Anderson
WBAW-AM-FM Barnwell
WLOW-FM Bluffton
WGCD Chester
WUJM-FM Goose Creek
WGSW Greenwood
WBHC-AM-FM Hampton
WYAK-FM Surfside Beach

South Dakota
KZMX-AM-FM Hot Springs
KORN Mitchell
KXRB Sioux Falls
KRCS-FM Sturgis
KKYA-FM Yankton
KYNT Yankton

Tennessee
WATX Algood
WGOW Chattanooga
WALV-FM Cleveland
WBAC Cleveland
WEKR Fayetteville
WHJM Knoxville
WWTN-FM Manchester
WWYN-FM McKenzie
WAMB Nashville

Texas
KNTS Abilene
KRUN-AM-FM Ballinger
KMIL Cameron
KCTX Childress
KCAR Clarksville
KSTA-AM-FM Coleman
KTSR-FM College Station
WTAW College Station
KSIX Corpus Christi
KAAM Dallas
KJZY-FM Denton
KEAS-AM-FM Eastland
KULP El Campo
KTSM El Paso
KAWA Floydada
KFLL-FM Floydada
KEES Gladewater
KTRH Houston
KLLL-AM-FM Lubbock
KJCS-FM Nacogdoches
KLIS-FM Palestine
KWED Seguin
KIKZ Seminole
KSEM-FM Seminole
KJIM Sherman
KCMC Texarkana
KSEV Tomball
KYZS Tyler
KISX-FM Whitehouse

Utah
KSOS-FM Brigham
KALL Salt Lake City
KSGI St. George

Vermont
WLFE-FM St. Albans
WWSR St. Albans

Virginia
WODY Bassett
WPKZ-FM Elkton
WQPO-FM Harrisonburg
WSVA Harrisonburg
WAGE Leesburg
WOLD-AM-FM Marion
WNRV Narrows
WNIS Norfolk
WPCE Portsmouth
WRNL-FM Richmond
WRIS Roanoke
WJLM-FM Salem

Washington
KLKI Anacortes
KPUG Bellingham
KOZI-AM-FM Chelan
KCLK-AM-FM Clarkston
KCLX Colfax
KYSN-FM East Wenatchee
KTCR Kennewick
KWIQ-FM Moses Lake
KWIQ-AM Moses Lake North
KQEU Olympia
KZXR-FM Prosser
KWNC Quincy
KOTY-FM Richland
KING Seattle
KIRO Seattle
KVI Seattle
KYXE Selah
KXLY-AM-FM Spokane

West Virginia
WJLS-AM-FM Beckley
WHLX-FM Bethlehem
WCHS Charleston
WKKW-FM Clarksburg
WKMM-FM Kingwood
WRNR Martinsburg
WRON-AM-FM Ronceverte
WBTH Williamson
WXCC-FM Williamson

Wisconsin
WJLW-FM De Pere
WRDN-AM-FM Durand
KFIZ Fond du Lac
WAUN-FM Kewaunee
WMZK-FM Merrill
WNOV Milwaukee
WOKY Milwaukee
WCOW-FM Sparta
WKLJ Sparta

Wyoming
KRAE Cheyenne
KODI Cody
KUGR Green River
KTRZ-FM Riverton
KTHE Thermopolis
KKLX-FM Worland
KWOR Worland

NBC Radio Network

Alabama
WSTH-FM Alexander City
WAVU Albertville
WQSB-FM Albertville
WKYD Andalusia
WHMA-FM Anniston
WASZ-FM Ashland
WAGG Birmingham
WAPI Birmingham
WENN-FM Birmingham
WGAD Gadsden
WQZK-FM Greenville
WAHR-FM Huntsville
WNPT-FM Linden
WZZX Lineville
WGOK Mobile
WYNI Monroeville
WLWI Montgomery
WRSM Sumiton
WNPT Tuscaloosa
WVNA-AM-FM Tuscumbia
WVSA Vernon
WYLS York

Alaska
KMBQ-FM Wasilla

American Samoa
WVUV Pago Pago

Arizona
KFYI Phoenix
KTNN Window Rock

Arkansas
KFCA Conway
KTOD-FM Conway
KAYZ-FM El Dorado
KELD El Dorado
KFAY Farmington
KWXI Glenwood
KHOZ-AM-FM Harrison
KBIS Little Rock
KPFM-FM Mountain Home

Major National Radio Networks

KDRS Paragould
KLQZ-FM Paragould
KWYN Wynne

California
KWST-FM Brawley
KLAU Capitola
KXDC-FM Carmel
KFLI Eureka
KMJ Fresno
KXBX-AM-FM Lakeport
KHJJ Lancaster
KLAC Los Angeles
KMPC Los Angeles
KTRB Modesto
KIDD Monterey
KBAI Morro Bay
KNWZ Palm Desert
KIOO-FM Porterville
KTIP Porterville
KSAC Sacramento
KRSO San Bernardino
KSDO San Diego
KNBR San Francisco
KSRO Santa Rosa
KUBA Yuba City

Canada
CKLW-AM-FM Windsor

Colorado
KYBG Aurora
KYBG-FM Castle Rock
KIIX Fort Collins
KQIL Grand Junction
KFKA Greeley
KRQS-FM Pagosa Springs
KGHF Pueblo

Connecticut
WREF Ridgefield

Delaware
WRKE-FM Ocean View

District of Columbia
WWRC Washington

Florida
WWOJ-FM Avon Park
WAFC-FM Clewiston
WZEP De Funiak Springs
WMMK-FM Destin
WIRA Fort Pierce
WMLO-FM Havana
WNZS Jacksonville
WDSR Lake City
WNFB-FM Lake City
WWTK Lake Placid
WONN Lakeland
WLBE Leesburg
WTOT Marianna
WQAM Miami
WPSO New Port Richey
WWBH New Smyrna Beach
WTMC Ocala
WOKC-AM-FM Okeechobee
WELE Ormond Beach
WPLK Palatka
WPAP-FM Panama City
WNFK-FM Perry
WPRY Perry
WGGO-FM Silver Springs
WSOS-FM St. Augustine
WTMP Tampa
WCWB-FM Trenton
WAMR Venice
WCTQ-FM Venice
WPCV-FM Winter Haven
WPAS Zephyrhills

Georgia
WNGC-FM Athens
WIGO Atlanta
WQXI Atlanta
WTUF-FM Boston
WHJX-FM Brunswick
WGRA Cairo
WEBS Calhoun
WPPI Carrollton
WCHM Clarksville
WRWH Cleveland
WVMG-AM-FM Cochran
WSTH Columbus
WKKN-FM Cordele
WOKA-AM-FM Douglas
WUFF-AM-FM Eastman
WBHB Fitzgerald
WOKF-FM Folkston

WKIG-AM-FM Glennville
WPLO Grayson
WHIE Griffin
WVOH-AM-FM Hazlehurst
WBTY-FM Homerville
WQCH Lafayette
WEGC-FM Leesburg
WBBT Lyons
WDEN-AM-FM Macon
WNEX Macon
WPEZ-FM Macon
WVFJ-FM Manchester
WDAX-AM-FM McRae
WLRR-FM Milledgeville
WNEA Newnan
WSFB Quitman
WTSH-FM Rockmart
WZOT Rockmart
WTSH-AM Rome
WLMX-FM Rossville
WJCL-FM Savannah
WSFT Thomaston
WTHO-FM Thomson
WADX Trenton
WAAC-FM Valdosta
WBGA-FM Waycross

Hawaii
KIPA Hilo
KHVH Honolulu

Idaho
KLCE-FM Blackfoot
KIDO Boise
KVNI Couer D'Alene
KKCH-FM Hayden

Illinois
KSGM Chester
WMAQ Chicago
WVON Chicago
WIAI-FM Danville
WFPS-FM Freeport
WEBQ Harrisburg
WMCW Harvard
WKKX-FM Jerseyville
WLPO LaSalle
WDDD-FM Marion
WRBT-FM Mt. Carmel
WYER Mt. Carmel
WGEM-AM-FM Quincy
WRWC-FM Rockton
WJBD-AM-FM Salem
WMAY Springfield

Indiana
WTRC Elkhart
WWWO-FM Hartford City
WIBC Indianapolis
WASK Lafayette
WMRI-FM Marion
WGTC-FM New Castle
WMDH-AM-FM New Castle
WAXI-FM Rockville
WAMW-AM-FM Washington

Iowa
KCHA-AM-FM Charles City
WOC Davenport
WHO Des Moines
KIOW-FM Forest City
KBKB-AM-FM Fort Madison
KCZY-FM Osage
KLEE Ottumwa
KSCJ Sioux City
KUOO-FM Spirit Lake
KWLO Waterloo

Kansas
KSOK Arkansas City
KERE Atchison
KAYS Hays
KWBW Hutchinson
KKAN Phillipsburg
KQMA-FM Phillipsburg
KMAJ-AM-FM Topeka
KNSS Wichita

Kentucky
WMDJ-FM Allen
WRVC-FM Ashland
WCBL-AM-FM Benton
WCTT Corbin
WLXG Lexington
WMDJ Martin

WYMC Mayfield
WOMI Owensboro
WKLW Paintsville
WBLG-FM Smith Grove

Louisiana
WJBO Baton Rouge
WASO Covington
WFPR Hammond
KHOM-FM Houma
KJEF-AM-FM Jennings
KVOL Lafayette
WTIX New Orleans
KVOL-FM Opelousas
KOKA Shreveport
KTIB Thibodaux
KYEA-FM West Monroe

Maine
WCXU-FM Caribou
WCXX Madawaska
WGAN Portland

Maryland
WNAV Annapolis
WCAO Baltimore
WALI Cumberland
WPGC Morningside
WMYJ-FM Pocomoke City
WYII-FM Williamsport

Massachusetts
WHDH Boston
WBSM New Bedford
WCTK-FM New Bedford
WHMP Northampton
WXTK-FM West Yarmouth
WTAG Worcester

Michigan
WAAM Ann Arbor
WBCK Battle Creek
WMTG Dearborn
WGPR-FM Detroit
WQBH Detroit
WOOD Grand Rapids
WIKB-AM-FM Iron River
WJPD-AM-FM Ishpeming
WJIM Lansing
WMTE-AM-FM Manistee
WDZR-FM Mt. Clemens
WUPQ-FM Newberry
WUPY-FM Ontonagon
WHAK Rogers City
WSGW Saginaw
WTLZ-FM Saginaw
WMKC-FM St. Ignace
WSJM St. Joseph
WKJC-FM Tawas City
WCHB Taylor

Minnesota
KXRA Alexandria
KAUS-AM-FM Austin
KLIZ Brainerd
WLKX-FM Forest Lake
WYRQ-FM Little Falls
KKOK-FM Morris
KMRS Morris
KNUJ New Ulm
KYMN Northfield
KDKK-FM Park Rapids
KPRM Park Rapids
KWEB Rochester
KSTP St. Paul
KQIC-FM Willmar
KWOA Worthington

Mississippi
WJWF-FM Artesia
WMBC-FM Columbus
WZQA-FM Flowood
WFOR Hattiesburg
WHER-FM Hattiesburg
WEEZ-FM Heidelburg
WOAD Jackson
WAML Laurel
WAPF McComb
WRQO-FM Monticello
WMIS Natchez
WWZD-FM New Albany
WWSL-FM Philadelphia
WPMX Tupelo

Missouri
KFUO-FM Clayton
KESM-AM-FM El Dorado Springs
KJCF Festus
KJMO-FM Jefferson City

Broadcasting & Cable Yearbook 1994
G-46

Major National Radio Networks

KMBZ Kansas City
KLID Poplar Bluff
KTXR Springfield
KJPW-AM-FM Waynesville

Montana
KBLG Billings
KRKX-FM Billings
KBLL-FM Helena
KBBZ-FM Kalispell
KDXT-FM Missoula
KJJR Whitefish

Nebraska
KCNI Broken Bow
KSYZ-FM Grand Island
KRVN-FM Lexington
KXNP-FM North Platte
KFAB Omaha
KSUX-FM Winnebago
KAWL York
KTMX-FM York

Nevada
KRRI-FM Boulder
KELY Ely
KKMR-FM Sparks
KSEL-AM-FM Sparks

New Hampshire
WDCR Hanover
WPNH-AM-FM Plymouth

New Jersey
WMID Atlantic City
WNNJ Newton

New Mexico
KQEO Albuquerque
KMGA-FM Albuquerque
KPER-FM Hobbs
KGRT-AM-FM Las Cruces
KSEL-AM-FM Portales

New York
WHRL-FM Albany
WNBF Binghamton
WECK Cheektowaga
WENY Elmira
WENT Gloversville
WGIX-FM Gouverneur
WIGS Gouverneur
WENU-FM Hudson Falls
WVBR-FM Ithaca
WGHQ Kingston
WYNY-FM Lake Success
WICY Malone
WSUL-FM Monticello
WEVD New York
WFAN New York
WNEW New York
WWRL New York
WCHN Norwich
WSLB Ogdensburg
WQBK Rensselaer
WHAM Rochester
WSTL South Glens Falls
WSYR Syracuse
WRUN Utica
WATN Watertown
WLSV Wellsville

North Carolina
WQNX Aberdeen
WCGC Belmont
WVBS-FM Burgaw
WKYK Burnsville
WDNC Durham
WLOE Eden
WKJX-FM Elizabeth City
WJNC Jacksonville
WKMT Kings Mountain
WKGK-FM Kinston
WAAV Leland
WLON Lincolnton
WAGR Lumberton
WJSK-FM Lumberton
WMYN Mayodan
WDEX Monroe
WKRK Murphy
WKBC North Wilkesboro
WCBQ Oxford
WPNC-AM-FM Plymouth
WAYN Rockingham
WSIC Statesville
WSVM Valdese
WSJS Winston-Salem

North Dakota
KMBR Bismarck
KQDY-FM Bismarck
KPOK Bowman
WDAY Fargo
KRRZ Minot

Ohio
WATH Athens
WCHI Chillicothe
WCKY Cincinnati
WERE Cleveland
WHK Cleveland
WMJI-FM Cleveland
WMNI Columbus
WCIT Lima
WIOI New Boston
WZIO-FM South Webster
WLQR-FM Toledo
WSPD Toledo
WYNT-FM Upper Sandusky
WKBN Youngstown
WHIZ-AM-FM Zanesville

Oklahoma
KSWO Lawton
KTMC-AM-FM McAlester
KPRW Oklahoma City
KRAD Perry
KWOX-FM Woodward

Oregon
KYTT-FM Coos Bay
KYKN Keizer
KUMA Pendleton
KDOV Phoenix

Pennsylvania
WESB Bradford
WCHA Chambersburg
WLEM Emporium
WQKY-FM Emporium
WLKK Erie
WHVR Hanover
WJAC Johnstown
WKYE-FM Johnstown
WJUN Mexico
WOYL Oil City
WRJS-FM Oil City
KYW Philadelphia
WDAS Philadelphia
WPHB-AM-FM Philipsburg
KDKA Pittsburgh
WARM Scranton
WRAK-AM-FM Williamsport

Rhode Island
WHJJ Providence

South Carolina
WANS Anderson
WTMA Charleston
WVOC Columbia
WEAC Gaffney
WUJM-FM Goose Creek
WFBC-AM-FM Greenville
WCRS Greenwood
WHHR Hilton Head
WAGL Lancaster
WKSY-FM Marion
WAJY-FM New Ellenton
WORD Spartanburg
WSSC Sumter
WGOG-AM-FM Walhalla

South Dakota
KGIM Aberdeen
KBRK Brookings
KIQK-FM Rapid City
KTOQ Rapid City

Tennessee
WJTZ Blountville
WCLE Cleveland
WUSY-FM Cleveland
WGSQ-FM Cookeville
WZYX Cowan
WUSJ-FM Elizabethtown
WGRV Greenville
WQQK-FM Hendersonville
WTNV-FM Jackson
WHJM Knoxville
WLIV Livingston
WCMT Martin
KJMS-FM Memphis
WEGR-FM Memphis
WLOK Memphis
WMC Memphis
WREC Memphis
WYNU-FM Milan
WSM-AM-FM Nashville
WXVO-FM Oliver Springs

Texas
KROO-FM Breckenridge
KOXE-FM Brownwood
KMXR-FM Corpus Christi
KLIF Dallas
KCOH Houston
KMMX-FM Lamesa
KKCL-FM Lorenzo
KCRS Midland
KSEV Tomball
KLLF Wichita Falls

Utah
KTKK Salt Lake City

Vermont
WTSA-AM-FM Brattleboro
WSYB Rutland

Virginia
WABN-AM-FM Abingdon
WDIC Clintwood
WKRE Exmore
WLRV Lebanon
WMEV-FM Marion
WMVA Martinsville
WNIS Norfolk
WSWV-AM-FM Pennington Gap
WXGI Richmond
WSLC Roanoke
WXZY-FM Ruckersville
WKDW Staunton
WUSQ-FM Winchester

Virgin Islands
WSTA St. Thomas

Washington
KXRO Aberdeen
KBFW Bellingham
KELA Centralia
KLOG Kelso
KQQQ Pullman
KALE Richland
KJR Seattle
KJRB Spokane
KMWX Yakima

West Virginia
WHAJ-FM Bluefield
WHIS Bluefield
WTCS Fairmont
WTKZ Huntington
WHJC Matewan
WLZT-FM Miami
WCLG Morgantown
WRRR-FM St. Mary's
WOVK-FM Wheeling
WWVA Wheeling

Wisconsin
WCLO Janesville
WJVL-FM Janesville
WKFX-FM Kaukauna
WIZM La Crosse
WTDY Madison
WMAM Marinette
WFMR-FM Menomonee Falls
WMEQ Menomonie
WMNE Menomonie
WJMT Merrill
WEMP Milwaukee
WNOV Milwaukee
WTMJ Milwaukee
WPKR-FM Omro
WOSH Oshkosh
WKPL-FM Platteville
WTOQ Platteville
WRJN Racine
WKKV-AM-FM Racine
WSPO Stevens Point
WDSM Superior
WTRW Two Rivers
WEZW-FM Wauwatosa

Wyoming
KLGT-FM Buffalo
KTRS-FM Casper
KRQU-FM Laramie

Broadcasting & Cable Yearbook 1994
G-47

Public Broadcasting - Radio

American Public Radio

American Public Radio will change its name to Public Radio International, as of July 1994.

Headquarters: 100 N. 6th St., Suite 900A, Minneapolis 55403. (612) 338-5000. FAX: (612) 330-9222.

Executives: Stephen Salyer, pres/CEO; Bruce Theriault, sr VP/dir net opns; Phelps S. Hawkins, sr VP/dir news & special events; Melinda Ward, sr VP/dir cultural progmg & dev; Timothy J. Engel, VP/dir finance & admin.; Douglas J. Eichten, VP/dir dev.

Directors: H. Brewster Atwater Jr., chmn/CEO General Mills Inc., Minneapolis; Dr. Joan Abrahamson, pres The Jefferson Institute, Los Angeles; William M. Dietel, vice chmn American Public Radio, Flint Hill, Va.; Dr. Claire Gaudiani, pres Connecticut College, New London, Conn.; Roger L. Hale, pres/CEO Tennant Co., Minneapolis; Susan Harmon, VP radio & admin North Texas Public Broadcasting, Dallas; S. Roger Horchow, Dallas; William H. Kling, pres Minnesota Public Radio, St. Paul, Minn.; Charles R. Longsworth, chmn The Colonial Williamsburg Foundation, Williamsburg, Va.; Jon B. Lovelace, chmn of bd Capital Research and Management Co., Los Angeles; William I. Miller, chmn Irwin Financial Corp., Columbus, Ind., & chmn American Public Radio; James Newton, professor Univ. of California-Irvine; Marita Rivero, VP/radio mgr WGBH Educational Foundation, Boston; Judith Rubin, commissioner Mayor's Commission on Protocol, City of New York; Stephen L. Salyer, pres/CEO American Public Radio, Minneapolis; Martin E. Segal, chmn emeritus Martin E. Segal Co., New York; Wallace Smith, pres USC Radio, & gen mgr. KUSC-FM, Los Angeles; John Tusa, pres Wolfson College, Cambridge, England.

American Public Radio (APR) distributes more hours of news, variety & mus progmg than any other public radio distributor. APR is a network that develops, funds, acquires & distributes public radio progmg from station-based, independent & international producers. APR has 476 affiliate stations nationwide.

Eastern Public Radio

Headquarters: 301 N. Beauregard St. #1417, Alexandria, Va. 22312-2914. (703) 658-4851. FAX: (703) 658-1742. Internet: MVDBOSCH and CAP.GWU.EDU.

Executive: Marjon van den Bosch, exec dir.

Officers: Kim Hodgson (chmn), WAMU-FM Washington; Ted Eldredge (vice chmn), WRTI-FM Philadelphia; Marjon van den Bosch (exec dir), Alexandria, Va.; Marita Rivero (treas), WGBH-FM Boston; Ralph Jennings, WFUV-FM New York; Kurt Anderson, WMNR-FM Monroe, Conn.; Brenda Hankey (sec), WMRA-FM Harrisonburg, Va.; David Othmer, VP bcstg WHYY-FM/TV Philadelphia.

National Public Radio (NPR)

Headquarters: 635 Massachusetts Ave. N.W., Washington 20001. (202) 414-2000.

Personnel: Delano E. Lewis, pres; Carl Matthusen, chmn.

This noncommercial, satellite-delivered radio system has nearly 480 public radio stns nationwide. NPR provides member stns with progmg, professional dev, promotional support, prog distribution, and representation in Washington on issues affecting bcstg. Progs include *All Things Considered, Morning Edition, Weekend Edition, Talk of the Nation, Car Talk, Fresh Air, Horizons, Afropop Worldwide, Performance Today, Blues Stage, Club del Sol, E-town, Jazz Set, Living on Earth, Rhythm Review & The Thistle & Shamrock.*

Radio Program Networks

American Forum Radio

Headquarters: 5025 Centennial Blvd., Colorado Springs 80919. (719) 528-7040. FAX: (719) 528-6544.

Executives: Skip Joeckel, VP affil svcs; Dave Rose, VP progmg.

American Forum Radio provides interactive talk progmg on a variety of topics.

American Sports Network

Headquarters: 5025 Centennial Blvd., Colorado Springs 80919. (719) 528-7040. FAX: (719) 528-6544.

Executives: Skip Joeckel, VP affil svcs; Dave Rose, VP progmg.

American Sports provides interactive sports progmg on a variety of topics.

Business Radio Network

Headquarters: 5025 Centennial Blvd., Colorado Springs 80919. (719) 528-7040. FAX: (719) 528-5170.

Executives: Skip Joeckel, VP affil svcs; Dave Rose, VP progmg.

Business Radio Networks provides business/financial news, consumer-oriented info & natl weather updates as well as interactive talk prog formats.

CNN Radio Network

Headquarters: One CNN Ctr., Box 105366, Atlanta 30348-5366. (404) 827-2750.

CNN Radio: Natl/international radio news net.

Principal executives: Tom Johnson, pres; Jon Petrovich, exec VP news; Len King, gen mgr CNN Radio Network; Ken Chamberlain, VP N.Y. bureau chief; Lou Dobbs, VP business news; Bill Headline, VP Washington bureau chief; Alma Knott, VP finance; Bill McPhail, VP sports; Kathy Christensen, dir library; Tom Hannon, dir/exec prod political unit; Virginia Tana Wong, dir per; Steve Haworth, dir pub rels.

Bureaus: Grayland Young, southeast; Jeff Flock, Chicago; Tony Clark, Dallas; Ed Garston, Detroit; Dave Farmer, Los Angeles; John Zarella, Miami, Fla.; Ken Chamberlain, New York; Greg LeFevre, San Francisco; Bill Headline, Washington; John Sweeney, Cairo; Ken Joutz, Frankfurt; Charles Hoff, Jerusalem; David Feingold, London; Mark Dulmage, Rome; John Lewis, Tokyo; Gary Strieker, Nairobi; Steve Hurst, Moscow.

CRC Radio Network (Cadena Radio Centro)

Headquarters: 1645 N. Vine St., Suite 220, Hollywood, Calif. 90028. (213) 463-3800. FAX (213) 463-5724.

Principal Executives: Carlos J. Aguirre, vice-chmn; Barrett L. Alley, pres; Raul A. Hernandez, VP/gen sls mgr; Carlos Rivas, CFO; Ilia Leon, VP affil rels dir.

CRC Sales Offices: New York (212) 696-9300; Los Angeles (213) 463-3800.

CRC: Seven days a week, 24-hours-a-day mus, features hourly news format via satellite net. Cadena Radio Centro: natl Spanish-language radio net. Comprised of 80 stns throughout the U.S., plus four international stns.

CBC Radio Network

Headquarters: Union Plaza Hotel, One Main St., Las Vegas 89101. (702) 798-1798. FAX: (702) 798-2922.

Principal Executives: David Papandrea, pres; Elaine Spieler, sls opns mgr; Jack Levin, political affrs advisor.

Political Advisors: Dr. Ray S. Cline, Washington, D.C.; Consul-General Victor Zazeraj, South Africa; Deputy Consul-General Tsuriel Raphael, Israel; Don Zimmerman, Dallas.

Advertising Sales: Elaine Spieler, Las Vegas. (702) 798-1798.

National Sales:
New York: Mark Goodman, LBS Communications Inc., 875 3rd Ave., New York 10022.

Los Angeles: LBS Communications Inc., 9220 Sunset Blvd., Suite 101-A, Los Angeles 90069. (213) 859-1055.

Chicago: LBS Communications Inc., 625 N. Michigan Ave., Suite 1200, Chicago 60611. (312) 943-0707.

CBC Radio Network: 48 hours per week of live talk radio on current events & timely interviews with nationally- & internationally-known guests via satellite on Satcom C5.

Children's Syndicated Radio Network

Headquarters: Box 294, Eaton Rapids, Mich. 48827. (517) 663-8442.

Principal Executives: Sandra L. Bailey-Bristol, pres/CEO; Monica Harris, personality & prog dir; John Sell, natl sls rep.

Motivation Station: One-hour children's prog offering mus & storytelling; children reporting news, weather, sports, health, fitness & nutrition, TV/movie/book reviews; Money Matters for Kids educationally, 800 number for call-ins with requests, comments, etc.; all available through ABC's satellite svcs or reel.

Family Stations Inc.

Headquarters: 290 Hegenberger Rd., Oakland, Calif. 94621. (510) 568-6200. Harold Camping, pres.

Christian progmg; mus & talk progs; news six days a week 24-hours daily. Nonprofit. 39 O & O's, shortwave, 10 languages. Satellite: Americom K-1 transponder #7.

GBI/Gear Broadcasting International Inc.

Headquarters: Box 23172, Weybosset St., Providence, R.I. 02903. (401) 331-6072; (401) 274-5121. News office: 94 Calverly St., Providence, R.I. 02908.

Executives: Edward R. Robalisky, chmn/pres; Jack G. Thayer, exec VP; G.A. Rainone, VP finance; Noel Howard, VP engrg.

Gear Syndicated Program Services: News This Week, News Pondering Commentaries, Magazine Reports on Radio, Sports Broadcast Capsule, Government Information Update, holiday mus progs, GBI on Entertainment, & Gear Science & Technology.

The SuperNetwork GBI provides news, talk, sports & entertainment progmg to wireless cable operators (MMDS), TVRO operators & radio stns in a delivered simulcasted format. Satellite: GTE Spacenet II.

IDB Communications Group Inc.

Headquarters: 10525 W. Washington Blvd., Culver City, Calif. 90232. (213) 870-9000. FAX: 213-240-3901.

Executives: Jeffrey P. Sudikoff, chmn & CEO; Edward R. Cheramy, pres; Peter F. Hartz, sr VP sls & mktg; Dave Anderson, VP opns.

Transmission & distribution svcs for domestic & international radio & data/voice communications. IDB is the largest U.S. reseller of satellite time. Facilities include IDB's teleports in Los Angeles, New York & Houston, The Sports Satellite Interconnect uplink net, transcontinental & oceanic fiber, "flyway" earth stn in the U.S. & extensive international links. Svcs include those for net, news, syndicated & special-event programming, plus teleconferencing, phone & fax support svcs. Remote packages from anywhere at any time.

Jones Satellite Networks

Headquarters: 9697 E. Mineral Ave., Englewood, Colo. 80112. (800) 876-3303.

Executives: Roy Simpson, exec VP & gen mgr; Phil Barry, VP progmg & opns.

Live 24-hour progmg, ratings & revenue driven.
U.S. Country: Mass appeal Country targeting 25-54 demos.
Adult Contemporary: A mix of the best recent songs with the most familiar titles from the 70s & 30s.
Soft Hits: Mus intensive soft A/C targeting the 35-44 audience.
CD Country: Personality driven Country Hits with lots of listener involvement.
Good Old time Oldies: The best hits from the 50s, 60s & early 70s.
FM Lite: A blend of instrumentals & vocals targeting the 40-54 audience.

Kidwaves Radio Network Inc.

Headquarters: 320 Walnut St., 2nd Fl., Philadelphia 19106. (215) 574-2920. FAX: (215) 574-1040.

Executives: Ragan A. Henry, chmn; Linda Katz & Marcia Moon, VP prog dirs.

Full-time satellite progmg svc providing children's progmg. Various shows target appropriate age groups: pre-school & elementary school children & parents. Mus, stories, features & interviews using a variety of nationally known hosts & talent. Progmg features combination of live disc jockeys & highly-produced taped shows. Not yet on air.

Moody Broadcasting Network

Headquarters: 820 N. LaSalle Blvd., Chicago 60610. (800) 621-7031; (312) 329-4433. FAX: (312) 329-4339.

Executives: Bob Norris, mgr bcst dev; Bob West, dir net dev; David Woodworth, admin affil dev.

Religious & educ stereo audio progmg; mus, talk, news & pub affrs 24 hours a day. The Moody Broadcasting Network has 278 radio affiliates in 49 states, Washington, D.C., Puerto Rico & the Virgin Islands, & on 48 cable systems serving 773,833 subscribers. Satellites: Spacenet IIIR, transponder 13 (FM-squared), & Satcom C-5 (Aurora II), transponder 10 (SCPC).

Spanish Information Service/Alfa Broadcasting

Headquarters: 7901 Carpenter Fwy., Dallas 75247. (214) 819-6351. FAX: (214) 819-6330.

Executives: Jose Luis Madrigal, pres/CEO; Doris Aguirre, gen sls mgr.

Bcsts 24-hour Spanish news, mus, sports, special progmg & entertainment. Concentrates on news from the U.S., Mexico & Latin America, & delivers news via satellite to 46 affiliates in 13 states nationwide via satellite.

Sun Radio Network
A subsidiary of Sound Communications, Inc.

Headquarters: 2870 Scherer Dr., Suite 100, St. Petersburg, Fla. 33716. (813) 572-9209. FAX: (813) 572-4735.

Executives: William Wardino, CEO/pres; Stan Anderson, VP/gen mgr; Carolyn Jones, VP/controller; Bill Muncey, chief engr.

Syndicated radio net svc, topical/service-oriented talk, satellite audio bcstg. No affiliation fee to qualified stns. Satellites: Satcom C-5, Trans. 15, Ch.11-1; Galaxy-2, Trans. 3, 65.3 audio.

Superadio Satellite Network

Headquarters: 1671 Worcester Rd., Framingham, MA 01701. (508) 626-2000.

Executives: John Garabedian, gen ptnr; Gary Burnstein, pres radio progmg; Kristen Carlson, dir mktg.

Open House Party: Delivered via satellite. A CHR mus weekend live prog svc. In-studio guests; listener interac-

Radio Program Networks

tion through "800" phone lines. Customized for local identity at each stn.

Super Mixx: Four hours of dance mus mixed back to back. Cleared by WQHT New York, KPWR Los Angeles & other top mkts. Mus from affil's playsheets & call out rsch. Unhosted, with pre-programmed coml & stn ID breaks. New prog each week.

Urban Mixx: *Slammin!* a mix prog for urban radio. Features currents, oldies/classics. Spin-off hours featuring dance hall/reggae, new jams, rap & world beat. Unhosted with pre-prorammed coml & stn ID breaks. Exclusive mkt access to our library of jams dating from 1978. Co-produced by WBLS New York & KKBT Los Angeles.

TNNR

Headquarters: 2644 McGavock Pike, Nashville 37214. (615) 871-6710.

Executives: Bob Meyer, gen mgr; Charlie Douglas, opns mgr; Jeff Lyman, net coord (615) 871-6725. Affil sls through Group W Satellite Communications: Lloyd Werner, sr VP (203) 965-6000; Steve Soule, VP affil rels; Peter Weisbard, VP adv sls.

TNNR syndicates *The Nashville Record Review,* a wkly top 40 country mus countdown show, hosted by TNN's *Crook & Chase.* Four hours in length on CD. Barter/exchange.

WFMT Fine Arts Network

Headquarters: 3 Illinois Ctr., 303 E. Wacker Dr., Chicago 60601. (312) 565-5000. FAX: (312) 565-5169.

Executives: David Levin, dir BSN, WFMT Fine Arts Network & WFMT Ideas Network; Jim Barker, gen sls mgr; Paul Gosiewski, finance dir; Jon Kavanaugh, dir corporate communications.

Satellite-delivered performing arts & spoken word progmg to over 900 coml & pub radio stns. Among the feature progs are concerts by major symphony orchestras; productions by opera companies; concerts from Europe; concerts & spoken word from the BBC; musical documentaries; folk mus; the *Studs Terkel Almanac; To The Best of Our Knowledge,* a three-hour magazine interview svcs; the Beethoven Satellite Network, a customized classical mus format svc, & periodic specials.

WLIR Jewish Radio Network

Headquarters: Box 489, Nanuet, N.Y. 10952. (914) 624-1300. FAX: (914) 624-2809.

Executives: Zev Brenner, pres; Philip W. Plack, gen mgr; Gary B. Duglin, opns & sls mgr; Yaakov Spivak, news dir; Michael Lobaito, chief engr; Gary Shiff, prod dir.

All Jewish Format: WLIR is the nation's only all Jewish radio stn featuring world Jewish news on the top of each hour, contemporary mus, talk, comedy, business & children's programs. Some of the stn's top rated shows include *Talkline wtih Zev Brenner, Curtis Sliwa, The Jewish Kids Quiz Program, The Singing Rabbi Sholomo Carlebach, The Torah Therapy Hour,* & the *Morning Shmooz.*

WLIR is satellite-delivered 24 hours a day on Satellite F2r, Transponder 18, 8.2 mhz to radio stns & cable systems throughout the U.S. & Canada.

Wall Street Journal Radio Network/ Dow Jones Radio Network

Headquarters: 200 Liberty St., 14th Fl., New York 10281. (212) 416-2381. FAX: (212) 416-4195.

Executives: Robert Rush, dir; Jonathan Krongard.

The Wall Street Journal Radio Network, designed for AM mus stns, provides 18 two-minute hourly business/financial newscasts each weekday & six one-minute weekend reports. Designed for FM mus stns, the Dow Jones Radio Network provides 16 one-minute newscasts daily focusing on money news & consumer trends. The net also provides six one-minute weekend reports. Both nets are satellite-delivered on Satcom C5.

Regional Radio Networks

AMI News/Skimedia Networks. 50 Vashell Way, Suite 300, Orinda, Calif. 94563. (510) 254-4450. FAX: (510) 254-6135. John Hamilton, pres; Rob Brown, VP/gen mgr.
Eastern Bureau: (800) 736-0370. Claire Diepenbrock.
Comprises 1,537 stns nationwide.

AgriAmerica Network. 401 Pennsylvania Pkwy., #300, Indianapolis 46280. (317) 848-4404. FAX: (317) 844-1243. G. Christopher Duffy, pres; John Newcomb, exec VP; Gary Truitt, gen mgr; Lew Middleton, affil rel.
Comprises 65 stns in Indiana. Represented by J.L. Farmakis.

Agrinet Farm Radio Network. Box 108, 179 Lovers Ln., Suite B, Elizabeth City, N.C. 27909. (919) 335-7294. FAX: (919) 335-2496. Bill Ray, pres; Gregory Gingery, VP; Lisa Ray, sls mgr.
Comprises 150 stns in Virginia, Maryland, Pennsylvania, New Jersey, West Virginia, North Carolina, South Carolina, Delaware, Massachusetts, Maine, Alabama, California, Florida, Georgia, Illinois, Indiana, Washington & Wyoming. Nationally distributed Agrinet prog.

Alaska Radio Network. 1777 Forest Park Dr., Anchorage 99503. (907) 272-7461. FAX: (907) 279-2112. Thomas E. Tierney, pres; John Ruby, gen mgr.
Comprises nine stns in Alaska. Represented by D&R Radio.

Allegheny Mountain Network. Box 204, State College, Pa. 16801. (814) 238-0792. FAX: (814) 684-1220. Cary H. Simpson, pres; John Salter, Betty F. Simpson, VPs; Robert H. Lynn, VP engrg; Ann G. Searer, business mgr.
Comprises nine stns in Pennsylvania. Represented by Dome & Associates.

American Ag Network. Box 1197, Pierre, S.D. 57501. (605) 224-9911. FAX: (605) 224-8984. Mark Swendsen, pres/gen mgr; Joel DeMent, sls mgr; Lyle Romine, NAFB farm dir.
Comprises 40 stns: 12 in South Dakota; 23 in North Dakota; five in Minnesota.

American Network Group Inc. 621 Mainstream Dr., Suite 230, Nashville 37228. (615) 742-6105. FAX: (615) 742-6124. John Casey, chmn/CEO; Bob Williamson, pres.
Owners of Tennessee Radio Network, Tennessee Ag-Net, Kentucky Ag-Net, South Carolina Network. See individual listings.

Arkansas Radio Network. Box 4189, Little Rock, Ark. 72214. (501) 661-7550. FAX: (501) 661-7620. Neal Gladner, VP/gen mgr; Ron Bredding, news dir.
Comprises 67 interconnected stns, all in Arkansas. Represented by McGavren Guild & State Reps.

Beasley Broadcast Group. 3033 Riviera Dr., Suite 200, Naples, Fla. 33940. (813) 263-5000. FAX: (813) 263-8191. George G. Beasley, chmn of bd; Simon T., pres/COO.
Comprises 15 stns in seven states: one in Arkansas, one in California, four in Florida, two in Illinois, one in Louisiana, four in North Carolina, two in Pennsylvania.

Beck-Ross Communications Inc. 100 Merrick Rd., Rockville Centre, N.Y. 11570. (516) 764-8999; (718) 343-1234. Martin F. Beck, chmn; James E. Champlin, pres; George H. Ross, sec/treas.
Comprises four stns: WHCN(FM) in Connecticut (Rep: Christal), WSNE(FM) in Massachusetts (Rep: Eastman), WBLI(FM) in New York (Rep: Katz) and gen ptnr of WCRS(FM) in Kentucky (Rep: Torbet).

Berkshire Broadcasting Co. Inc. 466 Curran Hwy., North Adams, Mass. 01247. (413) 663-6567. Donald A. Thurston, pres.
Comprises three stns in Massachusetts. Represented by Kettell-Carter (Boston).

Brownfield Network. (Division of Learfield Communications Inc.) Box 104180, 505 Hobbs Rd., Jefferson City, Mo. 65110-4180. (314) 893-7200. FAX: (314) 893-2321. Clyde G. Lear, pres; Derry Brownfield, farm dir; Chuck Zimmerman, gen mgr.
Comprises 175 stns in Illinois, Iowa, Missouri, Nebraska & Indiana.

Paul Bunyan Network. Paul Bunyan Bldg., 314 E. Front, Traverse City, Mich. 49684. (616) 947-7675. FAX: (616) 929-3988. Ross Biederman, pres/gen mgr radio stns; Jim Sofonia, chief engr; Jon Patrick, gen sls mgr; Jack O'Mallay, prog dir; Cordon & Jacob, atty.
Comprises five stns in Michigan. Represented by Katz Radio.

CRC Hispanic-Radio Network. (Cadena Radio Centro.) 1645 N. Vine, Suite 220, Hollywood, Calif. 90028. (213) 463-3800. FAX: (213) 463-5724. Carlos J. Aguirre, vice-chmn; Barrett L. Alley, pres; Raul A. Hernandez, VP/gen sls mgr; Ilia Leon, VP/affil rel mgr; Richard Santiago, news dir.
Comprised of 80 stns in: California; New York; Florida; Illinois; Texas; New Mexico; Arizona; Pennsylvania; Washington, D.C.; Massachusetts; Nevada; Utah; Oregon; Georgia; Washington; Rhode Island; Louisiana; Missouri; Oklahoma and Idaho.

CRN International Inc. Connecticut Radio Network One Circular Ave., Hamden, Conn. 06514. (203) 288-2002. FAX: (203) 281-3291. Barry Berman, pres; S. Richard Kalt, CRMC/exec VP; Patrick Kane, sr VP corporate dev; Richard Burman, VP/controller, Steve Kotchko, VP news & progmg; Gary E Zenobia, dir net opns; Paul Orio, dir affil rel.
Comprises 200 stns throughout the continental U.S.

Cadena Estereotempo Inc. Box 13427, Santurce, P.R. 00908. (809) 721-4020. FAX: (809) 722-6740. Alfredo R. de Arellano, pres; Sebastian Robiou, VP progmg; Ismael Nieves, VP sls; Jose L. Valentin, VP finance.
Comprises three stns in P.R. Represented by Katz.

California Agri-Radio Network. (Western Agri-Radio Networks.) 1320 S. 4th Ave., Yuma, Ariz. 85364. (800) 944-6977. FAX: (602) 782-7237. George Gatley, dir/ptnr; UNO Broadcasting Corp., ptnr.
Comprises 14 stns in California. Represented by Torbet Radio.

California Farm Network. 1601 Exposition Blvd., FB-10, Sacramento, Calif. 95815. (916) 924-4060. FAX: (916) 929-1680. Clark Biggs, mgr; Jim Taylor, adv mgr; Dave Kranz, communications supvr; Jim Morris, bcst specialist.
Comprises stns in California. 18 affils. Represented by Regional Reps.

Central Ag News Network. Box 6000, Eau Claire, Wisc. 54702-6000. (800) 866-9299. FAX: (715) 832-5329. Lindam Mann, net mgr; Keith Jones, gen mgr; Bob Bosold, farm dir.
Serves Wisconsin; 19 affils. Represented by Torbet Radio & Hyatt Ramsland.

Compu-Weather Inc. Box 1122, 29-50 Union St., Flushing, N.Y. 11354. (718) 961-4242. FAX: (718) 353-1294. Jeff Wimmer, pres; Todd Gross, VP; Peter Muldavin, sls mgr.

Delmarva Agrinet. Box 1408, 179 Lovers Ln., Suite B, Elizabeth City, N.C. 27909. (919) 335-7294. FAX: (919) 335-2496. Bill Ray, pres; Lisa Ray, sls mgr.
Comprises 65 stns in Virginia; West Virginia; Maryland; Washington, D.C.; Delaware; and New Jersey.

Florida Public Radio Network. 2561 Pottsdamer St., Tallahassee, Fla. 32301. (904) 487-3194. FAX: (904) 487-3293. Ben Wilcox, prod.

Florida's Radio Network Inc. 2500 Maitland Ctr. Pkwy., Suite 407, Maitland, Fla. 32751. (407) 661-1900. FAX: (407) 661-1940. James Poling, dir opns; Rick Green, gen mgr.
Represented by StateNets Inc. Comprises 58 stns in Florida.

Georgia Network. 550 Pharr Rd., Atlanta 30363. (404) 231-1888. FAX: (404) 237-5856. Robert Houghton, VP; Melinda Thompkins, gen mgr; Steve Youlious, sls mgr; Pete Konenkamp, news dir.
Comprises 143 stns in Georgia. Represented by Eastman.

Goetz Group. Fort Atkinson, Wis. 53538. (414) 563-2667. FAX: (414) 563-0315. Wayne Ripp, mgr net opns; Scott M. Trentadue, VP sls & mktg.
Comprises 70 stns in Wisconsin, Illinois & Michigan.

Goldman Group. Box 1139, Jamestown, N.Y. 14701. (716) 487-1151. FAX: (716) 664-9326. Simon Goldman, pres; Merrill Rosen, VP/gen mgr; Ora Larson, treas; Larry Saracki, sls mgr; Paul S. Goldman, Vermont Radio Division.
Comprises four stns: two in New York (WJTN/WWSE), two in Vermont (WVMT/WXXX). Represented by Republic & McGavren Guild.

Gulf Central Radio Network. Box 707, Columbus, Miss. 39703-0707. (601) 328-1420. FAX: (601) 328-1421. J.W. Furr Sr., principal.
Comprises four stns in Mississippi.

Hawkeye Network. (Division of Learfield Communications Inc.) Box 104180, Jefferson City, Mo. 65111-4180. (314) 893-7200. FAX: (314) 893-2321. Clyde G. Lear, pres; Roger Gardner, gen mgr.
Comprises 42 stns in Iowa.

Hometown Radio Network. Box 15146, Cleveland 44115. (216) 781-4070. FAX: (216) 781-7508. Sharon A. Morrow, corporate mgr.
Comprises 860 affils in: Delaware, Florida, Georgia, Iowa, Illinois, Indiana, Kansas, Kentucky, Maryland, Nebraska, North Carolina, Ohio, Oklahoma, Pennsylvania, South Carolina, Virginia, & West. Virginia.

ION Radio Network. Morristown Municipal Airport, Morristown, N.J. 07960. (201) 267-6800. FAX: (201) 267-0428. Stephen Pellettiere, pres.
Comprises 19 stns: five in New Jersey, six in New York, three in Pennsylvania, two in Maryland, two in Connecticut & one in R.I.

Illinois News Network. 430 W. Erie, Suite 505, Chicago 60610. (312) 915-0044. FAX: (312) 943-2620. Alex Seith, chmn; Andy Barrett, pres; Jim Roberts, dir opns; Philip O. Chasin, VP finance; Dan Keeney, dir news & progmg.
A statewide satellite-delivered net providing news, sports, weather, business & spec progmg. INN, 60 affils. Represented by StateNets Inc.

Indiana Broadcasters Group. Holiday Office Park, 644 Linn St., Suite 1228, Cincinnati 45203. (513) 651-1511. Joseph C. Hearn, VP.
Comprises 65 stns in Indiana. Represented by Regional Reps Corp.

Intermountain Farm/Ranch Network. 575 E. 4500 So., Suite B-200, Salt Lake City 84107. (801) 266-1480. FAX: (801) 266-2365. Kathy Bingham, gen mgr.
Comprises 102 stns, 21 in Colorado; nine in Idaho; 18 in Montana; nine in Nebraska; two in Nevada; one in New Mexico; two in North Dakota; one in South Dakota; 12 in Utah; 13 in Wyoming; five in Washington; nine in Oregon. Represented by Eastman Radio Inc.

Intermountain Network Inc. 575 East 4500 South, Suite B-200, Salt Lake City 84107. (801) 266-1480. FAX: (801) 266-2365. Ruth Hallett, CEO.
Comprises 221 stns. 41 in Colorado; two in North Dakota; two in Nevada; 18 in Idaho; one in South Dakota; 28 in Utah; 28 in Montana; 17 in Nebraska; 28 in Wyoming; six in New Mexico; 30 in Oregon; 19 in Washington; one in Arizona. Represented by Eastman Radio Inc.

KEDA Radio. 510 S. Flores, San Antonio 78204. (512) 226-5254. FAX: (512) 227-7937. Manuel G. Davila, pres; Madeline P. Davila, VP; Alberto P. Davila, gen mgr.
Comprises two stns in Texas, three affils. Represented by Caballero Spanish Media.

KFBK/KGBY. 1440 Ethan Way, Suite 200, Sacramento, Calif. 95825. (916) 929-5325. Rick Eytcheson, VP/gen mgr; Jan Shay, gen sls mgr; Betsy Braziel, prog mgr KFBK; Joyce Krieg, prom mgr KFBK; Robert John, prog dir KGBY; Melanie Polka, prom mgr KGBY.
Represented by Group W Radio Sales.

Kansas Agriculture Network. Box 119, Topeka, Kan. 66601-0119. (913) 272-2199. FAX: (913) 272-3536. Al Lobeck, gen mgr; Kathy Patton, farm dir; Ed O'Donnell, opns dir; Al Lobeck, VP radio.
Comprises 37 stns in Kansas. Represented by Katz Radio.

Kansas Information Network. Box 119, Topeka, Kan. 66601. (913) 272-2199. FAX: (913) 272-0117. Al Lobeck, gen mgr; Glenn Harmon, sls mgr; Ed O'Donnell, opns mgr; Ben Bauman, news dir.
Comprises 45 stns in Kansas. Represented by StateNets Inc.

Kentucky Ag-Net. (Subsidiary of Clear Channel Communications.) Box 1084, Louisville, Ky. 40201. (502) 582-3924. FAX: (502) 582-7393. Art Grunewald, gen sls mgr; Allen Aldridge, farm dir.
Comprises 40 stns carrying farm progmg in Kentucky. Live via-satellite.

Kentucky Network. (Subsidiary of Clear Channel Communications Inc.) 11001 Bluegrass Pkwy., Suite 390, Louisville 40299. (502) 267-6757. FAX: (502) 267-6218. Gary Elder, news dir; Art Grunewald, gen sls mgr; Alan Aldridge, agriculture net dir; Doug Ormay, sports dir.
Comprises 85 stns: 84 in Kentucky, one in West Virginia.

Regional Radio Networks

Kentucky News Network. Box 1984, Louisville, Ky. 40201. (502) 582-3924. FAX: (505) 582-7393. Art Grunewald, gen sls mgr; Gary Elder, news dir/opns mgr.
75 affils in Ky.

La Super Kadena. 117 Eleanor Roosevelt, Hato Rey, P.R. 00918. (809) 764-1090. FAX: (809) 764-3460. Reinaldo Royo, pres.
Comprises three stns in P.R. Represented by Katz.

Laird Group. Box 310, 810 Victoria St., Green Bay, Wis. 54305. (414) 468-4100. William C. Laird, pres; Michael Watts, gen sls mgr.
Comprising six stns, two in South Dakota; four in Wisconsin.

Linder Farm Network. 1340 N. 7th St., Box 838, Willmar, Minn. 56201. (612) 235-8695; (612) 235-1340. FAX: (612) 235-9111. Lynn Ketelsen, farm svc dir; H.J. (Bud) Hanson, sls mgr.
Comprises 14 stns, all in Minnesota. Represented by Katz Radio.

Louisiana Agri-News Network. 263 3rd St., 5th Fl., Baton Rouge 70801. (504) 383-8695. FAX: (504) 342-9950. Bill Rigell, pres; Rhett McMahon, VPs; Don Molino, farm dir.
Comprises 61 stns in Louisiana. Represented by McGavren Guild.

Louisiana Network Inc. 263 3rd St., 5th Fl., Baton Rouge 70801. (504) 383-8695. FAX: (504) 342-9950. Bill Rigell, pres/CEO; Rhett McMahon, VP; Stacy Long, sls mgr.
Comprises 84 stns in Louisiana. Represented by news network: StateNets Inc.; Agri-News Network: McGavren Guild.

The MNN Radio Networks Inc. 1370 Davern St., St. Paul, Minn. 55116. (612) 696-0123. FAX: (612) 696-0100. Don Wohlenhaus, pres; Timothy Shears, VP sls & mktg.
Comprises 80 stns in Minnesota, North Dakota, South Dakota, Iowa & Wisconsin. Represented by StateNets Inc. (retail) & self represented (agricultural).

Maine Radio Network Inc. Statehouse Station 70, Augusta, Me. 04333. (207) 287-1094. FAX: (207) 287-1099. Mal Leary, VP.
Comprises 22 stns in Maine.

Metronews Radio Network. Greer Bldg., Rt. 7, Morgantown, W. Va. 26505. (304) 296-0029. FAX: (304) 296-3876. Dale Miller, pres; Harvey Kercheval, VP news; Tony Caridi, VP sports; Jim Murphy, chief engr; Joe Parsons, VP sls.
Comprises West Virginia News (58 stns in West Virginia) & Mountaineer Sports Network (72 stns in West Virginia).

Michigan Farm Radio Network. Box 269, 233 Hurd St., Milan, Mich. 48160. (313) 439-1522. FAX: (313) 439-7794. Robert Driscoll, pres; John Stommen, VP admin & treas; Patrick Driscoll, exec dir/farm dir.
Comprises 29 stns in Michigan. Represented by J.L. Farmakis.

Mid-America Ag Network. 1632 S. Maze Rd., Wichita, Kan. 67209. (316) 721-8484. FAX: (316) 721-8276. Larry Steckline, pres/owner; Larry Steckline, Mike Dain, farm bcstrs; Greg Steckline, mgr; Don Shultz, sls mgr.
Comprises 44 stns in Colorado, Kansas, Nebraska and Oklahoma. Represented by Torbet Radio.

Mississippi Agri Network. 6310 I-55 N., Jackson, Miss. 39211. (601) 957-1700. FAX: (601) 956-5228. Steve Davenport, pres; Linda M. Tapp, VP; Frank Horn, sls mgr; John Winfield, agricultural dir.
Comprises 68 affils in Mississippi. Represented by McGavren Guild.

Mississippi News Network. 6310 I-55 N., Jackson, Miss. 39211. (601) 957-1700. FAX: (601) 956-5228. Steve Davenport, pres; Linda M. Tapp, VP; Frank Horn, sls mgr; Jim Bevers, news dir.
Comprises 77 affils in Mississippi. Represented by StateNets Inc.

Mississippi State Basketball Network. 6310 I-55 N., Jackson, Miss. 39211. (601) 957-1700. FAX: (601) 956-5228. Steve Davenport, pres; Linda M. Tapp, VP; Frank Horn, sls mgr.
Comprises 28 affils in Mississippi & one in Tennessee.

Mississippi State Football Network. 6310 I-55 N., Jackson, Miss. 39211. (601) 957-1700. FAX: (601) 956-5228. Steve Davenport, pres; Linda M. Tapp, VP; Frank Horn, sls mgr.
Comprises 44 stns in Mississippi, one in Tennessee & one in Louisiana.

Missourinet. (Division of Learfield Communications Inc.) Box 104180, 505 Hobbs Rd., Jefferson City, Mo. 65110. (314) 893-7200. Clyde G. Lear, pres; Steve Mays, VP news.
Serves Missouri - 75 affils.

Moon Radio Network. 2028 Club Pkwy., Norcross, Ga. 30093. (404) 939-5471. Russell F. Moon Jr., pres.
Comprises 27 stns in 10 states.

Network Indiana. 401 Pennsylvania Pkwy., #300, Indianapolis 46280. (317) 848-4404; (317) 632-3044. G. Christopher Duffy, pres; John Newcomb, exec VP; Scott Uecker, news dir; Emily Mantel, sls mgr; Lew Middleton, affil rels mgr.
Comprises 60 stns in Indiana.

New South Communications Inc. Box 5797, Meridian, Miss. 39302. (601) 693-2973. FAX: (601) 483-0826. Ed Holladay, pres.
Comprises four stns: one in Louisiana, two in Mississippi, one in Alabama. Represented by McGavren Guild.

North American Network Inc. 7910 Woodmont Ave., Suite 1400, Bethesda, Md. 28814. (301) 654-9810. FAX: (301) 654-9828. Tom Sweeny, pres; Lisa Brusio Coster, stn svc dir.
In all states, 85 nets comprising 2,800 stns.

North Carolina News Network. Box 12900, Raleigh, N.C. 27605. (919) 890-6030. FAX: (919) 890-6024. George Habel, gen mgr; Bev Holt, affil & opns mgr; Jerry Reckerd, sls mgr.
Comprises 90 stns in North Carolina. Represented by StateNets Inc.

North Dakota News Network. Box 1197, Pierre, S.D. 57501. (605) 224-9911. FAX: (605) 224-8984. Mark Swendsen, pres/gen mgr; Joel DeMent, sls mgr.
Comprises 24 stns in North Dakota. Represented by StateNets Inc.

Ohio Educational Broadcasting Network Commission. 2470 N. Star Rd., Columbus, Ohio 43221. (614) 421-1714. FAX: (614) 644-3112. Dave L. Fornshell, exec dir.
Comprising 12 television stns & 31 radio stns.

Oklahoma News Network. Oklahoma Agrinet, Box 1000, Oklahoma City 73101. (405) 840-5271. Tim West, gen mgr; Ron Hays, opns dir/farm dir.
Comprises 45 stns in Oklahoma. Represented by StateNets Inc.

Peach State Public Radio Network. 1540 Stewart Ave. S.W., Atlanta 30310. (404) 756-4730. FAX: (404) 756-4088. Richard Ottinger, exec dir; A.W. Bergeron, dir; Norman Bemelmans, prog dir.
Comprises nine stns in Georgia.

Pennsylvania Agrinet, Box 1408, 179 Lovers Ln., Suite B, Elizabeth City, N.C. 27909. (919) 335-7294. FAX: (919) 335-2496. Bill Ray, pres.
Comprises 40 stns.

Pittsburgh Country Network. 1439 Denniston Ave., Pittsburgh 15217. (412) 421-2600. FAX: (412) 421-6001.
Comprises three stns in Pennsylvania. Represented by Commercial Media Sales.

Progressive Farmer Network. Box 2000, 1004 N. Jackson St., Starkville, Miss. 39759. (601) 324-0949. FAX: (601) 324-0972. Jim Yancey, pres.
Comprises 55 stns. 12 in Arkansas, 13 in Louisiana, 17 in Mississippi, eight in Missouri & five in Tennessee.

RFD Illinois Radio Network. 1701 Towanda Ave., Bloomington, Ill. 61701. (309) 557-2598. (309) 557-2559. Alan Jarand, farm dir; Lou Hansen, bcst edit; Richard Verdery, adv sls mgr.
Comprises 97 stns in Illinois, one in Indiana, three in Iowa & two in Missouri. Represented by J.L. Farmakis Inc.

Radio Iowa. (Division of Learfield Communications Inc.) 2700 Grand Ave., Suite 103, Des Moines, Iowa 50312. (515) 282-1984. Clyde G. Lear, pres/CEO; Steve Mays, gen mgr.
Comprises 51 affils in Iowa.

Radio Pennsylvania Inc. (A Division of WITF Inc.) Box 2954, 1982 Locust Ln., Harrisburg, Pa. 17105. (717) 232-8400. FAX: (717) 232-7612. Stewart Chiefet, pres WITF Inc.; Kate Lohr, gen mgr; Gary Miller, news dir; Mark O'Neill, sports dir; Craig Rhodes, opns coord/traffic mgr; Scott LaMar, dir of affil rel; Linda Green, acct exec; John Bosak, dir engrg.
Bcsts state news, sports & features to affils in Pennsylvania. Comprises 80 stns. Represented by NASRN.

Ray Sports Radio Network. Box 1408, 179 Lovers Ln., Suite B, Elizabeth City, N.C. 27909. (919) 335-7294. FAX: (919) 335-2496. Bill Ray, pres; Bob DeBlois, sports dir.
Comprises 239 stns in New Jersey, Pennsylvania, Delaware, Maryland, Virginia, West Virginia, North Carolina and South Carolina.

South Carolina Network. (Subsidiary of American Network Group Inc., Nashville, Tenn.) 3710 Landmark Dr., Suite 100, Columbia, S.C. 29204. (803) 790-4300. FAX: (803) 790-4309. Tom Brabham, news dir; Don Williams, VP opns American Network Group; Greg Roberson, affil rel dir American Network Group.
Comprises 53 affils in South Carolina and 35 Univ. of South Carolina football affils.

South Dakota News Network. Box 1197, Pierre, S.D. 57501. (605) 224-9911. FAX: (605) 224-8984. Mark Swendsen, pres/gen mgr; Joel DeMent, sls mgr.
Comprises 17 stns in South Dakota. Represented by StateNets Inc.

Southeast Agrinet. 3621 N.W. 10th St., Ocala, Fla. 34475. (904) 629-7400. Gary Cooper, pres.
Comprises approx 50 stns in Georgia, Florida & Alabama. Satellite interconnected for farm radio progmg.

Southern Educational Communications Association. Box 50008, Columbia, S.C. 29250. (803) 799-5517. FAX: (803) 771-4831. Skip Hinton, pres.
Sixty-six TV members in 20 states & the U.S. Virgin Islands.

Southern Farm Network. 3012 Highwoods Blvd., Suite 200, Raleigh, N.C. 27604. (919) 876-0674. FAX: (919) 790-6457. Barbara Price, nat sls mgr; Joe Bell, gen mgr.

Southwest Agri-Radio Network. Western Agri-Radio Networks, 1320 S. 4th Ave., Yuma, Ariz. 85364. (800) 944-6077. FAX: (602) 782-7237. George Gatley, dir/ptnr; UNO Broadcasting Corp., ptnr.
Comprises 10 stns: eight in Arizona, two in California, one in Colorado. Represented by Torbet Radio.

Spanish Information Service. (Associated with Texas State Networks.) 7901 Carpenter Fwy., Dallas 75247. (214) 688-1133. FAX: (214) 637-3843. Jose Luis Madrigal, VP/gen mgr; Andy Barrett, gen sls mgr; Charles Staples, chief engr.
Comprises 53 stns in 10 states reaching 84% of U.S. Hispanic pop age 18 & older.

Suburban Radio Group. Box 888, Belmont, N.C. 28012. (704) 825-5272. FAX: (704) 825-4036. Robert R. Hilker, chmn/CEO; William R. Rollins, pres/COO.
Comprises eight stns: two in Georgia, two in North Carolina, two in Virginia, two in the Virgin Islands. Represented by Southern Spot Sales.

Temple Public Radio Network. Annenberg Hall, Temple Univ. (011-00), Philadelphia 19122. (215) 204-8405. FAX: (215) 204-4870. James S. White, VP pub affrs; George Ingram, assoc VP univ rel; W. Theodore Eldredge, gen mgr.
Comprises three stns in Pennsylvania and one in Delaware.

Tennessee Agri-Net. (Subsidiary of American Network Group Inc.) 621 Mainstream Dr., Suite 230, Nashville 37228. (615) 742-6100. FAX: (615) 742-6124. Dan Gordon, VP opns; agricultural dir; Greg Roberson, affil rel dir.
Comprises 50 stns in Tennessee.

Tennessee Radio Network. (Subsidiary of American Network Group Inc.) 621 Mainstream Dr., Suite 230, Nashville 37228. (615) 742-6100. FAX: (615) 742-6124. Robert J Williamson, pres; Dan Gordon, VP/net opns; Greg Roberson, affil rel dir.
Comprises 82 stns in Tennessee.

Texas Agribusiness Network. (Associated with Texas State Networks.) 7901 Carpenter Fwy., Dallas 75247. (214) 688-1133. FAX: (214) 689-1912. Charlie Seraphin, VP/gen mgr; John Buckley, gen sls mgr; Joe Short, dir affil rel; Erik Disen, dir engrg; Bob Cockrum, farm dir & chief engr; Lee McCoy, AG mktg specialist; Joe Short dir affil svcs.
Comprises 60 stns throughout Texas. Represented by StateNets Inc.

Texas AP Network. 4851 LBJ Fwy., Suite 300, Dallas 75244-6017. (214) 991-2020. FAX: (214) 991-7207. Amanda Barnett, supvr; Doug Kienitz, rgnl radio exec.
Approximately 40 affils full-svc, coml-free Associated Press radio net serving stns in Texas.

Regional Radio Networks

Texas State Network. 7901 Carpenter Fwy., Dallas 75247. (214) 688-1133. FAX: (214) 879-6330. Charlie Seraphin, VP/op mgr; John Buckley, gen sls mgr; Tina Nelson, news dir.

Provides newscasts & progs to 130 stns in Texas. Represented by StateNets Inc.

Tichenor Media System Inc. 100 Crescent Ct., Suite 1777, Dallas 75201. (214) 855-8882. FAX: (214) 855-8881. McHenry T. Tichenor Jr., pres; David Lykes, sr VP sls & mkg; Ricardo Alvarez del Castillo, VP opns.

Comprises 14 stns: 12 in Texas, two in Illinois. Represented by Katz Radio.

Tiger Network. (Division of Learfield Communications Inc.) Box 104180, Jefferson City, Mo. 65111-4180. (314) 893-7200. FAX: (314) 893-2321. Clyde G. Lear, pres; Roger Gardner, gen mgr; Keith Sampson, exec prod.

Comprises 55 stns in Missouri.

Tobacco Radio Network. Box 12800, 711 Hillsborough St., Raleigh, N.C. 27605. (919) 890-6046. FAX: (919) 890-6024. Ray Wilkinson, VP/gen mgr; Andy Roat, natl acct exec; Ken Tanner, farm edit.

Comprises stns in Alabama, Florida, Georgia, North Carolina, South Carolina & Virginia. Represented by TN Spot Sales.

Tribune Radio Networks. 435 N. Michigan Ave., Chicago 60611. (312) 222-3342. FAX: (312) 222-5165. Kenton Morris, gen mgr; Barbara Atsaves, mgr admin; Jack Rosenberg, mgr sports; Orion Samuelson, farm svcs dir; Max Armstrong, assoc farm svcs dir.

Network comprised of: Chicago Bears Network (43 stns), Chicago Cubs Network (63 stns), The Dave Wannstedt Show (38 stns), Pro Football Weekly (55 stns), The Thoroughbred Connection (47 stns), National Farm Report (330 stns), Farming America (230 stns), John Block Reports (175 stns), Agri-Voice Network (95 stns), Interstate Radio Network (58 stns). Represented by Christal.

University of Mississippi Baseball Network. 6310 I-55 N., Jackson, Miss. 39211. (601) 957-1700. FAX: (601) 956-5228. Steve Davenport, pres; Linda M. Tapp, VP; Frank Horn, sls mgr.

Comprises 12 affils all in Mississippi.

University of Mississippi Basketball Network. 6310 I-55 N., Jackson, Miss. 39211. (601) 957-1700. FAX: (601) 956-5228. Steve Davenport, pres; Linda M. Tapp, VP; Frank Horn, sls mgr.

Comprises 26 affils in Mississippi & one in Tennessee.

University of Mississippi Football Network. 6310 I-55 N., Jackson, Miss. 39211. (601) 957-1700. FAX: (601) 956-5228. Steve Davenport, pres; Linda M. Tapp, VP; Frank Horn, sls mgr.

Comprises 42 affils in Mississippi, one in Alabama & one in Tennessee.

University of Southern Mississippi Basketball Network. 6310 I-55 N., Jackson, Miss. 39211. (601) 957-1700. FAX: (601) 956-5228. Steve Davenport, pres; Linda M. Tapp, VP; Frank Horn, sls mgr.

Comprises 10 affils in Mississippi.

University of Southern Mississippi Football Network. 6310 I-55 N., Jackson, Miss. 39211. (601) 957-1700. FAX: (601) 956-5228. Steve Davenport, pres; Linda M. Tapp, VP; Frank Horn, sls mgr.

Comprises 25 affils in Mississippi & one in Alabama.

VSA Radio Network. 5376 Stewart Ln., San Angelo, Tex. 76904. (915) 944-1213. FAX: (915) 942-1027. Roddy Peeples, farm & ranch dir/own; Curt Lancaster, assoc farm & ranch dir; Don Atkinson, chief engr/dir mkt news.

Comprises 65 satellite-fed affils in Texas.

Virginia RFD. (A report on agriculture & consumer news.) Box 27552, Richmond, Va. 23261. (804) 225-7528. Norm Hyde, farm dir.

Comprises 30 stns in Virginia. Represented by NASRN sls.

Virginia News Network/Virginia. Box 643, Richmond, Va. 23205. (804) 697-6600. FAX: (804) 697-6601. Carl McNeil, gen mgr; Randy Davis, opns mgr; David Martin, sls mgr.

Serving Virginia News Network (55 stns). Lawn & Garden Network (32 stns in Pennsylvania, North Carolina, Maryland, Delaware, Ohio, Virginia & West Virginia). Represented by StateNets Inc.

Western Agri-Radio Networks. (dba California Agri-Radio Network & Southwest Agri-Radio Network.) 1320 S. 4th Ave., Yuma, Ariz. 85364. (800) 944-6077. FAX: (602) 782-7237. George Gatley, dir/ptnr; UNO Broadcasting Corp., ptnr.

Comprises 26 stns: 16 in California, eight in Arizona, one in Colorado, one in New Mexico. Represented by Torbet Radio.

Wisconsin Radio Network. (Division of Great Lakes Networks Inc.) 121 E. Main St., Madison, Wis. 53703. (608) 251-3900. FAX: (608) 251-7233. Alex Smith, chmn; Bob Jordan, gen mgr; Jeff Roberts, news dir/COO; Tim Van Houten, sports dir.

Statewide satellite-delivered net providing news, sports, business, weather, & spec progmg to 50 affils (49 in Wisconsin and one in Michigan).

Unwired Radio Networks

Note: Asterisk (*) denotes unwired television network. Others are unwired radio networks.

***ALIN-TV.** 149 Madison Ave., Suite 804, New York 10016. (212) 889-1337. FAX: (212) 213-6968. Alan Steinberg, chmn; John Giebel, pres; Alan Cohen, exec VP.
ALIN-TV offers natl coml participation on locally originated progmg on a lineup of ind TV stns.

Caballero Spanish Radio. 261 Madison Ave., Suite 1800, New York 10016. (212) 697-4120. Eduardo Caballero, pres.
Non-interconnected natl sls net specializing in Spanish mkts.

Intermountain Farm/Ranch Network. 575 East 4500 South, Suite B-200, Salt Lake City 84107. (801) 266-1480. FAX: (801) 266-2365. Kathy Bingham, gen mgr.
Comprises 102 stns: 21 in Colorado, nine in Idaho, 18 in Montana, nine in Nebraska, two in Nevada, one in New Mexico, two in North Dakota, one in South Dakota, 12 in Utah, 13 in Wyoming, five in Washington, nine in Oregon. Represented by Eastman Radio Inc.

Intermountain Network Inc. 575 East 4500 South, Suite B-200, Salt Lake City 84107. (801) 266-1480. FAX: (801) 266-2365. Greg Smith, pres; Kathy Bingham, gen mgr.
Comprises 221 stns: 41 in Colorado, two in North Dakota, two in Nevada, 18 in Idaho, one in South Dakota, 28 in Utah, 28 in Montana, 17 in Nebraska, 28 in Wyoming, six in New Mexico, 30 in Oregon, 19 in Washington, one in Arizona. Represented by Eastman Radio Inc.

Keystone Broadcasting System Inc. 22971 Nine Mile Rd., St. Clair Shores, Mich. 48080. (313) 774-4580. FAX: (313) 774-4889. Nicholas Gordon, chmn.
St. Clair Shores, Mich. 48081: Patt Media Sales, 21714 Lakeland. Detroit office.
Ridgefield, Conn. 06877: (203) 438-8868. FAX: (203) 438-1769. Lew Green, pres; Nicholas Gordon, chmn; Bill Gleason, VP.
Agency Commission: 15% on net stn time to accredited agencies; no cash discount. The stns can be bought separately. Minimum order: 20 stns. Stns may be purchased by state groups, rgns or full net. One contract, one itemized invoice & individual stn affidavits. Schedules, start dates, copy and/or live tags may vary from stn to stn. Rates for special combinations available on request.

Lotus Hispanic Reps. 50 E. 42nd St., New York 10017. (212) 697-7601. Richard Kraushaar, pres; Robert Albright, exec VP; Yvonne Luna, acct exec.
Stns in Arizona, California, Colorado, Connecticut, Florida, Illinois, New Mexico, Pennsylvania, Puerto Rico & Texas.

Canadian Radio Networks

Canadian Broadcasting Corp.

The Canadian Broadcasting Corp. (CBC) is a publicly owned corporation established by the Broadcasting Act (1936) of the Canadian Parliament to provide the natl bcstg svc in Canada in the two officially free languages, English and French. Under this legislation, the CBC is subject to regulations of the Canadian Radio-Television and Telecommunications Commission (CRTC).

Head Office: 1500 Bronson Ave., Ottawa, Ont.; Box 8478, Ottawa K1G 3J5. (613) 724-1200. TDD: (613) 733-8868. FAX: (613) 738-6887.

CBC Board of Directors: Patrick Watson, chairperson; Gerard Veilleux, pres/CEO; Gilles Boulet, John Crispo, Michel Doyon, Don Hamilton, Nancy L. Juneau, Sandra Kolber, Robert Kozminski, Thomas MacDonald, William H. Neville, Alain Paris, Brian Peckford, Thomas Wilson, Glen Wright.

Principal Officers: Gerard Veilleux, pres/CEO; Patrick Watson, chmn; Anthony S. Manera, sr VP resource mgmt & admin; Michael McEwen, sr VP radio svcs; Donna Logan, VP media accountability & rgnl bcst opns; Robert Hertzog, VP internal audit; Gerald A. Flaherty, VP/gen counsel/corporate sec; Steve Cotsman, VP fin & admin; Robert Pattillo, VP communications & pub affrs; Charles Gendron, VP human resources; John Shewbridge, VP bus affrs & corporate dev; Sheridan Scott, VP planning & regulatory affrs; Michael A. Hughes, exec dir MIS (Toronto); Louis-Paul Germain, gen mgr bcst centre dev project (Toronto); Charlotte O'Dea, sr dir corporate communications & pub affrs.

CBC Ombudsman: Bill Morgan, Box 500, Stn. "A," Toronto, Ont. M5W 1E6. (416) 975-2978; Mario Cardinal, 1400 René-Lévesque Blvd. E., Box 6000, Montreal H3C 3A8. (514) 597-4721.

Program Services: The CBC operates English and French AM & FM stereo nets. The progmg on these nets is almost all Canadian and virtually free of coml adv. CBC North bcsts radio and TV progs to Canada's north in English, French and seven native languages, serving the special needs of native & non-native groups in the Yukon, the Northwest Territories and northern Quebec. Radio Canada International is Canada's voice abroad. Bcstg on shortwave in seven languages, RCI's progmg reflects Canada's political, economic, social and cultural spectrum to an international audience. The heart of CBC's natl distribution system is Canada's Anik E2 satellite, carrying progmg through six different time zones. CBC's progmg is bcst over 669 AM & FM stns.

English Networks: Box 500, Stn. "A," Toronto, Ont. M5W 1E6. (416) 205-3311, TDD: (416) 205-6688.

Officers: Harold Redekopp, VP English radio; Jim Byrd, exec dir media opns; Sheila Hockin, actg sr dir bcst communications; Tom Curzon, sr dir media & pub rels.

French Networks: 1400 René-Lévesque Blvd. E., Box 6000, Montreal, Que. H3C 3A8. (514) 597-5970. TDD: (514) 597-6013.

Officers: Marcel Pepin, VP French radio; Claire Samson, gen mgr communications; Micheline Savoie, dir pub rels; Raymond Guay, dir net prom; Marcel Labelle, dir French rgnl communications.

CBC Engineering: 7925 Côte Saint Luc Rd., Montreal, Que. H4W 1R5. (514) 485-1031.

Officers: Brian D. Baldry, VP engrg; Claudette Lalonde, mgr tech info.

Radio Canada International: 1055 René-Lévesque Blvd. E., Box 6000, Montreal, Que. H3C 3A8. (514) 597-7555.

Officers: Terry Hargreaves, exec dir; Allan Familiant, prog dir.

Newfoundland Region: Ayre's Centre, Pippy Pl., Box 12010, Stn. "A," St. John's, Nfld. A1B 3T8. (709) 737-4140.

Officers: Ron Crocker, rgnl dir; John O'Mara, rgnl mgr communications.

Maritime Region: 5600 Sackville St., Box 3000, Halifax, N.S. B3J 3E9. (902) 420-8311.

Officers: W.K. Donovan, rgnl dir; Jessie Clarey, sr mgr eastern rgnl communications.

Atlantic Provinces: 250 Archibald St., Box 950, Moncton, N.B. E1C 8N8. (506) 853-6666.

Officers: Claude Bourque, rgnl dir French svcs; Robert Nadeau, rgnl mgr communications.

Quebec Region: 1400 René-Lévesque Blvd. E., Box 6000, Montreal, Que. H3C 3A8. (514) 597-5970.

Officers: Nicole Belanger, rgnl dir English svcs; John Yorston, rgnl mgr communications.

Quebec City & Eastern Quebec Region: 2475 Laurier Blvd., Box 10400, Ste-Foy, Que. G1V 2X2. (418) 654-1341.

Officers: Jacques D. Landry, dir French svcs; Ginette D'Aigle, mgr communications.

Ontario Region, English Services: Box 500, Stn. "A," Toronto, Ont. M5W 1E6. (416) 205-3311.

Officers: Norm Bolen, rgnl dir; Carol Jones, actg rgnl mgr communications (Ottawa).

Ontario Region, French Services: 250 Lanark Ave., Box 3220, Stn. "C," Ottawa, Ont. K1Y 1E4. (613) 724-1200.

Officers: Pierre Racicot, rgnl dir French svcs in Ontario & in the Outaouais; Maryse Lairot, actng rgnl mgr communications.

Manitoba Region: 491 Portage Ave., Box 160, Winnipeg, Man. R3C 2H1. English svcs: (204) 788-3222; French svcs: (204) 788-3141.

Officers: Marvin Terhoch, rgnl dir; Bridget A. Hoffer, sr mgr central rgnl communications; Gilbert Teffaine, rgnl dir French svcs; Huguette Le Gall, rgnl mgr communications.

Saskatchewan Region: 2440 Broad St., Regina, Sask. S4P 4A1. (306) 347-9540.

Officers: Brian Cousins, rgnl dir; Janice Carter, sr mgr western rgnl communications; Diane Rondeau, mgr communications.

Alberta Region: Box 55, Edmonton, Alta. T5J 2P4. (403) 468-7500.

Officers: Ron Smith, rgnl dir; Glenn Luff, rgnl mgr communications; Denis Lord, rgnl dir French svcs; Pierre Noel, communications mgr radio & TV.

British Columbia Region: Box 4600, Vancouver, B.C. V6B 4A2. (604) 662-6000.

Officers: John H. Kennedy, rgnl dir; Gilian Dusting, rgnl mgr communications; Pauline Sincennes, rgnl dir French svcs; Johanne Huard, actg rgnl mgr.

CBC North: 5002 Forrest Dr., Box 160, Yellowknife, N.W.T. X1A 2N2. (403) 920-5460.

Officers: Marie Wilson, rgnl dir/TV dir; Craig Yeo, rgnl mgr communications.

Radiomutuel Inc.

Head Office: 1717 René-Lévesque Blvd. E., Montreal, Que. H2L 4E8. (514) 529-3210. FAX: (514) 529-3219.

Principal Officer: Normand Beauchamp, CEO/chmn of bd; Paul Emile Beaulne, exec VP; Robert Leonard, VP sls.

Affiliates: CJMS Montreal; CKMF-FM Montreal; CJRP Quebec; CHIK-FM Quebec; CJTR Trois-Rivieres, Que.; CIGB-FM Trois-Rivieres, Que.; CJRS Sherbrooke, Que.; CIMO-FM Magog, Que.; CJRC Gatineau, Que.; CKTF-FM Gatineau, Que.; CJMM-FM Rouyn-Noranda, Que.; CJMV-FM Val d'Or, Que.; CKRS Jonquiere, Que.; CJAB-FM Chicoutimi, Que.

Telemedia Communications Inc.

1411 rue Peel, Montreal, Que. H3A 3L4. (514) 845-6291. FAX: (514) 845-6939.

Officers: P. de Gaspe Beaubien, chmn; R.J. McCoubrey, pres/CEO; C. Beaudoin, pres/VP/gen mgr CKAC & CITE Rock, Quebec.

Toronto, Ont. M4S 3C3: 40 Holly St. (416) 482-9383. FAX: (416) 482-9469.

Officers: D. Pagnutti, exec VP Ontario.

Radio News Services

ABC News. See ABC listing in Major National Television Networks and Major National Radio Networks, this section.

ABN/Associated Broadcast News Service. 2400 National Press Bldg., Washington 20045. (301) 320-4615. Robert C. Cody, exec edit.
ABN serves cable, radio & TV via satellite & syndication. Offers the consumer-oriented newsmagazine *FOCAL POINT* & segments therein, localized coverage of federal govt.

AMA Radio News. (American Medical Association.) 515 N. State St., Chicago 60610. (312) 464-4449. FAX: (312) 464-2450. Bruce K. Dixon, prod.
Medical news wraps by toll-free number & satellite (five per week). Mthy calendar mailing.

AMI News. 50 Vashell Way, Suite 300, Orinda, Calif. 94563. (510) 254-4456. FAX: (510) 254-6135. John Hamilton, pres; Rob Brown, VP sls & mktg. Eastern Bureau: (800) 736-0370. Claire Diepenbrock.
Phone- & tape-supplied features focusing on skiing, fishing, camping, travel & beach conditions with related news & info. Offered seasonally.

Accu-Weather Inc. 619 W. College Ave., State College, Pa. 16801. (814) 237-0309. FAX: (814) 238-1339. Joel N. Myers, pres; Sheldon Levine, natl sls mgr.
Coml weather svc providing exclusive Accu-Weather forecasts, top personalities & studio digital sound for TV & radio.

Africa News Service Inc. Box 3851, Durham, N.C. 27702. (919) 286-0747. FAX: (919) 286-2614. Reed Kramer, pres; Tami Hultman, exec edit; Bertie Howard, exec dir.
A news & info svc on African affrs.

Agence France-Presse. 1612 K St. N.W., Washington 20006. (202) 861-8535. FAX: (202) 861-8525. Philippe Gustin, rgnl dir for the Americas; Jacques Thomet, rgnl sls mgr for the Americas.
Produces a var of international news svcs, including text wires in six languages, photo wires, graphics & financial wires.

American Academy of Dermatology. Communications Dept., American Academy of Dermatology, Box 4014, 930 N. Meachum Rd., Schaumburg, Ill. 60168-4014. (708) 330-0230. FAX: (708) 330-0050. Bradford Claxton, exec dir.
Free 60-second radio spots on news about skin, hair & nails narrated by Chicago radio personality.

American Heart Association. 7272 Greenville Ave., Dallas 75231. (214) 706-1397. FAX: (214) 706-1341. Carol Floyd, bcst news edit; Howard L. Lewis, dir health & science news division.
TV: periodic satellite news feeds of medical rsch stories.

American Stock Exchange-Radio Amex. 86 Trinity Pl., New York 10006. (212) 306-1637. Tom Mariam; mgr Radio Amex.
Provides wkly talk show *Amex Business Talk* & stock mkt reports tailored for individual stns & nets.

American Urban Radio Networks. 463 7th Ave., New York 10018. (212) 714-1000. FAX: (212) 714-1563. Sydney L. Small & Ronald Davenport, co-chmns; Jack Bryant pres; Jerry Lopez, pres of progmg opns affil.
Black net news, sports, commentaries, pub affrs progs.

Associated Press Broadcast Division. 1825 K St. N.W., Washington 20006-1253. (202) 736-1100. (800) 821-4747. FAX: (202) 736-1199, news; (202) 736-1124, admin; (202) 736-1107, VP office. Jim Williams, VP/dir; Brad Kalbfeld, dep dir news progmg/mgng edit; Daryl Staehle, dep dir sls & mktg; Greg Groce, dir admin; Lee Perryman, dep dir; Wally Hindes, asst mgng edit opns; Sue Mosher, asst dir tech dev; Evelyn Cassidy, dir stn svcs; Ed Tobias, asst mgng edit news; Barbara Worth, asst mgng edit bcst wires; Bob Feldman, mktg mgr tech svcs; Dave Polyard, dir nets.
Real-time state, natl & international high-speed news wires; full-svc, coml-free radio nets; news mgmt software for TV & radio.

Associated Press Network News. See Associated Press listing in Major National Radio Networks, this section.

Athena Services Group. Box 1400, 2708 Elm St., Dubuque, Iowa 52004-1400. (319) 556-4000. Rita Daniels, pres; Thomas Churchill, chief meteorologist.
Provides 24-hour radio weathercasts & severe weather coverage. Digital audio, automated delivery & digital weathercast automation system available.

Audio-Video News. 3622 Stanford Cir., Falls Church, Va. 22041. (703) 354-6795. Connie Lawn, pres/chief correspondent.
Covers major natl, international & specialty stories for radio & TV stns in the U.S. & around the world.

BPI Entertainment News Wire. 100 Boylston St., Suite 210, Boston 02116. (617) 482-9447. FAX: (617) 482-9562. John Morgan, gen mgr; Don Gallagher, mgng edit; Judy Webb, sls mgr.
Advance news from BPI-owned publications.

The Berns Bureau. 400 N. Capitol St. N.W., #183, Washington, 20001. (202) 628-1430. FAX: (202) 628-1432. Matt Kaye, bureau chief; Cynthia Ingle, sr correspondent.
Complete "localized" coverage of Washington. Satellite & telephone transmission. Audio news releases. Govt, politics, farm, relg & other progmg for radio.

Black Radio Network Inc. (BRN). 166 Madison Ave., New York 10016. (212) 686-6850. FAX: (212) 686-7308. Diane Levy, pres; Roy Thompson, VP news dir; Bill Baldwin, bureau mgr New York; Peter Knight, VP sls; Sam Tucker, bureau mgr Washington; Sam Clark, bureau mgr Los Angeles.
Provides a daily actuality news svc emphasizing minority-oriented items.

British Information Services. 845 3rd Ave., New York 10022. (212) 745-0376. FAX: (212) 758-5395. Mark Hopkinson, head radio & TV division.
Provides daily news & feature audio svc filed by satellite from London at no cost to stns. Assists radio & TV crews visiting the U.K.

Broadcast Interview Source. 2233 Wisconsin Ave. N.W., Washington, 20007. (202) 333-4904. FAX: (202) 342-5411. Mitchell P. Davis, publisher; Stephanie Harshman, edit.
Publisher of *Annual Yearbook of Experts & Authorities & Spokespersons*.

Broadcast News Ltd. 36 King St. E., Toronto, Ont., Canada M5C 2L9. (416) 364-3172. FAX: (416) 364-8896. Wayne Waldroff, gen mgr; Michelle Poulin, business mgr; Rina Steuerman, satellite sls; Paul McDermott, gen exec eastern Canada; Jerry Fairbridge, mktg mgr.
Full wire & audio svcs (news agency), satellite delivery for prog syndicators.

Broadcast News Service. Box 1008, Boston 02103. P.J. Romano, dir.
Audio news & spec features.

The Business Radio Network Inc. 888 Garden of the Gods Rd., Colorado Springs 80907. (719) 528-7040. FAX: (719) 528-5170. Richard G. Grisar, CEO/pres; Dave Rose, VP progmg; Howard Price, VP sls & mktg; Skip Joeckel, VP affil; Donald Emanuel, VP corp dev.
Provides business, sports & entertainment news, 24 hours, seven days, on Business Radio Network, American Sports Radio Network & American Forum Network.

CBS News. See CBS listing in Major National Radio Networks, this section.

CNBC Business Radio. Unistar Radio Networks, 1675 Broadway, 17th Fl., New York 10019. (800) 225-3270; (212) 247-1600. FAX: (212) 247-0393. Bob Bartolomeo, dir affil rel.
Business news reports, twice an hour, 24 hours a day during the business week, plus weekend reports. Radio only.

CNN Headline News. Unistar Radio Networks, 1675 Broadway, 17th Fl., New York 10019. (212) 247-1600. FAX: (212) 247-0393.
Provides 24-hour audio from the CNN TV news ch for radio.

CNN Radio News. Unistar Radio Networks, 1675 Broadway, 17th Fl., New York 10019. (212) 247-1600. FAX: (212) 247-0393.
Top- and bottom-of-the-hour radio newscasts 24 hours a day, plus business, sports & lifestyle updates.

CNFP-TV Newsfilm Producers/Seacoast Films (CSEA-TV & Newsfilm City Hall) Pressroom 212, City Hall Desk, Philadelphia 19107-1684. (215) 686-3025; (215) 686-1776. Ron DeMarco, CEO/mgng edit.
Philadelphia 19124-4314: Claridge St. (215) 288-9325 exec office; (215) 990-2633 mobile unit.
All media svcs, print & bcst covering news, sports, entertainment, print, radio, TV, film & video. Satellite feeds.

CNW Broadcast. Waterpark Pl., 10 Bay St., Suite 914, Toronto, Ont., Canada M5J 2R8. (416) 863-9350. FAX: (416) 863-4825. Barry McQuillan, mgr bcst svcs.
Calgary, Alta., Canada T2P 3C7: Gulf Canada Sq., 401 9th Ave. S.W., Suite 635. (403) 269-7605. FAX: (403) 263-7888. TWX: 03-824872. John Mitchell, dir Prairie rgn.
Halifax, N.S., Canada B3J 3N4: Central Trust Tower, 1801 Hollis St., Suite 210. (902) 422-1411. FAX: (902) 422-3507. TWX: 019-21534. Brian Graham, mgr Atlantic Canada.
Montreal, Que., Canada H3G 1J1: 1350 Sherbrooke St. W., Suite 1025. (514) 842-2520. FAX: (514) 842-3745. TWX: 055-60936. Gunnel Pelleher, VP Quebec.
Ottawa, Ont., Canada K1P 5B9: 165 Sparks St., Suite 603. (613) 563-4465. FAX: (613) 563-0548. TWX: 053-3292. Don Hoskins, VP natl capital rgn.
Vancouver, B.C., Canada V6C 2TB: 750 W. Pender St., Suite 1103. (604) 669-7764. FAX: (604) 669-4356. TWX: 04-508529. Larry Cardy, VP western Canada.
Distributor of video & radio news releases, features, PSA & corporate prods via satellite & hard copy.

Capitol News Service. (Maine Radio Network.) The Statehouse, Stn. #70, Augusta, Me. 04333. (207) 287-1094. FAX: (207) 287-1099. Mal Leary, mgng edit.
Produced reports & actualities.

The Church of Jesus Christ Latter-day Saints (Mormons). 15 E. South Temple St., 2nd Fl., Salt Lake City 84150. (801) 240-4612. FAX: (801) 240-1167. Gerry Pond, mgr radio news & feature svc; Arnold Augustin, mgr TV news & feature svc; Don Russell, mgr electronic media mktg.
Offers free pub affrs, news & feature progmg for TV & radio; also guests for talk shows. Pub affrs progmg is not church-oriented.

Compu-Weather Inc. Box 1122, Flushing, N.Y. 11354. (718) 961-4242. Jeff Wimmer, pres; Todd Gross, VP; Peter Muldavin, sls mgr.
Weather forecasts, features, info & actualities for TV & radio.

Congressional Quarterly Inc. 1414 22nd St. N.W., Washington 20037. (202) 887-8500. FAX: (202) 728-1863. Andrew Barnes, chmn; Richard R. Edmond, pres; Neil Skene, edit/publisher; Robert W. Merry, exec edit; John J. Coyle, assoc publisher; Neil Brown, mgng edit.
Congressional Quarterly Weekly Report & News Service, editorial rsch reports, newsletters, seminars, rsch, reference volumes, paperbacks; daily & wkly congressional info publications.

Cornell Radio News Service. NB-13 MVR Hall, Cornell Univ. Media Services, Ithaca, N.Y. 14853. (607) 255-2190. FAX: (607) 255-1533. Nancy Fey, sr news prod; E.J. Miranda, news prod.
Closer Look wkly radio news feature series emphasizing health, consumer, social, technological & environmental issues. Short packages, actualities, topical features.

Digitized Radar Corp. Burke Lakefront Airport, Cleveland 44114. (216) 781-7396. FAX: (216) 781-7395. Gilbert A. Gomez, pres.
Color weather radar software specializing in color enhanced ground weather imagery, color weather radar & lightning displays for radio.

Ecumedia News Service. 475 Riverside Dr., Rm. 856, New York 10115. (212) 870-2312. FAX: (212) 870-2030. Roy Lloyd, exec dir.
Covers news of relg in voicers, actuals, commentaries & features on natl & international scene; interviews with religious leaders & newsmakers; for radio only.

Entertainment News Calendar. 250 W. 57th St., Suite 1527-105, New York 10107. (212) 421-1370. Evelyn Heyward, bureau chief.
Daily entertainment news svc.

Evening News Broadcasting Inc. Box 2777, Alexandria, Va. 22301. (703) 548-8007. Clayton Willis, pres/White House correspondent.
TV & radio news svcs.

Fairchild Broadcast News. Box 418, Hewlett, N.Y. 11557. (212) 686-6850. FAX: (212) 686-7308. Jay Levy, pres.
Gathers & disseminates news around the world.

Radio News Services

Feature-Net Radio Network. (Wholly-owned division of Liberty Hill Broadcasting.) 31800 N.W. Hwy., Suite 100, Farmington Hills, Mich. 48334. (313) 737-3000. Barry Zate, sr VP radio progmg; Leonard Jacobson, sr VP sports group; Ronald Zate, creative dir; Carol Cunningham, natl sls dir; Gina Ratliffe, stn svcs.
Custom radio features net: news, sports, entertainment & information. Short- & long-form progmg.

Hollywood News Calendar. 14755 Ventura Blvd., Suite 1562, Sherman Oaks, Calif. 91403. (213) 872-1507; (818) 986-8186. FAX: (818) 789-8047. Carolyn Fox, edit-in-chief; Susan Fox-Davis, edit.
Daily entertainment news svc.

Israel Broadcasting Service. 800 2nd Ave., New York 10017. (212) 867-7584. Myra Cohen, dir;
Free radio & TV progs & features from & about Israel.

Knight-Ridder Financial. 220 W. 89th St., Leawood, Kan. 66206. (913) 642-7373; (800) 248-0485. FAX: (913) 642-6488. David K. Ray, pres; Paul Tucker, CEO.
Electronic- & personal computer-based info for stns, & radio/TV nets involved in farm progmg.

Kyodo News Service. 50 Rockefeller Ctr., Suite 815, New York 10020. (212) 397-3723. FAX: (212) 397-3721. Hideaki Sakamoto, bureau chief; Toshi Mitsudome, mktg dir.
Real-time news svc, emphasizing economic, bus, sports & political coverage of Japan & Asia.

LANS (Los Angeles News Service). 1341 Ocean Ave., Suite 262, Santa Monica, Calif. 90401. (310) 399-6460. FAX: (310) 399-7541. Bob Tur, pres.
Provides helicopter reporting & video svcs for KNX Newsradio (CBS) and KCBS-TV.

Metro Weather Service Inc. 507-535 Rockaway Ave., Suite 3, Valley Stream, N.Y. 11581. (516) 568-8844; (800) 488-SUNNY. FAX: (516) 568-8853. Pat Pagano, pres.
Tailored weather forecasts for radio & TV. Feature reports: farming, marine, ski, long-range forecasts.

Mother Earth News. 24 E. 23rd St., 5th Fl., New York 10010. (212) 260-7210. FAX: (212) 260-7445. Owen Lipstein, ed dir.
Three-minute progs on back-to-nature, do-it-yourself, alt life-styles & other info.

Mutual Broadcasting System/Mutual Radio News. See Mutual Broadcasting System listing under Westwood Radio Network in Major National Radio Networks, this section.

NASDAQ Stock Market. 1735 K St. N.W., Washington 20006. (800) 777-6273. FAX: (202) 728-6993. Bob Ferri, dir media rel; Cameron Brown, mgr media svcs.
Free daily stock mkt reports tailored for loc & rgnl audiences. Voicers with NASDAQ mkt data & financial analysis.

NOAA/National Weather Service Headquarters. 1325 East-West Hwy., Silver Spring, Md. 20910. (301) 713-0622. FAX: (301) 713—0662. Ronald C. Lavoie, dir office of meteorology; James P. Travers, chief opns division; Donald R. Wernly, chief warning & forecast branch.
Bohemia, N.Y. 11716: 630 Johnson Ave. (516) 244-0100. Susan F. Zevin, dir eastern rgn.
Fort Worth, Tex. 76102: 819 Taylor St. (817) 334-2668. Harry S. Hassel, dir southern rgn.
Kansas City, Mo. 64106-2897: 601 E. 12th St. (816) 426-5400. Richard P. Augulis, dir central rgn.
Salt Lake City 84147: Box 11188, Federal Bldg., 125 S. State St. (801) 524-5122. Thomas D. Potter, dir western rgn.
Anchorage 99513-7575: 222 W. 7th Ave., #23. (907) 271-5136. Richard J. Hutcheon, dir Alaskan rgn.
Honolulu 96850-4493: Box 50027, 300 Ala Moana Blvd. (808) 541-1641. Richard H. Hagemeyer, dir Pacific rgn.
Weather & flood warnings, forecasts & related info for the media & gen public.

National Television News Inc. 6133 Kentland Ave., Woodland Hills, Calif. 91367. (818) 883-6121. FAX: (818) 883-0605. Howard Back, exec edit; Barbara Presson, stn rel mgr.
Oak Park, Mich. 48237: 13691 W. Eleven Mile Rd. (313) 541-1440. James O'Donnell, mgng edit; Joann Stevenson, opns mgr. (Detroit office.)
Planning & videotape prod & full natl or rgnl distribution of video news reports & public svc spots & related AV materials for radio-TV.

National Weather Network. Box 786, 916 Foley St., Jackson, Miss. 39205. (601) 352-6673. FAX: (601) 948-6052. Edward St. Pé, pres; Debbie St. Pé, treas; Dave Barber, opns mgr.
Custom weathercasts via satellite for TV only. Cash & barter.

Nemo News Service. 7179 Via Maria, San Jose, Calif. 95139. (408) 226-6339; (800) 243-8436. FAX: (408) 226-6403. Dick Reizner, own/assignment edit.
On-assignment coverage of news & sporting events for radio & TV stns worldwide.

News/Broadcast Network. 9431 W. Beloit Rd., Milwaukee 53227. (414) 321-6210. FAX: (414) 321-3608. James L. Hill, chmn; Michael Hill, pres.
Connecticut: (203) 972-1887. FAX: (203) 972-1508.
Chicago: (708) 963-4455. FAX: (708) 963-4487.
New York: (212) 889-0888. FAX: (212) 696-4611.
Washington: (703) 893-4577. FAX: (703) 893-6967.
Los Angeles: (909) 621-6903. FAX: (909) 621-9494.
Prod & distribution of radio news clips, actualities & pub affrs progs distributed by satellite, telephone & tape for TV & radio.

North American Network. 7910 Woodmont Ave., Suite 1400, Bethesda, Md. 20814. (310) 654-9810. FAX: (310) 654-9828. Tom Sweeney, pres; Julie Brown, VP opns; Steve Murphy, VP mktg; Lisa Brusio Coster, stn svcs mgr.
Audio news releases, talk show interviews, teleconferenced events, on-site coverage for corporations, govt agencies, assns.

Northern California News Satellite. 1121 L St., Suite 109, Sacramento, Calif. 95814. (916) 446-7890. FAX: (916) 446-7893. Steve Mallory, pres; Bill Branch, bureau chief.
Video wire svc providing daily news coverage, via satellite, of California's capitol for TV stns throughout the state.

Ohio State University Electronic News Services. 1125 Kinnear Rd., Columbus, Ohio 43212. (614) 292-8385; (800) 251-4636 (Ohio only). FAX: (614) 292-0154. Amy Murray, radio mgr; Kevin Jones, prod/videographer.
A 24-hour radio actualities svc: social, health & consumer features. Video of campus scenes inside & outside classes & laboratories, usually available at no chg.

Pacifica Network News. 702 H St. N.W., Washington, 20001. (202) 783-1620. FAX: (202) 393-1841. Julie Drizin, prod.
Half-hour nightly natl & international newscast distributed via satellite for radio only.

ProMedia. 170 Ludlow Ave, Northvale, N.J. 07647. (201) 768-7900; (800) 782-0700. FAX: (201) 768-7908. Frank Guida, VP prod; Phil Muro, asst prod.
Prod of comedy svcs for various radio formats.

Radio America. 1030 15th St. N.W., Suite 700, Washington, 20005. (202) 408-0944. FAX: (202) 404-1087. James C. Roberts, pres; Marc Lipsitz, VP; Brett Moss, news dir.
Short & long-form progs; spec series; documentaries; daily one hour news show. Radio only.

Radio Press News Services. Box 1122, El Cerrito, Calif. 94530. (510) 524-9559. FAX: (510) 524-9559. Joseph L. Levit, Ph.D., pres; Robert M. Master, M.Ph.A., edit-in-chief; T.J. Waters, spec events; R.A. Levit, edit foreign affrs.
Natl coverage, with spec unit for Northern California & Bay Area, in California & adjacent states. Multimedia news, *Travellands,* & *Vacationland.* Spec features, articles, transcriptions, video-features.

Radio Pulsebeat News. Box 418, Hewlett, N.Y. 11557. (212) 686-6850. FAX: (212) 686-7308. Jay R. Levy, pres/edit.
Gen actuality news svc.

Radio Weather Network. 2045 Riverside N., Baton Rouge 70802. (504) 928-4302. FAX: (504) 928-2102. Tony Doherty, pres.
Specialized weather forecasts, weather info svc bcst to radio stns; barter & paid.

Reuters America Inc. 1333 H St., Washington 20005. (202) 898-8410. FAX: (202) 898-8448. Steve Ginsburg, editor-in-chg (bcst svcs); Robert Doherty, bureau chief; Courtenay Carson, sls.
The Reuter Broadcast Report & Reuter Broadcast PLUS, featuring natl & international news, sports, business news, entertainment & weather.

Sheridan Broadcasting Network. 411 7th Ave., Suite 1500, Pittsburgh, Pa. 15219. (412) 456-4038. FAX: (412) 456-4040. Ronald R. Davenport, chmn; Jerry Lopes, VP news & sports.
New York 10036: One Times Sq. Plaza. (212) 575-0099. Glenn Bryant, sls mgr.
Chicago 60601: 75 E. Wacker Dr., Suite 700. (312) 558-9090. Drew Middleton, sls mgr.
Information, news, sports & entertainment of spec interest to blacks & other minorities.

Sidebar News International. 436 Valley Scent Ave., Scotch Plains, N.J. 07076-1163. (908) 322-8343. FAX: (908) 322-8902. Charles Homer, editorial dir.
News reports & progmg for TV, cable & radio.

Skywatch Weather Center. 347 Prestley Rd., Bridgeville, Pa. 15017. (800) SKY-WATCH. FAX: (412) 221-3160. Dick Mancini, pres; Dan Kryzwiecki, Stan Penkala, VPs; Stan Bostjancic, treas; Harry Green, sec.
Taped & live weathercasts targeted to the lstng area, in stn-specified formats. Featuring accuracy, clarity & mature voices.

Spanish Information Service. (Associated with Texas State Networks.) 7901 Carpenter Fwy., Dallas 75247. (214) 688-1133. FAX: (214) 637-3843. Jose Luis Madrigal, VP/gen mgr; Andy Barrett, gen sls mgr.
Comprises 53 stns in 10 states, reaching 84% of U.S. Hispanic pop over the age of 18.

Sportcom Associates/Motor Sports Radio (SM). 82 Zevan Rd., Johnson City, N.Y. 13790-4633. (607) 770-9165. FAX: (607) 770-9165. Paul Kaminski, CEO/news dir.
Bi-wkly preview & review of news, personalities & results of major auto racing, wkly road test feature on a barter basis for radio only. Galaxy 6 & Comerex single line phone distribution.

The Sports Network. 701 Masons Mill Business Park, Huntingdon Valley, Pa. 19006. (215) 947-2400. FAX: (215) 938-8466. Mickey Charles, pres; Steve Abbott, mgng edit; Phil Sokol, dir opns; John Sweeney, dir tech facilities.
Comprehensive sports wire svc. Sports real time, news, summaries, statistics & more. Designed for bcstrs.

SportsTicker. Harborside Financial Ctr., 600 Plaza Two, Jersey City, N.J. 07311. (201) 309-1200. FAX: (201) 860-9742. Peter Bavasi, pres; Rick Alessandri, VP admin; Joe Carnicelli, mgng edit; John Mastroberardino, gen mgr news opns; Louis Monaco, dir mktg svcs; John Buonaugurio, dir sls.
Instant scores & complete sports news coverage on all professional & major college events delivered to broadpage printer, newsroom computer or PC.

Standard Broadcast News. 2 St. Clair Ave. W., Toronto, Ont., Canada M4V 1L6. (416) 323-6824. FAX: (416) 323-6825. Steve Kowch, gen mgr; Cal Johnstone, natl news dir.
Ottawa, Ont., Canada K1P 5A4: 150 Wellington St., Suite 400. (613) 238-6585. Dwayne Desaulniers, parliamentary hill bureau chief.
Domestic & international audio & wire news svcs serving radio stns.

Standard Broadcast Wire. 2 St. Clair Ave. W., Toronto, Ont., Canada M4V 1L6. (416) 323-6824. FAX: (416) 323-6825. Steve Kowch, gen mgr; Paul Johnstone, natl news dir.
Ottawa, Ont., Canada K1P 5A4: 150 Wellington St., Suite 400. (613) 235-5010. Malcolm Bernard, bureau chief.
Wire svc for Canadian bcstrs, incorporating UPI Customcast for international coverage & Canadian staff, clients & stringers.

Studio M Productions. 8715 Waikiki Station, Honolulu 96830. (808) 734-3345; (800) 453-3345. FAX: (808) 734-3299. Mike Michaels, gen mgr.
Stringers for news, sports, features, remote bcsts, engrs, announcers, reporters & equipment, radio, TV, film & video.

TV Direct. See Associated Press listing in Major National Radio Networks, this section.

Texas News Service. 7901 Carpenter Fwy., Dallas 75247. (214) 688-1133. FAX: (214) 689-1912. Charlie Seraphin, pres/gen mgr; Joe Short, dir affil rel; Rick Wais, news dir.
Headline news svc of the Texas State Networks. Provides Texas news, sports & business headlines; natl & international headlines from ZapNews; Texas weather; features.

Trans World Communications Inc. Box 418, Hewlett, N.Y. 11557. (212) 686-6850. FAX: (212) 686-7308. Jay Levy, pres.
Produces audio news svcs for radio & TV bcstg.

Radio News Services

Frank Ucciardo. 538 Chestnut St., West Hempstead, N.Y. 11552. (516) 292-1403. FAX: (212) 643-8972.

Unistar News. Unistar Radio Networks, 1675 Broadway, 17th Fl., New York 10019 (212) 247-1600. FAX: (212) 247-0393. Rich Rieman, VP news & sports.

Top and bottom-of-the-hour radio newscasts 24 hours a day presented by anchors targeted to contemp demographics.

United Press International Inc. 1400 Eye St. N.W., Washington 20005. (202) 898-8000. FAX: (202) 789-3262. Robert Kennedy, pres/CEO; Steve Geimann, sr VP; Michael Aulabaugh, VP bcst svcs.

Chicago 60601: 202 N. Wabash. (312) 781-1600. Bob Kieckhefer, rgnl edit.

Los Angeles 90045: 6701 Center Dr. W. (310) 670-1100. Eric Kramer, rgnl edit.

New York 10001: 5 Penn Plaza. (212) 560-1100. William Morrissey, rgnl edit.

Atlanta 30367: 1819 Peachtree St. N.E. (404) 355-3700. David Mould, rgnl edit.

Full global text, audio, photo news & info svcs 24 hours a day.

Views and People in the News (VP News). 1212 5th Ave., New York 10029. (212) 876-6503. Gayle Gary, edit in chief.

Other offices located in Chicago, Los Angeles & San Francisco.

News svcs to radio stns currently having more than 100,000 subs; sells syndicated half-hour radio shows.

WINGS: Women's International News Gathering Service. Box 33220, Austin, Tex. 78764. (512) 416-9000. FAX: (512) 416-9000. Frieda Werden, prod.

Syndicate audiotape news & current affrs progs—both produced in-house & acquired—focus on women & hard news. Radio news svc.

WSI Corp. Four Federal St., Billerica, Mass. 01821. (508) 670-5000. FAX: (508) 670-5100. Mark Gildersleeve, pres; Don Freeland, media mkt mgr.

Art & animation capabilities, & real-time weather imagery products including composite radar imagery. Supply weather info to radio & TV.

The Wall Street Journal Radio Report. 200 Liberty St., New York 10281. (212) 416-2381. FAX: (212) 416-4195. Robert B. Rush, dir bcst svcs; Jonathan Krongard, mgr affil rel.

Hourly business & financial news reports transmitted live via satellite 24 times daily from the Journal's New York newsroom.

Washington International Teleport. 5600 General Washington Dr., Suite B-210, Alexandria, Va. 22312. (703) 914-0014. FAX: (703) 658-4919. Henry C. Clark, VP mktg sls; Andy Cassells, progmg booking mgr; Peter Browne, VP opns & engrg.

Domestic & international satellite transmission & reception svcs; transponder purchases, traf coord, portable equipment, loc microwave, fiber access, voice, data & video communication svcs.

WeatherData Inc. 825 N. Main, Wichita, Kan. 67203. (316) 265-9127. FAX; (316) 265-0371. Mike Smith, pres/certified consulting meteorologist; Steve Prior, mgr meteorology.

Forecasts for radio & TV, meteorology training, slides & videotape of weather & related phenomena.

Weather-One. (Wholly-owned division of Liberty Hill Broadcasting.) 31800 N.W. Hwy., Suite 100, Farmington Hills, Mich. 48334. (313) 737-3000. Barry Zate, sr VP; Richard Leiderman, chief forecaster.

Provides weather forecasting svc to radio stns, advanced storm warnings, agricultural & ski info.

Weather Services Corp. 131A Great Rd., Bedford, Mass. 01730. (617) 275-8860. FAX: (617) 275-9624. Peter R. Leavitt, CEO; Michael S. Leavitt, pres; John P. Murphy, sr VP; George J. Stamos, VP.

Weather by meteorologists for the exclusive use of radio stns.

Evan Weiner Productions. 370 Claremont Ave., Mount Vernon, N.Y. 10552. (914) 667-9070. FAX: (914) 667-3043. Evan Weiner, exec prod; Amy Bader, Gary Chester, Bob Huessler, on air talent; Shel Beugen, TV syndicator, (312) 944-4700, FAX: (312) 944-1582; Gary Chester, legal department; Don Barberino, prod, (203) 288-2597.

TV & radio prog prod. Sport commentaries & reporting. Current prog: *Sports: Beyond the Field*, sports issues show.

Western Information Network. 815 McBride Plaza, New Westminster, B.C., Canada V3L 2C1. (604) 524-9466. FAX: (604) 526-2430. Ray Dagg, pres; John Ashbridge, opns mgr; Trevor Pancoust, news dir; David Glasstetter, chief engr.

Live & prerecorded info & entertainment prog prod & satellite delivery to rgnl & natl Canadian radio nets.

Willis News Service. Box 2777, Alexandria, Va. 22301. (703) 548-8007. L. Clayton Willis, White House & Congressional correspondent/own.

TV, radio bcst & print media.

Zapnews. 4002 University Dr., Fairfax, Va. 22030. (800) 800-5100. FAX: (800) 800-9450.

World, natl & state news, sports & features written for immediate bcst. Compatible with newsroom computers & FAX machines.

Zondervan Radio Network. 5300 Patterson Ave. S.E., Grand Rapids, Mich. 49530. (616) 698-3417; (800) 727-8004. FAX: (616) 698-3439. Jonathan Petersen, dir.

International pub affrs svc of news, features, interviews, PSAs & commentaries of expert authors. Supplied on cassette every two weeks.

Radio Format Providers

ABC Radio Network. 12655 N. Central Expy., Suite 600, Dallas 75243. (214) 991-9200. FAX: (214) 991-1071. David Kantor, pres; David Hubschman, exec VP; Martin Raab, VP mktg; Robert Hall, sr VP.

Offers 10 live radio formats 24 hours a day; 1,000 plus subs. Spacenet 3 transponder.

Alternative Programing Inc. 3626 N. Hall, Suite 908, Dallas 75219. (800) 231-2818; (214) 521-4484. FAX: (214) 521-6808. Mickey Briggs, pres.

A var of formats offered on reel-to-reel, custom CD & cassette.

American Comedy Network. Park City Plaza, Bridgeport, Conn. 06604. (203) 384-9443. FAX: (203) 367-9346. Cliff Bia, pres.

Offers stns the National Features Service consisting of seven original features per week, 60-seconds to 90-seconds long. The bits include fake comls, song parodies, interactives & show openings.

American International Productions. Box 31000, Spokane, Wash. 99223. (509) 448-7400. FAX: (509) 448-3811. Thomas W. Read, pres; Melinda R.B. Read, VP.

Old-time radio shows & nostalgia specials.

American Urban Radio Networks. 411 7th Ave., Suite 1500, Pittsburgh 15219. (412) 456-4030; (800) 456-4211. FAX: (412) 456-4040. Jerry Lopes, pres prog opns & affiliations; Glenn Bryant, dir affil rels.

New York 10018: Executive Offices, 463 7th Ave., 6th Fl. (212) 714-1000. FAX: (212) 714-1563. Jack Bryant, pres.

Provides hourly news & sports, long-form talk & mus progmg as well as *USA Music Magazine*. Other alternative progmg includes *Coming Soon* movie review, *Straight Up* with Bev Smith & *White House Report* with veteran White House correspondent Bob Ellison.

America's Rock Network. 6577 E. Camino Vista, Suite 4, Anaheim Hills, Calif. 92807. (714) 921-9249. FAX: (714) 630-6778. Harvey Sheldon, pres.

Daily or wkly hard rock & heavy metal video format for TV & cable stns. On 77 CATV systems serving almost six million subs.

Toby Arnold & Assoc. 3234 Commander Dr., Carrollton, Tex. 75006. (214) 661-8201; (800) 527-5335. FAX (214) 250-6014. Toby Arnold, pres/CEO; Dolly Arnold, VP/COO; Larry Mangiameli, VP/creative dir.

Mus prod libraries for radio, TV & cable; custom stn ID's; news & image mus for radio, TV & cable.

Bailey Broadcasting Services. 3151 Cahuenga Blvd. W., Suite 200, Los Angeles 90068-1768. (213) 969-0011. FAX: (213) 969-8474. Lee Bailey, pres; Diane Blackmon Bailey, VP; Danielle Holland, stn rel.

Produces & syndicates daily & wkly entertainment—mus, info progs & specs.

Beethoven Satellite Network. 303 E. Wacker Dr., Chicago 60601. (800) USA-WFMT; (312) 565-5000. FAX: (312) 565-5169. David Levin, dir; Scott Kniper, prog dir; Carol Martinez, opns mgr; Jon Kavanaugh, dir corporate communications.

Provides classical mus progmg by satellite to more than 160 stns 82 hours per week; progs in one-hour modules with prog hosts & loc sound.

Bonneville Broadcasting System. 4080 Commercial Ave., Northbrook, Ill. 60062-1829. (800) 631-1600; (708) 291-0110. FAX: (708) 291-0841. John Patton, pres/CEO; Bud Stiker, exec VP; Walter Powers, VP opns; Ford Colley, VP consulting; Michael Krafcisin, VP opns & mktg svcs; Jon Radford, Joe Cassady, progmg consultants; Jeff Dear, prod mgr; Mindy Herman, office mgr.

Radio progmg, opns, mgmt, finance, duopoly & LMA consultants; progmg prod & distribution. *Signature Series* includes a var of formats. Auditorium mus testing. Talent bank & creative spot copywriting & prod svcs. Digital audio playback systems. Custom strategic mapping mkt analysis.

The Broadcast Group. 3333 K St. N.W., Suite 77, Washington 20007. (202) 337-3111. FAX: (202) 337-2567. Pegge Goertzen, pres; Chris Lauterbach, Matt Coates, prods.

Radio prod & distribution of progs including *Face Off* & *Leonard Maltin on Video*.

Broadcast Programming Inc. 2211 5th Ave., Seattle 98121. (206) 728-2741; (800) 426-9082. FAX: (206) 441-6582. Edith Hilliard, pres; John Carlile, mgr; Jay Albright, gen mgr BP Consulting Group; Jim LaMarca, sls mgr; Becky Brenner, progmg mgr; Keith Chambers, mktg mgr.

Radio mus formats on CD & reel-to-reel; offers 43 different formats plus custom mixes & complete digital 24-hour walk-away progmg & hardware.

Business Radio Network Inc. 888 Garden of the Gods Rd., Colorado Springs 80907. (719) 528-7040. FAX: (719) 528-5170. Richard G. Grisar, pres/CEO; Dave Rose, VP prgmg; Donald Emanuel, VP corporate dev; Howarad Price, VP sls & mktg; Skip Joeckel, VP affil.

Provides 24-hour business news & feature progmg. American Sports Radio, 24-hour sports talk & events. American Forum Network, 24-hour entertainment talk.

CBS RADIO NETWORKS

CBS Radio Networks. 51 W. 52nd St., New York 10019. (212) 975-4321. Frank Murphy, VP progmg.

This division currently offers two long-form progs—*Cruisin' America* & *On The Move*. Also syndicates *Byline Magazine*, which consists of 11 short-form features available on a cash basis.

CRN International. One Circular Ave., Hamden, Conn. 06514. (203) 288-2002. FAX: (203) 281-3291; (203) 288-8537. Barry Berman, pres; S. Richard Kalt, exec VP; Patrick E. Kane Sr., VP corporate dev; Paul Orio, dir affil rel.

Features include *Ski Watch*, a 60-second, daily update. Summer-oriented progmg includes *Beach Watch* & *Summer Watch*; Wimbeldon Radio Network. All progs are available on a barter basis.

Lita Cohen Radio Services. 309 Meadow Ln., Merion, Pa. 19066. (215) 667-7795. FAX: (215) 667-3996. Lita Cohen, pres.

Big Band Jump available to stns on cassette or tape with tones. All available on barter basis.

Concept Productions. 120 Main St., Roseville, Calif. 95678. (916) 782-7754; (800) 783-3454. FAX: (916) 786-8304. Dick Wagner, pres; Mary Wagner, VP.

Formats for live or automated radio stns on reels, DAT, or CDs: AC, CHR, gold, country, MOR. Also automation equipment.

Creative Radio Network. Box 7749, Westlake Village, Calif. 91361. (805) 379-4012. FAX: (805) 379-1741. Darwin Lamm, pres.

Radio mus prog for A/C—country & modern.

DC Audio. 1137 5th St. N.E., Washington 20002. (202) 544-2533. FAX: (202) 544-3048. John Dryden, pres; Luke Merriken, VP.

Offers *The Daily Feed*, news & satire, five segments per week at 90 seconds per segment.

DIR Broadcasting. 32 E. 57th St., New York 10022. (212) 371-6850. FAX: (212) 888-8650. Robert B. Meyrowitz, pres; D.R. Goven, dir affil rel.

Offers *King Biscuit Flour Hour*, a wkly one-hour prog delivered via CD, featuring live concert performances of top contemp recording artists.

Dialogue. (Progmg produced by the Woodrow Wilson International Center for Scholars.) 370 L'Enfant Promenade, Suite 704, Washington 20024. (202) 287-3000, ext. 325. FAX: (202) 287-3772. George Liston Seay, prod; Denis Saulnier, asst prod; John Tyler, tech dir.

Wkly half-hour prog of conversations on world politics, history & culture. Available to public & coml stns free of chg on CD or by satellite.

Eagle Media Productions Ltd. Box 430, N. Salem, N.Y. 10560. (914) 669-5277. Louis Adler, pres; Thalia Adler, VP/gen mgr.

Offers *Medical Journal* & *A Matter of Law*, 90-second features—barter; cassette delivery.

Euroline Communications. Box 362, 3727 S. 14th St., Sheboygan, Wis. 53081-0362. (414) 458-8880. FAX: (414) 458-3577. Dieter E. Helm, pres/own.

Contemp & traditional European mus in easy listening, light rock, classics & small combination formats for small-medium market FM & CATV.

Executive Broadcast Services. Box 60327, Colorado Springs, 80960. (800) 800-0107. FAX: (719) 579-6664. Skip Joekel, pres; Kelly Hilligoss, dir opns & mktg.

Mkts & sells a select line of progs, products & svcs to U.S. radio stns.

Far West Communications Inc. 120 N. Victory Blvd., Suite 106, Burbank, Calif. 91502. (818) 566-7003. FAX: (818) 566-7086. Paul Ward, pres/gen mgr; Skip Joeckel, mktg dir; Ron Blassnig, tech dir.

Formats: Gold Plus, 30 Plus, True Country, True Country II. Modern MOR progmg formats; Air Force One, Masterdisc audiophile mus libraries. CD, analog tape or DAT. Tape delivered to 71 subs.

Globe Productions. Box 20465, Roanoke, Va. 24018. (703) 344-3283. J.W. Sheperd, pres/own.

Full-svc automated easy listening featuring seven days of mus without a repeat—50/50 mix of vocals & instruments.

Fred Hall Production. Box 612478, S. Lake Tahoe, Calif. 96152. (916) 573-0709. FAX: (916) 573-0712. Fred Hall, pres; Clyde Hendricks, sls mgr.

Big Band prog *Fred Hall's Swing Thing* with celebrity guests, format Great Times, broad-based, 3,600-selection nostalgia library.

Hispanic Radio Network Inc. 112 W. San Francisco Ave., Suite 305, Santa Fe, N.M. 87501. (505) 984-0080. FAX: (505) 982-6889. Consuelo Luz, pres; Jeff Kline, gen mgr; Roberto Mondragon, news dir; Paul Orsinger, sls mgr.

Produces & syndicates four daily four-minute Spanish radio progs with natl, rgnl & statewide adv available free to stns.

The Specialist in Broadcast CD Music!

- Broadcast CD Music Libraries
- Weekly Top Hits U.S.A. on CD
- CD Christmas Library
- Music Rotation Software

**50 States & Canada:
800-521-2537**

Fax: 313-681-3936

Serving Broadcasters Since 1970.

Broadcasting & Cable Yearbook 1994

Radio Format Providers

Walter Cronkite's Twentieth Century
America's Great Journalist Looks Back at Significant Events on This Date in History
Delivered Seven Days a Week

When Radio Was... With ART FLEMING
The Best in Old-Time Radio! 5 hour-long show per week

THE MAN WHO DRAINED LAKE MICHIGAN AND FILLED IT WITH CHOCOLATE!!!

Stan Freberg Here
Satirical Commentary for the 90's Five times per week

ALL BARTER
Contact DAVID WEST at
(201) 385-6566
More Fine Radio Programming from DBA
DBA reserves the right of final selection of affiliates for any of its programs.

Jameson Broadcast Inc. 1700 Connecticut Ave. N.W., Suite 401, Washington 20009. (202) 328-3283. FAX: (202) 332-6810. Trulee Burns, VP.
 Specializes in short-form entertainment, info progs & promotions.

Joe Jones Productions. 10556 Arnwood Rd., Lake View Terrace, Calif. 91342. (818) 890-0730. FAX: (818) 899-4457. Joe Jones, pres/own; Marion Jones, VP/own; Dwayne Jones, gen mgr; Keith Jones, business mgr.
 Contemp & traditional New Orleans mus, rhythm & blues, Louisiana Cajun mus.

Jones Satellite Networks. 9697 E. Mineral Ave., Englewood, Colo. 80112. (800) 876-3303. FAX: (303) 784-8786. Roy Simpson, gen mgr/exec VP; Phil Barry, VP progmg & opns.
 Live 24-hour progmg; researched mus library; match-up playlist. Computer generated song-by-song list for every hour of every week. A/C, oldies, soft hits & CD country formats available.

KJAZ National Jazz Radio Network. 1131 Harbor Bay Pkwy., Alameda, Calif. 94502. (510) 769-4800. FAX: (510) 769-4849. Tim Hodges, gen mgr; Jim O'Dea, CFO; Steve Wade, dir mktg.
 Satellite-delivered bcstg of mainstream jazz mus for re-transmission by radio & cable affils.

MJI Broadcasting. 1290 Ave. of the Americas, 6th Fl., New York 10019. (212) 245-5010. FAX: (212) 586-1090. Joshua Feigenbaum, pres; Gary Krantz, VP/gen mgr; Julie Talbott, exec VP.
 Produces syndicated radio progs & specs for all formats, airing wkly on more than 2,000 stns & nets worldwide.

MRN Radio. 1801 International Speedway Blvd., Daytona Beach, Fla. 32114. (904) 254-6760. FAX: (904) 254-6716. John McMullin, pres/gen mgr; Allen Bestwick, asst gen mgr; David Hyatt, dir affils.
 Live bcsts of NASCAR stock car racing & related progs via satellite.

MediaAmerica Inc. 11 W. 42nd St., New York 10036. (212) 302-1100. FAX: (212) 302-6024. Ron Hartenbaum, chmn; Gary Schonfeld, pres.

Charles Michelson Inc. 9350 Wilshire Blvd., Suite 316, Beverly Hills, Calif. 90212. (310) 278-4546. FAX: (310) 278-7932. Charles Michelson, pres.
 Prog buyers for overseas TV stns. Distributors of half-hour radio progs. Cash not barter.

Musical Starstreams. Box 1989, Sedona, Ariz. 86339. (602) 204-1989. FAX: (602) 204-1990. Forest, prod/host.
 Musical Starstreams, is a wkly two-hour prog of progsv instrumental-based mus targeted to adults age 25-49.

The Nashville Network Radio. 2644 McGavock Pike, Nashville 37214. (615) 871-6710. FAX: (615) 871-6778. Jeff Lyman, net coord affil sls
 Syndicates one wkly radio feature, The Nashville Record Review. Hosted by Lorianne Crook & Charlie Chase.

Nashville Record Review. (Joint venture of Group W Satellite Communications & Opryland USA Inc.) Box 10210, 250 Harbor Plaza Dr., Stamford, Conn. 06904-2210. (203) 965-6000. FAX: (203) 965-6315. David Hall, VP/gen mgr TNN; Bob Meyer, group radio mgr Opryland USA Inc.; Lloyd Werner, sr VP sls & mktg GWSC; Steven Soule, VP affil rel GWSC; Peter Weisbard, VP sls GWSC; Steven Yanovsky, VP mktg; Cheryl Daly, VP pub rels GWSC.
 Nashville 37214: 2806 Opryland Dr. (615) 889-6840.
 Wkly four-hour countdown prog.

North American Network. 7910 Woodmont Ave., Suite 1400, Bethesda, Md. 20814. (301) 654-9810. FAX: (301) 654-9828. Tom Sweeney, pres; Steve Murphy, dir sls/stn svcs.
 Full-svc radio agency offering news feed, progs & PSAs; sets up interviews with experts & celebrities.

Old Time Radio National Archives Foundation. Box 31000, Spokane, Wash. 99223. (509) 484-7400. FAX: (509) 448-3811. Thomas Wilmot Read, pres.
 Old-time radio shows & nostalgia specials.

Olympia Networks Inc. 7745 Carondelet, St. Louis 63105-3315. (314) 727-8900. FAX: (314) 727-4115. Steve Bunyard, pres; Bill Latz, sr VP; John McElfresh, VP affil rel.
 Offers a var of comedy, sports & entertainment progmg.

Orange Productions. 105 Forest Ave., Narberth, Pa. 19072. (215) 667-8620. FAX: (215) 667-8939. Sid Mark, pres; Jon Harmelin, VP/gen mgr; Brian Marc, opns mgr.
 Prod & distribution of a wkly two-hour prog Sounds of Sinatra.

PIA Radio Network. 680 N. Lake Shore Dr., Suite 1230, Chicago 60611. (312) 943-8888. FAX: (312) 943-5464. Brad Saul, CEO; Sandy Kramer, chief opns.
 Produces & syndicates the College Football Game of the Week, DePaul Basketball, Chicago Bulls, White Sox, Pro Football This Week & three pub affrs progs.

Premiere Radio Networks. 15260 Ventura Blvd., Suite 500, Sherman Oaks, Calif. 91403. (818) 377-5300. FAX: (818) 377-5333. Steve Lahman, pres; Tim Kelly, exec VP; Kraig Kitchin, sr VP sls.
 Lineup includes Comedy Networks: CHR, AC, Country, Rock, Gold. Plain-Wrap Countdowns formats: CHR, AC, Urban, Country. Syndicated Morning Show: Gerry House & The House Foundation. Mediabase rsch formats: CHR, Rock, Urban, AC. Anti-Jingles & Pure Impact I & II Jingles. Short-form features include News from the Boonies, The Cla'ence Update of the Young and the Restless & On The Phone with Ti-Rone. All features & svcs offered on a barter basis & are available via satellite, disc, reel-to-reel tape, mailed script or telephone, depending on the prog.

Program Distributors. 403 W. Parker Rd., Jonesboro, Ark. 72403. (501) 972-5884. FAX: (501) 932-0892. Wayman Hatman, gen mgr.
 Nostalgic radio prod & distribution including Lum and Abner & Memorable Days of Radio.

Promedia. 170 Ludlow Ave., Northvale, N.J. 07647. (201) 768-7900; (800) 782-0700. FAX: (201) 768-7908. Beverly Padratzik, gen mgr; Frank Guida, VP prod.
 Supplier of radio comedy through mus parodies, spoof comls & spec IDs.

The Specialist in Broadcast CD Music!

- Broadcast CD Music Libraries
- Weekly Top Hits U.S.A. on CD
- CD Christmas Library
- Music Rotation Software

**50 States & Canada:
800-521-2537**
Fax: 313-681-3936

Serving Broadcasters Since 1970.

RPM Radio Programing and Management Inc. 4198 Orchard Lake Rd., Orchard Lake, Mich. 48323. (800) 521-2537; (313) 681-2660. FAX: (313) 681-3936. Thomas M. Krikorian, pres.
 Olympia Fields, Ill. 60461: 3521 Ithaca Rd. (800) 621-5699; (708) 748-9444. FAX: (708) 503-0001. Ray Lowy. Chicago office.
 Top Hits U.S.A. wkly CD svc & CD libraries including Solid Gold, Spectrum A/C & Country One. CD Christmas library.

Radio Express Inc. 3575 Cahuenga Blvd. W., Suite 390, Los Angeles 90068. (213) 850-1003. FAX: (213) 874-7753. Tom Rounds, pres; Lynn Anderson, VP sls; John Fudor, gen mgr/VP.
 Distributors outside the U.S. of American Top 40, Country Countdown, Hot Mix, Hitdisc, Golddisc, Hollywood Express, Love Songs, Production Libraries & Pow-

Radio Format Providers

erplay. Progs available by cash or barter. Libraries & products cash only.

Radio Spirits Inc. 1609 Barclay Blvd. Buffalo Grove, Ill. 60089. (708) 465-8245. FAX: (708) 465-8602. Carl Amari, CEO; Roy Millonzi, pres.

Radio producers of the nationally-syndicated old time radio prog *When Radio Was*. Complete digital recording studio features Sonic Solutions Digital Work Station with No-Noise.

SJS Entertainment Corp. 800 2nd Ave., 9th Fl., New York 10017. (212) 370-9460. FAX: (212) 983-1186. Steven Saslow, chmn; June Brody, pres.

Offers both wkly & mthy shows featuring classic rock, country, urban contemp & live concerts such as *In The Studio*.

Semaphore Entertainment Group. 32 E. 57th St., 7th Fl., New York 10022. (212) 371-6850. FAX: (212) 888-8650. Robert Meyrowitz, pres; D.R. Goven, dir affil rel.

Produces & distributes cable progmg.

Serendipity Nostalgia Quiz. 4775 Durham Rd., Guilford, Conn. 06437-3607. (203) 457-1039. Michael Paul Lund, pres; Robert Bradbury, gen mgr.

Featurette licensed to Big Band, nostalgia & easy listening stns across the country includes audio trivia incorporated into questions about radio & TV, mus personalities & nostalgia of all kinds.

Southcott Productions. Box 33185, Granada Hills, Calif. 91344. (800) 356-9107. FAX: (818) 368-4938. Chuck Southcott, own; Sammy Jackson, country consultant.

Provides adult MOR, adult country, & adult sacred mus formats.

Studio Center Corp. 200 W. 22nd St., Norfolk, Va. 23517. (804) 622-2111. FAX: (804) 623-5512. Warren M. Miller, CEO/exec prod; Robert Jump, pres/gen mgr.

Radio & TV coml prods. Sls on a cash basis.

Sun Radio Network. (Affiliate of Sound Communications Inc.) 2870 Scherer Dr. N., Suite 100, St. Petersburg, Fla. 33716-1024. (813) 572-9209. FAX: (813) 572-4735. Bill Wardino, pres.

Provides 20-hour radio net svc, news-talk, satellite audio bcstg; no affiliation fee to qualified stns.

TM Century Inc. 2002 Academy, Dallas 75234. (800) 937-2100. FAX: (800) 749-2121. P. Craig Turner, pres/CEO; Stuart McRae, VP sls; Richie Allen, VP.

GoldDiscs Mus Libraries, HitDisc wkly mus svc, jingles, TV prod, mus libraries, digital studio.

24 Karat Productions Inc. 566 S.E. Damask Ave., Port St. Lucie, Fla. 34983. (407) 340-4040; (800) 340-4142. Mark Prichard, pres/CEO; Gloria Prichard, exec VP/gen mgr; John Donahey, sls mgr.

A full-svc consultant for 25 years. Creates & distributes radio formats with complete consultant package including progmg, prom & sls. Also creator & developer of popular Music-1 format.

Talkline Communications Radio Network. Box 20108, Parkwest Station, New York 10025-1510. (212) 769-1925; (800) 628-TALK. FAX: (212) 799-4195. Zeb J. Brenner, pres.

Natl Jewish radio net featuring news & interviews with newsmaker guests & celebrities; live call-in format; live segments from Israel; satellite delivered. Available on barter.

Texas AP Network. 4851 LBJ Fwy., Suite 300, Dallas 75244. (214) 991-2020. FAX: (214) 991-7207. Amanda Barnett, supvr; Doug Kienetz, rgnl radio exec.

Full-svc, coml-free AP radio net serving more than 70 stns in Texas.

Unistar Radio Networks. 1675 Broadway, New York 10019. (212) 247-1600. FAX: (212) 247-0393. Bill Hogan, pres; Ed Salamon, pres progmg; Neil Sargent, VP affil rel; Kirk Stirland, VP affil rel.

Los Angeles 90078-4323: Box 4323.

Provides seven 24-hour satellite-delivered formats, wkly shows, specs: Don Imus, G. Gordon Liddy, Dot Mike, Donnie Simpson, CNN Radio & CNBC Radio.

United Press International. 1400 Eye St. N.W., 9th Fl., Washington 20005. (202) 898-8116; (202) 898-8240. FAX: (202) 898-8124. Mike Aulabaugh, VP bcstg; Howard Dicus, news dir.

Full-svc company offers a number of short-form info features to its affil radio stns.

WFMT Radio. 303 E. Wacker Dr., Chicago 60601. (312) 565-5000. FAX: (312) 565-5169. Norman Pellegrini, prog dir; Jim Barker, gen sls mgr; Daniel Schmidt, sr VP radio; Ray Nordstrand, dir dev.

Provides classical & folk mus, news & fine art progmg through United Video Inc. 24 hours per day. Serves 260 cable systems in 37 states with 1.2 million subs.

WLIR Radio. Box 489, Nanuet, N.Y. 10952. (914) 624-1300. FAX: (914) 624-2809. Zev Brenner, pres; Philip W. Plack, gen mgr; Gary B. Duglin, opns/sls mgr; Yaakov Spivak, news dir; Michael Lobaito, chief engr; Gary Shiff, prod dir.

Provides satellite-delivered Jewish progs including *World Jewish News* on the hour, contemp mus, talk, comedy, business & children's shows 24 hours per day.

Westwood One Radio Networks. 9540 Washington Blvd., Culver City, Calif. 90232. (310) 840-4383. FAX: (310) 840-4060. Norman J. Pattiz, CEO/chmn; Gregory P. Batusic, pres; Bruce E. Kanter, exec VP/CFO; Thomas A. Ferro, exec VP/gen mgr; Craig Whetstine, VP/dir affil rel; Andrew Denemark, dir progmg; Laurie Peters, dir pub rels; Bill Stolier, dir international affil rel; Rob Tonkin, dir artist rel, mktg & prom; Dwight Kuhlman, dir talent & mus mktg.

New York 10019: 1700 Broadway. (212) 237-2500. FAX: (212) 581-4699.

Arlington, Va. 22202: 1755 S. Jefferson Davis Hwy. (703) 413-8300. FAX: (703) 413-8445. Washington office.

Chicago 60601: 111 E. Wacker Dr., Suite 1321. (312) 938-0222.

Dallas 75231: 10000 N. Central Expy., Suite 1438. (214) 373-0022.

Troy, Mich. 48084: 3250 W. Big Beaver, Suite 125. (313) 649-6300. Detroit office.

Toronto, Ont., Canada M5V 1W5: 260 Richmond St. W., Suite 400. (416) 597-8529.

Produces & distributes syndicated radio progs, long & short form.

Winners News Network (WNN). 6699 N. Federal Hwy., Boca Raton, Fla. 33487. (407) 997-0074. FAX: (407) 997-0476. Howard Goldsmith, pres.

Exclusive worldwide 24-hour format of motivational speakers & self-help info.

Major National Television Networks

ABC

Capital Cities/ABC Inc.

Headquarters: 77 W. 66th St., New York 10023-6298. (212) 456-7777.

West Coast: 2040 Ave. of the Stars, Century City, Calif. 90067. (213) 557-7777.

Board of Directors: Thomas S. Murphy, Robert P. Bauman, Nicholas F. Brady, Warren E. Buffett, Frank T. Cary, John B. Fairchild, Leonard H. Goldenson, Frank S. Jones, Ann Dibble Jordan, John H. Muller Jr., Wyndham Robertson, M. Cabell Woodward Jr.

Officers: Thomas S. Murphy, chmn of bd/CEO; John B. Fairchild, exec VP; Robert A. Iger, exec VP/pres ABC Television Network Group; Ronald J. Doerfler, sr VP/CFO; Herbert A. Granath, sr VP/pres ABC Cable & International Broadcast Group; Michael P. Mallardi, sr VP/pres Broadcast Group; Phillip J. Meek, sr VP/pres Publishing Group; Stephen A. Weiswasser, sr VP/pres Multimedia Group; David Westin, VP/gen counsel; Allan J. Edelson, VP/controller/asst sec; Joseph M. Fitzgerald, VP investor rels; James M. Goldberg, VP/taxes; Robert T. Goldman, Andrew E. Jackson, VPs; Patricia J. Matson, VP corporate communications; Jeffrey Ruthizer, VP labor rels; David J. Vondrak, VP/treas; William J. Wilkinson, VP human resources; Philip R. Farnsworth, sec; Allen S. Bornes, asst treas.

Capital Cities/ABC Broadcast Group: Michael P. Mallardi, pres; Philip R. Beuth, VP/pres early morning & late night entertainment; Robert O. Niles, VP/dir engrg Broadcast Group; Lawrence J. Pollock, VP/pres TV stns.

ABC Television Network Group: Robert A. Iger, pres; Philip R. Beuth, VP/pres early morning & late night entertainment; Ted Harbert, pres ABC Entertainment; Dennis D. Swanson, pres ABC Sports; Pat Fili-Krushel, pres ABC Daytime; Jeanette B. Trias, pres children's progmg; Philip R. Beuth, pres early morning & late night entertainment; David Wstin, pres Production; Archie C. Purvis, pres Ambroco Media Group, Inc.; Dennis B. Kane, pres ABC & Kane Productions International; Brandon Stoddard, pres ABC Productions; Roone Arledge, pres ABC News; Mark Mandala, pres ABC TV Network; Preston Davis, pres bcst opns & engrg; Marvin F. Goldsmith, pres sls & mktg.

ABC Television Network: Mark Mandala, pres ABC TV Network; Mark D. Roth, VP opns; Stephen K. Nenno, VP prog admin; Maureen P. Dornal, VP/dir prog admin East Coast.

Television Network Sales: Marvin F. Goldsmith, pres sls & mktg; Robert Cagliero, exec VP/natl sls mgr; Lawrence S. Fried, exec VP/gen sls mgr; Robert S. Wallen, sr VP finance & admin; James F. Wasilko, sr VP prime time sls; Mary Ellen Holahan, VP/Detroit sls mgr; Mark C. Mitchell, VP eastern sls; Peter Scanlon, VP, prime time sls proposals; Edward J. Wollock, VP central sls; Michael R. Rubin, VP/dir central div; Daniel Barnathan, VP daytime sls; Gail A. Sullivan, VP/dir daytime sls; Charles W. Clark, VP sls western div; Charles A. Gabelmann, VP sls dev & mktg svcs; Madeline C. Nagel, VP sls & mktg; Harry H. Factor, VP promotional sls & account dev; William P. Cella, VP sports sls; Brian Sikorski, VP/dir sports sls; Cynthia Ponce Abrams, VP news & early am sls; Patrick J. McGovern, VP/dir news—early morning & late night sls; John J. Abbattista, VP revenue planning & admin.

ABC Entertainment: Edward W. Harbert, pres; Stuart J. Bloomberg, exec VP prime time; Kim Fleary, VP comedy series dev; Deborah Ellis Leoni, VP dramatic series dev; John Hamlin, VP variety & event specials; Brian McAndrews, VP current series progs; Judd Parkin, sr VP motion pictures for TV & miniseries; Barbara Lieberman, sr VP motion pictures for TV & miniseries; Alan Sternfeld, sr VP prog planning & scheduling; Donna Rosenstein, sr VP talent & casting; Ronald B. Sunderland, exec VP bus affrs & contracts; Mark Pedowitz, sr VP bus affrs; Barry Gordon, VP bus affrs West Coast; David L. Sherman, VP music & bus affrs; Ronald Pratz, VP bus affrs admin West Coast; Anthony S. Farinacci, VP bus affrs East Coast; P. Thomas Van Schaick, sr VP finance & admin; Eric Beattie, VP finance & admin West Coast; Mark C. Zakarin, sr VP mktg & concept specials; Stuart L. Brower, VP on-air prom; Chris Carlisle, VP special projects; Barbara Eddy, VP on-air graphics; Geoffrey S. Calnan, VP special projects; Pat Fili-Krushel, pres ABC daytime; Mary Alice Dwyer-Dobbin, exec VP ABC daytime; Terry Guarnier, VP daytime progmg East Coast; Amy Dorn Kopelan, VP direct response mktg & daytime progs; Charlotte Koppe, VP daytime progmg West Coast; William Herlihy, sr VP finance & admin early morning, daytime, children's & late night progmg; Dominick J. Nuzzi, VP prod East Coast; Edgar Hirst, VP prod West Coast; Tom Remiszewski, VP adv & prom ABC sports & daytime progs; Jeanette B. Trias, VP children's progs; Philip R. Beuth, pres ABC early morning & late night entertainment; Jim Wagner, VP adv & prom *Good Morning America*.

ABC News: Roone Arledge, pres; Paul Friedman, exec VP; Richard C. Wald, sr VP editorial quality; William N. Temple, sr VP finance; Alan Wurtzel, sr VP/mgr longform progmg; Michael Duffy, VP opns; William Moore, VP news opns Washington, D.C.; Steven Sadicario, VP bus affrs; Mimi Gurbst, VP news coverage; Don Dunphy Jr., VP affil news svcs; Joanna Bistany, VP/asst to the pres; Amy Entelis, VP talent recruitment & dev; William Nagy, VP prod control; Robin Sproul, VP news coverage Washington, D.C.

ABC Sports: Dennis Swanson, pres; Dennis Lewin, sr VP prod; Bob Apter, sr VP finance & admin; David Downs, VP progmg; Jack O'Hara, exec prod; Keith Ritter, VP mktg; Jonathan Leess, VP prod planning; Tom Remiszewski, VP adv & prom; Lydia Stephans, VP progmg.

Production: David Westin, pres Ambroco Media Group, Inc.; Archie C. Purvis, pres; Paul D. Coss, VP prog acquisitions & dev; Dennis B. Kane, pres ABC & Kane Productions International.

ABC Productions: Brandon Stoddard, pres; Michael Ross, sr VP bus affrs; Ada Goldberg, VP bus & legal affrs; Jeffrey Offsay, exec VP; Amy Adelson, sr VP creative affrs; John Schwartz, VP finance; Thomas H Brokek, sr VP prod; Jim Painten, VP prod; Ian Valentine, VP motion pictures for television; Gene Stein, VP comedy.

Broadcast Operations and Engineering: Preston A. Davis, pres; Michael Lang, VP business affrs; Neil MacLeod, VP admin, finance & planning; David Elliott, VP engrg svcs East Coast; Mary Frost Distler, VP gen mgr net opns East Coast; Elliott Reed, VP TV opns East Coast; Jim Truelove, VP bcst opns & engrg Washington, D.C. opns; Robert A. Young, VP bcst opns & engrg West Coast.

ABC Cable and International Broadcast Group: Herbert A. Granath, pres; John T. Healy, pres Capital Cities/ABC Video Enterprises International; Richard F. Spinner, mgng dir/CEO European opns; Jeremiah G. Sullivan, sr VP finance & admin.

Corporate Divisions:

Legal: Stephen A. Weiswasser, sr VP/pres Capital Cities & ABC Multimedia Group; Griffith Foxley, VP corporate legal affrs; Andrew E. Jackson, VP corporate affil; Jeffrey S. Rosen, VP litigation; Mark MacCarthy, VP Washington, D.C.; Larry M. Loeb, VP/gen counsel video enterprises & publishing; Samuel Antar, VP law & regulation; Charles L. Stanford, VP legal, bus affrs & bcstg; Jeffrey Ruthizer, VP labor rels.

Broadcast Standards & Practices: Christine Hikawa, VP; Harvey Cary Dzodin, VP coml standards; Brett White, VP prog standards.

Financial: Ronald J. Doerfler, sr VP/CFO; Allan J. Edelson, VP/controller; David J. Vondrak, VP/treas; Joseph M. Fitzgerald, VP investor rels; Mark Hasson, VP/asst controller; Kerry A. Carr, VP internal audit; James M. Goldberg, VP taxes; Andrew G. Governali, VP tax planning & admin; Alan S. Bornes, asst treas.

Administration: Robert T. Goldman, VP admin; Richard E. Hockman, VP real estate & construction; Roger Lund, VP admin West Coast; Bruce Phillips, VP design & dev, real estate & construction; Andrew Pucher, VP facilities & security East Coast; Marion Roder Capriglione, VP travel & conference admin.

Corporate Communications: Patricia J. Matson, VP corporate communications ABC Inc.; Julie Tarachow Hoover, VP corporate projects; Veronica Pollard, dir corporate communications.

Office of Corporate Initiatives: Charles Keller, VP corporate initiatives; Dr. John E. Harr, VP office of communications.

Human Resources: William J. Wilkinson, VP human resources; Anita Hecht, VP employee rels; Anthony D. Sproule, VP personnel West Coast; Warren Salerno, VP employee benefits.

Research: Peter Chrisanthopoulos, exec VP mktg & prom; Richard Montesano, sr VP mkt rsch; Frank J. Cuciti, VP planning & scheduling, on-air adv & prom; Henry DeVault, audience analysis; Lawrence J. Gianinno, VP prog rsch; Larry Hyams, VP audience analysis.

Affiliate Relations: George H. Newi, exec VP affil rels; Buzz Mathesius, VP/dir affil opns; Bryce Rathbone, VP/dir stn rels; Mike Nissenblatt, VP affil mktg & rsch svcs.

Public Relations & Affiliate Marketing Services: Pete Barrett, sr VP; Jerry Hellard, VP pub rels West Coast; Janice Gretemeyer, VP/dir pub rels East Coast; Alan R. Morris, VP/dir affil mktg svcs; Sherrie Berger, VP/dir prog publ & photography.

Business Affairs: Ronald V. Sunderland, exec VP bus affrs & contracts; Mark Pedowitz, sr VP bus affrs; Barry Gordon, VP bus affrs West Coast; Ronald Pratz, VP bus affrs admin West Coast; Anthony Farinacci, VP bus affrs East Coast; David Sherman, mus & bus affrs.

Capital Cities/ABC Publishing Group: 77 W. 66th St., New York 10023. Phillip J. Meek, pres; Ann Maynard Gray, VP/pres Diversified Publishing Group; David S. Loewith, VP/pres.

Specialized Publications:

Fairchild Publications (New York): John B. Fairchild, chmn/editorial dir; Michael F. Coady, pres.

Diversified Publishing Group: Ann Maynard Gray, pres.

Financial Services and Medical Group: Peter Derow, pres.

Daily Newspapers:

The Kansas City Star (Kansas City, Mo.): James H. Hale, chmn of bd/publisher.

Fort Worth Star-Telegram (Fort Worth, Tex.): Richard L. Connor, pres/publisher.

The Oakland Press (Pontiac, Mich.): Bruce H. McIntyre, pres/publisher.

Belleville News-Democrat (Belleville, Ill.): Gary L. Berkley, pres/publisher.

The Times Leader (Wilkes-Barre, Pa.): Dale A. Duncan, pres/publisher.

Major National Television Networks

Albany Democrat-Herald (Albany, Ore.): John Buchner, publisher.

The Daily Tidings (Ashland, Ore.): Michael O'Brien, publisher.

Milford Citizen (Milford, Ct.): Richard Backer, publisher.

St. Louis Daily Record (St. Louis): Sue Tedesco, publisher.

St. Louis Countian (St. Louis): Sue Tedesco, publisher.

St. Peter's Courier Post: Sue Tedesco, publisher.

Weekly Newspapers and Shopping Guides: Newspapers & shopping guides in eight states.

ABC Distribution Co.: Joseph Y. Abrams, pres; Carol Brokaw, VP sls opns & admin; Maria D. Komodikis, VP international TV sls; Michael J. Dragotto, VP theatrical/home video mktg.

ABC Television Network

Affiliated stations: 230. Note: Indented call letters indicate that station is a satellite of the preceding station.

KTXS Abilene, Tex.
WAKC Akron, Ohio
WTEN Albany, N.Y.
   WCDC Adams, Mass.
KOAT Albuquerque, N.M.
   KOVT Silver City, N.M.
KLAX Alexandria, La.
WATM Altoona, Pa.
KVII Amarillo, Tex.
   KVIH Clovis, N.M.
WOI Ames, Iowa
KIMO Anchorage
   KATN Fairbanks, Alaska
WLOS Asheville, N.C.
   WAXA Anderson, S.C.
WSB Atlanta
WJBF Augusta, Ga.
KAAL Austin, Minn.
KVUE Austin, Tex.
KBAK Bakersfield, Calif.
WJZ Baltimore
WVII Bangor, Me.
WBRZ Baton Rouge, La.
WOTV Battle Creek, Mich.
KSVI Billings, Mont.
   KCTZ Bozeman, Mont.
KBMT Beaumont, Tex.
WLOX Biloxi, Miss.
WMGC Binghamton, N.Y.
WBRC Birmingham, Ala.
KIVI Boise, Idaho
WCVB Boston
WBKO Bowling Green, Ky.
WKBW Buffalo, N.Y.
WVNY Burlington, Vt.
KFNB Casper, Wyo.
   KFNE Riverton, Wyo.
KCRG Cedar Rapids, Iowa
WCBD Charleston, S.C.
WCHS Charleston, W.Va.
WSOC Charlotte, N.C.
WTVC Chattanooga, Tenn.
WLS Chicago
WSVI Christiansted, V.I.
WKRC Cincinnati
WEWS Cleveland
KRDO Colorado Springs
KMIZ Columbia, Mo.
WOLO Columbia, S.C.
WTVM Columbus, Ga.
WSYX Columbus, Ohio
KIII Corpus Christi, Tex.
WFAA Dallas
WDTN Dayton, Ohio
WAND Decatur, Ill.
KUSA Denver
WXYZ Detroit
WDHN Dothan, Ala.
KDUB Dubuque, Iowa
WDIO Duluth, Minn.
   WIRT Hibbing, Minn.
WQOW Eau Claire, Wis.
KVIA El Paso
   KVIO Carlsbad, N.M.
WSJV Elkhart, Ind.
WENY Elmira, N.Y.
WJET Erie, Pa.
KEZI Eugene, Ore.
WTVW Evansville, Ind.
KATN Fairbanks, Alaska
WDAY Fargo, N.D.
   KBMY Bismarck, N.D.
   WDAZ Devils Lake, N.D.
   KMCY Minot, N.D.
WJRT Flint, Mich.

WPDE Florence, S.C.
KHBS Fort Smith, Ark.
   KHOG Fayetteville, Ark.
WPTA Fort Wayne, Ind.
KFSN Fresno, Calif.
WCJB Gainesville, Fla.
KJCT Grand Junction, Colo.
WZZM Grand Rapids, Mich.
KFBB Great Falls, Mont.
WBAY Green Bay, Wis.
WABG Greenville, Miss.
ZFB Hamilton, Bermuda
KOUS Hardin/Billings, Mont.
   KYUS Miles City, Mont.
WSIL Harrisburg, Ill.
   KPOB Poplar Bluff, Mo.
WHTM Harrisburg, Pa.
WHSV Harrisonburg, Va.
WGHP High Point, N.C.
KITV Honolulu
   KHVO Hilo, Hawaii
   KMAU Wailuku, Hawaii
KTRK Houston
WAAY Huntsville, Ala.
WRTV Indianapolis
WAPT Jackson, Miss.
WBBJ Jackson, Tenn.
WJKS Jacksonville, Fla.
KAIT Jonesboro, Ark.
KODE Joplin, Mo.
KJUD Juneau, Alaska
KMBC Kansas City, Mo.
KHGI Kearney, Neb.
   KWNB Hayes Center, Neb.
   KSNB Superior, Neb.
WKPT Kingsport, Tenn.
KTVO Kirksville, Mo.
WATE Knoxville, Tenn.
WXOW La Crosse, Wis.
KATC Lafayette, La.
WLAJ Lansing, Mich.
KTNV Las Vegas
KSWO Lawton, Okla.
WTVQ Lexington, Ky.
KATV Little Rock, Ark.
KABC Los Angeles
WHAS Louisville, Ky.
KAMC Lubbock, Tex.
WSET Lynchburg, Va.
WGXA Macon, Ga.
WKOW Madison, Wis.
WMUR Manchester, N.H.
WLUC Marquette, Mich.
KDRV Medford, Ore.
   KDKF Klamath Falls, Ore.
WHBQ Memphis
WTOK Meridian, Miss.
WPLG Miami
KMID Midland, Tex.
WISN Milwaukee
KSTP Minneapolis-St. Paul
   KSAX Alexandria, Minn.
   KRWF Redwood Falls, Minn.
KTMF Missoula, Mont.
WQAD Moline, Ill.
WHOA Montgomery, Ala.
WEVU Naples, Fla.
WKRN Nashville
WCTI New Bern, N.C.
WTNH New Haven, Conn.
WVUE New Orleans
WABC New York
WVEC Norfolk, Va.
WOAY Oak Hill, W. Va.
KOCO Oklahoma City
KETV Omaha
WFTV Orlando, Fla.
KESQ Palm Springs, Calif.

WMBB Panama City, Fla.
WEAR Pensacola, Fla.
WHOI Peoria, Ill.
WPVI Philadelphia
KTVK Phoenix
WTAE Pittsburgh
KPVI Pocatello, Idaho
   KJVI Jackson, Wyo.
   KKVI Twin Falls, Idaho
WMTW Portland, Me.
KATU Portland, Ore.
WPRI Providence, R.I.
WTVD Raleigh, N.C.
KOTA Rapid City, S.D.
   KHSD Lead, S.D.
   KDUH Scottsbluff, Neb.
   KSGW Sheridan, Wyo.
KRCR Redding, Calif.
KAEF Eureka, Calif.
KFWU Fort Bragg, Calif.
KOLO Reno
WRIC Richmond, Va.
WOKR Rochester, N.Y.
WREX Rockford, Ill.
KOVR Sacramento, Calif.
KQTV St. Joseph, Mo.
KTVI St. Louis
WMDT Salisbury, Md.
KTVX Salt Lake City
KSAT San Antonio, Tex.
KGTV San Diego
KGO San Francisco
KNTV San Jose, Calif.
KEYT Santa Barbara, Calif.
WWSB Sarasota, Fla.
WJCL Savannah, Ga.
WNEP Scranton, Pa.
KOMO Seattle
KTBS Shreveport, La.
KCAU Sioux City, Iowa
   KCAN Albion, Neb.
KSFY Sioux Falls, S.D.
   KABY Aberdeen, S.D.
   KPRY Pierre, S.D.
KXLY Spokane, Wash.
WGGB Springfield, Mass.
KSPR Springfield, Mo.
WIXT Syracuse, N.Y.
WTXL Tallahassee, Fla.
KTGM Tamuning, Guam
WTSP Tampa, Fla.
WBAK Terre Haute, Ind.
WNWO Toledo, Ohio
KTKA Topeka, Kan.
WGTU Traverse City, Mich.
   WGTQ Sault Ste. Marie, Mich.
KGUN Tucson, Ariz.
KTUL Tulsa, Okla.
KLTV Tyler, Tex.
   KTRE Lufkin, Tex.
WUTR Utica, N.Y.
KXXV Waco, Tex
WJLA Washington, D.C.
WWTI Watertown, N.Y.
WAOW Wausau, Wis.
KRGV Weslaco, Tex.
KARD West Monroe, La.
WPBF West Palm Bech, Fla.
WLOV West Point, Miss.
KAKE Wichita, Kan.
   KLBY Colby, Kan.
   KUPK Garden City, Kan.
WWAY Wilmington, N.C.
KAPP Yakima, Wash.
   KVEW Kennewick, Wash.
WYTV Youngstown, Ohio
KSWT Yuma, Ariz.

Major National Television Networks

CBS Inc.

Headquarters: 51 W. 52nd St., New York 10019. (212) 975-4321; 7800 Beverly Blvd., Los Angeles 90036. (213) 852-2345.

Officers: Laurence A. Tisch, chmn/pres/CEO; Jay L. Kriegel, sr VP; Martin D. Franks, VP Washington, D.C.; Mark B. Pearlman, VP planning & bus dev; Edward Grebow, sr VP opns & admin; Peter W. Keegan, sr VP finance; Louis J. Rauchenberger Jr., VP/treas; Keith Fawcett, asst treas; Dennis D'Oca, VP risk mgmt; Alvan L. Bobrow, VP/dir taxes; Anton W. Guitano, VP/gen auditor; James F. Sirmons, sr VP industrial rels; Leon Schulzinger, VP industrial rels East Coast; John M. McLean, VP industrial rels West Coast; Ellen O. Kaden, VP gen counsel/sec.

CBS Operations & Administration

Edward Grebow, sr VP opns & admin; Joan Showalter, sr VP human resources; Karen Beldegreen, VP compensation & policy per; Thomas F. McVeigh, VP per benefits; James Halsey, VP mgmt info systems CBS Inc.; John Lalli, VP opns; Thomas C. Maile, VP telecommunications; Robert Monaghan, VP admin svcs; Joseph A. Flaherty, sr VP technology; Dave White, VP special projects; Jay Fine, VP bcst opns East Coast; Brent Stranathan, VP bcst distribution; Andrew Barry, VP TV opns East Coast; Robert Mauro, VP prod mgmt; Charles Dages, VP engrg; Richard Streeter, VP systems engrg; Robert P. Seidel, VP bcst svcs engrg; Darcy Antonellis, VP tech opns; Charles Cappleman, VP bcst opns West Coast; Ken Cooper, VP facilities opns New York.

CBS Broadcast Group

Howard Stringer, pres; Beth Waxman Bressan, VP/asst to the pres; Matthew Margo, VP prog practices New York; Carol A. Altieri, VP prog practices Hollywood, Calif.; Peter A. Lund, exec VP CBS Broadcast Group/pres CBS Mktg div; George F. Schweitzer, sr VP mktg & communications; Ann Morfogen, VP media rels; Susan Tick, VP publ West Coast; Michael Mischler, VP adv & prom Los Angeles; Kathie Culleton, VP media & planning, adv & promotion; John Bradford Crum, VP affil adv & prom; John Luma, VP on-air prom; Jerold Goldberg, VP creative svcs; David F. Poltrack, sr VP planning & rsch; Michael Eisenberg, VP TV audience measurement & natl TV rsch; Arnold Becker, VP TV rsch Los Angeles; Charles Moschetto, VP TV rsch New York; Jay D. Gold, VP finance; Bruce C. Taub, VP financial planning; Frank Tinghitella, asst controller CBS Television Network; Gary McCarthy, VP finance Hollywood.

CBS Enterprises Division

James A. Warner, pres; Rainer Siek, sr VP sls & mktg CBS Broadcast International; David P. Berman, VP prod & admin CBS Broadcast International; Kenneth Ross, VP/gen mgr CBS Video, CBS Enterprises; Tom Newell, VP bus affrs & opns.

CBS Affiliate Relations Division

Anthony C. Malara, pres; Scott T. Michels, VP/dir.

CBS Entertainment Division

Jeff Sagansky, pres; Peter F. Tortorici, exec VP; Steve Warner, VP prog planning; Madalene Horne, VP current progs; Joe Voci, VP current comedy/dir comedy dev; Madeline Peerce, VP creative svcs & artist rels; Suzan Mischer, VP entertainment & info specials; John Matoian, sr VP motion pictures for TV & miniseries; Sunta Izzicupo, VP movies & miniseries; Andy Hill, exec VP CBS Entertainment Productions; Robert Gros Sr., sr VP CBS Entertainment Productions; Kelly S. Goode, VP series dev CBS Entertainment Productions; Timothy Flack, VP comedy prog dev; Jonathan Levin, VP dramatic prog dev; Lisa Freiberger, VP talent & casting; Lucy Johnson, VP daytime progs; Judy M. Price, VP children's progs & daytime specials; Rhoderic H. Perth, VP late night progs & non-net progmg; William B. Klein, sr VP bus affrs; Leola Gorius, VP bus affrs; Layne Britton, VP bus affrs West Coast; Sidney Lyons, VP bus affrs, long form contracts & acquisitions; James F. McGowan, VP bus affrs admin.

CBS Marketing Division

Peter A. Lund, exec VP CBS Broadcast Group/pres CBS Mktg Div; Mary Lou Jennerjahn, VP admin; Joseph Abruzzese, sr VP TV net sls; Daniel J. Koby, VP/group natl sls mgr; W. Scott McGraw, VP/dir sls & mktg; Duncan E. Ryder, VP/dir sls & mktg; John R. Kelly, VP/dir sls & mktg; John P. O'Sullivan, VP/dir sls & mktg; Martin B. Daly, VP/dir sls & mktg; Dorothy S. Schwartz, VP/group head planning, admin & mkt resources; Richard J. Blangiardi, VP new bus dev; Ann E. Harkins, VP sls svcs; Kenneth J. Wachtel, VP/dir sls planning & proposals; Bonnie Hiramoto, VP mkt resources; William G. Cecil, VP prog sls; John Gray, VP West Coast sls; John Ginway, VP central sls; Richard Masilotti, VP Detroit sls; JoAnn C. Ross, VP Olympic mktg & sls; Michael J. Nowacki, VP daytime & children's sls; Michael A. Guariglia, VP sports sls; Jane P. Davey, VP news sls; Brian F. Neuwirth, VP prime time & late night sls; Linda Rene, VP/dir prime time & late night sls; John K. Brooks, VP/dir sports sls.

CBS News Division

Eric Ober, pres; Joseph Peyronin, VP CBS News Prime Time/asst to pres; Donald E. DeCesare, VP opns; Lane Venardos, VP hard news & special events; John Frazee, VP news svcs; Linda Mason, VP pub affrs; James M. McKenna, VP finance & admin; Robert E. McCarthy, VP bus affrs; Barbara Cochran, VP/bureau mgr CBS News Washington, D.C.; Al Ortiz, VP/bureau chief London & Europe; Larry D. Cooper, VP news radio.

CBS Sports Division

Neal H. Pilson, pres; Jay B. Rosenstein, VP progmg; Len DeLuca, Jeremy Handelman, VPs prog planning; Rick Gentile, sr VP prod; Mark H. Harrington III, VP Olympics; James F. Harrington, VP prog admin & opns; Raymond Harmon, VP bus planning; Noel B. Berman, VP sports bus affrs & compliance.

CBS Television Stations

Johnathan Rodgers, pres; Jay Newman, VP opns & stn svcs; Philip S. Press, VP sls & mktg; Sam Stallworth, VP natl sls; Robert A. Finkel, VP finance, planning & stn svcs; Carl "Bud" Carey, gen mgr WCBS-TV; William Applegate, VP/gen mgr KCBS-TV; Steve Gigliotti, VP/gen mgr KCBS-TV; Robert McGann, VP/gen mgr WBBM-TV; John Culliton, VP/gen mgr WCCO-TV; Ken Rees, VP/stn mgr WCCO-TV; Eugene Lothery, VP/gen mgr WCAU-TV; Allen Y. Shaklan, VP/gen mgr WCIX-TV; R. Perry Kidder, VP/gen mgr WFRV-TV.

Affiliates Advisory Board: Bill Sullivan (chmn), KPAX-TV Missoula, Mont.; Ralph Gabbard (chmn-elect), WKYT-TV Lexington, Ky.; Howard Kennedy (sec/treas), KMTV Omaha, Neb.; David Lynch, WRGB Schenectady, N.Y.; Jack West, WSPA-TV Spartanburg, S.C.; Fred Barber, WRAL-TV Raleigh, N.C.; Buck Long, WKRG-TV Mobile, Ala.; Jack Dempsey, WJHL-TV Johnson City, Tenn.; David Sanks, WISC-TV Madison, Wis.; Paul Karpowicz, WISH-TV; Paul Fredricksen, KCCI-TV Des Moines, Iowa; Allan Howard, KHOU-TV Houston; Jim Lucas, KKTV Colorado Springs; Jim Putney, KVAL-TV Eugene, Ore.; Allan Cohen, KMOV-TV St. Louis; Ron Bergamo, KTSP-TV Phoenix. Active Past Chairmen: Joseph Carriere, KREX-TV Grand Junction, Colo.; Phil Jones, Meredith Corp. Des Moines, Iowa; Guy Main, WCIA Champaign, Ill.; Red Martin, WCAX-TV Burlington, Vt.; Mick Schafbuch, KOIN Portland, Ore.; Berry Smith, Schurz Communications South Bend, Ind.; Ben Tucker, Retlaw Enterprises Inc. Fresno, Calif. Standing Committee Chairmen: Mike Schafbuch (economic study, net affil agreement & retransmission consent study), KOIN Portland, Ore.; Ben Tucker (govt rels), Retlaw Enterprises Fresno, Calif.; Allan Howard (news), KHOU-TV Houston; Jim Lucas (news), KKTV Colorado Springs; Barry Barth (promotion), KREM-TV Spokane, Wash.; Bud Williamson (tech), WKBN-TV Youngstown, Ohio; Bill Murdoch, KSL-TV Salt Lake City; Jim Putney, KVAL-TV Eugene, Ore.

CBS-TV Network

Affiliated stations: more than 200. Note: Indented call letters indicate that the station is a satellite of the preceding station.

KTAB-TV Abilene, Tex.
KUAM Agana, Guam
WRGB Albany, N.Y.
KRQE Albuquerque
  KBIM-TV Roswell, N.M.
WBKB-TV Alpena, Mich.
WTAJ-TV Altoona, Pa.
KFDA-TV Amarillo, Tex.
KTVA Anchorage
WJSU-TV Anniston, Ala.
WAGA-TV Atlanta
WRDW-TV Augusta, Ga.
KTBC-TV Austin, Tex.
KERO-TV Bakersfield, Calif.
WBAL-TV Baltimore
WABI-TV Bangor, Me.
WAFB-TV Baton Rouge
KFDM-TV Beaumont, Tex.
KTVQ Billings, Mont.
WBNG-TV Binghamton, N.Y.
WBMG-TV Birmingham, Ala.
KXMB-TV Bismarck, N.D.
KBCI-TV Boise, Idaho
WHDH-TV Boston

KBTX-TV Bryan, Tex.
WIVB-TV Buffalo, N.Y.
WCAX-TV Burlington, Vt.
KXLF-TV Butte, Mont.
WWTV Cadillac, Mich.
  WWUP-TV Sault Ste. Marie, Mich.
KFVS-TV Cape Girardeau, Mo.
KGWC-TV Casper, Wyo.
  KGWL-TV Lander, Wyo.
  KGWR-TV Rock Springs, Wyo.
KGAN Cedar Rapids, Iowa
WCIA Champaign, Ill.
  WCFN Springfield, Ill.
WCSC-TV Charleston, S.C.
WBTV Charlotte, N.C.
WDEF-TV Chattanooga
KGWN-TV Cheyenne
  KSTF Scottsbluff, Neb.
  KTVS Sterling, Colo.
WBBM-TV Chicago
KHSL-TV Chico, Calif.
WCPO-TV Cincinnati
WJW-TV Cleveland
KKTV Colorado Springs
WLTX-TV Columbia, S.C.
WRBL Columbus, Ga.
WCBI-TV Columbus, Miss.
WBNS-TV Columbus, Ohio

KZTV Corpus Christi, Tex.
  KVTV Laredo, Tex.
KDFW-TV Dallas
WHIO-TV Dayton, Ohio
KMGH-TV Denver
KCCI-TV Des Moines, Iowa
WJBK-TV Detroit
WTVY Dothan, Ala.
KDLH Duluth, Minn.
KECY-TV El Centro, Calif.
KDBC-TV El Paso
WSEE-TV Erie, Pa.
KVAL-TV Eugene, Ore.
  KCBY-TV Coos Bay, Ore.
  KPIC Roseburg, Ore.
KVIQ-TV Eureka, Calif.
WEHT Evansville, Ind.
KTVF Fairbanks, Alaska
KXJB-TV Fargo, N.D.
WBTW Florence, S.C.
WINK-TV Fort Myers, Fla.
KFSM-TV Fort Smith, Ark.
WANE-TV Fort Wayne, Ind.
KJEO-TV Fresno, Calif.
KXGN-TV Glendive, Mont.
KREX-TV Grand Junction, Colo.
  KREZ-TV Durango, Colo.
  KREG-TV Glenwood Springs, Colo.

Major National Television Networks

KREY-TV Montrose, Colo.
KRTV Great Falls, Mont.
WFRV-TV Green Bay, Wis.
   WJMN Escanaba, Mich.
WFMY-TV Greensboro, N.C.
WXVT Greenville, Miss.
WNCT-TV Greenville, N.C.
KGBT-TV Harlingen, Tex.
WHP-TV Harrisburg, Pa.
WFSB Hartford, Conn.
KGMB Honolulu
   KGMD-TV Hilo, Hawaii
   KGMV Wailuku, Hawaii
KHOU-TV Houston
WOWK-TV Huntington, W.Va.
WHNT-TV Huntsville, Ala.
KIDK-TV Idaho Falls, Idaho
WISH-TV Indianapolis
WJTV Jackson, Miss.
   WHLT Hattiesburg, Miss.
WJXT Jacksonville, Fla.
KRCG-TV Jefferson City, Mo.
WJHL-TV Johnson City, Tenn.
WWMT Kalamazoo, Mich.
KCTV Kansas City, Mo.
WKXT-TV Knoxville, Tenn.
WKBT La Crosse, Wis.
WLFI-TV Lafayette, Ind.
KLFY-TV Lafayette, La.
WLYH-TV Lancaster, Pa.
WLNS-TV Lansing, Mich.
KLAS-TV Las Vegas
WKYT-TV Lexington, Ky.
   WYMT-TV Hazard, Ky.
KOLN Lincoln, Neb.
   KGIN Grand Island, Neb.
KTHV Little Rock, Ark.
KCBS-TV Los Angeles
WLKY-TV Louisville
KLBK-TV Lubbock, Tex.
WMAZ-TV Macon, Ga.
WISC-TV Madison, Wis.
KEYC-TV Mankato, Minn.
KIMT Mason City, Iowa
KTVL Medford, Ore.
WREG-TV Memphis

WCIX Miami
WITI-TV Milwaukee
WCCO-TV Minneapolis
   KCCO-TV Alexandria, Minn.
   KCCW-TV Walker, Minn.
KXMC-TV Minot, N.D.
   KXMA-TV Dickinson, N.D.
   KXMD-TV Williston, N.D.
KPAX-TV Missoula, Mont.
WKRG-TV Mobile, Ala.
KNOE-TV Monroe, La.
KMST Monterey, Calif.
WAKA-TV Montgomery, Ala.
WTVF Nashville
WWL-TV New Orleans
WCBS-TV New York
WTKR-TV Norfolk, Va.
KOSA-TV Odessa, Tex.
KWTV Oklahoma City
KMTV Omaha
WCPX-TV Orlando, Fla.
KVZK-TV Pago Pago, American Samoa
ZBM-TV Pembroke, Bermuda
WMBD-TV Peoria, Ill.
WCAU-TV Philadelphia
KTSP-TV Phoenix
KOAM-TV Pittsburg, Kan.
KDKA-TV Pittsburgh
WGME-TV Portland, Me.
KOIN Portland, Ore.
WAGM-TV Presque Isle, Me.
WLNE Providence, R.I.
KHQA-TV Quincy, Ill.
WRAL-TV Raleigh, N.C.
KTVN Reno
WTVR Richmond, Va.
WDBJ Roanoke, Va.
WROC-TV Rochester, N.Y.
WHBF-TV Rock Island, Ill.
WIFR Rockford, Ill.
KXTV Sacramento, Calif.
WEYI-TV Saginaw, Mich.
KMOV-TV St. Louis
WBOC-TV Salisbury, Md.
KSL-TV Salt Lake City
KLST San Angelo, Tex.

KENS-TV San Antonio, Tex.
KFMB-TV San Diego
KPIX San Francisco
KCOY-TV Santa Maria, Calif.
WTOC-TV Savannah, Ga.
WYOU Scranton, Pa.
KIRO-TV Seattle
KXII Sherman, Tex.
KSLA-TV Shreveport, La.
KMEG-TV Sioux City, Iowa
KELO-TV Sioux Falls, S.D.
   KDLO-TV Florence, S.D.
   KPLO-TV Reliance, S.D.
   KCLO-TV Rapid City, S.D.
KTNL-TV Sitka, Alaska
WSBT-TV South Bend, Ind.
WSPA-TV Spartanburg, S.C.
KREM-TV Spokane, Wash.
KOLR Springfield, Mo.
WTVH Syracuse, N.Y.
WCTV Tallahassee, Fla.
WTVT Tampa, Fla.
WTHI-TV Terre Haute, Ind.
WTOL-TV Toledo, Ohio
WIBW-TV Topeka, Kan.
KOLD-TV Tucson, Ariz.
KOTV Tulsa, Okla.
WCFT-TV Tuscaloosa, Ala.,
KMVT-TV Twin Falls, Idaho
KWTX-TV Waco, Tex.
WUSA-TV Washington, D.C.
WWNY-TV Watertown, N.Y.
WSAW-TV Wausau, Wis.
WPEC-TV West Palm Beach, Fla.
WDTV Weston, W. Va.
WTRF-TV Wheeling, W. Va.
KAUZ-TV Wichita Falls, Tex.
KWCH Wichita, Kan.
   KBSD-TV Ensign, Kan.
   KBSH-TV Hays, Kan.
   KBSL-TV Goodland, Kan.
WJKA Wilmington, N.C.
KIMA-TV Yakima, Wash.
   KLEW-TV Lewiston, Idaho
   KEPR-TV Pasco, Wash.
WKBN-TV Youngstown, Ohio

Fox Broadcasting Company

Headquarters: 10201 W. Pico Blvd., Los Angeles 90035. (213) 203-3266.

Branch Offices:

New York 10036: 1211 Ave. of the Americas, 3rd Fl. (212) 556-2400.

Chicago 60601: 205 N. Michigan Ave., Suite 48. (312) 946-0018.

Fox Broadcasting Company Executives: Rupert Murdoch, chmn/CEO Fox Inc.; Lucille S. Salhany, chmn Fox Broadcasting Co.; Sandy Grushow, pres Fox Entertainment Group; Gary Hoffman, sr VP Fox Broadcasting movies & miniseries; Margaret Loesch, pres Fox Children's Network; Van Gordon Sauter, pres Fox News; Preston Padden, exec VP affil rels; Tracy Dolgin, exec VP mktg; David Grant, exec VP net bus opns.

Senior Vice Presidents, Fox Broadcasting Company: Geoff Calnan, adv & prom; Andrew Fessel, rsch & mktg; Robert Greenblatt, drama dev; Larry Jacobson, finance; Ira Kurgan, bus affrs; Dan McDermott, current progs & specials; Jon Nesvig, sls; Tom Nunan, comedy dev; Pam Satterfield, media & affil prom; Stuart Smiley, creative dev; Eric Yeldell, legal affrs.

Fox Broadcasting Company Affiliates

Affiliated VHF stations: 19. Affiliated UHF stations: 121. Note: Indented call letters indicate that the station is a satellite of the preceding station. Fox owned and operated stations are marked in bold.

WFXL Albany, Ga.
WXXA Albany, N.Y.
KASA Albuquerque, N.M.
WNTZ Alexandria, La.
KCIT Amarillo, Tex.
KTBY Anchorage, Alaska
WATL Atlanta
WFXG Augusta, Ga.
KBVO Austin, Tex.
WBFF Baltimore
WGMB Baton Rouge
WXXV Biloxi, Miss.
   WDBB Birmingham, Ala.
   WTTO Birmingham, Ala.
   WNAL Gadsden, Ala.
KTRV Boise, Idaho
WFXT Boston
WGRB Bowling Green, Ky.
   WKNT Bowling Green, Ky.
WUTV Buffalo, N.Y.
WGKI Cadillac, Mich.
KOCR Cedar Rapids, Iowa

WRSP Champaign, Ill.
   WCCU Urbana, Ill.
WTAT Charleston, S.C.
WVAH Charleston, W.Va.
WCCB Charlotte, N.C.
WDSI Chattanooga, Tenn.
WFLD Chicago, Ill.
WXIX Cincinnati, Ohio
WOIO Cleveland, Ohio
KXRM Colorado Springs, Colo.
WACH Columbia, S.C.
WXTX Columbus, Ga.
WTTE Columbus, Ohio
KDAF Dallas
KLJB Davenport, Iowa
KJMH Davenport, Iowa
WRGT Dayton, Ohio
KDVR Denver, Colo.
KDSM Des Moines, Iowa
WKDB Detroit
WDAU Dothan, Ala.
KCIK El Paso, Tex.
WETG Erie, Pa.
KLSR Eugene, Ore.
WEVV Evansville, Ind.
KFBK Fairbanks, Alaska
KVRR Fargo, N.D.

KBRR Thiefriver Falls, Minn.
KJRR Jamestown, N.D.
KNRR Pembina, N.D.
WSMH Flint, Mich.
WCC Florence, S.C.
KMPH Fresno, Calif.
WFTX Ft. Myers, Fla.
KPBI Ft. Smith, Ark.
WFFT Ft. Wayne, Ind.
WOGX Gainesville, Fla.
WXMI Grand Rapids, Mich.
WGBA Green Bay, Wisc.
WNRW Greensboro, N.C.
   WGGT Greensboro, N.C.
   WHNS Greenville, N.C.
WFXI Greenville, N.C.
WPMT Harrisburg, Pa.
WTIC Hartford, Conn.
KHNL Honolulu, Hawaii
   KHBC Hilo, Hawaii
   KOGG Wailuku, Hawaii
KRIV Houston, Tex.
WZDX Huntsville, Ala.
WXIN Indianapolis
WDBD Jackson, Miss.
WAWS Jacksonville, Fla.
WWCP Johnstown, Pa.

Broadcasting & Cable Yearbook 1994

Major National Television Networks

KSHB Kansas City, Mo.
WKCH Knoxville, Tenn.
WLAX La Cross, Wisc.
   WEUX Eau Claire, Wisc.
KADN Lafayette, La.
KVHP Lake Charles, La.
WSYM Lansing, Mich.
KVVU Las Vegas
WDKY Lexington, Ky.
KLRT Little Rock, Ark.
KTTV Los Angeles
WDRB Louisville, Ky.
KJTV Lubbock, Tex.
WMSN Madison, Wisc.
WYVN Martinsburg, W.Va.
WPTY Memphis, Tenn.
WSVN Miami, Fla.
WCGV Milwaukee, Wisc.
KITN Minneapolis, Minn.
WPMI Mobile, Ala.
KCBA Monterey, Calif.
WCOV Montgomery, Ala.
WZTV Nashville, Tenn.
WNOL New Orleans, La.
WNYW New York
WTVZ Norfolk, Va.
KPEJ Odessa, Tex.

KOKH Oklahoma City, Okla.
KPTM Omaha, Neb.
WOFL Orlando, Fla.
KYOU Ottumwa, Iowa
KBSI Paducah, Ky.
WPGX Panama City, Fla.
WYZZ Peoria, Ill.
WTXF Philadelphia, Pa.
KNXV Phoenix, Ariz.
WPGH Pittsburgh, Pa.
WPXT Portland, Me.
KPDX Portland, Ore.
WNAC Providence, R.I.
WLFL Raleigh, N.C.
KAME Reno, Nev.
WRLH Richmond, Va.
WJPR Roanoke, Va.
   WVFT Roanoke, Va.
WUHF Rochester, N.Y.
WQRF Rockford, Ill.
KTXL Sacramento, Calif.
KSTU Salt Lake City
KIDY San Angelo, Tex.
KRRT San Antonio, Tex.
XETV San Diego, Calif.
KTVU San Francisco, Calif.
WTGS Savannah, Ga.

KCPQ Seattle, Wash.
KMSS Shreveport, La.
KTTW Sioux Falls, S.D.
   KTTM Huron, S.D.
KAYU Spokane, Wash.
KDEB Springfield, Mo.
KDNL St. Louis, Mo.
WSYT Syracuse, N.Y.
WTLH Tallahassee, Fla.
WFTS Tampa, Fla.
WUPW Toledo, Ohio
WGKI Traverse City, Mich.
WEMT Tri-Cities, Va.-Tenn.
KMSB Tucscon, Ariz.
KOKI Tulsa, Okla.
KFXK Tyler, Tex.
WFXV Utica, N.Y.
KWKT Waco, Tex.
WTTG Washington, D.C.
WFLX West Palm Beach, Fla.
KSAS Wichita, Kan.
   KAAS Salinas, Kan.
KJTL Wichita Falls, Tex.
WOLF Wilkes-Barre, Pa.
   WWLF Hazelton, Pa.
KCY Yakima, Wash.
   KBW Richland, Wash.

NBC

National Broadcasting Co.

Executive and Business Offices: GE Building, 30 Rockefeller Plaza, New York 10112. (212) 664-4444. Telegraphic Address: NATBROCAST, NY.

Washington Office: 4001 Nebraska Ave. N.W., Washington, D.C. 20001. (202) 885-4000.

Government Relations and Law Offices, Washington: 1331 Pennsylvania Ave., N.W., Suite 930 N., Washington, D.C. 20004. (202) 833-3600.

West Coast Offices: 3000 Alameda Ave., Burbank, Calif. 91523. (818) 840-4444.

Studios: GE Building, New York, Brooklyn, Burbank & Chicago. NBC-TV network originates progs from the TV studios at each of the owned & operated TV stn locations.

Corporate Affiliations: NBC is a subsidiary of General Electric Co.

President and Chief Executive Officer: Robert C. Wright.

President's Council: Richard Cotton, exec VP/gen counsel; Dick Ebersol, pres NBC sports; Randall Falco, pres opns & tech svcs; Andrew Lack, pres NBC news; Pierson Mapes, pres NBC TV net; Thomas Rogers, pres cable & bus dev; John Rohrbeck, pres NBC TV stns; Michael Sherlock, pres technology; Edward Scanlon, exec VP employee rels; Warren C. Jenson, sr VP finance; Judy Smith, sr VP corporate communications.

NBC Washington Government Relations Office: James Rowe III, VP Washington, D.C.

TV Stations: John Rohrbeck, pres; William Bolster, pres/gen mgr WNBC-TV New York; Allan Horlick, pres/gen mgr WRC-TV Washington, D.C.; Donald Browne, pres/gen mgr WTVJ Miami, Fla.; Reed Manville, pres/gen mgr KNBC-TV Los Angeles; Roger Ogden, pres/gen mgr KCNC-TV Denver; Pat Wallace, pres/gen mgr WMAQ-TV Chicago; Robert Finnerty, VP finance & opns; Kathryn Lenard, VP TVSD rsch.

NBC Legal & Standards Divison: Richard Cotton, exec VP/gen counsel; Stephen Stander, sr VP law New York; Ellen Agress, VP legal policy & planning; Anne Egerton, VP law West Coast; Patricia Langer, VP employment law.

Corporate Communications: Judy Smith, sr VP corporate communications; Beth Comstock, VP news information; Mary Neagov, VP corporate communications; Pat Schultz, VP corporate & media rels; Kathleen Tucci, VP talent rels & media svcs West Coast; Ed Markey, VP sports & special information projects.

NBC Finance: Warren C. Jensen, sr VP finance; E. James Greiner, sr VP finance opns, news, sports & entertainment; Arthur Angstreich, VP treasury & admin; John Baziotis, VP finance/controller; Harvey Brown, VP capital planning; Susan Costley, VP finance opns; Victor Garvey, VP corporate events & travel svcs; Edward Swindler, VP sls pricing & forecast; Kathleen Hurlie, VP/treas; John Eck, VP financial planning & analysis.

Personnel & Labor Relations: Edward Scanlon, exec VP; Bernard Gehan, VP labor rels West Coast; Day Krolik III, VP labor rels; Wayne Rickert, VP employee rels West Coast; Andria Alpert Romm, VP employee rels CNBC; Jeffrey Trullinger, VP organization & mgmt resources planning.

News Divison: Andrew Lack, pres NBC News; Therese Byrne, pres NBC news prod; Robert Horner, pres NBC News Channel; Jay Fine, VP tech opns & prod planning; Timothy J. Russert, sr VP/bureau chief Washington, D.C.; Jeffrey Gaspin, VP prog dev; Vera Mayer, VP info svcs; Elena Nachmanoff, VP talent dev; Bill Wheatley, Cheryl Goulds, VP news.

NBC Entertainment: Don Ohlmeyer, pres NBC West Coast; Warren Littlefield, pres NBC Entertainment; John Miller, exec VP adv, prom & event progmg; Lee Currlin, sr VP progmg & prog planning East Coast; Lindy DeKoven, sr VP miniseries & motion pictures for TV; Richard Ludwin, sr VP specials, var & late-night progs; Preston Beckman, VP prog planning & schedules; Danelle Black, VP prime time & daytime progs, East Coast; Jenness Brewer, VP print adv; Edward Frank, VP current comedy progs; Susan Lee, VP daytime progs; Linda Mancuso, VP Saturday morning & family progs; Vince Manze, VP adv & prom West Coast; Jeff Kreiner, VP adv & prom East Coast; Lori Openden, VP talent & casting; Brian Pike, VP drama dev; Martha Stanville, VP affil adv & prom svcs; Jamie Tarses, VP comedy dev; Jim Vescera, VP on-air prom; Stuart Weiss, VP prom creative svcs.

NBC Cable & Business Development: Thomas Rogers, pres; Roger Ailes, pres CNBC; Angela Purno, sr VP NBC cable ad sls, CNBC; Caroline Vanderlip, sr VP; Marty Yudkowitz, sr VP strategic dev; John Abernathy, VP finance & opns CNBC; Joseph Arnstein, VP sls central rgn CNBC; Susan Becker, VP sls NBC cable; Lyn Familant, VP mktg CNBC; Andy Friendly, VP prime time & prog dev & exec net prod CNBC; Laurence Grossman, VP natl sls CNBC; Edward Kurpis, VP finance & admin; Brian Lewis, VP media rels CNBC; John Luginbill, VP sls eastern central rgn CNBC; Peter Mann Jr., VP sls western rgn CNBC; Susan Packard, VP affil rels Midwest, West & Canada CNBC; Mike Reitman, VP tech opns CNBC; Adria Alpert Romm, VP employee rels CNBC; Todd Siegel, VP sls eastern territory CNBC; Laurence Smith, VP natl accts CNBC; Peter Sturtevant, VP bus news CNBC; Elizabeth Tilson, VP progmg "America's Talking"; Michael Wheeler, exec VP/gen mgr NBC cable;

David Zaslav, VP bus affrs/gen counsel CNBC; Bruce Ballard, rgnl VP affil rels East Coast.

NBC Productions & Enterprises: John Agoglia, pres NBC Enterprises/exec VP NBC prod; Michael Zinberg, pres creative affrs NBC prod; Susan Beckett, sr VP NBC Enterprises New York; Dennis Brown, sr VP film prod; Joe Bures, sr VP bus affrs; Gary Considine, VP tape prod opns; Todd Leavitt, sr VP NBC prod; Gerard Petry, sr VP finance & NBC prod bus opns; Frank Accarrino, VP entertainment prod opns East Coast; Dorothy Bailey, VP NBCP; Lorna Bitensky, VP prod bus affrs; Harold Brook, VP bus affrs; Leslie Maskin, VP bus affrs; Richard Nathan, VP prog & talent contracts; Jack O'Neill, VP entertainment prod opns West Coast; Jerry Reeves, VP MIS; Albert Spevak, VP prod & mktg bus affrs.

TV Network: Pierson G. Mapes, pres NBC-TV; Larry Hoffner, exec VP net sls; Alan Cohen, sr VP net mktg; Robert Niles, sr VP affil rels & prog rsch; Scott Bonn, VP client mktg; William Caufield, VP net sls planning & pricing; John Damiano, VP media, audience rsch & TV net svcs; Jean Dietz, VP TV affil corporate rels & mktg; Ron Dobson, VP daytime & late night sls; William Fouch, VP affil rels & entertainment; Barry Goodman, VP net mktg; James Hicks, VP mktg; James Bloom, VP affil rels news; Melvin Berning, VP news sls; Michael Mandelker, VP eastern sls; Bob Noonoo, VP telemarketing; Richard Plastine, VP gen mgr eastern sls; Richard Quackenboss, VP TV net opns; Thomas Rocco, VP sls dept; Richard Schade, VP central natl sls; Nicholas Schiavone, VP media & mktg rsch; Carl Schweinler, VP affil rels sports; Jonathan Spaet, VP sls eastern territory; J. Nicholls Spain Jr., VP Detroit sls; Keith Turner, VP sports sls; Gary Wold, VP/sls dir daytime & late night; Rosalyn Weinman, VP bcst standards & practices; Rick Gitter, VP adv standards & prog compliance.

Operations and Technical Services: Randall Falco, pres bcst & net opns; Michael Sherlock, pres technology; Leonard Garrambone, VP purchasing & bus svcs; Charles Jablonski, VP bcst & net engrg; Crawford McGill, VP bcst opns; Anthony Pedalino, VP facilities; David Schmerler, VP news prod opns; Peter Smith, VP engrg.

Sports: Dick Ebersol, pres; Peter Diamond, VP Olympic progmg; John Ertmann, sports negotiation; Keith Handyside, VP prod planning & opns; Richard Hussey, VP affil svcs & prog planning; Jonathan Miller, VP prog planning & dev.

NBC International: Matthew Ody, VP international sls; Mike Pevez, VP international sls & distribution.

Management Information Systems: Maurice Greenfield, VP; Gennaro Granito, VP database & support svcs; John Healy, VP application systems; Eric Koopman, VP opns & systems software.

Major National Television Networks

NBC-TV Network

Affiliated stations: 194.
KRBC-TV Abilene, Tex.
WALB-TV Albany, Ga.
WNYT Albany, N.Y.
KOB-TV Albuquerque
KALB-TV Alexandria, La.
KAMR-TV Amarillo, Tex.
KTUU-TV Anchorage
WXIA-TV Atlanta
WAGT Augusta, Ga.
KXAN-TV Austin, Tex.
KGET Bakersfield, Calif.
WMAR-TV Baltimore
WLBZ-TV Bangor, Me.
WVLA Baton Rouge
KTVZ Bend, Ore.
KWAB-TV Big Springs, Tex.
KULR-TV Billings, Mont.
WICZ-TV Binghamton, N.Y.
WVTM-TV Birmingham, Ala.
KFYR-TV Bismarck, N.D.
WVVA Bluefield, W.Va.
KTVB Boise, Idaho
WBZ-TV Boston
WCYB-TV Bristol, Va.
KVEO-TV Brownsville, Tex.
WGRZ-TV Buffalo, N.Y.
KTVM Butte, Mont.
KTWO-TV Casper, Wyo.
WICD Champaign, Ill.
WCIV Charleston, S.C.
WCNC-TV Charlotte, N.C.
WVIR-TV Charlottesville, Va.
WRCB-TV Chattanooga, Tenn.
WTOM-TV Cheboygan, Mich.
KKTU Cheyenne, Wyo.
WMAQ-TV Chicago
KCPM Chico, Calif.
WLWT Cincinnati
WBOY-TV Clarksburg, W.Va.
WKYC-TV Cleveland
KOMU-TV Columbia, Mo.
WIS-TV Columbia, S.C.
WLTZ Columbus, Ga.
WCMH Columbus, Ohio
KMTZ Coos Bay, Ore.
KRIS-TV Corpus Christi, Tex.
KWQC-TV Davenport, Iowa
WKEF Dayton, Ohio
WESH Daytona Beach-Orlando, Fla.
KCNC-TV Denver
WHO-TV Des Moines, Iowa
WDIV Detroit
KQCD-TV Dickinson, N.D.
KBJR-TV Duluth, Minn.
WEAU-TV Eau Claire, Wis.
KTVE El Dorado/Monroe, Ark.
WTSM-TV El Paso, Tex.
WETM-TV Elmira, N.Y.
WICU-TV Erie, Pa.
KMTR Eugene, Ore.
KIEM Eureka, Calif.
WFIE-TV Evansville, Ind.
KTHI-TV Fargo, N.D.
KOBF Farmington, N.M.
KNAZ-TV Flagstaff, Ariz.
WOWL-TV Florence, Ala.
WBBH Fort Myers, Fla.
KPOM-TV Fort Smith, Ark.
WKJG-TV Fort Wayne, Ind.
KXAS-TV Fort Worth-Dallas

KSEE Fresno, Calif.
KSNG Garden City, Kan.
WOOD-TV Grand Rapids, Mich.
KSNC Great Bend, Kan.
KTGF Great Falls, Mont.
WLUK-TV Green Bay, Wis.
WYFF-TV Greenville, S.C.
WHAG-TV Hagerstown, Md.
WNNE-TV Hanover, N.H.
WVIT Hartford, Conn.
KHAS-TV Hastings, Neb.
WDAM-TV Hattiesburg, Miss.
KTVH Helena, Mont.
KHAW-TV Hilo, Hawaii
KHON-TV Honolulu
KPRC-TV Houston
WSAZ-TV Huntington, W.Va.
WAFF Huntsville, Ala.
KIFI-TV Idaho Falls, Idaho
WTHR Indianapolis
WLBT-TV Jackson, Miss.
WTLV Jacksonville, Fla.
KETK-TV Jacksonville, Tex.
WJAC-TV Johnstown, Pa.
KSNF Joplin, Mo.
KCFW-TV Kalispell, Mont.
WDAF-TV Kansas City
KOTI Klamath Falls, Ore.
WBIR-TV Knoxville, Tenn.
KPLC-TV Lake Charles, La.
WGAL Lancaster, Pa.
WILX Lansing, Mich.
KGNS-TV Laredo, Tex.
KVBC Las Vegas
KIVV-TV Lead, S.D.
WLEX-TV Lexington, Ky.
WLIO Lima, Ohio
KARK-TV Little Rock, Ark.
KXAM-TV Llano, Tex.
KNBC-TV Los Angeles
WAVE Louisville, Ky.
KCBD-TV Lubbock, Tex.
WMGT Macon, Ga.
WMTV Madison, Wis.
KSNK McCook/Oberlin, Neb.
KOBI Medford, Ore.
WMC-TV Memphis
WGBC Meridian, Miss.
WTVJ Miami
KTPX Midland, Tex.
WTMJ-TV Milwaukee
KARE Minneapolis
KMOT Minot, N.D.
KECI-TV Missoula, Mont.
KDLT Mitchell/Sioux Falls, S.D.
WALA-TV Mobile, Ala.
WSFA Montgomery, Ala.
KLSB-TV Nacogdoches, Tex.
WSMV Nashville
WDSU-TV New Orleans
WNBC New York
WAVY-TV Norfolk, Va.
KNOP-TV North Platte, Neb.
KFOR-TV Oklahoma City
WOWT Omaha, Neb.
WPSD-TV Paducah, Ky.
KMIR-TV Palm Springs, Calif.
WJHG-TV Panama City, Fla.
WTAP-TV Parkersburg, W.Va.
WEEK-TV Peoria, Ill.
KYW-TV Philadelphia

KPNX Phoenix/Mesa, Ariz.
WPXI Pittsburgh
WPTZ Plattsburgh, N.Y.
KJAC-TV Port Arthur/Beaumont, Tex.
WCSH-TV Portland, Me.
KGW-TV Portland, Ore.
WJAR Providence, R.I.
WGEM-TV Quincy, Ill.
WRDC-TV Raleigh, N.C.
KEVN-TV Rapid City, S.D.
KRNV Reno, Nev.
WJFW-TV Rhinelander, Wis.
KNDU Richland, Wash.
WWBT Richmond, Va.
WSLS-TV Roanoke, Va.
KTTC Rochester, Minn.
WHEC-TV Rochester, N.Y.
WTVO Rockford, Ill.
KFAA-TV Rogers, Ark.
KOBR Roswell, N.M.
KCRA-TV Sacramento, Calif.
WNEM-TV Saginaw-Bay City, Mich.
KSDK St. Louis
KSBW Salinas, Calif.
KUTV Salt Lake City
KACB-TV San Angelo, Tex.
KMOL-TV San Antonio, Tex.
KNSD San Diego
KRON-TV San Francisco
KSBY San Luis Obispo, Calif.
WSAV-TV Savannah, Ga.
KING-TV Seattle
KTAL-TV Shreveport, La.
KTIV Sioux City, Iowa
WNDU-TV South Bend, Ind.
KHQ-TV Spokane, Wash.
WICS Springfield, Ill.
WWLP Springfield, Mass.
KYTV Springfield, Mo.
WTOV-TV Steubenville, Ohio
WSTM-TV Syracuse, N.Y.
WTWC Tallahassee, Fla.
WFLA-TV Tampa
KCEN-TV Temple, Tex.
WTWO Terre Haute, Ind.
WTVG Toledo, Ohio
KSNT Topeka, Kan.
WPBN-TV Traverse City, Mich.
KVOA-TV Tucson, Ariz.
KJRH-TV Tulsa, Okla.
WTVA Tupelo, Miss.
KAS-TV Twin Falls, Idaho
WKTV Utica, N.Y.
KAII-TV Wailuku, Hawaii
WRC-TV Washington, D.C.
WITN-TV Washington, N.C.
KWWL Waterloo, Iowa
WPTV West Palm Beach, Fla.
KSNW Wichita, Kan.
KFDX-TV Wichita Falls, Tex.
WMGM-TV Wildwood, N.J.
WBRE-TV Wilkes-Barre, Pa.
KUMV-TV Williston, N.D.
WECT Wilmington, N.C.
WXII Winston-Salem, N.C.
KNDO Yakima, Wash.
WFMJ-TV Youngstown, Ohio
KYMA Yuma, Ariz.
WHIZ-TV Zanesville, Ohio

Public Broadcasting - Television

Corporation for Public Broadcasting

Headquarters: 901 E St. N.W., Washington 20004-2037. (202) 879-9600. FAX: (202) 783-1019.

Chairmen: Sheila Tate, chmn, c/o CPB, 901 E St. N.W., Washington 20004-2037, (202) 879-9702; Martha Buchanan, vice chmn, c/o CPB, 901 E St. N.W., Washington 20004-2037, (202) 879-9702.

Directors: Honey Alexander, c/o CPB, 901 E St. N.W., Washington 20004-2037, (202) 879-9702, term ends 1996; Carloyn R. Bacon, exec dir O'Donnell Foundation, 1401 Elm St., Suite 3388, Dallas 75202, (214) 698-9915, term ends 1996; Diane D. Blair, Political Science Dept., University of Arkansas, Fayetteville, Ark. 72701, (501) 575-3356, term ends 1998; Martha Buchanan, 3814 Klingle Pl. N.W., Washington 20016, (202) 363-2886, term ends 1996; Ritajean Butterworth, 4815 Stanford Ave. N.E., Seattle 98105, (206) 525-5671, term ends 1997; Henry J. Cauthen, pres South Carolina Educational Television Commission, Box 11000, Columbia, S.C. 29211, (803) 737-3240, term ends 1994; Victor Gold, 6309 Beachway Dr., Falls Church, Va. 22044-1510, (703) 998-7711, term ends 1996; Lloyd Kaiser, 1204 Holton Rd., Oakmont, Pa. 15139, (412) 828-4364, term ends 1994; Sheila Tate, pres Powell Tate, 700 13th St. N.W., Suite 1000, Washington 20005, (202) 434-8502, term ends 1996.

Principal personnel: Richard W. Carlson, pres/CEO; Robert Coonrod, exec VP; Frederick L. DeMarco, sr VP system & stn dev; Paul E. Symczak, sr VP corp affrs/sec; Eugene Katt, sr VP progmg; Carolyn Reid-Wallace, sr VP education; Thomas Harvey, sr VP/gen counsel; Philip A. Smith, sr VP corp communications; Renee Ingram, dir budget/treas; Gerald F. Hogan, VP govt rel.

Educational Broadcasting Corp.

Headquarters: 356 W. 58th St., New York 10019. (212) 560-2000.

Owner and licensee of Thirteen/WNET in New York. Loc public TV stn & major source of progmg distributed nationally to 340 public TV stns by the Public Broadcasting Service.

Principal personnel: Dr. William F. Baker, pres/CEO; George L. Miles Jr., exec VP/COO; Edward A. Campo, controller; Ruth Ann Burns, VP/dir educ resources center; Harry Chancey, VP/dir progmg svcs; H. Melvin Ming, VP/chief admin off; Jonathan Olken, VP/dir mktg & communications/dir membership & dev.

Public Broadcasting Service

Headquarters: 1320 Braddock Pl., Alexandria, Va. 22314-1698. (703) 739-5000. FAX: (703) 739-0775.

National Press Relations/New York: 1790 Broadway, New York 10019-1412. (212) 708-3000. FAX: (212) 708-3009.

National Press Relations/Los Angeles: 3131 Los Feliz Blvd., #203, Los Angeles 90039. (213) 667-3488. FAX: (213) 667-3483.

Corporate Staff: Ervin S. Duggan, pres/CEO; Robert G. Ottenhoff, exec VP/COO; Jennifer Lawson, exec VP natl progmg & prom svcs; Sandra H. Welch, exec VP educ; Jonathan C. Abbott, sr VP dev & corporate rel; M. Peter Downey, sr VP prog bus affrs; John Grant, sr VP natl prog svc; Paula A. Jameson, sr VP/gen counsel/corporate sec; Howard N. Miller, sr VP bcst opns, engrg & computer svcs; Eric L. Sass, sr VP video mktg; Elizabeth A. Wolfe, sr VP/CFO/treas finance & admin; Carole Feld, VP prom & adv; Carlos V. Girod Jr., VP satellite technology; Jinny Goldstein, VP educ project dev; Nancy H. Hendry, VP/deputy gen counsel/asst corporate sec; Kathy Quattrone, VP progmg; Mark Richer, VP engrg & computer svcs; James Scalem, VP fund-raising progmg; Nanette Dudar, asst treas.

Board of Directors: Gerald L. Baliles Esq. (chmn), Hunton & Williams, Richmond, Va., representing WCVE Richmond; Maria Elena A. Flood (vice chmn), project dir Texas Tech Health Sciences Center, School of Medicine, El Paso, Tex. representing KCOS El Paso; Judy Stone (vice chmn), exec dir Alabama Public Television, Birmingham, Ala.; Charles R. Allen, gen mgr KAET, Arizona State University, Tempe, Ariz.; Walter H. Anderson, editor *Parade,* New York; Bill Arhos, pres KLRU, Capital of Texas Public Telecommunications Council, Austin, Tex.; Dr. William F. Baker, pres/CEO WNET, Educational Broadcasting Corp., New York; Ruben R. Cardenas, Esq., Cardenas, Whitis, Stephen, Corcoran & McLain, McAllen, Tex. representing KMBH Harlingen, Tex.; Dr. James W. Carey, Graduate School of Journalism, Columbia University, representing WILL Urbana, N.Y.; Fred C. Esplin, gen mgr KUED, University of Utah, Salt Lake City; Dr. Rosa Castro Feinberg, member Dade County School Board, Miami, Fla., representing WLRN Miami; Robert J. Flowers, sr VP Washington Mutual Savings Bank, Seattle, Wash. representing KCTS Seattle; Virginia G. Fox, exec dir Kentucky Educational Television Network, Lexington, Ky.; W. Wayne Godwin, pres/gen mgr WCET, Greater Cincinnati TV Educational Foundation, Cincinnati, Ohio; Peter J. Gomes, minister Memorial Church, Harvard University, Cambridge, Mass.; George H. Gruenwald, new prod dev consultant, Rancho Santa Fe, Calif.; Susan Howarth, exec dir Arkansas Education TV Network, Conway, Ark.; Ron Hull, stn mgr KUON, University of Nebraska, Lincoln, Neb.; Dr. Franklyn G. Jenifer, pres Howard University, Washington, representing WHMM Washington; Wilbert J. LeMelle, pres Phelps-Stokes Fund, New York; Dr. Arthur L. Johnson, VP community rel Wayne State University, Detroit, Mich., representing WTVS Detroit; Elmer W. Lower, university professor East Hampton, N.Y.; Mary Y. Matayoshi, vice chmn, c/o KHET - Hawaii Public Television, Honolulu; Jonathon Moore, sr assoc Carnegie Endowment for International Peace, Washington, representing WGBY Springfield, Mass.; Dr. Richard E. Ottinger, exec dir Georgia Public Telecommunications Network, Atlanta; James R. Pagliarini, CEO/gen mgr KNPB-TV, University of Nevada at Reno; Warren H. Phillips, former chmn of bd Dow Jones & Company Inc., New York; Dr. Thomas Hedley Reynolds, pres University of New England, Biddeford, Me., representing WCBB Lewiston, Me.; James Q. Riordan, former vice chmn Mobil Corp., New York; Sharon Percy Rockefeller, pres/CEO WETA-TV, Greater Washington Educational Telecommunications Association Inc., Washington; Noel T. Smith, stn mgr KNCT, Central Texas College, Killeen, Tex.; John F. Swope, pres Chubb Life American, Concord, N.H., representing New Hampshire Public Television; Marshall Turner, Taylor & Turner Associates Ltd., San Francisco, representing KQED San Francisco, Calif.; Milton P. Wilkins Jr., VP plant sciences div Monsanto Agricultural Co., St. Louis, Mo., representing KETC St. Louis.

Television Program Networks

Global Access Telecommunications Services
(Formerly Great American Broadcasting Co.)

Headquarters: 205 Portland St., 4th Fl., Boston 02114. (617) 367-0500; (800) 648-3333. FAX: (617) 720-0803.

Executives: Jack Morse, VP/gen mgr; Dick King, dir sls & mktg; Mary Beth Karr, bus mgr; Scott Lenahan, opns mgr; Carol McGrath, syndication mgr; Karla Silas, northeastern sls mgr; Susan Cecala, eastern rgnl sls mgr; Bud Turner, midwestern rgnl sls mgr; Carol Tucker, western rgnl sls mgr; Fred Healy, Tim Smith, Kathy Sohar, Lori Matte, satellite coords; Jessica Lynn, office mgr.

A full-svc telecommunications company offering complete worldwide satellite & fiber-optic svcs. Provides domestic & international video transmission svcs & transmission systems. Svcs include transponder time, fixed & transportable uplink svcs, fiber connectivity, syndication prog distribution, videoconferencing, news, sports & entertainment progmg & special events transmissions.

Branch Offices:
Boston 02114: 205 Portland St., 4th Fl. (617) 367-0500. FAX: (617) 720-0803. Dick King, dir sls (ext. 23).
Fairfax, Va. 22030: 11350 Random Hills Rd., Suite 800. (703) 934-6161. FAX: (703) 591-1937. Susan Cecala, eastern rgn.
Kansas City 64108: 3030 Summit. (816) 753-6217. FAX: (816) 932-9182. Bud Turner, midwestern rgn.
Encino, Calif. 91436: 16000 Ventura Blvd., 5th Fl. (818) 788-6868. FAX: (818) 788-6992. Carol Tucker, western rgn.

IDB Communications Group Inc.

Headquarters: 10525 W. Washington Blvd., Culver City, Calif. 90232. (213) 870-9000.

Executives: Jeffrey Sudikoff, chmn/CEO; Edward Cheramy, pres; Peter Hartz, sr VP sls & mktg; John Tagliaferro, pres IDB BROADCAST.

IDB BROADCAST, a unit of IDB Communications Group Inc., supplies transmission & distribution svcs for domestic & international radio, TV & data/voice communications. Svcs include those for net news, syndicated & special event progmg, plus teleconferencing, phone & fax support svcs. Includes Hughes Television Network TV sports svcs. IDB is the largest U.S. re-seller of satellite transponder time. Facilities include IDB's teleports in Los Angeles, New York & Houston, the Sports Satellite Interconnect uplink network, transcontinental & oceanic fiber & extensive international links.

Telemundo Group Inc.

Headquarters: 1740 Broadway, New York 10019. (212) 492-5500.

Principal Executives: Saul P. Steinberg, chmn of bd; Joaquin F. Blaya, pres/CEO; Peter J. Housman II, pres bus & corporate affrs; Jose C. Cancela, pres stn group/gen mgr WSCV.

Progmg includes hit movies, sitcoms, game shows, novellas, sports, info progs, news & var shows.

Univision

Headquarters: 605 3rd Ave., 12th Fl., New York 10158-0180. (212) 455-5200. FAX: (212) 867-6710.

Principal Executives: Univision Network: Jaime Davila, chmn/CEO; Ray Rodriguez, pres/COO; Doug Darfield, VP/dir rsch; Raul Torano, pres network sls; Mario Rodriguez, VP/dir progmg; Peter von Gal, VP/dir sls; Guillermo Martinez, VP/news dir; Milagros Carrasquillo, dir rsch; Stuart Livingston, VP/dir affil rels.

Sales Offices
Chicago 60611-4305: 401 E. Illinois St., Suite 325. (312) 321-8200. FAX: (312) 321-8223. Brian Pussilano, sls mgr.
Los Angeles 90045: 6701 Center Dr. W., 15th Fl., Los Angeles, Calif. (310) 338-0700. FAX: (310) 348-3619. Patricia Testa, sls mgr.
San Francisco 94124: 2200 Palou Ave. (415) 824-4384. FAX: (415) 824-1906. Rodolfo Balderrama, sls mgr.
Irvine, Calif. 92714: 2030 Main St., Suite 235. (714) 474-8585. FAX: (714) 474-8385. Steven Mandala, sls mgr.
Miami, Fla. 33178: 9405 N.W. 41st St. (305) 471-3900. FAX: (305) 471-4027. Evelyn Castillo, sls mgr.
Irving, Tex. 75039: 600 E. Colinas Blvd., Suite 566. (214) 869-0202; (214) 869-2635. Jack Hobbs, sls mgr.
Bingham Farms, Mich. 48025: 30700 Telegraph Rd., Suite 3640. (313) 540-5705. FAX: (313) 540-2419. Mark Brown, sls mgr (Detroit office).

Full range of Spanish-language progmg produced in the United States & throughout the Spanish-speaking world including movies, sporting events, newscasts, current affrs, children's progs, comedy & var shows.

Regional Television Networks

California Farm Network. 1601 Exposition Blvd., Sacramento, Calif. 95815. (916) 924-4360. FAX: (916) 923-5318. Clark Biggs, exec dir; Ron Miller, TV opns mgr.
Comprises KUZZ-TV Bakersfield, KAEF-TV Eureka, KSEE-TV Fresno, KIXE-TV Redding, KRCR-TV Redding, KSBW-TV Salinas, KFTL-TV San Leandro, KFMB-TV San Diego, KSBY-TV San Luis Obispo, KEYT(TV) Santa Barbara, KFWU(TV) Fort Bragg, KFTY-TV Santa Rosa, all Calif. Agrivision WS5, ch 17 (direct bcst satellite).

California-Oregon Broadcasting Inc. Box 5M, Medford, Ore. 97501. (503) 779-5555. Patricia C. Smullin, pres; Carol Anne Smullin Brown, VP; William B. Smullin, sec/founder; Doreeta Domke, VP.
Comprises KAEF(TV) Arcata & Eureka, KFWU-TV Fort Bragg & Ukiah, KRCR(TV) Redding, all Calif.; KLSR(TV) Eugene KOTI(TV) Klamath Falls & KOBI(TV) Medford, all Ore. Represented by John Blair & Co., Northwest.

Central Educational Network. 1400 E. Touhy Ave., Des Plaines, Ill. 60018. (708) 390-8700. FAX: (708) 390-9435. James A. Fellows, pres; Joan C. Lence, VP progmg; Helen Marie Boesche, VP finance & admin; Mark Gorelczenko, VP.
Comprises WSIU Carbondale, WTTW(TV) Chicago, WQPT-TV Moline, WTVP Peoria, WILL-TV Urbana, WEIU Charleston, CONVOCOM Springfield, all Ill.; WTIU(TV) Bloomington, WNIN(TV) Evansville, WFWA Fort Wayne, WFYI Indianapolis, WIPB Muncie, all Ind.; KBIN(TV) Council Bluffs, KDIN(TV) Des Moines, KTIN Fort Dodge, KIIN(TV) Iowa City, KYIN Mason City, KHIN(TV) Red Oak, KSIN(TV) Sioux City, KRIN Waterloo, all Iowa; KOOD(TV) Bunker Hill, KTWU Topeka, both Kan.; WTVS(TV) Detroit, WKAR-TV East Lansing, WFUM Flint, WGVU(TV) Grand Rapids, WNMU(TV) Marquette, WUCM(TV) University Center, all Mich.; KSMQ(TV) Austin, KTCA(TV) St. Paul, both Minn.; KETC St. Louis, Mo.; KTNE-TV Alliance, KMNE-TV Bassett, KHNE-TV Hastings, KLNE-TV Lexington, KUON-TV Lincoln, KRNE-TV Merriman, KXNE-TV Norfolk, KPNE-TV North Platte, KYNE Omaha, all Neb.; KBME(TV) Bismark, KDSE-TV Dickinson, KFME Fargo, KGFE Grand Forks, KSRE-TV Minot, KWSE Williston, all N.D.; WEAO-TV Akron, WNEO-TV Alliance, WOUB-TV Athens, WBGU-TV Bowling Green, WOUC-TV Cambridge, WOSU-TV Columbus, WPBO-TV Portsmouth, WGTE-TV, Toledo, all Ohio; WPSX University Park, Pa.; KDSD-TV Aberdeen, KESD-TV Brookings, KPSD-TV Eagle Butte, KQSD-TV Lowry, KZSD-TV, Martin, KTSD-TV Pierre, KBHE-TV Rapid City, KUSD-TV Vermillion, all S.D.; WHWC(TV) Eau Claire, WPNE(TV) Green Bay, WHLA(TV) LaCrosse, WHA-TV Madison, WMVS(TV) Milwaukee, WLEF(TV) Park Falls, WHRM(TV) Wausau, all Wis.; WMTJ-TV Rio Piedres, P.R.

Eastern Educational Television Network. 120 Boylston St., Boston 02116. (617) 338-4455. FAX: (617) 338-5369. Gene S. Nichols, exec dir.
Comprising WETA-TV, WHMM, both D.C.; WEDW(TV) Bridgeport, WEDY(TV) New Haven, WEDH(TV) Hartford, WEDN(TV) Norwich, all Conn.; WCBB(TV) Augusta, WMED-TV Calais, WMEB-TV Orono, WMEM-TV Presque Isle, all Me.; WGBH-TV Boston, WGBX-TV Boston, WGBY-TV Springfield, all Mass.; WENH-TV Durham, WEKW-TV Keene, WLED-TV Littleton, all N.H.; WNJT-TV Trenton, N.J.; WSKG(TV) Binghamton, WNED-TV Buffalo, WNET(TV) New York, WLIW-TV Plainview, WXXI(TV) Rochester, WMHT(TV) Schenectady, WCNY-TV Syracuse, WNPE-TV Watertown, all New York; WCET-TV Cincinnati, WVIZ-TV Cleveland, WPTD-TV Dayton, all Ohio; WLVT-TV Bethlehem-Allentown, WPSX-TV Clearfield, WITF-TV Harrisburg, WHYY-TV Philadelphia, WQED(TV) Pittsburgh, WVIA(TV) Scranton-Wilkes Barre, WQLN Erie, all Pa.; WSBE-TV Providence, R.I.; WMPT-TV Annapolis, WMPB(TV) Baltimore, WWPB(TV) Hagerstown, WCPB-TV Salisbury, all Md.

4X Network. Box 1686, 3425 S. Broadway, Minot, N.D. 58702. (701) 852-2104. FAX: (701) 838-9360. David Reiten, pres/gen mgr.
Comprises KXMB-TV Bismarck, KXMA-TV Dickinson, KXMC-TV Minot, KXMD-TV Williston, all N.D. Represented by Katz Continental.

KBS License L.P./S.D. Commuinications Inc. Box 12, Wichita, Kan. 67201. (316) 838-1212. FAX: (316) 838-3524. Mr. Sandy DiPasquale, pres/CEO KWCH-TV; Wayne Roberts, gen mgr KBSH-TV & KBSL-TV; Mr. Gayle Kiger, gen mgr KBSD-TV.
Comprises KBSD-TV Ensign-Dodge City, KBSL-TV Goodland, KBSH-TV Hays, KWCH-TV Wichita-Hutchinson, all Kan. Represented by TeleRep.

KLGT-TV. 1640 Como Ave., St. Paul, Minn. 55108. (612) 646-2300. FAX: (612) 646-1220. Linda Rios Brook, pres/gen mgr; Mark Gardner, VP/gen sls mgr; Larry Brook, VP/sls & mktg.
Represented by Adam Young.

KSN Television Group. Box 333, 833 N. Main St., Wichita, Kan. 67201. (316) 265-3333. FAX: (316) 292-1197. TWX: 910-741-6976. George Lilly, pres; Robert D. McCurdy, VP; Al Buch, VP/gen mgr.
Comprises KSNG Garden City, KSNC Great Bend, KSNT Topeka, KSNW Wichita, KSNK Oberlin, all Kan. Represented by Katz. Above television stns affild with NBC Television Network. Owned by SJL of Kansas Corp., Billings, Mont.

Kansas Television Network. Box 10, Wichita, Kan. 67201. (316) 943-4221. FAX: (316) 943-5160; (316) 943-5493 (traf & sls); (316) 943-5374. Jan McDaniel, pres/gen mgr; Steve South, VP/gen sls mgr.
Comprises KLBY-TV Colby, KUPK-TV Garden City, KAKE-TV Wichita, all Kan. Represented by Petry.

Keloland TV. Midcontinent Television of South Dakota, KELO TV Bldg., 501 S. Phillips St., Sioux Falls, S.D. 57102. (605) 336-1100. FAX: (605) 334-3447. TWX: 910-660-0552. N.L. Bentson, chmn; Mike Braker, VP/gen mgr.
Comprises KDLO-TV Florence, KPLO-TV Reliance, KELO-TV Sioux Falls, KCLO-TV Rapid City, all S.D. Represented by John Blair Co.

Meyer Television Network. 200 N. 4th St., Bismarck, N.D. 58501. (701) 255-5757. FAX: (701) 255-8220. Judith Ekberg Johnson, CEO/pres; Tom Barr, VP/gen mgr; Jerry Hegel, gen sls mgr; Penny Borg, gen sls mgr; Jim Sande, prog/opns mgr.
Comprises KFYR-TV Bismarck, KQCD-TV Dickinson, KMOT-TV Minot & KUMV-TV Williston, all N.D. Represented by Blair.

Minnesota Public Television Association (MPTA). c/o KTCA 172 E. 4th St., St. Paul, Minn. 55101. (612) 222-1717. Jack Willis, pres; George Jauss, tres; Ron Dougherty, sec.
Comprises KWCM-TV Appleton, KSMQ-TV Austin, KAWE-TV Bemidji, WDSE-TV Duluth, KTCA-TV Minneapolis-St. Paul, KTCI-TV Minneapolis-St. Paul, all Minn.; KFME Fargo, N.D.

Nebraska Television Network (NTV). Box 220, Kearney, Neb. 68848. (308) 743-2494. FAX: (308) 743-2644. Joe Grand, licensee; Steve Barry, asst licensee/gen mgr; Mitchell Bowles, dir adv, publ & prom; Dan Lab, business mgr; Al Zoebel, news dir; Jerry Fuehrer, chief engr; Jim Kettinger, prod mgr.
KSNB-TV4, Beatrice, Lincoln & York, KHGI-TV13, Kearney, Hastings & Grand Island, KWNB-TV North Platte & western Neb. and the trans of K02HB, K17CI, K11KV, K12KW, K13OM, K13NP, K13VO, K06EY. Represented by Katz Continental.

Ohio Educational Broadcasting Network Commission. 2470 N. Star Rd., Columbus, Ohio 43221. (614) 644-1714. Dave L. Fomshell, exec dir.
Comprises WEAO Akron, WNEO-TV Alliance, WOUB-TV Athens, WBGU-TV Bowling Green, WOUC-TV Cambridge, WCET Cincinnati, WVIZ-TV Cleveland, WOSU-TV Columbus, WPTD Dayton, WPTO Oxford, WPBO-TV Portsmouth, WGTE-TV Toledo, all Ohio.

Pacific Mountain Network. 1550 Park Ave., Denver 80218-1661. (303) 837-8000. FAX: (303) 837-9797. Joseph P. Zesbaugh, pres; Dana J. Rouse, VP progmg; Mary Lou Ray, VP learning svcs; Dan Flenniken, projects coord learning svcs; Midge Pierce, prog mgr; Lesley Sudders, dir business admin.
Comprises KAKM Anchorage, KYUK-TV Bethel, KUAC-TV Fairbanks, KTOO-TV Juneau, all Alaska; KAET Phoenix, KUAT-TV Tucson, both Ariz.; KEET Eureka, KVPT Fresno, KOCE-TV Huntington Beach, KCET Los Angeles, KIXE-TV Redding, KRCB-TV Rohnert Park, KVIE Sacramento, KMTP-TV San Francisco, KVCR-TV San Bernardino, KPBS-TV San Diego, KQED/KQEC San Francisco, KTEH San Jose, KCSM-TV San Mateo, all Calif.; KBDI-TV Denver, KRMA-TV Denver, KTSC Pueblo, all Colo.; KHET Honolulu, KMEB Wailuku, both Hawaii; KAID/KUID-TV/KISU-TV Boise, Idaho; KUSM, Bozeman, Mont.; KLVX Las Vegas, KNPB Reno, both Nev.; KNME-TV Albuquerque, KRWG-TV Las Cruces, KENW Portales, all N.M.; KOAC-TV/KTVR/KOAP-TV, Portland, KSYS Medford, all Ore.; KBYU-TV Provo, KUED Salt Lake City, both Utah; KWSU-TV Pullman, KCTS-TV Seattle, KSPS-TV Spokane, KTPS/KCKA Tacoma, KYVE-TV Yakima, all Wash.; KCWC-TV Cheyenne, Wyo.

Pennsylvania Public Television Network. Box 397, 24 Northeast Dr., Hershey, Pa. 17033. (717) 533-6010. FAX: (717) 533-4236. TWX: 910-380-4890. H. Sheldon Parker Jr., gen mgr.
Comprising WLVT-TV Allentown, WQLN-TV Erie, WITF-TV Harrisburg, WHYY-TV Philadelphia, WQED-TV Pittsburgh, WVIA-TV Scranton, WPSX-TV University Park, all Pa.

SJL Broadcast Management Corp. Box 2557, Billings, Mont. 59103. 3203 3rd Ave., N. Billings, Mont. 59101. (406) 256-0705. FAX: (406) 252-9144. Dave McCurdy, VP/controller.
Montecito, Calif. 93108: 633 Picacho Ln. (805) 969-9278. FAX: (805) 969-2399. George D. Lilly, pres.
Comprising KTVQ(TV) Billings, Mont.; WSTM-TV Syracuse, N.Y.; KSNW(TV) Wichita, KSNG(TV) Garden City, KSNC(TV) Great Bend, & KSNT(TV) Topeka, all Kan.; KSNK-TV McCook, Neb./Oberlin, Kan.; WJRT-TV Flint, Mich.; KOAM-TV Joplin, Mo./Pittsburg, Kan.; WTVG (TV) Toledo, Ohio.

Southern Educational Communications Association. Box 50008, Columbia, S.C. 29250. (803) 799-5517. FAX: (803) 771-4831. Skip Hinton, pres.
Comprises Ala. PTV; Ark. ETV; WCEU-TV, WEDU-TV, WFSU-TV, WLRN-TV, WSFP-TV, WSRE-TV, WUFT-TV, WUSF-TV, WXEL-TV; WBCC-TV, WJCT-TV, all Fla.; WPBA Atlanta; Ga. Public TV; KPTS-TV Wichita, Kan.; WKPC-TV Louisville, WKYU-TV Bowling Green, both Ky.; Ky. ETV; WYES-TV, WLAE-TV, both New Orleans; La. ETV; Miss. ETV; KCPT-TV Kansas City, KMOS-TV Warrensburg, KOZK-TV Springfield, all Mo.; N.H. PTV; WTVI-TV Charlotte, N.C.; N.C. Public TV; Okla. ETV; WYBE-TV Pa.; WSBE-TV R.I.; WJWJ-TV, WNSC-TV, WRET-TV, WRJA-TV, all S.C.; S.C. ETV; WDCN-TV, WLJT-TV, WTCI-TV, WSJK-TV, WKNO-TV, WCTE-TV, all Tenn.; KLRN-TV, KERA-TV, KAMU-TV, KNCT-TV, KTXT-TV, KEDT-TV, KCOS-TV, KLRU-TV, KMBH-TV, KOCV-TV, KCTF-TV, KUHT-TV, all Tex.; Vt. ETV; WBRA-TV, WCVE-TV, WHRO-TV, WNVC-TV, WNVT-TV, WVPT-TV, all Va.; WNPB-TV Morgantown, WSWP-TV Beckley, WPBY-TV Huntington, all W. Va.; WTJX-TV St. Thomas, V.I.

Wisconsin Public Television Network. 3319 W. Beltline Hwy., Madison, Wis. 53713-4296. (608) 264-9600. FAX: (608) 264-9622. Glenn A. Davison, exec dir.
Comprises WPNE(TV) Green Bay, WHLA-TV La Crosse, WHWC-TV Menomonie/Eau Claire, WLEF-TV Park Falls, WHRM-TV Wausau, all Wis. Affiliates: WHA-TV Madison, Wis.; WMVS(TV) Milwaukee; WDSE-TV Duluth, Minn.

Unwired Television Networks

Note: Asterisk (*) denotes unwired radio networks. Other is unwired television network.

ALIN-TV. 149 Madison Ave., Suite 804, New York 10016. (212) 889-1337. FAX: (212) 213-6968. Alan Steinberg, chmn; John Giebel, pres; Alan Cohen, exec VP.

ALIN-TV offers locally originated progmg on a line-up of leading ind stns providing natl participations on a daily basis. Specific nets are provided to zero in on target audience progmg: Prime, prime access, teen/young adult, late night entertainment, daytime, weekend entertainment, news, & kids.

*****Caballero Spanish Radio.** 261 Madison Ave., Suite 1800, New York 10016. (212) 697-4120. FAX: (212) 697-9151. Eduardo Caballero, pres.

Non-interconnected natl sls net specializing in Spanish mkts.

*****Keystone Broadcasting System Inc.** 22971 Nine Mile Rd., Saint Clair Shores, Mich. 48081. (312) 774-4580. Officers & Directors: Nicholas Gordon, chmn; James O'Boye, exec VP.

Saint Clair Shores, Mich. 48081: Patt Media Sales, 21714 Lakeland. Detroit office.

Westlake Village, Calif. 91362: 31220 La Baya Dr., Suite 110. (313) 445-0491. Tim McClintock.

Agency Commission: 15% on net stn time to accredited agencies; no cash discount. The stns can be bought separately. Minimum order: 20 stns. Stns may be purchased by state groups, rgns or full net. One contract, one itemized invoice & individual stn affidavits. Schedules, start dates, copy and/or live tags may vary from stn to stn. Rates for spec combinations available on request.

*****Lotus Hispanic Reps.** 50 E. 42nd St., New York 10017. (212) 697-7601. Richard Kraushaar, pres; Robert Albright, exec VP; Yvonne Luna, acct exec.

Stns in Arizona, California, Colorado, Connecticut, Washington D.C., Florida, Illinois, New Mexico, New York, Pennsylvania, Puerto Rico & Washington.

Canadian Television Networks

CTV Television Network Ltd.

Head Office: 42 Charles St. E., Toronto, Ont., Canada M4Y 1T5. (416) 928-6000. FAX: (416) 928-6265.

CTV Principal Officers and Department Executives: John M. Cassady, pres/CEO; Olga Cwiek, VP human resources, bus affrs & prog sls; Gary A. Maavara, VP sports & pub affrs; William D. McGregor, chmn; Gail Morrell, VP corporate communications; Eric Morrison, VP news; Peter O'Neill, corporate sec/dir strategic planning & pub affrs; Thomas Peddie, sr VP opns/CFO; Paul Robertson, sr VP sls & mktg; Joel Rotenberg, dir finance & accounting; Philip Wedge, VP progmg; Arthur Weinthal, VP entertainment progmg.

CTV Sales Offices:

Toronto M4Y 1T5: 42 Charles St. E. (416) 928-6049. FAX: (416) 928-5958.

Montreal H5B 1B7: Box 181, Place Bonaventure, 60 Elgin. (514) 878-3135. FAX: (514) 878-4554. Arthur Patterson, mgr.

Vancouver V6G 2Z6: 1500 W. Georgia St., Suite 790. (604) 669-1570. FAX: (604) 684-6169. Cora Barkman, mgr.

New York 10017: Telerep, One Dag Hammarskjold Plaza, 25th Fl. (212) 486-8746. FAX: (212) 644-3919. David B. Hills, VP sls dev.

Affiliates:

NTV-CJON, 446 Logy Bay Rd., St. John's, Nfld. A1C 5R6. (709) 722-5015. FAX: (709) 722-0023. Doreen Allen.

ATC-CKCW, 191 Halifax St., Moncton, N.B. E1C 8R6. (506) 857-2600. FAX: (506) 857-2618. Claire Wright.

CHRO, 10 Kimway Ave., Nepean, Ont. K2E 6Z6. (613) 228-2476. FAX: (613) 228-9406. Bob Hartwell.

CJBN, 102 10th St., Keewatin, Ont. P0X 1C0. (807) 547-2854. FAX: (807) 547-2236. Darryl Michaluk.

MCTV-North Bay, 245 Oak St. E., North Bay, Ont. P1B 8P8. (705) 476-3111. FAX: (705) 495-0922. Linda Holmes.

ATV-CJCB, 1283 George St., Sydney, N.S. B1P 1N7. (902) 562-5511. FAX: (902) 564-0495. Wilbur MacTavish.

CFCF 12, 405 Ogilvy Ave., Montreal H3N 1M4. (514) 273-6311. FAX: (514) 273-8986. John Murphy.

CFTO, 9 Channel Nine Dr., Toronto M1S 4B5. (416) 299-2000. FAX: (416) 299-2386. Cathy Huppe.

MCTV-Sudbury, 699 Frood Rd., Sudbury, Ont. P3C 5A3. (705) 674-8301. FAX: (705) 671-2444. Laird White.

MCTV-Sault Ste. Marie, 119 East St., Sault Ste. Marie, Ont. P6A 5M2. (705) 759-8232. FAX: (705) 759-7783. Helen Millen.

ATV-CJCH, 2885 Robie St., Halifax, N.S. B3J 2Z4. (902) 453-4000. FAX: (902) 454-3202. Anne Marie Varner.

CJOH, 1500 Merivale Rd., Ottawa, Ont. K2C 3G6. (613) 224-1313. FAX: (613) 224-0670. Ray Sapiano.

CKCO, 864 King St. W., Kitchener, Ont. N2G 4E9. (519) 741-4405. FAX: (519) 578-2021. Reg Sellner.

MCTV-Timmins, 681 Pine St. N., Timmins, Ont. P4N 7G3. (705) 264-4211. FAX: (705) 264-3266. Don Dewsbury.

CHFD, 87 North Hill St., Thunder Bay, Ont. P7A 5V6. (807) 344-9685. FAX: (807) 345-9923. Cynthia Makila Bonthron.

CKY, CKY Bldg., Polo Park, Winnipeg, Man. R3G 0L7. (204) 788-3340. FAX: (204) 783-4841. Tim Smith.

CITL, 5026 50th St., Lloydminster, Alta. T9V 1P3. (403) 875-3321. FAX: (403) 875-4704. Phil Manderson.

CFCN, Broadcast House, 80 Patina Rise S.W., Calgary, Alta. T3H 2W4. (403) 240-5690. FAX: (403) 240-5689. Brian Vos.

CHEK, 780 Kings Rd., Victoria, B.C. V8T 5A2. (604) 383-2435. FAX: (604) 384-7766. Barry Dodd.

CKCK, One Hwy. E., Regina, Sask. S4P 3E5. (306) 569-6375. FAX: (306) 522-0090. Rick Lewchuk.

CIPA, 22 10th St. W., Prince Albert, Sask. S6V 3A5. (306) 922-6066. FAX: (306) 763-3041. Cliff Horton.

CFRN, Broadcast House, 18520 Stony Plain Rd., Edmonton, Alta., T5P 4C2. (403) 483-3311. FAX: (403) 484-8016. Steve Lane.

CFQC, 216 1st Ave. N., Saskatoon, Sask. S7K 3W3. (306) 665-8600. FAX: (306) 665-9210. Bruce Acton.

CICC, 95 E. Broadway, Yorkton, Sask. S3N 0L1. (306) 783-3685. FAX: (306) 782-3433. Kim Balog.

BCTV, 7850 Enterprise St., Vancouver, B.C. V6B 4A3. (604) 444-9542. FAX: (604) 421-9427. Barry Thompson.

Canadian Broadcasting Corp.

The Canadian Broadcasting Corp. (CBC) is a publicly owned corporation established by the Broadcasting Act (1936) of the Canadian Parliament to provide the natl bcstg svc in Canada in the two official languages—English & French. Under this legislation, the CBC is subject to regulations of the Canadian Radio-television & Telecommunications Commission (CRTC).

Head Office: 1500 Bronson Ave., Box 8478, Ottawa, Ont. K1G 3J5. (613) 724-1200. TDD: (613) 733-8868. FAX: (613) 738-6887.

CBC Board of Directors: Patrick Watson, chmn; Gerard Veilleux, pres/CEO; Gillis Boulet, John Crispo, Michel Doyon, Don Hamilton, Nancy L. Juneau, Sandra Kolber, Robert Kozminski, Thomson MacDonald, William Neville, Alain Paris, Brian Peckford, Thomas Wilson, Glen Wright.

Principal Officers: Gerard Veilleux, pres/CEO; Patrick Watson, chmn; Anthony S. Manera, sr VP resource mgmt & admin; Michael McEwen, sr VP radio svcs; Donna Logan, VP media accountability & rgnl bcstg opns; Robert Hertzog, internal audit; Gerald Flaherty, Q.C., VP/gen counsel/corporate sec; Stephen Cotsman, VP finance & admin; Robert Pattillo, VP communications & pub affrs; Charles Gendron, VP human resources; John Shewbridge, VP bus affrs; Sheridan Scott, planning & regulatory affrs; Michael A. Hughes, exec dir mgmt info systems (Toronto); Louis-Paul Germain, gen mgr bcst centre dev project (Toronto); Charlotte O'Dea, sr dir corporate communications & pub affrs.

CBC Ombudsman: Bill Morgan, Box 500, Station "A," Toronto, Ont. M5W 1E6. (416) 975-2978; Mario Cardinal, 1400 René-Lévesque Blvd. E., Box 6000, Montreal, Que. H3C 3A8. (514) 597-4721.

Program Services: The CBC operates English & French TV nets. Prime-time TV progmg is 88-89% Canadian in content. More than 71% of the combined English & French progmg on Canadian TV is Canadian produced, approximately half by the CBC itself & the balance by outside prods & agencies. CBC operates Newsworld, a 24-hour natl satellite-to-cable English-language news & info svc. CBC North bcsts radio & TV progs to Canada's north in English, French & seven native languages, serving the special needs of native & non-native groups in the Yukon, Northwest Territories & northern Quebec. The heart of CBC's natl distribution system is Canada's Anik E2 satellite, carrying progmg through six different time zones. CBC's progmg is bcst over 857 TV stations.

English Networks: Box 500, Station "A", Toronto, Ont. M5W 1E6. (416) 975-3311, TDD: (416) 975-6688. Officers: Ivan Fecan, VP English TV networks; Tim Kotcheff, VP news, current affrs & Newsworld, TV; Jim Byrd, exec dir media opns; Sheila Hockin, acting sr dir bcst communications; Tom Curzon, sr dir media & PR.

French Networks: 1400 René-Lévesque Blvd. E., Box 6000, Montreal, Que. H3C 3A8. (514) 597-5970, TDD: (514) 597-6013. Officers: Guy Gougeon, VP French TV; Claire Samson, gen mgr communications; Micheline Savoie, dir net PR; Raymond Guay, dir net prom; Marcel Labelle, dir French rgnl communications; James Baer, gen mgr, TV5 (Consortium Quebec-Canada).

CBC Engineering: 7925 Cote St. Luc Rd., Montreal, Que. H4W 1R5. (514) 485-1031. Officers: Brian D. Baldry, VP engrg, Claudette Lalonde, mgr tech info.

Radio Canada International: 1055 René-Lévesque Blvd. E., P.O. Box 6000, Montreal, Que. H3C 3A8. (514) 597-7555. Officers: Terry Hargreaves, exec dir; Allan Familiant, prog dir.

Newfoundland Region: Ayre's Centre, Pippy Pl., Box 12010, Station "A", St. John's, Nfld. A1B 3T8. (709) 737-4140. Officers: Ron Crocker, rgnl dir; John O'Mara, rgnl mgr communications.

Maritime Region: 5600 Sackville St., Box 3000, Halifax, N.S. B3J 3E9. (902) 420-8311. Officers: W.K. Donovan, rgnl dir; Jessie Clarey, rgnl mgr communications.

Atlantic Provinces: 250 Archibald St., Box 950, Moncton, N.B. E1C 8N8. (506) 853-6666. Officers: Claude Bourque, rgnl dir French svcs; Robert Nadeau, rgnl mgr communications.

Quebec Region: 1400 René-Lévesque Blvd. E., Box 6000, Montreal, Que. H3C 3A8. (514) 597-5970. Officers: Nicole Belanger, rgnl dir English svcs; John Yorston, rgnl mgr communications.

Quebec City & Eastern Quebec Region: 2475 Laurier Blvd., Box 10400, Ste-Foy, Que. G1V 2X2. (418) 654-1341. Officers: Jacques D. Landry, dir French svcs; Ginette D'Aigle, mgr communications.

Ontario Region, English Services: Box 500, Station "A", Toronto, Ont. M5W 1E6. (416) 205-3311. Officers: Norm Bolen, rgnl dir; Carol Jones, rgnl mgr communications (Ottawa).

Ontario Region, French Services: 250 Lanark Ave., Box 3220, Station "C", Ottawa, Ont. K1Y 1E4. (613) 724-1200. Officers: Pierre Racicot, rgnl dir French svcs in Ontario & in the Outaouais; Maryse Lairot, actg rgnl mgr communications.

Manitoba Region: 491 Portage Ave., Box 160, Winnipeg, Man. R3C 2H1. English svcs: (204) 788-3222; French svcs: (204) 788-3141. Officers: Marvin Terhoch, rgnl dir; Bridget A. Hoffer, rgnl mgr mktg communications; Gilbert Teffaine, rgnl dir French svcs; Huguette LeGall, rgnl mgr communications.

Saskatchewan Region: 2440 Broad St., Regina, Sask. S4P 4A1. (306) 347-9540. Officers: Brian Cousins, rgnl dir; Janice Carter, sr mgr western rgnl communications; Lionel Bonneville, rgnl dir/dir TV French svcs; Diane Rondeau, mgr communications.

Alberta Region: Box 555, Edmonton, Alta. T5J 2P4. (403) 468-7500. Officers: Ron Smith, rgnl dir; Glenn Luff, rgnl mgr communications; Denis Lord, rgnl dir French svcs; Pierre Noel, communications mgr radio & TV.

British Columbia Region: Box 4600, Vancouver, B.C. V6B 4A2. (604) 662-6000. Officers: John H. Kennedy, rgnl dir; Gilian Dusting, rgnl mgr communications; Pauline Sincennes, rgnl dir French svcs; Johanne Huard, actg rgnl mgr.

CBC North: 5002 Forrest Dr., Box 160, Yellowknife, N.W.T. X1A 2N2. (403) 920-5460. Officers: Marie Wilson, rgnl dir/dir TV; Craig Yeo, rgnl mgr communications.

Global Television Network

Head Office: 81 Barber Green Rd., Don Mills, Ont. M3C 2A2. (416) 446-5311. FAX: (416) 446-5371.

Principal Officers: Stephen Gross, pres/CEO Canwest Global Communications Corp.; I.H. Asper, chmn/CEO Canwest Global Communications Corp.; Doug Bonar, VP news & opns Global Communications Ltd.; Doug Hoover, VP progmg Global Communications Ltd.; Tom Strike, VP finance Canwest Global Communications Corp.; James Sward, pres/CEO Global Communications Ltd.; Rodger Hone, VP mktg Global Communications Ltd.; Don Brinton, deputy chmn Canwest Global Communications Corp.; John Burgis, VP finance Global Communications Ltd.; Cam Johnson, treas Global Communications Ltd.

TVA

Head Office: 1600 de Maisonneuve Blvd. E., Montreal, Que. H2L 4P2. (514) 526-9251.

Principal Officer: Denis Lacroix, gen mgr.

Sales: Paul L'Anglais Inc., (514) 526-9251. FAX: (514) 526-6133 (Montreal); (416) 487-1551. FAX: (416) 489-2159 (Toronto).

Television Quatre Saisons

Head office: 405 Ogilvy Ave., Montreal, Que. H3N 2Y4. (514) 271-3535.

Principal officers: Jean A. Pouliot, chmn; Adrien D. Pouliot, vice chmn/CEO; Charles Belanger, pres/COO; Jean Fortier, exec VP/VP progmg & news; Ghyslain St. Pierre, VP engrg; Francois Laganiere, VP sls & mktg; Christiane Despres, traffic mgr; Daniel Asselin, news mgr; Luc Harvey, mgr progmg; Raymond Baril, rgnl sls mgr.

Affiliates: CFJP Montreal; CFAP Quebec; CFRS Jonquiere, Que.; CFKS Sherbrooke, Que.; CFKM Trois Rivieres, Que.; CFTF Riviere Du Loop, Que.; CFVS Val d'Or, Que.; CFGS Hull, Que.

Television News Services

ABC News. See ABC listing in Major National Television Networks, this section.

AMI News. 50 Vashell Way, Suite 300, Orinda, Calif. 94563. (510) 254-4456. FAX: (510) 254-6135. John Hamilton, pres; Rob Brown, VP/gen mgr. Eastern Bureau: (800) 736-0370. Claire Diepenbrock.
Phone- & tape-supplied features focusing on skiing, fishing, camping, travel & beach conditions with related news & info. Offered seasonally.

Accu-Weather Inc. 619 W. College Ave., State College, Pa. 16801. (814) 234-9601, ext. 400. FAX: (814) 238-1339. Joel N. Myers, pres; Sheldon Levine, natl sls mgr.
Coml weather svc provides high-resolution Ultra Graphix, lightning, NEXRAD, satellites, complete weather shows. Forecast briefing svc & satellite delivery available. Graphics creation, display, paint & animation system. Automatic crawl generation system for official warnings. TV & radio news svcs.

Africa News Service Inc. Box 3851, Durham, N.C. 27702. (919) 286-0747. FAX: (919) 286-2614. Reed Kramer, pres; Tami Hultman, exec edit.
A news & info svc on African affrs for TV, radio & print news svcs.

Agence France-Presse. 1612 K St. N.W., Washington 20006. (202) 861-8535. FAX: (202) 861-8525. Philippe Gustin, rgnl dir for the Americas; Jacques Thomet, rgnl sls mgr for the Americas; Pierre LeSourd, U.S. bureau chief.
Produces a var of international news svcs for radio & TV; including text wires in six languages, photo wires, graphics & financial wires.

All Points Broadcasting Co. Corporate & NewsBureau address: 538 Chesman St., West Hempstead, N.Y. 11552. (516) 292-1403. FAX: (212) 643-8972. J.J. Lombard, pres; Frank Ucciardo, VP; Thomas N. Traks, mngng edit; R.F. Burns, chief engr.
TV & radio news svcs syndication & direct bcst coverage for loc stns & nets.

All News Channel 1633 Broadway, 37th Fl., New York 10019. (212) 708-1315. FAX: (212) 708-3234. Jay Nordby, VP; Elizabeth Clayton, dir sls & mktg.
Chicago 60611: 401 N. Michigan Ave., Suite 1600. (312) 645-1122. Carl Schulz, VP sls.
A TV & cable 24-hour news svc with up-to-the minute natl, international, weather, sports, business & entertainment news.

American Heart Association. 7272 Greenville Ave., Dallas 75231. (214) 706-1397. FAX: (214) 706-1341. Carol Floyd, bcst news edit; Linda Carle, mgr bcst svcs.
TV: periodic satellite news feeds of medical rsch stories. Radio: rsch & life-style reports, distributed by tape & live copy.

The Associated Press. AP Broadcast News Ctr., 1825 K St. N.W., Washington 20006-1253. (800) 821-4747; (202) 736-1100. FAX: (202) 736-1199, news; (202) 736-1124, admin; (202) 736-1107, AP office. **Officers:** Louis D. Boccardi, pres/gen mgr; Jim Williams, VP/dir, (202) 736-1108. **News & Programming:** Brad Kalbfeld, deputy dir/mgng edit, (202) 736-1170; Ed Tobias, asst mgng edit news, (202) 736-1172; Wally Hindes, asst mgng edit progmg, (202) 736-1171; Barbara Worth, asst mgng edit bcst wires, (202) 736-1173; Steve Katz, chief supvr, (202) 736-9505; Kate McKenna, Lauri Schwartz, assignment edits, (202) 736-9520; Steve Cheney, graphics supvr, (202) 736-1182; Paul Courson, edit bus, (202) 736-9548; Dave Lubeski, dir sports, (202) 736-9540; Michael Weinfeld, edit entertainment, (202) 736-9515; George Mayo, chief engr, (202) 736-1161; Greg Crowley, asst chief engr, (202) 736-1162. **Sales & Marketing:** Daryl Staehle, dir sls & mktg, (202) 736-1145; Ed Bell, dir TV mktg, (202) 736-1146; Dave Polyard, dir nets, (202) 736-1150; Bob Feldman, mktg mgr technology svcs, (202) 736-1151. **Sales & Marketing—Regional Television Executives:** Nancy Shipley, Central, 230 N. Michigan Ave., Chicago 60601-5960, (312) 781-0500; Wayne Ludkey, West, 505 N. 2nd St., Suite 120, Phoenix 85004-3904, (602) 258-8934; Ron Merrill, Southwest, 4851 LBJ Fwy., Suite 300, Dallas 75244-6002, (214) 991-2627; Bob Young, Southeast, One CNN Ctr., S. Tower, Suite 500, Atlanta 30303-2705, (404) 522-8971. **Technology:** Lee Perryman, deputy dir, (202) 736-1135; Sue Mosher, asst dir technology dev, (202) 736-1136; John Morrissey, info systems mgr, (202) 736-1137; Lori McCafferty, prod mgr, (202) 736-1140. **Station Services:** Evelyn Cassidy, dir (202) 736-1152; Kelly Malone, mktg coord, (202) 736-1153. **Administration:** Greg Groce, dir (202) 736-1110; Wayne Chin, asst dir, (202) 736-1111.
AP Services for TV: Wires: APTV, AP NewsPower, AP Headlines, AP Specialty Wires. Graphics: AP GraphicsBank, AP GraphicsDirect, AP PhotoStream. Software: AP NewsCenter; AP NewsDesk; AP NewsDesk (LAN). Telephone Information Systems Resource: AP Audiotex. Data Delivery: AP Express.
For more information, see the listing for Associated Press Network News under Major National Radio Networks.

Athena Services Group. Box 1400, 2708 Elm St., Dubuque, Iowa 52004-1400. (319) 556-4000. Rita Daniels, pres; Thomas Churchill, chief meteorologist.
24-hour radio weathercasts & severe weather coverage standard. Digital audio, automated delivery & digital weathercast automation system available.

Audio-Video News. 3622 Stanford Cir., Falls Church, Va. 22041. (703) 354-6795. Connie Lawn, pres/chief correspondent.
Covers major natl, international & specialty stories for radio & TV stns in the U.S. & around the world.

BPI Entertainment News Wire. 100 Boylston St., Suite 210, Boston 02116. (617) 482-9447. FAX: (617) 482-9562. John Morgan, gen mgr; Don Gallagher, mngng edit; Judy Webb, sls mgr.
Advance news from BPI-owned publications serving radio & TV.

British Information Services. 845 3rd Ave., New York 10022. (212) 745-0376. FAX: (212) 758-5395. Mark Hopkinson, head radio/TV division.
Provides daily news/feature audio svc filed by satellite from London at no cost to stns for radio & TV. Assists radio & TV crews visiting the U.K.

Broadcast Interview Source. 2233 Wisconsin Ave. N.W., Washington 20007. (202) 333-4904. FAX: (202) 342-5411. Mitchell P. Davis, publisher; Stephanie Harshsman, edit.
Publisher of *Annual Yearbook of Experts & Authorities & Spokespersons*. Source book of interview contacts.

Broadcast News Ltd. 36 King St. E., Toronto, Ont., Canada M5C 2L9. (416) 364-3172. FAX: (416) 364-8896. Wayne Waldroff, gen mgr; Rina Steuerman, satellite sls; Paul McDermott, gen exec eastern Canada; Michelle Poulin, business mgr; Jerry Fairbridge, mktg mgr.
Full wire & audio svcs (news agency), satellite delivery for prog syndicators.

Broadcast News Networks. 78 Church St., Saratoga Springs, N.Y. 12866. (518) 899-6989. FAX: (518) 899-5620. Steven Rosenbaum, exec prod/pres; Martine Charles, VP mktg & dev; Betsy Green, VP sls & dev.
New York 10036: 460 W. 42nd St. (212) 768-3684. Steven Rosenbaum, exec prod/pres. Steven Rosenbaum.
TV prod & dev company specializing in newsmagazines (*Broadcast: New York, Broadcast News/New England*); live talk shows (*Taking Sides, Jerry & Judy*); documentaries (*Trial by Television for A&E*, etc.); news projects (*Dateline, CNN, Eye to Eye With Connie Chung, Front Page*, etc.) & specials.

Broadcast News & Production. Box 618700, Orlando, Fla. 32861. (407) 851-4672. FAX: (407) 298-2488. Paul M. Cicarelli, pres.
Photojournalists covering central Florida. Packages, live remotes, "B" roll & story origination.

Business News Broadcasting Corp. Box 247, Garrison, N.Y. 10524. (914) 424-3801. FAX: (212) 656-2824. Timothy J. Donovan, pres/exec prod; Ken Prewitt, mgng edit/anchor.
New York 10524: News Bureau & Studio, New York Stock Exchange, 11 Wall St. (212) 656-8123. Timothy Donovan, pres/exec prod.
TV svc providing consumer economics, hard business news, & features. All 90 seconds or less; morning, afternoon & evening daily.

CBS News. See CBS listing in Major National Television Networks, this section.

CNN and CNN Headline News. See CNN listing in Basic Cable Services, this section.

CNW Broadcast. Waterpark Pl., 10 Bay St., Suite 914, Toronto, Ont., Canada M5J 2R8. (416) 863-9350. FAX: (416) 863-4829. Barry McQuillan, mgr bcst svcs.

Calgary, Alta. T2P 3C7: Gulf Canada Sq. 401 9th Ave. S.W., Suite 635. (403) 269-7605. FAX: (403) 263-7888; TWX: 03-824872. Kim Blue, dir Prairie rgn.
Halifax, N.S. B3J 3N4: Central Trust Tower, 1801 Hollis St., Suite 210. (902) 422-1411. FAX: (902) 422-3507. TWX: 019-21534. Alison Lawrence, mgr Atlantic Canada.
Montreal H3G 1J1: 1350 Sherbrooke St. W., Suite 1025. (514) 842-2520. FAX: (514) 842-3745. TWX: 055-60936. Eve Malanson, VP Quebec.
Ottawa, Ont. K1P 5B9: 165 Sparks St., Suite 603. (613) 563-4465. FAX: (613) 563-0548. TWX: 053-3292. Dennis Hopkins, VP natl capital rgn.
Vancouver, B.C. V6C 2TB: 750 W. Pender St., Suite 1103. (604) 669-7764. FAX: (604) 669-4356. TWX: 04-508529. Larry Cardy, VP western Canada.
Distributor of video & radio news releases, features, PSA & corporate prods via satellite & hard copy.

The Church of Jesus Christ Latter-day Saints (Mormons). 15 E. Temple St., 2nd Fl., Salt Lake City 84150. (801) 240-1000. FAX: (801) 240-1167. Gerry Pond, mgr radio news/feature svc; Arnold Augustin, mgr TV news/feature svc; Don Russell, mgr electronic media mktg.
Offers free pub affrs, news & feature progmg; also guests for talk shows. Pub affrs progmg is not church-oriented.

Compu-Weather Inc. Box 1122, Flushing, N.Y. 11354. (718) 961-4242. FAX: (718) 353-1294. Jeff Wimmer, pres; Todd Gross, VP; Peter Muldavin, sls mgr.
TV & radio svc providing weather forecasts, features, info & actualities.

Congressional Quarterly Inc. 1414 22nd St. N.W., Washington 20037. (202) 887-8500. FAX: (202) 728-1863. Andrew Barnes, chmn; Andy Corty, vice chmn; Neil Skene, edit/publisher; Robert W. Merry, exec edit; John J. Coyle, assoc publisher; Neil Brown, mgng edit.
Congressional Quarterly Weekly Report & News Service, editorial rsch reports, newsletters, seminars, rsch, reference volumes, paperbacks; daily & wkly congressional info publications.

Conus Communications. 3415 University Ave., Minneapolis 55414. (612) 642-4645. Charles H. Dutcher III, pres/gen mgr; Ray Conover, dir engrg/VP; Tim Rudelli, VP Washington svcs.
Washington 20006: Conus Washington Northwest, 1825 K St. N.W., 9th Fl. (202) 467-5600. FAX: (202) 467-5610.
Satellite news-gathering system of affil stns nationwide utilizing transportable uplinks & exchanging news & progmg via Ku-band; news prog prod.

Entertainment News Calendar. 250 W. 57th St., Suite 1527-105, New York 10107. (212) 421-1370. FAX: (212) 563-3488. Evelyn Heyward, bureau chief; Carolyn Fox, publisher.
Daily entertainment news svc.

Evening News Broadcasting Co. Box 2777, Alexandria, Va. 22301. (703) 548-8007. Clayton Willis, pres/White House & Congressional correspondent.
TV, radio, & print news svc featuring documentaries, news reports & comls.

Golden Lamb Productions. New Britain Rd., East Chatham, N.Y. 12060 (518) 766-5950. FAX: (518) 766-5950. Dow Haynor, pres; Clint Whittemore, VP.
ENG, EFP crews, Betacam equipped; SNG available. Serves the Northeast, natl experience; 24-hour call; packages, live remotes, news & sports.

Hollywood News Calendar. 14755 Ventura Blvd., Suite 1562, Sherman Oaks, Calif. 91403. (213) 872-1507; (818) 986-8186. FAX: (818) 789-8047. Carolyn Fox, editor-in-chief; Susan Fox-Davis, edit.
Daily entertainment TV & radio news svc.

Independent Television News. 901 Battery St., Suite 220, San Francisco 94111. (415) 956-1703. FAX: (415) 956-2040. Linda Hannan, pres; Joan Tovey, VP prod.
Satellite uplinking capabilities. 20'x 40' studio for prod of cable progmg, teleconferences, live interviews, satellite press tours.

Independent Television News of London Ltd. 1726 M St. N.W., #703, Washington 20036. (202) 429-9080. FAX: (202) 429-8948. William Neely, bureau chief; David

Smith, correspondent; Kristine Kelleher, bureau mgr/prod; Marie Cerletty, prod.
London W1P3DE: ITN House, 48 Wells St. 011-441-637-2424. David Nicholas, edit.
Other branches: South Africa, Moscow. British TV news, Washington bureau.

Israel Broadcasting Service. 800 2nd Ave., New York 10017. (212) 867-7584. Myra Cohen, dir.
Free radio & TV progs & features from & about Israel.

Kyodo News Service. 50 Rockefeller Ctr., Suite 803, New York 10020. (212) 397-3723. FAX: (212) 397-3721. Hideaki Sakamoto, bureau chief; Toshi Mitsudome, mktg dir.
Real-time news svc, emphasizing economic, business, sports & political coverage of Japan and Asia.

LANS (Los Angeles News Service). 1341 Ocean Ave., Suite 262, Santa Monica, Calif. 90401. (310) 399-6460. FAX: (310) 399-7541. Bob Tur, pres.
Provides helicopter reporting & video svcs for KNX Newsradio (CBS) and KCBS TV.

Medialink. (Operated by Video Broadcasting Corp.) 708 3rd Ave., 21st Fl., New York 10017. (212) 682-8300. Laurence Moskowitz, pres; Graeme McWhirter, sr VP; Mark Manoff, VP sls; Nick Peters, VP mktg.
Chicago 60611: The Time & Life Bldg., 541 N. Fairbanks Ct. (312) 222-9850. FAX: (312) 222-9810.
Washington 20005: 1401 New York Ave. N.W., Suite 520., (202) 628-3800. FAX: (202) 628-2377.
Los Angeles 90028: 6430 Sunset Blvd. (213) 465-0111. FAX: (213) 465-9230.
London, England W1V5FB: 14 Sotto Sq. 44-71-439-1774. FAX: 44-71-439-1378.
International satellite feed & news video advisory svc. Accessible by computer/teleprinter in U.S. & European newsrooms.

Metro Weather Service Inc. 507-535 Rockaway Ave., Suite 3, Valley Stream, N.Y. 11581. (516) 568-8844; (800) 488-SUNNY. FAX: (516) 568-8853. Pat Pagano, pres.
Tailored weather forecasts for radio & TV. Feature reports: farming, marine, ski, long-range forecasts.

Miami Bureau. 4090 Laguna St., Suite A, Coral Gables, Fla. 33146. (305) 444-3303. FAX: (305) 441-0597. Mo Maghari, pres.
A 24-hour ind TV news, sport & entertainment svc.

Miami Television News Service. 7400 N. Kendall Dr., Suite 617, Miami, Fla. 33156. (305) 279-0414. FAX: (305) 279-0866. William Schmidt, pres.
Provides ENG crews to loc & out-of-town TV stns & foreign bcstrs. Shoot/edit uplink for out-of-town media.

Mighty Minute Programs. 840 Battery St., San Francisco 94111. (415) 788-1211. FAX: (415) 788-1139; (800) 988-1211. Andrew Meblin, pres; David Meblin, sr VP; Bob Kizer, VP sls mgr; Vivian Batty, Elaine Smith & Al Larson, sls.
Distributor/syndicator of TV news feature stories with personality authorities.

Nasdaq Stock Market. 1735 K St. N.W., Washington 20006. (800) 777-6273. FAX: (202) 728-6993. Bob Ferri, dir media rel; Cameron Brown, mgr media svcs; Jeff Salkin, mgr media svcs.
Radio: hourly 30-second ready-to-air reports on the financial mkts. TV: customized loc data.

NBC News. See NBC listing in Major National Television Networks, this section.

NOAA/National Weather Service Headquarters. 1325 East-West Hwy., Silver Spring, Md. 20910. (301) 713-0700. FAX: (301) 713-1598. Ronald L. Lavoie, dir office of meteorology; James P. Travers, chief opns division; Donald R. Wernly, chief warning & forecast branch.
Bohemia, N.Y. 11716: 630 Johnson Ave. (516) 244-0100. Susan F. Zevin, dir eastern rgn.
Fort Worth, Tex. 76102: 819 Taylor St. (817) 334-2668. Harry S. Hassel, dir southern rgn.
Kansas City, Mo. 64106-2897: 601 E. 12th St. (816) 426-5400. Richard P. Augulis, dir central rgn.
Salt Lake City 84147: Box 11188, Federal Bldg., 125 S. State St. (801) 524-5122. Thomas D. Potter, dir western rgn.
Anchorage 99513-7575: 222 W. Seventh Ave., #23. (907) 271-5136. Richard J. Hutcheon, dir Alaskan rgn.
Honolulu 96850-4493: Box 50027, 300 Ala Moana Blvd. (808) 541-1641. Richard H. Hagemeyer, dir Pacific rgn.
Weather & flood warnings, forecasts & related info for the media & gen public.

National Television News Inc. 6133 Kentland Ave., Woodland Hills, Calif. 91367. (818) 883-6121. Howard Back, exec edit; Barbara Presson, stn rels mgr.

Golden Lamb Productions
- *Location Production* -
Serving the Northeast from Upstate NY

ENG   SNG
EFP   Lives
News   Sports

Experienced Crews
New Britain Rd., E. Chatham, NY 12060
Phone (518) 766-5950   **Pager (518) 422-6772**

Oak Park, Mich. 48237: 13691 W. Eleven Mile Rd. (313) 541-1440. James O'Donnell, mng edit; Joann Stevenson, opns mgr. Detroit office.
Planning & videotape prod & full natl or rgnl distribution of video news reports & public svc spots & related AV materials for radio & TV.

N W N - T V
TV Weathercast Via Satellite
On/Air Weather Talent!
Localized, customized, TV weathercast for your market. Limited clients, now being accepted. Reserve your market for AM, PM, weekend, or drop-in weathercast.
Call National Weather Network: 601/352-6673
Edward St. Pe'

National Weather Network. Box 786, Jackson, Miss. 39205. (601) 352-6673. FAX: (601) 948-6052. Edward St. Pé, pres.
Customized, localized TV weathercasts with or without meteorologists. Barter/cash via Ku satellite.

Nemo News Service. 7179 Via Maria, San Jose, Calif. 95139. (408) 226-6339; (800) 243-8436. FAX: (408) 226-6403. Dick Reizner, own/assignment edit.
On-assignment coverage of news & sporting events for radio & TV stns worldwide.

Network Video Services Inc. 1600 Broadway, Suite 307, New York 10019. (212) 581-7108. FAX: (212) 582-9740. Francisco Ramirez, pres; H. Joseph Jackson, VP; Audie Colon, satellite/video transmission.
Eng/EFP crews w/wo prods, satellite/video transmission consultant, Betacam packages.

Nippon TV Network Corp. 50 Rockefeller Plaza, Suite 940, New York 10020. (212) 765-5076. FAX: (212) 265-8495.

Northern California News Satellite. 1121 L St., Suite 109, Sacramento, Calif. 95814. (916) 446-7890. FAX: (916) 446-7893. Steve Mallory, pres; Bill Branch, bureau chief.
A video wire svc providing daily news coverage, via satellite, of California's capitol for TV stns throughout the state.

Ohio State University Electronic News Services. 1125 Kinnear Rd., Columbus, Ohio 43212. (614) 292-8385; (800) 251-4636 (Ohio only). FAX: (614) 292-0154. Amy Murray, radio prod; Kevin Jones, prod/videographer.
A 24-hr radio actualities svc: social, health & consumer features for radio & TV. Video of campus scenes inside & outside classes & laboratories, usually available at no chg.

PVS (Professional Video Services Corp). 2030 M St. N.W., Suite 400, Washington 20036. (202) 775-0894; (800) 232-0894. FAX: (202) 775-1288. Robert L. Grevemberg, pres; Steve Tello, VP/gen mgr.
Complete teleprod svcs; ENG/EFP crews, rentals, interformat editing, studio, domestic & international satellite svcs; Ku-band/multicamera prod trucks, air-transportable earth stn; ImMIX editing. Radio & TV news svc.

Potomac Television. 500 N. Capitol St. N.W., 8th Fl., Washington 20001. (202) 783-8000. FAX: (202) 783-1132. Tom Kole, bureau chief.
New York 10001: Five Penn Plaza. (214) 714-7842. FAX: (214) 714-3319.
Washington coverage for loc TV news. Editing facilities, live shots, satellite capability.

Presson Perspectives. 600 Druid Rd. E., Clearwater, Fla. 34616. (813) 461-1885. FAX: (813) 443-1984. Gina Presson, pres/reporter/prod; Kristin Andersen, pro/writer; Liz Summer, reporter/prod; Rick Rockwell, prod/dev dir.
Specializing in TV news & documentary prod. Svcs include rsch, field prod, videography, postprod, & satellite feeds for radio & TV.

Radio Press News Service. Box 1122, El Cerrito, Calif. 94530. (510) 524-9559. FAX: (510) 524-9559. Joseph L. Levit, Ph.D., pres; Robert M. Master, M.Ph.A., edit-in-chief; T.J. Waters, spec events; R.A. Levit, edit foreign affrs/bk reveiw; Mark C. Rhadaman, photo & assignment edit.
Natl coverage, with spec unit for Northern California & Bay Area, of California & adjacent states. Multimedia news, *Travellands* & *Vacationland*. Special features, articles, transcriptions, video-features.

Reuters America Inc. 1333 H St., Washington 20005. (202) 898-8410. FAX: (202) 898-8448. Steve Ginsburg, editor-in-charge (bcst svcs); Robert Doherty, bureau chief; Courtenay Carson, sls.
The Reuter Broadcast Report & Reuter Broadcast PLUS, featuring natl & international news, sports, business news, entertainment & weather.

Reuters Television. Rockefeller Ctr., 630 5th Ave., Suite 700, New York 10111. (212) 698-4500. FAX: (212) 698-2367. Christopher Travers, exec VP; Richard Frisch, mktg mgr corporate video svcs.
London NW10 7EH: Visnews Ltd. (parent company), Visnews House, Cumberland Ave. 011-44-1-965-7733. Julian Kerr, mgng dir.
Worldwide TV news prod & transmission svcs for loc TV stns/prods. Camera crews, prod facilities, news bureaus, satellite svcs, video/slide archives.

The Seattle Bureau. 2700 Fourth Ave., Suite 607, Seattle 98121. (206) 448-2500. FAX: (206) 728-0878. David Oglevie, pres; Kevin Ely, VP opns.
ENG/EFP crews with BETACAM SP kits matched Ikegami HL-55s. Network experienced producers. Ku Satellite truck available.

Sidebar News International. 436 Valley Scent Ave., Scotch Plains, N.J. 07076-1163. (908) 322-8343. FAX: (908) 322-8902. Charles Homer, editorial dir.
News reports & progmg for TV, cable & radio.

Skywatch Weather Center. 347 Prestley Rd., Bridgeville, Pa. 15017. (800) SKY-WATCH. Dick Mancini, pres; Dan Kryzwiecki, Stan Penkala, VPs; Stan Bostjancic, treas; Harry Green, sec.
Taped & live weathercasts targeted to the lstng area, in stn-specified formats. Featuring accuracy, clarity & mature voices.

Southern California News Service. 466 N. Orange St., Suite 280, Redlands, Calif. 92374. (909) 335-1325; (800) 726-0382. Marc Curtis, pres.
TV news gathering & prod crews, stock footage, rsch.

Television News Services

The Sports Network. 701 Mason's Mill Business Park, Huntingdon Valley, Pa. 19006. (215) 947-2400. FAX: (215) 938-8466. Mickey Charles, pres; Steve Abbott, mng edit; Phil Sokol, dir opns; John Sweeney, dir tech facilities.

Comprehensive sports wire svc. Sports real time, news, summaries, statistics & more. Designed for bcstrs.

SportsTicker. Harborside Financial Ctr., 600 Plaza Two, Jersey City, N.J. 07311. (201) 309-1200. FAX: (201) 860-9742. Peter Bavasi, pres; Rick Alessandri, VP admin; Joe Carnicelli, mng edit; John Mastroberardino, gen mgr news opns; John Buonaugurio, dir sls; Lou Monaco, dir mktg svcs.

Instant scores & complete sports news coverage on all professional & major college events delivered to broad-page printer, newsroom computer or PC.

Standard Broadcast News. 2 St. Clair Ave. W., Toronto, Ont., Canada M4V 1L6. Admin: (416) 323-6832; News desk: (416) 323-6824; Audio desk: (416) 962-3392 or (800) 565-6625. FAX: (416) 323-6825; (800) 565-6995. Steve Kowch, gen mgr; Cal Johnstone, natl news dir; Nick Jalsevac, engr; Ben Lawson; systems engr; Darin Diehl, Kathy Miller, Andy Trklja, news supvrs; Glenn Wilkins, business edit; Pat Hewitt, features & entertainment.

Ottawa, Ont., Canada K1P 5A4: 150 Wellington St., Suite 400. (613) 238-6585. FAX: (613) 238-3806. Dwayne Desaulniers, bureau chief. Parliamentary Bureau. Halifax Bureau Chris Stover, correspondent.

Que., Canada G1R 5A4: c/o CJAD News, Tribue de la Presse, 1050 St. Augustine. (418) 644-4010. Pat Enborg, correspondent. Quebec City Bureau.

Queen's Park, Toronto, Ont., Canada. M7A 1A2: Legislative Bldg. Room 313 A, (416) 325-9544. FAX: (416) 325-7080. Hal Vincent, correspondent. Queen's Park Bureau.

Winnipeg, N.B., Canada. R3C OV8: 440 Broadway. (204) 942-5020. Don MacGillivray, Wilf Braun, correspondents. Winnipeg Bureau.

Regina, Sask., Canada S4S 0B3: 2405 Legislative Dr., room 329. (306) 352-0161. Kimberly Wihnan, Peter Mayne, correspondents. Regina Bureau.

Edmonton, Alta., Canada T5S 2E2: 100-18520 Stony Plain Rd. (403) 486-9106; (800) 661-1726. FAX: (403) 451-4795; (800) 661-3329. Bill Graveland, bureau chief; Steve Lambert & Bill Nation, correpondents; Ken Davis, Prairie coord (c/o CJCA, 10250 108th St., Edmonton, AB: 403-424-4618). Prairie Bureau.

Vancouver, B.C., Canada V5Z 4J6: 2440 Ash St. (604) 877-4469; (604) 665-4669. FAX: (604) 873-0877. Russ Byth, bureau chief. Vancouver Bureau.

Victoria, B.C., Canada V8V 1X4: Room 012, Parliament Bldg. (604) 382-2424. Mimi Robertson, correspondent. Victoria Bureau.

Wire & audio svc for Canadian bcstrs, utilizing, CBS, Reuters & UPI for international coverage.

The States News Service. 1333 F St. N.W., Washington 20004. (202) 628-3100;. (202) 638-2317. FAX: (202) 737-1653. Karen Grassmuch, deputy mng edit.

Specific news coverage by 25-member Washington staff designed for your viewing audience.

Studio M Productions. 8715 Waikiki Station, Honolulu 96830. (808) 734-3345; (800) 453-3345. FAX: (808) 734-3299. Mike Michaels, gen mgr.

Hollywood, Calif. 90038: 1041 N. Orange Dr., (213) 462-7372; (800) 762-7372.

Stringers for news, sports, features, remote bcsts, engrs, announcers, reporters & equipment, radio, TV, film & video.

TV Direct. See Associated Press listing in Major National Radio Networks this section.

Trans World Communications Inc. Box 418, Hewlett, N.Y. 11557. (212) 686-6850. FAX: (212) 686-7308. Jay Levy, pres.

Produces audio news svcs for radio & TV bcstg.

Frank Ucciardo. 538 Chestnut St., West Hempstead, N.Y. 11552. (516) 292-1403. FAX: (212) 643-8972.

United Press International Inc. 1400 Eye St. N.W., Washington 20005. (202) 898-8000. FAX: (202) 842-3625. L. Brusler Jackson, pres/CEO; Steve Giemann, VP/exec edit; Bob Martin, Washington bureau chief; Michael Aulabaugh, VP bcst svcs.

Chicago 60601: 202 N. Wabash. (312) 781-1600. Bob Kieckhefer, rgnl edit.

Los Angeles 90045: 6701 Center Dr. W. (310) 670-1100. Eric Kramer, rgnl edit.

New York 10001: Five Penn Plaza. (212) 560-1100. William Morrissey, rgnl edit.

Atlanta 30367: 1819 Peachtree St. N.E. (404) 355-3700. David Mould, rgnl edit.

Full global text, audio, photo news & info svcs 24 hours a day.

United States Catholic Conference. Department of Communication, Film/TV Review Svcs., 1011 1st Ave., Suite 1300, New York 10022. (212) 644-1880. FAX: (212) 644-1886. Gerri Pare, media reviews off; Henry Herx, dir office for film & bcstg, (212) 644-1894.

Filming & bcstng U.S. Catholic conferences for TV.

Video News Bureau Inc. 275 E. Commercial Blvd., Lauderdale-by-the-Sea, Fla. 33308. (305) 771-5999. FAX: (305) 491-1470. Jaf Fletcher, prod; James M. Fletcher, assoc prod/edit.

Electronic publ & pub rels for individuals & corporations.

WPIX Inc. 220 E. 42nd St, New York 10017. (212) 949-1100. FAX: (212) 986-1032. Michael Eigner, exec VP/gen mgr; Paul Bissonette, VP/stn mgr; Patrick Austin, sr VP finance/sls; John Corporon, sr VP news; Kathy Shepherd, VP prod/communications affrs; Julie Nunnari, VP progmg; Wendy Kaiser, dir creative svcs; Jane Perlman, VP rsch; Liz Goldberg, VP traf/opns; Claudia Gasparini, VP human resources; Elaine Huryn, VP planning; Fred Witte, controller; Frank Geraty, dir engrg; Michelle Leibowitz & Steve Berman, loc sls mgr; Vinnie Manzi, natl sls mgr.

WSI Corp. 4 Federal St., Billerica, Mass. 01821. (508) 670-5000. FAX: (508) 670-5100. Mark Gildersleeve, pres; Don Freeland, media mkt mgr.

Art & animation capabilities, & real-time weather imagery products including mosaic radar imagery. Supply weather info to TV & radio.

The Washington Bureau. 400 N. Capitol St. N.W., Suite 167, Washington 20001. (202) 347-6396. FAX: (202) 628-6295. Richard Tillery, bureau chief; Julia Rockler, deputy bureau chief.

Custom TV news coverage: ENG crews, producers & talent. Prod svcs: editing, studio, remote & satellite capabilities.

Washington International Teleport Inc. 5600 General Washington Dr., Suite B-210, Alexandria, Va. 22312. (703) 914-0014. FAX: (703) 658-4919. Stephen G. Tom, pres/CEO; Henry C. Clark, VP sls mktg; Peter Browne, VP engrg/opns.

Domestic & international satellite transmit & receive svcs; transponder purchase, traf coord, portable equip, loc microwave, fiber access, voice, data & video communication svcs.

Washington News Network. 400 N. Capitol St. N.W., Room 183, Washington 20001. (202) 628-4000. FAX: (202) 628-4015. Walter Gold, pres/gen mgr; Ward Lassoe, news dir.

Washington news bureau for more than 100 TV stns, rgnl nets & news progs nationwide. Provides reporter packages & vo/sots, crew hinges & hearing video transcripts. Full editing, studio & satellite facilities on Capitol Hill.

WeatherData Inc. 825 N. Main, Wichita, Kan. 67203. (316) 265-9127. FAX: (316) 265-0371. Mike Smith, pres/certified consulting meteorologist; Steve Pryor, mgr meteorology; Kristi Francis, dir business administration.

Forecasts for radio & TV, meteorology training, slides & videotape of weather & related phenomena.

Weathermean. 1390 Oak Ct., Boulder, Colo. 80304. (303) 443-7443. Dan Niemeyer, exec off.

Visual weather statistic for TV comparing current weather & forecasts to typical weather.

Evan Weiner Productions. 370 Claremont Ave., Mt. Vernon, N.Y. 10552. (914) 667-9070. FAX: (914) 667-3043. Evan Weiner, exec prod; Gary Chester, Amy Bader, Bob Muessler, talent; Don Barberino, prod *Sports Beyond the Field*.

TV & radio prog prod; sports commentaries & reporting; current prog: *Sports: Beyond the Field*, sports issues show.

Willis News Service. Box 2777, Alexandria, Va. 22301. (703) 548-8007. L. Clayton Willis, pres/White House correspondent/own/exec prod.

TV, radio bcst & print media; extensive tape & film library.

Worldwide Television News Corp. The Interchange, Oval Rd., Camden Lock, London, England NW1 7EP. (44) 71-410-5200. FAX: (44) 71-413-8302. Kenneth A. Coyte, pres; Robert E. Burke, exec VP; Terry O'Reilly, VP U.S. opns.

International TV svcs company, daily satellite news feeds to bcstrs worldwide, tech facilities, camera crew hire worldwide.

Zapnews. 4002 University Dr., Fairfax, Va. 22030. (800) 800-5100. FAX: (800) 800-9450. James R. Hood, pres/edit-in-chief; Joe Benton, exec edit; Ellen Ambrose, sls mgr.

World, natl & state news, sports & features written for immediate bcst. Compatible with newsroom computers & FAX machines.

Closed Circuit Television

Ambrose Video Publishing. 1290 Ave. of the Americas, Suite 2245, New York 10104. (212) 265-7272. William V. Ambrose, pres.
Video distribution to consumers (home) & non-theatrical (film & video) distribution to educ market. Subsidiaries:
Video Conference Networks Inc. 1271 Ave. of the Americas, New York 10020. (212) 541-5954. (Conference TV net, point-to-point & single location svcs.)
Management Television Systems Inc. 1271 Ave. of the Americas, New York 10020. (212) 541-5954. (Rental-leasing of color, B&W TV projection equipment.)
Amphicon Systems Inc. One Graphic Pl., Moonachie, N.J. (201) 641-3383. (Design, mfg, rsch & dev for MTS, above.)

Bramson Telecasting Service. 1501 Broadway, Rm. 2300, New York 10036. (212) 354-9575. E.M. Abramson, pres.
All phases of closed circuit TV.

Communications Systems Group/General Television. 13355 Capital Ave., Oak Park, Mich. 48237. (313) 399-2000. FAX: (313) 548-0028. Kurt Krinke, pres.
TV; audio; teleconferencing; training systems; design, sls & svc.

General Television Network. 13320 Northend, Oak Park, Mich. 48237. (313) 548-2500. Joan Binkow, CEO.
Sls & svc of closed circuit TV equipment & communications systems.

IDB Communications Group Inc. 10525 W. Washington Blvd., Culver City, Calif. 90232. (213) 870-9000. FAX: (213) 870-3400. Jeffrey Sudikoff, chmn/CEO; Edward Cheramy, pres; Peter Hartz, sr VP mktg & sls.
Domestic & international satellite transmission svcs for TV, radio & voice/data. Owns & operates New York & Los Angeles teleports, large fleet of transportable earth stns.

Kenneth R. Meades. Box 1469, Los Angeles 90053. (213) 669-9670. Kenneth R. Meades, own/mgr.
Consulting & systems design.

Pay Cable Services

BET-Action Pay Per View Network. 2425 W. Olympic Blvd., Suite 4050 W, Santa Monica, Calif. 90404. (310) 453-4500. FAX: (310) 453-2573. Curtis Symonds, pres/COO; Rodney M. Bagley, CFO; John Figueroa, VP mktg; Ron Norberg, sr VP sls; Andy Reimer, VP progmg.

Pay-per-view movie ch featuring action genre, ind film prods, events & major hit films.

Serving 5.8 million HH subs on 250 cable systems. Satellite: Galaxy I, transponder 2.

Cable Video Store. 532 Broadway, 7th Fl., New York 10012. (212) 941-1434. FAX: (212) 941-4746. Mark Graff, pres; Barry Teiman, VP progmg; Richard Kirby, dir opns; Steve Saril, VP affil sls & mktg.

A 24-hour, pay-per-view prog svc. Categories include top hits, spec events, comedy, action/adventure, horror/suspense, drama/romance & spec interest.

On 185 systems serving 2.3 million subs. Satellite: Telstar 303, transponder 9.

Cinemax. (Home Box Office.) 1100 Ave. of the Americas, New York 10036. (212) 512-1000. Michael Fuchs, chmn/CEO; Jeff Bewkes, pres.

A 24-hour premium svc offering select & broad-appeal films.

On 5,900 systems serving 6.3 million subs (includes non-cable affils). Satellites: Galaxy 1 (eastern feed); Galaxy 5 (western feed). Analog—Telstar 302; Digital—Galaxy 1; Multiplex svc (MAX2).

The Disney Channel. 3800 W. Alameda Ave., Burbank, Calif. 91505. (818) 569-7500. FAX: (818) 566-1358. John F. Cooke, pres.

Coml-free entertainment for the whole family.

On 7,000 cable systems serving approximately 7.08 million subs. Satellite: Galaxy 1, transponder 24 vertical (western feed); Galaxy 5, transponder 1 horizontal (eastern feed).

ENCORE. 4700 S. Syracuse Pkwy., Suite 1000, Denver 80237-2721. (303) 771-7700; FAX: (303) 741-3067. John J. Sie, chmn/CEO; Que Spaulding, sr VP mktg & sls; Warren S. Zeller, VP mktg; Mark Bauman, dir finance & admin.

A 24-hour premium svc featuring movies of the '60s, '70s & '80s uncut, unedited & coml-free.

On 1,090 cable systems serving approximately 3.9 million subs. Satellite: Galaxy 1, transponder 3.

ENCORE Thematic Multiplex. 4700 S. Syracuse Pkwy., Suite 1000, Denver 80237. (303) 771-7700. FAX: (303) 267-4098. John J. Sie, chmn/CEO; Mike Hale, sr VP progmg & opns.

A 24-hour premium svc that offers on-demand viewing options featuring uncut, coml-free movies classified by genre.

Home Box Office (HBO). 1100 Ave. of the Americas, New York 10036. (212) 512-1000. Michael J. Fuchs, chmn/CEO; Jeff Bewkes, pres/COO; John Billock, exec VP sls & mktg; Richard Plepler, sr VP corporate communications.

Rgnl offices in New York, Atlanta, Chicago, Philadelphia, Dallas, Denver, Los Angeles & San Francisco.

Features 24-hour var progmg including movies, specials, documentaries, sports, series & original progs.

On over 9,300 systems, serving 17.4 million subs (includes non-cable affils). Satellites: Galaxy 1 & 5 (eastern feeds); Galaxy 5 (western feed). Analog—Telstar 302; Digital—Galaxy 1; Multiplex svc (HBO2, HBO3).

Minority Broadcasting Corporation of America. World Trade Center, 2050 Stemmons Fwy., Suite 195, Dallas 75207. (214) 744-3934. FAX: (214) 748-6120. Alvin D. James, chmn; Van B. McClellan III, sr VP; Calvin Spencer, VP; Terome Burnett, VP administration; Dianne W. Atkins, dir natl sls; Crystal S. Browning, asst dir natl sls; Frankie Henderson, rgnl sls rep.

MBC Movie Network, a pay-TV svc, offers consulting on TV syndication & prog distribution, radio progs & prod svcs for start-up of TV, radio & cable nets; domestic & international.

Satellite: G-3; transponder 21.

The Movie Channel. (Showtime Networks Inc.) 1633 Broadway, New York 10019. (212) 708-1600. Winston H. "Tony" Cox, chmn/CEO SNI; Matthew Blank, pres/COO SNI; Jack Heim, exec VP sls & mktg SNI; Jim Miller, exec VP progmg SNI.

A 24-hour premium all-movie svc. Features on-air personalities & spec progmg slots.

Reaches a combined 10.7 million subs (Showtime Networks Inc.). Satellites: Satcom C-3, transponder 17 (eastern feed); Satcom C-4, transponder 22 (western feed).

New Culture Network. 2909 Stanton Ave., Silver Spring, Md. 20910. (301) 589-5691. FAX: (301) 589-9379. Charles Giffen, pres; David Thomas, VP mktg.

A 24-hour premium cable-exclusive progmg including films of all genres by American & international ind filmmakers.

PRISM. 225 City Ave., Bala Cynwyd, Pa. 19004. (215) 668-2210. FAX: (215) 668-9499. Dennis E. Patton, VP/gen mgr; Sam Schroeder, VP/asst gen mgr; Terri Morse sr mktg & sls dir; Daniel Ronayne, dir mktg; Lynn Lonker, prog dir.

Premium pay-TV net in the Philadelphia rgn. Offers first-run movies & loc professional & college sports.

Reaches 65 cable systems serving 400,000 subs. Via microwave.

Playboy TV. (Playboy Entertainment Group.) 9242 Beverly Blvd., Beverly Hills, Calif. 90210. (310) 246-4000. FAX: (310) 246-4050. Tony Lynn, pres; Richard Rosetti, pres prod; Michael Fleming, sr VP/gen mgr.

Sophisticated entertainment targeted to adults. Schedule consists of 75% original Playboy progs with the balance comprised of acquired progs & feature films.

On 625 cable systems serving 500,000 monthly subs & 9.5 million pay-per-view viewers. Satellite: Galaxy 5, transponder 2.

Pro Am Sports System Inc. 550 W. Lafayette Blvd., Detroit 48231. (313) 222-7277. FAX: (313) 223-2299. William J. Wischman Jr., gen mgr; Kathleen L. Hunt, bus mgr; Annette Mansfield, sr mgr affl rels & mktg; William P. Glenn, exec prod; Denise M. McGee, net mgr.

Cable Sports Network featuring Detroit Tigers, Pistons, Red Wings, Collegiate & Amateur sports affl with Prime Net.

Serving 800,000 subs on 250 cable systems. Satellite: Spacenet 3, transponder 11.

Request Television. 5619 DTC Pkwy., Suite 800, 9th Fl., Denver 80111. (303) 267-6100. FAX: (303) 267-6195. Hugh Panero, pres/CEO; Jeffrey Bernstein, VP mktg & progmg; Larry Smith, VP affil rels & sls; Dom Stasi, VP opns & technology.

Pay-per-view svc, including Request 1 through 5 available in addressable cable homes, offers movie titles plus spec events.

On cable systems serving more than 11 million subs. Satellites: GE Satcom C-4, transponder 16 (Request); GE Satcom C-4, transponder 2 (Request 2).

Sega Channel. 810 7th Ave., 32nd Fl., New York, 10019. (212) 484-6767. FAX: (212) 974-8790. Stanley B. Thomas Jr., pres/CEO; Paige Holmes, affil sls acct exec; Gail Williams, Howard Burkat.

A 24-hour premium ch that offers video games on demand & a video library accessible to subs.

SUR. (PanAmericana Television, USA.) 601 Brickell Key Dr., Suite 100, Miami, Fla., 33131. (305) 530-9987. FAX: (305) 373-7811. Hector Delgado Parker, pres; Manuel Iglesias, CEO.

Bcst direct via satellite. Progmg from 18 countries in Latin America.

Reaches four cable systems. Satellite: Spacenet 2, transponder 18.

Showtime Networks Inc. 1633 Broadway, 37th Fl., New York 10019. (212) 708-1600. FAX: (212) 708-1530. Winston H. "Tony" Cox, chmn/CEO; Matthew Blank, pres/COO; Jim Miller, exec VP progmg; Jack Heim, exec VP sls & affil mktg; Susan Denison, exec VP/gen mgr Showtime satellite nets; Gregory J. Ricca, exec VP/gen counsel; J. Nordby, VP All News Channel; Arthur G. Cooper, sr VP/CFO; Nancy R. Glauberman, VP corporate communications; Gregory J. Ricca, exec VP/gen counsel net groups; Ann Foley-Plunkett, sr VP progmg & creative opns, sr VP prog acquisitions & distribution; McAdory Litscomb, sr VP corp affrs.

A premium svc providing 24-hour var progmg including movies, championship boxing, var & comedy series, concerts & family progmg.

Showtime Networks Inc. (including The Movie Channel) reaches a combined 10.7 million subs. Satellites: Satcom C-3, transponder 15 (eastern feed); Satcom C-4, transponder 20 (western feed).

Spice. (Graff Pay-Per-View.) 532 Broadway, 7th Fl., New York 10012. (212) 941-1434. FAX: (212) 941-4746. Mark Graff, pres; Steve Saril, VP affil sls & mktg.

A 24-hour pay-per-view or sub svc. Offers a monthly package of up to 40 cable-version adult films.

On 200 cable systems serving 6.6 million subs. Satellite: Telstar 303, transponder 20.

TV Japan. (Japan Network Group Inc.) 1325 Ave. of the Americas, 8th Fl., New York 10019. (212) 262-3377. FAX: (212) 262-5577. Masakazu Ohtsu, CEO, Japan Network Group; Takao Yoneyama, pres.

An 18-hour premium svc. Daily direct bcst from Tokyo of popular progs from NHK & other bcsters, including news, sports, drama, educ & children's progmg.

On 17 cable systems serving 100,000 subs. Satellite: Satcom K-1, transponder 5; Prime Star.

TheatreVisioN. (Graff Pay-Per-View.) 532 Broadway, 7th Fl., New York 10012. (212) 941-1434. FAX: (212) 941-4746. Mark Graff, pres; Steven Saril, VP affil sls & mktg.

A 24-hour pay-per-view net offering up to eight chs of popular Hollywood movies & selected spec events.

Satellite: Telstar 303, transponders 1-8.

Viewer's Choice. 909 3rd Ave., 21st Fl., New York 10022. (212) 486-6600. FAX: (212) 688-9497. James O. Heyworth, pres/CEO; J. Robert Bedell, sr VP sls/mktg; Hilda Chazanovitz, VP mktg; James L. English, VP progmg; Samuel L. Yates, VP finance/COO; Sandra E. Landau, VP/gen counsel; Terry Taylor, rgnl VP west; David Intrator, rgnl VP east; Kim Cunningham, VP bus affrs.

Los Angeles 90067: 1888 Century Park East. (310) 785-9094; (310) 785-9194. FAX: (310) 785-9195; (310) 785-9769.

A pay-per-view net offering five chs of films, sports & entertainment events. Chs include: Viewers's Choice, HA Choice & Continuous Hits 1, 2 & 3.

Serving 11.5 million basic subs on more than 540 cable systems. Satellites: Satcom C-3, transponder 3; Satcom C-4, transponder 18.

World African Network. 5120 Goldleaf Cir., Suite 380, Los Angeles, 90056. (213) 299-3300. FAX: (213) 299-3344. Eugene D. Jackson, chmn/CEO; Phyllis Tucker Vinson Jackson, exec VP; Donna Clayburn, VP affil sls; Andre Hayes, dir sls; Dorothy Middleton, creative dir; Yvette Thompson, dir admin.

A 14-hour premium ch that will offer a comprehensive mix of classic & contemp films, TV, mus, sports, & original progmg from an African-American perspective.

Basic Cable Services

A&E Networks. 235 E. 45th St., New York 10017. (212) 210-1328. FAX: (212) 949-7147. Nickolas Davatzes, pres/CEO; Whitney Goit II, exec VP sls & mktg; Seymour H. Lesser, exec VP/CFO; Robert E. Igiel, sr VP consumer products; Daniel E. Davids, sr VP mktg; Brooke Bailey Johnson, VP progmg & prod; Abbe Raven, VP prod; Ronald M. Schneier, sr VP adv sls; Mary Ann Zimmer, VP legal & bus affrs; Ken Street, VP affil sls; Charles Maday, VP historical progmg.

Offers a mix of comedy, drama, documentaries & performing arts. A&E Networks also administers The History Channel (see listing).

A&E: serving 9,300 cable systems & 61 million subs. Satellite: Galaxy 5, transponder 23.

Alternate View Network. 400 Common St., Shreveport, La. 71101-2923. (318) 226-8776. FAX: (318) 227-9275. D.L. Dykes Jr., pres; George Nelson, chmn of bd; Roy M. Davis Jr., engr.

On 695 cable systems reaching more than 12 million total viewers.

Occasional uplink & prog prod.

American Movie Classics (AMC). (Rainbow Programming Service Holdings Inc.) 150 Crossways Park W., Woodbury, N.Y. 11797. (516) 364-2222. FAX: (516) 364-8929. Josh Sapan, pres; Kate McEnroe, VP/gen mgr American Movie Classics.

Sixty years of classic movies; uncut, unedited & coml-free.

Serving 4,100 cable systems & 45 million subs. Satellite: Satcom C-4, transponder 1.

America's Disability Channel. (Silent Network Inc.) 1777 N.E. Loop 410, Suite 300, San Antonio, 78217. (512) 824-7446. FAX: (512) 829-1388. TDD: (512) 824-1666. Dr. Bill Nichols, pres ADC; Ron Dickson, pres progmg & prod; Scott Senter, dir opns.

Info & entertainment progmg in sign language, voice & open captions, & sound for deaf & hearing-impaired audiences.

On 178 cable systems serving 14.7 million subs. Satellite: Satcom C-1, transponder 16.

Americana Television Network Inc. Box 398, 110 Wintergreen Rd., Branson, Mo. 65616. (417) 335-8600. FAX: (417) 335-2333. Stanley E. Hitchcock, chmn/CEO; Margaret C. Combs, COO; Joseph E. Sullivan, pres; Sharen Glassman, VP/CFO; Rene Ray, VP affil rels; Nan Olson, VP adv sls; Cecil Thomas, VP/gen sls mgr.

Original progs, documentaries & videos exploring our nation's mus, people & pastimes. Featuring American mus: bluegrass, blues, jazz, country, gospel & folk.

Serving 11.6 million subs on 751 cable systems. Satellite: C-3, transponder TBA.

Arts and Antiques Network (AAN). 3506 S. 16th St., Arlington, Va. 22204. (703) 553-0472. Douglas Ritter, pres; Warren Baise, VP.

Progmg related to cultural aspects of art & antiques. Live & taped coverage of cultural festivals & historical reenactments. Interactive auctions of art, antiques & collectibles. Launch in 4th quarter 1994.

Black Entertainment Television (BET). 1232 31 St. N.W., Washington 20007. (202) 337-5260. FAX: (202) 342-7882. Robert L. Johnson, pres/CEO; Debra Lee, exec VP; Curtis Symonds, VP affil sls & mktg; James Ebron, VP net sls.

Cable satellite net providing 24 hrs of Afro-American family progmg, including mus, sports, children's entertainment, news, pub affrs & specials.

Serves 2,745 cable systems & 36.8 million subs. Satellite: Galaxy 5, transponder 20.

THE BOX. 12000 Biscayne Blvd., Miami, Fla. 33181-2742. (305) 899-9000. FAX: (305) 892-3600. J. Patrick Michaels Jr., actg pres/CEO.

A 24-hr interactive, viewer-programmed TV net, which lets viewers select from a list of more than 300 available mus videos of all types.

Serves 16 million subs on 146 systems (includes LPTV households). Locally originated from each affil headend.

Bravo. (Rainbow Programming Holdings Inc.) 150 Crossways Park W., Woodbury, 11797. (516) 364-2222. FAX: (516) 364-7638. Josh Sapan, pres natl svcs; Kathleen Dore, VP/gen mgr; Jonathan Sehring, VP progmg.

Cable's cultural ch featuring fine films & performing arts.

Serving 11.5 million subs on 500 systems. Satellite: Satcom C-4, transponder 7.

C-SPAN (Cable Satellite Public Affairs Network). 400 N. Capitol St. N.W., Suite 650, Washington 20001. (202) 737-3220. FAX: (202) 737-3323. Brian P. Lamb, chmn/CEO; Robert Kennedy, Susan Swain, sr VPs; Terry Murphy, VP progmg.

Pub affrs progmg including live gavel-to-gavel coverage of the U.S. House of Representatives (C-SPAN) & Senate (C-SPAN 2).

Serving 59.6 million subs on 4,457 cable systems. Satellite: Satcom C-3, transponder 7.

CAL-SPAN/The California Channel. 1121 L St., Suite 502, Sacramento, Calif. 95814. (916) 444-9792. FAX: (916) 444-9812. Paul Koplin, pres.

Serving 2.8 million subs on 62 cable systems. Satelite: Satcom C-1, transponder 16.

CNBC. 2200 Fletcher Ave., Fort Lee, N.J. 07024. (201) 585-2622. FAX: (201) 585-6482. Roger Ailes, pres; Caroline Vanderlip, VP mktg & affil rels; Bruce Ballard, VP affil rels eastern rgn; Larry Smith, VP affil rels western rgn; Josh Grotstein, dir affil mktg; Paul Waters, dir loc adv sls.

Provides fast-breaking business & mkt news & consumer info.

Serving 49 million subs on 4,000 systems (includes non-cable affils). Satellite: Galaxy 5, transponder 13.

CNN-Cable News Network. Box 105366, One CNN Ctr., Atlanta 30348-5366. (404) 827-1700. Tom Johnson, pres; Burt Reinhardt, vice-chmn; Bob Furnad, exec VP; Ed Turner, exec VP news gathering; Lou Dobbs, sr VP/mngng editor business news; Gail Evans, sr VP/exec prod net bookings; Bill MacPhail, sr VP sports; Jane Maxwell, sr VP special events; Alma Sanders, sr VP finance & admin.

Live coverage of the world's news to a worldwide audience. Progmg encompasses in-depth coverage of major news stories & specialized daily reports on business, finance, medicine, nutrition, science, sports, weather, fashion & entertainment news.

Serving 61.7 million subs on 14,690 cable systems. Satellite: Galaxy 5, transponder 5.

Cable Health Club. 1000 Centerville Tpke., Virginia Beach, Va. 23467-4549. (804) 523-7301. FAX: (804) 523-7880. Steve Lentz, sr VP/mngng dir adv sls; Bob Hammer, dir sls & mktg IFE.

A 24-hr cable net providing viewers with hrly aerobics, fitness training & healthy living segments.

Satellite: Satcom C-4, transponder: 14.

Cable Satellite Entertainment Network. (Network One or N-1.) 6233 Variel Ave., Woodland Hills, Calif. 91367. (818) 704-5154. FAX: (818) 704-3934. Joseph D. Preston, chmn/CEO; Garrett Passon, pres/COO.

General entertainment progmg with interactive telephone direct-response proms.

Serving 3.4 million subs. Satellite: Satcom C1, transponder 11.

Caribbean Satellite Network. Bldg. G, Studio 10, 6175 N.W. 167th St., Miami, Fla. 33015. (305) 822-0484. FAX: (305) 822-9298. Delroy Cowan, pres/CEO; Dennis Krael, VP adv sls; Dawn Hill, exec VP worldwide dist.

A 24-hr source of Caribbean progmg including reggae, soca & other mus videoclips, as well as news, info, sports, comedy & specials.

Serving 8 million subs (including non-cable affils). Satellite: Galaxy 3, transponder 14.

The Cartoon Network. 1050 Techwood Dr. N.W., Atlanta 30318. (404) 885-2263. FAX: (404) 885-4301. Scott Sassa, pres, Turner Entertainment Networks; Betty Cohen, exec VP; Joshua Katz, sr VP mktg; Stephen Croncota, VP creative svcs; Mike Lazzo, dir progmg; Shirley Grisiatis, mgr pub rels.

A 24-hr cartoon net with selections from the Turner Entertainment Co. & Hanna-Barbera libraries, including Bugs Bunny, the Flintstones, Yogi Bear. For audiences of all ages.

Serving 6 million subs on 600 cable systems. Satellite: Galaxy 1, transponder 8.

Comedy Central. 1775 Broadway, New York 10019. (212) 767-8600. FAX: (212) 767-8582. Bob Creek, pres/CEO; Larry Divney, sr VP adv sls; Mitch Semel, sr VP progmg; Tony Fox, VP media rels.

Los Angeles 90067: 2049 Century Park E., Suite 4250. (310) 201-9500. FAX: (310) 201-9488.

A 24-hr all comedy TV net that covers stand-ups, sketch comedy, movies, talk shows, sitcoms, specials & classics (60% are original).

Serves more than 28 million subs on 2,679 cable systems. Satellites: Satcom C-3, transponder 21 (eastern feed); Galaxy 1, transponder 1 (western feed).

Country Music Television (CMT). (Group W Satellite Communications.) 250 Harbor Dr., Stamford, Conn. 06904. (203) 965-6000. David Hall, pres; Tom Griscom, chmn/pres Gaylord Community Group; Bob Baker, dir opns; Tracy Storey, prog mgr.

Nashville 37214: 2806 Opreyland Dr. (615) 871-5830. FAX: (615) 871-6698.

Country mus videos 24 hrs a day in stereo, featuring interviews & mus specials.

On 5,020 systems serving 19.6 million subs. Satellite: Satcom C-4, transponder 24.

Courtroom Television Network. 600 3rd Ave., 2nd Fl., New York 10016. (212) 973-2800. FAX: (212) 972-6258. Steven Brill, pres/editor-in-chief.

Provides 24-hr-a-day live & taped coverage of trials & legal news, supplemented by reporting & commentary.

On 700 cable systems serving 14.1 million subs. Satellite: Satcom C-3, transponder 6.

The Crime Channel. 13601 Ventura Blvd., Suite 103, Sherman Oaks, Calif. 91423. (818) 907-5769. FAX: (818) 907-5997. Arnie Frank, pres.

Crime-related progmg including entertaining, informational, nostalgic & educ progs.

Satellite: ASC-1, transponder 17.

Deep Dish TV. 339 Lafayette St., New York 10012. (212) 473-8933. FAX: (212) 420-8223. Kai Lumumba Barrow, exec dir; Ioannis Mookas, opns mgr.

Educ progmg two hrs a week, distributed to PBS & public access chs.

Serves 300 cable systems. Satellite: Satcom C-1.

The Discovery Channel. (Discovery Networks). 7700 Wisconsin Ave., Bethesda, Md. 20814. (301) 986-1999. FAX: (301) 986-4826. John S. Hendricks, chmn/CEO; Ruth L. Otte, pres/COO; Greg Durig, CFO; Greg Moyer, Chuck Gingold, sr VPs progmg; Tim Cowling, sr VP prod; Bill McGowan, sr VP adv sls; Clark Bunting, sr VP enterprises; Dawn McCall, VP.

Nonfiction progmg in the fields of science, nature, history, adventure & world exploration. Distributed to the U.S., northern Europe, Israel & Japan. (9 am-3 am ET daily.)

Carried on 9,860 cable systems serving 59.3 million subs. Satellites: Satcom C-4, transponder 21 (eastern feed); Galaxy 5, transponder 12 (western feed).

E! Entertainment Television. 5670 Wilshire Blvd., Los Angeles 90036-3709. (213) 954-2400. FAX: (213) 954-2620. Lee Masters, pres/CEO; Fran Shea, sr VP progmg; Christopher Fager, sr VP bus & legal affrs; William Keenan, sr VP/CFO; Debra Lieberman Green, sr VP affil sls; David T. Cassaro, sr VP adv sls.

A 24-hr cable net presenting major celebrities & current news from the entertainment world.

Serving 22 million subs through 1,060 cable systems. Satellite: Satcom C-3, transponder 23.

ESPN. ESPN Plaza, Bristol, Conn. 06010. (203) 585-2000. FAX: (203) 585-2213. Steven M. Bornstein, pres/CEO N.Y.; John S. Bonanni, sr VP adv sls N.Y.; Andrew P. Brilliant, sr VP/gen mgr ESPN international-N.Y.; Edwin M. Durso, exec VP net mktg & gen counsel N.Y.; Rosa M. Gatti, sr VP communications Conn.; Richard Glover, sr VP ESPN Enterprises N.Y.; Loren Matthews, sr VP progmg Conn.; Reginald R. Thomas, sr VP opns & engrg Conn..

New York 10158-0180: 605 3rd Ave. (212) 916-9200. Al Weider.

A 24-hr svc covering sports events, news & info, & lifestyle progmg.

Serves 61.9 million subs on 25,900 systems (including non-cable affils). Satellites: Galaxy 5, transponder 9 (primary); Galaxy 1, transponder 14 (alternate).

ESPN2. ESPN Plaza, Bristol, Conn. 06010-9454. (203) 585-2000. Steven M. Bornstein, pres/CEO; John Lack, exec VP mktg & progmg; George Bodenheimer, VP affil sls & mktg.

A 24-hr differentiated sports net that will feature more than 2,500 hrs per year of original progmg. Targeted to moderate sports viewers 18-34 years old.

Satellites: Galaxy 5, transponder 14 (primary); Galaxy 1, transponder 9 (alternate).

EWTN: The Catholic Cable Network. 5817 Old Leeds Rd., Birmingham, Ala. 35210. (205) 956-9537. FAX: (205) 965-0328. Mother M. Angelica, chmn; R. William Steltemeier, pres; Matt Scalici, VP engrg & satellite opns; Chris Harrington, VP opns & prod; Marynell Ford, VP mktg; Richard King, VP progmg.

A 24-hour Catholic cable net providing family-oriented, spiritual growth progmg featuring talk shows, wkly series & documentaries.

On 1,079 cable systems serving 32 million subs. Satellite: Galaxy 1, transponder 11.

Eastern Microwave. See WWOR-TV.

The ECO Channel. 9171 Victoria Dr., Ellicott City, Md. 21042. (410) 750-7291. Eric McLamb, founder/chmn/CEO; Cambodochine Dao, CFO; Brian A. Day, sr VP environmental policy; Tim Knipe, sr VP environmental opns.

A 24-hr ch offering contemp progmg regarding current trends, news, fiction & non-fiction about the environment. Launch in 4th quarter.

The Employment Channel. 1133 Broadway, Suite 1125, New York 10010. (212) 675-3811. FAX: (212) 675-4162. Broderick C. Byers, CEO/pres; Fred M. Bulah, VP opns; Leonard D. Jumpulsky, VP new bus dev.

Video employment ch that shows job listings, employment news & training, bus & entrepreneurial segments & educ info. Also available in Spanish, Japanese, Korean & Russian.

FX. Box 900, Beverly Hills, Calif. 90213. (310) 203-3474. FAX: (310) 203-2452. Anne M. Sweeney, chmn/CEO: Larry Jones, pres; Robert Fleming, sr VP finance & admin; Mindy Herman, VP bus & legal affrs: Elisabeth Murdoch, mgr prog acquisitions.

FXTV: Fitness and Exercise Television. Box 5767, Beverly Hills, Calif. 90209. (310) 271-5400. FAX: (310) 271-3479. Alan Mruvka, co-chmn; Larry Namer, co-chmn.

A 24-hr fitness & exercise net featuring virtually every type of exercise class, hosted by well-known instructors. Launch in July 1994.

Family Channel. 4549 1000 Centerville Tpke., Virginia Beach, Va. 23463-4549. (804) 523-7301. FAX: (804) 523-7880. Timothy B. Robertson, pres; Paul Krimsier, VP progmg; Steve Lentz, VP natl adv sls; Craig Sherwood, VP affil rels; Earl Weirich, VP pub rels; Terry Botwick, VP original progmg; Ron Harris, VP new ventures.

Family entertainment, original made-for-TV films, dramatic & comedy series, classic Westerns, specials & inspirational progs.

On 10,102 cable systems serving 57.4 million subs. Satellites: Galaxy 5, transponder 11 (eastern feed); Satcom C-3, transponder 1 (western feed).

FamilyNet. 6350 West Fwy., Fort Worth, Tex. 76150. (800) 8-FAMNET. FAX: (817) 737-7853. David Lewis, natl mktg dir; Deborah Key, gen mgr; Steve Roberson, sls.

Provides 24-hr family entertainment & inspirational progmg.

Satellite: Galaxy 7, transponder 14.

FoxNet. 11833 Mississippi Ave., Los Angeles 90025. (310) 447-7304. FAX: (310) 447-7334. Andy Murphy, VP cable affils; Katherine McGinity, asst.

A 24-hr basic svc. Cable affil to Fox Broadcasting Co. Serving 2 million subs on 733 cable systems. Satellite: Satcom C-1, transponder 19.

GEMS Television. 4380 N.W. 128th St., Opa Locka, Fla. 33054. (305) 769-4555. FAX: (305) 681-0412. W. Gary McBride, pres/CEO; M. Alexander Berger, COO; Mari Carmen Villanueva, dir progmg & prom.

A 16-hr Pan-American Spanish-language multichannel cable progmg svc targeted specifically to women. Progmg features novellas, miniseries, films & musicals.

Satellites: Intelsat 329; Spacenet 2.

GalaVision. (A subsidiary of UNIVISA.) 6701 Center Dr. W., 6th Fl., Los Angeles 90045. (310) 348-3640. FAX: (310) 348-3643. Jaime Davila, division pres; G.S. Livingston III, VP bcst opns.

A 24-hr Spanish-language net & basic cable svc that provides feature films, novellas, var specials, sports & news. Progmg is produced in Mexico & aired throughout the U.S., Mexico & Europe.

On 353 cable systems serving 4.2 million subs (includes SMATV sytems).

Satellites: Galaxy 1, transponder 20; Spacenet 2, transponder 10.

The Game Channel. 1000 Centerville Tpke., Virginia Beach, Va. 23454. (804) 523-7301. FAX: (804) 523-7249. Timothy Robertson, pres/CEO; Paul Krimsier, sr VP progmg; Mike Gwartney, dir progmg.

A full-time ch with a blend of original interactive game shows, phone games, video & audio games, & classic game shows.

The Game Show Channel. 10202 W. Washington Blvd., Culver City, Calif. 90232-3195. (310) 280-3092; (310) 452-3355. FAX: (310) 452-4077. Dick Block, project dir; Bob Boden, prog consultant (310-280-3042).

A 24-hr ch featuring classic & new game shows from Sony Pictures Entertainment, United Vidio & Mark Goodson Productions. Launch in 1994.

Gaming & Entertainment Network. Box 38306, Pittsburgh 15238-8306. (412) 782-2921. FAX: (412) 782-4242. Nelson L. Goldberg, pres/CEO; Willaim Heller, CFO; Carmella N. Acre, VP opns; Frederick I. Goldberg, VP dev.

Worldwide originator & communicator for the gaming & entertainment industries with live interactive players participation games, in-home shopping, simulcast racing & more, 24-hrs-a-day, seven days a week. Launch in 1994.

Global Village Network. 2030 M St. N.W., Suite 400, Washington 20036. (202) 393-3818. FAX: (202) 393-4805. Gloria Borland, chmn.

International bus & lifestyle progmg. Launch in late 1994.

Golden American Network Inc. 9250 Wilshire Blvd., Suite LL16, Beverly Hills, Calif. 90212. (310) 278-0088. FAX: (310) 278-1196. Bernard Weitzman, chmn; Charles Forman, senior VP; James Gates, VP prod & dev.

Prods original progs for the over 50 mkt. Currently available 10 one-hr progs, *Monty & Co.* starring Monty Hall & guests.

The Golf Channel. 1200 Corporate Dr., Suite 450, Birmingham, Ala. 35242-2940. (205) 995-0910. FAX: (205) 995-8171. Joseph E. Gibbs, pres/CEO; Robert Sutton, exec VP/COO; James L. Lowery, sr VP/CFO.

A 24-hr ch that offers a blend of professional tours, such as PGA, LPGA & Nike tours, as well as amateur tournaments. Launch in Spring 1994.

Satellite: Galaxy 1.

Headline News. Box 105366, One CNN Ctr., Atlanta Ga. 30348-5366. (404) 827-2608. FAX: (404) 827-3181. Tom Johnson, pres; Jon Petrovich, exec VP.

Provides viewers with a 30-minute news summary any time of the day or night. Each half-hr cycle covers the day's major news stories as well as bus, sports, medicine, entertainment, weather & human interest topics.

Serving 52.3 million subs on 6,700 cable systems. Satellite: Galaxy 5, transponder 22.

Health and Fitness Network. c/o WFIT TV 23, 10 Abbott Park, Providence, R.I. 02903. (401) 272-2558. FAX: (401) 751-2910. Philip R. DeSano, pres.

Health & fitness TV progs.

The Health Channel. 400 N. Capitol St. N.W., Washington 20001. (202) 508-4470. FAX: (202) 296-4649. Robert Fleshner, exec VP corp dev; Robert Grevemberg, exec VP facilities; Stephen Tello, sr VP facilities.

A 24-hr progmg svc aimed at giving viewers info about important devs in health, medicine & wellness. Launch in 2nd quarter 1994.

The History Channel. (A&E Networks.) 235 E. 45th St., New York 10017. (212) 661-4500. FAX: (212) 983-4370. Nickolas Davatzes, pres/CEO A&E Nets; Dan Davids, sr VP A&E & sr VP/gen mgr The History Channel; Charles Maday Jr., VP historical progmg.

A 24-hr ch that will feature historical documentaries, movies & miniseries. Launch in Oct. 1994.

Satellite: Satcom C-3, transponder 12.

Home Shopping Network Inc. Box 9090, Clearwater, Fla. 34618-9090. (813) 572-8585. FAX: (813) 572-8854. Gerald Hogan, pres.

A 24-hr live, discount shop-at-home TV svc for cable & bcst TV.

On 1,500 cable systems serving 21 million subs. Satellite: Satcom C-4, transponder 10.

Home Shopping Network II. Box 9090 Clearwater, Fla. 34618-9090. (813) 572-8585 ext. 7369. FAX: (813) 573-0866. Gerald Hogan, pres/CEO; Alan H. Gerson, exec VP.

A 24-hr shop-at-home svc featuring premium products.

On 471 cable systems serving 13 million subs. Satellite: Satcom C-3, transponder 10.

Horizons Cable Network. 125 Western Ave., Boston 02134. (617) 492-2777 ext. 3732. FAX: (617) 787-1639. Lawrence K. Grossman, pres; Diane Asadorian, principal.

A 24-hr ch covering events such as lectures & sympoisa from major museums, libraries & art centers. Launch in late 1994.

The Interactive Channel. 8140 Walnut Hill Ln., Suite 1000., Dallas 75231. (214) 369-8491. FAX: (214) 360-0737. Tim Peters, CEO; Scott Bedford, COO; John Reed, exec VP; John Neal, exec VP.

True multimedia interactive TV net deployable over traditional coaxial cable nets (parent company IT Network Inc.). Provides interactive media svcs to over 60 U.S. mkts. Launch in 1994.

Two trial cable systems served.

The International Channel. 12401 W. Olympic Blvd., Los Angeles 90064. (310) 826-2429. FAX: (310) 447-7916. George Leitner, sr VP/gen mgr; Craig McDonald, dir sls & mktg; Christine Ohama, dir community rels.

Foreign-language news, sports, drama & comedy from around the world.

Serving 4.7 million subs on 152 cable systems. Satellite: Satcom C-1, transponder 20.

Jewish Television Network. 9021 Melrose Ave., Suite 309, Los Angeles 90069. (310) 273-6841. FAX: (310) 273-6844. Jay Sanderson, exec dir.

Production & cablecasting of net-quality Jewish progmg in news, public affrs, education, arts & entertainment.

Serving 3 million subs on 15 cable systems.

Jones Computer Network. Box 3309, 9697 E. Mineral Ave., Englewood, Colo. 80155-3309. (303) 792-3111. FAX: (303) 792-5608. Glen R. Jones, pres/CEO, Jones International Ltd.: Greg Liptak, pres Mind Extension University; Gwenael S. Hagan, mgng dir Jones Computer Network: John Sadler, VP affil sls: Andy Holdgate, VP communications.

Progmg segment on Mind Extension University offering news & info about computers & new media. Independent ch in 1994.

Serving 23 million subs on 834 cable systems. Satellite: Galaxy 5, transponder 21.

KTLA. (United Video Inc.) 3801 S. Sheridan Rd., Tulsa, Okla. 74145. (800) 331-4806; (918) 665-6690. FAX: (918) 621-4720. Roy Bliss, pres; Jeff Treeman, sr VP/COO.

Los Angeles ind stn offers movies, news, specials & live sporting events, featuring the Los Angeles Angels & Dodgers baseball & LA Kings hockey.

Serving 5.5 million subs on 343 cable systems. Satellite: Spacenet 3, transponder 8.

KTVT. (United Video Inc.) 3801 S. Sheridan Rd., Tulsa, Okla. 74145. (800) 331-4806. FAX: (918) 621-4720. Roy Bliss, pres; Jeff Treeman, sr VP/COO.

Dallas-Fort Worth ind stn offers movies, news, specials, children's progmg, & live sporting events featuring Texas Ranger baseball & Mavericks NBA basketball.

Serving 2.4 million subs on 501 cable systems. Satellite: Spacenet 3, transponder 3.

The Learning Channel. (Discovery Networks). 7700 Wisconsin Ave., Bethesda, Md. 20814-3539. (301) 986-1999. FAX: (301) 986-4826. Dr. Harold E. Morse, chmn/CEO; Robert J. Shuman, pres/COO; Henry E. Schlenker, sr VP/COO; Robert Sestili, VP progmg; John M. McLaurin, VP mktg.

TLC offers adult educ progs.

On 1,628 cable systems serving 20.4 million subs. Satellite: Satcom C-3, transponder 2.

LIFETIME. Lifetime Astoria Studios, 36-12 35th Ave., Astoria, N.Y. 11106. (718) 482-4000. FAX: (718) 482-1903. Douglas W. McCormick, pres/CEO; Craig Harnett, group VP Hearst & ABC-VIACOM Entertainment Services (HAVES), & VP finance & technology; Judy Girard, group VP HAVES & sr VP progmg & prod LIFETIME;

Jane Tollinger, group VP HAVES & sr VP bus affrs, human resources & legal affrs Lifetime.

A 24-hr basic cable net that presents contemp, innovative progmg of specific interest to women.

Serving 57 million subs on 5,800 cable systems. Satellites: Satcom C-3, transponder 4 (western feed); Satcom C-4, transponder 4 (eastern feed).

MGA Communications. Box 40926, Washington 20016. (703) 522-1140; (800) 852-7766. FAX: (703) 522-7075. Max Gratzl, VP/COO.

Direct-response TV; prod, media placement & fulfillment mgmt.

MOR Music TV. 11500 9th St. N., Suite 120, St. Petersburg, Fla. 33716. (813) 579-4600. FAX: (813) 579-4667. Peter Forsythe, chmn; Ron Harris, pres/CEO; Edward M. Sherman, sr VP.

A 24-hr mus video ch playing the best videos from the 1950s-1990s. Sells CDs & cassettes of featured artists.

Serving 7 million subs on 165 cable systems. Satellite: Galaxy 5, transponder 10.

MTV Networks Inc. 1515 Broadway, New York 10036. (212) 258-7800. FAX: (212) 258-7955. Thomas E. Freston, chmn/CEO MTV nets; Gregory L. Ricca, exec VP/gen counsel; Carole Robinson, VP press rels MTV; Dwight Tierney, sr VP admin; Barry Kluger, sr VP pub rels MTV & VH-1.

A 24-hr mus video ch in stereo.

Serves 56.5 million subs on 8,290 cable systems. Satellites: Satcom C-4, transponder 17 (eastern feed); Satcom C-3, transponder 16 (western feed).

The Military Channel. 1230 Liberty Bank Ln., Louisville, Ky. 40222. (502) 425-8161. Fax: (502) 425-8597. L. Douglas Keeney, pres/CEO; Daniel P. Knopf, CFO/treas; Steven Titunik, VP military affrs; Tom Johnson, dir archival progmg; Dan Donnelly, dir affil rels.

Full-time cable TV net progmg war movies, documentaries, history progs, sports, news & aviation features. Launch in 1st quarter 1994.

Satellite: Satcom C-2.

Mind Extension University. Jones International Ltd., 9697 E. Mineral Ave., Englewood, Colo. 80112. (303) 792-3111. FAX: (303) 792-5608. Glenn R. Jones, founder/CEO; Gregory J. Liptak, pres; Donald A. Sutton, mgng dir; Dr. Pamela S. Pease, VP educ prog dev; Susan Harris, VP natl adv sls.

A 24-hr educ net providing distance educ progs from 23 of the nation's leading universities & institutions, including a bachelor's completion degree from the University of Maryland, MBA from Colorado State University & MA in educ & human dev from George Washington University. The Mind Extension Institute develops & distributes interactive video training progs focusing on customer svc, sls, safety & installation for cable TV system employees.

Satellite: Galaxy 5, transponder 21.

NASA Select Television. NASA Headquarters, Mail Code P-2, Washington 20546. (202) 358-1768. FAX: (202) 358-4360.

A 24-hr, govt-owned TV svc of the National Aeronautics and Space Administration, providing full coverage of shuttle missions, press conferences & other pub affr events. Also covers educ & informational progmg about the nations's space prog during non-mission times.

Satellite: Satcom F2-R, transponder 13.

National Empowerment Television (NET). 717 2nd St. N.E., Washington, 20002. (202) 544-3200. FAX: (202) 543-8425. Paul Weyrich, pres/CEO; Burton Pines, vice chmn/COO; Brian Jones, VP/gen mgr.

Unscrambled 24-hr ch that offers Washington-based pub affrs progmg, call- ins & interviews.

Satellite: Galaxy 7, transponder 20v.

National Jewish Television Network. Box 480, Wilton, Conn. 06897. (203) 834-3799. FAX: (203) 254-1413. Joel A. Levitch, pres; Aaron Etra, VP.

Informational, cultural & religious progmg for the Jewish community. Presented Sundays 1 pm-4 pm EST.

Serves 600 cable systems & more than 13 million subs. Satellite: Satcom F4-R, transponder 12.

Nationality Broadcasting Network. (NBN-Radio/TV.) 11906 Madison Ave., Lakewood, Ohio 44107. (216) 221-0330. FAX: (216) 221-3638. Miklos Kossanyi, pres; Sean Schompert, stn mgr; Attila Kossanyi, dir sls.

Provides internationally- & locally-produced nationality TV & radio progmg, spec progs & comls; also full-svc prod house.

Satellite: Space Net 1, transponder 23.

The New Inspirational Network. 9700 Southern Pine Blvd., Charlotte, N.C. 28273. (704) 525-9800. FAX: (704) 525-9899. David Cerullo, pres/CEO; Tom Hohman, VP cable affil rels; Judd Jackson, VP sls & mktg.

Provides 24-hr multi-faith progmg to the cable industry.

On more than 750 cable systems serving 7 million subs. Satellite: Galaxy 1, transponder 17.

NICK at NITE.

See Nickelodeon.

Nickelodeon. (MTV Networks Inc.) 1515 Broadway, New York 10036. (212) 258-8000. (212) 258-7736. FAX: (212) 258-7595. Tom Freston, chmn/CEO MTV Networks; Geraldine Laybourne, pres Nick/NAN.

Nickelodeon cable net targets kids. NICK at NITE provides entertainment svc for the TV generation.

Nickelodeon is on 9,171 cable systems. NICK at NITE is on 4,381 cable systems. Combined they serve 59 million subs. Satellites: Satcom C-4, transponder 3 (eastern feed); Satcom C-3, transponder 18 (western feed).

Nostalgia Television. 3575 Cahuenga Blvd. W., Suite 495, Los Angeles 90068. (213) 850-3000. FAX: (213) 969-8971. Michael E. Marcovsky, CEO; Charles V. Bush, pres/COO.

A 24-hr basic svc targeting active adults with entertainment, lifestyle, news & info progmg.

Serves 14.7 million subs on 764 systems. Satellite: Galaxy 1, transponder 22.

Our World Television. 3976 Park Blvd., San Diego, 92103. (619) 297-4975. FAX: (619) 688-0643 Ext. 77. Roy R. Snider, pres; Paul A. Farrell, VP.

A 24-hr ch that offers progmg for the gay & lesbian audience. Launch in 2nd quarter 1994.

Ovation-The Fine Arts Network. 211 N. Union St., Alexandria, Va. 22314. (703) 684-4828. FAX: (703) 684-4827. J. Carter Brown, chmn; Harold E. Morse, pres/CEO.

Advertiser-supported basic cable net featuring theater, concerts, dance performances, museum exhibits & cultural events from around the U.S. & the world. Launch in Nov. 1994.

Prevue Networks Inc. One Technology Plaza, 7140 S. Lewis Ave., Tulsa, Okla. 74136-5422. (918) 448-4000. FAX: (918) 663-6228. Joe D. Batson, pres; Daniel J. Sweeney, VP sls & mktg; James Smith, VP natl adv sls; Mary Prodger, VP progmg & prod; Chris Bourne, VP opns.

Prevue Channel: A system-specific, on-screen prog prom net that incorporates current listings on a scrolling grid with full-motion video previews for basic, pay & pay-per-view svcs to cable system subs. Prevue 1000: Offers the same features as the Prevue Channel but is designed for smaller systems. Sneak Prevue: A system-specific pay-per-view prom ch with full-motion video previews for pay-per-view. Prevue Networks Inc. is a part of the United Video Satellite Group.

All Prevue Networks svcs combined, including the Prevue Channel, Sneak Prevue, The EPG, EPG Jr., TPG & Cable Sportstracker reach 40 million homes in the U.S. & Canada. Satellite: Satcom C-4, transponder 8.

PrimeTime 24. 342 Madison Ave., Suite 1520, New York 10173. (212) 599-4440. FAX: (212) 599-2402. Janet Foster, pres; Karen Tardy, VP sls & mktg.

Net supersatation serving WABC-New York, WRAL (CBS)-Raleigh & WXIA (NBC)-Atlanta.

Satellites: F2 WRAL, transponder 2; F2 WABC, transponder 4; F2 WXIA, transponder 12.

The Promo Channel. Box 40926, Washington 20016. (800) 852-7766; (703) 522-1140. FAX: (703) 522-7075. Max Gartzl, VP/COO.

Mktg provider to the TV syndicator, specializing in satellite-telecast showcasing svcs for progmg inventory.

Q2 Network. 745 5th Ave., Suite 2403, New York 10151. (212) 371-4300. FAX: (212) 371-4837. Candice Carpenter, pres.

Home shopping, info & entertainment.

QVC. Goshen Corporate Park, 1365 Enterprise Dr., West Chester, Pa. 19380. (215) 430-1000. FAX: (215) 430-1051. Barry Diller, chmn/CEO; Michael C. Boyd, pres/COO; Douglas S. Briggs, exec VP progmg; William F. Costello, exec VP/CFO; Thomas Downs, exec VP customer svc; D. Bruce Sellers, exec VP affil rels; John F. Link, exec VP info systems & communications.

A 24-hr shop-at-home cable ch offering brand-name prods at discount.

Serves 46.2 million subs in 4,575 cable systems. Satellite: Satcom C-4, transponder 9.

The QVC Fashion Channel. (QVC Network.) Goshen Corporate Park, 1365 Enterprise Dr., West Chester, Pa. 19380. (215) 430-1022. FAX: (215) 431-6101. Barry Diller, chmn/CEO; Michael Boyd, pres/COO; D. Bruce Sellers, exec VP affil rels.

A 16-hr shop-at-home cable ch. Offers apparel, accessories, jewelry & other related prods.

On 415 cable systems serving 7.6 million subs. Satellite: C-3, transponder 8.

Recovery Net: The Wellness Channel. 7603 W. State St., Milwaukee 53213. (414) 771-2288. FAX: (414) 259-5006. Jonathan Katch, pres; Frederick L. D'Ambrosi, Dean Maytag, VPs; Diane Chase, dir info.

Progmg will address all aspects of physical & mental health including adddiction, nutrition & diseases. Launch date to be announced.

Romance Classics. 150 Crossways Park W., Woodbury, N.Y. 11797 (516) 364-2222. FAX: (516) 364-8924. Kate McEnroe, VP/gen mgr; Noreen O'Loughlin, VP mktg; Lisa Gamliel, dir mktg.

24-hr cable net featuring classic movies & TV progmg with a romantic theme.

Satellitte: C4, transponder 1.

Sci-Fi Channel. (USA Networks.) 1230 Ave. of the Americas, New York 10020. (212) 408-9100. FAX: (212) 408-8228. Kay Koplovitz, pres/CEO; Douglas Holloway, sr VP affil rels; Barry Schulman, VP progmg.

Dedicated to a broad range of science fiction & fact as well as fantasy & horror progs.

Serves 11 million subs. Satellite: Galaxy 5, transponder 4.

SCOLA. Box 619, McClelland, Iowa 51548-0619. (712) 566-2202. FAX: (712) 566-2502. Lee Lubbers S.J., pres/CEO; Francis Lajba, dir opns & mktg; Richard Kuhns, CFO; John Millar, prog dir.

A 24-hr educ ch that bcsts TV news retransmitted from 40 countries to more than 8,000 schools, colleges & universites throughout the Americas. Also available in German & French.

Reaches 4.5 million subs via 5,000 cable & non-cable affils. Satellite: ASC-1.

Shop Television Network. 1845 Empire Ave., Burbank, Calif. 91504. (818) 840-1400. FAX: (818) 845-4702. Michael E. Rosen, chmn/CEO.

Shopping ch.

STARNET. 1332 Enterprise Dr., Suite 200, West Chester, Penn. 19380. (215) 692-5900. FAX: (215) 692-6487. Allen McGlade, pres.

Automatic cross-ch tune-in promotion svc for basic, pay & pay-per-view delivered via satellite.

On 960 systems serving 23 million subs. Satellite: Satcom C-4, transponder 12.

StoryVision Network. National Bank Bldg., 14th Fl., 191 Lombard Ave., Winnipeg, Man., Canada R3B 0X1. (204) 942-1005. FAX: (204) 957-7647. Helmut Sass, pres; Greg Stetski, engr; Coleen Job, creative dir; Tannis Sass, prog dir.

A 24-hr children's net bcstg electronic storybooks that help improve reading skills.

Serving 2.5 million subs. Satellite: Galaxy 5, transponder 3 (subcarrier).

TBS. Box 105366, One CNN Ctr., Atlanta 30348-5366. (404) 827-1700. FAX: (404) 827-1947. Scott Sassa, pres Turner Entertainment Networks; Terry Segal, exec VP TBS; Kate McSweeny, Bill Cox, sr prog execs.

Cable net offering original documentaries, cable-exclusive sports, var specials, comedy series & movies.

On 16,139 cable systems serving 60.9 million subs. Satellite: Galaxy 1, transponder 18.

TBS Superstation. 1050 Techwood Dr., Atlanta Ga. 30318. (404) 827-1700. Terry Segal, exec VP/gen mgr; Kate McSweeny, VP progmg; Bill Cox, VP progmg; Pat Smith, VP creative svcs, TBS; Pat Mitchell, sr VP TBS Productions.

Basic cable svc specializing in popular movies, sports, comedies, kid's progmg, environmental specials & first-run prods.

Serving 60.2 million subs on 15,121 cable systems. Satellite: Galaxy 5, transponder 6.

TNN (The Nashville Network). (Group W Satellite Communications.) Box 10210, 250 Harbor Plaza Dr., Stamford, Conn. 06904-2210. (203) 965-6000. FAX: (203) 965-6315. Don Mitzner, pres; Lloyd Werner, sr VP sls & mktg; Steven Yanousky, VP mktg; Peter Weisbard, VP sls; Cheryl Daly, VP pub rels; Stephen Soule, VP affil rels.

Nashville 37214: 2806 Opryland Dr. (615) 889-6840.

Country mus entertainment & country lifestyle progmg. Entertainment svc offering original concert specials, exclusive sports coverage, entertainment news & interviews, info, live var & mus videos.

Carried on 13,421 cable systems serving 57.5 million subs. Satellite: Galaxy 5, transponder 18.

Basic Cable Services

TNT (Turner Network Television). 1050 Techwood Dr. N.W., Atlanta 30318. (404) 885-4389. FAX: (404) 885-4947. Scott Sassa, pres; Dennis Miller, exec VP; Allen Sabinson, sr VP prog dev; Neal Baseman, sr VP bus affrs.

Classic movies, original movies & miniseries, sports & children's progmg.

On 9,262 cable systems serving 59.9 million subs. Satellite: Galaxy 5, transponder 17.

TALK TV Network Inc. Box 54816, Phoenix 85078. (602) 585-1515. FAX: (602) 585-6101. Edwin Cooperstein, pres; Sondra Cooperstein, VP/treas; Richard C. Smith, sec.

A 24-hr, live, all-talk progmg cable ch.

Talkline Communications Television Network. Box 20108, Park West Stn., New York 10025-1510. (212) 769-1925; (800) 628-TALK. FAX: (212) 799-4195. Zev J. Brenner, pres.

Three hrs wkly of Jewish progs with newsmaker guests, celebrity interviews as well as informational progmg. Presented Sundays 2-4 pm EST & Fridays 11:30 am-12:30 pm EST.

On 825 cable systems serving over 13 million subs. Satellite: Satcom C-1, transponder 20.

Television Food Network (TVFN). c/o Pacesetter Communications, 159 W. 53rd St., Suite 17F, New York 10019. (212) 586-1731 FAX: (212) 759-1998. Renee Schonfeld, pres Pacesetter Communications.

A 24-hr ch focusing on all facets of food, fitness, health & nutrition.

Satellite: Galaxy 1, transponder 4.

The Travel Channel. 2690 Cumberland Pkwy, Suite 500, Atlanta 30339. (404) 801-2400. FAX: (404) 801-2441. Roger Williams, pres/COO; Michael Eckert, CEO; Norm Zeller, VP/natl adv sls mgr; Dalton Delan, VP progmg & prod; Dana Michaelis, VP affil sls.

A 24-hr travel-oriented news & entertainment net. Progs hosted by travel experts, authors, newsmakers & celebrities.

On 735 cable systems serving 17.5 million subs. Satellite: Satcom C-4, transponder 13.

Trinity Broadcasting Network (TBN Cable Network). 2900 Airport Fwy., Irving, Tex. 75062. (214) 313-1333. Paul Crouch, pres; Bob Higley, natl cable dir.

Tustin, Calif. 92680: 2442 Michelle Dr.

A 24-hr relg net featuring a var of progmg from a broad denominational representation.

Serving 20 million subs on 2,400 cable systems. Satellite: Galaxy 5, transponder 3.

Turner Classic Movies (TCM). 1050 Techwood Dr., Atlanta 30318. (404) 885-4339. FAX: (404) 885-4318. Scott Sassa, pres Turner Entertainment Group; Brad Siegel, exec VP Turner Network Television.

Features Hollywood's greatest movies of all time, 24-hr svc, coml free. Launch in April 1994.

U Network. NACB, 71 George St., Providence, R.I. 02912-1284. (401) 863-2225. FAX: (401) 863-2221. Glenn Gutmacher, exec dir/CEO; Gordon Kent, dev dir; David Singh, net dir.

Ch bcsts the best of America's student-produced & selected independently-produced works in all genres geared to a college-age audience (six hrs per week).

On 150 systems (also provides svc to LPTV & closed circuit TV affils). Satellite: SBS-6.

USA Networks. 1230 Ave. of the Americas, New York 10020. (212) 408-9100. FAX: (212) 408-3600. Kay Koplovitz, pres/CEO; Andrew Besch, sr VP mktg; Stephen Brenner, exec VP bus affrs & opns & gen counsel; Tim Brooks, VP rsch; Douglas Hamilton, CFO/VP finance; Douglas Holloway, sr VP affil rels; David Kenin, exec VP progmg; John Silvestri, exec VP adv sls.

All-entertainment net bcstg 24 hrs with world-premiere movies & series, sports specials & teen & children's progmg.

On 12,000 cable systems serving 60.124 million subs. Satellites: Galaxy 5 transponder 19 (eastern feed); Galaxy 1, transponder 21 (western feed).

Univision. 605 3rd Ave., 12th Fl., New York 10158. (212) 455-5200. FAX: (212) 867-7614. Stuart Livingston, VP/dir affil rels; Danny Huertas, West Coast affil rels; Vera Gonzalez, West Coast affil rels; Luly Estevez, East Coast affil rels.

Los Angeles 90045: 6701 Center Dr. W. (310) 338-0700. FAX: (310) 348-3643.

24-hr Spanish-language progmg featuring movies, novellas, sports & newscasts.

Serving 578,000 subs on 570 cable systems. Satellite: Galaxy 1, transponder 6.

VH1 (Video Hits One). (MTV Networks Inc.) 1515 Broadway, New York 10036. (212) 258-7860. FAX: (212) 258-7955. Ed Bennett, pres; Barry Kluger, sr VP media & net rels.

A 24-hr video mus ch featuring a var format of mus for a targeted age group of 25 to 49-year-olds.

Serves 47.4 million subs on 5,304 cable systems. Satellite: Satcom C-4, transponder 23.

VISN/ACTS. 5619 DTC Pkwy., Englewood, Colo. 80111-3000. (800) 522-5131. (303) 779-1161. FAX: (303) 488-3209. Nelson Price, CEO VISN Interfaith Satellite Network; Richard McCartney, CEO ACTS Satellite Network.

VISN's office: 74 Trinity Pl., Suite 915, New York 10006. (212) 602-9670. FAX: (212) 602-9679.

ACTS' office: 6350 W. Fwy., Fort Worth, Tex. 76150. (817) 737-4011. FAX: (817) 737-8209.

A 24-hr faith & values ch shared by VISN Network & ACTS Network. Offers a var of progmg including mus, talk, documentary, worship, sitcoms & movies.

VISN/ACTS serves 19.1 million subs on 1,249 systems. Satellite: Satcom C-3, transponder 5.

ValueVision. ValueVision International Inc., 5194 W. 76th St., Minneapolis 55439. (612) 831-1407. FAX: (612) 831-4870. Robert L. Johander, CEO; Nicholas M. Jaksich, pres.

A 24-hr home shopping svc.

On 70 systems serving 7 million subs. Satellite: Galaxy 1, transponder 12.

ViaTV. 10001 Kingston Pike, Suite 55, Knoxville, Tenn. 37922. (615) 671-1400. FAX: (615) 671-1980. Keith Halford, pres/CEO; Jay Walp, VP opns; John Padillo, CFO; Claude Broos, VP inventory control; Paul Kelley, exec prod.

Direct-response TV retailing for catalogers & manufacturers. Provides progmg, show hosts, formatting & pricing.

Satellite: G-3, transponder 1.

Video Jukebox Network Inc. 12000 Biscayne Blvd., Miami, Fla. 33181. (305) 899-9000. FAX: (305) 892-3600. J. Patrick Michaels CEO/actg pres; Luanne Simpson, CFO admin; Les Garland, VP progmg.

A 24-hr interactive mus video svc programmed locally by viewers.

On 150 systems reaching 16 million subs.

Viva Television Network Inc. 1028 Whiteknoll Dr., Los Angeles 90012. (213) 250-3049. FAX: (213) 250-3071. Mark J. Carreño, CEO; Guillermo Rodriguez, COO; Esteban de Icaza, VP.

A natl cable-exclusive Spanish-language progmg svc providing Latino audiences with entertainment, cultural & educ progmg (one hr per day).

Satellite: Satcom C-1, transponder 20 (via the International Channel).

WGN/UVI-TV. (United Video Inc.) 3801 S. Sheridan Rd., Tulsa, Okla. 74145. (918) 665-6690; (800) 331-4806. FAX: (918) 621-4720. Jeff Treeman, pres; Reuben Gant, VP sls; Anne Wilkerson, VP mktg; Sharon Metz, mgr customer svc.

Chicago ind: 235 sporting events with Chicago Cubs, White Sox, Bulls; blockbuster & classic films; children's shows, series, news & specials.

Serving 38.1 million subs on 14,354 cable systems. Satellite: Galaxy 5, transponder 7.

WPIX. (United Video Inc.) 3801 S. Sheridan Rd., Tulsa, Okla. 74145. (918) 665-6690; (800) 331-4806. FAX: (918) 621-4720. Jeff Treeman, pres; Reuben Gant, VP sls; Anne Wilkerson, VP mktg; Sharon Metz, mgr customer svcs.

New York ind stn featuring movies, specials, news, children's progmg & live sporting events including New York Yankees baseball & pre-season Giants & Jets football.

Serving 9.7 million subs on 637 cable systems. Satellite: Spacenet 3, transponder 5.

WSBK(TV). See WWOR-TV.

WWOR-TV. (EMI Communications.) 5015 Campus Wood Dr., E. Syracuse, N.Y. 13057. (315) 433-0022; (800) 448-3322. FAX: (315) 433-2342. Gil Korta, mktg & progmg; Laurie Silverman, dir corp mktg communications.

WWOR-TV (New York) & WSBK-TV (Boston) are 24-hr ind chs featuring sports, movies, news & specials.

On 1,566 systems serving more than 12 million subs. Satellite: Satcom C-4, transponder 15 (WWOR); Spacenet 3, transponder 3 (WSBK).

The Weather Channel. 2600 Cumberland Pkwy., Atlanta 30339. (404) 434-6800. FAX: (404) 801-2130. Michael Eckert, CEO; Rebecca Ruthven, VP affil sls & svc; Frank Garland, VP adv sls; Stan Hunter, sr VP progmg; Mark McKeen, dir engrg.

All-weather progmg 24 hrs a day; natl, international, rgnl & loc weather forecasts & features.

On 4,925 cable systems serving 53.4 million subs. Satellite: Satcom C-3, transponder 13.

Worship. The Christian Network Inc., 14444 66th St. N., Clearwater, Fla. 34618. (813) 536-0036. FAX: (813) 530-0671. James West, pres; Lee D. Nagelhout, VP progmg & affiliations; Mark MacGregor, dir relg rels.

Christian inspirational mus set to scenic videos. Callers may interact with prog host 24 hrs daily.

On 300 systems (includes LPTV affils). Satellite: ASC-1, transponder 12.

XTV. Independent Programming Network 6566 E. Cheney Dr., Scottsdale, Ariz., 85253. (602) 948-0381. FAX: (602) 443-0219. John D. Fletcher, pres; Kirk P. Kimerer, exec VP mktg & progmg; S. Otta Khera, exec VP pub affrs.

A 24-hr ch that offers short-formatted ind & student films, appealing to "Generation X," the age group 13-32. Launch in 2nd quarter 1994.

Z Music. 151 E. Ohio Ave., Lake Helen, Fla. 32744. (904) 228-1000. FAX: (904) 228-0785. Ken Yates, pres; John Roos, exec VP mktg; John Walker, exec VP finance & admin.

Offers videos from the Christian mus industry.

Serves 5.3 million subs on 263 systems. Satellite: Galaxy 1, transponder 15.

Automated Cable Channel Programmers

Data Broadcasting Corp. 1900 S. Norfolk St., Suite 150, San Mateo, Calif. 94403. (703) 571-1800. FAX: (415) 571-8507. B. Douglas Smith, pres; Fred McEnany, VP sls & mktg; Charles Thompson, VP info systems.

Real-time stock, option, commodity quotation svc & sports svc delivered via cable TV, FM frequency & bcst VBI to end user PCs.

Serving more than 17,000 subs on more than 700 systems.

Satellites: Satcom F3, transponder 11; Galaxy 3, transponder 24.

Prevue Networks Inc. One Technology Plaza, 7140 S. Lewis Ave., Tulsa, Okla. 74136. (918) 448-4000. Joe D. Batson, pres/COO; Daniel J. Sweeney, VP sls & mktg; James Smith, VP natl ad sls; Mary Prodger, VP progmg & prod; Chris Bourne, VP opns.

Prevue Channel is a system-specific, on-screen prog prom net that incorporates current listings on a scrolling grid with full motion video previews for basic, pay & pay-per-view svcs to cable system subs. Prevue 1000 is designed for smaller systems. Sneak Prevue is a system-specific pay-per-view prom ch with full motion video previews for pay-per-view.

All svcs—Prevue Channel, Sneak Prevue, The EPG, EPG Jr., TPG & Cable Sportstracker—reach 40 million homes in the U.S. & Canada.

Satellite: satellite C-4, transponder 8.

Texas Electronics Inc. Box 7225, Dallas 75209. (214) 631-2490; (800) 424-5651. FAX: (214) 631-4218.

Meteorological sensors, signal conditioning, dial, digital, recording displays. Wind direction & speed, barometric pressure, relative humidity, rainfall, temperature, solar radiation.

Tribune Information Services. 64 E. Concord St., Orlando, Fla. 32801. (800) 322-3068. FAX: (407) 839-5794. Timothy Brennan, VP electronic info products; Patricia Kettler, mgr electronic info products.

NewsPlus, BusinessPlus, SportsPlus. Available on 200 cable systems serving 8.1 million subs.

Satellite: Spacenet 3.

X*Press Information Services Ltd. Denver Corporate Center, Tower One, 4700 S. Syracuse Pkwy., Suite 1050, Denver 80237-2721. (303) 721-1062. Gerald E. Bennington, pres; Judy Spurgeon, VP business opns.

Audio Cable Programming Services

AEI Music Network. 3716 National Dr., Suite 210, Raleigh, N.C. 27612. (919) 571-1590. FAX: (919) 781-5056. Tommy Dunlap, systems rep.

Provides 24-hour coml-free mus svcs for audio background on alphanumeric/graphics chs, ad chs & FM band packages.

On 178 systems serving four million subs.

Satellites: Galaxy 1, transponder 3; GEK2, transponder 12.

The Beethoven Satellite Network. 303 E. Wacker Dr., Chicago 60601. (312) 565-5000. FAX: (312) 565-5169. David Levin, dir; Scott Kuiper, progmg dir; Don Mueller, distribution mgr; Carol Martinez, opns mgr.

Satellite-delivered classical mus format svc. Eleven hours daily serving 170 affils nationwide. Produced by WFMT-FM Chicago.

Satellite: Westar IV, transponder 2D (National Public Radio chs). Since 1986.

C-SPAN. 400 N. Capitol St. N.W., Suite 650, Washington 20001. (202) 737-3220. FAX: (202) 737-3323. Brian P. Lamb, chmn/CEO; Brian Lockman, VP net opns; Tom Patton, audio net mgr.

Audio svc 1: News progs from around the world & live events from nation's capital. Audio svc 2: The BBC World Service 24 hours a day.

On 55 systems serving 3.5 million subs.

Satellite: Galaxy III, transponder 24; audio 1, 5.22 audio subcarrier; audio 2, 5.40 audio subcarrier.

Cable Radio Network. 10487 Sunland Blvd., Sunland, Calif. 91040. (818) 352-7152. Michael Horn, CEO/pres; Jim Roope, VP opns; Don Tegeler, sls; Erin Farrell, dir mktg.

Used on the cable system's alphanumeric/text ch, part of the FM svc package & on the cable system's mus on hold. Provides 24-hour mus & talk svc with adult contemp, oldies, sports talk & specials.

On 95 cable systems nationwide serving seven million subs.

Satellite: Satcom 1R, transponder 15, audio subcarrier 7.235.

Digital Cable Radio. Bldg. One, 300 Welsh Rd., Suite 220, Horsham, Pa. 19044. (215) 784-5840. FAX: (215) 784-5869. David J. Del Beccaro, pres; Paul Clough, VP mktg; Jeremy Rosenburg, VP opns; Joe Capobianco, VP progmg; Tom Ferraro, VP affil rels eastern rgn; Pam Jensen, VP affil rels central rgn; Cathy Hetzel, VP affil rels western rgn.

Digital Cable Radio, a 24-hour coml- & interruption-free audio svc, features CD-quality sound in a var of mus formats & audio simulcast of five cable TV chs. Branch offices in Chicago, Los Angeles & Secaucus, N.J.

Satellite: Galaxy III, transponder 5.

Innovative Information Services Inc. 305 Mountain Dr., Suite F, Destin, Fla. 32541. (800) 653-7772. FAX: (904) 654-7775. Cynthia Creswell, CEO; Theodore Andros, VP/gen mgr; Steve de Shazo, sls mgr.

Complete turnkey audio svcs for cable companies & interconnects to eliminate unsold adv & create interactive adv.

International Cablecasting Technologies Inc./DMX. 11400 W. Olympic Blvd., Suite 1100, Los Angeles 90064-1507. (310) 444-1744. FAX (310) 444-1717. Jerold H. Rubinstein chmn/CEO; W. Thomas Oliver, pres/COO; Patti Dennis, CFO/corporate sec; Robert Manning, VP finance & bus dev.

Premium digital audio mus progmg, uninterrupted, coml free, 24-hour svc via satellite & cable.

Moody Broadcasting Network. 820 N. LaSalle Blvd., Chicago 60610. (800) 621-7031; (312) 329-4433. FAX: (312) 329-4339. Bob Norris, mgr bcst dev; Bob West, dir net dev; David Woodworth, administrator affil dev.

Provides 24-hour format of relg & educ progmg; mus, drama, talk, news & pub affrs.

On 48 cable systems serving 755,179 subs.

Satellites: Spacenet IIIR, transponder 7D (13-SCS); Satcom C1, transponder 10 (Alaska beam only-SCPC).

Radio Station WFMT-FM. 303 E. Wacker Dr., Chicago 60601. (312) 565-5000. FAX: (312) 565-5169. Dan Schmidt, sr VP radio; Norm Pellegrini, prog dir; Jim Barker, gen sls mgr.

Classical mus, news & fine arts progmg 24 hours a day from Chicago via United Video Inc.

On 235 cable systems in 35 states, serving more than 1.2 million subs.

Satellite: Galaxy 4, transponder 3.

Satellite Radio Network (KGOL). 525 N. Sam Houston Pkwy. E., Suite 525, Houston 77060-4017. (713) 999-1180; (800) 438-6311. FAX: (713) 999-0730. Mike Glinter, pres; Scott Ellis, prog dir/opns mgr.

Relg progmg 24 hours a day.

Sun Radio Network. (An affiliate of Sound Communications). 2870 Scherer Dr. N., Suite 100, St. Petersburg, Fla. 33716-1024. (813) 572-9209. FAX: (813) 572-4735. Bill Wardino, pres; Stan Anderson, gen mgr; Bill Muncey, chief engr.

News/talk progmg made available to cable systems & radio stns at no cost.

Satellite: SatCom C5, Channel 11-1, Audio 7-5.

Superaudio Cable Radio Service. Box 3309, 9697 E. Mineral Ave., Englewood, Colo. 80112. (303) 792-3111; FAX: (303) 790-0533. Jay Lewis, gen mgr; Chery Grund, dir affil sls; Dale Ogden, opn mgr; Sharon Sall, affil rels dir.

Basic Cable Audio svc offering nine chs of stereo mus & entertainment.

Satellite: Galaxy V, transponder 21. No video spectrum required.

WLIR Jewish Radio Network. Box 489, Nanuet, N.Y. 10952. (914) 624-1300. FAX: (914) 624-2809. Zev Brenner, pres; Philip W. Plack, gen mgr; Gary B. Duglin, opers & sls mgr; Yaakov Spivak, news dir; Michael Lobaito, chief engr; Gary Shiff, prod dir.

Net features satellite-delivered Jewish progs including Jewish world news at the top of each hour, contemp mus, talk, comedy, business & children's shows.

On radio stns & cable systems throughout the U.S. & Canada.

Satellite: F2r, transponder 18 (8.2 mHz).

The WFMT Fine Arts Network. 303 E. Wacker Dr., Chicago 60601. (312) 565-5000. FAX: (312) 565-5169. Dan Schmidt, VP radio; David Levin, dir; Don Mueller, distribution mgr; Carol Martinez, opns mgr.

Classical mus, spoken arts & fine arts prog series & specs. Satellite- & tape-delivered. Major symphony orchestras, grand opera from Chicago, exclusive BBC progmg, WFMT-produced archival & spoken-word progmg, live studio performances, folk mus.

Serving more than 900 radio outlets worldwide.

Satellite: Westar IV, transponder 2D (National Public Radio chs). Since 1976.

Regional Cable Television News Services

ChicagoLand Television News (CLTV). 2000 York Rd., Suite 114, Oak Brook, Ill. 60521. (708) 368-4000. FAX: (708) 571-0489. Robert Gremillion, VP/gen mgr; Jim Cushing Jr., VP bus affrs; Mike Adams, dir news & progmg; Max Kirkland, dir opns & engr; Ron Goldberg, dir sls.

Covers loc & rgnl news, sports news, weather & traf info on two cable systems serving 600,000 subs.

New England Cable News Channel. 160 Wells Ave., Newton, Mass. 02159. (617) 630-5000. Lawrence Meli, gen mgr.

New York 1 News. 460 W. 42nd St., New York 10036. (212) 465-0111. FAX: (212) 563-7632. Paul Sagan, VP news & progmg; Steve Paulus, news dir; Harlen Neugeboren, dir tech opns; Katherine Drew, Philip O'Brien, Tom Farkas, exec prods; Larry J. Fischer, pres Time Warner CityCable Advertisement (agent for NY 1 News).

A 24-hour, all-news cable ch devoted primarily to coverage of New York City & its neighborhoods.

News Channel 8. 7600-D Boston Blvd., Springfield, Va. 22153. (703) 912-5300. FAX: (703) 912-5599. John D. Hillis, pres/CEO; Wayne A. Lynch, news dir; Maria Zavarello, dir fin & admin; Brad Davis, dir sls; Tim Young, natl sls exec; Elane JaFolla, dir human resources; David Evans, dir opns & engr; Rick Young, dir audience dev.

A 24-hour rgnl news svc for Washington, D.C., suburban Maryland & northern Virginia on nine cable systems serving 675,000 subs.

News 12 Long Island. One Media Crossways, Woodbury, N.Y. 11797. (516) 496-1766. Patrick Dolan, news dir.

Orange County Newschannel. Box 11945, Santa Ana, Calif. 92711; 625 N. Grand Ave., Santa Ana, Calif. 92701. (714) 541-2626; (714) 565-3817. FAX: (714) 565-3650. Lewis Robertson, VP/gen mgr; Ed Casaccia, exec prod; Bob Coletti, gen sls mgr; John Miles, mktg & prom mgr.

A 24-hour news stn serving Orange County with loc news, sports, features & business on 11 cable systems serving 520,000 subs.

R News/ Greater Rochester Cablevision. 71 Mt. Hope Ave., Rochester, N.Y. 14620. (716) 325-1020. FAX: (716) 546-7946. Pete Dobrovitz, news dir; Gary Turner, asst news dir; Ed Buttaccio, assignment edit.

Cable Sports Services

Dimension Cable (ASPN). Box 37827, 17602 N. Black Canyon Hwy., Phoenix 85023. (602) 866-0072. FAX: (602) 863-3532. Greg Holmes, gen mgr; Ivan Johnson, VP community affrs; Steve Rizley, rgnl adv sls mgr; Suzee Smith, prog mgr.

Phoenix Suns basketball, San Francisco Giants baseball, collegiate & high school sports, etc.

On one cable system in the Phoenix metropolitan area serving 165,000 subs. Microwave.

ESPN Inc. 935 Middle St., Bristol, Conn. 06010. (203) 585-2000. FAX: (203) 585-2213. Steve Bornstein, pres/CEO.

ESPN offers a var of professional & amateur sports, including NFL & CFA football, college basketball & the NCAA tournament.

On 21,800 cable systems serving 56.3 million subs.

Empire Sports Network. 795 Indian Church Rd., West Seneca, N.Y. 14224. (716) 827-4289. FAX: (716) 827-4293. Rich Bradley, VP/gen mgr; John Domino, dir affil rels; Joe DelBalso, dir pub reis; Marc Honan, spec projects coord.

Rgnl sports net servicing western & central New York. Buffalo Bills progmg, Buffalo Sabres, AAA baseball & Syracuse University collegiate events.

Serving 500,000 subs on 24 cable systems. Satellite: Galaxy III, transponder 2.

Home Sports Entertainment of Dallas and Houston. 5251 Gulfton, Houston 77081. (713) 661-0078. FAX: (713) 661-8379. Dick Barron, exec VP; John McIntyre, dir opns; Joe Gagliardi, affil sls; Jack Stanfield, exec prod/prog dir.

Grand Prairie, Tex. 75050: Suite 260, 2080 N. State Hwy. (214) 988-9292. Ed Frazier, VP mktg. Mktg office.

Houston Rockets basketball, Houston Astros baseball, Texas Rangers baseball, Dallas Mavericks basketball, New Jersey Devils hockey, Southwest Conference collegiate sports, etc.

Home Team Sports (HTS). 7700 Wisconsin Ave, 2nd Fl., Bethesda, Md. 20814. (301) 718-3200. FAX: (301) 718-3300. Bill Aber, VP/gen mgr; Jody Shapiro, dir progmg; Jeff Wagner, gen mgr sls; Scott Broyles, communications & media rel.

More than 1,000 exclusive sporting events each year, including Orioles baseball, Capitals hockey, Bullets basketball & rgnl college action.

On 243 cable systems serving 2.4 million subs. Satellite: Spacenet III, transponder 12.

KBL Sports Network. 1301 Grandview Ave., Pittsburgh 15211. (412) 381-9500. FAX: (412) 381-9528. William Craig, gen mgr; David Brugnone, dir affil mktg & sls; George Simons, adv sls mgr; John Smith, controller.

Rgnl sports net available to cable companies in Pennsylvania, Ohio, West Virginia, western New York & Maryland. Progmg includes Pittsburgh Pirates, Penguins, & collegiate sports featuring University of Pittsburgh men's basketball.

Serving 1.4 million subs on 45 cable systems. Satellite: Spacenet II, transponder TX 10.

Madison Square Garden Network. Two Penn Plaza, 14th Fl., New York 10121. (212) 465-6000. FAX: (212) 465-6024. Robert Gutkowski, pres; Sid Amira, Martin Brooks, Doug Moss, sr VPs; Lee Berke, VP mktg; Peter Silverman, VP/exec prod; Paul Schneider, dir pub rels.

New York Knicks, Rangers & Yankees; college football & basketball games; boxing. Exclusive Garden events & original series progmg.

On more than 170 cable systems serving more than four million subs. Satellite: Satcom 4, transponder 6.

Midwest Sports Channel. 11th on the Mall, Minneapolis 55403. (612) 330-2637. FAX: (612) 330-2603. Kevin Cattoor, VP/gen mgr; Dave Garvin, dir sls; Kate Samoszuk, dir mktg & affil rel.

New England Sports Network (NESN) 70 Brookline Ave., Boston 02215. (617) 536-9233. FAX: (617) 536-7814. John W. Claiborne, VP/gen mgr; Robert B. Whitelaw, dir opns; Jerry McAuliffe, adv & sls dir; Sean P. McGrail, mktg dir; Donald J. Reilly, bus affrs dir; John P. Slattery, pub rels/adv; Michael B. Donovan, dir engrg.

NESN is a pay cable sports svc that delivers Boston Bruins, Red Sox & New England college sports as well as boxing, tennis, fishing, bowling & wrestling.

On 182 cable systems serving 411,125 subs. Satellites: Satcom F-4, transponder 13; GE C-3, transponder 14.

Prime Sports Network. 44 Cook St., Suite 600, Denver 80206. (303) 355-7777. FAX: (303) 377-3973. Bob Thompson, VP/gen mgr; Tim Griggs, dir adv & sls; Gretchen Bunn, dir affil mktg; Glenna Norvelle, dir prom; Mike Diamond, sr prod.

Rgnl sports net serving 18 states. Progmg includes Denver Nuggets, Utah Jazz, Minnesota Timberwolves & Indiana Pacers.

Serving 2.3 million subs on 450 cable systems. Satellites: Satcom C1, transponders 17 & 18; Satcom C3, transponder 11.

Prime Sports Northwest. 18 W. Mercer St., Suite 200, Seattle 98119. (206) 281-7800. FAX: (206) 283-6106. Clayton Packard, gen mgr; Theresa Cuthill, prog dir; Curtis Smith, dir mktg; Mark Jurgensen, natl sls mgr.

Coverage of PAC-10, Big Sky & other collegiate conference athletic events; professional and high school events to the Pacific Norhtwest rgn.

Serving 1.9 million subs on 250 cable systems. Satellite: Satcom C1, transponder 22 (scrambled).

Prime SportsChannel Networks. 3 Crossways Park W., Woodbury, N.Y. 11797. (516) 921-3764. FAX: (516) 364-1943. Daren Miller II, exec VP; Michael Ghibaudi, bus mgr.

Natl basic cable sports net covering NHL, U.S. National Soccer team, Univ. of Notre Dame, boxing, auto racing & more.

On 800 cable systems serving 12 million basic subs & 17 million affild basic subs. Satellite: Satcom IV, transponder 3,10.

Prime Ticket. 10000 Santa Monica Blvd., Los Angeles 90067. (310) 286-3800. FAX: (310) 286-3875; Sales FAX: (310) 286-3877. Tony Acone, asst chmn; Roger Werner, pres; John Jackson, progmg; Dan Corsini, exec VP progmg & prod.

Los Angeles Lakers basketball, Kings hockey, Lazers indoor soccer, Strings tennis; San Diego Soccers soccer; collegiate sports; etc.

Prime Ticket La Cadena Deportiva. 10000 Santa Monica Blvd., Los Angeles 90067. (310) 286-3800. FAX: (310) 286-3875. Roger L. Werner, Prime Ticket pres/CEO; Richard Ramirez, VP/gen mgr; Eva Rustos, dir affil mktg; Terry Planell, dir progmg.

Country's first all Spanish-language sports cable network.

Serving Southern Califomia, Arizona & Nevada. Satellite: GE Americom, Satcom C-1, transponder T.B.D.

Pro Am Sports System (PASS). Box 3040, 550 W. Lafayette, Detroit 48231-3040. (313) 222-7277. FAX: (313) 223-2299. William J. Wischman Jr., gen mgr; Kathleen L. Hunt, bus mgr; Annette Mansfield, sr mgr affil rel; William S. Moren, mgr mktg dev; Jody Hass, mgr affil dev; William P. Glenn, exec prod.

CableSports Network features Detroit Tigers, Pistons & Red Wings; Big 10 collegiate & amateur sports.

On 220 cable systems serving 750,000 subs. Satellite: Spacenet 3, transponder 11.

San Antonio Spurs. 100 Montana St., San Antonio 78203. (512) 554-7700. FAX: (512) 554-7701. Russ Bookbinder, exec VP; Lawrence Payne, sr VP bcstg.

Bcstg sponsorships, loc prom opportunities, corporate sponsorships. 225,000 subs.

San Diego Cable Sports Network. Cox Cable of San Diego, 5159 Federal Blvd., San Diego 92105. (619) 263-9251. FAX: (619) 266-5540. Marty Youngman, pay-per-view mgr.

San Diego Padres baseball, etc.

SportsChannel Chicago. 820 W. Madison, Oak Park, Ill. 60302. (708) 524-9444. FAX: (708) 524-9484. Jim Corno, VP/gen mgr; John Hokin, dir adv sls; Mary Collins, sr dir affil sls & mktg; John Tuohey, sr dir progmg & opns; Kelly Sullivan, dir creative svcs.

Rgnl all-sports cable net serving Illinois, Indiana & Iowa. Features Chicago Bulls, Blackhawks & White Sox games, & collegiate & high school sports.

On more than 141 cable systems serving 2.2 million subs. Satellite: C-1, transponder 13.

SportsChannel Cincinnati. 19 Garfield Pl., Suite 206, Cincinnati 45202. (513) 381-3900. FAX: (513) 381-6005. Jim Corno, VP midwest rgn; Mark London, dir affil sls; David Kline, gen mgr.

Rgnl all-sports cable net serving parts of Ohio, Indiana, Kentucky, Tennessee, Mississippi & North Carolina. Features Cincinnati Reds baseball, Univ. of Kentucky sports, Notre Dame games, the Big 10, Mid-American & Midwestern cities conferences, high school sports, talk shows & more.

SportsChannel Florida. 7900 Glades Rd., Suite 140, Boca Raton, Fla. 33434. (407) 477-0287. FAX: (407) 477-9276; (407) 997-2293. Jeffrey H. Genthner, VP/gen mgr; Steve A. Liverani, dir opns.

Features coverage of the NHL, the NBA's Miami Heat, the University of Florida Gators, University of South Florida Bulls, Jacksonville University Dolphins, Sun Belt Conference & Florida High School State championships.

SportsChannel New England. 10 Tower Office Park, Woburn, Mass. 01801. (617) 933-9300. FAX: (617) 933-4677. John Mohr, pres; Mitchell D. Freund, group VP/gen mgr; Stevan Reagan, asst gen mgr/dir opns; William O'Donnell, dir sls & mktg; Jeffrey Landis, dir pub rels.

Boston Celtics basketball, Hartford Whalers hockey, NHL, New York Mets (Conn. only); college football, hockey & professional tennis.

Satellite: Satcom F2R, transponder 23.

SportsChannel New York. 200 Crossways Park Dr., Woodbury, N.Y. 11797. (516) 364-3650. FAX: (516) 364-4020. Robert Pollichino, group VP/gen mgr; James Bates, asst gen mgr/dir sls & mktg; Jerry Passaro, exec prod/dir progmg; Rich Kahn, dir pub rels.

New York Islanders & Mets, New Jersey Nets & Devils, plus horse racing, college football, basketball & other sports specials.

On 121 cable systems serving more than 1.5 million subs. Satellite: Satcom 4, transponders 3 & 7.

SportsChannel Ohio. Metro Ctr., 6500 Rockside Rd., Suite 340, Independence, Ohio 44131. (216) 328-0333. FAX: (216) 328-0350. David Kline, VP/gen mgr; Michael Lehr, dir progmg & net opns; Michael Dolan, dir mktg & pub rels; Jim Cook, dir sls.

Live sports progmg: Cleveland Indians, Cleveland Cavaliers, Notre Dame & Ohio State athletics, Ohio high school basketball championships & more.

On 45 cable systems serving 1.2 million subs. Satellite: Satcom C3, transponder 16.

SportsChannel Pacific. 901 Battery St., Suite 204, San Francisco 94111. (415) 296-8900. FAX: (415) 296-9198. Michael Bair, VP/gen mgr; Mark Shuken, dir progmg & opns; Chris Geer, dir affil sls; Brett Benson, mktg mgr.

Rgnl & natl sports progmg including San Francisco Giants & Oakland Athletics baseball, Golden State Warriors basketball, San Jose Sharks, NHL hockey, PAC 10 football & basketball.

On 80 cable systems, serving 2 million subs. Satellite: Satcom C1.

SportsChannel Philadelphia. 225 City Line Ave., Bala Cynwyd, Pa. 19004. (215) 668-2210. FAX: (215) 668-9499. John R. Mohr, pres; Dennis E. Patton, gen mgr; Terri D. Morse, sr dir sls & mktg; Daniel Ronayne, dir mktg; Catherine O'R. Schmidt, dir pub rels; Ronald C. Bishop III, pub rels mgr.

Rgnl TV prgmg svc. Current properties include pre-Olympics event coverage, English League Soccer, Pro Boxing Tour, Team USA Soccer, NASCAR, Canadian Football League, American Hockey League. Also includes live coverage of Philadelphia Flyers ice hockey, Philadelphia '76ers basketball & Philadelphia Phillies baseball.

Serving 65 cable systems with 1.9 million total subs. Satellite: F2R, transponder 18.

SportSouth Network. Box 740080, One CNN Ctr., Atlanta 30374-0080. (404) 827-4100. FAX: (404) 827-4065. Blair Schmidt-Fellner, exec VP; Hunter Nickell, VP/gen mgr; Steve Pechman, VP gen sls mgr; Steve Craddock, VP/exec prod; Chris Killebrew, dir affil sls & mktg.

Atlanta Hawks & Charlotte Hornets basketball, SEC & SWC college football & basketball, Atlanta Braves baseball & more.

Cable Sports Services

Serving 3.6 million subs on 415 cable systems. Satellite: Spacenet 3, transponder 19.

Sunshine Network. 390 N. Orange Ave., Suite 1075, Orlando, Fla. 32801. (407) 648-1150. FAX: (407) 648-1679. Dave Almstead, VP/gen mgr; Amy Pempel, dir media rel; Thom Hastings, sr prod.

Rgnl sports cable net, affiliated with Prime Network, serving more than 3.1 million basic cable subs throughout Florida. Progmg includes Orlando Magic NBA basketball, Tampa Bay Lightning NHL hockey, Florida State & Univ. of Miami athletics, plus a wide var of sports from all Florida colleges & sports of natl & international significance provided by Prime Network.

VideoSeat Pay-Per-View. (Division of Host Communications Inc.) 546 E. Main St., Lexington, Ky. 40508. (606) 253-3230. FAX: (606) 254-1390. W. James Host, CEO; Charles L. Jarvie, COO; Gerald L Moore, CFO; Marc S. Kidd, pres natl sls; Mark Dyer, pres University Group; Richard A. Ford, pres publishing division; Susan L. Lester, dir mktg Video Group.

VideoSeat handles turnkey pay-per-view syndication of several top schools in college football, including, Auburn, Georgia, Mississippi St., South Carolina, & Tennessee. Systems in Alabama, Georgia, Mississippi, South Carolina & Tennessee.

Satellite: Galaxy 1, transponder 7 or 9; Satellite: Galaxy 3, transponder, various.

Canadian Cable Programming Services

Atlantic Satellite Network (ASN). Box 1653, 2885 Robie St., Halifax, N.S. B3J 2Z4. (902) 453-4000. FAX: (902) 454-3302. F.G. Shorratt, pres; G. Mudry, VP/gen mgr; J. Jay, prod supvr; A.M. Varner, prom dir; N. Fuller, sls mgr; R. Prat, prog mgr.

Movies, news & educational progs for weekend mornings.

Serves 51 cable systems. Satellite: Anik C-1.

CBC Newsworld. Box 500, Stn. A, Toronto, Ont. M5W 1E6. (416) 205-2950. FAX: (416) 205-6080. Michael Harris, pres; Janice Ward, asst to pres; Slawko Klym Kiw, sr exec prod/progmg.

Live 24-hour news & info net on basic cable in Canada.

CFMT-TV Toronto. (Multilingual Television Ltd.) 545 Lakeshore Blvd. W., Toronto, Ont. M5V 1A3. (416) 260-0047. FAX: (416) 260-0509. Tony Viner, pres; Jim MacDonald, VP sls; Tom Ayley, VP finance/CFO; Leslie Sole, exec VP; Farouk Muhammad, VP progmg.

Canadian Digital Radio (CDR). 5 Pl. Ville-Marie, Suite 1450, Montreal, Que. H3B 4R7 (514) 874-2656. FAX: (514) 874-0815. Alain Plante, VP/gen mgr; René Bourdages, gen mgr.

Mus svc offering 38 mus formats; CD quality; no coml s or DJs.

Satellite: SATCOM C-3.

Canadian Home Shopping Network. 1400 Castlefield Ave., Toronto, Ont. M6B 4H8. (416) 785-3500. FAX: (416) 785-1300. Ed duDomaine, pres/COO; Ralph Galley, VP mdse; Barbara Mallon, VP finance.

Live, shop-at-home televised retail svc, offering a var of consumer products. On 235 cable systems serving 5.7 million subs. Satellite: Anik, Ku-band, transponder T3.

Canadian Satellite Communications Inc. (CANCOM). 50 Burnhamthorpe Rd. W., 10th Fl., Mississauga, Ont. L5B 3C2 (416) 272-4960. FAX: (416) 272-3399. Sheelagh D. Whittaker, pres/CEO; Claude W. Lewis, exec VP; Louise Tremblay, sr VP/CFO; Susan Cornell, VP regulatory/corporate/native affrs.

Distributes TV signals to cable operators. DBS scrambled using OAK technology.

Over 2,323 cable headends serving 3 million households in Canada. Satellite: Anik E2.

Cathay International Television Inc. 494 W. 39th Ave., Vancouver, B.C. V5Y 2P7. (604) 321-5266. FAX: (604) 321-9625. Sing Kwan So, chmn; Joseph Chan.

A multilingual specialty progmg TV ch serving the greater Vancouver area. Provides a diversity of progs mainly in Chinese & Vietnamese.

19,000 total subscribers served.

Chinavision Canada Corp. 160 Duncan Mill Rd., Don Mills, Ont. M3B 1Z5. (416) 510-2850. FAX: (416) 510-2849. Peter Mann, receivership mgr.

All Chinese-language progmg. Serving more than 20 cable systems.

Digital Music Express - Canada. 7627 50th St., Edmonton, Alta. T6B 2W9. (403) 468-7115. FAX: (403) 463-0295. Heather Shaw, pres; Debra Avis, mktg mgr; Graham Duff, mgr/natl affil rel.

DMX audio svc; 25 formats; CD sound (16 bit, 44.1 kHz specifications).

Satellites: Anik E2; C3 Bank, TBA (Ku-band), T24 transponder.

The Family Channel. Box 787, BCE Pl., 181 Bay St., Toronto, Ont. M5J 2T3. (416) 956-2030. FAX: (416) 956-2035. Len Cochrane, pres/CEO; Darrel Atherley, VP sls/mktg; Nancy Auld, VP finances.

Pay TV net offering family entertainment based on 60% from the Disney Channel, 25% Canadian & 15% international progmg.

Approximately 550 cable systems serving 380,000 subs. Satellite: Anik E2, transponder 11(western feed); Anik E2, transponder 30(eastern feed).

Le Reseau des sports. 1755 Blvd. René-Lévesque E., Montreal, Que. H2K 4P6. (514) 599-2244. FAX: (514) 599-2299. Gerald Janneteau, pres; Jacques Boucher, VP progmg.

Provides 24-hour sports TV in French.

Satellite: Anik E2, transponder T-18.

The Movie Network - First Choice. Box 787, BCE Pl., First Choice Canadian Communications Corp., 181 Bay St. Suite 100, Toronto, Ont. M5J 2T3. (416) 956-2010. FAX: (416) 956-2018. Len Bramson, pres/COO; Lisa de Wilde, exec VP; Richard Miller, VP finance; Terry Markus, VP bus affrs; Dave Samuels, VP sls/mktg; Alison Clayton, VP progmg; Ellen Davidson, VP communications; Phyllis Yaffe, chmn Foundation to Underwrite New Drama (FUND).

English-language, general interest, pay TV net featuring movie titles.

On 231 cable systems serving 500,000 subs. Satellite: Anik E2, transponder 04.

MuchMusic. 299 Queen St. W., Toronto, Ont. M5V 2Z5. (416) 591-5757. FAX: (416) 340-7005. Moses Znaimer, pres/exec prod; Ron Waters, VP/gen mgr; David Kirkwood, dir sls/mktg.

A 24-hour, 7-day-a-week stereo video mus net.

Serving 1232 cable systems & 5.5 million subs. Satellite: Anik E2, transponder 3B.

MusiquePlus. 209 St. Catherine E., Montreal, Que. H2X IL2. (514) 284-7587. FAX: (514) 284-2803. Normand Beauchamp, pres; Pierre Lanctôt, sls dir; Pierre Marchand, exec dir.

Mus video TV net bcstg in Quebec, in French.

Approximately 116 cable systems serving 1.8 million subs. Satellite: Anik E2, transponder T20.

Superchannel. Allarcom Pay Television, 5324 Calgary Tr., Suite 200, Edmonton, Alta. T6H 4J8. (403) 437-7744. FAX: (403) 437-3188. Charles R. Allard, pres; Luther Haave, VP/gen mgr; Ric Davies, VP progmg; Don Joyner, VP mktg; Larry Burnett, VP finance.

Coml-free premium pay TV svc including movies, music & comedy specials, major sports events & boxing.

On 160 cable systems serving 220,000 subs. Satellite: Anik E2, transponder TR 12.

TSN-The Sports Network. 1155 Leslie St., Don Mills, Ont. M3C 2J6. (416) 449-2244. FAX: (416) 391-8210. Gordon Craig, pres/CEO; Jim Thompson, VP/gen mgr; Rick Brace, VP progrmg; Jake Scudamore, VP mktg; Ken Murphy, dir opns; Frank Bertolas, VP finance & admin.

24-hour sports ch distributed on basic cable in Canada. Covers all major & minor sports. On more than 2,000 systems serving 6 million subs.

TVOntario/Ontario Educational Communications Authority. Box 200, Stn. Q, Toronto, Ont. M4T 2T1. (416) 484-2600. Peter Herrndorf, chmn/CEO; Bill Roberts, sr dir gen/international affairs; Peter Bowers, COO.

Provides educ progmg to cable systems throughout Ontario.

Viewer's Choice Canada. Box 787, BCE Pl., 181 Bay St., Suite 100, Toronto, Ont. M5J 2T3. (416) 956-2050. FAX: (416) 956-2055. Len Bramson, pres/CEO; Stephen Tapp, VP/gen mgr; Elizabeth L. Snip, dir mktg; Susan Tucker, dir planning/dev.

Eastern Canada's pay-per-view net.

Vision TV: Canada's Faith Network. 315 Queen St. E., Toronto, Ont. M5A 1S7. (416) 368-3194. FAX: (416) 368-9774. Ron Keast, pres; Peter Flemington, dir progmg; John Dvorak, dir communications; Peter Palframan, dir finance.

Value-based dramas, documentaries, pub affrs & mus in addition to progs from specific faith communities.

On 216 cable systems serving over 5.5 million subs. Satellite: Anik E2, transponder T3; Digital video signal, natl Ku-band.

The Weather Network/MétéoMédia Inc. (A division of Pelmorex Communications Inc.) 1755 René-Lévesque Blvd. E., Suite 251, Montreal, Que. H2K 4P6. (514) 597-1700. FAX: (514) 597-1591. Pierre L. Morrissette, pres/CEO; David MacKinnon, VP opns; Robert A. Linney, VP progmg; Luc Perreault, dir affil rel.

Natl satellite-to-cable TV net bcstg in French (MétéoMédia) & English (The Weather Network) offering weather & environmental info 24 hours a day, 7 days a week.

On 410 headends serving 6.8 million subs. Satellite: Anik E2, transponder 1A.

YTV Canada Inc. 64 Jefferson Ave., Unit 18, Toronto, Ont. M6K 3H3. (416) 534-1191. FAX: (416) 533-0346. Kevin M. Shea, pres/CEO; Susan Ross, VP mktg; Suzan Grimmer, VP sls; Martin Abel, VP finance/CFO; Dale Taylor, VP progmg.

English-language basic cable specialty svc dedicated to children, teens & their families. On approximately 1200 cable systems serving an estimated 6.5 million subscribers. Satellite: Anik E2, transponder T29 12096 mHz horizontal polarization (eastern feed); transponder T10 11987 mHz vertical polarization (western feed).

Music Licensing Groups

American Society of Composers, Authors & Publishers (ASCAP). One Lincoln Plaza, New York 10023. (212) 595-3050. Morton Gould, pres; Arthur Hamilton, Irwin Z. Robinson, VPs.

Associated Production Music Sound Effects Libraries. 6255 Sunset Blvd., Suite 820, Hollywood, Calif. 90028. (213) 461-3211. FAX: (213) 461-9102. Cassie Lord, natl sls dir; Connie Reed, bcst sls dir.
 Supplying the Broadcast One, Two & Three prod mus & sound effects to radio & TV for use in promotions, programs, news & commercials.

BMI-Broadcast Music Inc. 320 W. 57th St., New York 10019. (212) 586-2000. FAX: (212) 489-2368.
 Frances W. Preston, pres/CEO; Robbin Ahrold, VP corporate rels; Del R. Bryant, VP performing rights; Richard J. Mack, VP opns; Thomas G. Annastas, VP gen licensing (nonbcst or cable); Marvin Berenson, VP counsel licensing; Larry Sweeney, VP telecommunications; Scott Andrews, Arnold Boatner, George Clay, Paul Cooper, Nereida Robles, Daniel Spears, rgnl dirs bcstg; Phil Graham, VP European writer/publisher rels.
 Nashville 37203: 10 Music Sq. E. (615) 259-3625.
 Hollywood, Calif. 90069: 8730 Sunset Blvd. (310) 659-9109.
 Licenses the public performance rights of musical compositions for more than 100,000 songwriters, composers & mus publishers; maintains reciprocal arrangements with more than 40 licensing organizations worldwide.

CPP-Belwin Inc. 15800 N.W. 48th Ave., Miami, Fla. 33014. (305) 620-1500. FAX: (305) 621-4869. Sandy Feldstein, pres.

European American Music Distributors Corp. Box 850, Valley Forge, Pa. 19482. (215) 648-0506. FAX: (215) 889-0242. Ronald L. Freed, pres.

The Harry Fox Agency Inc. 205 E. 42nd St., 18th Fl., New York 10017. (212) 370-5330. FAX: (212) 953-2384. Edward P. Murphy, pres/CEO; Bernard Kerner, VP finance; Yoshio Inomata, VP licensing.

Joe Jones Copyright Management. 10556 Arnwood Rd., Lake View Terrace, Calif. 91342. (818) 890-0730. FAX: (818) 899-4457. Joe Jones, pres/CEO; Marion Jones, sr VP/controller.
 Administers & issues music copyright licenses worldwide.

Makewde Agency/Joe Jones Intl. 10556 Arnwood Rd., Lake View Terrace, Calif. 91342. (818) 890-0730. FAX: (818) 899-4457. Marion Coleman, pres/CEO; Dwayne Jones, gen mgr; Keith Jones, VP spec projects; Detra Jones, VP admin.
 Mus license organization & admin.

Promusic Inc. 6555 N.W. 9th Ave., Suite 303, Fort Lauderdale, Fla. 33309. (800) 322-7879; (305) 776-2070. Alain Leroux, pres.

SESAC Inc. 55 Music Sq. E., Nashville 37203. (615) 320-0055. FAX: (615) 329-9627. Vincent Candilora, pres & COO; Deborah Houghton, VP cable & net licensing; Sheila Canovan, dir bcst licensing.
 New York 10019: 421 W. 54th St. (212) 586-3450. FAX: (212) 489-5699.
 Performing rights organization representing a diversity of copyrighted mus.

Society of Composers, Authors & Music Publishers of Canada (SOCAN). 41 Valleybrook Dr., Don Mills, Ont., Canada M3B 2S6. (416) 445-8700. FAX: (416) 445-7108. Michael Rock, gen mgr.
 SOCAN licenses the public performance of musico in Canada.

Videotext Operations

CompuServe. 5000 Arlington Ctr. Blvd., Columbus, Ohio 43220. (800) 848-8199; (614) 457-8600. FAX: (614) 457-0348.

On-line info net accessed by modem-equipped personal computer; svcs include communications, bus & finance, news & sports, travel, personal computing & consumer svcs, including a forum (bulletin bd) for bcst professionals.

Cowles Publishing Co. (Electronic Editions.) Box 2160, Spokane, Wash. 99210. (509) 459-5060. FAX: (509) 459-5234. Shaun L. O'Higgins, dir electronic publishing.

Provides classified adv, games, entertainment guide, bulletin bd, film times, & info-on-demand svcs.

Dow Jones Information Services. Box 300, Princeton, N.J. 08543-0300. (609) 520-4000. Carl Valenti, pres.

Dow Jones Information Svcs is a leading provider of electronically delivered bus news & financial info through computer, facsimile, radio, TV & telephone. Dow Jones Information Svcs is the electronic publishing arm of Dow Jones & Co. publisher of The Wall Street Jounal & Barron's.

International TeleText Communications Inc. 1307 S. Mary Ave., Suite 203, Sunnyvale, Calif. 94087. (408) 735-8833. FAX: (408) 738-3166. Robert H. Welch, CEO; Robert Evans, chief tech off.

Provides financial & news info svcs via Nationwide Wireless Network. Includes "15 minute delay" stock quotations & USA Today Decisionline at no chg to PC-based customers. Additional subscription svcs are available on the net. Custom data bcstg svcs for info providers & corporate customers.

San Francisco State University. Broadcast Communication Arts Department. 1600 Holloway Ave., San Francisco 94132. (415) 338-1788. FAX: (415) 338-1168. Ronald J. Compesi, chmn.

This 24-hour operational videotext-type svc on the Viacom Cablevision System has 90,000 users. Access by touch-tone telephone, no decoders needed. 3,500-page data base.

StarText. (Fort Worth Star-Telegram.) Box 1870, Fort Worth, Tex. 76101. (817) 390-7905. FAX: (817) 390-7797. Gerry J. Barker, dir mktg; Michael Holland, gen mgr.

Rgnl videotext svcs for computer owners in Fort Worth/Dallas.

Teletext Operations

International Teletext Communications Inc. 1307 S. Mary Ave., Suite 203, Sunnyvale, Calif. 94087. (408) 735-8833. FAX: (408) 738-3166. Robert H. Welch, CEO; Robert Evans, chief tech off.

Provides financial & news info svcs via Nationwide Wireless Network. Includes "15 minute delay" stock quotations & USA Today Decisionline at no chg to PC-based customers. Additional subscription svcs are available on the net. Custom data bcstg svcs for info providers & corporate customers.

KIRO Inc. 2807 3rd Ave., Seattle 98121. (206) 728-7777. FAX: (206) 728-8784. Paul Polzin, VP/dir engrg.

CBS affil, owned by Bonneville International Corp., transmits a teletext magazine.

KPIX-TV. 855 Battery St., San Francisco 94111. (415) 362-5550. FAX: (415) 765-8844. Richard Blantiardi, gen mgr; Randy Pringle, controller; Harry Fuller, news dir; Alan Buckner, sls mgr; Dave Phillips, bcst opns dir.

CBS affil TV bcstg stn.

KSL TeleText-5. 55 N. 300 W., Salt Lake City 84110-1160. (801) 575-5565. FAX: (801) 575-7548. Richard Linford, exec VP Bonneville International Corp.; David Webb, mgr.

An advertiser-supported NABTS news & info svc available through TV decoders or personal computers equipped with modems. Modem number is (801) 575-5911.

MA-Com Inc. 401 Edgewater Pl., Suite 560, Wakefield, Mass. 01880-6210. (617) 224-5615. FAX: (617) 224-5655. Al Rayfield, pres/COO; Tom Van der Slice, chmn/CEO; Peter Manno, VP sls & mktg.

Reuters Information Services Inc. 1700 Broadway, New York 10019. (212) 603-3300. FAX: (212) 603-3618. L. Brewster Jackson, sr VP media; John C. DePrez, natl sls mgr media.

Gen & financial news svcs for media & bus communities with international & domestic news plus real-time market data. Also historical databases.

Southern Satellite Systems Inc. 3530 Bomar Rd., Douglasville, Ga. 30135. (404) 949-6600. FAX: (404) 942-6653. Adam Grow III, gen mgr.

Satellite uplink/downlink facilities.

TVOntario. (Ontario Educational Communications Authority.) Box 200, Station Q, Toronto, Ont., Canada M4T 2T1. (416) 484-2600. FAX: (416) 484-6285. Peter Herrndorf, chmn/CEO; Bill Roberts, sr dir gen international affrs; Peter Bowers, COO; Patricia Fillmore, dir mktg & dev.

WGBH Boston. 125 Western Ave., Boston 02134. (617) 492-2777. FAX: (617) 787-0714.

PBS affil; focusing on potential pub applications of teletext & videotext. Also full-svc captioning agency, including teletext closed-captioning & a full prod facility.

WKRC Cincinnati. 1906 Highland Ave., Cincinnati 45219. (513) 763-5617. FAX: (513) 241-9444. Tom Oliver, chief engr.

ABC affil; regular questionnaires tracking teletext magazine usage & viewer response.

Subcarrier/VBI Services

Bonneville Market Information. 19 W. South Temple, Salt Lake City 84101. (800) 255-7374. FAX: (801) 532-3202. Charlie McQuinn, pres.

Real-time stock, commodity & option info via FM sideband & satellite; software & news svcs.

Green Consultants of Vero Beach Inc. 414 22nd St. S.E., Vero Beach, Fla. 32962. (407) 778-2573. Bert Green, pres.

Engrg & applied sciences of voice, data imaging communications & energy mgmt as related to cable/bcst business office automation.

IDB Communications Group Inc. 10525 W. Washington Blvd., Culver City, Calif. 90232-1922. (213) 870-9000. FAX: (213) 240-3911. Jeffrey P. Sudikoff, chmn/CEO; Edward R. Cheramy, pres; Peter Hartz, sr VP mktg & sls.

Domestic & international satellite transmission svcs for radio/TV/voice/data; New York & Los Angeles teleports; large fleet of transportable earth stns.

International Teletext Communications Inc. 1307 S. Mary, Sunnyvale, Calif. 94087. (408) 735-8833. FAX: (408) 738-3166. Robert Evans, pres.

Natl VBI teletext delivery svcs for TV stn rebcstg, private consumer & coml use. VBI-based data delivery applications.

LMC SatCom. 3530 Bomar Rd., Douglasville, Ga. 30135. (404) 949-6600. FAX: (404) 942-6653. Adam Grow, gen mgr/dir engrg; John Roberts, sls mgr.

Lotus Development Corp. 55 Cambridge Pkwy., Cambridge, Mass. 02142. (617) 577-8500. FAX: (617) 693-1299. Jim Manzi, pres.

Muzak. 400 N. 34th St., Suite 200, Seattle 98103. (206) 633-3000. FAX: (206) 633-6210. John R. Jester, pres; James F. Harrison, sr VP sls & mktg; Tom Gentry, VP/gen mgr DBS division.

Bcsts 12 chs of business mus, ad parting audio messages, ZNET data bcstg & occasional-use video via direct bcst satellite.

Telemet America Inc. 325 First St., Alexandria, Va. 22314. (703) 548-2042. Dr. F.G. Parsons, chmn.

Stock, option, commodities & news bcst by subcarrier to Pocket Quote & Radio Exchange receivers.

Section H
Services and Suppliers

Table of Contents

Table of Contents H-1
Technological Services
  Equipment Manufacturers and Distributors and Technical Services
    Subject Index H-2
    Alphabetical Index H-12
Professional Services
  Station and Cable Television Brokers H-59
  Consultants H-65
  Station Financing Services H-76
  Research Services H-79
  Engineering and Technical Consultants H-84
  Law Firms Active in Communications Law H-90
  Talent Agents and Managers H-102
  Employment and Executive Search Services H-103
  Professional Cards
    Engineering & Technical Consultants H-105
    Other Services H-107

Equipment Manufacturers, Distributors and Technical Services Subject Index

Companies are generally classified under their primary services and may be listed under one or more subject areas. Refer to the *Alphabetical Index* for complete company information.

ACOUSTICAL PANELS AND TREATMENT
Acoustic Systems
Alpha Audio Acoustics/Acoustical Solutions Inc.
Netwell Noise Control
RPG Diffusor Systems Inc.
Soundforms International

AMPLIFIERS
BEXT Inc.
BGW Systems Inc.
Protech Audio Corp.
Sascom Marketing Group

AMPLIFIERS, AUDIO
Audio Implements/GKC
BES Electronics Ltd.
BGW Systems Inc.
Benchmark Media Systems Inc.
Crown International
DYNAIR Electronics Inc.
ESE
Henry Engineering
Image Video Ltd.
JBL Professional
J.N.S. Electronics Inc.
Kintek Inc.
Protech Audio Corp.
RF Systems
RTS Systems
Sescom Inc.

AMPLIFIERS, RF
Acrodyne Industries Inc.
Augat Communications Products Inc.
Blonder-Tongue Laboratories Inc.
Continental Electronics Corp.
Crown International
EEV Inc.
Energy-Onix Broadcast Equipment Co. Inc.
Kahn Communications Inc.
Larcan Inc.
Link Electronics Inc.

AMPLIFIERS, VIDEO
DYNAIR Electronics Inc.
Digital Processing Systems Inc.
ESE
Link Electronics Inc.

ANALYZERS, DISTORTION, INTERMODULATION
Boonton Electronics Corp.
Potomac Instruments Inc.

ANIMATION SYSTEMS
Electric Image Inc.
Fast Forward Video
Videomedia Inc.
Wavefront Technologies Inc.

ANNOUNCEMENT SYSTEMS
Protech Audio Corp.

ANTENNAS AND ACCESSORIES
Antenna Concepts Inc.
Antenna Technology
Antenna and Tower Service Inc.
Blonder-Tongue Laboratories Inc.
Cablewave Systems Inc.
Channel Master
Cortland Cable Co. Inc.
ERI Electonics Research Inc.
Ellis Tower Co. Inc.
InSat Corp.
LDL Communications Inc.
Lindsay Specialty Products Ltd.
NSI
Norpak Corp.
S.W.R. Inc.
Telex Communications Inc.
Tennaplex Systems Ltd.
Tower Network Services

ANTENNAS, BROADCAST
Antenna Concepts Inc.
Antenna Technology
Antenna and Tower Service Inc.
Broadcast Equipment Sales & Engineering Inc.
Cablewave Systems Inc.
ERI Electonics Research Inc.
Emcee Broadcast Products
LDL Communications Inc.
Lindsay Specialty Products Ltd.
RF Systems
S.W.R. Inc.
Scala Electronic Corp.
Shively Laboratories Inc.
Television Technology Corp.
Tennaplex Systems Ltd.
Thomcast

ANTENNAS, EARTH STATION
Antenna Technology
Pinzone Communications Products Inc.
Radio Research Instrument Co. Inc.
Vertex Communications Corp.

ANTENNAS, INSTALLATION
Antenna and Tower Service Inc.
CTI Installations Inc.
Cambridge Products Corp.
EDX Engineering Inc.
ERI Electonics Research Inc.
Ellis Tower Co. Inc.
LDL Communications Inc.
Normex Telecom Inc.
S.W.R. Inc.
Swager Communications Inc.
Teletech Inc.
Tower Structures Inc.
Vertex Communications Corp.

ANTENNAS, TVRO
Blonder-Tongue Laboratories Inc.
Channel Master
Pinzone Communications Products Inc.

ATTENUATORS AND EQUALIZERS
Penny & Giles Inc.
Shallco Inc.

AUDIO ACCESSORIES
Auditronics Inc.
Channel Master
Cumming Corp.
Henry Engineering
Neutrik USA Inc.
Penny & Giles Inc.
PolyQuick
Professional Sound Corp.
Sescom Inc.
Sprague Magnetics Inc.
Switchcraft Inc.

AUDIO AMPS, AGC & LIMITERS
Professional Sound Corp.
Samson Technologies Corp.
Sescom Inc.

AUDIO CARTRIDGES
Fidelipac Corp.

AUDIO COMPRESSORS
Inovonics Inc.
Protech Audio Corp.
Sescom Inc.
Valley Audio Products Inc.

AUDIO CONSOLES
Amek/TAC U.S. Operations
Audioarts Engineering
Auditronics Inc.
Broadcast Electronics Inc.
Neotek Corp.
Pacific Recorders & Engineering Corp.
Professional Sound Corp.
Samson Technologies Corp.
Schafer World Communications Corp.
Soundcraft
Ultra Audio Pixtec
Wheatstone Corp.

AUDIO CONTROL CENTERS
Henry Engineering
Media Touch Systems Inc.
Protech Audio Corp.

AUDIO EQUIPMENT
360 Systems Broadcast Products Group
AKAI Digital/IMC
Amek/TAC U.S. Operations
Arrakis Systems Inc.
Audio Services Corp.
Avid Technology Inc.
BBE Sound Inc.
Crouse-Kimzey Co.
FM Systems Inc.
Gepco International
Inovonics Inc.
Lectrosonics Inc.
NVision Inc.
OptoDigital Design Inc.
Professional Sound Corp.
Protech Audio Corp.
Samson Technologies Corp.
Spectrum
Switchcraft Inc.
Telex Communications Inc.
Toner Cable Equipment Inc.
Wireworks Corp.

AUDIO JACKFIELDS, PRE-WIRED
ADC Telecommunications Inc.
Audio Accessories Inc.
Milestek Inc.
Penny & Giles Inc.
Switchcraft Inc.

AUDIO LIMITERS
Inovonics Inc.

AUDIO MIXERS AND RECORDERS
AMS Neve PLC
Allen & Heath
Amek/TAC U.S. Operations
Audioarts Engineering
Cooper Sound Systems
Graham-Patten Systems Inc.
Henry Engineering
Professional Sound Corp.
Professional Sound Services Inc.
Soundcraft
Soundtracs, PLC
Topham Audio Inc.
Ultra Audio Pixtec
Wheatstone Corp.

AUDIO MONITORING SYSTEMS
Auditronics Inc.
B&B Systems Inc.
J.N.S. Electronics Inc.

AUDIO NOISE REDUCTION SYSTEMS
Acoustic Systems
Avid Technology Inc.
Dolby Laboratories Inc.
Valley Audio Products Inc.

AUDIO PROCESSORS
Audioarts Engineering
BBE Sound Inc.
Cutting Edge Technologies
Inovonics Inc.
Modulation Sciences Inc.
Samson Technologies Corp.

Equipment Manufacturers, Distributors and Technical Services Subject Index

AUDIO REPLACEMENT HEADS
Sprague Magnetics Inc.

AUDIO ROUTING SWITCHES
360 Systems Broadcast Products Group
Burk Technology
J.N.S. Electronics Inc.
Link Electronics Inc.
NVision Inc.
Richmond Sound Design Ltd.
Ultra Audio Pixtec

AUDIO SIGNAL PROCESSING SYSTEMS
BBE Sound Inc.
Dolby Laboratories Inc.
Eventide Inc.
Fiber Options Inc.
Graham-Patten Systems Inc.
Inovonics Inc.
Kintek Inc.
Lectrosonics Inc.
Penny & Giles Inc.
Valley Audio Products Inc.

AUDIO SYSTEMS AND COMPONENTS
Audio Implements/GKC
Crown International
Math Associates Inc.
Parsons Audio

AUDIO TEST TAPES, GAUGES & EQUIPMENT
Audio Precision Inc.
Fidelipac Corp.
Taber Manufacturing and Engineering Co.
Valley Audio Products Inc.

AUDIO TRANSMISSION EQUIPMENT
Corporate Computer Systems
Tectan Inc.

AUDIOTAPE
National Audio Co. Inc.

AUDIOTAPE CARTRIDGE MACHINES
Broadcast Electronics Inc.

AUDIOTAPE DUPLICATING EQUIPMENT
National Audio Co. Inc.
Telex Communications Inc.

AUTOMATED NEWSROOM SYSTEMS
Associated Press Broadcast Services
BASYS Automation Systems Inc.
BDL-Audioscript Ltd.
Comprompter Inc.
Dynatech NewStar
Louth Automation
Media Computing Inc.

AUTOMATED RADIO
ADTEC Productions Inc.
Arrakis Systems Inc.
Kingdom Technology
Media Touch Systems Inc.
Radio Computing Services (RCS)
Sentry Systems
Schafer World Communications Corp.
Time Logic Inc.

AUTOMATED TELEPHONE & VOICE MAIL SYSTEMS
Scott Studios Corp.

AUTOMATIC CASSETTE LOADERS
Odetics Broadcast

AUTOMATIC TRANSMISSION SYSTEMS
Louth Automation
Odetics Broadcast
TE Consulting Inc.

AUTOMATION SYSTEMS
ADTEC Productions Inc.
BASYS Automation Systems Inc.
Broadcast Electronics Inc.
Enterprise Systems Group Inc.
Fidelipac Corp.
Jefferson-Pilot Data Services Inc.
Kingdom Technology
Louth Automation
MATCO
Media Computing Inc.
Media Touch Systems Inc.
Odetics Broadcast
Radio Computing Services (RCS)
Scott Studios Corp.
Sentry Systems
Sono-Mag Corp. (SMC)
Soundtracs, PLC
Superior Electronics Group Inc.
TE Consulting Inc.
Time Logic Inc.

AUTOMATION, SWITCHING AND CONTROL
ADTEC Productions Inc.
Kingdom Technology
Leightronix Inc.
Louth Automation
MATCO
Odetics Broadcast
Richmond Sound Design Ltd.
Scott Studios Corp.
TE Consulting Inc.

AUTOMATION, TV STATION
American Broadcast Systems Inc.
Dynatech NewStar
Image Video Ltd.
Inscriber Character Generator
Louth Automation
MATCO
Odetics Broadcast
Peter Storer & Associates Inc.
Time Logic Inc.

BASE INSULATORS
ERI Electonics Research Inc.

BATTERIES AND ACCESSORIES
ADCOUR
Allied Electronics Inc.
Alpha Technologies
Computer Power Inc.
Energy Plus Inc. & Rathbone Energy Systems Inc.
Frezzolini Electronics Inc.
Alan Gordon Enterprises Inc.

BLIMPS
Blimpy Floating Signs/Bend-A-Lite

BLOWERS AND FANS
Winsted Corp.

BOOMS AND CAMERAS
Alan Gordon Enterprises Inc.

BOOSTERS, TV
Channel Master

BROADCAST AUDIO PRODUCTS
360 Systems Broadcast Products Group
AMS Neve PLC
ASACA/Shibasoku Corp. of America
Audio Implements/GKC
Audio Processing Technology Ltd.
CBSI/Custom Business Systems Inc.
Cutting Edge Technologies
Dolby Laboratories Inc.
Eventide Inc.
Fidelipac Corp.
Frequency Measuring Service Inc.
Gepco International Inc.
Inovonics Inc.
Lectrosonics Inc.
Parsons Audio
RE America Inc.
RF Systems
Tectan Inc.
Telecast Fiber Systems Inc.
Telex Communications Inc.
Valley Audio Products Inc.
Wireworks Corp.

BROADCAST EQUIPMENT
AMS Neve PLC
Audio Broadcast Group
Audio Implements/GKC
Avid Technology Inc.
Crouse-Kimzey Co.
FM Systems Inc.
Gepco International
Henry Engineering
Image Video Ltd.
Intraplex Inc.
JVC Professional Products Co.
Kahn Communications Inc.
Link Electronics Inc.
Mark IV Sudio Broadcast & Production Group
Miranda Technologies Inc.
Modulation Sciences Inc.
POA/Paul Olivier & Associates Inc.
Rush Media Systems
Schafer World Communications Corp.
Technet Systems Group

BROADCAST & PROGRAM LOGGING RECORDERS
Eventide Inc.
Fast Forward Video

BROADCAST RF EQUIPMENT
Antenna Concepts Inc.
Comark Communications Inc.
Crown International
ERI Electonics Research Inc.
Frequency Measuring Service Inc.
Kahn Communications Inc.
RF Systems
RMS Electronics Inc.
Radio Resources & Services
Television Technology Corp.
Tennaplex Systems Ltd.

BROADCAST RADIO EQUIPMENT
Advanced Marketing
Audio Processing Technology Ltd.
Bradley Broadcast Sales
Broadcast Electronics Inc.
Cutting Edge Technologies
Henry Engineering
Kahn Communications Inc.
RE America Inc.
Radio Resources & Services
Sono-Mag Corp. (SMC)

BROADCAST STUDIO CONSTRUCTION, PREFAB
Acoustic Systems
Devlin Design Group
Mid Atlantic Radio Service
Newman-Kees Frequency Measurements
Northeastern Communications Concepts Inc.
Taber Manufacturing and Engineering Co.
Tower Structures Inc.
Video Integrators

BROADCAST STUDIO EQUIPMENT
Audio Processing Technology Ltd.
BDL-Audioscript Ltd.
Bradley Broadcast Sales
Dynatech Cable Products Group
ECHOLAB Inc.
Miranda Technologies Inc.
Nova Systems Inc.
O'Connor Engineering Labs
Pacific Recorders & Engineering Corp.
Parsons Audio
Radio Resources & Services
Teatronics International Inc. (TII)
Video Integrators

BROADCAST TV EQUIPMENT
Acrodyne Industries Inc.
Advanced Marketing
BEXT Inc.
Brek Connor Group Inc.
Canon U.S.A. Inc.
Comark Communications Inc.
Emcee Broadcast Products
Fast Forward Video
Frequency Measuring Service Inc.
Larcan Inc.
Miranda Technologies Inc.
O'Connor Engineering Labs
POA/Paul Olivier & Associates Inc.
Prime Image Inc.
Toshiba America Consumer Products

BROADCAST VIDEO PRODUCTS
ASACA/Shibasoku Corp. of America
Accom Inc.
Chromatek Scan Process Inc.
Cinema Products Corp.
Dynatech Cable Products Group
EEV Inc.
Electric Image Inc.

Equipment Manufacturers, Distributors and Technical Services Subject Index

Fast Forward Video
Fiber Options Inc.
Gepco International Inc.
Miranda Technologies Inc.
Network Video Services Inc.
P.C. & E. Lighting & Grip
Radio Resources & Services
Telecast Fiber Systems Inc.
Telemetrics Inc.
Videomedia Inc.

BULKTAPE DEGAUSSER

Data Security Inc.
Sprague Magnetics Inc.
Taber Manufacturing and Engineering Co.

BULKTAPE, AUDIO CASSETTE

DIC Digital

CATV EQUIPMENT AND SUPPLIES

American Laser Systems Inc.
Anixter Cable TV
Augat Communications Products Inc.
Blonder-Tongue Laboratories Inc.
C-COR Electronics Inc.
Cable Prep
Cadix International Inc.
Diamond Communication Products Inc.
FM Systems Inc.
Gepco International
Harmonic Lightwaves Inc.
Intelvideo Inc.
Just Drop Inc.
Lindsay Specialty Products Ltd.
MERET Optical Communications Inc.
RMS Electronics Inc.
Scientific-Atlanta Inc.
Spectrum
TV/Com International
Telecrafter Products
Toner Cable Equipment Inc.
WearGuard Corp.

CATV HYBRID MODULES

American Lightwave Systems Inc.

CATV POWER SUPPLIES

Alpha Technologies
Auto-Gen Electric Division
RMS Electronics Inc.

CABINETS, RACKS, PANELS

ADTEC Productions Inc.
Hi-Tech Furnishings
Major Engineering
Murphy Studio Furniture
Newark Electronics
Northeastern Communications Concepts Inc.
Storeel Corp.
Teatronics International Inc. (TII)
Winsted Corp.

CABLE AND ACCESSORIES

Allied Electronics Inc.
Cablewave Systems Inc.
Cambridge Products Corp.
Cortland Cable Co. Inc.
Gepco International Inc.
Just Drop Inc.
Milestek Inc.
Nemal Electronics International Inc.
Neutrik USA Inc.
Newark Electronics
RF Systems
James Thomas Engineering
Trompeter Electronics Inc
Wireworks Corp.

CABLE TERMINATION EQUIPMENT, AUDIO/VIDEO

Gepco International Inc.

CALIBRATORS, TV CAMERAS/MONITORS

Imero Fiorentino Associates Inc.
Frequency Measuring Service Inc.

CAMERA MOUNTS

Avtech Systems Inc.
Birns and Sawyer Inc.
Alan Gordon Enterprises Inc.
Production Consultants & Equipment
Shotmaker Dollies & Cranes
Telemetrics Inc.

CAMERA PAN/TILT HEADS

Broadcast Sports Technologies
CSI-Camera Support International
Canon U.S.A. Inc.
Alan Gordon Enterprises Inc.
Innovision Optics
O'Connor Engineering Labs
Pro Video & Film Equipment Group
Production Consultants & Equipment
Quickset International Inc.
Telemetrics Inc.

CAMERA TUBES

Avtech Systems Inc.
Daily Electronics Corp.
EEV Inc.
Richardson Electronics Ltd.

CAMERAS, PROJECTORS & ACCESSORIES

EEV Inc.
Alan Gordon Enterprises Inc.
Innovision Optics
Pro Video & Film Equipment Group
Toshiba America Consumer Products
VRI (Video Rentals Inc.)

CAPACITORS

BES Electronics Ltd.

CAPTIONING EQUIPMENT

Blue Feather Co.
Dynatech NewStar
Inscriber Character Generator

CARTRIDGE AUTOMATIC TAPE

Fidelipac Corp.
Odetics Broadcast

CARTRIDGE STORAGE RACKS

Murphy Studio Furniture

CASES

CSI-Camera Support International
Calzone Case Co.
Parsons Manufacturing Corp.
Plastic Reel Corp. of America
Star Case Manufacturing Co. Inc.

CASSETTE DUPLICATION, AUDIO/VIDEO

Leightronix Inc.
Telex Communications Inc.

CASSETTE, VIDEOTAPE EQUIPMENT AND ACCESSORIES

Data Security Inc.
Major Engineering
Plastic Reel Corp. of America

CASSETTES

DIC Digital
National Audio Co. Inc.
PolyQuick

CHARACTER GENERATORS

ADTEC Productions Inc.
Abekas Video Systems Inc.
Bio-Electronics Inc.
Brek Connor Group Inc.
Display Systems International Inc.
Dynatech Cable Products Group
Evertz Microsystems Ltd.
Inscriber Character Generator
Spectrum
Video Data Systems

CHRONOMETERS, CLOCKS

Chrono-Log Corp.

CLEANING ACCESSORIES, AUDIO/VIDEO

Data Security Inc.
Sprague Magnetics Inc.

CLOSED CAPTIONING SYSTEMS

Blue Feather Co.
EEG Enterprises Inc.
Gorman-Redlich Manufacturing Co.
Link Electronics Inc.

CLOSED CIRCUIT SYSTEMS

American Laser Systems Inc.
Math Associates Inc.
Print Products International

COAXIAL CABLES

Broadcast Equipment Sales & Engineering Inc.
Ellis Tower Co. Inc.
Gepco International Inc.
Just Drop Inc.
Milestek Inc.
Nemal Electronics International Inc.
Power & Telephone Supply Co.
Shively Laboratories Inc.
Trompeter Electronics Inc.
VueScan Inc.

COAXIAL CHANGEOVER UNITS, AUTOMATIC

Tennaplex Systems Ltd.

COAXIAL CONNECTORS

Augat Communications Products Inc.
Gilbert Engineering Co. Inc.
Just Drop Inc.
Milestek Inc.
Nemal Electronics International Inc.
Power & Telephone Supply Co.
RMS Electronics Inc.
S.W.R. Inc.
Switchcraft Inc.
Trompeter Electronics Inc.

COAXIAL PATCH PANELS

Augat Communications Products Inc.
Larcan Inc.
Milestek Inc.
Trompeter Electronics Inc.

COILS

BES Electronics Ltd.

COLOR CONTROL MONITORS

ASACA/Shibasoku Corp. of America

COMBINERS

Larcan Inc.
Shively Laboratories Inc.
Tennaplex Systems Ltd.

COMMUNICATIONS SYSTEMS

Audio Implements/GKC
EDX Engineering Inc.
Intraplex Inc.
LeBlanc Communications Inc.
Marti Electronics Inc.
Rush Media Systems
Technical Projects Inc.

COMPACT DISC EQUIPMENT

Scott Studios Corp.

COMPACT DISC MANUFACTURERS

DIC Digital
KAO Optical

COMPUTERS/BROADCAST EQUIPMENT CONTROL

Adrienne Electronics Corp.
American Broadcast Systems Inc.
Audio Processing Technology Ltd.
CBSI/Custom Business Systems Inc.
Enterprise Systems Group Inc.
Fast Forward Video
Imagine Products Inc.
International Teletext Communications Inc.
MATCO
Media Computing Inc.
Media Touch Systems Inc.
Radio Computing Services (RCS)
Scott Studios Corp.
Sentry Systems
Time Logic Inc.
Videomedia Inc.

COMPUTERS AND PERIPHERALS

BGW Systems Inc.
Business Systems Inc.
Computer Assisted Technologies
Energy Plus Inc. & Rathbone Energy Systems Inc.
Enterprise Systems Group Inc.
MARKETRON
Radio Computing Services (RCS)
Peter Storer & Associates Inc.
Teleflex Information Systems Inc.
Toner Cable Computer Systems

Equipment Manufacturers, Distributors and Technical Services Subject Index

CONNECTORS
Lemo U.S.A. Inc.

CONSOLE EQUIPMENT
Peter Albrecht Corp.
Audioarts Engineering
Teatronics International Inc. (TII)

CONSOLES
AMS Neve PLC
Arrakis Systems Inc.
Audioarts Engineering
Auditronics Inc.
Fidelipac Corp.
Hi-Tech Furnishings
Sascom Marketing Group
Soundcraft
Soundtracs, PLC
Winsted Corp.

CONSOLES, ON-AIR
Audioarts Engineering
Auditronics Inc.
Broadcast Equipment Sales & Engineering Inc.
Image Video Ltd.
Soundcraft
Wheatstone Corp.

CONSTRUCTION SERVICES
Peter Albrecht Corp.
B&B Systems Inc.
CTI Installations Inc.
Lakeside Associates Inc.
Mid Atlantic Radio Service
Normex Telecom Inc.
Swager Communications Inc.

CONTROL SYSTEMS
Fast Forward Video
Image Video Ltd.
MATCO
Richmond Sound Design Ltd.
Teatronics International Inc. (TII)
Videomedia Inc.

CONVERTERS, STANDARDS
Prime Image Inc.
Video International Development Corp.

CONVERTERS, TV
Magni Systems Inc.
TV/Com International
VueScan Inc.

COPY STANDS
Auditronics Inc.
Murphy Studio Furniture

COSTUMES AND PROPERTIES
Sacramento Theatrical Lighting

CUE SYSTEMS
COMTEK Inc.

CUSTOM CONSOLES
B&B Systems Inc.
Hi-Tech Furnishings

CUSTOM STUDIOS
Acoustic Systems
Hi-Tech Furnishings
Murphy Studio Furniture
POA/Paul Olivier & Associates Inc.
Pacific Recorders & Engineering Corp.

CYCLORAMA TRACKS
Peter Albrecht Corp.
Olesen

DATA COMMUNICATIONS SYSTEMS
EEG Enterprises Inc.
First Pacific Networks
International Teletext Communications Inc.
Jefferson-Pilot Data Services Inc.
MICOM Communications Corp.
Modulation Sciences Inc.
Norpak Corp.

DATA TRANSMISSION EQUIPMENT
Cambridge Products Corp.
First Pacific Networks
Norpak Corp.

DECODERS
Abekas Video Systems Inc.
Accom Inc.
Bio-Electronics Inc.
Gorman-Redlich Manufacturing Co.
Intelvideo Inc.
Microtime Inc.

DEHYDRATORS AND ACCESSORIES
Cablewave Systems Inc.
LDL Communications Inc.

DEMODULATORS AND MODULATORS
FM Systems Inc.
J.N.S. Electronics Inc.
NUCOMM Inc.

DESCRAMBLERS, PAY TV
TV/Com International
VueScan Inc.

DESIGN SERVICES, BROADCAST
Communications Design Associates Inc.
Murphy Studio Furniture
TE Consulting Inc.
Video Design Pro

DESIGNERS, PRODUCTION FACILITIES
Communications Design Associates Inc.
POA/Paul Olivier & Associates Inc.

DIGITAL AUDIO PROCESSING EQUIPMENT
Audio Processing Technology Ltd.
Avid Technlogy Inc.
CBSI/Custom Business Systems Inc.
Coastcom
Graham-Patten Systems Inc.
Great Lakes Data Systems Inc.
Lester Laboratories
NVision Inc.
OptoDigital Design Inc.
Radio Computing Services (RCS)
Valley Audio Products Inc.
WireReady Newswire Systems Inc.

DIGITAL AUDIO RECORDERS
360 Systems Broadcast Products Group
AKAI Digital/IMC
Audio Services Corp.
Digital Recorders Inc.
Fostex Corp. of America
Kingdom Technology
Magna-Tech Electronic Co. Inc.
Schafer World Communications Corp.
Sentry Systems
Wheatstone Corp.
WireReady Newswire Systems Inc.

DIGITAL AUDIO RECORDING & EDITING STATION
360 Systems Broadcast Products Group
AKAI Digital/IMC
AMS Neve PLC
Audio Broadcast Group
BASYS Automation Systems Inc.
CBSI/Custom Business Systems Inc.
Crouse-Kimzey Co.
Fostex Corp. of America
Kingdom Technology
Media Touch Systems Inc.
Pacific Recorders & Engineering Corp.
Parsons Audio
Radio Computing Services (RCS)
WireReady Newswire Systems Inc.

DIGITAL BROADCAST EQUIPMENT
360 Systems Broadcast Products Group
Accom Inc.
Advanced Marketing
American Lightwave Systems Inc.
Antenna Technology
Audio Broadcast Group
Audio/Digital
Broadcast Electronics Inc.
C-COR Electronics Inc.
CBSI/Custom Business Systems Inc.
California Digital Audio Systems Inc.
Coastcom
Fiber Options Inc.
InSat Corp.
Intraplex Inc.
J.N.S. Electronics Inc.
Lester Laboratories
MERET Optical Communications Inc.
RE America Inc.
Telos Systems

DIGITAL IMAGE PROCESSORS
Accom Inc.
Nova Systems Inc.

DIGITAL SPECIAL EFFECTS SYSTEMS
Abekas Video Systems Inc.
Commercial Electronics Ltd.
ECHOLAB Inc.
Eventide Inc.
Microtime Inc.
Toshiba America Consumer Products

DIGITAL VIDEO GRAPHICS AND ANIMATION SYSTEMS
Abekas Video Systems Inc.
Display Systems International Inc.

DIGITAL VIDEO PROCESSING EQUIPMENT
Accom Inc.
International Teletext Communications Inc.
Leitch/HEDCO - Leitch Inc.
OptoDigital Design Inc.
Prime Image Inc.
Scientific-Atlanta Inc.
TV/Com International

DIGITAL VIDEO PRODUCTION SYSTEMS
Microtime Inc.

DISTORTION ANALYZERS
Audio Precision Inc.
Boonton Electronics Corp.

DISTRIBUTION AMPLIFIERS
Benchmark Media Systems Inc.
Bio-Electronics Inc.
Chromatek Scan Process Inc.
ESE
J.N.S. Electronics Inc.
Leitch/HEDCO - Leitch Inc.
Lindsay Specialty Products Ltd.
TrueTime Inc.
Video Accessory Corp.
VueScan Inc.

DISTRIBUTION SYSTEMS
Lindsay Specialty Products Ltd.
Olesen

DOLLIES, INSTRUMENT CARTS, ETC.
Karl Heitz Inc.
Shotmaker Dollies & Cranes

DUMMY LOADS
Altronic Research Inc.
International Assn. of Satellite Users & Suppliers

DUPLICATORS
A&S Case Co. Inc.

EFP (ELECTRONIC FIELD PRODUCTION)
Cinema Products Corp.
Mobile Video Services Ltd.
Network Video Services Inc.

ENG EQUIPMENT AND ACCESSORIES
Audio Services Corp.
Canon U.S.A. Inc.
Cinema Products Corp.
DSC Laboratories
E-N-G Mobile Systems Inc.
FM Systems Inc.
Gepco International
InSat Inc.
Modulation Sciences Inc.
NSI
NUCOMM Inc.
Network Video Services Inc.
Professional Sound Services Inc.
Tectan Inc.
Telecast Fiber Systems Inc.
Telex Communications Inc.
Telos Systems
Topham Audio Inc.
Vertex Communications Corp.

Equipment Manufacturers, Distributors and Technical Services Subject Index

ENG VANS
E-N-G Mobile Systems Inc.
InSat Inc.
Mobile Video Services Ltd.
Phoenix E.N.G.
Shook Electronics USA Inc.

EARTH STATIONS
California Digital Audio Systems Inc.
InSat Inc.
Pinzone Communications Products Inc.
Vertex Communications Corp.

EDITING EQUIPMENT, SALES-RENTAL-SERVICE
Accom Inc.
Commercial Electronics Ltd.
Plastic Reel Corp. of America
VRI (Video Rentals Inc.)

EDITING FILM AND TAPE
Evertz Microsystems Ltd.
Time Logic Inc.

ELECTRONIC COMPONENTS
ADCOUR
Cambridge Products Corp.
Newark Electronics
Richardson Electronics Ltd.
Selco Products Co.
Switchcraft Inc.
TTE Inc.

ELECTRONIC EQUIPMENT
Boonton Electronics Corp.
EEV Inc.
Power & Telephone Supply Co.

EMERGENCY ALERTING SYSTEMS
Computer Power Inc.
Dynatech Cable Products Group
Gorman-Redlich Manufacturing Co.

EMERGENCY BROADCAST EQUIPMENT
Gorman-Redlich Manufacturing Co.

ENCODERS
Abekas Video Systems Inc.
Blue Feather Co.
Brek Connor Group Inc.
Dolby Laboratories Inc.
Gorman-Redlich Manufacturing Co.
Intelvideo Inc.
Kintek Inc.
TV/Com International

ENGINEERING SYSTEMS
B&B Systems Inc.
Bowen Broadcast Service Co. Inc.
Communications Design Associates Inc.
EDX Engineering Inc.

EQUALIZERS
JBL Professional

EQUIPMENT MAINTENANCE AND REPAIR
BEXT Inc.
Bowen Broadcast Service Co. Inc.
Mid Atlantic Radio Service
Newman-Kees Frequency Measurements
Specialized Communications
Television Technology Corp.

ERASERS, MAGNETIC TAPE
Data Security Inc.
Garner Industries

EXCITERS
Acrodyne Industries Inc.
BEXT Inc.
Crown International
LDL Communications Inc.

FACILITIES PLANNING
Communications Design Associates Inc.
Devlin Design Group
ERI Electronics Research Inc.
Lakeside Associates Inc.
Mid-State Communications
Video Design Pro

FIBER OPTIC CABLE AND ACCESSORIES
Cortland Cable Co. Inc.
Diamond Communication Products Inc.
Direct Broadcast Services Inc.
Fiber Options Inc.
Gepco International
Math Associates Inc.
Newark Electronics
Pirelli
Telecast Fiber Systems Inc.
VueScan Inc.

FIBER OPTIC TRANSMISSION SYSTEMS
ADC Telecommunications Inc.
American Lightwave Systems Inc.
Augat Communications Products Inc.
C-COR Electronics Inc.
DYNAIR Electronics Inc.
Direct Broadcast Services Inc.
Fiber Options Inc.
Harmonic Lightwaves Inc.
MERET Optical Communications Inc.
Math Associates Inc.
OptoDigital Design Inc.
Telecast Fiber Systems Inc

FIELD STRENGTH METERS
Holaday Industries Inc.
Potomac Instruments Inc.

FILM EQUIPMENT
BDL-Audioscript Ltd.
BHP Inc.
Birns and Sawyer Inc.
Cinema Products Corp.
Pro Video & Film Equipment Group
Production Consultants & Equipment
Spatial Technologies Inc.

FILM PRINTERS, MOTION PICTURES
BHP Inc.

FILM-TO-TAPE TRANSFER EQUIPMENT
Cinema Products Corp.
Evertz Microsystems Ltd.
L-W Athena Inc.
Options International Inc.
Time Logic Inc.

FILTERS AND DELAY LINES
TTE Inc.

FLOOR COVERING STAGES
Eddie Egan & Associates

FRAME SYNCHRONIZERS
Chromatek Scan Process Inc.
Digital Processing Systems Inc.
Leitch/HEDCO - Leitch Inc.
Microtime Inc.
Nova Systems Inc.
Prime Image Inc.

FREQUENCY MEASURING SERVICES
Antenna Concepts Inc.
Burkhardt Monitoring Service
Communications General Corp.
Frequency Measuring Service Inc.
Johnson Measurement Service
Phil McQuatters Frequency Measuring Service
Mid Atlantic Radio Service
Newman-Kees Frequency Measurements
Southwest Frequency Measurements
TrueTime Inc.
Ziehl Electronic Service

FREQUENCY MONITORS
Frequency Measuring Service Inc.
TrueTime Inc.

GENERATORS, ELECTRIC
Auto-Gen Electric Division
E-N-G Mobile Systems Inc.
Spectrum

GENERATORS, SIGNAL
Audio Precision Inc.
Bio-Electronics Inc.
Magni Systems Inc.

RE America Inc.
Video Accessory Corp.

GRAPHICS
Dynatech Cable Products Group
Electric Image Inc.
VCR Network

HDTV EQUIPMENT
ASACA/Shibasoku Corp. of America
Adrienne Electronics Corp.
Canon U.S.A. Inc.
Chromatek Scan Process Inc.
Comark Communications Inc.
LDL Communications Inc.
MERET Optical Communications Inc.
MYAT Inc.
Magni Systems Inc.
O'Connor Engineering Labs
TT Technologies Inc.
Toshiba America Consumer Products
Videomedia Inc.
Wheatstone Corp.

HEADEND SYSTEMS
Alpha Technologies
American Lightwave Systems Inc.
Anixter Cable TV
Harmonic Lightwaves Inc.
Lindsay Specialty Products Ltd.
TV/Com International
VueScan Inc.

HEADS, MAGNETIC FILM, MAGNETIC TAPE, DISK
International Electro-Magnetics Inc.
Sprague Magnetics Inc.
Taber Manufacturing and Engineering Co.

HEADS, REFURBISHING
International Electro-Magnetics Inc.
Sprague Magnetics Inc.
Taber Manufacturing and Engineering Co.

HEADSET AMPLIFIERS
Benchmark Media Systems Inc.
Clear-Com Intercom Systems Inc.
Olesen
R-Columbia Products Co. Inc.

HEADSETS, HEADPHONES
Audio Implements/GKC
Beyerdynamic
Clear-Com Intercom Systems Inc.
Olesen
R-Columbia Products Co. Inc.
RTS Systems
Sacramento Theatrical Lighting
Sennheiser Electronic Corp.
Technical Projects Inc.

HIGH DEFINITION TELEVISION (HDTV)
Comark Communications Inc.
Image Video Ltd.
Television Technology Corp.
Toshiba America Consumer Products

HYDRAULIC BORING EQUIPMENT
TT Technologies Inc.

ISO COUPLERS (AM & FM)
RF Systems

IMAGE ENHANCERS, TV
Intelvideo Inc.

INFRARED TRANSMISSION SYSTEMS
Sennheiser Electronic Corp.

INSTALLATION SERVICES
Anixter Cable TV
B&B Systems Inc.
CTI Installations Inc.
Comark Communications Inc.
Jefferson-Pilot Data Services Inc.
Lakeside Associates Inc.
Mid-State Communications
Newman-Kees Frequency Measurements
Normex Telecom Inc.
Swager Communications Inc.
TT Technologies Inc.
Taber Manufacturing and Engineering Co.
Technet Systems Group

INTERACTIVE TELEVISION
ActivCard Networks Inc.

INTERCOM SYSTEMS
Clear-Com Intercom Systems Inc.
R-Columbia Products Co. Inc.
RTS Systems
Sacramento Theatrical Lighting

JACK PANELS AND ACCESSORIES
ADC Telecommunications Inc.
BGW Systems Inc.
Gepco International Inc.
Nemal Electronics International Inc.
Penny & Giles Inc.

KLYSTRON AMPLIFIERS/LEAD OXIDE VIDICON
Daily Electronics Corp.
Penta Laboratories Inc.

KLYSTRONS
Daily Electronics Corp.
EEV Inc.
Penta Laboratories Inc.
Rush Media Systems
Television Technology Corp.
Thomson Components & Tubes Inc.

LED, VU AND S PANEL METERS
Benchmark Media Systems Inc.
ESE
Print Products International
Selco Products Co.
Sescom Inc.

LENSES, OPTICAL AND CAMERA
Angenieux Corp. of America
Canon U.S.A. Inc.
Innovision Optics
Production Consultants & Equipment
Spatial Technologies Inc.

LIGHTING DESIGN
Devlin Design Group
Imero Fiorentino Associates Inc.
Mole-Richardson Co.
Sacramento Theatrical Lighting
Teatronics International Inc. (TII)

LIGHTING EQUIPMENT
Peter Albrecht Corp.
Antenna and Tower Service Inc.
Bend-A-Lite Flexible Neon
Birns and Sawyer Inc.
Ellis Tower Co. Inc.
Imero Fiorentino Associates Inc.
Frezzolini Electronics Inc.
Full Compass Systems Ltd.
Lowel-Light Mfg Inc.
Mole-Richardson Co.
P.C. & E. Lighting & Grip
Production Consultants & Equipment
Sinar Bron Inc.
Teatronics International Inc. (TII)
James Thomas Engineering
Vantage Lighting Inc.
Westcott

LIGHTNING PROTECTION EQUIPMENT AND SYSTEMS
Alpha Technologies
Bend-A-Lite Flexible Neon
Cortana Corp.
EFI Electronics Corp.
Ellis Tower Co. Inc.
Lightning Master Corp.
Northern Technologies Inc.

LIGHTS, ON-AIR
Apollo Audio Visual/Lighting
Sinar Bron Inc.

LIGHTS, RECORDING
Apollo Audio Visual/Lighting
Sinar Bron Inc.

LIGHTS, STAGE
Apollo Audio Visual/Lighting
Bend-A-Lite Flexible Neon
Mole-Richardson Co.
Olesen
Pro Video & Film Equipment Group
Sacramento Theatrical Lighting

James Thomas Engineering
Vantage Lighting Inc.

LINE CONDITIONING
ADCOUR
Computer Power Inc.
Newark Electronics
Wil-Can Electronics Can Ltd.

LINE SURGE PROTECTORS
ADCOUR
Allied Electronics Inc.
EFI Electronics Corp.
Lightning Master Corp.
MCG Electronics Inc.
Wil-Can Electronics Can Ltd.

LOCKS
Telecrafter Products

LOGGING SYSTEM
Avid Technology Inc.
Datacount Inc.
Evertz Microsystems Ltd.
Imagine Products Inc.
Peter Storer & Associates Inc.

LOUDSPEAKERS AND ACCESSORIES
Auernheimer Labs and Co.
Renkus-Heinz Inc.

MACHINE CONTROL SYSTEMS
ADTEC Productions Inc.
Peter Albrecht Corp.
BASYS Automation Systems Inc.
Leightronix Inc.
MATCO
Media Computing Inc.
Video Data Systems

MASTER CONTROL SWITCHES
Ultra Audio Pixtec

METERS
Benchmark Media Systems Inc.
Weschler Instruments

MICROPHONES AND ACCESSORIES
Beyerdynamic
Karl Heitz Inc.
Professional Sound Corp.
R-Columbia Products Co. Inc.
Sennheiser Electronic Corp.
Sescom Inc.
Shure Brothers Inc.

MICROWAVE
Broadcast Sports Technologies
Direct Broadcast Services Inc.
International Association of Satellite Users & Suppliers
Keystone Communications
NSI
PMI/Producers Management Inc.

MICROWAVE AMPLIFIERS
NUCOMM Inc.
Radio Research Instrument Co. Inc.

MICROWAVE ANTENNAS
Broadcast Sports Technologies
Cablewave Systems Inc.
NSI
NUCOMM Inc.
Radio Research Instrument Co. Inc.
Scala Electronic Corp.

MICROWAVE EQUIPMENT
Broadcast Equipment Sales & Engineering Inc.
Broadcast Sports Technologies
E-N-G Mobile Systems Inc.
NSI
NUCOMM Inc.
Radio Research Instrument Co. Inc.

MICROWAVE TRANSMITTERS
Broadcast Sports Technologies
Channel Master
Emcee Broadcast Products
NUCOMM Inc.
Radio Research Instrument Co. Inc.

MOBILE COMMUNICATIONS
Arrowsmith Technologies Inc.
International Association of Satellite Users & Suppliers
Shook Electronics USA Inc.

MOBILE STUDIO EQUIPMENT
F&F Productions Inc.
Meyer Mobile Productions
Shook Electronics USA Inc.
Telecast Fiber Systems Inc.
Telos Systems

MOBILE UNITS-SALES/RENTAL
PMI/Producers Management Inc.

MOBILE VANS
E-N-G Mobile Systems Inc.
Energy Plus Inc. & Rathbone Energy Systems Inc.
F&F Productions Inc.
Meyer Mobile Productions
Shook Electronics USA Inc.

MODULATORS
Blonder-Tongue Laboratories Inc.
Continental Electronics Corp.

MOLDINGS
CableReady Inc.

MONITOR AMPLIFIERS
BGW Systems Inc.

MONITOR SPEAKERS
Renkus-Heinz Inc.

MONITORS, AUDIO AND VIDEO
Hoodman Corp.
JVC Professional Products Co.
Magni Systems Inc.
Network Video Services Inc.

MONOPOLES
Ellis Tower Co. Inc.
Tower Structures Inc.

MOTION CONTROL EQUIPMENT
Innovision Optics
Richmond Sound Design Ltd.

MOTION PICTURE EQUIPMENT
BHP Inc.
Birns and Sawyer Inc.
Cinema Products Corp.
Alan Gordon Enterprises Inc.
O'Connor Engineering Labs
Production Consultants & Equipment
Spatial Technologies Inc.

MOUNTING PRODUCTS
Display Devices Inc.
Math Associates Inc.

MULTIPLEXERS
AAVS-Advanced Audio Visual Systems
Coastcom
Intraplex Inc.
L-W Athena Inc.
MICOM Communications Corp.

MULTIPLEXING
MICOM Communications Corp.

NOISE REDUCTION SYSTEMS, VIDEO
Intelvideo Inc.
Netwell Noise Control
Nova Systems Inc.

OFFICE EQUIPMENT
Peter Storer & Associates Inc.

OPTICAL STORAGE
DIC Digital

OSCILLATORS
Potomac Instruments Inc.

PANELS
BGW Systems Inc.
Gepco International
Omni Craft Inc.

PASSIVE COMPONENTS
Elcom Systems Inc.
MYAT Inc.
Nemal Electronics International Inc.
Power & Telephone Supply Co.
S.W.R. Inc.
Thomson Components & Tubes Inc.

Equipment Manufacturers, Distributors and Technical Services Subject Index

PATCH CORDS
ADC Telecommunications Inc.
Audio Accessories Inc.
Nemal Electronics International Inc.
Neutrik USA Inc.
Penny & Giles Inc.
Trompeter Electronics Inc.

PAY TV EQUIPMENT AND SERVICES
Scientific-Atlanta Inc.
Video Data Systems

PEDESTALS
CSI-Camera Support International
Diamond Communication Products Inc.

PHASING EQUIPMENT
BES Electronics Ltd.
Kay Industries Inc.

PHONO EQUIPMENT AND E MICRO-TRAK
Telos Systems

PHOTOGRAPHIC EQUIPMENT
Bencher Inc.
Sinar Bron Inc.

PLASTICS AND INJECTION MOLDERS
Plastic Reel Corp. of America
Telecrafter Products

PLUGS AND CONNECTORS
ADC Telecommunications Inc.
Newark Electronics
Selco Products Co.

POLE LINE HARDWARE
Diamond Communication Products Inc.
Power & Telephone Supply Co.

PORTABLE AUDIO MIXERS
Cooper Sound Systems

PORTABLE LIGHT PLANTS
Auto-Gen Electric Division
Mole-Richardson Co.

PORTABLE POWER SUPPLIES
Auto-Gen Electric Division
Frezzolini Electronics Inc.

POSTPRODUCTION SYSTEMS
B&B Systems Inc.
Wavefront Technologies Inc.

POWER METERS
Boonton Electronics Corp.
Print Products International

POWER SUPPLIES AND ACCESSORIES
ADCOUR
Allied Electronics Inc.
Alpha Technologies
Computer Power Inc.
Print Products International
RMS Electronics Inc.

PRE-AMPS, MICROPHONE
Cooper Sound Systems
RTS Systems

PRESSURIZING EQUIPMENT AND ACCESSORIES
Cablewave Systems Inc.

PROFESSIONAL AUDIO EQUIPMENT
AKAI Digital/IMC
AMS Neve PLC
ASACA/Shibasoku Corp. of America
BBE Sound Inc.
Cooper Sound Systems
Crouse-Kimzey Co.
Dolby Laboratories Inc.
Eventide Inc.
Full Compass Systems Ltd.
Lectrosonics Inc.
NVision Inc.
Parsons Audio
Professional Sound Services Inc.
Topham Audio Inc.

PROFESSIONAL RECORDING EQUIPMENT
Cooper Sound Systems
Full Compass Systems Ltd.
Professional Sound Services Inc.
Soundcraft
Soundtracs, PLC
Topham Audio Inc.

PROFESSIONAL SOUND EQUIPMENT
BBE Sound Inc.
Bradley Broadcast Sales
Cooper Sound Systems
Full Compass Systems Ltd.
JBL Professional
Professional Sound Services Inc.
Topham Audio Inc.

PROFESSIONAL VIDEO EQUIPMENT
Advanced Marketing
BDL-Audioscript Ltd.
Brek Connor Group Inc.
Canon U.S.A. Inc.
Full Compass Systems Ltd.
Video Accessory Corp.

PROJECTORS, PROJECTION SYSTEMS
Cramer Production Co.
Display Devices Inc.

PROMOTION PRODUCTS
Communication Graphics Inc.
Faraone Communications
Video Data Systems

PROMPTING EQUIPMENT
BDL-Audioscript Ltd.
Comprompter Inc.
Listec Video Corp.

PUBLIC ADDRESS SYSTEMS
Full Compass Systems Ltd.

PUBLICATIONS, BROADCAST
Broadcast Engineering
Daniels Publishing Group Inc.

RF BRIDGING EQUIPMENT
Potomac Instruments Inc.

RF COAXIAL LOAD RESISTORS
Altronic Research Inc.
Television Technology Corp.
Trompeter Electronics Inc.

RF INSTRUMENTATION & COMPONENTS
Boonton Electronics Corp.
Cambridge Products Corp.
Potomac Instruments Inc.
RE America Inc.
Shively Laboratories Inc.
TTE Inc.

RACKS
Hi-Tech Furnishings
Omni Craft Inc.
Star Case Manufacturing Co. Inc.
Storeel Corp.
Winsted Corp.

RADAR SYSTEMS
Continental Electronics Corp.

RADIO EQUIPMENT
Kahn Communications Inc.

RADIO EQUIPMENT, 2-WAY
Mid-State Communications
R-Columbia Products Co. Inc.

RECEIVERS, SHORTWAVE, AM-FM TV, MULTIPLEX
Harmonic Lightwaves Inc.
Samson Technologies Corp.

RECORDERS, ACCESSORIES
Digital Recorders Inc.
PolyQuick
Stancil Corp.

RECORDERS, AUDIO
AKAI Digital/IMC
Bradley Broadcast Sales
Sono-Mag Corp. (SMC)
Stancil Corp.

RECORDERS, CASSETTE AUDIO LOGGING
Stancil Corp.

RECORDERS, VIDEO
Bowen Broadcast Service Co. Inc.

RECORDING STUDIOS
Acoustic Systems

RECORDING STUDIOS CONSTRUCTION, PREFAB
Acoustic Systems
Cramer Production Co.
Northeastern Communications Concepts Inc.

REELS, MAGNETIC TAPE
National Audio Co. Inc.
Plastic Reel Corp. of America
PolyQuick
Stancil Corp.

REMOTE BROADCAST EQUIPMENT
California Digital Audio Systems Inc.
Marti Electronics Inc.
Network Video Services Inc.
Telos Systems

REMOTE CONTROL
Broadcast Equipment Sales & Engineering Inc.
Broadcast Sports Technologies
Burk Technology
Leightronix Inc.
NSI
Potomac Instruments Inc.

REMOTE CONTROL SYSTEMS FOR TV CAMERAS
Avtech Systems Inc.
CSI-Camera Support International
TE Consulting Inc.

REMOTE CONTROL FOR VTRS
Adrienne Electronics Corp.
Imagine Products Inc.
Leightronix Inc.

RENTAL EQUIPMENT (BROADCAST AND CABLE)
Direct Broadcast Services Inc.
Innovision Optics
Mid-State Communications
PMI/Producers Management Inc.

REPAIR
Bowen Broadcast Service Co. Inc.
Emcee Broadcast Products
Sono-Mag Corp. (SMC)

RESEARCH AND EQUIPMENT
Peter Storer & Associates Inc.

RIGGING SYSTEMS
CTI Installations Inc.

ROBOTICS
Dynatech NewStar

ROUTING SWITCHERS
DYNAIR Electronics Inc.
Leitch/HEDCO - Leitch Inc.
NVision Inc.
Richmond Sound Design Ltd.

SATELLITE ANTENNAS
Antenna Technology
Pinzone Communications Products Inc.
Radio Research Instrument Co. Inc.
Rush Media Systems
Scientific-Atlanta Inc.
Vertex Communications Corp.

SATELLITE AUDIO SYSTEMS
California Digital Audio Systems Inc.
Kingdom Technology
Tectan Inc.

Broadcasting & Cable Yearbook 1994

Equipment Manufacturers, Distributors and Technical Services Subject Index

SATELLITE COMMUNICATIONS SYSTEMS
Antenna Technology
Fiber Options Inc.
International Assoc. of Satellite Users & Suppliers
International Teletext Communications Inc.
Intraplex Inc.
Keystone Communications
MICOM Communications Corp.
Pinzone Communications Products Inc.
Rush Media Systems
Vision Accomplished

SATELLITE NEWS VEHICLE
Direct Broadcast Services Inc.
Keystone Communications
Shook Electronics USA Inc.

SATELLITE RECEIVER
Blonder-Tongue Laboratories Inc.
California Digital Audio Systems Inc.
Keystone Communications

SATELLITE RESALE AND COMMON CARRIERS
GE American Communications Inc.
Keystone Communications

SATELLITE SERVICES
Direct Broadcast Services Inc.
GE American Communications Inc.
InSat Inc.
Keystone Communications
National Transcommunications Ltd.
PMI/Producers Management Inc.

SATELLITE TERMINALS
International Assoc. of Satellite Users & Suppliers

SCAN CONVERTERS
Chromatek Scan Process Inc.
National Transcommunications Ltd.
Video International Development Corp.

SCRAMBLERS, PAY TV
Leitch/HEDCO - Leitch Inc.

SECURITY SURVEILLANCE
Avtech Systems Inc.

SECURITY SYSTEMS
Avtech Systems Inc.

SERVICE, REPAIR AND MAINTENANCE
Bowen Broadcast Service Co. Inc.
CTI Installations Inc.
E-Z Trench Mfg. Co. Inc.
Newman-Kees Frequency Measurements
Normex Telecom Inc.
Teletech Inc.

SIGNAL GENERATORS
AAVS-Advanced Audio Visual Systems
DSC Laboratories
Digital Processing Systems Inc.
Magni Systems Inc.
Tektronix Inc.
Video Accessory Corp.

SIGNAL PROCESSOR
Amek/TAC U.S. Operations
BBE Sound Inc.
Nova Systems Inc.

SOUND EQUIPMENT
Audio Services Corp.
Wireworks Corp.

SOUND MIXERS
Amek/TAC U.S. Operations
Soundcraft
Soundtracs, PLC
Wheatstone Corp.

SOUND RECORDING EQUIPMENT
AKAI Digital/IMC
Audio Services Corp.
Bradley Broadcast Sales
JBL Professional
Quality Video Supply
Soundtracs, PLC

SOUND SYSTEMS
JBL Professional

SPEAKERS
JBL Professional

SPECIAL EFFECTS, AUDIOVISUAL
Electric Image Inc.
P.C. & E. Lighting & Grip
Richmond Sound Design Ltd.
Spatial Technologies Inc.
Wavefront Technologies Inc.

SPECIAL EFFECTS GENERATORS
Abekas Video Systems Inc.
ECHOLAB Inc.
JVC Professional Products Co.

SPECTRUM ANALYZERS
Print Products International
Tektronix Inc.

SPLICING EQUIPMENT, FILM, TAPE
PolyQuick

STANDARDS CONVERTERS
Prime Image Inc.

STANDBY POWER
ADCOUR
Auto-Gen Electric Division
Computer Power Inc.
RMS Electronics Inc.

STANDS, COMPUTER, A/V, TV ETC.
Winsted Corp.

STANDS, MICROPHONE
Sennheiser Electronic Corp.

STATION AUTOMATION
American Broadcast Systems Inc.
Enterprise Systems Group Inc.
Media Computing Inc.

STATUS MONITORING
Superior Electronics Group Inc.

STEREO EQUIPMENT, AUDIO
FM Systems Inc.

STEREO GENERATION EQUIPMENT
Kahn Communications Inc.
Modulation Sciences Inc.

STILL STORES
Brek Connor Group Inc.
Inscriber Character Generator

STILL STORES-DIGITAL
Digital Processing Systems Inc.
Leitch/HEDCO - Leitch Inc.

STORAGE FACILITIES
Hollywood Vaults Inc.
Major Engineering

STUDIO EQUIPMENT
Advanced Marketing
Peter Albrecht Corp.
BES Electronics Ltd.
Bradley Broadcast Sales
Crouse-Kimzey Co.
Parsons Audio
Spectrum

STUDIO FACILITIES
BES Electronics Ltd.
Communications Design Associates Inc.
Devlin Design Group
Lakeside Associates Inc.
Technet Systems Group

STUDIO FURNITURE
Arrakis Systems Inc.
Audio Broadcast Group
Devlin Design Group
Murphy Studio Furniture
Northeastern Communications Concepts Inc.
Pacific Recorders & Engineering Corp.

STUDIO SETS, CUSTOM
Devlin Design Group

SUB-CARRIER GENERATORS
Marti Electronics Inc.
Tectan Inc.

SWITCHES AND ACCESSORIES
Selco Products Co.
Switchcraft Inc.

SWITCHING EQUIPMENT, AUDIO
NVision Inc.
Tektronix Inc.
OptoDigital Design Inc.

SWITCHING EQUIPMENT, VIDEO
Bio-Electronics Inc.
ECHOLAB Inc.
OptoDigital Design Inc.
Video Accessory Corp.

TV EQUIPMENT
Larcan Inc.
POA/Paul Olivier & Associates Inc.

TAPE, AUDIO AND VIDEO
DIC Digital
Reproduction Technologies Inc.

TAPE CONDITIONER, AUDIO/VIDEO
Data Security Inc.

TAPE DUPLICATORS
Cramer Production Co.

TAPE EQUIPMENT AND ACCESSORIES
Reproduction Technologies Inc.

TAPE HEADS, AUDIO
International Electro-Magnetics Inc.
Reproduction Technologies Inc.

TAPE RECORDERS
Audio Services Corp.
Reproduction Technologies Inc.
Sono-Mag Corp. (SMC)

TELECINE
L-W Athena Inc.
Options International Inc.

TELECOMMUNICATIONS PRODUCTS
ADC Telecommunications Inc.
Augat Communications Products Inc.
Diamond Communication Products Inc.
Dolby Laboratories Inc.
EDX Engineering Inc.
First Pacific Networks
Intraplex Inc.
MICOM Communications Corp.
Power & Telephone Supply Co.
Telecrafter Products

TELECONFERENCING
American Lightwave Systems Inc.
C-COR Electronics Inc.
PMI/Producers Management Inc.

TELEMETRY TRANSMISSION LINKS
American Lightwave Systems Inc.
First Pacific Networks
Marti Electronics Inc.
Mid-State Communications

TELEPHONE CONTROL SYSTEMS
First Pacific Networks

TELEPHONE INTERFACE EQUIPMENT
First Pacific Networks
Telos Systems

TELEPROMPTERS
BDL-Audioscript Ltd.
Blue Feather Co.
Dynatech NewStar
Telescript Inc.

TEST EQUIPMENT
AAVS-Advanced Audio Visual Systems
ASACA/Shibasoku Corp. of America
Allied Electronics Inc.
Audio Precision Inc.
Boonton Electronics Corp.
Fluke Corp.
Holaday Industries Inc.

Equipment Manufacturers, Distributors and Technical Services Subject Index

International Assn. of Satellite Users & Suppliers
Link Electronics Inc.
Magni Systems Inc.
Modulation Sciences Inc.
Print Products International
RE America Inc.
Shallco Inc.
Superior Electronics Group Inc.
Tektronix Inc.

TIME BASE CORRECTORS

Broadcast Electronic Services
Prime Image Inc.
Tektronix Inc.
TrueTime Inc.

TIME CODE EQUIPMENT

Adrienne Electronics Corp.
Bio-Electronics Inc.
Chrono-Log Corp.
ESE
Evertz Microsystems Ltd.
Imagine Products Inc.
TrueTime Inc.

TIMERS

Chrono-Log Corp.
ESE

TOOLS AND ACCESSORIES

Anixter Cable TV
Cable Prep
Gilbert Engineering Co. Inc.
Just Drop Inc.
Milestek Inc.
Ripley Co., Cablematic Division
Telecrafter Products

TOWER DESIGN, MANUFACTURE

Aluma Tower Co. Inc.
Central Tower Inc.
LeBlanc Communications Inc.
Microflect Co. Inc.
Fred A. Nudd Corp.
Pi-Rod Inc.
Tower Specialties Inc.
Tower Structures Inc.
Utility Tower Co.

TOWER ERECTION

CTI Installations Inc.
Central Tower Inc.
ERI Installations Inc.
Lakeside Associates Inc.
LeBlanc Communications Inc.
Microflect Co. Inc.
Technet Systems Group
Teletech Inc.
Tower Specialties Inc.
Utility Tower Co.

TOWER INSPECTIONS

Central Tower Inc.
ERI Installations Inc.
LeBlanc Communications Inc.
Lightning Master Corp.
Microflect Co. Inc.
Fred A. Nudd Corp.
Teletech Inc.
Tower Network Services
Tower Specialties Inc.
Utility Tower Co.

TOWER MAINTENANCE

Central Tower Inc.
ERI Installations Inc.
LeBlanc Communications Inc.
Microflect Co. Inc.
Teletech Inc.
Tower Network Services
Tower Specialties Inc.

TOWER OBSTRUCTION LIGHTING AND CONTROLS

Antenna and Tower Service Inc.
ERI Installations Inc.
Hughey & Phillips Inc.
Microflect Co. Inc.
Racal-Decca Canada Ltd.
Tower Network Services

TOWER STRUCTURAL ANALYSIS

Central Tower Inc.
ERI Installations Inc.
LeBlanc Communications Inc.
Microflect Co. Inc.
Fred A. Nudd Corp.
Tower Network Services
Tower Specialties Inc.
Tower Structures Inc.

TOWERS, ACCESSORIES AND SERVICE

Antenna and Tower Service Inc.
Central Tower Inc.
ERI Installations Inc.
Fred A. Nudd Corp.
Racal-Decca Canada Ltd.
Swager Communications Inc.
Toner Cable Equipment Inc.
Tower Network Services
Tower Specialties Inc.
Tower Structures Inc.
United Ropeworks U.S.A. Inc./Phillystran

TRANSCODERS

Intelvideo Inc.

TRANSFORMERS

Allied Electronics Inc.
Computer Power Inc.
Neutrik USA Inc.
TTE Inc.

TRANSISTORS AND ICS

Richardson Electronics Ltd.

TRANSMISSION LINES

MYAT Inc.
Scala Electronic Corp.

TRANSMITTER SYSTEMS

Acrodyne Industries Inc.
C-COR Electronics Inc.
Continental Electronics Corp.
Emcee Broadcast Products
Energy-Onix Broadcast Equipment Co. Inc.
Math Associates Inc.
National Transcommunications Ltd.
Technet Systems Group

TRANSMITTERS

Acrodyne Industries Inc.
Continental Electronics Corp.
Energy-Onix Broadcast Equipment Co. Inc.
MERET Optical Communications Inc.
Samson Technologies Corp.

TRANSMITTERS, RADIO

Audio Broadcast Group
BEXT Inc.
Broadcast Electronics Inc.
Broadcast Equipment Sales & Engineering Inc.
Continental Electronics Corp.
Crown International
Digital Recorders Inc.
Energy-Onix Broadcast Equipment Co. Inc.
Nautel
Thomcast

TRANSMITTERS, TV

Acrodyne Industries Inc.
American Laser Systems Inc.
BEXT Inc.
Comark Communications Inc.
Emcee Broadcast Products
Larcan Inc.
Rush Media Systems
Thomcast

TRAVELING WAVE TUBES

Daily Electronics Corp.
Penta Laboratories Inc.
Thomson Components & Tubes Inc.

TRIPODS, PEDESTALS AND ACCESSORIES

Birns and Sawyer Inc.
CSI-Camera Support International
Diamond Communication Products Inc.
Just Drop Inc.
O'Connor Engineering Labs
Pro Video & Film Equipment Group
Quickset International Inc.
Sinar Bron Inc.

TUBES AND TUBE REBUILDING

Avtech Systems Inc.
Daily Electronics Corp.
Penta Laboratories Inc.
Richardson Electronics Ltd.
Thomson Components & Tubes Inc.
Vacuum Tube Industries Inc.

TURNKEY STUDIO SYSTEMS

Arrakis Systems Inc.
Audio Broadcast Group
Avid Technology Inc.
Lakeside Associates Inc.
Media Touch Systems Inc.
National Transcommunications Ltd.
Newman-Kees Frequency Measurements
POA/Paul Olivier & Associates Inc.
Pacific Recorders & Engineering Corp.
Technet Systems Group

TURNTABLES

Innovision Optics

USED BROADCAST EQUIPMENT

Pro Video & Film Equipment Group
System Associates

VBI EQUIPMENT

Norpak Corp.

VTR MODIFICATIONS

Specialized Communications

VACUUM CAPACITORS

Penta Laboratories Inc.
Richardson Electronics Ltd.

VANS AND MOBILE UNITS

E-N-G Mobile Systems Inc.
F&F Productions Inc.
PMI/Producers Management Inc.
Shook Electronics USA Inc.

VIDEO ACCESSORIES

Channel Master
PolyQuick
Quality Video Supply
Video Accessory Corp.

VIDEO CHARACTER GENERATORS

Brek Connor Group Inc.
Chrono-Log Corp.
Display Systems International Inc.
Dynatech Cable Products Group
Evertz Microsystems Ltd.
Great Lakes Data Systems Inc.
Inscriber Character Generator
Quality Video Supply
Video Data Systems

VIDEO DELAY LINES

Eventide Inc.

VIDEO DELAY SUBSYSTEMS

TTE Inc.

VIDEO DISC RECORDERS

Network Video Services Inc.

VIDEO EDITING EQUIPMENT

Broadcast Electronic Services
Editing Technologies Corp.
Imagine Products Inc.
Quality Video Supply
Radio Resources & Services
VRI (Video Rentals Inc.)
Videomedia Inc.

VIDEO EFFECTS GENERATORS AND ACCESSORIES

ECHOLAB Inc.
Microtime Inc.

VIDEO EQUIPMENT

DYNAIR Electronics Inc.
Quality Video Supply
Radio Resources & Services
Spatial Technologies Inc.
Spectrum
VRI (Video Rentals Inc.)

VIDEO GRAPHICS SYSTEMS

Bencher Inc.
Display Systems International Inc.

Electric Image Inc.
Wavefront Technologies Inc.

VIDEO PROCESSING EQUIPMENT

Chromatek Scan Process Inc.
Digital Processing Systems Inc.
Nova Systems Inc.

VIDEO PROJECTION SYSTEM, LARGE SCREEN

Cramer Production Co.

VIDEO ROUTING SWITCHERS

Adrienne Electronics Corp.
Advanced Marketing
DYNAIR Electronics Inc.
Digital Processing Systems Inc.
Quality Video Supply
TE Consulting Inc.

VIDEO SPECIAL EFFECTS SYSTEMS

ECHOLAB Inc.
Microtime Inc.
Wavefront Technologies Inc.

VIDEO TAPE RECORDERS

JVC Professional Products Co.
Toshiba America Consumer Products
VRI (Video Rentals Inc.)

VIDEO TAPE RECORDERS, PORTABLE

JVC Professional Products Co.
VRI (Video Rentals Inc.)

VIDEO TAPE SUPPLIERS

DIC Digital

WAVE GUIDES

MYAT Inc.
S.W.R. Inc.

WEATHER DATA DISPLAY SYSTEMS (WDDS)

Advanced Designs Corp.
Alden Electronics Inc.
Norpak Corp.
Video Data Systems

WEATHER RADAR AND GRAPHIC DISPLAYS, COLOR

Advanced Designs Corp.
Alden Electronics Inc.
Norpak Corp.

WIRELESS MICROPHONES AND COMMUNICATIONS SYSTEMS

American Laser Systems Inc.
Beyerdynamic
COMTEK Inc.
Clear-Com Intercom Systems Inc.
Lectrosonics Inc.
Professional Sound Services Inc.
R-Columbia Products Co. Inc.
Murry Rosenblum Sound Assoc. Inc.
Sennheiser Electronic Corp.
Topham Audio Inc.

WIRING PRODUCTS

Wireworks Corp.

Equipment Manufacturers and Distributors

A

AAA Printed Circuits Inc. 827 Black Oak Ridge Rd., Wayne, N.J. 07470. (201) 835-2765. FAX: (201) 835-2768. A. Sutaria, chmn; F.J. LaManna, admin exec.
Printed circuit bds.

ADC Telecommunications Inc. 4900 W. 78th St., Minneapolis 55435. (612) 938-8080. FAX: (612) 946-3292. William J. Cadogan, pres/CEO/COO.
Audio & video cable termination & circuit access equipment; products for optic access & transport integrated telephone/video over fiber, access & cross-connect of copper & fiber infrastructure.

ADCOUR. 18 Billings St., Sharon, Mass. 02067. (617) 784-8123. FAX: (617) 784-5563. Richard Jacobs, pres.
Batteries, chgrs, power supplies & power conditioning.

ADSCO Line Products. 100 Jackson at Comerce, Houston 77002; Box 1498, Houston 77251. (713) 223-1179; (800) 247-6484. FAX: (713) 223-5529. Randolph H. Smith, pres; A.B. "Barry" Wallace, VP.
Line hardware for CATV: guy strand, messengers, lashing wire/rods, formed groups/dead-ends & related line hardware.

ADTEC Productions Inc. 408 Russell St., Nashville, Tenn. 37206. (615) 256-6619. FAX: (615) 256-6593. Ron Johnson, dir mktg.
Jacksonville, Fla. 32216: 11315-2 St. Johns Industrial Pkwy. (904) 928-9604. Kevin Ancelin, VP opns.
Products offered: Loc origination controllers & systems, coml insertion controllers & systems, net delay recording.

AEG Bayly Inc. 167 Hunt St., Ajax, Ont., Canada L1S 1P6. (905) 683-8200. FAX: (905) 683-0186. Doug Carl, pres; Jerry Pullan, dir mktg.
Somerville, N.J. 08876-1269: Rt. 22 & Orr Dr. (908) 722-9800. Rainer Zopfy.
Solid state FM transmitters to 5 kw, automatic coaxial changeover units, sw transmitters.

AF Associates Inc. 100 Stonehurst Ct., Northvale, N.J. 07647. (201) 767-1200. FAX: (201) 784-8637. Tom Canavan, VP/gen mgr; Meryl E. Altman, VP systems; Marc Bressack, dir sls/cable TV systems.
Turnkey TV systems for bcst, cable & postprod facilities; RADAMEC EPO robotic camera systems.

Digital Audio Workstation
50 Simultaneous Stereo Segment Playback
2-Dimensional Project Creation - No Tracks!
-110dB Noise Floor
Turn To: **Micro Technology Unlimited**

AKG Acoustics Inc. 1525 Alvarado St., San Leandro, Calif. 94577. (510) 351-3500. FAX: (510) 351-0500. David M. Angress, VP sls & mktg; David Roudebush, corp mktg mgr.
Appleton, Wis. 54914: 1806 N. Blossom Dr. (414) 794-0044. Jeff Radke, rgnl mgr.
Bristol, Conn. 06010: 181-21 Sherbrooke St. (203) 589-4334. David "DJ" Bierut, eastern rgnl sls mgr.
Rsch, dev & mfg of microphones, headphones, accessories & professional audio products.

ALTA Group Inc. (Quanta Corp.) 180 Wright Brothers Dr., Suite 670, Salt Lake City 84116. (801) 328-8872. FAX: (801) 328-3668. Mark Siegel, western rgnl sls mgr.
Scotch Plains, N.J. 07076: 539 Willow Ave. (908) 322-6972. Michael Molinaro, eastern rgnl sls mgr.
Digital video prod systems including; TBC, digital & prod effects, image enhancement & audio/video switching.

AMCO Engineering Co. 3801 Rose St., Schiller Park, Ill. 60176. (708) 671-6670. FAX: (708) 671-9469. Edwin V. Anderson, pres; Joseph A. Mack, VP; Thomas Anderson, gen mgr; Tom Ligman, natl sls mgr.
Communication consoles; monitoring & computer desks, computer desktop cabinets, EMI cabinet; blowers & fans.

AMI Publishing. Box 35, 20 Wellington St. E., Aurora, Ont., Canada L4G 1H0. (905) 771-3800. FAX: (905) 853-5096. Shelagh Rogers, publisher; Barry Cobus, VP mktg & sls.
Several publications for companies involved in audio, AV, bcst, computers, film, video & mus.

AMS NEVE PLC. Billington Rd., Burnley, Lancashire, U.K. BB11 5ES. 44-282-457011. FAX: 44-282-39542. David Sim, head of sls.
Providing analog & digital editing, & mixers for the bcst film & mus recording industries.

ANTEC Communication Services. 2850 W. Gulf Rd., Rolling Meadows, Ill. 60008. (800) 252-2288; (708) 437-5777 FAX: (708) 439-8531. Marty Ingram, pres; Pete Wagener, VP.
Norcross, Ga. 30071: 2100-A Nancy Hanks Dr. (404) 840-7901. FAX: (404) 840-9702. Bob Santini, mgr. (Atlanta office.)
Bensenville, Ill. 60106: 888 Thomas Dr. (800) 544-5368; (708) 350-7788. FAX: (708) 350-7840. Pete Wagener, mgr.
Englewood, Colo. 80111: 8101 E. Prentice Ave., Suite 210. (303) 740-8949. FAX: (303) 740-9420. Matt Endsley, mgr. (Denver office.)
Iron Mountain, Mich. 49801: 1023 River Ave. (800) 624-8353; (906) 774-4111. FAX: (906) 774-6287. Marion Gammey, mgr.
Federal Way, Wash. 98003: 33710 9th Ave. S. (800) 438-9290; (206) 838-9552. FAX: (206) 838-9644. Michael Bridiges, mgr. (Seattle office.)
Wharton, N.J. 07885: 321 Richard Mine Rd. (800) 631-9603; (201) 328-0980. FAX: (201) 328-1267. John Dellasandro, mgr.
Irving, Tex. 75062: 102 Decker Ct., Suite 203. (800) 231-5006; (214) 717-4933. FAX: (214) 717-9722. Brent Viken, mgr. (Dallas office.)
Santa Ana, Calif. 92705: Bldg. F. 1936 Deere Ave., 219. (800) 854-0443; (714) 757-1630. FAX: (714) 757-1203. Rick Fahilga, mgr.
Earth stns, headend & distribution systems, converters & pay products, cables, hardware & fiber optic systems.

A.R.T.-Applied Research & Technology Inc. 215 Tremont St., Rochester, N.Y. 14608. (716) 436-2720. FAX: (716) 436-3942. Philip Betette, pres; Jim Bonis, mgr sls & mktg.
Digital audio signal processors & enhancement devices.

ARTI. 307 Orchard City Dr., Suite 204, Campbell, Calif. 95008. (408) 374-9044. FAX: (408) 374-3623. Michael Short, pres.
Media control net for computer control of videotape recorders, laser discs, switchers, cameras, etc.

A & S Case Co. Inc. 5260 Vineland Ave., North Hollywood, Calif. 91601. (818) 509-5920. FAX: (818) 509-1397. William B. Berry, pres; Kenneth W.E. Berry, treas.
Reusable shipping cases; computer & musical instrument cases.

ASACA/Shibasoku Corp. of America. 12509 Beatrice St., Los Angeles 90066. (310) 827-7144. FAX: (310) 306-1382. Teresa Baker, natl sls & mktg mgr; John Clemens, natl sls & engrg mgr.
Audio analyzers, high resolution auto set-up monitors, decoders, encoders, envelope delay measuring sets, erasable rewritable magneto optical audio files & still stores, GCR & HDTV equipment, high resolution auto set up monitors, generators, video cart systems & video noise meters.

ASC Audio Video Corp. 3816 Burbank Blvd., Burbank, Calif. 91505. (818) 843-7004. FAX: (818) 842-8945. Mark Chatinsky, pres; Stan Goldstein, opns mgr; Manferd Klemme, dir mktg.
Manufacturer of CASE video editing systems & the VIRTUAL recorder. Distributor of audio, video & computer products related to off-line video editing.

ATI-Audio Technologies Inc. 328 Maple Ave., Horsham, Pa. 19044. (215) 443-0330. FAX: (215) 443-0394. Samuel B. Wenzel, pres; Edward M. Mullin, VP.
Bcst audio, mic, line, distribution, interface & turntable amplifiers, power amps, on-air consoles & audio processors.

AVAB America Inc. 967 Howard St., San Francisco 94103. (415) 421-3562. FAX: (415) 777-2788. Hans J. Lau, pres.
Manufacturer of studio & theatrical lighting equipment; lighting controllers, dimmers, fixtures; distributor for Emil Niethammer luminaries.

AVCOM of Va. Inc. 500 Southlake Blvd., Richmond, Va. 23236. (804) 794-2500. FAX: (804) 794-8284. R. Andrew Hatfield, pres; Peter J. Gaglio, VP opns; Linda Abshire, sls mgr.
Manufacturer of portable analyzers, net analyzers, microwave sweep generators, satellite receivers, microwave video links & microwave accessories.

AVO Biddle Instruments. 510 Township Line Rd., Blue Bell, Pa. 19422. (215) 646-9200. FAX: (215) 643-2670. Paul Ochadlick, gen mgr.
Cable fault-locating equipment & other electrical testing instruments.

AVPC - Atlanta Video Production Center Inc. 1570 N. Side Dr. N.W., Suite 240, Atlanta 30318. (404) 355-3398; (404) 352-2958 edit. FAX: (404) 350-0302. Joseph Gora, pres.
Bcst video prod, postprod equipment & svcs; location EFP & multi-camera systems, crews & specialists.

AVX. 3900 Electronics Dr., Raleigh, N.C. 27604. (919) 878-6476. FAX: (919) 878-6218. Gary Burnett, purchasing; Richard Peoples, per mgr.
Glass, video delay subsystems, chroma keyers, borderliners, aperature correctors & custom subsystems.

Abekas Video Systems Inc. 101 Galveston Dr., Redwood City, Calif. 94063. (415) 369-5111. FAX: (415) 369-4777. William "Pete" Mountanos, pres/CEO; Rahoul K. Seth, exec VP/CFO; David N. Mayfield, VP opns.
Jericho, N.Y. 11753: 500 N. Broadway, Suite 101. (516) 939-9000. Ben Jamison, rgnl mgr.
Atlanta 30340: 3180 Presidential Dr., Suite G. (404) 451-0637. Earl Higgins, rgnl mgr.
Mount Prospect, Ill. 60056: 479 N. Business Ctr. Dr., Suite 107. (708) 699-9400. Gary Schutte, midwest rgnl mgr.
Dallas 75240: 6730 LBJ Fwy., Suite 2175. (214) 385-4544. Tom Hooper, southcentral rgnl mgr.
Burbank, Calif. 91505: 3500 W. Olive Ave., Suite 990. (818) 955-6446. Michael Bravin, sls.
Redwood City, Calif. 94063: 101 Galveston Dr. (415) 369-6791. Joe Falcone, rgnl mgr.
Digital special effects systems, disk recorders, still stores, character generators, video switchers & integrated prod systems. Designs, manufactures & markets state-of-the-art digital video products.

Abroyd Communications Ltd. 662 Colby Dr., Waterloo, Ont., Canada N2V 1A2. (519) 746-1743. FAX: (519) 746-0091. Albert J. Nightingale, P.E./pres; John T. Verlis, P.E./VP; Steve Williams, sls.
Designs & manufactures communication towers; manufactures & sells Lightning Dissipation Arrays & Chem-Rods from LEC.

Accom Inc. 1490 O'Brien Dr., Menlo Park, Calif. 94025. (415) 328-3818. FAX: (415) 327-2511. Junaid Sheikh, chmn.
Budd Lake, N.J. 07828: 17 Sunset Dr. (201) 691-7507. Ray Ostrom, rgnl mgr.
Elgin, Ill. 60123: 964 Glenmore Ln. (708) 742-6300. Steve Lose, rgnl mgr.
Palmdale, Calif. 93551: 41160 Summitview Way. (805) 722-4499. Mark Pinkel, rgnl mgr.
Digital video equipment for postprod.

Broadcasting & Cable Yearbook 1994
H-12

Three-Way Access To The Digital World.

Whether it's digital audio, digital video or machine control between VTRs and edit controllers, ADC's digital patch panels provide for the access, monitor and test of digital circuits throughout your studio or station.

Digital Video Panels
All ADC coax video jack panels are designed for composite analog, HDTV and serial digital video circuits, including D1, D2 and D3.

Digital Audio Panels
ADC's fully-normalled digital jackfields patch AES/EBU signals up to 100 meters. High-speed, data-grade cabling assures error-free transfer of the digital signal. The patented QCP split cylinder contact ensures gas-tight connections that can be reconfigured up to 200 times.

Machine Control Panels
ADC Patch By Exception bays allow you to cost-effectively increase the number of ports available for your edit controllers and handle data applications up to 20 Mb/s, including 10 Mb/s Ethernet, T1 and ISDN.

For more information on ensuring the quality of your digital signal with ADC's full line of digital patching products, call us at **1 800 726-4266.**

ADC Telecommunications

Equipment Manufacturers and Distributors

Accurate Sound Corp. 3475A Edison Way, Menlo Park, Calif. 94025. (415) 365-2843. FAX: (415) 365-3057. Ronald M. Newdoll, pres.
  High-speed tape duplicating & recording equipment; cassette audio logging recorders; audio & videotape conditioners; audio recorders.

Accu-Weather Inc. 619 W. College Ave., State College, Pa. 16801. (814) 237-0309. FAX: (814) 238-1339. Dr. Joel N. Myers, pres; Sheldon Levine, natl sls mgr.
  Pinpoint customized forecasts, graphics, satellite delivery, graphics computers, FirstWarn™ warning crawl system, Accu-Data data base.

Acoustic Systems. Box 3610, Austin, Tex. 78764. (800) 749-1460. FAX: (512) 444-2282. Jeff Schmitt, pres; John Hastings, dir mkt; David Michalek, controller; Chris Rowland, sls mgr.
  Prefabricated modular enclosures for construction of modular bcst & recording studios.

Acrodyne Industries Inc. 516 Township Line Rd., Blue Bell, Pa. 19422. (215) 542-7000; (800) 523-2596. FAX: (215) 540-5837. Marshall C. Smith, pres; Dan Traynor, VP/gen mgr; Timothy Hulick, VP engrg; Joe Wozniak, mgr sls & mktg.
  VHF & UHF transmitters & trans, 1 watt to 60 kw for domestic & international standards.

ActivCard Networks Inc. 245 Park Ave., 44th Fl., New York 10167. (212) 692-3535. FAX: (212) 661-5024. Ken Fineman, pres/CEO.
  Issy-Les-Moulineaux, France 92130: 2 Rue Maurice Hartmann. (011-331) 46-38-7373. Gilles Kremer, dir mktg.
  Interactive TV.

Adams-Smith. 34 Tower St., Hudson, Mass. 01749. (508) 562-3801. FAX: (508) 568-0404. S. Lake, prod specialist.
  Cambridge, U.K. CB7 4UB: Adams-Smith UK Ltd., Potter Group Center, Queen Adelaide. (353) 668109. (353) 668110. D. Godsmark.
  Burbank, Calif. 91506-2209: Adams-Smith Calif., 927 B Olive Ave. (818) 840-9588. FAX: (818) 840-0967. Rick Austin.
  Audio-for-video editing, tape synchronizing & time code equipment for prod & postprod.

AdExpress Co. 222 Sutter St., San Francisco 94109. (415) 274-4594. FAX: (510) 274-4545. Gerald S. Steele, pres; Thomas J. Stump, VP opns.
  Provides delivery system for ad insertion; traffic mgmt, verification & billing software for cable adv sls opns.

Adrienne Electronics Corp. 11994 Marjon Dr., Nevada City, Calif. 95959. (916) 265-8288. FAX: (916) 265-3805. Bruce Waggoner, pres.
  Small routing switchers, time code products & machine control products.

Advance Products Co. Inc. Box 2178, Wichita, Kan. 67201. (316) 263-4231. FAX: (316) 263-4245. Annette Schoenthaler, rgnl sls mgr.
  Mobile projector; TV & video tables & cabinets.

Advanced Audio Visual Systems (AAVS). 3200 Sencore Dr., Sioux Falls, S.D. 57107. (800) 769-2287; (605) 339-0100. FAX: (605) 335-6379. Doug Bowden, pres/CEO.
  Montreuil, France 93100: 222-226 rue de Rosny. (33) 1-48-57-27-21-64. David Abel, export dir.
  Brussels, Belgium 1080: 50 Koolmynen Kaai. (32) 2-4263788. Bill Finnerty, mktg specialist.
  Products offered: S310 Digital Video Analyzer; ACCESS 2000 multiplexer - a real-time electronic prog guide.

Advanced Designs Corp. 804 N. College Ave., Bloomington, Ind. 47404. (812) 333-1922. FAX: (812) 333-2030. Martin Riess, pres.
  DOPRAD III doppler radar system, weather data display system (WDDS), storm path analyzer.

Advanced Digital Imaging. 1250 N. Lakeview Ave., Unit O, Anaheim, Calif. 92807. (714) 779-7772. FAX: (714) 779-7773. Scott Auchmoody, pres.
  MacVAC video animation controller & the ADI digital disk recorder with RGB & DI in/out.

Advanced Marketing. Box 97, Redwood City, Calif. 94064. (415) 365-3944. FAX: (415) 365-1630. Frank Santucci, own.
  Sacramento, Calif. 95831: 1010B Florin Rd., Suite 233. (916) 392-6826. FAX: (916) 392-6907. Laurie Lewis, rgnl mgr.

D1/D2 encoders/decoders, audio/video DAs, analog encoders/decoders, routing switchers, ultimate, cameras, DVE, TBCs/synchronizers, disc recorders.

Advanced Research Technology Inc. 404 Apollo Ct., Richardson, Tex. 75081. (214) 644-1331. Roy I. Edenson, pres.
  TV bcst & TV products, systems, instrumentation & consulting svcs.

Advanced Videotech Corp. 1840 County Line Rd., Suite 201, Huntingdon Valley, Pa. 19006. (800) 233-0013; (215) 322-4600. FAX: (215) 322-4606. Stephen Rade, pres; Susan Rade, VP.
  All 2-way radio equipment.

Advent Communications Ltd. Alma Rd., Chesham, Bucks, England HP5 3HE. 44 494 774400. FAX: 44 494 791127. S. McGuinness, dir.
  Satellite systems; flyaway, transportable & fixed. Satellite communications products & equipment for TV, radio & communications.

Aerosonic Ltd. Unit 9, St. Giles Technology Park, Pool Rd., Newton, Powys, SY16 3AJ, Wales, UK. 0686 627355. FAX: 0686 627494. TELEX: 35851 CYM-EA G. James H. Steynor, mgng dir; Richard A. Amey, dir.
  Videotape quality assurance equipment including open reel VHS testers & multimedia signal evaluator.

Akai Digital/IMC. 1316 E. Lancaster, Fort Worth, Tex. 76102. (817) 336-5114. FAX: (817) 870-1271. Tommy Moore, pres; Tom Linklater, VP electronics; Ron Franklin, dir digital sls; James Martin, mkt mgr; Mike Roberts, AKI product mgr.
  Digital audio recording & editing systems.

Aladdin Media Products. 2 Research Dr., Branford, Conn. 06405. (203) 488-4267. FAX: (203) 483-7585.
  Custom mic flags & accessories.

Alamar Electronics USA Inc. 489 Division St., Campbell, Calif. 95008. (408) 866-9373. FAX: (408) 866-4367. Douglas A. Hurrell, pres; Frank J. Kovary, sls mgr; Frank Alioto, dir mktg & sls; Lynn Williams, engrg mgr.
  Wyomissing, Pa. 19610: 13 Kevin Ct. (215) 678-8711. FAX: (215) 678-8784. Frank J. Kovary, sls mgr.
  Stn automation: master control, net delay progmg, satellite resource mgmt, facility media data base mgmt, newsroom automation & remote machine control.

Peter Albrecht Corp. 6250 Industrial Ct., Greendale, Wis. 53129-2432. (414) 421-6630. FAX: (414) 421-9091. Paul G. Birkle, pres/CEO/chmn of bd; T.C. Ziolkowski, gen mgr/VP/sec.
  Motorized studio battens, plaks & other rigging systems. Cyclorama track & curtain systems designed & installed.

Alden Electronics Inc. 40 Washington St., Westboro, Mass. 01581. (508) 366-8851. Michael J. Porreca, weather systems sls mgr; Kevin A. Porreca, mgr coml weather division.

Color weather radar & graphic displays, facsimile weather chart recorders, satellite picture receivers, distribution of weather info via satellite.

Alesis. 3630 Holdrege Ave., Los Angeles 90016. (310) 558-4530. FAX: (310) 836-9192. Allen Wald, VP adv prom.
  Digital tape recording system, mixing consoles, digital & analog signal processing, amplification, drum machines, keyboards.

Alexander Batteries. Box 1508, 1511 S. Garfield Pl., Mason City, Iowa 50401. (800) 247-1821; (515) 423-8955. FAX: (515) 423-1644. Steve Alexandres, pres; John Alexandres, VP.
  McHenry, Ill. 60050: Box 365. 4410 W. Elm St. (815) 344-0666. Susan Grandt.
  Morrow, Ga. 30260: Box 220, 1235 E. Commerce Rd. (404) 968-4087. Ron Eggleston.
  Middlesex, N.J. 08846: Box 347, 283 Lincoln Blvd. (908) 271-5880. Jim Sapp.
  Minneapolis 55436: Box 35603. (612) 941-7697. Paul Ohlin. Paul Ohlin Sales Co.
  Denver 80223: 2020 Oneida St., No. 204. (303) 758-3051. Stan Reubenstein. Denver Aurora Marketing Co.
  San Diego 92128: Box 28880. (619) 480-4806. William Sapp Jr.
  Delta, B.C., Canada 2C8 V4G: No.3 7550 River Rd. (604) 946-0818. Jim Anderson. Traeger Distributors Ltd.
  Edmonton, Alta., Canada T5L 0M7: 12618 124th St. (403) 451-2355. Bruce Ramshaw. Allcan Electronics.
  St. Laurent, Que., Canada H4L 3V3: 605 Filiatrault. (514) 747-9939. Bob Montrevil Jr. Lexstar Battery Co. of Canada.
  Peterlee County Durham, U.K. SR8 2JE: Box 10. (0915) 872787. Alexander Batteries Ltd.
  Rechargeable NiCad in-board, on-board & battery belts; NiCad battery chgrs & analyzer/conditioners; portable radio & pager batteries.

All Mobile Video Inc. 221 W. 26th St., New York 10001. (212) 727-1234. FAX: (212) 255-6644. Anton Duke, CEO; Eric Duke, pres.
  Bcst video equipment rental including truck remotes & total carry-in packages. Complete studio facilities.

Allen Avionics Inc. 224 E. 2nd St., Mineola, N.Y. 11572. (516) 248-8080. FAX: (516) 747-6724. Richard Mintz, VP; Jim Lyons, VP; Eric Hausman, mgr sls & mktg.
  All passive components, video filters & delay lines, hum eliminators, LC filters & electromagnetic delay lines.

Allen & Heath. 8760 S. Sandy, Salt Lake City 84070. (801) 566-8800. FAX: (801) 566-7005. Lynn P. Martin, natl sls mgr; Michael Charles, sls coord.
  Audio mixing consoles for recording & live sound applications including automated consoles.

The Allen Products Co. 180 Wampus Ln., Milford, Conn. 06460. (203) 874-2563. FAX: (203) 877-6346. Ronald Bailer, pres.
  Photographic processing machine & accessories.

Allied Electronics Inc. 7410 Pebble Dr., Fort Worth, Tex. 76118. (800) 433-5700; (817) 595-3500. FAX: (817) 595-6470. David Yaniko, pres.
  Broad line distributor of electronic components.

Allied Tower Co. Inc. 12450 Old Galveston Rd., Webster, Tex. 77598. (713) 486-7691. FAX: (713) 486-6562. Max Bowen, pres; Gerald Penrose, VP; Doug W. Moore, sls mgr.
  Vinita, Okla. 74301: Box 945, 900 N. Wilson. (918) 256-5295. Terry Crawford, plant mgr.
  Design, fabrication & erection of FM, AM, TV & communication towers.

Allison Division/Cummins Allison Corp. Box 102, Indianapolis 46206-0102. (317) 244-2440. FAX: (317) 241-9518. Joseph H. Thomas, pres; Richard A. Lippitz, sr VP.
  Manufacturer of coupon payment systems for the financial community.

Allsop Inc. Box 23, Bellingham, Wash. 98227. (206) 734-9090. FAX: (206) 734-9858. Ivor Allsop, pres; Jim Allsop & Mike Allsop, VP's; Brian Matos, natl sls mgr.
  Cleaning accessories for audio & video, record care products & CD.

Alpack Associates. 261 Bloomfield Ave., Suite E, Verona, N.J. 07044 (201) 239-7100. FAX: (201) 239-9080. Les Weinstock.
  Standard & custom carrying/shipping cases for all bcst equipment. Hard & soft case styles available.

Equipment Manufacturers and Distributors

Alpha Audio Acoustics/Acoustical Solutions Inc. 2720 Enterprise Pkwy., Suite 101, Richmond, Va. 23294. (800) 782-5742. FAX: (804) 346-8808. Michael Binns, pres; Becky Colleran, mgr.
Sound & noise control materials to block outside noise & control studio acoustics.

Alpha One Communications & Leasing Inc. Box 777, 115 State Hwy. 193 (Macon Rd. Dr.), Collierville, Tenn. 38027-0777. (901) 853-8943. FAX: (901) 853-5881. Al F. Barzizza Jr., pres.
Used towers bought & sold: Cuax, antennas, tower leasing for TV & FM radio, two way & cable.

Alpha Technologies. 3767 Alpha Way, Bellingham, Wash. 98226. (206) 647-2360. FAX: (206) 671-4936. Fred Kaiser, pres; David Frankenfield, sls mgr.
Burnaby, B.C., Canada V5J 5E5: 5700 Sidley St. (604) 430-1476. Fred Kaiser, pres.
Manufacturer of power systems for coaxial & fiber optic nets. UPS systems, DC products, batteries & surge suppression.

Alpha Video & Electronics Co. 200 Keystone Dr., Carnegie, Pa. 15106. (412) 429-2000. Henry B. Lassige, pres; Terrance M. Lassige, VP.
O.B. vans, engr vans, VTR mods & upgrades, turnkey systems.

Altec Lansing Sound Products. Box 26105, Oklahoma City 73126-0105. (405) 324-5311. Jerry Spriggs, natl sls mgr.
Professional grade amplifiers & loudspeakers.

CALL TOLL FREE 1-800-482-LOAD
P.O. Box 249, Yellville, AR 72687 (501) 449-4093

ALTRONIC RESEARCH INC.

For (OMEGALINE) RF Coaxial Load Resistors

Altronic Research Inc. Box 249, Yellville, Ark. 72687. (800) 482-5623. FAX: (501) 449-6000. John Dyess, pres; Kenneth Hemphill, plant mgr.
Omegaline RF coaxial load resistors (dummy loads).

Aluma Tower Company Inc. Box 2806, Vero Beach, Fla. 32961-2806. (407) 567-3423. FAX: (407) 567-3432. Theodore E. Gottry, VP.
Aluminum crank-up towers, mobile van trailer towers, trailer towers with shelters.

Amek/TAC U.S. Operations. 10815 Burbank Blvd., North Hollywood, Calif. 91601. (818) 508-9788. FAX: (818) 508-8619. Carl Reavey, gen mgr; Steve Harvey, sls mgr.
Atlanta 30319: 2759 Skyland Dr. N.E. (800) 366-4811. Lewis Frisch, rgnl sls mgr.
Newton, Pa. 18940: 572 Atwood Ct. (215) 968-2059. Dave Lewty, rgnl sls mgr.
Amek & TAC (Total Audio Concepts) audio consoles for prod, postprod, audio recording, sound reinforcement & Medici signal processing equipment.

American Broadcast Systems Inc. 8222 Jamestown Dr., Suite 109B, Austin, Tex. 78758. (512) 837-3737. FAX: (512) 837-3791. Donald A. Forbes, pres/gen mgr.
MicroCart 100 PC/Windows-based TV cart system. MicroCart 50 basic on-air automation smart cart.

American Eurocopter Corp. 2701 Forum Dr., Grand Prairie, Tex. 75052-7099. (214) 641-0000. FAX: (214) 641-3550. Dave Smith, pres; Patrice Royer, VP mktg; Lynda Kate, mktg svcs mgr.
Servicing North American market; manufactures & sells complete line of single & twin engine turbine helicopters.

American Laser Systems Inc. Box 6944, Santa Barbara, Calif. 93160. (805) 967-0423. FAX: (805) 683-4382. Jackie Parker, pres.
Wireless Infrared transmission systems for short-haul link of CCTV & baseband video signals.

American Lightwave Systems Inc. 999 Research Pkwy., Meriden, Conn. 06450-8323. (203) 630-5700. FAX: (203) 630-5701. John Holobinko, VP mktg; Zee Shams, VP sls.
Bcst quality fiber optic transmission, single & multichannel systems. Audio, voice, data & video for bcstrs, CATV, educ & military applications. All fiber optics for digital VSB/AM, QAM video, telephony & data from master headend to sub nodes.

American Tower Services Inc. 1702 S. Val Vista Dr., Mesa, Ariz. 85204. (602) 267-1491. FAX: (602) 497-9871. Stephen D. Goebel, pres.
Tower foundation, erection, maintenance, inspections, structural analysis, soil analysis, path flashing svcs including instal & maintenance, antenna instal, portable bldgs.

American Winkomatic Sign & Signal. 6301 Best Friend Rd., Norcross, Ga. 30071. (404) 662-5400. FAX: (404) 263-8353. Don Griffin, pres.
Changeable outdoor electronic adv displays.

Amerivox Corp. 2208 N.W. Market St., Suite 4, Seattle, 98107. (206) 784-0081. FAX: (206) 784-8134. Donald G. McDaniel, pres; Michael P. McDaniel, VP bcst applications.
Listener info lines, loyal listener lines, interactive voice response systems, all sizes, 2-36 lines.

Ampex Systems Corp. 401 Broadway, Redwood City, Calif. 94063-3199. (415) 367-2011. FAX: (415) 367-2761. Ed Bramson, pres/CEO; George Merrick, exec VP; Bob Atchison, VP; Leslie E. Schenk, VP/CFO; Joel Talcott, VP/sec; Tom Wheeler, pres Ampex Recording Media Corp.
Allendale, N.J. 07401: 110 Commerce Dr. (201) 825-9600.
Rolling Meadows, Ill. 60008: 1600 Hicks Rd. (708) 590-5100.
Bethesda, Md. 20817: 10215 Fernwood Rd. (301) 530-8800.
San Fernando, Calif. 91340: 340 Parkside Dr. (818) 365-8627.
Dallas 75234: 3214 Belt Line Rd. (214) 620-9033.
Professional video recorders, cameras, switchers, special effects, graphics & editing systems; professional audio, video & data storage tapes; data storage systems.

Amplica Inc. 950 Lawrence Dr., Newbury Park, Calif. 91320. (805) 498-9671. FAX: (805) 498-4925. John Cole, pres.
Microwave amplifiers.

Amtel Systems Inc. 310 Judson St. Unit 6, Toronto, Ont., Canada M82 5T6. (416) 251-2748. FAX: (416) 251-3977. Peter McDonnell, pres; John McDonald, dir mktg; Ray Wilk, mgr R&D.
E-Pix non-linear editing systems, routing switches, bcst control systems, video conferencing.

Anchor Audio Inc. 913 W. 223rd St., Torrance, Calif. 90502. (310) 533-5984. FAX: (310) 533-6050. David Jacobs, pres; Jonathan Peirson, VP mktg.
Portable, powered P.A. systems & monitors.

Anders Inc. 77 Wolcott Rd., Simsbury, Conn. 06070. (203) 658-7666. FAX: (203) 651-5597. Virginia W. Andersen, chmn/treas; Donald W. Miner, pres.
Ultrasonic delay lines & Ultrasonic delay modules.

Anderson Radio Engineering Co. 202 Dayton School Rd., Easley, S.C. 29642. (803) 855-2327. Burton S. Anderson, own/operator.

The One Thing Thousands of Broadcasters Worldwide Have in Common.
JAMPRO ANTENNAS, INC.
(916) 383-1177

Andrew Corp. 10500 W. 153rd St., Orland Park, Ill. 60462. (708) 349-3300; (800) 255-1479. FAX: (708) 349-5943. F.L. English, pres/CEO.
VHF & UHF-TV transmitting, microwave & earth stn antennas, coaxial cable, waveguides, towers, equipment shelters & install svcs.

Angenieux Corp. of America. 12245 S.W. 132 Ct., Miami, Fla. 33186. (305) 256-6660. FAX: (305) 256-6657. Horst Stahl, VP/gen mgr; O.G. "Bud" Mills, rgnl sls mgr South.
Lenses & accessories for bcst TV cameras & cinematography.

Antenna Concepts Inc. 3234 Saddlehill Ct., Placerville, Calif. 95667. (916) 621-2015. FAX: (916) 622-3274. Mark A. Cunningham, pres.
Custom & standard low-, medium- and high-power omni or directional TV & FM bcst antennas.

Antenna Development. Box 1178, Hwy. 67 N., Poplar Bluff, Mo. 63901. (314) 686-1484. FAX: (314) 686-3856. James Gowen, pres; Pat Rains, accts mgr.
Satellite antenna manufacturer, models ADM-13', ADM-16', ADM-20', ADM-24' & ADM-26'. Solid & perforated aluminum antennas.

Antenna Technology. 1128 E. Greenway St., Mesa, Ariz. 85203. (602) 264-7275. FAX: (602) 898-7667. Gary Hatch, dir international sls & mktg; Scott Grone, Jason Hatch, Camilo Torres, area mgrs; Chuck Willman, dir mktg; Ron Kahle, controller.
Simulsat multibeam earth stns; parabolic antennas from 1.8 m to 32 m. Headend electronics, design & maintenance, used/refurbished equipment.
Simpson Pa. PA 18407: 289 Atlas St. (717) 282-3590. William Pryle, area mgr.

Antenna & Tower Service Inc. Box 33AA, Rt. 1, Sturgeon, Mo. 65284. (314) 474-7573. FAX: (314) 0474-7572. James E. Pickett, own; James M. Carey, VP.
Bcst towers sls & svc. Maintenance of AM, FM, TV, CATV, LPTV, 2-way, cellular mobile telephone & microwave.

Anton/Bauer Inc. One Controls Dr., Shelton, Conn. 06484. (203) 929-1100. FAX: (203) 929-9935. George Bauer, pres; Anton Wilson, exec VP; Michael Malcy, dir North American sls.
NiCad & silver zinc camera/VTR batteries, chgrs, lighting & diagnostic accessories.

Anvil Cases. (a subsidiary of Zero Corporation). 15650 Salt Lake Ave., City of Industry, Calif. 91745. (818) 968-4100. FAX: (818) 968-1703. Jim Biggers, VP sls & mktg; Bill Waskey, gen mgr.
Heavy-duty reuseable, custom & standard shipping cases & containers for all bcst equipment.

Aphex Systems Ltd. 11068 Randall St., Sun Valley, Calif. 91352. (818) 767-2929. FAX: (818) 767-2641. Marvin Caesar, pres; Paul Freudenberg, sls mgr; Donn Werrbach, VP engrg.
Compellor-intelligent AGC; Dominator II-precision multi-band peak limiter; aural exciter; expressor; expander/gate, digicoder FM stereo generator.

Apollo Audio Visual/Lighting. 60 Trade Zone Ct., Ronkonkoma, N.Y. 11779. (516) 467-8033. FAX: (516) 467-8036. H. Charlston, pres; Mark Becker, mktg.
Stage, studio, projection, display, graphic & micrographic lamps & full range of audio-visual equipment.

Argos Products Co. Inc. 600 S. Sycamore St., Genoa, Ill. 60135. (815) 784-6666. FAX: (815) 784-5110. John Colwell, pres; Richard Neville, VP sls.
Sound systems & components.

Argraph Corp. 111 Asia Pl., Carlstadt, N.J. 07072. (201) 939-7722. FAX: (201) 939-7782. Mark Roth, pres; Martin Lipton, sls mgr.
St. Louis 63110: 4916 Shaw Ave. (314) 773-0600.
Hayward, Calif. 94545: Argraph West, 2710 McCone. (510) 298-0575.
Anti-stat cleaning cloths, rechargeable batteries, bilora video tripods.

Aries Industries Inc. N63 W22641 Main St, Sussex, Wis. 53089. (414) 246-3900. FAX: (414) 246-7099. James T. Kunz, pres; Dick Schantz, gen mgr/VP.
Manufacture sewer televising equipment.

Armtec Industries Inc. 10 Ammon Dr., Manchester, N.H. 03103-7406. (603) 669-0940. FAX: (603) 669-0931. Charles Dockery, pres; Leon Demere, controller; Roberta Marino, mktg mgr.
Manufactures electronic components for industrial & marine fire detection systems & for aircraft manufacturers & aerospace progs.

Arrakis Systems Inc. 2619 Midpoint Dr., Fort Collins, Colo. 80525. (303) 224-2248. FAX: (303) 493-1076. Michael C. Palmer, pres; Jon Young, VP worldwide sls.
Audio consoles, digital audio & prod systems, prewired studios & studio furniture.

Equipment Manufacturers and Distributors

Arri Canada Inc. 23 Fraser Ave., Toronto, Ont., Canada M6K 1Y7. (416) 537-8440. FAX: (416) 531-5989. J. G. Sunday, pres.
Bcst prod equipment including ETC lighting controls, ARRI lighting, NAGRA audio & all professional accessories.

Arriflex Corp. 617 Rt. 303, Blauvelt, N.Y. 10913. (914) 353-1400. FAX: (914) 425-1250. Volker W. Bahnemann, pres; Juergen Schwinzer, VP camera; Charles Davidson, VP lighting.
Burbank, Calif. 91502: 600 N. Victory Blvd. (818) 841-7070. Bill Russell, western sls mgr.
Professional 16 mm, 35 mm & 65 mm film cameras, ARRI HMI, fresnel, studio fresnel & kit lighting, ARRI grip & Zeiss lenses.

Arrowsmith Technologies Inc. 1301 W. 25th St., Austin, Tex. 78705. (512) 474-6312. FAX: (512) 474-6389. Greg Kosmetsky, chmn; Gordon Graves, CEO; Curt Bilby, COO; Jack Matthews, VP mktg; Larry Drayer, engr.
Integrated field opns & fleet mgmt systems.

Artel Communications Corp. 22 Kane Industrial Dr., Hudson, Mass. 01749. (508) 562-2100. FAX: (508) 562-6942. Richard Santagati, pres/CEO; Bernard Baker, VP opns; Theresa Pratt, VP engrg; Kevin Conklin, dir mktg.
Fiber optic electronic transmission systems for video, audio, data & loc area net applications.

Asmara Overseas Shippers. 5568 Sepulveda Blvd., Culver City, Calif. 90230. (310) 398-0080. FAX: (310) 390-5250. Ashok Sadhwani, pres; Colin D'Abreo, sls exec.
Multi-standard TVs, VCRs & PAL camcorders for worldwide use.

Associated Broadcast Interest. 3205 Production Ave., Oceanside, Calif. 92054. (619) 433-5600. FAX: (619) 433-1590. Dennis John Nelson, own.
240 lines of new audio & transmission equipment. Also, many items of reconditioned & guaranteed equipment.

Associated Press Broadcast Services. 1825 K St. N.W., Washington 20006-1253. (202) 736-1100. FAX: (202) 736-1124. Jim Williams, VP/dir; Lee Perryman, dep dir; Sue Mosher, asst dir & tech svcs; John Morrissey, info systems mgr.
AP NewsDesk: Newsroom computer software prog for mngng TV & radio news & info resources.

Associated Production Music Sound Effects Libraries. 6255 Sunset Blvd., Suite 820, Hollywood, Calif. 90028. (213) 561-3211. FAX: (213) 461-9102. Cassie Lord, natl sls dir; Connie Reed, bcst sls dir.
Supplying the Broadcast One, Two & Three prod mus & sound effects to radio & TV for use in promos, progs, news & commercials.

Aston from Paltex. 2752 Walnut Ave., Tustin, Calif. 92680. (714) 838-8833. FAX: (714) 838-9619. Roger L. Bailey, mng dir; Earl M. Jamgochian, mktg mgr; Gary Hanfling, product specialist.
High resolution video character generators & gen purpose still stores.

Atlantic Inc. 10240 Matern Pl., Sante Fe Springs, Calif. 90670. (310) 903-9550. FAX: (310) 903-9053. Leo Dardashti, pres; Don Dolliver, VP sls.
Manufacturer of metal storage systems for CDs, cassettes, carts, VHS, Dats, 8mm.

Atlantic Sound Ltd. RR 2, New Glasgow, Pictou County, N.S., Canada B2H 5C5. (902) 752-8527. Peter W. Lann, mgr/own.
Professional bcstg, sound & lighting equipment.

Atlantic Video Inc. 650 Massachusetts Ave. N.W., Washington 20091-0904. (202) 408-0900. FAX: (202) 408-8496. Dong Moon Joo, pres; Christopher Cates, VP/gen mgr; Craig George, dir mktg.
Alexandria, Va. 22304: 150 S. Gordon St. (703) 823-2800. Lee Lindbloom, asst gen mgr.
Postprod, graphics, duplication, remote, satellite uplink, videoconferencing, sound stages.

Atlas/Soundolier, Atapco Security & Comunications Group. 1859 Intertech Dr., Fenton, Mo. 63026. (314) 349-3110; (800) 876-7337. FAX: (314) 349-1251. Bud Waters, natl sls mgr; Jeff Garstick, western sls mgr; Tony Satariano, eastern sls mgr; Jim Edwards, mgr mktg svcs; Colleen Sullivan, mgr adv & business communications.
Atlas Sound® brand microphone & equipment stands, accessories; equipment consoles, racks & cabinets; loudspeaker systems; signaling devices.

Audico Label Corp. 8343 W. Grand Ave., River Grove, Ill. 60171. (708) 456-0003. FAX: (708) 456-0418. Barbara Deletzke, pres.
Audio/video pressure sensitive lables, audiotape, audio rewinders, splicing tape, etc.

Audi-Cord Corp. 1845 W. Hovey Ave., Normal, Ill. 61761-4315. (309) 452-9461. FAX: (309) 452-0893. Andrew M. Rector, pres; Carol A. Pedigo, sls mgr.
Cartridge tape recorders & reproducers.

Audio Accessories Inc. Mill St., Marlow, N.H. 03456. (603) 446-3335. FAX: (603) 446-7543. M.B. Hall, pres; T.J. Symonds, opns mgr.
Jack panels, patch cords, telephone jacks & plugs, pre-wired jack panels (miniature & full-size) & video panels.

Studio Systems for FM & AM
- Delivered on time
- Within budget
- Outstanding workmanship
- Digital ready
- Pre-wires, turn-key

AUDIO BROADCAST GROUP
2342 S. Division
Grand Rapids, MI 49507
FAX 616-452-1652

Let's get our heads together!
1-800-999-9281

Audio Broadcast Group Inc. 2342 S. Division St., Grand Rapids, Mich. 49507. (800) 999-9281. FAX: (616) 452-1652. David Veldsma, CEO; Phyllis Freeman, COO; Dave Howland, VP sls & mktg; Jack Conners, sls & RF engr; Jerry Bufka, sls & customer svc.
Smithfield, N.C. 27577: 200 Fareway Dr., Suite 2, (800) 369-7623. FAX: (919) 934-8120. Cindy Edwards, sls rep, southeastern sls office.
Palmdale, Calif. 93550: 36956 Desert Willow Dr. (800) 858-9008. FAX: (805) 273-3321. Tony Mezey, sls rep, western sls office.
Audio bcst equipment supplier, bcst studio furniture; prewired studio systems; AM/FM transmitter & RF packages. Digital hard drive storage systems & work stns; Digital stn automation packages. Your single source supplier.

Audio/Digital. 8500 Balboa Blvd., Northridge, Calif. 91329. (818) 893-8411. FAX: (818) 893-3639. David Kimm, dir Soundcraft/Electronics Group; Bob Ofenstein, product mgr; Steve Bartlett, eletonic systems dev engr.
Manufacturer of digital sound reinforcement delays, bcst censure delays & digital crossovers.

Audio Implements/GKC. 3059 N. 124th St., Brookfield, Wis. 53005. (414) 784-0440. FAX: (414) 784-0858; TWX: 910-262-1159. Walter L. Kolb, own; Anita Brown, sec.
Acoustic coiled earpiece, receivers & cords, mic line & monitor amplifiers, used in conjunction with IFB system.

Audio Precision Inc. Box 2209, Beaverton, Ore. 97075. (503) 627-0832. Bob Metzler, pres; Thomas Mintner, dir sls & mktg.
System One, Portable One & ATS-1 audio test sets for bcst & satellite use.

Audio Processing Technology Ltd. Edgewater Rd., Belfast, Northern Ireland BT3 9JQ. (44) 232-371110.

FAX: (44) 232-371137. Dr. Stephen Smyth, mgng dir; John Knapton, European sls mgr; Steve Cheung, mgr sls & mktg.
Los Angeles 90028: 6255 Sunset Blvd. (213) 463-2963. Mike Smyth, opns mgr.
Apt-X digital audio compression system for professional applications such as storage & transmission.

Audio Services Corp. 10639 Riverside Dr., North Hollywood, Calif. 91602. (818) 980-9891. FAX: (818) 980-9911. Richard H. Topham Jr., pres; David Panfili, vp.
Las Vegas 89103: 4610 S. Polaris Ave. (702) 891-8555. Chris Bex, gen mgr.
Orlando, Fla. 32811: Topham Audio Inc. (407) 649-6444. FAX: (407) 648-1352. Joseph Guzzi, VP.
Wireless microphones, wireless & wired intercoms, IFB, telephone interfaces, analog & digital recorders, mixers, lavaliers, boompoles, microphones.

Audio Video Research. 65 Main St., Watertown, Mass. 02172. (617) 924-0660. FAX: (617) 924-0497. Octavio Brito, pres; Peter Solak, admin.
Hartford, Conn. 06818: 87 Church St. (203) 289-9475.
Professional audio & vis equipment.

Audioarts Engineering. (A division of Wheatstone Corp.) 7305 Performance Dr. Syracuse, N.Y. 13212. (315) 452-5000. FAX: (315) 452-0160. Gary C. Snow, pres; Andrew Calvanese, VP; Ramon Esparolini, sls mgr; Mark Kaltman, product mgr.
Manufacture of bcst audio consoles, studio furniture & audio signal processing equipment.

Audiolab Electronics Inc. 5831 Rosebud Ln., Bldg. C, Sacramento, Calif. 95841. (916) 348-0200. FAX: (916) 348-1512. Robert E. Stofan, pres; Ronald A. Stofan, mktg mgr.
Professional line of bulk tape degaussers for all formats of tape including: Beta SP, DAT 2" reels up to 16" dia.

Audiopak Inc. Box 3100, Winchester, Va. 22604. (703) 667-8125. FAX: (703) 667-6379. Nick Krassowski, pres; Gordon Stafford, VP sls.
Pismo Beach, Calif. 93449: 897 Oakpark Blvd., No. 278. (805) 481-8278. FAX: (805) 481-8279. Gordon Stafford, VP sls.
NAB type audio bcst cartridges & back lubricated audio tape.

Audio-Technica U.S. Inc. 1221 Commerce Dr., Stow, Ohio 44224. (216) 686-2600. Fred W. Nichols, sr VP; Ken Reichel, exec VP mktg; Phil Cajka, exec VP/CFO; Dean Slagle, VP opns.
Microphones audio & video accessories, phono cartridges, headphones, field prod mixers & loudspeaker systems.

Audiotechniques. 1600 Broadway, 8th Fl., New York 10019. (212) 586-5989. FAX: (212) 489-4936. Douglas Cook, pres.
Sls & svc parts for professional bcst audio equipment including Sony, Soundcraft, Trident, Dolby, ADC, Switchcraft, HME, Lydkraft, Adam-Smith & Otari.

Audio-Video Engineering Co. 65 Nancy Blvd., Merrick, N.Y. 11566. (516) 546-4239. FAX: (516) 623-7213. Olga M. Drucker, pres.
Video hum stop coil (hum bucker).

Audiovisual Inc. (A division of AVI Systems) 6253 Bury Dr., Eden Prairie, Minn. 55346. (612) 949-3700. FAX: (612) 949-6000. Joe Stoebner, pres; Joe Baer, sls.
Omaha, Neb. 68137: 11117 Mockingbird Dr. (402) 593-6500. Eldon Krein, rgnl mgr.
Urbandale, Iowa 50322: 2851 104th St., Suite D. (515) 254-9850. Steve Gassman, rgnl mgr.
Cameras, consoles, turntables, monitors, speakers, microphones, remote control, transmitters & exciters.

Auditronics Inc. 3750 Old Getwell Rd., Memphis 38118. (901) 362-1350. FAX: (901) 365-8629. Welton H. Jetton, CEO; Steve Sage, pres; Dave Evers, engrg prod mgr; Murray Shields, dir sls.
Audio consoles & assorted equipment for radio, TV bcsting & postprod.

Auernheimer Labs and Co. 4561 E. Florence Ave., Fresno, Calif. 93725. (209) 442-1048. Curly Auernheimer, own.
Loudspeaker systems; studio, monitor, control room & auditorium.

Augat Communications Products Inc. 23315 66th Ave. S., Kent, Wash. 98032. (206) 854-9802. FAX: (206) 813-1001. Larry E. Buffington, VP/gen mgr.

Equipment Manufacturers and Distributors

Designer & manufacturer of CATV connectors & amplifiers, optical nodes & telecom cross-connect products.

Augat Inc. Box 2510, 452 John Beitch Blvd., Attleboro Falls, Mass. 02763. (508) 699-7646. FAX: (508) 695-7010. Sid Hooper, mktg mgr; Ron Hoover, VP.
  Dip & pin grid sockets, card edge & dip connectors, transistor sockets, crystal sockets, test jacks, wire & cable.

Auratone Corp. Box 180698, Coronado, Calif. 92178-0698. (619) 297-2820. FAX: (619) 296-8734. J.A. Wilson, pres.
  Recording, bcst, monitor & reference loudspeaker systems. Sound reinforcement, background, foreground & sound distribution loudspeaker systems.

Aurora Systems. 2230 Martin Ave., Santa Clara, Calif. 95050. (408) 988-2000. FAX: (408) 986-0452. W. Tom Beams, pres/CEO; Damon Rarey, VP mktg & sls.
  Liberty paint & animation system for all silicon graphics workstations. Resolution from TV to HDTU to 8K by 8K for prepress.

Auto-Gen Electric Division. Box 895, Minden, La. 71058-0895. (318) 377-0844. FAX: (318) 377-2618. Emily V. Pepper, gen mgr; Robert M. Pepper, sls mgr; E. Michelle Bass, adv mgr.
  VEM/AC generators, power generators, portable light plants, standby gen-sets & accessories.

Autogram Corp. Box 456, 1500 Capital Ave., Plano, Tex. 75074. (214) 424-8585; (800) 327-6901. FAX: (214) 423-6334. Ernest T. Ankele Jr., pres.
  R/TV-12 twelve ch & R/TV-20 twenty ch consoles. Live assist, clock with temperature & stop watch, Pacemaker 6,8,10 Slide Pot, AC8, IC-10 Rotary Pot audio consoles, Mini-Mix 8 & Mini-Mix 12 Economy Consoles.

Automated Broadcast Controls. 13221 Rippling Brook Dr., Silver Spring, Md. 20906. (301) 871-1095. FAX: (301) 871-1097. Homer Guerra, pres; Tom Kitaguchi, exec VP.
  Bcst automation systems; multiple tape cartridge equipment; logging systems; FM stereo composite clipper, tone generator & detectors.

Automated Business Concepts. 10650 Treena St., Suite 201, San Diego 92131. (619) 566-8920. FAX: (619) 566-1039. John M. Caso, pres/CEO; Debbie K. Hart, VP.
  PC based multi-user traf, accounting, sls & mgmt, business systems for the radio industry.

Automated Drawing Systems Inc. 6855 Jimmy Carter Blvd., Suite 2200, Norcross, Ga. 30071. (404) 448-0977. FAX: (404) 242-8583. Jeffrey C. Eichler, pres.
  Mapperly, Nottingham, U.K. NG3-5QG: 613A Woodborough Rd. (0602) 856-348.
  Lynx Marketing, maps for sls penetration analysis, tiger files, maps showing addresses for census blocks.

Automatic Devices Company. 2121 S. 12th St., Allentown, Pa. 18103. (215) 797-6000. FAX: (215) 797-4088. John A. Samuels, pres.
  Cyclorama tracks, lighting tracks.

Avantek/H.P. 3175 Bowers Ave., Santa Clara, Calif. 95054-3294. (408) 727-0700. FAX: (408) 954-0633. Paul Sedlewicz, CEO/pres.
  Microwave transistors, MMICs & active components; specialized IC's for fiber-optic & other communications.

Avid Technology Inc. One Metropolitan Park W., Tewksbury, Mass. 01876. (800) 949-AVID; (508) 640-6789. FAX: (508) 851-0418. Anthony J. Mark, VP/gen mgr bcst prods; Mark P. Overington, dir worldwide sls bcst prods.
  New York 10022: 875 3rd Ave., 8th Fl. (212) 753-2843. Scott Greenberg, sls mgr
  Burbank, Calif. 91505: 3601 W. Olive Ave., Suite 450. (818) 557-2520. Martin Vann.
  Avid's networked bcst news prods are designed to facilitate the process of digital news gathering (DNG).

Avitel Electronics Corp. 3678 W. 2100 S., Salt Lake City 84120. (801) 977-9553. FAX: (801) 977-9674. Edward Scott, pres; Paul Treleaven, VP; Chris Cadzow, VP.
  Video & audio distribution amplifiers, time code generators, & readers & digital video patchpanels.

Avtech Systems Inc. 141 Ayers Ct., Teaneck, N.J. 07666. (201) 833-8777. FAX: (201) 833-4995. Fred M. Samuel, pres; Gloria Calandra, VP admin; David I. Samuel, VP sls.
  Closed circuit video equipment, components & accessories.

Aydin Microwave. 30 Great Oaks Blvd., San Jose, Calif. 95119. (408) 629-1100. FAX: (408) 224-4625. Mats Ofverberg, pres.

B

B&B Systems Inc. 28111 Ave. Stanford, Valencia, Calif. 91355. (805) 257-4853. FAX: (805) 257-8065. Dave Bartolone, pres; John Bradford, mgng.
  Design & instal of prod & postprod systems, manufacturer of audio monitoring products.

BAF Communications Corp. 16 Bourbon St., Peabody, Mass. 01960. (800) 633-8223; (407) 324-8250. FAX: (407) 324-7860. Charles G. Angelakis, pres/CEO.
  Lutz, Fla. 33549: 18251 Clear Lake Dr. (813) 949-7497. Bob King, VP sls & mktg.
  Williamsburg, Va. 23185: 106 Lake Dr. (800) 966-3822. James Vautrot, gen mgr bcst svcs.
  Cookhill, Warwickshire, U.K. B49 5JS: Oak Cottage, 2 Church Ln. 4452789-3070. Ian Dawson, European sls & engrg.
  Tuscon, Ariz. 85704: 6336 Oracle Rd., Suite 326-339. (602) 579-0543. Steven Rullison, western rgnl sls.
  Builder of satellite news vehicles, ENG & EFP vehicles; satellite transponder time broker & coordination svcs.

BAI Systems Inc. 20 Red Rose Dr., Levittown, Pa. 19056. (215) 547-7133. FAX: (215) 547-6021. John H. Bostwick, pres.
  Digital clock/timers, electronic customizing.

BARCO Inc. 1000 Cobb Place Blvd., Suite 100, Kennesaw, Ga. 30144. (404) 590-7900. FAX: (404) 590-8836. Guido Van Linden, pres; George Walter, product line mgr.
  Bcst, industrial, graphics & high quality monitors; routing switchers; Precision chroma decoders; professional modulators, demodulators, ch processors; satellite receivers & dishes; large screen video projection systems.

BASF Corporate Information Systems. Crosby Dr., Bedford, Mass. 01730. (617) 271-4000. FAX: (617) 275-2708. John Healion, pres.
  Professional audio/video products; audio/videotape & cassettes; computer floppy disks.

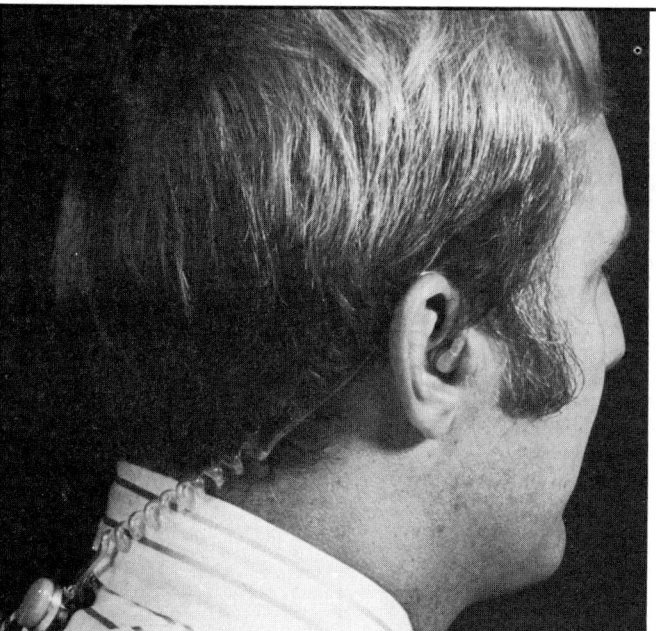

CALL OR WRITE TODAY

We carry a large supply of cords, receivers, monitor and mic-line amplifiers.

Please write or call for further information and printed material on our Audioclarifiers and amplifiers.

Audio Implements GKC is a small company located in Brookfield, Wisconsin, a suburb of Milwaukee. We invented this ear piece and have manufactured it **since 1967**. All major television networks use our products and have for many years. We hope to have the opportunity to be of service to you.

The On-Camera Audioclarifier is used mostly for talent. It comes with six different size ear tips or a custom ear piece. Both custom and tip models are also used for security and surveillance work.

AUDIO IMPLEMENTS
GKC Research & Development
3059 N. 124th STREET • BROOKFIELD, WISCONSIN 53005 USA
PHONE 414-784-0440 • TWX 910 262-1159 WISEARMOLD MIL
FAX 414-784-0858

Broadcasting & Cable Yearbook 1994

Equipment Manufacturers and Distributors

BASYS Automation Systems Inc. 5 Odell Plaza, Yonkers, N.Y. 10701. (914) 376-4800. FAX: (914) 376-0865. John Daly, VP admin & opns; John Chapman, VP customer svc.
 Atlanta 30328: Bldg. 12, Suite 350, 7000 Peachtree Dunwoody Rd. (404) 396-8752. Mike Casserly, VP news system sls.
 Sunnyvale, Calif. 94086: 501 Macara Ave. (408) 720-1236.
 Langley, Slough, England SL3 87U: Langley Business Centre, 11-49 Station Rd. (0753) 583333 David Lyon, CEO.
 Integrated automation solutions for TV, radio & cable bcstrs including newsroom computer systems & digital audio.

BBE Sound Inc. 5500 Bolsa Ave., Suite 245, Huntington Beach, Calif. 92649. (714) 897-6766. FAX: (714) 895-6728. Rob Rizzuto, natl sls mgr.
 Audio/video signal processors to eliminate phase & amplitude distortion.

BDL-Autoscript. A8 Poplar Business Park, 10 Prestons Rd., London, U.K. E14 9RL. 44-(0)71-538-1427. FAX: 44-(0)71-515-9529. Chris Lambert, mgng dir; Jinx Hayman, rental dir; Bill Babington, financial dir; Giles Dickenson, opns dir.
 Design & manufacture digital teleprompt systems, news, studio & location; sale or rental.

B.E.E.R. Inc./United States Broadcast. 2794 Circleport Dr., Erlanger, Ky. 41018. (606) 282-1802. FAX: (606) 282-1804. Peter Beckett, gen mgr.
 New & used TV/audio equipment, bcst batteries & chgrs.

BES Electronics Ltd. 5500 Tomken Rd., Unit #6, Mississauga, Ont., Canada L4W 2Z4. (416) 629-8444. FAX: (416) 276-0276. William R. Onn, pres/gen mgr.
 AM/FM bcst equipment from microphone to antenna; AM antenna tuning, phasing components & systems.

BEXT Inc. 739 5th Ave., Suite 7A, San Diego 92101. (619) 239-8462. FAX: (619) 239-8474; Anne de Fazio, pres/CEO; Dennis Pieri, VP.
 Transmitters, exciters, amplifiers, STLs, stereo generators, receivers, trans, boosters, low-power UHF, VHF & TV transmitters.

BGW Systems Inc. Box 5042, 13130 Yukon Ave., Hawthorne, Calif. 90250-5042. (310) 973-8090; (800) 468-AMPS. FAX: (310) 676-6713. Brian Wachner, pres; Barbara Wachner, VP; Joe DeMeo, mgr sls & mktg.
 Professional bcst & coml audio power amplifiers, signal processing power amplifiers & accessories.

BHP Inc. 1800 Winnemac Ave., Chicago 60640. (312) 989-2140. FAX: (312) 989-2144. John M. Ehrenberg, pres; George W. Darrell, exec VP.
 Motion picture laboratory equipment, film printers & accessories.

BIW Connector System Inc. 500 Tesconi Cir., Santa Rosa, Calif. 95401. (707) 523-2300. FAX: (707) 523-3567. Eckhard Konkel, mktg mgr.
 Cable connectors, assemblies & repair svcs for all bcst camera applications.

BMG/RCA Records. 1540 Broadway, New York 10036. (212) 930-4000. FAX: (212) 930-4015.
 Manufacture CDs, cassette tapes & video tapes.

BSM Systems Inc. Box 19007, Spokane, Wash. 99219-9007. (509) 747-5753. FAX: (509) 624-2941. Leon B. Skidmore, pres/gen mgr; Dick Jones, VP mktg.
 Audi/video routing switchers, audio/video distribution amps, telecommunications products.

BTS Broadcast Television Systems Inc. Box 30816, Salt Lake City 84130-0816. (801) 972-8000. FAX: (801) 972-6304. Michael D'Amore, dir business dev; Sonny Chaffin, VP opns; Dick Crippa, VP mktg & sls; Al Jensen, mgr mktg communications.
 Simi Valley, Calif. 93065: 94 W. Cochran St. (805) 584-4700. Dick Crippa, VP mktg & sls.
 Character generators, routing switchers, encoders/decoders, automation system, master control switchers, cameras, filmscanners, noise reducers, tape recorders.

Bald Mountain Laboratory. 230 Bellevue Rd., Troy, N.Y. 12180. (518) 279-9753. Robert S. Henry, own.
 Audio step generators, EBS tone generators, digital decibel meters.

Band Pro Film/Video Inc. 425 N. Moss St., Burbank, Calif. 91502. (818) 841-9655. FAX: (818) 841-7649. Amnon Band, own; Gary Pranckitas, gen mgr.
 New York 10010: 31 W. 21st St. (212) 627-3992. Amnon Band, own.
 Specialty items for film & video including chrosziel matteboxes, CAMS remote camera controllers, Sony cameras.

Barbervision. 9148 Exposition Dr., Los Angeles 90034. (310) 280-0363. FAX: (310) 280-0367. John Pagano, pres; Bruce Nelson, acct exec.
 Cable controlled camera booms; "Baby 20"- equipped for film or video.

Bec Technologies Inc. (Digital Transmission/Fiber) 9460 Delgates Dr., Suite 108, Orlando, Fla. 32837. (407) 855-8181. FAX: (407) 855-1653. Bob Proctor, pres/CEO.
 Seattle 98103-0891: Sales & Marketing, 1101 N. Northlake Way, Suite 100. (206) 632-2431. FAX: (206) 547-1421. Michael C. Creamer, VP sls & mktg.
 Digital audio sankes, A/D conversion & transmission, D/A conversion receivers & repeaters, microphone preamps, fiber optic transceivers.

Beers Associates Inc. 112 Turnpike Rd., Suite 302, Westboro, Mass. 01581. (508) 898-3200; (800) 84-BEERS. FAX: (508) 366-6815. Scott Beers, pres; Eric Pfaff, VP; Malcolm Beers, treas; Pamela Beers, admin.
 New York 10023: 124 W. 60th St. (212) 247-1505.
 South Orange, N.J. 07079: 348 S. Ridgewood Rd. (201) 763-5499.
 Baltimore 21234: 13 Kintore Ct. (410) 668-7189.
 TV bcst equipment.

Belar Electronics Laboratory Inc. Box 76, 119 Lancaster Ave., Devon, Pa. 19333. (215) 687-5550. FAX: (215) 687-2686. Arno Meyer, pres; David Hirsch, mktg dir.
 AM, FM, FM stereo, SCA, sw, TV, TV stereo modulation & frequency monitors.

Bencher Inc. 831 N. Central Ave., Wood Dale, Ill. 60191. (708) 238-1183. FAX: (708) 238-1186. Jere Benedict, pres; Robert Locher, VP; James Johanek, gen mgr.
 Photographic & video camera support systems & related accessories.

BENCHMARK...
The Finest Audio Products

Here's why ABC, NBC, NPR, the BBC, and WGBH'S Boston Symphony, among numerous others, rebuilt their facilities with audio and mic-pre distribution amplifiers from
BENCHMARK MEDIA SYSTEMS!
- *The very finest performance*
- *The broadest product line*
- *Customization available*
- *Competitive pricing*
- *Ease of installation*
- *Phenomenal reliability*
- *Excellent delivery times*

Discover these 21st century products.
Call Rory Rall, today!

Benchmark BENCHMARK MEDIA SYSTEMS, INC.
the measure of excellence! 1-800-262-4675, 315-437-6300

Benchmark Media Systems Inc. 5925 Court St. Rd., Syracuse, N.Y. 13206-1707. (315) 437-6300. FAX: (315) 437-8119. Allen H. Burdick, pres; Rory Rall, sls mgr.
 Audio processing & distribution systems, VU/PPM meters, interface/headphone amplifiers, microphone preamplifiers.

Bend-A-Lite Flexible Neon. Box 4357, Boynton Beach, Fla. 33424. (407) 738-5300. FAX: (407) 738-5055. Rick Schwartz, pres.
 Flexible neon that can be cut with scissors, cut section can be re-electrified. 110v, 12v, 220v, 24v, indoor/outdoor.

Benner-Nawman Inc. 3070 Bay Vista Ct., Unit B, Benicia, Calif. 94510. (707) 746-0500. FAX: (707) 745-0681. Edward R. Kientz, pres.
 Vandalia, Ill. 62471: Box 216, Van Tran Ave. (800) 851-4043. FAX: (618) 283-4440. Don Funk, dir opns.
 Wickenburg, Ariz. 85358: 3232 Sabin Brown Rd. (800) 528-5502. FAX: (602) 684-2813. Lon Brown, dir opns.
 Specialty tools for CATV & cable termination; distribution boxes (cabinets).

Bexel Corporation. 801 S. Main St., Burbank, Calif. 91506. (818) 841-5051. FAX: (818) 841-1572. David Trudeau, pres.
 Rental of video bcst equipment; sls of used video equipment, full svcs & maintenance of bcst & industrial equipment.

Beyerdynamic. 56 Central Ave., Farmingdale, N.Y. 11735. (516) 293-3200. FAX: (516) 293-3288. John Midgley, dir mktg; Mike Solomon, mktg mgr; Jim Hassel, svc mgr.
 Microphones, headsets, monitor headphones, studio & on-location wireless microphone systems.

Bio-Electronics Inc. Box 1468, Corrales, N.M. 87048. (505) 898-1455. FAX: (505) 898-0159. William J. Kent, VP opns.
 CG, black burst generators, DA's, video switchers, time code, video mixers, decoders.

Bird Electronic Corp. 30303 Aurora Rd., Solon, Ohio 44139-2794. (216) 248-1200. FAX: (216) 248-5426. J. Conway, pres; B. Bird, exec VP; W.L. Yochum, VP sls & mktg; T. Holt, dir engrg; Greg Johns, domestic sls mgr.
 Ojai, Calif. 93023: 621 W. Ojai Ave., Suite F. (805) 646-7255. George Churpek, rgnl sls mgr.
 RF directional wattmeters; power monitors; alarms; self, air & water-cooled loads; attenuators.

Birns and Sawyer Inc. 1026 N. Highland Ave., Hollywood, Calif. 90038. (213) 466-8211. FAX: (213) 466-7049. Marvin Stern, pres; Peter Anway, sls mgr; Mark Schweickart, rental mgr.
 Professional motion picture equipment such as Arriflex, Aaton, Tiffen, Lowell, LTM, Ronford, O'Connor, Harrison & Harrison & tech books.

Black Audio. Box 106, Ventura, Calif. 93002. (805) 653-5557. Bruce Black, pres.
 Remote recording up to 24 tracks for film, video, concerts, sports, radio & TV, theatre, etc.

Blimpy Floating Signs/Bend-A-Lite. Box 4357, Boynton Beach, Fla. 33424. (407) 738-5300; (800) 235-2201. FAX: (407) 738-5055. Richard Schwartz, pres.
 Giant blimps, hot air balloons & rooftop balloons. Complete custom dept for any shape or size, flexible neon in seven brilliant colors.

Mark Blinoff Inc. 1837 S.E. Harold St., Portland, Ore. 97202-4932. (503) 232-9787; (800) 929-5119. Mark Blinoff, gen mgr; Eric Norberg, VP progmg.
 Digital stereo audio tape package with video cue info suitable for automation or operator-assist.

Blonder-Tongue Laboratories Inc. Box 1000, One Jake Brown Rd., Old Bridge, N.J. 08857-1000. (908) 679-4000. FAX: (908) 679-4353. James A. Luksch, pres; Robert J. Palle', exec VP; Peter Pugielli, VP finance; Daniel Altiere, sr VP; Richard Colasurdo, VP purchasing.
 Fair Oaks, Calif. 95628: 4545 Shady Oaks Way. (916) 863-0452. Chuck Fitzer, western regl sls mgr.
 Cincinnati 45231: 9435 Galecrest Dr. (513) 931-0324. Edward Curreri, Midwest rgnl sls mgr.
 Old Bridge, N.J. 08857: One Jake Brown Rd. (90) 679-4000. Glenn Stawicki, eastern rgnl sls mgr.
 Muenchen, Germany Wuermtal Strasse 64, D-8000: (011) 49-89-714-1685. Ken Blunt, European sls.
 Manufacturer of coml cable equipment including satellite receivers, modulators, processors, amplifiers, combiners & passives.

Blue Feather Co. N8494 Poplar Grove Rd., New Glarus, Wis. 53574-0669. (608) 527-5077. FAX: (608) 527-5078. Jennifer Jarik, Jim Gladney, owners.

Equipment Manufacturers and Distributors

Portable IBM-compatible teleprompters with adaptable features.

Bogen Communications Inc. Box 575, 50 Spring St., Ramsey, N.J. 07446. (201) 934-8500. FAX: (201) 934-9832. John H. Ochtera, pres; Eron Nevo, VP finance; David Chambers, VP sls & mktg.
Audio amplifiers, mixer-preamplifiers, equalizers, power amplifiers; FM/AM tuners & receivers; intercom systems; public address & sound reinforcement systems; digital repeater products.

Bogen Photo Corp. 565 E. Crescent Ave., Ramsey, N.J. 07446. (201) 818-9500. FAX: (201) 818-9177. Susan Bogen-Zarrabi, pres; Bruce Landau, VP sls & mktg.
Professional video products including tripods, fluid heads, dollies & accessories.

Boonton Electronics Corp. 791 Rt. 10, Randolph, N.J. 07869. (201) 584-1077. FAX: (201) 584-3037. Richard Anlas, sls mgr; John Titterton, CFO; Charles Karen, dir opns; John Swank, dir engrg.
Electronic test & measuring equipment: microwave/RF power, RF Voltmeters, capacitance, inductance & modulation meters, signal generators.

Bowen Broadcast Service Company Inc. 8343 Lynn Haven Ave., El Paso, Tex. 79907. (915) 598-5556. Bill Bowen, pres.
TCR-100 refurbish prog, super long life canoe & sapphire guides, maintenance RCA quads.

Bradley Broadcast Sales. 8101 Cessna Ave., Gaithersburg, Md. 20879. (800) 732-7665. FAX: (301) 330-7178. Art Reed, gen mgr.
Radio control room; transmission equipment, professional sound equipment.

Brand-Rex Co. 1600 W. Main St., Willimantic, Conn. 06226. (203) 456-8000. FAX: (203) 450-7014. Carl Painter, pres; Richard Hall, VP sls; John Macchia, VP opns; Harry Tucker, VP mfg; James Anastasi, VP engrg; Thomas C. Ragion, VP/controller.
Wire & cable for telecommunications; electronic, audio & bcst interconnect.

Walter Brewer Corp. Box 35746, Tulsa, Okla. 74153-0746. (918) 493-7323. FAX: (918) 491-9817. Walter S. Brewer, pres; Robert Boltinghouse Jr., VP sls.
Lighting; studio & remote facilities design & install svcs. Distributor of full line lighting & grip equipment.

Broadcast Automation Inc. 3006 Edgewood Dr., Suite 13, Garland, Tex. 75042. (214) 487-5810. FAX: (214) 487-5810. Earl R. Bullock, pres.
New & remanufactured radio automation systems; live asst, new & used studio/prod equipment.

Broadcast Cartridge Service Inc. 15131 Triton Ln., Suite 108, Huntington Beach, Calif. 92649. (714) 898-7224. FAX: (714) 898-1753. Lora Crafton, pres.
Bcst audio tape cartridges, alignment tools, storage systems & accessories. Cartridge reloading svc.

Broadcast Data Consultants. 2189 Cleveland St., Suite 203, Clearwater, Fla. 34625. (813) 442-5566. FAX: (813) 443-5254. Neil Edwards, pres.
Fully integrated mus & traffic scheduling software. Features include automatic BMI reporting, audience mgmt & barter COP reporting. Single terminal or net PC.

Broadcast Electronic Services. Box 11005, 4668 Monument Point Dr., Jacksonville, Fla. 32239-1005. (904) 646-1630. FAX: (904) 641-1443. Tim Derstine, pres.
Betabox/GPI net 410, video-editing interface products for ENG & postprod; T.B.C. remote devices.

Broadcast Electronics Inc. Box 3606, 4100 N. 24th St., Quincy, Ill. 62305. (217) 224-9600. FAX: (217) 224-9607. John J. Nevin, pres; Bill Harland, dir domestic sls; Tim Bealor, dir mktg; Chuck Kelly, dir international sls; Dave Buck, audio sls mgr; David White, RF sls mgr; Rick Carpenter, dir RF studio engrg.
Audio consoles, cart machines, AM & FM transmitters, digital audio storage systems, satellite & prog automation.

Broadcast Engineering. Box 12901, Overland Park, Kan. 66282. (913) 341-1300. FAX: (913) 967-1905. Cameron Bishop, group VP; Dennis Triola, publisher; Tom Brick, mktg dir.

Brooklyn, N.Y. 11231: 210 President St., #4. (718) 802-0488. FAX: (718) 522-4571. Josh Gordon.
Chicago 60604: 55 E. Jackson, Suite 1100. (312) 435-2361. FAX: (312) 922-1408. Vytas Urbanas.
Santa Monica, Calif. 90401: 501 Santa Monica Blvd., Suite 401. (310) 393-9285. FAX: (310) 393-2381. Jason Perlman.
Deddington, Oxford, U.K. OX15 4TP: Intertec Publishing Corp. Roseleigh House, New St. (0869) 38794. FAX: (0869) 38040. Richard Woolley.
Shinjuku-ku, Tokyo Japan 162: Orient Echo Inc. 1101 Grand Maison, Shimomiyabi-Cho 2-18. (03) 3235-5961. FAX: (03) 3235-5852. Mashy Yoshikawa.
Frewville, S. Australia, Australia 5063: 109 Conyngham St., 799-522. FAX: 08 79 9522.
Agoura Hills, Calif. 91301: 5236 Colodny Ave., Suite 108. (818) 707-6476. FAX: (818) 707-2313. Duane Hefner.
New York, 10106: 888 7th Ave., 38th Fl., (212) 332-0628. FAX: (212) 332-0663. Joanne Melton.
Published for mgmt & engrg per bcst, prod, postprod, cable facilities worldwide.

Broadcast Equipment Sales & Engineering Inc. Box 20331, Jackson, Miss. 39289-1331. (601) 857-8573. FAX: (601) 857-2346. Jeffery Corkren, pres; Robert E. Buie Jr., VP/sls mgr; Tim Waltman, svc mgr; David T. Herring, comptroller.
Represent bcst equipment manufacturers; sls, svc, instal, turnkey designs & engrg; new & used equipment.

Broadcast International Group. 8280 N.W. 27th St., Suite 515, Miami, Fla. 33122. (305) 599-2112. FAX: (305) 599-1133. Ana Maria Sagastegui, pres.
Bcst TV equipment.

Broadcast Microwave Services Inc. 5795 Kearny Villa Rd., San Diego 92123. (619) 560-8601. FAX: (619) 560-1637. James W. Barnes, chmn/CEO; Dave MacKinney, dir mktg.
Microwave transmitters, receivers & antenna systems for vehicles, helicopters, autotrackers, receiving sites & STL/TSL intercity applications.

Broadcast Services Co. Reedy Creek Rd., Four Oaks, N.C. 27524. (919) 934-6869; (800) 525-1037. FAX: (919) 934-1537. Neal Davis, pres; Warren Grimes, controller; Kim Ferrell, order admin; Lorine Davis, accounting; Brian Gold, sls rep.
Palmdale, Calif. 93550: 1605 E. Palmdale Blvd., Suite G. (800) 523-1037. Tony Mezey, sls rep.
Video Products Division: Dennis Ford, Bill Gordon, sls reps. (800) 525-1037.
Full-svc supplier radio/video equipment, facility packages, lease svcs.

Broadcast Sports Technologies. 2135 Espey Ct., Suite 4, Crofton, Md. 21114. (410) 721-5151. FAX: (410) 721-6183. John Porter, pres; Peter Larson, VP pres.

Broadcast Store Inc. 1840 Flower, Glendale, Calif. 91201. (818) 551-5858. FAX: (818) 551-0686. Lou Claude, pres.
New York 10001: 460 W. 34th St., 4th Fl. (212) 268-8800. Richard Hydell, office mgr.
Audio/video bcst equipment; sellers & buyers for prod & postprod needs.

Broadcast Supply Worldwide. 7012 27th St. W., Tacoma, Wash. 98466. (800) 426-8434. FAX: (800) 231-7055. Irv Law, bd chmn; Bernice McCullough, pres; Tim Schwieger, VP mktg; Pat Medved, VP sls.
Blairstown, N.J. 07825: Box 298, Rd. 6. (800) 762-5566 Laura Tyson, eastern rgn sls.
Audio bcst equipment distributor: cartridges to consoles & transmitters. Over 200 product lines.

Broadcast Video Systems Ltd. 40 W. Wilmot St., Richmond Hill, Ont., Canada L4B 1H8. (416) 764-1584. FAX: (416) 764-7438. Bert Verwey, pres.
Encoders, decoders, transcoders, downstream keyers, safe area generators, ident generators, video delay lines & filters, procamps, VBI equipment, video routing switches.

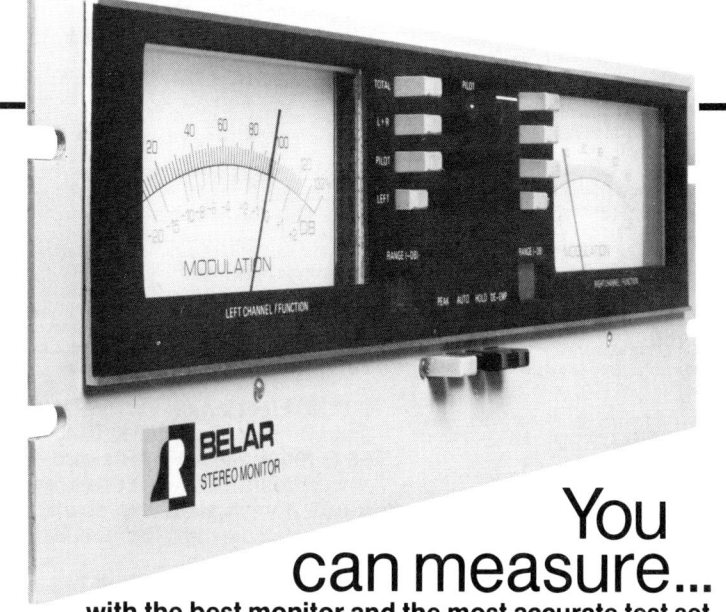

You can measure...
with the best monitor and the most accurate test set.

The FMM-2/FMS-2 series monitors provide an even greater degree of precision measurement than ever before... **You can measure** S/N below **90 dB, You can measure** crosstalk below **85 dB, You can measure** separations of better than **70 dB, You can measure** frequency response to better than **0.25 dB, You can measure** distortions to lower than **0.01%**, and much more... Our uncluttered panels and autoranging voltmeters make these measurements a dream.

BELAR ELECTRONICS LABORATORY, INC.
CALL 215-687-5550 FAX 215-687-2686
LANCASTER AVENUE AT DORSET, DEVON, PENNSYLVANIA 19333
Call or write for more information on Belar AM, FM, Stereo, SCA and TV monitors.

Equipment Manufacturers and Distributors

BROADCASTERS GENERAL STORE
A dealer and wholesale distributor for over 250 manufacturers of audio, video and RF equipment.
Phone 904-622-7700
Ocala, Florida

Broadcasters General Store Inc. 2480 S.E. 52nd St., Ocala, Fla. 34480. (904) 622-9058. FAX: (904) 629-7000. William Shute, CEO; David Kerstin, pres; Chris Shute, VP opns; Kandy Clark, rgnl office, (404) 425-0630.
Professional audio, video & RF equipment.

Broadcasting Frequency Monitor Service. Box 6161, Texarkana, Tex. 75505. (903) 838-6655. Donald W. Lynch, own.

Brooks Telecommunications Corp. 425 Woods Mill Rd. S., Suite 300, Town & Country, Mo. 63017. (314) 878-1616. FAX: (314) 878-3211. Robert A. Brooks, chmn/CEO; James C. Allen, pres; Jim A. Mofft, exec VP; John K. Brooks, sr VP; L.N. Lehman, sr VP/CFO.
International telecommunications infrastructure planning, design & consulting.

Bruel & Kjaer Instruments Inc. 2364 Park Central Blvd., Decatur, Ga. 30035. (404) 981-3998. FAX: (404) 593-3254. Randy Linville, VP; Will Kinard, adv mgr.
Livonia, Mich. 48150: 15873 Middlebelt Rd. (313) 522-8600. Mike Stephan, rgnl mgr.
Hoffman Estates, Ill. 60195: 555 W. Central Rd. (708) 358-7582. Fred Fey, rgnl mgr.
Orange, Calif. 92668: 721 N. Eckhoff. (714) 978-8066. Joe Weatherstone, rgnl mgr.
Instrumentation for sound, vibration, illumination, thermal comfort & signal analysis.

Bryston/Bryston Vermont Ltd. 979 Franklin Ln., Maple Glen, Pa. 19002. (800) 673-7899. FAX: (215) 628-2970. John Russell, pres.
Montpelier, Vt. 05602: Box 2255, RFD 4. (802) 223-6159. FAX: (802) 229-2210. John Russell, pres.
Audio amplifiers, pre-amplifiers, crossovers & microphone pre-amps.

Bryston Ltd. 57 Westmore Dr., Rexdale, Ont., Canada M9V 3Y6. (416) 746-1800. Brian W. Russell, pres; Christopher W. Russell, VP/engr.
Audio products, power amplifiers, line amplifiers, distribution amplifiers, preamplifiers, crossover, Dolby Nagra Interface, etc.

Bud Industries Inc. 4605 E. 355 St., Willoughby, Ohio 44094. (216) 946-3200. B.K. Haas, pres/VP mktg.
Open & welded racks; cabinets & accessories.

Buhl Optical. 1009 Beech Ave., Pittsburgh 15233. (412) 321-0076; (800) 245-4574. FAX: (412) 322-2640. Irv Stapsy, pres; Joe Pintavalle, mktg dir.
Biplexer, multiplexer for slide or film to video transfer; Raster "Masker" for "Talaria" light valve.

Burk Technology. 7 Lomar Dr., Pepperell, Mass. 01463. (508) 433-8877. FAX: (508) 433-8981. Peter C. Burk, pres; Phillip Halter, sls mgr.
Transmitter remote control systems including multi-site, unattended units & automatic transmitter control system.

Burkhardt Monitoring Service. Box 1411, Glen Allen, Va. 23060. (804) 261-1800. Edward E. Burkhardt, own.
Frequency measurement svc plus on site STL-Microwave-Modulation Monitor Calibrations.

Burle Industries Inc. 1000 New Holland Ave., Lancaster, Pa. 17601-5688. (717) 295-6000. FAX: (717) 295-6096. E. Burlefinger, pres/CEO; Carl Rintz, exec VP.
Electron tubes & devices; security cameras.

Burlington Audio/Video. 106 Mott St., Oceanside, N.Y. 11572. (516) 678-4414; (800) 331-3191. FAX: (516) 678-8959. Ruth Schwartz, pres; Rudy Schwartz, VP; Jan A. Schwartz, VP.
Distributors of all major brands of professional audio & video tape & accessories, custom loaded cassettes, splicing blocks, calibration tape, reels, boxes, etc.

Business Systems Inc. Box 26868, Greenville, S.C. 29616-1868. (803) 297-9290. William C. Cox, pres/CEO; Russell Bosko, exec VP.

In-house, real-time computerized billing & mgmt system featuring an interface to addressable converters & taps. Also interface to automated pay-per-view entry systems including ANI.

C

CADCO Inc. 2405 S. Shiloh Rd., Garland, Tex. 75041. (214) 271-3651. FAX: (214) 271-3654. Joe Drescoe, own; Jim Randolf pres; Bill Smith, VP mktg; Clayton McIntire, VP mftg.
Manufacturer of CATV & broadband communication products such as modulators, demodulators, signal processors, ch converters, trans & special application headend equipment, fixed-channel & frequency agile.

CATV Services Inc. 42307 Osgood Rd., Suite K, Fremont, Calif. 94539. (510) 226-4940. FAX: (510) 651-8545. Richard C. Richmond, pres.
Excess inventory professionals buy & sell; West Coast Wavetek sls & repair facility; full line distributor.

CBSI/Custom Business Systems Inc. Box 67, 20th & Winchester Ave., Reedsport, Ore. 97467. (800) 547-3930; (503) 271-3681. FAX: (503) 271-5721. I. Jerome Kenagy, pres; Stephen D. Kenagy, VP sls & mktg; John Kenagy, VP/CFO; Wes Lockard, engr; Bob Richardson, gen mgr; Bob Lundstrom, natl & international sls mgr; Ira Apple, Northeast U.S./Canada sls mgr; Al Hopwood & Jon Crossland, rgnl sls mgrs; Bunk Robinson, western sls mgr; Larry Keene, Elite Systems sls mgr; Joe MacDonald, product mgr Digital Audio Division.
Business software for bcst industry: Classic & Elite traffic & billing systems; InterAcct interactive accounting & gen ledger, mus library & scheduling; CustomRemote, interfaces, training & Digital Universe, (Digital Audio Division), advanced generation digital audio mgmt system, multiple-tasking & expandable.

CCA Electronics Corp. Box 426, 360 Bohannon Rd., Fairburn, Ga. 30213. (404) 964-3530. FAX: (404) 964-2222. Ronald Baker, pres; Steve McElroy, VP sls; Bill Brinegar, VP engrg.
Manufactures AM/FM & sw transmitters; parts support & repair svcs.

CCMS Inc. 1853 R.W. Berends Dr. SW, Wyoming, Mich. 49509. (616) 532-7250. FAX: (616) 532-8147. S. Michael Ross, pres; Judith K. Thome, VP.
Traffic mgmt & billing software for cable adv sls.

C-COR/COMLUX Inc. 47323 Warm Springs Blvd., Fremont, Calif. 94539-7462. (510) 440-0330 FAX: (510) 440-0218. Daniel Finch, pres; Dick Lawrence, natl sls mgr.
Vienna, Va. 22182: Eastern Region Sales Office, 8330 Boone Blvd., Suite 800. (703) 848-4624. Charles Coyle, eastern rgnl sls mgr.
San Francisco 94123: 2360 Chestnut St, Suite 111. (415) 923-9597. Robert Kasman, rgnl account exec.
Digital fiber optic transmission systems for the transmission of high quality video & audio data.

C-COR Electronics Inc. 60 Decibel Rd., State College, Pa. 16801. (814) 238-2461. FAX: (814) 238-4065. Richard E. Perry, chmn/pres/CEO; Jack B. Andrews, VP finance; John A. Hastings, dir sls; Richard Taylor, natl sls mgr; Richard Malkow, VP opns & mfg.
Fremont, Calif. 94539-7462: 47323 Warm Springs Blvd. (510) 440-0330. FAX: (510) 440-0218.
Palmyra, Pa. 17078: R.D. 1, Box 392. (717) 469-7285. Lee Stump.
Bloomington, Ind. 47401: 3404 Allendale Dr. (812) 334-2661. Robert Freedlund, rgnl account exec.
Plano, Tex. 75074: Suite 200, 555 Republic Dr. (214) 578-0071. Jim Rushing, rgnl sls exec.
Cable TV amplifiers & accesories; feedforward, power doubling & push/pull.

CCT Lighting Methods Inc. 1260 Lyell Ave., Rochester, N.Y. 14606. (716) 458-5790. FAX: (716) 458-5793. Albert H. Pfeiffer Jr., pres; Don Hindle, VP.
Manufacture theatrical lighting equip, spotlights, ellipsoidals, fresnels & floods.

CCTV Corp. 315 Hudson St., New York 10013. (212) 989-4433. FAX: (212) 463-9758. Harry Lefkowitz, chmn bd; Stephen Lefkowitz, pres.
Closed circuit TV cameras, monitors & accessories.

CEA-Computer Engineering Associates. 3922 Vero Rd., Baltimore 21227. (410) 247-5244. FAX: (410) 247-5407. Paul Keys, pres; Bill Baker, natl accounts exec.
CEA newsroom system—complete automation systems for radio & TV newsrooms.

CECO International Corp. 440 W. 15th St., New York 10011. (212) 206-8280. FAX: (212) 727-2144. Donald Kline, own/pres.
Motion picture & TV equipment; sls, rental, svc.

CED. 2500 N.W. 39th St., Miami, Fla. 33142. (305) 633-8020. FAX: (305) 633-6188. Sam Ascacci, pres; George Sabater, sls mgr.
MMDS, UHF, VHF & FM transmitters one w to 40 kw.

CEL Broadcast (USA). 1289 Hammerwood Ave., Sunnyvale, Calif. 94089. (408) 734-2917. FAX: (408) 745-1219. Robin Palmer, CEO.
2-D & 3-D DVE systems, standards converters, still store systems, encryption system.

CI Wescom. 201 Shelhouse Rd., Rantoul, Ill. 61866. (217) 893-8335. FAX: (217) 893-8362. Bill McDaniel, plant mgr.
Industrial battery chrgs, rectifiers, back-up systems & uninterruptible power supplies.

CMC Technology. (A division of Datatape Inc., a Kodak Co.) 2650 Lafayette St., Santa Clara, Calif. 95050. (408) 980-9800. FAX: (408) 988-7829. William Fitts, division VP & video opns.
Sony BVH1100 & BVH2000 upper drum refurbishing, VPR replacement heads.

CMX. 2230 Martin Ave., Santa Clara, Calif. 95050. (408) 988-2000. FAX: (408) 986-0452. W. Tom Beams, pres.
Design, mfg & mktg of linear & nonlinear video & film editing systems for bcstg TV, cable, video prod & post-prod, industrial mkts.

COASTCOM. 1151 Harbor Bay Pkwy., Alameda, Calif. 94502. (510) 523-6000. FAX: (510) 523-6150. E.M. "Ted" Buttner, pres; Diane Frank, gen mgr; Dennis Riemann, dir finance.
Manufacturer of T1 voice data net systems & digital prog chs for AM, FM & TV audio brdcstg.

COMTEK Inc. 357 W. 2700 S., Salt Lake City 84115. (801) 466-3463. FAX: (801) 484-6906. Steve Dupaix, sls dir.
Wireless microphones, wireless cueing systems & specialty wireless communications systems.

CONTEC International. Box 739, 1023 State St., Schenectady, N.Y. 12301. (518) 382-8000; (800) 382-2723. FAX: (518) 382-8452. Richard Monks, pres/COO.
Tampa, Fla. 33610: 5906 Breckenridge Rd., Suite A. (813) 623-1721. Russ Hersh, mgr.
Seattle 98148: 1250 S. 192nd St. (206) 244-5770. Bob Vick, mgr.
Bloomington, Ind. 47404: 2480 N. Curry Pike. (812) 330-8727. John Beard, mgr.
West Columbia, S.C. 29170: 1255 Boston Ave. (803) 794-3910. James Padgett, mgr.
Converter repair.

CORPLEX Systems Group. 6444 N. Ridgeway, Lincolnwood, Ill. 60645. (708) 673-5400. FAX: (708) 673-9201. Carter Ruehrdanz, pres.
Video prod & postprod equipment.

CS Communications Inc. 9825 Bridleridge Ct., Vienna, Va. 22181. (703) 938-5365. FAX: (703) 938-5823. Charles E. Sampson, pres.
Computer software billing system & engng svcs.

CSI-Camera Support Intl. Box 681, Woodland Hills, Calif. 91365. (818) 887-5430. FAX: (818) 887-5727. Bert I. Rosenberg, pres.
Camera support dollies, tripods, pan/tilt heads & accessories. ENG, EFP & studio application for bcst & industrial application.

C.T.E. International srl. Via Roberto Sevardi 7, 42100 Mancasale Reggio Emilia, Italy 522 516660/921212. FAX: 522 921248/586088. Mauro Tondelli, export coml dir; Giuseppe Coppola, export mgr; Enrico Antoniazzi, bcst sls mgr.
Radio & TV transmitters, studio links, antenna systems & passive components.

Broadcasting & Cable Yearbook 1994

Equipment Manufacturers and Distributors

CTI Installations Inc. 5688 Prospect Dr., Newburgh, Ind. 47630. (812) 858-2554. FAX: (812) 858-2522. Steve Rhinerson, pres; Brett Burnett, VP; Ray Ryan, chmn; Marvin Beasley, VP sls & mktg.
Tower instal, maintenance & inspection svcs; antenna instal for all FM & TV antennas; antenna rebuilding & field tuning.

Cabel-Con Inc. 5205 S. 31st Pl., Phoenix 85040. (800) 829-4529. Arvin N. Langham, pres.
Coaxial connectors for CATV.

Cable Leakage Technologies. 1111 International Pkwy., Suite 110, Richardson, Tex. 75081-2375. (214) 907-8100. FAX: (214) 907-2950. Wayne Havens, pres; Mike Ostteen, VP; Ken Eckenroth, VP engrg; Perry Havens, natl sls dir.
Digital RF tracking & mapping system used in CLI monitoring.

Cable Prep. (Ben Hughes Communication Products Co.) Box 373, 207 Middlesex Ave., Chester, Conn. 06412-0373. (203) 526-4337. FAX: (203) 526-2291. Deborah Morrow, pres; David Morrow, VP.
CABLE PREP hex crimp tools, coring & stripping/coring tools, accessories, drop cable stripping tool.

Cable Security Systems Inc. Box 2796, Opelika, Ala. 36801. (800) 288-1506; (205) 742-0050. FAX: (205) 742-0058. Curt B. Cope, pres; Mike W. Springer, VP sls.
The Beast: apartment boxes, metal & PVC molding, locks & locking systems.

Cable Services Company Inc. 2113 Marydale Ave., Williamsport, Pa. 17701. (717) 323-8518. FAX: (717) 322-5373. John Roskowski, pres; Gene Welliver, VP.
Turnkey fiber-optic & coaxial construction; distributor of CATV products.

Cable Services Group. 10825 Old Mill Rd. S., Omaha, Neb. 68154. (402) 222-4495. FAX: (402) 222-7572. Jay Oxton, pres; Jim Perkins, sr VP.
Lexington, Ky. 40511: 833 Nandino Blvd. (606) 271-7803. Connie Tanner, dir.
Complete sub info mgmt & data processing systems for the cable TV industry.

Cable Yellow Pages. 3430 Fujita St., Torrance, Calif. 90505. (310) 539-7038. FAX: (310) 530-5603. Neal Schnog, publisher.
Phone directory for cable TV systems (303 publications, bcst).

CableData. (A division of U.S. Computer Services). 11020 Sun Center Dr., Rancho Cordova, Calif. 95670-6184. (916) 636-5800. FAX: (916) 636-5645. Gerald Knapp, COO; Jim Castle, chmn.
Norcross, Ga. 30093: Eastern Svc. Ctr., 5300 Oakbrook Pkwy., Suite 250. (800) 331-9732. Joe LaGrossa, VP eastern opns.
Rancho Cordova, Calif. 95670: Western Svc. Ctr., 11020 Sun Center Dr. (800) 331-9728. Chuck Newkirk, VP western opns.
Dallas 75240: Dallas Svc. Ctr., 14180 Dallas Pkwy., Suite 200. (800) 331-9741. Ken Hill, dir.
Broomall, Pa. 19008: Philadelphia Svc. Ctr., 390 Reed Rd. (800) 331-9742. Ron Fishman, dir
Markham, Ont., Canada L3R 6B3: CableData Canada, 140 Renfrew Dr., Suite 103. (416) 477-3110. David Hunter, mng dir.
DDP sub mgmt & billing svcs, using Tandem (TM) computers; var of ancillary products are also available.

CableReady Inc. 470 E. 76th Ave., Bldg. 3 West, Denver 80229. (303) 288-8107. FAX: (303) 288-4769. Randy Holliday, pres; Susan Stockstill, natl sls mgr.
Painted steel molding with custom fittings backed by a 15-year warranty.

CableTek Center Products Inc. 1150 Taylor St., Elyria, Ohio 44035. (216) 365-3889. FAX: (216) 322-0321. Tim Reilly, sls dir.
Interior & exterior surface wiring products; terminal enclosures, residential enclosures, security products.

Cablewave Systems Inc. (A division of Radio Frequency Systems Inc.) 60 Dodge Ave., North Haven, Conn. 06473. (203) 239-3311. FAX: (203) 234-7718. George Gigas, pres; William Meola, natl sls mgr bcst; Charles Linke, VP sls & mktg; William Bayne, VP mfg.
Claremont, N.C. 28610: Box 310. (704) 459-9762. William Dixon, sls mgr.
Modesto, Calif. 95354: 1400 K St., Suite C-3. (209) 572-2525. Robert Parsons, sls mgr.
Rigid coaxial line (7/8" to 9/3/16"), FM antennas, FM, VHF/UHF IFTS, MMDS, TV antennas, dehydrators & instal accesories, RF & microwave antennas subsysts, instal & field svc.

Cadix International Inc. 5901-A Peachtree Dunwoody Rd., Suite 410, Atlanta 30328. (404) 804-9951. FAX: (404) 804-9949. Benjamin Lee, pres.
Fullerton, Calif. 92634: Box 6610. (714) 447-6911. Emmett Lee, sls mgr.
CATV design system.

Calaway Editing. (Beers Associates.) 180 Wright Brothers Dr., Suite 670, Salt Lake City 84116. (801) 366-7676. FAX: (801) 328-3668. Dave Carr, pres.
Designs, manufactures & markets high-performance, cost-effective editing equipment for use by video professionals in NTSC & PAL.

Calculated Industries Inc. 22720 Savi Ranch Pkwy., Yorba Linda, Calif. 92687. (714) 921-1800. FAX: (714) 921-2799. Henry Stricker, sls mgr.
Time code calculators that work in & convert between all time formats; drop/non-drop, multiple EPS rates for all SMPTE/PAL equations.

California Digital Audio Systems Inc. Box 120, Moorpark, Calif. 93020-0120. (805) 523-2310. FAX: (805) 523-0480. Linda Donahue, pres; Caryn Beemer, opns mgr.
Digital audio transmission systems via Ku- or C-band satellite or telco ISDN/Sw56. Ku flyaway systems, custom net control & Ku power control software. Featuring ComStream & CCS audio products.

California Microwave Inc. 985 Almanor Ave., Sunnyvale, Calif. 94086. (408) 732-4000. FAX: (408) 732-4244. Phil Otto, pres/chmn/CEO
Hauppage, N.Y. 11788: Satellite Transmissions Systems Inc. 125 Kennedy Dr. (516) 231-1919. David E. Hershberg, pres.
Satellite earth stns & equip for cable & bcst TV nets; mobile video/data earth stns.

California Switch and Signal Inc. 13717 S. Normandie Ave., Gardena, Calif. 90249. (310) 538-9830. FAX: (310) 327-2741. Ed Koshinski, sls mgr; Mark Poncher, mktg dir; JoAnn Brown, VP sls; Phil Haberman, VP/gen mgr.
San Diego 92126: 9466 Black Mountain Rd., Suite 233. (619) 231-6740.
Electromechanical devices with off-the-shelf delivery. Custom configurations, engraving & printing.

Calumet Professional Imaging. 890 Supreme Dr., Bensonville, Ill. 60106. (708) 860-7458; (800) CALUMET. FAX: (708) 860-7105. Kathy Houde, pres.

Calzone Case Co. 225 Black Rock Ave., Bridgeport, Conn. 06605. (203) 367-5766. FAX: (203) 336-4406. Joseph E. Calzone III, pres; Vincent J. Calzone, VP sls; Thomas M. Mackno, VP engrg.
Dallas 75220: 2919 Ladybird Ln. (214) 352-4620. Trisha Penna, gen mgr.
Pacoima, Calif. 91331: 12846 Pierce St. (818) 899-2547. Tim Lewis, gen mgr.
Manufacture standard & custom cases & containers for all industries. Feature Escort, Excalibur, Proline, Ultima & Convoy series.

Cambridge Products Corp. 920 River St., Windsor, Conn. 06095. (203) 688-0678. Irwin Scaman, pres; Richard Fischer, VP sls & mktg.
Coaxial connectors UHF & RF types.

The Camera Mart Inc. 456 W. 55th St., New York 10019. (212) 757-6977. FAX: (212) 582-2498. Shimon Ben-Dor, exec VP.
Evansville, Ind. 47715: 825 Royal Ave. (812) 476-6327. Joe Julian.
Sls, rental & repair of bcst & industrial quality video equipment.

CamMate. 2026 W. Campus Dr., Tempe, Ariz. 85282. (602) 438-1245. FAX: (602) 431-1421. Ron Mitchell, CEO.
12 to 20-foot camera booms.

Audio, Video & Broadcast Cables

2225 W. HUBBARD STREET, CHICAGO, IL 60612-1613
(312) 733-9555   FAX (312) 733-6416   (800) 966-0069

Canare Cable Inc. 511 5th St., Suite G, San Fernando, Calif. 91340. (818) 365-2446. FAX: (818) 365-0479. Barry Brenner, gen mgr.
"Star Quad" mic cable, quad-speaker cable, modular snake systems, cable reels, component video cable, video coaxial cable, 75 OHM BNC connectors, dual video patch bays, crimp tools & dies.

Canon U.S.A. Inc. (Broadcast Equipment Division Headquarters) 610 Palisade Ave., Englewood Cliffs, N.J. 07632. (201) 816-2915. FAX: (201) 816-9702. James Asai, dir/asst gen mgr.
Itasca, Ill. 60143: 100 Park Blvd. (708) 250-6231.
Irvine, Calif. 92718-3616: 15955 Alton Pkwy. (714) 753-4000. FAX: (714) 753-4337.
Mississauga, Ont., Canada L5T 1P7: Canon Canada Inc. 6390 Dixie Rd. (416) 678-2730.
Norcross, Ga. 30093: 5625 Oakbrook Pkwy. (404) 447-4290.
Irvine, Tex. 75063: 3200 Regent Blvd. (214) 830-9696.
Studio, field & ENG lenses & svc.

SAVE OUR PLANET, SAVE YOUR MONEY.
Our recycled evaluated video tapes are guaranteed as good as new for less than 1/2 the price. Order:
(800) 238-4300

Carpel Video Inc. 429 E. Patrick St., Frederick, Md. 21701. (800) 238-4300; (301) 694-3500. FAX: (301) 694-9510. Andy Carpel, pres.
Video tape wholesalers.

CASES UNLIMITED

Manufacturers of Custom Flightcases and Shipping Crates for virtually any application.

Tel: 201-669-CASE (2273)
Fax: 201-669-2826
1-3 Charles Street, Bldg. 135. 2nd Fl.
West Orange, NJ 07052

Cases Unlimited. Bldg. 135, 1-3 Charles St., 2nd Fl., West Orange, N.J. 07052. (201) 669-2273. FAX: (201) 669-2826. Paul DeVeau.
Manufacture custom flightcases & shipping crates for virtually any application.

Catel Telecommunications Inc. 1800 Stewart St., Santa Monica, Calif. 90404. (310) 315-1400. FAX: (310) 828-7167. Tom Elliott, dir opns; Ely Spater, dir mktg.
Products for transmission of audio, video & data signals in broadband coaxial cable or fiber optics systems.

Dwight Cavendish Company. 8242 McCormick Blvd., Skokie, Ill. 60076. (708) 673-0937. FAX: (708) 673-1389. Carter Ruehrdanz, pres.
Video cassette duplicators & duping accessories.

Celco Inc. 80 Sea Ln., Farmingdale, N.Y. 11735. (516) 249-3662. FAX: (516) 753-1020. Norman R. Wright, natl sls mgr.
London, U.K. SE6 32PN: Bellingham Rd. (1) 698-1027. Keith Dale, sls dir.
Lighting importers for CELCO bds & dimmers, power-drive trees, socapex connectors, Thomas trussing & lanterns.

Celwave R.F. 2 Ryan Rd., Marlboro, N.J. 07746. (908) 462-1880. FAX: (908) 462-6919. Richard P. Tallon, pres; Steven L. Aldinger, VP sls & mktg.
Phoenix 85004: 115 E. Watkins St. (602) 252-8058. Gary Marquis, admin mgr.
Schaumberg, Ill. 60173: Suite B, 941 N. Plum Grove Rd. (708) 843-7511. Gerald Anderson, rgnl mgr.
Base stns & mobile communications antenna systems, combining systems, duplexers & cavities.

Center City Film & Video. 1503-05 Walnut St., Philadelphia 19102. (215) 568-4134. FAX: (215) 568-6011. Frank Beazley, pres; Jordan Schwartz, chmn of bd; Dave Culver, VP/gen mgr.

Equipment Manufacturers and Distributors

Studio, remote, postprod 1" - Beta - 3/4" - ADO - Paint Box/Abekas 62/GV300 with E-Mem; film & tape DaVinci color correction, ADO repositioning & interactive motion control; D-2, D-3; AVID.

Central Dynamics Ltd. 147 Hymus Blvd., Pointe Claire, Que., Canada H9R 1G1. (514) 697-0810. FAX: (514) 697-0224. Pietro Censi, pres; John A. Boland; VP sls & mktg.
TV studio prod switchers, routing switchers, master control systems, distribution amplifiers, title keyers.

Central Tower Inc. 2855 Hwy. 261, Newburgh, Ind. 47630-8642. (800) 264-0595. FAX: (812) 853-6652. Ray Ryan, pres; Wayne Zinn, dir engrg; Marvin Beasley, VP sls & mktg; Scott Smith, gen mgr.
Manufacture towers for bcst, cellular & two-way; design & engr support structures; structural analysis; turnkey systems; antenna rebuilding; tower inspections.

Century Precision Optics. 10713 Burbank Blvd., North Hollywood, Calif. 91601. (818) 766-3715. FAX: (818) 505-9865. Steven E. Manios, VP; William J. Turner, gen mgr; Jeff Giordano, VP sls & mktg.
Wide angle & telephoto lens for video & motion picture cameras; lens accessories; lens svc.

Cezar Industries Ltd. dba Gateway USA. Box 4209, 3220 S. Higuera, Suite 200, San Luis Obispo, Calif. 93403-4209. (805) 541-4950. FAX: (805) 546-0145. Trone Miller, pres/CEO; Adrian A. Bray, VP finance/admin; Chad Stalsworth, VP engrg, rsch & dev.
International telecommunications enhanced svc provider.

Channel Master. (A division of Avnet Inc.) Box 1416, Industrial Park Dr., Smithfield, N.C. 27577. (919) 934-9711. FAX: (919) 989-2200. Syl Herlihy, pres; Buddy Mills, opns mgr; Wayne Abrams, controller; Richard Derrenbacher, mktg mgr; George Jusaites, dir adv.
Manufacturer of point-to-point microwave systems, satellite (TVRO) systems, coml broadband antennas & hardware.

Channel One Lighting Systems Inc. 1522 E. 6th St., Tulsa, Okla. 74120-4026. (918) 587-2663. FAX: (918) 587-9805. W. Blair Powell, pres.
Complete line of lighting equipment for TV, theatre & industrial applications; design, manufacture & distribute.

Channell Commercial Corp. Box 9022 26040 Ynez Rd., Temecula, Calif. 92591. (909) 694-9160; (800) 423-1863. FAX: (909) 694-9170. William H. Channell, pres; William H. Channell Jr., exec VP; Mike Loran, sls mgr; Gary Baker, finance.
Mississauga, Ont., Canada L5N 1A5: Channell Commercial Canada Ltd. 6341 Mississauga Rd. (416) 567-6751; (800) 387-8332. FAX: (416) 567-6756. Lynda Forsyth, opns admin.
Specialize in prods for underground construction. Plastic CATV enclosures; exclusive reps for Integral Corp. & fiber cable-in-duct; Carson Industries grade level boxes.

Channelmatic Inc. 821 Tavern Rd., Alpine, Calif. 91901. (619) 445-2691; (800) 766-7171. FAX: (619) 445-3293. Bill Killion, chmn; Paul Blevins, exec VP/CFO; Mike Watson, sr VP mktg & sls; Thomas Walsh, sr VP technology; Marc Yaxley, dir engrg.
Merrimac, Wis. 53561: S8268A Inspiration Dr. FAX: (608) 643-2445. Roger Heidenreich, rgnl sls mgr.
Hingham, Mass. 02043: 79 Central St. (617) 740-2102. Jim Sullivan, rgnl sls mgr.
Austin, Tex. 78759: Suite 104L, 11615 Angus Rd. (512) 343-0533. Rick DuRapau, rgnl sls mgr.
Ontario, Calif. 91764: 430 N. Vineyard, Suite 400. (714) 395-8540. FAX: (714) 395-8509. Kent Liday, rgnl sls mgr.
Redhook, N.Y. 12571: 9 Bard Ave. (914) 758-2680. FAX: (914) 758-2623. Dan Viles, rgnl sls mgr.
A/V switching distribution, control & automation; coml insertion products & systems; playback systems; custom time & tone switching systems.

Charles Industries Ltd. (Coil CATV Division) 5600 Apollo Dr., Rolling Meadows, Ill. 60008. (708) 806-6300. FAX: (708) 806-6231. Joseph T. Charles, pres.
Pedestals, custom security boxes, amplifier & TAP brackets-hardware, splicing vaults, taps, splitters & couplers.

Chenevert/Soderberg, Architects. 11750 Bricksome Ave., Suite B, Baton Rouge 70816. (504) 291-7884. FAX: (504) 296-5401. Norman J. Chenevert, AIA, proj mgr; Curtis D. Soderberg, AIA, proj mgr.
Architects, planners, interior designers & tech designers; specialize in new & renovated bcst/cable prod facilities.

Christie Electric Corp. 18120 S. Broadway, Gardena, Calif. 90248. (310) 715-1402. FAX: (310) 618-8368. Tom Christie, chmn; Raymond White, pres; Scott Marvel, dir mktg & sls.
CASP universal battery support systems & AC/DC power supplies.

Chromatek Scan Process Inc. 2049 Century Park E., Suite 2710, Los Angeles 90067. (310) 785-3810. FAX: (310) 785-3803. Yuji Ikushima, exec VP; Dale Rochon, VP mktg & sls.
Tokyo, Japan 150: Chromatek Inc. 8-18 Sakuragaoka Shibuya. 81-3-5458-2771. Daihei Ueno, pres/CEO.
Scan converters, HDTV-related equipments, multi-screen splitters.

Chrono-Log Corp. 2 W. Park Rd., Havertown, Pa. 19083. (215) 853-1130. FAX: (215) 853-3972. Arthur Freilich, pres.
WW synchronizer, digital clocks & time display systems, time code generators, video character generators.

Cine 60 Inc. 630 9th Ave., New York 10036. (212) 586-8782. FAX: (212) 459-9556. Paul Wildum, pres; Robert Kabo, mgr.

Hollywood, Calif. 90028: 1050 Cahuenga Blvd. (213) 461-3046. David Hermon, mgr.
Nickel-Cadmium battery belts, battery packs, chgrs, sun-guns & kits.

Cinema Products Corp. 3211 S. La Cienega Blvd., Los Angeles 90016. (310) 836-7991. FAX: (310) 836-9512. Ronald J. Lenney, pres; Jerry Kraus, mktg mgr; James Murphy, controller.
Professional prompters & camera support equipment, including Steadicam IIIA, EFP, vido SK & JR also film barcode reading systems including telecine & synchronizer systems.

Cipher Digital Corp. Box 427, Frederick, Md. 21705. (301) 695-0200. FAX: (301) 695-3622. Bob Tulloh, gen mgr.
Time code readers & generators in longitudinal & vertical interval formats.

Circuit Research Labs Inc. 2522 W. Geneva Dr., Tempe, Ariz. 85282. (800) 535-7648; (602) 438-0888. FAX: (602) 438-8227. Ron Jones, pres; Chuck Adams, engrg mgr.
Multiband audio AGCs, compressors & limiters for AM/FM; MTS processors, stereo generator & sw.

CLARK & ASSOCIATES

Broadcast Automation Systems

Digital Audio Storage Systems

Digital Audio Delay Systems

SMPTE/IRIG Time Code Cards

TEL: (309) 837-2244
FAX: (309) 833-5175

Clark & Associates
318 E. Calhoun
Macomb, IL 61455

Clark & Associates Ltd. 318 E. Calhoun, Macomb, Ill. 61455. (309) 837-2244. FAX: (309) 833-5175. William J. Clark, pres; Charles B. Owen, engrg.
Automation systems—single stns to large natl nets; digital audio storage systems 6-32 chs; SMPTE/IRIG PC cards.

Audio, Video & Broadcast Cables

2225 W. HUBBARD STREET, CHICAGO, IL 60612-1613
(312) 733-9555   FAX (312) 733-6416   (800) 966-0069

Clark Wire & Cable Co. Inc. 151 S. Pfingsten Rd., Unit B, Deerfield, Ill. 60015. (708) 272-9889. FAX: (708) 272-9564. Susan Clark, pres.
Audio, video, camera & speciality cable products for bcst industry.

Clear-Com Intercom Systems. 945 Camelia St., Berkeley, Calif. 94710. (510) 527-6666. FAX: (510) 527-6699. Bob Cohen, pres; Michael P. Goddard, natl sls mgr.

Central to:
- *Customer Needs*
- *Engineering*
- *Quality*
- *Fabrication*
- *Installation*
- *Specialized Services*

CENTRAL TOWER INC.

Central to All Your Tower Needs

2855 Hwy. 261 • Newburgh, IN 47630-8642
800-264-0595 • FAX 812-853-6652

Equipment Manufacturers and Distributors

Walnut Creek, Calif. 94596: Box 302. (503) 527-6666. Peter Giddings, mktg dir. (Export division office)

Single & multi-channel hardwire intercom systems for use in teleproduction. Wired & wireless partyline & point to point matrix intercom systems.

"Newsroom Hits Paydirt With The Environment"
— Broadcasting Magazine, June 1991

Now Broadcasters, put your money where your mouth is!

If you really do care about the environment and people, you should be using COARC Videotape.

F.Y.I.: We care about your needs, your bottomline, and our environment!

CoarcVideo

Videotape by people who really do care!

(800) 888-4451
FAX (518) 672-4048
Call us today, the world is waiting.

CoarcVideo. Box 2, Rt. 217, Mellenville, N.Y. 12544. (800) 888-4451; (518) 672-4451. FAX: (518) 672-4048. Edward Helfer, dir mktg; Alva Stalker, prod mgr.

Used by bcstrs, cable systems, duplicating houses, prod companies for environmentally-designed video tape reloaded products; provides Umatic & Betacam VHS tape, prog fulfullment svcs. CoarcVideo is part of the Coarc organization, which trains employees & provides various progs for the disabled.

Coaxial Dynamics Inc. 15210 Industrial Pkwy., Cleveland 44135. (216) 267-2233. FAX: (216) 267-3142. Joe Kluha, gen mgr; John R. Ittel, sls mgr.

RF wattmeters, terminations, RF load resistors, RF couplers & accessories.

Coherent Communications Systems Corp. 44084 Riverside Pkwy., Lansdowne, Va. 22075. (703) 729-6400. FAX: (703) 729-6152. D.L. McGinnis, pres; J. Skene, VP business dev; M. Pratt VP/gen mgr transmission prod division; G. Kephart, gen mgr teleconferencing; G. Stanton, VP finance & admin; D. Powell, mgr European division; S. Jolly, mgr Asia Pacific division.

Hauppauge, N.Y. 11788: 60 Commerce Dr. (516) 231-1550. G.S. Stanton, VP finance & admin.

Abingdon, Oxfordshire, England OX14 3Y3: 29 The Quandrant. 011-44-235-524-400. D. Powell, mgng dir.

Teleconferencing systems, digital echo cancellers, data over voice multiplexers, signaling systems, video conferencing, audio systems.

Cohu Inc. (Electronics Division.) Box 85623, 5755 Kearny Villa Rd., San Diego 92186-5623. (619) 277-6700. FAX: (619) 277-0221. Joe Olmstead Jr., natl sls mgr; Joe Barrett, OEM products mgr; Vijay Rana, international sls mgr.

Danville, Calif. 94526: 401 Pennington Pl. (510) 743-1456. FAX: (510) 743-0463. Gary Kuntz, mgr.

Lincoln, Neb. 68505: 420 Steinway Rd. (402) 488-8926. Bob Ruyle, mgr.

Binghamton, N.Y. 13904-9711: R.D. 7, 137 Colesville Rd. (607) 775-4437. FAX: (607) 775-3803. Ray Benck, mgr.

Ottawa, Ont., Canada K1G 4Z3: 2183 Thurston Dr. (613) 739-9068. David Purcell, mgr.

CCTV cameras & camera control systems, color, CCD, B/W.

Colorado Video Inc. Box 928, Boulder, Colo. 80306. (303) 530-9580. FAX: (303) 580-9569. Larry McClelland, pres.

Freeze-frame video for VBI or 7.5 khz audio subcarrier transmission; time-division video multiplexing/demultiplexing system.

ColorGraphics-Dynatech Broadcast Group. 6400 Enterprise Ln., Madison, Wis. 53719. (608) 274-5786. FAX: (608) 273-5686. Terry Kelly, corp VP; Kenneth W. Simmons, pres; Richard T. Daly, VP prod dev; Linda Post, gen mgr.

Video graphics systems for teleprod, postprod, news & weather graphics presentation systems.

Colortran Inc. 1015 Chestnut St., Burbank, Calif. 91506. (818) 843-1200. FAX: (818) 972-5599. Robert Sherman, pres; Mike Stephens, VP opns.

Totowa, N.J. 07512: East Coast Office, 40 B Commerce Way. (201) 256-7666. Bob Dente, rgnl sls mgr.

Mississauga, Ont., Canada L4Z 1N8: Canada Office, 400 Matheson Blvd., Units 1-3. (416) 890-0935. Paul Roscorla, rgnl sls mgr.

Lighting fixtures & control devices for theater, TV & architectural applications.

Columbine Broadcast Systems Inc. 1707 Cole Blvd., Golden, Colo. 80401. (303) 237-4000. FAX: (303) 237-0085. Wayne Ruting, pres/CEO; Mike Oldham, dir sls & mktg.

Fulham, London, U.K. S26 3DZ: 3 Hurlingham Sq., Peterborough Rd. 44-71-372-7676. Neil Hamilton, dir European opns.

Computer based automation solutions for radio, TV & cable industries including traf, master control, media, demographics, finance, archiving, admin, news & prod.

Comark Communications Inc. (A Thomson-CSF Co.) Box 506, Colmar, Pa. 18915. (215) 822-0777. FAX: (215) 822-9129. N.S. Ostroff, pres/CEO; Perry V. Priestly, international sls mgr; R.C. Kiesel, VP advanced dev; Richard E. Fiore Jr., natl sls mgr.

Southwick, Mass. 01077: Box 229. (413) 569-5939. A.H. Whiteside, VP engrg.

Inventor of inductive output tube (IOT) Dual Use UHF transmission technology.

Comex Worldwide Corp. 1657 N.W. 79th Ave., Miami, Fla. 33126. (305) 594-0850. FAX: (305) 591-7298. Jack A. Rickel, pres/CEO.

Design, furnish & install MMDS systems, point-to-point microwave & professional satellite systems.

Commercial Electronics Ltd. 1335 Burrard St., Vancouver, B.C., Canada V6Z 1Z7. (604) 669-5525. FAX: (604) 669-6347. H.H. von Tiesenhausen, pres.

Sls & engrg of bcst audio & video products & systems.

Commercial Radio Monitoring Co. 103 S.W. Market St., Lee's Summit, Mo. 64063. (816) 524-3777. FAX: (816) 524-3565. Gene McVay, CEO; Dale Crawford, mgr; W.R. Thorsen, coord field svc.

Frequency measurements & equipment calibraton.

Comm/Scope Inc. 1375 Lenoir Rhyne Blvd., Hickory, N.C. 28602. (800) 982-1708; (704) 324-2200. FAX: (704) 328-3400. Frank Drendel, pres/chmn of bd; Stan Lindsay, sr VP.

Coaxial & fiber optic cables including CRD & NEC approved drop cables, QR, P3 & CableGuard.

Communication Graphics Inc. 313 N. Redbud, Broken Arrow, Okla. 79012. (800) 331-4438; (918) 258-6502 (Okla). FAX: (918) 251-8223. Richard H. Lawrence, pres/gen mgr.

Screen printed decals for promotional uses & equipment markings; high gloss media folders.

Communications Data Services Inc. 6105-E Arlington Blvd., Falls Church, Va. 22044. (703) 534-0034.

FAX: (703) 534-7884. Richard P. Biby, pres; Richard L. Biby, VP.

Bcst-related computer svcs including Propogation Predications, FCC Data Files & Terrain data.

Communications Design Associates Inc. 1410 Providence Hwy., Norwood, Mass. 02062. (617) 551-8490. FAX: (617) 551-8491. Robert Hemenway, David Hutton, Stewart Randall & Greg Vincent, ptnrs.

Ind consultants to radio, TV, corporate & govt clients; designers of studios, prod, presentation & multi-media facilities.

Communications General Corp. 2685 Alta Vista Dr., Fallbrook, Calif. 92028-9683. (619) 723-2700. FAX: (619) 723-4000. Robert Gonsett, pres.

Mthy AM, FM & TV frequency measurements in the Southern California area, annual STL measurements, spectral measurements.

Communications Systems Group/General Television Network. 13355 Capital Ave., Oak Park, Mich. 48237. (313) 399-2000. FAX: (313) 548-0028. Kurt Krinke, pres.

TV, audio, teleconferencing systems design, sls & svc.

Compact Video Services Inc. 2813 W. Alameda Ave., Burbank, Calif. 91505. (818) 840-7000. FAX: (818) 846-5187. John Donlon, pres.

Postprod video & film svcs: editing, telecine, sound, duplication, satellite svcs, film lab, standard conversion tape to film transfers.

Comprehensive Video Supply Corp. 148 Veterans Dr., Northvale, N.J. 07647. (201) 767-7990. FAX: (201) 767-7377. Frank Taylor, natl sls mgr; Michael Lewis, product mgr.

PC-base editing system, character generator, software; full line video accessories, lighting, audio, test equipment.

Comprompter Inc. 1707 Main St., Suite 113, LaCrosse, Wis. 54601. (608) 785-1766. FAX: (608) 784-5013. Ralph King, pres.

Offers PC compatible computerized newsroom & prompting systems for radio, TV & industrial use.

CompuLink-Cable Services Group. 6200 S. Quebec, Suite 370, Englewood, Colo. 80111. (303) 488-8944. Pete Czornohus, pres; Judy Belisle, natl sls mgr.

Coml adv traffic & billing system; provides complete line of products for single systems through interconnects & corporate offices.

Computer Assisted Technologies. 333 E. 45th St., Suite 24A, New York 10017. (212) 687-BCAM. FAX: (212) 922-9521. Joseph Mahedy, pres.

Computer Concepts Corp. 8375 Melrose Dr., Lenexa, Kan. 66214. (800) 255-6350; (913) 541-0900. Greg L. Dean, chmn; Mark Bailey, pres.

In-house computer systems to automate traf, billing, gen ledger, script mgr, word processing & mus mgmt for radio; digital coml system.

Computer Power Inc. 124 W. Main St., High Bridge, N.J. 08829. (908) 638-8000. FAX: (908) 638-4931. Cheryl Borne, mktg mgr; Les Listwa, dir sls; Roger Love, CEO; Louis Massad, CFO; Todd Smith & Craig Sweetser, sls mgrs.

Carolina, Puerto Rico 00630: Box 3346. (809) 257-7000. Bob Thorpe, CEO.

Dorual, Que., Canada HP9 2R2: 517 Lepine Ave. (514) 631-9826. Gilbert LaCoste, CEO.

Stand-by & on-line static uninterruptible power systems, line conditioners & battery chgrs for the protection of bcstg equipment.

Computer Prompting Incaptioning Co. 3408 Wisconsin Ave. N.W., Suite 201, Washington 20016. (202) 966-0980; (800) 977-6678. FAX: (202) 966-0981. Dr. Dilip Som, pres; Sidney Hoffman, pres.

Computerized teleprompters & closed captioning systems running on IBM PCs, including laptops & compatibles. Optional closed captioning & newsroom system interface.

Computer Resolutions. 873 Wood Ave., Bridgeport, Conn. 06604. (203) 384-0742. FAX: (203) 384-0473. Carl Palmieri, pres.

PC & mainframe based traffic systems; both solutions offer multistation capability.

Comrex Corp. 65 Nonset Path, Acton, Mass. 01720. (508) 263-1800. FAX: (508) 635-0401. John F. Cheney, pres; Lynn E. Distler, VP.

Ealing, London U.K. W5 5LL: Comrex (UK) Ltd, 75 The Grove. (081) 579-9143. Ian Prowse, mgng dir.

Frequency extenders, digital audio codecs, telephone interface products, wireless IFB systems, TV aural monitors.

Broadcasting & Cable Yearbook 1994
H-23

Equipment Manufacturers and Distributors

Comsearch. 11720 Sunrise Valley Dr., Reston, Va. 22091. (703) 620-6300. FAX: (703) 476-2697. Michael Morin, pres; Kurt Oliver, mktg mgr.
 Richardson, Tex. 75080: 251 W. Renner Rd. (214) 680-1000. Jerry Mull, mktg mgr.
 Communication engrg svcs for mobile, microwave & satellite systems, including frequency, propagation & integration svcs.

ComSonics Inc. 1350 Port Republic Rd., Harrisonburg, Va. 22801. (703) 434-5965. FAX: (703) 434-9847. Dennis A. Zimmerman, pres/CEO; Donn E. Meyerhoeffer, dir opns; G. William McIntyre, dir finance; Raymond F. Schneider, dir engrg; Donald J. Sommerville, dir sls & mktg.
 Manufacture RF signal level meter & RF leakage detector & CATV repair facility.

Comstream Corp. 10180 Barnes Canyon Rd., San Diego 92121. (619) 458-1800. FAX: (619) 552-0488. John Puetz, mktg & prod mgr digital audio.
 Annapolis, Md. 21403: Eastern United States, 104 E. Bayview Dr. (410) 267-8040. FAX: (410) 267-8039. Charles Reutter.
 Hong Kong, China: Hong Kong Office, CD19 Cliffview Mansion. 852-559-6907. FAX: 852-858-6234. Michael Blair.
 Surrey, U.K. KT14 6NRE: Europe, 57 B Station Approach West Byfleet. 44-932-340-989. FAX: 44-932-341-266. Andrew Poole.
 Complete digital audio bcst net for compressed (MUSICAM) CD quality audio over satellite.

Comtech Antenna Corp. 3100 Communications Rd., St. Cloud, Fla. 34769. (407) 892-6411. Glenn Higgins, pres; Thomas Christy, VP mktg.
 Satellite antenna systems, sizes 3.0, 3.8, 5.0, 7.3 meters; Offsat(tm), 2 degree spacing antenna; 3.8, 5.0m & Offsat(tm) transportables.

Comwave. (A division of Communication Microwave Corp.) Box 69, 395 Oakhill Rd., Mountaintop, Pa. 18707. (717) 474-6751. FAX: (717) 474-5469. Stephen Koppelman, pres.
 Microwave transmitters, repeaters, amplifiers & ancillary equipment for MDS, ITFS, OFS, MMDS & total system capabilities.

Concept Productions. 120 Main St., Roseville, Calif. 95678. (916) 782-7754; (800) 783-3454. FAX: (916) 786-8304. Dick Wagner, pres; Mary Wagner, VP.
 Radio automation, CAPS, mus on DAT, spots on computer hard disk.

Concept W Systems Inc. 3302 W. 6th Ave., Emporia, Kan. 66801. (316) 342-7743. FAX: (316) 342-7405. J. Thomas Webb, CEO; C. Duane Woodmas, pres/chief engr.
 COMPLEX is a universally adaptable video/audio signals multiplexing system for ENG/EFP/SNG cameras used in remote applications.

Conifer Corp. Box 1025, 1400 N. Roosevelt, Burlington, Iowa 52601. (319) 752-3607. FAX: (319) 753-5508. John T. von Harz, pres; Gary Brotherson, VP; James Clark, sls mgr.
 Wireless cable (MMDS) & Instructional TV Fixed Service (ITFS) downconverters & antennas for receiving site.

Connect-Air International Inc. 50 37th St. N.E., Auburn, Wash. 98002. (206) 772-5033. FAX: (206) 939-4882. Michael D. Jones, pres; Ron Jones, sls mgr.
 Cable assemblies for most camera to VTR/CCU applications HL 79, ITC 730, etc.

Connectronics Corp. 300 Long Beach Blvd., Stratford, Conn. 06497. (203) 375-5577. FAX: (203) 375-5811. Richard J. Chilvers, pres.
 Audio wire & cable, patch bays & bodge plugs, cable reels.

Brek Connor Group Inc. 3405 S. 1470 W., Salt Lake City 84119. (801) 972-5900. FAX: (801) 975-0970. Randy E. Steele, pres.
 Professional & bcst character generators, still stores, audio-video distribution amplifiers & multi-layer keyers.

Conrac Display Products. 1724 S. Mountain Ave., Duarte, Calif. 91010. (818) 303-0095. FAX: (818) 303-5484. Ali Hussain, pres; Gusti L. Ives, dir mktg & sls.
 Colonia, N.J. 07067: Box 70. (908) 494-3113. Bernard Palmer, eastern rgnl sls mgr.
 St. Louis 63134: 6636 Carroll Lee. (314) 522-6922. Emery Bowser, central rgnl sls mgr.
 Manufacturer of a var of color & monochrome video monitors for bcst & computer graphic display.

Continental Electronics Corp. Box 270879, Dallas 75227. (214) 381-7161. FAX: (214) 381-4949. R. M. McDonald, pres; J.R. Faulkner, mktg mgr.
 Birmingham, Ala. 35226: Box 26509. (205) 822-1078. Dave Hultsman, rep.
 Evergreen, Colo. 80439: 7846 S. Centaur Dr. (303) 670-1049. Ken Perkins, rep.
 Streator, Ill. 61364: Box 575. (815) 672-8585. John Abdnour, district sls mgr.
 Apple Valley, Minn. 55124: 13783 Hanover Way. (612) 431-1313. Billy Emery, district sls mgr.
 Modesto, Calif. 95356: 3901 Rexford Ct. (209) 523-7505. Marvin Steelman, district sls mgr.
 Plano, Tex. 75086: Box 862008. (214) 423-3644. Steve H. Schott, district sls mgr.
 Seattle 98133: 19237 Aurora Ave. N. (206) 546-6546. John Schneider, rep.
 Columbus, N.C., 28722: Box 816. (704) 894-5433. Don Crain, district sls mgr.
 Specialists in AM, FM & SW radio transmitters, antenna systems & other RF equipment.

Control Concepts Corp. (a Subsidiary of Liebert Corporation) Box 1380, 328 Water St., Binghamton, N.Y. 13902-1380. (607) 724-2484; (800) 288-6169. FAX: (607) 722-8713. Patrick Gillette, pres; Oral R. Evans, VP special mkts.
 Power protection products for transmitters, studios & CATVs from transient & lightning induced voltages.

Control Technology Inc. 2950 S.W. 2nd Ave., Fort Lauderdale, Fla. 33315. (305) 761-1106; (800) 327-4121. FAX: (305) 764-3298. James C. Woodworth, pres.
 Sony, Auditronics, Technics, TFT, Ramsa; specialize in automation systems.

Convergence. 2752 Walnut Ave., Tustin, Calif. 92680. (714) 838-8833. FAX: (714) 838-9619. Roger L. Bailey, mng dir; Earl M. Jamgochian, mktg mgr.
 Heston-Middlesex, U.K. TW5 9NR: 7 Airlinks, Spitfire Way. 44-(0)81-756-1993.
 Videotape edit controllers.

Converter Parts Inc. Box 278, Rt. 20, Esperance, N.Y. 12066. (518) 875-6101. FAX: (518) 875-6388. Gary Rudolph, CEO; Rudy Moentmann, sls mgr; Paula Bever, office mgr; Tom Johnson, natl sls rep.
 Hand held remote converter parts - cosmetic & electronic; repair & refurbish converters.

Audio, Video & Broadcast Cables

2225 W. HUBBARD STREET, CHICAGO, IL 60612-1613
(312) 733-9555   FAX (312) 733-6416   (800) 966-0069

Cooper Industries/Belden Division. Box 1980, Richmond, Ind. 47375. 2200 U.S. Hwy. 27 S., Richmond, Ind. IN 47374. (317) 983-5200; (800) 235-3361. FAX: (317) 983-5294. Baker Cunningham, pres; John Valentine, dir mktg; Mike Murphy, dir sls.
 Precision video coaxial, triaxial cables, professional mus cables, ENG cables, audio snakes, RGB cables, 50 ohm transmission cables.

Cooper Power Systems. Box 2850, Pittsburgh 15230. (412) 269-6700. FAX: (412) 269-6761. W.D. Brewer, pres; William F. Oberschelp, VP sls & mktg; D.E. Cragen, VP opns; Neal Roth, rgnl sls mgr.
 Arlington, Tex. 76011: Box 5288. (817) 633-4861. J.M. Glenn, Joe Mann, rgnl mgrs.
 Millbrae, Calif. 94030: Box 849. (415) 692-4431. G.W. Ahlbrand, rgnl mgr.
 Glen Ellyn, Ill. 60137: Bldg. 8, 739 Roosevelt Rd., Suite 109. (708) 858-7100. L.P. Hellweg.
 Norcross, Ga. 30091: Box 1705. (404) 449-3723. J.L. Dennis, John Wright, rgnl mgrs.
 Golden, Colo. 80401-5256: Suite 305, 14618 W. 6th Ave. (303) 279-8870. Jim Quinn.
 Fogelsville, Pa. 18051-0280: Box 879. (215) 398-2365. Noel Lindsey.
 Electrical power transmission & distribution equipment - substn to the svc entrance.

Cooper Sound Systems. 31952 Paseo de Tania, San Juan Capistrano, Calif. 92675-3919. (714) 248-1361. FAX: (714) 248-5256. Andrew Cooper, own.
 Film & video location mixers & accessories, microphone preamplifiers & time code resolvers.

Convergent Media Systems Corp. 3490 Piedmont Rd., Suite 800, Atlanta 30305. (404) 262-1555. FAX: (404) 262-2055. K.F. Leddick, pres; James H. Black, exec VP.
 Transportable satellite uplinking & downlinking svcs. Includes facilities & transponder time for Ku & C-band applications.

Copperweld Bimetallics. 4 Gateway Ctr., Suite 2200, Pittsburgh 15222. (412) 263-3200. FAX: (412) 263-6998. John D. Turner, pres; J.F. Thomas, VP international sls; S. Levy, mktg mgr Bimetallics; Al Smith, VP opns.
 Copper-clad aluminium wire, copper-clad steel wire & aluminum-clad steel wire.

Corning Inc. (Telecommunications Products Division). MP-RO-03, Corning, N.Y. 14831. (607) 974-4476. FAX: (607) 974-7522. Melody Setter, mktg communications.
 Full line of single-mode & multimode optical fibers & optical splitters/couplers for cable TV applications.

Corporate Communications Consultants Inc. 64 Clinton Rd., Fairfield, N.J. 07004. (201) 226-5938. FAX: (201) 808-9117. Stanley J. Chayka, pres; Doris Adams, VP.
 Telecine color correctors & control systems; scene-by-scene computerized color correctors, comb filter decoders, remote controls for VTRs & telecines.

Corporate Computer Systems (CCS). 33 W. Main St., Holmdel, N.J. 07733. (908) 946-3800. FAX: (908) 946-7167. Tim Chase, pres; Larry Hinderks, VP; David Lin, product mgr.
 Digital audio codecs with band width up to 20 khz on 56/64 kbps digital carrier.

Cortana Corp. Box 2548, Farmington, N.M. 87499-2548. (505) 325-5336. FAX: (505) 326-2337. Evelyn Nott, pres; David Stockmar, VP.
 Stati-Cat Lightning Prevention System.

Cortland Cable Co. Inc. Box 330, 177 Port Watson St., Cortland, N.Y. 13045-0330. (607) 753-8276. FAX: (607) 753-3183. John Stidd, pres; Jack Dower, VP.
 Kevlar fiber antenna guys & ropes including eye splice end termination-potted sockets.

Costume Armour Inc./Christo Vac. Box 85, 2 Mill St., Cornwall, N.Y. 12518. (914) 534-9120. FAX: (914) 534-8602. Nino Novellino, pres.
 Period armor & weapons, vacuum-formed background panels, custom made props & sculpture.

Countryman Associates Inc. 417 Stanford Ave., Redwood City, Calif. 94063. (800) 669-1422; (415) 364-9988. FAX: (415) 364-2794. Carl Countryman, pres/chief engr.
 Very small precision electret condenser microphones for wide applications & the Type-85 Direct Box.

Cramer Productions Co. 355 Wood Rd., Braintree, Mass. 02184. (617) 849-3350. FAX: (617) 849-6165. Tom Martin, pres; Rich Sturchio, VP; Peter Ladue, Alex Frisbee, Steve Johnson, prod dirs; Maura MacMillan, opns mgr.
 Film & video prod svcs from design to presentation; staging svcs; video duplications.

Crouse-Kimzey Co. 4108 Amon Carter Blvd., #202, Fort Worth, Tex. 76155-2649. (817) 283-7700. FAX: (817) 283-8133. John Paul Kimzey, pres; Mark R. Bradford, VP/gen mgr.
 Annapolis, Md. 21401: Crouse-Kimzey of Annapolis, Box 6300. (410) 643-7700. FAX: (410) 643-8888. Kathleen Karas, gen mgr.
 Audio bcst equipment sls.

John Crowe Productions. 10 Greenway Plaza, Houston 77046. (713) 627-9270. FAX: (713) 871-9617. John T. Crowe, pres; Robert W. "Bob" Robinson, dir sls dev; Don Wilson, dir engrg; Dave Ernst, gen mgr.
 Irving, Tex. 75039: 6 Communications Complex, 6221 N. O'Connor, Suite 117. (214) 556-1816. FAX: (214) 556-2543. Dallas office.
 Multi-camera location prod company with 4-48' & 1-36' location prod trucks. ENG Package & full-svc offices in Houston & Dallas. Additional permanent facilities at the Summit in Houston.

Crown International. Box 1000, 1718 W. Mishawaka Rd., Elkhart, Ind. 46515-1000. (219) 294-8000. FAX: (219) 294-8FAX. Clyde Moore, pres/CEO; Gil Nichols, audio division mgr; Don Spragg, bcst division mgr.
 Amplifiers, preamplifiers, microphones & other audio equipment & FM bcst transmitters.

Equipment Manufacturers and Distributors

TV TO GO!

When your show hits the road we take your studio along for the ride.

Mobile services include editing, site checks, multi-track audio & crews.

The 26' truck is ideal for concerts, sports or pool coverage. Call for a demo tape.

Crystal Productions
A Division of Teletainment, Inc.
Chicago

1-800-899-CPTV
Available in the U.S. & Canada

Crystal Productions. 1024 Blouin Dr., Dolton, Ill. 60419. (708) 841-2622. FAX: (708) 841-2721. Tim Dwyer, opns mgr; Jeff Babick, prod mgr; Bob Liptack, chief engr.

Crystal Productions is a full-svc mobile prod company. One call to Crystal Productions puts you in touch with all mobile svcs. The list of svcs includes location scouting, microwave relay, satellite uplink, custom animation & postprod. The truck features five cameras, slo-motion playback, Chyron graphics & a var of recording formats. Experienced crews can be provided to staff all positions including Crane & Steadicam. Multi-track recording engrs are available for concerts or mus videos. The truck can be booked for prods in the U.S. & Canada.

Cumming Corp. 9620 Topanga Canyon Pl., Chatsworth, Calif. 91311-4132. (818) 882-0551. FAX: (818) 882-4835. Dave Happel, pres; Karen Chow, natl sls mgr.

Aereon brand dust & static control systems for telecine equipment.

Cummins-Allison Corp. Box 102, 2200 Production Dr., Indianapolis 46206-0102. (317) 244-2440. FAX: (317) 241-9518. Joseph H. Thomas, pres; Richard A. Lippitz, sr VP sls.

Coupon payment billing systems.

Cutting Edge Technologies. 2101 Superior Ave., Cleveland 44114. (216) 241-3343. FAX: (216) 241-4103. Frank Foti, pres.

AM & FM processors.

D

DBX. (A division of AKG Acoustics Inc.) 1525 Alvarado St., San Leandro, Calif. 94577. (510) 351-3500. FAX: (510) 351-0500. David Angress, VP sls & mktg; Amy Hemdon, corporate mktg mgr.

Bristol, Conn. 06010: 181-21 Sherbrooke St. (203) 589-4334. David "DJ" Bierut, eastern rgnl sls mgr.

Appleton, Wis. 54914: 1806 N. Blossom Dr. (414) 749-0044. Jeff Radke, central rgnl sls mgr.

Audio signal processing devices: compressor/limiters, De-essers, equalizers, gates, noise reduction.

DEDOTEC USA Inc. 410 Garibaldi Ave., Lodi, N.J. 07644. (201) 777-2771. FAX: (201) 777-5585. Paul Tepper, pres; Dedo Weigert, VP.

Low voltage high intensity lighting fixtures for film, video, ENG & EFP applications. Battery or AC operation.

D.H. Satellite. Box 239, 600 N. Marquette, Prairie du Chien, Wis. 53821. (608) 326-6041. FAX: (608) 326-4233. Mike Doll, VP; Randy Weeks, VP.

DIC Digital. 500 Frank W. Burr Blvd., Teaneck, N.J. 07666. (201) 692-7700. FAX: (201) 692-7757. Joseph Martinez, pres; Kevin Kennedy, mktg mgr.

Digital audio tape (DAT), 8mm video tape, Beta Cam SP tape, magneto optical disks.

DKW Systems Corp. 730, 9919-105 St., Edmonton, Alta. T5K 1B1. (403) 426-1551. FAX: (403) 428-0778. Alex Raczenko, CEO.

Dallas 75207: 4050 Infomart, 1950 Stemmons Fwy. (214) 746-5880. Ken Rozell, branch mgr.

Calgary, Alta., Canada TZP 1H4: 1060, 736 8th Ave. S.W. (403) 263-6081.

Bcst automation systems; live-assist digital audio mass storage; systems integration.

DSC Laboratories. 3565 Nashua Dr., Mississauga, Ont. L4V 1R1 (905) 673-3211. FAX: (905) 673-0929. D. Corley, pres; P. Corley, mktg; D. Beradi, sls.

Optical signal generators for camera alignment & postprod to SMPTE/NTSC & EBU/PAL Standards.

DVS GmbH. Krepenstrasse 8, Hanover 1, D-30165, Germany. 011-49-511-678070. FAX: +49-511-630070. S. Beyer, P. Spoer, H.U. Weidenbruch.

ISP200 & ISP400 RAM-based image sequence storage & display system for HDTV.

DX Communications Inc. 10 Skyline Dr., Hawthorne, N.Y. 10532. (914) 347-4040. FAX: (914) 347-3953. Koki Matsumotto, pres.

Satellite receivers & modulators.

DYMA Engineering Inc. Box 1535, 367 Main S.E., Las Lunas, N.M. 87031. (505) 865-6700. FAX: (505) 865-6776. Carroll G. Cunningham, pres.

Video & audio equipment, including RF gear & transmission line.

DYNAIR Electronics Inc. 5275 Market St., San Diego 92114. (619) 263-7711; (800) 854-2831 FAX: (619) 264-4181. E.G. Gramman, pres; H.P. Gruenstern, VP finance; C. Gallenson, dir engrg; Kelly Oletta, mktg & PR mgr; Mel West, VP opns.

Video, audio & data routing switchers, distribution amplifiers, fiber optic transmission equipment. D:A & A:D converters.

Dage-MTI Inc. 701 N. Roeske Ave., Michigan City, Ind. 46360. (219) 872-5514. FAX: (219) 872-5559. Arthur D. Sterling, pres; Paul L. Thomas, VP sls & mktg.

Closed circuit TV cameras & accessories.

Peter W. Dahl Co. Inc. 5869 Waycross, El Paso, Tex. 79924. (915) 751-2300. FAX: (915) 751-0768. Peter W. Dahl, pres; Gary L. Komassa, VP.

Heavy duty plate, power, filament, modulation transformers & reactors; single & three phase rectifiers.

Daily Electronics Corp. 10914 N.E. 39th St. # B-6, Vancouver, Wash. 98682. (206) 896-8856; (800) 346-6667. FAX: (206) 896-5476. Jim Grimes, pres.

Produces vacuum tubes: transmitting, camera, industrial, receiving & tube rebuilding.

Dalet Digital Media Systems. 1 Rue Cail, Paris, France 75010. 011 33 (1) 40380139. FAX: 33 (1) 42051866. Stephane Guez, gen mgr.

Digital audio PC-based nets for radio stns.

Daniels Publishing Group Inc. 9221 Flint St., Overland Park, Kan. 66214. (913) 492-9900. FAX: (913) 492-2085. Box 2056, Shawnee Mission, Kan. 66201. Charles H. Sheehan, chmn/CEO.

Publishers of electronic equipment, illustrated trade references & buyers guides plus tech & application manuals.

Data Security Inc. 729 Q St., Lincoln, Neb. 68508. (800) 225-7554. FAX: (402) 434-3291. Cary Gray, pres; Brian Boles, CEO.

Tape Enhancement Series features bulk tape deguassers & videotape cleaner/evaluators & dropout analyzers.

Datacount Inc. Box 3078, Opelika, Ala. 36801. (205) 749-5641. FAX: (205) 749-5666. Jerry L. Johnson, pres; Debbie Hamby, sls mgr.

PC-based system encompassing all aspects of logging, traf, co-op, billing, accts receivable & sls mgmt.

Data Guide Inc. Box 183, Giralda Farms, Madison, N.J. 07940-0183. (201) 514-5151. FAX (201) 514-5773. William Barcht, dir sls.

Electronic & info progmg guide.

Datatek Corp. 1121 Bristol Rd., Mountainside, N.J. 07092. (908) 654-8100. FAX: (908) 232-6381. Rick Rainey, sls.

Video/audio routing switchers, monitor switchers, machine control system, video/audio amplifiers, transmitter input equalizer.

Datum Inc. 1363 S. State College Blvd., Anaheim, Calif. 92806-5790. (714) 533-6333. FAX: (714) 533-6345. L.B. Horwitz, pres; Ray Waguespack, VP; Jim Madsen, VP.

Time code generators, readers, displays, encoders, search systems, distribution amplifiers, transmitters & receivers; design & manufacture precision frequency products & timing instruments.

Davis & Sanford Co. Inc. Box 1002, 24 Pleasant St., New Rochelle, N.Y. 10802. (914) 632-1636. E. Resk, pres.

Manufacture a wide range of tripods, heads & dollies for video & photographic use.

Delta Electronics Inc. Box 11268, 5730 General Washington Dr., Alexandria, Va. 22312. (703) 354-3350. FAX: (703) 354-0216. John Wright, pres; William R. Fox, VP engrg; Joseph S. Novak, VP mktg; Friedel Groene, VP mfg; Robert C. Stebbins, VP finance.

RF instrumentation: ammeters, operating impedance bridges, receiver generators, AM stereo exciters, monitors & audio processors.

DeSisti Lighting/DESMAR Corp. 1109 Grand Ave., North Bergen, N.J. 07047. (201) 319-1100. FAX: (201) 319-1104. Mario DeSisti, pres.

Professional lighting equipment & svcs. Quartz fresnels, softlights & cyc lights; HMI fresnels, softlights & sunguns; DeSisti rigging & light stands by Tre-D.

Devlin Design Group. 12526 High Bluff Dr., 3rd Fl., San Diego 92130. (619) 792-3676. FAX: (619) 942-2664. Dan Devlin, pres; Carol Vandervelden, design svcs mgr; Mike Newton, designer; Cindy Bradford, bcst consultant; David Smaw, lighting dir.

News sets & newsrooms - turnkey & design only; lighting direction; consultation.

Dialogic Communications Corp. Box 8, 1106 Harpeth Industrial Ct., Franklin, Tenn. 37065. (615) 790-2882. FAX: (615) 790-1329. Gene Kirby, pres; Mark Fuller, sls mgr; Charles Smith, VP engrg.

Interactive audio response voice processing equipment & software for pay-per-view, appointment confirmation, outage reporting, etc.

Diamond Communication Products Inc. 500 North Ave., Garwood, N.J. 07027. (908) 789-1400. Frank W. Pepe, pres; Gene Coll, VP; Howard Hoffman, western sls mgr; William Warner, eastern sls mgr.

Manufacture Poleline hardware aerial & drop systems, fiber optic hand holes & MMDS antenna mounting hardware.

Dictaphone Corp. (Special Markets Division). 3191 Broadbridge Ave., Stratford, Conn. 06497-2559. (203) 381-7000. FAX: (203) 381-7100. Marc C. Breslawsky, pres/CEO; Gordon F. Moore, Communications Recording Systems Division.

Multi-channel voice communications tape recorders (loggers).

Dielectric Communications. Box 949, Tower Hill Rd., Raymond, Me. 04071. (207) 655-4555. FAX: (207) 655-4669. Jim Beville, pres/gen mgr; Joseph Zuba, VP sls & mktg; Cole Plummer, VP engrg.

Voorhees, N.J., 08026: Dielectric Communications Antenna, 479 Gibbsboro Marlton Rds. (609) 435-3200.

Antennas, inside equipment, waveguide, transmission line, switches, loads, pressurization, custom applications.

Digital Audio Workstation
50 Simultaneous Stereo Segment Playback
2-Dimensional Project Creation - No Tracks!
-110dB Noise Floor

Turn To: **Micro Technology Unlimited**

Digidesign. 1360 Willow Rd., Suite 101, Menlo Park, Calif. 94025. (415) 688-0600. FAX: (415) 327-0777. Peter Gotcher, pres; Paul Lego, CFO; Paul Rice, VP sls; Tom Virden, VP mktg; David Olson, VP mfg.

Paris, France 75003: Digidesign France, 29 Blvd. Beaumarchais. 011-33-1-40270967. FAX: 011-33-1-40270965. Doug Provisor.

Los Angeles 90068: Digidesign Los Angeles, 3575 Chauenga Blvd. #220. (213) 874-3341. FAX: (213) 874-6323. Mick Walker.

Hoboken, N.J. 07030: Digidesign New York, 58 8th St., #1. (201) 659-2261. FAX: (201) 659-2184. Don Peebles.

Antioch, Tenn. 37013: Digidesign Tennessee, 701 Arbor Knoll Blvd. (615) 731-3650. FAX: (615) 731-3652. Ted Bahas.

Equipment Manufacturers and Distributors

Digital Arts. 4531 Empire Ave., #229, Burbank, Calif. 91505. (818) 972-2112. FAX: (818) 972-2115. Bruce Lyon, pres; Paul Phillips, sls admin.

Digital Broadcast Systems. 184 Mechanic St., Southbridge, Mass. 01550. (508) 764-4386. Richard R. LaVallee, pres; Paul J. Dobson, VP.
Astre: scheduling, prod on-air control software for logging 16-ch digital audio record/playback storage.

Digital Equipment Corp. 146 Main St., Maynard, Mass. 01754. (508) 493-5111. FAX: (508) 493-8780. Robert Palmer, pres.
Manufactures intractive computer systems.

Digital F/X Inc. 755 Ravendale Dr., Mountain View, Calif. 94043. (415) 961-2800. FAX: (415) 961-6990. Terry Brightner, sls dir.
Manufactures paint F/X digital graphics systems, the Composium digital component edit suite, the DDR-100, 100 second digital disk recorder, Video F/X, the Macintosh-based video editing system & Titleman, PostScript title generator. The leaders in integrated digital editing, graphics & audio solutions.

Digital Processing Systems Inc. 55 Nugget Ave., Unit 10, Scarborough, Ont., Canada M1S 3L1. (416) 754-8090. FAX: (416) 754-7046. John Fazackerley, chmn/CEO; Rui Luis, pres; Dr. Keith Lucas VP engrg.
Florence, Ky. 41042: 11 Spiral Dr., Suite 10. (606) 371-5533. (606) 371-3729. Brad Nogar, VP sls & mktg.
Video & audio equipment for bcst, prod & desktop video markets including TBCs, frame synchronizers, video disc recorders, color correctors & test equipment.

Digital Recorders Inc. Box 14068, Research Triangle Park, N.C. 27709-4068. (919) 361-2155; (800) 222-9583. FAX: (919) 361-2947. J. Phillip L. Johnston, pres; Drew Turner, VP TIS; Joanne Alpiser, sr account mgr.
Manufacture highway advisory bcst systems for low power AM radio; bcsts are for motorists.

Digitel Corp. 2816 Hagberg St., Duluth, Minn. 55811. (218) 727-0202. Jeffrey M. Stromquist, own.
Bcst remote control & automation control equipment.

Direct Brodcast Services Inc. 80 Red Schoolhouse Rd., Suite 220, Chestnut Ridge, N.Y. 10977-7032. (914) 426-3400. FAX: (914) 426-6059. Leo Rosenberg, pres; Jeffrey Wohl, VP.
Transmission svcs & rentals: Ku-band uplinking/downlinking, portable microwave, fiber optic systems.

Discreet Logic. 5505 Boul. St.- Laurent, # 5200 Montreal, Que. H2T1S6. (514) 272-0525. FAX: (514) 272-0585. Richard Szalwinski, pres.
Image processing & animation software running on silicon graphics hardware for the bcst & film market.

Display Devices Inc. 975 E. 58th Ave., Unit O, Denver 80216. (303) 297-1754. FAX: (303) 297-9072. Merv Perkins, pres.
CRT, LCD, slide projector motorized lifts & stationary mounts. Custom applications welcome.

The Display Source. 11420 Ferrell Dr., Suite 307, Dallas 75234. (214) 869-9040. FAX: (214) 432-9105. Brad Boa, pres; Dan South, VP sls.
Designs & manufactures modular & portable backdrops & displays.

Display Systems International Inc. 203 Mallin Crescent, Saskatoon, Sask., Canada S7K 7W8. (306) 934-6884. FAX: (306) 934-6447. Dale Lemke, pres.
Dayton, Pa. 16222: 147 W. Main St. (814) 257-8210. Buddy Dean, mktg mgr.
Low cost, high performance character generators/prod titlers; Spectraview, Spectraview II, Star & Elite 2000.

Ditch Witch. Box 66, Perry, Okla. 73077. (405) 336-4402. FAX: (405) 336-3458. Edwin Malzahn, pres.
Manufacture trenching, vibratory plow & trenchless technology equipment.

Di-Tech Inc. 48 Jefryn Blvd., Deer Park, N.Y. 11729. (516) 667-6300. FAX: (516) 595-1012. Tony Bolletino, mktg dir; Dan Mazur, sls.
Audio/video routing switchers, pulse distributor amplifiers, video equalizers, telephone control systems, audio monitor amplifiers & machine control systems.

Dolby Laboratories Inc. 100 Potrero Ave., San Francisco 94103. (415) 558-0200. FAX:(415) 863-1373; Ray M. Dolby, chmn; Bill Jasper, pres; Dick Bell, gen mgr, communications prods; Bill Mead, mktg dir, processing prods; Kevin Tam, mktg dir, communications prods.
Wootton Bassett, Wiltshire, England SN4 8QJ: (793) 842 100. Graham Carter, bcst projects mgr.
Audio noise reduction & signal processing equipment, digital audio STLs & codecs.

Dorrough Electronics. 5221 Collier Pl., Woodland Hills, Calif. 91364. (818) 999-1132. FAX: (818) 998-1507. Mike Dorrough.
Chatsworth, Calif. 91311: 20434 Corisco St. (818) 998-4886.
Audio processing for AM, FM & TV; FM stereo generator; audio level metering, both Peak & RMS. Stereo signal test equipment & video level meter.

Dow-Key Microwave Corp. 1667 Walter St., Ventura, Calif. 93003. (805) 650-0260. FAX: (805) 650-1734. E. Kjellberg, pres.
Microwave switches; coaxial RF relays & switches; high voltage relays.

R.L. Drake Co. Box 3006, Miamisburg, Ohio 45343. (513) 866-2421. FAX (513) 866-0806. Ron Wysong, pres/CEO; Mike Brubaker, VP sls; Phil Hawkins, coml products sls mgr.
Cable headend equipment including receivers, modulators, ch processors & accessories for reception & distribution of progmg.

M. Ducommun Co. 58 Main St., Warwick, N.Y. 10990. (914) 986-5757. FAX: (914) 986-7720. M. Ducommun Jr., pres.
Stopwatches for radio & TV; sls & svc.

Duncan Electronics Inc. 2865 Fairview Rd., Costa Mesa, Calif. 92626. (714) 545-8261. FAX: (714) 557-6240. H.H. Houdyshell, pres; James R. Colligan, mktg mgr.
Faders & attenuators: slide type with linear & audio output, single & dual ch.

Dynatech Cable Products Group. 4750 Wiley Post Way, Suite 145, Salt Lake City 84116. (801) 359-3205. FAX (801) 359-3554. Robert Shevlot, VP/gen mgr; Kenneth D. Lawson, VP sls & mktg.
Central Hong Kong, Dynatech Video Group, Asia Pacific. 19/F Kailey Tower, 16 Stanley St., 852-868-1993. Nick Lim, pres.
Turfstekerstraat 22, The Netherlands. Dynatech Broadcast Group, Graphics Division. Box 289, 1430 AG Aalsmeer. 011-31-2977-23473.
Character & graphics generators for both video prod & automated info display systems.

Dynatech NewStar. 6400 Enterprise Ln., Suite 200, Madison, Wis. 53719. (608) 274-8686. Robert E. Miller, pres; Kim Stribel, controller.
Automated newsroom systems.

E

ECHOLAB Inc. 175 Bedford Road, Burlington, Mass. 01803. (617) 273-1512. FAX: (617) 273-3275. Ted Whittaker, co-own.
Color special effects generators with memory.

EDX Engineering Inc. Box 1547, Eugene, Ore. 97440. (503) 345-0019. FAX: (503) 345-8145. H. R. Anderson, pres; D. J. Pinion, gen mgr.
Engrg software & svcs for AM, TV, FM bcst & communication svcs.

EEG Enterprises Inc. One Rome St., Farmingdale, N.Y. 11735. (516) 293-7472. FAX: (516) 293-7417. William Posner, pres; William Jorden, VP.
TV vertical blanking interval digital encoding & decoding equipment; line 21 closed-captioning; teletext; net communications & control.

EEV Canada Ltd. 67 Westmore Dr., Rexdale, Ont., Canada M9V 3Y6. (416) 745-9494. FAX: (416) 745-0618. J.A. Collard, pres; David Clissold, gen mgr.
TV camera tubes, spark gaps, surge arresters, vacuum capacitors, CCD cameras.

EEV Inc. 4 Westchester Plaza, Elmsford, N.Y. 10523. (914) 592-6050. FAX: (914) 682-8922. Jack Collard, pres; Mike Kirk, coml business mgr.
Buffalo, N.Y. 14221: 80 Post Rd. (716) 626-9055. Rick Bossert, natl sls mgr.
Manufacture UHF Klystrons, IOT & ESC power devices for TV transmitters; 1", $\frac{2}{3}$", 30 mm Leddicon camera tubes for studio, EFP & ENG cameras; Vidicon camera tubes for telecine & caption scanning; power tetrodes for AM/FM transmitters; CCD cameras for security surveillance.

EFI Electronics Corp. 2415 S. 2300 W., Salt Lake City 84119. (800) 877-1174. FAX: (801) 977-9009. Scott Nelson, pres/CEO; Mike Gilchrist, VP finance; David Bevan, VP opns.
Manufacture complete line of power protection systems for industrial, coml & computer applications.

EG&G Electro-Optics. 35 Congress St., Salem, Mass. 01970. (508) 745-3200. FAX: (508) 745-0894. Paul Beech, gen mgr; Ray Radford, mgr systems division; Joe Farrel, Lew Wetzel, sr sls engr.
High & medium intensity aviation obstruction lighting & beacons - FAA-approved; StrobeGuard; FlashGuard.

ENCO Systems Inc. 1866 Craigshire Dr., St. Louis 63146. (314) 453-0060. FAX: (314) 453-0061. Gene Novacek, pres.
Detroit (800) ENCO-SYS. Dave Turner, VP engrg.
Cleveland (800) ENCO-SYS. Nick Mues, VP/AI.
DAD486x-Intuitive graphic interfaces, digital audio delivery systems, custom software engrg for the bcst industry.

EON Corporation. 1941 Roland Clarke Pl., Reston, Va. 22091-1405. (703) 715-8600. FAX: (703) 715-8853. Michael Sheridan, pres; Lauren Battaglia, VP/gen counsel; Bob Chiaramonte, VP software & info systems; Len Smith, VP data products; Sanders Smith, VP bcst products.
Dev & mfg of wireless two-way interactive technology for consumers & businesses operating via radio frequency.

E-N-G Mobile Systems Inc. 2245 Via De Mercados., Concord, Calif. 94520. (510) 798-4060. FAX: (510) 798-0152. Dick A. Glass, pres; Ted Kendrick, VP; Tony Passer, customer svc.
Custom-designed ENG & EFP vehicles, rack-ready & turnkey systems; other mobile electronic systems; ENG system components.

EPE Technology. 1660 Scenic Ave., Costa Mesa, Calif. 92626. (714) 557-1636. Dennis Whittler, sec/treas.
Power conditioning products that protect computers & other equipment from power-related problems.

The One Thing Thousands of Broadcasters Worldwide Have in Common.
(916) 383-1177
JAMPRO ANTENNAS, INC.

ERI-Electronics Research Inc. 7777 Gardner Rd., Chandler, Ind. 47610. (812) 925-6000. Thomas B. Silliman P.E., pres; Robert W. Rose, VP electrical engrg; Ernest R Jones P.E., structural engrg; William J. Elmer, VP sls; David Davies, engrg sls & mktg.
FM & TV antennas, towers, filters, combiners, multiplexers & accessories. Structural & electrical consulting engrg svcs, tower & antenna instal & repair.

ERI-Installations Inc. 7777 Garner Rd., Chandler, Ind. 47610. (812) 925-6000. Thomas B. Silliman, pres; Max M. Brown, mgr.
Antenna & tower instal svc; antenna rebuilding, stand-by antennas, tower up-grades & gen maintenance; fully bonded & insured.

ESCO Communications Group. Box 6886, Fort Worth, Tex. 76115. (817) 295-8183. FAX: (817) 473-6993. C.W. Estes, pres; Rick Estes, VP; Joann Estes, sec/treas; Joe Wycoff, dir sls.
Tower mfg, site aquisition planning & dev. Antenna & transmission line sls & svc. Tower light monitoring.

ESE. 142 Sierra St., El Segundo, Calif. 90245. (310) 322-2136. FAX: (310) 322-8127. Jerrald D. Johnson, pres; Brian Way, mktg dir.
Solid state digital clocks, programmable timers, time code generators & readers, distribution amplifiers, programmable clocks.

ESV Inc. 525 Court St., Pekin, Ill. 61554. (800) 225-5378; (309) 347-6885. FAX: (309) 347-2535. Bernard W. Heberer Jr., pres; Roger Fahlberg, sls mgr, Michael Nachtrieb, sls rep.
Studio & projection lamps, gaffers tape, Ampex tapes, studio fixtures, colored gels & diffusion material.

E-Z Trench Mfg. Co. Inc. 1665 Hwy. 701 S., Loris, S.C. 29569. (803) 756-6444. FAX: (803) 756-6442. Roger Porter, pres.
Lightweight trenchers.

Equipment Manufacturers and Distributors

Eagle Comtronics Inc. 4562 Waterhouse Rd., Clay, N.Y. 13041. (315) 622-3402. FAX: (315) 622-3800. Alan E. Devendorf, pres; Joseph J. Ostuni, VP mktg & sls; Chester Syf, sls mgr.
CATV manufacturer & designer of traps, taps, scramble/descramble systems & converters.

East Coast Video Systems. 52 Ralph St., Belleville, N.J. 07109. (201) 751-5655. FAX: (201) 751-8731. Rich Bisignano, pres; Paul Krucik, VP engrg; Mary G. Nahra, VP sls.
Audio, video, data & control patch fields. TBC microprocessor control systems.

Eastman Kodak Co. 343 State St., Rochester, N.Y. 14650. (716) 724-4000. FAX: (716) 724-0663; Telex: 978481. Kay R. Whitmore, chmn, pres & CEO; Mike Benard, sr VP, dir communications & pub affrs; John R. McCarthy, sr VP/dir corporate rels; Paul L. Smith, sr VP/dir finance & admin.
Cameras, projectors, film; business sys, health sciences; graphic & motion picture products.

Echosphere Corp. 90 Inverness Cir. E., Englewood, Colo. 80112. (303) 799-8222. FAX: (303) 799-6222. Charles Ergen, pres; Brent Gale, dir bcst engrg.
Satellite reception systems.

Econco. 1318 Commerce Ave., Woodland, Calif. 95776. (916) 662-7553; (800) 532-6626. FAX: (916) 666-7760. Dave Elliott, pres; Debbie Storz, VP sls.
Rebuilds power transmitting tubes & klystrons.

Edcor Electronics. 7130 National Parks Hwy., Carlsbad, N.M. 88220. (505) 887-6790. FAX: (505) 887-6880. Larry Weston, pres.
Mixer & power amplifiers, automatic microphone mixers, audio microphone/line mixers, headphone amplifiers, programmable amplifiers, audio mixers & audio transformers.

The Edit Room. 5724 W. 3rd St., Suite 509, Los Angeles 90036. (213) 937-3500. FAX: (213) 937-3526. Harry Harris, pres.
Postprod sound editing digital, film & TV.

Editing Machines Corp. 5125 MacArthur Blvd., Suite 31, Washington 20016. (202) 362-3102. FAX: (202) 362-3240. Bill Ferster, pres; John Schwan VP sls.
Manufacture digital nonlinear editing products for the film & video industry.

Eddie Egan & Assoc. 156 S. Robertson Blvd., Los Angeles 90048. (213) 272-9282. FAX: (310) 275-6412. Daniel Egan, pres; Armand Egan, VP.
All types floor coverings for video stages: wood, vinyl, carpeting.

Editing Technologies Corp. 11992 Challenger Ct., Moorpark, Calif. 93021. (805) 529-7074. FAX: (805) 529-6744. Russell Srole, pres
Videotape editing systems.

Eigen Video. Box 848, Nevada City, Calif. 95959. (916) 265-2020. FAX: (916) 265-2792. George Foster, pres.
Digital image processors with optional floppy or Winchester disc storage. High-resolution video disc recorders.

Elan Enterprises Ltd. 502 E. St. Charles Rd., Carol Stream, Ill. 60188. (800) 331-8382. FAX: (708) 665-0296. Joe Johnsen Jr., pres; Jim Johnsen, sls mgr.
Redi-line electric generators.

Elantec Inc. 1996 Tarob Ct., Milpitas, Calif. 95035. (408) 945-1323; (800) 333-6314. FAX: (408) 945-9305. David O'Brien, pres/CEO; Ralph Granchelli, VP sls & mktg.
Braintree, Mass. 02184: Elantec Inc., 140 Wood Rd., Suite 410. (617) 849-9181. Patricia Wadden, rgnl sls mgr.
6 Lissenden Gardens, London, U.K. NW51LX. Gordon House Business Ctr, 1st Fl. 44-71-482-4596. Orit Josefi, European sls mgr.
High speed analog ICs, amplifiers, buffer, video asics.

Elcom Bauer. 6199 Warehouse Way, Sacramento, Calif. 95826. (916) 381-3750. FAX: (916) 381-4332. Paul Gregg, pres.
AM/FM transmitters, audio processing equipment, AM combining equipment.

Elcom Systems Inc. 932 Clint Moore Rd., Boca Raton, Fla. 33487. (407) 994-1774. FAX: (407) 994-1770. Leonard Pollachek, pres.
RF coaxial attenuators, terminations, couplers, double balanced mixers, detectors, DC-4.2 Ghz, impedance transformers.

Electric Image Inc. 117 E. Colorado Blvd., Suite 300, Pasadena, Calif. 91106. (818) 577-1627. FAX: (818) 577-2426. Jay Roth, pres/ CEO; Mark Granger, VP rsch & dev; Markus Houy, VP.
Electric Image Animation System 2.0 is a Macintosh/SGI-based 3D graphics software system for computer graphics & animation professionals.

Electro Impulse Laboratory Inc. Box 278, 1805 Corlies Ave., Neptune, N.J. 07753-0278. (908) 776-5800. FAX: (908) 776-6793. Mark Rubin, pres; Edward J. Kracum, chief engr.
Manufacture dry, forced air cooled FM dummy loads, RF calorimeters, wattmeters & attenuators.

Electro Sound Inc. 9130 Glenoaks Blvd., Sun Valley, Calif. 91352. (818) 504-3820. FAX: (818) 504-3828. Jim Williams, pres.
High speed audio tape duplicators, test equipment, automatic cassette loaders.

Electrohome Ltd. 809 Wellington St. N., Kitchener, Ont., Canada N2G 4J6. (519) 744-7111. FAX: (519) 744-7111. J.A. Pollock, chmn/CEO; W.M. Alguire, actg CFO/sec/treas.
Tonawanda, N.Y. 14150: 700 Ensminger Rd., Suite 112. (716) 874-3630.
Monitors: data graphics & projection systems; receivers, monitors.

Electroline Equipment Inc. 8750 8th Ave., Montreal, Que., Canada H1Z 2W4. (514) 374 6335. FAX: (514) 374-9370. Mitchell Olfman, pres/CEO.
Cable TV equipment, off premises addressable systems, passive devices, filters, amplifiers.

Electronic Script Prompting. 6129 Western, Clarendon Hills, Ill. 60514. (800) 543-0346; (708) 887-0346. FAX: (708) 887-0389. Frank Warner, pres.
Teleprompting; rental & sale.

Electronic Theatre Controls Inc. 3030 Laura Ln., Middleton, Wis. 53562. (608) 831-4116. FAX: (608) 836-1736. Fred Foster, pres.
New York 10010: Electronic Theatre Controls Inc. Northeast Regional Office, 1133 Broadway, Suite 1219. (212) 627-2272. Mark Vassallo, northeast rgnl mgr.
San Antonio 78250: Electronic Theatre Controls Inc, Southwest Regional Office, 9138 Autumn Whisper Rd. (512) 523-6310. John Massie, southwest rgnl mgr.
Entertainment lighting systems including control consoles, dimming equipment & interface products.

Electro-Voice Inc. 600 Cecil St., Buchanan, Mich. 49107. (616) 695-6831. FAX: (616) 695-1304. Paul McGuire, pres.
Microphones & accessories, monitor loudspeakers, mixers, signal processors, pub address systems, concert sound systems.

Elephant Replacement & Rehab Inc. Box 3626, 7980 Mercantile, North Fort Myers, Fla. 33917. (813) 995-7383. FAX: (813) 731-2153. Sam Abrams, pres.
Manufactures underground hydraulic boring machines & pipe splitting equipment for underground pipe replacement.

Ellis Tower Co. Inc. Box 23217, Fort Lauderdale, Fla. 33307. (305) 566-6432. FAX: (305) 566-6455. W.S. Ellis, pres; H.E. Blaksley, VP; C.S. Douglas, account exec.
Distributes & installs svcs towers, equipment bldgs & accessories.

Emcee Broadcast Products. Box 68, White Haven, Pa. 18661-0068. (717) 443-9575; (800) 233-6193. FAX: (717) 443-9257. James L. DeStefano, pres/CEO; Allan J. Harding, VP finance; Bob Nash, VP engr; John Saul, VP systems; Perry Spooner, VP international systems; Jim Zardo, sls & mktg mgr.
VHF/UHF transmitters - low & medium power; VHF/UHF trans - 1 w to 1kw; wireless cable & instructional TV; antenna & transmission systems; rsch & dev; systems analysis, field svc instal.

Emcor Products/Crenlo Inc. Box 4650, 1600 4th Ave. N.W., Rochester, Minn. 55901. (507) 289-3371. FAX: (507) 287-3405. Dan Estes, sls mgr; Thomas A. Regnier, adv coord.
Standard, modified standard & custom modular conventional EMI/RFI shielded enclosures & package blowers.

Emergency Alert Receiver Inc. Box 20629, New York 10025. (212) 222-7924. Jack Bergman, pres.
E.B.S. receivers for homes, schools, industry & loc officials.

Energy-Onix Broadcast Equipment Co. Inc. 752 Warren St., Hudson, N.Y. 12534. (518) 828-1690. FAX: (518) 828-8476. Bernard Wise, pres; Ernest A. Belanger, VP mktg.
Transmitters: FM solid state to 10KW, grounded grid triode to 50KW, AM & SW to 100KW.

Let *ERI®* Piece together your Antenna System Puzzle!

ERI® will provide a complete system, including . . .
ANTENNA, TOWER, LAMBDA™ SYSTEM and INSTALLATION

Call for a direct quotation
ERI® - Electronics Research, Inc.
(812) 925-6000

New SHPX antenna and Lambda™ Mounting System

Equipment Manufacturers and Distributors

THE AFFORDABLE ALTERNATIVE!™ BATTERIES AND CHARGERS

1-800-223-1775 PHONE   1-800-442-1775 FAX

Our sophisticated fast charging Battery Management Systems incorporate a built-in computer system, state of the art switching power supply technology, and a rugged interior/exterior aluminum enclosure for reliability and durability. Multi-port systems are currently designed for Nickel Cadmium and Nickel Metal Hydride cells but can be modified to any cell technology. Our Battery Management Charging Systems are very popular in the professional film, news and video markets for the total care and maintenance of rechargeable battery packs. We are a custom manufacturer of simple to complex battery charging systems for the computer, medical and other industries. Private label, design assistance, subassemblies and finished systems are all available.

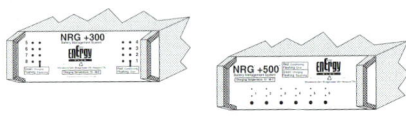

Custom Battery Assemblies, Micro-Processor Control Battery Management Charging Systems, Inverters (DC to AC), Power Supplies, PC'S & Notebooks by Zeos International.

PowersOnic	Panasonic	Eveready	Duracell	Varta	Sanyo	Gates
Sabi-Nife	Mercury	Alkaline	Lithium	Zinc-Air	Nickel Cadmium	Ni-Metal Hydride
Johnson Control	Prof. Video	Cam-Corder	Notebook Batteries	Cellular	Communications	OEM-Assm.
Lead Acid	Anton-Bauer	JVC/Cine 60	Battery Mngmt.	Charger Systems	Chrysler	Bio-Medical
Silver-Zinc	Frezzi/PAG	Alexander	Multiplex	Schlage	Shellock	I.E.N.S.
Nikon	Willi	H.P.	Topcon	Pentax	Kern	Sokkia
P.C.'S	Notebooks	Zeos Int.	U.S. Auto's	G.M.	Ford	Chrysler

Rathbone Energy Systems, Inc. & Energy Plus, Inc.
Shipping & Distribution • P.O. Box 1016 • 136 Old Huff Hollow Road • Newport, TN 37821
Sales & Service • 3220 New Rutledge Road • Kennesaw, GA 30144 • 404-975-8052 • 404-975-8915 FAX

Energy Plus Inc. & Rathbone Energy Systems Inc. Box 1016, 136 Old Huff Hollow Rd., Newport, Tenn. 37821. (404) 975-8052. FAX: (404) 975-8915. June Rathbone, CEO (RES Inc.); Ron Rathbone, CEO (Energy Plus Inc.); Nancy Wells, treas; Steve Owen, engrg VP (RES Inc.). Mfg, shipping & distribution.

Kennesaw, Ga. 30144: 3220 New Rutledge Rd. (800) 223-1775 (FAX also). Sls & svc.

In the industry of rechargable batteries, we supply chemical types including nickel cadmium, nickel hydride, lead acid, rechargable lithium, zinc-air & silver zinc. Primary batteries include alkaline, carbon-zinc, lithium, mercury & silver cell. Our Battery Management Charging Systems are very popular in the professional film, news & video markets for the total care & maintenance of rechargable battery packs. We can manufacture chargers & battery packs for any industry.

As a reseller for Zeos International Ltd., we provide PC & Notebook computers. Within the medical field, we actively participate in the manufacture of chiropractic support cushions & pillows. Within the corporate arena, we offer an auto-finder svc. We strive to create a purchasing environment that meets your needs. This includes 24/48-hour shipment of new products or repairs, warranties up to 24 mos, 20 day free trial period, competitive prices, free tech support & personal follow-up. We maintain the highest quality, svc, tech support & "confidence" for our customers.

The industries we currenty serve are professional video & film, television news, consumer camcorder, survey, computer, hotel, medical & the OEM markets. We work these markets through oem-v, distributors, dealers, manufacturer's reps, exporters & our own telephone sls & direct mktg departments.

"Environmentally conscious" is the theme of our company. As part of our mission to help protect the world we live in, we use recycled paper & recyclable plastic products wherever possible. We have accesss to facilities for the retreival of recyclable battery products.

Enghouse Systems Ltd. 80 Tiverton Ct., Suite 800, Markham, Ont., Canada L3R 0G4. (416) 477-1212. FAX: (416) 477-1466. Robert Kirby, pres; Gene Spence, exec VP.

Atlanta 30350: Enghouse Systems USA Inc., 8451 Dunwoody Pl. (404) 640-0055. FAX: (404) 642-0015. R. Bud Porter, VP.

CableCad (TM) - automated mapping & facilities mgmt software with integrated design capabilities for Cable TV companies.

Ensemble Designs. Box 993 Grass Valley, Calif. 95945. (916) 478-1830. FAX: (916) 478-1832. David S. Wood, pres; Cindy Zuelsdorf, mktg mgr.

TBC control systems, digital composite proc amp, D2 frame store, mac to video encoding/decoding.

Enterprise Electronics Corp. 1106 Gables Dr., Atlanta, 30319. (404) 261-8400. FAX: (404) 261-8400. Gene Rubin, sls mgr/meteorologist.

Doppler weather radar systems (rain & wind measurements) with PC-based graphics display & control.

Enterprise Systems Group Inc. Enterprise Systems Building, 5475 Tech Center Dr., Suite 300, Colorado Springs, 80919. (719) 548-1800. FAX: (719) 548-1818. Rick Schleufer, pres; George Beattie, sr VP; Rob McConnell, VP sls & mktg; Bob Lennon, VP opns; Clint Bulkley, VP finance & admin.

Full range of computer systems running on IBM AS/400 & System/38.

The Equipment Broker Inc. 514 Live Oak Circle Dr., Calabasas, Calif. 91302. (818) 752-3104. FAX: (818) 752-3105. Roy N. Isaia, pres.

Remote camera heads "Power-Pod/Pee-Pod," "Runford Baker" tripods & heads, camera cranes - "Cinerent carbon fiber," used cameras.

Euphonix Inc. 220 Portage Ave., Palo Alto, Calif. 94306. (415) 855-0400. FAX: (415) 855-0410. James Dobbie, CEO.

North Hollywood, Calif. 91602: Euphonix Sales & Marketing, 10647B Riverside Dr. (818) 766-1666. FAX: (818) 766-3401. Andy Wild, VP sls & mktg.

The Euphonix CSII digitally controlled analog audio mixing system.

Eventide Inc. 1 Alsan Way, Little Ferry, N.J. 07643. (201) 641-1200.

Audio & video delay lines, time compression & expansion, pitch change effects, digital reverb & effects processor, digital audio logger.

Evertz Microsystems Ltd. 3465 Mainway, Burlington, Ont. L7M 1A9. (416) 335-3700. FAX: (416) 335-3573. Dieter Evertz, pres; Alan Lambshead, VP/chief eng; Carter Lancaster, mktg.

LTC & VITC time code generators, readers, character inserters, trans, deleters, synchronizers, audio transport & VHS machine interfaces, clocks, timers & data displays, 16 & 35mm keykode readers, digital keyers, data list mgmt progs & data acquisition progs.

Excalibur Cable Communications Ltd. 8906 Telegraph Rd., Lorton, Va. 22079. (703) 550-8559. FAX: (703) 550-8840. K.E. Poth, pres.

Supply engrg design & instal data net systems.

The Express Group. 3518 3rd Ave., San Diego 92103. (619) 298-2834. FAX: (619) 298-4143. Byron Andrus, pres; George Andrus, sls mgr.

Design, fabricate & plan lighting of custom news sets, newsrooms & interview sets; custom & modular radio cabinetry.

F

F&F Productions Inc. 9675 4th St. N., St. Petersburg, Fla. 33702. (813) 576-7676. FAX: (813) 577-5011. George Orgera, pres; Robert W. Eisenstaedt, VP & gen mgr.

Remote prod svcs & television mobile units.

SCS Modified Radios

Receive hidden FM sideband programs on your very own modified radio! Explore the money-making possibilities of adding SCA to your station, or compare your station's subcarrier signal to others in your market. A great travel companion!

◆ G-E Superadio III with tunable, 57-92 kHz SCS module, $96.50 postpaid.

◆ G-E 3-5264 FM-AM-tape, new or factory serviced, modified with SCS, $72 ppd.

All radios are switchable from "FM" to "SCS," AC-DC. Other models available, as are quantity discounts!

◆ "FM Atlas" with FMaps and directories, showing stations having an SCS, FM station coverages, FM translators and more! 15th edition, 208-pp., $16 postpaid.

VISA – (218) 879-7676 – MASTERCARD
"FM Atlas," Box 336, Esko MN 55733-0336

FM Atlas—Publishing and Electronics. Box 336, Esko, Minn. 55733-0336. (218) 879-7676. Bruce Elving.

Tunable FM/SCS radios. Explore what is on FM subcarriers with your own radio or adapter kit, including adapters with LEDisplay.

FM Systems Inc. 3877 S. Main St., Santa Ana, Calif. 92707. (714) 979-3355; (800) 235-6960. FAX: (714) 979-0913. Frank McClatchie, pres.

Stereo performance meter, audio level master, digital video volt meter, video & audio modulation meters & multichannel subcarriers.

FM Technology Associates Inc. 30925 Vista View, Mount Dora, Fla. 32757. (904) 383-3682. FAX: (904) 383-4077. Howard L. Enstrom, pres; H. Larry Enstrom, VP.

FM & TV trans, multiple amplifiers, antennas, line, towers & accessories.

FOR.A Corp. of America. 313 Speen St., Natick, Mass. 01760. (508) 650-3902. FAX: (508) 651-8729. Jackson Kitahara, pres.

Cypress, Calif. 90630: 11095 Knott Ave., Suites A & B. (714) 894-3311.

Houston 77065: 11807 Yearling Dr. (713) 894-2668.

Video & audio bcst & postprod equipment; TBCs, color correctors, switchers, decoders/encoders & audio mixers.

FTC Inc. 155 W. 18th St., New York 10011. (212) 929-1156; (407) 422-8246. FAX: (212) 633-2301. Tony Foresta, pres; Kaye Armstong, sec of corp; Kirsten Fisher, prod mgr.

Remote video facility shooting studio & on-location prods in 1", 3/4" & Beta SP formats; specialized gear: Honda Goldwing Camera Bike, remote van.

FWT Inc. Box 8597, Fort Worth, Tex. 76124-0597; (817) 457-3060. FAX: (817) 429-6010. Ray Moore, VP mktg sls.

Towers, communications bldgs, standby power systems, mobile communications bldgs & fiber optics splicing trailers.

Equipment Manufacturers and Distributors

Digital Audio Workstation
50 Simultaneous Stereo Segment Playback
2-Dimensional Project Creation - No Tracks!
-110dB Noise Floor
Turn To: **Micro Technology Unlimited**

Fairlight ESP Pty. Ltd. Unit B, 5 Skyline Pl., Frenchs Forest, Sydney, Australia 2086. +61-2-212-6111. FAX: +61-2-975-1368. Kim Ryrie, chmn; John Lancken, sls mgr.
Digital audio workstation.

Faraone Communications Inc. 162 W. 56 St., Suite 1203. New York 10019 (212) 489-1313. Ted Faraone, pres; Teri Faraone, VP.
Media rel & publ svcs to entertainers, prods & distributors of radio & TV progs.

Faroudja Laboratories Inc. 750 Palomar Ave., Sunnyvale, Calif. 94086. (408) 735-1492. FAX: (408) 735-8571. Yves Faroudja, pres; Isabell Faroudja, VP.
NTSC encoder, NTSC decoder w/RGB, component & S-VHS outputs. VHP: vertical & horizontal detail processor. Component to RGB/RGB to component transcoder. SuperNTSC, line doubler.

Farpoint Technologies Inc. 1800 Water Pl., Suite 100, Atlanta 30339. (404) 956-0700. FAX: (404) 956-8781. Robert Tarabella, pres.
"Farpoint AccuPrompt"—MacIntosh based prompter system; "Farpoint Producer"—modular system for scripting, prompting, storyboarding & more.

Farrtronics Ltd. Rear Bldg., 39 Kent Ave., Kitchener, Ont. N2G 3R2. (519) 741-1010. FAX: (519) 578-2044. Norman Farr, pres; Andy Mooser, VP.
Intercom systems, IFB systems, distribution amplifiers, audio/video patchfields, beltpack party line systems & monitor packages.

Fast Electronic Sales Inc. 805 W. Orchard Dr., #4, Bellingham, Wash. 98225. (206) 671-3325. FAX: (206) 671-3860. H.H. von Tiesenhausen, pres; Kelly Michell, natl sls mgr.
Desktop video editing equipment includes: A/B Roll edit; digital special effects, frame synchronizers, etc.

Fast Forward Video. 18200-C W. McDurmott, Irvine, Calif. 92714. (714) 852-8404. FAX: (714) 852-1226. Paul Dekeyser, pres; Robert Riley, Jr., mgr; Eddeon Zarsadias, customer support.
Irvine, Calif. 92714: 18200-C W. McDurmott, (714) 852-8404. Eddeon Zarsadias, customer support.
Bandit-digital playback/recorder F-30 & F-22. Time code generators, readers & character inserters.

Feldmar Watch and Clock Center. 9000 W. Pico Blvd., Los Angeles 90035. (213) 272-1196. FAX: (310) 274-2081. Barney Feldmar, pres; Sol Meller, VP.
Stopwatches, clocks, watches, timers; sls & repairs.

Fermont Division. (Dynamic Corp. of America.) 141 N. Ave., Bridgeport, Conn. 06606. (203) 366-5211. W.F. Tuxbury, pres; R.T. Santry, dir mktg.
Emergency standby power & diesel generator sets. Co-generation plant modules.

Ferno-Washington Inc. 70 Weil Way, Wilmington, Ohio 45177. (513) 382-1451. FAX: (513) 382-1191. El Bourgraf, CEO; Wayne Smith, COO; Ed Vilchinsky, VP finance; Mark McMurphy, mkt mgr; George Reazer, VP mfg.
Carts designed to aid in the movement of heavy & bulky equipment.

Fiber Options Inc. 80 Orvillle Dr., Bohemia, N.Y. 11716. (516) 567-8320. FAX: (516) 567-8322. Robert DeLia, CEO; Fred E. Scott Jr., product mgr bcst systems.
Fiber-optic transmission systems for audio, video & control data.

Fidelipac Corp. Box 808, Moorestown, N.J. 08057. (609) 235-3900. FAX: (609) 235-7779. Robert S. Thanhauser, pres; Scott Martin, dir sls; Robert McNeill, sls mgr.
Audio cartridge machines, NAB bcst cartridges, 1/4" back-lubricated tape, studio warning lights, audio/video tape erasers, cartridge storage racks, accessories, bcst audio consoles, digital cartridge recording systems.

Filmline Technologies Inc. 43 Erna Ave., Milford, Conn. 06460. (203) 878-2433. FAX: (203) 876-1590. Allen W. Bradley, pres.
Motion picture film processors.

Film/Video Equipment Service Co. Inc. 800 S. Jason, Denver 80223. (303) 778-8616. FAX: (303) 778-8657. Dean D. Schneider, pres; Eric Altman, sls & mktg dir.

Wide angle lens attachments, film & video camera rental house, sls of lighting, camera support, pro audio & grip equip.

Imero Fiorentino Associates Inc. 33 W. 60th St., New York 10023. (212) 246-0600. FAX: (212) 246-6408. Imero Fiorentino, chmn of bd/pres; James Hartzer, exec VP/COO; William Marshall, VP facilities design.
Glendale, Calif. 91203: 229 N. Central Ave., (818) 551-9595. Carl Gibson, sr VP.
Prod, design, staging, lighting consultation & direction for TV, theatrical, concert & industrial prods; TV lighting & staging seminars; TV studio design.

First Pacific Networks. 601 W. California Ave., Sunnyvale, Calif. 94086. (408) 730-6600. FAX: (408) 730-6666. C.J. Brunet, chmn/CEO/pres; Rajiv Jaluria, COO; Ken Schneider, CFO; Daniel Tautges, VP international sls.
Local distribution technologies that enable switched voice, data & video communications over a single wire.

FirstCom/Music House/Chappell. (A division of Jim Long Companies Inc. A Zomba Company) 13747 Montfort Dr., Suite 220, Dallas 75240. (214) 934-2222; (800) 858-8880. FAX: (214) 404-9656. Jim Long, chmn; Cecelia Garr, pres/CEO.
Prod mus libraries, SFX, advertiser creative, IDs.

FitzCo Sound Inc. 2600 W. Wall, Midland, Tex. 79701. (915) 684-0861. FAX: (915) 682-9978. Michael Fitz-Gerald, pres.
Speakers, recorders, amplifiers, mixers, tape, microphones, headphones; sound reinforcement & bcst equipment.

Flash Technology. 55 Lake St., Nashua, N.H. 03060. (603) 883-6500. FAX: (603) 883-0205. William Somers, pres.
Brentwood, Tenn., 37024-3108: Box 3108, (615) 377-0600. Larry J. Montuori.
High intensity obstruction lights for tall structures. Medium intensity obstruction lights for structures up to 500 ft.

FloriCal Systems Inc. 4613-F N.W. 6th St., Gainesville, Fla. 32609-1781. (904) 372-8326. FAX: (904) 375-0859. Jim Moneyhun, pres.
TV stn automation, net tape delay, TV signal analysis, video matting & compositing.

Fluke Corp. Box 9090, Everett, Wash. 98206-9090. (206) 347-6100. FAX: (206) 356-5116. William G. Parzybok, chmn/CEO; George Winn, pres/COO.
Electronic test, measurement & control instrumentation.

Fostex Corp. of America. 15431 Blackburn Ave., Norwalk, Calif. 90650. (310) 921-1112. FAX: (310) 802-1964. Mr. Shinohara, pres; Bob Veri, exec VP/gen mgr; Steve Cunningham, VP sls & mktg.
Multitrack tape recorders, audio to video synchronizers, speakers, microphones, headphones, digital audio recorders & digital audio workstations.

Four Seasons Solar Products Corp. 5005 Veterans Memorial Hwy., Holbrook, N.Y. 11741. (516) 563-4000. FAX: (516) 563-4010. Chris Esposito, pres.

Freedon Systems Integrators. 405 S. Holland, Wichita, Kan. 67209. (316) 722-8100. FAX: (316) 722-8708. Terry Borchers, pres.
Single-channel & dual-channel video character generators & off-line editing terminals.

FREELAND PRODUCTS, INC.
75412 Highway 25
Covington, LA 70433
U.S.A.
Rebuilding Tubes Since 1940   800-624-7626
Pioneers in the Past   504-893-1243
Innovators for the Future   FAX 504-892-7323

Freeland Products Inc. 75412 Hwy. 25, Covington, La. 70433. (504) 893-1243; (800) 624-7626. FAX: (504) 892-7323. J. Harry Freeland, pres.
Rebuilding of TV & radio transmitter tubes.

Frequency Measuring Service Inc. Box 353, Commerce City, Colo. 80037. (303) 288-1482. Valerie E. Eldridge, pres; Howard S. Eldridge, tech dir.

Frezzolini Electronics Inc. 5-7 Valley St., Hawthorne, N.J. 07506. (201) 427-1160. FAX: (201) 427-0934. James J. Crawford, pres.
Sarasota, Fla. 34236: Frezzi-South. 767 John Ringling Blvd. (813) 366-3201. Jack Zink, sls.
High capacity NiCad batteries for all professional cameras & camcorders; advanced power supplies; microcomputer control chargers; ENG lighting & accessories.

Fuji Photo Film U.S.A. Inc. 555 Taxter Rd., Elmsford, N.Y. 10523. (914) 789-8100; (914) 789-8201. FAX: (914) 682-4955. Osamu Inoue, pres; Stan Bauer, VP/gen mgr; Joe Vissiailli, natl sls mgr professional products; Jim Hegadorn, tech svcs mgr; Tom Daly, professional products mgr; Brad Friedrich, dir mktg.
Itasca, Ill. 60143-1147: 1285 Hamilton Pkwy. (708) 773-7200. Dave Perrin, rgnl sls mgr.
Cypress, Calif. 90630: 6200 Phyllis Dr. (714) 372-4200. Don Jackson, rgnl sls mgr.
Norcross, Ga. 30092: 5461 Peachtree Industrial Blvd. (404) 417-4000. Jerry Lester, rgnl sls mgr.
South Hackensack, N.J. 07606: 3 Empire Blvd. (201) 935-6022. Thomas Volpicella, rgnl sls mgr.
Carrollton, Tex. 75006: 1628 W. Crosby Rd., Suite 100. (214) 466-9200. Stan Risetter, rgnl sls mgr.
Professional & industrial video tape & videocassettes.

Fujinon Inc. 10 High Point Dr., Wayne, N.J. 07470. (201) 633-5600. FAX: (201) 633-5216. Shoichi Takada, pres; John Newton, gen mgr; John Webb, natl sls mgr.
Carrolton, Tex. 75006: 2001 Midway, #114. (214) 385-8902. David Waddell, mktg mgr.
Carson, Calif. 90746: 129 E. Savarona Way. (310) 532-2861. John (Chuck) Lee, west coast sls mgr.
Miami 33196: 15181 SW 113th St. (305) 388-7399. Victor Luengo, Latin America sls mgr.
West Chicago 60185: 3N, 125 Springvale. (708) 231-7888. Bruce Wallace, rgnl sls mgr.
CTV, ENG, EFP lenses, optical systems, accessories.

Full Compass Systems Ltd. 5618 Odana Rd., Madison, Wis. 53719-1208. (800) 356-5844; (608) 271-1100. FAX: (608) 273-6336. Jonathan Lipp, pres.
Over 300 product lines for bcst, recording, entertainment, video & sound reinforcement industries.

Furman Sound Inc. 30 Rich St., Greenbrae, Calif. 94904. (415) 927-1225. FAX: (415) 927-4548. Jim Furman, pres; Joe Desmond, sls mgr; Gary Kephart, chief engr.
Rack-mount mixers, equalizers, compressors, crossovers, noise gates, patch bays, rack illumination modules, line voltage regulators/conditoners & headphone amplifiers.

Future Network Inc. 630 9th Ave., Suite 403, New York 10036. (212) 399-6090; (212) 333-3606. FAX: (212) 399-6092. Ken Washino, pres.
Fair Lawn, N.J. 07410: 18-01 Pollitt Dr. (201) 791-7079.
Manufactures & svcs audio/video distribution amplifiers, Video Duplication Control Systems, Broadcast Camera Control Systems & Computer Graphic Systems. Large video duplication svc.

G

G Prime Ltd. 1790 Broadway, 4th Floor, New York 10019-1412. (212) 765-3415. FAX: (212) 581-8938. Jerry L. Graham, pres; Russ O. Hamm, sls; Scott Jones, office mgr.
Importer & distributor of European professional audio equipment for the bcst & recording industries.

GE American Communications Inc. 4 Research Way, Princeton, N.J. 08540-6684. (609) 987-4000. FAX: (609) 987-4517. John F. Connelly, CEO/chmn of bd; Walter Braun, sr VP govt & tech opns; George Monaster, VP cable svcs; Andreas Georghiou, dir coml & bcst svcs.
Satellite distribution svcs for coml bcst & cable TV; prog syndicators, SNG, bcst radio distribution svcs.

GEC Marconi Communication Ltd. Marconi House, New St., Chelmsford-Essex, U.K. CM1 1PL. (011) 44-245-353-221. (011) 44-245-287-125. Geogio Ghiglione, mgmg dir.
Reston, Va. 22091: Marconi Communications Inc. 11800 Sunrise Valley Dr., 10th Fl. (703) 620-0333. FAX: (703)471-7368. L. Edward Marble, pres.
Full range bcst TV transmitters, studio products & satellite earth stn equipment.

G&M Power Products. 1544 Cassil Pl., Hollywood, Calif., 90028. (213) 462-3702. FAX: (213) 462-2932. Jim Tessmar, own; Rod Hines, sls.
Provide portable power supplies (batteries, cables & battery belts) to video, bcst & film mkts.

Equipment Manufacturers and Distributors

GML Inc. 7821 Burnet Ave., Van Nuys, Calif. 91405. (818) 781-1022. FAX: (818) 781-3828. George Massenburg, pres; Cary Fischer, dir sls & mktg; C.J. Flynn, gen mgr.
  Moving fader console automation with recall, parametric equalizers, microphone preamplifiers, compressor/limiters, rack mount mixers, distributor Focusrite audios consoles & peripherals.

GTE Spacenet. 1700 Old Meadow Rd., McLean, Va. 22102. (703) 848-1000. FAX: (703) 848-0004. Kathy Olson, dir human resources.
  Houston 77002: 101 Texas St., Suite 200.
  Dallas 75251: 12770 Coit Rd., Suite 722.
  Mountain View, Calif. 94043: 300 Ferguson Dr.
  Chicago 60601: 775 E. Wacker Dr., Suite 1510. (301) 251-4407.
  New York 10006: 71 Broadway, Suite 1200. (212) 775-1234.
  San Francisco 94111: 50 California St., Rm. 845.
  Voice, data, facsimile & video teleconferencing; international business svcs; VSATs.

Gabriel Electronics Inc. Box 70, Scarborough, Me. 04074-0070. (207) 883-5161. FAX: (207) 883-4469. Frank Gemme, VP.
  St.Louis 63146: 111 Westport Plaza, Suite 600. (314) 878-2982. Russell Lehr, sls engr.
  Santa Rosa, Calif. 95401: 131 Stony Cir.-Stony Pt. Business Park. (707) 576-1126. Garr Johnson, sls engr.
  Manufacture microwave antennas for point to point application in bcst, specialized common carriers & private coml nets.

Gala. (A division of Paco Corp.) 3185 Premiere Rue, Industrial Park, Hubert, J3Y 2R0. (514) 861-6768. FAX: (514) 861-9259. Pierre Gagnon, pres; Rene Bergeron, VP; Pierre LaForest, chmn of bd.
  Coronado, Calif. 92118: Box 1140. (619) 429-6092. Richard R. Haller.
  Theatrical rigging, revolving stages & orchestra lifts.

Gardiner Communications Corp. 3605 Security St., Garland, Tex. 75042. (214) 348-4747. FAX: (214) 341-1933. Jim Harris, pres; Annette Jensen, VP.
  Receivers, modulators, LNAs, LNBs, down converters & multicouplers.

Garner Industries. 4200 N. 48th St., Lincoln, Neb. 68504. (402) 434-9100. FAX: (402) 434-9133. Philip Mullin, pres; Scott McLain, prod mgr; Ross Faubel, asst prod mgr.
  Manufacture bulk tape erasers for audio, video & computer industries.

Gauss. 9130 Glen Oaks Blvd., Sun Valley, Calif. 91352. (213) 875-1900. FAX: (818) 767-4479. James R. Williams, pres.
  Professional loudspeakers & monitor systems; high speed audio tape duplicating equipment.

Take your station
to peak performance—

- **Telephone Systems & Hybrids**
- **Transmitter Remote Control**
- **AM & FM Audio Processing**
- **Digital Audio Storage**
- **Audio Routing & Distribution**

Gentner Communications Corporation
1825 Research Way • Salt Lake City, Utah 84119
TEL: (801) 975-7200 • FAX: (801) 977-0087

Gefen Systems. 6261 Variel Ave., Suite C, Woodland Hills, Calif. 91367. (818) 884-6294; (800) 545-6900. FAX: (818) 884-3108. Hagai Gefen, pres.
  SFX & prod mus locator software, searches for & plays CDs on NSM-3101-AC 100 CD Changer or Pioneer CAC-3000 300 CD Changer."M&E library & organizer system" (IBM/MAC based). Automated backround mus systems using multi CD players for business, bcst & homes.

Gemstar Development Corp. 135 N. Los Robles Ave. #870, Pasadena, Calif. 91101. (818) 792-5700. FAX: (818) 792-0257. Henry C. Yuen, CEO.
  VCR Plus+ (allows taping of a TV show in one step).

General Broadcast Supply Inc. HCR 31, Box 128, Deer, Ark. 72628-9606. (501) 428-5277. FAX: (501) 428-5267. Beverly Butler, VP.
  All bcst equipment items for AM/FM transmitters, studios, STL, towers & automation systems. Equipment appraisals.

General Cable Apparatus Div. 5600 W. 88th Ave., Westminster, Colo. 80030. (303) 427-3700. FAX: (303) 657-2205. Van J. Walbridge, pres.
  Aerial lifts for cable maintenance, placing & construction. Offices in Hayward, Calif.; Lithonia, Ga.; Frederick, Md.

General Camera Corp. 540 W. 36th St., New York 10018. (212) 594-8700. FAX: (212) 564-4918. Dick DiBona, pres; Milt Keslow, VP.
  16mm & 35mm motion picture & video equipment, lighting & grip equipment, generators, trucks, dollies & cranes.

General Electric Co. 3135 Easton Tpke., Fairfield, Conn. 06431. (203) 373-2211. FAX: (203) 373-2884. John F. Welch Jr., chmn/CEO.
  New York 10020: NBC, 30 Rockefeller Plaza. (212) 664-4444. Robert C. Wright, pres.
  Cleveland 44112: 4338 Nela Park. (216) 362-5600. FAX: (216) 266-2310. Keith T. S. Ward, quartz-stage studio prod mgr.

General Electrodynamics Corp. 8000 Calendar Rd., Arlington, Tex. 76017. (817) 572-0366. FAX: (817) 572-0373. D.E. Davis, pres; James G. Nelson, exec VP.
  Tubes, TV cameras, electronics, aircraft weighing equipment, contract weighing svcs, truck scales & load scales.

General Instrument Corp. 181 W. Madison St., 49th Fl. Chicago 60602. (312) 541-5000. FAX: (312) 541-8038. Daniel F. Akerson, chmn/CEO.
  Cable TV electronics, coaxial & fiber optic cables & satellite encryption systems.

General Television Network. 13355 Capital, Oak Park, Mich. 48237. (313) 599-2000. Dave Moore, pres.

General Videotex Corp.-Delphi. 1030 Massachusetts Ave., Cambridge, Mass. 02138. (617) 491-3393; (800) 695-4005. FAX: (617) 491-6642. Max Steinmann, chmn of bd; Daniel Bruns, pres/CEO.
  On-line svc & communications net providing electronic mail, real time conferencing & a full range of info svcs.

Generic Computer Systems. 357 N. Main St., Butler, Pa. 16001. (412) 283-1500. FAX: (412) 283-3005. Joel W. Rosenblum, own.
  Software does traffic, billing, aged trial balance & projections - bcster-owned.

Gennum Corp. Box 489, Station A, Burlington, Ont., Canada L7R 3Y3. (416) 632-2996. FAX: (416) 632-2055. H.D. Barber, pres/CEO; B. L. Nielsen, gen sls mgr; P.G.A. Moore, mgr video bcst prod.
  High performance integrated circuits, including switches & processing functions for analog & digital video applications.

Gentner Communications Corp. 1825 Research Way, Salt Lake City 84119. (801) 975-7200. FAX: (801) 977-0087. Russell Gentner, CEO; William U. Trowbridge, pres; Larry Banks, gen mgr.
  Manufacture audio telecommunications equipment for bcstg professional audio & teleconferencing.

Gepco International Inc. 2225 W. Hubbard St., Chicago 60612. (312) 733-9555. FAX: (312) 733-6416. Gary R. Geppert, pres; David Mecklenburger, CFO; Larry Smith Sr., VP tech & mktg; Greg Hansen, natl sls mgr.
  Ocala, Fla. 34480: Box 71157. (904) 732-4123. Todd Harrington, eastern rgnl sls.
  Audio & video cable products, bulk cable or cut lengths, breakout boxes, assemblies & synergistic interconnect products.

Gestetner Corp. Box 2656, 599 W. Putnam Ave., Greenwich, Conn. 06836. (203) 863-5555. FAX: (203) 863-5545. Chandran Rajaratnam, pres/CEO; Rick DeVincenzo, CFO.
  Copiers, duplicators & fax machines.

Gilbert Engineering Co. Inc. Box 23189, Phoenix 85063. (602) 245-1050. FAX: (602) 934-5160. Robert A. Spann, pres.
  Coaxial connectors for trunk, distribution & drop cables.

Glentronix. 90 Nolan Ct., Unit 7, Markham, Ont., Canada L3R 4L9. (905) 475-8494. FAX: (905) 475-0955. Patricia Kidd, pres; Raymond Quesnel, natl sls mgr.
  Studio video equipment, audio jackfield & test equipment.

Alan Gordon Enterprises Inc. 1430 Cahuenga Blvd., Hollywood, Calif. 90028. (213) 466-3561. Grant Loucks, pres; Wayne Loucks, sls mgr.
  Professional motion picture & video equipment; sls & rental.

Gorman-Redlich Manufacturing Co. 257 W. Union St., Athens, Ohio 45701. (614) 593-3150. FAX: (614) 592-3898. James T. Gorman, own.
  EBS encoders/decoders & receivers, digital antenna monitors, NOAA weather radios.

Graham-Patten Systems Inc. Box 1960, Grass Valley, Calif. 95945. (916) 273-8412; (800) 547-2489. FAX: (916) 273-7458. Val Marchus, pres/CEO; Mike Patten, VP engrg; Bill Rorden, VP rsch; Jim Ward, gen mgr; Tim Prouty, VP sls & mktg.
  Standard & custom designed equipment & systems for bcst, prod & postprod.

Grant Tower. 13064 Wisner Ave., Grant, Mich. 49327. (616) 834-5665. FAX: (616) 834-7870. Carroll Zerlaut, pres; Walter Knoch, office mgr; Terry Sharp, VP opns.
  Bcst tower erection & maintenance svc.

Grass Valley Group, Graphic System Division. 6 Forest Ave., Paramus, N.J. 07652-5214. (201) 845-8900. FAX: (201) 845-8063. Bob Wilson, pres; Terrence Pires, VP mktg.
  Video character generators, full-color paint systems, 3-D modeling & animation systems & still store image archiving systems.

The Grass Valley Group Inc. Box 1114, Grass Valley, Calif. 95945. (916) 478-3000. FAX: (916) 478-3187. Robert Wilson, exec VP; Robert Natwick, dir sls Americas.
  Woodland Hills, Calif. 91364: 21243 Ventura Blvd, Suite 143. (818) 999-2303.
  Rohnert Park, Calif. 94928: 613 Martin Ave., Suite 100A. (707) 585-8905.
  Miami, Fla. 33172: The Grass Valley Group Sud America. 8880 N.W. 20th St., Suite I. (305) 477-5583; (305) 477-5488.
  Tampa 33634: Florida Sales Office. 3929 Eden Roc Cir. E. (813) 884-0047.
  Silver Spring, Md. 20904: 12520 Prosperity Dr., Suite 110. (301) 622-6313.
  Burnsville, Minn., 55337: Minneapolis Sales Office. 14587 Grand Ave, Suite 211. (612) 435-1770.
  Elkhart, Ind. 46514: 810 W. Bristol St. (219) 264-0931.
  Tucker, Ga. 30084: 3554 Habersham at Northlake. (404) 493-1255.
  Paramus, N.J. 07652: 6 Forest Ave. (201) 845-7988.
  Arlington, Tex. 76017: 5628 Green Oaks Blvd. S.W., Suite A. (817) 483-7447.
  Granby, Conn. 06035: Box 839. (203) 653-3104.
  Hoffman Estates, Ill., 60195: Chicago rgnl office. 3100 W. Higgins Road, Suite 135. (708) 310-9190.
  Maple Valley, Wash. 98038: Northwest Sales Office. 26326 S.E. 237th.

Equipment Manufacturers and Distributors

Winchester-Hampshire, U.K. S023-9HE: GVG International Ltd., St. Thomas House. 7 St. Thomas St. 44-256-817817. Telex: U.K. 477766 GVC-EU.

Kowloon, Hong Kong 852-3-7874118: Grass Valley Group Asia. 1114 Houston Centre. (206) 486-5628.

Tokyo, Japan 170: Seiko Sunshine Bldg. XII, 1-30-6 Higashi-Ikebukuro Toshima-ku. 813-5992-0621.

Video switching, effects, timing, distribution & control equipment. Fiber optic audio, video & data communications systems.

Claude M. Gray. Box 602, Birmingham, Ala. 35201. (205) 822-1132. Claude M. Gray, consulting radio eng.

Gray Engineering Laboratories Inc. 504 W. Chapman Ave., Suite P, Orange, Calif. 92668. (714) 997-4151. Scott R. Gray, pres.

SMPTE time-code generators & readers, safe area generators, video-assisted film editing components.

The Great American Market. 826 N. Cole Ave., Hollywood, Calif. 90038. (213) 461-0200. FAX: (213) 461-4308. Joseph N. Tawil, own/gen mgr; Harry Beard, sls mgr.

Lighting equipment, portable & studio special effects & projections, control console, dimming & color filters.

Great Lakes Data Systems. Box 295, 1010 DeClark St., Beaver Dam, Wis. 53916. (414) 887-7651. FAX: (414) 887-7653. Larry Barbera, pres; J. Alonzo Rosado, exec VP.

Cardiff By The Sea, Calif. 92007: 119 Aberdeen Dr., Suite 3. (619) 753-1024; (800) 882-7950. J. Alonzo Rosado, exec VP.

PC based cable TV billing mgmt info systems with Pay-Per-View, ANI & ARU options.

Lynn Greenberg Electronic Teleprompting. 24506 Thistle Ct., Newhall, Calif. 91321. (805) 253-1987. FAX: (805) 253-3336. Lynn Greenberg, own.

Color computerized electronic teleprompting for all bcst & industrial uses.

Groton Computer Inc. (G.C.I.). 72 Oswegatchie Hills Rd., Niantic, Conn. 06357. (203) 739-7949. James Springer, systems mgr.

Logging, billing, affidavits, sls reports, projections & mo-end accounting.

Group W Satellite Communications. 250 Harbor Dr., Stamford, Conn. 06904. (203) 965-6388. FAX: (203) 965-6320. Don Mitzner, pres; Altan C. Stalker, VP/gen mgr; James Crowe, exec dir opns; Peter Concelmo, dir sls & mktg; Cheryl Daly, VP pub rels.

C- & Ku-band domestic & international transmission svc; connectivity to metro N.Y. via microwave & fiber; cable origination, bcst, business TV, transponder availability, studio & postprod.

Grumman Electronics Systems Corp. 1111 Stewart Ave., Bethpage, N.Y. 11714. (516) 575-0579. FAX: (516) 575-2311. Lorenzo, pres.

Ad insertion & program automation systems.

James Grunder & Associates Inc. 5925 Beverly St., Mission, Kan. 66202. (913) 831-0188. FAX: (913) 831-3427. James L. Grunder, pres; Jim Bendure, gen mgr; Nick Nichols, VP sls & mktg.

Scan rate converters, time base correctors, Hamlet audio & video signal measurement, waveform & vectorscopes.

Guicar Television Di G. Carracino. Via Faruffini, 25 20149 Milano, Italy (02) 462009. FAX: 02/4813310. Guido Carracino, own.

Video-library, ET 3D special effects: two subject groups include more than 50 1-minute bcst quality special effects for reel.

H

HAVE Inc. 309 Power Ave., Hudson, N.Y. 12534. (518) 828-2000. FAX: (518) 828-2008. Nancy Gordon, pres; Paul Swedenburg, VP.

Nashville 37214: 1313 Lincoya Bay Dr. (615) 889-9292. Agatha Brown, southern rgnl sls mgr.

Professional audio & video tape, equipment, accessories & supplies. Canare cable; connectors & adaptors. Duplication & postprod svc.

HM Electronics Inc. 6675 Mesa Ridge Rd., San Diego 92121. (619) 535-6000. FAX: (619) 452-7207. H.Y. Miyahira, pres; D.A. Kutz, exec VP; J.M. Hughes, VP mktg.

Intercom systems & wireless microphones.

Hallikainen & Friends Inc. 141 Suburban Rd., Bldg E4, San Luis Obispo, Calif. 93401-7590. (805) 541-0200. FAX: (805) 544-6715. Harold Hallikainen, pres; Frank Calabrese, VP.

Automatic & manual transmitter remote control equipment; audio equipment with AFV; remote satellite dish steering systems.

Hardigg Cases. Box 201, 393 N. Main St., South Deerfield, Mass. 01373. (413) 665-2163. FAX: (413) 665-8061. James S. Hardigg, pres.

Reusable shipping cases. Rugged 19" rack shock-mounted enclosures. Bcst equipment cases.

Harmonic Lightwaves Inc. 3005 Bunker Hill Lane, Santa Clara, Calif. 95054. (408) 970-9880. FAX (408) 492-0766. Anthony J. Ley, pres/CEO; Josef Berger, VP engr; Moshe Nazarathy, VP rsch & dev.

Stone Mountain, Ga. 30083: 5300 Memorial Dr., Suite 119, (404) 296-9005. Solomon Webb, dir North American sls.

Fiber optic telecommunication equipment for cable Television.

Harris Allied Broadcast Division. Box 4290, 3200 Wismann Ln., Quincy, Ill. 62305-4290. (217) 222-8200. FAX: (217) 224-1439. TELEX: 650-374-2978 HARIS UR. Joseph Huie, VP/gen mgr; Geoff Mendenhall, VP radio RF products; Jim Woods, VP radio studio prods; Frank Svet, VP engrg; Gustavo Ezcurra, VP world sls; Robert R. Weirather, dir advanced mktg; Gaylen C. Evans, dir domestic sls.

Richmond, Ind. 47375: Box 1487, 3712 National Rd. West. (317) 962-8596. FAX: (317) 962-8961. TELEX: 810-345-1394. Radio studio products.

Manufacture bcst RF equipment; distribute radio studio equipment. Worldwide systems supplier.

Harris-Farinon. 1691 Bayport Ave., San Carlos, Calif. 94070-5307. (415) 594-3666. FAX: (415) 594-3110. Denis Cote, VP mktg & sls.

New Rochelle, N.Y.: (914) 632-3800. Steve Von Rump, dir sls.

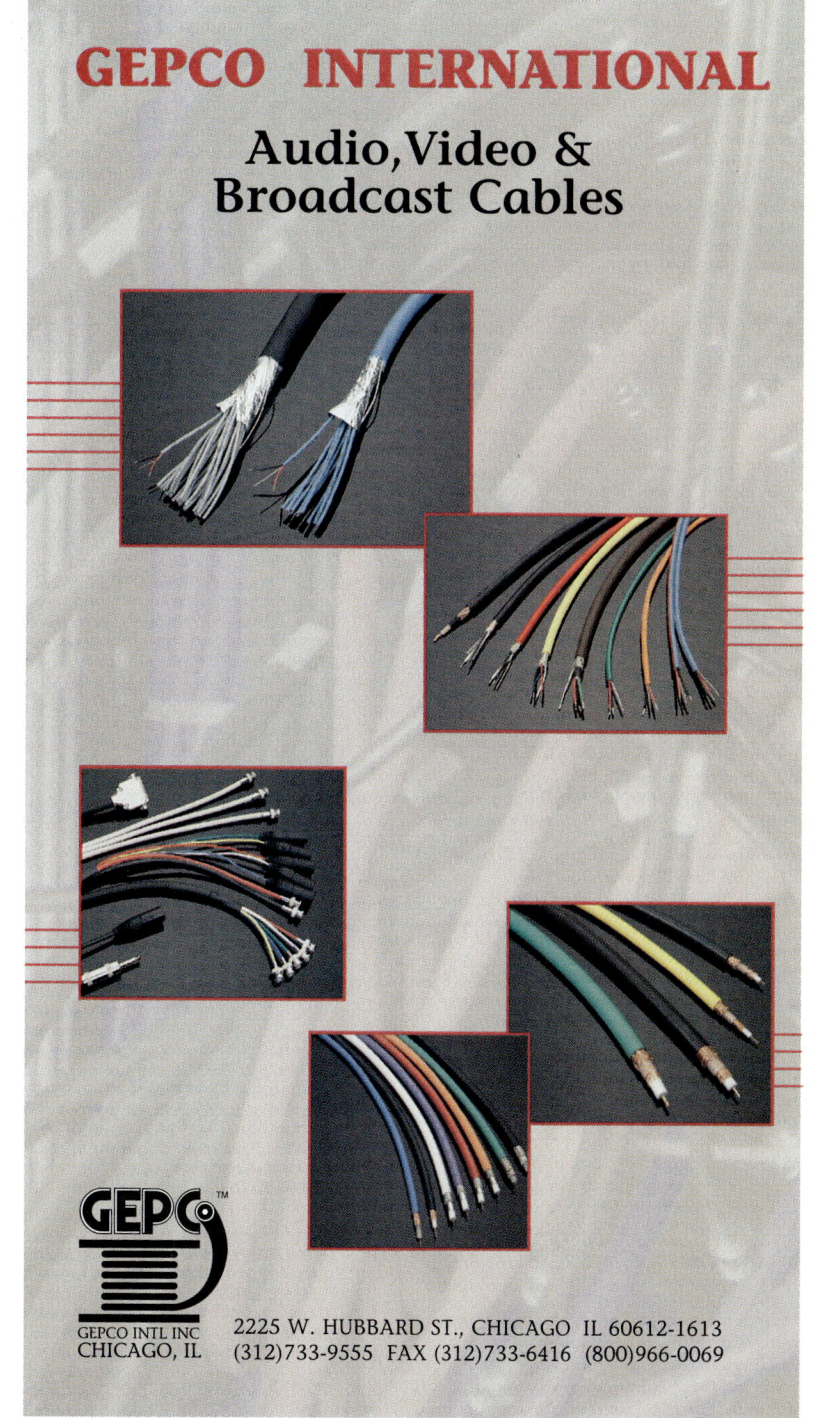

GEPCO INTERNATIONAL
Audio, Video & Broadcast Cables

GEPCO INTL INC CHICAGO, IL
2225 W. HUBBARD ST., CHICAGO IL 60612-1613
(312) 733-9555 FAX (312) 733-6416 (800) 966-0069

Equipment Manufacturers and Distributors

The Woodlands, Tex. 77380: (713) 363-4567. Chuck Geer, mgr southwest sls.
Microwave for intercity relay & satellites.

Harrison by GLW. 437 Atlas Dr., Nashville 37211. (615) 331-8800. FAX: (615) 331-8883. William B. Owen, pres; Ted Miller, VP opns; Ted Miller, VP sls & mktg.
Audio mixing consoles for on-air bcst, prod, video & film sound postprod, live sound & mus recording.

Karl Heitz Inc. Box 427, Woodside, N.Y. 11377. (718) 565-0004. FAX: (718) 565-2582. Karl Heitz, pres; Horacio Gonda, VP; Loretta Rosas, treas.
GITZO video & photo tripods; levelling balls with headlock, with & without rapid sliding or Cremaillere gearlift column for height adjustment; fluid & counter balanced heads & microphone fishpoles.

Henry Engineering. 503 Key Vista Dr., Sierra Madre, Calif. 91024. (818) 355-3656. FAX: (818) 355-0077. Hank Landsberg, own/pres.
The Matchbox & other audio interface, control interface & digital audio storage devices.

Hervic Corp. 16516 Arminta St., Van Nuys, Calif. 91406. (818) 781-1692. Richard Levinson, pres; William Levinson, VP.

Hessler Enterprises Inc. One Susan Dr. at Township Line, Elkins Park, Pa. 19117. (215) 379-2300. FAX: (215) 663-8839. Edwin S. Hessler, pres; Deena R. Hessler, VP.
Bcst forms: script sets, contracts, prog logs, invoices, labels, A/R statements & computer stock paper.

Hignite Tower Service. 9945 Arkansas St., Bellflower, Calif. 90706. (310) 925-1951. FAX: (310) 925-6171. John Hignite, own; Jackie Beneze, off mgr.
Tower engrg, erection, fabrication, maintenance & painting.

Hipotronics Inc. Box 414, Rt. 22, Brewster, N.Y. 10509. (914) 279-8091. FAX: (914) 279-2467.
High voltage DC power supplies & industrial grade voltage regulators for medium to high power applications.

Hitachi Denshi America Ltd. 150 Crossway Park Dr., Woodbury, N.Y. 11797. (516) 921-7200. FAX: (516) 921-0993. M. Matsuhashi, pres; B. Munzelle, VP mktg.
Atlanta 30360: 3039 Amwiler Rd. (404) 242-3636. Peter Conner, rgnl sls mgr.
Torrance, Calif. 90746: 371 Van Ness Way. (310) 328-6116.
Itaska, Ill. 60143: 250 E. Devon Ave., Suite 115. (708) 250-8050. R. Johnson, rgnl sls mgr.
Professional & industrial cameras, VTRs, monitors, test & measurement equipment.

High Tech Industries. 298 N. Smith Ave., Corona, Calif. 91720. (909) 279-5770. FAX: (909) 279-5773. Douglas J. Kanczuzewski, gen mgr.
Custom & standard prod, postprod & computer racks for TV & radio.

Hoagland Instruments Inc. Box 675, 26 Winthrop St., Melrose, Mass. 02176-0004. (617) 665-4428. FAX: (617) 665-3855. Robin Woodsum, pres.
Thermal & electronic time delay relays.

Hoffend & Sons Inc. 34 E. Main St., Honeoye, N.Y. 14471. (716) 229-5998. FAX: (716) 229-2746. Dr. Brun, pres; Bruce Downer, VP.
Engrg, mfg & install of studio rigging systems, motorized hoists, curtains, tracks, turntables & controls.

Hogg & Davis Inc. Box 405, 3800 Eagle Loop, Odell, Ore. 97044. (503) 354-1001. FAX: (503) 354-1080. F. Neil Hogg, pres.
Designs, manufactures & mkts cable pullers, carriers, reels & accessories.

Holaday Industries Inc. 14825 Martin Dr., Eden Prairie, Minn. 55344. (612) 934-4920. FAX: (612) 934-3604. Burton Gran, pres; David Baron, VP sls & mktg; William Rankin, VP engrg; David Thompson, VP mfg.
Non-ionizing radiation test equipment; low frequency survey meters; RF/microwave broadband field strength meters.

Holan Manufacturing Inc. 5500 W. 88th Ave., Westminster, Colo. 80030. (303) 657-2226. FAX: (303) 657-2205. William S. Robson, div mktg mgr; Dick Eskins, inside sls mgr; Dabo Dabasinkas, dir sls.
Manufacture aerial bucket trucks (insulated & non-insulated) for construction, maintenance & material handling. Holan & Telsta products are manufactured.

Hollywood Rentals. 7848 N. San Fernando Rd., Sun Valley, Calif. 91352. (818) 768-8018. FAX: (818) 768-1517.
Prod equipment & vehicle for film & video (rental); sale of new equipment & expendable items.

Hollywood Vaults Inc. 742 N. Seward St., Hollywood, Calif. 90038. (213) 461-6464. FAX: (805) 569-1657. David Wexler, pres; Julianna Wexler, VP.
Santa Barbara Calif. 93103: (corporate office of Hollywood Vaults Inc.) 1780 Prospect Ave., (805) 569-5336. Chris Robinson, office administrator.
State-of-the-art film & tape storage vault. Secure, climate-controlled with 24-hr self-svc access.

Holzberg Inc. Box 3323, Seabright, N.J. 07760. (908) 530-8555; (800) 242-7298. FAX: (908) 842-7552. Herb Holzberg, pres; Shirley Holzberg, sls.
Totowa, N.J. 07511: Box 322 (201) 256-0455. Andy Holzberg, sls mgr.
Routing & prod switching, audio & video studio & transmitting equipment, audio consoles, audio & video distribution, turnkey systems, computer radio bcst stns.

Homalite. (A division of Whitco Inc.) 11 Brookside Dr., Wilmington, Del. 19804. (302) 652-3686. FAX: (302) 652-4578. Kyle K. Whittaker, pres; J.K. Whittaker, PV.
Manufacture low-reflectance, contrast enhancement filters for use on CRTs, LEDs & other forms of info display.

Hoodman Corp. Box 816, Hermosa Beach, Calif. 90254. (310) 379-6391. FAX: (310) 372-6420. Mike Schmidt, pres.
TV sun shades & monitor hoods for glare free outdoor viewing.

Horita. Box 3993, Mission Viejo, Calif. 92690. (714) 489-0240. Gerald Hester, pres.
SMPTE time code readers, generators, inserters, PC tape logging software; color bar, black, sync generators; titler & distribution amplifiers.

Hotronic Inc. 1875 S. Winchester Blvd., Campbell, Calif. 95008. (408) 378-3883. FAX: (408) 378-3888. Andy Ho, pres; Linda Chang, sls & mktg mgr.
Time base corrector & frame synchronizer with freeze frame & field, digital effects, with wideband.

Howe Industries. Box 1059, Sanford, Fla. 32771-1059. (800) 322-1830. FAX: (407) 330-1317. Dale Coopock, natl accounts mgr.
Transit/shipping cases—custom manufactured to specifications; tool cases.

Hubcom Uplinks. 9675 4th St. N., St. Petersburg, Fla. 33702. (813) 577-7759; (813) 449-7295. FAX: (813) 577-5011. Lisa Robinson, dir sls & mktg.
Ind transmission company with 3 full redundant SNG vehicles for newsgathering; tech svc for uplink units.

Hughes Aircraft of Canada Ltd. 260 Saulteaux Crescent, Winnipeg, Man., Canada R3J 3T2. (204) 949-2400. FAX: (204) 889-1268. Ron Guimond, gen mgr; Tom Strauss, chief scientist.
Littleton, Colo. 80123: 7775 W. Ontario Pl. (303) 973-3869. Steve R. Dozier, western rgnl sls mgr.
Scranton, Pa. 18501: Box 1482. (717) 343-3564. Robert H. Stanton, eastern rgnl sls mgr.
Design & manufacture broadband microwave transmission systems for video, voice & data signal distribution.

Hughes Communications Inc. Box 92424, Los Angeles 90009. (310) 607-4511. FAX: (310) 607-4065. Stephen Petrucci, pres/CEO; Fred Judge, sr VP/COO; Jerald Farrell, sr VP; Eddy Hartenstein, pres (Direct TV Inc.).
Satellite communications: cable, bcst TV, radio distribution; international TV svcs; high-power DBS svcs; SNG; business TV; video time-sharing.

Hughey & Phillips Inc. Box 2167, 2162 Union Pl., Simi Valley, Calif. 93062. (805) 581-5591. FAX: (805) 581-5032. William P. Miller, pres; Peter H. Johnson, VP.
Tower lighting products.

I

I. DEN. 9620 Chesapeake Dr., #204, San Diego 92123. (619) 492-9239. FAX: (619) 279-2569. Pat O'Rourke, exec VP.
New Britain, Conn. 06053: I. DEN - Eastern rgnl sls office, 165A Brittany Farms Rd. (203) 827-8900
TBC, FS, DVE, HDTV Down Converter.

ICM (International Crystal Mfg.). Box 26330, Oklahoma City 73126. (405) 236-3741. FAX: (405) 235-1904. Royden Freeland, pres; Beth Meal; VP; Chuck Fithin, sls mgr.
Quartz crystals, crystal oven repair, two-way radio equipment & crystal oscillators.

IGM Communications. 4041 Home Rd., Bellingham, Wash. 98226. (206) 733-4567. FAX: (206) 734-7939. James F. Wells, pres; Rick Sawyer, opns mgr; Carl Peterson, sls mgr.
Prog automation controllers, custom audio control system, multiple cart playback machines.

InSat Corp. 6125 W. Sahara Ave., Suite 2D, Las Vegas 89102. (702) 368-3530. FAX: (702) 368-1054. John Spaziani, chmn; Andy Cauthen, CEO; Peter Mercer, project dir.
InSat Corporation is in the business of Digital Broadcast Satellite Technology: 1) Certified training instal prog; 2) instal & warranty work for client companies; 3) promoting DBS satellite technology & svcs to niche markets; 4) reseller VAR industry-related prods.

IPITEK. 2330 Faraday Ave., Carlsbad, Calif. 92008. (619) 438-8362. FAX: (619) 438-2412. James Bechtel, sr VP.
IPITEK designs, manufactures & markets innovative coml products, from components to systems. Products are based on state-of-the-art fiber optics & high-speed electronic technology.

IRIS Technologies Inc. 692 E. Pittsburg St., Greensburg, Pa. 15601. (412) 832-9855. FAX: (412) 832-8999. Jerry Salandro, CEO.
Video command - touch screen routing & switching system - 32x32 & 64x64.

ISS Engineering Inc. 992 San Antonio Rd., Palo Alto, Calif. 94303. (415) 424-0380. FAX: (415) 424-0405. Norman Gillaspie, pres; Lydia Gillaspie, VP mktg.
Birmingham, Ala. 35215: ISS East. 434 Westchester Dr. (800) 351-4477. John Coiro, VP sls.
Satellite receivers for radio & data transmission.

ITI Electronics Inc. 12 Kulick Rd., Fairfield, N.J. 07004. (201) 882-6405. Robert A. Stein, pres.
Prewired jackfields; patch panels; telephone line amplifiers.

ITT Cannon Electric. 1851 E. Deere Ave., Santa Ana, Calif. 92705. (714) 261-5300. FAX: (714) 757-8301. Roger Wolse, dir opns; Randy Lovelady, mktg dir; Wayne Zahlit, engrg dir.
Electronic connectors, interconnect systems & info card technology suppliers to a var of industries, including bcst & data communications companies.

ITT Electron Technology Division. Box 100, 3100 Charlotte Ave., Easton, Pa. 18044-0100. (215) 252-7331. FAX: (215) 258-6279. Travis Gerould, pres; Steven Black, mktg mgr.
Special purpose electron tubes & subsystems including TWTs, klystrons, power tubes, hydrogen thyratrons & power supplies.

Idontix. 510 N. Pastoria Ave., Sunnyvale, Calif. 94086-3520. (408) 739-2000. FAX: (408) 739-3308. Randy Fowler, pres.
Albuquerque 97110: 1306 Cagua N.E. (505) 265-7248.
Merrimac, Mass. 01860: 4 Grove St. (508) 346-9843.
Schaumburg, Ill. 60195: 200 W. Higgins Rd., #229. (708) 882-2022.
San Ramon, Calif. 94583: 2010 Crow Canyon Pl., No. 110. (510) 275-1743.
Bcst grade computer controlled component recording optical disc systems for still & coml mgmt.

Equipment Manufacturers and Distributors

Ikegami Electronics (USA) Inc. 37 Brook Ave., Maywood, N.J. 07607. (201) 368-9171. FAX: (201) 569-1626. Koichi Fukuda, pres; Thom Calabro, VP engrg; Masaaki Osada, VP finance; Larry Riddle, dir natl sls; John Chow, rgnl sls dir; Rodger A. Winchell, dir midwest sls; Robert J. Estony, mgr communications; Michael H. Steiker, mgr natl dealer sls; Lee Moreth, dir Latin America sls; Bob Low, sls mgr.
 Torrance, Calif. 90505: 23105 Kashiwa Ct. (310) 534-0050.
 Ft. Lauderdale, Fla. 33309: 5100 N.W. 33rd Ave. (305) 735-2203.
 Elmhurst, Ill. 60126: Units C4 & C5, 747 Church Rd. (708) 834-9774.
 Irving, Tex. 96814: 3 Dallas Communications Complex, 6309 N. O'Connor Rd., Suite 117. (214) 869-2363.
 Bcst/professional video cameras, monitors, microwave equipment, projection TV.

Image Logic Corp. 6807 Brennon Ln., Chevy Chase, Md. 20815. (301) 907-8891. FAX: (301) 652-6584. Woodrow Landay, pres.
 Log prod - automated videotape logging system: autocaption automated desktop closed captioning system.

Image Transform Inc. 4142 Lankershim Blvd., North Hollywood, Calif. 91602-2987. (800) 423-2652; (818) 985-7566. FAX: (818) 980-4268. John H. Donlon, pres; Gavin Schutz, VP engrg.
 Film to tape - all standards; tape to film - standards conversion; film laboratory; cassette duplication.

Image Video Ltd. 705 Progress Ave., Unit 46, Scarbrough, Ont., Canada M1H 2X1. (416) 438-3940. FAX: (416) 438-8465. Andy A. Vanags, pres.
 Buffalo, N.Y. 14206: 1051 Clinton St. (705) 855-2693.
 Digital audio/video routing switchers, digital to analog & analog to digital signal converters, digital audio storage & delay systems.

Imagine Products Inc. 581 S. Rangeline Rd., Suite B-3, Carmel, Ind. 46032-2149. (317) 843-0706. FAX: (317) 843-0807. Dan Montgomery, CEO/pres.
 PC software/hardware for logging, offline edit, EDL transfers & tape libraries. Timecode readers & VTR controls.

Imaging Automation. 7 Henry Clay Dr., Merrimac, N.H. 03054. (603) 598-3400. FAX: (603) 598-3422. Bruce Monk, pres.
 Supplier of optical-based systems for storing & retrieving documents & images.

Industrial Acoustics Co. 1160 Commerce Ave., Bronx, N.Y. 10462. (718) 931-8000. FAX: (718) 863-1138. Zachary Jaquett, dir communications dept; Robert Buelow, VP architectural dept; John Duda, sr consultant architectural dept.
 Staines-Middlesex, U.K. TW18 4XB: Walton House, Central Trading Estate. Simon White, dir mktg.
 Hong Kong, China: Honour Industrial Centre, 6 Sun Yip St., Suite 15, 15/F. 557-8633. Alvin Leung, pres.
 Complete acoustical environments for the bcstg industry plus unitary acoustical doors, windows & walls.

Industrial Equipment Representatives. 1685 Precision Park Ln., Suite E, San Diego 92173. (619) 428-2261; (619) 428-2262. FAX: (619) 428-3483. Alex Rodriguez, sls mgr; Juan Biosca, gen mgr.
 Bcst, TV & recording studios equipment & supplies.

Industrial/Midwec Capacitor Corp. 100511 Airport Rd., Scottsbluff, Neb. 69361. (308) 632-4127. FAX: (308) 632-2068. Rod Gensen, plant mgr.
 Film, oil & electrolytic capacitors; specialty toroids & filter nets.

Information Systems Development Inc. 3773 N.W. 126th Ave., Coral Springs, Fla. 33065. (305) 753-8220. FAX: (305) 341-7132. Wm. Peyton Lake, pres; Steve Reiss, VP sls.
 Atlanta 30319: 1400 Lake Hearn Dr., Suite 170. (404) 843-5738.
 "Cablemaster" customer mgmt & billing system running on IBM AS/400 platform; supports centralized or decentralized processing.

Information Transmissions Systems Corp. (ITS). 375 Valley Brook Rd., McMurray, Pa. 15317. (412) 941-1500. FAX: (412) 941-4603. Robert M. Unetich, pres; Jeffrey M. Lynn, VP mktg.
 VHF & UHF exciters for multichannel sound; LPTV, MMDS & ITFS transmitters.

J. Boyd Ingram & Associates. Box 73, Batesville, Miss. 38606. (601) 563-4664. J. Boyd Ingram, pres.

Innovative Technology International (ITI). (A division of Cross Keys Manufacturing Inc.) 204B Cross Keys Rd., Berlin, N.J. 08009. (609) 767-7806. FAX: (609) 767-7547. W. Gregg Fawthrop, pres.
 AM directional antenna systems equipment & design, dummy loads, field instal, RF components & ground screens.

Innovative Television Equipment (ITE). 2405 Empire Ave., Burbank, Calif. 91504. (818) 843-6715. FAX: (213) 849-1525. Tom Menke, sls mgr.
 TV camera support dollies, tripods, studio pedestals, pan/tilt heads, cases & microwave support equipment.

Innovision Optics. 1318 2nd St., Suite 31, Santa Monica, Calif. 90401. (310) 394-5510. FAX: (310) 395-2941. Mark Centkowski, pres; Keeva Kristal, sls.
 Taple-top technology includes camera lenses, motion control systems, camera support systems & lighting systems.

For more than 20 years . . .

. . . Inovonics has provided broadcasters with quality audio products at affordable prices.
 Without compromising performance, *simplicity of design* gives our equipment its superb specifications *and great sound!*
 Inovonics manufactures a broad range of audio processing, recording and instrumentation products, available from major domestic distributors and through a worldwide network of factory-authorized agents.
 For detailed technical information, simply write, FAX or call:

Inovonics, Inc.
1305 Fair Avenue • Santa Cruz, CA 95060
Tel: (408) 458-0552 • FAX: (408) 458-0554

Inovonics Inc. 1305 Fair Ave., Santa Cruz, Calif. 95060. (408) 458-0552. FAX: (408) 458-0554. James B. Wood, pres/chief engr; Ann Chaney, mgr.
 Manufacture bcst audio signal processing, sound recording & instrumentation equipment.

InSat Corp. 6125 W. Sahara Ave., Suite 2D, Las Vegas 89102. (702) 368-3530; FAX: (702) 368-1054. John Spaziani, chmn; Andy Cauthen, CEO; Peter Mercer, proj dir.
 InSat Corp. is in the business of Digital Broadcast Satellite technology: 1) Certified training installation program; 2) installation & warranty work for client companies; 3) promoting DBS satellite technology svcs to niche markets; 4) reseller VAR, industry-related products.

Inscriber Character Generator. 1131A Leslie St., 6th Fl., Toronto, Ont., Canada M3C 3L8. (416) 391-4500. FAX: (416) 391-1999. W. Weaver, Pres.
 Inscriber Character Generator system, subtitle, fontmaker & RTX real time titling.

Insulated Wire Inc. Microwave Products Division. 20 E. Franklin St., Danbury, Conn. 06810. (203) 791-1999. FAX: (203) 748-5217. Saverio T. Bruno, VP/gen mgr.
 High frequency, low loss microwave cable & cable assemblies featuring IW's Tuf-Flex Series to 60 GHz.

Integrated Technologies Inc. Box 7819, 2275 Van Story St., Suite 306, 2275 Vanstory St., Greensboro, N.C. 27403. (919) 852-0455. Michael Faulk, chmn; Harry Faulk, pres.
 Weather graphics, news graphics & 3-D animation systems.

Broadcasting & Cable Yearbook 1994
H-33

CALL
InSat

for:

SATELLITE TECHNOLOGY AND SERVICES :

Digital Broadcast Satellite Technology
•
Business Television
•
Certified System Installer Training Program
•
100 Regional Offices in USA and Canada
•
GPS Products
•
Satellite Locators
•
Spectrum Analyzers
•
Satellite Antennas
•
Satellite Receivers
•
Satellite Service
•

InSat has technical product development, marketing, and training specialists to meet your needs in satellite technololgy.

CALL US TODAY!

InSat Corporation

Las Vegas, Nevada, USA
(702) 368-3530
FAX (702) 368-1054

Equipment Manufacturers and Distributors

Intelliprompt. 1555 Cassil Pl. Los Angeles 90028. (213) 461-3113. FAX: (213) 461-1264. Ernest Boyden, pres.
New York 10001: 208 W. 29th St., Suite 503. (212) 629-6130. Duncan Chinnock, opns dir N.Y.
Toronto, Ont., Canada M5V 2M5: 30 Maude St. (416) 863-9535. Tony MacKinnon, opns dir Toronto.
Computerized color prompters for film, video, ENG & live speaking situations. Quick editing & telephone transfers.

Intelvideo Inc. 42 Arrow Head Dr., Stamford, Conn. 06903. (203) 322-5613. FAX: (203) 322-5613. John Rossi, pres.
Video processing equipment including color encoders, decoders, transcoders, color correctors, image enhancers & noise reducers.

Interactive Market Systems Inc. 11 W. 42nd St., New York 10036. (212) 789-3600. FAX: (212) 789-3636. Bev Andal, pres.
Chicago 60601: 360 N. Michigan, Suite 2010. (312) 372-3360. Carolyn Kidd Harper, mgr midwest opns.
Beverly Hills, Calif. 90010: 4751 Wilshire Blvd., Suite 202A. (213) 933-5491.
Toronto, Ont., Canada M5R 2A5: 1200 Bay St., Suite 405. (416) 961-2840. Carole MacDonald, VP/dir Canadian opns.
Honolulu 96822: 2144 Mott-Smith Dr. (808) 537-2063.
London, U.K. SW1 W0BS: 3537 Grosvenor Gardens House, Grosvenor Gardens. (001) 441-630-5033. Robert Hulks, exec VP.
Paris, France 75497: 15 Rue Fenelon. (011) 331-4878-1100.
Supply interactive on-line media mktg admin system for analysis of products demographics & media.

Interface Video Systems Inc. 1233 20th St. N.W., Washington 20036. (202) 861-0500. FAX: (202) 296-4492. Tom Angell, pres; Elise Reeder, VP opns; Ken Maruyama, VP creative svcs.
Full prod & postprod facility with location & studio shooting, offline & online suites, audio post, graphics & animation, duplication & standards conversion.

International Association of Satellite Users & Suppliers. (IASUS). Box DD, McLean, Va. 22101. (703) 759-2094. FAX: (703) 759-5094; Telex: (650) 338-5074. A. Fred Dassler, exec dir; Robert Veltman, dir.
Satellite earth stns & electronics, power systems, test equipment, microwave (LOS); mobile satellite terminals, C- & Ku-band uplink trucks.

International Cinema Equipment Co. 100 N.E. 39th St., Miami, Fla. 33137. (305) 573-7339. FAX: (305) 573-8101. Steve Krams, pres; Dara Reusch, VP.
16mm, 35mm, 70mm film projection equipment, film to tape transfer equipment, sound systems & editing equipment.

International Datacasting Corp. 2680 Queensview Dr., Ottawa, Ont., Canada K2B 8H6. (613) 596-4120. FAX: (613) 596-4863; (613) 596-9208. Kay Nishi, pres/CEO; Gary Carter, VP mktg & sls; Gen Oyama, exec VP/COO.
Norcross, Ga. 30092: IDC Communications Inc. 5555 Triangle Pkwy., Suite 140. (404) 446-9684. FAX: (404) 448-6396. Doug Kennedy, dir sls data; Bob Payne, dir sls audio.
Satellite communications systems for digital video, audio & data bcst applications.

International Electro-Magnetics. 350 N. Eric Dr., Palatine, Ill. 60067. (708) 358-4622. FAX: (708) 358-4623. Anthony Pretto, pres.
Standard replacement & custom recording heads for audio, video & film.

International Tapetronics Corp. Box 241, 2425 S. Main St., Bloomington, Ill. 61702-0241. (309) 828-1381; (800) 447-0414. FAX: (309) 828-1386. Charlie Bates, opns mgr; Michael J. Bove, midwest rgnl sls mgr.
Hendersonville, Tenn. 37075: 137 Allen Dr. (615) 826-0520. Raymond Updike, eastern rgnl sls mgr.
Audio tape cartridge machines, cartridges & accessories, audio routing switcher systems & remote controls, digital audio platforms, digital prog repeaters.

International Teletext Communications Inc. 1307 S. Mary Ave., Suite 203, Sunnyvale, Calif. 94087. (408) 735-8833. (408) 738-3166. Robert H. Welch, CEO; Robert Evans, chief tech off.
Provides financial & news info svcs via Nationwide Wireless Network. Includes "15 minute delay" stock quotations & USA Today Decisionline at no chg to its PC-based customers. Additional subscription svcs are available on the net. Custom data bcstg svcs for info providers & corporate customers.

Intraplex Inc. 3 Lyberty Way, Westford, Mass. 01886. (508) 692-9000. FAX: (508) 692-2200. John E Kelly, VP mktg; J. Peter Eadie, VP sls.
Digital STLs, digital prog audio equipment for transmission over TI, EI & fractional rate links.

J

JBL Professional. Box 2200, 8500 Balboa Blvd., Northridge, Calif. 91329. (818) 893-8411. Ronald H. Means, pres; Hope Neiman, exec VP mktg; Ken Lopez, VP sls.
Manufacture loudspeaker systems for bcstg, recording studios, theaters, concerts, stadiums & other applications.

JNJ Industries Inc. 195 E. Main St., Suite 303, Milford, Mass. 01757. (800) 554-9994; (508) 478-8757. FAX (508) 478-2221. Jack Volpe, pres; Gail Howe, VP sls & mktg; Richard Fountain, mktg mgr; Tom DeSisto, sls mgr; Lynda Picard, tech support mgr.
CFC-free solvents, presaturated cloth wipes, spray bottles, dry cloth wipes, lens wipes & swabs.

J.N.S. Electronics Inc. Box 32550, San Jose, Calif. 95152. (408) 729-3838. FAX: (408) 926-1003. John E. Leonard, Jr., pres.
Rosanna Victoria 3084, Australia J.N.S. Electronics Ltd. Box 85. 03-439-1000. R. T. Thompson, mgr.
Design, manufacture & sale of audio, video & RF products, including modular configured products & 8000 series rack frames, to the bcstg, communications & telecommunications industries.

JOA Cartridge Service. 448 E. Hancock St., Lansdale, Pa. 19446. (215) 362-8796. FAX: (215) 368-2336. Mark P. Molyneaux, own.

Bcst audio tape cartridges, audio, video tape & cassettes, tape accessories, DAT tape & cassettes, data storage diskettes & cassettes, optical disks, recordable CD's & reloading svc.

J&R Film Co. Inc. 1135 N. Mansfield Rd., Los Angeles 90038. (213) 467-3107. FAX: (213) 466-2201. Joe Paskal, pres; Jim Reichow, exec VP.
Chicago 60610: 416 W. Ontario. (312) 787-0622. Jeff McNeir, VP.
New York 10036: 636 11th Ave. (212) 247-0972. Bob Herman, VP.
Denver 80238: 8000 E. 40th Ave. (303) 321-1099. Randy Urlik, exec VP.
Film editing equipment; film & video shipping & storage; film to video transfer machine.

JVC Professional Products Co. 41 Slater Dr., Elmwood Park, N.J. 07407. (201) 794-3900. FAX: (201) 523-2077. Hajime Hazama, pres; Mike Yoshida, VP; Dave Walton, mktg mgr.
Pinebrook, N.J. 07058: I-80 at New Maple Ave. (201) 882-0900. Jim Turner, rgnl sls mgr.
Auroa, Ill. 60504-8149: 705 Enterprise St. (708) 851-7809. Chuck Evans, rgnl sls mgr.
Cypress, Calif. 90630: 5665 Corporate Ave. (714) 229-8024. Dennis Nymyer, rgnl sls mgr.
Full line of professional video equipment including VTRs, cameras, SEGs, audio mixers, editing controllers, CCV & digital audio.

The J-Lab Co. Box 6530, Malibu, Calif. 90264. (310) 457-4090. FAX: (310) 457-4494. Jerry Labarbera, pres.
Component accesories, battery operated video & audio D.A.s, camera controls, variable speed shutter devices, portable switchers.

Jackson Tool Systems. (subsidiary of Jackson Enterprises) 7555 Jacks Ln., Clayton, Ohio 45315. (513) 836-2641. FAX: (513) 836-0396. Richard L. Jackson, pres.
Aerial construction tools for cable, telephone & fiber.

Jamieson Film Co. 10425 Olympic Dr., Dallas 75220. (800) 527-2298; (214) 350-1283. FAX: (214) 357-2170. Gary W. Fuller, pres; Len Henderson, dir mktg.
Cinema film processors.

Jampro Antennas Inc. 6340 Skycreek Dr., Sacramento, Calif. 95828. (916) 383-1177. FAX: (916) 383-1187. James Olver, pres; Alex Perchevitch, VP.
Manufacture TV & FM bcst antennas, CP & horizontally polarized antennas, combining & filter systems & associated accessories.

Jefferson-Pilot Data Services Inc. 785 Crossover Ln., #141, Memphis 38117. (901) 762-8000. FAX: (901) 762-8038. Doug Rother, pres; Mike Jones, sr. VP rsch & dev; Bill Dodson, VP/CFO.
New York 10022: 919 3rd Ave., 5th Fl. (212) 838-4711. Harvey Kent, VP/gen mgr.
Provides comprehensive & innovative computer software

Jensen Tools Inc. 7815 S. 46th St., Phoenix 85044. (602) 968-6241. FAX: (602) 438-1690. Gary Treiber, mktg mgr.
Electronic tool kits & cases, tools & test equipment.

Jensen Transformers Inc. 10735 Burbank Blvd., North Hollywood, Calif. 91601. (213) 876-0059. FAX: (818) 763-4574. Bill Whitlock, pres.
Audio transformers, 990 operational amplifiers, audio amplifiers, microphone, preamplifiers, circuit analysis software for HP & 386 computers. Retro-fit electronics for Magna-tech film transports.

Jerrold Communications-General Instrument Corp. 2200 Byberry Rd., Hatboro, Pa. 19040. (215) 674-4800. FAX: (215) 672-5130. Hal Krisbergh, pres; Ed Breen, VP sls.
New York 10153: 767 5th Ave., 45th Fl. (212) 207-6200. Charles Cooper, rgnl mgr.
Englewood, Colo. 80111: 7100 E. Belleview Ave., Suite 101. (303) 740-6118. Matt Aden, rgnl mgr.
Carrollton, Tex. 75006: 2611 Westgrove Rd., Suite 108. (214) 248-7931. Tim Roberti, rgnl mgr.
Independence, Mo. 64055: Box 3063. (816) 537-6266.
Diamond Bar, Calif. 91765: 566 N. Diamond Bar. (714) 860-3600. Pete Wronski, rgnl mgr.
CATV headend & distribution equipment; sub terminals, addressable systems & interactive products.

Wireless Information Network in your TV station's VBI

Business Newswires ← → *Stock Market Quotes*
Financial Newspapers → *Electronic Newspapers*

Discover your station's wireless data potential

Excellent business opportunities await qualified stations

Int'l TeleText Communications, Inc.
1307 S. Mary Ave, Suite 203, Sunnyvale, CA 94087
408-735-8833   Fax 408-738-3166

Equipment Manufacturers and Distributors

E.F. Johnson Co. 438 Gateway Blvd., Burnsville, Minn. 55337. (612) 882-5500. FAX: (612) 882-5656. William Weskel, chmn; Robert H. Davies, vice chmn; Fred G. Hamer, VP sls & distribution.
Manufacture & market radio communication products, svcs & systems.

Johnson Measurement Service. 3497 Cornwall Dr. N.W., Canton, Ohio 44708. (216) 477-0635. David S. Johnson, own/engr; M. Jane Johnson, office mgr.
Bcst frequency measurements. Frequency counter calibrations.

Joslyn Jenning Corp. 970 McLaughlin Ave., San Jose, Calif. 95122. (408) 292-4025. Jim Berkeland, gen mgr; G.W. Walsh, controller; R. Doerr, dir opns.
High voltage vacuum & gas capacitors; relays, switches, single & three phase contactors & instruments.

Just Drop Inc. 500 Bi-County Blvd., Suite D-5, East Farmingdale, N.Y. 11735. (516) 753-5060. FAX: (516) 753-5068. Sy Guttenplan, pres.
Miami, Fla. 33172: 1950 N.W. 93 Ave., (305) 594-2969.
Natl stocking distributor for CATV & all drop material, connectors, wire, cable; telephone & data products; safety products & all MMDS items.

K

KAO Optical. 1857 Colonial Village Ln., Lancaster, Pa. 17601. (800) 525-6575. FAX: (717) 392-7897. John Stevens, dir CD-ROM dev; Tracy Files, sls svc mgr (audio); Maric Boddeker, west coast rgnl mgr; Joe D'Ambrosio, midwest rgnl mgr; Dennis Drake, northeast rgnl sls mgr (audio).
CD manufacturer specializing in printing fulfillment svcs & custom work in CD audio & CD-ROM.

KES. 101 Merritt Ave., Iron Mountain, Mich. 49801. (906) 774-6117. FAX: (906) 774-1755. Mike Amicangelo, sls mgr; Nancy Amicangelo, customer svc rep; Randy Proudfit, tech sls rep.
Full line of broadband system supplies including everything from the headend to converters for fiber as well as coax.

K&H Products Ltd. (Porta-Brace). Box 246 N., North Bennington, Vt. 05257. (802) 442-8171. FAX: (802) 442-9118. Robert Howe, pres.
Soft carrying cases for portable video equipment.

KTI. 1140 Sextonville Rd., Richland Center, Wis. 53581. (608) 647-8902. FAX: (608) 647-7394. Jim Atkinson, pres; Tom Prochnow, VP sls; Dawn Elliott, mktg & sls assoc.
Design & manufacture mesh satellite antennas ranging from 5'-16'. Makes antennas for headends.

Kahn Communications Inc. 222 Westbury Ave., Carle Place, N.Y. 11514. (516) 222-2221. Leonard R. Kahn, pres.
AM stereo exciter & receivers; RF-02 stereo monitor, POWER-side & Flatterer systems.

Kaitronics Corp. 859 Cowan Rd., Burlingame, Calif. 94010. (415) 697-9102. FAX: (415) 692-1828. Paul Tarrodaychik, VP.
News, routing, master control, switchers, computer controlled, video & audio data, NTSC, component, HDTV, RGB.

Kalun Communications Inc. 30 Todd Rd., Scarborough, Ont., Canada M1S 2J9. (416) 293-1346. FAX: (416) 297-4911. Paul Wong, pres.
RF test equipment- wideband sweep generator, etc. Video equipment-ch identification generator.

Kangaroo Video Products Inc. 10845 Wheatlands Ave., Suite C, Santee, Calif. 92071-2856. (619) 562-9696. FAX: (619) 449-7244. Steve Leiserson, pres; Kathy Gawlowski, prod mgr.
Engineered soft-sided cases for sensitive electronic equipment.

Kay Industries Inc. 604 N. Hill St., South Bend, Ind. 46617. (800) 348-5257. FAX: (219) 289-5932. Larry Katz, natl sls mgr; Bruce Marshall, mktg mgr.
Rotary phase converters for single phase to three phase power.

Kelly Broadcasting Co. 3 Television Cir., Sacramento, Calif. 95814-0794. (916) 446-3333. FAX: (916) 325-3731. John A. Serrao, gen mgr; Jerry Agresti, dir engrg.

Ketema Aerospace & Electronics Division. 790 Greenfield Dr., El Cajon, Calif. 92022. (619) 442-3451. FAX: (619) 440-1456. Tom Brooks, gen mgr.
Design build-to-print aerospace products, cryogenic lines, valves, burst discs, electric motors, actuators.

Keystone Communications. 6430 Sunset Blvd., Suite 1400, Los Angeles 90028. (213) 467-8900. FAX: (213) 465-8750. David E. Simmons, chmn; Barry McCann, VP sls & mktg; Charles A. Fedorko Jr., VP/gen mgr western rgn.
Ku-band uplink & prod truck, mobile microwave, extensive connectivity throughout the U.S., satellite transmission & uplinking svcs.

Kiddy-Fenwal Inc. 400 Main St., Ashland, Mass. 01721. (508) 881-2000. Robert T. Wickham, pres; David Citron, sls & mktg dir of control; Jean M Marshall, dir sls & fire suppression products.
High-speed fire protection systems.

Kingdom Technology. Box 1145, Fort Walton Beach, Fla. 32549-1145. (800) 695-4643. FAX: (904) 864-3195. David Benoit, own.
Stn controller automation system, digital audio system (DAS) for radio.

Kings Electronics Co. Inc. 40 Marbledale Rd., Tuckahoe, N.Y. 10707. (914) 793-5000. FAX: (914) 793-5092. Robert Dock, pres.
Video patch panels, patch cords, coaxial connectors, triaxial connectors, twinaxial connectors.

Kintek Inc. 224 Calvary St., Waltham, Mass. 02154. (617) 894-6111. FAX: (617) 647-4235. Zaki Abdun-Nabi, pres; David Blackmer, chmn.
Audio signal processing systems for stereo TV, FM & AM bcstg stns.

Kintronic Labs Inc. Box 845, Bristol, Tenn. 37621-0845. (615) 878-3141. FAX: (615) 878-4224. Louis A. King, CEO; Tom King, pres; Gwen King, VP sls.
Phasers, ATUs, transmitter combiners & multiplexers, RF filters, attenuators,

DESIGN, FABRICATION, INSTALLATION AND SUPPORT OF AM RADIO TRANSMISSION SYSTEMS, INCLUDING:
- DIRECTIONAL (DA) AM PHASORS AND TUNING UNITS (ATU'S)
- NON-DA OR DA MULTIPLEXED ANTENNAS
- ATU'S FOR AM STEREO
- TRANSMITTER COMBINERS
- ISOLATION UNITS FOR FM, STL,TSL,PAGING,CELLULAR, TRUNKING,ETC.
- DUMMY LOADS (1-300KW)
- TOWER DETUNING SKIRTS
- RF ATTENUATORS FOR PSA AND PSSA
- RIGID TRANSMISSION LINE AND ACCESSORIES
- FULL LINE OF RF COMPONENTS:
  - Fixed and Variable Inductors
  - RF Contactors
  - Lightning Protection Devices
  - Meter Jacks and Switches
  - Coaxial Cable Clamp Terminators
  - Static Drain and Lighting Chokes

BOX 845 BRISTOL TN 37621-0845
PHONE: 615-878-3141
FAX: 615-878-4224

There's Something In The Air...
JAMPRO
ANTENNAS, INC.

Complete Line of FM & TV Broadcast Antennas

RF Components, Filters & Combiners

CELEBRATING OVER 35 YEARS OF EXCELLENCE!
- *Innovative Engineering*
- *State of the Art Technology*
- *Rugged Construction*
- *Complete System Design*
- *Excellent Service*
- *Unbeatable Performance*
- *Reliability*

When Only The Best Will Do

6340 Sky Creek Drive, Sacramento, CA 95828 USA

(916) 383-1177
Fax (916) 383-1182

Equipment Manufacturers and Distributors

components & accessories; baluns, AM dummy loads & isocouplers; high power dipole curtain antennas, rigid & open wire transmission line.

Kliegl Brothers Lighting. 5 Aerial Way, Syosset, N.Y. 11791. (516) 937-3900. FAX: (516) 937-6042. Al Vitale, pres.
TV studio lighting & control equipment, portable lighting kits & HMI daylight units.

Kline Towers. Box 1013, Columbia, S.C. 29202. (803) 251-8000. FAX: (803) 739-3939. J.C. Kline, pres; R.C. White, gen mgr; David E. Monts, sls mgr; L.A. Foreman, VP engrg.
Designers, fabricators & erectors of TV, FM & other bcst towers & specialty structures.

Knowledge Industry Publications Inc. 701 Westchester Ave., White Plains, N.Y. 10604. (914) 328-9157. FAX: (914) 328-9093. Eliot Minsker, CEO; John Nolan, COO; Janet Moore, sr VP.
Magazines, books, trade shows & seminars.

Knox Video. 8547 Grovemont Cir., Gaithersburg, Md. 20877. (301) 840-5805. FAX: (301) 840-2946. Philip K. Edwards, pres; Roland D. Blood, VP.
Character generators & routing switchers.

Kuhnel Co. Inc. 155 Harmony Rd., Mickleton, N.J. 08056. (609) 423-4277. FAX: (609) 423-5105. Mary Kuhnel, pres.
Instal & maintenance of antennas & towers.

L

LBA Technology Inc. Box 8026, 210 W. 4th St., Greenville, N.C. 27835. (919) 757-0279. FAX: (919) 752-9155. Lawrence Behr, pres; Jay Batista, VP mktg; Phil Morse, gen mgr.
Folded unipole antennas, detuning systems, tuning units & associated products.

LDL Communications Inc. 14440 Cherry Lane Ct., Suite 201, Laurel, Md. 20707. (301) 498-2200. FAX: (301) 498-7952. G.J. Wilson, pres; R.J. Tattershall, VP antenna sls & mktg.

AM ANTENNA SYSTEMS

- **High Efficiency** Folded Unipoles
- **Economical** Antenna Tuning Units
- **Effective** Detuning Systems

PLUS

- Coax, components, and systems for AM, FM, Shortwave and TV, designed and built to international standards.

EXPANDED AM BAND SYSTEMS! SINGLE TOWER & SHARED TOWER AVAILABLE

FAST SERVICE!
800-522-4464
919-757-0279
919-752-9155 FAX

LBA Technology, Inc.
An LBA Group Company
Worldwide Engineering Services
Se Habla Español

Consult us for all your RF needs.

Faribault, Minn. 55021: 21644 Evans Trail. (507) 332-6703. Jeffrey N. Clarine, central rgnl mgr.
San Mateo, Calif. 94401: 323 N. San Mateo Dr. (415) 347-9700. David A. Hill, western rgnl mgr.
Warwick, R.I. 02888: 39 Posnegansett. (401) 461-0999. J. Robert Palmer, eastern rgnl mgr.
Design, supply & instal bcst transmitters, antennas & towers.

L.E.A. Dynatech Inc. 6520 Harney Rd., Tampa, 33610. (813) 621-1324. FAX: (813) 621-8980. Ronald R. Mazik, pres; David J. Breiter, VP/CFO.
Manufacturer transient voltage surge suppression.

LEE Colortran Inc. 1015 Chestnut St., Burbank, Calif. 91506. (818) 843-1200. FAX: (818) 954-8520. Robert Sherman, pres; John Fuller, sr VP sls & mktg.
Totowa, N.J. 07512: 40 Commerce Way, Unit B. (201) 256-7666. William Liento, sr VP sls & mktg.
Manufacture luminaires, dimming & control equipment for film, TV, theatre & environmental lighting mkts.

LMC SatCom Inc./Atlanta International Teleport. 3530 Bomar Rd., Douglasville, Ga. 30135. (404) 949-6600. FAX: (404) 942-6653. Adam Grow, gen mgr/dir engrg; John Roberts, sls mgr.

LNR Communications Inc, 180 Marcus Blvd., Hauppauge, N.Y. 11788. (516) 273-7111. FAX: (516) 273-7119. Dr. Frank Arams, VP mktg; Frank X. Kelly, dir mktg.
Satellite communications equipment manufacture; digital satellite communication systems incorporating audio, video, voice, data, fax via Corku-Band satellites.

LPB Inc. 28 Bacton Hill Rd., Frazer, Pa. 19355. (215) 644-1123. FAX: (215) 644-8651. Edward W. Devecka, pres; John E. Devecka, sls mgr; James D. Beissel Jr., opns mgr.

Canoga Park, Calif. 91303: 20944 Sherman Way, Suite 213. (818) 340-4590.

St. Michaels, Md. 21663: Box 88. (410) 745-3977. Richard H. Crompton, applications engr.

Bcst equipment: audio consoles, travelers advisory systems, AM transmitters, pre-sunrise transmitters, carrier current systems, hearing impaired systems.

LRC Electronics. Box 111, 901 South St., Horseheads, N.Y. 14845. (607) 739-3844. FAX: (607) 739-0106. Leonard DeRenzo Jr., VP mkt dev.
Coaxial connectors, jumper cables, heat shrink & crimp tools.

LTM Corp. of America. 11646 Pendelton St., Sun Valley, Calif. 91352-2501. (818) 767-1313. FAX: (818) 767-1442. Herb Breitling, pres.
New York 10018: LTM Corp. of America-N.Y., 353 W. 39th St., Suite 202. (212) 268-2667. Bob Wierzbicki, rental mgr.
Davie, Fla., 33329-2905: LTM Corp. of America-Florida, Box 292905. (305) 680-2667. Beth Nardin, sls mgr.
HMI & quartz lighting fixtures for film & video prod; fresnels, open face, par, fiber optic & soft lights from 100w to 18,000w.

L-W Athena Inc. 2215 1st St., # 109, Simi Valley, Calif. 93065. (805) 522-3284. FAX: (805) 522-3316. David G. Greve, pres.
Manufacture analytical equipment, Telecine systems & film to tape transfer systems.

Lakeside Associates Inc. 9272 Jeronimo Rd., Suite 123C, Irvine, Calif. 92718. (714) 770-6601. FAX: (714) 770-6575. Carl J. Yanchar, pres.
Acoustical design, facility design, consultation, systems design, studio construction & instal.

Lang Video Communications. 8446 N.W. 61st St., Miami, Fla. 33166. (305) 477-4947. FAX: (305) 594-3832. Mel Lang, pres.
New & used TV equipment broker. Transmitter systems.

Larcan Inc. 228 Ambassador Dr., Mississauga, Ont., Canada L5T 2J2. (416) 564-9222. FAX: (416) 564-9244. P.C. Turner, pres.
Laurel, Md., 20707: (LDL Communications Inc.), 14440 Cherry Lane Ct., Suite 201. (301) 498-2200. J. Wilson, pres.
VHF & UHF TV transmitters, FM radio transmitters; diplexers; combiners; filters & antennas.

Laumic Inc. 432 W. 45th St., New York 10036. (212) 586-6161. FAX: (212) 245-0974. Stuart Mann, gen mgr.

Sls, rental, svc & training for bcst & industrial equipment; systems designed & installed.

Lazar Diode Inc. 1130 Somerset St., New Brunswick, N.J. 08901. (908) 249-7000. FAX: (908) 249-9165. Larry Cramer, pres; Peter Schneider, exec VP; Michael J. Robertson, VP; Sanny C. Blumenthal, controller.
Gallium arsenide based semiconductor optical prods.

LeBlanc Communications Inc. 2301 Bridgeport Dr., Sioux City, Iowa 51111. (712) 252-4101; (800) 831-0974. FAX: (712) 252-2803. John W. Miller, exec VP; Walter M. Podousky, exec VP; P. Paul Gorski, VP mfg; Rick Elliott, sls mgr.
Dallas 75243: N. Central Plaza III, Suite 150. 12801 N. Central Expwy., LCI U.S. Headquarters & Structures Division Headquarters.
Sacramento, Calif. 95815: 1600 Tribute Rd., 14 Telcom Division Headquarters.
Sioux City, Iowa 51102-3807: Box 3807. Sioux City Manufacturing Plant.
St. Peters, Mo. 63376: (St.Louis Office.) Box 76905. 105 Boone Hills Dr.
Lewisberry, Pa. 17339: (Harrisburgh Office.) 571 Industrial Dr.
Clackamas, Ore. 97015: (Portland Office.) 15635 S.E. 114th St., Suite 211.
Dickinson, Tex. 77539: (Houston Office.) R.R. One, Box 647.
Suffolk, Va. 23439-1387: Box 1387.
Sioux City, Iowa 51111-1001: 2301 Bridgeport Dr.
Aiea, Hawaii 96701: (Honolulu Office.) 99-899 Iwaena St., Unit III.
Guyed, self-support, monopole towers & systems integration of cellular, microwave, bcst & trunked lines.

Leader Instruments Corp. 380 Oser Ave., Hauppauge, N.Y. 11788. (516) 231-6900. FAX: (516) 231-5295. S. Hirota, pres; R. Sparks, dir sls.
Cypress, Calif. 90630: 6484 Commerce Dr. (714) 527-9300.
Electronic test equipment for video, audio, RF, microwave, oscilloscopes & gen use.

Leaming Industries. 15339 Barranca Pkwy., Irvine, Calif. 92718. (714) 727-4144. FAX: (714) 727-3650. Robert F. Leaming, pres; Keith G. Rauch, sr VP.
Audio transmission equipment; STL & SCPC equipment; FM stereo processors; BTSC stereo generators; FM stereo modulators; audio AGC amplifiers.

Leasametric. (Instrument Rental Division) 1164-A Triton Dr., Foster City, Calif. 94404. (800) 553-2255. Marshall Hart, pres; Gerald Drozd, VP controller.
Media, Pa. 19063: Lafayette Bldg., 103 Chesley Dr., Suite 6. (800) 553-2255. Joel Sacco, rgnl mgr.
Test rental equipment including CATV sweep analyzers, signal level meters, video generators, monitors & cable fault locators.

Lectrosonics Inc. Box 15900, Rio Rancho, N.M. 87174. (505) 892-4501. FAX: (505) 892-6243. John Arasim Jr., pres; Larry E. Fisher, VP engrg; Bruce C. Jones, VP mktg & sls.
Wireless microphone systems for bcst, motion picture & tele-prod applications. Automatic sound system mixing & control.

Leightronix Inc. 2330 Jarco Dr., Holt, Mich. 48842. (517) 694-5589. FAX: (517) 694-4155. Jeff Possanza, dir sls & mktg.
Real time event controllers for VCR & switcher automation. Telephone remote equipment control.

Leitch/Hedco-Leitch Inc. 920 Corporate Ln., Chesapeake, Va. 23320. (804) 548-2300; (800) 231-9673. FAX: (804) 548-4088. John Walter, pres/gen mgr; Gary Stephens, sls mgr; Steve Miller, VP sls.
Greg Schriener, western rgnl sls mgr (714-459-1990).
Audio & video distribution amplifier, sync generators, clock systems & timers, synchronizers, test equipment, still storage, scramblers & descramblers. Audio, video, digital & data routing switchers, terminations, serial digital products.

Lemco Tool Corp. R.R. 2, Box 330A, Cogan Station, Pa. 17728. (717) 494-0620. FAX: (717) 494-0860. Glenn G. Miller, pres.
Designers & manufacturers of mechanical tools, equipment & materials for the construction & maintenance of CATV systems.

Lemo U.S.A. Inc. Box 11488, Santa Rosa, Calif. 95406. (707) 578-8811; (800) 444-5366. FAX: (707) 578-0869. Samuel M. Sokolik, gen mgr; Carol Taylor, customer svc mgr.
Multicontact, coaxial, triaxial, thermocouple, environmentally sealed, high voltage & audio patching connectors. Custom designs, patch panels & cable assemblies welcome.

Broadcasting & Cable Yearbook 1994
H-36

YOU CAN RELY ON LPB®

*Everyone knows the LPB Signature Series is the industry standard for rugged reliability.
The LPB tradition of durable, reliable, easy-to-use consoles continues in our new linear fader consoles.*

**Industry Standard
LPB Signature III Series**

With over 3,000 units in operation worldwide, the LPB Signature III console represents a standard others are still unable to match. The Signature Series has proved its ability to perform on 6 continents, in settings ranging from metropolitan to jungle. With an incredible record of ruggedness and easy maintenance, it's no wonder over half of the Signature console owners have more than one. Features include 3 inputs per channel, two output buses and plug-in electronics. LPB Signature III consoles are available in 6, 8, 10, and 12 channel stereo and 6, 8, and 10, channel mono models.

The LPB 7000 Series takes the standards of the Signature III a step further, adding more features than any other console in its price range. With front panel switches rated for 5,000,000 operations, gold contacts, plug-in modular electronics and more, the LPB 7000 Series has the durability radio and TV stations worldwide expect from LPB. Features include two inputs per channel, three stereo output buses with one mono-mixdown standard and two more optional, user configurable muting and remote starts, and much more. Available in 12 and 18 channel stereo models.

**All New
LPB 7000 Series**

*It doesn't matter which LPB board you choose, you'll get a console you can count on 24 hours a day.
One you'll keep for a long time. Ask any LPB console user – they're all around you.*

LPB®

28 Bacton Hill Road • Frazer, PA 19355 • (215) 644-1123 • Fax (215) 644-8651

Equipment Manufacturers and Distributors

Lester Laboratories. 9500 Forest Ln., Suite 102, Dallas 75243-5914. (214) 503-0958. FAX: (214) 503-6709. Gary Rilling, VP mktg.
Digital fiber optic transmission systems - DAS-2000, DAS-500.

Digital Audio Workstation
50 Simultaneous Stereo Segment Playback
2-Dimensional Project Creation - No Tracks!
-110dB Noise Floor
Turn To: **Micro Technology Unlimited**

Lexicon Inc. 100 Beaver St., Waltham, Mass. 02154-8425. (617) 736-0300. FAX: (617) 891-0340. Ronald P. Noonan, pres; Harvey L. Schein, VP/treas; Charles Bagnaschi, VP engrg; Steve Kramp, VP sls & mktg.
West Los Angeles, Calif. 90064: 2323 Cornith Ave. (213) 479-2771. Scott Esterson, rgnl mgr.
Manufacture digital audio reverberation & effects processors; time compression/expansion processors; digital audio prod & editing systems.

Lexidyne. Box 5295, Pittsburgh Pa. 15206. (412) 661-4526. Lewis J. Scheinman, pres.
Computer & electronic equipment cleaning supplies including lint-free wipers, disposable clothing, contamination-free chemicals.

Libra Corp. 1954 E. 7000 S., Salt Lake City 84121. (800) 453-3827. FAX: (801) 942-0095. William A. Maasberg, own; Carl Champagne, pres; Bob Seekly, VP mktg.
Accounting software for radio: billing affidavits & sls analysis.

Lightning Deterrent Corp. (A division of ODE-Guard Corp.) Box 595, Wilmington, Ill. 60481. (815) 458-4044;

(800) 776-7150. FAX: (815) 458-3057. Donald F. Hudalla, pres; Richard A. Tarney, sls & mktg.
Lightning & static deterrent equipment designed, individually manufactured & engineered.

Lightning Eliminators & Consultants Inc. 6687 Arapahoe Rd., Boulder, Colo. 80303. (303) 447-2828. FAX: (303) 447-8122. Roy B. Carpenter Jr., CEO.
Designer & manufacturer of lightning strike prevention, grounding & power conditioning systems.

Lightning Master Corp. Box 6017, 1920 Sherwood St., Clearwater, Fla. 34618-6017. (813) 447-6800. FAX: (813) 461-3177. Bruce A. Kaiser, pres; Dale R. Haygood, VP mfg; Tom West, VP sls & mktg.
Madison, Miss. 39110: (Jackson Office.) 118 Stonemill Dr. (800) 946-4646. Tom West, VP sls & mktg.
Grapevine, Tex. 76051-7810: (Ft. Worth Office.) 2104 Brookgate Dr., (817) 331-1776. Larry Conrad, natl sls mgr.
Structural lighting protection equipment, transient voltage surge suppression, bonding & grounding products & consulting svcs.

LIGHTNING PREVENTION SYSTEMS
The Highest Level of Lightning Protection DESIGNED To Save You Money

Lightning Prevention Systems. 204B Cross Keys Rd., Berlin, N.J. 08009. (609) 767-7209. FAX: (609) 767-7547. W. Gregg Fawthrop, pres.
Manufacture equipment that prevents bcst & communications towers from being struck by lightning. Also, ground screens, grounding equipment & consultation.

Lindsay Specialty Products Ltd. 50 Mary St. W., Lindsay, Ont., Canada K9V 4S7. (705) 324-2196. FAX: (705) 324-5474. John Thomas, pres; D.T. Atman, dir mktg; A.G. Zimmerman, sls mgr; Brian Ward, key account mgr.
Full line of receiver antennas, LPTV transmit antennas, 2-way communications antennas, CATV actives & passives.

Link Electronics Inc. 753 Enterprise St., Cape Girardeau, Mo. 63701. (314) 334-4433. FAX: (314) 334-9255. Bob Henson, pres; Ellen Henson, exec VP; James Timberlake, VP opns; Dave Aufdenberg; customer serv mgr; Dallas Hickerson, engr mgr.
Middletown, Md. 21769: 7303 Poplar Ln. (301) 371-5588. Tony Mattia, rgnl mgr.
Manufacture Sync Generators, system timing, audio & video DAs, Power Amps, encoders, decoders, video processing & test equipment, video presence detector, closed caption encoder/decoder.

Lipsner Smith Co. 4700 Chase Ave., Lincolnwood, Ill. 60646. (708) 677-3000; (800) 323-7520. FAX: (708) 677-1311. Ray L. Short Jr., pres; Thomas A. Tisch, VP mktg.
Ultrasonic film cleaners; film rewinders; film viewers.

Listec Video Corp. 40-3 Oser Ave., Hauppauge, N.Y. 11788-3809. (516) 273-3020. FAX: (516) 435-4544. Joanne Camarda, pres; Jack Littler, chmn.
Manufacturer PC & Apple based prompting software & electronic firmware. Studio/field on-camera & conference prompter displays. Traditional script drive tables.

Logica Inc. 5 Penn Plaza, New York 10001. (212) 629-3456. FAX: (212) 631-0269. Bill Engo, pres.
Involved in mktg of Prestel systems, selling own teletext systems & consulting.

Logitek. 3320 Bering Dr., Houston 77057. (713) 782-4592; (800) 231-5870. FAX: (713) 782-7597. Tag Borland, pres.

Audio consoles, amplifiers, preamplifiers, LED audio displays, distribution amplifiers, audio level indicators, serial controlled consoles.

Loral Fairchild Imaging Sensors. 1801 McCarthy Blvd., Milpitas, Calif. 95035. (408) 433-2500. FAX: (408) 433-2508. Joe Milelli, gen mgr; Jim Johnson, sls mgr.
Charge-coupled devices, linear area image sensors, cameras, video delay lines.

Loral Microwave-Narda. 435 Moreland Rd., Hauppauge, N.Y. 11788. (516) 231-1700. FAX: (516) 231-1711. Bernard Leibowitz, pres; Bob Damiano, VP engrg; John Crawford, sr VP opns; John Mega, VP finance & admin.
Portable RF/microwave test instruments, power density meters, coaxial power monitors & meters.

Loral TerraCom. 9020 Balboa Ave., San Diego 92123. (619) 278-4100. FAX: (619) 292-1140. Gus Schneidau, pres; Mike Lapadula, VP mktg; Brian Mertes, VP engrg.
HF, UHF & microwave communications & tactical radio equipment.

Louth Automation. 545 Middlefield Rd., Suite 160, Menlo Park, Calif. 94025-3443. (415) 329-9498. FAX: (415) 329-9530. Ken Louth, CEO; Hayley Ditzler, VP.
ADC-100 stn automation, NEWSTRAK- newsroom automation.

Lowel-Light Mfg. Inc. 140 58th St., Brooklyn, N.Y. 11220. (718) 921-0600. FAX: (718) 921-0303. Ross Lowell, pres; Marvin Seligman, CEO; Amy Carter, east coast sls rep; Don Youngberg, midwest sls; Dale Marks, sls rep; Toni Pearl, dealer liaison.
Film, video & still photography lighting equipment, kits & accessories for the professional.

Luxor Corp. 2245 Delaney Rd., Waukegan, Ill. 60087. (708) 244-1800. FAX: (800) 327-1698. Donald L. Nichoalds, chmn; Robert T. Raw, gen mgr; Greg Hunigan, natl sls mgr; Brian Kumkoske, sls mgr.
Computer stands, A/V equipment stands, conference room furniture, TV stands, library & office furniture.

Lyon Lamb Video Animation Systems Inc. 4531 Empire Ave., Suite 229. Burbank, Calif. 91505. (818) 843-4831. FAX: (818) 843-6544. Bruce Lyon, pres; Christine Lyon, VP.
Frame accurate animation controllers, RGB to NTSC & PAL scan converters.

M

M/A-Com MAC. 401 Edgewater Pl., Wakefield, Mass. 01880. (617) 272-9600. FAX: (617) 224-5655. Thomas A. Vanderslice, CEO; Allan L. Rayfield, COO/pres.
RF Microwave & millimeter wave components & subsystems.

MARKETRON. 101 Lincoln Center Dr., Suite 300, Foster City, Calif. 94404. (415) 341-4004. FAX: (415) 341-8197. Jerry Cronin, pres; Gary Davidson, exec VP; Michael D. Rooney, dir mktg.
Woodland Hills, Calif. 91364: 21031 Ventura Blvd., Suite 1020. (818) 347-6400. Gary Davidson, exec VP.
Bcst software application for radio/TV rsch & sls, for nets & syndicators. Radio/TV traffic, mgmt & accounting.

MATCO Inc. 15000 Stetson Rd., Los Gatos, Calif. 95030-9706. (408) 353-2670. FAX: (408) 353-8781. David Harbert, pres; Rita Harbert, VP/gen mgr.
Playback automation, coml insertion & machine control systems for bcst, cable & coml, industrial & medical.

MATH Associates Inc. (A subsidiary of General Microwave Corporation) (516) 226-8950. FAX: (516) 226-8966 Sherman A. Rinkel, pres; Irwin Math, VP/tech dir; Ellen Math, VP communications & mktg.

MCG Electronics Inc. 12 Burt Dr., Deer Park, N.Y. 11729. (516) 586-5125. FAX: (516) 586-5120. Michael J. Coyle, pres; Don Worden, sls mgr.
Surge protectors for AC power, telephone, signal & data lines.

MCL Inc. 501 S. Woodcreek Rd., Bolingbrook, Ill. 60440-4999. (708) 759-9500. FAX: (708) 759-5018. Frank P. Morgan, CEO.
Satellite communication fixed & mobile transmitter systems in C-band, Ku-band, DBS & millimeter-wave.

LINK ELECTRONICS

STARFLEX
Sophisticated Distribution System

LINK'S SECRET IS A UNIVERSAL SYSTEM FRAME
The Starflex system is designed for flexibility and system requirements for present and future expansion. The 3000 frame will accept stereo or mono audio DA's, video DA's, system timing, sync pulse gen., test set signal generators, transcoding, and master black in the same frame.

A master timebase module supplies the timing pulse for all system timing modules to maintain accurate SC/H phase and H timing.

LINK ELECTRONICS, INC. 753 ENTERPRISE STREET
CAPE GIRARDEAU, MO 63701 Phone 314 334 4433

Equipment Manufacturers and Distributors

MEMEX Software Inc. 1661 W. 8th Ave., Suite 303, Vancouver, B.C., Canada V6J 1T8. (604) 731-0831. FAX: (604) 736-6431. Warren L. McKay, pres; Patrick Payne, VP mktg; Umberto Sverdrup, client svcs.
Integrated TV mgmt software from progmg & traffic to prod & opns & more.

MERET Optical Communications Inc. 1800 Stewart St., Santa Monica, Calif. 90404. (310) 828-7496. FAX: (310) 828-7567. Xin Cheng, mngng dir; Eli Spater, VP/sls & mktg; Alan Davis, bcst sls mgr.
Baltimore 21208: 7313 Park Heights Ave., #101. (410) 764-6720. William Berry, northeastern rgnl sls mgr.
Clarkston, Ga. 30021: 1145 Cimarron Ct. (404) 296-3565. Ed Ballance, southeastern rgnl sls mgr.
Single & multimode fiber optic HDTV, NTSC & PAL transmission systems designed for ENG, sports & entertainment applications.

MICOM Communications Corp. 4100 Los Angeles Ave., Simi Valley, Calif. 93063. (805) 583-8600. FAX: (805) 583-1997. Barry Phelps, CEO; Gil Cabral, pres; Fran Good, CFO.
Guilford, Surrey, England GU1 4UD: 7 River View, Walnut Tree Close. 44-483-451960. FAX: 44-483-451883. Ken Burrough, rgnl mgr/contact. (European office)
Fullerton, Calif. 92631: 2600 E. Nutwood Ave., Suite 210. (714) 992-6702. Fax: (714) 992-6769. Dann Allen, rgnl mgr/contact; Kelly Boozell, admin.
Redmond, Wash. 98052: 15600 Redmond Way, Suite 200. (206) 883-4137. FAX: (206) 867-0955. Terry McFadden, rgnl mgr/contact.
Santa Clara, Calif. CA 95054: 5201 Great America Pkwy., Suite 306. (408) 986-0890. FAX: (408) 986-0962. Joseph Bloyd, rgnl mgr/contact; Sue Colandone, admin Techmart.
Irving, Tex. 75062: 102 Decker Ct., Suite 250. (214) 650-9000. FAX: (214) 650-0731. Mike Miehe, rgnl mgr/contact; Diana Chambers, admin.
Naperville, Ill. 60563: 184 Shuman Blvd., Suite 200. (708) 717-2999. FAX: (708) 717-9432. Jim Monk, rgnl mgr/contact.
St. Louis 63146: 11756 Borman Dr., Suite 200. (314) 432-0330. FAX: (314) 432-0849. Steve Gleason, rgnl mgr/contact; Carol Davis, admin.
Atlanta 30339: 2839 Paces Ferry Rd., Suite 340. (404) 435-2999. FAX: (404) 435-0663. Steve White, rgnl mgr/contact; Belinda Allen, admin. (Southern Region)
Hackensack, N.J. 07601: 411 Hackensack Ave. (201) 342-5110. FAX: (201) 342-8443. Terry Carlisano, rgnl mgr/contact; Lorraine McDonnell, admin. (Mid-Atlantic Region)
Newton, Mass. 02159: 75 Wells Ave., Suite 4. (617) 527-4010. FAX: (617) 527-2710. Janet Lunig, rgnl mgr/contact; Anne Downes, admin. (New England Region)
Manufactures products that integrate data, voice, fax & loc area net over low speed leased lines.

MTC Production Center 250 S. Robertson, Beverly Hills, Calif. 90211. (310) 854-8500; (800) 252-0100. FAX: (310) 854-8509. Theresa Stauring, gen mgr.
Bosch Telecine, DaVinci Color Corrector, multi-format on-line editing; off-line editing, audio sweetening; 2D & 3D computer graphics.

MYAT Inc. Box 425, 380 Chestnut St., Norwood, N.J. 07648-0425. (201) 767-5380. FAX: (201) 767-4147. Philip A. Cindrich, pres; Donald S. Aves, chief engr.
Rigid coaxial transmission lines, components & accessories.

MZB/Gray Inc. Bldg. 6, 6221 N. O'Connor, Suite 110, Irving, Tex. 75039. (214) 869-4500. FAX: (214) 869-4895. Richard W. Bock, pres; Kelly McCaddon, VP.
Houston 77036: 5750 Bintliff, Suite 217. (713) 782-8611. Karen Westbrook.
Madison, Ala. 35758: 190 Lime Quarry Rd., #105. (205) 461-0900. Walter Bridges. (Huntsville office.)
Mobile, Ala. 36606: 2866 Dauphin St., Suites F&G. (205) 476-2051. Kevin McDuff & Brenda Hobby.
Gainesville, Fla. 32606: 1031 N.W. 91st Ter. (904) 332-2435. Jerome Hoffman.
Orlando, Fla. 32806: 1605 S. Bumby Ave. (407) 896-7414.
Harahan, La. 70123: 5441 Pepsi St. (504) 733-7265. Travis Carter. (New Orleans office.)
Leander, Tex. 78641: Box 1190. (512) 259-0009. Dan Bock. (Austin office.)
Irving, Tex. 75039: 6221 N. O'Connor, Suite 110. (214) 869-4500.
Sales, rentals, svc & instal of professional video & bcst equipment.

Mac Panel Co., Audio Tape Division. Box 7728, 551 W. Fairfield Rd., High Point, N.C. 27264. (919) 861-3100. FAX: (919) 861-6280. Joseph L. Craycroft Jr., bd chmn; John Craycroft, pres.
Electrical & mechanical interface systems; military & coml.

Macrovision Corp. 700 E. El Camino Real, Suite 200, Mountain View, Calif. 94040. (415) 691-2900. FAX: (415) 691-2999. John Ryan, chmn; Joseph Swyt, pres; Bill Krepick, VP sls & mktg; Whit Jackson, sls mgr Encryption systems.
Oxbridge, Middlesex, U.K. UB8 1JN: Macrovision UK Ltd., One Kings Yard, High St. (44) 895-251602. Alistair Knox, mngng dir.
Shijuku-ku, Tokyo 160, Japan: Macrovision Services Corp. Shinjuku 1-7-2-602. 81-33-350-4050. Joe Ishimoda.
Video anticopy & scrambling systems for videocassettes, pay-per-view cable, satellite TV & video conferencing.

Magna-Tech Electronic Co. Inc. 630 9th Ave., New York 10036. (212) 586-7240. FAX: (212) 265-3638. Ernesto Aguilar, pres.
Film recorders & reproducers; 16 & 35mm projectors, telecine film followers, time code generators & readers.

Magnavox CATV Systems Inc. 100 Fairgrounds Dr., Manlius, N.Y. 13104. (315) 682-9105. FAX: (315) 682-9006. Dieter Brauer, pres/CEO; Alan Kernes, VP sls; Michael Senken, VP finance; Thoman Towne, VP opns.
Amplifiers, line extenders, fiber optic receivers & transmitters, status monitoring, headend equipment, passives, subpassives, connectors.

Magnefax International Inc. Rt. 1, Box 764, Rogers, Ark. 72756. (501) 925-1818. FAX: (501) 925-1841. Dennis W. Tallakson, pres.
Audio tape duplicating equipment & audio degaussers.

Magni Systems Inc. 9500 S.W. Gemini Dr., Beaverton, Ore. 97005. (503) 626-8400. FAX: (503) 626-6225. Victor L. Kong, chmn/CEO; Steve Talley, mktg support mgr.
Video test & measurement equipment, waveform monitors, vectorscopes, test signal generators & PC graphics to video encoders.

Magnum Towers Inc. 9370 Elder Creek Rd., Sacramento, Calif. 95829. (916) 381-5053. FAX: (916) 381-2144. Lawrence Smith, pres.
Radio, TV & microwave towers.

Major Engineering. Box 1024, Temple City, Calif. 91780. (818) 309-9470. Ronald Major, own.
Custom built, multi-format, video cassette storage system for high density storage.

The Management. Box 1-36457, Fort Worth, Tex. 76136. (817) 625-9761. FAX: (817) 624-9741. Peter R. Charlton, pres; Debra Charlton, VP.
Computer software for radio/TV traffic & billing, mus selection & digital audio record & play.

Marantz Professional Products. 1000 Corporate Blvd., Suite D, Aurora, Ill. 60504. (708) 820-4800. FAX: (708) 820-8103. Fred Hackendahl, pres.
Portable tape recorders & accessories.

Marathon Products Company. Box 623, 69 Sandersdale Rd., Charlton, Mass. 01507. (508) 248-3157; (508) 853-0988. Richard D. Myers Sr., pres.
Endless loop magnetic tape audio cartridges; maintenance accessories for tape cartridge transports (torque testers & speed indicators).

Marcom. Box 66507, Scotts Valley, Calif. 95066. (408) 438-4273. FAX: (408) 438-6617. Martin Jackson, pres.
FM, AM, TV & microwave transmitting equipment; install & maintenance.

Marconi Communication Systems Ltd. Marconi House, New St., Chelmsford-Essex, U.K. CM1 1PL. (011) 44-245-353-221. Geogio Ghiglione, gen admin.
Reston, Va. 22091: Marconi Communications Inc. 11800 Sunrise Valley Dr., 10th Fl. (703) 620-0333. FAX: (703)471-7368. L. Edward Marble, pres.
Full range bcst & TV transmitters, studio products & satellite earth stn equipment.

$ports + MARTI = Revenue

RPT-30 RPU Transmitter

Marti has been bringing back live sports remote broadcasts for over 34 years. Put Marti's proven reliability to work for you.

VISA   MasterCard

MARTI Electronics
1501 N. Main, Cleburne, TX 76031
Phone: (817) 645-9163   FAX: (817) 641-3869

Equipment Manufacturers and Distributors

Marconi Instruments. 3 Pearl Ct., Allendale, N.J. 07401. (201) 934-9050. FAX: (201) 934-9229. Carl A. Pepple, pres; John Garthwaite, mgr inside sls.
Test & measurement instrumentation.

Maritz Performance Improvement. 1000 Town Ctr., Suite 1200, Southfield, Mich. 48075. (313) 948-4500. FAX: (313) 948-4958. Mike Craven, VP Detroit area mgr; Jim Moore, VP/mktg mgr.
Detroit 42843: 600 Rennaisance Ctr., Suite 1700 (313) 948-4500. (313) 948-4777.
Communications, film/video training, business meetings, A/V.

Mark IV Sudio Broadcast & Production Group. 9900 Baldwin Pl., El Monte, Calif. 91731. (800) 877-1771. Rick Sanchez, mktg mgr.
Altec Lansing, Electro-Voice, Vega, DDA, Midas, Klark Teknik, Dynacord & Gauss, Electro-Sound.

Mark IV Vega. 9900 Baldwin Pl., El Monte, Calif. 91731. (818) 442-0782. FAX: (818) 444-1342. Gary J. Stanfill, pres; Kenneth M. Bourne, dir mktg.
Wireless microphones & walkaround intercom systems; signal, control & monitoring products.

Marketing Resources Plus. 555 Twin Dolphin Dr., Suite 350, Redwood City, Calif. 94065. (415) 595-1800. FAX: (415) 595-3410. Dennis McNeill, pres; Jeff Nelson, VP/sls dir; Brian Brady, VP rsch & sls.
Microcomputer software for TV.

Marshall Electronics. Box 2027, Culver City, Calif. 90230. (310) 390-6608. FAX: (310) 391-8926. Henry Shultz, pres; Leonard Marshall, VP.
Wire cable & connectors; Mogami, Tajimi & Sound Runner brands.

Marti Electronics. 1501 N. Main, Cleburne, Tex. 76033. (817) 645-9163. FAX: (817) 641-3869. M.E. McClanahan, pres; Dan Rau, sls dir.
Composite, dual mono & digital STL systems, remote pickup systems, telemetry links.

MicroSound™
Digital Audio Workstations
Edit & Assemble Audio as Projects
(exactly as you want to work)
With Creative Freedom As Never Before
... And On Budget!

* Place Audio Freely in your Projects **Without the Limitations of Tracks**
* Play Up to 50 Stereo Segments Together at any Time in the Project, With up to 2900 Segments in a Project
* Make Non-Destructive Edits to Sample Precision, Modifyable Any Time
* Acclaimed Ease-of-Use Dramatically Increases Productivity IMMEDIATELY
* Sync-Lock to Video or Any SMPTE
* 16/18 bit A/D/A, 2-4 Channels in/out
* -110dB Sonically Clear Audio Quality
* Ready-to-Use Workstations $7K - $15K
* Peripherals to Add to Your 386/486 Computer from $3K to $7K

Micro Technology Unlimited
PO Box 21061 - 6900 Six Forks Rd.
Raleigh, NC, USA 27619-1061
(919) 870-0344 Fax: (919) 870-7163
"Quality Digital Audio Since 1977"

Matrox Video Products Grp. 1055 St. Regis Blvd., Dorval, Que., Canada H9P 2T4. (514) 685-2630. FAX: (514) 685-2853. Lorne Trottier, pres; Ed Dwyer, VP sls & mktg.
Full range of desktop video prod systems.

Matthews Studio Equipment Group/ITE. 2405 Empire Ave., Burbank, Calif. 91504-3399. (818) 843-6715. FAX: (213) 849-1525. Carlos DeMettos, CEO; Edward Phillips, COO; Tom Menke, sls mgr.
TV camera support dollies, tripods, studio pedestals, pan & tilt heads, cases & microwave support equipment.

Maxell Corp. of America. 2208 Rt. 208, Fairlawn, N.J. 07410. (201) 794-5900. FAX: (201) 796-8790. Herb Matsumoto, pres; James Ringwood, VP prof prod; John Selvaggio, natl bcst mgr; Patricia Byrne, prod mgr.
Northbrook, Ill. 60062: 3305 Commercial Ave. (708) 480-7650. Dan Maida, natl duplicator mgr.
Irvine, Calif. 92714: 8 Bahia. (714) 263-0929. Tim Purnell, western rgnl mgr.
Blank audio & video recording tape for professional bcstrs & duplicators.

Maze Broadcast Inc. Box 100186, Birmingham, Ala. 35210. (205) 956-2227. FAX: (205) 956-5027. Rick Maze, pres; Vira J. Maze, sec.
Remarketers of TV & video equipment.

McCurdy Radio Industries Ltd. 108 Carnforth Rd., Toronto, Ont., Canada M4A 2L4. (800) 267-8800. FAX: (416) 751-6455. Paul Hudson, pres; Dan Kupieg, sls mgr.
Buffalo, N.Y. 14206: 1051 Clinton St.
Automation systems, radio consoles, audio test sets & monitors, disc audio storage systems.

Phil McQuatters Frequency Measuring Service. 601 S. Bunker Hill Dr., San Bernardino, Calif. 92410-2751. (909) 884-1526. Phil McQuatters, own.
Bcst frequency measurements of AM, FM & TV.

Media Computing Inc. 3506 E. Meadow Dr., Phoenix 85032-2718. (602) 482-9131. FAX: (602) 992-6572. Michael D. Rich, pres; Kathryn A. Hulka, VP; Larry L. Baum, tech opns mgr.
PC-based automation software for news (T.E.N.), graphics & elections (ANGIS), equipment control (PROtec).

Media Concepts Inc. 331 N. Broad St., Philadelphia 19107. (215) 923-2545. FAX: (215) 928-0750. Ed Harding, pres.
Video duplication, international video standards coversion, film & slide to tape transfers, time code burnins & audiocassette duplication.

Media Expressions Inc. 18 Alston Ct., Marlboro, N.J. 07746. (908) 536-4449.

Media Touch Systems Inc. 50 Northwestern Dr., Unit 11, Salem, N.H. 03079. (603) 893-5104. FAX: (603) 893-6390. John M. Connell, pres.
Software-based digital audio & control systems networked with traffic & mus systems. Complete automation or live assist using touch-screen technology.

Medialink. 708 3rd Ave., New York 10017. (212) 682-8300. FAX: (212) 953-9444. Laurence Moskowitz, pres.
Los Angeles 90028: 6430 Sunset Blvd. (213) 465-0111.
London, U.K. WC2E 7LJ: 38 Maiden Ln. 44-71-240-3923. Jim Gold.
Distribution of satellite feed news & video news release advisories via professional newswire.

Mediasoft Inc. 7510 Broadway Ext., Suite 206, Oklahoma City 73116. (405) 842-8165. FAX: (405) 843-5682. Bob Alfson, pres.
Microcomputer products & svcs.

Megadata Corp. 35 Orville Dr., Bohemia, N.Y. 11716-2598. (516) 589-6800. FAX: (516) 589-6858. Y.N. Bachana, pres; John R. Keller, VP.
Manufacture wireless communication devices, including plug-in radio modems (voice & data) for PCs & compatibles.

Megastar Inc. 701 Desert Ln., Suite 4, Las Vegas 89106. (702) 386-2844. Nigel Macrae, pres.
Design & install of integrated satellite nets. Reseller, earth stns, earth stn equip & microwave equip.

Melita Electronic Labs Inc. 6630 Bay Cir., Norcross, Ga. 30071. (404) 446-7800. FAX: (404) 446-2409; (404) 409-4444. Aleksander Szlam, pres/CEO.
Morristown, N.J. 08057: 720 E. Main St. (609) 235-1771. John Baum, natl acct exec.
Dallas 75238: 3778 Realty Rd. (609) 235-1771. Randy Pugh, natl acct exec.
Automated telephone call processing products.

Memtek Products/Memorex Audio & Video. Box 901021, Fort Worth, Tex. 76101. (817) 878-6700. FAX: (817) 878-6743. Linda Lambert, gen mgr; Tom Mitchko, natl sls mgr.
Memorex video & audio products.

Merlin Engineering Works Inc. 1888 Embarcadero Rd., Palo Alto, Calif. 94303. (415) 856-0900; (800) 227-1980. FAX: (415) 858-2302. John Streets, pres.
Bcst VTRs, custom VTRs & accessories, VTR automation systems, stereo audio encoders, standard converters.

Metz Engineering. R.R. 1, Box 181, Crescent, Iowa 51526. (712) 545-3222. FAX: (712) 545-9111. Joanne M. Metz, own; John P. Metz III, dir opns & tech svcs.
Tower maintenance.

Meyer Mobile Productions. 200 N. 4th St., Bismark, N.D. 58501. (800) 472-5458. FAX: (701) 255-8220. Jim Sande, prod mgr.
28' Multi-camera bcst truck, Betacam SP VTRs, DVE, A/B roll edit, 24 ch audio bd, wireless IFB & 7kw generator.

Mic Flags by Aladdin. 2 Research Dr., Branford, Conn. 06405. (203) 488-4267. FAX: (203) 483-7585. Terry N. Parsons, pres.
Mic flags, camera plates, desk name plates, badges, awards, banners, interior signs.

Micro Communications Inc. Box 4365, 438 Kelley Ave., Grenier Field, Manchester, N.H. 03108-4365. (603) 624-4351. FAX: (603) 624-4822. Thomas J. Vaughan, pres; Howard Bouldry, VP/gen mgr; Dennis Heymans, mktg mgr; Jennie Allen, inside sls.
Waveguide & coaxial transmission lines; complete RF system packages for UHF, VHF, FM & LPTV panel antennas; antennas for UHF, VHF & FM.

Micro Controls Inc. Box 728, Burleson, Tex. 76028. (817) 295-0965. Jeff E. Freeman, pres.
AM & FM bcstg equipment.

Micro Technology Unlimited. 6900 Six Forks Rd., Raleigh, N.C. 27615. (919) 870-0344. FAX: (919) 870-7163. David B. Cox, pres.
MTU has produced crystal transparent quality Digital Audio Workstations since 1979. MicroSound ™ Workstations provide truly unique Project-Editing ™, up to 50 audio events playing simultaneously, instant performance & reliability for a fearlessly creative environment. We work closely with our clients so they work on schedule & on budget.

Microdyne Corp. Box 7213, 491 Oak Rd., Ocala, Fla. 34472. (904) 687-4633. FAX: (904) 687-0561. Phillip Cunningham, pres; Bill Lennox, VP engrg.
Manufacturer of satellite receiving systems, antennas, telemetry receiving systems & ancillary equipment.

Microflect Co. Inc. 3575 25th St. S.E., Salem, Ore. 97302. (503) 363-9267. FAX: (503) 363-4613. Richard Kreitzberg, pres; John J. Kranitz, mktg mgr.
Towers, microwave passive repeaters, waveguide support systems, tech svc.

Microlex International. Bldg. 50, Brooklyn Navy Yard, Brooklyn, N.Y. 11205. (718) 486-5900. FAX: (718) 237-2050. J. Deutch, dir.
Exporter of major-brand industrial electronic components & equipment to communications facilities & overseas distributors.

Microlog Corporation. 20270 Goldenrod Ln., Germantown, Md. 20876. (301) 428-9100. FAX: (301) 540-5557. Joe Lynn, CEO; Dick Tompson, pres; John Stabb, rgnl sls mgr; Jack Moroz, govt & coml sls mgr.
Automated outbound/inbound voice messaging systems & svc bureau; interactive voice response to mainframe computer.

Micron Audio Products Ltd. 410 Garibaldi Ave., Lodi, N.J. 07644. (201) 777-7223. FAX: (201) 777-5585. Paul Tepper, pres.
Complete line of micron wireless microphone systems for film, TV, ENG, EFP & stage applications; SQN portable location audio mixers.

Microspace Communications Corp. 3100 Highwoods Blvd., Raleigh, N.C. 27604. (919) 850-4500. FAX: (919) 850-4518. Keith N. Smith, VP/gen mgr; Steve D. Grissom, consultant.

Equipment Manufacturers and Distributors

Domestic & international data & audio transmissions to small, inexpensive satellite earth stns.

Microtime. 1280 Blue Hills Ave., Bloomfield, Conn. 06002. (203) 242-4242. FAX: (203) 242-3321. David E. Acker, pres; Mark Podesla, mktg mgr.
Real time digital video prod workstations, true 3-D digital video effects systems, frame synchronizers, decoders.

Microwave Filter Co. Inc. 6743 Kinne St., East Syracuse, N.Y. 13057. (315) 437-3953; (800) 448-1666. FAX: (315) 463-1467. Carl Fahrenkrug, pres; Robert Portmess, VP mfg; Dick Jones, VP finance.
Filters, traps, custom nets for TV, radio, CATV, wireless cable, LAN, mobile radio.

Microwave Radio Corp. 20 Alpha Rd., Chelmsford, Mass. 01824. (508) 250-1110. FAX: (508) 256-5215. Frederick P. Collins, chmn/CEO; Robert J. Morrill, pres/COO; Edward W. Dahn, sr VP; David Glidden, dir corporate communications.
Field sls offices: Northeast: Robert Morrissette, (508) 250-1110; Southeast: George Hardy, (404) 623-6114; Central: Eric McCulley, (508) 433-5470; West: Carl Guastaferro, (408) 927-9161.
Offers a comprehensive line of microwave transmitter, receivers & antennas including the FLR/FLH series of radio systems (from 2 to 13 GHz) for long-haul applications, the MicroLink III & 23CX 18/23 GHz short-haul systems & the ProStar Series of TXs, RXs & antennas for portable opns from 2 to 40 GHz; var of digital microwave communications systems.

Mid Atlantic Radio Service. Box 11502, Wilmington, Del. 19850. (302) 323-0338. David W. Schmidt, own/operator.
AM, FM & TV frequency measurement svcs & contract engrg svcs.

Mid-State Communications Inc. 47 Berry St. Extension, Fitchburg, Mass. 01420. (508) 342-9697. FAX: (508) 342-8020. Norman L. Rivers, pres.
FCC applications, site acquisition, systems design.

Midwest CATV. 94 Inverness Ter. E., Suite 310, Englewood, Colo. 80112. (303) 799-4343. FAX: (303) 643-4797. Erika Bell, VP; Jim McCulley, VP sls.
Full-line, full-svc stocking distributor of CATV, LAN & Broadband equipment with warehouses nationwide.

Midwest Communications. Box 487, 7055 Production Ct., Florence, Ky. 41022-0487. (606) 781-2200. FAX: (606) 781-3987. J.C. Adrick, exec VP.
Video, audio, RF, satellite CATV products & systems.

Milestek Inc. 1 Lake Trail Dr., Argyle, Tex. 76226. (817) 455-7444; (800) 524-7444. FAX: (817) 455-2111. Frank J. Miles, pres.
Connectors including both 50 OHM & 75 OHM BNCs, cabling, patching & tools for coaxial cable.

Miller Fluid Heads (USA) Inc. 410 Garibaldi Ave., Lodi, N.J. 07644. (201) 473-9592. FAX: (201) 473-9693. Art Kramer, pres; Grant Clementson, CEO.
Pan & tilt fluid heads, tripods & camera support accessories.

Minolta Corp. 101 Williams Dr., Ramsey, N.J. 07446. (201) 818-3571. FAX: (201) 825-4374. Hiro Fuji, pres.
CRT & LCD color analyzing instrumentation.

Miralite Communications Inc. 4040 MacArthur Blvd., Suite 307, Newport Beach, Calif. 92660. (714) 474-1900. FAX: (714) 474-1885. Fred Fourcher, pres; Tim Anderson, VP.
Satellite earth stns systems.

Miranda Technologies Inc. 5695 Chemin St. Francois Rd., St-Laurent, Que., Canada H4S 1W6. (514) 333-1772. FAX: (514) 333-9828. Christian Tremblay, pres; Yvan Ouellet, dir sls & mktg.
Digital video products for prod & postprod: serializers, digital-to-analog converters, NTSC encoders, etc.

Jay Mitchell Associates. Box 1285, Fairfield, Iowa 52556. (515) 472-4087. FAX: (515) 472-6457. Jay Mitchell, pres.

Mitsubishi Electric Sales America. 800 Cottontail Ln., Somerset, N.J. 08873. (714) 220-1464. C.E. Phillips, exec VP; Jerry M. Astor, mktg dir.
Portable video tape recorder systems.

Mobile Satellite Link Corp. 322 Quaker Ridge Rd., Timonium, Md. 21093. (410) 252-7614. Dennis F. Dunn, pres.

Mobile Video Services Ltd. 1620 Eye St. N.W., Washington 20006. (202) 331-8882. Lawrence VanderVeen, pres; Steve Meeks, sls & mktg.
Complete EFP & ENG svcs, multi-camera trucks, editing teleco & satellite transmission svcs available.

Mobile-Cam Products. 340-F Vernon Way, El Cajon, Calif. 92020. (619) 441-1295. FAX: (619) 441-9263. William Black, pres; Fred Phillips, VP/treas.
Designs & builds TV news & prod vehicles; suburbans, vans, cab & chassis trucks.

Modern Telecommunications Inc. 885 2nd Ave., New York 10017. (212) 355-0510. FAX: (212) 759-7465. Bill Dalessandro, pres.

Modular Audio Products. One Roned Rd., Shirley, N.Y. 11967. (516) 345-3100. FAX: (516) 345-3106. S. Summer, pres; Kenneth Zajick, VP.
Audio distribution, preamps, limiters, etc. in rack & module form.

Modular Computer Systems Inc. (MODCOMP). 1650 W. McNab Rd., Fort Lauderdale, Fla. 33309; Box 6099, Fort Lauderdale, Fla. 33340-6099. (305) 974-1380. FAX: (305) 977-1900. Mike Black, dir mktg.
Minicomputer systems, hardware & software.

Modulation Sciences Inc. 12A World's Fair Dr., Somerset, N.J. 08873. (800) 826-2603. FAX: (908) 302-0206. Eric Small, pres; Arthur Constantine, VP sls & mktg.
Generators & reference decoders for multichannel TV sound; modulation monitors; audio processors & subcarrier generators for FM bcst. Stereo spatial image enlarger. RDS/RBDS generators.

Audio, Video & Broadcast Cables

2225 W. HUBBARD STREET, CHICAGO, IL 60612-1613
(312) 733-9555   FAX (312) 733-6416   (800) 966-0069

Mohawk Wire & Cable Corp. 9 Mohawk Dr., Leominster, Mass. 01453. (508) 537-9961. FAX: (508) 537-4358. Paul Olson, pres; Joseph R. Fichtl, VP sls & mktg; David Richardson, dir sls admin; Scott Penabaker, inside sls mgr.
Manufactures cables in PVC & Plenum constructions for application in data tele-communications, computer & electronic equipment industries.

Mole-Richardson Co. 937 N. Sycamore Ave., Hollywood, Calif. 90038-2384. (213) 851-0111. FAX: (213) 851-5593. Warren K. Parker, pres; Howard R. Bell, VP sls.
Lighting equipment for the motion picture, TV, video & still photographic industries.

Moseley Associates Inc. 111 Castilian Dr., Santa Barbara, Calif. 93117-3093. (805) 968-9621. FAX: (805) 685-9638. R. Douglas Hogg, pres/dir engrg; Jamal Hamdani, VP/dir mktg; John Primeau, dir mfg; Bruce Tarr, CFO.
Remote control systems; AM & FM stereo STLs; aural RPLs; data transmission systems.

Motor Capacitors Inc. 6655 Avondale Ave., Chicago 60631. (312) 631-0713. FAX: (312) 774-8778. Terry Noone, pres.
Motor-run, motor-start, metallized, oil-filtered, high voltage, film, electrolytic & power capacitors & R.C. nets.

Motorola AM Stereo. 3701 W. Algonquin Rd., 6th Fl., Rolling Meadows, Ill. 60008-3120. (708) 576-3592. FAX: (708) 576-5479. Frank Hilbert, mgr.
Motorola's latest generation C-Quam AM stereo exciters & modulation monitors & AM stereo receiver info.

Motorola Communications & Electronics Inc. 1301 E. Algonquin Rd., Schaumburg, Ill. 60196. (708) 576-5000. FAX: (708) 576-6601. Mort Topfer, exec VP/gen mgr.
Remote pickup & land mobile radio systems; studio & field prod cueing & communications systems; base stns; mobile & portable transceivers; radio pagers; CCTV systems.

Multi-Image Systems. 2812 Hegan Ln., Chico, Calif. 95928. (916) 345-4211. FAX: (916) 345-7737. Kathryn Schifferle, CEO; Craig Vitt, VP technology; John Schifferle, pres; Kathy Biehl, VP sls.
Multimedia prod systems for cable TV, bcst, training, education & corporate TV.

Multi Products International. 250 Lackawanna Ave., West Paterson, N.J. 07424. (201) 890-1344. FAX: (201) 890-1677. Howard Longin, pres; Irwin Wolberg, VP sls & mktg.
Matching, transformers, splitters, taps, ground blocks, attenuators, stainless steel devices, other CATV passives.

Multisonics. 3162 E. Lapoma, Unit E, Anaheim, Calif. 92806. (714) 255-1055. FAX: (714) 255-1088. Donald Griffin, pres; Jeff Momaney, western rgnl sls mgr.
Brea, Calif. 92621: 950 W. Central Ave., Suite C. (714) 255-1055. FAX: (714) 255-1088. Jeff York, branch sls mgr.
Fort Worth, Tex. 76118: 7431-C Dogwood Park. (817) 284-1471. FAX: (817) 589-7208. Rick Campbell, gen mgr.
Norcross, Ga. 30071: 6301 Best Friend Rd. (404) 662-5400. FAX: (404) 263-8353. David Low, eastern rgnl sls mgr.
Santa Clara, Calif. 95054-2704: 3510 Bassett St.
Traffic control equipment.

Murphy Studio Furniture. 4153 N. Bonita St, Spring Valley, Calif. 91977. (619) 698-4658. FAX: (619) 698-1268. Dennis W. Murphy, pres.
Design & construction-studio furniture for radio, TV & prod facilities. Five modular lines. Custom designs.

Musco Mobile Lighting Ltd. Box 73, Hwy. 63 S., Oskaloosa, Iowa 52577. (515) 673-0491. FAX: (515) 673-3996. David Crookham, gen mgr.
Mobile location lighting utilizing 6K HMIs; remote control of pan, tilt & focus.

N

NDG Phoenix Inc. 4641 Montgomery Ave., Suite 415, Bethesda, Md. 20814. (301) 718-8880. FAX: (301) 718-8883. Paul Paruensky, mngng ptnr; Steven Carr, dir bcst prod; Douglas Weiss, systems designer.

Communicate with us!

Microflect offers the most comprehensive line of antenna support structures, waveguide support systems, and microwave passive repeaters. Send for your *free* copy of our capabilities brochure for more information.

3575 25th St. SE • Salem, Oregon 97302
P.O. Box 12985 • Salem, OR 97309-0985
(503) 363-9267 • FAX (503) 363-4613

Equipment Manufacturers and Distributors

Proprietary software for bcst facility mgmt; computerized library systems, desktop graphic systems.

NEC America Inc. Broadcast Equipment Department, 1555 Walnut Hill Ln., Irving, Tex. 75038. (214) 518-4120; (214) 751-7000. FAX: (214) 751-7001. K. Matsumoto, dir; K. Hirayama, video engrg mgr.
 VUES on-line digital editing system (video).

NII (Norsat International Inc.). 12886 78th Ave., #302, Surrey, B.C., Canada V3W 8E7 (604) 597-6200. FAX: (604) 597-6214. John C. Anderson, pres; Dale Belsher, CFO.
 Bellingham, Wash. 98226: 4208 Meridian, #2. (206) 671-1373. R. Jones, mgr.
 South Carlton, Lincolnshire, U.K. LN1 2RH: Cedars Farm. (011) 44 522 730 800. Stan Muller.
 Electronics to receive bcst audio, video & data info from satellites, bcst systems & optical fiber.

NSI. 9050 Red Branch Rd., Columbia, Md. 21045. (410) 964-8400. FAX: (410) 964-9661. Stephen Neuberth, pres.
 Microwave antennas & remote controls for ENG applications; high performance antennas for point-to-point microwave links.

NTV-International Co. 50 Rockefeller Plaza, Rm. 845, New York 10020. (212) 489-8390. FAX: (212) 489-8395. Nobero Katsura, VP engrg.

NUCOMM Inc. 101 Bilby Rd., Bldg. #2, Hackettstown, N.J. 07840. (908) 852-3700. FAX: (908) 813-0399. Dr. John B. Payne, pres; David O. Thomas, dir sls & mktg.
 Microwave transmitters, receivers & accessories for both portable & fixed sight applications. Modulators/demodulators & color bar generators.

NVision Inc. Box 1658, Nevada City, Calif. 95959. (916) 265-1000. FAX: (916) 265-1010. Birney D. Dayton, pres; William E. Amos, VP; Charles S. Meyer, VP.
 Sherman Oaks, Calif. 91423-3143: 13571 Rye St., Suite 3. (818) 788-5245 Lon Neumann, rgnl sls mgr.
 Digital audio & data distribution, conversion, routing & transmission equipment for prod/postprod applications.

NWL Capacitors. Box 10416, Riviera Beach, Fla. 33419-0416. (407) 848-9009. FAX: (407) 848-9011. Bill King, exec VP.

Nady Systems Inc. 6701 Bay St., Emeryville, Calif. 94608. (510) 652-2411. FAX: (510) 652-5075. John Nady, pres.
 Wireless products for bcst, film, video, stage, fixed instals. Consumer audio & communication equipment.

Nakamichi America Corp. 955 Francisco St., Torrance, Calif. 90502. (310) 538-8150. FAX: (310) 719-9661.
 Professional cassette decks for bcst, prod studio & duplication facilities; DAT also available.

Nalpak Video Sales Inc. 1937 C Friendship Dr., El Cajon, Calif. 92020. (619) 258-1200. FAX: (619) 258-0925. Robert S. Kaplan, pres; Debra S. Kaplan, VP.
 West Orange, N.J. 07052: Box 270, WOB. (201) 485-3684. FAX: (201) 485-8784. Les Weinstock, mgr.
 Packaging & shipping devices, cases, tripak, test charts, travel-karts & cablemaster velcro cable straps.

National Audio Co. Inc. Box 3657, Glenstone Station, Springfield, Mo. 65808. (417) 863-1925. FAX: (417) 863-7825. Steve Stepp, pres; Maxine Bass, sec/treas.
 Ampex audio & video tapes, custom loaded audio cassettes. Fidelipac NAB cartridges. Telex Duplicators.

National Steel Erectors Corp. Box 709, Muskogee, Okla. 74402. (918) 683-6511. FAX: (918) 683-0888. B.R. Bayless, pres; Gary Lehman, exec VP.
 Erection of radio, TV & microwave towers, including turnkey construction from design to completion.

National Supervisory Network. Box 578, 20 Eagle Rd., Suite 310, Avon, Colo. 81620. (303) 949-7774; (800) 345-8728. FAX: (303) 949-9620. Muffy Montemayor, pres/gen mgr; C. William Sepmeier, VP.
 Off-premise control svcs for radio & TV facilities via satellite; provides 24-hour, FCC legal monitoring & command of transmitter plant, EBS, studio conditions & other parameters, complete opns logs, trend analysis & equipment performance reports.

National Transcommunications Ltd. Crawley Ct., Winchester, Hampshire, U.K. SO21 2QA. 44-962-822243. FAX: 44-962-822374. Dr. John Forrest, CEO; John Okas, business dev dir; Derek Chambers, opn dir; Ronald McKellar, financial dir.
 Bcst transmission svcs & systems, satellite linking, telecommunications, spectrum & net mgmt, rsch & dev & consulting.

National Video Service. 6800 Siera Ct., Suite D, Dublin, Calif. 94568. (510) 803-1440. FAX: (510) 803-0227. Jack E. Dixon, pres.
 TCR-100 cartridges; custom length VHS & Beta cassettes; Sony video tape products.

National Video Services Inc. 18 Commerce Rd., Newtown, Conn. 06470. (203) 270-0677. FAX: (203) 270-9619. Gregg M. Johnstone, pres; Harry Davies, sec/treas.
 Distribution of video equipment for corporate & industrial use; design & install of TV studios; mfg of video equipment; rsch & engrg.

Nautel. (Nautical Electronic Laboratories Ltd.) Hackett's Cove, R.R. 1, Tantallon, N.S., Canada B0J 3J0. (902) 823-2233. FAX: (902) 823-3183; D.J. Grace, pres; J.B. Jensen, mgr sls & mktg.
 Bangor, Me. 04401: Nautel Maine Inc. 201 Target Industrial Cir.
 Solid state AM/FM bcst transmitters.

Neilson-Hordell Ltd. Unit 18, Central Trading Estate, Staines, Middlesex, U.K. TW18 4XE. 784-45-6456. FAX: 784-45-9657. G. Peter Neilson, sls dir; R.O. Holden, financial dir; Nigel Holden, mgr.
 Manufacture animation & special effects equipment for professional film & video.

L.E. Nelson Sales Corp. (Thorn-EMI Studio & Theatre Lamps) 4225 Fidus Dr., Unit 110, Las Vegas 89103. (702) 367-3656. FAX: (702) 367-7058. L.E. Nelson, pres; J.M. Nelson, VP western rgnl.
 Elmwood Park, N.J. 07407: 20 Bushes Ln. (201) 794-6700. Dan Imfeld, VP eastern rgn.
 Studio lamps, quartz (tungsten-halogen) from 25 w to 10 kw & projection lamps.

Audio, Video & Broadcast Cables
2225 W. HUBBARD STREET, CHICAGO, IL 60612-1613
(312) 733-9555   FAX (312) 733-6416   (800) 966-0069

Nemal Electronics International Inc. 12240 NE 14th Ave., North Miami, Fla. 33161. (305) 899-0900. FAX: (305) 895-8178. Benjamin L. Nemser, pres.
 Manufacturer of electronic cable, connectors, assemblies & interconnect products for use in bcst applications.

Neotek Corp. 1154 W. Belmont, Chicago 60657. (312) 929-6699. FAX: (312) 975-1700. Craig Connally, pres; Tom Der, dir sls support.
 Complete line of audio control consoles for mus recording, bcst & video postprod applications.

Netwell Noise Control. 6125 Blue Circle Dr., Minnetonka, Minn. 55343. (800) 638-9355. FAX: (612) 939-9836. Mark Rustad, pres.
 Acoustical noise control products.

Network Video Services Inc. 1600 Broadway, Suite 307, New York 10019. (212) 581-7108. FAX: (212) 582-9740. Francisco Ramirez, pres; Joseph Jackson, VP opns.
 Prod svcs, editing, audio-visual presentation rentals.

Neumade Products Corp. Box 5001, Norwalk, Conn. 06854. (203) 866-7600. FAX: (203) 866-7522. R.N. Jones, CEO; Jeff Buchanan, sls mgr.
 Film handling & editing equipment; storage facilities for film, slides, video tape, overhead & opaque projectors; motion picture projection systems.

Neutrik Instrumentation/Amber 3520 Griffith St., St. Laurent, Que., Canada H4T 1A7. (514) 344-5220; (800) 661-6388 (U.S.) FAX: (514) 344-5221. Vincent DeSouza, sls mgr.
 Audio test & measurement equipment, including distortion analyzers, generators, spectrum analyzers, acoustic testers.

Neutrik USA Inc. 195 Lehigh Ave., Lakewood, N.J. 08701. (908) 901-9488. FAX: (908) 901-9608. James E. Cowan, VP/gen mgr.
 Audio connectors; plugs & jacks.

New Century Communications Inc. Rex Craft Bldg., Avoca, Pa. 18641. (717) 693-4249. FAX: (717) 451-0125. Franklin B. Gillespie, CEO; John P. Gibbons, VP; Joseph S. Babkowski, dir.
 Cable billing & customer svc software systems on IBM AS/400, IBM RS/6000 & PCs.

New York City Lites. 2315 Broadway, Suite 402, New York 10024. (212) 799-2445. FAX: (212) 787-2167. Deke Hazirjian, pres.
 Lighting design for video & TV.

Newark Electronics. (A Premier Company) 4801 N. Ravenswood Ave., Chicago 60640-4496. (800) 367-3573. FAX: (312) 275-9050. Bruce Johnson, pres; James Spotz, VP sls & mktg; Robert Ralston, VP purchasing.
 Distributor of all types of bcst cable, assemblies, connectors & electronic component parts. Branches throughout the U.S., Canada, U.K. & Germany.

Newman-Kees Frequency Measurements, Engineering, & Installations. 8611 Slate Rd., Evansville, Ind. 47720. (812) 963-3294. Frank Hertel, own/operator; Sandy Hertel, accounting/billing.
 RF & frequency measurements for AM, FM & TV coml users via air or on location. Audio/video svc & installs.

News Maker Systems. 3930 Quailwood St., Moorpark, Calif. 93021. (805) 529-7223. FAX: (805) 529-2586. Dean Kolkey, pres; Tony Chick, VP dev.
 PC-based electronic newsroom automation computer system.

News Technology Corp. Farmers & Merchants Bank, 201 Castro St., 4th Fl., Mountain View, Calif. 94041. (415) 965-7722. FAX: (415) 965-1516. Peter Kolstad, pres.
 TV electronic systems, radio news computers, special projects.

Nexus Display Systems Corp. 8668 Commerce Ct., Burnaby, B.C., Canada V5A 4N7. (604) 421-1424. FAX: (604) 421-4032. Alan McInnes, pres; Ken Cazakoff, VP engrg; Rob V. Kragelj, VP sls & mktg; Chris Chettle, dir sls; Carle Proskin, project mgr.
 Video display systems, character generators, VCR automation systems & photo classified adv systems.

Nexus Engineering Corp. 7725 Lougheed Hwy., Burnaby, B.C., Canada V5A 4V8. (604) 420-5322. FAX: (604) 420-5941. J.Basil Peters, chmn/CEO; Peter van der Gracht, pres; Ayman Ghafir, dir international sls.
 Bellevue, Wash. 90048: (206) 644-2371.
 TV RF signal processing equipment, low & medium power TV transmission products, two-way data, video & voice satellite transmission & reception equipment; video display systems, high frequency power products, cable TV amplifiers & fiber optic transmission systems.

Nexus Production. 10 E. 40th St., 18th Fl., New York 10016. (212) 679-2180. Alfred Muller, pres; John C. Jorgensen, treas/VP engrg.
 Videotape postprod editing of entertainment progs & comls. CMX, D2, 1", BSP, Quantel Paintbox, Abekas A64, kaleidoscope, superscribe, ADO IMC animation stand, D2 digital mixing & EMC non-linear editing.

Nigel B Furniture. 10655 Vanowen St., Burbank, Calif. 91505. (818) 769-9824. FAX: (818) 769-9965. Nigel Brent, own.
 Rack mount furniture for the bcst, TV, audio & postprod industries.

Norac Industrial Services Inc. Box 3472, Auburn, Me. 04212-3472. (800) 366-3912; (207) 783-4042 Paul R. Caron, pres.
 Diesel generators for standby & primary AC power, 15 kw-1000 kw.

Nordic Software. Box 6007, Lincoln, Neb. 68506-0007. (402) 488-5086. FAX: (402) 488-2914. Jim Wrenholt, pres.
 Complete traffic & billing system for radio stns. Includes RadioView software & Macintosh hardware.

Norlight. 275 N. Corporate Dr., Brookfield, Wis. 53045. (414) 792-9700. FAX: (414) 792-7717. Peter Marsh, VP sls & mktg.
 Fiber optic transmission of bcst level video.

Normex Telecom Inc. 55 Montpellier Blvd., St. Laurent, Que., Canada H4N 2G3. (514) 748-7811. FAX: (514) 744-2797. Jacques Coutellier, pres; Jerome Masson, VP/gen mgr; Raymond Cadieux, project mgr.
 Etobicoke, Ont., Canada M8Z 1N1 775 The Queensway. (416) 503-004. FAX: (416) 503-0006 Timothy A. Laurain, instal supvr.
 Mgmt, instal & maintenance svcs for studios, radio/TV transmitters, satellite systems & CATV.

Equipment Manufacturers and Distributors

Norpak Corporation. 10 Hearst Way, Kanata, Ont., Canada K2L 2P4. (613) 592-4164. FAX: (613) 592-6560. James Carruthers, pres; Ted McClelland, mktg mgr.
NABTS VBI data bcstg systems; VBI weather radar info delivery systems; teletext systems.

North Consumer Products. 2664-B Saturn St., Brea, Calif. 92621. (714) 524-1655; (800) 421-3841. FAX: (714) 524-1944. Tom Farrell, sls mgr; Kitty German, customer svc reps.
SaF-T-Climb fall prevention system for use on antennas, towers & bcstg/receiving structures.

North Hills, A PORTA Systems Company. 575 Underhill Blvd., Syosset, N.Y. 11791. (516) 682-7740. FAX: (516) 682-4655. Steve Muth, VP.
Video isolation transformers, humbuckers, baluns, impedance matching transformers & power splitters.

Northeast Broadcast Lab Inc. Box 1179, South Glens Falls, N.Y. 12803. (518) 793-2181. FAX: (518) 793-7423. Bill Bingham, pres; Gary Crowder sls mgr.
Laurel, Md. 20707: 16025 Dorset Rd. (800) 643-6325.
Plano, Tex. 75023: Box 867717. (214) 612-2053; (800) 729-0494. FAX: (214) 612-2145. "Doc" Masoomian.
Complete AM & FM bcst systems: equipment sls, svc & instal.

Northeast Towers Inc. 14 Milford St., Burlington, Conn. 06013. (203) 673-6644. FAX: (203) 675-7232. Stephen Savino Jr., pres.
AM, FM, TV, CATV & microwave towers; ground systems; maintenance, materials, turnkey installs, specialty coatings & strobes.

Northeastern Communications Concepts Inc. 16 E. 42nd St., New York 10017. (212) 972-1320. Alfred W. D'Alessio, pres; Joseph J. Maguire, project mgr; Richard J. Koziol, sr engr.
Bcst design svcs, studio furniture, custom audio equipment, custom data systems/components, cabinets, racks, panels, recording studios construction & prefab.

Northern Magnetics Inc. 718 Washington N., Minneapolis 55416. (612) 333-3071. FAX: (612) 333-3978. Robert R. Rocheleau, VP.
Sls & svc of magnetic recording heads.

Northern Power Systems. Box 659, One N. Wind Rd., Moretown, Vt. 05660. (802) 496-2955. FAX: (802) 496-2953. John Kueffner, VP; Clint Coleman, VP engrg.
Remote power systems based on renewable energy inputs (wind/solar); hybrid power systems.

Northern Technologies Inc. Box 610, 23123 E. Mission Ave., Liberty Lake, Wash. 99019. (800) 727-9119. FAX: (509) 927-0435. Tom Watson, Greg Matthews, bcst div mgrs.
Full line of transient control systems for AC, dataline & telephone, including; UPS systems & regulators.

Northern Telecom Ltd. World Headquarters, 3 Robert Speck Pkwy., Mississauga, Ont., Canada L4Z 3C8. (905) 897-9000; (905) 452-2000. FAX: (905) 566-3318. Jean Monty, pres/CEO.
Supplier of telecommunications equipment.

Northwest Mobile Television. 12698 Gateway Dr., Seattle 98168. (800) 242-0642; (206) 242-0642. FAX: (206) 241-6042. Larry Huisinga, opns mgr.
Equipment includes: 40' & 34' trailers. Philips LDK-26 cameras with 44X lenses, Ikegami HL-79EAL cameras, Grass Valley switchers, Sony BVH-2000 & BVH-3100 1" VTR's, Chyron 4100 EXB with CCM, Abekas A-53D, Yamaha audio mixers, RTS intercom & IFB, Sony BVE-900 edit on bd.

Northwest Monitoring Service. Box 70144, Eugene, Ore. 97401. (503) 345-2236. James C. Bradley, own.
Mthy frequency measurements for AM-FM-TV. Mobile svc includes California, Oregon, Washington, Idaho & Nevada.

Nortronics Co. Inc. 1000 Superior Blvd., Wayzata, Minn. 55391. (800) 325-2853. FAX: (612) 476-7316. James A. Tusing, dir sls.
Recording tape heads & mounting accessories for bcst cartridges & reel-to-reel recorders.

Nova Systems Inc. 50 Albany Turnpike, Canton, Conn. 06019. (203) 693-0238. FAX: (203) 693-1497. Stephen Kreinik, pres; Tedd Jacoby, VP mktg.
Digital time base correctors, frame synchronizers, encoders, decoders, transcoders, audio & video distribution amplifiers, switchers, computer/video interface & signal processors.

Fred A. Nudd Corp. Box 577, 1743 Rt. 104, Ontario, N.Y. 14519. (315) 524-2531. FAX: (315) 524-4249. Fred Nudd, pres; Tom Nudd, VP/dir sls & engrg.
Designs, manufactures, erects, inspects, maintains & analyzes communications towers.

Nytone Inc. 2424 S. 900 W., Salt Lake City 84119. (801) 973-4090. FAX: (801) 973-0176. George H. Balding, pres.
Provides 35mm slide scanner with 750 lines of resolution, fade between pan & zoom, complete movement to slides.

O

OKRA Marketing Corp. 6301 Benjamin Rd., Tampa 33634. (813) 886-3318; (800) ASK-OKRA. FAX: (813) 882-0329. John P. Kelly, pres/CEO.
Design & construct mktg mgmt decision database systems & solutions.

OSAR Inc. 4324 S.W. 35th Terr., Gainesville, Fla. 32608. (904) 375-2713.
Automation control systems.

OSRAM Sylvania. 100 Endicott St., Danvers, Mass. 01923. (800) 544-4828. FAX: (716) 668-6254. Anthony Pucillo, dir mktg & sls; Scott Sheidy, mktg mgr.
Danvers, Mass. 01923: 10 Hutchinson Dr. Wayne E. Steinhoff, rgnl sls mgr.
Elk Grove Village, Ill. 60007: 800 Devon Ave. Richard C. Ready, rgnl sls mgr.
Atlanta 30349: 5169 Pelican Dr. Peter C. Lyons, rgnl sls mgr.
Santa Clara, Calif. 95054: 3945 Freedom Cir., Suite 230. Richard A. Sarno, rgnl sls mgr.
Manufacture lamps for studios, theatre & TV as well as other applications.

O'Connor Engineering Labs. 100 Kalmus Dr., Costa Mesa, Calif. 92626. (714) 979-3993. FAX: (714) 957-8138. Joel Johnson, VP; Cary Clayton, VP sls.
Muncy, Pa. 17756: 406 S. Broadway. (717) 546-3099. Thomas Breneisen.
New York 10010: 104 E. 25th St. (212) 460-9471. Andrew Duncan, VP.
Manufacture camera support equipment including fluid heads, tripods & accessories.

Odetics Broadcast. 1515 S. Manchester Ave., Anaheim, Calif. 92802-2907. (714) 774-2200; (800) 243-2001. FAX: (714) 535-8532. David Lewis, VP coml products & bcst div; Bill Keegan, dir sls & mktg.
Reading, Berkshire, U.K. RG3 1EA: Odetics U.K. Ltd. 58 Portman Rd. 44 734 560 564. Robert Stopford, dir sls & mktg.
Automated library management video cart machines & integrated products for the TV industry.

Olesen. (A division of Entertainment Resources Inc.) Box 348, Hollywood, Calif. 90078-0348. (213) 461-4631. FAX: (213) 464-0444. Marjorie Romans, pres; Helene Romans, asst sls mgr.
Las Vegas 89103: 4221 Fidus Dr., #105. (702) 876-0117.
All prod supplies & equipment for TV & theatre; live & taped.

Olivetti Office USA. 765 U.S. Hwy 202 S., Bridgewater, N.J. 80807. (908) 526-8200. FAX: (908) 526-8405. Leon Harris, pres; William Lubrano, VP mktg.

Omicron Video. 21818 Lassen St., Unit H, Chatsworth, Calif. 91311-3680. (818) 700-0742. FAX: (818) 700-0313. Kimiharu Akiyama, pres, Omicron Japan.
Yokohama, Japan: (045)-353-6277. Kenji Suetsugu, pres.
Video/audio distribution equipment. Computer graphics/HDTV distribution equipment.

Omni Craft Inc. 14319 High Rd., Lockport, Ill. 60441. (815) 838-1285. FAX: (815) 838-7852. Preston Wakeland, pres.
Custom made engraved aluminum connector panels & rack rails.

Omniflight Helicopters Inc. 4650 Airway Pkwy., Dallas 75248. (214) 233-6464. FAX: (214) 490-1487. Hans Hilhuysen, pres; Mark D. Wittman, exec VP.
Chicago 60638: Midway Airport, 5040 W. 63rd St. (312) 585-9800. Jim Dau, gen mgr.
Baltimore 22120: Box 15440. Martin State Airport. (410) 391-7722. Mike Aslaksen, VP.
Helicopters for ENG use.

Omnimount Systems. 1501 W. 17th ST., Tempe, Ariz. 85281-6225. (602) 829-8000. FAX: (602) 756-9000. Alexander Cyrell, pres; Stacy Ward, sls.
Mounting assemblies for hanging speakers, monitors, security equipment. Weight loads from ounces to hundreds of pounds.

Omnimusic. 6255 Sunset Blvd., Hollywood, Calif. 90028. (213) 962-6494. FAX: (213) 962-4556. Jerry Burnham, dir natl sls & customer svc.
Digitally-produced mus & sound effect libraries for TV, radio & cable featuring real instruments in various styles & orchestrations.

Online Computer Systems Inc. 20251 Century Blvd., Germantown, Md. 20874. (301) 428-3700; (800) 922-9204. FAX: (301) 428-2903.

Opamp Labs Inc. 1033 N. Sycamore Ave., Los Angeles 90038. (213) 934-3566. FAX: (213) 462-6490. B. Losmandy, pres/chief engr.
Amplifiers: audio, video, microphone, line & power. Audio oscillators & transformers. Power supplies, net audio/video feed boxes, audio/video routing switches.

Optical Disc Corp. 12150 Mora Dr., Sante Fe Springs, Calif. 90670. (310) 946-3050. FAX: (310) 946-6030. Richard Wilkinson, pres; Donald Hayes, VP international sls & mktg; John Browne, VP domestic sls & mktg; John Winslow, VP disc mfg.
Recordable laser video discs, videodisc recording systems & other aux equipment. Compact disc & Videodisc mastering systems.

Options International Inc. 1110 17th Ave. S., Suite C, Nashville 37212. (615) 327-8090. FAX: (615) 321-1326. Donna Reid, Telecine mktg & sls; Peter Leatherland, CFO.
Distributor of various telecine accessories & upgrades for bcst purposes.

OptoDigital Design Inc. 8920 Business Park Dr., #135, Austin, Tex. 78759. (512) 338-4707. FAX: (512) 794-9997. Rod Herman, pres; Barry Thornton, VP mktg & engrg; Emory Straus, dir sls.
Audio & video digital fiber optic connectivity for prod, ENG & bcst. Video/audio processors.

Orban. (A division of AKG Acoustics Inc.) 1525 Alvarado St., San Leandro, Calif. 94577. (510) 351-3500. FAX: (510) 351-0500. David Angress, VP sls & mktg, Howard Mullinack, mgr bcst mktg; Jesse Maxenchs, rgnl mgr western hemisphere.
Optimod-AM, -TV & -FM, all mono or stereo, plus studio audio processing devices. 4000A Transmission Limiter.

Ortel Corp. 2015 W. Chestnut St., Alhambra, Calif. 91803. (818) 281-3636. FAX: (818) 281-8231. Bill Moore, VP sls; Israel Ury, chief tech off; Wim Selder, pres/CEO.
Fiberoptic communications products for satellite ground stns.

Allen Osborne Associates Inc. 756 Lakefield Rd. J, Westlake Village, Calif. 91361. (805) 495-8420. FAX: (805) 373-6067. Jim Osborne, mktg & sls.
Pneumatic masts systems for remote ENG; fixed or mobile radio communications.

Osram Corp. 110 Bracken Rd., Montgomery, N.Y. 12549. (914) 457-4040. FAX: (914) 457-4142. Robert E. Hojnacke, dir (Photo Optics Lighting Group); David G. Olsen, mktg mgr (Photo Optic Lighting Group).
Van Nuys, Calif. 91406: 7658 Haskell Ave. (818) 988-2007.
Lighting for stage, studio, film & video prod.

Otari Corporation. 378 Vintage Park Dr., Foster City, Calif. 94404. (415) 341-5900. FAX: (415) 341-7200. Jack Soma, pres; John Carey, mktg mgr; James Goodman, natl sls mgr.
Chofu-shi, Tokyo, Japan 4-33-3: Kokuryocho. 3481-8600. FAX: 3481-8633. Masayuki Hosoda, pres;

Equipment Manufacturers and Distributors

Shinichi Higashino, dir; Mamoru Gonda, dir; Norikatsu Soma, mgr international division.
   Meerbusch, Osterath, Germany 2: Otari Deutschland GmbH. Rudolf-Diesel-Strasse 12 D-4005. FAX: (02159)50861. Shunji Koizumi, gen mgr.
   Slough, Berkshire, U.K. SL3 6EP: Otari (U.K.) Ltd. Unit 13, Elder Way, Waterside Dr., Langley. (0753) 580777. Hisao Suzuki, gen mgr.
   Aljunied Industrial Complex, Singapore 1438: Otari Singapore Pte Ltd. 625 Aljunied Rd., Suite 07-05. 743-7711. Tomohiro Yoshizawa, gen mgr.
   Audio recorders, from 1/4" mono to 32-track (analog & digital); audio/video tape loaders, hub winders & hub leaderers; high speed audio/video duplicators; audio mixing consoles.

Owens Tower Co. Box 640, Stephenville, Tex. 76401. (817) 968-3921. FAX: (817) 965-7981. Marvin Owens, own.
   Any communications tower-related work; erection, install & some maintenance.

P

P.C.& E. 2235 DeFoor Hills Rd., Atlanta 30318. (404) 609-9001. Doug Smith, pres; Randy Napier, mgr.
   Equipment rental, grip & process trailers; rental & sls - lighting, expendables & cameras.

PEP Inc. 25 W. 54th St., New York 10019. (212) 246-2490. FAX: (212) 765-5988. James B. Tharpe, mgr.
   Glasgow, W. Va. 25086-0177: Box 177, (304) 595-3340. Sally K. Bramble, mgr.
   Shotlister- windows software that increases productivity in postprod & jog box-edit with audio in search jog & edit pre-roll. Sony DVR-10, DVR-18 & Betaeam-SP machines.

PESA Switching Systems. (A division of PESA Chiron Group) 2550 Hollywood Way, Suite 209, Burbank, Calif. 91505. (818) 563-4566. FAX: (818) 563-4568. Bob McCormick, gen mgr.
   Melville, N.Y. 11747: 2655 Pagnoli Rd. (800) 328-1008. Robert Mcalpine.
   Routing switchers, character generators, intercoms, terminal equipment, monitors & transmitters.

PMI/Producers Management Inc. 180 Church Rd., King of Prussia, Pa. 19406. (215) 768-1770. FAX: (215) 768-1773. Brian Powers, pres; Rob Schmoll, VP/gen mgr.
   Full-svc mobile TV prod company, providing mobile units, crews, satellite svcs, lighting, staging, etc., for sports, entertainment, teleconferences, worldwide.

POA/Paul Olivier & Associates Ltd. Box 410, 701 County Line Rd., Palmer Lake, Colo. 80133. (719) 488-2270. FAX: (719) 488-2648. Paul Olivier, pres; Dale Hill, sec/treas; Howard Phillips, dir engrg; Jeff Stanfield, dir products grp.
   TV bcst equipment, design engrg, fabrication, turnkey TV systems, bcst & cable consulting svcs, mobile units.

PORTAC Inc. 8547 Grovemont Cir., Gaithersburg, 20877. (301) 840-8407. FAX: (301) 840-2946. Philip Edwards, pres; Kevin Lapidus, prod mgr.
   Electronic bulletin bd for video messages. VCR control units.

PSB Engineering. 118 Dougharty Rd. W., Heidelberg, Victoria, Australia 3081. (03) 457-6044. FAX: (03) 459-2372. David Buchanan, dir engrg; Charles Sapiano, dir sls & svc.
   NAB cartridge machines, professional CD players, svc & spares for all Consolidated Electronics products.

PTS Electronics Corp. 5233 Hwy. 37 S., Bloomington, Ind. 47401. (812) 824-9331. FAX: (812) 824-2848. Jeff Hamilton, pres.
   Arvada, Colo. 80002: 4941 Allison St. (303) 423-7080.
   CATV electronic repair-computerized test equipment.

Pace Micro Technology Ltd. Victoria Rd., Saltaire, Shipley, West Yorkshire, U.K. BD18 3LF. 44-(0)274-532000. FAX: 44-(0)274-532010. David Hood, chmn/joint mng dir; Barry Rubery, joint mng dir; Steve Listor, sls & mktg dir; Robert Fleming, opns dir; Steven Jones, coml dir; John Knapp, financial dir; Graham Mitchell, engrg dir; Barry Wilson, materials dir.
   Shipley, West Yorkshire, U.K. BD18 3LF: Victoria Rd. (0)274-532000. Keith Wiggins, group gen mgr.
   Satellite TV bcst reception equipment plus accessories; data communications equipment.

Pacific Recorders & Engineering Corp. 2070 Las Palmas Dr., Carlsbad, Calif. 92009. (619) 438-3911. FAX: (619) 438-9277. Jack Williams, pres; Mike Dosch, gen mgr; Dave Pollard, sls mgr.
   Langenfeld, W. Germany D4018: Thum & Marh Audio, Konrad Adenauer, Platz 6-8. 021-734-7960.
   Design & manufacture radio studio equipment & systems.

Pacific Tower Co. 4334 N.E. 148th Ave., Portland, Ore. 97230. (503) 254-1055. Gilbert J. Nielsen, pres.
   Tower sls & erection for TV, radio & microwave; obstruction lighting; ground systems.

Packaged Lighting Systems Inc. Box 285, 29 Grant St., Walden, N.Y. 12586. (914) 778-3515; (800) 836-1024, order dept. FAX: (914) 778-1286. Lillian Hilzen, pres; Hy Hilzen, dir of technology.
   Factory prewired, self-contained TV studio systems complete with lighting, dimming, grid & power distribution.

Paltex International. 2752 Walnut Ave., Tustin, Calif. 92680. (714) 838-8833. FAX: (714) 838-9619. Roger L. Bailey, mgng dir.
   Heston, Middlesex, U.K. TW5 9NR: 7 Airlinks Spitfire Way. 44 (0) 81-756-1993. Gerald Bailey, opr dir.
   Video prod & postprod equipment.

Panasonic Broadcast and Television Company. One Panasonic Way, Panazip 4B-7, Secaucus, N.J. 07094. (201) 348-7671. FAX: (201) 392-6558. Stanley Basara, pres; Kurt Narita, VP.
   Washington: Sales: (703) 759-6900; Svc.: (202) 362-7265.
   Norcross, Ga. 30093: 1854 Shackleford Ct., Suite 250. (404) 717-3786; (404) 717-6772.
   Arlington Heights, Ill. 60005: 425 E. Algonquin Rd. (317) 852-3715; (708) 981-7325.
   Fort Worth, Tex. 76155: 4500 Amon Carter Blvd. (817) 685-1132.
   Burbank, Calif. 91505: 201 N. Hollywood Way, Suite 108. (818) 562-1579; (818) 562-1501/1502.
   MII VCR, D3 1/2 inch digital VCR, digital processed camera, Cart (MARC) - analog & digital, tape.

Pandora International Ltd. The White House, Mile End Green, Dartford, Kent, U.K. DA2 8EB. 44-47470-8182. FAX: 44-47470-6433. Aine Marsland, mgng dir; Martin Greenwood, tech dir.
   Burbank, Calif. 91505: 3900 W. Alameda Ave., Suite 1700. (818) 972-1737. FAX: (818) 972-9021. Dave Schnuelle, VP.
   Film transfer color correction systems & digital color processor.

Parallex. 12200 Briarwood, Suite 150, Englewood, Colo. 80112. (303) 799-6532. FAX: (303) 799-6739. Dale E. Kline, pres.
   Cable TV sub mgmt, billing, office automation & computerized mktg svc.

Parsons Audio. 192 Worcester St., Wellesley Hills, Mass. 02181. (617) 431-8708. FAX: (617) 431-8710. Mark Parsons, own; Andy Beaudet, bcst sls.
   Equipment sls: Sony, Wheatstone, Yamaha, Dolby, Audio Precision, Digidesign, Roland, Denon RTS, etc.

Parsons Manufacturing Corp. 1055 O'Brien Dr., Menlo Park, Calif. 94025. (415) 324-4726. FAX: (415) 324-3051. A.R. Parsons, pres; S. Wurzer, sls mgr.
   Instrument carrying cases, shipping cases; molded plastic, retracting wheels, recessed hardware.

Patch Bay Designation Co. Box 250278, Glendale, Calif. 91225-0279. (818) 241-5585. FAX: (818) 507-5050. Dale Lookholder, pres.
   Patch bay labeling for the audio/video industries; switch label film inserts.

Paulmar Industries Inc. Box 638, Antioch, Ill. 60062. (708) 395-2080. FAX: (708) 395-2475. Robert F. Menary, pres; Randy D. Kick, VP.
   Automatic film & video inspection machines, film & video supplies & computer scheduling systems.

Payview Ltd. GPO, Box 3000, Kowloon, Hong Kong, (011) 852-3-365111. George Ho, chmn; John Thompson, US consultant.
   Addressable, highly secure baseband decoding systems in modular components.

Peavey Audio Media Research. (A division of Peavey Electronics Corp.) Box 2898, Meridian, Miss. 39302-2898. (601) 483-5372. FAX: (601) 486-1278. Hartley Peavey, CEO; Melia Peavey, pres.
   Recording prod & audio products, SMPTE/MIDI synchronization signal processing, reference monitors, microphones & prod mixing consoles.

Peerless Sale Co. 1980 Hawthorne Ave., Melrose Park, Ill. 60160. (708) 865-8870. (800) 729-0307 (sls). FAX: (708) 865-2941. Walter Snodell, pres; Frank Briggs, mktg dir; Dustin Vallaly, sls dir; Therese Cleary, mgr customer svc.
   Mounting hardware including stands, carts & brackets for floor, furniture, wall & ceiling applications.

Peirce-Phelps Inc./AVSD. 2000 N. 59th St., Philadelphia 19131. (215) 879-7171; (800) 862-6800. FAX: (215) 878-5252. Henry S. Grove III, VP; Frank Brady, sls mgr.
   Camp Hill, Pa. 17011: 490 S. St. John's Church Rd. (717) 761-0204.
   Gaithersburg, Md. 20878: 7-7 Metropolitan Ct. (301) 948-5266; (800) 648-5266. FAX: (301) 948-9747. Herb Lee, sls mgr.
   San Diego 92121-3805: Sorrento Towers, 5355 Mira Sorrento Pl., Suite 100. (619) 597-7507. FAX: (619) 597-7417. Andrew Hudson, mgr.
   Audio/video sls & svcs; construction & maintainence of teleconferencing rooms; ENG, prod vans & studios.

Penn Fabrication (U.S.A.) Inc. 5316 Kazuko Ct., Moorpark, Calif. 93021. (805) 529-4962. FAX: (805) 529-0232. Phil Stratford, pres.
   Pompton Plains, N.J. 07444: Penn Fabrication Inc. 230 W. Pkwy, Unit 8. (201) 839-7777. Richard Stratford.
   Houston 77095: 9772 Whithorn Dr. (713) 855-9772. Alan Theobold.
   Hardware & accesories for flightcase, rack & speaker cabinets, stagelights & trussing.

Penny & Giles Inc. 2716 Ocean Park Blvd., Suite 1005, Santa Monica, Calif. 90405-5209. (310) 393-0014. FAX: (310) 450-9860. Neal Handler, sls office mgr.
   S. Wales, U.K. NP2 2YD: Blackwood, Gwent. (44) 495-228000. David McLain, VP.
   Studio faders; joystick controllers & T-Bar controllers for video effects generators; MIDI mgr & interface.

Penta Laboratories Inc. 21113 Superior St., Chatsworth, Calif. 91311. (818) 882-3872. FAX: (818) 882-3968. Gary Madvin, chmn; Steve Sanett, CEO.
   Electron tubes distribution & mfg.

Pentagon Industries Inc. 5115 N. Sheridan Rd., Chicago 60640. (312) 271-8300. FAX: (312) 271-0027. L.M. Khan, pres; John Vinci, gen mgr.
   High-speed, bcst quality cassette audio tape duplicators; mus cassette changer.

Pentax Corp. 35 Inverness Dr. E., Englewood, Colo. 80112. (303) 799-8000. FAX: (303) 790-1131. Masa Tanaka, pres; Joe Graham, VP; Warren Wright, Cosmicar sls mgr.
   Specialized video optics for CCTV & surveillance applications. 8mm & VHS format video camcorders.

Performance Cable TV Products. Box 947, Roswell, Ga. 30077. (404) 475-3192. Jud Williams, own.
   Standby power supplies, AC power supplies & battery testers.

Perma Power Electronics Inc. 5601 W. Howard St., Niles, Ill. 60714. (312) 763-0763. FAX: (312) 763-8330. Don Roth, natl sls mgr; Rick Jeffrey, VP mktg & sls.
   Portable sound systems & power line protection (surge suppressors, conditioners, standby power systems); FAX & VCR cable surge suppressors.

Perrott. 7201 Lee Hwy., Falls Church, Va. 22046. (800) 933-6422; (703) 532-0700. FAX: (703) 536-3204. W.D. Mallon, pres/COO; Michael T. Mallon, sls mgr.
   Full-svc battery company. Complete line of batteries & chgrs for engrg equipment.

Pesa Chyron Group. (Comprised of Pesa Switching Systems, Chyron Graphics, CMX Editing Systems, Aurora Paint Systems) 265 Spagnoli Rd., Melville, N.Y. 11747. (516) 845-2026. FAX: (516) 845-3895. Antonio Diaz Borja, chmn; Peter J. Lance, vice chmn/pres; Isaac Hersly, exec VP; John A. Poserina, VP/treas; Ron Witko, VP North American sls; Larry Mincer, VP computer display systems; Steve Sloane, VP international sls; David Buckler, VP client dev.
   Burbank, Calif. 91505: The Ctr. at Burbank Airport, 2550 Hollywood Way, Suite 209. (818) 563-4566. FAX: (818) 563-4568. Karl Arnemann, Chyron rgnl sls; Ed Bolger, CMX sls.
   Atlanta 30303: One CNN Ctr., South Towers, Suite 1240. (404) 880-9004. FAX: (404) 880-9104. Ryad Kahale, Chyron rgnl sls.
   Designs, manufactures & mkts complementary product lines for the bcst TV, cable, video prod, postprod, industrial & multimedia mkts.

Equipment Manufacturers and Distributors

Phasetek Inc. 550 California Rd., Unit 11, Quakertown, Pa. 18951. (215) 536-6648. FAX: (215) 536-7180. Kurt Gorman, pres; David Gorman, VP mktg; Matthew Nelson, plant mgr.

Manufactures AM/MW antennas, phasing equipment, antenna tuning units, diplexers, dummy loads, RF inducters & components.

Philips Broadband Networks. 100 Fairgrounds Dr., Manlius, N.Y. 13104. (800) 448-5171. Dieter Brauer, pres.

Manufactures microprocessor-controlled AM & FM fiberoptic transmission systems for CATV & interactive video & audio.

Philips Components. Providence Pike, Slatersville, R.I. 02876. (401) 762-9000. FAX: (401) 767-4493. J. Stewart, gen mgr MSO; Dennis Horowitz, pres; M. Janssen, R.I. site mgr; John Burnette, VP sls.

Roswell, Ga. 30076: 920 Holcomb Bridge Rd., Suite 400. (Atlanta office.)

Rolling Meadows, Ill. 60008: 3601 Alonquin Rd., Richardson, Tex. 75080: 1755 N. Collins, Suite 201. (Dallas office.)

Los Altos, Calif. 94022: 4546B10 El Camino Real, Suite 189. (San Jose office.)

Camera tubes, UHF klystrons (depressed collector & ABC), RF & CATV hybrid modules & semiconductors.

Phoebus Manufacturing. 2800 3rd St., San Francisco 94107. (415) 550-1177. FAX: (415) 550-2655. John Tedesco, pres/own; Scott Branson, natl sls mgr.

Manufactures theatrical & motion picture lighting equipment.

Phoenix E.N.G. 6832 Roxhill Ln., Cincinnati 45236. (513) 891-1444. Jenifer Braun, Kevin Jordan, principals.

"One man band" live trucks & vans - 4-wheel-drive.

Phoenix Systems. (Breen Systems Management Inc.) Box 507, 18 Blair Park Rd., Williston, Vt. 05495. (802) 879-4212. FAX: (802) 878-1717. James J. Breen, pres; Heidi L. Gloyd, client support specialist.

Hardware & software for bcstg traf, billing, accounts receivable & mgmt information.

Photo Research. Box 2192, 9330 De Soto Ave., Chatsworth, Calif. 91311. (818) 341-5151. FAX: (818) 341-7070. Chris Layne, controller.

Brightness photometers, footcandle meters, telephotometers, spectroradiometers, spectral & spatial scanners.

Photomart Cine-Video Inc. 6327 S. Orange Ave., Orlando, Fla. 32809. (407) 851-2780. FAX: (407) 851-2553. Cloyd Taylor, pres; Charles Sutyak, sec/treas.

Sales, svc, rental of film, audio & grip equipment for bscst & prod.

Pico Products Inc. 6315 Fly Rd., E. Syracuse, N.Y. 13057. (315) 437-1711. FAX: (315) 437-7525. Everett Keech, CEO/chmn of bd; George Knapp, pres; Robert J. Greiner Jr., VP sls & mktg.

Manufactures SMATV, private cable, CATV signal distributon & security devices.

PINNACLE

Pinnacle Systems Inc. 870 W. Mande Ave., Sunnyvale, Calif. 94086. (408) 720-9669. FAX: (408) 720-9674. Mark L. Sanders, pres/CEO; Ajay Chopra, VP engrg; Walter Werdmuller, VP sls.

Manufacture digital video effects & graphics work stns.

Digital video effects & graphics.

Pinzone Communications Products Inc. Box 540, 14985 Cross Creek Park, Newbury, Ohio 44065. (216) 564-9093. FAX: (216) 564-8066. Basil F. Pinzone Jr., pres.

Turnkey satellite uplinks & downlinks; systems & nets; VIMCAS stereo vertical interval audio encoding system; Pinzone CPG AM anti-skywave antenna.

Pioneer Communications of America Inc. 600 E. Crescent Ave., Upper Saddle River, N.J. 07458. (201) 327-6400. FAX: (201) 327-9379. Tom Haga, pres; Ken Hosoda, treas; Jerry Landskron, sr VP admin; Paul Dempsey, VP.

Columbus, Ohio 43228: 2200 Dividend Dr. (614) 876-0771. John Unverzagt, dir engrg. (Engineering office.)

Set-top & remote controlled tunable converters; one & two way addressable converters & control systems.

Pioneer Technology Corp. 1021 N. Lake St., Burbank, Calif. 91502. (818) 842-7165. FAX: (818) 842-0921. Donald E. Stults, pres; B.J. Seeley, VP.

Motion picture cameras, animation, optical effects, printers, lab equipment, projection equipment, telecine projectors, sound dubbing projectors, 35mm cameras, etc.

Pi-Rod Inc. Box 128, 1200 N. Oak Rd., Plymouth, Ind. 46563. (219) 936-4221. FAX: (219) 936-6796. Myron C. Noble, pres; Ron Hanson, VP opns; Wayne Lauer, VP finance; Brown Sander, VP mktg.

Radio, TV, microwave & communications towers.

Pirelli Cables North America - Communications Division. 700 Industrial Dr., Lexington, S.C. 29072-3799. (803) 951-4800. FAX: (803) 957-4628. Raymond Robinson, VP/gen mgr; Craig Lemrow, mktg mgr; Robert Hauptner, natl sls mgr.

Surrey, B.C., Canada V3W 2WI: (604) 591-3311. Lynette Yakimovitch, customer svc mgr.

ISO-9001 registered manufacturer of fiber optic cables for the CATV industry.

Plastic Reel Corp. of America. Brisbin Ave., Lyndhurst, N.J. 07071. (201) 933-5100. FAX: (201) 933-9468. Benjamin Zuk, pres.

North Hollywood, Calif. 91605: 8140 Webb Ave. (818) 504-0400. Carole Pinker, VP.

Chicago 60611: 1302 W. Randolph. (312) 942-1950.

Video & audio tape reels & boxes, video cassette mailing & storage boxes & video supplies.

Plateau Digital Technology. 12001 Mathis Way, Grass Valley, Calif. 95949. (916) 268-0190. FAX: (916) 268-3986. Richard Adams, pres.

Video digital waveform, vectorscope, noise, measure & test, portable & accurate.

PolyQuick. 1231 Rand Rd., Des Plaines, Ill. 60016-3402. (708) 390-7744. FAX: (708) 390-9886. Ed Kaiser, pres.

Audio & video spot reels, tape, recording & dubbing supplies

Portland Instrument. 6120 San Fernando Rd., Glendale, Calif. 91201. (818) 500-0269. FAX: (818) 240-1828. Marsha Fuller, pres; Dick Herbert, gen mgr.

Audio line monitors & switchers, intercom, party line & IFB systems, specialized & gen purpose audio modules.

Potomac Instruments Inc. 932 Philadelphia Ave., Silver Spring, Md. 20910. (301) 589-2662; FAX: (301) 589-2665. David G. Harry, COO.

Antenna monitors, field strength meters, audio test equipment, remote control systems.

Power Guard Inc. Box 2796, Opelika, Ala. 36803. (205) 742-0050. (800) 288-1507. FAX: (205) 742-0058. Curt B. Cope, CEO; Jerry Schultz, pres.

Standby & non-standby power supplies, surge protection devices & batteries for CATV.

Power & Telephone Supply Co. 2701 Union Extended, Suite 300., Memphis 38112. (901) 324-6116. FAX: (901) 320-3084. Jim Pentecost, pres; Laburn Dye, VP communication division; Sonny Dickinson, VP CATV.

Atlanta 30336: Box 43223, 530 Interchange Dr. N.W. (404) 691-6813. FAX: (404) 699-1625. Don Skinner.

Reamstown, Pa. 17567: Box 244, Route 272. (215) 267-4991. FAX: (215) 267-4367. Don Skinner.

Lexington, N.C. 27292: Box 1856, 2107 Greensboro Rd. N. (704) 249-0256. FAX: (704) 249-7475. Don Skinner.

Des Moines, Iowa, 50321: 3107 SW 61st St., Bldg. D. (515) 244-4375. FAX: (515) 244-4757. Tommy Browder.

Memphis 38112: Box 12383, 2668 Yale Ave. (901) 324-6116. FAX: (901) 320-3082. Tommy Doddridge.

Houston 77043: 1055 W. Sam Houston Pkwy. N., Suite 110. (713) 461-8444. FAX: (713) 461-5964. Sonny Dickinson.

Broadcasting & Cable Yearbook 1994
H-45

PHASETEK INC.
550 CALIFORNIA RD. UNIT 11
QUAKERTOWN, PA 18951
PHONE: (215) 536-6648
FAX: (215) 536-7180

CUSTOM MANUFACTURED:
ANTENNA PHASING SYSTEMS
CONTROL SYSTEMS
AM/MF ANTENNA TUNING UNITS
DIPLEXERS (NDA/DA & EXPANDED BAND)
TRIPLEXERS
TRANSMITTER COMBINERS
DUMMY LOADS (WITH MATCHING NETWORK)
TOWER DETUNING UNITS
BROADBAND MATCHING NETWORKS

EXPERIENCE

PHASETEK'S experienced staff of engineers and production personnel are dedicated to provide the broadcast industry the highest quality, custom designed phasing equipment.

RELIABLE/DEPENDABLE RF COMPONENTS & PARTS:
VARIABLE & FIXED INDUCTORS
VARIABLE & FIXED VACUUM CAPACITORS
FIXED MICA CAPACITORS
RF CONTACTORS
VACUUM RF CONTACTORS
TEST JACKS & ACCESSORIES
STATIC DRAIN & LIGHTING CHOKES
ISOLATION INDUCTORS
SAMPLING LOOPS
DIAL COUNTERS AND COUPLERS
TRANSMISSON LINE TERMINATIONS
RIBBON CLIPS & TUBING CLAMPS
HORN GAPS
TOROIDAL CURRENT TRANSFORMERS
AND MORE

PHASETEK'S manufacturing facility and components expertise are available to design and fabricate any type of inductor or special R.F. component.
Our engineering and production staff's years of experience and commitment to quality are available to fill any special requirements.

OTHER SERVICES AVAILABLE:
PHASING SYSTEM DESIGN
ENGINEERING & TECHNICAL FIELD SUPPORT
AM & FM INSTALLATIONS

Equipment Manufacturers and Distributors

Nashville 37207: 3412 Ambrose Ave. (615) 226-0321. FAX: (615) 227-0124. Joel Wright.
Knoxville, Tenn. 37921: 3414 Kenson Rd. (615) 588-7570. FAX: (615) 588-0659. Overton Lea Jr.
Jackson, Tenn. 38301: 1645 North Pkwy. (901) 423-0071. FAX: (901) 423-0073. Jim Oakley.
Neenah, Wis. 54956: 987 Ehlers Rd. (414) 725-5454. FAX: (414) 725-6162. Jack Reynolds.
Tigard, Ore. 97224: 16666 S.W. 72nd, Bldg. 12. (503) 620-4909. FAX: (503) 620-9074. Andy Baker. (Portland branch.)
Provides communication products including data & TV.

Powermark Case Corp. 12441 W. 49th Ave., #5, Wheat Ridge, Colo. 80033. (303) 421-7912; (800) 342-3246. FAX: (303) 424-0482. David Marks, pres.
Airline approved shipping & carrying cases. Local transport cases.

Powr-Ups Corporation. One Roned Rd., Shirley, N.Y. 11967. (516) 345-3100. FAX: (516) 345-3106. Steven E. Summer, pres.
DC-motor controls.

Practel Sales International. 35 Jacobsen Cres., Holden Hill, South Australia, Australia 5088. +61-8-2663433. FAX: +61-8-2661031. Neville Woodcock, mgng dir.
Video/audio routing & distribution equipment, SNG & ENG systems.

Precise Manufacturing Co. Inc. 520 S. Price Rd., Tempe, Ariz. 85281. (602) 967-0030; (800) 821-0862. FAX: (602) 967-1143. James C. Gavin, pres/CFO; Harold Wedell, VP.
Cable TV transmission equipment & integrated school mgmt systems.

Precision Design. 27106 46th Ave., Kent, Wash. 98032-7147. (206) 852-5070. FAX: (206) 852-5046. Brian Hayashi, pres.
Portable-remote audio mixers.

Prime Image Inc. 19943 Via Escuela, Saratoga, Calif. 95070. (408) 867-6519. FAX: (408) 926-7294. William B. Hendershot III, pres; Roberta Hendershot, exec VP; Keith Moeller, VP engng; James Aldrich, VP mfg.
Designs & manfactures affordable top quality video time base correctors, synchronizers, prod switchers & electronic still stores.

Print-Products Intl. 8931 Brookville Rd., Silver Spring, Md. 20910. (800) 638-2020. FAX: (800) 545-0058. Eric J. Wurst, opns mgr; Scott MacDonald, sls mgr.
Equipment, tools & supplies for electronic prod, maintenance & svc.

PrismaGraphics Inc. Box 703, Milwaukee 53201. (414) 342-6464; (800) 325-1089. FAX: (414) 342-0932. Richard Schmaelzle, pres; Ben Olson, mktg specialist.
Printer manufacturer specializing in presentation folders, media kits, sls kits & videocassette packaging.

Pro Battery Company Inc. 3941 Oakcliff Industrial Ct., Atlanta 30340. (404) 449-5900; FAX: (404) 449-5457. Eugene Sherry, pres; Judy Peter, VP sls; Tom Hilborn, natl sls mgr; John L. Faucette, COO.
Primary, secondary, bcst & custom battery applications; chgrs & bulbs.

Pro Video & Film Equipment Group. 11419 Mathis St., Dallas 75234. (214) 869-0011. FAX: (214) 869-0145. Norm Bleicher, CEO; Bill Reiter, pres .
Used equipment dealer specializing in video, bcst, film, lighting & audio. Consignment, leasing & appraisal svcs available.

Production Consultants & Equipment. 2235 DeFoor Hills Rd. Atlanta 30318. (404) 609-9001; (800) 537-4021. Doug Smith, pres/own; Rick Dooley, opns mgr; Randy Nappier, mgr lighting & grip division; Rita Braswell, VP camera division; Web Bailey, mgr sls.
Motion picture equipment rental: Arriflex cameras; lighting & grip truck fleet, camera cars, three sound stages.

Professional Sound Corporation. 24932 Kearny Ave, #4, Valencia, Calif. 91355. (805) 295-9395. FAX: (805) 295-8398. Ron Meyer, pres; Chris Palmer, international sls & mktg.
Design & manufacture portable sound products for film & video. U.S. rep for VDB, SEEM, SONOSAX & Rycote.

Professional Sound Services Inc. 311 W. 43rd St., Suite 910, New York 10036. (212) 586-1033. FAX: (212) 586-0970. Joe Guzzi, VP.

Wireless microphones, wireless & wired intercoms, IFB, telephone interfaces, analog & digital recorders, mixers, lavaliers, boompoles.

Professional Video Transmission Services. 2030 M St., N.W., Suite 704, Washington 20036. (202) 775-1290. FAX: (202) 775-4363. Al Levin, pres; Nelson Crumling, mgr opns.
Complete mobile facilities; Ku-band uplink trucks, multi-camera prod with interformat editing, internationally compliant fully redundant Ku air transportable uplink.

Profit Plus Broadcasting. 58 Redwood Dr., Kentfield, Calif. 94904. (415) 331-3200. FAX: (415) 331-4066. Phil Page, pres.
Provides computer software for radio stns, including Traffic Plus & Great Plains Accounting. All PC-based & Novell networkable.

Promotion Manager Software. 16 Cornell Pl., Rye, N.Y. 10580. (212) 745-8776. Chris Bungo, pres; Rocco Macri, VP/mktg & sls.
A comprehensive software package designed specifically for radio's prom & mktg dirs.

Prostar. 12831 Royal Dr., Stafford, Tex. 77477. (713) 240-2800. FAX: (713) 240-1447. John C. Parks, pres; D. Scott Hofmann, dir engrg & sls; Brent Shannon, dir opns.
Provides leased satellite signal encryption for business & entertainment.

Protech Audio Corp. One Flowerfield, Suite 24 St. James, N.Y. 11780-1503. (516) 584-5855. FAX: (516) 584-5904. William Murphy, pres.
Professional audio preamps, power amps & signal processors.

Q

QEI Corporation. Box 805, One Airport Dr., Williamstown, N.J. 08094. (609) 728-2020; (800) 334-9154. FAX: (609) 629-1751. Charles H. Haubrich, pres; John J. Pilman, VP engrg; Jeff R. Detweiler, domestic sls mgr.
FM transmitters 10w to 35 kw, cat-link digital STL/TSL, digital stereo generator, 691 FM modulation monitor & test set.

QSC Audio Products Inc. 1617 MacArthur Blvd., Costa Mesa, Calif. 92626-1468. (714) 754-6175. FAX: (714) 754-6174. Barry Andrews, CEO; Pat N. Quilter, VP engrg; John Andrews, COO; Pete Kalman, dir sls; Randy Curlee, dir mktg.
Professional power audio amplifiers, audio computer control & professional audio amplifier accessories.

Tel - (603) 893-7707
Fax - (603) 893-7714

Model 8000 - Create your own color video logos and display them anywhere with the Model 800!
Model 2000 - Off-air or cable demod with built-in proc amp, stereo audio and RS-232 control!
Model 1500 - Same as above without proc amp.

QSI Systems Inc. Box 718, 7(B) Raymond Ave., Unit 8, Salem, N.H. 03079. (603) 893-7707. FAX: (603) 893-7714. Alfred J. Smilgis, pres; Peter R. Smilgis, VP.
Color bar generators with source identification, Safe Area generators, Sync Processing amplifier countdown generator, auto switchover; Demod Tumers; Microwave AGC meter character generator RS232; Auto switchover & logo generators.

Q-TV. 104 E. 25th St., New York 10010. (212) 460-9050. FAX: (212) 529-9679. Gordon Greenfield, pres; George Andros, VP.
Los Angeles 90036: 7350 Beverly Blvd. (213) 936-6195. John Maffe, gen mgr.
Computer prompter software. 9", 12" & 15" on camera prompters. Lightweight flat panel prompters.

Qintar Inc. 700 Jefferson Ave., Ashland, Ore. 97520-3703. (503) 488-5500. FAX: (503) 488-5567. Randall Tishkoff, pres.
Active & passive devices for CATV, SMATV, MATV & phone, including amplifiers, filters, connectors & wall plates.

Quality Tower Erectors Inc. 2280 10th St. S.E., Largo, Fla. 34641. (813) 585-6176. FAX: (813) 581-3277. Robert F. Diamond, pres.

Maintenance, erection, antenna systems, microwave, cellular, painting & turnkey svc; tower site rental.

Quality Video Supply. 76 Frederick St., Hackensack, N.J. 07602. (800) 431-6000. FAX: (201) 487-1930. Shelly Goldstein, pres.
Video & audio equipment supplies & accessories for industrial & professional businesses.

Quanta Corp. 180 Wright Brothers Dr., Suite 670, Salt Lake City 84116. (801) 328-8872. FAX: (801) 328-3668. David Keller, pres; Brent Bullock, natl sls mgr; Ken Lawson, CATV products mktg mgr.
Chattanooga 37405-1403: 1833 Auburndale Dr. (615) 266-6937. FAX: (615) 266-2353. George M. Cudabac, southern rgnl sls mgr.
San Jose, Calif. 95126: 535 Race St. (408) 295-8814. FAX: (408) 295-6909. Dave Orr, gen mgr, Calaway Editing Systems.
Aalsmeer, The Netherlands 1430 AG: Postbus 289. (31) 2977-23473. FAX: (31) 2977-44158. David Hughes, dir of international opns.
Manufactures character generators, editing systems & cable related products.

Quantel Inc. 85 Old Kings Hwy. N., Darien, Conn. 06820. (203) 656-3100. FAX: (203) 656-3459. George Grasso, CEO; Ken Ellis, sr VP/COO.
Atlanta 30341: 2971 Flowers Rd. S., No. 106. (404) 457-1266. FAX: (404) 457-4048. Jack Houman.
Farmington Hills, Mich. 48331: 27947 Trailwood Ct. (313) 553-0670. FAX: (313) 553-0746. Larry Biehl.
Foster City, Calif. 94404: 1493 Beach Park Blvd. (415) 726-1077. FAX: (413) 349-5674. Eric Thorne.
Los Angeles 90028: 6255 Sunset Blvd., Suite 1505. (213) 962-6198. FAX: (213) 962-5840. Tom McGowan, Mark Grasso, Gordon Banta.
New York 10019: 111 W. 57th St., 9th Fl. (212) 977-4877. FAX: (212) 977-6539. Jim Longstreth, Rich Alexander.
Montgomery, Tex. 77356: 3802 Knollcrest. (409) 582-6645. FAX: (409) 582-2269. Glen Green.
Design & manufacture digital special effects equipment.

Quick-Set Inc. 3650 Woodhead Dr., Northbrook, Ill. 60062. (708) 498-0700. FAX: (708) 498-1258. Larry Pope, VP sls & mktg.
Instrument positioning equipment.

Quickset International Inc. 3650 Woodhead Dr., Northbrook, Ill. 60062. (708) 498-0700. FAX: (708) 498-1258. Dale Rice, pres; Lawrence Pope, VP sls & mktg.
Manufacturer & distributor of Pan/Tilt & tripod platforms.

R

R-Columbia Products Co. Inc. 2008 St. Johns Ave., Highland Park, Ill. 60035. (708) 432-7915. FAX: (708) 432-9181. I. Rozak, pres; Ed Hill, sls mgr.
Headphones with & without microphone; cameraman headphones, wired & wireless headphones, ultralight headphones & IFB/ENG telephones.

RCA Broadcast Parts/GE Support Services. 158 Gaither Dr., Mt. Laurel, N.J. 08054. (609) 866-3147. FAX: (609) 866-3146. Ron Ettinger, prog mgr.
Studio & transmission equip; replacement parts support through 35,000-line item inventory; 24-hr emergency svc; tech assistance; manuals & training.

RCS Traffic. 402 S. Ragsdale, Suite 206, Jacksonville, Tex. 75766. (800) 251-6677; (903) 586-0557. FAX: (903) 586-6751. Bill Keenan, VP mktg.
Supplies a complete Management Information Systems for radio. Software is portable & will run on any MS-DOS, Windows, OS/2 or UNIX system & includes traffic, scheduling, A/R & logging. Prospect Management, Newsroom, Co-op/Copy & Financial systems. Interface with any automation system including Master Control & RCS Works. True multi-user systems, e-mail, remote communications & PC, Macintosh, Novell net or dumb terminal connectivity.

RE America Inc. 31029 Center Ridge Rd., Westlake, Ohio 44145. (216) 871-7617. FAX: (216) 871-4303. J.P. McHale, pres; P. Andrew Bosworth, VP sls & mktg; Soren Pilhman, VP.
Digital audio/video bcst products, RDS coders, stereo generators, audio analyzers & CODECS.

RF Specialties Group. (RF Specialties of Missouri) 22406 N.E. 159th St., Kearney, Mo. 64060: (816) 635-5959. FAX: (816) 635-4508. Chris Kreger, own.

Equipment Manufacturers and Distributors

Pittsburgh 15239: RF Specialties of Pennsylvania Inc. 121 Conneaut Dr. (412) 733-1994. FAX: (412) 327-9336. Tom Monahan.

Seattle 98133: RF Specialties of Washington Inc. 19237 Aurora Ave. N. (206) 546-6546. FAX: (206) 546-2633. John Schneider.

Santa Barbara, Calif. 93105: RF Specialties of California. 3463 State St. Suite 229. (805) 682-9429. FAX: (805) 682-4396.

Valparaiso, Fla. 32508: RF Specialties of Florida. 271 Grandview. (904) 678-8943. FAX: (904) 729-2744. Bill Turney.

Amarillo, Tex. 96106: RF Specialties of Texas. 804 S. Rusk. (806) 372-4518. FAX: (806) 373-8036. Don Jones & Tim Hawks.

Full line radio bcst equipment suppliers. AM & FM transmitters, towers, lines & antenna systems, studios, microwave & digital systems.

RF Systems. (A division of Audiolab Electronics Inc.) 5831 Rosebud Ln., Bldg. C., Sacramento, Calif. 95841. (916) 348-0200. FAX: (916) 348-1512. Robert E. Stofan, pres.

RF products including STL antennas, ATUs, AM phasing units & isocouplers.

RF Technologies Corp. 238 Goddard Rd., Lewiston, Me. 04240. (207) 777-7778. FAX: (207) 777-7784. George M. Harris P.E., pres; Peter Robicheau, VP tech design; Lisa Johnson, mktg admin.

Designs & manufactures high pwr bcst RF nets & components for FM & TV bcstrs. Products include; antennas, diplexers, combiners, filters, switches, coax & waveguides.

RF Technology Inc. 16 Testa Pl., South Norwalk, Conn. 06854. (203) 866-4283. FAX: (203) 853-3513. Charles Bobbins, pres; Patrick Bradbury, VP.

Fairhope, Ala. 36532: 16 Orange Ave. (205) 928-9459. Grady Jackson, southern rgnl mgr.

Microwave products in 2, 2.5, 7, 13, 18, 40 ghz freq; transmitters, receivers, power amplifiers & antennas.

RMS Electronics Inc. 41-51 Hartz Way, Secaucus, N.J. 07094. (201) 601-9191. FAX: (201) 601-0011. Gary Napolitano, pres; Fred Mucciardi, VP; Bernadette Bishop, controller.

Manufacture power supplies; distribute cable TV supplies.

RPG Diffusor Systems Inc. 651-C Commerce Dr., Upper Marlboro, Md. 20772. (301) 249-0044. FAX: (301) 249-3912. Peter D'Antonio, pres/CEO; Troy B. Jensen, gen mgr.

Wall, ceiling & freestanding diffusors, absorbors, variable acoustics modules & performance shells.

RTS Systems. (A division of Telex Communications Inc.) 2550 N. Hollywood Way, Suite 207, Burbank, Calif. 91505-1055. (818) 566-6700. FAX: (818) 843-7953. John Hale, pres; Murray Porteous, gen sls mgr.

Union Lake, Mich. 48386: RTS Systems (Midwest Office), 9628 Mandon Rd. (313) 360-0430. Rick Fisher, sls mgr.

Wyckoff, N.J. 07481: RTS Systems (East Coast Office), 336 Village Pl. (201) 891-6525. Michael Guthrie, sls mgr.

Intercommunication systems, IFB systems, pro-audio amplifiers, mic & phono preamplifiers.

RACAL-DECCA CANADA LTD.
TOWER INSULATORS and
LIGHTING TRANSFORMERS
RACAL   Phone: (905) 405-1144
        Fax: (905) 405-1150

Racal-Decca Canada Inc. 7510 Airport Rd., Mississauga, Ont., Canada L4T 2H5. (905) 405-1144. FAX: (905) 405-1150. Patrick Warr, gen mgr; John Molloy-Vickers, tech mgr.

Racal-Decca Canada Inc.

- GUY STRAIN INSULATORS
- BASE INSULATORS*
- ISOLATION TRANSFORMERS
- TRANSFORMER ENCLOSURES
- STATIC DRAIN RESISTORS
- CUSTOM DESIGNED INSULATORS

*Base Insulators can be adapted for direct mounting of Isolation Transformers.

Racal-Decca
Canada Inc.
Insulators Division

7510 Airport Road, Mississauga, Ontario L4T 2H5, Canada
Telephone: (905) 405-1144 Fax: (905) 405-1150

Base & guyline insulators, static drain devices, tower lighting transformers, replacements for obsolete insulators.

Radiation Systems Inc. 1501 Moran Rd., Sterling, Va. 20166. (703) 450-5680. FAX: (703) 450-4706. Richard E. Thomas, chmn/CEO; H.J. Arnold, engrg VP; Mark Fuston, CFO; Marvin Shoemake, William Thomas, VPs; Doss McComas, VP international mktg.

Rockway, N.J. (201) 627-5981.

Largo, Fla. (813) 541-6688.

Des Plaines, Ill. 60018: (Mark Antennas Division) (708) 298-9420. FAX: (708) 615-7946. Mary Erhardt, pres.

Wortham, Tex. (817) 765-3304.

Richardson, Tex. (214) 907-9599; (214) 690-8865.

Duluth, Ga. (404) 497-8800.

Sterling, Va. (703) 450-7030; (703) 450-5680.

Rochester, Kent, U.K. 0634-71554.

Mithcham Junction, Surrey, U.K. (081) 648-9461.

Designs, manufactures, markets, installs, intergrates & maintains an extensive line of high quality microwave, satellite & radar antennas, antenna subsystems and/or turnkey terminals for communications, surveillance & radar applications.

Radio Aids Inc. 4266 N. 525 W., LaPorte, Ind. 46350. (219) 879-2215. Robert J. Swanson, chief eng; Ruth Swanson, office mgr.

Radio Computing Services (RCS). 2 Overhill Rd., Suite 100, Scarsdale, N.Y. 10583. (914) 723-8567. FAX: (914) 723-6651. Andrew M. Economos, pres; Lee Facto, VP/gen mgr.

Cincinnati 45248: 6120 Harrison Ave. (513) 574-5414. Dan Allen, VP north central sls.

Rockville, Md. 20852: 11100 Whisperwood Ln. (310) 897-3633. Allan Ginsburg, natl sls mgr.

Raleigh, N.C. 27607: 505 Oberlin Rd. (919) 839-4151. Steve Peppard, VP.

Pensacola, Fla. 32513: 9420 Scenic Hwy. (904) 479-2339. Jim Colley, southeastern sls.

Dallas 75225: 4136 Hanover. (214) 369-0597. Carl Barringer, VP south central sls.

Yuba City, Calif. 95933: (916) 674-3830. Dean Cull, western sls.

North Vancouver, Canada 278 W. 5th St. (604) 988-3915. Paul McKnight, GM RCS Canada.

Computer systems for radio progmg, rsch, traf, sls & digital audio prod & bcst.

Radio Design Labs. Box 1286, Carpinteria, Calif. 93014. (805) 684-5415. FAX: (805) 684-9316. Joel Bump, pres; Jerry Clements, VP.

Full line of mic & line level amplifiers, mixers, DAs & processors.

Radio Engineering Industries Inc. 6534 L St., Omaha, Neb. 68117. (402) 339-2200. FAX: (402) 339-1704. Bob Hayes, pres.

Sls & svc of bcst equipment, amplifiers, paging systems, SCA & coml sound equipment.

Radio Research Instrument Co. Inc. 584 N. Main St., Waterbury, Conn. 06704. (203) 753-5840. FAX: (203) 754-2567. P.J. Plishner, pres; E.B. Doyle, exec VP.

Provide radar systems, threat emitters & spare parts; complete maintenance facility for repair.

Radio Resources & Services. 1201 S. Sharp St., Baltimore, 21230. (800) 547-2346. FAX: (410) 783-4635.

Radio bcst equipment & audio supplies (RF & audio), pro audio equipment, rental test equipment & quality pre-owned radio & video equipment.

Radio Systems Inc. Box 458, Bridgeport, N.J. 08014. (609) 467-8000. FAX: (609) 467-3044. Daniel Braverman, pres; Gerrett Conover, sls mgr.

Audio consoles, cart machines, audio distribution amplifiers, timers, low power AM transmitters & bcst DAT machines.

Ram Broadcast Systems. Box 3100, Barrington, Ill. 60011-3100. (800) 779-7575; (708) 382-7575. FAX: (708) 382-8818. Ron Mitchell, pres.

Switchers (audio & video) mixers, intercom systems, audio/video DAs, systems engrg & custom cabinetry.

Ramko Research Inc. 3501 Sunrise Blvd., #4, Rancho Cordova, Calif. 95742. (916) 635-3600. FAX: (916) 635-0907. Ray Kohfeld, pres; Dave Baldwin, customer svc/tech; Mike Pardee, natl sls coord.

Audio consoles, audio/data router, distribution amplifiers. Programmable audio systems, mic, line & turntable amplifiers; full-line audio.

Broadcasting & Cable Yearbook 1994
H-47

Equipment Manufacturers and Distributors

Rangertone Research Inc. 115 Roosevelt Ave., Belleville, N.J. 07109. (201) 751-6833. FAX: (201) 751-9741. George P. Zazzali, pres; Daniel J. Zazzali, VP.
Audio-visual equipment.

Rank Cintel Inc. 25358 Ave. Stanford, Valencia, Calif. 91355. (805) 294-2310. FAX: (805) 294-1019. Arnold Taylor, pres; Jerry Ramsey, VP engrg; D. Edmonson, VP finance; Charles Morganti, eastern rgnl sls mgr; Raymond Bard, western rgnl sls mgr.
Schaumburg, Ill. 60173: 830 E. Higgins Rd., Suite 130. (708) 240-2620. Charles Morganti, eastern sls mgr.
Valley Cottage, N.Y. 10989: 704 Executive Blvd. (914) 268-8911. Henson Alexander, svc mgr.
Flying spot & digital CCD telecines; 4:2:2 still store, graphic animation system & image transmission systems.

Raven Screen Corp. 112 Spring St., Monroe, N.Y. 10950. (212) 534-8408; (212) 534-8409. FAX: (914) 782-1840. Martin Soss, pres.
Manual, motorized & custom projection screens & materials.

Raychem Corp. 300 Constitution Dr., Menlo Park, Calif. 94025. (415) 361-2288. FAX: (415) 361-4693. Lynn Chapman, CATV mgr.
Coaxial connectors, environmental sealing products, antenna de-icers.

Reach Electronics Inc. Box 308, 1311 W. Pacific, Lexington, Neb. 68850. (308) 324-6661. FAX: (308) 324-4985. Jim Longly, VP; Robert Payne, sls mgr.
Subcarrier Authorization (SCA) pagers & paging terminals.

Rebo Group. 530 W. 25th St., New York 10001. (212) 989-9466.

Recortec Inc. 1290 Lawrence Stn. Rd., Sunnyvale, Calif. 94089-2220. (408) 734-1290. FAX: (408) 734-2140. Dr. Lester H. Lee, pres.
Manufacturer of magnetic tape cleaners, rewinders, testers & duplicators.

Recoton Corporation. 46-23 Crane St., Long Island City, N.Y. 11101. (718) 392-6442. FAX: (718) 784-1080. Herbert Borchardt, chmn; Robert Borchardt, pres; Peter Wish, exec VP; George Calvi, sr VP mktg & sls; Peter Dayton, VP sls.
MTS stereo & SAP decoders to convert monaural TV & VCRs to receive stereo TV & bi-lingual bcsts.

Reel-O-Matic Systems Inc. Box 95309, Oklahoma City, 73143. (405) 672-0000. FAX: (405) 672-7200. John Schrott, pres; Terry Simmons, VP.
Equipment to re-spool, coil, measure & distribute cable.

Rees Associates Inc. 3817 N.W. Expwy., Suite 500, Oklahoma City 73112. (405) 942-7337. FAX: (405) 948-1261. Frank W. Rees Jr., pres.
Offices in: Dallas, Houston, Los Angeles, Oklahoma City, St. Petersburg, Fla.
Bcst & prod facility design; studio design; equipment planning; facility business plans; consulting.

Register Data Systems. Box 980, Perry, Ga. 31069. (912) 987-2501; (800) 521-5222. FAX: (912) 987-7595. Lowell L. Register, pres; Brad Harrison, sls mgr.
Digital audio automation systems for live assist & satellite, traffic & billing software packages for radio & TV.

Reliable Electric/Utility Products. 11333 W. Addison, Franklin Park, Ill. 60131. (708) 455-8010. FAX: (708) 451-5685. Mike Corkran, VP/gen mgr; Jim Zipper, dir engrg; Mike Cochran & Dennis DelCampo, mktg dirs.
CATV enclosures, security enclosures, protection devices, pole line hardware & connectors.

Renkus-Heinz Inc. 17191 Armstrong Ave., Irvine, Calif. 92714. (714) 250-0166. FAX: (714) 250-1035. Harro K. Heinz, pres; Carl Dorwaldt, sls mgr.
H.F. compression drivers, horns, woofers, speaker systems, amplifiers, "smart" processor-controlled speaker systems.

Reproduction Technologies Inc. Box 790, 110 E. Vistula St., Bristol, Ind. 46507. (219) 848-5233. FAX: (219) 848-5333. Michael Stoll, pres.

Research Technology International Inc. 4700 Chase Ave., Lincolnwood, Ill. 60646. (708) 677-3000; (800) 323-7520. FAX: (708) 677-1311. Ray L. Short Jr., pres; Thomas A. Tisch, VP mktg.
Videotape evaluator & cleaners; magnetic dropout counters; degaussers film editing & maintenance systems; video & film editing, storage & care, supplies & furniture.

Reuters Ltd. 1700 Broadway, 2nd Fl. New York 10019. (212) 603-3300. Glen Renfrew, mgr (North America); Desmond Maberley, mgng edit.
Chicago 60606: 311 S. Wacker Dr., Suite 1100. (312) 922-6038. Geoffrey Atkins, chief.
Washington 20005: 1333 H St. N.W., Suite 410. (202) 898-8300. Bruce Russell, chief.
Kansas City, Mo. 64112: 4800 Main. (816) 561-8671. Bob Martin.
Los Angeles 90071: 445 S. Figueroa, Suite 2100. (213) 380-2014. Ronald Clarke, chief.
Toronto, Ont., Canada M5H 3T9: Standard Life Centre, 121 King St. West, 20th Fl. (416) 869-3600. Peter Thomas, mgr Canada.
Montreal, Que., Canada H3A 2A5: 2020 Rue Universite, Suite 1020. (514) 282-0705. William Miller.
Ottawa, Ont., Canada K1P 5P8: 165 Sparks St., Booth Bldg. (613) 235-6745. Antony Parry, financial correspondent; John Rogers, gen news.
Supplier of natl, world & business news & info to media & professionals.

Richardson Electronics Ltd. 40 W 267 Keslinger Rd., LaFox, Ill. 60147. (708) 208-2200; (800) 348-5580. FAX: (708) 208-2550. TELEX: 283461. Edward Richardson, CEO; Dennis Gandy, Leonard Prange, VPs; David Gilden, VP international sls; Ad Ketelaars, VP European sls; Bob Prince, VP North American sls.
Woodland Hills, Calif. 91364: 21243 Ventura Blvd. (818) 594-5600; (800) 348-5580. FAX: (818) 594-5650.
Valley Stream, N.Y. 11580: 50 W. Hawthorne. (516) 872-4440; (800) 882-3397. FAX: (516) 872-4454.
Dallas 75240: 6360 L.B.J. Fwy. (214) 239-3680; (800) 348-5580. FAX: (818) 594-5650.
Mountain View, Calif. 94041: 444 Castro St., Suite 407. (415) 960-6900; (800) 348-5580. FAX: (818) 594-5650.
Winter Park, Fla. 32789: 140 N. Orlando Ave. (407) 644-1453; (800) 348-5580. FAX: (407) 645-3961.
Norwell, Mass. 02061: 167 Washington St. (617) 871-5162; (800) 348-5580. FAX: (617) 871-4654.
Mississauga, Ont., Canada L5T 1X6: 6185 Tomken Rd., Units 3-5. (800) 348-5580; (905) 795-6300. FAX: (905) 795-6350.
East Rochester, N.Y. 14445: 349 W. Commercial St., Suite 2265. (716) 264-1100; (800) 348-5580. FAX: (716) 264-1100.
Bellevue, Wash. 98004: 1400 112th Ave. S.E. (206) 646-7224; (800) 348-5580. FAX: (206) 646-7293.
Montgomeryville, Pa. 18936: 1380 Welsh Rd. (215) 628-0805; (800) 348-5580. FAX: (215) 643-4750.
Lincoln, U.K. LN2 4DT: Inspring House, Searby Rd. (0522) 542631. FAX: (0522) 545453. TELEX: 56175 REEL UK.
Argenteuil Cedex, France. France 95108: Richardson Electronique S.A. Direction Commerciale, 119 Ave. du Marais, Batiment Sophocle, Park des Algorithmes. (1) 34-26-4000. FAX: (1) 34-26-4020. TELEX: 606550 F RICH TUB.
Sesto Fiorentino, Italy. Italy 50019: Richardson/G.E.B. Electronics. Viale L. Aristo, 492/G. (055) 4201030. FAX: (055) 4210726; Numero Verde 1678-62138. TELEX: 571403 GEBTD.
Madrid, Spain. Spain 28045: Richardson Electronics Iberica S.A. Calle Hierro, 10 Planta Nave, 10 Edificio Legazpi. 528-3700. FAX: 467-5468. TELEX: 44932 REISA.
Puchheim, Germany. Germany W-8039: Richardson Electronics GmBH. Benzstrasse 28, Bau B. 089/80 02 13-1. FAX: 089/80 02 13-8.
Tokyo, Japan. Japan 110: Richardson Electronics Japan Co. Ltd. Tachibana Bldg., 1-22-3 Chome, Negishi Taito-Ku. (81) 3874-9933. FAX: (81) 3874-9944
St. Laurent, Que., Canada H4L 5G4: 685 Blvd. Decarie, Suite 310. (514) 748-1770; (800) 348-5580. FAX: (514) 748-1808.
Singapore, Suite 01-587 1233: Richardson Electronics Pte. Ltd. Block 25, 25 Bendemeer Rd. 298-4974. FAX: 297-2459. TELEX: 33471.
Export: Valley Stream, N.Y. 11580: 50 W. Hawthorne. (800) 882-3397; (800) TUBE EXPORT; (516) 872-4440. FAX: (516) 872-4454.
Distribution & manufacture of electron tubes & semiconductors.

Richmond Sound Design Ltd. 1234 W. 6th Ave., Vancouver, B.C., Canada V6H 1A5. (604) 664-5860. FAX: (604) 732-1234. C.B. Richmond, pres; K.D. Bell, PE gen mgr; M. Williams, project mgr.
Automated multichannel audio for live shows & theatre; show controllers.

Ripley Company, Cablematic Division. 46 Nootis Hill Rd., Cromwell, Conn. 06416. (203) 635-2200. FAX: (203) 635-3631. Chris Havelson, mktg mgr.
Complete line of cable preparation tools for CATV & telecommunications.

Riser-Bond Instruments. 5101 N. 57th St., Lincoln, Neb. 68507. (402) 466-0933. FAX: (402) 466-0967. Marshall B. Borchert, pres; Walter R. Campbell, VP sls & mktg.
Aurora, Neb. 68818: Box 188. (402) 694-5201. Deb Nissen, rgnl sls mgr.
Electronic test equipment; cable fault locators; time domain reflectometer.

Roadrunner Cases Inc. 447 E. Gardena Blvd., Gardena, Calif. 90248. (213) 770-4444. FAX: (310) 538-9560. Howard Chatt, pres.
Carrying, shipping & storage cases for all bcst equipment.

Rodelco Electronics Corp. 111 Haynes Ct., Ronkonkoma, N.Y. 11779. (516) 981-0900. FAX: (516) 981-1792. Joseph M. Rodgers, gen mgr.
Television trans; VHF & UHF.

Rodman-Brown & Associates. 1544 Lighthouse Dr., Naperville, Ill. 60565. (708) 983-0977. FAX: (708) 968-1234. Ted Czarnecki, prod mgr.
Traffic, billing, sls mgmt & accounting software for radio stns. Digital automation maker.

Rohde & Schwarz Inc. 4425 Nicole Dr., Lanham, Md. 20706-4352. (301) 459-8800. FAX: (301) 459-2810. Scott Elkins, VP mktg; John A. Pannucci; VP finance & admin.
Video test & measurement instruments; bcst & CATV demodulators; remote monitoring systems for transmitters.

Rohn. Box 2000, Peoria, Ill. 61656. (309) 697-4400. FAX: (309) 697-5612. Donald Rohn, pres; Richard Kleine, VP mktg; Mike Fleissner, natl sls mgr bcst products.
Worton, Md. 21678: Box 106. (410) 778-4441. FAX: (410) 778-3096. Ken L. Cordrey, eastern division sls mgr.
Plano, Tex. 75075: 555 Republic, Suite 22. (214) 422-5131. FAX: (214) 422-4800. Larry Grimes, southwest division sls mgr.
Atlantic, Iowa 50022: Box 461. (712) 243-1993. FAX: (712) 243-1993. Verle Miller, central division sls mgr.
Woodstock, Ga. 30188: Box 259. (404) 591-5683. FAX: (404) 591-5731.
Towers (up to 2000') & shelters for communication industry. Complete instal or material only.

RolandCorp U.S. 7200 Dominion Cir., Los Angeles 90040. (213) 685-5141. FAX: (213) 722-0911. Dennis Houlihan, pres; Mark Malborn, VP.
Electronic musical instruments, synchronization devices, signal processors, sound reinforcement, mus software & computer peripherals.

Rosco Laboratories Inc. 36 Bush Ave., Port Chester, N.Y. 10573. (914) 937-1300. FAX: (914) 937-5984. Stan Miller, pres; Stan Schwartz, exec VP.
Hollywood, Calif. 90038: 1135 N. Highland Ave. (213) 462-2233. FAX: (213) 462-3338. Jim Meyer, mgr.
Lighting filters & diffusers.

Roscom Inc. Box 1208, Roswell, Ga. 30077-1208. (404) 992-2230. FAX: (404) 992-6538. Bob Stewart, pres.
Bellvue, Colo. 80512: 6301 Jackpine Dr. (303) 482-9254. FAX: (303) 482-6123. John Shideler.
Radio bcst equipment; studios, transmitters, towers, antennas, COAX, STL, remote controls, processing, monitoring, automation.

Roscor Corp. 1061 Feehanville Dr., Mount Prospect, Ill. 60056. (708) 299-8080. FAX: (708) 299-4206. Paul Roston, pres; Mitch Roston, exec VP; Howard Ellman, VP sls; Edward Jones, VP finance.
West Allis, Wis. 53214: 11350 W. Theodore Trecker Way. (414) 476-2600. Ned White, branch mgr.
Farmington Hills, Mich. 48331: 27260 Haggerty Rd., A12. (313) 489-0090. Robert Zeichner, branch mgr.

Equipment Manufacturers and Distributors

Professional audio/video & RF presentation equipment. Turnkey engrg & instal svcs.

Murry Rosenblum Sound Assoc.Inc. 21-36 33rd Rd., Long Island City, N.Y. 11106. (718) 728-2654. FAX: (718) 728-2654. Murry Rosenblum, pres.
Audio limited wireless microphones - small UHF & VHF plain & diverse, high power transmitter.

Ross, Clarke & Associates. 76 S. Bayles Ave., Port Washington, N.Y. 11050. (516) 944-6599. FAX: (516) 767-7369. Walter J. Clarke, sr ptnr; Terry A. Shantz, ptnr.
Wayne, Pa. 19087: 130 Conestoga Rd. (215) 687-0291
Consulting engrs; tower engrg, design & construction mgmt.

Ross Video Ltd. Box 220, 8 John St., Iroquois, Ont., Canada K0E 1K0. (613) 652-4886. FAX: (613) 652-4425. John Ross, pres; Steve Horvath, mgr mktg & sls.
Video prod switchers, 10 to 30 inputs.

Rush Media Systems. Box 12354, Research Triangle Park, N.C. 27709. (919) 851-1926. FAX: (919) 851-1190. Carroll Ogle, pres.
Procuring, servicing, instal, sale of bcstg & satellite equipment. Leasing plans available.

Ruslang Corp. 320 Dewey St., Bridgeport, Conn. 06605. (203) 384-1266. FAX: (203) 384-1267. Frank Ruskay Jr., pres; Paul D. Ruskay, VP.
Cabinetry, consoles & racks for video switching & editing equipment & reel to reel recorders.

S

SAIC/Information Display Systems Division. 1710 Goodridge Dr., Mclean, Va. 22102. (703) 821-4300. FAX: (703) 356-7085. Scott Williams, Eidophor div mgr/asst VP.
Eidophor large screen projectors. Rental source & sole North American distributor.

SCA Data Systems Inc. 225 Arizona Ave., Suite 350, Santa Monica, Calif. 90401. (310) 576-0655. FAX: (310) 576-0566. Steven J. Davis, pres; Corinne Weber, opns mgr; Lawrence J. Karr, chmn; Mark Medow, tech advisor.
SCA audio & data receivers & generators, SCA paging & RDS generators.

SIMPAC. Box 7745, 20 Purple Sage, Irvine, Calif. 92715. (714) 846-0765. James Fallgatter, exclusive distributor.
Provides cart rack storage for radio & TV stns, libraries & control rooms.

S&L Plastics. 2860 Bass Pike, Nazareth, Pa. 18064. (215) 759-0280. FAX: (215) 759-0650. James D. Guiducci, pres.
Thermo plastic products.

SL Waber Inc. (Subsidiary of SL Industries) 520 Fellowship Rd., Suite 306, Mt. Laurel, N.J. 08054. (609) 866-8888. FAX: (609) 866-1945. Arthur Blumenthal, pres.
Multiple outlet strips, surge & noise suppressors & uninterruptible power supplies.

SPOTCATS. (Division of STEP Corp.) 8699 W. Chester Pike, Upper Darby, Pa. 19082. (800) 536-1515. (215) 446-1515. FAX: (215) 789-4353. Saul Meyer, chief Spot-Cat.
Traffic & billing software for radio, TV & LPTV.

ST Microsonics Corp. 265 Essex St., Weymouth, Mass. 02188. (617) 337-4200. FAX: (617) 337-4208. Douglas K. McConnell, pres; Anthony R. Pellegrino, dir opns.
Video delay modules 1H & 2H, glass delay lines 1H & 2H.

S.W.R. Inc. (Systems With Reliability) Cambria County Industrial Park, Ebensburg, Pa. 15931. (814) 472-5436. FAX: (814) 472-5552. Edward J. Edmiston, pres; Douglas A. Ross, dir engrg.
Manufacturers of TV & FM transmit antennas, rigid coax, waveguide & associated accessories.

The First Name In Automation
Genesis Digital Audio System By Schafer World Communications
A Totally New Beginning For Audio

GENESIS DIGITAL AUDIO™

You Can Trust Your Station's Programming Integrity To Schafer

schafer WORLD COMMUNICATIONS CORPORATION
P.O. Box 31
Marion, Virginia 24354-0031

Phone: 703-783-2000   FAX: 703-783-2064

NO MORE FEEDBACK! AUTOMATICALLY...

Our line of patented digital signal processors offer automatic feedback control, more gain before feedback, increased sound clarity - even digital filtering. Call us today for more details.

4637 N.W. 6th St. • Gainesville, FL 32609 USA
Phone: (904) 371-3829 • Fax: (904) 371-7441

Sabine Musical Manufacturing Co. Inc. 4637 NW 6th St., Gainesville, Fla. 32609. (904) 371-3829. FAX: (904) 371-7441. Doran Oster, pres; Robert Rothschild, dir sls & mktg; Gary Miller, dir engrg.
Manufacture digital signal processing equip for sound systems. Makers of the patented FBX Feedback Exterminator.

Sachs Communications Inc. 745 Avoca Ave, Montreal Que., Canada H9P 1G4. (514) 636-6560. FAX: (514) 631-4306. Jack Sachs, pres; Bernie Klein, gen mgr.
Champlain, N.Y. 12919-9703: 30 W. Service Rd. (800) 267-2247.
Atlanta 30120: 211 Stonewall St. (706) 382-4114. FAX: (706) 386-5482.
Manufacture quality products for aerial construction & sub instal hardware for the Cable TV & telephone industry.

Sachtler Corporation of America. 55 N. Main St., Freeport, N.Y. 11520. (516) 867-4900. FAX: (516) 623-6844. Eric D. Falkenberg, exec VP.
Burbank, Calif. 91505: 3316 W. Victory Blvd. (818) 854-4446.
Complete line of camera support equipment for ENG, EFP, O.B. & the new generation of studio cameras. Lighting for news, prod & studio open-face technology & fresnel.

Sacramento Theatrical Lighting. 950 Richards Blvd., Sacramento, Calif. 95814. (800) 283-2785. FAX: (916) 447-5012. Don Parsons, rental mgr; Tina Miranda, sls mgr.
Specialists in studio & location lighting, grip equipment, draperies, rigging & grid work. Consultation & prod svcs; sls & rentals.

Sadelco Inc. 75 W. Forest Ave., Englewood, N.J. 07631. (201) 569-3323. FAX: (201) 569-6285. Harry L. Sadel, pres; Les Kaplan, VP mktg.
Signal level m; calibrators & bridges.

Saki Magnetics Inc. 26600 Agoura Rd., Calabasas, Calif. 91302. (818) 880-4054. FAX: (818) 880-6242. Eugene Sakasegawa, chmn; Richard Drake, pres; Trevor Boyer, dir mktg & sls.
Manufacturer of metal & ferrite tape recording heads for professional audio & aerospace mkts.

Samson Technologies Corp. Box 9068, Hicksville, N.Y. 11802-9068. (516) 932-3810. FAX: (516) 932-3815. Douglas Bryant, pres/chief engr; Scott Goodman, CEO; Jack Knight, natl sls mgr Hartke Systems & Zoom; David Olivier, natl sls mgr Samson Audio & Samson Wireless; Bob Caputo, natl sls mgr Sountracs & Behringer; Kevin Moran, export mgr.
Manufacture wireless microphones, mixing consoles, power amplifiers & audio products. Distributor of Soundtracs consoles, Behringer audio processing, Hartke speakers & Zoom effects processors.

Sansui USA. 1290 Wall St., W., Lyndhurst, N.J. 07071. (201) 460-9710. FAX: (201) 460-9064. Norm Gahler, VP.
Carson, Calif. 90746: Box 4687, 17150 S. Margay Ave. (201) 460-9064.
Consumer & professional audio equipment.

Sanyo-Fisher (USA) Corp. 21350 Laffen St., Chadsworth, Calif. 91311. (818) 998-7322. FAX: (818) 998-3533. Paul Dearcy, VP mktg; David Claus, mktg mgr.
Recorders, mus systems & video tape systems.

David Sarnoff Research Center. (Subsidiary of SRI International) CN 5300, Princeton, N.J. 08543-5300. (609) 734-2000. FAX: (609) 734-2221. James E. Carnes, pres/COO.
Contract rsch facility for all principal areas of electronics: consumer electronics & info sciences, mfg & materials & solid state divisions.

Sascom Marketing Group. 635 Weyburn Sq., Pickering, Ont., Canada L1V 3V3. (416) 420-3946. FAX: (416) 420-0178. Curt Smith, pres.
Boisbriand, Que., Canada J7G 2G5: 865 Cournoyer. (514) 433-1677. Marc Vincent.
Optifile; Raindirk; Lafont; Demeter; Omniphonics; Professional Monitor Company; Larking; the Vitalizer.

Satellite Systems Corp. 101 Malibu Dr., Virginia Beach, Va. 23452. (804) 463-3553. FAX: (804) 463-3891. Fred Poteet, pres.
SCPC & video subcarrier satellite systems for radio, SNG & data bcst nets.

Satellite Transmission Systems Inc. (Subsidiary of California Microwave Inc.) 125 Kennedy Dr., Hauppage, N.Y. 11788. (516) 231-1919. FAX: (516) 231-1896. David E. Hershberg, pres; Gary Gomes, VP mktg & business dev; Kenneth A. Miller, exec VP.
Annapolis Junction, Md. 20701: 10820 Annapolis Junction Rd. (410) 792-2225. Nelson Ward, gen mgr.
Melbourne, Fla. 32901: 1615 W. Nassa Blvd. (407) 768-8490. Roger Parsons, VP.

Broadcasting & Cable Yearbook 1994
H-49

Equipment Manufacturers and Distributors

Turnkey satellite earth stns & nets, SNG & Fly Away electronics, ground communications equipment & M&C systems. Manufacture & implement full line of earth stn net monitor & control systems.

Scala Electronic Corp. Box 4580, Medford, Ore. 97501. (503) 779-6500. FAX: (503) 779-3991. Ellis Feinstein, pres; Dan Fowler, mktg mgr.
Antennas for LPTV, STL, CATV, trans, RPU, TSL, FM/TV monitoring, MMDS/ITFS & wireless cable.

Schafer Digital. 201 Lathrop Way, Suite C, Sacramento, Calif. 95815. (800) 831-1021; (916) 646-3444. FAX: (916) 646-3493. Jim Hansen, pres.
Digital automation systems & digital satellite automation systems for radio.

Schafer International. 17804 Cabela Dr., San Diego, 92127. (619) 673-8080. FAX: (619) 673-8210. Paul C. Schafer, pres; Susana Haikalis, mgr.
All equipment & parts including digital audio storage systems for radio & TV stns - primarily in Mexico.

FIRST NAME IN AUTOMATION

schafer
WORLD COMMUNICATIONS CORPORATION

HAS THE LATEST IN "DIGITAL AUDIO"
IN NEW PC AUTOMATION SYSTEMS
for Satellite, CD or Live Assist

PO Box 31, Marion, Va. 24354-0031
703-783-2000   FAX: 703-783-2064

Schafer World Communications Corp. Box 31, Marion, Va. 24354. (703) 783-2000. FAX: (703) 783-2064. Bob Dix, pres; Ann Dix, VP; Kevin Soos, customer svc mgr.
"GENESIS" Total digital automation systems using hard disc to store digital audio, with instant access of coms, jingles, IDs, promos, liners, etc., including controlling up to eight satellite nets for full automation or live assist. Complete CD HD digital automation systems. Schafer also has audio consoles & other equipment.

Schmid Telecommunication America Inc. 15 W. 26th St., New York 10010. (212) 213-2099. FAX: (212) 779-7305. Tom Newman, pres.
SIAT - Short Interval Audio Test System; RESCO - Remote Monitoring & Control System.

Schneider Corp. of America. 400 Crossways Park Dr., Woodbury, N.Y. 11797. (516) 496-8500. FAX: (516) 496-8524. Ron Leven, Dwight Lindsay, sr VPs. Craig Marcin, tech mgr.
Sls, svc & rentals for ENG, EFP & field camera lenses & filters.

Schuessler Case Company Inc. Box 276, Tarrytown, N.Y. 10591. (914) 631-4766. H. Pilzer, pres.
Shipping cases, cabinets & cans for film & tape; custom made fibre cases.

Scientific-Atlanta Inc. (Broadband Communications Group) 4386 Park Dr., Norcross, Ga. 30093. (800) 722-2009. James McDonald, pres/CEO; Jay Levergood, pres Broadband Communications Group; Gary Trimm, pres sub systems division; Robert McIntyre, pres transmission systems division.
A complete line of cable TV sub & transmission products.

Scientific Radio Systems Inc. 367 Orchard St., Rochester, N.Y. 14606. (716) 235-2040. FAX: (716) 235-7827. J. Robert Clement, pres; F.W. Brown, dir opns.
HF SSB/ISB, VHF AM/FM, MF CW communications equipment; LF/MF beacons; HF packet radio; selective call & voice privacy equipment.

Scott Studios CDRA. 13375 Stemmons Fwy, #200, Dallas 75234. (800) 330-3004. FAX: (214) 620-2707. Dave Scott, pres.
Radio automation systems; digital audio.

ScreenLight & Grip. 16 Holmen St. Boston 02134. (617) 783-3862. FAX: (617) 783-3862. Guy Holt, own.
Location lighting & prod svcs, equipment rental, trucks, vans, etc.

Second Chance Body Armor Inc. Box 578, 7919 Cameron St., Central Lake, Mich. 49622-0573. (616) 544-5721; (800) 253-7090. FAX: (616) 544-9824. Pamela M. Hinz, natl sls mgr.
Leading body armor manufacturer now offering ballistic protection for news media reporters & photographers.

Selco Products Co. 7580 Stage Rd., Buena Park, Calif. 90621. (714) 521-8673; (714) 739-1507. William J. Wilkinson, gen mgr; Celeste Favata, mktg dir.
VU & peak prog; collet & push-on knobs; bi-metal snap disc thermostats for amplifiers, etc.

Sencore Inc. 3200 Sencore Dr., Sioux Fall, S.D. 57107. (605) 339-0100. FAX: (605) 339-0317. George Gonos, VP sls & mktg; Brad Johnson, mktg mgr.
Electronic test equipment for svc & performance testing of consumer electronics & CATV/MATV equipment.

Sennheiser Electronic Corp. Box 987, 6 Vista Dr., Old Lyme, Conn. 06371. (203) 434-9190. FAX: (203) 434-1759. Andrew Brakhan, pres; Inge Hieret, sr VP. Burbank, Calif. 91505: 4116 W. Magnolia Blvd. (818) 845-7366 Matt Robertson, VP.
Microphones, headphones, boomsets, wireless microphones & infrared products.

Sentry Systems. 2211 5th Ave., Seattle 98121. (800) 426-9082. FAX: (206) 441-6582. Bob Arnold, gen mgr; Matt Meany, Allen Range, customer svc.
Radio bcst PC controller for live assist, satellite or full automation controlling CD players, carts, digital audio, R-DAT & reel.

Sescom Inc. 2100 Ward Dr., Henderson, Nev. 89015. (702) 565-3400. FAX: (702) 565-4828. Franklin J. Miller, pres.
Audio interfacing equipment, audio transformers & modules.

Setcom Corp. 1400 N. Shoreline Blvd., Mountain View, Calif. 94043. (415) 965-8020. FAX: (415) 965-1193. L. Kent Schwartzman, pres; Stephen Kilczewski, sls mgr.
Portable & fixed position intercom systems, bcst intercom & portable radio headsets.

Seton Name Plate Corp. Box 1331, New Haven, Conn. 06505. (800) 243-6624; (203) 488-8059. Richard L. Fisk, VP/gen mgr; Vincent Prigitano, dir opns.
Signs, tags, labels, pipe markers, valve tags & nameplates to meet OSHA/ANSI specifications.

Shallco Inc. Smithfield Industrial Park, Box 1089, Smithfield, N.C. 27577. (919) 934-3135. FAX: (919) 934-3298. Michael D. Sutton, pres; Jason S. Shallcross, VP.
Variable & fixed audio attenuators.

Sharp Electronics Corp. (LCD Products Division) Sharp Plaza, Mail Stop One, Mahwah, N.J. 07430-2135. (201) 529-8731. FAX: (201) 529-9636. Ron Colgan, gen mgr; Bruce Pollack, natl mktg mgr.
Carson, Calif. 90810: 20600 S. Alameda St. (310) 637-9488. T. Smock, rgnl sls mgr.
Lawrenceville, Ga. 30245: 725 Old Norcross Rd. (404) 995-0717. R. Parker, rgnl sls mgr.
Romeoville, Ill. 60441: 1300 Naperville Dr. (312) 759-8555. R. Miller, rgnl sls mgr.
LCD-based video projection systems, computer projection panels & direct-view flat-panel TV/monitors.

Shintron Co. Inc. 45 Winthrop St., Concord, Mass. 01742. (508) 371-7500. FAX: (508) 371-7554. Sam Asano, pres.
Routing switchers, distribution amplifiers, time code, component video, PC accessories & compugraphics to video.

WHEN ONLY THE BEST WILL DO.

JAMPRO ANTENNAS, INC.

(916) 383-1177

Shively Laboratories Inc. 86 Harrison Rd., Bridgton, Me. 04009. (207) 647-3327. FAX: (207) 647-8273. Charles Peabody, VP mktg; Robert A. Surette, mgr RF engr; Jonathan R. Clark, mktg mgr.
FM bcstg antennas, rigid coax, diplexers & combiners, RF filters & pressurization units.

Shook Electronics, USA Inc. Bldg. 200, 18975 Marbach Ln., San Antonio, 78266. (512) 651-5700. FAX: (512) 651-5220. Edwin L. Shook, pres & CEO; Ron Crockett, exec VP.
Mobile TV prod, ENG & SNV vehicles. Rack ready or turnkey delivery.

Shotmaker Dollies & Cranes. 28145 Ave. Crocker, Valencia, Calif. 91355. (818) 761-5414. FAX: (818) 761-5455. Rick Dinkel, exec VP/gen mgr.
Panther camera dollies, cranes, jib arms & track.

Shure Brothers Inc. 222 Hartrey Ave., Evanston, Ill. 60202. (708) 866-2200. S.N. Shure, chmn bd; J.H. Kogen, pres; R. Gilbert, VP sls; N. Calvert, mktg communications mgr.
Cabled & wireless microphones, automatic microphone systems, field prod equipment, sound reinforcement systems, teleconferencing systems.

Siecor Corp. Box 489 Siecor Park, Hickory, N.C. 28603. (704) 327-5000. FAX: (704) 327-5973. Joseph D. Hicks, pres/CEO; S. Lyons, CATV sls mgr.
Manufacture optical fiber cables & accessories for video, data & voice communication applications.

Siemens Audio Inc. 7 Parklawn Dr., Bethel, Conn. 06801. (203) 744-6230. FAX: (203) 792-7863. Michael Mayrobnig, exec VP.
Manufacture analog & digital recording for the bcst, video post-prod, film & mus recording & mastering industries.

Sierra Automated Systems & Engineering Corp. 2112 N. Glenoaks Blvd. Burbank, Calif. 91504. (818) 840-6749. FAX: (818) 840-6751. Edward O. Fritz, pres; Al Salci, VP; Giovanni Morales, gen mgr.
Audio switching & mixing systems maunufacturer. Mix-Minus/IFB, satellite distribution & switching, automated switching & distribution, studio intercom, on-air routing & teleconferencing.

Sifford Video Services Inc. Box 101510, 121 Lyle Ln., Nashville 37210. (615) 248-1010. FAX: (615) 244-5712. Gary Comstubble, pres; Lawson Turk, VP.
Hollywood, Fla. 33020: 2815 Evans St. (305) 920-5054. FAX: (305) 920-0059. Carole Williams.
Video tape duplication; standards conversion & distribution; specialized packaging; custom work.

Sigma Electronics Inc. Box 448, East Petersburg, Pa. 17520-0448. (717) 569-2681. FAX: (717) 569-4056. Oong Choi, pres; Bob Hivner, gen mgr.
Chino Valley, Ariz. 86323: Western Regional Office, Box 417. (602) 636-0228. Kent Porter, VP mktg.
Terminal equipment for professional TV studio: distribution; routing switchers & test & sync signals.

Signal Monitoring Service. Box 208, Mt. Vernon, Ohio 43050. (614) 397-5643. Robert (Bob) Bowman, own/operator.

Simplicity Tool Corp./SITCO. Box 20456, 10330 N.E. Marx St., Portland, Ore. 97220-1139. (503) 253-2000. FAX: (503) 253-2009. Gustave Berliner, pres; Markus Burcker, VP.
CATV, MATV antennas.

Sinar Bron Inc. 17 Progress St., Edison, N.J. 08820. (908) 754-5800. FAX: (908) 754-5807. Michael Mayer, pres; William D. Andrews, VP.
Pro-Cyc prefabricated coves for infiniti wall in video & photo studios & studio lighting/ HMI.

Sinclair Imaging Systems. 871 Mountain Ave., Springfield, N.J. 07081. (201) 376-1272. FAX: (201) 376-0903. George Sinclair, pres.
Still photo transmission, electric picture mgmt systems & weather satellite systems.

Equipment Manufacturers and Distributors

Singer Products Inc. 1840 W. 49th St., Suite 402, Hialeah, Fla. 33012. (305) 558-3000. FAX: (305) 558-2801. Jaime Rojas, chmn.
AM/FM transmitters, audio/video & TV equipment mobile microwave communications, fiber optics, cables, instrumentation.

Skotel Corp. 3730 Matte Blvd., Brossard, Que., Canada J4Y 2Z2. (514) 444-2088; (800) 361-4999 (USA). FAX: (514) 444-2083. Stephen Scott, pres; Joyce Scott, sls coord; Pardo Vitulli, customer svcs.
Time & film code readers & generators; VBI data communications.

Snell & Wilcox Inc. 1289 Hammerwood Ave., Sunnyvale, Calif. 94089. (408) 734-1688. FAX: (408) 734-4760. Halfon Hamaoui, CFO.
Petersfield, Hampshire, UK GU33 5AZ: Snell & Wilcox Ltd., Durford Mill. 44-0-730-821-188; 44-0-730-821-199. David Youlton, chmn; David Lambert, gen mgr.
Standards converters (from phase correlation motion detection to 2-field), test pattern generators, decoders, encoders, time base correctors, color correctors.

Software Specialists Inc. 1037 Rt. 173, Caledonia, Ill. 61011. (815) 885-3500. FAX: (815) 399-8148. Audrey L. Zeifelhofer, pres.
Bcstg sls traffic & accounting software package. Custom computer progmg.

Solid State Logic Inc. 320 W. 46th St., New York 10036. (212) 315-1111. FAX: (212) 315-0251. Piers Plaskitt, CEO.
Los Angeles 90028: 6255 Sunset Blvd. (213) 463-4444. Phil Wagner, VP western opns.
Automated audio consoles for mus, audio postprod, bcst & film. Digital audio work stations.

Solutec Ltd. (H.A.). 4360 D'Iberville St., Montreal, Que., Canada H2H 2L8. (514) 522-8960. FAX: (514) 598-7808. Gilles Fortin, pres.
Automated bcstg systems; audio level meter color keyed in video; audio distribution amplifier.

Sonex Acoustical Products. (A division of Illbruck Inc.) 3800 Washington Ave. N., Minneapolis 55412. (612) 520-3620. FAX: (612) 521-5639. Russell Leighton, division mgr; Eric Johnson, natl sls mgr.
Acoustical treatment or soundproofing of bcst studios.

Sono-Mag Corporation (SMC). 1833 W. Hovey Ave., Normal, Ill. 61761. (309) 452-5313. FAX: (309) 452-2521. William E. Moulic Jr., pres; Jon A. Housour, VP; Thomas D. Rousey, VP; A.W. Mapel, sec/treas.
Bcst automation systems, using carousels, compact disc multi-players & DAT players. Computer-assisted bcst equipment.

Sontec Electronics. Audio Dr., Goldbond, Va. 24094. (703) 626-7256. FAX: (703) 626-7257. Burgess Macneal, pres.
Audio processing & disc mastering; parts & svc for ITI audio equipment.

Sony Corp. of America. 123 W. Tryon, Teaneck, N.J. 07666. (201) 833-5200. FAX: (201) 833-5850. C.F. Taylor, VP.
Paramus, N.J. 07652: 15 Essex Rd. (201) 368-5111. C.C. Taylor, rgnl mgr.
Lanham, Md. 20706: 9001 Business Pkwy. (301) 577-9080. D. Doherty, rgnl mgr.
Norcross, Ga. 30071: 3175A Northwoods Pkwy. (404) 263-8015. R. Bowers, rgnl mgr.
Irving, Tex. 75063-2658: 3201 Premier, Suite 100. (214) 550-5303. N. Nicholson, rgnl mgr.
Itasca, Ill. 60143: 1200 N. Arlington Heights Rd. (708) 773-6046. T. Younce, rgnl mgr.
Burbank, Calif. 91505: 2820 W. Olive Ave., Suite A. (818) 841-8711. Tom Deyo, rgnl mgr.
San Jose, Calif. 95135: 655 River Oaks Pkwy. (408) 432-9191. Dave Stuart, rgnl mgr.
Boulder, Colo. 80301: 5665 Flatirons Pkwy. (303) 444-0016. D. Urry, rgnl mgr.
Bcst cameras, camcorders, editors, monitors, 1/2" & 1" VTRs, digital VTRs, multicassette systems & switchers.

Sound Designers Studio. 424 W. 45th St., New York 10036-3565. (212) 757-5679. FAX: (212) 265-1250. Gene Perla, mgr.
Electronic equipment racking systems, console automation systems & digital recording facilities.

Sound Technology Inc. 1190 Dell Ave., Suite G, Campbell, Calif. 95008. (408) 378-6540. FAX: (408) 378-6847. Sonny Funke, gen mgr.
Audio & acoustical test equipment.

Soundcraft. Box 2200, JBL Professional, 8500 Balboa Blvd., Northridge, Calif. 91329. (818) 893-8411. David Kimm, dir Soundcraft/Electronics Group; Ed Bigger, sls mgr.
Audio mixing consoles for recording, theatre, concert sound reinforcement & bcstg.

Soundforms International. Box 150431, San Rafael, Calif. 94915. (415) 455-9704. FAX: (415) 455-9705. Phil Neal, Spencer Nilsen, owns.
Portable, lightweight, modular sound control systems for bldg sound booths, walls or free-standing gobos.

Soundtracs, PLC. 91 Ewell Rd., Surbiton, Surrey, UK KT6 6AH. 081-399-3392; 081-390-8101. FAX: 081-399-6821; 081-390-9918. Todd Wells, mgng dir; John Carroll, sls & mktg dir; John Stadius, tech.
Glenrothes, Scotland KY7 4PA: Unit 0 (East), Baird Rd., Eastfield IND.EST. 0592-630499. FAX: 0592-630236.
Audio mixing consoles & Tracmix 2 automation system.

Southern Broadcast Services. Box 740, 210 Hillwood Park S., Alabaster, Ala. 35007. (205) 663-7108. FAX: (205) 663-7108.
Tower erection, antenna instal & maintenance svcs.

Southwest Frequency Measurements. 11508 Big Trail, Austin, Tex. 78759. (512) 345-5931. Ben F. Green, operator; Frieda M. Green, sec.

Spatial Technologies Inc. 801 N. La Brea Ave., Suite 104, Hollywood, Calif. 90038-3340. (213) 772-8425. FAX: (818) 592-0987. Daniel L. Symmes, pres.
Provides 3-D bcst TV processes. Supplies equipment, consultation & 3-D glasses.

Specialized Communication. 907 Maryland Ave., Hagerstown, Md. 21740. (301) 790-0103. FAX: (301) 790-0173. David Linetsky, svc mgr.
Ind svc ctr providing warranty & non-warranty svc on bcst video tape machines.

Spector Entertainment Group Inc. 6349 Palomar Oaks Ct., Carlsbad, Calif. 92009-1428. (619) 438-9080. FAX: (619) 438-0968. TWX: 182076 VSA TBI. Eric M. Spector, exec VP; Evan M. Spector, VP opns.
Offers international audio, video & data communications between U.S., Canada, Mexico & Latin America; private TV nets; 12 C-band transportable uplinks.

Spectra Sonics. 3750 Airport Rd., Ogden, Utah 84405. (801) 392-7531. William G. Dilley, pres; Gregory D. Dilley, VP.
Professional audio prod, including; power amplifiers, compressors, limiters, portable speaker system, mixers & line/distribution amplifiers.

Spectrum. 803 Forest Ridge, Suite 108, Bedford, Tex. 76022. (800) 628-0088. FAX: (817) 354-8445. Doug Sherar, sls mgr.
Full line supplier for headend, distribution, drop materials & audio/video equipment.

Sprague Magnetics Inc. 15720 Stagg St., Van Nuys, Calif. 91406. (818) 994-6602; (800) 553-8712. FAX: (818) 994-2153. Dorothy Sprague, pres; John Austin, VP.
Long-wearing cart, film, reel-to-reel tape heads, refurbishment svcs, replacement parts, alignment tapes & accessories.

Sprint Tele Media. 6600 College Blvd., Suite 310, Overland Park, Kan. 66211. (800) 735-5900. FAX: (913) 661-8008. Adrian Toader, VP/gen mgr; Nick Sample, dir natl sls; Ralph Reed, dir mktg/new business dev.
Interactive voice & fax svcs, used for polling, proms & productivity enhancement.

Stage Equipment & Lighting Inc. 12231 N.E. 13th Ct., Miami, Fla. 33161. (305) 891-2010. FAX: (305) 893-2828. Vivian Gill, pres; Michael Grosz, VP; Rick Rudolph, VP.
Orlando, Fla. 32811: 4600 S.W. 36th St. (407) 425-2010. FAX: (407) 648-2604. Mike Collins, tech consultant.
Film, video, theatrical lighting, grip & related support equipment.

Stahl Metal Products Division, The Scott & Fetzer Co. 3201 W. Lincoln Way, Wooster, Ohio 44691. (216) 264-7441. FAX: (216) 264-0891. Bob McBride, pres; Steve Denison, sls mgr.
Cardington, Ohio 43315: (419) 864-6871. Robert Sparks, plant mgr.
Durant, Okla. 74701: (405) 924-5575. David Norman, plant mgr.
Merced, Calif. 95340: (209) 383-4336.

DATELINE:
ATHENS BEIJING DAMASCUS DETROIT SARAJEVO TEL AVIV

When photographers cover news-breaking stories involving drugs, hostages, terrorism, international or home-town street wars...life-threatening conditions exist!

Second Chance body armor, industry leader with over 575 documented 'saves' of American law officers wearing their product, offers their street-wise and battlefield ballistic technology and their manufacturing capabilities to news reporters and news photographers.

- FLEXIBLE
- LIGHTWEIGHT
- WORKABLE
- DEPENDABLE

Call or write today for more information on this opportunity to inVEST in safety!

SECOND CHANCE
P.O.Box 578
Central Lake, MI 49622
800-253-7090
FAX: 616-544-9824

Equipment Manufacturers and Distributors

Stainless Inc./SG Communications.
Stainless Inc., 210 S. 3rd St., North Wales, Pa. 19454. (215) 699-4871. FAX: (215) 699-9597. Eugene F. Stluka, pres; John L. Windle, VP. Design, fabrication & erection of TV, radio & microwave towers. Tower inspection & maintenance, engrg studies, modifications, HDTV analysis.
SG Communications Services, Box 76269, Atlanta 30358-1269. (404) 824-7865; (404) 475-0247. William T. Rushton, pres; Daniel E. Ferguson, VP sls & mktg. Turnkey tower svcs, maintenance, erection, system design, antenna installation, reharness, HDTV planning, surveys, modifications, strobe/lighting systems.

Stancil Corp. 2644 S. Croddy Way, Santa Ana, Calif. 92704. (714) 546-2002; (800) 782-6245. FAX: (714) 546-2092. Michael D. Custer, CEO.
Voice logging recorders, multichannel, 1 to 64 tracks, 24-hour recording time.

Standard Communications Corp. Box 92151, Los Angeles 90009. (310) 532-5300. FAX: (310) 515-7197. Mark Thomas, pres.
Rebcst satellite TV receivers & cable headend products.

Standard Frequency Measuring Service 2092 Arrowood Pl., Cincinnati 45231. (513) 851-4964. Louis A. Williams Jr., P.E., consulting engr; Pat Williams, office mgr.

Stanton Magnetics Inc. 101 Sunnyside Blvd., Plainview, N.Y. 11803. (516) 349-0235. FAX: (516) 349-0230. Walter O. Stanton, pres; Pete Bidwell, VP professional products; Jean Kapen, mgr adv & prom.
Professional cartridges & styli for the recording & bcst industries, including announcers earphone & preamplifier.

Stantron. (A division of Zero Enclosures) 12224 Montague St., Pacoima, Calif. 91331. (818) 890-3445. FAX: (818) 890-4460. Jack Frickle, gen mgr.
Modular video center desks, consoles, cabinets, racks for video prod & postprod dubbing & editing.

Star Case Manufacturing Co. Inc. 648 Superior, Munster, Ind. 46321. (219) 922-4440; (800) 822-STAR. FAX: (219) 922-4442. Dennis Toma, pres; Ralph G. Hoopes, VP.
Flight cases (protective casement); Carry Star, ATA Star, Super Star, Ultra Star, EM5

Starliner Mobile Video. 525 Mildred Ave., Primos, Pa. 19018. (215) 626-6500. FAX: (215) 626-2638. Stan Leshner, VP mobile svcs.
48' mobile unit with Ikegami 323 & 323P cameras; Chyron 4100EXB; A42 & A53 & Sony 1" VTRs; & BVW 75's. Available in U.S. & Canada.

State Labs Inc. Bldg. 50, Brooklyn Navy Yard, Brooklyn, N.Y. 11205. (718) 486-5900. FAX: (718) 237-2050. Sender Deautsch, chmn/pres; Jay Deautsch, sec/treas.
Electronic tubes, semiconductors, diodes, Klystrons, transistors, integrated circuits, CRTs, magnetrons.

Steenbeck Inc. 9554 Vassar Ave., Chatsworth, Calif. 91311. (818) 998-4033. FAX: (818) 998-6992. H. McCall, chmn of bd; W. Bass, pres; D. Macaulay, sec; R.C. Macaulay, treas, Bob Campos, sls mgr.
Motion picture film editing tables with capability to transfer film to video.

Stellar Communications. Box 1120, 227 S. Vann, Vinita, Okla. 74301. (918) 256-7883. FAX: (918) 256-2558. Tom Snow, pres; Kevin Gajavn, VP opns.
Engineer, manufacture & install of guyed & self-supporting towers for AM, FM, TV, MW & cellular.

Michael Stevens & Partners Ltd. Invicta Works, Elliot Rd., Bromley, Kent, England BR2 9NT. 081-460-7299. FAX: 081-460-0499. Michael Stevens, mgng dir.
Professional audio equipment for the audio & video bcst industries.

Stoner Communications Inc. 300 8th St., Lakeside, Ore. 97449-9634. (503) 759-3103. FAX: (503) 759-3206. Elwood Cousins, pres.
AM & sw radio receivers & antennas.

Storeel Corp. Box 80523, Atlanta 30341. (404) 458-3280. FAX: (404) 457-5585. Carolyn S. Galvin, pres; R.D. Lauter, sls mgr.
Woodland Hills, Calif. 91364: 4608 Coyle Pl. (818) 346-9722. William Johnston, sls rep.
Allentown, Pa. 18102: 132 N. 11th St. (215) 437-2251. Kent Kjellgren, sls rep.
Woburn Mass. 01801: Multi Comm. 54 Cummings Park, Suite 314. (617) 932-0298. Matthew J. Bellomo, sls rep.
Van Nuys Calif. 91402: MT&T. 14417 Chase St., Suite 331. (818) 781-1500. Penelope Russell, sls rep.
Space efficient storage for all formats of tape & film; double-drive systems for longer lengths; set-up trucks; CD storage.

Peter Storer & Associates Inc. 11019 N. Towne Sq. Rd., Suite 7, Mequon, Wis. 53092. (414) 241-9005. FAX: (414) 241-9036. Peter Storer, pres.
Program Manager System - micro-computer system, full turnkey, instal & training, includes prog analysis, film amortization, scheduling, episode usage & rating info.

Strand Lighting Inc. 18111 S. Sante Fe Ave., Rancho Dominguez, Calif. 90221. (310) 637-7500. FAX: (310) 632-5519. Jim Griffith, pres.
Studio & remote lighting & control equipment.

Strata Marketing. 540 N. Lake Shore Dr., Chicago 60611. (312) 222-1555. FAX: (312) 222-2510. Bruce Johnson, pres; Roger Skolnik, VP; Marianne Dollear, dir opns.
Computer software for quantitative & qualitative radio, TV & nwspr media.

Strong International. c/o Ballantyne of Omaha Inc., 4350 McKinley St., Omaha, Neb. 68112. (402) 453-4444. FAX: (402) 453-7238. R.H. Echtenkamp, pres; John P. Wilmers, VP.
35/70mm projection equipment, xenon lamphouse systems, platters, xenon bulbs, follow spotlights.

Digital Audio Workstation
50 Simultaneous Stereo Segment Playback
2-Dimensional Project Creation - No Tracks!
-110dB Noise Floor

Turn To: **Micro Technology Unlimited**

Studer Editech. 1370 Willow Rd., Menlo Park, Calif. 94025. (415) 326-7030. FAX: (415) 326-7039. Guy W. McNally, CEO; Gerry Kearby, VP sls & mktg.
Disc-based digital audio recording & editing systems for prod & postprod applications.

Studer Editech Corp. 1865 Air Lane Dr., Suite 12, Nashville 37210. (615) 391-3399. FAX: (615) 391-5974. Bill Muggler, exec VP; Doug Beard, dir tech & mktg svc; Thomas M. Jenny, VP/gen mgr.
New York 10036: 1120 Ave. of the Americas. (212) 626-6734. Thorsteinn Thorsteinsson.
Van Nuys, Calif. 91406: 16102 Hart St. (818) 780-4234. Vencil Wells, western rgnl mgr.
Bcst audio recorders, TV audio consoles, Dyaxis Digital Audio workstns, SMPTE synchronizing equipment, telephone interfaces, amplifiers & speakers.

Studio Technologies Inc. 5520 W. Touhy Ave., Skokie, Ill. 60077. (708) 676-9177. FAX: (708) 982-0747. Gordon Kapes, pres.
Microphone pre-amplifiers, stereo simulators & recognition units, telephone & hard-wired IFB communications systems. Matrix switchers for digital audio workstations.

Studio Technology. Pennsylvania Ave., Suite 4, Malvern, Pa. 19355. (215) 640-1229. FAX: (215) 640-5880. Vince Fiola, dir.
Bcst furniture; design & instal svcs.

Subito Studios. 367 N. Hwy. 101, Solana Beach, Calif. 92075. (619) 259-9339. FAX: (619) 755-6562. Cam MacMillan, own/exec prod.
Design & prod of bcst 3-D computer graphics. Logo animation, stn packages. All tape formats supported. Prods of Subito Studio Video Graphic Library.

Summit Software Systems Inc. 1966 13th St., Suite 200, Boulder, Colo. 80302. (303) 443-9866. FAX: (303) 443-9934. Paul Adams, pres.
PC-based traf, sls, billing, accounts receivable, accounts payable, payroll & gen ledger for single or multi-stns & single or multi-users.

Superior Electronics Group Inc. 6432 Parkland Dr., Sarasota, Fla. 34243. (813) 756-6000. FAX: (813) 758-3800. Chris Krehmeyer, pres; Brett Price, dir opns.
Automated remote test equipment; 40 Mhz to 1 Ghz for cable & TV industry.

Superior Satellite Engineers. 2320 Sierra Meadows, Rocklin, Calif. 95677. (916) 624-8214. FAX: (916) 624-9146. Doyle G. Catlett, own/mgr.
Complete satellite antenna systems & svc for cable & bcst TV.

Swager Communications Inc. Box 569, Angola, Ind. 46703. (219) 495-5165. FAX: (219) 495-4205. Dan J. Swager, pres; Lee Swager, VP; Tim Swager, sec/treas.
Designs, fabricates, installs & maintains AM, FM, TV, CATV & microwave communication towers.

Swintek Enterprises Inc. 965 Shulman Ave., Santa Clara, Calif. 95050. (408) 727-4889. FAX: (408) 727-3025. William P. Swintek, pres.
Wireless headsets & radio microphones.

Switchcraft Inc. 5555 N. Elston Ave., Chicago 60630. (312) 631-1234. FAX: (312) 792-2129. Keith A. Bandolik, pres; William M. Pagett, dir sls; William Coulter, dir mktg; Barbara Higgens, mgr mktg communications.
Plugs, audio/video patchcords & panels, jacks, audio/video accessories, cable assemblies, switches & din connectors.

Symetrix Inc. 4211 24th Ave. W., Seattle 98199. (206) 282-2555. FAX: (206) 283-5504. Jon Bosaw, pres/dir sls & mfg; Walt Lowery, customer svc.
Digital & analog audio signal processing. Telephone interface devices.

Synchronous Communications Inc. 1885 Lundy Ave., Suite 102, San Jose, Calif. 95131. (408) 943-0222. FAX: (408) 943-0269. Albert R. Johnson, pres.
Fiber optic video links for bcst & CATV use. FDM up to 24 video chs per fiber.

Stainless, inc.
sg communications
A Stainless Company

Looking for Answers?
We Can Help!

HDTV Planning Study

Stainless/SG is a Turnkey Tower Service Co. Specializing in:
- System Design
- Structural Analysis
- Engineering Studies
- Project Management
- Tower Fabrication
- Full Service Maintenance
- Lighting Systems
- Inspections/Surveys

24 Hour Emergency Service
17 Service Locations Nationwide

Expect The Best for All Your Tower Needs Call Today!

1-800-824-7865

Equipment Manufacturers and Distributors

Syrcuits International Inc. Box 514, Liverpool, N.Y. 13088. (315) 451-7200. FAX: (315) 652-2418. Jack E. Weller, pres.
Matrix System (addressable trap system), addressable converter descrambler system, SPS Positive Scrambler, basic add-on descramblers.

System Associates. Box 3631, Culver City, Calif. 90231. (310) 836-1111. FAX: (310) 836-5996. Billy H. Seidel, pres; Walter A. Shubin, VP.
Used bcst TV equipment.

Systemation Corporation. 337 N. Water St., Decatur, Ill. 62523. (217) 428-9744. FAX: (217) 423-9744. Steve Bellinger, pres; Monte Throneburg, VP software dev; Robert Wille, plant mgr; Bernie Brobst, sls mgr.
Broken Hill, Australia: (61) 808-8188. David Tunkin.
Digital or analog automation, remotes, telephone audio storage & retrieval, sls tracking, logging & invoicing for radio/TV.

T

TALX Corporation. 1850 Borman Ct., St. Louis 63146. (314) 434-0046. FAX: (314) 434-9205. William W. Canfield, pres; Gary Lowe, Michael E. Smith, John E. Tubbesing, VPs.
Boston 02109: 10 Post Office Sq., Suite 600S. (617) 423-4231. Michael G. George, rgnl acct mgr.
Irvine, Calif., 92715: 4199 Campus Dr., Suite 550. (714) 725-9335. Ron Metrakos, rgnl acct mgr.
Interactive voice response.

CABLESCAN
SIMPLY THE FINEST MEDIA SALES
SOFTWARE AVAILABLE.
FROM TAPSCAN, INNOVATORS
IN SALES PRESENTATION
SOFTWARE FOR NEARLY
A DECADE.

TAPSCAN
INCORPORATED

3000 RIVERCHASE GALLERIA, SUITE 850
BIRMINGHAM, ALABAMA 35244
205-987-7456

TAPSCAN Inc. 3000 Riverchase Galleria, Suite 850, Birmingham, Ala. 35244. (205) 987-7456. FAX: (205) 733-6263. Jim Christian, chmn/CEO; Dave Carlisle, pres/COO.
Manhatten Beach, Calif. 90266: 1112 Ocean Dr., Suite 301. (310) 376-6242.
Waltham, Mass. 02154: 1601 Trapelo Rd. (617) 890-1901.
Chicago 60611: 980 N. Michigan Ave., Suite 1400. (312) 642-8985.
Toronto, Ont., Canada M2N 6C6: 5075 Yonge St., Suite 404. (416) 221-9944.
Vancouver, B.C., Canada V5R 5W2: 3665 Kingsway, Suite 300. (604) 439-0087.
Software for electronic media, primarily radio & TV, designed to address the needs of media selling, buying, planning, progmg & mgmt.

T.C. Electronic of Denmark. c/o Virtual Designs Ltd., 717 Lakefield Rd., Suite C, Westlake Village, Calif. 91361. (805) 373-1828. FAX: (805) 379-2648. Edward G. Simeone, U.S. mgng dir; Bob Rufkahr, natl sls mgr; Vince Basse, bcst sls.
AES/EBU test equipment, digital signal procsessors, programmable one-third octave equalizers, high resolution digital delays.

T-C Specialties Co. Box 192, Coudersport, Pa. 16915. (814) 274-8060; (800) 458-6074. FAX: (814) 274-0690. Daniel C. Major, pres; Bill Crown, VP prod; Judy Tucker, sls.
Coupon billing systems & related software; mail presort/barcoding; custom textile silkscreening.

TCI: Tele-Communications Inc. 5619 Denver Tech Pkwy., Englewood, Colo. 80111-3000. Box 5630, Denver CO 80217. (303) 267-5500. Larry Romrell, pres; Robert Lemming, exec VP; Russ Johnson, VP engrg; Chris C. Thomas, VP opns; Ben Summers, dir net dev.
Microwave for net TV & radio carrier's carrier, transportable uplinks & downlinks, permanent instals, govt svcs, remote site voice & data svcs.

TDK Electronics Corp. 12 Harbor Park Dr., Port Washington, N.Y. 11050. (516) 625-0100. FAX: (516) 625-0171. Takashi Tsujii, pres.

TE Consulting Inc. 18 Michael Rd., Framingham, Mass. 01701. (508) 877-6494; (800) 832-8353. FAX: (508) 788-0324. E.O. Tunmann, pres.
Studio automation, coml insertion, HDTV video stereo audio matrix routing equipment, video remote access system.

TEAC America Inc. 7733 Telegraph Rd., Montebello, Calif. 90640. (213) 726-0303. FAX: (213) 727-7656. Norio Tamura, pres; Gary S. Beckerman, exec VP; Hajime Yamaguchi, sr VP.
Consumer audio/video & professional recording equipment, airborne video recorder, instrumentation data recorders, computer peripherals/floppy disks, tape backup & industrial optical disk recorders & playback.

TECH-SA-PORT. Box 5295, 120 S. Whitfield St., Pittsburgh 15206-5295. (412) 661-1620. FAX: (413) 361-5103. Lewis J. Scheinman, pres.
Computer & electronic equipment cleaning supplies, including lint-free wipers, contamination-free chemicals & spray dusters.

TELEPAK San Diego. 4783 Ruffner St., San Diego 92111. (619) 268-8559. FAX: (619) 268-1790. Linda Stepp, mgr.
Soft carrying cases custom-designed to manufacturer's equipment specifications.

T.F.T. Inc. 3090 Oakmead Village Dr., Santa Clara, Calif. 95051. (408) 727-7272; (800) 347-3383. FAX: (408) 727-5942. Joseph C. Wu, pres; Darryl E. Parker, dir mktg; Perry Kirk, domestic sls; Vivian Marinko, rgnl sls mgr.
Digital & analog STLs, reciters & synchronous boosters, modulation monitors, RPU, EBS.

3M. Bldg 223-3N-01, 3M Ctr., St. Paul, Minn. 55144-1000. (612) 733-1110. Ted F. Colangelo, sls & mktg mgr.
Columbus, Ohio 43229: 6530 Singletree Dr. (614) 885-3310. Richard S. Armstrong, sls mgr.
Stormscope Weather Mapping Systems — passive thunderstorm detection & avoidance instrument.

360 Systems. 18740 Oxnard St., Suite 302, Tarzana, Calif. 91356. (818) 342-3127. FAX: (818) 342-4372. Robert Easton, pres; Don Bird, gen mgr.
Digital audio recorders/reproducers, audio routing switchers.

TM Century Inc. 2002 Academy, Dallas 75234. (800) 937-2100. FAX: (800) 749-2121. Craig Turner, CEO/pres.
CD software; digicart; digital studion systems; autosegue; TV prod; jingles.

TOA Electronics Inc. 601 Gateway, Suite 300, South San Francisco 94080. (415) 588-2538. FAX: (415) 588-3349. Mr. Nishiyama, pres.
Sound & communication equipment for coml sound & MI industries.

TSM Inc. 709 Executive Blvd., Valley Cottage, N.Y. 10989. (914) 268-0100. FAX: (914) 268-0113. Robert Gonnelli, pres; Gary Rotondelli, mktg mgr.
Sun Valley, Calif. 91352-4022: 8115-B Clybourn Ave. (818) 767-0306; (818) 767-0772. Glenn Sakata, western rgnl sls mgr.
Sunrise, Fla. 33351: 10208 N.W. 47th St. (305) 572-4344. Robert Polan, southern rgnl sls mgr.
Remote camera control systems. Pneumatic studio pedestals, pan & tilt heads, lightweight tripods & heads.

TT Technologies Inc. 1771 Mallette Rd., Aurora, Ill. 60505. (708) 851-8200. FAX: (708) 851-8299. Chris Brahler, pres; Dave Holcomb, VP.
Grundomat; Grundoram.

T and T Tower Services. 6924 Cleveland Ave., Lincoln, Neb. 68507. (402) 466-8007. FAX: (402) 489-4210. Ralph M. Tomjack, gen mgr.
Tower svcs include painting, erections & inspections.

TTE Inc. 2251 Barry Ave., Los Angeles 90064-1400. (800) 776-7614. FAX: (800) 473-2791. Stephen J. Sodaro, VP sls & mktg.
LC filters to 3000 MHz, balun & matching transformers, combiners, active filters to 1 mhz. RF & microwave filters DC-3000 MHz, video splitters.

TV/Com International. 16516 Via Esprillo, San Diego 92127. (619) 451-1500. FAX: (619) 451-1505. Hank Hanselaar, pres/CEO; Anthony J. Wechselberger, exec VP; Todd Easterling, dir mktg; Mark Brady, VP sls.
Addressable systems & converter/decoders for CATV & decorders for satellite systems & digital compression products.

TV Data. 3201 N.E. Loop 820, Suite 150, Fort Worth, Tex. 76137. (817) 847-0980. FAX: (800) 736-3885. Robert Newell, COO; Anna Addison, opns dir.
International supplier of TV listings for publications.

Taber Mfg. & Engr. Co. 13230 Evening Creek Dr. S., Suite 208, San Diego 92128. (619) 679-2015. FAX: (415) 858-2302. Veldon F. Leverich, pres.
Audio & video replacement heads & refurbishment, metal tape degaussers, standard tape degaussers, radio & TV stn systems; design & consulting.

Talk-a-Phone Co. 5013 N. Kedzie Ave., Chicago 60625. (312) 539-1100. FAX: (312) 539-1241. S. Shanes, exec VP; Dan F. Kagan, sls mgr.
Intercommunication systems.

Tamron Industries Inc. Box 388, 99 Seaview Blvd., Port Washington, N.Y. 11050. (516) 484-8880. FAX: (516) 484-8906. Hank Nagashima, pres; John Van Steenberg, eastern sls mgr; Brad Swain, western sls mgr.
Lenses for 35mm SLR cameras & still projectors, CCTV lenses, ENG lenses, Fotovix film video processors & camcorders.

Tannoy/TGI North America Inc. 300 Gage Ave., Unit #1, Kitchener, Ont., Canada N2M 2C8. (519) 745-1158. FAX: (519) 745-2364. Bill Calma, mktg mgr.
Tannoy reference audio monitors. Bruel & Kjear series 4000 professional microphones.

Tape Storage Systems (Tripp Comm. Sales). Box 5267, Walnut Creek, Calif. 94596. (510) 256-6006. FAX: (510) 256-6007. Ted Tripp, pres; R.H. Kearns, gen mgr.
Cabinets & shelving storage for; audio, video & DAT Tape, CDs, CD-ROM, Denon, Bernoulli & opticals.

Tapeswitch Corp. of America. 100 Schmitt Blvd., Farmingdale, N.Y. 11735. (516) 694-6312. FAX: (516) 694-6304. John O'Meara, pres; Ed Duhon, VP; Phyllis Rampulla, adv mgr.
Safety light curtains, sensing mats, edges, ribbon switches, electronic zone controllers, sensing bumpers, safety & protection equipment.

Teatronics International Inc. (TII). 3183 Duncan Rd., San Luis Obispo, Calif. 93401. (805) 544-3555. Tom Henderson, pres.
Dallas 95229: Box 781211. (214) 247-1077. Frank Scarlata, VP sls & mktg
Lighting control & power distribution systems for stage, studio & remote applications.

Tech Laboratories Inc. 500 10th St., Palisades Park, N.J. 07650. (201) 944-2221. FAX: (201) 944-1653. Berna Miciongoli, pres; Earl M. Bjorndal, VP.
Attenuators: rotary, fixed balanced/unbalanced ladder, pi, etc; rotary swithces; electrical & electronical subcontract.

Technet Systems Group
A Division of Steve Vanni Associates, Inc.
Broadcast Equipment   Turn-keyed Systems
P.O. Box 422   Tel: 603-483-5365
Auburn, N.H. 03032   Fax: 603-483-0512

Technet Systems Group. (A division of Steve Vanni Associates Inc.) Box 422, Auburn, N.H. 03032. (603) 483-5365. FAX: (603) 483-0512. Steve Vanni, mgr sls division; Bob Smith, mgr instal division; Kim Meisinger, mgr tower division.

Equipment Manufacturers and Distributors

Sandown N.H. 03873: Box 225. (603) 887-5858. Joe Soucise, mgr.
Bcst equipment supplier & distributor for radio & TV, specializing in complete turnkey packages including planning, design, equipment, instal, towers & FCC licensing.

Technical Projects Inc. Box 3247, Barrington, Ill. 60010. (800) 562-5872. FAX: (708) 381-4360. Glenn Mullis, pres; Sibbelina Mullis, sec.
Headset intercom communications, master stns, power supplies, headsets for video cameras, transceiver adaptor.

Technichrome. 701 Desert Ln., Suite 4, Las Vegas 89106. (702) 386-2844. FAX: (702) 388-1250. Nigel Macrae, pres.
Audio/video cartridges, jack panels & accessories, tape evaluators & video tape.

Techni-Tool Inc. 5 Apollo Rd., Plymouth Meeting, Pa. 19462. (215) 825-4990. FAX: (215) 828-5623. Paul Weiss, pres; Stuart Weiss, VP; William Bezar, gen mgr.
Hand tools, kits & eases; solder & desolder equipment; ESD products; cleanroom products.

Technology Service Corp. 2950 31st St., Santa Monica, Calif. 90405. (310) 450-9755. FAX: (310) 452-3175. Raymond Durand, mgr coml opns.
Weather presentation systems.

Tectan Inc. Box 271872, 1900 Bates Ave., Suite J, Concord, Calif. 94527. (510) 798-2222. FAX: (510) 798-2224. Paul A. Rivard, pres; Robert J. Nowacek, VP.
Designs & manufactures RBDS equipment & high performance audio transmission equipment. Products include frequency agile subcarrier systems for TV audio, SCPC systems for radio nets & RBDS encoders.

Tekskil Industries Inc. 108-15290-103A Ave., Surrey, B.C., Canada V3R 7A2. (604) 589-1100. FAX: (604) 589-1185. John Veenstra, pres; Rick Jones, VP.
Teleprompters: electronic & computer.

Tektronix Inc. Box 500, Mail Stn. 58-699, Beaverton, Ore. 97077. (503) 627-1555. FAX: (503) 627-5801. Dan Castles, VP/gen mgr Television Division; Austin Basso, dir sls & mktg; Larry Harrington, TV measurments & processing business unit mgr; Margaret Craig, TV displays & RF/cable business unit mgr.
Manufacture test & measurement equipment for audio, bcst, cable & telecommunications industries. Sls offices located in Santa Clara, Calif. (408-496-0800); Englewood, Colo. (303-799-1000); Gaithersburg, Md. (301-948-7151); Lexington, Mass. (617-861-6800); Irvine, Calif. (714-660-8080); Huntsville, Ala. (205-830-9212); Irving, Tex. (214-401-1666); Norcross, Ga. (404-449-4770); Blue Bell, Pa. (215-825-6400); Walnut Creek, Calif. (510-932-4949); Woodbridge, N.J. (908-636-8616); Rolling Meadows, Ill. (708-259-7580); Maitland, Fla. (407-249-1600); Woodland Hills, Calif. (818-999-1711); Kirkland, Wash. (206-821-9100).

Telco Plastics Ltd. Box 596, 7820 Pyott Rd., Crystal Lake, Ill. 60039. (815) 459-7400. FAX: (815) 459-7409. Paul Johnson, gen mgr.
Custom injection molder.

Telcom Research. 3375 N. Service Rd., A7, Burlington, Ont., Canada L7N 3G2. (416) 336-2450. FAX: (416) 336-1487. Tom Banting, pres; Rose Ting, VP.
SMPTE/EBU time code generators, readers; character inserters, LTC-VITC & VITC-LTC trans. Logging, off-line & EDL software.

Telecast Fiber Systems Inc. 102 Grove St., Worcester, Mass. 01605. (508) 754-4858. FAX: (508) 752-1520. Richard A. Cerny, pres; Eugene E. Baker, VP.
Fiber optic video & audio systems for outside bcsting, including ENG & EFP.

Telecorp Systems Inc. 1000 Holcomb Woods Pkwy., Suite 410A, Roswell, Ga. 30076. (404) 587-0700; (800) 347-9907 ext 567. FAX: (404) 587-0589. Larry Bradner, CEO; Steve Nusrallah, pres; Roger Reece, VP mktg.
ARVs & ANI svcs for PPV order processing; predictive dialing systems for telemktg & collections.

Telecrafter Products. 12687 W. Cedar Dr., Lakewood Colo. 80228-2031. (800) 257-2448; FAX: (303) 986-1042. Peter G. Mangone, pres.; Carol M. Gordon, sls mgr.
CATV drop instal & security products, including RB-2 Clip Gun & cable clips, cable markers, drop enclosures, security seals.

Teledyne Systems Co. 19601 Nordhoff St., Northridge, Calif. 91324. (818) 886-2211. FAX: (818) 701-7299. Kenneth D. Crawford, VP; Douglas Philips, VP.
Film & video cameras for the military; video to film recorders; optics & optical systems.

Teleflex Information Systems Inc. 7736 McCloud Rd., Greensboro, N.C. 27409-9324. (910) 605-3100. FAX: (910) 605-3111. Alan Neely, COO; Ken Eldridge, mgr sls & mktg.
Flexcell- billing & customer information. Mgmt software system for the telecommunications & cable industry.

Telemation. 8745 E. Orchard Rd., Suite 500, Greenwood Village, Colo. 80111. (303) 290-8000. FAX: (303) 290-6560. Dan Boyd, gen mgr; Kathy Hagan, opns mgr.
Full-svc video prod & postprod. D-2, 1", Beta-SP & 3/4" formats. Graphics, soundstage, grip truck, crews & duplication.

Tele-Measurements Inc. 145 Main Ave., Clifton, N.J. 07014-1078. (201) 473-8822. FAX: (201) 473-0521. William E. Endres, pres.
Bcst video equipment, tapes TV systems, teleconferencing, maintenance support, CCTV & rentals.

TELEMETRICS INC. 6 Leighton Pl., Mahwah, N.J. 07430. (201) 848-9818. FAX: (201) 848-9819. Anthony C. Cuomo, pres; Anthony E. Cuomo, mgr; Albert Chan & Haig Soojian, engrs.
Camera pan & tilt systems; triax camera control systems.

Telemundo Productions Inc. 2470 W. 8th Ave., Hialeah, Fla. 33010. (305) 883-7951. FAX: (305) 884-4722. Juaquin Blayr, sr VP/COO; Al Lewerenz, chief engr.
Prod capabilities & svcs. Uplink & video transmission. C-band & Ku-band uplink & downlink. Ku-band transportable, mobile prod vehicles, studio facilities & editing. Fiber & microwave also available.

Teleplex Inc. 6100 N. Keystone Ave., Suite 600, Indianapolis, Ind. 46220. (617) 935-8610; (617) 257-2085. FAX: (617) 933-4512. Tom L. Fitch, CEO/pres; Lois E. Clark, VP.
Produce precision electronics, components, FM stn combiners, custom FM radio antenna arrays & TV antenna systems.

Telescript Inc. 445 Livingston St., Norwood, N.J. 07648. (201) 767-6733. FAX: (201) 784-0323. Kay Hyde, mgr.
Lawrence, Kan. 66049: Telescript W. 1100 Centennial. (913) 843-6631. Jim Stringer, mgr.
IBM & compatibles prompting progs. Lightweight, high resolution 12" & 17" monitor prompters.

Telesource Communication Services Inc. Box 7132, Phoenix 85011. (602) 265-1232. FAX: (602) 248-8028. Roland C. Fleming, pres; Robert J. Early.
Computerized election reporting svc.

Tele-Tech Electronics Ltd. 920 Denison St., Unit 11, Markham, Ont., Canada L3R 3K5. (416) 499-3242; (416) 475-5646. FAX: (416) 475-5684. John Kirkpatrick, pres.
London, Ont., Canada N5Z 3M7: 931 Leathorne St. Paul Sharpe, mgr.
Toronto, Ont., Canada M5V 2H2: 134 Peter St., 3rd Fl. (519) 685-6561. Rick Noel, mgr.
Total bcst & post-prod audio & video sls svc & rental; equipment & supplies.

Teletech Inc. 23400 Michigan Ave., Dearborn, Mich. 48124. (313) 562-6873. Kenneth W. Hoehn, VP; Keith Johnson, field svcs mgr; Mark W. Dobronski, sr engr.
Scottsdale, Ariz. 85258: 8010 Morgan Terr. (602) 991-6000. Mark Dobronski, engr.
Turnkey studio & facility construction; tower erection & maintenance; antenna instal for AM, FM, TV, LPTV & microwave.

Television Engineering Corp. 580 Goddard Ave., Chesterfield, Mo. 63005. (314) 532-4700. FAX: (314) 536-2465. Jack Vines, pres.
Builds, designs & installs all sizes of custom ENG & EFP vehicles & bcst equipment.

Television Equipment Associates Inc. Box 393, S. Salem, N.Y. 10590. (914) 763-8893. FAX: (914) 763-9158. Bill Pegler, pres.
Video & pulse delays, video filters, headsets & intercom systems.

Television Technology Corp. 650 S. Taylor Ave., Louisville, Colo. 80027. (303) 665-8000; (800) 882-1099. FAX: (303) 673-9900. Byron W. St. Clair, chmn of bd; Dirk B. Freeman, pres; Russ Erickson, sls mgr.
High power UHF TV transmitters, low power TV transmitters & trans, FM transmitters & trans & AC line surge protectors.

Telex Communications Inc. 9600 Aldrich Ave. S., Minneapolis 55420. (612) 884-4051. John Hale, pres.
Wired & wireless microphones; headphones & headsets; intercoms; audio duplicators & copiers.

Telfax Communications. 2501 N. Loop Dr., Ames, Iowa 50010. (515) 296-9911. FAX: (515) 296-9910. Craig J. Pringle, pres.
Telephone remote bcst audio mixers; audio routing switchers; cellular remote units.

Telos Systems. 2101 Superior Ave., Cleveland 44114. (216) 241-7225. FAX: (216) 241-4103. Steve Church, pres.
Manufacturer of equipment for the telephone-to-broadcast interface.

Teltron Inc. 2 Riga Ln., Birdsboro, Pa. 19508. (215) 582-2711. FAX: (215) 582-0851. Arthur H. Mengel, CEO.
Camera tubes for monochrome, color & special purpose applications; view finder CRTs.

Tenco Tower Co. 9723 Folsom Blvd., Suite A, Sacramento, Calif. 95827. (916) 638-8833. Donald Joseph Tenns, pres.
Instal, maintenance & sls of towers, antennas & hardware for bcst, cable & communications industry.

Tennaplex Systems Ltd. 21 Concourse Gate, Unit #1, Nepean, Ont., Canada K2E 7S4. (613) 226-5870. FAX: (613) 727-1247. Manfred Muenzel, pres.
Broadband FM & TV panel antenna & combiners for all pattern & power requirements.

Tentel Corp. 4475 Golden Foothill Pkwy., El Dorado Hills, Calif. 95762. (916) 939-4005. FAX: (916) 939-4114. Wayne Graham, gen mgr; John Chavers, prod mgr.
Tape tension & spindle height gauges for video cassette recorders; head protrusion & eccentricity gauges; dial torque gauges.

Texas Electronics Inc. Box 7225, Dallas 75209. (214) 631-2490. FAX: (214) 631-4218. Joe Williams, pres; Jim Young. engrg sls.
Manufacture meteorological instruments & controls.

Texscan/MSI Corp. 124 N. Charles Lindbergh Dr., Salt Lake City 84116. (801) 359-0077. David Nicholas, VP/gen mgr; John A. Boland, dir sls & mktg; Dennis Gourley, industrial sls mgr.
Character generators, coml insertion systems, graphics & image capture systems & playback systems.

Theatre Service & Supply Corp. 1792 Union Ave., Baltimore 21211. (410) 467-1225. FAX: (410) 467-1289. Richard A. Antisdel, pres.
Manufacture studio & theatrical curtains & track systems; distributor of lighting & theatrical hardware.

Theatrical Services Inc. 128 S. Washington, Wichita, Kan. 67202. (316) 263-4415. FAX: (316) 263-9927. Stephen A. Wolf, pres; Tom Johnson, VP.
Manufacture & distribute studio lighting & control equipment, studio cycloramas, curtains & track.

Thermodyne International Ltd. 20850 S. Alameda St., Long Beach, Calif. 90810. (310) 603-1976. FAX: (310) 603-1929. Gary S. Ackerman, VP.
Reusable shipping cases; rack mounted operating cases.

James Thomas Engineering. 201 Sherlake Rd., Knoxville, Tenn. 37922. (615) 690-5397. FAX: (615) 694-0899. Mike Garl, pres.
Pinvin, Worcester, England: Station Approach, Pershore Trading Estate. 038655 3002. Graham Thomas, pres.
Manufacture & distribute spun aluminum PAR fixtures, modular aluminum trussing, ground support, pre-wired lamp bars, spot banks & lighting accessories. Distributes Socapex & VEAM multipin connectors & cable. Assembles custom multicables, breakouts & distributes boxes to specifications. Distribute olflex cables.

THOMCAST. One rue de L'Hautil, ConFlans - Ste. Honorine, France 78702. 33-1-34-90-31-00. FAX: 33-1-34-90-30-00. Marc Russell, pres; William Tschol, VP sls.
Provides TV & FM transmitters.

Thomson Broadcast Inc. Box 5266, 49 Smith St., Englewood, N.J. 07631. (201) 569-1650. FAX: (201) 569-1511. Bob Heron, gen mgr.
Studio EFP, ENG color TV cameras. Digital postprod equipment, color correctors, mixers, switchers, HDTV.

Thomson Components & Tubes Inc. 40 G Commerce Way, Totowa, N.J. 07511. (201) 812-9000. FAX: (201) 812-9050. E. L. Stern, CEO; V.M Pastore, mktg mgr.
Power grid triodes & tetrodes, cavities, klystrons & travel wave tubes.

Thomson Consumer Electronics Inc. (GE/RCA). 600 N. Sherman Dr., Indianapolis 46201. (317) 267-5000. FAX: (317) 231-4056. Joseph P. Clayton, exec VP; Joseph Donahue, sr VP tech; F.V. McCann, mgr pub rel;

Equipment Manufacturers and Distributors

Thomson S.A. (parent company), 173 Blvd. Houssman, Paris La Defense, 92045, Cedex 67, France.
Manufacture 7 mkt TVs, VCRs, camcorders, audio & communications products.

Thorn-EMI Studio Lamps/L.E. Nelson Sales Corp. 4225 Fidus Dr., Suite 110, Las Vegas 89103. (702) 367-3656. L.E. Nelson, pres; J.M. Nelson, VP western rgn.
Elmwood Park, N.J. 07407: 20 Bushes Ln. (201) 794-6700. Dan Imfeld, VP eastern rgn.
Thorn-EMI studio lamps.

Tiffen Manufacturing Corp. 90 Oser Ave., Hauppauge, N.Y. 11788. (516) 273-2500; (800) 645-2522. FAX: (516) 273-2557. Steve Tiffen, pres/CEO; Ira Tiffen, sr VP Rsch & Dev; Jack Bonura, VP/motion picture & TV division.
Photographic filters & lens accessories for motion picture, still photography, video, A/V products, Davis & Sanford tripods & support systems.

Times Fiber Communications Inc. 358 Hall Ave., Wallingford, Conn. 06492. (203) 265-8500. FAX: (203) 265-8422. John Forde, pres.
Chatham, Va. 24531: Box 119A, Rt. 2. (804) 432-2681. Tom Currie.
Phoenix 85063: Box 14975. (602) 278-5576. Les Judd.
Optical fibers & cables for CATV; One ghz & 600 mhz coaxial drop & semiflex cable F-connectors. Supplier to U.S. & international cable mkts.

Time Logic Inc. 11992 Challenger Ct., Moorpark, Calif. 93021. (800) 238-1055. FAX: (805) 529-6744. Jim Lindelien, pres.
Auomation systems for TV bscters & radio stns. Editing systems for telecine.

Time Manufacturing Co. Box 20368, Waco, Tex. 76702. (817) 776-0900. FAX: (817) 776-7531. Charles H. Wiley, pres.
Truck mounted hydraulic aerial work platforms (bucket trucks).

Tinsley Laboratory Inc. 3900 Lakeside Dr., Richmond, Calif. 94806. (510) 222-8110. FAX: (510) 223-4534. Robert Aronno, pres.
Gyrozoom image stabilizing lens, GX3 integrated CCD camera & stabilizing system.

Toner Cable Computer Systems. 969 Horsham Rd., Horsham, Pa. 19044. (215) 675-2053; (800) 523-5947. Robert L. Toner, pres.

Toner Cable Equipment Inc. 969 Horsham Rd., Horsham, Pa. 19044. (215) 675-2053; (800) 523-5947. FAX: (215) 675-7543. Robert L. Toner, pres; Karen M. Toner, computer division mgr; B.J. Toner, export sls mgr.
International distributor and/or manufacturer of a complete line of CATV & wireless cable equipment.

Topham Audio Inc. 4403 Vineland Rd., Suite B3, Orlando, Fla. 32811. (407) 649-6444. FAX: (407) 648-1352. Joseph Buzzi, VP; Bryan Hanni, rental mgr; Steve Terlep, sls mgr.
Rental sls & svc of professional audio for film, video, TV & post prod. Specialize in wireless communication equipment.

Torpey Controls & Engineering Ltd. 98-2220 Midland Ave., Scarborough, Ont., Canada M1P 3E6. (416) 298-7788. FAX: (416) 298-7789. R.J. Torpey, pres.
Master clock systems, digital & analog slave clocks, timers, video time & temperature equipment.

Toshiba America Consumer Products. 202 Carnegie Ctr., Suite 102, Princeton, N.J. 08540. (609) 951-8500. FAX: (609) 951-9172. Gregory DePriest, VP; Mikhak Tsinberg, sr rsch mgr.
HDTV products: HD-VCR (Analog-UniHi), HD monitor (projection & CRT), NTSC to HDTV upconverter, HD-CCD color camera, HD horizon system.

Tower Inspection Inc. Box 709, Muskogee, Okla. 74402-0709. (918) 683-8915. FAX: (918) 683-0888. Gary G. Lehman, pres; Barry R. Bayless, VP.
Inspection svcs during construction; maintenance inspection, painting & repairs of radio, microwave & TV towers.

Tower Network Services. 4130 N.W. 10th Ave., Fort Lauderdale, Fla. 33309. (305) 771-7180. FAX: (305) 771-7195. James Tiner, pres; Thomas Bull, VP opns; Steve Wanstall, chief engr Strobe Division; Ken French, opns mgr Atlanta division; Ray Flory, opns mgr Dallas division.
Atlanta Division (404-699-2620); Dallas Division (214-891-0555).
Tower, antenna, transmission line & strobe light svcs nationwide. Expert tower inspections.

Tower Specialties Inc. Box 649, Waycross, Ga. 31502-0649. (912) 285-2133. FAX: (912) 283-4224. C.G. Balwanz, chmn; Shirley Balwanz, pres; Ricky Balwanz, VP; Rudy Mora, VP; Carrol O'Bara, gen mgr.
Design, engr, fabricate, erect, maintain & paint communication towers of all sizes & types.

Tower Structures Inc. 1869 Nirvana Ave., Chula Vista, Calif. 91911. (619) 421-1181. FAX: (619) 421-0533. Steven Hopkins, pres; Donald G. Weirauch, VP.
Tower design & construction of transmitter bldgs, instal of bcst, microwave & satellite antennas.

Trans-American Video Inc. 1541 N. Vine St., Hollywood Calif. 90028. (213) 466-2141.

Transcom Corp. Box 26744, Elkins Park, Pa. 19117; 1077 Rydal Rd., Suite 101, Rydal, Pa. 19046. (215) 884-0888. FAX: (215) 884-0738. Martin Cooper, pres.
Provide used AM & FM transmitters & new bcst equipment packages.

Transtector Systems Inc. Box 300, 10701 Airport Dr., Hayden Lake, Idaho 83835. (800) 635-2537; (208) 772-8515. FAX: (208) 772-6619. Bruce Braskich, pres/COO; T.F. Wobker, VP corporate mktg.
Transient overvoltage protection; power quality consulting svcs; college-accredited power-quality assurance educ courses.

Treise Engineering Inc. 1941 1st St., San Fernando, Calif. 91340. (818) 365-3124. FAX: (818) 361-8019. Thomas C. Treise, pres/gen mgr.
Motion picture film processing machines, sound track applicators, temperature control systems, accessories & spare parts.

Tremetrics Inc. 2215 Grand Ave. Pkwy., Austin, Tex. 78728. (512) 251-1400. FAX: (512) 251-1596. Dr. Patrick Howard, gen mgr; H.M. Schwartz, sls mgr.
VLF/LF receivers to determine exact frequency of studio precise oscillators.

Trident Audio USA. 3091 N. Lima St. Burbank, Calif, 91504. (818) 972-1050. FAX: (818) 972-1058. Wayne Freeman, pres; Phil Wagner, natl sls mgr.
Audio mixing consoles for mus, bcst, recording & postproduction.

Tri-Ex Tower Corp. Box 5009, Visalia, Calif. 93278. (209) 651-2171. Edward A. Marue, pres; Robert Vargas, exec VP.
Freestanding, guyed, microwave & trailer towers.

Trilogy Communications Inc. 2910 Hwy. 80 E., Pearl, Miss. 39208. (601) 932-4461. FAX: (601) 939-6637. S. Shinn Lee, pres.
Manufacturer of CATV coaxial cable.

Trimm Inc. (A division of Newton Instrument Co.) Box 489, Libertyville, Ill. 60048. (708) 362-3700. FAX: (708) 680-3888. G. Wallace Newton, pres; Richard D. Neidl, sls mgr.
Manufacture audio/coaxial jacks & plugs, patchcords, prewired jackfields, fuse panels & terminal blocks.

Triple Crown Electronics Inc. 4560 Fieldgate Dr., Mississauga, Ont., Canada L4W 3W6 (905) 629-1111. Fax: (905) 629-1115. Charles J. Evans, pres; Karl Poirier, VP corporate dev.
TV Exciters, 5-10-20 watt LPTV trans & transmitters, TV modulators, demodulators, processors & satellite receivers.

Triplett Corp. One Triplett Dr., Bluffton, Ohio 45817. (419) 358-5015. FAX: (419) 358-7956. Warren Hess, pres.
Panel instruments & test equipment.

Tripp Communications Sales - TCS. Box 5267, Walnut Creek, Calif. 94596. (510) 256-6006. FAX: (510) 256-6007. Ted Tripp, pres; Bob Kearns, regnl mgr sls & mktg.
High density video tape storage, cabinets & roll-around trucks. Cabinets feature built-in dividers.

Trompeter Electronics Inc. Box 5069, 31186 La Baya Dr., Westlake Village, Calif. 91362-4047. (818) 707-2020; (800) 217-2020. FAX: (818) 706-1040. Jack M. Kantola, pres; Ray Calvin, VP sls & mktg.
Patch fields in WECO, RCA coax & audio; BNC, TNC & F connectors & accessories.

TrueTime Inc. 3243 Santa Rosa Ave., Santa Rosa, Calif. 95407. (707) 528-1230. FAX: (707) 527-6640. John L. Van Groos, pres/gen mgr; Rick Dielman, VP/sls mgr.
Time & frequency receivers traceable to NIST & USNO. Complete line of time code instrumentation.

Tulsat/Automation Techniques. 1575 N. 105th E. Ave., Tulsa, Okla. 74116. (918) 836-2584; (800) 331-5997. FAX: (918) 836-8281. David Chymiak.
Manufacture satellite receiver & accessories for coml & cable use. Repair coml videociphers.

Tunnel Radio of America Inc. 600 W. Hillsboro Blvd., Suite 27, Deerfield Beach, Fla. 33441. (305) 480-2727. FAX: (305) 480-8501. Roger Skinner, pres.
Broadcast systems (AM or FM) for use in vehicular tunnels.

Turner Production Field Operations. Box 105264, 1050 Techwood Dr., Atlanta 30348-5264. (404) 885-4115. FAX: (404) 885-4060. Ted Turner, CEO Turner Broadcasting System; Scott Sassa, pres Turner Entertainment Network.
Two 45' mobile units, with or without crews; 9 cam, 7 tape, ESS, DVE, Chyron; single-cam EFP, multi-format; RF cam.

U

UEC Skyvan. Box 21480, Oklahoma City 73156. (405) 755-9703. FAX: (405) 755-6829. James Neuburger, pres.
Aerial buckets: articulating & telescoping, truck & van mounted, working height ranges from 33 to 43 ft.

URDC Measurement Inc. 2477 E. 7000 S., Suite 101B, Salt Lake City 84121. (801) 942-8175. FAX: (801) 942-8074. Jerry Deal, pres; Kellie Saxton, sls mgr; Trent Saxton, VP.
Battery conditioning & analyzing equipment for NiCad rechargeable battery packs.

UREI. (Subsidiary of JBL Professional) 8500 Balboa Blvd., Northridge, Calif. 91329. (818) 893-8411. FAX: (818) 893-3639. Gary Hardesty, dir systems group; Bob Ofenstein, prod mgr; Steve Bartlett, electronic systems dev engr.
Manufacture audio signal processing equipment designed for sound reinforcement, recording & bcstg.

U.S. Audio. 100 Boxart St., Rochester, N.Y. 14612. (716) 663-8820. FAX: (716) 865-8930. Michael Laiacona, pres; Bonnie Gardner, VP/treas.
Mix-6 audio mixers, presspower active pressbox, AS-4 & AS-8 active splitters; P-12 & P-45 power amplifiers.

U.S. Concord. 270 RT. 206, Bldg. A, Flanders, N.J. 07836. (201) 927-0253. FAX: (201) 927-3771. Bob Burtis, sls mgr.
Minneapolis 55437: 8400 Normandale Lake. (612) 921-8498.
Pembroke Pines, Fla. 33027: No. One, 129 S.W. Ave. (305) 436-0440.
Oakbrook, Ill. 60521: 1100 Jorie Blvd., Suite 220. (708) 990-3180.
Irvine, Calif. 92715: 18201 Von Karmin Ave., Suite 1190. (714) 863-9795.
Postprod & radio/TV equipment financing.

U.S. Electronics Components Corp. 585 N. Bicycle Path, Suite 52, Port Jefferson Station, N.Y. 11776. (516) 331-2552. FAX: (516) 331-1833. Lee Greenbaum, pres; Scott Zajdel, dir sls.
Amherst, N.Y. 14226. 3960 Harlem Rd., (716) 839-3803. Scott Zajdel, dir sls.
Manufacture & distribute cable TV equipment.

U.S. Tape & Label Corp. 1561 Fairview Ave., St. Louis 63132. (314) 423-4411. FAX: (314) 423-2964. Jim Eiseman, pres.
Custom printed bumper strips & window labels for the bcst industry.

Ultimate Support Systems Inc. Box 470, Fort Collins, Colo. 80522. (303) 493-4488. FAX: (303) 221-2274. Darrell Schoenig, own; Jim Dismore, CEO.
Strong, lightweight speaker & lighting tripods.

Ultimatte Corp. 20554 Plummer St., Chatsworth, Calif. 91311. (818) 993-8007. FAX: (818) 993-3762. Paul Vlahos, pres; Alan Dadourian, chief engr; Gary Jacobson, sls mgr; Doug Mowinckel, adv mgr.

Equipment Manufacturers and Distributors

Video compositing devices for comls & live bcst, prod & postprod, computerized tripod head.

Ultra Audio Pixtec. (A division of Audio International Inc.) Box 910, Beverly Hills, Calif. 90213. (310) 276-2727. FAX: (310) 276-2726. Oliver Berliner, gen mgr.
Audio consoles, mixers & recorders, routing switches & master control switches.

Union Connector Co. Box H, 300 Babylon Tpke., Roosevelt, N.Y. 11575. (516) 623-7461. FAX: (516) 623-7476. Richard W. Wolpert, pres; Alan T. Wolpert, Vp.
Electrical connectors, power distribution systems, portable power cabinets & custom switchgear.

Union Electronic Distributors. 16012 S. Cottage Grove Ave., S. Holland, Ill. 60473. (708) 333-4100; (800) 648-6657. FAX: (708) 339-2777. John F. Cecich, pres; Steve H. Cecich, VP; Ted Pappas, dist sls mgr.
Wholesale distributor of O.E.M. bcst parts, headphones, earsets, microphones, test equipment, tools & audio/video processing equipment.

Unique Business Systems. 2901 Ocean Park Blvd., Suite 215, Santa Monica, Calif. 90405. (800) 669-4827. FAX: (310) 396-6114. Pradeep Batra, pres; Sanjit Singh, sls rep.
Trevose, Pa. 19053: 4628 Street Rd. (215) 364-9465. David Harty, sls rep.
Oak Brook, Ill. 60521: 600 Enterprise Dr., Suite 101. (708) 954-2860. Mike Budz, mgr.
Asset mgmt software to track rental equipment.

Uni-Set Corp. 449 Ave. A, Rochester, N.Y. 14621. (716) 544-3820. FAX: (716) 544-1110. Ronald D. Kniffin, pres.
Modular studio staging system for settings; riser, tops & ramp system; uni-set system.

Unisys Corp. 2 Enterprise Dr., Shelton, Conn. 06484. (203) 926-2800. FAX: (203) 926-2820. Jim Liska, account exec.
Cable info business systems. Unisys hardware: A1, A4, A6, A10, A12, A17 & IBM PC compatibles.

United Ad Label Co Inc. 650 Columbia St., Brea, Calif. 92622. (800) 423-4643; (714) 990-2700. FAX: (800) 423-8488. Cheryl Hall, prod mgr; David Rudeman, business mgr.

REBUILT TRANSMITTING POWER TUBES

- New Tube Warranty
- Guaranteed Satisfaction
- Off Shelf Delivery
- Fraction of New Price

PARTIAL LIST OF TYPES

125A	5682	6623	8550
207	5736	6696	8680
356	5770	6697	8752
880	5771	6803	8795
891	5891	6804	BR1121
891R	5918	6920	BR1176
892	5919	7007	23185
892R	6421	7480	23431
893AR	6421F	7560	3CX10,000H3
1089	6422	7804	3CX15,000H3
5667	6424	7806	3CX20,000H3
5671	6425F	7807	4CX5,000A
5681	6427	8333	4CX15,000A

- **Duds Purchased Or Rebuilt**
- **Send For Quote**

VACUUM TUBE INDUSTRIES, INC.
506 North Warren Avenue
P.O. Box 2009
Brockton, Massachusetts 02405
Area Code 508 Tel. 584-4500
Outside Mass.
(800) 528-5014 ext. 73
Fax #508-584-0096 Dept. BY

Video & audio tape format labels, tape mgmt labels, labelling software.

United Media. 4771 E. Hunter, Anaheim, Calif. 92807. (714) 777-4510. FAX: (714) 777-2434. Leslie K. Ricci, sls mgr.
Manufacture video editing equipment. Provide editing equipment with a product line that ranges from the beginner up to the experienced operator. UMI 400, 500 & 600 series. New desktop PC-based products include; VAC 100 Series Animation Controller Board, PC Editor Series & MultiVision System (MVS), a PC-based Windows video edit capable of linear & non-linear editing.

United Press International. 203 N. Wabash, Suite 600, Chicago 60601. (312) 781-1600. FAX: (312) 781-1603. Mary Kreiter, rgnl edit.
Dallas 75234: 13900 Midway Rd. (214) 980-8350. Jack Klinge, nat sls mgr cable.
A 24-hour automated & individually customized cable info svc with an extensive news (state & natl), sports, financial, features & weather menu.

United Ropeworks U.S.A. Inc./Phillystran. 151 Commerce Dr., Montgomeryville, Pa. 18936. (215) 368-6611. FAX: (215) 362-7956. W. Wynne Wister III, gen mgr.
Phillystran HPTG; electrically transparent, maintenance free tower guy system; specially designed systems for high power applications.

Unitel Mobile Video. 4100 Steubenville Pike, Pittsburgh 15205. (412) 922-2250. FAX: (412) 922-5380. R.L. Couser, pres; Susan E. Devlin, VP.
Burbank, Calif. 91505: 2231 N. Hollywood Way. (818) 846-0046. Susan Devlin, VP.
Six 45' & one 35' mobile studios fully equipped for video & sound recording; multi-track record capable.

Universal Manufacturer. Box 338, Ward, Ark. 72176. (501) 843-6517. FAX: (501) 843-9755. John Gaunt, pres. TV-CATV only
Manufacture satellite antennas for TVRO industry.

UniVision Inc. Box 4125, Missoula, Mont. 59806. (406) 721-8876; (800) 729-8876. Jim Green, pres.

Utah Scientific Inc. 4750 Wiley Post Way, Salt Lake City 84116. (801) 575-8801. FAX: (801) 575-3299. Ken Schwank, pres.
Audio/video routing & distribution systems, master control switchers, machine control systems, video prod switchers, stn automation.

Utility Tower Company. Box 12369, 3200 N.W. 38th, Oklahoma City 73157. (405) 946-5551. FAX: (405) 947-8466. G. Nelson, pres; Ron Nelson, sls; Joe M. James, sls & engr.
Design, fabrication & erection of radio, TV, cellular & microwave towers. Engrg studies & mods of existing towers. Tower inspections & maintenance.

V

VCR Network. 7888 Ostrow St., #A, San Diego 92111. (619) 569-4000. FAX: (619) 569-0505. Lenny Magill, pres.
Computer graphic library packages, backrounds & textures, animated & moving backrounds.

VGV Inc. 2400 N.E. Waldo Rd., Gainesville, Fla. 32609. (904) 372-0270. FAX: (904) 378-5320. Norman White, pres; Bill Park, dir sls & mktg.
Composite digital video switchers.

VIDESSENCE Inc. 980 David Rd., Burlingame, Calif. 94010. (415) 697-7033. FAX: (415) 697-7032. Paul Costa, pres & CEO.
Pittsburgh 15106: VIDESSENCE - East, 916 Washington Ave. (412) 279-9921 Sam Cevcone, pres.
TV lighting systems of patented technology. Products enhance video quality & are solid state in design.

VIF International. Box 1555, Mountain View, Calif. 94042. (408) 739-9740; (800) 848-4428. FAX: (408) 739-0809. N.L. MacKechnie, pres; Gordon MacKechnie, advisor international rel.
Audio tape recorder spare parts & accessories, motor remanufacturing.

VRI (Video Rentals Inc). Box 426, 183 Oak Tree Rd., Tappan, N.Y. 10983. (800) 255-2874; (914) 365-0748. Alan Schneider, dir opns; Bill Ebell, sr VP.
New York 10019: 423 W. 55th St. (212) 582-4400.
Rental of bcst video equipment including cameras, editing systems, graphics & VTRS.

Vacuum Tube Industries Inc. Box 2009, 506 N. Warren Ave., Dept. BY, Brockton, Mass. 02405-2009. (508) 584-4500 ext 73; (800) 528-5014 ext 73. FAX: (508) 584-0096, Dept. BY. Sheldon Nitenson, pres; Gene Tosti, VP.
Rebuild transmitting power tubes.

Valley Audio Products Inc. 9020 W. 51st Terr. Merriam, Ks. 66203. (913) 432-3388. FAX: (913) 432-9412. David Anderson, pres.
Digital audio signal processors & analog audio signal processor including limiters, compressors, noise gates, expanders, equalizers, de-essers, mic preamplifiers & VCAs.

Van Nostrand Radio Engineering Service. 3931 Lehigh Blvd., Decatur, Ga. 30034-5813. (404) 987-2221. W.L. Van Nostrand, co-own.
Melbourne Beach, Fla. 32951-0458: Box 510458. (407) 723-1250. Samuel B. Boor, co-own.

Vantage Lighting Inc. 175 Paul Dr., San Rafael, Calif. 94903. (800) 445-2677. FAX: (415) 507-0502. Marc Allsman, pres; Peter Allsman, sec/tres.
Webster, N.Y. 14580: Box 289. (800) 442-2852. Marty Phiefer, rgnl mgr.
Replacement lamps including stage, studio, projection audio-visual, HMI, Xenon.

Varian. (EIMAC Division.) 301 Industrial Way, San Carlos, Calif. 94070. (415) 592-1221. FAX: (415) 592-9988. Fred Koehler, VP/gen mgr; Janet Relyea, mktg mgr.
Salt Lake City 84104: 1678 S. Pioneer Rd. (801) 972-5000. Werner Brunhart, gen mgr.
Power grid tubes, cavity amplifiers. X-ray subsystems.

Varian Associates Inc. 3045 Hanover St., H-110, Palo Alto, Calif. 94304. (415) 493-4000. FAX: (415) 493-0307. Frederick Schaefer, mktg mgr.
Palo Alto, Calif. 94304: 811 Hansen Way. (415) 424-5267. Richard Born, VP/gen mgr.
San Carlos, Calif. 94070: 301 Industrial Way. (415) 592-1221. Fred Koehler, VP/gen mgr.
Manufacture components for medical, communications, scientific, industrial & defense mkts worldwide.

Veetronix Inc. 1311 W. Pacific, Lexington, Neb. 68850. (308) 324-4600. FAX: (308) 324-4985. Eddie Howerter, asst VP sls.
Keyboard & panel reed switches & keycaps with in-house tooling.

Vega. (A Mark IV Company) 9900 Baldwin Place, El Monte, Calif. 91731. (818) 442-0782; (800) 877-1771. FAX: (818) 444-1342. Gary J. Stanfill, pres; Kenneth M. Bourne, dir mktg; Eugene Johnson, natl sls mgr.
Signaling, monitoring & control products & systems.

Vermeer Manufacturing Co. Box 200, Pella, Iowa 50219. (515) 628-3141. FAX: (515) 628-3614. Robert Vermeer, chmn/CEO; Mary Andringa, pres/COO.
Cable plows, trenchers, backhoes & stump cutters.

Vertex Communications Corp. 2600 Longview St., Kilgore, Tex. 75662. (903) 984-0555. FAX: (903) 984-1826. J.R. Vardeman, pres; A.D.Branum, sr VP.
Ellicott City, Md. 21043: 5151 Crystal Springs Dr. (410) 461-4759. FAX: (410) 461-1547. George W. Gilbert, VP mkt dev.
Haslemere,Surrey, U.K. GU27 2QE: Vertex International Limited Clembro House, Weydown Rd. 011-4442-8661-100. 011-4442-8661-000. Barry K. Watson, VP business dev. (Europe)
Design, engrg & mfg firm specializing in radio frequency earth stn antennas.

Vertigo Technology Inc. 1030 W. Georgia St., Suite 1010, Vancouver, B.C., Canada V6E 2Y3. (604) 684-2113. FAX: (604) 684-2108. Jim Stewart, pres, Linda Fawcus, VP mktg & sls.
Vancouver, B.C., Canada V6B 2X6: 1134 Homer St., Suite 301. (604) 684-2113. Linda Fawws, VP mktg & sls.
3D Computer animation & visization software for silicon graphics computers.

Vicon Industries Inc. 525 Broadhollow Rd., Melville, N.Y. 11747. (516) 293-2200. FAX: (516) 293-2627. Ken Darby, pres/CEO; Dick Adam, VP international sls.
Precision camera positioning systems & equipment.

Vid-Comm Enterprises Inc. 5669 W. Howard St., Niles, Ill. 60714. (708) 647-0007. Timothy Tutt, pres.
Manufacture telestrator & computer peripherals.

Broadcasting & Cable Yearbook 1994
H-56

Equipment Manufacturers and Distributors

Video Accessory Corp. 2450 Central Ave., Suite H, Boulder, Colo. 80301. (800) 821-0426. FAX: (303) 440-8878. Norm Baer, CEO; Dr. Jack R. Baird, pres; Kirk Fowler, VP mktg; Carolyn Tremer, prod mgr.
Black Burst generators, Pattern generators, Sync generators, distribution amplifiers, video line isolators, switches & alarms.

Video Associates Lab Inc. 4926 Spicewood Springs Rd., Austin, Tex. 78759-8422. (512) 346-5781. FAX: (512) 346-9407. Henry B. Mistrot, CEO.
MicroKey desktop audio/video add-in products for IBM compatible personal computers.

Video Central Inc. 76 9th Ave., Suite 433, New York 10011. (212) 633-9200. FAX: (212) 564-1861. Yosef Yosifove, pres.
Orlando, Fla. 32819: 5422 Carrier Dr. #207, (407) 363-1913. Lee Golinello, mgr.
Sales of professional & bcst video equipment. Capability of designing systems.

Video Communications Inc. Box 215, Feeding Hills, Mass. 01030-0215. (413) 786-7955. FAX: (413) 786-4663. W. Lowell Putnam, pres.
Computer systems for TV stns including sls, traffic & accounting. Report processor & progmg system.

Video Data Systems. 630 Old Willets Path, Hauppauge, N.Y. 11788. (516) 231-4400. FAX: (516) 231-4405. William Leventer, pres; Stephen Seiden, VP.
Manufacture titlers, character generators, teleprompters, automated display & control systems; real-time programmable controllers.

Video Design Pro. 749 Carver Rd., Las Cruces, N.M. 88005. (505) 524-8959. FAX: (505) 524-9669. Dr. Walter Black, principal; Randy Scott, tech mgr.
Cable documentation & systems design software to reduce design & install time & costs 50-90%.

Video Integrators. 230 N. Potomac St., Suite 1A, Hagerstown, Md. 21740. (301) 739-1662. FAX: (301) 739-1662. Dave Clayberg, sls mgr.
Design & instal of video edit systems & custom video furniture.

Video International Development Corp. 65-16 Brook Ave., Deerpark, N.Y. 11729. (516) 243-5414. FAX: (516) 243-4314. Gerhard Freitag, pres; Bernd Bressel, gen mgr.
Barsinghausen, Germany. 30890: Ulmenweg II. (05105) 81144. S. Freitag, VP.
Westlake Village, Calif. 91359: Box 3125. (805) 529-7499. Stan Paris, sls mgr.
Digital TV standards converters with 4 field-4-line interpolation for bcst & industrial use.

Video One Inc. 10625 Chandler Blvd., North Hollywood, Calif. 91601. (818) 980-0704. FAX: (818) 980-4331. Robert G. Kaufmann, pres; Kevin E. Hamburger, VP.
Remote TV prod facilities.

Video Protection Co. Box 1131, Grand Rapids, Mich. 49501. (616) 453-5599; (800) 722-9010. FAX: (616) 453-6830. Rick Kamel, pres.
Externally worn protective garments for TV & radio news crews. Customized barricade tape to protect live remotes.

VideoLab. 15050-Q S.W. Koll Pkwy., Beaverton, Ore. 97006. (503) 644-7657. FAX: (503) 644-8678. Tom Anderson, pres.
Time code retrofits for Sony 3/4" industrial VTRs. Interface retrofit for RS-422 control of Sony type 5, 7, 9 industrial 3/4" VTRs.

Videomagnetics Inc. 725 Geiger Ct., Colorado Springs 80915. (719) 591-5757. FAX: (719) 591-0027. Tony B. Korte, pres.
Video head refurbishing for 1" C format Ampex, Sony & Hitachi machines; 2" quad; tape degaussers; Rebuilt AMPEX scanners for all VCR's.

Videomedia. 175 Lewis Rd., #23, San Jose, Calif. 95111. (408) 227-9977. FAX: (408) 227-6707. Donald Bennett, CEO; Bill Stickney, VP.
Datchet, Berkshire, U.K. S13 9EG: Unit 7 Portland Business Ctr., Manor House Ln. (0753) 681596. Brian Conner, sls mgr.
V-LAN(TM) compatible products for desktop video, professional dedicated video & animation systems.

Videotek Inc. 243 Shoemaker Rd., Pottstown, Pa. 19464. (215) 327-2292. FAX: (215) 327-9295. Philip Steyaert, pres; Peter H. Choi, VP; Robert Vanzyl, VP opns; Richard R. Hollowbush, VP tech svcs.
Color monitors, waveform monitors, combination waveform monitor/vectorscope, routing switchers, audio monitor, demodulator, distribution amplifiers, sync generators, timing equipment, RGB monitors & prod switchers.

Videotron Ltee. 2000 Berri St., Montreal Que., Canada H2L 4V7. (514) 281-1232. FAX: (514) 985-8794. Claude Chagnon, pres.
Cable TV & a multimedia system called Videoway - a terminal connected to cable TV offering to subs a multitude of svcs.

Videssence. 980 David Rd., Burlinggame. 94010. (415) 697-7032. FAX: (415) 697-7032. Paul Costa, pres.
Cosmetics for TV. All products are formulated from RGB based pigments. Complete airbrush cosmetic departments.

Vidicraft Inc. 8770 S.W. Nimbus Ave., Beaverton, Ore. 97005. (503) 626-1918. FAX: (503) 644-9887. Steve Johnson, pres.
Audio/video enhancement products & switchers.

Viewsonics Inc. 6454 E. Rogers Cir., Boca Raton, Fla. 33487. (407) 998-9594. FAX: (407) 998-3712. Abram Ackerman, pres; Cynthia Brown, gen mgr.
Amplifiers, security systems, apartment boxes, combiners, LAN, CATV & MMDS components.

Viking Cases. 10480 Oak St. N.E., St. Petersburg, Fla. 33716. (800) 237-8560. Arthur W. Stemler, pres; William W. Strickland, VP gen mgr; Bruce S. Stemler, VP mfg.
Heavy duty reusable shipping cases, lightweight carrying cases & EIA rack cases.

VISION ACCOMPLISHED INC.

Vision Accomplished Inc. 550 Maulhardt Ave., Oxnard, Calif. 93030. (805) 981-8740. FAX: (805) 981-8738.
Transportable & flyaway satellite transmission; mobile/TVRO's; studio/remote prod; transmission mgmt.

Vision Database Systems. 853 Donald Ross Rd., Juno Beach, Fla. 33408. (407) 694-2211. FAX: (407) 694-2220. Emil Bonaduce, pres.
PC-based tele-classifed ad creation; display & billing system.

Vision 1250 EEIG. 32 Ave. Albert Lancaster, Bruxelles, Belgium 1180. 32-2-374-6821. FAX: 32-2-374-5471. Michel Oudin, dir gen; Franco Visintin, deputy dir gen; Brian Scott, deputy dir gen; Sylvie Gormezano, sec gen.
HDTV facilities on 1250/50 standard.

Voltage Electronics. 1740 Evergreen St., Duarte, San Fernando, Calif. 91010. (818) 303-3737. FAX: (818) 303-2767. Keith Levitt, gen mgr.
Temporary & portable power distibution.

VueScan Inc. 1143 W. Newport Ctr. Dr., Deerfield Beach, Fla. 33442. (305) 427-5000; (800) 327-4966. FAX: (305) 427-0934. Gary J. Balsam, pres; Ronald N. Bandel, VP.
Sao Paulo Brasil VueScan Do Brasil Comercio Ltda. 011-725-3500 Luciane Pinto, office mgr.
Buenos Aires Argentina VueScan Argentina, S.A. 541-788-0600. Carlos Behrensen, gen mgr.
Stocking distributor for General Instrument, Scientific Atlanta, Lectro, Comm/Scope. Converter repairs.

W

WDZ Radio/Systemation. 337 N. Water, Decatur, Ill. 62523. (217) 423-9744. FAX: (217) 423-9764. Steve Bellinger, pres; Bernie Brobst, VP.
Automation, traffic, sls & accounting.

WILL-BURT Co., TMD Masts. Box 900, Orrville, Ohio 44667. (216) 682-7015. FAX: (216) 684-1190. Harry E. Featherstone, CEO; Don Barlow, sls mgr.
Telescoping mast used to position antennas, lights & cameras to heights of 20' to 134'.

WSI Corp. 4 Federal St., Billerica, Mass. 01821. (508) 670-5000. FAX: (508) 670-5100. Mark Gildersleeve, pres; Don Freeland, TV mkt mgr; Janis Farnham, sls mgr.
Real-time weather info svc with NOWrad live radar imagery, satellite imagery, weather graphics, worldwide data & NWS DIFAX.

WUAB Productions. 8443 Day Dr., Cleveland 44129. (216) 845-6043. FAX: (216) 845-6061. Jim Stunek, prod mgr; Sharon Ohlson, prod coord.
Full studio facilities; GVG 300 switcher, CMX 3100B edit, 1", 3/4", Beta formats; Abekas digital F/X; Artstar graphics; remote packages.

Wallach & Associates Inc. 3441 76th St., Cleveland 44127. (216) 441-0166. FAX: (216) 441-1872. Jim Jacobs, pres.
Cabinets, racks & mobile units for storage & filing of audio & video tapes, records, films, filmstrips & slides.

Walton Electronics Inc. 4324 S.W. 35th Ter., Gainesville, Fla. 32608. (904) 376-5658. Lloyd Walton, pres.
Instal & bcst svcs.

Ward-Beck Systems Ltd. 841 Progress Ave., Scarborough, Ont., Canada M1H 2X4. (416) 438-6550; FAX: (416) 438-3865. Eugene L. Johnson, mng dir.
Danvers, Mass. 01923: 10 Page St. (508) 777-7228. William McFadden, sls rep.
Professional audio mixing consoles. Communications systems, microprocessor & discrete control. Audio distribution amplifiers.

The Waterford Group. 307 Orchard City Dr., Suite 202, Campbell, Calif. 95008. (408) 374-8450. FAX: (408) 374-9560. Robert S. Kelly Jr., pres; Richard J. Reilly, VP.
Complete video systems-digital video work stations, cameras, beta/D-2-D-1, VTRs, microwave, TV stn automation, microwave, video printers.

Wave Front Technologies. 3020 Old Rankch Pkwy., Suite 170, Seal Beach, Calif. 90740. (310) 799-0011. FAX: (310) 799-1070. Achim von der Nuell, pres; Nick Tesi, natl sls mgr.
New York, 10020: 1270 Ave. of the Americas. (212) 247-1950.
3D graphics animation & visualization software for video, film or HDTV.

Wavefront Technologies Inc. 530 E. Montecito St., Santa Barbara, Calif. 93103. (805) 962-8117. FAX: (805) 963-0782. Larry Barels, chmn; Michael McCloskey, COO/CFO; Don Brittain, VP advanced rsch; Dave Swan, VP sls & mktg; Martin Plaehn, VP business product dev; Mark Sylvester, VP product mktg.
Branch offices: Atlanta, Chicago, Los Angeles, New York, San Francisco, Washinton, D.C., Frankfurt, Ghent, London, Milan, Paris & Tokyo.
3D animation software, visization software, post prod effects for film & video software.

Wavetek Corp. Communications Division. 5808 Churchman Bypass, Indianapolis 46203. (317) 788-9351. FAX: (317) 788-5999. Derek Morikawa, gen mgr; Russ Byrd, product mktg mgr; Mike Richardson & Tony Shortt, rgnl sls mgrs.
Electronic test equipment for communications, education, design, dev, maintenance, prod & rsch activities.

WearGuard Corporation. (A member of the ARA Group) Box 9105, Hingham, Mass., 02043. (800) 888-2900 x5835. FAX: (617)-982-0761 Dottie Paradis, acct mgr.
Offers a comprehensive line of work clothing & identity apparel serving the cable industry.

WeatherBank Inc. 5 Triad Ctr., Suite 315, Salt Lake City 84180. (801) 530-3131. FAX: (801) 530-3174. Steven A. Root, pres/CEO.
Satellite delivered weather info, audio forecasting svcs, consulting to all industries.

Wegener Communications Inc. 11350 Technology Cir., Duluth, Ga. 30136. (404) 623-0096. Robert Placek, pres; C. Troy Woodbury, Jr., treas/COO.
Design & manufacture satellite audio, video & data transmission systems for cable TV, radio & TV bcst & data communication industries.

Weircliffe. 2752 Walnut Ave., Tustin, Calif. 92680. (714) 838-8833. FAX: (714) 838-9619. Roger L. Bailey, CEO & chmn; Jim Owen, prod specialist.
Exeter, U.K. EX4 2AG: 44-3-927-2132. Geoff Bailey, mngng dir.
Video/audio tape degaussers.

Wescam. (A division of Istec Inc.) 1810 Hwy. 6 N., Hamilton, Ont., Canada L9J 1H2. (416) 529-5132. FAX: (416) 529-5311. Mark Chamberlain, pres; John Bastedo, gen mgr.
Pasadena, Calif.: 9687 Saluda Ave. (818) 248-2100. Dave Daunt, Steve Koster, Hans Bjemo, Wescam operators.

Broadcasting & Cable Yearbook 1994

H-57

Equipment Manufacturers and Distributors

Pasadena, Calif. 91103: Pasadena Camera Rental. 49 E. Walnut St. (818) 796-3300. FAX: (818) 584-4099. Steve Kaplow.

West Melbourne, Fla. 32904: C.R.M. Group. 270 East Dr., Suite A. (407) 727-1428. FAX: (407) 727-8315. Ed Silva; Terry O'Rourke.

Shepperton, Middlesex, U.K. TW17: Aerial Camera Systems, Lee International Studios. Studios Rd. (0932) 564-885. FAX: (0932) 568-030. Matthew Allwork, Susie Allwork.

Paris 75019: Societe Francaise De Production. 36 rue des Alouettes. 33-1-4003-57-12. FAX: 33-1-4240-75-75 Michel Benaim.

Brussels B-1040: Wim Robberechts & Co S.A. 46 Rue Colonel Bourg. 32-2-735-00-08. FAX: 32-2-735-20-05. Wim Robberechts.

Issogne, (AO), Italy: Eli Alpi S.P.A. Fraz. Mure 11020. (0125) 960471. FAX: (0125) 960575. J.P. Marafante.
Gyrostabilized camera systems.

Weschler Instruments. 16900 Foltz Pkwy., Cleveland 44136. (216) 238-2550. FAX: (216) 238-0660. Gary Gonzales, sls mgr.
Digital surface mount panel meters & digital/bargraph panel instruments (replacement to analog).

Westcott. Box 1596, Toledo, Ohio 43603. (419) 243-7311. FAX: (419) 243-8401. Thomas A. Waltz, pres.
Lightweight, portable & collapsible light control equipment: silks & solids, scrims, Illuminator TM reflectors, umbrellas & light modifiers.

Western CATV Distributors Inc. 3430 Fujita St., Torrance, Calif. 90505. (310) 539-8030; (800) 551-2288. FAX: (310) 530-5603. William Ewing, pres; Chris Ewing, gen mgr.
Amplifiers, headend equipment, cable, drop material, connectors, passives, tools, traps, enclosures, test equipment, power supplies, etc.

Western Tele-Communications Inc. Box 5630, Denver 80217. (303) 267-5500. FAX: (303) 488-3215. Larry Romrell, pres; Robert Lemming, exec VP.
Digital transmission svcs & video.

Western Wireless Works. Box 4500, Apache Junction, Ariz. 85278. (602) 380-1000. FAX: (602) 986-1442. Richard Haskey, opns mgr; Patricia Woods, mgr tech svcs; Rudy Petracci, engr.

For the personal touch needed to make equipment purchases an endurable event

Our 24th Year

• Technical Assistance
• Product Demonstrations
• Support-After-the-Sale

Digital Still Storage
High Quality Monitors
Switching Equipment
Cameras/Stabilization
Transmission/Patching
Coax Terminations
Data Communications

WILTRONIX

(800) 848-7870
(301) 258-7676

16850 Oakmont Avenue
P.O. Box 364
Washington Grove, MD 20880

Communications system engrg, turnkey construction, RF phasing equipment, custom electronics & studio cabinetry.

Westinghouse Electric Corp. 111 Schilling Rd., Hunt Valley, Md. 21030. (410) 765-1000.
Solid-state bcst transmitter.

Westlake Audio, Professional Products Manufacturing Group. 2696 Lavery Ct., Unit 18, Newbury Park, Calif. 91320. (805) 499-3686. FAX: (805) 498-2571. Glenn Phoenix, pres; Robert Pursell, mktg admin.
Audio monitors & accessories.

Westlake Audio, Professional Sales Group. 7265 Santa Monica Blvd., Los Angeles 90046. (213) 851-9800. FAX: (213) 851-0182. Deborah Rally, gen mgr; Arnold Toshner, sls mgr; Steve Burdick, studio mgr.
Los Angeles 90046: 8447 Beverly Blvd. (213) 654-2155. Steve Burdick.
Newbury Park, Calif. 91320: 2696 Lavery Ct., Unit 18. (805) 499-3686. Glenn Phoenix, pres.
Professional audio equipment, recording studios, rentals & studio design.

Wheatstone Corporation. 7305 Performance Dr., Syracuse, N.Y. 13212-3449. (315) 452-5000. FAX: (315) 452-0160. Gary C. Snow, pres; Andrew Calvanese, VP; Ramon Esparolini, sls mgr.
Manufacture bcst audio consoles, studio furniture, audio signal processing equipment & audio computer hard disc system.

Wheelit Inc. Box 352800, Toledo, Ohio 43635-2800. (419) 531-4900. FAX: (419) 531-6415. John M. Skilliter, VP sls.
Video prod carts (folding & non-folding), video display stands.

Whirlwind. Box 12692, 100 Boxart St., Rochester, N.Y. 14612. (716) 663-8820. FAX: (716) 865-8930. Michael Laiacona, pres; Bonnie Gardner, VP/treas.
Audio/video, cable & interface systems for bcst, coml & industrial applications; complete custom assembly facilities; interface specialty products.

White Mountain Cable Construction Corp. Box 459, Rte. 4, Epsom, N.H. 03234. (800) 233-7350; (603) 736-4766. FAX: (603) 736-8163. Dennis Nolin, pres; David Pouliotte, VP.
Provides coaxial, telephone & fiber optics cable construction. Also strands mapping, engineering svcs & FO splicing & testing.

Wil-Can Electronics Can Ltd. 920 Denison St., Unit 11, Markham, Ont. Canada L3R 3K5. (416) 475-5629. FAX: (416) 475-5684. William J. "Bill" Black, pres.
Designers, manufacturers & consultants. Lightning & high energy transient control. Svc & products.

Wiltronix Inc. Box 364, 16850 Oakmont Ave., Washington Grove, Md. 20880. (301) 258-7676. FAX: (301) 963-8624. Dwight Wilcox, pres; Ellen Packard, mktg mgr; Dave Wilcox sls mgr.
Annapolis, Md. 21401: 106 McKendree Ave. (301) 261-1857. Dave Wilcox.
Bcst prod, processing & transmission (audio, video, data), LAN/WAN test, internetworking.

Winfield Scott & Associates. Box 1149, Grapevine, Tex. 76051. (800) 346-1766; (817) 540-1823. W. Scott Webb, chief assoc.
Central City, Colo. 80427: Box 369. (817) 488-0197.

Winsted Corp. 10901 Hampshire Ave. S., Minneapolis 55438. (612) 944-8556. FAX: (612) 944-1546. C.E. Johnson, pres; G.R. Hoska, VP.
Editing & prod consoles, space saving tape & film storage systems.

WireReady Newswire Systems Inc. Chiswick Industrial Park 31 H Union Ave., Sudbury, Mass. 01776. (800) 833-4459; (508) 443-8181. FAX: (508) 443-5988. David Gerstmann, mktg & sls.
WireReady newsroom; CartReady digital & audio software systems.

Wireworks Corporation. 380 Hillside Ave., Hillside, N.J. 07205. (908) 686-7400; (800) 642-9473. FAX: (908) 686-0483. Gerald J. Krulewicz, pres; Larry J. Williams, comptroller; Angela Kelly, customer svc mgr.
Audio/video & audio/video combination cabling assemblies for bcst mkt. Cable Testers also.

Wohler Technologies Inc. 713 Grandview Dr., S. San Francisco, Calif. 94080. (415) 589-5676. FAX: (415) 589-1355. Will C. Wohler, pres.
Single rackspace, self-powered stereo, audio monitor speaker systems & other related audio products.

Wolf Coach Inc. 7 B St., Auburn Industrial Park, Auburn, Mass. 01501. (508) 791-1950. FAX: (508) 799-2384. Richard Wolf, pres/gen mgr; Mark A. Leonard, natl sls rep.
News vans, satellite vehicles, prod trailers, vehicle based microwave, satellite uplink & audio/video systems.

Frank Woolley & Co. Inc. 529 Franklin St., Reading, Pa. 19602. (215) 374-8335. FAX: (215) 374-3214. Frank L. Woolley, pres; Alison M. Whalen, VP.
Video animation system.

World Tower Co. Inc. Box 405, Mayfield, Ky. 42066. (502) 247-3649. FAX: (502) 247-0909 M.N. Sholar, pres; Jeff Sholar, VP.
Manufacture & erect bcst & CATV towers; microwave & cellular.

World Video Inc. Box 117, Boyertown, Pa. 19512. (215) 754-6700. John P. Koser, pres; John A. Taylor, VP.
Audio prog monitors; audio monitor & amplifiers; video timer & titler; screen spiltter; pattern generators.

X

Xedit Corp. (Editall Tape Splicing Systems) 218-31 97th Ave., Queens Village, N.Y. 11429. (718) 464-9400. FAX: (718) 464-9435. Claude M. Karczmer, pres.
Thirty-two models of tape splicing blocks (CA-24), for audio, video, digital & required accessories. Test equipment—drift & flutter meter.

Y

YEM America Inc. 19951 Mariner Ave., #200, Torrance, Calif. 90503. (310) 793-1288. FAX: (310) 371-5108. Yasushi Yamashita, pres.
Computer-to-video automatic scanconcerter, digital EDTV decoder to produce RGB31.468KHz Rubidium dual sync generator.

Yale Electronics. 6616 Sunset Blvd., Hollywood, Calif. 90028. (213) 465-3186. FAX: (213) 465-5630. Valerie Anne Yale, pres; Rebecca Wellborn, proj admin.
Provides cable, connectors, electronic parts & components for bcst, audio/video applications & Yaleflex audio snake cable.

Yamaha Corporation of America. 6600 Orangethorpe Ave., Buena Park, Calif. 90620. (714) 522-9011. FAX: (714) 522-4023. Masahiko Arimoto, pres.
Portable keyboards, synthesizers & drums.

Z

Zenith Electronics Corp. 1000 Milwaukee Ave., Glenview, Ill. 60025. (708) 391-7702. FAX: (708) 391-8569. Cable Products Division: John Bowler, pres; Dean DeBiase, sr VP sls & mktg; Vito Brugliera, VP mktg & product planning; Michael Long, dir engrg; John Taylor, dir pub rel.
Full line of CATV converters; MMDS systems; cable & pay TV systems for PAL & SECAM international mkts; PC-based system controllers; accessories.

Ziehl Electronic Service. 8611 Dale Rd., Gasport, N.Y. 14067. (716) 772-7800. Richard F. Ziehl, own.
Frequency measurement svc.

Zonal Ltd. Holmethorpe Ave., Holmethorpe Estate, Redhill, Surrey, U.K. RH1 2NX. 0737-767171. FAX: 0737-767610. A. Heise, mng dir; S. Malek Jahanian, dir sls.
Professional 35mm & 16mm sound recording film, audio tape & audio cassette products.

Station and Cable Television Brokers

AVPRO Inc. Box 176, Kennebunk, Me. 04043. (207) 985-3511. Lewis M. Marcy, pres; James M. Marcy, VP.
Media brokerage nationwide: TV, radio, nwsprs, cable.

AMERICAN RADIO BROKERS, INC.
MOST TRUSTED NAME IN MEDIA BROKERAGE
CHESTER P. COLEMAN / PRESIDENT
FOR THE BEST STATIONS FOR SALE FROM THIS AREA
CALL — 415/441-3377
1255 POST STREET / SUITE 625 / SAN FRANCISCO, CA 94109

American Radio Brokers Inc/SFO. Cathedral Hill Office Bldg., 1255 Post St., Suite 625, San Francisco 94109. (415) 441-3377. Chester P. Coleman, pres; Terry Engle, broker; Kathleen O'Donnell, office mgr; Richard "Julio" Haskey, tech dir; Warren Earl, consultant; Perry Pasu, financial mgr; Marlo Holmes, dir Alaskan opns.
Alaska: KABN Radio Facilities. (907) 892-8300.
Full-svc media brokerage of Pacific & western states radio & TV stns. Mgmt consultants, LMAs, bankruptcy, sls & appraisals.

Americom Radio Brokers Inc. 8401 Old Courthouse Rd., Suite 140, Vienna, Va. 22182. (202) 737-9000. FAX: (202) 737-9000. Thomas P. Gammon, pres; Daniel T. Gammon, mng ptnr.
Radio stn brokerage & financing.

Henry Ansbacher Inc. 280 Park Ave. E., 20th Fl., New York 10017. (212) 688-5544. FAX: (212) 922-1740. William J. McCluskey, pres.
London, U.K. EC3A 5AN: Henry Ansbacher Ltd., Media Division. Priory House, One Mitre Sq. (011) 4471-283-2500. FAX: (212) 688-6110. Fraser Jennings, chmn.
Merger, acquisition & evaluation svcs in media industry.

Associated Broadcasters. Box 42566, Cincinnati 45242. (513) 791-5982. FAX: (513) 489-5553. Irv Schwartz, mng dir; R. Galen, rsch admin.
Legal & filing svcs in turnkey packages; consulting & appraisal svcs available.

Barger Broadcast Transactions. 7800 N.W. I-10, Suite 330, San Antonio 78230. (210) 340-7080. FAX: (210) 340-1775. John W. Barger, principal.
Media brokerage, loc mktg agreements, financial placements, appraisals, mgmt/financial consulting.

Baugh & Associates. 6013 Quemsdo N.E., Albuquerque 87109. (505) 828-0950. FAX: (505) 888-0868. Ken Baugh, pres.
Fair Acres, N.M. 88033: Box 205. (505) 526-5349. Walter Rubens, assoc.
Marana, Ariz. 85653: 17762 W. Cocoraque Rd. (602) 682-6007. Bill Mitchell, assoc.
Brokers for radio & TV.

Beckerman Associates Inc. 14001 Miramar Ave., Madeira Beach, Fla. 33708. (813) 391-2824. FAX: (813) 398-2945. Milton B. Beckerman, co-own.
Tampa 33682: Box 82784. (813) 971-2061. Lincoln A. Mayo, assoc.
Media brokerage, appraisals for bcst & print. Consulting, concerning media sls & acquisitions.

We work hard to make you look lucky.

Frank Boyle & Co.
Brokerage - Mergers - Appraisals
2001 West Main Street, Stamford, Ct. 06902
203-969-2020

Bill-David Associates Inc. 2508 Fair Mount St., Colorado Springs 80909. (719) 636-1584. Bill Martin, broker.
Radio & TV stn brokerage, appraisals, mgmt consultants.

Blackburn & Co. Inc. 201 N. Union St., Suite 340, Alexandria, Va. 22314. (703) 519-3703. FAX: (703) 519-9756. James W. Blackburn Jr., chmn; Richard F. Blackburn, pres; Jack V. Harvey, Joseph M. Sitrick, Neil Rockoff, Tony Rizzo, Susan Byers, Richard Sharpe.

Frank Boyle & Co. 2001 W. Main St., Suite 280, Stamford, Conn. 06902. (203) 969-2020. FAX: (203) 969-3498. Frank Boyle, pres; Jim Boyle, VP cable division; Mary C. Downey, VP opns.
Radio, TV & cable media brokerage, consulting, mergers & acquisitions.

Broadcast Media Associates. 316 California St., Suite 700, Reno, Nev. 89509. (800) 237-3777. Clifford M. Hunter, pres.
Radio/TV/cable brokerage in the western states. Confidential mktg for radio, TV & LPTV properties; valuation, packages & financial analysis; consultants to sellers & brokers.

Broadcast Media Corp. Box 42513, 3939 McKinley N.W., Washington 20015. (202) 364-1019. FAX: (202) 363-5524. Randall H. Blair, pres.
Consulting to buyers & sellers of radio & TV properties.

Broadcast Media Partners. 8750 E. Evans Rd., Scottsdale, Ariz. 85260. (602) 998-7031. Ted Nicholson, ptnr.
Murrieta, Calif. 92562: 3855 Lochinvar Ct. (909) 698-1131. FAX: (909) 696-0998. F. Patrick Nugent, ptnr. (Los Angeles office.)
Brokerage svcs, valuations, due diligence, Far East consulting, court-approved takeover specialists.

Broadcasting Asset Management Corp. 1450 N. Astor St., 6th Fl., Chicago 60610. (312) 649-9029. FAX: (312) 348-5831. Jack Minkow, pres.
Radio stn & group stn brokerage, mergers, acquisition analysis, appraisals, feasibility studies & mgmt consulting.

Broadmark Capital Corp. 3030 Pacific 1st Ctr., 1420 5th Ave., Seattle 98101-2333. (206) 623-1200. FAX: (206) 623-2213. Gerald B. Dennon, VP.
Radio & TV brokerage svcs; mergers & acquisitions; investment banking.

The Jesse Neal Browder Co. Inc. Box 2197, Rt. 2, Lexington, Ga. 30648. (706) 743-8661. Neal Browder, broker.
Stn brokerage & appraisals specializing in the southeastern market.

Bulkley Media Inc./Bulkley Capital. 8333 Douglas Ave., Suite 777, Dallas 75225. (214) 692-5476. FAX: (214) 692-9309. G. Bradford Bulkley, pres/CEO.
Investment banking; mergers, acquisitions & private placements of debt & equity capital.

George Burns & Co. 6965 El Camino Real, Suite 105-229, Rancho La Costa, Calif. 92009. (619) 746-7993. FAX: (619) 739-8303. George Burns, chmn; Larry Lakoduk, pres; Todd Stewart, VP progmg.
Radio mgmt & consulting.

Business Broker Associates. 5555 Hixson Pike, Suite 203, Chattanooga 37343. (615) 756-7635; FAX: (615) 843-3421. C. Alfred Dick, own/broker.
Media broker for radio, TV & cable systems.

LAUREN A. COLBY
301-663-1086
COMMUNICATIONS ATTORNEY
Special Attention to Difficult Cases

Capstone Communications Inc. Box 331, Saddle River, N.J. 07458. (201) 934-5990. FAX: (201) 934-0192. Josh Mayberry, pres; Carol G. Mayberry, VP.
Brokerage, appraisals (fair market value), rsch consultation & stn mktg with confidentiality ensured.

Robert A. Chaisson Inc. 39 Locust Ave., New Canaan, Conn. 06840. (203) 966-6333. FAX: (203) 966-1924. Robert A. Chaisson, pres.
Brokerage of radio & TV sls & acquisitions.

S.R. Chanen & Co. Inc./Media Technology Capital Corp. 3300 N. 3rd Ave., Phoenix 85013. (602) 234-1411. FAX: (602) 266-0236. Steven R. Chanen, chmn; Ronald Halvorson, VP finance/CFO; Donald E. New, pres acquisitions & investments.
Investment banking, brokerage & financial advisory svcs for the communications & entertainment industry.

Chapin Enterprises. 751 NBC Ctr., Lincoln, Neb. 68508. (402) 475-5285. FAX: (402) 434-4181. Dick Chapin, pres.

The Chapman Co. Inc. 8431 Immokolee Rd., Ft. Pierce, Fla. 34951-4012. (407) 460-1597; FAX: (407) 460-1596. John D. Chapman, pres.
Brokers for the sale & acquisition of radio & TV.

Station and Cable Television Brokers

Donald K. Clark Inc. Box 340617, Tampa 33694. (813) 949-9311. FAX: (813) 949-2846. Donald K. Clark, pres; Anne Clark, VP.
Brokers for the sale & acquisition of radio & TV.

Communication Resources Unlimited Inc. Media Brokers. 3727 E. 31st St., Tulsa, Okla. 74135-1506. (918) 743-8300. FAX: (918) 749-3348. Tom Belcher, pres; Eileen Belcher, VP; Barbara Terry, sec/treas.
Brokerage svcs for radio & TV stns & cable TV systems.

Communications Equity Associates Inc. 101 E. Kennedy Blvd., Suite 3300, Tampa 33602. (813) 222-8844. FAX: (813) 225-1513. J. Patrick Michaels Jr., chmn/CEO; Harold D. Ewen, dir; H. Gene Gawthrop, exec VP/COO; Jeanette Tully, VP; Glenn Serafin, VP radio division.
New York 10152: 375 Park Ave., Suite 3808. (212) 319-1968. Don Russell, pres CEA Inc.; Dave Unger, VP.
TV bcst stn & radio bcst stn sls, acquisitions, trades, securing of financial debt & equity; stn fair market evaluations.

The Connelly Co. Inc. 5401 W. Kennedy Blvd., Suite 480, Tampa 33609. (813) 287-0906. FAX: (813) 289-0906. Robert J. Connelly, Richard S. Levy, Robert J. (Rob) Connelly, brokers.
Brokers, consultants & recovery unit to banks & financial institutions.

Crisler Capital Co. 600 Vine St., Suite 2710, Cincinnati 45202. (513) 381-7775. FAX: (513) 381-8808. R. Dean Meiszer, pres; Richard C. Crisler, chmn; Stephen E. Kaufmann, VP.
Chicago 60611: Ward L. Quaal Co. 401 N. Michigan Ave., Suite 3140. (312) 644-6066. FAX: (312) 644-3733.
Acquisition, merger, appraisal & financial svcs to radio, TV, nwspr, cable & other media-related industries.

Daniels & Associates. 3200 Cherry Creek S. Dr., Suite 500, Denver 80209. (303) 778-5555. FAX: (303) 778-5599. Phil Hogue, chmn; Brian Deevy, pres; Timothy David, exec VP.
New York 10153: 767 5th Ave. (212) 935-5900. FAX: (212) 832-2784. Gregory Ainsworth, sr VP; Michael Garstin, exec VP.
Provides brokerage svcs to cable TV & bcstg industries.

Eden Broadcast Services Inc. Box 647, 397 Periwinkle Rd., Eden, N.C. 27289-0647. (919) 623-7300. FAX: (919) 623-7300. Gene E. Ward Sr., pres.
Radio sls & appraisals.

Emerald Coast Radio Corp. Box 817, Destin, Fla. 32540. (904) 837-0101. FAX: (904) 837-7621. Tim Fulmer, Steve Riggs, co-owners.
Media brokerage, consultation, appraisals, etc.

William A. Exline Inc. 4340 Redwood Hwy., Suite F-230, San Rafael, Calif. 94903. (415) 479-3484. FAX: (415) 479-1574. Andrew P. McClure, pres; W. Dean LeGras, VP; Miramae M. Welch, assoc; William A. Exline, consultant.
Complete brokerage, consulting & appraisal svcs for radio & TV properties.

Norman Fischer & Associates Inc. 1209 Pkwy., Austin, Tex. 78703. (512) 476-9457. FAX: (512) 476-0540. Norman Fischer, pres.
Brokerage in radio, TV & cable. Consultation in mgmt & opns, appraisals, feasibility studies, expert testimony, financial planning & assistance.

Force Communications & Consultants. 580 Centre View Blvd., Crestiview Hills, Ky. 41017. (606) 344-8881. FAX: (606) 344-8616. John L. Pierce, Harold W. Gore, John E. Lauer, ptnrs.
Atlanta 30062: 200 N. Cobb Pkwy., Suite 114. (404) 528-1421. Harold W. Gore, ptnr.
Atlanta 30326: 3343 Peachtree Rd., Suite 200. (404) 841-6487. John E. Lauer, ptnr.
Radio, TV, cable sls & appraisals.

Milton Q. Ford & Associates Inc. 4006 Baronne Way, Memphis 38117. (901) 767-7980. Milton Q. Ford, pres.
Media broker.

Richard A. Foreman Associates. 330 Emery Dr. E., Stamford, Conn. 06902-2210. (203) 327-2800. FAX: (203) 967-9393. Richard A. Foreman, pres; Richard W. Kozak, assoc; Susan Brenner, admin asst.
Specializing in cash-positive radio & TV stns in major growth markets.

Michael Fox Auctioneers Inc. 3835 Naylors Ln., Baltimore 21208. (410) 653-4000. FAX: (410) 653-4069. William Z. Fox, chmn; David S. Fox, pres.
Auction sls of bcst properties.

Lazard Freres & Co. One Rockefeller Plaza, New York 10020. (212) 632-6154. FAX: (212) 632-6060. Steven Rattener, Luis Rinaldini, gen ptnrs; David Lee, VP; Michael Price, gen ptnr.
Acquisitions, investitures & financings for media companies.

Success is the Best Recommendation...

Norman Fischer & Associates, Inc.
Media Brokerage • Appraisals • Management Consultants
1209 Parkway • Austin, Texas 78703 • (512)476-9457

Norman Fischer, President

Over 20 years experience - A full service brokerage firm successfully representing buyers and sellers throughout the U.S.

GAMMON MEDIA BROKERS, INC.

Gammon Media Brokers Inc. 8280 Greensboro Dr., 7th Fl., McLean, Va. 22102. (703) 761-5020. FAX: (703) 761-5022. James A. Gammon, pres.
Brokerage & strategy advice to sellers & buyers of radio & TV properties.

Clifton Gardiner & Associates Inc. Box 5559, 0082 E. Beaver Blvd., Avon, Colo. 81620. (303) 949-4485. FAX: (303) 949-0266. Clifton H. Gardiner, pres.
Brokerage, financial svcs for the bcst & cable industries.

Cliff Gill Enterprises Inc. Box 1468, Hemet, Calif. 92546. (909) 927-8099. FAX: (909) 927-1083. Cliff Gill, pres; Dave Drubeck, VP; Kay Gill, sec/business mgr.
Brokers; coord for National Consortium of Media Brokers with offices in Los Angeles, San Francisco, Denver, Kansas City, Chicago & Philadelphia.

W. John Grandy
BROADCASTING BROKER
117 Country Club Drive
San Luis Obispo, CA 93401
Phone: (805) 541-1900
Fax: (805) 541-1906

W. John Grandy. Broadcasting Broker. 117 Country Club Dr., San Luis Obispo, Calif. 93401. (805) 541-1900. FAX: (805) 541-1906. W. John Grandy, pres; Dale Cowle, assoc.
Rancho Mirage, Calif. 92260: 90 Magdelena Dr. (619) 324-8451. Dale Cowle, assoc.
Brokers of radio & TV stns, cable appraisers, consultants.

Charles Greene Associates. 4380 Georgetown Sq. Rd., Suite 1010A, Atlanta 30338. (404) 452-8891. FAX: (404) 452-8892. Charles L. Greene, pres.
Cable TV brokerage svcs, including sls, acquisitions, appraisals & financing.

HPC Puckett & Co. 12626 High Bluff Dr., Suite 250, San Diego 92130-2072. (619) 793-7008. FAX: (619) 793-7233. Thomas Puckett, chmn.
Topeka, Kan. 66611: 2201 S.W. 29th St. (913) 273-0017.
Communications brokerage & investment banking.

Hadden & Associates. Media Brokers. 1385 Ayerswood Ct., Winter Springs, Fla. 32708. (407) 365-7832. FAX: (407) 366-8801. Doyle Hadden, pres/CEO.
Communications brokerage, consulting, financial assistance, appraisals.

Margret Haney of Graham-Haney. 2995 Woodside Rd., Woodside, Calif. 94062. (415) 325-5552. FAX: (415) 325-5556. Margret Haney, pres; Sondra Carver, J.D. law & taxes.
Media adv, buying, brokerage & consultation.

WILLIAM A. EXLINE, INC

MEDIA BROKERS
CONSULTANTS

Andrew P. McClure
President

Where integrity and results go hand in hand.

W. Dean LeGras
Vice President

William A. Exline
Consultant

WILLIAM A. EXLINE, INC

MEDIA BROKERS
CONSULTANTS

4340 Redwood Highway • Suite F 230
San Rafael, California 94903
TEL (415) 479-3484 • FAX (415) 479-1574

Miramae M. Welch
Associate

Station and Cable Television Brokers

Hardesty & Associates. 115 Retiro Way, San Francisco 94123. (415) 563-4411. John F. Hardesty, pres.
Acquisitions, divestitures, appraisals, financing & consulting.

Henson Media Inc. 2335 Bonnycastle Ave., Louisville, Ky. 40205. (502) 456-2200; FAX: (502) 456-2200. Ed Henson, pres.
Radio & TV brokers specializing in the Midwest & upper Southeast areas.

The Ted Hepburn Co. 325 Garden Rd., Palm Beach, Fla. 33480. (407) 863-8995. FAX: (407) 863-8997. Ted Hepburn, pres; Todd Hepburn, VP.
Cincinnati 45243: Box 43263. (513) 271-5400. FAX: (513) 271-5413. Todd Hepburn, VP.
Radio, TV & cable brokerage; appraisals; tax consultation through assn with Grant Thornton C.P.A.s.

Hickman Associates. Drake Manor, 29 Manor Dr., Newton, N.J. 07860. (201) 579-5232. FAX: (201) 579-6010. Ron Hickman, pres; Barbara Hickman, VP.
Media brokerage svcs, including mergers, acquisitions, appraisals & financial assistance. Consultants and recovery svc to assist banks & financial institutions.

R. Miller Hicks & Co. 1011 W. 11th St., Austin, Tex. 78703. (512) 477-7000. FAX: (512) 477-9697. R. Miller Hicks, pres.

Mel Hodell, Media Broker Inc. 5196 Benito St., Suite 11, Montclair, Calif. 91763. (909) 626-6440. FAX: (909) 624-8852. Mel Hodell, pres.
Daily & wkly nwsprs, & print publications sls, appraisals, consultation.

Hoffman Schutz Media Capitol Inc. 42 Monmouth Hills, Highlands, N.J. 07732. (212) 297-0620. Anthony M. Hoffman, pres; David E. Schutz, VP.
Debt & equity financing, appraisals, restructurings & litigation support.

Hogan-Feldmann Inc. 4463 Bergamo Dr., Encino, Calif. 91426. (818) 986-3201. FAX: (818) 986-2259. Arthur B. Hogan, pres.
Media brokers & consultants.

The Holt Corp. 961 Marcon Blvd., Suite 400, Allentown, Pa. 18103. (215) 264-4040. FAX: (215) 266-6464. Arthur H. Holt, pres; Christine E. Borger, exec VP/CFO; Bernhard M. Fuhrmann, sr VP.
Brokerage, consulting, appraisals.

Bruce Houston Associates Inc. 2251 Hunter Mill Rd., Vienna, Va. 22181. (703) 938-1016. FAX: (703) 938-6078. Bruce Houston, pres.
Media brokers for radio & TV.

J. C. & A. 5821 Fairview Rd., Suite 200, Charlotte, N.C. 28209. (704) 554-6809. FAX: (704) 554-9713. Eugene B. Johnson, pres.
Investment banker & brokers for media companies.

Johnson Communication Properties Inc. 4780 Regents Walk, Minneapolis 55331. (612) 474-1100; (612) 474-3332. Jerry Johnson, pres.
Radio & TV broker.

Jorgenson Broadcast Brokerage. 2700 W. M.L. King Blvd., Suite 400, Tampa 33607. (813) 877-3000. FAX: (813) 877-4849. Mark W. Jorgenson, pres.

Colorado Springs 80906: 2910 Electra Dr. (719) 630-3111. FAX: (719) 630-1871. Joseph Bennett McCoy III.
Confidential, nationwide brokerage of bcst properties.

Kalil & Co. Inc. 3444 N. Country Club, Suite 200, Tucson, Ariz. 85716. (602) 795-1050. FAX: (602) 322-0584. Frank C. Kalil, pres; Kelly F. Callan, Fred Kalil, Richard L. Beesemyer, Frank J. Higney, VPs.
Media brokerage firm dealing in radio, TV & cable. Handles exclusive listings, confidential searches & workouts.

Kelley Associates Inc. 2419 Elmwood Cir. N., Wichita Falls, Tex. 76308. (817) 692-7722. Boyd Kelley, pres.

Kepper, Tupper & Fugatt Inc. Box 636, 803 N. Front St., McHenry, Ill. 60051-0636. (815) 344-0242. FAX: (815) 344-0298. William Kepper, chmn; Michael L. Fugatt, pres.
Ridgefield, Conn. 06877: 183 Haviland Ave. (203) 431-3864. FAX: (203) 431-3366. John B. Tupper, pres.
Media brokerage firm specializing in confidential radio, TV & cable transactions. Svcs include appraisals & placement of financing.

Kozacko Media Services. Box 948, Elmira, N.Y. 14902. (607) 733-7138. FAX: (607) 733-1212. Richard L. Kozacko, pres; John C. Clancy, assoc.
Gaithersburg, Md. 20878: Box 3306. (301) 977-2023. Bruce M. Kanner, assoc.
Cape Elizabeth, Me. 04107: One Canterbury Way. (207) 799-8804. Melvin L. Stone, VP.
Sarasota, Fla. 34238: Box 39010. (813) 966-3411. W. Donald Roberts Jr., assoc.
Appraisals & current market evaluations of radio & TV stns; bcst stn acquisition brokers.

H.B. LaRue, Media Brokers. 9454 Wilshire Blvd., Suite 628, Beverly Hills, Calif. 90212. (310) 275-9266. FAX: (310) 274-4076. Hugh Ben LaRue, pres; Joy Thomas, VP; Marc Spinelli, West Coast office mgr; Larissa Alexandra, western rgn sls mgr.
New York 10021: 500 E. 77th St., Suite 1909. (212) 288-0737. Hugh Ben La Rue, pres; Elke Breyer, East Coast office mgr.
Media brokerage for TV, radio & CATV. Appraisals & feasibility studies.

Joe M. Leonard Jr. & Associates Inc. Box 222, Gainesville, Tex. 76241. (817) 665-4076. Joe M. Leonard Jr., pres.
Brokerage of radio & TV.

The Stephen T. Lindberg Co. 9815 E. Crestline Cir., Englewood, Colo. 80111. (303) 694-1637. Stephen T. Lindberg, pres/CEO.
Representation of ind owners of cable systems, MSOs, radio & TV stns in sls & acquisitions of operating assets.

Magna Carta Realty Corp. 1500 S.W. 5th Ave., Suite 2602, Portland, Ore. 97201. (503) 221-1122. FAX: (503) 299-6500; (800) 635-1772. Armand J. Santilli, pres.
Media brokers/finders, real estate investment bankers & brokers.

Jack Maloney Inc. 28 Shore Dr., Huntington, N.Y. 11743. (516) 549-2656. Jack Maloney, pres.
Provides confidential svc to buyers & sellers in the radio & TV business.

James A. Martin Associates. Box 798, 3061 Cranston Dr., Dublin, Ohio 43017. (614) 889-9747. FAX: (614) 889-2659. Jim Martin, pres; A.M. Tenney, CFO.
Media brokerage & investment banking: sr debt $1-$15 million, acquisition, bid option divestiture or refinance.

Reggie Martin & Associates Inc. Box 294, Roaring Gap, N.C. 28668-0294. (919) 363-3891. Reggie Martin, pres.

Four Offices To Assist You With All Your Broadcast Ownership Planning

Portland, ME
Sarasota, FL
Washington, DC
Elmira, NY

Richard L. Kozacko
President

Brokerage

Appraisals

Consulting

Feasibility Studies

KOZACKO-HORTON COMPANY
BROKERS AND CONSULTANTS

607.733.7138
FAX: 607.733.1212

P.O. Box 948
Elmira, NY 14902

Station and Cable Television Brokers

W. Edward McClenahan & Associates Inc. 561 Dryden Pl., Charlottesville, Va. 22903. (804) 977-4096. W. Edward McClenahan, pres.

Edward R. McKenna. 5600 Wisconsin Ave., Suite I-502, Chevy Chase, Md. 20815. (301) 986-1118. Edward R. McKenna, pres.
   Radio brokerage & consulting.

R.E. Meador & Associates. Box 36, Lexington, Mo. 64067. (816) 259-2544. FAX: (816) 259-6424. Ralph E. Meador, pres.
   Acquisitions, sls, mktg studies & appraisal svcs in central & midwestern states.

Media Acquisitions Inc. 429 Chapel Hill Rd., Marshall, N.C. 28753. (704) 656-2038. Robert E. Brown, pres; Arlene Brown, mgr.
   Media brokerage/consulting.

Media Services Group Inc. 2111 Wilson Blvd., Suite 700, Arlington, Va. 22201. (703) 351-5025; FAX: (703) 351-0361. Millard S. Younts, pres; Mona Wargo, mktg dir.
   Overland Park, Kan. 66212: 10575 Riley. (913) 383-2260. FAX: (913) 383-3152. Bill Lytle, VP.
   Berwyn, Pa. 19312: 179 St. Clair Cir. (215) 695-9339. FAX: (215) 695-9340. Kevin Cox, VP.
   Logan, Utah 84321: Box 744. (801) 753-8090. FAX: (801) 753-1394. Greg Merrill, VP.
   Jacksonville, Fla. 32250: 3948 3rd. St. (904) 285-3239. FAX: (904) 285-5618. George Reed, VP.
   Providence, R.I. 02903: 170 Westminster St., Suite 701. (401) 454-3130. FAX: (401) 454-3131. Robert J. Maccini, VP.
   Mergers, acquisitions, financing, valuations & consultation for radio & TV.

Media Venture Partners. 1650 Tysons Blvd., Suite 790, McLean, Va. 22102. (703) 827-2727. FAX: (703) 827-2728. Brian E. Cobb, Elliot B. Evers, Charles E. Giddens, Randall E. Jeffrey, ptnrs.
   Orlando, Fla. 32835: 7479 Conroy Rd., Suite C. (407) 295-2572. Randall E. Jeffrey.
   San Francisco 94133: 50 Francisco St., Suite 450. (415) 391-4877. Elliot B. Evers, ptnr.
   Cincinnati 45241: 4055 Executive Park Dr., Suite 413. (513) 769-4477. George I. Otwell, ptnr.
   Radio & TV brokerage svcs; mergers & acquisitions.

Mediacor. 1860 N. Talbott Pl., Waynesboro, Va. 22980-2224. (703) 942-1314. FAX: (703) 942-1314. Gary E. Kirtley, mng ptnr.
   Bcst brokers, appraisers & financial consultants; progmg & sls consultation.

Mitchell & Associates. 1939 Bayou Dr., Shreveport, La. 71105. (318) 868-5409. John Mitchell, pres.
   Media brokers, appraisers & consultants.

George Moore & Associates Inc. 12900 Preston Rd., Suite 1040, Dallas 75230. (214) 661-8970. FAX: (214) 661-8967. W. James Moore, pres; Charles J. Hagen, VP.
   Brokerage of radio, TV & cellular telephone properties & franchises; asset & market appraisals prepared for owners, buyers & lenders.

Gordon P. Moul & Associates Inc. Box 42, York Haven, Pa. 17370. (717) 266-4212. FAX: (717) 266-0780. Gordon Moul, pres.
   Bcst brokers & consultants.

O'Grady & Associates. Drawer D, Goshen, N.Y. 10924-0708. (914) 294-9515. FAX: (914) 294-9515. James F. O'Grady Jr., pres; Jane A. O'Grady, Anne Mary Diana, VPs.
   Jensen Beach, Fla. 34957-4308: 4460 N.E. Ocean Blvd., Suite H-2. (407) 225-0920. FAX: (407) 225-0920.
   Confidential media brokerage svcs; consultants & appraisals.

Packerland Consultants & Sales. 248-C N. Campbell Rd., Oshkosh, Wis. 54901. (414) 235-2625. Allen Embury, pres.

Donald A. Perry Associates Inc. Summerville Plantation, Box 857, Gloucester, Va. 23061. (804) 877-4367. FAX: (804) 693-2885. Donald A. Perry, pres; W. Kelvin Bowles, Patricia Gibbs, VPs; Brinton Belyea, engrg.
   Cable TV, investment banking, brokerage, appraisal & all related svcs.

The Proctor Group Inc. 980-FM 1746, Woodville, Tex. 75979. (409) 429-3679. FAX: (409) 429-5257. Gerald R. Proctor, pres; David P. Garland, VP.
   Radio, TV, cable brokerage.

Questcom Radio Brokerage Inc. 18310 Montgomery Village Ave., Suite 220, Gaithersburg, Md. 20879. (301) 963-3000. FAX: (301) 963-9572. Donald R. Bussell, pres.
   Denver 80202: 1444 Wazee St., Suite 120. (303) 534-3939. FAX: (303) 534-3322. Marc O. Hand, VP.
   Radio stn brokerage specialists concentrating in top 150 markets; offers assistance with financing of transactions; provides radio stn work-out svcs to financially troubled radio companies, their investors & lenders. Our firm is a registered FDIC & RTC broker/appraiser.

Radioactivity Inc. 1043 Jefferson Ave., Suite B-12, Atlanta, 30344. (404) 767-1840. FAX: (404) 767-1840. Dain L. Schult, pres; Craig Pak, sr VP finance; Joe Pedicino, VP mgmt; Hugh Roberts, VP mgmt.
   Atlanta 30344: 982 Winburn Dr. (404) 766-0312. Craig Pak, sr VP finance.
   Exlusive "FSBO" svc for small market owners; AM small market specialists; specializes in all types of appraisals.

Stan Raymond & Associates Inc. Box 8231, Longboat Key, Fla. 34228. (813) 383-9404. FAX: (813) 383-9132. Stan Raymond, pres.
   Financial svcs, media brokers, appraisers & consultants specializing in the Southeast.

Read & Read. Box 31000, Spokane, Wash. 99223-3016. (509) 448-7400. FAX: (509) 448-3811. Thomas W. Read, pres; Melinda Read, VP.
   Sun Valley, Idaho 83353: Box 2542. (509) 448-3811. FAX: (509) 448-3811.
   Frequency studies, applications, brokerage svcs & consultants.

Regenhold Auction Consultants Inc. 611 S. Myrtle Ave., Suite B, Clearwater, Fla. 34616. (813) 461-1666. Rickey H. Regenhold, pres.
   Radio stn & real estate auctions.

Gerald D. Reilly Associates. 12 Taconic Rd., Greenwich, Conn. 06830. (203) 622-0599. Gerald D. Reilly, pres/own.

Gordon Rice Associates. Box 20398, Charleston, S.C. 29413. (803) 884-3590. FAX: (803) 785-6829. Gordon Rice, pres.
   Brokerage svcs, appraisals & investment analysis for radio & TV.

WILLIAM R. RICE CO.
Brokers, Appraisers, Consultants

9102 N. Meridian, Suite 500 Indianapolis, IN 46260

Tel (317) 844-7390   Fax (317) 848-8973

William R. Rice Co. 9102 N. Meridian St., Suite 500, Indianapolis 46260. (317) 844-7390. FAX: (317) 848-8973. William R. Rice, own.
   Media brokerage, financial svcs, consultation, & appraisals (FDIC- & RTC-accepted appraiser).

Cecil L. Richards Inc. Box 9037, McLean, Va. 22102-0037. (703) 821-2552. FAX: (703) 821-2553. Cecil L. Richards, pres; Loyola C. Richards, admin asst.

Riley Representatives. 14330 Midway Rd., Dallas 75244. (214) 788-1630. Jack Riley.

Roehling Broadcast Services Ltd. 7021 Harmon Ct., Indianapolis 46227. (317) 889-1025. FAX: (317) 788-3490. Edward W. Roehling, pres; Dennis A. Roehling, VP; Sandra A. Roehling, sec/treas.
   Brokerage, appraisal, mgmt & sls consulting. Svcs are primary, with narration & video svcs offered.

Ray H. Rosenblum. Media Broker. Box 38296, Pittsburgh 15238. (412) 362-6311. Ray H. Rosenblum, pres; Helen Faye Rosenblum, VP.
   York Haven, Pa. 17370: Box 42. (717) 266-4212. Gordon Moul, assoc.
   Media brokerage, appraising, financing & consulting for radio & TV stns in Pennsylvania, Ohio, New York, West Virginia, Maryland, Michigan & Indiana.

Robert W. Rounsaville & Associates. 3104 E. Shadowlawn Ave. N.E., Atlanta 30305. (404) 261-3000. FAX: (404) 261-1500. Robert W. Rounsaville, pres.
   Radio & TV brokerage.

Rowan Media Brokers & Consultants. 16225 Meadow Ridge Way, Encino, Calif. 91436. (818) 783-0505. FAX: (818) 783-0909. Roy Rowan, pres.
   Specializing in radio-TV brokerage & appraisals in the western states, Alaska & Hawaii.

Rumbaut & Associates. 1160 Stillwater Dr., Tower Suite, Miami Beach, Fla. 33141. (305) 868-7000. FAX: (305) 868-7865. Julio Rumbaut, pres.
   Washington 20036: 1900 L St. N.W., Suite 500. (202) 293-2828. FAX: (202) 466-9042.

NEW ENGLAND MEDIA, INC.
BROKERS • APPRAISERS • CONSULTANTS

102 ROUTE 7, ST. ALBANS, VT 05478
(P) 802-524-5963 (F) 802-527-1450

New England Media Inc. 102 Swanton Rd., St. Albans, Vt. 05478. (802) 524-5963. FAX: (802) 527-1450. David R. Kimel, pres; Michael Rice, VP.
   Mansfield Center, Conn. 06250: 99 Highland Rd. (203) 456-1111. Mike Rice, VP.
   Media brokers, consultants & appraisers specializing in radio & TV in the Northeast.

William B. Schutz, Jr.
media broker

P.O. Box 404 • St. Michaels, MD 21663
Phone (301)745-3900 • Fax (301)745-5929

Brokerage • Appraisals • Financing

Putting buyers and sellers in sync with one another.

Station and Cable Television Brokers

Media brokers & consultants in all facets of the TV & radio industries.

Sailors & Associates. 5784 Lake Forrest Dr., Suite 252, Atlanta 30328. (404) 250-1897. FAX: (404) 250-9322. Don F. Sailors, pres.
Media brokerage & financing specializing in radio, TV & cable.

Satterfield & Perry Inc. 3062 Robb Cir., Denver 80215-7067. (303) 239-6670. FAX: (303) 231-9562. Al Perry, chmn.
Bala Cynwyd, Pa. 19004: Two Bala Plaza, Suite 300. (215) 668-1168. FAX: (215) 688-9447. Jack F. Satterfield, pres; John Weidman Jr., VP. (215) 660-7760.
Englewood, Colo. 80111: 5172 S. Ironton Way. (303) 740-8424. Bob Austin, VP.
Overland Park, Kan. 66207: 4918 W. 101st Terr. (913) 649-5103. Douglas Stephens, VP.
Point Pleasant, Pa. 18950: Box 248, River Point Rd. (215) 297-0625. George Pleasants, VP.
Radio, TV, & cable broker, mgmt consultant, appraiser, expert witness & accounts receivable funding.

John W. Saunders. 17101 Kuykendahl Rd., Suite 100, Houston 77068. (713) 444-4477. FAX: upon request. John W. Saunders, own.
Nationwide radio brokerage & appraisals. Buyers or sellers represented on a confidential, professional & personal basis. Top 10 to small markets.

William B. Schutz Jr. Box 404, St. Michaels, Md. 21663. (410) 745-3900. FAX: (410) 745-5929. William B. Schutz Jr.
Brokerage, appraisals & stn financing.

Barry Sherman & Associates. 7640 Tremayne Pl., Suite 204, McLean, Va. 22102. (703) 821-0877. Barry Sherman, pres.
Brokers/negotiators for purchase/sale of TV, radio, cable; provide financial svcs including equity, debt, mezzanine, appraisals.

Gordon Sherman & Associates Inc. 2255 Glades Rd., Suite 237W, Boca Raton, Fla. 33431-7383. (407) 998-0628. FAX: (407) 998-8006. Gordon Sherman, pres; Alan E. Sherman, VP.
Media brokers, consultants & appraisers for radio, TV & cable.

Burt Sherwood & Associates Inc. 6415 Midnight Pass Rd., Suite 206, Sarasota, Fla. 34242. (813) 349-2165; FAX: (813) 349-2356. Burt Sherwood, pres; Ellen Lyle, VP.
Vienna, Va. 22182: 9300 Arabian Ave. (703) 242-4276. Ellen Lyle, VP.
Northbrook, Ill. 60062: 4171 Dunde Rd., Suite 269. (708) 272-4970. Burt Sherwood, pres.
Radio, TV & LPTV brokerage & appraisals.

Barry Skidelsky, Esq. 655 Madsion Ave., 19th Fl., New York 10021. (212) 832-4800. FAX: (212) 486-8668. Barry Skidelsky, Esq.

Legal, financial & mgmt counsel re-purchase/sale; LMA/duopoly; bankruptcy trustee/receiver; expert witness; closings & more.

Sklar Communications Inc. 205 West End Ave., #11U, New York 10023. (212) 769-1839. FAX: (212) 799-2536. Sydelle Sklar, pres.

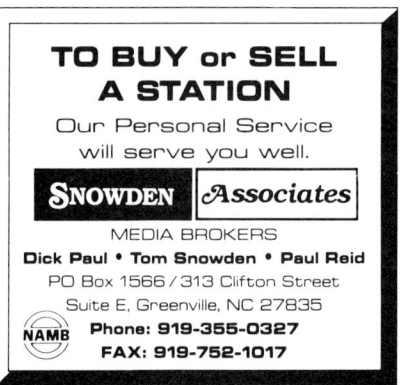

Snowden Associates. Box 1566, 313 Clifton St., Suite E, Greenville, N.C. 27835. (919) 355-0327. FAX: (919) 752-1017. J.T. "Tom" Snowden Jr., pres; Dick Paul, Paul E. Reid, assocs; Martha Snowden, office mgr.
Brokers, consultants & appraisers to the bcst industry.

Ray Stanfield & Associates. 16360 Roscoe Blvd., Suite 109, Van Nuys, Calif. 91406. (818) 893-3199. FAX: (818) 893-8020. Ray M. Stanfield, pres; James F. Mergen, assoc.
Nationwide brokers, consultants & appraisers for radio & TV stns.

Star Media Group Inc. 17304 Preston Rd., Suite 265, Dallas 75252. (214) 713-8500. FAX: (214) 713-8150. William J. Steding, Paul T. Leonard, Peter S. Handy, mgng dirs.
Specializing in portfolio planning, brokerage svcs & merchant banking.

Howard E. Stark. 575 Madison Ave., 10th Fl., New York 10022. (212) 355-0405. Howard E. Stark, pres.
Media broker—mergers & acquisitions in the communications field.

John D. Stebbins Co. Box 30, Lake Forest, Ill. 60045. (708) 234-4534. John D. Stebbins, pres.

Gary Stevens & Co. 49 Locust Ave., Suite 107, New Canaan, Conn. 06840. (203) 966-6465. FAX: (203) 966-6522. Gary Stevens, mgng dir.
Bcst mergers, acquisitions, investment banking svcs.

Stonemark Corp. 1370 Stewart St., Seattle 98111. (206) 628-8989. FAX: (206) 628-0839. William V. May, pres; Catherine Eldora, mktg; Jeffrey C. Baker; Timothy J. Dunton; Gregory Shade, VPs.
Specializing in business brokerage, acquisition searches, capital arrangement & debt placement for bcst properties as well as other industries.

Thoben-Van Huss & Associates Inc. 1010 E. 86th St., Suite 44C, Indianapolis 46204-1301. (317) 580-0094. FAX: (317) 580-0097. Phillip M. Thoben, pres; William K. Van Huss, chmn.
Brokerage & debt placement svcs for bcst & cable industries.

The Thorburn Co. 5465 Young Deer Dr., Cumming, Ga. 30130. (404) 781-8740. FAX: (404) 781-8741. Robert M. Thorburn, pres; Martha Thorburn, sec/treas.
Appraisals, brokerage, financial & mgmt consulting for radio, TV & cable.

Edwin Tornberg & Co. Inc. Box 55298, Washington 20011. (202) 291-8700. FAX: (202) 829-1590. Edwin Tomberg, pres.
Appraisals, brokerage, financial & mgmt consulting for radio, TV & cable.

The Venture Group Ltd. 1206 Laskin Rd., Suite 201, Virginia Beach, Va. 23451. (804) 491-5444. FAX: (804) 491-0828. Laurence I. Peterson, pres.
Intermediaries in the sale, merger & acquisition of radio & TV stns.

Ed Walters & Assocs. Box 3697, Barrington, Ill. 60011. (708) 304-8993. Ed Walters, pres; Michael Walters, VP.

J.N. Wells & Co. 21 W. 075 Monticello Rd., Lombard, Ill. 60148. (708) 916-6491. FAX: (708) 629-8411. Joseph N. Wells, pres; Jonathon S. Wells, Lloyd Q. Swenson, VPs.
Brokerage & investment banking svcs to bcstg, CATV, publishing, & the media & communications industries.

H. Walter Westman/Media Broker. 2386 Bal Harbour Dr., Venice, Fla. 34293. (813) 497-3325. H. Walter Westman, own.
Broker/negotiator for purchase/sale of TV, radio, cable; provides financial svcs including equity, debt & appraisals.

Whitley Media. 12770 Colt Rd., Suite 1111, Dallas 75251-1348. (214) 788-2525. FAX: (214) 788-2514. Bill Whitley, pres.
Bcst brokerage & appraisals.

Professional and confidential services in the sale of Radio and TV stations in the Southeast . . .

THE WHITTLE AGENCY
Media Brokerage
Gary Whittle

12716 Lindley Drive • Raleigh, NC 27614
(919) 848-3596 • FAX: (919) 848-0519

The Whittle Agency. 12716 Lindley Dr., Raleigh, N.C. 27614. (919) 848-3596. FAX: (919) 848-0519. Gary L. Whittle, pres.
Total media brokerage svcs including sls/appraisals of radio stns in the Carolinas, Virginia & the Southeast.

Wilkins Communications Network Inc. Box 444, Spartanburg, S.C. 29304. (803) 585-1885. Robert L. Wilkins, pres.

Willis & Co. 645 Church St., Suite 400, Norfolk, Va. 23510. (804) 624-6500. FAX: (804) 624-6515. L.E. Willis Sr., pres.

Wood & Co. Inc. 431 Ohio Pike, Suite 210N, Cincinnati 45255. (513) 528-7373. Larry C. Wood, pres; M.A. Dennis, rsch analyst; K.A. Gerard, analyst.
Nationwide brokerage svc to buyers & sellers of TV & radio properties.

Consultants

A

AVI Communications Inc. 6311 N. O'Connor Rd., LB 154, Irving, Tex. 75039. (214) 484-5345. FAX: (214) 484-3057. Patrick Shaughnessy, pres.
Produces *The Television Sales Training System*, a 19-volume video series complete with workbooks & exams designed to develop new business for TV stns.

Abt Associates Inc. 55 Wheeler St., Cambridge, Mass. 02138. (617) 492-7100. FAX: (617) 492-5219. Wendell J. Knox, pres/CEO.
Bethesda, Md. 20814: 4800 Montgomery Ln. (301) 913-0500. FAX: (301) 652-7530.
Chicago 60606: 101 N. Wacker Dr., Suite 400. (312) 332-3300. FAX: (312) 621-3840.
Market rsch, strategic planning, mgmt consulting, audience rsch & segmentation; customer satisfaction progs, quality of svc progs.

Accend Broadcast Services. Box 742, Olney, Md. 20832. (301) 924-5700. FAX: (301) 570-8916. Michael J. Weiner, pres/CEO.
Mktg & mgmt issues; talent training workshops & coaching.

AdMedia Corporate Advisors Inc. 866 3rd Ave., 26th Fl., New York 10022. (212) 759-1870. FAX: (212) 888-4960. Robert H. Huntington, Paul F. McPherson, mgng dirs.
Investment bankers & strategic advisors to bcstg, publishing, adv & mktg svcs companies.

Advocates Associates Inc. 180 Mohegan Tr., South Windsor, Conn. 06074-3823. (203) 644-2100. Sherman Tarr, pres.
Govt rels, pub affrs, lobbying, AV concepts, assn & trade group communications.

Air Science Consultants. 347 Prestly Rd., Bridgeville, Pa. 15017. (412) 221-6002; (800) SKY-WATCH. FAX: (412) 221-3160. Richard J. Mancini, pres.
Specially formatted weathercasts from the Skywatch Weather Center.

Aircasting Corp. Box 182, Scottsdale, Ariz. 85252. (602) 840-7341; (602) 840-1763. Richard B. Gilbert, pres/gen mgr; Alma C. Gilbert, VP/project mgr.
Consulting svcs for AM-FM-TV FCC applications, construction, finance, progmg & opns. Turnkey capability.

Jay Albright. 2211 5th Ave., Seattle 98121. (206) 728-2741. FAX: (206) 441-6582. Jay Albright, gen mgr BP Consulting Group; John Sherman, VP.
Specializes in prog consulting to country mus stns.

Allen Financial Services Media Division. Box 2480, Huntington Beach, Calif. 92647. (714) 898-4250. FAX: (818) 996-0796. Cole Allen, pres; Barbara Russell, collection mgr.
Specializes in the collection of coml accounts for suppliers & facilities in the bcst & film markets.

John P. Allen. Airspace Consultant. Box 1008, Fernandina Beach, Fla. 32035-1008. (904) 261-6523. FAX: (904) 277-3651. John P. Allen, own.
Conducts FAA aeronautical evaluations as specified in Subpart C of Part 77 of the Federal Aviation Regulations.

American Cablecom. 95 Morgan St., Stamford, Conn. 06905-5435. (203) 323-7800. FAX: (203) 323-3972. Rick Perrone, pres.
Cable TV svcs; system audits, sls mktg, construction, mgmt.

American Radio Brokers Inc/SFO. Cathedral Hill Hotel Office Bldg., 1255 Post St., Suite 625, San Francisco 94109. (415) 441-3377. Chester P. Coleman, pres; Kathleen O'Donnell, off mgr; Richard "Julio" Haskey, tech dir; Warren Earl, consultant.

Big Lake, Alaska 99652: c/o K.A.B.N. Radio Facilities. (907) 892-8300. Marlo Holmes, dir Alaskan opns.

Stn reviews, mgmt consulting, appraisals, market analysis & assistance for new, nonbcst owns.

Anderson Productions Ltd. 51 W. 81st St., Suite 1B, New York 10024. (212) 769-2501. FAX: (212) 769-2993. Steven C.F. Anderson, pres/exec prod; Vasso S. Anderson, VP mktg.
TV prog prod & consulting firm specializing in info progmg for cable TV, industry & education.

Nick Anthony & Associates. 399 Great Oaks Tr., Wadsworth, Ohio 44281. (216) 336-4570. FAX: (216) 336-0312. Nick Anthony, pres; Diane Agnesi, office mgr.
Mktg, progmg & motivational consultant.

Apex Incentive Travel. 11301 Olive Blvd., St. Louis, Mo. 63141. (314) 997-1500; (800) 325-6181. FAX: (314) 997-3224. Michael Jordan, pres; John Hoelker, dir opns; Renae Scales-Smith, incentive sls mgr.
Corporate & leisure travel, specializes in promotional packages & incentive progs. Apex has four offices in St. Louis and one in Copper Mt., Colo.

Apollo Radio Ltd. 350 Park Ave., New York 10022. (212) 750-4590. FAX: (212) 750-4531. William L. Stakelin, pres.
Consulting for investment purposes.

The Aspen Institute Program on Communications and Society. 1755 Massachusetts Ave. N.W., Suite 501, Washington 20036. (202) 736-5818. FAX: (202) 986-1913. Charles M. Firestone, dir; Katharina Kopp, prog coord.
Public policy seminars & reports.

Associated Essentials. Box 8135, Chicago 60680. (312) 224-5612. Frank Howard Jr., pres; R.C. Hillsman, VP.
Consultants to the radio, TV, CATV, mus video, teleconferencing, film/video & entertainment industries.

Atlantic Communications Inc. Box 3700, Winter Springs, Fla. 32708. (407) 365-4321. FAX: (407) 695-9282. Russell D. Bredholt, pres.
Mktg & communications strategies; mktg rsch.

Audience Research & Development (AR&D). 8828 Stemmons Fwy., Suite 600, Dallas 75247. (214) 630-5097; FAX: (214) 630-4951. Willis Duff, pres/CEO; William W. Taylor, COO; Ed Bewley, chmn; Jim Willi, exec VP client svcs; Jerry Florence, VP rsch; Sandra Connell, VP placement svcs.
Rsch & consultation in loc TV progmg specializing in news. Prog dev, per search, performance coaching, promotion, strategic planning, mktg & sls rsch for bcst TV.

The Austin Co. 3650 Mayfield Rd., Cleveland 44121. (216) 382-6600. FAX: (216) 291-6684. J. William Melsop, pres/CEO; John R. Owen, planning dir bcstg facilities.
Branches: Atlanta; Cleveland; Des Plaines, Ill.; Houston; Kansas City, Mo.; Santa Ana, Calif.; Seattle; South Plainfield, N.J.
Consulting, architectural design, engrg & construction svcs for TV, cable & radio bcstg facilities.

The Avery Co. 11300 Beech Ridge Ct., Fairfax, Va. 22030. (703) 352-3787. Ben Avery, pres.
Media consultation; pub affrs; earned media.

B

BCI/Protocol Inc. 5160 Parkstone Dr., Suite 190, Chantilly, Va. 22021. (703) 222-8300. FAX: (703) 222-0205. R.F. Graves, pres.
Provides specialized telecommunications engrg & consulting svcs.

BIA Consulting & BIA Publications Inc. Box 17307, Washington 20041. (703) 818-2425. FAX: (703) 803-3299. Thomas J. Buono, pres/CEO; William Redpath C.P.A./A.S.A., VP; Peter Bowman, mgr; Mark O'Brien, mgr publications; Debra Metcalf, asst VP mktg.
Appraisers, valuation experts & financial consultants of bcstg & cable business. Publisher of *Investing in Radio*, *Investing in Television* Duncan's Radio yearbook & the TV yearbook.

BP Consulting Group. 2211 5th Ave., Seattle 98121. (206) 728-2741; (800) 426-9082. FAX: (206) 441-6582. Jay Albright, gen mgr; John Sherman, sls; Jim LaMarca, sls; Becky Brenner (Country), Ron Harris (CHR/AOR), consultants; Alison Link, admin.
Radio mgmt & progmg consulting; market & ratings analysis, format search, mus & perceptual rsch, focus groups, staff training & playlists.

BTMI (Broadcast Trustee Management Inc.). 1090 Vermont Ave. N.W., Suite 800, Washington 20005. (202) 408-7036. FAX: (202) 408-1590. Paul W. Robinson Jr., pres.
Financial-asset mgmt, valuation, mktg, restructuring & recovery consultation svcs.

Bargmann Bowen & Kemp Inc. Box 218, Rochester, Vt. 05767. (802) 767-3597. FAX: (802) 767-3589. Henry Bargmann, Carroll G. Bowen, Don Kemp, principals.
Rutland, Vt. 05701: 42½ Center St. (802) 747-4400. FAX: (802) 747-4925.
Voice, data, video equipment, svc, nets, planned, evaluated, specified, implemented.

Joseph Barnes & Associates. 95 Colton Ln., Martinez, Calif. 94553. (510) 372-9495. FAX: (510) 372-9497. Joseph Barnes, pres; Kimberly Allen, creative svcs dir.
TV news consulting in all areas: content, talent, promotion, mktg, seminars.

Beckerman Associates Inc. 14001 Miramar Ave., Madeira Beach, Fla. 33708. (813) 391-2824. FAX: (813) 398-2945. Milton B. Beckerman, co-own.

Tampa 33682: Box 82784. (813) 971-2061. Lincoln A. Mayo, assoc.

Media brokerage, appraisals for bcst & print. Consulting concerning media sls & acquisitions.

Lawrence Behr Associates Inc. 210 W. 4th St., Greenville, N.C. 27835. (919) 757-0279. FAX: (919) 752-9155. Lawrence Behr, CEO; Win Donat, pres; Robert Broudenburg, VP.
Mgmt & tech consulting svcs for AM, FM, TV, telecommunications, cellular, & paging systems; project mgmt & evaluation.

The Benchmark Co. 1705 S. Capital of Texas Hwy., Suite 305, Austin, Tex. 78746. (512) 327-7010. FAX: (512) 328-1464. Rob Balon, pres; Paige Blount, dir rsch.
Full-svc bcst consulting company featuring benchmark phone surveys & the confrontation analysis system, which replaces focus groups.

The Benton Group. Box 5076, Vancouver, Wash. 98668. (206) 737-0296. FAX: (206) 737-0299. Donald Benton, pres; Mitchell Morgan, VP.
Yellow-page & newspr conversion, books for kids, specialized sls training progs & seminars.

Beveridge Institute of Sales & Sales Management. Box 511, Crystal Lake, Ill. 60039-0511. (815) 477-7797; (800) 227-4332 (out of state). FAX: (815) 477-0000. Dirk Beveridge, pres.
Sls & sls mgmt performance & productivity improvement progs; training workshops.

Blackburn & Co. Inc. 201 N. Union St., Suite 340, Alexandria, Va. 22314. (703) 519-3703. FAX: (703) 519-9756. James W. Blackburn Jr., chmn; Richard F. Blackburn, pres.
Acquisition svcs of all kinds including appraisals, brokerage & finance.

Block Communications Group Inc. 2910 Neilson Way, Suite 503, Santa Monica, Calif. 90405-5323. (310) 452-3355. FAX: (310) 452-4077. Richard C. Block, pres.
Consulting specializing in new cable svcs, bcstg stns, syndicated progmg distribution & mktg, serving domestic & international clients.

Bonneville Broadcasting System. 4080 Commercial Ave., Northbrook, Ill. 60062-1829. (800) 631-1600; (708) 291-0110. FAX: (708) 291-0841. John Patton, pres/CEO; Bud Stiker, exec VP; Walter Powers, VP opns; Ford Colley, VP consulting; Michael Krafcisin, mktg svcs; Dave Verdery, prog dir Easy Listening; Jon Radford, Joe Cassady, progmg consultants; Jeff Dear, prod mgr; Mindy Herman, office mgr.

Consultants

Howard Burkat Communications

Two decades of consulting, marketing, creative services, and recruiting for domestic and international cable and broadcasting.

Howard Burkat, President

11 Rectory Lane Scarsdale, New York 10583 Telephone 914·723·2657 Fax 914·472·6225

Full-svc radio progmg, opns, mgmt, finance, duopoly & LMA consultants. Progmg prod & distribution. Signature Series formats: Hot A/C (WMXV); Mainstream A/C (KBIG); Soft A/C (KOIT); Verdery Environment, Easy Mix, ULTRA, Classic Easy (Easy Listening); Paul Christy's Bonneville Gold (Oldies); Bonneville Country (Hit Country). TrueSource Adult Contemporary Compact Disc mus libraries. Monthly ChartBreakers CD Service. At-Cost auditorium mus testing. Talent Bank & Creative Svcs divisions provide talent resources & creative spot copywriting/prod svcs. Digital audio playback systems. Custom Strategic Mapping market analysis.

Bortz & Co. Inc. 1515 Arapahoe St., Suite 1425, Denver 80202. (303) 893-9902. Paul I. Bortz, pres; Mark C. Wyche, James M. Trautman, Lee A. Clayton, VPs.
TV stn mgmt consulting & fair market evaluations; cable financial & market analysis; corporate strategic planning.

Broad Street Ventures. Box 151, Riverside, Conn. 06878. (203) 637-4605. Richard L. Geismar, pres; Fred E. Walker, exec VP.
Financial & mgmt consulting for bcst industries.

Broadcast Alert. 6077 Far Hills Ave., Suite 101, Centerville, Ohio 45459. (513) 885-2137. FAX: (513) 885-2138. Chris Smallwood, pres; C. Radcliffe, VP.
Informs subs of new filing opportunities for radio & TV.

Broadcast-Cable Associates. 12 Lakeview Dr., Lynnfield, Mass. 01940. (617) 595-87900. FAX: (617) 595-8110. Paul McCarthy, gen mgng ptnr.
Indianapolis 46205: 2102 E. 52nd St. (317) 257-2882. FAX: (317) 257-2166. Michael Ruggiero, ptnr.
Negotiations with cable systems for retransmission consent carriage, preferred ch assignments & arrangements for TV stns. Conducts significant viewership studies to erase distant signal copyright liability & prove effective competition for cable systems.

Broadcast Direct Marketing Inc. 2041 S.W. 3rd Ave., Coral Gables, Fla. 33146-3609. (305) 858-9524. FAX: (305) 859-8777. Courtney R. Thompson, pres/CEO; John Doscher Jr., mktg & sls.
Chicago: (708) 382-5525.
Los Angeles: (818) 782-9524.
Custom strategic direct mktg progs; complete promotion & adv svcs including direct mail, telemarketing, data base, custom publishing, sls training, interactive phone/prom.

Broadcast Marketing Corp. 1633 Broadway, 38th Fl., New York 10019. (212) 246-8000. Lee Wolfman, CEO; Harvey Markovitz, pres/COO; Jeff Wolfman, exec VP; Sandy Aronowitz, sr VP/media dir; Shearon Grierson, sr VP client svcs; Ram Akella, sr VP reciprocal trading.
Media buying (all formats), media planning, barter, syndication, travel svcs, remarketing excess inventories.

Broadcast Media Associates. 316 California Ave., Suite 700, Reno, Nev. 89509. (800) 237-3777. Clifford M. Hunter, pres.
Mgmt consulting, mktg studies, bcst investment analysis, sls training & positioning.

Broadcast Media Corp. Box 42513, Washington 20015. (202) 364-1019. FAX: (202) 363-5524. Randall H. Blair, pres.

Full-svc mgmt & financial counseling to the bcst industry with emphasis on radio turnarounds, problems & start-ups; investment banking svc.

Broadcast News Development. 4959 Deepwood Ct., St. Louis, Mo. 63128. (314) 487-1190. FAX: (314) 487-8427. Fred Burrows, pres.
Complete TV bcst news consulting, rsch & talent search svcs.

Broadcasting Asset Management Corp. 1450 N. Astor St., 6th Fl., Chicago 60610. (312) 280-9172. FAX: (312) 348-5831. Jack Minkow, pres.
Merger & feasibility studies, acquisition analyses, capital structuring, brokerage, mgmt procurement & consulting.

Broadcasting Unlimited Inc. 35 Main St., Wayland, Mass. 01778. (508) 653-7200. FAX: (508) 653-4088. Jay Williams Jr., pres; Shauna Arruda, dir opns; Lou Josephs, rsch dir; Steve Gallagher, mgr progmg & promotion.
Strategic planning for audience & revenue growth through direct mktg, telemarketing, interactive technology & data base mgmt svcs.

Howard Burkat Communications. 11 Rectory Ln., Scarsdale, N.Y. 10583. (914) 723-2657. FAX: (914) 472-6225.
Mktg, promoting & consulting for TV, cable, radio & video, domestic & international, including campaigns, ads, brochures, rsch, plans, analysis & recruiting.

Burkhart/Douglas & Associates Inc. 6500 River Chase Cir. E., Atlanta 30328. (404) 955-1550. FAX: (404) 955-6220. Kent Burkhart, chmn; Dwight Douglas, pres.
New formats. Media consultants to radio stns & nets, cable TV, & audio & product mktg. LMA liaisons & negotiators.

Alan Burns & Associates. 11705 Sumacs St., Oakton, Va. 22124. (703) 648-0000. FAX: (703) 264-1710. Alan Burns, pres; Donna Burns, VP.
Progmg & mktg consultants.

George Burns & Co. 6965 El Camino Real, Suite 105-229, Rancho La Costa, Calif. 92009. (619) 746-7993. FAX: (619) 739-8303. George Burns, chmn; Larry Lakoduk, pres; Todd Stewart, VP progmg.
Radio mgmt & consulting.

Burns Media Consultants Inc. Box 6210, Malibu, Calif. 90264. (310) 457-1599. FAX: (310) 457-8367. George A. Burns, pres; Sandra Kasberger, VP.
Custom radio/TV rsch. One-on-one interviewing, strategic market studies, format search, auditorium mus testing, telephone studies, on-going rsch consultation.

Butterfield Communications Group. 87 Blanchard Rd., Cambridge, Mass. 02138. (617) 354-2227. David C. Butterfield, pres.
Sls, mktg, operational & financial counsel; The Benchmark Study of loc TV & radio sls force performance; custom rsch & reports.

C

LAUREN A. COLBY
301-663-1086
COMMUNICATIONS ATTORNEY
Special Attention to Difficult Cases

CLC Consulting. 340 N. Saint Asaph St., Alexandria, Va. 22314. (703) 836-1399. FAX: (703) 836-0717. Chase Libbey.

C.R.N. Media Inc. 124 W. 60th St., Suite 33-F, New York 10023. (212) 765-2587. FAX: (212) 586-8797. Tom Shovan, pres.
Radio stn net/syndication consultants. Svcs include mgmt & prog consulting, exec recruitment, financial planning, market, sls & format analysis.

CTIC Associates. 1700 Shaker Church Rd. N.W., Olympia, Wash. 98502. (206) 866-2080. FAX: (206) 866-1866. Harold Horn, pres.
Waterford, Va. 22190. Box 37, (703) 882-3032. James Reeve, dir tech svcs; Deborah Grindle, sr financial analyst.
Provides consulting svcs for municipal clients regarding cable TV & communications: financial, tech, utilization, renewal, compliance.

Cable Audit Associates Inc. 8101 E. Prentice Ave., Suite 604, Englewood, Colo. 80111. (303) 694-0444. FAX: (303) 694-2559. Alan Davis, pres/CEO; Irvin Hirschhorn, VP.
Progmg license fee audits of cable operators, MMDS, SMATVs & TVRO middlemen.

Cable Management Services. 4059 River Rd., Schenectady, N.Y. 12309-1518. (518) 785-9325. FAX: (518) 785-9325. Paul Schonewolf, George Williams, principals.
Full-svc mgmt consulting in finance, opns, engrg & mktg to cable TV operators & lenders, domestically & internationally.

Capitol Hill-Media Site/Facilities Selection Group. 1666 K St. N.W., Suite 1010, Washington 20006. (202) 833-5800. FAX: (202) 223-0996. James Connelly, Tim Hague, contacts.
Consulting coml real estate svcs, tenant/client representation, construction/financial analysis, turnkey lease/sale assumptions; roof & bldg zoning surveys, metropolitan Washington.

Michael A. Carraher. Qualitative Research Consultant. 204 Dupont St., Philadelphia 19127. (215) 487-2061. FAX: (215) 487-2359. Michael A. Carraher, pres.
Specialist in focus groups, in-depth interviews. Motivational, exploratory & progmg dev studies showing "what is" & "how to."

Cashdollar Inc. 4409 Kings Row, Muncie, Ind. 47304. (800) 552-8113. FAX: (317) 289-7963. Stephen Cashdollar, pres.
Sls training; sls seminars & consulting advisory svcs.

Robert A. Chaisson Inc. Indian Waters Dr., New Canaan, Conn. 06840. (203) 966-6333. FAX: (203) 966-1294. Robert A. Chaisson, pres.
Radio & TV sls & acquisitions.

Chenevert/Soderberg, Architects. 11750 Bricksome Ave., Suite B, Baton Rouge 70816. (504) 291-7884. FAX: (504) 296-5401. Curtis D. Soderberg, AIA, pres; Norman J. Chenevert, AIA, sec/treas.
Architects, planners & tech designers specializing in new & renovated bcst/cable prod facilities.

Christian TV Services of Ellicottville. Box 209, 18 Elizabeth St., Ellicottville, N.Y. 14731-0209. (716) 699-2549. FAX: (716) 699-2683. Rev. George A. Thayer, pres/CEO; Robert A. Thayer, VP/admin dir; Joyce E. Thayer, VP/sec/treas; Roger A. Thayer, VP progmg & prod; Randall A. Thayer, VP distribution & mktg.
TVRO consultant for relg cable & satellite organizations, churches & nets. Some prod & recording distribution of progs.

Clark-Mann & Associates. 203 Columbus Ave., San Francisco 94133. (415) 421-0220. FAX: (415) 421-0417. William D. Clark, pres/CEO.
London, U.K. WIR 51A: 500 Chesham House, 150 Regent St. (071) 439-6228. FAX: (071) 734-4166. William D. Clark, pres.

Broadcasting & Cable Yearbook 1994
H-66

Consultants

Full-svc adv agency & pub rels firm with background in bcst & print.

Jerry Clifton's New World Communications Co. Inc. 6127 Calle Vera Cruz, La Jolla, Calif. 92037. (619) 456-8059. Jerry Clifton, pres.
Complete prog consultation in the "contemporary" field including CHR, adult contemp & urban contemp.

Cole Appraisal Services Inc. Box 1185, Herndon, Va. 22070-1185. (703) 471-5117. FAX: (703) 471-5075. David H. Cole, pres.
Purchase price allocation appraisals, IRS support work, litigation support, asset-based lending appraisals, residual value forecasting, acquisition consulting & insurance valuations.

Coltrin & Associates. 1212 Ave. of the Americas, 10th Fl., New York 10036. (212) 221-1616. FAX: (212) 221-7718. Steve Coltrin, chmn/CEO; Sherril W. Taylor, vice chmn/chmn exec committee.
Consultant svcs to bcst mgmt, mktg sls, promotion rsch; New York & Washington representation in corporate, govt & pub rels.

The Comedy Center Inc. Box 1992, Wilmington, Del. 19899. (302) 656-2209. FAX: (302) 656-4710. Dan White, edit.
Topical humor, one-liners & quips; publishes *Current Comedy*, a semi-monthly newsletter.

Commonwealth Information Services Inc. Box 6497, 724 Thimble Shoals Blvd., Newport News, Va. 23606. (800) 888-2274; (804) 873-3200. FAX: (800) 873-9752. Terry C. Fuller, sr VP sls.
Nationwide collection svcs div.

Communication Bridges. 180 Harbor Dr., Suite 204A, Sausalito, Calif. 94965. (415) 331-3133. FAX: (415) 331-3141. Jon Leland, pres/creative dir.
Desktop video & animation, special effects & computer-based prod system design. Experience with creative svc depts & corporate communications.

Communication Design Associates Inc. 1410 Providence Hwy, Norwood, Mass. 02062. (617) 551-8490. FAX: (617) 551-8491. Robert Hemenway, David Hutton, Stewart Randall, Greg Vincent, ptnrs.
Independent consultants to radio, TV, corporate & govt clients. Designers of studios, prod, presentation & multimedia facilities.

Communication Resources Unlimited Inc. 3727 E. 31st St., Tulsa, Okla. 74135-1506. (918) 743-8300. FAX: (918) 749-3348. Tom Belcher, pres.
Media consultants to radio, TV & cable specializing in acquisitions, mergers & sls.

Communication Trends Inc. 300 Northcreek, Suite 550, 3715 Northside Pkwy. N.W., Atlanta 30327. (404) 262-2900. FAX: (404) 266-3645. Toni Augustine, chmn/pres; Arthur A. Dwyer, exec VP/COO; Elizabeth Maury, VP/business mgr; Teresa Huyck, VP media.
Mktg & adv for cable, direct bcst, & bcst communications industry & related technologies.

Communications Equity Associates. 101 E. Kennedy Blvd., Suite 3300, Tampa 33602. (813) 222-8844. FAX: (813) 225-1513. J. Patrick Michaels Jr., chmn/CEO; Glenn Serafin & Jeanette Tully, VPs/Radio; H. Gene Gawthrop, COO; Harold Even, vice-chmn.
New York 10152: CEA Inc., 375 Park Ave., Suite 3808. (212) 319-1968. Donald Russell, pres.
Berwyn, Pa. 19312: 1235 Westlakes Dr., Suite 140. (215) 251-0650. Thomas MacCrory, sr VP.
Denver 80111: 5613 DTC Pkwy., Suite 300. (303) 694-3090. Bob Berger, VP western opns.
Central, Hong Kong: 3402-04 One Exchange Sq., 8 Connaught Pl. (852) 845-5504. Sarah Rechin, mgng dir.
London, England EC3P 3AJ: 32 St. Mary at Hill. 44-71-623-8844. Lisa-Gaye Shearing, mgng dir.
Munich, Germany D-80539: Maximilianstrasse 30/II. 49-89-293317. Dr. Stephan Goetz, mgng dir.
Provides investment banking, brokerage, regulatory affrs & mgmt svcs for bcst, CATV & related communications industries.

Communications Resources Inc. 1271 Ave. of the Americas, Suite 4662, New York 10020. (212) 315-5600. FAX: (212) 315-5602 Ellen Berland Gibbs, pres.
Strategic planning & financial consulting to bcst, cable & nwspr companies, including merger & acquisition, investment banking & investment mgmt.

Cole Appraisal Services, Inc.

Appraisals

Litigation Support

Consulting

Dedicated to providing True Value in Client service.

David H. Cole, ASA
Senior Member: American Society of Appraisers

P.O. Box 1185
Herndon, VA 22070-1185

(703) 471-5117
FAX (703) 471-5075

Communications & Systems Analysis. 1800 N.W. 187th St., Miami, Fla. 33056. (305) 628-3600. FAX: (305) 628-3700. David Honig, pres.
EEO/affirmative action prog planning & consulting.

CommuniProbe. Box 9190, Seattle 98109. (206) 285-4479. Robert Schultz, dir.
Audience & mktg consultant for CATV & new electronic media; serving systems, MSOs, prog prods adv.

Comsearch. 251 W. Renner Pkwy., Suite 170 Richardson, Tex. 75080. (214) 680-1000. FAX: (214) 680-9802. Dick Smith, dir business info svcs.
Reston, Va. 22091: 11720 Sunrise Valley Dr., (703) 620-6300. FAX: (703) 476-2787. Michael Morin, pres; Harry Stemple, chmn/CEO.
Provides frequency coord, site selection, RFI measurements, path surveys, & protection for satellite earth stn dishes & terrestrial microwave facilities.

Concept Videos. Box 30408, Bethesda, Md. 20824. (301) 656-0842. FAX: (301) 656-0835. William Connell, pres.
Political media campaigns; direct-mktg videos; TV spot prod.

Conley & Associates. Box 3220, 3333 E. Broadway, Suite 1106, Bismarck, N.D. 58502. (701) 222-3902. FAX: (701) 222-4815. Christopher J. Conley, mgng gen ptnr; Candace Christianson, gen ptnr.
Consultants in the area of strategic planning, appraisals, finance, opns, engrg, mktg, human resources & public/govt rels.

Connelly Co. Inc. 5401 W. Kennedy Blvd., Suite 480, Tampa 33609. (813) 287-0906. FAX: (813) 289-0906. Robert J. Connelly, Richard S. Levy, Robert J. "Rob" Connelly, brokers.
Brokers, consultants & recovery unit to assist banks & financial institutions.

Charles M. Conner & Associates. 1437 Chardonnay, Houston 77077. (713) 870-9594. C.M. Conner, pres.
Consulting svc; radio adv sls (loc). Spot, prog, special promotions. Custom design packages, introductory seminars & expediting consultant.

Consolidated Communications Cunsultants. 1837 S.E. Harold St., Portland, Ore. 97202-4932. (503) 232-9787. Eric G. Norberg, pres/edit/publisher; Jane A. Kenney, rsch dir.
Provide progmg, sls & mktg assistance for radio stns (AM mass-appeal, A/C stns a specialty).

Contemporary Communications. Box 1787, Cleveland, Miss. 38732. (601) 846-1787. FAX: (601) 843-0494. Larry G. Fuss, pres.
Progmg, opns & mgmt consulting for small- & medium-market radio stns; tech svcs; FCC compliance; computer software svcs.

Convergent Media Systems. 3490 Piedmont Rd., Suite 800, Atlanta 30305. (404) 262-1555. FAX: (404) 262-2055. Murray Holland, pres; Jim Miles, VP; Jeff Hicks, VP corporate dev; Beverly Markos, VP mktg; Bill Wheless, CFO; Jeff Freemyer, VP strategic planning; Bryan Allen, VP opns & engrg.
Provider of video & data technologies to support the communication & training needs of companies; svcs include consultation, design, instal, net & systems mgmt; systems integration in the following areas: special event & business TV, desktop video, video prod, videoconferencing, interactive multimedia.

The Co-Op Connection. 4547 Kraft Ave., North Hollywood, Calif. 91602. (818) 763-1427. Lois Weiss, pres.
Specialists to the bcst industry in co-op & vendor sls training progs.

JCC — JAN CRAWFORD, PRESIDENT

JAN CRAWFORD COMMUNICATIONS
RT. 1, BOX 22-A, Paris, VA 22130
703-592-3166   FAX 703-592-3633

Jan Crawford Communications. Box 22-A, Rt. 1, Paris, Va. 22130. (703) 592-3166. FAX: (703) 592-3633. Jan Crawford, pres.
Media strategy & placement in FCC law, regarding Democratic political candidates & issues.

Cross Communications Co. 1881 Ninth St., Suite 302, Boulder, Colo. 80302-5151. (303) 444-7799. FAX: (303) 444-4687. Thomas B. Cross, dir.
Provides mgmt & product/svc consulting in teleconferencing, intelligent bldgs. Loc area nets, modems, telecommunications, annual conferences & in-depth rsch reports.

Cross-Country Communications. Box 535, Suffern, N.Y. 10901. (914) 368-1720. Joe Capobianco, pres.
Progmg/creative svcs for international electronic media; market analysis; feasibility studies; appraisals; product dev/implementation in all formats.

Cross The Road Productions. Box 801763, Santa Clarita, Calif. 91380. (818) 954-0214; (805) 254-8069. FAX: (805) 255-6015. Ron Lewis, own; Linda Mansfield, dir svcs; Sam Lawson, engrg; Mike Lundy, prod.
Burbank, Calif. 91502: 269 Alameda, Suite D.
Radio prog prod/consultants; bcst coml prod; produces special progmg for syndication.

Custom Audience Consultants. Box 6878, Arlington, Va. 22206. (703) 671-6303. FAX: (703) 354-8164. Sam Paley, pres; Karren Oakley, VP opns.
Full-svc rsch company; sls, mgmt & progmg, including diary analysis for radio & TV.

D

DDS Sales Training. 5904 W. 35th St., Sioux Falls, S.D. 57106. (605) 361-9923. FAX: (605) 361-1828. Darrell Solberg, pres.
Radio sls training & consulting; mgmt training & consulting; mktg/adv seminars for businesses.

DES Associates. 42 Monmouth Hills, Highlands, N.J. 07732. (908) 291-9807. David E. Schutz, pres; Anthony Hoffman, VP.

DIS Consulting Corp. 12 E. 46th St., Suite 5A, New York 10017. (212) 867-6060. FAX: (212) 867-6579. Douglas I. Sheer, pres.

Broadcasting & Cable Yearbook 1994
H-67

Consultants

Mktg consultant to bcst equipment manufacturers; copublishers of *Broadcast Equipment Marketplace Report (BEM)*.

Mgmt consultation, acquisition analysis & consultation, including financial & market evaluations, dev of mktg & operational plans, focus group rsch.

Daniels & Associates. 3200 Cherry Creek S. Dr., Suite 500, Denver 80209. (303) 778-5555. FAX: (303) 778-5599. Bill Daniels, chmn Daniels Communications Inc.; Phillip Hogue, chmn/CEO; Brian Deevy, pres/COO; Timothy David, exec VP.

New York 10153: Daniels & Associates, 767 5th Ave. (212) 935-5900. FAX: (212) 832-2784. Greg Ainsworth, sr VP; Michael Garstin, exec VP/sr mgng dir.

Provides both mergers & acquisitions, & corporate financial svcs to the CATV & bcstg industries.

Jonathan David. 1515 N. Court House Rd., Suite 301, Arlington, Va. 22201. (703) 276-9007. FAX: (703) 276-9008. Jonathan David.

International consultant specializing in business activities with Eastern European countries, including import & export with a focus on developing effective contacts with loc officials.

E. Alvin Davis & Associates Inc. 9851 Forest Glen Dr., Cincinnati 45242. (513) 984-5000. FAX: (513) 984-5072. E. Alvin Davis, pres; Ted McAllister, VP.

Advice & counsel to radio stns/groups in all areas of progmg & mktg including format selection, positioning, adv & execution.

The Deer River Group. 2000 L St. N.W., Suite 200, Washington 20036. (202) 659-3331. Robin B. Martin, pres/CEO; Erwin G. Krasnow Esq., gen counsel.

Wayland, Mass. 01778: 35 Main St. (508) 653-7200. Jay P. Williams Jr., COO.

Provide aquisition consulting svcs including private briefing seminars, advice on structuring deals, investment banking & due diligence assistance.

Design Publishers Inc. International Satellite Directory, 800 Siesta Way, Sonoma, Calif. 95476. (707) 939-9306. FAX: (707) 939-9235. Silvano Payne, publisher.

Publishers of the 1,200-page *International Satellite Directory,* complete source for all info on the satellite industry.

Direct Mail Express Inc. 2441 Bellevue Ave., Daytona Beach, Fla. 32114. (904) 257-2500. FAX: (904) 257-2570. Mike Panaggio, own.

High-impact direct mail campaigns, data base mgmt, audience rsch via cluster-targeted mktg, market exclusive.

Ditingo Media Enterprises. 100 Park Ave., New York 10017. (212) 308-8810. Vincent M. Ditingo, pres.

Media & mktg consulting, corporate writing, books, profiles, articles, speeches, brochures, video scripts, newsletters & periodicals for bcstg & cable.

Dominionet Inc. 1860 N. Talbott Pl., Waynesboro, Va. 22980. (703) 942-1314. FAX: (703) 942-1314. Gary E. Kirtley, pres.

Bcst appraisals, acquisition evaluations, sls & progmg analysis; interim mgmt; FMV appraisals.

Dornself Broadcast Group. 6075 Lincoln Dr., Edina, Minn. 55436-1638. (612) 933-7100. H.W. "Hank" Dornself, pres; Pat Perkins, assoc.

Consultants in tax matters & appraisals, financial & accounting, aquisitions, mergers, private placements, due diligence, workouts, strategic planning & motivational studies.

Willard Leo Dougherty Teach Me Time Sales. 2424-A Dunwoody Crossing, Dunwoody, Ga. 30338. (404) 451-3075. Willard Leo Dougherty, own.

Coaching specialists in the fundamentals of bcst adv time sls.

Drake-Chenault. (A division of Broadcast Programming.) 2211 5th Ave., Seattle 98121. (206) 728-2741; (800) 426-9082. FAX: (206) 441-6582. Edith Hilliard, VP/gen mgr; John Carlile, VP mktg; Jay Albright, consultant.

Radio stn format consulting & rsch. Wkly playlists, mus "safe" lists for most formats, mus rsch, focus groups, market analysis.

Duncan's American Radio Inc. Box 90284, Indianapolis 46290. (317) 844-0988; (317) 630-2888. James H. Duncan Jr., pres.

Publishes books about the radio industry, including *American Radio* (four editions per year), *American Radio-Small Market Edition, Radio Revenue Shares and Audience Shares, The Facilities of Amercian Radio, Duncan's Radio Market Guide & Duncan's Radio Group Directory.*

E

East Coast Video Systems. 52 Ralph St., Belleville, N.J. 07109. (201) 751-5655. FAX: (201) 751-8731. Richard Bisignano, pres; Paul M. Krucik, VP engrg; Mary Nahra, VP sls.

Video & audio system consultation, design, instal & training; serving cable systems, corporate, bcst & teleprod facilities.

Bill Elliott Broadcast Consultant. Box 1256, Port Richey, Fla. 34673-1256. (813) 849-3477. Bill Elliott, pres.

Mgmt & progmg, adv sls & mktg.

Enterprise Appraisal Co. 489 Devon Park Dr., Wayne, Pa. 19087. (215) 687-5855. FAX: (215) 971-0760. Jack C. Emery, pres; C. David Ungruhe, exec VP; William E. Benbow, sr VP.

Branch offices in New York & Washington.

Evaluates communications-oriented assets, such as equipment & real estate, for TV, CATV, radio, cellular systems, & satellites.

Executive Broadcast Services. Box 60327, Colorado Springs 80960. (800) 800-0107. FAX: (719) 579-6664. Skip Joeckel, pres; Kelley Hilligoss, dir opns & mktg.

Markets & sells a select line of progs, products & svcs to U.S. radio stns.

Executive Communications Inc. 700 Springdale Woods Dr., Macon, Ga. 31210. (912) 477-5931. Ron Leppig, pres.

Loc sls consulting for TV & radio stns, cable TV systems. Provides source for sls strategy & sls support, sls seminars; start-up & turnaround specialists.

Executive Decision Systems Inc. 6421 W. Weaver Dr., Littleton, Colo. 80123-3815. (303) 795-9090. FAX: (303) 795-9090. Dr. Philip Jay LeNoble, chmn/CEO; Donna LeNoble, pres/COO.

Provide sls & mgmt training focusing on generating long-term, loc direct business.

William A. Exline Inc. 4340 Redwood Hwy., Suite F230, San Rafael, Calif. 94903. (415) 479-3484. FAX: (415) 479-1574. Andrew P. McClure, pres; W. Dean LeGras, VP; Miramae M. Welch, assoc; William A. Exline, consultant.

Gen mgmt, financial rsch, appraisal, receiverships & bankruptcies.

The Express Corp. 3518 3rd Ave., San Diego 92103. (619) 298-2834. FAX: (619) 298-4143. Byron Andrus, pres.

Design, fabrication, instal & lighting of news environments, newsrooms, interview & talkshow sets. Six lines of modular studio cabinets for radio stns worldwide.

F

FM Atlas Publishing and Electronics. Box 336, Esko, Minn. 55733-0336. (218) 879-7676. Bruce F. Elving, own; Carol J. Elving, office mgr.

FM radio directory, rsch on FM-SCS & FM trans, FM-SCS receivers, *FMedial* newsletter.

Fair West Direct. 6020 Cornerstone Ct. W., Suite 100, San Diego 92121. (619) 552-0777. FAX: (619) 552-0098. Reg Johns, pres; Greg Fredrick, sr VP; George Johns, VP.

Direct & data base mktg systems for bcstg.

Faraone Communications Inc. 162 W. 56th St., Suite 1203, New York 10036. (212) 489-1313. Jennie Faraone, chmn; Ted Faraone, pres.

Media rels, press rels, image bldg & pub svc campaigns.

Faries & Associates. 67 Central Ave., Los Gatos, Calif. 95032. (408) 354-7308. FAX: (408) 395-6670. David A. Faries, mgng ptnr; Michael A. Faries, Jason D. Faries, assocs.

Corporate pub rels, investor rels, mktg communications, business intelligence, mgmt consulting.

Federal Engineering Inc. Redwood Plaza II, 10600 Arrowhead Dr., Fairfax, Va. 22030. (703) 359-8200. FAX: (703) 359-8204. Ronald F. Bosco, pres; P. Freedenberg, exec VP.

Strategic planning, coverage analysis, new product definition, market rsch, competitive anaylsis, rates & tariffs, bcst stn design, mergers & acquisitions, expert testimony, regulatory support.

Ferraro Communications Inc. 130 Bowdoin St., Boston 02108. (617) 367-6390. Tom Ferraro, pres.

Concept, script & prod/dir series for coml, radio, film & videotape prods.

Imero Fiorentino Associates Inc. 33 W. 60th St., New York 10023. (212) 246-0600. FAX: (212) 246-6408. Imero Fiorentino, chmn/pres; Jim Hartzer, exec VP/COO; Anthony Salerno Jr., VP prod; William Marshall, VP facilities design.

Glendale, Calif. 91203: 229 N. Central Ave. (818) 551-9595. Renee Howard, dir opns.

Prod, design, staging, lighting consultation, & direction for bcst TV & cable; TV studio facilities design; seminars on TV lighting & staging techniques.

FirstCom Broadcast Services. (A division of Jim Long Companies Inc., a Zomba Company.) 13747 Montfort Dr., Suite 220, Dallas 75240. (214) 934-2222; (800) 858-8880. FAX: (214) 404-9656. Jim Long, chmn; Cecelia Garr, pres/CEO.

Mus, prod & effects libraries; creative sls consulting.

Norman Fischer & Associates Inc. 1209 Pkwy., Austin, Tex. 78703. (512) 476-9457. FAX: (512) 476-0540. Norman Fischer, pres.

Brokerage in radio, TV & cable, consultation in mgmt & opns, appraisals, feasibility studies, expert testimony, financial planning & assistance.

Flagship Communications Inc. 11916 Glen Valley Rd., Brecksville, Ohio 44141. (216) 526-6017. Joel Rose, pres.

TV & radio prog consultation. Specializing in AM talk progmg.

FloriCal Systems. 4613 N.W. 6th St., Suite F, Gainesville, Fla. 32609-1781. (904) 372-8326. FAX: (904) 375-0859. Jim Moneyhun, pres.

Manufacturer of TV automation, control & effects.

Focal Press. 80 Montvale Ave., Stoneham, Mass. 02180. (617) 438-8464. FAX: (617) 438-8103. Karen Speerstra, publishing dir; Frank Satlow, tech publisher; Marie Lee, edit.

Publishes professional tech books in bcstg, film, video, AV, theater & photography.

Richard A. Foreman Associates Inc. 330 Emery Dr. E., Stamford, Conn. 06902. (203) 327-2800. FAX: (203) 967-9393. Richard A. Foreman, pres; Susan Brenner, admin asst; Richard W. Kozak, assoc.

Fair market evaluations & asset appraisals, media brokerage, stn financing, mgmt/prod consultation.

Robert H. Forward & Associates. 560 San Gorgonio St., San Diego 92106. (619) 223-7878. Robert H. Forward, pres.

Film prod & gen mgmt consultants.

Franey, Parr & CBA. 9901 Business Pkwy., Suite B, Lanham, Md. 20706. (301) 459-0055. FAX: (301) 459-5405. Bill Franey, CEO.

Insurance, bonding & benefits admin.

Fremer & Associates Inc. 15060 Ventura Blvd., Suite 225, Sherman Oaks, Calif. 91403. (818) 783-6028. FAX: (818) 382-3020. Lisa Fremer, ptnr.

Accounting, business mgmt, consulting, investment advisory svcs, prod, taxation, TV packaging, touring—domestic & international.

G

Clifton Gardiner & Associates Inc. Box 5559, 82 E. Beaver Creek Blvd., Avon, Colo. 81620. (303) 949-4485. FAX: (303) 949-0266. Clifton H. Gardiner, pres.

Brokerage, consulting & financial svcs for the bcst & cable TV industries.

Garrett Media Services. 1119 San Antonio, El Paso, Tex. 79901. (915) 533-4700. FAX: (915) 533-3640. Garrett W. Haston, pres; Michele A. Haston.

Dave Gifford International. 1143 Taos Hwy., Santa Fe, N.M. 87501. (505) 989-7007. FAX: (505) 988-1991. David W. Gifford, own/pres.

Sls turnarounds & troubleshooting. Sls, mgmt, & adv seminars. New account sls & client dev. Takeover counsel to first stn owns.

Gilbert Communications. 4101 Legends Way, Maryville, Tenn. 37801. (615) 977-6633. Robert W. Gilbert, sr consultant.

Full-svc radio/TV news consulting, writing seminars, staff motivation, news policy formulation, profit center strategy, *Broadcast News Handbook.*

Global Communications Consultants. 747 Wire Rd., Auburn, Ala. 36830. (205) 826-0390. H.D. Norman, pres; John Schramm, exec VP.

Pub rels & listener/viewer promotions for the media. Mail-order mktg.

Consultants

Green Consultants of Vero Beach Inc. 414 22nd St. S.E., Vero Beach, Fla. 32962. (407) 778-2573. Bert Green, pres.
Engrg & applied sciences for voice, data & imaging communications & energy mgmt as related to cable & bcst.

Greenwood Performance Systems. 3010 S. Harvard, Suite 210, Tulsa, Okla. 74114. (800) 331-9115. FAX: (918) 743-8451. Jim Rhea, pres.
Bcst-specific sls staff/mgmt training, seminars & courses including sls mgmt consultation, strategic studies, compensation, motivation & evaluation.

H

Hague & Co. 540 Frontage Rd., Suite 3020, Northfield, Ill. 60093-1201. (708) 441-7200. FAX: (708) 441-7262. Lee Hague, pres.
Corporate planning & acquisitions in TV, radio, CATV, nwsprs, magazines.

Halper & Associates. 304 Newbury St., Suite 506, Boston 02115. (617) 786-0666. FAX: (617) 786-1809. Donna L. Halper, pres; Jon Jacobik, computer consultant.
Radio progmg & mgmt consulting, market studies, format changes, mus library software. Staff training, motivation. Specialize in small- & medium-markets, new owners, turnarounds.

Margret Haney of Graham-Haney. 2995 Woodside Rd., Woodside, Calif. 94062. (415) 325-5552. FAX: (415) 325-5556. Margret Haney, pres; Sondra Carver, J.D. law & taxes.
Media adv, buying, brokerage & consulting.

Happi Associates. Sales/Programming/Management Consultants. Box 110892, Nashville 37211. (615) 331-8570; (800) 624-0018. FAX: (615) 331-8571. Skeeter Dodd C.R.M.C., VP/gen mgr.
Sls & mgmt assistance & motivation for radio, cable TV & business; progmg & format; AM specialist.

Hardesty & Associates. 115 Retiro Way, San Francisco 94123. (415) 563-4411. John F. Hardesty, pres.
Stn valuations including asset allocation appraisals, stn cost analysis, sls & promotion consultancy, financing advice.

Richard Harper Associates Inc. 9454 Wilshire Blvd., Suite 600, Beverly Hills, Calif. 90212. (310) 271-1133. Richard Harper, pres; Royal Harper, VP.
Appraisals & evaluations of motion pictures; worldwide licensing experts; per picture allocations; revenue forecasts; expert witness svcs.

Harris Marketing Group. 3422 Flair Dr., Dallas 75229. (214) 902-8552. FAX: (214) 956-9885. Bob Harris, pres.
Sls mktg, promotion consultants; direct-mail coupon books; scratch & match games, vendor, grocery mktg, food broker & food manufacturer progs.

Harrison, Bond & Pecaro. 1201 Connecticut Ave. N.W., Suite 450, Washington 20036-2605. (202) 775-8870. FAX: (202) 775-0175. Susan D. Harrison, James R. Bond Jr., Timothy S. Pecaro, John S. Sanders, Jeffrey P. Anderson.
Economic consulting, fair market valuations, asset allocation appraisals, feasibility studies, expert testimony.

William Hatfield. 212 Whitestone Rd., Silver Spring, Md. 20901. (301) 593-0184. William Hatfield, pres.
Fixed & mobile communications systems for voice & data.

Jack Hayes & Associates. (A division of INTERSTAR RADIO.) Box 12143, La Jolla, Calif. 92039-2143. (619) 229-8307. FAX: (619) 229-8308. Jack Hayes, pres; Kevin Barrett, VP.
San Diego 92122: Major Market Sweepers ID's, Sweepers, Promotion Production Co., 7770 Regents Rd., #393. (619) 990-5225.
Bcst consultants; CHR, sports/talk/news clients in all major markets; progmg, positioning, rsch.

Norman Hecht Research Inc. Box 698, 33 Queens St., Syosset, N.Y. 11791. (516) 496-8866. FAX: (516) 496-8165. Norman Hecht, pres; Richard Feldman, sr VP/gen mgr; Harvey Morrow, VP media rsch; Dennis Regan, VP progmg rsch.
Mktg rsch & consulting, specializing progmg, news & talent rsch, image & promotion, ratings analysis, new media, cable, VDT/VOD.

HOFFMAN SCHUTZ MEDIA CAPITAL

20 YEARS OF SERVICE TO THE COMMUNICATIONS INDUSTRY

Appraisals • Financing • Restructuring • Litigation Support

Anthony M. Hoffman **David E. Schutz**

42 Monmouth Hills • Highlands, New Jersey • 07732
(212) 297-0620

Bob Henabery Associates Inc. 136 E. 55th St., New York 10022. (212) 753-6513. FAX: (212) 888-6982. Bob Henabery, pres.
Radio progmg consulting svcs.

Bill Hennes & Associates. 130 Minges Hills Dr., Battle Creek, Mich. 49017. (616) 979-8926. Bill Hennes, pres; David Nelson, VP sls training.
Progmg, sls & mgmt consulting.

Hi Ho Productions. Box 8135, Chicago 60680. (312) 224-5612. Frank Howard Jr., pres; R.C. Hillsman, VP.
Consultants to radio, TV, CATV & video.

R. Miller Hicks & Co. 1011 W. 11th St., Austin, Tex. 78703. (512) 477-7000. FAX: (512) 477-9697. R. Miller Hicks, pres.
Brokerage, financing, mgmt consulting.

Hilding Communications. Box 1700, Morgan Hill, Calif. 95038-1700. (408) 842-2222. Eric R. Hilding, own.
Offers progmg, sls & mktg consultation, gen bcst consulting, FM ch studies, complex FM substitution proposals, site locations, 301 application engrg.

James C. Hirsch Communications Services. 447 Westover Rd., Stamford, Conn. 06902. (203) 324-2911. James C. Hirsch, own.
Bcstg/communications consulting svcs for adv & mktg progs, pub affrs, surveys & special projects, consulting & rsch implementation.

Hoffman Schutz Media Capital Inc. 42 Monmouth Hills, Highlands, N.J. 07732. (212) 297-0620. Anthony M. Hoffman, pres; David E. Schutz, VP.
Debt & equity financing, appraisals, restructurings & litigation support.

Host Communications. Box 3071, 546 E. Main St., Lexington, Ky. 40596. (606) 253-3230. FAX: (606) 233-1099. W. James Host, CEO; Marc Kidd, pres; Mike Wells, prod.
College sports bcstg & TV syndications; publishing & sports mktg.

The Howard-Sloan-Koller Group. 353 Lexington Ave., 11th Fl., New York 10016. (212) 661-5250. FAX: (212) 557-9178. Edward R. Koller Jr., pres; Karen Danziger, exec VP.
Executive search & consulting in the cable, info & publishing industries.

The Larry Howe Group. Dallas Communications Complex, 6311 N. O'Connor Rd., Suite N28, LB21, Irving, Tex. 75039-3510. (214) 869-7628. Larry W. Howe, pres.
Strategic project mgmt to new communications ventures; svcs include business feasibility studies, market assessment, funding & gen mgmt; focus on CATV, communications & entertainment sectors.

Don Hurt & Associates. Box 5550, Winter Park, Fla. 32793. (407) 679-8718. FAX: (407) 679-9146. Don Hurt, own.
Specializing in retail bcst sls training, radio & TV; emphasis on vendor support training & dev.

Mark F. Hutchins Broadcasting Services Inc. Box 6418, Brattleboro, Vt. 05302-6418. (802) 258-4500. FAX: (802) 254-6683. Mark F. Hutchins, pres; David L. Underhill, VP.
Computerized sls-oriented coverage maps.

I

Imagemaker Productions. Box 82, Neillsville, Wis. 54456. (715) 743-2883. Mark T. Moennig, pres.
Palatine, Ill. 60067: 965 N. Cove Dr. (708) 359-4455. Gregory Moennig, co-prod.
PSA prod for radio/TV.

Incentive Travel Co. 3025 Ashley Phosphate Rd., North Charleston, S.C. 29418. (803) 760-1311; FAX: (803) 760-2333. Larry Kirby, pres.
Bcst incentive trips worldwide; all major sporting events; owned & operated by bcstrs.

Innovative Audience Research Inc. 122 Purcell Dr., Alameda, Calif. 94502. (510) 523-2458. FAX: (510) 523-2458. Mike Silverstein, pres; Susan B. Silverstein, exec VP.
Strategic planning in news, progmg & promotion impacting sweep book ratings in 17 TV metered markets.

Innovative Information Services Corp. 305 Mountain Dr., Suite F, Destin, Fla. 32541. (904) 654-4772. Ty Andros, VP/gen mgr.
Produces consumer info directory.

J

Joe Jones & Marion Jones Co. 10556 Arnwood Rd., Lake View Terrace, Calif. 91342. (818) 890-0730. FAX: (818) 899-4457. Joe Jones, consultant; Marion Jones, exec VP/admin, mktg & audience rsch counsel.
Consultant to cable bcstg, motion picture, video, mus publishing, recording & entertainment industries.

Jones Satellite Audio Inc. Box 3309, 9697 E. Mineral Ave., Englewood, Colo. 80155-3309. (800) 876-3303; (303) 792-3111. FAX: (303) 792-3951; (303) 799-0551. T.J. Lambert, sr VP; Phil Barry, VP opns & progmg.
Five 24-hour satellite-delivered formats with no net commercials & CD library included with svc: Country, Adult Contemporary, Soft Hits, Goldies & Easy Listening.

Mike Joseph. 11 Punchbowl Dr., Westport, Conn. 06880. (203) 227-8326.
Monitoring, market & record rsch, targeting, recommendations, updates, sound design, staff search, reprogmg, custom-tailored on-scene work, retainer.

K

K-B Ltd. Box 25548, Milwaukee 53225. (414) 781-0188. FAX: (414) 781-5313. John Kompas, chmn; Jackie Biel, pres/CEO.
Rsch in LPTV: mktg feasibility studies, demographic analysis; rsch assistance to companies entering the LPTV market & stn representation.

Charles Kadlec & Associates. 1255 23rd St. N.W., Washington 20037. (202) 857-2950. FAX: (202) 857-2900. Charles H. Kadlec, pres.
Evaluation, tax allocation, litigation support, financial workout support, acquisition/divestiture consulting, market & economic analyses.

Kagan Capital Management Inc. 126 Clock Tower Pl., Carmel, Calif. 93923-8734. (408) 624-1536. FAX: (408) 625-3225. Paul Kagan, dir.
Investment & portfolio mgmt for media execs, companies & pension plans.

Broadcasting & Cable Yearbook 1994

Consultants

How Much Is Your Broadcast Property Worth?

If you're interested in valuing your broadcast property...or someone else's...call or write Paul Kagan or Bruce Bishop Cheen, the broadcasting industry's premier appraisers.

 Kagan Media Appraisals, Inc.
We Value Your Business.

126 Clock Tower Place, Carmel, CA 93923
Tel. 408-624-1536 • Fax 408-624-3105

Kagan Media Appraisals Inc. 126 Clock Tower Pl., Carmel, Calif. 93923-8734. (408) 624-3105. FAX: (408) 624-3105. Paul Kagan, chmn/pres; Robin Flynn, VP; Bruce Bishop Cheen, VP bcst appraisals.

Kagan Media Appraisals Inc. specializes in the valuation & appraisal of media & communications properties. As part of the Kagan Group of Companies, we maintain the industry's most comprehensive data base of stn values, so we know what yesterday's stns sold for, what buyers are paying today & what they are likely to pay tomorrow. Svcs include: fair market valuations, expert witness testimony, asset appraisals, ESOP valuations, fairness opinions, minority interest valuations, financial feasibility studies, strategic planning, custom rsch & reports, & consulting.

Paul Kagan Associates Inc. 126 Clock Tower Pl., Carmel, Calif. 93923-8734. (408) 624-1536. FAX: (408) 625-3225. Paul Kagan, pres.
Specializing in financial & investment rsch. Media financial newsletters & data base reports.

Kagan Seminars Inc. 126 Clock Tower Pl., Carmel, Calif. 93923-8734. (408) 624-1536. FAX: (408) 625-3225. Paul Kagan, pres; Genni Russell, seminar dir.
Seminars on media topics.

Kalba International Inc. 23 Sandy Pond Rd., Lincoln, Mass. 01773. (617) 259-9589. FAX: (617) 259-1460. Kas Kalba, pres; Pat Kalba, VP; Y. Braunstein, Pacific dir; G. Amyot, European mgr (Paris).
Rsch, planning & advisory svcs in telecommunications, bcstg & cable TV areas; specializes in international ventures & interactive multimedia.

Kane Reece Associates Inc. 399 Thornall St., Metro Park, N.J. 08837-2236. (908) 494-3700. FAX: (908) 494-8798. John "Jack" E. Kane, Norval D. Reece, Robert E. Ott, principals.
Asset appraisals, business enterprise evaluations, due diligence, engrg expert testimony, property tax control, & related financial & tech consulting svcs.

Allan Kaplan Enterprises. 6 Parkview Circle, Court Madera, Calif. 94925. (415) 927-7757. FAX: (415) 927-4637. Allan Kaplan, pres.
Mus & film consultant: mktg, communications, business dev.

Harry Kovsky Inc. Cedarlawn Rd., Irvington, N.Y. 10533. (914) 591-8244. FAX: (914) 591-7748. Harry Kovsky, pres.

Specialists in content & format analysis of loc & net TV news & entertainment progs, promotion analysis, ratings analysis & audience promotional rsch.

Kozacko Media Services. Box 948, 800 Underwood Ave., Elmira, N.Y. 14902. (607) 733-7138. FAX: (607) 733-1212. Richard L. Kozacko, pres; Melvin L. Stone, Bruce M. Kanner, VPs; John C. Clancy, W. Donald Roberts Jr., assocs.
Gaithersburg, Md. 20878: Box 3306. (301) 977-2023. Bruce M. Kanner.
Cape Elizabeth, Me. 04107: One Canterbury Way. (207) 799-8804. Melvin L. Stone.
Sarasota, Fla. 34238: Box 39010. (813) 966-3411. W. Donald Roberts.
Appraisals & current market valuations of radio & TV stns. Bcst acquisition planning.

L

Landsman Media Inc. 7 N. Airmont Rd., Suite 6, Suffern, N.Y. 10901. (914) 368-4810. FAX: (914) 368-4812. Dean Landsman, pres.
Mgmt consultation, acquisition analysis & consultation, including financial & market evaluations, dev of mktg & operational plans & focus group rsch.

The F.H. Laurier Design Group. 800 Brickell Ave., Suite 200, Miami, Fla. 33131. (305) 372-5225. FAX: (305) 375-9470. Francisco H. Laurier, pres; J. Raul Conde R.A.
Architecture, space planning, interior design, graphic design & signage, mktg & pub rels, purchase & instal, moving consultation & coord.

Lawson & Associates Architects. 4919 Bethesda Ave., Bethesda, Md. 20814. (301) 654-1600. FAX: (301) 654-1601. Bruce Lawson, A.I.A.; Garret Nicholson, R.A.
Consulting architectural design & construction mgmt svcs for TV & cable industry; facility planning, design & coord of construction svcs.

Lawson Media. 6008 Skyline Cir., West Linn, Ore. 97068. (503) 650-9695. FAX: (503) 657-7442. Alan Lawson, pres.
Radio progmg consultant specializing in adult AOR & NAC formats.

Tony Lease Incentive Tours. 806 S.W. Broadway, Portland, Ore. 97205. (800) 545-1010; (503) 295-2000. FAX: (503) 295-2102. Tony Lease, pres; June Hope Lease, exec VP.
Laguna Niguel, Calif. 92677: Box 7531. (714) 249-6867. Becky Cerato, exec asst mgr.
Branch offices in California & Hong Kong.
Bcst incentive tour company producing & operating tours for sls incentive plans; "Travel Secrets" radio informercial available on barter.

Let's Talk. (A division of BP Consulting Group.) 2211 5th Ave., Seattle 98121. (206) 728-2741. FAX: (206) 441-6582. Jay Albright, gen mgr; John Sherman, VP.
Specializing in prog consulting for country mus stns.

Lieber & Associates. 2 N. Riverside Plaza, Suite 2400, Chicago 60606. (312) 276-6891. Mitchell Lieber, pres.
Consulting svcs for cable TV customer svc centers, 800 number adv & data base mktg.

The Stephen T. Lindberg Co. 9815 E. Crestline Cir., Englewood, Colo. 80111. (303) 694-1637. FAX: (303) 771-8737. Stephen T. Lindberg, pres/CEO.
Consults ind owns of cable systems, MSOs, radio & TV stns in sls & acquisitions of operating assets.

Lipson & Co. 1900 Ave. of the Stars, Suite 2810, Los Angeles 90067. (310) 277-4646. FAX: (310) 277-8585. Howard R. Lipson, pres; Eiji Katayama, sr VP; Harriet L. Lipson, VP radio, cable & adv.
Specializes in international & domestic bcstg (TV & radio), cable, entertainment, adv, mktg, financial, mdse & licensing, recruiting.

Scott Lockwood Enterprises. 22706 Aspan St., Suite 703, Lake Forest, Calif. 92630. (714) 241-1111. Scott Lockwood, pres/CEO.
Prog consultation.

Lontos Sales & Motivation Inc. Box 2874, Laguna Hills, Calif. 92654. (714) 831-8861. FAX: (714) 831-8645. Pam Lontos, pres.
Keynote speeches, all-day seminars, in-stn sls consulting, audio sls tapes; specializes in radio, TV & cable sls.

Lund Consultants to Broadcast Management Inc. 1330 Millbrae Ave., Millbrae, Calif. 94030-2829. (415) 692-7777. FAX: (415) 692-7799. John C. Lund, pres; June H. Lund, exec VP; Russ Schell, Randy Scovil, assoc consultants; Laura Martorana, rsch assoc.
Customized progmg/mgmt consulting. Format design/implementation. Specialists: A/C, AOR, CHR, Oldies, Country, News/Talk. Market/stn evaluation. Music Manager ® software.

M

MJM Research & Programming. 11539 W. 83rd St. Lenexa, Ks. 66214. (800) 945-4656; (913) 888-3366. FAX: (913) 888-4423. C.C. McCartney, pres; Clark Roberts, VP.
Provides hook-tape prod, listener screening, fielding & tabulation for all mus testing, perceptual studies, focus groups & promotional telemarketing.

M.O.R. Media. 21-54 44th Dr., Long Island City, N.Y. 11101. (718) 786-3703; (800) 827-1722. FAX: (718) 786-3870. Steve Warren, gen mgr; Paul Siebold, office mgr; Lisa Stephens, receptionist; Ruth A. Meyer, assoc.
MOR/Pop standard format consulting, progmg, promotion, sls; special attention to AM turnarounds; distributes "Great Entertainers" MOR mus library/format.

Frank N. Magid Associates Inc. One Research Ctr., Marion, Iowa 52302. (319) 377-7345. FAX: (319) 377-5861. Frank N. Magid, CEO; Bruce Northcott, pres; Daniel Bormann, VP/chief admin off; Steve Ridge, group VP; Dick Haynes, VP rsch; Joe George, group VP; Mackie Morris, VP Magid Institute; Frank Biancuzzo; VP mktg & creative svcs; Steven Cagle, David L. Smith, VP entertainment.
London, U.K. W1R 5FA: 500 Chesham House, 150 Regent St. FAX: 011-44-71-431-6937. Charles Munro, mgr European opns; Brent Magid, dir international mktg.
Specialists in rsch-driven consultation to TV, radio, print & cable communicators all over the world; svcs include prog evaluation, talent search & coaching, The Magid Institute, & the Magid Network.

Mahlum & Nordfors, McKinley, Gordon. 2505 3rd Ave., Suite 219, Seattle 98121. (206) 441-4151. FAX: (206) 441-0478. John Mahlum, pres; Patrick A. Gordon A.I.A., principal; John E. Petterson A.I.A., tech project mgr.
Design, tech consulting, feasibility & facilities studies, cost analysis & construction admin for TV/radio stns; prod & equipment storage facilities; & film studios.

Malarkey-Taylor Associates Inc. (MTA/EMCI). 1130 Connecticut Ave. N.W., Suite 325, Washington 20036. (202) 835-7800. FAX: (202) 835-7811. Andrew Roscoe, CEO; Martin Malarkey, chmn; Archer Taylor, sr VP engrg; Robert M. Jones, pres; Andrew R. Gefen, VP financial svcs; Samuel Book, pres rsch.
Middlesex, London, U.K. UBD 7BD: 6 Chapel House Business Ctr. 152-156 High St. (011) 44-0-895-431-329. FAX: (011) 44-071-233-7163. Beverly Drumm-Schall, dir.
Cable, cellular, paging, bcstg consultants, fair market appraisals, asset evaluations, due diligence, engrg, market rsch, mgmt, expert testimony.

Marketing and Creative Services. (A division of Frank N. Magid Associates Inc.) One Research Ctr., Marion, Iowa 52302. (319) 377-7345. FAX: (319) 377-5861. Frank N. Magid, CEO; Bruce Northcott, pres; Steve Ridge, VP consultation; Frank Biancuzzo, VP mktg group; Charles Munro, mgr European opns.
Mktg/promotion rsch & consultation.

The Marshall Company. 2121 Ave. of the Stars, Suite 3120, Los Angeles 90067. (310) 552-6577. FAX: (310) 553-4911. Sherrie Marshall, pres.
Washington 20036: (202) 775-8469.
Specializing in strategic planning, regulatory policy & acquisition advice for communication companies.

Marshall & Stevens Inc. 600 Commonwealth Ave., Suite 700, Los Angeles 90005. (213) 385-1515. FAX: (213) 386-8911. Robert Kerslake, CEO; John Glenn, VP Pacific rgn.
Philadelphia 19103-9977: 1700 Market St., Suite 1510. (215) 561-5600. FAX: (215) 557-7280. Wiley Scott, VP Atlantic rgn.

Consultants

Other branch offices: Baltimore; Chicago; Dallas; Detroit; Houston; Kansas City, Mo.; New York; Portland, Ore.; San Francisco; Stamford, Conn.; St. Louis, Mo.; Tampa.
Appraisals & valuations of tangible & intangible assets—real estate, machinery & equipment; & enterprise valuations.

Pat Martin & Associates. 4359 S. Howell Ave., Suite 106, Milwaukee 53207-5056. (414) 482-1959. FAX: (414) 483-1980. Pat Martin, pres.
Radio stn start-ups & turnarounds; problem solving for difficult bcst situations.

Matlock Media Services Inc. Box 328, Eagle, Idaho 83616. (208) 939-2452. FAX: (208) 939-0361. Stephen J. Matlock, pres.
Telecommunications integration consulting.

Maxagrid International Inc. 3939 Belt Line Rd., Suite 250, Dallas 75244. (214) 241-2110. FAX: (214) 241-2174. Jim Tiller, pres/CEO; Shane Fox, COO; Fred Mueller, dir rsch/dev.
Developer of bcst yield & revenue mgmt systems; specializing in continued enhancement, dev, preparation & mktg of bcst Reservation & Yield Mgmt Systems.

Maxwell Media Group. 6053 Bunker Hill, Pittsburgh 15206. (412) 441-2020. FAX: (412) 661-9377. Bill Maxwell, pres.
Specialists in buying high-volume printed materials for direct-mail or other high-volume needs.

Mazer & Associates. 3452 Grayton Rd., Detroit 48224. (313) 885-5686. John Mazer Jr., pres.
Radio & TV progmg svcs; market rsch; format design; talent evaluation; license renewal preparation; labor rels; mgmt & admin consulting.

W. Edward McClenahan & Associates Inc. 561 Dryden Pl., Charlottesville, Va. 22903. (804) 977-4097. W. Edward McClenahan, pres.
Mgmt, sls, FCC application consulting; financing, business plans, & media brokerage.

McHugh & Hoffman Inc. 8301 Greensboro Dr., Suite 490, McLean, Va. 22102. (703) 506-8900. FAX: (703) 506-8905. John E. Bowen III, CEO; Jacques de Suze, pres; Franklin Graham.
Communications consultants: audience rsch, news & entertainment prog dev, mktg & promotion strategies, stn organization & mgmt. Svcs available internationally.

McKinsey & Co. 55 E. 52nd St., New York 10022. (212) 446-7000. FAX: (212) 446-8575. Frederick Gluck, mgr.

McManus International Inc. 425 E. 63rd St., New York 10021. (212) 888-7456. FAX:(212) 644-0328. Tom McManus, pres.
Consulting & representational svcs for domestic & international prods, distributors & rsch companies.

McNulty Consultants. 1926 E. 34th Ave., Spokane, Wash. 99203. (509) 535-5168. Wayne F. McNulty, pres.
Mgmt & financial assistance for operating & purchasing TV & radio stns. Bottom-line mgmt, all phases of stn & group opns.

Kenneth R. Meades. Box 1469, Los Angeles 90053. (213) 669-9570. Kenneth R. Meades, own.
Mgmt & tech consulting for small bcstrs & cable operators.

Media Advertising Credit Services. 11600 Sunrise Valley Dr., Reston, Va. 22091. (703) 648-1248. FAX: (703) 620-1386. Robert J. Kasabian, pres; Gary H. Bugge, VP opns.
Media credit reports, investigations, collections, education & fraud alerts.

Media Communications Group. 580 Centre View Blvd., Crestview Hills, Ky. 41017. (606) 344-8886. FAX: (606) 344-8562. John L. Pierce, CEO; Mark Roberts, pres; Sandy Collar, VP.
Representing, consulting & mgmt svcs to radio stns nationwide.

Media Economics. 69 N. Sheridan Ave., Bethpage, N.Y. 11714. (516) 931-0248. Layton W. Franko, Ph.D., pres.
Market analysis, forecasting, pricing, planning, sports economics & business rsch for TV, cable & radio industries.

Media & Marketing. 11288 Ventura Blvd., Suite 462, Studio City, Calif. 91604. (818) 753-9510. FAX: (818) 753-9320. Mel Lambert, creative dir.
Consulting svc for the audio industry.

Media Perspectives. 606 Cooper Landing Rd., Bldg. A, Suite 4B, Cherry Hill, N.J. 08002. (609) 482-7979. FAX: (609) 482-0957. Steven G. Apel, pres.
Progmg & mktg counseling through applied audience & advertiser rsch.

Media Sales South. 5609 Brooke Ridge Dr., Atlanta 30338. (404) 393-3393. FAX: (404) 551-9285. Nick Imbornone, pres.
Specialists in selling large- & medium-market radio stn properties.

Media Services Group Inc. 2111 Wilson Blvd., Suite 700, Arlington, Va. 22201. (703) 351-5025. FAX: (703) 351-0361. Millard S. Younts, pres; Mona Wargo, mktg dir.
Overland Park, Kan. 66212: 10575 Riley. (913) 383-2260. FAX: (913) 383-3152. Bill Lytle, VP.
Berwyn, Pa. 19312: 179 St. Clair Cir. (215) 695-9339. FAX: (215) 695-9340. Kevin Cox, VP.
Logan, Utah 84321: Box 744. (801) 753-8090. FAX: (801) 753-1394. Greg Merrill, VP.
Jacksonville, Fla. 32250: 3948 3rd St. (904) 285-3239. FAX: (904) 285-5618. George Reed, VP.
Providence, R.I. 02903: 170 Westminster St., Suite 701. (401) 454-3130. FAX: (401) 454-3131. Robert J. Maccini, VP.
Mergers, acquisitions, financing, valuations, consultation for radio & TV.

Media Travel Services. 1119 San Antonio, El Paso, Tex. 79901. (915) 533-4700. FAX: (915) 533-3640. Michelle A. Haston, VP.
Full-svc, licensed & bonded travel svcs, specializing in discount group tours, promotions, giveaways & incentive packages (air, cruises, hotel).

The Mediacenter. 501 Madison Ave., 10th Fl., New York 10022. (212) 207-8480. FAX: (212) 207-8485. Barbara Ann Zeiger, ptnr.
Chicago 60625: Box 25448. (312) 539-3991. Timothy Cornillie, ptnr.
Promote increased mktg professionalism among TV execs & mgrs; provide sls support tools that identify & dev new adv budgets.

Millar Co. Inc. Box 700, Cullman, Ala. 35056. (205) 734-4888. FAX: (205) 734-8600. Randy Millar, pres; Brett Miller, cable specialist.
Specialists in restructuring radio through sls & mktg techniques, systems & computerization.

Cheryl D. Miller Design. 145 Huguenot St., Suite 405, New Rochelle, N.Y. 10801. (914) 576-7444. FAX: (914) 576-9722. Cheryl D. Miller, pres/own.
Art direction/graphic design for TV & videotape prods, including logos, computer graphics, print animation, promotion items & set design.

Jay Mitchell Associates. Box 1285, Fairfield, Iowa 52556. (515) 472-4087. FAX: (515) 472-6457. Jay I. Mitchell, pres; Lori Morgan, opns mgr.
Mgmt progmg & mktg consulting; voice IDs, mus formats, speech & voice training; market analysis.

George Moore & Associates Inc. 1040 N. Dallas Bank Tower, Dallas 75230. (214) 661-8970. FAX: (214) 661-8967. W. James Moore, pres.
Brokerage of radio, TV & CATV properties; asset & market appraisals; introduction to institutional financing sources.

Timothy Moore & Co. 2900 M St., Washington 20007. (202) 333-4318. FAX: (202) 342-0418. Timothy Moore, pres.
Govt affrs, pub rels, mktg firm for bcst/cable. Expertise in FCC, Congress, copyright, political, HDTV & event planning.

Multi Market Media. 14677 Midway Rd., Suite 200, Dallas 75244. (214) 392-7571. FAX: (214) 392-7316. Terry Doane, VP.
Mktg svcs, including promotions, corporate event & sport sponsorships; media buying; radio & TV syndications.

Music Director Programing Service. Box 51978, Indian Orchard, Mass. 01151. (413) 783-4626. FAX: (413) 783-3168. Budd Clain, gen mgr; Rick Grade, country consultant; Rich Bosse, chief engr.
Consulting to radio stns progmg adult contemp, CHR & country formats; complete mus libraries offered on CD, DAT or reel-to-reel.

Myers Reports. 322 Rt. 46 W., Parsippany, N.J. 07054. (201) 882-6602. Jack Myers, pres; Leah Reznick, VP.
Conducts syndicated & proprietary rsch for media companies; publication scvs & creative scvs.

N

National Strategies Inc. 888 17th St. N.W., 12th Fl., Washington 20006. (202) 429-8744. FAX: (202) 296-2962. David Aylward, pres.
Public policy strategies dev, business & investment dev.

National Supervisory Network. Box 578, 20 Eagle Rd., Suite 310, Avon, Colo. 81620. (303) 949-7774; (800) 345-8728. FAX: (303) 949-9620. Muffy Montemayor, pres; C. William Sepmeier, VP engrg.
Vision svcs for audio distribution via satellite, centralized prod & mgmt, & off-premise transmitter & EBS control.

NeoData Services Inc. 2840 S. 123rd Ct., Omaha, Neb. 68144. (402) 330-6100. FAX: (402) 330-5739. Larry Jones, pres; Jim Schinco, VP.
Telemarketing svcs including sls, lead generation, direct mail follow-up & recorded voice messages.

New England Media Inc. 102 Rt. 7, St. Albans, Vt. 05478. (802) 524-5963. FAX: (802) 527-1450. David R. Kimel, pres; Michael Rice, VP; Robert I. Kimel, consultant.
Mansfield Center, Conn. 06250: 99 Highland Rd. (203) 456-1111. Michael Rice, VP.
Media brokers, consultants & appraisers specializing in radio & TV in the Northeast.

New York Communications. 207 S. State Rd., Upper Darby, Pa. 19082. (215) 352-5505. FAX: (215) 352-6225. Michael Davis, pres. (Philadelphia office.)
Consulting on all aspects of mktg, adv & promotion of loc news progs for TV stns.

Newberger, Greenberg & Associates. 370 N. Westlake Blvd., Suite 100, Westlake Village, Calif. 91362. (818) 446-4100. FAX: (805) 446-4111. Rick Newberger & George Greenberg, principals.
Advisory firm to media companies specializing in planning, financing & implementing new endeavors & technologies related to progmg & distribution.

YOU HAVE QUESTIONS:

Which Radio Format?
What Music?
Talents?
Promotions?
News-Talk?

THE LUND CONSULTANTS
have answers...

- 16 Year Success Record
- All Formats
  A/C, Oldies,
  Country, CHR,
  AOR, AM Specialists
- All Market Sizes

CALL JOHN LUND TODAY!
415-692-7777

THE LUND CONSULTANTS
TO BROADCAST MANAGEMENT, INC.

Consultants

Newbrough Associates Inc. Box 1822, Des Moines, Iowa 50306-1822. (515) 244-8909. FAX: (515) 986-9338. Bill Newbrough, pres.
Gen mgmt consulting & episodic mgmt svcs for mass communications organizations. Specialties: electronic journalism, mus radio, organizational dev & telephone mass calling.

NewCity Associates Inc./The Center for Sales Strategy. 1304 DeSoto Ave., Suite 404, Tampa 33606. (813) 254-5455. FAX: (813) 254-9222. Steve Marx, pres; Jim Hopes, VP; Dolly Heims, admin mgr.
Comprehensive consulting & training svcs for radio & TV stns in sls, mktg & mgmt, exclusively on a long-term, multi-year basis.

Noll & Associates. 4000 Bridgeway, Suite 205, Sausalito, Calif. 94965. (415) 332-5640. FAX: (415) 332-1261. Kennen Williams, pres/gen mgr.
Mgmt svcs consultation including training, TVSP progs, exec search, incentive travel & media placement.

Northlake Audio Inc. Box 161, Angie, La. 70426-0161. (504) 735-0097. Melvin Hall, pres; Purvis Hall, VP; Elaine Ferguson, sec/treas.

Northwest Broadcasting Co. Box 847, Barrington, Ill. 60011-0847. (708) 381-3209. Michael H. Krafcisin, pres.
Mgmt, progmg, opns & engrg consultation to radio stns.

M.S. Novik. 300 W. 23rd St., New York 10011. (212) 255-4385. M.S. Novik, own.
Public svc bcst consultant.

O

Off-Premise Control Service. National Supervisory Network, Box 578, 20 Eagle Rd., Suite 310, Avon, Colo. 81620. (303) 949-7774; (800) 345-8728. FAX: (303) 949-9620. Muffy Montemayor, pres; C. William Sepmeier, VP engrg.
Integrated opns net including off-premise control, audio distribution nets & centralized prod.

The Omnia Group. 601 South Blvd., Tampa 33606. (800) 525-7117. FAX: (813) 254-8558. Dale P. Smrekar, VP; Barbara Bauer, exec VP.
Same day response on bcst industry-validated selection personality tests; mission statements & goal setting, employee performance evaluation & mgmt techniques.

Orion Asia Pacific Corp. 2440 Research Blvd., Rockville, Md. 20850. (301) 258-8101. FAX: (301) 258-8119. John G. Puente, chmn; W. Neil Bauer, pres; C. Elliott Bardsley, VP business dev.
International telecommunication svcs in Asia Pacific region, specializing in private nets via satellite.

Ott & Associates. 9225 Chatham Grove Ln., Suite D, Richmond, Va. 23236. (804) 276-7202. Rick Ott, pres.
Problem solving, consultation in complete confidentiality. Management consulting.

P

PMA Marketing Inc. 4359 S. Howell, Suite 106, Milwaukie, Wis. 53207. (414) 482-2638. FAX: (414) 483-1980. Pat Martin, pres.
Buy & sell new & used bcst equipment.

PROSTAR. 12831 Royal Dr., Stafford, Tex. 77477. (713) 240-2800. John C. Parks, pres; D. Scott Hofmann, dir engrg; Brent Shannon, dir opns.
Provides leased satellite encryption systems for business, entertainment & sports usage.

Packer Communications. 19785 W. 12 Mile Rd., Suite 380, Southfield, Mich. 48076. (313) 569-8710; (313) 569-8000. Michael Packer, consultant.
Talk radio & news radio consultant; progmg, mktg, & audience rsch featuring Packer Communications Core Audience Tracker.

Palazzo deMix. 747 Bellevue Ave. E., Seattle 98102. (206) 324-9549. FAX: (206) 324-4348. Richard Roberts, pres.
Stn identity design & consultation svcs. On-air, print, outdoor, graphics, syndicated animation packages, movie & news opns, & radio spots.

Patrick Communications Corp. 13321 Ridgewood Dr., Ellicott City, Md. 21042. (301) 596-9814. FAX: (301) 596-9442. W. Lawrence Patrick, pres.
Business planning, market rsch, strategic planning, financing & opns consulting.

Donald A. Perry & Associates Inc. Box 857, Summerville Plantation, Gloucester, Va. 23061. (804) 877-4367. Donald A. Perry, pres; W.K. Bowles, Patricia Gibbs, VPs; Brinton Belyea, VP engrg.
Mgmt, brokerage & appraisal svcs to the cable TV industry.

The Personal Laboratory Inc. 733 Summer St., Stamford, Conn. 06901. (203) 325-4348. King Whitney Jr., pres; Irene Salese, Joanna Steinberg, VPs.
Consultants on per selection & recruitment.

Pollack Media Group. 984 Monument St., Suite 105, Pacific Palisades, Calif. 90272. (310) 459-8556. FAX: (310) 454-5046. Jeff Pollack, chmn/CEO; Tommy Hadges, pres; Carol Holt, VP opns.
International bcst progmg advisory firm, all facets of progmg, positioning, mktg, adv, rsch, mus & engrg. All formats.

BUSINESS EXPERTS
· Research & Data
· On-Site Media Interviews

POORMAN & GROUP
717-748-7000
143-147 E. Main St., Lock Haven, PA 17745

Poorman & Co. 143-147 E. Main St., Lock Haven, Pa, 17745. (717) 748-7000. FAX: (717) 748-7700. Stephen P. Poorman, pres.
Pennsylvania & Texas-based mgmt consulting firm offers "no-charge" interviews to radio & TV stns relating to business & real estate issues. Specializes in organizing & mgng financially distressed businesses.

Price Waterhouse Valuation Services. 200 E. Randolph Dr., Chicago 60601. (312) 540-2690. FAX: (312) 565-1458. Stephen M. Carr, dir.
Los Angeles 90071-2889: 400 S. Hope St. (213) 236-3000. James H. Dezart, ptnr.
Provides planning & accounting advice for acquisitions & divestitures, for financial reporting, & for income tax purposes; estimates for various purposes.

Primo Newservice Inc. Box 116, 182 Sound Beach Ave., Old Greenwich, Conn. 06870-0116. (203) 637-0044. FAX: (203) 698-0812. Albert T. Primo, pres; Kenn Venit, VP/sr consultant; Fred Landau, dir bcst opns.
TV news consulting, specialized rsch, news mgmt & talent career counseling & placement, talent coaching & prog dev, all mkts.

W.L. PRITCHARD & CO., INC.
CONSULTING ENGINEERS IN TELECOMMUNICATIONS
REGISTERED PROFESSIONAL ENGINEERS

DR. WILBUR PRITCHARD
PRESIDENT

7315 WISCONSIN AVE., #520E   TEL: (301) 654-1144
BETHESDA, MARYLAND 20814   FAX: (301) 654-1814

Pritchard Company Inc. 7315 Wisconsin Ave., Suite 520E, Bethesda, Md. 20814. (301) 654-1144. FAX: (301) 654-1818. Robert Nelson.
Registered, professional consulting engrs in telecommunications.

Q

The Ward L. Quaal Co. 401 N. Michigan Ave., Suite 3140, Chicago 60611. (312) 644-6066. FAX: (312) 644-3733. Ward L. Quaal, pres/own.
Gen mgmt consultants specializing in svcs to bcstg & allied arts.

R

The R Corp. 1950 Landings Blvd., Suite 110, Sarasota, Fla. 34231. (813) 924-2400. FAX: (813) 924-1650. Rod Warner, pres.
Consulting to cable & bcstg on mktg; contract door-to-door sls for cable opns.

R.F. Technologies Engineering Corp. 238 Goddard Rd., Lewiston, Me. 04240. (800) 634-4075; (207) 777-7778. FAX: (207) 777-7784. George M. Harris P.E., principal.
Provides file engrg & svc for TV & FM antennas, transmission lines, diplexers & combiners.

The Specialist in Broadcast CD Music!

- Broadcast CD Music Libraries
- Weekly Top Hits U.S.A. on CD
- CD Christmas Library
- Music Rotation Software

ULTRASONIC-Q RADIO DISC FOR BROADCAST ONLY

COMPACT DISC DIGITAL AUDIO

50 States & Canada:
800-521-2537
Fax: 313-681-3936

rpm RADIO PROGRAMMING AND MANAGEMENT, INC.
Serving Broadcasters Since 1970.

RPM Radio Programming & Management. 4198 Orchard Lake Rd., Orchard Lake, Mich. 48323. (313) 681-2660; (800) 521-2537. FAX: (313) 681-3936. Thomas M. Krikorian, pres.
Olympia Fields, Ill. 60461: 3521 Ithaca Rd. (800) 621-5699; (708) 748-9444. FAX: (708) 503-0001. Ray Lowy.
Top Hits U.S.A. wkly CD svc & CD libraries including Solid Gold, Spectrum A/C & Country One; CD Christmas library.

RRN Inc. 111 5th Ave., #1300, New York 10003-1005. (212) 995-9800. FAX: (212) 995-9848. Anthony S. Niskanen, pres; Patricia M. Barnes, opns mgr.
Provides licensed promotions for bcst & print media including the *69 Cent/Dollar* promotion & the *SMARTcash* & *Seed Money CHALLENGE* progs.

Radio Management Consulting. 1514 Lynn Dr., Lancaster, Ohio 43130. (614) 687-1080. FAX: (614) 687-1086. Gregory J. Eyerman, pres.
FCC Compliance Program: EEO, public files, political regulations, ownshp reports, license renewal assistance.

Radio Marketing Concepts Inc. Box 800497, Dallas 75380-0497. (214) 490-3311. FAX: (214) 458-7226. Norman Goldsmith, pres.
Sls & mktg consultation, evaluation, analysis; customized sls mgr progs in goal setting, planning, reportage, evaluation, compensation, training, sls seminars.

The Radio Marketing Dept. Inc. 155 Sun Valley Way, Morris Plains, N.J. 07950. (201) 993-8717. FAX: (201) 984-5115. Ilene Adams, pres.
Mktg, direct mail, telemarketing, sls promotions, event planning, creative design, data base mgmt.

Radioactivity Inc. 1043 Jefferson Ave., Suite B-12, Atlanta 30344. (404) 767-1840. FAX: (404) 767-1840. Dain L. Schult, pres; Hugh Roberts, VP mktg; Craig Pak, sr VP finance; Joe Pedicino, VP mgmt.
Atlanta 30344: 982 Winburn Dr. (404) 766-0312. Craig Pak, sr VP finance.
Comprehensive mgmt consultation including turnkey prog for first-time buyers; turnaround & bank workouts.

Rattigan Radio Services. 3409 Wilshire Rd., Portsmouth, Va. 23703. (804) 484-3017. FAX: (804) 484-0336. Jack M. Rattigan, pres; Adelaide C. Rattigan, VP admin.
Provides consultation, evaluation, analysis, customized sls mgmt progs in goal setting, time mgmt, consultant selling, servicing after the sale, repeat business, collections; personalized sls training seminar/workshops & follow-up consulting to radio stns.

The Raven Group. Box 309, Concord, Mass. 01742. (508) 369-1878. FAX: (508) 369-2009. Anne W. Branscomb, pres.

Consultants

Rees Associates Inc. 3817 Northwest Expressway, Suite 500, Oklahoma City 73112-1499. (405) 942-REES. FAX: (405) 948-1261. Clyde Leroy James, exec VP; William H. Yost, VP sls.
Other branches: Dallas; Houston; Los Angeles. FAX: (800) 525-REES.
Bcst & prod facility design; architectural svcs; facility business plans; interior design; studio design; equipment planning, consulting.

Restivo Communications. 107 S. West St., Suite 199, Alexandria, Va. 22314. (703) 461-0767. Peter J. Restivo, pres.
Bcst & media consultants; publishers of *Television & Radio Newsletter*.

Reymer & Associates Inc. 20300 Civic Ctr. Dr., Suite 201, Southfield, Mich. 48076. (313) 354-4950. FAX: (313) 354-0918. Arnold S. Reymer, pres; Joe Kirik, VP consulting.
Complete bcst news svc, consulting for stns & groups, audience rsch.

Robert E. Richer. 48 Mountain Rd., Farmington, Conn. 06032-2341. (203) 677-9688. FAX: (203) 677-9639. Robert E. Richer, own.
Small- to medium-market U.S. radio mgmt consulting, & gen European radio consulting.

Dan Robinson Broadcasting. One Horizon Rd., Fort Lee, N.J. 07024. (201) 886-0287. Dan Robinson, pres.
Prog & media consultant.

George Rodman Associates. 3785 Via Nona Marie, Suite 310, Carmel, Calif. 93923. (408) 626-1630. FAX: (408) 625-1250. George T. Rodman, pres; Sally M. Rodman, VP/client svcs mgr.
Provides stns, nets, groups & prog suppliers with mktg counseling, promotion materials including adv campaigns, logos, on-air design, TV spots, animation.

Rogers Consulting Services. 4600 Drake Rd., Cincinnati 45243. (513) 561-4420. FAX: (513) 561-4420. Lawrence H. Rogers II, own/operator; Barbara E. Harris, mgr.
TV & allied communications; appraisals, acquisitions & sls; financial analysis, organization, per, labor rels, mktg, financial & pub rels.

Ray H. Rosenblum. Box 38296, Pittsburgh, Pa. 15238. (412) 362-6311. Ray H. Rosenblum, pres; Helen Faye Rosenblum, VP.
Consultant & appraiser for radio & TV stns & political candidates with focus on mgmt, sls, promotions, news & pub rels.

Martin Rubenstein Associates. 4700 29th Pl. N.W., Washington 20008. (202) 244-1292. FAX: (202) 244-1292. Martin Rubenstein, principal.
General & financial domestic & international consultation in bcstg, new technologies, communications & allied arts.

Rubin-Frey Communications Inc. 847A 2nd Ave., Suite 131, New York 10017. (212) 213-1755. FAX: (212) 213-1643. Albert Rubin, pres; Charles Frey, exec VP.
Video prod, VNRs, B Rolls, training films, & educational & medical videos.

Rumbaut & Associates. 1160 Stillwater Dr., Tower Suite, Miami Beach, Fla. 33141. (305) 868-7000. FAX: (305) 868-7865. Julio Rumbaut, pres.
Washington 20036: 1900 L Street N.W., Suite 500. (202) 293-2828. FAX: (202) 466-9042.
Media brokers & consultants in all facets of the TV & radio industries.

S

S C Research International Inc. 12 E. 46th Street, Suite 5A, New York 10017. (212) 867-6060. FAX: (212) 867-6579. Douglas I. Sheer, Desmond C. Chaskelson, co-dirs.
Syndicated reports & custom rsch for manufacturers & investors in bcstg, professional video & audio; publishers of *Broadcast Equipment Marketplace (BEM)*, *Professional Video Marketplace (PFM)*, *Professional Multi-Media Marketplace (PMM)*, *European Telemedia Marketplace (ETM)*, *Asian Telemedia Marketplace (ATM)*.

SRCS/Markits. 17 Royal Rd., Bangor, Me. 04401. (207) 942-5548. FAX: (207) 942-5548. J. Stephen Robbins, pres.
Client-directed mktg prog for coml bcst properties (radio & TV).

Satterfield & Perry Inc. 3062 Robb Cir., Denver 80215-7067. (303) 239-6670. FAX: (303) 231-9562. Al Perry, chmn.
Bala Cynwyd, Pa. 19004: 2 Bala Plaza, Suite 300. (215) 668-1168. FAX: (215) 688-9447. Jack F. Satterfield, pres; John Weidman Jr., VP. (215) 660-7760.
Englewood, Colo. 80111: 5172 S. Ironton Way. (303) 740-8424. Bob Austin, VP.
Overland Park, Kan. 66207: 4918 W. 101st Terr. (913) 649-5103. Douglas Stevens, VP.
Point Pleasant, Pa. 18950: Box 248, River Point Rd. (215) 297-0625. George Pleasants, VP.
Radio, TV & cable broker; mgmt consultant, appraiser, expert witness & accounts receivable funding.

Sawyer Miller Group. 14 E. 60th St., New York 10022. (212) 755-1700. FAX: (212) 755-0673. David Sawyer, chmn; Jack Leslie, pres.

William B. Schutz Jr. Box 404, St. Michaels, Md. 21663. (410) 745-3900. FAX: (410) 745-5929.
Mgmt consulting, brokerage, appraisals & stn financing.

Shane Media Services. 2450 Fondren, Suite 112, Houston 77063. (713) 952-9221. FAX: (713) 952-1207. Ed Shane, Chuck Dickemann, Pamela Shane, Cheryl Broz, consultants; Laura English, dir mktg.
Strategic mgmt, progmg & rsch consultation, country, news, talk, alternative rock formats.

Barry Sherman & Associates. 7640 Tremayne Pl., Suite 204, McLean, Va. 22102. (703) 821-0877. Barry Sherman, pres.
Full-svc media brokerage & bcst mgmt consulting, including international coml bcst interests, bcst sls training, sls motivation consulting, investment consulting, appraisals & fair market valuation.

Bill Sims Partners. 1311 Calle Nava, Santa Fe, N.M. 87501. (505) 982-2668. FAX: (505) 988-3437. Bill Sims, mgmt consultant.
Small- & medium-market checkup, start-up experts; overall radio stn dev; build from CP to achieve maximum value.

Barry Skidelsky Esq. 655 Madison Ave., 19th Fl., New York 10021. (212) 832-4800. FAX: (212) 486-8668. Barry Skidelsky, atty/consultant.
Full-svc assistance for stn purchase & sale, start-up & imporvement; mgmt & lender consultation; trustee & arbitration.

George Skinner Associates Inc. Box 532, Old Greenwich, Conn. 06870-0532. (203) 329-3168. George D. Skinner, pres.
Complete consultation in all phases of TV news, plus prod, writing, corporate video.

Skye Broadcasting Services. 94 Beacon St., Hartford, Conn. 06105. (203) 236-4453. William L. Fleming, pres.
Investment banking/financial consultant to bcstrs; assists in structuring mergers, acquisitions & refinancings; arranges equity, debt or other funds needed.

Bill Slatter & Associates. 514 S. Union St., Natchez, Miss. 39120. (601) 446-6347. FAX: (601) 445-6623. Bill Slatter, pres; Denver Slatter, VP.
Personal rep or agent for on-air news per; talent coaching.

Smith and Co. 5910 John Hancock Ctr., 175 E. Delaware Pl., Chicago 60611. (312) 822-0123. James A. Smith, pres.
Market evaluation; ongoing consultation, positioning, progmg, rsch, mktg, mus, news, per selection & motivation, ratings analysis.

Smith/Davis Communication Research. Box 182, 158 Rolling Ridge Rd., Amherst, Mass. 01002. (413) 256-6925. FAX: (413) 256-6926. Leslie K. Davis Ph.D., James R. Smith Ph.D., mgng gen ptnrs.
Media rsch mktg. Bcst, cable, pay cable, print. Audience rsch & mktg, content analysis, promotion, competitive strategies, mgmt consulting.

Sound Decisions. 2051 Glenhill Rd., Colorado Springs 80906-3352. (719) 471-4125; (800) 552-2545. FAX: (719) 473-4546. Bobby Christian, pres.
Focus groups, one-on-one focus studies, format search, progmg consultation, auditorium mus tests, software for in-house mus rsch.

Soundtrack. 162 Columbus Ave., Boston 02116-5222. (617) 542-7272. FAX: (617) 542-7222. Jeanne McGrail, opns mgr.
Prod & custom mus of all kinds; specializing in contemp styles.

Southern Surveys. 1551 Olde Mill Pl., Marietta, Ga. 30066. (404) 924-3584. Rick Phillips, pres.
Radio qualitative one-on-one rsch, auditorium mus testing, perceptual rsch, artist loyalty studies, data processing.

Stacey, Lawson Associates Ltd. 5-1420 Youville Dr., Ottawa, Ont., Canada K1C 7B3. (613) 830-6985. FAX: (613) 830-8124. Wayne A. Stacey P.E., pres; Robert D.F. Lawson P.E., VP.
Govt regulations, CRTC/DOC applications, bcst rsch, bcst consulting, engrg svcs, demographic studies.

Stadlen Radio Associates Inc. 3123 Adirondack Dr. N.E., Cedar Rapids, Iowa 52402-3309. (319) 365-0410. FAX: (319) 365-0567. Richard W. Stadlen, pres.
Consultation svcs to radio stns in all market sizes; specializing in AC, lite AC, & oldies.

Jack Steck Associates. 1527 Dorchester Rd., Havertown, Pa. 19083. (215) 789-0966. Jack Steck, pres; Florence Steck, VP.
Bcst prog consultants, stage prod, pub rels.

Stein, Roe & Farnham. One S. Wacker Dr., Chicago 60606. (312) 368-7700. FAX: (312) 368-8074. Joe Stein, ptnr.
Investment counsel & mutual fund mgmt. Offices in Chicago; Cleveland; Fort Lauderdale, Fla.; Scottsdale, Ariz.; Minneapolis; New York; & Puerto Rico.

Gary Stevens & Co. 49 Locust Ave., Suite 107, New Canaan, Conn. 06840. (203) 966-6465. FAX: (203) 966-6522. Gary Stevens, pres.
Bcst mergers, acquistions & investment banking svcs.

Stone Communications Inc. One Canterbury Way, Cape Elizabeth, Me. 04107. (207) 799-8804. FAX: (207) 767-4379. Melvin L. Stone, pres.
Associate of Kozacko-Horton, media brokers.
Media brokers, mgmt consultants, mergers, acquisitions, radio, TV, cable.

Stonick Recruitment Inc. 10160 Grove Ln., Cooper City, Fla. 33328. (305) 680-6322. FAX: (305) 680-6327. Chris Stonick, pres; Laurie Stonick, VP.
A natl radio sls consulting firm bringing "recruitment adv" to radio (Strictly New Business Development).

Peter Storer & Associates Inc. 11019 N. Towne Sq. Rd., Suite 7, Mequon, Wis. 53092. (414) 241-9005. FAX: (414) 241-9036. Peter Storer Jr., pres.
Design & implementation of custom microcomputer applications.

Rupert Stow Associates. 18 Tuthill Point Rd., East Moriches, N.Y. 11940. (516) 878-8663. FAX: (516) 874-8809. Rupert Stow, pres.
Consultant in high definition/video.

Strategy Research Corp. 100 N.W. 37th Ave., Miami, Fla. 33125. (305) 649-5400. FAX: (305) 649-6312. Richard Tobin, pres; Raul J. Lopez, sr VP.
Irvine, Calif. 92715: 2082 Michelson Dr., Suite 100. (714) 752-6331. Dave Thomas, VP/gen mgr. Los Angeles office.
Full-svc mktg rsch company specializing in the Hispanic market; focus group testing, awareness usage tracking studies, media ratings.

Consultants

Structural System Technology Inc. 6867 Elm St., McLean, Va. 22101. (703) 356-9765. FAX: (703) 448-0979. J. Cabot Goudy, pres.
Structural engrg studies, analysis, design, mods, inspections & erections of towers & antenna structures.

Joe Sullivan & Associates Inc. Box 612, 44210 County Rd. No. 48, Southold, N.Y. 11971. (516) 765-5050. FAX: (516) 765-1662. Joseph J. Sullivan Jr., pres; Barbara Sullivan, VP.
Exec search & recruitment in bcstg & cable TV for sr-level positions with incomes in excess of $70,000 per year.

Synergistic Technologies Inc. 3 Parkway Ctr., Suite 102, Pittsburgh, Pa. 15220. (412) 928-0448. FAX: (412) 928-0451. John A. Luff, pres; Mark Albright, dir sls & mktg.
Provides consultation, facility design, instal & tech support for all aspects of video & audio communications; nationally & internationally.

Szabo Associates Inc. Media Collection Specialists. 3355 Lenox Rd., 9th Fl., Atlanta 30326. (404) 266-2464. FAX: (404) 266-2165. Peter F. Szabo, pres; C. Robin Szabo, VP.
Experts in creditor & debtor rights; consulting media properties in the accounts receivable process.

T

3-H Cable Communications Consultants. 502 E. Main St., Auburn, Wash. 98002-5502. (206) 935-9040. FAX: (206) 932-4284. Lon A. Hurd, VP/dir; Miles H. Overholt, sr consultant.
Cable franchise administration, negotiation, renewal, tech evaluation, community needs assessment & franchise fee audits.

TM Century Inc. 2002 Academy, Dallas 75234. (800) 937-2100. FAX: (800) 749-2121. P. Craig Turner, pres/CEO.
Progmg consultation, mus rotation software, automated playback, mus on CD, TV & jingle prod.

TRA Communications Consultants Inc. 600 W. Hillsboro Blvd., Suite 27, Deerfield Beach, Fla. 33441. (305) 480-2727. FAX: (305) 480-8501. J.R. Skinner, pres/chmn of bd; Loren M. Matthews, chief engr.
FCC application preparation for new FM, TV & LPTV stns; consulting for new start-ups, acquisitions, turnarounds or stn appraisal & sls for AM, FM, TV, LPTV.

TTC-The Telemarketing Co. 479 N. Business Center Dr., Mount Prospect, Ill. 60056. (708) 635-1500. FAX: (708) 635-8738. Mary Shanley, pres; George P. Parker, natl acct exec; Robert Aloisio, opns mgr.
Chicago 60634: 3945 N. Neenah. (312) 545-0407. Georgiann Mimler, opns mgr.
Round Lake, Ill. 60073: 314A Nippersink Rd. (708) 546-2090. Michael Martin, opns mgr.
Telemarketing Agency providing svcs to cable industry selling new svc & upgrades.

David Tait Appraisal Co. 1848 Laurel Canyon Blvd., Los Angeles 90046-2029. (213) 654-8420. FAX: (213) 656-1854. David Tait, CRA-admin/principal; Doby A. Rose, ASA, sr assoc.
Fair market value appraisals of radio/TV/CATV for purchase allocation, finance, estate planning, ESOPs, bankruptcy.

Tape Network Inc. 1305 Glenwood, Delano, Calif. 93215-2040. (805) 725-2345. FAX: (805) 725-2609. Richard Palmquist, pres.
Consulting, equipment package (audio only) & mus for 24-hour daily sacred mus.

TeamRadio. 2980 Cobb Pkwy., Bldg. 192, Suite 915, Atlanta 30339-3158. (404) 720-7762. FAX: (404) 720-7862. Steven A. Downes, mgng ptnr; Theodore C. Eselgroth, ptnr.
TeamRadio represents proven consultants, svcs & prods covering all areas of radio stn opns.

Tele-Measurements Inc. 145 Main Ave., Clifton, N.J. 07014-1078. (201) 473-8822. FAX: (201) 473-0521. William E. Endres, pres; Douglas W. Cook, VP sls; Alan Bjornsen, VP projects.
Bcst, professional video equipment, videotape, TV systems, teleconferencing, ongoing maintenance support, CCTV, equipment rentals.

Teletech Inc. 23400 Michigan Ave., Suite 615, Dearborn, Mich. 48124. (313) 562-6873. FAX: (313) 562-8612. Kenneth W. Hoehn, VP; Keith Johnson, field svcs mgr; Mark W. Dobronski, sr engr.
Antenna site mgmt; tower, studio & antenna construction & maintenance; frequency searches; FCC application preparation; EMI, radiation & microwave studies.

Television by Design Inc. 3277 Roswell Rd., Suite 714, Atlanta 30305. (404) 355-3277. FAX: (404) 355-3226. Jay Antzakas, pres; Melanie Goux, dir design.
Creators of electronic graphic design; consultants on vis design, equipment & opns for TV stns.

Television Consulting Service. 8033 Sunset Blvd., Suite 559, Los Angeles 90046. (213) 874-3991. FAX: (213) 874-0898. Ron Krueger, pres.
Bcst consultants to TV stns, prods, cable TV, group owns & operators, both domestic & international.

Telsa Inc. (Telecommunications Site Acquisitions Inc.) Box 32223 3500 Whitehaven Pkwy. N.W., Washington 20007. (202) 333-1985. (202) 342-9500. Gregory B. Daly, pres.
Site selection & investigations, site purchase/lease negotiations, demographic projections, bcst coverage gaps for new allocations & areas to locate, & interference studies for wireless cable. Transmitter site selection for FCC applicants, area to locate for allocations, site investigations, lease negotiation, construction.

Time Warner Telecommunications Inc. 1776 Eye St. N.W., Suite 850, Washington 20006. (202) 331-7478. FAX: (202) 331-1731. Dennis R. Patrick, CEO.
Develops new technologies & focuses on the use of the radio spectrum in mobile communications applications.

Edwin Tornberg & Co. Inc. Box 55298, Washington 20011. (202) 291-8700. Edwin Tornberg, pres.
Negotiators for purchase & sale of radio, TV stns & CATV systems; appraisers & financial advisers; mgmt consultants.

Trained Ear Ltd. 520 N. Michigan Ave., Suite 1700, Chicago 60611. (312) 527-5547. Robert Barnes-Watts, pres.
Recruitment of radio personalities; U.S. & international talent search svc.

Transcomm Inc. 6521 Arlington Blvd., Suite 214, Falls Church, Va. 22042. (703) 532-3160. Dr. Norman C. Lerner, pres.
Financial/economic analysis, market rsch, pricing studies & regulatory economics.

21st Century International Media Corp. 2955 80th Ave. S.E., Suite 202, Mercer Island, Wash. 98040. (206) 236-2111. FAX: (206) 236-2397. Peter D. Scheurmier, pres/COO; Fred Wright, VP sls.
South Port, Conn. 06490: Box 504. (203) 255-3333. FAX: (203) 259-6789. Christo Jackson, mgr eastern rgn.
Business & mgmt consulting, training, long-term strategic planning, organizations analysis, mktg positioning; seminars on goal setting, leadership, mgmt skills, sls training. Retail training.

24 Karat Productions Inc. 566 S.E. Damask Ave., Port St. Lucie, Fla. 34983. (407) 340-4040; (800) 340-4142. Mark Prichard, pres/CEO; Gloria Prichard, exec VP/gen mgr; John Donahey, sls mgr.
A full-svc consultant for 25 years. Creates & distributes radio formats with complete consultant package including progmg/promotion & sls. Also creator & developer of popular Music-1 format.

U

Jon Ulmer & Associates. 2176 Highpoint Rd., Snellville, Ga. 30278. (404) 979-3031. John R. Ulmer, owner.
Accounting, computer & financial management consulting.

V

Veronis, Suhler & Associates Inc. 350 Park Ave., New York 10022. (212) 935-4990. FAX: (212) 935-0877. John J. Veronis, chmn; John S. Suhler, pres; Marvin L. Shapiro, W. Dillaway Ayres, mgng dirs (radio, TV & cable); Robert J. Broadwater, mgng dir (corporate finance); Maro Sodi, mgng dir (International Group); Jeffrey T. Stevenson, pres VS&A Communications Partners L.P.
Investment bankers specializing in mergers & acquisitions for the communications.

Video Communication Resource Inc. 100 Amaral St., Riverside, R.I. 02915-2226. (401) 435-6416. FAX: (401) 434-8380. John Lamberti, pres.
Video post-production.

A.G. Visk. 2973 Evans Oaks Ct., Atlanta 30340. (404) 939-5657. Tony Visk, pres/own.
Promotional concepts, scripts & publications for the bcstg & entertainment industries.

W

WW Associates. 229 Quaker Rd., Chappaqua, N.Y. 10514. (914) 238-4375. FAX: (914) 238-1213. Jim Wiesenberg, principal.
International new media dev, strategic planning & acquisition assistance, cable & wireless MMDS expertise, PPV event & movie studio liaison.

Al-Ward Enterprises. 5530 Rab St., La Mesa, Calif. 91942-2461. (619) 460-9831. Alma C. Jaeger, pres; Edward J. Jaeger, exec VP/gen mgr; Edward C. Jaeger, VP.
Stn opns; consultant, progmg & sls, & engrg.

Charles Warner. 608 W. Stewart Rd., Columbia, Mo. 65203. (314) 882-6883. FAX: (314) 882-9002. Charles Warner, principal.
Mgmt consulting. Sls training seminars, hiring, training, compensation, MBO seminars.

Washington Information Group Ltd. Box 19352, 20th St. Station, Washington 20036. (202) 463-7323. FAX: (202) 463-8633. Douglas House, pres.
Customized business rsch. Competitive intelligence, public & private company rsch, industry & market studies. Strictly confidential; free consultation.

Wessels, Arnold & Henderson. 901 Marquette Ave., Minneapolis 55402-3280. (612) 373-6100. FAX: (612) 373-6280. William Henderson, mgng ptnr.
Investment banking & institutional brokerage.

Western Wireless Works. Box 4500, Apache Junction, Ariz. 85278. (602) 380-1000. FAX: (602) 986-1442. Richard Haskey, opns mgr; Patricia Woods, mgr tech svcs; Rudy Petracci, engr.
Feasibility studies, consulting svcs for AM-FM applications. Design telecommunication facilities. Turnkey capable. Facilities evaluation & appraisal. FCC Filings.

Edward Wetter & Co. Inc. 1000 Chesapeake Dr., Havre de Grace, Md. 21078. (410) 939-5555. Edward Wetter, pres.
Appraisals, financial & operational analysis, mgmt consulting.

The Wexler Group. 1317 F St. N.W., Suite 600, Washington 20004. (202) 638-2121. FAX: (202) 638-7045. Anne Wexler, chmn; Joseph W. Waz Jr., sr VP/gen counsel.
Consulting firm specializing in govt rels & pub affrs with strong emphasis on mass media, telecommunications, copyright, & trade.

Ron White. (Radio Programming Consultant.) 5053 Ocean Blvd., Suite 129, Sarasota, Fla. 34242. (813) 349-1916. FAX: (813) 346-3299. Ron White, own.
Radio progmg, positioning & mktg: format design, mus selection & scheduling, presentation, promotion.

Wilkin Communications. Box 2500, Atascadero, Calif. 92423. (805) 545-9628. FAX: (805) 461-1914. Eugene W. Wilkin, pres; R.A. Zapata, exec VP.
Full-svc consulting, from feasibility studies to daily progmg, turnkey "start-ups," prog rsch, negotiation, scheduling for existing stns; full range of financial svcs.

Consultants

Wind River Broadcast Center. 117 E. 11th St., Loveland, Colo. 80537. (303) 669-3442; (800) 669-3993. Jim McDonald, gen mgr.
 FCC compliance issues. Firm also makes FCC filings, designs & constructs studio & transmitter facilities & solves engrg problems.

Wishnow Group Inc. 82 Bubier Rd., Marblehead, Mass. 01945-3640. (617) 631-2444. FAX: (617) 639-1346. Jerrold D. Wishnow, pres; Charlayne Murrell, VP/project supvr; Christine Herbes-Sommers, project supvr.
 Positions bcst clients as community svc leaders.

The Wold Organization Ltd. 814 Amherst Ave., Los Angeles 90049-5292. (310) 826-0487. FAX: (310) 447-5954. Robert N. Wold, chmn/pres.
 Communications consulting svcs.

Walter Wulff & Associates. Airspace Consultants. Box 77028, Atlanta 30357. (404) 881-6786. FAX: (404) 881-6786. Walter H. Wulff, CEO.
 Conducts FAA tower studies & EMI evaluations.

Walter S. Wydro Consultants. The Atrium, 4 Terry Dr., Suite 10, Newtown, Pa. 18940. (215) 860-2288. FAX: (215) 860-5502. Walter S. Wydro, Alicia Thorne, B. Nuss, Anne Zielanski.
 Bcstg & CATV systems: mgmt, audits, appraisals, engrg, due diligence, financial svcs, expert testimony, & strategic planning.

Z

Joseph D. Zaleski Inc. 15 Jacob Arnold Rd., Morristown, N.J. 07960. (201) 455-8872. FAX: (201) 455-8873. Joseph D. Zaleski, pres.
 Sls & mktg consultation for prog prods, distributors, bcstrs, cable nets; prog/cost evaluation.

Zarecki Radio Consulting. 129 Brookside, Danbury, Conn. 06811. (203) 748-8411. FAX: (203) 798-1970. Tom Zarecki, pres.
 Morning show repair, prog dir training, small- & medium-markets format selection; consulting experience in 68 markets (39 states), nationwide since 1982.

Zate & Co. 31800 N.W. Hwy., #100, Farmington Hills, Mich. 48334. (313) 737-3000. Barry Zate, Ronald Zate, sr VPs; Ron Wittebols, stn svcs.
 Consulting for radio progmg, talent & admin svcs; on-site seminars, problem targeting & complete strategic planning for the communications industry.

Zeitgeist Inc. 9903 Santa Monica Blvd., #431, Beverly Hills, Calif. 90212. (310) 553-7788. FAX: (310) 553-7799. Sam Lee, pres; L.V. Heath, Sandra B. Lee, VPs.
 Holbrook, N.Y. 11741: Box 600.
 Century City, Calif. 90067: 1801 Century Park E., Suite 1810.
 Brokers for all bcst media svcs, urban specialists; adv, telemarketing & sls consulting.

Station Financing Services

HOFFMAN SCHUTZ MEDIA CAPITAL

20 YEARS OF SERVICE TO THE COMMUNICATIONS INDUSTRY

Appraisals • Financing • Restructuring • Litigation Support

Anthony M. Hoffman   **David E. Schutz**

42 Monmouth Hills • Highlands, New Jersey • 07732
(212) 297-0620

AT&T Capital Corp. 400 Perimeter Center Terr., Suite 900, Atlanta 30346. (404) 804-6403. FAX: (404) 804-6440. Samuel D. Bush, account off.
Provides sr debt financing for radio, TV & cable.

Act III Broadcasting Inc. 1999 Ave. of the Stars, Suite 500, Los Angeles 90067. (310) 553-3636. FAX: (310) 553-3928. Richard Ballinger, pres; John DeLorenzo, exec VP; Bill White, VP sls; George Pamicza, VP engrg; Melanie Abrams, controller.

AdMedia Corporate Advisors Inc. 866 3rd Ave., 26th Fl., New York 10022. (212) 759-1870. FAX: (212) 888-4960. Georgiana G. Kingsbury, mgr dir bcst.
Full range of investment banking svcs, including mergers, acquisitions & divestitures; recapitalization, financial analysis & counsel, debt or equity financing through private or public channels, including LBOs & ESOPs.

Aetna Life & Casualty Co. 151 Farmington Ave., Hartford, Conn. 06156. (203) 273-0123. John D. Loewenberg, pres info technology.

Allied Capital Corp. 1666 K St. N.W., Suite 901, Washington 20006. (202) 331-1112. FAX: (202) 659-2053. David Gladstone, chmn; C. Cabel Williams III, pres; Susan Gallagher, Tom Westbrook, VPs.

American Broadcast Financial Corp. 4359 S. Howell Ave., Suite 106, Milwaukee 53207. (414) 482-1959. FAX: (414) 483-1980. Patrick Lopeman, pres.
Equipment leasing & financial consulting svcs.

American Security Bank N.A. 1501 Pennsylvania Ave. N.W., Washington 20005. (202) 624-4198. FAX: (202) 624-7979. Frank P. Bramble, chmn of bd/CEO; Walter R. Fatzinger Jr., pres.

BancBoston Capital Inc. 100 Federal St., Boston 02110. (617) 434-5181; (617) 434-2509. FAX: (617) 434-1153. Sanford Anstey, mgng dir.
Active, experienced financing source of mezzanine & equity capital for media companies with over $90 million invested in these businesses.

BIA Consulting. Box 17307, Dulles International Airport, Washington 20041. (703) 818-BIA5. FAX: (703) 803-FAXX. Thomas J. Buono, A.S.A., pres/CEO; William Redpath C.P.A./A.S.A., VP; Peter Bowman, mgr financial analysis; Debra Metcalf, asst VP mktg.
Financial consultants to the communications industry; fair market valuations, tax appraisals, acquisition consulting, litigation support, investment publications.

BTMI. 1090 Vermont Ave. N.W., Suite 800, Washington 20005. (202) 408-7036. FAX: (202) 408-1590. Paul Robinson, pres; Mary D. Ames, CFO.

Barclays Bank Plc. 222 Broadway, 11th Fl., New York 10038. (212) 412-2917; (212) 412-7562; (212) 412-7561. FAX: (212) 412-7511. Frank Izzo, dir communications group.

Berkery, Noyes & Co. 50 Broad St., New York 10004. (212) 668-3022; FAX: (212) 363-7077. Joseph W. Berkery, pres; Dwight Johnson, VP; Marie Salerno, assoc.
Assists with mergers, acquisitions & divestitures; financial analysis & counsel; debt or equity financing through private or public channels, including LBOs & ESOPs.

Blackburn & Co. Capital Markets Group. 201 N. Union St., Suite 340, Alexandria, Va. 22314. (703) 519-3703. FAX: (703) 519-9756. James Blackburn Jr., chmn; Richard F. Blackburn, pres; Susan K. Byers.

Broadcast Financial Services. 1119 E. San Antonio St., El Paso, Tex. 79901. (915) 533-4700. FAX: (915) 533-3640. Garrett W. Haston, pres.
Provides accounts receivable financing.

Bulkley Media Inc./Bulkey Capital. 8333 Douglas Ave., Suite 777, Dallas 75225. (214) 692-5476. FAX: (214) 692-9309. G. Bradford Bulkley, pres.

Burr, Egan, Deleage & Co. One Post Office Sq., Suite 3800, Boston 02109. (617) 482-8020. FAX: (617) 482-1944. Craig L. Burr, William P. Egan, Brian W. McNeill, gen ptnrs.
 San Francisco 94111: One Embarcadero Ctr., Suite 4050. (415) 362-4022. FAX: (415) 362-6178. TELEX: 289397 BEDCO UR. Jean Deleage, Timothy Dibble, Robert Benbow, gen ptnrs.

CEA Inc. 375 Park Ave., Suite 3808, New York 10152. (212) 319-1968. FAX: (212) 319-4293. Donald Russell, pres; Stuart Goldfarb, sr VP/gen counsel; James Dunleavy, VP; Evan Blum, financial analyst; William Lisecky, asst VP.
Investment banking & brokerage.

Canadian Imperial Bank of Commerce. 425 Lexington Ave., New York 10017. (212) 856-4000. FAX: (212) 856-4035. Allyn W. Keiser, exec VP/gen mgr U.S.; Donald W. Stephenson, sr VP U.S.; Robert J. Munch, sr VP corporate finance U.S.; Peter G. Smith, sr dir communications & entertainment.
 San Francisco 94111: Embarcadero Ctr. W. Tower, 275 Battery St., Suite 1840. (415) 399-5700.
 Los Angeles 90071: 300 S. Grand Ave., Suite 2700. (213) 617-6200.
 Denver 80202: One Denver Pl., 999 18th St., Suite 925. (303) 292-0439.
 Atlanta 30339: Two Paces W., 2727 Paces Ferry Rd., Suite 1200. (404) 319-4999.
 Chicago 60606: 200 W. Madison St., Suite 2300. (312) 368-1160.
 New York 10005: Wall Street Box 181, 22 William St. (212) 825-7000.
 Portland, Ore. 97207: 315 S.W. 5th Ave. (503) 242-9240.
 Pittsburgh 15219: U.S. Steel Bldg., 600 Grant St., Suite 5670. (412) 456-2200.
 Dallas 75201: 3200 Lincoln Plaza, 500 N. Akard. (214) 954-3200.
 Houston 77010: Two Houston Ctr., 909 Fannin St., Suite 1200. (713) 658-8400.
 Seattle 98111: Box 100, 801 2nd Ave. (206) 223-7951.

Chemical Bank. 277 Park Ave., New York 10172. (212) 310-6027. FAX: (212) 750-9629. Thomas Pergola, VP/unit mgr.

Chesley, Maddox & Associates Inc. 575 Madison Ave., New York 10023. (216) 241-0905. FAX: (216) 241-0905. Chesley Maddox-Dorsey, pres.

Communications Capital Inc. 25 Tudor City Pl., New York 10017. (212) 986-0966. Blair Walliser, pres; Wade Barnes, VP.

Communications Equity Associates. 101 E. Kennedy Blvd., Suite 3300, Tampa 33602. (813) 222-8844. FAX: (813) 225-1513. J. Patrick Michaels Jr., chmn/CEO; H. Gene Gawthrop, exec VP/COO; Brad A. Gordon, VP/CFO; Glenn Serafin, VP radio; Jeanette Tully, VP.
 New York 10152: 375 Park Ave., Suite 3808. (212) 319-1968. Don Russell, pres CEA Inc.
 Berwyn, Pa. 19312: 1235 Westlakes Dr., Suite 140. (215) 251-0650. Thomas MacCrory, group VP. Philadelphia office.
 London, U.K. EC3P 3AJ: 32 St. Mary at Hill. 44-71-623-8844. Lisa-Gaye Shearing, mgng dir.
 Central, Hong Kong: 3402-04 One Exchange Sq., 8 Connaught Pl. 852-845-5504. Sarah Rechin, mgng dir.
 Munich, Germany D-80539: Maximilianstrasse 30/11. 49-89-293-317. Dr. Stephan Goetz, mgng dir.
Provides investment banking, brokerage & consulting svcs for bcst, CATV, cellular & related communications industries.

Continental Illinois National Bank and Trust Co. of Chicago. 231 S. LaSalle St., Chicago 60697. (312) 828-7831. FAX: (312) 987-5896. Thom C. Theobald, chmn.

Daniels & Associates. 3200 Cherry Creek S. Dr., Suite 500, Denver 80209. (303) 778-5555. FAX: (303) 778-5599. Phillip Hogue, chmn/CEO; Brian Deevy, pres/COO.
 New York 10153: 767 5th Ave. (212) 935-5900. FAX: (212) 832-2784. Greg Ainsworth, sr VP.
Provides investment banking svcs to the CATV & bcstg industries.

The Deer River Group. 2000 L St. N.W., Suite 200, Washington 20036. (202) 659-3331. Robin B. Martin, pres/CEO; Erwin G. Krasnow, gen counsel.
 Wayland, Mass. 01778: 35 Main St. (508) 653-7200. Jay P. Williams, COO.
Assist bcst execs in acquiring stns, securing financing; financial consultant to single stn & group owners.

Fahnestock & Co. Inc. 110 Wall St., 10th Fl., New York 10005. (212) 668-8175. FAX: (212) 425-2028. John E. Palmer, exec VP.

Financial Technology Research Corp. 88 Fulton St., Suite 517, New York 10038. (212) 791-3583. FAX: (212) 791-4236. Neal R. Bruckman, pres; Ira J. Victor, exec VP.
 Woodland Hills, Calif. 91346: 21724 Ventura Blvd., Suite 204. (818) 594-3310.
Financial corporate svcs, including acquisition financing, equity funding & initiation of international joint ventures for bcstrs, networks, cable operators & progmg syndicators.

Financing for Science International Inc. 10 Waterside Dr., Farmington, Conn. 06032-3065. (203) 676-1818. FAX: (203) 676-1814. Barry R. Bronfin, Sc.D., chmn/pres; Robert D. Pomeroy Jr., VP mktg; Kevin P. Kickery, VP natl sls; Daniel J. Nadis, VP corporate dev & portfolio mgmt; Joseph J. Artuso, VP natl progs.
Lease financing of technology-based equipment, generally valued at $500,000 to $20,000,000, to a variety of industries in the high-tech arena.

First National Bank of Chicago. One First National Plaza, Suite 0629, Chicago 60670. (312) 732-6950. FAX: (312) 732-8587. Richard L. Elmendorf.

Broadcasting & Cable Yearbook 1994

Station Financing Services

First Union National Bank of N.C. One First Union Center-0735, 19th Fl., Charlotte, N.C. 28288. (704) 374-4897. FAX: (704) 374-4092. William S. Laporte III, Paul Thomason, VPs.
Secured financing for acquisition and/or recapitalization of bcst properties.

Norman Fischer & Associates Inc. 1209 Parkway, Austin, Tex. 78703. (512) 476-9457. FAX: (512) 476-0504. Norman Fischer, pres.
Harlingen, Tex.: 802 E. Harrison. (512) 428-3736. Mal Kasanoff, assoc.
Brokerage in radio, TV & cable; consultation in mgmt & opns, appraisals, feasibility studies, expert testimony, financial planning & assistance.

Fleet Equity Partners. 111 Westminster St., Providence, R.I. 02903. (401) 278-6770. FAX: (401) 278-6387. Robert M. Van Degna, Habib Y. Gorgi, gen ptnrs; Riordon B. Smith, Michael A. Gorman, VPs; Bernard V. Buonanno III, assoc; Donald E. Bates, advisor.
Albany, N.Y. 12207: Peter D. Kiernan Plaza. (518) 447-4445. William P. Phelan, ptnr.
Source of equity capital to well-managed, positive cash flowing companies.

Fleet Mezzanine Capital Inc. 50 Kennedy Plaza, Providence, R.I. 02903. (401) 278-6274. Michael Rogers, VP.

William L. Fleming Inc. 94 Beacon St., Hartford, Conn. 06105-4103. (203) 236-4453. William L. Fleming, pres.
Investment banking; financial consultant to bcstrs. Assist in structuring mergers, acquisitions & refinancings. Arrange equity, debt or other funds needed.

Richard A. Foreman Associates. 330 Emery Dr. E., Stamford, Conn. 06902-2210. (203) 327-2800. FAX: (203) 967-9393. Richard A. Foreman, pres; Richard W. Kozak, assoc.

Franke & Co. Inc. 2525 E. Camelback, Suite 800, Phoenix 85016. (602) 956-8611. W.A. Franke, pres.
Investment banking, financing & consulting, negotiation for principals, investment properties acquisition.

Furman, Selz. 230 Park Ave., 13th Fl., New York 10169. (212) 309-8200. Raymond J. Timothy, sr mgng dir.

GE Capital Corp. 335 Madison Ave., 12th Fl., New York 10017. (212) 370-8000. FAX: (212) 983-8767. William Schink, sr VP.

Clifton Gardiner & Assoc. Inc. Box 5559, 0082 E. Beaver Creek Blvd., Avon, Colo. 81620. (303) 949-4485. FAX: (303) 949-0266. Clifton H. Gardiner, pres.

General Electric Capital Corp. 260 Long Ridge Rd., Stanford, Conn. 06927. (203) 357-3100. FAX: (203) 357-3933. Pat Yoder, mktg mgr; Jim McKay, coml finance.
Westport, Conn. 06880: 1221 Post Rd. E. (203) 222-6000. William Burke, VP.

Hague & Co. 540 Frontage Rd., Suite 3020, Northfield, Ill. 60093-1201. (708) 441-7200. FAX: (708) 441-7200. Lee Hague, pres.

Heller Financial Inc. (Media Business Division.) 500 W. Monroe St., Chicago 60661. (312) 441-7000; (312) 441-7345. Douglas W. Zylstra, VP.

R. Miller Hicks & Co. 1011 W. 11th St., Austin, Tex. 78703. (512) 477-7000. FAX: (512) 477-9697. R. Miller Hicks, pres.

Hoffman Schutz Media Capital Inc. 42 Monmouth Hills, Highlands, N.J. 07732. (212) 297-0620; Anthony M. Hoffman, pres; David E. Schutz, VP.

Hungerford, Aldrin, Nichols & Carter, C.P.A.s. 2910 Lucerne Dr. S.E., Grand Rapids, Mich. 49546. (616) 949-3200. FAX: (616) 949-7720. Clifford A. Aldrin C.P.A., ptnr bcst svcs.

JB Financial Advisors Inc. 14595 Avion Pkwy., Suite 500, Chantilly, Va. (703) 818-8115. FAX: (703) 803-3299. George E. Johnson, pres; Thomas J. Buono, exec VP.
Investment banking svc including "placement of debt & equity" advice in capital structure & merger & acquisition issues.

Paul Kagan Associates. 126 Clock Tower Pl., Carmel, Calif. 93923-8734. (408) 624-1536. FAX: (408) 625-3225. Bruce Bishop Cheen, VP bcst; Larry Gerbrandt, VP cable.

MFR Financial Resources Inc. 1532-A Brookhollow Dr., Santa Ana, Calif. 92705. (714) 540-0302. FAX: (714) 557-1556. Bart Fenmore, pres; Eric Fenmore, VP.
Accounts receivable funding for radio/TV stns.

Chesley Maddox & Associates Inc. 575 Madison Ave., 10th Fl., New York 10022. (212) 605-0553. FAX: (212) 308-9834. Chesley Maddox, pres.

McKinley Capital Partners. 712 5th Ave., New York 10019. (212) 956-2234. FAX: (212) 956-8407. Robert E. Beacham, mng dir; William M. Osborne III, pres; Ronald O. Drake Jr., financial analyst.
Investment banking & merchant banking for bcst, cable & related media industries.

Media Capital Inc. Box 12837, San Luis Obispo, Calif. 93406. (805) 543-9214. FAX: (805) 543-9243. Michael B. Hesser, pres.
Assist in finding, evaluating, financing & structuring acquisitions. Also, consulting, mgmt & sls.

Media Services Group Inc. 2111 Wilson Blvd., Suite 700, Arlington, Va. 22201. (703) 351-5025. FAX: (703) 351-0361. Millard S. Younts, pres; Mona Wargo, mktg dir.
Overland Park, Kan. 66212: 10575 Riley. (913) 383-2260. FAX: (913) 383-3152. Bill Lytle, VP.
Logan, Utah. 84321: Box 744. (801) 753-8090. FAX: (801) 753-1394. Greg Merrill.
Berwyn, Pa. 19312: 179 Saint Clair Ctr. (215) 695-9339. FAX: (215) 695-9340. Kevin C. Cox, VP.
Providence, R.I. 02903: 170 Westminster St., Suite 701. (401) 454-3130. FAX: (401) 454-3131. Robert J. Maccini, VP.
Jacksonville Beach, Fla. 32260: 3948 S. 3rd St., #191. (904) 285-3239. FAX: (904) 285-5618. George R. Reed, VP.
Mergers, acquisitions, financing, valuations, consultation for radio & TV.

Minority Broadcast Investment Corp. 1001 Connecticut Ave. N.W., Suite 622, Washington 20036. (202) 293-1166. FAX: (202) 293-1181. Walter Threadgill, pres/CEO.

National Broadcast Finance Corp. Box 3167, 27 Harrison St., New Haven, Conn. 06515. (203) 389-6000. FAX: (203) 389-6020. David C. Cherhoniak, pres.
Specialized investment banking & financial consulting including raising debt & equity for bcst acquisitions & refinancings.

Oppenheimer & Co. Inc. Oppenheimer Tower, One World Financial Center, New York 10281. Mark A. Leavitt, mgng dir (212-667-5028); Cary H. Thompson, sr VP (310-445-0106).

Park Leasing Co. Box 1719, Des Moines, Iowa 50306. (515) 288-1023. FAX: (515) 281-2185. Tom Bernau, pres; Steve Davis, VP.

Phoenix Cable Inc. 10 S. Franklin Tpke., Suite 100-B, Ramsey, N.J. 07446. (201) 825-9090. FAX: (201) 825-8794. James Feeney, Ron Demer, exec VPs.
Atlanta, 30324-5218: 641 E. Morningside Dr. N.E. (404) 872-2406. Ron Demer, exec VP.
Sacramento, Calif. 95827: 10316 Placer Ln. (916) 366-3830. Leslie Sorg Parker, VP.
Cable TV systems ownership, system mgmt svcs, & lease & debt financing svcs.

The Proctor Group Inc. 980 FM 1746, Woodville, Tex. 75979. (409) 429-3679. FAX: (409) 429-5257. Gerald R. Proctor, pres; David Garland, VP.
Brokerage & financial svcs to the bcst, cable & communications industries.

Rodgers Group Inc. Box 1577, Martinsville, Ind. 46151. (317) 342-3394. David A. Rodgers, pres.

Sanders & Co. 1900 Emery St. N.W., Suite 206, Atlanta 30318. (404) 355-6800. FAX: (404) 355-7600. William H. Sanders, pres.
Private placements of debt & equity for bcstrs & cable operators.

Satterfield & Perry Inc. 3062 Robb Cir., Denver 80215-7067. (303) 239-6670. FAX: (303) 231-9562. Al Perry, chmn.
Radio, TV & cable broker, mgmt consultant, appraiser, expert witness & accounts receivable funding.

William B. Schutz Jr. Box 404, St. Michaels, Md. 21663. (410) 745-3900. FAX: (410) 745-5929. William B. Schutz Jr, pres.

Barry Sherman & Associates. 7640 Tremayne Pl., Suite 204, McLean, Va. 22102. (703) 821-0877. Barry Sherman, pres.

THE RADIO FINANCE SPECIALISTS

- New Financings
- Refinances
- Smaller Markets
- Restructures

SIGNAL PROPERTIES
99 State St., Brooklyn Hts., N.Y. 11201
(718) 643-5825

Signal Properties. 99 State St., Brooklyn Heights, N.Y. 11201. (718) 643-5825. Mark Uncapher, mgng dir.
Radio finance specialists: new financings, refinances, restructures & smaller markets.

The Sillerman Companies. 150 E. 58th St., New York 10155. (212) 980-4455. FAX: (212) 832-5121. Robert F.X. Sillerman, chmn/CEO.
Capital investments in radio & TV stns & investment banking svcs (sr/mezzanine financing & acquisitions/divestitures) for portfolio companies.

OPPENHEIMER & CO., INC.

Investment Bankers to the Media and Communications Industry

Oppenheimer Tower
One World Financial Center, New York, NY 10281

Mark A. Leavitt, Managing Director
(212) 667-5028

Cary H. Thompson, Senior Vice President
(310) 445-0106

Oppenheimer & Co., Inc.

New York, Atlanta, Boston, Chicago, Fort Lauderdale,
Houston, Los Angeles, St. Louis, Seattle, London

Station Financing Services

Barry Skidelsky, Esq. 655 Madison Ave., 19th Fl., New York 10021. (212) 832-4800. FAX: (212) 486-8668. Barry Skidelsky, Esq.
Legal & consultation svcs available: bcst loans & investments; bankruptcy trustee/receiver.

Society National Bank. (Media Finance Division.) 127 Public Sq., 6th Fl., Cleveland 44114. (216) 689-5787. FAX: (216) 689-4666. Kathleen Mayher, sr VP/mgr.
Financing for media: TV, radio, cable, nwsprs & bcstg.

The Stebbins Co. Box 30, Lake Forest, Ill. 60045. (708) 234-4534. John D. Stebbins, pres.

Stonemark Corp. 1370 Stewart St., Seattle 98109. (206) 628-8989. FAX: (206) 628-0839. William V. May, pres.

Specializing in business brokerage, debt placement & equity arrangement related to bcst properties as well as other industries.

Syndicated Communications Inc. (SYNCOM). 8401 Colesville Rd., Silver Spring, Md. 20910. (301) 608-3203. FAX: (301) 608-3307. Terry L. Jones, pres; Duane C. McKnight, Anthony L. Williams, VPs.

TA Communications Partners. 75 State St., Boston 02109. (617) 345-7200. FAX: (617) 345-7201. David D. Croll, mgng ptnr; Richard H. Churchill, Stephen F. Gormley, James F. Wade, ptnrs; Christopher S. Gaffney, John G. Hayes, Peter O. Claudy, assocs.

Thoben-Van Huss & Associates Inc. 1010 E. 86th St., Suite 44C, Indianapolis 46240-1301. (317) 580-0094.

FAX: (317) 580-0097. William K. Van Huss, chmn; Phillip M. Thoben, pres.

Edwin Tornberg & Co. Inc. Box 55298, Washington 20011. (202) 291-8700. Edwin Tornberg, pres.

Waller Capital Corp. 30 Rockefeller Plaza, Suite 4350, New York 10112. (212) 632-3600. FAX: (212) 632-3607. John W. Waller III, chmn/CEO; Andrew J. Armstrong Jr., pres; Richard H. Patterson, John T. Woodruff; sr VPs.
Financing & investment svcs to cable TV industry, specializing in cable TV mergers & acquisitions, buyout financing, raising debt & equity.

Wood & Co. Inc. 431 Ohio Pike, Suite 210N, Cincinnati 45255. (513) 528-7373. Larry C. Wood, pres; M.A. Dennis, rsch analyst; K.A. Gerard, analyst.

Research Services

A & A Research. 690 Sunset Blvd., Kalispell, Mont. 59901. (406) 752-7857. FAX: (406) 752-0194. Judith Doonan, pres; Dr. E.B. Eiselein, rsch dir.
Qualitative & quantitative audience surveys for small- & medium-market radio stns, TV stns & cable.

Admar Research Co. Inc. 225 Park Ave. S., New York 10003. (212) 677-1700. FAX: (212) 260-2170. Henry D. Ostberg, chmn; Robert Wilkowitz, exec VP.
Adv rsch, concept evaluation, product testing & tracking studies; specializes in rsch for legal purposes.

The Adult Contemporary Music Research Letter. 1837 S.E. Harold St., Portland, Ore. 97202-4932. (503) 232-9787; (800) 929-5119. FAX: (503) 232-9787. Eric G. Norberg, pres/edit/publisher; Jane A. Kenney, rsch dir.
Rsch audience appeal, new & current adult contemp mus, reported in wkly newsletter. Book of oldies rsch also available.

Advanced Research Services. 22548 Pacific Coast Hwy, Suite 303, Malibu, Calif. 90265. (310) 456-6454. FAX: (310) 456-6508. Scott V. Tallal, pres.
Dallas 75205: 4201 Edmondson Ave. (214) 520-2000. Bill Brown.
New York 10022: 400 E. 59th St. (212) 355-1564. David Friedman.
Full-svc audience rsch firm specializing in computer-assisted telephone surveys (with digital audio capture) for cable & bcst TV.

Aim Music Research. 2119 E. Crocus Dr., Phoenix 85022. (602) 992-0310. FAX: (602) 443-1025. Tom Moran, pres.
Music rsch & software sls for radio stns.

Alpine Media Inc. Box 1197, Alpine, N.J. 07620. (201) 784-1068. FAX: (201) 784-3863. Michael Nigris Jr., pres.
Radio stn acquisition/mgmt consultants. Market analysis, liaison with financial institutions, preparations of business plans, feasibility studies & financial planning.

The Arbitron Co. 142 W. 57th St., New York 10019. (212) 887-1300. FAX: (212) 887-1401. Stephen B. Morris, pres; Robert Hyland, VP sls & mktg/TV net & stn svcs; Jay Guyther, VP sls & mktg/radio stn svcs.
Chicago 60611: 211 E. Ontario St., Suite 1400. (312) 266-4150. Debbie Buckley, midwestern mgr radio stn svcs; Barbara C. Czachorski, VP midwestern advertiser/agency svcs; James E. Mocarski, VP midwestern TV stn svcs.
Atlanta 30328: 9000 Central Pkwy., Suite 300. (404) 551-1400. Robert Bourquard, VP sls/dev/cable system svcs; Sanders Hickey, southeastern mgr radio stn svcs; Lisa Segall, southeastern mgr adv radio stn svcs; Christopher Werner, southeastern mgr TV stn svcs.
Dallas 75240: One Galleria Tower, 13355 Noel Rd., Suite 1120. (214) 385-5388. Sharon Rickel, southwestern mgr adv/agency svcs; Julie Girocco, southwestern mgr TV stn svcs; Patti Shannon, southwestern mgr radio stn svcs.
San Francisco 94111: One Maritime Plaza, Suite 1000. (415) 393-6925. Marvin Korach, western mgr radio stn svcs.
Los Angeles 90036: 5670 Wilshire Blvd., Suite 600. (213) 932-6500. Ken Hansely, western mgr TV stn svcs; Brad Bedford, Pacific southwestern mgr radio stn svcs; John Ferrari, western mgr adv/agency svcs; David Bright, western mgr TV stn svcs.
Laurel, Md. 20707: The Arbitron Building, 312 Marshall Ave. (301) 497-4600. Marshall L. Snyder, VP field opns & mktg svcs; David Lapovsky, VP rsch & data collection; Patricia Duggan, mgr client svcs.
West Chester, Pa. 19380: 1385 Enterprise Dr. (215) 692-5300.
TV & cable ratings, coml monitoring reports, product sls tracking info. Coml monitoring svc (Media Watch).

Audience Research & Development (AR&D). 8828 Stemmons, Suite 600, Dallas 75247. (214) 630-5097. FAX: (214) 630-4951. Willis Duff, pres/CEO; William W. Taylor, COO; Ed Bewley, chmn; Jim Willi, exec VP client svcs; Jerry Florence, VP rsch; Sandra Connell, VP placement svcs.
Rsch & consultation in loc TV progmg specializing in news. Prog dev, personnel search, performance coaching, promotion, strategic planning, mktg & sls rsch for bcst TV.

BBM Bureau of Measurement. 1500 Don Mills Rd., Suite 305, Don Mills, Ont., Canada M3B 3L7. (416) 445-9800. FAX: (416) 445-8644. Owen A. Charlebois, pres/CEO; David Chambers, VP finance/admin; Tom Clement, VP opns; Duncan McKie (ComQuest), VP/gen mgr; Brian Parish, VP radio; Ken Purdye, VP TV; Michael Wallace, VP MIS. Directors: Rodger Hone (Global TV Net, Toronto), chmn; Michel Arpin (Radiomutuel, Montreal), sec/treas; Sunni Boot, FCB-Ronalds-Reynolds, Toronto; Peter Elwood, Lever Bros Ltd., Toronto; Yvon Chouinard, Diffusion Power Inc., Montreal; Elmer Hildebrand, Golden West Broadcasting, Altona; Paul Martel, Paul Martel Inc., Montreal; Jim McLaughlin, radio exec chmn, Moffat Communications Ltd., Winnipeg; Greg Mudry, TV exec chmn, CITY-TV, Toronto; Doug Newell, N.Y.P. & N., Toronto; Kate Potter, Labatt Breweries of Canada, Toronto; Don Smith, Westcom TV Group, Vancouver; James T. Webb, CHYM/CKGL, Kitcher.
Montreal, Que. Canada H3B 1P5: 615 René-Lévesque Blvd., Suite 750. (514) 878-9711. FAX: (514) 878-4210. Robert Langlois, VP Quebec svcs.
Vancouver, B.C. Canada V6J 4S5: 1755 W. Broadway, Suite 305. (604) 731-1444. FAX: (604) 731-6692. Terry Dinsmore, dir western svcs.
Media rsch for radio & TV.

Joseph Barnes & Associates. 95 Colton Ln., Martinez, Calif. 94553. (510) 372-9495. FAX: (510) 372-9497. Joseph Barnes, pres; Kim Allen, office mgr.
Media mgmt consulting, mktg & training.

The Benchmark Co. 1705 S. Capital of Texas Hwy., Suite 305, Austin, Tex. 78746. (512) 327-7010. FAX: (512) 328-1464. Rob Balon, pres/CEO; Paige Blount, rsch dir.
Rsch & mktg for the bcst industry.

Berry Best Services Ltd. 1990 M St. N.W., Suite 740, Washington 20036. (202) 293-4964. FAX: (202) 293-0287. Thomas L. Berry, pres; Randy G. Berry, VP.
FCC rsch, hard-copy & full electronic distribution of FCC news releases, public notices & texts; on-line FCC data bases.

Bethlehem Publishing. 322 E. 50th St., New York 10022. (212) 832-7170. FAX: (212) 826-3169. Martin Herbst, publisher; Robert Herbst, Sarah Leaf, editors; Annette Chow, sls/mktg.
Bethlehem, N.H. 03547: 2 Edelweiss Dr. Prod office.
Publishes Media Market Guide, a source for media costs for all markets, & TV Datatrak, a complete TV & cable directory.

Billie Research Corp. 3909 National Dr., Suite 230, Burtonsville, Md. 20866. (301) 421-0140. FAX: (301) 421-1652. Jay Billie, pres.
Custom audience rsch & analysis for mgmt, progmg & sls purposes.

Bolton Research Corp. 250 W. Lancaster Ave., Philadelphia 19301. (215) 640-4400. FAX: (215) 647-4623. Ted Bolton, pres; Larry Rosin, VP/gen mgr; Lou Partick, dir rsch/progmg; Joe Lenski, rsch dir; Lisa Hennelly, mktg dir.
Perceptual rsch studies; marketplace positioning; mus rsch; format opportunity studies, focus groups.

Broadcast Media Associates. 316 California Ave., Suite 700, Reno, Nev. 89509. (800) 237-3777. Clifford M. Hunter, pres.
Custom market rsch including focus groups, perceptual studies, mus testing & format search.

Broadcast News Service. Box 1008, Boston 02103. P.J. Romano, dir.
Public opinion rsch, interviewing surveys, recording & bcst svcs.

Broadcast Research & Consulting Inc. Box 728, Port Washington, N.Y. 11050. (516) 883-8486. FAX: (516) 883-3090. Herbert Altman, pres.
Syndicated svcs: news & entertainment talent search, net anchor index. Natl & loc market rsch studies & consultation for bcstrs covering progs, movies, news, promotion, stn image & new electronic media.

Broadcast Service Bureau Inc. Box 10038, Rockville, Md. 20849-0038. (301) 762-8180. FAX: (301) 656-3053. John C. Keating, pres; Kevin W. Keating, VP; Sophie J. Steinberg, sec.
Publication, with updates of FCC Rules & Regulations, parts 0, 1, 2, 5, 13, 17, 73, 74, 76 & 78. Emphasis on bcst needs.

Bruskin/Goldring Research Inc. 100 Metroplex, Edison, N.J. 08817. (908) 572-7300. FAX: (908) 572-7980. Richard B. Hare, pres/COO; Marvin Baiman, sr VP; Barbara Berkowitz, Robert Golden, Joel Henkin, Paula Coll, client svc VPs.
Chicago 60610: 820 N. Orleans. (312) 440-5252. Jeff Kay, VP.

WHAT IF...?

LOOKING FOR ANSWERS?
We can provide actionable data to help you better position your market share and increase sales.

With our expertise in the broadcast industry and our qualitative and quantitative research capabilities we provide the answers!

- Hispanic Audience Ratings
- Copy/Promotion Testing
- Market Profile Studies
- Programming/Format Research
- Station Audience Profiles
- Coincidentals
- TV Overnights
- Ratings of On-Air Personalities

Call us! **1-800-741-5441**

Strategy Research Corporation
100 N.W. 37th Avenue, Miami, Florida 33125
Successful Marketing Requires Strategy

Custom-designed surveys for bcst industry on loc, rgnl & natl basis; loc & net radio & TV, cable/pay TV/DBS, videocassette & videodisc; natl omnibus studies; telephone & personal interviews.

George Burns & Co. 6965 El Camino Real, Suite 105-229, Rancho La Costa, Calif. 92009. (619) 746-7993. FAX: (619) 739-8303. George Burns, chmn; Larry Lakoduk, pres; Todd Stewart, VP progmg.
Radio mgmt & consulting.

Burns Media Consultants Inc. Box 6210, Malibu, Calif. 90264. (310) 457-1599. FAX: (310) 457-8367. George A. Burns, pres; Sandra Kasberger, VP.
Custom radio/TV rsch. One-on-one interviewing, strategic market studies, format search, auditorium mus testing, telephone studies, ongoing rsch consultation.

Canadian Facts. 1075 Bay St., Toronto, Ont., Canada M5S 2X5. (416) 924-5751. FAX: (416) 923-7085. Donald Monk, pres; Michael Lopresti, VP.
Montreal, Que., Canada H3G 2B3: 1411 Crescent St. (514) 288-6894. FAX: (514) 288-0777. Michel Gauvreau, VP.
Vancouver, B.C., Canada V6E 4A4: 1130 W. Pender St., Suite 600. (604) 668-3344. FAX: (604) 668-3333. Peter Forward, VP.
Ottawa, Ont., Canada K1P 5W6: Place de Ville Tower B, 112 Kent St., Suite 2010A. (613) 232-4408. FAX: (613) 232-7102. Susan O'Hara, VP.
Full range of custom-designed & syndicated market rsch svcs.

Capitol Hill-Media Site/Facilities Selection Group. 1666 K St. N.W., Suite 1010, Washington 20006. (202) 833-5800. FAX: (202) 223-0996. James Connelly, dir.
Consulting coml real estate svcs, tenant/client representation, construction/financial analysis, turnkey lease/sale assumptions; roof & bldg zoning surveys.

Carolina Global Maps Inc. Box 8026, Greenville, N.C. 27835. (800) 248-6277; (919) 757-2511. FAX: (800) 321-6277. Lawrence Behr, pres; LuAnn Moore, gen mgr.
Earth-science rsch & bcst-related topographic maps.

Michael A. Carraher. Qualitative Research Consultant. 204 Dupont St., Philadelphia 19127. (215) 487-2061. FAX: (215) 487-2359. Michael A. Carraher.
Specialist in focus groups, in-depth interviews. Motivational, exploratory & progmg dev studies showing "what is" & "how to."

Center for Radio Information. 19 Market St., Cold Spring, N.Y. 10516. (914) 265-4459; (800) 359-9898. FAX: (914) 265-2715. Maurie Webster, pres; Susan Rebentisch, VP admin; Scott Webster, VP dev.
Radio scan, PC data bases, market/probe, radio/link, mailing labels, phone lists, mktg file, net analysis, TV data bases, DB audits.

Claritas. 201 N. Union St., Suite 200, Alexandria, Va. 22314. (703) 683-8300. FAX: (703) 683-8309. Gary Hill, pres; Terry Pittman, VP.

Broadcasting & Cable Yearbook 1994

Research Services

New York 10036-8088: 11 W. 42nd St., 12th Floor. (212) 789-3580. Frank Pinnizotto, VP.
Los Angeles 90036-3603: 5757 Wilshire Blvd., Suite 201. (213) 954-3200. Sol Ortasse, mgr.
Chicago 60604-4302: 332 S. Michigan Ave., Suite 102. (312) 986-2650. Eric Garrett, mgr.
Dallas 75244-3127: 14679 Midway Rd. (214) 980-0198. Deborah Diot, VP.
Mktg data & software designed expressly for cable systems & for advertisers, & ad agencies.

Mark Clements Research Inc. 516 5th Ave., New York 10036. (212) 221-2470. FAX: (212) 221-7628. Mark Clements, pres; E.L. Reiter, exec VP.
Mktg, mgmt & product rsch; economic & progmg studies for TV & radio.

Coleman Research Inc. 2209 Century Dr., Raleigh, N.C. 27812. (919) 571-0000. FAX: (919) 571-9999. Jon Coleman, pres; Pierre Bouvard, VP.
Perceptual rsch including progmg, mktg & sls studies; continuing consultation.

Commtek Communications. 8330 Boone Blvd., Suite 600, Vienna, Va. 22182. (703) 827-0511. FAX: (208) 356-6179. David Wolford, CEO/publisher; Phil Swann, editorial dir; Pamella D. Waite, COO.
Rio Rancho, N.M. 87124: 561 Quantum Rd. N.E. (505) 892-2800. Reggie Burch, sls mgr.
Publisher of *Satellite Orbit Magazine*, a TV listing guide for TVRO owns.

Comsearch. 251 W. Renner Pkwy., Suite 170, Richardson, Tex. 75080. (214) 680-1000. FAX: (214) 680-9802. Richard Smith, dir.
Reston, Va. 22091: 11720 Sunrise Valley Dr. (703) 620-6300.
Computerized allocation studies, ch analysis, trans-interference analysis, system design, detailed coverage prediction, FCC application preparation, site location, mktg rsch.

Dr. Charles Connolly. 4012 Phoenix St., Ames, Iowa 50014-3918. (515) 292-4384. FAX: (515) 292-4384. Dr. Charles Connolly, exec dir.
Gen public ascertainment/issues surveys. Market rsch telephone surveys; progmg/news rsch for TV, radio, CATV. Focus groups, accelerated staff training; creative staff dev.

Co-op Resource Center. (A division of Media Monitors Inc.) Box 55592, Indianapolis 46205. (317) 547-1362. FAX: (317) 549-0331. John R. Curtis, pres/CEO.
Co-op consultants & co-op data base mgrs offering "fastlink" on-line electronic data systems.

Crossley Surveys Inc. 275 Madison Ave., New York 10016. (212) 692-9320. FAX: (212) 687-8387. Franklin B. Leonard, pres; Staats M. Abrams, sr VP.
Custom mktg rsch studies for media & marketers.

Custom Audience Consultants. Box 6878, Arlington, Va. 22206. (703) 671-6303. FAX: (703) 354-8164. Sam Paley, pres.
Full-svc rsch company; sls, mgmt & progmg, including diary analysis for radio & TV.

Dataworld Inc. Box 30730, Bethesda, Md. 20824. (301) 652-8822; (800) 368-5754. FAX: (301) 656-5341. Claude G. Grech, VP mktg; Robert E. Richards, sls; John T. Neff, sls.
Comprehensive data bases for AM, FM, TV, LPTV & wireless cable; coverage maps; on-line 24-hour remote access.

Duncan's American Radio Inc. Box 90284, Indianapolis 46290. (317) 844-0988; (317) 630-2888. FAX: (317) 571-0032. James H. Duncan Jr., pres; Vaun Thygerson, rsch assoc.
Publishes books about the radio industry, including *American Radio* (four editions per year), *American Radio-Small Market Edition*, *Duncan's Radio Market Guide* & *Duncan's Radio Group Directory*. Also *Radio Audience Shares and Revenue Share* & *The Technical Facilities of American Radio*.

Electronic Media Rating Council. 509 Madison Ave., Suite 1112, New York 10022. (212) 754-3343. FAX: (212) 754-6430. Richard Weinstein, exec dir; Thomas McClendon, chmn bd of dirs; Kathryn Lenard, vice-chmn, bd of dirs.
Determines criteria & standards, administers an audit system for accreditation of audience measurement svcs to assure conformance with criteria, standards & procedures developed.

Jay Eliasberg. 200 E. 74th St., New York 10021. (212) 772-2959. Jay Eliasberg, own.

Entertainment Partners. 2600 W. Olive Ave., Burbank, Calif. 91505. (818) 569-5100; (818) 955-6000. FAX: (312) 467-1113. Robert Draney, CEO; Jack Peterson, pres.
Branches in New York & Los Angeles.

Executive Broadcast Services. Box 60327, Colorado Springs 80960. (800) 800-0107. FAX: (719) 579-6664. Skip Joeckel, pres; Kelley Hilligoss, dir opns/mktg.
Markets & sells a select line of progs, products & svcs to U.S. radio stns.

FM Atlas Publishing. Box 336, Esko, Minn. 55733-0336. (218) 879-7676. Bruce F. Elving, Ph.D., own; Carol Elving, office mgr; Dan Granholm, technician.
FM radio directory & *FMedia!* newsletter; rsch on utilization of FM/SCA & FM trans; SCA-modified radios, TV/SAP receivers.

FMR Associates Inc. 6045 E. Grant Rd., Tucson, Ariz. 85712. (602) 886-5548. FAX: (602) 886-9307. Bruce Fohr, pres; Jesse DeVaney, dir rsch; Lynn Moore, project dir; Bob Goode, mng ptr EARS systems.
Cave Creek, Ariz. 85331: Box 1783. (602) 488-2500. Bob Goode, mngng ptnr.
Perceptual progmg studies, wkly callout, EARS Music Studies, format opportunity & vulnerability positioning studies; TV coml testing. Electronic progmg simulation tests.

FPS Document ReSearch and Retrieval. (A division of Washington Information Group Ltd.) Box 19352, 20th St. Station, Washington 20036-0352. (202) 463-7323. FAX: (202) 463-8633. Doug House, pres.
Find & retrieve applications, filings & other documents at FCC, courts & other state & federal agencies. Same-day svc available.

Fair Press Services. (A division of Washington Information Group.) 1926 N Street N.W., 3rd Fl., Washington 20036. (202) 463-7323. FAX: (202) 463-8633. Justin Wilt, dir.
Communication rsch & FCC document subscription svc offers daily delivery of public notices, releases & texts, plus applications, filings customized svcs.

Faroudja Research. 750 Palomar Ave., Sunnyvale, Calif. 94086. (408) 735-1492. FAX: (408) 735-8571. Yves Faroudja, pres; Isabell Faroudja, VP.
FCC document subscription prog offers 45 categories of public notices, releases, texts; same-day svc available.

Global Research Institute. 747 Wire Rd., Auburn, Ala. 36830. (205) 826-0390. H.D. Norman, pres; Enrico Valdez, VP; Cherry Foster, gen mgr.
Mktg, data & media studies. International radio & TV audience measurement & progmg consultants.

Melvin A. Goldberg Inc./Communications. 17 North Dr., Great Neck, N.Y. 11021. (516) 482-0166. FAX: (516) 482-0166. Melvin A. Goldberg, chmn; Norma N. Goldberg, pres.
Consultation: communications rsch, TV, radio, cable, ratings, surveys & market rsch.

Hagen Media Research. Box 40542, Washington 20016-0542. (703) 534-3003. FAX: (703) 534-3073. Don Hagen, pres.
Perceptual rsch for radio. Designs, conducts & interprets qualitative & quantitative studies. Focus groups, telephone surveys, one-on-one sessions, mus tests.

William R. Hamilton & Staff Inc. 5335 Wisconsin Ave. N.W., Suite 700, Washington 20015. (202) 686-5900. FAX: (202) 686-7080. William R. Hamilton, pres
News rsch, mktg rsch & pub opinion surveys relating to prog evaluation, licensing, new products, & high-tech telecommunications.

Peter D. Hart Research Associates Inc. 1724 Connecticut Ave. N.W., Washington 20009. (202) 234-5570. FAX: (202) 232-8134. Peter D. Hart, CEO; Geoffrey Garin, pres; Fred Hartwig, Tom Rhiele, Frederich Yang, VPs.
Audience rsch; polling for on-air use; bcst, cable, ETV, radio rsch svcs including market surveys, political communication & cable referenda rsch.

Hartford Gunn Institute. 1400 E. Touhy Ave., Suite 260, Des Plaines, Ill. 60018-3305. (708) 390-8703. FAX: (708) 390-9435. James Fellows, pres; Michael Hobbs, sr fellow.
Policy rsch & dev for public telecommunications.

William Hatfield. 212 Whitestone Rd., Silver Spring, Md. 20901. (301) 593-0184. William Hatfield, pres.

Norman Hecht Research Inc. Box 698, 33 Queens St., Syosset, N.Y. 11791. (516) 496-8866. FAX: (516) 496-8165. Norman Hecht, pres; Richard Feldman, sr VP/gen mgr media rsch; Harvey Morrow, VP media rsch; Dennis Regan, VP TV rsch.
Market rsch & consulting firm specializing in progmg, news & talent rsch, image studies, ratings analysis, adv effectiveness, cable MSO & cable net rsch & dev, & strategic sls.

Kenneth Hollander Associates Inc. 3490 Piedmont Rd., Suite 920, Atlanta 30305. (404) 231-4077. FAX: (404) 231-0763. Kenneth Hollander, pres.

Hungerford, Aldrin, Nichols & Carter, C.P.A.s. 2910 Lucerne Dr. S.E., Grand Rapids, Mich. 49546. (616) 949-3200. FAX: (616) 949-7720. Clifford A. Aldrin, C.P.A., ptnr bcst svcs.
Radio & TV revenue report preparation & year-end accounting/auditing svcs.

Innovative Audience Research Inc. 122 Purcell Dr., Alameda, Calif. 94502. (510) 523-2458. FAX: (510) 523-2458. Mike Silverstein, pres; Susan B. Silverstein, exec VP.
Strategic planning in news, progmg & promotion, impacting sweep book ratings in TV metered markets.

Institute For Research On Public Policy/Institut De Recherche En Politiques Publiques. 1470 Peel St., Suite 200, Montreal, Que., Canada H3A 1T1. (514) 985-2461. FAX: (514) 985-2559. Monique Jerome-Forget, pres.
Ottawa, Ont., Canada K1P 5E6: 250 Albert St., 13th Fl. (613) 238-2296. David Runnalls, dir.
Environment & sustainable dev progmg.

Intermedia Analyses Inc. 8 Shadow Rd., Upper Saddle River, N.J. 07458. (201) 327-6223. FAX: (201) 934-0192. Carol G. Mayberry, pres.
Strategies/analyses for buying and/or selling radio, optimizing revenue or investment.

Joe Jones. 10556 Amwood Rd., Lake View Terrace, Calif. 91342. (818) 890-0730. FAX: (818) 899-4457. Joe Jones, pres.
Mktg & audience rsch counsel.

Marion Jones. 10556 Arnwood Rd., Lake View Terrace, Calif. 91342. (818) 890-0730. FAX: (818) 899-4457. Marion Jones, pres.
Radio audience rsch for small- & medium-market stns.

K-B Ltd. Box 25548, Milwaukee 53225. (414) 781-0188. FAX: (414) 781-5313. John Kompas, chmn; Jackie Biel, pres/CEO.
Rsch in LPTV: mktg feasibility studies, demographic analysis. Rsch assistance to companies entering the LPTV market & stn representation.

KIDSNET. 6856 Eastern Ave. N.W., Suite 208, Washington 20012. (202) 291-1400. FAX: (202) 882-7315. Karen W. Jaffe, exec dir.
Computerized data base of info on children's progmg; prog-related study guides; mthy print & electronic publications.

Paul Kagan Associates Inc. 126 Clock Tower Pl., Carmel, Calif. 93923-8734. (408) 624-1536. FAX: (408) 625-3225. Paul Kagan, pres.
Specializing in financial & investment rsch. Media financial newsletters & data base reports.

Mark Kassof & Co. 150 S. 5th Ave., Suite B, Ann Arbor, Mich. 48104. (313) 662-5700. FAX: (313) 662-3255. Mark Kassof, pres.
Strategic audience rsch to pinpoint radio stn's most profitable format strategy; focus groups, auditorium mus testing, promotional testing.

M.A. Kempner Inc. 11800 Fountainside Cir., Boynton Beach, Fla. 33437. (800) 327-4994. FAX: (305) 360-7252. Marv Kempner, pres; H. Brant, engrg.
Scientific interactive polling equipment: Escape/600, telephone poll, TV-POWWW interactive electronic games, animated cartoons.

Korbel Marketing. 220 Gardenview Rd., San Antonio 78213. (512) 366-4210. FAX: (512) 366-4323. Susan Korbel, own.
Full-svc mktg rsch including stn image, consumer attitudes & media use.

Landsman Media Inc. 7 N. Airmont Rd., Suite 6, Suffern, N.Y. 10901. (914) 368-4810. FAX: (914) 368-4812. Dean F. Landsman, pres.
Prog feasibility; market analysis; focus groups; format & sls testing, including sls dept image studies.

Lowry & Co. Inc. 6302 E. Monte Cristo Ave., Scottsdale, Ariz. 85254. (602) 483-0586. FAX: (602) 443-1025. Robert M. Lowry, pres.
Full-svc rsch & prog consultation.

Research Services

Lund Media Research. 1330 Millbrae Ave., Millbrae, Calif. 94030. (415) 692-7777. FAX: (415) 692-7799. John C. Lund, pres.

Perceptual, focus group, sls, music research, RADIO MARKETING ASCERTAINMENT evaluates stn/competitive progmg. New stn/duopoly positioning. FORMAT DESIGN/implementation/marketing.

M Street Journal. 304 Park Ave. S., 7th Floor, New York 10010. (800) 248-4242; (212) 473-4668. FAX: (212) 473-4626. Robert Unmacht, pres/edit; Pat McCrummen, dir mktg.

Summary of FCC data & format changes. Publishes the *M Street Journal* & *M Street Radio Directory*.

MJM Research Inc. 11539 W. 83rd Terr., Lenexa, Kan. 66214. (800) 945-4656; (913) 888-3366. FAX: (913) 888-4423. C.C. McCartney, pres; Clark D. Roberts, VP.

Provides hook-tape prod, listener screening, fielding, & tabulation for all mus testing, perceptual studies, focus groups & promotional telemarketing.

Magazine Publishers of America. 919 3rd Ave., 22nd Fl., New York 10022. (212) 872-3700. FAX: (212) 888-4217. Donald Kummerfeld, pres; James R. Guthrie, exec VP mktg dev.

Washington 20036: 1211 Connecticut Ave. N.W. (202) 296-7277. George Gross, exec VP govt affrs.

Southfield, Mich. 48075: 4000 Town Ctr., Suite 675. (313) 352-8020. Charles Lee, VP automotive mktg.

Educational seminars; surveys members on various topics; extensive library on magazine publishing; monitors issues in the magazine industry. Publications: *Newsletter of Research, Newsletter of International Publishing, Washington Newsletter* & *Magazine Newsletter*.

Frank N. Magid Associates Inc. One Research Ctr., Marion, Iowa 52302. (319) 377-7345. FAX: (319) 377-5861. Frank N. Magid, CEO; Bruce Northcott, pres; Richard Haynes, VP rsch; Daniel Bormann, VP/chief admin off; Steve Ridge, Joe George, group VPs.

Audience & readership rsch. Talent & promotions testing utilizing VCResponse telefocus interviewing, agency/
advertiser studies, & sls rsch. New product dev & rsch stn positioning.

Market & Audience Research Group Inc. 11044 N.W. 8th Ct., Pompano Beach, Fla. 33071. Dorothy E. (Dot) Stein, pres.

Dresher, Pa. 19025: 245 Westwind Way. (215) 643-9135. Sharon R. Wolf, sr consultant.

TV rsch for sls, mktg & mgmt. Survey design available for custom studies, news, promotion, sls effectiveness.

Market Opinion Research. 31700 Middlebelt, Farmington Hills, Mich. 48334. (313) 737-5300. FAX: (313) 737-5326. James Buckley, VP media studies.

Market rsch, strategic planning, viewer satisfaction, economic modeling, audience analysis, data base mapping for TV & radio stns, cable TV franchises.

Marketing Resources Plus. 555 Twin Dolphin Blvd., Suite 350, Redwood City, Calif. 94065. (415) 595-1800. FAX: (415) 595-3410. Eugene F. Sokol, VP.

East Lansing, Mich. 48823: 1111 Michigan Ave., Suite 301. (517) 336-8787. FAX: (517) 351-4481. Brian Brady, sls mgr Broadcast Management Plus.

Broadcast Management Plus: Complete personal computer-based sls rsch. Proposal system for stns to sell time to agencies & advertisers.

MarketVision Research Inc. 4500 Cooper Rd., Cincinnati 45242-5617. (513) 791-3100. FAX: (513) 791-3103. Donald G. McMullen, pres; Robert V. Miller, Rex Repass, sr VPs.

Full-svc rsch firm. Specialized division for design, execution & analysis of bcst audience rsch.

Marquest Research. 400 Front St., Beaufort, N.C. 28516. (919) 728-3699. FAX: (919) 728-3180. Paul Rule, pres; Tyrus C. Ragland, VP.

Loc & natl cable, bcst & print surveys. Coincidentals, audience ratings & profiles, sub surveys, focus groups, interviewing/tabulation svcs.

Marshall Marketing & Communications Inc. 1699 Washington Rd., Suite 500, Pittsburgh 15228. (412) 854-4500. FAX: (412) 854-5030. Craig A. Marshall, pres; Thomas J. Burkhart, VP/gen mgr target dollars division; Katherine A. Marikos, VP retail & media svcs; Rochelle Kaecher, VP mktg & promotion; Richard Kinzler, VP opns.

Dayton, Ohio 45429: 4809 Silverwyck Dr. (513) 293-3218. Ira Slakter, VP mktg target dollar division.

Spokane, Wash. 99223: 3672 E. 33rd St. (509) 536-6317. Rick Hamm, rgnl mktg mgr.

Chicago 60610: 55 W. Goeth St. (312) 642-0065. Mary Kearns, rgnl mktg mgr.

Orlando, Fla. 32835: 1445 Saddleridge Dr. (407) 299-3510. Bruce Hahn, rgnl mktg mgr.

Sls dev rsch; custom-designed, market-specific data; consumer behavior; demographic data; media usage & psychographic "Vals 2" prog (lifestyle rsch/SRI International).

McNulty Research Inc. 21010 Center Ridge, Cleveland 44116. (216) 331-7236. Thomas M. McNulty, Ph.D., pres.

Market rsch to bcst cable industries. News, progmg, promotion, sls.

Kenneth R. Meades. Box 1469, Los Angeles 90053. (213) 669-9570. Kenneth R. Meades, own.

Market studies, progmg, engrg studies.

Media Monitors Inc. Box 55592, 2511 E. 46th St., Suite L, Indianapolis 46205. (317) 547-1362. FAX: (317) 549-0331. John R. Curtis, pres; John L. Selis, VP opns.

Radio, nwspr & magazine monitoring company. Political news clipping; creative review for natl advertisers' radio spots.

Media Perspectives. 606 Cooper Landing Rd., Bldg. A, Suite 4B, Cherry Hill, N.J. 08002. (609) 482-7979. FAX: (609) 482-0957. Steven G. Apel, pres.

Researches audience tastes & perceptions, employs advanced analytical techniques to guide bcstrs in constructing strategic progmg & mktg plans.

Mediamark Research Inc. 708 3rd Ave., 8th Fl., New York 10017. (212) 599-0444. FAX: (212) 682-6284. Alain J. Tessier, chmn; David C. Bender, pres/COO.

Chicago 60611: 500 N. Michigan Ave. (312) 329-0901. Scott Turner, VP.

Los Angeles 91604: 12001 Ventura Pl., Suite 300. (818) 506-5626. Selena Barzon, mgr western rgn.

Syndicated rsch: product, demographics for TV, radio, cable. Custom recontact surveys.

MediAnalysis. Box 39034, 4539 Alton Pl. N.W., Washington 20016. (202) 966-3303. James R. Bonfils, pres.

Coml monitoring of major stns in Baltimore. Reports published up to three times mthy.

Metro Radio Ratings. 11543 W. 83rd Terr. Lenexa, Ks. 66214. (800) 879-1729; (913) 888-1729. FAX: (913) 888-4423. Bill Lochman, mktg dir.

Telephone-response audience measurement. Complete quantitative & qualitative data on listener behavior within 24 hours from tabulation. Large, reliable samples measured in quarter-hour shares & ratings estimates.

Miller, Kaplan, Arase & Co. 10911 Riverside Dr., North Hollywood, Calif. 91602. (213) 877-6171. FAX: (818) 769-3100. George Nadel Rivin, C.P.A., ptnr in chg of bcst svcs.

Financial consulting, accounting & tax svcs including purchase price allocations & market revenue report preparation.

Jay Mitchell Associates. Box 1285, Fairfield, Iowa 52556. (515) 472-4087. Jay Mitchell, pres; Lori Morgan, opns mgr; Dawn Bergendahl, speech/language therapist; Jeffrey Hedquist, sweeper/IDs.

Mgmt, mktg & progmg consulting; market analysis & rsch. Voice IDs, mus formats, speech & voice training.

Myers Reports. 322 Rt. 46 W., Suite 130, Parsippany, N.J. 07054. (201) 808-7333. FAX: (201) 882-3651. Jack Myers, pres; Leah Reznick, VP.

Conducts syndicated & proprietary rsch for media companies: pub rels svcs, creative svcs.

Nathan Associates Inc. 2101 Wilson Blvd., Suite 1200, Arlington, Va. 22201. (703) 516-7700. FAX: (703) 351-6162. Gary L. French, Stephen A. Schneider, VPs.

Economic & mgmt consultants specializing in mktg & survey rsch, bus & property valuation & financial viability analysis.

National Broadcast Finance Corp. Box 3167, 27 Harrison St., New Haven, Conn. 06515. (203) 389-6000. FAX: (203) 389-6020. David C. Cherhoniak, pres.

National Economic Research Associates Inc. 50 Main St., White Plains, N.Y. 10606. (914) 448-4000. FAX: (914) 448-4040. Richard Rapp, pres; Judith Greenman, sr VP.

Washington 20036: 1800 M St. N.W., Suite 600 S. (202) 466-3510. Peter Max, sr VP.

Los Angeles 90071: 555 S. Flower St., Suite 4100. (213) 628-0131. Gary Dorman, sr VP.

Cambridge, Mass. 02142: One Main St. (617) 621-0444. William Taylor, sr VP.

Philadelphia 19102: 1515 Market St. (215) 546-2744. Eugene Ericksen, special consultant.

San Francisco 94111: 4 Embarcadero Ctr. (415) 291-1000. John Landon, sr VP.

New York 10036: 1166 Ave. of the Americas, 31st Fl. (212) 345-3000. Lewis Perl, sr VP; Linda McLaughlin, VP.

Ithaca, N.Y. 14850: 308 N. Cayuga St. (607) 277-3007. Alfred E. Kahn, special consultant.

Seattle 98101: 3411 One Union Sq., 600 University St. (206) 623-8037. Virginia Perry-Failor, sr analyst.

London, U.K. W1N 9AF: 15 Stratford Pl. 71-629-6787. Dermot Glynn, mgng dir.

Madrid, Spain 28014: Antonio Maura, 7. 1-521-0020. David Robinson, dir gen.

Economic consultant to bcst & cable TV companies on economic, public policy & business strategy issues.

National Research Consultants. 8633 Arbor Dr., El Cerrito, Calif. 94530. (510) 524-9559. Joseph L. Levit Ph.D./Sc Dipl., pres; Robert A. Levit, Ph.D./J.D., Robert M. Master, Ph.D., VPs.

Gaithersburg, Md. 20879: 401 C Blue Silk Ln. (301) 963-2014. Dr. Robert A. Levit, VP.

Consultant svcs, multimedia, criminology, survival consultants, scientific, tech, electronic, land, sea, air, space, & human factor svcs.

Nielsen Media Research. 1290 Ave. of the Americas, New York 10104. (212) 708-7500. FAX: (212) 708-7795. John A. Dimling, pres/COO; John A. Loftus, VP communications; Robert Lane, VP finance; Peter Sinisgalli, sr VP opns; David H. Harkness, sr VP planning & dev; Robert J. "Rusty" Taragan, sr VP loc svcs; Tom Hargreaves, VP & eastern sls mgr NSI; Toni Smith, sr VP & dir mktg Nielsen Television Index; L. Randall Yates, sr VP natl svcs.

Atlanta 30338-4767: 1200 Ashwood Pkwy., Suite 135. (404) 396-8879. Michael Stack, rgnl mgr.

Chicago 60601-5914: 205 N. Michigan Ave., Suite 2315. (312) 819-5530. Ron Meyer, VP/western sls mgr.

YOU HAVE QUESTIONS...

LUND MEDIA RESEARCH has answers...

Ascertain opportunities for ratings & revenue.
Full Service Radio Research Facilities

- Perceptual
- Music Research
- Format Opportunity

CALL JOHN LUND TODAY:
415-692-7777

- Focus Groups
- Sales Research
- Programming Evaluation

LUND MEDIA RESEARCH

Broadcasting & Cable Yearbook 1994

Research Services

Dallas 75248-4645: 15303 Dallas Pkwy., Suite 550/LB65. (214) 458-5520. John R. Norris, VP/southwestern rgnl mgr.
Los Angeles 90010: 3731 Wilshire Blvd., Suite 940. (213) 386-7316. Jane Ryan, rgnl mgr.
San Francisco 94111: 423 Washington St., 5th Fl. (415) 397-7774. Catherine Herkovic, northwestern rgnl mktg mgr.
Fremont, Calif. 94538: 2201 Walnut Ave. (510) 745-7200. Steve L. Dyer, VP/western rgnl mgr.
Audience measurement for net, loc, syndication, cable TV & home video. Metered market ratings in top markets & individual loc market reports in all markets; natl syndicated prog ratings; loc syndicated prog ratings; daily, wkly, & mthy net prog ratings; telephone coincidentals; New Media Services, Monitor Plus.

Edward J. Noonan, Marketing & Opinion Research. 373-A Pine Rd., Ormond Beach, Fla. 32176. (904) 673-7145. Edward J. Noonan, pres.
Advertising rsch, consumer/dealer surveys, financial studies, focus groups, mktg rsch, political polls, shopping studies, TV/radio audience surveys.

The Olson Co. (A division of Mark D. Olson Law Offices Media Research.) Box 12, 410 W. Badillo St., 2nd Fl., Los Angeles 90053. (818) 915-3333. FAX: (818) 331-1111. Mark D. Olson, pres.
Specialized ratings analysis & audience measurement for radio, TV & corporate mgmt. Exclusive provider of Synchronous Statistics & Pattern Research tracking more than 395,000 audience trends. Other expertise includes longitudinal studies of upscale consumers.

Paragon Research. 550 S. Wadsworth Blvd., Suite 401, Denver 80226. (303) 922-5600. FAX: (303) 922-1589. Roger Wimmer, pres; Chris Porter, exec VP; Mike Henry, VP.
Custom rsch: focus groups, auditorium mus tests, perceptual studies, tracking, auditorium format analyses.

Pike & Fischer Inc. 4600 East-West Hwy., Suite 200, Bethesda, Md. 20814-1438. (301) 654-6262. FAX: (301) 654-6297. John Sukenik, chmn; U. Joseph Hecker, pres; Robert E. Emeritz, VP/exec edit.
Publishers of communications law reporting svcs, including *Radio Regulation, Broadcast Rules Service, Cable TV Rules Service, Broadcast & Cable Rules on disk* & *Broadcast Forms on disk*.

Professional Research Services Inc. 6806 S. Terrace Rd., Tempe, Ariz. 85283. (602) 839-4003. FAX: (602) 839-1505. Dale Bennett, pres/gen mgr; Donna Bennett, exec VP; Bill Sasnett, opns mgr.
Customized radio audience telephone surveys, confidential results. Actual call sheets, sep coincidental/recall & total share figures. Twenty-one demographic categories.

RAD
Marketing and RadioBase

RAD Marketing and Radiobase. 167 Crary-on-the-Park, Mount Vernon, N.Y. 10550. (212) 274-0640. FAX: (212) 274-0646. Bob Dadarria, pres; Marc Dadarria, VP; Kathy Kruver, Hank Tooley, account execs.
RAD Marketing began with the unique idea of being able to provide marketers of any size with the largest, most ideal audience available. Through a variety of strategic mktg svcs, RAD Marketing can help companies identify & reach a market for their product—which can range from soup to soap, radio stations to cable nets & more. If you're looking for a unique & guaranteed method of locating your market, RAD Marketing can offer strategic solutions to your mktg needs. Other svcs include: Age Segmentation, Audio Duping/Voice-Overs, Brand-Name Modeling, Billing Insert Programs, Cable TV Direct, Computer Enhancement of Mailing Lists, Computerization, Custom Database Design, Date Entry, Direct Mail, Radio, TV, Fulfillment and Reporting, Fundraising, Laser Printing, List Management, List Order Fulfillment, Local Area Markets, Mapping, Merge Purge, Product Models—Regional/National, Product & Promotional Sweepstakes, RadioBase, Sweepstakes Mail Pick-Up Control, and TV Commerical Duping.

Radio Computing Services Inc. 2 Overhill Rd., Suite 100, Scarsdale, N.Y. 10583. (914) 723-8567. FAX: (914) 723-6651. Andrew M. Economos, pres; Lee Facto, VP/gen mgr.
Cincinnati 45248: 6020 Harrison Ave., Suite One. (513) 574-5414. FAX: (513) 574-5007. Dan Allen, VP.
Computer software for bcstrs, mus scheduling, rsch, data bases, yield mgmt, audio logging, digital audio systems.

Radio Expenditure Reports. (A division of Competetive Media Reports.) 740 W. Boston Post Rd., Mamaroneck, N.Y. 10543. (914) 381-6277. FAX: (914) 381-2457. Joseph McCallion, pres.
Supplier of natl & loc expenditure radio data, as well as loc multimedia report.

Radio Track. (A division of Broadcast Data Systems.) 1515 Broadway, New York 10036. (212) 536-5307. FAX: (212) 536-5310. Martin R. Feeley, pres; Joe Wallace, VP/gen mgr.
Radio Track electronically monitors airplay of stns nationwide. Data available on-line within hours of actual bcst.

Radio TV Reports Inc. 4701 Willard Ave., Chevy Chase, Md. 20815. (301) 656-4068. FAX: (301) 718-2651. Bob Lee, gen mgr.
Novi, Mich. 48375: 42400 Grand River Ave. (313) 344-1177. Detroit office.
Los Angeles 90028: (213) 466-6124. 6255 Sunset Blvd.
Chicago 60601: 35 Wacker St. (312) 542-2020.
Provides transcripts, digests & analyses of radio & TV news & comment; surveys of prog content; monitoring of comls; tape & cassette recordings; photoboards; film conversions; kinescopes.

Rantel Research. Box 681, Laurel, Md. 20725. (301) 490-8700. FAX: (410) 880-4190. David Tate, pres; Charles E. Helene, Steven A. Smith, VPs.
Perceptual & mktg segmentation rsch for radio, TV & cable, using advanced analytical techniques.

Research Communications Ltd. 990 Washington St., Suite 105, Dedham, Mass. 02026. (617) 461-1818. FAX: (617) 461-0909. Dr. Valerie Crane, pres; Tom Birk, exec VP.
TV & radio rsch on newscasts, progmg, mktg, bcst & cable multi-site natl/international testing.

The Research Group. 1100 Olive Way, Suite 1200, Seattle 98101. (206) 624-3888. FAX: (206) 624-5086. William C. Moyes, chmn; Larry B. Campbell, pres/COO.
Colorado Springs 80906: 660 Southpointe Ct., Suite 300. (719) 540-0100.
Mktg rsch & strategic planning svcs for radio stns in the U.S., Canada, Europe & Asia; full range of rsch svcs available.

Research Systems Corp. 110 Walnut St., Evansville, Ind. 47708. (812) 425-4562. FAX: (812) 425-2844. Mark Gleason, sr VP mktg.
Integrated systems to manage adv productivity. ARS, adv rsch system; Outlook, coml wearout model; CATS, comprehensive adv tracking system; FIRSTEP, adv strategy testing system.

Response Analysis Corp. Box 158, 377 Wall St., Princeton, N.J. 08542. (609) 921-3333. FAX: (609) 921-2611. James Fouss, pres; Diane Schrayer Linck, exec VP.
Market rsch & consulting; complete in-house facilities & professional staff for custom survey rsch.

Reymer & Associates Inc. 20300 Civic Center Dr., Suite 201, Southfield, Mich. 48076. (313) 354-4950. FAX: (313) 354-0918. Arnold S. Reymer, pres.

Qualitative, quantitative surveys & focus groups for TV/radio stns & cable. In-depth audience rsch on stn image, news, on-air personalities, audience segments & promotion.

Rules Service Co. 7615 Standish Pl., Rockville, Md. 20855. (301) 424-9402. FAX: (301) 762-7853. Mary Umlauf, pres; Joan Lombardi, VP; Pam Hertel, edit.
FCC rules & regulations updated in loose-leaf svcs, includes 0, 1, 2, 5, 13, 15, 17, 18, 19, 21, 22, 25, 73, 74, 76, 78, 80, 87, 90, 94, 95, 97 & 100.

SRI Gallop. 300 S. 68th St., Lincoln, Neb. 68510. (402) 489-9000. FAX: (402) 486-6402. James K. Clifton, pres; John Wood, group pres bcstg; Gale Muller, VP radio.
Minneapolis 55426: 1360 Interchange Bldg. (612) 545-9660. John Wood, group pres bcstg.
Specialized rsch in the areas of news, promotion effectiveness, image studies, positioning & progmg.

Satellite Services International. 800 Siesta Way, Sonoma, Calif. 95476. (707) 939-9306. FAX: (707) 939-9235. Kathryn Sanderson, pres; Silvano Payne, publisher; John Jordahn, VP sls.
Provide video training tapes for satellite communications.

Paul A. Scipione. Marketing Research and Consumer Psychology. 5 Burr Dr., Metuchen, N.J. 08840. (908) 548-2266. FAX: (908) 548-8871. Dr. Paul Scipione, sr ptnr.
Loc market profiles; acquisition analyses; public opinion surveys; listener profiles for advertisers & agencies; progmg & talent surveys.

Herschel Shosteck Associates Ltd. 10 Post Office Rd., Silver Spring, Md. 20910. (301) 589-2259. FAX: (301) 588-3311. Dr. Herschel Shosteck, pres.
Telecommunication economics & market analysis emphasizing cellular. Market rsch of cellular industry published quarterly. International consultation on demand, svc & equipment competition, distribution chs, economic & market effects of privatization, liberalization, competition, deregulation & market acceptance of Ct-2, Ct-3, DECT & PCN technologies. Newly published study on digital & next generation cellular technologies.

Simmons Market Research Bureau. 420 Lexington Ave., New York 10170. (212) 916-8900. FAX: (212) 916-8918. Ellen Cohen, pres; Stan Simon, VP electronic media sls.
Chicago 60611: 900 N. Michigan Ave. (312) 951-4400. Greg Clausen, VP.
Study of media & markets; comprehensive measurement of media & product usage.

Sindlinger & Co. Inc. 405 Osborne Ln., Wallingford, Pa. 19086. (215) 565-0247. FAX: (215) 565-3204. Albert E. Sindlinger, chmn of bd; Nellie Sindlinger, pres; Martin J. Sikorka, VP/edit.
Daily polling to determine consumer attitudes; microeconomic forecasting.

Lee Slurzberg Research Inc. 158 Linwood Plaza, Suite 318, Fort Lee, N.J. 07024-3704. (201) 461-6100. Lee Slurzberg, pres; Bill Healy, VP; Nancy Miller, field dir.
Ad-hoc custom studies for consumer, business-to-business, media companies, cable companies, adv agencies. Subspecialty in Hispanic mktg rsch for media—Spanish & Anglo.

Smith and Co. 5910 John Hancock Ctr., 175 E. Delaware Pl., Chicago 60611. (312) 822-0123. James A. Smith, pres.
Full-svc customized rsch. Mus, progmg, sls perceptual. Individual interview or group interview by telephone.

Sound Decisions. 2051 Glenhill Rd., Colorado Springs 80906-3352. (800) 552-2545; (719) 471-4125. FAX: (719) 473-4546. Bobby Christian, pres.
Auditorium mus tests, software for in-house mus rsch, one-on-one focus studies, focus groups, format search, progmg consultation.

Spectrum Research. 1808 Landmark One, Cherry Hill, N.J. 08034. (609) 795-7990. FAX: (609) 795-6013. Peter Mokover, pres.
Focus groups, lifestyle studies, strategic market studies, mus testing. Custom rsch for radio & TV.

Spot Quotations & Data Inc. 100 Clearbrook Rd., Elmsford, N.Y. 10523. (914) 347-5900. FAX: (914) 345-9244. Neil Klar, pres; Raymond DiStase, CEO.
Publishers of mthy SQAD-TV & quarterly SPARC-Radio, Cost-Per-Point & CPM reports. SQAD/PC computer system available for easy data analysis. Windows & DOS.

Starch INRA Hooper Inc. 566 E. Boston Post Rd., Mamaroneck, N.Y. 10543. (914) 698-0800. FAX: (914) 698-0485. William J. Wilson, pres.

Research Services

New York 10017: 205 E. 42nd St. (212) 599-0700. Edward Keller, exec VP.
Adv, mktg & public opinion rsch.

StationBase Co. 814 E. Harvard Ave., Gilbert, Ariz. 85234. (800) 359-2818. Denise "Dee" McVicker, own.
Mailing labels or computer diskettes of AM, FM & TV stns.

Statistical Research Inc. 111 Prospect St., Westfield, N.J. 07090. (908) 654-4000. Gale D. Metzger, pres; Maura Clancey, dir client svcs.
Natl & net audience measurement, radio, TV, cable audience rsch, consumer & mktg surveys.

Strata Marketing Inc. 540 N. Lake Shore Dr., Chicago 60611. (312) 222-1555. FAX: (312) 222-2510. Bruce W. Johnson, pres.
TV, radio & media ratings analysis. DOS- & Microsoft Windows-based software systems for stns & agencies.

Strategy Research Corp. 100 N.W. 37th Ave., Miami, Fla. 33125. (305) 649-5400. FAX: (305) 649-6312. Richard Tobin, pres; Raul Lopez, sr VP media rsch; Terry D'Angona, sr VP media mktg.
Irvine, Calif. 92715: 2082 Michelson Dr., Suite 301. (714) 752-6331. Dave Thomas, VP/gen mgr. Los Angeles office.
Radio/TV Hispanic audience ratings, natl & loc; market studies, stn profiles, focus groups, product usage/awareness, progmg/format rsch, copy testing. Specialization in ethnic rsch.

Stratford Research. Box 167581, 2965 Pickle Rd., Toledo, Ohio 43616. (419) 698-1166. FAX: (419) 693-7514. Lew Dickey, pres; John Dickey, Bill Hansen, Michael Hedges, VPs.
Radio rsch: Brand Marketing System, format opportunities, mus evaluation, target audience media usage, partisan consumer profile. TV rsch: syndicated progmg testing, strategic vulnerability studies for news.

T.A.P.E. (Consultancy) Ltd. 111 Regent's Park Rd., London, U.K. NW1 8UR. (01) 586-8546. Michael Firman, chmn; Brian Abrahams, mgng dir; Tom McManus, North American rep; Susan Tirsch, Los Angeles rep.
New York 10021: 425 E. 63rd St. (212) 888-7456. Tom McManus, domestic & international rep.
Los Angeles 90212: 9601 Charleville Rd. (310) 276-3766. Susan Tirsch, Los Angeles rep.
Prog evaluation, promotion & mktg svc for prods, distributors & TV programmers.

TGM Evaluations Inc. 1821 Featherwood St., Silver Spring, Md. 20904. (301) 622-4842. Thomas G. Moon, pres.
Analysis of ratings & rsch data for radio mgmt, mktg, sls & progmg; custom rsch svcs; complete rsch consultation for radio.

TVQ Inc. (A division of Marketing Evaluations Inc.) 14 Vanderventer Ave., Port Washington, N.Y. 11050. (516) 944-8833. FAX: (516) 944-3271. Steven Levitt, pres; Henry Schafer, exec VP; Carol Heller, VP TVQ svcs.
Syndicated marketed rsch surveys measuring familiarity & appeal of TV progs, performers, characters, magazine titles, company & brand names & sports personalities.

Tapscan Inc. 3000 Riverchase Galleria, Suite 850, Birmingham, Ala. 35244. (205) 987-7456. FAX: (205) 733-6263. Jim Christian, chmn/CEO; Dave Carlisle, pres/COO.
Manhattan Beach, Calif. 90266: 1112 Ocean Drive, Suite 301. (213) 376-6242.
Waltham, Mass. 02154: 1601 Trapelo Rd. (617) 890-1901.
Chicago 60611: 980 N. Michigan Ave., Suite 1400. (312) 214-3910.
Toronto, Ont., Canada M4T 1N5: Tapscan of Canada. 5075 Yonge St., Suite 404. (416) 221-9944.
Vancouver, B.C., Canada V5R 5W2: 3665 Kingsway, Suite 300, (604) 439-0087.
Software for electronic media, primarily radio & TV. Designed to address the needs of media selling, buying, planning, progmg & mgmt.

The Tarrance Group. 14405 Walters Rd., Suite 200, Houston 77014. (713) 444-9010. FAX: (713) 444-6993. Michael Baselice, VP.
Audience rsch svcs for radio, TV & cable. News, progmg, positioning, survey & promotion rsch.

Teen-age Research Unlimited. 601 Skokie Blvd., Northbrook, Ill. 60062. (708) 564-3440. FAX: (708) 564-0825. Peter Zollo, pres.
Twice annually, syndicated study of the teen market with optional custom/proprietary questions. Custom rsch in teenage markets.

Telecommunications Site Acquisitions Inc, (TELSA). Box 32223, 3500 Whitehaven Pkwy., Washington 20007-0523. (202) 333-1985. Gregory B. Daly, pres.
Frequency searches, gen FCC rsch, demographic & economic studies, & mktg projections for a number of telecommunications opportunities.

Teletech Inc. 23400 Michigan Ave., Dearborn, Mich. 48124. (313) 562-6873. FAX: (313) 562-8612. Kenneth W. Hoehn, VP; Keith Johnson, field svcs mgr; Mark W. Dobronski, sr engr.
Frequency searches, FCC application preparation.

VNU Operations. 12350 N.W. 39th St., Coral Springs, Fla. 33065. (305) 753-6043. FAX: (305) 755-1233. Eddie Ibrahim, gen mgr.
Englewood Cliffs, N.J. 07632: 560 Sylvan Ave. (201) 871-0011. Craig N. Harper, sr VP.
Atlanta 30339: 2110 Powers Ferry Rd., Suite 460. (404) 955-6317.
Rolling Meadows, Ill. 60008: 5105 Tollview Dr., Suite 208. (708) 392-5353. Jill Snyder, VP natl agencies. Chicago office.

Dallas 75240: 14800 Quorum Dr., Suite 530. (214) 934-3805. Larry Gorick, VP western rgn.
Los Angeles 90036: 5757 Wilshire Blvd. (213) 954-3230. Julie Goldsmith, VP western rgn.
Allentown, Pa. 18052: 1541 Alta Dr. (215) 821-9122. Kathi Stinner, mgr.
Louisville, Ky. 40218: 1941 Bishop Ln. (502) 451-0224. Terry Ferg, mgr.
San Antonio, Tex. 78217: Bldg. F, 4944 Research Dr. (512) 558-1500. Peter Shields, mgr. 2391 N.E. Loop, Suite 410. (512) 657-2500. Juan Hernandez, mgr.
Sarasota, Fla. 34236: 1751 Mound St., Suite 205. (512) 657-2500. Kathleen Michor, mgr.
Radio audience ratings reports, including qualitative, product & svc usage of radio listeners.

Videodex Inc. Box 11, Pound Ridge, N.Y. 10576. Allan V. Jay, pres.
TV audience analysis & test markets.

VideoProbeIndex Inc. Box 9190, Seattle 98109. (206) 285-4479. Robert Schultz, pres; Gloria Mamber, VP; Teresa Baker, dir field opns.
Significant viewing survey specialists for cable systems & stns filing with FCC for special relief copyright, must carry, re-transmission, syndex & net non-duplication.

Washington Information Group Ltd. Box 19352, 20th St. Station, Washington 20036-0352. (202) 463-7323. FAX: (202) 463-8633. Doug House, pres.
Customized bus rsch on client-specified aspects of the bcstg industry, including competitor intelligence on companies, products, svcs & markets.

Western International Media. (CABLESTAT/CABLECALL.) 8544 Sunset Blvd., Los Angeles 90069. (310) 854-4880. FAX: (310) 652-4703. Cheryl Idell, VP/dir rsch.
CABLESTAT is a loc audience measurement svc; CABLECALL is a listing of U.S. cable systems that offer loc ad avail.

Willhight Research Inc. 2104 S.W. 152nd, Suite 4, Seattle 98166. (206) 431-8430. FAX: (206) 431-0603. James A. Willhight, pres; David Hastings, VP mktg/sls dir; Travis Gamble, treas/opns dir; Nicole Herron, prod dir; Gene Robinson, rsch dir; Travis Gamble, treas.
Radio ratings; A.Q.H. & cumulative figures. Qualitative data; respondent based; market specific. Phone methodology; detailed software.

Winona Market Research Bureau Inc. 8200 Humboldt Ave. S., Minneapolis 55431-1486. (612) 881-5400. FAX: (612) 881-0763. Adam Phillips, CEO.
Full-svc custom rsch design through analysis. Facilities include 200-position WATS phones with CRTs & complete computer capabilities.

Worldwide Marketing Leadership Panel. 332 Rt. 46 W., Parsippany, N.J. 07054. (201) 808-7333. FAX: (201) 882-3651. Jack Myers, chmn.
Provides feedback & counsel to media companies. Publishes books & newsletters on adv.

Engineering and Technical Consultants

Asterisk (*) indicates membership in the Association of Federal Communications Consulting Engineers.

Advanced Broadcast Consultants Inc. Box 386, Pitman, N.J. 08071. (609) 589-7635. FAX: (609) 589-2586. Joseph S. Sherman, pres; Helen A. Sherman, sec/treas.
Engrg applications for FCC construction permits & licensing of coml & educ facilities. AM directional design & proofs. Phasor design.

Advanced Technology Systems Inc. 7646 Lee Hwy., Falls Church, Va. 22042-2807. (703) 204-1171. FAX: (703) 204-1176. John J. Renner, pres.
Engrg & cost analyses pertinent to planning, evaluation, regulation & purchase of telecommunications nets & svcs.

John P. Allen. Airspace Consultant. Box 1008, Fernandina Beach, Fla. 32035-1008. (904) 261-6523. FAX: (904) 277-3651. John P. Allen, own.
Conducts FAA aeronautical evaluations as specified in Subpart C of Part 77 of federal aviation regulations.

Anderson Radio Engineering. 202 Dayton School Rd., Easley, S.C. 29642. (803) 855-2327. Burton S. Anderson, own/operator.

Alvin H. Andrus P.E. 351 Scott Dr., Silver Spring, Md. 20904. (301) 384-5374. *Alvin H. Andrus, consulting engr.
AM, FM & TV applications, hearing exhibits; AM directional proofs; microwave & ITFS studies.

Aviation Systems Associates Inc. 23430 Hawthorne Blvd., Suite 200, Torrance, Calif. 90505. (310) 378-3299. FAX: (310) 791-1546. Jack Chevalier, pres; Gary Allen, exec VP; Dan Tenold, Tom Binczak, Barney Linden, aviation consultants; Martin Elliott, P.E.
Aviation consultants, EMI analysis, legal assistance & representation before FAA, state & local aeronautical agencies & zoning agencies.

BB&K Associates Inc. 42 1/2 Center St., Rutland, Vt. 05701. (802) 747-4400. FAX: (802) 747-4925. Don Kemp, pres.

BDS. (A subsidiary of MLJ.) 5203 Leesburg Pike, Suite 800, Falls Church, Va. 22041. (703) 824-5666. FAX: (703) 824-5672. Mark Steinwinter, dir; Allison DeLawder, asst dir.

Bcst data bases updated daily; PC engrg software; on-line access; FCC rsch.

John Barnett & Associates. 4415 Harbinger, Mesquite, Tex. 75150. (214) 279-5336. John Barnett Jr., P.E., pres.
AM, FM, TV engrg, FCC applications, DA proofs, field strength measurements.

John H. Battison, P.E., & Associates. Consulting Radio Engineers. 2684 State Rt. 60, Loudonville, Ohio 44842. (419) 994-3849. John H. Battison, P.E.
All FCC svcs: AM, FM, TV, LPTV, applications, liscensing, DA-proofs, ITFS & MMDS expert witness svcs.

Becker & Madison. 1915 Eye St. N.W., 8th Fl., Washington 20006. (202) 833-4422. FAX: (202) 296-7458. Richard Becker, pres; Paul Madison, VP; Siamak Harandi, engr.
Legal & engrg svcs for bcstg, cable TV, cellular, paging, microwave & private radio.

Franklyn R. Beemish & Co. 400 Roosevelt Ave., Freeport, N.Y. 11520. (516) 867-8510. FAX: (516) 867-8007. Franklyn R. Beemish, pres.
Engrg & architectural consulting. Facilities & systems design, space planning & project mgmt.

Lawrence Behr Associates Inc. Box 8026, Greenville, N.C. 27835. (919) 757-0279. FAX: (919) 752-9155. Lawrence Behr, CEO; Win Donat, pres; James Reineke, VP bus dev; Kathryn Tesh, Jeff May, engrs.
Consulting svcs for AM, FM, TV & CATV including frequency searches, FCC applications, measurements & proofs, procurement & construction mgmt. U.S. & international.

The Benchmark Co. 1705 S. Capital of Texas Hwy., Suite 305, Austin, Tex. 78746-6551. (512) 327-7010. FAX: (512) 328-1464. Rob Balon, pres/CEO; Paige Blount, rsch dir.
Mkt rsch for the bcst industry.

Serge Bergen, P.E. 7503 Amkin Ct., Clifton, Va. 22024. (703) 250-2691. *Serge Bergen, P.E., sr ptnr; William V. Tranavitch Jr., ptnr; David Ingram, tech consultant.
Engrg svcs: AM, FM, TV.

Bernard Associates. 143 Palmers Hill Rd., Stamford, Conn. 06902-2111. (203) 348-0804. Bernard Eichwald, P.E.

Clarence M. Beverage. (Communications Technologies Inc.) Box 1130, Marlton, N.J. 08053. (609) 985-0077. FAX: (609) 985-8124. Clarence M. Beverage, pres.

Richard L. Biby, P.E. Communications Engineering Services P.C. 6105 G, Arlington Blvd., Falls Church, Va. 22044. (703) 534-7880. FAX: (703) 534-7884. Richard L. Biby, pres; Richard P. Biby, E.I.T. Engr; Mark B. Peabody, engrg aide.
Bcst & land mobile engrg consulting svcs.

The Herbert Boyer Co. 14 E. 77th St., New York 10021. (212) 744-7558. FAX: (212) 249-5270. Herbert Boyer, pres; Donald W. Franz, sr VP; Gary M. Fey, Donald W. Franz, Joseph E. Griffith & James H. Hollyer, engrs.
Altanta 30339: 3317 Cochise Dr. (404) 432-0004. William F. Parsons, sr VP. Engrs: William F. Parsons.
Consulting svc to operators and manufacturers of CATV equipment for equipment evaluation, design criteria & mktg requirements. Acquisition & new venture studies. Exec searches.

W.H. Bradley, P.E. Consulting Radio & TV Engineer. 300 W. 41st St., Sand Springs, Okla. 74063. (918) 245-5444. William H. Bradley, registered P.E.; William C. Bradley, radio engr.
FCC engrg applications for bcstg, AM, FM, TV & aux field engrg & measurement svcs.

Broadcast Data Services. (A subsidiary of Moffet, Larson & Johnson Inc.) 5203 Leesburg Pike, Suite 800, Falls Church, Va. 22041. (703) 824-5666. FAX: (703) 824-5672. Mark Steinwinter, dir; Allison DeLawder, asst dir.
Bcst data bases updated daily; PC engrg software; on-line access; FCC rsch.

Broadcast Engineering & Equipment Maintenance Co. (BEEM Co.) 2322 S. 2nd Ave., Arcadia, Calif. 91006. (818) 446-3468. Joel T. Saxberg, own.
FCC applications, shadow maps, AM directionals, field work, studio & transmitter installations.

Broadcast Signal Lab. 64 Richdale Ave., Cambridge, Mass. 02140-2629. (617) 864-4298. Rick Levy, David P. Maxson.
AM, FM, TV-STL frequency measurements, spectrum analysis, NIR surveys, interference searches, FCC applications.

Bromo Communications Inc. 1331 Ocean Blvd., Suite 201, St. Simons Island, Ga. 31522. (912) 638-5608. FAX: (912) 638-5690. William G. Brown, pres; Clifton G. Moor, sec/treas; Richard S. Graham Jr., Jefferson Brock, VP. Engrs: William G. Brown, Clifton G. Moor, R. Stuart Graham, Jefferson G. Brock, Robert L. Purcell.
Washington: (202) 429-0600.
AM, FM & TV allocations, including field installations.

John F.X. Browne & Associates P.C. 525 Woodward Ave., Suite 100, Bloomfield Hills, Mich. 48304. (313) 642-6226. FAX: (313) 642-6027.
Washington: (202) 293-2020. *John F.X. Browne, P.E., pres; *Russell C. Harbaugh Jr., P.E., *Leonard W. Eden, Louis J. Raymo & Joseph Huk, engrs.
Bcst consulting AM/FM, TV, MMDS/ITFS, IVDS, PCS & satellite systems. FCC/FAA applications, filings & studies.

Richard W. Burden Associates. 20944 Sherman Way, Suite 213, Canoga Park, Calif. 91303. (818) 340-4590. Richard W. Burden, proprietor.
Bcst tech svcs, facilities design, Traveller's Information Service (TIS) & Education FM (EDFM) applications.

MAPS
IMMEDIATE DELIVERY
NATIONWIDE COVERAGE
TOPOS - AERIAL PHOTOS
1-800-248-MAPS
Carolina Global Maps, Inc.

Carolina Global Maps Inc. Box 8026, Greenville, N.C. 27835. (800) 248-6277. FAX: (800) 321-6277. Lawrence Behr, pres; Lu Ann Moore, gen mgr; Brooke Norris, mktg coord.
All USGS & DMA maps, NOS/NOAA charts; international topographic series, aerial photography, raised relief maps, business & mktg maps.

William B. Carr & Associates Inc. 1805 Burleson-Retta Rd., Burleson, Tex. 76028. (817) 295-1181. FAX: (817) 295-9347. *William B. Carr, pres.
Feasibility studies, FCC applications, field measurements, hearing & site evaluations for the bcst & land mobile svc.

Chu Associates Inc. Box 2387 Littleton, Mass. 01460. (508) 456-3282. FAX: (508) 456-8455. Steve Best.
Design, dev & manufacture communication ants.

Ciccoricco, Francis A. 73 Ogden Rd., Groton, N.Y. 13073. (607) 838-3110.

Cohen, Dippell & Everist P.C. 1300 L. St. N.W., Suite 1100, Washington 20005. (202) 898-0111. FAX: (202) 898-0895. *Sudhir K. Khanna, P.E., sec/treas; *Warren M. Powis, P.E., VP; *Donald G. Everist P.E., pres.
Professional engrg svcs to the bcstg industry U.S. & worldwide.

Jules Cohen & Associates Inc. 1725 De Sales St. N.W., Suite 600, Washington 20036. (202) 659-3707. FAX: (202) 659-0360. *Robert W. Denny Jr., P.E., pres; Engrs: *Richard Mertz, *Michael Rhodes, *Susan Crawford, *Jules Cohen, *Bernard R.Segal, P.E. consultants; *Charles N. Miller, P.E., *Alan R. Rosner; David Helinski, engr.

BROADCAST TECHNOLOGY SERVICES

Call the RF Experts!

- AM-FM-TV applications, FCC matters
- Frequency and allocation studies
- Field engineering, project management
- Wireless Cable (ITFS, MMDS)
- Microwave paths, interference solutions
- Radiation hazard compliance
- HDTV, DIGITAL, FM, PCN, paging and other new technologies

-Worldwide Services-
919-757-0279
919-752-9155 FAX

Lawrence Behr Associates, Inc.

30 Years of Excellence

An LBA Group Company

Engineering and Technical Consultants

Frequency allocation surveys; AM proofs; TV picture quality surveys; radiation hazard measurements; AM, FM & TV FCC applications. Also cellular & PCS/PCN services available.

Frank S. Colligan & Associates. 5111 Westpath Ct., Bethesda, Md. 20816. (301) 229-5577. Frank S. Colligan, pres.

Commercial Electronics. Box 70, Greenbrier, Ark. 72058. (501) 680-2332. FAX: (501) 679-4500. Raymond W. Loewy, own/chief engr.
  AM, FM, & TV recording, studio installation & maintenance. Emergency transmitter repair.

Commercial Radio Co. One Duttonsville School Dr., Cavendish, Vt. 05142. (802) 226-7582. FAX: (802) 226-7738. Daniel W. Churchill, pres/gen mgr; Toni M. Churchill, VP; Daniel W. Churchill & Andre S. LaPlante, engrs; Charles T. Shaffer, shop mgr.
  Custom bcst engrg; AM, FM & sw bcst equipment sls & svc specializing in transmitting components.

Communications Design Associates Inc. 1410 Providence Hwy., Norwood, Mass. 02062. (617) 551-8490. FAX: (617) 551-8491. Robert Hemenway, David Hutton, Stewart Randall, partners; Greg Vincent, ptnrs.
  Ind consultants to radio, TV, corporate and government clients. Designers of studios, prod, presentation & multimedia facilities.

Communications Engineering. 80 Worcester Rd., Etobicoke, Ont., Canada M9W 1K7. (416) 674-0224. FAX: (416) 675-6425. Ralph von Eppinghoven, gen mgr.
  Consulting engrg svcs with emphasis on design, installation & testing of CATV systems, fiber-optic nets, broadband loc area nets & baseboard video systems.

Communications Engineering Services P.C. 6105-G Arlington Blvd., Falls Church, Va. 22044. (703) 534-7880. FAX: (703) 534-7884. *Richard L. Biby, P.E., consulting engr.
  Bcst & mobile communications engrg consulting svcs.

Communications General Corp. 2685 Alta Vista Dr., Fallbrook, Calif. 92028-9683. (619) 723-2700. FAX: (619) 723-4000. Robert F. Gonsett, E.E., pres.
  Bcst engrg consulting, AM/FM/TV applications, field engrg & RF radiation hazard studies. Specializes in southwestern U.S., Hawaii & Mexico.

Communications Technologies Inc. Box 1130, 65 Country Club Ln., Marlton, N.J. 08053. (609) 985-0077. FAX: (609) 985-8124. Clarence M. Beverage, pres; Clarence M. Beverage, Laura M. Mizrahi & James W. Pollock, P.E., engrs.
  Bcst engrg consulting svcs with emphasis on RF systems design & preparation of applications consistent with FCC rules & policies.

Comsearch. 11720 Sunrise Valley Dr., Reston, Va. 22091. (703) 620-6300. FAX: (703) 476-2697. Michael Morin, pres; Kurt Oliver, sls mgr.
  A complete communications engrg svc organization specializing in frequency mgmt & propagation engrg.

ComSonics Inc. 1350 Port Republic Rd., Harrisonburg, Va. 22801. (703) 434-5965. FAX: (703) 434-9847. Dennis A. Zimmerman, pres/CEO; Donn E. Meyerhoeffer, dir opns; G. William McIntyre, dir finance; Raymond J. Schnieder, dir engrg; Don J. Sommerville, dir mktg & sls.
  Microprocessor controlled signal level meters, RF leakage detection and CATV repair facility.

Contemporary Communications. Box 1787, Cleveland, Miss. 38732. (601) 846-1787. FAX: (601) 843-0494. Larry G. Fuss, pres.
  FM, TV, STL & RPU applications; FM upgrades; computerized frequency searches; site selection assistance.

Cottrill & Holland Inc. 714 S.W. 12th Ave., Fort Lauderdale, Fla. 33312. (305) 522-3303. FAX: (305) 522-3355. Douglass L. Holland, pres/dir engrg.
  Ant, tower, studio & RF facilities design & construction, extended mgmt, tech consultants & planners.

Courtright Engineering Inc. 132 E. Griswold Rd., Phoenix 85020. (602) 944-0461. *M. Courtright, Ph.D., P.E., pres.
  Professional bcst & electrical engrg svcs, including FCC applications, RF radiation hazard studies, computer-aided studies & facility electrical design.

C.P. Crossno & Associates. Consulting Engineers. Box 180312, Dallas 75218. (214) 321-9140. FAX: (214) 321-9146. *Charles Paul Crossno, P.E., own/mgr. Engrs: *Charles Paul Crosso, P.E.
  Full comm consulting svcs, ant design & aerial radiation measurements.

William Culpepper & Associates Inc. 900 Jefferson Dr., Charlotte, N.C. 28270. (704) 365-9995. *William A. Culpepper, pres.
  AM, FM & TV engrg svcs.

D.B. Communications Inc. 4401 East-West Hwy., Suite 308, Bethesda, Md. 20814. (301) 654-0777. FAX: (301) 652-8641. Darrell E. Bauguess, pres; Rita Capobianchi, opns dir.

DCI Communications Inc. 30 Anderson Rd., Katonah, N.Y. 10536. (914) 232-6565. FAX: (301) 652-8641. Timothy Dwight, pres.
  Custom CAD-designed electronic products ranging from printed circuit boards to stand-alone equipment. Audio, video, digital, analog & control systems.

DSI Communications Inc. Box 626, 627 Blvd. Kenilworth, N.J 07033. (908) 245-4833. FAX: (908) 245-0011. Alfred D'Alssandro, Joseph Giardina, ptnrs.
  Full-svc engrg specializing in video & RF systems.

Datel Corp. 1515 N. Court House Rd., Suite 301, Arlington, Va. 22201. (703) 276-9007. FAX: (703) 276-9008. Jonathan David, pres; William R. Meintel, VP. Engr: William R. Meintel, engr.
  Domestic & international consulting engrg; FCC applications, measurements; complete stn & environmental hazard inspections; computer software dev; extensive experience in TV/radio matters in Eastern Europe & Latin America.

John J. Davis & Associates. Box 128, Sierra Madre, Calif. 91025-0128. (818) 355-6909. FAX: (818) 355-4890. *John J. Davis, pres/engr.
  Primary focus on FM & TV ch allocation studies & applications; facility upgrades, FM & TV translator applications, tower site mgmt.

Dettra Communications Inc. Box 18864, Washington 20036-8864. (202) 965-4664. FAX: (202) 965-4666. John E. Dettra Jr., pres; Manuel Mayobre Jr., Maurice Rea, Maurizio Fiorio, John Dettra III, engrs.
  Applications & hearing exhibits for bcst, paging, mobile telephone, cellular, microwave & private radio svcs; MMDS/ITFS; FCC rsch & consulting.

Devlin Design Group. 12526 High Bluff Dr., 3rd Fl., San Diego Calif. 92130. (619) 792-3676. FAX: (619) 942-2664. Dan Devlin, pres; Carol Vandervelden, design svcs mgr; Mike Newton, designer; Cindy Bradford, bcst consultant; David Smaw, lighting dir.
  News sets, newsrooms, turnkey & design only, lighting direction, consultation.

The Downtown Group. 242 W. 27th St., New York 10011. (212) 675-9506. Vin Gizzi, Peter Willcox, Mark Winkelman, ptnrs.
  Design of tech facilities: architecture, acoustics, engrg, testing. Typical projects include edit rooms, stages, recording studios & support facilities.

du Treil, Lundin & Rackley Inc. (A subsidiary of A.D. Ring P.C.) 240 N. Washington Blvd., Suite 700, Sarasota, Fla. 34236. (813) 366-2611. FAX: (813) 366-5533. *L. Robert du Treil, pres; *John A. Lundin, VP; *Ronald D. Rackley, sec/treas.
  Tech consulting for the communications industry.

ERI - Electronics Research Inc. 108 Market St., Newburgh, Ind. 47630. (812) 853-3318. FAX: (812) 858-5706. Thomas B. Silliman, P.E., pres; Robert Rose, rsch & dev; Bill Elmer, sls; Ernest R. Jones, P.E., structural engrg; David Davies, mktg. Engrs: *Manuel Sone, *Thomas B. Silliman, P.E., Ernest Jones, P.E.; Robert Rose; Jim Kemman; Dan Dowdle; Majid Farahanna, MS C.E.; Manuel Sone, MS E.E.; Tom Hayes BS E.E.; David Davies, BS M.E.
  Manufactures & installs coml bcst omni & directional ants, towers, filters, combiners, multiplexers. Structural analysis also available.

East Coast Video Systems. 52 Ralph St., Belleville, N.J. 07109. (201) 751-5655. FAX: (201) 751-8731. Richard Bisignano, pres; Paul M. Krucik, VP engrg; Mary Nahra, VP sls.
  Video & audio system consultation, design, installation & training; serving cable systems, corporate, bcst & teleprod facilities.

Bill Elliott, Broadcast Consultant. Box 1256, Port Richey, Fla. 34673-1256. (813) 849-3477. Bill Elliott, pres.
  AM & FM stn design & construction, maintenance progs, purchase evaluations; specializes in quality audio & RF.

Howard L. Enstrom. 30925 Vista View, Mount Dora, Fla. 32757. (904) 383-3682. FAX: (904) 383-4077. Howard L. Enstrom, pres; H. Larry Enstrom, VP.
  Feasibility studies, frequency searches, system design & FCC applications for FM & TV translators.

Evans Associates. 216 N. Green Bay Rd., Thiensville, Wis. 53092. (414) 242-6000; (414) 242-6045. *Ralph E. Evans Sr., P.E., ptnr; Ralph E. Evans III, E.E., ptnr; Lawrence B. Evans, MS comp svs/ptnr; *Benjamin Evans, E.E., ptnr; Wendi Walsh, E.E., staff engr; Robert Gorjance, field engr.
  Telecommunications consulting engrs, net design, FCC applications, frequency coordination, fieldwork for AM, FM, TV, CATV, ITFS, microwave relay facilities.

Executive Broadcast Services. Box 60327, Colorado Springs 80960. (719) 579-6664. Skip Joeckel, pres; Kelley Hilligoss, dir opns/mktg.
  Markets & sells a select line of progs, products & svcs to U.S. radio stns.

FM Technology Associates Inc. 30925 Vista View, Mount Dora, Fla. 32757. (904) 383-3682. FAX: (904) 383-4077. Howard L. Enstrom, pres; H. Larry Enstrom, VP; Howard L. Enstrom, engr.
  FM trans engrg, FCC application work & equipment supply; gen consulting.

Federal Engineering Inc. 10600 Arrowhead Dr., Fairfax, Va. 22030. (703) 359-8200. FAX: (703) 359-8204. Ronald F. Bosco, pres; Philip J. Freedenberg, exec VP.
  Bcst, fiber optics, satellite, microwave, mobile radio, cable networking, telephone switching & distance learning technologies.

Charles S. Fitch, P.E. 45 Sarah Dr., Avon, Conn. 06001. (203) 673-7260. Charles S. Fitch, P.E.
  FCC allocations & applications, facility design, system design, construction supervision, field surveys, facility appraisals & inspections, computer progmg.

Paul Dean Ford. Broadcast Engineering Consultant. 6 E. Colorado Ave., Casey, Ill. 62420. (217) 932-4869. *Paul Dean Ford, P.E., own/engr.
  AM, FM, TV & LPTV studies & allotments, FCC applications & field svc.

Freedman, Mel. 1479 Mountain View Rd., Hughson, Calif. 95326. (209) 883-2611. FAX: (209) 883-4727. Mel Freedman, consulting radio engr.

Independent Consultation, Design & Project Management Services For Broadcast, Production and Presentation Facilities

"Services designed to fit your requirements."

Communications Design Associates, Inc.

1410 Providence Highway
Norwood, MA 02062-5099
Voice: (617) 551-8490
Fax: (617) 551-8491

Engineering and Technical Consultants

George M. Frese, P.E. 1011 Denis Ct., East Wenatchee, Wash. 98802. (509) 884-4558. *George M. Frese, P.E., consulting engr/own.

Thomas B. Friedman. Box 5036, San Luis Obispo, Calif. 93403. (805) 544-2247. FAX: (805) 544-7356. Thomas B. Friedman, own.
FM application svcs.

Gallagher & Associates. 13226 Clopper Rd., Hagerstown, Md. 21742. (301) 790-2611. FAX: (301) 790-2062. *Charles I. Gallagher, P.E., own; Matthew B. Gallagher, engr.
Professional engrg svcs to the bcstg industry.

Global Engineering Group. 747 Wire Rd., Suite 100A, Auburn, Ala. 36830. (205) 826-0390. H.D. Norman, pres; Will Rudd, VP.
Tech consultants for turnkey, superpower, MW, SW, LW radio stns worldwide. Site-to-finish svcs.

Gray, Claude M. Box 602, Birmingham, Ala. 35201. (205) 822-1132.
Consulting radio engr.

W. Richard Green & Associates. (Consulting Telecommunications Engineers.) 3200 Wilkinson Rd., Cameron Park, Calif. 95682. (916) 677-7417. FAX: (916) 677-0971. W. Richard Green, own.
Rsch & design of AM, FM, TV & microwave ant systems; computerized & aeronautical RF path propagation studies; AM, FM, TV & microwave allocations & applications.

Frederick G. Griffin P.C. 3229 Waterlick Rd., Lynchburg, Va. 24502. (804) 237-2044. FAX: (804) 237-6063. *Frederick G. Griffin, P.E., pres; Engrs: Bernhard L. Klein, Eugene Langone, P.E.
Feasibility studies, systems engrg, equipment specifications, physical facilities planning, contract negotiations, project mgmt, analysis & certifications, I-NET design.

Guidestar Corp. 10600 Arrowhead Dr., Fairfax, Va. 22030. (703) 352-5700. FAX: (703) 359-8204. Ronald F. Bosco, dir; Philip J. Freedenberg, dir.
Mktg communications & PR specifically tailored to serving the telecommunications & info processing marketplaces.

Peter V. Gureckis & Associates. 10410 Windsor View Dr., Potomac, Md. 20854. (301) 299-5383. FAX: (301) 299-5604. Peter V. Gureckis, own/engr.
AM, FM, TV, low-power TV applications & field svcs.

Gurman, Kurtis, Blask & Freedman Chartered. 1400 16th St. N.W., Suite 500, Washington 20036. (202) 328-8200. FAX: (202) 462-1784. Michael K. Kurtis, Herbert C. Harris, Leonard M. Garavalia, Frank A. Rondinelli, James C. Egyud & Brent R. Shirey.
Preparation of bcst, wireless cable, cellular, paging, microwave, SMR & private radio applications; stn & system design & construction; consulting.

HN Engineering Inc. 1160 Douglas Rd., Burnaby, B.C., Canada V5C 4Z6. (604) 294-3401. FAX: (604) 299-6712. H. Grant McCormick, pres; Peter Hostinsky, VP admin & finance; Bruce W. Granholm, VP mkt; Peter A. Niblock, chief engr; T.J. Babock & K.R. Jones, engrs.
Tech design, licensing & implementation of AM, FM, TV & CATV systems.

Wm. Watt Hairston Communications Consulting. 10 Music Cir. E., Nashville 37203. (615) 242-4827. FAX: (615) 242-4826. William W. Hairston, Douglas P. Remmington.
Bcst consulting & svc.

Hammett & Edison Inc. Box 280068, San Francisco 94128-0068. (415) 342-5200; (202) 396-5200. FAX: (415) 342-8482. William F. Hammett, P.E., mgng dir; Consultants: *Robert L. Hammett, P.E.; *Edward Edison, P.E. Engrs: Dane E. Ericksen, P.E.; Gerhard J. Straub, P.E.; Stanley Salek; Robert Weller.
Design & FCC filings: AM, FM, TV, STL, cable. Specialties: AM directionals/diplexers, NIER(RFR) predictions & measurements, FM/TV computer propagation studies, field strength measurements, facilities appraisals, FAA EMI analysis.

F.W. Hannel & Associates. 911 Edward St., Henry, Ill. 61537. (309) 364-3903. FAX: (309) 364-3775. F.W. Hannel.

Hatfield & Dawson, Consulting Engineers Inc. 4226 6th Ave. N.W., Seattle 98107. (206) 783-9151. FAX: (206) 789-9834. B. F. Dawson, III, pres; J.B. Hatfield, sec/treas; T.M. Eckels, VP; *James B. Hatfield, P.E., *Benj. F. Dawson III, P.E., *Thomas M. Eckels, P.E., Paul W. Leonard, P.E., L.S.C. Enslow, Stephen S. Lockwood, E.I.T., engrs.
Telecommunications & radio physics engrg, including bcst, electromagnetic compatibility, NIER measurement & analysis, ant & propagation analysis & design.

Dave Hebert & Associates. Box 2442, Pasco, Wash. 99302. (509) 545-9672. Page: (509) 545-2847. Dave Hebert, pres; Mark Guenther.
Specializing in RF & transmitters, transmitter plant maintenance, minor tower work & audio performance.

Charles A. Hecht & Associates Inc. 16 Doe Run, Pittstown, N.J. 08867. (908) 730-7959. FAX: (908) 730-7408. Charles A. Hecht, pres; Don Neumuller, engr.
Radio engrg svcs including FCC studies & applications, directional ant design, fieldwork; specialists in audio processing optimization.

Hi Ho Productions. Box 8135, Chicago 60680. (312) 224-5612. Frank Howard Jr., pres; R.C. Hillsman, exec VP; Engrs: J. Hillsman, N. Hillsman.
Consulting engrs to radio, TV cable & video industries.

Hilding Communications. Box 1700, Morgan Hill, Calif. 95038-1700. (408) 842-2222. Eric Hilding, own.
FM channel studies, complex FM substitution proposals, site locations, 301 applications engrg, general bcst consulting.

R.L. Hoover. Consulting Telecommunications Engineer. 11704 Seven Locks Rd., Potomac, Md. 20854. (301) 983-0054. *Robert Lloyd Hoover, P.E., own.
Professional engrg consulting for AM, FM & TV applications & testimony. Radiation hazard analyses & testimony.

Hutcheson, Guy C. 1100 W. Abram St., Arlington, Tex. 76013. (817) 261-8721.

Mark F. Hutchins Broadcasting Services Inc. Box 6418, Brattleboro, Vt. 05302-6418. (802) 254-4500. FAX: (802) 254-6683. Mark F. Hutchins, pres/engr; David L. Underhill, VP/engr.
Stn design, construction, proofs. Field studies: Spectrum analysis, NRSC compliance. Computerized terrain analysis, coverage maps, RF path profiles & shadowing studies.

IDB Systems. 3236 Skylane Dr., Carrollton, Tex. 75006. (214) 407-7700. FAX: (214) 407-7787. Eric Silverthorn, gen mgr.
Satellite communication earth stn products & turnkey systems.

Independent Broadcast Consultants Inc. 110 County Rd. 146, Trumansburg, N.Y. 14886-9721. (607) 273-2970. FAX: (607) 387-6364. William Sitzman, pres; M.F. Sitzman, VP; George Soltysik, P.E., N.L. Hollenbeck, R.A. Lynch & A.J. MacLaren, engrs.
AM, FM & TV applications, specializing in AM allocation studies & broadband AM directional ant design.

J. Boyd Ingram & Associates. Box 73, Batesville, Miss. 38606. (601) 563-4664. FAX: (601) 563-9002. J. Boyd Ingram, pres; A.E. Jennings, John P. Ingram, assocs.
Tech consultation, facility construction & repair.

George Jacobs & Associates Inc. 8701 Georgia Ave., Suite 410, Silver Spring, Md. 20910. (301) 587-8800. FAX: (301) 587-8801. *George Jacobs, P.E., pres; Robert German & Anne Case, engrs.
Specialists in conceptional design, application filing & frequency mgmt for FCC-licensed international sw bcst stns. Consultative liaison with foreign bcst stns & organizations.

Vir James P.C. 965 S. Irving St., Denver 80219. (303) 937-1900. FAX: (303) 937-1902. *Timothy C. Cutforth, P.E., pres.
AM/FM/TV allocation studies & applications, AM directional ant design & tune-up, conductivity measurements.

Jenel Systems and Design Inc. 6700 Spokane Pl., Plano, Tex. 75023. (214) 491-1442. FAX: (214) 491-1442 Elmer Smalling III, CEO/pres; Bradley Rinklin, VP sls; B.J. Jones, Broda McAlister, Howard Halcomb, engrs.
Studio, post, acoustic, earth stn, design, trucks, TV system design from planning to turnkey construction.

Irv Joel & Associates. 528 River Rd., Teaneck, N.J. 07666. (201) 692-0010. FAX: (201) 836-6865. Irv Joel, pres.
System design, facilities design & supvr, spec project engrg, maintenance progs, training seminars, systems profiles.

Carl T. Jones Corp. 7901 Yarnwood Ct., Springfield, Va. 22153. (703) 569-7704. FAX: (703) 569-6417. *Carl T. Jones Jr., P.E., pres; Herman E. Hurst Jr., communications svs mgr; Michael A. Nicolay, EMC measurement & design mgr; Jon J. Bondanella, Daniel P. Cavegn, Charles R. Fenton, William J. Getz, David W. Goldsworthy, Cynthia M. Jacobson, Robert S. Rubin, James D. Sadler, engrs.
Consulting engrs specializing in bcstg & CATV technical design & regulatory filings. Maintain EMC/EMI testing laboratory.

Joe Jones. 10556 Arnwood Rd., Lake View Terrace, Calif. 91342. (818) 890-0730. FAX: (818) 899-4457. Joe Jones, pres/ptnr; Marion Jones, VP/ptnr; Dwayne Jones, opns mgr/ptnr; Keith Jones, asst to pres/ptnr.
Svc to bcstg & telecasting industries with emphasis on FCC-regulated aspects.

Jones Satellite Audio Inc. 8250 S. Akron, Suite 205, Englewood, Colo. 80112. (800) 876-3303; (303) 799-4010. FAX: (303) 799-0551. J. Chris Aschenbeck, group VP; T.J. Lambert, sr VP; Phil Barry, VP progmg.

R.L. Kennedy & Associates. Box 141, Waynesville, N.C. 28786. (704) 648-3283. FAX: (704) 648-7177. Richard L. Kennedy, proprietor.
Engrg consultation for radio, TV, ITFS & microwave application. Terrain analysis, site evaluation, system design, NEIR evaluation & measurements, construction oversight.

Kershner, Wright & Hagaman P.C. 5730 General Washington Dr., Alexandria, Va. 22312. (703) 354-3363. FAX: (703) 354-0216. *Stephen W. Kershner, pres; *Boynton G. Hagaman, VP. Engrs: Thomas G. Lavedas, James P. Cahill.
Ant communications consulting engrs specializing in VLF-HF.

Kessler & Gehman Associates Inc. 507 N.W. 60th St., Suite C, Gainesville, Fla. 32607. (904) 332-3157. FAX: (904) 332-6392. *Robert Gehman Jr., P.E., pres; William Kessler, P.E., VP; Keith G. Blanton & Jeffrey C. Gehman, engrs.
Studies, system design, FCC applications, bidding documents & contract monitoring for bcst, ITFS, wireless cable, microwave & mobile communications systems.

J. Gordon Keyworth. Stinson Lake Rd., Rumney, N.H. 03266. (603) 786-2203. J. Gordon Keyworth, P.E.
AM, FM, TV, LPTV engrg svcs, frequency allocation surveys, FCC applications. AM, FM & TV applications.

Kirksey, Terrell W. 5703 Westminster Dr., Austin, Tex. 78723. (512) 928-0617. Terrell W. Kirksey, P.E.
Preparation of engrg material for FCC applications & field measurements on radio stns.

Steve Kramer, P.E. (Consulting Engineers). 10500 Bighorn Tr., Suite 100, McKinney, Tex. 75070. (214) 529-5123. FAX: (214) 542-3725. Steve Kramer, P.E., pres; Brian A. Urban, Jerry Yacuzzi, J. Griffith & Mark Seglem, engrs.
Complete AM, FM, TV, LPTV engrg svcs: FCC applications, field engrg, directional ant adjustments, FAA tower height problem airspace studies.

Stanley Lapin Associates Inc. Box 2606 VDS, Charlotte Amalie, V.I. 00803. (809) 774-4059. FAX: (809) 774-4069. Stanley P. Lapin, P.E., pres.
FM, TV, MDS, MMDS, ITFS stn design, including FCC applications.

Lappas & Lindberg Co. 403 S. Wego Tr., Mt. Prospect, Ill. 60056; 141 W. Jackson Blvd., Suite 2172, Chicago 60604. (708) 392-8265; (312) 922-4123. FAX: (708) 392-8099. Frank G. Lappas, C.E., own.
Aeronautical consultants for communications industry, experienced in dealing with tall tower construction & negotiations with FAA.

Lechman & Johnson Inc. 16201 Trade Zone Ave., Suite 106, Upper Marlboro, Md. 20772. (301) 390-0900. FAX: (301) 249-2953. Peter Lechman, pres; Thomas J. Johnson, VP.
Bcst consulting on FCC matters; field engrg; AM, FM, TV facilities & common carrier engr problems.

Lightning Eliminators & Consultants Inc. 6687 Arapahoe Rd., Boulder, Colo. 80303. (303) 447-2828. FAX: (303) 447-8122. Roy B. Carpenter Jr., CEO; Ralph L. Auer, VP mktg; Darwin N. Sletten, chief engr.

Engineering and Technical Consultants

Consulting & engrg svcs in lightning prevention; grounding & power, signal, telephone & data line conditioning.

Lohnes and Culver. 8309 Cherry Ln., Laurel, Md. 20707-4830. (301) 776-4488. FAX: (301) 776-4499. *Robert D. Culver, ptnr; Frederick D. Veihmeyer, ptnr; D. Scott Turpie, engr.
Communication consulting engrg svc for bcst & related fields. Design, application, optimization, system evaluation & expert representation svcs.

Robert M. Lund Broadcast. Broadcast Consultants. 34 Loma Dr., Auburn, Mass. 01501. (508) 832-2611; (508) 832-9224. Robert M. Lund, own/engr.
AM, FM, TV, LPTV, MMDS, Public Safety Radio frequency searches, allocation studies, system design, FCC applications, AM directionals & cable TV signal availability analysis.

Cecil Lynch Consulting Engineers. 2460 Illinois Ave., Modesto, Calif. 95358. (209) 523-3955. FAX: (209) 522-5287. Cecil Lynch, P.E., CEO; Gerald L. Moore, tech assoc.
Bcst engrg, stn appraisals, customized computer progmg svc, GPS surveying & RFR measurements.

Dwight R. Magnuson. Box 2761, 30 Market Sq. Mall, Knoxville, Tenn. 37901. (615) 525-6358. FAX: (615) 525-6358. Dwight R. Magnuson, P.E.
Consulting engrg for FM, TV & LPTV; including frequency searches, allocations & FCC applications.

Magrill & Associates. 6212 S.W. 8th Pl., Gainsville, Fla. 32607. (904) 331-5999. FAX: (904) 331-6999. Kyle Magrill, own.
AM/FM frequency searches, applications & petitions. Radio stn field svcs & construction. Audio processor enhancements.

Malarkey-Taylor Associates Inc. 1130 Connecticut Ave., Suite 325, Washington 20036. (202) 835-7800. FAX: (202) 835-7811. Andrew Roscoe, CEO; Robert M. Jones, pres; Samuel H. Book, VP rsch div; Archer S. Taylor, sr consultant.
Yiewsley, W. Drayton, Middlesex, U.K. UB7 7BD: 6 Chapel House Business Centre, 152-156 High St.
Cable & wireless communication consultants specializing in appraisals, litigation support, tech due diligence, opns review, compliance requirements, product & system evaluations.

D.L. Markley & Associates Inc. 2104 W. Moss Ave., Peoria, Ill. 61604. (309) 673-7511. FAX: (309) 673-8128. *Donald L. Markley, P.E., pres; Phyllis Markley, sec/treas; Jeremy Ruck, engr.
AM, FM, TV & microwave applications, construction & measurements. Allocation studies, non-ionizing radiation measurements.

Marsand Inc. 400 Paint Pony Tr. N., Fort Worth, Tex. 76108. (817) 246-8384. FAX: (817) 246-4772. *Matthew A. Sanderford Jr., P.E./pres; David Sanderson, EIT, engr.
Turnkey installations, CAD-VIDCAD wiring documentation, FM & TV proof-of-performance, FCC consulting & applications, due diligence evaluations, RF trouble shooting & transmitter upgrade conversions.

Maynard, Frank J. 44683 Mansfield Dr., Novi, Mich. 48375. (313) 344-2965. Frank J. Maynard, own.
Radio & TV engrg svcs & applications.

McClanathan & Associates Inc. Box 939, Portland, Ore. 97207. (503) 246-8080. FAX: (503) 246-6304. *Robert A. McClanathan, P.E., pres; Frank Baker & John Barney, engrs.
Professional electrical engrs for radio & TV FCC applications, computer svcs, field engrg & construction svcs.

The McKinley-Gordon Architects PSC. 2505 3rd Ave., #219, Seattle 98121-1445. (206) 464-1880. FAX: (206) 464-0728. John Petterson, principal bcst facility design; Patrick A. Gordon, pres.

MidAmerica Electronics Service Inc. 410 Mt. Tabor Rd., New Albany, Ind. 47150. (812) 945-1209. FAX: (812) 945-1859. Peter C.L. Boyce, pres; Larry A. Young, sec; Peter C.L. Boyce & Robert Picklesimer, engrs.
AM & FM field engrg svcs, ant measurements, AM stereo installation & proof of performance, AM & FM spectrum analysis, NRSC compliance measurements, new construction & rebuilds.

Mid-State Communications Inc. 47 Berry St. Extension, Fitchburg, Mass. 01420. (508) 342-8965. FAX: (508) 342-8020. Norman L. Rivers, pres.
FCC applications, frequency searches, systems design.

Laura M. Mizrahi. Communications Technologies Inc., Box 1130, Marlton, N.J. 08053. (609) 985-0077. FAX: (609) 985-8124. Laura M. Mizrahi, VP.

Moffet, Larson & Johnson Inc. (MLJ). Two Skyline Pl., 5203 Leesburg Pike, Suite 800, Falls Church, Va. 22041. (703) 824-5660. FAX: (703) 824-5672. Richard Burke, VP/COO; Wallace E. Johnson, P.E.; Michael Degitz, Jeffrey M. Bixby, John Kean, William Hamman, Juan A. Portillo & C.G. Perry III, engrs.
Full-svc engrg for all telecommunication svcs: bcst, CATV, cellular, common carrier, private radio; includes allocation studies, applications, fieldwork, system design, etc.

George E. Molnar Jr. P.E. Box 832, Notre Dame, Ind. 46556. (219) 288-8816. George E. Molnar Jr., P.E., own.
Consulting & engrg for radio & TV.

Montana Engineering Inc. 345 Carlaw Ave., 2nd Fl., Toronto, Ont., Canada M4M 2T1. (416) 463-2155. FAX: (416) 463-3436. Lou Montana, pres.
Facility design, system engrg, project mgmt & feasibility analysis.

Lawrence L. Morton Associates. 1231 Mesa Oaks Ln., Mesa Oaks/Lompoc, Calif. 93436-2309. (805) 733-4275. FAX: (805) 733-4793. *Lawrence L. Morton, P.E., principal; *Lawrence L. Morton, P.E., engr.
Telecommunications engrg consulting svcs for AM, FM, TV & LPTV. Computerized engrg svcs, field svcs, FCC applications.

Mueller Broadcast Design. 613 S. La Grange Rd., La Grange, Ill. 60525. (708) 352-2166. FAX: (708) 352-2170. Mark A. Mueller, own.
AM/FM tech consultant, custom bcst equipment, automation.

Mullaney Engineering Inc. 9049 Shady Grove Ct., Gaithersburg, Md. 20877. (301) 921-0115. FAX: (301) 590-9757. *John J. Mullaney, pres/engr; *John H. Mullaney, P.E., engr; *R. Morgan Burrow Jr., P.E., engr.
Engrg planning for AM, FM, TV, LPTV, MMDS, ITFS & cellular.

Multicomm Sciences International Inc. 266 W. Main St., Denville, N.J. 07834. (201) 627-7400. FAX: (201) 625-1002. *Victor J. Nexon, P.E., pres; S.L. Crimmins, treas; Victor Nexon Jr., VP; *Victor J. Nexon, P.E., engr.

E. Harold Munn Jr. & Associates Inc. Box 220, 100 Airport Rd., Coldwater, Mich. 49036-0220. (517) 278-7339. FAX: (517) 278-6973. Wayne S. Reese, pres; Engrs: Virgil M. Royer, Donald Baad.
AM, FM, TV, LPTV & CATV engrg consulting svc, including applications, field tuning & problem solving.

David Newborg & Associates Inc. 10 Pontiac Dr., Medford, N.J. 08055. (609) 983-3150. David S. Newborg, pres.
Project mgmt plan & supervise installation of transmitters, ants & towers. Equipment appraisals, transmitter, ant & microwave mktg plans.

Northeast Broadcast Lab Inc. Box 1179, South Glens Falls, N.Y. 12803. (518) 793-2181. FAX: (518) 793-7423. William Bingham, pres.
Radio studio, transmission systems & equipment; qualified bcst engrg personnel.

Warren Only Group. Box 614, Oceanview, N.J. 08230. (609) 624-0265. Warren Only, pres.
Telecommunications consultant; AM, FM & TV FCC applications & field engrg. Satellite uplink coord; C- & Ku-band applications, satellite systems design.

Leonard L. Oursler Jr., E.E. 110 W. Warnock St., Princeton, Ind. 47670. (812) 385-2336. Leonard L. Oursler Jr., E.E.

Owl Engineering Inc. 1306 W. County Rd. F, Suite 105, Arden Hills, Minn. 55112. (612) 631-1338. FAX: (612) 631-3502. *Garrett G. Lysiak, P.E., ptnr; Diane Stewart Lysiak, M.A., ptnr; *Garrett G. Lysiak, P.E., Michael Radovich & Gary Wilson, engrs.
Telecommunications consulting engrg svcs, applications, facilities specifications svcs, field engrg svcs, maintenance & FCC compliance svcs.

POA Ltd. (Systems & Products Groups). Box 410, 701 Country Line Rd., Palmer Lake, Colo. 80133. (719) 488-2270. FAX: (719) 488-2648. Paul Olivier, pres; Dale Hill, sec/treas; Howard Phillips, dir engrg.
Full-svc video & bcst systems consulting, design engrg, fabrication, installation, training, equipment procurement & turnkey system integration.

Pacific Radio Electronics. 969 N. La Brea, Los Angeles, Calif. 90038. (213) 969-2035. FAX: (213) 969-2035. Alan Phillips, pres.

O.D. Page, P.E. Professional Engineers and Consultants. 7536 Spring Lake Dr., Bethesda, Md. 20817. (301) 469-6688. FAX: (301) 469-6688. O.D. Page, P.E., own; William C. Hsiao & Kenneth Taschner, engrs.
Franchising & refranchising; system appraisals; feasibility studies; budgets & projections; evaluation of physical plant; system design, contracting, supervision of construction, proof of performance.

Peters, Arthur K. Consulting Engineers. 7020 N.W. 11th Pl., Gainesville, Fla. 32605. (904) 331-0149. FAX: (904) 331-8026. *A.K. Peters, P.E., pres.

Phase One Communications Inc. 3452 Lake Lynda Dr., Suite 115, Orlando, Fla. 32817. (407) 381-4895. FAX: (407) 381-8560.
Tech consulting svcs for all telecommunications svcs including FCC applications, allocation studies, site acquisition.

William F. Pohts Telecommunications. 225 Denfield Dr., Alexandria, Va. 22309. (703) 360-7193. FAX: (703) 360-0309. William F. Pohts, consulting engr.
Consulting engr specializing in the emerging technologies in telecommunications & electronic systems.

James W. Pollack, P.E. Communications Technologies Inc., Box 1130, Marlton, N.J. 08053. (609) 985-0077. FAX: (609) 985-8124.

Rimma Posin. 3712 Carmel Ave. Irvine, Calif. 92714. (714) 857-9639. Consulting for cable; FCC applications.

W.L. Pritchard & Co. Inc. 7315 Wisconsin Ave., Suite 520E, Bethesda, Md. 20814. (301) 654-1144. FAX: (301) 654-1814. W.L. Pritchard, pres; Robert A. Neslon, Ph.D., VP; Ellen Hoff, VP; Rodney Moore, engr.
Consulting engrg & economics in telecommunications, particularly satellites, microwave, wireless cable, microwave radio & related systems.

RF Technologies Corp. 238 Goddard Rd., Lewiston, Me. 04240. (207) 777-7778. FAX: (207) 777-7784. *George M. Harris P.E., pres tech sls; Peter Robicheau, VP tech design; Lisa Johnson, mktg admin.
Designs & manufactures high power bcst RF nets & components for FM & TV bcstrs. Products include ants, diplexers, combiners, filters, switches, coax & waveguides.

Radio/TV Engineering Co. 1416 Hollister Ln., Los Osos, Calif. 93402. (805) 934-5471. Norwood J. Patterson, dir engrg; G. Dawn Patterson, exec asst; Engrs: Sherwood Patterson, G. Dawn Patterson.
AM, FM, FCC applications, directional ant design. Serving bcstrs for over 35 years.

Radiotechniques Engineering Corp. Box 367, 402 10th Ave., Haddon Heights, N.J. 08035-0367. (609) 546-8008. FAX: (609) 546-1841. Edward A. Schober, P.E., pres; Edward A. Schober, Peter Moncure & Darlene Newill, engrs.
AM, FM, TV, digital audio bcst, boosters. FCC equipment, field & systems engrg. RF, financial, opns & acoustical design.

Radio-TV Engineering Co. 1416 Hollister Ln., Los Osos, Calif. 93402-2940. (805) 528-1996. FAX: (805) 528-1982. Norwoc J. Patterson, pres/dir engrg; Gloria D. Patterson, sec/asst engr. Engrs: Sherwood Patterson, G. Dawn Patterson.
AM, FM, TV, FCC applications & directional ant design.

Response Reward Systems. 945 Treasure Ln., Vero Beach, Fla. 32963. (407) 234-5440. Henry Von Kohorn, CEO.
Patented technology for instant electronic crediting and/or dispensing of coupons in homes of TV, radio & telephone contestants.

A.D. Ring P.C. 240 N. Washington Blvd., Suite 700, Sarasota, Fla. 34236. (813) 366-2611. FAX: (813) 966-5533. *John A Lundin, pres; *L. Robert du Treil, VP; *Ronald D. F ckley, sec/treas; *Howard T. Head, *Marvin Blumberg, *Ogden Prestholdt & *Harold L. Kassens, consultants.
Full-svc professional engrg firm.

Rosenthal Engineering. Box 1650, San Luis Obispo, Calif. 93406. (805) 541-0910. Doren Rosenthal, pres.

Rosner Television Systems Inc. 17 Mitchell Dr., Kings Point, N.Y. 11024-1237. (516) 466-4172. FAX: (516) 466-4172. I.S. Rosner, pres; R. Rosner, VP; I.S. Rosner, engr.
Mgmt consulting, design & engrg svcs in radio, TV & communications.

Royce International Consulting Engineers. Renaissance Tower, 801 K St., 27th Fl., Sacramento, Calif. 95814-3500. (916) 442-1000. FAX: (916) 448-1655. E.R. Stolz II, pres/engr.

Engineering and Technical Consultants

FM & TV applications & construction; site & equipment acquisition; tech consulting svcs; qualified expert court witness.

Rubin, Bednarek & Associates. 1350 Connecticut Ave. N.W., #610, Washington 20036. (202) 296-9380. FAX: (202) 296-9383. Philip A. Rubin, pres; Robert A. Bednarek, VP; Alan Gearing, sr assoc; G. William Meeker, sr assoc.

Experts bcst TV & radio, satellites, cellular, DAB, PCS & other new media technologies. Familiar with FCC rules & regulations.

SG Communications Services. Box 76269, Atlanta, 30358-1269. (800) 824-7865. FAX: (404) 475-0247. William T. Rushton, pres; Daniel E. Ferguson, VP sls & mktg.

Turnkey tower svcs, maintenance, erection, system design, ant instal, reharness, HDTV planning, surveys, mod, strobe lighting systems.

D.W. Sargent Broadcast Service Inc. 804 Richard Rd., Cherry Hill, N.J. 08034. (609) 667-8573. FAX: (609) 667-1409. Dean W. Sargent, pres/treas; H.L. Sargent, sec; Dean W. Sargent & Lucci Roth, engrs.

Ant system design & measurements for FM & TV. FM master ant system design.

T.Z. Sawyer Technical Consultants. 6204 Highland Dr., Chevy Chase, Md. 20815. (301) 913-9287. FAX: (301) 913-5799. Timothy Z. Sawyer, pres.

FCC applications for AM, FM, TV LPTV & auxiliary svcs; AM directional ant design; AM, FM, & TV ant measurements; allocation studies; site surveys & inspections.

Merl Saxon. Consulting Radio Engineers. 622 Hoskins St., Lufkin, Tex. 75901. (409) 634-9558. Merl Saxon, own; Peter Mergens, engr.

Pagosa Springs, Colo. 81147: Box 1465. (303) 731-5641.

Ant design, tune-up & measurement for ND & DA opn. Transmitter problems & phasor design.

Frederic D. Schottland, P.E. 3201 Landmark Dr., #1105, Clearwater, Fla. 34621-1920. (813) 784-2770. *Frederic D. Schottland, P.E., own.

Radio bcstg engrg.

Sellmeyer Engineering. Box 356, McKinney, Tex. 75069. (214) 542-2056. FAX: (214) 542-2056. *J.S. (Jack) Sellmeyer, P.E., own.

AM, FM, TV applications, hearing support, directional ant design & adjustment; facilities planning specialized equipment design.

Shoolbred Engineers Inc. 1049 Morrison Dr., Charleston, S.C. 29403. (803) 577-4681. Robert A. Shoolbred, pres.

Shortwave Engineering. 1300 WWCR Ave., Nashville 37218. (615) 255-1300. George McClintock, pres; Watt Hairston, chief engr.

Consulting & contract engrg for AM, FM & sw radio.

Silliman and Silliman. 8601 Georgia Ave., Suite 910, Silver Spring, Md. 20910. (301) 589-8288. FAX: (301) 589-8291. *Robert M. Silliman, P.E., ptnr; *Thomas B. Silliman, P.E., ptnr; Susan N. Crawford, engr; Margaret Evans & Cathy A. Ozdany, staff.

Consulting engrs specializing in AM, FM & TV allocations, field assistance & EMR matters.

W. Lee Simmons & Associates Inc. One St. Augustine Pl., Hilton Head Island, S.C. 29928. (800) 277-5417; (803) 785-4445. FAX: (803) 842-3371. W. Lee Simmons, pres/engr; Sonja B. Simmons, sec/treas.

Consulting on AM, FM, TV applications, MATV, CATV, MDS & cellular.

Sisk Engineering Inc. Box 249, Fulton, Miss. 38843. (601) 862-2233. FAX: (601) 862-2233. Olvie E. Sisk, engr.

Specializing in RF systems & allocation work.

Skilling Ward Magnusson Barkshire Inc. 1301 5th Ave., Suite 3200, Seattle 98101-2699. (206) 292-1200. FAX: (206) 292-1201. Jon D. Magnusson, CEO; Arthur J. Barkshire, pres; Tony Tschanz, sr VP. Engrs: Ramon D. Upsahl, VP; Alan K. Gordon, design engr.

Tower inspection, wind rating, tower retrofit, concept studies, design, contract documents & construction mgmt.

Carl E. Smith. Consulting Engineers. Box 807, 2324 N. Cleve-Mass Rd., Bath, Ohio 44210-0807. (216) 659-4440. FAX: (216) 659-9234. Al Warmus, P.E., pres; Roy Stype, VP; Al Warmus, P.E., Roy Stype, Jerry Smith, Elmer Steingass, Mark Moceri, Derek Gorman & Roger Stevens, engrs.

AM, FM, TV & LPTV engrg, FCC applications, ant systems adjustments. Sls: towers, ants, transmission line & phasing equipment. Turnkey installations.

Carl E. Smith Electronics. 8200 Snowville Rd., Cleveland 44141. (216) 526-4386. FAX: (216) 526-9205. Carl E. Smith, own, P.E.

Radio, TV & sw consulting. Propagation studies, directional ant designs & expert court witness.

Frederick A. Smith Associates. Rt. 1, Box 284B, Elloree, S.C. 29047. (803) 897-2815. FAX: (803) 897-2815. Frederick A. Smith, P.E., pres; Cameron E. Smith, P.E., VP; Cameron E. Smith, P.E., engr.

Communication systems design, microwave path surveys, ant impedance measurements. U.S. & foreign.

Smith & Powstenko. 1233 20th St. N.W., Suite 502, Washington 20036. (202) 293-7742. FAX: (202) 296-2429. Neil Smith, ptnr; Jeanne Smith, ptnr; Neil M. Smith, Jeanne Smith & Kevin T. Fisher, engrs.

Tech consultants to AM, FM, TV, & LPTV stns; FCC applications; allocations studies; RF measurements; expert witness testimony.

Arthur A. Snowberger, P.E. 674 Marion St., Hagerstown, Md. 21740. (301) 733-7454. Arthur A. Snowberger, P.E., own.

AM, FM, TV engrg & fieldwork.

Southern Broadcast Services. Box 740, 210 Hillwood Park S., Alabaster, Ala. 35007. (205) 663-3709. FAX: (205) 663-7108.

Tower erection, ant & line installation, maintenance svcs.

Frederick L. Spaulding, P.E. Consulting Engineer. 883 San Simeon Dr., Mountain View, Calif. 94043. (415) 961-5018. Frederick L. Spaulding, consulting engr.

Full-svc radio & TV consulting engrg & fieldwork. Advanced modulation testing & analysis.

StarTrack Communications. 303 E. Monroe, Fairfield, Iowa 52556. (515) 472-5620. James W. Morrow, engr.

C- and Ku-band TVRO 3-7 meters, fully automated remote control, uplinks & downlinks for TV, radio, data, CATV.

David Steel & Associates Inc. Box 440, Chester, Md. 21619. (410) 643-7950. FAX: (410) 643-7991. *David Steel Sr., P.E., pres.

Complete bcst engrg, including TV, FM & wireless cable.

Steiger, Hurray & Associates Inc. 6816 Westview Dr., Cleveland 44141-2924. (216) 526-7187. Robert J. Steiger, pres; Jack Hurray, VP/treas; Robert J. Steiger & Jack Hurray, engrs.

Consulting engr svcs.

Walter J. Stiles & Associates. 4032 W. Krall Ave., Phoenix 85019. (602) 934-8522. FAX: (602) 842-2762. Walter J. Stiles, pres; Don Jackson; David Cavileer; Walter Stiles III.

FCC applications AM, FM & TV, proof of performances, design & construction of facilities, progmg, sls & mgmt consultation.

J.M. Stitt & Associates Inc. 621 Mehring Way, Suite 1907, Cincinnati, 45202. (513) 621-9292. James Stitt, pres; Steve Miller, associate.

Engrg consultants, facility design & instal, contract engrg svcs & acoustical consultants.

Structural Systems Technology Inc. 6867 Elm St., McLean, Va. 22101. (703) 356-9765. FAX: (703) 448-0979. J. Cabot Goudy, P.E., pres; Fred W. Purdy, P.E., VP opns; Kaveh Mehmama, P.E., VP engrg.

Structural engrg studies, analysis, design, modifications, inspections & erections of towers & ant structures.

Chester J. Stuart. Consulting Communications Engineer. Box 1236, Susanville, Calif. 96130-1236. (916) 257-2702. FAX: (916) 257-7994. Chester J. Stuart, own; Roland V. Stuart, assoc.

Consulting engr svcs to radio & TV stns.

Suffa & Cavell Inc. 10300 Eaton Pl., Suite 450, Fairfax, Va. 22030. (703) 591-0110. FAX: (703) 591-0115. *William P. Suffa, P.E., VP/sec/engr; Garrison C. Cavell, pres/engr; John Philip Davis, Robert M. Gates, Athony H. Mimiaga, engrs.

Domestic, international bcst & communications engrg; system & facility inspection, design, evaluation; bid & construction mgmt, energy exposure analysis, interference resolution, propagation analysis, applications & pleading support; power systems design.

Superior Satellite Engineers. 2320 Sierra Meadows, Rocklin, Calif. 95677. (916) 624-8214. FAX: (916) 624-9146. Doyle Catlett, pres. Engr: John Kernkamp.

Sls of remote steerable satellite ant & related products.

TABCON. 12856 S. 114th East Ave., Broken Arrow, Okla. 74011. (918) 369-2559. William E. Davis, P.E., own. Engrs: William E. Davis. P.E.

Bcst engrg AM, FM & TV; applications, installations, field svc.

3D Video Corp. 5240 Medina Rd., Woodland Hills, Calif. 91364-1913. (818) 769-6752. FAX (818) 592-0987. Daniel L. Symmes, pres; Alan Williams, dir mktg.

Hollywood, Calif. 90038-3340: 801 N. LaBrea Ave., Suite 104.

Supplies 3-D bcst TV process: equipment, consultation & 3-D glasses.

TRA Communications Consultants. 600 W. Hillsboro Blvd., Suite 27, Deerfield Beach, Fla. 33441. (305) 480-2727. FAX: (305) 480-8501. J. Rodger Skinner Jr., pres; Loren M. Matthews, chief engr.

Ch searches & application preparation for LPTV & FM.

TTF Lighting Consultants Inc. 8900 Yellow Brick Rd., Baltimore, Md. 21237. (410) 391-8001. FAX: (410) 391-4084. Russell Morris, pres; Mark Firley, VP; Mark Conners.

Rental & sls of lighting equipment, studio consultation & design; rental of lighting packages for outside bcsts.

Technet Systems Group, a division of Steve Vanni Associates Inc. Box 422, Auburn, N.H. 03032. (603) 483-5365. FAX: (603) 483-0512. Steve Vanni, pres/mgr sls div; Bob Smith, mgr installation div; Kim Meisinger, mgr tower div.

Bcst equipment supplier/distributor for radio & TV, specializing in complete turnkey packages including planning, design, equipment, installation, towers & FCC licensing.

Tecomm Systems Inc. 6455 Guide Meridian Rd., Lynden, Wash. 98264. (206) 738-9209. FAX: (206) 738-9209. Peter A. Niblock, P.E., pres/chief engr; Peter Hostinsky, VP finance & admin; H. Grant McCormick, bcst mgr/engr; Bruce W. Granholm, VP mktg & engr.

Telecommunications consulting engrg svcs for AM, FM, TV bcst & CATV systems, studio to transmitter links & studio systems.

Telecommunications Site Acquisitions Inc. (TelSA). Box 32223, Washington 20007-0523. (202) 342-7700; (800) USA-SITE. FAX: (202) 342-9500; (800) USA-TOWER. Gregory B. Daly, pres.

Teletech Inc. 23400 Michigan Ave., Dearborn, Mich. 48124. (313) 562-6873. FAX: (313) 562-8612. Kenneth W. Hoehn, VP; Keith Johnson, field svc mgr; Mark W. Dobronski, sr engr.

Scottsdale, Ariz. 85261: Box 4221. (602) 991-6000.

Engrg consultants: AM, FM, TV, LPTV; FCC applications/filings, FAA filings, aeronautical studies; tower erection, maintenance & inspections; ant site dev & mgmt; directional ant design & proof of performance; contract engrg svcs.

Cullen B. Tendick. Consulting Radio Engineer. Box 679, Honaunau, Hawaii 96726. (808) 328-2466. Cullen B. Tendick, consulting radio engr.

AM, FM & TV measurements & allocations.

Thomforde, C.J. 2615 4th Ave. N., Grand Forks, N.D. 58203. (701) 775-7084. C.J. Thomforde, pres.

Uplink Engineering Inc. 714 S.W. 12th Ave., Fort Lauderdale, Fla. 33312. (305) 522-3303; FAX: (305) 522-3355. Douglass L. Holland, pres/dir engrg.

Ant, tower, studio & RF facilities design & construction; FCC & FAA application preparation.

Steve Vanni Associates Inc. Box 422, Auburn, N.H. 03032. (603) 483-5365. FAX: (603) 483-0512. Steve Vanni, pres.

Tech consulting, systems design, project mgmt; complete turnkey svcs including equipment & towers through Technet Systems Group.

Thomas J. Vaughan & Associates. Consulting Engineers. Box 440, Rye Beach, N.H. 03871. (603) 624-4351. FAX: (603) 624-4822. *T.J. Vaughan, principal; M. Winsor, structural engr; H. McClure, systems/propagation engr.

HDTV propagation & tower feasibility studies, custom ant designs & site selection.

Douglas L. Vernier. 1600 Picturesque Dr., Cedar Falls, Iowa 50613. (319) 266-8402. FAX: (319) 266-9212. Doug Vernier, pres/engr.

Bcst engrg & consultation; ch searches, FCC applications, allocations, radio & TV systems design, coverage analysis & bcst engrg software.

Engineering and Technical Consultants

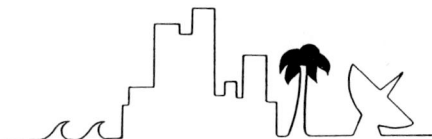

VISION ACCOMPLISHED INC.

Vision Accomplished Inc. 550 Maulhardt Ave., Oxnard, Calif. 93030. (805) 981-8740. FAX: (805) 981-8738.

Transportable & flyaway satellite transmission; mobile/TVROs; studio/remote production; transmission mgmt.

Visual Edge Technology. 306 Potrero Ave., Sunnyvale, Calif. 94086. (408) 245-1100. FAX: (408) 245-1107. Austin Vanchieri, pres.

Large format digital printing systems.

Weisman Consultants Inc. 5000 Dufferin St., Suite 210, Downsview, Ont., Canada M3H 5T5. (416) 736-7453. FAX: (416) 736-4372. Simon Weisman, P.E., pres.

Structural evaluation, design review, design & analysis software for guyed & self-supporting towers.

Western Wireless Works. Box 4500, Apache Junction, Ariz. 85278. (602) 380-1000. FAX: (602) 986-1442. Richard Haskey, opns mgr; Patricia Woods, mgr tech svcs. Rudy Petracci, engr.

D.C. Williams P.E. Consulting Radio Engineer. Box 1888, Carson City, Nev. 89702. (702) 885-2400. FAX: (702) 885-8705. *D.C. Williams, P.E., pres.

Registered professional engr specializing in allocations, ant system design, applications, construction, evaluation & measurement of AM & FM directional facilities.

Louis A. Williams Jr. & Associates. 2092 Arrowood Pl., Cincinnati 45231. (513) 851-4964. *Louis A. Williams Jr., P.E.; Pat Williams, office mgr.

FCC filings, frequency searches, RFR hazard measurements & analysis, field strength measurments, tech assistance & other measurement svcs.

Willoughby & Voss. Box 701190, San Antonio, 78270-1190. (210) 525-1111. FAX (210) 490-2779. Lyndon H. Willoughby, own.

AM, FM, TV, STL, translator applications, directional antenna design, field svcs, allocations, site studies, system planning, frequency searches, facility inspection, non-ionized radiation studies.

Wind River Broadcast Center. 117 E. 11th St., Loveland. Colo. 80537. (303) 669-3442; (800) 669-3993. FAX: (303) 667-0047. Jim McDonald.

Offers prods & svcs to aid in establishing & maintaining a sound, up-to-date tech operation & effective tools to comply with FCC rules.

Wold International Inc. 3440 Motor Ave., Suite 200, Los Angeles 90034. (310) 842-6900; (310) 842-6903. Robert E. Wold, chmn/pres; Richard H. Caldwill, exec VP.

Design, implementation & mgmt of international & domestic transmission systems using satellite, optical fiber technologies.

Charles Wooten. Broadcast Engineering. Box 4183, Panama City, Fla. 32401. (904) 265-9970. FAX: (904) 769-6164. Charles T. Wooten, own.

Turnkey installations (AM, FM studios & transmitters), tech appraisals, emergency repairs, upgrades.

Walter Wulff & Associates. Aviation Consultants. Box 77028, Atlanta 30357. (404) 881-6786. Walter H. Wulff, pres.

Conducts FAA obstruction evaluation studies, FM electro magnetic interference analysis & communications consulting engrs.

Walter S. Wydro Consultants. The Atrium, Four Terry Dr., Suite 10, Newtown, Pa. 18940. (215) 860-2288. FAX: (215) 860-5502. Walter S. Wydro, pres/own; Alicia A. Thome, VP; Barry Nuss & Walt Wydro, engrs.

Telecommunications engrg svcs with emphasis on bcstg, cable & pay TV; FCC filings, franchising; two-way interactive, site system evaluation, lab product testing & evaluation; litigation expertise.

Law Firms Active in Communications Law

This listing includes attorneys practicing before the FCC as reported by radio and television stations, brokers, consultants and the attorneys themselves. Many, but not all, are members of the Federal Communications Bar Association.

A

Abdo & Abdo. 710 Northstar W., 625 Marquette Ave., Minneapolis 55402-1702. (612) 333-1526. FAX: (612) 342-2608.

Accinelli Law Offices. 10795 Woodbine St., Los Angeles 90034-5401. (310) 202-7682. FAX: (310) 202-6592. Thomas F. Accinelli.

Adams, Duque & Hazeltine. 777 S. Figueroa St., 10th Fl., Los Angeles 90017-2513. (213) 620-1240. FAX: (213) 896-5500. Jeffrey L. Shumway.

Akerman, Senterfitt & Eidson. Box 231, Firstate Tower, 17th Fl., Orlando, Fla. 32802-0231. (407) 843-7860. FAX: (407) 843-6610. Tom Cardwell, atty.

Akin, Gump, Strauss, Hauer & Feld. 1333 New Hampshire Ave. N.W., Suite 400, Washington 20036. (202) 887-4000. FAX: (202) 887-4288. James P. Denvir, Diane Conley.

Alagia, Day, Marshall, Mintmire & Chauvin. 444 S. 5th St., Louisville, Ky. 40202. (502) 585-4131. Stanley L. Chauvin Jr.

Aldredge, Sawnie R. Box 120713, 1018 17th Ave. S., Suite 3, Nashville 37212. (615) 327-9377. FAX: (615) 327-9379.

Allen & Harold, PLC. 10610-A Crestwood Dr., Manassas, Va. 22110. (703) 361-2278; (800) 433-2636. FAX: (703) 361-0594. Robert G. Allen, Douglas W. Harold Jr., Robert L. Galbreath.

M. Allen & Associates. 1133 Ave. of the Americas, 45th Fl., New York 10036. (212) 768-7184. FAX: (212) 768-8366. Marv Allen

Ament, Gerald. 2861 Woodwardia Dr., Los Angeles 90077-2136. (310) 444-8330. FAX: (310) 444-8550.

Anderson, Kill, Olick & Oshinsky. 2000 Pennsylvania Ave. N.W., Washington 20006. (202) 728-3103. FAX: (202) 728-3199. Barry J. Fleishman.

Andrews, John E. Box 5326, Santa Monica, Calif. 90409-5326. (310) 396-0689.

Archilla-Roig, Efrain. Box 1240, Humacao, Puerto Rico 00792-1240. (809) 852-1240. FAX: (809) 852-1280.

Ardi, Dennis. 725 S. Figueroa St., 21st Fl., Los Angeles 90017-5524. (213) 239-0376. FAX: (213) 239-0381.

Arent, Fox, Kintner, Plotkin & Kahn. 1050 Connecticut Ave. N.W., Washington 20036-5339. (202) 857-6000. FAX: (202) 857-6395. Theodore David Frank, Susan A. Marshall, Vonya B. McCann, Gerald P. McCartin, Harry M. Plotkin, Thomas Schattenfield, George H. Shapiro, Marilyn D. Sonn, Peter Tannenwald, David F. Tillotson, Mitchell Lazarus, Kathleen L. Franco, Andrew C. Cooper.

Other offices: Vienna, Va.; Bethesda, Md.; New York; Budapest, Hungary; Jeddah, Saudi Arabia.

Arnold & Porter. 1200 New Hampshire Ave. N.W., Washington 20036. (202) 872-3990. FAX: (202) 728-2130. L. Reed Miller, Norman M. Sinel, Richard M. Firestone, Robert A. Garrett, Stephanie M. Phillipps, Patrick J. Grant, Marcia Cranberg, Bruce A. Adams, Caroline H. Little, Terri A. Southwick, William E. Cook.

Arrow, Edelstein, & Laird. 32 E. 57th St., New York 10022-2513. (212) 371-7111; (212) 245-4580. Allen H. Arrow.

Arter & Hadden. 1801 K St. N.W., Suite 400K, Washington 20006-1301. (202) 775-7100. FAX: (202) 857-0172. Ptnrs: Howard M. Liberman, Gerald Steven-Kittner. Assocs: Peter H. Doyle, Timothy Lockhart, Robert M. McDowell, Laura D. Montgomery, James U. Troup.

Asbill, Junkin, & Myers. 1615 New Hampshire Ave. N.W., Washington 20009. (202) 234-9000. FAX: (202) 332-6480. Matthew Myers.

Asbury, Philip S. 309 S. Broad St., Philadelphia 19107-5813. (215) 985-0911. FAX: (215) 985-1195.

Askoff, Richard A. National Exchange Carrier Association. 100 S. Jefferson Rd., Whippany, N.J. 07981. (201) 884-8000. FAX: (201) 884-8469.

Association of Independent Television Stations Inc. (INTV). 1320 19th St. N.W., Suite 300, Washington 20036. James B. Hedlund, pres; David L. Donovan, VP legal & legislative affrs; Jim Popham, VP gen counsel.

Auger, Adrien R. U.S. Federal Communications Commission, 1250 23rd St. N.W., Rm. 10, Washington 20554. (202) 632-4887. FAX: (202) 632-1411.

Ausley, McMullen, McGehee, Carothers & Proctor. Box 391, 227 S. Calhoun St., Tallahassee, Fla. 32301. (904) 224-9115. FAX: (904) 222-7952. John P. Fons.

B

BET (Black Entertainment Television). 1232 31st St. N.W., Washington 20007-3402. (202) 337-5260. Debra L. Lee.

Baca, Rudolfo Lujan. U.S. Federal Communications Commission, 1919 M. St. N.W., Rm. 814, Washington 20554. (202) 632-7557.

Baker, Barwick, Ravenel & Bender. Box 8057, 1730 Main St., Columbia, S.C. 29201-2820. (803) 799-9091. FAX: (803) 779-3423. Charles Baker, sr law ptnr.

Baker, Beverly G. U.S. Federal Communications Commission, Private Radio Bureau, 2025 M St. N.W., Washington 20554. (202) 632-6942.

Baker & Hostetler. 1050 Connecticut Ave. N.W., Suite 1100, Washington 20036. (202) 861-1500. FAX: (202) 861-1783. Donald P. Zeifang, (202) 861-1624; Bruce W. Sanford, (202) 861-1626; Kenneth C. Howard Jr., (202) 861-1580; David N. Roberts, (202) 861-1739.

Baker & McKenzie. 815 Connecticut Ave. N.W., Suite 900, Washington 20006. (202) 452-7083. FAX: (202) 452-7072; (202) 452-7073; (202) 452-7074. Ernest T. Sanchez.

Baker, Worthington, Crossley, Stansberry & Woolf. 1700 Nashville City Ctr., 511 Union St., Nashville 37219. (615) 726-5600. FAX: (615) 726-0464. C. Michael Norton.

Law Offices of Ruth S. Baker-Battist. 1828 L St. N.W., Suite 805, Washington 20036. (202) 223-7630; (301) 718-8866.

Baraff, Koerner, Olender & Hochberg P.C. 5335 Wisconsin Ave. N.W., Suite 300, Washington 20015. (202) 686-3200. FAX: (202) 686-8282. B. Jay Baraff; James A. Koerner; Robert L. Olender; Philip R. Hochberg; Mark J. Palchick; James E. Meyers; Robert Bennett Lubic, counsel.

Barb & Hart. 9060 Santa Monica Blvd., Beverly Hills, Calif. 90210. (310) 859-6644. Robert A. Kline.

Barkan & Barkan Co. 150 E. State St., Columbus, Ohio 43215. (614) 461-1551. FAX: (614) 461-6434. Gregory L. Patterson.

Barna, Allen A. U.S. Federal Communications Commission, 1919 M St. N.W., Rm. 518, Washington 20554. (202) 632-1370.

Barron, Newburger P.C. 900 Congress Ave., Suite 200, Austin, Tex. 78701. (512) 476-9103. FAX: (512) 476-9253. Barbara M. Barron.

Barton & Douglas. Wisconsin Bldg., 4000 Albemarle St. N.W., Suite 204, Washington 20016. (301) 229-1645. FAX: (703) 979-1487.

Basch, Richard H. 10 E. 44 St., 7th Fl., New York 10017-3606. (212) 867-1200.

Bass, Berry & Sims. 2700 First American Ctr., Nashville 37238. (615) 742-6200. John L. Unger.

Bassett, Gerry, Friend, Koenig & Sapronov. 2970 Clairmont Rd., Suite 600, Atlanta 30329. (404) 325-8196. FAX: (404) 325-0324. Walt Sapronov.

Bayer, Theodore R. 9400 S. Dadeland Blvd., Suite 300, Miami, Fla. 33156-2811. (305) 670-6300. FAX: (305) 670-4847.

Bechtel & Cole, Chartered. 1901 L St. N.W., Suite 250, Washington 20036. (202) 833-4190. FAX: (202) 833-3084. Gene A. Bechtel, Harry F. Cole, Ann C. Farhat.

Becker, London, Kossow. 1841 Broadway, Suite 600, New York 10023. (212) 541-7070. FAX: (212) 541-7080. Mortimer Becker, Daniel H. Kossow.

Becker & Madison, Chartered. 1915 Eye St. N.W., 8th Fl., Washington 20006. (202) 833-4422. FAX: (202) 296-7458. Richard S. Becker, James S. Finerfrock, Paul Madison.

Behr & Robinson. 2049 Century Park E., 26th Fl., Los Angeles 90067. (310) 556-9200. FAX: (310) 556-9229.

Bell, Boyd & Lloyd. 1615 L St. N.W., Suite 1200, Washington 20036. (202) 466-6300. FAX: (202) 463-0678. Thomas R. Gibbon.

BellSouth Corp. 1155 Peachtree St. N.E., Suite 1800, Atlanta 30367. (404) 249-2641. FAX (404) 249-5901. William Barfield.

Belvin, Lauren. U.S. Federal Communications Commission, 1919 M St. N.W., Rm. 808, Washington 20554. (202) 632-6405. FAX: (202) 632-7092.

Benson & Siman. 1207 17th Ave. S., 3rd Fl., Nashville 37212-2801. (615) 320-6116. FAX: (615) 320-6194.

Berger, Jerome. 767 5th Ave., New York 10011. (212) 447-6464; (212) 777-8220. FAX: (212) 661-0989.

Law Offices of Jeff Berke. 11766 Wilshire Blvd., Suite 550, Los Angeles 90025-6538. (310) 312-0221. FAX: (310) 478-3020. Jeff Berke, Esquire.

Berkowitz, Adam C. William Morris Agency. 1350 6th Ave., New York 10019. (212) 586-5100. FAX: (212) 246-3583.

Berland, Ava Holly. U.S. Federal Communications Commission, 1919 M St. N.W., Rm. 616, Washington 20554. (202) 632-6990. FAX: (202) 632-0149.

Bernick & Lifson. The Colonnade, 5500 Wayzata Blvd., Suite 1200, Minneapolis 55416-1270. (612) 546-1200. FAX: (612) 546-1003. Thomas D. Creighton.

At last! An attorney who's been there!
15 years of programming, sales and management experience.

BARRY SKIDELSKY

Attorney/Consultant

- full-service assistance for station start-up, purchase and sale
- new-buyer education (private seminar) • facilities improvement
- FCC hearings • financing • bankruptcy trustee • tax • corporate
- employment contracts • EEO • lender and management consultation

655 Madison Avenue, 19th floor, New York, NY 10021, (212) 832-4800

Protect yourself. Call the industry's lawyer.
Creative solutions to your most difficult problems.

Law Firms Active in Communications Law

Berry, Dunbar, Daniel, O'Connor & Jordan. Box 11645, Columbia, S.C. 29211; 1200 Main St., Columbia, S.C. 29201. (803) 765-1030. FAX: (803) 799-5536. James V. Dunbar Jr.

Besozzi, Gavin & Craven. 1901 L St. N.W., Suite 200, Washington 20036. (202) 293-7405. Paul C. Besozzi, Stephen Diaz Gavin, J. Jeffrey Craven, Thomas L. Siebert.

Birch, Horton, Bittner & Cherot. 1155 Connecticut Ave., Suite 1200, Washington 20036. (202) 659-5800. FAX: (202) 659-1027. J. Geoffrey Bentley, Eric A. Eisen, Elisabeth H. Ross, Thomas L. Albert, Jesse A. Halvorsen.

Bishop, Payne, Williams & Werley. 500 W. 7th St., Suite 1800, Ft. Worth, Tex. 76102-4787. (817) 335-4911. FAX: (817) 870-2631. Philip R. Bishop, Thomas J. Williams.

Blackwell, Sanders, Matheny, Weary & Lombardi. 2 Pershing Sq., 2300 Main St., Suite 1100, Kansas City, Mo. 64108. (816) 274-6847. FAX: (816) 274-6914. Robert E. Marsh.

Blasinsky, Mary R. 14400 Butternut Ct., Rockville, Md. 20853. (301) 871-1024.

Bleiweiss, Irene. U.S. Federal Communications Commission - Audio Services Division, 1919 M St. N.W., Rm. 302, Washington 20554. (202) 632-6485. Irene Bleiweiss.

Bloomfield, David. 5700 Wilshire Blvd., Los Angeles 90036. (213) 965-5850. FAX: (213) 965-5853.

Blooston, Mordkofsky, Jackson & Dickens. 2120 L St. N.W., Suite 300, Washington 20037. (202) 659-0830. Arthur Blooston, Harold Mordkofsky, Robert M. Jackson, Benjamin H. Dickens Jr., John A. Prendergast, Jerald J. Duffy, ptnrs; Jeremiah Courtney, of counsel.

Blumberg, Grace Ganz. 405 Hilgard Ave., Los Angeles 90024-1476. (310) 825-1334.

Blume, Elbaum & Collins. Corporate Ctr. W., 433 S. Main St., Suite 111, West Hartford, Conn. 06110. (203) 561-0000. FAX: (203) 561-1555. Daniel Blume.

Blumenfeld & Cohen. 1615 M St. N.W., Suite 700, Washington 20036. (202) 955-6300. FAX: (202) 955-6460. Jeffrey Blumenfeld, Neil S. Ende, Glenn B. Manishin, Suzanne B. Pope, John DiBene, Mary E. Wand, Charon J. Harris.

Law Offices of Hal L. Bodner. 7985 Santa Monica Blvd., Suite 109-397, West Hollywood, Calif. 90046. (213) 656-9378. Hal L. Bodner.

Boelter & Perry. 330 Washington St., Suite 400, Marina Del Rey, Calif. 90292-5130. (310) 822-5037. FAX: (310) 823-4325. Al Boelter.

Bogle & Gates. 2 Union Sq., 601 Union St., Suite 4700, Seattle 98101-2346. (206) 682-5151. FAX: (206) 621-2660.

William R. Booker III. 4615 N. 19th St., Arlington, Va. 22207-2045. (703) 524-3381. William R. Booker III.

Boose, Casey, Ciklin, Lubitz, Martens, McBane & O'Connell. Northbridge Tower, Suite 1900, 515 N. Flagler Dr., West Palm Beach, Fla. 33401. (407) 832-5900. FAX: (407) 833-4209. Lynda Waldron, per dir.

Booth, Freret & Imlay. 1233 20th St. N.W., Suite 204, Washington 20036. (202) 296-9100. FAX: (202) 293-1319. Julian P. Freret, Christopher D. Imlay.

Bordelon, Hamlin & Theriot. 701 S. Peters St., New Orleans 70130. (504) 524-5328. FAX: (504) 523-1071. Regina Wedig.

Borsari & Kump P.C. Box 19205, 2000 L St. N.W., Suite 200, Washington 20036. (202) 775-1100. FAX: (202) 775-1625. John A. Borsari, Edward R. Kump.

Borsari & Paxson. 2033 M St. N.W., Suite 630, Washington 20036. (202) 296-4800. FAX: (202) 296-4460. George R. Borsari Jr., Anne Thomas Paxson.

Boult, Cummings, Conners & Berry. Box 198062, 222 3rd Ave. N., Nashville 37219. (615) 252-2363. FAX: (615) 252-2380. Daniel R. Loftus.

Bowie, Nolan A. Temple Univ., Dept. of Radio, TV & Film, 448 W. School House Ln., Philadelphia 19144. (215) 204-8394.

Law Offices of Timothy K. Brady. Box 986, 7113 Peach Ct., Suite 208, Brentwood, Tenn. 37027-0986. (615) 371-9367. Timothy K. Brady.

Brann & Isaacson. Box 3070, 184 Main St., Lewiston, Me. 04243. (207) 786-3566. FAX: (207) 783-9325. Alfred C. Frawley.

Branscomb, Anne Wells. Box 309, Concord, Mass. 01742. (508) 369-1878. Anne Wells Branscomb

Branson, Robert E. Post-Newsweek Stations Inc., 1150 15th St. N.W., Washington 20071. (202) 334-4615. Robert E. Branson.

Brantley, Robert. U.S. Federal Communications Commission, 1919 M St. N.W., Rm. 332, Washington 20554. (202) 632-4504. FAX: (202) 632-0158.

Brass, Eric A. WGBH TV & Radio. 125 Western Ave., Boston 02134-1098. (617) 492-2777 ext. 4405. FAX: (617) 782-7969.

Breakstone, Douglas M. 36 Mill Plain Rd., Suite 209, Danbury, Conn. 06811. (203) 748-6400. FAX: (203) 748-7696. Douglas M. Breakstone.

Brecher, Howard A. 220 E. 42nd St., 6th Fl., New York 10017. (212) 907-1500. FAX: (212) 661-2807.

Brenner, Daniel L. National Cable Television Association. 1724 Massachusetts Ave. N.W., Washington 20036. (202) 775-3664. FAX: (202) 775-3603. Daniel L. Brenner.

Brickfield, Burchette & Ritts. West Tower, 8th Fl., 1025 Thomas Jefferson St. N.W., Suite 915, Washington 20007. (202) 342-0800. Peter Mattheis

Brinig & Bernstein. 1818 N St. N.W., Suite 200, Washington 20036. (202) 331-7050. FAX: (202) 331-9306. F. Joseph Brinig, Lawrence Bernstein.

Frederic E. Brown, Attorney at Law. Box 71718, Fairbanks, Alaska 99707. (907) 452-3452. Frederic E. Brown.

Brown, Herman, Scott, Dean & Miles. 200 Fort Worth Club Bldg., 306 W. 7th St., Fort Worth, Tex. 76102-4905. (817) 332-1391. FAX: (817) 870-2427. Morton L. Herman.

Brown, J. Bruce. U.S. Chamber of Commerce, 1615 H St. N.W., Washington 20026. (202) 463-5337.

Brown, Nietert, & Kaufman, Chartered. 1920 N St. N.W., Suite 660, Washington 20036. (202) 887-0600. FAX: (202) 457-0126. Richard L. Brown, Robyn S. Nietert, David J. Kaufman, Eric S. Kravetz, Lorretta K. Tobin.

Brown, Pamela J. Corporation for Public Broadcasting. 901 E St. N.W. Washington 20004. (202) 879-9701.

Brown & Schwaninger. 1835 K St. N.W., Suite 650, Washington 20006. (202) 223-8837. FAX: (202) 659-0071. Dennis C. Brown, Robert H. Schwaninger Jr, Kathlee, A. Kaercher.

Brown, Stephen S. 106 Avondale St., Houston 77006-3314. (713) 522-8686.

Brown, Steve Ames. Box 14515, 69 Grand View Ave., San Francisco 94114-2741. (415) 647-7700.

Law Offices of Tom Watson Brown. 2110 Cain Tower, 229 Peachtree St. N.E., Atlanta 30303. (404) 525-3311. Tom Watson Brown.

Bryan Cave. 700 13th St. N.W., Suite 700, Washington 20005. (202) 508-6000. FAX: (202) 508-6200. Edward S. O'Neill, John R. Wilner, John G. Johnson Jr., Carl W. Northrop, Jack R. Smith, Caroline B. Kahl, Rebecca L. Dorch, Sandra K. Danner, E. Ashton Johnston.

Bubar, James S., Attorney at Law. 1050 17th St. N.W., Suite 830, Washington 20036. (202) 223-2060. FAX: (202) 955-3111. James S. Bubar.

Law Offices of Robert J. Buenzle. 12110 Sunset Hills Rd., Suite 450, Reston, Va. 22090. (703) 715-3006. FAX: (703) 476-0218. Robert Buenzle.

Bullivant, Houser, Bailey, Pendergraff & Hoffman. 300 Pioneer Tower, 888 S.W. 5th Ave., Portland, Ore. 97204. (503) 228-6351. FAX: (503) 295-0915. Carol O'Connell.

Bulmash, Jay S. Box 580, Seal Beach, Calif. 90740-0580. (310) 430-1437. FAX: (310) 431-0455.

Burns, Barbara. Greater Media Inc. Box 1059, 2 Kennedy Blvd. East Brunswick, N.J. 08816-1248. (908) 247-6161.

Burton & Associates P.C. 5301 Hollister St., Houston 77040-6119. (713) 462-3838. FAX: (713) 462-4848. Louis W. Burton.

Bustard, R. David. 7401 Hemlock Ln., Sarasota, Fla. 34241. (813) 366-5282.

Byelas & Neigher. 1804 Post Rd. E., East Westport, Conn. 06880. (203) 259-0599. FAX: (203) 255-2570. Alan Neigher.

C

Cade & Vaughn-Carrington. 600 New Hampshire Ave. N.W., Suite 1111, Washington 20037. (202) 333-2946. FAX: (202) 625-0662. Debra M. Vaughn-Carrington.

Cades, Schutte, Fleming & Wright. Box 939, 1000 Bishop St., Honolulu 96808. (808) 521-9200. FAX: (808) 531-8738. Jeffrey S. Portnoy.

Cahill, Gordon & Reindel. 1990 K St. N.W., Suite 950, Washington 20006. (202) 862-8950. FAX: (202) 862-8958. Donald J. Mulvihill, Kathy Silberthau Strom.
  New York 10005: 80 Pine St. (212) 701-3000. Floyd Abrams, H. Richard Schumacher.

Calfee, Halter & Griswold. 800 Superior Ave., Suite 1800, Cleveland 44114. (216) 622-8200. FAX: (216) 241-0816.

Callister, Duncan & Nebeker. Kennecott Bldg., Suite 800, Salt Lake City 84133. (801) 530-7300. FAX: (801) 364-9127. Dorothy C. Pleshe.

Cameron, John F. 566 S. Perry St., Montgomery, Ala. 36102. (205) 263-0322.

Cameron & Mittleman. 56 Exchange Terr., Providence, R.I. 02903-1766. (401) 331-5700. FAX: (401) 331-5787. E. Colby Cameron, David L. Mayer, Amy L. Mower.

Capell, Howard, Knabe & Cobbs. Box 2069, 57 Adams Ave., Montgomery, Ala. 36102-2069. (205) 241-8000. FAX: (205) 265-7454. Robert S. Richard.

Carey, Nancy B. MRC Telecommunications, 275 N. Corporate Dr., Brookfield, Wis. 53045-5818. (414) 792-7730. FAX: (414) 792-7733. Nancy B. Carey, pres.

Caridi Entertainment. 250 W. 57th St., Suite 1416, New York 10107-0001. (212) 581-2277. FAX: (212) 581-2278. Carmella Caridi, Peter Hargrove.

Carlisle & Lecates. 415 S.E. 12th St., Fort Lauderdale, Fla. 33316-1999. (305) 764-4000. FAX: (305) 525-9604. William Lecates.

Carr, Morris & Graeff. 1120 G St. N.W., Washington 20005. (202) 789-1000. FAX: (202) 628-3834. Lawrence E. Carr III.

Carter, Ledyard & Milburn. 1350 I St. N.W., Suite 870, Washington 20005. (202) 898-1515. FAX: (202) 898-1521. Robert L. Hoegle, Timothy J. Fitzgibbon, Thomas F. Bardo.

Peter A. Casciato P.C. 1500 Sansome St., Suite 201, San Francisco 94111. (415) 291-8661. FAX: (415) 291-8165. Peter A. Casciato.

Cass, Ronald A. 36 Forest St., Wellesley Hills, Mass. 02181. (617) 237-9790. FAX: (617) 353-5995.

Edward de R. Cayia, P.A. 432 N.E. 3rd Ave., Fort Lauderdale, Fla. 33301-3234. (305) 765-1400.

Chadbourne & Parke. 1101 Vermont Ave. N.W., Suite 900, Washington 20005. (202) 289-3000. FAX: (202) 289-3002. Keith Martin.
  New York 10112: 30 Rockefeller Plaza. (212) 408-5100.
  Los Angeles 90017: 601 S. Figueroa St. (213) 892-1000.

Chapman & Moran. 3 Landmark Sq., Stamford, Conn. 06901. (203) 353-8000. Brian E. Moran, John Haven Chapman.

Charnay, John B. 900 Exposition Blvd., Los Angeles 90007-3307. (213) 744-3538. John B. Charnay.

Chasen & Lichter. 1740 Broadway, New York 10019-4315. (212) 582-0888. Rosaland Lichter.
  Santa Fe, N.M. 87501: Chasen & Lichter, 230 Montoya Cir. (505) 982-1122. FAX: (505) 982-1191.

Chesser, James P. MWC America Bldg. 1710 Grand Ave., Nashville 37212-2206. (615) 321-3020. FAX (615) 321-8575.

Chetkof, Gary H. 118 Tinker St., Woodstock, N.Y. 12498. (914) 679-7266. FAX: (914) 679-5395.

Chrystie & Berle. 1925 Century Park E., Suite 2200, Los Angeles 90067-2723. (310) 788-7700. FAX: (310) 201-0436.

Clark, Klein & Beaumont. 1600 First Federal Bldg., 1001 Woodward Ave., Detroit 48226-1962. (313) 965-8300. FAX: (313) 962-4348. David E. Nims.

Law Firms Active in Communications Law

Clark & Stant. 900 One Columbus Ctr., Virginia Beach, Va. 23462. (804) 499-8800 - main office; (804) 473-5380. FAX: (804) 473-0395.

Clark, Waldemar H. Box 821, 3008 Rolling Acres Pl., Valrico, Fla. 33594-5651. (813) 681-6204.

Claro & Claro. 6305 Waterford Blvd., Suite 410, Oklahoma City 73118-1120. (405) 843-4074. FAX: (405) 843-4371. John A. Claro.

Clarvit, Richard N. 1313 N.E. 125th St., North Miami, Fla., 33161. (305) 893-4135. FAX: (305) 893-4173.

Coffman, Gordon C. U.S. Federal Communications Commission, 1919 M St. N.W., Rm. 610, Washington 20554. (202) 632-7220. Gordon C. Coffman.

Cohen & Berfield P.C. 1129 20th St. N.W., Suite 507, Washington 20036. (202) 466-8565. FAX: (202) 785-0934. Lewis I. Cohen, Morton L. Berfield, John J. Schauble.

Cohen, Eric J. 301 Bainbridge St., Philadelphia 19147-1543. (215) 574-2900. FAX: (215) 440-7367. Eric J. Cohen.

Cohen, Swados, Wright, Hanifin, Bradford & Brett. 70 Niagara St., Buffalo, N.Y. 14202. (716) 856-4600. FAX: (716) 856-5228. Thomas J. Hanifin.

Colby, Lauren A. Box 113, 10 E. 4th St., Frederick, Md. 21701. (301) 663-1086. FAX: (301) 695-8734.

Cole, Raywid & Braverman. 1919 Pennsylvania Ave. N.W., Suite 200, Washington 20006. (202) 659-9750. FAX: (202) 452-0067. John P. Cole Jr., Wesley R. Heppler, James F. Ireland III, Robert L. James, Joseph R. Reifer, David M. Silverman, Burt A. Braverman, Frances J. Chetwynd, Paul Glist, Steven J. Horvitz, Robert G. Scott, Susan W. Westfall, Theresa A. Zeterberg, John D. Thomas.

Collier, Shannon, Rill & Scott. 3050 K St. N.W., Washington 20007. (202) 342-8400. FAX: (202) 333-5534. T. Michael Jankowski, Daniel J. Harrold, Paul D. Cullen, James R. Loftis III.

Collins, Kathleen J. U.S. Federal Communications Commission, 1919 M St. N.W., Rm. 658, Washington 20554. (202) 632-0935.

Conner & Chopnick. 12 E. 41st St., 6th Fl., New York 10017. (212) 696-1050. FAX: (212) 696-1059.

Conrad, Diane W. 2623 Myrtle Springs Ave., Dallas 75220-2514. (214) 358-2623. FAX: (214) 358-0185.

Cook, Yancey, King & Galloway. Box 22260, Shreveport, La. 71120-2260. (318) 221-6277.

Cooper, Epstein & Hurewitz. 345 N. Maple Dr., Suite 200, Beverly Hills, Calif. 90210. (310) 278-1111. FAX: (310) 271-0307.

Cooper, White & Cooper. 201 California St., 17th Fl., San Francisco 94111. (415) 433-1900. FAX: (415) 433-5530. Walter W. Hansell, Mark P. Schreiber, Karen L. Holm, Jed E. Solomon.

The Cooter Law Firm. Alleco Bldg. Allegney Cir., Cheverly, Md. 20781. (301) 322-6600. FAX: (301) 322-6613.

Corber, Brian L. Box 44212, Panorama City, Calif. 91402. (818) 786-7133. Brian L. Corber.

Law Offices of Bernard R. Corbett. 1750 Pennsylvania Ave. N.W., Suite 1201, Washington 20006. (202) 393-0300. FAX: (202) 393-0363.

Cordon & Kelly. Box 6648 Annapolis, Md. 21401. (202) 293-2300; (410) 280-6290. FAX: (410) 626-1794. Dennis J. Kelly; Alfred C. Cordon, of counsel (both D.C. Bar only).

Cornell, Diane J. U.S. Federal Communications Commission, 1919 M St. N.W., Rm. 534, Washington 20554. (202) 632-3214. FAX: (202) 634-1382.

Corn-Revere, Robert L. U.S. Federal Communications Commission, 1919 M St. N.W., Rm. 802, Washington 20554. (202) 632-7557.

Law Offices of Jeremiah Courtney. 2120 L St. N.W., Washington 20037. (202) 659-0830. FAX: (202) 828-5568.

Couzens, Michael. 385 8th St., 2nd Fl., San Francisco 94103. (415) 621-4030.

Covington & Burling. Box 7566, 1201 Pennsylvania Ave. N.W., Washington 20044. (202) 662-6000. FAX: (202) 662-6291. Paul J. Berman, Jonathan Dewey Blake, E. Edward Bruce, Michael T. Buckley, Edgar F. Czarra Jr., Nicholas W. Fels, Francis R. Hawkins Jr., Janet E. Milne, Gregory M. Schmidt.

Cowan, Liebowitz & Latman P.C. 605 3rd Ave., New York 10158. (212) 503-6200. FAX: (212) 986-2390. Sidney I. Liebowitz, Simon Gerson, Dorothy R. Whitney.

Crane, David W. 2787 E. Oakland Park Blvd., Suite 404, Fort Lauderdale, Fla. 33306. (305) 565-4848. FAX: (305) 565-4866.

Law Offices of Henry E. Crawford. 1150 Connecticut Ave. N.W., Suite 900, Washington 20036. (202) 862-4395. FAX: (202) 659-3493. Henry Crawford.

Cromer & Mabry. Box 11675, 1225 Pickens St., Columbia, S.C. 29201-3427. (803) 799-9530. FAX: (803) 799-9533. J. Lewis Cromer.

Crooks, Leonard William. 300 Poydras, Suite 1026, New Orleans 70130. (504) 528-9221.

Crowell & Moring. 1001 Pennsylvania Ave. N.W., Washington 20004-2505. (202) 624-2500. FAX: (202) 628-5116. John I. Stewart Jr., Linda K. Smith, John T. Scott III, Robert M. Halperin, William D. Wallace.

Culp, Guterson & Grader. One Union Sq., 27th Fl., 600 University St., Seattle 98101-3143. (206) 624-7141. FAX: (206) 624-5128. Richard C. Yarmuth.

D

D'Ancona & Pflaum. 30 N. LaSalle St., Suite 2900, Chicago 60602. (312) 580-2050. FAX: (312) 580-0923. Paul H. Vishny, Joel D. Rubin (312) 580-2080.

Dantes, David C. 6922 Hollywood Blvd., Los Angeles 90028-6117. (213) 463-1199. FAX: (213) 461-7151.

Law Offices of George E. Darby. Box 61450, Honolulu 96839-1450. (808) 955-1445. FAX: (808) 955-2936.

Daronco, Peter J. U.S. Federal Communications Commission, 2025 M St. N.W., Rm. 5202, Washington 20554. (202) 632-6497.

David, Jonathan. 1515 N. Courthouse Rd., Suite 301, Arlington, Va. 22201. (703) 276-9007. FAX: (703) 276-9008.

Davis, Miner, Barnhill & Galland. 14 W. Erie St., Chicago 60610-3811. (312) 751-1170. FAX: (312) 751-0438. Allison S. Davis.

Davis, T. Martin. 212 Center St., 10th Fl., Little Rock, Ark. 72201-2429. (501) 374-1229. FAX: (501) 374-5463.

Davis, Wright, & Tremaine. 2600 Century Sq., 1501 4th Ave., Seattle 98101-1688. (206) 622-3150. FAX: (206) 628-7040. P. Cameron Devore, Marshall Nelson, Daniel Waggoner, Bruce E.H. Johnson, Craig A. Gannett, Richard S. Wyde.
Portland, Ore. 97201: 2300 First Interstate Tower, 1300 S.W. 5th Ave. (503) 241-2300. FAX: (503) 778-5299. Duane A. Bosworth.
Washington 20004-2608: 701 Pennsylvania Ave. N.W., Suite 600. (202) 508-6600. FAX: (202) 508-6699. Edward Cohen, Caryn L. Zimmerman, Stuart F. Pierson.

Day, Berry & Howard. City Place I, Hartford, Conn. 06103-3499. (203) 275-0122. FAX: (203) 275-0343. Robert P. Knickerbocker, Jr.

DeBare, Charles A. 47 E. 88th St., New York 10128-1152. (212) 348-7109.

Debevoise & Plimpton. 875 3rd Ave., New York 10022. (212) 909-6000. James C. Goodale, John G. Koeltl, Bruce Keller.

Washington 20004: 555 13th St. N.W., Suite 1100-E. (202) 383-8000. Robert R. Bruce, Jeffrey P. Cunard, Mark D.

Decker, Jones, McMackin, McClane, Hall & Bates. 301 Commerce St., Suite 2400, Fort Worth, Tex. 76102-4140. (817) 336-2400. FAX: (817) 336-2181; (817) 332-3043. Jeffrey W. Storie.

Defeis, Elizabeth F. Seton Hall University Law School, 1111 Raymond Blvd., Newark, N.J. 07102. (201) 642-8500.

Del, Rubel, Shaw, Mason & Derin. 2029 Century Park, Suite 3910, Los Angeles 90067-3025. (310) 770-2000. FAX: (310) 772-2777.

Delsack, Kurt. 4695 MacArthur Ct., Suite 1040, Newport Beach, Calif. 92660. (714) 553-8002. FAX: (714) 752-2464. Kurt Delsack.

Denechaud & Denechaud. 1412 Pere Marquette Bldg., New Orleans 70112. (504) 522-4756. FAX: (504) 568-0783. Charles I. Denechaud III.

Devine, Millimet & Branch. Box 719, 111 Amherst St., Manchester, N.H. 03101-1809. (603) 669-1000. FAX: (603) 669-8547. Karen Solomon McGinley.

Dickerson, Dickerson, Lieberman & Consul. 330 S. 3rd St., Suite 1130, Las Vegas 89101. (702) 388-8600. FAX: (702) 388-0210. Luke Puschnig.

Dickler, Gerald. 230 Park Ave., New York 10169. (212) 687-4020. FAX: (212) 557-9810.

Dickstein, Shapiro & Morin. 2101 L St. N.W., Washington 20037. (202) 785-9700. FAX: (202) 887-0689. Walter J. Walvick.

Dieguez, Richard P. 192 Garden St., Suite 2, Roslyn Heights, N.Y. 11577. (516) 621-6424. FAX: (516) 621-6469. Richard P. Dieguez.

Dierker, Robert A. Library of Congress, 101 Independence Ave S.E., Washington 20540. (202) 707-6151. FAX: (202) 707-1567.

Dinkspiel, Donovan & Reder. One Embarcadero Ctr., Suite 2701, San Francisco 94111. (415) 788-1100. FAX: (415) 397-5949. David Michael Wilson.

Doherty, Rumble & Butler. 150 S. 5th St., Suite 3500, Minneapolis 55402. (612) 340-5555. FAX: (612) 340-5584. C. Robert Beattie, Allan I. Silver, Keyna P. Skeffington, Don W. Niles.
Washington 20036: 1625 M St. N.W. (202) 293-0555. Helen Starr, Communications Law Dept.

Donnella, Michael A. 295 N. Maple Ave., Basking Ridge, N.J. 07920-1002. (201) 762-2484.

Donrey Media Group. Box 17017, 3600 Wheeler, Fort Smith, Ark. 72917. (501) 785-7810. FAX: (501) 785-9430. David M. Olive.

William S. Dorman & Associates. 1146 E. 64th St., Tulsa, Okla. 74136-2239. (918) 747-1080. FAX: (918) 747-1105.

Dorsey & Whitney. 220 S. 6th St., Minneapolis 55402. (612) 340-2600. Gary M. Johnson.

Dow, Lohnes & Albertson. 1255 23rd St. N.W., Washington 20037. (202) 857-2500. FAX: (202) 857-2900. Corinne M. Antley, Michael D. Basile, Raymond G. Bender Jr., John R. Feore Jr., Todd D. Gray, Ralph W. Hardy Jr., Werner K. Hartenberger, Thomas J. Hutton, John S. Logan, Arnold P. Lutzker, Richard D. Marks, B. Dwight Perry, Suzanne M. Perry, Laura H. Phillips, J. Christopher Redding, Kevin F. Reed, Michael Schooler, Kenneth S. Salomon, Daniel W. Toohey, James A. Treanor, David J. Wittenstein, Nancy L. Wolf, D'Wana Speight, Peter Feinberg, Brenda L. Fox, J.G. Harrington, Leonard Kennedy, Elizabeth McGeary, Margaret Miller.
Atlanta 30346: One Ravinia Dr., Suite 1600. (404) 901-8800.

Dowd, Diane. 3220 N St., Suite 176, Washington 20007. (202) 342-0719.

Downs, Bertis E. Box 625, Athens, Ga. 30603-0625. (404) 353-6689.

Dreilinger, David A. 31 W. 56th St., New York 10019-3902. (212) 245-4680. David A. Dreilinger.

Dreyfuss, Kenneth R. 1901 Brickell Ave., Suite B901, Miami, Fla. 33129. (305) 227-2155. FAX: (305) 227-2156. Kenneth R. Dreyfuss.

Law Office of David M. Drucker. Box 255, Evergreen, Colo. 80439. (303) 674-7047. FAX: (303) 751-5993.

Dunham, Corydon B. Counsel. Cahill, Gordon & Reindel, 1990 K St. N.W., Suite 950, Washington 20006.

(202) 862-8950. FAX: (202) 862-8958. Corydon B. Dunham.

Dwyer, James Jr. 2100 Electronics Ln., Fort Myers, Fla. 33912. (813) 489-1600. FAX: (813) 489-1622.

Dyer, Ellis, Joseph & Mills. 600 New Hampshire Ave. N.W., Suite 1000, Washington 20037. (202) 944-3040. FAX: (202) 944-3068. James Ellis.

E

Easley & Willits, P.A. 1655 Palm Beach Lakes Blvd., Suite 800, West Palm Beach, Fla. 33401. (407) 684-7300. H. Michael Easley, sr ptnr.

Eaton, Peabody, Bradford & Veague. Box 1210, Fleet Ctr. Exchange, Bangor, Me. 04402. (207) 942-0111. FAX: (207) 942-3040.

Edstrom, Thomas H. 6352 Vineland Ave., Suite 160, North Hollywood, Calif. 91606. (213) 464-4463.

Edwards & Angell. 101 Federal St., Boston 02110-1810. (617) 439-4444. FAX: (617) 439-4170. Elizabeth H. Munnell, Stephen O. Meridith.
Specializing in communications finance, mergers & acquisitions; representing operators, as well as institutions & investor groups, which lend to, or invest in, cable & bcst industries.

Effros, Stephen R. Box 1005, Fairfax, Va. 22030-1005. (703) 691-8875. FAX: (703) 691-8911. Stephen R. Effros.

Elam, Burke & Boyd. Box 1539, Key Financial Ctr., 10th Fl., 702 W. Idaho St., Boise, Idaho 83701. (208) 343-5454. FAX: (208) 384-5844. William Batt.

Elias, Edward G. 1720 Merriman Rd., Akron, Ohio 44313-5252. (216) 867-4920. FAX: (216) 869-6682.

Ende, Neil. 1615 M St. N.W., Washington 20036-3209. (202) 955-6300. FAX: (202) 955-6460.

Epstein, Levy & Levinsohn P.C. 1780 Broadway, Suite 1200, New York 10019. (212) 765-5038. FAX: (212) 262-2937. Robert J. Epstein.

Ezor, A. Edward. 201 S. Lake Ave., Suite 505, Pasadena, Calif. 91101-3004. (818) 568-8098.

F

Faegre & Benson. 400 Capital Sq., 400 Locust St., Des Moines, Iowa 50309. (515) 248-9000. FAX: (515) 248-9010. Michael A. Giudicessi.

Farmer, Shirley. One Lincoln Plaza, New York 10023-7129. (212) 787-6566.

Farquhar, Michele. U.S. Federal Communications Commission, 1919 M St. N.W., Room 832, Washington 20554. (202) 632-6996.

Farrand, Cooper & Bruiniers P.C. 235 Montgomery St., Suite 1035, San Francisco 94104. (415) 399-0600. FAX: (415) 677-2950. Wayne B. Cooper, Terence L. Bruiniers, Stephen R. Farrand.

Farrow, Bramson, Chavez & Baskin. 2125 Oak Grove Rd., Suite 120, Walnut Creek, Calif. 94598. (510) 945-0200. FAX: (510) 945-8792. Harold R. Farrow, Robert M. Bramson, Anne M. Ronan.

Feldman, Lindsey S. 100 Wilshire Blvd., 20th Fl., Santa Monica, Calif. 90401. (310) 393-5345. FAX: (310) 395-8782. Lindsey S. Feldman.

Ferris & Britton. 1855 1st Ave., Suite 300, San Diego 92101. (619) 233-3131. William M. Winter, Alfred G. Ferris.

Fields & Director. 1001 Pennsylvania Ave. N.W., Suite 250 N., Washington 20004. (202) 628-7000.

Fine & Associates. 335-337 Decatur St., Vieux Carre, New Orleans 70130-1023. (504) 581-5152. FAX: (504) 581-5152, ext. 124. David Fine.

Fine & Block. 2060 Mt. Paran Rd. N.W., Suite 106, Atlanta 30327. (404) 261-6800. A.J. Block Jr.

Finkelstein, Thompson & Loughlan. 2828 Pennsylvania Ave. N.W., Suite 200, Washington 20007. (202) 337-8000. FAX: (202) 965-9363. Douglas G. Thompson Jr.

Law Offices of Charles M. Firestone. 1755 Massachusetts Ave. N.W., Suite 501, Washington 20036. (202) 736-5810. FAX: (202) 986-1913. Charles M. Firestone.

Firestone, Richard M. U.S. Federal Communications Commission, 1919 M St. N.W., Rm. 500, CCB, Washington 20554. (202) 632-7000; (202) 632-6910.

Fischbein, Badillo, Wagner, & Hzler. 909 3rd Ave., New York 10023-7129. (212) 826-2000. David G. Lubell.

Fisher, Wayland, Cooper & Leader. 1255 23rd St. N.W., Suite 800, Washington 20037-1170. (202) 659-3494. FAX: (202) 296-6518. Ben C. Fisher; Grover C. Cooper; Martin R. Leader; Richard R. Zaragoza; Clifford M. Harrington; Kathyrn R. Schmeltzer; David D. Oxenford; Ann K. Ford; Bruce D. Jacobs; Eliot J. Greenwald; Carroll John Yung; John Joseph McVeigh; Scott R. Flick; Francisco R. Montero; Gregory L. Masters; Matthew P. Zinn; Robert C. Fisher; Lauren Ann Lynch; Brian J. Carter; Kelly D. Yaksich; Glenn S. Richards; John M. Burgett; Sharon L. Tasman; Theresa A. Smyth; Julie Arthur Garcia; John Q. Hearne, of counsel.

Fishkin, Kenneth R. 50 Milk St., 20th Fl., Boston 02109-5002. (617) 423-5800. Kenneth R. Fishkin.

Fitch & Tourse. One Bowdin Sq., Boston 02114. (617) 557-3700. FAX: (617) 557-3799. Melvin B. Miller.

Fitelson, Lasky, Aslan & Couture. 551 5th Ave., New York 10176-0001. (212) 586-4700. FAX: (212) 949-6746. Jerold L. Couture.

Fleischman & Walsh. 1400 16th St. N.W., Washington 20036. (202) 939-7900. FAX: (202) 745-0916. Aaron I. Fleischman, Charles S. Walsh, Arthur H. Harding. Stuart F. Feldstein, Richard Rubin, Jeffry L. Hardin, Stephen A. Bouchard, R. Bruce Beckner, Robert J. Keller, Howard S. Shapiro, Christopher G. Wood, Seth A. Davidson, Matthew D. Emmer, Jonathan R. Spencer, David D. Burns, Jill Kleppe McClelland, Mark J. O'Connor, Steven N. Teplitz, Peter T. Noone.

Fletcher, Heald & Hildreth. 1300 N. 17th St., 11th Fl., Rosslyn, Va., 22209. Box 33847, Washington 20036. (703) 812-0400. FAX: (703) 812-0486. Richard Hildreth, Howard Weiss, Marvin Rosenberg, James P. Riley, Edward W. Hummers Jr., Leonard R. Raish, Vincent J. Curtis Jr., George Petrutsas, James G. Ennis, Patricia A. Mahoney, Thomas J. Dougherty Jr., Frank R. Jazzo, Barry Lambergman, Anne Goodwin Crump, Lonna M. Thompson, Paul Feldman, Kathleen Victory, M. Veronica Pastor, Cathryn Kleiman, Edward A. Caine, Charles H. Kennedy.

Fletcher, Michael W. 6500 Wilshire Blvd., 17th Fl., Los Angeles 90048-3103. (213) 852-1000. FAX: (213) 651-2577.

Foley & Lardner. First Wisconsin Plaza, One S. Pinckney St., Madison, Wis. 53703-2808. (608) 257-5035. FAX: (608) 258-4258. Robert M. Whitney.

Foley, Robert M. 1150 Connecticut Ave. N.W., Suite 900, Washington 20036. (202) 223-6464. FAX: (202) 331-3206.

Saul Foos & Associates. 867 N. Dearborn St., 1st Fl., Chicago 60610-3371. (312) 642-0454. FAX: (312) 266-7145. Saul Foos.

Milton Q. Ford & Associates Inc. 4006 Baronne Way, Memphis 38117. (901) 767-7980.

Forman, Sandra G. 20 Winthrip, Boston 02110. (617) 542-0050.

Formato, Richard A. 116 Stiles Rd., Boylston, Mass. 01505. (508) 869-6077. FAX: (508) 869-2890. Richard A. Formato, Esquire.

Forrest, Herbert E. 8706 Bellwood Rd., Bethesda, Md. 20817. (202) 514-2809. Herbert E. Forrest.

Fowler, Measle & Bell. Kincaid Towers, 300 W. Vine St., Suite 650, Lexington, Ky. 40507-1660. (606) 252-6700. FAX: (606) 255-3735. Elizabeth S. Feamster.

Fox, Timothy. Box 5510, North Little Rock, Ark. 72119. (501) 377-7366.

Frankl, Kenneth R. 45 Christopher St., New York 10014. (212) 924-4275.

Franklin/Waterman Entertainment. 2644 30th St., 1st Fl., Santa Monica, Calif. 90405-3009. (310) 452-9100. FAX: (310) 452-1771. Franklin Burton.

Franzblau, Dratch & Friedman. 3 ADP Blvd., Roseland, N.J. 07068. (201) 992-3700.

Freer & Alagia, Chartered. 1000 Thomas Jefferson St. N.W., Suite 600, Washington 20007. (202) 965-6565. FAX: (202) 965-4839. Robert E. Freer Jr., Claybome E. Chavers.

Friedman, Howard D. 525 Rt. 73 S., Suite 200, Marlton, N.J. 07067. (609) 596-1021. FAX: (609) 596-6060.

Friedman, Rob. 348 W. Crestview Ave., Boalsburg, Pa. 16827. (814) 466-7745. FAX: (814) 863-8044. Rob Friedman, atty/consultant.

Frisby, Michael L. 280 S. Beverly Dr., Beverly Hills, Calif. 90212-3907. (310) 858-8330. FAX: (310) 859-9339.

Frost, Mark E. Box 153, Glens Falls, N.Y. 12801-0153. (518) 792-1126.

Frumkin, Shralow & Cerullo P.C. 1760 Market St., 12th Fl., Philadelphia 19103. (215) 636-0400. FAX: (215) 636-0523. Abraham H. Frumkin, M. Melvin Shralow, Martin J. Cerullo, Edward DeMarco Jr.

G

Gammon & Grange P.C. 8280 Greensboro Dr., 7th Fl., McLean, Va. 22102-3807. (703) 761-5000. FAX: (703) 761-5023. James A. Gammon, George R. Grange II, A. Wray Fitch III, Richard M. Campanelli, H. Robert Showers, Nancy Oliver LeSourd, Michael J. Woodruff, Peter F. Rathbun.

Gantt, John B. 1025 Thomas Jefferson St. N.W., Suite 500 E, Washington 20007. (202) 944-3212.

Ganz, Hollinger & Towe. 1394 3rd Ave., New York 10021-0465. (212) 517-5500. FAX: (212) 772-2720. Terri Towe.

Gardere & Wynne. Thanksgiving Tower, 1601 Elm St., Suite 3000, Dallas 75201-4761. (214) 999-3000. FAX: (214) 999-4967.

Gardner, Carton & Douglas. East Tower, 1301 K. St. N.W., Suite 900, Washington 20005. (202) 408-7100. FAX: (202) 289-1504. Francis E. Fletcher Jr., M. Scott Johnson, Edward P. Taptich, James S. Blaszak, Grier C. Raclin, John E. Fiorini III, Charles C. Hunter, Patrick J. Whittle, James K. Edmundson, Russell H. Fox, Mark Van Bergh, Laura C. Mow, Kevin S. DiLallo, Pamela C. Cooper, Catherine M. Withers, Peter D. Shields.

Law Offices of Michael R. Gardner P.C. 1150 Connecticut Ave. N.W., Suite 710, Washington 20036. (202) 785-2828. FAX: (202) 785-1504. Michael R. Gardner, Charles R. Milkis.

Allen Garner. 320 E. McCarty St., Jefferson City, Mo. 65101-3115. (314) 634-6313. FAX: (314) 634-6329.

Gartrell, Alexander & Gebhardt. 8601 Georgia Ave., Suite 805, Silver Spring, Md. 20910. (301) 589-2222. FAX: (301) 589-2523. James L. Bearden, J. Darrell Peterson, Stephanie Bradley.

Garvey, Schubert & Barer. 1191 2nd Ave., 18th Fl., Seattle 98101-2939. (206) 464-3939. FAX: (206) 464-0125. Keven J. Davis.

Gay, Maher, & Brown. 111 Broadway, 7th Fl., New York 10006. (212) 587-0300. FAX: (212) 732-1522.

Geer, Dr. LouAnn S. Univ. of California, John E. Anderson Graduate School of Management, 405 Hilgard Ave., Los Angeles 90024-1481. (310) 206-4052.

Gelfan, Gregory. Paramount Pictures, 5555 Melrose Ave., Los Angeles 90038. (213) 956-5000. FAX: (213) 956-2007.

Gerst, Heffner, Carpenter & Precup. 1700 K St., Suite 1107, Washington 20006. (202) 659-0026. John D. Heffner. (202) 293-3319.

Thomas G. Gherardi P.C. 1229 19th St. N.W., Washington 20036. (202) 223-1535. FAX: (202) 429-4912. Thomas Gherardi

Gibbs & Bressler. 1995 Broadway, New York 10023-5882. (212) 595-3514. FAX: (212) 595-3388. Bud H. Gibbs, Martin J. Bressler.

Gibson, Dunn & Crutcher. 333 S. Grand Ave., Suite 4600, Los Angeles 90071-3197. (213) 229-7000. FAX: (213) 229-7520. Ginger G. Bauer.
Washington 20036. 1050 Connecticut Ave. N.W., Suite 900. (202) 955-8500. Robert A. McConnell.

Gilbert, George T. 270 1st Ave., New York 10009-2619. (212) 213-1234. FAX: (212) 213-1245. George T. Gilbert

Gilbert & Gilbert. 10 E. 40th St., Suite 2105, New York 10016-0200. (212) 532-3140. FAX: (212) 532-3143. Harry R. Olsson Jr.

Arthur L. Ginsburg. Northern Arizona Univ., 45 Sedona View Dr., Sedona, Ariz. 86336. (602) 282-2374. Arthur L. Ginsburg, professor of communication.

Ginsburg, Feldman & Bress, Chartered. 1250 Connecticut Ave. N.W., Suite 800, Washington 20036. (202) 637-9000. FAX: (202) 637-9155. E. William Henry, Henry M. Rivera, Rodney L. Joyce, Helen N. Lavergne, Dan J. Alpert, Ann Bavender, Claudia B. Koeppel.

Law Firms Active in Communications Law

Robert A. Ginsburg P.C. 377 Main St., West Haven, Conn. 06516. (203) 934-2647. Robert A. Ginsburg.

Glover, Jerry W. 5400 N. Saint Louis Ave., Chicago 60625-4623. (312) 583-5000.

Gold, Marks, Ring & Pepper. 1800 Ave. of the Stars, Suite 300, Los Angeles 90067-4205. (310) 914-7977. Bernard Donnenfeld.

Gold, Rotatori, Schwartz & Gibbons Co. 1500 Leader Bldg., Cleveland 44114. (216) 696-6122. FAX: (216) 696-3214. William P. Gibbons.

Goldberg, Godles, Wiener & Wright. 1229 19th St. N.W., Washington 20036. (202) 429-4900. FAX: (202) 429-4912. Henry Goldberg, Joseph A. Godles, Jonathan L. Wiener, Henrietta Wright, Mary J. Dent, Daniel S. Goldberg, Thomas G. Gherardi.

Golden & Golden. 10521 Judicial Dr., Suite 305, Fairfax, Va. 22030. (703) 691-8530. FAX: (703) 691-1367. Richard A. Golden.

Golden Jubilee Commission on Telecommunications. 3001 Veazey Terr. N.W., Washington 20008. (202) 244-4525; (202) 955-4687. FAX: (202) 955-4642. Max D. Paglin, exec dir.

Goldfarb & Associates. 918 16th St. N.W., Suite 400, Washington 20006-2998. (202) 466-3030. FAX: (202) 293-3187. Ronald Goldfarb.

Glenn A. Goldstein, Attorney at Law. One Commerce Sq., 2005 Market St., 21st Fl., Philadelphia 19103. (215) 241-5061. FAX: (215) 241-1857. Glenn A. Goldstein, Esq.

Goldstein & Phillips. One Embarcadero Ctr., 8th Fl., San Francisco 94111. (415) 981-8855.

Goldstein & Schrank. 300 E. 42nd St., 7th Fl., New York 10017. (212) 972-6161. Stewart Schrank.

Goodkind, Labaton & Rudoff. 100 Park Ave, New York 10007. (212) 490-2332. FAX: (212) 818-0477. Brian Kaplin.

Graham & James. One Maritime Plaza, 3rd Fl., San Francisco 94111. (415) 954-0200. Fax: (415) 391-2493. Rachelle B. Chong, Richard L. Goldberg.

Grambow, Martin E. 1667 K St. N.W., Washington 20006-1605. (202) 293-8568. FAX: (202) 833-3297. Martin E. Grambow, VP/gen atty.

Law Offices of Jeffrey L. Graubart. 2029 Century Park E., #2020, Los Angeles 90067-3041. (310) 788-2650. FAX: (310) 788-2657. Jeffery L. Graubart, principal.

Gray, Harris & Robinson. Box 3068, 201 E. Pine St., Suite 1200, Orlando, Fla. 32801-2798. (407) 843-8880. FAX: (407) 244-5690.

Greater Media Inc. Fox Television Stations Inc., 2 Kennedy Blvd., East Brunswick, N.J. 08816. (908) 247-6161. FAX: (908) 247-4956. Philip P. Jimenez, corporate counsel; Thomas Milewski, Barbara Burns.

Greensfelder, Hemker & Gale. 1800 Equitable Bldg., 10 S. Broadway, St. Louis 63102-1774. (314) 241-9090. FAX: (314) 241-8624. Gerald R. Ortbals, John Moticka.

Greenspan, David J. 733 9th Ave., New York 10019-7289. (212) 757-4555. David Greenspan, dir business affrs.

Greiter, Pegger & Kofler. Maria Theresien-Strasse 24, A-6020, Innsbruck, 22 Austria (43-5222) 31811. (43) 512-571811; (43) 512-571812; (43) 512-588646. FAX: (43) 512-584925; (43) 512-571152. TELEX: 5-33889. TWX: 3522-314. Ivo Greiter.

Grinker, Ronald L. 7605 Production Dr., Cincinnati 45237-3208. (513) 761-7770. FAX: (513) 761-7772.

Law Office of Milton J. Grossman. 1730 K St. N.W., Suite 1000, Washington 20006. (202) 347-7002. FAX: (202) 223-9183. Milton J. Grossman.

Groveman, Amy. Cablevision Systems Corp., One Media Crossways, Woodbury, N.Y. 11797. (516) 364-8450. FAX: (516) 496-1780.

Grubb, Jay G. 5350 Wendy Rd., Sykesville, Md. 21784-6859. (410) 781-4858. FAX: (410) 781-6734. Jay G. Grubb.

Grubman, Indursky, Schindler & Goldstein P.C. 152 W. 57th St., New York 10019. (212) 554-0400. FAX: (212) 554-0444.

Gullett, Sanford, Robinson & Martin. Box 19888, 230 4th Ave. N., Nashville 37219-2187. (615) 244-4994. FAX: (615) 256-6339; (615) 242-8219. John D. Lentz.

Gundy, Nathan Murray. 14 Briar Leaf Ct., Catonsville, Md. 21228. (202) 898-0899.

Gurman, Kurtis, Blask & Freedman, Chartered. 1400 16th St. N.W., Suite 500, Washington 20036. (202) 328-8200. FAX: (202) 462-1784. Louis Gurman, Michael K. Kurtis, Jerome K. Blask, William D. Freedman, Richard M. Tettelbaum, Doame Kiechel, Robert Hoggarth, Andrea Miano, Colleen Eagen.

Gust Rosenfeld. 3300 Bank One Ctr., Phoenix 85073-3300. (602) 254-7457. FAX: (602) 254-4878. Tom Chauncey II; John Escher, Tucson office.

Gustlin, Golob & Bragin. 11755 Wilshire, Suite 1400, Los Angeles 90025-1520. (310) 477-1050. FAX: (310) 477-1010.

Guy, Patrick W. Lifetime Television, 3612 35th Ave., Astoria, N.Y. 11106-1227. (718) 482-4000. Patrick W. Guy, VP business & legal affrs.

H

Haderlein, John A. 3413 N. Lincoln Ave., Chicago 60657-1101. (312) 472-2888. Patrick W. Guy, VP business & legal affrs.

Michael Robert Hafitz. 107 Appleton St., #1, Boston 02116. (617) 536-7536. FAX: (617) 266-1649. Michael Robert Hafitz.

Haley, Bader & Potts. 4350 N. Fairfax Dr., Suite 900, Arlington, Va. 22203-1633. (202) 331-0606; (703) 841-0606. FAX: (703) 841-2345. Michael H. Bader, William J. Byrnes, John Crigler, James E. Dunstan, John Wells King, Theodore D. Kramer, David G. O'Neil, John M. Pelkey, William J. Potts Jr., Richard M. Riehl, Susan H. Rosenau, Dawn M. Scairrino, Lee W. Shubert, Henry A. Solomon, Richard H. Strodel, Melodie A. Virtue.

Hall, Dickler, Lawler, Kent & Friedman. 909 3rd Ave., New York 10022. (212) 339-5400. FAX: (212) 935-3121. Jeffrey S. Edelstein.

Halpern, Steven J. 440 Martin Ln., Beverly Hills, Calif. 90210. (310) 550-7137.

Handman, Stanley H. 10160 Cielo Dr., Beverly Hills, Calif. 90210-2037. (310) 276-7503. FAX: (310) 276-1559.

Hansen, Jacobson & Teller. 450 N. Rockbury Dr., 8th Fl., Beverly Hills, Calif. 90210-3200. (310) 271-8777. FAX: (310) 276-8310. Stephen P. Warren.

Law Offices of Kenneth E. Hardman P.C. 1255 23rd St. N.W., Suite 830, Washington 20037. (202) 223-3772. FAX: (202) 833-2416.

Harris, Barrett, Mann & Dew. Drawer 1441, St. Petersburg, Fla. 33731. (813) 892-3100. FAX: (813) 898-0227.

Harris, Beach & Wilcox. 1816 Jefferson Pl. N.W., Washington 20036-2505. (703) 528-1600. James R. Cooke.
 Buffalo, N.Y. 14202: 50 Fountain Plaza, Suite 1260. (716) 854-5300. Henry W. Killeen, III.
 Rochester, N.Y. 14604: 130 E. Main St. (716) 232-4440. Frances E. Carafell.

Harris & Berlin. 53 W. Jackson Blvd., Suite 640, Chicago 60604-3606. (312) 939-4404. FAX: (312) 939-8630. Gerald R. Berlin.

Harrison, Regina. U.S. Federal Communications Commission, 2025 M St. N.W., Rm. 8002, Washington 20554. (202) 632-7792.

Hartman, Steven H. Nabisco Inc., 7 Campus Dr., Parsippany, N.J. 07054-0311. (201) 682-5000, ext. 6163. FAX: (201) 682-6103.

Hartsfield, Paul B. 1208 Princeton Dr. N.E., Albuquerque 87106-2617. (505) 266-9969.

Hasey, Mark S. 313 Soquel Ave., #A, Santa Cruz, Calif. 95062-2305. (408) 427-2112.

Hassett, Cohen & Beitchman. 990 Hammond Dr., Suite 990, Atlanta 30328. (404) 393-0990. FAX: (404) 904-9417. Lee B. Beitchman.

Hatcher, James A. Cox Enterprises, 1400 Lake Hearn Dr. N.E., Atlanta 30319. (404) 843-5000. James Hatcher.

Hawkins, Howard R. 80 Field Point Rd., Greenwich, Conn. 06830. (203) 661-7390. FAX: (203) 629-9589.

Law Offices of Richard J. Hayes. 13809 Black Meadow Rd., Spotsylvania, Va. 22553. (703) 972-2690. FAX: (703) 972-1309. Richard J. Hayes.
 Lincolnville Me. 04849: Box 200. (207) 789-5122. FAX: (207) 789-5123.

William K. Hayes. 5225 Wilshire Blvd., Los Angeles 90036-4301. (213) 938-2112. William K. Hayes. FAX: (213) 935-6591.

Hazel & Thomas. Box 120, 3110 Fairview Park, Suite 1400, Falls Church, Va. 22042-4503. (703) 641-4200. FAX: (703) 641-4340.

Head, James M. Turner Broadcating Systems, Box 105366, One CNN Ctr., Atlanta 30348. (404) 827-1700. FAX: (404) 827-1995.

Head & Johnson. 228 W. 17th Pl., Tulsa, Okla. 74119. (918) 587-2000. FAX: (918) 587-5603. Mark G. Kachigian.

Healy, John F. 8606 Cromwell Dr., Springfield. Va. 22151. (703) 978-9068.

Hearn, Edward R. 84 W. Santa Clara St., Suite 660, San Jose, Calif. 95113-1815. (408) 998-3400.

Hearne, John Q. 100 Wilshire Blvd., Suite 1000, Santa Monica, Calif. 90401. (310) 451-4430. FAX: (310) 451-1423.

Hebert & Spencer. 701 Laurel St., Baton Rouge 70802. (504) 344-2601. FAX: (504) 387-1714. Charles L. Spencer, mng ptnr.

Hecker, Stuart. 521 5th Ave., New York 10175. (212) 682-7070. FAX: (212) 949-9835.

Hedman, Gibson & Costigan. 1185 Ave. of the Americas, New York 10036. (212) 302-8989. FAX: (212) 302-8998.

Helland, Lauritz Sande. 3400 188th St. S.W., Lynnwood, Wash. 98037-4708. (206) 744-6107. Lauritz Sande Helland.

Heller, Ehrman, White & McAuliffe. 525 University Ave., 11th Fl., Palo Alto, Calif. (415) 324-7044. FAX: (415) 324-0638. Daniel L. Appelman.

Hendrickson, Thomas. 13 Dunleith Ct., Gaithersburg, Md. 20878-2516. (301) 963-9881. Thomas Hendrickson.

Henslee, William D. 2425 Pacific Coast Hwy., Malibu, Calif. 90265. (310) 456-4763. FAX: (310) 456-4063. William D. Henslee.

Hewitt, A. Kenneth. 1710 Resurgens Plaza, 945 E. Paces Ferry Rd., Atlanta 30326. (404) 814-0000. FAX: (404) 816-8900.

Hickey & Neuland. One Technology Dr., Suite I-803, Irvine, Calif. 92718-2319. (714) 453-7200. FAX: (714) 453-7212.

Law Offices of Dean George Hill & Welch. 1330 New Hampshire Ave. N.W., Suite 113, Washington 20036. (202) 775-0070. FAX: (202) 775-9026. Dean George Hill, Timothy E. Welch.

Hill & Knowlton. 901 31st St. N.W., Washington 20007. (202) 333-7400. FAX: (202) 333-1638. Mary Jo Manning.

Hillman, Adrienne. 41 E. 57th St., 15th Fl., New York 10022. (212) 593-5223. FAX: (212) 593-4633.

Michael J. Hirrel. 1300 New York Ave. N.W., Suite 200-E, Washington 20005. (202) 789-2182. FAX: (202) 289-8113. Michael J. Hirrel.

Hirst & Applegate. Box 1083, 200 Boyd Bldg., Cheyenne, Wyo. 82003-1083. (307) 632-0541. FAX: (307) 632-4999.

Hobbs, Strauss, Dean & Wilder. 1819 H St. N.W., Suite 800, Washington 20006. (202) 783-5100. FAX: (202) 296-8834. Charles A. Hobbs.

Hobson, James R. Donelan, Cleary, Wood & Maser P.C., 1275 K St. N.W., Suite 850, Washington 20005-4078. (202) 371-9500. James R. Hobson.

Hofbauer, Diane L. U.S. Federal Communications Commission, 1919 M St. N.W., Rm. 616, Washington 20554. (202) 632-6990.

Hogan & Hartson. Columbia Sq., 555 13th St. N.W., Washington 20004. (202) 637-5600. FAX: (202) 637-5910. Ptnrs: Marvin J. Diamond, Gardner F. Gillespie III, William S. Reyner Jr., Jay E. Ricks, Richard S. Rodin, David J. Saylor, Susan Wing, Joel S. Winnik. Associates: Karis A. Hastings, Steven J. Horvitz, Marissa G. Repp, Mace J. Rosenstein.

Holland & Hart. 1001 Pennsylvania Ave. N.W., Suite 310-S, Washington 20004. (202) 638-5500. FAX: (202) 638-5050. J. Peter Luedtke.

Holland & Knight. 888 17th St. N.W., Suite 900, Washington 20006. (202) 955-5550. FAX: (202) 955-5564. Janet R. Studley, Dennis Lane, Harold K. McCombs Jr.

Law Firms Active in Communications Law

Holmes, Mark Snyder. 530 W. O'Brien Dr., Argana, 96910. (671) 477-9334. FAX: (671) 477-7847. Mark Holmes.

Holtz, Edgar W. 555 13th St. N.W., Washington 20004-1109. (202) 637-6520. FAX: (202) 637-5910.

Law Office of David Honig. 1800 N.W. 187th St., Miami, Fla. 33056. (305) 628-3600. FAX: (305) 628-3700. David Honig, Ronda Robinson.

Hopkins & Sutter. 888 16th St. N.W., Washington 20006. (202) 835-8000. John P. Bankson Jr., Joe Dixon Edge, Neal M. Goldberg, Charles W. Petty, Steven C. Lambert, Malcolm P. Pfunder, John W. Petit.
 Chicago 60602: 3 First National Plaza. (312) 558-6600. Cordell J. Overgaard.

Hopper & Knoff C.P. 1610 Wymkoop St. Denver 80203. (303) 892-6000. FAX: (303) 892-0547. Michael L. Glaser.

Horack, Talley, Pharr & Lowndes. 2600 One First Union Ctr., 301 S. College St., Charlotte, N.C. 28202. (704) 377-2500. FAX: (704) 377-7566. Russell J. Schwartz.

Horgan, Michael Owen. 110 E. Robert Toombs Ave., Washington, Ga. 30673-1738. (706) 678-1987.

Horowitz, David Ernest. U.S. Federal Communications Commission, 2025 M St. N.W., Rm. 8002, Washington 20554. (202) 632-7792. FAX: (202) 653-9659.

Horton, June C. William Morris Agency, 151 El Camino Dr., Beverly Hills, Calif. 90212-2704. (310) 274-7451.

Howrey & Simon. 1299 Pennsylvania Ave. N.W., Washington 20006. (202) 783-0800. FAX: (202) 383-6610. Edward P. Henneberry.

Humphrey, Margot Smiley. 1150 Connecticut Ave. N.W., Washington 20036. (202) 467-5700.

Hutzler & Charne. 329 Prospect St., Ridgewood, N.J. 07450-5137. (201) 447-4327. James I. Charne.

I

Ice, Miller, Donadio & Ryan. Box 82001, One American Sq., Indianapolis 46282. (317) 236-2100. FAX: (317) 236-2219. Leonard J. Betley, Thomas H. Ristine.

Inghram & Inghram. Boatmen's Bank Bldg., 529 Hampshire, Suite 409, Quincy, Ill. 62301. (217) 222-7420. FAX: (217) 222-1653. John T. Inghram III, James R. Inghram.

Israel & Bray. 919 3rd Ave., 6th Fl., New York 10022-3902. (212) 319-3400. FAX: (212) 755-9685. Larry E. Bray.
 Mus industry & other entertainment-related matters (transactional).

Iwai, Motooka, Goto & Morris. Haseko Ctr., Suite 502, 820 Mililani St., Honolulu 96813. (808) 537-1935. FAX: (808) 528-5813.

J

Jackson & Campbell P.C. 1120 20th St. N.W., Suite 300-S, Washington 20036. (202) 457-1600. FAX: (202) 457-1678. James R. Michal.

Jatlow, David C. 2300 N St. N.W., Washington 20037. (202) 663-9082. FAX: (202) 331-8001.

Jeffer, Mangels, Butler & Marmaro. 2121 Ave. of the Stars, 10th Fl., Los Angeles 90067-5010. (310) 203-8080. FAX: (310) 203-0567. Michael S. Sherman, Allen D. Lenard, Patti C. Felker, Anthony L. Abner, Lindsey J. Bayman, Traci A. Dallas.

Jenner & Block. 601 13th St. N.W., 12th Fl., Washington 20005. (202) 639-6000. FAX: (202) 639-6066. Michael H. Salsbury, Anthony C. Epstein, Carl S. Nadler, John S. di Bene.

Johnson, Andrea L. 225 Cedar St., San Diego 92101. (619) 239-0391. FAX: (619) 696-9999.

Johnson, Charles F. 100 Universal City Plaza, Universal City, Calif. 91608-1002. (818) 777-2823. FAX: (818) 777-8274. Charles F. Johnson, co-exec prod.

Johnson & Gibbs P.C. 1301 K St. N.W., Suite 800 E, Washington 20005. (202) 682-4500. FAX: (202) 682-4674.

Johnston, Buchan & Dalfen. 275 Slater St., Suite 1700, Ottawa, Ont., Canada KIP 5H9. (613) 236-3882. FAX: (613) 230-6423; (613) 230-6762. Charles M. Dalfen; C. Christopher Johnston, Q.C.; Robert J. Buchan; Laurence J.E. Dunbar, Stephen P. Whitehead; J. Aidan O'Neill; Stephen B. Acker, Kathleen C. McNair; Christopher A. Taylor; Renee van Dieen.

Johnston, James H. 1133 Connecticut Ave. N.W., Suite 1000, Washington 20036. (202) 659-1911. FAX: (202) 833-8491. James H. Johnston.

Jones, Day, Reavis & Pogue. 1450 G St. N.W., Suite 700, Washington 20005-2088. (202) 879-3939. FAX: (202) 737-2832. Robert S. Foosaner, Randall B. Lowe, Christopher T. Rogers, Morgan E. O'Brien, Sherry F. Bellamy, Lawrence R. Krevor, John E. Hoover, Michael R. Carper, Joe Sims, Kathryn M. Fenton, Karl B. Anderson, Helen L. Liebman, Anthony C. Grigsby, Leonard G. Kriss, C. Victor Raiser, Raymond J. Wiacek.

Jones, Waldo, Holbrook & McDonough. 2300 M St. N.W., Suite 900, Washington 20037. (202) 296-5950. FAX: (202) 293-2509. Barry D. Wood, Merilyn Strailman, Ronald D. Maines.

Joyce & Jacobs. 2300 M St. N.W., Suite 130, Washington 20037. (202) 457-0100. FAX: (202) 457-0186. Frederick M. Joyce, Christine McLaughlin, Jill M. Lyon.

Law Offices of Leonard S. Joyce. 5335 Wisconsin Ave. N.W., Suite 300, Washington 20015. (202) 364-6970. FAX: (202) 686-8282. Leonard S. Joyce, William D. Silva, Shaun A. Maher.

Julian & Associates. 1038 N. LaSalle Dr., Chicago 60610. (312) 266-1500. FAX: (312) 337-1972. Paul T. Julian.

Julien, Jay I. 1501 Broadway, New York 10036-5503. (212) 221-7575.

K

Kalcheim, Elliott. 79 W. Monroe St., Chicago 60603-4901. (312) 782-7806. FAX: (312) 782-0238.

James L. Kaler Jr., Attorney at Law. 5101 River Rd., Suite 410, Bethesda, Md. 20816. (301) 654-0874. James L. Kaler Jr.

Kass, Skalet, Segan, Spevack & Van Grack P.C. 1050 17th St. N.W., Suite 1100, Washington 20036. (202) 659-6500. FAX: (202) 293-2608. Arnold D. Spevack.

Katine, Mitchell. 6671 Southwest Fwy., Suite 303, Houston 77074-2209. (713) 981-9595. FAX: (713) 981-8670.

Katz, Edward S. 747 Chesnut Ridge, Chesnut Ridge, 10977. (914) 425-0700.

Katz, Marvin. 75 Rockefeller Plaza, New York 10022. (212) 275-2950. FAX: (212) 275-2951.

Kay, Sheldon L. 30445 Northwestern Hwy., Farmington Hills, Mich. 48334. (313) 539-1111. Fax: (313) 539-1114.

Kaye, Scholer, Fierman, Hays & Handler. 901 15th St. N.W., Suite 1100, Washington 20005. (202) 682-3526. FAX: (202) 682-3580. Jason L. Shrinsky, Bruce A. Eisen, James M. Weitzman, Allan G. Moskowitz, Irving Gastfreund.

Keck, Mahin, & Cate. 77 W. Wacker Dr., 49th Fl., Chicago 60601-1693. (312) 634-7700. FAX: (312) 634-5000. Lewis J. Paper, Paul J. Sinderbrand, Robert Aldrich.
 San Francisco 94111: One Maritime Plaza, 23rd Plaza. (415) 392-7077. FAX: (415) 392-3969. Roger J. Metzler, Ronald K. Clausen.
 Washington 20005-3919: 1201 New York Ave. N.W., Penthouse Suite. (202) 789-3400. FAX: (202) 789-1158.

Kehoe, William A. III. U.S. Federal Communications Commission, 2000 L St. N.W., Rm. 257, Washington 20554. (202) 632-7500.

Keller & Heckman. 1001 G St. N.W., Suite 500 N, Washington 20001. (202) 434-4100. FAX: (202) 434-4646. Wayne V. Black, Martin W. Bercovici, Carole C. Harris, Michael F. Morrone, Christine Meagher Gill, Shirley S. Fujimoto, John B. Richards, C. Douglas Jarrett, Michael R. Bennet, Brian T. Ashby, Rick D. Rhodes.

Kelman, Edward M. 300 Park Ave., 19th Fl., New York 10022. (212) 371-9490. FAX: (212) 750-1356.

Kenkel & Associates. 1901 L St. N.W., Suite 200, Washington 20036. (202) 659-4401. FAX: (202) 457-0426. John B. Kenkel, Scott Cinnamon.

Kennedy, Vann M. 301 Artesian St., Corpus Christi, Tex. 78401. (512) 883-7070. FAX: (512) 882-8553.

Kensinger, Karl A. U.S. Federal Communications Commission, 1919 M St. N.W., Washington 20554. (202) 632-6460. Karl A. Kensinger, spec asst to chief mass media.

Kessler & Executives. 205 W. Wacker Dr., Chicago 60606-1216. (312) 372-1315. FAX: (312) 726-0265. Hal Ross Kessler.

Law Offices of John R. Kettle III. 248 Midland Ave., Montclair, N.J. 07042-3029. (201) 748-0072. FAX: (201) 509-0684. John R. Kettle.

Kilday, Mary Catherine. U.S. Federal Communications Commission, 1919 M St. N.W., Rm. 8202, Washington 20554. (202) 632-6968. Mary Catherine Kilday, asst-chief Enforcement Div MMB, FCC.

Kilpatrick & Cody. 700 13th St. N.W., Suite 800, Washington 20005. (202) 508-5800. FAX: (202) 508-5858. Frederick H. von Unwerth.

King & Ballow. 1200 Noel Pl., 200 4th Ave. N., Nashville 37219. (615) 259-3456. FAX: (615) 254-7907. Douglas R. Pierce, Mark E. Hunt, Casey DelCasino, Elizabeth B. Marney.

Kircher, Miriam. 1745 Cy Dr., Vienna, Va. 22180. (703) 242-1672. FAX: (703) 938-7134. Miriam Kircher.

Kirton, McConkie & Pullman. 60 E. S. Temple, Suite 1800, Salt Lake City 84111. (801) 328-3600. FAX: (801) 321-4893. Charles W. Dahlquist II.

Harold S. Klein, Esq. 36 W. 44th St., New York 10036-8102. (212) 575-2345. FAX: (212) 391-2181. Harold S. Klein, Esq.

Kleinberg & Lange. 1880 Century Park E., Suite 1150, Los Angeles 90067. (310) 551-9137. FAX: (310) 277-7145. Kenneth Kleinberg.

Kletter, Matthew L. 666 3rd Ave., 12th Fl., New York 10022. (212) 983-3896.

Klitzman, Stephen. U.S. Federal Communications Commission, 1919 M St. N.W., Rm. 808, Washington 20554. (202) 723-1876.

Koslyn, Pamela. 1230 N. Horn Ave., Suite 409, West Hollywood, Calif. 90069. (310) 657-2219; (310) 536-9351. Fax: (310) 536-0474.

Koteen & Naftalin. 1150 Connecticut Ave. N.W., Suite 1000, Washington 20036. (202) 467-5700. FAX: (202) 467-5915. Bernard Koteen, Alan Y. Naftalin, Arthur B. Goodkind, George Y. Wheeler, Rainer K. Kraus, Herbert D. Miller Jr., Margot Smiley Humphrey, Peter M. Connolly, Charles R. Naftalin, M. Anne Swanson, Gregory C. Staple.

Kraditor, Haber & Bienstock. 152 W. 57th St., 36th Fl. New York 10019. (212) 307-1800. FAX: (212) 307-5799.

Kramer, Levin, Naftalis, Nessin, Kamin & Frankel. 919 3rd Ave., New York 10022. (212) 715-9100. FAX: (212) 688-2119.

Krassner, Michael L. 100 Harrison St., 5th Fl., San Francisco 94105-1605. (415) 597-9850 FAX: (415) 597-9744. Michael L. Krassner.

Krech, David H. U.S. Federal Communications Commission, Office of the Bureau Chief, Common Carrier Bureau, 1919 M St. N.W., Room 500, Washington 20554. (202) 632-6910. FAX: (202) 634-1382. David H. Krech.

L

Landay, David S. 56 W. 57th St., 4th FL., New York 10019. (212) 586-5600. David S. Landay; Cole Ellerd, client svcs.

Lang, Richert & Patch. 5200 N. Palm Ave., 4th Fl., Fresno, Calif. 93704-2225. (209) 436-6700. FAX: (209) 436-6689. William T. Richert.

Latham & Watkins. 1001 Pennsylvania Ave. N.W., Suite 1300-S, Washington 20004. (202) 637-2200. FAX: (202) 637-2201. Aileen R. Pisciotta, Eric L. Bernthal, Joseph Blum, Kevin C. Boyle, Gary M. Epstein, Mark S. Fowler, Reed E. Hundt, James F. Rogers, Bruce E. Rosenblum, Eric A. Stern, Joseph D. Sullivan, John D. Watson Jr.

Lautanen, Michelle R. 20th Century Fox. 10201 W. Pico Blvd., #88, Los Angeles 90067. (310) 838-5221. Michelle R. King.

Lawson, Belford V. III. Federal Communications Commission, 2025 M St. N.W., Rm. 8308, Washington 20554. (202) 632-6302. Belford V. Lawson III, MMB/PRD.

LeBoeuf, Lamb, Leiby & MacRae. 1875 Connecticut Ave. N.W., Suite 1200, Washington 20009. (202) 986-8000. FAX: (202) 986-8102. David R. Poe, Cherie R. Kiser.
 New York 10019: 125 W. 55th St. (212) 424-8000. Richard Berman, Vivian Polak.
 Boston 02110: 260 Franklin St. (617) 439-9500. Paul Connolly.

Law Firms Active in Communications Law

Harrisburg, Pa. 17108: Box 12105, Strawberry Sq., 320 Market St., Suite E-400. (717) 232-8199. Jim Cawley.

Newark, N.J. 07102-5311: One Gateway Ctr., Suite 603. (201) 643-8000. Hon. Fredrick B. Lacey.

Leeds, Martin N. 2920 Nielson Way, Suite 404, Santa Monica, 90405. (310) 450-5123.

Lefevre & Associates. 731 Emerson St., Palo Alto, Calif. 94301. (415) 328-0103. FAX: (415) 328-0106.

Leibowitz, David Evan. 1020 19th St. N.W., Suite 200, Washington 20036. (202) 775-0101. FAX: (202) 775-7253. David Evan Leibowitz.

Leibowitz & Spencer. One S.E. 3rd Ave., Suite 1450, Miami, Fla. 33131. (305) 530-1322. FAX: (305) 530-9417. Matthew L. Leibowitz, John M. Spencer, Joseph A. Belisle.

Washington 20036: 1000 Connecticut Ave. N.W., Suite 500.

Leighton & Regnery. 1667 K St. N.W., Suite 801, Washington 20006. (202) 955-3900. FAX: (202) 955-3770. Richard J. Leighton, Richard F. Mann, ptnrs; Amy N. Rodgers.

Leopold, Petrich & Smith. 2049 Century Park E., Suite 3110, Los Angeles 90067-3274. (310) 277-3333. FAX: (310) 277-7444. Daniel M. Mayeda.

Lettieri, Joan. JTL Entertainment, 2160 Century Park E., Suite 1205, Los Angeles 90067-2244. (310) 201-5000. FAX: (310) 201-5000. Joan T. Lettieri, Esq/CEO.

Leventhal, Senter & Lerman. 2000 K St. N.W., Suite 600, Washington 20006-1809. (202) 429-8970. FAX: (202) 293-7783. Norman P. Leventhal, Meredith S. Senter Jr., Steven Alman Lerman, Raul R. Rodriguez, Dennis P. Corbett, Barbara K. Gardner, Stephen D. Baruch, Sally A. Buckman, Brian M. Madden, Laura B. Humphries, Lynn M. Crakes, David S. Keir, A.B. Cruz III, Linda G. Morrison.

Levy, Thomas R. 300 E. 42nd St., 9th Fl., New York 10017-5947. (212) 682-6110. FAX: (212) 599-2484.

Lewis, Lewis, Clift & Ferraro. 39 Russ St., Hartford, Conn. 06106. (203) 278-2300. FAX: (203) 278-2301. Wyland Dale Clift.

Licht, Renee. U.S. Federal Communications Commission, 1919 M St. N.W., Rm. 614, Washington 20554. (202) 632-7020. Renee Licht.

Lieberman, Harry. 520 Post Oak Blvd., Houston 77027-9404. (713) 961-4215. FAX: (713) 960-8230.

Law Offices of John A. Ligon. Box 880, 128 Mount Hebron Rd., Upper Montclair, N.J. 07043. (201) 509-9192. FAX: (201) 509-9492.

Lilienthal & Fowler. Mills Tower, 220 Montgomery St., 15th Fl., San Francisco 94104-3402. (415) 956-5050. FAX: (415) 989-1137. Peter N. Fowler.

Lipscomb, Greg. 2127 California St. N.W., #802, Washington 20008-1844. (202) 634-4216. FAX: (202) 634-6625. Greg Lipscomb.

Liskey, John R. 1070 Trowbridge Rd., East Lansing, Mich. 48823. (517) 651-6198.

David Ben Liss P.C. 1622 41st St. N., McLean, Va. 22101-3347. (703) 534-4844. FAX: (703) 534-4622. David B. Liss.

Lockridge & Becker P.C. Box 107, Knoxville, Tenn. 37901. (615) 522-4194.

Loeb & Loeb. 345 Park Ave., New York 10154. (212) 407-4000. FAX: (212) 407-4990. Donald L.B. Baraf.

Los Angeles 90017-2475: 1000 Wilshire Blvd, Suite 1800. (213) 688-3400. Robert Thorne.

William R. Loftus. Nighswander, Martin & Mitchell P.A., 23 Bank St., Lebanon, N.H. 03766. (603) 448-3080. FAX: (603) 448-3236. William R. Loftus Esq., dir.

London, Michael B. 10452 Oletha Ln., Los Angeles 90077-2420. (310) 474-0577.

Lowe & Mahon. 2700 Q St. N.W., Washington 20007-5002. (202) 483-6777.

Lowenthal, Landau, Fischer & Bring. 250 Park Ave., New York 10177-0030. (212) 986-1116. FAX: (212) 906-0604. Stuart A. Shorenstein.

Lowndes, Drosdick, Doster, Kantor & Reed. Box 2809, 215 N. Eola Dr., Orlando, Fla. 32802-2809. (407) 843-4600. FAX: (407) 843-4060.

Lowry, Steven R. 8444 Wilshire Blvd., 8th Fl., Beverly Hills, Calif. 90211-3200. (213) 653-8444. FAX: (213) 655-1814.

Lukas, McGowan, Nace & Gutierrez, Chartered. 1819 H St. N.W., 7th Fl., Washington 20006. (202) 857-3500. FAX: (202) 842-4485. Russell D. Lukas; Gerald S. McGowan; David L. Nace; Thomas Gutierrez; George L. Lyon Jr.; Elizabeth R. Sachs; Pamela L. Gist; Marci E. Greenstein; Bob J. Goldberg; David A. LaFuria; J. Justin McClure; Hope Helpern; Marilyn Suchecki.

Lyons, Patrice A. 1401 16th St. N.W., Washington 20036. (202) 939-9666. FAX: (202) 338-3566.

M

Maddox & Hicks. Box 120511, 1101 17th Ave. S., Nashville 37212-2203. (615) 329-0086. FAX: (615) 327-9101. David L. Maddox, J. Rush Hicks Jr.

Madigan & Getzendanner. 30 N. LaSalle St., Suite 3906, Chicago 60602-2507. (312) 346-4321. FAX: (312) 346-5619. Michael J. Madigan, Vincent J. Getzendanner.

Madruga-Forti, Olga. 2025 M St. N.W., Suite 6008, Washington 20554. (202) 634-1800.

Mahoney, Hawkes & Goldings. 18 Dale Ave., Gloucester, Mass. 01930-5906. (508) 281-1310. Morris M. Goldings.

Boston 02110-3359: 40 Rowes Wharf. (617) 439-7600.

Malinen, Eric. U.S. Federal Communications Commission, 2025 M St. N.W., Rm. 5322, Washington 20554. (202) 632-7175.

Maloney & Burch. 1100 Connecticut Ave. N.W., Suite 1200, Washington 20036-4101. (202) 293-1414. FAX: (202) 293-1702. Barry Maloney, ptnr; Adrian Cronauer.

Mankoff, Hill, Held & Goldburg P.C. 3878 Oak Lawn Ave., 4th Fl., Dallas 75219. (214) 523-3700. FAX: (214) 523-3838. Joel Held, Billy B. Hill Jr., Steven C. Metzger.

Marchant, Byron F. U.S. Federal Communications Commission, 1919 M St. N.W., Rm. 844, Washington 20554. (202) 632-7117.

Margolin, James S. 4505 Madison Ave., Kansas City, Mo. 64111. (816) 751-0560. James S. Margolin.

Marino, Joseph A. U.S. Federal Communications Commission, 2000 L St. N.W., Washington 20554. (202) 632-7180. FAX: (202) 632-0195.

Donald E. Martin P.C. 2000 L St. N.W., Suite 200, Washington 20036. (202) 887-5070. FAX: (202) 833-3843. Donald E. Martin.

Matre, Cuni. 11260 Chester Rd., Suite 600, Cincinnati 45246-4054. (513) 771-6768. FAX: (513) 771-7681. James A. Matre; James F. O'Brien; assoc.

Matthews, A. Kimberly. 1140 Connecticut N.W., Washington 20036. (202) 293-3831. FAX: (202) 293-3836.

Matthews & Branscomb. One Alamo Ctr., Suite 800, 106 S. St. Mary's St., San Antonio 78205. (512) 226-4211. FAX: (512) 226-0521. J. Tullos Wells.

Mauro, Thomas A. c/o Fleit, Jacobson, Cohn, Price, Holman & Stern. 400 7th St. N.W., Suite 600, Washington 20004. (202) 638-6666.

May & Dunne, Chartered. 1000 Thomas Jefferson St. N.W., Suite 520, Washington 20007. (202) 298-6345. FAX: (202) 298-6375. Colby M. May, Joseph E. Dunne III.

McBride, Baker & Coles. Northwestern Atrium Ctr., 500 W. Madison St., 40th Fl., Chicago 60661-2511. (708) 769-0033. FAX: (708) 993-9350. Thomas R. Leavens.

McCampbell & Young P.C. Box 550, Suite 2021, Plaza Tower, Knoxville, Tenn. 37901-0550. (615) 637-1440. FAX: (615) 546-9731. Robert S. Stone.

McCarey, Wilma R. 3403 Miller Heights Rd., Oakton, Va. 22124. (703) 385-9766.

McCauley, Victoria M. U.S. Federal Communications Commission, 2025 M St. N.W., Rm. 8322, Washington 20554. (202) 634-6530.

McDonald, Hopkins, Burke & Haber Co. L.P.A. 2100 Bank One Ctr., 600 Superior Ave. E., Cleveland 44114-2653. (216) 348-5400. FAX: (216) 348-5474. Brian M. O'Neill.

McFadden, Evans & Sill. 1627 Eye St. N.W., Suite 810, Washington 20006. (202) 293-0700. FAX: (202) 659-5409. Douglas B. McFadden, Donald J. Evans, William J. Sill, Thomas L. Jones, William M. Barnard, Marianne H. LePera, Christine Crowe, Nancy Killian.

Paul J. McGeady. Morality in Media. 475 Riverside Dr., Rm. 239, New York 10115. (212) 870-3232. Paul J. McGeady; Robert J. Peters.

McGillan, James J. 1345 Woodside Dr., McLean, Va. 22102. (703) 847-2930. FAX: (703) 556-0111.

McGregor, Michael A. Indiana University, Dept. of Telecommunications, Radio-TV 204, 515 N. Park, Bloomington, Ind. 47405. (812) 885-6295.

McLaren, Teresa Greco. 411 S. Madison Ave., Pasadena, Calif. 91101-3382. (818) 568-0503.

McLeod, Frasor & Cone. Box 230, 111 E. Washington St., Walterboro, S.C. 29488. (803) 549-2516. Walton J. McLeod.

McManimon & Scotland. One Gateway Ctr., 18th Fl., Newark, N.J. 07102. (201) 622-1800. (201) 622-7333. Martin C. Rothfelder.

Washington 20004-2404: 1275 Pennsylvania Ave., N.W. (202) 638-3100. FAX: (202) 638-4222. Thomas A. Hart Jr., mgng ptnr; Bradford M. Stern.

McNair & Sanford P.A. 1155 15th St. N.W., Suite 400, Washington 20005. (202) 659-3900. FAX: (202) 659-5763. John W. Hunter.

McNamara, Robert H. U.S. Federal Communications Commission, 2025 M St. N.W., Washington 20554. (202) 632-7197.

Aimee Hueston McNulty. 256 Columbia Tpke., Suite 207, Florham Park, N.J. 07932-1510. (201) 377-0200.

Meisel, Myron S. 3264 Ellenda Ave., Los Angeles 90034-4403. (310) 474-5346.

Melnikoff, Stephen S. 1401 I St., N.W., Suite 1100, Washington 20005. (202) 326-8885. FAX: (202) 408-4806.

Mensch, Linda Susan. 431 S. Dearborn St., Suite 1302, Chicago 60605. (312) 922-2910. FAX: (312) 922-1865.

Messerli & Kramer. 150 S. 5th St., Suite 1800, Minneapolis 55402-4246. (612) 893-6650. FAX: (612) 672-3777. William F. Messerli.

Metzer, Hollis, Gordon, & Mortimer. 1275 K St. N.W., Suite 1000, Washington 20005. (202) 842-1600. FAX: (202) 682-2127. John W. Berresford.

Metzger, Wickersham, Knauss & Erb. Box 93, 111 Market St., Harrisburg, Pa. 17108. (717) 238-8187. Robert E. Yetter.

Meyer, Faller, Weisman & Rosenberg P.C. 4400 Jenifer St. N.W., Suite 380, Washington 20015. (202) 362-1100. FAX: (202) 362-9818. David E. Weisman, Alan S. Tilles, Lloyd C. Coward.

Meyers & Meyers. 180 N. LaSalle St., Suite 2630, Chicago 60601. (312) 201-1515. FAX: (312) 201-8085. Gail E. Meyers, Peter R. Meyers.

Midlen & Guillot, Chartered. 3238 Prospect St. N.W., Washington 20007. (202) 333-1500. FAX: (202) 333-6852. John H. Midlen Jr.; Gregory H. Guillot.

Milbank, Tweed, Hadley & McCloy. One Chase Manhattan Plaza, New York 10005. (212) 530-5000. FAX: (212) 530-5219. Bernard C. Topper Jr.

Law Offices Alvin S. Milder. 134 Greenfield Ave., Los Angeles 90049. (310) 472-6799. FAX: (310) 472-5652.

Milham, Julee L. 1110 Pinellas Bayway S., Tierra Verde, Fla. 33715-1506. (813) 867-4224. FAX: (813) 867-4242.

Miller, Canfield, Paddock & Stone. 1150 Connecticut Ave. N.W., 11th Fl., Washington 20036. (202) 429-5575. FAX: (202) 331-1118. Charles Andrew Weber.

Miller, Cassidy, Larocca & Lewin. 2555 M St. N.W., Washington 20037. (202) 293-6400. FAX: (202) 293-1827. Herbert J. Miller Jr., John Joseph Cassidy.

Miller & Holbrooke. 1225 19th St. N.W., Suite 400, Washington 20036. (202) 785-0600. FAX: (202) 785-1234. Larrine S. Holbrooke, Tillman L. Lay, William R. Malone, Nicholas P. Miller, Teresa D. Baer, Lisa S. Gelb, Frederick E. Ellrod III, Joseph Van Eaton.

Miller, Larry A. U.S. Federal Communications Commission, 2025 M St. N.W., Washington 20554. (202) 632-6402.

Miller & Miller P.C. 1990 M St. N.W., Suite 760, Washington 20036. (202) 785-2720. Samuel Miller, Jerrold D. Miller, John S. Neely.

Law Firms Active in Communications Law

Miller, Stephen M. 150 2nd Ave. N., Suite 400, Nashville 37201-1934. (615) 255-4447. FAX: (615) 244-7004.

Milne, J.L. U.S. Federal Communications Commission, 1919 M St. N.W., Washington 20554. (202) 634-1772.

Mintz, Levin, Cohn, Ferris, Glovsky and Popeo P.C. 701 Pennsylvania Ave. N.W., Washington 20004. (202) 434-7300. Diane B. Burstein, Charles D. Ferris, James A. Kirkland, Frank W. Lloyd, Bruce D. Sokler, Howard J. Symons.
Boston 02111: Keith A. Barrett Popeo.

Law Office of Paul J. Mirowski A.P.C. 1775 Hancock St., Suite 200, San Diego 92110. (619) 686-2777. Paul J. Mirowski.

Mitchell, Bisulca & Slaughter. 5025 Backlick Rd, #C, Annadale, Va. 22003-6044. (703) 941-9550. Andrew C. Bisulca, assoc.

Mitchell, Charles D. 920 South St., Vicksburg, Miss. 39180-3256. (601) 636-4545. FAX: (601) 634-0897.

Mitchell, Silberberg & Knupp. 11377 W. Olympic Blvd., Los Angeles 90064. (310) 312-2000. FAX: (310) 312-3000.

Moebes, Anne. Department of Commerce, 14th & Constitution Ave. N.W., Rm. 4713, Washington 20230. (202) 482-1816.

Molesky & Brown. 80 Grand Ave., Oakland, Calif. 94612-3725. (510) 987-7500. FAX: (510) 987-7575.

Monderer, Howard. 1331 Pennsylvania Ave. N.W., Washington 20004-1703. (202) 637-4536.

Mooney & Associates. 236 S., 300 E., Salt Lake City 84111-2502. (801) 364-5635. FAX: (801) 364-3406. Jerome Mooney.

Morris, Rathnau & De La Rosa. 100 W. Monroe St., Suite 1600, Chicago 60603. (312) 606-0876. Joseph A. Morris.

Morrison & Foerster. 2000 Pennsylvania Ave. N.W., Suite 5500, Washington 20006. (202) 887-1500. FAX: (202) 887-0763. Henry D. Levine, Diane S. Killory, Linda F. Calhoun, Susan H. Crandall, Debra L. Lagapa, Ellen G. Block.

Moss & Barnett, a Professional Assn. 4800 Norwest Ctr., 90 S. 7th St., Minneapolis 55402-4129. (612) 347-0300. FAX: (612) 339-6686. Michael J. Ahern, Michael J. Bradley, Howard S. Cox, Mitchell S. Cox, Michael L. Flanagan, Brian T. Grogan, Adrian E. Herbst, Richard S. Johnson, Ann K.Newhall, M. Cecilia Ray, Maureen A. Scott.

Law Firm of Peter Muller. 21 E. 66th St., New York 10021-5853. (212) 472-8884. FAX: (212) 861-7581.

Mullin, Rhyne, Emmons & Topel P.C. 1000 Connecticut Ave. N.W., Suite 500, Washington 20036. (202) 659-4700. FAX: (202) 872-0604. Eugene F. Mullin; Sydney White Rhyne; Nathaniel F. Emmons; Robert E. Levine; Howard A. Topel; Mark N. Lipp; Christopher A. Holt; Andrew H. Weissman. J. Parker Conner, counsel.

Murphy, Alexander. 4 E Miner St., Suite B, West Chester, Pa. 19382. (215) 431-1833. FAX: (215) 431-1267.

Murphy, Daniel R. 223 4th Ave., Pittsburgh, 15222-1713. (412) 642-4370. FAX: (412) 471-7067.

Murphy & Demory Ltd. 1101 30th St., N.W., Suite 200, Washington 20007. (202) 333-8300. FAX: (202) 965-0775.

Riley Marie Murphy, Attorney at Law. 1100 Poydras St., Suite 2590, New Orleans 70163. (504) 585-3775. Riley Marie Murphy, Michael Hale Wirpel.

Law Offices of Kevin Murray. 8721 Santa Monica Blvd., Suite 403, West Hollywood, Calif. 90069. (310) 652-5534. FAX: (301) 652-9176. Kevin Murray.

Todd W. Musburger Ltd. 142 E. Ontario St., Suite 500, Chicago 60611. (312) 664-2600. FAX: (312) 664-4137. Todd W. Musburger.

Law Offices of Richard S. Myers. 1090 Vermont Ave. N.W., Suite 800, Washington 20005. (202) 408-7032. FAX: (202) 371-0789. Sean P. Beatty, ESQ; James J. Keller, non-atty communications engr.

Myman, Abell, Fineman & Greenspan. 11777 San Vicente Blvd., Los Angeles 90049-5011. (310) 820-7717. Robert M. Myman.

N

Nadal, Mark S. U.S. Federal Communications Commission, 1919 M St. N.W., Rm. 544, Washington 20554. (202) 632-1301.

Nakamura, Kent Y. U.S. Federal Communications Commission, 2025 M St. N.W., Rm. 5002, PRB, Washington 20554. (202) 632-6940.

Naphtali, Ashirah S. 130-33 217th St., Laurelton, N.Y. 11413-1320. (718) 481-8688.

Nath, Michael J. Cedar Point, Sandusky, Ohio 44870. (419) 627-0933.

Nemeth, Valerie A. 619 S. Vulcan Ave., Suite 215, Encinitas, Calif. 92024-3652. (619) 944-4130.

Law Offices of Roger P. Newell. 130 Jane St., New York 10014. (212) 463-0517. FAX: (212) 463-7628.

David B. Newman & Associates P.C. Box 2728, Centennial Sq., La Plata, Md. 20646-2728. (301) 934-6100. FAX: (301) 934-5782.

Nichols, Keith. U.S. Federal Communicaitons Commission, 1250 23rd St., Plaza Level, Washington 20554. (202) 632-4887.

Entertainment Law Offices of Richard Niederberg. Box 1883, Studio City, Calif. 91614-0883. (213) 650-9600; (310) 247-9800; (818) 769-9000. FAX: (818) 985-9200. TELEX: 673-1611. Richard Niederberg.

Nielsen & Merksamer. 770 L St., Suite 800, Sacramento, Calif. 95814. (916) 446-6752. FAX: (916) 446-6106.

Nighswander, Martin & Mitchell P.A. 23 Bank St. Laconia, N.H. 03766. (603) 524-4121. Joseph Adrignola, admin.

Nilsson, Kent R. U.S. Federal Communications Commission, 1919 M St. N.W., Rm. 544, Washington 20554. (202) 632-1302.

Nixon, Hargrave, Devans & Doyle. One Thomas Cir. N.W., Suite 800, Washington 20005. (202) 457-5300. FAX: (202) 457-5355. Veronica M. Ahern; Robert A. Mazer; Albert Shuldiner; Richard D. Rochford Jr.; William S. Andrews.

Nixon, Wilbert E. Jr. U.S. Federal Communications Commission, 2025 M St. N.W., Rm. 6110, Washington 20554. (202) 634-1627. FAX: (202) 634-6625.

Nogi, Appleton, Weinburger & Wren P.C. 415 Wyoming Ave., Scranton, Pa. 18503. (717) 963-8880.

O

Ober, Kaler, Grimes & Shriver. 1850 M. St., Suite 280, Washington 20036. (202) 778-0878. FAX: (202) 788-0688. Frederick S. Hird Jr.

O'Connell & Aronowitz. 100 State St., Albany, N.Y. 12207. (518) 462-5601. FAX: (518) 462-2670. Peter Danziger; Neil H. Rivchin.

Daniel W. O'Connell. 120 E. Baltimore, Baltimore 21102. (410) 332-7500. FAX: (410) 332-7582. Daniel W. O'Connell.

O'Connell, Matthew M. 405 Lexington Ave., 54th Fl., N.Y. 10174-0002. (212) 697-2280. FAX: (212) 697-2249. Matthew O'Connell, Sr. VP/Gen Counsel, Osborn Communications Corp.

O'Connell, Susan Lee. U.S. Federal Communications Commission, 1919 M St. N.W., Rm. 534, Washington 20554.

O'Connor & Hannan. 1919 Pennsylvania Ave. N.W., Suite 800, Washington 20006. (202) 887-1400. FAX: (202) 466-2198. David L. Hill, Audrey P. Rasmussen.

O'Donnell, Fox & Gartner P.C. 880 3rd Ave., 9th Fl., New York 10022. (212) 319-0600. Leonard W. Tuft.

Oettinger, Elmer R. 58 Oakwood Dr., Chapel Hill, N.C. 27514-5652. (919) 942-1048.

Ogden, Murphy & Wallace. 2100 Westlake Ctr. Tower, 1601 5th Ave., Seattle 98101-1686. (206) 447-7000. FAX: (206) 447-0215. James A. Murphy.

O'Laverty, Cheri S. 12121 Wilshire Blvd., Los Angeles 90025-1123. (310) 207-9706.

Oliver, Linda L. U.S. Federal Communications Commission, 1919 M St. N.W., Rm. 832, Washington 20554. (202) 632-6996.

Law Offices of Mark D. Olson. Box 5009, Covina, Calif. 91723-5004. (818) 915-3333. FAX: (818) 331-1111.

Oman, Roy Erik. U.S. Federal Communications Commission, 1919 M St. N.W., Rm. 332, Washington 20554. (202) 632-3954.

O'Melveny & Myers. 555 13th St. N.W., Suite 500 W., Washington 20004. (202) 383-5300. FAX: (202) 383-5414. John H. Beisner, F. Amanda DeBusk.

O'Neil, Cannon & Hollman. Bank One Plaza, Suite 1400, 111 E. Wisconsin Ave., Milwaukee 53202-4803. (414) 276-5000. FAX: (414) 276-6581. Faye L. Calvey.

O'Neill & Athy P.C. 1310 19th St. N.W., Washington 20036. (202) 466-6555. FAX: (202) 466-6596. Christopher P. O'Neill.

Oppenheim, Louis J. 421 7th Ave., Suite 1410, New York 10001-2002. (212) 695-0300. FAX: (212) 695-1318.

O'Reilly, Ranchillio, Nitz, Andrews & Turnbull. 12900 Hall Rd., Suite 350, Sterling Heights, Mich. 48313-1151. (313) 726-1000. FAX: (313) 726-1560. Neil J. Lehta.

Orr & Reno. Box 709, One Eagle Sq., Concord, N.H. 03301-4903. (603) 224-2381. FAX: (603) 224-2318. William L. Chapman.

Orten & Hindman. 1125 17th St., Suite 2310, Denver 80202. (303) 292-9999. FAX: (303) 292-9898. Thomas J. Hindman.

Outlaw, Rondrew A. 19126 Magnolia St., Suite 201, Huntington Beach, Calif. 92646. (714) 963-6022. (714) 962-1851.

Overton, John B. 2401 Marinship Way, Sausalito, Calif. 94965-2854. (415) 331-2889.

Ovian, Douglas Alan. 55 Bobby Ln., Manchester, Conn. 06040. (203) 649-8118.

Law Offices of James L. Oyster. Rt. 1, Box 203-A, Castleton, Va. 22716. (703) 937-4800. FAX: (703) 937-2148.

P

Page, Scranton, Harris, McGlamry & Chapman P.C. Box 1199, 1043 3rd Ave., Columbus, Ga. 31994. (706) 324-0251. Cecil M. Cheves.

Palmer & Dodge. One Beacon St., Boston 02108. (617) 573-0100. FAX: (617) 227-4420. John Taylor Williams, Neil P. Arkuss, F. Andrew Anderson, Robert Duggan, Laurie S. Gill, Eric F. Menoyo, Thane D. Scott, George Ticknor.

Pankopf, Arthur. 7819 Hampden Ln., Bethesda, Md. 20814-1108. (301) 657-8790.

Papajohn, John N. 1807 Windmill Ln., Alexandria, Va. 22307-1946. (703) 768-4443.

Pardo & Pardo P.A. 5963 Biscayne Blvd., Miami, Fla. 33137. (305) 751-6711.

Partnoy, Robert W. 120 W. 74th St., New York 10023-2324. (212) 877-1269.

The Partridge Group. Meeting House Farm, Lincoln, Va. 22078. (703) 338-3750. B. Waring Partridge III.

Patton, Boggs & Blow. 2550 M St. N.W., Suite 900, Washington 20037. (202) 457-5227. FAX: (202) 457-6315. Penelope S. Farthing, Thomas H. Boggs Jr., Ray M. O'Hara.

Pauker, Molly. Fox Television Stations Inc. 5151 Wisconsin Ave. N.W., Washington 20016-4124. (202) 244-5151.

Paul, Hastings, Janofsky & Walker. 1050 Connecticut Ave. N.W., 12th Fl., Washington 20036. (202) 223-9000. Ralph B. Everett; Bruce D. Ryan.

Paul, Weiss, Rifkind, Wharton & Garrison. 1615 L St. N.W., Suite 1300, Washington 20036. (202) 223-7300. FAX: (202) 223-7420. Phillip L. Spector; Jeffrey H. Olson.

Pearce & Durick. Box 400, 314 E. Thayer Ave., Bismarck, N.D. 58501-4018. (701) 223-2890. Patrick W. Durick; Larry L. Boschee.

Pearls, Ressegule, Kline, Barber & LeBous. Box 1864, Binghamton, N.Y. 13902-1864. (607) 724-3211. FAX: (607) 773-0093. Stuart M. Pearis Sr.

John D. Pellegrin, Chartered. 1140 Connecticut Ave. N.W., Suite 606, Washington 20036. (202) 293-3831. FAX: (202) 293-3836. John D. Pellegrin; A. Kimberly Matthews.

Law Firms Active in Communications Law

Penney, James A. 1201 3rd Ave., Suite 3600, Seattle 98101-3000. (206) 621-0906. FAX: (206) 623-9015. James A. Penney, VP/Gen Counsel.

Pepper & Corazzini. 1776 K St. N.W., Suite 200, Washington 20006. (202) 296-0600. Vincent A. Pepper, Robert F. Corazzini, Peter Gutman, John F. Garziglia, Neal J. Friedman, Ellen S. Mandell, William J. Franklin, Louise Cybulski, Robert L. Thompson.

Pepper, Hamilton & Scheetz. 2 Logan Sq., 18th & Arch Street, Suite 3000, Philadelphia 19103-2799. (215) 981-4000. FAX: (215) 981-4750. John McLamb Jr.
    Los Angeles 90017: 444 S Flower St. (213) 688-5600. Richard M. Brown.
    Washington 20036: 1300 19th St. N.W., (202) 828-1200. FAX: (202) 828-1665. William Warfield Ross.

Perez, Benjamin. Abacus Communications Co. 1801 Columbus Rd. N.W., Suite 101, Washington. 20009-2031. (202) 462-3680. FAX: (202) 462-3781. Benjamin Perez.

Perkins, Roy F. Jr. 1724 Whitewood Ln., Herndon, Va. 22070. (703) 435-9700. FAX: (703) 435-9701.

Larry D. Perry, Attorney at Law. 11464 Saga Ln., Suite 110, Knoxville, Tenn. 37931. (615) 927-8474. FAX: (615) 927-8474. Larry D. Perry, Esq.

Law Offices of George B. Peters Jr. 624 S. Milledge Ave., Suite 209, Athens, Ga. 30601. (706) 353-8633. FAX: (706) 549-7090.

Peterson, Dwight T. 1528 Walnut St., Philadelphia 19102. (215) 985-4484. FAX: (215) 985-0827.

Pettit, Robert L. Crowell & Morning, 1001 Pennsylvania Ave. N.W., Washington 20004-2595. (202) 624-2935.

Phillips, Anne Haase. 7550 E. McDonald Dr., Suite K, Scottsdale, Ariz. 85250-6026. (602) 991-5991. FAX: (602) 951-5295.

Phillips, Nizer, Benjamin, Krim & Ballon. 31 W. 52nd St., New York 10019-6118. (212) 977-9700. FAX: (212) 262-5152. Barry Rosenthal, atty.

Pierce, Stanley & Robinson. 600 W. 4th St., North Little Rock, Ark. 72114-5383. (501) 372-3131. FAX: (501) 372-3825. Robert Lee Pierce.

Pilafian, James. 1566 Coral Way, Suite 3, Miami, Fla. 33145. (305) 285-0144.

Pillsbury, Madison & Sutro. Box 7880, 225 Bush St., San Francisco 94120. (415) 983-1000.

Piper & Marbury. 1200 19th St. N.W., Suite 700, Washington 20036. (202) 861-3913. FAX: (202) 861-3963. Mark J. Tauber, Nora E. Garrote.

Pollock, Elliot B. 6333 N. Milwaukee, Suite 106, Chicago 60646. (312) 774-1860.

Pontius & Associates. 101 University Blvd., Denver 80206-4630. (303) 321-4597. FAX: (303) 321-4598.

Pope, Ballard, Shepard & Fowle Ltd. 69 W. Washington St., Suite 3200, Chicago 60602. (312) 214-4200. FAX: (312) 214-4601.

Popham, Haik, Schnolorich, Kaufman & Doty Ltd. 3300 Hyper Jaffrey Tower, Minneapolis 55402. (612) 333-4800. Thomas J. Barrett, Thomas K. Berg, Allen W. Hindraker, David A. Jones, Mark F. Palma, Wayne G. Popham, Lee E. Sheehy.

Popham, James J. Association of Independent Television Stations Inc., 1320 19th St. N.W., Suite 300, Washington 20036. (202) 887-1970. FAX: (202) 887-0950.

Law Offices of Dean George Popps. 1360 Beverly Rd., Suite 305, McLean, Va. 22101. (703) 734-0159. FAX: (703) 448-3515; (703) 448-1236. Dean George Popps.

Gene Posner & Associates. 152 W. Wisconsin Ave., Suite 404, Milwaukee 53203. (414) 276-7440. Gene Posner.

Powell, Goldstein, Frazer & Murphy. 191 Peach Tree St. N.E., 16th Fl., Atlanta 30303. (404) 572-6600. FAX: (404) 572-6999. Walter G. Moeling IV, Chris D. Molen, Kevin Conboy, James C. Rawls, V. Robert Denham Jr., W. Gordon Hamlin Jr., Robert C. Lewison, Stuart E. Eizenstat, Simon Lazarus III.
    Washington 20004: 1001 Pennsylvania Ave. N.W., 6th Fl. (202) 347-0066. FAX: (202) 624-7222. Jerome S. Breed.

Office of Janice Hill Powell. 7754 El Rito Way, Sacramento, Calif. 95831. (916) 428-7703.

Pratcher, Jackson, Livsey & Cox. 1133 Kensington Ave., Buffalo, N.Y. 14215-1611. (716) 838-4612 FAX: (716) 838-4828 Joseph M. Cox.

Preston, Gates, Ellis & Rouvelas Meeds. 1735 New York Ave. N.W., Suite 500, Washington 20006. (202) 628-1700. FAX: (202) 331-1024. Craig J. Gehring, John L. Longstreth, Drew D. Pettus, Allen Erenbaum.

Preston, Thorgrimson, Shidler, Gates, & Ellis. 5000 Columbia Seafirst Ctr., 701 5th Ave., Seattle 98104. (206) 623-7580. Gordon G. Conger.

Primestar Partners. 100 Presidential Blvd., Bala Cynwyd, Pa. 19004. (215) 660-6100. FAX: (215) 660-6112. Marcus Evans.

Prives, Melvin A. 20 Park Plaza, Boston 02116. (617) 542-6122. FAX: (617) 426-9236.

Proskauer, Rose, Goetz & Mendelsohn. 1585 Broadway, New York 10036. (212) 969-3000. FAX: (212) 969-2900. Bertram A. Abrams, Lawrence H. Budish.

Provosty, Sadler & Delaunay. Box 1791, Hibernia National Bank, 8th Fl., Alexandria, La. 71309-1791. (318) 445-3631. Ricky L. Sooter.

Pulis, Gregory M. Creative Artists Agency 9830 Wilshire Blvd. Beverly Hills, Calif. 90212. (310) 288-4545. FAX: (310) 288-5454.

Putbrese, Hunsaker & Ruddy. Box 539, 6800 Fleetwood Rd., Suite 100, McLean, Va. 22101. (703) 790-8400. FAX: (703) 827-9538. Keith E. Putbrese, David M. Hunsaker, John C. Trent.

R

Rapke, Eileen F. Creative Artists Agency. 9830 Wilshire Blvd., Beverly Hills, Calif. 90212-1804. (310) 288-4545. FAX (310) 288-5544.

Law Offices, Richard Warren Rappaport. 3970 Oaks Clubhouse Dr., Suite 208, Pompano Beach, Fla. 33069. (305) 972-2931. Richard Warren Rappaport.

Reboul, MacMurray, Hewitt, Maynard & Kristol. 1111 19th St. N.W., Suite 406, Washington 20036. (202) 429-0004. FAX: (202) 429-8743. James E. Magee.

Reddy, Begley & Martin. 1001 22nd St. N.W., Washington 20037. (202) 659-5700. FAX: (202) 659-5711. Dennis F. Begley; Harry C. Martin; Cheryl A. Kenny; Matthew H. McCormick; Andrew S. Kersting.

Reed, Smith, Shaw & McClay. 1200 18th St. N.W., Suite 1000, Washington 20036. (202) 457-6100. FAX: (202) 457-6113. Robert J. Aamoth, Harold David Cohen, James J. Freeman, William S. Green, Benjamin J. Griffin, Brian A. Johnson, Peter D. O'Connell, W. Theodore Pierson Jr., Judith St. Ledger-Roty, Mamie K. Sarver, J. Laurent Scharff, Trudie J. White, Lynn E. Shapiro, Nancy J. Thompson, Michael Wack, Matthew J. Harthun, Kathleen A. Kirby.

Reed, Victor P. 353 Sacramento St., Suite 1500, San Francisco 94111-3662. (415) 398-5212. FAX: (415) 362-1776.

Rees, Broome & Diaz. 8133 Leesburg Pike, 9th Fl., Vienna, Va. 22182. (703) 790-1911. FAX: (703) 790-1913. Peter S. Philbin.

Reid & Priest. 701 Pennsylvania Ave. N.W., Suite 800, Washington 20004. (202) 508-4000. FAX: (202) 508-4321. Tedson J. Meyers; Michael W. Faber; Tara K. Giunta; Michael D. Paul; Timothy J. Logue, space & telecommunications analyst.

Renouf & Polivy. 1532 16th St. N.W., Washington 20036. (202) 265-1807. FAX: (202) 265-1810. Katrina Renouf, Margot Polivy.

Resnick, Bernard Max. Bellevue Bldg., 6th Fl., Broad & Walnut St., Philadelphia 19102. (215) 790-1155. FAX: (215) 790-0509.

Reznick, Nina J. 28 E. 10th St., New York 10003-6201. (212) 473-6279.

Rhoades, McKee, Boer, Goodrich & Titta. 600 Waters Bldg., Grand Rapids, Mich. 49503. (616) 235-3500. Richard G. Leonard.

Rhodes, Andrew J. U.S. Federal Communications Commission, 1919 M St. N.W., Rm. 8010, Washington 20554. (202) 632-5414. FAX: (202) 653-9659.

Rice, David M. One Old Country Rd., Carle Place, N.Y. 11514. (516) 747-7979. FAX: (516) 741-3440.

Rich, Tracy S. NBC Inc. 3000 W. Alameda Ave., Burbank, Calif. 91523. (818) 840-4444.

Richards, Mary Beth. U.S. Federal Communications Commission, 1919 M St. N.W., Rm. 744, Washington 20554. (202) 632-7090.

Richardson, Julieanna L. Show Case Television Network/Channel 25. 1931 W. Diversey, Chicago 60614.

Rickell & Baun. 63 Kercheval, Gross Point Farms, Mich. 48243. (313) 886-0000. FAX: (313) 886-0405. John M. Rickell.

Riepen, Brian S. 1901 N. Akard St., Dallas 75201-2330. (214) 953-1560. FAX: (214) 953-1655.

Riezman & Blitz. Chromalloy Plaza, Suite 1028, 120 S. Central Ave., St. Louis. 63105-1705. (314) 727-0101. Frederick J. Berger.

Riker, Danzig, Scherer, Hyland & Perretti. One Speedwell Ave., Headquarters Plaza, Morristown, N.J. 07962. (201) 538-0800. FAX: (201) 538-1984.

Rivera, Michael Anthony. 2707 Barnes Ave., Bronx, N.Y. 10467. (718) 515-6756.

Robb & Henning. 515 Madison Ave., Suite 2100, New York 10022. (212) 752-5566. FAX: (212) 421-4036. Scott Hall Robb; Dovie F. Wingard; Gregory L. Howard, consultant.

Roberts & Eckard P.C. 1919 Pennsylvania Ave., Suite 222, Washington 20006. (202) 296-0533. FAX: (202) 296-0464. Lawrence Roberts; Linda J. Eckard; James S. Blitz; Kenneth M. Kaufman; Mary L. Plantamura; Pamela C. Cooper.

Roberts, Virgil. 1635 N. Cahuenga Blvd., 6th Fl., Los Angeles 90028-6240. (213) 461-0390.

Robins, Kaplan, Miller & Ciresi. 2800 LaSalle Plaza, 800 LaSalle Ave., Minneapolis 55402-2015. (612) 349-8500. FAX: (612) 339-4181. Kathleen A. Marron; Thomas A. Miller; Sarah A. Poulos; Ernest I. Reveal; Thomas J. Undlin.

Geoffrey K. Robinson. 800 West Ave., Suite 418, Miami Beach, Fla. 33139. (305) 531-1095. FAX: (305) 672-3073.

Robinson, Marvin A. 119 Gwynmont Dr., North Wales, Pa. 19454-1812. (215) 699-6691.

Robinson, Wil E. Box 723657, Atlanta 31139. (404) 859-9568. FAX: (404) 399-9671.

Roche, James T. 4141 N. Henderson Rd., Suite 824, Arlington, Va. 22203. (703) 528-9070.

Roddy, Carolyn Tatum. U.S. Federal Communications Commission, 1250 23rd St., Rm. 144, Washington 20554. (202) 632-4887.

Rogers, Robert G. Siemens Corp., 701 Pennsylvania Ave. N.W., Suite 720, Washington 20004. (202) 434-4800. FAX: (202) 737-0028.

Rogers, Wallett Bancroft. U.S. Federal Communications Commission, 1250 23rd St. N.W., Plaza Level, Washington 20554. (202) 632-4887. FAX: (202) 632-1411.

Rogers & Wells. 607 14th St. N.W., Washington 20005. (202) 434-0700. FAX: (202) 434-0800. A. Richard Metzger Jr., Charles A. Zielinski.

Romano, B. Alan. U.S. Federal Communications Commission, 2025 M St. N.W., Rm. 8010, Washington 20554. (202) 632-5414. FAX: (202) 653-9659.

Root, Henry W. 1541 Ocean Ave., Santa Monica, Calif. 90401-2110. (310) 395-6800. FAX: (310) 393-7777.

Rosenfeld, Meyer & Susman. 9601 Wilshire Blvd., 4th Fl., Beverly Hills, Calif. 90210-5288. (310) 858-7700. FAX: (310) 271-6430.

Rosenman & Colin. 575 Madison Ave., New York 10022. (212) 940-8800. Jerome S. Boros, Marvin R. Lange, Jerry Silber, Merril Mironer.
    Washington 20036: 1300 19th St. N.W. (202) 463-7177. Howard J. Braun, Jerold L. Jacobs, Diane L. Mooney, Shelley Sadowsky.

Ross & Hardies. 888 16th St. N.W., Suite 300, Washington 20006. (202) 296-8600. Stephen R. Ross; Raymond J. Kimball; John A. Howell; James A. Stenger; Kathryn A. Hutton; Jocelyn R. Roy.

Ross & Stevens. Firstar Plaza, One S. Pickney St., Madison, Wis. 53703. (608) 257-5353. Steven L. Ritt.

Rothman, Gordon, Foreman & Groudine P.C. 300 Grant Bldg., Pittsburgh 15219. (412) 338-1100. FAX: (412) 281-7304. Frederick A. Polner, Esq.

Rourke, Gerald S. 1155 Connecticut Ave. N.W., Suite 300, Washington 20036. (202) 467-8596. FAX: (301) 983-0776.

Rowlenson, Richard C. 2002 Pisgah Church Rd., Greensboro, N.C. 27455-3314.

Law Firms Active in Communications Law

Rubin, Winston, Diercks, Harris & Cooke. 1730 M St. N.W., Suite 412, Washington 20036. (202) 861-0870. FAX: (202) 429-0657. James L. Winston, Walter E. Diercks, Eric M. Rubin, Jeffrey Harris.

Ruger, Michael C. U.S. Federal Communications Commission, 2033 M St. N.W., Rm. 920, Washington 20554. (202) 416-0856. FAX: (202) 461-0898.

Runyon & Howard. 69 Main St., Peterborough, N.H. 03458. (603) 924-7276. FAX: (603) 924-4264. Al Phillips Runyon III.

Ryan, Louis Farthing. 150 W. Brambleton Ave., Norfolk, Va. 23510-2018.

Ryan, Swanson & Cleveland. 1201 3rd Ave., #3400, Seattle 98101-3034. (206) 464-4224. FAX: (206) 583-0359.

S

Sachs & Sax. Northern Trust Plaza, 301 Yamato Rd., Suite 4150, Boca Raton, Fla. 33431-4917. (407) 994-4499. Peter Sachs, Spence Sax, Larry Glickman.

Sacks & Zweig. Wilshire Bldg. 100 Wilshire Blvd., Suite 1300, Santa Monica, Calif. 90401-1110. (310) 451-3113. FAX: (310) 451-0089. Lee Sacks.

Sadler, Sullivan, Herring & Sharp P.C. Box 2679, Huntsville, Ala. 35804; 204 Gates Ave. S.E., Huntsville, Ala. 35801. (205) 534-4343. FAX: (205) 534-4370. Harold F. Herring.

Sahl, John Patrick. School of Law, University of Akron, Akron, Ohio 44325-2901. (216) 972-6753.

Salas, Magalie R. U.S. Federal Communications Commission, 1919 M St. N.W., Rm.622, Washington 20554. (202) 254-6530. FAX: (202) 632-0149.

Santarelli, Smith, & Carroccio. 1155 Connecticut Ave. N.W., 9th Fl., Washington 20036. (202) 466-6800. FAX: (202) 463-0969. Donald E. Santarelli, A. Thomas Carroccio.

Santoro, Edward J. 304 Maple Ave., South Plainfield, N.J. 07080. (908) 756-0785. FAX: (908) 756-0828.

Calvin C. Saunders. 67 Wall St., Suite 2411, New York N.Y. 10005. (212) 323-8014. FAX (212) 943-2300.

Janet Savage. 20th Television, 5515 Melrose Ave., Beverly Hills, Calif. 90038. (213) 467-9999, ext. 3702.

Schiffman & Blaustein & Miller. 18 W. 41st St., Suite 1605, New York 10017. (718) 436-2839. FAX: (212) 685-7106. Steven Mitchell Schiffman, Bruce R. Blaustein. London, England: Grady Miller.

Schimmel & Associates. 7322 S.W. Fwy., Suite 825, Houston 77074. (713) 988-7822. FAX: (713) 988-7916. Bruce I. Schimmel.

Schnader, Harrison, Segal & Lewis. 1111 19th St. N.W., Washington 20036. (202) 463-2900. FAX: (202) 296-8930; FAX: (202) 775-8741. Delbert D. Smith, Stefan M. Lopatkiewicz, Brigitte L. Adams.

Schned, Ellen J. Federal Communications Commission, Office of Legislative Affairs. 1919 M St. N.W., Suite 808, Washington 20554. (202) 632-6405. FAX: (202) 632-7092.

Gary P. Schonman. Federal Communications Commission, 2025 M St. N.W., Suite 7212, Washington 20554. (202) 632-6402. Gary P. Schonman.

Schreibman, Paul S. 142 1/2 S. Bedford Dr., Beverly Hills, Calif. 90212. (310) 247-1934.

Schrier, Helene T. U.S. Federal Communications Commission, 2000 L St. N.W., Washington 20554. (202) 632-3922.

Schuman, Kane, Felts, & Everngam, Chartered. 4804 Moorland Ln., Bethesda, Md. 20814. (301) 986-0200. FAX: (301) 986-7960. Sheldon Paul Schuman.

Schuster & Associates. 8327 N. Marina Pacifica, Long Beach, Calif. 90803-3814. (310) 596-5900. FAX:(310) 431-4540.

Schuster, Robert J. 2425 Olympic Blvd., Suite 4060 W., Santa Monica, Calif. 90404. (310) 453-5140. FAX: (310) 998-9201.

Law Offices of Philip L. Schwartz P.A. 633 Andrews Ave., Suite 203, Fort Lauderdale, Fla. 33301-1116. (305) 760-7770. FAX: (305) 760-7775.

Schwartz, Woods & Miller. 1350 Connecticut Ave. N.W., Suite 300, Washington 20036. (202) 833-1700. FAX: (202) 833-2351. Louis Schwartz, Robert A. Woods,

Lawrence M. Miller, Steven C. Schaffer, Malcolm G. Stevenson.

Schwartzman, Andrew Jay. 2000 M St. N.W., Suite 400, Washington 20036-3307. (202) 232-4300.

Robert A. Seidenberg, Attorney at Law. 61 Broadway, 18th Fl., New York 10006-2701. (212) 797-9100. FAX: (212) 797-9161.

Seligman, Harold. 1200 Post Oak Blvd., Suite 114, Houston 77056. (713) 961-0112. FAX: (713) 621-8825. Harold Seligman.

Sell & Melton. Box 229, 577 Mulberry St., Macon, Ga. 31297-2899. (912) 746-8521. FAX: (912) 745-6426. Edward S. Sell III.

Semmes, Bowen & Semmes. 1025 Connecticut Ave. N.W., Suite 500, Washington 20036. (202) 822-8250. FAX: (202) 822-8258. Barry A. Friedman, Gilbert B. Lessenco, Irving P. Cohen, Deborah H. Diehl, Annette R. Fries, Carl Wilson.

Seven Hundred Camp Street Associates. 700 Camp St., New Orleans 70130. (504) 528-9500. FAX: (504) 528-9500. Edward Anderson.

Severaid, Ronald H. 1780 Creekside Oaks Dr., Suite 125, Sacramento, Calif. 95833-3633. (916) 921-2567. FAX: (916) 925-4763.

Seward, Amanda M. 3400 Cahuenga Blvd., Hollywood, Calif. 90068-1376. (213) 969-1225. FAX: (213) 969-4195.

Seyfarth, Shaw, Fairweather & Geraldson. 2029 Century Park E., 33rd Fl., Los Angeles 90067. (310) 277-7200. (310) 201-5219. Mitchell Whitehead.

Law Offices of Thomas G. Shack Jr. 1150 Connecticut Ave. N.W., Suite 900, Washington 20036. (202) 293-5900. FAX: (202) 659-3493. Thomas G. Shack Jr.

Shafer, Nancy Chausow. 221 N. LaSalle, Suite 863, Chicago 60601. (312) 609-6600. FAX: (312) 609-6610.

Shanks & Blackstock. Box 1346, 2 Centre Sq., 625 S. Gay St., #250, Knoxville, Tenn. 37902-1669. (615) 637-2981. FAX: (615) 637-2017. Susan Esterle Shanks.

Shapiro, Burton J. 2147 N. Beachwood Dr., Los Angeles Calif. 90068-3462. (213) 469-9452. FAX (213) 469-9452

Shartsis, Friese & Ginsburg. One Maritime Plaza, Suite 1800, San Francisco 94111. (415) 421-6500. FAX: (415) 421-2922. Douglas Mo, Tracy L. Salisbury, Charles Rice.

Shaw, Curtis M. 6255 W. Sunset Blvd., Los Angeles 90028-7403. (213) 464-8424. FAX: (213) 466-1892.

Shaw, Pittman, Potts & Trowbridge. 2300 N St. N.W., Washington 20037. (202) 663-8000. FAX (202) 663-8007. Robert E. Conn, John Francis Dealy.

Shields, Dan W. 14 Parkway Dr., Englewood, Colo. 80110-4222.

Steven R. Shine Law Office. 2810 Beaver at Broadway, Suite B, Fort Wayne, Ind. 46807. (219) 745-1970. FAX: (219) 744-5411.

Richard R. Shreves, Esq. Box 684751, Austin, Tex. 78768-4751. (512) 444-1243. FAX: (512) 370-4041. Richard R. Shreves.

Shriver, Elizabeth. 4926 Hillbrook Ln. N.W., Washington 20016. (202) 362-7698.

Shukat, Hafer & Weber. 111 W. 57th St., Suite 1120, New York 10019-2211. (212) 245-4580. FAX: (212) 956-6471. Peter Shukat.

Shulman, Rogers, Gandel, Pordy & Ecker. 11921 Rockville Pike, Suite 300, Rockville, Md. 20852. (301) 230-5200. FAX: (301) 230-2891. Alan B. Sternstein.

Law Offices of Cynthia Siddall. 3325 Wilshire Blvd., Los Angeles 90010-1703 (213) 388-4001. FAX: (213) 388-0686. William Margolin.

Siddall, David R. U.S. Federal Communications Commission, Mass Media Bureau, 2025 M St. N.W., Rm. 7102-A, Washington 20554. (202) 653-8108. FAX: (202) 653-8773.

Siegal, Joel H. 1352 5th Ave, San Diego 92101. (619) 338-9555. FAX: (619) 236-0916.

Siegal, Kelleher & Kahn. 420 Franklin St., Buffalo, N.Y. 14202. (716) 883-3222. FAX: (716) 885-3369. Leroi Johnson.

Siegan & Weisman Ltd. 200 W. Adams, Suite 901, Chicago Ill. 60606. (312) 782-1212. FAX: (312) 782-3032. Joel Weisman, David Rosenberg, Keith M. Kanter.

Silfen & Glasser. 545 5th Ave., New York 10017-7299. (212) 986-0890. FAX: (212) 986-0880.

Silva, Silva & Herrera P.C. 1002 Magoffin, El Paso, Tex. 79901. (915) 544-0888. FAX: (915) 533-6582. Jose A. Silva Jr., Jorge C. Herrera.

Law Offices of William D. Silva. 5335 Wisconsin Ave. N.W., Suite 300, Washington 20015-2003. (202) 362-1711. FAX: (202) 686-8282. William D. Silva.

Simenowitz, Krasner & Pehar. 1001 Franklin Ave., Garden City, N.Y. 11530-2901. (516) 739-0830. FAX: (516) 739-2105. Steven H. Simenowitz.

Simpkens, John Paul. 1300 Robinson Bldg., 42 S. 15th St., Philadelphia 19102. (215) 568-8040. FAX: (215) 568-2467.

Siporin, Sheldon. 3165 Nostrand Ave., Brooklyn, N.Y. 11229-3211. (212) 869-3050.

Skadden, Arps, Slate, Meagher & Flom. 1440 New York Ave. N.W., Washington 20015. (202) 371-7000. FAX: (202) 393-5760. Thomas J. Casey, Warren G. Lavey, Jay L. Birnbaum, Simone Wu, Timothy Robinson, Richard Hindman, David Pawlik, James Fink.

BARRY SKIDELSKY
Attorney at Law
(212) 832-4800
See our ad on page **H-90**

Barry Skidelsky, Esq. 655 Madison Ave., 19th Fl., New York 10021. (212) 832-4800. FAX: (212) 486-8668. Barry Skidelsky.

Small, William L. Box 6395, Arlington, Va. 22206-0395.

Smallwood, Christopher C. 6077 Far Hills Ave., Suite 101, Centerville, Ohio 45459. (513) 885-2137. FAX: (513) 885-2138.

Smith, Barab & Simpson. 9606 Santa Monica Blvd., Beverly Hills, Calif. 90210. (310) 859-6644. FAX: (301) 859-6650. Martin J. Barab; Robert A. Kline.

Smith, Bernadette M. Box 93153, Atlanta 30377-0153. (404) 875-0133.

Law Office of Eric H. Smith. 1747 Pennsylvania Ave. N.W., 12th Fl., Washington 20006. (202) 833-4198. FAX: (202) 872-0546. Eric H. Smith, Maria S. Strong.

Eugene T. Smith. 715 G St. S.E., Washington 20003. (202) 347-2363.

Smith, Gill, Fisher & Butts. 1200 Main St., 35th Fl., Kansas City, Mo. 64105. (816) 474-7400. John F. Dodd.

Smith, Grant W. 9 Music Sq. W., Nashville 37203-3203. (615) 244-3696. FAX: (615) 256-4396.

Smith, J. Clay. School of Law, Howard University, 2900 Van Ness St. N.W., Washington 20008-1101. (202) 806-8028. FAX: (202) 806-8037.

Smithwick & Belendiuk P.C. 1990 M St. N.W., Suite 510, Washington 20036. (202) 785-2800. FAX: (202) 785-2804. Gary S. Smithwick, Arthur V. Belendiuk, Shaun A. Maher, Robert W. Healy, counsel.

Snyder & Snyder. 183 Main St. E., #1024, Rochester, N.Y. 14604. (716) 546-7258. FAX: (716) 546-8332. Sherwood M. Snyder.

Sodos & Kafkas. 1229 S. 41st St., Milwaukee 53215-1325. (414) 645-9800. FAX: (414) 645-6098.

Sokolow, David Simon. University of Texas School of Law, 727 E. 26th St., Austin, Tex. 78705-3224. (512) 471-8171. (512) 471-6988.

Solomon, David H. U.S. Federal Communications Commission, 1919 M St. N.W., Rm. 616, Washington 20554. (202) 632-6990. FAX: (202) 632-0149.

Solomon, Edward S. Box 98, 16 City Hall Pl., Plattsburgh, N.Y. 12901. (518) 561-8100. FAX: (518) 561-8555.

Norman E. Solomon & Associates. Box 120356, 1503 17th Ave. S., Nashville Tenn. 37212-0356. (615) 385-3434. FAX: (615) 385-3489. Norman E. Solomon. Media/bcst collections, debt liquidation.

Law Firms Active in Communications Law

Sommer & Associates P.C. 2300 N St. N.W., Suite 600, Washington 20037. (202) 663-9037. FAX: (202) 667-8050. Stephanie Sommer.

Sommer, Seymour. 9777 Wilshire Blvd., Beverly Hills, Calif. 90212-1910. (310) 858-4989. FAX (310) 858-0775.

Sommers, Schwartz, Silver & Schwartz P.C. 2000 Town Ctr., Suite 900, Southfield, Mich. 48075. (313) 355-0300. FAX: (313) 746-4001. Patrick B. McCauley.

Sonneman & Sonneman. 111 Riverfront, Suite 409, Winona, Minn. 55987. (507) 454-8885. FAX: (507) 454-8887. Karl W. Sonneman.

Sonnenschein, Gail A. Videofashion Inc., One W. 37th St, 5th Fl., New York N.Y. 10018-6221. (212) 869-4666. FAX (212) 869-8208.

Sonnenschein, Nath & Rosenthal. 800 Sears Tower, 233 S. Wacker Dr., Chicago 60606. (312) 876-3114. FAX: (312) 876-7934. David W. Maher, Samuel Fifer.

Sony Classical. 550 Madison Ave., 16th Fl., New York N.Y. 10022. (212) 833-4277. Linda Novak, entertainment atty.

Soocher, Stan. Entertainment Law & Finance, 111 8th Ave., 9th Fl., New York 10011-5201. (212) 463-5522.

Southmayd & Miller P.C. 1220 19th St. N.W., Suite 400, Washington 20036. (202) 331-4100. FAX: (202) 331-4123. Jeffrey D. Southmayd; Michael R. Miller; Robert Clifton Burns, counsel.

Spawn, Coy U. Jr. 1815 Bering Dr., Houston 77057-3109. (713) 782-2977.

Spiegel & McDiarmid. 1350 New York Ave. N.W., Suite 1100, Washington 20005-4798. (202) 879-4000. FAX: (202) 393-2866. James N. Horwood.

Lester W. Spillane, Attorney at Law. 268 Kaanapali Dr., Napa, Calif. 94558. (503) 977-0167. FAX: (707) 258-1956.

Spivak, Peter B. 3753 Penobscot Bldg., Detroit 48226. (313) 963-2070. FAX: (313) 965-9828.

Squire, Sanders & Dempsey. Box 407, 1201 Pennsylvania Ave. N.W., Washington 20044. (202) 626-6600. FAX: (202) 626-6780; Thomas J. Ramsey, David A. Nall, Lauren H. Kravetz, Herbert E. Marks, Stephen R. Bell, Joseph P. Markoski, James L. Casserly, Ann J. LaFrance, Radhika V. Karmarkar, Kerry E. Murray, Jody D. Newman.
  Cleveland 44114-1304: 4900 Society Ctr., 127 Public Sq. (216) 479-8500. FAX: (216) 479-8777. Terrence J. Clark, ptnr.

Law Offices of Marc R. Staenberg, A.P.C. 2530 Wilshire Blvd., 2nd Fl., Santa Monica, Calif. 90403. (310) 829-1700. FAX: (310) 829-2148. Marc R. Staenberg.

Steingard, Charles G. 2519 W. Jerome St., 3rd Fl., Chicago 60645. (312) 262-6314.

Stennett, Wilkinson & Ward. Box 22627, Jackson, Miss. 39225-2627. (601) 948-3000. FAX: (601) 948-3019. Gene Wilkinson.

Stephens, Louis C. 1547 Candlewick Ct., McLean, Va. 22101. (703) 356-9111.

Steptoe & Johnson. 1330 Connecticut Ave. N.W., Washington 20036. (202) 429-3000. FAX: (202) 429-9204. Philip L. Malet, Judith O'Neill, James McHugh.

Stevens, Sally L. River Rd., Lumberville, Pa. 18933. (212) 977-3823; (215) 297-8245. FAX: (215) 297-5106.

Stewart, Estes & Donnell. Third National Financial Ctr., Nashville 37219. (615) 244-6538. FAX: (615) 256-8386. Philip M. Kirkpatrick.

Stewart & Irwin. 2 Market Sq. Ctr., Suite 110, 251 E. Ohio St., Indianapolis 46204-2142. (317) 639-5454. FAX: (317) 632-1319. Richard E. Aikman.

Law Offices of Richard Augustin Storm III P.C. 2001 Park Pl. N., Suite 495, Birmingham, Ala. 35203. (205) 252-5725. FAX: (205) 323-6174.

Streibich & Seale. Bryton Tower, 1271 Popular Ave., Suite 101, Memphis 38104. (901) 722-8188. FAX: (901) 278-7126. Harold C. Streibich, William B. Seale, David A. Outlaw, Bruce A. Ralston, David A. Lee.

Strichartz, James L. 200 W. Mercer St., Seattle 98119-3958. (206) 282-8020. FAX: (206) 282-5041.

Stroock, Stroock & Lavin. 1150 17th St. N.W., Suite 600, Washington 20036. (202) 452-9250. FAX: (202) 293-2293.

Stryker, Tams & Dill. 2 Penn Plaza E., Newark, N.J. 07105-2293. (201) 491-9500. FAX (201) 491-9692. Dennis C. Linken.
  The firm is engaged in a wide-ranging regulatory, litigation & transactional law practice. A significant aspect of the firm's activities involves public utilities & cable television matters, wherein the firm practices regularly before municipal bodies, various state admin agencies & state & federal courts. The firm represents a number of communications clients, including primarily cable television, paging & telecommunication companies. In addition to its significant regulatory role on behalf of its clients, the firm has represented cable television, paging & cellular telephone companies with respect to their transactional needs, including sls & acquisitions & financing transactions with lenders. The firm has also represented banks with respect to their lending activities to communications companies.

Stults, Balber, Horton & Slotnik. 1370 Ave. of the Americas, 30th Fl., New York 10019. (212) 246-2400. FAX: (212) 765-4212. Theodore Striggles.

Suffness, Michael. 2419 Coit Rd., Suite A, Plano, Tex. 75075. (214) 985-1331. FAX: (214) 985-1315.

Sullivan & Worcester. 1025 Connecticut Ave. N.W., Suite 1000, Washington 20036. (202) 775-8190. FAX: (202) 293-2275. Eric Fishman, William L. Fishman.

Sutherland, Asbill & Brennan. 1275 Pennsylvania Ave. N.W., Washington 20004-2404. (202) 383-0100. FAX: (202) 637-3593. Anne P. Jones, Frank J. Martin Jr., David A. Gross, Timothy J. Cooney, Randolph J. May.

Swidler & Berlin, Chartered. 3000 K St. N.W., Suite 300, Washington 20002. (202) 424-7833. FAX: (202) 424-7645. Andy Lipman, Jean Kiddoo, Russell Blau, Helen Disenhaus, Catherine Wang, Ann Morton, Richard Rindler, Dana Frix, Robert Berger, Jonathan Canis, Margaret Charles, Charles Kallenbach, Russell Merbeth.

T

Tapia & Associates. 2715 M St. N.W., Suite 300, Washington 20007. (202) 298-8700. FAX: (202) 333-6732. Raul R. Tapia.

Law Office of Hugh Taylor. 900 17th St. N.W., #900, Washington 20006. (202) 331-5880. FAX: (202) 296-1682. Hugh P. Taylor.

Taylor, Jack. 1289 Lincoln Rd. Yuba City, Calif. 95991. (916) 671-6800. FAX (916) 671-6447.

Leslie Taylor Associates. 6800 Carlynn Ct., Bethesda, Md. 20817. (301) 229-9341.

Taylor, Ray L. 11608 Chayote St., Los Angeles 90049. (310) 476-6493. FAX: (310) 472-7257.

Taylor, Thiemann & Aitken. 908 King St., Suite 300, Alexandria, Va. 22314. (703) 836-9400. FAX: (703) 836-9409. Russell C. Powell.

Teitelbaum, Israel. 11301 Amherst Ave., Suite 202, Silver Spring, Md. 20902. (202) 933-3373. FAX: (202) 933-3651.

Tekulsky, Joseph D. 13570 Bayliss Rd., Los Angeles 90049-1813. (310) 476-8066.

Tharrington, Smith & Hargrove. Box 1151, Raleigh, N.C. 27602; 209 Fayetteville St. Mall, Raleigh N.C. 27601. (919) 821-4711. FAX: (919) 829-1583. Wade H. Hargrove, Mark J. Prak, Randall M. Roden, William A. Davis II, E. Hardy Lewis, Daniel W. Clark.

Thelen, Marrin, Johnson & Bridges. 2 Embarcardo Ctr., San Francisco 94111. (415) 392-6320. FAX: (415) 421-1068. John Foot.

Thomas, Ballenger, Vogelman & Turner. 124 S. Royal St., Alexandria, Va. 22314. (703) 836-3400. FAX: (703) 836-3549. John M. Ballenger.

Thompson, Adams, DeBast, & Helzer. 4500 S.W. Hall Blvd., Beaverton, Ore. 97005-0504. (503) 644-2146. FAX: (503) 646-2227. Richard G. Helzer.

Thompson, Hine & Florry. 10 W. Broad St., Suite 700, Columbus, Ohio 43215. (614) 469-3200. FAX: (614) 469-3250. George C. McConaughey.
  Washington 20036: 1920 N St. N.W., Suite 700. (202) 331-8800. Jon F. Kelly.

Thrasher, Dinsmore & Dolan. 100 7th St., Suite 150, Chardon, Ohio 44024-1079. (216) 285-2242. FAX: (216) 285-9423. Paul J. Dolan.

Tierney & Swift. 1200 18th St. N.W., Suite 210, Washington 20036. (202) 293-7979. FAX: (202) 293-7983. John L. Tierney, Richard F. Swift.

Tighe, M. Joan. 720 S. Orange Grove Blvd., Pasadena, Calif. 91105. (818) 441-3450.

Tobias, Jeffrey. Pike & Fischer Inc. 4600 East West Hwy., Suite 200, Bethesda, Md. 20814-1438. (301) 654-6262.

Law Offices of Victor J. Toth. 2719 Soapstone Dr., Reston, Va. 22091. (703) 476-5515. FAX: (703) 620-6086.

Trager & Trager P.C. 1305 Post Rd., Fairfield, Conn. 06430. (203) 255-6138. FAX: (203) 255-4162.

Trapp, Chastain & Ulterwyk. 390 N. Orange Ave., Suite 2100, Orlando, Fla., 32801. (407) 648-1418. FAX: (407) 422-6858. Richard Trapp.
  Tampa 33629-5901: 1810 S. MacDill Ave. (305) 764-4000.

Traylor, Michael S. 10474 Santa Monica Blvd., Suite 401, Los Angeles 90025. (310) 446-8891. (310) 446-8894.

Tribune Company. 435 N. Michigan Ave., Chicago Ill. 60611-4041. Joseph P Thornton. sr counsel. (312) 222-4123. FAX (312) 222-4206.

Troutman, Sanders. Nations Bank Plaza, 600 Peachtree St. Suite 5200, Atlanta Ga. 30308. (404) 885-3118. FAX: (404) 885-3900. Tench Coxe, Robert W. Webb, Alan P. Shor.

Troy & Gould. 1801 Century Park E., 16th Fl., Los Angeles 90067. (310) 553-4441. FAX: (310) 201-4746.

Trugman, Richard S. 9615 Brighton Way, Suite 320, Beverly Hills, Calif. 90210-5109. (310) 273-8834. FAX: (310) 273-8345.

Turner Publishing/TBS Productions. 1050 Techwood Dr., Atlanta 30318. (404) 885-4033. FAX: (404) 885-4066.

Edmund W. Turnley. 1105 16th Ave. S., Suite B, Nashville 37208. (615) 327-8772. Edmund W. Turnley.

Turtle, Joel S. 3210 21st St., San Francisco 94110. (415) 282-3600.

Tyrrell, Thomas C. Box 4450, New York 10101-4450. (212) 445-3907.

U

Umansky, Barry D. National Association of Broadcasters, 1771 N St. N.W., Washington 20036-2805. (202) 429-5430.

Mark Uncapher. 99 State St., Brooklyn Heights, N.Y. 11201. (718) 643-5825.

Unger, Zave M. 7616 137th St., Flushing, N.Y. 11367. (718) 268-5660.

V

Van Cott, Bagley, Cornwall & McCarthy. Box 45340, 50 S. Main St., Suite 1600, Salt Lake City 84144-0103. (801) 532-3333. FAX: (801) 534-0058. Maxilian A. Farbman.

Vance, Jackson, Simpson & Vance-Lewis. 1429 Walnut St., 8th Fl., Philadelphia 19102. (215) 665-8082. FAX: (215) 665-8086.

Vanias, A. Chavis. Box 9612, 1929 "A" Marion St., Columbia, S.C. 29290. (803) 799-2532. FAX: (803) 799-2532.

Varet, Marcis, & Fink. 53 Wall St., New York 10005. (212) 858-5300. FAX: (212) 858-5201. Robinson Markel.

Varnum, Riddering, Schmidt & Howlett. 171 Monroe St. N.W., Suite 800, Grand Rapids, Mich. 49503. (616) 459-4186. FAX: (616) 459-8468. Eric J. Schneidewind.

Vasak, Stephen. 2 University Plaza, Suite 205, Hackensack, N.J. 07601-6201. (201) 488-3737.

Vedder, Price, Caughman, Kammholz, & Day. One Dag Hammerskzold Plaza,, New York 10017. (212) 687-1140. FAX: (212) 223-1790.

Venable, Baetjer, Howard & Civiletti. 1800 Mercantile Bank Bldg., 2 Hopkins Plaza, Baltimore 21201. (410) 244-7400. H. Russell Frisby Jr.
  Washington 20005: 1201 New York Ave. N.W., Suite 1000. (202) 962-4800.

Law Firms Active in Communications Law

Verner, Liipfert, Bernhard, McPherson & Hand, Chartered. 901 15th St. N.W., Suite 700, Washington 20005. (202) 371-6000. FAX: (202) 371-6279. Erwin G. Krasnow, Thomas J. Keller, William H. Crispin, William E. Kennard, Michael E. Beller, Eric T. Werner, Dean R. Brenner, Lawrence R. Sidman, Michael Wroblewski, Kathy Smith.

Viera, Melie. Esq. 7355 N.W. 41st St., Miami, Fla. 33166-6713. (305) 593-6969. FAX: (305) 594-2780.

Voelker & Battard. 3850 N. Causeway Blvd., Suite 1330, Metairie, La. 70002. (504) 836-7055. FAX: (504) 836-7062. Richard L. Voelker Jr.

Volpe, Boskey & Lyons. 918 16th St. N.W., Suite 602, Washington 20006. (202) 737-6580.

Vorys, Sater, Seymour & Pease. Box 1008, 52 E. Gay St., Columbus, Ohio 43216-1008. (614) 464-6400. FAX: (614) 464-6350. Sheldon A. Taft, M. Howard Petricoff, Stephen M. Howard, James H. Gross, William D. Kloss, C. William O'Neill, William S. Newcomb Jr.
  Washington 20036: 1828 L St. N.W., Suite 1111. (202) 467-8800. FAX: (202) 467-8900.
  Cleveland 44114: 2100 One Cleveland Ctr., 1375 E. 9th St. (216) 479-6100. FAX: (216) 479-6060.
  Cincinnati 45201: Suite 2100, Atrium Two, 221 E. 4th St., Box 0236. (513) 723-4000. FAX: (513) 723-4056.

W

Wagner, Michael Francis. U.S. Federal Communications Commission, 1919 M St. N.W., Rm. 318, Washington 20554. (202) 632-3954.

Waller, Lansden, Dortch & Davis. 511 Union St., Suite 2100, Nashville 37219. (615) 244-6380. FAX: (615) 244-5686. William F. Carpenter.

Walsh, Robert P. Box 71, Battle Creek, Mich. 49016. (616) 963-3716.

Walton, Frederick H. Jr. 7214 Maple Ave., Chevy Chase, Md. 20815. (301) 652-9411.

Law Offices of Donald E. Ward. 1201 Pennsylvania Ave. N.W., 4th Fl., Washington 20004. (202) 626-6290. FAX: (202) 626-6292. Donald E. Ward.

Ware, Kenneth. 523 W. 150th St., Suite 6, New York 10031. (212) 862-1196.

Warner Bros. Warner Bros., 4000 Warner Blvd., Burbank, Calif. 91522. (818) 954-6000.

Law Offices of Harry P. Warner. 6455 Hayes Dr., Los Angeles 90048. (213) 931-2713.

Warner & Stackpole. 75 State St., Boston 02109. (617) 951-9000. FAX: (617) 951-9151. Steven Palmer.

Waxman, Jon M. 302 W. 12th, New York 10014. (212) 929-2562.

Weber, Frederic G. 631 N. First Ave., Phoenix 85003-1514. (602) 258-6161. FAX: (602) 252-9563.

Weber, Joseph Paul. U.S. Federal Communications Commission, 1919 M St. N.W., Rm. 644, Washington 20554. (202) 632-6450. FAX: (202) 634-7845.

Law Offices of Edward L. Weidenfeld. 1899 L St. N.W., 5th Fl., Washington 20036. (202) 785-2143. FAX: (202) 452-8938.

Weil, Gotshal & Manges. 1615 L St. N.W., Suite 700, Washington 20036. (202) 682-7000. FAX: (202) 857-0940. Bruce H. Turnbull.

Weinstein, Joel H. 90 Woodbridge Ctr. Dr., Suite 710, Woodbridge, N.J. 07095. (908) 750-0900. FAX: (908) 750-1222.

Weinstock, Bruce J. 12400 Wilshire Blvd., Los Angeles 90025-1019. (310) 207-0266. FAX: (310) 442-0181.

Weissmann, Wolff, Bergman, Coleman & Silverman. 9665 Wilshire Blvd., Suite 900, Beverly Hills, Calif. 90212-2316. (310) 858-7888. Eric Weissmann.

Werner, Robert L. 116 E. 68th St., New York N.Y. 10020. (212) 734-1866.

West, Joella. 4024 Radford Ave., Bldg. #3, Studio City, Calif. 91604-2101. (818) 760-5176. FAX: (818) 760-6328.

Westervelt, Johnson, Nicholl & Keller. First Financial Plaza, 411 Hamilton Blvd., 14th Fl., Peoria, Ill. 61602. (309) 671-3550. FAX: (309) 671-3588. Arthur G. Greenberg.

Westrick, Carole J. 900 Bridgeway, Sausalito, Calif. 94966. (415) 332-3265. FAX: (415) 332-3290.

The Wexler Group/Hill & Knowlton. 1317 F St. N.W., Suite 600, Washington 20004. (202) 638-2121. FAX: (202) 638-7045. Joseph W. Waz Jr.

Wheeler & Wheeler. 808 17th St. N.W., Washington 20006. (202) 467-0500. FAX: (202) 467-0502. Edward K. Wheeler.

Wheeler Wolf Law Firm. Box 2056, 116 N. 4th. St., Bismarck, N.D. 58501-4001. (701) 225-5300. Jack McDonald.

Whent, Christopher R. 270 Madison Ave., Suite 1410, New York 10016-0601. (212) 679-8710. FAX: (212) 686-2182.

White, Raymond A. U.S. Federal Communications Commission, Mass Media Bureau, 1919 M St. N.W., Rm. 8202, Washington 20554. (202) 632-7586. FAX: (202) 653-9659.

White, Verville, Fulton & Saner. 1156 15th St. N.W., Suite 1100, Washington 20005. (202) 659-2900. Peter S. Leyton.

Whitesell Law Offices. Box 336, Iowa Falls, Iowa 50126. (515) 648-4646. FAX: (515) 648-6283. John P. Whitesell.

Whitley, Jack W. 27 Pine Ave., Takoma Park, Md. 20912. (301) 270-4394.

Whitten, Phyllis A., General Attorney. Sprint Communications Co. 1850 M St. N.W., 1st. Fl., Suite 1100, Washington 20036 (202) 857-1030. FAX: (202) 822-8999.

Joan Wilbon & Associates. 1511 K St. N.W., Suite 405, Washington 20005. (202) 737-7458. FAX: (202) 347-5845. Joan Wilbon.

Wildman, Harrold, Allen & Dickson. 225 W. Wacker Dr., Suite 2800, Chicago 60606. (312) 201-2000. FAX: (312) 201-2555. George W. Overton.

Wiley, Rein & Fielding. 1776 K St., N.W., Washington 20006. (202) 429-7000. FAX: (202) 429-7049; FAX: (202) 429-7207. Danny E. Adams, William B. Baker, John L. Bartlett, James R. Bayes, William H. Berman, Robert J. Butler, Mimi W. Dawson, Kurt E. DeSoto, Carl R. Frank, Jerry V. Haines, David E. Hilliard, Katherine M. Holden, Jeffrey S. Linder, Philip V. Permut, John C. Quale, Carl R. Ramey, Lawrence W. Secrest III, R. Michael Senkowski, Richard E. Wiley, Edward A. Yorkgitis, Michael Yourshaw, Wayne D. Johnsen, Katherine A. King, Nancy J. Victory, Richard J. Bodorff, Eric DeSilva, Aliza F. Katz, Rachel Rothstein, Daniel E. Troy, Steven A. Augustino, Howard H. Bell, Lauren A. Brofazi, John I. Davis, Kenneth D. Ebanks, Donna C. Gregg, Rosemary C. Harold, Ken I. Kersch, Brad E. Mutschelknaus, Todd M. Stansbury, Diane Zipursky.

Law Offices of Michael J. Wilhelm. 1350 Connecticut Ave. N.W., Suite 905, Washington 20036. (202) 785-9117.

Wilkes, Artis, Hedrick & Lane. 1666 K St. N.W., Suite 1100, Washington 20006. (202) 457-7800. FAX: (202) 457-7814. John D. Lane, Ramsey L. Woodworth, Martin J. Gaynes, Robert M. Gurss.

Wilkinson, Barker, Knauer & Quinn. 1735 New York Ave. N.W., Suite 600, Washington 20006. (202) 783-4141. FAX: (202) 783-5851. Earl R. Stanley, Leon T. Knauer, L. Andrew Tollin, Michael D. Sullivan, Kenneth E. Satten, F. Thomas Moran, Kenneth D. Patrich, Lusia L. Lancetti, Christine V. Simpson, Kathryn A. Zachem, Werner J. Hein, Lawrence J. Movshin, Kelley A. Baione, Janet Fitzpatrick, Robert Kirk, Kim D, Larsen, Carolyn W. Malanga.

Willcox & Savage. Nations Bank Ctr., Norfolk, Va. 23510. (804) 628-5500. FAX: (804) 628-5566. Jeffrey H. Gray, Conrad M. Shumadine, Elizabeth Hoyes Esinhurt.

Willkie, Farr & Gallagher. 1155 21st St. N.W., Suite 600, Washington 20036. (202) 328-8000. Sue D. Blumenfeld, John L. McGrew, Philip Verveer, Theodore Whitehouse, Brian Conboy, Michael Hammer, Larry Atlas, Michele Pistone, Melissa Mewman, Frank Buono, Jennifer Donaldson, Brian Finley.

Wilmer, Cutler & Pickering. 2445 M St. N.W., Washington 20037-1420. (202) 663-6000. FAX: (202) 293-0074. Timothy N. Black, W. Scott Blackmer, Lloyd N. Cutler, Robert A. Hammond III, John H. Harwood, William T. Lake, Jonathan Jacob Nadler, Daniel Marcus, A. Douglas Melamed, William R. Richardson Jr., Joel Rosenbloom, J. Roger Wollenberg, Andrea Ann Timko, Patrick J. Carome, Kelly Klegar Levy, Julie C. Buchanan.

Wilner, Morton H. 2701 Chesapeake St. N.W., Washington 20008. (202) 362-3839. FAX: (202) 224-1250.

Wilson, Alexandra M. U.S. Federal Communications Commission, 2033 M St. N.W., Rm. 918, Washington 20036. (202) 416-0856.

Winkler & Belgrave P.C. 60 Park Pl., Suite 1703, Newark, N.J. 07102. (201) 624-5500. FAX: (201) 624-5980. Maury R. Winkler.

Winston & Strawn. 35 W. Wacker Dr., Chicago 60601-1695. (312) 558-5600. Ross Fishman.
  Washington 20005: 1400 L St. N.W., 8th Fl., (202) 371-5710. FAX: (202) 371-5950. William K. Keane.

Winthrop, Stimson, Putnam & Roberts. 1133 Connecticut Ave. N.W., Washington 20036. (202) 775-9800. FAX: (202) 833-8491 Stuart N. Brotman.

Wise, C, Michael. 338 S. High St., Columbus, Ohio 43215-4570. (614) 222-0530.

Wleklinski, Mark J. 1220 Oakland Blvd., Suite 200, Walnut Creek, Calif. 94596-3572. (510) 943-1191. FAX: (510) 943-3018.

Wolf, Greenfield & Sacks. Federal Reserve Plaza, 600 Atlantic Ave., Boston 02210-2206. (617) 720-3500. FAX: (617) 720-2441. Mark A. Fischer, Jay M. Fialkov, atty.

Wolf & Wolf. 9000 W. Sunset Blvd., #1005, Los Angeles 90069-5810. (310) 278-6060. David M. Wolf.

Wolfe, Richard C. 20803 Biscayne Blvd., Miami, Fla. 33180. (305) 935-6888. FAX: (305) 932-6043.

Wolff, Nancy E. 115 E. 57th St., New York 10022-2049. (212) 753-2224. FAX: (212) 826-0199.

Woodrow & Gruskin P.C. 999 18th St., Suite 3450, Denver 80202. (303) 296-1400. FAX: (303) 296-1924. Shalene Farley.

Wright & Tallisman P.C. 1200 G St. N.W., Suite 600, Washington 20005. (202) 393-1200. FAX: (202) 393-1240. Robert Benna.

Wyatt, Tarrant, Combs, Gilbert & Milom. 511 Union St., Suite 1500, Nashville 37219. (615) 244-0020.
  Louisville, Ky. 40202: Citizens Plaza, (502) 589-5235. Kimberly K. Greene.

Y

Young, Clement, Rivers & Tisdale. Box 993, 28 Broad St., Charleston, S.C. 29402. (803) 577-4000. FAX: (803) 724-6600. Robert L. Clement Jr., Thomas S. Tisdale.

Young, James R. 1310 N. Courthouse Rd., 11th Fl., Arlington, Va. 22201. (703) 974-3609. FAX: (703) 974-1951.

Law Offices of W. Randolph Young. 1050 17th St. N.W., Suite 1200, Washington 20036. (202) 785-8980. FAX: (202) 331-0174.

Z

Zaina, Lisa M. 21 Dupont Cir. N.W., Suite 700. Washington 20036. (202) 659-5990. FAX: (202) 659-4619.

Law Office of Arnold G. Ziegler P.C. 8700 Georgia Ave., Suite 304, Silver Spring, Md. 20910. (301) 588-7411. FAX: (301) 588-7420.

Zimmerman, Rosenfeld & Gersh. 9107 Wilshire Blvd., Suite 300, Beverly Hills, Calif. 90210-5531. (310) 278-7560. FAX: (310) 273-5602. Scott Zolke.

Zipperman, Jeff. Motloff. 8800 W. Sunset Blvd., Los Angeles 90069-2105. (310) 859-8800. FAX: (310) 657-1629.

Zoslov, Amy. U.S. Federal Communications Commission, Mass Media Bureau, 2025 M St. N.W., Rm. 8210, Washington 20554. (202) 632-3922. FAX: (202) 653-9659.

Zuckman, Harvey L. Leahy Hall, 620 Michigan Ave., N.E., Washington 20064. (202) 319-5140. FAX: (202) 319-4459.

Zukowski, Rogers, Flood & McArdle. 100 S. Wacker Dr., Suite 1502, Chicago 60606. (312) 407-7700. FAX: (312) 663-3689. Richard R. Zukowski, William J. O'Connor.

Talent Agents and Managers

Abrams, Rubaloff & Lawrence Inc. 8075 W. 3rd St., Suite 303, Los Angeles 90048. (213) 935-1700. FAX: (213) 932-9901. Richard Lawrence, pres.

Associated Essentials. Box 8135, Chicago 60680. (312) 224-5612. Attn R.C. Hillsman; Frank Howard Jr.; R. C. Hillsman, VP.

Sherlee Barish & Associates. 47 S. Palm Ave., Suite 201, Sarasota, Fla. 34236. (813) 952-0199. FAX: (813) 952-0466. Sherlee Barish, pres; Colleen Marone, asst to pres.
Representation: on-air TV news & news mgmt.

N.S. Bienstock. 1740 Broadway, 24th Fl., New York 10019. (212) 765-3040. FAX: (212) 757-6411. Richard A. Leibner, Carole Cooper, Steve Lefkowitz, Stuart Witt, Sherry Berman, George Hiltzik, agents.

Carolco Television. 432 Park Ave. S., New York 10016. (212) 685-6699. FAX: (212) 586-5697. John Ranck, pres.

Command Appearance. 8633 Arbor Dr., El Cerrito, Calif. 94530-2728. (510) 524-9559. FAX: (510) 524-9559. Joe Leavitt & Jeanne Leavitt, principals; Robert M. Master, M.Ph.A., talent exec/chief photographer; Mark C. Rhadaman, talent progression; T. Waters, talent/photography instruction.
Gaithersburg, Md. 20879: (510) 524-9559. Robert Levit, Ph.D.
Pageant specialists: dev, photography, instruction, testing, mgmt direction.

Diamond Artists Ltd. 215 N. Barrington Ave., Los Angeles 90049. (310) 472-7579; (310) 278-8146. FAX: (310) 472-2687. Abner J. Greshler, pres; Camille Harris, dir.
New York 10019: 119 W. 57th St. (212) Circle 7, ext. 3025. Camille Harris, dir.

Robert Eatman Enterprises Inc. (Talent Agency). Box 5824, Beverly Hills, Calif. 90209-5834. (310) 459-3728. FAX: (310) 459-0058. Robert Eatman, pres.
Representing TV newspersons, radio morning shows, prog directors, & TV personalities.

Ephraim & Associates P.C. 108 W. Grand Ave., Chicago 60610-4206. (312) 321-9700. FAX: (312) 321-3655. Donald M. Ephraim, pres; Joseph F. Coyne, VP; Eliot S. Ephraim, treas; David M. Ephraim, asst sec.

Jack Fields & Associates Inc. 10100 Santa Monica Blvd., Suite 700, Los Angeles 90067. (310) 277-4400. FAX: (310) 277-7820. Jack X. Fields, pres.

Glenn A. Goldstein, Esq. One Commerce Sq., 2005 Market St., 21st Fl., Philadelphia 19103. (215) 241-5061. FAX: (215) 241-1857. Glenn A. Goldstein, atty.

Reece Halsey Agency. 8733 Sunset Blvd., West Hollywood, Calif. 90069. (310) 652-2409. Dorris Halsey, own.

Shirley Hamilton Inc. 333 E. Ontario, Chicago 60611. (312) 787-4700. FAX: (312) 787-8456. Shirley Hamilton, pres; Lynne S. Hamilton, VP.

ICM Holding Inc. 40 W. 57th St., 18th Fl., New York 10019. (212) 556-5600. FAX: (212) 556-5665. Marvin Josephson, chmn of bd; Ralph Mann, vice-chmn.

International Creative Management Inc. 40 W. 57th St., New York 10019. (212) 556-5600. FAX (212) 556-5665. Jeff Berg, chmn; James Wiatt, pres.
Los Angeles 10019: 8899 Beverly Blvd. (310) 550-4000.
London, U.K. W1R 1RB: 76 Oxford St. (011) 44-71-636-6565.

Jennifer Jones Booking Agency. 523 Dumaine, Suite 6, New Orleans 70116. (504) 529-2543. FAX: (504) 529-2544. Jennifer Jones, pres.
B.A., P.M., P.R., business mgmt.

Joe Jones Management. 10556 Arnwood Rd., Lake View Terrace, Calif. 91342. (818) 890-0730. FAX: (818) 899-4457. Joe Jones, pres.
New Orleans 70119: 2114 New Orleans St. (504) 949-8969. Deborah Jones, branch mgr.
B.A., P.M., P.R., business mgmt.

MAKEDWE Booking Agency. 10556 Arnwood Rd., Lake View Terrace, Calif. 91342. (818) 890-0730. FAX: (818) 899-4457. Dwayne Jones, gen mgr; Marion Jones, chmn; Joe Jones, CEO-international.
B.A., P.M., P.R., business mgmt.

Media Alliance. Box 1984, Burlington, Conn. 06013. (203) 673-3044. W.F. LaPlante II, exec dir.

Miller Broadcast Management Inc. 708 N. Dearborn, Chicago 60610. (312) 266-6665. FAX: (312) 266-6632. Lisa Miller, pres.
Representing radio talent & mgmt.

William Morris Agency Inc. 1350 Ave. of the Americas, New York 10019. (212) 586-5100. FAX: (212) 246-3583. Jerry Kal, pres; Lou Weiss, exec VP Worldwide TV; Len Rosenberg, VP TV East Coast.
Beverly Hills, Calif. 90212: 151 El Camino Dr. (310) 274-7451. Jerry Katzman, VP TV West Coast.
Nashville 37215: 2325 Crestmoor Rd. (615) 385-0310. Jeffrey Beals.
London, U.K. W1V 5DG: 31/32 Soho Sq. (71) 434-2191. Steve Kenis, dir.

Navarro-Bertoni Casting & Assoc. Co. Ltd. 101 W. 31st St., Suite 2112, New York 10001. (212) 736-9272. FAX: (212) 465-2064. Esther Navarro, pres; Riccardo Bertoni, Beata Lynar, VPs.

Producer's Audition Hotline Inc. Box 742, Olney, Md. 20830. (301) 924-5700. FAX: (301) 570-8916. Michael J. Weiner, pres.
New York Hotline: (212) 593-4327.
Los Angeles Hotline: (213) 656-4327.
Mid-Atlantic Hotline: (301) 924-4327.
Specializing in voice talent.

Richard H. Roffman Associates. 697 West End Ave., New York 10025. (212) 749-3647. Richard H. Roffman, pres; Florence Morrison, exec VP; Don Lester, VP; Leo Blau, VP; Evelyn Neinken, talent coord.

Screen Children's Agency. 12444 Ventura Blvd., Suite 103, Studio City, Calif. 91604. (818) 985-6131. Irene Gallagher, own/talent agent.

Burt Shapiro Management. 2147 N. Beachwood Dr., Los Angeles 90067. (213) 469-9452. FAX: (213) 469-9452. Burt Shapiro, pres.

Siegan & Weisman Ltd. 200 W. Adams, Suite 901, Chicago 60606. (312) 782-1212. FAX: (312) 782-3032. Joel Weisman, pres.

Barry Skidelsky, Esq. 655 Madison Ave., 19th Fl., New York 10021. (212) 832-4800. FAX: (212) 486-8668. Barry Skidelsky, Esq.

Charles H. Stern Agency Inc. 11755 Wilshire Blvd., #2320, Los Angeles 90025. (310) 479-1788. Charles H. Stern, pres.

The Voicecaster. 1832 W. Burbank Blvd., Burbank, Calif. 91506. (818) 841-5300. FAX: (818) 841-2085. Robert Lloyd, own.

Wise Management Agency. 13603 Fawn Ridge Blvd., Tampa 33626. (813) 920-6959. FAX: (813) 920-7900. Douglas F. Simms, pres.

Carter Wright Enterprises. 6533 Hollywood Blvd., Suite 201, Los Angeles 90028. (213) 469-0944. FAX: (213) 464-3781. Carter Wright, pres; June Wright, VP; Lisa Andresen, ptnr.

Employment and Executive Search Services

Bornholdt Shives & Friends. 295 Madison Ave., Suite 1206, New York 10017. (212) 557-5252. FAX: (212) 557-5704. John N. Bornholdt, James M. Shives, gen ptnrs.
Exec recruiters to the communications industry.

Boydon Consulting Corp. 55 Madison Ave., Morristown, N.J. 07960. (201) 267-0980. FAX: (201) 267-6172. Peter R. Schmidt, pres; Leeda Marting, VP.
Worldwide sr mgmt exec search firm specializing in TV, radio, CATV & entertainment industry.

George Burns & Company. 6965 El Camino Real, Suite 105-229, Rancho La Costa, Calif. 92009. (619) 746-7993. FAX: (619) 739-8303. George Burns, chmn; Larry Lakoduk, pres; Todd Stewart, VP progmg.
Radio mgmt & consulting.

California Broadcasters Association. 1127 11th St., Suite 730, Sacramento, Calif. 95814. (916) 444-2237. FAX: (916) 444-2043. Vic Biondi, exec dir.

Bill Elliott, Broadcast Consultant. Box 1256, Port Richey, Fla. 34673-1256. (813) 849-3477. Bill Elliott, pres.
Radio, TV, cable job search & per recruitment—executive, talent & tech.

Entertainment Employment Journal. 7095 Hollywood Blvd., Suite 815, Hollywood, Calif. 90028. (213) 969-8500.
Bi-monthly newsletter providing career info & job listings with major & ind motion picture, TV & cable companies.

Fink & Blakely Associates. 900 N. Point St., Suite 410, San Francisco 94109. (415) 441-3777. FAX: (415) 775-4925. Neil Fink, pres; Larry Blakely, exec VP.
Meridian, Miss. 39305: 7753 State Blvd. Ext. (601) 693-5185. FAX: (601) 485-7117. Neil Fink, pres; Larry Blakely, exec VP; Sondra Albright, acct exec.
Executive search and mgmt consulting firm servicing the audio video, bcst, multi-media & related communications and high technology industries.

Don Fitzpatrick Associates. 408 Columbus Ave., Suite One, San Francisco 94133. (415) 954-0700. FAX: (415) 954-0820. Don Fitzpatrick, pres; Keitha Mashaw, VP; Patty Craig, Debra Wilson, talent coords.
TV news & progmg; talent & mgmt placement.

The Howard-Sloan-Koller Group. 353 Lexington Ave., 11th Fl., New York 10016. (212) 661-5250. FAX: (212) 557-9178. Edward R. Koller Jr., pres; Karen Danziger, exec VP.
Executive search & consultation in the cable, info & publishing industries.

JOBPHONE. Box 5048, Newport Beach, Calif. 92662. To hear job openings nationwide: (900) 726-5627 (JOBS), $1.99 per minute. To leave job openings: (212) 570-7440, free svc. Keith Mueller.
Natl TV/radio employment hotline.

Job Leads/Broadcast Employment Newsletter. 66 The Terrace, New York 10536. (914) 232-7926. Bernard M. Brickel, publisher & edit.
Wkly newsletter featuring positions in radio, TV & cable; all categories.

Joe Jones Search Co. 10556 Arnwood Rd., Lake View Terr., Calif. 91342. (818) 890-0730. FAX: (818) 899-4457. Joe Jones, exec of search; Marion Jones, pres/CEO.
Exec search & clearinghouse specializing in radio & the TV industry.

Korn/Ferry International. 1800 Century Park E., Suite 900, Los Angeles 90067. (310) 552-1834. FAX: (310) 553-6452. William D. Simon, mgng dir; Benjamin F. Ward, sr assoc.
Worldwide sr level mgmt exec search firm servicing all sectors of the entertainment industry.

Lipson & Co. 1900 Ave. of the Stars, Suite 2810, Los Angeles 90067. (310) 277-4646. FAX: (619) 792-5583. Howard R. Lipson, pres; Eiji Katayama, sr VP; Harriet L. Lipson, VP adv & mktg assoc.
Specialists in international & domestic bcstg (TV & radio), cable & entertainment, & related financial, professional AV & electronic recruiting. Svcs also for TV & film prod, mdse, licensing, computers.

The James Lloyd Group. Box 448, Jacksonville, Ore. 97530. (503) 899-8888. FAX: (503) 488-5627. Electronic mail address: MCI mail "JLLOYD". TELEX: 6502163932 MCI. James Lloyd, own.
Exec search for Christian Bcst; also publishing company for Christian media trade periodical.

Management Recruiters International. Box 1186, 121 Tarboro St., Rocky Mount, N.C. 27802-1186. (919) 442-8000. FAX: (919) 442-9000. Bob Manning, mgr; John McVickar, mgr.
Nationwide exec search for mgmt, sls mgmt, financial & mktg positions.

F.L. Mannix & Co. Inc. 10 Village Rd., Weston, Mass. 02193. (617) 894-9660. FAX: (617) 431-7940. F.L. Mannix, pres.
Exec search for the bcst industry.

Brad Marks International. 1888 Century Park E., #1040, Los Angeles 90067. (310) 286-0600. FAX: (310) 286-0479. Brad Marks, chmn/CEO; Leslie A. Hollingsworth, mgng dir.
We perform exec search at sr mgmt levels for communications, bcst, cable & media-related companies throughout the world. Our specialty areas include TV & film prod, progmg, sls, mktg, news, gen mgmt, financial svcs, postprod, adv & engrg.

Don Fitzpatrick Associates is the country's largest talent and management placement company for television news and programming. In addition to stations and networks across the country, our client list includes ABC Entertainment, TIME-Telepictures and Comedy Central.

Don Fitzpatrick Associates
1.900.776.6644
gives you instant access to television job openings...
and
Read DFA's electronic newsletter, SHOPTALK, for daily news, information and events happening in the broadcast industry!

DON FITZPATRICK ASSOCIATES....We're Loaded With Talent!

TV JOBS

408 Columbus Avenue, Suite #1 San Francisco, CA 94133-3978   415.954.0700   Fax 415.954.0820

Broadcasting & Cable Yearbook 1994
H-103

Employment and Executive Search Services

Media Executives. One Lewis Rd., Suite 6, Winchester, Mass. 01890. (617) 721-2121. FAX: (617) 721-1055. David F. Adams, pres; Steven Segal, assoc.
Mgmt consulting firm specializing in recruiting execs & mgrs for cable, radio, TV & other electronic media companies. Exec & mgmt placements in admin, sls, mktg, opns & progmg.

Media Grapevine. 7400 N. Oracle Rd., Suite 100Y, Tucson, Ariz. 85704-6342. (602) 797-2511; (900) 787-7800 ($1.99 per min.). Randy Rauch, pres; Tammy Hyatt, VP.
Weekly magazine & daily phone svc of current job openings for TV anchors, reporters, weather anchors, sports anchors, producers & entry level.

Media Management Resources Inc. 21982 Paradise Cir., Golden, Colo. 80401-9437. (303) 526-5500. FAX: (303) 526-5400. Michael S. Wein, pres; Bill Wein, VP opns.
Roswell, Ga. 30075: 3423 Johnson Ferry Rd. (404) 998-9991. FAX: (404) 552-0468. Paula Rothschild, dir.
Tucker, Ga. 29224: 174 Kenville Dr. (404) 717-1388. FAX: (404) 717-9135. Cindy Maddox, dir.
Marquette, Mich. 49855: 3050 Lakeshore Blvd. (906) 225-5507. FAX: (906) 225-5508. Tom Krieg, dir.
Birmingham, Ala. 35243: 2678 Altadena Rd. (205) 967-5927. FAX: (205) 967-8180. Robert McArdle, dir.
Exec search specializing in entertainment, information, telephone and media environments.
Golden, Colo. 80401-9437: Interim Management Solutions Inc. 21982 Paradise Cir. (303) 526-5500. FAX: (303) 526-5400. Thomas Forkin, VP.
Specialists in transition mgmt in telecommunications.
Englewood, Colo. 80111: Media Management Services Inc. 5429 South Krameria St. (303) 721-9788. FAX: (303) 771-1306. Dean Ericson, mgr dir; John Kerklo, Dan Carter, Paula Sullivan, Michael Wein, principals.
Full-svc consulting practice providing business support & technology svcs to select media & technology companies.

Media Marketing/THE HOT SHEET. Box 1476, Palm Harbor, Fla. 34682-1476. (813) 786-3603. FAX: (813) 787-5808. Dave Sanders, pres; Janet Ragan, exec VP; Kristine Disney, talent coord.
Full-svc consulting firm providing job listings nationwide; agent representation; free employment referral/placement; demo tape evaluations. Television, radio, corporate.

Medialine. Box 51909, Pacific Grove, Calif. 93950. (800) 237-8073; (408) 648-5204. Adrienne Laurent, pres; Kent Collins, VP; Mark Shilstone, office mgr.
Daily, updated voice mail listings for TV news, prod & prom openings.

Miller Broadcast Management Inc. 708 N. Dearborn, Chicago 60610. (312) 266-6665. FAX: (312) 266-6632. Lisa Miller, pres.
Employment & exec search svcs for radio talent & mgmt.

Robert Murphy Associates. 230 Park Ave., New York 10169. (212) 661-0460. Robert Murphy, pres; Tom Cook, exec VP; Paul Hill, sr VP; Rita Dreyfus, John Murry, Bruce Wheeler, pres; Steve Williams, VPs.
Exec search consultants to all areas of the communications industry.

National Black Media Coalition. Employment Resource Center, 38 New York N.E., Washington, 20002. (202) 387-8155. FAX: (202) 462-4469. Pluria Marshall, sr chmn; Carmen Marshall, exec dir.
Specialists in bcst, cable & print media positions. Consultation with industry on EEO/affirmative action matters.

National Broadcast Talent Coordinators. Box 20551, Birmingham, Ala. 35216. (205) 822-9144. Douglas Whitley, pres; Daisey Whitley, exec VP; Alma Dougherty, dir registrations.
Radio per placement in all size mkts across the U.S.; announcers, programmers, news dirs, sportscasters, prod, sls.

Newspeople. (Division of Reymer & Associates Inc.) 20300 Civic Center Dr., Suite 201, Southfield, Mich. 48076. (313) 354-4950. FAX: (313) 354-0918. Arnold S. Reymer, pres; Joe Karik, VP; Hal Downs, mgr.
Employment svcs for bcst newspeople, covering all newsroom positions, including talent, news mgmt.

Noll & Associates. 4000 Bridgeway, Suite 205, Sausalito, Calif. 94965. (415) 332-5640. FAX: (415) 332-1261. Kennen Williams, pres/gen mgr.
Mgmt svcs consultation including gen & gen sls mgmt exec search.

Primo People Inc. Box 116, Old Greenwich, Conn. 06870-0116. (203) 637-3653. FAX: (203) 598-0812. Fred Landau, dir bcst opns.
Placement of TV news & prog talent; placement of news & stn mgt per in all mkts.

Promotion Recruiters Inc. 11 Rectory Ln., Suite B, Scarsdale, N.Y. 10583. (914) 723-2657. FAX: (914) 472-6225. Howard Burkat, pres.
Search for stn, net & cable prom & mktg execs & producers, exclusively.

1-900-40-RTNDA Updated Daily
RTNDA Job Service
85 cents a minute. Listings free.
Call 202-659-6510 (Fax 202-223-4007).
Radio-Television News Directors Association
1000 Connecticut Ave., N.W., Suite 615
Washington, D.C. 20036

RTNDA Job Services. 1000 Connecticut Ave. N.W., Washington 20036. (202) 659-6510. FAX: (202) 223-4007.
Job svc phone line of the Radio-Television News Directors Association.

Screen Children's Agency. 12444 Ventura Blvd., Suite 103, Studio City, Calif. 91604. (818) 985-6131. FAX: (818) 985-8756. Irene Bayless Gallagher, talent agent/own.

Search Source Inc. Box 1161, Granite City, Ill. 62040. (618) 876-6060. FAX: (618) 876-6071. James R. McKechan, pres.
Search & recruitment of bcst professionals.

SearchWest Inc. 1888 Century Park E., Suite 2050, Los Angeles 90067. (310) 284-8888. FAX: (310) 284-3409. Don Dreifus, VP.
Exec search firm providing svcs to the upper-middle mgt & tech community.

Barry Skidelsky, Esq. 655 Madison Ave., 19th Fl., New York 10021. (212) 832-4800. FAX: (212) 486-8668. Barry Skidelsky, Esq.
Legal/employment svcs include contracts, terminations, EEO arbitration.

R.A. Stone & Associates. 14881 Quorum Dr., Suite 325, Dallas 75240. (214) 233-0483. FAX: (214) 991-4995. Robert A. Stone, pres.
Sr- & middle-mgmt exec search svcs for domestic & international TV, radio, cable, prod & related communications industries.

Stone & Youngblood/Target Recruiting. 304 Newbury St., Suite 210, Boston 02115. (617) 647-0070. FAX: (617) 647-0460. Stephen Sarkis, pres.
Exec search & recruitment for the communication industries, including radio, cable and bcst TV.

Joe Sullivan & Associates Inc. Box 612, 44210 County Rd. 48, Southold, N.Y. 11971. (516) 765-5050. Joseph J. Sullivan Jr., pres; Barbara Sullivan, VP.
Exec recruitment in bcstg, cable, entertainment & satellite industries for positions with incomes in excess of $70,000 per year.

Ron Sunshine Associates. Box 410514, St. Louis, Mo. 63141-0514. (314) 275-8808. FAX: (314) 275-8816. Ron Sunshine, pres; Barbara Blake, VP.
Radio, TV & cable middle & upper mgmt.

Trained Ear Ltd. 520 N. Michigan Ave., Suite 1700, Chicago 60611. (312) 527-5547. Bob Barnes-Watts, pres.
Placement of radio personalities; U.S. & international.

Warren, Morris & Madison Ltd. 2190 Carmel Valley Rd. Del Mar, Calif. 92014. (619) 481-3388. FAX: (619) 481-6221. Charles C. Morris, pres; Scott C. Warren, VP/sec.
Portsmouth, N.H. 03801: 132 Chapel St. (603) 431-7929. FAX: (603) 431-3460.
Natl & international exec/mgmt-level recruitment svcs in the cable TV, cellular, paging & bcst industries.

Steve Wyman & Associates Inc. 4201 Fairgreen Terr., Marietta, Ga. 30068. (404) 977-4410. FAX: (404) 578-0883. Steve Wyman, pres.
Exec search for bcst industry.

Youngs, Walker & Co. 1605 Colonial Pkwy., Inverness, Ill. 60067. (708) 991-6900. Carl Youngs, pres; Mike Walker, VP; Robert Epperly, consultant.
Exec recruitment on a retained basis for TV & radio stn mgmt levels & corporate positions.

Professional Cards
Engineering & Technical Consultants

---

du Treil, Lundin & Rackley, Inc.
A Subsidiary of A.D. Ring, P.C.
240 North Washington Blvd.
Suite 700
Sarasota, Florida 34236
(813) 366-2611
MEMBER AFCCE

Jules Cohen & Associates, P.C.
Consulting Electronics Engineers
Suite 600
1725 DeSales, N.W.
Washington, D.C. 20036
Telephone: (202) 659-3707
Telecopy: (202) 659-0360
Member AFCCE

**E. Harold Munn, Jr.
& Associates, Inc.**
Broadcast Engineering Consultants
Box 220
Coldwater, Michigan 49036
Phone: (517) 278-7339
Fax: (517) 278-6973

AFCCE
ASSOCIATION OF
FEDERAL COMMUNICATIONS
CONSULTING ENGINEERS
P.O. BOX 19333
WASHINGTON, D.C. 20036-0333
(301) 776-4488

SMITH and POWSTENKO
Broadcasting and Telecommunications
Consultants
Suite 502
1233 20th Street, N.W.
Washington, DC 20036
Tel: 202/293-7742 Fax: 202/296-2429

C.P. CROSSNO & ASSOCIATES
CONSULTING ENGINEERS
P.O. BOX 180312
DALLAS, TEXAS 75218
TELECOMMUNICATIONS (FCC, FAA)
CHARLES PAUL CROSSNO, P.E.
(214) 321-9140   MEMBER AFCCE

• FCC Data Bases
• FCC Applications and Field Engineering
• Frequency Searches and Coordination
• AM-FM-CATV-ITFS-LPTV
OWL ENGINEERING, INC.
Consulting Communications Engineers
1306 W. County Road F, St. Paul, MN 55112
(612) 631-1338 "Member AFCCE"

**COHEN, DIPPELL AND
EVERIST, P.C.**
CONSULTING ENGINEERS
1300 "L" STREET, N.W. SUITE 1100
WASHINGTON, D.C. 20005
(202) 898-0111
Member AFCCE

CARL T. JONES CORPORATION
CONSULTING ENGINEERS
7901 YARNWOOD COURT
SPRINGFIELD, VIRGINIA 22153
(703) 569-7704
MEMBER AFCCE

JOHN J. DAVIS & ASSOCIATES
BROADCASTING ENGINEERING
CONSULTANTS
P.O. Box 128
Sierra Madre, CA 91025-0128
818/355-6909 FAX: 818/355-4890
JOHN J. DAVIS, P.E.
Member AFCCE

STRUCTURAL SYSTEMS
TECHNOLOGY, INC.
J. Cabot Goudy, P.E.
PRESIDENT
TOWERS, ANTENNAS, STRUCTURES
New Tall Towers, Existing Towers
Studies, Analysis, Design Modifications,
Inspections, Erection, Etc
6867 Elm St., McLean, VA 22101 (703) 356-9765

Walter J. Stiles
Communications Consultant
4032 West Krall Ave.
Phoenix, AZ 85019
Phone: (602) 934-8522
FAX: (602) 842-2762

CHARLES A. HECHT & ASSOC., INC.
BROADCAST ENGINEERING CONSULTANTS
16 Doe Run
Pittstown, New Jersey 08867
(908) 730-7959 FAX (908) 730-7408

 FOR WORLDWIDE
SATELLITE
TRANSMISSION
SERVICES CONTACT:
IDB COMMUNICATIONS GROUP
10525 WEST WASHINGTON BLVD.
CULVER CITY, CA 90232-1922
213-870-9000 FAX: 213-240-3904

**JOHN F.X. BROWNE
& ASSOCIATES, P.C.**
525 Woodward Ave
Bloomfield Hills, MI 48013
(313) 642-6226
Washington Office
(202) 293-2020
Member AFCCE

COMMUNICATIONS TECHNOLOGIES INC.
BROADCAST ENGINEERING CONSULTANTS
Clarence M. Beverage
Laura M. Mizrahi
P.O. Box #1130, Marlton, NJ 08053
(609) 985-0077 • FAX: (609) 985-8124

F.A.A. Aeronautical Evaluations
John P. Allen
Airspace Consultant

Telephone   P.O. Box 1008
(904) 277-3651   Fernandina Beach, Florida 32035

Richard L. Biby, P.E.
COMMUNICATIONS
ENGINEERING
SERVICES, P.C.
6105-G ARLINGTON BLVD.
FALLS CHURCH, VIRGINIA
703-534-7880
Fax: 703-534-7884

Marsand, Inc.   Consulting Engineer
SBE - PBE
Matthew A. Sanderford, Jr., P.E.
President
Radio & TV Turnkey, Wiring Documentation
FCC filings, Xmtr & Klystron Upgrades,
Proof-of-Performance

400 Paint Pony Trail N.   Office: 817-246-6384
Fort Worth, Texas 76108   FAX 817-246-4772

**WILLIAM B. CARR
& ASSOCIATES, INC.**
WILLIAM B. CARR, P.E.
1805 BURLESON-RETTA ROAD
BURLESON, TEXAS
(817) 295-1181
Member AFCCE

HAMMETT & EDISON, INC.
CONSULTING ENGINEERS
Box 280068
San Francisco, California 94128
(415) 342-5200
(202) 396-5200
Member AFCCE

J.M. STITT & ASSOCIATES, INC.
BROADCAST & RECORDING STUDIO FACILITY DESIGNERS
ELECTRONIC MEDIA TECHNICAL CONSULTANTS
621 MEHRING WAY #1907
CINCINNATI, OH 45202 (513) 621-9292

Richard L. Vega, Jr.
President

PHASE ONE
COMMUNICATIONS, INC.
3452 Lake Lynda Drive, Suite 115
Orlando, Florida 32817
(407) 381-4895 • Fax (407) 381-8560

---

cottrill & holland, inc.
technical consultants and planners
to the communications industry.
Rita Cottrill   Doug Holland
714 S.W. 12th Avenue
Ft. Lauderdale, FL 33312
(305) 522-3303
FAX 522-3355

HATFIELD & DAWSON
CONSULTING ENGINEERS
4226 SIXTH AVE. N.W.
SEATTLE, WASHINGTON 98107
(206) 783-9151; Facsimile: (206) 789-9834
MEMBER AFCCE

SPECTRUM
ENGINEERING COMPANY
BILL CORDELL, P.E.
11211 Katy Freeway, Suite 390
Houston, Texas 77079
(713)984-8885 or (713)438-3838
Communications Engineering Consultants
Member AFCCE

KLINE TOWERS
Towers, Antenna Structures
Engineering & Installation
P.O. Box 1013
Columbia, S.C. 29202
803/251-8000 FAX: 803/739-3939

**George Jacobs
& Associates, Inc.**
Consulting Broadcast Engineers
Domestic & International
Member AFCCE
Suite 410   8701 Georgia Ave.
(301) 587-8800   Silver Spring, MD
FAX: (301) 587-8801   20910

EVANS ASSOCIATES
Consulting Communications Engineers
AM-FM-TV-CATV-ITFS Cellular
Broadcast Engineering Software
216 N. Green Bay Rd.
THIENSVILLE, WISCONSIN 53092
Phone (414) 242-6000
Member AFCCE

**CARL E. SMITH
CONSULTING ENGINEERS**
AM-FM-TV Engineering Consultants
Complete Tower and Rigging Services
*"Serving the Broadcast Industry
for over 50 Years"*
Box 807 Bath, Ohio 44210
(216) 659-4440

T. Z. Sawyer Technical Consultants
AM-FM-TV-LPTV
• FCC Applications & Exhibits   • Frequency Studies
• Experimental Authorizations   • Class Upgrades
• AM Directional Antennas   • STL Applications
• High Power Antenna Arrays   • Station Inspections
☎ 1-800-255-2632
FAX: (301) 913-5799 • 6204 Highland Dr. • Chevy Chase, MD 20815

SELLMEYER ENGINEERING
Consulting Engineers

P.O. Box 356
McKinney, Texas 75069
(214) 542-2056
Member AFCCE

Professional Cards
Engineering & Technical Consultants

SILLIMAN AND SILLIMAN
8601 Georgia Ave #910
Silver Spring, MD 20910
ROBERT M. SILLIMAN, P.E.
(301) 589-8288
THOMAS B. SILLIMAN, P.E.
(812) 853-9754
Member AFCCE

Charles T. Wooten
Broadcast Engineering
TURNKEYS — EMERGENCY SERVICE
Box 4183
Panama City, Florida 32401
904-265-9970

F.W. HANNEL & ASSOCIATES
Registered Professional Engineers
911 Edward Street
Henry, Illinois 61537
(309) 364-3903
Fax (309) 364-3775

Radio/Tv Engineering Company
"Serving Broadcasters over 35 Years"
Consultants: Norwood J. Patterson, Pres.
1416 Hollister Lane, Los Osos, Ca. 93402
Ph. (805) 528-1996 & Fax (805) 528-1982

Alvin H. Andrus, P.E.
Broadcast Consulting Engineer
351 Scott Drive
Silver Spring, MD 20904
(301) 384-5374
Member AFCCE

WILLOUGHBY & VOSS
BROADCAST TECHNICAL CONSULTANTS
P.O. BOX 701190
SAN ANTONIO, TX 78270-1190
PHONE (210) 525-1111
FAX (210) 490-2779

SG Communications
TV/FM RF Systems Specialists
RF System Measurements
Tower Erection & Maintenance
800-824-7865 Tucson, AZ
800-874-5449 Tampa, FL
215-699-6284 N. Wales, PA

Dave Hebert & Associates
"Services for the Broadcaster"
P.O. Box 2442
Pasco, Washington 99302
(509) 545-9672 • Pager 545-2847
SBE Certified Professional Broadcast Engineer
Amateur Extra - Class License WA7YKV
FCC General Radio Telephone License
Member - SBE, AES, ARRL

Mullaney Engineering, Inc.
Consulting Telecommunications Engineers
9049 Shady Grove Court
Gaithersburg, MD 20877
301-921-0115
FAX: 301-590-9757
Member AFCCE

KESSLER & GEHMAN ASSOCIATES, INC.
Telecommunications Consulting Eng.
507 N.W. 60th Street Suite C
Gainesville, Florida 32607
Phone: 904-332-3157
FAX: 904-332-6392

WILLIAM J. SITZMAN
PRESIDENT
INDEPENDENT BROADCAST CONSULTANTS, INC.
CONSULTING COMMUNICATIONS ENGINEERS
110 COUNTY RD. 146,
TRUMANSBURG, N.Y. 14886-9721
(607) 273-2970

W. RICHARD GREEN & ASSOCIATES
Consulting Telecommunications Engineers
FCC Applications • Field Engineering
Antenna Systems
3200 Wilkinson Road
Cameron Park, CA 95682
(916) 677-7417 • FAX 677-0071
Sacramento (916) 939-4099

LAWRENCE L. MORTON ASSOCIATES
1231 MESA OAKS LANE
MESA OAKS CALIFORNIA 93436
TELECOMMUNICATIONS ENGINEERS
LAWRENCE L. MORTON, P.E.
AM • FM • TV
APPLICATIONS • FIELD ENGINEERING
MEMBER AFCCE
(805) 733-4275 / FAX (805) 733-4793

LOHNES AND CULVER
CONSULTING RADIO ENGINEERS
8309 Cherry Lane
Laurel, MD 20707-4830
(301) 776-4488
Fax: (301) 776-4499   Since 1944
Member AFCCE

Communications Design Associates, Inc.
1410 Providence Highway
Norwood, MA 02062-5099
Voice: (617) 551-8490
Fax: (617) 551-8491

DSI COMMUNICATIONS INC
• Radio and Television System Design
• Transmitter and Studio Installation
• Microwave and Satellite Engineering and Installation
627 Boulevard
908-245-4833   Kenilworth, NJ 07033

COMPLETE TOWER SERVICES
SBS
P.O. BOX 740
210 HILLWOOD PK. S.
ALABASTER, AL 35007
(205) 663-3709
FAX: (205) 663-7108
TOWERS • ANTENNAS • GROUND SYSTEMS

JOHN H. BATTISON, P.E. & ASSOCIATES
CONSULTING RADIO ENGINEERS
Directional Antennas, FCC Applications
Field Work, Proofs, LPTV
Established 1954
2684 State Route 60
Loudonville, Ohio 44842
(419) 998-3849

PHONE (303) 937-1900
VIR JAMES, P.C.
BROADCAST ENGINEERING CONSULTANTS
965 S. IRVING ST.
DENVER, CO. 80219
TIM CUTFORTH, P.E.
PRESIDENT
DIRECTOR OF ENGINEERING
MEMBER AFCCE & NAB

Suffa and Cavell, Inc.
Consulting Engineers
10300 Eaton Place, Suite 450
Fairfax, VA 22030
(703) 591-0110 or (202) 332-0110
FAX: (703) 591-0115
Member AFCCE

MLJ Moffet, Larson & Johnson, Inc.
Consulting Telecommunications Engineers
Two Skyline Place, Suite 800
5203 Leesburg Pike
Falls Church, VA 22041
(703) 824-5660
FAX: 703-824-5672
Member AFCCE

BDS
BROADCAST DATA SERVICES
A Div. of Moffet, Larson & Johnson, Inc.
* AM, FM, TV, H-group databases
* Coverage, allocation and terrain studies
* FCC research
703 824-5666   FAX: 703 824-5672

Shoolbred Engineers, Inc.
Structural Consultants
Towers and Antenna Structures
Robert A. Shoolbred, P.E.
1049 Morrison Drive
Charleston, S.C. 29403 • (803) 577-4681

Professional Cards
Other Services

```
LIGHTNING
PREVENTION
SYSTEMS
PROTECT YOUR PROPERTY,
YOUR GREATEST INVESTMENT
204B Cross Keys Rd.
Berlin, NJ 08009    (609)767-7209
```

```
MICROWAVE
RADIO corporation
The Microwave Connection
Microwave Radio Corporation
20 Alpha Road
Chelmsford, MA 01824 USA
TEL:    (508) 250-1110
FAX:    (508) 256-5215
```

```
Broadcast Video Tape
Great Service • Excellent Prices
CoarcVideo™
New Quality Stock • Custom Reloads
BETACAM • U-MATIC • VHS
1-800-888-4451
```

A stellar performance...
Handel's National Directory for the Performing Arts™, 5th Edition

Formerly published by NDPA, Inc.

"Handel's continues to be the most inclusive national directory for the performing arts industry." — *CHOICE*

"Highly recommended." — *LIBRARY JOURNAL*

"A major comprehensive resource document for and about the performing arts." — *INSTRUMENTALIST*

NEW EDITION! FULLY REVISED AND EXPANDED!

Now available from R.R. Bowker® — completely revised and thoroughly updated — the new edition of **Handel's National Directory for the Performing Arts** provides detailed information on virtually every significant professional dance, music, and theater organization in the country, as well as educational institutions that offer training and degrees in the performing arts.

As versatile as the needs of your patrons, this comprehensive, two-volume directory features:

- Detailed information on dance, music and theatre organizations
- Complete listings of performing arts facilities
- Comprehensive information on universities, colleges, schools, and educational institutions
- Data on courses, faculty, degrees offered and financial assistance
- Up-to-date listings of key personnel
- Organized by state then city
- Cross-indexing for easy access
- Hundreds of new entries

Volume One
Performing Arts Organizations and Facilities

This volume contains detailed information on dance, music and theatre organizations and performing series. Organizations and facilities are listed geographically and cross-indexed by arts area. Listings contain the names of artistic and administrative management and board, paid staff, budget and attendance statistics, type of facility and stage, building costs, architect, resident groups, facility rental information and other relevant facts.

Volume Two
Performing Arts Education

This volume features comprehensive information on universities, colleges, schools, and institutions offering courses in dance, music and/or theatre listed alphabetically by state. Courses, degrees and certificates, department heads, technical training and financial assistance are detailed.

The 5th edition of HANDEL'S NATIONAL DIRECTORY FOR THE PERFORMING ARTS is the only complete national reference on the performing arts industry. Make sure it stars in your library.

January 1993 • c.1,800 pp. • 2-vol. set • 0-8352-3250-6 • $250.00
Available on Standing Order.

1-800-521-8110

R.R. BOWKER
A Reed Reference Publishing Company
121 Chanlon Road
New Providence, NJ 07974
BOWKER is a registered trademark of Reed Publishing (USA) Inc.

TURN TO US FOR NAMES THAT ARE NEWS.

(And over 81,000 other intriguing people.)

NEWS, KATHRYN ANNE, editor, educator, writer; b. McPherson County, Kans., Mar. 16, 1934; d. Henry J. and Mary J. (Kauffman) Goering; m. Albert D. Klassen Jr. (div. June 1976); children: Teresa C., Jean A., Eric P., Rachel S.; m. Francis W. News, Mar. 4, 1982. Student, Bethel Coll., 1952-54, Washburn U., 1964-67; BA, Roosevelt U., 1968; MA, Ind. U., 1971. Assoc. editor Holiday mag. Curtis Pub. Co., Indpls., 1973-74, mng. editor, 1974-77; travel page cons. Sat. Evening Post, 1976-77, Country Gentleman, 1976-77; editor Going Places mag. Chilton Publs., Radnor, Pa., 1977-79; mng. editor Réalités mag., 1979-81; Spring mag. Rodale Press, 1981-82; assoc. prof. communications Temple U., Phila., 1982–. Author: Great Escapes: An Executive's Guide to Fine Resorts, 1980. Recipient cert. of merit Atlantic Monthly, 1958, 1st Place Fellowship award Ind. U., Writers Conf., 1970, Golden Basset award, 1973, Chilton Editorial award, 1978. Office: Temple U Dept Journalism Philadelphia PA 19122

There are a lot of interesting people making news in this country. Groundbreaking, innovative and influential people with biographies packed with accomplishments. But, there is only one place to find them all together. It's *Marquis Who's Who in America*. As the one place more researchers turn to, it's become the foremost biographical reference book in America. It's accurate. It's trusted. And this year, it's better than ever. Now updated annually, the 1994 *Who's Who in America* features 13,000 new entries and over 55,000 updated ones.

And, to help find facts fast, we've included the Geographical/Professional Index volume at no extra cost.

Order your 1994 edition of *Marquis Who's Who in America* today and keep more than 81,000 of America's most newsworthy people in your office.

MARQUIS Who'sWho in America®

A REED REFERENCE PUBLISHING COMPANY

To order your 1994 edition, call 800-521-8110 today.

Section I
Associations, Events, Education and Awards

Table of Contents

Table of Contents.. I-1
Associations
  Major National Associations..................................... I-2
  National Associations.. I-8
  State and Regional Broadcast Associations........................ I-15
  State and Regional Cable Associations............................ I-17
  Union/Labor Groups.. I-18
Events
  Trade Shows
    Alphabetical Index.. I-20
    Trade Shows By Category..................................... I-21
Education
  Schools Specializing in Radio-Television-Cable.................... I-25
  Universities and Colleges.. I-27
Awards
  Major Broadcasting and Cable Awards........................... I-32

Major National Associations

Association of Independent Television Stations Inc.

Headquarters: 1320 19th St. N.W., Suite 300, Washington 20036. (202) 887-1970. FAX: (202) 887-0950.

Board of Directors: James B. Hedlund, pres INTV, Washington; Al DeVaney (INTV chmn), sr VP/gen mgr WPWR-TV Chicago; Kevin O'Brien (INTV vice-chmn), VP/gen mgr KTVU-TV Oakland, Calif.; Dennis J. Fitzsimmons (INTV sec), pres Tribune Television, Chicago; Richard Ballinger, pres/CEO Act III Broadcasting, New York; Linda Cochran, VP/gen mgr WSYT-TV Syracuse, N.Y.; Harvey Cohen, pres/gen mgr WDZL-TV Miami, Fla.; Michael A. Liff, KABB-TV San Antonio; James F. Major, VP/gen mgr WFTS-TV, Tampa; Sharon Moloney, VP/gen mgr WXTX-TV Columbus, Ga.; Patrick North, VP/gen mgr KPHO-TV Phoenix; Roger C. Ottenbach, gen mgr KCPQ-TV Tacoma, Wash.; David Pulido, VP/gen counsel ABRY Communications, Boston; Brooke Spectorsky, VP/gen mgr WUAB-TV Cleveland; J. Daniel Sullivan, pres/COO Clear Channel TV, Houston; Stuart Swartz, VP/gen mgr KMSP Minneapolis; E.D. Trimble, VP/gen mgr KTVT-TV Fort Worth, Tex.; Richard H. Williams, mgr WDCA-TV Washington.

Associate (Distributor) Board of Directors: John Claster, pres Claster TV Inc., Timonium, Md.; Derk Zimmerman, pres/CEO Group W Productions, Los Angeles.

Associate (Ex-Officio) Board of Directors: Randall E. Smith, exec VP/gen mgr WPHL-TV Philadelphia; Edward G. Aiken, pres/gen mgr WTOG-TV St. Petersburg, Fla.

INTV Staff: Susan Baurenfeind, asst to pres; David L. Donovan, VP legal/legislative affrs; James J. Popham, VP gen counsel; Alan Petronio, VP finance; Angela Giroux, dir congressional rels.

Cabletelevision Advertising Bureau Inc. (CAB)

Headquarters: 757 3rd Ave., New York 10017. (212) 751-7770. FAX: (212) 832-3268.

Executives: Greg Liptak, chmn; Thomas E. McKinney, pres/CEO; Robert H. Alter, vice-chmn; Paul Freas, treas; Donald Mitzner, sec; Ron Fischmann, sr VP local sls; Jonathon B. Sims, VP rsch; Vincent J. Fazio, sr VP finance & admin; Lynne Nordone, VP member svcs; Steve Raddock, VP communications; Richard Thorne, VP natl sls; Ella Blackman, controller.

Board of Directors: John J. Rigas, Adelphia Communications Corp.; Nickolas Davatzes, Arts & Entertainment Cable Network; Robert L. Johnson, Black Entertainment Television; William J. Bresnan, Bresnan Communications; Robert H. Alter, Thomas E. McKinney, Cabletelevision Advertising Bureau; Robert Fennimore, CNI; Thomas G. Baxter, Comcast Cable Communications Inc.; Robert A. Stengel, Continental Cablevision; Ajit Dalvi, Cox Cable Communications; John S. Hendricks, Discovery Networks Inc.; Steven M. Bornstein, ESPN; Frank J. Intiso, Falcon Cable TV; Timothy B. Robertson, The Family Channel; Leo J. Hindery Jr., Intermedia Partners; Greg Liptak, Jones Spacelink; H.F. Lenfest, The Lenfest Group; Douglas W. McCormick, Lifetime; Tom Freston, MTV Networks; Michael C. Burrus, Multimedia Cablevision; David R. Van Valkenburg, Multivision Cable TV; Robert D. Williams, National Cable Advertising; Daniel P. Cavallo, Newchannels Corp.; Ed Frazier, Prime Network; J.C. Sparkman, Tele-Communications Inc; Christopher B. Forgy, Times Mirror Cable TV; Paul W. Freas, TKR Cable; John Barbera, Turner Broadcasting System; Kay Koplovitz, USA Network; Michael J. Eckert, The Weather Channel; Theodore J. Cutler, Time Warner Cable; Joel Rudich, Coaxial Communications; F. Steven Crawford, E.W. Scripps; Garrett Girvan, Viacom Cable.

Canadian Cable Television Association (CCTA)

Headquarters: 360 rue Albert St., Suite 1010, Ottawa, Ont., Canada K1R 7X7. (613) 232-2631. FAX: (613) 232-2137.

Branch Office: Pacific Office: No. 2, 4695-53rd St., Delta, B.C., Canada V4K 2Y9. Wayne McLean, exec dir.

Executive Staff: Ken Stein, pres/CEO; Elizabeth Roscoe, sr VP pub affrs & regulatory dev; Harris Boyd, VP communications; Elizabeth McDonald, VP progmg svcs; Jay Thomson, VP legal & regulatory affrs; Gerry Wall, VP telecommunications; Antoine Boucher, dir tech; Mary Lemon, dir info svcs & regulatory rsch.

Executive Committee

Pierre Simon, chmn; Scott Colbran, sec/treas; Vera Piccini, Pacific vice-chair; Fred Wagman, Midwest/N.W.T. vice-chair; Paul Temple, Ontario vice-chair; Jacques Begin, Quebec vice-chair; Stuart Rath, Atlantic vice-chair; Ken Fowler, past chair; Noel Bambrough, strategic planning chair.

Board of Directors

President/CEO: Ken Stein. **Past Chmn (Ex-Officio):** Guy R. Beauchamp. **Trade Dir:** Dale Frew, dir Canadian opns General Instrument of Canada Inc., Jerrold Communications. **Atlantic Region:** Stuart Rath, pres Eastern Cablevision Ltd.; Mel Taylor, dir planning & progmg Cable Atlantic; Donald A. Durant, sr VP/CFO Fundy Cable Ltd.; Simon Compton, gen mgr Island Cablevision Ltd. **Quebec Region:** Jacques Begin, VP/gen dir Coneco Cable Inc.; Pierre Simon, pres Le Cable de Riviere-du-Loup Ltee; Guy Beaudry, VP corporate affrs Le Groupe Viedotron Ltee.; Andre de Chavigny, pres/COO CF Cable. **Ontario Region:** Paul Temple; Glenn I. Baxter, pres Nor-Del Cablevision Ltd.; Colin D. Watson, pres/CEO Rogers Cablesystems Ltd.; R. Scott Colbran, sr VP Maclean Hunter Cable TV; Gaston Germain, CEO Northern Cable Holdings Ltd.; Walter Weckers, sr VP cable CUC Broadcasting Ltd.; Rudi M. Engel, VP opns eastern rgn Rogers Cablesystems Ltd.; Robert Barker, pres Cablenet Ltd. **Midwest Region:** Vaughn Tozer, VP/gen mgr Videon Cable TV; Grant Pisko, exec VP Monarch Cable TV Ltd.; Jim Shaw Jr., sr VP Shaw Cablesystems Ltd.; Fred Wagman, gen mgr Regina Cablevision Cooperative. **Pacific Region:** John McKay, pres West Coast Cablevision Ltd.; Ken Fowler, sr VP planning Shaw Cablesystems Ltd.; Vera Piccini, VP mktg Rogers Cablesystems Western Region.

Community Antenna Television Association (CATA)

Headquarters: 3950 Chain Bridge Rd., Fairfax, Va. 22030; Box 1005, Fairfax, Va. 22030-1005 (mailing address). (703) 691-8875. FAX: (703) 691-8911. Stephen R. Effros, pres; Jim Ewalt, exec VP.

Officers: James DeSorrento (chmn), Triax Communications Corp.; Fred Nichols (vice-chmn), TCA Cable TV Inc.; Jim Hays III (sec/treas), Irvine Community TV Inc.

Staff: Stephen R. Effros, pres; James H. Ewalt, exec VP; Robert J. Ungar, VP/gen counsel; Rob Stoddard, VP communications; Lynn E. Grosz, VP industry training; Ellen Neill-Dore, dir special projects; G. Scott Souchock, dir publications; Susie Rosenbrook, office mgr; Janenne Springer, training prog registrar; Martha Tye, admin asst.

Directors: District 1 (Conn., Me., Mass., N.H., R.I., Vt.): Robert Sachs, dir; Michael Isaacs, vice dir. District 2 (Del., N.J., N.Y., Pa., Canada): Michael J. Rigas, dir; Cathy Brienza, vice dir. District 3 (D.C., Md., Va., W.V.): Bob Gordon, dir; James J. Jackman, vice dir. District 4 (Ala., Fla., Ga., N.C., S.C., Tenn.): Gary Blount, dir; Paul W. Freas, vice dir. District 5 (Ark., La., Miss., Okla., Tex.): Fred Nichols, dir; James E. Wilbanks, vice dir. District 6 (Ariz., Calif., Hawaii, Nev., N.M., Utah, Guam, Northern Marianas): Lee Holmes, dir; Leo J. Hindery Jr., vice dir. District 7 (Alaska, Colo., Idaho, Mont., Ore., Wash., Wyo.): John Whetzell, dir; James DeSorrento, vice dir. District 8 (Kan., Minn., Neb., N.D., S.D., Iowa): Richard Plunkett, dir; Mike Pohl, vice dir. District 9 (Ill., Mo., Wis.): Michael Burrus, dir; Gregory J. Liptak, vice dir. District 10 (Ind., Ky., Mich., Ohio): Jim Hays III, dir; Barry L. Babcok, vice dir.

Electronic Media Rating Council

Headquarters: 509 Madison Ave., Suite 1112, New York 10022. (212) 754-3343. FAX: (212) 754-6430.

Officers: Richard Weinstein, exec dir; Thomas McClendon (chmn EMRC Board), Cox Broadcasting, Atlanta; Kathy Lenard (chmn TV Committee), NBC, New York; Dr. Tom Evans (chmn Radio Committee), Westwood One, New York; Tim Brooks (chmn Cable Committee), USA Networks, New York.

National Association of Broadcasters (NAB)

Headquarters: 1771 N St. N.W., Washington 20036. Phone: (202) 429-5300.

Officers and Staff

President's Office: Edward O. Fritts, pres/CEO; Rory Benson, sr VP/special asst to pres/natl campaign coord.

Operations: John Abel, exec VP; Terri Rabel, VP.

Advertising: Randi Reiten, VP adv; Mack Rebholz, dir adv & event mktg opns.

Conventions and Exhibitions: Rick Dobson, sr VP conventions & exhibits; Lee Ann Burr, dir convention opns; Jack Chiasson, dir registration & svcs; Jennifer Nance, dir exhibit opns.

Finance & Administration: Kenneth D. Almgren, sr VP/CFO; Mary Dickson, sr VP; W. Bernard Burns, VP prod; Diane Goff, dir accounting svcs; Karen Alsbach, dir personnel.

Government Relations: James C. May, exec VP; Michael Waring, VP govt rels; Dan Phythyon, Stephen Jacobs, VPs congressional liaison; Tristan Warren, dir Senate liaison; Jill D'Andrea, dir admin & events; DeDe Ferrell, dir House liaison; Kathy Ramsey, bcstr Congressional rels; Lisa Keller, exec asst.

Major National Associations

Human Resource Development: Dwight Ellis, VP; J. Hatim Hamer, dir bcst progs.

Legal: Henry L. "Jeff" Baumann, exec VP/gen counsel; Barry Umansky, deputy gen counsel; Valerie Schulte, sr assoc gen counsel; Steven Bookshester, assoc gen counsel; Howard Woolley, VP regulatory affrs; Ben Ivins, asst gen counsel.

Library and Information Center: Susan Hill, VP.

Management and Marketing Information Systems: Michael Fitzmaurice, dir.

Meetings and Special Events: Kathy Muller, VP; Hilda Jannesson, dir housing.

Public Affairs and Communications: Walt Wurfel, sr VP; Gene Jeffers, VP PA&C; Lynn McReynolds, VP media rel; John Merli, sr dir member communications; Dos Schuette, sr dir creative svcs; John Groundwater, dir conventions mktg; Doug Wills, dir media rels.

Radio: John David, sr VP; Donna Leonard, VP radio membership; Susan Platt, VP radio opns.

Research & Information Group: Richard Ducey, sr VP; Mark Fratrik, VP/economist; Marcia De Sonne, dir tech assessment; Gerald Hartshorn, dir audience measurement & policy rsch; Brenda Helregel, dir convention rsch & analysis.

Science & Technology: Michael Rau, sr VP; Janet Elliott, dir opns; Lynn Claudy, VP.

Services: Teri Lepovitz, sr VP.

Television: Charles E. Sherman, sr VP; Sharon Goldener Kinsman, VP TV membership; Carolyn Wilkins, dir opns; Becky Lauer, dir TV prod.

Television & Radio Political Action Committee: Rae Ann Bevington, mgr.

Board of Directors

Chairman: Wayne Vriesman, Tribune Broadcasting Co., Chicago, Ill.

Past Chairman: Gary Chapman, LIN Television Corp., Providence, R.I.

President: Edward O. Fritts, NAB, Washington.

Radio Board of Directors

Radio Board Chairman: Robert Fox, KVEN/KHAY-FM Ventura, Calif.

Radio Board Vice Chairman: Skip Finley, WKYS-FM Washington, D.C.

District Representatives

Richard A. Ferguson, NewCity Communications, Bridgeport, Conn. (New England); John R. Quinn, WJDM Elizabeth, N.J. (N.Y.-N.J.); Jerry Lee, WBEB-AM-FM Philadelphia (Pa.); T. David Luther, WBTM/WAKG Danville, Va. (Del., D.C., Md., Va.); William R. Evans, WQXE-FM Elizabethtown, Ky. (W.Va., Ky.); Carl V. Venters Jr., Voyager Communications Group, Raleigh, N.C. (N.C., S.C.); Paul Levesque, Taylor Communications, Orlando, Fla. (Fla., P.R., V.I.); Raymond A. Saadi, KHOM-FM/KTIB-AM Houma, La. (La., Miss.); Houston Pearce, Radio South Inc., Tuscaloosa, Ala. (Ga., Ala.); Charles A. Blake, WIKY-AM-FM Evansville, Ind. (Ind.); C. Richard McBroom, WONW-AM/WNDH-FM/WZOM-FM Napoleon, Ohio (Ohio); Gene Millard, KFEQ St. Joseph, Mo. (Mo., Kan.); Ross Biederman, WTCM-AM-FM Traverse City, Mich. (Mich.); Don Seehafer, Seehafer Broadcasting Corp., Manitowoc, Wis. (Iowa, Wis.); Bayard H. Walters, The Cromwell Group, Nashville, Tenn. (Tenn., Ark.); Ray H. Lockart, KOGA-AM-FM Ogallala, Neb. (Colo., Neb.); Wayne Vriesman, Tribune Broadcasting Co., Chicago (Ill.); Dick Oppenheimer, Signature Broadcasting Co., Austin, Tex. (southern Tex.); J. Douglas Williams, KWOX-FM Woodward, Okla. (Okla., northern Tex.); Alan W. Harris, KUGR/KYCS Green River, N.Y. (Mont., Idaho, Wyo.); Paul C. Hedberg, Hedberg Broadcasting, Morris, Minn. (Minn., S.D., N.D.); James F. Taszarek, KTAR-AM/KKLT-FM Phoenix, Ariz. (Ariz., Nev., Utah, N.M.); David Benjamin, Community Pacific Broadcasting, Salinas, Calif. (northern Calif., Alaska); Robert Fox, KVEN/KHAY-FM Ventura, Calif. (southern Calif., Guam, American Samoa, Hawaii); Harold Greenberg, KMAS Shelton, Wash. (Ore., Wash.).

Designated Board Seats

Mark Bench, Bonneville International Corp.; Alan L. Box, EZ Communications Inc., Fairfax, Va.; Ricardo A. del Castillo, Tichenor Media System Inc., Dallas; Joseph M. Field, Entercom, Bala Cynwyd, Pa.; Skip Finley, WKYS-FM Washington; Randy Odeneal, Sconnix Broadcasting Group, Vienna, Va.; Carol Reilly, The Griffin Group, New York; Owen Weber, Summit Communications Group, Atlanta.

Network Representatives

William Hogan, Unistar Radio Networks, New York; Roy Simpson, Jones Satellite Networks, Englewood, Colo.; Nancy Widmann, CBS Radio, New York.

Television Board of Directors

Chairman: John C. Siegel, Chris-Craft/United Television, San Francisco.

Vice Chairman: G. William Ryan, Post Newsweek Stations Inc., Miami, Fla.

Elected Representatives

Ralph W. Gabbard, Kentucky Central TV Inc., WKYT-TV Lexington, Ky.; Kenneth L. Hatch, KIRO Inc., Seattle; Phil Jones, Meredith Corp., Des Moines, Iowa; Amy McCombs, KRON-TV San Francisco; Bruce C. McGorrill, Maine Broadcasting, Portland, Me.; Thomas A. Oakley, QNI Broadcast Group, Quincy, Ill.; Harry J. Pappas, Pappas Telecasting Companies, Visalia, Calif.; Clyde Payne, Benedek Group, WBKO-TV Bowling Green, Ky.; Tom Reiff, H&C Communications Inc., Houston; G. William Ryan, Post Newsweek Stations Inc., Miami, Fla.; John C. Siegel, Chris-Craft/United Television, San Francisco; Nicholas D. Trigony, Cox Broadcasting, Atlanta.

Designated Board Seat

Edward G. Aiken, Hubbard Broadcasting, WTOG St. Petersburg, Fla.; Elizabeth Murphy Burns, Morgan Murphy Stations, WISC-TV Madison, Wis.; Peter B. Desnoes, Burnham Broadcasting Co., Chicago; Richard M. Lobo, WTVJ Miami, Fla.; Edward T. Reilly, McGraw-Hill Broadcasting Co., New York; Patricia Smullin, California/Oregon Broadcasting; Ben Tucker, Retlaw Broadcasting, KMST Fresno, Calif.

Network Representatives

Martin D. Franks, CBS Inc., Washington; James Rowe, NBC, Washington; Mark MacCarthy, Capital Cities/ABC Inc., Washington.

NAB Committees

Advanced Television Task Force: Warren Williamson III (chmn), pres WKBN Broadcasting Corp., Youngstown, Ohio; Joseph A. Flaherty, sr VP tech CBS Inc., New York; William T. Hayes, mgr engrg WSAZ-TV Huntington, W. Va.; August C. Meyer, pres Midwest Television Inc., Champaign, Ill.; Howard Miller, sr VP bcst opns & engrg Public Broadcasting Service, Alexandria, Va.; Robert Niles, VP/dir engrg Capital Cities/ABC Inc., WPVI-TV Philadelphia; Harold E. Protter, sr VP strategic planning Koplar Communications, St. Louis; Frank Roberts, pres New York Times Broadcasting Group, Memphis; Andrew Setos, sr VP studio & bcst opns, & engrg Fox Broadcasting, Beverly Hills, Calif.; Michael Sherlock, pres opns & tech svcs NBC Inc., New York; Margita White (ex-officio), pres Association for Maximum Service Television, Washington; Charles Sherman, Michael Rau, staff liaisons; Lowry Mays, ExCom liaison.

AM Improvement Committee: Art Suberbielle (chmn), pres/gen mgr KANE-AM New Iberia, La.; Kenneth Brown, mgr allocations & licensing bcst engrg ABC Broadcast Operations & Engineering, New York; Vern Killion, dir engrg KRVN Lexington, Neb.; Harold M. Kneller Jr., pres/gen mgr WKII-AM Punta Gorda, Fla.; T. David Luther, pres WBTM/WAKG Radio, Danville, Va.; Tom Simmons, gen mgr KELO-AM-FM Sioux Falls, S.D.; Herb Squire, dir engrg WQXR, New York; Anthony Welch, pres/gen mgr WROD-AM Daytona Beach, Fla.; Michael Rau, staff liaison; Wayne Vriesman, ExCom liaison.

AMAX Task Force: John Quinn (chmn), pres/gen mgr WJDM Radio, Elizabeth, N.J.; Ron Frizzell, pres/gen mgr WLAM Radio, Lewiston, Me.; Thomas M. Kushak, pres/gen mgr WMAY/WNNS Radio, Springfield, Ill.; Ted Snider, pres Snider Corp., Little Rock, Ark.; Art Suberbielle, pres/gen mgr KANE Radio, New Iberia, La.; E. Glynn Walden, dir engrg Group W, Philadelphia; Michael Rau, staff liaison; Wayne Vriesman, ExCom liaison.

Cable Relations Task Force: Jerry P. Colvin (chmn), exec VP/gen mgr WTOV-TV Battle Creek, Mich.; Martin D. Franks, VP CBS Inc., Washington; Ralph W. Gabbard, pres/gen mgr Kentucky Central Television Inc., WKYT-TV Lexington, Ky.; James Keelor, pres Cosmos Broadcasting Corp., Greenville, S.C.; Richard M. Lobo, pres/gen mgr NBC Television Stations, WTVJ Miami, Fla.; Monte Loos, opns mgr KOTA-TV Rapid City, S.D.; LeRoy Paul, COO AFLAC Columbus, Ga.; W. Russell Withers Jr., pres Withers Broadcasting Co., Mount Vernon, Ill.; Vincent Young, chmn Young Broadcasting Inc., New York; Charles Sherman, Ben Ivins, staff liaisons; John Siegel, ExCom liaison.

Children's Television Committee: G. William Ryan (chmn), pres Post-Newsweek Stations Inc., Miami, Fla.; Marcellus Alexander, VP/gen mgr WJZ-TV Baltimore; Helen Boehm, VP Fox Children's Network, Fox Broadcasting Co., New York; Gail Brekke, gen mgr KITN-TV, Minneapolis; Beth Bressan, VP/asst to pres CBS Broadcast Group, New York; Robert Farrow, VP/gen mgr WFRV-TV Green Bay, Wis.; Jack Forehand, VP/gen mgr KENS-TV San Antonio; Timothy Gilbert, opns mgr WKBW-TV Buffalo, N.Y.; Kenneth L. Hatch, chmn/pres/CEO KIRO Seattle; Jeffrey Lee, pres/gen mgr WESH-TV Daytona Beach, Fla.; Lon Lee, VP/gen mgr KHQ-TV Spokane, Wash.; Karen Maser, dir community rel Capital Cities/ABC Inc., New York; Dr. Rosalyn Weinman, VP bcst standards & practices NBC, New York; Charles Sherman, staff liaison; Ron Townsend, ExCom liaison.

Congressional Relations Committee: Richard D. Novik (co-chmn), pres WKIP-AM/WRNQ-FM Poughkeepsie, N.Y.; Tom Oakley (co-chmn), Quincy Newspapers, Quincy, Ill.; Jack Clements, pres Mutual Broadcasting System, Arlington, Va.; Peter B. Desnoes, mng gen ptnr/CEO Burnham Broadcasting Co., Chicago; Skip Finley, pres/gen mgr Albimar Communications, WKYS-FM Washington; Wallace Jorgenson, exec VP Hubbard Broadcasting, Tampa; Bruce McGorrill, exec VP/CEO Maine Broadcasting, Portland, Me.; Harry J. Pappas, pres/CEO Pappas Telecasting Companies, Visalia, Calif.; Jerry Papenfuss, pres Result Radio Group, KAGE/KBRF/KBEW Winona, Minn.; Houston Pearce, pres Radio South Inc., Tuscaloosa, Ala.; Tom Reiff, pres bcst group H&C Communications Inc., Houston; Edward T. Reilly, pres McGraw-Hill Broadcasting Co., New York; Patricia Smullin, pres California/Oregon Broadcasting, Medford, Ore.; Nicholas D. Trigony, pres bcst div Cox Broadcasting Co., Atlanta; Ben Tucker, pres Retlaw Broadcasting, Fresno, Calif.

Network Affiliates Liaison: Martin Franks, VP CBS Inc., Washington; James Rowe, VP NBC, Washington; James May, staff liaison; John Siegel, ExCom liaison.

Copyright Committee: Leavitt J. Pope (chmn), pres/CEO WPIX Inc., New York; Edward Aiken, pres/gen mgr Hubbard Broadcasting Inc., WTOG-TV St. Petersburg, Fla.; John F. Carpenter, gen sls mgr WDSU-TV New Orleans; Robert B. Giese, VP/counsel govt rels; Doug Kiel, pres WTMJ Inc., Milwaukee; James Rowe, VP NBC, Washington; Ben Ivins, staff liaison; Ron Townsend, ExCom liaison.

Digital Audio & Satellite Sound Broadcasting Task Force: Alan Box (chmn), pres EZ Communications Inc., Fairfax, Va.; Jack Adamson, sr VP Bonneville International Corp., Broadcast House, Salt Lake City; Ron Davenport, chmn American Urban Radio Network, Pittsburgh; Joseph M. Field, pres/CEO Entercom, Bala Cynwyd, Pa.; Dean Goodman, exec VP radio Gilmore Broadcasting Corp., WLVE-FM Miami; David Hicks, pres/CEO Hicks Broadcasting Corp., WKFR-WKMI Kalamazoo, Mich.; Ray H. Lockhart, pres/CEO KOGA-AM-FM Oglalla, Neb.; Randy Odeneal, pres Sconnix Broadcasting Group, Vienna, Va.; Carl V. Venters Jr., chmn Voyager Communications Group, Raleigh, N.C.; Stephen Edwards (Canadian rep), VP corporate engrg & tech Rogers Broadcasting Ltd., Toronto, Ont. Canada; Michel Tremblay, sr VP Canadian Association of Broadcasters, Ottawa, Ont. Canada; Carlos Aguirre Gomez (Mexican rep), pres Cardena Radio Centro, Mexico; Don Wilkinson (technical advisor), Fisher Broadcasting Inc., Seattle; Art Suberbielle, (AM improvement liaison), pres/gen mgr KANE Radio, New Iberia, La.; Michael Rau, staff liaison; Bob Fox, ExCom liaison.

DAB Task Force Technical Advisory Group: Donald Wilkinson (chmn), Fisher Broadcasting, Seattle; J. Talmage Ball, VP engrg Bonneville International Corp., Salt Lake City; Bob Donnelly, gen mgr satellite system ABC Radio Network, New York; J. Eric Hoehn, tech dir Contemporary Media Broadcasting Group, KFMZ Columbia, Mo.; Alan D. Kirschner, dir engrg Westwood One Companies, New York; Andy Laird, VP engrg radio group Heritage Media Corp., Bellevue, Wash.; Donald Lockett, dir engrg National Public Radio, Washington; Charles Morgan, VP/dir engrg Susquehanna Radio Corp., York, Pa.; Dave Murray, WWNZ Orlando, Fla.; Milford Smith, VP engrg Greater Media Inc., East Brunswick, N.J.; Dennis Snyder, chief engr WJOY/WOKO Radio, Burlington, Vt.; Michael Rau, staff liaison; Bob Fox, ExCom liaison.

Engineering Conference and Advisory Committee: Charles Dages (chmn), VP engrg CBS Television Network, New York; Harvey Arnold, assoc dir engrg The University of North Carolina Center for Public Television, Research Triangle Park, N.C.; James Ary, VP radio engrg Great American Communications, WTVN/WLVQ Columbus, Ohio; Margaret Bryant, engrg mgr WMAQ Chicago; Jerry Butler, WETA-TV Washington; Carl W. Davis, VP engrg Voyager Communications Inc., Raleigh, N.C.; Louis Libin, sr staff engr communications svcs NBC, New York; Fred R. Morton Jr., VP dir engrg KMGZ-FM Lawton, Okla.; Bob Ogren, VP engrg & opns LIN Television Corp., Providence, R.I.; Gerald Robinson, VP engrg Hearst Broadcasting, Milwaukee; Tony Uyttendaele, dir engrg dev & advanced systems Capital Cities/ABC Inc., New York; Jerry Whitaker (SBE rep to the Engineering Conference & Advisory Committee), tech writer Beaverton, Ore.; Michael Rau, staff liaison; John Siegel, ExCom liaison.

Financial Advisory Committee: David Benjamin (chmn), pres/CEO Community Pacific Broadcasting, Monterey, Calif.; Richard Benedek, pres Benedek Broadcasting Corp., New York; Skip Fenley, pres WKYS-FM Washington; Alan W. Harris, pres KUGR/KYCS Green River, Wyo.; Edward T. Reilly, pres McGraw-Hill Broadcasting Co., New York; Ben Tucker, pres Retlaw Broadcasting, Fresno, Calif.; Kenneth Almgren, staff liaison; Wayne Vriesman, ExCom liaison.

Financial Liaison Task Force: Skip Finley (co-chmn), pres WKYS-FM Washington; Milton Maltz (co-chmn), chmn/CEO Malrite Communications Group Inc., Cleveland; Ragan Henry, CEO Ragan Henry Broadcast Group, Philadelphia; Robin B. Martin, pres/CEO The Deer River Group, Washington; L. Lowry Mays, pres/CEO Clear Channel Communications, San Antonio; Ken O'Rorke, VP mktg Communications Equity Associates Inc., Tampa; Rick Reider, CEO WestGroup Broadcasting, Ft. Collins, Colo.; Carl V. Venters Jr., chmn Voyager Communications Group, Raleigh, N.C.; Owen Weber, exec VP Summit Communications Group, Atlanta; John David, John Abel, Eddie Fritts, staff liaisons; Wayne Vriesman, ExCom liaison.

FM Transmission Committee: Alan D. Kirschner (chmn), dir engrg Westwood One Companies, New York; Steve Davis, dir engr KMOD-FM Clear Channel Radio, Tulsa, Okla.; Richard Mertz, dir engrg United Broadcasting, WJZE-FM Washington; Dave Murray, tech dir WWNZ Radio, Orlando, Fla.; David Reaves, chief engr WHTZ-FM Secaucus, N.J.; Michael Rice, pres Contemporary Media Broadcasting, St. Peters, Mo.; Milford K. Smith Jr., VP engrg Greater Media Inc., East Brunswick, N.J.; Jim Stagnitto, dir engrg WMXV-FM New York; Michael Rau, staff liaison; Bob Fox, ExCom liaison.

Future of Broadcasting (Radio): Bill Clark (chmn), pres Shamrock Broadcasting, Burbank, Calif.; Mark Bench, VP/gen mgr WMXV-Radio New York; Bob Callahan, pres ABC Radio Networks, New York; Jack Clements, pres Mutual Broadcasting, Arlington, Va.; Richard Ferguson, pres NewCity Communications, Bridgeport, Conn.; William Figenshu, sr VP bcstg/pres radio Viacom Broadcasting, New York; Edward T. Hardy, VP/gen mgr Scripps Howard Broadcasting, KUPL-AM-FM Portland, Ore.; C. Richard McBroom, pres/gen mgr WONW-AM/WNDH-FM Napoleon, Ohio; Carol M. Reilly, dir media mktg & svcs The Griffin Group, New York; William Shearer, pres/gen mgr KGFJ Radio, Los Angeles; Jim Thompson, pres Group W Radio, Westinghouse Broadcasting Co., New York; Bayard H. Walters, pres Cromwell Group, Nashville; Nancy Widmann, pres CBS Radio, New York; John David, John Abel, Michael Rau, Rick Ducey, staff liaisons; Wayne Vriesman, ExCom liaison.

Future of Broadcasting (TV): John Siegel (chmn), VP Chris Craft/United Television, San Francisco; Edward G. Aiken, pres WTOG-TV St. Petersburg, Fla.; Elizabeth Murphy Burns, pres Morgan Murphy Stations, WISC-TV Duluth, Minn.; Michael Conly, sr VP Harte Hanks Communications, San Antonio; Peter B. Desnoes, mgng gen ptnr/CEO Burnham Broadcasting Co., Chicago; Andrew Fisher, exec VP affil Cox Broadcasting, Atlanta; Ralph W. Gabbard, pres/gen mgr Kentucky Central Television Inc., Lexington, Ky.; John E. Hayes, VP TV Providence Journal Co., WCNC Charlotte, N.C.; Edward J. Koplar, pres/CEO Koplar Communications, St. Louis; Amy McCombs, pres/gen mgr KRON-TV San Francisco; Bruce C. McGorrill, exec VP/CEO Maine Broadcasting, Portland, Me.; Travis Rockey, pres Cordillera Communications, Spokane, Wash.; G. William Ryan, pres/CEO Post-Newsweek Stations Inc., Miami, Fla.; Charles Sherman, John Abel, Michael Rau, Rick Ducey, staff liaisons; Ron Townsend, ExCom liaison.

HDTV World: James McKinney (chmn), chmn ATSC, Washington; Wendell Bailey, VP science & tech NCTA, Washington; Julius Barnathan, consultant tech & strategic planning Capital Cities/ABC Inc., New York; Steven Bonica, pres Panasonic Broadcast & TV Systems Co., Secaucus, N.J.; William Connolly, chmn Sony High Definition Facilities Inc., Culver City, Calif.; Allen Cooper, VP tech evaluation & planning Motion Picture Association of America, Washington; Greg DePriest, VP ATV tech Toshiba America Consumer Products, Princeton, N.J.; Joseph Flaherty, sr VP tech CBS Inc., New York; Dr. Keiichi Kubota, sr scientist NHK General Bureau for America, New York; Howard Miller, sr VP bcst opns & engrg Public Broadcasting Service, Alexandria, Va.; William Sawchuk, dir gen bcst tech rsch Communications Research Centre, Ottawa, Ont. Canada; Jerry Schneider, mgr trade show & TV studio TV div, Tektronix Inc., Beaverton, Ore.; Michael Sherlock, pres opns & tech svcs NBC Inc., New York; Altan Stalker, VP/gen mgr opns & engrg Westinghouse Broadcasting Co., Stamford, Conn.; Rupert Stow, East Moriches, N.Y.; Dr. Masao Sugimoto, counselor, Pioneer Electronic Corp., Tokyo, Japan; George T. Waters, dir technical dept European Broadcasting Union, Geneva, Switzerland; Dan Wells, VP bus dev Comsat Video Enterprises, Clarksburg, Md.; Margita White, pres Association for Maximum Service Television, Washington; Michael Rau, Chuck Sherman, Rick Dobson, staff liaisons; John Siegel, ExCom liaison.

Hundred Plus Markets Television Committee: Elizabeth Murphy Burns (chmn), pres Morgan Murphy Stations, WISC-TV Duluth, Minn.; Ray Alexander, gen mgr KRGV-TV Weslaco, Tex.; Richard Benedek, pres Benedek Broadcasting Corp., New York; Nora L. Guzewicz, pres WICZ-TV, Vestal, N.Y.; Mark Ledbetter, gen mgr WTVA-TV, Tupelo, Miss.; Bruce Liljegren, gen mgr KEZI-TV Eugene, Ore.; Joe Macione, stn mgr WCYB-TV Bristol, Va.; Charles Stauffer, gen mgr KCOY-TV Santa Maria, Calif.; Charles Webb, VP/gen mgr WVVA-TV Bluefield W. Va.; Charles Sherman, staff liaison; Ron Townsend, ExCom liaison.

Insurance Committee: Donna McDonald (chairperson), corporate risk specialist Nationwide Communications, Columbus, Ohio; Deborah Kaczmarzyk, dir corporate dev LIN Broadcasting, Providence, R.I.; Ronald L. Lindwall, sr VP finance Benedek Broadcast Corp., Rockford, Ill.; George Nelson, VP Morgan Murphy Group, WISC-TV Madison, Wis.; Colleen Roach, CFO Citadel Communications Co., Bronxville, N.Y.; Teri Lepovitz, staff liaison; Bob Fox, ExCom liaison.

Multimedia World Executive Committee: Philip Dodds (chmn), exec dir Interactive Multimedia Association, Annapolis, Md.; Stewart Alsop, editor-in-chief Infoworld Magazine, San Mateo, Calif.; Stanley Baron, mgng dir TV tech NBC Television Network, New York; William Comcowich, VP Effective Communication Arts Inc., New York; Bert Gall, dir tech mgmt multimedia systems Philips Consumer Electronics, Eindhoven, The Netherlands; Robert Henninger, pres/CEO Henninger Video, Arlington, Va.; Hal Josephson, dir industry rels The 3DO Co., San Mateo, Calif.; Lisa LeBlanc, mktg communications mgr Avid Technology Inc., Tewksbury, Mass.; Robert Lippincott, dir multimedia products Lotus Development Corp., Cambridge, Mass.; Thomas Lopez, chmn Mammoth Micro Productions, Seattle; Georgia McCabe, dir worldwide commercial CD imaging, Eastman Kodak, Rochester, N.Y.; Howard Miller, sr VP bcst opns & engrg Public Broadcasting Service, Alexandria, Va.; Bernie Mitchell, natl mktg mgr prof CD-I, Philips Consumer Electronics, Knoxville, Tenn.; Dr. Stephen Molyneux, independent consultant, Telford, England; Robert Pearson, dir interactive media prod mktg Sun Microsystems, Mountain View, Calif.; John Sabol, asst to chmn Microsoft Corp., Redmond, Wash.; Kirk Shorte, sr prod mktg mgr QuickTime Technologies Apple Computer, Cupertino, Calif.; Steven Solazzo, dir multimedia Fireworks Partners, IBM Corp., Atlanta; Geoff Tully, sr VP Multimedia Pioneer Communications of America Inc., Upper Saddle River, N.J.; Debbie Vodenos, assoc publisher InMotion Magazine, Potomac, Md.; Michael Rau, staff liaison.

Radio Show Committee: Jim Thompson (chmn), pres Group W Radio, Westinghouse Broadcasting Co., New York.

Management Subcommittee: Bill Stakelin (chmn), pres/CEO Apollo Radio Ltd., New York; William Figenshu, sr VP bcstg/pres radio Viacom Broadcasting, New York; Maureen Lesourd, pres/gen mgr WRQX-FM Washington; Ray Saadi, VP/gen mgr KTIB/KHOM Houma, La.; Carl V. Venters Jr., chmn Voyager Communications Group, Raleigh, N.C.; Al Vicente, VP/gen mgr WGNA-AM-FM Albany, N.Y.; J. Douglas Williams, pres/gen mgr KWOX-FM Woodward, Okla.

Programming Subcommittee: Bob Dunphy (chmn), VP progmg WMXV-FM New York; Ted Bolton, pres Bolton Research Corp., Paoli, Pa.; J.D. Freeman, VP/gen mgr KMLE-FM Phoenix; Barbara A. Prieto, prog dir WKYS-FM Washington; Joel Reish, VP progmg & rsch Entercom, Bala Cynwyd, Pa.; Don Seehafer, pres Seehafer Broadcasting Corp., Manitowoc, Wis.

Sales Subcommittee: Rod Calarco (chmn), VP CBS Owned FM Radio Stations, New York; David Gingold, pres/COO Barnstable Broadcasting Inc., Waltham, Mass.; Jennifer McCann, gen mgr WSSH-AM-FM Woburn, Mass.; Chuck Mefford, sr VP Midwest Family Broadcasting, Petoskey, Mich.; Darryl Trent, Group W Radio, Fort Washington, Pa.; Cynthia Weiner, gen mgr KRZY/KRST, Albuquerque, N.M.; John David, staff liaison; Lowry Mays, ExCom liaison.

On-Air Initiatives Committee: Jeanne Bohn (chmn), public svc dir WSOC-TV Charlotte, N.C.; Art Brooks, exec dir Arizona Broadcasters Association, Phoenix; Charlie Eads, VP/gen mgr KSHO-AM/KGAL-FM Albany, Ore.; Don Gale, VP news & pub affrs Bonneville International Corp., Salt Lake City; Susan Haspel, dir community rel & public svc, New York; Dr. Judy Karst, gen mgr KRRV-AM-FM Alexandria, La.; Joseph Lewin, gen mgr WRIC-TV Richmond, Va.; Dick Lobo, pres/gen mgr WTVJ Miami, Fla.; Nick Miller, VP mktg radio Great American Broadcasting, Cincinnati; Ray Saadi, mgng ptnr KHOM-FM/KTIB-AM Houma, La.; Shaun Sheehan, VP Tribune Broadcasting Co., Washington; Alan Sprague, New Hampshire Association of Broadcasters, Bedford, N.H.; Richard Wachtel, pres/gen mgr Shenandoah Communications Inc., Martinsburg, W. Va.; Karole White, exec dir Michigan Association of Broadcasters, Lansing, Mich.

On-Air Initiatives Committee (Ex-Officio): Eva Kasten, VP The Advertising Council, Washington; Wally Snyder, pres American Advertising Federation, Washington; John Kamp, VP American Association of Advertising Agencies, Washington; John Highbush, VP communications American Red Cross, Washington; DeWitt Helm, pres Association of National Advertisers, New York; Bernadette McGuire, dir rsch Association of American Public TV Stations, Washington; Tina Van Dusen, VP communications Canadian Association of Broadcasters, Ottawa, Ont., Canada; Ramiro Mora, gen mgr CIRT (Mexican Association of Broadcasters), Mexico; Janet Brown, exec dir Commission on Presidential Debates, Washington; Doris Matsui, Congressional Families Action for Breast Cancer Awareness, Alexandria, Va.; Caroline McMillan, Congressional Families Action for Breast Cancer Awareness, Alexandria, Va.; Nancy Murkowski, pres Congressional Families for Drug-Free Youth, Washington; Ron Trethric, chief demand reduction section, Drug Enforcement Administration, Arlington, Va.; Scott Nelson, special agent Federal Bureau of Investigation, Washington; Jim Small, mgr pub rels Major League Baseball, New York; Milo Kirk, pres Mothers Against Drunk Driving, Dallas; Fred Kroger, National AIDS Information & Educational Program, dir Centers for Disease Control, Atlanta; Carolyn Blitz, National Basketball Association, New York; Terry Schiavone, exec dir National Commission Against Drunk Driving, Washington; Candace Romig, National Conference of State Legislatures, Denver; Betty Herron, pres National Federation of Parents for Drug-Free Youth, St. Louis; Gene Upshaw, pres/exec dir National Football League Players Association, Washington; M.J. Jacobson, National Geographic Society, Washington; Jennifer Davis, special asst National Governors' Association, Washington; Marion Blakely, admin National Highway Traffic Safety Administration, Washington; Michael Y. Townsend, exec VP Partnership for A Drug-Free America, New York; George Hyde, exec VP Radio Advertising Bureau, New York; Herta Feely, exec dir Safe Kids, Washington; Jerry Sachs, TEAM, Landover, Md.; Sunshine Janda Overkamp, VP communications United Way of America, Alexandria, Va.; Mike Brown, dir pub affrs U.S. Conference of Mayors, Washington; Barry Tron, dir America 2000, U.S. Department of Education, Washington; Alixe Glen, asst sec for pub affrs U.S. Department of Health & Human Services, Washington; Johanna Schneider, deputy asst sec for pub affrs, Washington; Linda Leinbach Mays, Vote America, Washington; Rory Benson, staff liaison; John Siegel, ExCom liaison.

Radio Members & Board Composition Committee: Dick Oppenheimer (chmn), pres/COO Signature Broadcasting Co., Austin, Tex.; Bob Callahan, pres ABC Radio Networks, New York; James Champlin, pres/CEO Beck Ross Communications Inc., Rockville Centre, N.Y.; Steve Downes, gen mgr WCHK-AM-FM Canton, Ga.; Harold Greenberg, pres/gen mgr KMAS-AM Shelton, Wash.; William L. McElveen, pres/gen mgr WTCB-FM Columbia, S.C.; Gene Millard, gen mgr KFEQ-AM St. Joseph, Mo.; David Rose, COO Business Radio Network, Colorado Springs; David Shepherd, pres/gen mgr KWIX-AM/KRES-FM Moberly, Mo.; John David, staff liaison; Wayne Vriesman, ExCom liaison.

Radio Operators Caucus Liaison: Randy Odeneal, gen ptnr Sconnix Broadcasting Group, Vienna, Va.; John David, staff liaison; Lowry Mays, ExCom liaison.

Regulatory Review Committee: Richard W. Osborne (chmn), pres/gen mgr WKXL-AM-FM Concord, N.H.; Kirk M. Anderson, VP KHWY Radio, Las Vegas; Jerry Colvin, pres/gen mgr WOTV-TV Battle Creek, Mich.; Mark Crump, gen mgr KDXU-AM/KZEZ-FM St. George, Utah; Donald W. Cuthrell Jr., pres Hong-Cuthrell Communications Inc., WLLL/WGOL Richmond, Va.; Katherine K. Dolley, pres/gen mgr WQCB-FM Brewer, Me.; Harriet Lange (CAE), exec dir Kansas Association of Broadcasters, Topeka, Kan.; Kenneth Maness, pres/gen mgr WJCW/WQUT Gray, Tenn.; Mary Quass, pres/gen mgr Quass Broadcasting, KHAK-AM-FM Cedar Rapids, Iowa; J. Shannon Sweatte, VP/gen mgr KVI/KPLZ Seattle; J.T. Whitlock, exec dir WLBN/WLSK Radio, Lebanon, Ky.; Barry Umansky, staff liaison; Bob Fox, ExCom liaison.

Research Committee: W. Tom Simmons (chmn), gen mgr KELO-AM-FM Sioux Falls, S.D.; Lyle Banks, pres/gen mgr WAVY-TV Portsmouth, Va.; Peter Chrisanthopoulos, exec VP rsch, mktg & promotion Capital Cities/ABC Inc., New York; John Damiano, VP media & audience rsch/TV net svcs NBC, New York; Dave Kennedy, sr VP Susquehanna Broadcasting Co., York, Pa.; Thomas McClendon, VP bcstg div Cox Enterprises Inc., Atlanta; David F. Poltrack, sr VP planning & rsch CBS TV net, CBS Inc., New York; Roy Shapiro, VP/gen mgr KYW-AM/WMMR-FM Philadelphia; Tom Tolar, pres/gen mgr WRCB-TV Chattanooga, Tenn.; Carroll Ward, VP progmg WTVM-TV Columbus, Ga.; Rick Ducey, staff liaison; Gary Chapman, ExCom liaison.

Research Committee on Local Radio Audience Measurement (COLRAM): David Kennedy (chmn), sr VP Susquehanna Broadcasting Co., York, Pa.; Ross Biederman, pres WTCM-AM-FM Traverse City, Mich.; Charles Blake, VP/gen mgr WIKY-AM-FM Evansville, Ind.; Amos C. Brown III, stn mgr WTUX/WTLC Indianapolis; Glen Bryant, VP media mkt & rsch Sheridan Broadcasting Network, New York; Terry Drucker, dir rsch CBS Radio, New York; Jerry Lee, pres WEAZ-FM Bala Cynwyd, Pa.; Mike Levine, VP/sls mgr WNNJ-AM-FM Newton, N.J.; Bill McClenaghan, sr VP rsch/dev ABC Radio Network, New York; Robert Miller, stn mgr WKMI-WKFR Kalamazoo, Mich.; Bob Neil, exec VP radio Cox Broadcasting Co., Atlanta; Owen Weber, exec VP Summit Communications Group, Atlanta; Jane Shapiro (ex-officio), dir rsch Radio Advertising Bureau, New York; Richard Weinstein, (ex-officio) exec dir Electronic Media Rating Council, New York; Rick Ducey, staff liaison; Wayne Vriesman, ExCom liaison.

Research Subcommittee on Local TV Audience Measurement (COLTAM): Thomas McClendon (chmn), VP bcstg div Cox Enterprises Inc., Atlanta; Fred Barber, VP/gen mgr WRAL-TV Raleigh, N.C.; Lawrence Clamage, sr VP TV, Anchor Media, St. Petersburg, Fla.; Gary Corbitt, rsch dir WJXT-TV Jacksonville, Fla.; Brian Fiori, dir rsch KRON-TV San Francisco; Kathryn Lenard, VP rsch NBC, New York; Gary Nielsen, pres/gen mgr WOKR-TV Rochester, N.Y.; Dr. Jack Wakshlag, dir rsch CBS-TV Stations, New York; Richard Weinstein, exec dir Electronic Media Rating Council, New York; Harold Simpson (ex-officio), sr VP rsch Television Bureau of Advertising, New York; Rick Ducey, staff liaison; Gary Chapman, ExCom liaison.

Resource Development Committee: Edward Jones (chmn), gen mgr WHMM-TV Washington; Rene DeLaRosa, pres/gen mgr KIQI San Francisco; Art Mobley, pres KMJK-FM Phoenix; Denise Oliver, VP progmg Unistar Radio Network, New York; Tony Rodriguez, pres KSSA-AM-FM Dallas; Larry Saunders, chmn WPEX/WWDE Hampton, Va.; William Saunders, pres/own WPAL Charleston, S.C.; Celia Shaw, VP/gen mgr WCIV-TV Charleston, S.C.; Dwight Ellis, staff liaison; Eddie Fritts, ExCom liaison.

Small/Medium Market Radio Committee: Small Markets: W. Leroy Schneck (co-chmn), pres/gen mgr WNAE/WRRN Warren, Pa.; Larry Bevins, gen mgr WVOW-AM-FM Logan, W. Va.; Bruce Grassman, co-own/gen mgr WTCH/WOWN Shawano, Wis.; John O. Kimel, pres WWSR/WLFE St. Albans, Vt.; Dennis Martin, gen mgr KATE/KRGR Radio, Albert Lea, Minn.; C. Richard McBroom, pres/gen mgr WONW/WNDH Napoleon, Ohio; Mylene Walden, gen mgr KIHR/KCGB Hood River, Ore.; Medium Markets: Houston Pearce (co-chmn), pres Radio South Inc., Tuscaloosa, Ala.; Curtis W. Brown, KTTS-AM-FM Springfield, Mo.; Julie Gade, gen mgr KZKX-FM Lincoln, Neb.; Bill Evans, pres/gen mgr WQXE-FM Elizabethtown, Ky.; Bill Hickman, gen mgr WMFM-FM Hattiesburg, Miss.; Sharon MacWilliams, gen mgr WALL/WKOJ Middletown, N.Y.; George Swift, pres KLCL/KHLA Lake Charles, La.; John David, staff liaison; Bob Fox, ExCom liaison.

TELCO Entry Task Force: Nicholas D. Trigony (chmn), pres bcst div, Cox Broadcasting Co., Atlanta; Andrew Banks, mgng dir ABRY Communications, Boston; John Behnke, chmn Fisher Broadcasting Inc., Seattle; Michael Bock, VP TV, Guy Gannett Broadcasting Services, Portland, Me.; Rodney H. Brady, pres/CEO Bonneville International Corp., Salt Lake City; Michael Finkelstein, pres Renaissance Communications, Greenwich, Conn.; Dennis FitzSimons, pres Tribune Television, Tribune Broadcasting Co., Chicago; Jonathan Klein, pres Group W Television, Westinghouse Broadcasting Co., Philadelphia; Benjamin McKeel, VP TV, Nationwide Communications, Columbus, Ohio; John Quinn, pres/gen mgr WJDM-AM Elizabeth, N.J.; Gary Schmedding, VP bcstg Lee Enterprises, Davenport, Iowa; Paul Virciglio, VP/gen mgr WNEM-TV, Saginaw, Mich.; Anita Wallgren, VP Great American Broadcasting Co., Cincinnati; John Abel, Jim May, Jeff Baumann, Charles Sherman, staff liaisons; Ron Townsend, ExCom liaison.

Television Group Advisory Committee: Harry J. Pappas (chmn), pres/CEO Pappas Telecasting Companies, Visalia, Calif.; Stuart Beck, pres Granite Broadcasting Corp., New York; Lawrence A. Busse, pres Busse Broadcasting Corp., Kalamazoo, Mich.; James A. Kizer, VP opns Federal Broadcasting Co., WLUC Negaunee, Mich.; H. Lewis Klein, pres Gateway Communications, Bala Cynwyd, Pa.; Pat Servodidio, pres Multimedia Broadcasting Co., Cincinnati; Marvin Shirley, VP Allbritton Communications, Washington; Berry Smith, sr VP bcstg Schurz Communications Inc., South Bend, Ind.; J. Daniel Sullivan, pres/COO Clear Channel Communications, Houston; Royce Yudkoff, mgng dir ABRY Communications, Boston; Charles Sherman, staff liaison; Ron Townsend, Excom liaison.

Distinguished Service Award Recipients: 1953: David Sarnoff; 1954: William S. Paley; 1955: former NAB President Mark Ethridge; 1956: Robert E. Kintner; 1957: Herbert Hoover; 1958: Frank Stanton; 1959: Robert W. Sarnoff; 1960: Clair R. McCollough; 1961: former NAB President Justin Miller; 1962: Edward R. Murrow; 1963: Bob Hope; 1964: Donald H. McGannon; 1965: Leonard H. Goldenson; 1966: Sol Taishoff; 1967: Chet Huntley and David Brinkley; 1968: Lowell Thomas; 1969: John Fetzer; 1970: Rosel Hyde; 1971: former NAB President Neville Miller; 1972: Billy Graham; 1973: Ward Quaal; 1974: Richard Chapin; 1975: George Storer; 1976: Julian Goodman; 1977: Harold Krelstein; 1978: J. Leonard Reinsch; 1979: Jack Harris; 1980: Donald Thurston; 1981: Arch Madsen; 1982: Walter Cronkite; 1983: former NAB President Vincent Wasilewski; 1984: Elton Rule; 1985: Wilson Wearn; 1986: Grant Tinker; 1987: Martin Umansky; 1988: Mark Fowler; 1989: James E. Duffy; 1990: Bill Smullin; 1991: Thomas Murphy; 1992: Ronald Reagan; 1993: Dick Clark.

National Association of Television Program Executives International (NATPE)

Address: 2425 W. Olympic Blvd., Suite 550E, Santa Monica, Calif. 90404. (310) 453-4440. FAX: (310) 453-5258.

Other Offices: London, England W1R 5FA: Chesham House, Suite 500, 150 Regent St. (71) 494-3633. FAX: (71) 734-4166. Peter Lord. Santiago 9 Chile: Providencia 929 P.H. Casilla 7-9. (562) 251-8665. FAX: (562) 274-1512. Osvaldo Barzelatto.

Executive Committee: Lou Gattozzi, chmn/CEO WJW-TV Cleveland; Russell Meyerson, first vice chmn/treas Media General Broadcast Group, Tampa; Carolyn Worford, second vice chmn/sec WJBK-TV Detroit; Pat Patton, immediate past chmn KMBC-TV Kansas City; Steve Goldman, assoc member rep Paramount Television, Los Angeles; Bruce Johansen, pres/COO NATPE International, Los Angeles; A. Philip Corvo, exec VP NATPE International, Los Angeles.

Board of Directors

Class of 1994: Jayne Adair, KDKA-TV Pittsburgh; Philip Jones, Central Television Enterprises, London; Gene Lothery, WCAU-TV Philadelphia; Greg Meidel, Twentieth Century Television, Los Angeles.

Class of 1995: Pat Fili-Krushel, ABC, New York; Phil Jones, Meredith Corp., Des Moines, Iowa; Ed Wilson, Columbia Pictures Television, Los Angeles.

Class of 1996: Matt Mixon, WFSB-TV Hartford, Conn.; Craig Smith, KING-TV Seattle; Lynn Stepanian, WESH-TV Orlando, Fla.; John Rohr, Blair Television, New York; John Ryan, Worldvision Enterprises, New York.

Officers/Consultants: Ron Gold, sr VP mktg NATPE International, Los Angeles; Nick Orfanopoulos, sr VP conferences NATPE International, Los Angeles; Peter Lord, European mgr, London, England; Osvaldo Barzelatto, Latin American rep, Santiago, Chile; Leroy Bobbitt, legal counsel, Loeb & Loeb, Los Angeles; Dick Barovick, legal counsel, Loeb & Loeb, New York; Mickey Gardner, Washington counsel, Washington; Dick Lippin, pub rels The Lippin Group, Los Angeles & New York.

National Cable Television Association Inc. (NCTA)

Headquarters: 1724 Massachusetts Ave. N.W., Washington 20036. (202) 775-3550.

Executives: Decker S. Anstrom, pres; Pamela J. Turner, VP govt rel; Daniel L. Brenner, VP law & regulatory policy; Wendell Bailey, VP science & tech; Suzanne Hayes, VP progmg & mktg; Cynthia B. Brumfield, VP rsch & policy analysis; Jadz Janucik, VP assn affrs; Barbara O. York, VP industry affrs.

Executive committee: Robert Miron; James O. Robbins; Joseph J. Collins, immediate past chmn; Richard D. Roberts, chmn; Brian L. Roberts, sec; Amos B. Hostetter Jr.; John Malone; Larry W. Wangberg, vice-chmn; Tony H. Cox; William J. Bresnan; R.E. Turner, treas.

NCTA Officers and Board of Directors

John W. Goddard, Viacom Cable, Box 13, Pleasanton, Calif. 94566-0811. (510) 463-0987. FAX: (510) 463-3241.

Major National Associations

Robert Miron, Newhouse Broadcasting Corp., Box 4872, Syracuse, N.Y. 13221. (315) 463-7677. FAX: (315) 463-4127.

Jerry D. Lindauer, Prime Cable, One American Ctr., Suite 3000, 600 Congress Ave., Austin, Tex. 78701. (512) 476-7888. FAX: (512) 476-4869.

James O. Robbins, Cox Cable Communications, 1400 Lake Hearn Dr., Atlanta 30319. (404) 843-5811. FAX: (404) 843-5777.

James S. Cownie, New Heritage Associates, 2600 Grand Ave., Suite 301, Des Moines, Iowa 50312. (515) 246-4450. FAX: (515) 246-8210.

Decker Anstrom (pres), National Cable Television Association, 1724 Massachusetts Ave. N.W., Washington 20036. (202) 775-3655. FAX: (202) 775-3695.

Brian L. Roberts (sec), Comcast Corp., 1234 Market St., 16th Fl., Philadelphia 19107. (215) 981-7501. FAX: (215) 981-7779.

Gregory Bryan Blow, Rainbow Cablevision, 733 N. Second St., Ajo, Ariz. 85321. (602) 387-7033. FAX: (602) 387-5114.

William J. Bresnan, Bresnan Communications Co., 709 Westchester Ave., White Plains, N.Y. 10604. (914) 997-5656. FAX: (914) 997-6871.

Joseph J. Collins (immediate past chmn), Time Warner Cable, 300 First Stamford Pl., Stamford, Conn. 06902-6732. (203) 328-0601. FAX: (203) 328-0677.

Winston "Tony" H. Cox, Showtime Networks Inc., 1633 Broadway, 37th Fl., New York 10019. (212) 708-1461. FAX: (212) 708-1391.

Frank M. Drendel, Comm/Scope Inc., 1375 Lenoir-Rhyne Blvd., Hickory, N.C. 28602. (704) 323-4881. FAX: (704) 324-2760.

John D. Evans, Hauser Communications, 2707 Wilson Blvd., Arlington, Va. 22201. (703) 358-2770. FAX: (703) 524-6146.

Michael J. Fuchs, Home Box Office, 1100 Ave. of the Americas, New York 10036. (212) 512-1364. FAX: (212) 512-5088.

Alan Gerry, Cablevision Industries Inc., Box 311, Liberty, N.Y. 12754. (914) 295-2700. FAX: (914) 295-2701.

Amos B. Hostetter Jr., Continental Cablevision Inc., The Pilot House, Lewis Wharf, Boston 02110. (617) 742-9500 ext 221. FAX: (617) 742-0530.

Marvin L. Jones, Marvin Jones Associates Inc., 8101 E. Prentice Ave., Suite 500, Englewood, Colo. 80111. (303) 721-5407. FAX: (303) 721-5415.

Kay Koplovitz, USA Networks, 1230 Ave. of the Americas, 20th Fl., New York 10020. (212) 408-2700. FAX: (212) 408-8863.

Dr. John C. Malone, Tele-Communications Inc., Terrace Tower II, 5619 DTC Pkwy., Englewood, Colo. 80111. (303) 267-5201. FAX: (303) 488-3200.

John J. Rigas, Adelphia Communications Corp., Box 472, Coudersport, Pa. 16915. (814) 274-9830. FAX: (814) 274-8631.

Richard D. Roberts (chmn), TeleCable Corp., Box 2098, Norfolk, Va. 23501. (804) 624-5002. FAX: (804) 624-5838.

Jack C. Clifford, Colony Communications Inc., 75 Fountain St., Providence, R.I. 02902. (401) 277-7151. FAX: (401) 274-2076.

June E. Travis, Rifkin & Associates Inc., 360 S. Monroe St., Suite 600, Denver 80209. (303) 333-1215. FAX: (303) 322-3553.

R.E. "Ted" Turner (treas), Turner Broadcasting System Inc., Box 105366, Atlanta 30348-5366. (404) 827-1700. FAX: (404) 827-5655.

Larry W. Wangberg (vice-chmn), Times Mirror Cable Television, 2381 Morse Ave., Irvine, Calif. 92714-6233. (714) 660-0500, ext. 232. FAX: (714) 660-7715.

John "Dubby" O. Wynne, Landmark Communications Inc., 150 W. Brambleton Ave., Norfolk, Va. 23510. (804) 446-2007. FAX: (804) 446-2489.

Donald Sbarra, Multimedia Cablevision Inc., 701 E. Douglas, Wichita, Kan. 67202. (316) 262-4270. FAX: (316) 262-2309.

Henry W. Harris, MetroVision Inc., 115 Perimeter Ctr. Pl., Suite 550, Atlanta 30346. (404) 394-8837. FAX: (404) 698-0228.

James A. Hirshfield Jr., Summit Communications Inc., 3633 136th Pl. S.E., Suite 107, Bellevue, Wash. 98006. (206) 747-4600, ext. 104. FAX: (206) 644-4621.

Lee C. Howley, North Coast Cable of Bratenahl Inc., 3400 Lakeside Ave., Cleveland 44114. (216) 566-5458. FAX: (216) 566-0463.

Glenn R. Jones, Jones Intercable Inc., 9697 E. Mineral Ave., Englewood, Colo. 80112. (303) 792-3111. FAX: (303) 784-8510.

Joseph S. Gans Sr., Cable TV Co., 217 E. 9th St., Hazelton, Pa. 18201. (717) 455-4251. FAX: (717) 459-0963.

Timothy B. Robertson, The Family Channel, 1000 Centerville Tpke., Virginia Beach, Va. 23463. (804) 523-7151. FAX: (804) 523-7880.

John M. Egan, ANTEC, 2850 W. Golf Rd., Rolling Meadows, Ill. 60008. (708) 439-4444. FAX: (708) 439-8527.

Don D. Jordan, KBLCOM Inc., 5 Post Oak Park, 440 Post Oak Pkwy., Houston 77027. (713) 629-3001. FAX: (713) 629-3065.

James A. Kofalt, Cablevision Systems Corp., One Media Crossways, Woodbury, N.Y. 11797. (516) 496-1333. FAX: (516) 364-8501.

James A. Monroe, Apache Cablevision, 9795 E. Caron St., Scottsdale, Ariz. 85258. (602) 391-1904. FAX (602) 451-7712.

Marc B. Nathanson, Falcon Cable TV, 10900 Wilshire Blvd., 15th Fl., Los Angeles 90024. (310) 474-6512. FAX: (310) 470-2091.

Steven J. Simmons, Simmons Communications Inc., One Landmark Sq., Suite 1400, Stamford, Conn. 06901. (203) 359-0455. FAX: (203) 353-1649.

J.C. Sparkman, Tele-Communications Inc., Terrace Tower II, 5619 DTC Pkwy., Englewood, Colo. 80111. (303) 267-5247. FAX: (303) 488-3200.

James M. Hoak, Crown Media Inc., One Galleria Tower, 13355 Noel Rd., Suite 1650, Dallas 75240. (214) 960-4802. FAX: (214) 960-4866.

National Cable Television Cooperative Inc.

Headquarters: 14809 W. 95th St., Lenexa, Kan. 66215. (913) 599-5900. FAX: (913) 599-5903.

Executives: Michael L. Pandzik, pres; David M. Clark, VP, Frank J. Hughes, VP natl accts.

Officer: Linda Stuchell, chmn.

NCTC Board Members: James Brown, Wometco; Peter Callais, Callais Cablevision; Ray Miller, Cablevision Industries; Linda Stuchell, Harron Communications; Paul Mass, Cablesouth; Dan Simons, Columbine Cablevision; Gene Hager, Antietam Cable; Elizabeth Burke, People's Broadband Communications; Robert Knoke, W.K. Communications.

Staff: Julie Cooke, hardware svcs; Dorothy Pinkelman, acct supvr; Kathy Svoboda, prog supvr; Martha Dixon, Brian Jones, prog assts; Julaire Sterbach, special projects.

Radio Advertising Bureau

Headquarters: 304 Park Ave. S., New York 10010. (212) 387-2100. FAX: (212) 254-8713.

Chicago Office: 625 N. Michigan Ave., Chicago 60611. (312) 751-3456. FAX: (312) 587-9529.

Detroit Office: 21 Kercheval Ave., Suite 232, Grosse Point Farms, Mich. 48236. (313) 885-5454. FAX: (313) 885-2192.

Los Angeles Office: 5670 Wilshire Blvd., Suite 910, Los Angeles 90036. (213) 938-3228. FAX: (213) 938-8174.

Officers

Paul Fiddick (chmn), pres radio group Heritage Media Group; Gary Edens (vice-chmn), chmn Edens Broadcasting; John Dille (chmn finance committee), pres Federated Media; Gary H. Simpson (sec), pres Allegheny Mountain Network, Tyrone, Pa.; Gary Fries, pres/CEO; Wayne Cornils, exec VP svcs; Ron Ruth, exec VP stns; Judy Carlough, exec VP mktg; George Hyde, exec VP training; Harley Park, sr VP/CFO; Ken Costa, VP radio info; Roann Evans, VP new bus resources; Ed O'Halloran, VP mktg; Chuck Shepard, VP opns; Laura Morandin, VP communications; Mike Mahone, VP training; J.D. MacKay, VP mktg (Chicago); Mike Quaid, VP stns; Lynn Christian, sr VP stns West Coast rgn (Los Angeles).

Board of Directors

Paul W. Fiddick (chmn), pres radio group Heritage Media Corp., Dallas; Gary Edens (vice-chmn), chmn Edens Broadcasting; John Dille (finance chmn), pres Federated Media, Elkhart, Ind.; Cary H. Simpson (sec), pres Allegheny Mountain Network, Tyrone, Pa.; Stephen P. Bellinger, pres Prairieland Broadcasters, Decatur, Ill.; Randy Bongarten, exec VP WNCN Radio New York; Don Bouloukos, pres owned radio stns WABC, New York; Carl C. Brazell, pres Command Communications, New York; Richard D. Buckley (nomination committee chmn), pres Buckley Broadcasting, Greenwich, Conn.; Rod Calarco, VP CBS-owned FM stns, New York; Robert Callahan, pres ABC Radio Networks, New York; Arthur W. Carlson, pres Susquehanna Broadcasting Co., York, Pa.; James E. Champlin, pres Beck-Ross Communications, Rockville Centre, N.Y.; Richard W. Chapin, pres Chapin Enterprises, Lincoln, Neb.; Bill Clark, pres Shamrock Broadcasting, Burbank, Calif.; Dave Crowl, pres radio group Great American Broadcasting, Cincinnati; Lee Davis, pres/gen mgr CUB Radio Inc., Manitowoc, Wis.; Steve Edwards, pres/gen mgr South Central Communications, Nashville; Skip Finley, pres/gen mgr WKYS Radio, Washington; Mickey Franko, VP radio Nationwide Communications, Columbus, Ohio; Gary R. Fries, pres/CEO Radio Advertising Bureau, New York; David Gingold, pres Barnstable Broadcasting, Waltham, Mass.; Les Goldberg, pres The Interep Radio Store, New York; Merrell Hansen, exec VP Gannett Radio Division, St. Louis; Richard Harris, pres WSPB Radio, Sarasota, Fla.; Gordon Hastings, pres Katz Radio Group, New York; Kenneth Hatch, pres/CEO KIRO Inc., Seattle; William J. Hogan, pres/gen mgr Unistar, New York; Ken Johnson, pres Capitol Broadcasting, Mobile, Ala.; Bob L. Lawrence, exec VP/COO Jacor Communications, Cincinnati; Bob Lind, VP radio group Capitol Broadcasting, Raleigh, N.C.; Jerry Lyman, pres/CEO Lyman Radio Corp., Bethesda, Md.; Glenn Mahone (RAB counsel), Reed, Smith, Shaw & McClay, Pittsburgh; Phil Marella, pres/chmn Pinnacle Broadcasting, New York; Herb McCord, pres/CEO Granum Communications, New York; Gunther Meisse, pres/gen mgr WVNO/WRGM Radio, Mansfield, Ohio; David H. Morris (chmn by-laws committee), pres Texas Coast Broadcasters, Houston; Norman Pattiz, chmn/CEO Westwood One Inc., Culver City, Calif.; Allen Shaw, pres TA Communications, Winston-Salem, N.C.; Lester M. Smith, CEO Kaye-Smith Enterprises, Bellevue, Wash.; Jeffrey Smulyan, COB, Emmis Broadcasting, Indianapolis; Dean Sorenson, pres Sorenson Broadcasting, Sioux Falls, S.D.; William Stakelin, pres Apollo Radio Group, New York; Jim Taszarek, VP/gen mgr KTAR/KKLT Radio, Phoenix; John Tenaglia, pres/CEO TK Communications, Fort Lauderdale, Fla.; James B. Thompson, pres Liberty Broadcasting, Chatham, N.J.; Nicholas J. Verbitsky, chmn/CEO Bentley Broadcasting Co., New York; Wayne Vriesman, VP radio group Tribune Broadcasting Co., Chicago; Ray Watson, VP/gen mgr KXL Radio, Portland, Ore.; Nancy C. Widmann, pres CBS Radio, New York; Thomas L. Young, pres/gen mgr Young Radio Inc., Napa, Calif.

Board Committees

Executive Committee: Paul Fiddick (chmn), Richard Buckley, James Champlin, Bill Clark, John Dille, Gary Edens, Skip Finley, Gary Fries, Herb McCord, Cary Simpson, Dean Sorenson, Nancy Widmann.

Finance Committee: John Dille (chmn), Randy Bongarten, Bob Callahan, Dave Crowl, Gary Edens, Merrell Hansen, Herb McCord, Gunther Meisse.

Local Sales & Services Committee: Jerry Lyman (chmn), Mark Bench, Rod Calarco, Lee Davis, John

Major National Associations

Dille, Ken Johnson, Phil Marella, Gunther Meisse, David Morris, Cary Simpson, Dean Sorenson, Ray Watson.

Membership Committee: Jim Champlin (chmn), Don Bouloukos, Bill Clark, Dave Crowl, John Dille, Gary Edens, Mickey Franko, Merrell Hansen, Gordon Hastings, Bill Hogan, Bob Lind, Phil Marella, Herb McCord, Gunther Meisse, Allen Shaw, Cary Simpson, Jeff Smulyan, Jim Thompson, Nick Verbitsky, Nancy Widmann, Tom Young.

National Marketing Committee: Bill Clark (chmn), Mark Bench, Randy Bongarten, Don Bouloukos, Carl Brazell, Rod Calarco, Robert Callahan, James Champlin, Skip Finley, Mickey Franko, Les Goldberg, Gordon Hastings, Bill Hogan, Herb McCord, Norm Pattiz, Jeff Smulyan, Bill Stakelin, John Tenaglia, James Thompson, Nicholas Verbitsky, Wayne Vriesman, Nancy Widmann.

Research Committee: Skip Finley (chmn), Steve Bellinger, Randy Bongarten, Carl Brazell, Robert Callahan, Steve Edwards, David Gingold, Les Goldberg, Bob Lawrence, Glenn Mahone, David Morris, Norm Pattiz, Bill Stakelin, Jim Taszarek, John Tenaglia, Wayne Vriesman, Ray Watson.

Training & Education Committee: Merrell Hansen (chmn), Steve Bellinger, Dave Crowl, Gary Edens, Steve Edwards, David Gingold, Ken Johnson, Bob Lawrence, Bob Lind, Jerry Lyman, Glenn Mahone, Allen Shaw, Dean Sorenson, Jim Taszarek, Tom Young.

Radio-Television News Directors Association

Headquarters: 1000 Connecticut Ave. N.W., Suite 615, Washington 20036. (202) 659-6510. FAX: (202) 223-4007.

Officers: Marci Burdick (chmn), WYTV-TV Springfield, Mo.; Bill Yeager, Metro News Network, Philadelphia; David Bartlett (pres), RTNDA, Washington; Lou Prato (treas), Medill News Service, Washington; Gary Hanson (past chmn), WKBN-TV Youngstown, Ohio.

Regional Directors: John Sears, KPTV Portland, Ore., rgn 1; Vickie Jenkins, KOIT-AM San Francisco, rgn 2; Marie Curkan-Flanagan, KOCO-TV Oklahoma City, Okla., rgn 4; Mark Millage, KELO-TV Sioux Falls, S.D., rgn 5; David Busiek, KCCI-TV Des Moines, Iowa, rgn 6; Scot Witt, WDCB-FM Glen Ellyn, Ill., rgn 7; Dan Acklen, WUAB-TV Cleveland, rgn 8; James Smith, KPLC-TV Lake Charles, La., rgn 9; James Whiteaker, WMC-TV Memphis, rgn 10; Paul Douglas, WTIC-AM Hartford, Conn., rgn 11; Bernie Gershon, WCBS Radio New York, rgn 12; Robert Garcia, CBS Radio Washington, rgn 13; Richard Moore, WSB-TV Atlanta, rgn 14; Ron Johnston, CKCO-TV Kitchener, Ont., Canada, RTNDA Canada rep; Al Gibson, Broadcast News Ltd., Toronto, Ont., Canada, international rep.

Directors-at-large: Mike Cavender, WTSP-TV Tampa/St. Petersburg, Fla.; Jon Petrovich, CNN Headline News, Atlanta; Marsha Taylor, WDBO-AM Orlando, Fla.; Loren Tobia, KMTV Omaha, Neb.

Ex Officio: Tony Harmon, Texas Tech (AEJMC); Don Gale, Bonnesville International (NCEW); Ernest Gudule, KWGN-TV Denver (NAHJ); Sheila Stanback, CNBC-TV Fort Lee, N.J. (NABJ); David Louie, KGO-TV San Francisco (AAJA); Raul Ramirez, KQED-FM San Francisco (NLGJA); Laverne Sheppard, FMC, Pocatello, Idaho (NAJA).

Staff: Leslie Breen, dir progs; Joe Tiernan, edit; Kathleen Hilburn, asst to pres; Michele Fitzgerald, dir membership; Sandy Doherty, dir finance & admin; Ron Bardach, dir adv sls; Wendy Dressel, mgr meetings & special events; Stephanie Sweeney, admin asst; Tammy Rawls.

Active Members: About 1,200 radio and TV news directors.

Total Members: About 3,600.

Television Bureau of Advertising (TVB)

Headquarters: 850 3rd Ave., New York 10022-5892. (212) 486-1111. FAX: (212) 935-5631.

Officers

Ave Butensky, pres; Jack Sander, chmn; David Allen, treas; Ed Reilly, chmn/ex-officio; Joseph C. Tirinato, sr VP natl sls & mktg; Thomas A. Conway, sr VP dir retail mktg; Ronni Faust, VP communications; Harold Simpson, VP rsch; Sheila O'Leary, VP prod; Sam McPherson, CFO.

Board of Directors: David Allen, pres Petry Television Sales, New York; Barry Baker, pres/CEO River City TV Broadcasting, St. Louis; Francis P. Brady, pres TV group Viacom Broadcasting; Ave Butensky, pres Television Bureau of Advertising, New York; Andrew Fisher, exec VP affil Cox Enterprises, Atlanta; Dennis FitzSimons, pres Tribune Television, Chicago; Peter Goulazian, pres/CEO Katz Corp., New York; John Hayes, VP bcstg Providence Journal Co., Providence, R.I.; Steve Herson, pres/gen mgr TeleRep Inc., New York; Phil Jones, pres Meredith Broadcasting Corp., Des Moines, Iowa; Timothy McAuliff, pres/CEO John Blair Communications, New York; James Moroney, VP/gen mgr KOTV Tulsa, Okla.; Jack Oken, pres MMT Sales Inc., New York; Lawrence J. Pollock, pres Capital Cities/ABC-owned TV stns, Philadelphia; Edward T. Reilly, pres McGraw-Hill Broadcasting Co. Inc., New York; John Rohrbeck, pres NBC Television Stations, New York; Peter Ryan, pres Harrington, Righter & Parsons Inc., New York; G. William Ryan, pres Post-Newsweek Stations Inc., Miami, Fla.; Jack Sander, pres/gen mgr WAGA-TV Atlanta; Shelly Schwab, pres MCA-TV, Universal City, Calif.; A. Pat Serrodidio, pres Multimedia Broadcasting, Cincinnati; Paul Wise, dir sls KPLR-TV St. Louis; Henry K. Yaggi III, pres/gen mgr WUSA Washington.

Committees

Executive Committee (board of directors): Jack Sander, chmn; Ave Butensky, pres; Tim McAuliff, VP; David Allen, treas; Edward T. Reilly, chmn ex-officio; Barry Baker, Andrew Fisher, members-at-large.

Sales Advisory Committee: Rick Keilty (chmn), dir sls & mktg KHOU Houston; William Fine (ex-officio), local sls mgr WCVB Boston; Nancy Dodson, mgr Blair TV, Los Angeles; Bill Spell, gen sls mgr WSB Atlanta; Bill Ballard, gen sls mgr WTXF, Philadelphia; Jeff Block, gen sls mgr KTVU Oakland, Calif.; Kent Beckwith, gen sls mgr WOKR Rochester, N.Y.; Darrell Brown, gen sls mgr KGTV San Diego; Thomas Calato, gen sls mgr WOFL Orlando, Fla.; Lisa Churchville, gen sls mgr WMAQ Chicago; Kathy Clements-Hill, gen sls mgr WFAA Dallas; Joe Collins, gen sls mgr KNSD San Diego; John Cottingham, gen sls mgr WTOL Toledo, Ohio; Karl Davis, gen sls mgr WNYT Albany, N.Y.; Chuck DeVendra, gen sls mgr WKRC Cincinnati; Helen Feinbloom, dir sls WDCA-TV Washington, D.C.; Gil Fitts, local sls mgr WTVD Raleigh, N.C.; Tim Frame, gen sls mgr WRIC Richmond, Va.; Chris Gallu, gen sls mgr, Knoxville, Tenn.; Phil Johnson, dir sls WDKA Pittsburgh; Kathleen Keefe, gen sls mgr WFSB Hartford, Conn.; Donna Kirner, gen sls mgr WISC Madison, Wis.; Steve Langford, gen sls mgr WAVE Louisville, Ky.; Jack Lyons, gen sls mgr WFLA Tampa; Phyllis Ned, local sls mgr KETV Omaha, Neb.; Janet Noll, gen sls mgr WJZY Charlotte, N.C.; Judy Obernier, local sls mgr WPLG Miami, Fla.; Ted Pearce, gen sls mgr WDIV-TV Detroit; Michael Renda, gen sls mgr WLWT Cincinnati; John Riedl, gen sls mgr KABC Los Angeles; Rick Rogala, gen sls mgr KTVI St. Louis; John Tamerlano, gen sls mgr WKYC Cleveland; Fran Tivald, gen sls mgr WJZ Baltimore; Paul Trelstar, gen sls mgr KPNX Phoenix; Mike Vrabac, gen sls mgr KJRH Tulsa, Okla.; John Washington, gen sls mgr KING Seattle; Allen Wiese, natl sls mgr KWQC Davenport, Iowa.

National Sales Advisory Committee: Timothy McAuliff (chmn), pres/CEO Blair Communications; Arthur Scott, pres Adam Young Co.; Sam Stallworth Jr., VP natl sls CBS Television; John Watkins, pres Capital Cities/ABC natl sls; Joel Segall, VP/gen sls mgr Group W Television Sales; Peter Ryan, pres Harrington, Righter & Parsons; Thomas F. Olson, pres Katz Television Group; Jack Oken, pres MMT Sales Inc.; John Heise, pres Petry Television Inc.; L. Donald Robinson, pres/CEO Seltel Inc.; Steve Herson, pres/gen mgr TeleRep Inc.

National Associations

Academy of Canadian Cinema & Television. 158 Pearl St., Toronto, Ont., Canada M5H 1L3. (416) 591-2040. FAX: (416) 591-2157. Maria Topalovich, exec dir.

Academy of Religious Broadcasting. 500 Wall St., Suite 415, Seattle 98121-1588. (206) 441-6110. J. Graley Taylor, exec dir.

Acoustical Society of America. 500 Sunnyside Blvd., Woodbury, N.Y. 11797. (516) 576-2360. FAX: (516) 349-7669. Charles E. Schmid, exec dir.

Advertiser Syndicated Television Association. 1756 Broadway, New York 10019. (212) 245-0840. FAX: (212) 245-0842. Mike Shaw (Buena Vista), pres; Bob Cesa (20th TV), VP; Tim Duncan, exec dir.

Directors: Rich Goldfarb (Turner); Brian Byrne (Byrne); Dan Cosgrove (Group W); Clark Morehouse (Warner), pres emeritus.

The Advertising Council Inc. 261 Madison Ave., New York 10016-2303. (212) 922-1500. FAX: (212) 922-1676. Philip H. Grier Jr. (Interpublic Group of Companies), chmn/CEO; Ruth A. Wooden, pres; Elinor U. Biggs, sr VP financial dev; Robert D. Schultz, sr VP media dev; Donna Feiner, VP/dir media admin; Paula A. Veale, dir pub rels.

Washington 20036: 1730 Rhode Island Ave. N.W., Suite 414. (202) 331-9153. FAX: (202) 331-9790. Eva Kasten, exec VP.

Chicago 60611: 740 Rush St. (312) 751-8055. FAX: (312) 280-3179. Robert Zabel, mng dir.

Advertising Research Foundation Inc. 641 Lexington Ave., New York 10022. (212) 751-5656. FAX: (212) 319-5265. Michael J. Naples, pres.

Alliance of Motion Picture and Television Producers. 15503 Ventura Blvd., Sherman Oaks, Calif. 91436. (818) 995-3600. FAX: (818) 382-1793. J. Nicholas Counter II, pres; Kathleen Grotticelli, CFO; Carol A. Lombardini, VP legal affrs.

American Advertising Federation. 1101 Vermont Ave. N.W., Suite 500, Washington 20005. (202) 898-0089. FAX: (202) 898-0159. Julie Dolan, sr VP; Janel McKenna, VP club svcs.

American Association of Advertising Agencies (AAAA). 666 3rd Ave., New York 10017. (212) 682-2500. FAX: (212) 953-5665. O. Burtch Drake, exec VP/COO; Harry Paster, exec VP consulting.

Beverly Hills, Calif. 90211: 8383 Wilshire Blvd, Suite 342. (213) 658-5750. Jerry L. Gibbons, sr VP.

Washington 20036: 1899 L St. N.W. (202) 331-7345. Hal Shoup, exec VP.

Broadcast Administration Policy Committee: JoAnn Kessler (Grey Advertising Inc.), chmn; Dorothy C. Forget, AAAA staff rep.

Broadcast Administration Subcommittee—Central: Diane Sievers (Bozell Inc.), chmn; Dorothy C. Forget, AAAA staff rep.

Broadcast Administration Subcommittee—South: Janice Mock (Tracy-Locke), chmn; Dorothy C. Forget, AAAA sec.

Broadcast Administration Subcommittee—Los Angeles: Linda Daubson (Saatchi & Saatchi), chmn; Dorothy C. Forget (AAAA), sec/staff rep.

Broadcast Administration Policy Subcommittee—San Francisco: Sharon Rundberg (McCann-Erickson), chmn; Dorothy C. Forget, AAAA staff rep.

Broadcast Networks and Programming Committee: Steve Grubbs (BBDO), chmn; Beverly T. Plyer, AAAA sec.

American Center for Children's Television. 1400 E. Touhy Ave., Suite 260, Des Plaines, Ill. 600018-3305. (708) 390-6499. FAX: (708) 390-9435. James Fellows, pres; David Kleeman, dir.

Board of Governors: David Britt (Children's Television Workshop); Bruce L. Christensen (Public Broadcasting Service); John Cooke (The Disney Channel); James Dowdle (Tribune Broadcasting Co.); James A. Fellows (Central Educational Network); John Ford (The Learning Channel); Geraldine Laybourne (Nickelodeon/Nick at Nite); Eugene Katt (Corporation for Public Broadcasting); William J. McCarter (WTTW/Chicago); Judy Price (CBS Entertainment); Mr. Sterling C. Quinlan (Mediatech); Ame Simon.

American Cinema Editors Inc. 1041 N. Formosa Ave., West Hollywood, Calif. 90046. (213) 850-2900. FAX: (213) 850-2922. Michael Hoggan, pres; Doug Ibold, VP; George Hively, sec; Jack Tucker, treas.

Directors: Charles Bornstein, Daniel Cahn, Tina Hirsh, David Rosenbloom, Eric Sears, Bernie Gribble, Mark Goldblatt.

American Composers Alliance. 170 W. 74th St., New York 10023. (212) 362-8900. FAX: (212) 874-8605. Rosalie Calabrese, exec dir; Richard Hervig, pres.

American Electronics Association. 5201 Great America Pkwy., Suite 520, Santa Clara, Calif. 95054. (408) 987-4200. FAX: (408) 970-8565. 1225 Eye St., Washington 20054. (202) 682-9110; (202) 682-9111. J.R. Iverson, pres/CEO; Mike McQuade, sr VP member svcs; John Hatch, VP pub rels; John Mancini, sr VP natl mktg; William Philips, sr VP finance; Pat Hubbard, sr VP memberships; John Baumeister, VP mktg svcs; William Kist, sr VP international; John Stern, VP Asian opns; Tim Elliott, VP sls.

American Film Marketing Association. 12424 Wilshire Blvd., Suite 600, Los Angeles 90025. (310) 447-1555. FAX: (310) 447-1666. Pamela Pickering, chmn; Jonas Rosenfield, pres; Tim Kittleson, exec VP.

American Hispanic Owned Radio Association (AHORA). 230 Truxtun Ave., Bakersfield, Calif. 93301. (805) 324-4411. FAX: (805) 327-9459. Mary Helen Barro, pres; Eduardo Gomez, VP; Amancio V. Suarez Sr., sec/treas.

Directors: Raul Alarcon Jr., Manuel Davila, Rene de la Rosa, Zenon Ferrufino, Ernesto V. Portillo, Miguel A. Villarreal Jr, Eduardo Gomez, Mary Helen Barro, Amancio V. Suarez Sr.

American Marketing Association. 250 S. Wacker Dr., Suite 200, Chicago 60606. (312) 648-0536. FAX: (312) 993-7542. Michael Wukitsch, interim pres.

American Medical Televison. 515 N. State St., Chicago 60610. (312) 464-4420. FAX: (312) 464-4190. Wendy M. Borrow, pres; Leona Doyle, VP opns.

Director: Daniel Mjolsness, dir sls & mktg.

American Meteorological Society. 45 Beacon St., Boston 02108. (617) 227-2425. FAX: (617) 742-8718. Dr. Richard E. Hallgren, exec dir; Robert T. Ryan, pres; Dr. Warren M. Washington, pres-elect.

American Radio Relay League. 225 Main St., Newington, Conn. 06111. (203) 666-1541. FAX: (203) 665-7531 (general); (203) 665-1166 (publications). George S. Wilson, pres; Rodney J. Stafford, 1st VP; David Sumner, exec VP/sec; Perry Williams, Washington area coord; Christopher Imlay, gen counsel.

Washington 20036: 1920 N St. N.W., Suite 520. (202) 296-9107.

American Society of Composers, Authors & Publishers (ASCAP). One Lincoln Plaza, New York 10023. (212) 621-6000. FAX: (212) 721-0955. John Lofrumento, COO; Morton Gould, pres; Sammy Cahn, Jay Morganstern, VPs; Gloria Messinger, mng dir; Arnold Broido, treas.

(See listing under Music Licensing Groups, Section G).

American Society of Media Photographers (ASMP). 14 Washington Rd., Suite 502, Princeton Junction, N.J. 08550-1033. (609) 799-8300. FAX: (609) 799-2233. Richard Weisgrau, exec dir; Bruce Bland, deputy exec dir; Matt Heron, pres; Robert Rathe, 1st VP; Regan Bradshaw, 2nd VP.

Directors: Allan Abromowitz, Jay Asaquini, Dennie Cody, Enrico Ferorelli, Lou Jacobs Jr., Peter B. Kaplan, Dan Klumpp, Dan Luce, David MacTavish, Jay Maisel, Tery Pagos, Margo Pinkerton, Roger Ressmeyer, Vince Streano.

American Society of TV Cameramen Inc. (U.S. affiliate of International Society of Videographers.) Box 296, Washington St., Sparkill, N.Y. 10976. (914) 359-5569 (1 pm-4 pm Eastern Time). Robert M. Zweck, pres; Morton Morje, exec sec; Greg Suhm, international rep Latin America; Clem Laurie, European rep U.K.; Monique Ajrab, European rep France; Buddy Fleck, corporate sec; Steve Jambeck, dir member svcs; Greg Beasley, dir Cammy awards/special projects; Nicole Zweck Spanos, assoc dir Cammy Awards; Jan Kasoff, membership dir; Janet Doka, dir seminars/professional training.

Directors: R.M. Zweck (NBC), chmn; V.T. Jocelyn (Fox TV); F. Melchiorre (ABC); S. Bress (CBS); P. Basil (NBC); Buddy Fleck.

American Sportscasters Association. 5 Beekman St., Suite 814, New York 10038. (212) 227-8080. FAX: (212) 571-0556. Louis O. Schwartz, pres; Curt Gowdy, VP; Jack Brickhouse, sec/treas.

Directors: Dick Enberg, chmn of bd; Jack Brickhouse, Don Dunphy, Curt Gowdy, Louis O. Schwartz.

American Sportscasters Charitable Trust. 5 Beekman St., Suite 814, New York 10038. (212) 227-8080. Jack Brickhouse, Louis O. Schwartz, trustees.

American Women in Radio and Television Inc. 1101 Connecticut Ave. N.W., Suite 700, Washington 20036. (202) 429-5102. FAX: (202) 223-4579. Sondra Lee, natl pres; Linda Tremere, pres-elect; Donna Cantor, exec dir; Cris Stovall, sec/treas.

Armed Forces Broadcasters Association. Box 335, Sun Valley, Calif. 91353-0335. (409) 544-5000. Peter Barrett, pres.

Armed Forces Communications and Electronics Association. 4400 Fair Lakes Ct., Fairfax, Va. 22033-3899. (703) 631-6100. FAX: (703) 631-4693. Gerald Ebker, chmn of bd; Major General M. Padden (USAF retired), exec VP/treas; Admiral James B. Busby IV (USN retired), international press.

Directors: John Spargo, exhibits mgr; Colonel Clem Clement (USAF retired), dir intelligence; Rear Admiral William J. Holland Jr. (USN retired), pres AFCEA Educational Foundation.

Associated Press Broadcasters Inc. (APB). 1825 K St. N.W., Suite 710, Washington 20006-1253. (202) 736-1100. FAX: (202) 736-1124. Roger Ogden (KCNC-TV Denver), pres; Kenneth Maness (WJCW/WQUT Gray, Tenn.), pres-elect; John Corporon (WPIX-TV New York), VP TV; Treeda Smith (WRVQ-FM Richmond, Va.), VP radio; Scott Herman (KYW-TV Philadelphia), sec; Francis A. Martin III (Chronicle Broadcasting Co.), ex-officio.

Directors: Allan Buch (KSNW-TV Wichita, Kan.); Terry Duffie (WKMX-FM Enterprise, Ala.); Dan Halyburton (KLIF-AM/KPLX-FM Dallas); Mike Kettenring (WSMV-TV Nashville); Adrienne Laurent (KMST-TV Monterey, Calif.); Robert Rogers (KENS-TV San Antonio); Richard Moore (WSB-TV Atlanta); Kenneth L. Hatch (KIRO-AM/KSEA-FM/KIRO-TV Seattle); Carol Rueppel (WDIV-TV Detroit); Eric Seidel (WGST-AM Atlanta); William R. Sanders (KICD-AM/FM Spencer, Iowa); Fred Lark (KXLO-AM/KLCM-FM Lewiston, Mont.); Dave Maurer (WSGW-AM/WIOG-FM Saginaw, Mich.).

Association for Education in Journalism and Mass Communication. (AEJMC). University of South Carolina, 1621 College St., Columbia, S.C. 29208-0251. (803) 777-2005. Jennifer H. McGill, exec dir.

Association for Maximum Service Television Inc. 1776 Massachusetts Ave. N.W., Suite 310, Washington 20036. (202) 861-0344. FAX: (202) 861-0342. Margita White, pres; Julian L. Shepard, VP/gen counsel; Victor Tawil, VP; April Lee, admin mgr.

Directors: Rodney H. Brady (Bonneville International Corp., Salt Lake City); Bud Carey (WCBS-TV New York); John G. Conomikes (The Hearst Corp., New York); James E. Crowther (H & C Communications, Houston); James C. Dowdle (Tribune Broadcasting Co., Chicago); Ken J. Elkins (Pulitzer Broadcasting Co., St. Louis); Stanley S. Hubbard (Hubbard Broadcasting, St. Paul); Ward L. Huey Jr. (A.H. Belo Corp, Dallas); Philip A. Jones (Meredith Corp., Des Moines, Iowa); Bill Korn (Group W/Westinghouse Bcstg Co., New York); Michael P. Mallardi (Capital Cities/ABC Inc., New York); Benjamin D. McKeel (Nationwide Commuications, Columbus, Ohio); Leroy Paul (AFLAC Broadcast Div., Columbus, Ga.); Fred Paxton (WPSD-TV Paducah, Ky.); Edward T. Reilly (McGraw-Hill Broadcasting Co., New York); John H. Rohrbeck (NBC Television Stations, New York); G. William Ryan (Post-Newsweek Stations, Miami, Fla.); Dudley S. Taft (Taft Broadcasting Co., Cincinnati); Nicholas D. Trigony (Cox Broadcasting, Atlanta); Cecil L. Walker (Gannett Broadcasting, Arlington, Va.); W.P. Williamson III (WKBN Broadcasting Corp., Youngstown, Ohio); Steve Goldman (Paramount Communications, Los Angeles); John P. Zanotti (Great American Communications Co., Cincinnati).

Association of American Railroads. American Railroads Bldg., 50 F St. N.W., Washington 20001. (202) 639-2100. FAX: (202) 639-2806. Edwin L. Harper, pres/CEO; John J. Hartnett, VP communications; Carol B. Perkins, dir media svcs.

Association of America's Public Television Stations. 1350 Connecticut Ave. N.W., Suite 200, Washington 20036. (202) 887-1700. FAX: (202) 293-2422. David J. Brugger, pres; Richard Grefe, VP; Marilyn Mohrman-

Gillis, gen counsel; Bernadette McGuire, dir rsch & planning; Nancy F. Neubauer, dir communications.
Directors: William McCarter (WTTW), chmn; Robert M. Greber (Pacific Stock Exchange); Hope Green (Vermont ETV); Ronald C. Bornstein (WHA Madison, Wis.); David J. Brugger (America's Public Television Stations); Burnill F. Clark (KCTS); Arthur Mallory (KOZK Springfield); Robert H. Ellis (KAET Tempe, Ariz.); John Maxey II (Mississippi ETV Jackson); Charlotte Hill (KLVX Las Vegas); Barbara M. Hoffman (WKPC Louisville); Dr. Robert F. Larson (WTVS Detroit); Maynard Orme (Oregon Public Broadcasting, Portland); George L. Miles Jr. (Thirteen/WNET New York); Arthur J. Singer (New Hampshire Public TV); Eric C. Smith (WFSU Tallahassee, Fla.); Joseph N. Traigle (Louisiana Public Broadcasting); Jeff Clarke (KUHT Houston); Elsie Garner (WEDU Tampa., Fla.); Victor Miramontes (KLRN San Antonio); Karen Sherrin (WFUM Flint, Mich.).

Association of Canadian Advertisers Inc. 180 Bloor St. W., Suite 803, Toronto, Ont., Canada M5S 2V6. (416) 964-3805. FAX: (416) 964-0771. Patrick McDougall, pres; Maurice Brisebois, VP.

Association of Cinema & Video Laboratories Inc. 7375 Woodward Ave., Detroit 48202. (313) 871-2222. FAX: (313) 871-4120. James Merkle, pres; Frank Ricotta, 1st VP; Gail Ringer, 2nd VP; Rich Vedvick, treas; George Hutchison, sec.
Directors: Ray Balousek, Robert Redd, Robert Smith, Lambert Levy, Stan Nalski.

Association of Federal Communications Consulting Engineers. Box 19333, 20th St. Station, Washington 20036-0333. (703) 824-5660. Charles G. Perry III, pres; Robert D. Culver, VP; William P. Suffa, sec; Robert W. Denny Jr., treas.
Executive Committee: John A. Lundin, Carl T. Jones Jr., Charles I. Gallagher, Sudhir K. Kahanna, Warren M. Powls.

Association of Independent Television Stations Inc. See listing under Major National Associations, this section.

Association of National Advertisers Inc. (ANA). 155 E. 44th St., New York 10017. (212) 697-5950. FAX: (212) 661-8057. Officers: Richard Garvey, chmn; Janet L. Soderstrom, vice-chmn; DeWitt F. Helm Jr., pres; Frank J. Mortenson, VP/sec/controller.
DeWitt F. Helm, Jr. (ANA); Richard S. Bartlett (Eastman Kodak Co.); Tom Campanella (Paramount Pictures); Richard A. Costello (General Electric Co.); David R. Drescher (Fruit of the Loom Inc.); John J. Flieder (Allstate Insurance Co.); Linda S. Graebner (Dole Food Co. Inc.); Robert Klugman (Coors Brewing Co.); Peggy Mitchell-King (American Express Co. Inc.); John R. Morrison (Coca-Cola U.S.A.); James C. Relly (IBM); John B. Vanderzee (Ford Motor Co.); Robert W. Watson (AT&T); L. Ross Love (Procter & Gamble Worldwide); Philip Guarascio (General Motors Corp.); John E. Ruhaak (United Airlines); Maurice L. Kelley Jr. (SmithKline Beecham Consumer Brands); Carol M. Mabe (Hanes Hosiery Inc.); Celeste A. Clarke (Kellogg Co.); Ronald O. Cox (Wm. Wrigley Jr. Co.); Russell Elliot (Schering-Plough HealthCare Products Inc. & Schering-Plough HealthCare Products Advertising Corp.); Rodger E. Godbeer (Colgate-Palmolive Co.); Michael W. Gunn (American Airlines Inc.); Gary S. Moss (Campbell Soup Company); Victor Galef (SEI Corp.).
Corporate Communications Committee: Richard Costello (General Electric Co.), chmn. Radio Advertising Committee: David Drew (Anheuser-Busch's Media Group Inc.), chmn. Print Advertising Commitee: Duncan Maurer (The House of Seagram), chmn. TV Advertising Committee: James Van Cleave (Proctor & Gamble Co.), chmn. ANA Members of ANA-AAAA Joint Policy Committee for Broadcast Talent Union Relations: George Feld (Revlon Inc.), co-chmn; JoAnn Kessler (Grey Advertising), co-chmn.
Directors: Bill Kelsey, Jay Doudna, Brenda Homickle, Marcia Jonke, Lynn Brewer, Beth Jones, Bob Wall, Jim Cashin, Bob Brummond, Gwendolyn Bedford, Kelly Brand, Lynn Chadwick.

Association of Regional Religious Communicators. 1542 Pullan Ave., Cincinnatti 45223. (513) 541-5900. Richard Jameson, exec sec.

The Audio Engineering Society Inc. 60 E. 42nd St., New York 10017. (212) 661-8528. FAX: (212) 682-0477. Richard Cabot, pres; Louis Fielder, pres-elect; Floyd E. Toole, past pres; Ken Pohlmann, VP eastern rgn U.S./Canada; Don Keele, VP central rgn U.S./Canada; Laurel Cash-Jones, VP western rgn U.S./Canada; Don Popescu, VP European rgn; Subir Pramanik, VP international rgn; Ronald D. Streicher, sec; Leo de Gar Kulka, treas; Donald J. Plunkett, exec dir; Sandra J. Requa, exec assist; Daniel von Recklinghausen.
Governors: Marshall Buck, David Clark, Elizabeth Cohen, Roger Furness, David Griesinger, Tim Shelton, John Strawn, Rhonda Wilson.

British Film Institute. 21 Stephen St., London, U.K. W1P 1PL. 071-255 1444. FAX: 071-436 7950. Sir Richard Attenborough C.B.E., chmn; Wilf Stevenson, dir; Ian Christie, head distribution; Michael Prescott, asst dir; Colin MacCabe, head rsch & info; Clyde Jeavons, curator National Film Archive; Jurgen Berger, controller BFI South Bank.
Wilf Stevens, dir.

Broadcast Cable Credit Association Inc. 701 Lee St., Suite 1030, Des Plaines, Ill. 60016. (708) 827-9330. FAX: (708) 827-1653. Neil Best (Meredith Broadcasting, New York), pres; Anthony Grego (Westinghouse Broadcasting, New York), VP; Lew Munzer (WPOC-FM Baltimore), sec; Diane Vickers (WDIV-TV Detroit), treas; Buz Buzogany (BCFM Des Plaines, Ill.), exec dir.
Directors: Carolyn Alford (Group W Productions, Los Angeles); Barbara Burger (Interep Radio Store, New York); Joseph Capitani (Univision Television Group Inc., Secaucus, N.J.); Frank DeFrancesco (Noble Broadcasting, Chicago); Gail Kurzer (WPLG-FM Columbus, Ohio); William S. Murray (Tribune Broadcasting, Chicago); Jim Strawn (Summit Communications Group, Atlanta); Andy Weinberg (Katz Communications Inc., New York); Fred Witte (WPIX-TV New York).

Broadcast Cable Financial Management Association. 701 Lee St., Suite 1010, Des Plaines, Ill. 60016. (708) 296-0200. FAX: (708) 296-7510. Buz Buzogary (BCFM Des Plaines, Ill.), exec dir; James M. Strawn (Summit Communications Group, Atlanta), pres; William S. Murray (Tribune Broadcasting, Chicago), VP; Frank DeFrancesco (Noble Broadcasting, Chicago), sec; Carolyn Alford (Group W Productions, Los Angeles), treas.
Directors: Wanda Borges (Teitelbaum, Braveman & Borges, New Hyde Park, N.Y.); Gerald Agema (Tribune Broadcasting, Chicago); Sandra Clark (KATC-TV Lafayette, La.); Richard Graham (Cap Cities/WABC-TV New York); Paul McTear Jr. (Providence Journal Broadcasting, Providence, R.I.); Art Reitmayer (CKNW/CFMI Radio, New Westminster, B.C., Canada); Ralph Bender (La. TV Broadcasting Co., Baton Rouge); James Bond (Harrison, Bond & Pecaro, Washington); Peter Howe (Ernst & Young, New York); Catherine Nierle (Post Newsweek Stations, Washington); Andrea Schaffell (Turner Entertainment Networks, Atlanta); Carolyn Alford (Group W Productions, Los Angeles); Ronald Eckhart (Greater Media-Cable Division, East Brunswick, N.J.); Bruce Chastine (WSOC-TV Charlotte, N.C.); Daniel Ehrman Jr. (Gannett Broadcasting, Arlington, VA.); Byrne Hopkin (Bonneville International Corp., Salt Lake City); Kevin Reymond (Viacom Broadcasting, New York); Michael Sileck (River City Broadcasting, St Louis); Wesley Spencer (Group W Radio, New York).

Broadcast Designers' Association. 350 Townsend St., Suite 422, San Francisco 94107. (415) 543-6330. FAX: (415) 543-6332. Lynn Myers, BDA administrator.
Kathy Thaden, pres; Larne Higgins, VP; Wendy Lambert, sec; Lori Pate, treas.

Broadcast Education Association. 1771 N St. N.W., Washington 20036-2891. (202) 429-5355. James Smith (SUNY-NEW PALTZ, New Paltz, N.Y.), chmn; Ramsey Elliott (Fuller-Jeffrey Broadcasting, Granite Bay, Calif.), vice-chmn; Lynne Gross (Pepperdine University, Malibu, Calif.), sec/treas; J. William Poole (WFLS AM/FM Fredericksburg, Va.), immediate past chmn; Louisa Nielsen, exec dir.
Directors: Gary Chapman (LIN Television Corp., Providence, R.I.); Joe Foote (Southern Illnois University, Carbondale, Ill.); Roger Hadley (Oklahoma Baptist University, Shawnee, Okla.); Joe Levin (WRIC-TV Richmond, Va.); Michael McGregor (Indiana University, Bloomington, Ind.); Gay Russell (Grossmont College, El Cajon, Calif.); Kent Sidel (University of South Carolina, Columbia, S.C.); Dennis Upah (WEEK-TV East Peoria, Ill.).

Broadcast Music Inc. (BMI). 320 W. 57th St., New York 10019. (212) 586-2000. FAX: (212) 582-5972. Frances W. Preston, pres/CEO; Robbin Ahrold, VP corporate rels; Thomas G. Annastas, VP gen licensing; Marvin Berenson, sr VP/gen counsel; Del Bryant, sr VP performing rights & writer/publisher rels; Edward W. Chapin, VP human resources/sec; Charlie Feldman, VP New York writer/publisher rels; Phil Graham, VP European writer/publisher rels; Richard Mack, sr VP opns; Joe Moscheo, VP special projects; Rick Riccobono, VP writer/publisher rels, Los Angeles; Ekkehart Schnabel, VP international; Alan H. Smith, VP rsch & info; Roger Sovine, VP Nashville; Larry Sweeney, VP telecommunications; Fred Willms, sr VP/CFO; Theodora Zavin, sr VP/special counsel; John Shaker, sr VP licensing.
Directors: K. James Yager, chmn; James G. Babb; Joseph A. Carriere; Harold C. Crump; Ken J. Elkins; J. Clinton Formby; Philip A. Jones; Clifford M. Kirtland Jr.; Francis A. Martin III; Robert L. Pratt; Frances W. Preston; Donald A. Thurston; George V. Willoughby.
Los Angeles 90069: 8730 Sunset Blvd. (310) 659-9109.
Nashville 37203: 10 Music Sq. E. (615) 291-6700.

Broadcast Pioneers. 320 W. 57th St., New York 10019. (212) 830-2581. James Delmonico, pres; Ed DeGray, exec dir.

Broadcast Pioneers Library. 1771 N St. N.W., Washington 20036. (202) 223-0088. Vincent J. Curtis Jr., pres; Catharine Heinz, VP/sec; Harold Niven, VP; Norman B. Blumenthal, treas; Ramsey L. Woodworth, gen counsel.
Directors: Norman B. Blumenthal, John F. Behnke, Arthur W. Carlson, Gary R. Chapman, Vincent J. Curtis Jr., Stanley S. Hubbard, Pierson G. Mapes, Joseph J.B. Ryan, Harry B. Smart, William L. Stakelin, Lawrence B. Taishoff, Albert Warren, Millard S. Younts.
Trustees: Joseph E. Baudino, Layne R. Beaty, Joseph H. Berman, John F. Dille Jr., Wallace B. Dunlap, Edward O. Fritts, Ellen M. Genet, Jack V. Harvey, Catharine Heinz, Donald H. Kirkley Jr., Erwin G. Krasnow, Lawrence Laurent, Carl E Lee, Clair R. McCollough, Roger A. Neuhoff, Harold Niven, Tom E. Paro, Clark Pollock, Ward L. Quaal, Richard M. Schmidt Jr., Sylvester L. Weaver, Virginia Pate Wetter; G. Richard Shafto, sr advisor.

Broadcast Technology Society of the Institute of Electrical and Electronics Engineers. 330 Independence Ave. S.W., Room 4242, Washington 20547. (202) 619-3771. FAX: (202) 619-3484. Gerald A. Berman (VOA), pres; E. Bruce Hunter (VOA), VP; Lynn Claudy (NAB), sec; Garrison Cavell (Suffa & Cavell Inc.), treas; George B. Grills, awards chmn; Roger Radcliff (Ohio University), education chmn; Charles R. Allen (WTXX-TV Waterbury, Conn.), membership chmn; John D. Tollefson (WJLA-TV Washington), newsletter edit; Alan Godber, standards chmn; Edmund A. Williams (PBS, Engineering Department), symposium chmn; Philip A. Rubin (Rubin, Bednarek & Associates), transactions edit.

Broadcasters Foundation Inc. 320 W. 57th St., New York 10019. (212) 830-2581. James Delmonico, pres; Ed DeGray, exec dir.

Broadcasters Hall of Fame. 1171 Morningview Dr., Tallmadge, Ohio 44278. (216) 633-2334. Jean Hartz, chmn of bd; Fred Boy, chmn of bd emeritus; Hank Pawlak, pres.
Directors: George Mamas, exec VP; Mary Ann Bock, Don Dempsey, VPs.

Broadcasting Industry Council to Improve American Productivity. 1771 N St. N.W., Washington 20036. (202) 429-5330. FAX: (202) 429-5406. Don LeBrecht, exec dir; Jerry Lee, chmn; Ken Almgren, treas; George Borsari, counsel.
Directors: Jack Clements (Mutual Broadcasting); L. Lowry Mays (Clear Channel Broadcasting); Walter May (WPKE Radio); Gerald Udwin (Westinghouse Broadcasting & Cable); Gary Chapman (LIN Broadcasting).

Cable in the Classroom. 1900 N. Beauregard St., #108, Alexandria, Va. 22311. (703) 845-1400. FAX: (703) 845-1409. Bobbi L. Kamil Ph.D., exec dir; Megan Stevens Hookey, assoc dir.

Cable TV Public Affairs Association. 9101 Cherry Ln., Suite 204, Laurel, Md. 20708. (301) 206-5393. FAX: (301) 206-9112. Mary Pittelli, exec dir.

Cable Television Administration & Marketing Society (CTAM). 635 Slaters Ln., Suite 250, Alexandria, Va. 22314. (703) 549-4200. FAX: (703) 684-1167. Char Beales, pres/COO; William Ascani, VP opns; Corrine Beller, VP mktg.

Cable Television Laboratories Inc. 1050 Walnut St., #500, Boulder, Colo. 80302. (303) 939-8500. FAX: (303) 939-9189. Dr. Richard R. Green, pres/CEO; Baryn S. Futa, COO.
Directors: Dr. John C. Malone, chmn; James Doolittle, treas; Brian Roberts, sec.

Cabletelevision Advertising Bureau Inc. (CAB). See listing under Major National Associations, this section.

Canadian Association of Broadcast Consultants. c/o Yves Hamel & Associates, 3772 Kent Ave., Montreal, Que., Canada H3S 1N3. (514) 733-6107. FAX: (514) 733-4760. P. LaBarre, pres; F. Hamel, sec/treas.

The Canadian Association of Broadcast Representatives Inc. 48 St. Clair Ave. W., 12th Fl., Toronto, Ont., Canada M4V 2Z2. (416) 961-4770. FAX: (416) 960-9067.

Directors: Leon Hildebrandt, pres; Leigh Kelk, past pres; Ed Voltan, VP TV; Marc Parts, VP radio; Tim Steele, sec/treas; Keith Morrison, dir at large.

The Canadian Association of Broadcasters. Box 627, Station B, Ottawa, Ont., Canada K1P 5S2; 306-350 Sparks St., Ottawa, Ont., Canada K1R 7S8. (613) 233-4035. FAX: (613) 233-6961.

CAB Executive Committee: Bill Coombes (Fraser Valley Radio Group, Chilliwack, B.C.), chair; Liette Champagne (Communication Telemedia Inc., Montreal, Que.), chair Radio; Duff Roman (CHUM Ltd., Toronto, Ont.), vice-chair Radio; Douglas Holtby (WIC Western International Communications Ltd., Vancouver, B.C.), chair TV; Louis Audet (Cogeco Inc., Montreal, Que.), vice-chair TV; Peter Liba (CKND-TV/STV Winnipeg, Man.), immediate past chair; Anthony Viner (Rogers Broadcasting Limited, Toronto, Ont.), treas; Bruce Cowie (Sumwapta Broadcasting Ltd., Edmonton, Alta.), special delegate.

CAB Executive Staff: Michael McCabe, pres/CEO; Michel Tremblay, exec VP; Jane Logan, VP radio; Robert Scarth, VP TV; Tina VanDusen, VP communications; Sharon Orr, VP mktg & member svcs; Peter H. Miller, legal counsel; Arlene Keis, dir industry human resource dev; Jessie A. McLean, dir finance & administration; Sylvie Bissonnette, coord special events; Michael Buzzell, communications & info coord.

Canadian Association of Ethnic (Radio) Broadcasters. 622 College St., Toronto, Ont., Canada M6G 1B6. (416) 531-9991. FAX: (416) 531-6654. Johnny Lombardi (CHIN Toronto, Ont.), pres; Jack Stark (CJVB Vancouver, B.C.), 1st VP; Roger Charest (CKER Edmonton, Alta.), 2nd VP; Andrew Mielewczyk (CFMB Montreal, Que. & CKJS Winnipeg, Man.), sec/treas.

Canadian Cable Television Association (CCTA). See listing under Major National Associations, this section.

Canadian Film and Television Production Association (CFTPA). 175 Bloor St. E., Suite 806, N. Tower, Toronto, Ont., Canada M4W 3R8. (416) 927-8942. FAX: (416) 922-4038. Sandra MacDonald, pres; Mireille Watson, dir industrial rels & membership.

Directors: Gwen Iveson, Charles Falzon, Micheline Charest, R. Stephen Ellis, Doug Dales, Andrew Cochran, Kevin DeWalt, Harold Tichenor, Douglas Barrett, Bill Gray, Tom Berry, Gord Haines, Jackie Scott, Richard Borchiver, Susan Cavan, Richard Davis, Steve Levitan, Joan Scott, Annabel Slaight, Andy Thomson.

The Caption Center. 125 Western Ave., Boston 02134. (617) 492-9225. FAX: (508) 562-0590. Brad Botkin, opns dir; Trisha O'Connell, mktg dir; Larry Goldberg, dir.

Caribbean Broadcasting Union (CBU). Wilkins Lodge, 2 Mile Hill, St. Michael, Barbados, West Indies. (809) 429-9146. FAX: (809) 429-2171.

Management Committee: Vic Fernandes (Barbados Rediffusion Service Ltd., River Rd., St Michael, Barbados), pres; Ronald Abraham (Marpin Television Co. Ltd., Turkey Ln., Roseau, Dominica), VP TV; Neil Giuseppi (Trinidad Broadcasting Co. Ltd., 11B Maraval Rd., Port-of-Spain, Trinidad), VP radio; Michael Thompson (Broadcasting Corporation of the Bahamas, 3rd Terr. E., Centreville, Nassau, Bahamas), VP engrg.

Members: Lester Spaulding (Radio Jamaica Ltd., 32 lyndhurst Rd., Kingston 5, Jamaica), Sam Taitt (Caribbean Broadcasting Corp., Pine, St. Michael, Barbados), Claude Robinson (Jamaica Broadcasting Corp., 5-9 S. Odeon Ave., Kingston 10, Jamaica), Rene Villanueva (LOVE-FM, 33 Freetown Rd., Belize City, Belize), Grenfell Kissoon (Trinidad & Tobago Television, 11A Maraval Rd., Port-of-Spain, Trinidad).

Center For Communication Inc. 570 Lexington Ave., 21st Fl., New York 10022. (212) 836-3050. FAX: (212) 836-2773. Irina Posner, exec dir; Catherine Williams, prog dir.

Directors: Burton B. Staniar, chmn; Frank Stanton, chmn emeritus.

Classical Music Broadcasters Association. 335 Powell St., San Francisco 94102. (415) 986-2151. FAX: (415) 834-0219. Bruce E. Beebe (KKHI AM/FM San Francisco), pres; Simona McCrae, VP; Rick Marschner, treas; Tom Beauvois, sec.

Clear Channel Broadcasting Service. 1776 K St. N.W., Washington 20006. (202) 429-7020. Wayne Vriesman (WGN-AM), pres.

Legal counsel: John L. Bartlett, David E. Hilliard (Wiley, Rein & Fielding).

Engrg counsel: Harold L. Kassens (A.D. Ring & Associates).

Engrg consultants: John H. DeWitt Jr., George F. Leydorf, Johnie S. Campbell.

Commonwealth Broadcasting Association. CBA Secretariat, Broadcasting House, London, U.K. W1A 1AA. (01) 580-4468, ext. 5022. Mohammed Ibrahim, pres; Stuart Revill, secretary-general.

Members of Standing Committee: Mohammed Ibrahim (NTA Nigeria), pres; S.K. Kapoor (AIR India), VP progs/administration; Neville Lane (TVNZ New Zealand), VP engrg; John Birt (BBC Britain), David Hill (ABC Australia), Sir Alkan Tololo (PNGNBC Papua, New Guinea), Ted Makgekgenene (RB Botswana), Sunil Sarath Perera (SLRC Sri Lanka), Claudette Manchester (ZIZRT St. Kitts, Nevis), Philip Okundi (KBC Kenya), Gerard Veilleux (CBC Canada).

Community Antenna Television Association (CATA). See listing under Major National Associations, this section.

Community Broadcasters Association (CBA). Box 9556, Panama City, Fla. 32417. (904) 234-2773. FAX: (904) 234-1179. Jud Colley, pres; Woody Jenkins, VP; Sherwin Grossman, sec; D.J. Everett, treas.

Directors: D.J. Everett (Kentucky New Era Inc.); John Kompas (Kompas/Biel & Associates); Woody Jenkins (Great Oaks Broadcasting Inc.); Jud Colley (Beach TV); Sherwin Grossman (Sherjan Broadcasting); Robert Raff (Montgomery Publications Inc.); Enrique Perez (WSBL Tampa).

Concert Music Broadcasters Association. 11300 Rockville Pike, Rockville, Md. 20852. (301) 468-1800. FAX: (301) 468-0491. Catherine Meloy, pres.

Directors: Peter Newman, Simona McCray, George Stokes, Bruce Beebe, Mary Kading.

Council of Better Business Bureaus Inc. 4200 Wilson Blvd., 8th Fl., Arlington, Va. 22203. (703) 276-0100. FAX: (703) 525-8277. James H. McIlhenny, pres.

Country Music Association Inc. One Music Cir. S., Nashville 37203. (615) 244-2840. FAX: (615) 726-0314. Edwin W. Benson Jr., exec dir.

Country Radio Broadcasters Inc. 50 Music Sq. W., #702, Nashville 37203-3228. (615) 327-4487. FAX (615) 329-4492. Ed Salamon, pres; Frank Mull, exec dir.

The assn holds an annual country radio seminar.

Detroit Museum of Broadcasting. 31800 Northwestern Hwy., Suite 100, Farmington Hills, Mich. 48334. (313) 737-3000. Ronald Zate.

Direct Marketing Association. 11 W. 42nd St., New York 10036-8096; 6 E. 43rd St., New York 10017. (212) 768-7277. FAX: (212) 599-1268. Jonah Gitlitz, pres/CEO.

Washington 20036: 1101 17th St. N.W., Suite 900. (202) 347-1222.

Electrical and Electronic Manufacturers Association of Canada. 10 Carlson Ct., Suite 500, Rexdale, Ont. Canada M9W 6L2. (416) 674-7410. FAX: (416) 674-7412. William Hethrington, chmn; Norman Aspin, pres.

Electronic Industries Association (EIA). 2001 Pennsylvania Ave. N.W., Washington 20006. (202) 457-4900. FAX: (202) 457-4985. Peter F. McCloskey, pres; John J. Kelly, VP/sec/gen counsel.

Directors: Elizabeth A. Hartnett, VP admin & finance; Dan C. Heinemeier, VP govt division; O.E. Lussier, VP components group; Kevin C. Richardson, VP govt rels; Mark V. Rosenker, VP pub affr; Gary J. Shapiro, group VP Consumer Electronic Group.

Electronic Media Rating Council. See listing under Major National Associations, this section.

Electronic Representatives Association. 20 E. Huron St., Chicago 60611. (312) 649-1333. FAX: (312) 649-9509.

Executive Committee: W. David McCoy, chmn of bd; Timothy Eyerman, CPMR, pres; Glenn Alverson, sr VP fiscal & legal; Clark Moulthrop, CPMR, sr VP education; Ray Hall, exec VP/CEO; Roger Ponto, sr VP membership; Jess Harper, CPMR, sr VP industry, principal & govt rels.

Electronic Service Dealers Association. 4621 N. Kedzie Ave., Chicago 60625. (312) 463-2499. FAX: (312) 463-8000. George J. Weiss, exec dir; Frank J. Stillson, pres; Joseph Issak, treas.

FCBA (Federal Communications Bar Association). 1150 Connecticut Ave. N.W., Suite 1050, Washington 20036. (202) 833-2684. FAX: (202) 833-1308. Alan C. Campbell, pres; S. White Rhyne, pres-elect; Henry M. Rivera, sec; Alexandra M. Wilson, asst sec; Jean L. Kiddoo, treas; Paula G. Friedman, asst treas; James H. Herbert, exec dir; Lisa Levy Koppel, admin dir.

Executive Committee: Robert A. Beizer, Scott Cinnamon, Diane J. Cornell, Arthur B. Goodkind, Robert L. Pettit, Michelle N. Plotkin, John C. Quale, Lawrence Roberts, Gregory M. Schmidt, Mark Van Bergh, James L. Winston.

Richard R. Zaragoza, delegate to American Bar Association.

Federation of Australian Commercial Television Stations. 44 Avenue Rd., Mosman, Australia N.S.W. 2088. (02) 960-2622. FAX: (02) 969-3520. Tony Brannigin, gen mgr.

Federation of Australian Radio Broadcasters. Box 299, Unit 10, Garden Mews, 82-86 Pacific Hwy., St. Leonards, N.S.W., Australia 2065. (02) 906-5944. FAX: (02) 906-5128. Tony King, chief exec/contact.

Foundation for American Communications (FACS). 3800 Barham Blvd., Suite 409, Los Angeles 90068. (213) 851-7372. FAX: (213) 851-9186. John E. Cox Jr., pres; Peter C. McCarty, sr VP opns; Douglas Ramsey, sr VP progs; Edward P. Bassett (dir School of Communications, Univ. of Washington), chmn of bd.

Hollywood Radio & Television Society. 5315 Laurel Canyon Blvd., Suite 202, North Hollywood, Calif. 91607. (818) 769-4313. FAX: (818) 509-1262. Gene Herd, exec dir.

ITA. 505 8th Ave., 12th Fl. A, New York 10018. (212) 643-0620. FAX: (212) 643-0624. Henry Brief, exec VP; Charles Van Horn, exec dir.

Institute of Electrical and Electronics Engineers Inc. 345 E. 47th St., New York 10017. (212) 705-7900. FAX: (212) 752-4929. John H. Powers, gen mgr.

Interactive Services Association. 8403 Colesville Rd., Suite 865, Silver Spring, Md. 20910. (301) 495-4955. FAX: (301) 495-4959. Robert L. Smith Jr., exec dir.

Intercollegiate Broadcasting System. Box 592, Vails Gate, N.Y. 12584. (914) 565-6710. FAX: (914) 561-6932. Jeff Tellis, pres; Fritz Kass, treas; Norman Prusslin, chmn; Dr. George Abraham, vice-chmn; David W. Borst, vice-chmn/sec.

Directors: John Vernile, Diana Ades, Greg Adamo, John Murphy, Thom O'Hair, Stuart A. Shorenstein, Steven C. Schaffer, Michael Butscher.

International Advertising Association. (The global partnership of advertisers, agencies & media.) 342 Madison Ave., Suite 2000, New York 10173-0073. (212) 557-1133. FAX: (212) 983-0455. Mustapha Assad, world pres; Norman Vale, dir gen; Richard Corner, exec dir.

International Association of Broadcasting (IAB). Calle Yi, 1264-Montevideo, Uruguay. 90-4456/90-0053/98-5408. TELEX: UY 843, Cables: AIRRADIO. Luiz Eduardo Borgerth, pres; Hector Aurengual, dir gen; Alberto Gollan, 1st VP; Fernando Eleta Casanova, 2nd VP; Genaro Delgado Parker, treas.

Titular Board Members: Joaquim Mendoca, Ricardo Londono, Oscar Pizarro Romero, Eugenino Galdon, Ramon de Rato Figaredo, Donald Smullin, Luciano Mecarozzi, Andres Garcia Lavin, Hugo Romay Salvo, Felix Cardona Moreno.

Deputy Board Members: Evaristo R.E. Alonso, Martin Rodriguez Brizuela, Emilio Amadei Beringhs, Fernando E. Correa, Samuel Duque Rozo, Ricardo Bezanilla Renovales, Javier Gimeno de Priede, Pedro Antonio Martin, Walter Canals, Eugenio Porta, Juan Jose Espejo Puente, Jose Gabriel Diaz, Fernando Gonzalez del Campo, Atilio Fracois, Alfredo Vetancourt.

International Association of Satellite Users & Suppliers (IASUS). 45681 Oakbrook Ct., Unit 107, Sterling, Va. 22107. (703) 759-2094. FAX: (703) 759-5094. A. Fred Dassler, exec dir; Robert D. Smith, comptroller; Robert Veltman, sec.

Directors: Larry Steinman, Leonard Graziplene.

The International Council of The National Academy of Television Arts and Sciences. 142 W. 57th St., 16th Fl., New York 10019. (212) 489-6969. FAX: (212) 489-6557. Renato Pachetti, chmn; David Louie, vice-chmn/VP; Richard Dunn, vice-chmn; Kay Koplovitz, vice-chmn; Richard Carlton, exec dir; Donald Taffner, treas; George Dessart, sec.

Presidents: Dave Howell (Arizona); Jim Kitchell (Atlanta); Alan Koenig (Boston); Scott Craig (Chicago); Rich O'Dell (Cleveland); Durry Jones (Columbus/Dayton/Cincinnati, Ohio); Mike Halpin (Colorado); Dennis Carnevale (Detroit); Mike Boylan (Miami, Fla.); Mike Duncan (Nashville); Paul Noble (New York); Janice Selinger (Philadelphia); Allan Cohen (St. Louis); Sue Strom (San Diego); John Odell (San Francisco); Don McCune (Seattle); Sue Ann Staake (Washington).

International Federation of Advertising Agencies Inc. (IFAA). 7979 S. Tanuam Tr., Suite 172, Sarasota, Fla. 32082. (813) 366-2902. Robert Pinne, pres; Fred Sandven, exec VP; James Anderson, VP; Kenneth Hill, sec; Frank Callahan, treas.

International Institute of Communications. Tavistock House S., Tavistock Sq., London, U.K. WC1H 9LF. (44) 71-388-0671. FAX: (44) 71-380-0623. Carol Joy, exec dir; Alain Gourd, pres.

International Radio and Television Foundation Inc. 420 Lexington Ave., Suite 1714, New York 10170. (212) 867-6650. FAX: (212) 867-6653. Thomas E. McKinney (Cabletelevision Advertising Bureau Inc.), pres; Stephen B. Labunski, exec sec.

International Radio and Television Society Inc. 420 Lexington Ave., Suite 1714, New York 10170. (212) 867-6650. FAX: (212) 867-6653. Peter A. Lund (CBS/Broadcast Group), pres; Dick Ebersol (NBC Sports), 1st VP; Stephen H. Coltrin (Coltrin & Associates), VP; Gerald M. Levin (Time Warner Inc.), VP; Douglas W. McCormick (Lifetime Television), VP; Thomas E. McKinney (Cabletelevision Advertising Bureau), VP; James A. Rose (Blair Television), VP; Peter F. Ryan (Harrington, Righter & Parsons Inc.), VP; Jack Higgins (Katz Continental Television), sec; Donn H. O'Brien, sr VP/treas; Eric Stubin (TeleRep), asst sec; Stephen B. Labunski, exec dir; Joyce M. Tudryn, assoc exec dir.

International Teleproduction Society. 350 5th Ave., #2400, New York 10018. (212) 629-3266. FAX: (212) 629-3265. Michael Cunningham (Western Images, San Francisco), pres; Ron Burnett (Sunset Post, Calif.), exec VP; Janet Luhrs, exec dir.

Iota Beta Sigma. Box 592, Vails Gate, N.Y. 12584-0592. (914) 565-6710. FAX: (914) 561-6932. Jeff Tellis, exec dir.

League of Advertising Agencies. 2 S. End Ave., Suite 4-C, New York 10280. (212) 945-4990. Michael Sloser, pres; Richard Ross, VP; Mary C. Boland, exec dir.

The Media Institute. 1000 Potomac St. N.W., Suite 301, Washington 20007. (202) 298-7512. FAX: (202) 337-7092. Patrick D. Maines, pres; Richard T. Kaplar, VP.

Montreal International Festival of New Cinema and Video. 3726 St. Laurent Blvd., Montreal, Que., Canada H2X 2V8. (514) 843-4725. FAX: (514) 843-4631. Claude Chamberlan, Dimitri Eipides, dirs.

Mortgage Bankers Association of America (MBA). 1125 15th St. N.W., Washington 20005. (202) 861-6500. Stephen B. Ashley (CMB), pres; Joe K. Pickett, pres elect.

Motion Picture Association of America. 1600 Eye St. N.W., Washington 20006. (202) 293-1966. FAX: (202) 293-7674. Jack J. Valenti, pres.

Encino, Calif. 91436: 15503 Ventura Blvd. (818) 995-3600.

Motion Picture Export Association of America. 15503 Ventura Blvd., Encino, Calif. 91436. (818) 995-6600. FAX: (818) 382-1799. Jack Valenti, chmn/CEO; Myron Karlin, pres/COO; Willaim Billick, exec VP/gen counsel; William Murray, VP theatrical & TV; Harlan Moen, sr VP Europe & Africa; Harry Stone, sr VP Latin America; Stephen A. Clug, VP Far East & Australia.

Museum of Broadcast Communications. Michigan Ave. & Washington St., Chicago 60602-3407. (312) 629-6000. FAX: (312) 629-6009. Bruce DuMont, pres; Arthur C. Nielsen, chmn; Gerald W. Agema, VP/treas; Richard C. Christian, E. Ronald Culp, Chuck Schaden, Lynne Harvey, VPs; Wally Gair, sec.

Directors: Steve Allen, Tom Baur, Frances Bergen, J. Byron Felter Jr., Marvin J. Dickman, James Dowdle, Gary Pradarelli, Stephen P. Durchslag, Beverley Blettner, Hitoshi Ohashi, Red Quinlan, Brad Saul, Dennis Swanson, Dempsey Travis, Joseph M. Swiderski III, Mary Francais Fagan, John Gehron, Gary Horton, Bruce Huber, Arnold Levy, Charles H. Martin III, Essee Kupcinet, Lisa Emerick, Stedman Graham, Eric Harkna, Tony Weisman.

Museum is free to public. Hours: Mon-Sat 10 am-4:30 pm, Sun 12-5 pm.

The Museum of Television & Radio. 25 W. 52nd St., New York 10019-6101. (212) 621-6600. FAX: (212) 621-6700. Frank A. Bennack Jr. (The Hearst Corporation), chmn bd of trustees; Robert M. Batscha, pres.

Trustees: Frank A Bennack Jr. (The Hearst Corporation); Robert M. Batscha (The Museum of Television & Radio); Alan Alda; Ralph M. Baruch; Candice Bergen; Frank J. Biondi Jr. (Viacom International Inc.); Steven Bochco (Steven Bocho Productions); Richard W. Carlson (Corporation for Public Broadcasting); Thomas Carter (Thomas Carter Company); Martin S. Davis (Paramount Communications Inc.); Barry Diller; Leonard H. Goldenson (Capital Cities/ABC Inc.), trustee emeritus; Ralph Guild (The Interep Radio Store); Bill Haber (Creative Artists Agency Inc.); Gustave M. Hauser (Hauser Communications Inc.); Donald R. Keough (The Coca-Cola Company); Henry A. Kissinger (Kissenger Associates Inc.); Kay Koplovitz (USA Network); Norman Lear (Act III Communications), trustee emeritus; Arthur L. Liman (Paul, Weiss, Rifkind, Wharton & Garrison); J. Bruce Llewellyn (Queen City Broadcasting); Burt Manning (J. Walter Thompson Company); Dina Merrill; Thomas S. Murphy (Capital Cities/ABC Inc.); Edward N. Ney (Burson-Marsteller); William C. Paley; Norman J. Pattiz (Westwood One Inc.); Robert W. Sarnoff, trustee emeritus; Michael P. Schulhof (Sony USA Inc.); Sid Sheinberg (MCA Inc.); Noble Smith (Edward John Noble Foundation); Burton B. Staniar (Westinghouse Broadcasting Company Inc.); Frank Stanton, trustee emeritus; Marlo Thomas; Grant A. Tinker; Laurence A. Tisch (CBS Inc.); R.E. Turner (Turner Broadcasting System Inc.); Barbara Walters (ABC News); Lou Weiss (William Morris Agency Inc.); Robert C. Wright (NBC Inc.).

N.A.S.A.—Network Affiliated Station Alliance. c/o Benjamin Tucker, Box 5455, Fresno, Calif. 93755. (209) 222-2411. FAX: (209) 222-5593. Ben Tucker, CBS affil assn co-chmn; Patsy Smullin, NBC affil assn co-chmn; Edward Reilly, ABC affil assn co-chmn.

NHL Broadcasters Association. c/o Dick Irvin, 109 Brigadoon Dr., Pointe Claire, Que., Canada H9R 1J2. (514) 695-7011. Chuck Kaiton (Hartford Whalers), pres; Jim Robson (Vancouver Canucks), VP; Mike Emrick (New Jersey Devils), VP; Dick Irvin (Montreal Canadians), sec/treas.

National Academy of Cable Programming. 1724 Massachusetts Ave. N.W., Washington 20036. (202) 775-3611. FAX: (202) 775-3689. John S. Hendricks, chmn; Larry W. Wangber, vice-chmn; Suzanne Hayes, exec dir; Robert J. Wussler (Turner Broadcasting System), treas; Shelley Duvall (Think Entertainment), sec.

The National Academy of Television Arts & Sciences. 111 W. 57th St., Suite 1020, New York 10019. (212) 586-8424. FAX: (212) 586-8424. Michael Collyer, chmn of bd; David Louie, vice-chmn; John Cannon, pres; Alice Marshal, VP; Sue Ann Staake, sec; Malachy Wienges, treas.

Arizona: Dr. John E. Craft, pres.
Atlanta: Darryl Cohen, pres.
Boston: Hubert Jessup, pres.
Chicago: Allen Hall, pres.
Cleveland: Rich O'Dell, pres.
Colorado: Julie Lucas, pres.
Columbus/Dayton/Cincinnati: Julie S. Weindel, pres.
Detroit: Dennis Carnevale, pres.
Miami: Mike Boylan, pres.
Nashville: Dr. Ed Kimbrell, pres.
New York: Paul Noble, pres.
Philadelphia: Roger LaMay, pres.
St. Louis: Allan Cohen, pres.
San Diego: Terry C. Williams, pres.
San Francisco: John Odell, pres.
Seattle: Alice Marshall, pres.
Washington: Sue Ann Staake, pres.

National Academy of Television Journalists. Box 52995, Atlanta 30355. (404) 262-9155. Neil F. Bayne, pres; Dave Walker, exec dir.

National Association of Black Journalists (NABJ). 11600 Sunrise Valley Dr., Reston, Va. 22091. (703) 648-1270. FAX: (703) 476-6245. Dorothy Gilliam, pres.

National Association of Black Owned Broadcasters Inc. (NABOB). 1730 M St. N.W., Suite 412, Washington 20036. (202) 463-8970. FAX: (202) 429-0657. James L. Winston, exec dir/gen counsel.

Directors: Pierre M. Sutton, chmn; Bennie Turner, pres; Mutter D. Evans, 1st VP; Andrew A. Langston, 2nd VP; Sydney L. Small, treas; Lois E. Wright, counsel to the bd; Michael Carter, sec.

Regional reps: Skip Finley, Northeast; Greg A. Davis, Southeast; James Wolfe, Midwest; Joseph Stroud, TV rep.

National Association of Broadcasters. See listing under Major National Associations, this section.

National Association of College Broadcasters (NACB). 71 George St., Providence, R.I. 02912-1824. (401) 863-2225. FAX: (401) 863-2221. Glenn Gutmacher, exec dir; JoAnn Forgit, assn dir; Jeff Southard, special project dir; Gordon Kent, dir dev; Michael Hummel, mus mktg dir; David Singh, net dir; James Dellaria, special projects coord.

Directors: Mike Aitken (Grossmont College, El Cajon, Calif.); Nancy Kaplan (Hofstra University, Hempstead, N.Y.); Steven Klinenberg (Think Tank Entertainment, Los Angeles); Sarah Hahnet (University of Wisconsin, Stevens Point, Wis.); Cristina Currier (Stonehill College, North Easton, Mass.); Michael Steiner (Columbia College, Chicago).

Advisory Board: Eleanor Applewhaite (WNET-TV New York); Walter Cronkite, Frank Stanton, Robert Morton (CBS New York); Anne Edwards, consultant; Michael Fuchs, Sheila Shayon (HBO New York); Marc Guild, Ralph Guild (Interep Radio Store, New York); Vartan Gregorian (Brown University, Providence, R.I.); Doug Herzog (MTV Networks, New York); Bob Guccione Jr. (SPIN, New York); Quincy Jones (Quincy Jones Entertainment, Los Angeles); Oedipus (WBCN-FM Boston); Bob Pittman (Time Warner, New York); Chuck Sherman (NAB Washington); Ted Turner (Turner Broadcasting System, Atlanta); Richard Wiley (Wiley, Rein & Fielding, Washington); Garth Ancier (Garth Ancier Productions, Los Angeles); Renko Isowa (Unicom U.S.A., New York); George Lucas (Lucas Film Ltd., San Rafael, Calif.); Cory Tepper (Meyer, Faller, Weisman & Rosenberg, Washington).

Board of Trustees: Garth Ancier (Garth Ancier Productions, Los Angeles); David Bartis (HBO Independent Productions, Los Angeles); Steven Klinenberg, Douglas Liman (Think Tank Entertainment, Los Angeles); Gary Toyn (Target Marketing, Ogden, Utah).

National Association of Hispanic Journalists. 529 14th St. N.W., Suite 1193, Washington 20045. (202) 662-7145. FAX: (202) 662-7144. Diane Alverio, pres; Ernest Gurule, VP bcst; Mileta Garza, VP print; Mike Martinez, treas; Laramie Trevino, sec.

At large officers: Gilbert Bailon, Cheryl Brownstein-Santiago, Bertha Coombs-Sague.

Directors: Ivonne Garcia, dir rgn 1; Patricia Dvarte, dir rgn 2; Rolando Arrieta, dir rgn 3; Nancy San Martin, dir rgn 4; Dino Chiecchi, dir rgn 5; Rodrigo A. Sierra, dir rgn 6; Don Rodriquez, dir rgn 7; Julio Moran, dir rgn 8.

National Association of Media Brokers Inc. 6210 Iroquois Ct., Odessa/Tampa, Fla. 33556. (813) 920-0800. Tim Menowsky, pres; James W. Blackburn Jr., treas.

National Association of Radio Reading Services. 2100 Wharton St., Suite 140, Pittsburgh 15203. (412) 488-3944. FAX: (412) 488-3953. William Pasco, pres; John Mulvihill, 1st VP; Mike Duke, 2nd VP; Sally Oremland, sec; David W. Judy, treas.

Directors: Bill Kelsey, Jay Doudna, Brenda Homickle, Marcia Jonke, Lynn Brewer, Beth Jones, Bob Wall, Jim Cashin, Bob Brummond, Gwendolyn Bedford, Kelly Brand, Lynn Chadwick.

National Association of Retail Dealers of America. 10 E. 22nd St., Suite 310, Lombard, Ill. 60148. (708) 953-8950. FAX: (708) 953-8957. Marty Wolf, chmn of bd; Con Maloney, pres; Ron Romero, 1st VP; Terry Oates, 2nd VP; Ed Knodle, exec dir; Joe Bookwalter, sec; Robert Kramer, treas.

Directors: David Borsani, Jack Clarke, Robert Cremer, Jim Feeney, Mike Fischer, Bill Fisher, Jerry Plavin, C.W. Conn, Tom Peterson, Dale Plass, Jim Renier, Ken Stucky, Elly Valas.

National Association of State Radio Networks Inc. 263 3rd St., 5th Fl., Baton Rouge 70801. (504) 383-8695. FAX: (504) 342-9950.

Directors: George Habel, pres; Tim Shears, pres-elect; Neal Gladner, VP; Andy Barrett, sec; Joe Parsons, treas; Stacy Long, dir; Bill Rigell, post pres.
Chicago: Tom Dobrez.
Atlanta: Ann MacDonald.

National Association of Telecommunications Officers and Advisors. 1301 Pennsylvania Ave. N.W., Washington 20004. (202) 626-3160. FAX: (202) 626-3143. William Squadron, pres; Susan Littlefield, VP; Mike Reardon, sec/treas.

Directors: Michael Hunt, Jonathan Kramer, Cheryl Pasalic, John Risk, Tom Robinson.

National Association of Television Program Executives International (NATPE). See listing under Major National Associations, this section.

National Association of Theatre Owners Inc. (NATO). 4605 Lankershim Blvd., Suite 340, North Hollywood, Calif. 91602. (818) 506-1778. FAX: (818) 506-0269. Mary Ann Grasso, exec dir; Jerome Forman, chmn; Willaim Karpozian, pres.

National Association of Weathercasters. AMF Building, #612252, DFW International Airport, Tex. 75261. (817) 860-2241. FAX: (214) 502-2656. Dr. Charles E. Coldwell, dir; Dr. David Briggs, membership committee; Douglas P. Watson, sec.

National Black Media Coalition. 38 New York Ave. N.E., Washington 20002. (202) 387-8155. FAX: (202) 462-4469. Pluria W. Marshall, chmn; Carmen Marshall, exec dir.

The National Broadcasting Society. Alpha Epsilon Rho, College of Journalism, University of South Carolina, Columbia, S.C. 29208. (803) 777-3324. FAX: (803) 777-3324. Jamie M. Byrne, natl pres; John Lopiccolo, natl treas.

National Cable Television Association Inc. (NCTA). See listing under Major National Associations, this section.

National Cable Television Center. Level B, Sparks Bldg., University Park, Pa. 16802-5203. (814) 865-1875. FAX: (814) 863-7808.

Directors: William D. Arnold, Yolanda G. Barco, William J. Bresnan, Bradford E. Choate, Frank Drendel, Joseph S. Gans Sr., Shirley S. Hendrick, Glenn R. Jones, George J. McMurtry, Sanford F. Randolph, Leslie H. Read, Michael J. Rigas, William W. Ricker, James H. Ryan, James H. "Trey" Smith, Richard D. Taylor.

National Cable Television Cooperative Inc. See listing under Major National Associations, this section.

National Cable Television Institute. 801 W. Mineral Ave., Littleton, Colo. 80120-4501. (303) 797-9393; (303) 797-9394. Roland Hieb, chmn; Byron Leech, pres; Don Oden, dir admissions.

National Captioning Institute (NCI). 5203 Leesburg Pike, Falls Church, Va. 22041. (703) 998-2416. FAX: (703) 998-2458. Dr. Edward C. Merrill, pres; Jane Edmondson, VP prog mktg; Lily P. Bess, VP external affrs; Don Thieme, exec dir pub rels.

Directors: Eileen Smith, exec dir consumer mktg; Len Novick, exec dir opns; Gerald Freda, dir engrg svcs; Linda Randall, dir off-line captioning; Amnon Salomon, dir systems dev; Eric Kirkland, dir business dev; Dave Orphan, dir live captioning; Renee Simmons, dir prog mktg; Gary Chase, dir consumer product engrg.

National Catholic Association for Broadcasters/Communicators. 901 Irving Ave., Dayton, Ohio 45409-2316. (513) 229-2303. FAX: (513) 229-2300. Sr. Angela Ann Zukowski, pres; Rev. Bernard Bonnot, 1st VP; Bernard Rocheleau, 2nd VP; Sr. Judy Zielinski, sec; William G. Halpin, treas; Sr. Nancy Kinross, natl office coord.

National Committee for UHF Television. Box 8603, Virginia Beach, Va. 23450. (804) 425-3305. FAX: (804) 491-8812. Scott Hessek, pres; Allan Winters, VP.

National Council for Families & Television. 3801 Barham Blvd., Suite 300, Los Angeles 90068. (213) 876-5959. FAX: (213) 851-6180. Tricia McLeod Robin, pres; Richard Krafsur, edit *Television & Family* magazine.

Board of Trustees Officers: Marian Rees, Bill Allen, Marcy Carsey, co-chmn; Gerald M. Levin, sec/treas.

National Education Association. 1201 16th St. N.W., Washington 20036. (202) 833-4000. FAX: (202) 822-7292. Don Cameron, exec dir; Bill Martin, dir communications svcs.

National Electrical Manufacturers Association (NEMA). 2101 L St. N.W., Washington 20037. (202) 457-8400. Malcolm E. O'Hagan, pres.

National Federation of Community Broadcasters (NFCB). 666 11th St. N.W., Suite 805, Washington 20001. (202) 393-2355. Lynn Chadwick, pres; David LePage, VP member svcs; Douglas K. Bostrom, dir member svcs.

Directors: Lynn Chadwick (NFCB Washington); Joe Orozco (KIDE Hoopa, Calif.); Marty Durlan (KGNU Boulder, Colo.); Marcos Martinez (KUNM Albuquerque); Jeff Colebrook (WERV Blue Hill Falls, Me.); Dottie Talmage (KVNF Paonia, Colo.); Molly M. Romero (Omaha, Neb.); Barry Forbes (KPFT Houston).

National Federation of Local Cable Programmers. 666 11th St. N.W., Suite 806, Washington 20001-4542. (202) 393-2650. FAX: (202) 393-2653. T. Andrew Lewis, exec dir, Anthony Riddle, chmn; Julie Omelchuck, vice-chmn; Kari Peterson, sec; Carl Kucharski, treas.

Directors: Jeiona Boneham, Pamela O'Brown, Alan Bushong, Paul Congo, Sue Diciple, Ann Flynn, Hap Haasch, James Howood, Paul LeValley, Anne Mitchell, Sharon Mooney, Fernando Moreno, Gerry Pauleen, Penelope Place, Nantz Richard, Richard Turner, Greg Vawter, Deb Vinsel, LaMonte Ward, Rika Welshs.

National Federation of Press Women Inc. Box 99, Blue Springs, Mo. 64013. (816) 229-1666. Gwen White, pres; Ruth Anna, 1st VP; Linn Rounds, 2nd VP; Donna Hunt, 3rd VP; Vivien Sadowski, treas; Ella Wright, sec; Lois Wolfe, exec dir.

Progs, svcs & contest categories for female & male professionals in all media.

National Informational Marketing Association (NIMA). 1201 New York Ave. N.W., Suite 1000, Washington 20005. (202) 962-8342. FAX: (202) 962-8300. Helene Blake, exec dir; David Savage, dir communications; Jeff Knowles, gen counsel; Justina Brewer, exec asst; David Bennett, dir member svcs.

Directors: Douglas Bornstein (Douglas Communications); David Chaladoff (Universal Direct Television); Jeffery Engler (USA Direct); Jeff Glickman (First Class Marketing); Michael Hammond (National Media Corp.); Tim Hawthorne (Hawthorne Communications); Lynn Kintz (Fitness Quest); Nancy Langston (Nancy Langston & Associates); David Marsh (American Telecast Corp.); Greg Renker (Guthy-Renker Corp.); Arthur Toll (The Regal Group); Gene Williams (Power Media Marketing Group); Katie Williams (Williams Television Time); Helene Blake, NIMA exec dir; Jeffrey D. Knowles, NIMA gen counsel.

National League of Cities. 1301 Pennsylvania Ave. N.W., Washington 20004. (202) 626-3160. FAX: (202) 626-3043. Donald J. Borut, exec dir; Frank Shafroth, dir policy/federal rels; Randy Arndt, dir media rels.

National Museum of Communications Inc. 2001 Plymouth Rock Dr., Richardson, Tex. 75081. (214) 690-3636. FAX: (214) 644-2473. Chris Christian, chmn; William J. Bragg, founder.

Directors: Andy Bell, Tom McCartin, Clay Dobson.

National Newspaper Association. 1627 K St., Suite 400, Washington 20006. (202) 466-7200. FAX: (202) 331-1403. Sam M. Griffin Jr., chmn; Tonda F. Rush, CEO; Charlotte Schexnayder, pres; Frank Garred, VP.

Directors: Raymond Gross, Joseph Biddle II, Jack Fishman, William E. Shaw, Dalton C. Wright, Michael Sellett, Michael Parta, Roy Eaton, Sue Dutson, William P. Monroe, John M. Andrist, Charles Wribel, Sam Spencer.

National Press Club. 529 14th St. N.W., Washington 20045. (202) 662-7500. FAX: (202) 662-7512. Clayton W. Boyce, pres; Sonja Hillgren, chmn bd of governors; Bill Vose, gen mgr; Barbara Vandegrift, librarian.

National Religious Broadcasters. 7839 Ashton Ave., Manassas, Va. 22110. (703) 330-7000. FAX: (703) 330-7100. E. Brandt Gustavson, pres; David W. Clark, chmn; Michael Glenn, dir conventions; Michael Kisha, dir finance; Ron J. Kopczick, dir communications; Patricia Mahoney, dir membership.

National Retail Federation. 100 W. 31st St., New York 10001. (212) 244-8780. FAX: (212) 594-0487. Joseph E. Antonini, chmn of bd; Bernard F. Brennan, 1st vice-chmn of bd; John J. Shea, 2nd vice-chmn of bd; Daryl Routzahn, 3rd vice-chmn of bd; Thomas A. Hays, chmn finance committee; Francis R. Stawbridge III, chmn nominating committee; Harold E. Sells, chmn natl retail institute; John J. Schultz, exec dir/pres retail svcs division; Tracy Mullin, pres govt & pub affrs; Phillip T. Davidson, corporate sec.

National Telemedia Council Inc. 120 E. Wilson St., Madison, Wis. 53703. (608) 257-7712. FAX: (608) 257-7714. Marieli Rowe, exec dir.

Officers: Dr. Marti Tomas Izral, pres; Susan Dreyfus Fosdick, VP; Rev. Stephen J. Umhoefer, treas; Joanna Overn, sec; Joseph E. Meagher, past pres.

National Translator Association. Box 628, Riverton, Wyo. 82501. (307) 856-3322. FAX: (307) 856-0707. Darwin Hillberry, pres; Kent Parsons, Doug Maupin, VPs; Bill Ball, sec/treas.

National Video Credit Managers Association. Box 40120, Cleveland 44140. (216) 835-2477. FAX: (216) 835-4594. Marilyn Swadling, coord.

Network Television Association. 825 7th Ave., 4th Fl., New York 10019. (212) 456-1781. FAX: (212) 456-1780. Marcella Rosen, pres/CEO; Steve Singer, sr VP/dir rsch; Julie Pinkwater, sr VP/dir mktg; Susan Sewell, VP/dir pub rels.

Directors: Pierson Mapes, pres NBC; John Damiano, VP Media NBC; Larry Hoffner, exec VP sls NBC; Mark Mandala, pres ABC; Marvin Goldsmith, pres sls ABC; Joseph Abruzzese, sr VP CBS sls; Peter Lunde, exec VP CBS; David Poltrack, sr VP planning CBS; Peter Chrisanthapoulis.

New York Market Radio Broadcasters Association (NYMRAD). 51 E. 42nd St., Suite 416, New York 10017. (212) 808-4330. FAX: (212) 986-3242. Sanford Josephson, exec dir; Debra Beagan, mgr member svcs.

Directors: Mark Bench (WMXV); Bob Bruno (WOR); Tom Chiusano (WXRK); Peter Doyle (McGavren Guild); Maureen LeSourd (WQCD); Bill Hogan (Unistar); James Morley (WEZN); Charles Warfield (WRKS); Rona Landy (WLTW); Maire Mason (WCBS-FM); Mitch Dolan (WPLJ); Don Bouloukos (WABC); Steve Cardullo (WYNY); Dan Griffin (WCBS-AM); Gene Hobicorn (WPAT-AM/FM); Joel Hollander (WFAN); David Lampol (WBLS); Warren Maurer (WINS); Fran Sharp (WBBR); Kevin Smith (WNEW-FM); Gary Starr (WINE/WRKI).

Newspaper Association of America. The Newspaper Center, 11600 Sunrise Valley Dr., Reston, Va. 22091. (703) 648-1000. FAX: (703) 620-4557. Cathleen Black, pres/CEO; Len Forman, exec VP/COO.

Senior Vice Presidents: Nicholas Cannistraro Jr., sr VP/chief sls & mktg; George R. Cashau, sr VP technology; Kathleen Criner, sr VP industry dev & diversity; James E. Donahue, sr VP communications; Reggie R. Hall, sr VP assn mktg svcs; Mary Anne Kanter, sr VP/CFO finance & administration; John F. Sturm, sr VP govt, legal & policy; Rosalind G. Stark, sr VP NAA Foundation.

Officers: Donald Newhouse (Advance Publications, Newark), chmn exec committee; Charles T. Brumback (Tribune Co., Chicago), vice-chmn exec committee; Uzal H. Martz Jr. (*Republican*, Pottsville, Pa.), sec exec committee; John J. Curley (Gannett Co. Inc., Arlington, Va.), treas exec committee.

Executive Board: Alejandro José Aguirre (Diario Las Americas, Miami, Fla.); Frank Batten (Landmark Communications Inc., Norfolk, Va.); James K. Batten (Knight-Ridder Inc., Miami, Fla.); Frank A. Bennack Jr. (The Hearst Corp., New York), exec committee; Frank A. Blethen (*The Seattle Times*); J. Stewart Bryan III (Media General Inc., Richmond, Va.); Daniel B. Burke (Capital Cities/ABC New York); David C. Cox (Cowles Media Co., Minneapolis); Fred D. Crisp Jr. (The News & Observer Publishing Co., Raleigh, N.C.); Robert W. Decherd (A.H. Belo Corp., Dallas); Richard E. Diamond (*Staten Island Advance*, New York); Sandra C. Hardy (Calkins Newspapers, Levittown, Pa.), exec committee; Joe Hladky (The Gazette Co., Cedar Rapids, Iowa), exec committee; Michael W. Johnston (Thomson Newspapers Corp., Toronto, Ont., Canada); James C. Kennedy (Cox Enterprises Inc., Atlanta); David Laventhol (*Los Angeles Times*); Lawrence A. Leser (E.W. Scripps Co., Cincinnati); Standford Lipsey (*The Buffalo News*, Buffalo, N.Y.); Sam S. McKeel (*Chicago Sun-Times*); William S. Morris III (Morris Communications Corp., Augusta, Ga.); W. Curtis Riddle (*Lansing State Journal*, Lansing, Mich.); Scott C. Schurz (*The Herald-Times*, Bloomington, Ind.); Arthur O. Sulzberger Jr. (*The New York Times*); William O. Taylor (*The Boston Globe*); Richard J. Warren (*Bangor Daily News*, Bangor, Me.).

Board Of Governors: Alejandro José Aguirre, Robert W. Althus, Andrew E. Barnes, Walter E. Bartlett, Frank Batten, James K. Batten, Frank A. Bennack Jr., Frank A. Blethen, Henry H. Bradley, Charles T. Brumback, J. Stewart Bryan III, Daniel B. Burke, Susan Burman, Michael Busse, Crawford C. Carroll Jr., Cathy B. Coffey, Alfred E. Corey Jr., David C. Cox, Fred D. Crisp Jr., John J. Curley, James C. Currow, Robert W. Decherd, Richard E. Diamond, James E. Doughton, Douglas B. Fox, Larry Franklin, Richard D. Gottlieb, Stephen Hamblett, Sandra C. Hardy, Dale Harris, Robert H. Hartmann, Joe Hladky, Robert M. Jelenic, Michael W. Johnston, James C. Kennedy, Beverly A. Klein, Lynn Wood Lange, David Laventhol, Lawrence A. Leser, Stanford Lipsey, Uzal H. Martz Jr., Cathy Melton, Sam S. McKeel, William S. Morris III, Donald E. Newhouse, Erwin R. Potts, Michael E. Pulitzer, Orage Quarles III, W. Curtis Riddle, Carlton F. Rosenburgh, Frank E. Russell, Scott C. Schurz, W. Dean Singleton, Fred W. Smith, Arthur O. Sulzberger Jr., John W. Sweeney III, William O. Taylor, Richard T. Thieriot, Eivind Thomsen, R. David Threshie, Jerome S. Tilis, J. David Tipton, Richard J. Warren, Jack A. Williams, John F. Wolfe, Clydette S. Womack.

Nonprescription Drug Manufacturers Association. 1150 Connecticut Ave. N.W., Washington 20036. (202) 429-9260. FAX: (202) 223-6835. James D. Cope, pres.

North American Broadcast Section of the World Association for Christian Communication. 1300 Mutual Bldg., Detroit 48226. (313) 962-0340. Rev. Ed Willingham, business mgr.

North American National Broadcasters' Association (NANBA). Secretariat, 1500 Bronson Ave., Ottawa, Ont., Canada K1G 3J5. (613) 738-6553. FAX: (613) 738-6887. Michael McEwen (CBC), pres; Mary Frost (ABC),

VP; Jorge Kanahuati (Televisa), VP; Spencer Moore (NANBA), sec gen.

Directors: John A. Frazee (CBS); Paul E. Symczak (CPB); Philip Wedge (CTV); Ron Gnidziejko (NBC); Eason Jordan (TBS).

North American Telecommunications Association. 2000 M St., Suite 550, Washington 20036. (202) 296-9800. Edwin B. Spievack, pres.

Ohio State Awards. Ohio State University, 2400 Olentangy River Rd., Columbus, Ohio 43210-1027. (614) 292-0185. FAX: (614) 292-7625. Dale K. Ouzts, dir; Phyllis Madry, awards mgr.

Pacific Pioneer Broadcasters. Box 4866, North Hollywood, Calif. 91607. (213) 461-2121. Jack Smith, pres; Ralph Edwards, chmn of bd; Art Gilmore, vice-chmn; John Harlan, VP; Loyd Sigmon, VP; Barbara Fuller, sec; Robert H. Ahmanson, treas; Betty Emery Cooley, asst treas.

Directors: Ray Angona, Sam Benson, Chuck Cecil, Sue Clark Chadwick, Robert Dwan, Dorothy Gardiner, Kay Irwin, Eddy King, Milt Klein, Robert M. Light, Shirley Mitchell, Joel Malone, Jack Narz, Don Page, R.H. Peck, Lee Ray, Phil Reed, Ralph Story, Chuck Southcott, Gil Stratton, Ted Toll.

Promax International. 6255 Sunset Blvd., Suite 624, Los Angeles 90028-7426. (213) 465-3777. FAX: (213) 469-9559. James B. Chabin (BPME Los Angeles), pres; Joan Voukides (Cablevision, Woodbury, N.Y.), chmn; Nancy Smith (Global Television Network, Ont., Canada), chmn-elect; John Calver (KMBC-TV Kansas City, Mo.), vice-chmn/treas; Gregg Balko, dir conferences/membership.

Directors: Janet Magleby (KJR/KLTX-Radio Seattle); Bob Klein (Klein, Los Angeles); Brad Crum (CBS/Broadcast Group, Los Angeles); Sandy Martin, (KSHB-TV Kansas City, Mo.); Rich Brase (KSDK St. Louis); Lou Bortone, (WBMX-FM Boston); Tim Miller (NBC Television, New York); Peter Smith, (Pulitizer Broadcasting Co., St. Louis); Lloyd P. Trufelman (Trylon Associates Inc., New York); Barbara Bowman (ABC-TV); Micki Byrnes (Cannell Communications); Doug Friedman (Genesis Entertainment); Chris Mosely (The Discovery Channel); Rod Rightmire (Indiana University); Rita Scarfone (Worldvision Enterprises Inc.).

Promotion Marketing Association of America. 257 Park Ave., 11th Fl., New York 10001. (212) 420-1100. FAX: (212) 533-7622. Christopher J. Sutherland, exec dir; Bonnie Carlson, pres/chmn of bd.

Public Radio in Mid-America (PRIMA). c/o Jeff Stoll (WHIL-FM), Box 160326, Mobile, Ala. 36616. (205) 460-2395. FAX: (205) 460-2773. Craig Beeby (WOSU-FM Stillwater, Okla.), pres; Michael Lazar (WNIU-FM DeKalb, Ill.), treas; Jeff Stoll (WHIL-FM Mobile, Ala.), sec; Patricia Cahill (KCUR-FM Kansas, Mo.), past pres.

Directors: Patricia Cahill (KCUR-FM Kansas City, Mo.); Bruce Haines (WBNI-FM Fort Wayne, Ind.); Dori Gain (WIUM-FM Macomb, Ill.).

Public Relations Society of America. 33 Irving Pl., New York 10003-2376. (212) 995-2230. FAX: (212) 995-0757. Harland W. "Hal" Warner, pres; Joseph A. Vecchione, pres-elect; Luis W. Morales, sec; John R. Beardsley, treas.

Directors: Rosalee A. Roberts, David M. Bicofsky, Jerry L. Bryan, Mary Lynn Cusick, Janice M. Newman, Guy E. Brown II, Frances M. Driscoll, Debra A. Miller, Anna L. West; Elizabeth Ann Kovacs, exec VP.

Assembly Delegates-at-Large: Michael D. Bardin, Amanda Brown-Olmstead.

Canadian Public Relations Society Delegate-at-Large: Carla Gates-Morris.

Public Relations Journal, Editor/Director Publications: Susan L. Bovet.

Publishers Information Bureau. 919 3rd Ave., 22nd Fl., New York 10022. (212) 752-0055. FAX: (212) 888-4217. James Guthrie, exec dir.

Radio Advertising Bureau. See listing under Major National Associations, this section.

Radio and Television News Directors Foundation. 1000 Connecticut Ave. N.W., Suite 615, Washington 20036. (202) 659-6510. FAX: (202) 223-4007. David Bartlett (RTNDA), pres exec committee; Robert A. Bruner, VP exec committee; Colonel Barney Oldfield, treas exec committee; Louis F. Prato (Medill News Service), sec exec committee.

Trustees: Thomas P. Bier (WISC-TV); George Glazer (Hill & Knowlton Inc.); Robert A. Priddy (MissouriNet), exec committee; Ron Townsend (Gannett Television Group); J. Spencer Kinard (KXIV-TV); Jeffrey Marks (WLBZ-TV); Gene P. Mater (International Media Fund); Patricia Diaz Dennis (Sullivan & Cromwell); Gary L. Hanson (WKBN-TV); Carole Simpson (ABC News); Tenold R. Sunde; Gary Wordlaw (WJLA-TV).

Radio and Television Research Council. c/o Headquarter Group, Attn: R. Sharpe, 245 5th Ave., New York 10016. (212) 481-3038. FAX: (212) 481-3071. Terry Drucker, pres; Michele Buslik, pres-elect; Alan Torkes, sec/treas.

Radio Marketing Bureau. 146 Yorkville Ave., Toronto, Ont., Canada M5R 1C2. (416) 922-5757; (416) 922-6542. Brian W. Jones, pres/CEO; Robin Glenny, VP mktg & sls; Ginny Townsen, VP loc sls & svcs; Tony Leadman, sr VP Ottawa; Cathy Hamel, controller; Terry Hibbard, rsch mgr.

Directors: Don Pagnutti, chmn; Bill Herz, vice-chmn; Merv Russell, sec/treas; Brian W. Jones, Jim MacLeod, Yvon Chouinard, Patrick Grierson, Warren Holte, Larry Lamb, Michael McCabe, Gary Miles, Joe Mulvihill, Jim Waters, Owen Charlebois, Bryan Edwards, John Gorman, Clint Forster, Jim MacLeod.

Radio Network Association Inc. 51 W. 52nd St., 17th Fl., New York 10019. (212) 777-0045. FAX: (212) 777-0353. Robert P. Kipperman (CBS Radio Networks), chmn; William J. Hogan (Unistar Radio Networks), vice-chmn; Rick Devlin, pres; Robert Callahan (ABC Radio Networks), treas; Greg P. Batusic, (Westwood One/Mutual), sec.

Radio Regulation Board (RRB). International Telecommunication Union, Place des Nations, CH-1211 Geneva, 20, Switzerland. (+41-22) 730-5784. FAX: (+41-22) 730-5785. M. Miura, chmn; M. Harbi, vice-chmn; W.H. Bellchambers, G.C. Brooks, V.V. Kozlov, members.

The RRB is a five-member bd elected at the ITU Plenipotentiary Conference, Nairobi, 1982, responsible for mgmt of the radio frequency spectrum & the geostationary-satellite orbit in conformity with the international radio regulations.

Radio-Television Correspondents' Association. S-325, U.S. Capitol, Washington 20510. (202) 224-6421.

Executive Committee: Brian Lockman (C-SPAN), chmn; John Bisney (Unistar Radio Network); Aaron S. Cohen (Radio News Washington); William W. Headline (CNN); Cokie Roberts (ABC News/NPR); Louise L. Schiavone (Associated Press Broadcast); Linda J. Scott (CONUS Communications).

Radio-Television News Directors Association. See listing under Major National Associations, this section.

Radio Television News Directors Association (Canada). 2175 Shephard Ave. E., Suite 110, Toronto, Ont., Canada M2J 1W8. (416) 491-1670. FAX: (416) 491-1670. Gary Ennett (CFPL Radio London), pres; Tom Mark (CJJR FM/CHRX), VP radio; Dave McGinn (CJOH-TV Ottawa), VP TV; Al Gibson (Broadcast News), sec/treas.

Recording Industry Association of America Inc. (RIAA). 1020 19th St. N.W., Suite 200, Washington 20036. (202) 775-0101. FAX: (202) 775-7253. Jason S. Berman, pres; Hilary B. Rosen, exec VP; David E. Leibowitz, gen counsel; Tim Sites, VP.

Directors: Jerry Moss, Chris Wright, Al Teller, Clive Davis, Joseph Smith, Clarence Avant, Mo Ostin, Jheryl Busby, Dick Griffey, Zach Horowitz, Tommy Mottola, Doug Morris, Bob Krasnow, Sal Licata, Hale Milgrim, Jason Berman, Joseph Galente, Mel Ilberman, Eric Kronfeld, Richard Palmese, Joel Schoenfeld, Mike Bone, Myron Roth, Dave Johnson.

Royal Television Society, North America Inc. c/o KAET-TV, Arizona State University, Tempe, Ariz. 85287-1405. (602) 965-7661. FAX: (602) 965-1000. Peter J. Marshall, pres; Roger J. Carter, sec.

Directors: Alan Godber, Jonathan A. Crane.

Satellite Broadcasting and Communications Association of America (SBCA). 225 Reinekers Ln., Suite 600, Alexandria, Va. 22314. (703) 549-6990. FAX: (703) 549-7640. Charles C. Hewitt, pres; Andrew R. Paul, sr VP govt affrs; Alan E. Burgess, dir opns; Magaret A. Parone, dir communications.

Directors: H. Taylor Howard, chmn; Rik Hawkins, Gordon D. Main, Stanley E. Hubbard II, Susan Denison.

Society of Broadcast Engineers Inc. Box 20450, Indianapolis 46220. (317) 253-1640. FAX: (317) 253-0418. John L. Poray C.A.E., exec dir; Richard Farquhar, pres.

Society of Cable Television Engineers Inc. 669 Exton Commons, Exton, Pa. 19341. (215) 363-6888. FAX: (215) 363-5898. William W. Riker, pres; Tom Elliot, chmn; Walt Ciciora Ph.D., eastern vice-chmn; Pam Nobles, western VP; Norrie Bush, sec; Bill Arnold, treas.

Directors: Steve Allen, Jennifer Hays, Robert Schaeffer, Terry Bush, Jack Trower, Hugh McCarley, Michael Smith, Bernie Czarnecki, Wendell Bailey, Wendell Woody.

Society of Environmental Journalists (SEJ). 9425 Stenton Ave., Suite 209, Philadelphia, Pa. 19118. (215) 247-9710. FAX: 247-9712. Beth Parke, exec. dir.

Directors: Jim Detjen (*Philadelphia Inquirer*), pres; Emilia Askari (*Detroit Free Press*) & Rae Tyson (*USA Today*), VPs; Steve Curwood (National Public Radio's *Living On Earth)*, treas; Kevin Carmody *(Charlottesville Daily Progress)*, sec.

Other Directors: Marla Cone (*Los Angeles Times*); Julie Edelson (Inside Washington Publishers); Randy Loftis (*Dallas Morning News*); Mike Mansur (*Kansas City Star*); Tom Meersman (*Minneapolis Star News*); Wevonneda Minis (*Post Courier*); David Ropeik (WCVB-TV Boston); Teya Ryan (Turner Broadcasting).

Society of Motion Picture and Television Engineers. 595 W. Harstdale Ave., White Plains, N.Y. 10607. (914) 761-1100. FAX: (914) 761-3115. Irwin W. Young, pres; Blaine Baker, past pres; Stanley N. Baron, exec VP; Kenneth P. Davis, engrg VP; David L. George, editorial VP; Charles H. Jablonski, financial VP; Edward P. Hobson II, conference VP; John A. Carlson, sections VP; Peter A. Dare, sec/treas; Lynette A. Robinson, exec dir; Carol King, press rels.

Society of Professional Journalists. Box 77, 16 S. Jackson, Greencastle, Ind. 46135. (317) 653-3333. FAX: (317) 653-4631. Ernie Ford, exec dir; Paul McMasters, pres; Reginald Stuart, sec/treas.

Twelve rgnl dirs, natl officers elected annually, four student reps.

Society of Satellite Professionals International. 2200 Wilson Blvd., #102-258, Arlington, Va. 22201. (703) 522-7745. FAX: (703) 528-4084. Karl Savatiel (NJ), chmn; LaRene Tondro (Washington), exec dir; Peter Marshall (Washington), pres; Irl "Bucky" Marshall (Englewood), VP U.S. chapters; Kimithy Vaughan (Los Angeles), VP international liaison; Harley Shuler, VP member svcs; Monica Morgan, VP membership; Susan Irwin, sec; Clifford M. Harrington (Washington), treas.

The Songwriters Guild of America. 276 5th Ave., New York 10001. (212) 686-6820. FAX: (212) 481-3680. George David Weiss, pres; Lewis M. Bachman, VP; Richard Adler, 1st VP; Vic Mizzy, 2nd VP; Ray Evans, 3rd VP; Rick Carnes, 4th VP; Ervin Drake, sec; Gretchen Adamson, asst sec; William Harbach, treas; Donald Kahn, asst treas; George Wurzbach, natl projects dir.

Hollywood, Calif. 90028: 6430 Sunset Blvd. (213) 462-1108. Aaron Meza, rgnl dir.

Nashville 37212: 1222 16th Ave. S., Suite 25. (615) 329-1782. Kathy Hyland, rgnl dir.

Station Representatives Association. 230 Park Ave., New York 10169. (212) 687-2484. FAX: (212) 972-4372. Jerome Feniger, mgng dir; Tim McAuliff, pres; Tom Olson, VP TV; Don Macfarlane, VP radio; David Kaufman, sec; Lee Lahey, treas.

Telecommunications Research and Action Center. (Formerly NCCB.) Box 12038, Washington 20005. (202) 462-2520. Minie Rajwar, contact.

Directors: Everett Parker, Henry Geller, Willhelmina Cooke, David Mitchell, Robert J. Stein, Andy Schwartzman.

Television Bureau of Advertising (TVB). See listing under Major National Associations, this section.

Television Bureau of Canada. 890 Yonge St., Suite 700, Toronto, Ont., Canada M4W 3P4. (416) 923-8813. FAX: (416) 923-8739. Cameron Fellman, pres; R. Dilworth, VP mktg.

Television Critics Association. c/o The News Herald, 38879 Mentor Ave., Willoughby, Ohio 44094. (216) 951-7274. FAX: (216) 975-2293. David Glasier (*News Herald*), pres; Tom Feran (*Cleveland Plain-Dealer*), VP; Bob Cartwright (*Wichita Eagle*), sec; Rodi Alexander, treas.

Directors: Phil Rosenthal, Eric Kohanic, Gail Shister, Tom Walter.

Television Operators Caucus. 901 31st St. N.W., Washington 20007-4423. (202) 944-5109. Mary Jo Manning, coord.

Television Publicity Executives Committee. 7449 Melrose Ave., Los Angeles 90046. (213) 655-8970. FAX: (213) 655-8147. Connie Stone, CEO; George Faber, sec.

Committee Members: Sue Binford VP corporate & media affrs NBC; Marcy De Veaux, assoc dir PBS; Doug Duitsman; George Faber, dir pub rels Viacom Entertainment Group; Larry Goldman, ptnr Bender Goldman Helper; Bob Crutchfield, sr VP publ, adv & promotion Universal TV; Cliff Dektar, sr VP The Lippin Group; Marian Effinger, VP adv, publ & prom Walt Disney TV;

National Associations

Libby Gill, VP publ Columbia Pictures TV; James A. Gordon, VP pub rels Steven Bochco Productions; Ben Halpern; Diane Passarelli, VP publ, adv & prom Stephen Cannell Productions; Kim Reed, VP publ, adv & promotion MGM/TV; Penelope Selwyn, sr VP adv, publ & promotion Warner Brothers TV; Susan Tick, VP publ West Coast CBS Broadcast Group; Cynthia Lieberman, dir publ Twentieth TV; Russell Patrick, exec VP Stone/Hallinan Associates Inc.; Dee Schroder, sr VP entertainment TV Rogers & Cowan; David Stapf, VP publ Lorimar TV; Betsy Wagner, VP pub rels Fox Broadcasting Co.; Gene Walsh; Bob Wright, VP pub rels West Coast Capital Cities/ABC Inc.; John Wentworth, VP publ Paramount TV; Richard Licata, VP media rels HBO; Linda Alexander, VP press rels MTV Networks; Robin McMillan, VP pub rels Showtime; Alison Hill, VP pub rels Turner Broadcasting.

Theatre Authority Inc. 16 E. 42nd St., New York 10017. (212) 682-4215. FAX: (212) 682-8407. Helen Leahy, exec dir; Jane Powell, pres; John H. Sucke, 1st VP; Terry Walker, 2nd VP; Robert Bruyr, 3rd VP; Rod McKuen, 4th VP; Joan Greenspan, treas; Alan D. Olsen, recording sec.

TA is a regulatory nonprofit organization authorized by the five performers' unions to represent the entertainers who donate their time & talent to live & televised benefits sponsored by bona fide charities. The performers unions are Actors' Equity Association, American Guild of Musical Artists, American Guild of Variety Artists, American Federation of Television and Radio Artists, The Screen Actors Guild, as well as the Actors Fund of America & other guilds.

Hollywood, Calif. 90028: Theatre Authority West Inc., 6464 Sunset Blvd. George Ives, pres; Judith Bailey, exec dir.

U.S. Advanced Television Systems Committee (ATSC). 1750 K St. N.W., Suite 800, Washington 20006. (202) 828-3130. FAX: (202) 828-3131. James C. McKinney, chmn; Robert Hopkins, exec dir.

More than 50 members representing TV nets, manufacturers' assns & others.

U.S. Catholic Conference, Dept. of Communications. 3211 4th St. N.E., Washington 20017-1194. (202) 541-3320. FAX: (202) 541-3129. Richard W. Daw, sec for communications.

Veteran Wireless Operators Association Inc. Office of the Secretary, 46 Murdock St., Fords, N.J. 08863. (908) 225-2539. Hon. Barry M. Goldwater, honorary pres; David Kintzer, pres; Robert E. Stuhler, 1st VP; Henry Paulisen, 2nd VP; Edward F. Pleuler Jr., sec; Herman Arond, treas; Rev. Peter Larom, chaplain.

Directors: F.T. Cassidy, chmn; J.Z. Alexander, P. Anselmo, W.R. Benson, T.B. DeMeis, A. Ehrlich, E.S. Johnson, S. Margolis, H. Paulisen, J.M. Shaw, D.S. Stivison, R.E. Stuhler, D.I. Temple, D.W. Winter.

Veterans Bedside Network (of the Veterans Hospital Radio & TV Guild). 250 W. 54th St., 9th Fl., New York 10019. (212) 757-8657. FAX: (212) 757-8659. Douglas Lutz, pres/administrator; Wallace I. Green, exec VP; Jerry Katz, treas; Megen Spanierman, sec.

Directors: John Martello, Dennis Bigelow, Helen Veden, Laurie Beckelman, Paul W. Bucha, Gerard Byrne, Peter Eldridge, Robert S. Grimes, Peggy Kerry, Barbara Legeti, John Eric Smith, Vic Tardino Jr., Marc Valenti.

Western States Advertising Agencies Association. 6404 Wilshire Blvd., Suite 1111, Los Angeles 90048. (213) 655-1951. FAX: (213) 655-8627. Carol Golden, exec dir.

Wireless Cable Association. 1155 Connecticut Ave. N.W., Suite 700, Washington 20036. (202) 452-7823. FAX: (202) 452-0041. Robert L. Schmidt, pres.

Women In Cable. 500 N. Michigan Ave., Suite 1400, Chicago 60611. (312) 661-1700. Pamela Vickers Williams, exec dir.

Directors: Diane Blackwood, pres; Ann Carlsen, VP; Coleen Abdoulah, sec; Patti Rowe, treas; Ruth Warren, past pres.

Women In Communications Inc. 2101 Wilson Blvd., Suite 417, Arlington, Va. 22201. (703) 528-4200. FAX: (703) 528-4205. Anne S. Greenberg, pres; Roni D. Posner, exec dir.

Women In Film Foundation. 6464 Sunset Blvd., Suite 530, Hollywood, Calif. 90028. (213) 463-6040. FAX: (213) 463-0963. Meredith MacRae, chmn; Bonny Dore, vice-chmn; Rita Dillon, vice-chmn/treas.

The World Teleport Association. 2 World Trade Center, Suite 2150, New York 10048. (212) 432-2028. FAX: (212) 432-6356. Barker Herr, chmn.

Directors: Tadayoshi Yomada, chmn; Brian Lawrence, vice-chmn.

State and Regional Broadcast Associations

Alabama Broadcasters Association. 1316 Alford Ave., Suite 201, Birmingham, Ala. 35226. (205) 979-1690. FAX: (205) 979-9981. Ben K. McKinnon, exec dir; Tina Currier, admin sec.

Alaska Broadcasters Association. Box 102424, Anchorage 99510. (907) 258-2424. FAX: (907) 258-2414. Bruce Sloan, pres; Tom Busch, VP; Carol Schatz, sec/treas.
Directors: B.G. Randlett, Dennis Bookey, Mark Byford, Gary Donovan, Kellie Law, Peter Van Nort, Jack McKain, Alice Walsh, Dennis Egan.

Arizona Broadcasters Association. 3101 N. Central Ave., Suite 560, Phoenix 85012. (602) 274-1418. FAX: (602) 631-9853. Art Brooks, exec dir.

Arkansas Broadcasters Association. Suite 201, 2024 Arkansas Valley Dr., Little Rock, Ark. 72212. (501) 227-7564. FAX: (501) 223-9798. Neal Gladner, pres; Jim Earls, past pres.

California Broadcasters Association. 1127 11th St., Suite 730, Sacramento, Calif. 95814. (916) 444-2237. FAX: (916) 444-2043. Victor J. Biondi, exec dir; Lillie Player, exec asst.
Directors: Amy McCombs, pres; Dino Corbin, pres-elect.

Colorado Broadcasters Association. 1660 Lincoln, Suite 2202, Denver 80264. (303) 894-0911. FAX: (303) 830-8326. Douglas R. Wayland, exec dir; Julie Patterson, admin asst.

Connecticut Broadcasters Association. Box 678, Glastonbury, Conn. 06033. (203) 633-5031. FAX: (203) 657-2491. Paul K. Taff, exec dir.

Florida Association of Broadcasters. 109 E. College Ave., Tallahassee, Fla. 32301. (904) 681-6444. FAX: (904) 222-3957. Clarence McKee, chmn; C. Patrick Roberts, pres; George Mills, chmn-elect; Richard Lobo, vice-chmn TV; Dean Goodman, vice-chmn radio; Bill Petersen, treas; Julz Graham, exec asst.

Georgia Association of Broadcasters Inc. 8010 Roswell Rd., Suite 260, Atlanta 30350. (404) 395-7200. FAX: (404) 395-7235. William G. Sanders, exec dir.

Hawaii Association of Broadcasters. Box 91049, Honolulu 96838-1049. Lee Hacohen, pres.

Idaho State Broadcasters Association. 405 S. 8th St., Suite 365, Boise, Idaho 83702-7100. (208) 345-3072. FAX: (208) 345-8046. Connie Searles, exec dir.

Illinois Broadcasters Association. 1125 S. 5th St., Springfield, Ill. 62704. (217) 753-2636. FAX: (217) 753-8443. Wally Gair, exec dir; Dennis Upah, pres; Jack Everette, sr VP; Dan Fabian, VP radio; Jim Grimes, VP TV; John Vitanovec, treas.

Indiana Broadcasters Association Inc. 11595 Meridian St., Suite 300, Carmel, Ind. 46032. (317) 573-2995. FAX: (317) 573-2994. Linda Compton, exec dir; Doug Padgett, VP TV; Paul Karpowitz, sec/treas; Mike Corken, pres; Mike Day, VP AM radio; Louis Disinger, VP FM radio; Dick Lange, pres-elect.

Iowa Broadcasters Association. Box 71186, Des Moines, Iowa 50325. (515) 224-7237. FAX: (515) 224-6560. Sue Toma, exec dir.

Kansas Association of Broadcasters. 800 S.W. Jackson St., Suite 818, Topeka, Kan. 66612-1216. (913) 235-1307. FAX: (913) 233-3052. Harriet J. Lange CAE, exec dir; Lea Firestone, pres.

Kentucky Broadcasters Association. Box 680, Old Springfield Rd., Lebanon, Ky. 40033. (502) 692-6888; (502) 692-3126. FAX: (502) 692-6003. J.T. Whitlock, exec dir/treas; Steve Newberry, pres; Corkey Norcia, pres-elect; Bob Scherer, past pres; Dr. Charles Anderson, Jere Pigue, TV dirs; David Wickinson, PBS dir; Carl Nathe, assoc dir; Walter E. May, NAB radio bd; Ralph Gabbard, NAB TV dir; Sam B. Thomas, Frankfort Lobbyist.
Directors: District 1, Jim Freeland; District 2, Leonard Norcia; District 3, Christopher D. Baker; District 4, Tom Isaac; District 5, Steve Newberry; District 6, Dan Dorsett; District 7, Louise Wesley; District 8, Walt Williams; District 9, Dick Martin Jr.; District 10, Randy Thompson.

Louisiana Association of Broadcasters. 8762 Quarters Lake Rd., Baton Rouge 70809. (504) 922-9150. FAX: (504) 922-7750. Louise Lowman, exec dir; Joseph Varholy (KLFY-TV), pres; Tom Deal (KNOE/KNOE-FM), pres-elect; George Swift (KLCL/KHLA-FM), past pres; Tom Gay (KCTO/KCTO-FM), treas; Dan Hollingsworth (KRUS/KXKZ-FM), radio VP.
Directors: Alan Cartwright, KSLA-TV; Mike Mitchell, KPEL/KTDY-FM; Wayne Barnett, WDSU-TV; Nancy David, WBIU/KRVE-FM; Karl DeRouen, KEUN-AM; Stephen Levet, WCKW/WCKW-FM; Ray Saadi, KTIB/KHOM-FM; Taylor Thompson, KSYL/KQID-FM; Charles Spencer, LAB general counsel Herbert & Spencer.

Maine Association of Broadcasters. 75 Sewall St., Augusta, Me. 04330. (207) 623-3870. FAX: (207) 623-3870. Carolynn Sumner Hood, exec dir; Dennis Curley, pres; William Devin, pres-elect; Kevin Keogh, 2nd VP; Bob Rice, sec/treas.
Directors: Jo Ann Small Fisher, District 1; Alan Anderson, District 2; James Bartlett, District 3; Catherine Donovan, District 4.

Maryland-District of Columbia-Delaware Broadcasters Association Inc. One E. Chase St., Suite 1129, Baltimore 21202. (410) 385-0224. FAX: (410) 783-1875. Chip Weinman, pres; Tom Bresnaham, VP; Charles Walus, treas.

Massachusetts Broadcasters Association Inc. 22 Amherst Rd., Beverly, Mass. 01915. (508) 921-6400. FAX: (508) 921-6400. Robert S. Mehrman, exec dir.

Michigan Association of Broadcasters. 819 N. Washington Ave., Lansing, Mich. 48906. (517) 484-7444. FAX: (517) 484-5810. Karole L. White, exec dir; Philip C. Lamka (WWWM-FM Detroit), pres; Thomas Scanlan (WGTU/WGTQ-TV Traverse City), VP/pres-elect; John Cravens (WHYT-FM Detroit), treas; Patrick J. Mullen (WXMI-TV Grand Rapids), past pres.
Directors: James A. Jensen, Liggett Broadcasting Inc.; Nancy Sinclair, WSTD-FM Sterling/Standish; Stephen C. Trivers, WQSN-AM/WQLR-FM Kalamazoo; Eric S. Land, WEYI-TV Saginaw; Timothy Achterhoff, WMUS-AM/FM Muskegon; Gilbert L. Buettner, WWMT-TV Kalamazoo; Grace Gilchrist, WXYZ-TV Detroit; Patricia MacDonald-Garber, WMBN-AM/FM Petoskey; Ross Woodstock, WLNS-TV Lansing; Thomas Cleary, J. Michael Busch, Charles F. Benson, Michigan Legislative Consultants.

Minnesota Broadcasters Association. Box 16030, 3517 Raleigh Ave. S., St. Louis Park, Minn. 55416-0030. (612) 926-8123. FAX: (612) 926-9761. James Wychor, exec dir; John Mayasich (Hubbard Bcstg, Twin Cities), pres; Wayne Eddy (KYMN AM Stereo, Northfield), pres-elect; Ken Rees (WCCO-TV Twin Cities), VP; Jo Guck Bailey (Pro Radio Group, Mankato), treas; Pat Niekamp (KAAL-TV Austin), sec; Lew Latto (WAKX/KXTP Duluth), past pres.
Directors: Susan Anderson, KSAX-TV Alexandria; Sharon Flaherty, WKKQ/WTBX Hibbing; Hank Price, KARE-TV Twin Cities; Roseanne Rybeck, KROC AM/FM Rochester; Rand Gottlieb, pres TCRB Twin Cities/ex-officio; Billy Emery, Continental Electronics Corp, Apple Valley.

Mississippi Association of Broadcasters. 15 Northtown Drive, Suite A, Jackson, Miss. 39211. (601) 957-9121. FAX: (601) 957-9121. Jackie Lett, exec dir.

Missouri Broadcasters Association. Box 104445, 1803 Sun Valley Dr., Jefferson City, Mo. 65110-4445. (314) 636-6692. FAX: (314) 636-8258. Ted Griffin, exec VP; Rod Orr, pres; John Rose, pres-elect; John Zimmer, sec/treas.
Directors: District 1, Merrell Hansen, KUSA-KSD St. Louis; John Beck, KSHE St. Louis; District 2, Ron Carter, KMBZ/KLTH Kansas City; Charlotte English, KSHB-TV Kansas City; District 3, Shellby Hendee, KMRN Cameron; District 4, Dennis Polk, KSIS/KSDL/KXKX Sedalia; District 5, Jerry Montgomery, KODE-TV Joplin; District 6, Robert C. Eckman, KALM-KAMS Thayer; District 7, Steve Engles, KBSI-TV Cape Girardeau.

Montana Broadcasters Association. Box 503, Helena, Mont. 59624. (406) 442-3961. FAX: (406) 442-3987. Robert Precht, pres; Ron Davis, VP; Jim Senst, sec/treas.
Directors: Jerry Black, Don Bradley, Dan Michael; Jack Hyyppa.

Nebraska Broadcasters Association. 12020 Shamrock Pl., Suite 333, Omaha, Neb. 68154. (402) 333-3034. Richard Palmquist, exec dir.

Nevada Broadcasters Association. c/o Las Vegas Chamber of Commerce, 711 E. Desert Inn Rd., Las Vegas 89109. (702) 735-2450. FAX: (702) 735-2011. Mark Smith, exec dir.

New Hampshire Association of Broadcasters. 10 Chestnut Dr., Bedford, N.H. 03110. (603) 472-9800. FAX: (603) 472-9803. B. Allan Sprague, exec VP; Gary Howard, pres; Cynthia Fenneman, 1st VP.

New Jersey Broadcasters Association. 7 Centre Dr., Suite One, Jamesburg, N.J. 08831. (609) 860-0111. FAX: (609) 860-0110. Philip H. Roberts, pres; Pat Delsi (WSSJ Camden), chmn; Howard Green (WMGM-TV Atlantic City), vice-chmn; John Quinn (WJDM Elizabeth), past chmn; Shirley Carter, Harry Mitchell.
Joseph J. Knox Jr., John Forsythe, Dick Taylor, Penny Pinsker, exec bd; Peter Arnow, Anthony Marano, John Morris, bd members; Thomas J. Milewski, assoc member rep; Charles A. Hecht, engrg member rep.

New Mexico Broadcasters Association. 790-9D Tramway Ln. N.E., Albuquerque 87122. (505) 856-6748. FAX: (505) 856-6748. Dee Schelling, exec dir; Betty King (KBIM-AM/FM Roswell), pres.

New York State Broadcasters Association Inc. 115A Great Oaks Office Park, Albany, N.Y. 12203. (518) 456-8888. FAX (518) 456-8943. Joseph A. Reilly, pres; Sharon Van Loan, admin dir.

North Carolina Association of Broadcasters. Box 627, Raleigh, N.C. 27602. (919) 821-7300. FAX: (919) 829-1583. Wade H. Hargrove, gen counsel; Rees Poag, pres; Laura Ridgeway, exec mgr; Teresa Calton, membership svcs.

North Dakota Broadcasters Association. Box 5324, Grand Forks, N.D. 58206. (701) 775-3537. FAX: (701) 775-3537. Chuck Bundlie, exec dir; Bob Simmons (KNDK-AM/FM Langdon), pres; John Hrobesky (KTHI-TV Fargo), pres-elect.

Northern California Broadcasters Association. 131 Stewart St., Suite 301, San Francisco, Calif. 94105. (415) 546-NCBA. FAX: (415) 546-6290. Thomas Martz, exec VP/gen mgr; Jennifer Evert, project coord.
Directors: Pat McNally (KITS), pres; Harvey Stone (KBLX), VP; Don Marion, treas.

Ohio Association of Broadcasters Inc. 88 E. Broad St., Suite 1780, Columbus, Ohio 43215. (614) 228-4052. FAX: (614) 228-8133. Dale V. Bring, exec VP; Judy Cahill Masters, asst.

Oklahoma Association of Broadcasters. 6520 N. Western, Suite 104, Oklahoma City 73116. (405) 848-0771. FAX: (405) 848-0772. Carl C. Smith, exec dir; Ed Smith, pres.

Oregon Association of Broadcasters. Box 20037, Portland, Ore. 97220. (503) 257-3041. FAX: (503) 257-3041. Gordon Bussey, exec dir; Greg Walden (KIHR Hood River), pres; Mike Cheney (KBND Bend), VP; Bruce Liljegren (KEZI-TV Eugene), sec/treas.

Pennsylvania Association of Broadcasters. Box 4669, Harrisburg, Pa. 17111-0669. (717) 534-2504. FAX: (717) 533-1119. Richard E. Wyckoff, pres.

Radio Broadcasters Association of Puerto Rico. Cabian Plaza, Suite 212, San Juan, P.R. 00909-1837. (809) 724-8150. FAX: (809) 722-2667. Jose A. Ribas Dominicci, exec dir; Huberto Biaggi, pres.

Rhode Island Broadcasters Association. c/o WNRI Radio, 786 Diamond Hill Rd., Woonsocket, R.I. 02895. (401) 769-6925. Roger Bouchard (WNRI), exec dir; William Campbell, pres.

South Carolina Broadcasters Association. College of Journalism & Mass Communications, University of South Carolina, Columbia, S.C. 29208. (803) 777-6783. FAX: (803) 777-4103. Dr. Richard M. Uray, exec mgr; Jack West (WSTA AM/FM/TV Spartanburg), pres.

South Dakota Broadcasters Association. 1018 S. Lyndale, Sioux Falls, S.D. 57105. (605) 334-2682. Joe Cooper, exec dir; Tom Simmons (KELO AM/FM), pres; Steve Herman (KDLT TV), pres-elect.
Directors: Monte Loos, KOTA TV; Michael Schweitzer, KBJM AM; Joe Shields, KORN/KQRN; Darrell Gill, KOLY AM/FM; Bill Holst, KYNT/KKYA; Bob Faehnm, KSDR AM/FM; Gary Pierone, KEVN TV; Billy Emery, Continental Electronics.

Southern California Broadcasters Association. 5670 Wilshire Blvd., Suite 910, Los Angeles 90036. (213) 938-3100. FAX: (213) 938-8600. Gordon F. Mason, pres; Carol D. Senor, VP mktg; Susan Lorenz, dir pub affrs.

State and Regional Broadcast Associations

Directors: Trip Reeb, chmn; Doyle Rose, vice-chmn; Dave VanDyke, sec; Howard Anderson, treas.

Southern Educational Communications Association. Box 50008, Columbia, S.C. 29250. (803) 799-5517. FAX: (803) 771-4831. Judy Stone (Public TV Alabama), chmn; Susan Howarth, vice-chmn; Joann Winik (KLRN San Antonio), sec; Noel Smith (KNCT Killeen, Tex.), treas.

Tennessee Association of Broadcasters. Box 101015, Nashville 37224-1015. (615) 399-3791. FAX: (615) 361-3488. Whit Adamson, exec dir.

Texas Association of Broadcasters. 1907 N. Lamar, Suite 300, Austin, Tex. 78705. (512) 322-9944. (512) 322-0522. Ann Arnold, exec dir; J.R. Curtis Jr. (KFRO/KLSQ Longview), pres; Allan Howard (KHOU-TV Houston), VP; Vesta Brandt (KNUZ/KQUE FM Houston), sec; W.R. Buchanan (KSHN Liberty), treas; Jeff Rosser (KDFW-TV Dallas), chmn; Joe Jerkins (KVUE-TV Austin), past pres.

Directors: Roger Ashley, KTMD Houston; Bill Carter, KIDY-TV San Angelo; Larry Gunter, KYKS Lufkin; Jerry Hanszen, KGAS Carthage; John Hare, WBAP Ft. Worth; Bill Hill, WOAI AM San Antonio; Ken Lane, KVRP Haskell; Daniel Lesmeister, KCEN-TV Temple; Gregg Lindahl, KLRX Dallas; Tom Michalk, KBMT Beaumont; Richard Pearson, KTSM El Paso; Douglas Raab, KTXZ Austin; Craig Reinenger, KKYR-FM Texarkana; Brad Streit, KLTV-TV Tyler; Jane Wallace, KXAN-TV Austin; Tom Dee Whitehead, KTTX/KWHI Brenham; David Wrinkle, KBST AM/FM Big Springs; Tom Hooper, Steve Krant, assoc bd members; Augie Grant, Gerry Haskins, education bd members.

Utah Broadcasters Association. 1600 S. Main St., Suite 1600, Salt Lake City 84115. (801) 486-9521. FAX: (801) 484-7294. Dale Zabriskie, exec dir; Dana Horner, pres; Tom Anderson, VP.

Vermont Association of Broadcasters. 15 W. Patterson St., Barre, Vt. 05641. (802) 476-8789. FAX: (802) 479-5893. Alan H. Noyes, exec dir; Dennis Snyder, teas; David Kimel (WLFE), pres; Eric Michaels (WDEV), VP; Karen Marshall (WECF), sec.

Directors: Steve Puffer (WYKR), at large; Ken Jarvis (WCAX TV), past pres.

Virginia Association of Broadcasters. 620 Stage Coach Rd., Charlottesville, Va. 22902. (804) 977-3716. FAX: (804) 979-2439. Peter Easter C.A.E., exec dir.

Virginia Public Radio Association. c/o WVTF, 4235 Electric Rd. S.W., Roanoke, Va. 24014. (703) 857-8900. FAX: (703) 857-7578. Steve Mills, chmn.

Washington Area Broadcasters Association. c/o WJLA-TV, 3007 Tilden St. N.W., Washington 20008. (202) 364-7808. FAX: (202) 364-1943. Skip Finley (WKYS), chmn; Hank Yaggi (WUSA-TV), vice-chmn; Tom Herwitz (WTTG-TV), treas; Marion Thompson (WJLA-TV), exec sec.

Washington State Association of Broadcasters. 924 Capitol Way S., Suite 104, Olympia, Wash. 98501. (206) 705-0774. FAX: (206) 705-0873. Mark Allen, exec dir.

West Virginia Broadcasters Association. 2120 Weberwood Dr., S. Charleston, W. Va. 25303-3099. (304) 344-3798. FAX: (304) 345-3798. Marilyn Fletcher, exec dir; Larry Bevins (WVOW AM/FM Logan), pres; Don Ray (WSAZ-TV Huntington), VP; Jack W. Fritz II (WKYG/WXKX Parkersburg), sec/treas; Susan Adkins, exec asst; Leo MacCourtney (WOWK-TV Huntington), past pres.

Directors: Paul McNeill, WHIS/WHAJ Bluefield; Mike Smith, WDTV-TV Bridgeport; Harvey Kercheval, WAJR/WVAQ Morgantown; Ron Bishop, WDMX Vienna; Yogi Yoder, WEPM/WKMZ Martinsburg.

Wisconsin Broadcasters Association. 44 E. Mifflin St., Suite 900, Madison, Wis. 53703. (608) 255-2600; (800) 236-1922. FAX: (608) 256-3986. John M. Laabs, pres; Susan Knaack (WAPL/WHBY Appleton), chmn; David Sanks (WISC TV Madison), vice-chmn TV; Robert Dailey (WCLO/WJVL Janesville), vice-chmn radio; Martin Green (WAXX/WAYY Eau Claire), sec; Howard Ritchie (WISN TV Milwaukee), treas.

Directors: John Bartel, Bill Fyffe, Bruce Grassman, Chuck Roth, Steve Sinicropi, Tommy Lee Bychinski, Byron Knight, Dave Raven, Mike Schuch.

Wyoming Association of Broadcasters. 1807 Capitol Ave., Cheyenne, Wyo. 82003. (307) 632-7622. FAX: (307) 638-3469. Ray Lansing, exec dir/treas; Ray Mapel, pres; Jim Caroll, 1st VP; Bob Grammens, 2nd VP.

Directors: Faith Harris; Steve Lawrence; Kent Smith, Dave Lerner.

Cheyenne, Wyo. 82001: 1805 Capitol Ave., Suite 201.

State and Regional Cable Associations

Alabama Cable Television Association. Box 20683, Montgomery, Ala. 36120. (205) 834-2282. FAX: (205) 834-4908. Earl Hines, pres.; Don Richey, VP; Tommy Hill, sec/teas; Michael D'Ambra, past pres; Mary John Garret Martin, exec dir.

Alaska CATV Association. 5151 Fairbanks, Anchorage 99503. (907) 562-3455. FAX: (907) 561-4397. Gary Haynes, pres; Greg Stevens, VP.

Arizona Cable Television Association. 3610 N. 44th St., Suite 240, Phoenix 85018. (602) 955-4122. FAX: (602) 955-4505. Susan Bitter Smith, exec dir; Gregg Holmes, pres.

Arkansas Cable Television Association. Box 21061, Little Rock, Ark. 72221. (501) 221-1477. FAX: (501) 224-2282. Bob Blount, exec dir; Harold Sudbury, pres; Dwight Harlan, pres elect.

Cable Television Association of Maryland, Delaware & District of Columbia. 2530 Riva Rd. #316, Annapolis, Md. 21401. (410) 266-9111. FAX: (410) 266-6133. Wayne O'Dell, pres; Patricia A. Rodriguez, asst; J. Edward Davis Esq., legal counsel.
  Directors: Rich Angerman, chmn; Gary Massaglia, 1st vice chmn; John Eddy, 2nd vice chmn; Euan Fannell, treas; Jon Danielsen, sec; Steve Burch, past chmn.
  Directors-at-Large: Tony Peduto, Marian Phillips, Roger Wells, David Wilson.
  Associate Directors: Christine Appleby, Michael Ortman.

Cable Television Association of New York Inc. 126 State St., 3rd Fl., Albany, N.Y. 12207. (518) 463-6676. FAX: (518) 463-0574. Richard F. Alteri, pres; Robert Merrilees, chmn; Mary Beth Mooney, dir pub affrs.

Cable Television Operators of Oklahoma. 301 N. 63rd, Suite 400, Oklahoma City, Okla. 73116. (405) 843-8855. FAX: (405) 843-8934. James (Jim) E. Walker, exec dir & gen counsel; Jerald Stone, pres.

California Cable Television Association. Box 11080, Oakland, Calif. 94611. (510) 428-2225. FAX: (510) 428-0151. Spencer R. Kaitz, pres; Dennis Mangers, sr VP.
  Sacramento, Calif. 95814: 1121 L St., Suite 400. (916) 446-7732. FAX: (916) 446-1605.

Colorado Cable TV Association. 1600 Sherman, Suite 1110, Denver 80203. (303) 863-0084. FAX: (303) 863-0522. Stephen Durham, pres.
  Littleton, Colo. 80123: 7580 S. Pierce St., Suite 7. (303) 978-9838; (303) 979-8819; (303) 466-8990. FAX: (303) 972-9417. James Honiotos, pres.
  Englewood, Colo. 80112: 6859 S. Tucson Way. (303) 790-0386. FAX: (303) 790-4938. Stephen Dougherty, sec/treas.
  Denver, 80223: 1617 S. Acoma. (303) 778-2978, ext. 615. FAX: (303) 778-2912. Steven Kniffen, VP.

Florida Cable Television Association. Box 10383, Tallahassee, Fla. 32302. (904) 681-1990. FAX: (904) 681-9676. Steve Wilkerson, pres; Bob Brillante, VP; Rich Gunter, chmn.

Georgia Cable Television Association. 6175 Barfield Rd., Suite 220, Atlanta 30328. (404) 252-4371. FAX: (404) 252-0215. Nancy Horne, exec dir.

Hawaii Cable Television Association. 7 Waterfront Plaza, Suite 400, 500 Ala Mona Blvd., Honolulu 96813. (808) 526-0159. FAX: (808) 522-9490. Hardy Hutchinson, exec dir; Robert Trott, pres.

Idaho Cable Television Association. 1365 N. Orchard, Suite 268, Boise, Idaho 83706. (208) 376-7836. FAX: (208) 376-5814. JoAn Condie, exec dir; Sharon Becker, pres.
  Directors: Kevin Sharrai, Ed Aronson, Jim Uebelher, Vince Thompson. Joan Rickett, assoc member.

Illinois Cable Television Association. 2400 E. Devon, Suite 317, Des Plaines, Ill. 60018. (708) 297-4520. FAX: (708) 297-3865. Gary J. Maher, pres.

Indiana Cable Television Assoc. Inc. 300 N. Meridian, Suite 1800, Indianapolis 46204. (317) 237-3330. FAX: (317) 237-3337. Phillip E. Bainbridge, exec dir/gen counsel; Charles T. Hiltunen, III, dir opns & govt affrs; J. Satterfield, pres.

Iowa Cable TV Association. 1400 Dean Ave., Des Moines, Iowa 50316. (515) 266-5522. FAX: (515) 265-6480. Thomas P. Graves, exec VP.

Kansas CATV Association. Box 4006, Lawrence, Kan. 66046-1006. (913) 841-0073. FAX: (913) 841-4975. Linda Jurgensen, pres; Ron Marnell, exec sec/treas.

Kentucky CATV Association. Box 415, Burkesville, Ky. 42717. (502) 864-5352. FAX: (502) 864-3110. Patsy Judd, exec dir; Ed Mount, pres.

Louisiana Cable Television Association. 256 East Blvd., Baton Rouge 70802. (504) 387-5960. FAX: (504) 383-6705. Dr. C.P. "Tony" Currier, exec dir/state lobbyist; Dick Kirby, pres; Sam Holland, VP.

Michigan Cable TV Association. 615 W. Ionia St., Lansing, Mich. 48933. (517) 482-2622. FAX: (517) 482-1819. Colleen M. McNamara, exec dir; Tom Bjorklund, pres.

Mid-America Cable TV Association. Box 3306, Lawrence, Kan. 66046. (913) 841-9241. FAX: (913) 841-4975. Jim Perry, pres; Richard Hook, 1st VP; Vic Davis, sec/treas/counsel; Rob Marshall, exec dir.

Minnesota CATV Association. 450 N. Syndicate, Suite 185, St. Paul, Minn. 55104. (612) 641-0268. FAX: (612) 641-0319. Richard Sjoberg, pres; Michael C. Martin, exec dir.

Mississippi CATV Association. Box 726, Petal, Miss. 39465. (601) 582-3525. FAX: (601) 865-9476. Mildred E. Smith, exec dir; Ray Clemons, pres.

Missouri Cable Television Association. 705 N.W. 44th St., Kansas City, Mo. 64116. (816) 453-3392. FAX: (816) 453-6435. Charles Broomfield, exec dir.

Montana Cable Television Association. Box 5502, Helena, Mont. 59604. (406) 442-1060. FAX: (406) 443-5843. Joe Hoiland, pres; Steve Proper, VP; Tom Glendenning, sec/treas.

Nebraska Cable Communications Association. 5011 Capitol Ave., Omaha, Neb. 68132. (402) 551-8456. James D. Brown Jr., pres; Richard Bates, sec/treas; Mike Kohler, exec dir.

Nevada State CATV Association. Box 1802, Carson City, Nev. 89702. (702) 852-2253. FAX: (702) 852-2253. MANUAL. Deanna Lawrence, exec dir; Dick Fairbanks, pres; Brian Sullivan, VP; Bob Nelsen, sec/treas.

New England Cable TV Association Inc. 100 Grandview Rd., Suite 201, Braintree, Mass. 02184. (617) 843-3418. FAX: (617) 849-6267. Paul R. Cianelli, pres; Thomas K. Steel Jr., VP/gen counsel; William D. Durand, VP opns/legal counsel.

New Jersey Cable Television Association. 132 W. State St., Trenton, N.J. 08608. (609) 392-3223. FAX: (609) 394-8768. Nancy H. Becker, exec dir; Pat McCall, pres/chmn of bd.

New Mexico Cable Television Association. Box 2264, Santa Fe, N.M. 87504. (505) 983-5885. FAX: (505) 983-1169. Raymond W. Davenport, exec dir; Jim Howard, pres.

North Carolina CATV Association. Box 1151, Raleigh, N.C. 27602. (919) 821-4711. FAX: (919) 829-1583. Wade H. Hargrove, gen counsel; Randall Roden, counsel; Larry Ott, pres; Rob Bridges, VP; Jack Stanley, sec; Bill Hysell, treas; Bill Carey, past pres; Wade H. Hargrove, Ed Palumbo, Ruth Thompson, Barry Wilson, gen counsels; Gene Swithenbank, assoc rep; Randy Fraser, govt rels chmn.
  Directors: Adrian Cox, Tommy Edwards, Bob Melton.

North Central Cable Television Association. 450 N. Syndicate, Suite 185, Saint Paul, Minn. 55104. (612) 641-0268. FAX: (612) 641-0319. Michael C. Martin, exec dir.

North Dakota Cable Television Association. c/o Westmarc Cable, Box 130, Wahpeton, N.D. 58074. (701) 642-5355; (701) 223-4000. FAX: (701) 642-4816. Darcy Gjestvang, pres.

Ohio Cable Television Association. 50 W. Broad St., Suite 1118, Columbus, Ohio 43215. (614) 461-4014. FAX: (614) 461-9326. Carol A. Caruso, exec VP; James K. Anderson, pres.

Oregon Cable Television Association. 960 Liberty St. S.E., Suite 200, Salem, Ore. 97301. (503) 362-8838. FAX: (503) 399-1029. Michael W. Dewey, exec dir; Roger Harris, pres; Bob Smith, VP; Dave Stang, sec/treas. Board Members: Joe Bonica, Bryon Allen, Sandra Coleman, Teri Scott, Dave Young.

Pennsylvania Cable Television Association. 119 Pine St., Harrisburg, Pa. 17101. (717) 234-2190. FAX: (717) 234-1887. Joseph S. Gans III, chmn; Charles A. Morrow, vice chmn; Martin F. Brophy, treas; Susan C. Yee, sec; Gerard F. Boyle, immediate past chmn; Mary Fincham, Harold Etsell, Jr., Stanley H. Greene, Carol Rosebrough, T. Ronald Barckhoff, Ty Conner, Larry Kisslinger, Robert Lawrence, Ronald Podlesny, Jon Scott, Alane Sica; Stanley T. Singer, pres; William J. Cologie, dir communications.
  Directors: Mary Fincham, Harold Etsell, Jr., Stanley H. Greene, Carol Rosebrough, T. Ronald Barckhoff, Ty Conner, Larry Kisslinger, Robert Lawrence, Ronald Podlesny, Jon Scott, Alane Sica.

Rocky Mountain Cable Television Association. 121 S. Martin Luther King Blvd. Las Vegas 89106. (702) 384-8084. FAX: (702) 383-0614. Harris Bass, exec VP.

South Carolina Cable Television Association. 6175 Barfield Rd., Suite 220, Atlanta 30328. (404) 252-2454. FAX: (404) 252-0215. Nancy Horne, exec dir.

South Dakota Cable Television Association. Box 356, Pierre, S.D. 57501. (605) 229-1775. FAX: (605) 229-0478. Steve Holmvig, pres; Steve Shirber, VP; Doug Duba, sec/treas.

Southern Cable TV Association Inc. 6175 Barfield Rd., Suite 220, Atlanta 30328. (404) 255-1608. FAX: (404) 252-0215. C.W. Goodhall (Continental Cablevision), pres; Michael D'Ambra (ATC-Birmingham Division), VP; Dean Deyo (Memphis Cable TV), past pres.
  Directors: Richard Shows (Comcast of the Shoals, Florence, Ala.); Mike Wilson (Storer Cable Communications, Little Rock, Ark.); Joe Brewster (Cox Cable University City, Gainesville, Fla.); Harris L. Bagley (TriTek, Atlanta); Alan Reed (Union CATV, Sturgis, Ky.); Dick Kirby (Cablevision of Baton Rouge); Ray G. Clemons (Post-Newsweek Cable, Gulfport, Miss.); Bruce Mears (Multimedia, Rocky Mount, N.C.); Vic Nicholls (TeleCable of Greenville, S.C.); Gary Blount (Mid-South-Cable TV Inc., McKenzie, Tenn.); Frank Bowers (Cable Hampton Roads, Virginia Beach, Va.); Don Kersey (TeleScripps Cable Co., Bluefield, W.V.); Jim Hall Jr. (Showtime Networks Inc., Atlanta), assoc dir; Rick Jubeck (Trilogy Communications, Woodstock, Ga.), assoc dir; Alex Best (Cox Cable Communications, Atlanta), dir engrg; Nancy Horne (Southern Cable Television Association, Atlanta), exec dir.

Tennessee Cable TV Association. Stouffer Tower, 611 Commerce St., Suite 2706, Nashville 37203. (615) 256-7037. FAX: (615) 254-9710. Dan Walter, exec dir; Gordon Wilson, pres.

Texas Cable TV Association. Box 13518, Austin, Tex. 78711. (512) 474-2082. FAX: (512) 474-0966. W.D. Arnold, pres.

Utah Cable Television Association. 50 S. 600 East, Salt Lake City 84102. (801) 364-8759. FAX: (801) 364-0786. Randall Lee, chmn; Becky Ruley, vice chmn; David Spatafore, exec dir.

Virginia Cable Television Association. 300 W. Franklin St., Richmond, Va. 23220. (804) 780-1776. FAX: (804) 225-8036. Richard H. Carlton, exec dir; Donald A. Perry, pres; Charles G. Dopp, VP; Troy L. Fitzhugh, sec; Regina Craig Martin, treas.
  Directors: Franklin R. Bowers; William T. Day; Donald E. Deal; Ronald C. DeForrest; John D. Evans; H.W. Goodall; John P. Lewis (ex-officio); Thomas E. Waldrop; Mark Mayhook; Joseph L. Price. Associate Members: Pam K. Stewart, Mary Lou Swann.

Washington State Cable Communications Association. 4301 S. Pine St., Suite 446, Tacoma, Wash. 98409-7264. (206) 473-9697. FAX: (206) 473-9698. Bruce Frickleton CAE, exec dir; Fred Comer, pres; Jack Gradwohl, pres-elect; Diane Lachel, treas.
  Directors: Bill Lawson, Nancy Ervin, Jim Elliot, Tim Klinefelter, Ron Asplund.

West Virginia Cable Television Association. 10 Hale St., Charleston, W. Va. 25301. (304) 345-2917. FAX: (304) 342-1285. Mel Yapp, pres; Terry White, VP; Brenda McNutt, sec; Charlie Bradley, treas.
  Directors: Linda Arnold, exec dir; Beverly Midkiff, asst dir.

Wisconsin Cable Communications Association. 44 E. Mifflin St., No. 301, Madison, Wis. 53703. (608) 256-1683. FAX: (608) 256-6222. Tom Hanson, exec dir; Bob Guell, pres.

Wyoming CATV Association. Box 640, Laramie, Wyo. 82070-0640. (307) 672-5841. FAX: (307) 672-5844. Jim Wilhelm, pres; Randy Rediker, VP; Curtis Syme, sec/treas.

Union/Labor Groups

Asterisk (*) indicates organizations affiliated with Associated Actors & Artistes of America.

Actors' Equity Association (AEA).* (AFL-CIO.) 165 W. 46th St., New York 10036. (212) 869-8530. FAX: (212) 719-9815. Ron Silver, pres; Alan Eisenberg, exec sec.
 Los Angeles 90028: 6430 Sunset Blvd. (213) 462-2334. George Ives, western rgnl dir.
 San Francisco 94104: 235 Pine St. (415) 391-3838. Anne Sabastian.
 Chicago 60601: 203 N. Wabash Ave. (312) 641-0393. Fergus G. Currie, midwest rgnl dir.
 Orlando, Fla. 32821: 10369 Orangewood Blvd. (407) 345-8600. Richard Delahanty, dir.

Affiliated Property Craftsmen Local 44. (IATSE, AFL-CIO.) 11500 Burbank Blvd., North Hollywood, Calif. 91601. (818) 769-2500. FAX: (818) 769-1739.
 Philadelphia 19103: Local 1, 12 N. 21st St. (215) 564-1251. Mort Borrow, pres.

American Federation of Labor-Congress of Industrial Organizations. 815 16th St. N.W., Washington 20006. (202) 637-5020. FAX: (202) 637-5058. Lane Kirkland, pres; Thomas R. Donahue, sec/treas; Rex Hardesty, info dir.

American Federation of Musicians, United States & Canada. 1501 Broadway, Suite 600, New York 10036. (212) 869-1330; FAX: (212) 764-6134. Mark Tully Massagli, pres; Stephen R. Sprague, sec/treas; Ray Petch, VP Canada; Steve Young, VP.
 Don Mills, Ont., Canada M3C 2E9: 75 The Donway W., Suite 1010. (416) 391-5161; Ray Petch, VP.

American Federation of Television & Radio Artists (AFTRA).* (AFL-CIO.) 260 Madison Ave., New York 10016. (212) 532-0800. FAX: (212) 532-2242; (212) 545-1238 (N.Y. loc). Shelby Scott, natl pres; Stephen Burrow, N.Y exec dir; Mike Baker, N.Y. loc pres.
 Los Angeles 90028: 6922 Hollywood Blvd. (213) 461-8111. Mark Alan Farber, exec dir.
 Chicago 60601: 75 E. Wacker St, 14th Fl. (312) 372-8081. Paul Wagner, exec dir.

American Guild of Musical Artists.* 1727 Broadway, New York 10019. (212) 265-3687. Regina Resnik, pres; Louise K. Gilmore, natl exec sec.
 Branch offices in Los Angeles, Chicago, San Francisco, New Orleans, Seattle, Dallas, Washington, Boston, Philadelphia & Toronto.

American Guild of Variety Artists. (AFL-CIO.) 184 Fifth Ave., New York 10010. (212) 675-1003. Rod McKuen, exec pres; Eileen Collins, exec VP; Frances Gaar, exec sec/treas.
 Chalmette, La. 70044: Box 54, 1936 Seelos Ct. (504) 277-4112. Tina Marie, rgnl VP.
 Los Angeles 91607: 4741 Laurel Canyon Blvd. (819) 508-9984.

Associated Actors & Artistes of America.* (AFL-CIO.) 165 W. 46th St., New York 10036. (212) 869-0358. FAX: (212) 869-1746. Theodore Bikel, pres; Alan Eisenberg, exec sec; John H. Sucke, treas.

Broadcast-Television Recording Engineers Local 45. 6255 Sunset Blvd., Suite 721, Hollywood, Calif. 90028. (213) 851-5515. FAX: (213) 466-1793. James Jackson, business mgr/financial sec; Charles Guzzi, pres.

Cinema Lodge 1185, International Association of Machinists (IAM). (AFL-CIO.) 21414 S. Loma Dr., Los Angeles 90026. (213) 483-6630. FAX: (213) 413-8534. Max Chavez, pres.

Communications Workers of America (CWA). (AFL-CIO.) 501 3rd St. N.W., Washington 20001-2797. (202) 434-1100. FAX: (202) 434-1279. Jeff Miller, dir internal communications.

Directors Guild of America Inc. (DGA). 7920 Sunset Blvd., Los Angeles 90046. (310) 289-2000. FAX: (310) 289-2029. Glenn Gumpel, exec dir; Gene Reynolds, pres; Sheldon Leonard, sec/treas.
 New York 10019: 110 W. 57th Fl. (212) 581-0370. Alan Gordon, eastern exec sec.

Illustrators & Matte Artists Local 790. (IATSE.) 13949 Ventura Blvd., Suite 301, Sherman Oaks, Calif. 91423. (818) 784-6555. Joseph Musso, pres; Thomas Cranham, VP; Camille Abbott, sec/treas; Marjo Bernay, bus rep.

International Alliance of Theatrical Stage Employees & Moving Picture Machine Operators of the United States & Canada. (IATSE.) 1515 Broadway, Suite 601, New York 10036. (212) 730-1770. FAX: (212) 921-7699. Alfred W. Ditolla, pres; Thomas C. Short, gen sec/treas.
 Sherman Oaks, Calif. 91423: 13949 Ventura Blvd., Suite 300. (818) 905-8999. FAX: (818) 905-6297. Harry J. Floyd, asst to pres.

International Brotherhood of Electrical Workers (IBEW). (AFL-CIO.) 1125 15th St. N.W., Washington 20005. (202) 833-7000. FAX: (202) 467-6316. J.J. Barry, international pres; Jack F. Moore, international sec; Reginald Gilliam, dir bcst & recording dept.
 St. Louis 63104: Local 4, 1547 S. Broadway, (314) 647-2288. Michael Pendergast, business mgr.
 North Hollywood, Calif. 91601: Local 40, 5643 Vineland Ave. (818) 762-4379. Tim Dixon, business mgr.
 Hollywood, Calif. 90028: Local 45, 6255 Sunset Blvd., Suite 721. (213) 851-5515. James E. Jackson.
 Daly City, Calif. 94015: Local 202, 333 Gellert Blvd., Suite 116. (415) 755-9400. F. DuCharme, business mgr.
 Upper Marlboro, Md. 20772: Local 1200, 9660 Marlboro Pike. (301) 868-2703. Lillian Firmani, business mgr.
 New York 10036: Local 1212, 230 W. 41st St. (212) 354-6770. Michael G. Deleso, business mgr.
 Chicago 60631: Local 1220, 8619 W. Bryn Mawr, Suite 6. (312) 693-0001. Jessica Logan.
 Newton Highlands, Mass. 02161: Local 1228 (Boston), 1194 Walnut St. (617) 964-4450. Kenneth Flanagan, business mgr.

International Photographers Guild of the Motion Pictures and Television Industries. 7715 Sunset Blvd., Suite 300, Los Angeles 90046. (213) 876-0160. FAX: (213) 876-6383. George Spiro Dibie, pres; Bruce C. Doering, George J. Toscas, business reps.

International Sound Technicians, Cinetechnicians, Television Engineers, Studio Projectionists and Video Projection Technicians Local 695. (IATSE, MPMO.) 5439 Cahuenga Way, N. Hollywood, Calif. 91601. (818) 985-9204; (213) 877-1052. FAX: (818) 760-4681. Frank H. Meadows, business rep/exec dir.

International Union of Electronic, AFL-CIO. (AFL-CIO.) 1126 16th St. N.W., Washington 20036. (202) 296-1200. FAX: (202) 785-4563. William H. Bywater, pres; Edward Fire, sec/treas.
 Jenkintown, Pa. 19046: 100 Old York Rd. (215) 886-9860. Michael Giardino, district pres.
 Saugus, Mass. 01906: 335 Central St. (617) 233-4807. Robert Scott, district pres.
 East Rutherford, N.J. 07073: 355 Murray Hill Pkwy. (201) 933-9494. Sal Ingrassia, district pres.
 Little Rock, Ark. 72209: 8803 Oman Rd. (501) 565-3488. George Clark, district pres.
 Dayton, Ohio 45439: 3461 Office Park Dr. (513) 294-1491. Michael Bindas, district pres.
 Fort Wayne, Ind. 46825: 9006 Coldwater Rd. (219) 489-7092. Thomas Rebman, district pres.

Labor Institute of Public Affairs. (AFL-CIO.) 815 16th St. N.W., Suite 206, Washington 20006. (202) 637-5334. FAX: (202) 637-5058. Bill Wagner, exec dir; Bob Trussell, prod dir.

Laboratory Film/Video Technicians Local 683. (IATSE, AFL.) Box 7429, Burbank, Calif. 91510-7429. (818) 955-9720. FAX: (818) 955-5834. James E. Choice, pres; Brian Ralph, business rep; David R. Tucker, sec/treas.

Make-Up Artist & Hairstylists Local 706. (IATSE, AFL-CIO.) 11519 Chandler Blvd., North Hollywood, Calif. 91601. (818) 984-1700. Howard J. Smit, business rep.

Motion Picture Costumers Local 705. (IATSE, AFL-CIO.) 1427 N. La Brea Ave., Hollywood, Calif. 90028. (213) 851-0220. FAX: (213) 851-9062. Robert Ellsworth, business rep; Sandra Berke Jordan, sec/treas; Mort Schwartz, pres.

Motion Picture Editors Guild. (IATSE, AFL-CIO.) 7715 W. Sunset Blvd., Hollywood, Calif. 90046. (213) 876-4770. FAX: (213) 876-0861 Ronald G. Kutak, exec dir.

Motion Picture Screen Cartoonists Local 839. (IATSE, AFL-CIO.) 4729 Lankershim Blvd., North Hollywood, Calif. 91602. (818) 766-7151. FAX: (818) 506-4805. Karen Storr, pres; Steve Hulett, business rep.

Motion Picture Set Painters & Sign-writers Local 729. (IATSE). 11365 Ventura Blvd., Suite 202, Studio City, Calif. 91604. (818) 984-3000. FAX: (213) 877-0671. Carmine A. Palazzo, business rep/sec/treas.

Motion Picture Studio Electrical Technicians Local 728. (IATSE, MPMO, AFL-CIO.) 14629 Nordhoff St., Panorama City, Calif. 91402. (213) 851-3300. FAX: (818) 891-5288. Dean Bray, business rep; Ron Cickle, treas.

Motion Picture Studio Grips Local 80. (IATSE, AFL-CIO.) 6926 Melrose Ave., Los Angeles 90038. (213) 931-1419. FAX: (213) 931-6014. Fred Albrecht, pres; Tom Davis, VP; Jim Buck, business rep; Patrik Hoff, sec/treas.

Musicians' Union Local 47. (AFM, AFL-CIO.) 817 N. Vine St., Hollywood, Calif. 90038-3779. (213) 462-2161. FAX: (213) 461-5260. Bill Peterson, pres; Richard Totusek, VP; Serena Kay Williams, sec; Chase Craig, treas.

National Association of Broadcast Employees & Technicians. (AFL-CIO, NABET.) 7101 Wisconsin Ave., Suite 800, Bethesda, Md. 20814. (301) 657-8420. FAX: (301) 657-9478. James P. Nolan, international pres; John S. Clark III, international VP; William Bryan, international sec/treas.
 New York 10106: Local 11, 888 7th Ave., Suite 4511. (212) 757-3065. John S. Clark, international VP.
 Burbank, Calif. 91506: Local 53, 1918 W. Burbank Blvd. (818) 846-0490. Richard T. Smith, pres.
 Chicago 60604: 224 S. Michigan Ave., Suite 330. William J. Bryan, international sec/treas.

The Newspaper Guild. (AFL-CIO, CLC.) 8611 2nd Ave., Silver Spring, Md. 20910. (301) 585-2990. FAX: (301) 585-0668. Charles Dale, pres, Linda Foley, sec/treas.
 Nepean, Ont., Canada K2E 7V7: 30 Concourse Gate, Unit 103. (613) 727-0990. John Bryant, Canadian dir.

Office & Professional Employees International Union Local 174 (OPEIU). (AFL-CIO.) 120 S. Victory Blvd., #201, Burbank, Calif. 91502-2801. (818) 842-5572. Jan Bilson, pres; Linda Contraris, sec; Jay Lester, business rep.

Scenic & Title Artists Local 816. (IATSE.) 13949 Ventura Blvd., Suite 308, Sherman Oaks, Calif. 91423. (818) 906-7822.

Screen Actors Guild. (AFL-CIO.) 5757 Wilshire Blvd., Los Angeles Calif. 90036. (213) 549-6400. FAX: (213) 549-6603. Ken Orsatti, natl exec dir; Gerald Wilson, controller; Mark Locher, natl dir communications.
 Phoenix 85016: 1616 E. Indian School Rd., Suite 330. (602) 265-2712.
 Atlanta 30305: 455 E. Paces Ferry Rd. N.E., Suite 334. (404) 239-0131.
 Boston 02108: 11 Beacon St., Suite 512. (617) 742-2688.
 Cleveland 44115: (AFTRA) Caretaker, 1030 Eulid Ave., Suite 429. (216) 579-9305.
 Houston 77057: 2650 Fountainview, Suite 326. (713) 972-1806.
 New York 10036: 1515 Broadway, 44th Fl. (212) 944-1030. FAX: (212) 944-6774.
 Chicago 60601: 75 E. Wacker Dr., 14th Fl. (312) 372-8081.
 Miami, Fla. 33156: 7300 N. Kendall Dr., Suite 620. (305) 670-7677. FAX: (305) 670-1813.
 Kissimmee, Fla. 34741: 3393 W. Vine St., Orlando (407) 239-7720. FAX (407) 847-5833.
 Denver 80222: 950 S. Cherry St., Suite 502. (303) 757-6226.
 Dallas 75206: 6060 N. Central Expwy. (214) 363-8300.
 Honolulu 96814: 949 Kapiolani Blvd., Suite 105. (808) 538-6122.
 San Diego 92111: 7827 Convoy Ct., Suite 400. (619) 278-7695.
 Minneapolis 55401: (AFTRA) Caretaker, 708 N. 1st St., Suite 343A. (612) 371-9120.
 Nashville 37212: Box 121087. (615) 327-2958.
 Philadelphia 19102: 230 S. Broad St., 10th Fl. (215) 545-3150.
 St. Louis, 63101: 906 Olive St., Suite 1006. (314) 231-8410.
 San Francisco 94104: 235 Pine St., 11th Fl. (415) 391-7510.
 Seattle 98109: (AFTRA) Caretaker, 601 Valley St., Suite 200. (206) 282-2506.

Union/Labor Groups

Chevy Chase, Md. 20815: 5480 Wisconsin Ave., Suite 201. (301) 657-2560. Washington office.
Lathrup Village, Mich. 48076: 28690 Southfield Rd., Suite 290 A&B. (313) 559-9540.

Script Supervisors Local 871. (IATSE.) 7061 B. Hayvenhurst Ave., Van Nuys, Calif. 91406. (818) 782-7063. FAX: (818) 782-5483. Casandra Barrere, pres; John L. Coffey, business rep.

Service Employees International Union. Box 17916, 1247 W. 7th St., Los Angeles 90017. (213) 680-9567. FAX: (213) 488-0328. Jim Zellers, pres.

Set Designers & Model Makers Local 847. (IATSE.) 13949 Ventura Blvd., Suite 301, Sherman Oaks, Calif. 91423. (818) 784-6555. Cate Bangs, pres; Bill Newmon, VP; Susan Feller-Otto, sec/treas; Marjo Bernay, business rep.

Society of Motion Picture & Television Art Directors Local 876. 11365 Ventura Blvd., Suite 315, Studio City, Calif. 91604. (818) 762-9995. Gene Allen, exec dir.

Story Analysts Local 854. (IATSE, AFL-CIO.) 13949 Ventura Blvd., Suite 301, Sherman Oaks, Calif. 91423. (818) 784-6555. Walter Hanley Jr., pres; Christopher E. Vogler, VP; Don Leonard, sec/treas; Marjo Bernay, business rep.

United Electrical, Radio & Machine Workers of America. 2400 Oliver Bldg., 535 Smithfield St., Pittsburgh 15222. (412) 471-8919. (412) 471-8999. John H. Hovis, gen pres; Amy R. Newell, gen sec/treas; Robert B. Kingsley, dir organization.

United Scenic Artists Local 829. (Art Directors/Scenic Designers/Costume Designers/Scenic Artists.) 16 W. 61st St., 11th Fl., New York 10023. (212) 581-0300. FAX: (212) 977-2011. Domingo Rodreguez, pres.
Chicago 60603: 176 W. Adams St. (312) 857-0829. John Derdall, rgnl business rep.
Los Angeles 90036: 5410 Wilshire Blvd., Suite 407. (213) 965-0957. Charles Berliner, rgnl business rep.

Writers Guild of America East Inc. (WGAE). 555 W. 57th St., New York 10019. (212) 767-7800. FAX: (212) 582-1909. Herb Sargent, pres; Mona Mangan, exec dir.

Writers Guild of America West Inc. (WGAW). 8955 Beverly Blvd., West Hollywood, Calif. 90048. (310) 550-1000. FAX: (310) 550-8185. Frank Pierson, pres; Carl Gottliev, VP; John Wells, sec/treas; Brian Walton, exec dir.

Trade Shows Alphabetical Index

Annual Country Radio Seminar (Public/Trade), see Radio, TV and Cable.

Armed Forces Communications and Electronics Association (AFCEA) International Convention and Exposition, see Communications.

Association for Multi-Image International Inc. Exposition (Public/Trade), see Radio, TV and Cable.

Atlantic Cable Show, see Radio, TV and Cable.

Audio Engineering Society Convention (Public/Trade), see Engineering.

BroadcastAsia94, See Radio, TV and Cable.

Broadcast Financial Management Associates, see Radio, TV and Cable.

Broadcast Promotion and Marketing Executives and Broadcast Designers Associations Conference and Exposition, see Advertising and Marketing.

CABLEXPO, see Radio, TV and Cable.

Cable '94, see Radio, TV and Cable.

Cable and Satellite '94, see Radio, TV and Cable.

Cable-Tec Expo, see Radio, TV and Cable.

Cable Television Advertising Bureau Inc. Cable Advertising Conference (Public/Trade), see Advertising and Marketing.

Canadian Association of Broadcasters Convention (Public/Trade), see Radio, TV and Cable.

Eastern Cable Television Trade Show, see Radio, TV and Cable.

Great Lakes Cable Expo, see Radio, TV and Cable.

High Frequency Power Conversion (Public/Trade), see Radio, TV and Cable.

HomeMedia, see Radio, TV and Cable.

INFOCOMM-International, see Communications.

ITS Annual Forum, see Communications.

Image World, see Communications.

Image World International, see Communications.

International Wireless Communications Expo/Fall, see Communications.

International Wireless Communications Expo/Spring, see Communications.

Interwire, see Communications.

KBA Fall Convention, see Radio, TV and Cable.

Low Power Communication Television, see Radio, TV and Cable.

Multimedia '94 (Public/Trade), see Communications.

National Association of Broadcasters Annual Convention and International Exposition, see Radio, TV, Cable.

National Association of Television Program Executives Annual Program Conference, see Radio, TV and Cable.

National Cable Television Association Annual Convention and Exposition, see Radio, TV and Cable.

National Conference of College Broadcasters, see Radio, TV and Cable.

National Religious Broadcasters Media Exposition (Public/Trade), see Radio, TV and Cable.

New Media Expo, see Communications.

News/Tech '94, see Radio, TV and Cable.

Public Relations Society of America, see Advertising and Marketing.

RAB '94 Managing Sales Conference, see Radio, TV and Cable.

Radio Management, Programming, Sales and Engineering Convention/Exposition, see Radio, TV and Cable.

SBCA Satellite Show, see Communications.

Satellite Communications Users Conference, see Communications.

ShowBiz Expo, see Radio, TV and Cable.

Society of Motion Picture and Television Engineers Annual Technical Conference and Equipment Exhibition (Public/Trade), see Engineering.

TeleCon XII (Public/Trade), see Communications.

The Texas Show, see Radio, TV and Cable.

Video Software Dealers Association Convention, see Communications.

VISCOMM (Visual Communications Expo), see Communications.

WCA '94, see Radio, TV and Cable.

The 1994 Western Show, see Radio, TV and Cable.

Trade Shows by Category

Advertising and Marketing

Broadcast Promotion and Marketing Executives and Broadcast Designers Associations Conference and Exposition. SHOW MANAGEMENT: NATPE, 2425 W. Olympic Blvd., Suite 550 E., Santa Monica, Calif. 90404. Contact: Nick Orfanapoulos. (310) 453-4440. FAX: (310) 453-5258. SHOW SPONSOR: BPME and BDA, 6255 Sunset Blvd., Suite 624, Los Angeles 90028. Contact: Gregg Balko. (213) 465-3777. SHOW MANAGEMENT STATEMENT: To bring broadcast promoters and designers in the electronic media together in one show. DATE AND LOCATION: 1994—June 8-11, Ernest N. Morial Convention Center, New Orleans. PROFILE OF EXHIBITORS: Music video production; computer animation and graphics hardware; station design and image packages; advertising premiums and incentives. PROFILE OF ATTENDEES: BPME—Serves those individuals responsible for the marketing, advertising, promotion and publicizing of television stations, networks, production companies, radio stations and cable systems on a national level. BDA—Consists of an international membership of art directors, designers and graphic artists. SHOW HISTORY: Last Show: 1993—June 13-16, Walt Disney World Dolphin Hotel, Orlando, Fla.

Cable Television Advertising Bureau Inc. Cable Advertising Conference (Public/Trade). SHOW MANAGEMENT: Cable Television Advertising Bureau Inc., 757 3rd Ave., New York 10017. Contact: Vincent J. Fazio. (212) 751-7770. FAX: (212) 832-3268. SHOW SPONSOR: Same as show management. SHOW MANAGEMENT STATEMENT: The Cable Television Advertising Bureau's Cable Advertising Conference provides a forum for key issues in the realm of cable advertising. DATE AND LOCATION: 1994—Apr. 10-12, Marriott Marquis Hotel, New York. (Show held in same city every year.) PROFILE OF EXHIBITORS: Cable programming services and hardware/software suppliers. PROFILE OF ATTENDEES: Cable-system operators, network personnel, advertising executives, agencies and corporate clients. SHOW HISTORY: First Year of Show: 1982. Last Show: 1993—Apr. 18-20, Marriott Marquis Hotel, New York.

Public Relations Society of America. SHOW MANAGEMENT: Public Relations Society of America, 33 Irving Pl., New York 10003. Contact: Cathy Tulloch. (212) 995-2230. FAX: (212) 995-0757. SHOW SPONSOR: Same as show management. SHOW MANAGEMENT STATEMENT: Updates latest technology and techniques of public relations. DATE AND LOCATION: 1994—Nov. 13-16, Baltimore Convention Center, Baltimore. PROFILE OF EXHIBITORS: Suppliers of goods and services to the public relations industry, such as software, hardware and clipping services. PROFILE OF ATTENDEES: Public relations practitioners. SHOW HISTORY: Annual. First Year of Show: 1948. Last Show: 1992—Oct. 25-28, Hyatt Regency Crown Center and Westin Crown Center Hotel, Kansas City, Mo.

Communications

Armed Forces Communications and Electronics Association (AFCEA)/U.S. Naval Institute Western Conference & Exposition. SHOW MANAGEMENT: Spargo (J.) and Associates, 4400 Fair Lakes Ct., Fairfax, Va. 22033. Contact: Beth Cain. (703) 631-6200. FAX: (703) 818-9177. TELEX/TWX: 901-114. SHOW SPONSOR: Armed Forces Communications and Electronics Association (AFCEA), 4400 Fair Lakes Ct., Fairfax, Va. 22033. Contact: Beth Cain. (703) 631-6200. TELEX/TWX: 901114 AFCEA. SHOW MANAGEMENT STATEMENT: The International Convention and Exposition is produced to maintain and improve the technical cooperation and understanding between the government, armed forces and industry in the planning, design, procurement, production, maintenance and operation of communications, electronics, computer science, command, control and imagery equipment. Exhibitors are limited to firms, organizations and agencies whose exhibits are in harmony with the purpose of the AFCEA Technical Exposition. DATES AND LOCATION: 1995—Feb. 18-20; 1996—Feb. 14-16. San Diego Convention Center, San Diego. (Show held in same city every year.) PROFILE OF EXHIBITORS: Over 300 product categories, including antennas, avionics, communications components/systems, computers, fiber optics, graphics, HF radio, microwave, power supplies, radar, satellites, software, telecommunications, tempest, word processors. PROFILE OF ATTENDEES: Persons who engineer, procure, manage, operate and maintain communications, computer, and command and control equipment, systems and services. Includes career officers and managers from throughout government and industry. Attendees from more than 50 nations. SHOW HISTORY: Held annually in June. First Year of Show: 1946. Last Show: 1993—June 6-8, San Diego Convention Center, San Diego.

INFOCOMM-International. SHOW MANAGEMENT: International Communications Industries Association, 3150 Spring St., Fairfax, Va. 22031-2399. Contact: Terence M. Bolls. (703) 273-7200. FAX: (703) 278-8082. SHOW SPONSOR: International Communications Industries Association. SHOW MANAGEMENT STATEMENT: The Exposition of the video, computer, A/V, presentation and multimedia communications industry. DATE AND LOCATION: 1995—June 15-17, Dallas Convention Center, Dallas. PROFILE OF EXHIBITORS: Manufacturers of video, computer and audio-visual based communications and information products; producers of software programs for all technologies represented. PROFILE OF ATTENDEES: Dealers who sell video, computer graphics, presentation systems and installations to professional users of these media; production and postproduction companies, advertising and public relations agencies, laboratories and other users of video and related technologies; corporate, government and military executives who depend on effective presentations to communicate and train successfully; educators who use communications technology in the classroom, media center, lab and library. SHOW HISTORY: Formerly called the National Audio-Visual Convention and Exhibit; held annually; different location each year; frequently-used cities include Anaheim, Atlanta, Dallas, Las Vegas and New Orleans. First Year of Show: 1983. Last Show: 1993—Jan. 14-16, Ernest N. Morial Convention Center, New Orleans.

ITS Annual Forum. SHOW MANAGEMENT: Flagg Management Inc., Box 4440, New York 10163. Contact: Russell E. Flagg. (212) 286-0333. FAX: (212) 286-0086. SHOW SPONSOR: Same as show management. DATES AND LOCATIONS: 1994—July; 1995—July. Sites to be announced. PROFILE OF EXHIBITORS: Suppliers of film/video and sound equipment, systems and services. Specialization in postproduction systems, such as electronic paint boxes to enhance images, and electronic systems to enhance sound. PROFILE OF ATTENDEES: Production and postproduction facilities, broadcasting, AV departments of corporations, and international film/video and sound production operations. General managers, principals, and their key staff who operate and produce. SHOW HISTORY: Inaugurated in 1988, this forum has developed into the postproduction event for management buying and using postproduction equipment and systems. First Year of Show: 1988.

Image World. SHOW MANAGEMENT: Knowledge Industry Publications, 701 Westchester Ave., White Plains, N.Y. 10604. Contact: Benita Roumanis. (914) 328-9157. FAX: (914) 328-9093. SHOW SPONSOR: Same as show management. SHOW MANAGEMENT STATEMENT: Image World, featuring video expo and the CAMMP-computer animation, graphics, multimedia and presentations, provides industry professionals with the opportunity to see, test and compare equipment and services and also to enroll in a comprehensive seminar program covering a wide array of topics. Seminars fall into four categories: Interactive Multimedia, Creative Video, Desktop Graphics and Design, and Desktop Video. DATE AND LOCATION: 1994—Sept. 19-24, Jacob K. Javits Convention Center of New York, New York. SHOW HISTORY: Formerly called Video Expo, Image World is held in 4-5 cities across the country every year.

Image World International. SHOW MANAGEMENT: Knowledge Industry Publications, 701 Westchester Ave., White Plains, N.Y. 10604. Contact: Benita Roumanis. (914) 328-9157. FAX: (914) 328-9093. SHOW SPONSOR: Same as show management. SHOW MANAGEMENT STATEMENT: This is a seminar program and exposition for video users in business, industry, education, government, medicine, broadcast or cable TV, and nonprofit organizations. DATE AND LOCATION: 1994—Dec. 7-9, site to be announced. PROFILE OF EXHIBITORS: Manufacturers and distributors of video production equipment and suppliers of video production services. PROFILE OF ATTENDEES: Video users in business, industry, education, government, medicine, broadcast or cable TV, and nonprofit organizations. SHOW HISTORY: First Year of Show: 1985.

International Wireless Communications Expo/Fall. SHOW MANAGEMENT: Cardiff Publishing Co., 6300 S. Syracuse Way, Suite 650, Englewood, Colo. 80111. Contact: April DeBaker. (303) 220-0600. FAX: (303) 770-0253. SHOW SPONSOR: Communications Magazine and Marketing Magazine, 6300 S. Syracuse Way, Suite 650, Englewood, Colo. 80111. SHOW MANAGEMENT STATEMENT: The exposition is geared towards the information needs of the mobile communications professional. The event showcases the newest innovative technology available in the communications industry. Products on display will include mobile/portable radios and phones, cellular systems and services, mobile data, paging equipment, antennas, test equipment, tone signaling/control equipment, tower systems and products, auxiliary equipment, and special services. DATE AND LOCATION: 1994—Oct. 19-21, Tampa Convention Center, Tampa, Fla. PROFILE OF EXHIBITORS: Manufacturers and service organizations within the land mobile radio specialties of cellular technology, paging, mobile/portable radios, antennas and accessories, test equipment, and more. PROFILE OF ATTENDEES: Owners and officers from land mobile radio dealerships, RCCs and cellular system operators. Participation from the Caribbean and South America. SHOW HISTORY: Formerly known as Land Mobile Expo East. Held annually in the fall. First Year of Show: 1982. Last Show: 1993—Sept. 21-23, Pennsylvania Convention Center, Philadelphia.

International Wireless Communications Expo/Spring. SHOW MANAGEMENT: Cardiff Publishing Co., 6300 S. Syracuse Way, Suite 650, Englewood, Colo. 80111. Contact: April DeBaker. (303) 220-0600. FAX: (303) 770-0253. SHOW SPONSOR: Communications Magazine and Marketing Magazine, 6300 S. Syracuse Way, Suite 650, Englewood, Colo. 80111. DATES AND LOCATIONS: 1994—Apr. 13-15, Las Vegas Convention Center, Las Vegas; 1995—Apr. 25-27, Sands Exposition and Convention Center, Las Vegas; 1996—Apr. 30-May 2, Sands Exposition and Convention Center, Las Vegas; 1997—Apr. 2-4, Sands Exposition and Convention Center, Las Vegas; 1998—Apr. 20-22, Sands Exposition and Convention Center, Las Vegas. SHOW HISTORY: Formerly known as National Land Mobile Expo. Held annually in the spring in rotating western cities. First Year of Show: 1977. Last Show: 1993—Mar. 23-25, Anaheim Convention Center, Anaheim, Calif.

Interwire. SHOW MANAGEMENT: Wire Association International, Box H, Guilford, Conn. 06437. Contact: S.M. Pascarelle. (203) 453-2777. FAX: (203) 453-8384. SHOW SPONSOR: Same as show management. SHOW MANAGEMENT STATEMENT: Interwire show provides a marketplace for the wire and cable industry. It is a trade show for wire manufacturers, fabricators, suppliers, and other buyers and users with administrative, engineering, technical and purchasing personnel in attendance from the United States, Europe and Asia. Product classifications include wire machinery, spring machinery, fasteners and fabricators, fiber optics, chemicals and coatings, accessories, and other wire-related products. DATES AND LOCATIONS: 1994—June 5-9, Ontario Exhibit Hall/Westin Hotel, Detroit; 1995—Mar. 25-31, Georgia World Congress Center, Atlanta. SHOW HISTORY: First Year of Show: 1981.

Multimedia '94 (Public/Trade). SHOW MANAGEMENT: Multimedia Trade Shows, Inc., 70 Villarboit Crescent, Unit 7, Concord, Ont., Canada L4K 4C7. Contact: Jai Cole. (416) 324-3233; (416) 660-2491. FAX: (416) 660-2492. SHOW MANAGEMENT STATEMENT: The show provides an annual marketplace for equipment, supplies and services for creative professionals, including photographers, illustrators, film and video producers, directors and technicians, art directors, computer designers and graphic designers in Canada. Multimedia '94 incorporates VICOM, the electronic design show and showcase on production. DATE AND LOCATION: 1994—May 26-28, Toronto. (Show held in same city every year.) PROFILE OF EXHIBITORS: Computers, software, monitors, CD Rom, video projection systems, color pre-press, training and education centers; presentation media, laser disk, electronic imaging, photography, film and video. PROFILE OF ATTENDEES: Photographers, illustrators, videographers, art directors, computer graphic designers, graphic designers, executive officers, owners. Most attendees are from central Canada with a representation from coast to coast. SHOW HISTORY: Annual. First Year of Show: 1985.

New Media Expo. SHOW MANAGEMENT: The Interface Group, 300 1st Ave., Needham, Mass. 02194. Contact: Richard L. Schweb. (617) 449-6600. FAX: (617) 449-6953. SHOW SPONSOR: Same as show management. DATE AND LOCATION: 1994—Apr.12-14, Los Angeles Convention and Exhibition Center, Los Angeles. (Show held in same city every year.) PROFILE OF EXHIBITORS: Manufacturers and distributors of hardware, software, communications technology, consumer electronics and information products. PROFILE OF ATTENDEES: Corporate executives, marketing specialists, program and software developers, communications executives, distribution specialists, publishers, advertising and media executives. SHOW HISTORY: First Year of Show: 1994.

SBCA Satellite Show. SHOW MANAGEMENT: Satellite Broadcasting Communications Association, 225 Reinekers Ln., Alexandria, Va. 22314. Contact: Laurie McCall. (703) 549-6990. FAX: (312) 782-3617. SHOW SPONSOR: Same as show management. SHOW MANAGEMENT STATEMENT: The show is held to display satellite reception equipment and programming services and to provide educational seminars on various industry topics. DATE AND LOCATION: 1994—Aug. 4-6, Orange County Convention Center, Orlando, Fla. PROFILE OF EXHIBITORS: Satellite equipment manufacturers and software and program providers. PROFILE OF ATTENDEES: Satellite equipment retailers and distributors. SHOW HISTORY: Held twice a year. First Year of Show: 1982. Last Show: 1992—Aug. 6-8, Baltimore Convention Center, Baltimore.

Satellite Communications Users Conference. SHOW MANAGEMENT: Cardiff Publishing Co., 6300 S. Syracuse Way, Suite 650, Englewood, Colo. 80111. Contact: Barb Binge. (303) 220-0600. FAX: (303) 770-0253. SHOW SPONSOR: Satellite Communications Magazine, 6300 S. Syracuse Way, Suite 650, Englewood, Colo. 80111. SHOW MANAGEMENT STATISTICS: The conference is designed to provide a showcase for a range of products used in private satellite networks, including data transmission, teleconferencing, and video conferencing. Equipment displayed is also pertinent to broadcasters and cable systems. An extensive conference schedule is dedicated to regulatory concerns, new technologies and applications, and competitive forces in the industry. DATES AND LOCATIONS: 1994—Sept. 19-21, Sheraton, Washington; 1995—Sept. 20-22. San Jose McEneny Convention Center, San Jose, Calif. PROFILE OF EXHIBITORS: Manufacturers of earth-station hardware and satellite hardware, suppliers of satellite services and corporate communications services. PROFILE OF ATTENDEES: Corporate officers, communications department managers and engineers from Fortune 1000 firms using satellite communications extensively in operation. National and international draw. SHOW HISTORY: Held annually in the fall with rotating locations. First Year of Show: 1979. Last Show: 1992—Nov. 16-18, Sheraton/Washington Hotel, Washington.

TeleCon XIV (Public/Trade). SHOW MANAGEMENT: Applied Business Telecommunications, 2401 Crow Canyon Rd., Suite 310, Box 5106, San Ramon, Calif. 94583. Contact: Patrick S. Portway. (510) 820-5563. FAX: (510) 820-5894. SHOW SPONSOR: Same as show management. SHOW MANAGEMENT STATEMENT: TeleCon XIV, the Annual Teleconferencing Users Conference, celebrates its 14th year as a conference and trade show on advanced forms of communications applied to business and education. Business television, two-way videoconferencing, video phones, audio-graphic, computer and interactive multimedia systems. Teleconferencing is now a billion-dollar-a-year business. TeleCon is the marketplace and initial training ground for this growing industry's leaders. DATES AND LOCATIONS: 1994—Oct. 12-14, Anaheim Convention Center, Anaheim, Calif.; 1995—Nov. 13-15, San Jose Convention Center, San Jose, Calif. SHOW HISTORY: First Year of Show: 1981.

Video Software Dealers Association Convention. SHOW MANAGEMENT: Video Software Dealers Association, 303 Harper Dr., Moorestown, N.J. 08057-3229. Contact: Donna Ward, Director of Meetings and Conventions. (609) 231-7800. FAX: (609) 231-9791. SHOW MANAGEMENT STATEMENT: This convention provides a forum of communications for the video industry. Video retailers and distributors have the opportunity to meet face to face with their peers, studio representatives and other suppliers. Movie studios are able to announce new releases and sales programs. Educational seminars enable the retailer, distributor and manufacturer to better understand each other and to gather useful information to help run their businesses. DATES AND LOCATIONS: 1994—July 24-27, Las Vegas Convention Center, Las Vegas; 1995—July 9-12, Las Vegas Convention Center, Las Vegas. (Show held in same city every year.) PROFILE OF EXHIBITORS: Producers of prerecorded video software, media, accessory manufacturers, video distributors. PROFILE OF ATTENDEES: Producers of prerecorded video software, media, accessory manufacturers, video distributors, video retail specialists and mass merchandisers of prerecorded video. SHOW HISTORY: First Year of Show: 1982. Last Show: 1993—July 26-29, Las Vegas Convention Center, Las Vegas.

VISCOMM (Visual Communications Expo). SHOW MANAGEMENT: CMC, 200 Connectivut Ave., Norwalk, Conn. 06856-4990. Contact: Eileen Baird, Group Show Dir. (203) 852-0500. FAX: (203) 831-8446. SHOW SPONSOR: Same as show management. SHOW MANAGEMENT STATEMENT: VISCOMM is an amalgamation of four different trade shows and conferences focusing on visual communications. These are Photo, the international conference and exhibition for professional photographers; Prolab, the international event for commercial and minilabs; Grafix, the international conference for graphic design professionals; Corporate Video Expo, the international event for corporate video communicators. DATE AND LOCATION: 1994—Oct. 28-30, Jacob K. Javits Convention Center of New York, New York. (Show held in same city every year.) PROFILE OF EXHIBITORS: Manufacturers, suppliers and distributors of commercial lab equipment, products, services, professional photographic equipment and products. Electronic design and hardware, software, peripherals, typesetting equipment, stock photography, paper companies, furniture, book and magazine publishers. Audio recorders, color copiers, film recorders, image capturing devices, LCD panels, monitors, presentation systems and software, printers, recorder manufacturers, suppliers and distributors. PROFILE OF ATTENDEES: Photolab professionals, owners, managers, technicians, graphic designers, art/creative directors, illustrators, production managers, professional photographers specializing in fashion, still life, corporate, industrial, editorial, advertising and illustration photography. Training directors, meeting planners, presentation managers, audio-visual directors and video/graphics managers. SHOW HISTORY: First Year of Show: 1992.

Engineering

Audio Engineering Society Convention (Public/Trade). SHOW MANAGEMENT: Audio Engineering Society (AES), 60 E. 42nd St., New York 10165. Contact: Donald Plunkett, Executive Director. (212) 661-8528. FAX: (212) 682-0477. SHOW MANAGEMENT STATEMENT: Show provides an annual marketplace for professional audio equipment. Attendees are audio engineers. DATE AND LOCATION: 1994—Nov.10-13, Moscone Convention Center, San Francisco.

Society of Motion Picture and Television Engineers Annual Technical Conference and Equipment Exhibition (Public/Trade). SHOW MANAGEMENT: Society of Motion Picture and Television Engineers, 595 W. Hartsdale Ave., White Plains, N.Y. 10607. Contact: Al Ehrlich. (914) 761-1100. FAX: (914) 761-3115. SHOW SPONSOR: Same as show management. SHOW MANAGEMENT STATEMENT: The show provides an annual marketplace for equipment and supplies for production, engineering and purchasing personnel in worldwide professional motion-picture and broadcast-television industries. Product classification includes radio, television and cable production, postproduction, laboratory, and field-production equipment. DATES AND LOCATIONS: 1994—Oct. 13-16, Los Angeles Convention and Exhibition Center, Los Angeles; 1995—Oct., site to be announced. PROFILE OF EXHIBITORS: Manufacturers, dealers, distributors of professional television-broadcast and motion-picture equipment. PROFILE OF ATTENDEES: International broadcast-television and professional motion-picture-engineering executives. SHOW HISTORY: Annual meeting and exhibit for motion-picture industry (1916) and television industry (1950). Set Rotation Pattern: West Coast odd-numbered years, East Coast even-numbered years.

Radio, TV and Cable

Annual Country Radio Seminar (Public/Trade). SHOW MANAGEMENT: Country Radio Broadcasters, 50 Music Sq. W., Suite 604, Nashville 37203. Contact: Frank Mull. (615) 327-4487. FAX: (615) 327-4499. SHOW SPONSOR: Same as show management. DATE AND LOCATION: 1993—Mar. 2-5, Ryman Exhibit Hall/Opryland Hotel, Nashville. (Show held in same city every year.) PROFILE OF EXHIBITORS: Manufacturers, distributors or suppliers of a product or service for any of the following categories: advertising and promotions; audio equipment, automation and control; broadcasting engineering; recording equipment; wire, cable, satellite and microwave systems. PROFILE OF ATTENDEES: Independent station owners; CEOs of major station groups; general managers and their sales managers, program directors, operations managers, news directors and engineers. SHOW HISTORY: First Year of Show: 1969. Last Show: 1993—Mar. 3-6, Ryman Exhibit Hall/Opryland Hotel, Nashville.

Association for Multi-Image International Inc. Exposition (Public/Trade). SHOW MANAGEMENT: Association for Multi-Image International Inc., 10008 N. Dale Mabry Hwy., Suite 113, Tampa 33618-4424. Contact: Marilyn Kulp, Executive Director. (813) 960-1692. FAX: (813) 962-7911. SHOW SPONSOR: Same as show management. SHOW MANAGEMENT STATEMENT: The purpose is to bring together individuals who are actively engaged in the field of multi-image production and utilization to enhance their individual and cooperative creativity and production, and to promote the use of multi-image as a medium for education, communication and entertainment. DATE AND LOCATION: 1994—Aug. 22-26, New Orleans Hilton Riverside and Towers, New Orleans. PROFILE OF EXHIBITORS: Audio-visual. PROFILE OF ATTENDEES: Producers and manufacturers of audio-visual shows and equipment. SHOW HISTORY: First Year of Show: 1978. Set Rotation Pattern: East Coast, central, West Coast.

Atlantic Cable Show. SHOW MANAGEMENT: Slack Inc., 6900 Grove Rd., Thorofare, N.J. 08086. Contact: Rhonda A. Moy. (609) 848-1000. FAX: (609) 853-5991. SHOW MANAGEMENT STATEMENT: A regional meeting sponsored by the Maryland/Delaware/District of Columbia, New Jersey, New York and Pennsylvania associations. Registrants are primarily system owners/operators, managers, engineers, technicians, marketing managers, local programmers, and vendors. DATES AND LOCATION: 1994—Oct. 4-6; 1995—Oct. 10-11; 1996—Oct. 1-3; 1997—Oct. 7-9. Atlantic City Convention Center, Atlantic City, N.J. (Show held in same city every year.) PROFILE OF EXHIBITORS: Cable-related companies and products. PROFILE OF ATTENDEES: System owners/operators, managers, engineers, technicians, marketing managers, local programmers, and vendors. SHOW HISTORY: First Year of Show: 1982. Last Show: 1993—Oct. 5-7, Atlantic City Convention Center, Atlantic City.

BroadcastAsia94. SHOW MANAGEMENT: Singapore Exhibition Services Pte Ltd., 11 Dhoby Ghaut, #15-09 Cathay Bldg., Singapore 0922. (65) 338 4747. FAX: (65) 339 5651. TELEX: RS 28733 SINGEX. SHOW MANAGEMENT STATEMENT: Held concurrently with: CommunicAsia94 (the 8th Asian International Electronic Communication and Information Technology Exhibition and Conference); MobileCommAsia94 (the Asian International Cellular, Radio and Satellite Communications Exhibition and Conference); NetworkAsia94 (the Asian International Networking Exhibition and Conference). DATE AND LOCATION: 1994—June 1-4, World Trade Centre, Singapore.

Broadcast Financial Management Associates. SHOW MANAGEMENT: BFMA, 701 Lee St., Suite 1010, Des Plaines, Ill. 60016-4555. Contact: Kathy Lynch. (708) 296-0200. FAX: (708) 296-7510. DATES AND LOCATIONS: 1994 —May 22-25, Sheraton Harbor Island East, San Diego; 1995—May 21-24, Mirage Hotel and Casino, Las Vegas.

CABLEXPO. SHOW MANAGEMENT: Canadian Cable Television Association, 360 Albert St., Suite 1010, Ottawa, Ont., Canada K1R 7X7. Contact: C. Thompson. (613) 232-2631. FAX: (613) 232-2137. DATES AND LOCATIONS: 1994—May 16-18, Montreal Convention Centre, Montreal; 1995—May 29-31, World Trade and Convention Centre, Halifax, N.S. PROFILE OF EXHIBITORS: Cable television hardware and software. PROFILE OF ATTENDEES: Canadian cable operators and Canadian government regulators. SHOW HISTORY: Set Rotation Pattern: East-West pattern; Canada only. Last Show: 1992—June 1-3, Vancouver Trade and Convention Centre, Vancouver, B.C.

Cable '94. SHOW MANAGEMENT: National Cable Television Association, 1724 Massachusetts Ave. N.W., Washington, D.C. 20036. Contact: NCTA Industry Affairs Dept. (202) 775-3669. FAX: (202) 775-3692. SHOW MANAGEMENT STATEMENT: Showcases state-of-the-art technology, programming, and a full array of other significant businesses relevant to the cable television industry. Provides a full complement of substantive sessions addressing the latest in technology, future business, public policy, programming, finance, marketing and management issues. DATE AND LOCATION: 1994—May 22-25, Ernest N. Morial Convention Center, New Orleans.

Cable and Satellite '94. SHOW MANAGEMENT: Reed Exhibitions, Radcliffe House, Blenheim Court, Solihull, U.K. CONTACT: Stephen de Looze, Exhibition Director. 44 (0)21 705 6707. FAX: 44 (0)21 705 4380. SHOW MANAGEMENT STATEMENT: Attracts an international audience associated with both the cable and satellite industries, entertainment technologies, and broadcast/receiving. DATE AND LOCATION: 1994—April 11-13.

Cable-Tec Expo. SHOW MANAGEMENT: Society of Cable Television Engineers, 669 Exton Commons, Exton, Pa. 19341. Contact: Anna Riker. (215) 363-6888. FAX: (215) 353-5898. SHOW SPONSOR: Same as show management. SHOW MANAGEMENT STATEMENT: The SCTE Conference and Exposition brings together engineers, technicians and technical executives from the United States who represent cable systems, MSOs, and independent operators. DATES AND LOCATIONS: 1994—June 15-18, St. Louis Convention Center, St. Louis; 1995—June 14-17, Las Vegas Convention Center, Las Vegas; 1996—June 19-22, Henry B. Gonzalez Convention Center, San Antonio. PROFILE OF EXHIBITORS: Construction equipment, signal distribution, cable casting, transmission/receiving, test equipment, microwave/MDS, digital systems, system testing quality control, and other related hardware. PROFILE OF ATTENDEES: Engineers, technicians, executives of MSOs, and independent operators. SHOW HISTORY: The annual SCTE Show was established concurrently with the rotating Annual Engineering Conference to fulfill the growing need to address the technical end of the cable television industry. First Year of Show: 1983. Last Show: 1992—June 14-17, Henry B. Gonzalez Convention Center, San Antonio.

Canadian Association of Broadcasters Convention (Public/Trade). SHOW MANAGEMENT: Canadian Association of Broadcasters, Box 627, Stn. B, Ottawa, Ont., Canada K1P 5S2. Contact: Sylvie Bissonnette. (613) 233-4035. FAX: (613) 233-6961. DATES AND LOCATIONS: 1994—Nov. 5-9, Winnipeg Convention Centre, Winnipeg, Mant.; 1995—Oct. 28-Nov. 1, Ottawa Congress Centre, Ottawa; 1996—Oct. 26-30, Edmonton Convention Centre, Edmonton, Alta.; 1997—Nov. 2-4, Montreal Convention Centre, Montreal, Que. PROFILE OF EXHIBITORS: Companies who provide products or services to Canadian broadcast (radio-TV) operators. PROFILE OF ATTENDEES: Senior management, owners and engineers. SHOW HISTORY: Set Rotation Pattern: East/West rotation. Last Show: 1992—Nov. 1-4, Vancouver Trade and Convention Centre, Vancouver, B.C.

Eastern Cable Television Trade Show. SHOW MANAGEMENT: Convention and Show Management Co., 6175 Barfield Rd., Suite 220, Atlanta 30328. Contact: Nancy Horne. (404) 252-2454. SHOW SPONSOR: Southern Cable Television Association, 6175 Barfield Rd., Suite 220, Atlanta 30328. Contact: Nancy Horne. (404) 252-2454. SHOW MANAGEMENT STATEMENT: The Annual Eastern Cable Television Trade Show and Convention provides a forum and product showcase for the cable television industry in the eastern half of the United States. Product classifications include cable hardware and satellite receiving equipment, cable programming, cable software, cable financial and consulting services. DATES AND LOCATIONS: 1994—Aug. 1-3; 1995—Aug. 27-29; 1996—Aug. 27-29. Atlanta Market Center (Merchandise Mart, Apparel Mart, Gift Mart, INFORUM), Atlanta. (Show held in same city every year.) PROFILE OF EXHIBITORS: Suppliers to the cable television industry, including cable hardware, software, programming, and general services such as financing and consulting. PROFILE OF ATTENDEES: Cable television system operators from throughout the eastern United States SHOW HISTORY: First Year of Show: 1963. Last Show: 1993—Aug. 25-27, Atlanta Market Center, Atlanta.

Great Lakes Cable Expo. SHOW MANAGEMENT: Great Lakes Cable Television Association, 6910 N. Shadeland Ave., Suite 206, Indianapolis 46220. Contact: Debbie Locklear. (317) 845-8100. FAX: (317) 578-0621. SHOW SPONSOR: Same as show management. SHOW MANAGEMENT STATEMENT: The Great Lakes Cable Expo provides an annual marketplace for regional cable TV operators, technicians, owners and executives of the Illinois, Indiana, Michigan, Ohio and Wisconsin areas. It is one of the five regional cable television shows in the United States. DATES AND LOCATIONS: 1994—Sept. 20-22; 1995—Aug. 29-31. Sites to be announced. PROFILE OF EXHIBITORS: Suppliers of cable television products and services; hardware manufacturers, constructors and programmers. PROFILE OF ATTENDEES: Cable television system employees. SHOW HISTORY: First Year of Show: 1982. Set Rotation Pattern: Indiana, Ohio and Michigan. Last Show: 1992—Sept. 13-17, Cleveland Convention Center, Cleveland.

High Frequency Power Conversion (Public/Trade). SHOW MANAGEMENT: Intertec International Inc., 2472 Eastman Ave., Suite 34, Ventura, Calif. 93003. (805) 650-7070. FAX: (805) 650-7079. TELEX/TWX: 182218. SHOW HISTORY: First Year of Show: 1985.

HomeMedia. SHOW MANAGEMENT: American Expositions Inc., 110 Greene St., Suite 703, New York 10012. Contact: Victor Harwood. (212) 226-4141. DATE AND LOCATION: 1994—Feb. 7-9, Beverly Hilton Hotel, Los Angeles. (Show held in same city every year.) PROFILE OF EXHIBITORS: Computer hardware and software interactive television and other interactive entertainment technologies. PROFILE OF ATTENDEES: Executives, producers and developers in high tech and entertainment industry. SHOW HISTORY: Last Show: 1993—Mar. 3-5, Beverly Hilton Hotel, Los Angeles.

KBA Fall Convention. SHOW MANAGEMENT: Kentucky Broadcasting Association, Radio Station Rd., Lebanon, Ky. 40033. Contact: J.T. Whitlock, Executive Director. (502) 692-3126. FAX: (502) 692-6003. SHOW MANAGEMENT STATEMENT: This convention is held twice a year. Its purpose is to further train broadcasters on both legal aspects of broadcasting as well as sales and management. DATE AND LOCATION: 1994—Oct. 6-8, Radisson Plaza, Lexington, Ky. PROFILE OF EXHIBITORS: Electronics, computers, programs syndications, broadcast suppliers (radio and TV). PROFILE OF ATTENDEES: Owners and management throughout the state of Kentucky. SHOW HISTORY: Biannual, spring in Louisville, Ky. (Apr.); fall in Lexington, Ky. (Oct.) First Year of Show: 1953.

Low Power Communication Television. SHOW MANAGEMENT: BFMA, 701 Lee St., Suite 1010, Des Plaines, Ill. 60016-4555. (708) 296-0200. FAX: (708) 296-7510. Contact: Eddie Barker. DATE AND LOCATION: 1994—cancelled.

National Association of Broadcasters Annual Convention and International Exposition. SHOW MANAGEMENT: National Association of Broadcasters, 1771 N St. N.W., Washington 20036. Contact: Rick Dobson. (202) 429-5300. FAX: (202) 429-5343. SHOW MANAGEMENT STATEMENT: The convention is an annual gathering of broadcast professionals; sessions cover all aspects of broadcasting, both technical and management oriented. DATES AND LOCATION: 1994—Mar. 21-24; 1995—Apr. 10-13; 1996—Apr. 15-18. Las Vegas Convention Center, Las Vegas. (Show held in same city every year.) PROFILE OF EXHIBITORS: Manufacturers and distributors of broadcast hardware and software. PROFILE OF ATTENDEES: Owners and managers of broadcast properties. Department of Commerce Certificates: This show will be promoted overseas by the United States Department of Commerce under the Foreign Buyer Program. SHOW HISTORY: First Year of Show: 1922. Last Show: 1993—Apr. 19-22, Las Vegas Convention Center, Las Vegas.

National Association of Television Program Executives Annual Program Conference. SHOW MANAGEMENT: NATPE, 2425 W. Olympic Blvd., Suite 550 E, Santa Monica, Calif. 90404. Contact: Nick Orfanopoulos, N.P. Conferences. (310) 453-4440. FAX: (310) 453-5258. TELEX/TWX: 276674 NATPUR. SHOW SPONSOR: Same as show management. SHOW MANAGEMENT STATEMENT: This show provides an annual marketplace for syndicated television programs, first-run and/or off-network programs. DATES AND LOCATIONS: 1994—Jan. 24-28, Miami Beach Convention Center, Miami Beach, Fla.; 1995—Jan. 16-20, Sands Expo and Convention Center, Las Vegas; 1996—Jan. 15-19, Sands Expo and Convention Center, Las Vegas; 1997—Jan. 20-24, Ernest N. Morial Convention Center, New Orleans; 1998—Jan. 19-23, Ernest N. Morial Convention Center, New Orleans. PROFILE OF EXHIBITORS: Major studios, independent television and film producers, distributors and syndicators. PROFILE OF ATTENDEES: Television programmers, distributors, syndicators and foreign programmers. SHOW HISTORY: First Year of Show: 1984. Last Show: 1992—Jan. 21-24, New Orleans Convention Center, New Orleans.

National Cable Television Association Annual Convention and Exposition. SHOW MANAGEMENT: Dobson and Associates Ltd., 1225 19th St. N.W., Washington 20036. Contact: E. Dan Dobson. (202) 775-3606. FAX: (202) 775-1028. SHOW SPONSOR: Same as show management. SHOW MANAGEMENT STATEMENT: The National Cable Television Association Convention and Exposition provides a marketplace for the equipment, programming and supplementary services for cable systems and personnel. Categories of exhibits include cable TV headend, distribution, studio and related equipment; satellite TVRO equipment; cable programming services; marketing, consulting and brokerage firms; insurance and financial institutions; office management, office automation and communications firms, including car, computer and office-system manufacturers; vehicles, furnishings, publications and program guides. DATES AND LOCATIONS: 1994—May 22-25, Ernest N. Morial Convention Center, New Orleans; 1995—May 7-10, Dallas Convention Center, Dallas. PROFILE OF EXHIBITORS: All industries related to cable television including manufacturers of cable and studio equipment, programmers, publications, financial services, and all support services. PROFILE OF ATTENDEES: Include multiple system operators, independent operators, programmers, equipment manufacturers, investment and financial institutions. SHOW HISTORY: Held annually on a rotating basis. First Year of Show: 1950. Last Show: 1993—June 6-9, Moscone Convention Center, San Francisco.

National Conference of College Broadcasters. SHOW MANAGEMENT: National Association of College Broadcasters Inc., 71 George St., Providence, R.I. 02912-1824. Contact: Mike Hummel. (401) 863-2225. FAX: 863-2221. SHOW SPONSOR: Same as show management. SHOW MANAGEMENT STATEMENT: The National Conference serves anyone and everyone affiliated with college radio and TV facilities—both broadcast stations and cable outlets—or interested in careers in media. We offer more than 80 seminars, panels, hands-on workshops, roundtables by media professionals, college broadcasters and faculty presenters. Keynote addresses given by major industry figures. Exhibitors are primarily equipment and program suppliers, record labels, publications and other associations seeking to reach college radio and TV and establish brand loyalties among those who represent a large percentage of tomorrow's media professionals. DATE AND LOCATION: 1994—Nov. 11-13, Rhode Island Convention Center, Providence, R.I. PROFILE OF EXHIBITORS: Broadcast and cable equipment manufacturers, record labels/program suppliers, and other associations. PROFILE OF ATTENDEES: Those who build, manage and operate (student, staff and faculty), program (DJs and producers) and staff (students and community volunteers) college radio or TV facilities. SHOW HISTORY: Annual show held in November, usually in Providence, R.I. First Year of Show: 1988. Last Show: 1993—Nov. 11-14, Omni Biltmore Hotel, Providence, R.I.

National Religious Broadcasters Media Exposition (Public/Trade). SHOW MANAGEMENT: National Religious Broadcasters, 7839 Ashton Ave., Manassas, Va. 22110. Contact: Michael Glenn. (703) 330-7000. FAX: (703) 330-7100. SHOW SPONSOR: Same as show management. SHOW MANAGEMENT STATEMENT: The NRB Media Exposition is an annual gathering of manufacturers and distributors of broadcast equipment, computers, radio and TV programs, consultant services, gospel music, publishing and other related items to the religious communications industry. Attendees include radio and TV executives, ministers, denominational executives, musicians, advertising executives, educators and Christian bookstore owners. PROFILE OF EXHIBITORS: Manufacturers and distributors of consumer and broadcast audio and video equipment, computers, radio and television programs, publishers, and miscellaneous items relating to the religious field. PROFILE OF ATTENDEES: National and international: 48% management, 20% program production, 16% sales and advertising, 8% technical/engineering, 2% education, 6% miscellaneous "by industry". Radio 43%, TV Cable 17%, print 14%, video 8%, church 7%, music 5%, miscellaneous 4%, film 2%. SHOW HISTORY: First Year of Show: 1968. Last Show: 1994—Jan. 29-Feb. 1, Sheraton Washington Hotel, Washington.

News/Tech '94. SHOW MANAGEMENT: BFMA, 701 Lee St., Suite 1010, Des Plaines, Ill. 60016-4555. Contact: Eddie Barker. (708) 296-0200. FAX: (708) 296-7510. SHOW SPONSOR: Radio-Television News Directors Association (RTNDA), 1717 K. St. N.W., Washington 20006. (214) 631-1278. SHOW MANAGEMENT STATEMENT: The News/Tech exposition is held annually in conjuction with the association's international conference. News directors and producers make up the major portion of attendees. General managers and chief engineers attend in increasing numbers due to the nature of the exhibits. In addition to the equipment exhibitors, program syndicators, news services and public relations divisions of corporations and associations are also in the exhibit hall. DATE AND LOCATION: 1994—

Trade Shows By Category

Sept., Los Angeles Convention and Exhibition Center, Los Angeles. PROFILE OF EXHIBITORS: Hardware and software manufacturers, suppliers, programmers, syndicators, public relations for companies and associations. PROFILE OF ATTENDEES: News directors, producers of local and network news operations, cable, engineers and associated professionals. SHOW HISTORY: Exhibit hall was established in 1975; held in mid-September except in presidential election years when it is held in early December. First Year of Show: 1945. LAST SHOW: 1992—Sept., Henry B. Gonzalez Convention Center, San Antonio.

RAB '94 Managing Sales Conference. SHOW MANAGEMENT: Radio Advertising Bureau, 304 Park Ave. S., New York 10010. Contact: Wayne Cornils. (212) 254-4800. SHOW SPONSOR: Same as show management. SHOW MANAGEMENT STATEMENT: RAB Managing Sales Conference represents more than 3,500 member radio stations, radio station sales managers, broadcast groups, radio networks, station representatives, network executives, and associated industry organizations from the 50 states. DATE AND LOCATION: 1994—Feb. 17-20, Loews Anatole Dallas, Dallas. PROFILE OF EXHIBITORS: Manufacturers, distributors or suppliers of a product or service for any of the following categories: computer/software programs; radio and TV products; radio networks; specialty advertising; program syndication; sales and marketing research; sales consulting. No hardware suppliers. PROFILE OF ATTENDEES: Radio station sales managers, general managers, network executives and group heads from throughout the United States. SHOW HISTORY: First Year of Show: 1980. Last Show: 1993—Feb. 4-7, Loews Anatole Dallas, Dallas.

Radio Management, Programming, Sales and Engineering Convention/Exposition. SHOW MANAGEMENT: National Association of Broadcasters, 1771 N. St. N.W., Washington 20036. Contact: Rick Dobson. (202) 429-5300; (202) 429-5409. FAX: (202) 429-5343. SHOW SPONSOR: Same as show management. SHOW MANAGEMENT STATEMENT: The Radio Convention is attended by 7,000 radio-industry personnel from throughout the United States and other countries—independent station owners, CEOs of major station groups, general managers, program directors, operations managers, news directors, and engineers. DATE AND LOCATION: 1994—Sept., site to be announced. PROFILE OF EXHIBITORS: Manufacturers, distributors and suppliers of hardware, supplies and services used in managing, programming, sales and engineering of radio stations. PROFILE OF ATTENDEES: Radio station personnel: owners, general sales, operations and business managers, program and promotion directors, engineers. SHOW HISTORY: First Year of Show: 1984. Last Show: 1992—Sept. 10-12, Ernest N. Morial Convention Center, New Orleans.

ShowBiz Expo. SHOW MANAGEMENT: Live Time, Inc., 2122 Hillhurst Ave., Los Angeles 90027. Contact: Nalini Lasiewicz. (213) 668-1811. FAX: (213) 668-1033. TELEX/TWX: (213) 668-1033. SHOW MANAGEMENT STATEMENT: ShowBiz Expo is an annual, regional, business and production trade show for the video, film and legitimate theatre industries. The show draws producers, directors, writers, MIS executives, artists, post-production editors, cameramen, studio executives. SBE exhibits showcase a broad and diverse range of equipment, products and services used in production and postproduction for entertainment professionals. Trade associations participate in hosting seminars and will be distributing free VIP passes to trade members. The event emphasizes a cross-pollination of entertainment and media professionals. DATES AND LOCATIONS: 1994—Jan. 11-13; 1995—June 14-20. Los Angeles Convention and Exhibition Center, Los Angeles. (Show held in same city every year.) PROFILE OF EXHIBITORS: Film and video production services, vertical computer software, film equipment manufacturers, video equipment, computer graphics, special effects, film commissions, lighting gear, financial services, theatrical bondsmen, postproduction sound and editing services. PROFILE OF ATTENDEES: Production companies, producers, production managers, directors, creative directors, writers, artists, studio personnel, MIS executives, postproduction technicians, accountants, etc. SHOW HISTORY: Established in June 1984 as Micro Show and renamed ShowBiz Expo in 1985 when it grew to include other products and services for the entertainment industry. New technologies remain a big emphasis. Over 50 trade organizations and guilds participate with seminars, information tables, and mailings to members. First Year of Show: 1984. Last Show: 1993—June 5-7, Los Angeles Convention and Exhibition Center, Los Angeles.

The Texas Show. SHOW MANAGEMENT: Texas Cable TV Association, 506 W. 16th St., Austin, Tex. 78701. Contact: William D. Arnold. (512) 474-2082. FAX: (512) 474-0966. SHOW SPONSOR: Same as show management. SHOW MANAGEMENT STATEMENT: This is a trade show and convention for the cable television industry. DATE AND LOCATION: 1994—Feb., Henry B. Gonzalez Convention Center, San Antonio. (Show held in same city every year.) PROFILE OF EXHIBITORS: Those associated with cable TV, hardware and software. PROFILE OF ATTENDEES: Cable operators, trade press, persons interested in cable television. SHOW HISTORY: Annual show held in February. First Year of Show: 1960. Last Show: 1992—Feb. 26-28, Henry B. Gonzalez Convention Center, San Antonio.

WCA '94. The 7th Annual Wireless Cable Association International Inc. Convention. SHOW SPONSOR: Wireless Cable Association International Inc., Box 1025, Burlington, Iowa 52601. Contact: Convention Services. (319) 752-8336. FAX: (319) 753-5508. SHOW MANAGEMENT STATEMENT: The Wireless Cable Association International Convention is devoted exclusively to the wireless cable industry and includes exhibits, seminars and keynote speakers. DATE AND LOCATION: 1994—June 20-23. Las Vegas Hilton, Las Vegas.

The 1994 Western Show. SHOW MANAGEMENT: Trade Associates Inc., 6001 Montrose Rd., Suite 900, Rockville, Md. 20852. Contact: Deborah Grosso. (301) 468-3210. FAX: (301) 468-3662. SHOW SPONSOR: California Cable Television Association (CCTA), 4341 Piedmont Ave., Box 11080, Oakland, Calif. 94611. Contact: Susan Petoletti. (415) 428-2225. SHOW MANAGEMENT STATEMENT: The Western Cable Television Show attracts major buyers/users of cable products and services who are cable operators, MSO executives, system engineers, producers and other cable professionals with interests in programming and hardware and software technology. DATE AND LOCATION: 1994—Nov. 30-Dec. 2, Anaheim Convention Center, Anaheim, Calif. (Show held in same city every year.) PROFILE OF EXHIBITORS: Cable suppliers and operators of the cable industry. PROFILE OF ATTENDEES: Cable operators, MSO executives, system engineers, owners and financial officers. SHOW HISTORY: First Year of Show: 1968. Last Show: 1993—Dec. 1-3, Anaheim Convention Center, Anaheim, Calif.

Schools Specializing in Radio-Television-Cable

This list includes only those schools that specialize in professional or technical courses in broadcasting. Many colleges and universities also offer courses in radio and television. Current information on colleges and universities that offer degrees in radio and television is covered in *Universities and Colleges,* beginning on page I-27.

American School of Broadcasting. 1788 Morse Rd., Columbus, Ohio 43229. (614) 785-9272. FAX: (614) 431-5684. William D. Antonelli, chmn.
Courses offered include Radio/TV, (600 hours, six months); disc jockey; news/sportscasting; copywriting; prod; progmg; promotions; cablecasting; LPTV; TV news anchor/sports/weather; FCC rules & regulations; time sls. Lifetime placement svc.

Ameritech Colleges Inc. 6843 Lennox Ave., Van Nuys, Calif. 91405. (818) 901-7311. FAX: (818) 901-7815. Jari Simpson, pres; Tauni Murphy, dir.
Courses offered include electronics/computer maintenance, word processing, secretarial, & computerized accounting. Health claims examination.

Andrews University. Berrien Springs, Mich. 49104. (616) 471-3303. FAX: (616) 471-7771. Richard Lesher, pres; Delmar Davis, VP academic affrs; Luanne Bauer, communication dept chair.
B.A. degrees offered in communications, journalism & mass media, & pub rels.

Antonelli Media Training Center Inc. 150 5th Ave., New York 10011. (212) 206-8063. Martin C. Antonelli, pres.
Courses offered include TV time sls, mgr training, & sls improvement prog for loc sls staffs.

The Art Institute of Pittsburgh. 526 Penn Ave., Pittsburgh 15222. (800) 275-2470. FAX: (412) 263-6666. Sandra Vanhyle, pres; Connie Moore, mus/video bus prog dir.
Courses offered include audio recording & prod, video prod, bcst media feature writing, script writing, legal issues, concert prod/sound, radio/studio prod, filmmaking.

Broadcast Center. 7720 Forsyth Blvd., St. Louis 63105. (314) 862-8181. Douglas H. Huber, pres; Linda Havite, VP.
Training in mktg & time sls, coml & prog prod, bcst journalism & bcst performance. Training includes voice training & dev for bcstg; announcing training including news, comls, DJ & sportscasting; news & coml copywriting.

Broadcast Professionals, The Complete School of Radio Broadcasting. 11507-D S.W. Pacific Hwy., Portland, Ore. 97223-8632. (503) 244-5113. Rosemary Reynolds, dir; Keith Allen, exec dir.
Preparation for entry-level employment in all aspects of radio bcstg, including combo DJ, announcing, news writing & reporting, progmg, mus directing, promotion, copywriting & prod, sls, FCC rules & equipment operation. Career College Association accredited. Financial aid available for those who qualify. Nine-month prog.

Broadcasting Institute of Maryland. 7200 Harford Rd., Baltimore 21234. (410) 254-2770; (800) 942-9246. FAX: (410) 254-5357. John C. Jeppi Sr., pres; John C. Jeppi Jr., bus mgr; Dean R. Kendall, dir education.
Courses offered include comprehensive course in radio & TV bcstg; majors available in radio, TV, news & sports.

Carolina School of Broadcasting. 7003 Wallace Rd., Suite 100, Charlotte, N.C. 28212-6815. (704) 532-9748. Ken D. FuQuay, dir; Alyson M. Young, asst dir; Cris Remme, dir mktg.
Courses offered include "Broadcasting: Non-Technical" (group sessions) and "Lab Course" (in-stn training); announcing, prod, copywriting, news, coml prod, sls, admin. Daytime Group sessions meet Monday-Friday for four mos. Optional in-stn training, full- or part-time as determined by stn & student. Closed circuit TV facilities & stereo control room; resident training in studio & stn opns at coml radio & TV stns in North Carolina, South Carolina, Virginia & Tennessee.

Cleveland Institute of Electronics. 1776 E. 17th St., Cleveland 44114. (216) 781-9400. FAX: (216) 781-0331. John R. Drinko, pres; Dan Hadorn, VP info mgmt.
Offers an Associate in Applied Science degree in electronics, tech engrg, & bcst engrg. FCC license preparation.

Clover Park Technical College. 4500 Steilacoom Blvd. S.W., Tacoma, Wash. 98499-4098. (206) 589-5884. Alson E. Green Jr., pres; John L. Mangan, radio bcstg instructor.
Bcst training since 1954. Comprehensive 12-month course in all aspects of radio stn opn prepares students for entry-level employment. Course includes staff experience at 39-kw KVTI(FM). Supplemental courses in sportscasting (play-by-play) & rsch. Operated by the State Board for Community & Technical Colleges as an area vocational-technical school servicing both adult & high school students.

Columbia Broadcasting Center. 613 4th St., Suite 203, Santa Rosa, Calif. 95404. (707) 576-7542. Richard Rynders, dir.
Courses offered: radio bcstg, prod, copywriting, adv sls & promotions.

Columbia College-Hollywood. 925 N. LaBrea Ave., Hollywood, Calif. 90038. (213) 851-0550. FAX: (213) 851-6401. Kurt Wolfe, dir admissions; Bernard H. Hunt, VP student svcs; Frank Zuniga, academic dean; Allan Rossman, pres.
Courses offered include TV prod, directing, studio & product lighting, camera opn, newscast prod, videotape recording & editing, adv, copywriting, screenwriting, cable stn operation & progmg, cinematography, film editing & direction, sound mixing, & bcst engrg. Two- & four-year degree progs.

Columbia School of Broadcasting. 5808 Columbia Pike, Bailey's Crossroads, Va. 22041-2007. (703) 820-2020. Roy E. Blair, pres/school dir. Washington, D.C. office.
Courses offered include radio announcing (in English & Sp), & basic radio prod. Also TV announcing workshop. Offers comprehensive training for entry-level bcstg positions.

Columbia School of Broadcasting - Indiana. 1815 N. Meridian St., Suite 101, Indianapolis 46202. (317) 923-1550. FAX: (317) 924-9953. Alberta R. Rodd, pres; Bruce Henderson, office mgr.
Courses offered include bcstg for radio, & on-camera TV films. Also actg workshops.

Columbia School of Broadcasting. 46-001 Kam Hwy., Suite 216, Kaneohe, Hawaii 96744. (808) 236-7333. Dennis McCann, dir.
Courses offered in radio/TV announcing.

Columbia School of Broadcasting. 3705 Southwest Trafficway, Kansas City, Mo. 64111. (816) 561-3422. Thom Brent, pres.

Columbia School of Broadcasting. 5050 Poplar Ave., Suite 1500, Memphis 38157. (901) 682-0606. Larry Gullett, dir.
Courses offered in radio announcing (newscasting, sportscasting, disc jockey), voice-overs, & interview/talk shows.

Connecticut School of Broadcasting Inc. Radio Park, Farmington, Conn. 06032. (203) 232-9988. Dick Robinson, pres; Sara Robinson, VP; Hank Tenney, dir.
Stratford, Conn. 06497: 2874 Main St. (203) 378-5155. Tim Clark, dir.
North Palm Beach, Fla. 33408: 525 Northlake Blvd. (407) 842-2000. Donna Marie Cavalier, dir.
Wellesley Hills, Mass. 02181: 49 Walnut Park. (617) 235-2050. Bud Stone, exec dir.
Rochelle Park, N.J. 07662: 151 W. Passaic St. (201) 587-1212. Jeff Dreisbach, dir.
Atlanta 30067: Bldg. 1472-100, 1355 Terrell Mill Rd. (404) 951-0033. FAX: (404) 984-9113. Bill Pearson, pres.
Courses offered include radio & TV announcing (day & evening classes), history of communications, copywriting, bcst performance, bcst mgmt, control room procedures, FCC license preparation, DJ, VJ, sports, news, weather, prod, & sls.

Franciscan University of Steubenville. Franciscan Way, Steubenville, Ohio 43952. (614) 283-3771. FAX: (614) 283-6452. James E. Coyle Jr., assoc professor; David J. Schaefer, asst professor.
Four-year radio & TV Bachelor degree.

Grantham College of Engineering. Box 5700, 34641 Grantham College Rd., Slidell, La. 70469-5700. (504) 649-4191. FAX: (504) 649-4183. Donald J. Grantham, pres; Donna L. Stradley, dir student svcs.
Courses offered include electronics engrg tech & computer engrg tech by correspondence, leading to ASET & BSET degrees.

Specs Howard School of Broadcast Arts Inc. 16900 W. Eight Mile Rd., Suite 115, Southfield, Mich. 48075. (313) 569-0101. FAX: (313) 569-8059. Specs Howard, exec dir; Dick Kernan, VP.
Courses offered include radio & TV bcstg & prod; electronics technology. Accredited by NATTS.

ICS/School of Electronics. (Division of National Education Corp.) Scranton, Pa. 18515. (717) 342-7701. FAX: (717) 349-9072. Ralph J. Kurtz, course mgr; Russell Bilby, consultant.
Diploma courses include basic electronics, electronics tech, basic computer progmg, TV/VCR repair or personal computer repair. Center for Degree Studies offers specialized Associate degree in electronics tech & electrical, mechanical, civil & industrial engrg tech; specialized Associate degree in business mgmt, mktg, finance, accounting or applied computer science.

Institute For Communications Law Studies. The Catholic University School of Law, 620 Michigan Ave. N.E., Washington 20064. (202) 319-5140. FAX: (202) 319-4459. Harvey L. Zuckman, dir.
Courses offered: First Amendment problems, bcstg & cable regulations, FCC practices & procedures, new communications technologies & the law, communication common carrier regulations, international regulations of tele-communications, copyright problems of the media, & entertainment law. Internships are offered with major communications organizations including FCC & NAB.

International College of Broadcasting. 6 S. Smithville Rd., Dayton, Ohio 45431. (513) 258-8251. FAX: (513) 258-8714. Michael A. LeMaster, pres; James Dunn, dir.
Courses offered include radio, TV, camera operation, CATV, disc jockey, news, sports, audio/recording engrg. Associate degree in communication arts in radio & TV.

Long Island University. C.W. Post Campus, Brookville, N.Y. (516) 299-2395. FAX: (516) 626-9730. Dr. David Steinberg, pres; Dr. Walter S. Jones, VP academic affrs.
Courses & specializations offered include Introduction to Bcstg, Foundations in Bcstg, basic & advanced audio prod, basic & advanced TV prod, bcst journalism specialization, Issues & Trends in Bcstg, cable & satellite communications, sls & rsch, TV workshops, TV law specialities, bcst classics, pub rels specialization.
Classes conducted in video, audio & computer prod facilities, including the Visual & Performing Arts Computer Lab & WCWP-FM.

Mississippi State University. Drawer 5167, Broadcast Meteorology Program, Department of Geosciences, Mississippi State Univ., Mississippi State, Miss. 39762-5167. (601) 325-2908. FAX: (601) 325-2907. Mark S. Binkley, dir.
Courses offered include meteorology, physical geography, climatology, world geography, severe weather, applied climatology, statistical climatology, satellite & radar meteorology, natural hazards & processes, synoptic meteorology I & II, water resources, thermodynamic meteorology. These & other classes are offered on-campus leading to B.S. & M.S. degrees.

NEI College of Technology. 825 41st Ave. N.E., Columbia Heights, Minn. 55421. (612) 781-4881. FAX: (612) 781-4884. Charles R. Dettmann, pres.
Courses offered include Associate degrees in electronics, computers, radio-TV, industrial electronics, digital electronics, TV, & aviation electronics. Also certificate progs.

National Education Center. Brown Institute Campus, 2225 E. Lake St., Minneapolis 55407. (612) 721-2481. FAX: (612) 721-2179. Steve Marks, pres; Michael A. Hatch, department head; Robert Beringer, placement dir; Bonnie Hugeback, assoc school dir.
Courses offered include RTV announcing, sls, bcst adv, bcst journalism, audio prod, TV prod, TV engrg & editing, sports announcing, audio engrg. Associate of

Schools Specializing in Radio-Television-Cable

Applied Science degree in radio-TV bcstg. Certificate in Radio/TV bcstg.

National Radio Institute. 4401 Connecticut Ave. N.W., Washington 20008. (202) 244-1600.

New England School of Broadcasting. One College Cir., Bangor, Me. 04401. (207) 947-6083. George E. Wildey, pres; Ben Haskell, dir; Hope Eaton, coord; Nelson Jewell, admissions dir.

Courses offered include announcing, bcst sls, writing for bcst, TV prod, sound recording, voice & diction, news & sports reporting, adv & pub rels, & public speaking.

New School for Social Research. 2 W. 13th St., New York 10011. (212) 229-8903. FAX: (212) 229-5357. Jonathan Fanton, pres; Elizabeth Dickey, dean; Linda Dunn, chmn communications dept.

Courses offered include TV writing workshops, writing for TV, films & radio; TV prod workshop; voice & speech for theater & TV; seminars on TV comls; writing TV comls. Offers certificate in film/TV studies, BA, BA/MA, MA in media studies.

Northeast Broadcasting School. Pledge of Allegiance Bldg., 142 Berkeley St., Boston 02116. (617) 267-7910. FAX: (617) 236-7883. Howard E. Horton, pres; Peter L. Miller, CEO; Robert M. Matorin, dean.

Courses offered include radio, TV prod, speech, bcst news, radio prod, coml copywriting, bcst sls, sportscasting, performing for TV, rock mus for DJs, bcst technology, audio recording, & MIDI prod.

Northwest Technical College - KSRQ-FM. Thief River Falls Campus. 1301 Hwy. 1 E., Thief River Falls, Minn. 56701. (218) 681-6364; (800) 222-2884. FAX: (218) 681-5519. Orley Gunderson, dir; Howard Rokke, gen mgr/instructor; Donald Jorstad, stn mgr.

Courses offered include 110-credit prog in radio & TV bcstg working on a 24,000-kw educ FM stn. A 54-credit prog earns a diploma; additional 56 credits earns an A.A.S. degree in media communications.

Palomar College. 1140 W. Mission Rd., San Marcos, Calif. 92069-1487. (619) 744-1150; (619) 727-7529. Dr. George Boggs, supt; Rob Branch, asst professor radio & TV communications.

Offers hands-on & theoretical course work in bcstg; Associate in Arts (A.A.) Degree or Certificate of Achievement in Radio & Television.

School of Communication Arts. 2526 27th Ave. S., Minneapolis 55406. (612) 721-5357. FAX: (612) 721-6642. Roger Klietz, pres; Kathy Dale, VP.

Courses offered include video prod & technology, applied photography, business computers, computer art & animation, & computer graphic design.

Southwest School of Broadcasting. 1031 E. Battlefield, Suite 212B, Springfield, Mo. 65807. (417) 883-4060. Johnie F. Jones, VP.

Courses offered include gen bcstg, FCC licensing.

Technical Career Institutes. 320 W. 31st St., New York 10001. (212) 594-4000. FAX: (212) 629-3937. Henry Moss, pres; Edward Leff, dean of faculty/VP.

Technical courses offered in electronics engrg, air conditioning & refrigeration, & office mgmt. Associate degree progs.

Trans American School of Broadcasting. One Point Pl., Suite One, Madison, Wis. 53719. (608) 829-2728. Ed Hutchings, pres; Chris Hutchings, dir.

Courses offered include announcing, audio prod, recording & mus technology, TV prod, copywriting, journalism, voice improvement, progmg, & bcst adv sls. Accredited by the Career College Assn.

Western Wisconsin Technical College. 6th & Vine Sts., La Crosse, Wis. 54602. (608) 785-9107. FAX: (608) 785-9407. Jack Jennerjahn, mgr Instructional Media Center.

Courses offered include photography, computer graphics, TV prod, video editing, operation & maintenance of media equipment, audio prod, & all parts of the Associate degree in Visual Communications Science.

Universities and Colleges

Universities and Colleges Offering Degrees in Broadcasting

Alabama
Alabama A and M U.; Normal 35762. BA.
Alabama, U. of; Tuscaloosa 35487-0152. PhD.
Alabama at Birmingham, U. of; Birmingham 35294. BA-BS.
Auburn U.; Auburn 36849. MA-MS.
Jacksonville State University; Jacksonville 36265. BA-BS.
Montevallo, U. of; Montevallo 35115. BA-BS.
North Alabama, U. of; University Stn. 35632-0001. BA-BS.
Troy State University; Troy 36082. BS-BA.

Alaska
Alaska, U. of; Fairbanks 99775-0940. BA-BS.

Arizona
Arizona State U.; Tempe 85287-1305. MA-MS.
Arizona, U. of; Tucson 85721. MA-MS.
Northern Arizona U.; Flagstaff 86004. BA-BS.

Arkansas
Arkansas at Fayetteville, U. of; Fayetteville 72701. MA.
Arkansas at Little Rock, U. of; Little Rock 72204. BA-BS.
Arkansas State U.; Jonesboro 72467. MA-MS.
John Brown U.; Siloam Springs 72761. BA-BS.
Central Arkansas, U. of; Conway 72032. BA-BS.
Harding U.; Searcy 72143. BA-BS.
Southern Arkansas U.; Magnolia 71753. BA-BS.

California
California Polytechnic State U.; San Luis Obispo 93407. BA.
California State U., Chico; Chico 95927. BA-BS.
California State U., Fresno; Fresno 93740-0046. MA-MS.
California State U., Fullerton; Fullerton 92634-4080. MA-MS.
California State U., Hayward; Hayward 94542. BA-BS.
California State U., Long Beach; Long Beach 90840-2803. BA-BS.
California State U., Los Angeles; Los Angeles 90032. BA.
California State U., Northridge; Northridge 91330. MA-MS.
California State U., Sacramento; Sacramento 95819-6070. MA-MS.
California State U., San Jose; San Jose 95192. BA.
California, U. of; Los Angeles 90024-1641. PhD.
Humboldt State U.; Arcata 95521. BA-BS.
La Verne, U. of; La Verne 91750. BA-BS.
Loyola Marymount U.; Los Angeles 90045. MA-MS.
Pepperdine U.; Malibu 90263. MA-MS.
San Diego State U.; San Diego 92182-0417. MA-MS.
San Francisco State U.; San Francisco 94132. MA-MS.
San Francisco, U. of; San Francisco 94117. MA-MS.
San Jose State U.; San Jose 95192-0098. BA-BS.
Santa Clara U.; Santa Clara 95053-2999. BA-BS.
Southern California College; Costa Mesa 92626. BA-BS.
Southern California, U. of; Los Angeles 90089-1695. MA-MS.

Colorado
Colorado State U.; Fort Collins 80523. MA-MS.
Colorado, U. of; Boulder 80309. PhD.
Denver, U. of; Denver 80208. MA-MS.

Connecticut
Eastern Connecticut State U.; Willimantic 06226. BA-BS.
Western Connecticut State College; Danbury 06810. BA.

District of Columbia
American U.; Washington 20016. MA-MS.
Howard U.; Washington 20059. PhD.
Mount Vernon College; Washington 20007. BA.
George Washington U.; Washington 20052. BA-BS.

Florida
Central Florida, U. of; Orlando 32816. BA-BS.
Edward Waters College; Jacksonville 32209. BA.
Florida A&M U.; Tallahassee 32307. BA.
Florida Atlantic U.; Boca Raton 33431. BA-MA.
Florida Southern College; Lakeland 33802. BA-BS.
Florida State U.; Tallahassee 32306-4021. PhD.
Florida, U. of; Gainesville 32601. PhD.
Miami, U. of; Coral Gables 33124. MA-MS.
South Florida, U. of; Tampa 33620. BA.
West Florida, U. of; Pensacola 32514. MA-MS.

Georgia
Augusta College; Augusta 30910. BA-BS.
Clark Atlanta College; Atlanta 30314. BA.
Georgia State U.; Atlanta 30303. MA-MS.
Georgia, U. of; Athens 30602. PhD.

Hawaii
Hawaii, U. of; Honolulu 96822. BA.

Idaho
Idaho, U. of; Moscow 83843. BA-BS.

Illinois
Bradley U.; Peoria 61625. BA-BS.
Columbia College; Chicago 60605. BA.
Eastern Illinois U.; Charleston 61920. MA-MS.
Governors State U.; Park Forest South 60466. MA.
Illinois Benedictine College; Lisle 60532. BA-BS.
Illinois State U.; Normal 61761. BA.
Illinois, Urbana-Champaign, U. of; Urbana 61801. MA-MS.
Lewis University; Romeoville 60441. BA.
Loyola University of Chicago; Chicago 60611. BA-BS.
North Central College; Naperville 60566-7063. BA-BS.
Northern Illinois U.; Dekalb 60115. MA-MS.
Northwestern U.; Evanston 60208. PhD.
Principia College; Elsah 62028. BA-BS.
St. Francis, College of; Joliet 60435. BA.
Saint Xavier College; Chicago 60655. BA-BS.
Sangamon State U.; Springfield 62794-9234. MA-MS.
Southern Illinois U. at Carbondale; Carbondale 62901. MA-MS.
Southern Illinois U. at Edwardsville; Edwardsville 62026. MA-MS.
Western Illinois U.; Macomb 61455. MA-MS.
Wheaton College and Graduate School; Wheaton 60187. MA-MS.

Indiana
Anderson U.; Anderson 46012. BA-BS.
Ball State U.; Muncie 47306. BA-BS.
Butler U.; Indianapolis 46208. MA-MS.
DePauw U.; Greencastle 46135. BA-BS.
Evansville, U. of; Evansville 47702. BS.
Indiana State U.; Terre Haute 47809. MA-MS.
Indiana U.; Bloomington 47405. PhD.
Indianapolis, U. of; Indianapolis 46227. BA-BS.
Notre Dame, U. of; Notre Dame 46556. MA-MS.
Purdue U.; West Lafayette 47907. PhD.
Purdue U., Calumet; Hammond 46323. MA-MS.

Iowa
Buena Vista College; Storm Lake 50588. BA-BS.
Drake U.; Des Moines 50311. BA-BS.
Grand View College; Des Moines 50316. BA-BS.
Iowa State U.; Ames 50011. MA-MS.
Iowa, U. of; Iowa City 52242. PhD.
Morningside College; Sioux City 50588. BA.
Northern Iowa, U. of; Cedar Falls 50614-0139. BA-BS.

Kansas
Fort Hays State U.; Hays 67601-4099. MA-MS.
Kansas State U.; Manhattan 66506-1501. MA-MS.
Kansas, U. of; Lawrence 66045. MA-MS.
Pittsburg St. U.; Pittsburg 66762. BA-BS.
Washburn U.; Topeka 66621. BA-BS.
Wichita State U.; Wichita 67208-1595. MA-MS.

Kentucky
Eastern Kentucky U.; Richmond 40475-0941. BA.
Kentucky, U. of; Lexington 40506-0042. PhD.
Louisville, U. of; Louisville 40292. BA.
Morehead State U.; Morehead 40351-1689. MA-MS.
Murray State U.; Murray 42071. MA-MS.
Northern Kentucky U.; Highland Heights 41076. BA-BS.
Western Kentucky U.; Bowling Green 42104. BA-BS.

Louisiana
Grambling State U.; Grambling 71245. BA-BS.
Louisiana State U.; Baton Rouge 70803. MA-MS.
Loyola U. of New Orleans; New Orleans 70118. BA-BS.
McNeese State U.; Lake Charles 70609-0335. BA-BS.
Nicholls State U.; Thibodaux 70310. BA-BS.
Northeast Louisiana U.; Monroe 71209. BA.
Southeastern Louisiana U.; Hammond 70402. BA-BS.
Southwestern Louisiana, U. of; Lafayette 70504-3650. MA-MS.
Xavier U.; New Orleans 70125. BA-BS.

Maine
Maine, U. of; Orono 04469. BA-BS.
St. Joseph's College; North Windham 04062. BA-BS.

Maryland
Frostburg State U.; Frostburg 21532. BA-BS.
Goucher College; Towson 21204. BA-BS.
Maryland, U. of; College Park 20742. PhD.
Morgan State U.; Baltimore 21239-4093. BA-BS.

Universities and Colleges

Notre Dame of Maryland, College of; Baltimore 21210. BA.
Towson State U.; Towson 21204. MA-MS.

Massachusetts
Boston College; Chestnut Hill 02167. BA-BS.
Boston U.; Boston 02215. MA-MS.
Bridgewater State College; Bridgewater 02325. BA-BS.
Curry College; Milton 02186. BA.
Emerson College; Boston 02116. MA-MS.
Massachusetts, U. of; Amherst 01003. PhD.
Mt. Ida College; Newton Centre 03159. BA-BS.
Northeastern U.; Boston 02115. MA-MS.
Pine Manor College; Chestnut Hill 02167. BA-BS.

Michigan
Calvin College; Grand Rapids 49546. BA-BS.
Central Michigan U.; Mt. Pleasant 48859. MA-MS.
Detroit Mercy, U. of; Detroit 48221. BA.
Eastern Michigan U.; Ypsilanti 48197. BA-BS.
Ferris State U.; Big Rapids 49307. BS.
Michigan State U.; East Lansing 48824. BA-BS.
Northern Michigan U.; Marquette 49855. BA.
Wayne State U.; Detroit 48202. PhD.
Western Michigan U.; Kalamazoo 49008-5090. BA-BS.

Minnesota
Bemidji State U.; Bemidji 55601. BA-BS.
Minnesota, U. of; Minneapolis 55455. PhD.
Northwestern College; St. Paul 55113. BA-BS.
St. Cloud State U.; St. Cloud 56301-4498. BA-BS.
St. Scholastica, College of; Duluth 55811. BA-BS.
St. Thomas at St. Paul; St. Paul 55105. BA-BS.
Winona State U.; Winona 55987. BA-BS.

Mississippi
Jackson State U.; Jackson 39217. MS.
Mississippi State U.; Mississippi State 39762. BA-BS.
Mississippi U. for Women; Columbus 38701. BA.
Mississippi, U. of; University 38677. MA-MS.
Southern Mississippi, U. of; Hattiesburg 39406-5141. BA-BS.

Missouri
Avila College; Kansas City 64145-9990. BA.
Central Missouri State U.; Warrensburg 64093. MA-MS.
Evangel College; Springfield 65802. BA-BS.
William Jewell College; Liberty 64068. BA-BS.
Lindenwood Colleges; St. Charles 63301. BA.
Missouri Southern State College; Joplin 64801-1595. BA-BS.
Missouri, U. of; Kansas City 64110. BA.
Missouri-Columbia, U. of; Columbia 65205. PhD.
Missouri-St. Louis, U. of; St. Louis 63121. BA-BS.
Northwest Missouri State U.; Maryville 64468. BA-BS.
Park College; Parkville 64152. BA.
St. Louis U.; St. Louis 63108. MA.
Southeast Missouri State U.; Cape Girardeau 63701. BA-BS.
Southwest Missouri State U.; Springfield 65804. MA-MS.

Montana
Montana State U.; Bozeman 59717. BA.
Montana, U. of; Missoula 59812. BA-BS.

Nebraska
Creighton U.; Omaha 68178. BA-BS.
Hastings College; Hastings 68901. BA.
Nebraska at Kearney, U. of; Kearney 68849. BA-BS.
Nebraska at Lincoln, U. of; Lincoln 68588. MA-MS.
Nebraska at Omaha, U. of; Omaha 68182-0112. MA-MS.

Nevada
Nevada at Las Vegas, U. of; Las Vegas 89154. MA-MS.

New Hampshire
Franklin Pierce College; Rindge 03461. BA-BS.

New Jersey
Jersey City State College; Jersey City 07305. BA.
Montclair State College; Upper Montclair 07043. MA-MS.
William Paterson College; Wayne 07470. MA.
Seton Hall U.; South Orange 07079. BA.
Trenton State College; Trenton 08619. BA.

New Mexico
Eastern New Mexico U.; Portales 88130. MA-MS.
New Mexico State U.; Las Cruces 88003. BA-BS.

New York
Brooklyn College; Brooklyn 11210. MA-MS.
Buffalo State College; Buffalo 14222. BA-BS.
Canisius College; Buffalo 14208. BA-BS.
Columbia U.; New York 10027. MA-MS.
Fordham U.; Bronx 10458. BA.
Hofstra U.; Hempstead 11550. BA-BS.
Iona College; New Rochelle 10801. BA. Yonkers 10701. BA.
Ithaca College; Ithaca 14850. BA-BS.
Lehman College, CUNY; Bronx 10468. BA-BS.
Long Island U.; Brooklyn 11201. BA.
Marist College; Poughkeepsie 12601. BA.
Mount Saint Vincent, College of; Riverdale 10471. BA-BS.
New Rochelle, College of; New Rochelle 10801. BA.
New York at Brockport, State U. of; Brockport 14420. BA-BS.
New York at Fredonia, State U. of; Fredonia 14063. BA-BS.
New York Institute of Technology; New York 10023. MA.
New York at New Paltz, State U. of; New Paltz 12561. BA-BS.
New York at Oneonta, State U. of; Oneonta 13820-4015. BA-BS.
New York at Oswego, State U. of; Oswego 13126. BA-BS.
New York at Plattsburgh, State U. of; Plattsburgh 12901. BA.
New York U.; New York 10003. BA.
Niagara U.; Niagara 14189. BA-BS.
Pace U.; Pleasantville 10570. BA-BS.
Queens College, CUNY; Flushing 11367. MA-MS.
St. John Fisher College; Rochester 14618. BA.
St. John's U.; Jamaica 11439. BA.
Staten Island, The College of; Staten Island 10301. BA.
Syracuse U.; Syracuse 13244-2100. PhD.

North Carolina
Appalachian State U.; Boone 28608. BA-BS.
East Carolina U.; Greenville 27858. BA-BS.
Elon College; Elon College 27244. BA-BS.
North Carolina State U.; Raleigh 27695-8104. BA-BS.
North Carolina at Chapel Hill, U. of; Chapel Hill 27599. MA-MS.
Pembroke State U.; Pembroke 28372. BA-BS.
Shaw U.; Raleigh 27611. BA.
Wake Forest U.; Winston-Salem 27109. BA-BS.
Western Carolina U.; Cullowhee 28723. BA-BS.

North Dakota
Minot State College; Minot 58701. BA.
North Dakota, U. of; Grand Forks 58202-8118. MA-MS.

Ohio
Akron, U. of; Akron 44325-1003. BA-BS.
Ashland College; Ashland 44805. BA.
Bowling Green State U.; Bowling Green 43403. PhD.
Capital U.; Columbus 43209. BA-BS.
John Carroll U.; University Heights 44118. BA-BS.
Cedarville College; Cedarville 45314. BA-BS.
Cincinnati, U. of; Cincinnati 45221. BA-BS.
Dayton, U. of; Dayton 45409. BA.
Franciscan U. of Steubenville; Steubenville 43952-6701. BA-BS.
Kent State U.; Kent 44242. MA-MS.
Marietta College; Marietta 45750. BA.
Miami U.; Oxford 45056. MA-MS.
Muskingum College; New Concord 43762. BA-BS.
Ohio Northern U.; Ada 45810. BA-BS.
Ohio State U.; Columbus 43210. PhD.
Ohio U.; Athens 45701. PhD.
Otterbein College; Westerville 43081. BA.
Toledo, U. of; Toledo 43606. BA.
Wright State U.; Dayton 45435. BA.
Xavier U.; Cincinnati 45207. BA.
Youngstown State U.; Youngstown 44555. BA.

Oklahoma
Cameron U.; Lawton 73505. BA-BS.
Central Oklahoma, U. of; Edmond 73034-0197. MA-MS.
Langston U.; Langston 73050. BA.
Oklahoma Baptist U.; Shawnee 74801. BA-BS.
Oklahoma Christian U. of Science and Arts; Oklahoma 73136-1100. BA-BS.
Oklahoma City U.; Oklahoma City 73106. BA.
Oklahoma State U.; Stillwater 74078-0195. MA-MS.
Oklahoma, U. of; Norman 73019. MA-MS.
Tulsa, U. of; Tulsa 74104. BA.

Oregon
Lewis and Clark College; Portland 97219. BA-BS.
Southern Oregon State College; Ashland 97520. MA-MS.

Pennsylvania
Bloomsburg U.; Bloomsburg 17815. BA-BS.
California U. of Pennsylvania; California 15419. BA-BS.
Duquesne U.; Pittsburgh 15282-1601. MA-MS.
Elizabethtown College; Elizabethtown 17022-2298. BA-BS.
Geneva College; Beaver Falls 15010. BA.
King's College; Wilkes-Barre 18711. BA.
Kutztown U.; Kutztown 19530. MA-MS.
LaSalle U.; Philadelphia 19141. BA-BS.
Lycoming College; Williamsport 17701. BA-BS.
Mansfield U.; Mansfield 16933. BA-BS.
Pennsylvania State U.; University Park 16802. PhD.
Scranton, U. of; Scranton 18510. BA-BS.
Shippensburg U.; Shippensburg 17257. BA-BS.
Slippery Rock U.; Slippery Rock 16057. BA-BS.
Susquehanna U.; Selinsgrove 17870. BA-BS.

Universities and Colleges

Temple U.; Philadelphia 19122. PhD.
Villanova U.; Villanova 19085-1699. BA-BS.
Westminster College; New Wilmington 16172. BA-BS.
York College of Pennsylvania; York 17403. BA-BS.

South Carolina
South Carolina, U. of; Columbia 29208. MA-MS.
Winthrop College; Rock Hill 29733-0001. BA-BS.

South Dakota
Sioux Falls College; Sioux Falls 57105. BA-BS.
South Dakota State U.; Brookings 57006. BA.
South Dakota, U. of; Vermillion 57069. MA-MS.

Tennessee
East Tennessee State U.; Johnson City 37614. BA-BS.
Freed-Hardeman College; Henderson 38340. BA-BS.
Memphis State U.; Memphis 38152. MA-MS.
Middle Tennessee State U.; Murfreesboro 37132. BA-BS.
Southern College of Seventh-day Adventists; Collegedale 37315. BA.
Tennessee at Chattanooga, U. of; Chattanooga 37403. BA-BS.
Tennessee at Knoxville, U. of; Knoxville 37996. PhD.
Tennessee at Martin, U. of; Martin 38230. BA-BS.

Texas
Abilene Christian U.; Abilene 79699-7568. MA-MS.
Angelo State U.; San Angelo 76909. BA-BS.
Stephen F. Austin State U.; Nacogdoches 75962. MA-MS.
Baylor U.; Waco 76798. MA-MS.
East Texas State U.; Commerce 75428. BA-BS.
Houston, U. of; Houston 77204-4072. MA-MS.
Sam Houston State U.; Huntsville 77340. BA-BS.
Incarnate Word College; San Antonio 78209. MA.
Howard Payne U.; Brownwood 76801. BA-BS.
St. Thomas at Houston, U. of; Houston 77006-4137. BA-BS.
Southern Methodist U.; Dallas 75275. BA-BS.
Southwestern Adventist College; Keene 76059. BA-BS.
Southwest Texas State U.; San Marcos 78666. BA.
Texas A&I U.; Kingsville 78363. BA-BS.
Texas A&M U.; College Station 77843-4111. BA-BS.
Texas Christian U.; Fort Worth 76129. MA-MS.
Texas State U.; Commerce 75428. BA.
Texas Tech U.; Lubbock 79409. MA-MS.
Texas at Arlington, U. of; Arlington 76019. BA-BS.
Texas at Austin, U. of; Austin 78712. PhD.
Texas at El Paso, U. of; El Paso 79968. MA-MS.
Texas Wesleyan College; Fort Worth 76105. BA.
Texas Woman's U.; Denton 76204. BA.
Trinity U.; San Antonio 78212. BA-BS.
Wayland Baptist U.; Plainview 79072. BA-BS.
West Texas State U.; Canyon 79016. BA-BS.

Utah
Brigham Young U.; Provo 84602. MA-MS.
Utah State U.; Logan 84321. BA-BS.
Utah, U. of; Salt Lake City 84112. PhD.
Weber State U; Ogden 84408-1903. BA-BS.

Vermont
Castleton State College; Castleton 05735. BA-BS.

Virginia
Hampton U.; Hampton 23668. BA-BS.
James Madison U.; Harrisonburg 22807. BA-BS.
Liberty U.; Lynchburg 24506. BA.
Norfolk State U.; Norfolk 23504. MA-MS.
Radford U.; Radford 24124. MA-MS.
Regent U.; Virginia Beach 23464. PhD.
Virginia Polytechnic Institute & State U.; Blacksburg 24061. BA.
Washington and Lee U.; Lexington 24450. BA-BS.

Washington
Central Washington U.; Ellenburg 98926. BA-BS.
Eastern Washington U.; Cheney 99004. BA-BS.
Gonzaga U.; Spokane 99258. BA-BS.
Walla Walla College; College Place 99324. BA.
Washington State U.; Pullman 99164-2520. MA-MS.
Washington, U. of; Seattle 98195. PhD.
Western Washington U.; Bellingham 98225. BA.

West Virginia
Bethany College; Bethany 26032. BA-BS.
Marshall U.; Huntington 25755. MA-MS.
Salem-Teikyo U.; Salem 26426. BA.
West Virginia U.; Morgantown 25606-6010. MA-MS.

Wisconsin
Beloit College; Beloit 53511. BA-BS.
Marquette U.; Milwaukee 53233. MA-MS.
Wisconsin-Eau Claire, U. of; Eau Claire 54701. BA-BS.
Wisconsin-La Crosse, U. of; LaCrosse 54601. BA.
Wisconsin-Madison, U. of; Madison 53706. PhD.
Wisconsin-Milwaukee, U. of; Milwaukee 53201. MA-MS.
Wisconsin-Oshkosh, U. of; Oshkosh 54901. BA-BS.
Wisconsin-Platteville, U. of; Platteville 53818-3099. BA-BS.
Wisconsin-River Falls, U. of; River Falls 54022. BA-BS.
Wisconsin-Stevens Point, U. of; Stevens Point 54481. MA.
Wisconsin-Whitewater, U. of; Whitewater 53190. BA-BS.

Wyoming
Wyoming, U. of; Laramie 82071. MA-MS.

Universities and Colleges Offering Broadcasting Courses

Delaware
Delaware-South, U. of; Georgetown 19947.

Idaho
Idaho State U.; Pocatello 83209.

Massachusetts
Endicott College; Beverly 01915.

Missouri
Stephens College; Columbia 65215.

Montana
Eastern Montana College; Billings 59103.

New Hampshire
New Hampshire, U. of; Durham 03824.

New York
Cornell U.; Ithaca 14805.
Rochester Institute of Technology; Rochester 14623.
New York at Geneseo, State U. of; Geneseo 14454.

North Carolina
Duke U.; Durham 27706.

Ohio
Capital U.; Columbus 43209.
Ohio U. at Zanesville; Zanesville 43701.

Oregon
Linfield College; McMinnville 97128.

Pennsylvania
East Stroudsburg U.; East Stroudsburg 18301.

Texas
North Texas, U. of; Denton 76203-3108.

Virginia
Virginia Commonwealth U.; Richmond 23284.

Wisconsin
St. Norbert College; DePere 54115.
Wisconsin Superior, U. of; Superior 54880.

Two-Year Colleges Offering Programs in Broadcasting

Alabama
Alexander City Junior College; Alexander City 35010.
Calhoun Community College; Decatur 35602.
Chattahoochee Valley State Community College; Phenix City 36867.
Gadsden State Community College; Gadsden 35902-0227.
Gadsden State Junior College; Gadsden 35999.
Jefferson State Community College; Birmingham 35215.

Alaska
Prince William Sound Community College; Valdez 99681.

Arizona
Arizona Western College; Yuma 85364.
Phoenix College; Phoenix 85013.

California
Bakersfield Community College; Bakersfield 93305.
Butte College; Oroville 95926.
Chalbot College; Hayward 94545.
College of the Desert; Palm Desert 92260.
Cosumnes River College; Sacramento 95823.
Fullerton College; Fullerton 92634.
Grossmont College; El Cajon 92020.
Laney College; Oakland 94607.
L.A. Pierce College; Woodland Hills 91371.
Long Beach City College; Long Beach 90808.
Los Angeles City College; Los Angeles 90029.
Merced College; Merced 95340.
Modesto Junior College; Modesto 95350.
Moorpark College; Moorpark 93021.
Mt. San Antonio Community College; Walnut 91789.

Universities and Colleges

Orange Coast College; Costa Mesa 92626.

Palomar College; San Marcos 92069.

Pasadena City College; Pasadena 91106.

Rancho Santiago College; Santa Ana 92706.

Rio Hondo College; Whittier 90608.

Saddleback College; Mission Viejo 92692.

San Bernardino Valley College; San Bernardino 92410.

San Diego, City College of; San Diego 92101.

San Francisco, City College of; San Francisco 94112.

San Joaquin Delta College; Stockton 95207.

San Jose City College; San Jose 95128.

San Mateo, College of; San Mateo 94402.

Santa Monica College; Santa Monica 90405.

Santa Rosa Junior College; Santa Rosa 95401.

Southwestern College; Chula Vista 92010.

Taft College; Taft 93268.

Yuba College; Marysville 95901.

Florida

Art Institute of Fort Lauderdale; Fort Lauderdale 33316-3000.

Broward Community College; Davie 33314.

Florida Community College at Jacksonville; Jacksonville 32202.

Florida Junior College; Jacksonville 32202.

Gulf Coast Community College; Panama City 32401.

Lake City Community College; Lake City 32055.

Lake-Sumter Community College; Leesburg 32748.

Miami-Dade Community College; Miami 33176.

Palm Beach Junior College; Lake Worth 33461.

Pensacola Junior College; Pensacola 32504.

St. Petersburg Junior College; St. Petersburg 33710.

Santa Fe Community College; Gainesville 32601.

Georgia

Abraham Baldwin Agricultural College; Tifton 31794.

Dekalb Community College; Clarkston 30021.

Gainesville Junior College; Gainesville 30503.

Idaho

Ricks College; Rexburg 83440.

Illinois

Black Hawk College; Moline 61265.

Illinois Eastern Community Colleges-Campus of Wabash Valley College; Mt. Carmel 62863.

Kennedy-King College; Chicago 60621.

Lakeland College; Mattoon 61938.

Lewis & Clark Community College; Godfrey 62035.

Lincoln College; Lincoln 62656.

Parkland College; Champaign 61853.

Wm. Rainey Harper College; Palatine 60067.

Thornton Community College; South Holland 60473.

John Wood Community College; Quincy 62301.

Indiana

Defense Information School; Fort Benjamin Harrison 46216-6200.

Vincennes U.; Vincennes 47591.

Iowa

Iowa Central Community College; Fort Dodge 50501.

Iowa Lakes Community College; Estherville 51334.

Scott Community College; Bettendorf 52722.

Kansas

Barton County Community Junior College; Great Bend 67530.

Cloud County Community College; Concordia 66901.

Colby Community College; Colby 67701.

Garden City Community College; Garden City 67846.

Hutchinson Community College; Hutchinson 67501.

Kentucky

Ashland Community College; Ashland 41101.

Henderson Community College; Henderson 42420.

Somerset Community College; Somerset 42501.

Maryland

Anne Arundel Community College; Arnold 21012.

Baltimore, Community College of; Baltimore 21216.

Cantonsville Community College; Baltimore 21224.

Essex Community College; Baltimore 21237.

Hagerstown Jr. College; Hagerstown 21740.

Harford Community College; Bel Air 21015.

Montgomery College; Rockville 20850.

Massachusetts

Dean Junior College; Franklin 02038.

Endicott College; Beverly 01915.

Graham Junior College; Boston 02215.

Mt. Wachusett Community College; Gardner 01440-1000.

Michigan

Delta College; University Center 48710.

Kellog Community College; Battle Creek 49015.

Lansing Community College; Lansing 48901.

Oakland Community College-Orchard Ridge Campus; Farmington 48024.

St. Clair County Community College; Port Huron 48060.

Minnesota

Anoka-Ramsey Community College; Coon Rapids 55433.

Area Vocational Technical Institute; Thief River Falls 56701.

Brainerd Community College; Brainerd 56401.

Brainerd/Staples Regional Technical College; Staples 56479.

Duluth Area Vocational Technical Institute; Duluth 55811.

Northwestern College; Roseville 55113.

Rochester Community College; Rochester 55901.

Staples Technical College; Staples 56479.

Mississippi

Mississippi Gulf Coast Jr. College, Jefferson Davis Campus; Gulfport 39501.

Northwest Mississippi Jr. College; Senatobia 38668.

Missouri

Missouri Western State College; St. Joseph 64507.

St. Louis Community College at Florissant Valley; St. Louis 63135.

St. Louis Community College at Forest Park; St. Louis 63110.

Nebraska

Central Technical Community College; Hastings 68901.

Northeast Nebraska Technical Community College; Norfolk 68701.

New Jersey

Brookdale Community College; Lincroft 07738.

Mercer County Community College; Trenton 08690.

New Mexico

New Mexico Military Institute; Roswell 88201-5173.

New York

Adirondack Community College; Queensbury 12804.

Alfred State College; Alfred 14802.

Herkimer County Community College; Herkimer 13350.

Monroe Community College; Rochester 14623.

Nassau Community College; Garden City 11530.

Niagara County Community College; Sanborn 14132.

Onondaga Community College; Syracuse 13215.

Suffolk County Community College; Selden 11784.

Ulster County Community College; Stone Ridge 12486.

North Carolina

Central Carolina Community College; Sanford 27330.

Isothermal Community College; Spindale 28160.

Lenoir Community College; Kingston 28501.

Wilkes Community College; Wilkesboro 28697.

North Dakota

Dickinson State College; Dickinson 58601.

Ohio

International College of Broadcasting; Dayton 45431.

Ohio U.; Zanesville 43701.

Washington State Community College; Marietta 45750.

Toledo, U. of; Toledo 43606-3390.

Oklahoma

Claremore College; Claremore 74017.

Northern Oklahoma College; Tonkawa 74653.

Rose State College; Midwest City 73110.

Oregon

Mt. Hood Community College; Gresham 97030.

Portland Community College; Portland 97219.

Pennsylvania

Bucks County Community College; Newtown 18940.

Community College of Beaver County; Monaca 15061.

Luzerne County Community College; Nanticoke 18634.

Northampton County Community College; Bethlehem 18017.

South Carolina

Tri County Technical College; Pendleton 29670.

South Dakota

Black Hills State U.; Spearfish 57799-9003.

Universities and Colleges

Tennessee
Jackson State Community College; Jackson 38301.
Trevecca Nazarene College; Nashville 37210.
Volunteer State Community College; Gallatin 37066.

Texas
Alvin Community College; Alvin 77511.
Amarillo College; Amarillo 79178.
Central Texas College; Killeen 76540-9990.
Navarro College; Corsicana 75110.
Odessa College; Odessa 79760.
San Antonio College; San Antonio 78212-4299.
San Jacinto College; Pasadena 77505.
Western Texas College; Snyder 79549.

Utah
Defense Information School; Ft. Benjamin Harrison 46216-6200.
Dixie College; St. George 84770.

Vermont
Castleton State College; Castleton 05735.

Virginia
Northern Virginia Community College; Annandale 22003.
Virginia Western Community College; Roanoke 24015.

Washington
Bellevue Community College; Bellevue 98007.
Yakima Valley College; Yakima 98902.

West Virginia
Bethany College; Bethany 26032.
West Virginia State College; Institute 25112.

Wisconsin
Gateway Technical College; Kenosha 53142-1690.
Milwaukee Area Technical College; Milwaukee 53203.

Wyoming
Central Wyoming College; Riverton 82501.

Major Broadcasting and Cable Awards

AAAS-Westinghouse Science Journalism Awards. The American Association for the Advancement of Science (AAAS) offers five awards of $2,500 each for outstanding reporting on the sciences & their applications. Included are life, physical & social sciences, engineering, mathematics, & policy issues grounded in science or technology. Items exclusively related to health or clinical medicine are not included. Separate categories for radio & TV. Contest period for 1994 awards: July 1, 1993, through June 30, 1994. Entries must be postmarked before July 13, 1994. Contact: Nan Broadbent, AAAS, 1333 H St. N.W., Washington 20005.

ACTS Awards. Given annually by the ACTS Satellite Network Inc. to local ACTS affiliates for achievement in local promotion, production, management & community service. All winners receive bronze medallions displaying the ACTS logo. Recipients are chosen from entries submitted by cable & broadcast affiliates throughout the nation. Covers the period from Jan. 1 through Dec. 31 of the same year. Deadline for entries: Feb. 1. Contact: Deborah Key, ACTS Satellite Network Inc., 6350 West Fwy., Fort Worth, Tex. 76150. (817) 737-3241. FAX: (817) 737-7853.

Academy of Television Arts and Sciences Emmy Awards. The Emmys are awarded by the Academy of Television Arts & Sciences for outstanding achievement in the following areas: programs, performing, directing, writing, editing, sound, technical direction/electronic camera, lighting, animation/graphics, choreography, cinematography, art direction, music, costume design, costumers, makeup & hairstyling. Emmys & citations may also be awarded for outstanding achievement in engineering development & casting. To be considered, all achievements must have been broadcast or cablecast to 50% or more of the national nighttime audience in the awards year under consideration. Deadline: Apr. 1. Contact: John Leverence, Awards Director, Academy of Television Arts & Sciences, 5220 Lankershim Blvd., North Hollywood, Calif. 91602.

American Legion Fourth Estate Award. Awarded annually to a member of the electronic or print media for excellence in journalism. Entries must document significant public impact. Recipient must accept the award in person during the American Legion National Convention. A $1,500 stipend is included to compensate for expenses incurred in accepting the award. Eligibility period: Jan. 1 through Dec. 31 annually. Deadline: Jan. 31 annually. Contact: The American Legion National Headquarters, Public Relations Division, Box 1055, Indianapolis 46206.

American Speech-Language-Hearing Association National Media Awards for Journalists. ASHA's Media Awards recognize outstanding contributions by broadcast journalists to the public's knowledge & understanding of speech, language & hearing disorders; their impact on the ability to communicate; & the role of speech-language pathologists & audiologists in treating them. Material must have been broadcast between June 1, 1993, & May 31, 1994. Deadline for entries: June 30, 1994. Contact: Mary Schreder, Public Information ASHA Coordinator, 1994 Media Awards for Journalists, Public Information Dept., American Speech-Language-Hearing Association, 10801 Rockville Pike, Rockville, Md. 20852. (301) 897-5700.

American Women in Radio and Television Inc. Awards. The Commendation Awards recognize network programs, local programs & commercials for excellence in portraying a positive & realistic image of women. The Silver Satellite Award honors an individual who has made outstanding contributions to the industry. AWRT Achievement Award pays tribute to a member who has earned the recognition of her peers & strengthened the role of women in the industry through her exceptional contribution to AWRT & the community. The Sid Guber Award assists a student of the performing arts. The Chapter of the Year Award is presented each year to the active AWRT chapter that demonstrates the greatest contribution to the growth, development & visibility of AWRT in the broadcast industry; service to the chapter's membership & community; & dedication & commitment to the goals & objectives of AWRT. The Star Awards are presented each year to three individuals, stations or companies in radio, TV & cable on the basis of their sensitivity & commitment to issues & concerns of women. Deadline for entries: Dec. 31, 1994. Contact: Diane Walden, Director of Advertising & Public Relations, AWRT, 1101 Connecticut Ave. N.W., Suite 700, Washington 20036. (202) 429-5102. FAX: (202) 857-1111.

Armstrong Awards. Given annually to radio stations (AM & FM) & networks for "programming innovations & creative use of radio." This can be anything from innovative new program formats to creative documentataries to compelling new reports. There are three categories: commercial stations & networks; public stations & networks; college stations & networks. In addition, a fourth category entitled "technical innovation" goes to innovators in the field of telecommunications taken in its broadest sense—e.g., radio, television, computers, telephony, lasers, satellites. First place winners in each category receive a plaque made of brass & bronze on wood. Second place & honorable mention runners-up receive certificates suitable for framing. Established in 1964, the awards are administered & sponsored by the Armstrong Memorial Research Foundation in cooperation with Columbia University. The annual awards program covers the period from Jan. 1 to Dec. 31. Deadlines for entries: June 15. Contact: Matthew Field, Chairman Awards Committee, Armstrong Foundation, Columbia University, S.W. Mudd Hall, 500 W. 120th St., Room 1311, New York 10027. (212) 854-8703.

Batten Fellowship Program. For full-time journalists from any medium with at least three years of experience to earn an MBA in a full-time, two-year program, & who intend to pursue a career in media management. Must be a U.S. citizen & meet all requirements as an entering MBA student. Three Batten fellowships can be awarded annually. Tuition, fees & stipend for living expenses provided. Deadline for entries: March 15. Contact: Director of Financial Aid, The Darden School, University of Virginia, Box 6550, Charlottesville, Va. 22906.

The William Benton Fellowships in Broadcast Journalism. The Benton Fellowships Program at the University of Chicago offers the nation's most promising broadcast journalists nine months to study fundamental issues that underlie the news. Twelve Benton Fellows are chosen annually on the basis of applications & recommendations. They receive stipends normally equal to their full current salaries & financial assistance for relocation. Deadline for entries: Feb. 1. Contact: Director, William Benton Fellowships in Broadcast Journalism, The University of Chicago, 5737 University Ave., Chicago 60637. (312) 702-3435.

Howard W. Blakeslee Awards. Given annually for creative efforts in any medium of mass communication judged to have contributed most to public understanding of progress in research, & the prevention, care & treatment of heart & circulatory diseases; $1,000 & citation. Eligibility period: previous calendar year. Deadline for entry: Feb. 1. Contact: Howard W. Blakeslee Awards, American Heart Association, National Center, 7272 Greenville Ave., Dallas 75231. (214) 706-1340. FAX: (214) 369-3685.

Broadcast Cable Financial Management Association "Avatar" Award. Given annually in the spring to an individual for outstanding contributions to the communications industry & to local community affairs. Candidates are generally nominated by BCFM members, but nominations from other sources are considered. Submit a letter detailing the candidate's qualifications, as well as a rationale for consideration by BCFM Avatar Awards Committee. The award consists of a plaque & a contribution by BCFM of a maximum of $1,000 to a charitable, educational or other type of institution of the recipient's choice, subject to BCFM board approval. Contact: BCFM, Buz Buzogany, Executive Director, Broadcast Cable Financial Management Association, 701 Lee St., Suite 1010, Des Planes, Ill. 60016-4555. (708) 296-0200.

Broadcast Designers Association Award. An annual juried exposition to reward & encourage excellence in video design. Eligible entries must be created within the preceding calendar year. Winners who qualify for the show receive BDA Gold, Silver or Bronze Award at the discretion of the judges. The Gold & Silver awards are presented during a special program at the annual BDA Seminar, held in early June. Broadcast designers may submit entries in categories of on-air, scenic, multimedia & print. Non-BDA members are encouraged to enter. The entire show is available to schools & professional organizations on request. Deadline: Jan. 5, 1995. Contact: Lynn Myers, BDA Administrator, 350 Townsend St., #422, San Francisco 94107. (415) 543-6330. FAX: (415) 543-6332.

Broadcast Education Association. The BEA offers broadcasting scholarships in cooperation with the National Association of Broadcasters (NAB) to honor broadcasters & the broadcast industry. Scholarships will be awarded for a period of one scholastic year, normally two semesters or three quarters, for study in the junior or senior year or for study in graduate school. There should be substantial evidence of superior academic performance & potential to be an outstanding contributor to the field. The applicant must, under any scholarship, pursue a course of study for a degree in a university or college that is an institutional member of the BEA. Scholarships offered are as follows: Harold E. Fellows Memorial Scholarships, four scholarships of $1,250 each for study in any area of broadcasting. The applicant or parent must be, or have been, an employee or have engaged in a formal internship at a NAB member radio, TV station or network; James Lawrence Fly Scholarships, one scholarship of $2,500 offered to juniors, seniors, graduate students & law students presented by the law firm of Fly, Shuebruk, Gaguine, Boros, Shulkind & Braun; Walter Patterson Scholarships, two scholarships of $1,250 each awarded to students working for a career in radio; Broadcast Pioneers, two scholarships of $1,250 each offered to juniors, seniors & graduate students studying any area of broadcasting; Shane Media Scholarships, one scholarship of $3,000 for study in a career in radio, presented by Shane Media Services, Houston; Vincent T. Wasilewski Scholarship, one scholarship of $2,500 awarded to a junior, senior or graduate student studying any area of broadcasting, presented by Patrick Communications Corp., Columbia, Md. Application forms require personal and academic data, broadcast experience & other activity records & a written statement of goals & references. Deadline to call for applications: Dec. 15. Deadline to submit applications: Jan. 15. Contact: BEA, 1771 N St. N.W., Washington 20036. (202) 429-5354. Louisa A. Nielsen, Executive Director.

Broadcast Promotion & Marketing Executives International Gold Medallion Awards. Awards recognize excellence in the fields of audience, news & sales, promotion & publicity, & special projects undertaken by radio or TV stations, networks, program distributors or cable systems. Eighty-nine categories are divided into work done by & for: TV stations, radio stations, networks, program distributors, cable systems & cable networks. Entry categories encompass work done for on-air, print, outdoor, publicity, special projects & direct mail. Finalists are notified prior to annual conference & expo in June. Deadline for entries: February 1995. Entries must run between Jan. 1, 1994 & Dec. 31, 1994. Contact: Steve Ferger, BPME, 6255 Sunset Blvd., Suite 624, Los Angeles 90028. (213) 465-3777. FAX: (213) 469-9559.

Heywood Broun Award. A $2,000 award for outstanding journalistic achievement is given "in the spirit of Heywood Broun." Eligibility period: preceding calendar year. Deadline for entry: early Jan. Contact: David Eisen, Research & Information Director, The Newspaper Guild, 8611 2nd Ave., Silver Spring, Md. 20910.

CableACE Awards. Recognizes outstanding achievement in the cable industry on both the national & local level. Local awards for 35 categories are given out annually at the NCTA Convention. National awards are given out in January, for 85 categories. Industry awards include the Golden CableACE (awarded annually for a special project), the Governor's Award (given, when applicable, to an individual), and the Creator's Award (given, when applicable, to a network). Deadline for national awards is in August. Deadline for local awards varies upon the date of the NCTA Convention. Contact: Howard Marcantel, Competitions Director, 1724 Massachusetts Ave. N.W., Washington 20036. (202) 775-3611. FAX: (202) 775-3689.

Russell L. Cecil Arthritis Writing Awards. Given each year by the Arthritis Foundation for outstanding writing about arthritis in TV, radio, newspapers & magazines. Eligibility period: preceding calendar year. Deadline for entries: Feb. 15. Contact: Lisa M. Newbern, Cecil Awards, Arthritis Foundation, 1314 Spring St. N.W., Atlanta 30309. (404) 872-7100. FAX: (404) 872-0457.

Clarion Awards. Sponsored by Women in Communications Inc. Open to all media. More than half of an entry must have been published, broadcast or implemented between Jan. 1 & Dec. 31. Entry forms will be available in December. Winners will receive Clarion Award plaques at the annual Women in Communications Inc. National Professional Conference. There are more than 80 categories in the areas of photography, newspapers, magazines, brochures, newsletters, public relations, marketing, audiovisual productions, radio, television & advertising. Deadline: early March. Contact: Margaret Jenkins, Women in Communications Inc., 2101 Wilson Blvd., Suite 417, Arlington, Va. 22201. (703) 528-4200.

The New CLIO Awards. Given annually for best U.S. & international TV, cinema, cable, print & radio advertising. CLIO statues for best, certificates of recognition for finalists. Open to all commercials introduced in prior year. Deadline: Jan 15, 1995. Awarded: June 20, 1995. Contact: James Smyth, CEO, CLIO, 400 Madison Ave., Suite 1208, New York 10017. (212) 593-1900. FAX: (212) 754-0581.

College Television Programming Awards. Annual national award scholarships are presented to student broadcast & cable producers for outstanding works in various entertainment & educational program genres. The awards are also designed to encourage talented producers to stay in the film & video production field. Works must have been completed in the preceding year (Oct.-Sept.) in either film or video, but not necessarily aired on a college TV station/channel. Awards are presented at the National Conference of College Broadcasters in November. Entry deadline: Oct. 2. Contact: Glenn Gutmacher, NACB, 71 George St., Providence, R.I. 02912-1824. (401) 863-2225. FAX: (401) 863-2221.

Corporation for Public Broadcasting. CPB presents the following awards annually: Public Television Local Program Awards recognize excellence in local programming in public TV. Public Radio Program Awards recognize excellence in radio programming at the local or national level. The Ralph Lowell Award is presented to an individual who has made outstanding contributions to public TV. The Edward R. Murrow Award is presented to an individual for outstanding contributions to public radio. Deadlines vary to coincide with the annual meetings of the public radio & TV licensees. The Local Radio Development Awards are given for excellence in marketing & fund-raising. For information about the first four awards, contact Station Relations, CPB, 901 E St. N.W., Washington 20004-2006. (202) 879-9771.

Crystal Radio Award. Annual award given by the NAB to 10 radio stations for excellence in community service. Stations apply to the NAB for consideration by an independent panel of judges. Deadline for entry each year is Feb. 8. Winners are announced at the NAB's spring convention. Entry forms may be obtained by contacting William Peak, NAB Radio, 1771 N St. N.W., Washington 20036-2891. (202) 429-5422.

Alfred I. duPont-Columbia University Awards. The Silver Batons are given annually for outstanding work in news & public affairs during the year. Categories for judging include network, local & cable TV as well as radio & independent productions. Local TV station entries are judged in categories according to market size—major market: ADI 1-10; medium market: ADI 11-50; small market: ADI 51 & smaller. Awards may also be made to individual journalists, programs, stations or series at the jurors' discretion. The Gold Baton, honoring the program judged to have made the greatest contribution to the public's understanding of important issues or news events, may also be made at the jurors' discretion. A board of screeners made up of news & public affairs professionals, many of whom are former winners, reviews all of the entries & designates finalists, with specific recommendations to the jurors who then select the winners. Entry forms are available in May & may be obtained by contacting the awards office. The eligibility period is July 1, 1993, through June 30, 1994. Deadline for entry: July 15, 1994. Contact: Lesley Kuchek, Administrative Assistant, Alfred I. duPont Center for Broadcast Journalism, Columbia University, School of Journalism, Rm. 701, New York 10027. (212) 280-5047.

Freedoms Foundation Awards. Given annually to radio & TV stations that develop or feature constructive activities to bring about a better understanding of America. Subjects may be drug abuse educucation, ecology projects, patriotic programs, respect for the law, economic education, moral & spiritual values, human dignity, brotherhood & responsible citizenship. Principal award of honor medal & additional honor medals. Substantiating materials must include a script or synopsis. Information needed is date the feature was aired or released, name of sponsor (station, network &/or company/organization), full address(es) & the CEO. If sponsor is a station, it is helpful to know the network affiliation. Eligibility period: May 1, 1993 to May 1, 1994. Nominations must be received by May 1. Contact: E. Katherine Wood-Jacobs, Awards Department, Rt. 23, Freedoms Foundation at Valley Forge, Valley Forge, Pa. 19481. (215) 933-8825.

Gabriel Awards. Given annually by Unda-USA (the National Catholic Association of Broadcasters and Communicators) to honor TV & radio programs, feature segments, spots & stations that serve viewers & listeners through the positive, creative treatment of issues of concern to humankind & enrich their audiences through a value-centered vision of humanity. Program categories in TV: entertainment, information, children's (for 14 years-of-age & under), religious, programming in the arts, coverage of a single news story, community service programs, PSAs & short features. Program categories in radio: arts/entertainment, news/information, religious, coverage of a single news story, community awareness campaign, PSAs & short features. Also awards for Station of the Year & Personal Achievement Award. Deadline for entries: July 13. Contact: Unda-USA, National Catholic Association for Broadcasters and Communicators, 901 Irving Ave., Dayton, Ohio 45409-2316. (513) 229-2303. FAX: (513) 229-2300.

Gavel Awards. Given annually by the American Bar Association in recognition of outstanding public service by United States newspapers, wire services, magazines, book publishers, news syndicates, theater, radio, TV & motion pictures for increasing public understanding of the American system of law & justice. Awards for media organizations are in the form of individually-inscribed gavels. Gavel Award certificates are given to individuals identified as playing key roles in the creation of winning entries. The Gavels are presented at the ABA's annual meeting in August to the CEO of the award-winning organization; the certificates are mailed directly to the winners. Eligible materials must have been published, broadcast or produced during the period from Jan. 1 through Dec. 31., & entries must be received no later than Feb. 1, for all materials. Request official order form prior to submitting entries. TV programs are considered in several classifications: network programs, syndicated programs, local &/or independent programs, local noncommercial programs & cable. All entries must be submitted in the form of 3/4" video cassettes. Radio programs considered in six classifications. Maximum of five entries per media organization. Write for entry form & rules brochure. Deadline: early Feb. Contact: Peggy O'Carroll, Staff Liaison, Gavel Awards, American Bar Assn., 750 N. Lake Shore Dr., Chicago 60611. (312) 988-6137.

General Motors Cancer Research Foundation International Biomedical Journalism Prizes. A $10,000 cash prize & a limited-edition work of art are awarded in each of three categories: newspaper or wire services, periodical & broadcast. Winners are selected annually. Deadline on or before midnight, Jan. 31 of the year following the contest year. Contact: General Motors Cancer Research Foundation, 11-132 General Motors Bldg., 3044 W. Grand Blvd., Detroit 48202.

Global Media Awards. The Global Media Awards are given by The Population Institute to those who have drawn attention to population issues & problems. There are 15 categories, including best columnist, best radio program, best TV documentary & best individual reporting effort. Nominees can include institutions or journalists, & previous winners are eligible. Entries should be made in writing, along with justification for entry & photo of nominee, by Sept. 15, 1995. For more information, contact Media Awards Coordinator, The Population Institute, 107 2nd St. N.E., Washington 20002. (202) 544-3300. FAX: (202) 544-0068.

Green Eyeshade Award. Excellence in Journalism awards for journalists working in print, radio & television for eleven southeastern states: Georgia, Florida, Alabama, Tennessee, Mississippi, North & South Carolina, West Virginia, Kentucky, Arkansas, and Louisiana. Entries must have run between Jan. 1, 1994 & Dec. 31, 1994. Entries must be received by midnight, Friday, Jan. 8, 1995. Contact Kat Yancey, SPJ Chapter Manager, 3425 Regalwoods Dr., Altanta 30340.

Hall of Fame Award. Worldwide in scope. Given to anyone who has made an outstanding contribution to the art of broadcasting. Candidate must have been deceased at least two years prior to annual meeting of Broadcast Pioneers in spring of each year. Nomination must be accompanied by short biography & statement of achievement. Contact: Ed DeGray, Executive Director, Broadcast Pioneers, 320 W. 57th St., New York 10019. (212) 830-2581. FAX: (212) 956-2059.

Health Journalism Awards. Given annually by the American Chiropractic Association to recognize journalists in every medium & reward those who have distinguished themselves in health reporting. The categories of competition include newspapers, consumer magazines, TV, radio, student publication & productions, trade, professional or special interest publications & audiovisuals. Each winner will receive a cash award of $200 & an ACA distinguished journalism plaque. Special recognition plaques also go to runners-up. Deadline for entries: Apr. 1 for works published or produced during the preceding calendar year. Contact: Abbe Fischler, Director of Communications, ACA Headquarters, 1701 Clarendon Blvd., Arlington, Va. 22209. (703) 276-8800. FAX: (703) 243-2593.

Sidney Hillman Foundation Prize Awards. Given annually by the Sidney Hillman Foundation for contributions in the fields of daily or periodical journalism, nonfiction, radio & TV. Themes would include the protection of individual civil liberties, improved race relations, a strengthened labor movement, the advancement of social welfare & economic security, greater world understanding & related problems. Contributions must be published or produced under professional auspices in 1994. Final scripts must be submitted in connection with radio & TV awards. Films, tapes & records should not be submitted until requested. Prizes of $1,000 are awarded. Deadline for entries: Jan. 15, 1995. Contact: Mary Contini, Awards Coordinator, The Sidney Hillman Foundation, 15 Union Square, New York 10003. (212) 242-0700. FAX: (212) 255-7230.

Hugo Awards. The Annual Chicago International Film Festival, Oct. 8-24. Gold & Silver Hugo statues awarded annually in 15 different categories, including talk shows, drama for TV, documentaries & children's programming, as well as ten special achievement categories. Open to all TV film commercials & documentary & entertainment programs telecast worldwide. Deadline: July 31. Contact: Entry Coordinator, Chicago International Film Festival Inc., 415 N. Dearborn, Chicago 60610. (312) 644-3400.

IRE Annual Awards for Investigative Reporting. The IRE Awards for Investigative Reporting are given for initiative, originality & persistence in breaking down secrecy in matters of public importance in the following categories: a network or syndicated TV program, TV stations in the top 20 markets, TV stations under top 20 markets, newspapers with less than 75,000 circulation, newspapers with greater than 75,000 circulation, radio, books, magazines. Awards are for work done in the preceding calendar year. Official entry form available through Investigative Reporters and Editors. $15 fee per entry. Deadline: Jan 15. Contact: Tracy Barnett, Acting Director, IRE, 100 Neff Hall, UMC-Journalism, Columbia, Mo. 65211.

IRE Tom Renner Award for Crime Reporting. Given to the best investigative reporting in print, broadcast or book form, covering organized crime or other criminal acts. $1,000 cash award for work done in the preceding calendar year. Deadline: January 15. Contact: Tracy Barnett, Acting Director, IRE, 100 Neff Hall, UMC-Journalism, Columbia, Mo. 65211.

The Interep Radio Store National College Radio Awards. Scholarships to individuals & cash awards to stations are sponsored by The Interep Radio Store of New York for outstanding station operations, promotion & programming on college radio in various award categories. The program is designed to inspire college broadcasters to excel in various aspects of college radio station operations & to encourage them to pursue radio as a career. Awards are presented at the National Conference of College Broadcasters in November. Entry deadline: Oct. 2. Contact: Glenn Gutmacher, NACB, 71 George St., Providence, R.I. 02912-1824. (401) 863-2225. FAX: (401) 863-2221.

International Broadcasting Awards. Given to "world's best" radio & TV commercials broadcast in 1994. New additional categories in both radio & TV, including broadcast entertainment promotion & best spot promoting environmental awareness. Format requirements: TV—3/4" videocassette; radio—5" reel, 7 1/2 IPS or audiocassette. Deadline for entries: Jan. 22, 1995. Call for entries by Nov. 1994. Entry fee: $95 single TV entry, $75 single radio entry. Contact: Gene Herd, Associate Executive Director, Hollywood Radio & Television Society, 5315 Laurel Canyon Blvd., Suite 202, North Hollywood, Calif. 91607. (818) 769-4313. FAX: (818) 509-1262.

The International Emmy Awards of the International Council of the National Academy of Television Arts & Sciences. Recognizing excellence in programs made outside the United States, presented annually in New York City. Six program categories: drama, documentary, arts documentary, performing arts, popular arts, children & young people. Deadline for entries: mid-September. Contact: Linda Alexander, Program Manager, The International Council of NATAS, 142 W. 57th St., 16th Fl., New York 10019. (212) 489-6969. FAX: (212) 489-6557. TWX: 275766.

International Radio & Television Society Gold Medal Award. A gold medal is presented each year to an outstanding individual or corporate entity in radio, TV, cable, broadcast advertising or related fields. Contact: International Radio & Television Society, 420 Lexington Ave., New York 10170.

Iris Awards. Presented each January by NATPE International. Outstanding locally-produced TV programs in six categories are awarded at the annual program convention. Deadline: Oct. 11. Contact: Phil Corvo, NATPE, 2425 Olympic Blvd., Suite 550E, Santa Monica, Calif. 90404. (310) 453-4440.

Max Karant Awards for Excellence in Aviation Journalism. The Max Karant Awards for Excellence in Aviation Journalism will be given for fair & insightful coverage of general aviation. There are three entry categories: print, TV & radio. A $1,000 award will be given in each category based on works published or broadcast in the previous year only. Call for details. Pat Rishel, AOPA, (Aircraft Owners and Pilots Association), 421 Aviation Way, Frederick, Md. 21701. (301) 695-2157.

The Frank Kelley Journalistic Award. Through this award, the American Association of Professional Landmen is recognizing those in the broadcast media who exhibit excellence & responsibility in reporting oil & gas development & issues to the public. The winner will receive $500 in cash & a walnut-and-bronze plaque. All entries must have been produced & aired in the United States & Canada between May 1, 1993, & May 1, 1994. Deadline: May 15, 1994. Contact: AAPL, 4100 Fossil Creek Blvd., Fort Worth, Tex. 76137-2791.

Robert F. Kennedy Journalism Awards. Given annually for outstanding broadcast, print, cartoon & photojournalism coverage of the problems of the disadvantaged in American society & outstanding coverage in the American press of the disadvantaged abroad by a foreign correspondent. Separate professional & student categories. Entries must have been broadcast or published during the preceding calendar year. The awards program is sponsored by an independent committee of broadcast & print journalists who annually choose a panel of judges from within the profession. Deadline: late Jan. Contact: Erin P. Scully, Director. 1206 30th St. N.W., Washington 20007. (202) 333-1880.

The Livingston Awards for Young Broadcast and Print Journalists. Three $5,000 prizes are given for the best coverage of local, national & international news by journalists aged 35 or younger in any U.S.-owned medium. Deadline for entries: early Feb. Contact: Charles R. Eisendrath or Barbara Tucker, The Livingston Awards, Wallace House, 620 Oxford Rd., 2080 Frieze, Univ. of Michigan, Ann Arbor, Mich. 48104. (313) 998-7575.

Marconi Radio Award. Named after the inventor and Noble Laureate, Guglielmo Marconi, the NAB's Marconi Radio Awards honor stations & personalities for their excellence in & contributions to radio. Nomination forms available in the spring for awards of the past calendar year. Contact: William Peak, Awards Coordinator, NAB Radio, 1771 N St. N.W., Washington 20036. (202) 429-5422.

Mark of Excellence. Annual competition recognizing outstanding college journalists in each SPJ region (first, second & third places) with the first-place winners competing at the national level for one award in each category; open to all students; self-nomination; judged by panels of professionals. Five new categories—radio newscast, television news photography, television feature photography, television sports photography & television newscast—are being added this year for a total of 27 categories. Fee per entry is $5 for members, $10 for non-members. Deadline is late January, regional awards presented at regions' spring conferences, national awards presented at convention. Contact: Peggy Tennis, SPJ, Box 77, 16 S. Jackson, Greencastle, Ind. 46135. (317) 653-3333. FAX: (317) 653-4631.

The Lowell Mellett Award for Improving Journalism through Critical Evaluation. The award was established by the Mellett Fund for a Free and Responsible Press in 1978 & was transferred to the School of Communications of The Pennsylvania State University in 1984. The award, like the fund, is named in honor of the distinguished Scripps-Howard editor & syndicated columnist who died in 1960. The Mellett Award seeks to recognize distinguished contributions from whatever source to the improvement of print & broadcast journalism by means of responsible analysis or critical evaluation, & to encourage new & innovative approaches to constructive journalism or media criticism. Examples of the kind of work the award is intended to recognize include that of media ombudsmen, journalism reviews, books & broadcasts, & academic & other research studies. The first-place prize is $1,000. The winner will be selected by judges drawn from journalism education & practice. It will be given for work done in the calendar year 1993. Deadline for entries: early March. Contact: Karen Freeman, Director Mellett Award, School of Communications, Pennsylvania State University, 210 Carnegie Bldg., University Park, Pa. 16802.

Michigan Journalism Fellows. The University of Michigan awards mid-career fellowships for professional or personal development; $25,000 plus tuition. Print, photo & broadcast mediums. Eligibility extends to any full-time word or image journalist with five years' experience whose work either as an employee or free-lance appears regularly in U.S.-controlled print or broadcast media. Individuals may nominate themselves, or be proposed by employers. Open to U.S. citizens only. Eligibility period: academic year (Sept.-April). Deadline: February 1. Contact: Charles R. Eisendrath, Director, Michigan Journalism Fellows, Wallace House, 620 Oxford Rd., University of Michigan, Ann Arbor, Mich. 48104.

Millennium Award. Salutes innovative strategies that companies in the cable industry are implementing to recruit, train, motivate & retain high-quality employees—today & into the next millenium. All workforce programs currently in place are eligible for review. Deadline: July 1, 1994. Contact: Pamela Williams, 500 N. Michigan Ave., Suite 1400, Chicago 60611. (312) 661-1700.

Paul Miller Washington Reporting Fellowships. Fellowships are sponsored by The Freedom Forum of Arlington, Va. The fellowships were created in honor of the late Paul Miller, former chairman of the Gannett Foundation & Gannett Co. Inc. The program is designed to help Washington-based bureau chiefs & staffers develop locally-oriented news stories in the nation's capital. Fifteen fellows spend two days a month for 12 months meeting with experienced Washington journalists & visiting the places where local news originates, thus learning newsgathering skills, associating with prominent news makers & establishing contacts with behind-the-scenes news sources. Candidates must be journalists currently or about to be assigned to Washington by any regional or national newspapers, wire services, radio or TV stations maintaining Washington bureaus. Applicants must submit a 500-word statement describing the benefits they would derive from the program & a statement from their employers endorsing the application & affirming that the applicants will be allowed to attend all sessions. All applications for 1994-1995 program must be postmarked no later than Jan. 15, 1995. Selection will be based on applicant's apparent potential to provide superior coverage of locally-oriented news in Washington for readers & audiences across the country. Contact: Brian Buchanan, Director, 1101 Wilson Blvd., Arlington, Va. 22209. (703) 528-0800. FAX: (703) 284-2879.

Missouri Medals. Given annually since 1930 for lifetime accomplishments in the field of journalism—in news, advertising, photography, education, radio, TV & graphics. Missouri Medals are based on records of performance over many years rather than upon a single instance of journalistic achievement. Deadline for nominations, which must be accompanied by significant supporting material: Apr. 1. Contact: Dean, School of Journalism, Box 838, University of Missouri-Columbia, Columbia, Mo. 65205. (314) 882-4821.

The Mobius Advertising Awards. 24th Annual International Awards Competition for TV, cinema & radio commercials, print advertising & package design. Eligible are any commercials produced or aired during the 12 months preceding the festival's annual Oct. 1 deadline. Newly produced, previously produced, currently appearing or reintroduced advertising is eligible. Contact: J.W. Anderson, Chairman; Patricia Meyer, Executive Director, 841 N. Addison Ave., Elmhurst, Ill. 60126. (708) 834-7773. FAX: (708) 834-5565.

NBC Fellowships for Minorities. Five fellowships are distributed among institutions near each of the NBC TV stations in New York; Washington; Burbank, Calif.; Cleveland; & Chicago. Contact: Judy Sullivan, Administration, 30 Rockefeller Plaza, New York 10112. (212) 664-5255.

Alliance For Community Media Hometown Video Festival Awards. Awards are given to the best of public, educational & government access programming in 37 categories from over 2,000 international entries. Eligibility period: March 7, 1994 to March 6, 1995. Deadline: March, 1995. Contact: Programs Managers, the Buskey Group, 666 11th St. N.W., Suite 806, Washington 20001-4542. (916) 441-6277.

NPPA Annual TV Photography and Editing Contest. Presented annually for the best news stories produced in spot, general, sports, feature, new feature, documentary & in-depth series classes. News Photography Station of the Year & News Photographer of the Year are also included. Editing categories are: under deadline, general news-cuts only, general news-super booth, editor's feature & sports editing. Stories are submitted on BETA & 3/4" tape format. Deadline: Postmarked by January 31. Contact: Robert J. Sprouls, Contest Chairman, 6452 Streamside Ct., Indianapolis 46278-1964. (317) 291-5690.

National Academy of Television Arts & Sciences "Emmy" Awards. Recognizes outstanding achievements in all phases of daytime TV, including programming, directing, writing, performing, etc. The National Academy of Television Arts & Sciences also presents the Sports Emmy & the Engineering Development awards, covering the entire previous year. Contact: Trudy Wilson, Awards Manager, (212) 586-8424. FAX: (212) 246-8129. For deadline information contact Richard Thrall, Chairman National Awards, 111 W. 57th St., New York 10019.

National AP Broadcasters Awards. Presented annually by Associated Press Broadcasters Inc., an advisory board of directors to the broadcast division of The Associated Press, in recognition of journalistic excellence among AP TV & radio members. Entrants must first win similar AP awards on the state level. Eligibility period: previous calendar year. Contact the state AP bureau or APB Awards, Associated Press, 1825 K St. N.W., Suite 710, Washington 20006-1253. (202) 736-1100; (800) 821-4747.

National Association of Broadcasters (NAB) Distinguished Service Award. Plaque awarded annually to any broadcaster, whether or not actively engaged in the operations-end of the broadcasting industry, who has made a significant & lasting contribution to the American system of broadcasting by virtue of singular achievement or continuing service for, or on behalf of, the industry. The recipient is required to be present at the convention to receive the award. Established in 1953, the award is presented at the annual convention. Contact: NAB Distinguished Service Award, 1771 N. St. N.W., Washington 20036. (202) 429-5422. FAX: (202) 775-3523.

National Association of Broadcasters (NAB) National Radio Award. Established in 1984, this annual award is presented to an individual for a significant or ongoing contribution to the radio industry either as a performer or in a leadership position. The winner is selected by the NAB's executive committee. Applications are not accepted for this award, which is presented at the NAB's fall radio convention. Contact: William Peak, Awards Coordinator, NAB Radio, 1771 N St. N.W., Washington 20036-2891. (202) 429-5422. FAX: (202) 775-3523.

National Association of Broadcasters (NAB) Radio & Television Engineering Achievement Awards. Annual award presented to owners, officers or employees of any company, subsidiary or division whose primary business is broadcasting or is directly in support of broadcasting, including employees of the federal government directly engaged in broadcast engineering work. The candidates for the two awards shall be recognized on the basis of a single significant contribution, or contributions, made over a period of time for significant advancements in broadcasting engineering. A contribution may include inventions, the development of new techniques, leadership in broadcast engineering issues, or the dissemination of technical knowledge & literature. Deadline for entries: Nov. 29. Contact: NAB Science & Technology, 1771 N St. N.W., Washington 20036. (202) 429-5346. FAX: (202) 775-4981.

National Association of Broadcasters (NAB) Service to Children Television Awards. Annual awards program established by the NAB to recognize outstanding achievement in locally-produced children's TV programming & outreach activities. Entries are solicited in the spring & awards are presented in the fall. All entries are judged by a panel of individuals recognized for their contributions to children's issues & TV. Contact: John Porter,

NAB Television Department, 1771 N St. N.W., Washington 20036. (202) 429-5368.

National Awards for Education Reporting. Given annually for the best reporting on education, the awards are presented in 18 categories, including separate categories for TV, cable and radio. First Prize $250. Grand Prize for Distinguished Education Reporting $1,000. Sponsored by the Education Writers Association (EWA), the national professional association for education reporters, the selections are made by an independent judging panel coordinated by the University of Maryland College of Journalism. Awards are presented at the EWA National Seminar. Eligibility period: calendar year 1994. Deadline for entries: January 18, 1995. Contact: EWA, 1001 Connecticut Ave. N.W., Suite 310, Washington 20036. (202) 429-9680. FAX: (202) 872-4016.

National Federation of Community Broadcasters Community Radio Program Awards. Given annually to recognize outstanding programming for community-oriented radio. Open to all radio producers—commercial or public radio, independent or station-based. Deadline for entries: Jan. 10, 1995, for programs that were broadcast during the previous year. Estimated entry fee: $20 (one hour maximum per entry). Contact: NFCB Program Awards, 666 11th St. N.W., Suite 805, Washington 20001. (202) 393-2355.

National Headliners Club Awards. Given annually for radio & TV network news broadcasting & individual news stations, public service, documentary & investigative reporting from the previous calendar year. Winners receive medallions at awards dinner in Atlantic City, N.J. Deadline for entry: Jan. 15, 1995. Contact: Charles C. Reynolds, Executive Director, National Headliners Club, Devins Ln., Pleasantville, N.J. 08232. (609) 645-1234; (609) 272-7141.

National Mass Media Brotherhood Awards. Given by National Conference of Christians & Jews to pay tribute to mass media for outstanding creative work promoting better mutual understanding & cooperation among Americans of different religions, races & ethnic origins. Material must have appeared during the calendar year preceding the judging. Contact: Chris Bugby, Director Public Relations, Brotherhood Media Awards, National Conference of Christians & Jews, 71 5th Ave., New York 10003. (212) 206-0006.

The New York Festivals - International Radio Programming & Promotion Awards. Held in June 1995, this annual international competition encompasses radio news, information & entertainment programming plus radio advertising & PSAs. Eligibility period covers March 1, 1994 through March 1, 1995. Deadline for entries: Feb.-March 1995. Contact: Bilha Goldberg, Festival Director, The New York Festivals, 655 Ave. of the Americas, New York 10010. (914) 238-4481. FAX: (914) 238-5040.

The New York Festivals - International TV Programming & Promotion Awards. Held in January 1995, this annual international competition encompasses TV news, documentaries, entertainment & children's programming in addition to TV advertising & PSAs. Eligibility covers Aug. 1, 1993 through Aug. 5, 1994. Deadline for entries: Aug. 5, 1994. Contact: Bilha Goldberg, Festival Director, The New York Festivals, 655 Ave. of the Americas, New York 10010. (914) 238-4481. FAX: (914) 238-5040.

The Ohio State Awards. Annually recognizes excellence in education, information & public affairs broadcasting. Any agency, organization or institution producing, broadcasting or cablecasting a radio or TV program, which is presented in English & the primary intent of which is to educate (instruct, inform or enrich understanding) rather than entertain, may enter. The competition is sponsored by the Institute for Education by Radio-Television under the auspices of The WOSU Stations of The Ohio State University. For the 1995 competition only: Entries must have been broadcast/cablecast between July 1993 & Dec. 31, 1994. Deadline for entries: Jan. 10, 1995. Contact: Phyllis Madry, Ohio State Awards Manager, 2400 Olentangy River Rd., Columbus, Ohio 43210-1027. (614) 292-0185.

The Ollie Award. Eight Ollie Awards are given every other year for excellence in children's television. They are given without category for overall quality, to national & local, cable & broadcast, public & commercial programs. The winners are selected at a three-day conference that is the premier professional meeting for people who work with children's TV. Eligibility: Two years prior to the entry deadline (for 1995—July 1, 1993 to June 30, 1995). Deadline: July 1, 1995. Contact: David Kleeman, Director, American Center for Children's Television, 1400 E. Touhy, Suite 260, Des Plaines, Ill. 60018-3305.

Overseas Press Club Awards. Given annually in news media categories, awards include: Amy & Eric Burger Award for the best reporting dealing with the topics of human rights or foreign affairs, reported or interpreted from daily newspapers or wire services; Robert Capa Gold Medal for best photographic reporting or interpretation from abroad requiring exceptional courage & enterprise, radio spot news from abroad, radio interpretation of foreign news, TV spot news reporting from abroad, TV interpretation or documentary on foreign affairs, magazine reporting from abroad, magazine interpretation of foreign affairs, cartoon on foreign affairs, or book on foreign affairs; Olivier Rebbot Award for best photography in magazines & books; & the Madeline Dane Ross Award for international reporting demonstrating concern for humanity (any medium). Winners receive illuminated scrolls. Covers entries from Jan. 1, 1994, through Dec. 31, 1994. Deadline: Jan. 30, 1995. Contact: Mary E. Novick, Manager, Overseas Press Club Awards, 310 Madison Ave., Suite 2116, New York 10017. (212) 983-4655.

George Foster Peabody Award. Given annually & covering year prior to presentation, for radio, TV & cable achievement in the following fields: news, entertainment, education, programs for children, documentaries & public service. Deadline for entry or recommendation: Jan. 15. Contact: Dr. Barry L. Sherman, Director, Peabody Awards, Henry W. Grady School of Journalism, University of Georgia, Athens, Ga. 30602. (706) 542-3787.

George Polk Awards. The basic criteria for these awards is dissemination of a new story, coverage, resourcefulness in gathering information & skill in relating the story. Categories vary somewhat from year to year, but it has been customary to give awards in foreign, national & local reporting (in print & broadcasting), news photography & criticism. Documentary films & books based on investigative reporting or dealing specifically with the field of journalism also may be considered for awards. From time to time, awards are made for a body of work. Two copies of news or feature stories, radio or TV tapes, should be submitted. Packaging is not a consideration: the simpler, the better. There are no entry fees or application forms. Entries will not be returned. Deadline for entry: Jan. 7, 1995. Contact: Sidney Offit, Curator, George Polk Awards, Long Island University, The Brooklyn Center, University Plaza, Brooklyn, N.Y. 11201.

RTNDA Edward R. Murrow Awards. Given by the Radio-TV News Directors Association to TV & radio news departments for spot news coverage, continuing coverage, investigative reporting, news series & documentary, & overall excellence. Stations compete on regional level before consideration on national level. Covering calendar year. Deadline for entry: Jan. 15. Contact: Wendy Dressel, RTNDA, 1000 Connecticut Ave. N.W., Suite 615, Washington 20036.

The Radio Creative Fund Radio Mercury Awards. The Radio Mercury Awards recognize creative excellence in radio advertising. The prize package is the largest in the advertising industry, with nearly $200,000 in cash awards. The top prize, the Mercury Gold Award, includes a $100,000 check. Paid radio advertisements which aired on a U.S. radio station during the calendar year are eligible for review. Deadline: Feb. Contact: Laura Morandin, the Radio Advertising Bureau, 304 Park Ave. S., New York 10010.

Scripps Howard Foundation - Jack R. Howard Awards. Given by the Scripps Howard Foundation to any journalistic program or series of programs. Judging criteria for these awards will be journalistic excellence, relevance to area served, courage to enlighten the public, writing skills, quality of production, & results that may have been generated. The format & length of entries is not restricted. The competition is open to any single radio or TV station or cable systems originating local programs in the United States or its territories. Networks are not eligible. TV entries must be submitted on 3/4" videotape cassettes only. Radio entries must be submitted on audiocassette only. Eligibility period: the preceding calendar year. The categories are large market TV (1-50), small market TV (51 & up), large market radio (1-50), small market radio (51 & over). A bronze plaque & $2,000 are awarded to the winner in each category. Eligibility period: the preceding calendar year. Deadline: Jan. 31. Entry form required. No entry fee. Contact: Mary Lou Marusin, Scripps Howard Foundation, Box 5380, Cincinnati 45201. (513) 977-3035.

Scripps Howard Foundation - Charles E. Scripps Awards. Given by the Scripps Howard Foundation, recognizes a newspaper and/or TV, radio station or cable system for the most outstanding effort in the preceding year to combat illiteracy in their communities. Judges will look at the scope of the campaigns, the commitment of the newspaper and/or broadcast cable station to overcome illiteracy, its efficacy in bringing it to the attention of the public, & personal involvement of the staff. Cash prizes of $2,500 & a bronze plaque will be awarded to each winner. Prizes will be given to the editor of the newspaper and/or the general manager of the station for distribution to those on the staff who contributed significantly to the winning entry. Additionally, Scripps Howard Foundation will donate $5,000 to a literacy project or program in the community served by each award winner. The agencies receiving this special grant will be designated by the editor of the winning newspaper and/or the general manager of the station. Submitted material must have been published or broadcast during 1994 or deal with activities that took place in 1994. Entries must be received no later than Feb. 14, 1995. Entry form required; no entry fee. Contact: Mary Lou Marusin, Executive Director, Scripps Howard Foundation, Box 5380, Cincinnati 45201. (513) 977-3035.

Sigma Delta Chi Distinguished Service Awards. Annual competition honoring the best in print & broadcast journalism in the nation during the previous year; judged by panels of professionals. A new category, Informational Graphics Reporting, is being added this year, making the total number of categories 27. The entry fee is $60. The deadline is early January; winners announced in the spring & awards are presented at the convention. Awards are plaque & bronze medallion. Contact: Peggy Tennis, SPJ, Box 77, 16 S. Jackson, Greencastle, Ind. 46135. (317) 653-3333. FAX: (317) 653-4631.

Silver Anvil Awards. Given annually by Public Relations Society of America Inc. to recognize outstanding public relations programs of preceding year. Deadline for entry: early March. Contact: Carla Both, Public Relations Society of America Inc., 33 Irving Place, 3rd Fl., New York 10003. (212) 995-2230.

Society of Motion Picture & Television Engineers Awards. Citation for Outstanding Service to the Society recognizes individuals for dedicated service to the Society. The Presidential Proclamation recognizes individuals of established & outstanding status & reputation in the motion picture & TV industries worldwide. The Agfa-Gevaert Gold Medal Award recognizes the individual's outstanding leadership, inventiveness and/or other achievements in research, development or engineering of new techniques &/or equipment that result in a significant improvement to interface between motion picture film & TV imaging systems, whereby the combined advantages contribute to further development of visual communications systems. Eastman Kodak Medal Award recognizes outstanding contributions that lead to new or unique educational programs using motion pictures, TV, high-speed & instrumental photography, or other photographic sciences. The award recognizes developments in equipment, systems or instructional applications that advance the educational process at any or all levels. The John Grierson International Gold Medal Award recognizes significant technical achievements related to the production of documentary motion picture films. The Journal Award recognizes the outstanding paper originally published in the Journal of the Society during the previous calendar year. The Technicolor/Herbert T. Kalmus Gold Medal Award recognizes outstanding contributions in the development of color films, processing, techniques or equipment useful in making color motion pictures for theater or TV use. The Alexander M. Poniatoff Gold Medal for Technical Excellence recognizes outstanding technical excellence of contributions in research or development of new techniques and/or equipment that advance audio or TV magnetic recording & reproduction. The Samuel L. Warner Memorial Award recognizes outstanding contributions in design & development of new & improved methods and/or apparatus for sound-on-film motion pictures, including any step in the process. The Progress Award recognizes outstanding technical contribution to the process of engineering phases of the motion-picture and/or TV industries. The David Sarnoff Gold Medal Award recognizes outstanding contributions in the development of new techniques or equipment that improve the engineering phases of TV, including theater TV. The Fuji Gold Medal Award recognizes outstanding engineering achievements in the design & development of new or enhanced techniques and/or equipment that have contributed significantly to the advancement of photographic or electronic image origination. Deadline for entries: Jan. 15. Contact: Ly-

Major Broadcasting and Cable Awards

nette Robinson, Executive Director, Society of Motion Pictures and Television Engineers, 595 W. Hartsdale Ave., White Plains, N.Y. 10607.

Television Bureau of Advertising Awards. Annual competitions sponsored by the National Auto Dealers Association (NADA) for dealer & dealer association TV commercials. Deadline for entry: Nov. 15, 1994. Contact: Television Bureau of Advertising, 850 3rd Ave., 10th Fl., New York 10022. (212) 486-1111. FAX: (212) 935-5631.

Television Directorial Awards. Given in six categories: comedy shows; dramatic shows, night; musical & variety; sports; documentary/actuality; dramatic specials. Programs must be one hour or longer. Deadline for entries: Dec. 28, 1994. Contact: Directors Guild of America Inc., 7920 Sunset Blvd., Los Angeles 90046. (310) 289-2038. FAX: (310) 289-2024.

The U Festival of Student Film, Video, Television and Animation - National Programming Awards. Annual national festival awarding the best U.S. student-produced works in various entertainment & educational program genres, including paid production internships at networks & other professional media companies, & over $3,000 in cash prizes. The awards are also designed to encourage talented producers to pursue careers in video-oriented media. Works must have been completed between Oct. 1993 & Sept. 1994 to be eligible for the fall 1994 competition. Awards are presented at a gala industry ceremony during the National Conference of College Braodcasters each November. Entry deadline: Fri., Oct. 8, 1994. Contact: Glenn Gutmacher, NACB, 71 George St., Providence, R.I. 02912-1824. (401) 863-2225. FAX: (401) 863-2221.

Voice of Democracy Scholarship Program. Nationwide audio essay competition for 10th-, 11th- & 12th-grade students. The program is sponsored annually by the Veterans of Foreign Wars of the United States & its Ladies Auxiliary during the fall term of each school year. National scholarship awards amounting to $89,500 are made. Deadline for completion of school competition: Nov. 15. Contact: Local VFW Post, high school counselor or Voice of Democracy Program, VFW National Headquarters, 406 W. 34th St., Kansas City, Mo. 64111.

Ida B. Wells. Presented annually by the University of Kansas, The National Association of Black Journalists & the National Conference of Editorial Writers to executives of broadcast or print journalism organizations for exemplary leadership in providing minorities opportunities in journalism. Deadline for entries: May 1. Send nominations to: Sam Adams, William Allen White School of Journalism and Mass Communication, University of Kansas, 208 Stauffer-Flint Hall, Lawrence, Kan. 66045-2350. (913) 864-4755. FAX: (913) 864-5318.

Western Heritage Awards (The Wrangler). The Western Heritage Awards, sponsored by the National Cowboy Hall of Fame, are presented annually to outstanding works which tell great stories of the American West with accuracy & high artistic quality. The bronze "Wrangler" award is presented in 15 categories of Western literature, music, TV & film. TV categories (5) include: TV drama, documentary/docudrama, factual narrative, news features & TV feature film. All eligible works must be produced &/or aired between January 1 & December 31 of the applicable calendar year. Deadline: December 31. Contact: Dana Sullivan, Director Public Relations, National Cowboy Hall of Fame, 1700 N.E. 63rd St., Oklahoma City 73111.

Women at Work Broadcast Awards. Recognizes excellence in broadcast journalism & entertainment TV about working women's issues. Yearly themes for awards. Contact: Trudy Perry Singletary, National Commission on Working Women, 1325 G St. N.W., Lower Level, Washington 20005. (202) 737-5764. FAX: (202) 638-4885.

Section J
Books, Periodicals, Videos

Table of Contents

Table of Contents J-1
Books
   Books on Broadcasting, Cable and Mass Media,
      An Annotated Bibliography J-2
   Books on Broadcasting and Cable J-7
Periodicals
   Periodicals on Broadcasting, Cable and Mass Media,
      An Annotated Bibliography J-16
   Periodicals on Broadcasting and Cable J-18
Videos on Broadcasting and Cable J-31

Books on Broadcasting, Cable and Mass Media
An Annotated Bibliography

Compiled by Christopher H. Sterling, Professor and Director, National Center for Communication Studies, George Washington University.

This bibliography organizes and annotates a selection of the most recent (generally published in or since 1990) books on broadcasting, cable, mass media and peripheral areas of interest. The books are listed once under one of the subject headings under **United States** or **Foreign/International**. Citations are current to December 1993. Consult previous editions of *Broadcasting & Cable Yearbook* for older titles (generally, those more than five years old).

United States

Titles are listed under one of these headings: general and reference; history; biography; organization and economics; policy regulation; journalism; entertainment; public (non commercial) broadcasting; audience and research; newer media systems; technology; production and performance.

GENERAL AND REFERENCE

Block, Eleanor S., and James K. Bracken. **Communications and the Mass Media: A Guide to the Reference Literature.** Englewood, CO: Libraries Unlimited, 1991. 198 pp. $40.00. Very useful guide to the growing number of reference sources on all of the media.

Blum, Eleanor, and Frances Goins Wilhoit. **Mass Media Bibliography: An Annotated Guide to Books and Journals for Research and Reference.** Urbana, IL: University of Illinois Press, 1990. 344 pp. $49.95. Latest edition of the single best overall guide with author, title, and subject indexes to some 2,000 titles.

Brown, Les, ed. **Les Brown's Encyclopedia of Television.** Detroit, MI: Gale Research, 1992 (3rd ed.). 723 pp. $39.95. First issued in 1977 and last revised in 1982 (each time by a different publisher), this valuable handbook is back and updated with some 900 entries on industry people, programs, organizations, technologies, regulation, etc.

Diamant, Lincoln. **The Broadcast Communications Dictionary.** Westport, CT: Greenwood Press, 1989. 260 pp. $35.00. Now covering some 6,000 terms, this is updated from a work last issued a decade ago by another publisher.

Duncan, James, Jr. **American Radio.** Indianapolis, IN: Duncan's American Radio Inc., 1974-date, bimonthly regular issues. Price varies with edition. Based on Arbitron data, these compilations provide a summary of market information: stations, formats, rates, audience size, and the like. See also Duncan's **Radio Market Guide**, issued annually, for more inclusive reference material. Both are invaluable references.

Electronic Market Data Book. Washington, D.C.: Electronic Industries Association, annual. 120 pp. $150.00. Invaluable standard collection of historical statistics over the past two decades on all types of consumer and general communication electronics along with world trade data. (Note: see also the free booklet Consumer Electronics, published annually by EIA's Consumer Electronics Division, and drawn from this longer publication.)

Ellmore, R. Terry. **NTC's Mass Media Dictionary.** Lincolnwood, IL: NTC Business Books, 1991. 668 pp. $39.95. Covers some 20,000 terms across all of the media.

Elving, Bruce F. **FM Atlas.** (Box 336, Esko, MN 55733-0336), 1992. 192 pp. $10.95, paper. Fourteenth edition of a regularly-updated useful handbook of the fast-changing world of FM radio, first published more than two decades ago. It covers all FM stations in North America, their programming, facilities, and the like, including pages of maps locating stations.

Greenfield, Thomas Allen. **Radio: A Reference Guide.** Westport, CT: Greenfield, 1989. 200 pp. $39.95. Good topical chapters assess what is known and written about all aspects of radio.

Head, Sydney W., Christopher H. Sterling, and Lemuel B. Schofield. **Broadcasting in America: A Survey of Electronic Media.** Boston: Houghton Mifflin, 1994 (7th ed.). 650 pp. Standard text covering history, technology, economics, programming, audience, regulation of broadcasting, cable and newer services—plus an extensive annotated guide to further reading.

Jones, Glenn R. **Jones' Dictionary of Cable Television Terminology Including Related Computer & Satellite Definitions.** Englewood, CO: Jones International, 1988. 100 pp. Defines some 1,600 terms.

Penney, Edmund F. **The Facts on File Dictionary of Film and Broadcast Terms.** New York: Facts on File, 1991. 251 pp. $29.95/$14.95. Includes some 2,500 definitions.

Rubin, Rebecca, et al. **Communication Research: Strategies and Resources.** Belmont, CA: Wadsworth, 1993 (3rd ed.). 318 pp. Basic guide to research in the mass communication field. Invaluable guide for students lost in (or even near) the library.

Signorelli, Nancy, ed. **A Sourcebook on Children and Television.** Westport, CT: Greenwood Press, 1991. 216 pp. $45.00. Best current survey of the literature.

Sova, Harry, and Patricia Sova, eds. **Communication Serials 1992-93.** Sovacomm Inc. (Box 64697, Virginia Beach, VA 23464-0697). 1,100 pp. $129.00. Full details on some 2,700 periodical titles, past and present, in the performing arts and communications. There is no other source like this—unique and invaluable.

Weiner, Richard. **Webster's New World Dictionary of Media and Communications.** New York: Prentice-Hall, 1990. 533 pp. $29.95. Some 30,000 definitions combining print and electronic (and film) media.

HISTORY (see also Entertainment and Biography)

Altschuler, Glenn C., and David I. Grossvogel. **Changing Channels: America in *TV Guide*.** Champaign, IL: University of Illinois Press, 1992. 224 pp. $21.95. A history of the important weekly, along with some discussion of its impact and what it says about America's long affair with television.

Auletta, Ken. **Three Blind Mice: How the TV Networks Lost Their Way.** New York: Random House, 1991. 642 pp. $25.00. Detailed narrative on the changing ownership of each of the networks since the mid-1980s, and some of the impacts of those changes.

Barnouw, Erik. **Tube of Plenty: The Evolution of American Television.** New York: Oxford University Press, 1990 (2nd rev. ed.). 607 pp. $34.95/$13.95. A standard one-volume condensation and updating of his three-volume history (published 1966-70). Strong in material on news and documentaries.

Brooks, Tim, and Earle Marsh. **The Complete Directory to Prime Time Network TV Shows 1946-Present.** New York: Ballantine, 1992 (5th ed.). 1,209 pp. $19.00. Most inclusive and descriptive of several available historical guides. Includes annual network schedules. (See also Gianakos, below.)

Dayan, Daniel, and Elihu Katz. **Media Events: The Live Broadcasting of History.** Cambridge, MA: Harvard University Press, 1992. 306 pp. Argues that TV coverage of major news events has become a kind of ritual. The authors use six examples from the 1960s and 1970s to illustrate their points.

Gianakos, Larry J. **Television Drama Series Programming.** Metuchen, NJ: Scarecrow Press, 1978-92, 6 vols. 4,099 pp. $316.50 set. Definitive and detailed guide to each individual episode of all network drama series, from 1947 through 1986. (See also Brooks and Marsh, above.)

Godfrey, Donald G. **Reruns on File: A Guide to Electronic Media Archives.** Hillsdale, NJ: Lawrence Erlbaum, 1992. 322 pp. $59.95. Unique guide to what is available in both public and private archives in the way of recorded material on radio and television. Arranged by state and then by specific collection, each listing includes from one page to several covering the organization, contact person, general formats held, program types held, subject content description (for major collections this is a lengthy and detailed section), special interests of the collection, and its accessibility (including hours, copying, etc.).

Hilliard, Robert L., and Michael C. Keith. **The Broadcast Century: A Biography of American Broadcasting.** Stoneham, MA: Focal Press, 1992. 330 pp. An informal and illustrated history told in chronological fashion, with many contributed comments from important pioneering figures.

MacDonald, J. Fred. **One Nation Under Television: The Rise and Decline of Network TV.** New York: Pantheon, 1990. 335 pp. $24.95. Well-written history focusing on programs and programming, exploring reasons and the trend from success to today's competitive tension.

McChesney, Robert W. **Telecommunications, Mass Media, & Democracy: The Battle for the Control of U.S. Broadcasting, 1928-1935.** New York: Oxford, 1993. 393 pp. $45.00. Study of how little input the public (or, according to the author, the public interest) had in development of the 1934 Communications Act.

Schiffer, Michael Brian. **The Portable Radio in American Life.** Tucson, AZ: University of Arizona Press, 1991. 259 pp. $45.00/$24.95. A social/technical history of the portable radio from the 1920s well into the 1960s with lots of photos and reproductions of ads. But most interestingly, what we have here is an archeologist writing an archeology of a fairly modern device—a social history of the changing shape and function of the portable in changing American society.

Slide, Anthony, ed. **The Television Industry: A Historical Dictionary.** Westport, CT: Greenwood, 1991. 374 pp. $59.50. More than 1,000 narrative entries cover important organizations, networks, owners, studios, etc., often with further sources listed.

Stempel, Tom. **Storytellers to the Nation: A History of American Television Writing.** New York: Continuum, 1992. 307 pp. $24.95. Appears to be the first study of its kind—a history of television from the writers' point of view based on interviews with some 40 writers.

Sterling, Christopher H., and John M. Kittross. **Stay Tuned: A Concise History of American Broadcasting.** Belmont, CA: Wadsworth, 1990 (2nd ed.). 715 pp. Balanced treatment of radio and television development through periods, covering structure and size, economic aspects, educational broadcasting, programming, audience research and characteristics, and changing policies. Appendices include annotated bibliography, chronology and tables of historical data.

Watson, Mary Ann. **The Expanding Vista: American Television in the Kennedy Years.** New York: Oxford University Press, 1990. 273 pp. $22.95. Excellent social history of all aspects of television in the early 1960s, covering entertainment and news programming, emerging satellite technology, policy and regulation, etc.

BIOGRAPHY (see also History)

Bibb, Porter. **It Ain't As Easy As It Looks: Ted Turner's Amazing Story.** New York: Crown, 1993. 468 pp. $25.00 First biography in over a decade, this offers a detailed look at the cable mogul's life before and since CNN and TBS.

Garay, Ronald. **Gordon McLendon: The Maverick of Radio.** Westport, CT: Greenwood Press, 1992. 264 pp. $45.00. The first detailed study of one of modern radio's important pioneers.

Goldberg, Robert, and Gerald Jay Goldberg. **Anchors: Brokaw, Jennings, Rather and the Evening News.** New York: Birch Lane Press/Carol, 1990. 399 pp. $19.95. Combines biography of the three (and others) plus useful behind-the-scenes information on how the process works—and is changing on the network level.

Goldensen, Leonard. **Beating the Odds: The Untold Story Behind the Rise of ABC: The Stars, Struggles and Egos that Transformed Network Television.** New York: Scribner's, 1991. 495 pp. $24.95. The informal memoirs of the longtime head of ABC.

Lewis, Tom. **Empire of the Air: The Men Who Made Radio.** New York: HarperCollins, 1991. 300 pp. $24.95. Narrative biography of three key pioneers: Lee de Forest, Edwin Howard Armstrong, and David Sarnoff.

Marc, David, and Robert J. Thompson. **Prime Time Movers: From *I Love Lucy* to *L.A. Law*—America's Greatest TV Shows and the People Who Created**

Them. Boston: Little, Brown, 1992. 336 pp. $22.95. Study of 25 key television producers and their products.

Shawcross, William. **Murdoch**. New York: Simon & Schuster, 1992. 492 pp. $27.50. Well-written biography detailing both the man and his many worldwide companies and media holdings.

Smith, Sally Bedell. **In All His Glory: The Life of William S. Paley, the Legendary Tycoon and his Brilliant Circle**. New York: Simon & Schuster, 1990. 782 pp. $29.95. Well-reviewed and wonderfully readable biography of the longtime head of CBS which tells a good deal about the rise of radio and television broadcasting.

ORGANIZATION AND ECONOMICS

Keith, Michael C. **Selling Radio Direct**. Stoneham, MA: Focal Press, 1992. 117 pp. $11.95, paper. Brief and to-the-point advice to selling in a tough economy.

Keith, Michael C., and Joseph M. Krause. **The Radio Station**. Boston: Focal Press, 1993 (3rd ed.). 315 pp. $29.95. All aspects of operating and programming the modern commercial station sales format, news, research, promotion, traffic and billing, production, engineering and consultants.

Krasnow, Erwin G., et al. **Buying or Building a Broadcast Station in the 1990s**. Washington, DC: National Association of Broadcasters, 1991. 98 pp. $50, paper. Most detailed guide available, this is the third edition with some new sections and considerable updating.

Morgan, Bradley J., ed. **Radio and Television Career Directory**. Detroit: Visible Ink/Gale Research, 1993 (2nd ed.). 334 pp. $17.95, paper. Just what the budding prospect needs to have close at hand.

Owen, Bruce, and Steven S. Wildman. **Video Economics**. Cambridge, MA: Harvard University Press, 1992. 364 pp. $38.00. The economics of network television, cable and VCRs are details in terms of supply and demand and traditional and new models of program choice. The final 100 pages focus on public policy alternatives, including public and children's TV.

Pringle, Peter K., et al. **Electronic Media Management**. Boston: Focal Press, 1991 (2nd ed.). 403 pp. Covers radio, television and related media services, and all aspects of running them: personnel, sales, programming, community relations, regulation, and changing technologies.

Vogel, Harold L. **Entertainment Industry Economics: A Guide for Financial Analysis**. New York: Cambridge University Press, 1990 (2nd. ed.). 432 pp. $35.00. Includes, among other services, television and radio, cable, and movie/television programming. Only book of its kind.

Warner, Charles, and Jack Buchman. **Broadcast and Cable Selling**. Belmont, CA: Wadsworth, 1993 (updated 2nd ed.). 447 pp. All types and approaches to selling time over the air and on cable.

POLICY AND REGULATION

Bensman, Marvin R. **Broadcast/Cable Regulation**. Lanham, MD: University Press of America, 1990. 211 pp. $14.75, paper. A useful and well-indexed guide to specific important cases, stressing recent years, and arranged alphabetically by topic or subject sections, rather than the chronology of earlier editions.

Carter, T. Barton, et al. **The First Amendment and the Fifth Estate: Regulation of Electronic Mass Media**. Mineola, NY: Foundation Press, 1993 (3rd ed.). 891 pp. This is a combination text/case book for broadcasting and cable which is annually updated with a pamphlet. The 14 chapters cover all aspects of law and administrative regulation.

Creech, Kenneth C. **Electronic Media Law and Regulation**. Stoneham, MA; Focal Press, 1993. 404 pp. $34.95, paper. Broadscale text introducing most aspects of broadcast and cable control.

Emord, Jonathan W. **Freedom, Technology, and the First Amendment**. San Francisco: Pacific Research Institute, 1991. 335 pp. $29.95/$14.95. Twenty-three chapters define the core values of the First Amendment, discuss the First Amendment standard and (longest section) assess how to protect those core values in a new media age with many chapters on broadcast and cable concerns. Charts, tables, notes.

Federal Communications Commission. **Annual Report**. Washington, DC: Government Printing Office, annual. Pagination and price varies. Provides good overview of FCC structure, recent cases and overall electronic media regulation with some statistics on licensing.

Federal Communications Commission. **Code of Federal Regulations: Title 47—Telecommunications**. Washington, DC: Government Printing Office, annual. Issued in five volumes (the fourth, covering parts 70-79, is of most direct concern to broadcasters while the fifth, parts 80-end, includes the many new cable regulations), this is the annually-updated full printing of all FCC rules and regulations.

Federal Communications Commission. **The Communications Act of 1934, As Amended**. Washington, DC.: Government Printing Office, regularly updated. Pagination and price varies. Should be on hand at every station and cable system in the country. Recent printings include provisions of the 1984 and 1992 cable acts as Title VI.

Ferris, Charles, et al. **Cable Television Law: A Video Communications Guide**. New York: Matthew Bender, 1983 (regular updates). 3 vols. A standard guide to cable and newer media regulation by Congress, the FCC, and local government entities including the 1984 Cable Act and recent cases, and updated usually twice a year.

Ginsburg, Douglas H., et al. **Regulation of the Electronic Mass Media: Law and Policy for Radio, Television, Cable, and the New Video Technologies**. St. Paul, MN: West Publishing, 1991 (2nd ed.). 657 pp. "Casebook" combining text with important excerpts of FCC and court decisions.

Hilliard, Robert L. **The Federal Communications Commission: A Primer**. Stoneham, MA: Focal Press, 1991. 115 pp. $11.95. Useful short guide to how the agency is organized and works.

Hixon, Richard F. **Mass Media and the Constitution: An Encyclopedia of Supreme Court Decisions**. New York: Garland, 1989. 600 pp. $85.00. Important reference work which covers some 200 cases and is well indexed. Not a bad argument settler either!

Rosini, Neil J. **The Practical Guide to Libel Law**. New York: Praeger, 1991. 256 pp. $29.95. A three-step guide to staying out of trouble!

Strong, William S. **The Copyright Book: A Practical Guide**. Cambridge, MA: MIT Press, 1993 (4th ed.). 288 pp. $22.50. A very useful guide designed for ready everyday use and covering most important aspects of cable.

JOURNALISM (see also Production)

Bliss, Edward Jr. **And Now the News: The Story of Broadcast Journalism**. New York: Columbia University Press, 1991. 400 pp. $34.95. First full-length narrative overview of radio and television news.

Campbell, Richard. **60 Minutes and the News: A Mythology for Middle America**. Champaign, IL: University of Illinois Press, 1991. 279 pp. $29.95. Assesses the appeal of the long-running and top-rated documentary series.

Cook, Philip, Douglas Gomery and Lawrency Lichty, eds. **The Future of News: Television, Newspapers, Wires, Newsmagazines**. Baltimore: Johns Hopkins University Press, 1992. 261 pp. $34.50/$13.95. Collection of 15 insightful papers including those arguing more TV may mean less news, the blurring of network vs. local news distinctions, and the rise of talk-show journalism. Useful context places television within other news media.

Diamond, Edwin, and Stephen Bates. **The Spot: The Rise of Political Advertising on Television**. Cambridge, MA: MIT Press, 1992 (3rd ed.). 418 pp. $14.95, paper. Updates this now-standard history first issued in 1984 and revised in 1988—this volume appears in presidential election years! The authors have added material on the 1988 campaign for this third edition.

Dobkin, Bethami A. **Tales of Terror: Television News and the Construction of the Terrorist Threat**. New York: Praeger, 1992. 144 pp. $42.95. Content analysis of evening television news from 1981-87 to detail how television reacts to terrorist events and threats.

Donovan, Robert J., and Ray Scherer. **Unsilent Revolution: Television News and American Life 1948–1991**. New York: Cambridge University Press, 1992. 357 pp. Valuable assessment of four decades of political newsmaking divided into two parts: a review of coverage of 12 specific news events followed by a broader contextual review of TV news impacts.

Frank, Reuven. **Out of Thin Air**. New York: Simon & Schuster, 1991. 429 pp. $24.95. Former head of NBC News relates his own story and, through it, the story of TV news in a well-written and insightful narrative.

Greenberg, Bradley S., and Walter Gantz, eds. **Desert Storm and the Mass Media**. Cresskill, NJ: Hampton Press, 1993. 447 pp. $24.95, paper. Twenty-eight academic papers assess virtually all aspects of media coverage of the early 1991 conflict.

Henson, Robert. **Television Weathercasting: A History**. Jefferson, NC: McFarland, 1990. 193 pp. $35.00. The first book on the subject reviews history and how the process works today, with profiles of key figures across the country.

Hirsch, Alan. **Talking Heads: Political Talk Shows and the Star Pundits**. New York: St. Martin's Press, 1991. 249 pp. $17.95. Reviews the professional lives of the best-known national personalities.

Hitchcock, John R. **Sportscasting**. Stoneham, MA: Focal Press, 1991. 106 pp. $11.95. Practical guide to the techniques, skills and operations necessary.

Johnston, Carla B. **Election Coverage: Blueprint for Broadcasters**. Stoneham, MA: Focal Press, 1991. 105 pp. $11.95. Issues, ethics, and options for quality electoral coverage are detailed.

Matelski, Marilyn J. **TV News Ethics**. Stoneham, MA: Focal Press, 1991. 79 pp. $11.95. Based on a survey of media managers, this outlines major issues and potential approaches.

Musberger, Robert B. **Electronic News Gathering: A Guide to ENG**. Stoneham, MA: Focal Press, 1991. 80 pp. $11.95. Concepts and techniques needed to research, write, shoot, edit, and deliver an ENG story.

Soley, Lawrence C. **The News Shapers: The Sources Who Explain the News**. New York: Praeger, 1992. 175 pp. Examines 1987–88 network newscasts and their fairly narrow sample of "experts" upon whom networks relied to explain news events.

Stempel, Guido H. III, and John W. Windhauser, eds. **The Media in the 1984 and 1988 Presidential Campaigns**. Westport, CT: Greenwood Press, 1991. 232 pp. $39.95. Survey of newspaper, network, and newsmagazine content.

Stone, Vernon A. **Let's Talk Pay in Television and Radio News**. Chicago: Bonus Books, 1993. 194 pp. One of the few public sources that details career patterns and salary averages, ranges and trends in broadcast news, as seen by a longtime expert.

Weaver, David H., and G. Cleveland Wilhoit. **The American Journalist: A Portrait of the U.S. News People and their Work**. Bloomington, IN: Indiana University Press, 1991 (2nd ed.). 240 pp. $29.95. Based on surveys of print and electronic journalists in the 1980s and a similar study done a decade earlier, this is a review of characteristics and background of journalists today.

ENTERTAINMENT (see also History)

Alley, Robert S., and Irby B. Brown. **Murphy Brown: Anatomy of a Sitcom**. New York: Dell Delta Books, 1990. 286 pp. $10.95. Useful behind-the-scenes look at the successful sitcom and what makes it tick.

Bruce, Steve. **Pray TV: Televangelism in America**. New York: Routledge, 1990. 272 pp. $16.95, paper. One of the better analyses of where the televangelists came from, their role and impact.

Eastman, Susan Tyler, ed. **Broadcast/Cable Programming: Strategies and Practices**. Belmont, CA: Wadsworth, 1993. 588 pp. Fourth edition of a basic text first published in 1981, this is completely updated to include such things as the implications of compression technology on programming, public television's radically new process of program selection, and the role of the Fox network. The book's 17 chapters are divided into five major parts: programming resources and constraints, broadcast television, cable programming, commercial radio, and public broadcasting (radio and television) strategies. This remains the most complete and current overview of a constantly changing process.

Fuller, Linda K. **The Cosby Show: Audiences, Impact, and Implications**. Westport, CT: Greenwood Press, 1992. 256 pp. $47.95. Provides a broad overview of the top-rated NBC program, exploring how the show went together, why it was so popular, and something of its impact. Fuller details the background of the Cosby phenomenon, the economics of the program, politics and legalities, production of the series, audiences, kudos and criticisms of the programs, and the sociocultural implications of *The Cosby Show.*

Halper, Donna L. **Full-Service Radio: Programming for the Community.** Stoneham, MA: Focal Press, 1991. 103 pp. $11.95. The details on stations programming news, information and music—middle-of-the-road stations.

Kuney, Jack. **Take One: Television Directors on Directing.** New York: Praeger, 1990. 191 pp. $39.95/ $14.95. Ten interviews with key directors on all aspects of the craft.

Matelski, Marilyn J. **Daytime Television Programming.** Stoneham, MA: Focal Press, 1991. 82 pp. $11.95. Practical understanding of daytime TV formats, viewer demographics and programming strategy.

Shapiro, Mitchell E. **Television Network Daytime and Late-Night Programming, 1959-1989.** Jefferson, NC: McFarland, 1990. 264 pp. $39.95. Companion to the two following volumes.

Shapiro, Mitchell E. **Television Network Prime-Time Programming, 1948-1988.** Jefferson, NC: McFarland, 1989. 750 pp. $45.00. Reference work arranged by day of the week and including charts showing network program changes. See also above and below titles.

Shapiro, Mitchell E. **Television Network Weekend Programming, 1959-1990.** Jefferson, NC: McFarland, 1992. 464 pp. $42.50. Companion to volumes above.

PUBLIC (NONCOMMERCIAL) BROADCASTING

Corporation for Public Broadcasting. **Annual Report.** Washington, DC: CPB, annual. Trends in public radio and television, and overall financial statistics.

Quality Time? The Report of the Twentieth Century Fund Task Force on Public Television. New York: Twentieth Century Fund, 1993. 188 pp. The latest analysis of what is right and wrong with the CPB-PBS system established in the late 1960s, with a detailed set of recommendations and a useful background report.

Robertson, Jim. **Televisionaries: In Their Own Words Public Television's Founders Tell How It All Began.** Tabby House Books (4429 Shady Lane, Charlotte Harbor, FL 33980), 1993. 285 pp. $29.95. Oral history originally done for CPB is here made into a continuous narrative shedding much light on the transition from "educational" to "public" television and the key figures in that change.

Zigerell, James. **The Uses of Television in American Higher Education.** New York: Praeger, 1991. 186 pp. $39.95. Telecourses and other kinds of distant learning are assessed.

AUDIENCE AND RESEARCH

America's Watching: Public Attitudes Toward Television. Washington, DC: National Association of Broadcasters, 1991. 40 pp. Updates a Roper survey done regularly since 1959, and finding most people like and trust most of what they see most of the time.

Bryant, Jennings, ed. **Television and the American Family.** Hillsdale, NJ: Lawrence Erlbaum, 1990. 385 pp. Seventeen papers on uses of TV by families, portrayal of families on TV shows, effects of TV on families, mediating TV's impact, and public policy issues.

Buzzard, Karen. **Electronic Media Ratings: Turning Audiences into Dollars and Sense.** Stoneham, MA: Focal Press, 1992. 119 pp. $12.95, paper. Brief survey of a complicated area including why ratings in the first place, gathering the data, survey methods, calculating the results, interpreting the ratings, network TV ratings, local TV ratings, radio ratings, cable and VCR ratings, etc.

Dobrow, Julia R., ed. **Social and Cultural Aspects of VCR Use.** Hillsdale, NJ: Lawrence Erlbaum, 1990. 219 pp. Eleven papers on how "watching TV" now means many different things.

Heeter, Carrie, and Bradley Greenberg. **Cableviewing.** Norwood, NJ: Ablex, 1989. 321 pp. $24.95. First book-length treatment of most aspects of audience use of cable television and its changing patterns.

Houston, Aletha C., et al. **Big World, Small Screen: The Role of Television in American Society.** Lincoln, NE: University of Nebraska Press, 1992. 195 pp. $25.00. Important summary of scholarly findings on impacts of television as seen in multi-year project by an American Psychological Association task force. It reviews in detail the research literature of the past decade.

Kubey, Robert, and Mihaly Csikszentmihalyi. **Television and the Quality of Life: How Viewing Shapes Everyday Experience.** Hillsdale, NJ: Lawrence Erlbaum, 1990. 287 pp. $39.95/$19.95. A research-based study which updates much of what is known of TV's short- and longer-term impact. One of the more important recent studies.

Neuman, W. Russell. **The Future of the Mass Audience.** New York: Cambridge University Press, 1992. 202 pp. $12.95, paper. Conclusion of a five-year study arguing that national mass media will continue to be important services, despite growth of newer media.

Schrag, Robert L. **Taming the Wild Tube: A Family's Guide to Television and Video.** Chapel Hill, NC: University of North Carolina Press, 1990. 165 pp. $19.95/$9.95. Written to parents, this brief guide reviews much of the best on-air and video programming available and offers guidance generally.

Webster, James G., and Lawrence W. Lichty. **Ratings Analysis: Theory and Practice.** Hillsdale, NJ: Lawrence Erlbaum, 1991. 290 pp. Excellent and clearly-written guide to the mysteries of how the ratings companies and systems work.

Wimmer, Roger D., and Joseph R. Dominick. **Mass Media Research: An Introduction.** Belmont, CA: Wadsworth, 1994 (4th ed.). 497 pp. The research process, procedures and elements including lab and experimental design, survey work, field and related methods, content analysis, statistical methods, and research applications.

NEWER MEDIA SYSTEMS

Brotman, Stuart N. **Telephone Company and Cable Television Competition: Key Technical, Economic, Legal and Policy Issues.** Norwood, NJ: Artech House, 1990. 509 pp. $60.00. Only book focusing on the controversy.

De Sonne, Marcia L. **Advanced Broadcast/Media Technologies: Market Developments and Impacts in the '90s and Beyond.** Washington, DC: National Association of Broadcasters, 1992. 149 pp. $40.00. Divided into sections on technologies that enhance broadcasting, competitive technologies, and those of transition and new business opportunities. Useful glossary, too.

De Sonne, Marcia L. **Digital Audio Broadcasting: Status Report and Outlook,** and **Digital Audio Broadcasting: 1991 Market and Policy Developments.** Washington, DC: National Association of Broadcasters, 1991. 69 pp. and 101 pp. $40.00 each. Examples of current reports from the trade association on the rapid developments in DAB field.

Dobrow, Julia R. **Social and Cultural Aspects of VCR Use.** Hillsdale, NJ: Lawrence Erlbaum, 1990. 219 pp. $29.95. Eleven original papers review the growing impact of the ubiquitous VCR here and abroad.

Grant, August, et al, eds. **Communication Technology Update.** Austin, TX: Technology Futures Inc., annual. 350 pp. Some 40 useful short papers on the most current media-related technologies.

Hudson, Heather E. **Communication Satellites: Their Development and Impact.** New York: Free Press, 1990. 338 pp. $24.95. One of the better historical treatments with much on applications. (Winner of 1990 NAB/BEA Book of the Year award.)

Inglis, Andrew F. **Satellite Technology: An Introduction.** Stoneham, MA: Focal Press, 1991. 110 pp. $11.95. Basic introduction in clear language to satellite operation and setting up of mobile earth stations.

Levy, Mark R., ed. **The VCR Age: Home Video and Mass Communication.** Newbury Park, CA: Sage, 1989. 274 pp. $16.95. Thirteen research papers on the uses and roles of the VCR here and in Britain.

Pool, Ithiel de Sola. **Technologies without Boundaries.** Cambridge, MA: Harvard University Press, 1990. 283 pp. $27.50. Final work by the famous MIT political scientist, edited after his death by Eli Noam. Discusses dramatic changes underway and coming due to the many new services coming on line.

Walker, James R., and Robert V. Bellamy, Jr, eds. **The Remote Control in the New Age of Television.** Westport, CT: Greenwood, 1993. 288 pp. $55.00. Collects 16 academic papers on all aspects of remotes including history, individual use of the devices, group viewing and remote use, the impact of remote use on programming, and critical perspectives.

TECHNOLOGY

Harrington, Thomas P. **The Hidden Signals on Satellite TV.** Columbus, OH: Universal Electronics, 1991 (3rd ed.). 238 pp. $20.00. Aimed at radio amateurs, this is a useful source of data on satellite systems of all kinds.

Jackson, K.G., and G.B. Townsend. **TV and Video Engineer's Reference Book.** Stoneham, MA: Focal Press, 1991. 700 pp. Detailed reference in 60 chapters on all aspects of broadcast technology.

LeBow, Irwin. **The Digital Connection: A Layman's Guide to the Information Age.** New York: Freeman/Computer Science Press, 1991. 261 pp. $15.95. Just that—the basics in clear and non-technical fashion.

Long, Mark, comp. **World Satellite Almanac: The Global Guide to Satellite Transmission and Technology.** Winter Beach, FL: MLE Inc., 1992 (3rd ed.). 1,050 pp. Descriptive chapters plus a lot of valuable reference material on communication satellites worldwide, including coverage maps and other technical details.

National Association of Broadcasters Engineering Handbook. Washington, DC: National Association of Broadcasters, 1992. 1,345 pp. $235.00 The eighth edition of a book first issued in 1935 and last revised in 1985. Other than HDTV and DAB (neither had matured sufficiently for inclusion, say the editors), all the latest developments are here in detailed text and diagrams. Revisions of this basic reference are coming more often—an indicator of the pace of change.

Noll, A Michael. **Television Technology: Fundamentals and Future Prospects.** Norwood, MA: Artech House, 1988. $48.00. To-the-point text and facing-page simplified graphics for a clear and comprehensive overview.

Pierce, John R., and A. Michael Noll. **Signals: The Science of Tele-Communications.** New York: Freeman, 1990 (2nd ed.). 247 pp. $32.95. Excellent combination of history and clear description of wired and wireless communication process.

Prentiss, Stan. **HDTV: High-Definition Television.** Blue Ridge Summit, PA: TAB Books, 1990. 232 pp. $16.95, paper. One of the first book-length treatments of the hot technical topic of the 1990s, this combines broadscale background and information on the standards-setting process with specific information on the competing systems.

PRODUCTION AND PERFORMANCE

Alten, Stanley R. **Audio in Media.** Belmont, CA: Wadsworth, 1990 (3rd ed.). 644 pp. The fullest treatment of all aspects of audio in all media.

Armer, Alan A. **Directing Television and Film.** Belmont, CA: Wadsworth, 1990 (2nd ed.). 386 pp. All aspects, including varied approaches for different kinds of programs.

Benedict, Larry and Susan. **The Video Demo Tape: How to Save Money Making a Tape that Gets You Work.** Stoneham, MA: Focal Press, 1992. 220 pp. $24.95, paper. A husband-wife team of free-lance actors and producers describes how to make the media work *for* you. Includes sections on editing, shooting, technical considerations, and distribution—invaluable reading for those seeking initial jobs. Glossary.

Browne, Steven E. **Film-Video Terms and Concepts.** Stoneham, MA: Focal Press, 1992. 181 pp., paper. Useful reference by a practiced professional with extensive production credits and several books. Making extensive use of diagrams and photos (as well as clever symbols to help readers find what they seek), he introduces several hundred terms with brief descriptions and, especially handy, careful discussion of how video and film overlap and where they differ. Diagrams, photos.

Gross, Lynne S., and Larry W. Ward. **Electronic Moviemaking.** Belmont, CA: Wadsworth, 1991. 313 pp. Album-sized, well-illustrated guide to all aspects of preproduction, production, and postproduction process.

Halper, Donna L. **Radio Music Directing.** Stoneham, MA: Focal Press, 1991. 100 pp. $11.95. Quick survey of radio operations in music area focusing on music director's roles.

Hausman, Carl. **Institutional Video: Planning, Budgeting, Production, and Evaluation.** Belmont, CA: Wadsworth, 1991. 295 pp. The video department, planning programs, scripting, budgeting, evaluation, making the actual program, specialized applications, etc.

Hawes, William. **Television Performing: News and Information.** Stoneham, MA: Focal Press, 1991. 94 pp.

$11.95. Useful guide for news personnel and others (community experts, private citizens) needing to appear on the air.

Hilliard, Robert L. **Writing for Television and Radio**. Belmont, CA: Wadsworth, 1991 (5th ed.). 484 pp. Covers all kinds of writing, both fiction and non-fiction formats.

Hyde, Stuart W. **Television and Radio Announcing**. Boston: Houghton-Mifflin, 1991 (6th ed.). 576 pp. The standard text fully updated and reorganized, with a new chapter on careers in the field. Many examples, as well as "spotlight" profiles on key figures in the industry.

Keith, Michael C. **Radio Production: Art and Science.** Stoneham, MA: Focal Press, 1990. 255 pp. The radio producer, studios and equipment, planning-mixing-editing, production in format radio, and production in noncommercial radio.

Millerson, Gerald. **TV Scenic Design Handbook**. Stoneham, MA: Focal Press, 1989 (3rd ed.). 249 pp. Basic well-illustrated instructions from design to scene construction, shoestring operations, and scenic effects.

Millerson, Gerald. **Television Production**. Stoneham, MA: Focal Press, 1990 (12th ed.). 566 pp. One of the standard full-featured texts now brought fully up to date.

O'Donnell, Lewis B., et al. **Modern Radio Production**. Belmont, CA: Wadsworth, 1990 (2nd ed). 258 pp. Basic entry-level text on all aspects of the topic.

Orlik, Peter B. **Broadcast/Cable Copyrighting**. Boston: Allyn & Bacon, 1990 (4th ed.). 746 pp. The most current comprehensive handbook on writing copy for radio and TV.

Viera, Dave. **Lighting for Film and Electronic Cinematography.** Belmont, CA: Wadsworth, 1993. 336 pp. Combines text and illustrations in chapters on basic lighting concepts, lighting setups, fundamentals of exposure (four chapters), lighting applications (five chapters), electronic cinematography (two chapters) and a final section offering lighting analyses of selected shots. Photos (some color), diagrams, appendices, glossary, bibliography, index.

Zettl, Herbert. **Sight, Sound, Motion: Applied Media Aesthetics**. Belmont, CA: Wadsworth Publishing, 1990 (2nd ed.). 408 pp. The only book of its kind—combines production experience/guidance with a theory of media aesthetics in text and illustration.

Zettl, Herbert. **Television Production Handbook.** Belmont, CA: Wadsworth Publishing, 1992 (5th ed.). 647 pp. $51.95. A standard text first issued in 1961 and now with two-color printing throughout plus eight pages of full-color inserts. New chapters on the role of the director in preproduction and production/postproduction.

Foreign and International

Includes the best of current English-language book material on mass media in other parts of the world. The emphasis is on material from the 1990s, so previous *Broadcasting & Cable Yearbook* listings should be consulted for older titles. Citations are found under one of the following headings: general and reference; policy and law; world journalism; Britain and Western Europe; Eastern Europe and the former Soviet Union; general Third World; The Middle East and Africa; Asia and Oceania; the Americas; and international propaganda. Where available, periodical addresses are included.

GENERAL AND REFERENCE

Fortner, Robert S. **International Communication: History, Conflict, and Control of the Global Metropolis.** Belmont, CA: Wadsworth, 1993. 390 pp. Illustrated chapters discuss international communication in general, a theoretical perspective on the global metropolis, technical dimensions of international communication, the birth and early years of international communication (1835-1913), exploiting new possibilities (1914-1932), the triumph of international propaganda (1933-45), developments since 1946, the periphery versus core (big and little countries and news flow questions), political and economic turmoil in the past five years, and the future of international communication.

Globalization of Mass Media. Washington: Government Printing Office, 1993. 228 pp. $20.00, paper. Report by the National Telecommunications and Information Administration focusing on transnational developments and the role of American firms.

Johnston, Carla B. **International Television Co-Production: From Access to Success**. Stoneham, MA: Focal Press, 1992. 108 pp. $11.95, paper. Useful analysis of why co-production, samples of co-production, legal and political/economic realities, the production process and culture, acquisition and distribution, opportunities and contacts—plus resource lists.

Lewis, Peter M., and Jerry Booth. **The Invisible Medium: Public, Commercial and Community Radio.** Washington, DC: Howard University Press, 1990. 245 pp. $24.95. One of the few studies of world *radio* broadcast systems, this includes material on American, British, Australian, Italian, French and Third World radio.

Mytton, Graham, ed. **Global Audiences: Research for Worldwide Broadcasting 1993.** London: John Libbey, 1993. 240 pp. $48.00, paper. The first in what is projected as a new annual, this is based on the respected research work done by the BBC under the author's direction. Includes studies from all parts of the world.

Noam, Eli, and Joel Millonzi, eds. **The International Market in Film and Television Programs.** Norwood, NJ: Ablex, 1993. 202 pp. $45.00/$24.50. Nine academic papers from various authors in different countries assess the growing world market in programming.

Passport to World Band Radio. Penns Park, PA: International Broadcasting Services, Inc., annual. 440 pp., paper. Useful combination of descriptive text, equipment reviews and listings, and detailed directory of major world shortwave broadcasters.

Smith, Anthony. **The Age of Behemoths: The Globalization of Mass Media Firms.** Washington, DC: Brookings/Twentieth Century Fund, 1991. 83 pp. Good essay by a British expert on the economic trend to increasingly centralized control.

Traveller's Guide to World Radio. New York: Billboard/Watson-Guptill, annual. 178 pp. $9.95, paper. Guide to English-language programming in 51 cities worldwide.

Unesco. **Statistical Yearbook**. Paris: Unesco, annual. Pagination and price varies. The standard compendium of statistics on (among many other things) radio and television in virtually every country of the world.

Unesco. **World Communication Report**. Paris: Unesco, 1989. 551 pp. $81.00, paper. Not cheap, but provides a wealth of information on all media around the world, based on reports from each nation. Dozens of tables, bibliographies, sources of further information. Planned for regular revision.

Unesco. **World Media Handbook: 1990 Edition Selected Country Profiles**. Paris: Unesco/Lanham, MD: Unipub, 1990. 299 pp. $38.00. Brief tabular listings by country of media and their owners, cultural indicators, etc. To be revised every other year.

World Radio & Television Receivers. BBC World Service, International Broadcasting and Audience Research (Bush House, Box 76, London WC2B 4PH). 50 pp. Annually revised accounting of receivers and VCRs in virtually all countries, including number per 100 persons.

World Radio & TV Handbook. New York: Billboard Publications, annual. Pagination and price varies. The standard guide with text, tables, and charts on hours, frequencies, and programs of domestic and international shortwave and television broadcasting.

POLICY AND LAW

International Telecommunication Union. **Report by the ITU on Telecommunication and the Peaceful Uses of Outer Space.** Geneva: ITU, 1962-date, annual. Best regular review of satellite research and developments in all involved countries.

Office of Technology Assessment. **The 1992 World Administrative Radio Conference: Technology and Policy Implications**. Washington: Government Printing Office, 1993. 190 pp. $11.00, paper. Useful survey of how the worldwide process of spectrum allocation works.

Savage, James G. **The Politics of International Telecommunications Regulation.** Boulder, CO: Westview Press, 1990. 240 pp. Good current overview of how the ITU and related entities operate today.

Stewart, M. LeSeuer. **To See the World: The Global Dimension in International Direct Television Broadcasting by Satellite.** Norwell, MA: Kluwer Academic, 1991. 630 pp. Legal study of United Nations and other policy arenas grappling with national rights vs. international technology.

Wallenstein, Gerd. **Setting Global Telecommunication Standards: The Stakes, The Players & the Process**. Norwood, MA: Artech House, 1990. 256 pp. $66.00. The most focused treatment of a complicated and little-understood process—seeking agreement on worldwide technical standards.

WORLD JOURNALISM

Gaunt, Philip. **Making the Newsmakers: International Handbook on Journalism Training**. Westport, CT: Greenwood, 1992. 256 pp. $49.95. Unesco-sponsored study details training needs, programs, and facilities in 70 countries—the first such assessment in over three decades.

Merrill, John C., ed. **Global Journalism: Survey of International Communication.** White Plains, NY: Longman, 1991 (2nd ed.). 401 pp. Useful anthology covering both press and electronic media by region plus chapters on overall trends and controversies.

Reporters Sans Frontieres: Freedom of the Press Throughout the World. London: John Libbey, annual. 250 pp. Detailed country-by-country assessment of press freedom in virtually every country of the world, including electronic as well as print media.

Sussman, Leonard R. **Power, the Press and the Technology of Freedom: The Coming Age of ISDN.** Lanham, MD: Freedom House, 1990. 514 pp. $24.95. A worldwide review of news media developments and how technology is changing the government/media equation.

Wallis, Roger, and Stanley Baran. **The Known World of Broadcast News: International News and the Electronic Media**. New York: Routledge, 1990. 267 pp. $59.95/$16.95. Compares and contrasts American and British approaches to broadcast news, and discusses international broadcasters. Charts and tables.

BRITAIN AND WESTERN EUROPE

Blue Book of British Broadcasting. Tellex Monitors (47 Gray's Inn Rd., London WC1X 8PR). 600 pp. About $65. Annual directory of radio and television stations, personnel, and organizations in the U.K.

Avery, Robert K., ed. **Public Service Broadcasting in a Multichannel Environment: The History and Survival of an Ideal.** White Plains, NY: Longman, 1993. 211 pp. Collection of academic papers comparing and contrasting public service broadcasting in seven countries and the U.S.

Blumler, Jay G., and T.J. Nossiter, eds. **Broadcasting Finance in Transition: A Comparative Handbook.** New York: Oxford University Press, 1991. 443 pp. $49.95. Useful collection of contributed chapters on developed nations' broadcast systems, most in Europe, and how their financial support is changing.

Collins, Richard. **Satellite Television in Western Europe.** London: John Libbey, 1992 (2nd ed.). 125 pp. $35.00. Chapters on the history, organization, funding, audience and applications of satellite TV program delivery.

Donow, Kenneth. **European Media Markets: Commercial and Public Media in 15 Countries**. Washington, DC: National Association of Broadcasters, 1992. 342 pp. $199.00, paper. Invaluable report on all aspects of radio, television, cable, and satellite television trends throughout Western Europe.

Film and Television Yearbook. British Film Institute (127 Charing Cross Rd., London WC2H OEA). Price and pagination varies. An annual review of trends, films, programs, and people.

Hills, Jill, with Stylianos Papathanassopoulos. **The Democracy Gap: The Politics of Information and Communication Technologies in the United States and Europe.** Westport, CT: Greenwood, 1991. 216 pp. $45.00. Combines consideration of the broadcast and broader telecommunications markets and their changes.

Jankowski, Nick, et al. **The People's Voice: Local Radio and Television in Europe**. London: John Libbey, 1992. 274 pp. $45.00. Eighteen papers discuss two decades' development, including 11 chapters on specific countries.

MacDonald, Barrie. **Broadcasting in the United Kingdom: A Guide to Information Sources**. London: Mansell (in the U.S.: Cassell, PCS, 360 W. 31st St., New York 10011), 1993 (2nd ed.). $100.00. 316 pp. Would that more countries had such a resource—a very useful guide by a longtime BBC and then IBA librarian provides considerable detail on traditional (book and recording) and less-traditional (on-line and archive) sources.

Books on Broadcasting, Cable and Mass Media

Noam, Eli. **Television in Europe.** New York: Oxford University Press, 1991. 395 pp. $39.95. Valuable survey of each country plus useful assessment of continent-wide trends. Useful background and valuable insight.

OECD. **Competition Policy and a Changing Broadcast Industry.** Paris/Washington: Organization for Economic Cooperation and Development, 1993. 296 pp. $50.00, paper. Excellent and detailed survey of broadcasting in OECD member countries (most in Europe) reviewing the winds of change sweeping the industry and continent.

OECD. **Telecommunications and Broadcasting: Convergence or Collision?** Paris/Washington: Organization for Economic Cooperation and Development, 1992. 287 pp. $60.00, paper. Seven general chapters assess trends across Europe, followed by 150 pages of detailed per-country information.

Pilati, Antonio. **Media Industry in Europe.** London: John Libbey, 1993. 246 pp. $48.00, paper. Intended as the first of an annual series, this anthology details early 1990s' developments across Europe and provides in-depth studies of several selected countries.

Sepstrup, Preben. **Transnationalization of Television in Western Europe** London: John Libbey, 1990. 132 pp. $35.00. Conceptualization of TV program flows and their impacts, showing a lively industry. Explores where the transnational trend comes from and where it's going.

Tunstall, Jeremy, and Michael Palmer. **Liberating Communications: Policy Making in Britain and France.** New York: Basil Blackwell, 1990. 342 pp. $49.95. Good analysis of just how much the government's role is changing in both countries, including both electronic media and telecommunications.

Tunstall, Jeremy, and Michael Palmer. **Media Moguls.** New York: Routledge, 1991. 258 pp. $17.95, paper. Useful study of the major British, French, Italian and German media owners.

Tunstall, Jeremy. **Television Producers.** London and New York: Routledge, 1993. 235 pp. Interview-based study of some 250 British TV producers detailing their work and environment.

Wedell, George, and Philip Crookes, eds. **Radio 2000: The Opportunities for Public and Private Radio Services in Europe.** London: John Libbey, 1991. 274 pp. Useful report reviewing the fast-changing world of radio in all of Europe (including the East), including statistics and a bibliography.

EASTERN EUROPE AND THE FORMER SOVIET UNION

Androunas, Elena. **Soviet Media in Transition: Structural and Economic Alternatives.** Westport, CT: Praeger, 1993. 167 pp. $49.95. Useful first-person study of the dramatic changes in the past several years by a Russian with extensive experience in the West.

Broadcast Diversity in Eastern Europe: Challenges for the 1990's. International Communications Studies Program (Center for Strategic and International Studies, 1800 K St. N.W., Washington, DC 20036). 1990. 321 pp. $48.00. Transcript of conference held in November 1990 combining European and American experts on all aspects of broadcasting and newer technologies in Central and Eastern Europe.

Eastern Europe: Please Stand By—Report of the Task Force on Telecommunications and Broadcasting in Eastern Europe. Washington, DC: Advisory Committee on International Communications and Information Policy, Department of State. About 100 pp. Timely overview of systems in transition, based on visits early in 1990 to most former "Eastern Bloc" countries.

Emerging Voices: East European Media in Transition. New York: Gannett Center for Media Studies/Columbia University, 1990. 101 pp. Based on on-site investigations in Poland, Czechoslovakia, Hungary, and Yugoslavia.

GENERAL THIRD WORLD

Boyd, Douglas, et al. **Videocassette Recorders in the Third World.** White Plains, NY: Longman, 1989. 300 pp. A collection of research articles on the spread and uses of VCRs in developing nations shows how important the VCR has become in a few years.

Casmir, Fred L., ed. **Communications in Development.** Norwood, NJ: Ablex, 1991. Conceptual base, role of media in development, Latin American examples, and role of communication in already-developed nations.

Hachten, William. **The Growth of Media in the Third World: African Failures, Asian Successes.** Ames: Iowa State University Press, 1993. 129 pp. A longtime researcher in Third World media seeks patterns in why some countries develop and others seem not to.

Mowlana, Hamid, and Laurie J. Wilson. **The Passing of Modernity: Communication and the Transformation of Society.** White Plains, NY: Longman, 1990. 240 pp. Useful theoretical overview of media impact in development process, reviewing many studies over past two decades.

Reeves, Geoffrey. **Communication and the "Third World."** New York: Routledge, 1993. 277 pp. $17.95, paper. Argues for a new way of assessing media impact by more use of research by people living in the countries in question rather than relying so heavily on Western researchers.

Sussman, Gerald, and John A. Lent, eds. **Transnational Communications: Wiring the Third World.** Newbury Park, CA: Sage, 1991. 326 pp. $39.95. Thirteen papers, some on specific countries, with a focus on interrelationships among developed and developing nations.

THE MIDDLE EAST AND AFRICA

Boyd, Douglas A. **Broadcasting in the Arab World: A Survey of Radio and Television in the Middle East.** Ames: Iowa State University Press, 1993 (2nd ed.). 390 pp. $37.95. Country-by-country details as well as a regional overview and information on trans-border broadcasts.

Hawk, Beverly G., ed. **Africa's Media Image.** New York: Praeger, 1992. 280 pp. $49.95. Collects 20 papers, many by African scholars, exploring the image of Africa in print and broadcast media here and elsewhere. Five of them detail the South African story.

ASIA AND OCEANIA

B&T Yearbook. Sydney: Greater Publications, annual. Directory of radio and television stations, networks, newspapers, and ad agencies in Australia.

Lull, James. **China Turned On: Television, Reform and Resistance.** New York: Routledge, 1992. 230 pp. $49.95/$16.95. Examines the unique role of television in the events of 1989 and since in China including the expanding role of television, people's use of TV, reform on prime-time television, popular culture and censorship, viewing habits and cultural consequences.

NHK Handbook. Tokyo: Nippon Hoso Kyokai, annual. Review of programs, structure, audience research and other developments of the public corporation running radio and TV networks.

Pacific Telecommunications Conference Proceedings [title varies]. Honolulu: PTC/University of Hawaii Press, annual. Pagination and price varies. Papers from the annual conference which is usually heavy on satellite communications and other aspects of telecommunications among Pacific Rim nations.

Studies of Broadcasting. Nippon Hoso Kyokai Theoretical Research Center (2-1-1 Atago, Minatu-ku, Tokyo 105, Japan). Annual in English. Research studies issued since 1963 and devoted mainly to work in and on Japan.

THE AMERICAS
(for the U.S., see first part of this bibliography)

Canadian Radio Television and Telecommunications Commission Annual Report. Ottawa: CRTC. The counterpart to our FCC. Report covers regulatory actions and industry developments in broadcasting and common carrier telecommunications.

Lent, John A. **Mass Communications in the Caribbean.** Ames: Iowa State University Press, 1990. 398 pp. $36.95. Wonderfully detailed description and assessment both by country and by overall regional topical approach.

Skidmore, Thomas E., ed. **Television, Politics, and the Transition to Democracy in Latin America.** Baltimore: Johns Hopkins University Press, 1993. 188 pp. $25.00. Academic papers from a 1990 conference at the Smithsonian argue the positive role of television coverage of elections and politics in several Latin nations.

INTERNATIONAL PROPAGANDA

Board for International Broadcasting. **Annual Report.** Washington, DC: Government Print Office, annual. Statistics and developments at Radio Free Europe, and Radio Liberty.

Wasburn, Philo C. **Broadcasting Propaganda: International Radio Broadcasting and the Construction of Political Reality.** New York: Praeger, 1992. 208 pp. $45.00. Combines history and theory to assess the role of such broadcasting before and since 1945 with a case study of services toward the end of the Cold War.

Wood, James. **History of International Broadcasting.** Piscataway, NJ: IEEE Service Center, 1992. 258 pp. $60.00. Focus on transmission developments in worldwide short-wave as well as program trends, reviewing trends from the 1920s to date.

Books on Broadcasting and Cable

A list of books on radio and television broadcasting, mass media, satellites and cable television from R.R. Bowker's *Books in Print* data base. This listing is limited to more recent books, those published between 1989 through 1993, and is meant to complement the annotated book listing, and may or may not include those titles.

Advanced Methods for Satellite & Deep Space Communications: Proceedings of an International Seminar Organized by Deutsche Forschungsanstalt fur Luft-und Raumfahrt, Bonn, Germany, Sept. 1992. Hagenauer, J., editor. Pub Date: 1992. 210 pp. Binding: Paper. Price: $51.00. ISBN: 0-387-55851-9.
Springer-Verlag New York Inc., New York.

Advanced Technology in Satellite Communication Antennas: Electrical & Mechanical Design. Kitsuregawa, Takashi, editor. Pub Date: 1990. 415 pp. Binding: Hardcover. Price: $59.00. ISBN: 0-89006-387-7.
Artech House Inc., Norwood, MA.

The Adventures of Amos 'n' Andy: A Social History of an American Phenomenon. Ely, Melvin P. Pub Date: 1992. 322 pp. Binding: Paper. Price: $12.95. ISBN: 0-02-909503-4.
Free Press, New York.

Affirmation & Denial: Construction of Femininity on Indian Television. Krishnan, Prabha and Dighe, Anita. Pub Date: 1990. 128 pp. Binding: Hardcover text edition. Price: $22.50. ISBN: 0-8039-9643-8.
Sage Publications Inc., Thousand Oaks, CA.

AgeWise: A Case Study of a Public Access Cable Television Program. Taylor, Tom T., III, McCrossen, Melinda and Lansky, David. Pub Date: 1989. 140 pp. Binding: Paper. Price: $19.95. ISBN: 0-9622710-3-9.
AgeWise Publishing, Portland, OR.

Airwaves Over Alaska: Story of Pioneer Broadcaster Augie Hiebert. Chlupach, Robin A. Foreword by Cronkite, Walter. Illus. Pub Date: 1992. 266 pp. Binding: Hardcover. Price: $19.95. ISBN: 0-942381-09-2.
Sammamish Press, Issaquah, WA.

All About Satellite TV: A Technical Guide for Home Dish Owners. Fincke, Karl. Scott, James E., editor. Pub Date: 1993. 128 pp. Binding: Paper. Price: $9.95. ISBN: 1-879804-01-8.
Fortuna Communications Corp., Fortuna, CA.

All Talk: The Talkshow in Media Culture. Munson, Wayne. Pub Date: 1993. 288 pp. Binding: Hardcover. Price: $34.95. ISBN: 0-87722-995-3.
Temple University Press, Philadelphia.

All That Glitters: A Newsperson Explores the World of Television. Cook, Coleen. Pub Date: 1992. Binding: Hardcover text edition. Price: $15.99. ISBN: 0-8024-0736-6.
Moody Press, Chicago.

The American Film Institute Guide to College Courses in Film & Television. American Film Institute Staff. Edition: 8th. Pub Date: 1992. 304 pp. Binding: Paper. Price: $20.00. ISBN: 0-13-025594-7.
Prentice Hall General Reference & Travel, New York.

The American Radio Industry & Its Latin American Activities, 1900-1939. Schwoch, James. Pub Date: 1990. 176 pp. Binding: Hardcover. Price: $29.95. ISBN: 0-252-01690-4.
University of Illinois Press, Champaign, IL.

The American Trojan Horse: U.S. Television Confronts Canadian Economic & Cultural Nationalism. Berlin, Berry. Pub Date: 1990. Binding: Hardcover. Price: $45.00. ISBN: 0-313-27508-4.
Greenwood Publishing Group Inc., Westport, CT.

An Assessment of Potential Markets for Small Satellites. Stern, Lawrence H., Lacobie, Kevin J. and Zygmont, Zenon X. Introductions by Morgan, Stephen L. and Miller, Michael W. Pub Date: 1989. 111 pp. Binding: Paper. Price: $25.00. ISBN: 0-9625101-0-6.
Virginia's Center for Innovative Technology, Herndon, VA.

Associated Press History of Television. Goldstein, Norm. Pub Date: 1991. Binding: Hardcover. Price: $19.99. ISBN: 0-517-02011-4.
Outlet Book Co. Inc., Avenal, NJ.

At the Hinge of History: A Reporter's Story. Harsch, Joseph C. Foreword by Fromm, Joseph. Illus. Pub Date: 1993. 240 pp. Binding: Hardcover. Price: $29.95. ISBN: 0-8203-1515-X.
University of Georgia Press, Athens, GA.

Audience Research Sourcebook. Hartshorn, Gerald, editor. Illus. Pub Date: 1991. 192 pp. Binding: Paper. Price: $50.00 reference guide. ISBN: 0-89324-113-X.
National Association of Broadcasters, Washington, DC.

Audio Control Handbook. Oringel, Robert S. Illus. Edition: 6th. Pub Date: 1989. 304 pp. Binding: Paper. Price: $32.95. ISBN: 0-240-80015-X.
Focal Press, Stoneham, MA.

AutoCAD Onstage: A Computer-Aided Design Handbook for Theater, Film & Television. Rose, Rich. Illus. Pub Date: 1991. 280 pp. Binding: Hardcover. Price: $29.95. ISBN: 1-55870-165-6. Binding: Paper. Price: $19.95. ISBN: 1-55870-164-8.
Betterway Books, Cincinnati, OH.

Autonomy for the Electronic Media: A National Debate on the Prasar Bharati Bill. Thomas, T. K., editor. Pub Date: 1990. 172 pp. Binding: Hardcover text edition. Price: $27.50. ISBN: 81-220-0188-2.
Advent Books Inc., New York.

BCTV: Bibliography on Cable Television. Communications Library Staff. Connelly, Theodore S., editor. Pub Date: 1992. 100 pp. Binding: Paper. Price: $35.00. ISBN: 0-934339-18-X.
Communications Library, San Francisco.

BCTV: Bibliography on Cable Television—1989. Communications Library Staff. Pub Date: 1989. 100 pp. Binding: Paper. Price: $35.00. ISBN: 0-934339-15-5.
Communications Library, San Francisco.

BCTV: Bibliography on Cable Television—1990. Communications Library Staff. Connelly, Theodore S., editor. Pub Date: 1990. 100 pp. Binding: Paper. Price: $35.00. ISBN: 0-934339-16-3.
Communications Library, San Francisco.

BCTV: Bibliography on Cable Television—1991. Communications Library Staff. Connelly, Theodore S., editor. Pub Date: 1991. 100 pp. Binding: Paper. Price: $35.00. ISBN: 0-934339-17-1.
Communications Library, San Francisco.

BCTV: Bibliography on Cable Television—1993. Connelly, Theodore S., editor. Pub Date: 1993. 100 pp. Binding: Paper. Price: $35.00. ISBN: 0-934339-19-8.
Communications Library, San Francisco.

BCTV: Bibliography on Cable Television—1994. Communications Library Staff. Connelly, Theodore S., editor. Pub Date: 06/1994. 100 pp. Binding: Paper. Price: $40.00. ISBN: 0-934339-20-1.
Communications Library, San Francisco.

BIB Television Programming Source Books, 1992-93, Vol. 1: Films A–L. Holland, Heidi, editor. Edition: rev. Pub Date: 1992. 725 pp. Binding: Paper. Price: $455.00 incl Vol. 2. ISBN: 0-912920-69-6.
North American Publishing Co., Philadelphia.

BIB Television Programming Source Books, 1992-93, Vol. 2: Films M-Z. Holland, Heidi, editor. Edition: rev. Pub Date: 1992. 725 pp. Binding: Paper. Price: $455.00 incl. Vol. 1. ISBN: 0-912920-70-X.
North American Publishing Co., Philadelphia.

BIB Television Programming Source Books, 1992-93, Vol. 3: Film Packages. Holland, Heidi, editor. Edition: rev. Pub Date: 1992. 725 pp. Binding: Paper. Price: $455.00 incl. Vols. 1-3. ISBN: 0-912920-71-8.
North American Publishing Co., Philadelphia.

BIB Television Programming Source Books, 1992-93, Vol. 4: Series. Holland, Heidi, editor. Edition: rev. Pub Date: 1992. 725 pp. Binding: Paper. Price: $345.00. ISBN: 0-912920-72-6.
North American Publishing Co., Philadelphia.

BIB Television Programming Source Books, 1992-93: Films A–L; Films M–Z; Film Packages; Series, 4 Vols. Holland, Heidi, editor. Edition: rev. Pub Date: 1992. 2,900 pp. Binding: Paper. Price: $745.00. ISBN: 0-912920-68-8.
North American Publishing Co., Philadelphia.

BIB World Guide to Television & Programming 1991-92. Holland, Heidi, editor. Illus. Edition: rev. Pub Date: 1991. 800 pp. Binding: Paper. Price: $245.00. ISBN: 0-912920-65-3.
North American Publishing Co., Philadelphia.

BIB World Guide to Television & Programming 1993. Holland, Heidi and Sass, Perry. Illus. Pub Date: Date not set. 600 pp. Binding: Paperback text edition. Price: $295.00. ISBN: 0-912920-75-0.
North American Publishing Co., Philadelphia.

BICC PLC & Sterling Greengate Cable Co. Ltd: Monopolies & Mergers Commission Report. Pub Date: 1990. 69 pp. Binding: Paper. Price: $18.00. ISBN: 0-10-111312-9.
UNIPUB, Lanham, MD.

BPI Cable Contacts, 1993. Pub Date: 1992. 686 pp. Binding: Hardcover. Price: $150.00. ISBN: 0-8230-8544-9.
BPI Media Services, New York.

BPI Radio Contacts, 1993. Pub Date: 1992. 686 pp. Binding: Hardcover. Price: $195.00. ISBN: 0-8230-8542-2.
BPI Media Services, New York.

BPI TV News Contact, 1993. Pub Date: 1992. 330 pp. Binding: Hardcover. Price: $150.00. ISBN: 0-8230-8547-3.
BPI Media Services, New York.

BPI Television Contacts, 1993. Pub Date: 1992. 686 pp. Binding: Hardcover. Price: $195.00. ISBN: 0-8230-8546-5.
BPI Media Services, New York.

Basic TV Reporting: Media Manuals. Yorke, Ivor. Pub Date: 1990. 168 pp. Binding: Paper. Price: $24.95. ISBN: 0-240-51283-9.
Focal Press, Stoneham, MA.

Battle Lines: The American Media & the Intifada. Lederman, Jim. Pub Date: 1992. 384 pp. Binding: Hardcover. Price: $29.95. ISBN: 0-8050-1602-3.
Holt, Henry, & Co. Inc., New York.

The Battle for the Control of U.S. Broadcasting, 1930–1935. McChesney, Roberet W. Pub Date: 1993. Binding: Hardcover. Price: $45.00. ISBN: 0-19-507174-3.
Oxford University Press Inc., New York.

The Battle to Control Broadcast News: Who Owns the First Amendment? Donahue, Hugh C. Pub Date: 1989. 240 pp. Binding: Hardcover. Price: $24.95. ISBN: 0-262-04099-9.
MIT Press, Cambridge, MA.

The Beast, the Eunuch & the Glass-Eyed Child: Television in the 80's. Powers, Ron. Pub Date: 1990. Binding: Hardcover. Price: $24.95. ISBN: 0-15-111251-7.
Harcourt Brace & Co., San Diego.

The Beast, the Eunuch, & the Glass-Eyed Child: Television in the 80's & Beyond. Pub Date: 1991. Binding: Paper. Price: $13.00. ISBN: 0-385-41821-3.
Doubleday & Co. Inc., New York.

Behind the Scenes at the Local News. Goald, Robert S. Pub Date: Date not set. Binding: Hardcover. Price: $149.50 incl. 1/2" VHS Video, 120 mins. ISBN: 0-240-80153-9. Binding: Paper. Price: $149.50 incl. 1/2" VHS Video, 120 mins. ISBN: 0-240-80153-9.
Focal Press, Stoneham, MA.

Behind the Tube: History of Broadcasting. Inglis, Andrew F. Illus. Pub Date: 1990. 552 pp. Binding: Hardcover. Price: $42.95. ISBN: 0-240-80043-5.
Focal Press, Stoneham, MA.

Beyond the BBC: Broadcasters & the Public in the 1980s. Madge, Tim. Pub Date: 1989. 190 pp. Binding: Hardcover. Price: $65.00. ISBN: 0-333-39427-5.
International Specialized Book Services, Portland, OR.

Books on Broadcasting and Cable

Big World, Small Screen: The Role of Television in American Society. Huston, Aletha C., Donnerstein, Edward, Fairchild, Halford, Feshbach, Norma D., Katz, Phyllis A., Murray, John P., Rubenstein, Eli A., Wilcox, Brian L. and Zuckerman, Diana. Illus. Pub Date: 1992. 196 pp. Binding: Hardcover. Price: $25.00. ISBN: 0-8032-2357-9. Binding: Paper. Price: $12.00. ISBN: 0-8032-7263-4.
University of Nebraska Press, Lincoln, NE.

Black & White in Colour: Black People in British Television since 1936. Pines, Jim, editor. Illus. Pub Date: 1992. 256 pp. Binding: Hardcover. Price: $55.00. ISBN: 0-85170-329-1. Binding: Paper. Price: $22.95. ISBN: 0-85170-328-3.
Indiana University Press, Bloomington, IN.

Border Radio: Quacks, Yodelers, Pitchmen, Psychics, & Other Amazing Broadcasters of the American Airwaves. Fowler, Gene and Crawford, Bill. Foreword by Jack, Wolfman. Illus. Pub Date: 1990. 294 pp. Binding: Paper. Price: $13.95. ISBN: 0-87910-142-3.
Limelight Editions, New York.

British Film Institute Broadcasting Debate, 7 Bklts. Pub Date: 1990. Binding: Paper. Price: $57.50. ISBN: 0-253-31193-4 (set).
Indiana University Press, Bloomington, IN.

British Television Drama in the 1980s. Brandt, George W., editor. Illus. Pub Date: 1993. 284 pp. Binding: Hardcover. Price: write for info. ISBN: 0-521-41726-0. Binding: Paper. Price: write for info. ISBN: 0-521-42723-1.
Cambridge University Press, New York.

Broadcast Blues: Dispatches from the Twenty-Year War Between a Television Reporter & His Medium. Burns, Eric. Pub Date: 1993. 288 pp. Binding: Hardcover. Price: $22.00. ISBN: 0-06-019032-9.
HarperCollins Publishers Inc., New York.

Broadcast—Cable Programming: Strategies & Practices. Eastman, Susan T. Edition: 4th. Pub Date: 1993. 588 pp. Binding: Hardcover text edition. Price: write for info. ISBN: 0-534-16662-8.
Wadsworth Publishing Co., Belmont, CA.

The Broadcast Century: A Biography of American Broadcasting. Hilliard, Robert L. and Keith, Michael C. Illus. Pub Date: 1992. 304 pp. Binding: Hardcover. Price: $39.95. ISBN: 0-240-80046-X.
Focal Press, Stoneham, MA.

The Broadcast Communications Dictionary. Diamant, Lincoln, editor. Edition: 3rd. Pub Date: 1989. 266 pp. Binding: Hardcover. Price: $49.95. ISBN: 0-313-26502-X.
Greenwood Publishing Group Inc., Westport, CT.

The Broadcast Communications Dictionary. Diamant, Lincoln. Edition: 3rd. Pub Date: 1991. Binding: Paper. Price: $27.95. ISBN: 0-8442-3325-0.
NTC Publishing Group, Lincolnwood, IL.

Broadcast Newswriting. Cohler, David K. Pub Date: 1990. 288 pp. Binding: Paperback text edition. Price: write for info. ISBN: 0-13-083528-5.
Prentice Hall, Englewood Cliffs, NJ.

Broadcast Talk. Scannell, Paddy, editor. Pub Date: 1992. 224 pp. Binding: Hardcover text edition. Binding: Paperback text edition. Price: $55.00. Price: $19.95. ISBN: 0-8039-8374-3. ISBN: 0-8039-8375-1.
Sage Publications Inc., Thousand Oaks, CA.

Broadcast Technology Report, 1990. Fitzmaurice, Michael. Pub Date: 1990. 56 pp. Binding: Paper. Price: $40.00. ISBN: 0-89324-082-6.
National Association of Broadcasters, Washington, DC.

Broadcast Technology Worktext. Ebersole, Samuel. Illus. Pub Date: 1991. 256 pp. Binding: Paper. Price: $26.95. ISBN: 0-240-80122-9.
Focal Press, Stoneham, MA.

Broadcast Transmission Engineering Practice. Wharton, Metcalfe, Shaun and Platts, Geoff C. Illus. Pub Date: 1992. 279 pp. Binding: Hardcover. Price: $115.00. ISBN: 0-240-51335-5.
Focal Press, Stoneham, MA.

Broadcast Voice Handbook: How to Polish Your On-Air Delivery. Utterback, Ann. Illus. Pub Date: 1990. 265 pp. Binding: Hardcover. Price: $26.95. ISBN: 0-929387-16-3.
Bonus Books Inc., Chicago.

A Broadcaster's Guide to Special Events & Sponsorship Risk Management. Everett, Daryl, editor. Pub Date: 1991. 61 pp. Binding: Hardcover. Price: $40.00 reference guide. ISBN: 0-89324-115-6.
National Association of Broadcasters, Washington, DC.

Broadcasting: Cable & Beyond. Dominick, Joseph R. Pub Date: 1990. Binding: Hardcover text edition. Price: $35.43. ISBN: 0-07-017547-0.
McGraw-Hill Inc., New York.

Broadcasting—Cable & Beyond: An Introduction to Modern Electronic Media. Dominick, Joseph R., Sherman, Barry L. and Copeland, Gary A. Edition: 2nd. Pub Date: 1992. Binding: Hardcover text edition. Price: write for info. ISBN: 0-07-017817-8.
McGraw-Hill Inc., New York.

Broadcasting & Cable Yearbook 1993, 2 Vols. Bowker, R.R., Staff, editor. Pub Date: 1993. 2,014 pp. Binding: Paper. Price: $159.95. ISBN: 0-8352-3315-4 (set).
Bowker, R.R., New Providence, NJ.

Broadcasting & Cable Yearbook 1994, 2 Vols. Bowker, R.R., Staff, editor. Pub Date: 03/1994. 2,100 pp. Binding: Paper. Price: write for info. ISBN: 0-8352-3438-X (set).
Bowker, R.R., New Providence, NJ.

Broadcasting Finance in Transition: A Comparative Handbook. Blumler, Jay G. and Nossiter, T. J., editors. Pub Date: 1991. 416 pp. Binding: Hardcover. Price: $55.00. ISBN: 0-19-505089-4.
Oxford University Press Inc., New York.

Broadcasting in America, Brief. Head, Sydney and Sterling, Christopher. Pub Date: 1991. Binding: Hardcover. Price: write for info. ISBN: 0-395-54445-9.
Houghton Mifflin Software, School & College Division, Boston.

Broadcasting in America: A Survey of Electronic Media. Head, Sydney and Sterling, Christopher. Edition: 6th. Pub Date: 1989. Binding: Hardcover text edition. Binding: Supplementary materials (study guide). Price: $51.96. Price: $16.76. ISBN: 0-395-43253-7. ISBN: 0-395-52936-0.
Houghton Mifflin Co., Boston.

Broadcasting in the Arab World: A Survey of the Electronic Media in the Middle East. Boyd, Douglas A. Illus. Edition: 2nd. Pub Date: 1993. 360 pp. Binding: Hardcover text edition. Price: $39.95. ISBN: 0-8138-0468-X.
Iowa State University Press, Ames, IA.

Broadcasting in Australia. Illus. Pub Date: 1989. 126 pp. Binding: Paperback text edition. Price: $19.95. ISBN: 0-644-06923-6.
Australian Government Publishing Service, New York.

Broadcasting in Australia. Illus. Pub Date: 1992. 350 pp. Binding: Paper. Price: $34.95. ISBN: 0-685-53607-6.
Australian Government Publishing Service, New York.

Broadcasting in India. Chatterji, P. C. Edition: 2nd. Pub Date: 1992. 228 pp. Binding: Hardcover. Price: $29.95. ISBN: 0-8039-9107-X.
Sage Publications Inc., Thousand Oaks, CA.

Broadcasting in the United Kingdom: A Guide to Information Sources. MacDonald, Barrie. Edition: 2nd. Pub Date: 1993. 304 pp. Binding: Hardcover text edition. Price: $100.00. ISBN: 0-7201-2086-1.
Cassell Publishing, New York.

Broadcasting It!: An Encyclopaedia of Homosexuality in Film, Radio, & TV in the UK, 1923-1993. Howes, Keith. Foreword by Bennett, Alan. Pub Date: 1993. 216 pp. Binding: Hardcover text edition. Binding: Paperback text edition. Price: $56.00. Price: $20.00. ISBN: 0-304-32700-X. ISBN: 0-304-32702-6.
Cassell Publishing, New York.

Broadcasting Law: A Comparative Study. Barendt, Eric M. Pub Date: 1993. 300 pp. Binding: Hardcover. Price: $45.00. ISBN: 0-19-825254-4.
Oxford University Press Inc., New York.

Broadcasting: The New Law. Reville, Nicholas. Pub Date: 1991. Binding: Paper. Price: $36.00. ISBN: 0-406-00137-5.
Butterworth U.S., Legal Publishers Inc., U.S. Headquarters, Salem, NH.

Broadcasting & Telecommunication: An Introduction. Bittner, John. Edition: 3rd. Pub Date: 1991. Binding: Hardcover. Price: $32.00. ISBN: 0-13-083239-1.
Prentice Hall, Englewood Cliffs, NJ.

Building Bridges with Cable: A Survey of Local Cable System Operators & MSO Executives. Reymer and Gersin Associates Staff. Pub Date: 1990. 130 pp. Binding: Paper. Price: $40.00. ISBN: 0-89324-087-7.
National Association of Broadcasters, Washington, DC.

The Business Television Directory, 1991. Warren Publishing Inc. Staff. Irwin, Susan, editor. Pub Date: 1990. 300 pp. Binding: Hardcover. Price: write for info. ISBN: 0-911486-59-3.
Warren Publishing Inc., Washington, DC.

The Business Television Directory, 1992 Edition. Warren Publishing Inc. Staff. Irwin, Susan, editor. Edition: 4th, rev. Pub Date: 1992. 236 pp. Binding: Hardcover. Price: write for info. ISBN: 0-911486-63-1.
Warren Publishing Inc., Washington, DC.

Buying or Building a Broadcast Station in the 1990s. Krasnow, Erwin G., Bentley, Geoffrey and Martin, Robin B. Pub Date: 1991. 108 pp. Binding: Hardcover. Price: write for info.
National Association of Broadcasters, Washington, DC.

Buying TV & Radio Airtime: A Money-Saving Method That Puts You in Control. Scanlan, Timothy J. Pub Date: 1991. 80 pp. Binding: Hardcover. Price: $85.00. ISBN: 1-880112-01-9.
Evergreen Media Inc., Lynnwood, WA.

CATV & Fiber Optics. IGIC Staff. Pub Date: 1990. 250 pp. Binding: Paper. Price: $1995.00. ISBN: 0-918435-67-6.
Information Gatekeepers Inc., Boston.

CBS News Index, 1986: Key to the Television News Broadcasts. Pub Date: 1989. 983 pp. Binding: Hardcover. Price: $125.00. ISBN: 0-685-46003-7.
University Microfilms Inc., Ann Arbor, MI.

CNN: The Inside Story: How a Band of Mavericks Changed the Face of Television News. Whittemore, Hank. Illus. Pub Date: 1990. 356 pp. Binding: Hardcover. Price: $22.95. ISBN: 0-316-93761-4.
Little, Brown & Co., New York.

The Cable Re-Regulation Handbook. Meyers, James E. Pub Date: 1994. 525 pp. Price: $295.
Thompson Publishing Group, Washington, DC.

Cable Spot Advertising Directory, 1993. National Register Publishing Staff. Pub Date: 1993. 763 pp. Binding: Paper. Price: $125.00. ISBN: 0-87217-948-6.
National Register Publishing, New Providence, NJ.

Cable & Station Coverage Atlas, 1991. Warren Publishing Inc. Staff. Warren, Albert, editor. Illus. Pub Date: 1991. 628 pp. Binding: Hardcover. Price: $345.00. ISBN: 0-911486-45-3.
Warren Publishing Inc., Washington, DC.

Cable & Station Coverage Atlas, 1992 Edition. Warren Publishing Inc. Staff. Warren, Albert, editor. Illus. Edition: 26th, rev. Pub Date: 1992. 650 pp. Binding: Hardcover. Price: write for info. ISBN: 0-911486-55-0.
Warren Publishing Inc., Washington, DC.

Cable & Station Coverage Atlas: 1993 Edition. Warren Publishing Inc. Staff. Taliaferro, Michael, editor. Illus. Edition: rev. Pub Date: 1993. Binding: Hardcover. Price: $360.00. ISBN: 0-911486-68-2.
Warren Publishing Inc., Washington, DC.

The Cable Statistics Book: 1993 Edition. Warren Publishing Inc. Staff. Taliaferro, Michael, editor. Illus. Edition: rev. Pub Date: 1993. Binding: Hardcover. Price: $95.00 supplement. ISBN: 0-911486-71-2.
Warren Publishing Inc., Washington, DC.

Cable Television Law: Living with Re-regulation, 2 Vols. Pub Date: 1991. 1,471 pp. Binding: Paperback text edition. Price: $30.00. ISBN: 0-685-49929-4 (set).
Practising Law Institute, New York.

Cable Television: A Source Guide. Pub Date: 1991. Binding: Library binding—adult. Price: $75.00. ISBN: 0-8490-4911-3.
Gordon Press Publishers, New York.

Cable Television Technology & Operations. Bartlett, Eugene R. Pub Date: 1990. Binding: Hardcover text edition. Price: $49.95. ISBN: 0-07-003957-7.
McGraw-Hill Inc., New York.

Canned Laughter: The Best Stories from Radio & Television's Golden Years. Hay, Peter. Pub Date: 1992. 304 pp. Binding: Hardcover. Price: $22.95. ISBN: 0-19-506836-X.
Oxford University Press Inc., New York.

Books on Broadcasting and Cable

Captain Kangaroo: America's Gentlest Hero. Keeshan, Robert and Bergman, Carl. Pub Date: 1989. Binding: Hardcover. Price: $17.95. ISBN: 0-318-42491-6.
Doubleday & Co. Inc., New York.

Career Opportunities in Television, Cable & Video. Reed, Maxine K. and Reed, Robert M. Edition: 3rd. Pub Date: 1991. 272 pp. Binding: Paper. Price: $14.95. ISBN: 0-8160-2341-7.
Facts on File Inc., New York.

Careers in Video: Getting Ahead in Professional Television. Jurek, Ken. Pub Date: 1989. 265 pp. Binding: Hardcover. Price: $34.95. ISBN: 0-86729-169-9.
Knowledge Industry Publications Inc., White Plains, NY.

Changing Channels: America in TV Guide. Altschuler, Glenn C. and Grossvogel, David I. Illus. Pub Date: 1992. 232 pp. Binding: Hardcover. Price: $21.95. ISBN: 0-252-01779-X.
University of Illinois Press, Champaign, IL.

Changing Channels: Issues & Realities in Television News. Jacobs, Jerry. Pub Date: 1990. 165 pp. Binding: Paperback text edition. Price: $19.95. ISBN: 0-87484-946-2.
Mayfield Publishing Co., Mountain View, CA.

Channels of Belief: Religion & American Commercial Television. Ferre, John P., editor. Pub Date: 1990. 152 pp. Binding: Hardcover text edition. Price: $19.95. ISBN: 0-8138-0639-9.
Iowa State University Press, Ames, IA.

China Turned On: Television, Reform & Resistance. Lull, James. Illus. Pub Date: 1991. 208 pp. Binding: Hardcover. Price: $49.95. ISBN: 0-415-05215-7. Binding: Paper. Price: $16.95. ISBN: 0-415-05216-5.
Routledge, New York.

Commons Sense: A Viewer's Guide to the British House of Commons. Watson, Patrick. Pub Date: 1992. 48 pp. Binding: Paper. Price: $3.95. ISBN: 0-685-60089-0.
C-Span, Washington, DC.

The Communication Satellites: Their History & Future. Hudson, Heather E. Pub Date: 1990. 288 pp. Binding: Hardcover text edition. Price: $29.95. ISBN: 0-02-915320-4.
Free Press, New York.

Communication Services Via Satellite: A Handbook for Design, Installation & Service Engineers. Lewis, G. E. Illus. Edition: 2nd. Pub Date: 1992. 400 pp. Binding: Hardcover. Price: $64.95. ISBN: 0-7506-0437-9.
Butterworth-Heinemann, Stoneham, MA.

Communications Law, 1990: A Course Handbook, 3 Vols. Pub Date: 1990. Binding: Hardcover. Price: $85.00. ISBN: 0-685-48534-X (set).
Practising Law Institute, New York.

Communications Receivers: The Vacuum Tube Era, 50 Glorious Years, 1932-1981. Moore, Raymond S. Illus. Edition: 2nd, rev. Pub Date: 1992. 116 pp. Binding: Paper. Price: $17.95. ISBN: 0-9618882-1-0.
RSM Communications Inc., Walpole, MA.

Comparing Broadcast Systems: The Experiences of Six Industrialized Nations. Browne, Donald R. Illus. Pub Date: 1989. 464 pp. Binding: Hardcover text edition. Price: $39.95. ISBN: 0-8138-0113-3.
Iowa State University Press, Ames, IA.

Competing Video Media: A Market-by-Market Guide, 1993. Warren Publishing Inc. Staff. Taliaferro, Michael, editor. Illus. Edition: rev. Pub Date: 1993. Binding: Hardcover. Price: $95.00 supplement. ISBN: 0-911486-72-0.
Warren Publishing Inc., Washington, DC.

The Complete Guide to American Film Schools & Cinema & Television Courses. Pintoff, Ernest. Pub Date: 04/1994. 624 pp. Binding: Paper. Price: $15.00. ISBN: 0-14-017226-2.
Viking Penguin, New York.

Contemporary Radio Programming Strategies. MacFarland, David T. Pub Date: 1990. 224 pp. Binding: Paperback text edition. Price: $22.50. ISBN: 0-8058-0665-2.
Erlbaum, Lawrence, Associates Inc., Hillsdale, NJ.

Contemporary Theatre, Film, & Television, Vol. 7. Gale Research Inc. Staff. Hubbard, Linda, editor. O'Donnell, Owen, editor. Pub Date: 1989. Binding: Hardcover. Price: $120.00. ISBN: 0-8103-2070-3.
Gale Research Inc., Detroit.

Contemporary Theatre, Film & TV, Vol. 9. Pub Date: 1991. Binding: Hardcover. Price: $120.00. ISBN: 0-8103-2072-X.
Gale Research Inc., Detroit.

Contemporary Theatre, Film & TV, Vol. 10. Pub Date: 1992. Binding: Hardcover. Price: $120.00. ISBN: 0-8103-2073-8.
Gale Research Inc., Detroit.

Contemporary Theatre, Film & TV, Vol. 11. Pub Date: 1993. Binding: Hardcover. Price: $120.00. ISBN: 0-8103-2074-6.
Gale Research Inc., Detroit.

Contemporary Theatre, Film & TV, Vol. 12. Pub Date: 08/1994. Binding: Hardcover. Price: $120.00. ISBN: 0-8103-6902-8.
Gale Research Inc., Detroit.

Conventional Wisdom: A Television Viewer's Guide to the 1992 National Political Conventions. Alpert, Eugene. Pub Date: 1992. 36 pp. Binding: Paper. Price: $6.95. ISBN: 1-881846-00-8.
C-Span, Washington, DC.

The Cosby Show: Audiences, Impact, & Implications. Fuller, Linda K. Pub Date: 1992. Binding: Hardcover. Price: $47.95. ISBN: 0-313-26407-4.
Greenwood Publishing Group Inc., Westport, CT.

A Country Practice: Quality Soap. Moran, Albert and Tulloch, John. Pub Date: 1990. Binding: Hardcover. Price: $45.00. ISBN: 0-86819-142-6.
State Mutual Book & Periodical Service, Limited, New York.

Cousin Cliff: Forty Magical Years in Television. Hollis, Tim. Illus. Pub Date: 1991. 152 pp. Binding: Paper. Price: $14.95. ISBN: 0-9628798-0-0.
Campbell's Publishing, Adamsville, AL.

Covering the Environmental Beat: An Overview for Radio & TV Journalists. Prato, Lou. Media Institute Staff, editor. Pref. by Maines, Patrick D. Bartlett, David. Pub Date: 1991. 113 pp. Binding: Paper. Price: $9.95. ISBN: 0-937790-47-8.
Media Institute, The, Washington, DC.

Covering the World: International Television News Services—Essay. Friedland, Lewis A. Pub Date: 1992. Binding: Hardcover. Price: $8.95. ISBN: 0-87078-345-9.
Twentieth Century Fund Press/Priority Press Publications, New York.

Creating Special Effects for TV & Video. Wilkie, Bernard. Illus. Edition: 2nd. Pub Date: 1992. 182 pp. Binding: Hardcover. Price: $34.95. ISBN: 0-240-51316-9.
Focal Press, Stoneham, MA.

Creative Radio Production. Siegel, Bruce. Illus. Pub Date: 1992. 304 pp. Binding: Paper. Price: $39.95. ISBN: 0-240-80070-2.
Focal Press, Stoneham, MA.

Cultural Rights: Technology, Legality, & Personality. Lury, Celia. Pub Date: 1993. Binding: Hardcover. Price: write for info. ISBN: 0-415-03155-9. Binding: Paper. Price: write for info. ISBN: 0-415-09578-6.
Routledge, New York.

Days of Vision: Working with David Mercer: Television Drama Then & Now. Taylor, Don. Pub Date: 1990. 282 pp. Binding: Hardcover. Price: $31.95. ISBN: 0-413-61510-3.
Heinemann, Portsmouth, NH.

Daytime Television Programming. Matelski, Marilyn. Pub Date: 1991. 96 pp. Binding: Paper. Price: $14.95. ISBN: 0-240-80087-7.
Focal Press, Stoneham, MA.

Defense Beat: The Dilemmas of Defense Coverage. Thompson, Loren, editor. Pub Date: 1991. 208 pp. Binding: Hardcover text edition. Price: $29.95. ISBN: 0-669-21842-1.
Free Press, New York.

Dictionary of Teleliteracy: A Personal Guide to Television from 1948 to the Present. Bianculli, David. Illus. Pub Date: 1993. 288 pp. Binding: Hardcover. Price: $24.95. ISBN: 0-8264-0577-0.
Continuum Publishing Co., New York.

Digital Communications by Satellite: Modulaton, Multiple Access & Coding. Bhargava, Vijay K., Haccoun, David, Matyas, Robert and Nuspl, Peter P. Pub Date: 1991. 592 pp. Binding: Hardcover text edition. Price: $84.50. ISBN: 0-89464-629-X.
Krieger Publishing Co., Melbourne, FL.

Digital Satellite Communications. Ha, Tri T. Edition: 2nd. Pub Date: 1990. 172 pp. Binding: Hardcover text edition. Binding: Laboratory manuals. Price: $65.00. Price: $19.95 student's solutions manual. ISBN: 0-07-025389-7. ISBN: 0-685-46983-2.
McGraw-Hill Inc., New York.

Digital Satellite Communications Systems & Technologies: Military & Civil Applications. Ince, Nejat, editor. Pub Date: 1992. 624 pp. Binding: Library binding—adult. Price: $138.50. ISBN: 0-7923-9254-X.
Kluwer Academic Publishers, Norwell, MA.

ENG: Television News & the New Technology. Yoakam, Richard D. and Cremer, Charles F. Foreword by Pettit, Tom. Illus. Edition: 2nd. Pub Date: 1989. 400 pp. Binding: Paperback text edition. Price: $22.95. ISBN: 0-394-37102-X.
Random House Inc., New York.

Electoral Coverage. Johnston, Carla. Pub Date: 1991. 112 pp. Binding: Paper. Price: $14.95. ISBN: 0-240-80088-5.
Focal Press, Stoneham, MA.

Electronic Golden Calf: Images, Religion & the Making of Meaning. Goethals, Gregor T. Pub Date: 1990. 225 pp. Binding: Hardcover. Price: $21.95. ISBN: 1-56101-007-3. Binding: Paper. Price: $11.95. ISBN: 1-56101-002-2.
Cowley Publications, Boston.

Electronic Hearth: Creating an American Television Culture. Tichi, Cecelia. Illus. Pub Date: 1992. 272 pp. Binding: Paper. Price: $9.95. ISBN: 0-19-507914-0.
Oxford University Press Inc., New York.

Electronic Media Management. Pringle, Peter K. Edition: 2nd. Pub Date: 1990. 336 pp. Binding: Paper. Price: $32.95. ISBN: 0-240-80050-8.
Focal Press, Stoneham, MA.

Electronic Media Programming: Strategies & Decision Making. Carroll, Raymond L. and Davis, Donald M. Pub Date: 1993. Binding: Hardcover text edition. Price: write for info. ISBN: 0-07-010298-8.
McGraw-Hill Inc., New York.

Electronic News Gathering: A Guide to ENG. Musburger. Pub Date: 1991. 96 pp. Binding: Paper. Price: $14.95. ISBN: 0-240-80079-6.
Focal Press, Stoneham, MA.

Empire of the Air: The Creation of Radio. Lewis, Tom. Illus. Pub Date: 1991. 352 pp. Binding: Hardcover. Price: $25.00. ISBN: 0-06-018215-6.
HarperCollins Publishers Inc., New York.

Empire of the Air: The Men Who Made Radio. Lewis, Tom. Illus. Pub Date: 1993. 432 pp. Binding: Paper. Price: $13.00. ISBN: 0-06-098119-9.
HarperCollins Publishers Inc., New York.

European Coproduction in Film & Television. Becker, Jurgen and Rehbinder, Manfred, editors. Pub Date: 1989. 178 pp. Binding: Paper. Price: $21.00. ISBN: 3-7890-1779-5.
International Book Import Service Inc., Huntsville, AL.

The Evil Eye: The Unacceptable Face of Television. Playfair, Guy L. Pub Date: 1991. 192 pp. Binding: Hardcover. Price: $29.95. ISBN: 0-224-02791-3.
Trafalgar Square, North Pomfret, VT.

Expanding Free Expression in the Marketplace: Broadcasting & the Public Forum. Caristi, Dom. Pub Date: 1992. Binding: Hardcover. Price: $45.00. ISBN: 0-89930-720-5.
Greenwood Publishing Group Inc., Westport, CT.

Expanding Vista: American Television in the Kennedy Years. Watson, Mary Ann. Illus. Pub Date: 1990. 304 pp. Binding: Hardcover. Price: $22.95. ISBN: 0-19-505746-5.
Oxford University Press Inc., New York.

FCC Exam Guide. Whitehouse, Bart. Illus. Pub Date: 1991. 225 pp. Binding: Paperback text edition. Price: $16.95. ISBN: 0-89100-387-8.
IAP Inc., Casper, WY.

Facts on File Dictionary of Film & Broadcast Terms. Penney, Edmund F. Pub Date: 1992. 272 pp. Binding: Paper. Price: $14.95. ISBN: 0-8160-2782-X.
Facts on File Inc., New York.

The Facts on File Dictionary of Film & Broadcast Terms. Penney, Edmund F. Pub Date: 1991. 304 pp. Binding: Hardcover. Price: $29.95. ISBN: 0-8160-1923-1.
Facts on File Inc., New York.

Federal Telecommunications Law. Kellogg, Michael K., Thorne, John and Huber, Peter W. Pub Date: 1992.

Books on Broadcasting and Cable

862 pp. Binding: Hardcover. Price: $145.00. ISBN: 0-316-48676-0.
Little, Brown & Co., New York.

Fields in Vision: Television Sport & Cultural Transformation. Whannel, Garry. Pub Date: 1992. 288 pp. Binding: Hardcover. Price: $69.95. ISBN: 0-415-05382-X. Binding: Paper. Price: $16.95. ISBN: 0-415-05383-8.
Routledge, New York.

Fifties Television: The Industry & Its Critics. Boddy, William. Illus. Pub Date: 1990. 304 pp. Binding: Paper. Price: $14.95. ISBN: 0-252-06299-X.
University of Illinois Press, Champaign, IL.

Film & Television Handbook, 1992. Leafe, David, editor. Illus. Pub Date: 1992. 332 pp. Binding: Paper. Price: $28.95. ISBN: 0-85170-317-8.
Indiana University Press, Bloomington, IN.

Fixed & Mobile Terminal Antennas. Kumar, Akhileshwar. Pub Date: 1991. 528 pp. Binding: Hardcover text edition. Price: $88.00. ISBN: 0-89006-438-5.
Artech House Inc., Norwood, MA.

Framing the Past: The Historiography of German Cinema & Television. Murray, Bruce A. and Wickham, Christopher J., editors. Illus. Pub Date: 1992. 384 pp. Binding: Hardcover. Price: $34.95. ISBN: 0-8093-1756-7.
Southern Illinois University Press, Carbondale, IL.

Fred Allen's Radio Comedy. Havig, Alan. Pub Date: 1992. Binding: Paper. Price: $16.95. ISBN: 0-87722-810-8.
Temple University Press, Philadelphia.

From Whistle Stop to Sound Bite: Four Decades of Politics & Television. Mickelson, Sig. Pub Date: 1989. 196 pp. Binding: Hardcover. Price: $42.95. ISBN: 0-275-92351-7. Binding: Paper. Price: $16.95. ISBN: 0-275-92632-X.
Greenwood Publishing Group Inc., Westport, CT.

Full Service Radio. Halper, Donna L. Illus. Pub Date: 1990. 112 pp. Binding: Paper. Price: $14.95. ISBN: 0-240-80083-4.
Focal Press, Stoneham, MA.

The Future of Television. Doyle, Marc. Pub Date: 1992. 208 pp. Binding: Hardcover. Price: $39.95. ISBN: 0-8442-3461-3.
NTC Publishing Group, Lincolnwood, IL.

Gale Directory of Publications & Broadcast Media '94 & Update. Winklepleck. Pub Date: 04/1994. Binding: Hardcover. Price: write for info. ISBN: 0-8103-8063-3.
Gale Research Inc., Detroit.

Gale Directory of Publications & Broadcast Media '93 & Update. Winklepleck. Pub Date: 1993. Binding: Hardcover. Price: write for info. ISBN: 0-8103-7999-6.
Gale Research Inc., Detroit.

Gale Directory of Publications & Broadcast Media '94 & Update. Winklepleck. Pub Date: 1993. Binding: Hardcover. Price: $315.00. ISBN: 0-8103-8059-5.
Gale Research Inc., Detroit.

Gale Directory of Publications & Broadcast Media '94, Vol. 1. Winklepleck. Pub Date: 1993. Binding: Hardcover. Price: write for info. ISBN: 0-8103-8060-9.
Gale Research Inc., Detroit.

Gale Directory of Publications & Broadcast Media '94, Vol. 2. Winklepleck. Pub Date: 1993. Binding: Hardcover. Price: write for info. ISBN: 0-8103-8061-7.
Gale Research Inc., Detroit.

Gale Directory of Publications & Broadcast Media '94, Vol. 3. Winklepleck. Pub Date: 1993. Binding: Hardcover. Price: write for info. ISBN: 0-8103-8062-5.
Gale Research Inc., Detroit.

The Game Behind the Game: High Pressure, High Stakes in Sports Television. O'Neil, Terry. Pub Date: 1989. Binding: Hardcover. Price: $17.95. ISBN: 0-06-016019-5.
HarperCollins Publishers Inc., New York.

Games & Sets: The Changing Face of Sport on Television. Barnett, Steven. Illus. Pub Date: 1990. 224 pp. Binding: Hardcover. Price: $39.95. ISBN: 0-85170-267-8. Binding: Paper. Price: $17.95. ISBN: 0-85170-268-6.
Indiana University Press, Bloomington, IN.

Gavel to Gavel: A Guide to the Televised Proceedings of Congress. Green, Alan. Pub Date: 1992. 64 pp. Binding: Paper. Price: $3.95. ISBN: 1-881846-02-4.
C-Span, Washington, DC.

Gender Politics & MTV: Voicing the Difference. Lewis, Lisa A. Pub Date: 1992. Binding: Paper. Price: $16.95. ISBN: 0-87722-942-2.
Temple University Press, Philadelphia.

The Golden Age of Television: Notes from the Survivors. Wilk, Max. Illus. Pub Date: 1990. 288 pp. Binding: Paper. Price: $12.95. ISBN: 1-55921-000-1.
Moyer Bell, Wakefield, RI.

Gordon McLendon Maverick of Radio. Pub Date: 1992. 256 pp. Binding: Hardcover. Price: $45.00. ISBN: 0-313-26676-X.
Greenwood Publishing Group Inc., Westport, CT.

The Great God Unclothed: or The Five Myths of Television Power. Davis, Douglas. Pub Date: 1993. 256 pp. Binding: Hardcover. Price: $20.00. ISBN: 0-671-73963-8.
Simon & Schuster Trade, New York.

Guide to Broadcasting Stations. Darrington, Philip, editor. Edition: 20th. Pub Date: 1989. Binding: Paper. Price: $32.95. ISBN: 0-434-90309-4.
Butterworth-Heinemann, Stoneham, MA.

Hake's Guide to TV Collectibles. Hake, Ted, editor. Illus. Pub Date: 1990. 200 pp. Binding: Paper. Price: $14.95. ISBN: 0-87069-571-1.
Chilton Book Co., Radnor, PA.

Hard to Get: Fast Talk & Rude Questions Along the Interview Trail. Collins, Nancy. Pub Date: 1992. 368 pp. Binding: Paper. Price: $11.00. ISBN: 0-06-097433-8.
HarperCollins Publishers Inc., New York.

Hi-Ho, Steverino: My Adventures in the Wonderful Wacky World of Television. Allen, Steve. Pub Date: 1992. Binding: Hardcover. Price: $19.95. ISBN: 0-942637-55-0.
Barricade Books Inc., New York.

Hidden Agendas: The Politics of Religious Broadcasting in Britain 1987–1991. Quicke, Andrew and Quicke, Juliet. Pub Date: 1993. 276 pp. Binding: Paper. Price: $14.99. ISBN: 0-9635509-0-X.
Dominion Kings Grant Publishing Inc., Virginia Beach, VA.

Highway Radio, 1989: A Guide to Tuning in on America's Highways. Stank, William J. Illus. Pub Date: 1989. 112 pp. Binding: Paper. Price: $4.95. ISBN: 0-9621334-1-8.
ArcTrek Publishing, Allentown, PA.

History of International Broadcasting. Wood, James. Pub Date: 1992. 264 pp. Binding: Hardcover text edition. Price: $59.00. ISBN: 0-86341-281-5.
Institution of Electrical Engineers, Piscataway, NJ.

Hollywood & Broadcasting: From Radio to Cable. Hilmes, Michele. Pub Date: 1990. 264 pp. Binding: Hardcover. Price: $24.95. ISBN: 0-252-01709-9.
University of Illinois Press, Champaign, IL.

Hollywood in the Age of Television. Balio, Tino. Pub Date: 1990. 384 pp. Binding: Hardcover text edition. Binding: Paperback text edition. Price: $60.00. Price: $21.95. ISBN: 0-04-445837-1. ISBN: 0-04-445836-3.
Routledge, Chapman & Hall Inc., New York.

Hollywood vs. America. Medved, Michael. Pub Date: 1993. 400 pp. Binding: Paper. Price: $12.00. ISBN: 0-06-092435-7.
HarperCollins Publishers Inc., New York.

Home Satellite TV Installation & Troubleshooting Manual. Baylin, Frank and Gale, Brent. Illus. Edition: 3rd, rev. Pub Date: 1992. 356 pp. Binding: Paper. Price: $30.00. ISBN: 0-917893-12-3.
Baylin Publications, Boulder, CO.

Honey, I'm Home!: Sitcoms, Selling the American Dream. Jones, Gerard. Pub Date: 1993. Binding: Paper. Price: $13.95. ISBN: 0-312-08810-8.
Saint Martin's Press Inc., New York.

Horizontal Hold: The Making & Breaking of a Network Pilot. Paisner, Daniel. Illus. Pub Date: 1992. 256 pp. Binding: Hardcover. Price: $18.95. ISBN: 1-55972-148-0.
Carol Publishing Group, New York.

How CNN Fought the War: A View from the Inside. Smith, Perry M. Illus. Pub Date: 1991. 256 pp. Binding: Hardcover. Price: $18.95. ISBN: 1-55972-083-2. Binding: Paper. Price: $12.95. ISBN: 1-55972-090-5.
Carol Publishing Group, New York.

How to Find a Job in Television, Radio or Cable. Elliott, Bill. Pub Date: 1993. 44 pp. Price: $24.95.
Elliott Broadcast Consultants, Port Richey, FL.

How to Get a Job in Radio: Proven Techniques to Save Time, Money & Get You on the Airwaves! Stucker, Steve. Illus. Pub Date: 1990. 100 pp. Binding: Paper. Price: $12.95. ISBN: 0-9627970-3-0.
Stucker Productions, Albuquerque, NM.

How to Launch Your Career in TV News. Leshay, Jeff. Pub Date: 1993. 144 pp. Binding: Paper. Price: $14.95. ISBN: 0-8442-4138-5.
NTC Publishing Group, Lincolnwood, IL.

How to Watch TV News. Postman, Neil and Powers, Steve. Pub Date: 1992. 160 pp. Binding: Paper. Price: $10.00. ISBN: 0-14-013231-7.
Viking Penguin, New York.

How the World Was One: Toward the Tele-Family of Man. Clarke, Arthur C. Pub Date: 1992. Binding: Hardcover. Price: $22.50. ISBN: 0-553-07440-7.
Bantam Books Inc., New York.

The ITV Encyclopedia of Adventure. Rogers, Dave. Pub Date: 1990. 593 pp. Binding: Hardcover. Price: $125.00. ISBN: 1-85283-217-7.
State Mutual Book & Periodical Service, Limited, New York.

Image As Artifact: The Historical Analysis of Film & Television. O'Connor, John E. Pub Date: 1990. 356 pp. Binding: Paper. Price: $29.50. ISBN: 0-89464-313-4.
Krieger Publishing Co., Melbourne, FL.

Images & Industry: Television Drama Production in Australia. Moran, Albert, editor. Pub Date: 1990. Binding: Hardcover. Price: $49.00. ISBN: 0-86819-073-X.
State Mutual Book & Periodical Service, Limited, New York.

Imitations of Life: A Reader on Film & Television Melodrama. Landy, Marcia, editor. Illus. Pub Date: 1991. 619 pp. Binding: Hardcover text edition. Binding: Paperback text edition. Price: $45.00. Price: $19.95. ISBN: 0-8143-2064-3. ISBN: 0-8143-2065-1.
Wayne State University Press, Detroit.

Information Superhighways: The Economics of Advanced Public Communication Networks. Egan, Bruce L. Pub Date: 1991. 270 pp. Binding: Hardcover text edition. Price: $59.00. ISBN: 0-89006-474-1.
Artech House Inc., Norwood, MA.

Inside Family Viewing: Ethnographic Research on Television's Audiences. Lull, James. Pub Date: 1991. 208 pp. Binding: Hardcover. Price: $49.95. ISBN: 0-415-04414-6. Binding: Paper. Price: $17.95. ISBN: 0-415-04997-0.
Routledge, New York.

Integrated Broadband Networks: The Public Policy Issues. Elton, M. C. Pub Date: 1991. Binding: Hardcover. Price: $80.00. ISBN: 0-444-89068-8.
Elsevier Science Publishing Co. Inc., New York.

International Callsign Directory: Your Guide for Identifying Broadcasting & Utilities Stations Heard on Longwave, Shortwave, & VHF-UHF. Van Horn, Gayle. Grove, Bob, editor. Pub Date: 1992. 256 pp. Binding: Hardcover. Price: $24.95. ISBN: 0-944543-04-9.
Grove Enterprises Inc., Brasstown, NC.

International Communications Satellite Systems Conference, 14th: Proceedings. Pub Date: 1992. Binding: Hardcover. Price: $250.00. ISBN: 0-685-59647-8.
American Institute of Aeronautics & Astronautics, Washington, DC.

The International Politics of Television. Quester, George H. Pub Date: 1990. 304 pp. Binding: Hardcover text edition. Binding: Paper. Price: $49.95. Price: $24.95. ISBN: 0-669-20992-9. ISBN: 0-669-24456-2.
Free Press, New York.

International Regulation of Satellite Communication. Smith, Milton L. Pub Date: 1990. Binding: Library binding—adult. Price: $100.00. ISBN: 0-7923-0580-9.
Kluwer Academic Publishers, Norwell, MA.

International Satellite Directory, 1989. Payne, Silvano, editor. Illus. Edition: 4th. Pub Date: 1989. 1,200 pp. Binding: Hardcover. Price: $240.00. ISBN: 0-936361-04-2.
Design Publishers, Sonoma, CA.

International Satellite Directory, 1990. Payne, Silvano, editor. Illus. Edition: 5th. Pub Date: 1990. Binding: Hardcover. Price: $240.00. ISBN: 0-936361-05-0.
Design Publishers, Sonoma, CA.

International Television & Video Almanac, 1993. Monush, Barry, editor. Pub Date: 1993. Binding: Hardcover. Price: $85.00. ISBN: 0-900610-49-2.
Quigley Publishing Co. Inc., New York.

The Internationalisation of Television. Negrine, Ralph and Papathanassopolous, Stylianos. Pub Date: 1991.

Books on Broadcasting and Cable

Binding: Hardcover text edition. Price: $54.00. ISBN: 0-86187-761-6.
Saint Martin's Press Inc., New York.

Inventing American Broadcasting, 1899–1922. Douglas, Susan J. Illus. Pub Date: 1989. 400 pp. Binding: Paperback text edition. Price: $15.95. ISBN: 0-8018-3832-0.
Johns Hopkins University Press, Baltimore.

The Invisible Medium: Commercial, Public & Community Radio. Lewis, Peter and Booth, Jerry, editors. Pub Date: 1990. 250 pp. Binding: Hardcover. Price: $24.95. ISBN: 0-88258-032-9. Binding: Paper. Price: $14.95. ISBN: 0-88258-106-6.
Howard University Press, Washington, DC.

Is Anyone Responsible?: How Television Frames Political Issues. Iyengar, Shanto. Illus. Pub Date: 1991. 160 pp. Binding: Hardcover. Price: $19.95. ISBN: 0-226-38854-9.
University of Chicago Press, Chicago.

Ku-Band Satellite TV: Theory, Installation & Repair. Baylin, Frank and Gale, Brent. Illus. Edition: 3rd. Pub Date: 1990. 432 pp. Binding: Paper. Price: $29.95. ISBN: 0-917893-10-7.
Baylin Publications, Boulder, CO.

Law & Space Telecommunications. Lyall, Francis. Pub Date: 1989. Binding: Hardcover text edition. Price: $99.95. ISBN: 1-85521-039-8.
Ashgate Publishing Co., Brookfield, VT.

Lee De Forest & the Fatherhood of Radio. Hijiya, James A. Illus. Pub Date: 1992. 184 pp. Binding: Hardcover. Price: $32.50. ISBN: 0-934223-23-8.
Lehigh University Press.

Les Brown's Encyclopedia of Television. Brown, Les. Edition: 3rd. Pub Date: 1991. 723 pp. Binding: Paper. Binding: Paper. Price: $22.95. Price: $44.95. ISBN: 0-8103-9420-0. ISBN: 0-8103-8871-5.
Visible Ink Press.

Life After Television: The Coming Transformation of Media & American Life. Gilder, George. Rukeyser, William S., editor. Kiser, Anthony C., editor. Illus. Pub Date: 1990. 88 pp. Binding: Hardcover. Price: $11.95. ISBN: 0-9624745-2-5.
Whittle Communications, Knoxville, TN.

Listening In: The First Decade of Canadian Broadcasting, 1922–1932. Vipond, Mary. Pub Date: 1992. 448 pp. Binding: Hardcover. Price: $49.95. ISBN: 0-7735-0917-8.
University of Toronto Press, Cheektowaga, NY.

Live Via Satellite: The Amazing Story of How COMSAT Changed the World. Tedeschi, Anthony M. Pub Date: 1989. 224 pp. Binding: Hardcover. Price: $19.95. ISBN: 0-87491-922-3.
Acropolis Books, Herndon, VA.

Logics of Television: Essays in Cultural Criticism. Mellencamp, Patricia, editor. Pub Date: 1990. 318 pp. Binding: Hardcover. Price: $35.00. ISBN: 0-253-33617-1. Binding: Paper. Price: $14.95. ISBN: 0-253-20582-4.
Indiana University Press, Bloomington, IN.

Make-Believe Media: Politics of Film & Television. Parenti, Michael. Pub Date: 1991. Binding: Hardcover. Price: $19.95. ISBN: 0-312-05894-2.
Saint Martin's Press Inc., New York.

The Making of Exile Cultures: Iranian Television in Los Angeles. Naficy, Hamid. Pub Date: 1993. 320 pp. Binding: Hardcover text edition. Binding: Paper. Price: $44.95. Price: $18.95. ISBN: 0-8166-2084-9. ISBN: 0-8166-2087-3.
University of Minnesota Press, Minneapolis.

Making Sense of Television: The Psychology of Audience Interpretation. Livingstone, Sonia M. Illus. Pub Date: 1990. 390 pp. Binding: Hardcover text edition. Price: $51.00. ISBN: 0-08-036760-7.
Pergamon Press Inc., Tarrytown, NY.

Making a TV Series: The Bellamy Project. Moran, Albert. Pub Date: 1990. Binding: Hardcover. Price: $45.00. ISBN: 0-86819-061-6.
State Mutual Book & Periodical Service, Limited, New York.

Managing Electronic Media. Czech-Beckerman, Elizabeth. Pub Date: 1991. 96 pp. Binding: Paper. Price: $14.95. ISBN: 0-240-80072-9.
Focal Press, Stoneham, MA.

Mapping Hegemony: Television News & Industrial Conflict. Goldman, Robert and Rajagopal, Arvind, editors. Pub Date: 1991. 272 pp. Binding: Hardcover text edition. Binding: Paper. Price: $47.50. Price: $24.95. ISBN: 0-89391-697-8. ISBN: 0-89391-819-9.
Ablex Publishing Corp., Norwood, NJ.

Market for Cable TV Hardware & Associated Technologies (U.S.). Pub Date: 1991. 459 pp. Binding: Hardcover. Price: $2950.00. ISBN: 0-685-61719-X.
Frost & Sullivan Market Intelligence, Mountain View, CA.

Market for Cable Television (CATV) Services & Associated Equipment (Europe). Pub Date: 1990. 350 pp. Binding: Hardcover. Price: $4750.00. ISBN: 0-685-61726-2.
Frost & Sullivan Market Intelligence, Mountain View, CA.

Market for Military Satellite Communications (U.S.). Pub Date: 1991. 340 pp. Binding: Hardcover. Price: $2450.00. ISBN: 0-685-61951-6.
Frost & Sullivan Market Intelligence, Mountain View, CA.

The Meaning of the Medium: Perspectives of the Art of Television. Henderson, Katherine U. and Mazzeo, Joseph A., editors. Pub Date: 1990. Binding: Hardcover. Price: $42.95. ISBN: 0-275-93390-3.
Greenwood Publishing Group Inc., Westport, CT.

Media Events: The Live Broadcasting of History. Dayan, Daniel and Katz, Elihu. Illus. Pub Date: 1992. 320 pp. Binding: Hardcover. Price: $29.95. ISBN: 0-674-55955-X.
Harvard University Press, Cambridge, MA.

The Media Game: American Politics in the Television Age. Ansolabehere, Stephen, Behr, Roy and Iyengar, Shanto. Pub Date: 1992. Binding: Paper. Price: write for info. ISBN: 0-02-359965-0.
Macmillan Publishing Co. Inc., New York.

The Media Show: The Changing Face of the News, 1985-1990. Diamond, Edwin. Illus. Pub Date: 1991. 230 pp. Binding: Hardcover. Price: $19.95. ISBN: 0-262-04125-1.
MIT Press, Cambridge, MA.

Medium Rare: The Evolution, Workings & Impact of Commercial Television. Papazian, Ed. Edition: rev. Pub Date: 1991. 578 pp. Binding: Paper. Price: $35.00. ISBN: 0-9621947-1-9.
Media Dynamics, New York.

Milestones in Motion-Picture & Television Technology—The SMPTE 75th Anniversary Collection. Friedman, Jeffrey, editor. Foreword by Haney, Frank J. Introduction by Baker, Blaine. Pub Date: 1991. 241 pp. Binding: Hardcover. Price: $25.00. ISBN: 0-940690-19-5.
Society of Motion Picture & Television Engineers, White Plains, NY.

Missed Opportunities: The Story of Canada's Broadcasting Policy. Raboy, Marc. Pub Date: 1990. 472 pp. Binding: Library binding—adult. Binding: Paper. Price: $49.95. Price: $22.95. ISBN: 0-7735-0743-4. ISBN: 0-7735-0775-2.
University of Toronto Press, Cheektowaga, NY.

The Movie of the Week: Private Stories—Public Events. Rapping, Elayne. Pub Date: 1992. 208 pp. Binding: Hardcover. Price: $39.95. ISBN: 0-8166-2017-2. Binding: Paper. Price: $14.95. ISBN: 0-8166-2018-0.
University of Minnesota Press, Minneapolis.

Movies on TV & Videocassette, 1991–1992. Scheuer, Steven H. Pub Date: 1990. Binding: Paper. Price: $5.95. ISBN: 0-553-28801-6.
Bantam Books Inc., New York.

Movies on TV & Videocassette, 1992–1993. Scheuer, Steven H., editor. Pub Date: 1992. Binding: Hardcover. Price: $14.99. ISBN: 0-517-09465-7.
Outlet Book Co. Inc., Avenal, NJ.

Music You Can See: The MTV Story. Nance, Scott. Pub Date: 1993. Binding: Paper. Price: $14.95. ISBN: 1-55698-355-7.
Movie Publisher Services Inc., Las Vegas.

NAB Engineering Conference Proceedings, 1991. Illus. Pub Date: 1991. 512 pp. Binding: Hardcover. Price: $70.00. ISBN: 0-89324-107-5.
National Association of Broadcasters, Washington, DC.

NAB Guide for Broadcast Station Chief Operators. NAB Staff. Pub Date: 1991. 82 pp. Binding: Hardcover. Price: $60.00 guide. ISBN: 0-89324-105-9.
National Association of Broadcasters, Washington, DC.

NAB Legal Guide to Broadcast Law & Regulation 1991 Supplement. Green, William S., editor. Pub Date: 1991. 264 pp. Binding: Hardcover. Price: $130.00. ISBN: 0-89324-109-1.
National Association of Broadcasters, Washington, DC.

NAB Proceedings, 1990: Forty-Fourth Annual Broadcast Engineering Conference. Pub Date: 1990. 552 pp. Binding: Paper. Price: $70.00. ISBN: 0-89324-086-9.
National Association of Broadcasters, Washington, DC.

NBC Handbook of Pronunciation. Ehrlich, Eugene and Hand, Raymond, Jr. Edition: 4th. Pub Date: 1991. 544 pp. Binding: Paper. Price: $13.00. ISBN: 0-06-273056-8.
HarperCollins Publishers Inc., New York.

NCTA Technical Papers 1989. Rutkowski, Katherine, editor. Illus. Pub Date: 1989. 320 pp. Binding: Hardcover. Price: $40.00. ISBN: 0-940272-16-4.
National Cable Television Association, Washington, DC.

NCTA Technical Papers 1992. Rutkowski, Katherine, editor. Illus. Pub Date: 1992. 509 pp. Binding: Hardcover. Price: $50.00. ISBN: 0-940272-20-2.
National Cable Television Association, Washington, DC.

National Public Radio: The Cast of Characters. Collins, Mary. Liebling, Jerome, photographer. Illus. Pub Date: 1993. 172 pp. Binding: Hardcover text edition. Price: $39.95. ISBN: 0-929765-19-2.
Seven Locks Press, Arlington, VA.

National Radio Guide, 1990: The Official Guide to Radio Stations of Your Choice. Wood, Steven N. and Fry, John M. Pub Date: 1990. 125 pp. Binding: Paper. Price: $5.95. ISBN: 0-9625470-0-X.
WF Innovations Inc., Mesa, AZ.

National Radio Publicity Outlets, No. 7. Edition: rev. Pub Date: 1989. 544 pp. Binding: Paper. Price: $119.75. ISBN: 0-925133-03-5.
Morgan-Rand Publishing Co., Philadelphia.

Nervous Laughter: Television Situation Comedy & Liberal Democratic Ideology. Hamamoto, Darrell Y. Illus. Pub Date: 1991. 189 pp. Binding: Hardcover. Price: $45.00. ISBN: 0-275-92861-6. Binding: Paper. Price: $14.95. ISBN: 0-275-94050-0.
Greenwood Publishing Group Inc., Westport, CT.

The New European Satellite Smorgasbord: Dishing Up the Policies, Politics & Technologies of the 1990s. Bruno, Susan, editor. Illus. Pub Date: 1992. 293 pp. Binding: Paperback text edition. Price: $35.00. ISBN: 0-89206-196-0.
Center for Strategic & International Studies, Washington, DC.

The New News vs. the Old News: Press & Politics in the 1990s. Rosen, Jay and Taylor, Paul, editors. Pub Date: 1992. Binding: Paper. Price: $9.95. ISBN: 0-87078-344-0.
Twentieth Century Fund Press/Priority Press Publications, New York.

New Technology Developments Impacting Broadcasting Businesses, Markets, & Operations. Pub Date: 1990. 110 pp. Binding: Paper. Price: $40.00. ISBN: 0-89324-084-2.
National Association of Broadcasters, Washington, DC.

Newnes Guide to Satellite TV: Installation, Reception & Repair. Stephenson, D. J. Illus. Edition: 2nd. Pub Date: 1991. 256 pp. Binding: Hardcover. Price: $34.95. ISBN: 0-7506-0215-5.
Butterworth-Heinemann, Stoneham, MA.

News & Journalism in the UK: A Textbook. McNair, Brian. Pub Date: 1993. Binding: Hardcover. Price: write for info. ISBN: 0-415-06022-2. Binding: Paper. Price: write for info. ISBN: 0-415-06023-0.
Routledge, New York.

The News Shapers: The Sources Who Explain the News. Soley, Lawrence C. Pub Date: 1992. 184 pp. Binding: Hardcover. Price: $42.95. ISBN: 0-275-94033-0.
Greenwood Publishing Group Inc., Westport, CT.

News that Matters: Television & American Opinion. Iyengar, Shanto and Kinder, Donald R. Illus. Pub Date: 1989. 200 pp. Binding: Paper. Price: $10.95. ISBN: 0-226-38857-3.
University of Chicago Press, Chicago.

Books on Broadcasting and Cable

Newsroom Management: A Guide to Theory & Practice. Giles, Robert H. Illus. Edition: 6th. 742 pp. Pub Date: 1992. Repr. of 1987 edition. Binding: Hardcover. Price: $29.95. ISBN: 0-685-44396-5.
Media Management Books Inc. 615 Lafayette Blvd., Detroit 48226. (313) 222-2247.

Management is a subject of growing importance to media executives. NEWSROOM MANAGEMENT introduces a framework for managing others. It is a useful reference that lays out theories & strategies for resolving the issues that confront executives in every media organization. This book can be an important resource for the executive who seeks a larger understanding of how to manage human behavior.

Next Time I Want to Come Back as a Yellow Bird. Burdick, Richard S. Blackman, Sushila, editor. Illus. Pub Date: 1992. 240 pp. Binding: Hardcover. Price: $24.95. ISBN: 0-936417-30-7.
Axelrod Publishing of Tampa Bay, Tampa.

Now the News: The Story of Broadcast Journalism. Bliss, Edward. Pub Date: 1991. Binding: Hardcover. Price: $34.95. ISBN: 0-231-04402-X.
Columbia University Press, New York.

Official CBS Viewers Guide to the 1992 Winter Olympics. Rosenthal, Michael. Pub Date: 1991. Binding: Paper. Price: $3.95. ISBN: 0-918223-90-3.
Pindar Press, New York.

Official NBC Viewers Guide to the 1992 Summer Olympics. Rosenthal, Michael. Pub Date: 1992. Binding: Paper. Price: $14.95. ISBN: 0-918223-92-X.
Pindar Press, New York.

On the Air. Carlson, Mark. McGar, Kerri, illustrator. Carlson, Mark, illustrator. Illus. Pub Date: 1991. 64 pp. Binding: Paper. Price: $16.95. ISBN: 0-910303-23-1.
Writers Publishing Service Co., Seattle.

On the Radio: Music Radio in Britain. Barnard, Stephen. Pub Date: 1989. 176 pp. Binding: Hardcover. Price: $90.00. ISBN: 0-335-15284-8. Binding: Paper. Price: $34.00. ISBN: 0-335-15130-2.
Taylor & Francis Inc., Washington, DC.

One Nation Under Television. MacDonald, J. Fred. Pub Date: 1990. Binding: Hardcover. Price: $24.95. ISBN: 0-394-58018-4.
Pantheon Books, New York.

One Nation Under Television: The Rise & Decline of Network TV. MacDonald, J. Fred. Pub Date: 1993. 300 pp. Binding: Paperback text edition. Price: $18.95. ISBN: 0-8304-1362-6.
Nelson-Hall Inc., Chicago.

Opportunities in Broadcasting Careers. Ellis, Elmo. Illus. Edition: 2nd. Pub Date: 1992. 160 pp. Binding: Hardcover. Price: $13.95. ISBN: 0-8442-4003-6. Binding: Paper. Price: $10.95. ISBN: 0-8442-4004-4.
NTC Publishing Group, Lincolnwood, IL.

Opportunities in Cable Television Careers. Bone, Jan. Pub Date: 1992. Binding: Hardcover. Price: $13.95. ISBN: 0-8442-4026-5. Binding: Paper. Price: $10.95. ISBN: 0-8442-4027-3.
NTC Publishing Group, Lincolnwood, IL.

Orion Video & Television Blue Book, 1991. Pub Date: 1990. Binding: Hardcover. Price: $129.00. ISBN: 0-932089-47-X.
Orion Research, Scottsdale, AZ.

The Pay-Per-View Book: 1993 Edition. Warren Publishing Inc. Staff. Taliaferro, Michael, editor. Illus. Edition: rev. Pub Date: 1993. Binding: Hardcover. Price: $95.00 supplement. ISBN: 0-911486-73-9.
Warren Publishing Inc., Washington, DC.

The Perfect Machine: Television & the Bomb. Nelson, Joyce. Illus. Pub Date: 1991. 192 pp. Binding: Library binding—adult. Binding: Paper. Price: $39.95. Price: $12.95. ISBN: 0-86571-234-4. ISBN: 0-86571-235-2.
New Society Publishers, Philadelphia.

The Persian Gulf TV War. Kellner, Douglas. Pub Date: 1992. 460 pp. Binding: Hardcover text edition. Binding: Paperback text edition. Price: $60.50. Price: $19.95. ISBN: 0-8133-1614-6. ISBN: 0-8133-1615-4.
Westview Press, Boulder, CO.

Personal Contacts: TV Stations & Cable Systems, 1993. Warren Publishing Inc. Staff. Taliaferro, Michael, editor. Illus. Edition: rev. Pub Date: 1993. Binding: Hardcover. Price: $95.00 supplement. ISBN: 0-911486-69-0.
Warren Publishing Inc., Washington, DC.

Perspectives on Radio & TV: Telecommunications in the United States. Smith, F. Leslie. Edition: 3rd. Pub Date: 1990. 588 pp. Binding: Hardcover text edition. Price: $55.50. ISBN: 0-06-046301-5.
HarperCollins College, New York.

The Pied Pipers of Rock 'n' Roll. Smith, Wes. Illus. Pub Date: 1989. 304 pp. Binding: Hardcover. Price: $16.95. ISBN: 0-929264-69-X.
Longstreet Press Inc., Marietta, GA.

Pioneering Television. Takayanagi, K. Illus. Pub Date: 1993. Binding: Hardcover. Price: $18.75. ISBN: 0-911302-66-2.
San Francisco Press Inc., San Francisco.

Pluralism, Politics & the Marketplace: The Regulation of West German Broadcasting in the 1980s. Porter, Vincent and Hasselbach, Suzanne. Illus. Pub Date: 1991. 240 pp. Binding: Hardcover. Price: $74.50. ISBN: 0-415-05394-3.
Routledge, New York.

Popular Television in Britain: Essays in Cultural History. Corner, John, editor. Illus. Pub Date: 1990. 224 pp. Binding: Hardcover. Price: $49.95. ISBN: 0-85170-269-4. Binding: Paper. Price: $19.95. ISBN: 0-85170-270-8.
Indiana University Press, Bloomington, IN.

The Portable Radio in American Life. Schiffer, Michael B. Illus. Pub Date: 1991. 260 pp. Binding: Hardcover. Price: $45.00. ISBN: 0-8165-1259-0.
University of Arizona Press, Tucson, AZ.

The Portable Radio in American Life. Schiffer, Michael B. Illus. Pub Date: 1992. 259 pp. Binding: Paper. Price: $24.95. ISBN: 0-8165-1284-1.
University of Arizona Press, Tucson, AZ.

Power & Television in Latin America: The Dominican Case. Menendez, Antonio V. Pub Date: 1992. Binding: Hardcover. Price: $47.95. ISBN: 0-275-94275-9.
Greenwood Publishing Group Inc., Westport, CT.

Practical Application of SPC in the Wire & Cable Industry. Relyea, Douglas B. Illus. Pub Date: 1990. 176 pp. Binding: Paper. Price: $21.50. ISBN: 0-527-91643-9.
Quality Resources, White Plains, NY.

Prime-Time Families: Television Culture in Post-War America. Taylor, Ella. Illus. Pub Date: 1991. 208 pp. Binding: Paper. Price: $14.00. ISBN: 0-520-07418-1.
University of California Press, Berkeley, CA.

Prime Time & Misdemeanors: Investigating the 1950s TV Quiz Scandal—A D.A.'s Account. Stone, Joseph and Yohn, Tim. Illus. Pub Date: 1992. 370 pp. Binding: Hardcover. Price: $22.95. ISBN: 0-8135-1753-2.
Rutgers University Press, New Brunswick, NJ.

Prime Time, Our Time: America's Life & Times Through the Prism of Television. McCrohan, Donna. Pub Date: 1990. 384 pp. Binding: Hardcover. Price: $19.95. ISBN: 1-55958-005-4.
Prima Publishing, Roseville, CA.

Prime Time, Prime Movers: The Inside Story of the Inside People Who Made American Television. Marc, David and Thompson, Robert J. Illus. Pub Date: 1992. 304 pp. Binding: Hardcover. Price: $22.95. ISBN: 0-316-54589-9.
Little, Brown & Co., New York.

Prime-Time Society: An Anthropological Analysis of Television & Culture. Kottak, Conrad P. Pub Date: 1990. 247 pp. Binding: Paperback text edition. Price: write for info. ISBN: 0-534-12498-4.
Wadsworth Publishing Co., Belmont, CA.

Prime-Time Television: Content & Control. Cantor, Muriel B. and Cantor, Joel M. Edition: 2nd. Pub Date: 1991. 160 pp. Binding: Hardcover text edition. Paperback text edition. Price: $31.95. Price: $15.50. ISBN: 0-8039-3169-7. ISBN: 0-8039-3170-0.
Sage Publications Inc., Thousand Oaks, CA.

Prime Times, Bad Times: A Personal Drama of Network TV. Joyce, Ed. Pub Date: 1989. 560 pp. Binding: Paper. Price: $9.95. ISBN: 0-385-26102-0.
Doubleday & Co. Inc., New York.

Principles of Communications Satellites. Gordon, Gary D. and Morgan, Walter L. Pub Date: 1993. 544 pp. Binding: Hardcover. Price: $69.95. ISBN: 0-471-55796-X.
Wiley, John, & Sons Inc., New York.

Prior Consent to International Direct Satellite Broadcasting. Fisher, David I. Pub Date: 1990. Binding: Library binding—adult. Price: $90.00. ISBN: 0-7923-0692-9.
Kluwer Academic Publishers, Norwell, MA.

Private Network Business Satellite Systems Market (U.S.). Pub Date: 1990. 302 pp. Binding: Hardcover. Price: $4200.00. ISBN: 0-685-61722-X.
Frost & Sullivan Market Intelligence, Mountain View, CA.

Producer's Masterguide, 1993: The International Production Manual for Motion Picture, Broadcast TV, Commercials, Cable & Video Industries Throughout the U.S., Canada, UK, Caribbean, Israel, Europe, Australia, Japan, Philippines & Mexico. Bension, Shmuel. Edition: 13th. Pub Date: 1993. 400 pp. Binding: Paper. Price: $115.00. ISBN: 0-935744-12-6.
Producer's Masterguide, New York.

Questions of Broadcasting. Hood, Stuart and O'Leary, Garret. Pub Date: 1990. 237 pp. Binding: Hardcover. Price: $29.95. ISBN: 0-413-62220-7.
Heinemann, Portsmouth, NH.

Quiz Craze: America's Infatuation with the Radio & Television Game Shows. DeLong, Thomas A. Pub Date: 1991. 328 pp. Binding: Hardcover. Price: $22.95. ISBN: 0-275-94042-X.
Greenwood Publishing Group Inc., Westport, CT.

Radio Broadcast Technician. Rudman, Jack. Pub Date: 1991. Binding: Paper. Price: $20.00. ISBN: 0-8373-0682-5.
National Learning Corp., Syosset, NY.

Radio Broadcasting from 1930-1990: An Annotated Bibliography. Carothers, Diane F. Pub Date: 1991. 640 pp. Binding: Hardcover. Price: $60.00. ISBN: 0-8240-1209-7.
Garland Publishing Inc., New York.

Radio Financing: A Guide to Lenders & Investors. Martin, Robin B. and Krasnow, Erwin G. Pub Date: 1990. 51 pp. Binding: Paper. Price: $40.00. ISBN: 0-89324-090-7.
National Association of Broadcasters, Washington, DC.

Radio in Australia. Potts, John. Illus. Pub Date: 1989. 189 pp. Binding: Paper. Price: $19.95. ISBN: 0-86840-331-8.
International Specialized Book Services, Portland, OR.

Radio in Rural Guatemala: Three Case Studies. Lowrey, Wilson H. Pref. by Hester, Al. Illus. Pub Date: 1990. 150 pp. Binding: Paperback text edition. Price: $5.95. ISBN: 0-943089-01-8.
University of Georgia, Henry W. Grady School of Journalism & Mass Communication, Center for International Mass Communication Training & Research, Athens, GA.

Radio Music Directing. Halper, Donna L. Illus. Pub Date: 1991. 112 pp. Binding: Paper. Price: $14.95. ISBN: 0-240-80081-8.
Focal Press, Stoneham, MA.

Radio Mystery & Adventure & Its Appearances in Film, Television & Other Media. Harmon, Jim. Pub Date: 1992. 302 pp. Binding: Library binding—adult. Price: $45.00. ISBN: 0-89950-663-1.
McFarland & Co. Inc., Publishers, Jefferson, NC.

Radio Production: The Art & Science. Keith, Michael C. Pub Date: 1990. 272 pp. Binding: Paper. Price: $34.95. ISBN: 0-240-80017-6.
Focal Press, Stoneham, MA.

Radio Recombination Lines: Twenty Five Years of Investigation. Gordon, M. A. and Sorochenko, R. L., editors. Pub Date: 1990. Binding: Library binding—adult. Price: $107.00. ISBN: 0-7923-0804-2.
Kluwer Academic Publishers, Norwell, MA.

Radio: A Reference Guide. Greenfield, Thomas A. Pub Date: 1989. 185 pp. Binding: Hardcover. Price: $45.00. ISBN: 0-313-22276-2.
Greenwood Publishing Group Inc., Westport, CT.

Radio Research: An Annotated Bibliography 1975-1988. Langham, Josephine and Chrichley, Janine. Pub Date: 1990. 368 pp. Binding: Hardcover text edition. Price: $69.95. ISBN: 0-566-07130-4.
Ashgate Publishing Co., Brookfield, VT.

Books on Broadcasting and Cable

Radio Sound Effects: Who Did It & How, in the Era of Live Broadcasting. Mott, Robert L. Pub Date: 1992. 336 pp. Binding: Library binding—adult. Price: $39.95. ISBN: 0-89950-747-6.
McFarland & Co. Inc., Publishers, Jefferson, NC.

The Radio Station. Keith, Michael C. and Krause, Joseph M. Illus. Edition: 3rd. Pub Date: 1993. 315 pp. Binding: Paper. Price: $34.95. ISBN: 0-240-80159-8.
Focal Press, Stoneham, MA.

Radio Station Manager. Rudman, Jack. Pub Date: 1991. Binding: Paper. Price: $24.00. ISBN: 0-8373-2935-3.
National Learning Corp., Syosset, NY.

Radio Station Operations: Management & Employee Perspectives. O'Donnell, Lewis B., Hausman and Benoit. Pub Date: 1989. 409 pp. Binding: Paperback text edition. Price: write for info. ISBN: 0-534-09540-2.
Wadsworth Publishing Co., Belmont, CA.

Radio & TV Journalism. Shrivastava, K. M. Pub Date: 1990. 290 pp. Binding: Hardcover text edition. Price: $35.00. ISBN: 81-207-0439-8.
Apt Books Inc., New York.

Radio & Television Career Directory: A Practical One-Stop Guide to Getting a Job in Public Relations. Morgan, Bradley J., editor. Edition: 2nd. Pub Date: 1993. 300 pp. Binding: Hardcover. Price: $29.95. ISBN: 0-8103-5612-0.
Gale Research Inc., Detroit.

Radio & Television: A Selected, Annotated Bibliography; Supplement Two: 1982-1986. Pringle, Peter K. and Clinton, Helen E. Pub Date: 1989. 249 pp. Binding: Hardcover. Price: $27.50. ISBN: 0-8108-2158-3.
Scarecrow Press Inc., Metuchen, NJ.

Radio & Television Towers: Maintaining, Modifying & Leasing. Frock, Jane P. Edition: 2nd. Pub Date: 1990. 54 pp. Binding: Hardcover. Price: $30.00. ISBN: 0-89324-079-6.
National Association of Broadcasters, Washington, DC.

Radio on Wheels: Eastern Edition. Rocheleau, Paul. Pub Date: 1991. Binding: Paper. Price: $8.95. ISBN: 0-425-12860-1.
Berkley Publishing Group, New York.

Radio on Wheels: Western Edition. Rocheleau, Paul. Pub Date: 1991. Binding: Paper. Price: $8.95. ISBN: 0-425-12861-X.
Berkley Publishing Group, New York.

RadiOutlook II: New Forces Shaping the Industry. McLean, Austin, editor. Pub Date: 1991. 143 pp. Binding: Hardcover. Price: $40.00. ISBN: 0-89324-112-1.
National Association of Broadcasters, Washington, DC.

Raymond Williams on Television: The Culture of Television. Williams, Raymond. O'Connor, Alan, editor. Pub Date: 1989. 256 pp. Binding: Paper. Price: $14.95. ISBN: 0-415-02627-X.
Routledge, New York.

Redeeming Television: How TV Changes Christians—How Christians Can Change TV. Schultze, Quentin J. Pub Date: 1992. 204 pp. Binding: Paper. Price: $8.99. ISBN: 0-8308-1383-7.
InterVarsity Press, Downers Grove, IL.

Regulation of the Electronic Mass Media: Law & Policy for Radio, Television, Cable & the New Video Technologies. Ginsburg, Douglas H., Botein, Michael H. and Director, Mark D. Pub Date: 1991. 657 pp. Binding: Hardcover text edition. Price: $41.95. ISBN: 0-314-82946-6.
West Publishing Co., College & School Division, Saint Paul, MN.

The Remote Control in the New Age of Television. Walker, James R. and Bellamy, Robert V., editors. Pub Date: 1993. Binding: Hardcover. Price: $55.00. ISBN: 0-275-94396-8.
Greenwood Publishing Group Inc., Westport, CT.

Remote Control: Television Audiences & Cultural Power. Seiter, Ellen, Borchers, Hans, Kreutzner, Gabriele and Warth, Eva-Maria, editors. Pub Date: 1991. 272 pp. Binding: Paper. Price: $15.95. ISBN: 0-415-06505-4.
Routledge, New York.

Reporting on Risk: How the Mass Media Portray Accidents, Diseases, Disasters & Other Hazards. Singer, Eleanor and Endreny, Phyllis M. Pub Date: 1993. 288 pp. Binding: Hardcover. Price: $24.95. ISBN: 0-87154-801-1.
Russell Sage Foundation, New York.

Reruns on File: Using Broadcast Archives. Godfrey, Donald G. Pub Date: 1991. 322 pp. Binding: Hardcover text edition. Binding: Paperback text edition. Price: $59.95. Price: $29.95. ISBN: 0-8058-1146-X. ISBN: 0-8058-1147-8.
Erlbaum, Lawrence, Associates Inc., Hillsdale, NJ.

Rewriting Network News—Wordwatching Tips from 345 TV & Radio Scripts. Block, Mervin. Illus. Pub Date: 1990. 221 pp. Binding: Hardcover. Price: $24.95. ISBN: 0-929387-15-5.
Bonus Books Inc., Chicago.

Rex Reed's Guide to Movies on TV & Video. Reed, Rex. Pub Date: 1992. 640 pp. Binding: Paper. Price: $6.99. ISBN: 0-446-36206-9.
Warner Books Inc., New York.

Sally: Unconventional Success. Raphael, Sally Jesse and Proctor, Pam. Pub Date: 1990. Binding: Hardcover. Price: $17.95. ISBN: 0-688-06992-4.
Morrow, William, & Co. Inc., New York.

Satellite Communication System: Systems, Techniques & Technology. Maral, G. and Bousquet, M. David, S., translator. Edition: 2nd. Pub Date: 1993. 688 pp. Binding: Hardcover. Price: $79.95. ISBN: 0-471-93032-6.
Wiley, John, & Sons Inc., New York.

Satellite Communication Systems II. Pub Date: 1991. Binding: Hardcover text edition. Price: $99.00 casebound. ISBN: 0-86341-229-7.
Institution of Electrical Engineers, Piscataway, NJ.

Satellite Communication Systems Engineering. Pritchard, Wilbur L., Suyderhoud, Henri G. and Nelson, Robert A. Edition: 2nd. Pub Date: 1992. 544 pp. Binding: Hardcover. Price: $58.00 casebound. ISBN: 0-13-791468-7.
Prentice Hall General Reference & Travel, New York.

Satellite Communications. Roddy, Dennis. Pub Date: 1989. 352 pp. Binding: Hardcover text edition. Price: $50.00 casebound. ISBN: 0-13-791303-6.
Prentice Hall, Englewood Cliffs, NJ.

Satellite Communications. Gagliardi, Robert M. Edition: 2nd. Pub Date: 1990. Binding: Hardcover text edition. Price: $69.95. ISBN: 0-442-22745-0.
Van Nostrand Reinhold, New York.

Satellite Communications: the First Quarter Century of Service. Rees, David W. Pub Date: 1990. Binding: Hardcover text edition. Price: $54.95. ISBN: 0-471-62243-5.
Wiley, John, & Sons Inc., New York.

Satellite Communications in North America (U.S.): Commercial Systems. Pub Date: 1992. 200 pp. Binding: Hardcover. Price: $2900.00. ISBN: 0-685-61717-3.
Frost & Sullivan Market Intelligence, Mountain View, CA.

Satellite Communications: Mobile & Fixed Services. Miller, Michael J., Vucetic, Branka and Berry, Les, editors. Pub Date: 1993. 432 pp. Binding: Library binding—adult. Price: $97.50. ISBN: 0-7923-9333-3.
Kluwer Academic Publishers, Norwell, MA.

Satellite Communications: A Practical Guide. Dalgleish, D. I. and Johnson, E. C. Pub Date: 1989. Binding: Hardcover. Price: $86.00. ISBN: 0-86341-132-0.
Institution of Electrical Engineers, Piscataway, NJ.

Satellite Communications: Self Study Course Package. Pratt, Timothy. Illus. Pub Date: 1989. Binding: Hardcover. Price: $299.00 includes study guide, solutions manual, final exam and textbook. ISBN: 0-87942-459-1.
Institute of Electrical & Electronics Engineers Inc., Piscataway, NJ.

Satellite Experimenter's Handbook. Davidoff, Martin. Pub Date: 1990. Binding: Hardcover. Price: $20.00. ISBN: 0-87259-318-5.
American Radio Relay League Inc., Newington, CT.

Satellite Installation Handbook. Long, Mark and Keating, Jeffrey. Illus. Pub Date: 1993. 256 pp. Binding: Hardcover. Price: $29.95. ISBN: 0-929548-11-6.
MLE Inc., Fort Lauderdale, FL.

Satellite TV & DBS Systems. Wood, James. Illus. Pub Date: 1993. 288 pp. Binding: Hardcover. Price: $79.95. ISBN: 0-240-51338-X.
Focal Press, Stoneham, MA.

Satellite Technology: An Introduction. Inglis, Andrew F. Pub Date: 1991. Binding: Paper. Price: $14.95. ISBN: 0-240-80078-8.
Focal Press, Stoneham, MA.

Satellite Television Source Book. Reitz, Ken. Illus. Pub Date: 1991. 100 pp. Binding: Paper. Price: $20.00. ISBN: 0-9627654-0-6.
Xenolith Press, Louisa, VA.

Satellites & Radio Broadcasting: Historical Review & Market Developments. Pub Date: 1991. 65 pp. Binding: Hardcover. Price: $60.00. ISBN: 0-89324-118-0.
National Association of Broadcasters, Washington, DC.

Scaring Myself Again: Far-Flung Adventures of a TV Journalist. Abel, Allen. Pub Date: 1993. 249 pp. Binding: Paper. Price: $12.00. ISBN: 0-00-637908-7.
HarperCollins Publishers Inc., New York.

Science Fiction TV from Twilight Zone to Deep Space Nine. Van Hise, James. Pub Date: 1993. Binding: Paper. Price: $14.95. ISBN: 1-55698-362-X.
Movie Publisher Services Inc., Las Vegas.

Scott Guides Travelers National Radio Entertainment Guide, 1990. Scott, Jim and Murdock, Phelps D., Jr. Pub Date: 1989. 350 pp. Binding: Paper. Price: $6.95. ISBN: 0-317-94036-8.
Scott Guides Inc., Kansas City, MO.

Screen Gems: A History of Columbia Pictures Television from Cohn to Coke, 1948-1983. Perry, Jeb H. Pub Date: 1991. 385 pp. Binding: Hardcover. Price: $42.50. ISBN: 0-8108-2487-6.
Scarecrow Press Inc., Metuchen, NJ.

Secrets of Successful QSL'ing. Dexter, Gerry L. Edition: 2nd. Pub Date: 1992. 120 pp. Binding: Paper. Price: $12.95. ISBN: 0-936653-36-1.
Tiare Publications, Lake Geneva, WI.

Seeing & Believing: The Influence of Television. Philo, Greg. Pub Date: 1990. 240 pp. Binding: Hardcover. Price: $65.00. ISBN: 0-415-03620-8. Binding: Paper. Price: $17.95. ISBN: 0-415-03621-6.
Routledge, New York.

Selling the Sixties: The Pirates & Pop Music Radio. Chapman, Robert. Pub Date: 1992. 256 pp. Binding: Hardcover. Price: $39.95. ISBN: 0-04-445881-9.
Routledge, Chapman & Hall Inc., New York.

Seventy-Fifth Anniversary Book—From Spark to Space. Pub Date: 1989. Binding: Hardcover. Price: $10.00. ISBN: 0-87259-259-6.
American Radio Relay League Inc., Newington, CT.

Show Biz with an Attitude. Fleiss, Mike and Silver, Michael. Illus. Pub Date: 1993. 160 pp. Binding: Paper. Price: $7.95. ISBN: 0-8431-3574-3.
Price Stern Sloan Inc., Los Angeles.

Six O'Clock High: Making Television News. Lechter, Michael and Musberger, R., editors. Pub Date: 1993. Binding: Hardcover. Binding: Supplementary materials. Price: $40.00 (booklet includes video). Price: write for info-video. ISBN: 1-56321-106-8. ISBN: 1-56321-105-X.
Erlbaum, Lawrence, Associates Software & Alternate Media Inc., Hillsdale, NJ.

The Six O'Clock President: A Theory of Presidential Press Relations in the Age of Television. Smoller, Fredric T. Pub Date: 1990. 176 pp. Binding: Hardcover. Price: $42.95. ISBN: 0-275-93598-1.
Greenwood Publishing Group Inc., Westport, CT.

Sixty Minutes & the News: A Mythology for Middle America. Campbell, Richard. Foreword by Carey, James W. Illus. Pub Date: 1991. 304 pp. Binding: Hardcover. Price: $29.95. ISBN: 0-252-01777-3.
University of Illinois Press, Champaign, IL.

Smart-Daaf Boys: The Inventors of Radio & Television & Nathan B. Stubblefield, 4 Vols., Vol. 1. Stubblefield-Cory, Troy, Sova, Mark A. and Cory, Josie. Pub Date: 1993. Binding: Hardcover. Price: $80.00. ISBN: 1-883644-00-3 (set).
Television International Publishers, Universal City, CA.

A Social History of British Broadcasting, Vol. 1, 1922-1939: Serving the Nation. Scannell, Paddy and Cardiff, David. Pub Date: 1991. 400 pp. Binding: Hardcover text edition. Price: $69.95. ISBN: 0-631-17543-1.
Blackwell Publishers, Cambridge, MA.

Sound Effects: Radio, TV & Film. Mott, Robert L. Illus. Pub Date: 1990. 222 pp. Binding: Paper. Price: $34.95. ISBN: 0-240-80029-X.
Focal Press, Stoneham, MA.

The Sound Studio. Nisbett, Alec. Illus. Edition: 5th. Pub Date: 1993. 480 pp. Binding: Paper. Price: $39.95. ISBN: 0-240-51292-8.
Focal Press, Stoneham, MA.

Books on Broadcasting and Cable

Sounds in the Air: The Golden Age of Radio. Finkelstein, Norman H. Pub Date: 1993. 144 pp. Binding: Hardcover. Price: $14.95. ISBN: 0-684-19271-3.
Macmillan Children's Book Group, New York.

Spacebridges: Television & U.S.-Soviet Dialogue. Brainerd, Michael, editor. Pub Date: 1989. 120 pp. Binding: Library binding—adult. Binding: Paperback text edition. Price: $31.75. Price: $19.00. ISBN: 0-8191-7432-7. ISBN: 0-8191-7433-5.
University Press of America, Lanham, MD.

Sport & the Mass Media: National & European Identities. Blain, Neil, Boyle, Raymond and O'Donnell, Hugh. Pub Date: 1993. 256 pp. Binding: Paperback text edition. Price: write for info. ISBN: 0-7185-1451-3.
Saint Martin's Press Inc., New York.

Sports on Television: A New Ball Game for Broadcasters. Wyche, Mark C., Trautman, James M. and Bortz, Paul I. Pub Date: 1990. 99 pp. Binding: Paper. Price: $80.00. ISBN: 0-89324-089-3.
National Association of Broadcasters, Washington, DC.

Sportscasting. Hitchcock, John R. Pub Date: 1991. 116 pp. Binding: Paper. Price: $14.95. ISBN: 0-240-80062-1.
Focal Press, Stoneham, MA.

Stars of TV Shows. Robinson, Philip L. Pub Date: 1991. Binding: Hardcover. Price: $6.95. ISBN: 0-8059-3180-5.
Dorrance Publishing Co. Inc., Pittsburgh.

State Responsibility & the Direct Broadcast Satellite. Taishoff, Marika N. Pub Date: 1992. 220 pp. Binding: Hardcover. Price: $45.00. ISBN: 0-86187-700-4.
Saint Martin's Press Inc., New York.

Stay Tuned: A Concise History of American Broadcasting. Sterling, Christopher H. and Kittross, John M. Edition: 2nd. Pub Date: 1990. 705 pp. Binding: Hardcover text edition. Price: write for info. ISBN: 0-534-11905-0.
Wadsworth Publishing Co., Belmont, CA.

TV & Cable Sales Reps & Interconnects: 1993 Edition. Warren Publishing Inc. Staff. Taliaferro, Michael, editor. Illus. Edition: rev. Pub Date: 1993. Binding: Hardcover. Price: $95.00 supplement. ISBN: 0-911486-74-7.
Warren Publishing Inc., Washington, DC.

TV Dimensions. Illus. Pub Date: 1989. 300 pp. Binding: Hardcover. Price: $105.00. ISBN: 0-317-93251-9.
Media Dynamics, New York.

TV Dimensions '90. Pub Date: 1990. 371 pp. Binding: Hardcover. Price: $65.00. ISBN: 0-685-45454-1.
Media Dynamics, New York.

TV Dimensions '91. Papazian, Ed and Williams, Carol, editors. Pub Date: 1991. 360 pp. Binding: Paper. Price: $125.00. ISBN: 0-685-48874-8.
Media Dynamics, New York.

The TV Guide TV Book. TV Guide Editors. Weiner, Ed. Illus. Pub Date: 1992. 256 pp. Binding: Paper. Price: $9.95. ISBN: 0-06-096914-8.
HarperCollins Publishers Inc., New York.

The TV & Movie Business: An Encyclopedia of Careers, Technologies, & Practices. Rachlin, Harvey. Illus. Pub Date: 1991. 320 pp. Binding: Hardcover. Price: $21.00. ISBN: 0-517-57578-7.
Crown Publishing Group, New York.

TV News: Building a Career in Broadcast Journalism. White, Ray. Illus. Pub Date: 1989. 151 pp. Binding: Paper. Price: $19.95. ISBN: 0-240-80036-2.
Focal Press, Stoneham, MA.

TV News Ethics. Matelski, Marilyn. Illus. Pub Date: 1991. 96 pp. Binding: Paper. Price: $14.95. ISBN: 0-240-80089-3.
Focal Press, Stoneham, MA.

TV News, Urban Conflict & the Inner City. Cottle, Simon. Pub Date: 1993. 240 pp. Binding: Hardcover text edition. Price: write for info. ISBN: 0-7185-1447-5.
Saint Martin's Press Inc., New York.

TV Newscast Processes & Procedures. Schihl, Robert J. Pub Date: 1991. 176 pp. Binding: Paper. Price: $26.95. ISBN: 0-240-80094-X.
Focal Press, Stoneham, MA.

TV Station & Cable Ownership Directory: 1993 Edition. Warren Publishing Inc. Staff. Taliaferro, Michael, editor. Illus. Edition: rev. Pub Date: 1993. Binding: Hardcover. Price: $95.00 supplement. ISBN: 0-911486-70-4.
Warren Publishing Inc., Washington, DC.

TVRO Technology. Prentiss, Stanton R. Pub Date: 1989. 320 pp. Binding: Hardcover text edition. Price: $39.00 casebound. ISBN: 0-13-933326-6.
Prentice Hall, Englewood Cliffs, NJ.

Tales of Terror: Television News & the Construction of the Terrorist Threat. Dobkin, Bethami A. Pub Date: 1992. 144 pp. Binding: Hardcover. Price: $42.95. ISBN: 0-275-93981-2.
Greenwood Publishing Group Inc., Westport, CT.

Talk on Television: Audience Participation & Public Debate. Livingstone, Sonia and Lunt, Peter. Pub Date: 1993. Binding: Hardcover. Price: write for info. ISBN: 0-415-07737-0. Binding: Paper. Price: write for info. ISBN: 0-415-07738-9.
Routledge, New York.

Talk Show & Entertainment Program Processes & Procedures. Schihl, Robert. Pub Date: 1991. 112 pp. Binding: Paper. Price: $26.95. ISBN: 0-240-80092-3.
Focal Press, Stoneham, MA.

Talk Show "Selects": Top TV & Radio News—Talk Contacts. Davis, Mitchell P. and Pazienza, Marc, editors. Pub Date: 1990. 312 pp. Binding: Hardcover. Price: $185.00. ISBN: 0-934333-08-4.
Broadcast Interview Source, Washington, DC.

Talk Shows & Hosts on Radio: A Directory Including Show Titles & Formats, Brief Biographical Sketches of Hosts & Locators. Brewer, Annie M. and Brewer, Donald E., editors. Pub Date: 1992. Binding: Paper. Price: $24.95. ISBN: 0-9632341-0-2.
Whitefoord Press, Dearborn, MI.

Tele-Advising: Therapeutic Discourse in American Television. White, Mimi. Pub Date: 1992. 218 pp. Binding: Hardcover. Price: $29.95. ISBN: 0-8078-2055-5. Binding: Paper. Price: $10.95. ISBN: 0-8078-4390-3.
University of North Carolina Press, Chapel Hill, NC.

Telecommunications & Broadcasting: Convergence or Collision? Pub Date: 1992. 288 pp. Binding: Paper. Price: $60.00. ISBN: 92-64-13764-5.
Organization for Economic Cooperation & Development, Washington, DC.

Tele-ology: Studies in Television. Hartley, John. Pub Date: 1992. 240 pp. Binding: Hardcover. Price: $52.50. ISBN: 0-415-06817-7. Binding: Paper. Price: $15.95. ISBN: 0-415-06818-5.
Routledge, New York.

Telephone Co. & Cable Television Competition. Brotman, Stuart N. Illus. Pub Date: 1990. 532 pp. Binding: Paper. Price: $60.00. ISBN: 0-89006-461-X.
Artech House Inc., Norwood, MA.

Teletheory: Grammatology in the Age of Video. Luper, Gregory L. Pub Date: 1989. 256 pp. Binding: Hardcover. Price: $45.00. ISBN: 0-415-90120-0. Binding: Paper. Price: $14.95. ISBN: 0-415-90121-9.
Routledge, New York.

Televising Democracies. Franklin, Bob, editor. Pub Date: 1992. 288 pp. Binding: Hardcover. Price: $69.95. ISBN: 0-415-07021-X. Binding: Paper. Price: $22.00. ISBN: 0-415-07022-8.
Routledge, New York.

Television, Audiences, & Cultural Studies. Morley, David. Pub Date: 1993. 304 pp., hardcover; 272 pp., paper. Binding: Hardcover. Price: $69.95. ISBN: 0-415-05444-3. Binding: Paper. Price: $16.95. ISBN: 0-415-05445-1.
Routledge, New York.

Television & Cable Factbook, 1991, 2 Vols., No. 59. Warren Publishing Inc. Staff. Warren, Albert, editor. Illus. Pub Date: 1991. 4,600 pp. Binding: Paper. Price: write for info. ISBN: 0-911486-46-1 (set).
Warren Publishing Inc., Washington, DC.

Television & Cable Factbook, No. 60: Cable & Services, 1992. Warren Publishing Inc. Staff. Warren, Albert, editor. Illus. Edition: 60th, rev. Pub Date: 1992. 2,000 pp. Binding: Paper. Price: $375.00. ISBN: 0-911486-58-5.
Warren Publishing Inc., Washington, DC.

Television & Cable Factbook, Vol. One: Stations, 1992 Edition. Warren Publishing Inc. Staff. Warren, Albert, editor. Illus. Edition: 60th, rev. Pub Date: 1991. 1800 pp. Binding: Paper. Price: $375.00. ISBN: 0-911486-57-7.
Warren Publishing Inc., Washington, DC.

Television, Cable & Radio: A Communications Approach. Willis, Edgar E. and Aldridge, Henry B. Pub Date: 1991. 544 pp. Binding: Hardcover text edition. Price: write for info. ISBN: 0-13-898065-9.
Prentice Hall, Englewood Cliffs, NJ.

Television & the Crisis of Democracy. Kellner, Douglas. Pub Date: 1990. 287 pp. Binding: Hardcover text edition. Binding: Paperback text edition. Price: $58.50. Price: $18.95. ISBN: 0-8133-0548-9. ISBN: 0-8133-0549-7.
Westview Press, Boulder, CO.

Television & the Drama of Crime. Sparks, Richard. Pub Date: 1992. 192 pp. Binding: Hardcover. Price: $85.00. ISBN: 0-335-09328-0. Binding: Paper. Price: $32.00. ISBN: 0-335-09327-2.
Taylor & Francis Inc., Washington, DC.

Television Field Production & Reporting. Shook, Frederick. Pub Date: 1989. 416 pp. Binding: Hardcover text edition. Price: $40.95. ISBN: 0-582-28633-6.
Longman Publishing Group, White Plains, NY.

The Television Gray Market. Eisenson, Henry L. Illus. Pub Date: 1993. 160 pp. Binding: Paper. Price: $23.75. ISBN: 1-56866-037-5.
Index Publishing Group, San Diego.

Television: Identifying Propaganda Techniques. O'Sullivan, Carol. Illus. Pub Date: 1990. 32 pp. Binding: Publisher library binding. Price: $10.95. ISBN: 0-89908-606-3.
Greenhaven Press Inc., San Diego.

Television in America. Comstock, George. Edition: 2nd. Pub Date: 1991. 237 pp. Binding: Hardcover text edition. Binding: Paperback text edition. Price: $31.95. Price: $15.50. ISBN: 0-8039-3338-X. ISBN: 0-8039-3339-8.
Sage Publications Inc., Thousand Oaks, CA.

Television in Europe. Noam, Eli. Illus. Pub Date: 1992. 408 pp. Binding: Hardcover. Price: $45.00. ISBN: 0-19-506942-0.
Oxford University Press Inc., New York.

The Television Industry: A Historical Dictionary. Slide, Anthony. Pub Date: 1991. 392 pp. Binding: Hardcover. Price: $59.50. ISBN: 0-313-25634-9.
Greenwood Publishing Group Inc., Westport, CT.

Television & Its Audience. Barwise, Patrick and Ehrenberg, Andrew. Pub Date: 1989. 224 pp. Binding: Hardcover text edition. Binding: Paperback text edition. Price: $39.95. Price: $16.95. ISBN: 0-8039-8154-6. ISBN: 0-8039-8155-4.
Sage Publications Inc., Thousand Oaks, CA.

Television-Merging Multiple Technologies. King, Carol, editor. Foreword by Haney, Frank J. Pref. by Smith, Clyde D. Pub Date: 1990. 436 pp. Binding: Paper. Price: $35.00. ISBN: 0-940690-17-9.
Society of Motion Picture & Television Engineers, White Plains, NY.

Television News Anchors: An Anthology of Profiles of the Major Figures & Issues in United States Network Reporting. Fensch, Thomas, editor. Pub Date: 1993. 320 pp. Binding: Library binding—adult. Price: $35.00. ISBN: 0-89950-769-7.
McFarland & Co. Inc., Publishers, Jefferson, NC.

Television & Nuclear Power: Making the Public Mind. Wober, Mallory. Dervin, Brenda, editor. Pub Date: 1992. 320 pp. Binding: Hardcover text edition. Binding: Paperback text edition. Price: $59.50. Price: $29.50. ISBN: 0-89391-676-5. ISBN: 0-89391-836-9.
Ablex Publishing Corp., Norwood, NJ.

The Television PA's Handbook. Rowlands, Avril. Edition: 2nd. Pub Date: 1993. Binding: Hardcover. Price: $14.95. ISBN: 0-240-51353-3.
Focal Press, Stoneham, MA.

Television Performance. Hawes, William. Pub Date: 1991. 104 pp. Binding: Paperback text edition. Price: $14.95. ISBN: 0-240-80056-7.
Focal Press, Stoneham, MA.

Television & the Public Interest: Vulnerable Values in West European Broadcasting. Blumler, Jay G., editor. Pub Date: 1992. 240 pp. Binding: Hardcover. Price: $55.00. ISBN: 0-8039-8649-1. Binding: Paper. Price: $22.50. ISBN: 0-8039-8650-5.
Sage Publications Inc., Thousand Oaks, CA.

Television Studies: Textual Analysis. Burns, Gary and Thompson, Robert J., editors. Pub Date: 1989. 268 pp. Binding: Hardcover. Price: $49.95. ISBN: 0-275-92745-8.
Greenwood Publishing Group Inc., Westport, CT.

Television Weathercasting: A History. Henson, Robert. Illus. Pub Date: 1990. 205 pp. Binding: Library binding—adult. Price: $35.00. ISBN: 0-89950-492-2.
McFarland & Co. Inc., Publishers, Jefferson, NC.

The Television Yearbook. Lovece, Frank. Pub Date: 1992. 272 pp. Binding: Paper. Price: $12.95. ISBN: 0-399-51702-2.
Putnam Publishing Group, The, New York.

Books on Broadcasting and Cable

TeleVisionaries: In Their Own Words, Public Television's Founders Tell How It All Began. Robertson, Jim. Illus. Pub Date: 1992. 288 pp. Binding: Hardcover. Price: $29.95. ISBN: 0-9627974-8-0.
Tabby House Books, Charlotte Harbor, FL.

The Third Programme: A Literary History. Whitehead, Kate. Illus. Pub Date: 1989. 272 pp. Binding: Hardcover. Price: $55.00. ISBN: 0-19-812893-2.
Oxford University Press Inc., New York.

Three Blind Mice: How the TV Networks Lost Their Way. Auletta, Ken. Pub Date: 1991. Binding: Hardcover. Price: $24.50. ISBN: 0-394-56358-1.
Random House Inc., New York.

Three Decades of Television: A Catalog of Television Programs Acquired by the Library of Congress, 1949-1979. Rouse, Sarah and Loughney, Katharine, editors. Illus. Pub Date: 1989. 716 pp. Binding: Hardcover text edition. Price: $51.00. ISBN: 0-16-003989-4.
United States Government Printing Office, Washington, DC.

To Pay or Not to Pay: New Broadcasting-Related Services. Pub Date: 1990. 160 pp. Binding: Paperback text edition. Price: $14.95. ISBN: 0-644-10917-3.
Australian Government Publishing Service, New York.

Total Television: A Comprehensive Guide to Programming from 1948 to the Present. McNeil, Alex. Illus. Edition: 3rd. Pub Date: 1991. Binding: Paper. Price: $19.00. ISBN: 0-14-015736-0.
Viking Penguin, New York.

The Trouble Is Not In Your Set: A History of Television in the World—& in Cincinnati—with a World of Characters. Kelly, Mary A. Illus. Pub Date: 1990. 350 pp. Binding: Hardcover. Price: write for info. ISBN: 0-9627159-0-5.
Kelly, Mary Ann, Covington, KY.

Tube of Plenty: The Evolution of American Television. Barnouw, Erik. Illus. Edition: 2nd, rev. Pub Date: 1990. 624 pp. Binding: Paper. Price: $14.95. ISBN: 0-19-506484-4.
Oxford University Press Inc., New York.

Tuned In: Television in American Life. DeGrane, Lloyd, photographer. Introduction by Brashler, William. Foreword by Viskochil, Larry A. Illus. Pub Date: 1991. 96 pp. Binding: Hardcover. Price: $24.95. ISBN: 0-252-01809-5. Binding: Paper. Price: $11.95. ISBN: 0-252-06222-1.
University of Illinois Press, Champaign, IL.

Turning Up the Volume on International Radio. Garcia, Michael O., editor. Pub Date: 1991. 261 pp. Binding: Paperback text edition. Price: $35.00. ISBN: 0-89206-197-9.
Center for Strategic & International Studies, Washington, DC.

Two Way Radio & Broadcast Equipment: Troubleshooting & Repair. Carr, Joseph J. Pub Date: 1989. 320 pp. Binding: Hardcover text edition. Price: $44.00 casebound. ISBN: 0-13-935348-8.
Prentice Hall, Englewood Cliffs, NJ.

Understanding Mobility: Guide to Wireless & Personal Communications. Ajayi, A'isha M. Pub Date: 08/1994. Binding: Hardcover. Price: write for info. ISBN: 0-471-54926-6.
Wiley, John, & Sons Inc., New York.

Understanding Television. Goodwin, Andrew and Whannel, Garry, editors. Illus. Pub Date: 1990. 208 pp. Binding: Hardcover. Price: $59.95. ISBN: 0-415-01671-1. Binding: Paper. Price: $16.95. ISBN: 0-415-01672-X.
Routledge, New York.

Unholy Alliances: Working the Tawana Brawley Story. Taibbi, Mike and Sims-Phillips, Anna. Pub Date: 1989. 375 pp. Binding: Hardcover. Price: $18.95. ISBN: 0-15-188050-6.
Harcourt Brace & Co., San Diego.

U.S. & Canadian Electronic Wire & Cable Manufacturers: 1990 Competitive Analysis. Bender, Amadee. Illus. Pub Date: 1990. 200 pp. Binding: Paper. Price: $1800.00. ISBN: 1-878218-11-5.
World Information Technologies Inc., Northport, NY.

Unsilent Revolution: Television News & American Public Life, 1948-1991. Donovan, Robert and Scherer, Ray. Pub Date: 1992. 500 pp. Binding: Hardcover. Price: $54.95. ISBN: 0-521-41829-1. Binding: Paper. Price: $17.95. ISBN: 0-521-42862-9.
Cambridge University Press, New York.

Variety Source, Book I: Broadcast-Video. Matelski, Marily J. and Thomas, David O. Pub Date: 1990. 136 pp. Binding: Paper. Price: $19.95. ISBN: 0-240-80067-2.
Focal Press, Stoneham, MA.

Video Economics. Owen, Bruce M. and Wildman, Steven S. Illus. Pub Date: 1992. 384 pp. Binding: Hardcover. Price: $35.00. ISBN: 0-674-93716-3.
Harvard University Press, Cambridge, MA.

View at Your Own Risk. Wheeler, Joe L. Pub Date: 1993. Binding: Hardcover. Price: write for info. ISBN: 0-8280-0725-X.
Review & Herald Publishing Association, Hagerstown, MD.

Waiting for the Banana Peel: We Did It Live, the Early TV Shows of Dick Van Dyke & Fran Adams. Kearton, Fran. Parker, Diane, editor. Pub Date: 1993. 250 pp. Binding: Hardcover. Price: $22.95. ISBN: 0-88247-977-6.
R & E Publishers Inc., Saratoga, CA.

Wales in Vision: The People & Politics of Television. Hannan, Patrick. Pub Date: 1990. 164 pp. Binding: Hardcover. Price: $45.00. ISBN: 0-86383-549-X.
State Mutual Book & Periodical Service, Limited, New York.

War & Television. Cumings, Bruce. Pub Date: 1992. Binding: Hardcover. Price: $29.95. ISBN: 0-86091-374-0.
Routledge, Chapman & Hall Inc., New York.

The Washington Radio Guide. Baker, Steven H. Baker, Mary A., editor. Pub Date: 1989. 28 pp. Binding: Paper. Price: $6.98. ISBN: 0-9625176-0-7.
Pocket Guides Inc., Charlottesville, VA.

We Keep America on Top of the World: Television Journalism & the Public Sphere. Hallin, Daniel C. Pub Date: 1993. 208 pp. Binding: Hardcover. Binding: Hardcover. Price: write for info. ISBN: 0-415-09142-X. ISBN: 0-415-09143-8.
Routledge, New York.

Weather Radio: A Complete Guide to Receiving NOPP, Volmet, Weather Fax, Weather Satellites & Other Weather Information Sources. Curtis, Anthony R. Pub Date: 1992. 126 pp. Binding: Hardcover. Price: $14.95. ISBN: 0-936653-32-9.
Tiare Publications, Lake Geneva, WI.

Wheelin' on Beale: The Story of the Nation's First All-Black Radio Station. Cantor, Louis. Illus. Pub Date: 1992. 272 pp. Binding: Hardcover. Price: $19.95. ISBN: 0-88687-633-8.
F&W Inc., NJ.

When Television Was Young: Primetime Canada 1952-1967. Rutherford, Paul. Pub Date: 1990. 638 pp. Binding: Hardcover. Price: $65.00. ISBN: 0-8020-5830-2. Binding: Paper. Price: $29.95. ISBN: 0-8020-6647-X.
University of Toronto Press, Cheektowaga, NY.

Who's Who—Qui Est Qui, 1991–92: In Canadian Film & Television—Au Cinema et a la Television au Canada. Academy of Canadian Cinema and Television Staff. Pub Date: 1991. 640 pp. Binding: Paper. Price: $49.95. ISBN: 0-88920-210-9.
Humanities Press International Inc., Atlantic Highlands, NJ.

Who's Who in Television—1991–92: Writers, Directors, Producers & the Networks. Gregg, Rodman W., editor. Edition: rev. Pub Date: 1991. 210 pp. Binding: Paper. Price: $16.95. ISBN: 0-941710-12-2.
Packard Publishing, Beverly Hills, CA.

Why Viewers Watch: A Reappraisal of Television's Effects. Fowles, Jib. Pub Date: 1992. 253 pp. Binding: Hardcover. Price: $46.00. ISBN: 0-8039-4076-9. Binding: Paper. Price: $19.95. ISBN: 0-8039-4077-7.
Sage Publications Inc., Thousand Oaks, CA.

Wireless Communication in the United States: The Early Development of American Radio Operating Companies. Mayes, Thom L. Goodnow, Arthur C., editor. Merriam, Nancy A., editor. Merriam, Robert W., editor. Illus. Pub Date: 1989. 248 pp. Binding: Paperback text edition. Price: $29.95. ISBN: 0-9625170-0-3.
New England Wireless & Steam Museum Inc., East Greenwich, RI.

Women Dimension on Television: Policy, Personnel & Programme. Joshi, Ila. Pub Date: 1991. Binding: Hardcover. Price: $17.50. ISBN: 81-7022-360-1.
South Asia Books, Columbia, MO.

Working in TV News: The Insider's Guide. Filoreto, Carl and Setzer, Lynn. Pub Date: 1993. 192 pp. Binding: Paper. Price: $12.95. ISBN: 0-914457-50-0.
Mustang Publishing, Memphis, TN.

World Satellite Almanac, 1992. Edition: 3rd. Pub Date: 1991. 1,072 pp. Binding: Hardcover. Price: $149.95 leatherbound. ISBN: 0-929548-06-X.
MLE Inc., Fort Lauderdale, FL.

The World Satellite Almanac: The Complete Guide to Satellite Transmission & Technology. Long, Mark. Birkill, Stephen J., editor. Pref. by Clarke, Arthur C. Illus. Edition: 3rd. Pub Date: 1992. 1,072 pp. Binding: Paper. Price: $99.95. ISBN: 0-929548-04-3.
MLE Inc., Fort Lauderdale, FL.

World Satellite Annual, 1990. Long, Mark, illustrator. Pub Date: 1989. 432 pp. Binding: Paper. Price: $39.95. ISBN: 0-685-21883-X.
MLE Inc., Fort Lauderdale, FL.

World Satellite Annual, 1991. Pub Date: 1990. 608 pp. Binding: Paper. Price: $49.95. ISBN: 0-929548-03-5.
MLE Inc., Fort Lauderdale, FL.

World Satellite Communications in Developing Countries (Worldwide). Pub Date: 1992. Binding: Hardcover. Price: $3700.00. ISBN: 0-685-61727-0.
Frost & Sullivan Market Intelligence, Mountain View, CA.

World Satellite Directory, 1989. Payne, Silvano, editor. Illus. Edition: 2nd. Pub Date: 1989. 225 pp. Binding: Hardcover. Price: $175.00. ISBN: 0-936361-10-7.
Design Publishers, Sonoma, CA.

World Satellite Directory, 1990. Payne, Silvano, editor. Illus. Edition: 3rd. Pub Date: 1990. Binding: Hardcover. Price: $125.00. ISBN: 0-936361-11-5.
Design Publishers, Sonoma, CA.

The World of Satellite TV: International Edition for Asia, the Middle East, & the Pacific Rim. Long, Mark and Keating, Jeffrey. Introduction by Howard, H. Taylor. Illus. Pub Date: 1992. 220 pp. Binding: Paper. Price: $19.95. ISBN: 0-929548-08-6.
MLE Inc., Fort Lauderdale, FL.

World of Satellite TV: International Edition for Europe & Africa. Long, Mark and Keating, Jeffrey. Illus. Pub Date: 1993. Binding: Paper. Price: $24.95. ISBN: 0-929548-10-8.
MLE Inc., Fort Lauderdale, FL.

World of Satellite TV: North & South America. Long, Mark and Keating, Jeffrey. Illus. Edition: 6th. Pub Date: 1992. 308 pp. Binding: Paperback text edition. Price: $24.95. ISBN: 0-929548-07-8.
MLE Inc., Fort Lauderdale, FL.

World Satellite TV & Scrambling Methods: The Technicians' Handbook. Baylin, Frank, Maddox, Richard and McCormac, John. Illus. Pub Date: 1990. 356 pp. Binding: Paper. Price: $39.95. ISBN: 0-917893-11-5.
Baylin Publications, Boulder, CO.

The World Television Industry: An Economic Analysis. Dunnett, Peter J. S. Pub Date: 1990. 240 pp. Binding: Hardcover. Price: $55.00. ISBN: 0-415-00162-5.
Routledge, New York.

Writing Broadcast News: Shorter, Sharper, Stronger. Block, Mervin. Pub Date: 1989. 231 pp. Binding: Hardcover. Price: $24.95. ISBN: 0-933893-20-5.
Bonus Books Inc., Chicago.

Writing for Television & Radio. Hilliard, Robert L. Edition: 5th. Pub Date: 1991. 485 pp. Binding: Paperback text edition. Price: write for info. ISBN: 0-534-14262-1.
Wadsworth Publishing Co., Belmont, CA.

Writing Style Differences in Newspaper, Radio, & Television News. Fang, Irving. Bridwell-Bowles, Lillian, editor. Prior, Paul, editor. Pub Date: 1991. 40 pp. Binding: Paper. Price: $4.50. ISBN: 1-881221-00-8.
University of Minnesota, Center for Interdisciplinary Studies of Writing, Minneapolis.

Yearbook of Experts, Authorities & Spokespersons: Encyclopedia of Sources. Davis, Mitchell P. Illus. Edition: 11th. Pub Date: 1993. Binding: Paper. Price: $47.50. ISBN: 0-934333-18-1.
Broadcast Interview Source, Washington, DC.

Periodicals on Broadcasting, Cable and Mass Media
An Annotated Bibliography

Compiled by Christopher H. Sterling, Professor and Director, National Center for Communication Studies, George Washington University.

This bibliography details a selection of important English-language periodicals presently published here and abroad. They appear in sections on American and Foreign/International publications—each further divided between trade and academic/commentary/law titles. Where possible, year of inception and publisher addresses are provided. For yearbooks and other annuals, see the earlier annotated bibliography of books.

Useful Guides to Periodicals

Communication Abstracts. (1978) Quarterly. (Sage Publications, 2455 Teller Rd., Newbury Park, CA 91320). Abstracts articles from some 250 journals (plus some books), most of them scholarly.

Index to Journals in Mass Communication. (1988) Annual. (Carpelan Publishing, Box 2726, Riverside, CA 92516). Provides an author and subject index to the 20 most important scholarly journals.

Topicator. (1965) Monthly with annual index (Topicator, Clackamas, OR). Subtitled "Classified Article Guide to the Advertising/Communications/Marketing Periodical Press," this offers selective indexing of nearly 20 business and scholarly journals.

International Telecommunication Union. **List of Periodicals** and **List of Annuals.** Geneva: International Telecommunication Union, annual. Issued by the ITU's Central Library, these are computer-printed non-annotated listings by title with geographical indexes.

Slide, Anthony. **International Film, Radio, and Television Journals.** Westport, CT: Greenwood, 1985. 429 pp. More than 150 titles past and present are profiled in detail.

Sova, Harry, and Patricia Sova. **Communication Serials 1992-93.** (Sovacomm Inc., Box 64697, Virginia Beach, VA 23464-0697). $129. A huge book detailing some 3,000 titles (primarily American) in 38 subject categories with multiple indexes. The best single source of information.

American—Trade

Advertising Age. (1929) Weekly. (Crain Communications Inc., 740 Rush St., Chicago 60611). The standard trade paper for advertising in all its forms.

BM/E's Television Engineering. (1965, title has varied) Monthly. (Broadband Publications, 375 Park Ave., New York 10016). Technical and management-oriented articles on broadcasting and cable.

Billboard. (1894) Weekly. (Billboard Publications, One Astor Plaza, 1515 Broadway, New York 10036). News of the music and recording industries, including radio.

Broadcast Engineering: Journal of Broadcast Technology. (1959) Monthly. (Intertec Publishing, 9800 Metcalf, Overland Park, KS 66212). Technical news and features on broadcasting and cable equipment, systems and technologies.

Broadcasting & Cable. (1931, title has varied) Weekly. (Broadcasting, 1705 DeSales St. N.W., Washington, DC 20036). Standard news magazine of broadcasting, cable and related electronic media.

Broadcasting and the Law. (1971) Bimonthly. (Broadcasting and the Law Inc., One S.E. 3rd Ave, Suite 1450, Miami, FL 33131). Current information about changing rules and regulations of day-to-day concern to broadcasters.

Cablevision. (1975) Biweekly. (Capital Cities/ABC Diversified Publishing Group, 825 7th Ave., New York 10019). News magazine for cable industry with departments and feature articles.

Cash Box. (1941) Weekly. (Cash Box, 330 W. 58th St., New York 10019). Trade paper for popular music business.

Communications Daily. (1981) Daily. (Warren Publishing, 2115 Ward Ct. N.W., Washington, DC 20037). Newsletter covering all electronic media and telecommunications, stressing policy developments in Washington, DC.

Current. (1982) Biweekly. (Current Publishing, 2311 18th St. N.W., Washington, DC 20009). Newspaper of public radio and television, dealing with national and local levels.

Electronic Media. (1982) Weekly. (Crain Communications, 740 Rush St., Chicago 60611). News and features on radio, television and cable, especially programming.

Multichannel News. (1980) Weekly. (Diversified Publishing Group, 825 7th Ave., New York 10019). Newspaper on MMDS and related broadband services.

Pay TV Newsletter. Biweekly. (Paul Kagan Associates, 126 Clock Tower Place, Carmel, CA 93923). Covers all developments in pay cable and pay-per-view and related services.

Public Broadcasting Report. Biweekly. (Warren Publishing, 2115 Ward Ct. N.W., Washington, DC 20037). Developments at CPB, NPR, PBS, funding, programming, and stations.

R&R: Radio and Records. (1971) Weekly. (Radio & Records, 1930 Century Park W., Los Angeles 90067). Tabloid trade paper on radio industry focusing on music trends, stressing record news and listings.

RTNDA Communicator. (1971) Monthly. (Radio-Television News Directors Association, 1717 K St. N.W., Suite 615, Washington, DC 20006). News about news broadcasting, broadcast and cable journalists, and freedom of expression.

Radio Only. Monthly. (Inside Radio Inc. 1930 E. Marlton Pike, Suite S-93, Cherry Hill, NJ 08003). Radio management, sales and programming.

Satellite Week. Weekly. (Warren Publishing, 2115 Ward Ct. N.W., Washington, DC 20037). All aspects of domestic and international satellite developments.

Television Digest. (1945) Weekly. (Warren Publishing, 2115 Ward Ct. N.W., Washington, DC 20037). Standard trade periodical stressing regulation and industry developments, and consumer electronics.

TV Guide. (1953) Weekly. (Murdoch Magazines, 4 Radnor Corporate Ctr., Matsanford Rd., Box 500, Radnor, PA 19088). Viewer guide to broadcast and cable service programs with about 100 regional editions.

Variety. (1905) Weekly. (Variety Inc. 475 Park Ave. S., New York 10016). Standard show business trade paper.

Via Satellite. (1986) Monthly. (Phillips Publishing, 7811 Montrose Rd., Potomac, MD 20854). News and features on satellite organizations, technologies and policy.

Video Week. Weekly. (Warren Publishing, 2115 Ward Ct. N.W., Washington, DC 20037). Company and sales information on consumer videocassette market.

American—Academic/Commentary/Law

Columbia Journalism Review. (1962) Bimonthly. (Graduate School of Journalism, Columbia University, New York 10027). Premier journal of critical analysis of all American news media.

Comm/Ent: A Journal of Communications and Entertainment Law. (1977) Quarterly. (Hastings College of Law, University of California, 200 McAllister St., San Francisco 94102). Specialized legal journal on all aspects of communications/entertainment law and policy.

Communication Booknotes. (1969, title has varied) Bimonthly. (Ctr. for Advanced Study in Telecommunications, Ohio State University, 210E Baker Systems, Columbus, OH 43210). Annotated bibliography of new books and periodicals in electronic media, information and telecommunications.

Communications and the Law. (1979) Bimonthly. (Meckler Publishing, 520 Riverside Ave., Westport CT 06880). Articles on government policy and regulation of communication.

Critical Studies in Mass Communication. (1984) Quarterly. (Speech Communication Association, 5105 Backlick Rd., Suite E, Annandale, VA 22003). Scholarly journal covering all media and stressing "critical" methodology.

Entertainment Law Reporter. Monthly. (Entertainment Law Reporter Publishing, 2210 Wilshire Blvd., No. 311, Santa Monica 90403). News of legal developments in electronic media and entertainment.

Federal Communications Law Journal (1937, title has varied). Three times a year. (UCLA School of Law, 405 Hilgard Ave., Los Angeles 90024). Scholarly legal articles on communications policy concerns.

Journal of Broadcasting and Electronic Media. (1956) Quarterly. (Broadcast Education Association, 1771 N St. N.W., Washington, DC 20036). Scholarly articles on history, process and effects, policy, and economics of broadcasting and cable.

Journal of Communication. (1951) Quarterly. (School of Journalism, University of Maryland, College Park, MD). Research studies, commentary, reviews and analysis on all aspects of mass communication and telecommunication.

Journal of Radio Studies. (1992) Annual. (Martin Lo-Monaco, Communications, Nassau Community College, Garden City, NY 11530-6793). A new journal which will work toward twice-a-year or quarterly publication. The first (1992) volume includes six papers on contemporary research and the future of radio, three on radio history, a three-part symposium on country music radio, and more. The second issue (1993) is devoted to a symposium on the state of AM radio.

Journalism Quarterly. (1924) Quarterly. (Association for Education in Journalism and Mass Communication, School of Journalism, University of South Carolina, Columbia, SC). Oldest American scholarly journal which now devotes considerable space to electronic media issues. Useful book review section.

Media Law Reporter. (1977) Weekly. (Bureau of National Affairs Inc., 1231 25th St. N.W., Washington, DC 20037). Reference service with full texts of federal and state court decisions and selected FCC and related rulings.

Media Studies Journal. (1987, title has varied) Quarterly. (Freedom Forum Media Studies Ctr., 2950 Broadway, Columbia University, New York 10027). Excellent journal combining research and serious comment, usually focused on a specific topic each issue.

SMPTE Journal. (1930) Monthly. (Society of Motion Picture and Television Engineers, 595 W. Hartsdale Ave., White Plains, NY 10607). Technical articles, sometimes including historical material.

Television News Index and Abstracts. (1972) Monthly. (Vanderbilt Television News Archive, Vanderbilt University, 110 21st Ave. S., Suite 704, Nashville, TN 37240). Detailed content listing of network evening news and related programs with subject, person and place indexing.

Television Quarterly. (1962) Quarterly. (National Academy of Television Arts and Sciences, 110 W. 57th St., New York 10019). Commentary, opinions, and historical articles.

Foreign/International—Trade

BRITAIN AND EUROPE

Broadcast. (1973) Weekly. (International Thomson Business Publications, 7 Swallow Pike, London W1 7AA) Begun in 1959 as *Television Mail,* this is the key trade periodical for British broadcasting covering all aspects of radio and television, BBC and commercial services.

Cable and Satellite Europe. (1984) Monthly. (Cable & Satellite Magazine Ltd., London). Detailed news reports on these services in Britain and Europe.

Combroad. (1966) Quarterly. (Commonwealth Broadcasting Association, Broadcasting House, London W1A 1AA). Technical, policy, and program developments in member countries of the British Commonwealth, especially in Africa.

Eastern European & Soviet Telecom Report. (1990) Monthly. (EESTR, 2940 28th St. N.W., Washington, DC

20008). Newsletter covering the rapid and dramatic changes including privatizing of electronic media.

London Calling. (1939) Monthly. (BBC, Box 76, Bush House, London WC2B 4PH.) Magazine of BBC World Service with articles and detailed wavelength charts and program listings.

Music and Media. Weekly. (Music & Media, Box 50558, 1007 DB Amsterdam, Netherlands). Covers music news and rankings from 18 European markets.

Radio Times. (1923) Weekly. (BBC, 35 Marylebone High St. London W1M 4AA). BBC listener guide with detailed program listings and articles.

TV World. (1977) Monthly. (International Thomson Business Publishing, London). Focuses on television program production, sales and distribution.

World Broadcasting Information (title has varied). Daily. (News and Publications, BBC Monitoring Service, Caversham Park, Reading, England RG4 8TZ). This is a daily subscription service divided into four parts (you can get one or all): USSR, Eastern Europe, India and Far East, and Middle East/Africa/Latin America. For each, the BBC issues a daily summary and a weekly economic report. The material is based on BBC monitoring and reproduces complete texts of important material.

AUSTRALIA AND CANADA

B&T Advertising, Marketing and Media Weekly. Weekly. (Greater Publications, Sydney, Australia). All aspects of Australian print and electronic media news.

Broadcaster. (1942) Monthly. (Northern Miner Press, 7 Labatt Ave., Toronto, Ont. M5A 3P2). All aspects of Canadian radio and television broadcasting. Directory issues listing stations and systems, plus related firms and associations are issued in the spring and fall.

Cable Communications Magazine. Monthly. (Ter-Sat Media Publications, 4 Smetana Dr. Kitchner, Ont. N2B 3B8). All aspects of Canadian cable television in Canada and elsewhere.

OTHER COUNTRIES

Arab States Broadcasting Union Review. Quarterly. (Asian Broadcasting Union, Cairo, Egypt). Covers all aspects of radio and television, and sometimes other media (satellite uses especially), of Arab nations.

Asian Broadcasting. Bimonthly. (Syme Media Enterprises Ltd., Hong Kong). Programming and business aspects of radio and television, plus technical overview covering the region from Egypt to Japan.

Broadcasting Abroad. (1989) Monthly. (Cahners Publishing Company, a Div. of Reed Reference Publishing, 1705 DeSales St. N.W., Washington DC 20036). News articles on broadcasting outside of the U.S.

Foreign/International—Academic/Commentary/Law

The Asian Broadcasting Technical Review. Bimonthly. (Asia-Pacific Broadcasting Union, Box 1164, Pantai, Kuala Lumpur 22-07, Malaysia). Technical developments and equipment trends among Asian member nations.

Development Communication Report. (1976) Quarterly. (Clearinghouse on Development Communication, 1815 N. Fort Myer Dr., Suite 600, Arlington, VA 22209). Descriptions of research projects and practical applications of media in Third World countries.

EBU Review. (1951) Monthly. There are two of these, each published bimonthly in English and French editions. One edition focuses on production, programming, administration and law (Ancienne Route 17A, Case Postale 67, CH-1218 Grand-Saconnex, Geneva, Switzerland). The other edition deals with technical developments in audio and video (EBU Technical Centre, Ave. Albert Lancaster 32, B-1180 Brussels, Belgium). A combined subscription to what is, in effect, a monthly from two locations, can be ordered from the Geneva office.

European Journal of Communication. (1986) Quarterly (Sage Publications, 6 Bonhill St., London EC2A 4PU). Scholarly journal covering all media.

Gazette. (1955) Three times a year. (Kluwer Academic Publishers, Dordrecht, The Netherlands). Reliable scholarly journal on all aspects of the world press, especially studies of content trends and developing nations' use of media. Useful for bibliographies and articles on trends in developing areas.

InterMedia. (1973) Bimonthly. (International Institute of Communications, Tavistock House South, Tavistock Square, London WC1H 9LF). News and features on European and international developments, usually a section of related articles. Good book review section.

Media Asia. (1974) Quarterly. (Asian Mass Communication Research & Information Centre, 39 Newton Rd., Singapore 1130). Articles on media trends and policies in the Far East.

Media Bulletin. (1984) Quarterly. (European Institute for the Media, University of Manchester, Manchester, England M13 9PL). Detailed news and related book reviews on radio, television, and newer services from all of Europe.

Media, Culture and Society. (1979) Quarterly. (Sage Publications, 6 Bonhill St., London EC2A 4PU). Scholarly forum for research on all aspects of media; issues often focus on specific topic.

Media Information Australia. Quarterly. (Australian Film, Television, and Radio School, Box 126, North Ryde, N.S.W. 2113). Articles, essays, book and periodical reviews, and material on regulation of Australian (and other) media.

Nordicom Review of Nordic Mass Communication Research. (Nordic Documentation Ctr. for Mass Communication Research, Department of Political Science, University of Goteborg, Box 5048, S-402, 21 Goteborg, Sweden). Major Scandinavian research journal; reviews of research projects; literature.

Satellite Communication: An International Journal. Quarterly. (Elsevier Sciences Publishing, Box 211, 1000 AE Amsterdam, Netherlands). Technical, financial, and legal research articles on satellite communications.

Telecommunication Journal. (1934) Monthly. (International Telecommunication Union, Place de Nations, CH-1211 Geneva 20, Switzerland). English, French and Spanish editions. The official publication of the ITU, this includes technical, standards and policy material on common carrier and media issues, as well as details on the CCIR, CCITT and IFRB.

Telecommunications Policy. (1976) Bimonthly. (Journals Fulfillment Dept., Butterworths, 80 Montvale Ave., Stoneham, MA 02180). Scholarly articles on policy and regulation of common carrier and electronic media with worldwide coverage (emphasis is on Western Europe and the U.S.) and useful material on new media and industry structure.

Television. (1931) Bimonthly. (Royal Television Society, London). One of the oldest television periodicals in the world, this is a wide-ranging journal on policy, programs and technology, focusing on British television.

Periodicals on Broadcasting and Cable

A listing of magazines and periodicals, reports, annuals and journals on broadcasting, mass media, radio, satellites and television from the *Ulrich's International Periodicals Directory* data base. This list is limited to serials and periodicals published in the United States. This periodical listing is meant to complement the annotated periodicals listing, and may or may not include those titles. Abbreviations used in the entries are included in the *List of Abbreviations* in the front of this book.

ABC News Index. ISSN: 0891-8775. Research Publications Inc. (Woodbridge), 12 Lunar Dr., Drawer AB, Woodbridge, CT 06525. Telephone: 203-397-2600. FAX: 203-397-3893. Frequency: q. (with a. cumulation). Year First Published: 1986. Back issues available. Price: $185.
Index to transcripts of ABC-TV news programs available in microfiche.

A & E Program Guide. Editor(s): Paulette McLoud. Sponsoring Organization: Arts & Entertainment Channel, 235 E. 45th St., New York 10017. Telephone: 212-661-4500. Frequency: m. Price: $18.

AFTRA. Editor(s): Dick Moore. Sponsoring Organization: American Federation of Television and Radio Artists, 260 Madison Ave., 7th Fl., New York 10016-2401. Frequency: q. Year First Published: 1968. Special Features: adv, bk rev, charts, illus. Circulation: 80,000. Price: Free.

AMSAT Journal. Editor(s): Paul Urie. Sponsoring Organization: Radio Amateur Satellite Corp., 850 Sligo Ave., No. 600, Silver Spring, MD 20910. Telephone: 301-589-6062. Frequency: w. Year First Published: 1981. Back issues available. Circulation: 6,000. Price: U.S. $30; Canada $36; elsewhere $45.

APRA News. Editor(s): Mark W. Dobronski. Sponsoring Organization: American Private Radio Association Inc., Box 4221, Scottsdale, AZ 85261-4221. Telephone: 602-947-1100. FAX: 602-947-3131. Frequency: m. Circulation: 9,000.

ARA Log. ISSN: 0001-2289. Editor(s): W.R. Steinberg. Sponsoring Organization: American Radio Association, 26 Journal Sq., Suite 1501, Jersey City, NJ 07306. Frequency: 2/yr. Year First Published: 1949. Special Features: adv, bk rev, charts, illus, stat. Circulation: 3,000. Price: Membership only.

ARRL License Manual Series. Sponsoring Organization: American Radio Relay League Inc., 225 Main St., Newington, CT 06111. Telephone: 203-666-1541. FAX: 203-665-7531. Frequency: q. Price: $6.

ARRL Repeater Directory. ISSN: 0190-3632. Editor(s): Jay Mabey. Sponsoring Organization: American Radio Relay League Inc., 225 Main St., Newington, CT 06111. Telephone: 203-666-1541. FAX: 203-665-7531. Frequency: a. Circulation: 55,000. Price: $6.

A-V Advisor. Editor(s): Bill Weber, 66 12th St., Atlanta 30309. Telephone: 404-876-7841. FAX: 404-875-5258. Frequency: m.

AV Video: Production and Presentation Technology. ISSN: 0747-1335. Editor(s): Phillip Kurz. Montage Publishing Inc., Knowledge Industry Publications Inc., 701 Westchester Ave., White Plains, NY 10604. Telephone: 914-328-9157. Frequency: m. Year First Published: 1978. Special Features: adv. Back issues available. Circulation: 60,000. Price: $48.
Covers all facets of the audio-video industry: video, presentation media, computer-graphic, audio and interactive products and services. Also provides practical "how to" information as well as a special section on media management; includes computer-generated art.

Academy Players Directory. Editor(s): Patricia L. Citrano. Sponsoring Organization: Academy of Motion Picture Arts and Sciences, 8949 Wilshire Blvd., Beverly Hills, CA 90211. Telephone: 310-247-3000. FAX: 310-859-9351. Frequency: 3/yr. Price: $65 per mo.

Across the Dial. R.R. Bowker, A Reed Reference Publishing Co., 121 Chanlon Rd., New Providence, NJ 07974. Telephone: 908-665-2823. FAX: 908-771-9317. Frequency: irreg., 6th ed. 1989.
Guide to radio and TV stations in the U.S. and Canada; provides format and call letters of radio stations arranged by state, city, then call letters. Enables automotive travelers and visitors to tune in to desired stations. TV stations are also listed by state and city with channel numbers.

Ad-Tier Newsletter. Editor(s): Lloyd Trufelman. Cabletelevision Advertising Bureau (CAB), 757 3rd Ave., New York 10017. Telephone: 212-751-7770. Frequency: m. Year First Published: 1981. Circulation: 2,100. Price: Membership.
Information on cable advertising.

Advanced Wireless Communications. ISSN: 1058-7713. Editor(s): Ed Warner. Capitol Publications Inc., Telecom Publishing Group, 1101 King St., Suite 444, Box 1455, Alexandria, VA 22313-2055. Telephone: 800-327-7205. FAX: 703-739-6490. Frequency: 24/yr. Year First Published: 1990. Price: $446 (foreign $470).
Covers the business of personal communications, digital cellular, digital radio, miniature paging, in-flight phones, local loop alternatives, low-orbit satellites, specialized mobile radio, spectrum allocation, telepoint, vehicle location, wireless payphones, wireless PBXs and LANs, and other next-generation wireless technologies.

Agencies: What the Actor Needs to Know. Editor(s): Lawrence Parke. Acting World Books, Box 3044, Hollywood, CA 90078. Telephone: 818-905-1345. Frequency: bi-m. Year First Published: 1984. Special Features: tr lit. Circulation: 5,000. Price: $40.
Update of franchised talent agencies in Hollywood, with full descriptions of representation and staffs; also includes appraisals by industry consultants.

Amateur Radio Service Master File Updates. Sponsoring Organization: Federal Communications Commission, U.S. National Technical Information Service, 5825 Port Royal Rd., Springfield, VA 22161. Telephone: 703-487-4630. Frequency: m. Price: $290 per mo. U.S., Canada, Mexico; elsewhere $580.
Contains only additions and changes to the master file, not the master file. Limited to only those requiring a new license to be issued (approximately 95 percent of the changes).

American Film & Video Review. Editor(s): John A. Baird Jr. Sponsoring Organization: American Educational Film and Video Center, Eastern College, St. Davids, PA 19087. Telephone: 215-341-5935. Frequency: a. Year First Published: 1962. Circulation: 30,000. Price: Free.

American Radio. ISSN: 0738-8675. Editor(s): James H. Duncan Jr. Duncan's American Radio Inc., Box 90284, Indianapolis 46290. Telephone: 317-630-2888. Frequency: q. Year First Published: 1976. Circulation: 4,000. Price: Varies.

Applause: The Magazine of WHYY TV12 and 91FM. Sponsoring Organization: WHYY, Inc., RJR Associates Inc., 150 N. 6th St., Philadelphia 19106. Telephone: 215-351-0511. Frequency: m. Year First Published: 1988. Price: $40.

Art on Screen: The Newsletter of Film & Video on the Visual Arts. ISSN: 1062-9459. Editor(s): Susan Delson. Sponsoring Organization: Program for Art on Film, NY 10021. Telephone: 212-988-4876. FAX: 212-628-8963. Frequency: 3/yr. Year First Published: 1992. Circulation: 8,000 (controlled). Price: Free to qualified personnel.
Disseminates information on the presentation of the visual arts in film, video, television and interactive computer programs, including news of the program's activities and services and new releases on film and video. Also international.

Asia Cable. Editor(s): John Vezmar. Box 307, Lake Oswego, OR 97034-0035. Frequency: bi-m.

Aviation Master File. Sponsoring Organization: Federal Communications Commission, U.S. National Technical Information Service, 5825 Port Royal Rd., Springfield, VA 22161. Telephone: 703-487-4630. Frequency: q. Price: $20 per mo. in U.S., Canada, Mexico; elsewhere $40.
Contains radio license data of aircraft records in FAA number sequence. Cross-reference indexes are also included by fleet and name licensees.

BIB Channels: What's New in Domestic and International Television Programming and Syndication. North American Publishing Co., 401 N. Broad St., Philadelphia 19108. Telephone: 215-238-5300. FAX: 215-238-5457. Frequency: q. Year First Published: 1992. Price: $75.
Features the latest program availabilities.

BIB Television Programming Source Books. ISSN: 1056-6104. Editor(s): Heidi Holland. North American Publishing Co., 401 N. Broad St., Philadelphia 19108. Telephone: 215-238-5300. FAX: 215-238-5457. Frequency: a. Year First Published: 1989.

B M-E. ISSN: 0005-3201. Editor(s): Jerry Walker. Broadband Publications, c/o Broadband Information Bureau, 375 Park Ave., New York 10016. Telephone: 212-685-5320. Frequency: m. Year First Published: 1964. Special Features: adv, bk rev, bibl, charts, illus. Circulation: 30,000. Price: $24.

BM-E: The Source Issue. Broadband Publications, c/o Broadband Information Bureau, 375 Park Ave., New York 10016. Telephone: 212-685-5320. Frequency: a. Price: $5.
Lists manufacturers and distributors of equipment in the radio and TV broadcasting industries.

BPME Image. Editor(s): Dominick Morra. Broadcasters Promotion & Marketing Executives Inc., 6255 Sunset Blvd., Suite 624, Los Angeles 90028. Telephone: 213-465-3777. FAX: 213-469-9559. Frequency: m. Year First Published: 1985. Special Features: adv, bk rev, index. Circulation: 1,600 (controlled). Price: membership.
Directed to radio and TV stations, cable systems, cable, radio, TV networks.

Back Stage-Shoot. Editor(s): Peter Caranicas. BPI Communications, 1515 Broadway, 17th Fl., New York 10036. Telephone: 212-764-7300. FAX: 212-536-5321. Frequency: w. Year First Published: 1990. Circulation: 18,100. Price: $65.
For the commercial production and advertising industries. Special feature issues cover industry events such as the Clio Awards, NAB Convention, ITS Convention and SMPTE.

Backstage: The Performing Arts Weekly. Editor(s): Sherry Eaker. BPI Communications, 1515 Broadway, 17th Fl., New York 10036. Telephone: 212-764-7300. FAX: 212-536-5318. Frequency: w. Year First Published: 1960. Special Features: adv, bk rev, play rev, illus, tr lit. Reprint service available from UMI. Circulation: 25,000. Price: $65.
Presents news stories, informative columns, reviews, previews of upcoming theatre seasons, listings of agents, casting directors, rehearsal spaces, personal managers, acting coaches, and notices for stage, screen, television and cabaret.

Bacon's Radio-TV Directory: Broadcast Media, Personnel and Programs. ISSN: 0891-0103. Bacon's Publishing Co. Inc., 332 S. Michigan Ave., Suite 900, Chicago 60604. Telephone: 312-922-2400. FAX: 312-922-3127. Frequency: a. (plus q. update). Circulation: 6,000. Price: $250.
Directory of all U.S. broadcast media.

Better Radio and Television. ISSN: 0006-0194. Editor(s): Frank Orme. Sponsoring Organization: National Association for Better Broadcasting, 7918 Naylor Ave., Los Angeles 90045. Telephone: 213-641-4903. Frequency: q. Year First Published: 1960. Special Features: bk rev, illus. Circulation: 2,500. Price: $6.

Bibliography on Cable Television. ISSN: 0742-4914. Sponsoring Organization: Communications Institute, CA 94147-2139. Telephone: 415-626-5050. Frequency: a. Year First Published: 1975. Special Features: index, cum index: 1975-1991. Back issues available. Price: $35.
Open-ended, non-cumulative bibliography on access, advertising and marketing, audience and subscribers, programming, finance, law, technology and other issues of cable television.

Blue Lights. Editor(s): Vicki Werkley. Sponsoring Organization: Spotlight Starman, 16563 Ellen Springs Dr., Lower Lake, CA 95457. Frequency: bi-m.
Covers TV and videotapes.

Board for International Broadcasting Annual Report. Sponsoring Organization: Board for International Broadcasting, 1201 Connecticut Ave. N.W., Suite 400, Washington, DC 20036. Telephone: 202-254-8040. Frequency: a.

Bowker's Complete Video Directory: Combining Variety's Extensive Listing of Currently Available Entertainment Titles with Education and Special Interest Videos for Home, School and Business. ISSN: 1051-290X. R.R. Bowker, A Reed Reference Publishing Co., 121 Chanlon Rd., New Providence, NJ 07974. Telephone: 908-464-6800. FAX: 908-665-6688. Frequency: a. Year First Published: 1990. Price: $205 for complete set; $105 for Vol.1; $130 for Vols. 2 & 3.
For libraries, schools and video resource centers. Covers over 85,000 videos, in all formats available, including VHS, Beta, 3/4 U-matic, 8mm and laser disc.

Broadcast Banker-Broker. ISSN: 0889-2644. Editor(s): Paul Kagan, Sharon Armbrust. Paul Kagan Associates Inc., 126 Clock Tower Place, Carmel, CA 93923. Telephone: 408-624-1536. Frequency: m. Year First Published: 1984. Price: $495.
Covers equity and debt financing for radio and TV. Includes an analysis of interest rates and cash flow.

Broadcast Cable Financial Journal. Editor(s): Peter M. Duvel. Sponsoring Organization: Broadcast Cable Financial Management Association, 701 Lee St., Suite 1010, Des Plaines, IL 60016. Telephone: 708-296-0200. FAX: 708-296-7510. Frequency: bi-m. Year First Published: 1972. Special Features: index. Circulation: 1,500. Price: $42.
For professional financial and business managers of broadcasting and cable properties.

Broadcast Engineering: Journal of Broadcast Technology. ISSN: 0007-1994. Intertec Publishing Corp., 9800 Metcalf, Overland Park, KS 66212-2215. Telephone: 913-341-1300. FAX: 913-967-1898. Frequency: m. Year First Published: 1959. Special Features: bk rev, charts, illus, stat, tr lit, index. Reprint service available from UMI. Circulation: 35,193. Price: $50 (free to qualified personnel).

Broadcast Engineering (Spanish Language Edition). Intertec Publishing Corp., 9800 Metcalf, Overland Park, KS 66212-2215. Telephone: 913-341-1300. FAX: 913-967-1898. Frequency: s-a. Year First Published: 1988. Special Features: adv. Circulation: 9,016.
For management and technical personnel at radio and TV studios, recording studios and government agencies throught the Americas and in Spain and Portugal.

Broadcast Engineering Equipment Reference Manual. Editor(s): Carl Bentz. Intertec Publishing Corp., 9800 Metcalf, Overland Park, KS 66212-2215. Telephone: 913-888-4664. FAX: 913-541-6697. Frequency: a. Year First Published: 1981. Back issues available. Circulation: 35,193. Price: $20 (free to qualified personnel).

Broadcast Investor: The Newsletter on Radio-TV Station Finance. ISSN: 0146-0110. Editor(s): Paul Kagan, Sharon Armbrust. Paul Kagan Associates Inc., 126 Clock Tower Place, Carmel, CA 93923. Telephone: 408-624-1536. Frequency: m. Year First Published: 1975. Special Features: charts, index. Price: $575.
Covers investments in private radio and TV stations plus public broadcast companies. Gives analysis of cash flow multiples, valuations of stations and companies.

Broadcast Investor Charts: Monthly Service Showing Price Movements of Broadcast Stocks Over Two-Year Spans. ISSN: 0736-9069. Paul Kagan Associates Inc., 126 Clock Tower Place, Carmel, CA 93923. Telephone: 408-624-1536. FAX: 408-625-3225. Frequency: m. Year First Published: 1983. Special Features: charts. Reprint service available. Price: $395.
Chart service on stock price movements of 41 publicly held broadcast companies for the past two years.

Broadcast Stats. ISSN: 0749-2936. Editor(s): Paul Kagan. Paul Kagan Associates Inc., 126 Clock Tower Place, Carmel, CA 93923. Telephone: 408-625-3225. Frequency: m. Year First Published: 1984. Price: $450.

Broadcasting Abroad. ISSN: 1064-6124. Cahners Publishing Co. (Washington), Division of Reed Publishing (USA) Inc., 1705 DeSales St. N.W., Washington, DC 20036. Telephone: 202-659-2340. FAX: 202-429-0651. Frequency: q. Circulation: 7,500 (controlled).
An international publication dedicated to providing global information on radio, television, cable and satellites.

Broadcasting & Cable. Editor(s): Donald West. Cahners Publishing Co. (Washington), Division of Reed Publishing (USA) Inc., 1705 DeSales St., N.W., Washington, DC 20036. Telephone: 202-659-2340. FAX: 202-429-0651. Frequency: w. Year First Published: 1931. Special Features: adv, bk rev, charts, illus, stat, cum index: 1972-1981. Reprint service available from UMI. Circulation: 30,000. Price: $99 (foreign $300).
Covers the broadcasting and cable industries in-depth, including news/reports on radio, TV, cable and satellite. Features legislative updates, radio and TV ownership changes, new stations, facilities changes, band allocations and more.

Broadcasting & Cable Yearbook. R.R. Bowker, A Reed Reference Publishing Co., 121 Chanlon Rd., NJ 07974. Telephone: 908-665-2823. FAX: 908-771-7725. Frequency: a. Year First Published: 1935. Special Features: adv. Circulation: 15,000. Price: $159.95.
Comprehensive guide to the broadcasting and cable industries. Contains listings of U.S. and Canadian radio stations, television stations, top cable MSOs, satellites, service providers, market data and trade shows. Includes yellow pages.

Broadcasting & Cable International. Editor(s): Don West. 1705 DeSales St. N.W., Washington, DC 20036. Telephone: 202-659-2340. Frequency: q. Price: Complimentary with subscription to *Broadcasting & Cable.*
Full coverage of industry trends.

Broadcasting & Cable's TV International. Editor(s): Meredith Amdur, Peter Checketts. 2455 Teller Rd., Thousand Oaks, CA 91320. Telephone: 805-499-0721, ext. 289. FAX: 805-499-0871. Frequency: bi-w. Price: $495.
In-depth news and analysis of the global television business. Newsletter focuses on programming, ratings, distribution, finance, cable, satellite, co-production, regulation, new media technology, joint ventures, etc.

Broadcasting and the Law. ISSN: 0161-5823. Editor(s): John Spencer. Broadcasting and the Law Inc., One S.E. 3rd Ave., Suite 1450, Miami, FL 33131-1715. Telephone: 800-933-IFCC. FAX: 305-530-9417. Frequency: s-m. Year First Published: 1970. Special Features: index. Circulation: 7,000. Price: $120.
Provides current information about regulations and all aspects of station operations to help cut legal costs.

Business Radio. ISSN: 0746-8911. Editor(s): A.E. Goetz. Sponsoring Organization: National Association of Business and Educational Radio Inc. (NABER), 1501 Duke St., Alexandria, VA 22314. Telephone: 703-739-0300. FAX: 703-836-1608. Frequency: 10/yr. Year First Published: 1965. Special Features: adv, bk rev, illus. Circulation: 3,000. Price: $65.
Offers information of interest to two-way radio dealers, owners, towers and site managers, operators of private carrier paging and specialized mobile radio systems, technicians, system users and manufacturers.

Business Television Directory. ISSN: 1052-3138. Sponsoring Organization: Telehealth Associates, 11 Willow St., Needham, MA 02192. Frequency: a. Year First Published: 1988.

CCIR Plenary Assembly (17th Dussledorf Germany, 1990). Sponsoring Organization: International Telecommunication Union, U.S. National Technical Information Service, 5285 Port Royal Rd., Springfield, VA 22161. Telephone: 703-487-4630. FAX: 703-321-8547. Frequency: quadrennial. Price: $1,659.

CD-ROM World: The Optical Media Review for Information Professionals. ISSN: 1066-274X. Editor(s): Norman Desmarais. Meckler Publishing Corp., 11 Ferry Lane W., Westport, CT 06880-5808. Telephone: 203-226-6967. Frequency: m. (except July-Aug. combined). Year First Published: 1986. Price: $87.

CINCOM: Courses in Communications. ISSN: 0742-3632. Sponsoring Organization: Communications Institute, Communications Library, Lockbox 5891, San Francisco 94147-2139. Telephone: 415-626-5050. Frequency: a. Year First Published: 1983. Special Features: bk rev. Circulation: 5,000. Price: $35.
Contains over 1,200 accredited American, Asian, Canadian, European and Middle Eastern IHEs offering courses and degrees in communications, data telecom, telephony, telecommunications and CATV.

CMJ New Music Report. ISSN: 0890-0795. Editor(s): Robert Haber. College Media Inc., 245 Great Neck Rd., 3rd Fl., Great Neck, NY 11021-3308. Telephone: 516-466-6000. FAX: 516-466-7159. Frequency: w. Year First Published: 1978. Special Features: adv, bk rev, film rev. Back issues available. Circulation: 3,000. Price: $250.

CPB Report. Sponsoring Organization: Corp. for Public Broadcasting, 901 E St., N.W., Washington, DC 20004-2037. Telephone: 202-879-9600. FAX: 202-783-1039. Frequency: bi-w. Year First Published: 1969. Special Features: bk rev. Circulation: 4,000.

CQ: The Radio Amateurs' Journal. ISSN: 0007-893X. Editor(s): A.M. Dorhoffer. CQ Communications Inc., 76 N. Broadway, Hicksville, NY 11801. Telephone: 516-681-2922. FAX: 516-681-2926. Frequency: m. Year First Published: 1945. Special Features: adv, bk rev, charts, illus. Circulation: 113,309. Price: $24.50 (Canada and Mexico $25; elsewhere $27).
For radio amateurs who are actively involved in operating, building and using amateur radio equipment and related devices.

CTVD: Cinema-T V-Digest: A Quarterly Review of the Serious, Foreign-Language Cinema-TV-Press. ISSN: 0007-9219. Editor(s): Ben Hamilton. Hampton Books, Box 5936, Columbia, SC 29250-5936. Telephone: 803-276-6870. Frequency: irreg. Year First Published: 1962. Special Features: adv, bk rev, film rev, illus. Back issues available. Circulation: 550. Price: $3 for four mos. (foreign $4).

CVC Report. Editor(s): Mitchell Rowen. Creative Video Consulting, 648 Broadway, New York 10012-2314. Telephone: 212-533-9870. FAX: 212-473-3772. Frequency: s-m.

Cable in the Classroom: Teaching with Television. ISSN: 1054-5409. Editor(s): Robert Moses. IDG Peterborough, 80 Elm St., Peterborough, NH 03458. Telephone: 603-924-0100. Frequency: m. Year First Published: 1989. Circulation: 30,000.
Directed to teachers interested in bringing television into the classroom as an educational medium.

Cable Contacts (Year). ISSN: 1053-9026. BPI Communications Inc. (Schenectady), BPI Media Services, 210 Canal Sq., Schenectady, NY 12305. Telephone: 518-374-7640. FAX: 518-374-7889. Frequency: a. (plus m. updates and toll-free phone-in verification service). Price: $150.

Cable Guide. Editor(s): Allan Wratg. TV Syndicated Market, 309 Lakeside Dr., Horsham, PA 19044. Telephone: 215-443-9300. Frequency: m. Year First Published: 1982. Special Features: adv. Back issues available. Circulation: 4,200,000. Price: $14.
Listing of programs on cable and pay TV. Includes feature articles and interviews.

Cable Plus. Editor(s): Becki Barton. TV Host Inc., Box 1665, 3953 Jonestown Rd., Harrisburg, PA 17109. Telephone: 717-657-1700. FAX: 717-657-2921. Frequency: s-m. Year First Published: 1980. Special Features: adv. Circulation: 70,000. Price: $24.

Cable Spot Advertising Directory. National Register Publishing, A Reed Reference Publishing Co., 121 Chanlon Rd., New Providence, NJ 07974. Telephone: 908-464-6800. FAX: 908-665-6688. Frequency: a. Year First Published: 1983. Price: $125.
Provides information on cable advertising opportunities, including detailed information on more than 700 cable systems.

Cable and Station Coverage Atlas. Editor(s): Albert Warren. Warren Publishing Inc., 2115 Ward Ct., N.W., Washington, DC 20037. Telephone: 202-872-9200. FAX: 202-293-3435. Frequency: a. Year First Published: 1966. Special Features: index. Price: $360.

Cable TV Advertising: The Newsletter on Sale of Commercial Time by Cable TV Systems. ISSN: 0270-885X. Editor(s): Larry Gerbrandt. Paul Kagan Associates Inc., 126 Clock Tower Place, Carmel, CA 93923, Telephone: 408-624-1536. Frequency: m. Year First Published: 1980. Special Features: charts, index. Price: $475.
Examines the sale of commercial time by cable TV systems and networks. Includes local and national ad sales, case studies and projections.

Cable TV Banker-Broker: The Newsletter on Bank, Insurance, Commercial Loans to Cable Operators. ISSN: 0893-2131. Editor(s): Paul Kagan. Paul Kagan Associates Inc., 126 Clock Tower Place, Carmel, CA 93923. Telephone: 408-624-1536. FAX: 408-625-3225. Frequency: m. Year First Published: 1982. Special Features: charts, index. Price: $595.
Covers sources of funding for cable TV. Analysis of bank, insurance and bridge loans. Case studies of financing strategies.

Cable TV Facts. Cabletelevision Advertising Bureau (CAB), 757 3rd Ave., New York 10017. Telephone: 212-751-7770. Frequency: a. Year First Published: 1983. Price: $3.50.

Cable TV Financial Databook: Sourcebook for All Key Financial Data on Cable TV. ISSN: 0736-8143. Editor(s): Eleanor Wylde Morrice. Paul Kagan Associates Inc., 126 Clock Tower Place, Carmel, CA 93923. Telephone: 408-624-1536. Frequency: a. Year First Published: 1980. Special Features: adv, charts, stat. Back issues available. Price: $130.

Cable TV Franchising: The Newsletter on Federal-State-City Regulation of Cable Television. ISSN: 0731-0269. Editor(s): John Mansell. Paul Kagan Associates Inc., 126 Clock Tower Place, Carmel, CA 93923. Telephone: 408-624-1536. Frequency: m. Year First Published: 1975. Special Features: charts, index. Price: $450.

Newsletter on franchise awards and renewals and legal battles with cities and states. Includes listing of most cable TV rate increases.

Cable TV Investor: The Newsletter on Investments in Cable TV Systems and Publicly Held Cable TV Stocks. ISSN: 0731-0250. Editor(s): Paul Kagan, Sharon Armbrust. Paul Kagan Associates Inc., 126 Clock Tower Place, Carmel, CA 93923. Telephone: 408-624-1536. FAX: 408-624-1536. Frequency: m. Year First Published: 1969. Special Features: charts, index. Price: $695.

Provides analysis of cash flow multiples and value per subscriber.

Cable TV Investor Charts: Service Showing Price Movements on Cable TV Stocks Over Two-Year Spans. ISSN: 0732-7757. Paul Kagan Associates Inc., 126 Clock Tower Place, Carmel, CA 93923. Telephone: 408-624-1536. FAX: 408-625-3225. Frequency: m. Year First Published: 1982. Special Features: charts. Price: $395.

Chart service on stock price movements of 41 publicly-held cable TV companies. Each chart shows two years of stock price activity.

Cable TV Law Reporter. ISSN: 0749-7652. Paul Kagan Associates Inc., 126 Clock Tower Pl., Carmel, CA 93923. Telephone: 408-624-1536. Frequency: m. Year First Published: 1984. Price: $425.

Issues concerning cable TV. Includes anti-trust, first amendment, franchising, taxation, copyright, rate regulation, privacy and international law.

Cable TV and New Media Law & Finance. Editor(s): Michael Botein, David M. Rice. Leader Publications Inc., New York Law Publishing Co., 111 8th Ave., Suite 900, New York 10011. Telephone: 800-888-8300. FAX: 212-463-5523. Frequency: m. Year First Published: 1983. Special Features: bk rev. Price: $195.

Interprets and analyzes the latest developments in cable and video.

Cable TV Programming: The Newsletter on Programs for Pay Cable TV and Analysis of Basic Cable Networks. ISSN: 0278-503X. Editor(s): Paul Kagan. Paul Kagan Associates Inc., 126 Clock Tower Place, Carmel, CA 93923. Telephone: 408-624-1536. FAX: 408-625-3225. Frequency: m. Year First Published: 1981. Special Features: charts, index. Reprint service available. Price: $550.

Covers the economics of basic and pay TV program networks. Gives case studies of cable system program valuations.

Cable TV Station Authorization Report. Sponsoring Organization: Federal Communications Commission, U.S. National Technical Information Service, 5825 Port Royal Rd., Springfield, VA 22161. Telephone: 703-487-4630. Frequency: q. Price: $25 per mo. in U.S., Canada, Mexico; elsewhere $50.

Lists by call letters and locations the cable television stations authorized to broadcast programs.

Cable TV Station Distribution File. Sponsoring Organization: Federal Communications Commission, U.S. National Technical Information Service, 5825 Port Royal Rd., Springfield, VA 22161. Telephone: 703-487-4630. Frequency: s-a. Price: $25 per mo. in U.S., Canada, Mexico; elsewhere $40.

Cable TV Tax Letter: Newsletter on Cable TV Tax Shelters. ISSN: 0730-6202. Editor(s): John Mansell. Paul Kagan Associates Inc., 126 Clock Tower Place, Carmel, CA 93923. Telephone: 408-624-1536. Frequency: m. Year First Published: 1981. Special Features: charts, index. Price: $525.

Provides analysis of public and private cable limited partnerships.

Cable TV Technology: The Newsletter on Technical Advances, Construction of New Systems and Rebuild of Existing Systems. ISSN: 0276-5713. Editor(s): John Mansell. Paul Kagan Associates Inc., 126 Clock Tower Place, Carmel, CA 93923. Telephone: 408-624-1536. Frequency: m. Year First Published: 1981. Special Features: charts, index. Price: $550.

Covers addressability updates and projections.

Cable Theft Newsletter. Skybridge Publishing Inc., c/o Schreff, 9 Fontier Rd., Cos Cob, CT 06807-1208. Frequency: m. Price: $72.

Cable Update. Editor(s): Betty Ann Kane. Miller & Holbrooke Information Services, 1225 19th St., N.W., Suite 400, Washington, DC 20036. Telephone: 202-785-8827. FAX: 202-785-1234. Frequency: m. Year First Published: 1979. Special Features: bk rev, bibl, index. Back issues available. Circulation: 300. Price: $300.

Contains reports, analysis and documents related to cable television and telecommunications of interest to state and local franchising authorities, municipal cable officers, libraries and other interested persons.

Cable Video Briefs. Skybridge Publishing Inc., c/o Schreff, 9 Frontier Rd., Cos Cob, CT 06807-1208. Frequency: m. Price: $72.

Cable World. ISSN: 1042-7228. Editor(s): Peggy Ziegler. Cable World Associates, 1905 Sherman St., Suite 1000, Denver 80203. Telephone: 303-837-0900. FAX: 303-837-0915. Frequency: w. Year First Published: 1989. Special Features: adv. Circulation: 11,000 (controlled). Price: $55.

Business news magazine for the cable television industry. Includes in-depth reports on trends and issues affecting the cable business.

Cablefax. Editor(s): Lesley Barnes. Transmedia Partners, 50 S. Steele St., Suite 500, Denver 80209. Telephone: 303-355-2101. FAX: 303-355-2144. Frequency: d. (5/w.). Year First Published: 1990. Special Features: adv. Circulation: 1,421. Price: $279.95.

Covers industry news, legislation, finance, acquisitions, programming, hardware and personnel.

Cablesports Newsletter. Editor(s): Dantia Gould. QV Publishing Inc., Meadowbrook Office Park, Box 2000, York, ME 03909. Telephone: 207-363-6222. FAX: 207-363-6182. Frequency: w. Year First Published: 1983. Special Features: adv. Back issues available. Price: $325.

Covers trends in the televising of sports.

CableVision: The Analysis and Features Bi-Weekly of the Cable Television Industry. ISSN: 0361-8374. Editor(s): Craig Leddy. Capital Cities-ABC Inc., Diversified Publishing Group, 825 7th Ave., New York 10019. Telephone: 212-887-8400. FAX: 212-887-8585. Frequency: s-m. Year First Published: 1975. Special Features: adv, bk rev. Circulation: 13,600. Price: $55.

Covers all fields related to cable television management: programming, pay per view, marketing and promotion, advertising sales, technology, operations, customer service and policy and business.

Caption. Editor(s): Morgan Bramlet. Sponsoring Organization: National Captioning Institute Inc., 5203 Leesburg Pike, Falls Church, VA 22041. Telephone: 703-998-2450. Frequency: a. Year First Published: 1980. Circulation: 100,000 (controlled). Price: Free.

Chicago Film & Video News. Editor(s): Donna B. Proske. Real Estate News Corp., 2600 W. Peterson Ave., Chicago 60659-4031. Telephone: 312-465-7246. FAX: 312-465-7218. Frequency: bi-m. Special Features: adv.

Children's Video Report. ISSN: 0883-6922. Editor(s): Martha Dewing. Box 3228, Princeton. NJ 08543-3228. Telephone: 609-452-7980. FAX: 609-452-7151. Frequency: 8/yr. Year First Published: 1985. Circulation: 1,200. Price: $60.

Reports on children and video from experts on child development and media.

Choices Satellite TV: Your Guide to Satellite Pay Per View Entertainment. Fortuna Communications Corp., Box 308, Fortuna, CA 95540. Telephone: 707-725-6951. FAX: 707-725-4311. Frequency: m. Year First Published: 1991. Special Features: adv, film rev. Circulation: 40,000. Price: $18.

City County Communications. Editor(s): Mary Floyd. Sponsoring Organization: Innovation Groups Inc., Box 16645, Tampa 33687. Telephone: 813-622-8484. FAX: 813-664-0051. Frequency: q. Year First Published: 1987. Special Features: adv, bk rev, video rev. Circulation: 2,600. Price: $19.

Studies videos, cable TV, radio, communication programs, training programs on video and multimedia computer presentations, and means of communication between local government, employees and the public.

Clandestine Confidential. Editor(s): Gerry L. Dexter. R.R. 4, Box 110, Lake Geneva, WI 53147. Telephone: 414-248-4845. Frequency: bi-m. Year First Published: 1984. Special Features: bk rev. Back issues available. Circulation: 100. Price: $10 (foreign $13).

Contains information about schedules, backers and locations of clandestine political broadcasters.

College Broadcaster. Editor(s): Richard L. Smith. Sponsoring Organization: National Association of College Broadcasters, 71 George St., 2nd Fl., Providence, RI 02912. Telephone: 401-863-2225. FAX: 401-863-3700. Frequency: 8/yr. Special Features: adv. Circulation: 5,100.

Comedy Writers Association Newsletter. Sponsoring Organization: Comedy Writers Association, Robert Makinson, Ed. & Pub., Box 023304, Brooklyn, NY 11202-0066. Telephone: 718-855-5057. Frequency: q. Year First Published: 1989. Special Features: adv, bk rev. Back issues available. Price: $18.

Creation and marketing of jokes, scripts and humorous stories.

Comedy Writers Bulletin. Robert Makinson, Ed. & Pub., Box 023304, Brooklyn, NY 11202-0066. Telephone: 718-855-5057. Frequency: a. Year First Published: 1980. Circulation: 50. Price: $9.

Communication Arts International. ISSN: 0010-3500. Editor(s): Dr. E. Von Rothkirch. Sponsoring Organization: International Association of Independent Producers, Box 1933, Washington, DC 20013. Frequency: q. Year First Published: 1954. Special Features: adv, bk rev, film rev, play rev, charts, illus, mkt, pat, stat, tr lit. Circulation: 7,000. Price: $6 to non-members.

Communication Disciplines in Higher Education: A Directory. Editor(s): Garland C. Elmore. Sponsoring Organization: Association for Communication Administration, 5105-F Backlick Rd., Annandale, VA 22003. Telephone: 703-750-0533. Frequency: a., latest 1993 ed. Year First Published: 1987. Price: $30.

Lists academic programs and faculty in radio, television, film and related media.

Communications Daily: The Authoritative News Service of Electronic Communications. ISSN: 0277-0679. Editor(s): Albert Warren. Warren Publishing Inc., 2115 Ward Ct. N.W., Washington, DC 20037. Telephone: 202-872-9200. FAX: 202-293-3435. Frequency: 5/w. Year First Published: 1981. Price: $2,380 (foreign $2,520).

Communications Engineering and Design. ISSN: 0191-5428. Editor(s): Roger Brown. Capital Cities-ABC Inc. (Denver), 600 S. Cherry St., Suite 400, Denver 80222. 303-393-6654. Frequency: m. Year First Published: 1975. Special Features: adv, bk rev, illus. Circulation: 14,500. Price: $48.

Written and edited for cable television engineering and technical personnel.

Communications: For the Professional in Land Mobile Radio. ISSN: 0010-356X. Editor(s): George Dennis. Cardiff Publishing Co., 6300 S. Syracuse Way, Suite 650, Englewood, CO 80111. Telephone: 303-220-0600. Frequency: m. Year First Published: 1963. Special Features: adv, bk rev, charts, illus, index. Reprint service available from UMI. Circulation: 20,466. Price: $29 (foreign $42).

Serves the mobile communications industry with features on regulatory, business, technology and marketing issues.

Communications Quarterly: A Journal of Communications Technology. ISSN: 1053-9344. Editor(s): Terry Littlefield. CQ Communications Inc., 76 N. Broadway, Hicksville, NY 11801. Telephone: 516-681-2926. FAX: 516-681-2926. Frequency: q. Year First Published: 1990. Circulation: 6,828. Price: $29.95 (foreign $39.95).

Technically-oriented amateur radio magazine that offers in-depth coverage of the science of communications.

Communications Technology. ISSN: 0884-2272. Editor(s): Rikki T. Lee. Sponsoring Organization: Society of Cable Television Engineers, Communications Technology Publications Corp., Transmedia Partners, 50 S. Steele, Suite 700, Denver 80209. Telephone: 303-792-0023. Frequency: m. Year First Published: 1984. Special Features: adv, charts, illus, index. Back issues available. Circulation: 13,000. Price: Free.

Covers cable TV engineering and technology.

Community Radio News. Editor(s): Lynn Chadwick. Sponsoring Organization: National Federation of

Community Broadcasters, 666 11th St. N.W., Suite 805, Washington, DC 20001. Telephone: 202-393-2355. Frequency: m. Year First Published: 1974. Special Features: adv. Back issues available. Circulation: 500. Price: $75 to non-members.
Covers public radio policy and issues. Includes information on programming, fundraising, management, volunteer coordination, and production.

Community Television Review. Sponsoring Organization: Alliance for Community Media, 666 11th St., N.W., Suite 806, Washington, DC 20001-4542. Telephone: 202-393-2560. FAX: 202-393-2653. Frequency: 6/yr. Year First Published: 1977. Special Features: adv, bk rev. Back issues available. Circulation: 8,500. Price: $25.

Contacts: The Media Pipeline for Public Relations People. Editor(s): Madeleine Gillis. Sponsoring Organization: CAP Communications Associates Ltd., 35-20 Broadway, Astoria, NY 11106. Telephone: 718-721-0508. Frequency: w. Year First Published: 1970. Special Features: cum index. Back issues available. Circulation: 5,000. Price: $287.
Outlines the information needs of editors, writers and producers of magazines (consumer & trade), newspapers, TV & radio, providing contact information.

Critical Studies in Mass Communication. ISSN: 0739-3180. Editor(s): Sari Thomas. Sponsoring Organization: Speech Communication Association, 5105 Backlick Rd., Bldg. E., Annandale, VA 22003. Telephone: 703-750-0533. Frequency: q. Year First Published: 1984. Special Features: adv, cum index. Circulation: 2,800. Price: $75 membership.

Current (Washington, 1982). Editor(s): Steve Behrens. Current Publishing Committee, 2311 18th St. N.W., Washington, DC 20009. Telephone: 202-265-8310. FAX: 202-265-8314. Frequency: bi-w. Year First Published: 1976-1980 (Oct.); resumed Mar. 1982. Special Features: adv, bk rev, illus. Circulation: 6,000. Price: $70.
Covers public television, public radio and noncommercial telecommunications.

Cyrano's Journal. ISSN: 0740-5405. Editor(s): D.P. Greanville. Sponsoring Organization: New England Communications Task Force Inc., Box 68, Westport, CT 06881. Frequency: q. Year First Published: 1982. Special Features: adv, bk rev, film rev, abstr, bibl, charts, illus, index. Back issues available. Circulation: 15,000. Price: $18 to individuals; libraries $24.

DAB Report. Warren Publishing Corp., 2115 Ward Ct., N.W., Washington, DC 20037. Telephone: 202-872-9200. FAX: 202-293-3435. Frequency: fortn.
Covers digital radio broadcasting.

DX Monitor. ISSN: 0899-9732. Editor(s): Ralph Sanserino. Sponsoring Organization: International Radio Club of America, 12072 Elk Blvd., Riverside, CA 92505-3835. Frequency: 34/yr. Year First Published: 1964. Special Features: adv, bk rev, charts, illus. Back issues available. Circulation: 275. Price: $27.
Covers the hobby of listening to distant stations on the AM broadcast band.

DX Reporter. Sponsoring Organization: Association of DX Reporters, 7008 Plymouth Rd., Baltimore 21208. Frequency: m. Year First Published: 1982. Special Features: bk rev. Circulation: 160. Price: $19 (Canada and Mexico $20; elsewhere $22).
Active HF utility and hamband DXers.

Daily Variety: News of the Entertainment Industry. ISSN: 0011-5509. Editor(s): Peter P. Pryor. Sponsoring Organization: Daily Variety Ltd., Cahners Publishing Co. (New York), Entertainment Division, Division of Reed Publishing (USA) Inc., 475 Park Ave. S., New York 10016-6901. Telephone: 212-779-1999. Frequency: d. (Mon.-Fri.). Year First Published: 1933. Special Features: adv, bk rev, film rev, music rev, play rev, tele rev, charts. Circulation: 23,373. Price: $129 (foreign $239).

Daytime Digest. Sterling's Magazines Inc., 355 Lexington Ave., New York 10017. Telephone: 212-396-5965. FAX: 212-396-1365. Frequency: m. Special Features: adv. Price: $2.50 per mo.
Focuses on TV personalities.

Daytime TV. Sterling's Magazines Inc., 355 Lexington Ave., New York 10017. Telephone: 212-396-5965. FAX: 212-391-1400. Frequency: m. Special Features: adv. Price: $2.50 per mo.
Edited to entertain female readers by focusing on TV personalities.

Daytime TV Presents. Editor(s): Jason Bonderoff. Sterling's Magazines Inc., 355 Lexington Ave., New York 10017. Telephone: 212-396-5965. FAX: 212-396-1365. Frequency: bi-m. Year First Published: 1969. Special Features: adv. Price: $2.50 per mo.
Concentrates on TV personalities.

Daytime TV's Greatest Stories. Sterling's Magazines Inc., 1754 15th St., No. 6, Santa Monica, CA 90404. Telephone: 213-396-5965. FAX: 213-396-1365. Frequency: bi-m. Special Features: adv. Price: $2.50 per mo.
Provides material of an entertaining and diversionary nature for women. Devoted to TV personalities.

Desktop Video World. ISSN: 1067-7720. Editor(s): Louis R. Wallace. TechMedia Publishing Inc., IDG Co., 80 Elm St., Peterborough, NH 03458. Telephone: 603-924-0100. FAX: 603-924-4066. Frequency: bi-m. Year First Published: 1993. Circulation: 40,000. Price: $24.
Covers the convergence of computers and video, providing information on desktop video hardware and software for major platforms for videographers who are creating computer-enhanced videos. Includes graphics, animation, editing and imaging.

Destination Discovery. ISSN: 1065-1535. Sponsoring Organization: The Discovery Channel, Discovery Publishing, 7700 Wisconsin Ave., 7th Fl., Bethesda, MD 20814. Telephone: 301-986-0444. FAX: 301-986-4628. Frequency: m. Year First Published: 1985. Circulation: 200,000. Price: $19.95.

Detroit Film and Video News. Editor(s): Donna B. Proske. Real Estate News Corp., 2600 W. Peterson, Suite 100, Chicago 60659. Telephone: 312-465-7246. 312-465-7218. Frequency: q. Year First Published: 1990. Special Features: adv. Circulation: 3,500. Price: $7.50.
Reports on the industry's progress in the Detroit Metro area and throughout Michigan. Covers trends, equipment, innovations, new facilities, services and technology.

Digest of the UFVA. Editor(s): Steve Fore, Gerry Veeder. Sponsoring Organization: University Film Video Association, c/o Gerry Veeder, University of N. Texas, Radio, TV & Film Dept., Box 13108, Denton, TX 76203-3108. Telephone: 213-740-0832. Frequency: bi-m. Price: Membership.

Directory of Free Programs, Performing Talent and Attractions: The Promotional Sourcebook. ISSN: 0736-7759. Editor(s): Robert D. and Eileen E. Shelley, Box 1288, Champlain. NY 12919-1288. 514-443-3251. Frequency: a. Year First Published: 1983. Special Features: bk rev. Circulation: 500,273. Price: $49.95.

Directory of Religious Broadcasting. ISSN: 0731-0331. Editor(s): Marjorie Stevens. Sponsoring Organization: National Religious Broadcasters Inc., 7839 Ashton Ave., Manassas, VA 22110. Telephone: 703-330-7000. FAX: 703-330-7100. Frequency: a. Year First Published: 1972. Special Features: index. Reprint service available from UMI. Circulation: 3,000. Price: $49.95.
Covers the worldwide Christian religious broadcasting industry, listing more than 4,400 radio and television stations, program producers, manufacturers, and related suppliers and services.

Directory of Video Retailers. ISSN: 1053-9069. Editor(s): Steve Tolin. Palm Springs Media Inc., Box 2740, Palm Springs, CA 92263-2740. Telephone: 619-322-3050. Frequency: a. Year First Published: 1990. Price: $175.
Lists 100,000 U.S. retailers of video hardware and software.

Document Image Automation. ISSN: 1054-9692. Editor(s): Judith Paris Roth. Meckler Publishing Corp., 11 Ferry Lane W., Westport, CT 06880-5808. Telephone: 203-226-6967. Frequency: bi-m. Year First Published: 1981. Special Features: adv, bk rev. Price: $125.

Document Image Automation Update. ISSN: 1054-9706. Editor(s): William Saffady. Meckler Publishing Corp., 11 Ferry Lane W., Westport, CT 06880-5808. Telephone: 203-226-6967. Frequency: 12/yr. Year First Published: 1982. Price: $297.

Drama-Logue. Editor(s): Faye Bordy. Drama-Logue Inc., Box 38771, Los Angeles 90038. Telephone: 213-464-5079. Frequency: w. Year First Published: 1969. Special Features: adv, bk rev. Circulation: 75,000. Price: $55.

Duncan's Radio Market Guide. Editor(s): James H. Duncan. Duncan's American Radio Inc., Box 90284, Indianapolis 46290. Telephone: 317-630-2888. Frequency: a. Price: $295.

Early Warning Report. ISSN: 0193-3655. Editor(s): Albert Warren. Warren Publishing Inc., 2115 Ward Ct., N.W., Washington, DC 20037. Telephone: 202-872-9200. FAX: 202-293-3435. Frequency: m. Year First Published: 1975. Price: $10,004 (foreign $1,016).

Educators Guide to Free Videotapes. Editor(s): James L. Berger. Sponsoring Organization: Educators Progress Service Inc., 214 Center St., Randolph, WI 53956. Telephone: 414-326-3126. FAX: 414-326-3127. Frequency: a. Year First Published: 1954. Price: $24.95.

Electronic Media. ISSN: 0745-0311. Editor(s): David Klein. Crain Communications Inc. (Chicago), 740 Rush St., Chicago 60611-2590. Telephone: 312-649-5200. FAX: 312-649-5465. Frequency: w. Year First Published: 1982. Special Features: adv. Circulation: 26,753. Price: $69.
Written for the management of television and radio stations, broadcast networks, cable systems and the emerging electronic media, as well as advertising agency media executives, and producers and syndicators of programming.

Electronic Media Daily Fax. Editor(s): David Klein. Crain Communications Inc. (Chicago), 740 Rush St., Chicago 60611-2590. Frequency: 4/w. Year First Published: 1991. Special Features: adv. Circulation: 26,753. Price: $99.
Provides each day's breaking news, ratings results and other timely information.

Electronics Experimenters Handbook (Year). Editor(s): Brian Fenton. Gernsback Publications Inc., 500-B Bi-county Blvd., Farmingdale, NY 11735. Telephone: 516-293-3000. FAX: 516-293-3115. Frequency: a. Year First Published: 1983. Special Features: adv, bk rev, charts, illus. Back issues available; reprint service available from UMI. Circulation: 135,000. Price: $3.95.
Collection of reprinted articles from Electronics Now magazine. Feature articles include coverage on microcomputers, hardware and peripherals, as well as new product reviews.

Electronics Now: New Ideas in Electronics. Editor(s): Brian Fenton. Gernsback Publications Inc., 500-B Bi-county Blvd., Farmingdale, NY 11735. Telephone: 516-293-3000. FAX: 516-293-3115. Frequency: m. Year First Published: 1929. Special Features: bk rev, charts, illus, tr lit, index. Reprint service available from UMI. Circulation: 171,679. Price: $19.97.
Reports on microcomputers, the electronics industry, technology and service. Coverage includes feature articles, building projects, products reviews.

Eleven. Editor(s): Elizabeth Altick-McCarthy. Sponsoring Organization: WTTW-Chicago, 5400 N. St. Louis Ave., Chicago 60625-4623. Telephone: 312-509-5435. FAX: 312-583-3046. Frequency: m. Circulation: 170,000.

Emmy. ISSN: 0164-3495. Editor(s): Hank Rieger. Sponsoring Organization: Academy of Television Arts & Sciences, 5220 Lankershim Blvd., N. Hollywood, CA 91601-3107. Telephone: 818-754-2800. FAX: 818-761-2827. Frequency: bi-m. Year First Published: 1979. Special Features: adv, bk rev, illus. Circulation: 12,000. Price: $23.
Covers matters of interest to the television industry, including members of the academy.

Entertainment Law & Finance. ISSN: 0883-2455. New York Law Publishing Co., Marketing Dept., 111 8th Ave., New York 10011. Telephone: 212-741-8300. Frequency: m. Year First Published: 1985. Price: $175.
Legal and financial developments in music, film, theater, broadcasting, sports, publishing, video and related media arts.

Entertainment Law Reporter: Motion Pictures, Television, Radio, Music, Theater, Publishing, Sports. ISSN: 0270-3831. Editor(s): Lionel S. Sobel. Entertainment Law Reporter Publishing Co., 2210 Wilshire Blvd., No. 311, Santa Monica, CA 90403. Telephone: 310-829-9335. Frequency: m. Year First Published: 1979. Special Features: adv, bk rev, index. Circulation: 825. Price: $175.

Entertainment, Publishing and the Arts Handbook. ISSN: 0739-1897. Editor(s): Michael Meyer, John David Viera. Clark-Boardman-Callaghan Co. Ltd., 375 Hudson St., New York 10014. Telephone: 212-929-7500. FAX: 212-924-0460. Frequency: a. Price: $79.50.

Episodes (New York). Editor(s): Joanne Berg. Sponsoring Organization: Capital Cities-ABC Inc., 77 W. 66th St., New York 10023. Telephone: 212-456-6070. FAX: 212-456-6059. Frequency: bi-m. Year First Published: 1990. Special Features: adv. Circulation: 1,000,000. Price: $7.95.

Covers the lives and lifestyles of ABC daytime soap opera celebrities. Takes readers behind the scenes at the soaps.

Equipment Directory of Audio-Visual, Computer and Video Products. ISSN: 0884-2124. Editor(s): Kim Williams. Sponsoring Organization: International Communications Industries Association Inc., 3150 Spring St., Fairfax, VA 22031-2399. Telephone: 703-273-7200. Frequency: a. Year First Published: 1953. Special Features: charts, illus, stat, index. Circulation: 12,000. Price: $60 to commercial non-members.

Espectacular. Telephone: 215-455-8400. FAX: 215-455-8402. Frequency: m. Year First Published: 1987. Special Features: adv. Price: $20.
Covers entertainment news and events.

Etin. Editor(s): Jerry Cochrane. Sponsoring Organization: National Association of Regional Media Centers, Grant Wood AEA, 4401 6th St. S.W., Cedar Rapids, IA 52404. Telephone: 319-399-6741. FAX: 319-399-6457. Frequency: 8/yr. Year First Published: 1974. Special Features: adv. Circulation: 400. Price: Membership.
Informs members of current activities in the film and video world.

Euromedia Investor. ISSN: 1041-3014. Editor(s): Paul Kagan. Paul Kagan Associates Inc., 126 Clock Tower Place, Carmel, CA 93923. Telephone: 408-624-1536. FAX: 408-625-3225. Frequency: m. Year First Published: 1988. Price: $525.
Economic analysis of European cable and pay TV, with valuations of public and private companies involved in international media.

F Media!. ISSN: 0890-6718. Editor(s): Bruce F. Elving. FM Atlas Publishing, Box 24, Adolph, MN 55701. Telephone: 218-879-7676. Frequency: m. Year First Published: 1987. Circulation: 300. Price: $30 for six mos.
Contains fact and opinion about FM radio and related technologies.

FM Engineering Data Base. Sponsoring Organization: Federal Communications Commission, U.S. National Technical Information Service, 5825 Port Royal Rd., Springfield, VA 22161. Telephone: 703-487-4630. Frequency: m. Also available on diskette. Price: $360 per mo. in U.S., Canada, Mexico; elsewhere $720.
Presents records for existing and proposed stations, allocations, rulemaking petitions and proposals, as well as translators and boosters.

FM Engineering Data Base In Order by State. Sponsoring Organization: Federal Communications Commission, U.S. National Technical Information Service, 5825 Port Royal Rd., Springfield, VA 22161. Telephone: 703-487-4630. Frequency: m. Price: $20 per mo. in U.S., Canada, Mexico; elsewhere $40.
Includes vacant assignments, proposed rulemaking and foreign facilities.

FM Guide. ISSN: 0014-5971. Hampton International Communications Inc., 211 E. 43rd St., Suite 1306, New York 10017. Frequency: m. Year First Published: 1962. Special Features: adv, film rev, play rev. Circulation: 72,000. Price: $10.

Faces International. Editor(s): Nikki Laurel. GSG Publishing Inc., 10537 Santa Monica Blvd., 2nd Fl., Los Angeles 90025-4907. Telephone: 213-475-4990. FAX: 213-475-3935. Frequency: q. Year First Published: 1980. Special Features: adv. Circulation: 15,000. Price: $20.

Facets Features. ISSN: 0736-3745. Editor(s): Milos Stehlik. Facets Multimedia Inc., 1517 W. Fullerton Ave., Chicago 60614. Telephone: 312-281-9075. FAX: 312-929-5437. Frequency: bi-m. Year First Published: 1975. Special Features: adv, bk rev, film rev, illus. Circulation: 50,000. Price: $12.
Covers the world of international films and video, including new foreign, independent and classic releases.

Family Radio News. Editor(s): Richard Homeres. Sponsoring Organization: Family Stations Inc., 290 Hegenberger Rd., Oakland, CA 94621. Telephone: 800-543-1495. FAX: 510-633-7983. Frequency: q. Year First Published: 1966. Special Features: charts, illus. Circulation: 100,000. Price: Free.
Contains articles about the ministry of Family Radio as well as the program guide for the stations served.

Feedback. ISSN: 0147-4871. Editor(s): Jim Fletcher. Sponsoring Organization: Broadcast Education Association, 1771 N St., N.W., Washington, DC 20036-2891. Telephone: 202-429-5355. Frequency: q. Year First Published: 1977. Special Features: bk rev. Circulation: 1,000. Price: Membership only.
Provides a forum for the exchange of ideas among members on subjects relevant to educational programs and the industry.

Fiesta en Video. Editor(s): Ira Shuli, 331 Jeffrey Rd., Peterborough. NH 03458. Telephone: 603-924-7271. Frequency: m. Year First Published: 1990. Special Features: adv, film rev. Circulation: 100,000.
Lists new and available video movies in Spanish or with Spanish subtitles.

1590 Broadcaster. 1590 Broadcasting Corp., 502 W. Hollis St., Box 548, Nashua, NH 03061. Telephone: 603-889-1590. FAX: 603-883-4344. Frequency: w. Year First Published: 1964. Back issues available. Circulation: 63,500 (controlled). Price: $20.

Film & Video: The Production Magazine. ISSN: 1041-1933. Editor(s): David Swartz. Optic Music Inc., 8455 Beverly Blvd., Suite 508, Los Angeles 90048. Telephone: 213-653-8053. FAX: 213-653-8190. Frequency: m. Year First Published: 1984. Special Features: adv. Back issues available. Price: $50 (N. America $75; elsewhere $90).
Covers all areas of the production and post-production process within the teleproduction, commercial, music video and motion picture industries.

Film & Video Finder. Sponsoring Organization: National Information Center for Educational Media, Plexus Publishing Inc., 143 Old Marlton Pike, Medford, NJ 08055-8750. Telephone: 609-654-4888. FAX: 609-654-4309. Frequency: irreg., 3rd ed., 1991. Year First Published: 1987. Price: $295.
Lists 92,000 films and videos by subject heading outline and index. Includes subject section by title and distributor code, producers and distributors.

Film Literature Index ISSN: 0093-6758. Sponsoring Organization: Film and Television Documentation Center, State University of New York at Albany, Richardson 390C, 1400 Washington Ave., Albany, NY 12222. Telephone: 518-442-5745. FAX: 518-442-5232. Frequency: q. Year First Published: 1973. Special Features: bk rev, bibl. Circulation: 500. Price: $325 (foreign $350) includes bound a. cum.; bound a. cum. only $125 (foreign $135).
Indexes international periodical literature on film, television and video, by author and subject.

Film Threat Video Guide. Editor(s): David E. Williams. Sponsoring Organization: Film Threat Video, 2805 W. Magnolia, Burbank, CA 91505. Telephone: 818-848-8971. FAX: 818-848-5956. Frequency: 4/yr. Year First Published: 1991. Special Features: adv, illus. Circulation: 30,000. Price: $12 (foreign $22).
Source for what's new and unusual on video.

Fine Tuning. Editor(s): Steve Tighe. Channel 10-36 Friends Inc., Box 122, Milwaukee 53201. Telephone: 414-278-1468. FAX: 414-225-1895. Frequency: m. Year First Published: 1983. Special Features: adv. Circulation: 56,000. Price: $3.

Flip. Editor(s): Sue Kossoy. Flip Magazines Inc., 801 2nd Ave., New York 10017. Telephone: 212-661-7878. Frequency: m. Year First Published: 1990. Circulation: 100,000. Price: $12.95.
Covers movie and television celebrities and music groups popular with teenagers. Includes news about "Dance Party USA."

Florida State University Instructional Support Center: Film and Video. Editor(s): Peggy Stewart. Sponsoring Organization: Florida State University, Tallahassee, FL 32306-1019. Telephone: 904-644-2820. FAX: 904-644-3783. Frequency: biennial. Year First Published: 1954. Circulation: 5,000. Price: $5.

Folio (Berkeley). Editor(s): Richard Wolinsky. Sponsoring Organization: Pacifica Foundation, 1929 Martin Luther King Jr. Way, Berkeley, CA 94704. Telephone: 510-848-6767. FAX: 510-848-3812. Frequency: m. (except Sep.). Year First Published: 1949. Special Features: adv, bk rev. Back issues available. Circulation: 23,000. Price: $45.
Program guide for listener-sponsored KPFA-FM Pacifica community radio station.

Folio (North Hollywood). Editor(s): Jill Smolin. Sponsoring Organization: KPFK-FM (Pacifica Radio), 3729 Cahuenga Blvd., W., N. Hollywood, CA 91604. Telephone: 818-985-2711. Frequency: m. Year First Published: 1959?. Special Features: adv. Back issues available. Circulation: 16,000. Price: $50 membership.

Follow Up File. ISSN: 0888-3955. Editor(s): Steve Hess. Editorial Services Inc., 24 Vinka Ln., Irvington, NY 10333-2333. 914-591-6526. Frequency: w. Year First Published: 1975. Special Features: index. Back issues available. Price: $144.
News idea service for radio and TV stations, newspapers and magazines.

Free Press Network. Editor(s): Michael Grossberg. Sponsoring Organization: Free Press Association, Box 15548, Columbus, OH 43215. Telephone: 614-291-1441. Frequency: q. Year First Published: 1982. Special Features: adv, bk rev. Back issues available. Circulation: 400. Price: $25.
Debates First Amendment issues and reports on controversies in the area of communication.

Friction. Momentum Publishing Inc., Mavety Media Group Ltd., 462 Broadway, Suite 4000, New York 10013. Telephone: 212-966-8400. Frequency: m. Price: $36.

GBH: The Members' Magazine. Editor(s): Diane Dion. Sponsoring Organization: WGBH Educational Foundation, 125 Western Ave., Boston 02134. Telephone: 617-492-2578. Frequency: m. Year First Published: 1987. Special Features: adv. Circulation: 175,000. Price: Membership.
Program guide and magazine for members of WGBH, Boston's PBS and NPR station. All editorial is program-related and explores issues, events and people associated with station programming, which includes the arts, history and public affairs.

GMV. Editor(s): Ron Merrell. PSN Publications, United Newspapers Publications Ltd., 2 Park Ave., 18th Fl., New York 10016. Telephone: 212-213-3444. FAX: 212-213-3484. Frequency: m. Year First Published: 1989. Circulation: 8,335. Price: $30.
For video professionals in federal, state and city government and the military.

Gene Perret's Round Table: A Gathering Place for Comedy Writers and Humorists. Editor(s): Linda Perret, 2135 Huntington Dr., Suite 205, San Marino. CA 91031. Telephone: 818-796-4823. Frequency: m. Year First Published: 1981. Special Features: bk rev. Back issues available. Circulation: 200. Price: $49.95.

Get Ready Sheet. ISSN: 0148-7566. Sponsoring Organization: Mid-York Library System, c/o S.V. Wawraszek, Ed., 1600 Lincoln Ave., Utica, NY 13502. Telephone: 315-735-8328. Frequency: bi-w. Year First Published: 1976. Special Features: adv. Circulation: 1,300. Price: $28.

Giorno Poetry Systems LP's, CD's, Cassettes & Giorno Video Pak Series. Editor(s): John Giorno. Giorno Poetry Systems Institute Inc., 222 Bowery, New York 10012. Telephone: 212-925-6372. FAX: 212-966-7574. Frequency: s-a. Year First Published: 1967. Circulation: 17,000.
Poets working with performance, music and video.

Global Communications: The Magazine of Mobile Radio Products and Technology. ISSN: 0195-2250. Editor(s): Vibeke Holmes. Cardiff Publishing Co., 6300 S. Syracuse Way, Suite 650, Englewood, CO 80111. Telephone: 303-220-0600. Frequency: q. Year First Published: 1979. Reprint service available from UMI. Circulation: 10,000. Price: $19 (foreign $27).
Focuses on the international applications of radio technology.

Great American Video Business Newsletter. ISSN: 1051-6050. Editor(s): Vernon Parrish. V. Parrish Publishing, 1900 S. Eads St., Arlington, VA 22202. Telephone: 703-892-1993. Frequency: m. Year First Published: 1990. Special Features: adv. Price: $60.
Provides issue analysis, feature stories, market evaluations, business and product news, and strategies for the video businessperson.

HD World Review: Journal for High Definition and Advanced Television Technology. ISSN: 1055-6931. Editor(s): Corey Carbonara. Meckler Publishing Corp., 11 Ferry Lane W., Westport, CT 06880-5808. Telephone: 203-226-6967. Frequency: q. Year First Published: 1990. Price: $97.
Provides articles on television standards, government regulation of television, and technological trends in the HDTV area.

HDTV Report. ISSN: 1055-9280. Editor(s): Chris McConnell. Phillips Publishing Inc., 7811 Montrose Rd., Potomac, MD 20854. Telephone: 301-340-2100. FAX: 301-424-4297. Frequency: fortn. Year First Published: 1991. Price: $447.
Provides current information on developments in the U.S., Europe and Japan in all areas of the race toward all-digital television, including displays, transmission, production and broadcasting and computers.

Hastings Communications and Entertainment Law Journal (Comm-Ent). ISSN: 1061-6578. Editor(s): David S. Nagy. Sponsoring Organization: University of California, San Francisco, Hastings College of Law, 200

McAllister St.,San Francisco CA 94102-4978. Telephone: 415-565-4731. FAX: 415-565-4814. Frequency: q. Year First Published: 1977. Special Features: adv, bk rev, abstr, bibl, cum index every five yrs. Back issues available.; reprint service available from UMI,WSH. Circulation: 1,200. Price: $20 (foreign $22).

Covers telecommunications, broadcasting, cable and other non-broadcast video, the print media, defamation, advertising, the arts, entertainment, sports, computers and high-tech information services, copyright, patent, trademark and privacy.

Hola-Magazine. Editor(s): Mario G. Duenas. Spanish Publications Inc., 6802 Bintliff, Houston 77227-7923. Telephone: 713-774-4652. FAX: 713-774-4666. Frequency: w. Year First Published: 1977. Back issues available. Circulation: 60,000. Price: Free.

Television entertainment guide.

Hollywood Acting Coaches and Teachers Directory. Editor(s): Lawrence Parke. Acting World Books, Box 3044, Hollywood, CA 90078. Telephone: 818-905-1345. Frequency: q. Year First Published: 1984. Special Features: tr lit. Circulation: 2,000.

Contains a directory of all Hollywood acting instruction programs; includes biographies of instructors, articles about studying acting.

Hollywood Reporter Studio Blu-Book Directory. ISSN: 0278-419X. Editor(s): Alex Ben Block. H.R. Industries Inc., 6715 Sunset Blvd., Hollywood, CA 90028. Telephone: 213-469-8770. FAX: 213-464-7411. Frequency: a. Year First Published: 1978. Special Features: bk rev. Circulation: 3,000. Price: $55.

Home Shopping Investor. ISSN: 0890-1155. Paul Kagan Associates Inc., 126 Clock Tower Pl., Carmel, CA 93923. Telephone: 408-624-1536. FAX: 408-624-1536. Frequency: m. Year First Published: 1986. Price: $495.

Tracks home video retailing services with trends in TV merchandising, retailing and advertising. Covers industry profit margins, revenues and public stocks.

Home Viewer Magazine. Editor(s): Bruce Apar. Home Viewer Publications Inc., 8380 Old York Rd., Suite 404, Philadelphia 19117-1543. Telephone: 215-629-1558. Frequency: m. Year First Published: 1984.

Horn Speaker: The Newspaper for the Hobbyist of Vintage Electronics and Sound. ISSN: 0898-6959. Jim Cranshaw, Ed. & Pub., Box 1193, Mabank, TX 75147. Telephone: 214-848-0304. Frequency: m. (10/yr.). Year First Published: 1972. Special Features: adv, bk rev, bibl, illus, tr lit. Circulation: 1,500. Price: $12.50.

Discusses radios and phonographs for historical and collecting purposes.

IEEE Transactions on Broadcasting. ISSN: 0018-9316. Editor(s): Phil Rubin. Sponsoring Organization: IEEE, Institute of Electrical and Electronics Engineers Inc., 345 E. 47th St., New York 10017-2394. Telephone: 212-705-7366. FAX: 212-705-7682. Frequency: q. Year First Published: 1955. Special Features: bk rev, abstr, illus, index. Price: $50 to non-members.

Examines broadcast transmission systems engineering, including the design and utilization of equipment.

IEEE Transactions on Circuits and Systems for Video Technology. ISSN: 1051-8215. Editor(s): Ming Liou. Institute of Electrical and Electronics, Engineers Inc., 345 E. 47th St., New York 10017-2394. Telephone: 908-981-1393. FAX: 908-981-9667. Frequency: q. Year First Published: 1991. Price: $100 to non-members.

Covers video processing algorithms, real-time implementation, VLSI architecture and technology, and related topics.

INTV Newsletter. Editor(s): Lawrence Laurent. Sponsoring Organization: Association of Independent Television Stations Inc., INTV, 1200 18th St. N.W., Washington, DC 20036. Telephone: 202-887-1970. FAX: 202-887-0950. Frequency: bi-w. Year First Published: 1972. Special Features: bk rev. Circulation: 500. Price: qualified personnel only.

News for association members.

IRTS Gold Medal Journal. Sponsoring Organization: International Radio and Television Society Inc., 420 Lexington Ave., Suite 531, New York 10170. Telephone: 212-867-6650. FAX: 212-867-6653. Frequency: a. Year First Published: 1964. Special Features: adv. Price: Membership.

Imaging News. Capitol Publications Inc., Telecon, Publishing Group, 1101 King St., Suite 444, Box 1455, Alexandria, VA 22313-2055. Telephone: 800-327-7505. FAX: 703-739-6490. Frequency: 24/yr. Price: $380 (foreign $404).

Covers videoconferencing, high-resolution imaging and broadband services.

In Focus (Los Angeles). Editor(s): Russell Leong, Joyce Nako. Sponsoring Organization: Friends of Visual Communications, 263 S. Los Angeles St., Suite 307, Los Angeles 90012. 213-687-4848. Frequency: q. Year First Published: 1984. Special Features: film rev, video rev, illus. Circulation: 3,000. Price: $25 membership.

For supporters of Asian-American work in visual communications.

In Her Own Image: Films and Videos Empowering Women for the Future—A Media Network Guide. Sponsoring Organization: Alternative Media Information Center, Media Network, 39 W. 14th St., Suite 403, New York 10011. Telephone: 212-929-2663. FAX: 212-929-2732. Frequency: biennial. Special Features: illus.

Describes 82 films and videos listed by eight categories, indexed by subject, region, audience and title. Entries give title, producer, director, length, available language versions, year released, name of distributor, format and cost.

In Motion (Annapolis): Film and Video Production Magazine. ISSN: 0889-6208. Editor(s): Allison Dollar. In Motion Inc., 1203 West St., Annapolis, MD 21401. Telephone: 410-269-0605. FAX: 410-263-4615. Frequency: m. Year First Published: 1981. Special Features: adv. Back issues available. Circulation: 15,000. Price: $27.95.

Reports on equipment, trends and people in the film and video production industry. Covers production, post-production, talent and production support services as well as surveys of segments of the industry.

Independent Film and Video Monthly. ISSN: 0731-5198. Editor(s): Patricia Thomson. Sponsoring Organization: Association of Independent Video and Filmmakers Foundation for Independent Video & Film, 625 Broadway, 9th Fl., New York 10012. Telephone: 212-473-3400. FAX: 212-677-8732. Frequency: m. (10/yr.). Year First Published: 1978. Special Features: adv, bk rev. Back issues available. Circulation: 30,000. Price: $45 to individuals; libraries $75.

Covers the technical, legislative, marketing and artistic facets of film and video production (especially independent production), with book reviews, conference reports and announcements of festivals.

Independent Television. Editor(s): William H. Dunlap. Sponsoring Organization: Association of Independent Television Stations Inc., Crain Communications Inc. (New York), 220 E. 42nd St., New York 10017. Telephone: 212-210-0291. FAX: 212-210-0400. Frequency: q. Year First Published: 1990. Special Features: adv.

Inside Radio: The Latest News, Trends and Management Information. Editor(s): Jerry Del Colliano. Inside Radio Inc., 1930 E. Marlton Pike, Suite S-93, Cherry Hill, NJ 08003. Telephone: 609-424-6800. Frequency: d. Year First Published: vol.12, 1987. Price: $225.

Insiders Sportsletter. Editor(s): Louis O. Schwartz. Sponsoring Organization: American Sportscasters Association Inc., 5 Beekman St., Suite 814, New York 10038. Telephone: 212-227-8080. FAX: 212-571-0556. Frequency: bi-m. Year First Published: 1981. Special Features: adv, bk rev. Back issues available. Circulation: 2,500. Price: Membership.

Interlit. ISSN: 0020-5575. Editor(s): Gladys J. Peterson. David C. Cook Foundation, 850 N. Grove Ave., Elgin, IL 60120. Telephone: 708-741-2400. Frequency: q. Year First Published: 1964. Special Features: bk rev. Circulation: 7,000. Price: $2.50 (free to qualified personnel).

International Bluegrass. Editor(s): Jon Hartley Fox. Sponsoring Organization: International Bluegrass Music Association, 207 E. 2nd St., Owensboro, KY 42303. Telephone: 502-684-9025. FAX: 502-686-7863. Frequency: bi-m. Year First Published: 1985. Special Features: bk rev. Back issues available. Circulation: 1,000. Price: $20.

News, articles and how-to features aimed at bluegrass-music people working in radio.

International Cable. Editor(s): Robert Diddlebock. Transmedia Partners, 50 S. Steele, Suite 500, Denver 80209. Telephone: 303-355-2101. FAX: 303-355-2144. Frequency: bi-m. Year First Published: 1971. Special Features: adv, bk rev, charts, illus. Circulation: Controlled. Price: Free to qualified personnel.

International Callbook. Sponsoring Organization: Radio Amateur Callbook Inc., 1695 Oak St., Lakewood, NJ 08701-5925. Frequency: a. Year First Published: 1920. Special Features: adv. Price: $30 includes update Service Editions.

International Directory of Film and TV Documentation Centers. Editor(s): Frances Thorpe. Sponsoring Organization: International Federation of Film Archives, Gale Research Inc., St. James Press, 845 Penobscot Bldg., Detroit 48226-4232. Telephone: 800-877-4253. Frequency: irreg. Year First Published: 1988. Special Features: bk rev. Price: $45.

Describes more than 100 major collections (in over forty countries) of published and unpublished material relating to television and film.

International Telecommunications Energy Conference Proceedings. ISSN: 0275-0473. Sponsoring Organization: IEEE, Institute of Electrical and Electronics, Engineers Inc., 345 E. 47th St., New York 10017-2394. Telephone: 212-705-7900. FAX: 212-705-7682. Frequency: a. Year First Published: 1978.

Details state-of-the-art and future developments in the field of power supply for equipment and services.

International Television News. Editor(s): Deborah Moore. Sponsoring Organization: International Television Association, Fred Wehrli, Pub., 6311 N. O'Connor Rd., LB-51, Irving, TX 75039. Telephone: 214-869-1112. FAX: 214-869-2980. Frequency: m. Year First Published: 1970. Special Features: adv, bk rev. Circulation: 8,500. Price: Membership.

Carries articles about industry issues and trends for video professionals in the non-broadcast arena. Details association events.

International Television & Video Almanac: Reference Tool of the Television and Home Video Industries. Editor(s): Barry Monush. Sponsoring Organization: Quigley Publishing Co., 159 W. 53 St., New York 10019. Telephone: 212-247-3100. FAX; 212-489-0871. Frequency: a. Year First Published: 1956. Price: $85.

Journal of Broadcasting and Electronic Media. ISSN: 0883-8151. Editor(s): Jim Potter. Sponsoring Organization: Broadcast Education Association, 1771 N St. N.W., Washington, DC 20036. Frequency: q. Year First Published: 1956. Special Features: bk rev, charts, index, cum index every 25 yrs. Reprint service available from UMI, WSH. Circulation: 2,200. Price: Varies.

Scholarly journal of communication and electronic media research, including media uses, effect, regulation, history, organization, advertising, technology, news and entertainment.

Journal of College Radio. ISSN: 0010-1133. Editor(s): Jeffrey N. Tellis. Sponsoring Organization: Intercollegiate Broadcasting System Inc., Box 592, Vails Gate, NY 12584-0592. Telephone: 914-565-6710. FAX: 914-561-6932. Frequency: 4/yr. Year First Published: 1941-1982; 1984-1987; resumed 1989. Special Features: adv, bk rev, abstr, charts, illus, tr lit. Circulation: 2,500. Price: $12.

Contains articles for and about college radio stations.

Journal of Film and Video. ISSN: 0742-4671. Sponsoring Organization: University Film and Video Association, c/o Georgia State University, Dept. of Communication, Atlanta 30303. Frequency: q. Year First Published: 1947. Special Features: film rev, index, cum index. Back issues available. Circulation: 1,300. Price: $15 (foreign $24).

Scholarly articles on film and video.

KCTS-Nine. ISSN: 1050-513X. Editor(s): Linda Johns, 2505 2nd Ave., Suite 602, Seattle 98121-2384. Telephone: 206-441-8415. FAX: 206-441-8325. Frequency: m. Year First Published: 1987. Special Features: adv. Circulation: 150,000.

Television program guide distributed to contributors to KCTS-9, with additional articles on arts, travel and personalities.

KPBS on Air. Sponsoring Organization: KPBS-TV and FM Radio, San Diego State University, San Diego 92182-0001. Telephone: 619-293-3490. FAX: 619-293-3494. Frequency: m. Year First Published: 1969. Special Features: adv. Circulation: 59,033. Price: $35.

Contains radio and TV listings and highlights of San Francisco's cultural events, leisure activities and dining establishments.

Kagan Census of Cable and Pay TV: Semi-Annual Compilation of Basic Cable and TV Subscribers. ISSN: 0732-2283. Editor(s): Antonio Iniguez. Paul Kagan Associates Inc., 126 Clock Tower Place, Carmel, CA 93923. Telephone: 408-624-1536. FAX: 408-625-3225. Frequency: s-a. Year First Published: 1975. Special Features: adv, charts, stat. Back issues available. Price: $450.

LPTV Reporter: Translator & Low Power TV News & Affairs. Sponsoring Organization: Television Center Inc., Box 9, Phoenicia, NY 12464. Frequency: m. Year

First Published: 1981. Special Features: adv, bibl, charts, illus, index. Back issues available. Circulation: 1,500. Price: $65.

Ladyslipper Catalog and Resource Guide of Records, Tapes, Compact Discs and Videos by Women. Editor(s): Laurie Fuchs. Sponsoring Organization: Ladyslipper Inc., Box 3124, Durham, NC 27715. Telephone: 919-682-5601. Frequency: a. Year First Published: 1976. Special Features: adv, film rev, index. Back issues available. Circulation: 250,000. Price: Free.

Lewis Letter on Cable Marketing. Editor(s): Eiken Willner. Sponsoring Organization: Lewis Associates Inc., 292 Main St., Great Barrington, MA 01230. Telephone: 413-528-9445. Frequency: m. Year First Published: 1977. Back issues available. Price: $95.

Marketing, public relations and advertising advice for cable companies.

Linking Up: An Idea Exchange for Cable Professionals. Editor(s): Sally Follem. Sponsoring Organization: National Cable Television Association, 1724 Massachusetts Ave. N.W., Washington, DC 20036. Telephone: 202-775-3550. Frequency: bi-m. Year First Published: 1989. Price: Membership only.

Location Update: The Magazine of Film and Video Production. Location Update Inc., 6922 Hollywood Blvd., Suite 612, Hollywood, CA 90028. Telephone: 213-461-8887. FAX: 213-469-3711. Frequency: m. Year First Published: 1985. Special Features: adv. Circulation: 30,000 (controlled). Price: $25.95 (foreign $49.95).

Covers elements that evolve when filming and video taping on local and distant location, as well as studios and soundstages.

Look-Listen Project Report. Editor(s): Marieli Rowe. Sponsoring Organization: National Telemedia Council Inc., 120 E. Wilson St., Madison, WI 53703. Telephone: 608-257-7712. Frequency: irreg. Year First Published: 1953. Circulation: 400. Price: Varies.

Lowdown. Editor(s): Ken Stryker. Sponsoring Organization: Longwave Club of America, 45 Wildflower Rd., Levittown, PA 19057. Frequency: m.

Lurzer's International Archive: Ads, TV and Posters World-Wide. ISSN: 0893-0260. Editor(s): Walter Lurzer, Ann Middlebrook. Sponsoring Organization: American Showcase, 915 Broadway, Suite 14, New York 10010-7108. Telephone: 212-673-6600. FAX: 212-673-9795. Frequency: bi-m. Year First Published: 1984. Special Features: adv, illus, tr lit. Back issues available. Circulation: 7,300. Price: $43.97.

Presents international TV commercials and print ad campaigns. Covers 24 categories of ads.

M Street Journal. ISSN: 1052-7109. Editor(s): Robert Unmacht. M Street Corp., 304 Park Ave. S., 7th Fl., New York 10010. Telephone: 212-473-4668. FAX: 212-473-4626. Frequency: w. Price: $99 (includes The M Street Radio Directory).

Reports on AM and FM stations' format, technical, call letter and ownership changes; covers major decisions and actions taken by the FCC regarding radio broadcasting each week.

M Street Radio Directory. ISSN: 1052-7117. Editor(s): Robert Unmacht. M Street Corp., 340 Park Ave. S., 7th Fl., New York 10010. Telephone: 212-473-4668. FAX: 212-473-4626. Frequency: a. Price: $32.95.

A guide to all radio stations in the U.S. and Canada.

MAIN. Sponsoring Organization: National Alliance for Media Arts and Culture, 1212 Broadway, No. 816, Oakland, CA 94612. Telephone: 510-451-2717. FAX: 510-834-3741. Frequency: m. Year First Published: 1991. Price: Membership only.

Made for Video. Editor(s): Phil Fora. Location Promotion Guide, Box 617024, Orlando, FL 32861-7024. Telephone: 407-295-1094. Frequency: bi-m. Year First Published: 1992. Circulation: 2,500.

Production-oriented news and information, for makers of feature films, documentaries and other items on video.

Marine Data Base. Sponsoring Organization: Federal Communications Commission, U.S. National Technical Information Service, 5825 Port Royal Rd., Springfield, VA 22161. Telephone: 703-487-4630. Frequency: q. Price: $3,000 for 1600 bpi in U.S., Canada, Mexico; elsewhere $6,000.

Contains data for applicants and licensees operating under the Marine (Telephone) Radio Service.

Marine Radio Station Master File. Sponsoring Organization: Federal Communications Commission, U.S. National Technical Information Service, 5825 Port Royal Rd., Springfield, VA 22161. Telephone: 703-487-4630. Frequency: q. Price: $25 per mo. in U.S., Canada, Mexico; elsewhere $40.

Data sorted in vessel name sequence. Cross-reference indexes included by name of licensee, call sign, state and city, treasury number.

Markee. Editor(s): Janet Karcher. HJK Publications Inc., 655 Fulton St., Suite 9, Sanford, FL 32771. Telephone: 407-324-1733. FAX: 407-324-1766. Frequency: m. Year First Published: 1986. Special Features: adv. Circulation: 13,800. Price: $24.

For the Southeast and Southwest film and video industries.

Marketing New Media. ISSN: 0743-2178. Editor(s): Paul Kagan. Paul Kagan Associates Inc., 126 Clock Tower Pl., Carmel, CA 93923. Telephone: 408-624-1536. FAX: 408-624-1536. Frequency: m. Year First Published: 1984. Price: $425.

Covers sales and promotion of cable TV, pay cable, SMATV, MDS, DBS and STV. Provides analysis of subscriber totals, detailed explanations of marketing techniques and tracks the trends in competitive media.

Media Guide (Cleveland). Sponsoring Organization: Federation for Community Planning, 614 Superior Ave. W., Suite 300, Cleveland 44113-1306. Telephone: 216-781-2944. FAX: 216-781-2988. Frequency: a. Year First Published: 1954. Circulation: 1,200. Price: $15.

Directory of local print and broadcast media along with advice on accessing media.

Media Sports Business. ISSN: 0889-0951. Editor(s): John Mansell. Paul Kagan Associates Inc., 126 Clock Tower Place, Carmel, CA 93923. Telephone: 408-624-1536. Frequency: m. Year First Published: 1982. Special Features: charts, index. Price: $425.

Newsletter on the economic power struggle among sports teams and the electronic media. Analysis of the value of sports media rights.

Media Studies Journal. ISSN: 1057-7416. Editor(s): Edward C. Pease. Sponsoring Organization: Columbia University, Freedom Forum Media Studies Center, 2950 Broadway, New York 10027. Telephone: 212-678-6600. FAX: 212-678-6661. Frequency: q. Year First Published: 1987. Special Features: bk rev. Back issues available. Circulation: 9,000. Price: $20.

For scholars, practitioners and informed commentators. Discusses mass communications issues of importance to the media and the public.

Millimeter: The Magazine of the Motion Picture and Television Production Industries. ISSN: 0164-9655. Editor(s): Alison Johns. Penton Publishing (New York), Pittway Co., 826 Broadway, New York 10003. Telephone: 212-477-4700. Frequency: m. Year First Published: 1973. Special Features: adv, bk rev, film rev. Circulation: 30,000. Price: $60.

Reports on the motion picture and TV production industries for production professionals involved in the commissioning, shooting and postproduction of commercials, programming and movies. Feature articles cover aspects of creative process.

Mobile Radio Technology. ISSN: 0745-7626. Editor(s): Don Bishop. Intertec Publishing Corp., 9800 Metcalf, Overland Park, KS 66212-2215. Telephone: 913-341-1300. FAX: 913-967-1898. Frequency: m. Year First Published: 1983. Special Features: adv, bk rev, tr lit. Circulation: 24,458. Price: $30 (free to qualified personnel).

Monitor Month: A Global Voice. Christian Science Publishing Society, One Norway St., Boston 02115. Telephone: 617-450-2000. Frequency: m.

Monitoring Times. ISSN: 0889-5341. Editor(s): Rachel Baughn. Grove Enterprises Inc., Box 98, Brasstown, NC 28902. Telephone: 704-837-9200. FAX: 704-837-2216. Frequency: m. Year First Published: 1982. Special Features: adv, bk rev, index. Back issues available. Circulation: 30,000. Price: $19.95.

News on radio communications, scanner monitoring, with loggings, international radio broadcast schedules, station, program, product, personality, technological profiles and technical advice.

Motion Picture, TV & Theatre Directory: For Services & Products. ISSN: 0580-0412. M.P.E. Publications Inc., Box 10591. Telephone: 212-245-0969. FAX: 212-245-0974. Frequency: s-a. Year First Published: 1960. Special Features: adv. Back issues available. Circulation: 73,200. Price: $15.90.

Directory of the motion picture and television industries. Primarily concerns preproduction, production and postproduction (products, services, equipment) of film and video.

Movie Marketplace. Editor(s): Robert Meyers. World Publishing Co., Century Publishing Co., 990 Grove St., Evanston, IL 60201-4370. Telephone: 708-491-6440. Frequency: bi-m. Year First Published: 1987. Special Features: adv. Circulation: 125,000. Price: $19.94 (foreign $24).

Includes feature articles and video listings of over 5,000 titles available for direct purchase.

Multicast: The Newsletter on Multipoint Distribution Service. ISSN: 0146-0099. Editor(s): George Eagle. Paul Kagan Associates Inc., 126 Clock Tower Place, Carmel, CA 93923. Telephone: 408-624-1536. Frequency: m. Year First Published: 1972. Special Features: charts, index. Price: $395.

Covers MDS, the FCC-regulated common carrier for pay TV and data services.

Multichannel News. ISSN: 0276-8593. Editor(s): Marianne Paskowski. Capital Cities-ABC Inc., Diversified Publishing Group, 825 7th Ave., New York 10019. Telephone: 212-887-8398. Frequency: w. Year First Published: 1980. Special Features: adv, index. Circulation: 15,000. Price: $65 (foreign $195).

Covers all the related fields of cable television industry: programming, pay per view, marketing and promotion, advertising sales, technology, operations, customer service, policy and business.

Multimedia and Videodisc Monitor. ISSN: 1054-7258. Editor(s): Rockley L. Miller. Future Systems Inc., Box 26, Falls Church, VA 22040. Telephone: 703-241-1799. FAX: 703-532-0529. Frequency: m. Year First Published: 1983. Special Features: adv, bk rev. Back issues available. Circulation: 3,000. Price: $347 to individuals; educational institutions $150.

Music Video Magazine. ISSN: 1065-0229. Editor(s): David Bernstein, Ed. & Pub., Box 17705, Irvine, CA 92713. Telephone: 714-262-9336. Frequency: m. Year First Published: 1991. Special Features: adv.

Provides coverage of the music video industry.

NABET News. ISSN: 0027-5697. Editor(s): John J. Krieger. Sponsoring Organization: National Association of Broadcast Employees and Technicians, AFL-CIO, 7101 Wisconsin Ave., Suite 800, Bethesda, MD 20814. Telephone: 301-659-8420. FAX: 301-657-9478. Frequency: bi-m. Year First Published: 1975. Special Features: illus. Circulation: 9,500. Price: $2.

NATPE Programmer. Editor(s): Bill Strubbe. Sponsoring Organization: National Association of Television Program Executives, 2425 Olympic Blvd., Suite 550E, Santa Monica, CA 90404-4030. Frequency: 10/yr. Year First Published: 1965. Special Features: adv. Circulation: 2,400. Price: $25.

NCTV News: Violence Should Always Be Gently But Firmly Protested. ISSN: 0739-6767. Editor(s): Dir. Dr. Carole Lieberman. Sponsoring Organization: National Coalition on Television Violence, Box 2157, Champaign, IL 61825. Telephone: 217-384-1920. Frequency: bi-m. Year First Published: 1980. Special Features: bk rev, film rev, tele rev, stat. Circulation: 11,000. Price: $25.

Discusses issues and events relating to efforts to monitor and minimize violence in film and television, with reports on coalition activities, research and surveys, significant legislation and ratings of specific films and TV programs.

NJN Guide. NJ Public Broadcasting, CN 777, Trenton, NJ 08625. Frequency: m. Price: $30.

NRC FM Radio Log. ISSN: 1054-7444. NRC Publications, Box 164, Mannsville, NY 13661-0164. Frequency: a. Year First Published: 1991.

NTCA Exchange. Editor(s): Lisa Westbrook. Sponsoring Organization: National Telephone Cooperative Association, 2626 Pennsylvania Ave. N.W., Washington, DC 20037. Telephone: 202-298-2300. FAX: 202-298-2320. Frequency: bi-m. Year First Published: 1982. Circulation: 4,200. Price: $10.

National News. Sponsoring Organization: Association of Independent Commercial Producers, Kaufman Astoria Studios, 12 West End Ave., 5th Fl., New York 10023-7841. Telephone: 718-392-2427. FAX: 718-361-9366. Frequency: q.

For those involved with various aspects of television commercial production.

National Radio Publicity Outlets. Editor(s): Russell Perkins. Morgan-Rand Publishing Co., 2200 Sansom St., Philadelphia 19103. Telephone: 215-557-8200. FAX: 215-557-8414. Frequency: s-a. Year First Published: 1972. Special Features: adv. Price: $90.

Network Futures & ProLog. Television Index Inc., 40-29 27th St., Long Island City, NY 11101. Telephone: 718-937-3990. Frequency: w. Price: $100.

New York Casting—Survival Guide and Datebook. Editor(s): Chip Brill. Peter Glenn Publications Inc., 42 W. 38th St., Suite 802, New York 10018. Telephone: 212-869-2020. FAX: 212-869-3287. Frequency: a. Year First Published: 1980. Special Features: adv. Price: $15.95.
Resource tool for performing artists.

NewMedia Age: Technologies for the Professional Communicator. Editor(s): Ben Calica. HyperMedia Communications Inc., 901 Mariners Island, Suite 365, San Mateo, CA 94404. Telephone: 415-573-5170. FAX: 408-773-8309. Frequency: q. Year First Published: 1991. Circulation: 40,000 (controlled). Price: $24 (Canada and Mexico $70; elsewhere $100).
Covers new products and technology trends in audio, video and computing.

News-Broadcast Network. Editor(s): Thomas Hill, 9431 Beloit Rd., Milwaukee 53227-4365. Telephone: 414-321-6210. FAX: 414-321-3608. Frequency: q. Circulation: 2,000.

NewsBank Review of the Arts: Film and Television. ISSN: 0737-3988. NewsBank Inc., 58 Pine St., New Canaan, CT 06840-5426. Telephone: 203-966-1100. FAX: 203-966-6254. Frequency: m. (plus q. and a. cum.). Year First Published: 1972. Price: Varies.

Nielsen Newscast. ISSN: 0468-1835. Editor(s): L. Frerk. Nielsen Media Research, Nielsen Plaza, Northbrook, IL 60062. Telephone: 708-498-6300. Frequency: s-a. Year First Published: 1950. Special Features: charts, illus. Circulation: 11,500. Price: Free.
TV audience data, trends, product improvements and media and advertising information.

Nielsen Report on Television. Editor(s): L. Frerk. Nielsen Media Research, Nielsen Plaza, Northbrook, IL 60062. Frequency: a. Year First Published: 1955. Reprint service available. Circulation: 27,000. Price: Free.
Summary of program audiences, trends and related data on cable and VCR usage.

North American Callbook. Sponsoring Organization: Radio Amateur Callbook Inc., 1695 Oak St., Lakewood, NJ 08701-5925. Frequency: a. Year First Published: 1920. Special Features: adv. Price: $28.
Now includes Canada, U.S. and Mexico.

ONSAT-America's Weekly Satellite Guide. Editor(s): Jim H. Cothran. Triple D Publishing Inc., 1300 S. DeKalb St., Box 2347, Shelby, NC 28151-2384. Telephone: 704-482-9673. Frequency: w. Year First Published: 1984. Special Features: adv. Circulation: 290,000. Price: $49.97.
Includes listings and articles concerning satellite TV programming.

Official Video Directory & Buyer's Guide. ISSN: 0890-782X. Editor(s): Steve Tolin. Palm Springs Media Inc., Box 2740, Palm Springs, CA 92263. Telephone: 619-322-3050. FAX: 619-322-1260. Frequency: a. Year First Published: 1987. Special Features: adv. Circulation: 6,000. Price: $125.
Sourcebook of suppliers and manufacturers of video hardware and software.

On Location Directory: The National Film & Videotape Production Directory. Editor(s): Steven Bernard. On Location Publishing, Box 4147, Torrance, CA 90510-4147. Frequency: a. Year First Published: 1977. Price: $75.

On Location Magazine: The Film & Videotape Production Magazine. ISSN: 0149-7014. Editor(s): Steven Bernard. On Location Publishing, Box 4147, Torrance, CA 90510-4147. Telephone: 213-467-1268. Frequency: m. Year First Published: 1977. Special Features: adv. Price: $66.

One to One (Fresno): The Journal of Creative Broadcasting. Editor(s): Jay Trachman. CreeYadio Services, Box 9787, Fresno, CA 93794. Telephone: 209-226-0558. FAX: 209-226-7481. Frequency: w. Year First Published: 1976. Special Features: adv, index. Back issues available. Circulation: 3,000. Price: $150.
Provides radio talent with guidance in delivery techniques; plus weekly humor, calendar and "Today in History" promotions, and artist biography.

One to One II. Editor(s): Linda Richardson. CreeYadio Services, Box 9787, Fresno, CA 93794. Telephone: 209-226-0558. FAX: 209-226-7481. Frequency: m. Year First Published: 1977. Back issues available. Circulation: 300. Price: $65.
Contains humorous items for on-air and public speaking.

Orbit Video. Editor(s): Phillip Swann. Orbit Publishing, CommTek Publishing Co. Inc., 8330 Boone Blvd., Suite 600, Vienna, VA 22180. Telephone: 703-827-0511. Frequency: m. Year First Published: 1989. Price: $28.
Contains reviews of approximately 100 new video releases, ratings that describe movie content and information on video equipment.

Orbiter. Sponsoring Organization: Society of Satellite Professionals International, 2200 Wilson Blvd., No. 102-258, Arlington, VA 22201. Telephone: 703-243-8948. Frequency: bi-m. Back issues available. Circulation: 800. Price: Membership.
Articles and news on the satellite industry.

PC Videolog. Phonolog Publishing, Trade Service Corp., 10996 Torreyana Rd., Box 85007, San Diego 92138. Telephone: 619-457-5920. Frequency: m. updates on diskette. Year First Published: 1988. Price: $240.

PRC News: A Weekly News in Brief for the Video Industry. ISSN: 0898-302X. Editor(s): Deborah Rolfe. Corbell Publishing, 2554 Lincoln Blvd., Suite 1015, Marina Del Rey, CA 90291. Telephone: 310-821-6675. FAX: 310-641-9769. Frequency: w. Year First Published: 1988. Special Features: adv, charts, illus. Back issues available; reprint service available. Circulation: 2,000. Price: $397.
Covers news, mergers and acquisitions, people on the move, calender of events, statistics, new releases and sell-through products.

Palmer Video Magazine. Editor(s): Susan Baar, Mary Schwartz. Palmer Video Corp., 1767 Morris Ave., Union, NJ 07083. Telephone: 908-686-3030. FAX: 908-686-2151. Frequency: m. Year First Published: 1981. Special Features: adv, video rev. Circulation: 203,915 (controlled). Price: $15.

Passport to World Band Radio. ISSN: 0897-0157. Editor(s): Lawrence Magne. Sponsoring Organization: International Broadcasting Services, Ltd., IBS Ltd., 825 Cherry Lane, Box 300, Penn's Park, PA 18943. Telephone: 215-794-3410. FAX: 215-794-3396. Frequency: a. Year First Published: 1984. Special Features: adv, charts. Circulation: 80,000. Price: $19.90.
Refers to news, sports and entertainment shortwave broadcasts available from abroad.

Pay-Per-View Update. Editor(s): Dantia Gould. QV Publishing Inc., Meadowbrook Office Park, Box 2000, York, ME 03909. Telephone: 207-363-6222. FAX: 207-363-6182. Frequency: s-m. Year First Published: 1983. Special Features: index. Back issues available. Price: $325.
Covers trends in pay-per-view television programming.

Pay TV Movie Log. Paul Kagan Associates Inc., 126 Clock Tower Plaza, Carmel, CA 93923. Telephone: 408-624-1536. FAX: 408-624-1536. Frequency: m.
Includes survey of movie product playing on eight cable services.

Pay TV Newsletter: The Newsletter on Developments in Pay Television. ISSN: 0146-0072. Editor(s): Larry Gerbrandt. Paul Kagan Associates Inc., 126 Clock Tower Place, Carmel, CA 93923. Telephone: 408-624-1536. Frequency: m. Year First Published: 1973. Special Features: charts, index. Price: $575.
Covers cable, over-the-air and direct satellite with analysis of the industry's subscribers, revenues and profits.

Perfect Vision. ISSN: 0895-4143. Editor(s): Harry Pearson. Pearson Publishing Enterprises, Box 357, Sea Cliff, NY 11579. Telephone: 516-676-2830. FAX: 516-676-5469. Frequency: 4/yr. Year First Published: 1986. Special Features: adv. Circulation: 13,000. Price: $22.

Performance Guide. Editor(s): Louis Marroquin, 1203 Lake St., Suite 200, Ft. Worth. TX 76102-4504. Telephone: 817-338-9444. Frequency: m.

Power Media Selects. ISSN: 1045-9545. Broadcast Interview Source, 2233 Wisconsin Ave., N.W., Washington, DC 20007. Telephone: 202-333-4904. Frequency: s-a. Year First Published: 1989. Price: $166.50.

Private Cable Plus Wireless Cable. Sponsoring Organization: National Satellite Publishing Inc., 1909 Ave. G, Box 1489, Rosenberg, TX 77471-2535. Telephone: 713-342-9826. FAX: 713-342-2488. Frequency: m. Year First Published: 1982. Circulation: 12,200. Price: $18 (foreign $95).

Producer. Editor(s): Ken McGorry. Testa Communications Inc., 25 Willowdale Ave., Port Washington, NY 11050. Telephone: 516-767-2500. FAX: 516-767-9335. Frequency: bi-m. Year First Published: 1990. Special Features: charts, illus, stat, tr lit. Back issues available. Circulation: 15,000. Price: $15.
For producers, directors, editors, videographers, composers–all creative people.

Psychotronic Video. Editor(s): Michael Weldon, 151 First Ave., New York 10003. Telephone: 212-533-0500. Frequency: 4/yr. Year First Published: 1991. Special Features: film rev, video rev. Price: $3.50 per mo.
Covers unusual film and video releases.

Public Broadcasting Report. ISSN: 0193-3663. Editor(s): Jeff Kole. Warren Publishing Inc., 2115 Ward Ct., N.W., Washington, DC 20037. Telephone: 202-872-9200. FAX: 202-293-3435. Frequency: bi-w. Year First Published: 1978. Special Features: index. Price: $390 (foreign $411).

Public Radio Legal Handbook. Sponsoring Organization: National Federation of Community Broadcasters, 666 11th St. N.W., Suite 805, Washington, DC 20001. Telephone: 202-393-2355. Frequency: irreg. Special Features: index. Price: $75 to non-members; members $50.
Reference checklist and explanation of the rules and regulations concerning regular station operation.

Public Television Transcripts. Index ISSN: 0897-9642. Research Publications Inc. (Woodbridge), 12 Lunar Dr., Drawer AB, Woodbridge, CT 06525. Telephone: 203-397-2600. FAX: 203-397-3893. Frequency: q. (with a. cumulation). Year First Published: 1987. Back issues available. Price: $175.
Index to transcripts of Public Television news programs available in microfiche.

Pyramid Film and Video Catalog. Editor(s): Julie Lawson. Sponsoring Organization: Pyramid Film & Video, Box 1048, Santa Monica, CA 90406-1048. Telephone: 310-828-7577. FAX: 310-453-9083. Frequency: biennial. Year First Published: 1960. Special Features: film rev. Circulation: 60,000. Price: Free.
Lists a variety of films and videos distributed by Pyramid.

QCWA Journal. Editor(s): J.C. Walsh. Sponsoring Organization: Quarter Century Wireless Association Inc., 159 E. 16th Ave., Eugene, OR 97401-4017. Telephone: 503-683-0987. FAX: 503-683-4181. Frequency: q. Year First Published: 1954. Special Features: adv, bk rev. Circulation: 9,500. Price: Membership.

QEXARRL Experimenters' Exchange. Editor(s): John Bloom. Sponsoring Organization: American Radio Relay League Inc., 225 Main St., Newington, CT 06111. Frequency: m. Circulation: 4,000. Price: $12 to members.

QST: Devoted Entirely to Amateur Radio. ISSN: 0033-4812. Editor(s): Mark Wilson. American Radio Relay League Inc., 225 Main St., Newington, CT 06111. Telephone: 203-666-1541. FAX: 203-665-7531. Frequency: m. Year First Published: 1915. Special Features: adv, bk rev, charts, illus, index. Reprint service available from UMI. Circulation: 160,000. Price: $30.

QT—Quarterly Two-Way Transmissions. Editor(s): Kenton Sturdevant. Forest Industries Telecommunications, 871 Country Club Rd., Suite A, Eugene, OR 97401-6009. Telephone: 503-485-8441. FAX: 503-485-7556. Frequency: q. Circulation: 5,000.

Quarterly Review of Film and Video. ISSN: 1050-9208. Editor(s): Michael Renov. Harwood Academic Publishers, 270 8th Ave., New York 10011. Telephone: 212-206-8900. FAX: 212-645-2459. Frequency: 4/yr. (in one vol., four mos./vol.). Year First Published: 1976. Special Features: bk rev, index. Reprint service available from UMI.

RCMA Journal. Editor(s): Carol Ruth. Sponsoring Organization: Radio Communications Monitoring Association, Box 542, Silverado, CA 92676. Frequency: m. Year First Published: 1975. Special Features: adv, bk rev, index. Circulation: 2,100. Price: $24 (foreign $28).

RCR Cellular Handbook. ISSN: 1060-0868. Editor(s): Nancy Kuehl. RCR Publications Inc., 777 E. Speer Blvd., Denver 80203-4214. Telephone: 303-832-6000. FAX: 303-832-5043. Frequency: biennial. Year First Published: 1977. Special Features: adv, index.
Provides information for the cellular communications industry, including listings of manufacturers, service providers, representatives, distributors and cellular operators.

RCR Paging Handbook. RCR Publications Inc., 777 E. Speer Blvd., Denver 80203-4214. Telephone: 303-832-6000. FAX: 303-832-5043. Frequency: biennial. Year First Published: 1977. Special Features: adv.

RTCA Digest. ISSN: 0193-4422. Sponsoring Organization: Radio Technical Commission for Aeronautics, RTCA Inc., 1140 Connecticut Ave. N.W., Suite 1020, Washington, DC 20036-4001. Telephone: 202-833-9339. FAX: 202-833-9434. Frequency: q. Year First Published: 1965. Circulation: 3,600.

RTNDA Communicator. ISSN: 0033-7153. Editor(s): Joe Tieman. Sponsoring Organization: Radio-Television News Directors Association, 1717 K St. N.W., Washington, DC 20006. Telephone: 202-659-6510. FAX: 202-223-4007. Frequency: m. Year First Published: 1946. Special Features: adv, bk rev, abstr, bibl, illus. Circulation: 4,200. Price: $65.

RTS Video Gazette. RTS, Box 93897, Las Vegas 89193-3897. Telephone: 702-896-1300. Frequency: m. Year First Published: 1985. Price: $15.

Industry insider's column of latest trends, new releases and information on pricing. Also covers obscure titles available for sale, including silents, serials, B movies in all genres, foreign and cult films.

RTTY Journal. ISSN: 0033-7161. Editor(s): Dale S. Sinner. RTTY Journal, 9085 La Casita Ave., Fountain Valley, CA 92708. Telephone: 714-847-5058. FAX: 714-892-2720. Frequency: 10/yr. Year First Published: 1953. Special Features: adv, bk rev, charts, illus, tr lit, index, cum index: 1956-1980. Circulation: 5,700. Price: $16 (foreign $32).

Covers amateur radio teletype, including RTTY, AMTOR, PACTOR, packet radio, news, hardware and software and other technical information affecting ham radio.

Radio Advertising Bureau Radio Facts. Sponsoring Organization: Radio Advertising Bureau, 304 Park Ave. S., 7th Fl., New York 10010. Telephone: 212-254-4800. FAX: 212-254-8713. Frequency: a. Circulation: 40,000. Price: $10 to non-members.

Statistical overview of the U.S. commercial radio industry. Includes comparison of radio advertising with that in other media.

Radio Advertising Bureau Retail Marketing Kit. Sponsoring Organization: Radio Advertising Bureau, 304 Park Ave. S., 7th Fl., New York 10010. Telephone: 212-254-4800. FAX: 212-254-8713. Frequency: m.

Radio Amateur's Handbook. ISSN: 0079-9440. Editor(s): Mark Wilson. Sponsoring Organization: American Radio Relay League Inc., 225 Main St., Newington, CT 06111. Telephone: 203-666-1541. FAX: 203-665-7531. Frequency: a. Year First Published: 1926. Special Features: illus, index. Circulation: 45,000. Price: $25 hardcover.

Radio Business Report. Box 782, Springfield. VA 22150. Telephone: 703-866-9300. FAX: 703-866-9306. Frequency: w. Year First Published: 1983. Special Features: adv. Circulation: 5,200. Price: $215 to non-members; members $189.

Covers radio and communications business and news for radio station and advertising personnel.

Radio-Chicago. ISSN: 1044-9647. Editor(s): Donna Walters. Radio-Chicago Inc., 431 S. Dearborn St., No. 1304, Chicago 60605-1152. Telephone: 312-939-5480. FAX: 312-341-0222. Frequency: q. Year First Published: 1989. Special Features: adv. Circulation: 15,000. Price: $12.

Covers radio personalities and events in the Chicago metropolitan market.

Radio Club of America Proceedings. ISSN: 0033-779X. Sponsoring Organization: Radio Club of America Inc., c/o John Morrisey, Ed., 45 S. 5th St., Park Ridge, NJ 07656. Telephone: 201-391-7664. Frequency: s-a. Year First Published: 1920. Special Features: adv, bk rev, illus, index. Circulation: 1,500. Price: $15 to non-members.

Radio Co-op Sources. Sponsoring Organization: Radio Advertising Bureau, 304 Park Ave. S., 7th Fl., New York 10010. Telephone: 212-254-4800. FAX: 212-254-8713. Frequency: a. Year First Published: 1978. Circulation: 5,000. Price: $15 membership.

Cooperative advertising fund directory for radio station salespeople.

Radio Contacts (Year). Editor(s): Mitch Tebo. BPI Communications Inc. (Schenectady), BPI Media Services, 210 Canal Sq., Schenectady, NY 12305. Telephone: 518-374-7640. FAX: 518-374-7889. Frequency: a. (plus m. updates and toll-free phone-in verification service). Year First Published: 1970. Price: $195.

Provides contact information for U.S. and Canadian radio stations, national networks, syndicators and their programming.

Radio Fun. ISSN: 1055-887X. Wayne Green Inc., 70 Rte 202 N., Peterborough, NH 03458. Telephone: 603-924-0058. FAX: 603-924-9327. Frequency: m. Year First Published: 1991. Circulation: 25,000. Price: $12.95.

Radio Handbook. ISSN: 0079-9467. Editor(s): William I. Orr. Prentice Hall Computer Publishing, 11711 N. College Ave., Suite 140, Carmel, IN 46032-3281. Telephone: 317-298-5400. Frequency: irreg., 23rd ed., 1986. Year First Published: 1935. Price: $39.95.

Radio Ink. Editor(s): Elaine Schmidt. Streamline Publishing Inc., 1501 Corporate Dr., Boynton Beach, FL 33426-6654. Telephone: 407-736-4416. FAX: 407-736-6134. Frequency: fortn. Year First Published: 1986. Special Features: adv, bk rev. Circulation: 9,000. Price: $99.

Provides news, interviews and features to help radio station owners, operators and managers.

Radio Only Magazine: The Monthly Management Tool. Editor(s): Jerry Del Colliano. Inside Radio Inc., 1930 E. Marlton Pike, Suite S-93, Cherry Hill, NJ 08003. Telephone: 609-424-6800. Frequency: m. Year First Published: 1978. Special Features: tr lit. Back issues available. Price: $75 (foreign $120).

Management information for radio executives and their sales representatives containing the latest trends and programming techniques.

Radio & Records. ISSN: 0277-4860. Radio & Records Inc., 1930 Century Park W., Los Angeles 90067. Telephone: 213-553-4330. FAX: 310-203-8727. Frequency: w. Year First Published: 1973. Special Features: adv. Circulation: 8,300. Price: $275.

Radio Resource. Editor(s): Rikki T. Lee. Pandata Corp., Box 24768, Denver 80224-0768. Telephone: 303-771-8616. FAX: 303-771-8605. Frequency: bi-m. Year First Published: 1987. Special Features: adv. Circulation: 35,000 (controlled).

Radio Resource International. Editor(s): Rikki T. Lee. Pandata Corp., Box 24768, Denver 80224. Telephone: 303-771-8616. FAX: 303-771-8605. Frequency: 2/yr. Year First Published: 1987. Price: Free to qualified personnel.

Covers the international mobile communication market.

Radio y TV Hispana. Telephone: 805-986-2202. Frequency: m. Year First Published: 1987. Circulation: 4,800. Price: $4 per mo.

Covers the Hispanic radio and television industry and personalities. Includes music charts and play lists.

Radio Technical Commission for Aeronautics Proceedings of the Annual Technical Symposium. Sponsoring Organization: Radio Technical Commission for Aeronautics, RTCA Inc., 1140 Connecticut Ave. N.W., Suite 1020, Washington, DC 20036-4001. Telephone: 202-833-9339. FAX: 202-833-9434. Frequency: a. Year First Published: 1955. Circulation: 750. Price: $25.

Radio and Television Career Directory. ISSN: 1062-0737. Editor(s): Bradley J. Morgan. Gale Research Inc., 835 Penobscot Bldg., Detroit 48226. Telephone: 313-961-2242. FAX: 313-961-6083. Frequency: irreg., 2nd ed., 1993. Year First Published: 1991. Price: $29.95; softcover $17.95.

Contains essays to help users find on-air and behind-the-scenes opportunities.

Radio World. ISSN: 0274-8541. Editor(s): Alex Zavistovich. Sponsoring Organization: Industrial Marketing Advisory Services Inc.,5827 Columbia Pike, Suite 310, Falls Church, VA 22041. Telephone: 703-998-7600. FAX: 703-998-2966. Frequency: s-m. Year First Published: 1977. Special Features: bk rev, tr lit. Back issues available. Circulation: 18,000.

Radio World International. ISSN: 0279-151X. Editor(s): Alan Carter. Sponsoring Organization: Industrial Marketing Advisory Services Inc.,5827 Columbia Pike, Suite 310, Falls Church, VA 22041. Telephone: 703-998-7600. FAX: 703-998-2966. Frequency: m. Year First Published: 1990. Special Features: adv. Back issues available. Circulation: 20,000. Price: Free.

Covers radio station technology, developments and applications. Geared toward radio station engineers, producers, technical staff and managers

Radioelectronics and Communications Systems. ISSN: 0033-7870. Editor(s): Ya.K. Trokhimenko. Sponsoring Organization: Politekhnichnyi Instytut, Allerton Press Inc., 150 5th Ave., New York 10011. Telephone: 212-924-3950. FAX: 212-463-9684. Frequency: m. Year First Published: 1977. Price: $900.

Religious Broadcasting. ISSN: 0034-4079. Editor(s): Ron J. Kopczick. Sponsoring Organization: National Religious Broadcasters Inc., 7839 Ashton Ave., Manassas, VA 22110. Telephone: 703-330-7000. FAX: 703-330-7100. Frequency: m. (11/yr.). Year First Published: 1969. Special Features: bk rev, charts, illus. Back issues available; reprint service available from UMI. Circulation: 9,933. Price: $24.

For Christian radio and television producers, station owners and operators and others interested in religious broadcasting.

Response TV. Editor(s): Jack Schember. Advanstar Communications Inc., 7500 Old Oak Blvd., Cleveland 44130. Telephone: 216-826-2839. FAX: 216-891-2726. Frequency: bi-m. Year First Published: 1992. Circulation: 16,000. Price: $29.95 (with Annual Directory $40).

Covers how to run your show, do two-minute commercials, as well as home-shopping networks and emerging interactive technologies.

Review of International Broadcasting. ISSN: 0149-9971. Glenn Hauser, Ed. & Pub., Box 1684, Enid, OK 73702-1684. Frequency: m. Year First Published: 1977. Special Features: adv, bk rev, charts, illus. Circulation: 2,000. Price: $18.

Rights and Liabilities of Publishers, Broadcasters and Reporters. Shepard's-McGraw-Hill Inc., Box 35300, Colorado Springs 80935-3530. Telephone: 800-525-2474. Frequency: two base vols. (plus a. suppl.). Year First Published: 1982. Price: $195.

Covers entire spectrum of media litigation: libel, privacy, compelled disclosure, media access, prior restraint, anti-trust law and commercial speech and advertising.

Ross Reports Television: New York Casting-National Script Contacts. ISSN: 0035-8355. Editor(s): Bd. Sponsoring Organization: Television Index Inc., 40-29 27th St., Long Island City, NY 11101. Telephone: 718-937-3990. Frequency: m. Year First Published: 1949. Price: $42.75.

SET Free: The Newsletter Against Television. Editor(s): Steve Wagner. Sponsoring Organization: Society for the Eradication of Television, Box 10491, Oakland, CA 94610-0491. Telephone: 510-763-8712. Frequency: q. Year First Published: 1982. Special Features: adv, bk rev. Circulation: 1,200. Price: $5 for 10 issues.

Contains news and updates about television's role in society with summaries of scholarly reports and empirical data.

SMATV News: The Newsletter on Economics of SMATV Systems Serving Multi-Unit Complexes. ISSN: 0734-5399. Editor(s): John Mansell. Paul Kagan Associates Inc., 126 Clock Tower Place, Carmel, CA 93923. Telephone: 408-624-1536. Frequency: m. Year First Published: 1982. Special Features: charts, index. Price: $425.

Covers the economic, technical, marketing and legal issues that affect SMATV.

SMPTE Journal. ISSN: 0036-1682. Editor(s): Jeffrey B. Friedman. Sponsoring Organization: Society of Motion Picture and Television Engineers, 595 W. Hartsdale Ave., White Plains, NY 10607-1824. Telephone: 914-761-1100. FAX: 914-761-3115. Frequency: m. Year First Published: 1916. Special Features: adv, bk rev, abstr, bibl, illus, index, cum index every five yrs. Reprint service available from UMI. Circulation: 10,500. Price: $75.

SSPI Update. Sponsoring Organization: Society of Satellite Professionals International, 2200 Wilson Blvd., No. 102-258, Arlington, VA 22201. Telephone: 703-243-8948. Frequency: m. Back issues available. Circulation: 800. Price: Membership.

Update covering society's events.

SWL. ISSN: 0162-5934. Editor(s): Stewart MacKenzie. Sponsoring Organization: American Shortwave Listeners Club, 16182 Ballad Ln., Huntington Beach, CA 92649-2204. Telephone: 714-846-1685. Frequency: m. Year First Published: 1959. Special Features: adv, bk rev, bibl, charts, illus, stat. Circulation: 600. Price: $20 (Canada and Mexico $22); students $18.

Contains logging of shortwave broadcast stations as reported by members. Includes feature articles on technology and equipment, club events and program schedules.

San Jose Film & Video Production Binder. Sponsoring Organization: San Jose Film & Video Commission, 333 W. San Carlos St., Suite 1000, San Jose, CA 95110. Telephone: 408-295-9600. FAX: 408-295-3937. Frequency: m. Year First Published: 1981. Circulation: 1,000. Price: $10.

Covers local crew personnel available for hire, sample of locations available for filming, general services and permit information.

Periodicals on Broadcasting and Cable

Satellite Orbit: The Magazine of the New Television. ISSN: 0732-7668. Editor(s): Phil Swan. CommTek Publishing Co. Inc., 8330 Boone Blvd., Vienna, VA 22182. Telephone: 703-827-0511. FAX: 703-356-6179. Frequency: m. Year First Published: 1982. Special Features: adv. Back issues available. Circulation: 389,000. Price: $52.

TV viewing guide for home satellite dish owners.

Satellite Retailer. Editor(s): David Melton. Triple D Publishing Inc., 1300 S. DeKalb St., Box 2384, Shelby, NC 28151-2384. Telephone: 704-482-9673. FAX: 704-484-8558. Frequency: m. Circulation: 10,700.

Trade journal for satellite TV installation, service and repair facilities.

Satellite TV Pre Vue. Editor(s): Sandy Jackson. Terra Publishing Inc., R.D. 1, Box 142, Center St. Ext., Salamanca, NY 14779. Telephone: 716-945-3488. Frequency: w. Year First Published: 1983. Special Features: adv. Circulation: 35,000. Price: $52.

Contains satellite television listings and articles.

Satellite TV Week. ISSN: 0744-7841. Editor(s): James E. Scott. Fortuna Communications Corp., Box 308, Fortuna, CA 95540. Telephone: 707-725-6951. FAX: 707-725-4311. Frequency: w. Year First Published: 1981. Circulation: 400,000. Price: $52.

Reports television program listings for satellite channels. Includes editorial coverage of issues affecting the satellite industry, as well as entertainment features, sports coverage, consumer electronics and personality interviews.

Satellite Week. ISSN: 0193-2861. Editor(s): Chris McCarter. Warren Publishing Inc., 2115 Ward Ct. N.W., Washington, DC 20037. Telephone: 202-872-9200. FAX: 202-293-3435. Frequency: w. Year First Published: 1979. Price: $811 (foreign $853).

SatVision Magazine. Sponsoring Organization: Satellite Broadcasting and Communications, Association of America, 225 Reinekers Lane, Suite 600, Alexandria, VA 22314-2322. Telephone: 703-549-6990. FAX: 703-549-7640. Frequency: m. Year First Published: 1987. Special Features: adv. Back issues available. Circulation: 10,000 (controlled). Price: $35.

Provides information for satellite television dealers.

Screen. ISSN: 0276-153X. Editor(s): Ruth L. Ratny, 720 N. Wabash Ave., Chicago 60611. Telephone: 312-664-5236. FAX: 312-664-8425. Frequency: w. Year First Published: 1979. Special Features: adv. Circulation: 15,000. Price: $70.

Covers film, video and AV production within the Chicagoland area: television commercials, industrial and corporate programs, audiovisuals, theatrical features.

Scriptwriters Market. ISSN: 0734-8592. Editor(s): Leslie Gates, David Buffum. Scriptwriters-Filmmakers Publishing Co., 8033 Sunset Blvd., No. 306, Hollywood, CA 90046. Telephone: 818-762-3726. Frequency: a. Year First Published: 1979. Special Features: adv. Circulation: 10,000. Price: $28.95.

Secure Signals. Editor(s): James S. Allen. Sponsoring Organization: National Cable Television Association, Office of Cable Signal Theft, 1724 Massachusetts Ave. N.W., Washington, DC 20036. Telephone: 202-775-3684. FAX: 202-775-3669. Frequency: q. Year First Published: 1986. Special Features: stat, tr lit. Circulation: 4,000. Price: Membership only.

Industry-oriented information covering legal and technical aspects of theft of cable television services and means of preventing losses.

73 Amateur Radio Today. ISSN: 1052-2522. Editor(s): David Cassidy. Wayne Greene Enterprises, Forest Rd., Hancock, NH 03449. Telephone: 603-525-4201. FAX: 603-525-4423. Frequency: m. Year First Published: 1960. Special Features: adv, bk rev, illus, index. Reprint service available from UMI. Circulation: 65,000. Price: $19.97.

Shoot Commercial Production Directory. Editor(s): Theresa Piti. BPI Communications Inc., 330 W. 42nd St., New York 10036. Telephone: 212-947-0020. FAX: 212-967-6786. Frequency: a. Year First Published: 1965. Special Features: adv. Circulation: 7,000. Price: $39.

Shortwave Directory: A Frequency Guide for the 10 kHz-30 mHz Spectrum. Grove Enterprises Inc., Box 98, Brasstown, NC 28902. Telephone: 704-837-9200. FAX: 704-837-2216. Frequency: irreg., 7th ed. Price: $15.95.

Includes international broadcasting and VLF with emphasis on two-way communications (utilities).

Shortwave Radio Today: The DX Radio Magazine for Active SWL'S. E. Janusz, Ed. & Pub., Box 149, Bricktown, NJ 08723. 903-255-9220. Frequency: m. Year First Published: 1971. Special Features: bk rev. Circulation: 700. Price: $23.

Provides up-to-date information on shortwave radio broadcasting, including schedules, rare catches of distant stations and general radio news.

Showbiz Magazine. Editor(s): Cheryl Gaw, 121 S. Martin Luther King Blvd., Las Vegas 89106-4309. Telephone: 702-383-7185. FAX: 702-382-1089. Frequency: w. Special Features: adv. Circulation: 142,000.

Skypix. Viare Publishing Co., 271 North Ave., No. 318, New Rochelle, NY 10801-5111. Telephone: 212-477-2200. FAX: 212-599-3176. Frequency: m. Year First Published: 1992. Special Features: film rev. Price: $12.95.

Feature articles and interviews of interest to satellite television viewers.

Soap Opera Digest. ISSN: 0164-3584. Editor(s): Meredith Berlin. K-III Magazines, 200 Madison Ave., New York 10016. Telephone: 212-332-0250. FAX: 212-447-4778. Frequency: 26/yr. Year First Published: 1975. Special Features: adv, illus. Reprint service available from UMI. Circulation: 1,300,000. Price: $45.90 (Canada $59.81; elsewhere $55.90).

Covers TV dramas, with synopses, interviews and news items, with lifestyle features on beauty, fashion, food and parenting topics.

Soap Opera Digest Presents. ISSN: 0899-1979. Editor(s): Roberta Capole. K-III Magazines, 200 Madison Ave., New York 10016. Telephone: 212-332-0255. Frequency: irreg. Year First Published: 1988. Reprint service available from UMI. Circulation: 500,000. Price: $2.50 per mo.

Each issue covers a particular soap opera theme.

Soap Opera Illustrated. K-III Magazines, 200 Madison Ave., New York 10016. Telephone: 212-447-4700. FAX: 212-447-4778. Frequency: bi-m. Year First Published: 1992.

Soap Opera Magazine. ISSN: 1057-9192. Editor(s): Joseph J. Policy. SOM Publishing Inc., 600 S. East Coast Ave., Lantana, FL 33462. Telephone: 407-586-1111. FAX: 407-582-0126. Frequency: w. Special Features: adv, illus. Price: $35.88.

Weekly record of daily television soap operas, featuring interviews with stars, previews and behind the scenes gossip.

Soap Opera Stars. Sterling's Magazines Inc., 355 Lexington Ave., New York 10017. Telephone: 212-396-5965. FAX: 213-396-1365. Frequency: bi-m. Special Features: adv. Price: $2.50 per mo.

Focuses on soap opera stars.

Soap Opera Update. ISSN: 0898-1485. Editor(s): Jerome Shapiro, Allison J. Waldman. 270 Sylvan Ave., Englewood Cliffs, NJ 07632-2513. Telephone: 201-569-6699. FAX: 201-592-0106. Frequency: 26/yr. Year First Published: 1988. Special Features: adv. Circulation: 300,000. Price: $52.

Soap Opera Weekly. K-III Magazines, 200 Madison Ave., New York 10016. Telephone: 212-447-4700. FAX: 212-447-4778. Frequency: w. Price: $56.68 (Canada $88.47).

News magazine devoted to the plots and personalities of TV dramas, with interviews and a variety of feature columns.

Sound & Video Contractor: The International Management and Engineering Journal for Sound and Video Contractors. ISSN: 0741-1715. Editor(s): Ted Uzzle. Intertec Publishing Corp., 9800 Metcalf, Overland Park, KS 66212-2215. Telephone: 913-341-1300. FAX: 913-967-1898. Frequency: m. Year First Published: 1983. Special Features: adv, tr lit. Circulation: 20,943. Price: $27 (free to qualified personnel).

Spec-Com Journal. ISSN: 0883-2560. Editor(s): M.J. Donovan. Sponsoring Organization: United States A TV Society, Spec-Com Communications and Publishing Group Ltd., Box 1002, Dubuque, IA 52004-1002. Telephone: 319-557-8791. FAX: 319-583-6462. Frequency: bi-m. Year First Published: 1967. Special Features: adv, bk rev. Circulation: 1,400. Price: $20.

Spectator (Los Angeles). ISSN: 1051-0230. Sponsoring Organization: University of Southern California, School of Cinema—Television, University Park, Los Angeles 90089-2211. Telephone: 213-740-3334. FAX: 213-740-9471. Frequency: bi-a. Year First Published: 1982. Special Features: bk rev. Price: $10 to individuals (foreign $15); institutions $20 (foreign $25).

Spot Radio Rates and Data. ISSN: 0038-9560. Editor(s): Randy Melcher. Sponsoring Organization: Standard Rate and Data Service, 2000 Clearwater Dr., Oak Brook, IL 60521. Telephone: 708-574-6000. FAX: 708-574-6541. Frequency: m. Year First Published: 1929. Special Features: adv. Price: $389.

Contains listings of radio stations arranged geographically.

Spot Radio Small Markets Edition. ISSN: 1066-2030. Editor(s): Randy Melcher. Sponsoring Organization: Standard Rate and Data Service, 2000 Clearwater Dr., Oak Brook, IL 60521. Telephone: 708-574-6000. FAX: 708-574-6541. Frequency: s-a. Year First Published: 1976. Special Features: adv. Price: $132.

Profiles commercial radio stations licensed to cities with less than 25,000 population.

Spot Television Rates and Data. ISSN: 0038-9552. Editor(s): Randy Melcher. Sponsoring Organization: Standard Rate and Data Service, 2000 Clearwater Dr., Oak Brook, IL 60521. Telephone: 708-574-6000. FAX: 708-574-6541. Frequency: m. Year First Published: 1947. Special Features: adv. Price: $369.

For planners and buyers of television advertising. Lists TV stations geographically. Includes programming information, personnel and other data.

Systems and Computers in Japan. ISSN: 0882-1666. Editor(s): C.H. Park. Sponsoring Organization: Institute of Electronics, Information and, Communications Engineers of Japan. Scripta Technica Inc., John Wiley & Sons Inc., 7961 Eastern Ave., Silver Spring, MD 20910. Telephone: 301-588-0484. FAX: 301-588-5278. Frequency: 14/yr. Year First Published: 1969. Special Features: adv, charts, illus, index. Back issues available. Circulation: 300. Price: $1,096 (Canada & Mexico $1,236; elsewhere $1,288.50).

Covers computer architecture, large system design, advanced digital circuitry, data transmission, interface device, data processing, signal and speech processing.

TA Report on Telecom Advertising & Publishing. Editor(s): Efrem Sigel. SIMBA-Communications Trends, 213 Danbury Rd., Box 7430, Wilton, CT 06897. Telephone: 203-834-0033. FAX: 203-834-1771. Frequency: fortn. Year First Published: 1985. Special Features: index. Back issues available. Price: $492 (foreign $525).

News of marketing and advertising campaigns by telecom companies, news of telecom publishers.

TV & Cable Publicity Outlets-Nationwide. ISSN: 1054-4259. Editor(s): Russell Perkins. Morgan-Rand Publishing Co., 2200 Sansom St., Philadelphia 19103. Telephone: 215-557-8200. FAX: 215-557-8414. Frequency: s-a. Year First Published: 1970. Circulation: 1,500. Price: $90.

TV Collector. ISSN: 0887-5847. Editor(s): Diane L. Albert. Sponsoring Organization: TVC Enterprises, Box 1088, 69 S. St., Easton, MA 02375. Telephone: 508-238-1179. Frequency: bi-m. Year First Published: 1976. Special Features: bk rev, video rev. Back issues available. Circulation: 2,000. Price: $17 in U.S.; Canada $19; Europe & S. America $25; elsewhere $27.

Provides in-depth articles, episode guides, interviews with stars of old TV series, actor profiles, tributes and interviews.

TV Dimensions. ISSN: 0884-1098. Media Dynamics, 322 E. 50th St., New York 10022. Frequency: a. Year First Published: 1984.

TV Executive: A Printed Marketplace for Programming and Production. ISSN: 0736-2986. Editor(s): Dom Serafini. TV Trade Media Inc., 216 E. 75th St., No. One W., New York 10021. Telephone: 212-288-3933. FAX: 212-734-9033. Frequency: 2/yr. Year First Published: 1983. Price: $20 (subscription includes Annual Directory Who's Who of Promo-Ad Executives).

Contains news and information about the TV industry with profiles, analysis and commentary.

TV Guide. ISSN: 0039-8543. Editor(s): Anthea Disney. Murdoch Magazines (Radnor), Four Radnor Corporate Center, 100 Matsonford Rd., Box 500, Radnor, PA 19088. Telephone: 800-628-7300. FAX: 215-688-3285. Frequency: w. Year First Published: 1953. Special Features: adv, bk rev, illus, 38-yr. cum index. Circulation: 15,800,000. Price: $39.52.

Personality profiles and articles on television and entertainment of national interest. Published in regional editions with comprehensive listing of local network and cable TV programs.

TV Host Monthly. Editor(s): Suzanne Stefanic. TV Host Inc., Box 1665, 3935 Jonestown Rd., Harrisburg, PA 17109. Telephone: 717-657-1700. FAX: 717-657-2921. Frequency: m. Circulation: 1,800,000. Price: $14.

TV Host Weekly. TV Host Inc., Box 1665, 3935 Jonestown Rd., Harrisburg, PA 17109. Telephone: 717-657-1700. FAX: 717-657-2921. Frequency: w. Circulation: 140,000. Price: $33.97.

TV Magazine. Editor(s): James B. Clark, 5900 W. Jefferson Blvd., Suite 100, Fort Wayne, IN 46804. Telephone: 219-436-5550. FAX: 219-432-6833. Frequency: w. Year First Published: 1973. Special Features: adv. Back issues available. Circulation: 10,000. Price: $19.90.

TV and Movie Screen. ISSN: 0041-4492. Editor(s): Fran Levine. Sterling's Magazines Inc., 355 Lexington Ave., New York 10017. Telephone: 212-949-6850. Frequency: bi-m. Year First Published: 1957. Special Features: adv, bk rev, film rev, record rev, illus. Price: $6.

TV News. Editor(s): Liz Farkas, 80 8th Ave., Suite 315, New York. NY 10011. Telephone: 212-243-6800. FAX: 212-243-7457. Frequency: w. Year First Published: 1973. Special Features: adv, bk rev, record rev. Circulation: 400,000.

TV News Contacts (Year). ISSN: 1051-3590. Editor(s): Mitch Tebo. BPI Communications Inc. (Schenectady), BPI Media Services, 210 Canal Sq., Schenectady, NY 12305. Telephone: 518-374-7640. FAX: 518-374-7889. Frequency: a. (plus m. updates and contact verification service). Year First Published: 1970. Price: $150.

TV News Magazine: Central Indiana, Eastern Illinois Television Listings. Editor(s): Jack Carter. Carter Publications Inc., 427 Gradle Dr., Box 313, Carmel, IN 46032-0313. Frequency: w. Year First Published: 1950. Special Features: adv. Circulation: 22,500. Price: $23.70.

TV y Novelas. Editor(s): Jesus Gallegos. Editorial America S.A., Vanidades Continental Bldg., 6355 N.W. 36th St., Virginia Gardens, FL 33166. Telephone: 305-871-6400. FAX: 305-871-8769. Frequency: bi-w. Year First Published: 1982. Special Features: adv. Circulation: 1,237,000. Price: $34.10.
Covers the soap operas and their stars.

TV Program Investor. ISSN: 0885-2340. Editor(s): Larry Gerbrandt. Paul Kagan Associates Inc., 126 Clock Tower Pl., Carmel, CA 93923. Telephone: 408-624-1536. Frequency: m. Year First Published: 1985. Price: $450.
Covers trends in TV program syndication, values of TV networks and programs, public stocks and private companies in the TV program business and analysis of mergers and acquisitions.

TV Superstar. Sterling's Magazines Inc., 355 Lexington Ave., New York 10017. Telephone: 212-949-6850. Frequency: 6/yr. Price: $7.50.

TV Technology. ISSN: 0887-1701. Editor(s): Marlene Lane. Sponsoring Organization: Industrial Marketing Advisory Services Inc., 5827 Columbia Pike, Suite 310, Falls Church, VA 22041. Telephone: 703-998-7600. FAX: 703-998-2966. Frequency: 13/yr. Year First Published: 1983. Special Features: adv. Reprint service available. Circulation: 45,000.

TV Times (St. Paul). Editor(s): Richard B. Beeson. TV Times Publications Inc., 1010 University Ave., St. Paul, MN 55104. Telephone: 612-646-9629. Frequency: w. Year First Published: 1967. Special Features: adv, illus. Circulation: 102,000. Price: $27.

TV Today. Editor(s): Cindy Price. Sponsoring Organization: National Association of Broadcasters, 1771 N St. N.W., Washington, DC 20036. Telephone: 202-429-5486. Frequency: w. Year First Published: 1933. Circulation: Controlled. Price: $48.

TVRO Dealer. Fortuna Communications Corp., 140 S. Fortuna Blvd., Fortuna, CA 95540. Telephone: 707-725-6591. FAX: 707-725-4311. Frequency: m. Year First Published: 1986. Circulation: 15,042. Price: $18.

Tape-Disc Directory (Year): For the Record, CD and Audio-Video Tape Industries. Editor(s): Susan Nunziata. Billboard Publications Inc. (New York), 1515 Broadway, 39th Fl., New York 10036. Telephone: 212-536-5025. FAX: 212-921-2486. Frequency: a. Special Features: adv. Circulation: 7,500. Price: $35.
Information on tape, audio and video professional equipment and manufacturers.

Techline: A Publication for the Cable Engineering Community. ISSN: 0896-3215. Editor(s): Katherine Rutkowski. Sponsoring Organization: National Cable Television Association, 1724 Massachusetts Ave. N.W., Washington, DC 20036. Telephone: 202-775-3550. Frequency: 10/yr. Year First Published: 1979. Special Features: bibl. Back issues available. Circulation: 3,200. Price: Membership only.
Geared to the U.S. cable television engineering community.

Technos: Quarterly for Education and Technology. ISSN: 1060-5649. Editor(s): Carole Novak. Sponsoring Organization: Agency for Instructional Technology, Box A, Bloomington, IN 47402-0120. Telephone: 812-339-2203. FAX: 812-333-4218. Frequency: q. Year First Published: 1966. Circulation: 3,500. Price: $20 to individuals; libraries $16; foreign $24.
Provides a forum for the discussion of ideas about the use of technology in education, with focus on reform.

Telcom Highlights International. Editor(s): George Knights. Box 1609, Paramus, NJ 07653-1609. Telephone: 201-265-7236. FAX: 201-261-0183. Frequency: w. Year First Published: 1978. Special Features: bk rev. Circulation: 450. Price: $425.

Tele Viewing. Paper Publishers Inc., 200 E. Wilcox, Sierra Vista, AZ 85635. Telephone: 602-458-3340. FAX: 602-458-9338. Frequency: s-w. Year First Published: 1975. Special Features: adv. Circulation: 37,200. Price: $12.

Telecommunications and Radio Engineering. ISSN: 0040-2508. Editor(s): Reuben C. Glass. Sponsoring Organization: Russian Society of Electronics and Communications Engineers, Scripta Technica Inc., John Wiley & Sons Inc., 7961 Eastern Ave., Silver Spring, MD 20910. Telephone: 301-588-0484. FAX: 301-588-5278. Frequency: m. Year First Published: 1962. Special Features: adv, bk rev, bibl, charts, illus. Circulation: 500. Price: $785 (foreign $897).
Covers digital and analog wire, radio, video and optical communications, facsimile, micro- and millimeter-wave communications, switching and coding theory, signal processing, voice and pattern recognition, antennae and waveguides.

Teleguia USA. Four Star Productions, 2585 Commerce Way, Los Angeles 90040. Telephone: 213-725-0141. FAX: 213-725-2521. Frequency: w. Year First Published: 1985. Special Features: film rev. Circulation: 179,000. Price: Free.
Guide to television broadcasts. Includes coverage of sports, food, entertainment, cars, health and beauty.

Telemedium. Editor(s): Marieli Rowe. Sponsoring Organization: National Telemedia Council Inc., 120 E. Wilson St., Madison, WI 53703. Telephone: 608-257-7712. Frequency: q. Year First Published: 1953. Special Features: bk rev. Circulation: 600. Price: Membership.

Television Broadcast. Editor(s): Ed Rosenthal. PSN Publications, United Newspapers Publications Ltd., Two Park Ave., 18th Fl., New York 10016. Telephone: 212-213-3444. FAX: 212-213-3484. Frequency: m. Year First Published: 1978. Special Features: adv, bk rev. Circulation: 30,653 (controlled). Price: $38 (free to qualified personnel).

Television & Cable Action Update: The Authoritative News Service of Actions Affecting Television Stations and Cable TV Activities. ISSN: 1061-5741. Warren Publishing Inc., 2115 Ward Ct. N.W., Washington, DC 20037. Telephone: 202-872-9200. Frequency: w. Year First Published: 1991. Special Features: stat. Back issues available. Price: $400 (foreign $500).
Highlights a weekly listing of new applications including permits, sales franchises, grants and regulatory changes.

Television and Cable Factbook. ISSN: 0732-8648. Editor(s): Albert Warren. Warren Publishing Inc., 2115 Ward Ct. N.W., Washington, DC 20037. Telephone: 202-872-9200. FAX: 202-393-3435. Frequency: a. Year First Published: 1945. Price: $395.

Television Contacts (Year). Editor(s): Mitch Tebo. BPI Communications Inc. (Schenectady), BPI Media Services, 210 Canal Sq., Schenectady, NY 12305. Telephone: 518-374-7640. FAX: 518-536-5351. Frequency: a. (plus m. updates and contact verification service). Year First Published: 1976. Circulation: 5,000. Price: $195.

Television Digest with Consumer Electronics. ISSN: 0497-1515. Editor(s): Albert Warren. Warren Publishing Inc., 2115 Ward Ct. N.W., Washington, DC 20037. Telephone: 202-872-9200. FAX: 202-293-3435. Frequency: w. Year First Published: 1945. Price: $802 (foreign $902).

Television Directors Guide. ISSN: 1055-0828. Lone Eagle Publishing Co., 2337 Roscomare Rd., #9, Los Angeles 90077-1815. Telephone: 213-471-8066. FAX: 213-471-4969. Frequency: a. Year First Published: 1990. Special Features: adv. Circulation: 2,500. Price: $29.95.
Lists television directors, their credits and contacts.

Television Index: Television Network Program and Production Reporting Service. ISSN: 0739-5531. Editor(s): Jonathan Miller. Sponsoring Organization: Television Index Inc., 40-29 27th St., Long Island City, NY 11101. Telephone: 718-937-3990. Frequency: w. Year First Published: 1949. Special Features: cum index. Price: $250.

Television International Magazine. Editor(s): Josie Cory. Sponsoring Organization: Television International Publications Ltd., Box 2430, Hollywood, CA 90028. Telephone: 818-795-8386. FAX: 818-795-8436. Frequency: bi-m. Year First Published: 1956. Special Features: adv, bk rev, bibl, illus. Circulation: 14,000. Price: $42.

Television News Index and Abstracts. ISSN: 0085-7157. Editor(s): Andrew H. Pfeiffer. Sponsoring Organization: Vanderbilt University, Vanderbilt Television News Archive, 110 21st Ave. S., Suite 704, Nashville 37240-0007. Telephone: 615-322-2927. FAX: 615-343-8250. Frequency: m. Year First Published: 1968. Special Features: abstr, index. Circulation: 250. Price: $550 to individuals; institutions $330; microfilm $110.
Guide to Vanderbilt's collection of network television evening news programs and other news broadcasts, including abstract and subject, person and place indexing.

Television Quarterly. ISSN: 0040-2796. Editor(s): Richard Pack. Sponsoring Organization: National Academy of Television Arts & Sciences, c/o Ed Eberung, 111 W. 57th St., New York 10019. Telephone: 212-586-8424. FAX: 212-246-8129. Frequency: q. Year First Published: 1962. Special Features: adv, bk rev. Reprint service available from UMI. Circulation: 11,500. Price: $25 (foreign $30).
Presents scholarly and professional views and interpretations of patterns and trends in the television industry and provides a critique of industry performance.

Television Sponsors Directory: Product Cross-Reference Directory. ISSN: 0049-3317. Editor(s): Roger C. Foss. Sponsoring Organization: Everglades Publishing Co., Drawer Q, Everglades, FL 33929. Frequency: q. Year First Published: 1970. Circulation: 1,200. Price: $19.40.

Television Writers Guide. Lone Eagle Publishing Co., 2337 Roscomare Rd., #9, Los Angeles 90077-1815. Telephone: 213-471-8066. FAX: 213-471-4969. Frequency: a. Special Features: adv. Circulation: 3,000. Price: $49.95.
Lists people who write for television. Includes contacts, credits, networks and genres.

Telocator. Editor(s): Dennis Connaughton. Sponsoring Organization: Telocator, 1019 19th St. N.W., Suite 1100, Washington, DC 20036. Telephone: 202-467-4770. Frequency: m. Year First Published: 1977. Special Features: adv, charts, illus, tr lit. Circulation: 3,500 (controlled). Price: $60.

Telocator Bulletin: News and Analysis for the Personal Communication Industry. ISSN: 1061-6438. Editor(s): David Williams. Telocator, 1019 19th St. N.W., Suite 1100, Washington, DC 20036-3396. Telephone: 202-467-4770. FAX: 202-467-6987. Frequency: w. Special Features: adv, illus. Circulation: 1,200. Price: $495.
Covers mobile and personal communication systems (such as paging, cellular telephone, mobile data communications and mobile satellite systems) as a business (rather than a science or technology) for executives and managers.

Tennessee Broadcaster. Sponsoring Organization: Tennessee Association of Broadcasters, Box 101015, Nashville 37224-1015. Frequency: m. Year First Published: 1978.

Total TV. TV Syndicated Market, 309 Lakeside Dr., Horsham, PA 19044. Telephone: 215-443-9300. Frequency: w. Year First Published: 1993. Circulation: 425,000.
System-specific cable guide.

Transmitter. Editor(s): Robert P. Bubniak. Sponsoring Organization: Armed Forces Broadcasters Association, 10888 La Tuna Canyon Rd., Sun Valley, CA 91352-2009. Telephone: 703-573-5078. Frequency: q. Year First Published: 1982. Special Features: adv, bk rev. Circulation: 800. Price: $20 membership.
Covers military broadcasting activities and projects. Provides a forum for ex-military broadcasters.

Transponder. ISSN: 1059-8286. Editor(s): Timothy L. Jackson. Terra Publishing Inc., RD 1, Box 142, Center

St. Ext., Salamanca, NY 14779. Telephone: 716-945-3488. Frequency: m. Year First Published: 1986. Special Features: adv. Circulation: 14,500 (controlled).
Trade magazine for the satellite television industry.

Twenty-four. Editor(s): Barbara Gibson. Community Communications Inc., 11510 E. Colonial Dr., Orlando, FL 32817. Telephone: 407-273-2300. FAX: 407-273-8462. Frequency: m. Circulation: 24,500.

Tyndall Report. Editor(s): Bruno Pajaczkowski. ADT Research, 135 Rivington St., New York 10002. Telephone: 212-674-8913. FAX: 212-979-7304. Frequency: bi-m. Year First Published: 1988. Back issues available. Circulation: 500. Price: $60.
Analysis of television news; monitors the nightly newscasts of the three U.S. broadcast networks with statistical data and commentary. Tracks trends in major news stories, social issues, domestic and foreign affairs and politics.

US Scanner News. Bob's Publications, 706 W. 43rd St., Vancouver, WA 98660. Frequency: m. Price: $18 (foreign $26).
For the scanner hobbyist.

Ultrahigh Speed and High Speed Photography, Photonics and Videography. ISSN: 1046-9311. Sponsoring Organization: International Society for Optical Engineering (SPIE), Box 98227, 1000 20th St., Bellingham, WA 98227-0010. Telephone: 206-676-3290. Frequency: a. Year First Published: 1983.

Unda-USA Newsletter. Sponsoring Organization: Unda-USA, National Catholic Association for Broadcasters and Allied Communicators c/o Patrick DiSalvatore, 5451 W. Rockwell Rd., Austintown, OH 44515. Frequency: bi-m. Year First Published: 1963. Special Features: bk rev, stat. Circulation: 500. Price: Membership.

Utility and Telephone Fleets. Editor(s): Alan Richter. Practical Communications Inc., Box 183, Cary, IL 60013-0183. Telephone: 708-639-2200. FAX: 708-639-9542. Frequency: 8/yr. Year First Published: 1987. Circulation: 18,000. Price: $20.
For fleet managers and maintenance supervisors employed by telephone companies, utilities, CATV operators, municipalities, public works and related contractors.

VCR Letter. ISSN: 8755-9927. Paul Kagan Associates Inc., 126 Clock Tower Pl., Carmel, CA 93923. Telephone: 408-624-1536. Frequency: m. Year First Published: 1984. Price: $425.
Covers the economics of the home video industry and its impact on pay TV. Analyzes developments in hardware, software and retailing.

VSDA Voice. Editor(s): L. MacAlpine. Sponsoring Organization: Video Software Dealers Association, 303 Harper Dr., Moorestown, NJ 08057. Telephone: 609-231-7800. FAX: 609-231-9791. Frequency: bi-m. Year First Published: 1983. Circulation: 5,000. Price: $19.95 (subscription includes supplement 3/yr).
Supplies information about association news, legislative and First Amendment issues, emerging technologies and commentary.

Variety's Video Directory Plus. R.R. Bowker, A Reed Reference Publishing Co., 121 Chanlon Rd., New Providence, NJ 07974. Telephone: 908-665-2867. FAX: 908-665-6688. Frequency: a. Available for MS-DOS. Price: $395.

Video Age International: The Business Journal of Film, TV Broadcasting, Cable, Pay TV, PPV, Home Video, DBS, Production. ISSN: 0278-5013. Editor(s): Dom Serafini. TV Trade Media Inc., 216 E. 75th St., Suite1W, New York 10021. Telephone: 212-288-3933. FAX: 212-734-9033. Frequency: 9/yr. Year First Published: 1981. Special Features: adv, bk rev. Circulation: 15,000. Price: $30 in N. America; elsewhere $45 (includes Who's Who).
International trade publication for the video industry including profiles, information and analysis.

Video Annual. ISSN: 1055-0062. ABC-Clio, 130 Cremona Dr., Box 1911, Santa Barbara, CA 93116-1911. Frequency: a. Year First Published: 1991.

Video Business. ISSN: 0279-571X. Editor(s): Bruce Apar. Capital Cities-ABC Inc., Diversified Publishing, 825 7th Ave., 6th Fl., New York 10019. Telephone: 212-887-8400. Frequency: w. Year First Published: 1981. Special Features: adv, charts, illus, stat. Back issues available. Circulation: 40,369. Price: $70.

Video Choice. Editor(s): Deborah Navas. Connell Communications Inc., 331 Jaffrey Rd., Peterborough, NH 03458. Telephone: 603-924-7271. FAX: 603-924-7013. Frequency: m. Year First Published: 1988. Special Features: adv. Circulation: 85,000. Price: $24.95.

Video Duplication Directory. Corbell Publishing, 2554 Lincoln Blvd., Suite 1015, Marina Del Rey, CA 90291. Telephone: 310-821-6675. FAX: 310-641-9769. Frequency: a., 2nd ed. Year First Published: 1992. Price: $167.
Complete guide to video duplicators in the United States and Canada.

Video Event. Connell Communications Inc., 331 Jaffrey Rd., Peterborough, NH 03458. Telephone: 603-924-7271. FAX: 603-924-7013. Frequency: m. Year First Published: 1988. Special Features: adv. Circulation: 400,000.
Gives reviews of the box office hits being released on video.

Video Extra. Editor(s): Bruce Apar. Home Viewer Publications Inc., 8380 Old York Rd., Suite 404, Philadelphia 19117-1543. Telephone: 215-629-1588. Frequency: m. Year First Published: 1984. Special Features: adv, bk rev, stat. Circulation: 25,000. Price: $18.

Video Film Music. Editor(s): David Deaton. Video Film Music Communications Inc., 5231 E. Memorial Dr., Suite 136, Stone Mountain, GA 30083. Telephone: 404-498-1729. Frequency: bi-m. Year First Published: 1992. Circulation: 20,000. Price: $5.95.

Video Industry Statistical Report. Editor(s): Deborah Rolfe. Corbell Publishing, 2554 Lincoln Blvd., Suite 1015, Marina Del Rey, CA 90291. Telephone: 310-821-6675. FAX: 310-641-9769. Frequency: a., 4th ed. Year First Published: 1989. Special Features: charts. Price: $295.
Provides statistics on pre-recorded video, blank tape, video hardware, VCRs, laser discs, 8mm and penetration data.

Video Insider. Editor(s): Tim Cornitius. AKF Communications Inc., 223 Conestoga Rd., Wayne, PA 19087. Telephone: 215-688-7030. FAX: 215-687-5543. Frequency: q. Year First Published: 1983. Special Features: adv. Circulation: 21,000. Price: $99.
Offers marketing and merchandising ideas for retailers, distributors and suppliers in the video industry.

Video Librarian. ISSN: 0887-6851. Editor(s): Randy Pitman. Video Librarian, Box 2725, Bremerton, WA 98310. Telephone: 206-377-2231. FAX: 206-373-6805. Frequency: m. (combined Jul.-Aug.). Year First Published: 1986. Special Features: bk rev, film rev. Back issues available. Circulation: 764. Price: $47 (Canada $52; elsewhere $69).
Articles, news and reviews on the subject of video in public and school libraries.

Video Magazine. ISSN: 1044-7288. Editor(s): James Barry. Reese Communications Inc., 460 W. 34th St., New York 10001. Telephone: 212-947-6500. FAX: 212-947-6727. Frequency: m. Year First Published: 1978. Special Features: adv, bk rev, illus, index. Reprint service available from UMI. Circulation: 450,000. Price: $15.

Video Marketing News. Editor(s): Kathleen Silvassy. Phillips Publishing Inc., 7811 Montrose Rd., Potomac, MD 20854. Telephone: 301-340-2100. FAX: 301-424-4297. Frequency: fortn. Year First Published: 1980. Special Features: stat. Back issues available. Price: $497.

Video Movies (Bremerton). ISSN: 1063-5106. Editor(s): Randy Pitman. Video Librarian, Box 2725, Bremerton, WA 98310. Telephone: 206-377-2231. FAX: 206-373-6805. Frequency: m. Year First Published: 1992. Special Features: video rev. Price: $42 (Canada $47; elsewhere $64).
Critical reviews of forthcoming video movie releases for libraries and collectors, with information on stars, original production date for theaters or TV, price, distributor and potential audience.

Video Networks. ISSN: 0738-7563. Editor(s): Marianne Yusavage. Sponsoring Organization: Bay Area Video Coalition, 1111 17th St., San Francisco 94107. Telephone: 415-861-3282. FAX: 415-861-4316. Frequency: bi-m. Year First Published: 1976. Special Features: adv. Back issues available. Circulation: 8,000. Price: $20.
Targets independent video producers and artists with valuable information and opportunities in production, exhibition, distribution and fund-raising.

Video Rating Guide for Libraries. ISSN: 1045-3393. Editor(s): Timothy O'Donnell. ABC-Clio, 130 Cremona, Box 1911, Santa Barbara, CA 93116-1911. Telephone: 805-968-1911. FAX: 805-685-9685. Frequency: q. Year First Published: 1990. Price: $126.

Provides evaluative reviews of special-interest, nontheatrical videos. Includes information on how to obtain the individual video.

Video Register and Teleconferencing Resources Directory. ISSN: 0190-3705. Editor(s): Margaret Csenge. Knowledge Industry Publications Inc., 701 Westchester Ave., White Plains, NY 10604. Telephone: 914-328-9157. FAX: 914-328-9093. Frequency: a. Year First Published: 1979. Special Features: adv. Price: $74.50.

Video Reserved Collection. Editor(s): M.S. Bram. TM Publishing Inc., 2609 S. Highland, Box 18000-5, Las Vegas 89109. Telephone: 702-796-9966. FAX: 702-796-5655. Frequency: 12/yr.

Video Source Book. ISSN: 0277-3317. Editor(s): Julia Furtan. Sponsoring Organization: National Video Clearinghouse Inc., Gale Research Inc., Dept. 77748, Detroit 48226. Telephone: 313-961-2242. FAX: 313-961-6083. Frequency: a. (plus s-a. supplement). Year First Published: 1979. Special Features: adv, index. Back issues available. Circulation: 6,000. Price: $230.
Describes more than 125,000 currently available videotapes and discs, including feature movies and instructional films.

Video Specialist Newsletter. Editor(s): James J. Lahm. J. Lahm Consultants Inc., 2630 Coronado Dr., Fullerton, CA 92635. Telephone: 714-738-8422. FAX: 714-738-4860. Frequency: m. Year First Published: 1981. Circulation: 300. Price: $144 (foreign $156).
Advisory news to retailers, manufacturers and executives in home video. Also covers industry trends, video dispensing machines, strategies, promotions and new products and services.

Video Systems: The Magazine for Video Professionals. ISSN: 0361-0942. Editor(s): Ned Soseman. Intertec Publishing Corp., 9800 Metcalf, Overland Park, KS 66212-2215. Telephone: 913-341-1300. FAX: 913-967-1898. Frequency: m. Year First Published: 1975. Special Features: adv, bk rev, illus. Reprint service available from UMI. Circulation: 31,477. Price: $45 (free to qualified personnel).

Video Technology News. ISSN: 1040-2772. Editor(s): Charlotte Wolter. Phillips Publishing Inc., 7811 Montrose Rd., Potomac, MD 20854. Telephone: 301-340-2100. FAX: 301-309-3847. Frequency: fortn. Price: $595.
Covers current developments in video technology, including broadcasting, cable, computers, satellites, consumer electronics and telecommunications and related business opportunities and trends.

Video Times (New York). Editor(s): Janette V. Rensburg, Fern R. Landburg. Sponsoring Organization: MPCS Video Industries Inc., 514 W. 57th St., New York 10019-2902. Frequency: q. Year First Published: 1982. Special Features: adv. Circulation: 70,000.

Video Viewing. View Publications, 4643 N. 12th St., Phoenix 85014. Telephone: 602-279-0841. FAX: 602-277-8491. Frequency: m. Year First Published: 1984. Price: Free.

Video Voice. Editor(s): P. Blumenthal. David Blumenthal Associates Inc., 30 E. 37th St., New York 10016. Telephone: 212-686-8550. Frequency: m. Year First Published: 1980. Price: $2.95.

Video Watchdog: The Perfectionist's Guide to Fantastic Video. Editor(s): Donna Lucas, Box 5283, Cincinnati 45205-0283. Telephone: 513-471-8989. Frequency: bi-m. Year First Published: 1990. Special Features: adv, bk rev, illus. Price: $35.
Reports on the condition of video movies in terms of original release, the directors, as well as other film and video-related subjects.

Video Week. ISSN: 0196-5905. Editor(s): Lisa Lilienthal. Warren Publishing Inc., 2115 Ward Ct. N.W., Washington, DC 20037. Telephone: 202-872-9200. FAX: 202-293-3435. Frequency: w. Year First Published: 1980. Price: $764 (foreign $806).

Videography. ISSN: 0363-1001. Editor(s): Brian McKernan. PSN Publications, United Newspapers Publications Ltd., Two Park Ave., 18th Fl., New York 10016. Telephone: 212-213-3444. FAX: 212-213-3484. Frequency: m. Year First Published: 1976. Special Features: adv. Circulation: 41,185. Price: $30.
For video professionals. Contains news, trends and analysis of the video industry, interviews with specialists, editorials, guest columns, and a calendar of meetings and shows.

VideoHound's Golden Movie Retriever. Gale Research Inc., 835 Penobscot Bldg., Detroit 48226. Telephone: 313-961-2242. FAX: 313-961-6083. Frequency: a. Year First Published: 1992. Price: $17.95.

Periodicals on Broadcasting and Cable

Videolog. ISSN: 0746-7680. Editor(s): Bonnie Dudley. Trade Service Corp., 10996 Torreyana Rd., San Diego 92121. Telephone: 619-457-5920. FAX: 619-457-1320. Frequency: w. Year First Published: 1981. Special Features: adv. Circulation: 5,250. Price: $252.

Bulletin of video industry news, containing reviews of video release listings.

Videolog Reporter. Editor(s): Bonnie J. Dudley. Phonolog Publishing Trade Service Corp., 10996 Torreyana Rd., Box 85007, San Diego 92138. Telephone: 619-457-5920. Frequency: w. Year First Published: 1981. Price: $252.

Videomaker: The Video Camera User's Magazine. ISSN: 0889-4973. Editor(s): Stephen Muratore. Videomaker Inc., Box 4591, Chico, CA 95927. Telephone: 916-891-8410. FAX: 916-891-8443. Frequency: m. Year First Published: 1986. Special Features: adv, bk rev, illus. Circulation: 90,000. Price: $22.50 (Canada $32.50; elsewhere $42.50).

Presents tools, tips and techniques for consumers and professionals involved with videomaking as a hobby, in business or in education.

Videopro: For the Business of Production. ISSN: 0746-3286. Editor(s): Steve Feldman. Vid-Pro Publishing, 902 Broadway, New York 10011. Telephone: 212-477-2200. Frequency: m. Year First Published: 1982. Special Features: adv. Back issues available. Circulation: 22,000. Price: $24.

Videos for Business and Training: Professional and Vocational Videos and How to Get Them. ISSN: 1043-9579. Editor(s): David Weiner. Gale Research Inc., 835 Penobscot Bldg., Detroit 48226-4094. Telephone: 313-961-2242. FAX: 313-961-6083. Frequency: irreg. Year First Published: 1989.

Voice of Prophecy News. Editor(s): Eldyn Karr. Sponsoring Organization: Voice of Prophecy Inc., Box 2525, Newbury Park, CA 91319. Telephone: 805-373-7657. FAX: 805-373-7701. Frequency: q. Year First Published: 1942. Special Features: bk rev. Back issues available. Circulation: 42,000. Price: Free to qualified personnel.

Reports on the North American activities of the oldest, continuously-aired religious radio broadcast since 1930.

WETA Magazine. Editor(s): Pat Good. Sponsoring Organization: WETA, 3700 S. Four Mile Run Dr., Arlington, VA 22206. Telephone: 703-845-8084. FAX: 703-379-5232. Frequency: m. Circulation: 125,000.

WIC News. Editor(s): C. Kane. Sponsoring Organization: Women In Cable, PM Haeger & Associates, 500 N. Michigan Ave., Suite 1400, Chicago 60611. Telephone: 312-661-1700. FAX: 312-661-0769. Frequency: bi-m. Year First Published: 1984. Special Features: bk rev. Circulation: 20,000. Price: $75.

Supports professional development opportunities and issues that concern working women in the cable industry.

Whitmark Magazine. Editor(s): Eric Hirschhorn. Sponsoring Organization: Whitmark Associates, 4120 Main St., Dallas 75226-1196. Telephone: 214-871-8901. Frequency: bi-m. Year First Published: 1968. Special Features: illus. Circulation: 12,000. Price: $12.

Reports from seven-state southwestern film-video industry on radio and television communications.

World Broadcast News. Editor(s): Gerald Walker. Intertec Publishing Corp., 9800 Metcalf, Overland Park, KS 66212-2215. Telephone: 913-341-1300. FAX: 913-967-1898. Frequency: m. (except July-Aug. combined). Circulation: 11,212 (controlled). Price: Free to qualified personnel.

World Guide to Television and Programming. ISSN: 1058-1944. North American Publishing Co., 401 N. Broad St., Philadelphia 19108. Telephone: 215-238-5300. FAX: 215-238-5474. Frequency: a.

World Radio TV Handbook. ISSN: 0144-7750. Editor(s): A.G. Sennitt. BPI Communications Inc. (New York), Affiliated Publications Inc., 1515 Broadway, 39th Fl., New York 10036. Telephone: 212-764-7300. FAX: 212-944-1719. Frequency: a. Year First Published: 1947. Circulation: 55,000. Price: $19.95.

Complete guide to international broadcasting.

World Scanner Report. ISSN: 1061-9240. Commtronics Engineering, Box 262478-C, San Diego 92196-2478. Frequency: m. Year First Published: 1991. Special Features: adv, bk rev. Price: $25.

Features do-it-yourself mods, soup-ups, hints and kinks for serious scanner needs.

Worldradio. Editor(s): Robin Wortley, Armand Noble. Worldradio Inc., 2120 28th St., Sacramento, CA 95818. Telephone: 916-457-3655. Frequency: m. Year First Published: 1971. Special Features: adv, bk rev, illus. Circulation: 26,600. Price: $14.

Articles for the amateur radio hobbyist.

Worldwide Directory of Film and Video Festivals and Events. Editor(s): Richard Calkins. Sponsoring Organization: Council on International Nontheatrical Events Inc., 1001 Connecticut Ave. N.W., Suite 1016, Washington, DC 20036. Telephone: 202-785-1136. FAX: 202-785-4114. Frequency: a. Year First Published: 1988. Circulation: 3,000. Price: $18.

Worldwide Videotex Update. ISSN: 0731-7891. Editor(s): Mark Wright. Worldwide Videotex, Box 138, Babson Park, Boston 02157. Telephone: 508-477-8979. Frequency: m. Year First Published: 1981. Back issues available. Circulation: 800. Price: $125.

Yearbook of Experts, Authorities & Spokespersons: An Encyclopedia of Sources. Editor(s): Mitchell P. Davis. Sponsoring Organization: Broadcast Interview Source, 2233 Wisconsin Ave. N.W., Washington, DC 20007. Telephone: 202-333-4904. FAX: 202-342-5411. Frequency: a. Year First Published: 1984. Special Features: adv. Circulation: 9,400. Price: $39.75.

Reviews 14,312 topics of interest to the media and provides contact names and phone numbers.

Videos on Broadcasting and Cable

A listing of videos on radio and television broadcasting, satellites and cable television from *Bowker's Complete Video Directory* data base.

Action & Violence. 1981. Getting the Most Out of TV Series. Color. 12 minutes. Made-for-video. New Dimension Media, Inc. Tel.: 503-484-7125. VHS $195.00.

Alex Segal: Former Director Discusses TV. The Lively Arts Series. 30 minutes. Contributions by John J. Beeston. Univ. of Southern California, Davidson Conference Center. Tel.: 213-743-5219. VHS $95.00.

Announcing & Presentation. Basic Radio Skills Series. Color. 28 minutes. Made-for-video. First Light Video Publishing. Tel.: 800-777-1576. VHS $149.00.

The Art of the Radio Advertising. Color. 20 minutes. Made-for-video. First Light Video Publishing. Tel.: 800-777-1576. VHS $119.00.

Basic Radio Skills Series. Color. Made-for-video. First Light Video Publishing. Tel.: 800-777-1576. VHS $695.00.

Basic Television Terms: A Video Dictionary. 1977. Color. 17 minutes. Narrated by Leonard Nimoy. Pyramid Film & Video. Tel.: 800-421-2304. VHS $195.00.

Behind Your Radio Dial & Westinghouse Presents. 1948. 45 minutes. Documentary. Video Yesteryear. Tel.: 800-243-0987. VHS $24.95. Beta $24.95.

Broadcast Journalism Lab. Instructional Video. Tel.: 419-475-5060. VHS $29.95.

Broadcast Journalism Lab Exercise. 1989. Color. 60 minutes. Instructional Video. Tel.: 419-475-5060. VHS $29.95.

Broadcast News: How It Works. 1988. Color. 26 minutes. Instructional Video. Tel.: 419-475-5060. VHS $39.95.

Camera Mountings. Color. 11 minutes. Films for the Humanities & Sciences. Tel.: 800-257-5126. VHS $129.00.

Careers in Broadcast News. 1989. Color. 35 minutes. Instructional Video. Tel.: 419-475-5060. VHS $39.95.

The Case Against Television. 1987. Color. 15 minutes. Barr Films, Inc. Tel.: 800-234-7878. VHS $230.00.

The Case Against Television. 1988. Color. 14 minutes. Barr Films, Inc. Tel.: 800-234-7878. VHS $230.00.

Characters We See on TV. Getting the Most Out of TV Series. Color. 12 minutes. Made-for-video. 1981. New Dimension Media, Inc. Tel.: 503-484-7125. VHS $195.00.

Childhood Socialization. Focus on Society Series. 30 minutes. A look at the role of television in childhood socialization. RMI Media Productions, Inc. Tel.: 800-821-5480. VHS $75.00.

Children & Television. Parents' Point of View Series. 30 minutes. Hosted by Nancy Thurmond. RMI Media Productions, Inc. Tel.: 800-821-5480. VHS $69.95.

Commercial Mania. Rhino Home Video. Tel.: 310-828-1980. VHS $29.95. Beta $29.95.

Commercials. Getting the Most Out of TV Series. Color. 12 minutes. Made-for-video. 1981. New Dimension Media, Inc. Tel.: 503-484-7125. VHS $195.00.

Consuming Hunger: Famine & the Media. Documentary. Maryknoll World Productions. Tel.: 914-945-0670. VHS $39.95.

Continuity & the Single Camera. Color. 25 minutes. Films for the Humanities & Sciences. Tel.: 800-257-5126. VHS $149.00.

Continuity: Tricks of the Trade. Color. 40 minutes. Films for the Humanities & Sciences. Tel.: 800-257-5126. VHS $149.00.

A Conversation with Sam Donaldson. Color. 30 minutes. Hosted by Bob Ray Sanders. Documentary. Eidos Productions, Inc. Tel.: 214-330-9795. VHS $50.00.

Deidre Hall: A Video Biography. 75 minutes. Documentary. June 1987. Columbia Tristar Home Video. Tel.: 818-972-8686. VHS $19.95. Beta $19.95.

Diary of a News Story. Inside Television News Series. Color. 11 minutes. Made-for-video. 1990. New Dimension Media, Inc. Tel.: 503-484-7125. VHS $125.00.

Ed McMahon, Supersalesman. Color. 28 minutes. Hosted by Phil Donahue. Films for the Humanities & Sciences. Tel.: 800-257-5126. VHS $149.00.

Editing. Basic Radio Skills Series. Color. 16 minutes. Made-for-video. First Light Video Publishing. Tel.: 800-777-1576. VHS $119.00.

Electronic Effects. Color. 37 minutes. Films for the Humanities & Sciences. Tel.: 800-257-5126. VHS $149.00.

The Electronic Rainbow: Television. 1977. Color. 23 minutes. Hosted by Leonard Nimoy. Pyramid Film & Video. Tel.: 800-421-2304. VHS $95.00.

The Era of Direct Broadcast Satellites. Color. 56 minutes. 1990. Shelburne Films. Tel.: 614-378-6297. VHS $149.00.

Ethics. Inside Television News Series. Color. 10 minutes. Made-for-video. 1990. New Dimension Media, Inc. Tel.: 503-484-7125.

Events That Shaped Our World. Great TV News Stories Series. Color. 30 minutes. Contributions by ABC News Team Staff. Made-for-television. MPI Home Video. Tel.: 800-323-0442. VHS $9.98.

Fifteen Years of MacNeil-Lehrer. 1990. Color. 60 minutes. Featuring Robert MacNeil and James Lehrer. CC. PBS Video. Tel.: 800-424-7963. VHS $49.95.

Fifteen Years with MacNeil-Lehrer. 65 minutes. Facets Multimedia, Inc. Tel.: 800-331-6197. VHS $19.95.

Getting the Most Out of TV. Color. 84 minutes. Made-for-video. 1981. New Dimension Media, Inc. Tel.: 503-484-7125. VHS $295.00.

The Great Gleason. 1987. Black and white. 90 minutes. Dec. 1987. MPI Home Video. Tel.: 800-323-0442. VHS $29.95. Beta $29.95.

The Great Radio Comedians. Color. CRM Films, L.P. Tel.: 800-421-0833. VHS $295.00.

Great TV News Stories: TWA Hijacking - 17 Days of Terror. 60 minutes. Sept 1989. MPI Home Video. Tel.: 800-323-0442. VHS $24.95. Beta $24.95.

Henson's Place: The Man Behind the Muppets. The Muppets Series. Color. 52 minutes. Contributions by Jim Henson. 1988. Public Media, Inc. Tel.: 800-323-4222. VHS $49.00.

The Home Satellite TV Installation Video Tape. 1986. Color. 44 minutes. Demonstrated by Frank Baylin. Baylin Publications, Inc. Tel.: 303-449-4551. VHS $29.95. Beta $29.95.

How a Radio Station Works. 1988. Color. 26 minutes. Documentary. Instructional Video. Tel.: 419-475-5060. VHS $39.95.

The Impact of Television. 20 minutes. Contributions by Clive M. Davis. 1980. Encyclopaedia Britannica Educational Corp. Tel.: 800-554-9862. VHS $300.00. Beta $300.00.

The Impact of Television: A Chautauqua Chronicle. 1989. Color. 60 minutes. Documentary. WNED-TV. Tel.: 716-881-5000. VHS $29.95.

In Conversation with Joan Collins. Color. 26 minutes. Horizon Entertainment Group, Inc. Tel.: 805-257-6054. VHS $9.95.

Installing Satellite Antennas. 1984. 31 minutes. Shelburne Films. Tel.: 614-378-6297. VHS $125.00. Beta $125.00.

An Introduction to the Studio. Color. 17 minutes. Films for the Humanities & Sciences. Tel.: 800-257-5126. VHS $149.00.

Jimmy Swaggart: Friday, February 19, 1988 & Monday, February 22, 1988. The Best of Nightline Series. Color. 30 minutes. Hosted by Ted Koppel. Made-for-television. MPI Home Video. Tel.: 800-323-0442. VHS $14.98.

Joan Does Dynasty. 1986. Color. 35 minutes. Women Make Movies, Inc. Tel.: 212-925-0606.

The Key Players. Inside Television News Series. Color. 11 minutes. Made-for-video. 1990. New Dimension Media, Inc. Tel.: 503-484-7125.

The Legal Considerations of Broadcast News. 1988. Color. 29 minutes. Instructional Video. Tel.: 419-475-5060. VHS $39.95.

Louis Farrakhan: Thursday, April 5, 1984. The Best of Nightline Series. Color. 30 minutes. Hosted by Ted Koppel. Made-for-television. MPI Home Video. Tel.: 800-323-0442. VHS $14.98.

Lucille Ball Dies: Wednesday, April 26, 1989. The Best of Nightline Series. Color. 30 minutes. Hosted by Ted Koppel. Made-for-television. MPI Home Video. Tel.: 800-323-0442. VHS $14.98.

MacNeil-Lehrer Newshour. 60 minutes. PBS Video. Tel.: 800-424-7963. VHS $34.95.

The Magic of TV. 1981. Getting the Most Out of TV Series. Color. 12 minutes. Made-for-video. New Dimension Media, Inc. Tel.: 503-484-7125. VHS $195.00.

The Making of a Documentary. Color. 21 minutes. Carousel Film & Video. Tel.: 212-683-1660. VHS $175.00.

The Making of a Live TV Show. 1977. Color. 24 minutes. Pyramid Film & Video. Tel.: 800-421-2304. VHS $295.00.

The Making of a Live Television Show. 1988. Color. 22 minutes. Documentary. Instructional Video. Tel.: 419-475-5060. VHS $39.95.

The Making of Television News. 1989. Color. 45 minutes. Instructional Video. Tel.: 419-475-5060. VHS $39.95.

The Making of the Television News. Color. 40 minutes. Films for the Humanities & Sciences. Tel.: 800-257-5126. VHS $149.00.

Media & Message—Television: The Electric Art. The Art of Being Human Series. 30 minutes. Documentary. RMI Media Productions, Inc. Tel.: 800-821-5480. VHS $59.95.

Motown: The Last Radio Station. Color. 60 minutes. MCA/Universal Home Video. Distributed by LaserDisc Corp. of America. Tel.: 310-835-6177. VHS; write for info. Beta; write for info.

Mountain Vision: Homegrown Television in Appalachian. 1991. Color. 29 minutes. Appalshop. Tel.: 800-545-7467. VHS $150.00.

Mr. Television. 30 minutes. Featuring Milton Berle. The Christophers. Tel.:212-759-4050. VHS $19.95.

Newswomen. Color. 28 minutes. Films for the Humanities & Sciences. Tel.: 800-257-5126. VHS $149.00.

Nixon-Wallace TV Election Spots, 1968. 1968. Color. 27 minutes. International Historic Films, Inc. Tel.: 800-726-1315. VHS $22.00. Beta $22.00.

Of Muppets & Men. The Muppets Series. Color. 52 minutes. 1988. Public Media, Inc. Tel.: 800-323-4222. VHS $49.00.

On TV. Color. 93 minutes. Video Publishing House, Inc. Tel.: 800-824-8889. VHS $295.00.

On Television: Public Trust or Private Property? 1988. Color. 50 minutes. Hosted by Edwin Newman. Public Media, Inc. Tel.: 800-323-4222. VHS $129.00.

On Television: The Violence Factor. Color. 58 minutes. Hosted by Edwin Newman. 1984. Public Media, Inc. Tel.: 800-323-4222. VHS $129.00.

People Make Programs. 1981. Getting the Most Out of TV Series. 12 minutes. New Dimension Media, Inc. Tel.: 503-484-7125.

Persistence of Vision: Monitoring the Media. 1987. Color. The Voyager Co. Tel.: 800-446-2001. VHS $39.95. Beta $39.95.

Persistence of Vision: Outside the Lines. 1987. Color. The Voyager Co. Tel.: 800-446-2001. VHS $39.95. Beta $39.95.

The Power of TV News. Inside Television News Series. Color. 10 minutes. Made-for-video. 1990. New Dimension Media, Inc. Tel.: 503-484-7125.

Videos on Broadcasting and Cable

Quarks. 1980. Color. 8 minutes. An analysis of broadcast television. The Kitchen. Tel.: 212-255-5793. VHS $75.00.

The Question of Television Violence. 1972. Color. 56 minutes. National Film Board of Canada. Tel.: 212-586-5131. VHS $450.00. Beta $450.00.

The Question of Television Violence. 1974. Color. 56 minutes. Phoenix/BFA Films & Video. Tel.: 800-221-1274.

Radio Interview. Basic Radio Skills Series. Color. 20 minutes. Made-for-video. First Light Video Publishing. Tel.: 800-777-1576. VHS $149.00.

Radio News. Basic Radio Skills Series. Color. 38 minutes. Made-for-video. First Light Video Publishing. Tel.: 800-777-1576. VHS $149.00.

Radio Production: Making a Radio Commercial. 1988. Color. 43 minutes. Narrated by Street Remley. Made-for-video. First Light Video Publishing. Tel.: 800-777-1576. VHS $149.00.

Radio Studio. Basic Radio Skills Series. Color. 31 minutes. Made-for-video. First Light Video Publishing. Tel.: 800-777-1576. VHS $149.00.

Radio Talkback. Basic Radio Skills Series. Color. 35 minutes. Made-for-video. First Light Video Publishing. Tel.: 800-777-1576. VHS $149.00.

Radio-TV Announcers. Miscellaneous Career Series. Color. Educational Images, Ltd. Tel.: 607-732-1090. VHS $39.95.

Radio Writing. Basic Radio Skills Series. Color. 47 minutes. Made-for-video. First Light Video Publishing. Tel.: 800-777-1576. VHS $149.00.

The Real World of TV. 1981. Getting the Most Out of TV Series. 12 minutes. New Dimension Media, Inc. Tel.: 503-484-7125.

The Satellite Sky. 1990. The American Experience Series. Color. 60 minutes. CC. PBS Video. Tel.: 800-424-7963. VHS $69.95.

Satellite TV Basics II. 1985. Color. 14 minutes. Shelburne Films. Tel.: 614-378-6297. VHS $99.00. Beta $99.00.

Script To Screen. Color. 39 minutes. Films for the Humanities & Sciences. Tel.: 800-257-5126. VHS $149.00.

Secrets of Effective Radio Advertising. Color. 75 minutes. Films for the Humanities & Sciences. Tel.: 800-257-5126. VHS $159.00.

Shaping News for the Consumer. 1975. Color. 17 minutes. Phoenix/BFA Films & Video. Tel.: 800-221-1274. VHS; write for info.

Shock Waves: Television in America. 1984. 32 minutes. Coronet, The Multimedia Co. Tel.: 800-621-2131. VHS $250.00. Beta $250.00.

Sixty Second Spot. 1974. Color. 25 minutes. Pyramid Film & Video. Tel.: 800-421-2304. VHS $95.00.

Speak up on Television. 30 minutes. 1986. Encyclopaedia Britannica Educational Corp. Tel.: 800-554-9862. VHS $395.00.

Sports Satellite TV. 1992. Color. 60 minutes. Made-for-video. July 1992. Quality Video, Inc. Tel.: 612-924-2322. VHS $7.99.

The Story of Television. 1956. Black and white; color. 27 minutes. Featuring David Sarnoff. Documentary. Video Yesteryear. Tel.: 800-243-0987. VHS $19.95. Beta $19.95.

Superboy Screen Tests. 1961. 22 minutes. Video Yesteryear. Tel.: 800-243-0987. VHS $19.95. Beta $19.95.

The Technical Side of TV. 1981. Getting the Most Out of TV Series. Color. 12 minutes. Made-for-video. New Dimension Media, Inc. Tel.: 503-484-7125. VHS $195.00.

The Techniques of Television Commercials. 1989. Color. 28 minutes. Instructional Video. Tel.: 419-475-5060. VHS $39.95.

TV Ads: Our Mini-Myths. 1977. Color. 16 minutes. Pyramid Film & Video. Tel.: 800-421-2304. VHS $295.00.

TV: Behind the Screen. 1978. Color. 16 minutes. Churchill Films. Tel.: 310-207-1330. VHS $79.00. Beta $79.00.

TV Evangelists: Monday, March 23, 1987 & Tuesday, March 24, 1987. The Best of Nightline Series. Color. 75 minutes. Hosted by Ted Koppel. Made-for-television. MPI Home Video. Tel.: 800-323-0442. VHS $14.98.

A TV Guide: Thinking about What We Watch. 1978. Color. 17 minutes. Churchill Films. Tel.: 310-207-1330. VHS $89.00. Beta $89.00.

TV News: Behind the Scenes. The World of Work Series. 27 minutes. Contributions by Sig Mickelson. Documentary. 1973. Encyclopaedia Britannica Educational Corp. Tel.: 800-554-9862. VHS $300.00. Beta $300.00.

TV News: Measure of the Medium. 1971. Color. 16 minutes. Phoenix/BFA Films & Video. Tel.: 800-221-1274. VHS; write for info.

Television Delivers People. 1973. Color. 6 minutes. The Kitchen. Tel.: 212-255-5793. VHS $75.00.

The Television Designer. Color. 27 minutes. Films for the Humanities & Sciences. Tel.: 800-257-5126. VHS $149.00.

The Television Newsman. 1976. Color. 28 minutes. Pyramid Film & Video. Tel.: 800-421-2304. VHS $350.00.

Television & the Presidency. Black and white; color. 98 minutes. Hosted by E.G. Marshall. Documentary. Social Studies Schl. Service. Tel.: 800-421-4246.

Televisionland. 1971. Color. 12 minutes. Pyramid Film & Video. Tel.: 800-421-2304. VHS $95.00.

Television's Vietnam: Impact of the Media & The Real Story. 120 minutes. Narrated by Charlton Heston. Documentary. SVS, Inc. Tel.: 212-757-4990. VHS $14.95. Beta $14.95.

Theme Song. 1973. Black and white. 30 minutes. Explores the intimacy of the television viewing situation. The Kitchen. Tel.: 212-255-5793. VHS $100.00.

Thirty Second Spots: TV Commercials for Artists. 1982. Color. 15 minutes. The Kitchen. Tel.: 212-255-5793. VHS $100.00.

Turn a Handle, Flick a Switch. 1983. Color. 14 minutes. Churchill Films. Tel.: 310-207-1330. VHS $220.00.

The Twenty-One-Inch World. Communications Skills Two—Advanced Series. 28 minutes. RMI Media Productions, Inc. Tel.: 800-821-5480. VHS $89.95.

Visual Effects for TV: The Battlefield. Color. 30 minutes. Films for the Humanities & Sciences. Tel.: 800-257-5126. VHS $149.00.

Webster Groves Revisited. Black and white. 53 minutes. Examines the effect of a televion broadcast on a small community. Carousel Film & Video. Tel.: 212-683-1660. VHS $250.00.

What Is News?: Inside Television News Series. Color. 14 minutes. Made-for-video. 1989. New Dimension Media, Inc. Tel.: 503-484-7125.

Who Is Sylvia?. 1978. Footsteps Series. Color. 29 minutes. Distributed by the National Audiovisual Center. Tel.: 301-763-1850. VHS $110.00. Beta $110.00.

Who Is Sylvia?: Learning Through TV. The Footsteps Series. 28 minutes. Perennial Education, Inc. Tel.: 800-323-9084. VHS $139.00. Beta $139.00.

Women As Seen on Television. Color. 11 minutes. Made-for-video. 1991. New Dimension Media, Inc. Tel.: 503-484-7125. VHS $195.00.

Writing Commentary. Color. 30 minutes. Films for the Humanities & Sciences. Tel.: 800-257-5126. VHS $149.00.

Writing for Radio. 1989. Color. 44 minutes. Made-for-video. First Light Video Publishing. Tel.: 800-777-1576. VHS $149.00.

Yap...How Did You Know We'd Like TV?. 1987. Color. 54 minutes. Documentary. Direct Cinema, Ltd. Tel.: 800-345-6748.

Index to Sections

A

Abbreviations xii

ABC
   Executives and Staff G-36, G-62
   Networks, Radio G-36
   Networks, TV G-62

Acknowledgements ii

ADIs
   Arbitron Market Atlas C-123
   Multi-City Cross-Reference C-201

Adult Contemporary
   Definition of Format B-529
   Format by Province B-540
   Format by State B-530
   Programming, Canada B-571
   Programming, U.S. B-543
   Special Programming, U.S. B-573

Advertisers Index K-9

Advertising
   Agency Directory F-2
   Associations, Media Societies I-2, I-8
   Professional Cards H-105

Affiliates (see appropriate network)

AFRTS (Armed Forces Radio
   and Television Service) B-449

Agencies
   Advertising F-2
   Canadian Government A-52
   State Cable Regulatory A-53
   U.S. Government A-50

Agents, Talent H-102

Agriculture & Farm
   Definition of Format B-529
   Format by Province B-540
   Format by State B-530
   Programming, Canada B-571
   Programming, U.S. B-546
   Special Programming, Canada B-589
   Special Programming, U.S. B-573

Allotments, FM B-475

AM Stations
   By Call Letters, Canada B-473
   By Call Letters, U.S. B-451
   By Frequencies, Canada B-525
   By Frequencies, U.S. B-486
   By Provinces, Canada B-540
   By States, U.S. B-530

American Broadcasting Co. G-36, G-62

American Indian
   Definition of Format B-529
   Format by State B-530
   Programming, U.S. B-546
   Special Programming, Canada B-589
   Special Programming, U.S. B-575

American Public Radio G-48

American Urban Radio Networks G-37

AOR (see Rock)

AP (Associated Press) G-38

Applying for a Broadcast Station A-30

Associated Press (AP) G-38

Association of Independent I-2
   Television Stations Inc.

Arabic
   Special Programming, Canada B-589
   Special Programming, U.S. B-575

Arbitron Metro Survey Area
   Ranking of Radio Markets B-598

Armed Forces Radio & TV Service (AFRTS) ... B-449

Armenian
   Special Programming, U.S. B-575

Artists Representatives H-102

Assignments of
   FM Stations, U.S. B-475
   TV Channels, U.S. C-120

Associations
   Major National I-2
   National I-8
   State and Regional Broadcast I-15
   State and Regional Cable I-17

Associations, Events, Education and Awards
   Table of Contents I-1

Attorneys, Communications H-90

Audience
   Radio B-605
   TV C-219
   Measurement Services H-79

Audio Cable Programming Services G-84

Automated Cable Channel Programmers G-83

Awards, Major Broadcasting and Cable I-32

B

Barter Service Companies F-9

Basic Cable Services G-79

Beautiful Music
   Definition of Format B-529
   Format by Province B-540
   Format by State B-530
   Programming, Canada B-571
   Programming, U.S. B-546
   Special Programming, U.S. B-575

Big Band
   Definition of Format B-529
   Format by Province B-540
   Format by State B-530
   Programming, Canada B-571
   Programming, U.S. B-547
   Special Programming, Canada B-589
   Special Programming, U.S. B-575

Black
   Definition of Format B-529
   Format by State B-530
   Programming, U.S. B-547
   Special Programming, Canada B-589
   Special Programming, U.S. B-575

Bluegrass
   Definition of Format B-529
   Format by State B-530
   Programming, U.S. B-547
   Special Programming, Canada B-589
   Special Programming, U.S. B-576

Blues
   Definition of Format B-529
   Format by State B-530
   Programming, U.S. B-548
   Special Programming, Canada B-589
   Special Programming, U.S. B-577

Books
   International J-5
   On Broadcasting J-2, J-7
   Relating to Radio, TV & Cable J-2, J-7

Books, Periodicals, Videos
   Table of Contents J-1

Brief History of Broadcasting and Cable xiii

Broadcast History xiii

Broadcast Station, Applying for A-30

Broadcasters in Cable D-66

Broadcasters State and Regional Associations .. I-15

Broadcasting
   Books on J-2, J-7
   Degrees in I-26
   History of xiii
   Major Awards I-32
   Periodicals on J-16, J-18
   Videos on J-31

Brokers H-59

Buying/Planning Services F-8

C

CAB (Cabletelevision Advertising Bureau Inc.) I-2

Cable
   Automated Channel Programmers G-83
   Basic Services G-79
   Books on J-2, J-7
   Broadcasters in D-66
   Brokers H-59
   Geographic Index to Systems D-55
   History of xiii
   Listings, Key to D-2
   MSOs D-3
   Networks G-78
   Pay Services G-78
   Penetration by Market D-68
   Periodicals on J-16, J-18
   Program Services G-78
   Regional Cable TV
     News Program Networks G-85
   Regional Associations I-17
   Regulations A-32
   Regulatory Agencies, State A-53
   Representatives, Canadian F-20
   Representatives, U.S. F-10
   Schools I-25
   Sports Services G-86
   State Associations I-17
   Systems D-3
   Table of Contents D-1
   Videos on J-31

Cable News Network (CNN) G-79

Cabletelevision Advertising Bureau Inc. (CAB) I-2

Call Letters
   Radio, Canadian AM by B-473
   Radio, Canadian FM by B-474
   Radio, U.S. AM by B-451
   Radio, U.S. FM by B-460
   TV, Canadian by C-93
   TV, U.S. by C-90

Canada
   AM Stations by Call Letters B-473
   AM Stations by Frequency B-525
   FM Stations by Call Letters B-474
   FM Stations by Frequency B-527
   Radio Station Directory B-427
   TV by Channel C-119
   TV Station Directory C-81

Canadian Broadcasting Corp. G-55, G-72

Canadian Cable Programming Services G-88

Canadian Cable Television Assn. (CCTA) I-2

Canadian Government Agencies A-52

Canadian Radio
   Formats by Province B-540
   Programming Formats B-571
   Special Programming B-589

Canadian Radio-Television and
   Telecommunications Commission A-52

Canadian Representatives F-20

Capital Cities/ABC Inc. G-36, G-62

Index to Sections

CATA (Community Antenna Television Assn.) I-2

CBS Inc.
Executives and Staff G-39, G-64
Networks, Radio G-36
Networks, TV G-62

CCTA (Canadian Cable Television Assn.) I-2

Channel Programmers, Automated Cable G-83

Channels
FM B-475
TV by, Canadian C-119
TV by, United States C-115

Charts
Arbitron ADI Market Atlas C-123
Bottom 50 Market Areas Ranked by
Percentage of Cable Penetration D-75
Cable Penetration by Market D-68
Comparable Record of Radio Station
Growth Since TV Began B-604
Comparable Record of TV Station Growth
Since TV Began C-218
Federal Communications Commission Staff.... A-2
Growth of Radio Broadcasting Pre-TV B-602
History of Station Sales Transactions A-95
How Network Delivery Varies by Market..... C-213
Multi-City ADI Cross-Reference C-201
Non-ADI Markets C-202
Radio Audiences B-605
Radio Markets Ranked by Arbitron
Metro Survey Area B-598
Radio Markets Ranked by Arbitron
Total Survey Area B-600
Radio Markets Ranked by Population....... B-600
Satellite Guide to the Sky E-3
Television Audiences C-219
TV Markets Ranked by Size C-203
TV Markets Ranked by Nielsen
Marketing Research Territory C-208
Top 50 Market Areas Ranked by
Cable TV Households D-73
Top 50 Market Areas Ranked by
Percentage of Cable Penetration D-72
Top 50 Market Areas Ranked by
TV Households D-74
Top 50 Cable MSOs D-76
Top 100 Companies C-210
U.S. and Canadian Radio
Programming Formats B-542
U.S. Radio Set Sales 1958-1991 .... B-603
U.S. Sales of Television
Receivers 1958-1991 .... C-217

Children
Definition of Format B-529
Format by State B-530
Programming, U.S. B-548
Special Programming, U.S. B-577

Chinese
Format by Province B-540
Programming, Canada B-571
Special Programming, Canada............. B-589
Special Programming, U.S. B-577

Citations and Awards I-32

Classic Rock
Definition of Format B-529
Format by Province B-540
Format by State B-530
Programming, Canada B-571
Programming, U.S. B-548
Special Programming, Canada............. B-589
Special Programming, U.S. B-577

Classical
Definition of Format B-529
Format by Province B-540
Format by State B-530
Programming, Canada B-571
Programming, U.S. B-548
Special Programming, Canada............. B-589
Special Programming, U.S. B-577

Closed Circuit TV G-77

CNN (Cable News Network)................ G-79

Codes, NAB TV-Radio A-49

Coding, ISCI A-48

College-Owned
Radio B-484
TV C-113

Colleges Offering Radio-TV-Cable Courses I-29

Colleges Offering Broadcasting Degrees I-27

Colleges Offering Two-Year Programs I-29

Comedy
Definition of Format B-529
Format by State B-530
Special Programming, U.S. B-578

Commerce Committees, House and Senate.... A-50

Common Carriers E-4

Communications, Canadian Department of..... A-52

Communications Law, Firms Active in H-90

Community Antenna Television Assn. (CATA) I-2

Congressional Committees................. A-50

Consultants
Management H-65
Technical, Engineering................... H-84

Contemporary Hit / Top 40
Definition of Format B-529
Format by Province B-540
Format by State B-530
Programming, Canada B-571
Programming, U.S. B-549
Special Programming, Canada B-589
Special Programming, U.S. B-578

Corporation for Public Broadcasting G-68

Country
Definition of Format B-529
Format by Province B-540
Format by State B-530
Programming, Canada B-571
Programming, U.S. B-550
Special Progrmming, Canada B-589
Special Programming, U.S. B-578

Croatian
Special Programming, Canada B-589
Special Programming, U.S. B-578

Cross-Ownership, Station A-118

Czech
Special Programming, U.S. B-578

D

DBS..................................... E-9

Definition of Radio Formats................ B-529

Degrees in Broadcasting I-27

Direct Broadcast Satellites E-9

Directories
Advertising Agencies F-2
Canadian Radio Stations................. B-412
Canadian TV Stations C-81
Miscellaneous Radio Services B-449
MSOs and Cable Systems D-3
U.S. Radio Stations B-3
U.S. TV Stations C-3

Disco
Definition of Format B-529
Format by Province B-540
Programming, Canada B-571
Programming, U.S. B-555
Special Programming, U.S. B-578

Distribution Services
Multichannel Multipoint E-17
Multipoint E-14

Distributors
Equipment H-2, H-12
Programs G-3, G-9

Diverse (see Variety)

DMA
By % Penetration D-72
Top 50 by Cable TV Households........... D-73
Top 50 by TV Households D-74
Bottom 50 by % Cable Penetration D-75

Drama/Literature
Definition of Format B-529
Format by Province B-540
Format by State B-530
Programming, Canada B-571
Programming, U.S. B-555
Special Programming, Canada............. B-589
Special Programming, U.S. B-578

E

Eastern Public Radio G-48

Education
Schools Specializing in Radio-TV-Cable,
Universities and Colleges Offering I-25
Degrees in Broadcasting.................. I-27

Educational Broadcasting Corp.............. G-68

Educational
Definition by Format B-529
Format by Province B-540
Format by State B-530
Programming, Canada B-571
Programming, U.S. B-555
Special Programming, Canada............. B-589
Special Programming, U.S. B-578

Electronic Media
Books on J-2, J-7
Periodicals on J-16, J-18

Electronic Media Rating Council............... I-2

Employment Services..................... H-103

Engineering Consultants H-84

Equipment Manufacturers, Distributors H-2, H-12

Ethnic (see Foreign Language)

Events
Trade Shows Alphabetical Index............ I-20
Trade Show by Category.................. I-21

Executive Search Services H-103

Experimental TV Stations C-111

F

Farm (See Agriculture & Farm)

Federal Communications Commission
Executives & Staff....................... A-2
Organization Chart A-3
Past Members............................ A-4
Rules Regulating Cable A-32
Rules Regulating Radio and TV A-5

Filipino
Format by State B-530
Programming, U.S. B-555
Special Programming, Canada............. B-589
Special Programming, U.S. B-578

Film Distributors for TV..................... G-3

Financial Consultants............ H-59, H-65, H-76

Financing, Station........................ H-76

Finnish
Special Programming, Canada............. B-589
Special Programming, U.S. B-578

FM Stations
Allotments............................ B-475
By Call Letters, Canada B-474
By Call Letters, U.S. B-460
By Frequency, Canada B-527
By Frequency, U.S. B-502
Channels B-475
Stations, U.S. B-3

Folk
Definition by Format B-529
Format by State B-530

Broadcasting & Cable Yearbook 1994
K-2

Index to Sections

Programming, U.S. B-555
   Special Programming, Canada B-589
   Special Programming, U.S. B-578
Foreign Language
   Definition of Format B-529
   Format by Province B-540
   Format by State B-530
   Programming, Canada B-571
   Programming, U.S. B-555
   Special Programming, Canada B-589
   Special Programming, U.S. B-579
Formats
   Definition for Radio B-529
   By State for Radio B-530
   By Province for Radio B-540
   Canadian Radio Programming B-571
   U.S. Radio Programming B-543
Fox Broadcasting Company G-65
French
   Format by Province B-540
   Format by State B-530
   Programming, Canada B-572
   Programming, U.S. B-556
   Special Programming, Canada B-589
   Special Programming, U.S. B-579
Frequencies
   Canadian AM B-525
   Canadian FM B-527
   United States AM B-486
   United States FM B-502

G

Geographic Index to Cable Systems D-55
German
   Programming, U.S. B-556
   Special Programming, Canada B-589
   Special Programming, U.S. B-579
Global Television Network G-73
Glossary of Terms xi
Gospel
   Definition of Format B-529
   Format by State B-530
   Programming, Canada B-572
   Programming, U.S. B-556
   Special Programming, Canada B-589
   Special Programming, U.S. B-580
Government Agencies
   Federal Communications Commission A-2
   House Committee on Commerce A-50
   Senate Committee on Commerce A-50
   Supreme Court A-50
Government, Canadian A-52
Greek
   Format by State B-530
   Programming, U.S. B-556
   Special Programming, Canada B-589
   Special Programming, U.S. B-581
Group Ownership of Stations A-96
Groups, Labor & Unions I-18
Growth of Broadcasting .... xiii, B-602, C-218
Guide
   Satellite E-3
   User's vii

H

Hebrew
   Special Programming, Canada B-589
   Special Programming, U.S. B-581
Hindi
   Special Programming, Canada B-589
   Special Programming, U.S. B-581
History
   Broadcasting and Cable xiii
House Committee on Commerce A-50

Hungarian
   Special Programming, Canada B-589
   Special Programming, U.S. B-581

I

Independent Media Buying/Planning Services ... F-8
Independent TV Stations, Assn. of I-2
Independent TV Stations, U.S. C-112
Index
   Advertisers K-9
   Cable Systems, Geographically D-55
   Equipment Manufacturers and Distributors
     and Technical Services Subject H-2
   Equipment Manufacturers and Distributors
     and Technical Services Alphabetical ... H-12
   Producers, Distributors, Production
     and Other Services Subject G-2
   Radio and TV by Province K-8
   Radio and TV by State K-8
   Sections K-1
   Trade Shows Alphabetical I-20
   Trade Shows Subject I-21
   Radio, TV & Cable Industries
     Yellow Pages .... Volume II
Industry Standard Coding
   Identification System (ISCI) A-48
Information Agency, U.S. A-51
International Stations in the U.S. B-449
Irish
   Special Programming, Canada B-589
   Special Programming, U.S. B-581
ISCI (Industry Standard Coding
   Identification System) A-48
Italian
   Programming, U.S. B-556
   Special Programming, Canada B-589
   Special Programming, U.S. B-581

J

Japanese
   Programming, U.S. B-556
   Special Programming, U.S. B-581
Jazz
   Definition of Format B-529
   Format by Province B-540
   Format by State B-530
   Programming, Canada B-572
   Programming, U.S. B-556
   Special Programming, Canada B-589
   Special Programming, U.S. B-581
Jewish
   Programming, U.S. B-557
   Special Programming, Canada B-589
   Special Programming, U.S. B-582

K

Key to Cable Listings D-2
Key to Radio Listings B-2
Key to Television Listings C-2
Korean
   Programming, U.S. B-557
   Special Programming, U.S. B-582

L

Labor Groups & Unions I-18
Land Lines (AT&T) E-2
Law and Regulation, Government Agencies
   and Ownership, Table of Contents A-1
Law Firms H-90
Lawyers, Communications H-90
License, How to Apply for A-30

Licensing, Music G-89
Lithuanian
   Special Programming, U.S. B-582
Low Power TV (LPTV) C-94

M

Magazine or Newspaper
   Cross-Ownership with Stations A-118
Magazine or Newspaper
   Ownership of Stations A-124
Magazines for Broadcasting Industry J-16, J-18
Major Broadcasting and Cable Awards I-32
Major National Associations
   Assn. of Independent Television Stations Inc. ... I-2
   Cabletelevision Advertising Bureau Inc. (CAB) ... I-2
   Canadian Cable Television Assn. (CCTA) ... I-2
   Community Antenna Television Assn. (CATA) ... I-2
   Electronic Media Rating Council I-2
   National Assn. of Broadcasters (NAB) ... I-2
   NATPE International (National Assn. of
     Television Program Executives) I-5
   National Cable Television Assn. Inc. (NCTA) I-5
   National Cable Television Cooperative Inc. I-6
   Radio Advertising Bureau I-6
   Radio-Television News Directors Assn. I-7
   Television Bureau of Advertising (TVB) I-7
Major Networks, Radio
   ABC G-36
   American Urban Radio Networks G-37
   Associated Press (AP) G-38
   CBS Inc. G-39
   National Public Radio G-48
   NBC G-45
   Unistar Radio Network G-42
   United Press International G-42
   USA Radio Network G-43
   Westwood One Inc. G-43
Major Networks, TV
   ABC G-62
   CBS G-64
   Corporation for Public Broadcasting G-68
   Educational Broadcasting Corp. G-68
   Fox Broadcasting Co. G-65
   NBC G-66
   Public Broadcasting Service G-68
Management Consultants H-65
Managers, Talent H-102
Manufacturers of Equipment H-2, H-12
Maps of TV Markets C-123
Market Research Services H-79
Markets
   ADI TV, Arbitron Market Atlas C-123
   ADI TV, Multi-City C-201
   Bottom 50 Ranked by Percentage of
     Cable Penetration D-75
   Non-ADI TV C-202
   Radio by Arbitron Metro Survey Area B-598
   Radio by Population B-600
   Top 50 MSOs D-76
   Top 50 Ranked by Percentage of
     Cable Penetration D-72
   Top 50 Ranked by Cable TV Households D-73
   Top 50 Ranked by TV Households D-74
   TV by Nielson Marketing Research
     Territory C-208
   TV by Size C-203
   TV (Maps) C-123
   TV Network Delivery Variations C-213
   TV Top 100 .... C-210
Media Buying/Planning Services F-8
Media, Electronic
   Books on J-2, J-7
   Periodicals on J-16, J-18
Media Societies, Groups I-2, I-8
Microwave E-12

Broadcasting & Cable Yearbook 1994

Index to Sections

Middle-of-the-Road (see MOR)

MOR (Middle-of-the-Road)
   Definition of Format B-529
   Format by Province B-540
   Format by State B-530
   Programming, Canada B-572
   Programming, U.S. B-557
   Special Programming, U.S. B-582

MSOs
   Top 50 .... D-76
   U.S. D-3

Multichannel Multipoint Distribution Services E-17

Multiple Station Owners A-96

Multiple Systems Operators D-3

Multiple Systems Operators, Top 50 .... D-76

Multipoint Distribution Services E-14

Music Licensing Groups G-89

Mutual Broadcasting System G-43

N

NAB (National Assn. of Broadcasters) I-2

National Associations I-2, I-8

National Assn. of Broadcasters (NAB) I-2
   Radio Code A-49
   TV Code A-49

National Assn. of Television Program Executives
   (NATPE International) I-5

National Broadcasting Co. G-43, G-66

National Cable Television Assn. Inc. (NCTA) I-5

National Cable Television Cooperative Inc. I-6

National Networks, Radio
   ABC G-36
   American Urban G-37
   Associated Press (AP) G-38
   CBS Inc. G-39
   National Public Radio G-48
   NBC G-45
   Unistar Radio Network G-42
   United Press International G-42
   USA Radio Network G-43
   Westwood One Inc. G-43

National Networks, TV
   ABC G-62
   CBS G-64
   Corporation for Public Broadcasting G-68
   Educational Broadcasting Corp. G-68
   Fox Broadcasting Co. G-65
   NBC G-66
   Public Broadcasting Service G-68

NATPE International (National Assn.
   of Television Program Executives) I-5

National Public Radio (NPR) G-48

NBC Inc.
   Executives and Staff G-45, G-66
   Networks, Radio G-45
   Networks, TV G-66

NCTA (National Cable Television Assn. Inc.) I-5

Network Audience in TV Markets C-213

Networks, Radio
   ABC G-36
   American Public Radio G-48
   American Urban Radio Networks G-37
   Associated Press (AP) G-38
   Canadian G-55
   CBS Inc. G-39
   Eastern Public Radio G-48
   Mutual Broadcasting System G-43
   National Public Radio G-48
   NBC G-45
   Radio Program G-49
   Regional Radio G-51
   Satellite E-2

Unistar G-42
Unwired G-54
USA Radio Network G-43
UPI G-42
Westwood One Inc. G-43

Networks, TV
   ABC G-62
   Cable G-78, G-79
   Canadian G-72
   CBS G-64
   Corporation for Public Broadcasting G-68
   Educational Broadcasting Corp. G-68
   Fox Broadcasting Company G-65
   NBC G-66
   Public Broadcasting Service G-68
   Regional TV G-70
   Satellite E-2
   TV Program G-69
   Unwired G-71

New Age
   Definition of Format B-529
   Format by State B-530
   Programming, U.S. B-558
   Programming, Canada B-572
   Special Programming, Canada B-589
   Special Programming, U.S. B-582

News
   Definition of Format B-529
   Format by Province B-540
   Format by State B-530
   Programming, Canada B-572
   Programming, U.S. B-558
   Special Programming, Canada B-589
   Special Programming, U.S. B-582

News Directors, Radio-TV Association I-7

News Services
   Radio G-56
   TV G-74

News/Talk
   Definition of Format B-529
   Format by Province B-540
   Format by State B-530
   Programming, Canada B-572
   Programming, U.S. B-559
   Special Programming, Canada B-589
   Special Programming, U.S. B-583

Newspaper or Magazine
   Cross-Ownership with Stations A-118

Newspaper or Magazine
   Ownership of Stations A-124

Non-ADI TV Markets C-202

Nostalgia
   Definition of Format B-529
   Format by Province B-540
   Format by State B-530
   Programming, Canada B-572
   Programming, U.S. B-560
   Special Programming, Canada B-589
   Special Programming, U.S. B-583

NPR (National Public Radio) G-48

O

Oldies
   Definition of Format B-529
   Format by Province B-540
   Format by State B-530
   Programming, Canada B-572
   Programming, U.S. B-561
   Special Programming, Canada B-589
   Special Programming, U.S. B-583

Operators, Multiple Systems D-3

Other (Program Format)
   Definition of Format B-529
   Format by Province B-540
   Format by State B-530
   Programming, Canada B-572
   Programming, U.S. B-562
   Special Programming, Canada B-589
   Special Programming, U.S. B-583

Owners and Operators, Satellite E-2

Ownership
   Group Stations A-96
   Magazine of Broadcast Station A-118
   Newspaper of Broadcast Station A-118
   Transfers of TV A-54

P

Pay Cable Services G-78

PBS (Public Broadcasting Service) G-68

Periodicals J-16, J-18

Periodicals, International J-17

Placement Services H-103

Polish
   Format by State B-530
   Programming, U.S. B-562
   Special Programming, Canada B-589
   Special Programming, U.S. B-583

Polka
   Definition of Format B-529
   Format by State B-530
   Programming, U.S. B-562
   Special Programming, U.S. B-584

Portuguese
   Format by State B-530
   Programming, U.S. B-562
   Special Programming, Canada B-589
   Special Programming, U.S. B-584

Production Services G-2, G-9

Professional Cards (Advertising) H-105, H-107

Professional Societies I-2, I-8

Program
   Consultants H-65
   Distribution G-2, G-9
   Producers G-2, G-9

Program Services, Cable G-78

Programming, Canada
   Adult Contemporary B-571
   Agricultural B-571
   AOR B-572
   Beautiful Music B-571
   Big Band B-571
   Black B-571
   Chinese B-571
   Classic Rock B-571
   Classical B-571
   Contemporary Hit B-571
   Country B-571
   Disco B-571
   Diverse B-572
   Drama B-571
   Educational B-571
   Ethnic B-571
   Farm B-571
   Foreign Language B-571
   French B-572
   Gospel B-572
   Jazz B-572
   Literature B-571
   Middle-of-the-Road (MOR) B-572
   New Age B-572
   News B-572
   News/Talk B-572
   Nostalgia B-572
   Oldies B-572
   Other B-572
   Progressive B-572
   Public Affairs B-572
   Religious B-572
   Rock B-572
   Sports B-572
   Talk B-572
   Top 40 .... B-571
   Variety B-572

Programming, U.S. Radio
   Adult Contemporary B-543
   Agricultural B-546
   American Indian B-546
   Arabic B-546
   AOR B-565
   Beautiful Music B-546
   Big Band B-547

Index to Sections

Black B-547
Bluegrass B-547
Blues B-548
Children B-548
Classic Rock B-548
Classical B-548
Contemporary Hit B-549
Country B-550
Disco B-555
Drama B-555
Diverse B-569
Educational B-555
Ethnic B-555
Farm B-546
Filipino B-555
Folk B-555
Foreign Language B-555
French B-556
German B-556
Gospel B-556
Greek B-556
Italian B-556
Japanese B-556
Jazz B-556
Jewish B-557
Korean B-557
Literature B-555
Middle-of-the Road (MOR) B-557
New Age B-558
News B-558
News/Talk B-559
Nostalgia B-560
Oldies B-561
Other B-562
Polish B-562
Polka B-562
Portuguese B-562
Progressive B-562
Public Affairs B-563
Reggae B-563
Religious B-563
Rock B-565
Spanish B-566
Sports B-567
Talk B-567
Top 40 . . . . . B-549
Urban Contemporary B-568
Variety B-569

Progressive
Definition of Format B-529
Format by Province B-540
Format by State B-530
Programming, Canada B-572
Programming, U.S. B-562
Special Programming, U.S. B-584

Programming Services, Table of Contents G-1

Promotion
Consultants H-65
Films F-21
Services F-21

Province, Radio Formats Listed by B-540

Public Affairs
Definition of Format B-529
Format by Province B-540
Format by State B-530
Programming, Canada B-572
Programming, U.S. B-563
Special Programming, Canada B-589
Special Programming, U.S. B-584

Public Broadcasting Service G-68

Public Relations Services F-21

Publications J-2, J-7, J-16, J-18

Publications, International J-5, J-17

Publicity Services F-21

R

Radio
Advertising Bureau I-6
Armed Forces B-449
Assignments of FM Stations B-475
Audience B-605
Call Letters, AM B-451
Call Letters, FM B-460
Canadian AM-FM Stations B-427
Code of NAB A-49
College-Owned B-484
Directory of Stations B-3
Equipment Manufacturers H-2, H-12
FM Allotments B-475
Format Providers G-59
Formats by State B-530
Formats by Province B-540
Formats, Defined B-529
Frequencies, AM B-486
Frequencies, FM B-502
Group Ownership A-96
Industry Yellow Pages . . . . . Volume II
International Stations B-449
Listings, Key to B-2
Markets B-591
Miscellaneous Services B-449
Networks, Regional G-51
Newspaper Ownership A-118
News Services G-56
Program Distributors G-2, G-9
Program Producers G-2, G-9
Programming, Canada B-571
Programming, U.S. B-543
Programming Chart B-542
Programming Formats B-529
Program Services G-36
Representatives, Canadian F-20
Representatives, U.S. F-10
School-Owned B-484
Schools I-25
Set Sales 1958-1991 . . . . . B-603
Special Programming, Canadian B-589
Special Programming, U.S. B-573
Stations on Air, by Market B-591
Table of Contents B-1
U.S. AM Stations B-486
U.S. FM Stations B-502
U.S. International B-449
Voice of America B-449

Radio Advertising Bureau I-6

Radio Free Europe B-449

Radio Liberty B-432

Radio & TV by State/Province, Index to K-8

Radio-TV & Telecommunications Commission of Canada A-52

Radio-TV News Directors Association I-7

Ranking of TV Markets C-203

Reggae
Definition of Format B-529
Format by State B-530
Programming, U.S. B-563
Special Programming, Canada B-589
Special Programming, U.S. B-584

Regional Radio Networks G-51

Regional TV Networks G-70

Regulations, Cable A-32

Regulations, FCC for Radio-TV A-5

Religious
Definition of Format B-529
Format by Province B-540
Format by State B-530
Programming, Canada B-572
Programming, U.S. B-563
Special Programming, Canada B-589
Special Programming, U.S. B-585

Representatives of
Artists H-102
Canadian Stations F-20
U.S. Stations F-10

Resale and Common Carriers, Satellite E-4

Research Services, Radio-TV H-79

Review 1992, Year in xxi

Rock/AOR
Definition of Format B-529
Format by Province B-540
Format by State B-530
Programming, Canada B-572
Programming, U.S. B-565
Special Programming, Canada B-590
Special Programming, U.S. B-586

Rules and Regulations, FCC A-5

Russian
Special Programming, U.S. B-586

S

Sales
Consultants H-65
of Stations in 1993 . . . . . A-90
of U.S. Radio Sets B-603
of U.S. TV Receivers C-217

Satellites
Direct Broadcast E-9
Guide to the Sky E-3
Owners, Operators E-2
Resale, Common Carriers E-4

Satellites and Other Carriers
Microwave E-12
Multichannel Multipoint Distribution Services . E-17
Multipoint Distribution Services E-14
Table of Contents E-1
Teleports E-10

School-Owned
Radio B-484
TV C-113

Schools, Radio, TV and Cable I-25

Scottish
Special Programming, Canada B-590
Special Programming, U.S. B-586

Sections, Index to K-1

Senate Committee on Commerce A-50

Serbian
Special Programming, Canada B-590
Special Programming, U.S. B-586

Services
Advertising F-2
Audio Cable Programming G-84
Automated Cable Channel Programmers G-83
Barter F-9
Basic Cable G-79
Brokers, Station and Cable TV H-59
Cable Programming G-78
Cable Sports G-86
Canadian Cable Programming G-88
Closed Circuit G-77
Communications Law, Firms Active in H-90
Consulting H-65
Distribution G-2, G-9
Employment H-103
Engineering Consultation H-84
Executive Search H-103
Financing, of Stations H-76
Market Research H-79
Marketing F-8, F-10, F-20, F-21
Media Buying/Planning F-8
Multichannel Multipoint Distribution E-17
Multipoint Distribution E-14
Music Licensing Groups G-89
Pay Cable G-78
Production G-2, G-9
Promotion F-21
Public Relations F-21
Publicity F-21
Rating & Research H-79
Radio Format Providers G-59
Radio News G-56
Radio Programming G-36
Research H-79
Subcarrier/VBI G-92
Talent, Agents and Managers H-102
Technical Consultation H-84
Teletext Operations G-91
TV News G-74
TV Programming G-62
Videotext Operations G-90

Services and Suppliers, Table of Contents H-1

Shows, Trade I-20, I-21

Broadcasting & Cable Yearbook 1994
K-5

Index to Sections

Slovak
Special Programming, U.S. B-586

Slovenian
Special Programming, U.S. B-586

Societies, Professional, Radio-TV I-2, I-8

Spanish
Format by State B-530
Programming, U.S. B-566
Special Programming, Canada B-590
Special Programming, U.S. B-586

Spanish-Language Stations, TV C-110

Special Programming, Canada
Agriculture B-589
American Indian B-589
AOR B-590
Arabic B-589
Big Band B-589
Black B-589
Bluegrass B-589
Blues B-589
Chinese B-589
Classic Rock B-589
Classical B-589
Contemporary Hit B-589
Country B-589
Croation B-589
Drama B-589
Educational B-589
Ethnic B-589
Farm B-589
Filipino B-589
Finnish B-589
Folk B-589
Foreign Language B-589
French B-589
German B-589
Gospel B-589
Greek B-589
Hebrew B-589
Hindi B-589
Hungarian B-589
Irish B-589
Italian B-589
Jazz B-589
Jewish B-589
Literature B-589
New Age B-589
News B-589
News/Talk B-589
Nostalgia B-589
Oldies B-589
Other B-589
Polish B-589
Portuguese B-589
Public Affairs B-589
Reggae B-589
Religious B-589
Rock B-590
Scottish B-590
Serbian B-590
Spanish B-590
Sports B-590
Talk B-590
Top 40 .... B-589
Ukrainian B-590
Vietnamese B-590
Women B-590

Special Programming, U.S.
Adult Contemporary B-573
Agriculture B-573
Albanian B-575
American Indian B-575
AOR B-586
Arabic B-575
Armenian B-575
Beautiful Music B-575
Big Band B-575
Black B-575
Bluegrass B-576
Blues B-577
Children B-577
Chinese B-577
Classic Rock B-577
Classical B-577
Comedy B-578
Contemporary Hit B-578
Country B-578
Croation B-578
Czech B-578
Disco B-578
Diverse B-588
Drama B-578
Educational B-578
Ethnic B-579
Farm B-573
Filipino B-578
Finnish B-578
Folk B-578
Foreign Language B-579
French B-579
German B-579
Gospel B-580
Greek B-581
Hebrew B-581
Hindi B-581
Hungarian B-581
Irish B-581
Italian B-581
Japanese B-581
Jazz B-581
Jewish B-582
Korean B-582
Literature B-578
Lithuanian B-582
Middle-of-the-Road (MOR) B-582
New Age B-582
News B-582
News/Talk B-583
Nostalgia B-583
Oldies B-583
Other B-583
Polish B-583
Polka B-584
Portuguese B-584
Progressive B-584
Public Affairs B-584
Reggae B-584
Religious B-585
Rock B-586
Russian B-586
Scottish B-586
Serbian B-586
Slovak B-586
Slovenian B-586
Spanish B-586
Sports B-587
Talk B-588
Top 40 .... B-578
Ukrainian B-588
Urban Contemporary B-588
Variety B-588
Vietnamese B-588
Women B-588

Sports
Definition of Format B-529
Format by Province B-540
Format by State B-530
Programming, Canada B-572
Programming, U.S. B-567
Special Programming, Canada B-590
Special Programming, U.S. B-587

State
Broadcast Associations I-15
Cable Associations I-17
Cable Regulatory Agencies A-53
Radio Formats Listed by B-530
TV Assignments by C-120

Station
Applications A-30
Brokers H-59
Cross-Ownership A-118
Financing H-76
Representatives F-10
Transactions, 40 Years of A-95
Transfers, TV A-54
Sales 1993 .... A-90

Stations
Broadcasting in Stereo, U.S. TV C-114
Directory of Canadian Radio B-427
Directory of U.S. Radio B-3
Experimental TV C-111
Group Ownership of A-96
Independent TV, U.S. C-112
Low Power TV (LPTV) C-94
Miscellaneous Radio B-449
Newspaper/Magazine
Cross-Ownership with A-118
Newspaper/Magazine Ownership of A-118
Programming on Canadian Radio B-571
Programming on U.S. Radio B-543
School-Owned Radio B-484
School-Owned TV C-113
Spanish-Language TV C-110
Special Programming on Canadian Radio ... B-589
Special Programming on U.S. Radio B-573
TV by Channel, Canadian C-119
TV by Channel, U.S. C-115

Stereo, U.S. TV Stations Broadcasting in C-114

Subcarriers/VBI Services G-92

Suppliers & Services H-1

Supreme Court A-50

Surveys & Market Research H-79

T

Table of Contents
Advertising and Marketing Services F-1
Associations, Events, Education, Awards I-1
Books, Periodicals, Videos J-1
Cable D-1
Law and Regulation, Government Agencies
and Ownership A-1
Main iii
Programming Services G-1
Radio B-1
Services and Suppliers H-1
Satellites and Other Carriers E-1
Television C-1

Table of FM Allotments B-475

Talent Agents and Managers H-102

Talk
Definition of Format B-529
Format by Province B-540
Format by State B-530
Programming, Canada B-572
Programming, U.S. B-567
Special Programming, Canada B-590
Special Programming, U.S. B-588

Technical Consultants H-84

Technical Services H-2, H-12

Teleports E-10

Teletext Operations G-91

Television
ADI Markets C-123
Advertising Bureau I-7
Assignments C-120
Audiences C-219
Bureau of Advertising I-7
Call Letters, U.S. C-90
Call Letters, Canada C-93
Channel Assignments C-120
Channels, Canada C-119
Channels, U.S. C-115
Closed Circuit G-77
College-Owned C-113
Commercial Producers G-2, G-9
Code of NAB A-49
Directory, Canadian C-81
Directory, U.S. C-3
Equipment Manufacturers H-2, H-12
Experimental C-111
Group Ownership A-96
Independent, U.S. C-112
Industry Yellow Pages .... Volume II
International Publications J-5, J-17
Listings, Key to C-2
Low Power (LPTV) C-94
Markets, by ADI C-123
Market Ranking C-203, C-208
Network Delivery C-213
Networks, Major National G-62
Networks, Regional G-70
News Services G-74
Newspaper Ownership A-118
Program Distributors G-2, G-9
Program Production Services G-2, G-9
Program Services G-2, G-62
Promotion Films F-21
Regional Networks G-70
Representatives, Canadian F-20
Representatives, U.S. F-10
Schools I-25
Spanish-Language Stations C-110

Broadcasting & Cable Yearbook 1994
K-6

Index to Sections

Station Sales A-54, A-90, A-95
Stations, Canadian C-81
Stations, U.S. C-3
Table of Contents C-1
Transfers of Ownership A-54

Television Bureau of Advertising (TVB) I-7

Television Quatre Saisons G-73

Terms, Glossary of xi

Top 50 MSOs D-76

Top 40 (See Contemporary Hit)

Trade Associations & Professional Groups I-18

Trade Shows Alphabetical Index I-20

Trade Shows Subject Index I-21

Transactions, 40 Years of Station A-95

Transfers of TV Ownership A-54

TVA (Network) G-73

TVB (Television Bureau of Advertising) I-7

U

Ukrainian
Special Programming, Canada B-590
Special Programming, U.S. B-586

Unions/Labor Groups I-18

University-Owned
Radio B-484
TV C-113

Universities Offering Radio-TV-Cable Courses . . . I-29

Universities Offering Broadcasting Degrees I-27

Universities Offering Two Year Programs I-29

Unistar Radio Networks G-42

United Press International (UPI) G-42

United States
Government Agencies A-50
Independent TV Stations C-112
International Radio B-449
Radio Markets B-591
Radio Programming Formats B-530
Radio Station Directory B-3
Special Programming B-573
TV Station Directory C-3
TV Stations Broadcasting in Stereo C-114
TV Stations by Calls C-90

Unwired Networks
Radio G-54
TV G-71

UPI (United Press International) G-42

Urban Contemporary
Definition of Format B-529
Format by Province B-540
Format by State B-530
Programming, U.S. B-568
Special Programming, U.S. B-588

USA Radio Network G-43

User's Guide vii

V

Variety/Diverse
Definition of Format B-529
Format by Province B-540
Format by State B-530
Programming, Canada B-572
Programming, U.S. B-569
Special Programming, U.S. B-588

Videos on Broadcasting J-31

Videotext G-90

Videotext Operations G-90

Vietnamese
Special Programming, Canada B-590
Special Programming, U.S. B-588

Viewing Habits C-219

Voice of America B-449

W

Westwood One Inc. G-43

Wireless Cable Operators E-13

Women
Format Defined B-529
Special Programming, Canada B-590
Special Programming, U.S. B-588

Y

Year in Review 1993 xxi

Yellow Pages, Radio, TV . . . . Volume II
& Cable Industries

Index of Radio and Television by State/Possession/Province

Alabama
Radio B-3
Television C-3

Alaska
Radio B-13
Television C-4

Arizona
Radio B-16
Television C-5

Arkansas
Radio B-22
Television C-6

California
Radio B-30
Television C-7

Colorado
Radio B-56
Television C-12

Connecticut
Radio B-63
Television C-13

Delaware
Radio B-67
Television C-14

District of Columbia
Radio B-68
Television C-14

Florida
Radio B-69
Television C-14

Georgia
Radio B-87
Television C-19

Hawaii
Radio B-101
Television C-21

Idaho
Radio B-103
Television C-22

Illinois
Radio B-107
Television C-22

Indiana
Radio B-121
Television C-25

Iowa
Radio B-131
Television C-26

Kansas
Radio B-139
Television C-28

Kentucky
Radio B-145
Television C-29

Louisiana
Radio B-156
Television C-30

Maine
Radio B-163
Television C-32

Maryland
Radio B-167
Television C-33

Massachusetts
Radio B-172
Television C-33

Michigan
Radio B-179
Television C-34

Minnesota
Radio B-192
Television C-37

Mississippi
Radio B-202
Television C-38

Missouri
Radio B-210
Television C-39

Montana
Radio B-221
Television C-41

Nebraska
Radio B-224
Television C-42

Nevada
Radio B-229
Television C-44

New Hampshire
Radio B-232
Television C-45

New Jersey
Radio B-235
Television C-45

New Mexico
Radio B-239
Television C-46

New York
Radio B-244
Television C-47

North Carolina
Radio B-263
Television C-50

North Dakota
Radio B-277
Television C-52

Ohio
Radio B-280
Television C-53

Oklahoma
Radio B-294
Television C-56

Oregon
Radio B-301
Television C-58

Pennsylvania
Radio B-308
Television C-59

Rhode Island
Radio B-325
Television C-61

South Carolina
Radio B-327
Television C-61

South Dakota
Radio B-335
Television C-63

Tennessee
Radio B-338
Television C-64

Texas
Radio B-351
Television C-66

Utah
Radio B-377
Television C-71

Vermont
Radio B-380
Television C-72

Virginia
Radio B-383
Television C-72

Washington
Radio B-394
Television C-74

West Virginia
Radio B-403
Television C-75

Wisconsin
Radio B-408
Television C-76

Wyoming
Radio B-418
Television C-78

Guam
Radio B-421
Television C-79

Puerto Rico
Radio B-422
Television C-79

Virgin Islands
Radio B-425
Television C-80

American Samoa
Radio B-421
Television C-79

Federated State of Micronesia
Radio B-421

Northern Mariana Islands
Radio B-421

Alberta
Radio B-427
Television C-81

British Columbia
Radio B-429
Television C-82

Manitoba
Radio B-432
Television C-82

New Brunswick
Radio B-433
Television C-83

Newfoundland
Radio B-434
Television C-83

Northwest Territories
Radio B-435
Television C-84

Nova Scotia
Radio B-435
Television C-84

Ontario
Radio B-436
Television C-84

Prince Edward Island
Radio B-442
Television C-87

Quebec
Radio B-443
Television C-87

Saskatchewan
Radio B-447
Television C-88

Yukon Territory
Radio B-448
Television C-89

Index to Advertisers

Advertiser	Page
ADC Telecommunications	H-12, H-13
AFCCE	H-105
AT&T	E-2
Abekas Video Systems Inc.	H-12
Agency for Instructional Technology	G-9
Alladin Media Products	H-14, Outsert
Allen, John P., Airspace Consultant	H-105
Alternate View Network	G-79
Altronic Research	H-15
American Radio Brokers	B-13, B-18, B-30, B-34, B-36, B-40, B-47, B-49, B-56, B-68, B-172, B-230, B-306, B-379, B-399, B-400, F-21, H-59, H-65
Andrus, Alvin H. P.E.	H-106
Associated Press	Inside Front Cover, Spine
Audio Broadcast Group	H-16
Audio Implements/G.K.C.	H-16, H-17
Avid Technology Inc.	G-10; Inside Back Cover
Battison, John H., P.E. & Associates	H-106
Baugh & Associates	H-59
Beckerman Associates Inc.	B-71, H-59, H-65
Behr, Lawrence Associates Inc.	H-84
Belar Electronics Laboratory Inc.	H-18, H-19
Benchmark Media Systems Inc.	H-18, Outsert
Blair Television (A subsidiary of John Blair Communications Inc.)	F-10
Boyle, Frank	H-59
Broadcast Data Services (BDS)	H-106
Broadcast Group, The	G-12
Broadcasters General Store	H-20
Broadcasting & Cable	C-43
Broadcasting & Cable International and Broadcasting & Cable TV International	Tab C, front; Tab J, back
Broadcasting & Cable Yearbook	Tab A, front
Browne, John F.X. & Associates, P.C.	H-105
Burkat, Howard Communications	H-66
CBS Radio Networks	G-59
CCA Electronics Corp.	H-20
C-COR Electronics Inc.	H-20
CRN International	G-59
Cable Networks Inc.	F-11
Cable Television Network of New Jersey	G-12
Cahners Mail List Services	Tab F, back
Capitol Satellite & Communications Systems Inc.	E-11
Carpel Video Inc.	H-21
Carolina Global Map	H-84
Carr, William B. & Associates Inc.	H-105
Cases Unlimited	H-21
Central Tower Inc.	H-22
Clark & Associates Ltd.	B-85, H-22
Clark Inc, Donald K.	H-60
CoarcVideo	H-23, H-107
Coaxial Dynamics Inc.	H-23
Cohen, Dippell & Everist	H-105
Cohen, Jules & Associates	H-105
Colby, Lauren A., Esq.	B-3, B-23, B-32, B-69, B-87, B-103, B-107, B-139, B-145, B-156, B-168, B-175, B-179, B-192, B-202, B-210, B-221, B-224, B-230, B-237, B-236, B-280, B-301, B-310, B-327, B-335, B-338, B-351, B-377, B-383, B-403, C-33, C-73, H-59, H-66, H-92
Cole Appraisal Services	H-67
Comark Communications Inc.	Tab H, front
Communications Design Associates Inc.	H-85, H-106
Communications Engineering Services P.C. (Richard L. Biby, P.E.)	H-105
Communications Resources Unlimited Inc.	H-60
Communications Technologies Inc.	H-105
Com/Tech Communications	G-14; Back Cover
Co-op Source Directory	Tab G, front
Cottrill & Holland Inc.	H-105
Crawford, Jan Communications	H-67
Crossno, C.P. & Associates	H-105
Crystal Productions	H-25
DSI Communications Inc.	H-106
Daily Variety	D-65
Davis, John J. & Associates	H-105
Design Publishers International	E-5
du Treil, Lundin & Rackley Inc.	H-105
ERI (Electronics Research Inc.)	H-26, H-27
ESCO	Tab H, back
Energy Plus Inc./Rathbone Energy Systems Inc.	H-28
Evans Associates	H-105
Exline, William A. Inc.	B-30, B-57, B-101, B-103, B-301, B-394, H-60, H-61
FM Atlas—Publishing and Electronics	H-28
Fischer, Norman & Associates	B-22, B-156, B-241, B-249, B-351, H-60
Fitzpatrick, Don & Associates	H-103
Freeland Products Inc.	H-29
Gammon Media Brokers	H-60
Gentner Communications	H-30
Gepco International	H-21, H-22, H-24, H-30, H-31, H-41, H-42
Giles, Robert	J-12
Golden Lamb Productions	Tab G, back; C-47, G-74, G-75
Gordon Communications	G-18
Grandy, W. John	H-60
Green, W. Richard & Associates	H-86, H-106
Group W Video Services	E-4
Hammett & Edison Inc.	H-105
Handel's National Directory for the Performing Arts	Tab I, front
Haney, Margret of Graham-Haney	B-42, B-50, C-11, H-60, H-69
Hannel, F.W. & Associates	H-106
Hatfield & Dawson	H-105
Hebert, Dave & Associates	H-106
Hecht, Charles A. & Associates Inc.	H-86, H-105
Hepburn, Ted Co.	H-62
Hitachi Denshi America	H-32
Hoffman Schutz Media Capital Inc.	H-62, H-69, H-76, H-77
Hughes Communications Inc.	Tab E, back; E-2, E-4
IDB Communications Group	E-4, G-49, G-105
I.N.I. Entertainment Group	G-19
Independent Broadcast Consultants Inc.	E-10, E-11, H-106
InSat Corp.	H-33
Interep	F-13
International Teletext Communications Inc.	H-34
Inovonics Inc.	H-33
Jacobs, George & Associates Inc.	H-105
James, Vir, P.C.	H-106
Jampro Antennas Inc.	H-15, H-26, H-34, H-35, H-50
Jefferson-Pilot Data Services	H-34
Jones, Carl T. Corp.	H-105
KGBT/KIWW	B-362
KITV	C-21
KLUZ-TV Channel 41	C-46
KOA Optical	H-35
KRRI(FM)	B-231
KWYR Radio	B-338
Kagan Media Appraisals	H-70
Katz Communications Inc.	F-13
Kessler & Gehman Associates Inc.	H-106
Keystone Communications	E-4, E-10
Killer Tracks	G-21
Kintronic Labs Inc.	H-35
Kline Towers	H-105
Kozacko Media Services	H-62
LBA Technology Inc.	H-36
LPB Inc.	H-36, H-37
Lester Laboratories	H-38
Lifetime Television Network	G-22, G-23
Lightning Prevention Systems	H-38, H-106
Link Electronics Inc.	H-38
Literary Market Place	Tab J, front
Lohnes & Culver	H-106
Lund Consultants to Broadcast Management Inc.	H-70, H-71
Lund Media Research	H-81

Broadcasting & Cable Yearbook 1994

Index to Advertisers

Advertiser	Page
Marks, Brad International	H-103
Marsand Inc.	H-105
Marti Electronics	H-39, H-40
Martindale-Hubbell Bar Register of Preeminent Lawyers	Tab A, back
Micro Technology Unlimited	H-12, H-25, H-29, H-38, H-40, H-52
Microflect Co. Inc.	H-40, H-41
Microwave Radio Corp.	H-107
Moffett, Larson & Johnson Inc.	H-106
Moore, Art Inc.	F-16
Morris Network of Alabama WDHN-TV 18	C-3
Morton, Lawrence L., P.E.	H-106
Mullaney Engineering Inc.	H-106
Munn Jr., E. Harold & Associates Inc.	H-105
National Weather Network	G-25, G-75
New England Media Inc.	H-63
92.5 The Flash	B-49
Omnimusic	B-41, C-9, G-25, G-43
Oppenheimer & Co. Inc.	H-77
Owl Engineering Inc.	H-105
Petry Television Inc.	F-16
Phase One Communications Inc.	H-105
Phasetek Inc.	H-45
Pike & Fischer Inc.	H-82
Pinnacle Systems Inc.	H-45
Population Institute, The	Tab D, front; Tab D, back
Poorman & Group	H-72
Potomac Instruments Inc.	H-45
Pritchard Co. Inc.	H-72
Professional Video Services (PVS)	E-6, E-7
QSI Systems Inc.	H-46
RAD Marketing and Radiobase	F-3, F-6, G-27, H-82
RPM Radio Programming & Management	G-59, G-60, H-72
RTNDA Job Services	H-104
Racal-Decca Canada Inc.	H-47
Radio Information Center	B-3, B-40, B-109, B-254
Radio, Ink.	Outsert
Radio Spirits Inc.	G-60, G-61
Radio WADO/Spanish Radio Network	See WADO
Radio/TV Engineering Co.	H-106
Redbooks	Tab F, front
Rice, William R. Co.	H-63
SG Communications	H-106
Sabine Musical Manufacturing Co. Inc.	H-49
Satterfield & Perry Inc.	B-59, B-214, B-318, B-352, C-12, C-60, H-64, H-73
Sawyer, T.Z. Technical Consultants	H-105
Schafer World Communications Corp.	H-49, H-50
Schutz Jr., William B.	H-63, H-64
Scientific-Atlanta	Tab C, back
Second Chance Body Armor	H-50, H-51
Sellmeyer Engineering	H-105
Shoolbred Engineering Inc.	H-106
Signal Properties	H-77
Silliman and Silliman	H-106
Skidelsky, Barry	H-90, H-99
Smith & Powstenko	H-105
Smith, Carl E. Consulting Engineering	H-105
Snowden Associates	H-64
Southern Broadcast Services	H-106
Spectrum Engineering Co.	H-105
Sportsticker	G-57, G-76
Stainless Inc./SG Communications	H-52
Standard Directories (Redbooks)	Tab F, front
Standard News	Tab B, back
Stiles, Walter J.	H-105
Stitt, J.M. & Associates Inc.	H-105
Strategy Research Corp.	H-79, H-83
Structural Systems Technology Inc.	H-105
Subito Studios	Outsert
Suffa & Cavell Inc.	H-88, H-106
Talkline	B-249, B-255
Tapscan Inc.	H-53
Target Radio Inc.	F-18
Technet Systems Group (A division of Steve Vanni Associates Inc.)	H-53
Telerep Inc.	F-18
Thorburn Co.	H-64
Trimm Inc. (A division of Newton Instruments Co.)	H-55
24 Karat Productions Inc.	G-61
Vacuum Tube Industries Inc.	H-56
Variety	C-57
Vision Accomplished	E-4, E-8, H-57, H-89
WADO(AM)	B-254
WBCU	B-334
WBSV-TV	C-18
WDHN-TV	C-3
WDTL Radio	B-203
WEVD Radio	B-254
WFTX-TV	C-18
WHIZ	B-294
WPMR FM/AM	B-317
WSLM	B-129
WTYM(AM)	B-315
WUSA	C-14
WVLK (AM) (FM)	B-150
WWGO-FM	B-80
WWOR TV	C-49
Whittle Agency	B-265, H-64
Who's Who in America	Tab I, back
Williams Radio Sales Inc.	F-19
Willoughby & Voss	H-106
Wiltronix	H-58
Wooten, Charles Broadcast Engineering	H-106
Working Press of the Nation	Tab E, front

Notes

Notes

Notes

Notes